NATIONAL
of Historic Places 1966 to 1994
REGISTER

The outbuildings on the Shields-Ethridge Farm in Jackson County, "represent the broadest assortment of 19th and early 20th–century domestic, agricultural, and industrial outbuildings known to exist on a single farm in Georgia." (James R. Lockhart, 1990)

NATIONAL
of Historic Places 1966 to 1994
REGISTER

Cumulative List Through January 1, 1994

National Park Service
Washington, D.C.

The Preservation Press
National Trust for Historic Preservation
Washington, D.C.

National Conference of State
Historic Preservation Officers
Washington, D.C.

The Preservation Press
National Trust for Historic Preservation
1785 Massachusetts Avenue, N.W.
Washington, D.C. 20036

The National Trust for Historic Preservation is the only private, nonprofit organization chartered by Congress to encourage public participation in the preservation of sites, buildings, and objects significant in American history and culture. In carrying out this mission, the National Trust fosters an appreciation of the diverse character and meaning of our American cultural heritage and preserves and revitalizes the livability of our communities by leading the nation in saving America's historic environments.

Support for the National Trust is provided by membership dues, contributions, and a matching grant from the National Park Service, U.S. Department of the Interior, under provisions of the National Historic Preservation Act of 1966. The opinions expressed here do not necessarily reflect the views or policies of the Interior Department.

Printed in the United States of America
97 96 95 94   5 4 3 2 1

ISBN 0-89133-254-5

Library of Congress Cataloging-in-Publication Data

National Register of Historic Places 1966 to 1994: cumulative list
through January 1, 1994
    p. cm.
    1. Historic sites—United States—Directories.   I. National
Trust for Historic Preservation.   II. United States.
National Park Service.
    E159.N3419   1991   973'.025—dc20   91-29186   CIP

The cumulative list included in this edition of the *National Register of Historic Places 1966 to 1994* has been compiled, edited, and provided to the Preservation Press in magnetic tape form by the National Park Service.

Design by Impressions, a division of Edwards Brothers, Inc.

Photo Credits:

Front cover: Wellesley Town Hall, Norfolk County, MA

Rear cover: Ohio and Erie Canal, Lock 39, Cuyahoga County,
          OH—Louise Taft Cawood, HAER, 1986.
         San Jose de Gracia Church, Las Trampas, Taos
          County, NM—Walter Smalling, Jr., HABS, 1980
         Brooklyn Bridge, New York City, NY—Jet Lowe,
          HAER, 1982
         Drayton Street, Savannah, Victorian Historic
          District, Chatham County, GA—Walter
          Smalling, Jr., HABS 1979

Contents

Exquisite woodwork is found throughout Shard Villa in Addison County, Vermont. (Max Peterson, 1987)

Introduction

America's historic places embody our unique character and identity. They tell a compelling story of the nation, the states, and communities throughout the country. Historic places represent important historical trends and events, reflect the lives of significant persons, illustrate distinctive architectural and engineering designs, and impart information about America's past.

Individually and collectively, historic places listed in the National Register of Historic Places evoke our nation's heritage. National Register documentation traces the history of towns and cities by recording the physical characteristics and significance of historic places. Clusters of farm buildings on agricultural land can be linked to a community's development. Historic bridges that were constructed across a state illustrate that state's efforts to improve transportation systems and commerce. The residence of a prominent writer offers insight into that person's creative process. The careers of architects, master builders, and other designers appear in examples of their work across a community, a region, or the nation. The migration and lifeways of America's cultural groups left their imprint on the landscape and in settlements. Historic places like these and numerous others constitute the nation's collective experience and memory.

What Is the National Register of Historic Places?

Expressly authorized by the National Historic Preservation Act of 1966, the National Register of Historic Places is the nation's official list of historic places worth preserving and is the centerpiece of a larger historic preservation program authorized by the Act. The National Park Service, under the Secretary of the Interior, administers the National Register of Historic Places in partnership with federal, tribal, state, and local governments, and private citizens.

The framers of the 1966 Act clearly envisioned a broad role for the National Register when they authorized the Secretary of the Interior to expand and maintain a National Register of Historic Places "composed of districts, sites, buildings, structures, and objects significant in American history, architecture, archaeology, engineering, and culture." In Section 1(b)(6), the 1966 Act states:

> The increased knowledge of our historic resources, the establishment of better means of identifying and administering them, and the encouragement of their preservation will improve the planning and execution of federal and federally assisted projects and will assist economic growth and development.

The preamble established the National Register within the context of community planning and development and visualized an active role for historic places in contemporary American life:

> the historical and cultural foundations of the Nation should be preserved as a living part of our community life and development in order to give a sense of orientation to the American people.

Before 1966, the Federal government recognized only places of national significance, many of which were publicly owned. The initial National Register list consisted of the relatively few historical units of the National Park System and National Historic Landmarks. All historical units of the National Park System continue to be automatically listed in the National Register; they are documented to identify those features and qualities deserving protection. Historical units of the National Park System include such places as Independence National Historical Park in Philadelphia, Pennsylvania, and the Harry S Truman National Historic Site in Independence, Missouri.

Authorized by the 1935 Historic Sites Act, National Historic Landmarks are designated by the Secretary of the Interior for their national significance in illustrating or representing American history and prehistory, such as the Upton Sinclair House in Los Angeles County, California. The National Park Service undertakes or sponsors thematic studies that support evaluation and documentation of potential National Historic Landmarks. When designated by the Secretary of the Interior, National Historic Landmarks not listed previously are entered into the National Register.

Since its inception in 1966, the National Register has broadened this federal recognition of historic places to include those important to the states and localities, such

National Register Listings by Ownership Category*

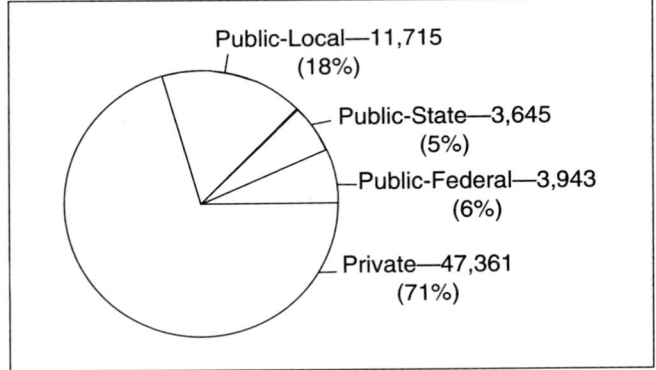

Public-Local—11,715 (18%)

Public-State—3,645 (5%)

Public-Federal—3,943 (6%)

Private—47,361 (71%)

*Some properties have more than one ownership category.

The Lower Central Business District in New Orleans is a visually and historically distinct area between the city's modern downtown and the Vieux Carre. (John C. Ferguson, 1990)

as the Fayetteville Historic District in Fayette County, West Virginia.

Currently, there are over 62,000 listings in the National Register that encompass more than 900,000 resources. Of the listings, 73 percent are buildings, 14 percent are districts, 7 percent are sites, 5 percent are structures, and less than 1 percent are objects. A **building** may be a house, barn, church, or hotel that is created principally to shelter human activity. A **structure**—distinguished from a building by its design for purposes other than human shelter—may be a bridge, tunnel, dam, boat, or railroad locomotive. A **site** is a location of a significant event; a prehistoric or historic occupation or activity; or a location that possesses historic, cultural, or archeological value regardless of the value of any existing structure. An **object** is primarily artistic in nature, or relatively small in scale and simply constructed, such as a sculpture, monument, boundary marker, or fountain. A **district** is a significant concentration of sites, buildings, structures, or objects united historically or aesthetically.

To be eligible for listing, a place must possess historical significance, as defined by the National Register Criteria for Evaluation. (National Register Criteria for Evaluation appear on page xix.) It may be associated with historic events or trends, such as a World War II fortification in Guam. It may be associated with significant persons, such as a district of prominent artists' and writers' homes in Santa Fe, New Mexico. Distinctive and representative examples of an architectural style, engineered design, or construction method include skyscrapers in Chicago and mining structures in Alaska. Archeological properties such as the Cedar Swamp Archeological District in Massachusetts qualify for the important information they may contain about the past.

Eighty-two percent of National Register listings are recognized for their architectural or engineering merits, 51 percent for their associations with significant events, 15 percent for their associations with important people, and 7 percent for the information they contain. Properties frequently meet more than one criterion.

In addition to actually listing historic places in the National Register, the National Park Service assists individuals, governments, and organizations in preparing National Register nominations. It sets standards and provides guidance and technical assistance for identifying, evaluating, and documenting significant places; and monitors adherence to the standards by reviewing nominations. The National Park Service also produces an array of educational materials about the National Register and the importance of historic places in defining the nation's character. It makes the large quantity of information on National Register listings available to the public for planning, management, research, and public education.

What Does Listing in the National Register Mean?

Over the past quarter-century, the National Register has fulfilled the broad role that the framers of the 1966 Act envisioned. While listing in the National Register signifies that a place has been documented to uniform national standards and meets the National Register Criteria for Evaluation, it has meaning that far transcends an honor roll of significant places. In the words of Joan K. Davidson, State Historic Preservation Officer of New York:

> The National Register of the 1990s turns out to be something quite different, indeed something vastly more consequential, than I had assumed. It has become a document of social history, an encyclopedia of material culture, a revelation of the nature of community—even, possibly, a guide for planning the future of the built environment in our state.[1]

Types of Properties Listed

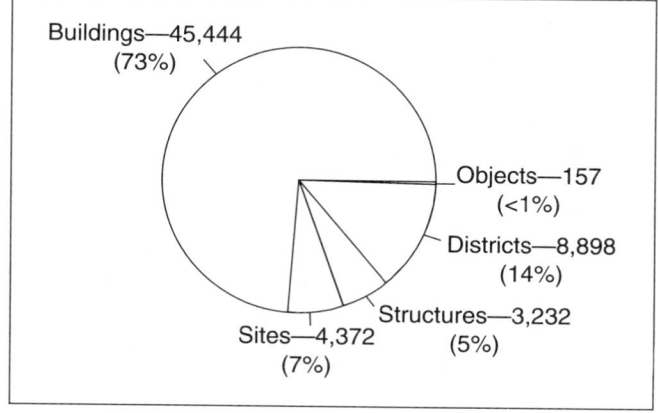

National Register documentation of historic properties becomes part of a national database and research resource available for planning, management, research, education, and interpretation. Listing furnishes authentication of the worth of a historic place and often influences a community's attitude toward its heritage.

Recognition

National Register listing honors a historic place by recognizing its importance to its community, state, or the nation. Marcella Sherfy, State Historic Preservation Officer of Montana, cites the effects of this recognition on the everyday decisions property owners and communities make about maintaining and preserving their historic properties:

> The National Register's understated but clear recognition for a broad range of locally significant resources delights Montanans who love their history. The process of listing itself deepens and broadens public support for preservation.[2]

National Register status for historic places often is cited in travel literature, tourism promotion, historical guides, real estate advertisements, and other publications aimed at the general public and is widely viewed as a decided advantage in the desirability of a place.

Federal Agency Responsibilities

The 1966 Act requires that federal agencies review any of their actions that may affect National Register-listed or eligible places and allow the Advisory Council on Historic Preservation, an independent federal agency, an opportunity to comment on the actions and their effects on the places. This ensures that the values of these places are considered in the planning of federal and federally assisted projects. Listed and eligible places are considered in decisions to issue surface coal mining permits, for example. More than 70,000 federal projects are reviewed annually. States provide more than 9,000 National Register eligibility opinions to federal agencies on an annual basis.

National Register documentation assists the federal government not only with the management and preservation, but also with the interpretation, of cultural resources under its control. NPS Chief Historian Edwin C. Bearss states:

> Equally important [to the cultural resource management mandate] is the value of National Register documentation as it has evolved since the 1970s to park interpreters. To enable NPS interpreters to hone their research, writing, and communication skills, the National Register has held several workshops at which NPS interpreters prepare lesson plans. By doing so, they develop skills that benefit the parks and add to their professional skills.[3]

By clarifying what within their jurisdiction is significant and why, National Register information assists Federal land managers as they administer their land, accommodate change in a manner respectful of historic places, and interpret the importance of historic places to the public.

Federal Financial Incentives

Owners of income-producing National Register properties may apply for federal investment tax credits for the rehabilitation of their properties. To date, this tax credit has spurred the revitalization of 25,000 buildings and $16 billion in private investment. Owners of properties listed in the National Register may be eligible for income and estate tax deductions for charitable contributions of partial interests in historic property (easements). Owners of National Register properties also may receive federal Historic Preservation Fund matching grants for restoration through state historic preservation offices, when they are available.

Many community organizations and owners make creative use of "layered funding" by combining National

In the White Rock Canyon Archeological District in Los Alamos County, New Mexico, 59 sites, each with petroglyphs, present information about centuries-old Anasazi and Tewa farming patterns. (Betty Lilienthal, 1991)

Register listing and historic preservation grants and tax incentives with Community Development Block Grants, local funding, foundation support, and special rate mortgage loans. For example, in Hardwick, Vermont, a combination of National Register listing, Historic Preservation Fund grants, federal preservation tax credits, and other federal financial incentives rehabilitated several buildings for use as housing for low– and moderate–income residents and revitalized the town's commercial center.

State and Local Governments Use the National Register

State and local governments actively use the National Register to preserve historic places. Describing historic places, documenting their significance, and registering them contribute important data to planning and decision making. The resulting information assists state and local governments in participating in Advisory Council on Historic Preservation review. The information also encourages citizens to take part in decisions about what to save as living parts of their communities and recognizes places that should be used in tourism and economic development. As Pamela Sterne King of the City of Birmingham, AL, observed:

... the National Register program has been a key—if not the key—component to effecting urban revitalization in Birmingham. Without it, historic buildings would not have been re-

habilitated and the essence of Birmingham preserved. In addition, National Register designations have provided a critical stimulus to neighborhoods and neighborhood leaders by helping them to access a wealth of community pride and, therefore, tackle even their most severe problems.[4]

Some states and localities use National Register listing as a basis for state or local historic preservation benefits and protection as in Arizona, which has a Historic Property Tax Reduction Program that provides for a 50 percent reduction in the real estate taxes for non-income-producing residential properties listed in the National Register.

National Register listing may precede local designation and serve as a precursor to local protection; or it may follow local designation and lend credibility to local decision making and affirm the goals of local preservationists and supportive politicians. Local governments also may incorporate information on historic places into municipal master plans. Based on a study of three local governments in Pennsylvania, Tanya M. Velt, a historian with the National Conference of State Historic Preservation Officers, summarized the contribution of the National Register program to local planning efforts:

National Register listing establishes an organizational infrastructure to guide local cultural resource management, compatible zoning and development planning, and historical and architectural review ordinances.[5]

Using the National Register and related governmental programs can enhance strong communities, transform de-

National Register Listings in Each State* (January 1, 1994)

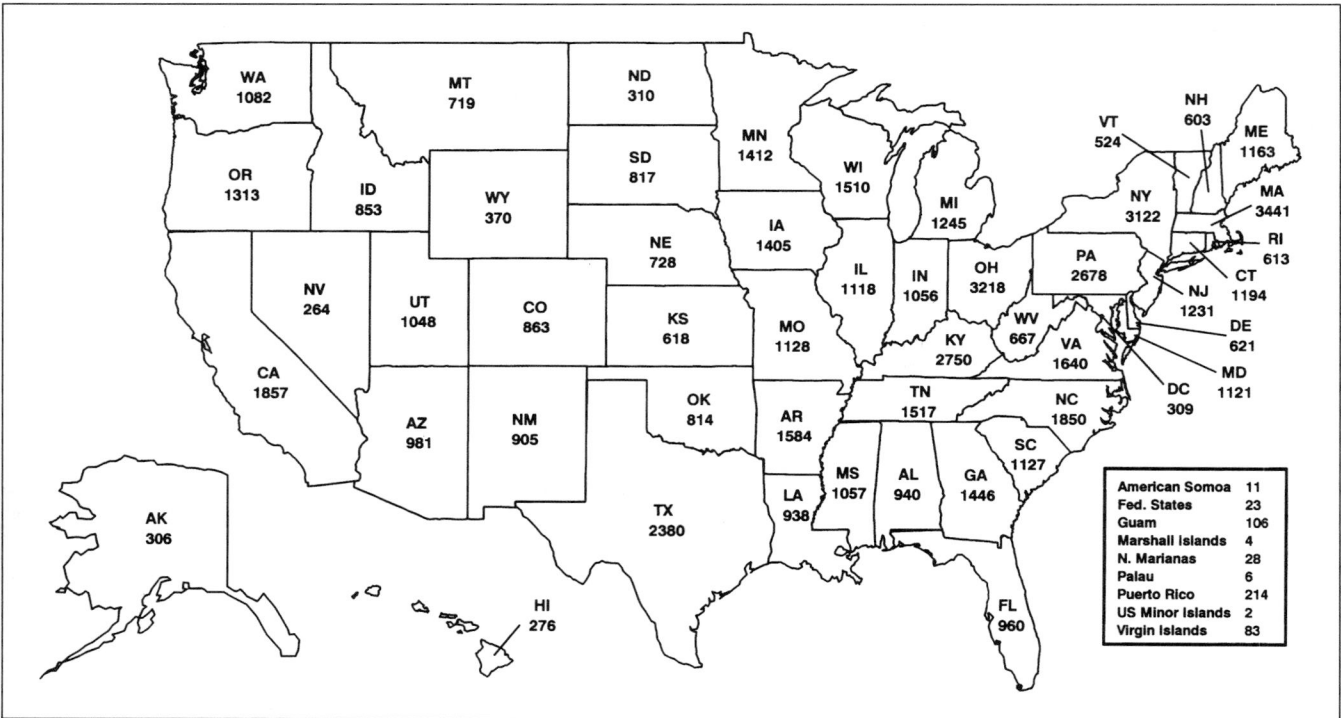

*Some properties may be counted multiple times because they are in more than one state.

Contributing Resources Included in National Register Listings in Each State (January 1, 1994)

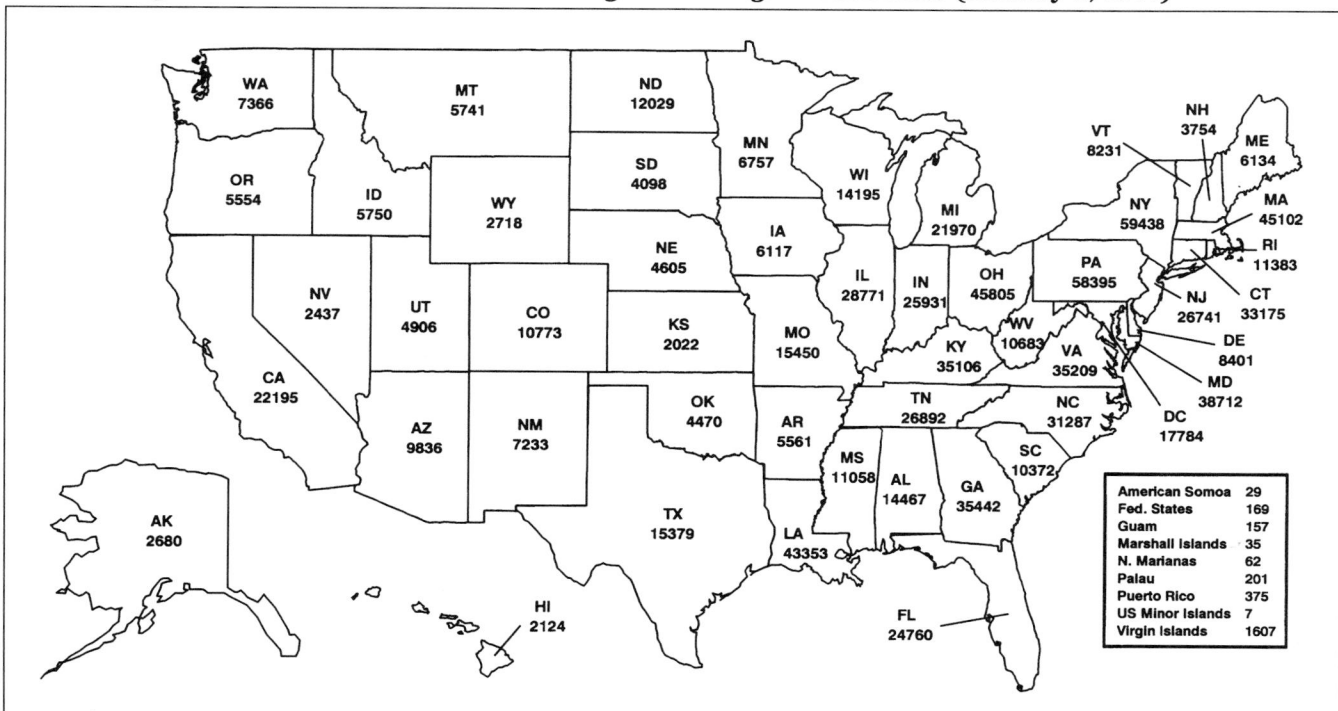

clining ones, and provide a strong sense of identity essential to the long-term health of communities. The community of Washington, Missouri, serves as a model of how a community develops a local historic preservation program: it conducted a survey of its downtown, has two districts listed in the National Register, developed a comprehensive plan for the downtown taking into account the National Register districts, and developed a design guidelines handbook. It also became a Certified Local Government, having adopted a local historic preservation ordinance, appointed a historical commission, initiated ongoing survey work, and held design and planning workshops. Since beginning this effort in the mid-1980s, Washington's downtown has experienced an economic revival.

G. Bernard Callan, Jr. of the National Alliance of Preservation Commissions summarized the role of the National Register for local governments:

> Local governments increasingly see National Register listing as more than a resource protection planning tool. It has become an economic development tool because it is frequently a requirement for local zoning advantages as well as federal, state, and local tax advantages. It has become a community development tool because it adds an increased sense of value to where people live and work.[6]

Historical Research Strategies

The scope of the National Register encourages the development of new research strategies and reinforces the

importance of studying state and local history. Places listed in the National Register and the documentation about them address such topics as the migration of cultural groups, the development of small railroad communities, and the evolution of educational facilities throughout a state. This kind of narrative history has a strong hold on the public's attention because it recasts community history into a collective and shared experience.

The establishment of the National Register coincided with the development of such new areas of historical research, as the study of local history, gender, ethnic and minority groups, and common, everyday life in the past. Historians also sought connections with other disciplines, such as anthropology, ethnography, and geography, to broaden the interpretation of historical data. For example, as Bernard L. Herman of the University of Delaware writes about the "new architectural history,"

> The National Register as a research strategy places buildings at the center of historical inquiry, and raises their significance from association with an individual, event, or style to their active role in signifying changing human relationships defined through interpretive categories such as class, ethnicity, occupation, environment, technology, and landscape. This is architectural history with a large agenda.[7]

An increasing number of historic preservation and applied history courses at the nation's colleges and universities are using the National Register. Students are introduced to the requirements of a National Register nomination, to sources and methods for conducting local

National Register Listings by Federal Agency

DEPARTMENT OF AGRICULTURE	22
Farmers Home Administration	3
Forest Service	594
Soil Conservation Service	2
DEPARTMENT OF COMMERCE	3
Economic Development Administration	1
DEPARTMENT OF DEFENSE	19
Air Force	41
Army	102
Army Corps of Engineers	170
Marine Corps	7
Navy	116
DEPARTMENT OF ENERGY	19
DEPARTMENT OF HEALTH AND HUMAN SERVICE	4
DEPARTMENT OF HOUSING AND URBAN DEVELOPMENT	7
DEPARTMENT OF THE INTERIOR	9
Bureau of Indian Affairs	31
Bureau of Land Management	328
Bureau of Mines	3
Bureau of Outdoor Recreation	1
Bureau of Reclamation	54
Fish and Wildlife Service	75
U.S. Geological Survey	1
National Park Service	1136
DEPARTMENT OF JUSTICE	4
DEPARTMENT OF LABOR	3
DEPARTMENT OF STATE	2
DEPARTMENT OF THE TREASURY	20
DEPARTMENT OF TRANSPORTATION	21
Coast Guard	295
DEPARTMENT OF VETERANS AFFAIRS	34
INDEPENDENT AGENCIES	
Federal Communications Commission	1
Federal Maritime Commission	1
General Services Administration	204
International Boundary & Water Commission	3
National Aeronautics & Space Administration	23
National Science Foundation	1
Nuclear Regulatory Commission	2
Small Business Administration	1
Smithsonian Institution	9
Tennessee Valley Authority	25
U.S. Postal Service	853
TOTAL FEDERAL AGENCY LISTINGS	4250

history research, and to the process of evaluating the significance of historic places. The results of the new research strategies are published in journals or in other publications and are making a major contribution to public appreciation of the American past.

Education and Interpretation

The power of historic places in relating the narrative history of the nation can transform established educational/interpretive systems. The National Register pro-gram already has played an important role in education at all levels. National Register documentation serves as the basis for the *Teaching with Historic Places* program of the National Park Service and the National Trust for Historic Preservation. *Teaching with Historic Places* is a heritage education program that develops educational materials to use in the classroom and trains teachers and preservationists to use historic places listed in the National Register to teach core curriculum requirements effectively; link the dramatic story of places to larger themes in history, social studies, and other subjects; and encourage basic and critical thinking skills.

John J. Patrick, professor of education at Indiana University and director of both the Social Studies Development Center and the Department of Education's ERIC Clearinghouse for Social Science/Social Education, has stated:

> There are prominent places or openings for content about historic places in the emerging social studies core curriculum exemplified by the National Standards Projects. Historic places are tangible forms of our legacy from preceding generations, and, like written primary sources, they embody and reflect the traditions, experiences, ideas, and controversies of our past.[8]

The National Register of Historic Places can be used to develop information on important historical themes and places them into the larger contexts of American history. For example, using the National Register Information System (NRIS) database and the Integrated Preservation Software (IPS), the National Park Service developed a book celebrating over 800 historic places listed in the National Register for associations with African American history, published by The Preservation Press of the National Trust for Historic Preservation. The publication can be used for a variety of educational and interpretive purposes, including the development of heritage trails linking such related historic places as African American colleges and universities and Civil Rights Movement locations.

National Register status confirms the significance of historic places and contributes to heritage tourism and interpretation efforts. Because historic places are increasingly popular travel destinations, tourism literature often notes when they are listed in the National Register. Appreciation of historic places leads to "sensitivity, awareness, understanding, appreciation, and commitment." As noted by Paul H. Risk, Director of the Center for Resource Communication and Interpretation, College of Forestry, at Stephen F. Austin State University in Nacogdoches, Texas:

> Cultural interpretation can provide a sense of regional and heritage pride which will enhance citizen concern, protection and preservation of resources, and give a sense of geographical awareness. Environmental, geographic, and his-

toric understanding helps us all become wholly integrated with the past, the present, and the future and it may be hoped, lessen the likelihood of remaking historic mistakes.[9]

Larry A. Kingsbury, forest archeologist and historian at the Payette National Forest, McCall, Idaho, cited the interpretive possibilities that resulted from the forest's efforts to live up to the letter and spirit of the 1966 Act. As an outgrowth of the forest's study of 19th century Chinese occupations and activities in the Warren Mining District and nomination of eligible properties to the National Register, the National Forest developed interpretive signs, exhibits, and publications. Chinese Americans and others have traveled from as far away as New York City and Hawaii to visit and learn about these National Register–listed historic places.[10]

How Are Places Listed in the National Register?

Although the National Register lists historic units of the National Park System and National Historic Landmarks, states and federal agencies nominate most places to the National Register. For the National Register program, the term "state" refers to the 50 states, the District of Columbia, American Samoa, Guam, Puerto Rico, the Virgin Islands, the freely associated states of Micronesia, and the Commonwealth of the Northern Mariana Islands. States nominate more than 93 percent and federal agencies approximately seven percent of the total.

Both states and federal agencies conduct surveys, identify historic resources, evaluate and document these places, and nominate eligible properties for National Register listing. Anyone may prepare a nomination and submit it to a state or federal historic preservation officer for consideration. Interested individuals should contact the appropriate State Historic Preservation Officer (see page ixx), or Federal Preservation Officer (see page xxvii) if the property is federally owned or controlled.

Nominations follow procedures described in National Register regulations 36 CFR 60. Nominating authorities notify property owners and public officials of proposed nominations and give owners of private property an opportunity to agree or object to a listing. For a state nomination, the state review board evaluates a property's significance and documentation, hears comments from interested parties, and recommends to the State Historic Preservation Officer whether or not to approve the nomination. The State Historic Preservation Officer then nominates the property on behalf of the state by forwarding the documentation to the National Park Service's National Register. If the property meets the criteria and owners have not objected, the National Register staff will list it. If the owner or the majority of owners of a privately

This house (ca. 1902) in the Fayetteville Historic District, West Virginia, was built for one of Fayette County's most outstanding citizens, Morris Harvey, who once served as the president of the Continental Divide Gold and Silver Company and whose philanthropy revitalized Barboursville College, now the Morris Harvey College of Arts and Sciences at the University of Charleston. (Courtney Proctor Cross, 1990)

owned property objects to the listing, the property may be found eligible for listing in the National Register, but not actually listed.

Nominations for historic places on federal land are prepared under the supervision of Federal Preservation Officers, who request the opinion of the appropriate State Historic Preservation Officers. The Federal Preservation Officer then may approve the nomination and forward it to the National Register.

Listing does **not** give the federal government control over private property. Private property owners can do anything they wish with their property subject to local land use controls, provided that no federal license, permit, or funding is involved. When there is federal involvement, the appropriate federal agency is responsible for giving the Advisory Council on Historic Preservation an opportunity to comment on the project and its effects on the property to ensure that historic and archeological properties are considered in the federal planning process. Owners have no obligation to open their properties to the

National Register of Historic Places Areas of Significance

Areas	Number	Percentage
Architecture	47744	76.8
Commerce	8058	12.9
Social History	6314	10.1
Politics/Government	6050	9.7
Industry	4631	7.4
Transportation	4464	7.1
Exploration/Settlement	4350	7.0
Education	3881	6.2
Agriculture	3378	5.4
Community Planning and Development	3346	5.3
Engineering	3181	5.1
Religion	2998	4.8
Prehistoric	2928	4.7
Military	2479	3.9
Art	1682	2.7
Landscape Architecture	1453	2.3
Historic—Non-Aboriginal	1315	2.1
Entertainment/Recreation	1255	2.0
Historic—Aboriginal	943	1.5
European	739	1.0
Black	677	1.0
Conservation	638	1.0
Communications	618	1.0
Law	538	<1.0
Literature	528	<1.0
Health/Medicine	513	<1.0
Economics	509	<1.0
Performing Arts	496	<1.0
Science	400	<1.0
Invention	362	<1.0
Native American	320	<1.0
Maritime History	316	<1.0
Other	145	<1.0
Hispanic	69	<1.0
Philosophy	59	<1.0
Asian	46	<1.0
Other—Ethnic	22	<1.0
Pacific-Islander	18	<1.0

public, to restore them, or even to maintain them, if they choose not to do so.

Local governments also play an important role in shaping the National Register. Of the more than 2,000 local governments that have preservation commissions today, more than 850 have become Certified Local Governments (CLGs). Certified Local Governments have a formal role in the National Register process, which includes commenting on the eligibility of properties to State Historic Preservation Officers and conducting surveys and preparing National Register nominations with grant assistance from state historic preservation offices.

The role of American Indian tribes, Alaska Native groups, and Native Hawaiian organizations in the National Register process was strengthened in several ways by the 1992 amendments to the 1966 Act. The Act now allows Indian tribes to assume any or all of the responsibilities of the State Historic Preservation Officer, including

the State Historic Preservation Officer's role in nominating properties on tribal lands to the National Register, if the Indian tribe's chief governing authority so requests and the tribe meets certain requirements in the Act. In addition, the Act now explicitly states that:

> Properties of traditional religious and cultural importance to an Indian tribe or Native Hawaiian organization may be determined to be eligible for inclusion on the National Register.

Many properties significant in the history of American Indians tribes, Alaska Native groups, and Native Hawaiians, such as schools, churches, community settlements, and traditional cultural properties already are listed in the National Register. Many more properties important to these groups will be listed or declared eligible, taking advantage of the new opportunities offered by the 1992 amendments. Both state and federal preservation officers must consult with these groups in assessing the cultural significance of properties and in determining whether to nominate such properties to the National Register.

How Can I Learn More About the National Register?

Each state historic preservation office and the National Park Service in Washington, D.C., keep on file detailed documentation on listed places. Every National Register nomination record includes a description of the current and historic appearance and condition of the place, a statement explaining its historical significance, maps, photographs, bibliography, and other information. Locations and other sensitive data about fragile resources are kept confidential.

Data on National Register properties also are automated in the National Register Information System (NRIS), maintained by the National Park Service. NRIS data offer profiles of National Register resources, information that can help in making planning decisions, researching topics related to the American landscape and our history, and developing educational and interpretive programs. The registration files themselves serve as important research resources.

To assist those engaged in identifying, evaluating, documenting, and registering historic places, the National Park Service produces the *National Register Bulletin* series of technical guidance. This series addresses such general questions as how to apply National Register criteria and how to complete registration forms, and also addresses the treatment of such specific types of resources as designed and rural landscapes, traditional cultural properties, mining properties, and historical archeological resources. The National Register continues to expand this series to cover other needed topics. To obtain copies of registration documentation, query the NRIS database, or

Structures are constructed for purposes other than housing human activities. This structure, a catwalk clinging to the cliff face of the Black Canyon (in the Lake Mead National Recreation Area, Nevada-Arizona), was designed to link two gauging stations responsible for measuring the Colorado River's flow in the 1930s. (William Tweed, 1976)

secure copies of *National Register Bulletins* or the National Register "starter kit," contact the National Register of Historic Places, Interagency Resources Division, National Park Service, P.O. Box 37127, Washington, D.C. 20013-7127; (202) 343-9559; FAX: (202) 343-1836. *Teaching with Historic Places* literature and an order form describing available lesson plans are available from The Preservation Press, National Trust for Historic Preservation, 1785

Massachusetts Avenue, N.W., Washington, DC 20036 (202) 673-4058 or 800-766-6847.

Information about historic places and copies of National Register nominations in each state may be obtained from the appropriate State Historic Preservation Officer (see page xxi) or from the National Register of Historic Places (see address in previous paragraph). Registration documentation, grouped by state, also is available on microfiche from Chadwyck-Healey, Inc., 1101 King Street, Suite 380, Alexandria, Virginia 22314, (800) 752-0515; FAX: (703) 683-7589.

Many places listed in the National Register also have been documented by the National Park Service's Historic American Buildings Survey/Historic American Engineering Record (HABS/HAER). To date, this program has recorded approximately 25,000 historic buildings and structures through measured drawings, photographs, and written documentation. The collections are available from the Prints and Photographs Division, Library of Congress, First and Independence Avenue, N.W., Washington, D.C. 20540.

What Information is Contained in This Book?

This volume includes all properties listed in the National Register of Historic Places between October 15, 1966 and December 31, 1993. It does not contain properties that have been determined eligible for the National Register but are not yet listed. Places are organized alphabetically by state, county, and property name. Each entry gives the following information:

1. property name as recorded in the National Register;
2. name of the multiple property submission with which the property was nominated, if applicable (MPS = Multiple Property Submission; MRA = Multiple Resource Area; TR = Thematic Resource); (Multiple property nominations were created to facilitate the nomination of groups of related properties in a defined area.)
3. address, if applicable;
4. town or vicinity;
5. date the property was listed in the National Register;
6. National Register criterion(ia) for which the property was accepted, in upper case lettering (A,B,C,D);
7. National Register criteria exception(s), if applicable, in lower case lettering (a,b,c,d,e,f,g);
8. identification of National Park Service properties and National Historic Landmarks, if applicable (NPS or NHL);

Sculptures like this playful Trachedon at Dinosaur Park near Rapid City, South Dakota, are classified as objects for National Register purposes. (John Rau, 1987)

9. the property's National Register Information System (NRIS) computer reference number (e.g. 89001385).

This volume also includes comprehensive lists of all State Historic Preservation Officers and Federal Preservation Officers.

Who Produced This Book?

The **National Park Service's** Interagency Resources Division administers the National Register of Historic Places for the Secretary of the Interior. The Interagency Resources Division houses all National Register registration forms, photographs, and maps, and manages the computer records of the National Register Information System. In addition, the Interagency Resources Division supports cultural resource survey and planning activities; directs the Certified Local Government program, the Micronesian preservation programs, the Tribal preservation programs, and the American Battlefield Protection Program; manages the National Park Service's Cultural Resources Geographic Information System; and directs pol-

icies by which the states and federal agencies fulfill their federal preservation responsibilities.

The **National Trust for Historic Preservation** published this book through its Preservation Press. The National Trust is the nation's leading private, non-profit preservation organization. Its mission is to encourage public participation in the preservation of sites, buildings, and objects significant in American history and culture.

The **National Conference of State Historic Preservation Officers** is the association of gubernatorially-appointed state officials who carry out the national historic preservation program in each state on behalf of the Secretary of the Interior and the National Park Service.

Notes

1. Quoted in David S. Gillespie, "Unlocking the Past: The National Register in New York." In *CRM: Using the National Register of Historic Places*, edited by Antoinette J. Lee and Tanya M. Velt, page 16. Washington, DC: U.S. Department of the Interior, National Park Service, 1994.

2. Marcella Sherfy, "Praise and Recognition: The National Register in Montana." In *CRM: Using the National Register of Historic Places*, pages 15, 20.

3. Edwin C. Bearss, "From Skeptic to Believer." In *CRM: Using the National Register of Historic Places*, pages 21–22.

4. Pamela Sterne King, Historic Preservation Planner, Department of Urban Planning, City of Birmingham, AL, to Chief of Registration, National Register of Historic Places, Interagency Resources Division, National Park Service, August 3, 1993.

5. Tanya M. Velt, Personal Communication, May 5, 1994.

6. G. Bernard Callan, Jr., Personal Communication, May 27, 1994.

7. Bernard L. Herman, "The New Architectural History." In *CRM: Using the National Register of Historic Places*, pages 6–7.

8. John J. Patrick, "Prominent Places for Historic Places: K–12 Social Studies Curriculum." In *CRM: Teaching With Historic Places*, edited by Beth Boland, pages 8–9. Washington, DC: U.S. Department of the Interior, National Park Service, 1993.

9. Paul H. Risk, "Interpretation: A Road to Creative Enlightenment." In *CRM: Using the National Register of Historic Places*, pages 37, 40.

10. Lawrence A. Kingsbury, "Chinese Properties Listed in the National Register: A Forest Service Initiative." In *CRM: Using the National Register of Historic Places*, pages 23, 25.

National Register Criteria for Evaluation

The quality of significance in American history, architecture, archeology, engineering and culture is present in districts, sites, buildings, structures, and objects that posess integrity of location, design, setting, materials, workmanship, feeling, and association, and:

A. that are associated with events that have made a significant contribution to the broad patterns of our history; or

B. that are associated with the lives of persons significant in our past; or

C. that embody the distinctive characteristics of a type, period, or method of construction, or that represent the work of a master, or that possess high artistic values, or that represent a significant and distinguishable entity whose components may lack individual distinction; or

D. that have yielded or may be likely to yield information important in prehistory or history.

Criteria Exceptions

Ordinarily, cemeteries, birthplaces or graves of historical figures, properties owned by religious institutions or used for religious purposes, structures that have been moved from their original locations, reconstructed historic buildings, properties primarily commemorative in nature, and properties that have achieved significance within the last fifty years shall not be considered eligible for the National Register. However, such properties will qualify if they are integral parts of districts that do meet the criteria or if they fall within the following categories:

a. a religious property deriving significance from architectural or artistic distinction or historical importance; or

b. a building or structure removed from its original location, but which is significant primarily for architectural value, or which is the surviving structure most importantly associated with a particular person or event; or

c. a birthplace or grave of a historical figure of outstanding importance if there is no other appropriate site or building directly associated with his productive life; or

d. a cemetery that derives its primary significance from graves of persons of transcendent importance, from age, from distinctive design features, or from association with historic events; or

e. a reconstructed building when accurately executed in a suitable environment and presented in a dignified manner as part of a restoration master plan, and when no other building or structure with the same association has survived; or

f. a property primarily commemorative in intent if design, age, tradition, or symbolic value has invested it with its own historical significance; or

g. a property achieving significance within the past fifty years if it is of exceptional importance.

Illinois (IL)

Mr. William L. Wheeler
Associate Director
Illinois Historic Preservation Agency
1 Old State Capitol Plaza
Springfield, Illinois 62701-1512
(217) 785-1153
FAX: (217) 524-7525

Indiana (IN)

Mr. Patrick R. Ralston
Director
Department of Natural Resources
402 West Washington Street
Indiana Government Center South,
    Room W256
Indianapolis, Indiana 46204
(317) 232-4020
FAX: (317) 232-8036

Iowa (IA)

Mr. David E. Crosson
Administrator
State Historical Society of Iowa
Capitol Complex
East 6th and Locust Streets
Des Moines, Iowa 50319
(515) 281-8837
FAX: (515) 242-0560

Kansas (KS)

Dr. Ramon S. Powers
Executive Director
Kansas State Historical Society
120 West 10th Street
Topeka, Kansas 66612
(913) 296-3251
FAX: (913) 296-1005

Kentucky (KY)

Mr. David L. Morgan
Executive Director
Kentucky Heritage Council
300 Washington Street
Frankfort, Kentucky 40601
(502) 564-7005
FAX: (502) 564-5820

Louisiana (LA)

Ms. Gerri J. Hobdy
Assistant Secretary
Office of Cultural Development
Department of Culture, Recreation and
    Tourism
P.O. Box 44247
Baton Rouge, Louisiana 70804
(504) 342-8200
FAX: (504) 342-8173

Maine (ME)

Mr. Earle G. Shettleworth, Jr.
Director
Maine Historic Preservation
    Commission
55 Capitol Street, Station 65
Augusta, Maine 04333-0065
(207) 287-2132
FAX: (207) 287-2335

Marshall Islands, Republic of the (RMI)

Ms. Carmen Bigler
Secretary of Interior and Outer Islands
    Affairs
P.O. Box 1454
Majuro Atoll
Republic of the Marshall Islands 96960
011-692-625-3413/3240/3264
FAX: 011-692-625-5353

Maryland (MD)

Mr. J. Rodney Little
Director of Historical and Cultural
    Programs
Department of Housing and Community
    Development
100 Community Place, Third Floor
Crownsville, Maryland 21032-2023
(410) 514-7600
FAX: (410) 514-7678

Massachusetts (MA)

Ms. Judith B. McDonough
Executive Director
Massachusetts Historical Commission
80 Boylston Street, Suite 310
Boston, Massachusetts 02116
(617) 727-8470
FAX: (617) 727-5128

Michigan (MI)

Dr. Kathryn B. Eckert
State Historic Preservation Officer
Michigan Historical Center
717 West Allegan Street
Lansing, Michigan 48918
(517) 373-0511
FAX: (517) 373-0851

Micronesia, Federated States (FSM)

Mrs. SeNellie P. Singeo
Historic Preservation Officer
Office of Administrative Services
Division of Archives and Historic
    Preservation
FSM National Government
P.O. Box PS 35
Palikir, Pohnpei, FSM 96941
011-691-320-2343
FAX: (691) 320-2597

*Includes four states, whose Historic
Preservation Officers are listed below:*

Mr. Andrew Kugfras
Yap SHPO
Office of the Governor
Colonia, Yap, FSM
W. Caroline Islands 96943
011-691-350-2194/2255
FAX: 691-350-2381

Mr. Elvis Killion O'Sonis
Chuuk SHPO
Department of Resources and
    Development
Moen, Chuuk, FSM
E. Caroline Islands 96942
011-691-330-3309
FAX: 691-330-2232

Mr. Yasuo I. Yamada
Director
Department of Land
Pohnpei State Government
P.O. Box 158
Kolonia, Pohnpei, FSM
E. Caroline Islands 96941
011-691-320-2715
FAX: 011-691-320-5706

Mr. Berlin Sigrah
Administrator
Division of History and Cultural
    Preservation
Department of Conservation and
    Development
Kosrae, FSM
E. Caroline Islands 96944
011-691-370-3078
FAX: 011-691-370-3003

Minnesota (MN)

Dr. Nina M. Archabal
Director
Minnesota Historical Society
345 Kellogg Boulevard West
St. Paul, Minnesota 55102-1906
(612) 296-2747
FAX: (612) 296-1004

Mississippi (MS)

Mr. Elbert Hilliard
Director
Mississippi Department of Archives and
    History
P.O. Box 571
Jackson, Mississippi 39205-0571
(601) 359-6850
FAX: (601) 359-6955

Missouri (MO)

Mr. David A. Shorr
Director
Department of Natural Resources
205 Jefferson
P.O. Box 176
Jefferson City, Missouri 65102
(314) 751-4422
FAX: (314) 526-2852

Montana (MT)

Ms. Marcella Sherfy
State Historic Preservation Officer
State Historic Preservation Office
1410 8th Avenue
P.O. Box 201202
Helena, Montana 59620-1202
(406) 444-7715
FAX: (406) 444-6575

Nebraska (NE)

Mr. Lawrence Sommer
Director
Nebraska State Historical Society
P.O. Box 82554
Lincoln, Nebraska 68501
(402) 471-4787
FAX: (402) 471-3100

Nevada (NV)

Mr. Ronald M. James
Supervisor
Historic Preservation Office
101 South Stewart Street
Capitol Complex
Carson City, Nevada 89710
(702) 687-6360

New Hampshire (NH)

Ms. Nancy Muller
Director
Division of Historical Resources
19 Pillsbury Street
P.O. Box 2043
Concord, New Hampshire 03302-2043
(603) 271-3483
FAX: (603) 271-3433

New Jersey (NJ)

Mr. Scott A. Weiner
Commissioner
Department of Environmental
    Protection and Energy
CN-402, 401 East State Street
Trenton, New Jersey 08625
(609) 292-2885
FAX: (609) 292-7695

New Mexico (NM)

Mr. Michael Romero Taylor
Director
Historic Preservation Division
Office of Cultural Affairs
Villa Rivera
228 E. Palace Avenue
Santa Fe, New Mexico 87503
(505) 827-6320
FAX: (505) 827-6338

New York (NY)

Ms. Joan K. Davidson
State Historic Preservation Officer
Office of Parks, Recreation and Historic
    Preservation
Agency Building #1, Empire State Plaza
Albany, New York 12238
(518) 474-0443
FAX: (518) 474-4492

North Carolina (NC)

Dr. William S. Price, Jr.
Director
Department of Cultural Resources
Division of Archives & History
109 East Jones Street
Raleigh, North Carolina 27601-2807
(919) 733-7305
FAX: (919) 733-8807

North Dakota (ND)

Mr. James E. Sperry
State Historic Preservation Officer
State Historical Society of North Dakota
North Dakota Heritage Center
612 E. Boulevard Avenue
Bismarck, North Dakota 58505
(701) 224-2667
FAX: (701) 224-3710

Northern Mariana Islands, Commonwealth of the (CM)

Mr. Michael A. Fleming
Historic Preservation Officer
Department of Community and Cultural
    Affairs
Northern Mariana Islands
Saipan, Mariana Islands 96950
011-670-233-9722/9556
FAX: 011-670-233-4058/5096

Ohio (OH)

Dr. W. Ray Luce
State Historic Preservation Officer
Ohio Historic Preservation Office
Ohio Historical Center
1982 Velma Avenue
Columbus, Ohio 43211-2497
(614) 297-2470
FAX: (614) 297-2546

Oklahoma (OK)

Mr. J. Blake Wade
Executive Director
Oklahoma Historical Society
2100 N. Lincoln Blvd.
Wiley Post Historical Building
Oklahoma City, Oklahoma 73105
(405) 521-2491
FAX: (405) 525-3272

Oregon (OR)

Mr. Robert L. Meinen
Director
State Parks and Recreation Department
1115 Commercial Street, N.E.
Salem, Oregon 97310-1001
(503) 378-5019
FAX: (503) 378-6447

Palau, Republic of

Ms. Victoria N. Kanai
Chief of Cultural Affairs
Ministry of Community and Cultural
    Affairs
P.O. Box 100
Koror, Republic of Palau 96940
011-680-488-2489
FAX: 011-680-488-1725/1662

Pennsylvania (PA)

Dr. Brent D. Glass
Executive Director
Pennsylvania Historical & Museum
    Commission
P.O. Box 1026
Harrisburg, Pennsylvania 17108
(717) 787-2891
FAX: (717) 783-1073

Puerto Rico, Commonwealth of (PR)

Dr. Arleen Pabón
State Historic Preservation Officer
Office of Historic Preservation
P.O. Box 82, La Fortaleza
San Juan, Puerto Rico 00901
(809) 721-2676/3737
FAX: (809) 723-0957

Rhode Island (RI)

Mr. Frederick C. Williamson
State Historic Preservation Officer
Rhode Island Historical Preservation
    Commission
Old State House
150 Benefit Street
Providence, Rhode Island 02903
(401) 277-2678
FAX: (401) 277-2968

South Carolina (SC)

Dr. George L. Vogt
Director
Department of Archives & History
P.O. Box 11669
Columbia, South Carolina 29211
(803) 734-8609
FAX: (803) 734-8820

South Dakota (SD)

Dr. Junius R. Fishburne
Director
South Dakota Historical Society
Cultural Heritage Center
900 Governors Drive
Pierre, South Dakota 57501
(605) 773-3458
FAX: (605) 773-6041

Tennessee (TN)

Mr. J. W. Luna
Commissioner
Department of Environment and
    Conservation
401 Church Street
L&C Tower 21st Floor
Nashville, Tennessee 37243-0435
(615) 532-0109
FAX: (615) 532-0120

Texas (TX)

Mr. Curtis Tunnell
Executive Director
Texas Historical Commission
P.O. Box 12276
Austin, Texas 78711-2276
(512) 463-6100
FAX: (512) 463-6095

Utah (UT)

Mr. Max J. Evans
Director
Utah State Historical Society
300 Rio Grande
Salt Lake City, Utah 84101
(801) 533-3500
FAX: (801) 533-3503

Vermont (VT)

Mr. Robert Martin
State Historic Preservation Officer
Agency of Development and
    Community Affairs
135 State Street, 4th Floor
Drawer 33
Montpelier, Vermont 05633-1201
(802) 828-3211
FAX: (802) 828-3206

Virgin Islands (VI)

Mr. Roy E. Adams
Commissioner
Department of Planning and Natural
    Resources
Suite 231, Nisky Center
No. 45A Estate Nisky
St. Thomas, Virgin Islands 00802
(809) 774-3320

Virginia (VA)

Mr. H. Alexander Wise, Jr.
Director
Department of Historic Resources
Commonwealth of Virginia
221 Governor Street
Richmond, Virginia 23219
(804) 786-3143
FAX: (804) 225-4261

Washington (WA)

Ms. Mary Thompson
Director
Office of Archeology & Historic
    Preservation
111 West 21st Avenue, KL-11
Olympia, Washington 98504
(206) 753-4011
FAX: (206) 586-0250

West Virginia (WV)

Mr. William M. Drennen, Jr.
Commissioner
West Virginia Division of Culture &
    History
Historic Preservation Office
1900 Kanawha Boulevard East
Charleston, West Virginia 25305-0300
(304) 558-0220
FAX: (304) 558-2779

Wisconsin (WI)

Mr. Jeff Dean
Director
Historic Preservation Division
State Historical Society of Wisconsin
816 State Street
Madison, Wisconsin 53706
(608) 264-6500
FAX: (608) 264-6404

Wyoming (WY)

Mr. John Keck
State Historic Preservation Officer
Wyoming State Historic Preservation
　Office
4th Floor Barrett Building
2301 Central Avenue
Cheyenne, Wyoming 82002
(307) 777-7697
FAX: (307) 777-6421

Federal Preservation Officers

Representatives with an asterisk * by their names have been designated by their department or agency as the authority to approve National Register nominations.

Agriculture, Department of

Agricultural Stabilization and Conservation Service

*Mr. James R. McMullen
Director
Conservation and Environmental
    Protection Division
Agricultural Stabilization and
    Conservation Service
P.O. Box 2415
Washington, D.C. 20013
(202) 720-6221

Farmers Home Administration

*Ms. Susan G. Wieferich
Senior Environmental Specialist
Farmers Home Administration
Room 6303
14th Street and Independence Avenue,
    S.W.
Washington, D.C. 20250
(202) 720-9619

Forest Service

*Mr. Evan I. DeBloois
Historic Preservation Officer
Forest Service
Auditors' Building
4 Central, P.O. Box 96090
Washington, D.C. 20090-6090
(202) 205-1427

Rural Electrification Administration

*Mr. Lawrence R. Wolfe
Environmental Policy Specialist
Electric Staff Division
Rural Electrification Administration
Room 1269
14th Street and Independence Avenue,
    S.W.
Washington, D.C. 20250
(202) 720-5093

Soil Conservation Service

*Mr. Michael J. Kaczor
National Archeologist
Economics and Social Sciences
    Division
U.S.D.A. Soil Conservation Service
P.O. Box 2890
Washington, D.C. 20013-2890
(202) 720-2307

Commerce, Department of

*Mr. Roger Jarrell
Chief
National Program Division
Office of Federal Property Programs
Department of Commerce
Room 1329
14th Street and Constitution Avenue,
    N.W.
Washington, D.C. 20230
(202) 482-6075

Economic Development Administration

*Mr. Frank Monteferrante
Associate Director of Environment
Economic Development Administration
Room 7019, Herbert Hoover Building
14th Street and Constitution Avenue,
    N.W.
Washington, D.C. 20230
(202) 482-4208

National Oceanic and Atmospheric Administration

*Mr. Joseph A. Uravitch
Chief
Sanctuaries and Reserves
Office of Ocean and Coastal Resource
    Management
National Oceanic and Atmospheric
    Administration
1305 East-West Highway
Silver Spring, Maryland 20901
(301) 713-3155

Defense, Department of

Air Force

*Mr. Allen P. Babbitt
Acting Deputy Assistant Secretary
Environment Safety and Occupational
    Health
SAF/MIQ
Room 5C 916, The Pentagon
Washington, D.C. 20330-1600
(703) 697-9297

Army

*Ms. Constance Werner-Ramirez
Historic Preservation Officer
Department of the Army
U.S. Army Engineering and Housing
    Support Center
Attn: CEHSC-FN
Fort Belvoir, Virginia 22060-5516
(703) 704-1570

Army Corps of Engineers

*Mr. William Klesch
Chief
Office of Environmental Policy
CECW-PO
U.S. Army Corps of Engineers
Pulaski Building
20 Massachusetts Avenue, N.W.
Washington, D.C. 20314-1000
(202) 272-0166

Navy and Marine Corps

*Dr. John Bernard Murphy
Navy Federal Preservation Officer
Office of the Assistant Secretary of the
    Navy
(Installations and Environment)
Washington, D.C. 20360-5000
(703) 602-2687

Education, Department of

Mr. Donald J. Fork
Coordinator
LSCA Title II
(OERI/LP/PLSS)
Department of Education
555 New Jersey Avenue, N.W.
Washington, D.C. 20208-1430
(202) 219-1312

Energy, Department of

Ms. Lois M. Thompson
Office of Environmental Guidance
  (EH-23)
Department of Energy
1000 Independence Avenue, S.W.
Washington, D.C. 20585
(202) 586-9581

Federal Energy Regulatory Commission

*Ms. Lois D. Campbell
Acting Secretary
Federal Energy Regulatory Commission
825 North Capitol Street, N.E.
Washington, D.C. 20426
(202) 208-0400

Health and Human Services, Department of

*Mr. Scott M. Waldman
Historic Preservation Officer
Department of Health and Human
  Services
Room 4714, Cohen Building
330 Independence Avenue, S.W.
Washington, D.C. 20201
(202) 619-0426

National Institutes of Health

*Mr. Ricardo C. Herring, AIA
National Institues of Health
Facilities Planning Office
Building 13, Room 2W48
Bethesda, Maryland 20892
(301) 496-5037

Housing and Urban Development, Department of

*Mr. Richard H. Broun
Director
Office of Environment and Energy
Department of Housing and Urban
  Development
Room 7240
451 Seventh Street, S.W.
Washington, D.C. 20410
(202) 708-2894

Interior, Department of

Bureau of Indian Affairs

*Mr. George Farris
Chief
Environmental Services
Office of Trust and Economic
  Development
Bureau of Indian Affairs
Department of the Interior
Room 4525-MIB
18th and C Streets, N.W.
Washington, D.C. 20245
(202) 208-4791

Bureau of Land Management

*Mr. John G. Douglas
Senior Archeologist
Bureau of Land Management (340)
Room 3360
18th and C Streets, N.W.
Washington, D.C. 20240
(202) 452-0330

Bureau of Reclamation

Mr. Ed Friedman
Bureau of Reclamation
Ecological Resources Division
Denver Office
P.O. Box 25007, D5650
Denver, Colorado 80225-0007
(303) 236-8098

Fish and Wildlife Service

*Mr. David L. Olsen
Assistant Director
Refuges and Wildlife
Fish and Wildlife Service
MS 3246-MIB
18th and C Streets, N.W.
Washington, D.C. 20240
(202) 208-5333

Minerals Management Service

*Ms. Melanie Stright
Archeologist
Branch of Environmental Operations
  and Analysis
Minerals Management Service
Mail Stop 4360, 381 Elden Street
Herndon, Virginia 22070
(703) 787-1736

National Park Service

*Mr. Edwin C. Bearss
Chief
History Division (418)
National Park Service
P.O. Box 37127
Washington, D.C. 22013-7127
(202) 343-8167

Office of Surface Mining

*Ms. Suzanne Hudak
Policy Analyst
Division of Regulatory Programs
Office of Surface Mining
1951 Constitution Avenue, N.W.
Washington, D.C. 20240
(202) 208-2700

Territorial and International Affairs

Ms. Nancy L. Fanning
Director
Territorial Liaisons
Room 4318
Territorial and International Affairs
Department of the Interior
Washington, D.C. 20240
(202) 208-6816

U.S. Geological Survey

*Mr. Norman E. Wingard
Environmental Affairs Program
U.S. Geological Survey
National Center, Mail Stop 423
12201 Sunrise Valley Dive
Reston,Virginia 22092
(703) 648-6828

Justice, Department of

*Mr. Bill Lawrence
Deputy Assistant Director
Justice Building Services
Department of Justice
Suite 2226, Ariel Rios Building
12th Street and Pennsylvania Avenue,
  N.W.
Washington, D.C. 20530
(202) 616-2417

Labor, Department of

*Mr. Michael F. O'Malley
Architect
Division of Administrative Services
Department of Labor
Room C-4513
200 Constitution Avenue, N.W.
Washington, D.C. 20210
(202) 535-8710

State, Department of

*Mr. James R. Slager
A/OPR/RPM/DC
Office of Real Property
Office of Operations
Department of State
Room 1878
2201 C Street, N.W.
Washington, D.C. 20520
(202) 736-7170

Transportation, Department of

*Mr. Stephen M. Shapiro
Historic Preservation Officer
Environmental Division (P-14)
Office of Transportation Regulatory
    Affairs
Department of Transportation
400 Seventh Street, S.W.
Washington, D.C. 20590
(202) 366-4866

Federal Aviation Administration

*Ms. Laurette V. Fisher
Environmental Specialist
Policy and Regulatory Division
Office of Environment (AEE-300)
Federal Aviation Administration
Room 432
800 Independence Avenue, S.W.
Washington, D.C. 20591
(202) 267-3561

Federal Highway Administration

*Mr. Charles Des Jardins
Chief
Environmental Quality Branch, HEP-42
Federal Highway Administration
400 Seventh Street, S.W.
Washington, DC 20590
(202) 366-9173

Federal Railroad Administration

*Ms. Marilyn Klein
Office of Policy
Room 8302, RRP-32
Department of Transportation
400 Seventh Street, S.W.
Washington, D.C. 20590
(202) 366-0358

Federal Transit Administration

*Mr. Don Emerson
Federal Transit Administration
Department of Transportation (TGM-22)
400 Seventh Street, S.W.
Washington, D.C. 20590
(202) 366-0096

U.S. Coast Guard

Mr. Thomas J. Granito
Chief
Environmental Section (G-ECV-2B)
Room 6109
Civil Engineering Division
U.S. Coast Guard
2100 Second Street, S.W.
Washington, D.C. 20593
(202) 267-1941

Treasury, Department of

*Mr. William M. McGovern
Environmental Programs Officer
Treasury Department Annex Building
Room 6140
Washington, D.C. 20220
(202) 622-0043

Veterans Affairs, Department of

*Ms. Karen Ronne Tupek
Historic Preservation Officer
Historic Preservation Office (086B)
Department of Veterans Affairs
810 Vermont Avenue, N.W.
Washington, D.C. 20420
(202) 233-3447

Independent Agencies

Environmental Protection Agency

*Mr. John Gerba
NEPD-EIA Specialist
Office of Enforcement
Office of Federal Activities (A-104)
Environmental Protection Agency
Waterside Mall, S.W.
Washington, D.C. 20460
(202) 382-5910

Federal Communications Commission

*Ms. Ava H. (Holly) Berland
Office of the General Counsel
Federal Communications Commission
Room 616
1919 M Street, N.W.
Washington, D.C. 20554
(202) 254-6530

Federal Deposit Insurance Corporation

*Mr. Stanley J. Poling
Director
Division of Supervision
Room 5028
Federal Deposit Insurance Corporation
550 17th Street, N.W.
Washington, D.C. 20429
(202) 898-6944

Federal Housing Finance Board

*Mr. Richard Tucker
Federal Housing Finance Board
Housing Finance Directorate
1777 F Street, N.W.
Washington, D.C. 20006
(202) 408-2848

Federal Emergency Management Agency

Mr. Alfred E. Warren
Chief
Records and Information Systems
    Management Division
Federal Emergency Management
    Agency
Room 316
500 C Street, S.W.
Washington, D.C. 20472
(202) 646-2641

General Services Administration

*Mr. Dale M. Lanzone
Director
Arts and Historic Preservation (PGA)
Public Buildings Service
General Services Administration
Room 1300
18th and F Streets, N.W.
Washington, D.C. 20405
(202) 501-1256

Interstate Commerce Commission

Ms. Elaine Kaiser
Chief
Section of Energy and Environment
Interstate Commerce Commission
12th and Constitution Avenue, N.W.
Washington, D.C. 20423
(202) 927-6248

Library of Congress

Mr. Alan Jabbour
American Folklife Center
Library of Congress
Washington, D.C. 20540-8100
(202) 707-6590

Metropolitan Washington Airports Authority

Mr. Frank D. Holly, Jr.
Metropolitan Washington Airports
    Authority
Engineering Division, MWAA
Washington National Airport
Washington, D.C. 20001-4901
(202) 685-8151

National Aeronautics and Space Administration

*Mr. Kenneth Kumor
Facilities Engineering Division
Code JXG, NASA Headquarters
Two Independence Square, S.W.
Washington, D.C. 20546
(202) 358-1112

National Capital Planning Commission

*Ms. Margot Stephenson
Historic Preservation Architect
National Capital Planning Commission
801 Pennsylvania Avenue, N.W.
Suite 301
Washington, D.C. 20576
(202) 724-0174

National Endowment for the Arts

*Ms. Karen L. Elias
National Endowment for the Arts
1100 Pennsylvania Avenue, N.W.
Room 522
Washington, D.C. 20506
(202) 682-5418

National Endowment for the Humanities

Ms. Bonnie Gould
National Endowment for the
    Humanities
1100 Pennsylvania Avenue, N.W.
Room 429
Washington, D.C. 20506
(202) 606-8358

National Science Foundation

Mr. George Mazuzan
Historian
Legislative Affairs Office
National Science Foundation
4201 Wilson Boulevard
Room 1245
Arlington, Virginia 22230
(703) 306-1070

Nuclear Regulatory Commission

*Ms. Hazel I. Smith
Nuclear Regulatory Commission
Mail Stop P1-22
One White Flint North
11555 Rockville Pike
Rockville, Maryland 20852
(301) 504-2075

Office of Personnel Management

*Mr. Jack L. Finglass
Agency Architect
Office of Personnel Management
Washington, D.C. 20415-0001
(202) 606-1703

Pennsylvania Avenue Development Corporation

*Ms. Jan Franklina
Historic Preservation Officer
Pennsylvania Avenue Development
    Corporation
Suite 1220 North
1331 Pennsylvania Avenue, N.W.
Washington, D.C. 20004
(202) 724-9091

Small Business Administration

*Ms. Annie McCluney
Office of Portfolio Management
Small Business Administration
409 Third Street, S.W.
Washington, D.C. 20416
(202) 205-6481

Smithsonian Institution

*Dr. Cynthia Field
Director
Office of Architectural History and
    Historic Preservation
Smithsonian Institution (A&I-2225)
Washington, D.C. 20560
(202) 357-2064

Tennessee Valley Authority

*Mr. Norman A. Zigrossi
President
Resource Group
400 West Summit Hill Drive
Knoxville, Tennessee 37902-1499
(615) 632-4765

U.S. Postal Service

*Mr. John S. Sorenson
Program Manager
Historic Preservation
U.S. Postal Service
Customer Service Facilities
475 L'Enfant Plaza
Washington, D.C. 20260-6235
(202) 268-3107

NATIONAL

of Historic Places 1966 to 1994

REGISTER

ALABAMA

Autauga County

Daniel Pratt Historic District, Roughly bounded by Northington Rd., 1st, 6th, Bridge, and Court Sts., Prattville, 8/30/84, A, B, C, 84000596

Montgomery—Janes—Whittaker House, S of Prattville off AL 14, Prattville vicinity, 10/25/74, C, 74000396

Baldwin County

Allen House [Creole and Gulf Coast Cottages in Baldwin County TR], Off CR 10 on N bank of Bon Secour River, Bon Secour, 12/20/88, C, 88002809

Bank of Fairhope [Fairhope MRA], 396 Fairhope Ave., Fairhope, 7/01/88, A, C, 88001008

Battles Wharf Historic District, US 98, Eastern Shore Blvd. roughly between Woolworth Ave. and Buerger La., Battles Wharf, 4/28/88, A, C, 88000107

Beckner House [Fairhope MRA], 63 S. Church St., Fairhope, 7/01/88, C, 88001007

Blakeley, Address Restricted, Bridgehead vicinity, 6/25/74, D, 74000397

Bloxham, Carl L., Building [Fairhope MRA], 327 Fairhope Ave., Fairhope, 6/30/88, C, g, 88001005

Bottle Creek Indian Mounds, Address Restricted, Stockton vicinity, 12/02/74, D, a, 74000398

Brodbeck—Zundel Historic District, US 98 Scenic Route and Old Marlow Rd., Point Clear, 4/28/88, C, 88000520

Captain Adams House [Creole and Gulf Coast Cottages in Baldwin County TR], 907 Captain O'Neal Dr., Daphne, 12/20/88, C, 88002810

Cullum, George W., House, 1915 Old County Rd., Daphne, 6/14/90, C, 90000930

Fairhope Bayfront District [Fairhope MRA], Roughly bounded by Blakeney, N. and S. Summit Sts., Fels Ave. and Mobile Bay, Fairhope, 7/01/88, A, C, 88001003

First Baptist Church [Rural Churches of Baldwin County TR], N side D'Olive St., Bay Minette, 8/25/88, C, a, 88001349

Fort Mims Site, Address Restricted, Tensaw vicinity, 9/14/72, A, D, 72000153

Fort Morgan, Western terminus of AL 180, Gasque vicinity, 10/15/66, A, NHL, 66000146

Gaston Building [Fairhope MRA], 336 Fairhope Ave., Fairhope, 7/01/88, A, C, 88001004

Golf, Gun & Country Club [Fairhope MRA], 651 Johnson Ave., Fairhope, 7/01/88, A, C, 88001002

Hamner House [Creole and Gulf Coast Cottages in Baldwin County TR], Oak Rd. off CR 6, Bon Secour, 12/20/88, C, 88002811

Latham United Methodist Church [Rural Churches of Baldwin County TR], E side Hwy. 59, Latham, 8/25/88, C, a, 88001350

Lebanon Chapel AME Church [Rural Churches of Baldwin County TR], Bounded by Young St. on the West and Middle St. on the North, Fairhope, 8/25/88, C, a, 88001351

McMillan House [Creole and Gulf Coast Cottages in Baldwin County TR], 1404 Captain O'Neal Ave., Daphne, 12/20/88, C, 88002812

Methodist Episcopal Church, South, 1608 Old County Rd., Daphne, 9/22/80, C, a, 80000679

Montgomery Hill Baptist Church [Rural Churches of Baldwin County TR], E side Hwy. 59 on CR 80, Tensaw, 8/25/88, C, a, d, 88001352

Montrose Historic District, Main (AL 42) and 2nd Sts., Montrose, 6/03/76, C, c, 76000310

Nelson House [Creole and Gulf Coast Cottages in Baldwin County TR], Hwy. 59, North, Latham, 12/20/88, C, 88002814

Nicholson House [Creole and Gulf Coast Cottages in Baldwin County TR], CR 6, Oyster Bay, 12/20/88, C, 88002813

Orrell House [Creole and Gulf Coast Cottages in Baldwin County TR], CR 6, Bon Secour, 12/20/88, C, 88002815

Point Clear Historic District, W side of US 98/Eastern Shore Blvd., Point Clear, 4/28/88, A, C, b, 88000515

Sand Island Light, SW of Fort Morgan off Mobile Point, Fort Morgan vicinity, 11/12/75, A, 75000305

School of Organic Education [Fairhope MRA], Bounded by Fairhope and Morphy Aves. and Bancroft and School Sts., Fairhope, 7/01/88, A, B, C, 88001010

St. Mark's Lutheran Church [Rural Churches of Baldwin County TR], W side CR 83, Elberta, 8/25/88, C, a, 88001353

St. Patrick's Catholic Church [Rural Churches of Baldwin County TR], E side Hwy. 90, Loxley, 8/25/88, C, a, 88001354

St. Paul's Episcopal Church [Rural Churches of Baldwin County TR], N side Oak Ave., Magnolia Springs, 8/25/88, C, a, 88001355

Starke, Lewis, House, 2103 Old County Rd., Daphne, 6/14/90, C, 90000929

Stockton Methodist Church [Rural Churches of Baldwin County TR], E side Hwy. 59, Stockton, 8/25/88, C, a, 88001356

Street House [Creole and Gulf Coast Cottages in Baldwin County TR], Wood Acres Rd. off CR 3, Point Clear, 12/20/88, C, 88002816

Svea Land Company Office, S. 6th St., Silverhill, 3/07/85, A, 85000443

Swift Presbyterian Church [Rural Churches of Baldwin County TR], Swift Church Rd., Miflin, 8/25/88, C, a, 88001357

Texas, The [Creole and Gulf Coast Cottages in Baldwin County TR], 306 Dryer Ave., Daphne, 12/20/88, C, b, 88002817

Twin Beach AME Church [Rural Churches of Baldwin County TR], S side of CR 44, Fairhope, 8/25/88, C, a, 88001358

U.S.S. TECUMSEH, NW of Fort Morgan in Mobile Bay, Fort Morgan vicinity, 5/14/75, A, 75000306

US Post Office [Fairhope MRA], 325 Fairhope Ave., Fairhope, 7/01/88, C, 88001001

Walker House [Creole and Gulf Coast Cottages in Baldwin County TR], 905 Captain O'Neal Dr., Daphne, 12/20/88, C, 88002818

White Avenue Historic District [Fairhope MRA], White Ave., Fairhope, 7/01/88, A, C, 88001009

Whittier Hall, 201 Magnolia Ave., Fairhope, 3/07/85, A, 85000442

Zurhorst House [Fairhope MRA], 200 Fels Ave., Fairhope, 7/01/88, C, 88001006

Barbour County

Bray-Barron House, N. Eufaula Ave., Eufaula, 5/27/71, C, 71000093

Cato House, 823 W. Barbour St., Eufaula, 5/27/71, B, 71000094

Clayton, Henry D., House, 1 mi. S of Clayton off AL 30, Clayton vicinity, 12/08/76, B, NHL, 76002259

Drewry-Mitchell-Moorer House, 640 N. Eufaula Ave., Eufaula, 4/13/72, C, 72000154

Fendall Hall, Barbour St., Eufaula, 7/28/70, C, 70000097

Kendall Manor, 534 W. Broad St., Eufaula, 1/14/72, C, 72000155

Kiels-McNab House, W. Washington St., Eufaula, 1/21/82, B, b, 82001996

Lore Historic District, Bounded by Eufaula Ave., and Browder, Livingston, and Barbour Sts., Eufaula, 12/12/73, A, C, 73000330

Lore, Seth and Irwinton Historic District (Boundary Increase), Roughly bounded by Browder St., Van Buren Ave., Washington St., and Sanford Ave., Eufaula, 8/14/86, A, B, C, 86001534

McNab Bank Building, Broad St., Eufaula, 6/24/71, B, C, 71000095

Miller-Martin Town House, Louisville Ave., Clayton, 12/16/74, A, C, 74000399

Petty—Roberts—Beatty House, 103 N. Midway, Clayton, 1/21/74, C, 74000400

Sheppard Cottage, E. Barbour St., Eufaula, 5/27/71, C, c, 71000096

Shorter Mansion, 340 N. Eufaula Ave., Eufaula, 1/14/72, B, C, 72000156

Sparks, Gov. Chauncy, House, 257 Broad St., Eufaula, 6/28/72, B, 72000157

Tavern, The, 105 Riverside Dr., Eufaula, 10/06/70, C, 70000098

Wellborn, Livingston Ave., Eufaula, 7/14/71, C, 71000097

Bibb County

Brierfield Furnace, W of Brierfield, Brierfield vicinity, 11/20/74, A, 74000401

Bibb County—Continued

Centreville Historic District, Walnut St., East and West Court Sq., Centreville, 10/19/78, A, C, a, f, 78000482

Davidson—Smitherman House, 167 Third Ave., Centreville, 1/06/88, B, C, 87001552

McKinney, Sarah Amanda Trott, House, AL 25 between Montevallo and Centreville, Six Mile, 5/29/92, C, 92000626

Montebrier, N of Brierfield on Mahan Creek, Brierfield, 4/02/73, C, 73000331

Blount County

Easley Covered Bridge [Blount County Covered Bridges TR], Spans Dub Branch, Oneonta vicinity, 8/20/81, A, C, 81000125

Horton Mill Covered Bridge [Blount County Covered Bridges TR], 5 mi. (8 km) N of Oneonta on Rte. 3, Oneonta vicinity, 12/29/70, A, C, g, 70000099

Nectar Covered Bridge [Blount County Covered Bridges TR], 8 mi. SW of Nectar, Nectar vicinity, 8/20/81, A, C, g, 81000124

Swann Covered Bridge [Blount County Covered Bridges TR], W of Cleveland, Cleveland vicinity, 8/20/81, A, C, g, 81000123

Bullock County

Bullock County Courthouse Historic District, N. Prairie St., Union Springs, 10/08/76, A, 76000312

Butler County

Blackwell, W. S., House [Greenville MRA], 211 Ft. Dale St., Greenville, 9/04/86, C, 86001751

Buell—Stallings—Stewart House [Greenville MRA], 205 Fort Dale St., Greenville, 9/04/86, B, C, 86001752

Butler Chapel A.M.E. Zion Church [Greenville MRA], 407 Oglesby, Greenville, 9/04/86, A, C, a, 86001755

Commerce Street Residential Historic District [Greenville MRA], 206, 212, 218, 301 E. Commerce St., Greenville, 8/28/86, B, C, 86001967

Confederate Park [Greenville MRA], E. Commerce St., Greenville, 9/04/86, A, C, a, 86001791

Dickenson House [Greenville MRA], 537 S. Conecuh St., Greenville, 9/04/86, C, 86001794

East Commerce Street Historic District [Greenville MRA], Roughly bounded by Cedar, Chestnut, Commerce, and Hickory Sts., Greenville, 11/04/86, A, C, 86001966

Evens—McMullan House [Greenville MRA], 303 Bolling St., Greenville, 9/04/86, C, 86001797

First Baptist Church [Greenville MRA], 707 South St., Greenville, 9/04/86, A, a, 86001799

First Presbyterian Church [Greenville MRA], 215 E. Commerce St., Greenville, 9/04/86, C, a, 86001801

Fort Dale—College Street Historic District [Greenville MRA], Roughly bounded by Ft. Dale, Hamilton, and N. College Sts., Greenville, 8/28/86, B, C, 86001974

Gaston—Perdue House [Greenville MRA], 111 Cedar St., Greenville, 9/04/86, B, C, 86001803

Graydon House [Greenville MRA], 507 Cedar St., Greenville, 9/04/86, C, 86001805

Greenville City Hall [Greenville MRA], E. Commerce St., Greenville, 11/04/86, A, C, g, 86001807

Greenville Public School Complex [Greenville MRA], 101 Butler Circle, Greenville, 9/04/86, A, C, 86001811

Hawthorne—Cowart House [Greenville MRA], 319 Bolling St., Greenville, 9/04/86, C, 86001853

Hinson House [Greenville MRA], 208 Oliver St., Greenville, 9/04/86, C, 86001854

House at 308 South Street [Greenville MRA], 308 South St., Greenville, 9/04/86, C, 86001856

Howard, John W., House and Outbuildings, AL 10E, Greenville vicinity, 9/04/92, C, d, 92001090

King Street Historic District [Greenville MRA], Roughly bounded by W. Commerce, Oliver, Milner, and King Sts., Greenville, 8/28/86, C, 86001971

Lane—Kendrick—Sherling House [Greenville MRA], 109 Ft. Dale St., Greenville, 9/04/86, A, B, C, 86001858

Little—Stabler House [Greenville MRA], 710 Fort Dale St., Greenville, 11/04/86, C, 86001861

McMullan—Skinner House [Greenville MRA], 204 Oliver St., Greenville, 9/04/86, C, 86001865

Oakey Streak Methodist Episcopal Church, Off SR 59, Greenville vicinity, 1/04/80, A, C, a, 80000680

Post Office Historic District [Greenville MRA], 100–115 W. Commerce and 101 E. Commerce Sts., Greenville, 11/04/86, A, C, 86001968

South Greenville Historic District [Greenville MRA], Roughly bounded by Walnut, S. Conecuh, Parmer, and Church and Harrison and Caldwell Sts., Greenville, 8/28/86, B, C, 86001965

South Street Historic District [Greenville MRA], Roughly bounded by South, Oliver, and McKenzie Sts., Greenville, 8/28/86, C, 86001972

Theological Building—A.M.E. Zion Theological Institute [Greenville MRA], E. Conecuh St., Greenville, 9/04/86, A, a, 86001867

Ward Nicholson Corner Store [Greenville MRA], 219 W. Parmer, Greenville, 11/04/86, A, B, a, 86001870

West Commerce Street Historic District [Greenville MRA], Roughly bounded by W. Commerce, Bolling, and Milner Sts., and L & N RR, Greenville, 8/28/86, A, C, 86001970

Wright—Kilgore House [Greenville MRA], 808 Walnut St., Greenville, 9/04/86, B, C, 86001873

Calhoun County

Aderholdt's Mill, Aderholdt's Mill Rd., Jacksonville vicinity, 12/29/88, A, C, 88003077

Anniston Cotton Manufacturing Company [Anniston MRA], 215 W. Eleventh St., Anniston, 10/03/85, A, C, 85002739

Anniston Electric and Gas Company Plant, Old, 2 W. Third St., Anniston, 5/16/91, A, C, 91000611

Anniston Inn Kitchen, 130 W. 15th St., Anniston, 5/08/73, A, C, 73000332

Anniston Transfer Company [Anniston MRA], 911 Wilmer Ave., Anniston, 10/03/85, C, 85002740

Bagley—Cater Building [Anniston MRA], 15 E. Tenth St., Anniston, 10/03/85, C, 85002864

Bank of Anniston [Anniston MRA], 1005 Noble St., Anniston, 10/03/85, A, C, 85002865

Caldwell Building, 1001 Noble St., Anniston, 3/01/82, B, C, 82001997

Calhoun County Courthouse [Anniston MRA], 25 W. Eleventh St., Anniston, 10/03/85, A, C, 85002866

Coldwater Creek Covered Bridge, Spans Coldwater Creek 0.5 mi. (0.8 km) from I 20, Coldwater, 4/11/73, A, C, 73000333

Crowan Cottage, 1401 Woodstock Ave., Anniston, 5/16/75, C, 75000307

Downtown Anniston Historic District [Anniston MRA], Roughly bounded by Moore Ave., 14th St., Wilmer Ave. and 9th St., Anniston, 5/30/91, A, C, 91000663

Downtown Jacksonville Historic District, Roughly bounded by College, Thomas, Coffee, and Spring Sts., Jacksonville, 5/13/86, A, C, 86001044

East Anniston Residential Historic District [Anniston MRA], Roughly, along Leighton and Christine Aves. from 11th St. to 22nd Sts. and Woodstock Ave. from 11th St. to Rocky Hollow, Anniston, 5/28/93, C, 93000418

First Presbyterian Church, 200 E. Clinton St., Jacksonville, 2/04/82, C, a, 82001999

Francis, Dr. J. C., Office, 100 Gayle St., Jacksonville, 11/20/70, B, 70000100

Glen Addie Volunteer Hose Company Fire Hall [Anniston MRA], Fourth St. and Pine Ave., Anniston, 10/03/85, A, 85002738

Glenwood Terrace Residential Historic District [Anniston MRA], Roughly bounded by Oak St., Jefferson Ave., lots on S side of Glenwood Terr. & N side of Orchard St., and Highland Ave., Anniston, 10/03/85, C, 85002867

Glover, Henry Burt, House [Anniston MRA], 1119 Leighton Ave., Anniston, 10/03/85, A, B, C, 85002868

Grace Episcopal Church [Anniston MRA], 1000 Leighton Ave., Anniston, 10/03/85, A, C, a, 85002869

Greenwood, Jct. Old Anniston—Gadsden Rd. and Co. Rd. 25, Alexandria vicinity, 3/09/89, C, 89000162

Hillside Cemetery [Anniston MRA], Highland Ave. between Tenth and Eleventh Sts., Anniston, 10/03/85, A, C, d, 85002870

Huger, Richard P., House [Anniston MRA], 1901 Wilmer Ave., Anniston, 10/03/85, B, C, 85002871

Janney Furnace, 1 mi. NW of Ohatchee off AL 62, Ohatchee vicinity, 9/28/76, B, 76000315

Calhoun County—Continued

Kilby House [Anniston MRA], 1301 Woodstock Ave., Anniston, 10/03/85, B, C, 85002872

Kress Building [Anniston MRA], 1106 Noble St., Anniston, 10/03/85, C, 85002873

Lyric Theatre, 1302 Noble St., Anniston, 5/22/80, A, 80000681

McKleroy-Wilson-Kirby House, 1604 Quintard Ave., Anniston, 8/30/84, A, C, 84000597

Montgomery Ward—Alabama Power Company Building [Anniston MRA], 1201 Noble St., Anniston, 10/03/85, C, 85002874

Mount Zion Baptist Church [Anniston MRA], 212 Second St., Anniston, 10/03/85, A, C, a, 85002875

Noble Cottage, 900 Leighton Ave., Anniston, 10/08/76, C, 76000313

Noble, Samuel, Monument [Anniston MRA], Eleventh St. and Quintard Ave., Anniston, 10/03/85, A, f, 85002876

Noble—McCaa—Butler House [Anniston MRA], 1025 Fairmont Ave., Anniston, 10/03/85, B, C, 85002877

Nonnenmacher Bakery [Anniston MRA], 36 W. Eleventh St., Anniston, 10/03/85, A, C, 85002878

Nonnenmacher House [Anniston MRA], 1311 Gurnee Ave., Anniston, 10/03/85, C, 85002879

Oak Tree Cottage [Anniston MRA], 721 Oak St., Anniston, 10/03/85, C, 85002880

Parker Memorial Baptist Church [Anniston MRA], 1205 Quintard Ave., Anniston, 10/03/85, C, a, 85002881

Parker-Reynolds House [Anniston MRA (AD)], 330 E. 6th St., Anniston, 2/19/82, B, C, 82001998

Peerless Saloon [Anniston MRA], 13 W. Tenth St., Anniston, 10/03/85, A, C, 85002882

Saint Paul's Methodist Episcopal Church [Anniston MRA], 1327 Leighton Ave., Anniston, 10/03/85, A, C, a, 85002884

Security Bank Building [Anniston MRA], 1030 Noble St., Anniston, 10/03/85, A, C, 85002885

Smith, Lansing T., House [Anniston MRA], 531 Keith Ave., Anniston, 10/03/85, B, 85002886

Snow, Dudley, House, 704 Snow St., Oxford, 2/04/82, B, C, 82002000

Southern Railway Depot, 200 N. Center Ave., Piedmont, 1/05/84, A, C, 84000599

St. Michael and All Angels Episcopal Church, W. 18th St., Anniston, 2/14/78, A, C, a, 78000483

Temple Beth-El [Anniston MRA], 301 E. Thirteenth St., Anniston, 10/03/85, C, a, 85002887

The Pines, SE corner of 5th St. and Lapsley Ave., Anniston, 5/13/91, C, 91000594

Tyler Hill Residential Historic District [Anniston MRA], Roughly bounded by E. Seventh, Knox and Goodwin and Lapsley Aves., E. Sixth St., and Leighton Ave., Anniston, 10/03/85, C, 85002888

U.S. Post Office, 1129 Noble St., Anniston, 11/13/76, A, C, 76000314

Union Depot and Freight House [Anniston MRA], 1300 Walnut Ave., Anniston, 10/03/85, A, C, 85002889

West Fifteenth Street Historic District, 416–712 W. Fifteenth St., Anniston, 5/30/91, A, C, 91000662

Wikle Drug Company [Anniston MRA], 1010 Noble St., Anniston, 10/03/85, A, C, 85002890

Woods, Alexander, House, 517 N. Pelham Rd., Jacksonville, 3/15/88, B, C, 87001651

Chambers County

Chambers County Courthouse Square Historic District, Roughly bounded by Alabama and 2nd Aves., and 1st St., LaFayette, 3/27/80, C, 80000682

County Line Baptist Church, E of Dudleyville, Dudleyville Vicinity, 8/19/82, C, a, 82002001

Oliver, Ernest McCarty, House, LaFayette St. N/US 431, LaFayette, 1/21/74, B, C, 74000402

Cherokee County

Cornwall Furnace, 2 mi. (3.2 km) N of Cedar Bluff, Cedar Bluff vicinity, 9/27/72, A, 72000158

Chilton County

Verbena, US 31, Verbena, 1/19/76, A, 76002238

Walker—Klinner Farm, 3.5 mi. E of Maplesville on AL 22, Maplesville, 10/15/87, A, C, 87001849

Choctaw County

Mount Sterling Methodist Church, Near jct. of CR 43 and CR 27, Mount Sterling, 5/08/86, C, a, 86000995

Clarke County

Alston-Cobb House, 120 Cobb St., Grove Hill, 4/30/79, C, 79000382

Dickinson House, 101 Dickinson Ave., Grove Hill, 9/13/78, C, 78000485

Fort Sinquefield, SE of Grove Hill, Grove Hill vicinity, 12/31/74, A, 74000403

Gainestown Schoolhouse, W. side Gainestown—Suggsville Public Rd. N of Good Hope Church, Gainestown, 10/01/92, C, 92000033

Wilson-Finlay House, N of Gainestown on Suggsville Rd., Gainestown vicinity, 7/12/78, C, 78000484

Woodlands, Off U.S. 84, Gosport, 4/28/80, C, 80000683

Clay County

Black, Hugo, House, S. 2nd St., E. (AL 77), Ashland, 10/09/73, B, 73000334

Clay County Courthouse, Courthouse Sq., Ashland, 11/21/76, C, 76000316

Cleburne County

Cleburne County Courthouse, Vickory St., Heflin, 6/22/76, A, C, 76000317

Morgan, John, House, 321 Ross St., Heflin, 8/05/93, C, 93000762

Shoal Creek Church, 4 mi. (6.4 km) NW of Edwardsville, on Forest Service Rd. 533 in Talladega National Forest, Edwardsville vicinity, 12/04/74, A, C, a, 74000404

Coffee County

Boll Weevil Monument, Main and College Sts., Enterprise, 4/26/73, A, f, 73000336

Coffee County Courthouse, Courthouse Sq., Elba, 5/08/73, C, 73000335

Pea River Power Company Hydroelectric Facility, S of Elba, Elba vicinity, 8/01/84, A, 84000602

Rawls Hotel, 116 S. Main St., Enterprise, 9/17/80, B, C, 80000684

Seaboard Coastline Depot, Corner of Railroad and W. College Sts., Enterprise, 8/07/74, A, C, 74000405

Colbert County

Barton Hall, 2.5 mi. (4 km) W of Cherokee on U.S. 72, Cherokee vicinity, 11/07/73, C, NHL, 73000337

Belmont, SE of Tuscumbia, Tuscumbia vicinity, 2/23/82, A, C, 82002003

Buzzard Roost, 3 mi. W of Cherokee on U.S. 72, Cherokee vicinity, 11/07/76, A, NPS, 76000157

Chambers—Robinson House, 910 Montgomery Ave., Sheffield, 5/14/93, C, 93000419

Christian, John and Archibald, House, Off US 72, Tuscumbia, 2/04/82, C, 82002004

Colbert County Courthouse Square Historic District, Roughly bounded by E. and W. 2nd, N. and S. Cave, E. and W. 6th, and N. and S. Indian Sts., Tuscumbia, 5/24/73, C, a, 73000338

Ivy Green, 300 W. North Common, Tuscumbia, 8/25/70, B, NHL, 70000101

Johnson's Woods, 801 E. North Commons, Tuscumbia, 5/04/88, C, 88000511

Johnson, John, House [Tidewater Cottages in the Tennessee Valley TR], Near jct. of Fosters Mill and River Rds., Leighton vicinity, 7/09/86, A, C, 86001537

La Grange Rock Shelter, Address Restricted, Leighton vicinity, 6/13/74, D, 74000406

Nitrate Village No. 1 Historic District, Roughly bounded by Wilson Dam Circle, Wheeler and Wilson Dam Aves., Fontana, and Pickwick Sts., Sheffield, 8/30/84, A, C, 84000603

Norman, Felix Grundy, House, 401 N. Main St., Tuscumbia, 4/12/84, C, 84000749

Colbert County—Continued

Oaks, The, SE of Tuscumbia off AL 157 on Ricks Lane, Tuscumbia vicinity, 11/07/76, C, 76000319

Old Brick Presbyterian Church, Old Brick Rd., N of Leighton, Leighton vicinity, 1/09/89, A, C, a, d, 88003078

Preuit Oaks, Cotton Town Rd., Leighton, 5/08/86, A, C, d, 86000997

Rather, John Daniel, House, 209 S. Cave St., Tuscumbia, 12/16/82, C, 82001603

Rock Creek Archeological District (ACt44, ACt45), Address Restricted, Maud vicinity, 6/26/90, D, NPS, 88003068

Tuscumbia Historic District, Roughly bounded by N. & E. Commons, Eight St. and Spring Rd., Hooks, W. 5th & S. Milton including Steel Bridge, Tuscumbia, 5/23/85, A, B, C, g, 85001158

Tuscumbia Landing Site, W of Sheffield, Sheffield vicinity, 6/10/82, A, 82002002

Wilson Dam, Tennessee River on AL 133, Florence vicinity, 11/13/66, A, g, NHL, 66000147

Winston, William, House, N. Commons St., Tuscumbia, 4/15/82, C, 82002005

Conecuh County

Louisville and Nashville Depot, SW end of Front St., Evergreen, 4/03/75, A, 75000308

Coosa County

Coosa County Jail, Off AL 22, Rockford, 6/20/74, C, 74000407

Oakachoy Covered Bridge, Over Oakachoy Cr. W of SR 259, Nixburg vicinity, 6/14/90, C, 90000928

Covington County

Andalusia Commercial Historic District, Roughly bounded by Coffee St., Seaboard RR tracks, and S. Three Notch St., Andalusia, 1/26/89, A, C, 88003238

Bank of Andalusia, 28 S. Court Sq., Andalusia, 1/28/89, C, 88003239

Central of Georgia Depot, 125 Central St., Andalusia, 8/30/84, A, C, 84000606

Covington County Courthouse and Jail, 101 N. Court Sq., Andalusia, 1/28/89, A, C, 88003240

First National Bank Building, 101 S. Cotton St., Andalusia, 8/26/82, A, C, 82002006

Shepard, William T., House, Poley Rd., Opp, 8/14/73, A, 73000339

Crenshaw County

Kirkpatrick House, W of Highland Home on U.S. 331, Highland Home vicinity, 2/25/75, A, 75000309

Cullman County

Ave Maria Grotto, St. Bernard Abbey, Cullman, 1/19/84, C, 84000610

Clarkson Bridge, W of Cullman, Cullman vicinity, 6/25/74, C, 74000408

Cullman Downtown Commercial Historic District, Roughly bounded by 4th and 1st Aves., 2nd and 5th Sts. SE, Cullman, 4/11/85, A, C, 85000738

Cullman Historic District, Roughly bounded by 1st and 8th Aves., 3rd and 9th Sts., Cullman, 8/30/84, A, C, 84000615

Greene, Ernest Edward, House, 105 6th Ave. SE., Cullman, 2/03/93, C, 92001828

Louisville and Nashville Railroad Depot, 309 1st Ave., NE, Cullman, 6/17/76, C, 76000320

Stiefelmeyer's, 202 1st Ave. SE, Cullman, 12/22/83, C, 83003444

Dale County

Claybank Log Church, E. Andrews Ave., Ozark, 11/07/76, C, a, 76000321

Holman, J. D., House, 409 E. Broad St., Ozark, 2/19/82, B, C, 82002007

Oates-Reynolds Memorial Building, Oates St., Newton, 6/13/74, A, 74000409

Dallas County

Adams Grove Presbyterian Church, S side of Cahaba-Greenville Rd., Cahaba vicinity, 6/05/86, C, a, d, 86001239

Antique Store [Plantersville MRA], Off AL 22, Plantersville, 1/29/87, A, C, 86003662

Brown Chapel African Methodist Episcopal Church, 410 Martin Luther King, Jr. St., Selma, 2/04/82, A, C, a, g, 82002009

Cahaba, 11 mi (17.6 km) SW of Selma at jct. of Cahaba and Alabama Rivers, Selma vicinity, 5/08/73, A, 73000341

Carlowville Historic District, 17 Mi. (27 km) S of Selma on AL 89, Selma vicinity, 1/18/78, C, 78000487

Christian Church and Parsonage [Plantersville MRA], Off AL 22, Plantersville, 1/29/87, C, a, 86003664

Dallas County Courthouse, 109 Union St., Selma, 6/20/75, C, 75000310

Doctor's Office [Plantersville MRA], Jct. of First Ave. N of Oak St. and First Ave., Plantersville, 1/29/87, C, 86003663

Driskell—Martin House [Plantersville MRA], NW jct. of Cherry St. and First Ave., Plantersville, 1/29/87, C, 86003661

First Baptist Church, 709 Martin Luther King, Jr. St., Selma, 9/20/79, A, C, a, g, 79000383

Icehouse Historic District, Roughly bounded by Jefferson Davis and Dallas Aves., Union and Lapsley Sts., and Valley Cr., Selma, 6/28/90, A, C, 90000886

Marshall's Grove, AL 22, Selma vicinity, 2/04/82, C, 82002010

Morgan, John Tyler, House, 719 Tremont St., Selma, 9/27/72, B, 72000159

Old Town Historic District, Roughly bounded by the Alabama River, Jefferson Davis Ave., Pettus, Broad, and Franklin Sts., Selma, 5/03/78, A, C, g, 78000486

Plattenburg, Wesley, House, 601 Washington St., Selma, 2/03/93, C, 92001827

Riverdale, NE of Selma on River Rd., Selma vicinity, 9/10/79, C, 79000384

Riverview Historic District, Roughly bounded by Selma Ave., Satterfield and Lapsley Sts. and the Alabama R., Selma, 6/28/90, A, C, 90000887

Skinner, Marcus Meyer, House, 2612 Summerfield Rd., Selma, 8/27/87, B, C, 87001418

St. Luke's Episcopal Church, S of Browns, Browns vicinity, 3/25/82, A, C, a, 82002008

St. Paul's Episcopal Church, 210 Lauderdale St., Selma, 3/25/75, C, a, 75000311

Sturdivant Hall, 713 Mabry St., Selma, 1/18/73, C, 73000340

Summerfield District, Selma-Summerfield and Marion Rds., Centenary and College Sts., Summerfield, 3/01/82, A, C, 82002011

Todd House [Plantersville MRA], S side of Oak St. W of First Ave., Plantersville, 1/29/87, C, 86003665

U.S. Post Office Building, 908 Alabama Ave., Selma, 3/26/76, C, 76000322

Valley Creek Presbyterian Church, N of Selma on Valley Creek Rd., Selma vicinity, 5/28/76, C, a, 76000323

Water Avenue Historic District, Water Ave., Selma, 12/26/72, A, C, 72000160

De Kalb County

Alabama Builder's Hardware Manufacturing Company Complex (Boundary Increase), 203–204 8th St., NE., Fort Payne, 10/13/92, A, 92000637

Alabama Builders' Hardware Manufacturing Company, 204 Eighth St. NE, Fort Payne, 5/08/86, A, 86000999

Alabama Great Southern Railroad Passenger Depot, NE 5th St., Fort Payne, 9/10/71, A, 71001070

Cherokee Plantation, 100 Cherokee Dr. N. E., Fort Payne, 11/29/84, B, C, 84000384

Fort Payne Boom Town Historic District, Roughly Gault St. from 4th St. NE. to 6th St. NE., Fort Payne, 4/21/89, A, C, 89000308

Fort Payne Main Street Historic District, Roughly Gault Ave. from 2nd St. NE. to 2nd St. NW., Fort Payne, 4/21/89, A, C, 89000307

Fort Payne Opera House, 510 Gault Ave. N, Fort Payne, 4/28/70, A, 74002262

Fort Payne Residential Historic District, Roughly bounded by Forrest Ave. and Elm St., Fifth St. NW, Grand and Alabama Aves., and Fourth St. SW and Second St. NW, Fort Payne, 5/04/88, A, C, a, 88000444

De Kalb County—Continued

Mentone Springs Hotel, AL 117, Mentone, 10/20/83, A, 83003445

Winston Place, Off AL 117, Valley Head, 3/19/87, A, 87000476

Elmore County

Alabama State Penitentiary, NE of Wetumpka on US 231, Wetumpka, 5/08/73, A, 73000342

East Wetumpka Commercial Historic District, Roughly, Company St. from Spring St. to E. Bridge St. and E. Bridge and Commerce Sts. from Main to Hill Sts., Wetumpka, 2/20/92, A, C, 92000055

First Presbyterian Church Of Wetumpka, W. Bridge St., Wetumpka, 10/08/76, C, a, 76000324

First United Methodist Church, 308 Tuskeena St., Wetumpka, 2/15/73, A, C, a, 73000343

Fort Toulouse, 4 mi (6.4 km) SW of Wetumpka at confluence of the Coosa and Tallapoosa rivers, Wetumpka vicinity, 10/15/66, A, NHL, 66000148

Hickory Ground, Address Restricted, Wetumpka vicinity, 3/10/80, D, 80000685

Robinson Springs United Methodist Church, AL 14 and AL 143, Robinson Springs, 3/01/82, A, C, a, 82002012

Tallassee Commercial Historic District, Roughly, 3 blocks on S side Barnett Blvd. between old River Rd. and DuBois St., Tallassee, 3/06/92, C, 92000072

Wetumpka L & N Depot, Coosa St., Wetumpka, 7/01/75, A, 75000312

Escambia County

Brewton Historic Commercial District, AL 3 and US 31, Brewton, 3/15/82, A, C, 82002013

Commercial Hotel—Hart Hotel, 120 Palafox St., Flomaton, 5/22/86, A, 86001160

Etowah County

Alabama City Library, 1 Cabot Ave., Gadsden, 12/27/74, C, 74000410

Eleventh Street School, 1026 Chestnut St., Gadsden, 5/10/84, A, 84000616

Forrest Cemetery Chapel and Comfort Station, 1100 S. 15th St., Gadsden, 9/03/92, C, a, 92001069

Gadsden Times-News Building, Fourth and Chestnut Sts., Gadsden, 1/11/83, A, 83002967

Gunn, Charles, House, 872 Chestnut St., Gadsden, 2/19/93, C, 93000052

Hood, Col. O. R., House, 862 Chestnut St., Gadsden, 5/08/86, B, C, 86001000

Legion Park Bowl, 336 1st St., S., Gadsden, 9/28/88, C, 88001581

U.S. Post Office, 600 Broad St., Gadsden, 6/03/76, C, g, 76000325

U.S. Post Office, 401 4th St., Attalla, 6/21/83, A, C, 83002968

Fayette County

Fayette County Courthouse District, Roughly area between Peyton and Caine Sts., and Luxapalilla St. and railroad tracks, Fayette, 4/30/76, C, g, 76000326

Franklin County

Alabama Iron Works, S of Russellville off U.S. 43, Russellville vicinity, 8/03/77, A, 77000203

Overton Farm, 4 mi (6.4 km) NW of Hodges, Hodges vicinity, 10/03/73, A, C, D, 73000344

Greene County

Anthony, David Rinehart, House [Antebellum Homes in Eutaw TR], 307 Wilson Ave., Eutaw, 4/02/82, C, 82002015

Boligee Hill, SE of Boligee, Boligee vicinity, 2/19/82, A, B, C, 82002014

Braune, Gustave, House [Antebellum Homes in Eutaw TR], 236 Prairie St., Eutaw, 4/02/82, C, 82002016

Cockrell, Samuel W., House [Antebellum Homes in Eutaw TR], 210 Wilson St., Eutaw, 12/06/82, C, 82001618

Coleman, John, House [Antebellum Homes in Eutaw TR], 1160 Mesopotamia St., Eutaw vicinity, 12/06/82, C, 82001617

Coleman-Banks House, 430 Springfield Rd., Eutaw, 12/18/70, C, 70000102

Davis, Attoway R., Home [Antebellum Homes in Eutaw TR], 305 Main St., Eutaw, 4/02/82, C, b, 82002017

Elliott, John W., House [Antebellum Homes in Eutaw TR], 244 Prairie St., Eutaw, 4/02/82, C, 82002018

First Presbyterian Church, Main St. and Wilson Ave., Eutaw, 12/16/74, A, C, a, 74000411

Glenville [Antebellum Homes in Eutaw TR], 200 Scears St., Eutaw vicinity, 4/02/82, C, 82002019

Gray, Rev. John H., House [Antebellum Homes in Eutaw TR], 709 Mesopotamia St., Eutaw vicinity, 4/02/82, C, 82002020

Greene County Courthouse, Courthouse Sq., Eutaw, 3/24/71, C, 71000098

Greene County Courthouse Square District, U.S. 11 and AL7, Eutaw, 12/31/79, A, C, 79000385

Gullett, Benjamin D., House [Antebellum Homes in Eutaw TR], 317 Main St., Eutaw, 4/02/82, C, 82002021

Hale, Stephen Fowler, House [Antebellum Homes in Eutaw TR], 223 Wilson St., Eutaw, 4/02/82, C, 82002022

Jones, William C., House [Antebellum Homes in Eutaw TR], 507 Mesopotamia St., Eutaw, 4/02/82, C, 82002023

Kirkwood, 111 Kirkwood Dr., Eutaw, 5/17/76, C, 76000327

Meriwether, Dr. Willis, House [Antebellum Homes in Eutaw TR], 243 Wilson Ave., Eutaw, 4/02/82, C, b, 82002024

Murphy, Samuel R., House [Antebellum Homes in Eutaw TR], 1150 Mesopotamia St., Eutaw vicinity, 4/02/82, C, 82002025

Perkins, William, House [Antebellum Homes in Eutaw TR], 89 Spencer St., Eutaw, 4/02/82, C, 82002026

Pierce, William F., House, 309 Womack Ave., Eutaw, 11/17/83, C, 83003446

Pippen, Littleberry, House [Antebellum Homes in Eutaw TR], 431 Springfield St., Eutaw, 4/02/82, C, 82002027

Reese, Edwin, House [Antebellum Homes in Eutaw TR], 244 Wilson Ave., Eutaw, 4/02/82, C, 82002028

Rogers, William A., House [Antebellum Homes in Eutaw TR], 1149 Mesopotamia St., Eutaw vicinity, 4/02/82, C, 82002029

Rosemount, 1 mi. (1.6 km) NW of Forkland, Forkland vicinity, 5/27/71, C, 71000099

Schoppert, Phillip, House [Antebellum Homes in Eutaw TR], 230 Prairie St., Eutaw, 4/02/82, C, 82002030

St. John's-In-The-Prairie, SR 4, Forkland, 11/20/75, C, a, 75000313

Thornhill, NW of Forkland, Forkland vicinity, 5/10/84, A, C, 84000618

Vaughan, Iredell P., House [Antebellum Homes in Eutaw TR], 409 Wilson St., Eutaw, 4/02/82, C, b, 82002031

Webb, William Peter, House [Antebellum Homes in Eutaw TR], 401 Main St., Eutaw, 4/02/82, C, 82002032

White, Asa, House [Antebellum Homes in Eutaw TR], 314 Mesopotamia St., Eutaw, 4/02/82, C, 82002033

Wills, William B., House, 108 Ashby Dr., Eutaw, 9/22/83, C, b, 83002969

Wilson, Catlin, House [Antebellum Homes in Eutaw TR], 237 Wilson Ave., Eutaw, 4/02/82, C, 82002034

Wright, Daniel R., House [Antebellum Homes in Eutaw TR], 501 Pickens St., Eutaw, 4/02/82, C, 82002035

Hale County

Erwin, John, House, 705 Erwin Dr., Greensboro, 1/18/78, B, C, 78000488

Greensboro Historic District, Main St. between Hobson and 1st, Greensboro, 8/13/76, A, C, 76000328

Hatch House, Jct. of AL 14 and Norfleet Rd., Hale vicinity, 10/11/91, C, 91001483

Hatch, Alfred, Place at Arcola, Rt. 1, CR #2, Gallion vicinity, 1/06/88, C, 87001784

Magnolia Grove, W end of Main St., Greensboro, 4/11/73, B, C, 73000345

McGehee-Stringfellow House, NW of Greensboro on SR 30, Greensboro vicinity, 9/17/80, A, C, 80000686

Hale County—Continued

Millwood, Roughly bounded by Millwood Pond, Co. Rd. 17, and Black Warrior River, Greensboro vicinity, 9/26/89, A, C, 89000314

Moundville, 1 mi. (1.6 km) W of Moundville on SR 21, Moundville vicinity, 10/15/66, D, NHL, 66000149

St. Andrew's Church, U.S. 80, Prairieville, 11/07/73, C, a, NHL, 73000347

Tanglewood, About 11 mi. N of Greensboro off AL 23, Greensboro vicinity, 4/11/73, A, B, C, 73000346

Henry County

Kennedy House, 300 Kirkland St., Abbeville, 1/05/78, C, 78000489

Seaboard Coast Line Railroad Depot, Broad St., Headland, 9/04/80, A, C, 80000687

Houston County

Alabama Midland Railway Depot, Midland St., Ashford, 9/12/85, A, C, 85002163

Dothan Municipal Light and Water Plant, 126 N. College St., Dothan, 10/03/91, A, g, 90001315

Dothan Opera House, 103 N. St. Andrews St., Dothan, 12/16/77, C, 77000204

Federal Building and U.S. Courthouse, 100 W. Troy St., Dothan, 12/31/74, C, 74000412

Main Street Comerical District, E. Main, Foster, St. Andrews, Crawford, and Troy Sts., Dothan, 4/21/83, C, 83002984

Purcell-Killingsworth House, Main St., Columbia, 12/16/82, A, C, 82001616

Jackson County

Brown-Proctor House, 208 S. Houston St., Scottsboro, 9/16/82, B, 82002036

College Hill Historic District, 306–418 and 405–411 College Ave., Scottsboro, 3/30/83, C, 83002970

Fort Harker, S of AL 117, Stevenson, 5/02/77, A, D, 77000205

Public Square Historic District, Roughly bounded by Appletree, Andrews, Willow and Caldwell Sts., Scottsboro, 4/15/82, A, 82002037

Rosecrans, Gen. William, Headquarters, Myrtle Pl., Stevenson, 7/12/78, A, C, 78000490

Russell Cave National Monument, 8 mi. (12.8 km) W of Bridgeport via U.S. 72, CR 91 and 75, Bridgeport vicinity, 10/15/66, A, D, NPS, 66000150

Stevenson Historic District, Irregular pattern along RR tracks, Stevenson, 9/13/78, A, C, 78000491

Stevenson Railroad Depot and Hotel, Main St., Stevenson, 5/13/76, A, 76000329

Jefferson County

Age-Herald Building, 2107 5th Ave. N, Birmingham, 8/30/84, A, C, 84000620

Agee House, 1804 Twelfth Ave. S, Birmingham, 8/28/86, C, 86001962

Alabama Penny Savings Bank, 310 18th St. N, Birmingham, 3/10/80, A, C, 80004471

Alabama Theatre, 1811 3rd Ave., N, Birmingham, 11/13/79, A, C, 79000386

Anderson Place Historic District, Roughly bounded by Fourteenth Ave. S, Eighteenth St. S, Sixteen Ave. S, and Fifteenth St. S, Birmingham, 8/28/86, C, 86001981

Anderson Place Historic District (Boundary Increase), Roughly, 16th Ave. S. from 15th St. to a line S from 18th St., Birmingham, 5/15/91, C, 91000592

Arlington, 331 Cotton Ave., SW, Birmingham, 12/02/70, A, C, 70000103

Automotive Historic District, Roughly bounded by First Ave. N., 24th St. S., Fifth Ave. S. and 20th St. S., Birmingham, 5/30/91, A, C, 91000661

Avalon, 3005–3015 Highland Ave. and 3000–3020 13th Ave. S, Birmingham, 3/07/85, A, C, 85000444

Bank of Ensley, 19th St. and Ave. E, Birmingham, 6/21/84, A, 84000623

Birmingham, Railway, Light and Power Building, 2100 N. 1st Ave., Birmingham, 3/11/80, A, C, 80000688

Blessed Sacrament Academy, 1525 Cotton Ave., SW, Birmingham, 11/28/80, A, C, a, 80000689

Bottega Favorita, 2240–2244 Highland Ave., Birmingham, 8/28/86, C, 86001952

Bradshaw House, 2154 Highland Ave., Birmingham, 4/28/80, B, C, 80000690

Brown, Dr. A. M., House, 319 N. 4th Ter., Birmingham, 6/20/74, B, C, 74000413

Caldwell-Milner Building, 2015 1st Ave., N, Birmingham, 11/08/79, A, C, 79000387

Chestnut Hill Historic District, Roughly bounded by Highland Ave. and Thirty-first St., Birmingham, 6/12/87, C, 87000940

Claridge Manor Apartments [Apartment Hotels in Birmingham, 1900–1930, TR], 1100 27th St. S, Birmingham, 5/17/84, C, 84000625

Continental Gin Company, 4500 5th Ave., S., Birmingham, 11/20/80, A, C, g, 80000691

Crittenden Building, 1914 3rd Ave. N, Birmingham, 12/30/81, A, C, g, 81000126

Cullom Street—Twelfth Street South Historic District, Roughly bounded by Eleventh Ave., Twelfth St. S, Cullom St., and Thirteenth St. S, Birmingham, 8/21/86, A, C, 86001890

Downtown Bessemer Historic District, Roughly bounded by 21st St. N., Carolina Ave., 19th St. N., 5th Ave. N. and the Southern RR tracks, Bessemer, 7/15/92, A, C, 92000852

Downtown Birmingham Historic District, Roughly bounded by 3rd Ave., 24th St., 1rst Ave., and 20th St., Birmingham, 2/11/82, A, C, 82002039

Downtown Birmingham Historic District (Boundary Increase), 312–322 21rst St. N and 1923 3rd. Ave., Birmingham, 2/21/85, A, C, 85000305

Downtown Birmingham Retail and Theatre Historic District, Roughly bounded by 3rd Ave. North, 20th St. North, Morris Ave., and 17th St. North, Birmingham, 5/05/89, A, C, 89000315

Dr. Pepper Syrup Plant, 2829 Second Ave., S., Birmingham, 9/06/90, A, 90001317

Empire Building, 1928 1st Ave., N, Birmingham, 3/19/82, A, C, 82002040

Enslen House, 2737 Highland Ave., Birmingham, 3/13/75, B, C, 75000314

Episcopal Church of the Advent, 20th St. and 6th Ave. N, Birmingham, 3/30/83, C, a, 83002972

Exclusive Furniture Shop, 704 29th St., S, Birmingham, 8/30/84, C, 84000626

Fire Station No. 10 [Historic Fire Stations of Birmingham MPS], 4120 2nd Ave. S., Birmingham, 10/25/90, C, 90001556

Fire Station No. 11 [Historic Fire Stations of Birmingham MPS], 1250 13th St. N., Birmingham, 10/25/90, C, 90001557

Fire Station No. 12 [Historic Fire Stations of Birmingham MPS], 15 57th St. S., Birmingham, 10/25/90, A, C, 90001558

Fire Station No. 15 [Historic Fire Stations of Birmingham MPS], 1345 Steiner Ave., SW., Birmingham, 10/25/90, C, 90001559

Fire Station No. 16 [Historic Fire Stations of Birmingham MPS], 1621 Ave. G, Birmingham, 10/25/90, C, 90001560

Fire Station No. 19 [Historic Fire Stations of Birmingham MPS], 7713 Division Ave., Birmingham, 10/25/90, A, C, 90001561

Fire Station No. 22 [Historic Fire Stations of Birmingham MPS], 3114 Clairmont Ave., Birmingham, 10/25/90, A, C, 90001562

Fire Station No. 3 [Historic Fire Stations of Birmingham MPS], 2210 Highland Ave., Birmingham, 10/25/90, A, C, 90001554

Fire Station No. 6 [Historic Fire Stations of Birmingham MPS], 317 15th St. N., Birmingham, 10/25/90, C, 90001555

First Christian Church Education Building, 2100 7th Ave. N, Birmingham, 2/15/80, C, a, 80000692

First National-John A. Hand Building, 17 N. 20th St., Birmingham, 9/29/83, A, C, 83002976

First Presbyterian Church, 2100 4th Ave., N, Birmingham, 12/28/82, C, a, 82001604

First United Methodist Church, 6th Ave. and 19th St., N, Birmingham, 12/27/82, C, a, 82001605

Five Mile Creek Bridge, 1 mi. NE of McCalla off U.S. 11, McCalla vicinity, 2/28/73, A, C, 73000350

Five Points South Historic District, Roughly bounded by 10th and 15th Aves., 19th and 21st Sts., Birmingham, 3/16/83, A, C, 83002973

Five Points South Historic District (Boundary Increase), Roughly bounded by Twelfth Ave., Nineteenth St., Thirteenth Ave., and Seventeenth St., Birmingham, 8/28/86, C, 86001984

Five Points South Historic District (Boundary Increase II), Roughly bounded by 15th Ave. S., 20th St. S., 16th Ave. S. and 18th St., Birmingham, 5/15/91, C, 91000593

Forest Park, Roughly bounded by Highland Golf Course, 38th St. and Cherry Sts., Clairmont and

Jefferson County—Continued

Linwood Rds., and Overlook Ave., Birmingham, 11/21/80, C, 80000693

Fourth Avenue Historic District, 1600–1800 blks of 4th Ave. N and part of the 300 blks of 17th and 18th Sts. N, Birmingham, 2/11/82, A, C, 82002041

Fox Building, 19th St. and 4th Ave., Birmingham, 8/11/80, B, C, 80000694

Glen Iris Park Historic District, 1–20 Glen Iris Park, Birmingham, 8/30/84, A, C, 84000628

Hanover Court Apartments, 2620 Highland Ave., Birmingham, 4/20/88, C, 88000446

Heaviest Corner on Earth, 1st Ave., N and 20th St., N, Birmingham vicinity, 7/11/85, A, C, 85001502

Highland Avenue Historic District, 2000 block thru 3200 block 11th Court S., Birmingham, 11/17/77, B, C, 77000206

Highland Plaza Apartments [Apartment Hotels in Birmingham, 1900–1930, TR], 2250 Highland Ave., S, Birmingham, 5/17/84, C, 84000630

Hotel Redmont, 2101 Fifth Ave., N, Birmingham, 1/27/83, C, 83002974

Ideal Department Store Building, 111 19th St., N, Birmingham, 5/02/85, C, 85000918

Jefferson County Courthouse, 716 21st St., N, Birmingham, 12/27/82, C, 82001606

Kress, S. H., and Company Building, 3rd Ave. and 19th St., Birmingham, 1/04/82, A, C, g, 82002042

Lakeview School, 2800 Clairmont Ave., Birmingham, 11/17/77, A, C, 77000207

Loveman, Joseph, & Loeb Department Store, 214–224 19th St., N, Birmingham, 4/14/83, A, C, 83002971

Manchester Terrace, 720–728 S. 29th St., Birmingham, 3/22/89, C, 89000163

McAdory Building, 2013 1st Ave., N, Birmingham, 11/14/79, C, 79000388

McAdory, Thomas, House, 214 Eastern Valley Rd., Bessemer, 12/26/72, C, 72000161

Morris Avenue Historic District, 2000–2400 blocks of Morris Ave., Birmingham, 4/24/73, A, C, 73000349

Morris Avenue-First Avenue North Historic District, 2000–2400 blks. of Morris Ave. and 2100–2500 blks. of First Ave. N., Birmingham, 1/09/86, A, C, 86000009

Nabers, Morrow and Sinnige, Building, 109 20th St. N, Birmingham, 9/22/80, B, C, 80000695

Oak Hill Cemetery, 1120 N. 19th St., Birmingham, 7/13/77, C, d, 77000208

Orlando Apartments, 2301 Fifteenth Ave. S., Birmingham, 5/15/90, C, 90000309

Owen Plantation House, S of Bessemer on Eastern Valley Rd., Bessemer vicinity, 10/22/76, C, 76000330

Owen, Dr. Thomas McAdory, House, 510 N. 18th St., Bessemer, 1/21/82, B, 82002038

Phelan Park Historic District, Roughly bounded by 13th Ave. S., 14th St. S., 16th Ave. S., and 13th Pl. S., Birmingham, 1/26/89, A, C, 88003241

Powell School, 2331 6th Ave., N, Birmingham, 6/17/76, A, C, 76000331

Pratt City Carline Historic District, Ave. U from Ave. A to Carline and Carline from Ave. W to 6th St., Birmingham, 3/02/89, A, C, 89000118

Quinlan Castle, 2030 9th Ave., S, Birmingham, 9/13/84, C, 84000632

Red Mountain Suburbs Historic District, Roughly bounded by Crest and Argyle and Altamont, Country Club, Salisbury, and Lanark Rds., Birmingham (also in Mountain Brook), 10/03/85, A, B, C, 85002719

Redmont Garden Apartments, 2829 Thornhill Rd., Mountain Brook, 8/05/93, C, 93000761

Reed, William, House, 888 Twin Lake Dr., Birmingham, 10/01/87, A, B, C, 87001778

Rhodes Park, Roughly bounded by S. 10th, S. 13th and Highland Aves. S. 28th and S. 30th Sts., Birmingham, 4/15/82, A, C, 82002043

Rickwood Field, 1137 2nd Ave. W., Birmingham, 2/01/93, A, 92001826

Ridgely Apartments [Apartment Hotels in Birmingham, 1900–1930, TR], 608 21st St., N, Birmingham, 5/17/84, C, 84000634

Sadler House, 3 mi. S of McCalla on Eastern Valley Rd., McCalla vicinity, 4/23/75, C, 75000315

Saint Andrew's Episcopal Church, 1164 Eleventh Ave. S, Birmingham, 8/28/86, C, a, 86001959

Second Presbyterian Church, Tenth Ave. and Twelfth St. S, Birmingham, 9/11/86, C, a, 86002616

Sixteenth Street Baptist Church, 6th Ave. and 16th St., Birmingham, 9/17/80, A, C, a, g, 80000696

Sloss Blast Furnace Site, 1st Ave. at 32nd St., Birmingham, 6/22/72, A, C, NHL, 72000162

Smith, Joseph Riley, Historic District, 300–400 blks. of Tenth Ave., 100–400 blks. of Ninth Ct., 944 Fourth St. W, and 948 Third St. W, Birmingham, 10/10/85, C, 85002898

Smithfield Historic District, Roughly bounded by Eighth Ave. N, Sixth St. N, Fourth Terr. N, and First St. N, Birmingham, 10/15/85, A, C, 85002899

Southern Railroad Depot, 933 Thornton Ave., NE, Leeds, 6/30/83, C, 83002975

Southern Railway Terminal Station, 1905 Alabama Ave., Bessemer, 2/28/73, A, C, 73000348

St. Paul's Catholic Church, 2120 3rd Ave. N, Birmingham, 12/27/82, C, a, 82001607

Steiner Bank Building, 2101 1st Ave. N, Birmingham, 6/25/74, B, C, 74000414

Thomas Historic District, Roughly area between 1st and 8th Sts., N of Village Creek and W of St. Louis and San Francisco Railroad tracks, Birmingham, 3/02/89, A, C, 89000119

U.S. Post Office, 1800 5th Ave., N, Birmingham, 6/03/76, C, 76000332

Vulcan, Vulcan Park, US 31 S, Birmingham, 7/06/76, C, b, e, f, 76000333

Waters Building, 209–211 22nd St. N, Birmingham, 3/11/80, A, C, 80000697

Watts Building, 2008 3rd Ave., N, Birmingham, 9/17/79, C, 79000389

West End Masonic Temple, 1346 Tuscaloosa Ave., Birmingham, 8/27/87, A, C, 87001417

West Park, 5th Ave. N and 16th St., Birmingham, 5/24/84, A, 84000636

Whilldin Building, 513–517 21st St., N, Birmingham, 3/25/82, C, 82002044

Wimberly-Thomas Warehouse, 1809 First Ave. S, Birmingham, 10/03/85, A, C, 85002718

Windham Construction Office Building, 528 8th Ave., N, Birmingham, 8/09/84, A, 84000638

Woodlawn City Hall, 5525 First Ave., N, Birmingham, 6/30/88, A, C, 88000990

Woodlawn Comercial Historic District, Area around jct. of 1st Ave. N. and 55th Pl., Birmingham, 1/25/91, A, C, 90002179

Woodward Building, 1927 1st Ave., N, Birmingham, 6/30/83, A, C, 83002977

Wylam Fire Station [Historic Fire Stations of Birmingham MPS], NE Corner 8th Ave. and Huron St., Birmingham, 10/25/90, A, C, 90001563

Zinszer's Peter, Mammoth Furniture House, 2115, 2117 and 2119 2nd Ave., N, Birmingham, 9/23/80, B, C, 80000698

Lamar County

Bankhead, James Greer, House, Wolf Rd., Sulligent, 2/13/75, B, C, 75000316

Lauderdale County

Armistead, Peter F., Sr., House [Tidewater Cottages in the Tennessee Valley TR], Waterloo Rd., Florence vicinity, 7/09/86, A, C, b, 86001540

Coffee High School, 319 Hermitage Dr., Florence, 2/04/82, A, 82002045

Coulter, George, House, 420 S. Pine St., Florence, 1/21/82, C, 82002046

Courtview, Court St., Florence, 6/13/74, A, C, 74000415

Karsner-Carroll House, 303 N. Pine St., Florence, 3/31/70, C, 70000104

Koger, William, House [Tidewater Cottages in the Tennessee Valley TR], Smithsonia-Rhodesville Rd., Smithsonia vicinity, 7/09/86, A, C, 86001542

Larimore House, Mars Hill Rd./US 8, Box 344, Florence, 11/21/74, A, C, 74000416

Martin, James, House, 1400 Cypress Mill Rd., Florence, 12/09/81, B, C, 81000128

Old Natchez Trace (310–2A), 15 mi. NW of Florence on AL 20, Florence vicinity, 11/07/76, A, NPS, 76000156

Patton, Gov. Robert, House, Sweetwater and Florence Blvd., Florence, 6/17/76, B, C, 76000335

Rosenbaum House, 117 Riverview Dr., Florence, 12/19/78, C, g, 78000492

Sannoner Historic District, Includes both sides of N. Pine and N. Court from Tuscaloosa Ave. to University of Alabama, Florence, 1/01/76, C, 76000336

Seven Mile Island Archeological District, Address Restricted, Florence vicinity, 4/16/79, D, 79003352

Southall Drugs, 201 N. Court St., Florence, 8/21/80, C, 80000699

Lauderdale County—Continued

Walnut Street Historic District, N. Walnut between Hermitage and Tuscaloosa, Florence, 12/12/76, A, C, 76000337

Walnut Street Historic District (Boundary Increase), 415–609 N. Poplar St. (odd numbers), Florence, 3/04/93, C, 92001836

Water Tower, Seymore St., Florence, 4/28/80, C, 80000700

Wesleyan Hall, Morrison Ave., Florence, 6/20/74, A, C, 74000417

Wilson Park Houses, 209, 217, and 223 E. Tuscaloosa St., Florence, 1/25/79, A, C, 79000390

Wood Avenue Historic District, N Wood Ave. roughly bounded by Tuscaloosa and Hawthorne Sts., Florence, 10/10/78, C, 78000493

Lawrence County

Archeological Site No. 1LA102, Address Restricted, Haleyville vicinity, 12/14/85, D, 85003117

Bride's Hill [Tidewater Cottages in the Tennessee Valley TR], Lock Rd., Wheeler vicinity, 7/09/86, A, C, 86001544

Courtland Historic District, Roughly bounded by Clinton, Madison, Van Buren, Jefferson, Ussery, Tennessee, Monroe and Academy Sts., Courtland, 5/13/91, A, C, 91000597

Goode-Hall House, N of Town Creek of AL 101, Town Creek vicinity, 10/01/74, C, 74000418

Holland, Thomas, House, Off Alt. US 72 S of Hillsboro, Hillsboro vicinity, 10/01/91, C, 91001478

McMahon, John, House, Jct. South Lane & Jefferson St., Courtland, 12/11/87, A, C, 87001454

Wheeler, Joseph, Plantation, E of Courtland off AL 20, Courtland vicinity, 4/13/77, B, 77000209

Lee County

Auburn Players Theater, College Ave. at Thach St., Auburn, 5/22/73, A, C, a, 73000351

Auburn University Historic District, Auburn University campus, Auburn, 6/03/76, A, C, 76000338

Burton, Robert Wilton, House, 315 E. Magnolia St., Auburn, 5/08/80, B, C, 80000701

Ebenezer Missionary Baptist Church, Thach St. and Auburn Dr. S, Auburn, 4/21/75, A, B, a, 75000317

Geneva Street Historic District, Roughly bounded by S. Seventh, Glenn, Stowe, Geneva, and S. Tenth Sts., and Ave. C, Opelika, 9/15/87, C, 87000981

Lee County Courthouse, S. 9th St. between Aves. A and B, Opelika, 7/23/73, A, C, 73000353

Loachapoka Historic District, Both sides of AL 14 in Loachapoka, Loachapoka, 5/11/73, A, C, 73000352

Lowther House Complex, Lee Co. Rd. 318, Smiths Station vicinity, 9/16/93, C, 93000986

McLain, Dr. Andrew D., Office and Drug Store, Main and Crawford Sts., Salem, 2/03/83, C, 83002978

Noble Hall, 3 mi. N of Auburn on Shelton Mill Rd., Auburn vicinity, 3/24/72, C, 72000163

Old Main and Church Street Historic District, Roughly bounded by E. Drake Ave., Western RR of Alabama, N. Gay St., N. College St. and Bragg Ave. and Warrior Ct., Auburn, 10/19/78, B, C, 78003194

Old Rotation, Auburn University, Auburn, 1/14/88, A, 87002390

Railroad Avenue Historic District, Roughly bounded by 7th and 10th Sts., 1st Ave. and Ave. B, Opelika, 8/30/84, A, C, 84000640

Scott-Yarbrough House, 101 DeBardeleben St., Auburn, 4/16/75, B, C, 75000318

Spring Villa, 6 mi. (9.6 km) SE of Opelika on Spring Villa Rd., Opelika vicinity, 1/03/78, C, 78000494

Summers Plantation, 475 Lee Rd. 181, Opelika vicinity, 2/21/91, C, d, 91000095

U.S. Post Office, 701 Ave. A, Opelika, 11/18/76, C, 76000339

U.S. Post Office, 144 Tichenor Ave., Auburn, 6/21/83, C, 83002979

Yarbrough, Franklin, Jr., Store, Co. Hwy. 68, Beaulah vicinity, 6/29/89, A, C, 89000309

Limestone County

Athens State College Historic District, 202–212 and 311 N. Beaty St., central campus area roughly bounded by Beaty, Pryor and Hobbs Sts., Athens, 2/14/85, A, C, 85000254

Belle Mina, S of Belle Mina on the Mooresville-Elkton Rd., Belle Mina vicinity, 10/31/72, B, C, 72000164

Blackburn House, W of Athens, Athens vicinity, 9/20/84, C, 84000643

Donnell, Robert, House, 601 S. Clinton St., Athens, 9/19/73, B, 73000354

Houston, George S., Historic District, Roughly 2nd Ave., Jefferson St., McClellan St., Marion St., Hobbs St., Madison St., Washington St., and Houston St., Athens, 7/20/89, C, 89000943

Houston, Governor George Smith, House, 101 N. Houston St., Athens, 5/15/86, B, C, 86001043

Mooresville, Off U.S. 72 (AL 20), Mooresville, 4/13/72, C, 72000165

Old Athens, Alabama Main Post Office, 310 W. Washington St., Athens, 2/18/82, A, C, 82002047

Robert Beaty Historic District, Roughly bounded by Louisville and Nashville RR, Forrest, East, and Washington Sts., Athens, 8/30/84, A, C, 84000646

Sulphur Trestle Fort Site, 1 mi. S of Elkmont, Elkmont vicinity, 5/08/73, A, 73000355

Woodside, SW of Belle Mina, Belle Mina vicinity, 2/19/82, A, C, 82002048

Lowndes County

Calhoun School Principal's House, CR 33, Calhoun, 3/26/76, B, 76000340

Lowndes County Courthouse, Washington St., Hayneville, 6/24/71, A, 71000100

Lowndesboro, N of U.S. 80, Lowndesboro, 12/12/73, A, C, a, 73000356

Williamson, James Spullock, House, AL 31, Sandy Ridge, 1/05/89, C, 88003123

Macon County

Archeological Site No. 1MC110, Address Restricted, Tuskegee vicinity, 12/14/85, D, 85003118

Atasi Site, Address Restricted, Shorter vicinity, 4/18/77, D, 77000210

Creekwood, Society Hill Rd., 0.4 mi. N of Co. Hwy. 10, Creekstand vicinity, 4/13/89, C, 89000310

Grey Columns, 399 Old Montgomery Rd., Tuskegee, 1/11/80, C, NPS, 80000364

Macon County Courthouse, E. Northside and N. Main Sts., Tuskegee, 11/17/78, A, C, 78000495

Main Street Historic District, Main St., Tuskegee, 3/12/84, A, C, 84000650

North Main Street Historic District, 600, 615, 616 N. Main, 101, 110 E. Water, 700 Water, 701 Maple and 811 N. Maple Sts., Tuskegee, 3/07/85, A, C, 85000445

Tuskegee Institute National Historic Site, 1 mi. NW of Tuskegee on U.S. 80, Tuskegee vicinity, 10/15/66, A, B, f, NHL, NPS, 66000151

Madison County

Beckers Block [Downtown Huntsville MRA], 105–111 N. Jefferson St., Huntsville, 9/22/80, A, C, 80000703

Bibb, James H., House, 11 Allen St., Madison, 4/12/84, A, C, 84000651

Big Spring [Downtown Huntsville MRA], W. Side Sq., Huntsville, 9/22/80, A, 80000704

Building at 105 N. Washington Street [Downtown Huntsville MRA], 105 N. Washington St., Huntsville, 5/23/84, A, C, 84000653

Buildings at 104–128 S. Side Sq. [Downtown Huntsville MRA], 104–128 S. Side Sq., Huntsville, 9/22/80, A, C, 80004472

Burritt, William, Mansion, 3101 Burritt Dr., SE., Huntsville, 5/29/92, C, 92000627

Butlers' Store, 5498 Main Dr., New Hope, 8/31/92, C, 92001089

Church of the Visitation [Downtown Huntsville MRA], 222 N. Jefferson St., Huntsville, 9/22/80, A, 80000705

Clemens House, Clinton Ave. at Church St., Huntsville, 10/16/74, B, C, 74000419

Dallas Mill, 701 Dallas Ave., Huntsville, 9/18/78, A, C, 78000496

Madison County—Continued

Domestic Science Building, Alabama Agricultural and Mechanical University campus, Normal, 4/11/73, A, 73000358

Donegan Block [Downtown Huntsville MRA], 105–109 N. Side Sq., Huntsville, 9/22/80, C, 80000706

Downtown Chevron Station [Downtown Huntsville MRA], 300 E. Clinton Ave., Huntsville, 9/22/80, C, 80000707

Dunnavant's Building [Downtown Huntsville MRA], 100 N. Washington St., Huntsville, 9/22/80, C, 80000708

Episcopal Church of the Nativity, 212 Eustis St., Huntsville, 10/09/74, A, C, a, NHL, 74000420

Everett Building [Downtown Huntsville MRA], 115–123 N. Washington St., Huntsville, 9/22/80, C, 80000709

First National Bank, West Side Sq., Huntsville, 10/25/74, A, C, 74000421

Flint River Place, 1997 Jordan Rd., Huntsville vicinity, 1/18/82, C, 82002050

Halsey Grocery Warehouse [Downtown Huntsville MRA], 301 N. Jefferson St., Huntsville, 9/22/80, C, 80000710

Halsey, W. L., Warehouse [Downtown Huntsville MRA], 300 N. Jefferson St., Huntsville, 9/22/80, C, 80000711

Henderson National Bank [Downtown Huntsville MRA], 118 S. Jefferson St., Huntsville, 9/22/80, C, g, 80000712

Hotel Russel Erskine [Downtown Huntsville MRA], 123 W. Clinton Ave., Huntsville, 9/22/80, A, C, 80000713

Humphreys, David C., House, 510 Clinton Ave., W., Huntsville, 8/03/77, A, B, 77000211

Hundley House, 401 Madison St., Huntsville, 5/22/78, B, C, 78000497

Hundley Rental Houses [Downtown Huntsville MRA], 108 Gates St. and 400 Franklin St., Huntsville, 9/22/80, B, C, 80000714

Hutchens, Terry, Building [Downtown Huntsville MRA], 102 W. Clinton Ave., Huntsville, 9/22/80, A, C, 80000715

Hutchens, W. T., Building [Downtown Huntsville MRA], 100–104 S. Jefferson St., Huntsville, 12/28/83, C, 83004374

Kelly Brothers and Rowe Building [Downtown Huntsville MRA], 307 N. Jefferson St., Huntsville, 9/22/80, C, 80000716

Kildare-McCormick House, 2005 Kildare St., Huntsville, 7/15/82, A, C, 82002051

Kress Building [Downtown Huntsville MRA], 107 S. Washington St., Huntsville, 9/22/80, C, 80000717

Leech-Hauer House, 502 Governors Dr., Huntsville, 12/08/78, C, 78000498

Lincoln School, 1110 N. Meridian St., Huntsville, 12/27/82, C, 82001608

Lombardo Building [Downtown Huntsville MRA], 315 N. Jefferson St., Huntsville, 9/22/80, C, 80000718

Mason Building [Downtown Huntsville MRA], 115 E. Clinton Ave., Huntsville, 9/22/80, C, 80000719

May and Cooney Dry Goods Company [Downtown Huntsville MRA], 205 E. Side Sq., Huntsville, 9/22/80, A, C, 80000720

McCartney-Bone House, 3 mi. NE of Maysville on Hurricane Rd., Maysville vicinity, 12/16/77, C, 77000213

McCrary House, NE of Huntsville, Huntsville vicinity, 6/01/82, A, C, 82002052

Milligan Block [Downtown Huntsville MRA], 201–203 E. Side Sq., Huntsville, 9/22/80, C, 80000721

Neutral Buoyancy Space Simulator, George C. Marshall Space Flight Center, Huntsville, 10/03/85, A, C, g, NHL, 85002807

New Market Presbyterian Church, 1723 New Market Rd., New Market, 8/25/88, C, a, 88001348

New Market United Methodist Church, 310 Hurricane Rd., New Market, 6/14/90, C, a, 90000919

Old Town Historic District, Roughly bounded by Dement and Lincoln Sts., and Randolph and Walker Aves., Huntsville, 7/18/78, C, a, 78000499

Otey, William Madison, House, S of Meridianville, Meridianville vicinity, 1/19/82, A, C, 82002056

Phelps-Jones House, 6112 Pulaski Pike, Huntsville, 2/19/82, A, C, 82002053

Propulsion and Structural Test Facility, George C. Marshall Space Flight Center, Huntsville, 10/03/85, A, C, g, NHL, 85002804

Rand Building [Downtown Huntsville MRA], 113 N. Side Sq., Huntsville, 9/22/80, C, 80000722

Randolph Street Church of Christ [Downtown Huntsville MRA], 210 Randolph Ave., Huntsville, 9/22/80, C, a, 80000723

Redstone Test Stand, George C. Marshall Space Flight Center, Huntsville vicinity, 5/13/76, A, C, g, NHL, 76000341

Robinson, John, House, 2709 Meridian St. N, Huntsville, 10/06/77, C, 77000212

Robinson, Mrs. William, House, 401 Quietdale Dr. NE, Huntsville, 2/04/82, C, 82002054

Saturn V Dynamic Test Stand, George C. Marshall Space Flight Center, Huntsville, 10/03/85, A, C, g, NHL, 85002806

Saturn V Space Vehicle, Tranquility Base, Huntsville, 11/22/78, A, g, NHL, 78000500

Schiffman Building [Downtown Huntsville MRA], 231 E. Side Sq., Huntsville, 9/22/80, C, 80000724

Southern Railway System Depot, 330 Church St., Huntsville, 9/10/71, A, C, 71000101

Steele-Fowler House, 808 Maysville Rd., Huntsville, 6/20/74, A, C, a, 74000422

Steger House, 3141 Maysville Rd., Huntsville vicinity, 6/01/82, B, C, 82002055

Struve-Hay Building [Downtown Huntsville MRA], 117–123 N. Jefferson St., Huntsville, 9/22/80, C, 80000725

Times Building [Downtown Huntsville MRA], 228 E. Holmes Ave., Huntsville, 9/22/80, A, C, 80000726

Twickenham Historic District, Roughly bounded by Clinton Ave., California St., Newman Ave.

and S. Green St., and Franklin St., Huntsville, 1/04/73, C, 73000357

U.S. Courthouse and Post Office [Downtown Huntsville MRA], 101 E. Holmes Ave., Huntsville, 2/24/81, C, g, 81000129

Urguhart House, 8042 Pulaski Pike, Huntsville vicinity, 2/13/92, C, 92000034

Vaught House, 701 Ward Ave., Huntsville, 12/15/81, C, 81000130

White-Turner-Sanford House, 601 Madison St., Huntsville, 4/12/84, A, C, 84000655

Whitman-Cobb House, Winchester Rd., New Market, 1/18/82, C, 82002057

Withers-Chapman House, 2409 Gaboury Lane, NE, Huntsville, 12/08/78, C, 78000501

Yarbrough Hotel [Downtown Huntsville MRA], 127–129 N. Washington St., Huntsville, 9/22/80, A, C, 80000727

Marengo County

Altwood [Plantation Houses of the Alabama Canebrake and Their Associated Outbuildings MPS], W of Marengo Co. Rd. 51, S of jct. with Co. Rd. 54, Faunsdale vicinity, 7/13/93, C, b, 93000598

Ashe Cottage, 307 N. Commissioners Ave., Demopolis, 10/19/78, C, b, 78000502

Bluff Hall, 405 N. Commissioners Ave., Demopolis, 7/28/70, B, C, 70000105

Cedar Crest [Plantation Houses of the Alabama Canebrake MPS], E. side Marengo Co. Rd. 51, .5 mi. S. of Co. Rd. 54, Faunsdale vicinity, 8/05/93, C, b, 93000763

Cedar Grove Plantation [Plantation Houses of the Alabama Canebrake and Their Associated Outbuildings MPS], Marengo Co. Rd. E of jct. with AL 25, Faunsdale vicinity, 7/13/93, C, 93000599

Cedar Haven [Plantation Houses of the Alabama Canebrake and Their Associated Outbuildings MPS], Marengo Co. Rd. 61 SE of jct. with AL 25, Faunsdale vicinity, 7/13/93, C, 93000600

Confederate Park, Bounded by Main, Capitol, Walnut, and Washington Sts., Demopolis, 10/29/75, C, 75000319

Cuba Plantation [Plantation Houses of the Alabama Canebrake and Their Associated Outbuildings MPS], Marengo Co. Rd. 54 W of jct. with AL 25, Faunsdale vicinity, 7/13/93, C, 93000601

Curtis House, 510 N. Main, Demopolis, 4/11/77, C, 77000214

Demopolis Historic Business District, Roughly bounded by Capital and Franklin Sts., Desnanette and Cedar Aves., Demopolis, 10/25/79, A, C, 79000391

Demopolis Public School, 601 S. Main Ave., Demopolis, 10/28/83, A, C, 83003453

Faunsdale Plantation [Plantation Houses of the Alabama Canebrake and Their Associated Outbuildings MPS], Marengo Co. Rd. 54 just W of jct. with AL 25, Faunsdale vicinity, 7/13/93, A, C, 93000602

Marengo County—Continued

Foscue-Whitfield House, W of Demopolis on U.S. 80, Demopolis vicinity, 1/21/74, C, 74000423

Gaineswood, 805 S. Cedar St., Demopolis, 1/05/72, C, NHL, 72000167

Glover Mausoleum, Riverside Cemetery, Demopolis, 1/21/74, C, c, 74000424

Half-Chance Bridge, SR 39 over the Chickasaw Bogue Creek, Dayton vicinity, 9/14/72, C, 72000166

Jefferson Historic District, AL 28, Jefferson, 11/13/76, C, 76000342

Lyon-Lamar House, 102 S. Main Ave., Demopolis, 1/21/74, B, C, 74000425

Old Courthouse, 300 W. Cahaba Ave., Linden, 1/18/74, C, 74000426

US Post Office, 100 W. Capitol St., Demopolis, 7/28/84, A, C, 84000657

White Bluff, Arch St., Demopolis, 8/25/70, A, 70000106

Marion County

Pearce's Mill, E of Hamilton on SR 253, Hamilton vicinity, 10/08/76, B, 76000343

Marshall County

Albertville Depot, E. Main St., Albertville, 2/20/75, A, 75000320

Henry, Albert G., Jr., House, 308 Blount Ave., Guntersville, 4/13/89, C, 89000291

Henry-Jordan House, 301 Blount Ave., Guntersville, 9/04/79, C, 79003351

Saratoga Victory Mill, 1821 Gunter Ave., Guntersville, 4/12/84, A, C, 84000659

U.S. Post Office, 107 W. Main St., Albertville, 6/21/83, C, 83002980

Mobile County

Ashland Place Historic District, Roughly bounded by Springhill and Ryan Aves., Old Shell Rd., and Levert Ave., Mobile, 6/23/87, A, C, g, 87000935

Askew, Wade, House [Spanish Revival Residences in Mobile MPS], 103 Florence Pl., Mobile, 7/12/91, C, 91000858

Austin, Hiram B., House, AL 163 at 12 mi. marker, Mon Louis Island vicinity, 2/11/88, C, b, 88000106

Azalea Court Apartments, 1820 Old Government St., Mobile, 2/11/88, C, 88000108

Barr's Subdivision Historic District, Roughly along US 45 and Howard St. between LeBaron and State, Citronelle, 1/25/90, A, C, 89002452

Barton Academy, 504 Government St., Mobile, 2/16/70, A, C, 70000107

Battle House Royale, 26 N. Royal St., Mobile, 8/19/75, C, 75000322

Beal-Gaillard House [19th Century Spring Hill Neighborhood TR], 111 Myrtlewood Lane, Mobile, 10/18/84, A, C, 84000078

Bellingrath Gardens and Home, S of Theodore off AL 59, Theodore vicinity, 10/19/82, C, g, 82001609

Bishop Manor Estate, Argyl Rd., St. Elmo, 2/14/85, C, 85000255

Bragg-Mitchell House, 1906 Springhill Ave., Mobile, 9/27/72, B, C, 72000168

Brisk & Jacobson Store, 51 Dauphin St., Mobile, 3/14/73, C, 73000361

Carlen House, 54 S. Carlen St., Mobile, 6/12/81, A, C, 81000131

Carolina Hall, 70 S. McGregor St., Mobile, 1/18/73, C, 73000362

Cavellero House, 7 N. Jackson St., Mobile, 10/07/82, C, 82001610

Center-Gaillard House [19th Century Spring Hill Neighborhood TR], 3500 The Cedars, Mobile, 10/18/84, A, C, 84000081

Central Core Historic District, Roughly State and Le Baron Sts. from Mobile to Second Sts., Citronelle, 1/25/90, A, C, 89002424

Church Street East Historic District, Roughly bounded by Conti, Water and Claiborne, Eslava, and Warren and Bayou Sts., Mobile, 12/16/71, C, 71000102

Church Street Historic District (Boundary Increase), Roughly bounded by Broad, Conti, Water, Claiborne, and Canal Sts., Mobile, 1/13/84, C, b, 84000663

Citronelle Railroad Historic District, Roughly Center and Main from Union to Faye, Citronelle, 1/25/90, A, C, 89002421

Clark, Willis G., House, E of US 45 S of Citronelle, Citronelle vicinity, 1/25/90, B, C, 89002454

Cleveland, U. J., House, 551 Charles St., Mobile, 5/21/93, C, 93000420

Coley Building, 56 St. Francis St., Mobile, 10/22/82, C, 82001611

Collins-Marston House [19th Century Spring Hill Neighborhood TR], 4703 Old Shell Rd., Mobile, 10/18/84, A, C, 84000083

Collins-Robinson House [19th Century Spring Hill Neighborhood TR], 56 Oakland Ave., Mobile, 10/18/84, A, C, 84000087

Common Street District, 959–1002 Dauphin St. and 7–19 Common St., Mobile, 2/04/82, A, C, 82002058

Convent and Academy of the Visitation [Historic Roman Catholic Properties in Mobile MPS], 2300 Springhill Ave., Mobile, 4/24/92, C, a, d, 91000844

Convent of Mercy [Historic Roman Catholic Properties in Mobile MPS], 753 St. Francis St., Mobile, 4/24/92, C, a, 91000845

Dahm House, 7 N. Claiborne St., Mobile, 1/05/84, C, 84000665

Davis Avenue Branch, Mobile Public Library, 564 Davis Ave., Mobile, 12/22/83, C, 83003459

Davis—Oak Grove District, W side of Oak Grove Rd. just N of Kali Oka Rd., Mauvila vicinity, 5/03/88, A, C, a, 88000445

De Tonti Square Historic District, Roughly bounded by Adams, St. Anthony, Claiborne,

and Conception Sts., Mobile, 2/07/72, C, 72000169

Denby House, 558 Conti St., Mobile, 1/05/84, C, 84000668

Ellicott Stone, 1 mi. S of Bucks off U.S. 43, Bucks vicinity, 4/11/73, A, 73000359

Emanuel AME Church, 656 Saint Michael St., Mobile, 5/29/87, C, a, 87000853

Emanuel Building, 100 N. Royal St., Mobile, 3/21/78, A, C, 78000503

Fearn, George, House [Spanish Revival Residences in Mobile MPS], 1806 Airport Blvd., Mobile, 7/12/91, C, 91000855

Fire Station No. 5, 7 N. Lawrence St., Mobile, 12/22/83, C, 83003462

First National Bank, 68 St. Francis St., Mobile, 11/17/78, A, C, 78000504

Fort Conde-Charlotte, Church and Royal Sts., Mobile, 5/21/69, A, D, 69000033

Fort Gaines, S of Mobile on E end of Dauphin Island, Mobile vicinity, 12/12/76, A, C, 76000348

Fort Louis De La Louisiane, Address Restricted, Bay Minette vicinity, 5/06/76, D, 76000344

Gates-Daves House, 1570–1572 Dauphin St., Mobile, 6/20/74, C, 74000427

Georgia Cottage, 2564 Springhill Ave., Mobile, 9/14/72, B, 72000170

Government Street Presbyterian Church, 300 Government St., Mobile, 10/05/92, C, a, NHL, 92001885

Grand Bay Historic District, Jct. of Dezauche Ln. and Freeland, Grand Bay, 6/28/90, A, 90000918

Greene-Marston House, 2000 Dauphin St., Mobile, 1/11/83, C, 83002966

Gulf, Mobile, and Ohio Passenger Terminal, Beauregard and St. Joseph Sts., Mobile, 8/15/75, C, 75000323

Hawthorn House, 352 Stanton Rd., Mobile, 5/21/84, C, 84000671

Horst, Martin, House, 407 Conti St., Mobile, 6/21/71, C, 71000103

Hunter House, 504 St. Francis St., Mobile, 3/07/85, B, C, 85000446

Indian Mound Park, Restricted Address, Dauphin Island vicinity, 8/14/73, D, NHL, 73000360

Jossen, Joseph, House, 109 N. Conception St., Mobile, 5/29/92, C, 92000628

Kirkbride House, 104 Theater St., Mobile, 12/12/73, C, 73000363

Leatherbury, George, House, Shell Belt Rd. SE of Sans Souci Beach, Coden, 6/14/90, C, 90000917

Leinkauf Historic District, Roughly bounded by Government, S. Monterey, Eslava, Lamar, and S. Monterey Sts., Mobile, 6/24/87, A, C, g, 87000936

Levy, George, House [Spanish Revival Residences in Mobile MPS], 107 Florence Pl., Mobile, 7/12/91, C, 91000861

Lindsey, Martin, House, 3112 Bayfront Rd., Mobile, 1/24/91, C, 90002176

Lower Dauphin Street Historic District, 171–614 Dauphin St., Mobile, 2/09/79, A, C, 79000392

Lower Dauphin Street Historic District (Boundary Increase), Dauphin St. from Water to Dearborn Ave., Mobile, 2/19/82, A, C, 82002059

Mobile County—Continued

Magee, Jacob, House, CR 45 N of Kushla Mcleod Rd., Kushla vicinity, 2/12/88, A, C, 88000112

Magnolia Cemetery including Mobile National Cemetery, Ann and Virginia Sts., Mobile, 6/13/86, A, C, d, 86003757

Meaher-Zoghby House, 5 N. Claiborne St., Mobile, 1/05/84, C, 84000672

Megginson, Ernest, House [Spanish Revival Residences in Mobile MPS], 143 Florence Pl., Mobile, 7/12/91, C, 91000860

Metzger House, 7 N. Hamilton St., Mobile, 1/05/84, C, 84000675

Middle Bay Light, Middle of Mobile Bay, Mobile Bay, 12/30/74, C, 74000429

Miller-O'Donnell House, 1102 Broad St., Mobile, 2/19/82, A, C, 82002060

Mobile City Hall, 111 S. Royal St., Mobile, 12/03/69, A, C, NHL, 69000034

Mobile City Hospital, 900–950 St. Anthony St., Mobile, 2/26/70, A, C, 70000108

Monterey Place, 1552 Monterey Pl., Mobile, 1/05/84, A, C, 84000680

Morrison, James Arthur, House [Spanish Revival Residences in Mobile MPS], 159 Hillwood Rd., Mobile, 7/12/91, C, 91000863

Mount Vernon Arsenal—Searcy Hospital Complex, Coy Smith Hwy. 1/2 mi. W of AL 43, Mt. Vernon vicinity, 5/26/88, A, B, C, 88000676

Murphy High School, 100 S. Carlen St, Mobile, 11/04/82, A, C, 82001612

Nanna Hubba Bluff, Address Restricted, Stockton vicinity, 10/01/74, D, 74000430

Neville House, 255 St. Francis St., Mobile, 1/05/84, C, 84000682

Oakleigh, 350 Oakleigh St., Mobile, 5/27/71, B, C, 71000104

Oakleigh Garden Historic District, Roughly bounded by Government, Marine, Texas, and Ann Sts., Mobile, 4/13/72, A, C, 72000171

Oakleigh Garden Historic District (Boundary Increase), Roughly bounded by Selma St., Broad St., Texas St. and Rapier Ave., Mobile, 1/30/91, C, a, 90002175

Old Dauphin Way Historic District, Roughly bounded by Springhill Ave., Broad, Goverment, and Houston Sts., Mobile, 8/30/84, C, g, 84000686

Paterson House, 1673 Government St., Mobile, 5/15/86, C, 86001065

Paterson, J. E., House [Spanish Revival Residences in Mobile MPS], 118 Florence Pl., Mobile, 7/12/91, C, 91000859

Patton, Dave, House, 1252 Martin Luther King, Jr. Ave., Mobile, 6/12/87, B, C, 87000937

Pfau-Creighton Cottage [19th Century Spring Hill Neighborhood TR], 3703 Old Shell Rd., Mobile, 10/18/84, A, C, 84000120

Phillips House, 53 N. Jackson St., Mobile, 1/05/84, C, 84000689

Pincus Building, 1 S. Royal St., Mobile, 12/12/76, C, 76000345

Portier, Bishop, House, 307 Conti St., Mobile, 2/26/70, B, C, a, 70000109

Protestant Children's Home, 911 Dauphin St., Mobile, 6/18/73, A, C, 73000364

Saint Francis Xavier Roman Catholic Church [Historic Roman Catholic Properties in Mobile MPS], 2034 St. Stephens Rd., Mobile, 7/03/91, C, a, 91000842

Saint Joseph's Roman Catholic Church [Historic Roman Catholic Properties in Mobile MPS], 808 Springhill Ave., Mobile, 7/03/91, C, a, 91000841

Saint Matthew's Catholic Church [Historic Roman Catholic Properties in Mobile MPS], 1200 S. Marine St., Mobile, 7/03/91, C, a, 91000840

Saint Paul's Episcopal Chapel [19th Century Spring Hill Neighborhood TR], 4051 Old Shell Rd., Mobile, 10/18/84, A, C, a, 84000123

Saint Vincent de Paul [Historic Roman Catholic Properties in Mobile MPS], 351 S. Lawrence St., Mobile, 4/24/92, C, a, 91000839

Scottish Rites Temple, 351 St. Francis St., Mobile, 1/05/84, C, 84000694

Semmes, Raphael, House, 804 Government St., Mobile, 2/26/70, B, C, a, 70000110

Sodality Chapel [19th Century Spring Hill Neighborhood TR], 4307 Old Shell Rd., Mobile, 10/18/84, A, C, a, 84000122

South Lafayette Street Creole Cottages, 20, 22, and 23 S. Lafayette St., Mobile, 11/07/76, C, 76000346

Spotswood, Robert L., House [Spanish Revival Residences in Mobile MPS], 1 Country Club Rd., Mobile, 7/12/91, C, 91000854

Spring Hill College Quadrangle, 4307 Old Shell Rd., Mobile, 8/17/73, A, C, a, 73000365

St. Francis Street Methodist Church, 15 N. Joachim St., Mobile, 1/05/84, A, C, a, 84000690

St. Louis Street Missionary Baptist Church, 108 N. Dearborn St., Mobile, 10/08/76, A, a, 76000347

State Street A.M.E. Zion Church, 502 State St., Mobile, 9/06/78, A, C, a, 78000505

Stewart, Amelia, House, 137 Tuscaloosa St., Mobile, 5/29/92, C, 92000629

Stewartfield [19th Century Spring Hill Neighborhood TR], 4307 Old Shell Rd., Mobile, 10/18/84, A, C, 84000124

Stone Street Baptist Church, 311 Tunstall St., Mobile, 8/08/85, C, a, 85001749

Stone Street Cemetery [Historic Roman Catholic Properties in Mobile MPS], 1700 Martin Luther King, Jr., Blvd., Mobile, 7/03/91, C, a, d, 91000843

Thompson, N. Q. and Virginia M., House, 105 LeBaron, Citronelle, 1/25/90, C, 89002453

Trinity Episcopal Church, 1900 Dauphin St., Mobile, 8/20/90, C, a, b, 90001240

Tschiener House, 1120 Old Shell Rd., Mobile, 1/18/82, A, C, 82002061

U.S. Marine Hospital, 800 St. Anthony St., Mobile, 6/27/74, A, C, 74000428

USS ALABAMA (battleship), Battleship Pkwy., Mobile, 1/14/86, A, g, NHL, 86000083

USS DRUM (submarine), Battleship Pkwy., Mobile, 1/14/86, A, g, NHL, 86000086

VanderSys, Arthur, House [Spanish Revival Residences in Mobile MPS], 119 Florence Pl., Mobile, 7/12/91, C, 91000857

VanderSys, Jacob, House [Spanish Revival Residences in Mobile MPS], 129 Florence Pl., Mobile, 7/12/91, C, 91000862

Vickers and Schumacher Buildings, 707–709 and 711 Dauphin St., Mobile, 12/22/83, C, 83003474

Walker, Joseph M., House [Spanish Revival Residences in Mobile MPS], 104 Florence Pl., Mobile, 7/12/91, C, 91000856

Weems House, 1155 Springhill Ave., Mobile, 10/07/82, C, 82001613

Monroe County

Old Monroe County Courthouse, Courthouse Sq., Monroeville, 4/26/73, A, B, C, 73000366

Robbins Hotel, AL 265, Beatrice, 8/26/87, A, 87000858

Montgomery County

Alabama State Capitol, Goat Hill, E end of Dexter Ave., Montgomery, 10/15/66, A, NHL, 66000152

Bell Building, 207 Montgomery St., Montgomery, 12/15/81, C, 81000132

Brame House, 402–404 S. Hull St., Montgomery, 9/17/80, B, 80000728

Brittan, Patrick Henry, House, 507 Columbus St., Montgomery, 12/13/79, B, C, 79000393

Building 800—Austin Hall, Second St., Maxwell AFB, Montgomery vicinity, 3/02/88, A, C, 87002178

Building 836—Community College of the Air Force Building, Maxwell Blvd., Maxwell AFB, Montgomery vicinity, 3/02/88, A, C, 87002182

Cassimus House, 110 N. Jackson St., Montgomery, 8/13/76, B, C, 76000349

City of St. Jude Historic District, 2048 W. Fairview Ave., Montgomery, 6/18/90, A, C, a, g, 90000916

Cloverdale Historic District, Roughly bounded by Norman Bridge & Cloverdale Rd., Fairview & Felder Aves. and Boultier St., Montgomery, 9/12/85, C, a, 85002161

Cottage Hill Historic District, Roughly bounded by Goldthwaite, Bell, Holt, and Clayton Sts., Montgomery, 11/07/76, C, 76000350

Court Square Historic District, 21–35 Court St., 1–2 Dexter Ave., 18–24 N. Court St., and Court Sq., Montgomery, 3/01/82, A, C, 82002062

Court Square-Dexter Avenue Historic District (Boundary Increase), Roughly Dexter Ave., Perry, Court, and Monroe Sts., Montgomery, 8/30/84, C, 84000697

Davis, Jefferson, Hotel, Catoma and Montgomery Sts., Montgomery, 3/13/79, A, C, 75000324

Dexter Avenue Baptist Church, 454 Dexter Ave., Montgomery, 7/01/74, B, a, g, NHL, 74000431

Dowe Historic District, 320 and 334 Washington Ave. and 114–116 S. Hull St., Montgomery, 12/29/88, C, 88003076

Edgewood, 3175 Thomas Ave., Montgomery, 4/24/73, C, e, 73000367

Montgomery County—Continued

First White House of the Confederacy, 644 Washington Ave., Montgomery, 6/25/74, A, b, 74000432

Garden District, Roughly bounded by Norman Bridge Rd., Court St., Jeff Davis, and Fairview Aves., Montgomery, 9/13/84, C, 84000698

Gay House, 230 Noble Ave., Montgomery, 3/15/75, C, 75000325

Gerald-Dowdell House, 405 S. Hull St., Montgomery, 4/28/80, C, 80000729

Governor's Mansion, 1142 S. Perry St., Montgomery, 7/03/72, B, C, g, 72000172

Grace Episcopal Church, Pike Rd., Mount Meigs, 2/19/82, A, C, a, 82002067

Harrington Archaeological Site, Address Restricted, Montgomery vicinity, 1/25/79, D, c, 79000394

Jackson, Jefferson Franklin, House, 409 S. Union St., Montgomery, 5/17/84, A, B, 84000711

Jones, Gov. Thomas G., House, 323 Adams Ave., Montgomery, 12/08/78, B, 78000506

Lower Commerce Street Historic District, Roughly bounded by RR tracks, Commerce, N. Court, and Bibb Sts., Montgomery, 3/29/79, A, C, g, 79000395

Lower Commerce Street Historic District (Boundary Increase), Roughly bounded by RR tracks, N. Court, Commerce, Coosa, and Tallapoosa Sts., Montgomery, 2/25/82, A, C, 82002063

Lower Commerce Street Historic District (Boundary Increase), Roughly bounded by Central of Georgia RR tracks, N. Lawrence St., Madison Ave., and Commerce St., Montgomery, 1/15/87, A, C, g, 86001529

Maxwell Air Force Base Senior Officer's Quarters Historic District, West Dr., N. Juniper & S. Juniper Sts., Inner Circle, Center Dr., Sequoia, & East Dr., Maxwell Air Force Base, Montgomery vicinity, 3/02/88, B, C, 87002177

McBryde-Screws-Tyson House, 433 Mildred St., Montgomery, 11/28/80, B, C, 80000730

Montgomery Union Station and Trainshed, Water St., Montgomery, 7/24/73, A, C, NHL, 73000368

Muklassa, Address Restricted, Montgomery vicinity, 8/28/73, D, 73000369

Murphy House, The, 22 Bibb St., Montgomery, 3/24/72, C, 72000173

North Lawrence-Monroe Street Historic District, 132–148, 216, 220 Monroe St. and 14, 22, 28–40, 56 N. Lawrence St., Montgomery, 8/30/84, A, 84000712

Old Ship African Methodist Episcopal Zion Church, 483 Holcombe St., Montgomery, 1/24/91, C, a, 90002177

Opp Cottage, 33 W. Jefferson Davis Ave., Montgomery, 5/04/76, C, 76000351

Ordeman-Shaw Historic District, Bounded by McDonough, Decatur, Madison, and Randolph Sts., Montgomery, 5/13/71, B, C, b, 71000105

Pastorium, Dexter Avenue Baptist Church, 309 S. Jackson St., Montgomery, 3/10/82, B, C, a, g, 82002064

Pepperman House, 17 Mildred St., Montgomery, 3/01/82, C, 82002065

Perry Street Historic District, Bounded roughly by McDonough St. on E, Sayre St. on W, Washington St. on N, and Donaldson St. on S, Montgomery, 12/16/71, C, 71000106

Powder Magazine, End of Eugene St., Montgomery, 4/13/73, A, 73000370

Sayre Street School, 506 Sayre St., Montgomery, 2/19/82, A, C, 82002066

Scott Street Firehouse, 418 Scott St., Montgomery, 2/12/81, A, 81000133

Semple House, 725 Monroe St., Montgomery, 9/27/72, B, C, 72000174

Shepherd Building, 312 Montgomery St., Montgomery, 5/22/86, C, 86001106

Shine, Jere, Site, Address Restricted, Montgomery vicinity, 12/08/78, D, 78000507

Smith—Joseph—Stratton House, 302 Alabama St., Montgomery, 4/11/85, B, C, 85000736

South Perry Street Historic District, Roughly Perry St. between Washington St. and Dexter Ave., Montgomery, 8/30/84, C, 84000713

St. John's Episcopal Church, 113 Madison Ave., Montgomery, 2/24/75, A, C, a, 75000326

Stay House, 631 S. Hull St, Montgomery, 9/10/79, C, 79000396

Steiner-Lobman and Teague Hardware Buildings, 184 and 172 Commerce St., Montgomery, 1/31/79, C, 79000397

Thigpen, Dr. C. A., House, 1412 S. Perry St., Montgomery, 12/13/77, B, C, 77000215

Tulane Building, 800 High St., Montgomery, 3/21/79, B, C, 79000398

Tyson-Maner House, 469 S. McDonough St., Montgomery, 5/10/79, C, 79000399

Winter Building, 2 Dexter Ave., Montgomery, 1/14/72, A, B, C, 72000175

Yancey, William Lowndes, Law Office, Adams and Perry Sts., Montgomery, 11/07/73, B, NHL, 73000371

Morgan County

Albany Heritage Neighborhood Historic District, Roughly bounded by Gordon Dr., Summerville Rd., Jackson, 8th, Moulton, 6th, and 4th Aves., Decatur, 2/03/83, C, 83002981

Bank Street Historic District, Bank St., Decatur, 3/27/80, A, C, 80000731

Bank Street-Old Decatur Historic District (Boundary Increase), Roughly bounded by Bank, Market, Well and Lee Sts., Decatur, 5/16/85, B, C, 85001067

Cotaco Opera House, 115 Johnson St. SE, Decatur, 4/29/86, A, 86000914

Dancy, Col. Francis, House, 901 Railroad St., NW, Decatur, 4/28/80, C, 80000732

Forest Home, E of Trinity, Trinity vicinity, 11/21/80, B, C, 80000733

Murphey, Dr. William E., House [Tidewater Cottages in the Tennessee Valley TR], Off US 72, Trinity vicinity, 7/09/86, A, C, 86001547

Rhea-McEntire House, 1105 Sycamore St., Decatur, 8/30/84, A, C, 84000715

Rice, Green Pryor, House [Tidewater Cottages in the Tennessee Valley TR], Jct. of Madison and Monroe Sts., Somerville vicinity, 7/09/86, A, C, 86001546

Somerville Courthouse, SR 36, Somerville, 3/24/72, C, 72000177

Southern Railway Depot, 701 Railroad St., NW, Decatur, 3/10/80, A, C, 80004470

State Bank Building, Decatur Branch, 925 Bank St., NE, Decatur, 3/24/72, A, C, 72000176

Westview, S of Decatur, Decatur vicinity, 1/18/82, B, C, 82002068

Perry County

Chapel and Lovelace Hall, Marion Military Institute, AL 14, Marion, 9/13/78, A, C, a, 78000508

Fairhope Plantation, US 80 1 mi. E of Uniontown city limits, Uniontown vicinity, 5/29/92, C, 92000630

First Congregational Church of Marion, 601 Clay St., Marion, 12/17/82, A, C, a, 82001614

Green Street Historic District, 203–751 W. Green St., Marion, 5/30/79, C, 79000400

Henry House, S. Washington St., Marion, 9/25/86, C, 86002744

Judson College Historic District, Roughly bounded by E. Lafayette, Curb, Mason and Washington Sts., Marion, 2/03/93, A, C, g, 92001825

Kenworthy Hall, AL 14, W of Marion, Marion vicinity, 8/23/90, C, 90001318

Marion Female Seminary, 202 Monroe St., Marion, 10/04/73, A, 73000372

Phillips Memorial Auditorium, Lincoln Ave. and Lee St., Marion, 2/13/90, A, C, g, 88003243

Pitts' Folly, Old Cahaba Rd., Uniontown, 8/09/84, C, 84000717

President's House, Marion Institute, 110 Brown St., Marion, 5/14/79, B, C, 79000401

Siloam Baptist Church, 503 Washington St., Marion, 12/27/82, C, a, 82001615

West Marion Historic District, Roughly bounded by W. Lafayette St., Washington St., Murfree Ave., College St. and Margin St., Marion, 4/22/93, A, C, 92001844

Westwood, N of Uniontown off AL 61, Uniontown vicinity, 11/21/74, C, 74000433

Westwood (Boundary Increase), AL 61, Uniontown, 3/15/84, C, 84000719

Westwood Plantation(Boundary Increase), Bounded roughly by Hwy. 80, Hwy. 61, Rabbit Yard Rd., and Old Uniontown RR Spur, Uniontown, 12/10/84, C, D, 84000488

Pickens County

Aliceville Elementary and High School, 420 3rd Ave., NE, Aliceville, 5/09/80, A, C, 80000734

Ball, Parks E., House, NW of Aliceville, Aliceville vicinity, 1/18/82, C, 82002069

Pickens County—Continued

Hill, Hugh Wilson, House, 201 Phoenix, Carrollton, 4/13/89, C, 89000292

MONTGOMERY (snagboat), Tom Bevill Visitor Center, Pickensville, 11/28/83, A, C, b, NHL, 83003521

Old Jail, NE corner of Church St. and 1st Ave., Gordo, 12/17/74, A, C, 74000434

Stewart-Blanton House, AL 86, Carrollton, 5/23/85, B, C, a, 85001130

Pike County

College Street Historic District, W. College St. between Pine and Cherry Sts., Troy, 8/13/76, C, 76000352

Troy High School, 436 Elm St., Troy, 8/30/84, A, 84000721

Randolph County

McCosh Grist Mill, SE of Rock Mills on McCosh Mill Rd., Rock Mills vicinity, 11/21/76, A, 76000353

Roanoke Downtown Historic District, Roughly bounded by White, Main, W. Point, La Monte, Chestnut & Louina Sts., Roanoke, 2/03/93, A, C, 85003683

Russell County

Apalachicola Fort, Address Restricted, Holy Trinity vicinity, 10/15/66, A, D, NHL, 66000931

Bass-Perry House, 4 mi. NE of Seale on U.S. 431, Seale vicinity, 1/19/76, C, 76000355

Brooks-Hughes House [Phenix City MRA], 1010 Sandfort Rd., Phenix City, 11/03/83, C, 83003477

Brownville-Summerville Historic District [Phenix City MRA], Roughly bounded by 15th and 23rd Sts., and 6th and 11th Aves., Phenix City, 11/03/83, A, C, 83003479

Floyd-Newsome House [Phenix City MRA], 900 22nd St., Phenix City, 11/03/83, C, 83004373

Fort Mitchell Site, Address Restricted, Fort Mitchell vicinity, 6/13/72, A, D, d, NHL, 72000178

Fort No. 5, W of Phenix on Opelika Hwy., Phenix City vicinity, 5/06/76, A, 76000354

Girard High School [Phenix City MRA], Sandfort Rd., Phenix City, 11/03/83, A, C, 83003480

Girard Historic District [Phenix City MRA], Roughly bounded by 8th Pl., 10th St., 5th and 8th Aves., Phenix City, 11/03/83, A, C, 83003481

Glenn-Thompson Plantation, S of Pittsview on U.S. 431, Pittsview vicinity, 4/09/80, A, B, C, 80000735

Glennville Historic District, S of Pittsview, Pittsview vicinity, 8/07/79, A, C, d, 79000402

Kid Alley Residential Historic District [Phenix City MRA], 11th Ave. at 9th Pl., Phenix City, 11/03/83, C, 83003482

Lower Twentieth Street Residential Historic District [Phenix City MRA], 20th St. from 2nd to 6th Aves., Phenix City, 11/03/83, A, C, 83003483

Morgan-Curtis House [Phenix City MRA], 1815 Abbott Dr., Phenix City, 11/03/83, A, B, 83003484

Pitts, Samuel R., Plantation, E of US 431, S of Southern RR tracks, Pittsview vicinity, 6/25/92, C, b, 92000819

Russell County Courthouse at Seale, Courthouse Sq., Seale, 5/23/74, A, 74000436

Shapre-Monte House [Phenix City MRA], 726 6th Ave., Phenix City, 11/03/83, C, 83003485

Smith Residential Historic District [Phenix City MRA], 20th St., 7th Ave., and 6th Court, Phenix City, 11/03/83, C, 83003486

Snow Valley Residential Historic District [Phenix City MRA], 11th and 12th Sts. at 11th Ave., Phenix City, 11/03/83, C, 83003487

Upper Twentieth Street Residential Historic District [Phenix City MRA], 1201–1217 W. 20th St., Phenix City, 11/03/83, C, 83003488

Shelby County

Alabama Girls' Industrial School, Bounded by Middle Campus Dr., Oak, Bloch and Middle Sts., Montevallo, 12/11/78, A, 78000509

Columbiana City Hall, Main St., Columbiana, 10/29/74, A, 74000437

King House, University of Montevallo campus, Montevallo, 1/14/72, C, 72000179

University of Montevallo Historic District (Boundary Increase), Roughly bounded by Bloch St., Farmer St., Flowerhill Dr., King St., Valley St., and Middle St., Montevallo, 10/17/90, A, C, 90001529

St. Clair County

Ash, John, House, US 411 W of jct. with US 231, Ashville vicinity, 10/01/91, C, 91001479

Bothwell, Dr. James J., House, Hartford Ave., Ashville, 2/04/82, A, C, 82004612

Fort Strother Site, Address Restricted, Ohatchee vicinity, 7/24/72, B, D, 72001440

Green, Jacob, House, E of Ashville on SR 33, Ashville vicinity, 1/20/80, C, 80004238

Inzer House, Hartford Ave., Ashville, 12/04/73, B, C, 73002127

Looney House, 5 mi. W of Ashville on Greenport Rd., Ashville vicinity, 12/31/74, A, C, b, 74002179

Newton, Rev. Thomas, House, S of US 411, W of jct. with US 231, Ashville vicinity, 10/11/91, A, C, 91001480

Presley Store, 601 Main St., Springville, 1/11/83, C, 83002982

Robinson, Judge Elisha, House, US 231 S of jct. with AL 23, Ashville, 5/13/91, C, 91000595

St. Clair Springs, AL 23, St. Clair Springs, 4/26/76, A, 76002140

Sumter County

Coffin Shop [Gainesville MRA], McKee and Monroe Sts., Gainesville, 10/29/85, A, b, 85002930

Colgin Hill [Gainesville MRA], Off AL 39, Gainesville, 10/03/85, C, 85002924

Fort Tombecbee, Address Restricted, Epes vicinity, 10/02/73, A, D, NHL, 73000373

Gainesville Historic District [Gainesville MRA], Roughly bounded by North Carolina, Church and School and Lafayette Sts., end of town grid, and Webster St., Gainesville, 10/03/85, C, a, 85002925

Gibbs House [Gainesville MRA], SW of Spruce and Webster Sts., Gainesville, 10/03/85, C, 85002926

Main—Yankee Street Historic District [Gainesville MRA], Roughly bounded by Main, Washington, and School Sts., Gainesville, 10/03/85, C, 85002927

Mobley, Col. Green G., House, Webster and Pearl Sts., Gainesville, 1/18/82, C, 82002070

Oakhurst, Gainesville—Lacy's Ford Rd. approx. 3 mi. SW of AL 116, Emelle, 1/06/87, C, 86003563

Park and Bandstand [Gainesville MRA], State and McKee Sts., Gainesville, 10/29/85, A, C, 85002929

Sumter County Courthouse, US 11, Livingston, 3/24/72, A, C, 72000180

Watson, Laura, House [Gainesville MRA], Epes Rd., Gainesville, 10/03/85, C, 85002928

Talladega County

Averiett, Benjamin H., House [Benjamin H. Averiett Houses TR], AL 8, Sylacauga vicinity, 8/28/86, B, C, 86002034

Averiett, William, House [Benjamin H. Averiett Houses TR], Off AL 8, Sylacauga vicinity, 8/28/86, B, C, 86002038

Boxwood, 406 E. North St. E, Talladega, 6/09/83, C, 83002983

Curry, J. L. M., House, 3 mi. NE of Talladega on AL 21, Talladega vicinity, 10/15/66, B, NHL, 66000154

Elston House, 10 mi. N of Talladega on Turner's Mill Rd., Talladega vicinity, 10/08/76, C, 76000357

First Presbyterian Church, 130 North St. E, Talladega, 11/17/83, C, a, 83003489

Goodwin—Hamilton House [Benjamin H. Averiett Houses TR], Marble Valley Rd., Sylagauca vicinity, 8/28/86, B, C, 86002041

Idlewild, AL 5, 0.1 mi. N of AL 21, Talladega vicinity, 10/15/93, C, 93001012

Jemison House Complex, S of jct. of Chocolocco and Cheaha Creeks, Eastaboga vicinity, 10/01/90, C, 90001507

Talladega County—Continued

Kymulga Mill And Covered Bridge, 4.5 mi. NE of Childersburg on SR 46, Childersburg vicinity, 10/29/76, A, C, 76000356

Lawler—Whiting House, AL 21 S of Talladega, Talladega, 5/22/86, B, C, 86001157

Silk Stocking District, Roughly Bounded by Coffee, 2nd, McMillan, and Court Sts., Talladega, 12/13/79, C, 79000403

Swayne Hall, Talladega College campus, Talladega, 12/02/74, A, NHL, 74002223

Talladega College Historic District, Jct. of Battle St. and Martin Luther King Dr., Talladega, 8/23/90, A, C, a, 90001316

Talladega Courthouse Square Historic District, Courthouse Sq., Talladega, 10/18/72, A, C, 72000181

Talladega Courthouse Square Historic District (Boundary Increase), Roughly bounded by N. East and E. North and S. East, Coffee and Spring Sts., Talladega, 6/30/88, A, C, 88000471

Watters, William, House, Co. Hwy. 8, Sylacauga, 9/25/87, C, 87001652

Welch—Averiett House [Benjamin H. Averiett Houses TR], AL 8, Sylacauga vicinity, 8/28/86, B, C, 86002044

Tallapoosa County

Coley, A. J. and Emma E. Thomas, House, 416 Hillabee St., Alexander City, 1/03/91, C, 90002109

Horseshoe Bend National Military Park, Tallapoosa River, 12 mi. N of Dadeville on AL 49, Dadeville vicinity, 10/15/66, A, NPS, 66000060

Tuscaloosa County

Alabama Insane, Hospital, University Blvd., Tuscaloosa, 4/18/77, A, B, C, 77000216

Audubon Place Historic District, 1515–1707 (odd) University Blvd. & #8–37 Audubon Pl., Tuscaloosa, 7/11/85, A, C, 85001517

Bama Theatre-City Hall Building, 600 Greensboro Ave., Tuscaloosa, 8/30/84, A, C, g, 84000746

Battle-Friedman House, 1010 Greensboro Ave., Tuscaloosa, 1/14/72, C, 72000184

Byler Road, 11 mi. N of Northport, off U.S. 43, Northport vicinity, 11/19/74, A, 74000438

Caplewood Drive Historic District, Roughly bounded by Caplewood Dr., and University Blvd., Tuscaloosa, 5/30/85, A, C, 85001159

Carson Place, 610 - 36th Ave., Tuscaloosa, 3/07/85, C, 85000448

City National Bank, 2301 University Blvd., Tuscaloosa, 3/07/85, C, 85000449

Collier-Overby House, SE corner of 9th St. and 21st Ave., Tuscaloosa, 7/14/71, B, C, 71000107

Downtown Tuscaloosa Historic District, Roughly bounded by Fourth St., Twenty-second Ave., Seventh St., and Greensboro Ave., Tuscaloosa, 5/15/86, A, C, 86001084

Downtown Tuscaloosa Historic District (Boundary Increase), Roughly bounded by University Blvd., 21st Ave., 6th St. and 22nd Ave., Tuscaloosa, 1/26/89, A, C, 88003242

Druid City Historic District, Roughly bounded by Queen City Pk., Sixteenth St., Fifteenth St., and Twenty-first Ave., Tuscaloosa, 2/24/75, C, 75000327

First African Baptist Church, 2621 9th St., Tuscaloosa, 9/28/88, A, C, a, g, 88001580

Fitch House, 3404 Sixth St., Tuscaloosa, 7/22/87, C, 87001027

Foster Home/Sylvan Plantation, Off US 11, Tuscaloosa, 3/07/85, B, C, d, 85000451

Gorgas-Manly Historic District, On the University of Alabama campus, Tuscaloosa, 7/14/71, A, B, C, 71000108

Guild-Verner House, 1904 University Ave., Tuscaloosa, 12/04/73, B, 73000374

Hassell, John, House, Rt. 1 Watermelon Rd., Northport vicinity, 3/07/85, C, 85000447

Jemison, Robert, Servants' House, 2303 13th St., Tuscaloosa, 11/29/90, C, 90001808

Jemison-Vandegraaff House, 1305 Greensboro Ave., Tuscaloosa, 4/19/72, C, 72000185

Murphy—Collins House, 2601 Paul Bryant Dr., Tuscaloosa, 1/28/93, A, 92001824

Northport Historic District, 25th, 26th, 28th and 30th Aves., Main, 5th, and 6th Sts., Northport, 5/01/80, A, C, a, 80000736

Old Observatory, N of University Blvd., on University of Alabama campus, University, 1/14/72, A, C, 72000187

Old Tuscaloosa County Jail, 2803 6th St., Tuscaloosa, 11/28/79, C, 79000404

Pinehurst Historic District, 215 and 305 Seventeenth Ave., 1–28 Pinehurst Dr., and 6–9 N. Pinehurst Dr., Tuscaloosa, 6/05/86, A, C, 86001229

President's Mansion, University of Alabama campus, Tuscaloosa, 1/14/72, A, C, 72000186

Queen City Pool and Pool House, Jct. of Queen City Ave. and Riverside Dr., Tuscaloosa, 9/10/92, A, C, g, 92001088

Searcy House, 2606 8th St., Tuscaloosa, 4/21/75, B, 75000328

Searcy House, 815 Greensboro Ave., Tuscaloosa, 9/14/84, C, 84000748

Shirley, James, House, 512 Main Ave., Northport, 3/24/72, C, 72000183

Tannehill Furnace, 3 mi. E of U.S. 11, Abernant vicinity, 7/24/72, A, 72000182

Wheeler House, 2703 7th St., Tuscaloosa, 4/28/80, C, 80000737

Wilson-Clements House, 1802 20th Ave., Northport, 4/11/85, C, 85000737

Walker County

Bankhead House, 1400 7th Ave., Jasper, 6/18/73, B, 73000375

Boshell's Mill, N of Townley on AL 124, Townley vicinity, 5/30/75, A, 75000329

First United Methodist Church, 1800 3rd Ave., Jasper, 2/14/85, C, a, 85000257

Gilchrist House, 12 mi. SW of Cordova on Pleasantfield-Evansbridge Rd., Cordova vicinity, 3/24/72, C, 72000188

Stephenson House, Cobb St., Oakman, 9/18/78, B, C, 78000510

Walker County Hospital, 1100 7th Ave., Jasper, 5/30/85, A, 85001160

Washington County

McIntosh Log Church, S of McIntosh off U.S. 43, McIntosh vicinity, 11/20/74, C, a, 74000439

Old St. Stephens Site, Address Restricted, St. Stephens vicinity, 12/29/70, A, D, 70000111

Wilcox County

Beck, William King, House, AL 28 N side, 3.2 mi. N of jct. with AL 10, Camden vicinity, 5/21/93, C, 93000421

Bethea, Tristram, House, AL 28 and CR 22, Camden vicinity, 7/11/85, A, B, C, 85001501

Hawthorn House, 9 - N. Broad St., Pine Apple, 3/07/85, B, C, 85000452

Liberty Hall, AL 221, Camden, 1/05/84, C, 84000751

Liddell Archeological Site, Address Restricted, Camden vicinity, 11/17/78, D, 78000511

Wilcox County Courthouse Historic District, Irregular pattern along Broad St., Camden, 1/18/79, A, B, C, 79000405

Wilcox Female Institute, Church St., Camden, 4/03/75, A, 75000330

Winston County

Archeological Site No. 1WI50, Address Restricted, Haleyville vicinity, 12/14/85, D, 85003119

Houston Jail, Off U.S. 278 on SR 63, Houston, 6/05/75, C, 75000331

Winston County Courthouse, Addison Rd., Double Springs, 8/27/87, A, C, 87001416

ALASKA

Aleutian Islands Borough-Census Area

Adak Army Base and Adak Naval Operating Station, Roughly bounded by Cape Adagdak, Scabbard Bay, and Shagak Bay, Adak Station, 2/27/87, A, g, NHL, 87000841

Anangula Archeological District, Address Restricted, Nikolski vicinity, 6/02/78, D, NHL, 78000512

Ananiuliak Island Archeological District, Address Restricted, Ananiuliak Island vicinity, 3/24/72, D, 72001580

Atka B–24D Liberator, Address Restricted, Atka vicinity, 7/26/79, A, g, 79000407

Attu Battlefield and U.S. Army and Navy Airfields on Attu, Attu Island, Aleutian Islands, 2/04/85, A, NHL, 85002729

Cape Field at Fort Glenn (Umnak Island), NE section of Umnak Island, Fort Glenn, 5/28/87, A, g, NHL, 87001301

Chaluka Site, Address Restricted, Nikolski vicinity, 10/15/66, D, NHL, 66000155

Church of the Holy Ascension [Russian Orthodox Church Buildings and Sites TR (AD)], In Unalaska, Unalaska, 4/15/70, A, C, a, NHL, 70000112

Dutch Harbor Naval Operating Base and Fort Mears, U.S. Army, Amaknak Island, Unalaska, 2/04/85, A, NHL, 85002733

Fur Seal Rookeries, St. Paul and St. George Islands, Pribilof Islands, 10/15/66, A, a, g, NHL, 66000156

Holy Resurrection Church [Russian Orthodox Church Buildings and Sites TR], In Belkofski, Belkofski, 6/06/80, A, C, a, 80000739

Japanese Occupation Site, Kiska Island, Kiska Island, Aleutian Islands, 2/04/85, A, g, NHL, 85002732

Port Moller Hot Springs Village Site, Address Restricted, Port Moller vicinity, 4/20/79, D, 79000408

Sitka Spruce Plantation, N of Unalaska on Amaknak Island, Unalaska vicinity, 2/14/78, A, NHL, 78000513

St. Alexander Nevsky Chapel [Russian Orthodox Church Buildings and Sites TR], In Akutan, Akutan, 6/06/80, A, C, a, 80000738

St. George the Great Martyr Orthodox Church [Russian Orthodox Church Buildings and Sites TR], On St. George Island, St. George Island, 6/06/80, A, C, a, g, 80000743

St. John the Theologian Church [Russian Orthodox Church Buildings and Sites TR], In Perryville, Perryville, 6/06/80, A, C, a, 80000741

St. Nicholas Chapel [Russian Orthodox Church Buildings and Sites TR], In Sand Point, Sand Point, 6/06/80, A, C, a, g, 80000742

St. Nicholas Church [Russian Orthodox Church Buildings and Sites TR], In Nikolski, Nikolski, 6/06/80, A, C, a, 80000740

Sts. Peter and Paul Church [Russian Orthodox Church Buildings and Sites TR], On St. Paul Island, St. Paul Island, 6/06/80, A, C, a, 80000744

Temnac P–38G Lightning, Address Restricted, Aleutian Islands, 6/26/79, A, g, 79000406

Anchorage Borough-Census Area

A. E. C. Cottage No. 23, 618 Christensen Dr., Anchorage, 6/11/90, A, 90000825

Alex, Mike, Cabin, Off AK 1, Eklutna, 9/08/82, A, B, g, 82002071

Anchorage Cemetery, 535 E. 9th Ave., Anchorage, 4/26/93, A, d, 93000320

Anchorage City Hall, 524 W. 4th Ave., Anchorage, 12/02/80, A, B, C, g, 80000745

Anderson, Oscar, House, 4th Ave. extended, Anchorage, 6/13/78, B, C, b, 78000514

Beluga Point Site, Address Restricted, Anchorage vicinity, 3/30/78, D, 78000515

Campus Center, Wesley Dr., Anchorage, 6/22/79, A, g, 79000409

Crow Creek Consolidated Gold Mining Company, NE of Girdwood, Girdwood vicinity, 9/13/78, A, 78000517

David, Leopold, House, 605 W. Second Ave., Anchorage, 7/24/86, B, C, 86001900

Eklutna Power Plant, NE of Anchorage, Anchorage vicinity, 6/20/80, C, g, 80000746

Federal Building-U.S. Courthouse, 601 W. 4th Ave., Anchorage, 6/23/78, A, B, C, g, 78000516

Fourth Avenue Theatre (AHRS Site No. ANC–284), 630 W. 4th Ave., Anchorage, 10/05/82, B, C, g, 82001620

Indian Valley Mine, Address Restricted, Indian vicinity, 10/25/89, A, b, 89001762

KENI Radio Building, 1777 Forest Park Dr., Anchorage, 4/18/88, C, g, 88000380

Kimball's Store, 500 and 504 W. Fifth Ave., Anchorage, 7/24/86, A, 86001901

Old St. Nicholas Russian Orthodox Church [Russian Orthodox Church Buildings and Sites TR (AD)], Eklutna Village Rd., Eklutna, 3/24/72, A, a, 72000189

Pioneer School House, 3rd Ave. and Eagle St., Anchorage, 12/03/80, A, b, 80000747

Potter Section House, Off AK 1, Anchorage, 12/06/85, A, 85003113

Wasilla Community Hall, 215 Main St., Wasilla, 9/08/82, A, C, 82002072

Wendler Building, 400 D. St., Anchorage, 6/24/88, A, B, C, b, 82004973

Bethel Borough-Census Area

First Mission House, 291 Third Ave., Bethel, 10/30/90, A, a, b, 90001551

Kolmakov Redoubt Site, Address Restricted, Sleetmute vicinity, 2/15/74, A, D, 74002322

St. Jacob's Church [Russian Orthodox Church Buildings and Sites TR], In Napaskiak, Napaskiak, 6/06/80, A, C, a, 80000748

St. Nicholas Russian Orthodox Church [Russian Orthodox Church Buildings and Sites TR], Lower Kuskokim R., Kwethluk, 4/15/91, A, C, a, 91000385

St. Seraphim Chapel [Russian Orthodox Church Buildings and Sites TR], In Lower Kalskag, Lower Kalskag, 6/06/80, A, C, a, 80004586

St. Sergius Chapel [Russian Orthodox Church Buildings and Sites TR], In Chuathbaluk, Chuathbaluk, 6/06/80, A, C, a, 80004585

Sts. Constantine and Helen Chapel [Russian Orthodox Church Buildings and Sites TR], In Lime Village, Lime Village, 6/06/80, A, C, a, 80004583

Bristol Bay Borough-Census Area

Archeological Site 49 MK 10, Address Restricted, Kanatak vicinity, 6/23/78, D, NPS, 78000425

Brooks River Archeological District, Address Restricted, Naknek vicinity, 2/14/78, D, NHL, NPS, 78000342

Elevation of Holy Cross Church [Russian Orthodox Church Buildings and Sites TR], In South Naknek, South Naknek, 6/06/80, A, C, a, 80000755

Fure's Cabin, Katmai National Park and Preserve, King Salmon vicinity, 2/07/85, C, NPS, 85000187

Kijik Historic District, Address Restricted, Nondalton vicinity, 1/29/79, D, 79000410

Old Savonoski Site, Address Restricted, Naknek vicinity, 6/23/78, D, NPS, 78000344

Savonoski River Archeological District, Address Restricted, Naknek vicinity, 6/23/78, D, NPS, 78000525

St. John the Baptist Chapel [Russian Orthodox Church Buildings and Sites TR], In Naknek, Naknek, 6/06/80, A, C, a, 80000750

St. Nicholas Chapel [Russian Orthodox Church Buildings and Sites TR], In Ekuk, Ekuk, 6/06/80, A, C, a, 80000749

St. Nicholas Chapel [Russian Orthodox Church Buildings and Sites TR], In Nondalton, Nondalton, 6/06/80, A, C, a, 80000751

St. Nicholas Chapel [Russian Orthodox Church Buildings and Sites TR], In Pedro Bay, Pedro Bay, 6/06/80, A, C, a, 80000753

St. Nicholas Church [Russian Orthodox Church Buildings and Sites TR], In Pilot Point, Pilot Point, 6/06/80, A, C, a, 80000754

Transfiguration of Our Lord Chapel [Russian Orthodox Church Buildings and Sites TR], In Nushagak, Nushagak, 6/06/80, A, C, a, 80000752

Dillingham Borough-Census Area

Archeological Site 49 AF 3, Address Restricted, Kanatak vicinity, 2/17/78, D, NPS, 78000276

Kaguyak Village Site, Address Restricted, Kanatak vicinity, 6/23/78, D, NPS, 78000274

Kukak Village Site, Address Restricted, Kanatak vicinity, 7/20/78, D, NPS, 78000343

Pilgrim 100B Aircraft, Dillingham Municipal Airport, Dillingham, 8/07/86, A, 86002230

St. Nicholas Chapel [Russian Orthodox Church Buildings and Sites TR], In Igiugig, Igiugig, 6/06/80, A, C, a, 80004579

Takli Island Archeological District, Address Restricted, Kanatak vicinity, 5/23/78, D, NPS, 78000275

Fairbanks North Star Borough-Census Area

Chatanika Gold Camp, Mile 27 3/4, Steese Hwy., Chatanika, 10/16/79, A, g, 79003753

Chena Pump House, Chena Pump Rd., Fairbanks vicinity, 3/17/82, A, g, 82004900

Chugwater Site, Address Restricted, North Pole vicinity, 11/23/79, D, 79003754

Clay Street Cemetery (AHRS Site No. FAI–164), 7th Ave. and Riverside Dr., Fairbanks, 10/25/82, A, d, g, 82001619

Davis, Mary Lee, House, 410 Cowles St., Fairbanks, 9/31/82, C, 82004901

Discovery Claim on Pedro Creek, Mile 16.5 Steese Hwy., Fairbanks vicinity, 5/13/92, A, B, 92000498

Ester Camp Historic District, Off AK 3, Ester, 5/06/87, A, b, 87000703

Federal Building, Cushman St. and 3rd Ave., Fairbanks, 8/02/78, C, g, 78003422

Goldstream Dredge No. 8, Mile 9, Steese Hwy., Goldstream Valley, Fairbanks vicinity, 2/28/84, A, C, b, 84000637

Harding Railroad Car, Alaskaland, Fairbanks, 4/06/78, B, b, g, 78003423

Hinckley-Creamer Dairy, Between Farmer's Loop and College Rd., Fairbanks, 4/13/77, A, g, 77001572

Immaculate Conception Church, 115 N. Cushman St., Fairbanks, 4/03/76, A, a, b, 76002278

Joslin, Falcon, House, 413 Cowles St., Fairbanks, 4/29/80, B, C, 80004567

Lacey Street Theatre, 504 Second Ave., Fairbanks, 6/14/90, A, C, 90000878

Ladd Field, Address Unknown, Fairbanks vicinity, 2/04/85, A, g, NHL, 85002730

Main School, Jct. of Seventh Ave. and Cushman St., Fairbanks, 9/27/90, A, C, 90001472

Masonic Temple, 809 1st Ave., Fairbanks, 6/03/80, A, C, 80004568

NENANA (steamer), Alaskaland, Fairbanks, 6/27/72, A, C, b, g, NHL, 72001581

Nabesna Gold Mine Historic District, Base of White Mountain, Nabesna, 5/25/79, B, 79003755

Oddfellows House, 825 1st Ave., Fairbanks, 6/03/80, A, C, g, 80004569

Rainey's Cabin, University of Alaska campus, College, 11/20/75, B, g, 75002158

Rose Building, 520 Church St., Fairbanks, 5/11/92, A, C, b, 92000444

Sullivan Roadhouse, W of Delta Junction, Delta Junction vicinity, 8/10/79, A, 79003756

Thomas, George C., Memorial Library, 901 1st Ave., Fairbanks, 2/23/72, A, NHL, 72001542

Wickersham House, Alaskaland, Fairbanks, 4/27/79, B, b, 79003757

Haines Borough-Census Area

Eldred Rock Lighthouse, S of Haines off Sullivan Island, Haines vicinity, 12/30/75, A, C, 75000332

Fort William H. Seward, S of Haines at Port Chilkoot, Haines vicinity, 4/11/72, A, NHL, 72000190

Government Indian School, 1st St., Haines, 2/08/80, A, 80000756

Pleasant Camp, NW Building, Haines at Mile 40, Haines Hwy., Haines vicinity, 7/05/73, A, 73000376

Porcupine District, W of Haines at Mile 35, Haines Hwy., Haines vicinity, 11/13/76, A, g, 76000358

Juneau Borough-Census Area

Alaska Governor's Mansion, 716 Calhoun St., Juneau, 11/07/76, A, C, g, 76000359

Alaska Steam Laundry, 174 S. Franklin St., Juneau, 2/17/78, A, C, 78000527

Alaskan Hotel, 167 S. Franklin St., Juneau, 10/25/78, A, C, 78000526

Bergmann Hotel, 434 3rd St., Juneau, 7/28/77, B, 77000217

Davis, J. M., House, 202 6th St., Juneau, 8/31/82, A, C, 82002073

Fort Durham Site, Address Restricted, Taku Harbor vicinity, 5/05/78, A, D, NHL, 78000529

Frances House, 137 6th St., Juneau, 6/07/85, C, b, 85001187

Fries Miners' Cabins, 500 blk., Kennedy St., Juneau, 9/08/88, A, 88001347

Gruening, Ernest, Cabin, Mile 26, Glacier Hwy., NW of Juneau, Juneau vicinity, 6/08/92, B, g, 92000633

Holy Trinity Church, 325 Gold St., Juneau, 10/19/78, A, a, 78000528

Jualpa Mining Camp, 1001 Basin Rd., Juneau, 8/05/93, A, g, 93000733

Mayflower School, St. Ann's and Savikko Sts., Douglas, 11/21/88, A, 88002534

St. Nicholas Russian Orthodox Church [Russian Orthodox Church Buildings and Sites TR (AD)], 326 5th St., Juneau, 9/19/73, A, a, 73000377

Twin Glacier Camp, Along the Taku River, Juneau vicinity, 5/20/88, A, 88000556

Valentine Building, 202 Front St., Juneau, 5/30/85, A, C, 85001275

Wickersham House, 213 7th St., Juneau, 11/21/76, B, g, 76000360

Kenai Peninsula Borough-Census Area

Alaska Central Railroad: Tunnel No. 1, N of Seward, Seward vicinity, 11/28/77, A, 77001576

Alaska Nellie's Homestead, Mile 23, Seward Hwy., Lawing vicinity, 4/03/75, B, 75002159

Ballaine House, 437 3rd Ave., Seward, 7/12/78, B, 78003429

Brown & Hawkins Store, 205, 207, 209 Fourth Ave., Seward, 6/23/88, A, B, 88000710

Chugachik Island Site, Address Restricted, Homer vicinity, 8/19/76, D, 76002279

Church of the Assumption of the Virgin Mary [Russian Orthodox Church Buildings and Sites TR (AD)], Mission and Overland Sts., Kenai, 5/10/70, A, C, a, NHL, 70000898

Coal Village Site, N of Port Graham, Port Graham vicinity, 11/21/78, A, 78003424

Cooper Landing Historic District, AK 1, Cooper Landing, 8/21/86, A, 86001475

Cooper Landing Post Office, Sterling Hwy., Cooper Landing, 5/23/78, A, 78003425

Diversion Tunnel, At Lowell Creek, Seward, 11/23/77, A, C, g, 77001577

Government Cable Office, 218 6th Ave., Seward, 1/04/80, A, 80004574

Hirshey Mine, SE of Hope on Palmer Creek Rd., Hope vicinity, 9/13/78, A, 78003419

Holm, Victor, Cabin, SW of Kenai on Cohoe Rd. at Kasilof River, Kenai vicinity, 4/13/77, A, 77001573

Holy Transfiguration of Our Lord Chapel [Russian Orthodox Church Buildings and Sites TR (AD)], Sterling Hwy., Ninilchik, 5/22/78, A, a, 78003426

Hope Historic District, Mile 17, Hope Rd., Hope, 4/25/72, A, 72001583

Lauritsen Cabin, N of Moose Pass off AK 1, Moose Pass vicinity, 10/16/79, A, 79003761

Moose River Site, Address Restricted, Sterling vicinity, 12/20/78, D, 78003427

Selenie Lagoon Archeological Site, Address Restricted, Port Graham vicinity, 10/16/74, D, 74002321

Seward Depot, 501 Railway Ave., Seward, 7/16/87, A, C, b, 87000652

St. John the Baptist Church [Russian Orthodox Church Buildings and Sites TR], In Angoon, Angoon, 6/06/80, A, C, a, 80004589

St. Nicholas Chapel [Russian Orthodox Church Buildings and Sites TR], In Seldovia, Seldovia, 6/06/80, A, C, a, 80004588

St. Peter's Episcopal Church, 2nd Ave. and Adams St., Seward, 12/21/79, A, C, a, 79003762

Sts. Sergius and Herman of Valaam Church [Russian Orthodox Church Buildings and Sites TR], In English Bay, English Bay, 6/06/80, A, C, a, 80004587

Swetman House, 325 5th Ave., Seward, 2/17/78, C, b, 78003430

Kenai Peninsula Borough-Census Area—Continued

Van Gilder Hotel, 307 Adams St., Seward, 12/02/80, A, 80004575

Ziegler House, 623 Grant St., Ketchikan, 5/30/85, C, 85001161

Ketchikan Gateway Borough-Census Area

Alaska Totems, Between Park and Deermount Aves., Ketchikan, 6/21/71, C, b, 71001090

Burkhart-Dibrell House, 500 Main St., Ketchikan, 9/08/82, B, C, 82004902

Chief Kashakes House, Mile 2.5 S. Tongass Hwy., Saxman, 4/26/93, A, C, b, 93000338

First Lutheran Church, 1200 Tongass Ave., Ketchikan, 5/18/87, A, a, 87000716

Gilmore Building, 326 Front St., Ketchikan, 9/27/89, A, 89001415

Ketchikan Ranger House, 309 Gorge St., Ketchikan, 7/16/87, A, C, 87000645

Saxman Totem Park, S. Tongass Hwy., Saxman, 8/07/79, C, e, g, 79003758

The Star, 5 Creek St., Ketchikan, 4/26/93, A, 93000336

Totem Bight State Historic Site, W side of Revillagigedo Island, Ketchikan vicinity, 10/27/70, A, C, e, g, 70000916

Walker-Broderick House, 541 Pine St., Ketchikan, 8/31/82, B, C, 82004903

Kodiak Island Borough-Census Area

AHRS Site KOD–207, Address Restricted, Kodiak vicinity, 12/01/78, D, 78003428

American Cemetery, Upper Mill Bay, Kodiak, 4/10/80, A, d, 80004570

Ascension of Our Lord Chapel [Russian Orthodox Church Buildings and Sites TR], In Karluk, Karluk, 6/06/80, A, C, a, 80004580

Erskine House, Main St. and Mission Rd., Kodiak, 10/15/66, C, NHL, 66000954

Fort Abercrombie State Historic Site, Miller Point, 5 mi. from Kodiak, Kodiak Island, 10/27/70, A, g, 70000917

Holy Resurrection Church [Russian Orthodox Church Buildings and Sites TR (AD)], Mission Rd. and Kashevaroff St., Kodiak, 12/12/77, C, a, g, 77001574

KOD–171 Site, Address Restricted, Larsen Bay vicinity, 8/13/81, D, 81000707

KOD–233 Site, Address Restricted, Larsen Bay vicinity, 8/13/81, D, 81000708

Kodiak 011 Site, Address Restricted, Kodiak vicinity, 7/21/80, D, 80004571

Kodiak Naval Operating Base and Forts Greely and Abercrombie, Address unknown, Kodiak vicinity, 2/04/85, A, g, NHL, 85002731

Nativity of Holy Theolokos Church [Russian Orthodox Church Buildings and Sites TR], In Afognak, Afognak, 6/06/80, A, C, a, 80004577

Nativity of Our Lord Chapel [Russian Orthodox Church Buildings and Sites TR], In Ouzinkie, Ouzinkie, 6/06/80, A, C, a, 80004582

Protection of the Theotokos Chapel [Russian Orthodox Church Buildings and Sites TR], In Akhiok, Akhiok, 6/06/80, A, C, a, 80004590

Sts. Sergius and Herman of Valaam Chapel [Russian Orthodox Church Buildings and Sites TR], Spruce Island, Mok's Lagoon, Ouzinkie vicinity, 6/06/80, A, C, a, 80004581

Three Saints Site, Address Restricted, Old Harbor vicinity, 2/23/72, A, D, NHL, 72001541

Matanuska-Susitna Borough-Census Area

Bailey Colony Farm [Settlement and Economic Development of Alaska's Matanuska—Susitna Valley MPS], 3150 N. Glenn Hwy., Palmer vicinity, 6/21/91, A, C, b, 91000775

Berry House [Settlement and Economic Development of Alaska's Matanuska—Susitna Valley MPS], 5805 N. Farm Loop Rd., Palmer vicinity, 6/21/91, A, C, 91000779

Cunningham-Hall Pt–6, Nc–692W, S of Palmer at Mile 40, Glen Hwy., Palmer vicinity, 12/29/78, A, g, 78000531

Curry Lookout, Atop Curry Ridge, Mile 137.2, Parks Hwy., Talkeetna vicinity, 4/27/92, A, 92000424

Fairview Inn, Main St., Talkeetna, 5/07/82, A, 82004905

Herried House [Settlement and Economic Development of Alaska's Matanuska—Susitna Valley MPS], 4400 N. Palmer—Fishook Hwy., Palmer vicinity, 6/21/91, A, C, 91000778

Hyland Hotel [Settlement and Economic Development of Alaska's Matanuska—Susitna Valley MPS], 333 W. Evergreen, Palmer vicinity, 6/21/91, A, 91000774

Independence Mines, W of Palmer, Palmer vicinity, 10/09/74, A, g, 74000440

Knik Site, About 15 mi. SW of Wasilla, Knik Rd., Wasilla vicinity, 7/24/73, A, 73000379

Matanuska Colony Community Center [Settlement and Economic Development of Alaska's Matanuska—Susitna Valley MPS], Roughly bounded by S. Colony, E. Firewood, S. Eklutna, E. Elmwood, S. Denali and a line N of properties on E. Dahlia, Palmer, 6/21/91, A, C, b, 91000773

Palmer Depot, AK 1, Palmer, 1/09/78, A, g, 78000530

Patten Colony Farm [Settlement and Economic Development of Alaska's Matanuska—Susitna Valley MPS], Mi. 39.9 Glenn Hwy., across from State Fairground, Palmer vicinity, 6/21/91, A, C, b, 91000776

Puhl House [Settlement and Economic Development of Alaska's Matanuska—Susitna Valley

MPS], 13151 E. Scott Rd., Palmer vicinity, 6/21/91, A, C, 91000777

Rebarchek, Raymond, Colony Farm, S of Palmer off Glenn Hwy., Palmer vicinity, 10/03/78, A, g, 78000532

Talkeetna Historic District, Roughly bounded by C, First, D and Front Sts., Talkeetna, 4/26/93, A, 93000321

Tangle Lakes Archeological District (Boundary Decrease), Address Restricted, Glennallen vicinity, 8/12/93, D, 93000713

Teeland's Country Store, Mile 42 George Parks Hwy. and Knik Rd., Wasilla, 11/14/78, B, 78000533

United Protestant Church, S. Denali and Elmwood Sts., Palmer, 4/10/80, A, B, C, a, g, 80000757

Wasilla Depot, Parks Highway and Knik Rd., Wasilla, 12/16/77, A, 77000218

Wasilla Elementary School, Off AK 3, Wasilla, 2/05/80, A, a, g, 80000758

Nome Borough-Census Area

Anvil Creek Gold Discovery Site, 4.25 mi. N of Nome on Seward Peninsula at Anvil Creek, Nome vicinity, 10/15/66, A, NHL, 66000159

Berger, Jacob, House, 1st Ave., Nome, 8/03/77, B, C, g, 77000219

Cape Nome Mining District Discovery Sites, Address unknown, Nome vicinity, 6/02/78, A, NHL, 78000535

Cape Nome Roadhouse, E of Nome at Mile 14, Nome-Council Hwy., Nome vicinity, 12/12/76, A, 76000361

Discovery Saloon, 1st and D Sts., Nome, 4/03/80, A, 80000759

Fairhaven Ditch, Address Restricted, Deering vicinity, 9/23/87, C, NPS, 87001579

Fort St. Michael, At St. Michael Bay, St. Michael, 11/10/77, A, 77000221

Gambell Sites, Address Restricted, St. Lawrence Island vicinity, 10/15/66, D, NHL, 66000160

Iyatayet Site, Address Restricted, Cape Denbigh Peninsula vicinity, 10/15/66, D, NHL, 66000158

Lindblom, Erik, Placer Claim, N of Nome, Nome vicinity, 11/21/76, A, B, 76000362

Norge Storage Site, Grantley Harbor, Teller, 10/09/74, A, 74000441

Pilgrim Hot Springs, E of Teller on Kugarock Rd., Teller vicinity, 4/11/77, A, a, 77000223

Snow Creek Placer Claim No. 1, N of Nome at Snow Gulch, Nome vicinity, 9/28/76, A, 76000363

Solomon Roadhouse, Nome-Council Hwy., Solomon, 9/17/80, A, b, 80000760

St. Michael Redoubt Site, Address Restricted, St. Michael vicinity, 11/10/77, D, 77000222

Wales Sites, Address Restricted, Wales vicinity, 10/15/66, D, NHL, 66000161

North Slope Borough-Census Area

Aluakpak, Location unknown at this time, Wainright vicinity, 3/18/80, A, 80004555

Anaktuuk, Address Restricted, Wainright vicinity, 3/18/80, D, 80004556

Atanik, Address Restricted, Wainright vicinity, 3/18/80, D, 80004557

Avalitkuk, Address Restricted, Wainright vicinity, 3/18/80, D, g, 80004558

Birnirk Site, Address Restricted, Barrow vicinity, 10/15/66, D, NHL, 66000953

Gallagher Flint Station Archeological Site, Address Restricted, Sagwon vicinity, 6/16/78, D, NHL, 78003208

Ipiutak Archeological District, Address Restricted, Point Hope Peninsula vicinity, 5/25/79, D, 79000411

Ipiutak Site, Address Restricted, Point Hope Peninsula vicinity, 10/15/66, D, NHL, 66000157

Ivishaat, Address Restricted, Wainright vicinity, 3/18/80, D, 80004559

Kanitch, Address Restricted, Wainright vicinity, 3/18/80, D, 80004560

Leffingwell Camp Site, 58 mi. W of Barter Island on Arctic Coast, Flaxman Island, 6/21/71, B, NHL, 71001093

Napanik, Address Restricted, Wainright vicinity, 3/18/80, D, 80004561

Negilik Site, Address Restricted, Wainright vicinity, 4/15/80, D, 80004562

Point Barrow Refuge Station, Browersville, Barrow, 12/02/80, A, 80004563

Rogers-Post Site, 13 mi. SW of Barrow, Barrow vicinity, 4/22/80, B, b, f, g, 80004564

Utkeagvik Church Manse, Off Momegan St., Barrow, 10/06/83, C, a, 83003447

Uyagaagruk, Address Restricted, Wainright vicinity, 3/18/80, D, 80004565

Northwest Arctic Borough-Census Area

Cape Krusenstern Archeological District, Address Restricted, Kotzebue vicinity, 11/07/73, D, NHL, NPS, 73000378

Onion Portage Archeological District, Address Restricted, Kiana vicinity, 6/20/72, D, NHL, NPS, 72000191

Prince of Wales-Outer K. Borough-Census Area

Duncan, Father William, House, 5th Ave. and Atkinson St., Metlakatla, 2/23/72, A, 72001582

Storehouse No. 3, NE of Ketchikan at Halibut Bay Estuary, Ketchikan vicinity, 12/07/77, A, C, 77001575

Storehouse No. 4, International St., Hyder, 8/13/76, A, 76002280

Sitka Borough-Census Area

Alaska Native Brotherhood Hall, Katlean St., Sitka, 2/23/72, A, NHL, 72000192

American Flag Raising Site, Castle Hill, Sitka, 10/15/66, A, NHL, 66000162

Cable House and Station, Lincoln St., Sitka, 6/04/79, A, 79000412

Emmons House, 601 Lincoln St., Sitka, 12/16/77, B, 77000224

Hanlon—Osbakken House, 419 Lincoln St., Sitka, 4/27/92, C, 92000404

Mills House, 315 Seward St., Sitka, 1/31/78, C, 78000536

Mills, W. P., House, 1 Maksoutoff St., Sitka, 12/16/77, C, 77000226

Murray Apartments and Cottages, 200, 204 and 206 Seward, Sitka, 4/27/92, A, e, 92000402

Old Sitka Site, 6 mi. N (9.6 km) of Sitka on Starrigavan Bay, Sitka vicinity, 10/15/66, A, NHL, 66000166

Russian Bishop's House [Russian Orthodox Church Buildings and Sites TR (AD)], Lincoln and Monastery Sts., Sitka, 10/15/66, A, C, a, NHL, NPS, 66000025

Russian-American Building No. 29, 202–204 Lincoln St., Sitka, 5/28/87, A, NHL, 87001282

See House, 611 Lincoln St., Sitka, 3/30/78, B, a, 78000537

Sheldon Jackson Museum, Lincoln St., Sitka, 2/23/72, A, 72000193

Sitka National Historical Park, 106 Metlakatla St., Sitka, 10/15/66, A, C, f, NPS, 66000164

Sitka Naval Operating Base and US Army Coastal Defenses, Japonski Island, Sitka vicinity, 8/11/86, A, g, NHL, 86003559

Sitka Pioneers' Home, Katkian Ave. and Lincoln St., Sitka, 10/18/79, A, C, g, 79000413

St. Michael's Cathedral [Russian Orthodox Church Buildings and Sites TR (AD)], Lincoln and Maksoutoff District, , Sitka, 10/15/66, A, C, a, e, NHL, 66000165

St. Peter's Church, 611 Lincoln St., Sitka, 1/31/78, A, C, a, 78000538

US Coast Guard and Geodetic Survey Seismological and Geomagnetic House, 210 Seward St., Sitka, 11/25/86, A, C, 86003234

Skagway-Yakutat-Angoon Borough-Census Area

Cape Spencer Lighthouse, S of Yakutat at entrance of Cross Sound, Glacier Bay National Monument, Yakutat, 12/04/75, A, g, 75002160

Chilkoot Trail, Mile 0 to U.S./Canada Border, Skagway vicinity, 4/14/75, A, NHL, NPS, 75002120

Klondike Goldrush National Historical Park, P.O. Box 517, Skagway, 6/30/76, A, C, NPS, 76002189

New Russia Site, SW of Yakutat on Phipps Peninsula, Yakutat vicinity, 2/23/72, A, NHL, 72001593

Skagway Historic District and White Pass, Head of Taiya Inlet on Lynn Canal, Skagway and vicinity, 10/15/66, C, NHL, NPS, 66000943

Southeast Fairbanks Borough-Census Area

Big Delta Historic District, Richardson Hwy., Mile 274.5 at jct. of Tanana and Delta Rivers, Delta Junction vicinity, 3/20/91, A, e, 91000252

Eagle Historic District, Mile 0, Taylor Hwy., Eagle, 10/27/70, A, NHL, 70000919

Kink, The, E of Fairbanks, part of N fork of Fortymile River, Fairbanks vicinity, 11/20/75, A, C, 75002161

Rika's Landing Roadhouse, Mile 252, Richardson Hwy., Big Delta, 9/01/76, A, g, 76000364

Steele Creek Roadhouse, Fortymile River, Eagle vicinity, 4/29/80, A, C, 80004576

Valdez-Cordova Borough-Census Area

Bering Expedition Landing Site, S of Katalla on Kayak Island, Katalla, 7/20/77, B, NHL, 77001542

Cape St. Elias Lighthouse, S of Katalla on Kayak Island, Katalla vicinity, 12/18/75, A, 75002157

Chilkat Oil Company Refinery Site, Katalla Rd., Katalla vicinity, 9/06/74, A, g, 74002320

Chisana Historic District, Extending W 1/4 mi. from SE end of Chisana Airstrip and parallel to Johnson Creek, Chisana, 11/29/85, A, C, NPS, 85002999

Chitina Tin Shop, Main St., Chitina, 6/11/79, A, 79003763

Copper River and Northwestern Railway, Beginning at Chitina and following the Copper River to Tasnuna River, Chitina vicinity, 4/24/73, A, C, 73002275

Cordova Post Office and Courthouse, 2nd St., Cordova, 8/02/77, C, 77001571

Dakah De'nin's Village Site, Address Restricted, Chitina vicinity, 4/09/79, D, 79003764

Gahona Roadhouse, Mile 205, Glenn Hwy., Gahona, 8/03/77, A, 77001579

Kennecott Mines, SE of Kennecott Glacier on N bank of National Creek, Kennecott vicinity, 7/12/78, A, g, NHL, 78003420

McCarthy General Store, Kennecott and Sholai Sts., McCarthy, 1/31/78, A, 78003421

McCarthy Power Plant, At McCarthy Creek, McCarthy, 4/26/79, A, 79003752

Palugvik Archeological District, Address Restricted, Cordova vicinity, 10/15/66, D, NHL, 66000957

Reception Building, 2nd and B Sts., Cordova, 4/09/80, B, 80004566

Red Dragon Historic District, Lake St., Cordova, 8/31/82, A, C, a, 82004899

Sourdough Lodge, AK 4 (Richardson Hwy.), Gakona vicinity, 10/01/74, A, NHL, 74002264

Valdez-Cordova Borough-Census Area— Continued

St. Michael the Archangel Church [Russian Orthodox Church Buildings and Sites TR], In Cordova, Cordova, 6/06/80, A, C, a, 80004578

Tangle Lakes Archeological District, Address Restricted, Paxson vicinity, 11/12/71, D, 71001091

Wrangell-Peterburg Borough-Census Area

CHUGACH (Ranger Boat), Federal Government Dock, Wrangell Narrows, Petersburg, 1/21/92, A, C, 91001937

Chief Shakes Historic Site, Shakes Island, Wrangell, 10/27/70, A, C, e, g, 70000918

ETOLIN CANOE, Tongass National Forest, Wrangell vicinity, 6/05/89, C, D, 88001061

Saint Philip's Episcopal Church, 446 Church St., Wrangell, 5/06/87, A, B, a, 87000654

Sons of Norway Hall, Indian St., Petersburg, 7/10/79, A, 79003765

Wrangell Public School, 2nd and Bevier Sts., Wrangell, 5/16/78, A, 78003432

Yukon-Koyukuk Borough-Census Area

Beiderman, Ed, Fish Camp [Yukon River Lifeways TR], Left bank of the Yukon River 1/2 mi. down across from the Kandick River, Eagle vicinity, 7/20/87, A, NPS, 87001204

Central House, Mile 128, Steese Hwy., Central, 7/31/78, A, C, g, 78003431

Christ Church Mission, In Anvik, Anvik, 5/08/80, A, B, a, b, d, g, 80004572

Dry Creek Archeological Site, Address Restricted, Lignite vicinity, 9/06/74, D, NHL, 74000442

Ewe Creek Ranger Cabin No. 8 [Patrol Cabins, Mount McKinley National Park TR], 5 mi. downstream on the Savage River from Park Hwy. near Ewe Creek, Denali National Park & Preserve, 11/25/86, A, NPS, 86003217

Igloo Creek Cabin No. 25 [Patrol Cabins, Mount McKinley National Park TR], Near Igloo Creek at Mile 34.1 N of Park Rd., Denali National Park & Preserve, 11/25/86, A, NPS, 86003208

Lower East Fork Ranger Cabin No. 9 [Patrol Cabins, Mount McKinley National Park TR], 25 mi. downstream on the E fork of the Toklat River from Parrk Rd., Denali National Park & Preserve, 11/25/86, A, NPS, 86003214

Lower Toklat River Ranger Cabin No. 18 [Patrol Cabins, Mount McKinley National Park TR], 30 mi. N on Toklat River from Park Rd., Denali National Park & Preserve, 11/25/86, A, NPS, 86003222

Lower Windy Creek Ranger Cabin No. 15 [Patrol Cabins, Mount McKinley National Park TR], E of Mile 324 on Alaska Railroad, Denali National Park & Preserve, 11/25/86, A, NPS, 86003229

McGregor, George, Cabin [Yukon River Lifeways TR], Left bank of the Yukon River 2 mi. down from Coal Creek, Eagle vicinity, 7/21/87, A, g, NPS, 87001199

Mission Church, E fork of Chandalar River, Arctic Village, 4/11/77, C, a, 77001578

Moose Creek Ranger Cabin No. 19 [Patrol Cabins, Mount McKinley National Park TR], 5 mi. N of Mile 73.8 on Park Rd., Denali National Park & Preserve, 11/25/86, A, NPS, 86003231

Mount McKinley National Park Headquarters District, Mi. 3.4 McKinley Park Hwy., Unknown, 10/23/87, A, C, g, NPS, 87000975

Nenana Depot, A St., Nenana, 8/10/77, A, 77000229

Old Mission House, Ft. Yukon, Fort Yukon, 11/07/78, A, a, g, 78000539

Presentation of Our Lord Chapel [Russian Orthodox Church Buildings and Sites TR], In Nikolai, Nikolai, 6/06/80, A, C, a, 80004584

Riley Creek Ranger Cabin No. 20 [Patrol Cabins, Mount McKinley National Park TR], 5 mi. cross-country and W of Mile 336 on Alaska RR, Denali National Park & Preserve, 11/25/86, A, NPS, 86003225

Ruby Roadhouse, Olson St., Ruby, 5/20/82, A, g, 82004898

Sanctuary River Cabin No. 31 [Patrol Cabins, Mount McKinley National Park TR], On Sanctuary River at Mile 22.7 S of Park Rd., Denali National Park & Preserve, 11/25/86, A, NPS, 86003206

Slaven, Frank, Roadhouse [Yukon River Lifeways TR], Left bank of the Yukon River 1/4 mi. from the mouth of Coal Creek, Eagle vicinity, 7/20/87, A, NPS, 87001202

Sushana River Ranger Cabin No. 17 [Patrol Cabins, Mount McKinley National Park TR], 10 mi. cross-country and N of Mile 25 on Park Rd., Denali National Park & Preserve, 11/25/86, A, NPS, 86003227

Susitna River Bridge, N of Gold Creek, Gold Creek vicinity, 9/15/77, C, 77000227

Tanana Mission, E of Tanana, Tanana, 8/03/77, A, C, a, d, g, 77000230

Teklanika Archeological District, Address Restricted, Toklat vicinity, 1/31/76, D, NPS, 76000171

Toklat Ranger Station—Pearson Cabin No. 4 [Patrol Cabins, Mount McKinley National Park TR], Near the main branch of the Toklat River at Mile 53.8 W of Park Rd., Denali National Park & Preserve, 11/25/86, A, NPS, 86003207

Tolovana Roadhouse, Sled Rd., Nenana vicinity, 10/07/88, A, 88000402

Upper East Fork Cabin No. 29 [Patrol Cabins, Mount McKinley National Park TR], Near the E fork of the Toklat River at Mile 43 S of Park Rd., Denali National Park & Preserve, 11/25/86, A, NPS, 86003209

Upper Toklat River Cabin No. 24 [Patrol Cabins, Mount McKinley National Park TR], Near main branch of Toklat River at Mile 53.7, W of park rd., Denali National Park & Preserve, 11/25/86, A, NPS, 86003211

Upper Windy Creek Ranger Cabin No. 7 [Patrol Cabins, Mount McKinley National Park TR], 6 mi. W of Cantwell S of Windy Creek, Denali National Park & Preserve, 11/25/86, A, NPS, 86003219

Woodchopper Roadhouse [Yukon River Lifeways TR], Left bank of the Yukon River 1 mi. up from Woodchopper Creek, Eagle vicinity, 7/20/87, A, NPS, 87001201

Yukon Island Main Site, Address Restricted, Yukon Island vicinity, 10/15/66, D, NHL, 66000955

AMERICAN SAMOA

Eastern District

Blunts Point Naval Gun, Matautu Ridge, Pago Pago vicinity, 4/26/73, A, g, NHL, 73002128

Courthouse of American Samoa, Near Pago Pago Harbor, Fagatogo, 2/12/74, C, 74002180

Government House, Togotogo Ridge, Pago Pago, 3/16/72, A, C, g, NHL, 72001443

Navy Building 38, Pago Pago Harbor, Fagatogo, 3/16/72, A, C, 72001441

Navy Building 43, Pago Pago Harbor, Fagatogo, 3/16/72, C, 72001442

US Naval Station Tutuila Historic District, Between Togotogo Ridge and W side of Pago Pago Harbor, on waterfronts of Fagatogo and Utulei villages, Fagatogo and Utulei, 6/20/90, A, g, 90000854

Western District

A'a Village (AS-34-33), Address Restricted, Tapua'ina vicinity, 11/19/87, D, 87001956

Aasu, Near the village of Aasu, Aasu, 4/13/72, A, 72001444

Atauloma Girls School, W edge of Afao, Afao, 3/16/72, A, C, a, 72001445

Fagalele Boys School, S of Leone, Leone vicinity, 3/16/72, A, C, a, 72001446

Tataga—Matau Fortified Quarry Complex (AS-34-10), Address Restricted, Leone vicinity, 11/19/87, A, D, 87001957

Established in 1900 and converted to civilian use in 1951, the U.S. Naval Station Tutuila is significant for its role in the military and governmental history of American Samoa. (Erwin N. Thompson, 1988)

ARIZONA

Apache County

Allentown Bridge [Vehicular Bridges in Arizona MPS], Indian Rt. 9402 over Puerco River, milepost 9.1, Houck vicinity, 9/30/88, A, C, 88001617

Butterfly Lodge, Forest Rd. 245 E of AZ 373, Apache NF, Greer vicinity, 6/17/92, B, g, 92000686

Canyon de Chelly National Monument, E side of Chinle, Chinle, 8/25/70, A, D, NPS, 70000066

Casa Malpais Site, Address Restricted, Springerville vicinity, 10/15/66, D, NHL, 66000936

Colter Ranch Historic District, Jct. of 4th St. and School Bus Rd., Eagar vicinity, 7/09/93, B, 93000626

Eagar School, 174 S. Main St., Eagar, 7/22/93, A, 93000624

Eagar Townsite Historic District, Roughly bounded by Central Ave., Main St., 1st Ave. and Eagar St., 2nd Ave and Harless St., 3rd Ave. and Eagar St., Eagar, 7/23/93, A, 93000625

Flattop Site, Address Restricted, Adamana vicinity, 7/12/76, D, NPS, 76000214

Hubbell Trading Post National Historic Site, W side of Ganado, Ganado, 10/15/66, A, C, NHL, NPS, 66000167

Isaacson Building, 37 Commercial St., St. Johns, 9/12/83, B, C, 83002997

Kin Tiel, Address Restricted, Chambers vicinity, 5/22/78, A, D, 78000540

Lake Mountain Lookout Complex [National Forest Fire Lookouts in the Southwestern Region TR], Off Vernon McNary Rd., McNary vicinity, 1/28/88, A, C, 87002453

Los Burros Ranger Station, Forest Rd. 20, McNary vicinity, 10/23/86, A, 86002854

Newspaper Rock Petroglyphs Archeological District, Address Restricted, Adamana vicinity, 7/12/76, A, D, NPS, 76000185

PS Knoll Lookout Complex [National Forest Fire Lookouts in the Southwestern Region TR], Apache-Sitgreaves National Forest, Maverick vicinity, 1/28/88, A, C, g, 87002451

Painted Desert Inn, W of Navajo in Petrified Forest National Park, Navajo vicinity, 10/10/75, A, C, g, NPS, 75000217

Petrified Forest Bridge [Vehicular Bridges in Arizona MPS], Petrified Forest Park Rd. over Rio Puerco, Navajo vicinity, 9/30/88, A, C, NPS, 88001616

Puerco Ruin and Petroglyphs, Address Restricted, Adamana vicinity, 7/12/76, D, NPS, 76000208

Querino Canyon Bridge [Vehicular Bridges in Arizona MPS], Old US 66 over Querino Canyon, Houck vicinity, 9/30/88, A, C, 88001623

Sanders Bridge [Vehicular Bridges in Arizona MPS], Indian Rt. 9402 over the Puerco River, Sanders, 9/30/88, A, C, 88001618

St. Michael's Mission, N of Window Rock off AZ 264, Window Rock vicinity, 5/29/75, A, a, 75000335

Thirty-Fifth Parallel Route, 25 mi. E of Holbrook Off I 40, Holbrook vicinity, 12/06/77, A, NPS, 77000129

Twin Buttes Archeological District, Address Restricted, Adamana vicinity, 7/12/76, D, NPS, 76000952

Water Canyon Administrative Site [Depression-Era USDA Forest Service Administrative Complexes in Arizona MPS], Forest Rd. 285 S of Springerville, Apache—Sitgreaves NF, Springerville vicinity, 6/10/93, A, C, 93000511

Cochise County

Barfoot Lookout Complex [National Forest Fire Lookouts in the Southwestern Region TR], Buena Vista Peak, Portal vicinity, 1/28/88, A, C, 87002463

Bear Spring House, Guardhouse, and Spring, S of Bowie off Apache Pass Rd., Bowie, 3/18/83, A, C, 83002985

Bisbee Historic District, US 80, Bisbee, 7/03/80, A, C, 80004487

Bisbee Woman's Club Clubhouse, 74 Quality Hill, Bisbee, 1/31/85, A, 85000145

Briscoe, Benjamin E., House [Willcox MRA], 358 N. Bowie, Willcox, 5/27/87, C, 87000737

Cima Park Fire Guard Station [Depression-Era USDA Forest Service Administrative Complexes in Arizona MPS], In Chiricahua Wilderness NE of Douglas, Coronado NF, Douglas vicinity, 6/10/93, A, C, 93000514

Cochise Hotel, Off U.S. 666, Cochise, 10/22/76, A, 76000370

Coronado National Memorial, 30 mi. SW of Bisbee, Bisbee vicinity, 10/15/66, A, B, f, NPS, 66000168

Council Rocks Archaeological District, Address Restricted, St. David vicinity, 1/16/87, D, 86003666

Crowley House [Willcox MRA], 175 S. Railroad Ave., Willcox, 8/06/87, B, C, 87000748

Double Adobe Site, Address Restricted, Douglas vicinity, 10/15/66, D, NHL, 66000169

Douglas Historic District, Roughly bounded by Pan American, H, and F Aves. along 8th, 10th, 11th, 12th, and 13th Sts. and G Ave., Douglas, 1/31/85, A, C, 85000146

Douglas Municipal Airport, E end of 10th Ave., Douglas, 12/30/75, A, g, 75000336

Douglas Residential Historic District, Roughly bounded by Twelfth St., Carmelita Ave., Seventh St., and East Ave., Douglas, 7/31/86, A, C, 86002095

Douglas Sonoran Historic District, Roughly bounded by the W side of H Ave. between

Sixth and Ninth Sts., Douglas, 8/26/87, A, C, 87001793

Douglas Underpass [Vehicular Bridges in Arizona MPS], US 80 under Southern Pacific RR, milepost 366.1, Douglas, 9/30/88, A, C, 88001609

Dragoon Springs Stage Station Site, Address Restricted, Dragoon vicinity, 5/07/79, A, D, 79000415

El Paso and Southwestern Railroad YMCA, 1000 Pan American Ave., Douglas, 3/01/84, A, C, 84000647

El Paso and Southwestern Railroad Passenger Depot—Douglas, Fourteenth St. and H Ave., Douglas, 4/16/86, A, C, 86000792

Faraway Ranch Historic District, AZ 181, Dos Cabezas vicinity, 8/27/80, A, B, C, NPS, 80000368

Fort Bowie National Historic Site, 12 mi. S of Bowie, Bowie vicinity, 7/29/72, A, C, f, NHL, NPS, 72000194

Fort Huachuca, 3.6 mi. W of Sierra Vista, Sierra Vista vicinity, 11/20/74, A, NHL, 74000443

Gadsden Hotel, 1046 G. Ave., Douglas, 7/30/76, A, C, g, 76000371

Garden Canyon Archeological Site, Address Restricted, Sierra Vista vicinity, 10/29/75, D, 75000338

Garden Canyon Petroglyphs, Address Restricted, Sierra Vista vicinity, 7/30/74, D, 74000444

Grand Theatre, 1139–1149 G. Ave., Douglas, 7/30/76, A, C, 76000372

Gung'l, John, House [Willcox MRA], 210 S. El Paso Ave., Willcox, 5/27/87, C, 87000749

Hereford Bridge [Vehicular Bridges in Arizona MPS], Hereford Rd. over the San Pedro River, Hereford, 9/30/88, A, C, 88001659

Hooker Town House [Willcox MRA], 235 E. Stewart, Willcox, 5/27/87, B, C, 87000736

Johnson—Tillotson House [Willcox MRA], 124 N. Curtis, Willcox, 8/06/87, C, 87000743

Lehner Mammoth-Kill Site, Address Restricted, Hereford vicinity, 5/28/67, D, NHL, 67000002

Mee, Joe, House [Willcox MRA], 265 W. Stewart, Willcox, 8/06/87, C, 87000739

Monte Vista Lookout Cabin [National Forest Fire Lookouts in the Southwestern Region TR], Monte Vista Peak, Elfrida vicinity, 1/28/88, A, C, 87002468

Morgan House [Willcox MRA], 2442 E. Maley, Willcox, 8/18/87, B, C, 87000746

Muheim House, 207 Youngblood Ave., Bisbee, 1/23/79, B, C, 79000414

Naco Border Station, 106 D St., Naco, 2/19/91, A, C, 91000026

Naco-Mammoth Kill Site, Address Restricted, Naco vicinity, 7/21/76, D, 76002285

Norton, John H., and Company Store, 180 N. Railroad Ave., Willcox, 3/31/83, C, 83002987

Pearce General Store, Ghost Town and Pearce Rd., Pearce, 11/16/78, A, C, 78000541

Cochise County—Continued

Phelps Dodge General Office Building, Copper Queen Plaza, intersection of Main St. and Brewery Gulch, Bisbee, 6/03/71, A, NHL, 71000109

Portal Ranger Station [Depression-Era USDA Forest Service Administrative Complexes in Arizona MPS], Forest Rd. 42A SW of Portal, Coronado NF, Portal vicinity, 6/10/93, A, C, 93000517

Quiburi, Address Restricted, Fairbank vicinity, 4/07/71, A, C, D, 71000110

Railroad Avenue Historic District [Willcox MRA], Roughly bounded by Curtis Ave., Stewart St., Southern Pacific RR tracks, and Grant St., Willcox, 5/27/87, A, 87000751

Rustler Park Fire Guard Station [Depression-Era USDA Forest Service Administrative Complexes in Arizona MPS], SE of Chiricahua NM, Coronado NF, Douglas vicinity, 6/10/93, A, C, 93000518

San Bernardino Ranch, 17 mi. E of Douglas on the international boundary, Douglas vicinity, 10/15/66, A, B, C, D, NHL, 66000170

Saxon, Harry, House [Willcox MRA], 308 S. Haskell, Willcox, 5/27/87, C, 87000750

Schwertner House [Willcox MRA (AD)], 124 E. Stewart St., Willcox, 8/25/83, A, C, 83002986

Silver Peak Lookout Complex [National Forest Fire Lookouts in the Southwestern Region TR], Coronado National Forest, Portal vicinity, 1/28/88, A, C, g, 87002469

Soto, Pablo, House [Willcox MRA], 108 E. Stewart, Willcox, 8/18/87, B, C, 87000744

St. Paul's Episcopal Church, Safford and 3rd Sts., Tombstone, 9/22/71, A, B, C, a, 71000111

Stafford Cabin, 30 mi. SE of Willcox in Chiricahua National Monument, Willcox vicinity, 3/31/75, A, NPS, 75000171

Tombstone City Hall, 315 E. Fremont St., Tombstone, 2/01/72, C, 72000195

Tombstone Courthouse, 219 E. Toughnut, Tombstone, 4/13/72, A, C, 72000196

Tombstone Historic District, U.S. 80, Tombstone, 10/15/66, A, NHL, 66000171

US Post Office and Customs House—Douglas Main [Historic US Post Offices in Arizona, 1900–1941, TR], 601 Tenth St., Douglas, 12/03/85, A, C, 85003104

Willcox Women's Club [Willcox MRA], 312 W. Stewart, Willcox, 5/27/87, A, C, 87000740

Wilson, J. C., House [Willcox MRA], 258 E. Maley, Willcox, 8/18/87, B, C, 87000747

Coconino County

Abandoned Route 66, Ash Fork Hill [Historic US Route 66 in Arizona MPS], N of I-40 between Ash Fork and Williams, Ash Fork vicinity, 5/19/89, A, g, 89000380

Abandoned Route 66, Parks (1921) [Historic US Route 66 in Arizona MPS], W of Parks, Parks vicinity, 5/19/89, A, g, 89000377

Abandoned Route 66, Parks (1931) [Historic US Route 66 in Arizona MPS], E of Parks, Parks vicinity, 5/19/89, A, g, 89000378

Arizona Lumber and Timber Company Office [Flagstaff MRA], 1 Riordan Rd., Flagstaff, 4/30/86, A, C, 86000900

Ash Fork Steel Dam, E of Ash Fork off U.S. 66, Ash Fork vicinity, 7/30/76, C, 76000373

Ashurst House, 417-421 W. Aspen Ave., Flagstaff, 11/29/84, A, B, C, 84000529

Bank Hotel, Santa Fe and Leroux St., Flagstaff, 12/07/77, C, 77000232

Big Springs Lookout Tower [National Forest Fire Lookouts in the Southwestern Region TR], Kaibab National Forest, Big Springs, 1/28/88, A, C, 87002478

Big Springs Ranger Station [Depression-Era USDA Forest Service Administrative Complexes in Arizona MPS], Along Ryan Rd., Kaibab NF, Big Springs vicinity, 6/10/93, A, C, 93000519

Brannen—Devine House [Flagstaff MRA], 209 E. Cottage, Flagstaff, 4/30/86, C, 86000912

Brow Monument, N. Kaibab Ranger District, Kaibab National Forest, Big Springs vicinity, 7/13/87, A, 87001159

Buck Mountain Lookout Tower [National Forest Fire Lookouts in the Southwestern Region TR], Coconino National Forest, Buck Mountain, 1/28/88, A, C, g, 87002460

Bullethead [Snake Gulch Rock Art MPS], Address Restricted, Fredonia vicinity, 11/21/92, C, D, 92001544

C & M Garage [Flagstaff MRA], 204 S. Milton Rd., Flagstaff, 4/30/86, A, C, 86000908

CHARLES H. SPENCER Hulk, Address Restricted, Lee's Ferry vicinity, 10/15/89, A, C, D, NPS, 89001593

Cameron Suspension Bridge [Vehicular Bridges in Arizona MPS (AD)], Carries US 89 over the Little Colorado River, Cameron vicinity, 6/05/86, A, C, 86001206

Camp Clover Ranger Station [Depression-Era USDA Forest Service Administrative Complexes in Arizona MPS], Off US 66/89 SW of Williams, Kaibab NF, Williams vicinity, 7/16/93, A, C, 93000520

Campbell, H. E., House [Flagstaff MRA], 215 Leroux, Flagstaff, 4/30/86, B, C, 86000910

Canyon Diablo Bridge [Vehicular Bridges in Arizona MPS], Abandoned grade of US 66 over Diablo Canyon, Winona vicinity, 9/30/88, A, C, 88001664

Canyon Padre Bridge [Vehicular Bridges in Arizona MPS], Abandoned grade of US 66 over Padre Canyon, Flagstaff vicinity, 9/30/88, A, C, 88001666

Checkered Men [Snake Gulch Rock Art MPS], Address Restricted, Fredonia vicinity, 11/21/92, C, D, 92001546

Clark, J. M., House, 503 N. Humphreys St., Flagstaff, 12/05/84, C, 84000446

Coconino County Hospital Complex [Flagstaff MRA], Ft. Valley Rd., Flagstaff, 4/30/86, A, C, 86000905

Cooper Ridge Lookout Tree [National Forest Fire Lookouts in the Southwestern Region TR], N of

jct. of Alt. US 89 and AZ 67, Kaibab NF, Fredonia vicinity, 1/13/92, A, C, 91001962

Corral Lake Lookout Tree [National Forest Fire Lookouts in the Southwestern Region TR], Roughly 30 mi. SE of Fredonia, Kaibab NF, Fredonia vicinity, 1/13/92, A, C, 91001954

Coyote Range, N of Flagstaff on US 180, Flagstaff vicinity, 5/14/84, A, C, 84000641

Dead Indian Canyon Bridge [Vehicular Bridges in Arizona MPS], Abandoned grade of US 64 over Dead Indian Canyon, Desert View vicinity, 9/30/88, A, C, 88001603

Dry Park Lookout Cabin and Storage Sheds [National Forest Fire Lookouts in the Southwestern Region TR], Kaibab National Forest, Big Springs vicinity, 1/28/88, A, C, 87002479

El Tovar Hotel, Grand Canyon National Park, Rte. 8A, Grand Canyon, 9/06/74, A, C, NHL, NPS, 74000334

El Tovar Stables, Off Grand Canyon National Park Rte. 8A, Grand Canyon, 9/06/74, A, C, NPS, 74000336

Elden Pueblo, Address Restricted, Flagstaff vicinity, 10/24/86, A, C, D, 86002853

Fern Mountain Ranch, N of Flagstaff, Flagstaff vicinity, 3/29/78, A, 78000542

First Baptist Church, 123 S. Beaver St., Flagstaff, 12/23/91, C, a, 91001576

First Methodist Episcopal Church and Parsonage, 127 W. Sherman St., Williams, 11/29/84, A, C, a, 84000403

Flagstaff Armory [Flagstaff MRA], 503 S. Milton, Flagstaff, 4/30/86, C, 86000903

Flagstaff Townsite Historic Residential District [Flagstaff MRA], Roughly bounded by Cherry, Humphreys and Sitgreaves Sts., Railroad Ave., and Toltec and Aztec Sts., Flagstaff, 4/30/86, A, C, 86000897

Fracas Lookout Tree [National Forest Fire Lookouts in the Southwestern Region TR], Roughly 30 mi. SE of Fredonia, Kaibab NF, Fredonia vicinity, 1/13/92, A, C, 91001955

Francis, D. M., House [Flagstaff MRA], 1456 Meade Ln., Flagstaff, 4/30/86, B, C, 86000902

Grand Canyon Inn and Campground, North Rim, Grand Canyon National Park, 9/02/82, A, C, NPS, 82001872

Grand Canyon Lodge, North Rim on Bright Angel Point, Grand Canyon National Park, 9/02/82, A, C, g, NHL, NPS, 82001721

Grand Canyon North Rim Headquarters, North Rim, Grand Canyon, 9/02/82, A, C, g, NPS, 82001722

Grand Canyon Park Operations Building, Off West Rim Dr., Grand Canyon National Park, 5/28/87, C, NHL, NPS, 87001412

Grand Canyon Power House, Off West Rim Dr., Grand Canyon National Park, 5/28/87, C, NHL, NPS, 87001411

Grand Canyon Railroad Station, Grand Canyon National Park Rte. 8A, Grand Canyon, 9/06/74, A, C, NHL, NPS, 74000337

Grand Canyon Village Historic District, AZ 64, Grand Canyon, 11/20/75, A, C, b, g, NPS, 75000343

Coconino County—Continued

Grandview Lookout Tower and Cabin [National Forest Fire Lookouts in the Southwestern Region TR], Off Coconino Rim Rd., Twin Lakes, 1/28/88, A, C, 87002482

Grandview Lookout Tree [National Forest Fire Lookouts in the Southwestern Region TR], S of Grandview Pt., Grand Canyon NP, in Kaibab NF, Grand Canyon vicinity, 1/13/92, A, 91001945

Grandview Mine, Grand Canyon National Park, Grand Canyon, 7/09/74, A, NPS, 74000347

Head Hunters [Snake Gulch Rock Art MPS], Address Restricted, Fredonia vicinity, 11/21/92, C, D, 92001548

Hermits Rest Concession Building, Grand Canyon National Park, Grand Canyon, 8/07/74, A, C, NPS, 74000335

Homestead, The, 3 mi. N of Flagstaff on U.S. 180, Flagstaff vicinity, 5/27/75, C, g, 75000341

House at 310 South Beaver [Flagstaff MRA], 310 S. Beaver, Flagstaff, 4/30/86, C, 86000913

House at 720 Grand Canyon Avenue [Flagstaff MRA], 720 Grand Canyon Ave., Flagstaff, 4/30/86, B, C, 86000909

Hull Cabin Historic District, 1.5 mi. S of Grand Canyon South Rim, Kaibab National Forest, Grand Canyon South Rim vicinity, 10/23/85, A, B, C, 85003370

Hull Tank Lookout Tree [National Forest Fire Lookouts in the Southwestern Region TR], SE of Grandview Pt., Grand Canyon NP, in Kaibab NF, Grand Canyon vicinity, 1/13/92, A, C, 91001947

Jacob Lake Lookout Tower [National Forest Fire Lookouts in the Southwestern Region TR], Grand Canyon Hwy., Jacob Lake, 1/28/88, A, C, 87002477

Jacob Lake Ranger Station, N. Kaibab Ranger District off AZ 67, Kaibab National Forest, Jacob Lake vicinity, 7/13/87, A, 87001151

Kendrick Lookout Cabin [National Forest Fire Lookouts in the Southwestern Region TR], Kaibab National Forest, Pumpkin Center vicinity, 1/28/88, A, C, 87002480

Koch, I. B., House [Flagstaff MRA], 7 Riordan Rd., Flagstaff, 4/30/86, B, C, 86000901

La Cuidad de Mexico Grocery [Flagstaff MRA], 217 S. San Francisco, Flagstaff, 4/30/86, C, 86000906

La Iglesia Metodista Mexicana, El Divino Redentor [Flagstaff MRA (AD)], 319 S. San Francisco St., Flagstaff, 1/30/85, A, C, a, b, 85000147

Laws Spring, Kaibab National Forest, Williams vicinity, 7/05/84, A, 84000645

Lee Butte Lookout Tower and Cabin [National Forest Fire Lookouts in the Southwestern Region TR], Woods Canyon, Happy Jack vicinity, 1/28/88, A, C, 87002461

Lees Ferry, SW of Page at Colorado River, Page vicinity, 3/15/76, A, NPS, 76000374

Little Mountain Lookout Tree [National Forest Fire Lookouts in the Southwestern Region TR],

Roughly 30 mi. SE of Fredonia, Kaibab NF, Fredonia vicinity, 1/13/92, A, C, 91001950

Lonely Dell Ranch Historic District, SW of Page in Glen Canyon National Recreation Area, Page vicinity, 5/19/78, B, NPS, 78000277

Lowell Observatory [Flagstaff MRA (AD)], 1 mi. W of Flagstaff on Mars Hill, Flagstaff vicinity, 10/15/66, A, B, NHL, 66000172

Mary Jane Colter Buildings (Hopi House, The Lookout, Hermit's Rest, and the Desert View Watchtower), Several locations along the South Rim, Grand Canyon National Park, 5/28/87, A, C, NHL, NPS, 87001436

Merriam, C. Hart, Base Camp Site, 20 mi. NW of Flagstaff in Coconino National Forest, Flagstaff vicinity, 10/15/66, B, NHL, 66000173

Midgley, W. W., Bridge [Vehicular Bridges in Arizona MPS], Alt. US 89 over Wilson Canyon, milepost 375.7, Sedona vicinity, 3/31/89, A, C, 88001614

Milligan House, 323 W. Aspen, Flagstaff, 11/29/84, B, C, 84000389

Moqui Lookout Cabin [National Forest Fire Lookouts in the Southwestern Region TR], Coconino National Forest, Blue Ridge, 1/28/88, A, C, 87002457

Moqui Ranger Station [Depression-Era USDA Forest Service Administrative Complexes in Arizona MPS], Off US 180 N of Tusayan, Kaibab NF, Tusayan vicinity, 6/10/93, A, C, 93000521

Mormon Lake Lookout Cabin [National Forest Fire Lookouts in the Southwestern Region TR], Coconino National Forest, Mormon Lake vicinity, 1/28/88, A, C, 87002459

Museum of Northern Arizona Exhibition Building, 3001 N. Fort Valley Rd., Flagstaff, 4/27/93, A, B, C, 93000305

Navajo National Monument, 30 mi. SW of Kayenta, Kayenta vicinity, 10/15/66, C, D, NPS, 66000176

Navajo Steel Arch Highway Bridge [Vehicular Bridges in Arizona MPS (AD)], SW of Lee, Lee's Ferry vicinity, 8/13/81, A, C, 81000134

North End Historic Residential District [Flagstaff MRA], Roughly bounded by Hunt, San Fransisco and Verde, Elm and Cherry, and Beaver and Humphreys Sts., Flagstaff, 4/30/86, A, C, 86000899

Northern Arizona Normal School Historic District, Northern Arizona University, US 89, Flagstaff, 5/22/86, A, C, 86001107

Nuvakwewtaqa, Address Restricted, Winslow vicinity, 8/02/77, D, 77000233

O'Neill, Buckey, Cabin, Off AZ 64 in Grand Canyon National Park, Grand Canyon, 10/29/75, B, g, NPS, 75000227

Old Headquarters, 2 mi. E of Flagstaff in Walnut Canyon National Monument, Flagstaff vicinity, 3/31/75, A, NPS, 75000220

Our Lady of Guadaloupe Church [Flagstaff MRA], 302 S. Kendrick, Flagstaff, 4/30/86, C, a, 86000907

Pendley Homestead Historic District, US 89-A, 7 mi. N of Sedona, Sedona vicinity, 12/23/91, A, 91001857

Presbyterian Church Parsonage [Flagstaff MRA], 15 E. Cherry, Flagstaff, 4/30/86, C, a, 86000911

Prochnow House [Flagstaff MRA], 304 S. Elden, Flagstaff, 4/30/86, C, 86000898

Promontory Butte Lookout Complex [National Forest Fire Lookouts in the Southwestern Region TR], Rim Rd., Apache-Sitgreaves National Forest, Beaver Park vicinity, 1/28/88, A, C, 87002455

Pumphouse Wash Bridge [Vehicular Bridges in Arizona MPS], US 89 over Pumphouse Wash, milepost 387.4, Flagstaff vicinity, 9/30/88, A, C, 88001605

Railroad Addition Historic District [Flagstaff MRA (AD)], Roughly bounded by Santa Fe RR tracks, Agassiz and Beaver Sts., Birch and Aspen Aves., Flagstaff, 1/18/83, A, C, g, 83002989

Railroad Addition Historic District (Boundary Increase) [Flagstaff MRA], Roughly bounded by Santa Fe RR tracks, San Francisco St., alley S of Phoenix Ave., and Beaver St., Flagstaff, 6/17/86, A, C, 86001360

Ranger's Dormitory, Off AZ 64 in Grand Canyon National Park, Grand Canyon, 9/05/75, A, C, NPS, 75000219

Ridge Ruin Archeological District, Address Restricted, Flagstaff vicinity, 4/20/92, B, D, 92000339

Riordan Estate, 2 Kinlichi Knoll, Flagstaff, 2/28/79, B, C, 79000416

Rock Family [Snake Gulch Rock Art MPS], Address Restricted, Fredonia vicinity, 11/21/92, C, D, 92001550

Rocketeers [Snake Gulch Rock Art MPS], Address Restricted, Fredonia vicinity, 11/21/92, C, D, 92001547

Rural Route 66, Brannigan Park [Historic US Route 66 in Arizona MPS], Forest Rd. 146 E of Parks to Brannigan Park, Parks vicinity, 5/19/89, A, g, 89000375

Rural Route 66, Parks [Historic US Route 66 in Arizona MPS], Forest Rd. 146 between Beacon Hill and Parks, Parks vicinity, 5/19/89, A, g, 89000374

Rural Route 66, Pine Springs [Historic US Route 66 in Arizona MPS], Forest Rd. 108 at Pine Springs Ranch, Williams vicinity, 5/19/89, A, g, 89000379

South Beaver School, 506 S. Beaver St., Flagstaff, 8/06/87, A, C, 87001342

Summit Mountain Lookout Tree [National Forest Fire Lookouts in the Southwestern Region TR], Off Perkinsville Rd. SE of Williams, Kaibab NF, Williams vicinity, 1/13/92, A, 91001948

Superintendent's Residence, Off Rte. 8A, in Grand Canyon National Park, Grand Canyon, 9/06/74, A, NPS, 74000450

Tater Point Lookout Tree [National Forest Fire Lookouts in the Southwestern Region TR], Forest Rd. 240 E of AZ 67, S of Alt. US 89, Kaibab NF, Fredonia vicinity, 1/13/92, A, C, 91001946

Taylor Cabin Line Camp, Sycamore Canyon Wilderness Area, Sedona, 7/16/85, A, 85001580

Telephone Hill Lookout Tree [National Forest Fire Lookouts in the Southwestern Region TR],

Coconino County—Continued

Off AZ 67 S of jct. with Alt. US 89, Kaibab NF, Fredonia vicinity, 1/13/92, A, C, 91001952

Tipover Lookout Tree [National Forest Fire Lookouts in the Southwestern Region TR], NW of N. Rim Entrance Station, Grand Canyon NP, in Kaibab NF, Fredonia vicinity, 1/13/92, A, C, 91001953

Trans-Canyon Telephone Line, Grand Canyon National Park, Grand Canyon along Bright Angel & North Kaibab Trails from South Rim to Roaring Springs & South Kaibab Trail to Tipoff, Grand Canyon vicinity, 5/13/86, A, C, g, 86001102

Tusayan Lookout Tree [National Forest Fire Lookouts in the Southwestern Region TR], W of US 180, SW of Tusayan, Kaibab NF, Tusayan vicinity, 1/13/92, A, C, 91001951

Tusayan Ruins, Grand Canyon National Park, Grand Canyon National Park vicinity, 7/10/74, D, NPS, 74000285

Tutuveni, Address Restricted, Cameron vicinity, 12/03/86, D, a, 86003283

Twins [Snake Gulch Rock Art MPS], Address Restricted, Fredonia vicinity, 11/21/92, C, D, 92001545

Urban Route 66, Williams [Historic US Route 66 in Arizona MPS], Bill Williams Ave. between Sixth St. and Pine St., Williams, 5/19/89, A, g, 89000376

Volunteer Lookout Cabin [National Forest Fire Lookouts in the Southwestern Region TR], Kaibab National Forest, Bellemont vicinity, 1/28/88, A, C, g, 87002481

Walnut Canyon Bridge [Vehicular Bridges in Arizona MPS], Townsend-Winona Hwy., Winona vicinity, 9/30/88, A, C, 88001660

Walnut Canyon Dam, SE of Flagstaff, Flagstaff vicinity, 1/18/79, A, C, g, 79000417

Walnut Canyon National Monument, 8 mi. E of Flagstaff off U.S. 66, Flagstaff vicinity, 10/15/66, D, NPS, 66000174

Water Reclamation Plant, S of Grand Canyon National Park, Rte. 8A, Grand Canyon, 9/06/74, A, C, g, NPS, 74000348

Weatherford Hotel, 23 N. Leroux St., Flagstaff, 3/30/78, A, 78000543

White Man Cave [Snake Gulch Rock Art MPS], Address Restricted, Fredonia vicinity, 11/21/92, C, D, 92001543

Williams Historic Business District, Roughly bounded by Grant and Railroad Aves., and 1st and 4th Sts., Williams, 12/20/84, A, C, 84000436

Willow Springs, Address Restricted, Cameron vicinity, 12/03/86, A, D, 86003285

Wilson, Charles, Jr., House [Flagstaff MRA], 100 Wilson Dr., Flagstaff, 4/30/86, C, 86000904

Winona, Address Restricted, Winona vicinity, 10/15/66, D, NHL, 66000177

Wise Men [Snake Gulch Rock Art MPS], Address Restricted, Fredonia vicinity, 11/21/92, C, D, 92001549

Woody Mountain Lookout Tower [National Forest Fire Lookouts in the Southwestern Region

TR], Rogers Lake, Flagstaff vicinity, 1/28/88, A, C, 87002458

Wupatki National Monument, 30 mi. N of Flagstaff off U.S. 89, Flagstaff vicinity, 10/15/66, C, D, NPS, 66000175

Gila County

Archeological Site No. AR-03-12-06-1130(TNF) [Bandelier's, Adolph F. A., Archeological Survey of Tonto Basin, Tonto National Forest, MPS], Address Restricted, Punkin Center vicinity, 4/21/89, A, B, 89000273

Archeological Site No. AR-03-12-06-1131(TNF) [Bandelier's, Adolph F. A., Archeological Survey of Tonto Basin, Tonto National Forest, MPS], Address Restricted, Punkin Center vicinity, 4/21/89, A, B, 89000274

Besh-Ba-Gowah, S of Globe, Globe vicinity, 5/09/84, A, D, 84000648

Black River Bridge [Vehicular Bridges in Arizona MPS], Indian Rt. 9 over Black River, Carrizo vicinity, 9/30/88, A, C, 88001619

Cline Terrace Platform Mound (AR-03-12-06-132 TNF) [Bandelier's, Adolph F. A., Archeological Survey of Tonto Basin, Tonto National Forest, MPS], Address Restricted, Punkin Center vicinity, 4/21/89, A, B, 89000269

Coolidge Dam, SW of San Carlos, San Carlos vicinity, 10/29/81, A, C, 81000135

Cordova Avenue Bridge [Vehicular Bridges in Arizona MPS], Cordova Ave. over Bloody Tanks Wash, Miami, 3/31/89, A, C, 88001690

Diamond Point Lookout Cabin [National Forest Fire Lookouts in the Southwestern Region TR], Tonto National Forest, Tonto Village vicinity, 1/28/88, A, C, g, 87002493

Dominion Hotel, S. Broad St., Globe, 5/22/78, A, 78000545

Elks Building [Globe Commercial and Civic MRA], 155 W. Mesquite, Globe, 8/06/87, A, 87000860

Fossil Creek Bridge [Vehicular Bridges in Arizona MPS], Forest Service Rd. over Fossil Creek, Strawberry vicinity, 9/30/88, C, 88001620

Gila County Courthouse [Globe Commercial and Civic MRA], Oak and Broad Sts., Globe, 5/27/75, A, C, 75000347

Gila Pueblo, S of Globe, Globe vicinity, 11/17/77, B, D, e, 77000235

Gila Valley Bank and Trust Building [Globe Commercial and Civic MRA], 292 N. Broad St., Globe, 8/06/87, C, 87000861

Globe Downtown Historic District [Globe Commercial and Civic MRA], Broad St. between Cedar and Tebbs, Globe, 5/28/87, A, C, 87000862

Globe Mine Rescue Station, 1330 N. Broad St., Globe, 6/07/90, A, 90000875

Holy Angels Church [Globe Commercial and Civic MRA (AD)], 231 S. Broad St., Globe, 12/01/83, C, a, 83003448

Houston Mesa Ruins, Address Restricted, Payson vicinity, 9/04/86, D, 86002191

Inspiration Avenue Bridge [Vehicular Bridges in Arizona MPS], Inspiration Ave. over Bloody Tanks Wash, Miami, 3/31/89, A, C, 88001691

International House [Globe Commercial and Civic MRA], 636–638 N. Broad St., Globe, 3/31/88, C, 88000233

Keystone Avenue Bridge [Vehicular Bridges in Arizona MPS], Keystone Ave. over Bloody Tanks Wash, Miami, 3/31/89, A, C, 88001692

Kinishba Ruins, Address Restricted, Whiteriver vicinity, 10/15/66, C, D, NHL, 66000180

Miami Avenue Bridge [Vehicular Bridges in Arizona MPS], Miami Ave. over Bloody Tanks Wash, Miami, 3/31/89, A, C, 88001693

Natural Bridge Lodge, Off AZ 87, Payson vicinity, 8/21/86, A, 86001558

Oak Creek Platform Mound (AR-03-12-06-714 TNF) [Bandelier's, Adolph F. A., Archeological Survey of Tonto Basin, Tonto National Forest, MPS], Address Restricted, Punkin Center vicinity, 4/21/89, A, B, 89000271

Park Creek Platform Mound (AR-03-12-06-1044 TNF) [Bandelier's, Adolph F. A., Archeological Survey of Tonto Basin, Tonto National Forest, MPS], Address Restricted, Punkin Center vicinity, 4/21/89, A, B, 89000272

Pinal Ranger Station [Depression-Era USDA Forest Service Administrative Complexes in Arizona MPS], S of Globe, Tonto NF, Globe vicinity, 6/10/93, A, C, 93000526

Pleasant Valley Ranger Station [Depression-Era USDA Forest Service Administrative Complexes in Arizona MPS], S of AZ 288, Tonto NF, Young vicinity, 6/10/93, A, C, 93000527

Reppy Avenue Bridge [Vehicular Bridges in Arizona MPS], Reppy Ave. over Bloody Tanks Wash, Miami, 9/30/88, A, C, 88001689

Roosevelt Dam [Vehicular Bridges in Arizona MPS (AD)], Salt River, 31 mi. NW of Globe on AZ 88, in Tonto National Forest, Globe vicinity, 10/15/66, A, C, NHL, 66000178

Salt River Bridge [Vehicular Bridges in Arizona MPS], AZ 288 over Salt River, milepost 262.4, Roosevelt vicinity, 9/30/88, A, C, 88001604

Salt River Canyon Bridge [Vehicular Bridges in Arizona MPS], US 60 over Salt River, milepost 292.9, Carrizo vicinity, 9/30/88, A, C, 88001608

Schoolhouse Point (AR-03-12-06-13(TNF) [Bandelier's, Adolph F. A., Archeological Survey of Tonto Basin, Tonto National Forest, MPS], Address Restricted, Roosevelt vicinity, 4/21/89, A, B, 89000267

St. John's Episcopal Church [Globe Commercial and Civic MRA (AD)], 175 E. Oak St., Globe, 11/22/77, A, C, a, g, 77000234

Tonto National Monument Archeological District, Address Restricted, Roosevelt vicinity, 10/15/66, D, NPS, 66000081

Tonto National Monument, Lower Ruin (AZ U:8:047A ASM) [Bandelier's, Adolph F. A., Archeological Survey of Tonto Basin, Tonto National Forest, MPS], Off AZ 188, Roosevelt vicinity, 4/21/89, A, B, NPS, 89000265

Tonto National Monument, Upper Ruin (AZ U:8:048 ASM) [Bandelier's, Adolph F. A., Archeological Survey of Tonto Basin, Tonto Na-

Gila County—Continued

tional Forest, MPS], Off AZ 188, Roosevelt vicinity, 4/21/89, A, B, NPS, 89000266

US Post Office and Courthouse—Globe Main [Historic US Post Offices in Arizona, 1900–1941, TR; Globe Commercial and Civic MRA (AD)], Hill and Sycamore Sts., Globe, 12/03/85, A, C, 85003106

Graham County

Arizona Bank and Trust [Safford MRA], 429 Main, Safford, 2/09/88, A, C, 87002557

Bingham, Richard, House [Safford MRA], 1208 Ninth Ave., Safford, 2/09/88, C, 87002556

Brooks, Paul, House [Safford MRA], 1033 Fifth Ave., Safford, 2/09/88, C, 87002559

Buena Vista Hotel [Safford MRA], 322 Main, Safford, 2/09/88, A, C, 87002560

Columbine Work Station [Depression-Era USDA Forest Service Administrative Complexes in Arizona MPS], AZ 366 SW of Safford, Coronado NF, Safford vicinity, 6/10/93, A, C, 93000516

Cross, T. D., House [Safford MRA], 918 First Ave., Safford, 2/09/88, C, 87002563

Davis, William Charles, House [Safford MRA], 301 Eleventh St., Safford, 2/09/88, C, 87002565

Graham County Courthouse, 800 Main St., Safford, 5/25/82, A, C, 82002077

Heliograph Lookout Complex [National Forest Fire Lookouts in the Southwestern Region TR], Coronado National Forest, Old Columbine vicinity, 1/28/88, A, C, 87002467

Horowitz, Joe, House [Safford MRA], 118 Main, Safford, 2/09/88, C, 87002566

House at 611 Third Avenue [Safford MRA], 611 Third Ave., Safford, 2/09/88, C, 87002568

Kearny Campsite and Trail, NE of Safford off U.S. 666, Safford vicinity, 10/09/74, A, 74000454

Marijilda Canyon Prehistoric Archeological District, Address Restricted, Safford vicinity, 10/02/88, D, 88001572

O'Brien, Mathew, House [Safford MRA], 615 First Ave., Safford, 2/09/88, C, 87002570

Oak Draw Archeological District, Address Restricted, Safford vicinity, 11/25/92, D, 92001564

Oddfellows Home [Safford MRA], 808 Eighth Ave., Safford, 5/12/88, C, 87002571

Olney, George A., House [Safford MRA], 1104 Central, Safford, 2/09/88, B, C, 87002574

Packer, Alonzo Hamilton, House [Safford MRA], 1203 Central, Safford, 2/09/88, C, 87002575

Point of Pines, Address Restricted, Morenci vicinity, 10/15/66, D, NHL, 66000182

Power's Cabin, NW of Willcox in Coronado National Forest, Willcox vicinity, 8/13/75, A, C, 75000348

Ridgeway, David, House [Safford MRA], 928 Central, Safford, 2/09/88, C, 87002576

Safford High School [Safford MRA], 520 Eleventh St., Safford, 2/09/88, A, C, 87002577

Sierra Bonita Ranch, SW of Bonita, Bonita vicinity, 10/15/66, B, NHL, 66000181

Southern Pacific Railroad Depot [Safford MRA], 808 Central, Safford, 2/09/88, A, C, 87002578

Talley, Hugh, House [Safford MRA], 1114 Third Ave., Safford, 2/09/88, C, 87002580

Talley, William, House [Safford MRA], 219 Eleventh St., Safford, 2/09/88, C, 87002581

Webb Peak Lookout Tower [National Forest Fire Lookouts in the Southwestern Region TR], Off AZ 366, Old Columbine vicinity, 1/28/88, A, C, 87002464

Welker, James R., House [Safford MRA], 1127 Central, Safford, 2/09/88, C, 87002582

West Peak Lookout Tower [National Forest Fire Lookouts in the Southwestern Region TR], Coronado National Forest, Bonita vicinity, 1/28/88, A, C, 87002466

Wickersham, David, House [Safford MRA], 1101 Fifth Ave., Safford, 2/09/88, C, 87002583

Williams, Dan, House [Safford MRA], 603 Relation, Safford, 2/09/88, C, 87002584

Wilson, J. Mark, House [Safford MRA], 712 Relation, Safford, 2/09/88, C, 87002585

Woman's Club [Safford MRA], 215 Main, Safford, 5/12/88, A, C, 87002586

Greenlee County

Bear Mountain Lookout Complex [National Forest Fire Lookouts in the Southwestern Region TR], Apache-Sitgreaves National Forest, Mogollon Rim, 1/28/88, A, C, g, 87002452

Billingsley, Benjamin F., House, 202 Main St., Duncan, 8/25/83, B, C, 83002998

Black Gap Bridge [Vehicular Bridges in Arizona MPS], Old Safford Rd., 7.8 mi. SW of Clifton, Clifton vicinity, 9/30/88, A, C, 88001627

Clifton Casa Grande Building, 8 Park Ave., Clifton, 6/26/79, A, B, C, 79003445

Clifton Townsite Historic District, Confluence of Chase Creek and the San Francisco River, Clifton, 3/01/90, A, C, D, 90000339

Gila River Bridge [Vehicular Bridges in Arizona MPS], Old Safford Rd., 6.8 mi. SE of Clifton, Clifton vicinity, 9/30/88, A, C, 88001628

Park Avenue Bridge [Vehicular Bridges in Arizona MPS], Park Ave. over the San Francisco River, Clifton, 9/30/88, A, C, 88001661

Potter, Dell, Ranch House, N of Clifton, Clifton vicinity, 8/03/77, A, C, 77000236

Solomonville Road Overpass [Vehicular Bridges in Arizona MPS], Old Safford Rd., 3.6 mi. S. of Clifton, Safford vicinity, 9/30/88, A, 88001625

Solomonville Road Overpass [Vehicular Bridges in Arizona MPS], Old Safford Rd., 4.5 mi. S of Clifton, Clifton vicinity, 9/30/88, A, 88001626

La Paz County

Eagletail Petroglyph Site, Address Restricted, Hyder vicinity, 9/28/88, D, 88001570

Maricopa County

1931 Tempe Bridge, Mill Ave., Tempe, 8/13/81, A, C, 81000137

6th Avenue Hotel-Windsor Hotel [Phoenix Commercial MRA], 546 W. Adams, Phoenix, 9/04/85, A, 85002041

Adams School, 800 W. Adams St, Phoenix, 11/29/79, A, C, 79000418

Administration/Science Building [Tempe MRA], ASU Campus (Bldg. 11), Tempe, 9/04/85, A, C, 85002169

Alchesay Canyon Bridge [Vehicular Bridges in Arizona MPS], AZ 88 over Alchesay Canyon, milepost 241.1, Roosevelt vicinity, 9/30/88, A, 88001615

Alhambra Hotel, 43 S. Macdonald, Mesa, 7/31/91, A, 91000982

Anchor Manufacturing Co. [Phoenix Commercial MRA], 551 S. Central, Phoenix, 9/04/85, A, 85002042

Anderson, Helen, House, 149 W. McDowell Rd., Phoenix, 11/30/83, A, C, 83003449

Andre Building, 401–403 S. Mill Ave., Tempe, 8/10/79, A, C, 79000419

Arizona Academy—North Hall and South Hall [Educational Buildings in Phoenix MPS], 1325 N. 14th St., Phoenix, 8/12/93, A, 93000813

Arizona Citrus Growers Association Warehouse [Phoenix Commercial MRA], 601 E. Jackson, Phoenix, 9/04/85, A, 85002043

Arizona Compress & Warehouse Co. Warehouse [Phoenix Commercial MRA], 215 S. 13th St., Phoenix, 9/04/85, A, 85002044

Arizona State Capitol Building, 1700 W. Washington St., Phoenix, 10/29/74, A, C, 74000455

Arvizu's El Fresnal Grocery Store [Phoenix Commercial MRA], 310 E. Buchanon, Phoenix, 9/04/85, A, 85002046

B. B. Moeur Activity Building [Tempe MRA], ASU Campus (Bldg. 37), Tempe, 9/11/85, A, C, g, 85002171

Baird, F. S., Machine Shop [Phoenix Commercial MRA], 623 E. Adams, Phoenix, 9/04/85, A, 85002047

Bayless, J. B., Store No. 7 [Phoenix Commercial MRA], 825 N. 7th St., Phoenix, 9/04/85, A, 85002048

Beet Sugar Factory, 5243 W. Glendale Ave., Glendale, 1/30/78, A, 78000548

Bethlehem Baptist Church [Religious Architecture in Phoenix MPS], 1402 E. Adams St., Phoenix, 8/10/93, C, a, 93000744

Blount Addition Historic District [Roosevelt Neighborhood MRA], N side of W. Culver St. between Central and Third Aves., Phoenix, 2/27/86, C, 86000265

Borden Milk Co. Creamery and Ice Factory [Tempe MRA], 1300-1360 E. Eigth St., Tempe, 10/10/84, A, C, 84000171

Boulder Creek Bridge [Vehicular Bridges in Arizona MPS], AZ 88 over Boulder Creek, Tortilla Flat vicinity, 3/31/89, A, C, b, 88001599

Brazaletes Pueblo Site, Address Restricted, Carefree vicinity, 1/17/75, D, 75000349

Maricopa County—Continued

Brophy College Chapel [Religious Architecture in Phoenix MPS], 4701 N. Central Ave., Phoenix, 8/10/93, C, a, 93000747

Brown's Pharmacy [Phoenix Commercial MRA], 1000 E. Pierce, Phoenix, 9/04/85, A, 85002049

Cactus Inn [Wickenburg MRA], 158 Yavapai, Wickenburg, 7/10/86, A, 86001576

Cartwright School [Educational Buildings in Phoenix MPS], 5833 W. Thomas Rd., Phoenix, 8/12/93, A, 93000739

Cashion Archeological Site, Address Restricted, Cashion vicinity, 12/19/78, D, 78000547

Celora Stoddard/Lon Harmon House [Roosevelt Neighborhood MRA], 801 N. 1st Ave., Phoenix, 11/30/83, A, B, C, 83003451

Central School, 10304 N. 83rd Ave., Peoria, 5/12/82, A, C, 82002080

Chambers Transfer & Storage Co.-Central Warehouse [Phoenix Commercial MRA], 15–39 E. Jackson, Phoenix, 9/04/85, A, 85002051

Chambers Transfer & Storage Co. [Phoenix Commercial MRA], 309 S. 4th Ave., Phoenix, 9/04/85, A, 85002052

Chelsea Place Historic District [Roosevelt Neighborhood MRA], Roughly bounded by W. Lynwood and W. Willetta Sts. between Central and 3rd Aves., Phoenix, 11/30/83, A, C, 83003452

City Hall and Jail [Wickenburg MRA], 117 Yavapai, Wickenburg, 7/10/86, A, 86001577

Concrete Block House [Roosevelt Neighborhood MRA], 614 N. 4th Ave., Phoenix, 11/30/83, B, C, 83003455

Concrete Block House [Roosevelt Neighborhood MRA], 640 N. 6th Ave., Phoenix, 11/30/83, A, C, 83003456

Concrete Block House [Roosevelt Neighborhood MRA], 618-620 N. 4th Ave., Phoenix, 11/30/83, A, C, 83003457

Copeland & Tracht Service Station [Phoenix Commercial MRA], 1702 W. Van Buren, Phoenix, 9/04/85, A, 85002054

Coronado Neighborhood Historic District, Roughly bounded by Virginia Ave., Fourteenth St., McDowell Rd., and Seventh St., Phoenix, 2/13/86, A, C, 86000206

Coronado Neighborhood Historic District (Boundary Increase), Roughly bounded by 13th St., Coronado Rd., 14th St. and Monte Vista Rd., and W side 13th St. between Monte Vista and Oak, Phoenix, 12/08/93, A, C, 91002029

Craig Mansion, 131 E. Country Club Dr., Phoenix, 8/18/92, C, 92001013

Curtis Cottage [Prescott Territorial Buildings MRA], 125 S. McCormick, Prescott, 5/04/93, A, C, 93000344

Douglas, Lewis, House, 815 E. Orangewood Ave., Phoenix, 2/08/85, B, 85000188

Dunbar School [Educational Buildings in Phoenix MPS], 707 W. Grant, Phoenix, 8/12/93, A, 93000740

Dunlap, Charles H., House [Roosevelt Neighborhood MRA], 650 N. 1st Ave., Phoenix, 11/30/83, B, C, 83003466

Durand Grocery [Phoenix Commercial MRA], 901 Grand Ave., Phoenix, 10/01/85, A, 85002891

El Zaribah Shrine Auditorium, 1502 W. Washington St., Phoenix, 3/09/89, A, C, 89000168

Elias-Rodriguez House [Tempe MRA], 927 E. 8th St., Tempe, 5/07/84, C, 84000684

Elizabeth Seargeant-Emery Oldaker House [Roosevelt Neighborhood MRA], 649 N. 3rd Ave., Phoenix, 11/30/83, B, C, 83003472

Elliott House [Tempe MRA], 1010 Maple Ave., Tempe, 5/07/84, C, 84000693

Ellis-Shackelford House [Roosevelt Neighborhood MRA], 1242 N. Central Ave., Phoenix, 11/30/83, B, C, 83003475

Encanto—Palmcroft Historic District (Boundary Increase), Holly St. from 15th Ave. to 12th Ave. and 12th from Holly to Encanto Blvd., Phoenix, 6/10/92, A, C, 92000670

Encanto-Palmcroft Historic District, Bounded by N. 7th and N. 15th Aves., McDowell and Thomas Rds., Phoenix, 2/16/84, A, C, 84000696

Evans House, 1108 W. Washington St., Phoenix, 9/01/76, C, 76000375

Farmer-Goodwin House, 820 Farmer Ave., Tempe, 12/26/72, A, C, 72000197

Firestone [Phoenix Commercial MRA], 302 W. Van Buren, Phoenix, 10/01/85, A, 85002892

First Baptist Church, 302 W. Monroe St., Phoenix, 2/08/82, A, C, a, 82002081

First Church of Christ Scientist [Religious Architecture in Phoenix MPS], 924 N. First St., Phoenix, 8/10/93, C, a, 93000745

First National Bank of Glendale Building, 6838 N. 58th Dr., Glendale, 8/25/83, A, C, 83002991

First Presbyterian Church [Religious Architecture in Phoenix MPS], 402 W. Monroe St., Phoenix, 8/10/93, C, a, 93000746

Fish Creek Bridge [Vehicular Bridges in Arizona MPS], AZ 88, milepost 223.50, Tortilla Flat vicinity, 9/30/88, A, C, 88001600

Fort McDowell, Indian Rt. 1, off AZ 87, Yavapai Indian Reservation, Fort McDowell, 8/27/92, D, a, d, 92001050

Fortaleza, Address Restricted, Gila Bend vicinity, 6/23/69, D, 69000035

Frankenberg House, 129 E. University Dr., Tempe, 1/29/81, C, 81000138

Franklin School [Educational Buildings in Phoenix MPS], 1625 W. McDowell Rd., Phoenix, 8/12/93, A, 93000814

Fry Building-Baxter Block [Phoenix Commercial MRA], 146 E. Washington, Phoenix, 9/04/85, A, 85002056

Garcia School [Wickenburg MRA (AD)], Yavapai St. and US 89, Wickenburg, 4/01/82, A, C, 82002087

Garfield Methodist Church [Religious Architecture in Phoenix MPS], 1302 E. Roosevelt St., Phoenix, 8/10/93, C, a, 93000743

Gates, Neil H., House, 4602 N. Elsie Ave., Phoenix, 8/11/86, C, 86002646

Gatlin Site, Address Restricted, Gila Bend vicinity, 10/15/66, D, NHL, 66000183

Gerardo's Building [Phoenix Commercial MRA], 421 S. 3rd St., Phoenix, 9/04/85, A, 85002057

Gibbes, Carter W., House, 2233 N. Alvarado, Phoenix, 8/25/83, C, 83002992

Gila Bend Overpass [Vehicular Bridges in Arizona MPS], Bus. Rt. 8 over Southern Pacific RR, Gila Bend, 9/30/88, A, C, 88001607

Gilbert Elementary School, Elliot and Gilbert Rds., Gilbert, 6/16/80, A, C, 80000762

Gillespie Dam Highway Bridge [Vehicular Bridges in Arizona MPS (AD)], NW of Gila Bend, Gila Bend vicinity, 5/05/81, A, C, 81000136

Glendale Townsite—Catlin Court Historic District, Roughly bounded by Gardenia, 58th, Myrtle, 57th, Palmaire and 59th Aves. and 58th Dr., Glendale, 6/09/92, A, C, 92000680

Glendale Woman's Club Clubhouse, 7032 N. 56th Ave., Glendale, 7/27/89, A, 89001003

Gonzales-Martinez House [Tempe MRA], 320 W. 1st St., Tempe, 5/07/84, C, 84000708

Goodwin Building [Tempe MRA], 512-518 S. Mill Ave., Tempe, 5/07/84, B, C, 84000710

Grace Lutheran Church [Religious Architecture in Phoenix MPS], 1124 N. 3rd St., Phoenix, 8/12/93, C, 93000835

Grady Gammage Memorial Auditorium [Tempe MRA], NE Corner of Mill and Apache, Tempe, 9/11/85, C, g, 85002170

Green, Mary and Moses, House [Tempe MRA], W of Carver St., Tempe, 2/13/85, A, C, 85000406

Grunow, Lois, Memorial Clinic [Phoenix Commercial MRA], 926 E. McDowell, Phoenix, 9/04/85, A, 85002065

Hackett, Roy, House, 401 and 405 Maple St., Tempe, 12/04/74, A, C, 74000458

Hanny's [Phoenix Commercial MRA], 44 N. 1st St., Phoenix, 9/06/85, A, C, g, 85002058

Harrington-Birchett House [Tempe MRA], 202 E. 7th St., Tempe, 5/07/84, C, 84000716

Hassayampa River Bridge [Vehicular Bridges in Arizona MPS], Old US 80 over the Hassayampa River, Hassayampa, 9/30/88, A, C, 88001658

Hayden, C. T., House [Tempe MRA], 3 W. 1st St., Tempe, 10/10/84, A, C, 84000173

Heard Building [Phoenix Commercial MRA], 112 N. Central, Phoenix, 9/04/85, A, B, 85002059

Hedgpeth Hills Petroglyph Site, Address Restricted, Phoenix vicinity, 2/16/84, D, 84000718

Hiatt House [Tempe MRA], 1104 Ash Ave., Tempe, 5/07/84, C, 84000720

Higuera Grocery [Phoenix Commercial MRA], 923 S. Second Ave., Phoenix, 10/01/85, A, 85002893

Hohokam-Pima Irrigation Sites, Address Restricted, Phoenix vicinity, 10/15/66, D, NHL, 66000184

Hotel St. James [Phoenix Commercial MRA], 21 E. Madison, Phoenix, 9/04/85, A, 85002061

Hotel Westward Ho [Phoenix Commercial MRA (AD)], 618 N. Central Ave., Phoenix, 2/19/82, A, C, 82002082

House at 160 Apache [Wickenburg MRA], 160 Apache, Wickenburg, 7/10/86, C, 86001578

House at 170 Center [Wickenburg MRA], 170 Center, Wickenburg, 7/10/86, C, 86001579

Maricopa County—Continued

House at 185 Washington [Wickenburg MRA], 185 Washington, Wickenburg, 7/10/86, C, 86001580

Humbert, William K., House, 2238 N. Alvarado Rd., Phoenix, 12/01/83, C, 83003476

Hurley Building [Phoenix Commercial MRA], 536, 544–548 W. McDowell & 1601 N. 7th Ave., Phoenix, 9/04/85, A, 85002062

Immaculate Heart of Mary [Religious Architecture in Phoenix MPS], 909 E. Washington St., Phoenix, 8/10/93, C, a, 93000742

Industrial Arts Building [Tempe MRA], ASU Campus (Bldg. 4), Tempe, 9/04/85, A, C, 85002168

Jacobs House [Wickenburg MRA], 355 N. Jefferson, Wickenburg, 7/10/86, C, 86001581

Kaler House, 301 W. Frier Dr., Phoenix, 12/17/92, A, C, 92001686

Kenilworth Elementary School, 1210 N. 5th Ave., Phoenix, 3/25/82, A, C, 82002083

Kenilworth Historic District [Roosevelt Neighborhood MRA], Roughly bounded by W. Lynwood and W. Willetta Sts. between 3rd and 7th Aves., and W. Culver between 5th and 7th Aves., Phoenix, 11/30/83, A, C, 83003478

King's Rest Hotel Motor Court [Phoenix Commercial MRA], 801 S. Seventeenth Ave., Phoenix, 8/26/87, A, C, 87001882

Knights of Pythias Building [Phoenix Commercial MRA], 829 N. 1st Ave., Phoenix, 9/04/85, A, 85002063

Laird, Hugh, House [Tempe MRA], 821 S. Farmer, Tempe, 5/07/84, B, C, 84000726

Lewis and Pranty Creek Bridge [Vehicular Bridges in Arizona MPS], AZ 88, milepost 224.60, Tortilla Flat vicinity, 9/30/88, A, C, 88001601

Lightning Delivery Co. Warehouse [Phoenix Commercial MRA], 425 E. Jackson, Phoenix, 9/04/85, A, 85002064

Long, Samuel C., House, 27 E. 6th St., Tempe, 11/28/80, C, 80000765

MacLennan House [Wickenburg MRA], 338 Jefferson, Wickenburg, 7/10/86, B, C, b, 86001582

Main Building, Tempe Normal School [Tempe MRA], ASU Campus, Tempe, 1/07/85, A, C, 85000052

Maricopa County Courthouse, 125 W. Washington St., Phoenix, 2/10/89, A, C, 88003237

Masonic Hall [Wickenburg MRA], 108 Tegner, Wickenburg, 7/10/86, A, C, 86001583

Matthews Hall [Tempe MRA], ASU Campus (Bldg. 172), Tempe, 1/11/85, A, C, 85000053

McClintock, James H., House, 323 E. Willetta St., Phoenix, 10/04/90, B, 90001525

Mesa Grande, Address Restricted, Mesa vicinity, 11/21/78, D, 78000549

Mesa Journal—Tribune FHA Demonstration Home, 22 E. First Ave., Mesa, 12/29/88, B, 88003056

Mesa Woman's Club, 200 N. Macdonald, Mesa, 8/05/91, A, 91000995

Midvale Archeological Site, Address Restricted, Chandler vicinity, 6/14/90, D, 90000933

Miller Block [Tempe MRA], 418-422 Mill Ave., Tempe, 5/07/84, C, 84000727

Miranda, Jesus, Homestead [Tempe MRA], 1992 E. University, Tempe, 5/07/84, C, 84000729

Moeur, W. A., House [Tempe MRA], 850 Ash Ave., Tempe, 5/07/84, B, 84000730

Monroe School, 215 N. 7th St., Phoenix, 8/26/77, A, C, 77000237

Mormon Flat Bridge [Vehicular Bridges in Arizona MPS], AZ 88 over Willow Creek, Tortilla Flat vicinity, 9/30/88, A, C, 88001598

Morristown Store, US 89 NW of Castle Hot Springs Rd., Morristown vicinity, 8/12/91, A, 91001003

Morrow-Hudson House [Tempe MRA], 1203 E. Alameda Dr., Tempe, 5/07/84, B, C, 84000733

Mullen, C. P., House [Tempe MRA], 918 Mill Ave., Tempe, 5/07/84, C, 84000734

Municipal Light Plant [Wickenburg MRA], 245 N. Washington, Wickenburg, 7/10/86, A, 86001584

Oakland Historic District, Roughly bounded by Fillmore St., 19th Ave., Van Buren St. and Grand Ave., Phoenix, 7/10/92, A, 92000847

Old Barber Shop [Wickenburg MRA], 68 Frontier, Wickenburg, 7/10/86, A, C, 86001585

Old Brick Post Office [Wickenburg MRA], 144 N. Frontier, Wickenburg, 7/10/86, A, 86001586

Ong Yut Geong Wholesale Market [Phoenix Commercial MRA], 502 S. 2nd St., Phoenix, 9/04/85, A, 85002066

Ong's, Jim, Market [Phoenix Commercial MRA (AD)], 1110 E. Washington St., Phoenix, 7/08/82, A, C, 82002084

Orpheum Theater [Phoenix Commercial MRA], 209 W. Adams, Phoenix, 9/04/85, A, 85002067

Osborn, William Lewis, House, 1266 W. Pierce Ave., Phoenix, 5/15/91, C, 91000544

Our Lady of Mount Carmel Catholic Church, College and University Ave., Tempe, 1/30/78, C, a, 78000552

Overland Arizona Co. [Phoenix Commercial MRA], 12 N. Fourth Ave., Phoenix, 10/01/85, A, 85002896

Painted Rocks, W of Theba, Theba vicinity, 11/25/77, D, 77000238

Park of the Canals, Along Horne Rd. N from Utah Ditch S to Mesa-Consolidated Canal, Mesa, 5/30/75, D, 75000350

Pay'n Takit #13 [Phoenix Commercial MRA], 1402 E. Van Buren, Phoenix, 9/04/85, A, 85002068

Pay'n Takit #25 [Phoenix Commercial MRA], 1753–1755 W. Van Buren, Phoenix, 9/05/85, A, 85002070

Pay'n Takit #5 [Phoenix Commercial MRA], 1012 N. 7th Ave., Phoenix, 9/04/85, A, 85002069

Petersen Building, 409-413 S. Mill Ave., Tempe, 3/18/80, A, C, 80000766

Petersen, Niels, House, Southern Ave. and Priest St., Tempe, 1/05/78, C, 78000553

Phoenix Carnegie Library And Library Park, 1101 W. Washington St., Phoenix, 11/19/74, A, C, 74000456

Phoenix Homesteads Historic District, Roughly bounded by Flower & Twenty-eight Sts., Pinchot Ave., & Twenty-sixth Sts., Phoenix, 10/13/87, A, C, 87001430

Phoenix LDS Second Ward Church [Roosevelt Neighborhood MRA], 1120 N. 3rd Ave., Phoenix, 11/30/83, A, C, a, 83003492

Phoenix Seed & Feed Company [Phoenix Commercial MRA], 411 S. 2nd St., Phoenix, 9/04/85, A, 85002071

Phoenix Townsite, Bounded by 6th, 7th, Monroe, and Adams Sts., Phoenix, 11/07/78, C, 78000550

Phoenix Union Colored High School, 415 E. Grant St., Phoenix, 5/02/91, A, 91000543

Phoenix Union High School Historic District, 512 E. Van Buren, Phoenix, 7/15/82, A, C, 82002085

Pierce, Harry E., House [Roosevelt Neighborhood MRA], 632 N. 3rd Ave., Phoenix, 11/30/83, B, C, 83003493

Pieri-Elliot House, 767 E. Moreland St., Phoenix, 12/29/83, C, 83003500

Pine Creek Bridge [Vehicular Bridges in Arizona MPS], AZ 88, milepost 233.50, Tortilla Flat vicinity, 9/30/88, A, C, 88001602

Portland Street Historic District [Roosevelt Neighborhood MRA], W. Portland St. between 3rd and 7th Aves., Phoenix, 11/30/83, A, B, C, 83003491

President's House [Tempe MRA], ASU campus, Tempe, 1/07/85, C, 85000054

Professional Building [Phoenix Commercial MRA], 137 N. Central, Phoenix, 1/08/93, A, C, 85003563

Pueblo Grande Ruin, 4619 E. Washington Ave., Phoenix, 10/15/66, A, D, NHL, 66000185

Rancho Joaquina House, 4630 E. Cheery Lynn Rd., Phoenix, 7/09/84, C, 84000786

Redden, Byron, House [Tempe MRA], 948 Ash Ave., Tempe, 5/07/84, C, 84000738

Redden, Lowell, House [Tempe MRA], 333 Carver St., Tempe, 2/13/85, C, 85000407

Rehbein Grocery [Phoenix Commercial MRA], 1231 Grand Ave., Phoenix, 10/01/85, A, 85002895

Rohrig School [Tempe MRA], 2328 E. University Dr., Tempe, 10/10/84, C, 84000175

Roosevelt Historic District [Roosevelt Neighborhood MRA], Roughly bounded by Portland and Fillmore Sts., Central and 7th Aves., Phoenix, 11/30/83, A, B, C, 83003490

Rosson, Dr. Roland Lee, House, 139 N. 6th St., Phoenix, 6/03/71, C, 71000112

Safeway Pay 'n Takit [Wickenburg MRA], 42 N. Tegner, Wickenburg, 7/10/86, A, 86001587

Sahuaro Ranch, N. 58th Dr., Glendale, 3/07/80, A, 80000763

San Carlos Hotel [Phoenix Commercial MRA (AD)], 202 N. Central Ave., Phoenix, 12/08/83, A, C, 83003498

San Marcos Hotel, 1 San Marcos Pl., Chandler, 4/29/82, C, 82002078

Santa Fe Railroad Depot [Wickenburg MRA], 215 N. Frontier, Wickenburg, 7/10/86, A, 86001588

Scott, Robert, House, 2230 E. Grandview St., Mesa, 7/08/82, C, b, 82002079

Scudder, B. H., Rental House [Tempe MRA], 919 S. Maple Ave., Tempe, 5/07/84, C, 84000740

Security Building [Phoenix Commercial MRA], 234 N. Central, Phoenix, 9/12/85, A, 85002081

Maricopa County—Continued

Shell Oil Co. [Phoenix Commercial MRA], 425 S. 16th Ave., Phoenix, 9/04/85, A, 85002073

Shride House [Wickenburg MRA], 57 Tegner, Wickenburg, 7/21/86, C, 86001589

Skeleton Cave Massacre Site, Address Restricted, Apache Junction vicinity, 2/21/91, A, 91000100

Spangler—Wilbur House, 128 N. MacDonald St., Mesa, 11/01/93, C, 93001141

St. Mary's Church, 231 N. 3rd St., Phoenix, 11/29/78, C, a, 78000551

Steinegger Lodging House [Phoenix Commercial MRA], 27 E. Monroe, Phoenix, 6/19/86, A, 86001369

Storage Warehouse [Phoenix Commercial MRA], 429 W. Jackson, Phoenix, 9/04/85, A, 85002074

Storms House [Wickenburg MRA], 130 Center, Wickenburg, 7/10/86, C, 86001590

Story, F. Q., Neighborhood Historic District, Mc-Dowell Rd., Seventh Ave., Roosevelt St. and Sixteenth Ave., Phoenix, 3/24/88, A, C, 88000212

Story, F. Q., Neighborhood Historic District (Boundary Increase), Roughly bounded by 17th Ave., Culver St., 15th Ave. and Lynwood St., also lots on Roosevelt St. and McDowell Rd., Phoenix, 4/27/93, A, C, 92001834

Stoughton, Ralph H., Estate, 805 W. South Mountain Ave., Phoenix, 7/03/85, A, C, 85001475

Strauch House, 148 N. Macdonald, Mesa, 7/31/91, C, 91000983

Sun Mercantile Building [Phoenix Commercial MRA], 232 S. 3rd St., Phoenix, 9/04/85, A, 85002075

Sun-Up Ranch, W. Frontage Rd. off Black Canyon Hwy./I-17, New River, 5/23/88, A, 88000558

Sunflower Ranger Staiton [Depression-Era USDA Forest Service Administrative Complexes in Arizona MPS], AZ 87 W of Punkin Center, Tonto NF, Punkin Center vicinity, 6/10/93, A, C, 93000528

Taliesin West, N of jct. of Shea Blvd. and 108th St., Scottsdale vicinity, 2/12/74, B, C, g, NHL, 74000457

Tempe Beach Stadium [Tempe MRA], Ash at 1st St., Tempe, 1/07/85, A, 85000055

Tempe Concrete Arch Highway Bridge [Tempe MRA], Mill Ave. and Salt River, Tempe, 5/07/84, C, 84000743

Tempe Cotton Exchange Cotton Gin Seed Storage Building [Tempe MRA], 215 W. 7th St., Tempe, 5/07/84, A, 84000744

Tempe Hardware Building, 520 S. Mill Ave., Tempe, 6/26/80, A, C, 80000767

Title and Trust Building [Phoenix Commercial MRA], 112 N. 1st Ave., Phoenix, 9/04/85, A, 85002076

Titus, Frank, House, 1310 N. Hayden Rd., Scottsdale, 5/13/82, C, 82002086

Tweed, Judge Charles Austin, House, 1611 W. Fillmore Ave., Phoenix, 5/14/87, C, 87000775

U.S. Post Office, 522 N. Central Ave., Phoenix, 2/10/83, A, C, g, 83002993

Union Station [Phoenix Commercial MRA], Fourth Ave. and Southern Pacific RR tracks, Phoenix, 11/25/85, C, 85003056

Upton, George B., House [Wickenburg MRA], 171 Washington, Wickenburg, 7/10/86, C, 86001592

Valley Plumbing & Sheet Metal [Phoenix Commercial MRA], 530 W. Adams, Phoenix, 10/01/85, C, 85002894

Vernetta Hotel [Wickenburg MRA], 1 Apache St., Wickenburg, 7/10/86, A, C, 86001593

Victoria Place Historic District, 700 blk. E. McKinley St., Phoenix, 4/18/88, A, C, 88000384

Vienna Bakery, 415 S. Mill Ave., Tempe, 6/30/80, A, C, 80000764

Walker, Harry, House [Tempe MRA], 118 E. 7th St., Tempe, 5/07/84, C, 84000745

Walker, J. W., Building-Central Arizona Light & Power [Phoenix Commercial MRA], 10 N. 3rd Ave. & 300 W. Washington, Phoenix, 9/04/85, A, 85002077

Webster Auditorium, 1201 N. Galvin Pkwy., Phoenix, 6/14/90, A, 90000823

West End Hotel [Phoenix Commercial MRA], 701 W. Washington, Phoenix, 10/01/85, A, 85002897

Western Wholesale Drug Co. Warehouse [Phoenix Commercial MRA], 101 E. Jackson, Phoenix, 9/04/85, A, 85002078

White, E. M., Dairy Barn [Tempe MRA], 1810 E. Apache, Tempe, 10/10/84, C, 84000176

Whitney, J. T., Funeral Home [Phoenix Commercial MRA], 330 N. 2nd Ave., Phoenix, 9/04/85, A, 85002079

Whittier, John G., School [Educational Buildings in Phoenix MPS], 2004 N. 16th St., Phoenix, 8/12/93, A, 93000741

Wickenburg High School Gymnasium [Wickenburg MRA], 252 S. Tegner, Wickenburg, 7/10/86, A, C, 86001594

Wickenburg High School and Annex [Wickenburg MRA], 250 S. Tegner, Wickenburg, 7/10/86, A, C, 86001595

Wickenburg Ice and Cold Storage [Wickenburg MRA], 48 S. Coconino, Wickenburg, 7/10/86, C, 86001596

Willo Historic District, Roughly bounded by Central Ave., McDowell Rd., 7th Ave. and Thomas Rd., Phoenix, 1/09/91, A, C, 90002099

Wisdom House [Wickenburg MRA], 48 Kerkes, Wickenburg, 8/06/87, C, 87001590

Woodland Historic District, Roughly bounded by Van Buren St., Seventh Ave., Adams St. and 15th Ave., Phoenix, 7/10/92, A, 92000839

Wrigley, William, Jr., Winter Cottage, 2501 E. Telawa Trail, Phoenix, 8/16/89, B, C, 89001045

Yaun Ah Gim Groceries [Phoenix Commercial MRA], 1002 S. Fourth Ave., Phoenix, 7/08/86, A, 86001553

Mohave County

AT & SF Locomotive [Kingman MRA], City Park, Kingman, 5/14/86, A, 86001113

AT & T Building [Kingman MRA], Pine and Third Sts., Kingman, 5/14/86, C, 86001114

Anderson, Max J., House [Kingman MRA], 523 Pine St., Kingman, 5/14/86, C, 86001110

Anderson, R. L., House [Kingman MRA], 703 E. Beale, Kingman, 5/28/87, B, C, 87001160

Antelope Cave, Address Restricted, Colorado City vicinity, 10/10/75, D, 75000351

Armour and Jacobson Building [Kingman MRA], 426–430 Beale St., Kingman, 5/14/86, B, C, 86001112

Big House, Main Rd., Moccasin, 10/20/83, A, C, 83003497

Bighorn Cave, Address Restricted, Oatman vicinity, 9/28/88, D, 88001571

Black, Arthur F., House, 707 Cerbat Ave., Kingman, 12/09/93, B, 93001324

Blakeley, William G., House [Kingman MRA], 503 Spring St., Kingman, 5/14/86, B, C, 86001115

Blakely, Ross H., House [Kingman MRA], 519 E. Spring St., Kingman, 1/07/88, C, 86003763

Bonelli House [Kingman MRA (AD)], Spring and 5th Sts., Kingman, 4/24/75, C, 75000352

Brown, Duff T., House [Kingman MRA], 524 E. Oak St., Kingman, 5/14/86, C, 86001116

Building at 218 Spring [Kingman MRA], 218 Spring St., Kingman, 5/14/86, C, 86001117

Camp Beale Springs, Address Restricted, Kingman vicinity, 7/18/74, A, D, 74000459

Carr, Raymond, House [Kingman MRA], 620 E. Oak St., Kingman, 5/14/86, C, 86001118

Dennis, Foster S., House [Kingman MRA], Second and Park, Kingman, 5/14/86, C, 86001119

Desert Power & Water Co., Electric Power Plant [Kingman MRA], Bounded by AT & SF RR tracks, Spillway Ln., Park and First Sts., Kingman, 5/14/86, A, 86001137

Durlin Hotel, Main St., Oatman, 8/25/83, C, 83002988

Elk's Lodge No. 468 [Kingman MRA], Fourth and Oak Sts., Kingman, 5/14/86, A, C, 86001138

Elliott, S. T., House [Kingman MRA], 537 Spring St., Kingman, 5/14/86, C, 86001139

Gates, J. M., House [Kingman MRA], 714 E. Oak St., Kingman, 5/14/86, B, C, 86001140

Grand Wash Archeological District, Address Restricted, Lake Mead vicinity, 2/08/80, D, NPS, 80000369

Gruninger, W. A., Building [Kingman MRA], 424 Beale St., Kingman, 5/14/86, C, 86001141

Gymnasium [Kingman MRA], First St., Kingman, 5/14/86, C, 86001142

Hoover Dam [Vehicular Bridges in Arizona MPS (AD) D], E of Las Vegas on U.S. 93, Boulder City, vicinity, 4/08/81, A, C, NHL, 81000382

Horse Valley Ranch, Lake Mead National Recreation Area, Littlefield vicinity, 4/12/84, A, NPS, 84000781

House at 105 Spring St. [Kingman MRA], 105 Spring St., Kingman, 5/14/86, C, 86001143

House at 519 Golconda [Kingman MRA], 519 Golconda, Kingman, 5/14/86, C, 86001148

House at 527 Pine [Kingman MRA], 527 Pine St., Kingman, 5/14/86, C, 86001145

House at 536 Park [Kingman MRA], 536 Park, Kingman, 5/14/86, C, 86001146

Mohave County—Continued

House at 809 Grand View [Kingman MRA], 809 Grand View, Kingman, 5/14/86, C, 86001144

Householder, Ross E., House [Kingman MRA], 431 Spring St., Kingman, 5/14/86, B, C, 86001149

Hubbs House [Kingman MRA (AD)], 4th and Golconda Sts., Kingman, 6/15/78, C, 78000554

IOOF Building [Kingman MRA], 208 N. Fifth St., Kingman, 5/14/86, A, C, 86001150

Kayser, George R., House [Kingman MRA], 604 E. Oak St., Kingman, 5/14/86, C, 86001151

Kingman Commercial Historic District [Kingman MRA], 300 and 400 blks. of Andy Devine Ave., Kingman, 5/14/86, A, C, 86001153

Kingman Grammar School [Kingman MRA], Pine St., Kingman, 5/14/86, A, C, 86001154

Lefever House [Kingman MRA], 525 E. Oak St., Kingman, 5/14/86, C, 86001162

Little Red School [Kingman MRA], 219 N. Fourth St., Kingman, 5/14/86, A, C, 86001156

Livingston, Dr. David S., House [Kingman MRA], 222 Topeka, Kingman, 5/14/86, C, 86001158

Lovin & Withers Investment House [Kingman MRA], 722 E. Beale St., Kingman, 5/14/86, C, 86001161

Lovin and Withers Cottages [Kingman MRA], Eighth and Topeka, Kingman, 5/14/86, A, C, 86001159

Mahoney, W. P., House [Kingman MRA], 155 E. Walnut, Kingman, 5/14/86, C, 86001163

Masonic Temple [Kingman MRA], 212 N. Fourth St., Kingman, 5/19/86, C, g, 86001164

Mohave County Courthouse and Jail [Kingman MRA (AD)], 310 N. 4th St., Kingman, 8/25/83, C, 83002990

Mohave County Hospital [Kingman MRA], W. Beale between Grand View and First St., Kingman, 5/14/86, C, 86001165

Old Trails Bridge [Vehicular Bridges in Arizona MPS], Abandoned US 66 over the Colorado River, Topock, 9/30/88, A, C, 88001676

Pipe Spring National Monument, AZ 389, Moccasin vicinity, 10/15/66, A, f, NPS, 66000186

Saint John's Methodist Episcopal Church [Kingman MRA], Spring and Fifth Sts., Kingman, 5/14/86, C, a, 86001170

Saint Mary's Catholic Church [Kingman MRA], Third and Spring Sts., Kingman, 5/14/86, C, a, 86001166

Sand Hollow Wash Bridge [Vehicular Bridges in Arizona MPS], Old US 91 over Sand Hollow Wash, Littlefield vicinity, 9/30/88, A, C, 88001657

Sargent, Mrs. M. P., House [Kingman MRA], 426 Topeka, Kingman, 5/14/86, C, 86001167

Sullivan, G. H., Lodging House [Kingman MRA], 218 E. Oak, Kingman, 5/14/86, C, 86001168

Tyrell House [Kingman MRA], 133 Beale St., Kingman, 5/14/86, C, 86001172

US Post Office [Kingman MRA], 310 N. Fourth St., Kingman, 5/14/86, A, 86001173

Van Marter Building [Kingman MRA], 423–427 Beale St., Kingman, 5/14/86, C, 86001174

Walker, O. E., House [Kingman MRA], 906 Madison, Kingman, 5/14/86, C, 86001175

White, Dr. Toler R., House [Kingman MRA], 509 Spring St., Kingman, 5/14/86, C, 86001176

Williams, E. B., House [Kingman MRA], 513 E. Oak St., Kingman, 5/14/86, B, C, 86001177

Willow Beach Gauging Station, Lake Mead National Recreation Area, Willow Beach, vicinity, 3/21/86, A, C, NPS, 86000587

Wright, J. B., House [Kingman MRA], 317 Spring St., Kingman, 5/14/86, C, a, 86001178

Ziemer, Charles, House [Kingman MRA], 507 E. Oak St., Kingman, 5/14/86, B, C, 86001179

Navajo County

Agate House Pueblo, Petrified Forest National Park, Holbrook vicinity, 10/06/75, D, NPS, 75000170

Awatovi Ruins, W of Jeddito, Keams Canyon vicinity, 10/15/66, D, NHL, 66000187

Brigham City, N of Winslow, Winslow vicinity, 6/09/78, A, D, 78000558

Cedar Canyon Bridge [Vehicular Bridges in Arizona MPS], US 60 over Cedar Canyon, milepost 323.4, Show Low vicinity, 9/30/88, A, C, 88001612

Chevelon Creek Bridge [Vehicular Bridges in Arizona MPS (AD)], Chevelon Creek, SE of Winslow, Winslow vicinity, 12/08/83, A, C, 83003454

Chevelon Ruin, Address Restricted, Winslow vicinity, 3/01/84, D, 84000778

Corduroy Creek Bridge [Vehicular Bridges in Arizona MPS], US 60 over Corduroy Creek, milepost, 328.3, Show Low vicinity, 9/30/88, A, C, 88001613

Deer Springs Lookout Complex [National Forest Fire Lookouts in the Southwestern Region TR], Apache-Sitgreaves National Forest, Mogollon Rim, 1/28/88, A, C, 87002454

Flake, James M., House, Stinson and Hunt Sts., Snowflake, 7/14/71, A, C, 71000113

Fort Apache Historic District, S of Whiteriver off AZ 73 on Fort Apache Indian Reservation, Whiteriver vicinity, 10/14/76, A, g, 76000377

Freeman, John A., House, Main and Freeman Sts., Snowflake, 11/25/80, B, C, 80000768

Grasshopper Ruin, Address Restricted, Cibecue vicinity, 2/17/78, A, D, 78000555

Holbrook Bridge [Vehicular Bridges in Arizona MPS], AZ 77 over the Little Colorado River, Holbrook, 3/31/89, A, C, 88001685

Holbrook Bridge [Vehicular Bridges in Arizona MPS], Abandoned grade of US 70 over the Little Colorado River, 4.2 mi. SE of Holbrook, Holbrook vicinity, 9/30/88, A, C, 88001686

Homolovi Four (IV), Address Restricted, Winslow vicinity, 6/04/86, D, 86001243

Homolovi I Ruin, Address Restricted, Winslow vicinity, 6/04/84, D, 84000776

Homolovi II, Address Restricted, Winslow vicinity, 8/02/83, D, 83002994

Homolovi III, Address Restricted, Winslow vicinity, 3/01/84, D, 84000756

Hulet, John R., House, Hulet Ave. and Smith St., Snowflake, 3/25/80, B, C, 80000769

Inscription Rock, E of Keams Canyon off AZ 264, Keams Canyon vicinity, 4/06/78, A, 78000557

Jack's Canyon Bridge [Vehicular Bridges in Arizona MPS], Abandoned AZ 99 over Jack's Canyon SE of Winslow, Winslow vicinity, 9/30/88, A, C, 88001678

La Posada Historic District, 200 E. Second St., Winslow, 3/31/92, A, C, 92000256

Lithodendron Wash Bridge [Vehicular Bridges in Arizona MPS], 13.2 mi. NE of Holbrook on I-40 Frontage Rd., Holbrook vicinity, 9/30/88, A, C, 88001687

Little Lithodendron Wash Bridge [Vehicular Bridges in Arizona MPS], 15.8 mi. NE of Holbrook on I-40 Frontage Rd., Holbrook vicinity, 9/30/88, A, C, 88001688

Navajo County Courthouse, Courthouse Sq., Holbrook, 7/31/78, C, 78000556

Old Oraibi, Hopi Indian Reservation, Oraibi vicinity, 10/15/66, D, NHL, 66000188

Painted Desert Inn, Off US 40, Petrified Forest National Park, 5/28/87, A, C, g, NHL, NPS, 87001421

Painted Desert Petroglyphs and Ruins Archeological District, Address Restricted, Holbrook vicinity, 6/24/76, D, NPS, 76000215

Pinedale Ranger Station [Depression-Era USDA Forest Service Administrative Complexes in Arizona MPS], Forest Rd. 130 (formerly AZ 260), Apache—Sitgreaves NF, Pinedale vicinity, 6/10/93, A, C, 93000510

Sapp, Sidney, House, 215 W. Hopi, Halbrook, 3/13/86, B, C, 86000362

Shumway School, Off AZ 77, Shumway, 1/29/79, A, C, 79000420

Smith, Jesse N., House, 203 W. Smith Ave., Snowflake, 7/14/71, C, 71000114

Snowflake Stake Academy Building, Ballard and Hulet Aves., Snowflake, 3/25/80, A, C, 80000770

St. Joseph Bridge [Vehicular Bridges in Arizona MPS], 4.4 mi. SE of Joseph City on Joseph City-Holbrook Rd., Joseph City vicinity, 9/30/88, A, C, 88001633

Standing Fall House, Address Restricted, Black Mesa vicinity, 11/01/85, D, 85003480

Stinson-Flake House, Freeman Ave and Stinson St., Snowflake, 3/10/82, A, C, 82001621

Winslow Bridge [Vehicular Bridges in Arizona MPS], AZ 87 over Little Colorado River, milepost 344.9, Winslow vicinity, 3/31/89, A, C, 88001611

Winslow Commercial Historic District, Roughly bounded by 3rd, Williamson Ave., 1st, and Warren Ave., Winslow, 4/20/89, A, C, 89000316

Winslow Residential Historic District, Kinsley Ave. from Oak to Aspinwall, Winslow, 4/28/89, A, C, 89000296

Winslow Underpass [Vehicular Bridges in Arizona MPS], AZ 87 under Atchison, Topeka and Santa Fe RR, milepost 342.1, Winslow, 9/30/88, A, C, 88001610

Woodruff Bridge [Vehicular Bridges in Arizona MPS], 4 mi. S of Woodruff on Woodruff-Snow-

Navajo County—Continued

flake Rd., Woodruff vicinity, 9/30/88, A, C, b, 88001630

Pima County

Air Force Facility Missile Site 8 (571-7) Military Reservation, 1580 W. Duval Mine Rd., Green Valley, 12/03/92, A, C, g, 92001234

Arizona Inn, 2200 E. Elm St., Tucson, 4/05/88, A, B, C, 88000240

Armory Park Historic Residential District, E. 12th St. to 19th St., Stone Ave. to 2nd Ave., Tucson, 7/30/76, A, C, 76000378

Barrio Libre, Roughly bounded by 14th, 19th, Stone and Osborne Sts., Tucson, 10/18/78, A, C, 78000565

Blixt—Avitia House [Menlo Park MPS], 830 W. Alameda St., Tucson, 3/30/92, C, 92000251

Boudreaux—Robison House [Menlo Park MPS], 101 N. Bella Vista Dr., Tucson, 3/30/92, C, 92000253

Bray—Valenzuela House [Menlo Park MPS], 203 N. Grande Ave., Tucson, 3/30/92, C, 92000255

Bull Pasture, E of Lukeville on Organ Pipe Cactus National Monument, Lukeville vicinity, 9/01/78, A, D, NPS, 78000380

Cannon, Dr. William Austin, House, 1189 E. Speedway, Tucson, 10/25/82, B, 82001663

Cavalry Corrals [Fort Lowell MRA], N. Craycroft Blvd., Tucson, 12/13/78, A, 78003359

Cienega Bridge [Vehicular Bridges in Arizona MPS], 5.3 mi. SE of Vail on Marsh Station Rd., Vail vicinity, 9/30/88, A, C, 88001642

Cocoraque Butte Archeological District, Address Restricted, Tucson vicinity, 10/10/75, D, 75000355

Colonia Solana Residential Historic District, Roughly bounded by Broadway Blvd., S. Randolph Way, Camino Campestre, and S. Country Club, Tucson, 1/04/89, A, C, 88002963

Colossal Cave Preservation Park Historic District, Jct. of Old Spanish Trail and Colossal Cave Rd., Vail, 7/10/92, A, C, 92000850

Copper Bell Bed and Breakfast [Menlo Park MPS], 25 N. Westmoreland Ave., Tucson, 3/30/92, C, 92000254

Cordova House, 173–177 N. Meyer Ave., Tucson, 5/04/72, C, 72000198

Coronado Hotel, 410 E. 9th St., Tucson, 11/30/82, A, C, 82001622

Desert Laboratory, W of Tucson off W. Anklam Rd. on Tumamoc Hill, Tucson vicinity, 10/15/66, A, NHL, 66000190

Dodson—Esquivel House [Menlo Park MPS], 1004 W. Alameda St., Tucson, 3/30/92, C, 92000252

El Camino Del Diablo, NW of Lukeville, Lukeville vicinity, 12/01/78, A, D, 78000560

El Conquistador Water Tower, Broadway and Randolph Way, Tucson, 6/20/80, C, 80000771

El Encanto Estates Residential Historic District, Roughly bounded by Country Club Rd., Broad-

way Blvd., Fifth St., & Jones St., Tucson, 1/29/88, A, C, g, 87002284

El Presidio Historic District, Roughly bounded by W. 6th, W. Alameda Sts., N. Stone and Granada Aves., Tucson, 9/27/76, C, D, 76000379

El Tiradito, 221 S. Main St., Tucson, 11/19/71, A, b, f, 71000115

Empire Ranch, 6 mi. E of Greaterville, Greaterville vicinity, 5/30/75, A, 75000354

Fort Lowell Park [Fort Lowell MRA], N. Craycroft Blvd., Tucson, 12/13/78, D, 78003358

Fourth Avenue Underpass [Vehicular Bridges in Arizona MPS], Fourth Ave., Tuscon, 9/30/88, A, C, 88001654

Gachado Well and Line Camp, E of Lukeville in Organ Pipe Cactus National Monument, Lukeville vicinity, 11/02/78, A, C, NPS, 78000348

Growler Mine Area, N of Lukeville, Lukeville vicinity, 11/14/78, A, D, NPS, 78000350

Gunsight Mountain Archeological District, Address Restricted, Three Points vicinity, 6/21/91, D, 90000996

Iron Horse Expansion Historic District, Roughly bounded by Eighth St., Euclid Ave., Hughes and Tenth Sts., and N. Fourth and Hoff Aves., Tucson, 6/19/86, A, C, 86001347

Lemmon Rock Lookout House [National Forest Fire Lookouts in the Southwestern Region TR], Coronado National Forest, Tucson vicinity, 1/28/88, A, C, 87002465

Los Robles Archeological District [Hohokam Platform Mound Communities of the Lower Santa Cruz River Basin c. A.D. 1050–1450 MPS], Address Restricted, Red Rock vicinity, 5/11/89, D, 89000337

Lowell Ranger Station [Depression-Era USDA Forest Service Administrative Complexes in Arizona MPS], Off Sabino Canyon Rd. NE of Tucson, Coronado NF, Tucson vicinity, 6/10/93, A, C, 93000529

Manning Cabin, 10 mi. E of Tucson in Saquaro National Monument, Tucson vicinity, 3/31/75, A, NPS, 75000169

Manning, Levi H., House, 9 Paseo Redondo, Tucson, 7/27/79, A, C, 79000421

Matus, Antonio, House and Property, 856 W. Calle Santa Ana, Tucson, 7/22/91, A, C, 91000900

Men's Gymnasium, University of Arizona, E. Fourth St., University of Arizona campus, Tucson, 10/04/90, A, C, 90001526

Milton Mine, NW of Lukeville, Lukeville vicinity, 9/01/78, A, g, NPS, 78000351

Officer's Quarters [Fort Lowell MRA], N. Craycroft Blvd., Tucson, 12/13/78, C, 78003366

Old Adobe Patio, 40 W. Broadway, Tucson, 6/03/71, C, 71000117

Old Library Building, University of Arizona campus, Tucson, 11/28/79, A, C, 79000422

Old Main, University of Arizona, University of Arizona campus, Tucson, 4/13/72, A, C, 72000199

Pima County Courthouse, 115 N. Church St., Tucson, 6/23/78, C, g, 78000566

Post Trader's Store and Riallito House [Fort Lowell MRA], 5425 E. Fort Lowell Rd., Tucson, 12/13/78, C, 78003367

Post Trader's Storehouse [Fort Lowell MRA], 5354 E. Fort Lowell Rd., Tucson, 12/13/78, A, C, 78003368

Quartermaster Storehouse [Fort Lowell MRA], 5479 E. Fort Lowell Rd., Tucson, 12/13/78, A, C, 78003369

Quartermaster's Corrals [Fort Lowell MRA], N. Craycroft Rd., Tucson, 12/13/78, A, 78003370

Rillito Racetrack—Chute, 4502 N. First Ave., Tucson, 6/12/86, A, g, 86001322

Rincon Mountain Foothills Archeological District, Address Restricted, Tucson vicinity, 10/16/79, D, NPS, 79000252

Ronstadt House, 607 N. 6th Ave., Tucson, 2/26/79, A, B, C, 79000423

Ronstadt—Sims Adobe Warehouse [Spring, John, MRA], 911 N. 13th Ave., Tucson, 5/11/89, A, C, 88002133

Sabedra—Huerta House [Spring, John, MRA], 1036–1038 N. 13th Ave., Tucson, 11/10/88, A, C, 88002132

San Pedro Chapel, 5230 E. Ft. Lowell Rd., Tucson, 4/28/93, A, C, a, g, 93000306

San Xavier del Bac, 9 mi. S of Tucson via Mission Rd., Tucson vicinity, 10/15/66, A, C, a, NHL, 66000191

Santa Ana del Chiquiburitac Mission Site, Address Restricted, Tucson vicinity, 9/18/75, D, 75000357

Schwalen—Gomez House [Menlo Park MPS], 217 N. Melwood Ave., Tucson, 3/30/92, B, 92000250

Site No. HD 13-11 [Fort Lowell MRA], E. Fort Lowell Rd., Tucson, 12/13/78, A, 78003373

Site No. HD 13-13 [Fort Lowell MRA], E. Fort Lowell Rd., Tucson, 12/13/78, A, 78003372

Site No. HD 13-4 [Fort Lowell MRA], N. Craycroft Blvd., Tucson, 12/13/78, A, 78003376

Site No. HD 4-8A [Fort Lowell MRA], E. Fort Lowell Rd., Tucson, 12/13/78, A, 78003374

Site No. HD 5-26 [Fort Lowell MRA], 5495 E. Fort Lowell Rd., Tucson, 12/13/78, A, 78003360

Site No. HD 7-0A [Fort Lowell MRA], 5429 E. Fort Lowell Rd., Tucson, 12/13/78, A, 78003361

Site No. HD 7-13 [Fort Lowell MRA], 5531 E. Fort Lowell Rd., Tucson, 12/13/78, A, 78003365

Site No. HD 9-28 [Fort Lowell MRA], 5668 E. Fort Lowell Rd., Tucson, 12/13/78, A, 78003363

Site Nos. HD 12-4/12-8 [Fort Lowell MRA], E. Fort Lowell Rd., Tucson, 12/13/78, A, 78003375

Site Nos. HD 5-28/5-25 [Fort Lowell MRA], 3031 N. Craycroft Blvd., Tucson, 12/13/78, A, 78003364

Site Nos. HD 9-11/9-2 [Fort Lowell MRA], 5651 E. Fort Lowell Rd., Tucson, 12/13/78, A, 78003362

Sixth Avenue Underpass [Vehicular Bridges in Arizona MPS], Sixth Ave., Tucson, 9/30/88, A, C, 88001655

Smith, Professor George E. P., House, 1195 E. Speedway, Tucson, 6/03/82, A, B, C, 82002090

Sosa—Carrillo—Fremont House, 145–153 S. Main St., Tucson, 6/03/71, C, 71000116

Southern Pacific Railroad Locomotive No. 1673, Himmel Park, Tucson, 1/09/92, A, 91001918

Speedway—Drachman Historic District, Roughly bounded by Lee St., Park Ave., Speedway

Pima County—Continued

Blvd., 7th Ave., Drachman St., and 2nd Ave., Tucson, 9/21/89, A, C, 89001460

Spring, John, Neighborhood Historic District [Spring, John, MRA], Roughly bounded by W. Speedway Blvd., N. Ninth Ave., W. Fifth St., N. Main Ave., W. Second St., and N. Tenth St., Tucson, 5/11/89, A, C, 88002131

Stone Avenue Underpass [Vehicular Bridges in Arizona MPS], Stone Ave., Tucson, 9/30/88, A, C, 88001656

Sutherland Wash Archeological District, Address Restricted, Tucson vicinity, 8/15/88, D, 88000228

Sutherland Wash Rock Art District, Address Restricted, Tucson vicinity, 10/19/93, C, D, 93001107

U.S. Post Office and Courthouse, 55 E. Broadway, Tucson, 2/10/83, A, C, 83002995

University Heights Elementary School, 1201 N. Park Ave., Tucson, 10/06/83, A, C, 83003494

University of Arizona Campus Historic District, Roughly bounded by E. Second St., N. Cherry Ave., E. Fourth St., and Park Ave., Tuscon, 6/13/86, A, C, g, 86001254

Upper Davidson Canyon Archeological District, Address Restricted, Sonoita vicinity, 1/03/92, D, 91001891

Valencia Site (BB:13:15; BB:13:74), Address Restricted, Tucson vicinity, 5/17/84, D, 84000762

Velasco House, 471–475–477 S. Stone Ave. and 522 S. Russell St., Tucson, 3/05/74, A, B, C, 74000460

Ventana Cave, Address Restricted, Santa Rosa vicinity, 10/15/66, D, NHL, 66000189

Victoria Mine, N of Lukeville, Lukeville vicinity, 9/01/78, A, NPS, 78000349

Warner, Solomon, House and Mill, 350 S. Grand Ave., Tucson, 6/03/76, A, 76000380

West University Historic District, Roughly bounded by Speedway Blvd., 6th St., Park and Stone Aves., Tucson, 12/10/80, A, C, 80004240

Wright, Harold Bell, Estate, 850 N. Barbara Worth, Tucson, 1/18/85, B, 85000081

Pinal County

Acadia Ranch, AZ 77, Oracle, 2/22/84, A, C, 84000765

Adamsville Ruin, Address Restricted, Florence vicinity, 8/25/70, D, 70000114

All Saint's Church, AZ 77, Oracle, 5/03/84, C, a, 84000768

American Flag Post Office Ranch, 5 mi. SE of Oracle, Oracle vicinity, 6/20/79, A, C, 79000426

Arballo, Ramon, House [Florence MRA], 405 Park St., Florence, 8/01/86, C, 86002623

Avenenti, Encarnacion, House [Florence MRA], 203 Butte St., Florence, 7/13/87, C, 87001592

Bayless, Earl, House [Casa Grande MRA], 211 N. Cameron, Casa Grande, 4/16/85, B, C, 85000878

Baylis, Wilbur O./Grasty House [Casa Grande MRA], 221 N. Cameron, Casa Grande, 4/16/85, C, 85000879

Bien/McNatt House [Casa Grande MRA], 208A W. 1st St., Casa Grande, 4/16/85, A, C, 85000880

Butte-Cochran Charcoal Ovens, 16 mi. E of Florence N of Gila River, Florence vicinity, 5/30/75, A, 75000358

C. H. Cook Memorial Church, Church St., Sacaton, 8/28/75, C, a, 75000359

Carminatti—Perham House [Florence MRA], Sixth and Florence Sts., Florence, 8/01/86, C, 86002624

Casa Grande Hotel [Casa Grande MRA], 201 W. Main Ave., Casa Grande, 4/16/85, A, C, 85000881

Casa Grande National Monument, Casa Grande National Monument, Coolidge vicinity, 10/15/66, A, C, D, NPS, 66000192

Casa Grande Stone Church [Casa Grande MRA (AD)], Florence Blvd. and N. Park Ave., Casa Grande, 6/15/78, C, a, 78000567

Casa Grande Union High School and Gymnasium [Casa Grande MRA], 420 E. Florence Blvd., Casa Grande, 2/03/86, A, C, 86000821

Casa Grande Woman's Club Building [Casa Grande MRA (AD)], 407 N. Sacaton St., Casa Grande, 3/21/79, A, 79000425

Central Creditors Association Building [Casa Grande MRA], 118 N. Sacaton, Casa Grande, 4/16/85, C, 85000882

Colton, Albert and Freeman, H. H., House [Florence MRA], 1500 Willow St., Florence, 8/01/86, C, 86002625

Coolidge Woman's Club, 240 W. Pinkley Ave., Coolidge, 10/04/90, A, 90001524

Cruz Trading Post [Casa Grande MRA], 200 W. Main St., Casa Grande, 4/16/85, A, C, 85000883

Day, Judge William T., House [Casa Grande MRA], 310 W. 1st St., Casa Grande, 7/25/85, A, B, C, 85001624

Devil's Canyon Bridge [Vehicular Bridges in Arizona MPS], Abandoned US 60 over Devil's Canyon, Superior vicinity, 9/30/88, A, C, 88001681

Devine, Ed and Lottie, House [Florence MRA], 1200 Central St., Florence, 8/01/86, C, 86002626

First Florence Courthouse, 5th and Main Sts., Florence, 7/30/74, A, C, 74000461

Fisher Memorial Home [Casa Grande MRA], 300 E. 8th St., Casa Grande, 4/16/85, C, 85000884

Florence Townsite Historic District, Roughly bounded by 3rd & Florence Sts., Butte and Central Aves., and Chase/Ruggles Ditch, Florence, 10/26/82, A, C, 82001623

Florence Union High School [Florence MRA], S. Main St., Florence, 6/22/87, C, 87001306

Ha-ak Va-ak Intaglio Site, Address Restricted, Sacaton vicinity, 9/06/79, D, 79000427

Harvey—Niemeyer House [Florence MRA], 1613 Main St., Florence, 8/01/86, C, 86002627

Henry, C. D., House [Florence MRA], 1520 Willow St., Florence, 8/01/86, C, 86002628

Hohokam-Pima National Monument, 20 mi. S of Phoenix on Interstate 10, Gila River Indian Reservation, 7/19/74, A, C, D, NPS, 74002221

Huffman, Dr. George, House [Florence MRA], 507 E. Butte St., Florence, 8/01/86, C, 86002629

Johnson's Grocery Store [Casa Grande MRA], 301 N. Picacho, Casa Grande, 4/16/85, A, C, 85000885

Kelvin Bridge [Vehicular Bridges in Arizona MPS], Florence-Kelvin Hwy. over the Gila River, Kelvin, 9/30/88, A, C, 88001646

Kratzka, Gus, House [Casa Grande MRA], N. Maricopa and 3rd St., Casa Grande, 4/16/85, B, C, 85000886

Laundry Building [Casa Grande MRA], Rear of 309 W. 8th, Casa Grande, 4/16/85, A, 85000887

Lehmberg, Dr. H. B., House [Casa Grande MRA], 929 N. Lehmberg, Casa Grande, 4/16/85, B, C, 85000888

Littlefield, Inez and Davis, Bea, House [Florence MRA], 1913 Elizabeth St., Florence, 8/01/86, C, 86002630

Lorona, Andronico, Second House [Florence MRA], 704 Silver St., Florence, 8/01/86, C, 86002631

Manjarres House [Florence MRA], 203 Silver St., Florence, 8/06/87, A, C, 87001591

McClellan Wash Archeological District [Hohokam Platform Mound Communities of the Lower Santa Cruz River Basin c. A.D. 1050–1450 MPS], Address Restricted, Picacho vicinity, 5/11/89, D, 89000336

Meehan/Gaar House [Casa Grande MRA], 202 W. 1st St., Casa Grande, 4/16/85, B, C, 85000890

Mineral Creek Bridge [Vehicular Bridges in Arizona MPS], Old US 77 over Mineral Creek, Kelvin, 9/30/88, C, 88001648

Period Revival House [Casa Grande MRA], 905 N. Lehmberg, Casa Grande, 7/25/85, C, 85001623

Pierson, Adrian, House [Florence MRA], E. Sixth St. and US 89, Florence, 7/13/87, C, 87001593

Pinal County Courthouse, Pinal and 12th Sts., Florence, 8/02/78, A, C, 78000568

Pioneer Market [Casa Grande MRA], 119 Florence St., Casa Grande, 4/16/85, A, C, 85000919

Prettyman's Meat Market and Grocery/Brigg's Jeweler [Casa Grande MRA], 114 W. Main St., Casa Grande, 4/16/85, A, 85000891

Price, W. Y., House [Florence MRA], 1612 Willow St., Florence, 8/01/86, C, 86002632

Queen Creek Bridge [Vehicular Bridges in Arizona MPS], Old Florence Hwy. over Queen Creek, Florence Junction vicinity, 9/30/88, A, C, 88001643

Queen Creek Bridge [Vehicular Bridges in Arizona MPS], Abandonded US 60 over Upper Queen Creek Canyon, Superior vicinity, 9/30/88, A, C, 88001679

Sacaton Dam Bridge [Vehicular Bridges in Arizona MPS], Gila River Indian Reservation Rd., Sacaton vicinity, 9/30/88, A, C, 88001621

Saint Anthony's Church and Rectory [Casa Grande MRA], 215 N. Picacho, Casa Grande, 4/16/85, C, a, 85000892

San Tan Canal Bridge [Vehicular Bridges in Arizona MPS], Gila River Indian Reservation Rd., Sacaton vicinity, 9/30/88, A, C, 88001622

Shonessy Building/Don Chun Wo Store [Casa Grande MRA], 121 W. Main Ave., Casa Grande, 4/16/85, B, C, 85000893

Pinal County—Continued

Shonessy House [Casa Grande MRA], 115 W. Main Ave., Casa Grande, 4/16/85, B, C, 85000894

Stone Bungalow [Casa Grande MRA], 515 E. 3rd St., Casa Grande, 4/16/85, C, 85000895

Stone Warehouse [Casa Grande MRA], 119 Florence St. in rear, Casa Grande, 4/16/85, C, 85000896

Thompson, Boyce, Southwestern Arboretum, 2 mi. W of Superior on U.S. 60, Superior vicinity, 3/26/76, A, B, D, 76000381

Truman—Randall House [Florence MRA], 2010 S. Main St., Florence, 7/13/87, C, 87001594

Vasquez House [Casa Grande MRA], 114 E. Florence Blvd., Casa Grande, 4/16/85, C, 85000897

Ward's Variety Store [Casa Grande MRA], 112 N. Sacaton, Casa Grande, 4/16/85, C, 85000898

Warner, P. C., First House [Florence MRA], 310 Third St., Florence, 8/01/86, C, 86002633

White House [Casa Grande MRA], 901 N. Morrison, Casa Grande, 4/16/85, C, 85000899

Wilson, C. J. (Blinky), House [Casa Grande MRA], 223 W. 10th, Casa Grande, 4/16/85, B, C, 85000900

Winkelman Bridge [Vehicular Bridges in Arizona MPS], Old AZ 77 over the Gila River, Winkelman, 9/30/88, A, C, 88001649

Santa Cruz County

10 Cottages on Short Street [Nogales MRA], 117–126 Short, Nogales, 8/29/85, C, 85001873

Arizona-Sonora Manufacturing Company Machine Shop [Nogales MRA], Grand Ave. at Arroyo Blvd., Nogales, 8/29/85, A, C, 85001851

Atascosa Lookout House [National Forest Fire Lookouts in the Southwestern Region TR], Coronado National Forest, Tubac vicinity, 1/28/88, A, C, 87002462

Bowman Hotel [Nogales MRA], 314–316 Grand Ave., Nogales, 8/29/85, A, C, 85001852

Bowman, W. G., House [Nogales MRA], 112 Sierra, Nogales, 8/29/85, C, 85001850

Burton Building [Nogales MRA], 322–324 Grande, Nogales, 8/29/85, A, C, 85001848

Cady Hall, 346 Duquesne St., Patagonia, 12/02/92, A, C, a, 92001635

Calabasas, N of Nogales, Nogales vicinity, 6/03/71, A, D, a, NHL, 71000118

Canelo Ranger Station [Depression-Era USDA Forest Service Administrative Complexes in Arizona MPS], Forest Rd. 52B N of Canelo, Coronado NF, Canelo vicinity, 6/10/93, A, C, 93000513

Canelo School, 18 mi. SE of Sonoita on AZ 93, Canelo vicinity, 7/31/91, A, 91000981

Cranz, Frank F., House [Nogales MRA], 408 Arroyo, Nogales, 8/29/85, B, C, 85001849

Crawford Hill Historic Residential District [Nogales MRA], Roughly bounded by Oak St., Terrace Ave., Compound St., & Interstate 19 & Grindell, Nogales, 8/29/85, A, B, C, a, 85001874

Dunbar, George, House [Nogales MRA], 118 Sierra, Nogales, 8/29/85, B, C, 85001853

Finley, James, House, 7.2 mi. SW of Patagonia in Coronado National Forest, Patagonia vicinity, 11/19/74, A, C, 74000462

Guevavi Mission Ruins, 6 mi. N of U.S.-Mexican border, Nogales vicinity, 11/05/71, A, B, D, a, NHL, 71000119

Harrison, Sen. James A., House [Nogales MRA], 449 Morley, Nogales, 8/29/85, B, C, 85001854

Hotel Blanca [Nogales MRA], 701 Morley, Nogales, 8/29/85, C, 85001861

House at 220 Walnut Street [Nogales MRA], 220 Walnut St., Nogales, 8/29/85, C, 85001856

House at 334–338 Walnut Street [Nogales MRA], 334–338 Walnut St., Nogales, 8/29/85, C, 85001857

House at 665 Morley Avenue [Nogales MRA], 665 Morley Ave., Nogales, 8/29/85, C, 85001858

Kitchen, Pete, Ranch, 3.5 mi. N of Nogales off U.S. 89, Nogales vicinity, 2/20/75, B, C, 75000360

Kress, S. H., & Co., Building [Nogales MRA], 119–121 Morley, Nogales, 8/29/85, C, 85001859

Las Dos Naciones Cigar Factory [Nogales MRA], 331 Morley, Nogales, 8/29/85, A, C, 85001860

Marsh Heights Historic District [Nogales MRA], Roughly bounded by Court St., Summit Ave., S. Court St., and Morley Ave., Nogalez, 10/29/85, C, 85003407

Marsh, George B., Building [Nogales MRA], 213–225 Grand, Nogales, 8/29/85, B, 85001855

Mediterranean Style House [Nogales MRA], 124 Walnut, Nogales, 8/29/85, C, 85001862

Mediterranean Style House [Nogales MRA], 116 Walnut, Nogales, 8/29/85, C, 85001863

Miller, Hugo, House [Nogales MRA], 750 Petrero, Nogales, 8/29/85, C, 85001864

Montezuma Hotel [Nogales MRA], 217 Morley, Nogales, 8/29/85, A, 85001867

Nogales Electric Light, Ice & Water Company Power House [Nogales MRA], 498 Grand, Nogales, 8/29/85, A, 85001865

Nogales High School [Nogales MRA], 209 Plum, Nogales, 8/29/85, A, C, 85001866

Nogales Steam Laundry Building [Nogales MRA], 223–219 East, Nogales, 8/29/85, A, C, 85001868

Noon, A. S., Building [Nogales MRA], 246 Grande, Nogales, 8/29/85, A, C, 85001871

Old Nogales City Hall and Fire Station [Nogales MRA (AD)], 223 Grand Ave., Nogales, 4/03/80, A, 80000772

Old Tubac Schoolhouse, Address unknown at this time, Tubac, 11/10/70, A, C, 70000115

Piscorski, Jose, Building [Nogales MRA], 315 Morley, Nogales, 8/29/85, C, 85001870

Ruby, N of U.S./Mexico border between Ruby and Montana peaks, Ruby and Vicinity vicinity, 4/28/75, A, 75000361

Santa Cruz Bridge No. 1 [Vehicular Bridges in Arizona MPS], South River Rd. over the Santa Cruz River, Nogales vicinity, 9/30/88, A, C, 88001635

Santa Cruz County Courthouse, Court and Morley Sts., Nogales, 12/07/77, C, 77000239

Three Mediterranean Cottages on Pajarito Street [Nogales MRA], 102–104 Pajarito, Nogales, 8/29/85, C, 85001872

Tubac Presidio, Broadway and River Rd., Tubac, 12/02/70, A, D, 70000116

Tumacacori Museum, Tumacacori National Monument, Tumacacori, 5/28/87, C, NHL, NPS, 87001437

Tumacacori National Monument, 18 mi. N of Nogales on I 19, Tumacacori, 10/15/66, A, C, D, a, f, NPS, 66000193

US Custom House [Nogales MRA], Jct. of International and Terrace Sts., Nogales, 8/06/87, A, C, 87001344

US Post Office and Immigration Station—Nogales Main [Historic US Post Offices in Arizona, 1900–1941, TR], Hudgin St. and Morley Ave., Nogales, 12/03/85, A, C, 85003107

Wise, J. E., Building [Nogales MRA], 134 Grande, Nogales, 8/29/85, A, B, 85001869

Yavapai County

Beaver Creek Ranger Station [Depression-Era USDA Forest Service Administrative Complexes in Arizona MPS], Off I-17 NE of Rimrock, Coconino NF, Rimrock vicinity, 6/10/93, A, C, 93000512

Blumberg House [Prescott Territorial Buildings MRA], 143 N. Mt. Vernon, Prescott, 12/14/78, B, C, 78003217

Brinkmeyer House [Prescott Territorial Buildings MRA], 605 W. Gurley, Prescott, 12/14/78, C, 78003218

Broadway Bridge [Vehicular Bridges in Arizona MPS], Broadway St. over Bitter Creek, Clarkdale, 9/30/88, A, C, 88001651

Building at 826 North Main Street [Cottonwood MRA], 826 N. Main St., Cottonwood, 9/19/86, C, 86002147

Burmister/Timerhoff House [Prescott Territorial Buildings MRA], 116 S. Mt. Vernon, Prescott, 12/14/78, C, 78003219

Childs—Irving Hydroelectric Facilities, From E. bank of Verde R. NE to Stehr Lake and along Fossil Cr., Coconino/Tonto NF, Camp Verde vicinity, 8/09/91, A, C, 91001023

Clark House [Prescott Territorial Buildings MRA], 109 N. Pleasant, Prescott, 12/14/78, C, b, 78003220

Clark Memorial Clubhouse, Off N. 9th St., Clarkdale, 10/29/82, B, C, 82001662

Clear Creek Church, 3.5 mi. SE of Camp Verde, Camp Verde vicinity, 8/06/75, A, C, a, 75000362

Clear Creek Pueblo and Caves, Address Restricted, Camp Verde vicinity, 2/10/75, D, 75000363

Clemenceau Public School [Cottonwood MRA], 1 N. Willard St., Cottonwood, 9/19/86, A, 86002149

Copper Creek Guard Station [Depression-Era USDA Forest Service Administrative Complexes in Arizona MPS], NE of Black Canyon

Yavapai County—Continued

City, Tonto NF, Black Canyon City vicinity, 6/10/93, A, C, 93000525

Courthouse Plaza Historic District [Prescott Territorial Buildings MRA], Roughly Bounded by Gurley, Montezuma, Cortez and Goodwin Sts., Prescott, 12/14/78, A, C, 78003583

Crown King Ranger Station [Depression-Era USDA Forest Service Administrative Complexes in Arizona MPS], W of Crown King, Prescott NF, Crown King vicinity, 6/10/93, A, C, 93000522

Day House [Prescott Territorial Buildings MRA], 212 E. Gurley, Prescott, 12/14/78, C, 78003222

Detwiler House [Prescott Territorial Buildings MRA], 310 N. Alarcon, Prescott, 12/14/78, C, 78003223

Drake House [Prescott Territorial Buildings MRA], 137 N. Mt. Vernon, Prescott, 12/14/78, B, C, 78003224

Dunning, Charles H., Log Cabin, 811 Boulder Dr., Prescott, 8/26/93, C, 93000870

East Prescott Historic District [Prescott Territorial Buildings MRA], Roughly bounded by Atchison, Topeka, and Santa Fe Railroad tracks, N. Mt. Vernon St., Carleton St. and N. Alarcon St., Prescott, 10/02/89, A, C, 89000165

Edens House [Cottonwood MRA], 1015 N. Cactus St., Cottonwood, 9/19/86, C, 86002150

Elks Building and Theater [Prescott Territorial Buildings MRA], 117 E. Gurley, Prescott, 12/14/78, C, 78003226

Fewke's Fort Below Aztec Pass (AR-03-09-06-23) [Prehistoric Walled Hilltop Sites of Prescott National Forest and Adjacent Regions MPS], Address Restricted, Prescott vicinity, 1/20/89, D, 88003186

First Congregational Church and Parsonage [Prescott Territorial Buildings MRA], 216–220 E. Gurley, Prescott, 12/14/78, C, a, 78003227

Fisher/Goldwater House [Prescott Territorial Buildings MRA], 240 S. Cortez, Prescott, 12/14/78, B, C, 78003228

Fort Verde District, Bounded by Hance, Coppinger, and Woods Sts., Camp Verde, 10/07/71, A, B, C, 71000120

Fort Verde District (Boundary Increase), Roughly N and E of Hance and Coppinger Sts. to Verde Ditch, Camp Verde, 9/19/77, A, 77001556

Fredericks House [Prescott Territorial Buildings MRA], 202 S. Pleasant, Prescott, 12/14/78, B, C, 78003229

Gage/Murphy House [Prescott Territorial Buildings MRA], 105 S. Alarcon, Prescott, 12/14/78, C, 78003230

Gardner, James I., Store [Prescott Territorial Buildings MRA], 201 N. Cortez, Prescott, 1/09/85, A, C, 85000056

Goldwater, Henry, House, 217 E. Union St., Prescott, 3/25/82, C, 82002091

Groom Creek School, Senator Hwy. SE of Prescott, Prescott NF, Prescott vicinity. 11/18/92, A, 92001568

Hassayampa Hotel, 122 E. Gurley St, Prescott, 11/29/79, A, C, 79000429

Hatalacva Ruin, Address Restricted, Clarkdale vicinity, 7/24/74, D, 74000463

Hawkins House [Prescott Territorial Buildings MRA], 122 S. Mt. Vernon, Prescott, 12/14/78, B, C, 78003232

Hazeltine House [Prescott Territorial Buildings MRA], 202 S. Mt. Vernon, Prescott, 12/14/78, C, 78003233

Head House [Prescott Territorial Buildings MRA], 309 E. Gurley, Prescott, 12/14/78, C, 78003234

Hell Canyon Bridge [Vehicular Bridges in Arizona MPS], Abandoned US 89 over Hell Canyon, Drake vicinity, 9/30/88, A, C, 88001682

Hill House [Prescott Territorial Buildings MRA], 144 S. Park, Prescott, 12/14/78, C, 78003235

Hill, Sam, Hardware [Prescott Territorial Buildings MRA], 154 S. Montezuma, Prescott, 12/14/78, A, C, 78003252

Hill, Samuel, Hardware Company Warehouse, 232 N. McCormick St., Prescott, 9/13/84, A, C, 84000772

Hotel Vendome, 230 S. Cortez, Prescott, 11/25/83, A, C, 83003495

Hyde Mountain Lookout House [National Forest Fire Lookouts in the Southwestern Region TR], Prescott National Forest, Camp Wood vicinity, 1/28/88, A, C, 87002491

Indian Peak Ruin (AR-03-09-06-116) [Prehistoric Walled Hilltop Sites of Prescott National Forest and Adjacent Regions MPS], Address Restricted, Prescott vicinity, 1/20/89, D, a, 88003185

Iron Turbine Windmill, 415 W. Gurley St., Prescott, 7/09/81, C, 81000139

Jerome Historic District, Jerome, Jerome, 11/13/66, A, NHL, 66000196

Kay-El-Bar Ranch, N of Wickenburg on Rincon Rd., Wickenburg vicinity, 5/22/78, A, B, 78000572

Kenwill Apartments [Prescott Territorial Buildings MRA], 119–127 E. Goodwin St., Prescott, 1/21/88, B, C, 87002494

Lawler-Hetherington Double House [Prescott Territorial Buildings MRA], 223 E. Union, Prescott, 12/14/78, B, C, 78003237

Little Hell Canyon Bridge [Vehicular Bridges in Arizona MPS], Abandoned US 89 over Little Hell Canyon, Drake vicinity, 9/30/88, A, C, 88001684

Loy Butte Pueblo, Address Restricted, Sedona vicinity, 2/10/75, D, 75000367

Lynx Creek Bridge [Vehicular Bridges in Arizona MPS], 5.9 mi. E of Prescott on Old Black Canyon Hwy., Prescott vicinity, 9/30/88, A, C, 88001641

Lynx Creek District, E of Prescott, Prescott vicinity, 8/31/78, B, C, D, 78000571

Marks House [Prescott Territorial Buildings MRA], 203 E. Union, Prescott, 12/14/78, C, 78003239

Martin/Ling House [Prescott Territorial Buildings MRA], 125 N. Pleasant, Prescott, 12/14/78, C, 78003240

Master Mechanic's House [Cottonwood MRA], 333 S. Willard St., Cottonwood, 9/19/86, C, 86002152

Mayer Apartments, Central Ave. SW of Ash St., Mayer, 7/13/89, B, 89000860

Mayer Business Block, Oak St. and Central Ave., Mayer, 7/13/89, B, 89000859

Mingus Lookout Complex [National Forest Fire Lookouts in the Southwestern Region TR], Prescott National Forest, Mingus vicinity, 1/28/88, A, C, 87002490

Montezuma Castle National Monument, 40 mi. S of Flagstaff on I-17, Flagstaff vicinity, 10/15/66, C, D, NPS, 66000082

Morin House [Prescott Territorial Buildings MRA], 134 N. Mt. Vernon, Prescott, 12/14/78, C, 78003242

Mormon Church, 126 N. Marina St., Prescott, 12/22/83, A, C, a, 83003496

Morrison House [Prescott Territorial Buildings MRA], 300 S. Marina, Prescott, 12/14/78, C, 78003243

Mount Union Lookout Cabin [National Forest Fire Lookouts in the Southwestern Region TR], Prescott National Forest, Potatoe Patch vicinity, 1/28/88, A, C, 87002489

Mulvenon Building [Prescott Territorial Buildings MRA], 230 W. Gurley St., Prescott, 4/15/93, A, 93000287

Old Governor's Mansion, 400 block of W. Gurley, Prescott, 9/10/71, A, C, 71000121

Otis House [Prescott Territorial Buildings MRA], 113 N. Pleasant, Prescott, 12/14/78, C, 78003245

Palace Station District, 23 mi. S of Prescott in Prescott National Forest, Prescott vicinity, 4/30/76, A, 76000382

Perkinsville Bridge [Vehicular Bridges in Arizona MPS], Perkinsville—Williams Rd. over Verde River, Ash Fork vicinity, 3/31/89, A, C, b, 88001671

Perry Mesa Archeological District, Address Restricted, Phoenix vicinity, 11/20/75, D, 75000364

Peter House [Prescott Territorial Buildings MRA], 211 E. Union, Prescott, 12/14/78, C, 78003247

Pine Crest Historic District, Roughly bounded by San Carlos St., Coronado Ave., and Yavapai, Apache, and Mohave Drs., Prescott, 8/10/89, A, C, 89001074

Poland Tunnel, W of Poland off AZ 69, Poland vicinity, 3/29/78, A, C, 78000570

Prescott Public Library, 125 E. Gurley St., Prescott, 5/28/75, C, 75000365

Roberts House [Prescott Territorial Buildings MRA], 136 N. Pleasant, Prescott, 12/14/78, C, 78003249

Robinson, A. W., Building [Prescott Territorial Buildings MRA], 115 N. Grove, Prescott, 12/14/78, C, 78003250

Sacred Heart Catholic Church and Rectory [Prescott Territorial Buildings MRA], 208 N. Marina, Prescott, 12/14/78, C, a, 78003251

Sacred Mountain, Address Restricted, Rimrock vicinity, 3/04/75, D, 75000366

Santa Fe, Prescott and Phoenix Railroad Depot, Cortez St., Prescott, 2/08/88, A, C, 82004978

Yavapai County—Continued

Sewall House [Prescott Territorial Buildings MRA], 220 N. Mt. Vernon, Prescott, 12/14/78, C, 78003253

Shekels House [Prescott Territorial Buildings MRA], 226 S. Cortez, Prescott, 12/14/78, C, 78003254

Sisters of Mercy Hospital Convent, 220 Grove Ave., Prescott, 2/19/82, A, C, a, 82002092

Sloan House [Prescott Territorial Buildings MRA], 128 N. Mt. Vernon, Prescott, 12/14/78, B, C, 78003255

Smelter Machine Shop [Cottonwood MRA], 360 S. Sixth St., Cottonwood, 9/19/86, A, 86002154

Strahan House [Cottonwood MRA], 725 E. Main St., Cottonwood, 9/19/86, C, 86002157

Superintendent's Residence [Cottonwood MRA], 315 S. Willard, Cottonwood, 10/14/86, A, C, 86002159

Sycamore Cliff Dwelling, Address Restricted, Sedona vicinity, 9/28/90, D, 90001455

Sycamore Ranger Station [Depression-Era USDA Forest Service Administrative Complexes in Arizona MPS], Forest Rd. 68F SW of Camp Verde, Prescott NF, Camp Verde vicinity, 6/10/93, A, C, 93000523

Thompson Ranch [Cottonwood MRA], 2874 US Alt. 89, Cottonwood, 9/19/86, A, 86002162

Tuzigoot National Monument Archeological District, Address Restricted, Clarkdale vicinity, 10/15/66, C, D, NPS, 66000194

US Post Office and Courthouse—Prescott Main [Historic US Post Offices in Arizona, 1900–1941, TR], 101 W. Goodwin Ave., Prescott, 12/03/85, A, C, 85003108

UVX Smelter Operations Complex [Cottonwood MRA], 361 S. Willard, Cottonwood, 9/19/86, A, 86002164

Verde River Bridge [Vehicular Bridges in Arizona MPS], 2.7 mi. S of Paulden on Sullivan Lake Rd., Paulden vicinity, 9/30/88, A, C, 88001639

Verde River Sheep Bridge, N of Carefree on Verde River, Carefree vicinity, 11/21/78, A, C, g, 78000569

Walker Charcoal Kiln, SE of Prescott in Prescott National Forest, Prescott vicinity, 10/08/76, A, 76000383

Walnut Creek Bridge [Vehicular Bridges in Arizona MPS], Forest Service Rd. over Walnut Creek, Simmons vicinity, 3/31/89, A, C, b, 88001673

Walnut Creek Ranger Station [Depression-Era USDA Forest Service Administrative Complexes in Arizona MPS], NW of Prescott, Prescott NF, Prescott vicinity, 6/10/93, A, C, 93000524

Walnut Grove Bridge [Vehicular Bridges in Arizona MPS], 3.5 mi. NW of Walnut Grove on Wagoner Rd., Walnut Grove vicinity, 9/30/88, A, C, 88001637

Wells House [Prescott Territorial Buildings MRA], 303 S. Cortez, Prescott, 12/14/78, C, 78003257

West Prescott Historic District [Prescott Territorial Buildings MRA], Roughly bounded by Gurley Dr., Park Ave., Country Club Dr., Vista Dr., and Coronado Ave., Prescott, 8/10/89, A, C, 89001075

Wilder House [Prescott Territorial Buildings MRA], 346 S. Montezuma, Prescott, 12/14/78, B, C, 78003259

Willard House [Cottonwood MRA], 114 W. Main, Cottonwood, 9/19/86, B, C, 86002166

Wingfield, Robert W., House, Montezuma Castle Hwy., Camp Verde vicinity, 2/03/86, B, C, 86000146

Woolsey Ranchhouse Ruins, N of Humboldt off AZ 69, Humboldt vicinity, 11/07/77, A, B, 77000240

Yavapai County Courthouse, Courthouse Sq., Prescott, 4/13/77, C, 77000241

Yuma County

Antelope Hill Highway Bridge [Vehicular Bridges in Arizona MPS (AD)], NW of Tacna spanning the Gila River, Tacna vicinity, 6/28/79, A, C, 79003444

Balsz House [Yuma MRA], 475 2nd Ave., Yuma, 12/07/82, C, 82001624

Blaisdell Slow Sand Filter Washing Machine, N. Jones St., Yuma, 1/18/79, A, 79000430

Brinley Avenue Historic District [Yuma MRA], 29-96 W. 2nd St., 198-200 S. Main, 201 S. 1st, and 102-298 Madison Aves., Yuma, 12/07/82, A, C, 82001625

Brown House [Yuma MRA], 268 S. 1st Ave., Yuma, 12/07/82, C, 82001626

Brownstetter House [Yuma MRA], 627 Orange Ave., Yuma, 12/07/82, C, 82001627

Cactus Press—Plaza Paint Building [Yuma MRA], 30–54 E. Third St., Yuma, 4/24/87, C, 87000613

Caruthers House [Yuma MRA], 441 2nd Ave., Yuma, 12/07/82, C, 82001628

Connor House [Yuma MRA], 281 S. 1st Ave., Yuma, 12/07/82, C, 82001629

Dougle Roof House [Yuma MRA], 553 4th Ave., Yuma, 12/07/82, C, 82001631

Dressing Apartments [Yuma MRA], 146 1st Ave., Yuma, 12/07/82, C, 82001630

Ewing, Frank, House [Yuma MRA], 700 2nd Ave., Yuma, 12/07/82, B, C, 82001632

Ewing, Ruth, House [Yuma MRA], 712 2nd Ave., Yuma, 12/07/82, C, 82004844

Fourth Avenue Junior High School [Yuma MRA], 450 S. 4th Ave., Yuma, 12/07/82, C, 82001633

Fredley Apartments [Yuma MRA], 406 2nd Ave., Yuma, 12/07/82, C, 82001634

Fredley House [Yuma MRA], 408 2nd Ave., Yuma, 12/07/82, C, 82001635

Gandolfo Theater [Yuma MRA], 200 S. 1st Ave., Yuma, 12/07/82, A, 82001636

Griffin, Alfred, House [Yuma MRA], 641 1st Ave., Yuma, 12/07/82, C, 82001637

Harquahala Peak Observatory, E of Wenden off U.S. 60, Wenden vicinity, 10/03/75, A, 75000370

Hodges, Peter B., House [Yuma MRA], 209 Orange Ave., Yuma, 12/07/82, C, 82001638

Hotel del Ming [Yuma MRA], 300 Gila St., Yuma, 12/07/82, A, C, 82001639

Jackson, W. B., House [Yuma MRA], 572 1st Ave., Yuma, 12/07/82, C, 82001640

Kent, Jerry, House [Yuma MRA], 450 3rd Ave., Yuma, 12/07/82, C, 82001641

Lee Hotel [Yuma MRA], 390 Main St., Yuma, 4/12/84, C, 84000750

Levy, Henry, House [Yuma MRA], 602 2nd Ave., Yuma, 12/07/82, C, 82001642

Marable, George, House [Yuma MRA], 482 Orange Ave., Yuma, 12/07/82, C, 82001643

Martinez Lake Site (AZ-050-0210), Address Restricted, Fisher's Landing vicinity, 9/10/87, D, 87001446

Masonic Temple [Yuma MRA], 153 S. 2nd Ave., Yuma, 4/12/84, C, 84000752

Mayhew, Carmelita, House [Yuma MRA], 660 1st Ave., Yuma, 12/07/82, C, 82001644

McPhaul Suspension Bridge [Vehicular Bridges in Arizona MPS (AD)], W of Dome, Dome vicinity, 8/13/81, A, C, 81000140

Methodist Episcopal Church [Yuma MRA], 256 S. 1st Ave., Yuma, 12/07/82, A, C, a, 82001645

Methodist Parsonage [Yuma MRA], 248 S. 1st Ave., Yuma, 12/07/82, B, C, 82001646

Mexican Consulate [Yuma MRA], 129 W. 4th St., Yuma, 12/07/82, C, c, 82001647

Ming, A.B., House [Yuma MRA], 468 Orange Ave., Yuma, 12/07/82, C, 82001648

Mohawk Valley School, 5151 South Ave. 39 East, Roll, 12/29/86, A, 86003525

Norton House [Yuma MRA], 226 S. 1st Ave., Yuma, 12/07/82, B, 82001649

Ocean To Ocean Bridge [Vehicular Bridges in Arizona MPS (AD)], Penitentiary Ave, Yuma, 9/11/79, A, C, 79000431

Old La Paz, Address Restricted, Ehrenberg vicinity, 8/25/70, A, D, 70000117

Old Presbyterian Church, SW of Parker on 2nd Ave., Parker vicinity, 6/03/71, A, D, a, 71000122

Ortiz House [Yuma MRA], 206 S. 1st Ave., Yuma, 12/07/82, C, 82001650

Pancrazi House [Yuma MRA], 432 S. Madison Ave., Yuma, 12/07/82, B, C, 82001651

Parker Jail, N side of Agency Rd. in Pop Harvey Park, Parker, 4/03/75, A, 75000369

Pauley Apartments [Yuma MRA], 490 W. 1st St., Yuma, 12/07/82, C, 82001652

Power Apartments [Yuma MRA], 20 W. 3rd St., Yuma, 12/07/82, C, 82001653

Riley, Clara Smith, House [Yuma MRA], 734 2nd Ave., Yuma, 12/07/82, C, 82001654

Ripley Intaglios, Address Restricted, Ehrenberg vicinity, 11/20/75, D, 75000368

Roosevelt School [Yuma MRA], 201 6th St., Yuma, 12/07/82, C, 82001655

Russell-Williamson House [Yuma MRA], 652 2nd Ave., Yuma, 12/07/82, C, 82001656

San Carlos Hotel [Yuma MRA], 106 1st St., Yuma, 4/12/84, C, 84000754

San Ysidro Hacienda, Address Restricted, Yuma vicinity, 10/10/75, A, D, 75000371

Sears Point Archaeological District, Address Restricted, Gila Bend vicinity, 10/16/85, D, 85003150

Yuma County—Continued

Smith, J. Homer, House [Yuma MRA], 600 5th Ave., Yuma, 12/07/82, B, C, 82001658

Southern Pacific Freight Depot [Yuma MRA], Main St., Yuma, 4/24/87, A, C, 87000614

Southern Pacific Railroad Depot, Gila St., Yuma, 6/22/76, A, C, 76000384

St. Paul's Episcopal Church [Yuma MRA], 637 2nd Ave., Yuma, 12/07/82, C, a, 82001657

Stoffela Store/Railroad Exchange [Yuma MRA], 447 S. Main St., Yuma, 12/07/82, A, C, 82001659

US Post Office—Yuma Main [Historic US Post Offices in Arizona, 1900–1941, TR], 370 W. Third St., Yuma, 12/03/85, A, C, 85003109

Yuma Century Heights Conservancy Residential Historic District, Roughly bounded by 4th Ave.,

8th St., 1st and Orange Aves., Yuma, 10/11/88, A, C, a, 88001834

Yuma City Hall [Yuma MRA], 181 W. 1st St., Yuma, 12/07/82, A, C, 82001660

Yuma County Courthouse [Yuma MRA], 168 S. 2nd Ave., Yuma, 12/07/82, A, C, 82001661

Yuma Crossing and Associated Sites, Banks of the Colorado River, Yuma, 11/13/66, A, NHL, 66000197

The Childs-Irving Hydroelectric Facilities (ca. 1908–09 and 1915–16) complex is a notable example of a continuously operating engineered power delivery system in the state of Arizona. (Courtesy Arizona State Parks, 1980)

ARKANSAS

Arkansas County

Arkansas County Courthouse—Southern District, Courthouse Sq., DeWitt, 11/20/92, C, 92001620

Arkansas County Courthouse—Northern District, Jct. of E. 3rd and S. College Sts., SW corner, Stuttgart, 11/20/92, C, 92001621

Arkansas Post National Memorial, 8 mi. SE of Gillett on AR 1 and 169, Gillett vicinity, 10/15/66, A, f, NHL, NPS, 66000198

First United Methodist Church [Thompson, Charles L., Design Collection TR], Jct. of Jefferson and Cross Sts., DeWitt, 9/04/92, C, a, 92001158

Halliburton House, 300 W. Halliburton St., DeWitt, 11/05/74, B, 74000464

Menard—Hodges Mounds (3AR4), Address Restricted, Nady vicinity, 10/31/85, D, a, NHL, 85003542

Riceland Hotel, Third and Main Sts., Stuttgart, 5/21/86, C, 86001105

Roland Site, Address Restricted, Tichnor vicinity, 5/02/75, D, 75000372

St. Charles Battle Site, Jct. of AR 1 and the White River, St. Charles, 12/02/74, A, 74000465

Standard Ice Company Building, 517 S. Main St., Stuttgart, 7/02/79, A, C, 79003433

Ashley County

Crossett Experimental Forest Building No. 2 [Facilities Constructed by the CCC in Arkansas MPS], AR 133 S of Crossett, Crossett vicinity, 10/20/93, A, 93001084

Crossett Experimental Forest Building No. 6 [Facilities Constructed by the CCC in Arkansas MPS], AR 133 S of Crossett, Crossett vicinity, 10/20/93, A, 93001085

Crossett Experimental Forest Building No. 8 [Facilities Constructed by the CCC in Arkansas MPS], AR 133 S of Crossett, Crossett vicinity, 10/20/93, A, 93001086

Dean House [Thompson, Charles L., Design Collection TR], Off US 165, Portland, 12/22/82, C, 82000797

First United Methodist Church, 204 S. Main, Hamburg, 4/27/92, C, a, 92000388

Hamburg Presbyterian Church, Jct. of Cherry and Lincoln Sts., Hamburg, 5/14/91, C, a, 91000589

Naff House, Jct. of 3rd Ave. and Fir St., NW corner, Portland, 7/24/92, C, 92000957

Pugh House [Thompson, Charles L., Design Collection TR], Off US 165, Portland, 12/22/82, C, 82000798

Watson House, 300 N. Cherry, Hamburg, 12/28/77, C, 77000242

Watson-Sawyer House, 502 E. Parker St., Hamburg, 12/06/75, B, C, 75000373

Wiggins Cabin, City Park, Crossett, 9/30/82, C, b, 82002093

Williams, Dr. Robert George, House, AR 8 and 209, Parkdale, 10/04/84, C, 84000002

Baxter County

Big Flat School Gymnasium [Public Schools in the Ozarks MPS], Co. Rd. 121 S of jct. with AR 14, Big Flat, 11/19/93, A, C, 93001255

Buford School Building [Public Schools in the Ozarks MPS], AR 126, Buford, 9/04/92, A, 92001128

Case—Shiras—Dearmore House, 351 E. 4th St., Mountain Home, 2/03/92, B, 91000580

Casey House, Fairgrounds off U.S. 62, Mountain Home, 12/04/75, B, C, 75000374

Cotter Bridge [Historic Bridges of Arkansas MPS], US 62, over the White River, Cotter, 4/04/90, A, C, 90000518

North Fork Bridge [Historic Bridges of Arkansas MPS], AR 5, over North Fork of the White River, Norfork, 4/09/90, A, C, 90000512

Old Joe [Rock Art Sites in Arkansas TR], Address Restricted, Norfolk vicinity, 5/04/82, D, 82002094

Wolf, Jacob, House, On AR 5, W of fork of the White and North Fork Rivers, Norfork, 4/13/73, C, 73000380

Benton County

Adar House [Benton County MRA], Off AR 59, Sulfur Springs vicinity, 3/25/88, C, 87002358

Alden House [Benton County MRA], Rt. 1, Bentonville, 1/28/88, C, 87002378

Alfrey-Brown House, 1001 S. Washington St., Siloam Springs, 10/04/84, C, 84000003

Applegate Drugstore, 116 1st St., Rogers, 6/23/82, A, C, 82002095

Bank of Gentry [Benton County MRA], Main St., Gentry, 1/28/88, C, 87002416

Bank of Rogers Building, 114 S. 1st St., Rogers, 6/23/80, A, C, 80000773

Banks House [Benton County MRA], AR 72, W of Hiwassee, Hiwassee vicinity, 1/28/88, C, 87002365

Bartell, Fred, House [Benton County MRA], 324 E. Twin Springs St., Siloam Springs, 1/28/88, C, 87002429

Beasley Homestead [Benton County MRA], US 71, Bethel Heights, 1/28/88, C, 87002375

Bella Vista Water Tank [Benton County MRA], Jct. of Suits Us Dr. and Pumpkin Hollow Rd., Bella Vista vicinity, 8/14/92, A, C, 92000985

Benton County Courthouse [Benton County MRA], 106 S.E. A St., Bentonville, 1/28/88, C, 87002340

Benton County Jail [Benton County MRA], 212 N. Main St., Bentonville, 1/28/88, C, 87002334

Benton County National Bank, 123 W. Central, Benton City, 9/01/83, C, 83001156

Bentonville High School [Benton County MRA], 410 N.W. Second St., Bentonville, 1/28/88, C, 87002339

Bentonville Third Street Historic District [Benton County MPS], Roughly, 3rd St. SE. from Main St. to C St. SE., Bentonville, 11/12/93, C, 93001202

Bentonville Train Station [Benton County MRA], 414 S. Main St., Bentonville, 1/28/88, A, C, 87002337

Bentonville West Central Avenue Historic District [Benton County MPS], W. Central Ave. between SW. A and SW. G Sts., Bentonville, 10/22/92, C, 92001349

Bertschy House [Benton County MRA], 507 N.W. Fifth St., Bentonville, 1/28/88, C, 87002336

Blackburn House [Benton County MRA], 220 N. Fourth St., Rogers, 1/28/88, B, C, 87002402

Blackwell—Paisley Cabin [Benton County MRA], Suits-Us Dr., Bella Vista, 1/28/88, A, C, 87002351

Blake House [Benton County MRA], 211 S.E. A St., Bentonville, 1/28/88, C, 87002324

Bogan Cabin [Benton County MRA], Cedarcrest Mountain, Bella Vista, 1/28/88, A, C, 87002352

Bogart Hardware Building [Benton County MRA], 112 E. Central, Bentonville, 1/28/88, C, 87002329

Bolin Barn and Smokehouse [Benton County MRA], SE of Gravette on Spavinaw Creek Rd., Gravette vicinity, 1/28/88, C, 87002359

Braithwaite House [Benton County MRA], Old Bella Vista Hwy., Bentonville, 1/28/88, C, 87002314

Bratt—Smiley House [Benton County MRA], University and Broadway, Siloam Springs, 1/28/88, C, 87002428

Breedlove House and Water Tower [Benton County MRA], Rt. 4, Bentonville vicinity, 1/28/88, A, C, 87002326

Bryan House No. 2 [Benton County MRA], 321 E. Locust St., Rogers, 1/28/88, C, 87002396

Campbell House [Benton County MRA], 714 W. Third St., Rogers, 1/28/88, C, 87002391

Carl House [Benton County MRA], 70 Main St., Gentry, 1/28/88, C, 87002422

Coal Gap School [Public Schools in the Ozarks MPS], Co. Rd. 920, Larue vicinity, 9/04/92, A, 92001123

Coats School [Benton County MRA], Spavinaw Creek Rd., Maysville vicinity, 1/28/88, C, 87002370

Connelly—Harrington House [Benton County MRA], 115 E. University, Siloam Springs, 1/28/88, C, 87002386

Council Grove Methodist Church [Benton County MRA], Osage Mills Rd., Osage Mills, 1/28/88, C, a, 87002377

Benton County—Continued

Craig—Bryan House [Benton County MRA], 307 W. Central, Bentonville, 1/28/88, C, 87002320

Daniels House [Benton County MRA], 902 E. Central, Bentonville, 1/28/88, C, 87002317

Deaton Cabin [Benton County MRA], Suits Us Rd., Bella Vista, 1/28/88, A, C, 87002348

Douglas House [Benton County MRA], 8 mi. off of AR 12, Vaughn vicinity, 1/28/88, C, 87002372

Drane House [Benton County MRA], 1004 S. First St., Rogers, 1/28/88, C, 87002389

Duckworth—Williams House [Benton County MRA], 103 S. College, Siloam Springs, 1/28/88, C, 87002385

Elliott House, 303 SE 3rd St., Bentonville, 1/20/78, C, 78000573

First National Bank [Benton County MRA], 109 E. University, Siloam Springs, 1/28/88, C, 87002431

Freeman—Felker House [Benton County MRA], 318 W. Elm St., Rogers, 1/28/88, C, 87002399

Gailey Hollow Farmstead [Benton County MRA], 1/4 mi. E of Logan intersection, Logan Community vicinity, 1/28/88, C, 87002381

German Builder's House [Benton County MRA], 315 E. Central, Siloam Springs, 1/28/88, C, 87002426

Goforth—Saindon Mound Group, Address Restricted, Siloam Springs vicinity, 1/23/86, D, 86000099

Green Barn [Benton County MRA], McClure St., Lowell, 1/28/88, C, 87002368

Gypsy Camp Historic District [Benton County MRA], Off AR 59, Siloam Springs vicinity, 1/28/88, A, C, 87002425

Hagler—Cole Cabin [Benton County MRA], Mt. Pisqua Dr., Bella Vista, 1/28/88, A, C, 87002342

Henry—Thompson House [Benton County MRA], 302 S.E. Second St., Bentonville, 1/28/88, C, 87002327

Hiwassee Bank Building [Benton County MRA], Main St., AR 279, Hiwassee, 1/28/88, C, 87002366

House at 305 E. Ashley [Benton County MRA], 305 E. Ashley, Siloam Springs, 1/28/88, C, 87002427

Illinois River Bridge [Benton County MRA], 6 mi. E of Siloam Springs, Siloam Springs, 1/28/88, C, 87002420

Jackson House [Benton County MRA], 207 W. Central, Bentonville, 1/28/88, C, 87002331

James House [Benton County MRA], Rt. 2, Rogers vicinity, 1/28/88, C, 87002332

Jones House [Benton County MRA], 220 Bush St., Sulphur Springs, 1/28/88, C, 87002363

Juhre, Charles, House [Benton County MPS], 406 N. 4th St., Rogers, 2/25/93, C, 93000091

Kansas City—Southern Depot—Decatur [Historic Railroad Depots of Arkansas MPS], AR 59, Decatur, 6/11/92, A, C, 92000606

Kefauver House [Benton County MRA], 224 W. Cherry St., Rogers, 1/28/88, C, 87002405

Kindley House [Benton County MRA], 503 Charlotte St., Gravette, 1/28/88, C, 87002356

Koons House [Benton County MRA], 409 Fifth St., Bentonville, 1/22/88, C, 87002330

Lakeside Hotel, 119 W. University St, Siloam Springs, 11/15/79, A, C, 79000432

Lamberton Cabin [Benton County MRA], 8 North Mountain, Bella Vista, 1/28/88, A, C, 87002343

Lane Hotel [Benton County MRA], 121 W. Poplar St., Rogers, 1/28/88, C, 87002411

Lillard—Sprague House [Benton County MRA], Pleasant Grove Rd., Rogers, 1/28/88, C, 87002398

Linebarger House [Benton County MRA], 606 W. Central, Bentonville, 1/28/88, B, C, 87002335

Macon—Harrison House [Benton County MRA], 209 N.E. Second St., Bentonville, 1/28/88, B, C, 87002333

Markey House [Benton County MRA], Rt. 1, Garfield vicinity, 1/28/88, C, b, 87002354

Massey Hotel, U.S. 71, Bentonville, 12/01/78, A, C, 78000574

Maxwell—Hinman House [Benton County MRA], 902 N.W. Second St., Bentonville, 1/28/88, C, 87002322

Maxwell—Sweet House [Benton County MRA], 114 S. College, Siloam Springs, 1/28/88, C, 87002388

McCleod House [Benton County MRA], Rt. 1, Springdale, 1/28/88, C, 87002355

McIntyre House [Benton County MRA], Logan Rd., Logan Community vicinity, 1/28/88, C, 87002382

Merrill House [Benton County MRA], 617 S. Sixth, Rogers, 1/28/88, C, 87002404

Methodist Church [Benton County MRA], AR 112 and AR 264, Cave Springs, 1/28/88, C, a, 87002373

Miller Homestead [Benton County MRA], 1/2 mi. E of AR 94, Pea Ridge, 1/28/88, C, 87002362

Mitchell House [Benton County MRA], 115 N. Nelson, Gentry, 1/28/88, C, 87002423

Monte Ne, Off AR 94, Monte Ne, 2/17/78, B, C, g, 78000575

Morris House [Benton County MRA], 407 S.W. Fourth St., Bentonville, 1/28/88, C, 87002316

Mutual Aid Union Building, 2nd and Poplar Sts., Rogers, 10/14/76, A, C, 76000385

Myler House [Benton County MRA], 315 N. Third St., Rogers, 1/28/88, C, 87002393

New Home School and Church [Benton County MRA], S of Bella Vista on McKisic Creek Rd., Bella Vista vicinity, 1/28/88, C, a, d, 87002357

Norwood School [Benton County MRA], Norwood Rd. and AR 16, Norwood Community vicinity, 1/28/88, C, 87002384

Oklahoma Row Hotel Site, AR 94 Spur at shore of Beaver Lake, Monte Ne, 5/20/92, B, C, 91001668

Osage Creek Bridge [Benton County MRA], 4 1/2 mi. N of Tontitown, Tontitown, 1/28/88, C, 87002418

Osage Mills Dam [Benton County MRA], N of Osage Mills on Little Osage Creek, Osage Mills, 1/28/88, A, C, 87002376

Parks—Reagan House [Benton County MRA], 410 W. Poplar St., Rogers, 1/28/88, C, 87002395

Pea Ridge National Military Park, US 62, Pea Ridge, 10/15/66, A, f, NPS, 66000199

Pharr Cabin [Benton County MRA], 2 North Mountain, Bella Vista, 1/28/88, A, C, 87002346

Piercy Farmstead [Benton County MRA], Osage Mills Rd., Osage Mills, 1/28/88, C, 87002379

Pinkston—Mays Store Building [Benton County MRA], 107–109 Lackston St., Lowell, 1/28/88, C, 87002367

Princedom Cabin [Benton County MRA], Lookout Dr., Bella Vista, 1/28/88, A, C, 87002347

Quell House [Benton County MRA], 222 S. Wright, Siloam Springs, 1/28/88, C, 87002387

Raney House [Benton County MRA], 1331 Monte Ne, Rogers, 1/28/88, C, 87002403

Rice House [Benton County MRA], 501 N.W. A St., Bentonville, 1/28/88, C, 87002325

Rice, James A., House, 204 SE 3rd St., Bentonville, 11/01/84, C, 84000177

Rife Farmstead [Benton County MRA], Osage Mills Rd., Osage Mills, 1/28/88, C, 87002380

Rife House [Benton County MRA], 1515 S. Eighth St., Rogers, 1/28/88, C, 87002406

Rocky Branch School [Benton County MRA], 200 N. Hwy. 303, Prairie Creek vicinity, 3/25/88, C, b, 87002360

Rogers City Hall [Benton County MRA], 202 W. Elm St., Rogers, 1/28/88, A, C, 87002409

Rogers Commercial Historic District (Boundary Increase) [Benton County MPS], Roughly bounded by Walnut, First, Poplar and Second Sts., Rogers, 9/30/93, C, 93001028

Rogers Post Office Building [Benton County MRA], 120 W. Poplar St., Rogers, 1/28/88, C, 87002408

Roy's Office Supply Building [Benton County MRA], 110 E. Central, Bentonville, 1/28/88, C, 87002328

Sager, Simon, Cabin, John Brown University campus, Siloam Springs, 1/30/76, B, C, 76000386

Sellers Farm [Benton County MRA], Old Hwy. on State Line, Maysville, 1/28/88, C, 87002369

Shady Grove School [Benton County MRA], AR 94, Pea Ridge vicinity, 1/28/88, C, 87002361

Shiloh House [Benton County MRA], Off Kibler St., Sulphur Springs, 1/28/88, C, 87002364

Shores Warehouse [Benton County MRA], Main St., Cave Springs, 1/28/88, C, 87002374

Siloam Springs Train Station [Benton County MRA], E. Jefferson, Siloam Springs, 1/28/88, A, C, 87002413

Spavinaw Creek Bridge [Benton County MRA], 4 mi. N of Decatur on CR 29, Decatur vicinity, 1/28/88, C, 87002414

Stack Barn [Benton County MRA], AR 94 Spur, Monte Ne, 1/28/88, C, 87002353

Stockton Building [Benton County MRA], 113 N. Broadway, Siloam Springs, 1/28/88, C, 87002432

Stroud House [Benton County MRA], 204 S. Third St., Rogers, 1/28/88, C, 87002400

Sunset Hotel [Benton County MRA], W of US 71, Bella Vista, 8/14/92, A, 92000986

Sutherlin Cabin [Benton County MRA], 4 North Mountain, Bella Vista, 1/28/88, A, C, 87002344

Terry Block Building, 101-103 N. Main St., Bentonville, 5/13/82, B, C, 82004613

Benton County—Continued

Thurmond House [Benton County MRA], 407 Britt, Siloam Springs, 1/28/88, C, 87002430

Vinson House [Benton County MRA], 1016 S. Fourth, Rogers, 1/28/88, C, 87002392

Walnut Street Historic District [Benton County MRA], Walnut St., Rogers, 1/28/88, C, 87002412

War Eagle Bridge, Carries CR 98 over War Eagle Creek, War Eagle, 11/19/85, A, C, 85003497

Wasson House [Benton County MRA], Main St., Springtown, 1/28/88, C, 87002371

Wonderland Cave [Benton County MRA], Dertmoor Rd., Bella Vista, 1/28/88, A, 87002313

Young, Col., House [Benton County MRA], 1007 S.E. Fifth St., Bentonville, 1/28/88, C, 87002319

Boone County

Bergman High School [Public Schools in the Ozarks MPS], Co. Rd. 48, Bergman, 9/10/92, A, 92001203

Boone County Courthouse, Courthouse Sq., Harrison, 7/21/76, A, C, 76000387

Boone County Jail, Central Ave. and Willow St., Harrison, 12/12/76, A, C, 76000388

Everton School [Public Schools in the Ozarks MPS], Main St., Everton, 9/10/92, A, 92001205

Missouri and North Arkansas Depot—Bellefonte [Historic Railroad Depots of Arkansas MPS], SE corner of Center St. and Keeter Dr., Bellefonte, 6/11/92, A, C, 92000601

Valley Springs School [Public Schools in the Ozarks MPS], 1 School St., Valley Springs, 9/10/92, A, 92001204

Bradley County

Adams-Leslie House, S of Warren, Warren vicinity, 8/09/79, B, C, 79000433

Bailey House, 302 Chestnut St., Warren, 8/28/75, B, C, 75000375

Bradley County Courthouse and Clerk's Office, Courthouse Sq., Warren, 12/12/76, A, C, 76000389

Ederington House, 326 S. Main St., Warren, 6/21/84, C, 84000660

Martin, Dr. John Wilson, House, 200 Ash St., Warren, 12/27/90, C, D, 90001948

Warren and Ouachita Valley Railway Station, 325 W. Cedar St., Warren, 8/03/77, A, C, e, 77000244

Calhoun County

Boone's Mounds, Address Restricted, Calion vicinity, 4/14/80, D, 80000774

Calhoun County Courthouse, Courthouse Sq., Hampton, 12/12/76, A, C, 76000390

Dunn House, W of Hampton on AR 4, Hampton vicinity, 5/04/76, B, 76000391

Keller Site, Address Restricted, Calion vicinity, 10/29/79, D, 79000434

Ouachita River Lock and Dam No. 8, SE of Calion, Calion vicinity, 12/19/83, A, C, 83003458

Carroll County

Beaver Bridge [Historic Bridges of Arkansas MPS], AR 187, over the White River, Beaver, 4/09/90, A, C, 90000730

Berryville Agriculture Building [Public Schools in the Ozarks MPS], S of Freeman Ave., E of Linda St., N of W. College Ave. and W of Ferguson St., Berryville, 9/10/92, A, 92001214

Berryville Gymnasium [Public Schools in the Ozarks MPS], S. of Freeman Ave., E of Linda St., N of W. College Ave. and W of Ferguson St., Berryville, 9/10/92, A, 92001215

Carroll County Courthouse, Eastern District, Public Sq., Berryville, 8/27/76, A, C, 76000392

Chaney, James C., House, AR 68, Osage, 11/20/89, B, C, D, 89002012

Crawford, W. D., House, E of Co. Rd. 27, about 1 mi. N of jct. with Co. Rd. 98, Cisco vicinity, 11/20/92, B, C, 92001613

Dog Branch School, S of US 412, approximately 3 mi. E of Osage, Osage vicinity, 9/08/92, C, 92001177

Eureka Springs Historic District, Most Eureka Springs and its environs, Eureka Springs, 12/18/70, A, C, 70000118

Eureka Springs Historic District (Boundary Increase), S. Main, Eureka Springs, 1/29/79, A, C, 79003730

Lake Leatherwood Recreational Facilities [Facilities Constructed by the Civilian Conservation Corps in Arkansas MPS], End of Co. Rd. No. 61, Eureka Springs vicinity, 8/12/92, A, C, 90001942

Mulladay Hollow Bridge [Historic Bridges of Arkansas MPS], Co. Rd. 61, over Mulladay Hollow Creek, Eureka Springs vicinity, 4/06/90, A, C, 90000531

Stamps Store, Old Hwy 68 near its jct. with AR 68, Osage, 9/05/90, C, 90001380

Winona Church and School, Rockhouse Rd., Winona Springs, 6/05/91, C, a, 91000688

Yell Masonic Lodge Hall, Off AR 68, Carrollton, 11/01/84, A, C, a, 84000178

Chicot County

American Legion Post No. 127 Building, Jct. of Cherry and Armstrong Sts., NE corner, Eudora, 10/08/92, C, 92001350

Anderson, Dr. A. G., House, Jct. of Duncan and Main Sts., Eudora, 7/24/92, C, 92000929

Bunker House, AR 159 W of jct. with US 65/82, Lake Village, 11/20/92, C, 92001622

Carlton House, 434 S. Lakeshore Dr., Lake Village, 6/05/91, C, 91000692

Epstein, Sam, House [Ethnic and Racial Minority Settlement of the Arkansas Delta MPS], 488 Lake Shore Dr., Lake Village, 9/21/92, B, 92001226

Lakeport Plantation, About 3 mi. SE of Shives, off AR 142, Shives vicinity, 11/20/74, C, 74000466

Landi, A., General Merchandise Building [Ethnic and Racial Minority Settlement of the Arkansas Delta MPS], AR 8, Grand Lake, 10/08/92, A, 92001347

Liberto, P. and J.—Rosa Portera Building [Ethnic and Racial Minority Settlement of the Arkansas Delta MPS], Main St., Eudora, 10/08/92, A, 92001348

New Hope Missionary Baptist Church Cemetery, Historic Section [Ethnic and Racial Minority Settlement of the Arkansas Delta MPS], St. Marys St., Lake Village, 9/21/92, A, d, 92001227

Tushek, John, Building, 108 Main St., Lake Village, 8/05/93, C, 93000811

Walker House [Thompson, Charles L., Design Collection TR], 606 Main St., Dermott, 12/22/82, C, 82000799

Clark County

Bank of Amity, Old, NW corner of town square, Amity, 6/05/91, C, 91000690

Barkman, James E. M., House, 406 N. 10th St., Arkadelphia, 7/30/74, C, 74000467

Bayou Sel, Address Restricted, Arkadelphia vicinity, 9/10/74, B, D, 74000468

Benjamin Mercantile Building, 410 Main St., Arkadelphia, 9/05/90, B, C, D, 90001378

Boaz, Dr., House, AR 26, Clear Spring vicinity, 1/28/92, C, 91002014

Bozeman House, W of Arkadelphia on AR 26, Arkadelphia vicinity, 11/14/78, B, C, 78000576

Clark County Courthouse, 4th and Crittenden Sts., Arkadelphia, 12/01/78, A, C, 78000577

Clark County Library, 609 Caddo St., Arkadelphia, 11/05/74, A, C, 74000469

Clear Springs Tabernacle, Jct. of AR 26 and Bobo Rd., Okolona vicinity, 2/13/92, C, a, 92000057

Domestic Science Building [Thompson, Charles L., Design Collection TR], 11th and Haddock, Arkadelphia, 12/22/82, C, 82000800

Estes, Horace, House, 614 E. Main St., Gurdon, 9/21/93, C, 93000487

Flanagin Law Office, 320 Clay St., Arkadelphia, 12/22/77, B, 77000245

Gurdon Jail, W. Joslyn and Front Sts., Gurdon, 11/13/89, A, 89001959

Habicht—Cohn—Crow House, Eighth and Pine, Arkadelphia, 10/03/85, C, 85002717

Hudson-Jones House, E of Arkadelphia on SR 2, Arkadelphia vicinity, 9/30/82, B, C, 82002096

Kirksey, Loy, House, Co. Rd. 59 W of De Gray Lake, Fendley vicinity, 2/03/92, C, 91000586

Little Missouri River Bridge [Historic Bridges of Arkansas MPS], Co. Rd. 179, over the Little Missouri River, Prescott vicinity, 4/09/90, A, C, 90000536

Magnolia Manor, 0.6 mi. SW of jct. of I-30 and AR 51, Arkadelphia, 9/27/72, C, 72000200

Clark County—Continued

Missouri—Pacific Railroad Depot—Arkadelphia [Historic Railroad Depots of Arkansas MPS], S. Fifth St., Arkadelphia, 6/11/92, A, C, 92000599

Missouri—Pacific Railroad Depot—Gurdon [Historic Railroad Depots of Arkansas MPS], NW of jct. of N. First and E. Walnut Sts., Gurdon, 6/11/92, A, C, 92000609

Ross Site (3CL401), Address Restricted, Whelen Springs vicinity, 10/10/85, D, 85003133

Sandidge, June, House, 811 Cherry St., Gurdon, 2/25/93, C, 93000093

Clay County

Baynham House, Stephens St., Success, 8/31/78, B, 78000579

Chalk Bluff, N of St. Francis, St. Francis vicinity, 10/29/74, A, B, 74000470

Knob School—Masonic Lodge, AR 141, Knob, 5/30/91, C, 91000679

Oliver House, 203 W. Front St., Corning, 12/08/78, B, C, b, 78000578

Pfeiffer House and Carriage House, 10th and Cherry Sts., Piggott, 6/10/82, B, g, 82002097

Sheeks House, 502 Market St., Corning, 8/22/75, B, 75000376

Waddle House, S. Erwin, Success, 3/28/77, B, 77000246

Cleburne County

Cleburne County Courthouse, Courthouse Sq., Heber Springs, 7/12/76, A, C, 76000393

Crosby, Dr. Cyrus F., House, 202 N. Broadway St., Heber Springs, 11/19/93, C, 93001258

Frauenthal, Clarence, House, 210 N. Broadway St., Heber Springs, 11/19/93, C, 93001256

King, Hugh L., House, 110 W. Spring St., Heber Springs, 9/08/92, C, 92001224

Quitman High School Building [Public Schools in the Ozarks MPS], AR 25, Quitman, 9/04/92, A, 92001126

Quitman Home Economics Building [Public Schools in the Ozarks MPS], 2nd Ave., Quitman, 9/04/92, A, 92001127

Winkley Bridge, E of Heber Springs at Little Red River, Heber Springs vicinity, 10/09/84, A, C, 84000020

Cleveland County

Barnett-Attwood House, NE of New Edinburg, New Edinburg vicinity, 7/29/77, B, C, 77000247

Cleveland County Clerk's Building, Fairgrounds, Rison, 1/31/76, A, b, 76000394

Cleveland County Courthouse, Main and Magnolia, Rison, 4/11/77, A, C, 77000248

Marks' Mills Battlefield Park, Jct. of AR 8 and AR 97, Fordyce vicinity, 1/21/70, A, f, 70000119

Mount Olivet Methodist Church, Fairgrounds off AR 35, Rison, 12/01/75, A, C, a, b, 75000377

Columbia County

Allen, W. H., House, NW of Spotville off AR 98, Spotville vicinity, 10/14/76, C, 76000395

Bank of Waldo [Thompson, Charles L., Design Collection TR], Locust and Main Sts., Waldo, 12/22/82, C, 82000801

Caraway Hall, Southern Arkansas University, Adjacent to E. Lane Dr., Magnolia, 2/25/93, C, 93000088

Columbia County Courthouse, Court Sq., Magnolia, 4/15/78, C, 78000580

Columbia County Jail [Thompson, Charles L., Design Collection TR], Calhoun & Jefferson Sts., Magnolia, 12/22/82, C, 82000802

Couch, Harvey C., School, NE of jct. of Co. Rd. 11 (Calhoun Rd.) and Co. Rd. 25, Calhoun, 6/08/93, C, 93000482

Couch—Marshall House, 505 W. Monroe St., Magnolia, 7/24/92, C, 92000955

Frog Level, Address unknown at this time, Bussey vicinity, 9/22/72, C, 72000201

Longino, Dr. H. A., House, 317 W. Main St., Magnolia, 6/14/82, C, 82002098

Louisiana and Northwest Railroad Depot—Magnolia [Historic Railroad Depots of Arkansas MPS], N side of Main St., between Clay and Walnut Sts., Magnolia, 6/11/92, A, 92000614

Mt. Prospect Methodist Church, Jct. of Co. Rds. 446 and 61, Richland, 3/22/90, C, a, 90000428

Old Alexander House, NE of Magnolia, Magnolia vicinity, 1/18/79, C, 79000435

Ozmer House, Southern Arkansas University farm, US 82 Bypass, Magnolia vicinity, 11/20/86, C, b, 86003226

Smith, William H., House, N of jct. of AR 98 and Co. Rd. 85, Atlanta, 11/27/92, C, 92001630

Turner, Kate, House, 709 W. Main St., Magnolia, 8/26/82, C, 82002099

Conway County

Aycock House, 410 W. Church St., Morrilton, 5/13/76, C, 76000397

Cafeteria Building—Cleveland School [Public Schools in the Ozarks MPS], Co. Rd. 511, Cleveland vicinity, 9/10/92, A, 92001194

Cedar Creek Bridge [Historic Bridges of Arkansas MPS], Off AR 154, over Cedar Creek at Roosevelt Lake, Petit Jean State Park, 4/09/90, A, C, 90000520

Coca-Cola Building [Thompson, Charles L., Design Collection TR], 211 N. Moose, Morrilton, 12/22/82, C, 82000803

Conway County Courthouse, Moose St. at Church St., Morrilton, 11/13/89, C, 89001960

Conway County Library, 101 W. Church St., Morrilton, 4/15/78, C, 78000581

Cox House, Bridge St., Morrilton, 10/22/74, C, 74000471

First National Bank of Morrilton [Thompson, Charles L., Design Collection TR], Main at Moose St., Morrilton, 12/22/82, C, 82000804

Grotto, Petit Jean No. 8 [Rock Art Sites in Arkansas TR], Address Restricted, Oppelo vicinity, 5/04/82, D, 82002100

Hardison Shelter, Petit Jean No. 3 [Rock Art Sites in Arkansas TR], Address Restricted, Oppelo vicinity, 5/04/82, D, 82002101

Indian Cave, Petit Jean No. 1 [Rock Art Sites in Arkansas TR], Address Restricted, Oppelo vicinity, 5/04/82, D, 82002102

Moose House, 711 Green St., Morrilton, 10/22/74, B, C, 74000472

Morrilton Male and Female College, E. Church St., Morrilton, 8/03/79, C, 79000436

Morrilton Railroad Station, Railroad Ave. between Division and Moose Sts., Morrilton, 9/13/77, C, 77000249

Petit Jean No. 10 [Rock Art Sites in Arkansas TR], Address Restricted, Oppelo vicinity, 5/04/82, D, 82002103

Petit Jean No. 11 [Rock Art Sites in Arkansas TR], Address Restricted, Oppelo vicinity, 5/04/82, D, 82002104

Petit Jean No. 4 [Rock Art Sites in Arkansas TR], Address Restricted, Oppelo vicinity, 5/04/82, D, 82002105

Petit Jean No. 5 [Rock Art Sites in Arkansas TR], Address Restricted, Oppelo vicinity, 5/04/82, D, 82002106

Petit Jean No. 6 [Rock Art Sites in Arkansas TR], Address Restricted, Oppelo vicinity, 5/04/82, D, 82002107

Petit Jean No. 7 [Rock Art Sites in Arkansas TR], Address Restricted, Oppelo vicinity, 5/04/82, D, 82002108

Petit Jean No. 9 [Rock Art Sites in Arkansas TR], Address Restricted, Oppelo vicinity, 5/04/82, D, 82002109

Petit Jean State Park—Administration Office [Facilities Constructed by the CCC in Arkansas MPS], AR 154 E of Bench Mark 914, Petit Jean State Park, Winrock vicinity, 5/28/92, A, C, 92000520

Petit Jean State Park—Blue Hole Road District [Facilities Constructed by the CCC in Arkansas MPS], Blue Hole Rd., Petit Jean State Park, Winrock vicinity, 5/28/92, A, C, 92000513

Petit Jean State Park—Cabin No. 16 [Facilities Constructed by the CCC in Arkansas MPS], Campground access rd., Petit Jean State Park, Winrock vicinity, 5/28/92, A, C, 92000522

Petit Jean State Park—Cabin No. 1 [Facilities Constructed by the CCC in Arkansas MPS], Campground access rd., Petit Jean State Park, Winrock vicinity, 5/28/92, A, C, 92000523

Petit Jean State Park—Cabin No. 6 [Facilities Constructed by the CCC in Arkansas MPS], Campground access rd., Petit Jean State Park, Winrock vicinity, 5/28/92, A, C, 92000524

Petit Jean State Park—Cabin No. 9 [Facilities Constructed by the CCC in Arkansas MPS], Campground access rd., Petit Jean State Park, Winrock vicinity, 5/28/92, A, C, 92000525

Conway County—Continued

Petit Jean State Park—Cedar Falls Trail Historic District [Facilities Constructed by the CCC in Arkansas MPS], Adjacent to main access rd., Petit Jean State Park, Winrock vicinity, 5/28/92, A, C, 92000514

Petit Jean State Park—Concrete Log Bridge [Facilities Constructed by the CCC in Arkansas MPS], AR 154 S of Bench Mark 914, Petit Jean State Park, Winrock vicinity, 5/28/92, A, C, 92000519

Petit Jean State Park—Culvert No. 1 [Facilities Constructed by the CCC in Arkansas MPS], AR 154, Petit Jean State Park, Winrock vicinity, 5/28/92, A, C, 92000518

Petit Jean State Park—Lake Bailey-Roosevelt Lake Historic District [Facilities Constructed by the CCC in Arkansas MPS], E and N of AR 154, Petit Jean State Park, Winrock vicinity, 5/28/92, A, C, 92000515

Petit Jean State Park—Mather Lodge [Facilities Constructed by the CCC in Arkansas MPS], Main access rd., Petit Jean State Park, Winrock vicinity, 5/28/92, A, C, 92000521

Petit Jean State Park—Office Headquarters [Facilities Constructed by the CCC in Arkansas MPS], AR 154, approximately 500 ft. S of Bench Mark 914, Petit Jean State Park, Winrock vicinity, 5/28/92, A, C, 92000516

Petit Jean State Park—Water Treatment Building [Facilities Constructed by the CCC in Arkansas MPS], On dirt access rd. S of jct. with AR 154, approximately 800 ft. E of Bench Mark 914, Petit Jean State Park, Winrock vicinity, 5/28/92, A, C, 92000517

Plumerville School Building [Public Schools in the Ozarks MPS], Arnold St., Plumerville, 9/10/92, A, a, 92001193

Plummer's Station, S of Plummerville on Gap Creek, Plummerville vicinity, 8/11/75, A, B, 75000378

Rockhouse Cave, Petit Jean No. 2 [Rock Art Sites in Arkansas TR], Address Restricted, Oppelo vicinity, 5/04/82, D, 82002110

Saint Anthony's Hospital, 202 E. Green St., Morrilton, 3/28/86, A, a, g, 86000581

Sims Hotel, Center of Plummerville, Plummerville, 8/28/75, A, C, 75000379

Trinity Lutheran Church, 7.2 mi. S of Atkins off AR 154, Atkins vicinity, 12/13/76, C, a, 76000396

Craighead County

Bay Mounds, Address Restricted, Bay vicinity, 2/14/78, D, 78000582

Bell House, 303 W. Cherry St., Jonesboro, 11/07/76, C, 76000398

Berger-Graham House, 1327 S. Main St., Jonesboro, 10/10/85, C, 85003006

Frierson House, 1112 S. Main St., Jonesboro, 4/24/73, A, B, C, 73000381

St. Francis River Bridge [Historic Bridges of Arkansas MPS], AR 18, over the St. Francis River, Lake City, 4/09/90, A, C, 90000515

West Washington Avenue Historic District, 500-626 W Washington Ave., Jonesboro, 10/22/82, A, C, 82000805

Crawford County

Brown, Dr. Charles Fox, House, 420 Drennan St., Van Buren, 9/06/78, B, C, 78000583

Bryan House, 105 Fayetteville St., Van Buren, 1/09/78, B, C, 78000584

Burns, Bob, House, 821 Jefferson St., Van Buren, 4/30/76, B, 76000399

Cedarville School Building [Public Schools in the Ozarks MPS], Co. Rd. 523, Cedarville, 9/10/92, A, 92001217

Clarke—Harrell—Burson House, 603 Parkview, Van Buren, 5/14/91, B, C, D, 91000582

Drennen-Scott House, Drennen Reserve, N. 3rd St., Van Buren, 9/10/71, C, 71000123

Dunham, Joseph Starr, House, 418 Broadway, Van Buren, 5/03/76, B, C, 76000400

High Rock Petroglyph Shelter [Rock Art Sites in Arkansas TR], Address Restricted, Rudy vicinity, 5/04/82, D, 82002111

Lee Creek Bridge [Historic Bridges of Arkansas MPS], AR 220, over Lee Creek, Cove City vicinity, 4/09/90, A, C, 90000504

Lee Creek Bridge [Historic Bridges of Arkansas MPS], AR 59, over Lee Creek, Natural Dam, 4/06/90, A, C, 90000508

Mills, Henry Clay, House, 425 N. 15th St., Van Buren, 12/16/77, A, 77000250

Mount Olive United Methodist Church, Lafayette and Knox Sts., Van Buren, 7/30/76, A, C, a, 76000401

Mountainburg High School [Public Schools in the Ozarks MPS], AR 71, Mountainburg, 9/10/92, A, 92001216

Mulberry Home Economics Building [Public Schools in the Ozarks MPS], Church St., Mulberry, 9/10/92, A, 92001218

Van Buren Historic District, Main St., bounded by Cane Hill St. and the Arkansas River, Van Buren, 4/30/76, A, C, 76000402

Wilhauf House, 109 N. 3rd St., Van Buren, 8/27/74, C, 74000473

Yoes, Col. Jacob, Building, Front St., Chester, 6/05/75, A, C, 75000380

Crittenden County

Crittenden County Bank and Trust Company, Military Rd., Marion, 4/19/84, A, C, 84000662

Crittenden County Courthouse, 85 Jackson St., Marion, 8/03/77, C, 77000251

Dabbs Store, 1320 S. Avalon, West Memphis, 5/17/82, A, C, 82002112

Missouri Pacific Depot, Main and Commerce Sts., Earle, 3/06/86, A, C, 86000383

Cross County

Deadrick, Capt. Isaac N., House, NW of jct. of US 64 and AR 163, Levesque, 9/16/93, A, B, 93000964

Grace Episcopal Church, 614 E. Poplar St., Wynne, 3/05/92, C, a, 92000106

Missouri—Pacific Depot—Wynne [Historic Railroad Depots of Arkansas MPS], SW of jct. of N. Front St. and E. Hamilton Ave., Wynne, 6/11/92, A, C, 92000623

Parkin Indian Mound, Address Restricted, Parkin vicinity, 10/15/66, D, NHL, 66000200

Woman's Progressive Club, Rowena St. and Merriman Ave., Wynne, 3/27/90, A, C, 90000430

Dallas County

Amis House [Dallas County MRA], 2nd St., Fordyce, 10/28/83, C, 83003460

Atchley, Henry, House [Dallas County MRA], Off AR 8, Dalark, 10/28/83, C, 83003461

Bank of Carthage [Thompson, Charles L., Design Collection TR], AR 229, Carthage, 12/22/82, C, 82000806

Bird Kiln, 6 mi. SW of Leola off AR 9, Leola vicinity, 5/29/75, A, 75000381

Brazeale Homestead [Dallas County MRA], SE of AR 128, Pine Grove, 10/28/83, A, C, 83003463

Brewster House [Dallas County MRA], US 79, Fordyce, 10/28/83, C, 83003464

Butler-Matthews Homestead [Dallas County MRA], SW of Tulip off AR 9, Tulip vicinity, 10/28/83, A, C, 83003465

Charlotte Street Historic District [Dallas County MRA], Roughly bounded by Holmes, Charlotte, Broadway, and E. College Sts., Fordyce, 9/14/87, B, C, 87001348

Cotton Belt Railroad Depot—Fordyce [Historic Railroad Depots of Arkansas MPS], SW corner of Main and First Sts., Fordyce, 6/11/92, A, C, 92000608

Culbertson Kiln, E of Princeton on Stark Bland Rd., Princeton vicinity, 5/29/75, A, 75000382

Dallas County Courthouse [Dallas County MRA], 3rd and Oak Sts., Fordyce, 3/27/84, A, C, 84000677

Elliott House [Dallas County MRA], 309 Pine St., Fordyce, 3/27/84, C, 84000681

Fielder House [Dallas County MRA], US 79B, Fordyce, 10/28/83, B, C, 83003467

First Presbyterian Church [Dallas County MRA], AR 79B, Fordyce, 10/28/83, C, a, 83003468

First United Methodist Church [Dallas County MRA], E. 4th and Spring Sts., Fordyce, 10/28/83, C, a, 83003469

Fordyce Home Accident Ins. Co. [Thompson, Charles L., Design Collection TR], 300 Main, Fordyce, 12/22/82, C, 82000807

Garrison Place [Dallas County MRA], S of AR 48, Carthage vicinity, 10/28/83, C, 83003470

Goodgame, Capt., House [Dallas County MRA], AR 128, Holly Springs, 10/28/83, C, 83003471

Dallas County—Continued

Hampton Springs Cemetery (Black Section) [Dallas County MRA], Off AR 48, Carthage vicinity, 10/28/83, A, d, 83003473

Knight, Ed, House [Dallas County MRA], Off AR 128, Pine Grove, 10/28/83, C, 83003524

Koonce Building [Dallas County MRA], 3rd St., Fordyce, 10/28/83, C, 83003525

Mallett, George W., House [Dallas County MRA], Off AR 8, Princeton, 10/28/83, B, C, 83003526

Mt. Carmel Methodist Church [Dallas County MRA], AR 9, Jacinto, 10/28/83, C, a, 83003528

Mt. Zion Methodist Church [Dallas County MRA], NE of Carthage, Carthage vicinity, 10/28/83, C, a, 83003529

Old Fordyce Post Office [Dallas County MRA], E. 2nd St., Fordyce, 10/28/83, C, 83003530

Princeton Cemetery [Dallas County MRA], Off AR 9, Princeton vicinity, 3/27/84, A, d, 84000872

Princeton Methodist Church [Dallas County MRA], AR 9, Princeton, 10/28/83, C, a, 83003533

Rock Island Railway Depot [Dallas County MRA], 3rd St., Fordyce, 10/28/83, A, 83003534

Russell, John, House [Dallas County MRA], 904 Charlotte St., Fordyce, 10/28/83, C, 83003535

Sardis Methodist Church [Dallas County MRA], NE of Pine Grove off AR 128, Sparkman, 10/28/83, C, a, 83003540

Smith, Jessie B., House [Dallas County MRA], Off US 79, Fordyce, 10/28/83, C, 83003541

Thomas Homestead [Dallas County MRA], Off AR 7, Fairview, 3/27/84, A, C, 84000895

Tulip Cemetery [Dallas County MRA], Off AR 9, Tulip, 10/28/83, A, d, 83003543

Waters House [Thompson, Charles L., Design Collection TR], 515 Oak St., Fordyce, 12/22/82, C, 82000808

Welch Pottery Works, Address Restricted, Tulip vicinity, 5/12/75, A, 75000383

Wommack Kiln, SE of Wave on Wave Rd., Wave vicinity, 6/10/75, A, 75000384

Wynne House [Dallas County MRA], 4th St., Fordyce, 10/28/83, C, 83003544

Desha County

Arkansas City High School, Robert S. Moore and President Sts., Arkansas City, 10/04/84, C, 84000005

Desha County Courthouse, Robert S. Moore Ave., Arkansas City, 7/12/76, A, C, 76000403

McKennon—Shea House, 206 Waterman St., Dumas, 6/08/93, B, 93000485

Merchants & Farmers Bank [Thompson, Charles L., Design Collection TR], Waterman and Main Sts., Dumas, 12/22/82, C, 82000809

Missouri—Pacific Railroad Depot—McGehee [Historic Railroad Depots of Arkansas MPS], Railroad St., McGehee, 6/11/92, A, C, 92000616

Parnell—Sharpe House, 302 N. Second St., McGehee, 9/28/89, C, 89001594

Rohwer Relocation Center Memorial Cemetery, AR 1, Rohwer vicinity, 7/06/92, A, d, NHL, 92001882

Rohwer Relocation Center Site, AR 1, Rohwer, 7/30/74, A, g, 74000474

Thane House [Thompson, Charles L., Design Collection TR], Levy and First Sts., Arkansas City, 12/22/82, C, 82000810

Drew County

Cavaness, Garvin, House, 404 S. Main St., Monticello, 5/23/80, C, 80000775

Grubbs, Champ, House, AR 172 W of New Hope, New Hope vicinity, 11/20/92, C, 92001619

Hardy, Robert Lee, House, 207 S. Main St., Monticello, 4/26/82, C, 82002113

Hotchkiss House, 509 N. Boyd St., Monticello, 12/12/76, C, 76000404

Lambert House, 204 W. Jackson St., Monticello, 12/22/83, C, 83003545

Monticello North Main Street Historic District, Irregular pattern along Westwood Ave. and N. Main St., Monticello, 2/18/79, C, a, 79000437

Selma Methodist Church, N of AR 4 in town of Selma, Selma, 9/22/72, A, C, a, 72000202

Veasey—DeArmond House, AR 81, 15 mi. N of Monticello, Lacey vicinity, 9/14/89, C, 89001424

Faulkner County

Blessing Farmstead, N of Enola, Barney vicinity, 9/05/90, C, D, 90001369

Brown House [Thompson, Charles L., Design Collection TR], 1604 Caldwell St., Conway, 12/22/82, C, 82000811

Cadron Settlement, Address Restricted, Conway vicinity, 5/17/74, A, D, 74000475

Farmers State Bank [Thompson, Charles L., Design Collection TR], 1001 Front St., Conway, 12/22/82, C, 82000812

Faulkner County Jail, Courthouse Sq., Conway, 7/20/78, A, C, 78000585

First Baptist Church [Thompson, Charles L., Design Collection TR], Davis and Robinson Sts., Conway, 12/22/82, C, a, 82000813

First United Methodist Church, Jct. of Prince and Clifton Sts., NW corner, Conway, 11/20/92, C, a, 92001623

Frauenthal & Schwarz Building, 824 Front St., Conway, 10/23/92, C, 92000956

Fraunthal House [Thompson, Charles L., Design Collection TR], 631 Western, Conway, 12/22/82, C, 82000814

Galloway Hall [Thompson, Charles L., Design Collection TR], Hendrix College campus, Conway, 12/22/82, C, 82000953

Guy High School Gymnasium [Public Schools in the Ozarks MPS], AR 25, Guy, 9/10/92, A, 92001196

Guy Home Economics Building [Public Schools in the Ozarks MPS], AR 25, Guy, 9/10/92, A, 92001197

Halter, Frank U., House, 1355 College Ave., Conway, 8/29/80, C, 80000776

Harton House, 1821 Robinson Ave., Conway, 5/25/79, B, C, 79000438

Liberty School Cafeteria [Public Schools in the Ozarks MPS], AR 36 N of jct. with US 64, Hamlet, 9/10/92, A, 92001195

Martin Hall [Thompson, Charles L., Design Collection TR], Hendrix College campus, Conway, 12/22/82, C, 82000815

Patton House, AR 25, Wooster, 9/30/93, C, 93001026

President's House [Thompson, Charles L., Design Collection TR], Hendrix College campus, Conway, 12/22/82, C, 82000816

Smith, S. G., House [Thompson, Charles L., Design Collection TR], 1837 Caldwell St., Conway, 12/22/82, C, 82000853

Springfield Bridge, CR 222 at Cadron Creek, Springfield vicinity, 7/21/88, A, C, 88000660

Franklin County

Center Cross School [Public Schools in the Ozarks MPS], Co. Rd. 95, W of Altus, Altus vicinity, 10/08/92, A, a, 92001351

First Methodist Episcopal Church, South, 503 W. Commercial St., Ozark, 9/04/92, C, a, 92001154

Franklin County Courthouse, Southern District, AR 22, Charleston, 10/18/76, A, C, 76000407

Franklin County Jail, 3rd and River Sts., Ozark, 6/23/82, C, 82002114

German—American Bank, Jct. of Franklin and Main Sts., Altus, 9/13/90, C, 90001448

Missouri—Pacific Depot—Altus [Historic Railroad Depots of Arkansas MPS], AR 64, Altus, 7/08/92, A, 92000597

Missouri—Pacific Depot—Ozark [Historic Railroad Depots of Arkansas MPS], S of jct. of River and First Sts., Ozark, 6/11/92, A, C, 92000598

O'Kane—Jacobs House, Rossville Rd., Altus, 5/14/91, C, 91000585

Our Lady of Perpetual Help Church, N of Altus, Altus vicinity, 5/03/76, A, C, a, 76000406

The Cabins, W of Ozark on AR 219, Ozark vicinity, 4/13/77, A, C, 77000253

Wiederkehr Wine Cellar, N of Altus at St. Mary's Mountain, Altus vicinity, 5/02/77, A, C, 77000252

Fulton County

County Line School and Lodge, NW of Gepp on E side of Baxter-Fulton county line, 2 mi. S of state line, Gepp vicinity, 3/27/75, A, a, 75000386

Kansas City, Fort Scott and Memphis Railroad Depot [Historic Railroad Depots of Arkansas MPS], SE of Burlington Northern RR tracks on Mammoth Spring State Park access road, Mammoth Spring, 6/11/92, A, C, 92000617

Morris, T. H., House, Jct. of 6th and Bethel Sts., Mammoth Springs, 9/13/90, C, 90001462

Saint Andrews's Episcopal Church, AR 9, Mammoth Spring, 11/26/86, C, a, b, 86002944

Garland County

Bathhouse Row, Central Ave. between Reserve and Fountain Sts., in Hot Springs National Park, Hot Springs, 11/13/74, A, C, NHL, NPS, 74000275

Belding—Gaines Cemetery, US 270, Hot Springs vicinity, 2/25/93, B, 93000089

Brown, W. C., House, 2330 Central Ave., Hot Springs, 10/16/86, B, C, 86002862

Camp Clearfork Historic District [Facilities Constructed by the CCC in Arkansas MPS], S of US 270, W of Crystal Springs, Ouachita NF, Crystal Springs vicinity, 10/21/93, A, C, 93001079

Carpenter Dam, 1398 Carpenter Dam Rd., Hot Springs vicinity, 9/04/92, A, 92001083

Charlton Bathhouse [Facilities Constructed by the CCC in Arkansas MPS], N of US 270, W of Crystal Springs, Ouachita NF, Crystal Springs vicinity, 10/20/93, A, C, 93001080

Charlton Spillway—Dam [Facilities Constructed by the CCC in Arkansas MPS], N of US 270, W of Crystal Springs, Ouachita NF, Crystal Springs vicinity, 10/21/93, A, C, 93001081

Citizens Building, 723 Central Ave., Hot Springs, 8/09/79, A, C, 79000440

Couchwood [Arkansas Sculptures of Dionicio Rodriguez TR], Address Restricted, Shorewood Hills vicinity, 12/04/86, C, g, 86003582

Doherty House, 705 Malvern Ave., Hot Springs, 11/14/78, A, C, 78000587

First Presbyterian Church [Thompson, Charles L., Design Collection TR], 213 Whittington, Hot Springs, 12/22/82, C, a, 82000817

Fordyce House [Thompson, Charles L., Design Collection TR], 746 Park Ave., Hot Springs, 12/22/82, C, 82000818

Forest Service Headquarters Historic District [Facilities Constructed by the CCC in Arkansas MPS], S of jct. of Winona and Indiana Sts., Hot Springs, 10/20/93, A, 93001089

Garland County Courthouse, Ouachita and Hawthorne Aves, Hot Springs, 12/06/79, A, C, 79000441

Green, Harley E., House, N of Bear, Bear vicinity, 7/19/79, A, C, 79000439

Hot Springs Central Avenue Historic District, Central Ave., from Prospect to Park Sts., Hot Springs, 6/25/85, A, C, 85001370

Hot Springs High School, Oak St. between Orange and Olive Sts., Hot Springs, 1/28/88, C, 87002495

Interstate Orphanage [Thompson, Charles L., Design Collection TR], 339 Combs, Hot Springs, 12/22/82, C, 82000832

Iron Springs Dam [Facilities Constructed by the CCC in Arkansas MPS], AR 7 N of Jessieville, Ouachita NF, Jessieville vicinity, 10/21/93, A, C, 93001090

Iron Springs Shelter No. 1 [Facilities Constructed by the CCC in Arkansas MPS], AR 7 N of Jessieville, Ouachita NF, Jessieville vicinity, 10/20/93, A, C, 93001091

Iron Springs Shelter No. 2 [Facilities Constructed by the CCC in Arkansas MPS], AR 7 N of Jessie-

ville, Ouachita NF, Jessieville vicinity, 10/20/93, A, C, 93001092

Jones School, Linwood and Hobson Aves., Hot Springs, 5/05/88, C, 88000517

Klein, George, Tourist Court Historic District, 501 Morrison St., Hot Springs, 6/08/93, C, 93000480

Little Switzerland [Arkansas Sculptures of Dionicio Rodriguez TR], Address Restricted, Shorewood Hills vicinity, 12/04/86, C, g, 86003584

Martin, William H., House, 815 Quapaw Ave., Hot Springs, 6/11/86, C, 86001320

Mayberry Springs, US 270, Crystal Springs vicinity, 9/05/90, C, D, 90001379

Medical Arts Building, 236 Central Ave., Hot Springs, 11/30/78, C, g, 78000588

Missouri—Pacific Railroad Depot—Hot Springs [Historic Railroad Depots of Arkansas MPS], Jct. of Broadway and Market St., Hot Springs, 6/11/92, A, C, 92000611

Moore, W. H., House, 906 Malvern St., Hot Springs, 3/27/90, C, 90000429

Old Post Office, Convention Blvd., Hot Springs, 4/12/90, C, 90000547

Park Hotel [Thompson, Charles L., Design Collection TR], 210 Fountain, Hot Springs, 12/22/82, C, 82000819

Passmore House, 846 Park Ave., Hot Springs, 10/08/76, A, C, 76000408

Rivera Hotel [Thompson, Charles L., Design Collection TR], 719 Central, Hot Springs, 12/22/82, C, 82000820

Rix, Charles N., House, 628 Quapaw Ave., Hot Springs, 10/15/92, B, 92001393

Short-Dodson House, 755 Park Ave., Hot Springs, 5/03/76, C, 76000409

South Fork Bridge [Historic Bridges of Arkansas MPS], Off AR 128, over South Fork, Fountain Lake vicinity, 4/09/90, A, C, 90000521

St. Luke's Episcopal Church [Thompson, Charles L., Design Collection TR], Spring and Cottage Sts., Hot Springs, 12/22/82, C, a, 82000821

Stitt House, 824 Park Ave., Hot Springs, 5/03/76, B, C, 76000410

Wade Building [Thompson, Charles L., Design Collection TR], 231 Central, Hot Springs, 12/22/82, C, 82000822

Wildwood, 808 Park Ave., Hot Springs, 10/08/76, B, C, 76000411

Williams-Wootton House, 420 Quapaw Ave., Hot Springs, 11/30/78, B, C, 78000589

Grant County

Butler, Dr. John L., House, 313 Oak St., Sheridan, 10/09/86, B, C, 86002848

Jenkins' Ferry Battleground, NE of Leola on AR 46, Leola vicinity, 1/21/70, A, 70000120

Oak Grove School, US 270, 6 mi. E of Sheridan, Oak Grove Community, 6/14/91, C, a, 91000693

Greene County

Crowley's Ridge State Park—Dining Hall [Facilities Constructed by the CCC in Arkansas MPS],

Employee housing area access rd., Crowley's Ridge State Park, Walcott vicinity, 5/28/92, A, C, 92000536

Crowley's Ridge State Park—Bathhouse [Facilities Constructed by the CCC in Arkansas MPS], Main service center area access rd., Crowley's Ridge State Park, Walcott vicinity, 5/28/92, A, C, 92000537

Crowley's Ridge State Park—Comfort Station [Facilities Constructed by the CCC in Arkansas MPS], Campground and cabin area access rd., Crowley's Ridge State Park, Walcott vicinity, 5/28/92, A, C, 92000538

Crowley's Ridge State Park—Bridge [Facilities Constructed by the CCC in Arkansas MPS], Main service center area access rd., Crowley's Ridge State Park, Walcott vicinity, 5/28/92, A, C, 92000540

Eight Mile Creek Bridge [Historic Bridges of Arkansas MPS], AR 135, over Eight Mile Creek, Paragould, 4/06/90, A, C, 90000524

Greene County Courthouse, Courtsquare, Paragould, 8/11/76, A, C, 76000412

Jackson—Herget House, 206 S. 4th St., Paragould, 7/24/92, B, C, 92000907

National Bank of Commerce Building, 200 S. Pruett St., Paragould, 5/14/93, C, 93000423

Old Bethel Methodist Church, W of Paragould off AR 141, Paragould vicinity, 4/19/78, A, C, a, 78000590

Hempstead County

Brundidge Building, W. Second St., Hope, 3/27/90, C, 90000431

Carrigan House, 704 W. Avenue B, Hope, 7/20/78, B, C, 78000591

Columbus Presbyterian Church, AR 73, Columbus, 11/17/82, C, a, 82000823

Confederate State Capitol, Main St., Washington, 5/19/72, A, C, 72000203

Ethridge House, 511 N. Main St., Hope, 12/01/93, B, 93001259

Foster House [Thompson, Charles L., Design Collection TR], 303 N. Hervey St., Hope, 12/22/82, C, 82000825

Foster House, 420 S. Spruce St., Hope, 6/05/91, C, 91000683

Goodlett Gin, 3 mi. W of Ozan on AR 4, Ozan vicinity, 1/17/75, A, C, 75000387

Greening, E. S., House, 707 E. Division St., Hope, 7/09/87, C, 87001147

Jacques, Dr. Thomas S., House, NW of McCaskill, McCaskill vicinity, 11/03/89, C, b, 89001940

McRae House [Thompson, Charles L., Design Collection TR], 1113 E. 3rd St., Hope, 12/22/82, C, 82000826

McRae, K. G., House, 3rd and Edgewood Sts., Hope, 5/04/76, B, C, 76000413

Missouri—Pacific Railroad Depot—Hope [Historic Railroad Depots of Arkansas MPS], N of jct. of E. Division and Main Sts., Hope, 6/11/92, A, C, 92000610

Hempstead County—Continued

Ozan Methodist Church, Mulberry St., Ozan, 11/04/82, C, a, 82000827

Royston, Grandison D., House, Alexander St., SW of Columbus St., Washington, 6/21/71, B, C, 71000124

St. Mark's Episcopal Church, 3rd and Elm Sts., Hope, 5/06/76, A, C, a, 76000414

Ward—Jackson House, 122 N. Louisiana, Hope, 9/14/89, C, 89001421

Washington Historic District, Boundaries correspond to original 1824 plat of city, Washington, 6/20/72, A, C, a, b, 72000204

Hot Spring County

Bank of Malvern, 212 S. Main St., Malvern, 3/13/87, A, C, 87000425

Blakely House, W of Social Hill on AR 84, Social Hill vicinity, 5/03/76, A, C, 76002142

Clark House [Thompson, Charles L., Design Collection TR], 1324 S. Main St., Malvern, 12/22/82, C, 82000828

Gatewood House, 235 Pine Bluff St., Malvern, 7/24/92, C, 92000928

Jones Mill Site (3HS28), Address Restricted, Jones Mill vicinity, 9/12/88, D, 87001385

Lake Catherine Quarry, Address Restricted, Malvern vicinity, 9/11/75, D, 75000388

Lake Catherine State Park—Cabin No. 2 [Facilities Constructed by the CCC in Arkansas MPS], Cabin area access rd., Lake Catherine State Park, Shorewood Hills vicinity, 5/28/92, A, C, 92000526

Lake Catherine State Park—Cabin No. 3 [Facilities Constructed by the CCC in Arkansas MPS], Cabin area access rd., Lake Catherine State Park, Shorewood Hills vicinity, 5/28/92, A, C, 92000527

Lake Catherine State Park—Bridge No. 2 [Facilities Constructed by the CCC in Arkansas MPS], AR 171 W of Slunger Cr., Lake Catherine State Park, Shorewood Hills vicinity, 5/28/92, A, C, 92000528

Lake Catherine State Park—Nature Cabin [Facilities Constructed by the CCC in Arkansas MPS], Camping area access rd., Lake Catherine State Park, Shorewood Hills vicinity, 5/28/92, A, C, 92000535

Missouri—Pacific Railroad Depot—Malvern [Historic Railroad Depots of Arkansas MPS], First St., Malvern, 6/11/92, A, C, 92000615

Morrison Plantation Smokehouse, Off I-30, Saginaw vicinity, 12/28/77, A, C, 77000254

Old Rockport Bridge, W of Rockport across Ouachita River, Rockport vicinity, 10/07/82, A, C, 82000829

Remmel Dam, Remmel Dam Rd., Jones Mill vicinity, 9/04/92, A, C, 92001084

Strauss House [Thompson, Charles L., Design Collection TR], 528 E. Page St., Malvern, 12/22/82, C, 82000830

Howard County

Boyd, Adam, House, E of Center Point on AR 26, Center Point vicinity, 5/13/76, A, C, 76000415

Clardy-Lee House, AR 26, Center Point, 11/10/77, C, 77000255

DeQueen and Eastern Railroad Depot—Dierks [Historic Railroad Depots of Arkansas MPS], E of Herman Ave., Dierks, 6/11/92, A, C, 92000607

Ebenezer Campground, N of Center Point off AR 4, Center Point vicinity, 3/26/76, A, a, 76000416

First Christian Church, N. Main St., Nashville, 11/04/82, C, a, 82000831

First Presbyterian Church, 2nd and Hempstead Sts., Nashville, 5/04/76, C, a, 76000418

Holt, Elbert W., House, 902 N. Main St., Nashville, 9/20/84, C, 84000901

Holt, Flavius, House, Kohler St., Nashville, 12/01/78, A, C, 78000593

Howard County Courthouse, Jct. of N. Main St. and Bishop St., Nashville, 6/14/90, C, 90000902

Memphis, Paris, and Gulf Depot, AR 27, Mineral Springs, 12/04/78, A, C, 78000592

Missouri—Pacific Railroad Depot—Nashville [Historic Railroad Depots of Arkansas MPS], S of E. Hempstead St., between S. Front and S. Ansley Sts., Nashville, 6/11/92, A, C, 92000618

Nashville American Legion Building, AR 27 W of Main St., Nashville, 9/13/90, C, 90001463

Russey House, S of Center Point on AR 4, Center Point vicinity, 5/04/76, A, C, 76000417

Womack-Parker House, Off AR 4, Nashville, 12/01/78, A, C, 78000594

Independence County

Adler House [Thompson, Charles L., Design Collection TR], 292 Boswell St., Batesville, 12/22/82, C, 82000833

Batesville Commercial Historic District, Main and Central Sts., Batesville, 10/07/82, A, C, 82000834

Batesville Commercial Historic District (Boundary Increase), Main St. from N of Central to 1 block N of Church, Batesville, 10/05/90, A, C, 90001097

Batesville East Main Historic District, Main St. between 7th and 11th Sts., Batesville, 12/22/83, A, C, 83003546

Bethel African Methodist Episcopal Church, 895 Oak St., Batesville, 10/16/86, A, a, 86002875

Cook-Morrow House, 875 Main St., Batesville, 7/29/77, C, 77000256

Dearing House, AR 122, Newark, 5/03/76, A, C, 76000419

Desha, Franklin, House, Address Restricted, Desha, 10/09/86, A, B, 86002844

Dickinson, Edward, House, 672 E. Boswell St., Batesville, 11/26/86, C, 86002907

Dondy Building [Thompson, Charles L., Design Collection TR], 154 S. Third, Batesville, 12/22/82, C, 82000824

Garrott House, 561 E. Main St., Batesville, 6/24/71, C, 71000125

Glenn House, 653 Water St., Batesville, 5/02/75, A, C, 75000389

Goff Petroglyph Site [Rock Art Sites in Arkansas TR], Address Restricted, Salado vicinity, 5/04/82, D, 82002117

Handford, Charles R., House, 658 E. Boswell St., Batesville, 5/02/75, B, C, 75000390

Handford, James S., House, 659 E. Boswell St., Batesville, 5/02/75, B, C, 75000391

Jamestown School [Public Schools in the Ozarks MPS], N of AR 230, Jamestown, 9/04/92, A, 92001106

Locust Grove School [Public Schools in the Ozarks MPS], AR 230 S of jct. with AR 25, Locust Grove, 9/04/92, A, 92001107

Luster Urban Farmstead, 487 N. Central Ave., Batesville, 9/16/83, A, C, 83001158

Mitchell House [Thompson, Charles L., Design Collection TR], 1138 Main St., Batesville, 12/22/82, C, 82000835

Moorefield School [Public Schools in the Ozarks MPS], N side of Ham St., Moorefield, 9/04/92, A, a, 92001109

Morrow Hall, 7th and Boswell Sts., Batesville, 10/18/72, A, C, a, 72000205

Pfeiffer House, US 167, Pfeiffer, 5/01/89, C, 89000172

Spring Mill, NW of Batesville on AR 69, Batesville vicinity, 3/01/74, A, C, 74000477

St. Paul's Parish Church [Thompson, Charles L., Design Collection TR], 5th and Main, Batesville, 12/22/82, C, a, 82000836

Thida Grove School [Public Schools in the Ozarks MPS], Co. Rd. 20, Thida, 9/04/92, A, 92001108

Warner, Capt. John T., House, 822 E. College St., Batesville, 9/02/82, B, 82002115

Wheel Store, The, River and Broad Sts., Batesville, 12/08/88, A, 88002822

Wyatt Petroglyphs [Rock Art Sites in Arkansas TR], Address Restricted, Desha vicinity, 5/04/82, D, 82002116

Wycough-Jones House, 683 Water St., Batesville, 5/02/75, A, C, 75000393

Izard County

Boswell School [Public Schools in the Ozarks MPS], End of Co. Rd. 196, Boswell, 9/18/92, C, a, 92001178

Calico Rock Historic District, Roughly bounded by Main, Rodman, and Walnut Sts., and Peppersauce Alley, Calico Rock, 11/19/85, A, C, 85003499

Calico Rock Historic District (Boundary Increase), W side of Rodman St. at Missouri-Pacific Railroad tracks, Calico Rock, 10/26/89, A, C, 88002827

Calico Rock Home Economics Building [Public Schools in the Ozarks MPS], 2nd St., Calico Rock, 9/10/92, A, 92001200

Izard County Courthouse, AR 69 (Courthouse Square), Melbourne, 9/30/93, A, C, 93001025

Izard County—Continued

Melbourne Home Economics Building [Public Schools in the Ozarks MPS], School Dr., Melbourne, 9/10/92, A, 92001201

Philadelphia Methodist Church, N of Melbourne, Melbourne vicinity, 9/29/76, A, C, a, 76000420

Rector Log Barn, Co. Rd. 218, 1.23 mi. NW of jct. with AR 9, Melbourne vicinity, 6/03/93, C, 93000488

Smith, Sylvester, Farmstead, S of Co. Rd. 10, approximately 3/4 mi. NE of jct. with Co. Rd. 13, Boswell vicinity, 9/08/92, B, C, 92001222

Jackson County

Arkansas Bank & Trust Company, 103 Walnut St., Newport, 10/16/86, A, C, 86002859

Empie-Van Dyke House, 403 Laurel, Newport, 12/28/77, C, 77000257

First Presbyterian Church [Thompson, Charles L., Design Collection TR], 4th and Main Sts., Newport, 12/22/82, C, 82000837

Gregg House [Thompson, Charles L., Design Collection TR], 412 Pine St., Newport, 12/22/82, C, 82000838

Hickory Grove Church and School, N of Jacksonport, Jacksonport vicinity, 5/23/78, A, a, 78000595

Jackson County Courthouse, U.S. 67, Newport, 11/18/76, C, 76000421

Jackson County Jail, 503 3rd St., Newport, 8/10/79, A, C, 79003432

Jacksonport State Park, Between Dillard St. and the White River, Jacksonport, 1/21/70, D, 70000121

Missouri—Pacific Depot—Newport [Historic Railroad Depots of Arkansas MPS], NW of jct. of Walnut and Front Sts., Newport, 6/11/92, A, C, 92000619

New Home School Building, Co. Rd. 69, NW of Swifton, Swifton vicinity, 10/08/92, C, 92001357

Newport American Legion Community Hut, Remmel Park, N of Remmel Ave., Newport, 12/10/92, A, C, 92001672

Newport Bridge [Historic Bridges of Arkansas MPS], US 67, over the White River, Newport, 4/09/90, A, C, 90000503

Newport Junior & Senior High School [Thompson, Charles L., Design Collection TR], Remmel Park, Newport, 12/22/82, C, 82000839

Rock Island Depot—Weldon [Historic Railroad Depots of Arkansas MPS], AR 17, Weldon, 6/11/92, A, 92000621

Jefferson County

Austin House [Thompson, Charles L., Design Collection TR], 704 W. 5th Ave., Pine Bluff, 12/22/82, C, 82000842

Boone-Murphy House, 714 W. 4th Ave., Pine Bluff, 2/18/79, A, B, C, b, 79000442

Caldwell Hall [Thompson, Charles L., Design Collection TR], University Drive, Pine Bluff, 12/22/82, C, 82000843

Collier House [Thompson, Charles L., Design Collection TR], 1227 W. 5th St., Pine Bluff, 12/22/82, C, 82000844

Dilley House, 656 Laurel St., Pine Bluff, 8/03/77, B, C, 77000258

Dollarway Road, S of Redfield off U.S. 65, Redfield vicinity, 5/17/74, A, C, 74000480

Du Bocage, 1115 W. 4th St., Pine Bluff, 6/24/74, C, 74000478

Elms, The, S of Altheimer, Altheimer vicinity, 7/07/78, C, 78000596

Ferguson House, 902 E. 4th Ave., Pine Bluff, 1/18/78, A, C, 78000598

Fox House [Thompson, Charles L., Design Collection TR], 1303 S. Olive St., Pine Bluff, 12/22/82, C, 82000845

Gibson—Burnham House, 1326 Cherry St., Pine Bluff, 6/05/91, C, 91000694

Gracie House [Thompson, Charles L., Design Collection TR], Off AR 88, New Gascony, 12/22/82, C, 82000846

Hospital and Benevolent Ass'n [Thompson, Charles L., Design Collection TR], 11th and Cherry, Pine Bluff, 12/22/82, C, 82000841

Hotel Pines, Main St. and W. 5th Ave., Pine Bluff, 8/10/79, A, C, 79000443

Howson House [Thompson, Charles L., Design Collection TR], 1700 S. Olive St., Pine Bluff, 12/22/82, C, 82000847

Hudson House [Thompson, Charles L., Design Collection TR], 304 W. 5th St., Pine Bluff, 12/22/82, C, 82000848

Hudson-Grace-Borreson House, 716 W. Barraque, Pine Bluff, 6/24/71, C, 71000126

Johnson House [Thompson, Charles L., Design Collection TR], 315 Martin St., Pine Bluff, 12/22/82, C, 82000849

Katzenstein House [Thompson, Charles L., Design Collection TR], 902 W. 5th St., Pine Bluff, 12/22/82, C, 82000850

Knox, R. M., House, 1504 W. 6th St., Pine Bluff, 6/05/75, B, C, 75000395

Lake Dick, 4 mi. S of Altheimer off AR 88, Altheimer vicinity, 7/03/75, A, g, 75000394

Lee, R. E., House, 1302 W. 2nd Ave., Pine Bluff, 6/08/82, C, 82002118

MacMillan-Dilley House, 407 Martin Ave., Pine Bluff, 12/12/76, C, 76000422

Masonic Temple, 4th and State St., Pine Bluff, 11/30/78, A, C, 78000599

Merchants and Planters Bank Building, 100 Main St., Pine Bluff, 8/01/78, C, 78000600

Nichol House [Thompson, Charles L., Design Collection TR], 205 Park Pl., Pine Bluff, 11/12/93, C, 93001201

Parkview Apartments, 300 W. 13th Ave., Pine Bluff, 5/01/89, A, B, C, 89000335

Pine Bluff Fifth Avenue Historic District, 5th Ave., Pine Bluff, 10/29/80, A, C, 80000777

Plum Bayou Homesteads, N of Pine Bluff, E of Arkansas River, includes town of Wright and environs, Pine Bluff vicinity, 6/05/75, A, g, 75000396

Prigmore House, 1104 W. Fifth Ave., Pine Bluff, 4/10/86, C, 86000720

Puddephatt House [Thompson, Charles L., Design Collection TR], 1820 S. Olive St., Pine Bluff, 12/22/82, C, 82000851

Roselawn, SW of Altheimer off AR 88, Altheimer vicinity, 5/23/78, C, 78000597

Roth-Rosenzweig House, 717 W. 2nd Ave., Pine Bluff, 12/12/76, C, 76000423

Russell House [Thompson, Charles L., Design Collection TR], 1617 S. Olive St., Pine Bluff, 12/22/82, C, 82000852

Sorrells, Walter B., Cottage, Off AR 104, Pine Bluff, 8/04/86, A, C, 86002276

Temple House [Thompson, Charles L., Design Collection TR], 1702 S. Oak St., Pine Bluff, 12/22/82, C, 82000840

Trinity Episcopal Church, 3rd and Oak Sts., Pine Bluff, 7/30/74, A, C, a, 74000479

Trulock-Cook House, 703 W. 2nd Ave., Pine Bluff, 2/21/79, B, C, 79000444

Trulock-Gould-Mullis House, 704 W. Barraque St., Pine Bluff, 1/03/78, C, 78003199

Union Station, E. 4th Ave. and State St., Pine Bluff, 12/14/78, A, 78000601

Yauch-Ragar House, 625 State St., Pine Bluff, 1/20/78, B, C, 78000602

Johnson County

Big Piney Creek Bridge [Historic Bridges of Arkansas MPS], AR 123, over Big Piney Creek, Hagersville vicinity, 4/09/90, A, C, 90000506

Clarksville High School Building No. 1 [Public Schools in the Ozarks MPS], Main St., Clarksville, 9/10/92, A, 92001202

Davis House [Thompson, Charles L., Design Collection TR], 212 Fulton St., Clarksville, 12/22/82, C, 82000854

Dunlap House [Thompson, Charles L., Design Collection TR], 101 Grandview, Clarksville, 12/22/82, C, 82000855

First Presbyterian Church, 212 College Ave., Clarksville, 5/13/91, C, a, 91000588

Johnson County Courthouse, Jct. of Main and Fulton Sts., Clarksville, 6/14/91, C, 91000680

King's Canyon Petroglyphs [Rock Art Sites in Arkansas TR], Address Restricted, Clarksville vicinity, 5/04/82, D, 82002119

McKennon House [Thompson, Charles L., Design Collection TR], 115 Grandview, Clarksville, 12/22/82, C, 82000856

McKennon, Capt. Archibald S., House, 215 N. Central, Clarksville, 1/02/76, B, C, 76000424

Missouri—Pacific Depot—Clarksville [Historic Railroad Depots of Arkansas MPS], W of College St. between Cherry and Main Sts., Clarksville, 6/11/92, A, C, 92000604

Munger, Raymond, Memorial Chapel—University of the Ozarks, W of AR 103, University of the Ozarks campus, Clarksville, 6/08/93, C, a, 93000489

Science Hall, University of the Ozarks, University of the Ozarks campus, W of AR 103, Clarksville, 1/21/93, C, 92001830

Johnson County—Continued

Serpent Cave [Rock Art Sites in Arkansas TR], Address Restricted, Clarksville vicinity, 5/04/82, D, 82002120

Lafayette County

Conway Cemetery, W of Bradley, Bradley vicinity, 11/23/77, B, c, 77000259

King-Whatley Building, 2nd and Maple Sts., Lewisville, 3/30/78, A, C, 78000603

Lafayette County Courthouse, Bounded by Third, Spruce, Fourth and Maple Sts., Lewisville, 2/25/93, C, 93000085

Lawrence County

Cache River Bridge [Historic Bridges of Arkansas MPS], AR 25, over the Cache River, Walnut Ridge vicinity, 4/09/90, A, C, 90000523

Clover Bend High School, AR 228, Clover Bend, 8/17/83, A, 83001159

Clover Bend Historic District, Jct. of AR 228 and Co. Rd. 1220, Clover Bend, 9/17/90, A, C, 90001368

Ficklin—Imboden House [Powhatan MPS], Third and Main Sts., Powhatan, 10/16/89, A, C, 88003206

French, Alice, House, AR 28, Clover Bend vicinity, 1/11/76, B, b, 76000425

Hatcher, Dr. John Octavius, House, 210 Third St., Imboden, 10/23/92, C, 92001358

Home Economics—F. F. A. Building, City Park Dr., Portia, 6/14/90, A, C, 90000901

Missouri—Pacific Depot—Walnut Ridge [Historic Railroad Depots of Arkansas MPS], SW. 1st St., Walnut Ridge, 6/11/92, A, C, 92000622

Portia School, City Park, Portia, 12/13/78, C, 78000604

Powhatan Courthouse, Address unknown at this time, Powhatan, 2/16/70, C, 70000122

Powhatan Jail [Powhatan MPS], SR 25, Powhatan, 10/16/89, C, 88003205

Powhatan Methodist Church, AR 25, Powhatan, 11/23/77, A, a, 77000260

Powhatan Schoolhouse, AR 25, Powhatan, 7/31/78, A, 78000605

Smithville Public School Building [Public Schools in the Ozarks MPS], AR 117, Smithville, 1/14/93, A, 92001219

St. Louis—San Francisco Overpass [Historic Bridges of Arkansas MPS], US 62, over the Spring River, Imboden, 4/09/90, A, C, 90000513

Telephone Exchange Building [Powhatan MPS], First and Main Sts., Powhatan, 10/16/89, A, C, 88003207

Lee County

Elks Club, 67 W. Main St., Marianna, 7/27/79, A, C, 79000445

Louisiana Purchase Survey Marker, SE of Blackton at corner of Monroe and Phillips counties, Blackton vicinity, 2/23/72, A, NHL, 72000206

McClintock House, 82 W. Main St., Marianna, 12/28/77, C, 77000261

McClintock House [Thompson, Charles L., Design Collection TR], 43 Magnolia, Marianna, 12/22/82, C, 82000857

Lincoln County

Crow House, 7 mi. SE of Star City, Star City vicinity, 6/29/76, A, C, 76000426

Crow, Oscar, House, 404 Washington St., Star City, 10/08/92, C, 92001343

Mt. Zion Presbyterian Church, AR 81, Relfs Bluff, 1/21/88, C, a, 87002496

Little River County

Cowling, Judge Jefferson Thomas, House, 611 Willow St., Ashdown, 12/08/88, B, C, 88002823

Little River County Courthouse, Main and 2nd Sts., Ashdown, 9/29/76, C, 76000427

Reed, Will, Farm House, Main St., Alleene, 7/14/78, C, 78000606

Logan County

Anhalt Barn, Co. Rd. 68, New Blaine vicinity, 2/25/93, C, 93000087

Bank of Booneville Building, 1 W. Main St., Booneville, 4/26/78, A, C, 78000608

Chicago, Rock Island, and Pacific Railroad Depot, Off AR 10, Blue Mountain, 2/14/78, C, b, 78000607

Elizabeth Hall, Off AR 22, New Blaine, 5/04/76, A, C, 76000428

Farmers and Merchants Bank—Masonic Lodge, 288 N. Broadway, Booneville, 11/19/93, C, 93001257

Gill, Tolbert E., House, AR 22 W of jct. with AR 109, Paris, 9/30/93, C, 93001024

Jack Creek Bathhouse [Facilities Constructed by the CCC in Arkansas MPS], FS Rd. 141 SW of Sugar Grove, Ouachita NF, Sugar Grove vicinity, 10/21/93, A, C, 93001093

Logan County Courthouse, Eastern District, Courthouse Sq., Paris, 7/30/76, C, 76000429

Logan County Jail, Old, 204 N. Vine St., Paris, 11/19/93, C, 93001254

Magazine City Hall—Jail, NW of jct. of Garland and Priddy Sts., Magazine, 6/08/93, C, 93000483

New Blaine School, Jct. of AR 22 and Spring Rd., New Blaine vicinity, 8/18/92, C, 92001007

New Liberty School [Public Schools in the Ozarks MPS], S of AR 22, Liberty, 9/10/92, A, 92001220

Rock Island Railroad Depot—Booneville [Historic Railroad Depots of Arkansas MPS], S of First St. and W of Broadway, at the N end of

Rhyne Ave., Booneville, 6/11/92, A, C, 92000603

Saint Anthony's Catholic Church, N of AR 22, Ratcliff, 8/21/86, A, a, 86001885

Walker, Evelyn Gill, House, 18 S. Spruce St., Paris, 9/16/93, C, 93000985

Lonoke County

Ashley-Alexander House, N of Scott, Scott vicinity, 6/18/76, B, C, 76000431

Boyd, Thomas Sloan, House, 220 Park Ave., Lonoke, 1/01/76, A, C, 76000430

Carlisle Rock Island Depot, Jct. of Main St. and Court Ave., Carlisle, 6/14/90, A, C, 90000905

Dortch Plantation, NE of Scott off AR 130 at Bearskin Lake, Scott vicinity, 12/06/75, B, C, 75000397

Dortch Plantation (Boundary Increase), NE of Scott off AR 130 at Bearskin Lake, Scott vicinity, 3/21/79, A, C, g, 79003777

Eagle House [Thompson, Charles L., Design Collection TR], 217 Ash St., Lonoke, 12/22/82, C, 82000858

Fletcher, W. P., House, 604 W. Fourth St., Lonoke, 9/05/90, B, C, 90001373

Lonoke County Courthouse, N. Center St., Lonoke, 6/08/82, C, 82002121

Rock Island Depot, U.S. 70 and Center St., Lonoke, 10/04/84, A, C, 84000006

Sears House, SE of jct. of AR 38 and AR 319, Austin vicinity, 8/05/92, C, 92000952

Shull House [Thompson, Charles L., Design Collection TR], 418 Park, Lonoke, 12/22/82, C, 82000859

Toltec Mounds, Address Restricted, Scott vicinity, 1/12/73, D, NHL, 73000382

Trimble House [Thompson, Charles L., Design Collection TR], 518 Center St., Lonoke, 12/22/82, C, 82000860

Walls House [Thompson, Charles L., Design Collection TR], 406 Jefferson St., Lonoke, 12/22/82, C, 82000861

Wheat House [Thompson, Charles L., Design Collection TR], 600 Center St., Lonoke, 12/22/82, C, 82000862

Woodlawn School Building, NW of jct. of Bizzell Rd. and AR 31, Woodlawn, 2/25/93, C, 93000086

Madison County

Alabam School, S of Alabam at jct. of AR 68 and AR 127, Alabam vicinity, 7/14/76, A, a, 76000432

Bank of Kingston, 101 Public Sq., Kingston, 3/25/82, A, C, 82002122

Enterprise School [Public Schools in the Ozarks MPS], SE of jct. of Co. Rds. 8 and 192, Thorney vicinity, 9/10/92, A, 92001192

Madison County Courthouse, 1 Main St., Huntsville, 11/19/93, A, C, 93001253

Marion County

Aggie Hall [Public Schools in the Ozarks MPS], Co. Rd. 9, Bruno, 9/04/92, A, 92001115

Aggie Workshop [Public Schools in the Ozarks MPS], AR 235 Spur, Bruno, 9/04/92, A, 92001113

Bruno School Building [Public Schools in the Ozarks MPS], Co. Rd. 9, Bruno, 9/04/92, A, 92001112

Buffalo River State Park, Buffalo National River, Yellville vicinity, 10/20/88, C, NPS, 78003461

Carter—Jones House, 30 Carter St., Yellville, 7/21/87, C, 87000979

Cold Springs School [Public Schools in the Ozarks MPS], Cold Spring Hollow, just E of Buffalo R., Big Flat vicinity, 10/29/92, A, NPS, 92001494

Cowdrey House, 1 Valley St., Yellville, 7/20/78, B, C, 78000609

Eros School Building [Public Schools in the Ozarks MPS], Co. Rd. 9, Eros, 9/04/92, A, 92001110

Fairview School Building [Public Schools in the Ozarks MPS], Co. Rd. 203, Fairview, 9/04/92, A, 92001116

Hirst—Mathew Hall [Public Schools in the Ozarks MPS], AR 235 Spur, Bruno, 9/04/92, A, 92001114

Layton Building, 1110 Mill St., Yellville, 4/26/78, C, 78000610

Pea Ridge School Building, E of Co. Rd. 6, approximately 4 mi. S of Bruno, Bruno vicinity, 6/08/93, C, 93000486

Pyatt School Building [Public Schools in the Ozarks MPS], Co. Rd. 12, Pyatt, 9/04/92, A, 92001111

Rush Historic District, Rush Rd., Yellville vicinity, 2/27/87, A, C, D, NPS, 87000105

Sunburst Shelter [Rock Art Sites in Arkansas TR], Address Restricted, Summit vicinity, 5/04/82, D, 82002123

Miller County

Averitt House, US 71 W side, 6 mi. S of Texarkana, Mount Pleasant vicinity, 7/24/92, C, 92000958

Bottoms House, 500 Hickory, Texarkana, 6/08/82, C, 82002124

Canaan Baptist Church, Jct. of Laurel and 10th Sts., Texarkana, 6/14/90, C, a, 90000903

Dean House, 1520 Beech St., Texarkana, 12/12/76, B, C, 76000433

First Methodist Church [Thompson, Charles L., Design Collection TR], 400 E. 6th, Texarkana, 12/22/82, C, a, 82000863

Foulke, Claude, House, 501 Pecan St., Texarkana, 4/22/82, C, 82002125

Garrison, Augustus M. House, 600 Pecan St., Texarkana, 3/25/82, C, 82002126

Kiblah School, Rt. 1, Doddridge vicinity, 11/20/89, A, 88003210

Kittrell House [Thompson, Charles L., Design Collection TR], 1103 Hickory St., Texarkana, 12/22/82, C, 82000864

Orr School, 831 Laurel St., Texarkana, 7/30/76, B, 76000434

Red River Bridge [Historic Bridges of Arkansas MPS], US 82, over the Red River, Garland City, 4/04/90, A, C, 90000517

Ritchie Grocery Building, Jct. of Front and Olive Sts., Texarkana, 6/14/90, C, 90000900

Texarkana Union Station, State Line and Front St., Texarkana, 11/19/78, A, C, 78000611

Whitmarsh, Alvah Horace, House, 711 Pecan St., Texarkana, 8/29/80, C, 80000778

Wynn—Price House, Price St., Garland vicinity, 1/23/92, C, 90001950

Mississippi County

Bank of Osceola [Osceola MRA], 207 E. Hale St., Osceola, 8/06/87, C, 87001352

Blytheville Greyhound Bus Station, 109 N. Fifth St., Blytheville, 8/17/87, C, g, 87000447

Blytheville, Leachville and Arkansas Southern Railroad Depot—Leachville [Historic Railroad Depots of Arkansas MPS], NE corner of 2nd and McNamee Sts., Leachville, 6/11/92, A, C, 92000612

Chickasawba Mound (3M55), Address Restricted, Blytheville vicinity, 11/16/84, D, 84000217

City Hall [Osceola MRA], 316 W. Hale St., Osceola, 8/06/87, C, 87001350

Dyess Colony Center, AR 297, Dyess, 1/01/76, A, g, 76000435

Eaker Site, Address Restricted, Blytheville vicinity, 11/25/92, D, 91001048

Florida Brothers Building [Osceola MRA], 319 W. Hale St., Osceola, 8/06/87, A, C, 87001355

Hale Avenue Historic District [Osceola MRA], Roughly bounded by Hale Ave., Poplar St., Ford Ave., and Walnut St., Osceola, 9/14/87, A, C, 87001349

Keiser School, Jct. of Main and School Sts., SE corner, Keiser, 10/08/92, C, 92001342

Mississippi County Courthouse, Hale and Poplar Aves., Osceola, 12/13/78, C, 78000612

Mississippi County Jail [Osceola MRA], 300 S. Poplar St., Osceola, 8/06/87, C, 87001356

Nodena Site, Address Restricted, Wilson vicinity, 10/15/66, D, NHL, 66000201

Old Bell Telephone Building [Osceola MRA], 100 blk. of Ash St., Osceola, 8/06/87, A, C, 87001353

Osceola Times Building [Osceola MRA], 112 N. Poplar St., Osceola, 8/06/87, A, B, 87001351

Planters Bank Building [Osceola MRA], 200 E. Hale St., Osceola, 8/06/87, C, 87001354

Zebree Homestead, Address Restricted, Buckeye vicinity, 5/02/75, D, 75000398

Monroe County

Anderson Boarding House [Clarendon MRA], 201 Main St., Clarendon, 11/01/84, C, 84000180

Bank of Clarendon [Clarendon MRA], 125 Court St., Clarendon, 11/01/84, C, 84000183

Bateman-Griffith House [Clarendon MRA], 316 Jefferson St., Clarendon, 11/01/84, C, 84000184

Baytown Site, Address Restricted, Indian Bay vicinity, 5/13/76, D, 76000440

Black, William, Family House, 311 W. Ash St., Brinkley, 12/12/76, C, 76000437

Bondi Brothers Store [Clarendon MRA], 104 Madison St., Clarendon, 11/01/84, A, 84000185

Bounds Building [Clarendon MRA], 105 Second St., Clarendon, 11/01/84, C, 84000186

Capps House, Co. Rd. 48 E of jct. with SR 17, Lawrenceville vicinity, 6/21/90, C, D, 90000877

Clarendon Methodist-Episcopal Church South [Clarendon MRA], 121 Third St., Clarendon, 11/01/84, C, a, 84000187

Cumberland Presbyterian Church, 120 Washington St., Clarendon, 7/30/76, A, C, a, 76000438

Ellas-McKay House, 404 N. Wells St., Clarendon, 12/08/78, C, 78000613

Ewan Building [Clarendon MRA], 124-128 Second St., Clarendon, 11/01/84, C, 84000188

Galloway, Orth C., House, 504 Park St., Clarendon, 5/23/80, C, 80000779

Gazzola and Vaccaro Building [Thompson, Charles L., Design Collection TR], 131-133 W. Cypress, Brinkley, 12/22/82, C, 82000865

Goldman and Son Store [Clarendon MRA], 101 Main St., Clarendon, 11/01/84, C, 84000189

Highway 79 Bridge [Clarendon MRA], U.S. 79 and White River, Clarendon, 11/01/84, C, 84000190

Holly Grove Historic District, Main and Pine Sts., Holly Grove, 2/02/79, A, 79000446

Holly Grove Presbyterian Church, 310 Second St., Holly Grove, 5/13/91, C, a, 91000581

Jefferies Building [Clarendon MRA], 122 Madison St., Clarendon, 11/01/84, C, 84000191

Jefferies-Craptree House [Clarendon MRA], 300 Jefferson St., Clarendon, 11/01/84, B, C, 84000192

Lick Skillet Railroad Work Station Historic District, Jct. of E. Cypress St. and New Orleans Ave., Brinkley, 6/01/92, A, C, 92000558

Lo Beele House [Thompson, Charles L., Design Collection TR], 312 New York Ave., Brinkley, 12/22/82, C, 82000866

Manning, Lee and Moore Law Office [Clarendon MRA], 109 Court St., Clarendon, 11/01/84, B, C, b, 84000193

Marston House [Clarendon MRA], 429 Main St., Clarendon, 11/01/84, C, 84000194

Merchants and Planters Bank [Thompson, Charles L., Design Collection TR], 214 Madison, Clarendon, 12/22/82, C, 82000867

Midland Depot [Clarendon MRA], 205 Midland St., Clarendon, 11/01/84, A, 84000195

Monroe County Courthouse, Courthouse Sq., Clarendon, 10/14/76, C, 76000439

Monroe County Jail, 2nd and Kendall, Clarendon, 4/11/77, A, C, 77000262

Moore-Jacobs House, 500 N. Main St., Clarendon, 9/29/83, C, b, 83001160

Mount Zion Missionary Baptist Church, 409 S. Main St., Brinkley, 11/04/86, A, a, 86002951

New South Inn [Clarendon MRA], 132-164 Second St., Clarendon, 11/01/84, C, 84000196

Monroe County—Continued

Palmer House, SE of Blackton off U.S. 49, Blackton vicinity, 5/04/76, B, C, 76000436

Rusher Hotel, 127 W. Cedar, Brinkley, 7/18/86, A, C, 86001664

St. John the Baptist Catholic Church, Jct. of New Orleans and W. Ash St., SW corner, Brinkley, 10/02/92, C, a, 92001283

Walls, James A., House, Off AR 17, Holly Grove, 6/09/80, B, C, 80000780

Montgomery County

Collier Springs Shelter [Facilities Constructed by the CCC in Arkansas MPS], FS Rd. 177 NE of Norman, Ouachita NF, Norman vicinity, 10/20/93, A, C, 93001083

Crystal Springs Camp Shelter [Facilities Constructed by the CCC in Arkansas MPS], FS Rd. 177 E of AR 27, Ouachita NF, Norman vicinity, 10/21/93, A, C, 93001087

Crystal Springs Dam [Facilities Constructed by the CCC in Arkansas MPS], FS Rd. 177 E of AR 27, Ouachita NF, Norman vicinity, 10/21/93, A, C, 93001088

Huddleston Store and McKinzie Store, AR 88, Pine Ridge, 10/04/84, A, B, b, 84000007

Montgomery County Courthouse, Court Sq., Mount Ida, 8/27/76, A, 76000441

Norman Town Square, Bounded by AR 8 and 8th, Gurdon and 7th Sts., Norman, 2/25/93, C, 93000092

Reeves-Melson House, SE of Montgomery adjacent to branch of Mazarn Creek, Bonnerdale vicinity, 12/05/85, A, 85003069

Womble District Administration House No. 1 [Facilities Constructed by the CCC in Arkansas MPS], US 270 N side, E of Mt. Ida, Mt. Ida vicinity, 10/20/93, A, C, 93001101

Nevada County

Bemis Florist Shop [Thompson, Charles L., Design Collection TR], 117 E. Second, Prescott, 12/22/82, C, 82000868

Carolina Methodist Church, Co. Rd. #10 E of jct. with Kirk Rd., Poison Springs SF, Rosston vicinity, 1/03/91, C, a, 90001947

McRae, D. L., House [Thompson, Charles L., Design Collection TR], 424 E. Main St., Prescott, 12/22/82, C, 82000869

McRae, T. C., House [Thompson, Charles L., Design Collection TR], 506 E. Elm St., Prescott, 12/22/82, C, 82000870

Missouri Pacific Depot, 300 W. 1st St. North, Prescott, 11/17/78, C, 78000614

Prairie De Ann Battlefield, N and S of Hwy. 24 and SW of Prescott, Prescott vicinity, 3/22/74, A, 74000481

Wortham Gymnasium, AR 200, Oak Grove, 4/19/90, A, C, 90000667

Newton County

Big Buffalo Valley Historic District, Buffalo National River, Ponca vicinity, 7/29/87, A, C, NPS, 87000110

Buffalo River Bridge [Historic Bridges of Arkansas MPS], AR 7, over the Buffalo River, Pruitt, 4/09/90, A, C, 90000509

Dr. Hudson Sanitarium Agricultural Building Historic District, AR 327 S of jct. with AR 74, Jasper vicinity, 10/08/92, B, C, 92001345

Harp Creek Bridge [Historic Bridges of Arkansas MPS], AR 7, over Harp Creek, Jasper vicinity, 4/09/90, A, C, 90000519

Parker—Hickman Farm Historic District, Buffalo National River, Erbie vicinity, 8/11/87, A, C, NPS, 87001029

Villines Mill, N of Boxley on AR 43, Boxley vicinity, 7/31/74, A, 74000482

Ouachita County

Bragg House, W of Camden on AR 4, Camden vicinity, 3/01/74, A, B, 74000487

Elliott-Meek House, 761 Washington St., Camden, 3/01/74, A, C, 74000483

Graham-Gaughan-Betts House, 710 Washington St., Camden, 10/18/74, C, 74000484

Holt-Poindexter Store Building, Ouachita County Rd., Stephens vicinity, 10/23/86, A, 86002948

Leake-Ingham Building, 926 Washington St., NW, Camden, 5/02/75, A, C, b, 75000399

Lester And Haltom No. 1 Well Site, NE of Stephens on Old Wire Rd., Stephens vicinity, 4/03/76, A, 76000442

McCollum-Chidester House, 926 Washington St., NW, Camden, 6/24/71, C, 71000127

Missouri—Pacific Railroad Depot—Camden [Historic Railroad Depots of Arkansas MPS], SW corner of Main and First Sts., Camden, 6/11/92, A, C, 92000605

Oakland Farm, S of Camden at Tate and Oakland Sts., Camden vicinity, 3/24/78, B, 78003062

Old Camden Post Office, 133 Washington St., SW, Camden, 5/02/77, A, C, 77000263

Ouachita County Courthouse, 145 Jefferson Ave., Camden, 11/13/89, C, 89001958

Poison Spring State Park, NW of Camden, Chidester vicinity, 12/03/69, A, 69000036

Powell, Benjamin T., House, 305 California Ave., Camden, 1/21/74, A, C, 74000485

Richmond-Tufts House, NW of Camden on AR 24, Camden vicinity, 12/02/77, B, 77000264

Smith, Rowland B., House, 234 Agee St., Camden, 1/21/74, C, 74000486

Tate's Barn, 902 Tate St., Camden, 11/09/72, C, 72000207

Perry County

Camp Ouachita Girl Scout Camp Historic District [Facilities Constructed by the CCC in Arkansas MPS], Area surrounding and N of Lake Sylvia, Ouachita NF, Paron vicinity, 2/03/92, A, C, 90001826

Cypress Creek Bridge [Historic Bridges of Arkansas MPS], Co. Rd. 64, over Cypress Creek, Perry vicinity, 4/09/90, A, C, 90000537

Perry County Courthouse, Main and Pine Sts., Perryville, 7/06/76, A, C, 76000443

Perryville American Legion Building, Plum and Main Sts., Perryville, 9/05/90, C, 90001377

Phillips County

Allin House, 515 Columbia St., Helena, 6/04/73, B, C, 73000383

Almer Store, 824 Columbia St., Helena, 10/18/74, A, C, 74000488

Altman House, 1202 Perry St., Helena, 1/21/88, C, 87002497

Barlow-Coolidge House, 917 Ohio St., Helena, 8/19/75, B, C, 75000402

Battery A Site, Battle of Helena, NW of jct. of Adams and Columbia Sts., Helena, 8/18/92, A, 92001012

Battery B Site, Battle of Helena, NE of jct. of Liberty St. and Summit Rd., Helena, 8/18/92, A, 92001011

Battery C Site, Clark and York Sts., Helena, 12/01/78, A, 78000615

Battery D, Military Rd., Helena, 9/17/74, A, 74000489

Beech Street Historic District, Roughly bounded by McDonough, Columbia, Beech, Elm, Perry and College, Helena, 1/30/87, C, 86003314

Centennial Baptist Church, York and Columbia Sts., Helena, 3/26/87, B, C, a, 87000518

Cherry Street Historic District, Along Cherry St. between Porter and Elm Sts., Helena, 8/17/87, A, C, 86003546

Coolidge House, 820 Perry St., Helena, 9/08/83, C, 83001161

Estevan Hall, 653 S. Biscoe St., Helena, 10/22/74, A, B, 74000491

First Baptist Church, Jct. of Pine and Carruth Sts., Marvell, 5/13/91, C, a, 91000587

Helena Depot, Natchez and Missouri Sts., Helena, 11/05/87, A, C, 87000877

Helena Library and Museum, 623 Peach St., Helena, 12/06/75, A, C, g, 75000400

Horner, Sidney H., House, 626 Porter St., Helena, 12/04/75, C, 75000401

Keesee House, 723 Arkansas St., Helena, 9/08/83, C, 83001162

Kitchens, Richard L., Post No. 41, 409 Porter St., Helena, 9/30/76, A, C, 76000444

Moore-Hornor House, 323 Beech St., Helena, 6/04/73, A, 73000384

Perry Street Historic District, Perry St. between Pecan and Franklin and Pecan St. from Porter to Perry, Helena, 11/26/86, C, a, 86002954

Phillips County Courthouse, 622 Cherry St., Helena, 7/15/77, C, 77000265

Pillow, Jerome Bonaparte, House, 718 Perry St., Helena, 5/07/73, C, 73000385

Phillips County—Continued

Ready, E. S., House, 929 Beech St., Helena, 1/01/76, C, 76000445

Short, William A., House, 317 Biscoe St., Helena, 4/18/85, C, 85000833

Short-Deisch House, 409 Biscoe St., Helena, 10/18/74, C, 74000490

Straub, William Nichols, House, 531 Perry St., Helena, 4/18/85, C, 85000834

Tappan, James C., House, 717 Poplar St., Helena, 6/04/73, B, C, 73002270

Tappan, Maj. James Alexander, House, 727 Columbia St., Helena, 9/09/74, B, C, 74000493

West House, 229 Beech St., Helena, 9/08/83, C, 83001163

White House [Thompson, Charles L., Design Collection TR], 1015 Perry St., Helena, 12/22/82, C, 82000871

Pike County

Conway Hotel, 108 Courthouse Sq., Murfreesboro, 3/06/86, A, 86000384

Crater Of Diamonds State Park, SE of Murfreesboro, Murfreesboro vicinity, 6/18/73, A, 73000386

O'Neel-Blackburn House, W of Daisy off U.S. 70, Daisy vicinity, 5/03/76, A, C, 76000446

Pike County Courthouse, Courthouse Sq., Murfreesboro, 10/16/86, A, C, 86002863

Rosenwald School, AR 26, Delight vicinity, 9/17/90, A, C, 90001381

Poinsett County

Marked Tree Lock and Siphons, On the St. Francis River, Marked Tree vicinity, 5/02/88, A, C, g, 88000431

Modern News Building, 216 N. Main St., Harrisburg, 6/18/76, A, 76000447

Poinsett Community Club, Main & Poinsett Sts., Trumann, 10/09/86, A, C, 86002847

Poinsett County Courthouse, Bounded by Market, East, Court, and Main Sts., Harrisburg, 11/03/89, C, 89001876

Rivervale Inverted Siphons, Just SW of AR 135 across Little R., Rivervale, 3/22/91, A, C, 91000339

Polk County

Bard Springs Bathhouse [Facilities Constructed by the CCC in Arkansas MPS], FS Rd. 106 NW of Athens, Caney Cr. Wildlife Management Area, Ouachita NF, Athens vicinity, 10/20/93, A, C, 93001073

Bard Springs Dam No. 1 [Facilities Constructed by the CCC in Arkansas MPS], FS Rd. 106 NW of Athens, Caney Cr. Wildlife Management Area, Ouachita NF, Athens vicinity, 10/21/93, A, C, 93001074

Bard Springs Dam No. 2 [Facilities Constructed by the CCC in Arkansas MPS], FS Rd. 106 NW of Athens, Caney Cr. Wildlife Management Area, Ouachita NF, Athens vicinity, 10/21/93, A, C, 93001075

Bard Springs Picnic Shelter [Facilities Constructed by the CCC in Arkansas MPS], FS Rd. 106 NW of Athens, Caney Cr. Wildlife Management Area, Ouachita NF, Athens vicinity, 10/20/93, A, C, 93001076

Bee Mountain Fire Tower [Facilities Constructed by the CCC in Arkansas MPS], FS Rd. 30 NE of Vandervoort, Ouachita NF, Vandervoort vicinity, 10/20/93, A, C, 93001078

Bogg Springs Hotel, AR 84, Bogg Springs, 9/30/93, A, C, 93001023

Ebenezer Monument, Jct. of 9th and Church Sts., Mena, 1/30/92, A, 91000689

Foster, C. E., House, AR 88 N. side, W of jct. with AR 272, Mena vicinity, 2/25/93, C, 93000084

Janssen Park, Off AR 8, Mena, 12/13/79, A, 79000448

Mena Kansas City—Southern Depot, W of jct. of Pickering Ave. and Mena St., Mena, 6/05/91, A, C, 91000685

Mountain Fork Bridge [Historic Bridges of Arkansas MPS], Co. Rd. 38, over Mountain Fork Creek, Mena vicinity, 4/09/90, A, C, 90000540

National Guard Armory, Jct. of DeQueen and Maple Sts., Mena, 6/05/91, C, 91000682

Old Post Office, 520 N. Mena St., Mena, 6/05/91, C, 91000686

Polk County Courthouse, Jct. of Church Ave. and DeQueen St., NE corner, Mena, 11/20/92, C, 92001618

Scoggin House, 1215 Port Arthur Ave., Mena, 7/20/78, B, C, 78000616

Shady Lake Bathhouse [Facilities Constructed by the CCC in Arkansas MPS], Co. Rd. 64, Caney Cr. Wildlife Management Area, Ouachita NF, Athens vicinity, 10/20/93, A, C, 93001097

Shady Lake Caretaker's House [Facilities Constructed by the CCC in Arkansas MPS], FS Rd. 38, Caney Cr. Wildlife Management Area, Ouachita NF, Athens vicinity, 10/20/93, A, C, 93001098

Shady Lake Dam [Facilities Constructed by the CCC in Arkansas MPS], Co. Rd. 64, Caney Cr. Wildlife Management Area, Ouachita NF, Athens vicinity, 10/20/93, A, 93001099

Shady Lake Picnic Pavilion [Facilities Constructed by the CCC in Arkansas MPS], FS Rd. 38, Caney Cr. Wildlife Management Area, Ouachita NF, Athens vicinity, 10/20/93, A, C, 93001100

Shaver, Judge Benjamin, House, 501 12th St., Mena, 12/06/79, A, B, C, 79003431

St. Agnes Catholic Church, Jct. of 8th and Walnut Sts., Mena, 6/05/91, C, 91000696

State Line Marker, 17 mi. NW of Mena on AR 88, Mena vicinity, 11/18/76, A, 76000448

Tall Peak Fire Tower [Facilities Constructed by the CCC in Arkansas MPS], FS Rd. 38A NW of Athens, Caney Cr. Wildlife Management Area, Ouachita NF, Athens vicinity, 10/20/93, A, C, 93001077

Pope County

Caraway Hall—Arkansas Tech University [Public Schools in the Ozarks MPS], N. Arkansas St., Russellville, 9/10/92, A, C, 92001213

Center Valley Well House [Public Schools in the Ozarks MPS], AR 124, Center Valley, 9/10/92, A, 92001206

Crow Mountain Petroglyph [Rock Art Sites in Arkansas TR], Address Restricted, Dover vicinity, 5/04/82, D, 82004838

Galla Creek Bridge [Historic Bridges of Arkansas MPS], Old AR 64 over Galla Cr., Pottsville, 2/25/93, C, 93000090

Girls' Domestic Science and Arts Building—Arkansas Tech University [Public Schools in the Ozarks MPS], E of N. El Paso St., Russellville, 9/18/92, A, 92001212

Hughes Hall—Arkansas Tech University [Public Schools in the Ozarks MPS], W. M St., Russellville, 9/18/92, A, 92001210

Koen, Henry R., Forest Service Building, 605 W. Main St., Russellville, 12/11/89, A, C, 89001628

Missouri—Pacific Depot—Atkins [Historic Railroad Depots of Arkansas MPS], US 64, Atkins, 6/11/92, A, C, 92000600

Missouri—Pacific Depot—Russellville [Historic Railroad Depots of Arkansas MPS], N of jct. of C St. and Denver Ave., Russellville, 6/11/92, A, C, 92000620

Mountain View School [Public Schools in the Ozarks MPS], AR 326, Russellville, 9/10/92, A, 92001207

Physical Education Building—Arkansas Tech University [Public Schools in the Ozarks MPS], Jct. of N. El Paso and W. O Sts., SE corner, Russellville, 9/10/92, A, C, 92001211

Potts' Inn, Main and Center Sts., Pottsville, 6/22/70, B, 70000123

White, John W., House, 1509 W. Main St., Russellville, 5/05/88, C, 88000524

White, W. J., House, 1412 W. Main St., Russellville, 12/13/78, C, 78000617

Williamson Hall—Arkansas Tech University [Public Schools in the Ozarks MPS], N. El Paso St., Russellville, 9/18/92, A, C, 92001208

Wilson Hall—Arkansas Tech University [Public Schools in the Ozarks MPS], N. El Paso St., Russellville, 9/18/92, A, C, 92001209

Wilson House, 214 E. 5th St., Russellville, 3/29/78, B, C, 78000618

Prairie County

Bethel House [Thompson, Charles L., Design Collection TR], Erwin and 2nd Sts., Des Arc, 12/22/82, C, 82000872

Bethell, Bedford Brown, House, 2nd and Curran Sts., Des Arc, 12/04/78, B, C, 78000619

Prairie County—Continued

DeValls Bluff First Baptist Church, Jct. of Prairie and Mason Sts., SE corner, DeValls Bluff, 11/20/92, C, a, 92001616

First Presbyterian Church, Jct. of Main and 5th Sts., Des Arc, 6/14/90, C, a, 90000897

Frith-Plunkett House, 8th and Main Sts., Des Arc, 6/10/82, A, C, 82002127

Prairie County Courthouse, Main St., Des Arc, 4/18/77, C, 77000266

Rock Island Depot, US 70, Hazen, 12/22/87, A, 87002285

White River Bridge at DeValls Bluff [Historic Bridges of Arkansas MPS], US 70, over the White River, DeValls Bluff, 4/09/90, A, C, 90000514

Pulaski County

ARKANSAS II (riverboat), S end of Locust St. on David D. Terry Lake, North Little Rock, 6/14/90, C, 90000899

Albert Pike Memorial Temple [Little Rock Main Street MRA], 700–724 Scott St., Little Rock, 11/13/86, C, 86003118

All Souls Church, Off AR 130, Scott, 8/12/77, A, C, a, 77000275

Argenta Historic District, Roughly, Melrose Cir. and Willow St. S to W. 4th St., and Main St. from W. 6th St. to W. 3rd St., North Little Rock, 3/15/93, A, 93000094

Arkansas Power & Light Building, Jct. of Ninth St. and Louisiana St., Little Rock, 9/14/92, C, g, 92001156

Arkansas State Capitol, 5th and Woodlane Sts., Little Rock, 6/28/74, A, C, 74000494

Associated Reformed Presbyterian Church [Thompson, Charles L., Design Collection TR], 3323 W. 12th St., Little Rock, 12/22/82, C, a, 82000874

BPOE Elks Club [Thompson, Charles L., Design Collection TR], 4th and Scott Sts., Little Rock, 12/22/82, C, 82000880

Back House [Thompson, Charles L., Design Collection TR], 1523 Cumberland St., Little Rock, 12/22/82, C, 82000875

Baer House [Thompson, Charles L., Design Collection TR], 1010 Rock St., Little Rock, 12/22/82, C, 82000876

Baker House, 109 5th St., North Little Rock, 12/06/78, C, 78000627

Bechle Apartment Building, 1000 E. 9th St., Little Rock, 10/02/78, B, C, 78003201

Bechle House, 1004 E. 9th St., Little Rock, 2/02/79, B, C, 79000449

Beyerlein House [Thompson, Charles L., Design Collection TR], 412 W. 14th St., Little Rock, 12/22/82, C, 82000878

Blass, Gus, Department Store [Little Rock Main Street MRA], 318–324 Main St., Little Rock, 11/13/86, A, C, 86003122

Boone House [Thompson, Charles L., Design Collection TR], 4014 Lookout, Little Rock, 12/22/82, C, 82000879

Bragg, Richard, House, 305 E. 16th St., Little Rock, 7/22/79, B, C, 79000450

Bruner House, 1415 Cantrell Rd., Little Rock, 4/11/77, B, C, 77000267

Buhler House, 1820 Fair Park Blvd., Little Rock, 4/25/88, C, 88000433

Bush House [Thompson, Charles L., Design Collection TR], 1516 Ringo St., Little Rock, 12/22/82, C, 82000877

Capital Hotel, 117 W. Markham St., Little Rock, 7/30/74, A, C, 74000495

Central Presbyterian Church [Thompson, Charles L., Design Collection TR], 1921 Arch St., Little Rock, 12/22/82, C, a, 82000881

Cherry House [Pre-Depression Houses and Outbuildings of Edgemont in Park Hill MPS], 217 Dooley Rd., North Little Rock, 6/01/92, A, C, 92000562

Cherry—Luter Estate, 521 W. Scenic Dr., North Little Rock, 9/04/92, C, 92001155

Chisum House, 1320 Cumberland, Little Rock, 12/04/75, C, 75000403

Choctaw Route Station, E. 3rd at Rock Island RR., Little Rock, 5/06/75, A, C, 75000404

Compton-Wood House, 800 High St., Little Rock, 5/07/80, B, C, 80000781

Cook House, 116 W. 7th St., North Little Rock, 11/19/93, C, 93001250

Cornish House [Thompson, Charles L., Design Collection TR], 1800 Arch St., Little Rock, 12/22/82, C, 82000882

Crestview Park [Arkansas Sculptures of Dionicio Rodriguez TR], Address Restricted, North Little Rock, 12/04/86, C, 86003583

Croxson House [Thompson, Charles L., Design Collection TR], 1901 Gaines St., Little Rock, 12/22/82, C, 82000883

Curran Hall, 615 E. Capitol St., Little Rock, 1/01/76, B, C, 76000453

Darragh House [Thompson, Charles L., Design Collection TR], 2412 Broadway, Little Rock, 12/22/82, C, 82000884

Deane House, 1701 Arch St., Little Rock, 9/05/75, B, C, 75000405

Dunaway House [Thompson, Charles L., Design Collection TR], 2022 Battery, Little Rock, 12/22/82, C, 82000885

Dunbar Junior and Senior High School and Junior College, Wright Ave. and Ringo St., Little Rock, 8/06/80, A, C, g, 80000782

Edgemere Street Bridge [Historic Bridges of Arkansas MPS], Edgemere St., at Lake No. 3, North Little Rock, 4/09/90, A, C, 90000533

Engelberger House, 2105 N. Maple St., North Little Rock, 6/14/90, C, 90000895

England House [Thompson, Charles L., Design Collection TR], 2121 Arch St., Little Rock, 12/22/82, C, 82000886

England, Joseph E. Jr., House [Pre-Depression Houses and Outbuildings of Edgemont in Park Hill MPS], 313 Skyline Dr., North Little Rock, 6/01/92, A, C, 92000566

Exchange Bank Building [Thompson, Charles L., Design Collection TR], 423 Main St., Little Rock, 10/23/86, C, 86002896

Farrell House [Thompson, Charles L., Design Collection TR], 2111 Louisiana, Little Rock, 12/22/82, C, 82000887

Farrell House [Thompson, Charles L., Design Collection TR], 2115 Louisiana, Little Rock, 12/22/82, C, 82000888

Farrell House [Thompson, Charles L., Design Collection TR], 2121 Louisiana, Little Rock, 12/22/82, C, 82000889

Farrell House [Thompson, Charles L., Design Collection TR], 2109 Louisiana, Little Rock, 10/11/84, C, 84000103

Faucette Building, 4th and Main Sts., North Little Rock, 12/06/78, B, 78000628

Faucette, James Peter, House, 316 W. 4th St., North Little Rock, 1/04/78, B, C, 78000629

Federal Reserve Bank Building [Thompson, Charles L., Design Collection TR], 123 W. Third St., Little Rock, 10/23/86, C, 86002895

First Church of Christ, Scientist, 20th and Louisiana Sts., Little Rock, 10/04/84, C, a, 84000008

First Missionary Baptist Church, 701 S. Gaines St., Little Rock, 9/29/83, C, a, 83001164

First Presbyterian Church [Little Rock Main Street MRA], 123 E. Eighth St., Little Rock, 11/13/86, C, a, 86003124

First Presbyterian Church Manse, 415 N. Maple St., North Little Rock, 11/19/93, C, 93001251

First United Methodist Church, 723 Center St., Little Rock, 10/09/86, A, C, a, 86002845

Fletcher House [Thompson, Charles L., Design Collection TR], 909 Cumberland St., Little Rock, 12/22/82, C, 82000890

Florence Crittenton Home [Thompson, Charles L., Design Collection TR], 3600 W. 11th St., Little Rock, 12/22/82, C, 82000891

Fones House, 902 W. 2nd St., Little Rock, 8/19/75, B, C, 75000406

Fordyce House, 2115 S. Broadway, Little Rock, 8/06/75, B, C, 75000407

Forrey-Smith Apartments [Thompson, Charles L., Design Collection TR], 409 Ringo St., Little Rock, 12/22/82, C, 82000892

Forrey-Smith Apartments [Thompson, Charles L., Design Collection TR], 1019 W. 4th St., Little Rock, 12/22/82, C, 82000893

Fort Logan H. Roots Military Post, Scenic Hill Dr., North Little Rock, 9/04/74, A, C, 74000498

Fowler, Absalom, House, 502 E. 7th St., Little Rock, 6/04/73, B, C, 73000387

Frank, Joseph M., House, 912 W. Fourth, Little Rock, 10/03/85, B, C, 85002716

Frauenthal House [Thompson, Charles L., Design Collection TR], 2008 Arch St., Little Rock, 12/22/82, C, 82000895

French-England House [Thompson, Charles L., Design Collection TR], 1700 Broadway, Little Rock, 12/22/82, C, 82000896

Frenchman's Mountain Methodist Episcopal Church And Cemetery, W of Cato on Cato Rd., Cato vicinity, 10/22/76, A, C, a, d, 76000450

Fulk Building [Little Rock Main Street MRA], 300 Main St., Little Rock, 11/13/86, A, C, 86003121

Gans, Solomon, House, 1010 W. 3rd St., Little Rock, 3/29/84, A, C, 84000905

Pulaski County—Continued

Garland, Augustus, House, 1404 Scott St., Little Rock, 6/10/75, B, C, c, 75000408

Gazette Building, 112 W. 3rd St., Little Rock, 10/22/76, A, C, 76002239

George, Alexander, House, 1007 E. 2nd St., Little Rock, 5/28/76, A, B, C, 76000454

Governor's Mansion Historic District, Bounded by the Mansion grounds, 13th, Center, Gaines, and 18th Sts., Little Rock, 9/13/78, C, 78000620

Governor's Mansion Historic District (Boundary Increase), Roughly bounded by Louisiana St., Twenty-Third St. & Roosevelt Rd., Chester and State Sts., & Thirteenth & Twelfth Sts., Little Rock, 5/19/88, C, a, 88000631

Hall House [Thompson, Charles L., Design Collection TR], 32 Edgehill, Little Rock, 12/22/82, C, 82000897

Halliburton Town Houses, 1601 and 1605 Center St., Little Rock, 12/12/76, C, 76000455

Hanger Cotton Gin, Harper Rd. and Gates Lane, Sweet Home, 10/08/76, A, C, 76000463

Hanger, Frederick, House, 1010 Scott St., Little Rock, 3/15/74, B, C, 74000496

Hardy House [Thompson, Charles L., Design Collection TR], 2400 Broadway, Little Rock, 12/22/82, C, 82000898

Harris House, SE of Hensley off AR 365, Hensley vicinity, 1/01/76, B, C, 76000451

Healey and Roth Mortuary Building [Thompson, Charles L., Design Collection TR], 815 Main, Little Rock, 12/22/82, C, 82000899

Hemingway House [Thompson, Charles L., Design Collection TR], 1720 Arch St., Little Rock, 12/22/82, C, 82000900

Hempfling, Barth, House, 507 Main St., North Little Rock, 10/16/86, A, C, 86002860

Herschell—Spillman Carousel, War Memorial Park midway, Little Rock, 12/01/89, C, 89002065

Hillcrest Historic District, Bounded by Woodrow, Jackson and Markham Sts. and N. Lookout Rd., Little Rock, 12/18/90, A, C, 90001920

Hillcrest Historic District (Boundary Increase), Roughly bounded by Evergreen, Harrison, Lee and Jackson Sts., Little Rock, 10/08/92, A, C, 92001356

Hodge—Cook House, 620 N. Maple St., North Little Rock, 11/19/93, C, 93001252

Hornibrook House, 2120 S. Louisiana St., Little Rock, 7/30/74, C, 74000497

Hotze House, 1619 Louisiana St., Little Rock, 8/11/75, C, 75000409

Howell-Garner-Monfee House, 300 W. 4th St., North Little Rock, 1/04/78, C, 78000630

Immaculate Heart of Mary Church [Thompson, Charles L., Design Collection TR], N of North Little Rock off AR 365, North Little Rock vicinity, 12/22/82, C, a, 82000901

Immaculate Heart of Mary School, Off AR 365, N of Blue Hill Rd., Marche vicinity, 9/16/93, C, a, 93000965

Ish House, 1600 Scott St., Little Rock, 1/03/78, B, C, 78000621

Jeffries House [Pre-Depression Houses and Outbuildings of Edgemont in Park Hill MPS], 415 Skyline Dr., North Little Rock, 6/01/92, A, C, 92000567

Johnson House [Thompson, Charles L., Design Collection TR], 514 E. 8th St., Little Rock, 12/22/82, C, 82000902

Johnson House [Thompson, Charles L., Design Collection TR], 516 E. 8th St., Little Rock, 12/22/82, C, 82000903

Johnson House [Thompson, Charles L., Design Collection TR], 518 E. 8th St., Little Rock, 12/22/82, C, 82000904

Jones, Arthur J., House, 814 Scott St., Little Rock, 1/01/76, B, C, b, 76000456

Kahn—Jennings House, 5300 Sherwood St., Little Rock, 9/08/92, C, 92001223

Keith House [Thompson, Charles L., Design Collection TR], 2200 Broadway, Little Rock, 12/22/82, C, 82000905

Kleiber House [Pre-Depression Houses and Outbuildings of Edgemont in Park Hill MPS], 637 Skyline Dr., North Little Rock, 6/01/92, A, C, 92000561

Knoop, Werner, House, 6 Ozark Point, Little Rock, 8/03/90, C, 90001147

LaFayette Hotel, 525 S. Louisiana St., Little Rock, 9/30/82, C, 82002128

Lake No. 1 Bridge [Historic Bridges of Arkansas MPS], Avondale Rd., over Lake No. 1, North Little Rock, 4/09/90, A, C, 90000534

Lakeshore Drive Bridge [Historic Bridges of Arkansas MPS], Lakeshore Dr. at Lake No. 3, North Little Rock, 4/09/90, A, C, 90000532

Lakewood Park [Arkansas Sculptures of Dionicio Rodriguez TR], Address Restricted, North Little Rock, 12/04/86, C, 86003586

Leiper-Scott House, 312 S. Pulaski St., Little Rock, 5/01/80, C, 80000783

Lincoln Avenue Viaduct [Historic Bridges of Arkansas MPS], AR 10, over the Missouri-Pacific Railroad, Little Rock, 4/09/90, A, C, 90000731

Little Rock Boys Club [Thompson, Charles L., Design Collection TR], 8th & Scott Sts., Little Rock, 12/22/82, C, 82000906

Little Rock Central Fire Station, 520 W. Markham St., Little Rock, 10/18/79, C, 79000451

Little Rock City Hall, 500 W. Markham St., Little Rock, 10/18/79, C, 79000452

Little Rock High School, 14th and Park Sts., Little Rock, 8/19/77, A, g, NHL, 77000268

Little Rock Y.M.C.A., 524 Broadway St., Little Rock, 7/22/79, A, C, a, 79000456

Little Rock, The, On S bank of the Arkansas River at foot of Rock St., Little Rock, 10/06/70, A, 70000124

MacArthur Park Historic District, Roughly bounded by Ferry, McGowan, McAlmont, 16th, Bragg, 15th, Scott, 9th, Cumberland, and 5th Sts., Little Rock, 7/25/77, A, B, C, 77000269

Main Building, Arkansas Baptist College, 1600 High St., Little Rock, 4/30/76, A, B, C, 76000457

Manees, E. O., House, 216 W. 4th St., North Little Rock, 8/06/75, B, 75000413

Mann, George R., Building, 115 E. 5th St., Little Rock, 12/29/83, C, 83003547

Marre, Angelo, House, 1321 Scott St., Little Rock, 6/15/70, B, C, 70000128

Marshall House [Thompson, Charles L., Design Collection TR], 2009 Arch St., Little Rock, 12/22/82, C, 82000907

Marshall Square Historic District, Bounded by 17th, McAlmont, 18th, and Vance Sts., Little Rock, 8/10/79, A, C, 79000453

Matthews House, 406 Goshen, North Little Rock, 9/29/83, A, B, C, 83001165

Matthews, Justin, Jr., House, 257 Skyline Dr., North Little Rock, 12/18/90, C, 90001933

Matthews—Bradshaw House [Pre-Depression Houses and Outbuildings of Edgemont in Park Hill MPS], 524 Skyline Dr., North Little Rock, 6/01/92, A, C, 92000568

Matthews—Bryan House [Pre-Depression Houses and Outbuildings of Edgemont in Park Hill MPS], 320 Dooley Rd., North Little Rock, 6/01/92, A, C, 92000560

Matthews—Dillon House [Pre-Depression Houses and Outbuildings of Edgemont in Park Hill MPS], 701 Skyline Dr., North Little Rock, 6/01/92, A, C, 92000563

Matthews—Godt House [Pre-Depression Houses and Outbuildings of Edgemont in Park Hill MPS], 248 Skyline Dr., North Little Rock, 6/01/92, A, C, 92000565

Matthews—MacFadyen House [Pre-Depression Houses and Outbuildings of Edgemont in Park Hill MPS], 206 Dooley Rd., North Little Rock, 6/01/92, A, C, 92000569

McDonald-Wait-Newton House, 1406 Cantrell Rd., Little Rock, 7/14/78, B, C, 78000622

McGuire, Thomas R., House, 114 Rice St., Little Rock, 12/19/91, C, 91001858

McKenzie House, 4911 AR 161, Scott, 3/05/92, C, b, 92000105

McLean House [Thompson, Charles L., Design Collection TR], 470 Ridgeway, Little Rock, 12/22/82, C, 82000908

Mehaffey House [Thompson, Charles L., Design Collection TR], 2101 Louisiana, Little Rock, 12/22/82, C, 82000909

Mitchell House [Thompson, Charles L., Design Collection TR], 1415 Spring St., Little Rock, 12/22/82, C, 82000910

Moore Building [Thompson, Charles L., Design Collection TR], 519–523 Center St., Little Rock, 10/23/86, C, 86002894

Moore House [Thompson, Charles L., Design Collection TR], 20 Armistead, Little Rock, 12/22/82, C, 82000911

Mopac Station, Markham and Victory St., Little Rock, 6/17/77, A, 77000270

Mosaic Templars of America Headquarters Building, 900 Broadway, Little Rock, 4/19/90, A, B, C, 90000634

Mount Holly Cemetery, 12th St. and Broadway, Little Rock, 3/05/70, A, d, 70000125

Mount Holly Mausoleum [Thompson, Charles L., Design Collection TR], 12th and Broadway, Little Rock, 12/22/82, C, 82000912

Mount Zion Baptist Church, 900 Cross St., Little Rock, 3/27/87, C, a, 86003230

Pulaski County—Continued

Nash House [Thompson, Charles L., Design Collection TR], 409 E. 6th St., Little Rock, 12/22/82, C, 82000913

Nash House [Thompson, Charles L., Design Collection TR], 601 Rock St., Little Rock, 12/22/82, C, 82000914

North Little Rock City Hall, 3rd and Main Sts., North Little Rock, 8/06/75, A, C, 75000414

North Little Rock High School, 101 W. 22nd St., North Little Rock, 2/25/93, C, 92001625

North Little Rock Post Office [Thompson, Charles L., Design Collection TR], 420 N. Main St., North Little Rock, 12/22/82, C, 82000915

Old Central Fire Station, 506 Main St., North Little Rock, 12/22/77, C, 77000274

Old Post Office Building and Customhouse, 2nd and Spring Sts., Little Rock, 5/07/73, C, 73000388

Old Statehouse, 300 W. Markham St., Little Rock, 12/03/69, A, C, 69000037

Owings House [Pre-Depression Houses and Outbuildings of Edgemont in Park Hill MPS], 563 Skyline Dr., North Little Rock, 6/01/92, A, C, 92000564

Park Hill Fire Station and Water Company Complex, 3417–3421 Magnolia St., North Little Rock, 11/19/93, A, C, 93001248

Pearson-Robinson House, 1900 Marshall St., Little Rock, 7/24/78, B, C, 78000623

Peoples Building & Loan Building, 213–217 W. 2nd St., Little Rock, 9/02/82, C, 82002129

Pettefer, Harry, House, 105 E. 24th St., Little Rock, 10/19/78, B, C, 78000624

Pike, Albert, Hotel, 7th and Scott Sts., Little Rock, 11/21/78, C, g, 78000625

Pike-Fletcher-Terry House, 411 E. 7th St., Little Rock, 8/21/72, B, C, 72000208

Porter, Lamar, Athletic Field, Jct. of Johnson and 7th Sts., Little Rock, 12/06/90, C, 90001827

Pruniski House, 345 Goshen Ave., North Little Rock, 2/09/90, C, 90000116

Pugh, T. R., Memorial Park [Arkansas Sculptures of Dionicio Rodriguez TR], Address Restricted, North Little Rock, 12/04/86, C, 86003585

Pulaski County Courthouse, 405 W. Markham St., Little Rock, 10/18/79, C, 79000454

Ragland House, 1617 Center St., Little Rock, 6/17/77, B, C, 77000271

Rapillard House, 123 W. 7th St., North Little Rock, 11/19/93, C, 93001249

Reichardt House, 1201 Welch St., Little Rock, 5/02/75, B, C, 75000410

Reid House [Thompson, Charles L., Design Collection TR], 1425 Kavanaugh St., Little Rock, 12/22/82, C, 82000916

Remmel Apartments [Thompson, Charles L., Design Collection TR], 409-411 W. 17th St., Little Rock, 12/22/82, C, 82000917

Remmel Apartments [Thompson, Charles L., Design Collection TR], 1708-1710 Spring St., Little Rock, 12/22/82, C, 82000918

Remmel Apartments [Thompson, Charles L., Design Collection TR], 1704-1706 Spring St., Little Rock, 12/22/82, C, 82000919

Remmel Flats [Thompson, Charles L., Design Collection TR], 1700-1702 Spring St., Little Rock, 12/22/82, C, 82000920

Retan House [Thompson, Charles L., Design Collection TR], 2510 Broadway, Little Rock, 12/22/82, C, 82000921

Retan, Albert, House, 506 N. Elm St., Little Rock, 12/03/80, A, C, 80000784

Robinson, Joseph Taylor, House, 2122 Broadway, Little Rock, 8/28/75, B, g, 75000411

Rock Island—Argenta Depot, 4th and Hazel, North Little Rock, 9/21/89, A, C, 89001403

Rogers House [Thompson, Charles L., Design Collection TR], 400 W. 18th St., Little Rock, 12/22/82, C, 82000922

Rose Building [Little Rock Main Street MRA], 307 Main St., Little Rock, 11/13/86, A, C, 86003119

Rose, U. M., School [Thompson, Charles L., Design Collection TR], Izard and W. 13th St., Little Rock, 12/08/88, C, 88002820

Roselawn Memorial Park Gatehouse [Thompson, Charles L., Design Collection TR], 2801 Asher, Little Rock, 12/22/82, C, d, 82000923

Runyan, J. P., House, 1514 S. Schiller, Little Rock, 8/18/92, B, C, 92001067

Safferstone House [Thompson, Charles L., Design Collection TR], 2205 Arch St., Little Rock, 12/22/82, C, 82000925

Saint Andrews Catholic Cathedral [Little Rock Main Street MRA], 617 Louisiana St., Little Rock, 11/13/86, C, a, 86003117

Sanders House [Thompson, Charles L., Design Collection TR], 2100 Gaines St., Little Rock, 12/22/82, C, 82000924

Schaer House [Thompson, Charles L., Design Collection TR], 1862 Arch St., Little Rock, 12/22/82, C, 82000926

Second Street Bridge [Historic Bridges of Arkansas MPS], Second St., over the Missouri-Pacific Railroad, Little Rock, 4/09/90, A, C, 90000528

Skillern House [Thompson, Charles L., Design Collection TR], 2522 Arch St., Little Rock, 12/22/82, C, 82000927

Snyder House [Thompson, Charles L., Design Collection TR], 4004 S. Lookout, Little Rock, 12/22/82, C, 82000928

St. Edwards Church [Thompson, Charles L., Design Collection TR], 823 Sherman, Little Rock, 12/22/82, C, a, 82000929

St. Joseph's Home, Camp Robinson Rd. off AR 176, North Little Rock, 5/04/76, B, C, a, 76000462

Stewart House [Thompson, Charles L., Design Collection TR], 1406 Summit St., Little Rock, 12/22/82, C, 82000930

Taborian Hall, 9th and State Sts., Little Rock, 4/29/82, A, 82002130

Tavern, The, 214 E. 3rd St., Little Rock, 3/05/70, A, C, 70000126

Taylor Building [Little Rock Main Street MRA], 304 Main St., Little Rock, 11/13/86, A, C, 86003123

Ten Mile House, N of Mabelvale on AR 5, Mabelvale vicinity, 6/22/70, C, 70000129

Terminal Hotel, Victory and Markham Sts., Little Rock, 11/17/78, A, C, 78003200

Terminal Warehouse Building, 500 E. Markham St., Little Rock, 4/29/82, C, 82002131

Terry, William L., House, 1422 Scott St., Little Rock, 1/01/76, B, C, 76000459

Thompson, Ada, Memorial Home, 2021 S. Main, Little Rock, 8/03/77, A, C, 77000272

Thurston House [Thompson, Charles L., Design Collection TR], 923 Cumberland St., Little Rock, 12/22/82, C, 82000931

Trapnall Hall, 423 E. Capitol Ave., Little Rock, 4/13/73, B, C, 73000389

Trinity Episcopal Cathedral, 310 W. 17th St., Little Rock, 5/13/76, A, C, a, 76000460

Turner House [Thompson, Charles L., Design Collection TR], 1701 Center St., Little Rock, 12/22/82, C, 82000932

Turner-Ledbetter House, 1700 S. Louisiana St., Little Rock, 6/18/87, C, 87000978

U.S. Arsenal Building, MacArthur Park, 9th and Commerce Sts., Little Rock, 7/28/70, A, 70000127

Union Life Building, 212 Center St., Little Rock, 9/25/81, C, 81000141

Van Frank Cottages, 515–519 E. Fifteenth St. and 1510 Park Ln., Little Rock, 10/21/85, C, 85003476

Vanetten House [Thompson, Charles L., Design Collection TR], 1012 Cumberland, Little Rock, 12/22/82, C, 82000933

Vaughn House [Thompson, Charles L., Design Collection TR], 2201 Broadway, Little Rock, 12/22/82, C, 82000934

Vinson House, 2123 Broadway, Little Rock, 5/06/76, C, 76000461

Walnut Grove Methodist Church, W of Little Rock on Walnut Grove Rd., Little Rock vicinity, 9/28/77, A, C, a, 77000273

Ward, Zeb, Building, 1001–1003 W. Markham St., Little Rock, 4/19/78, B, C, 78000626

Ward-Hays House, 1008 W. 2nd St., Little Rock, 8/11/75, B, C, 75000412

Waters, Charles Clary, House, 2004 W. 22nd St., Little Rock, 8/10/79, B, C, 79000455

Waterside Street Bridge [Historic Bridges of Arkansas MPS], Waterside St. near jct. with Jacksonville Blvd., North Little Rock, 6/14/90, A, C, 90000888

White-Baucum House, 201 S. Izard St., Little Rock, 2/29/80, C, 80000785

Williamson House [Thompson, Charles L., Design Collection TR], 325 Fairfax St., Little Rock, 11/15/84, C, 84000238

Winfield Methodist Church [Thompson, Charles L., Design Collection TR], 1601 Louisiana, Little Rock, 12/22/82, C, a, 82000935

Woodruff, William, House, 1017 E. 8th St., Little Rock, 3/21/89, B, 89000173

Worthen Bank Building [Little Rock Main Street MRA], 401 Main St., Little Rock, 11/13/86, A, C, 86003125

Pulaski County—Continued

YMCA—Democrat Building [Thompson, Charles L., Design Collection TR], E. Capitol & Scott Sts., LIttle Rock, 6/11/92, C, 87001544

Young House [Pre-Depression Houses and Outbuildings of Edgemont in Park Hill MPS], 436 Skyline Dr., North Little Rock, 6/01/92, A, C, 92000559

Randolph County

Bates, Daniel V., House, U.S. 67, Pocahontas, 12/27/79, C, 79000457

Black River Bridge [Historic Bridges of Arkansas MPS], US 67, over the Black River, Pocahontas, 4/09/90, A, C, 90000522

Old Davidsonville State Historic Monument, NE of Black Rock on Black River, Black Rock vicinity, 1/18/74, A, 74000499

Old Randolph County Courthouse, Broadway and Vance St., Pocahontas, 4/24/73, C, 73000390

Old Union School, 504 Old Union Rd., Birdell vicinity, 11/12/93, C, 93001203

Saline County

Clary, J. W. and Ann Lowe, House, 305 N. East St., Benton, 2/19/93, C, 93000053

Gann Building, 218 S. Market St., Benton, 10/21/75, B, C, 75000415

Gann House, S. Market St., Benton, 1/02/76, B, C, 76000464

Hughes Mound Site (3SA11), Address Restricted, Benton vicinity, 10/10/85, D, 85003134

Hunter, Andrew, House, W of Bryant on AR 5, Bryant vicinity, 12/12/76, B, a, 76000466

Missouri—Pacific Railroad Depot—Benton [Historic Railroad Depots of Arkansas MPS], Adjacent to jct. of S. East and E. Hazel Sts., Benton, 6/11/92, A, C, 92000602

Old River Bridge, SW of Benton at River Rd. and Saline River, Benton vicinity, 9/15/77, C, 77000277

Pleasant Hill Methodist Church, Jct. of Lawson and Lake Norrell Rds., Pleasant Hill, 6/05/91, C, a, 91000684

Rucker House, AR 183 and Gibbons Rd., Bauxite vicinity, 6/16/88, A, 88000744

Saline County Courthouse, Courthouse Sq., Benton, 11/22/76, C, 76000465

Saline River Bridge [Historic Bridges of Arkansas MPS], Co. Hwy. 365, over the Saline River, Benton, 4/09/90, A, C, 90000529

Shoppach House, 508 N. Main St., Benton, 10/10/75, A, B, C, 75000416

Walton, Dr. James Wyatt, House, 301 W. Sevier, Benton, 12/22/77, C, 77000276

Scott County

Cold Spring [Facilities Constructed by the CCC in Arkansas MPS], Scott Co. Rd. 93 NE of Waldron, Ouachita NF, Waldron vicinity, 10/21/93, A, C, 93001082

Forrester, John T., House, 115 Danville St., Waldron, 12/08/80, C, 80000786

Mount Pleasant Methodist Church, AR 248, Waldron vicinity, 6/05/86, C, a, 86001207

Poteau Work Center [Facilities Constructed by the CCC in Arkansas MPS], Poteau Work Center Access Rd., off AR 80, Waldron, 10/20/93, A, 93001094

Poteau Work Center Residence No. 2 [Facilities Constructed by the CCC in Arkansas MPS], Poteau Work Center Access Rd., off AR 80, Waldron, 10/20/93, A, 93001095

Powder Magazine [Facilities Constructed by the CCC in Arkansas MPS], Co. Rd. 96 N of Blue Ball, Ouachita NF, Blue Ball vicinity, 10/20/93, A, 93001096

Scott County Courthouse, Address Unavailable, Waldron, 11/13/89, C, 89001971

Searcy County

3SE33, Address Restricted, Silver Hill vicinity, 6/29/76, D, 76000468

Aday—Stephenson House [Searcy County MPS], Pine St., Marshall, 12/02/93, C, 93001365

American Legion Post No. 131 [Searcy County MPS], Center St. W of jct. with Walnut St., Leslie, 12/02/93, A, C, 93001369

Bank of Marshall Building [Searcy County MPS], Jct. of Main and Center Sts., SE corner, Marshall, 10/04/93, A, C, 93000974

Bartley, Guy, House [Searcy County MPS], Jct. of Elm and Fifth Sts., NE corner, Leslie, 12/02/93, C, 93001372

Bates Tourist Court [Searcy County MPS], Fair St., Marshall, 10/04/93, C, 93000979

Bromley—Mills—Treece House [Searcy County MPS], Main St., Marshall, 10/04/93, C, 93000966

Bryan, Noah, Store [Searcy County MPS], SW corner of Glade and Main Sts., Marshall, 8/18/93, A, C, 93000760

Campbell Post Office—Kuykendall General Store [Searcy County MPS], Co. Rd. 73 NW of Oxley, Oxley vicinity, 12/02/93, C, 93001364

Clay, Dr., House [Searcy County MPS], Jct. of Walnut and Center Sts., Leslie, 12/02/93, C, 93001368

Cooper's Bluff [Rock Art Sites in Arkansas TR], Address Restricted, Snowballs vicinity, 5/04/82, D, 82002132

Cotton, Dr. J. O., House [Searcy County MPS], Jct. of AR 66 and High St., SE corner, Leslie, 12/02/93, C, 93001366

Daniel, Dr. Sam G., House [Searcy County MPS], N side of Nome St., one block W of Courthouse Square, Marshall, 8/18/93, A, C, 93000759

Dugger and Schultz Millinery Store Building [Searcy County MPS], Jct. of Glade and Nome Sts., SW corner, Marshall, 10/04/93, C, 93000973

Farmers Bank Building [Searcy County MPS], Jct. of Main and Walnut Sts., Leslie, 8/18/93, A, C, 93000753

Fendley, Bud, House [Searcy County MPS], 201 Spring St., Marshall, 8/18/93, C, 93000816

Ferguson Gas Station [Searcy County MPS], Jct. of Center and US 65, SE corner, Marshall, 10/04/93, C, 93000967

Ferguson, T. M., House [Searcy County MPS], Canaan St., Marshall, 10/04/93, C, 93000972

Ferguson, Zeb, House [Searcy County MPS], US 65, Marshall, 10/04/93, C, 93000968

Gates—Helm Farm [Searcy County MPS], Co. Rd. 13, approximately 1 mi. N of jct. with Co. Rd. 250, Snowball vicinity, 8/18/93, C, 93000817

Hatchett, Columbus, House [Searcy County MPS], N side of jct. of Main and Hazel Sts., Leslie, 8/18/93, C, 93000756

Henley, Benjamin Franklin, House, Off US 65, St. Joe vicinity, 12/05/85, C, 85003070

Hollabaugh, Dr. Cleveland, House [Searcy County MPS], Oak St., Leslie, 12/02/93, C, 93001371

Lay, S. A., House [Searcy County MPS], Jct. of Glade St. and US 65, Marshall, 10/04/93, C, 93000971

Leslie—Rolen House [Searcy County MPS], Jct. of Cherry and High Sts., Leslie, 8/18/93, C, 93000815

Luna, Anthony, House [Searcy County MPS], Jct. of Main and Spring Sts., SW corner, Marshall, 10/04/93, C, 93000975

Lynch, Thomas, House [Searcy County MPS], Co. Rd. 52, approximately 2.5 mi. N of Morning Star, Morning Star vicinity, 8/18/93, C, 93000757

Marshall, Sam, House [Searcy County MPS], Co. Rd. 163, Morning Star vicinity, 10/04/93, C, 93000980

Mays General Store, Front St., Gilbert, 9/01/83, A, 83001166

McCall, J. M., House [Searcy County MPS], Spring St., Marshall, 10/04/93, C, 93000970

McCall, Vinie, House [Searcy County MPS], Spring St., Marshall, 10/04/93, C, 93000969

Miller, J. C., House [Searcy County MPS], Jct. of Oak and High Sts., NW corner, Leslie, 12/02/93, C, 93001370

Missouri and North Arkansas Depot—Leslie [Historic Railroad Depots of Arkansas MPS], SW end of Walnut St., Leslie, 6/11/92, A, C, 92000613

Passmore, Charley, House [Searcy County MPS], Campus St., Marshall, 10/04/93, C, 93000978

Redman, Oscar, Building [Searcy County MPS], 119 E. Main St., Marshall, 8/18/93, A, C, 93000758

Reeves, W. F., House [Searcy County MPS], Short St., Marshall, 10/04/93, C, 93000977

Robinson, Dr., House [Searcy County MPS], Walnut St. E of jct. with Center St., Leslie, 12/02/93, C, 93001367

Searcy County—Continued

Sanders—Hollabaugh House [Searcy County MPS], Church St., Marshall, 10/04/93, C, 93000976

Searcy County Courthouse, Courthouse Sq., Marshall, 10/21/76, A, 76000467

St. Joe Missouri and North Arkansas Railroad Depot [Historic Railroad Depots of Arkansas MPS], US 65, S side, St. Joe, 9/16/93, A, C, 93000988

Thomas, Greene, House [Searcy County MPS], W of Co. Rd. 55, 0.25 mi. S of jct. with Co. Rd. 74, Leslie vicinity, 8/18/93, C, 93000755

Treat Commercial Building [Searcy County MPS], Oak St. NW side, between High and 4th Sts., Leslie, 8/18/93, A, C, 93000752

Treece, Jasper E., Building [Searcy County MPS], W of Co. Rd. 55, approximately 0.5 mi. S of jct. with AR 74, Baker vicinity, 8/18/93, C, 93000754

Sebastian County

Atkinson-Williams Warehouse, 320 Rogers Ave., Fort Smith, 12/13/79, A, 79000458

Bonneville House, 318 N. 7th St., Fort Smith, 9/22/71, C, 71000128

Bracht, Karl Edward, House, 315 N. 13th St., Fort Smith, 5/02/79, A, C, 79000459

Breckinridge, C. R., House, 504 N. 16th St., Fort Smith, 8/07/79, B, 79000460

Christ the King Church [Thompson, Charles L., Design Collection TR], Greenwood Ave. at S. S St., Ft. Smith, 12/22/82, C, a, 82000936

Clayton, W. H. H., House, 514 N. 6th St., Fort Smith, 9/04/70, B, 70000130

Commercial Hotel, 123 N. 1st St., Fort Smith, 5/07/73, C, 73000391

Ferguson-Calderara House, 214 N. 14th St., Fort Smith, 12/11/79, B, C, 79000461

Fort Smith Masonic Temple, 200 N. 11th St., Fort Smith, 11/20/92, C, 92001624

Fort Smith National Historic Site, Address unknown at this time, Fort Smith, 10/15/66, A, f, NHL, NPS, 66000202

Fort Smith's Belle Grove Historic District, Address unknown at this time, Fort Smith, 7/16/73, A, C, 73000392

Foster, Josiah, Building, 222 Garrison Ave., Fort Smith, 1/20/78, A, C, 78000631

Jenny Lind Bridge [Historic Bridges of Arkansas MPS], Howard Hill School Rd., Jenny Lind vicinity, 4/06/90, A, C, 90000530

Knoble, Joseph, Brewery, N. 3rd and E Sts., Fort Smith, 3/24/72, B, 72000209

McLeod, Angus, House, 912 N. 13th St., Fort Smith, 12/08/78, C, 78000632

Milltown Bridge [Historic Bridges of Arkansas MPS], Co. Rd. 77, 1.5 mi. W of Milltown, Milltown vicinity, 4/06/90, A, C, 90000527

Murphy, William J., House, 923 N. 13th St., Fort Smith, 8/07/79, B, C, 79000462

Rogers, Horace Franklin, House, 2900 Rogers Ave., Fort Smith, 5/02/79, B, C, 79000463

Sebastian County Courthouse—Ft. Smith City Hall, 100 S. 6th St., Fort Smith, 6/08/93, C, 93000484

Shaw, Tillman, House, 500 S. Nineteenth St., Fort Smith, 5/16/88, C, 88000561

Sparks, James, House, 201 N. 14th St., Fort Smith, 9/14/72, C, 72000210

West Garrison Avenue Historic District, 100–525 Garrison Ave., Fort Smith, 4/26/79, A, C, 79000464

Sevier County

Hayes Hardware Store, 314 DeQueen St., DeQueen, 12/03/80, A, C, 80000787

Little Cossatot River Bridge [Historic Bridges of Arkansas MPS], Co. Rd. 139H, over the Little Cossatot River, Lockesburg vicinity, 4/06/90, A, C, 90000538

Locke—Nall House, Off US 59/71 N of Lockesburg, Lockesburg vicinity, 5/01/89, C, 89000340

Sharp County

Cochran Store [Evening Shade MRA], Main St., Evening Shade, 6/02/82, A, C, 82002133

Coger House [Evening Shade MRA], Main St., Evening Shade, 6/02/82, C, 82002134

Crystal River Tourist Camp, Jct. of US 167 and Cave St., Cave City, 6/06/91, C, 91000620

Davidson, Sam, House [Evening Shade MRA], Cammack St., Evening Shade, 6/02/82, C, 82002135

Edwards, W. A., House [Evening Shade MRA], Main St., Evening Shade, 6/02/82, B, C, 82002136

Herrn House [Evening Shade MRA (AD)], W. Main St., Evening Shade, 9/29/76, C, 76000469

Maxville School Building [Public Schools in the Ozarks MPS], US 167 N of Cave City, Cave City vicinity, 9/10/92, A, 92001199

McCaleb, John, House [Evening Shade MRA], Main St., Evening Shade, 6/02/82, B, C, 82002137

Metcalfe House [Evening Shade MRA], Gin Dr., Evening Shade, 6/02/82, B, C, 82002138

Poughkeepsie School Building [Public Schools in the Ozarks MPS], AR 58 S of Co. Rd. 137, Poughkeepsie, 9/10/92, A, 92001198

Shaver, Charles W., House [Evening Shade MRA], Court St., Evening Shade, 9/30/82, C, 82002139

Shaver, John W., House [Evening Shade MRA], Main St., Evening Shade, 6/02/82, B, C, 82002140

Stokes House [Evening Shade MRA], Cammack St., Evening Shade, 6/02/82, C, 82002141

Williford Methodist Church, NW of jct. of Ferguson and Hail Sts., Williford, 11/27/92, C, a, 92001629

Woodland Courts, NW of jct. of Dawson and Old CC Rds., Hardy, 11/27/92, C, 92001634

St. Francis County

Forrest City High School, Rosser St., Forrest City, 10/08/92, C, 92001341

Mann House [Thompson, Charles L., Design Collection TR], 422 Forest St., Forrest City, 12/22/82, C, 82000937

Smith House [Thompson, Charles L., Design Collection TR], Memphis Ave., Wheatly, 12/22/82, C, 82000938

St. Francis River Bridge [Historic Bridges of Arkansas MPS], US 70, over the St. Francis River, Madison vicinity, 4/09/90, A, C, 90000516

Stone, William, House, Jct. of AR 306 and Ellis Ln., SE corner, Colt, 10/08/92, C, 92001346

Stuart Springs, Stuart St., Forrest City, 8/03/77, A, 77001502

Stone County

Abernathy, Jessie, House [Stone County MRA], Off AR 14, Marcella, 9/17/85, B, C, 85002216

Alco School [Public Schools in the Ozarks MPS], Just N of AR 66, Alco, 9/04/92, A, 92001125

Anderson, Clarence, Barn [Stone County MRA], AR 66, Newnata, 9/17/85, C, 85002217

Anderson, George, House [Stone County MRA], W of Big Springs, Big Springs, 9/17/85, C, 85002218

Avey, John, Barn [Stone County MRA], Off AR 66, Big Springs, 9/17/85, C, 85002219

Bettis, John, House [Stone County MRA], AR 14, Pleasant Grove, 9/17/85, C, 85002220

Bluff Springs Church and School [Stone County MRA], 3.5 miles W of Onia, Onia vicinity, 9/17/85, A, C, a, 85002210

Bonds House [Stone County MRA], Co. Rd. 2 E of Meadow Cr., Fox vicinity, 2/03/92, C, 91000691

Brewer's Mill [Stone County MRA], AR 66, Mountain View, 9/17/85, A, 85002221

Brewer, A. B., Building [Stone County MRA], AR 66, Mountain View, 10/25/85, C, 85003395

Brewer, John F., House [Stone County MRA], AR 9, Mountain View, 10/25/85, C, 85003398

Brown, Samuel, House [Stone County MRA], Off AR 9, West Richwoods, 9/17/85, C, 85002204

Case, C. B., Motor Co. Building [Stone County MRA], AR 66, Mountain View, 9/17/85, A, C, 85002222

Clark-King House [Stone County MRA], NE of Mountain View, Mountain View vicinity, 9/17/85, B, C, a, 85002234

Commercial Hotel [Stone County MRA], Off AR 66, Mountain View, 9/17/85, A, 85002223

Copeland, Henry, House [Stone County MRA], AR 14, Pleasant Grove, 9/17/85, C, 85002224

Copeland, Wesley, House [Stone County MRA], SE of Timbo, Timbo vicinity, 9/17/85, C, 85002208

Davis Barn [Stone County MRA], W of Pleasant Grove, Pleasant Grove vicinity, 9/17/85, C, 85002225

Stone County—Continued

Dew Drop Inn [Stone County MRA], Off AR 66, Mountain View, 9/17/85, A, 85002231

Dillard, William, Homestead [Stone County MRA], Near White River, Round Bottom, 9/17/85, A, C, 85002214

Doughtery, H. J., House [Stone County MRA], AR 14, Marcella, 9/17/85, C, 85002232

Farmers and Merchants Bank [Stone County MRA], AR 66, Mountain View, 9/17/85, C, 85002228

Ford, Zachariah, House [Stone County MRA], Near White River, Pleasant Grove vicinity, 9/17/85, C, 85002206

Fox Pictograph [Rock Art Sites in Arkansas TR], Address Restricted, Fox vicinity, 5/04/82, D, 82002143

Gammill, Orvall, Barn [Stone County MRA], NW of Big Springs, Big Springs, 9/17/85, C, 85002229

Gray, Walter, House [Stone County MRA], Off AR 14, Melrose, 9/17/85, B, C, 85002212

Guffey, Joe, House [Stone County MRA], AR 110, Old Lexington, 9/17/85, C, 85002211

Hess, Binks, House and Barn [Stone County MRA], Off AR 14, Marcella, 9/17/85, C, 85002227

Hess, Thomas E., House, AR 14, Marcella, 12/27/83, A, C, 83003548

Hess, Thomas M., House [Stone County MRA], Off AR 14, Marcella, 9/17/85, B, C, 85002226

Jeffery, Miles, Barn [Stone County MRA], Off AR 5, Optimus vicinity, 9/17/85, C, 85002215

Lackey General Merchandise and Warehouse [Stone County MRA], AR 66, Mountain View, 9/17/85, A, C, 85002233

Lackey, George W., House [Stone County MPS], Jct. of King and Washington Sts., Mountain View, 10/02/90, B, 90000992

Lancaster, Fred, Barn [Stone County MRA], Near White River, Round Bottom, 9/17/85, C, 85002213

Lancaster, John L., House [Stone County MRA], Off AR 66, Mountain View, 9/17/85, A, B, C, 85002235

Luber School [Public Schools in the Ozarks MPS], Co. Rd. 214, Luber, 9/04/92, A, 92001124

Mabry, H. S., Barn [Stone County MRA], Near Johnson Creek, East Richwoods, 9/17/85, A, C, 85002236

Marcella Church & School [Stone County MRA], AR 14, Marcella, 9/17/85, A, C, a, 85002237

Martin, Owen, House [Stone County MRA], AR 14, Marcella, 10/25/85, C, 85003397

McCarn, Noah, House [Stone County MRA], AR 5, Mountain View vicinity, 9/17/85, C, 85002238

Morris, Jim, Barn [Stone County MRA], AR 66, Timbo, 9/17/85, C, 85002209

Pictograph Cave [Rock Art Sites in Arkansas TR], Address Restricted, Mountain View vicinity, 5/04/82, D, 82002144

Pruitt, Pinky, Barn [Stone County MRA], AR 14, St. James, 9/17/85, C, 85002239

Roasting Ear Church and School [Stone County MRA], NE of Onia, Onia vicinity, 9/17/85, A, C, a, 85002230

Smith, C. L., & Son General Store [Stone County MRA], AR 66, Mountain View, 9/17/85, C, 85002240

Stegall General Store [Stone County MRA], AR 66, Mountain View, 9/17/85, C, 85002241

Stone County Courthouse, Courthouse Sq., Mountain View, 9/29/76, C, 76000470

Stone County Recorder Building [Stone County MRA], Off AR 66, Mountain View, 9/17/85, C, 85002242

Taylor-Stokes House [Stone County MRA], Off AR 14, Marcella vicinity, 9/17/85, C, 85002207

Turkey Creek School [Stone County MRA], AR 9, Turkey Creek, 10/25/85, C, 85003396

West Richwoods Church & School [Stone County MRA], AR 9, West Richwoods, 9/17/85, A, C, a, 85002205

Union County

Bank of Commerce, 200 N. Washington St., El Dorado, 3/25/82, A, C, 82002145

El Dorado Apartments, 420 Wilson Pl., El Dorado, 12/01/83, A, C, 83003549

El Dorado Junior College Building, 300 S. West Ave., El Dorado, 9/13/78, A, C, 78000633

Exchange Bank, Washington and Oak Sts., El Dorado, 12/16/86, A, C, 86003304

First Presbyterian Church, 300 E. Main, El Dorado, 5/14/91, C, a, 91000579

McDonald, D., House, 800 S. Broadway, Smackover, 12/27/90, C, 90001949

McKinney, Henry Crawford, House, 510 E. Faulkner, El Dorado, 9/01/83, B, C, 83001157

Mount Moriah Masonic Lodge No. 18, Off AR 172, Lisbon, 3/13/87, A, C, a, 87000442

Municipal Building, 204 N. West Ave., El Dorado, 6/30/83, A, C, 83001167

Murphy, Charles H., Sr., House, 900 N. Madison Ave., El Dorado, 9/08/83, B, C, 83001168

Ouachita River Bridge [Historic Bridges of Arkansas MPS], US 167, over the Ouachita River, Calion, 4/09/90, A, C, 90000507

Rainey, Matthew, House, 510 N. Jackson St., El Dorado, 11/06/74, C, b, 74000501

Rialto Theatre, 117 E. Cedar St., El Dorado, 8/21/86, C, 86001888

SAU at Dorado [Thompson, Charles L., Design Collection TR], Summit at Block Sts., El Dorado, 12/22/82, C, 82000939

Smackover Historic Commercial District, 601–628 Broadway, Smackover, 6/14/90, A, C, 90000884

Smith, Joel, House, Jct. of US 167 and Co. Rd. 5, El Dorado, 8/31/90, C, D, 90001220

Smith—McCurry House, AR 15 N side, 3.5 mi. E of El Dorado, El Dorado vicinity, 10/15/92, B, C, 92001394

Union County Courthouse, Union Sq., El Dorado, 6/30/83, A, C, 83001169

Van Buren County

Collums—Baker House, US 65 E side, approximately 1/2 mi. S of town limits, Bee Branch vicinity, 11/24/92, C, 92001282

Damascus Gymnasium [Public Schools in the Ozarks MPS], AR 285, Damascus, 9/04/92, A, 92001122

Edgemont Shelter [Rock Art Sites in Arkansas TR], Address Restricted, Shirley vicinity, 5/04/82, D, 82002146

Lynn Creek Shelter [Rock Art Sites in Arkansas TR], Address Restricted, Fairfield Bay vicinity, 3/21/78, D, 78000634

Stobaugh House, AR 9, 0.5 mi. SW of Choctaw, Choctaw vicinity, 7/06/76, A, B, C, 76000471

Van Buren County Courthouse, Jct. of Griggs and Main Sts., Clinton, 5/13/91, C, 91000584

Washington County

Agriculture Building—University of Arkansas, Fayetteville [Public Schools in the Ozarks MPS], Campus Dr., Fayetteville, 9/04/92, A, C, 92001098

Bariola Farm, 329 Ardemagni Rd., Tontitown, 3/05/92, A, C, 92000096

Blackburn House [Canehill MRA], Main at College Sts., Canehill, 11/17/82, C, 82000940

Borden House, NE of Prairie Grove on U.S. 62, Prairie Grove vicinity, 3/17/77, A, 77000278

Brown Bluff (3WA10), Address Restricted, Woolsey vicinity, 6/24/87, D, 86002946

Business Administration Building—University of Arkansas, Fayetteville [Public Schools in the Ozarks MPS], Campus Dr., Fayetteville, 9/04/92, A, C, 92001099

Canehill Cemetery [Canehill MRA], SR 13, Canehill, 11/17/82, A, d, 82000941

Canehill College Building [Canehill MRA], McClellan and College St., Canehill, 11/17/82, A, C, 82000942

Carnell, Ella, Hall [Thompson, Charles L., Design Collection TR], Arkansas Ave. and Maple St., Fayetteville, 12/22/82, C, 82000943

Carroll, A. R., Building [Canehill MRA], Main St., Canehill, 11/17/82, A, C, 82000944

Chemistry Building—University of Arkansas, Fayetteville [Public Schools in the Ozarks MPS], Campus Dr., Fayetteville, 9/04/92, A, C, 92001100

Chi Omega Greek Theatre—University of Arkansas, Fayetteville [Public Schools in the Ozarks MPS], Dickson St., Fayetteville, 9/04/92, A, C, 92001101

Combs, Nathan, House, Address Restricted, Fayetteville vicinity, 12/12/76, B, C, 76000472

Dodson Memorial Building [Public Schools in the Ozarks MPS], Jct. of Pleasant St. and Emma Ave., NE corner, Springdale, 9/04/92, A, 92001118

Durham School [Public Schools in the Ozarks MPS], Co. Rd. 183, Durham, 9/04/92, A, 92001121

Washington County—Continued

Earle House [Canehill MRA], AR 45, Canehill, 11/17/82, B, C, 82000945

Edmiston, D. N., House [Canehill MRA], Main St., Canehill, 11/17/82, C, 82000946

Edmiston, John, House [Canehill MRA], Off AR 45, Canehill vicinity, 11/17/82, B, C, 82000947

Edmiston, Zeb, House [Canehill MRA], Main St., Canehill, 11/17/82, C, 82000948

Fayetteville Confederate Cemetery, Rock St., approximately 800 feet N of jct. with Willow St., Fayetteville, 6/03/93, A, d, 93000481

Fishback School [Public Schools in the Ozarks MPS], AR 68N, Springdale, 9/04/92, A, 92001120

Frisco Depot, 550 W. Dickson St., Fayetteville, 12/08/88, A, C, 88002819

Gordon, Troy, House, 9 E. Township Rd., Fayetteville, 12/01/78, C, 78000635

Gregg House, 339 N. Gregg St., Fayetteville, 9/17/74, B, C, 74000502

Guisinger Building, E. Mountain St., Fayetteville, 9/20/84, A, C, 84000910

Happy Hollow Farm, CR 10, Fayetteville, 8/06/86, B, 86002241

Headquarters House, 118 E. Dickson St., Fayetteville, 6/24/71, B, 71000129

Hemingway House and Barn, 3310 Old Missouri Rd., Fayetteville, 8/12/82, C, 82002148

Home Economics Building—University of Arkansas, Fayetteville [Public Schools in the Ozarks MPS], W of Campus Dr., Fayetteville, 9/04/92, A, C, 92001102

House at 712 N. Mill Street, 712 N. Mill St., Springdale, 9/04/92, C, 92001157

Jackson House, 1500 Mission Hwy. (AR 45), Fayetteville, 8/17/82, A, C, 82002149

Johnson Barn, Cato Springs Rd. N of Round Top Mtn., Fayetteville vicinity, 6/21/90, C, 90000896

Johnson House and Mill, W of Johnson on Johnson Rd., Johnson vicinity, 12/12/76, B, C, 76000473

Kantz House, E of Fayetteville at 2650 Mission St., Fayetteville vicinity, 11/14/80, B, C, 80000788

Lake-Bell House, N of Prairie Grove, Prairie Grove vicinity, 11/08/74, C, 74000504

Lewis Brothers Building, 1 S. Block, Fayetteville, 8/17/87, A, C, 86003334

Magnolia Company Filling Station, 492 W. Lafayette St., Fayetteville, 11/15/78, C, 78000636

McClellan, E. W., House [Canehill MRA], SW of Canehill off AR 45, Canehill vicinity, 11/17/82, A, C, 82000949

Men's Gymnasium—University of Arkansas, Fayetteville [Public Schools in the Ozarks MPS], Garland Ave., Fayetteville, 9/04/92, A, C, 92001103

Methodist Manse [Canehill MRA], Main and Spring Sts., Canehill, 11/17/82, A, C, a, 82000950

Moore House [Canehill MRA], NW of Canehill on SR 13, Canehill, 11/17/82, C, 82000951

Mount Nord Historic District, Mount Nord Ave., Fayetteville, 9/16/82, B, C, 82002150

Old Main, University of Arkansas, Arkansas Ave., Fayetteville, 6/15/70, A, C, 70000131

Old Post Office, City Sq., Fayetteville, 8/27/74, C, 74000503

Prairie Grove Battlefield Park, Within a triangle formed by North Rd. on the NW and U.S. 62 on the S, Prairie Grove, 9/04/70, A, 70000133

Prairie Grove Battlefield (Boundary Increase), US 62 N side, E of Prairie Grove, Prairie Grove vicinity, 11/09/92, A, 92001523

Pyeatte Mill Site [Canehill MRA], S of Canehill on AR 45, Canehill vicinity, 11/17/82, A, 82000954

Pyeatte, Henry, House [Canehill MRA], N of Canehill on AR 45, Canehill vicinity, 11/17/82, C, 82000952

Rabbits Foot Lodge, 3600 Silent Grove Rd., Springdale, 9/11/86, B, C, g, 86002421

Ridge House, 230 W. Center St., Fayetteville, 11/02/72, B, C, 72000211

Routh—Bailey House, Old Wire Rd. 3 mi. E of Fayetteville, Fayetteville vicinity, 9/28/89, C, 89001592

Shiloh Church, Huntsville and Main Sts., Springdale, 6/05/75, A, a, 75000418

Shiloh Historic District, Roughly bounded by Spring Creek, Shiloh, Johnson, Mill, and Spring Sts., Springdale, 8/31/78, B, C, 78000640

Smith, Tom, House, AR 74 W of jct. with AR 295, NE of Elkins, Elkins vicinity, 10/08/92, B, C, 92001344

Southern Mercantile Building, 107 E. Buchanan, Prairie Grove, 6/14/90, A, C, 90000898

Spring Valley School District 120 Building [Public Schools in the Ozarks MPS], Co. Rd. 379, Spring Valley, 9/04/92, A, a, 92001119

Stone House, 207 Center St., Fayetteville, 9/04/70, C, 70000132

Student Union Building—University of Arkansas, Fayetteville [Public Schools in the Ozarks MPS], Jct. of Campus Dr. and Maple St., SE corner, Fayetteville, 9/04/92, A, C, 92001104

Tilley, John, House, W of Prairie Dr. on Rhea's Mill Rd., Prairie Grove vicinity, 11/02/78, B, C, 78000639

Tontitown School Building [Public Schools in the Ozarks MPS], AR 412, Tontitown, 9/04/92, A, 92001117

United Presbyterian Church of Canehill [Canehill MRA], Main St., Canehill, 11/17/82, A, C, a, 82000955

Vest, John S., House, 21 N. West St., Fayetteville, 11/27/79, C, 79003103

Villa Rosa, 617 W. Lafayette, Fayetteville, 12/27/90, B, C, D, 90001946

Wade-Heerwagen House, 338 Washington Ave., N, Fayetteville, 6/15/78, A, C, 78000637

Walker House, Knerr Rd., Fayetteville, 6/10/75, B, C, 75000417

Walker, Vol, Library—University of Arkansas, Fayetteville [Public Schools in the Ozarks MPS], Campus Dr., Fayetteville, 9/04/92, A, C, 92001105

Washington County Courthouse, College Ave. and E. Center St., Fayetteville, 2/23/72, A, C, 72000212

Washington County Jail, College and County Aves., Fayetteville, 12/01/78, A, C, 78000638

Washington-Willow Historic District, Roughly bounded by College and Walnut Aves., Rebecca and Spring Sts., Fayetteville, 5/23/80, A, B, C, 80000789

Waters—Pierce Oil Company Building [Thompson, Charles L., Design Collection TR], West St., Fayetteville, 12/08/88, C, 88002821

Welch, William, House [Canehill MRA], Main St., Canehill, 11/17/82, A, C, 82000956

Wilson-Pittman-Campbell-Gregory House, 405 E. Dickson St., Fayetteville, 5/06/80, C, 80000790

Wyman Bridge [Historic Bridges of Arkansas MPS], Co. Rd. 38, over West Fork of the White River, Fayetteville vicinity, 4/09/90, A, C, 90000526

White County

Abington, William Thomas, House [White County MPS], Center St. SW of jct. with AR 367, Beebe, 7/11/92, C, 91001350

Ackins House [White County MPS], Jct. of AR 31 and AR 305, Floyd vicinity, 7/11/92, C, 91001322

American Legion Hall [White County MPS], Jct. of Race and Spruce Sts., Searcy, 9/13/91, A, C, 91001186

Andrews, Col. Ralph, House [White County MPS], 517 W. Center St., Beebe, 9/05/91, C, 91001253

Arnold Farmstead [White County MPS], Off Maple St. S of Deener Cr., Searcy, 9/13/91, C, 91001187

Baldock House [White County MPS], Jct. of S. Elm St. and W. Woodruff Ave., Searcy, 9/05/91, C, 91001239

Bank of Searcy [White County MPS], 301 N. Spruce St., Searcy, 9/05/91, C, 91001228

Beebe Jail [White County MPS], E of jct. of N. Main and Illinois Sts., Beebe, 9/13/91, A, 91001251

Beebe Railroad Station, Center St., Beebe, 12/11/79, A, C, 79000465

Beebe Theater [White County MPS], Center St., Beebe, 9/05/91, C, 91001265

Bell House [White County MPS], 302 W. Woodruff Ave., Searcy, 9/05/91, C, 91001201

Berry House [White County MPS], 208 Hickory, Beebe, 9/05/91, C, 91001262

Big Four School [White County MPS], Co. Rd. 383 S of jct. with AR 258, Providence vicinity, 7/10/92, A, C, 91001192

Black, Benjamin Clayton, House, 300 E. Race St., Searcy, 11/20/74, B, C, 74000505

Bloom House [White County MPS], Jct. of N. Maple and Academy Sts., Searcy, 9/05/91, C, 91001176

Blunt House Livestock Barn [White County MPS], Co. Rd. 357 E of jct. with AR 157, Midway vicinity, 7/10/92, C, 91001363

Boggs, James William, House [White County MPS], Austin St. between South and Torrence Sts., Pangburn, 9/05/91, C, 91001298

Bone, Luke, Grocery—Boarding House [White County MPS], Jct. of Main and Market Sts., Bald Knob, 9/13/91, C, 91001275

White County—Continued

Booth, Green, House [White County MPS], Jct. of S. Pecan St. and W. Center Ave., Searcy, 9/05/91, C, 91001202

Booth—Weir House [White County MPS], W. First St., McRae, 9/05/91, B, 91001345

Brooks House [White County MPS], 704 E. Market St., Searcy, 7/10/92, C, 91001217

Brown House [White County MPS], Elm St., Bald Knob, 9/13/91, C, 91001268

Brown, Joe, House and Farmstead [White County MPS], Co. Rd. 529 NW of Little Red, Little Red vicinity, 9/13/91, C, 91001338

Burnett House [White County MPS], Co. Rd. 766 NW of Searcy, Searcy vicinity, 7/11/92, C, 91001337

Caldwell House [White County MPS], Jct. of E. 2nd and Smith Sts., McRae, 9/05/91, C, 91001347

Campbell—Chrisp House [White County MPS], 102 Elm St., Bald Knob, 9/05/91, C, 91001280

Cary House [White County MPS], Jct. of Searcy and Short Sts., Pangburn, 7/10/92, C, 91001293

Chandler House [White County MPS], Jct. of Co. Rds. 327 and 379, Stevens Creek vicinity, 7/10/92, C, 91001310

Childers Farmstead [White County MPS], E of AR 367 S of McRae, McRae vicinity, 7/11/92, C, 91001349

Churchill—Hilger House [White County MPS], Jct. of Main and Searcy Sts., Pangburn, 9/05/91, B, C, 91001301

Cobb, Pattie, Hall [White County MPS], 900 E. Center, Harding University, Searcy, 9/05/91, A, C, 91001209

Cooley, Sam, Barn [White County MPS], Co. Rd. 96 SE of Bald Knob, Bald Knob vicinity, 7/11/92, C, 91001282

Coward House [White County MPS], 1105 N. Maple St., Searcy, 7/10/92, C, 91001229

Cremane House [White County MPS], Co. Rd. 95 W of Bradford Lake, Bradford, 7/10/92, C, 91001320

Critz, Col. John, Farm, Springhouse [White County MPS], Co. Rd. 818 W of jct. with Co. Rd. 41, Center Hill vicinity, 7/10/92, C, 91001333

Cross House [White County MPS], 410 S. Main St., Beebe, 7/10/92, C, 91001259

Cumberland Presbyterian Church [White County MPS], Jct. of Race and Spring Sts., Searcy, 7/10/92, C, a, 91001225

Cypert, Jesse N., Law Office [White County MPS], 104 E. Race St., Searcy, 7/12/92, B, C, 91001179

Darden-Gifford House, N of Rosebud off AR 5, Rosebud vicinity, 1/01/76, B, C, 76000474

Deener House [Thompson, Charles L., Design Collection TR], 310 E. Center Ave., Searcy, 12/22/82, C, 82000957

Doniphan Lumber Mill Historic District [White County MPS], Around Doniphan Lake off AR 367, Doniphan, 9/13/91, C, 91001196

Doss House [White County MPS], 408 N. Main St., at Louisiana St., Beebe, 7/10/92, C, 91001264

Doyle, David, House No. 2 [White County MPS], Jct. of Co. Rd. 953 and AR 5, El Paso, 9/05/91, C, 91001302

Edie, James W., House [White County MPS], Jct. of Jackson and Washington Sts., Judsonia, 9/05/91, C, 91001189

El Paso Bank [White County MPS], Co. Rd. 3 E of jct. with AR 5, El Paso, 9/05/91, C, 91001303

Elm Street House [White County MPS], Elm St., Bald Knob, 9/13/91, C, 91001269

Emmer, Joe, House [White County MPS], Co. Rd. 47, Holly Springs vicinity, 7/12/92, C, 91001327

First Christian Church [White County MPS], Jct. of N. Main and E. Market Sts., Searcy, 7/12/92, C, a, 91001198

First United Methodist Church [White County MPS], Jct. of Main and Market Sts., Searcy, 7/12/92, C, a, 91001206

Floyd Cotton Gin [White County MPS], Jct. of AR 31 and AR 305, Floyd vicinity, 7/12/92, A, C, 91001324

Fox Motel House [White County MPS], AR 367, Bald Knob, 7/12/92, C, 91001267

Freeman, Wood, House No. 1 [White County MPS], 702 Arch St., Searcy, 9/05/91, C, 91001185

Freeman, Wood, House No. 2 [White County MPS], 703 W. Race St., Searcy, 9/05/91, C, 91001181

Frizell, Dr., House [White County MPS], Jct. of US 67 and Elm St., Bradford, 7/12/92, C, 91001318

Garrard, Lizzie, House [White County MPS], N. Cypress St., Beebe, 9/05/91, C, 91001263

Gooden, Milt, House [White County MPS], Co. Rd. 83 SE of Bald Knob, Bald Knob vicinity, 7/13/92, C, 91001281

Gordon, Leonard, Homestead, Hexagonal Grain Crib [White County MPS], Co. Rd. 69, Twentythree vicinity, 7/21/92, C, 91001311

Gravel Hill Baptist Church [White County MPS], Gravel Hill Road, Gravel Hill, 7/21/92, C, a, 91001323

Gray House [White County MPS], Jct of Co. Rds. 758 and 46, Crosby vicinity, 7/21/92, C, 91001334

Gray, Louis, Homestead, Barn [White County MPS], AR 157 E of Plainview, Plainview vicinity, 7/21/92, C, 91001194

Gray, Rufus, House [White County MPS], Jct. of Austin and South Sts., Pangburn, 9/05/91, C, 91001294

Gray—Kincaid House [White County MPS], Jct. of Co. Rds. 46 and 759, Crosby vicinity, 7/21/92, C, 91001335

Griffithville School [White County MPS], AR 11 W of jct. with AR 385, Griffithville, 7/13/92, A, C, 91001357

Hale, Thomas Jefferson, General Merchandise Store [White County MPS], Jct of Co. Rds. 62 and 433, Vinity Corner, 7/21/92, A, C, 91001358

Hall, Fred, House [White County MPS], Jct. of 2nd and W. Searcy Sts., Kensett, 9/05/91, C, 91001222

Hammond, Mary Alice, House [White County MPS], Co. Rd. 839 W of jct. with AR 367, Searcy, 7/21/92, C, b, 91001204

Harper, Roy, House [White County MPS], Co. Rd. 16 E of jct. with AR 5, Romance vicinity, 7/21/92, C, 91001304

Hartsell, Morris, Farmstead [White County MPS], AR 157, Steprock vicinity, 9/13/91, C, 91001340

Hassell House [White County MPS], Jct. of S. Elm St. and W. Woodruff Ave., Searcy, 9/05/91, C, 91001205

Hays, Brady, Homestead [White County MPS], US 167 S of Denmark, Denmark vicinity, 9/13/91, A, C, 91001312

Henson, Alfred W., House, 111 Main St., Judsonia, 10/23/86, B, C, 86002938

Herring Building [White County MPS], Jct. of E. First and Smith Sts., McRae, 9/05/91, A, C, 91001348

Hickmon, Marshall, Homestead [White County MPS], AR 87, Bradford, 7/21/92, C, 91001317

Hickmon, U. L., Hardware Store [White County MPS], Jct. of Main and Second Sts., Bradford, 9/05/91, A, C, 91001316

Hicks, Ida, House [White County MPS], 410 W. Arch St., Searcy, 9/05/91, C, 91001180

Hicks-Dugan-Deener House, 306 E. Center St., Searcy, 4/18/85, C, 85000835

Hilger, Louis N., Homestead, Livestock Barn [White County MPS], Co. Rd.374 W of jct. with AR 157, Providence vicinity, 7/21/92, C, 91001191

Hill Farm [White County MPS], N of US 67 SW of Beebe, Beebe vicinity, 7/21/92, C, 91001258

Hoag House [White County MPS], Jct. of AR 157 and AR 367, Judsonia vicinity, 7/21/92, C, 91001236

Holly Grove School [White County MPS], Co. Rd. 379 N of jct. with Co. Rd. 327, Stevens Creek vicinity, 7/13/92, A, C, 91001309

Honey Hill Christian Union Church [White County MPS], S of AR 36 SW of Searcy, Searcy vicinity, 7/21/92, C, a, 91001352

Hoofman Farmstead Barn [White County MPS], Between Plainview and the Little Red R., Searcy vicinity, 7/22/92, C, 91001188

Hoofman, Arthur W., House [White County MPS], Jct. of E. Race and N. Cross Sts., Searcy, 7/22/92, C, 91001184

Hoofman, Tobe, Farmstead [White County MPS], AR 371 N of jct. with AR 157, Providence vicinity, 7/22/92, C, 91001228

Hopewell District No. 45 School [White County MPS], AR 258 W of Lake Bald Knob, Hopewell vicinity, 7/13/92, A, C, a, 91001283

Hunt House [White County MPS], 707 W. Center St., Searcy, 9/13/91, C, 91001207

Hunt, Thomas, House [White County MPS], AR 157 N of Plainview, Plainview vicinity, 7/22/92, C, 91001193

Hutchinson, L. D., House [White County MPS], AR 31 N of jct. with AR 305, Floyd vicinity, 7/22/92, C, 91001325

James, Dr., House [White County MPS], Jct. of W. Center and S. Gum Sts., Searcy, 9/13/91, C, 91001241

Jameson—Richards Cafe [White County MPS], AR 367 E of jct. with Vine St., Bald Knob, 9/05/91, C, 91001266

White County—Continued

Jameson—Richards Gas Station [White County MPS], Jct. of AR 367 and Vine St., Bald Knob, 9/05/91, C, 91001279

Joiner House [White County MPS], 708 Market St., Searcy, 7/22/92, C, 91001214

Jones, Mark P., House [White County MPS], Jct. of Center and Fir Sts., Searcy, 9/05/91, C, 91001197

Judsonia Bridge [Historic Bridges of Arkansas MPS], Co. Rd. 66, over the Little Red River, Judsonia, 4/09/90, A, C, 90000535

Judsonia Community Building Historic District [White County MPS], Jct. of Judson Ave. and 6th St., Judsonia, 9/05/91, A, C, 91001234

Judsonia High School Gymnasium [White County MPS], Roadman Ave., Judsonia, 9/13/91, A, C, 91001232

Kelly, C. D., House [White County MPS], Jct. of Main and Adams Sts., Judsonia, 9/05/91, C, 91001190

Kimbrough, S. A., House [White County MPS], 302 E. Illinois St., Beebe, 9/05/91, C, 91001252

Klotz, Henry W., Sr., Service Station [White County MPS], W. First St., Russell, 9/13/91, A, C, 91001273

Klotz, Henry, Sr., House [White County MPS], First St., Russell, 7/22/92, C, 91001285

Larned, Capt., House [White County MPS], AR 157 N of US 64, Judsonia vicinity, 7/22/92, C, 91001235

Lattimer House [White County MPS], Jct. of Oak and Market Sts., Searcy, 9/05/91, C, 91001215

Laws—Jarvis House [White County MPS], 409 N. Main St., Beebe, 7/22/92, C, 91001256

Lea, Harvey, House [White County MPS], Co. Rd. 70, Russell, 7/13/92, C, 91001270

Leggett House [White County MPS], AR 124 E of Little Red, Little Red, 7/13/92, C, 91001339

Lemay House [White County MPS], 305 S. Cypress St., Beebe, 7/20/92, C, 91001254

Letona Hotel [White County MPS], Off AR 310, Letona, 9/13/91, A, C, 91001329

Lightle House [Thompson, Charles L., Design Collection TR], 605 Race Ave., Searcy, 12/22/82, C, 82000958

Lightle House [White County MPS], Co. Rd. 76, Searcy vicinity, 7/20/92, C, 91001224

Lightle House [White County MPS], 107 N. Elm St., Searcy, 9/05/91, C, 91001244

Lightle, Ben, House [White County MPS], Jct. of N. Locust and E. Market Sts., Searcy, 9/05/91, C, 91001216

Lightle, William H., House [White County MPS], 601 E. Race St., Searcy, 9/05/91, B, C, 91001226

Little, Jim, House [White County MPS], Walnut St. E of jct. with Front St., Bradford, 9/05/91, C, 91001315

Livestock and Equipment Barn, Glenn Homestead [White County MPS], AR 124 NE of Pangburn, Pangburn vicinity, 7/20/92, C, 91001287

Lone Star School [White County MPS], E of Big Mingo Cr., Lone Star vicinity, 7/20/92, C, 91001355

Lovell, Dr., House [White County MPS], Walnut St. E of jct. with Main St., Bradford, 7/20/92, C, 91001314

Maddox, E. D., Farm Chicken House [White County MPS], Co. Rd. 36 E of jct. with AR 5, Rosebud, 7/20/92, C, 91001359

Marsh, Walter, House [White County MPS], Jct. of Maple and Torrence Sts., Pangburn, 9/05/91, C, 91001288

Marsh, Wesley, House [White County MPS], Jct. of AR 16 and AR 305, Letona vicinity, 7/20/92, C, 91001328

Martindale Corn Crib [White County MPS], AR 310, Letona, 7/20/92, C, 91001330

Mason House [White County MPS], W. Main St. W of jct. with Walnut St., Bradford, 7/20/92, C, 91001319

Mayfair Hotel [White County MPS], Jct. of Spring and Center Sts., Searcy, 9/05/91, A, C, 91001242

McAdams House [White County MPS], Jct. of Maple and South Sts., Pangburn, 9/05/91, C, 91001289

McAdams, Dr., House [White County MPS], Jct. of Maple and Searcy Sts., Pangburn, 9/13/91, C, 91001300

McDonald, Emmett, House [White County MPS], Co. Rd. 443 SE of McRae, McRae vicinity, 7/20/92, A, C, 91001368

McRae Jail [White County MPS], E. First St., McRae, 7/20/92, A, 91001344

Methodist Episcopal Church, South [White County MPS], Jct. of Main and Center Sts., Bald Knob, 7/20/92, C, a, 91001278

Miller, Emmett, House [White County MPS], AR 371 E of Plainview, Plainview vicinity, 7/20/92, C, 91001237

Mills House [White County MPS], 200 W. Searcy St., Kensett, 9/05/91, C, 91001220

Missouri—Pacific Depot [White County MPS], Jct. of Market and Ramey Sts., Bald Knob, 7/20/92, C, 91001276

Moody House [White County MPS], 104 Market St., Bald Knob, 7/20/92, C, 91001277

Moore House [White County MPS], 405 Center St., Searcy, 9/13/91, C, 91001210

Morris House, Rte. 1, Bradford, 12/04/78, B, C, 78000641

Morris Institute Dairy Barn [White County MPS], Co. Rd. 41 S of jct. with Co. Rd. 818, Crosby vicinity, 7/20/92, C, 91001332

National Guard Armory Building [White County MPS], Jct. of Race and N. Locust Sts., Searcy, 9/13/91, A, C, 91001178

Neaville, J. A., House [White County MPS], AR 385 N of jct. with AR 11, Griffithville, 7/22/92, C, 91001356

New Mt. Pisgah School [White County MPS], Between Mt. Pisgah and Little Cr., New Mt. Pisgah vicinity, 7/20/92, A, C, 91001331

Nimmo Clubhouse [White County MPS], Co. Rd. 65 at Little Red R., Nimmo vicinity, 7/22/92, C, 91001360

O'Neal, Howard, Barn [White County MPS], Co. Rd. 73 S of Russell, Russell vicinity, 7/20/92, C, 91001286

Pangburn, Austin, House [White County MPS], Jct. of Main and Austin Sts., Pangburn, 9/05/91, C, 91001290

Paschall House [White County MPS], Jct. of N. Oak and E. Center Sts., Searcy, 9/05/91, C, 91001203

Patman House [White County MPS], Jct. of Mountain and Jackson Sts., Pangburn, 9/05/91, C, 91001292

Pemberton House [White County MPS], 601 N. Cypress St., Beebe, 9/05/91, C, 91001255

Pence—Carmichael Farm, Barn and Root Cellar [White County MPS], Off AR 31 E of Romance, Romance vicinity, 7/20/92, C, 91001305

Plummer House [White County MPS], 314 Alabama St., Beebe, 7/22/92, C, 91001247

Powell Clothing Store [White County MPS], 201 N. Main St., Beebe, 9/05/91, C, 91001249

Prince House [White County MPS], Co. Rd. 68 NW of Velvet Ridge, Velvet Ridge vicinity, 7/22/92, C, 91001307

Ransom, Edward, Farmstead, Livestock and Equipment Barn [White County MPS], Co. Rd. 359 W of jct. with US 167, Midway, 7/22/92, C, 91001361

Rascoe House [White County MPS], 702 Main St., Searcy, 7/23/92, C, 91001213

Ray, Sam, House [White County MPS], AR 305 NE of jct. with Co. Rd. 47, Clay vicinity, 7/23/92, C, 91001296

Rhew, J. C., Co. Packing Shed [White County MPS], Co. Rd. 376 NE of Providence, Providence vicinity, 7/23/92, A, C, 91001343

Rialto Theater [White County MPS], Jct. of Race and Spring Sts., Searcy, 9/13/91, C, 91001231

Robertson Drugstore [White County MPS], Jct. of Spring and Arch Sts., Searcy, 9/13/91, B, C, 91001245

Robertson House [White County MPS], Jct.of 2nd and Dandridge Sts., Kensett, 9/05/91, C, 91001221

Rock Building [White County MPS], Co. Rd. 370 S of jct. with AR 157, Plainview vicinity, 7/23/92, C, 91001195

Rodgers, Porter, Sr., House [White County MPS], Jct. of N. Oak and E. Race Sts., Searcy, 9/05/91, C, 91001230

Rogers, Bob, House [White County MPS], Jct. of S. Spring St. and W. Woodruff Ave., Searcy, 9/13/91, C, 91001219

Roper House [White County MPS], Hill Street, McRae, 9/05/91, C, 91001346

Russell Jail [White County MPS], Off Elm St., Russell, 7/23/92, A, 91001271

Scott—Davis House [White County MPS], Co. Rd. 15 SW of Romance, Romance vicinity, 7/20/92, C, 91001306

Searcy City Hall [White County MPS], Jct. of Gum and Race Sts., Searcy, 9/05/91, A, C, 91001227

Searcy Post Office [White County MPS], Jct. of Gum and Arch Sts., SW corner, Searcy, 7/20/92, A, C, 91001200

Sears, Dean L. C., House [White County MPS], 805 E. Center St., Searcy, 7/20/92, C, 91001208

Sellers House [White County MPS], 702 W. Center St., Beebe, 9/05/91, C, 91001261

White County—Continued

Shue House [White County MPS], 108 Holly St., Beebe, 9/05/91, C, 91001257

Shutter, John, House [White County MPS], Jct. of Austin and Main Sts., Pangburn, 9/05/91, C, 91001299

Simpson, Stanley, Farmstead Picking Sled [White County MPS], Co. Rd. 390 W of jct. with AR 157, Providence, 9/13/91, A, C, 91001342

Smith House [White County MPS], 607 W. Arch Ave., Searcy, 9/05/91, C, 91001218

Smith, A. J., House [White County MPS], AR 385, Griffithville, 9/05/91, C, 91001223

Smith—Moore House [White County MPS], 901 N. Main St., Beebe, 7/20/92, C, 91001246

Smyrna Methodist Church [White County MPS], AR 36 E of Center Hill, Center Hill vicinity, 7/20/92, C, a, 91001336

Snipes, Dr. Emmett, House [White County MPS], Jct. of E. Market and N. Locust Sts., Searcy, 9/05/91, C, 91001243

St. Richard's Catholic Church [White County MPS], Jct. of Hickory and Cleveland Sts., Bald Knob, 7/20/92, C, a, 91001274

Staggs—Huffaker Building [White County MPS], Jct. of N. Main and W. Illinois Sts., Beebe, 9/05/91, C, 91001250

Stipe Cotton Gin [White County MPS], Jct. of Florida and Cypress Sts., Beebe, 7/20/92, A, C, 91001248

Storm Cellar, William Howell House [White County MPS], Co. Rd. 47 E of jct. with AR 305, Clay, 7/20/92, C, 91001295

Thomas House [White County MPS], Co. Rd. 751 NW of Fourmile Hill, Fourmile Hill vicinity, 7/23/92, C, 91001326

Thompson House [White County MPS], Co. Rd. 328 behind Holly Grove Cemetery, Stevens Creek vicinity, 7/23/92, C, 91001341

Thrasher, John, Homestead [White County MPS], Off Co. Rd. 359 W of jct. with US 167, Midway vicinity, 7/23/92, C, 91001362

Titus House [White County MPS], 406 E. Center St., Searcy, 9/05/91, C, 91001240

Trinity Episcopal Church [White County MPS], Jct. of N. Elm and Market Sts., Searcy, 7/23/92, C, a, 91001199

Van Meter, R. L., House [White County MPS], Jct. of Wade and 14th Sts., Judsonia, 9/05/91, C, 91001233

Walker Homestead Historic District [White County MPS], Co. Rd. 56 E of jct. with AR 267, Garner vicinity, 7/20/92, A, C, 91001351

Walker, Otha, Homestead [White County MPS], AR 36, West Point vicinity, 7/23/92, C, 91001354

Ward—Stout House [White County MPS], Jct. of Front and Walnut Sts., Bradford, 9/05/91, C, 91001313

Watkins House [White County MPS], 1208 E. Race St., Searcy, 9/05/91, C, 91001182

Watkins, Tom, House [White County MPS], Jct. of Oak and Race Sts., Searcy, 9/05/91, C, 91001183

Watson, William Henry, Homestead [White County MPS], Co. Rd. 68 S of Denmark, Denmark vicinity, 7/20/92, C, 91001308

Weber House [White County MPS], Elm St., Russell, 9/05/91, C, 91001272

Westbrooke, Lipsy, House [White County MPS], 809 W. Center St., Beebe, 7/23/92, C, 91001260

Whisinant, Albert, House [White County MPS], AR 16 N of Mountain Home, Mountain Home vicinity, 7/23/92, C, 91001297

White County Courthouse, Court Sq., Searcy, 8/03/77, A, C, 77000279

Wilburn House [White County MPS], 707 E. Race St., Searcy, 9/05/91, C, 91001177

Williams House [White County MPS], Jct. of Co. Rd. 54 and AR 267, Searcy vicinity, 7/23/92, C, 91001353

Williams, Arthur, Homestead, Feed Storage Shed [White County MPS], Falwell Rd., Bradford vicinity, 7/23/92, C, 91001321

Wood, Jack, House, Judson Ave., Judsonia, 11/02/89, C, 89001939

Woodson, Arthur W., House [White County MPS], 1005 W. Arch Ave., Searcy, 9/05/91, C, 91001211

Woodson, Dalton, House [White County MPS], 1007 W. Arch Ave., Searcy, 9/05/91, C, 91001212

Wright, Avanell, House [White County MPS], Jct. of Main and Pine Sts., Pangburn, 9/05/91, C, 91001291

Wright, Jim, Farmstead Historic District [White County MPS], AR 258 E of jct. with AR 323, Bald Knob vicinity, 9/05/91, C, 91001284

Woodruff County

Augusta Bridge [Historic Bridges of Arkansas MPS], US 64, over the White River, Augusta, 4/09/90, A, C, 90000505

Augusta Presbyterian Church, Third and Walnut Sts., Augusta, 10/16/86, A, C, a, 86002873

Ferguson House, 416 N. 3rd St., Augusta, 12/06/75, B, C, 75000419

Woodruff County Courthouse [Thompson, Charles L., Design Collection TR], 500 N. 3rd St., Augusta, 12/22/82, C, 82000959

Yell County

Achmun Creek Bridge [Historic Bridges of Arkansas MPS], Co. Rd. 222, over Achmun Creek, Ola vicinity, 4/09/90, A, C, 90000539

First Presbyterian Church, Second and Quay Sts., Dardanelle, 7/09/87, C, a, 87001156

Kimball House, 713 N. Front St., Dardanelle, 6/23/82, C, 82002151

Mitchell House, SR 80 W of Watson Branch, Waltreak, 6/07/90, C, D, 90000876

Mt. Nebo State Park—Pavilion [Facilities Constructed by the CCC in Arkansas MPS], N of AR 155, Mount Nebo State Park, Dardanelle vicinity, 5/28/92, A, C, 92000542

Spring Lake Bridge [Historic Bridges of Arkansas MPS], AR 307, over Bob Barnes Branch, Belleville vicinity, 6/21/90, A, C, 90000510

Steamboat House, 601 N. Front St., Dardanelle, 6/05/75, C, 75000420

Yell County Courthouse, 209 Union St., Dardanelle, 9/08/92, C, 92001176

CALIFORNIA

Alameda County

Abbey, The, Joaquin Miller Rd. and Sanborn Dr., Oakland, 10/15/66, B, NHL, 66000204

Alameda City Hall, Santa Clara Ave. and Oak St., Alameda, 10/14/80, C, 80000791

Alameda Free Library, 2264 Santa Clara Ave., Alameda, 6/25/82, C, 82002152

Alameda High School, 2200 Central Ave., Alameda, 5/12/77, C, g, 77000280

Anna Head School for Girls, 2538 Channing Way, Berkeley, 8/11/80, A, B, C, 80000795

Bank of Italy, 2250 1st St., Livermore, 11/16/78, C, 78000648

Berkeley Day Nursery, 2031 6th St., Berkeley, 9/15/77, C, 77000281

Berkeley Public Library, 2090 Kittredge St., Berkeley, 6/25/82, C, 82002156

Berkeley Women's City Club, 2315 Durant Ave., Berkeley, 10/28/77, C, 77000282

Boone's University School, 2029 Durant Ave., Berkeley, 11/01/82, A, C, 82000994

CITY OF OAKLAND (USS HOGA), FDR Memorial Pier, Jack London Sq., Oaklnad, 6/30/89, A, g, NHL, 89001429

California Hall [Berkeley, University of California MRA], Oxford St., Berkeley, 3/25/82, C, 82004638

California Hotel, 3443–3501 San Pablo Ave., Oakland, 6/30/88, C, 88000969

California Nursery Co. Guest House, California Nursery Co., Niles Blvd. at Nursery Ave., Fremont, 5/06/71, A, C, 71000130

Cameron-Stanford House, 1426 Lakeside Dr., Oakland, 6/13/72, A, C, 72000213

Casa Peralta, 384 W. Estudillo Ave., San Leandro, 1/04/82, C, 82002168

Chamber of Commerce Building, 2140–2144 Shattuck Ave. & 2071–2089 Center St., Berkeley, 8/29/85, A, C, 85001916

Church of the Good Shepherd-Episcopal, 1001 Hearst St. at Ninth St., Berkeley, 12/01/86, A, C, a, 86003361

City Hall, 2134 Grove St., Berkeley, 9/11/81, C, 81000142

Clay Building, 1001–1007 Clay St., Oakland, 11/20/78, A, C, 78000650

Cloyne Court Hotel, 2600 Ridge Rd., Berkeley, 12/24/92, C, 92001718

Cohen, Alfred H., House, 1440 29th Ave., Oakland, 6/19/73, C, 73000394

College Women's Club, 2680 Bancroft Way, Berkeley, 1/21/82, A, C, 82002157

Corder Building, 2300–2350 Shattuck Ave., Berkeley, 1/11/82, A, C, 82002158

Croll Building, 1400 Webster St., Alameda, 10/04/82, A, B, C, 82000960

Doe Memorial Library [Berkeley, University of California MRA], Oxford St., Berkeley, 3/25/82, A, C, 82004639

Drawing Building, Hearst Ave., University of California campus, Berkeley, 11/18/76, A, C, 76000475

Dunns Block, 725 Washington St., Oakland, 11/15/78, C, 78000652

Dunsmuir House, Peralta Oaks Ct., Oakland, 5/19/72, C, 72000214

Durant Hall [Berkeley, University of California MRA], Oxford St., Berkeley, 3/25/82, A, C, 82004640

Edwards, George C., Stadium, Jct. of Bancroft Way and Fulton St., UC Berkeley campus, Berkeley, 4/01/93, A, C, 93000263

Elliston, 463 and 341 Kilkare Rd., Sunol, 6/19/85, A, B, C, 85001327

Faculty Club [Berkeley, University of California MRA], Oxford St., Berkeley, 3/25/82, A, C, 82004641

Federal Realty Building, 1615 Broadway, Oakland, 1/02/79, C, 79000467

First Church of Christ, Scientist, 2619 Dwight Way, Berkeley, 12/22/77, C, a, NHL, 77000283

First Presbyterian Church Sanctuary Building, 2001 Santa Clara Ave., Alameda, 11/25/80, C, 80000792

First Unitarian Church, 2401 Bancroft Way, Berkeley, 12/10/81, A, C, a, 81000143

First Unitarian Church of Oakland, 685 14th St., Oakland, 6/16/77, A, C, a, 77000284

Founders' Rock [Berkeley, University of California MRA], Oxford St., Berkeley, 3/25/82, A, f, 82004642

Fox Court, 1472–1478 University Ave., Berkeley, 2/04/82, C, 82002159

Fox-Oakland Theater, 1807–1829 Telegraph Ave., Oakland, 2/02/79, A, C, 79000468

Garfield Intermediate School, 1414 Walnut St., Berkeley, 6/14/82, A, C, 82002160

Giannini Hall [Berkeley, University of California MRA], Oxford St., Berkeley, 3/25/82, C, 82004643

Girton Hall, Off College Ave. next to Cowell Hospital, University of California, Berkeley campus, Berkeley, 9/26/91, A, C, b, 91001473

Golden Sheaf Bakery, 2069–2071 Addison St., Berkeley, 3/31/78, A, C, 78000644

Greek Orthodox Church of the Assumption, 9th and Castro Sts., Oakland, 5/22/78, A, C, a, b, 78000651

Haviland Hall, University of California Campus, Berkeley, 2/01/82, C, 82002161

Hearst Greek Theatre [Berkeley, University of California MRA], Oxford St., Berkeley, 3/25/82, C, 82004644

Hearst Gymnasium for Women [Berkeley, University of California MRA], Oxford St., Berkeley, 3/25/82, C, 82004645

Hearst Memorial Mining Building [Berkeley, University of California MRA], Oxford St., Berkeley, 3/25/82, C, 82004646

Heathcote—MacKenzie House, 4501 Pleasanton Ave., Pleasanton, 10/29/91, A, 91001538

Hilgard Hall [Berkeley, University of California MRA], Oxford St., Berkeley, 3/25/82, C, 82004647

Hillside School, 1581 Leroy Ave., Berkeley, 10/29/82, C, 82000961

Kahn's Department Store, 1501–39 Broadway, Oakland, 3/30/89, C, 89000194

Kottinger, John W., Adobe Barn, 200 Ray St., Pleasanton, 9/12/85, B, C, 85002305

Lake Merritt Wild Duck Refuge, Lakeside Park, Grand Ave., Oakland, 10/15/66, A, NHL, 66000205

Liberty Hall, 1483–1485 8th St., Oakland, 3/30/89, A, C, 89000199

Lightship WAL-605, RELIEF, Oakland Estuary in Brrooklyn Basin, Oakland, 12/20/89, A, C, g, NHL, 89002462

Locke House, 3911 Harrison St., Oakland, 4/07/89, C, 89000258

Loring House, 1730 Spruce St., Berkeley, 7/13/89, C, 89000857

M.V. SANTA ROSA, Howard Terminal, Oakland, 5/29/79, C, 79000469

Madison Park Apartments, 100 9th St., Oakland, 4/01/82, C, 82002164

Main Post Office and Federal Building, 201 13th St., Oakland, 10/23/80, C, 80000796

Masonic Temple, 2105 Bancroft Way and 2295 Shattuck Ave., Berkeley, 7/15/82, C, 82002162

Masonic Temple and Lodge, 1329–31 Park St. and 2312 Alameda Ave., Alameda, 3/25/82, A, C, 82002153

McCrea House, 3500 Mountain Blvd., Oakland, 2/11/82, C, 82002165

Meek Mansion and Carriage House, 240 Hampton Rd., Hayward, 6/04/73, B, C, 73000393

Mills Hall, Mills College campus, Oakland, 10/14/71, A, C, 71000132

Mission San Jose, Mission Blvd. at Washington Blvd., Fremont, 7/14/71, A, a, 71000131

Murphy, D. J., House, 291 McLeod St., Livermore, 4/06/78, B, C, b, 78000649

North Gate Hall [Berkeley, University of California MRA], Oxford St., Berkeley, 3/25/82, C, 82004648

Oakland City Hall, 1421 Washington St., Oakland, 9/15/83, A, C, 83001170

Oakland Hotel, 260 13th St., Oakland, 9/04/79, A, C, 79000470

Oakland Iron Works-United Works, and the Remillard Brick Company, 552–592 2nd St., Oakland, 8/25/83, A, C, 83001171

Oakland Public Library, 659 14th St., Oakland, 8/11/83, A, C, 83001173

Oakland YWCA Building, 1515 Webster St., Oakland, 9/20/84, A, C, 84000755

Pacific Gas & Electric Company Building, 1625 Clay and 551 Seventeenth Sts., Oakland, 7/17/86, C, 86001665

Alameda County—Continued

Pacific Press Building, 1117 Castro St., Oakland, 4/14/75, A, C, 75000421

Paramount Theatre, 2025 Broadway, Oakland, 8/14/73, A, C, g, NHL, 73000395

Pardee House, 672 11th St., Oakland, 5/24/76, B, C, 76000476

Park Street Historic Commercial District, Roughly bounded by Oak St., Park, Lincoln, and Encinal Aves., Alameda, 5/12/82, A, C, 82002154

Patterson, George Washington, Ranch—Ardenwood, 34600 Newark Blvd., Fremont, 11/29/85, A, C, 85003043

Peralta House, 561 Lafayette Ave., San Leandro, 11/22/78, C, 78000654

Peralta, Antonio Maria, House, 2465 34th Ave., Oakland, 11/17/77, A, C, b, 77000285

Peterson House, 1124 Talbot Ave., Albany, 3/11/82, C, 82002155

Phi Delta Theta Chapter House, 2717 Hearst Ave., Berkeley, 1/11/83, C, a, 83001172

Ravenswood, S of Livermore on Arroyo Rd., Livermore vicinity, 6/26/79, A, B, C, 79000466

Room 307, Gilman Hall, University of California, University of California at Berkeley campus, Berkeley, 10/15/66, A, g, NHL, 66000203

Sather Gate and Bridge [Berkeley, University of California MRA], U.C.Berkeley, Berkeley, 3/25/82, C, 82004649

Sather Tower [Berkeley, University of California MRA], Oxford St., Berkeley, 3/25/82, C, 82004650

Security Bank and Trust Company Building, 1000 Broadway, Oakland, 7/26/82, A, C, g, 82002166

Senior Hall, University of California, Berkeley campus, Berkeley, 11/05/74, C, 74000506

South Hall [Berkeley, University of California MRA], Oxford St., Berkeley, 3/25/82, C, 82004651

St. John's Presbyterian Church, 2640 College Ave., Berkeley, 8/07/74, C, a, 74000507

St. Joseph's Basilica, 1109 Chestnut St., Alameda, 9/18/78, C, a, 78000642

State Asylum for the Deaf, Dumb and Blind, Bounded by Dwight Way, City line, Derby and Warring Sts., Berkeley, 10/14/82, A, C, 82000962

Studio Building, 2045 Shattuck Ave., Berkeley, 4/06/78, C, 78000645

The Bellevue-Staten, 492 Staten Ave., Oakland, 12/27/91, A, C, 91001896

Thorsen, William R., House, 2307 Piedmont Ave., Berkeley, 11/20/78, C, 78000646

Toverii Tuppa, 1819 10th St., Berkeley, 7/12/78, A, C, 78000647

Treadwell Mansion and Carriage House, 5212 Broadway, Oakland, 7/15/77, A, C, 77000286

Trinity Church, 525 29th St., Oakland, 2/04/82, C, a, 82002167

Tupper and Reed Building, 2275 Shattuck Ave., Berkeley, 1/21/82, C, 82002163

U.S. Post Office, 2000 Milvia St., Berkeley, 1/29/81, C, g, 81000144

USS POTOMAC (yacht), 1660 Embarcadero, Oakland, 2/20/87, A, B, g, NHL, 87000068

Union Iron Works Powerhouse, 2308 Webster St., Alameda, 1/10/80, A, C, 80000793

Union Iron Works Turbine Machine Shop, 2200 Webster St., Alameda, 4/10/80, A, C, 80000794

University High School, 5714 Martin Luther King Jr. Way, Oakland, 10/02/92, A, C, 92001300

University House [Berkeley, University of California MRA], Oxford St., Berkeley, 3/25/82, C, 82004652

Washington Union High School, 38442 Fremont Blvd., Fremont, 10/05/81, A, C, 81000145

Wellman Hall [Berkeley, University of California MRA], Oxford St., Berkeley, 3/25/82, A, C, 82004653

Wetmore House, 342 Bonita Ave., Piedmont, 4/14/78, B, C, 78000653

Wheeler Hall [Berkeley, University of California MRA], Oxford St., Berkeley, 3/25/82, A, C, 82004654

White Mansion, 604 E. 17th St., Oakland, 10/31/80, C, 80000797

Amador County

Amador County Hospital Building, 708 Court St., Jackson, 2/23/72, A, C, 72000215

Butterfield, John A., House, 115 Broadway, Jackson, 9/11/86, C, 86002412

Chichizola Family Store Complex, 1316–1330 Jackson Gate Rd., Jackson vicinity, 8/14/92, A, 92000979

DePue, Grace Blair, House and Indian Museum, 215 Court St., Jackson, 5/07/82, A, C, 82002169

Fiddletown, Off CA 49, Fiddletown, 6/07/78, A, C, 78000655

Five Mile Drive—Sutter Creek Bridge, Five Mile Drive, Ione vicinity, 4/11/86, C, 86000734

Indian Grinding Rock, Address Restricted, Volcano vicinity, 5/06/71, D, 71000133

Ione City Centenary Church, 150 W. Marlette St., Ione, 5/26/77, A, C, a, 77000287

Kennedy Tailing Wheels, Jackson Gate Rd., Jackson, 7/07/81, A, C, 81000146

Knight's Foundry and Shops, 13 Eureka St., Sutter Creek, 7/01/75, A, B, C, 75000423

Preston Castle, N of Ione on Preston Ave., Ione vicinity, 7/30/75, A, C, 75000422

Saint Sava Serbian Orthodox Church, 724 N. Main, Jackson, 3/06/86, A, C, a, 86000385

Scully Ranch, Marlette St., Ione, 11/21/78, A, C, 78000656

St. George Hotel, 2 Main St., Volcano, 9/07/84, A, C, 84000757

Sutter Creek Grammar School, Between Broad and Cole Sts., Sutter Creek, 12/12/76, A, C, 76000477

Butte County

Allen—Sommer—Gage House, 410 Normal St., Chico, 4/13/77, C, 77000288

Bidwell Mansion, Sowillenno Ave., Chico, 3/24/72, A, B, C, 72000216

Centerville Schoolhouse, 2 mi. NE of Paradise on Humbug Rd., Paradise vicinity, 3/24/72, A, 72000219

Chapman, A. H., House, 256 E. 12th St., Chico, 1/28/82, A, C, 82002170

Durham, W. W., House, 2280 Durham—Dayton Rd., Durham, 4/02/92, B, 92000316

Honey Run Covered Bridge, Honey Run Humbug Rd., Chico vicinity, 6/23/88, A, C, 88000920

Inskip Hotel, 6 mi. N of Stirling on Skyway (Old Humbug Rd.), Stirling City vicinity, 5/02/75, A, 75000425

Lee, Fong, Company, Address Restricted, Oroville vicinity, 3/11/82, A, D, 82002173

Magalia Community Church, Stirling Hwy., Magalia, 1/11/82, A, a, 82002172

Mud Creek Canyon, Address Restricted, Chico vicinity, 8/14/73, D, 73000396

Oroville Chinese Temple, 1500 Broderick St., Oroville, 7/30/76, A, C, a, 76000478

Oroville Commercial District (old), Montgomery, Myers and Huntoon Sts. and Miner Alley, Oroville, 7/28/83, A, C, 83001174

Oroville Inn, 2066 Bird St., Oroville, 9/13/90, A, C, 90001431

Patrick Ranch House, 3 mi. SE of Chico off U.S. 99E, Chico vicinity, 2/23/72, C, 72000217

Patrick Rancheria, Address Restricted, Chico vicinity, 2/23/72, D, 72000218

Silberstein Park Building, 426, 430, 434 Broadway, Chico, 2/17/83, C, 83001175

South of Campus Neighborhood, Bounded by W. 2nd, Normal, W. 6th and Cherry Sts., Chico, 6/24/91, A, C, 91000636

Southern Pacific Depot, 430 Orange St., Chico, 1/29/87, A, 87000001

St. John's Episcopal Church, 230 Salem St., Chico, 1/21/82, C, a, b, 82002171

Stansbury House, 307 W. 5th St., Chico, 6/05/75, C, 75000424

State Theatre, 1489 Myers St., Oroville, 9/13/91, A, C, 91001383

US Post Office—Chico Midtown Station [US Post Office in California 1900-1941 TR], 141 W. 5th St., Chico, 1/11/85, C, 85000122

US Post Office—Oroville Main [US Post Office in California 1900-1941 TR], 1735 Robinson St., Oroville, 1/11/85, C, 85000123

Calaveras County

Altaville Grammar School, 125 N. Main St., Altaville, 8/24/79, A, C, 79000471

Angels Hotel, Main St. at Birds Way, Angels Camp, 3/24/72, B, 72000220

Calaveras County Bank, 1239 Main St., Angels Camp, 8/01/85, A, C, 85001683

Calaveras County Courthouse, Main St., San Andreas, 2/28/72, A, B, 72000221

Choy, Sam, Brick Store, Bird Way, Angels Camp, 9/20/84, A, C, 84000759

Douglas Flat School, NE of Vallecito on SR 4, Douglas Flat, 5/24/73, A, C, b, 73000397

Calaveras County—Continued

Honigsberger Store, 665 Main St., Copperopolis, 4/02/92, A, C, 92000310

Murphys Grammar School, Jones St., Murphys, 6/08/73, A, C, 73000398

Murphys Hotel, Main and Algiers Sts., Murphys, 11/23/71, A, 71000134

Reed's Store, 679 Main St., Copperopolis, 4/02/92, A, C, 92000309

Synder, John J., House, 247 W. St. Charles St., San Andreas, 8/02/84, C, 84000760

Thorn House, 87 E. St. Charles St., San Andreas, 2/23/72, A, B, C, 72000222

Utica Mansion, 1103 Bush St., Angels Camp, 5/31/84, A, C, 84000764

Colusa County

Colusa Carnegie Library [California Carnegie Libraries MPS], 260 Sixth St., Colusa, 12/10/90, A, C, 90001816

Colusa Grammar School, 425 Webster St., Colusa, 6/13/78, C, 78000657

Colusa High School and Grounds, 745 10th St., Colusa, 8/13/76, C, 76000479

Grand Island Shrine, 8 mi. S of Colusa on CA 45, Colusa vicinity, 12/31/74, B, C, a, 74000508

Nowi Rancheria, Address Restricted, Grimes vicinity, 3/24/71, D, 71000135

Contra Costa County

Alvarado Park, Jct. of Marin and Park Aves., Richmond vicinity, 4/09/92, A, C, 92000313

Black Diamond Mines, Somersville Rd. SE of Antioch, Antioch vicinity, 10/02/91, A, C, D, 91001425

Clayton Vineyards-DeMartini Winery, 5919 Clayton Rd., Clayton, 8/30/84, A, B, C, 84000767

Contra Costa County Courthouse Block, 625 Court St., Martinez, 12/28/89, A, C, 89002113

Contra Costa County Hall of Records, 725 Court St., Martinez, 9/13/91, A, C, 91001385

East Brother Island Light Station, On East Brother Island W of Point San Pablo, Richmond vicinity, 2/12/71, A, C, 71000138

Eugene O'Neill National Historic Site, 1.5 mi. W of Danville, Danville vicinity, 5/06/71, B, g, NHL, NPS, 71000137

Fernandez, Bernardo, House, 100 Tennent Ave., Pinola, 4/11/73, B, C, 73000399

Ford Motor Company Assembly Plant, 1414–1422 Harbour Way, S., Richmond, 6/23/88, A, C, 88000919

Galindo, Don Francisco, House, 1721 Amador Ave., Concord, 5/20/88, B, C, 88000553

Hard, Roswell Butler, House, 815 W. First St., Antioch, 9/30/93, A, B, C, 93001020

Hendrick, William T., House, 218 Center Ave., Pacheco, 9/08/83, A, 83001176

Hercules Village, Kings, Railroad, Santa Fe and Hercules Aves., Talley Way, Bay and Pinole Sts., Hercules, 8/22/80, A, 80000799

Hershell-Spillman Merry-Go-Round, E of Berkeley in Tilden Regional Park, Berkeley vicinity, 9/29/76, C, 76000480

John Muir National Historic Site, 4202 Alhambra Ave., Martinez, 10/15/66, A, B, C, b, NHL, NPS, 66000083

Marsh, John, House, 6 mi. W of Byron on Marsh Creek Rd., Byron vicinity, 10/07/71, A, B, C, 71000136

Moraga Adobe, 24 Adobe Lane, Orinda, 3/16/72, C, 72000223

New Hotel Carquinez, 410 Harbour Way, Richmond, 5/07/92, A, C, 92000466

Old Borges Ranch, 1035 Castlerock Rd., Walnut Creek vicinity, 7/07/81, A, 81000147

Pacheco, Don Fernando, Adobe, 3119 Grant St., Concord, 6/06/80, B, C, 80000798

Point Richmond Historic District, Off CA 17, Richmond vicinity, 11/05/79, C, 79000472

Port Costa School, Plaza El Hambre, Port Costa, 5/25/88, A, C, 88000563

Rodgers, Patrick, Farm, 315 Cortsen Rd., Pleasant Hill, 3/22/91, A, B, 91000305

Shadelands Ranch House, 2660 Ygnacio Valley Rd., Walnut Creek, 8/29/85, A, C, 85001915

Shannon—Williamson Ranch, RR 1/Lone Tree Way, Antioch, 1/29/87, A, C, 87000003

Winehaven, Point Molate, Richmond, 10/02/78, A, C, D, 78000658

Del Norte County

Cresent City Lighthouse, A St., Battery Point Island, Crescent City, 9/15/83, A, C, 83001177

Endert's Beach Archeological Sites, Address Restricted, Crescent City vicinity, 6/30/77, A, D, NPS, 77000121

Mus-yeh-sait-neh Village and Cultural Landscape Property, Address Restricted, Gasquet vicinity, 10/25/93, A, D, 93001109

O'Men Village Site, Address Restricted, Klamath vicinity, 6/30/77, D, NPS, 77000120

Old Requa, Address Restricted, Redwood National Park vicinity, 12/16/74, D, d, 74000509

Point St. George Site, Address Restricted, Crescent City vicinity, 5/17/76, D, c, 76000481

Radar Station B-71, W of Klamath, Klamath vicinity, 4/19/78, A, C, g, NPS, 78000282

Redwood Highway, W of Klamath, Klamath vicinity, 12/17/79, A, C, NPS, 79000253

St. George Reef Light Station [Light Stations of California MPS], NW Seal Rock, approximately 6 nautical mi. off coast from Point St. George, Crescent City vicinity, 12/09/93, A, C, 93001373

Yontocket Historic District, Address Restricted, Fort Dick vicinity, 12/18/73, A, D, a, 73000400

El Dorado County

Baldwin Estate, NW of US 50 and CA 89 jct. on N side of CA 89, South Lake Tahoe, 4/01/87, C, 87000496

Baley Hotel, N of Pilot Hill on CA 49, Pilot Hill vicinity, 12/18/78, C, 78000660

Coloma, 7 mi. NW of Placerville on CA 49, Placerville vicinity, 10/15/66, A, NHL, 66000207

Combellack-Blair House, 3059 Cedar Ravine, Placerville, 2/14/85, C, 85000259

Confidence Hall, 487 Main St., Placerville, 1/04/82, A, C, 82002174

Crawford Ditch, Address Restricted, Pleasant Valley vicinity, 10/21/91, A, C, 91001522

Eddy Tree Breeding Station, 2480 and 2500 Carson Rd., Placerville, 3/31/87, A, C, 87000485

Episcopal Church of Our Saviour, 2979 Coloma St., Placerville, 11/17/77, A, C, a, 77000291

Fountain-Tallman Soda Works, 524 Main St., Placerville, 9/13/84, C, 84000770

Hattie (Gold Bug), Priest and Silver Pine Mines and Stampmill, 2501 Bedford Ave., Placerville, 11/15/85, A, D, 85003522

Heller Estate, NW of US 50 and CA 89 jct. on N side of CA 89, South Lake Tahoe, 4/01/87, C, 87000497

Lombardo Ranch, 1709 Carson Rd., Placerville, 9/30/77, A, C, 77000292

Pearson, John, Soda Works, 594 Main St., Placerville, 12/12/85, A, 85003326

Pope Estate, NW of US 50 and CA 89 jct. on N side of CA 89, South Lake Tahoe, 4/01/87, B, C, 87000495

Sugar Pine Point State Park, 3 mi. S of Homewood on CA 90, Homewood vicinity, 3/30/73, C, D, 73000401

Tahoe Meadows, US 50 between Ski Run Blvd. and Park Ave., South Lake Tahoe, 3/29/90, A, C, 90000555

Fresno County

Bank of Italy, 1015 Fulton Mall, Fresno, 10/29/82, C, 82000963

Brix, H. H., Mansion, 2844 Fresno St., Fresno, 9/15/83, A, C, 83001178

Coalinga Polk Street School, S. 5th and E. Polk Sts., Coalinga, 5/06/82, A, C, 82002175

Einstein House, 1600 M St., Fresno, 1/31/78, A, B, C, a, 78000662

Forestiere Underground Gardens, 5021 W. Shaw Ave., Fresno, 10/28/77, A, B, C, g, 77000293

Fresno Bee Building, 1555 Van Ness Ave., Fresno, 11/01/82, A, C, 82000964

Fresno Brewing Company Office and Warehouse, 100 M St., Fresno, 1/05/84, A, C, 84000773

Fresno Republican Printery Building, 2130 Kern St., Fresno, 1/02/79, A, C, 79000474

Gamlin Cabin, NW of Wilsonia, Wilsonia vicinity, 3/08/77, A, C, NPS, 77000123

Holy Trinity Armenian Apostolic Church, 2226 Ventura St., Fresno, 7/31/86, A, C, a, 86002097

Kearney, M. Theo, Park and Mansion, 7160 Kearney Blvd., Fresno, 3/13/75, A, B, C, 75000426

Kindler, Paul, House, 1520 E. Olive Ave, Fresno, 10/29/82, C, 82000965

Knapp Cabin, W of Cedar Grove in Kings Canyon National Park, Cedar Grove vicinity, 12/20/78, A, NPS, 78000291

Fresno County—Continued

Maulbridge Apartments, 2344 Tulare St., Fresno, 5/06/82, C, 82002176

Meux House, 1007 R St., Fresno, 1/13/75, C, 75000427

Old Administration Building, Fresno City College, 1101 University Ave., Fresno, 5/01/74, A, C, 74000510

Old Fresno Water Tower, 2444 Fresno St., Fresno, 10/14/71, A, C, 71000139

Orange Cove Santa Fe Railway Depot, 633 E. Railroad Ave., Orange Cove, 8/29/78, A, 78000668

Pantages, Alexander, Theater, 1400 Fulton St., Fresno, 2/23/78, A, B, C, g, 78000663

Physicians Building, 2607 Fresno St., Fresno, 11/20/78, A, C, 78000664

Reedley National Bank, 1100 G St., Reedley, 2/28/85, A, C, 85000352

Reedley Opera House Complex, 10th and G Sts., Reedley, 4/05/84, A, C, 84000774

Rehorn House, 1050 S St., Fresno, 1/08/82, C, 82002177

Romain, Frank, House, 2055 San Joaquin St., Fresno, 1/11/82, A, B, C, 82002178

Santa Fe Hotel, 935 Santa Fe Ave., Fresno, 3/14/91, A, 91000287

Santa Fe Passenger Depot, 2650 Tulare St., Fresno, 11/07/76, A, C, 76000482

Shorty Lovelace Historic District, E of Pinehurst on Kings Canyon National Park, Pinehurst vicinity, 1/31/78, A, C, g, NPS, 78000293

Southern Pacific Passenger Depot, 1033 H St., Fresno, 3/21/78, A, C, 78000665

Stoner House, 21143 E. Welson Ave., Sanger vicinity, 10/17/85, B, C, 85003145

Tower Theatre, 1201 N. Wishon Ave., Fresno, 9/24/92, C, 92001276

Twining Laboratories, 2527 Fresno St., Fresno, 3/26/91, B, C, 91000308

Warehouse Row, 722, 744, and 764 P St., Fresno, 3/24/78, A, C, 78000666

Y.W.C.A. Building, 1660 M St., Fresno, 9/21/78, A, C, 78000667

Glenn County

Gianella Bridge, CA 32, Hamilton City, 7/08/82, A, C, g, 82004614

US Post Office—Willows Main [US Post Office in California 1900-1941 TR], 315 W. Sycamore St., Willows, 1/11/85, C, 85000124

Humboldt County

Alford—Nielson House, 1299 Main St., Ferndale, 1/23/86, C, 86000100

Andreasen, F. W.—John Rossen House, Port Kenyon Rd. and Bush St., Ferndale vicinity, 9/25/89, A, C, 89000855

Bald Hills Archeological District, Address Restricted, Orick vicinity, 7/09/82, A, D, NPS, 82001723

Bald Hills Archeological District Extension (Boundary Increase), Address Restricted, Orick vicinity, 11/04/85, D, NPS, 85003481

Bank of Eureka Building, 240 E St., Eureka, 4/12/82, A, C, 82002180

Bank of Loleta, 358 Main St., Loleta, 2/28/85, A, C, 85000354

Benbow Inn, 445 Lake Benbow Dr., Garberville, 9/15/83, C, 83001179

Berding, A., House, 455 Ocean Ave., Ferndale, 1/04/83, C, 83001180

Carlotta Hotel, Central Ave., Carlotta, 5/23/78, A, C, 78000671

Carnegie Free Library, 636 F St., Eureka, 1/23/86, A, C, 86000101

Clark, William S., House, 1406 C St., Eureka, 1/14/88, B, C, 87002394

De-No-To Cultural District, Address Restricted, Hoopa vicinity, 4/24/85, A, D, 85000901

Eureka Historic District, Roughly, First, Second and Third Sts., between C and N Sts., Eureka, 10/15/91, A, C, 91001523

Eureka Inn, 7th and F Sts., Eureka, 2/11/82, A, C, 82002181

Fern Cottage Historic District, 2099 Centerville Rd., Ferndale vicinity, 1/07/88, A, C, 87002294

Fernbridge, CA 211, Fernbridge, 4/02/87, C, 87000566

Ferndale Public Library [California Carnegie Libraries MPS], 807 Main St., Ferndale, 12/10/90, A, C, 90001815

First and F Street Building, 112 F St., Eureka, 7/12/74, A, C, 74000511

Grizzly Bluff School, E of Ferndale on Grizzly Bluff Rd, Ferndale vicinity, 11/27/79, A, C, 79000476

Gunther Island Site 67, Address Restricted, Eureka vicinity, 10/15/66, D, NHL, 66000208

Gushaw-Mudgett House, 820 9th St., Fortuna, 1/11/82, B, C, 82002184

Holy Trinity Church, Parker and Hector St., Trinidad, 8/06/80, A, 80004608

Hotel Arcata, 708 9th St., Arcata, 1/05/84, A, C, 84000775

Humboldt Bay Life-Saving Station, S of Samoa on Samoa Rd, Samoa vicinity, 10/30/79, A, C, 79000477

Humboldt Bay Woolen Mill, 1400 Broadway, Eureka, 6/25/82, A, C, 82002182

Jacoby Building, 791 8th St., Arcata, 6/17/82, A, C, 82002179

Janssen, E., Building, 422 1st St., Eureka, 7/16/73, A, B, C, 73000402

Lower Blackburn Grade Bridge, NW of Bridgeville on CA 36, Bridgeville vicinity, 6/25/81, A, C, 81000148

McDonald, D. C., Building, 108 F St., Eureka, 11/17/82, A, C, 82000966

McFarlan, George, House, 1410 2nd St., Eureka, 11/15/78, A, C, 78000672

Odd Fellows Hall, 123 F St., Eureka, 5/03/78, A, C, 78000673

Old Jacoby Creek School, 2212 Jacoby Creek Rd., Bayside, 2/28/85, C, 85000353

Phillips House, 71 E. Seventh St., Arcata, 10/24/85, A, C, 85003373

Punta Gorda Light Station, 10.5 mi. SW of Petrolia, Petrolia vicinity, 9/01/76, A, g, 76000483

Pythian Castle, 1100 H St., Arcata, 2/20/86, A, C, 86000263

Rectory, Catholic Church of the Assumption, 563 Ocean Ave., Ferndale, 2/11/82, A, C, a, b, 82002183

Ricks, Thomas F., House, 730 H St., Eureka, 10/02/92, A, C, 92001302

Schorlig House, 1050 12th St., Arcata, 11/20/78, A, 78000670

Shaw House, 703 Main St., Ferndale, 9/13/84, B, C, 84000777

Simpson—Vance House, 904 G St., Eureka, 7/17/86, C, 86001668

Stone House, 902 Fourteenth St., Arcata, 2/27/86, C, 86000267

Trinidad Head Light Station [Light Stations of California MPS], Trinidad Head, Trinidad vicinity, 9/03/91, A, C, 91001098

Tsahpek, Address Restricted, Eureka vicinity, 12/05/72, D, 72000224

U.S. Post Office and Courthouse, 5th and H Sts., Eureka, 2/10/83, A, C, 83001181

Whaley House, 1395 H St., Arcata, 12/31/79, C, b, 79000475

Imperial County

Desert View Tower [Twentieth Century Folk Art Environment in California TR], SW of Ocotillo, Ocotillo vicinity, 8/29/80, C, 80000801

Stonehead (L-7) [Earth Figures of California—Arizona Colorado River Basin TR], Address Restricted, Yuma vicinity, 5/01/87, D, 87001026

US Post Office—El Centro Main [US Post Office in California 1900-1941 TR], 230 S. 5th St., El Centro, 1/11/85, C, 85000125

Winterhaven Anthropomorph and Bowknot, L-9 [Earth Figures of California—Arizona Colorado River Basin TR], Address Restricted, Winterhaven vicinity, 10/25/85, C, D, 85003429

Winterhaven Anthropomorph (L-8) [Earth Figures of California—Arizona Colorado River Basin TR], Address Restricted, Yuma vicinity, 5/01/87, D, 87001025

Yuha Basin Discontiguous District, Address Restricted, Plaster City vicinity, 5/24/82, D, 82002185

Yuma Crossing and Associated Sites, Banks of the Colorado River, Winterhaven, 11/13/66, A, NHL, 66000197

Inyo County

Big and Little Petroglyph Canyons, Address Restricted, China Lake vicinity, 10/15/66, C, D, NHL, 66000209

Coso Hot Springs, Address Restricted, Little Lake vicinity, 1/03/78, A, C, D, 78000674

Inyo County—Continued

Death Valley Junction Historic District, CA 127 and CA 190, Death Valley Junction, 12/10/80, A, B, C, 80000802

Death Valley Scotty Historic District, NE of Olancha on CA 72 in Death Valley National Monument, Olancha vicinity, 7/20/78, A, C, NPS, 78000297

Eagle Borax Works, Death Valley National Monument, Furnace Creek, 12/31/74, A, NPS, 74000338

Fossil Falls Archeological District, Address Restricted, Little Lake vicinity, 7/09/80, D, 80004492

Harmony Borax Works, Death Valley National Monument, Stovepipe Wells vicinity, 12/31/74, A, NPS, 74000339

Laws Narrow Gauge Railroad Historic District, NE of Bishop, Bishop vicinity, 10/01/81, A, 81000149

Leadfield, Death Valley National Monument on Titus Canyon Trail, Death Valley, 6/10/75, A, NPS, 75000221

Manzanar War Relocation Center, 6 mi. S of Independence on CA 395, Independence vicinity, 7/30/76, A, g, NHL, 76000484

Pawona Witu, Address Restricted, Bishop vicinity, 10/14/75, D, 75000428

Saline Valley Salt Tram Historic Structure, N of Keeler between Gordo Peak and New York Butte, Keeler vicinity, 12/31/74, A, C, 74000514

Skidoo, Death Valley National Monument, Wildrose District, Death Valley, 4/16/74, A, g, NPS, 74000349

Kern County

Bakersfield California Building, 1707 Eye St., Bakersfield, 3/10/83, C, 83001183

Bandit Rock, SW of Inyokern near jct. of CA 14 and 178, Inyokern vicinity, 10/31/75, A, B, 75000431

First Baptist Church, 1200 Truxtun Ave., Bakersfield, 1/02/79, C, a, 79000478

Fort Tejon, 3 mi. NW of Lebec, Lebec vicinity, 5/06/71, A, 71000140

Fort, The, Ash and Lincoln Sts., Taft, 7/22/81, A, C, b, 81000151

Green Hotel, 530 James St., Shafter, 3/16/89, A, b, 89000204

Gross, Courtlandt, House, 18600 Courtlandt Ct., Tehachapi vicinity, 3/22/87, B, C, g, 87000669

Jastro Building, 1800 19th St., Bakersfield, 9/22/83, A, C, 83001182

Kern Branch, Beale Memorial Library, 1400 Baker St., Bakersfield, 4/01/81, C, 81000150

Last Chance Canyon, Address Restricted, Johannesburg vicinity, 12/05/72, D, 72000225

Long Canyon Village Site, Address Restricted, South Lake vicinity, 4/14/80, D, 80000803

Rogers Dry Lake, Edwards Air Force Base, Mojave Desert, 10/03/85, A, NHL, 85002816

Santa Fe Passenger and Freight Depot, 150 Central Valley Hwy., Shafter, 1/19/82, C, b, 82002187

Tevis Block, 1712 19th St., Bakersfield, 3/29/84, A, C, 84000780

Walker Pass, 60 mi. NE of Bakersfield on CA 178, Bakersfield vicinity, 10/15/66, A, B, NHL, 66000210

Kings County

Hanford Carnegie Library, 109 E. 8th St., Hanford, 12/17/81, A, C, 81000152

Kings County Courthouse, 114 W. 8th St., Hanford, 9/21/78, A, C, 78003063

Taoist Temple, No. 12 China Alley, Hanford, 6/13/72, A, a, 72000226

Witt Site, Address Restricted, Kettleman City vicinity, 5/06/71, D, 71000141

Lake County

Anderson Marsh Archeological District, Address Restricted, Lower Lake vicinity, 8/24/78, A, D, 78000676

Archeological Site No. Ca-Lak-711, Address Restricted, Anderson Springs vicinity, 5/25/79, D, 79000479

Borax Lake—Hodges Archeological Site, Address Restricted, Clearlake vicinity, 10/03/91, D, 91001424

Lake County Courthouse, 255 N. Main St., Lakeport, 10/28/70, C, 70000134

Patwin Indian Site, Address Restricted, Clearlake Oaks vicinity, 2/23/72, D, 72000227

Lassen County

Roop's Fort, N. Weatherlow St., Susanville, 5/02/74, A, B, C, 74000516

Willow Creek Rim Archeological District, Address Restricted, Litchfield vicinity, 12/21/78, D, 78000677

Los Angeles County

500 Varas Square—Government Reserve, Address Restricted, Los Angeles vicinity, 3/12/86, A, C, 86000326

Adamson House, 23200 W. Pacific Coast Highway, Malibu, 10/28/77, C, g, 77000298

Adobe Flores, 1804 Foothill St., South Pasadena, 6/18/73, A, 73000404

Al Malaikah Temple, 655 W. Jefferson Blvd., Los Angeles, 4/02/87, A, C, 87000577

Alvarado Terrace Historic District, Alvarado Terr., Bonnie Brae and 14th Sts., Los Angeles, 5/17/84, A, C, 84000783

American Trona Corporation Building, Pacific Ave., Los Angeles, 8/30/84, C, 84000785

Angelus Mesa Branch [Los Angeles Branch Library System TR], 2700 W. Fifty-second St., Los Angeles, 5/19/87, A, C, 87001005

Angelus Temple, 1100 Glendale Blvd., Los Angeles, 4/27/92, A, B, a, NHL, 92001875

Antelope Valley Indian Museum, 15701 East Ave., Lancaster, 2/26/87, A, C, 87000509

Atchison, Topeka, and Santa Fe Railroad Station, 110 W. 1st St., Claremont, 7/15/82, C, 82002188

Auditorium [Torrance High School Campus TR], 2200 W. Carson, Torrance, 10/13/83, A, C, 83003499

Aztec Hotel, 311 W. Foothill Blvd., Monrovia, 5/22/78, C, 78000691

Bailey, Jonathan, House, 13421 E. Camilla St., Whittier, 8/29/77, B, 77000304

Baldwin Hills Village, 5300 Village Green, Loa Angeles, 4/01/93, A, C, 93000269

Banning House, 401 E. M St., Wilmington, 5/06/71, C, 71000160

Barnsdall Park, 4800 Hollywood Blvd., Los Angeles, 5/06/71, C, 71000143

Batchelder House, 626 S. Arroyo Blvd., Pasadena, 12/14/78, A, C, 78000695

Battery John Barlow and Saxton, Fort MacArthur, San Pedro, 5/04/82, A, C, 82002200

Battery Osgood-Farley, Fort MacArthur Upper Reservation, San Pedro, 10/16/74, A, C, 74000526

Bentz, Louise C., House, 657 Prospect Blvd., Pasadena, 12/02/77, C, 77000299

Bernard, Susana Machado, House and Barn, 845 S. Lake St., Los Angeles, 9/04/79, C, 79000482

Beverly Wilshire Hotel, 9528 Wilshire Blvd., Beverly Hills, 6/12/87, C, 87000908

Blacker, Robert R., House, 1177 Hillcrest Ave., Pasadena, 2/06/86, C, 86000147

Bolton Hall, 10116 Commerce Ave., Tujunga, 11/23/71, A, C, 71000159

Bolton, Dr. W. T., House, 370 W. Del Mar Blvd., Pasadena, 7/09/80, C, 80004491

Bowen Court, 539 E. Villa St., Pasadena, 6/17/82, C, 82002194

Bradbury Building, 304 S. Broadway, Los Angeles, 7/14/71, C, NHL, 71000144

Britt, Eugene W., House, 2141 W. Adams Blvd., Los Angeles, 5/17/79, C, 79000483

Broadway Theater and Commercial District, 300–849 S. Broadway, Los Angeles, 5/09/79, A, C, 79000484

Bryan Court [Bungalow Courts of Pasadena TR], 427 S. Morengo Ave., Pasadena, 4/16/86, C, 86000790

Bryson Apartment Hotel, 2701 Wilshire Blvd., Los Angeles, 4/07/83, C, 83001184

Bullock's Wilshire Building, 3050 Wilshire Blvd., Los Angeles, 5/25/78, B, C, 78000685

Bunche, Ralph J., House, 1221 E. 40th Pl., Los Angeles, 5/22/78, B, 78000686

Cahuenga Branch [Los Angeles Branch Library System TR], 4591 W. Santa Monica Blvd., Los Angeles, 5/19/87, A, C, 87001006

Carroll Avenue, 1300 Block, Carroll Ave. between Edgeware and Douglas Sts., Los Angeles, 4/22/76, A, C, 76000488

Los Angeles County—Continued

Casa de Parley Johnson, 7749 Florence Ave., Downey, 3/20/86, C, 86000449

Catholic-Protestant Chapels, Veterans Administration Center, Eisenhower Ave., Los Angeles, 2/11/72, C, a, 72000229

Cedar Avenue Complex, 44843 (44855), 44845 and 44851 Cedar Ave., 606 Lancaster Blvd., and Old Jail (no address), Lancaster, 9/30/93, A, C, 93001017

Centinela Adobe, 7634 Midfield Ave., Los Angeles, 5/02/74, A, C, 74000522

Christmas Tree Lane, Santa Rosa Ave. between Woodbury Ave. and Altadena Dr., Altadena, 9/13/90, A, 90001444

Citizens Publishing Company Building, 9355 Culver Blvd., Culver City, 2/12/87, A, B, C, 87000082

Civic Center Financial District, E. Colorado Blvd. and Marengo Ave., Pasadena, 10/29/82, A, C, 82000967

Clarke Estate, 10211 Pioneer Blvd., Santa Fe Springs, 1/04/90, C, 89002267

Colonial Court [Bungalow Courts of Pasadena TR], 291-301 N. Garfield Ave., Pasadena, 7/11/83, C, 83001185

Colonial House, 1416 N. Havenhurst Dr., West Hollywood, 4/15/82, A, C, 82002190

Colorado Street Bridge, Colorado Blvd., Pasadena, 2/12/81, A, C, 81000156

Congregation B'nai B'rith, 3663 Wilshire Blvd., Los Angeles, 12/21/81, C, a, 81000154

Cottage Court [Bungalow Courts of Pasadena TR], 642-654 S. Margeno Ave., Pasadena, 7/11/83, C, 83001186

Court [Bungalow Courts of Pasadena TR], 497-503 1/2 N. Madison Ave., Pasadena, 7/11/83, C, 83001187

Court [Bungalow Courts of Pasadena TR], 744-756 1/2 S. Marengo Ave., Pasadena, 7/11/83, C, 83001188

Court [Bungalow Courts of Pasadena TR], 732-744 Santa Barbara St., Pasadena, 7/11/83, C, 83001189

Crossroads of the World, 6671 Sunset Blvd., Hollywood, 9/08/80, C, g, 80000805

Culbertson, Cordelia A., House, 1188 Hillcrest Ave., Pasadena, 9/12/85, C, 85002198

Cypress Court [Bungalow Courts of Pasadena TR], 623-641 N. Madison Ave., Pasadena, 7/11/83, C, 83001190

Dana, Richard Henry, Branch [Los Angeles Branch Library System TR], 3320 Pepper St., Los Angeles, 5/19/87, A, C, 87001007

De Neve, Felipe, Branch [Los Angeles Branch Library System TR], 2820 W. Sixth St., Los Angeles, 5/19/87, A, C, 87001008

DeWenter Mansion, Guest House and Grounds, 6100 Brydon Rd., La Verne, 11/05/92, C, 92001559

Derby, James Daniel, House, 2535 E. Chevy Chase Dr., Glendale, 12/14/78, C, 78000682

Diamond Apartments, 321 Diamond St., Redondo Beach, 3/26/92, A, 92000260

Doheny Estate/Greystone, 905 Loma Vista Dr., Beverly Hills, 4/23/76, C, 76000485

Dominguez Ranch Adobe, 18127 S. Alameda St., Compton, 5/28/76, C, a, 76000486

Don Carlos Court [Bungalow Courts of Pasadena TR], 374-386 S. Marengo Ave., Pasadena, 7/11/83, C, 83001191

Drum Barracks, 1053 Carey St., Wilmington, 2/12/71, A, 71000161

Eagle Rock Branch Library [Los Angeles Branch Library System TR], 2224 Colorado Blvd., Los Angeles, 5/19/87, A, C, 87001004

Edison Historic District, 611, 637, and 500 blk. of W. Second St., Pomona, 8/13/86, A, C, 86001477

El Greco Apartment, 817 N. Hayworth Ave., Los Angeles, 11/03/88, C, 88002017

El Molino Viejo, 1120 Old Mill Rd., Pasadena, 5/06/71, A, C, 71000154

Engine Co. No. 27, 1355 N. Cahuenga Blvd., Los Angeles, 9/24/85, A, C, 85002559

Engine Company No. 28, 644-646 S. Figuara St, Los Angeles, 11/16/79, C, 79000485

Engine House No. 18, 2616 S. Hobart Blvd., Los Angeles, 10/29/82, C, 82000968

Ennis House, 2607 Glendower Ave., Los Angeles, 10/14/71, C, 71000145

Episcopal Church of the Ascension, 25 E. Laurel Ave., Sierra Madre, 8/19/77, A, C, a, 77000303

Euclid Court [Bungalow Courts of Pasadena TR], 545 S. Euclid Ave., Pasadena, 7/11/83, C, 83001193

Evanston Inn, 385-395 S. Marengo Ave., Pasadena, 9/13/84, A, C, 84000787

Exposition Park Rose Garden, Exposition Park, jct. of Exposition Blvd. and Vermont Ave., Los Angeles, 3/28/91, C, 91000285

Federal Reserve Bank of San Francisco, 409 W. Olympic Blvd., Los Angeles, 9/20/84, C, 84000843

Fenyes Estate, 470 W. Walnut St. & 160 N. Orange Grove Blvd., Pasadena, 9/05/85, C, 85001983

Fern Avenue School, 1314 Fern Ave., Torrance, 2/20/92, A, C, 92000067

Fire Station No. 23, 225 E. 5th St., Los Angeles, 6/09/80, A, C, 80000809

First National Bank of Long Beach, 101-125 Pine Ave., Long Beach, 9/13/90, C, 90001432

First Trust Building and Garage, 587-611 E. Colorado Blvd. and 30-44 N. Madison Ave., Pasadena, 6/12/87, C, 87000941

Freeman, Samuel, House, 1962 Glencoe Way, Los Angeles, 10/14/71, C, 71000146

Fremont, John C., Branch [Los Angeles Branch Library System TR], 6121 Melrose Ave., Los Angeles, 5/19/87, A, C, 87001009

Friday Morning Club, 938-940 S. Figueroa St., Los Angeles, 5/17/84, A, C, 84000865

Friendship Baptist Church, 80 W. Dayton St., Pasadena, 11/20/78, A, C, a, 78000696

Gamble House, 4 Westmoreland Pl., Pasadena, 9/03/71, C, NHL, 71000155

Gano, Peter, House, 718 Crescent Ave., Avalon, 9/15/83, A, C, 83001194

Garbutt House, 1809 Apex Ave., Los Angeles, 7/22/87, B, C, 87001174

Garfield Building, 403 W. 8th St., Los Angeles, 6/25/82, C, 82002191

Garfield House, 1001 Buena Vista St., South Pasadena, 4/24/73, C, 73000405

Gartz Court [Bungalow Courts of Pasadena TR], 270 N. Madison, Pasadena, 8/25/83, C, 83001195

Glendora Bougainvillea, Bennett and Minnesota Aves., Glendora, 2/07/78, A, C, 78000683

Golden Gate Theater, 5170-5188 E. Whittier Blvd., Los Angeles, 2/23/82, A, C, 82002192

Granada Shoppes and Studios, 672 S. Lafayette Park Pl., Los Angeles, 11/20/86, C, 86003320

Greenwood, Barbara, Kindergarten, Hacienda Pl. and McKinley Ave., Pomona, 9/18/78, B, b, 78000697

Guaranty Building, 6331 Hollywood Blvd, Hollywood, 9/04/79, A, C, g, 79000481

HUGHES FLYING BOAT (HERCULES), Berth 121, Pier E, Port of Long Beach, Long Beach, 11/26/80, B, C, g, 80004493

Hacienda Arms Apartments, 8439 Sunset Blvd., West Hollywood, 12/15/83, C, 83003531

Hale House, Heritage Sq., 3800 N. Homer St., Highland Park, Los Angeles, 9/22/72, C, b, 72000230

Hale Solar Laboratory, 740 Holladay Rd., Pasadena, 1/23/86, A, B, C, g, NHL, 86000103

Hangar One, 5701 W. Imperial Hwy., Los Angeles, 7/30/92, A, 92000959

Haskett Court, 824-834 E. California Blvd., Pasadena, 2/25/82, C, 82002195

Hawkins—Nimocks Estate-Patricio Ontiveros Adobe, 12100 Telegraph Rd., Santa Fe Springs, 12/31/87, A, B, C, D, 82004982

Heinsbergen Decorating Company Building, 7415 Beverly Blvd., Los Angeles, 9/20/84, B, C, 84000873

Highland Park Masonic Temple, 104 N. Avenue 56, Los Angeles, 1/18/90, A, C, 89002268

Highland Park Police Station, 6045 York Blvd., Los Angeles, 3/22/84, A, C, 84000874

Highland—Camrose Bungalow Village, Jct. Highland and Camrose Ave., Los Angeles, 3/16/89, C, 89000198

Holly Street Livery Stable, 110 E. Holly St, Pasadena, 10/25/79, A, 79000491

Hollywood Boulevard Commercial and Entertainment District, 6200-7000 Hollywood Blvd., N. Vine St., N. Highland Ave. and N. Ivar St., Los Angeles, 4/04/85, A, C, 85000704

Hollywood Masonic Temple, 6840 Hollywood Blvd., Hollywood, 2/28/85, A, C, 85000355

Hollywood Melrose Hotel, 5150-70 Melrose Blvd., Los Angeles, 7/08/92, C, 92000834

Hollywood Studio Club, 1215 Lodi Pl., Hollywood, 11/25/80, A, C, 80000806

Home Economics Building [Torrance High School Campus TR], 2200 W. Carson, Torrance, 10/13/83, A, C, 83003536

Home Laundry, 432 S. Arroyo Pkwy., Pasadena, 6/18/87, B, C, 87000980

Horatio West Court, 140 Hollister Ave., Santa Monica, 4/11/77, A, C, 77000302

Hotel Green, 99 S. Raymond Ave., Pasadena, 3/23/82, A, C, 82002196

Los Angeles County—Continued

House at 530 S. Marengo Avenue, 530 S. Marengo Ave., Pasadena, 9/13/79, C, 79000492

Hubble, Edwin, House, 1340 Woodstock Rd., San Marino, 12/08/76, B, NHL, 76000494

Humaliwo, Address Restricted, Malibu vicinity, 9/01/76, D, d, 76000492

Irving, Washington, Branch [Los Angeles Branch Library System TR], 1803 S. Arlington Ave., Los Angeles, 5/19/87, A, C, 87001010

Jackson, Helen Hunt, Branch [Los Angeles Branch Library System TR], 2330 Naomi St., Los Angeles, 5/19/87, A, C, a, 87001011

Jardinette Apartments, 5128 Marathon St., Los Angeles, 12/29/86, C, 86003524

Jefferson Branch [Los Angeles Branch Library System TR], 2211 W. Jefferson Blvd., Los Angeles, 5/19/87, A, C, 87001012

Johnston, Darius David, House, 12426 Mapledale St., Norwalk, 11/02/78, A, C, 78000693

Jordan, Orin, House, 8310 S. Comstock Ave., Whittier, 7/28/80, B, 80000815

Keyes Bungalow, 1337 E. Boston St., Altadena, 11/14/78, B, C, 78000678

LANE VICTORY, Berth 4, Port of San Pedro, San Pedro, 12/14/90, A, C, g, NHL, 90002222

La Belle Tour, 6200 Franklin Ave., Hollywood, 1/22/88, A, C, 87002291

La Casa Alvarado, 1459 Old Settlers Lane, Pomona, 4/19/78, A, C, 78000698

La Casa Primera de Rancho San Jose, 1569 N. Park Ave., Pomona, 4/03/75, C, 75000436

Las Casitas Court [Bungalow Courts of Pasadena TR], 656 N. Summit Ave., Pasadena, 7/11/83, C, 83001196

Leonis Adobe, 23537 Calabasas Rd., Calabasas, 5/29/75, A, C, 75000433

Lincoln Heights Branch [Los Angeles Branch Library System TR], 2530 Workman St., Los Angeles, 5/19/87, A, C, 87001013

Lincoln, Abraham, Elementary School, 1200 N. Gordon Ave., Pomona, 8/03/89, C, 89000935

Little Rock Creek Dam, 4.5 mi. S of Pearland off CA 138, Pearland vicinity, 4/15/77, A, C, 77000301

Little Tokyo Historic District, 301–369 First and 106–120 San Pedro Sts., Los Angeles, 8/22/86, A, C, a, g, 86001479

Lloyd, Harold, Estate, Address Restricted, Beverly Hills vicinity, 2/09/84, B, C, 84000876

Longfellow-Hastings House, 85 S. Allen Ave., Pasadena, 3/02/82, C, b, 82002197

Longley, Howard, House, 1005 Buena Vista St., South Pasadena, 4/16/74, C, 74000527

Lopez Adobe, 1100 Pico St., San Fernando, 5/06/71, A, C, 71000157

Los Angeles Central Library, 630 W. 5th St., Los Angeles, 12/18/70, C, 70000136

Los Angeles Harbor Light Station, Los Angeles Harbor (San Pedro Breakwater), Los Angeles, 10/14/80, A, 80000810

Los Angeles Memorial Coliseum, 3911 S. Figueroa St., Los Angeles, 7/27/84, A, NHL, 84003866

Los Angeles Pacific Company Ivy Park Substation, 9015 Venice Blvd., Los Angeles, 3/25/81, A, C, 81000155

Los Angeles Plaza Historic District, Roughly bounded by Spring, Macy, Alameda and Arcadia Sts., and Old Sunset Blvd., Los Angeles, 11/03/72, A, C, a, e, 72000231

Los Angeles Union Passenger Terminal, 800 N. Alameda St., Los Angeles, 11/13/80, A, C, g, 80000811

Los Cerritos Ranch House, 4600 Virginia Rd., Long Beach, 4/15/70, C, NHL, 70000135

Lovell House, 4616 Dundee Dr., Los Angeles, 10/14/71, C, g, 71000147

Lukens, Theodore Parker, House, 267 N. El Molino Ave., Pasadena, 3/29/84, B, C, 84000879

Lummis House, 200 E. Ave. 43, Los Angeles, 5/06/71, A, B, C, 71000148

Lynwood Pacific Electric Railway Depot, 11453 Long Beach Blvd., Lynwood, 9/25/74, A, C, 74000524

Machell—Seaman House, 2341 Scarff St., Los Angeles, 6/23/88, C, 88000922

Main Building [Torrance High School Campus TR], 2200 W. Carson, Torrance, 10/13/83, A, C, 83003538

Malabar Branch [Los Angeles Branch Library System TR], 2801 Wabash Ave., Los Angeles, 5/19/87, A, C, 87001014

Marengo Gardens [Bungalow Courts of Pasadena TR], 982, 986, 990 S. Marengo Ave. and 221-241 Ohio St., Pasadena, 7/11/83, C, 83001197

McNally's Windemere Ranch Headquarters, San Esteban and San Cristobal Dr., La Mirada, 7/20/78, A, B, 78000684

Memorial Branch [Los Angeles Branch Library System TR], 4645 W. Olympic Blvd., Los Angeles, 5/19/87, A, C, 87001015

Menlo Avenue—West Twenty-ninth Street Historic District, Bounded by Adams Blvd., Ellendale, Thirtieth Ave., and Vermont, Los Angeles, 2/12/87, A, C, 87000139

Millard House, 645 Prospect Crescent, Pasadena, 12/12/76, C, 76000493

Miller and Herriott House, 1163 W. 27th St., Los Angeles, 11/16/79, C, 79000486

Million Dollar Theater, 307 S. Broadway, Los Angeles, 7/20/78, A, C, 78000687

Miltimore House, 1301 S. Chelten Way, South Pasadena, 3/24/72, C, 72000235

Mission Court [Bungalow Courts of Pasadena TR], 567 N. Oakland Ave., Pasadena, 7/11/83, C, 83001198

Mission San Fernando Rey de Convento Building, 15151 San Fernando Mission Blvd., Los Angeles, 10/27/88, A, C, a, 88002147

Moneta Branch [Los Angeles Branch Library System TR], 4255 S. Olive St., Los Angeles, 5/19/87, A, C, 87001016

Montecito Apartments, 6650 Franklin Ave., Los Angeles, 7/18/85, C, 85001592

Mooers, Frederick Mitchell, House, 818 S. Bonnie Brae St., Los Angeles, 6/03/76, C, 76000489

Mount Lowe Railway, N of Altadena in Angeles NF, Altadena vicinity, 1/06/93, A, B, C, 92001522

Mount Pleasant House, Heritage Sq., 3800 Homer St., Los Angeles, 12/12/76, A, C, b, 76000490

Muir, John, Branch [Los Angeles Branch Library System TR], 1005 W. Sixty-fourth St., Los Angeles, 5/19/87, A, C, 87001017

National Bank of Whittier Building, 13002 E. Philadelphia St., Whittier, 12/30/82, A, C, 82000969

Natural History Museum, 900 Exposition Blvd., Los Angeles, 3/04/75, C, 75000434

Newcomb House, 675–677 N. El Molino Ave., Pasadena, 9/02/82, C, 82002198

Nicholson, Grace, Building, 46 N. Los Robles Ave., Pasadena, 7/21/77, A, B, C, 77000300

North Hollywood Branch [Los Angeles Branch Library System TR], 5211 N. Tujunga Ave., Los Angeles, 5/19/87, A, C, 87001018

Oaklawn Bridge and Waiting Station, Between Oaklawn and Fair Oaks Aves., South Pasadena, 7/16/73, C, 73000406

Oaks, The, 250 N. Primrose Ave., Monrovia, 4/06/78, A, C, 78000692

Odd Fellows Temple, 175 N. Los Robles Ave., Pasadena, 8/01/85, C, 85001682

Old Pasadena Historic District, Roughly bounded by Pasadena, Fair Oaks, Raymond Aves., Arroyo Pkwy., Del Mar Blvd., and Corson St., Pasadena, 9/15/83, A, C, 83001200

Old Santa Susana Stage Road, Address Restricted, Chatsworth vicinity, 1/10/74, A, D, 74000517

Orange Grove Court [Bungalow Courts of Pasadena TR], 745 E. Orange Grove Blvd., Pasadena, 7/11/83, C, 83001199

Oviatt, James, Building, 617 S. Olive St., Los Angeles, 8/11/83, A, C, 83004529

Pacific Electric Railroad Bridge, Torrance Blvd. and Bow St., Torrance, 7/13/89, C, 89000854

Pacific Electric Railway Company Substation No. 8, 2245 N. Lake Ave., Altadena, 11/09/77, A, C, 77000295

Paddison Ranch Buildings, 11951 Imperial Hwy., Norwalk, 6/23/78, A, C, 78000694

Palmer, Minnie Hill, House, Chatsworth Park South, Chatsworth, 9/04/79, A, 79000480

Palmetto Court [Bungalow Courts of Pasadena TR], 100 Palmetto Dr., Pasadena, 7/11/83, C, 83001201

Palomares, Ygnacio, Adobe, Corner of Arrow Hwy. and Orange Grove Ave., Pomona, 3/24/71, C, 71000156

Parkhurst Building, 185 Pier Ave., Santa Monica, 11/17/78, A, 78000699

Pasadena Civic Center District, Roughly bounded by Walnut and Green Sts., Raymond and Euclid Aves., Pasadena, 7/28/80, A, C, 80000813

Pasadena Playhouse, 39 S. El Molino Ave., Pasadena, 11/11/75, A, C, 75000435

Patio del Moro, 8225–8237 Fountain Ave., West Hollywood, 9/11/86, C, 86002418

Pegler, John Carlton, House, 419 E. Highland Ave., Sierra Madre, 10/20/88, A, B, C, 88002019

Pellissier Building, 3780 Wilshire Blvd., Los Angeles, 2/23/79, A, C, g, 79000488

Phillips Mansion, 2640 W. Pomona Blvd., Pomona, 11/06/74, B, C, 74000525

Pico, Pio, Casa, 6003 Pioneer Blvd., Whittier, 6/19/73, B, 73000408

Los Angeles County—Continued

Pico, Romulo, Adobe, 10940 Sepulveda Blvd., Mission Hills, 11/13/66, C, e, 66000211

Pitzer House, 4353 N. Towne, Claremont, 9/04/86, B, C, 86002192

Plaza Substation, 10 Olvera St., Los Angeles, 9/13/78, A, 78000689

Point Fermin Lighthouse, 805 Paseo Del Mar, San Pedro, 6/13/72, A, 72000234

Point Vicente Light, Rancho Palos Verdes, Long Beach, 10/31/80, C, 80000808

Pomona Fox Theater, 102–144 3rd St., Pomona, 2/19/82, A, C, 82002201

Pomona YMCA Building, 350 N. Geary Ave., Pomona, 3/06/86, A, C, 86000408

Prospect Historic District, Prospect Blvd., Square, Crescent, and Terrace, Rosemont Ave., Armada and Fremont Drs., and La Mesa Pl., Pasadena, 4/07/83, C, 83001202

Puvunga Indian Village Sites, Address Restricted, Long Beach vicinity, 1/21/74, D, 74000521

Puvunga Indian Village Sites (Boundary Increase), Address Restricted, Long Beach, 5/22/82, D, 82000429

Queen Anne Cottage and Coach Barn, 301 N. Baldwin Ave., Arcadia, 10/31/80, C, 80000804

RALPH J. SCOTT, Berth 85, San Pedro, 6/30/89, A, B, C, NHL, 89001430

RMS QUEEN MARY, Pier J, 1126 Queensway Hwy., Long Beach, 4/15/93, A, g, 92001714

Ralphs Grocery Store, 1142–54 Westwood Blvd., Los Angeles, 7/30/92, A, C, 92000969

Ramsay—Durfee Estate, 2425 S. Western Ave., Los Angeles, 7/24/89, C, a, 89000821

Rancho El Encino, 16756 Moorpark St., Encino, 2/24/71, C, 71000142

Rancho Los Alamitos, 6400 Bixby Hill Rd., Long Beach, 7/07/81, A, C, D, b, 81000153

Redondo Beach Original Townsite Historic District, N. Gertruda Ave., Carnelian St., N. Guadalupe Ave. and Diamond St., Redondo Beach, 6/30/88, A, C, 88000970

Redondo Beach Public Library, 309 Esplanade St., Redondo Beach, 3/12/81, C, 81000158

Reeve, Jennie A., House, 4260 Country Club Dr., Long Beach, 6/21/84, C, 84000883

Rialto Theatre, 1019–1023 Fair Oaks Ave., South Pasadena, 5/24/78, A, C, 78000700

Rindge, Frederick Hastings, House, 2263 Harvard Blvd., Los Angeles, 1/23/86, C, 86000105

Rives, James C., House, 10921 S. Paramount Blvd., Downey, 5/22/78, C, 78000681

Robinson, Virginia, Estate, 1008 Elden Way, Beverly Hills, 11/15/78, A, C, 78000679

Rogers, Will, House, 14253 Sunset Blvd., Los Angeles, 2/24/71, B, g, 71000149

Ronda, 1400–1414 Havenhurst Dr., West Hollywood, 2/28/85, C, 85000356

Rose Bowl, The, 991 Rosemont Ave., Brookside Park, Pasadena, 2/27/87, A, NHL, 87000755

Rose Court [Bungalow Courts of Pasadena TR], 449-457 S. Hudson Ave., Pasadena, 7/11/83, C, 83001203

Rowland, John A., House, 16021 E. Gale Ave., Industry, 7/16/73, A, C, 73000403

Russian Village District, 290–370 S. Mills Ave. and 480 Cucamonga Ave., Claremont, 12/28/78, A, C, g, 78000680

S.S. CATALINA, Berth 96, Los Angeles Harbor, San Pedro, 9/01/76, A, C, g, 76000495

Saddle Rock Ranch Pictograph Site, Address Restricted, Malibu vicinity, 2/12/82, D, 82004617

San Dimas Hotel, 121 San Dimas Ave., San Dimas, 3/16/72, C, 72000233

San Fernando Building, The, 400–410 S. Main St., Los Angeles, 7/31/86, A, C, 86002098

San Gabriel Mission, Junipero St. and W. Mission Dr., San Gabriel, 5/06/71, C, a, 71000158

San Rafael Rancho, Bonita Dr., Glendale, 12/12/76, A, C, 76000487

Santa Monica Looff Hippodrome, 276 Santa Monica Pier, Santa Monica, 2/27/87, A, NHL, 87000766

Sara-Thel Court [Bungalow Courts of Pasadena TR], 618-630 S. Marengo Ave., Pasadena, 7/11/83, C, 83001192

Schindler, R. M., House, 833 N. Kings Rd., West Hollywood, 7/14/71, C, 71000150

Scripps College for Women, Columbia and 10th St., Claremont, 9/20/84, C, 84000887

Second Church of Christ, Scientist, 946 W. Adams Blvd., Los Angeles, 4/02/87, A, C, a, 87000576

Security Trust and Savings, 6381-85 Hollywood Blvd., Hollywood, 8/18/83, A, C, 83001204

Sinclair, Upton, House, 464 N. Myrtle Ave., Monrovia, 11/11/71, B, g, NHL, 71000153

Singer Building, 16 S. Oakland Ave. and 520 E. Colorado Blvd., Pasadena, 5/16/85, C, 85001066

Smith Estate, 5905 El Mio Dr., Los Angeles, 10/29/82, C, 82000971

Smith, Ernest W., House, 272 S. Los Robles Ave., Pasadena, 1/14/88, C, 87002397

Somerville Hotel, 4225 S. Central Ave., Los Angeles, 1/17/76, A, g, 76000491

South Bonnie Brae Tract Historic District, 1026–1053 S. Bonnie Brae St. and 1830–1851 W. Eleventh St., Los Angeles, 1/14/88, C, b, 87002401

South Marengo Historic District, S. Marengo Ave., Pasadena, 6/02/82, C, 82002199

South Pasadena Historic District, Roughly bounded by Mission and El Centro Sts., and Fairview and Meridian Aves., South Pasadena, 7/21/82, A, 82002202

South Serrano Avenue Historic District, 400 blk. of S. Serrano Ave., Los Angeles, 1/28/88, A, C, 87002407

Southern Pacific Railroad Station, 11825 Bailey St., Whittier, 5/22/78, A, 78000701

Sowden, John, House, 5121 Franklin Ave., Los Angeles, 7/14/71, C, g, 71000151

Space Flight Operations Facility, Jet Propulsion Laboratory, Pasadena, 10/03/85, A, C, g, NHL, 85002814

Spring Street Financial District, 354–704 S. Spring St., Los Angeles, 8/10/79, A, C, 79000489

St. James Park Historic District, Roughly bounded by 21st and 23 Sts., Mount St. Mary's College, W. Adams Blvd. and Union Ave., Los Angeles, 9/27/91, A, B, C, 91001387

Standard Oil Building, 7257 Bright Ave., Whittier, 6/09/80, A, C, 80000816

Stevenson, Robert Louis, Branch [Los Angeles Branch Library System TR], 803 Spence St., Los Angeles, 5/19/87, A, C, 87001021

Stimson House, 2421 S. Figueroa St., Los Angeles, 3/30/78, C, a, 78000690

Storer House, 8161 Hollywood Blvd., Los Angeles, 9/28/71, C, g, 71000152

Stoutenburgh House, 255 S. Marengo Ave., Pasadena, 11/25/80, A, C, 80000814

Straight, Charles E., House, 4333 Emerald Ave., La Verne, 7/08/92, A, B, C, 92000833

Streetcar Depot, Pershing and Dewey Aves., Los Angeles, 2/23/72, C, 72000232

Sunset Towers, 8358 Sunset Blvd., West Hollywood, 5/30/80, C, 80000812

Sweetser Residence, 417 E. Beryl St., Redondo Beach, 9/05/85, C, 85001984

Temple Mansion, 15415 E. Don Julian Rd., Industry, 12/02/74, C, 74000518

Title Guarantee and Trust Company Building, 401-411 W. 5th St., Los Angeles, 7/26/84, C, 84000891

Toberman, C. E., Estate, 1847 Camino Palmero, Hollywood, 9/15/83, A, C, 83001205

Torrance School [Torrance High School Campus TR], 2200 W. Carson, Torrance, 10/13/83, A, C, 83003542

Tuna Club of Avalon, 100 St. Catherine Way, Catalina Island, Avalon, 4/02/91, A, C, 91000338

Twentieth Street Historic District, 912–950 20th St. (even numbers), Los Angeles, 7/22/91, C, 91000915

Twenty-Five Foot Space Simulator, Jet Propulsion Laboratory, Pasadena, 10/03/85, A, C, g, NHL, 85002812

US Post Office—Beverly Hills Main [US Post Office in California 1900-1941 TR], 469 N. Crescent Dr., Beverly Hills, 1/11/85, C, 85000126

US Post Office—Burbank Downtown Station [US Post Office in California 1900-1941 TR], 125 E. Olive Ave., Burbank, 1/11/85, C, g, 85000127

US Post Office—Glendale Main [US Post Office in California 1900-1941 TR], 313 E. Broadway St., Glendale, 1/11/85, C, 85000128

US Post Office—Hollywood Station [US Post Office in California 1900-1941 TR], 1615 N. Wilcox Ave., Los Angeles, 1/11/85, C, g, 85000130

US Post Office—Long Beach Main [US Post Office in California 1900-1941 TR], 300 Long Beach Blvd., Long Beach, 1/11/85, C, 85000129

US Post Office—Los Angeles Terminal Annex [US Post Office in California 1900-1941 TR], 900 Alameda St., Los Angeles, 1/11/85, C, g, 85000131

US Post Office—San Pedro Main [US Post Office in California 1900-1941 TR], 839 S. Beacon St., San Pedro, 1/11/85, C, g, 85000132

Van Buren Place Historic District, 2620–2657 Van Buren Pl., Los Angeles, 8/10/89, B, C, 89001103

Van Nuys Branch [Los Angeles Branch Library System TR], 14553 Sylvan Way, Los Angeles, 5/19/87, A, C, 87001019

Vasquez Rocks, Agua Dulce Rd., Agua Dulce, 6/22/72, D, 72000228

Los Angeles County—Continued

Venice Branch [Los Angeles Branch Library System TR], 610 California Ave., Los Angeles, 5/19/87, A, C, 87001020

Venice Canal Historic District, Roughly bounded by Grand, Carroll, Eastern, and Sherman canals, Los Angeles, 8/30/82, A, 82002193

Vermont Square Branch [Los Angeles Branch Library System TR], 1201 W. Forty-eighth St., Los Angeles, 5/19/87, A, C, 87001022

Villa Bonita, 1817 Hillcrest Rd., Hollywood, 9/12/86, C, 86001950

Villa Francesca, 1 Peppertree Dr., Rancho Palos Verdes, 10/02/86, A, C, 86002796

Villa Verde, 800 S. San Rafael, Pasadena, 9/13/84, C, 84000896

Vista del Arroyo Hotel and Bungalows, 125 S. Grand Ave., Pasadena, 4/02/81, C, 81000157

Washington Building, 9720–9732 Washington Blvd., Culver City, 5/28/91, B, C, 91000635

Watts Station, 1686 E. 103rd St., Los Angeles, 3/15/74, A, C, 74000523

Watts Towers of Simon Rodia, 1765 E. 107th St., Los Angeles, 4/13/77, A, C, g, NHL, 77000297

Weaver, Henry, House, 142 Adelaide Dr., Santa Monica, 12/27/89, C, 89002114

Well No. 4, Pico Canyon Oil Field, 9.5 mi. N of San Fernando, W of U.S. 99, San Fernando vicinity, 11/13/66, A, NHL, 66000212

Whitley Heights Historic District, Roughly bounded by Franklin, Highland, Cahuenga, and Fairfield Aves., Hollywood, 8/19/82, A, C, g, 82002189

Wilmington Branch [Los Angeles Branch Library System TR], 309 W. Opp St., Los Angeles, 5/19/87, A, C, 87001023

Wilshire Branch [Los Angeles Branch Library System TR], 149 N. Saint Andrews Pl., Los Angeles, 5/19/87, A, C, 87001024

Wilson, Warren, Beach House, 15 Thirtieth St., Venice, 7/17/86, A, C, 86001666

Wilton Historic District, S. Wilton Pl., S. Wilton Dr., and Ridgewood Pl., Los Angeles, 7/24/79, C, 79000490

Woman's Club of Redondo Beach, 400 S. Broadway, Redondo Beach, 4/19/84, A, C, 84000900

Woodbury—Story House, 2606 N. Madison Ave., Altedena, 12/30/93, B, C, 93001463

Workman Adobe, 15415 Don Julian Rd., Industry, 11/20/74, A, C, 74000519

Workman Family Cemetery, 15415 E. Don Julian Rd., Industry, 11/20/74, B, C, d, 74000520

Wright, Lloyd, Home and Studio, 858 N. Doheny Dr., West Hollywood, 4/06/87, C, g, 87000562

Wrigley, William, Jr., Summer Cottage, 76 Wrigley Rd., Avalon, 8/15/85, C, 85001785

Wynyate, 851 Lyndon St., South Pasadena, 4/24/73, B, C, 73000407

Madera County

Madera County Courthouse, 210 W. Yosemite Ave., Madera, 9/03/71, A, C, 71000162

Marin County

Alexander-Acacia Bridge, Alexander Ave. between Acacia and Monte Vista Aves., Larkspur, 1/05/84, C, 84000903

Angel Island, SE of Tiburon in San Francisco Bay, Tiburon vicinity, 10/14/71, A, C, D, 71000164

Barrett, William G., House, 156 Bulkley, Sausalito, 6/17/80, C, 80004490

Boyd House, 1125 B St., San Rafael, 12/17/74, C, f, 74000528

Bradford House, 333 G St., San Rafael, 6/06/80, A, B, C, 80000818

China Camp, 247 N. San Pedro Dr., San Rafael, 4/26/79, A, C, D, 79000493

Dixie Schoolhouse, 2255 Las Gallinas Ave., San Rafael, 12/26/72, A, C, b, 72000236

Dollar, Robert, Estate, 1408 Mission Ave., San Rafael, 12/11/72, A, B, C, 72000237

Dollar, Robert, House, 115 J St., San Rafael, 7/23/91, B, C, 91000920

Dolliver House, 58 Madrone Ave., Larkspur, 5/22/78, A, B, C, f, 78000703

Fashion Shop and Stephen Porcella House, 800 Grant Ave. and 1009 Reichert Ave., Novato, 6/25/80, A, D, 80000817

Forts Baker, Barry, and Cronkhite, S of Sausalito off U.S. 101, Sausalito vicinity, 12/12/73, A, NPS, 73000255

Green Brae Brick Yard, 125 E. Sir Francis Drake Blvd., Larkspur, 3/24/78, A, C, D, 78000704

Griswold House, 639 Main St., Sausalito, 9/12/85, C, 85002306

Larkspur Downtown Historic District, 234-552 1/2 Magnolia Ave., Larkspur, 10/07/82, C, 82000972

Lyford's Stone Tower, 2034 Paradise Dr., Tiburon, 12/02/76, A, C, 76000497

Marin County Civic Center, Jct. of N. San Pedro Rd. and Civic Center Dr., San Rafael, 7/17/91, C, g, NHL, 91002055

McNear, Erskine, B., House, 121 Knight Dr., San Rafael, 1/11/82, A, B, C, a, 82002204

Miller Creek School Indian Mound, Address Restricted, San Rafael vicinity, 10/14/71, D, d, 71000163

Muir Beach Archeological Site, Address Restricted, Marin City vicinity, 1/26/81, D, NPS, 81000097

Olema Lime Kilns, 4 mi. SE of Olema on CA 1, Olema vicinity, 10/08/76, A, NPS, 76000217

Outdoor Art Club, 1 W. Blithedale Ave., Mill Valley, 11/16/78, A, C, 78000705

Pierce Ranch, Point Reyes National Seashore, Inverness vicinity, 12/06/85, A, C, D, NPS, 85003324

Point Bonita Light Station [Light Stations of California MPS], Point Bonita, Sausalito, 9/03/91, A, C, 91001099

Point Reyes Lifeboat Rescue Station, 1927, Drake's Bay, Point Reyes National Seashore, Inverness vicinity, 11/07/85, A, g, NHL, NPS, 85002756

Point Reyes Light Station [Light Stations of California MPS], Point Reyes National Seashore, Point Reyes vicinity, 9/03/91, A, C, 91001100

Rancho Olompali, Address Restricted, Novato vicinity, 1/12/73, A, C, D, 73000409

Rey, Valentine, House, 428 Golden Gate Ave., Belvedere, 4/22/82, C, 82002203

San Rafael Improvement Club, 1800 5th Ave., San Rafael, 3/29/84, A, C, 84000907

Sausalito Woman's Club, 120 Central Ave., Sausalito, 4/15/93, A, 93000272

Schreiber, Brock, Boathouse and Beach, 12830 Sir Francis Drake Blvd., Inverness, 7/07/78, A, C, g, 78000702

Station KPH Operating Station, 18500 CA 1, Marshall, 7/24/89, A, 89000819

Station KPH, Marconi Wireless Telegraph Company of America, 18500 CA 1, Marshall, 7/24/89, A, 88003223

Steamship TENNESSEE Remains, Address Restricted, Marin City vicinity, 4/15/81, A, D, NPS, 81000102

Tomales Presbyterian Church and Cemetery, 11 Church St., Tomales, 8/01/75, A, C, a, d, 75000437

Mariposa County

Acting Superintendent's Headquarters, Yosemite National Park, Wawona, 6/09/78, A, b, NPS, 78000362

Ahwahnee Hotel, Yosemite Valley, Yosemite National Park, 2/15/77, C, NHL, NPS, 77000149

Bagby Stationhouse, Water Tanks and Turntable, CA 140, El Portal, 4/13/79, A, b, NPS, 79000316

Big Gap Flume, E of Groveland off CA 120 in Stanislaus National Forest, Groveland vicinity, 5/12/75, A, 75000438

Camp Curry Historic District, Yosemite Valley, Yosemite National Park, 11/01/79, A, C, NPS, 79000315

Coulterville Main Street Historic District, Main St., Coulterville, 3/12/82, A, C, 82002205

El Portal Archeological District, Address Restricted, Mariposa vicinity, 8/18/78, D, NPS, 78000359

Glacier Point Trailside Museum, E of El Portal in Yosemite National Park, El Portal vicinity, 4/04/78, A, C, NPS, 78000357

Hetch Hetchy Railroad Engine No.6, CA 140, El Portal, 1/30/78, A, NPS, 78000360

Hodgdon Homestead Cabin, Yosemite National Park, Wawona, 6/09/78, A, C, NPS, 78000356

Jorgenson, Chris, Studio, Pioneer Yosemite Historic Center, Yosemite National Park, 4/13/79, B, NPS, 79000280

Le Conte Memorial Lodge, Yosemite Valley, Yosemite National Park, Curry Village, 3/08/77, A, C, b, NHL, NPS, 77000148

Mariposa County Courthouse, 5088 Bullion St., Mariposa, 12/07/77, A, C, 77000306

Mariposa County High School Auditorium, 5074 Old Highway N., Mariposa, 5/02/91, C, 91000547

Mariposa Grove Museum, SE of Wawona in Yosemite National Park, Wawona vicinity, 12/01/78, A, C, g, NPS, 78000381

Mariposa County—Continued

Mariposa Town Historic District, Roughly bounded by Charles, 11th, Jones and 4th Sts., Mariposa, 5/15/91, A, B, C, 91000560

McCauley and Meyer Barns, N of El Portal in Yosemite National Park, El Portal vicinity, 6/15/78, A, C, NPS, 78000353

McGurk Cabin, S of Yosemite Village, Yosemite Village vicinity, 6/04/79, A, NPS, 79000281

Merced Grove Ranger Station, N of El Portal in Yosemite National Park, El Portal, 6/15/78, C, g, NPS, 78000358

Rangers' Club, Yosemite Valley, Yosemite National Park, 5/28/87, A, C, NHL, NPS, 87001414

St. Joseph Catholic Church, Rectory and Cemetery, 4983–4985 Bullion St., Mariposa, 4/16/91, A, C, a, d, 91000424

Track Bus No. 19, CA 140, El Portal, 5/22/78, A, NPS, 78000363

Wawona Hotel and Pavilion, On CA 41 in Yosemite National Park, Wawona, 10/01/75, A, C, NPS, 75000223

Yosemite Transportation Company Office, N of Wawona in Yosemite National Park, Wawona vicinity, 6/09/78, A, C, NPS, 78000355

Yosemite Valley Archeological District, Address Restricted, Yosemite Village vicinity, 1/20/78, D, NPS, 78000361

Yosemite Valley Bridges, 8 Bridges over Merced River, Yosemite National Park, Yosemite Village vicinity, 11/25/77, C, NPS, 77000160

Yosemite Valley Chapel, Off CA 140, Yosemite National Park, 12/12/73, C, a, b, NPS, 73000256

Yosemite Valley Railroad Caboose No. 15, CA 140, El Portal, 5/22/78, A, NPS, 78000352

Yosemite Village Historic District, E of El Portal in Yosemite National Park, El Portal vicinity, 3/30/78, A, C, NPS, 78000354

Mendocino County

Arena Cove Historic District [Point Arena MPS], Arena Cove, Point Arena, 9/13/90, A, 90001363

Buckridge Ranch House [Point Arena MPS], On the Garcia River near Buckridge Rd., Point Arena vicinity, 9/13/90, C, 90001359

Con Creek School, 2 mi. N of Boonville on CA 128, Boonville vicinity, 10/18/79, C, b, e, 79000498

FROLIC (brig), NE of Pt. Cabrillo, Caspar vicinity, 5/16/91, A, D, 91000565

Getchell, O. W., House, CA 1, Anchor Bay vicinity, 10/03/80, C, 80000819

Gillmore, E. P. and Clara, House [Point Arena MPS], 40 Mill St., Point Arena, 9/13/90, C, 90001355

Groshon, Sid, House [Point Arena MPS], 50 Mill St., Point Arena, 9/13/90, C, 90001356

Held—Poage House, 603 W. Perkins St., Ukiah, 1/07/88, B, C, 87002292

Hofman, Charles, House, 308 S. School St., Ukiah, 9/30/93, B, C, 93001022

Hoyt—Scott House [Point Arena MPS], 10 Riverside Dr., Point Arena, 9/13/90, C, 90001354

Italian Hotel [Point Arena MPS], 105 Main St., Point Arena, 9/13/90, A, 90001361

Iverson House [Point Arena MPS], 40 Iverson Ave., Point Arena, 9/13/90, C, 90001353

Ketchum, Billy, House [Point Arena MPS], 10 Scott Pl., Point Arena, 9/13/90, C, 90001358

Lovejoy Homestead, N of Branscomb, Branscomb vicinity, 4/26/78, A, C, 78000719

Main Street Historic Commercial District [Point Arena MPS], 165–265 Main St., Point Arena, 9/13/90, A, 90001364

Manchester Schoolhouse, 19750 CA 1, Manchester, 6/26/79, A, C, b, 79000499

Mendocino and Headlands Historic District, Bounded roughly by the Pacific Ocean on the W and S, Little Lake St. on the N, and CA 1 on the E, Mendocino, 7/14/71, A, C, 71000165

Milano Hotel, 38300 Highway One S, Gualala, 6/23/78, A, C, 78000720

Morse, LeGrand, House [Point Arena MPS], 365 Main St., Point Arena, 9/13/90, B, 90001362

Palace Hotel, 272 N. State St., Ukiah, 10/02/79, A, C, 79003458

Palmer, Annie, House [Point Arena MPS], 284 Main St., Point Arena, 9/13/90, C, 90001357

Point Arena High School [Point Arena MPS], 200 Lake St., Point Arena, 9/13/90, A, 90001365

Point Arena Light Station [Point Arena MPS], Lighthouse Rd., Point Arena vicinity, 7/16/91, A, C, 90002189

Point Arena Rancheria Roundhouse [Point Arena MPS], On the Garcia River at end of Rancheria Rd., Point Arena vicinity, 9/13/90, A, a, 90001360

Point Cabrillo Light Station [Light Stations of California MPS], 45300 Lighthouse Rd., Caspar vicinity, 9/03/91, A, C, 91001092

Point Cabrillo Site, Address Restricted, Pine Grove vicinity, 2/23/72, D, 72000238

Round Valley Flour Mills, Main and Greely Sts., Covelo, 11/10/80, C, D, 80000820

St. Paul's Methodist Episcopal Church [Point Arena MPS], 40 School St., Point Arena, 9/13/90, A, a, 90001366

Sun House, 431 S. Main St., Ukiah, 9/02/81, B, C, 81000161

Town Creek Archeological Site, Address Restricted, Covelo vicinity, 5/17/76, D, 76000498

Weller House, 524 Stewart St., Fort Bragg, 7/19/76, A, C, 76000499

Willits Carnegie Library [California Carnegie Libraries], 85 E. Commercial St., Willits, 1/07/93, A, C, 92001756

Merced County

Bank of Los Banos Building, 836, 840, 842 and 848 6th St., Los Banos, 8/24/79, C, 79000500

Bloss Mansion, 1020 Cedar Ave., Atwater, 9/03/81, B, C, 81000162

Buhach Grammar School, 2606 N. Buhach Rd., Merced vicinity, 4/07/83, C, 83001206

Cook, Maj. George Beecher, House, 356 W. 21st St., Merced, 9/15/83, C, 83001207

Kaehler-Rector House, 408 W. 25th St., Merced, 1/04/82, C, 82002206

Leggett House, 352 W. 22nd St, Merced, 10/25/79, C, 79000501

Leggett, Thomas H., House, 346 W. 21st St., Merced, 7/08/82, C, 82002207

Merced County Courthouse, W. 21st and N Sts., Merced, 10/29/75, C, 75000441

Merced County High School, 2125 M St., Merced, 5/31/84, A, C, 84000909

San Luis Gonzaga Archeological District, Address Restricted, Los Banos vicinity, 5/07/73, D, 73000412

Tioga Hotel, 1715 N St., Merced, 10/03/80, C, 80000821

U.S. Post Office, 401 W. 18th St., Merced, 2/10/83, A, C, 83001208

Modoc County

Anklin Village Archeological Site, Address Restricted, Canby vicinity, 6/03/76, D, 76000500

Black Cow Spring, Address Restricted, Canby vicinity, 7/09/74, D, NPS, 74000341

Core Site, Address Restricted, Canby vicinity, 4/08/74, D, 74000531

Cuppy Cave, Address Restricted, Canby vicinity, 7/12/74, D, NPS, 74000342

Fern Cave Archeological Site, Address Restricted, Tule Lake vicinity, 5/29/75, D, NPS, 75000224

Lava Beds National Monument Archeological District, Address Restricted, Tulelake vicinity, 3/21/91, A, B, D, NPS, 75002182

Mildred Ann Archeological Site, Address Restricted, Canby vicinity, 6/03/76, D, 76000501

NCO Railway Depot, East and 3rd Sts., Alturas, 2/28/85, A, C, b, 85000357

Nevada-California-Oregon Railway Co. General Office Building, 619 N. Main St., Alturas, 9/06/74, C, 74000529

Petroglyph Point Archeological Site, Address Restricted, Tulelake vicinity, 5/29/75, C, D, NPS, 75000178

Sacred Heart Catholic Church, 507 E. 4th St., Alturas, 6/30/83, A, C, a, 83001209

Seven Mile Flat Site, Address Restricted, Devil's Garden Ranger District vicinity, 12/24/74, D, NPS, 74000340

Skull Ridge, Address Restricted, Canby vicinity, 7/09/74, D, NPS, 74000287

Skull Spring, Address Restricted, Canby vicinity, 7/09/74, D, NPS, 74000288

Mono County

Bodie Historic District, 7 mi. S of Bridgeport on U.S. 395, then 12 mi. E on secondary rd., Bridgeport vicinity, 10/15/66, A, NHL, 66000213

Mono County Courthouse, Main St., Bridgeport, 3/01/74, A, C, 74000536

Monterey County

Asilomar Conference Grounds, Asilomar Blvd., Pacific Grove, 2/27/87, A, NHL, 87000823

Berwick Manor and Orchard, NW of Carmel Valley, Carmel Valley vicinity, 11/17/77, A, B, b, 77000309

Black, Samuel M., House, 418 Pajaro St., Salinas, 9/20/84, C, 84000911

Bontadelli, Peter J., House, 119 Cayuga St., Salinas, 7/15/80, C, 80000823

Boronda, Jose Eusebio, Adobe, Boronda Rd. and W. Laurel Dr., Salinas vicinity, 3/20/73, C, 73000413

Buck, Frank LaVerne, House, 581 Pine Ave., Pacific Grove, 9/11/86, B, C, 86002401

Carmel Mission, Rio Rd., Carmel, 10/15/66, A, C, a, NHL, 66000214

Centrella Hotel, 612 Central Ave., Pacific Grove, 10/29/82, A, 82000973

Community Church of Gonzales, 301 4th St., Gonzales, 9/15/83, A, C, a, 83001210

Cueva Pintada, Address Restricted, King City vicinity, 2/13/75, D, 75000445

Deetjen's Big Sur Inn, CA 1 N of Castro Cr., Big Sur vicinity, 9/13/90, A, 90001464

Dutton Hotel, Stagecoach Station, King City-Jolon Rd., Jolon vicinity, 10/14/71, C, 71000166

El Castillo, Address Restricted, Monterey vicinity, 11/23/71, A, D, 71000167

Finch, James W., House, 410 Monroe St., Monterey, 10/19/82, C, 82000974

Gabilan Lodge No. 372—Independent Order of Odd Fellows, 117 Fourth St., Gonzales, 10/02/86, A, C, 86002813

Gil, Jose Mario, Adobe, Hunter Liggett Military Reservation, Jolon, 6/07/74, B, C, 74000537

Gosby House Inn, 643 Lighthouse Ave., Pacific Grove, 12/02/80, C, 80000822

Jeffers, Robinson, House, 26304 Ocean View Ave., Carmel, 10/10/75, B, C, 75000444

King City Joint Union High School Auditorium, N. Mildred Ave., NW of jct. with Broadway St., King City, 7/23/91, C, 91000917

Kirk Creek Campground, Address Restricted, Lucia vicinity, 12/31/74, D, 74000538

Krough House, 146 Central Ave., Salinas, 1/18/82, C, 82002209

Larkin House, 464 Calle Principale, Monterey, 10/15/66, C, NHL, 66000215

Los Coches Rancho, 1 mi, (1.6 km) S of Soledad on U.S. 101, Soledad vicinity, 1/31/79, C, D, 79000502

Merritt, Josiah, Adobe, 386 Pacific St., Monterey, 11/22/77, A, C, 77000311

Milpitas Ranchhouse, S of King City, King City vicinity, 12/02/77, B, g, 77000310

Monterey Old Town Historic District, Boundary undetermined at this time, Monterey, 4/15/70, A, C, NHL, 70000137

Nesbitt, Sheriff William Joseph, House, 66 Capitol St., Salinas, 2/19/82, A, C, 82002210

Olvida Penas, 1061 Majella Rd., Pebble Beach, 4/03/78, C, 78000721

Outlands in the Eighty Acres, 25800 Hatton, Carmel By-the-Sea, 3/23/89, C, 89000228

Point Pinos Lighthouse, Asilomar Blvd. and Lighthouse Ave., Pacific Grove, 7/14/77, A, C, 77000312

Point Sur Light Station [Light Stations of California MPS], Morro Rock on Point Sur, 0.5 mi. W of CA 1, Big Sur vicinity, 9/03/91, A, C, 91001097

Porter—Vallejo Mansion, 29 Bishop St., Pajaro, 1/04/90, B, C, 89002273

Post, Joseph W., House, CA 1, Big Sur vicinity, 9/12/85, B, C, 85002196

Rancho Las Palmas, S of Salinas at 200 River Rd., Salinas vicinity, 11/20/78, B, C, 78000722

Rancho San Lucas, 1 3/4 mi. SW of jct. of Paris Valley Rd. and Rancho San Lucas entry rd., San Lucas, 5/06/91, B, 91000530

Royal Presidio Chapel, 550 Church St., Monterey, 10/15/66, A, C, NHL, 66000216

San Antonio de Padua Mission, NW of Jolon off Del Venturi Rd., Jolon vicinity, 4/26/76, C, a, 76000504

Sargent, B. V., House, 154 Central Ave., Salinas, 10/20/80, C, 80000824

Site Number 4 Mnt 85, Address Restricted, Greenfield vicinity, 10/29/76, D, 76000502

Stevenson House, Houston St. between Pearl and Webster Sts., Monterey, 1/07/72, A, B, 72000239

Tidball Store, Jolon Rd., Jolon, 12/12/76, A, 76000503

Trimmer Hill, 230 6th St., Pacific Grove, 6/28/82, C, 82002208

U.S. Customhouse, Calle Principal at Decatur St., Monterey, 10/15/66, C, NHL, 66000217

Napa County

Aetna Springs Resort, 1600 Aetna Springs Rd., Pope Valley, 3/09/87, A, C, 87000341

Alexandria Hotel and Annex, 840–844 Brown St., Napa, 1/11/82, C, 82002212

Andrews, William, House, 741 Seminary St., Napa, 6/18/92, C, 92000789

Atkinson House, 8440 St. Helena Hwy., Rutherford, 9/13/90, A, C, 90001443

Bale Mill, 3 mi. NW of St. Helena off CA 128, St. Helena vicinity, 6/22/72, A, C, 72000240

Bank of Napa, 903 Main St. and 908 Brown St., Napa, 6/18/92, C, 92000785

Brannan, Sam, Cottage, 109 Wapoo Ave., Calistoga, 8/18/83, C, 83001211

Buford House, 1930 Clay St., Napa, 11/11/77, C, 77000314

Chateau Chevalier, 3101 Spring Mountain Rd., St. Helena, 6/12/87, A, C, 87000926

Churchill Manor, 485 Brown St., Napa, 4/18/77, C, 77000315

Earl, Thomas, House, 1221 Seminary St., Napa, 8/18/92, B, 92000996

Elmshaven, 125 Glass Mountain Ln., St. Helena, 11/04/93, B, a, NHL, 93001609

Eshcol Winery, 1160 Oak Knoll Ave., Napa, 7/16/87, A, C, 87001155

Far Niente Winery, S of Oakville at 1577 Oakville Grade, Oakville vicinity, 2/28/79, A, C, 79000507

First National Bank, 1026 First St., Napa, 9/24/92, C, 92001277

First Presbyterian Church, 1333 3rd St., Napa, 6/05/75, A, C, a, 75000446

Francis, James H., House, 1403 Myrtle St., Calistoga, 1/31/79, C, 79000503

French Laundry, 6640 Washington St., Yountville, 4/19/78, C, 78000728

Goodman Library, 1219 1st St., Napa, 1/21/74, C, 74000539

Goodman, George E., Jr., House, 492 Randolph St., Napa, 4/01/93, C, 93000270

Goodman, George E., Mansion, 1120 Oak St., Napa, 4/15/93, C, 93000261

Gordon Building, 1130 1st St., Napa, 9/12/85, B, C, 85002197

Greystone Cellars, 2555 Main St., St. Helena, 8/10/78, B, C, 78000725

Groezinger Wine Cellars, 6525 Washington St., Yountville, 2/04/82, B, C, 82002218

Hackett House, 2109 1st St., Napa, 4/19/84, C, 84000913

Hatt Building, 5th and Main Sts., Napa, 5/02/77, A, 77000316

Helios Ranch, 1575 St. Helena Hwy., St. Helena, 5/09/85, B, C, 85001014

Henessey, Dr. Edwin, House, 1727 Main St., Napa, 8/28/86, B, C, 86001976

Kee, Sam, Laundry Building, 1245 Main St., Napa, 10/01/74, A, C, 74000540

Kreuzer Ranch, 167 Kreuzer Lane, Napa vicinity, 2/11/82, A, C, 82002214

Krug, Charles, Winery, St. Helena Hwy., St. Helena, 11/08/74, A, B, C, 74000542

Larkmead Winery, NW of St. Helena at 1091 Larkmead Lane, St. Helena vicinity, 2/01/82, A, C, 82002215

Lisbon Winery, 1720 Brown St., Napa, 3/01/79, A, C, 79000505

Manasse Mansion, 443 Brown St., Napa, 11/14/78, B, C, 78000723

Manasse, Edward G., House, 495 Coombs St., Napa, 4/15/93, B, 93000271

Migliavacca House, Division St., Napa, 3/30/78, C, b, 78000724

Mount View Hotel, 1457 Lincoln Ave., Calistoga, 4/12/82, A, B, C, g, 82002211

Napa County Courthouse Plaza, Bounded by Coombs, Second, Brown and Third Sts., Napa, 6/18/92, A, C, 92000778

Napa Opera House, 1018–1030 Main St. on E side, Napa, 10/25/73, A, 73000414

Napa Valley Railroad Depot, Lincoln Ave. and Fair Way, Calistoga, 4/18/77, A, 77000313

Nichelini Winery, E of St. Helena at 2950 Sage Canyon Rd, St. Helena vicinity, 8/24/79, A, C, 79000508

Noyes Mansion, 1750 First St., Napa, 6/18/92, C, 92000788

Oakville Grocery, 7856 St. Helena Hwy., Oakville, 7/22/93, A, 93000664

Old Napa Register Building, 1202 1st St., Napa, 2/19/82, A, C, 82002213

Napa County—Continued

Palmer, Judge Augustus C., House, 1300 Cedar St., Calistoga, 1/31/79, C, 79000504

Pinkham, Capt. George, House, 529–531 Brown St., Napa, 6/18/92, B, 92000786

Pope Street Bridge, Pope St., over the Napa River, St. Helena, 10/05/72, C, 72000241

Rhine House, 2000 Main St., St. Helena, 2/23/72, C, 72000242

Rovegno, Charles, House, 6711 Washington St., Yountville, 9/13/91, C, 91001384

Semorile Building, 975 1st St., Napa, 11/21/74, B, C, 74000541

St. Helena Catholic Church, Oak and Tainter Sts., St. Helena, 5/23/78, C, a, 78000726

St. Helena High School, 437 Main St., St. Helena, 5/22/78, C, 78000727

St. Helena Public Library, 1360 Oak Ave., St. Helena, 1/19/79, C, 79000509

Suscol House, S of Napa on Old Suscol Ferry Rd., Napa vicinity, 2/28/79, A, C, b, 79000506

Taylor, Duckworth and Company Foundry Building, 1345 Railroad Ave., St. Helena, 1/21/82, A, C, 82002216

US Post Office—Napa Franklin Station [US Post Office in California 1900-1941 TR], 1352 2nd St., Napa, 1/11/85, C, 85000133

Veterans Home of California Chapel, CA 29, Yountville, 2/13/79, A, C, a, 79000510

Webber, John Lee, House, 6610 Webber St., Yountville, 1/19/82, A, B, C, b, 82002219

William Tell Saloon and Hotel, 1228 Spring St., St. Helena, 5/07/82, A, 82002217

Winship-Smernes Building, 948 Main St., Napa, 7/29/77, C, 77000317

Wulff, Capt. N. H., House, 549 Brown St., Napa, 8/18/92, B, 92000994

Yount, Eliza G., House, 423 Seminary St., Napa, 9/24/92, C, 92001279

Nevada County

Boca Dam [Newlands Reclamation TR], S end of Boca Resevoir, Truckee vicinity, 3/25/81, A, C, g, 81000712

Bridgeport Covered Bridge, SW of French Corral over S. Yuba River, French Corral vicinity, 7/14/71, A, C, 71000168

Donner Camp, 2.6 mi. W of Truckee on U.S. 40, Truckee vicinity, 10/15/66, A, NHL, 66000218

Empire Mine, SE of Grass Valley at 338 E. Empire St., Grass Valley vicinity, 12/09/77, A, C, 77000318

Grass Valley Public Library [California Carnegie Libraries MPS], 207 Mill St., Grass Valley, 3/26/92, A, C, 92000267

Kruger House, 10292 Donner Pass Rd., Truckee, 6/17/82, A, B, C, 82002220

Malakoff Diggins-North Bloomfield Historic District, Graniteville Star Route, North Bloomfield, 4/11/73, A, C, a, b, 73000418

Marsh, Martin Luther, House, 254 Boulder St., Nevada City, 4/11/73, C, 73000415

Meadow Lake Petroglyphs, Address Restricted, French Lake vicinity, 5/06/71, D, 71000169

Mount St. Mary's Academy and Convent, Church and Chapel Sts., Grass Valley, 5/03/74, A, a, 74000543

National Exchange Hotel, 211 Broad St., Nevada City, 10/25/73, A, C, 73000416

Nevada Brewery, 107 Sacramento St., Nevada City, 9/12/85, A, C, 85002303

Nevada City Downtown Historic District, Roughly bounded by Spring, Bridge, Commercial, York, Washington, Coyote, and Main Sts., Nevada City, 9/23/85, A, C, 85002520

Nevada City Firehouse No. 2, 420 Broad St., Nevada City, 5/03/74, C, 74000544

Nevada City Free Public Library [California Carnegie Libraries MPS], 211 N. Pine St., Nevada City, 12/10/90, A, C, 90001809

Nevada Theatre, Broad and Bridge Sts., Nevada City, 3/14/73, A, C, 73000417

Ott's Assay Office, 130 Main St., Nevada City, 4/14/75, A, 75000447

Sargent, Aaron A., House, 449 Broad St., Nevada City, 6/20/80, A, B, C, 80000825

Orange County

Ainsworth, Lewis, House, 414 E. Chapman Ave., Orange, 3/13/81, A, C, 81000163

Backs, Ferdinand, House, 225 N. Claudina St., Anaheim, 10/14/80, C, 80000826

Balboa Inn, 105 Main St., Newport Beach, 4/11/86, A, C, 86000730

Balboa Pavilion, 400 Main St., Balboa, 5/17/84, A, C, 84000914

Bank of Balboa—Bank of America, 611 E. Balboa Blvd., Newport Beach, 7/24/86, A, C, 86001903

Bradford, A. S., House, 136 Palm Circle, Placentia, 10/03/78, B, C, 78000730

Brea City Hall and Park, 401 S. Brea Blvd., Brea, 5/24/84, A, C, 84000917

Builders Exchange Building, 202–208 N. Main St., Santa Ana, 4/29/82, A, 82002223

Carnegie Library, 241 S. Anaheim Blvd., Anaheim, 10/22/79, A, 79000511

Casa Romantica, 415 Avenida Granada, San Clemente, 12/27/91, B, 91001900

Casa de Esperanza, 31806 El Camino Real, San Juan Capistrano, 10/01/90, A, B, 90001484

Chapman Building, 110 E. Wilshire Ave., Fullerton, 9/22/83, B, C, 83001212

Christ College Site, Address Restricted, Irvine vicinity, 4/16/93, D, 93000300

Clark, Dr. George C., House, California State University campus, Fullerton, 12/12/76, B, C, b, 76000506

Crystal Cove Historic District, NW of Laguna Beach, Laguna Beach vicinity, 6/15/79, A, C, 79000514

Culver, C. Z., House, 205 E. Palmyra, Orange, 3/20/86, B, C, 86000458

Downtown Santa Ana Historic Districts (North, Government/Institutional and South, Retail), Roughly bounded by Civic Center Dr., First,

Ross, and Spurgeon Sts., Santa Ana, 12/19/84, A, C, 84000438

Easley, Oscar, Block, 101 El Camino Real, San Clemente, 2/17/83, C, 83001213

Elephant Packing House, 201 W. Truslow Ave., Fullerton, 9/21/83, A, B, 83001214

Esslinger Building, 31866 Camino Capistrano, San Juan Capistrano, 5/16/88, C, g, 88000557

Fairview Indian Site, Address Restricted, Costa Mesa vicinity, 6/27/72, D, 72000243

Forster, Frank A., House, 27182 Ortega Hwy., San Juan Capistrano, 9/11/86, C, 86002405

Frances Packing House, NE of Irvine, Irvine vicinity, 8/02/77, A, C, 77000319

Fullerton Union Pacific Depot, 100 E. Santa Fe Ave., Fullerton, 10/12/83, A, C, 83003551

Harmon-McNeil House, 322 E. Chestnut St., Santa Ana, 11/07/85, A, C, 85002764

Harrison House, 27832 Ortega Hwy., San Juan Capistrano, 8/21/79, C, 79000515

Hetebrink House, 515 E. Chapman, Fullerton, 7/01/93, C, 93000597

Hotel San Clemente, 114 Avenida Del Mar, San Clemente, 8/31/89, A, B, C, 89001149

Howe-Waffle House and Carriage House, Sycamore and Civic Center Dr., Santa Ana, 4/13/77, A, C, 77000320

Huntington Beach Municipal Pier, Main St. and Ocean Ave., Huntington Beach, 8/24/89, A, C, 89001203

Irvine Bean and Growers Association Building, 14972 Sand Canyon Ave., Irvine, 1/13/86, A, C, g, 86000068

Irvine Blacksmith Shop, 14952 Sand Canyon Ave., Irvine, 3/20/86, A, B, C, 86000452

Irvine Park, 21401 Chapman Ave., Orange vicinity, 4/07/83, C, 83001215

Key, George, Ranch, 625 Bastanchury Rd., Placentia, 4/21/75, B, C, 75000449

Kraemer, Samuel, Building (American Savings Bank/First National Bank), 76 S. Claudina St, Anaheim vicinity, 6/16/83, C, 83001217

Kroger-Melrose District, Roughly bounded by Lincoln Ave., S. Kroger, W. Broadway and S. Philadelphia, Anaheim, 6/19/85, A, C, 85001326

Lighter-than-Air Ship Hangars, Valencia and Redhill Aves., Santa Ana, 4/03/75, A, g, 75000451

Los Rios Street Historic District, 31600-31921 Los Rios St., San Juan Capistrano, 4/04/83, A, C, 83001216

Lovell Beach House, 1242 W. Ocean Front, Newport Beach, 2/05/74, C, g, 74000545

Mariona, 2529 S. Coast Hwy., Laguna Beach, 3/29/84, C, 84000922

Melrose-Backs Neighborhood Houses, 226 and 228 E. Adele and 303, 307, 317, 321 N. Philadelphia, Anaheim, 4/03/86, A, B, C, 86000783

Minter, George W., House, 322 W. 3rd St., Santa Ana, 6/09/80, B, C, b, 80000830

Mission San Juan Capistrano, Camino Capistrano and Ortega Hwy., San Juan Capistrano, 9/03/71, A, B, C, D, a, 71000170

Modjeska House, Modjeska Canyon Rd., Modjeska, 12/11/72, A, B, C, NHL, 72000244

Montanez Adobe, 31745 Los Rios St., San Juan Capistrano, 4/21/75, B, C, a, 75000450

Orange County—Continued

Muckenthaler House, 1201 W. Malvern Ave., Fullerton, 5/31/80, C, 80000829

Newland House, 19820 Beach Blvd., Huntington Beach, 10/24/85, A, B, C, 85003374

Nixon, Richard, Birthplace, 18061 Yorba Linda Blvd., Yorba Linda, 12/17/71, B, c, NHL, 71000171

Odd Fellows Hall, 309-311 N. Main St., Santa Ana, 8/18/83, A, C, 83001218

Old Backs House, 215 N. Claudina St., Anaheim, 10/14/80, A, C, b, 80000827

Olive Civic Center, 3030 N. Magnolia Ave., Orange, 10/07/93, A, C, 93001038

Orange County Courthouse, 211 W. Santa Ana Blvd., Santa Ana, 8/29/77, A, C, 77000321

Orange Intermediate School—Central Grammar School, 370 N. Glassell St., Orange, 4/13/93, A, C, 93000282

Orange Union High School, 333 N. Glassell St., Orange, 4/14/75, A, C, g, 75000448

Pacific Electric Railway Company Depot, 18132 Imperial Hwy., Yorba Linda, 10/25/79, A, 79000517

Pacific Electric Sub-Station No. 14, 802 E. 5th St., Santa Ana, 9/22/83, A, C, 83001219

Parker House, 163 S. Cypress St., Orange, 8/10/89, A, B, C, 89000975

Parra, Miguel, Adobe, 27832 Ortega Hwy., San Juan Capistrano, 9/11/78, A, C, 78000731

Pickwick Hotel, 225 S. Anaheim Blvd., Anaheim, 12/31/79, A, 79000513

Pierotti, Attlio and Jane, House, 1731 N. Bradford Ave., Fullerton, 9/02/93, B, C, 93000907

Plaza Historic District, Roughly bounded by Maple and Almond Aves., Orange and Olive Sts., Orange, 3/19/82, A, C, 82002221

Plaza, The, Chapman Ave. and Glassell St., Orange, 12/20/78, A, C, 78000729

Plummer, Louis, Auditorium, 201 E. Chapman Ave., Fullerton, 9/30/93, A, C, 93001019

Rankin Building, 117 W. 4th St., Santa Ana, 2/24/83, C, 83001220

San Clemente Beach Club, Avenida Boca De La Playa, San Clemente, 4/09/81, A, C, 81000164

Santa Ana City Hall, 217 N. Main St., Santa Ana, 11/10/82, C, 82000975

Santa Ana Fire Station Headquarters No. 1, 1322 N. Sycamore St., Santa Ana, 7/10/86, A, C, 86001549

Santa Fe Railway Passenger and Freight Depot, 140 E. Santa Fe Ave., Fullerton, 2/05/92, A, C, 91002031

Santora Building, 207 N. Broadway, Santa Ana, 12/27/82, C, 82000976

Seal Beach City Hall, 201 8th St., Seal Beach, 8/11/83, A, C, 83001221

Serrano, Jose, Adobe, 21802 Serrano Rd., El Toro, 5/24/76, A, C, D, 76000505

Smith and Clark Brothers Ranch and Grounds, 18922 Santiago Blvd., Villa Park, 9/22/83, A, C, 83001222

Smith-Tuthill Funeral Parlors, 518 N. Broadway, Santa Ana, 5/19/78, A, C, 78000732

Southern Counties Gas Co., 207 W. 2nd St., Santa Ana, 7/28/83, C, 83001223

Spurgeon Block, 206 W. 4th St, Santa Ana, 8/31/79, B, C, 79000516

St. Francis by-the-Sea American Catholic Church, 430 Park Ave., Laguna Beach, 6/30/88, A, B, C, a, 88000978

St. John's Lutheran Church, 185 S. Center St., Orange, 10/16/91, C, a, 91001520

Stanton, Phillip Ackley, House, 2200 W. Sequoia Ave., Anaheim, 11/21/80, A, B, C, 80000828

Stevens, Sherman, House, 228 W. Main St., Tustin, 1/05/84, B, C, 84000926

Truxaw-Gervais House, 887 S. Anaheim Blvd., Anaheim, 10/29/82, C, 82000977

US Post Office Station—Spurgeon Station [US Post Office in California 1900-1941 TR], 605 Bush St., Santa Ana, 1/11/85, C, 85000134

VIRGINIA (sloop), Dana Point Youth & Group Facility, W. basin, Dana Point Harbor, Dana Point, 4/02/91, C, 91000337

Walkers Orange County Theater, 308 N. Main St., Santa Ana, 2/19/82, A, C, 82002224

Wright, George L., House, 831 N. Minister St., Santa Ana, 11/12/82, C, 82000978

Yorba, Domingo Adobe and Casa Manuel Garcia, 31781 Camino Capistrano, San Juan Capistrano, 2/04/82, A, C, 82002222

Yost Theater—Ritz Hotel, 301-307 N. Spurgeon St., Santa Ana, 1/23/86, A, C, 86000107

Young Men's Christian Association—Santa Ana-Tustin Chapter, 205 W. Civic Center Dr., Santa Ana, 3/25/93, A, C, 93000237

Placer County

Dutch Flat Historic District, Main and Stockton Sts., Dutch Flat, 3/28/73, A, C, 73000419

Griffith House, 7325 English Colony Way, Penryn, 12/19/78, A, B, C, 78000733

Griffith Quarry, Taylor Rd., Penryn, 10/20/77, A, B, D, 77000322

Haman House, 424 Oak St., Roseville, 11/17/76, C, 76000507

Lake Tahoe Dam [Newlands Reclamation TR], SR 89 at Truckee River, Tahoe City, 3/25/81, A, C, 81000713

Lincoln Public Library [California Carnegie Libraries MPS], 590 Fifth St., Lincoln, 12/10/90, A, C, 90001814

Michigan Bluff—Last Chance Trail, From Michigan Bluff NE to Last Chance, Michigan Bluff vicinity, 6/26/92, A, C, 92000854

Newcastle Portuguese Hall, Taylor Rd., Newcastle vicinity, 3/25/82, A, b, 82002225

Old Auburn Historic District, Roughly bounded by Maple, Commercial, Court, Washington, Spring, and Sacramento Sts., Auburn, 12/29/70, A, C, 70000138

Outlet Gates and Gatekeeper's Cabin, U.S. 89 at mouth of Truckee River, Tahoe City, 12/13/72, C, 72000245

Strap Ravine Nisenan Maidu Indian Site, Address Restricted, Roseville vicinity, 1/08/73, D, d, 73000420

Summit Soda Springs, SE of Soda Springs, Soda Springs vicinity, 12/15/78, A, B, C, 78000734

Watson Log Cabin, 560 N. Lake Blvd, Tahoe City, 8/24/79, A, C, 79000518

Plumas County

Lakes Basin Petroglyphs, Address Restricted, Gold Lake vicinity, 5/06/71, D, 71000172

Plumas-Eureka Mill, Jamison Mines District, W of Blairsden off Alt. U.S. 40 in Plumas-Eureka State Park, Blairsden vicinity, 7/16/73, A, 73000421

Warner Valley Ranger Station, N of Chester in Lassen Volcanic National Park, Chester vicinity, 4/03/78, A, C, NPS, 78000364

Riverside County

Administration Building, Sherman Institute, 9010 Magnolia Ave., Riverside, 1/09/80, A, C, 80000831

All Souls Universalist Church, 3657 Lemon St., Riverside, 9/18/78, B, C, a, 78000736

Andreas Canyon, Address Restricted, Palm Springs vicinity, 1/08/73, D, 73000422

Arlington Branch Library and Fire Hall, 9556 Magnolia Ave., Riverside, 7/22/93, A, C, 93000668

Armory Hall, 252 N. Main St., Lake Elsinore, 1/29/92, A, C, 91002032

Barker Dam, SE of Twentynine Palms in Joshua Tree National Monument, Twentynine Palms vicinity, 10/29/75, A, NPS, 75000173

Blythe Intaglios, Addres Restricted, Blythe vicinity, 8/22/75, A, D, a, 75000452

Buttercup Farms Pictograph, Address Restricted, Perris vicinity, 5/03/76, D, 76000509

Carnegie, Andrew, Library, 8th and Main Sts., Corona, 6/29/77, A, C, 77000324

Chinatown, Brockton and Tequesquite Aves., Riverside, 3/01/90, A, D, 90000151

Coachella Valley Fish Traps, Restricted Address, Valerie vicinity, 6/13/72, C, D, 72000247

Crescent Bathhouse, 201 W. Graham Ave., Lake Elsinore, 7/30/75, C, 75000453

Desert Queen Mine, S of Twentynine Palms in Joshua Tree National Monument, Twentynine Palms vicinity, 1/17/76, A, g, NPS, 76000216

Federal Post Office, 3720 Orange St., Riverside, 11/20/78, C, 78000737

First Church of Christ, Scientist, 3606 Lemon St., Riverside, 9/22/92, C, a, 92001250

Gilman Ranch, 1937 W. Gilman St., Banning, 11/17/77, A, B, D, 76000508

Harada House, 3356 Lemon St., Riverside, 9/15/77, A, NHL, 77000325

Heritage House, 8193 Magnolia Ave., Riverside, 2/28/73, C, 73000423

Jensen, Cornelius, Ranch, 4350 Riverview Dr, Rubidoux, 9/06/79, A, B, C, 79000519

Martinez Historical District, Off SR 86, Torres-Martinez Indian Reservation, 5/17/73, C, D, 73000425

Riverside County—Continued

Masonic Temple, 3650 11th St., Riverside, 6/06/80, C, 80000832

McCoy Spring Archeological Site, Address Restricted, Blythe vicinity, 5/10/82, D, 82002226

Mission Court Bungalows, 3355–3373 Second St. and 3354–3362 First St., Riverside, 7/08/93, C, 93000549

Mission Inn, 3649 7th St., Riverside, 5/14/71, C, NHL, 71000173

Murrieta Creek Archeological Area, Address Restricted, Temecula vicinity, 4/24/73, D, d, 73000424

North Chuckwalla Mountain Quarry District, Address Restricted, Desert Center vicinity, 8/24/81, D, 81000165

North Chuckwalla Mountains Petroglyph District Ca-Riv 1383, Address Restricted, Desert Center vicinity, 9/03/81, D, 81000166

Old YWCA Building, 3425 7th St., Riverside, 1/28/82, A, C, 82002227

Riverside Municipal Auditorium and Soldier's Memorial Building, 3485 7th St., Riverside, 3/31/78, C, 78000738

Riverside-Arlington Heights Fruit Exchange, 3391 7th St., Riverside, 6/09/80, A, C, 80000833

Ryan House and Lost Horse Well, S of Twentynine Palms in Joshua Tree National Monument, Twentynine Palms vicinity, 6/05/75, A, C, NPS, 75000175

San Pedro, Los Angeles, & Salt Lake RR Depot, 3751 Vine St., Riverside, 4/18/77, A, C, 77000326

Simon's, M. H., Undertaking Chapel, 3610 11th St., Riverside, 6/09/80, C, 80000834

Southern Hotel, 445 D St., Perris, 10/15/92, A, C, 92001384

Sutherland Fruit Company, 3191 Seventh St., Riverside, 4/11/86, A, C, 86000732

Tahquitz Canyon, Address Restricted, Palm Springs vicinity, 10/31/72, A, C, D, 72000246

University Heights Junior High School, 2060 University Ave., Riverside, 6/24/93, A, C, 93000547

Woman's Improvement Club Clubhouse, 1101 S. Main St., Corona, 11/03/88, A, C, 88002014

Sacramento County

Alkali Flat Central Historic District, Roughly E and F Sts. between 9th and 12th Sts., Sacramento, 7/26/84, A, C, b, 84000929

Alkali Flat North Historic District, D and 11th Sts., Sacramento, 4/19/84, A, C, 84000933

Alkali Flat West Historic District, E, F, and 8th Sts., Sacramento, 7/26/84, A, C, 84000936

Alta Mesa Farm Bureau Hall, 10195 Alta Mesa Rd., Wilton vicinity, 1/07/87, A, 86003577

Blue Anchor Building, 1400 10th St., Sacramento, 2/03/83, C, 83001224

Brewster House, 206 5th St., Galt, 6/23/78, C, 78000740

Brighton School, 3312 Bradshaw Rd., Sacramento, 4/03/81, A, C, 81000168

California Governor's Mansion, 16th and H Sts., Sacramento, 11/10/70, A, C, 70000139

California State Capitol, Between 10th and 16th and L and N Sts., Sacramento, 4/03/73, A, C, 73000427

Calpak Plant No. 11, 1721 C St., Sacramento, 5/17/84, A, 84000939

Capitol Extension District, Capitol Mall, Sacramento, 5/24/84, A, C, 84000944

Cohn House, 305 Scott St., Folsom, 1/21/82, C, 82002228

Coolot Company Building, 812 J St., Sacramento, 9/20/78, A, C, 78000742

Crocker, E. B., Art Gallery, 216 O St., Sacramento, 5/06/71, A, C, 71000176

Delta Meadows Site, Address Restricted, Locke vicinity, 11/05/71, D, 71000175

Dunlap's Dining Room, 4322 Fourth Ave., Sacramento, 4/02/92, A, B, 92000308

Eastern Star Hall, 2719 K St., Sacramento, 1/07/93, A, C, 92001757

Elk Grove Historic District, 8986–9097 Elk Grove Blvd. also School, Gage and Grove Sts., Elk Grove, 3/01/88, A, C, a, b, 87002410

Fire Station No. 6, 3414 4th Ave., Sacramento, 4/25/91, A, C, 91000484

Firehouse No. 3, 1215 19th St., Sacramento, 10/29/91, A, C, 91001537

Folsom Depot, 200 Wool St., Folsom, 2/19/82, A, C, D, 82002229

Folsom Powerhouse, Off Folsom Blvd. in Folsom Lake State Recreation Area, Folsom, 10/02/73, A, C, NHL, 73000426

Goethe House, 3731 T St., Sacramento, 2/19/82, C, 82002230

Greene, John T., House, 3200 H St., Sacramento, 4/15/82, C, 82002231

Heilbron House, 704 O St., Sacramento, 12/12/76, C, 76000511

Hotel Regis, 1024-1030 K St, Sacramento, 10/29/82, C, 82000979

Hotel Senator, 1121 L St., Sacramento, 5/30/79, A, C, 79003459

Howe, Edward P., Jr., House, 2215 21st St., Sacramento, 2/19/82, C, 82002232

Hubbard-Upson House, 1010 F St., Sacramento, 12/02/77, B, C, 77000327

I Street Bridge, CA 16, Sacramento, 4/22/82, A, C, 82002233

Imperial Theatre, Market St., Walnut Grove, 10/29/82, A, g, 82000980

Indian Stone Corral, Address Restricted, Orangevale vicinity, 4/16/75, D, 75000456

Isleton Chinese and Japanese Commercial Districts, Bounded by River Rd. and Union, E and H Sts., Isleton, 3/14/91, A, C, 91000297

J Street Wreck, At the foot of J St., in the Sacramento R., Sacramento, 5/16/91, A, D, 91000562

Joe Mound, Address Restricted, Sacramento vicinity, 10/14/71, D, 71000177

Johnson, J. Neely, House, 1029 F St., Sacramento, 9/13/76, B, C, 76000512

Kuchler Row, 608–614 10th St., Sacramento, 6/25/82, A, C, 82002234

Lais, Charles, House, 1301 H St., Sacramento, 2/28/85, C, 85000358

Libby McNeil and Libby Fruit and Vegetable Cannery, 1724 Stockton Blvd., Sacramento, 3/02/82, A, C, 82002235

Locke Historic District, Bounded on the W by the Sacramento River, on the N by Locke Rd., on the E by Alley St., and on the S by Levee St., Locke, 5/06/71, A, C, NHL, 71000174

Merrium Apartments, 1017 14th St., Sacramento, 9/13/90, A, C, 90001386

Mesick House, 517 8th St., Sacramento, 1/21/82, C, 82002236

Nisenan Village Site, Address Restricted, Carmichael vicinity, 3/21/78, D, 78000739

Old Sacramento Historic District, Jcts. of U.S. 40, 50, 99, and CA 16 and 24, Sacramento, 10/15/66, A, NHL, 66000219

Old Tavern, 2801 Capitol Ave., Sacramento, 9/15/83, A, C, 83001225

Pony Express Terminal, 1006 2nd St., Sacramento, 10/15/66, A, NHL, 66000220

Rosebud Ranch, N of Hood, Hood vicinity, 12/31/79, C, 79000521

Ruhstaller Building, 900 J St., Sacramento, 1/21/82, C, 82002237

Sacramento Air Depot Historic District, McClellan Air Force Base, North Highlands vicinity, 1/21/92, A, C, 91001969

Sacramento Bank Building, 3418 Broadway, Sacramento, 1/21/82, A, C, 82002238

Sacramento City Library [California Carnegie Libraries MPS], 828 I St., Sacramento, 7/30/92, A, C, 92000967

Sacramento Memorial Auditorium, 16th and J Sts., Sacramento, 3/29/78, A, C, 78000743

Slocum House, 7992 California Ave., Fair Oaks, 1/31/79, A, B, 79000520

Southern Pacific Railroad Company's Sacramento Depot, 5th and 1 Sts., Sacramento, 4/21/75, A, C, g, 75000457

Stanford-Lathrop House, 800 N St., Sacramento, 12/09/71, A, B, C, NHL, 71000178

Sutter's Fort, 2701 L St., Sacramento, 10/15/66, A, NHL, 66000221

Tower Bridge, CA 275 across Sacramento River, Sacramento, 6/24/82, A, C, g, 82004845

Travelers' Hotel, 428 J St., Sacramento, 10/19/78, A, C, 78000744

U.S. Post Office, Courthouse and Federal Building, 801 I St., Sacramento, 1/25/80, C, g, 80000835

Utah Condensed Milk Company Plant, 621 3rd St., Galt, 8/03/78, A, 78000741

Van Voorhies House, 925 G St., Sacramento, 11/17/77, B, C, 77000328

Wagner, Anton, Duplex, 701 E St., Sacramento, 11/10/80, C, 80000836

Walnut Grove Chinese-American Historic District, Bounded by C, Tyler, and Bridge Sts., and River Rd., Walnut Grove, 3/22/90, A, C, 90000484

Walnut Grove Commercial/Residential Historic District, Browns Alley and River Rd., Walnut Grove, 4/12/90, A, B, C, 90000551

Walnut Grove Gakuen Hall, Pine and C Sts., Walnut Grove, 6/17/80, A, 80000837

Walnut Grove Japanese-American Historic District, Bounded by Winnie St., Tyler St., C St.,

Sacramento County—Continued

and River Rd., Walnut Grove, 3/22/90, A, C, 90000483

Wetzlar, Julius, House, 1021 H St., Sacramento, 3/31/83, C, 83001226

Witter, Edwin, Ranch, 3480 Witter Way, Sacramento, 3/14/91, A, B, C, 91000284

Woodlake Site, Address Restricted, Sacramento vicinity, 5/06/71, D, 71000179

San Benito County

Anza House, 3rd and Franklin Sts., San Juan Bautista, 4/15/70, C, NHL, 70000140

Castro, Jose, House, S side of the Plaza, San Juan Bautista, 4/15/70, C, NHL, 70000141

Chalone Creek Archeological Sites, Address Restricted, Soledad vicinity, 8/31/78, D, NPS, 78000365

Downtown Hollister Historic District, Roughly bounded by Fourth, East, South and Monterey Sts., Hollister, 8/14/92, A, 92000974

Hawkins, Joel and Rena, House [Hollister MPS], 801 South St., Hollister, 7/28/93, C, 93000669

Hollister Carnegie Library [California Carnegie Libraries MPS], 375 Fifth St., Hollister, 3/26/92, A, C, 92000269

Marentis House, 45 Monterey St., San Juan Bautista, 9/13/84, C, 84000951

Monterey Street Historic District, Monterey St. and intersecting streets between 5th and B Sts., Hollister, 1/07/93, C, 92001740

Rozas House, 31 Polk St., San Juan Bautista, 4/12/82, A, C, 82002243

San Juan Bautista Plaza Historic District, Buildings surrounding plaza at Washington, Mariposa, and 2nd Sts., San Juan Bautista, 12/08/69, C, a, NHL, 69000038

Wilcox, Benjamin, House, 315 The Alameda, San Juan Bautista, 2/19/82, C, 82002244

San Bernardino County

A. K. Smiley Public Library, 125 W. Vine St., Redlands, 12/12/76, A, C, 76000513

Aiken's Wash National Register District, Address Restricted, Baker vicinity, 5/24/82, D, 82002239

Archeological Site CA SBR 3186, Address Restricted, Silver Lake vicinity, 2/10/81, D, 81000170

Archeological Site No. D-4 [Earth Figures of California—Arizona Colorado River Basin TR], Address Restricted, Needles vicinity, 10/25/85, C, D, 85003435

Archeological Site No. E-21 [Earth Figures of California—Arizona Colorado River Basin TR], Address Restricted, Parker vicinity, 10/25/85, C, D, 85003430

Bitter Spring Archaeological Site (4-SBr-2659), Address Restricted, Barstow vicinity, 12/20/82, D, 82000981

CA SBr 1008A, CA SBr 1008B, CA SBr 1008C, Address Restricted, Johannesburg vicinity, 5/24/82, A, D, 82002241

Calico Mountains Archeological District, Address Restricted, Yermo vicinity, 3/30/73, A, D, g, 73000430

Carnegie Public Library Building, 380 N. La Cadena Dr., Colton, 6/23/88, A, C, 88000894

Cow Camp, SW of Twentynine Palms in Joshua Tree National Monument, Twentynine Palms vicinity, 10/29/75, A, NPS, 75000228

Crowder Canyon Archeological District, Address Restricted, San Bernardino vicinity, 6/16/76, A, D, 76000514

Fontana Farms Company Ranch House, Camp No. 1, 8863 Pepper St., Fontana, 11/01/82, A, C, 82000982

Fontana Pit and Groove Petroglyph Site, Address Restricted, Fontana vicinity, 4/17/80, C, D, 80000838

Frankish Building, 200 S. Euclid Ave., Ontario, 8/11/80, A, C, 80000839

Harvey House Railroad Depot, Santa Fe Depot, Barstow, 4/03/75, A, C, 75000458

Hofer Ranch, 11248 S. Turner Ave., Ontario, 7/08/93, A, C, 93000596

Keys Desert Queen Ranch, SW of Twentynine Palms in Joshua Tree National Monument, Twentynine Palms vicinity, 10/30/75, A, B, g, NPS, 75000174

Mill Creek Zanja, Sylvan Blvd. E to Mill Creek Rd., Redlands and vicinity, 5/12/77, A, 77000329

Moyse Building, 13150 7th St., Chino, 2/31/79, A, 79000522

Old San Antonio Hospital, 792 W. Arrow Hwy., Upland, 1/02/80, A, B, C, a, 80000840

Ontario State Bank Block, 300 S. Euclid Ave., Ontario, 1/08/82, A, C, 82002242

Pioneer Deep Space Station, Goldstone Deep Space Communications Complex, Fort Irwin, 10/03/85, A, C, g, NHL, 85002813

Piute Pass Archeological District, Address Restricted, Needles vicinity, 8/14/73, A, C, D, 73000429

Rains, John, House, 7869 Vineyard Ave., Cucamonga, 4/24/73, A, C, D, 73000428

Redlands Central Railway Company Car Barn, 746 E. Citrus Ave., Redlands, 1/03/91, A, 90002119

Redlands Santa Fe Depot District, Roughly bounded by Stuart Ave., N. 5th St., Redlands Blvd., Eureka St. and the SFRR tracks, Redlands, 10/29/91, A, C, 91001535

Rodman Mountains Petroglyphs Archeological District, Address Restricted, Barstow vicinity, 5/10/82, D, 82002240

Squaw Spring Archeological District, Address Restricted, Red Mountain vicinity, 7/28/81, D, 81000169

Topock Maze Archeological Site, Address Restricted, Needles vicinity, 10/05/78, A, D, 78000745

US Post Office—Downtown Station [US Post Office in California 1900-1941 TR], 390 W. 5th St., San Bernardino, 1/11/85, C, 85000136

US Post Office—Redlands Main [US Post Office in California 1900-1941 TR], 201 Brookside Ave., Redlands, 1/11/85, C, g, 85000135

Upland Public Library [California Carnegie Libraries MPS], 123 E. D St., Upland, 12/10/90, A, C, 90001817

Wall Street Mill, S of Twentynine Palms in Joshua Tree National Monument, Twentynine Palms vicinity, 11/12/75, A, g, NPS, 75000176

Washington, Henry, Survey Marker, S of Big Bear City in San Bernadino National Forest, Big Bear City vicinity, 5/12/75, A, 75000459

Yorba-Slaughter Adobe, 5.5 mi. S of Chino at 17127 Pomona Rincon Rd., Chino vicinity, 7/07/75, A, C, 75000460

San Diego County

Anza Borrego-Palo Verde Site, S-2 [Earth Figures of California—Arizona Colorado River Basin TR], Address Restricted, Borrego Springs vicinity, 10/25/85, C, D, 85003431

Anza Borrego-Sin Nombre, S-4 [Earth Figures of California—Arizona Colorado River Basin TR], Address Restricted, Borrego Springs vicinity, 10/25/85, C, D, 85003432

Anza Borrego-Spit Mountain Site, S-3 [Earth Figures of California—Arizona Colorado River Basin TR], Address Restricted, Borrego Springs vicinity, 10/25/85, C, D, 85003433

BERKELEY, B St. Pier, San Diego, 12/14/90, A, C, NHL, 90002220

Baker, Pearl, Row House [Lilian Rice-Designed Buildings in Rancho Santa Fe MPS], 6122 Paseo Delicias, Rancho Santa Fe, 9/30/93, C, 93001018

Balboa Park, CA Quadrangle 41, San Diego vicinity, 12/22/77, C, NHL, 77000331

Bancroft, Hubert H., Ranchhouse, Bancroft Dr. off CA 94, Spring Valley, 10/15/66, B, NHL, 66000227

Bandy House, 638 S. Juniper, Escondido, 1/12/93, C, 92001754

Beach, A.H., House, 700 S. Juniper, Escondido, 12/30/93, C, 93001462

Bear Valley Archeological Site, Address Restricted, Pine Valley vicinity, 7/30/74, D, 74000547

Bingham, Samuel, House [Lilian Rice Designed Buildings in Rancho Santa Fe MPS], 6427 La Plateada, Rancho Santa Fe, 8/05/91, C, 91000942

Braun, Charles A., House, 790 Vale View Dr., Vista, 1/05/86, C, 86000010

Brick Row, A Ave. between 9th and 10th Sts., National City, 7/16/73, C, 73000431

Burnham—Marston House, 3563 Seventh Ave., San Diego, 9/22/86, B, C, 86002665

Cabrillo National Monument, 10 mi. from San Diego off U.S. 10, near S tip of Point Loma, San Diego vicinity, 10/15/66, A, B, f, NPS, 66000224

California Quadrangle, Balboa Park-El Prado Area, San Diego, 5/17/74, A, C, a, 74000548

San Diego County—Continued

Carlsbad Santa Fe Depot, 400 Carlsbad Village Dr. (Elm Ave.), Carlsbad, 9/30/93, A, C, 93001016

Carmichael, Norman and Florence B., House [Lilian Rice Designed Buildings in Rancho Santa Fe MPS], 6855 La Valle Plateada, Rancho Santa Fe, 8/05/91, C, 91000941

Castle, The, W of Ramona, Ramona vicinity, 3/30/78, C, 78000749

Chaplain's House, 836 Washington St., San Diego, 11/24/78, C, b, 78000750

Christiancy, George A. C., House [Lilian Rice Designed Buildings in Rancho Santa Fe MPS], 17078 El Mirador, Rancho Santa Fe, 8/05/91, C, 91000943

Clotfelter, Reginald M. and Constance, Row House [Lilian Rice Designed Buildings in Rancho Santa Fe MPS], 6112 Paseo Delicias, Rancho Santa Fe, 8/05/91, C, 91000939

Coulter House, 3162 2nd Ave., San Diego, 9/30/83, C, 83001227

Eagles Hall, 733 Eighth Ave., San Diego, 10/04/85, A, 85002723

Edgemoor Farm Dairy Barn, 9064 Edgemoor Dr., Edgemoor Geriatric Hospital, Santee, 5/16/85, A, C, 85001065

El Prado Complex, Balboa Park, San Diego, 12/12/76, A, C, 76000515

Estudillo House, 4000 Mason St., San Diego, 4/15/70, C, NHL, 70000143

Fages-De Anza Trail-Southern Emigrant Road, Anza-Borrego State Park, Borrego Springs vicinity, 1/29/73, A, D, 73002252

Ford Building, Balboa Park, Palisades Area, San Diego, 4/26/73, A, C, g, 73000433

Gaslamp Quarter Historic District, Bounded by RR tracks, Broadway, 4th, and 6th Sts., San Diego, 5/23/80, A, C, 80000841

Grand-Horton Hotel, 332, 328 and 334 F St., San Diego, 6/20/80, A, C, 80000842

Granger Hall, 1700 E. 4th St., National City, 3/18/75, A, C, b, 75000465

Grant, U.S. Hotel, 326 Broadway St, San Diego, 8/27/79, A, C, 79000523

Guajome Ranch House, 2.5 mi. NE of Vista, Vista vicinity, 4/15/70, C, NHL, 70000145

Haines, Alfred, House, 2470 E St., San Diego, 7/30/92, B, C, 92000966

Hawthorne Inn, 2121 1st Ave., San Diego, 3/30/82, C, 82002245

Heilman Villas, 1060, 1070, 1080, 1090 Seventh St. and 706–720 (even nos.) Orange Ave., Coronado, 4/08/92, C, 92000319

Hotel Charlotta, 637 S. Upas, Escondido, 1/07/93, A, 92001752

Hotel Del Coronado, 1500 Orange Ave., Coronado, 10/14/71, C, NHL, 71000181

Howell House, 103 W. Eighth St., Escondido, 11/20/92, C, 92001612

Independent Order of Odd Fellows Building, 526 Market St., San Diego, 1/31/78, A, C, 78000751

Initial Point of Boundary Between U.S. and Mexico, S of Imperial Beach off Monument Rd., San Diego, 9/06/74, A, 74000550

Johnson-Taylor Ranch Headquarters, E of San Diego and Black Mountain Rd., San Diego vicinity, 10/31/80, A, C, 80000843

Kinsey, Martha, House, 1624 Ludington Ln., La Jolla, 8/07/92, C, 92000968

Kuchamaa, SE of San Diego at the US—Mexico border, Tecate vicinity, 10/06/92, A, a, 92001268

La Jolla Women's Club, 715 Silverado St., La Jolla, 11/05/74, A, C, 74000546

Las Flores Adobe, Stuart Mesa Rd., about 7 mi. N of jct. with Vandergrift Blvd., Camp Pendleton, 11/24/68, C, NHL, 68000021

Las Flores Estancia, Jct. of Pulgas and Stuart Mesa Rds., Camp Pendleton, 5/20/93, A, D, 93000391

Las Flores Site, Address Restricted, Camp Pendleton vicinity, 8/19/75, D, d, 75000464

Lee, Robert E., Hotel, 815 3rd Ave. and 314 F St., San Diego, 5/31/80, A, C, 80000844

Libby, Charles, House, 636 Rockledge St., Oceanside, 7/12/78, C, b, 78000748

Long-Waterman House, 2408 1st Ave., San Diego, 6/14/76, C, 76000516

Marine Corps Recruit Depot Historic District, S of jct. of Barnett Ave. and Pacific Hwy., San Diego, 1/31/91, A, C, 90001477

Marston, George W., House, 3525 7th Ave., San Diego, 12/16/74, C, 74000552

McClintock Storage Warehouse, 1202 Kettner Blvd., San Diego, 10/03/80, A, C, 80000845

Medico-Dental Building, 233 A St., San Diego, 9/04/79, C, 79000524

Mission Beach Roller Coaster, 3000 Mission Blvd., San Diego, 12/27/78, A, C, NHL, 78000753

Mission Brewery, 1715 Hancock St., San Diego, 7/06/89, A, C, 89000805

Mission San Diego de Alcala, 5 mi. E of Old Town San Diego on Friars Rd., San Diego vicinity, 4/15/70, A, a, NHL, 70000144

Moylan, Maj. Myles, House, 2214–2224 2nd Ave., San Diego, 3/22/84, B, C, 84001181

Naval Air Station, San Diego, Historic District, Naval Air Station, North Island, N. shore, San Diego, 5/21/91, A, C, 91000590

Oak Grove Butterfield Stage Station, 13 mi. NW of Warner Springs on CA 79, Oak Grove, 10/15/66, A, NHL, 66000222

Oceanside City Hall and Fire Station, 704 and 714 Third St., Oceanside, 6/07/89, C, 89000257

Old Mission Dam, N side of Mission St.-Gorge Rd., San Diego, 10/15/66, A, C, NHL, 66000225

Old Point Loma Lighthouse, Included in Cabrillo National Monument, San Diego, 6/27/74, A, C, NPS, 74000350

Old Town San Diego Historic District, Jct. of US 5 and US 80, San Diego, 9/03/71, A, 71000182

Olivenhain Town Meeting Hall, 423 Rancho Santa Fe Rd., Olivenhain, 12/17/93, A, 93001395

Panama Hotel, 105 W. F St., San Diego, 3/22/84, C, 84001182

Park Place Methodist Episcopal Church South, 508 Olive St., San Diego, 9/15/83, A, C, a, 83003432

Pythias Lodge Building, 211 E St. and 870 3rd Ave., San Diego, 4/08/81, A, C, 81000171

Rancho De Los Kiotes, 4758 Palomar Airport Rd., Carlsbad, 3/31/92, B, 92000261

Rancho Santa Fe Land and Improvement Company Office [Lilian Rice Designed Buildings in Rancho Santa Fe MPS], 16915 Avenida de Acacias, Rancho Santa Fe, 8/05/91, C, 91000940

Red Rest and Red Roost Cottages, 1187 and 1179 Coast Blvd., La Jolla, 3/15/76, C, 76002247

Rice, Lilian Jenette, House [Lilian Rice Designed Buildings in Rancho Santa Fe MPS], 16780 La Gracia, Rancho Santa Fe, 8/05/91, C, 91000946

Robinson Hotel, 2032 Main St., Julian, 6/23/78, A, 78000747

Rockwell Field, North Island, San Diego, 5/21/91, A, C, 75002185

Ruiz-Alvarado Ranch Site, Address Restricted, San Diego vicinity, 1/22/82, A, D, 82002246

STAR OF INDIA, San Diego Embarcadero, San Diego, 11/13/66, A, NHL, 66000223

San Diego Civic Center, 1600 Pacific Hwy., San Diego, 5/16/88, A, C, g, 88000554

San Diego Presidio, Presidio Park, San Diego, 10/15/66, A, NHL, 66000226

San Diego Rowing Club, 525 E. Harbor Dr, San Diego, 8/30/79, A, 79000525

San Luis Rey Mission Church, 4 mi. E of Oceanside on CA 76, Oceanside vicinity, 4/15/70, C, a, NHL, 70000142

Santa Fe Depot, 1050 Kettner St., San Diego, 6/26/72, A, C, 72000248

Santa Margarita Ranchhouse, Off Vandergrift Blvd., Camp Pendleton, 5/06/71, A, C, 71000180

Scripps, George H., Memorial Marine Biological Laboratory, 8602 La Jolla Shores Dr., La Jolla, 11/10/77, A, NHL, 77000330

Shaffer, Charles A., House [Lilian Rice Designed Buildings in Rancho Santa Fe MPS], 5610 La Crescenta, Rancho Santa Fe, 8/05/91, C, 91000944

Sorrento Valley Site, Address Restricted, San Diego vicinity, 10/21/75, D, d, 75000466

Spreckels Theatre Building, 123 W. Broadway, San Diego, 5/28/75, A, C, 75000467

St. Matthew's Episcopal Church, 521 E. 8th St., National City, 10/25/73, A, C, a, 73000432

Sweet, A. H., Residence and Adjacent Small House, 435 W. Spruce and 3141 Curlew Sts., San Diego, 4/16/87, B, C, 87000621

Table Mountain District, Address Restricted, Jacumba vicinity, 10/28/83, D, 83003593

Terwilliger, Claude and Florence, House [Lilian Rice Designed Buildings in Rancho Santa Fe MPS], 5880 San Elijo, Rancho Santa Fe, 8/05/91, C, 91000945

Thomas House, 208 E. Fifth Ave., Escondido, 12/30/92, B, 92001684

Torrey Pines Gliderport, W of Torrey Pines Rd., bordering Torrey Pines Scenic Dr. and S and W of Torrey Pines Golf Course, San Diego, 7/12/93, A, 93000578

U.S. Courthouse, 325 W. F St., San Diego, 1/29/75, C, g, 75000468

U.S. Inspection Station/U.S. Custom House, Virginia and Tijuana Sts., San Ysidro, 2/10/83, A, C, 83001228

San Diego County—Continued

US Inspection Station—Tecate, CA 188, Tecate, 2/14/92, A, C, 91001748

US Post Office—Downtown Station [US Post Office in California 1900-1941 TR], 815 E St., San Diego, 1/11/85, C, g, 85000137

Verlaque, Theophile, House, 645 Main St., Ramona, 8/07/91, A, C, 91000548

Villa Montezuma, 1925 K St., San Diego, 5/06/71, A, C, 71000183

Warner's Ranch, 4 mi. S of Warner Springs, Warner Springs vicinity, 10/15/66, A, B, NHL, 66000228

Watts Building, 520 E St., San Diego, 4/26/79, A, C, 79000526

San Francisco County

ALMA (Scow Schooner), 2905 Hyde St. (Hyde St. Pier), San Francisco, 10/10/75, A, C, NHL, NPS, 75000179

APOLLO (Storeship), NW corner of Sacramento and Battery Sts., San Francisco, 5/16/91, A, D, 91000561

Alcatraz, Alcatraz Island, San Francisco Bay, San Francisco, 6/23/76, A, g, NHL, NPS, 76000209

Aquatic Park Historic District, Bounded by Van Ness Ave., Hyde and Polk Sts., San Francisco, 1/26/84, A, C, NHL, NPS, 84001183

Atherton House, 1990 California St., San Francisco, 1/31/79, C, 79000527

Audiffred Building, 1–21 Mission St., San Francisco, 5/10/79, C, 79000528

BALCLUTHA, Pier 41 East, San Francisco, 11/07/76, A, NHL, NPS, 76000178

Bank of Italy, 552 Montgomery St., San Francisco, 6/02/78, B, NHL, 78000754

Beach Chalet, 1000 Great Hwy., San Francisco, 7/22/81, C, 81000172

Belden, C. A., House, 2004-2010 Gough St., San Francisco, 8/11/83, C, 83001229

Belt Railroad Engine House and Sandhouse, Block bounded by Lombard, Sansome, and the Embarcadero, San Francisco, 2/13/86, A, C, 86000207

Building at 1735–1737 Webster Street, 1735–1737 Webster St., San Francisco, 3/08/73, C, b, 73000444

Building at 1813–1813B Sutter Street, 1813–1813B Sutter St., San Francisco, 3/08/73, C, b, 73000443

Building at 1840–1842 Eddy Street, 1840–1842 Eddy St., San Francisco, 3/08/73, C, b, 73000437

Building at 33–35 Beideman Place, 33–35 Beideman Pl., San Francisco, 3/08/73, C, b, 73000435

Building at 45–57 Beideman Place, 45–57 Beideman Pl., San Francisco, 3/08/73, C, b, 73000436

Bush Street-Cottage Row Historic District, 2101-2125 Bush St., 1-6 Cottage Row, and 1940-1948 Sutter St., San Francisco, 12/27/82, C, 82000983

C.A. THAYER, San Francisco Maritime State Historic Park, San Francisco, 11/13/66, A, NHL, NPS, 66000229

Calvary Presbyterian Church, 2501–2515 Fillmore St., San Francisco, 5/03/78, C, a, 78000755

Chambord Apartments, 1298 Sacramento St., San Francisco, 9/20/84, C, 84001184

City of Paris Building, 181-199 Geary St., San Francisco, 1/23/75, A, C, 75000471

Dallam-Merritt House, 2355 Washington St., San Francisco, 4/19/84, A, C, 84001185

Delane House, 70 Buena Vista Terr., San Francisco, 10/29/82, C, 82000984

EUREKA, San Francisco Maritime State Historic Park, 2905 Hyde St., San Francisco, 4/24/73, A, C, g, NHL, NPS, 73000229

Edwards, Frank G., House, 1366 Guerrero St., San Francisco, 10/29/82, B, C, 82000986

Engine House No. 31, 1088 Green St., San Francisco, 1/07/88, C, 87002290

Farallone Islands, 28 mi. W of San Francisco, San Francisco vicinity, 3/08/77, A, 77000332

Federal Reserve Bank of San Francisco, 400 Sansome St., San Francisco, 7/31/89, A, C, 89000009

Ferry Station Post Office Building, Embarcadero at Mission St., San Francisco, 12/01/78, A, C, 78000756

Feusier Octagon House, 1067 Green St., San Francisco, 3/24/74, C, 74000554

Fillmore-Pine Building, Address Restricted, San Francisco, 1/11/82, C, 82002247

Fleishhacker, Delia, Memorial Building, Zoo Rd. and Sloat Blvd., San Francisco, 12/31/79, A, C, g, 79000529

Flood, James C., Mansion, California and Mason Sts., San Francisco, 11/13/66, B, NHL, 66000230

Fort Mason Historic District, Portion of Fort Mason N and E of Franklin St. and McArthur Ave., San Francisco, 4/25/72, C, 72000109

Fort Mason Historic District (Boundary Increase), Bounded by Van Ness Ave., Bay and Laguna Sts., San Fransisco, 4/23/79, A, C, g, NPS, 79000530

Fort Miley Military Reservation, Off CA 1, San Francisco, 5/23/80, A, g, NPS, 80000371

Fort Point National Historic Site, N tip of San Francisco Peninsula on U.S. 101 and I 480, San Francisco, 10/16/70, A, C, NPS, 70000146

GRIFFING'S, FREDERICK, (ship), Address Restricted, San Francisco vicinity, 2/01/82, A, D, 82002248

Geary Theatre, 415 Geary St., San Francisco, 5/27/75, A, C, 75000472

Girls Club, 362 Capp St., San Francisco, 11/06/79, B, C, 79000531

Golden Gate Park Conservatory, Mount Link, N of John F. Kennedy Dr. at E end of Golden Gate Park, San Francisco, 10/14/71, C, 71000184

Goodman Building, 1117 Geary Blvd., San Francisco, 6/18/75, C, 75000473

HERCULES (tugboat), Maritime Unit, Hyde St. Pier, National Maritime Museum, San Francisco, 1/17/75, A, C, g, NHL, NPS, 75000225

Haas-Lilienthal House, 2007 Franklin St., San Francisco, 7/02/73, C, 73000438

Hale Brothers Department Store, 901 Market St., San Francisco, 12/18/86, C, 86003492

Hallidie Building, 130 Sutter St., San Francisco, 11/19/71, C, 71000185

Haslett Warehouse, 680 Beach St., San Francisco, 3/28/75, A, C, NPS, 75000172

Herald Hotel, 308 Eddy St., San Francisco, 10/29/82, C, 82000985

House at 1239–1245 Scott Street, 1239–1245 Scott St., San Francisco, 3/08/73, C, b, 73000441

House at 1249–1251 Scott Street, 1249–1251 Scott St., San Francisco, 3/08/73, C, b, 73000442

House at 1254–1256 Montgomery Street, 1254–1256 Montgomery St., San Francisco, 1/31/79, C, 79000532

House at 1321 Scott Street, 1321 Scott St., San Francisco, 3/08/73, C, b, 73000439

House at 1331–1335 Scott Street, 1331–1335 Scott St., San Francisco, 3/08/73, C, b, 73000440

House at 584 Page Street, 584 Page St., San Francisco, 9/12/85, C, 85002195

International Hotel, 848 Kearny St., San Francisco, 6/15/77, A, 77000333

Jackson Brewing Company, 1475–1489 Folsom St. and 319–351 11th St., San Francisco, 4/08/93, A, C, 93000284

Jackson Square Historic District, Roughly bounded by Broadway on N, Sansome St. on E, Washington St. on S, and Columbus Ave. on W, San Francisco, 11/18/71, A, C, 71000186

Jessie Street Substation, 222–226 Jessie St., San Francisco, 9/06/74, C, 74000555

KING PHILIP (ship) and REPORTER (schooner) Shipwreck Site, Address Restricted, San Francisco vicinity, 5/08/86, A, C, D, NPS, 86001014

Koshland House, 3800 Washington St., San Francisco, 1/05/84, A, C, 84001186

Krotoszyner, Dr. Martin M., Medical Offices and House, 995–999 Sutter St., San Francisco, 8/15/85, B, C, 85001784

LEWIS ARK (Houseboat), Hyde St. Pier, San Francisco, 11/08/79, C, g, NPS, 79000256

Liberty Street Historic District, Roughly 15-188 Liberty St., San Francisco, 9/15/83, C, 83001230

Lotta Crabtree Fountain, Market, Geary, and Kearny Sts., San Francisco, 6/20/75, B, C, f, 75000475

Lower Nob Hill Apartment Hotel District, Roughly, 590–1209 Bush, 680–1156 Sutter and 600–1099 Post Sts. and the intersecting cross streets, San Francisco, 7/31/91, A, C, 91000957

Lydia, The, Address Restricted, San Francisco vicinity, 7/16/81, D, 81000173

Market Street Theatre and Loft District, 982–1112 Market, 973–1105 Market, 1 Jones, and 1–35 Taylor Sts., San Francisco, 4/10/86, A, C, 86000729

McElroy Octagon House, 2645 Gough St., San Francisco, 2/23/72, C, b, 72000250

McMullen, John, House, 827 Guerrero St., San Francisco, 9/15/83, A, C, 83001231

Mills Building and Tower, 220 Montgomery St. and 220 Bush St., San Francisco, 4/13/77, C, 77000334

Mish House, 1153 Oak St., San Francisco, 5/21/79, C, b, 79000534

Mission Dolores, 320 Dolores St., San Francisco, 3/16/72, A, C, a, d, 72000251

San Francisco County—Continued

Moss Flats Building, 1626 Great Hwy., San Francisco, 2/24/83, C, 83001232

Myrtle Street Flats, 234–248 Myrtle St., San Francisco, 6/14/76, C, 76000520

NIANTIC (Storeship), NW corner of Clay and Sansome Sts., San Francisco, 5/16/91, A, D, 91000563

National Carbon Company Building, 599 8th St., San Francisco, 8/25/83, C, 83001233

Old Ohio Street Houses, 17–55 Osgood Pl., San Francisco, 5/31/79, C, 79000535

Old U.S. Mint, 5th and Mission Sts., San Francisco, 10/15/66, A, C, NHL, 66000231

Pacific Gas and Electric Company Substation J, 565 Commercial and 568 Sacremento Sts., San Francisco, 12/29/86, A, C, 86003514

Paige Motor Car Co. Building, 1699 Van Ness Ave., San Francisco, 2/24/83, C, 83001234

Park View Hotel, 750 Stanyan St., San Francisco, 8/11/83, A, C, 83001235

Payne, Theodore F., House, 1409 Sutter St., San Francisco, 6/11/80, C, 80000847

Phelps, Abner, House, 1111 Oak St., San Francisco, 5/23/79, A, C, b, 71000187

Pioneer Trunk Factory—C. A. Malm & Co., 2185–2199 Folsom and 3180 18th Sts., San Francisco, 3/05/87, A, C, 86003727

Pioneer Woolen Mills and D. Ghirardelli Company, 900 N. Point St., San Francisco, 4/29/82, A, C, 82002249

Point Lobos Archeological Sites, Address Restricted, San Francisco, 11/07/76, A, D, NPS, 76000176

Presidio, Northern tip of San Francisco Peninsula on U.S. 101 and I-480, San Francisco, 10/15/66, A, NHL, NPS, 66000232

Pumping Station No. 2 San Francisco Fire Department Auxiliary Water Supply System, N end of Van Ness Ave, San Francisco, 5/13/76, A, C, g, NPS, 76000177

Quarters 1, Yerba Buena Island, Naval Training Station, 1 Whiting Way, Yerba Buena Island, San Francisco, 9/10/91, A, C, 91001380

Rincon Annex, 101–199 Mission St., San Francisco, 11/16/79, C, g, 79000537

Russian Hill—Macondray Lane District, Roughly 900–982 Green, 1918–1960 Jones, 15–84 Macondray & 1801–1809 Taylor, San Francisco, 1/07/88, A, B, C, 87002286

Russian Hill—Paris Block Architectural District, Roughly 1017–1067 Green St., San Francisco, 1/07/88, C, b, 87002288

Russian Hill—Vallejo Street Crest District, Roughly 1020-1032 Broadway, 1-49 Florence, 1728-1742 Jones, 1-7 Russian Hill Pl., 1629-1715 Taylor, & 1000-1085 Vallejo, San Francisco, 1/22/88, A, B, C, g, 87002289

SS JEREMIAH O'BRIEN National Historic Landmark, Pier 3, Fort Mason Center, San Francisco, 6/07/78, A, g, NHL, 78003405

SS RIO DE JANEIRO Shipwreck, Address Restricted, San Francisco vicinity, 11/03/88, A, C, D, 88002394

San Francisco Cable Cars, 1390 Washington St., San Francisco, 10/15/66, A, NHL, 66000233

San Francisco Civic Center Historic District, Roughly bounded by Golden Gate Ave., 7th, Franklin, Hayes, and Market Sts., San Francisco, 10/10/78, A, C, g, NHL, 78000757

San Francisco National Guard Armory and Arsenal, 1800 Mission St., San Francisco, 11/14/78, C, 78000758

San Francisco Port of Embarkation, US Army, Ft. Mason, San Francisco, 2/04/85, A, g, NHL, NPS, 85002433

Schoenstein and Company Pipe Organ Factory, 3101 20th St., San Francisco, 11/14/78, A, C, 78000759

Scott, Irving Murray, School, 1060 Tennessee St., San Francisco, 4/11/85, A, 85000714

Six-Inch Rifled Gun No. 9, Baker Beach, San Francisco, 2/07/79, A, NPS, 79000255

Southern Pacific Company Hospital Historic District, 1400 Fall St., San Francisco, 5/05/89, A, C, 89000319

St. Joseph's Church and Complex, 1401–1415 Howard St., San Francisco, 1/15/82, C, a, 82002250

St. Joseph's Hospital, 355 Buena Vista Ave. East, San Francisco, 5/09/85, A, C, a, 85001016

St. Paulus Lutheran Church, 999 Eddy St., San Francisco, 2/11/82, C, a, 82002251

Stadtmuller House, 819 Eddy St., San Francisco, 7/19/76, C, 76000523

The Real Estate Associates (TREA) Houses, 2503, 2524, 2530 and 2536 Clay Sts., San Francisco, 4/04/85, A, C, 85000705

Trinity Presbyterian Church, 3261 23rd St., San Francisco, 3/02/82, C, a, 82002252

Tubbs Cordage Company Office Building, Hyde St. Pier, San Francisco, 11/06/79, A, NPS, 79000254

U.S. Customhouse, 555 Battery St., San Francisco, 1/29/75, C, 75000476

U.S. Post Office and Courthouse, NE corner of 7th and Mission Sts., San Francisco, 10/14/71, C, 71000188

US Mint, 155 Hermann St., San Francisco, 2/18/88, A, g, 88000026

USS PAMPANITO (submarine), Fisherman's Wharf-Pier 45, San Francisco, 1/14/86, A, g, NHL, 86000089

Union Ferry Depot, Embarcadero at Market St., San Francisco, 12/01/78, A, C, 78000760

WAPAMA, San Francisco Maritime State Historic Park, 2905 Hyde St., San Francisco, 4/24/73, A, C, g, NHL, NPS, 73000228

Warren, Russell, House, 465-467 Oak St. and 368 Lily St., San Francisco, 12/12/83, C, 83003594

Westerfeld, William, House, 1198 Fulton St., San Francisco, 3/16/89, C, 89000197

Whittier Mansion, 2090 Jackson St., San Francisco, 4/26/76, C, 76000524

Wilford, Albert, Houses, 2121 & 2127 Vallejo St., San Francisco, 8/29/85, C, 85001914

YMCA Hotel, 351 Turk St., San Francisco, 2/06/86, A, C, 86000148

Yerba Buena Island Lighthouse [Light Stations of California MPS], Yerba Buena Island, San Francisco vicinity, 9/03/91, A, C, 91001096

San Joaquin County

Bank of Italy, 628 Central Ave., Tracy, 7/18/85, A, C, 85001591

Bank of Tracy, 801 Central Ave., Tracy, 6/03/80, A, C, 80000851

Cole's Five Cypress Farm, 11221 E. Eight Mile Rd., Stockton, 5/25/88, A, B, C, 88000578

Commercial and Savings Bank, 343 Main St., Stockton, 11/25/80, A, C, 80000849

El Dorado Elementary School, Harding Way and Pacific Ave., Stockton, 8/15/77, C, 77000335

Elks Building, 42 N. Sutter St., Stockton, 6/03/80, A, C, 80004606

Farmer's and Merchant's Bank, 11 S. San Joaquin St., Stockton, 10/09/80, A, C, 80000850

Fox California Theater, 242 E. Main St., Stockton, 6/27/79, C, 79000540

Gew, Wong K., Mansion, 345 W. Clay St., Stockton, 9/20/78, A, C, 78000761

Holt, Benjamin, House, 548 Park St., Stockton, 3/02/82, B, 82002254

Hotel Stockton, 133 E. Weber Ave., Stockton, 4/01/81, A, C, 81000174

I.O.O.F. Hall, Main St., Woodbridge, 4/22/82, A, C, 82002257

Locke House and Barn, 19960 W. Elliott Rd., Lockeford, 6/19/72, A, 72000252

Locke's Meat Market, 13480 CA 88, Lockeford, 2/19/82, A, C, 82002253

Lodi Arch, Pine St., Lodi, 9/17/80, A, C, 80000848

Morse—Skinner Ranch House, 13063 N. CA 99, Lodi, 8/21/86, C, 86001878

Nippon Hospital, 25 S. Commerce St., Stockton, 9/18/78, A, 78000762

Ohm, John, House, 31524 S. Kasson Rd., Tracy vicinity, 2/04/82, A, B, C, 82002256

Old Weber School, 55 W. Flora St., Stockton, 7/16/73, A, C, 73000445

Rodgers, Moses, House, 921 S. San Joaquin St., Stockton, 4/26/78, A, B, 78000763

Sperry Office Building, 146 W. Weber Ave., Stockton, 2/19/82, A, C, 82002255

Sperry Union Flour Mill, 445 W. Weber, Stockton, 1/31/79, A, C, 79000541

Stockton Savings and Loan Society Bank, 301 E. Main St., Stockton, 10/19/78, A, C, 78000764

Terminous Culling Chute, 14900 W. CA 12, Lodi vicinity, 4/19/84, A, C, 84001189

Tracy City Hall and Jail, 25 W. 7th St., Tracy, 10/18/79, A, C, 79000542

Tracy Inn, 24 W. 11th St., Tracy, 10/31/80, A, C, 80000852

Tretheway Block, 229 E. Weber St., Stockton, 10/29/82, C, 82000987

U.S. Post Office, 401 N. San Joaquin St., Stockton, 2/10/83, C, 83001236

West Side Bank, 47 W. 6th St., Tracy, 12/12/78, C, 78000765

San Joaquin County—Continued

Woman's Club of Lodi, 325 W. Pine St., Lodi, 5/20/88, A, C, 88000555

Woodbridge Masonic Lodge No. 131, 1040 Augusta St., Woodbridge, 4/20/89, A, C, 89000318

San Luis Obispo County

Administration Building, Atascadero Colony, 6500 Palma Ave., Atascadero, 11/17/77, A, C, 77000336

Angel, Myron, House, 714 Buchon St., San Luis Obispo, 11/22/82, B, 82000988

Archeological Site 4 SLO 834, Address Restricted, Atascadero vicinity, 2/25/82, D, 82004618

Arroyo Grande IOOF Hall, 128 Bridge St., Arroyo Grande, 3/22/91, C, 91000344

Brewster-Dutra House, 1803 Vine St., Paso Robles, 10/29/82, C, 82000989

Caledonia Adobe, 0.5 mi. S of 10th St., San Miguel, 7/14/71, A, C, 71000190

Call—Booth House, 1315 Vine St., Robles, 11/03/88, B, C, 88002031

Corral de Piedra, S of San Luis Obispo on Price Canyon Rd., San Luis Obispo vicinity, 5/22/78, B, D, 78000766

Dana Adobe, S end of Oak Glen Ave., Nipomo, 5/06/71, A, C, 71000189

Guthrie House, Burton and Center Sts., Cambria, 1/10/80, A, C, 80000853

Hearst San Simeon Estate, 3 mi. NE of San Simeon, San Simeon vicinity, 6/22/72, B, C, NHL, 72000253

Jack, Robert, House, 536 Marsh St., San Luis Obispo, 4/13/92, B, 92000312

Mission San Miguel, U.S. 101, San Miguel, 7/14/71, C, 71000191

Old Santa Rosa Catholic Church and Cemetery, Main St., Cambria, 10/29/82, A, C, a, d, 82000990

Pacific Coast Railway Company Grain Warehouse, 65 Higuera St., San Luis Obispo, 6/23/88, A, C, 88000921

Piedras Blancas Light Station [Light Stations of California MPS], CA 1 on Point Piedras Blancas, San Simeon vicinity, 9/03/91, A, C, 91001095

Port San Luis Site, Address Restricted, San Luis Obispo vicinity, 5/22/78, D, 78000767

Powerhouse, The, Jct. of S. Perimeter Rd. and Cuesta Ave., NE corner, San Luis Obispo, 7/30/93, A, C, 93000670

Price, John, House, Highland Dr. off Price Canyon Rd., Pismo Beach vicinity, 11/03/88, B, C, 88002013

Rancho Canada de los Osos y Pecho y Islay, Address Restricted, San Luis Obispo vicinity, 6/20/75, D, 75000477

San Luis Obispo Light Station [Light Stations of California MPS], Point San Luis, Avila Beach vicinity, 9/03/91, A, C, 91001093

Tribune—Republic Building, 1763 Santa Barbara St., San Luis Obispo, 6/24/93, A, B, b, 93000548

San Mateo County

Archeological Site SMA-151, Address Restricted, Princeton vicinity, 2/23/78, D, 78000771

Barron—Latham—Hopkins Gate Lodge, 555 Ravenswood Ave., Menlo Park, 8/28/86, A, C, 86001951

Bourn-Roth Estate, 3.7 mi. NW of Woodside off Canada Rd., Woodside vicinity, 8/28/75, A, B, C, D, 75000479

Burlingame Railroad Station, Burlingame Ave. and California Dr., Burlingame, 4/19/78, C, 78000769

Carolands, The, 565 Remillard Dr., Hillsborough, 10/21/75, C, 75000478

Casa de Tableta, 3915 Alpine Rd., Portola Valley, 8/14/73, A, 73000447

Church of the Nativity, 210 Oak Grove Ave., Menlo Park, 10/31/80, A, C, a, b, 80000855

De Sabla, Eugene J., Jr., Teahouse and Tea Garden, 70 De Sabla Ave., San Mateo, 7/30/92, A, C, 92000965

Dickerman Barn, Cabrillo Hwy., Pescadero vicinity, 1/11/82, A, C, 82002259

First Congregational Church of Pescadero, San Gregorio St., Pescadero, 10/31/80, C, 80000856

Green Gables—Fleischhacker, Mortimer, Country House, 329 Albin Ave., Woodside, 9/26/86, B, C, 86002396

Green Oaks Ranch House, 13 mi. S of Pescadero on CA 1, Pescadero vicinity, 11/21/76, A, C, 76000526

Hofmann, Arthur and Mona, House, 1048 La Cuesta Rd., Hillsborough, 8/05/91, C, 91000926

Independence Hall, 129 Albion Ave., Woodside, 8/03/78, A, C, b, 78000772

Johnston, James, House, Higgins-Purisima Rd., Half Moon Bay vicinity, 5/09/73, C, 73000446

Kohl Mansion, 2750 Adeline Dr., Burlingame, 2/03/82, C, 82002258

Lathrop House, 627 Hamilton St., Redwood City, 4/11/73, C, 73000448

Menlo Park Railroad Station, 1100 Merrill St., Menlo Park, 10/01/74, A, C, 74000556

Methodist Episcopal Church at Half Moon Bay, 777 Miramontes St., Half Moon Bay, 11/10/80, A, C, a, 80000854

Methodist Episcopal Church of Pescadero, 108 San Gregorio St., Pescadero, 3/10/82, A, C, a, 82002260

Mills, Robert, Dairy Barn, Higgins Purissima Rd., Half Moon Bay vicinity, 2/15/90, A, B, C, 90000120

Our Lady of the Wayside, 930 Portola Rd., Portola Valley, 11/22/77, A, C, a, 77000338

Pigeon Point Lighthouse, S of Pescadero at Pigeon Point off CA 1, Pescadero vicinity, 3/08/77, A, C, 77000337

Point Montara Light Station [Light Stations of California MPS], Jct. of 16th St. and CA 1, Montara vicinity, 9/03/91, A, C, 91001094

Portola Valley School, 775 Portola Rd., Portola Valley, 6/28/74, A, C, 74000557

Princeton Hotel, Capistrano Rd. and Prospect Way, Princeton, 1/31/79, A, C, 79000543

Ralston, William C., House, College of Notre Dame campus, Belmont, 11/15/66, B, a, NHL, 66000234

Redwood City Historic Commercial Buildings, Broadway and Main Sts., Redwood City, 11/07/77, A, C, 77000339

San Francisco Bay Discovery Site, 4 mi. W of San Bruno via Skyline Dr. and Sneath Lane, San Bruno vicinity, 5/23/68, A, NHL, 68000022

San Gregorio House, Old Stage Rd., San Gregorio, 5/06/77, A, C, 77000341

San Mateo County Courthouse, Broadway, Redwood City, 12/13/77, A, C, 77000340

Sanchez Adobe Park, Linda Mar Blvd., 1 mi. E of CA 1, Pacifica, 4/13/76, A, B, C, 76000525

Simmons, William Adam, House, 751 Kelly Ave., Half Moon Bay, 8/18/92, A, B, C, 92000995

Southern Pacific Depot, 21 E. Millbrae Ave., Millbrae, 9/01/78, A, C, b, 78000770

Southern Pacific Depot, 559 El Camino Real, San Carlos, 9/20/84, A, C, 84001191

US Post Main Office—San Mateo [US Post Office in California 1900-1941 TR], 210 S. Ellsworth St., San Mateo, 4/18/88, A, C, 88000443

Union Cemetery, 316 Woodside Rd., Redwood City, 8/25/83, D, d, 83001237

Watkins-Cartan House, 25 Isabella Ave., Atherton, 3/30/78, C, 78000768

Woodside Store, 471 Kings Mountain Rd., Woodside, 7/18/85, A, B, C, 85001563

Santa Barbara County

Campbell No. 2 Archeological Site, Address Restricted, Goleta vicinity, 1/25/93, D, 92001755

Eastern Sierra Madre Ridge Archeological District, Address Restricted, New Cuyama vicinity, 12/19/78, D, 78000779

El Paseo and Casa de la Guerra, 808–818 State St., 813–819 Anacapa St., and 9–25 E. de la Guerra St., Santa Barbara, 2/02/77, A, C, g, 77000346

Faith Mission, 409 State St., Santa Barbara, 1/11/82, A, C, a, 82002269

Gonzalez, Rafael, House, 835 Laguna St., Santa Barbara, 4/15/70, C, NHL, 70000149

Hammond's Estate Site, Address Restricted, Santa Barbara vicinity, 5/19/78, D, 78000782

Hill-Carrillo Adobe, 11 E. Carrillo St., Santa Barbara, 1/14/86, A, C, 86000778

Hope, Thomas, House, 399 Nogal Dr., Santa Barbara vicinity, 12/01/78, C, 78000783

Janssens-Orella-Birk Building, 1029–1031 State St., Santa Barbara, 7/16/87, A, C, 87001170

La Purisima Mission, 4 mi. E of Lompoc, near jct. of CA 1 and 150, Lompoc vicinity, 4/15/70, A, a, e, NHL, 70000147

Lompoc Public Library [California Carnegie Libraries MPS], 200 S. H St., Lompoc, 12/10/90, A, C, 90001818

Los Alamos Ranch House, 3 mi. W of Los Alamos on old U.S. 101, Los Alamos vicinity, 4/15/70, A, C, NHL, 70000148

Los Banos del Mar, 401 Shoreline Dr., Santa Barbara, 12/24/92, A, C, 92001726

Santa Barbara County—Continued

Madulce Guard Station and Site, 40 mi. N. of Santa Barbara, Santa Barbara vicinity, 12/11/79, C, e, 79000547

Minerva Club of Santa Maria, 127 W. Boone St., Santa Maria, 9/20/84, A, C, 84001193

Mission de la Purisima Concepcion de Maria Santisima Site, Bounded by Locust Ave., city limits, E and G Sts., Lompoc, 5/05/78, A, D, a, 78000775

Painted Cave, Address Restricted, Santa Barbara vicinity, 12/05/72, C, D, 72000256

Point Conception Light Station, U.S. Coast Guard Light Station, Santa Barbara vicinity, 2/25/81, A, D, 81000176

SS YANKEE BLADE, Address Restricted, Lompoc vicinity, 5/16/91, A, D, 91000564

San Marcos Rancho, Address Restricted, Santa Barbara vicinity, 4/26/79, D, 79000548

San Miguel Island Archeological District, Address Restricted, Santa Barbara vicinity, 9/12/79, A, D, NPS, 79000258

Santa Barbara County Courthouse, 1100 Anacapa St., Santa Barbara, 1/23/81, A, C, 81000177

Santa Barbara Island Archeological District, Address Restricted, Santa Barbara vicinity, 9/12/79, A, D, NPS, 79000259

Santa Barbara Mission, 2201 Laguna St., Santa Barbara, 10/15/66, A, C, a, NHL, 66000237

Santa Barbara Presidio, Roughly bounded by Carrillo, Garden, De la Guerra and Anacapa Sts., Santa Barbara, 11/26/73, A, C, D, e, 73000455

Santa Cruz Island Archeological District, Address Restricted, Santa Barbara vicinity, 1/30/80, D, NPS, 80000405

Sexton, Joseph and Lucy Foster, House, 5490 Hollister Ave., Santa Barbara, 2/05/92, B, C, 91002033

Space Launch Complex 10, Vandenberg Air Force Base, Lompoc, 6/23/86, A, g, NHL, 86003511

St. Vincent Orphanage and School Building, 925 De La Vina St., Santa Barbara, 6/02/82, A, C, 82002270

Steedman Estate, 1387 E. Valley Rd., Montecito, 1/29/87, C, 87000002

US Post Office—Santa Barbara Main [US Post Office in California 1900-1941 TR], 836 Anacapa St., Santa Barbara, 1/11/85, C, g, 85000138

Santa Clara County

Alviso Historic District, Boundaries unknown at this time, Alviso, 10/09/73, A, 73000449

Ashworth-Remillard House, 755 Story Rd., San Jose, 12/12/76, A, C, 76000529

Building at 27–29 Fountain Alley, 27–29 Fountain Alley, San Jose, 3/02/82, C, 82002265

Campbell Union Grammar School, 11 E. Campbell Ave., Campbell, 7/20/79, A, C, 79000544

Campbell Union High School Historic District, 1 W. Campbell Ave., Campbell, 8/17/89, A, C, 89001048

Christian Church of Gilroy, 160 5th St., Gilroy, 4/01/82, A, C, a, b, 82002261

Civic Art Gallery, 110 Market St., San Jose, 1/29/73, C, 73000453

Coyote Creek Archeological District, Address Restricted, Gilroy Hot Springs vicinity, 10/14/71, D, 71000192

De Anza Hotel, 233 W. Santa Clara St., San Jose, 1/21/82, A, C, 82002266

Dohrmann Building, 325 S. First St., San Jose, 2/20/86, C, 86000264

Downing, T. B., House, 706 Cowper St., Palo Alto, 10/30/73, C, 73000452

Dunker House, 420 Maple St., Palo Alto, 2/19/82, C, 82002264

East San Jose Carnegie Library [California Carnegie Libraries MPS], 1102 E. Santa Clara St., San Jose, 12/10/90, A, C, 90001813

First Unitarian Universalist Church, 160 N. 3rd St., San Jose, 11/17/77, A, C, a, 77000343

Forbes Mill Annex, CA 17, Los Gatos, 7/31/78, A, C, 78000776

Fraternal Hall Building, 140 University Ave. and 514 High St., Palo Alto, 2/15/90, A, C, 90000119

Galindo-Leigh House, 140 S. Peter Dr., Campbell, 8/22/80, C, 80000857

Gilroy Free Library, 195 Fifth St., Gilroy, 6/23/88, A, C, 88000923

Griffin, Willard, House and Carriage House, 12345 S. El Monte Ave., Los Altos vicinity, 4/13/77, A, C, 77000342

Hamilton, Capt. James A., House, 2295 S. Basom Ave., San Jose vicinity, 6/09/80, C, 80000864

Hanna-Honeycomb House, 737 Frenchman's Rd., Palo Alto vicinity, 11/07/78, A, C, g, NHL, 78000780

Hayes Mansion, 200 Edenvale Ave., San Jose, 8/01/75, A, C, 75000481

Hensley Historic District, Roughly bounded by Julian, 1st, 7th, and Empire Sts., San Jose, 6/21/83, C, D, 83001238

Holloway, Edgar, House, 7539 Eigleberry St., Gilroy, 1/28/82, B, C, 82002262

Hoover, Lou Henry, House, 623 Mirada Rd., Stanford, 1/30/78, B, C, NHL, 78000786

Hostess House, W of University Ave. underpass of El Camino Real, Palo Alto, 7/30/76, A, C, 76000528

Hotel Sainte Claire, 302 and 320 S. Market St., San Jose, 6/03/80, A, C, 80000865

Kee House, 2310 Yale St., Palo Alto, 4/11/85, B, C, 85000715

Kotani-En Garden, Address Restricted, Los Gatos vicinity, 11/07/76, C, 76000527

Landrum, Andrew J., House, 1219 Santa Clara St., Santa Clara, 2/19/82, C, 82002271

Lantarnam Hall, 12355 Stonebrook Dr., Los Altos Hills, 12/19/85, C, 85003189

Le Petit Trianon, De Anza College campus, Cupertino, 11/15/72, A, C, 72001552

Leib Carriage House, 60 N. Keeble Ave., San Jose, 6/02/80, C, e, 80000866

Lick, James, Mill, 305 Montague Expwy., Santa Clara, 3/02/82, A, C, 82002272

Live Oak Creamery, 88 Martin St., Gilroy, 3/11/82, A, 82002263

Los Gatos Historic Commercial District, 1–24 N. Santa Cruz Ave., 9–15 University Ave. and 14–198 W. Main St., Los Gatos, 9/13/91, A, C, 91001382

Malaguerra Winery, N. of Morgan Hill on Burnett Ave., Morgan Hill vicinity, 10/23/80, A, 80000858

Masson, Paul, Mountain Winery, Pierce Rd., Saratoga vicinity, 6/09/83, A, B, C, 83001239

McCullagh-Jones House, 18000 Overlook Rd., Los Gatos, 10/29/74, C, 74000558

Miller—Melone Ranch, 12795 Saratoga—Sunnyvale Rd., Saratoga, 4/01/93, A, C, 93000260

Milpitas Grammar School, 160 N. Main St., Milpitas, 7/22/93, A, C, 93000667

Moir Building, 227-247 N. 1st St., San Jose, 10/29/82, A, C, 82000991

Morse, Charles Copeland, House, 981 Fremont St., Santa Clara, 4/13/77, A, B, C, 77000347

New Almaden, 14 mi. S of San Jose on CR G8, San Jose vicinity, 10/15/66, A, NHL, 66000236

Norris House, 1247 Cowper St., Palo Alto, 7/24/80, B, C, a, 80000859

Norris, Frank, Cabin, 10 mi. W of Gilroy off CA 152, Gilroy vicinity, 10/15/66, B, NHL, 66000235

Old City Hall, 7410 Monterey St., Gilroy, 4/16/75, A, C, 75000480

Palo Alto Stock Farm Horse Barn, Fremont Rd., Stanford, 12/12/85, A, C, 85003325

Peralta, Luis Maria, Adobe, 184 W. St. John St., San Jose, 10/15/73, A, C, 73000454

Pettigrew House, Address Restricted, Palo Alto, 11/25/80, C, 80000860

Picchetti Brothers Winery, SW of Cupertino at 13100 Montebello Rd., Cupertino vicinity, 5/10/79, A, B, 79000545

Poverty Flat Site, Address Restricted, Morgan Hill vicinity, 2/23/72, D, 72000254

Professorville Historic District, Roughly bounded by Embarcadero Rd., Addison Ave., Emerson and Cowper Sts., Palo Alto, 10/03/80, A, C, 80000861

Ramona Street Architectural District, 518–581 Ramona St. and 255–267 Hamilton Ave., Palo Alto, 3/27/86, C, g, 86000592

Rengstorff, Henry A., House, 1737 Stierlin Rd., Mountain View, 6/13/78, A, C, 78000778

Roberto—Sunol Adobe, 770 Lincoln Ave., San Jose, 3/17/77, A, C, 77000344

Roma Bakery, 655 Almaden Ave., San Jose, 1/21/82, A, 82002267

Ross House, 693 S. 2nd St., San Jose, 10/29/82, C, 82000992

San Jose Downtown Historic District, E. Santa Clara, South First, Second, Third and E. San Fernando Sts., San Jose, 5/26/83, A, C, 83003822

Santa Clara Depot, 1 Railroad Ave., Santa Clara, 2/28/85, A, C, b, 85000359

Santa Clara Verein, 1082 Alviso St., Santa Clara, 1/19/84, A, C, 84001199

Southern Pacific Depot, 65 Cahill St., San Jose, 4/01/93, C, 93000274

Squire, John Adam, House, 900 University Ave., Palo Alto, 3/06/72, C, 72000255

St. James Square Historic District, Roughly bounded by N. 1st, N. 4th, E. St. James, and E.

Santa Clara County—Continued

St. John Sts., San Jose, 11/27/79, A, C, a, 79000546

St. Joseph's Roman Catholic Church, Market and San Fernando Sts., San Jose, 8/26/77, A, C, a, 77000345

Steinbeck, John, House, 16250 Greenwood Ln., Monte Sereno, 12/28/89, B, 89002117

Troy Laundry, 722 Almaden Ave., San Jose, 1/28/82, A, C, 82002268

U.S. Post Office, 380 Hamilton Ave., Palo Alto, 4/05/81, A, C, 81000175

Unitary Plan Wind Tunnel, Ames Research Center, Moffett Field, 10/03/85, A, C, g, NHL, 85002799

Villa Mira Monte, 17860 Monterey Rd., Morgan Hill, 5/25/78, B, C, 78000777

Villa Montalvo, 14800 Montalvo Rd., Saratoga, 5/01/78, A, C, 78000784

We and Our Neighbors Clubhouse, S of San Jose at 15460 Union Ave., San Jose vicinity, 12/20/78, A, 78000781

Welch-Hurst, 15800 Sanborn Rd., Saratoga vicinity, 9/18/78, B, 78000785

Wheeler Hospital, 650 Fifth St., Gilroy, 9/13/90, C, 90001442

Wilson House, 860 University St., Palo Alto, 1/02/80, C, 80000862

Winchester House, 525 S. Winchester Blvd., San Jose, 8/07/74, B, C, 74000559

Woodhills, S of Cupertino on Prospect Rd., Cupertino vicinity, 12/20/78, A, C, 78000773

Yung See San Fong House, 16660 Cypress Way, Los Gatos, 9/08/83, A, C, g, 83001240

de Lemos, Pedro, House, 100-110 Waverley Oaks, Palo Alto, 1/10/80, C, g, 80000863

Santa Cruz County

Bank of Santa Cruz County, 1502 Pacific Ave., Santa Cruz, 3/15/82, A, g, 82002273

Bayview Hotel, 8041 Soquel Dr., Aptos, 3/30/92, A, b, 92000259

Bockius, Godfrey M., House, 322 E. Beach St., Watsonville, 7/13/89, B, C, 89000937

Branciforte Adobe, 1351 N. Branciforte Ave., Santa Cruz, 1/31/79, A, D, 79000552

Brown, Allan, Site, Address Restricted, Santa Cruz vicinity, 6/25/81, D, 81000178

Carmelita Court, 315-321 Main St., Santa Cruz, 3/20/86, B, C, 86000456

Castro, Jose Joaquin, Adobe, NW of Watsonville at 184 Old Adobe Rd., Watsonville vicinity, 12/12/76, A, C, 76000531

Cope Row Houses, 412–420 Lincoln St., Santa Cruz, 1/28/82, A, C, 82002274

Davenport Jail, 1 Center St., Davenport, 4/27/92, A, 92000422

Felton Covered Bridge, Covered Bridge Rd., Felton, 6/19/73, A, C, 73000451

Felton Presbyterian Church, 6299 Gushee St., Felton, 4/06/78, C, a, 78000774

Garfield Park Branch Library [California Carnegie Libraries MPS], 705 Woodrow Ave., Santa Cruz, 3/26/92, A, C, 92000268

Glen Canyon Covered Bridge, Branciforte Dr., Santa Cruz vicinity, 5/17/84, A, C, b, 84001194

Golden Gate Villa, 924 3rd St., Santa Cruz, 7/24/75, C, 75000482

Hihn Building, 201 Monterey Ave., Capitola, 3/20/73, A, C, 73000450

Hinds, A. J., House, 529 Chestnut St., Santa Cruz, 8/25/83, B, C, 83001241

Hotel Metropole, 1111 Pacific Ave., Santa Cruz, 5/23/79, A, C, 79000553

Judge Lee House, 128 E. Beach St., Watsonville, 6/30/80, C, 80000868

Lettunich Building, 406 Main St., Watsonville, 9/24/92, A, C, 92001278

Live Oak Ranch, 105 Mentel Ave., Santa Cruz, 7/10/75, A, C, 75000483

Looff Carousel and Roller Coaster on the Santa Cruz Beach Boardwalk, Along Beach St., Santa Cruz, 2/27/87, A, NHL, 87000764

Madison House, 335 East Lake, Watsonville, 2/02/84, C, 84001195

Mansion House Hotel, 418-424 Main St., Watsonville, 8/18/83, A, C, 83001242

Mission Hill Area Historic District, Mission St., Santa Cruz, 5/17/76, A, C, D, 76000530

Neary-Rodriguez Adobe, 130-134 School St., Santa Cruz, 2/24/75, A, C, a, 75000484

Octagon Building, Corner of Front and Cooper Sts., Santa Cruz, 3/24/71, C, 71000193

Old Riverview Historic District, Blue Gum Ave., Capitola Ave., Riverview Ave., Riverview Dr., and Wharf Rd., Capitola, 1/22/88, A, C, 87000626

Phillipshurst-Riverwood, CA 9, Ben Lomond vicinity, 8/04/83, B, C, 83004369

Rispin Mansion, 2200 Wharf Rd., Capitola, 3/14/91, B, 91000286

Santa Cruz Downtown Historic District, Roughly Rincon St., Church St., Chestnut St., Walnut St., Cedar St., Laurel St., Myrtle St., and Lincoln St., Santa Cruz, 7/27/89, A, C, 89001005

Scott, Hiram D., House, 4603 Scotts Valley Dr., Scotts Valley, 4/13/77, A, B, C, b, 77000348

Six Sisters-Lawn Way Historic District, Roughly bounded by San Jose Ave., Capitola Ave., and Esplanade, Capitola, 5/01/87, A, C, 87000623

Stoesser Block and Annex, 331-341 Main St., Watsonville, 4/07/83, C, 83001243

US Post Office—Santa Cruz Main [US Post Office in California 1900-1941 TR], 850 Front St., Santa Cruz, 1/11/85, C, 85000139

Valencia Hall, Valencia Rd., Aptos vicinity, 9/20/84, A, B, C, 84001201

Venetian Court Apartments, 1500 Wharf Rd., Capitola, 4/02/87, A, C, 87000574

Veterans Memorial Building, 842–846 Front St., Santa Cruz, 4/27/92, A, C, 92000423

Watsonville City Plaza, Bounded by Main, Peck, Union, and E. Beach Cts., Watsonville, 8/22/83, A, C, 83001244

Watsonville-Lee Road Site, Address Restricted, Watsonville vicinity, 5/28/76, D, a, 76000532

Shasta County

Benton Tract Site, Address Restricted, Redding vicinity, 11/12/71, D, 71000197

Cottonwood Historic District, Off US 99, Cottonwood, 7/16/73, A, C, 73000456

Cow Creek Petroglyphs, Address Restricted, Millville vicinity, 11/05/71, D, 71000195

Dersch-Taylor Petroglyphs, Address Restricted, Millville vicinity, 10/14/71, D, 71000196

French Gulch Historic District, Along both sides of French Gulch Rd., French Gulch, 3/24/72, A, 72000257

Frisbie, Edward, House, 1246 East St., Redding, 3/29/90, B, C, 90000550

Horseshoe Lake Ranger Station, N of Chester in Lassen Volcanic National Park, Chester vicinity, 5/05/78, A, C, g, NPS, 78000292

Lake Britton Archeological District, Address Restricted, Burney vicinity, 4/14/75, D, 75000485

Loomis Vistor Center, Bldg. 43, Lassen Volcanic National Park, Manzanita Lake, 2/25/75, A, g, NPS, 75000177

Nobles Emigrant Trail, E of Shingletown in Lassen Volcanic National Park, Shingletown vicinity, 10/03/75, A, NPS, 75000222

Old City Hall Building, 1313 Market St., Redding, 11/14/78, A, C, 78000790

Olsen Petroglyphs, Address Restricted, Redding vicinity, 3/24/71, D, 71000198

Pine Street School, 1135 Pine St., Redding, 3/21/78, A, C, 78000791

Prospect Peak Fire Lookout, NE of Mineral, Mineral vicinity, 3/30/78, A, NPS, 78000295

Reading Adobe Site, Adobe Lane, 5 mi. E of the center of Cottonwood, Cottonwood vicinity, 7/14/71, B, D, 71000194

Shasta State Historic Park, U.S. 299, Shasta, 10/14/71, A, C, 71000199

Squaw Creek Archeological Site, Address Restricted, Redding vicinity, 9/03/81, D, 81000179

Summit Lake Ranger Station, NE of Mineral in Lassen Volcanic National Park, Mineral vicinity, 4/03/78, A, NPS, 78000296

Tower House District, Whiskeyton National Recreation Area, Whiskeytown, 7/02/73, A, NPS, 73000257

Tower House—Soo-Yeh-Choo-Pus, Address Restricted, French Gulch vicinity, 11/04/85, D, NPS, 85003483

Sierra County

1872 California-Nevada State Boundary Marker, NW of Verdi on CA/NV border, Unknown, vicinity, 8/27/81, A, 81000387

Foote's Crossing Road, Tahoe National Forest, Nevada City vicinity, 1/29/81, A, 81000180

Hawley Lake Petroglyphs, Address Restricted, Gold Lake vicinity, 5/06/71, C, D, 71000200

Kyburz Flat Site, Address Restricted, Loyalton vicinity, 11/12/71, D, 71000201

Sierra County—Continued

Sardine Valley Archeological District, Address Restricted, Truckee vicinity, 5/06/71, A, D, 71000202

Sierra County Sheriff's Gallows, Galloway Rd. and Courthouse Sq., Downieville, 2/15/90, A, C, 90000118

Stampede Site, Address Restricted, Verdi vicinity, 10/14/71, D, 71000203

Siskiyou County

Captain Jack's Stronghold, S of Tulelake, Lava Beds National Monument, Tulelake vicinity, 9/20/73, A, NPS, 73000259

Dunsmuir Historic Commercial District, Roughly bounded by Sacramento and Shasta Aves., Spruce and Cedar Sts. (both sides), Dunsmuir, 11/10/82, A, C, 82000993

Falkenstein, Lewis, House, 401 S. Gold Street, Yreka, 12/31/79, C, 79000554

Fort Jones House, Main St., Fort Jones, 4/22/76, A, C, 76000533

Harlow, William, Cabin, Elliot Cr. Rd. #1050, 1 mi. from Joe Bar Subdivision, Seiad Valley vicinity, 6/03/91, A, C, 91000699

Hospital Rock Army Camp Site, S of Tulelake, Lava Beds National Monument, Tulelake vicinity, 10/02/73, A, NPS, 73000227

Hotel Macdoel, Montezuma Ave. and Mt. Shasta St., Macdoel, 2/11/82, A, C, 82002275

Lower Klamath National Wildlife Refuge, Lower Klamath Lake, E of Dorris, Dorris vicinity, 10/15/66, A, NHL, 66000238

McCloud, Roughly bounded by Columbero Dr., Main St., W. Minnesota Ave., and Lawndale Ct., McCloud, 3/16/90, A, C, 90000444

Sawyers Bar Catholic Church, Klamath National Forest, Sawyers Bar, 7/07/78, A, C, a, d, 78000792

Shasta Inn and Week Lumber Company Boarding House, 829 and 877 N. Davis St., Weed, 11/10/80, A, 80000869

Thomas-Wright Battle Site, S of Tulelake in Lava Beds National Monument, Tulelake vicinity, 11/15/78, A, NPS, 78000366

West Miner Street-Third Street Historic District, 102–402 W. Miner St. and 122–419 3rd St., Yreka, 12/11/72, A, C, 72000258

White's Gulch Arrastra, E of Swayers Bar, Sawyers Bar vicinity, 12/22/78, D, 78000793

Yreka Carnegie Library [California Carnegie Libraries MPS], 412 W. Miner St., Yreka, 3/26/92, A, C, 92000270

Solano County

Benicia Arsenal, Army Point and I-680, Benicia, 11/07/76, A, C, 76000534

Benicia Capitol State Historic Park, 1st and G Sts., Benicia, 2/12/71, A, C, 71000204

Buck, Will H., House, 301 Buck Ave., Vacaville, 10/24/85, B, C, 85003372

Carr House, 165 E. D St, Benicia, 9/13/79, C, 79000555

Crooks Mansion, 285 W. G St., Benicia, 11/14/78, B, C, D, 78000795

DELTA KING, 3 mi. (4.8 km) N of Rio Vista on CA 84, Rio Vista vicinity, 3/31/78, A, 78000797

Fischer, Joseph, House, 135 G St., Benicia, 5/24/79, C, 79000556

Hastings Adobe, NE of Collinsville off CA 68, Collinsville vicinity, 6/13/72, B, 72000260

Mare Island Naval Shipyard, Mare Island, Vallejo, 5/15/75, A, NHL, 75002103

Martin, Samuel, House, 293 Suisun Valley Rd., Suisun vicinity, 5/26/77, B, C, D, 77000349

Old Masonic Hall, 106 W. J St., Benicia, 3/16/72, A, 72000259

Pena Adobe, 2 mi. SW of Vacaville on I-80, Vacaville vicinity, 1/07/72, B, 72000261

SS JEREMIAH O'BRIEN, E of Benicia at Suisun Bay, Benicia vicinity, 7/07/78, A, C, g, 78000796

STAMBOUL (Whaling Bark), Foot of W. 12th St., Benicia, 11/02/88, A, C, D, 88002030

Suisun Masonic Lodge No. 55, 623 Main St., Suisun City, 12/18/78, C, 78000798

Vacaville Town Hall, 620 E. Main St., Vacaville, 9/18/78, C, 78000799

Vallejo City Hall and County Building Branch, 734 Marin St., Vallejo, 11/07/76, C, 76000535

Vallejo Old City Historic District, Sonoma Blvd., and Monterey, Carolina, and York Sts., Vallejo, 3/20/73, C, 73000460

Sonoma County

Bodega Bay, Address Restricted, Bodega Bay vicinity, 12/18/73, D, 73000461

Buena Vista Vineyards—Buena Vista Vinicultural Society, 18000 Old Winery Rd., Sonoma, 7/24/86, B, C, 86001902

Burbank, Luther, House and Garden, 200 Santa Rosa Ave., Santa Rosa, 10/15/66, B, NHL, 66000241

Cloverdale Railroad Station, Railroad Ave., Cloverdale, 12/12/76, A, C, 76000536

Cnopius House, 726 College Ave., Santa Rosa, 4/12/82, B, C, 82002277

Dry Creek-Warm Springs Valleys Archeological District, Address Restricted, Healdsburg vicinity, 12/09/77, D, 77000350

Duncan's Landing Site, Address Restricted, Jenner vicinity, 11/12/71, D, 71000206

Fort Ross, N of Fort Ross on CA 1, Fort Ross vicinity, 10/15/66, A, e, f, NHL, 66000239

Fort Ross Commander's House, N of Fort Ross on CA 1, Fort Ross State Historical Monument, Fort Ross vicinity, 4/15/70, A, C, NHL, 70000150

Free Public Library of Petaluma, 20 Fourth St., Petaluma, 6/23/88, A, C, 88000925

Gables, The, 4257 Petaluma Hill Rd., Santa Rosa, 9/20/84, B, C, 84001206

Geyserville Union School, Main St., Geyserville, 10/24/79, A, C, 79000558

Gold Ridge Farm, W of Sebastopol, Sebastopol vicinity, 12/14/78, B, 78000803

Gould—Shaw House, 215 N. Cloverdale Blvd., Cloverdale, 9/10/92, A, B, C, 92001244

Guerneville Bridge, Rt. 116 over Russian River, Guerneville, 8/04/89, A, 89000945

Healdsburg Carnegie Library, 221 Matheson St., Healdsburg, 7/06/88, A, C, 88000924

Hicks House, 3160 Hicks Rd., Graton, 7/21/87, B, C, 87001157

Hinds Hotel, 306 Bohemian Hwy., Freestone, 1/31/79, C, 79000557

Hotel Chauvet, 13756 Arnold Dr., Glen Ellen, 2/15/90, A, 90000117

Hotel La Rose, 5th and Wilson Sts., Santa Rosa, 8/03/78, A, C, 78000802

Knipp and Stengel Ranch Barn, CA 1, Sea Ranch, 1/29/87, A, C, 87000005

Laughlin, James H. and Frances E., House, SE of Windsor on Lone Redwood Rd., Windsor vicinity, 4/26/79, B, C, 79000563

Llano Road Roadhouse, 4353 Gravenstein Hwy., S, Sebastopol vicinity, 5/22/78, A, C, 78000804

London, Jack, Ranch, 0.4 mi. W of Glen Ellen in Jack London Historical State Park, Glen Ellen vicinity, 10/15/66, B, c, NHL, 66000240

Lumsden, W. H., House, 727 Mendocino St., Santa Rosa, 8/11/83, C, 83001245

Madrona Knoll Rancho District, 1001 Westside Rd., Healdsburg, 4/02/87, A, B, C, 87000573

McDonald Mansion, 1015 McDonald Ave., Santa Rosa, 3/01/74, B, C, 74000560

Old Petaluma Opera House, 147–149 Kentucky St., Petaluma, 12/22/78, C, 78000801

Old Post Office, 425 7th St., Santa Rosa, 11/16/79, C, b, 79000559

Park Apartments, 300 Santa Rosa Ave., Santa Rosa, 4/26/79, C, 79000560

Petaluma Adobe, 4 mi. E of Petaluma on Casa Grande Rd., Petaluma vicinity, 4/15/70, B, C, NHL, 70000151

Petaluma Silk Mill, 420 Jefferson St., Petaluma, 3/06/86, A, C, 86000386

Petaluma and Santa Rosa Railway Powerhouse, 238–258 Petaluma Ave., Sepbastopol, 7/23/91, A, 91000918

Pinschower, Simon, House, 302 N. Main St., Cloverdale, 2/25/82, C, 82002276

Railroad Square District, Roughly bounded by 3rd, Davis, Wilson, and 6th Sts. and Santa Rosa Creek, Santa Rosa, 4/20/79, A, C, 79000561

Ranch Site, The, Address Restricted, Bodega Bay vicinity, 7/14/71, D, 71000205

Salt Point State Park Archeological District, Address Restricted, Stewarts Point vicinity, 3/24/71, D, 71000207

Shaw, Isaac E., Building, 219 N. Cloverdale Blvd., Cloverdale, 1/25/91, A, B, 90002155

Sonoma Depot, 284 1st St., W, Sonoma, 4/03/75, A, 75000488

Sonoma Grammar School, 276 E. Napa St., Sonoma, 11/28/80, A, C, 80000871

Sonoma Plaza, Center of Sonoma, Sonoma, 4/03/75, A, C, NHL, 75000489

Sonoma Plaza (Boundary Increase), Area S and E of town plaza, along Broadway and the N

Sonoma County—Continued

side of E. Napa St., Sonoma, 5/06/92, A, C, 92000293

Strout, George A., House, 253 Florence Ave., Sebastopol, 6/17/80, B, C, b, 80000870

Sweed, Philip, House, 301 Keokuk St., Petaluma, 6/18/92, B, C, 92000787

Sweet House, 607 Cherry St., Santa Rosa, 1/14/88, B, C, 87002415

US Post Office—Petaluma [US Post Office in California 1900-1941 TR], 120 4th St., Petaluma, 1/11/85, C, 85000140

Vallejo Estate, Corner of Spain and W. 3rd Sts., Sonoma, 6/29/72, B, 72000262

Walters Ranch, 6 mi. S of Healdsburg at 6050 Westside Rd., Healdsburg vicinity, 10/07/77, A, C, b, 77000351

Wasserman House, 930 Mendocino Ave., Santa Rosa, 1/31/79, B, C, 79000562

Watson School, 15000 Bodega Hwy., Bodega vicinity, 8/18/78, A, 78000800

Stanislaus County

Gold Dredge, S of La Grange, La Grange vicinity, 12/16/71, A, g, 71000208

Kingen Hotel [La Grange MRA], 30054 Yosemite Blvd., La Grange, 8/24/79, C, 79003465

Knights Ferry, On Stanislaus River 2 mi. from Stanislaus, Knights Ferry and vicinity, 4/23/75, A, C, 75000490

Louie's Place [La Grange MRA], 30048 Yosemite Blvd., La Grange, 8/24/79, A, C, 79003466

McHenry Mansion, 906 15th St., Modesto, 4/04/78, B, C, 78000805

Odd Fellows Hall [La Grange MRA], Yosemite Blvd., La Grange, 8/24/79, A, C, 79003467

Old Adobe Barn [La Grange MRA], Yosemite Blvd. and La Grange Rd., La Grange, 8/24/79, A, C, 79003462

Old La Grange Schoolhouse [La Grange MRA], La Grange Rd. and Floto St., La Grange, 8/24/79, A, C, 79003461

Patterson Branch Library [California Carnegie Libraries MPS], 355 W. Las Palmas Ave., Patterson, 12/10/90, A, C, 90001812

Shell Gas Station [La Grange MRA], Yosemite Blvd., La Grange, 8/24/79, C, 79003464

St. Louis Catholic Church [La Grange MRA], La Grange Rd. and Floto St., La Grange, 8/24/79, C, a, 79003460

Stage Stop [La Grange MRA], Yosemite Blvd. and La Grange Rd., La Grange, 8/24/79, C, 79003463

Turlock Carnegie Library [California Carnegie Libraries], 250 N. Broadway, Turlock, 1/07/93, A, C, 92001753

Turlock High School Auditorium and Gymnasium, 1574 E. Canal Dr., Turlock, 1/11/91, A, C, 90002141

U.S. Post Office, Twelfth and I Sts., Modesto, 2/10/83, A, C, 83001246

Whitmore, Daniel, House, 2928 Fifth St., Ceres, 4/05/89, B, C, 89000230

Wood, Walter B., House, 814 Twelfth St., Modesto, 5/20/88, B, C, 88000551

Tehama County

Cone and Kimball Building, 747 Main St., Red Bluff, 6/26/79, A, C, 79000564

Maywood Woman's Club, 902 Marin St., Corning, 10/02/92, A, 92001301

Molino Lodge Building, 3rd and C Sts., Tehama, 6/06/80, A, C, a, 80000874

Odd Fellows Building, 342 Oak St., Red Bluff, 12/12/76, C, 76000537

Old Bank of America Building, 710 Main St., Red Bluff, 7/28/80, A, C, 80000873

Park Headquarters, Lassen Volcanic National Park, Off CA 36, Mineral, 10/03/78, A, C, NPS, 78N00294

Saint Mary's Parish, 515 Main St., Red Bluff, 2/04/82, A, C, a, 82002278

Sulphur Creek Archeological District, Address Restricted, Mill Creek vicinity, 4/14/80, D, NPS, 80000370

Trinity County

Bowerman Barn, SW of Trinity Center on Guy Covington Dr., Trinity Center vicinity, 3/20/81, A, C, 81000181

Helena Historic District, N of U.S. 299 W, on North Fork of Trinity River, Helena, 5/24/84, A, C, D, 84001219

Lewiston Historic District, Roughly Deadwood, Turnpike, and Schoolhouse Rds., Lewiston, 4/17/89, A, B, C, 88000550

Weaverville Historic District, Both sides of Main St., Weaverville, 10/14/71, A, 71000209

Tulare County

Allensworth Historic District, Town of Allensworth and its environs along CA 43, Allensworth and vicinity, 2/23/72, A, B, a, 72000263

Ash Mountain Entrance Sign, N of Three Rivers in Sequoia National Park, Three Rivers vicinity, 4/27/78, A, C, b, g, NPS, 78000367

Bank of Italy Building, 128 E. Main St., Visalia, 4/01/82, A, C, 82002280

Barton-Lackey Cabin, N of Mineral King in Kings Canyon National Park, Mineral King vicinity, 3/30/78, A, NPS, 78000290

Cabin Creek Ranger Residence and Dormitory, SE of Wilsonia on Generals Highway in Sequoia National Park, Wilsonia vicinity, 4/27/78, C, g, NPS, 78000368

Cattle Cabin, NE of Three Rivers on Sequoia National Park, Three Rivers vicinity, 9/15/77, A, NPS, 77000150

Elster, C. A., Building, CA 190 and Tule River Dr., Springville, 3/25/82, A, B, C, 82002279

Exeter Public Library [California Carnegie Libraries MPS], 309 S. E St., Exeter, 12/10/90, A, C, 90001811

Generals' Highway Stone Bridges, N of Mineral King in Sequoia National Park, Mineral King vicinity, 9/13/78, C, NPS, 78000284

Giant Forest Lodge Historic District, NE of Three Rivers in Sequoia National Park, Three River vicinity, 5/05/78, A, C, NPS, 78000287

Giant Forest Village-Camp Kaweah Historic District, N of Three Rivers in Sequoia National Park, Three Rivers vicinity, 5/22/78, A, B, C, NPS, 78000311

Groenfeldt Site, Address Restricted, Three Rivers vicinity, 3/30/78, D, NPS, 78000288

Hockett Meadow Ranger Station, S of Silver City in Sequoia National Park, Silver City vicinity, 4/27/78, A, C, g, NPS, 78000369

Hospital Rock, Address Restricted, Three Rivers vicinity, 8/29/77, A, D, NPS, 77000122

Hyde House, 500 S. Court St., Visalia, 4/26/79, C, 79000565

Moro Rock Stairway, N of Three Rivers in Sequoia National Park, Three Rivers vicinity, 12/29/78, A, C, NPS, 78000283

Orosi Branch Library, 12662 Ave. 416, Orosi, 8/25/83, A, 83001247

Pear Lake Ski Hut, N of Mineral King on Sequioa National Park, Mineral King vicinity, 5/05/78, A, C, g, NPS, 78000285

Pogue Hotel, 32792 Sierra Dr. (CA 198), Lemoncove, 8/05/91, B, 91000927

Quinn Ranger Station, S on Mineral King on Sequoia National Park, Mineral King vicinity, 4/13/77, A, NPS, 77000118

Redwood Meadow Ranger Station, NE of Three Rivers in Sequoia National Park, Three Rivers vicinity, 4/13/78, C, g, NPS, 78000289

Smithsonian Institution Shelter, W of Lone Pine in Sequoia National Park, Lone Pine vicinity, 3/08/77, A, NPS, 77000119

Squatter's Cabin, NE of Three Rivers, Three Rivers vicinity, 3/08/77, A, NPS, 77000116

Tenalu, Address Restricted, Porterville vicinity, 9/04/86, C, 86002194

Tharp's Log, NE of Three Rivers, Three Rivers vicinity, 3/08/77, A, NPS, 77000117

The Pioneer, 27000 S. Mooney Blvd., Visalia, 5/05/77, A, 77000358

US Post Office—Porterville Main [US Post Office in California 1900-1941 TR], 65 W. Mill Ave., Porterville, 1/11/85, C, g, 85000141

US Post Office—Visalia Town Center Station [US Post Office in California 1900-1941 TR], 11 W. Acequia St., Visalia, 1/11/85, C, 85000142

Zalud House, 393 N. Hockett St., Porterville, 3/31/87, C, 86003681

Tuolumne County

Cady House, 72 N. Norlin St., Sonora, 2/25/82, A, C, b, e, 82002281

Chinaman Mortar Site, Address Restricted, Strawberry vicinity, 6/20/75, D, 75000492

Tuolumne County—Continued

City Hotel, 145 S. Washington St., Sonora, 6/30/83, A, C, 83001248

Columbia Historic District, 4 mi. NW of Sonora on CA 49, Sonora vicinity, 10/15/66, A, C, NHL, 66000242

Emporium, 735 Main St., Jamestown, 2/17/78, A, C, 78000817

Gamble Building and Miner's Bean Kettle, 17544 CA 120, Big Oak Flat, 3/22/91, A, C, 91000335

Great Sierra Mine Historic Site, W of Lee Vining in Yosemite National Park, Lee Vining vicinity, 5/24/78, A, C, NPS, 78000382

Great Sierra Wagon Road, N of Yosemite Village, Yosemite Valley vicinity, 8/25/78, A, C, NPS, 78000373

McCauley Cabin, W of Lee Vining at Tuolumne Meadows, Lee Vining vicinity, 3/08/77, C, NPS, 77000359

Niagara Camp, NE of Tuolumne in Stanislaus National Forest, Tuolumne vicinity, 6/06/75, A, C, g, 75000494

Parsons Memorial Lodge, Tuolumne Meadows, Yosemite National Park, 4/30/79, A, C, NHL, NPS, 79000283

Quail Site, Address Restricted, Long Barn vicinity, 3/10/75, D, 75000491

Soda Springs Cabin, SW of Lee Vining, Lee Vining vicinity, 4/19/79, A, B, NPS, 79000282

Sugg House, 37 Theall St., Sonora, 9/13/84, A, C, 84001210

Tioga Pass Entrance Station, SW of Lee Vining in Yosemite National Park, Lee Vining vicinity, 12/14/78, C, g, NPS, 78000372

Tuolumne County Courthouse, 41 W. Yaney Ave., Sonora, 9/17/81, A, C, 81000182

Tuolumne County Jail, 156 W. Bradford St., Sonora, 11/07/78, A, 78000822

Tuolumne Meadows, SW of Lee Vining in Yosemite National Park, Lee Vining vicinity, 11/30/78, A, C, g, NPS, 78000371

Tuolumne Meadows Ranger Stations and Comfort Stations, SW of Lee Vining in Yosemite National Park, Lee Vining vicinity, 12/18/78, A, C, NPS, 78000370

Ventura County

Anacapa Island Archeological District, Address Restricted, Port Hueneme vicinity, 9/12/79, A, D, NPS, 79000257

Anacapa Island Light Station [Light Stations of California MPS], Anacapa Island, Channel Islands National Park, Oxnard vicinity, 9/03/91, A, C, NPS, 91001101

Bard, Elizabeth, Memorial Hospital, 121 N. Fir St., Ventura, 11/11/77, A, C, 77000361

Bardsdale Methodist Episcopal Church, 1418 Bardsdale Ave., Fillmore, 8/28/86, A, C, a, 86001986

Berylwood, Ventura Rd., Port Hueneme, 9/15/77, A, B, C, b, 77000360

Burro Flats Painted Cave, Address Restricted, Santa Susana vicinity, 5/05/76, D, 76000539

Calleguas Creek Site, Address Restricted, Oxnard vicinity, 5/19/76, D, d, 76000538

Colony House, 137 Strathearn Pl., Simi, 9/18/78, A, C, b, 78000824

Dudley House, 4085 Telegraph Rd., Ventura, 5/12/77, A, C, 77000362

Ebell Club of Santa Paula, 125 S. Seventh St., Santa Paula, 7/20/89, A, B, C, 89000949

Faulkner, George Washington, House, 14292 W. Telegraph Rd., Santa Paula, 4/25/91, B, C, 91000485

Feraud General Merchandise Store, 2 and 12 W. Main St., Ventura, 1/23/86, A, C, 86000109

Franz, Emmanuel, House, 31 N. Oak St., Ventura, 6/25/82, A, C, 82002282

Glen Tavern Hotel, 134 N. Mill St., Santa Paula, 7/26/84, A, C, 84001225

Grand Union Hotel, 51 Ventu Park Rd., Newbury Park, 12/30/75, A, C, b, e, g, 75000495

Mission San Buenaventura and Mission Compound Site, Bounded by Poli St., Ventura and Santa Clara Aves., and Palm St., San Buenaventura vicinity, 4/10/75, A, D, a, 75000496

Olivas Adobe, 4200 Olivas Park Dr., Ventura, 7/24/79, A, C, 79000570

Oxnard Public Library, 424 S. C St., Oxnard, 7/27/71, A, C, 71000210

SS WINFIELD SCOTT (Steamship), Address Restricted, Anacapa Island vicinity, 9/12/88, A, C, D, NPS, 87002111

San Buenaventura Mission Aqueduct, 234 Canada Larga Rd., Ventura, 3/07/75, A, C, 75000497

San Miguel Chapel Site, Address Restricted, Ventura vicinity, 7/20/78, D, a, 78000826

Santa Paula Hardware Company Block—Union Oil Company, 1003 E. Main St., Santa Paula, 8/14/86, A, C, 86002619

Simi Adobe-Strathearn House, 137 Strathearn Pl., Simi vicinity, 5/19/78, A, B, C, 78000825

Ventura County Courthouse, 501 Poli St., Ventura, 8/19/71, C, 71000211

Ventura Theatre, 26 S. Chestnut, Ventura, 12/29/86, A, C, 86003523

Women's Improvement Club of Hueneme, 239 E. Scott St., Port Hueneme, 8/21/89, A, 89001150

Yolo County

Animal Science Building, University of California, West Quad and Peter J. Shields Ave., Davis, 6/17/86, A, C, 86001354

Beamer, R. H., House, 19 3rd St., Woodland, 8/02/82, B, C, 82002283

Canon School, 0.5 mi. N of Brooks, Brooks vicinity, 6/13/72, A, 72000264

Dresbach-Hunt-Boyer House, 604 2nd St., Davis, 9/13/76, A, C, 76000540

First Pacific Coast Salmon Cannery Site, On the Sacramento River, opposite the foot of K St., Broderick, 10/15/66, A, f, NHL, 66000938

Gibson, William B., House, 512 Gibson Rd., Woodland, 11/07/76, A, C, 76000542

I.O.O.F. Building, 723 Main St., Woodland, 2/25/82, A, C, 82002284

Moore, James, House, SW of Woodland, Woodland vicinity, 11/16/78, C, 78000827

Nelson Ranch, CA 18C between CA 113 and 102, Woodland vicinity, 7/17/72, A, C, 72000266

Porter Building, 501–511 Main St., Woodland, 11/30/78, A, C, 78000828

Rumsey Town Hall, CA 16 at Manzanita St., Rumsey, 6/19/72, A, 72000265

Southern Pacific Railroad Station, H and 2nd Sts., Davis, 11/07/76, A, C, 76000541

Tufts, Joshua B., House, 434 J St, Davis, 9/06/79, C, 79000571

Woodland Opera House, 320 2nd St., Woodland, 11/05/71, A, C, 71000212

Woodland Public Library, 250 1st St., Woodland, 9/28/81, A, C, 81000183

Yolo Branch Library [California Carnegie Libraries MPS], 200 Sacramento St., Yolo, 12/10/90, A, C, 90001810

Yuba County

Bok Kai Temple, Yuba River Levee at D St., Marysville, 5/21/75, A, C, a, 75000498

Hart Building, 423–425 4th St., Marysville, 1/28/82, A, C, 82002285

Johnson Ranch and Burtis Hotel Sites, Address Restricted, Wheatland vicinity, 7/22/91, A, D, 91000919

Oregon Creek Covered Bridge, 3 mi. NE of North San Juan over Oregon Creek, North San Juan vicinity, 5/30/75, A, 75000499

Packard Library, 301 4th St., Marysville, 12/18/78, C, 78000829

Ramirez, Jose Manuel, House, 220 5th St., Marysville, 1/17/76, A, C, 76000545

US Post Office—Marysville Main [US Post Office in California 1900-1941 TR], 407 C St., Marysville, 1/11/85, C, 85000143

Wheatland Masonic Temple, 400 Front St., Wheatland, 12/23/93, A, C, 93001396

Woodleaf Hotel, Marysville-La Porte Rd., Woodleaf, 4/09/75, A, C, 75000500

COLORADO

Adams County

Bowles House, 3924 W. 72nd Ave., Westminster, 11/03/88, A, C, 88002308

Harris Park School, 7200 Lowell Blvd., Westminster, 8/30/90, A, C, 90000868

Westminster University, 3455 W. 83rd Ave., Westminster, 8/10/79, A, C, a, 79000572

Alamosa County

Denver and Rio Grande Railroad Depot, 610 State St., Alamosa, 2/11/93, A, 93000034

Superintendent's Residence, Great Sand Dunes National Monument, CO 150, SW of Mosca, Mosca vicinity, 11/02/89, C, NPS, 89001761

Zapata Ranch Headquarters, 5303 CO 150, Mosca vicinity, 4/05/93, A, 93000199

Arapahoe County

Brown, David W., House, 2303 E. Dartmouth Ave., Englewood, 4/10/80, B, C, b, 80000875

Comanche Crossing of the Kansas Pacific Railroad, On Union Pacific Railroad tracks E of the Strasburg depot, Strasburg vicinity, 8/10/70, A, 70000152

Curtis School, 2349 E. Orchard Rd., Greenwood Village, 6/25/92, A, b, 92000808

DeLaney Barn, 200 S. Chambers Rd., Aurora, 2/09/89, A, C, 89000010

Gully Homestead, 200 S. Chambers Rd., Aurora, 1/09/86, A, C, b, g, 86000022

Littleton Town Hall, 2450 W. Main St., Littleton, 9/04/80, C, 80000876

Melvin School, 4950 S. Laredo St., Aurora, 1/05/84, A, C, b, 84000790

Seventeen Mile House, 8181 S. Parker Rd., Parker vicinity, 10/06/83, A, C, 83003501

Smith, William, House, 412 Oswego Ct., Aurora, 9/26/85, A, C, 85002565

Archuleta County

Chimney Rock Archeological Site, Address Restricted, Chimney Rock vicinity, 8/25/70, D, 70000153

Cumbres and Toltec Scenic Railroad, Between Antonito and Chama, NM, Antonito vicinity, 2/16/73, A, C, 73000462

Labo Del Rio Bridge [Vehicular Bridges in Colorado TR], Cty. Rd. F40 over Piedra River, Arboles vicinity, 6/24/85, C, b, 85001399

Baca County

Colorado Millennial Site, Address Restricted, Ruxton vicinity, 4/08/80, A, D, 80000877

Springfield Schoolhouse, 281 W. 7th Ave., Springfield, 10/05/77, A, C, 77000363

Bent County

Bent County Courthouse, Bounded by Carson and Bent Aves., 7th and 8th Sts., Las Animas, 1/02/76, A, C, 76000546

Boggsville, S of Las Animas on CO 101, Las Animas, 10/24/86, A, B, C, 86002841

Prowers Bridge [Vehicular Bridges in Colorado TR], Cty. Rd. 34, Prowers vicinity, 2/04/85, C, 85000189

Boulder County

Boulder Valley Grange No. 131, 3400 N. Ninety-fifth St., Lafayette vicinity, 12/07/87, A, C, 87002009

Bunce School, CO 7 S of Allenspark, Allenspark, 5/22/86, A, 86001109

Callahan, T. M., House, 312 Terry St., Longmont, 5/16/85, B, C, 85001064

Carnegie Library, 1125 Pine St., Boulder, 2/16/79, C, 79000573

Chautauqua Auditorium, Chautauqua Park, Boulder, 1/21/74, A, 74000562

Church of the Brethren, 17th Ave., Hygiene vicinity, 1/05/84, A, C, a, 84000794

Colorado Chautauqua, Chautauqua Park, Boulder, 3/21/78, A, 78000830

Congregational Church [Lafayette Coal Mining Era Buildings TR], 300 E. Simpson St., Lafayette, 5/20/83, A, a, 83001298

Denver Elevator—Grain Elevator [Louisville MRA], Tract 712 near CO 42, Louisville, 2/14/86, A, C, 86000212

Denver, Boulder and Western Railway Historic District, CO 72, Ward vicinity, 9/18/80, A, C, 80000882

Denver, Northwestern and Pacific Railway Historic District, SW of Eldora, Eldora vicinity, 9/30/80, A, C, 80000881

Dickens Opera House, 300 Main St., Longmont, 7/28/87, A, C, 87000702

Downtown Boulder Historic District, CO 19, Boulder, 12/03/80, A, C, 80000878

Eldora Historic District [Metal Mining and Tourist Era Resources of Boulder County MPS], Roughly Eaton Pl., 6th, Pearl, and 4th Sts., Huron Ave., 6th St., Eldorado Ave., and 7th St., Klondyke Ave. & Tenth St., Eldora, 10/04/89, A, C, 89000978

Empson Cannery, 15 3rd Ave., Longmont, 1/05/84, A, 84000796

First Congregational Church of Lyons, High and 4th Sts., Lyons, 12/12/76, A, C, a, 76000547

Ginacci House [Louisville MRA], 1116 LaFarge St., Louisville, 2/14/86, A, C, 86000213

Gold Hill Historic District [Metal Mining and Tourist Era Resources of Boulder County MPS], Roughly bounded by North St., Pine St., Boulder St., Gold Run St., and College St., Gold Hill, 8/03/89, A, C, 89000979

Highland School, 885 Arapahoe Ave., Boulder, 12/18/78, A, C, 78000831

Jacoe Store [Louisville MRA], 1001 Main St., Louisville, 2/14/86, A, C, 86000215

Jamestown Mercantile Building [Metal Mining and Tourist Era Resources of Boulder County MPS], Main St., Jamestown, 8/03/89, A, C, 89000985

Kullgren House [Lafayette Coal Mining Era Buildings TR], 209 E. Cleveland St., Lafayette, 5/20/83, A, C, 83001299

LaSalla House [Louisville MRA], 1124 Main St., Louisville, 2/14/86, C, 86000217

Lackner's Tavern [Louisville MRA], 1006 Pine, Louisville, 2/14/86, C, 86000220

Lafayette House [Lafayette Coal Mining Era Buildings TR], 600 E. Simpson St., Lafayette, 5/20/83, A, C, 83001300

Lewis House [Lafayette Coal Mining Era Buildings TR], 108 E. Simpson St., Lafayette, 5/20/83, A, 83001301

Little Church in the Pines [Metal Mining and Tourist Era Resources of Boulder County MPS], 414 Gold Run Rd., Salina, 8/03/89, C, a, 89000983

Longmont Carnegie Library, 457 Fourth Ave., Longmont, 11/03/92, A, C, 92001406

Longmont College, 546 Atwood St., Longmont, 8/12/87, A, C, 87001285

Longmont Fire Department, 667 4th Ave., Longmont, 5/16/85, A, 85001063

Longmont Power Plant, Old Apple Valley Rd., Lyons vicinity, 9/10/87, A, 87001553

Lyons Railroad Depot, 400 block of Broadway, Lyons, 12/02/74, A, 74000563

Lyons Sandstone Buildings, U.S. 36 and CO 7, Lyons, 4/29/80, A, C, 80000880

Miller House [Lafayette Coal Mining Era Buildings TR], 409 E. Cleveland St., Lafayette, 5/20/83, A, B, 83001291

Modoc Mill, N of Ward, Ward vicinity, 12/27/78, A, C, 78000833

National Fuel Company Store [Louisville MRA], 801 Main St., Louisville, 2/14/86, A, 86000222

Norlin Quadrangle Historic District, University of Colorado campus, Boulder, 3/27/80, A, C, 80000879

Northern Colorado Power Company Substation, 1590 Broadway, Boulder, 5/22/86, A, 86001108

Boulder County—Continued

Petrelli—DelPizzo House [Louisville MRA], 1016 Main St., Louisville, 2/14/86, C, 86000224

Rhoades House [Louisville MRA], 1024 Grant, Louisville, 2/14/86, C, 86000226

Robinson House [Louisville MRA], 301 Spruce, Louisville, 2/14/86, C, 86000228

Salina School [Metal Mining and Tourist Era Resources of Boulder County MPS], 536 Gold Run Rd., Salina, 8/03/89, A, C, 89000984

Snowbound Mine, Co. Rd. 52, Gold Hill vicinity, 8/03/89, A, C, 89000998

Squires-Tourtellot House, 1019 Spruce St., Boulder, 8/10/78, A, B, C, 78000832

St. Stephen's Episcopal Church, 1881, 470 Main St., Longmont, 2/24/75, A, C, a, 75000501

Stolmes House [Louisville MRA], 616 Front St., Louisville, 2/14/86, C, 86000229

Sunshine School [Metal Mining and Tourist Era Resources of Boulder County MPS], 355 Co. Rd. 83, Sunshine, 7/27/89, A, C, 89000982

Swedish Evangelical Lutheran Church of Ryssby, N. 63rd St., Boulder vicinity, 2/16/84, A, a, d, 84000797

Tego Brothers Drugstore—State National Bank of Louisville [Louisville MRA], 700 Main St., Louisville, 2/14/86, C, 86000230

Terrace, The [Lafayette Coal Mining Era Buildings TR], 207 E. Cleveland St., Lafayette, 11/03/87, A, C, g, 87001287

Thomas House [Louisville MRA], 700 Lincoln, Louisville, 2/14/86, C, 86000231

Thunder Lake Patrol Cabin [Rocky Mountain National Park MRA], Thunder Lake, Estes Park vicinity, 1/29/88, C, NPS, 87001124

US Post Office—Boulder Main [US Post Offices in Colorado, 1900–1941, TR], 1905 Fifteenth St., Boulder, 1/22/86, C, g, 86000164

Walker Ranch Historic District, W of Boulder, Boulder vicinity, 6/14/84, A, C, D, 84000798

Walker Ranch Historic District (Boundary Increase), 7.5 mi. W of Boulder off Flagstaff Rd., Boulder vicinity, 6/29/88, A, 88000756

Wall Street Assay Office [Metal Mining and Tourist Era Resources of Boulder County MPS], 6352 Four Mile Canyon Dr., Wallstreet, 8/03/89, A, C, 89000986

Wall Street Assay Office (Boundary Increase) [Metal Mining and Tourist Era Resources of Boulder County MPS], Area W and across Wall St. from Assay Office, Wall Street, 1/28/92, A, 91002028

Ward Congregational Church [Metal Mining and Tourist Era Resources of Boulder County MPS], 41 Modoc, Ward, 8/03/89, A, C, a, 89000981

Ward School [Metal Mining and Tourist Era Resources of Boulder County MPS], 66 Columbia, Ward, 8/03/89, A, C, 89000980

West Side Historic District, Roughly bounded by Fifth, Terry, Third, and Grant, Longmont, 1/07/87, C, 86002846

Wild Basin House [Rocky Mountain National Park MRA], Wild Basin, Estes Park vicinity, 1/29/88, C, NPS, 87001125

Wild Basin Ranger Station and House [Rocky Mountain National Park MRA], Wild Basin, Estes Park vicinity, 1/29/88, C, NPS, 87001126

Woodward-Baird House, 1733 Canyon Blvd., Boulder, 2/15/79, C, 79000574

Chaffee County

Bridge over Arkansas River [Vehicular Bridges in Colorado TR], U.S. Hwy 24, Buena Vista vicinity, 2/04/85, C, g, 85000190

Chaffee County Courthouse and Jail Buildings, 501 E. Main St, Buena Vista, 9/10/79, C, 79000575

Chaffee County Poor Farm, 8495 County Rd. 160, Salida vicinity, 5/16/85, A, 85001062

F Street Bridge [Vehicular Bridges in Colorado TR], F St., Salida, 2/04/85, C, 85000192

Grace Episcopal Church, Main and Park Ave., Buena Vista, 1/20/78, B, C, a, 78000834

Gray, Garret and Julia, Cottage, 125 E. 5th St., Salida, 9/12/80, B, C, 80000884

Heginbotham, W. E., House, 539 S. Baxter, Holyoke, 3/08/88, C, 88000170

Hortense Bridge [Vehicular Bridges in Colorado TR], CO 162, Nathrop vicinity, 2/04/85, A, C, 85000191

Hutchinson Ranch, 2 mi. E of Poncha Springs on U.S. 50, Poncha Springs vicinity, 5/11/73, A, C, 73000463

Littlejohn Mine Complex, SW of Granite, Granite vicinity, 12/27/78, A, C, 78000835

Manhattan Hotel, 225 F St., Salida, 4/21/83, C, 83001302

Ohio-Colorado Smelting and Refining Company Smokestack, NE of Salida at jct. of SR 150 and 152, Salida vicinity, 1/11/76, A, C, 76000548

Poncha Springs Schoolhouse, 330 Burnett St., Poncha Springs, 1/25/90, C, 89002375

Salida Downtown Historic District, Roughly bounded by Arkansas River, RR Track, 3rd and D Sts., Salida, 6/14/84, A, C, 84000800

St. Elmo Historic District, Pitkin, Gunnison, 1st., Main and Poplar Sts., St. Elmo, 9/17/79, A, C, 79000577

Vicksburg Mining Camp, 15 mi. NW of Buena Vista on SR 390, Buena Vista vicinity, 3/08/77, A, 77000364

Winfield Mining Camp, 15 mi. NW of Buena Vista, Buena Vista vicinity, 3/10/80, A, 80000883

Cheyenne County

Cheyenne County Courthouse, 51 S. 1st St., Cheyenne Wells, 7/27/89, A, C, 89000997

Cheyenne County Jail, 85 W. Second St., Cheyenne Wells, 6/16/88, A, C, 88000758

Clear Creek County

Alpine Hose Company No. 2, 507 5th St., Georgetown, 1/25/73, C, 73000464

Argo Tunnel and Mill, 2517 Riverside Dr., Idaho Springs, 1/31/78, A, 78000836

Evans, Anne, Mountain Home, Address Restricted, Evergreen vicinity, 1/28/92, B, C, 91001530

Evans-Elbert Ranch, Upper Bear Creek Rd., Idaho Springs vicinity, 9/11/80, A, C, 80000885

Georgetown Loop Railroad, Runs between Georgetown and Silver Plume, Georgetown vicinity, 12/18/70, A, C, 70000909

Georgetown-Silver Plume Historic District, I-70, Georgetown-Silver Plume vicinity, 11/13/66, A, NHL, 66000243

Grace Episcopal Church, Taos St., between 4th and 5th Sts., Georgetown, 8/14/73, A, C, a, 73000465

Hamill House, Argentine and 3rd Sts., Georgetown, 5/31/72, A, 72000267

Hotel de Paris, Alpine St., Georgetown, 4/28/70, B, C, 70000154

Idaho Springs Downtown Commercial District, Roughly bounded by Center Alley, 14th Ave., Riverside Dr., and Idaho St., Idaho Springs, 1/05/84, A, C, 84000801

Lebanon and Everett Mine Tunnels, NE of Silver Plume, adjacent to I-70 right-of-way, Silver Plume vicinity, 10/07/71, A, 71000214

McClellan House, 919 Taos St., Georgetown, 12/05/72, C, 72000268

Miner Street Bridge [Vehicular Bridges in Colorado TR], Miner St., Idaho Springs, 2/04/85, C, 85000193

Mint Saloon, 13 E. Park Ave. (US 40), Empire, 2/03/93, A, C, 92001845

Ore Processing Mill and Dam, 1 mi. SW of Georgetown off I-70, Georgetown vicinity, 5/06/71, A, 71000213

Peck House, 83 Sunny Ave., Empire, 3/25/93, A, C, 93000201

Silver Plume Depot, Off I-70, Silver Plume, 5/06/71, A, C, b, 71000215

Toll House, S side of Georgetown adjacent to I-70, Georgetown, 12/18/70, B, C, b, 70000155

Conejos County

Costilla Crossing Bridge [Vehicular Bridges in Colorado TR], Cty. Rd. over Rio Grande River, Antonito vicinity, 2/04/85, C, 85000194

Cumbres and Toltec Scenic Railroad, Between Antonito and Chama, NM, Antonito, vicinity, 2/16/73, A, C, 73000462

Engine No. 463, Off U.S. 285, Antonito, 5/12/75, A, C, 75000502

La Jara Depot, Broadway and Main Sts., La Jara, 5/12/75, A, C, 75000503

Pike's Stockade, 4 mi. E of Sanford on CO 136, Sanford vicinity, 10/15/66, A, B, f, NHL, 66000244

Warshauer Mansion, 515 River St., Antonito, 8/30/74, C, 74000564

Costilla County

Fort Garland, On CO 159, 1 block S of U.S. 10, Fort Garland, 2/26/70, A, 70000156

Plaza de San Luis de la Culebra, CO 159, San Luis, 12/22/78, A, C, 78000837

San Luis Bridge [Vehicular Bridges in Colorado TR], Off CO 159, San Luis, 2/04/85, C, 85000195

Smith-Gallego House, Main St., San Luis, 4/14/75, A, C, 75000504

Crowley County

Manzanola Bridge [Vehicular Bridges in Colorado TR], CO Hwy. 207, Manzanola vicinity, 6/24/85, C, b, 85001400

Custer County

Hope Lutheran Church, 310 S. 3rd St., Westcliffe, 1/31/78, A, a, 78000838

Mingus Homestead, Off CO 165 N of jct. with Ophir Cr. Rd., San Isabel NF, Beulah vicinity, 12/04/90, C, 90001791

National Hotel—Wolff Building, 201 Second St., Westcliffe, 11/05/87, C, 87001288

Westcliff School, 304 4th St., Westcliffe, 7/27/89, C, 89000999

Westcliffe Jail, 116 Second St., Westcliffe, 2/03/93, A, C, 92001846

Willows School, Willows Ln. (Co. Rd. 141) between Muddy Ln. (Co. Rd. 155) and Schoolfield Rd. (Co. Rd. 328), Westcliffe vicinity, 5/14/93, A, C, 93000413

Delta County

Curtis Hardware Store, 228 Grand Ave., Paonia, 10/19/89, A, C, 89001746

Delta Bridge [Vehicular Bridges in Colorado TR], U.S. Hwy 50, Delta, 2/04/85, A, C, 85000198

Delta County Bank Building, 301 and 305 Main St., Delta, 6/24/93, C, 93000577

Egyptian Theater, 452 Main St., Delta, 7/12/93, A, 93000575

Escalante Canon Bridge [Vehicular Bridges in Colorado TR], Cty. Rd. 650R, Delta vicinity, 2/04/85, A, C, b, 85000196

Ferganchick Orchard Rock Art Site, Address Restricted, Austin vicinity, 5/09/83, D, 83001304

First Methodist Episcopal Church of Delta, 199 E. Fifth St., Delta, 2/20/91, C, a, 91000069

Hotchkiss Bridge [Vehicular Bridges in Colorado TR], Cty. Rd. 3400R, Hotchkiss, 2/04/85, C, 85000199

Hotchkiss Hotel, 101 Bridge St., Hotchkiss, 9/20/84, A, 84000802

Roubideau Bridge [Vehicular Bridges in Colorado TR], Cty. Rd. G50R, Delta vicinity, 2/04/85, C, 85000197

US Post Office and Federal Building—Delta Main [US Post Offices in Colorado, 1900–1941, TR], 360 Meeker St., Delta, 1/24/86, A, C, g, 86000173

Denver County

14th Street Viaduct [Vehicular Bridges in Colorado TR], 14th St., Denver, 2/04/85, C, 85000200

19th Street Bridge [Vehicular Bridges in Colorado TR], 19th St., Denver, 2/04/85, C, 85000201

20th Street Viaduct [Vehicular Bridges in Colorado TR], 20th St., Denver, 2/04/85, A, C, 85000202

Alamo Placita Park [Denver Park and Parkway System TR], Roughly bounded by Speer Blvd., First Ave., and Clarkson St., Denver, 9/17/86, A, C, 86002242

All Saints Episcopal Church, 2222 W. 32nd Ave., Denver, 6/23/78, C, a, 78000839

Annunciation Church, 3601 Humboldt St., Denver, 6/21/90, A, C, a, 90000869

Arno Apartments, 325 E. Eighteenth Ave., Denver, 2/05/87, C, 87000009

Auraria 9th Street Historic District, 9th St. from Curtis to Champa St., Denver, 3/26/73, C, 73000466

Avoca Lodge, 2690 S. Wadsworth Blvd., Denver, 1/26/90, A, C, 89002373

Bailey House, 1600 Ogden St., Denver, 9/18/78, B, C, 78000840

Bancroft, Caroline, House, 1079–81 Downing St. and 1180 E. 11th, Denver, 8/29/90, B, C, g, 90001086

Bats Grocery Store, 4336 Clayton St., Denver, 1/28/88, A, C, 87002545

Beierle Farm [Denver International Airport MPS], Hudson Rd. just N of Irondale Rd., Watkins vicinity, 12/23/92, A, 92001673

Belcaro, 3400 Belcaro Dr., Denver, 2/10/75, B, g, 75000505

Berkeley Lake Park [Denver Park and Parkway System TR], Roughly bounded by N side of Berkeley Lake, Tennyson St., W. Forty-sixth Ave., and Sheridan Blvd., Denver, 9/17/86, A, C, 86002255

Boston Building, 828 17th St., Denver, 9/18/78, A, C, 78000841

Bouvier-Lothrop House, 1600 Emerson St., Denver, 9/04/80, A, C, 80000886

Bowman, William Norman, House—Yamecila, 325 King St., Denver, 3/14/91, A, C, a, 91000295

Brinker Collegiate Institute, 1725–1727 Tremont Pl., Denver, 10/28/77, A, 77000365

Broadway Bridge [Vehicular Bridges in Colorado TR], Broadway Ave., Denver, 2/04/85, C, 85000203

Brown Palace Hotel, 17th St. and Tremont Pl., Denver, 4/28/70, C, 70000157

Brown, J. S., Mercantile Building, 1634 18th St., Denver, 11/03/88, A, C, 88002375

Brown, Molly, House, 1340 Pennsylvania St., Denver, 2/01/72, C, 72000269

Buchtel Bungalow, 2100 S. Columbine St., Denver, 11/03/88, A, B, C, 88002383

Building at 1389 Stuart Street [West Colfax TR], 1389 Stuart St., Denver, 7/19/82, B, C, 82002287

Building at 1390 Stuart Street [West Colfax TR], 1390 Stuart St., Denver, 7/19/82, B, C, 82002288

Building at 1435 Stuart Street [West Colfax TR], 1435 Stuart St., Denver, 7/19/82, B, C, 82002289

Building at 1444 Stuart Street [West Colfax TR], 1444 Stuart St., Denver, 7/19/82, B, C, 82002290

Building at 1471 Stuart Street [West Colfax TR], 1471 Stuart St., Denver, 7/19/82, B, C, 82002291

Butters, Alfred, House, 1129 Pennsylvania, Denver, 10/29/82, B, C, 82004913

Byers-Evans House, 1310 Bannock St., Denver, 8/25/70, B, C, 70000158

Campbell, Richard Crawford, House, 909 York St., Denver, 7/03/79, A, C, g, 79000578

Carter-Rice Building, 1623-1631 Blake St., Denver, 9/20/84, C, 84000805

Cathedral of the Immaculate Conception, NE corner of Colfax Ave. and Logan St., Denver, 3/03/75, A, C, 75000506

Central Presbyterian Church, 1660 Sherman St., Denver, 11/21/74, C, a, 74000565

Chamberlin Observatory, 2930 E. Warren Ave., Denver, 3/27/80, A, C, 80000887

Chapel No. 1, Reeves St. on Lowry AFB, Denver, 5/06/82, A, C, a, g, 82002292

Chappell, Delos Allen, House, 1555 Race St., Denver, 6/03/82, B, C, a, 82002293

Cheesman Park [Denver Park and Parkway System TR], Roughly bounded by E. Thirteenth Ave., High St., E. Eigth Ave., and Franklin St., Denver, 9/17/86, A, C, 86002221

Cheesman Park Duplex, 1372 S. Pennsylvania St., Denver, 5/05/83, C, b, 83001306

Cheesman Park Esplanade [Denver Park and Parkway System TR], Roughly bounded by Eighth Ave., High St., Seventh Ave. Pkwy., and Williams St., Denver, 9/17/86, A, C, 86002218

Christ Methodist Episcopal Church, 2201 Ogden St., Denver, 11/07/76, A, 76000549

City Park [Denver Park and Parkway System TR], Roughly bounded by E. Twenty-third Ave., Colorado Blvd., E. Seventeenth Ave., and York St., Denver, 9/17/86, A, C, 86002190

City Park Esplanade [Denver Park and Parkway System TR], City Park Esplanade from E. Colfax Ave. to E. Seventeenth Ave., Denver, 9/17/86, A, C, 86002177

City Park Golf [Denver Park and Parkway System TR], Roughly bounded by E. Twenty-sixth Ave., Colorado Blvd., E. Twenty-third Ave., and York St., Denver, 9/17/86, A, C, 86002198

Civic Center Historic District, Roughly bounded by W. Colfax, E. Colfax, Grant, E. 14th, Broadway, E. 13th, W. 13th, Bannock, W. 14th, and Delaware, Denver, 2/27/74, A, C, f, 74002348

Clements Rowhouse, 2201-2217 Glenarm Pl., Denver, 9/12/80, C, 80000888

Clermont Street Parkway [Denver Park and Parkway System TR], Clermont St. Pkwy. from E. Third Ave. to E. Sixth Ave., Denver, 9/17/86, A, C, 86002215

Colorado Governor's Mansion, 400 E. 8th Ave., Denver, 12/03/69, C, 69000039

Denver County—Continued

Colorado State Capitol Annex Building and Boiler Plant, 1341 Sherman St., Denver, 6/24/91, A, C, 91000824

Cornwall Apartments, 1317 Ogden St., 912 E. 13th Ave., Denver, 10/08/76, B, C, 76000550

Country Club Historic District, Roughly bounded by 1st and 4th Aves., Race and Downing Sts., Denver, 7/10/79, A, C, 79000579

Country Club Historic District (Boundary Increase), Between Downing & University, E. 4th Ave. and N of Alameda Ave., Denver, 9/27/85, C, 85002587

Cranmer Park [Denver Park and Parkway System TR], Roughly bounded by E. Third Ave., Cherry St., E. First Ave., and Bellaire St., Denver, 9/17/86, A, C, 86002216

Crawford Hill Mansion, 969 Sherman St., Denver, 9/13/90, A, C, 90001417

Creswell Mansion, 1244 Grant St., Denver, 11/25/77, C, 77000366

Crocker, F. W., and Company Steam Cracker Factory, 1862 Blake St., Denver, 6/21/84, A, C, 84000808

Croke-Patterson-Campbell Mansion, 428–430 E. 11th Ave., Denver, 9/19/73, B, C, 73000467

Curry-Chucovich House, 1439 Court Pl., Denver, 6/09/78, B, C, 78000842

Curtis-Champa Streets District, Roughly bounded by Arapahoe, 30th, California, and 24th Sts., Denver, 4/01/75, C, 75000507

Curtis-Champa Streets Historic District (Boundary Increase), Roughly 30th, Stout, Downing and Arapahoe Sts., Denver, 9/22/83, C, 83001307

Daniels and Fisher Tower, 1101 16th St., Denver, 12/03/69, C, 69000040

Denver Athletic Club, 1325 Glenarm Pl., Denver, 11/14/79, A, C, 79000580

Denver City Cable Railway Building, 1801 Lawrence St., Denver, 7/02/79, A, C, 79000581

Denver City Railway Company Building, 1635 17th St., 1734-1736 Wynkoop St., Denver, 6/04/84, A, C, 84000810

Denver Civic Center Classroom Building, 1445 Cleveland Pl., Denver, 12/06/90, C, g, 90001346

Denver Dry Goods Company Building, 16th and California Sts., Denver, 1/09/78, A, 78000843

Denver Mint, W. Colfax Ave. and Delaware St., Denver, 2/01/72, A, C, 72000270

Denver Municipal Auditorium, 1323 Champa St., Denver, 10/16/91, A, 91001531

Denver Public Library, 1357 Broadway, Denver, 12/06/90, C, g, 90001345

Dow-Rosenzweig House, 1129 E. 17th Ave., Denver, 6/03/82, B, C, 82002294

Downing Street Parkway [Denver Park and Parkway System TR], Downing St. Pkwy. from E. Bayaud Ave. to E. Third Ave., Denver, 9/17/86, A, C, 86002228

Dunning-Benedict House, 1200 Pennsylvania St., Denver, 9/20/84, C, 84000811

Dunwoody, William J., House, 2637 W. 26th Ave., Denver, 4/11/79, B, C, 79000582

East Fourth Avenue Parkway [Denver Park and Parkway System TR], E. Fourth Ave. Pkwy. from Gilpin St. to Williams St., Denver, 9/17/86, A, C, 86002226

East Seventeenth Avenue Parkway [Denver Park and Parkway System TR], E. Seventeenth Ave. Pkwy. from Colorado Blvd. to Monaco St. Pkwy., Denver, 9/17/86, A, C, 86002200

East Seventh Avenue Parkway [Denver Park and Parkway System TR], E. Seventh Ave. Pkwy. from Williams St. to Colorado Blvd., Denver, 9/17/86, A, C, 86002217

East Sixth Avenue Parkway [Denver Park and Parkway System TR], E. Sixth Ave. Pkwy. from Colorado Blvd. to Quebec St., Denver, 9/17/86, A, C, 86002214

Elitch Theatre, W. 38th Ave. and Tennyson St., Denver, 3/21/78, A, B, C, 78000844

Elsner, John, House, 2810 Arapahoe St., Denver, 12/17/79, B, C, 79000583

Emmanuel Shearith Israel Chapel, 1201 10th St., Denver, 12/01/69, A, 69000041

Enterprise Hill Historic District, Bounded by 21st and 22nd Aves., Tremont and Glenarm Pls., Denver, 8/09/79, A, C, 79000584

Eppich Apartments, 1266 Emerson St., Denver, 1/05/84, C, 84000813

Equitable Building, 730 17th St., Denver, 1/09/78, C, 78000845

Evans Memorial Chapel, University of Denver campus, Denver, 12/27/74, A, b, 74000567

Evans School, 1115 Acoma St., Denver, 10/03/80, A, C, 80000889

Field, Eugene, House, 715 S. Franklin St., Denver, 11/01/74, B, C, b, 74000568

Fire Station No. 1, 1326 Tremont Pl., Denver, 11/14/79, A, C, 79000586

First Congregational Church, 980 Clarkson St., Denver, 11/16/87, C, a, 87002011

Fisher, William G., House, 1600 Logan St., Denver, 11/20/74, B, C, 74000569

Fitzroy Place, 2160 S. Cook St., Denver, 2/20/75, B, C, a, 75000508

Fleming-Hanington House, 1133 Pennsylvania, Denver, 10/29/82, C, 82001009

Flower, John S., House, 1618 Ogden St., Denver, 9/04/80, B, C, 80000890

Flower-Vaile House, 1610 Emerson St., Denver, 10/21/82, B, C, 82001010

Ford, Barney L., Building, 1514 Blake St., Denver, 6/24/76, B, 76000551

Ford, Justina, House, 3091 California St., Denver, 11/23/84, B, C, b, 84000244

Forest Street Parkway [Denver Park and Parkway System TR], Forest St. Pkwy. from Seventeenth Ave. to Montview Blvd., Denver, 9/17/86, A, C, 86002203

Foster, A. C., Building, 912 16th St., Denver, 1/09/78, B, C, 78000846

Foster, Ernest LeNeve, House, 2105 Lafayette St., Denver, 9/04/80, B, C, 80000891

Four-Mile House, 715 S. Forest St., Denver, 12/03/69, C, 69000042

Gebhard Mansion, 2253 Downing St., Denver, 10/01/92, C, 92001254

General Electric Building, 1441 18th St., Denver, 8/25/83, C, 83001308

Glenarm Place Historic Residential District, 2417-2462 Glenarm Pl., Denver, 8/25/83, C, 83001309

Grafton, The, 1001-1020 E. 17th Ave., Denver, 10/21/82, C, 82001011

Grant-Humphreys Mansion, 770 Pennsylvania St., Denver, 9/30/70, B, C, 70000160

Grimm, S. A., Block, 2031–2033 Curtis St., Denver, 6/25/92, C, 92000807

Guerrieri-Decunto House, 1650 Pennsylvania St., Denver, 9/10/79, B, C, 79000587

Hamburger, George, Block, 2199 Arapahoe, Denver, 1/25/90, C, 89002382

Hanigan—Canino Terrace, 1421–1435 W. Thirty-fifth Ave., Denver, 11/25/87, A, C, 87001289

Haskell House, 1651 Emerson St., Denver, 9/15/83, B, 83001310

Hendrie and Bolthoff Warehouse Building, 1743 Wazee, Denver, 2/09/88, A, C, 87002544

Highland Park [Denver Park and Parkway System TR], Roughly bounded by Highland Park Pl., Federal Blvd., and Fairview Pl., Denver, 9/17/86, A, C, 86002248

Highland Park Historic District, Bounded by Zuni St., Dunkeld Pl., Clay St., and 32nd Ave., Denver, 1/18/85, C, 85000082

Humboldt Street Historic District, Humboldt St. between E. 10th and E. 12th Sts., Denver, 12/29/78, B, C, 78000848

Hungarian Freedom Park [Denver Park and Parkway System TR], Roughly bounded by Speer Blvd., First Ave., and Clarkson St., Denver, 9/17/86, A, C, 86002244

Ideal Building, 821 17th St., Denver, 6/09/77, A, C, 77000367

Inspiration Point [Denver Park and Parkway System TR], Roughly bounded by W. Fiftieth Ave., Sheridan Blvd., W. Forty-ninth Ave., and Fenton St., Denver, 9/17/86, A, C, 86002259

Keating, Jeffery and Mary, House, 1207 Pennsylvania St., Denver, 10/22/80, B, C, 80000892

Kistler-Rodriguez House, 700 E. 9th Ave., Denver, 5/27/83, C, g, 83001311

Kittredge Building, 511 16th St., Denver, 12/02/77, C, 77000368

Lang, William, Townhouse, 1626 Washington St., Denver, 8/18/83, C, 83001312

Larimer Square, 1400 block of Larimer St., Denver, 5/07/73, A, C, 73000468

LeFevre, Owen E., House, 1311 York St., Denver, 8/13/76, B, C, 76000552

Littleton Creamery—Beatrice Foods Cold Storage Warehouse, 1801 Wynkoop St., Denver, 9/05/85, A, C, 85001952

Loretto Heights Academy, 3001 S. Federal Blvd., Denver, 9/18/75, A, B, C, a, 75000510

Masonic Temple Building, 1614 Welton St., Denver, 11/22/77, C, 77000369

McCourt, Peter, House, 1471 High St., Denver, 5/09/83, B, C, 83001313

McPhee and McGinnity Building, 2301 Blake St., Denver, 9/20/84, A, C, 84000816

Midwest Steel and Iron Works Company Complex, 25 Larimer St., Denver, 4/10/85, A, 85000858

Denver County—Continued

Moffat Station, 2105 15th St., Denver, 10/22/76, B, 76000553

Monaco Street Parkway [Denver Park and Parkway System TR], Monaco St. Pkwy. from E. First Ave. to Montview Blvd., Denver, 9/17/86, A, C, 86002207

Montclair Park [Denver Park and Parkway System TR], Roughly bounded by E. Twelfth Ave., Onieda St., and Richthofen Pkwy., Denver, 9/17/86, A, C, 86002213

Montgomery Court, 215 E. Eleventh Ave., Denver, 10/02/86, C, 86002810

Montview Boulevard [Denver Park and Parkway System TR], Montview Blvd. from Colorado Blvd. to Monaco St. Pkwy., Denver, 10/01/86, A, C, 86002205

Moore, Dora, Elementary School, E. 9th Ave. and Corona St., Denver, 6/09/78, B, C, 78000849

Neef, Frederick W., House, 2143 Grove St., Denver, 10/25/79, B, C, 79000588

Neusteter Building, 720 Sixteenth St., Denver, 11/30/87, A, C, 87002070

New Terrace, 900–914 E. Twentieth Ave., Denver, 2/05/87, C, 87000008

Niblock—Yacovetta Terrace, 1301–1319 W. Thirty-fifth Ave., Denver, 6/27/86, A, 86001450

Norman Apartments, 99 S. Downing St., Denver, 12/22/83, C, 83003509

Old Highland Business District, 15th and Boulder Sts., Denver, 7/17/79, A, C, 79000589

Orlando Flats, 2330 Washington St., Denver, 2/16/84, A, 84000818

Oxford Hotel, 1612 17th St., Denver, 4/17/79, A, C, 79000590

Pacific Express Stable, 2363 Blake St., Denver, 9/20/84, A, C, 84000821

Palmer, Judge Peter L. House, 1250 Ogden St., Denver, 10/21/82, C, 82001012

Palmer—Ferril House, 2123 Downing St., Denver, 11/03/92, B, g, 92001408

Paramount Theater, 519 16th St., Denver, 11/21/80, C, 80000893

Pearce-McAllister Cottage, 1880 Gaylord St., Denver, 6/20/72, C, 72000271

Peters Paper Company Warehouse, 1625–1631 Wazee St., Denver, 6/16/88, A, C, 88000757

Pierce-Haley House, 857 Grant St., Denver, 10/03/84, C, 84000583

Potter Highlands Historic District, Roughy bounded by W. Thirty-eighth, Zuni, and W. Thirty-second Sts., and Federal Blvd., Denver, 1/22/86, A, C, 86000097

Public Service Building, 910 15th St., Denver, 7/20/78, C, 78000851

Raymond, Wilbur S., House, 1572 Race St., Denver, 11/21/74, A, C, 74000570

Richthofen Castle, 7020 E. 12th Ave., Denver, 4/21/75, B, C, 75000511

Richthofen Monument [Denver Park and Parkway System TR], Richthofen Pkwy. at Oneida St., Denver, 9/17/86, A, C, 86002212

Richthofen Place Parkway [Denver Park and Parkway System TR], Richthofen Pl. Pkwy.

from Monaco St. Pkwy. to Oneida St., Denver, 9/17/86, A, C, 86002209

Rocky Mountain Hotel, 2301 7th St., Denver, 4/21/83, A, 83001314

Rocky Mountain Lake Park [Denver Park and Parkway System TR], Roughly bounded by I-70, Federal Blvd., W. Forty-sixth Ave., and Lowell Blvd., Denver, 9/17/86, A, C, 86002250

Root, Amos H., Building, 1501–1529 Platte St., Denver, 3/27/80, B, C, 80000894

Saint Thomas Theological Seminary, 1300 S. Steele, Denver, 7/27/89, A, C, a, 89001007

San Rafael Historic District, Roughly bounded by E. Twenty-sixth Ave., Downing St., E. Twentieth Ave., and Washington St., Denver, 6/20/86, C, 86001353

Schleier, George, Mansion, 1665 Grant St., Denver, 11/17/77, B, C, 77000370

Schlessinger House, 1544 Race St., Denver, 11/14/79, B, C, 79000591

Schmidt, George, House, 2345 7th St., Denver, 10/29/76, B, C, 76000554

Shorthorn Building, 2257 Larimer St., Denver, 11/14/79, B, C, 79000592

Smith House, 1801 York St., Denver, 9/26/85, C, 85002566

Smith's Irrigation Ditch, Washington Park, Denver, 10/08/76, C, 76000555

Smith, Pierce T., House, 1751 Gilpin St., Denver, 9/20/84, C, 84000823

South Marion Street Parkway [Denver Park and Parkway System TR], S. Marion St. Pkwy. from E. Virginia Ave. to E. Bayaud Ave. at Downing St., Denver, 9/17/86, A, C, 86002239

South Side—Baker Historic District, Roughly bounded by W. Fifth Ave., Broadway, W. Alameda Ave., and W. Fox St., Denver, 10/03/85, C, 85002932

Speer Boulevard [Denver Park and Parkway System TR], Speer Blvd. from W. Colfax Ave. to Downing St., Denver, 9/17/86, A, C, 86002240

Spratlen-Anderson Wholesale Grocery Company—Davis Brothers Warehouse, 1450 Wynkoop St., Denver, 12/03/85, C, 85003061

St. Andrews Episcopal Church, 2015 Glenarm Pl., Denver, 3/18/75, C, a, 75000512

St. Elizabeth's Church, 1062 11th St., Denver, 12/01/69, C, a, 69000043

St. Elizabeth's Retreat Chapel, 2825 W. 32nd Ave., Denver, 5/24/76, A, C, a, 76000556

St. John's Cathedral, 14th and Washington Sts., Denver, 8/01/75, B, C, a, 75000513

St. Joseph's Polish Roman Catholic Church, 517 E. 46th Ave, Denver, 4/21/83, A, a, g, 83001315

St. Joseph's Roman Catholic Church of Denver, 600 Galapago, Denver, 6/03/82, A, C, a, 82002295

St. Mark's Parish Church, 1160 Lincoln St., Denver, 9/18/75, A, C, a, 75000514

St. Patrick Mission Church, 3325 Pecos St., Denver, 11/14/79, A, B, C, a, 79000593

Stearns House, 1030 Logan St., Denver, 6/03/82, C, 82002296

Stonemen's Row Historic District, South side 28th Ave. between Umatilla and Vallejo Sts., Denver, 1/05/84, C, 84000824

Sugar Building, 1530 16th St., Denver, 2/17/78, A, B, 78000852

Sunken Gardens [Denver Park and Parkway System TR], Roughly bounded by Speer Blvd., W. Eighth Ave., Delaware, and Elati Sts., Denver, 9/17/86, A, C, 86002247

Swallow Hill Historic District, Roughly Bounded by Clarkson St., E. Seventeenth Ave., Downing St., E Colfax Ave., Denver, 1/07/88, C, 87002295

Tallmadge and Boyer Block, 2926-2942 Zuni St., Denver, 10/21/82, C, 82001013

Tears-McFarlane House, 1200 Williams St., Denver, 1/11/76, B, C, 76000557

Temple Emanuel, 24 Curtis St., Denver, 10/10/78, A, C, a, e, 78000853

Temple Emanuel, 1595 Pearl St., Denver, 11/25/87, C, a, 87001554

Thomas, H. H., House, 2104 Glenarm Pl., Denver, 5/30/75, B, C, 75000515

Tivoli Brewery Company, 1320–1348 10th St., Denver, 4/11/73, A, C, 73000469

Tramway Building, 1100 14th St., Denver, 1/05/78, A, B, C, 78000854

Treat Hall, E. 18th Ave. and Pontiac St., Denver, 8/10/78, A, C, 78000855

Trinity United Methodist Church, E. 18th Ave. and Broadway, Denver, 7/28/70, A, C, a, 70000161

U.S. Customhouse, 721 19th St., Denver, 10/16/79, C, g, 79000594

U.S. Post Office and Federal Building, 18th and Stout Sts., Denver, 3/20/73, C, 73000470

Union Station, 17th St. at Wynkoop, Denver, 11/20/74, A, C, 74000571

Union Warehouse, 1514 17th St., Denver, 6/03/82, A, C, 82002297

University Boulevard [Denver Park and Parkway System TR], University Blvd. from E. Iowa Ave. to E. Alameda Ave., Denver, 9/17/86, A, C, 86002237

Vine Street Houses, 1415, 1429, 1435, 1441, 1453 Vine St., Denver, 12/16/74, A, C, 74000572

Washington Park [Denver Park and Parkway System TR], Roughly bounded by E. Virginia Ave., S. Franklin St., E. Louisiana Ave., and S. Downing St., Denver, 9/17/86, A, C, 86002238

Weckbaugh House, 1701 E. Cedar Ave., Denver, 1/16/84, C, 84000826

West Forty-sixth Avenue Parkway [Denver Park and Parkway System TR], W. Forty-sixth Ave. Pkwy. from Stuart St. to Grove St., Denver, 9/17/86, A, C, 86002249

Westside Neighborhood, 1311–1466 Lipan St., 1305–1370 Kalamath St., 931–1126 W. 14th Ave., 1312–1438 Maraposa St., & 1008-1118 W. 13th Ave., Denver, 4/17/75, A, C, 75000516

Williams Street Parkway [Denver Park and Parkway System TR], Williams St. Pkwy. from E. Fourth Ave. to E. Eighth Ave., Denver, 9/17/86, A, C, 86002222

Wood-Morris-Bonfils House, 707 Washington St., Denver, 12/04/74, B, C, 74000573

Zang, Adolph J., House, 1532 Emerson St., Denver, 11/14/79, B, C, 79000596

Zang, Adolph, Mansion, 709 Clarkson St., Denver, 11/23/77, B, C, a, 77000371

Denver County—Continued

Zeitz Buckhorn Exchange, 1000 Osage St., Denver, 4/21/83, A, B, g, 83001292

Dolores County

Beaver Creek Massacre Site, Address Restricted, Dolores vicinity, 10/02/86, A, D, 86002670

Kauffman, William, House, Silver St., Rico, 10/29/82, C, 82001014

Rico City Hall, NE corner of Commercial and Mantz Sts., Rico, 12/31/74, A, C, 74000574

Douglas County

Bear Canon Agricultural District, S of Denver on both sides of CO 105 from CO 67 S to Jarre Creek, Denver vicinity, 10/29/75, A, C, 75000517

Castle Rock Depot, 420 Elbert St., Castle Rock, 10/11/74, A, C, b, 74000575

Castle Rock Elementry School, 3rd and Cantril Sts., Castle Rock, 9/20/84, C, 84000827

Church of St. Philip-in-the-Field and Bear Canon Cemetery, 5 mi. S of Sedalia on CO 105, Sedalia vicinity, 4/11/73, A, C, a, d, 73000471

Glen Grove School, N of Palmer Lake off Perry Park Rd., Palmer Lake vicinity, 11/05/74, C, 74000576

Hammar, Benjamin, House, 203 Cantril St., Castle Rock, 2/03/93, C, 92001847

Indian Park School, 10 mi. (16 km) W of Sedalia on CO 67, Sedalia vicinity, 2/08/78, A, 78000857

Kinner, John, House, 6694 Perry Park Rd., Sedalia vicinity, 10/11/74, B, C, 74000578

Pike's Peak Grange No. 163, 3093 CO 83, Franktown vicinity, 10/01/90, A, C, 90001502

Quick, Ben, Ranch and Fort, 6695 W. Plum Creek Rd., Palmer Lake vicinity, 10/01/74, A, B, C, 74000577

Roxborough State Park Archaeological District, Address Restricted, Waterton vicinity, 1/27/83, A, C, D, 83001316

Ruth Memorial Methodist Episcopal Church, 19670 E. Mainstreet, Parker, 5/01/89, A, C, a, 89000332

Sinclaire, Reginald, House, 6154 Perry Park Rd., Larkspur, 9/20/91, C, 91001418

Spring Valley School, E of Larkspur at Spring Valley and Lorraine Rds., Larkspur vicinity, 12/18/78, A, C, 78000856

Eagle County

Archeological Site 5EA484, Address Restricted, Basalt vicinity, 5/10/82, D, 82002299

Camp Hale Site, Address Restricted, Leadville vicinity, 4/10/92, A, g, 78003522

First Evangelical Lutheran Church, 400 2nd St., Gypsum, 6/24/93, C, a, 93000576

Red Cliff Bridge [Vehicular Bridges in Colorado TR], U.S. 24, Red Cliff vicinity, 2/04/85, C, g, 85000204

State Bridge [Vehicular Bridges in Colorado TR], Off CO 131, State Bridge, 6/24/85, A, C, 85001401

Waterwheel, SE of McCoy at Colorado River, McCoy vicinity, 4/11/77, A, 77000372

Woods Lake Resort, 11 mi. N of Thomasville at Woods Lake, Thomasville vicinity, 8/11/88, A, C, 88001226

Yarmony Archeological Site [Archaic Period Architectural Sites in Colorado MPS], Address Restricted, Radium vicinity, 5/28/91, C, D, 91000615

El Paso County

Alamo Hotel, 128 S. Tejon St., Colorado Springs, 9/14/77, A, 77000373

Atchison, Topeka and Santa Fe Passenger Depot, 555 E. Pikes Peak Ave., Colorado Springs, 9/10/79, C, 79000597

Barker House, 819 Manitou, Manitou Springs, 10/11/79, B, C, 79000604

Bemis, Judson Moss, House, 506 N. Cascade Ave., Colorado Springs, 9/14/79, B, C, 79000598

Black Forest School, 6770 Shoup Rd., Colorado Springs, 11/03/92, A, C, a, 92001407

Boulder Crescent Place Historic District, 9 and 11 W. Boulder St. and 312, 318, and 320 N. Cascade, Colorado Springs, 9/10/87, A, C, 87001555

Briarhurst, 404 Manitou Ave., Manitou Springs, 4/23/73, B, C, 73000473

Bridge over Fountain Creek [Vehicular Bridges in Colorado TR], Rt. 24, Manitou Springs, 2/04/85, A, C, 85000206

Burgess House, 730 N. Nevada Ave., Colorado Springs, 9/13/90, A, C, 90001418

Carlton House, Pine Valley, US Air Force Academy, Colorado Springs vicinity, 11/03/89, C, 89001785

Chambers Ranch, 3202 Chambers Way, Colorado Springs, 11/29/79, A, B, C, 79000599

City Hall of Colorado City, 2902 W. Colorado Ave., Colorado Springs, 6/03/82, A, C, a, 82002300

Claremont, 21 Broadmoor Ave., Colorado Springs, 4/13/77, C, 77000374

Cliff House, 306 Canon Ave., Manitou Springs, 3/27/80, A, C, 80000897

Colorado Springs Day Nursery, 104 E. Rio Grande St., Colorado Springs, 2/23/90, A, C, 90000304

Colorado Springs Fine Arts Center, 30 W. Dale St., Colorado Springs, 7/03/86, B, C, 86001455

Crystal Valley Cemetery [Manitou Springs MRA], Plainview Ave., Manitou Springs, 11/18/82, C, d, 82001015

Cutler Hall [Colorado College TR], 912 N. Cascade Ave., Colorado Springs, 7/03/86, A, C, 86001410

DeGraff Building, 116-118 N. Tejon, Colorado Springs, 8/18/83, C, 83001293

El Paso County Courthouse, 215 S. Tejon St., Colorado Springs, 9/29/72, A, C, 72000272

Emmanuel Presbyterian Church, 419 Mesa Rd., Colorado Springs, 5/17/84, C, a, 84000830

Evergreen Cemetery, 1005 S. Hancock Ave., Colorado Springs, 2/11/93, A, C, d, 93000035

First Congregational Church, 101 Pawnee Ave., Manitou Springs, 10/16/79, A, C, a, 79000606

First Presbyterian Church of Ramah, 113 S. Commercial St., Ramah, 7/07/88, C, a, 88001015

Giddings Building, 101 N. Tejon St., Colorado Springs, 4/21/83, B, C, 83001294

Glen Eyrie, 3280 N. 30th St., Colorado Springs, 4/21/75, B, C, a, 75000519

Gwynne—Love House, 730 N. Cascade Ave., Colorado Springs, 2/05/87, C, 87000010

Hagerman Mansion, 610 N. Cascade Ave., Colorado Springs, 9/20/84, B, C, 84000831

Keithley Log Cabin Development District [Manitou Springs MRA], Roughly bounded by Santa Fe Pl., Crystal Rd., and Spur Rd., Manitou Springs, 11/18/82, A, C, 82001016

Lewis, Inez Johnson, School, 146 Jefferson St., Monument, 11/03/88, A, 88002306

Manitou Bathhouse, 934 Manitou Ave., Manitou Springs, 8/01/79, A, C, 79000608

Manitou Springs Bridges (2) [Vehicular Bridges in Colorado TR], Park Ave. and Cannon Ave. over Fountain Creek, Manitou Springs, 6/24/85, C, 85001398

Manitou Springs Historic District [Manitou Springs MRA], Roughly bounded by El Paso Blvd., Ruxton Ave., US 24, and Iron Mt. Ave., Manitou Springs, 10/07/83, A, C, 83003516

McAllister House, 423 N. Cascade Ave., Colorado Springs, 8/14/73, B, C, 73000472

Midland Terminal Railroad Roundhouse, 600 S. 21st St., Colorado Springs, 7/10/79, A, C, 79000600

Miramont, 9 Capitol Hill, Manitou Springs, 4/11/77, B, C, a, 77000375

Montgomery Hall, Colorado College [Colorado College MPS], 1030 N. Cascade Ave., Colorado Springs, 9/13/90, A, C, 90001419

Navajo Hogan, 2817 N. Nevada Ave., Colorado Springs, 9/13/90, A, C, 90001420

North End Historic District, Roughly bounded by Monument Valley Wood, Nevada Ave., Madison and Unitah Sts., Colorado Springs, 12/17/82, A, C, 82001017

North Weber Street-Wahsatch Avenue Historic Residential District, N. Weber St. between Boulder and Del Norte St., and N. Wahsatch Ave. between St. Vrain and Columbia St., Colorado Springs, 2/08/85, C, 85000205

Old Colorado City Historic Commercial District, N side of Colorado Ave. from 24th St., W to 2611 Colorado Ave., also includes 115 S. 26 St. and 2418 W. Pikes Peak Ave., Colorado Springs, 11/02/82, A, C, 82001018

Old Livery Stable, 217 W. Missouri, Fountain, 3/02/79, C, 79000603

Palmer Hall [Colorado College TR], 116 E. San Rafael, Colorado Springs, 7/03/86, A, C, 86001412

Pikes Peak, 15 mi. W of Colorado Springs in Pike National Forest, Colorado Springs vicinity, 10/15/66, A, NHL, 66000245

El Paso County—Continued

Pioneer Cabin, 11 mi. N of Colorado Springs off I-25 on grounds of U.S. Air Force Academy, Colorado Springs vicinity, 1/27/75, C, 75000520

Plaza Hotel, 830 N. Tejon St., Colorado Springs, 9/01/83, C, 83001317

Rio Grande Engine No. 168, 9 S. Sierra Madre, Colorado Springs, 8/10/79, A, C, 79000601

Second Midland School, 815 S. 25th St., Colorado Springs, 9/12/80, A, C, 80000895

St. Mary's Catholic Church, 26 W. Kiowa St., Colorado Springs, 6/03/82, A, C, a, 82002301

Stockbridge House, 2801 W. Colorado Ave., Colorado Springs, 9/11/80, B, C, 80000896

US Post Office and Federal Courthouse—Colorado Springs Main [US Post Offices in Colorado, 1900–1941, TR], 210 Pikes Peak Ave., Colorado Springs, 1/22/86, A, C, 86000170

US Post Office—Manitou Springs Main [US Post Offices in Colorado, 1900–1941, TR], 307 Canon Ave., Mainitou Springs, 1/24/86, A, C, g, 86000181

Wheeler Bank, 717–719 Manitou Ave., Manitou Springs, 9/12/80, B, C, 80000898

Y.W.C.A., 130 E. Kiowa St., Colorado Springs, 9/10/79, A, C, 79000602

Elbert County

St. Mark United Presbyterian Church, 225 Main St., Elbert, 9/18/80, A, C, a, 80000899

Fremont County

Bridge No. 10/Adelaide Bridge [Vehicular Bridges in Colorado TR], Fremont Cty. Rd., Florence vicinity, 2/04/85, C, 85000208

Canon City Downtown Historic District, Roughly Main St. from 3rd to 9th Sts. and Macon Ave., Canon City, 10/20/83, A, C, 83003517

Canon City Downtown Historic District (Boundary Increase), 602 Macon Ave., Canon City, 2/06/86, A, C, 86000201

Canon City Municipal Building, 612 Royal Gorge Blvd., Canon City, 8/18/83, C, 83001318

First Presbyterian Church, Macon and 7th Sts., Canon City, 9/01/83, C, a, 83001319

Fourth Street Bridge [Vehicular Bridges in Colorado TR], 4th St., Canon City, 2/04/85, C, 85000207

Holy Cross Abbey, US 50, Canon City, 8/18/83, A, C, a, 83001320

Howard Bridge [Vehicular Bridges in Colorado TR], Off U.S. 50, Howard, 2/04/85, C, 85000209

McClure House, 323-331 Main St., Canon City, 9/14/79, B, C, 79000609

Portland Bridge [Vehicular Bridges in Colorado TR], SR 120, Portland, 2/04/85, C, 85000210

Robison Mansion, 12 Riverside Dr., Canon City, 10/11/84, A, C, 84000022

Royal Gorge Bridge and Incline Railway, NW of Canon City, Canon City vicinity, 9/02/83, A, C, 83001303

US Post Office and Federal Building—Canon City Main [US Post Offices in Colorado, 1900–1941, TR], Fifth St. and Macon Ave., Canon City, 1/22/86, C, 86000167

US Post Office—Florence Main [US Post Offices in Colorado, 1900–1941, TR], 121 N. Pikes Peak St., Florence, 1/22/86, A, C, 86000174

Garfield County

Battlement Mesa Schoolhouse, 7201 300 Rd., Battlement Mesa, 4/21/83, C, 83001295

Havemeyer-Willcox Canal Pumphouse and Forebay, W of Rifle, Rifle vicinity, 4/22/80, A, C, 80000900

Hotel Colorado, 526 Pine St., Glenwood Springs, 5/26/77, A, B, 77000376

Rifle Bridge [Vehicular Bridges in Colorado TR], Off SR 6/24 over Colorado River, Rifle, 2/04/85, C, 85000213

Satank Bridge [Vehicular Bridges in Colorado TR], Cty. Rd. 106, Carbondale vicinity, 2/04/85, C, 85000211

South Canon Bridge [Vehicular Bridges in Colorado TR], Cty. Rd. 134, Glenwood Springs vicinity, 2/04/85, C, 85000212

Starr Manor, 901 Palmer Ave., Glenwood Springs, 6/20/86, C, 86001350

Taylor, Edward T., House, 903 Bennett Ave., Glenwood Springs, 10/14/86, B, g, 86002807

US Post Office—Rifle Main [US Post Offices in Colorado, 1900–1941, TR], Railroad Ave. and Fourth St., Rifle, 1/24/86, C, g, 86000186

Gilpin County

Central City Opera House, Eureka St., Central City, 1/18/73, A, C, 73000474

Central City—Black Hawk Historic District On SR 119, Central City, 10/15/66, A, NHL, 66000246

Teller House, Eureka St., Central City, 1/18/73, C, 73000475

Winks Panorama, SW of Pinecliffe, Pinecliffe vicinity, 3/28/80, A, 80000901

Grand County

Cozens Ranch House, CO 40 1 1/2 mi. S of Fraser, Fraser, 6/09/88, A, B, C, 88000709

Dutchtown [Rocky Mountain National Park MRA], Ditch Rd., Grand Lake vicinity, 1/29/88, A, NPS, 76002292

Grand Lake Lodge, 15500 US 34, Grand Lake, 7/22/93, A, C, 93000663

Grand River Ditch [Rocky Mountain National Park MRA (AD)], N of Grand Lake, Grand Lake vicinity, 9/29/76, C, NPS, 76000218

Holzwarth Historic District [Rocky Mountain National Park MRA (AD)], N of Grand Lake on Trail Ridge Rd., Grand Lake vicinity, 12/02/77, A, g, NPS, 77000112

Kauffman House, NW corner of Pitkin and Lake Ave., Grand Lake, 11/21/74, B, C, 74000579

Lulu City Site [Rocky Mountain National Park MRA (AD)], N of Grand Lake on Trail Ridge Rd., Grand Lake vicinity, 9/14/77, A, NPS, 77001562

Milner Pass Road Camp Mess Hall and House [Rocky Mountain National Park MRA], Milner Pass Rd., Estes Park vicinity, 7/20/87, C, NPS, 87001130

Shadow Mountain Lookout [Rocky Mountain National Park MRA (AD)], SE of Grand Lake in Rocky Mountain National Park, Grand Lake vicinity, 8/02/78, A, C, g, NPS, 78000279

Timber Creek Campground Comfort Station No. 245 [Rocky Mountain National Park MRA], Timber Creek Campground, Estes Park vicinity, 1/29/88, C, g, NPS, 87001131

Timber Creek Campground Comfort Station No. 246 [Rocky Mountain National Park MRA], Timber Creek Campground, Estes Park vicinity, 1/29/88, C, g, NPS, 87001132

Timber Creek Campground Comfort Station No. 247 [Rocky Mountain National Park MRA], Timber Creek Campground, Estes Park vicinity, 1/29/88, C, g, NPS, 87001133

Timber Creek Road Camp Barn [Rocky Mountain National Park MRA], Timber Creek Rd., Estes Park vicinity, 7/30/87, C, NPS, 87001134

Timberline Cabin [Rocky Mountain National Park MRA], Fall River Rd., Estes Park vicinity, 1/29/88, A, C, NPS, 87001136

Yust, E. C., Homestead, S of Kremmling off CO 9, Kremmling vicinity, 10/29/82, C, 82001019

Gunnison County

Crystal Mill, Cty. Rd. 3, 7 mi. SE of Marble, Crystal vicinity, 7/05/85, A, 85001493

Curecanti Archeological District, Address Restricted, Gunnison vicinity, 8/15/84, D, NPS, 84000852

Fisher-Zugelder House and Smith Cottage, 601 N. Wisconsin St., Gunnison, 1/05/84, C, 84000853

Marble High School [Marble MPS], 412 Main St., Marble, 8/03/89, A, C, 89000989

Marble Mill Site, Park and W. 3rd Sts., Marble, 2/07/79, A, 79000610

Marble Town Hall [Marble MPS], 407 Main St., Marble, 8/03/89, A, C, b, 89000988

Parry, William D., House [Marble MPS], 115 Main St., Marble, 8/03/89, A, C, 89000987

St. Paul's Church [Marble MPS], 123 State St., Marble, 8/03/89, A, C, a, b, 89000990

Town of Crested Butte, Roughly bounded by Butte and Belleview Aves., 1st and 4th Sts., Creted Butte, 5/29/74, C, a, g, 74002279

Webster Building, 229 N. Main St., Gunnison, 5/17/84, A, C, 84000857

Hinsdale County

Lake City Historic District, CO 149, Lake City, 12/01/78, A, C, a, 78000859
Rose Lime Kiln, Co. Rd. 20 SW of Lake City, Lake City vicinity, 4/08/93, A, B, C, 93000293

Huerfano County

Francisco Plaza, 312 S. Main St., Le Veta, 10/23/86, A, C, 86002950
Huerfano County Courthouse and Jail, 400 Main St., Walsenburg, 4/23/73, C, 73000476
La Veta Pass Narrow Gauge Railroad Depot, Off U.S. 160, La Veta, 6/06/80, A, C, 80000902
Lamme Hospital, 314 S. Main St., La Veta, 12/10/93, A, 93001376

Jefferson County

Ammunition Igloo [Camp George West MPS], 15001 Denver W. Pkwy., Golden, 5/20/93, A, C, 93000379
Arvada Flour Mill, 5580 Wadsworth Blvd., Arvada, 4/24/75, A, C, 75000521
Astor House Hotel, 822 12th St., Golden, 3/01/73, A, C, 73000478
Bear Creek Canyon Scenic Mountain Drive [Denver Mountain Parks MPS], CO 74 section between Morrison and Idledale, Morrison vicinity, 11/15/90, A, C, 90001706
Bergen Park [Denver Mountain Parks MPS], CO 74 S of I-40, Evergreen vicinity, 11/15/90, A, C, 90001707
Blue Jay Inn, Hwy. 126, Buffalo Creek, 10/01/74, A, 74000580
Bradford House III Archeological Site, Address Restricted, Morrison vicinity, 4/08/80, D, 80000906
Camp George West Historic District [Camp George West MPS], 15000 S. Golden Rd., Golden vicinity, 2/11/93, A, C, 92001865
Colorado Amphitheater [Camp George West MPS], 15001 Denver W. Pkwy., Golden, 5/20/93, A, C, 93000378
Colorado National Guard Armory, 1301 Arapahoe St., Golden, 12/18/78, A, C, 78000860
Colorow Point Park [Denver Mountain Parks MPS], 900 Colorow Rd., Golden vicinity, 11/15/90, A, C, 90001712
Corwina Park, O'Fallon Park, Pence Park [Denver Mountain Parks MPS], Roughly, area SE of jct. of Kittredge and Myers Gulch Rds., Evergreen vicinity, 12/28/90, A, C, 90001708
Dedisse Park [Denver Mountain Parks MPS], 29614 Upper Bear Creek Rd., Evergreen vicinity, 11/15/90, A, C, 90001709
Evergreen Conference District, CO 74, Evergreen, 5/01/79, A, B, a, 79000611
Everhardt Ranch, SE of Evergreen, Evergreen vicinity, 5/07/80, A, 80000903

First Presbyterian Church of Golden—Unger House, 809 15th St., Golden, 3/14/91, A, C, a, 91000294
Genesee Park [Denver Mountain Parks MPS], 26771 Genesee Ln., Golden vicinity, 11/15/90, A, C, 90001710
Green Mercantile Store, NW of Buffalo Creek, Buffalo Creek vicinity, 10/01/74, A, 74000581
Green Mountain Ranch, S of Buffalo Creek on Hwy. 126, Buffalo Creek vicinity, 10/01/74, A, 74000582
Hildebrande Ranch, 7 mi. SW of Littleton off Deer Creek Canyon Rd., Littleton vicinity, 3/13/75, A, 75000524
Hiwan Homestead, Meadow Dr., Evergreen, 4/09/74, A, C, 74000583
Humphrey House, 620 S. Soda Creek Rd., Evergreen, 12/31/74, C, 74000584
Jewish Consuptives' Relief Society, 6401 W. Colfax Ave., Lakewood, 6/26/80, A, C, a, 80000905
La Hacienda, On SR off U.S. 285, Buffalo Creek, 7/20/73, A, C, 73000477
Lariat Trail Scenic Mountain Drive [Denver Mountain Parks MPS], Lookout Mountain Rd. S of US 6 to Golden Reservoir, Golden vicinity, 11/15/90, A, C, 90001711
Lookout Mountain Park [Denver Mountain Parks MPS], 987 1/2 Lookout Mountain Rd., Golden vicinity, 11/15/90, A, C, 90001713
Lorraine Lodge, SW of Golden, Golden vicinity, 1/18/84, C, 84000858
Magic Mountain Site, Address Restricted, Golden vicinity, 8/21/80, D, 80000904
Midway House, 9345 U.S. 285, Conifer vicinity, 9/18/90, A, C, 90001479
Morrison Historic District, CO 8, Morrison, 9/28/76, A, B, 76000561
Morrison Schoolhouse, 226 Spring St., Morrison, 9/04/74, A, 74000585
Mount Vernon House, About 1 mi. S of Golden city limits at jct. of I-70, CO 26 and Mount Vernon Canyon Rd., Golden vicinity, 11/20/70, A, C, 70000162
North Fork Historic District, Both sides of South Platte River from Pine to South Platte, in Red Pike National Forest, Pine and South Platte, 10/09/74, A, 74000586
Peterson House, E of Morrison on Morrison Rd., Morrison vicinity, 9/10/81, C, 81000184
Pioneer Sod House, 4610 Robb St., Wheat Ridge, 3/14/73, C, 73000479
Red Rocks Park District [Denver Mountain Parks MPS], 16351 Co. Rd. 93, Morrison, 5/18/90, A, C, 90000725
Richards Mansion, 5349 W. 27th Ave., Wheat Ridge, 9/15/77, B, C, 77000379
Rooney Ranch, S of Golden, jct. of Rooney Rd. and Alameda Pkwy., Golden vicinity, 2/13/75, A, C, 75000522
Russell-Graves House, 5605 Yukon St., Arvada, 5/09/83, B, C, 83001296
Stone House, S of Lakewood off of S. Wadsworth Blvd., Lakewood vicinity, 5/01/75, A, C, 75000523
Tower of Memories, 8500 W. Twenty-ninth Ave., Denver, 9/25/87, C, d, 87001725

Twelfth Street Historic Residential District, Roughly bounded by 11th, 13th, Elm, and Arapahoe Sts., Golden, 9/22/83, A, C, 83001321

Kit Carson County

Burlington State Armory, 191 14th St., Burlington, 9/20/84, A, C, 84000859
Elitch Gardens Carousel, Kit Carson County Fairgrounds, Burlington, 12/19/78, A, C, NHL, 78000861
Flagler Hospital, 311 Main Ave., P.O. Box 126, Flagler, 1/30/91, B, g, 90001421
Winegar Building, 494–498 Fourteenth St., Burlington, 5/22/86, B, 86001123

La Plata County

Colorado Ute Power Plant, 14th St. and Animas River, Durango, 9/29/83, A, C, 83001323
Durango Rock Shelters Archeology Site, Address Restricted, Durango vicinity, 2/11/85, A, D, 85000260
Durango-Silverton Narrow-Gauge Railroad, Right-of-way between Durango and Silverton, Durango, 10/15/66, A, C, NHL, 66000247
East Third Avenue Historic Residential District, E. 3rd. Ave. between 5th, and 15th Sts., Durango, 10/11/84, C, 84000024
La Plata County Fairgrounds, 2500 Main Ave., Durango, 8/12/91, A, C, 91001031
Main Avenue Historic District, Main Ave., Durango, 8/07/80, A, C, 80000907
Newman Block, 801–813 Main Ave., Durango, 10/15/79, B, C, 79000613
Spring Creek Archeological District, Address Restricted, Bayfield vicinity, 5/21/83, A, D, 83001322
Ute Mountain Ute Mancos Canyon Historic District, Address Restricted, Durango vicinity, 5/02/72, D, 72000273

Lake County

Dexter Cabin, 912 Harrison Ave., Leadville, 8/25/70, C, b, 70000163
Healy House, 912 Harrison Ave., Leadville, 8/25/70, C, 70000164
Interlaken Resort District, E of Twin Lakes off CO 82, Twin Lakes vicinity, 8/07/74, C, 74000587
Leadville Historic District, Town of Leadville, Leadville, 10/15/66, A, C, NHL, 66000248
Leadville National Fish Hatchery, W of Leadville, Leadville vicinity, 5/29/80, A, 80000908
Twin Lakes District, Both sides of CO 82, Twin Lakes, 7/30/74, A, C, b, 74000588

Larimer County

Ammons Hall, Colorado State University campus, Fort Collins, 6/15/78, A, 78000864

Larimer County—Continued

Anderson, Peter, House, 300 S. Howes St., Fort Collins, 10/25/79, B, C, 79000614

Andrews House, 324 E. Oak St., Fort Collins, 12/15/78, C, 78000865

Arrowhead Lodge, 34500 Poudre Canyon Hwy., Roosevelt NF, Bellvue, 5/27/92, A, C, 92000502

Avery House, 328 W. Mountain Ave., Fort Collins, 6/24/72, C, 72000274

Baker House, 304–304 1/2 E. Mulberry St., Fort Collins, 7/20/78, B, C, 78000866

Bear Lake Comfort Station [Rocky Mountain National Park MRA], Bear Lake, Estes Park vicinity, 1/29/88, C, g, NPS, 87001137

Bear Lake Ranger Station [Rocky Mountain National Park MRA], Bear Lake, Estes Park vicinity, 1/29/88, C, NPS, 87001138

Bimson Blacksmith Shop, 224 Mountain St., Berthoud, 7/23/81, A, B, C, 81000185

Botanical and Horticultural Laboratory, Colorado State University campus, Fort Collins, 9/18/78, A, C, 78003395

Bouton, Jay H., House, 113 N. Sherwood St., Fort Collins, 12/18/78, B, C, 78000867

Chasteen's Grove, W of Loveland off U.S. 34, Loveland vicinity, 9/06/78, A, C, 78000872

Colorado and Southern Railway Depot, 405 Railroad Ave., Loveland, 6/14/82, A, C, 82002303

Elkhorn Lodge, 530 W. Elkhorn Ave., Estes Park, 12/27/78, A, B, C, 78000862

Fall River Entrance Historic District [Rocky Mountain National Park MRA], Fall River Entrance, Estes Park vicinity, 1/29/88, C, NPS, 87001139

Fall River Pass Ranger Station [Rocky Mountain National Park MRA], Fall River Pass, Estes Park vicinity, 1/29/88, C, NPS, 87001140

Fall River Road [Rocky Mountain National Park MRA], Fall River Rd., Estes Park vicinity, 7/20/87, A, NPS, 87001129

Fern Lake Patrol Cabin [Rocky Mountain National Park MRA], Fern Lake, Estes Park vicinity, 1/29/88, C, NPS, 87001142

Fort Collins Municipal Railway Birney Safety Streetcar No. 21, 1801 W. Mountain Ave., Fort Collins, 1/05/84, A, 84000860

Fort Collins Post Office, 201 S. College Ave., Fort Collins, 1/30/78, C, 78000868

Fuller, Montezuma, House, 226 W. Magnolia St., Fort Collins, 12/15/78, C, 78000869

Glacier Basin Campground Ranger Station [Rocky Mountain National Park MRA], Glacier Basin, Estes Park vicinity, 7/20/87, C, NPS, 87001143

Homestead Meadows Discontiguous District, Address Restricted, Estes Park vicinity, 10/04/90, D, 90001476

Kissock Block Building, 115-121 E. Mountain Ave., Fort Collins, 5/16/85, A, C, 85001061

Laurel School Historic District, Off U.S. 287, Fort Collins, 10/03/80, A, C, 80000909

Leiffer House, S of Estes Park off CO 7, Estes Park vicinity, 8/02/78, C, NPS, 78000278

Lindenmeier Site, Address Restricted, Fort Collins vicinity, 10/15/66, D, NHL, 66000249

MacGregor Ranch, 180 MacGregor Ave., Estes Park vicinity, 7/31/89, A, C, 89001008

Maxwell, R. G., House, 2340 W. Mulberry St., Fort Collins, 9/29/80, B, C, 80000910

McHugh-Andrews House, 202 Remington St., Fort Collins, 12/27/78, B, C, 78000870

Mills, Enos, Homestead Cabin, S of Estes Park off CO 7, Estes Park vicinity, 5/11/73, B, 73000480

Moraine Lodge [Rocky Mountain National Park MRA (AD)], W of Estes Park off U.S. 36 on Bear Lake Rd., Estes Park vicinity, 10/08/76, A, NPS, 76000206

Old Town Fort Collins, Roughly bounded by College Ave., Mountain, Pine, Willow, and Walnut Sts., Fort Collins, 8/02/78, A, C, 78000871

Opera House Block/Central Block Building, 117-131 N. College Ave., Fort Collins, 2/08/85, A, C, 85000214

Park Theatre, 130 Moraine Ave., Estes Park, 6/14/84, A, C, 84000862

Rialto Theater, 228–230 E. Fourth Ave., Loveland, 2/17/88, A, C, 87002213

Robertson, T. H., House, 420 W. Mountain Ave., Fort Collins, 7/02/92, C, 92000811

Rocky Mountain National Park Utility Area Historic District [Rocky Mountain National Park MRA (AD)], Beaver Meadows Entrance Rd., Estes Park vicinity, 3/18/82, C, g, NPS, 82001717

Spruce Hall, Colorado State University campus, Fort Collins, 1/09/77, A, C, 77000381

Stanley Hotel, 333 Wonder View Ave., Estes Park, 5/26/77, A, C, 77000380

Stanley Hotel District, 333 Wonder View Ave., Estes Park, 6/20/85, B, C, 85001256

Trail Ridge Road [Rocky Mountain National Park MRA (AD)], Rocky Mountain National Park, Estes Park vicinity, 11/14/84, A, C, NPS, 84000242

Twin Sisters Lookout [Rocky Mountain National Park MPS], On Twin Sisters Peaks, Rocky Mountain National Park (ROMO), Estes Park vicinity, 12/24/92, C, NPS, 92001670

Vaille, Agnes, Shelter [Rocky Mountain National Park MPS], NW of Longs Peak along E. Longs Peak Trail, Rocky Mountain National Park (ROMO), Estes Park vicinity, 12/24/92, C, NPS, 92001669

Virginia Dale Stage Station, Off US 287, Virginia Dale, 9/26/85, A, C, 85002562

Waycott, Ernest, House, 1501 W. Mountain Ave., Fort Collins, 12/02/93, C, 93001363

White, William Allen, Cabins [Rocky Mountain National Park MRA (AD)], W of Estes Park of Moraine Park Visitor Center in Rocky Mountain National Park, Estes Park vicinity, 10/25/73, B, NPS, 73001944

Willow Park Patrol Cabin [Rocky Mountain National Park MRA], Fall River Rd., Estes Park vicinity, 7/20/87, C, NPS, 87001144

Willow Park Stable [Rocky Mountain National Park MRA], Fall River Pass, Estes Park vicinity, 7/20/87, C, NPS, 87001145

Las Animas County

Avery Bridges [Vehicular Bridges in Colorado TR], Cty. Rd. over Leitensdorfer Arroyo and Apishapa River, Hoehne and Aguilar vicinity, 6/24/85, C, 85001403

Baca House and Outbuilding, 300 block of Main St., Trinidad, 2/26/70, A, C, 70000165

Bloom, Frank G., House, 300 block of Main St., Trinidad, 2/26/70, C, 70000166

Bridge over Burro Canon [Vehicular Bridges in Colorado TR], CO 12, Madrid vicinity, 2/04/85, C, g, 85000216

Cokedale Historic District, Roughly bounded by Church, Maple, Pine, Elm, and Spruce Sts., Cokedale, 1/18/85, A, C, 85000083

Commercial Street Bridge [Vehicular Bridges in Colorado TR], Commercial St., Trinidad, 2/04/85, C, 85000217

Corazon de Trinidad, Roughly bounded by Purgatoire River on N and W, Walnut St. on E, and 3rd, W. 1st and Animas Sts. on S, Trinidad, 2/28/73, A, C, 73000482

Elson Bridge [Vehicular Bridges in Colorado TR], Cty. Rd. 36, El Moro vicinity, 2/04/85, C, 85000215

Jaffa Opera House, 100–116 W. Main St., Trinidad, 2/07/72, A, C, 72000275

Ludlow Tent Colony Site, Del Aqua Canyon Rd., Ludlow, 6/19/85, A, f, 85001328

Raton Pass, U.S. 85-87, CO/NM border, Trinidad, vicinity, 10/15/66, A, NHL, 66000474

Torres Cave Archeological Site, Address Restricted, Villegreen vicinity, 4/29/80, D, 80000911

US Post Office—Trinidad Main [US Post Offices in Colorado, 1900–1941, TR], 301 E. Main St., Trinidad, 1/22/86, C, 86000188

Logan County

First United Presbyterian Church, 130 S. 4th St., Sterling, 6/03/82, C, a, 82002304

Harris, W. C., House, 102 Taylor St., Sterling, 5/17/84, B, 84000864

I and M Building, 223 Main St., Sterling, 6/03/82, C, 82002305

Logan County Courthouse, Main St., Sterling, 2/28/79, C, 79000615

Luft, Conrad, Sr., House, 1429 CO 14, Sterling vicinity, 5/17/84, C, b, 84000866

St. Anthony's Roman Catholic Church, 329 S. 3rd St., Sterling, 6/03/82, C, a, 82002306

Sterling Union Pacific Railroad Depot, 113 N. Front St., Sterling, 2/06/86, A, C, b, 86000210

US Post Office, Federal Building, and Federal Courthouse—Sterling Main [US Post Offices in Colorado, 1900–1941, TR], Third and Popular Sts., Sterling, 1/22/86, C, 86000187

Mesa County

Black Bridge [Vehicular Bridges in Colorado TR], 25.30 Rd. over Gunnison River, Grand Junction, 2/04/85, C, 85000219

Mesa County—Continued

Bloomfield Site, Address Restricted, Whitewater vicinity, 1/20/83, D, 83001324

Clifton Community Center and Church, F and Main St., Clifton, 6/03/82, A, C, a, 82002307

Coates Creek Schoolhouse, D S Rd. 16 mi. W of Glade Park, Glade Park vicinity, 2/03/93, A, C, b, 92001839

Convicts' Bread Oven, W of Molina on CO 65, Molina vicinity, 12/31/74, A, 74000589

Cross Land and Fruit Company Orchards and Ranch, NE of Grand Junction at 3079 F Rd., Grand Junction vicinity, 3/28/80, A, C, 80000912

Denver and Rio Grande Western Railroad Depot, 119 Pitkin Ave., Grand Junction, 9/08/92, A, C, 92001190

Fifth Street Bridge [Vehicular Bridges in Colorado TR], U.S. Hwy. 50, Grand Junction, 2/04/85, C, 85000220

Fruita Bridge [Vehicular Bridges in Colorado TR], Cty. Rd. 17.50 over Colorado River, Fruita vicinity, 2/04/85, C, 85000218

Hotel St. Regis, 359 Colorado Ave., Grand Junction, 10/22/92, A, C, 92001410

IOOF Hall, Jct. of 4th St. and Curtis Ave., De Beque, 3/25/93, A, C, 93000200

Kettle-Jens House, 498 32nd Rd., Clifton, 5/06/83, C, 83001325

Margery Building, 519–527 Main St., Grand Junction, 2/24/93, A, C, 93000033

North Seventh Street Historic Residential District, 7th St. between Hill and White Aves., Grand Junction, 1/05/84, C, 84000870

U.S. Post Office, 400 Rood Ave., Grand Junction, 1/31/80, B, g, 80000913

Mineral County

Sevenmile Bridge [Vehicular Bridges in Colorado TR], County Rd. 6 miles SW of Creede, Creede, 7/11/85, C, b, 85001552

Wagon Wheel Gap Railroad Station, SE of Creede at Wagon Wheel Gap off CO 149, Creede vicinity, 9/27/76, B, 76000563

Moffat County

Chew, Rial, Ranch Complex [Dinosaur National Monument MRA], US 40, Dinosaur, 10/27/87, A, g, NPS, 86003392

Julien, Denis, Inscription [Dinosaur National Monument MRA], US 40, Dinosaur, 12/19/86, A, B, NPS, 86003395

Marcia (pullman car), 341 E. Victory Way, Craig, 6/20/75, B, f, 75000526

Old Ladore School, By Green River on SR 318, Brown's Park, 2/24/75, A, 75000525

State Armory, 590 Yampa Ave., Craig, 6/25/92, A, C, 92000810

Two-Bar Ranch, W of Maybell off CO 318, Maybell vicinity, 2/17/78, A, 78000873

Upper Wade and Curtis Cabin [Dinosaur National Monument MRA], US 40, Dinosaur, 12/19/86, A, NPS, 86003399

White-Indian Contact Site, Address Restricted, Sparks vicinity, 3/08/77, B, D, NHL, 77001561

Montezuma County

Anasazi Archeological District, Address Restricted, Dolores vicinity, 7/19/84, D, 84001273

Escalante Ruin, Address Restricted, Dolores vicinity, 11/20/75, B, D, 75000527

Hovenweep National Monument, NW of Cortez, Cortez vicinity, 10/15/66, A, D, NPS, 66000250

Lancaster, James A., Site, Address Restricted, Pleasant View vicinity, 4/14/80, C, D, 80000914

Lost Canyon Archeological District, Address Restricted, Mancos vicinity, 10/18/88, C, D, 88001909

Lowry Ruin, 30 mi. NW of Cortez via U.S. 160, Pleasant View vicinity, 10/15/66, D, NHL, 66000253

Mancos High School, 350 Grand Ave., Mancos, 12/23/91, A, C, 91001740

Mancos Opera House, 136 W. Grand Ave., Mancos, 1/07/88, A, C, 87002183

Mesa Verde Administrative District, Area at head of Spruce Canyon off park service road, Mesa Verde National Park, 5/28/87, C, NHL, NPS, 87001410

Mesa Verde National Park, 10 mi. E of Cortez on U.S. 160, Cortez vicinity, 10/15/66, A, C, D, NPS, 66000251

Mud Springs Pueblo, Address Restricted, Cortez vicinity, 10/29/82, D, 82001020

Pigge Site, Address Restricted, Pleasant View vicinity, 4/07/80, D, 80000915

Roy's Ruin [Great Pueblo Period of the McElmo Drainage Unit MPS], Address Restricted, Cortez vicinity, 1/31/92, A, D, 91002027

Southern Hotel, 101 S. Fifth St., Dolores, 2/23/89, A, 89000018

Yellowjacket Pueblo (5-MT-5), Address Restricted, Yellow Jacket vicinity, 9/28/85, D, 85002701

Yucca House National Monument, 12 mi. S of Cortez via U.S. 666, Cortez vicinity, 10/15/66, C, D, NPS, 66000252

Montrose County

D & RG Narrow Gauge Trestle, NE of Cimarron, Cimarron vicinity, 6/18/76, A, C, NPS, 76000172

Denver and Rio Grande Depot, 20 N. Rio Grande Ave., Montrose, 6/03/82, A, C, 82002308

Gunnison Tunnel, E of Montrose, Montrose vicinity, 7/22/79, A, C, 79000616

Hanging Flume, 5.7 mi. NW of Uravan on CO 141, Uravan, 5/15/80, A, 80000917

Lathrop, J. V., House, 718 Main St., Montrose, 7/08/88, C, 88001016

Montrose City Hall, 433 S. 1st St., Montrose, 6/03/82, A, C, 82002309

Townsend, Thomas B., House, 222 S. 5th St., Montrose, 9/17/80, B, C, 80000916

US Bureau of Reclamation Project Office Building, 601 N. Park Ave., Montrose, 11/27/91, A, C, 91001685

US Post Office—Montrose Main [US Post Offices in Colorado, 1900–1941, TR], 321 S. First St., Montrose, 1/22/86, C, 86000183

Ute Memorial Site, 2 mi. S of Montrose on U.S. 550, Montrose vicinity, 2/26/70, B, f, 70000167

Morgan County

All Saints Church of Eben Ezer, 120 Hospital Rd., Brush, 6/03/82, A, C, a, 82002310

Farmers State Bank Building, 300 Main St., Fort Morgan, 9/13/90, C, 90001422

Rainbow Arch Bridge [Vehicular Bridges in Colorado TR], CO 52, Fort Morgan vicinity, 2/04/85, C, 85000221

Sherman Street Historic Residential District, 400 and 500 blks. of Sherman St., Fort Morgan, 9/10/87, A, C, 87001286

US Post Office—Fort Morgan Main [US Post Offices in Colorado, 1900–1941, TR], 300 State St., Fort Morgan, 1/22/86, C, 86000177

Otero County

Bent's Old Fort National Historic Site, CO 194, La Junta vicinity, 10/15/66, A, e, NHL, NPS, 66000254

Finney, Dr. Frank, House, 608 Belleview Ave., La Junta, 5/17/84, C, 84000877

Hart, Wilson A., House, 802 Raton Ave., La Junta, 5/31/79, B, C, 79000617

Lincoln School, 300 block W. 3rd St., La Junta, 9/13/78, A, C, g, 78000874

North La Junta School, Jct. of CO 109 and CO 194, La Junta, 6/25/92, A, C, 92000809

Rourke, Eugene, House, 619 Carson St., La Junta, 5/09/83, C, 83001326

San Juan Avenue Historic District, San Juan Ave., La Junta, 8/27/80, B, C, 80000918

Sciumbato, Daniel, Grocery Store, 706 2nd St., La Junta, 5/17/84, C, 84000878

U.S. Post Office, 4th and Colorado Ave., La Junta, 7/12/76, C, 76000565

Ouray County

Beaumont Hotel, US 550, Ouray, 10/30/73, A, C, 73000483

Ouray City Hall and Walsh Library, 6th Ave. between 3rd and 4th Sts., Ouray, 4/16/75, C, 75000528

Ouray Historic District, US 550, Ouray, 10/06/83, A, C, 83003537

Park County

Boreas Railroad Station Site, Boreas Pass Rd. NW of Como, Pike NF, Como vicinity, 10/28/93, A, D, 93001108

Como Roundhouse, Railroad Depot and Hotel Complex, Off U.S. 285, Como, 5/20/83, A, C, 83003880

Estabrook Historic District, NE of Bailey, Bailey vicinity, 10/20/80, B, C, 80000919

Glenisle, Off US Hwy 285, Bailey vicinity, 1/18/85, A, C, 85000084

Park County Courthouse and Jail, 418 Main St., Fairplay, 5/25/79, A, C, 79000618

South Park Community Church, 6th and Hathaway Sts., Fairplay, 11/22/77, B, C, a, 77000382

South Park Lager Beer Brewery, 3rd and Front Sts., Fairplay, 6/25/74, B, 74000590

Summer Saloon, 3rd and Front Sts., Fairplay, 5/08/74, B, 74000591

Tarryall School, 31000 County Rd., Tarryall, 5/16/85, C, 85001060

Phillips County

First National Bank of Haxtun, 145 S. Colorado Ave., Haxtun, 7/01/86, C, 86001454

Pitkin County

Armory Hall, Fraternal Hall, 130 S. Galena St., Aspen, 6/05/75, A, 75000529

Ashcroft, Colorado, 12 mi. S of Aspen in White River National Forest, Aspen vicinity, 5/12/75, A, 75000533

Aspen Community Church, 200 N. Aspen St., Aspen, 5/12/75, A, C, a, 75000530

Boat Tow [Historic Resources of Aspen MPS], 700 S. Aspen St., Aspen, 6/22/90, A, C, 90000866

Bowles—Cooley House [Aspen MRA], 201 W. Francis St., Aspen, 3/06/87, B, C, 87000188

Callahan, Matthew, Log Cabin [Aspen MRA], 205 S. Third St., Aspen, 3/06/87, B, C, 87000150

Collins Block—Aspen Lumber and Supply [Aspen MRA], 204 S. Mill St., Aspen, 3/06/87, C, 87000191

Dixon—Markle House [Aspen MRA], 135 E. Cooper Ave., Aspen, 3/06/87, C, 87000165

Frantz, D. E., House [Aspen MRA], 333 W. Bleeker St., Aspen, 3/06/87, C, 87000152

Hallett, Samuel I., House [Aspen MRA], 432 W. Francis St., Aspen, 3/06/87, B, C, 87000155

Holden Mining and Smelting Co. [Historic Resources of Aspen MPS], 1000 Block W. Hwy. 82, Aspen vicinity, 6/22/90, A, D, 90000867

Hotel Jerome, 330 E. Main St., Aspen, 3/20/86, B, C, 86000459

Hyman-Brand Building, 203 S. Galena St., Aspen, 1/18/85, B, C, 85000085

Hynes, Thomas, House [Aspen MRA], 303 E. Main St., Aspen, 3/06/87, C, 87000157

Independence and Independence Mill Site, On CO 82, in White River National Forest, Ghost Town, 4/11/73, A, 73000484

La Fave Block [Aspen MRA], 405 S. Hunter St., Aspen, 3/06/87, C, 87000193

Maroon Creek Bridge [Vehicular Bridges in Colorado TR], CO 82, Aspen vicinity, 2/04/85, C, 85000222

New Brick—The Brick Saloon [Aspen MRA], 420 E. Cooper Ave., Aspen, 3/06/87, C, 87000185

Newberry House [Aspen MRA], 206 Lake Ave., Aspen, 3/06/87, C, 87000158

Osgood Castle, About 1 mi. S of Redstone on CO 133, Redstone vicinity, 6/28/71, B, C, 71000216

Osgood Gamekeeper's Lodge [Redstone MPS], 18679 CO 133, Redstone, 7/19/89, A, C, 89000933

Osgood-Kuhnhausen House, 0642 Redstone Blvd., Redstone, 8/18/83, A, C, 83001327

Pitkin County Courthouse, 506 E. Main St., Aspen, 5/12/75, A, C, 75000531

Redstone Coke Oven Historic District [Redstone MPS], CO 133 and Chair Mountain Stables Rd., Redstone vicinity, 2/07/90, A, C, 89002385

Redstone Historic District [Redstone MPS], Roughly along the Crystal River from Hawk Creek to 226 Redstone Blvd., Redstone, 7/19/89, A, B, C, 89000934

Redstone Inn, 0082 Redstone Blvd., Redstone, 3/27/80, B, C, 80000920

Riede's City Bakery [Aspen MRA], 413 E. Hyman Ave., Aspen, 3/06/87, C, 87000182

Sheely Bridge [Vehicular Bridges in Colorado TR], Mill Street Park, Aspen, 2/04/85, C, b, 85000223

Shilling—Lamb House [Aspen MRA], 525 N. Fifth St., Aspen, 3/06/87, C, 87000163

Smith—Elisha House [Aspen MRA], 320 W. Main St., Aspen, 1/19/89, C, 87002121

Smuggler Mine [Aspen MRA], Smuggler Mountain, Aspen, 5/18/87, A, C, 87000194

Waite, Davis, House [Aspen MRA], 234 W. Francis St., Aspen, 3/06/87, B, C, 87000160

Webber, Henry, House—Pioneer Park [Aspen MRA], 442 W. Bleeker St., Aspen, 3/06/87, B, C, 87000189

Wheeler Opera House, 330 E. Hyman Ave., Aspen, 8/21/72, A, C, 72000276

Wheeler-Stallard House, 620 W. Bleeker St., Aspen, 5/30/75, A, C, 75000532

Prowers County

Davies Hotel, 122 N. Main, Lamar, 10/19/78, C, 78000875

Douglas Crossing Bridge [Vehicular Bridges in Colorado TR], Cty. Rd. 28, Granada vicinity, 2/04/85, C, g, 85000224

Prowers County Building, 301 S. Main St., Lamar, 9/21/81, A, C, 81000186

US Post Office—Lamar Main [US Post Offices in Colorado, 1900–1941, TR], 300 S. Fifth St., Lamar, 1/22/86, C, 86000179

Pueblo County

Avondale Bridge [Vehicular Bridges in Colorado TR], Cty. Rd. 327, Avondale, 2/04/85, C, 85000225

Barndollar—Gann House, 1906 Court St., Pueblo, 11/07/85, C, 85002761

Baxter House, 325 W. 15th St., Pueblo, 2/17/78, B, C, a, 78000876

Beaumont, Allen, J., House, 425 W. 15th St., Pueblo, 8/18/83, C, 83001328

Black, Dr. John A., House Complex, 102 W. Pitkin Ave., Pueblo, 11/07/85, C, 85002760

Bowen Mansion, 229 W. 12th St., Pueblo, 1/09/78, B, C, 78000877

Butler House, 6916 Broadacre Rd., Pueblo vicinity, 8/16/84, A, B, C, 84000880

Carlile, James N., House, 44 Carlile Pl., Pueblo, 2/08/85, C, 85000297

Central High School, 431 E. Pitkin Ave., Pueblo, 11/14/79, B, C, 79000619

City Park Carousel, City Park, Pueblo, 4/21/83, A, C, b, g, 83001297

Colorado Building, 401–411 N. Main St., Pueblo, 4/17/92, A, C, 92000315

Colorado State Hospital Superintendent's House, 13th & Francisco Sts., Pueblo, 9/26/85, A, C, 85002563

Doyle Settlement, SE of Pueblo on Doyle Rd., Pueblo vicinity, 4/10/80, A, B, C, d, 80000922

Duke, Nathaniel W., House, 1409 Craig St., Pueblo, 2/08/85, B, C, 85000229

Edison School, 900 W. Mesa, Pueblo, 6/19/85, A, C, 85001330

First Congregational Church, 225 W. Evans, Pueblo, 2/08/85, C, a, 85000230

First Methodist Episcopal Church, 400 Broadway St., Pueblo, 11/14/79, A, C, a, 79000620

Fitch Terrace, 401, 403, 405, 407, 409, and 411 W. Eleventh St., Pueblo, 10/02/86, B, C, 86002809

Frazier, R. T., House, 2121 N. Elizabeth St., Pueblo, 6/19/85, A, C, 85001329

Galligan House, 501 Colorado Ave., Pueblo, 6/03/82, B, C, 82002311

Gast Mansion, 1801 Greenwood St., Pueblo, 6/03/82, B, C, 82002312

Goodnight Barn, W of Pueblo at CO 96W and Siloam Rd., Pueblo vicinity, 7/30/74, B, 74002278

Hazelhurst, 905 Berkley Ave., Pueblo, 12/15/78, B, C, 78000879

Henkel-Duke Mercantile Company Warehouse, 212-222 W. 3rd Ave., Pueblo, 5/17/84, A, C, 84000881

Huerfano Bridge [Vehicular Bridges in Colorado TR], U.S. Hwy 50, Boone vicinity, 2/04/85, A, C, 85000226

Indian Petroglyphs and Pictographs, Address Restricted, Penrose vicinity, 5/03/76, D, 76000566

King, Dr. Alexander T., House and Carriage House, 229 Quincy St. and 215 W. Routt Ave., Pueblo, 4/21/83, C, 83001329

McCarthy, T. G., House, 817 N. Grand Ave., Pueblo, 5/22/86, B, 86001122

McClelland Orphanage, 415 E. Abriendo Ave., Pueblo, 1/30/92, A, C, 91002043

Pueblo County—Continued

Mechanics Building/Masonic Building, 207-211 N. Main St., Pueblo, 6/16/83, C, 83001330

Nepesta Bridge [Vehicular Bridges in Colorado TR], Cty. Rd. 613, Boone vicinity, 2/04/85, C, 85000227

Orman-Adams House, 102 W. Orman Ave., Pueblo, 7/13/76, B, C, 76000567

Pitkin Place Historic District, S side of 300 block W. Pitkin Pl., Pueblo, 1/31/78, A, C, 78000880

Pryor, Frank, House, 1325 Greenwood St., Pueblo, 2/08/85, B, C, 85000231

Pueblo County Courthouse, 10th and Main Sts., Pueblo, 6/27/75, A, B, C, 75000534

Pueblo Federal Building, 421 N. Main St., Pueblo, 1/03/78, C, 78000881

Quaker Flour Mill, 102 S. Oneida St., Pueblo, 9/30/76, A, 76000568

Rice, Ward, House, 1825 Grand Ave., Pueblo, 11/07/85, C, 85002762

Rood Candy Company Building, 408-416 W. 7th St., Pueblo, 5/17/84, A, C, 84000882

Rosemount, 419 W. 14th St., Pueblo, 7/30/74, B, C, 74000592

Sacred Heart Church, 1025 N. Grand Ave., Pueblo, 2/21/89, C, a, 89000037

Sacred Heart Orphanage, 2316 Sprague St., Pueblo, 3/03/89, A, C, 89000038

St. Charles Bridge [Vehicular Bridges in Colorado TR], Cty. Rd. 65, Pueblo vicinity, 2/04/85, C, 85000228

Star Journal Model Home, 2920 High St., Pueblo, 2/16/84, C, 84000886

Stickney, Charles H., House, 101 E. Orman Ave., Pueblo, 2/08/85, B, C, 85000232

Streit, J. L., House, 2201 Grand Ave., Pueblo, 9/20/84, C, 84000892

Tooke—Nuckolls House, 38 Carlile Pl., Pueblo, 11/07/85, C, 85002763

Tutt Building, 421 Central Plaza, Pueblo, 8/18/83, C, 83001331

Union Avenue Historic Commerical District, Roughly bounded by RR tracks, Main St., Grand and Victoria Aves., Pueblo, 12/28/82, A, C, 82001021

Union Depot, Victoria and B Sts., Pueblo, 4/01/75, A, C, 75000535

Vail Hotel, 217 S. Grand Ave., Pueblo, 12/18/78, B, C, 78000882

Walter, Martin, House, 300 W. Abriendo Ave., Pueblo, 5/17/84, A, C, 84000894

White, Asbury, House, 417 W. 11th St., Pueblo, 10/11/84, B, 84000025

Young Women's Christian Association, 801 N. Santa Fe Ave., Pueblo, 3/24/80, A, C, g, 80000921

Rio Blanco County

Battle of Milk River Site, Address Restricted, Meeker vicinity, 8/22/75, A, D, 75000536

Canon Pintado, Address Restricted, Rangely vicinity, 10/06/75, A, B, D, 75000538

Carrot Men Pictograph Site, Address Restricted, Rangely vicinity, 8/22/75, A, D, 75000539

Collage Shelter Site, Address Restricted, Rangely vicinity, 8/27/80, D, 80000924

Duck Creek Wickiup Village, Address Restricted, Meeker vicinity, 11/20/75, C, D, 75000537

Fremont Lookout Fortification Site, Address Restricted, Rangely vicinity, 11/20/74, D, 74000593

Hay's Ranch Bridge [Vehicular Bridges in Colorado TR], Cty. Rd. 127, Meeker vicinity, 2/04/85, A, C, 85000233

Hotel Meeker, 560 Main St., Meeker, 5/07/80, B, C, 80000923

St. James Episcopal Church, 368 4th St., Meeker, 3/30/78, A, C, a, 78000883

Rio Grande County

El Monte Hotel, 925 First Ave., Monte Vista, 6/07/90, A, C, 90000870

Masonic Park Bridge [Vehicular Bridges in Colorado TR], Off CO 149, South Fork vicinity, 2/04/85, C, b, 85000236

Monte Vista Downtown Historic District, Jct. of First Ave. and Washington St., Monte Vista, 11/01/91, A, C, 91001612

Sutherland Bridge [Vehicular Bridges in Colorado TR], Off U.S. 160, Del Norte vicinity, 2/04/85, C, 85000234

US Post Office and Federal Building—Monte Vista Main [US Post Offices in Colorado, 1900–1941, TR], Washington and Second Ave., Monte Vista, 1/22/86, C, 86000182

Wheeler Bridge [Vehicular Bridges in Colorado TR], Off U.S. 160, Del Norte vicinity, 2/04/85, C, 85000235

Routt County

Bell Mercantile, 101–111 Moffat Ave., Oak Creek, 6/07/90, A, C, 90000871

Foidel Canyon School, NW of Oak Creek, Oak Creek vicinity, 5/09/83, A, C, g, 83001332

Four Mile Bridge [Vehicular Bridges in Colorado TR], Cty. Rd. 42, Steamboat Springs vicinity, 2/04/85, C, 85000237

Hahns Peak Schoolhouse, Main St., Hahns Peak, 2/15/74, A, 74000594

Hayden Depot, 300 W. Pearl St., Hayden, 10/22/92, A, 92001409

Rock Creek Stage Station, E of Toponas off CO 84, Toponas vicinity, 10/21/82, A, C, 82004860

Steamboat Springs Depot, 39265 Routt County Rd. 33B, Steamboat Springs, 12/20/78, A, C, 78000884

Saguache County

Capilla de San Juan Bautista, NW of La Garita, La Garita vicinity, 2/08/80, A, C, a, d, 80000926

Carnero Creek Pictographs, Address Restricted, La Garita vicinity, 6/05/75, D, 75000540

Creststone School, Cottonwood St. and Carbonate Ave., Creststone, 1/09/86, A, 86000011

Saguache Flour Mill, W of Saguache, Saguache vicinity, 9/18/78, B, C, 78000885

Saguache School and Jail Buildings, U.S. 285 and San Juan Ave., Saguache, 5/02/75, A, C, 75000541

San Juan County

Cascade Boy Scout Camp, Adjacent to Lime Creek Rd., San Juan National Forest, Durango vicinity, 9/08/88, A, C, 88001529

Silverton Historic District, US 550, Silverton, 10/15/66, A, NHL, 66000255

San Miguel County

Smuggler-Union Hydroelectric Power Plant, SE of Telluride at Bridal Veil Falls, Telluride vicinity, 12/27/79, A, C, 79000621

Telluride Historic District, Rt. 145, Telluride, 10/15/66, A, C, NHL, 66000256

Summit County

Breckenridge Historic District, Roughly bounded by Jefferson Ave., Wellington Rd., High and Main St., Breckenridge, 4/09/80, A, B, C, a, g, 80000927

Frisco Schoolhouse, 120 Main St., Frisco, 9/15/83, A, g, 83001333

Porcupine Peak Site, Address Restricted, Dillon vicinity, 8/01/80, D, 80000928

Slate Creek Bridge [Vehicular Bridges in Colorado TR], Cty. Rd. 1450 over Blue River, Slate Creek, 6/24/85, C, 85001402

Wildhack's Grocery Store-Post Office, 510 Main St., Frisco, 5/16/85, A, C, 85001059

Teller County

Cripple Creek Historic District, Rt. 67, Cripple Creek, 10/15/66, A, NHL, 66000939

Florissant School, 2009 Co. Rd. 31, Florissant, 10/01/90, C, 90001503

Goldfield City Hall and Fire Station, Victor Ave. and 9th St., Goldfield, 5/17/84, A, C, 84000897

Hornbek House, CR 1, Florissant vicinity, 12/08/81, C, NPS, 81000105

Midland Terminal Railroad Depot, 230 N. 4th St., Victor, 5/17/84, A, C, 84000899

Stratton's Independence Mine and Mill, Jct. of Rangeview Rd. and CO 67, Victor vicinity, 3/04/93, A, B, 93000054

Victor Downtown Historic District, Roughly bounded by Diamond Ave., Second, Portland and 5th Sts., Victor, 7/03/85, A, C, 85001463

Teller County—Continued

Victor Hotel, 4th St. and Victor Ave., Victor, 4/10/80, B, C, 80000929

Weld County

Ball, Elmer and Etta, Ranch [Historic Farms and Ranches of Weld County MPS], Weld Co. Rd. 69 W of Briggsdale, Briggsdale vicinity, 10/16/91, A, C, 91001533

Brush, Jared L., Barn [Historic Farms and Ranches of Weld County MPS], 24308 Weld Co. Rd. 17, Johnstown vicinity, 10/16/91, A, C, 91001532

First Baptist Church, Tenth Ave. at Eleventh St., NW corner, Greeley, 11/25/87, A, C, a, 87001510

Fort Vasquez Site, Address Restricted, Platteville vicinity, 9/30/70, A, B, D, 70000169

Glazier House, 1403 10th Ave., Greeley, 2/05/91, C, 91000002

Greeley High School and Grade School, 1015 8th St., Greeley, 7/23/81, A, C, 81000189

Greeley Union Pacific Railroad Depot, Jct. of 7th Ave. and 9th St., Greeley, 11/04/93, C, 93001180

Jurgens Site [Prehistoric Paleo-Indian Cultures of the Colorado Plains MPS], Address Restricted, Kersey vicinity, 7/18/90, D, 90001084

Keota Stone Circles Archeological District, Address Restricted, Keota vicinity, 7/28/81, D, 81000190

Lincoln School, 645 Holbrook St., Erie, 7/22/81, A, C, 81000188

Meeker Memorial Museum, 1324 9th Ave., Greeley, 2/26/70, B, 70000168

Milne Farm [Historic Farms and Ranches in Weld County MPS], 18457 CO 392, Lucerne vicinity, 2/03/93, A, C, 92001840

SLW Ranch [Historic Farms and Ranches in Weld County MPS], 27401 Weld Co. Rd. 58 1/2, Greeley vicinity, 3/15/91, A, C, 91000288

Sandstone Ranch, E of Longmont off CO 119, Longmont vicinity, 1/23/84, A, C, 84000904

United Church of Christ of Highlandlake, 16896 Weld CR 5, Mead vicinity, 2/10/89, C, a, 88002237

Weld County Courthouse, 9th St. and 9th Ave., Greeley, 1/09/78, A, C, 78000886

Woodbury, Joseph A., House, 1124 7th St., Greeley, 5/17/84, C, 84000908

Yuma County

Beecher Island Battleground, 16.5 mi. SE of Wray on Beecher Rd., Wray vicinity, 10/29/76, A, B, 76000569

Boggs Lumber and Hardware Building, 125 N. Main St., Eckley, 1/18/85, C, 85000086

Lett Hotel, 204 S. Ash, Yuma, 1/25/90, A, C, 89002378

Constructed at the historical entry to Salida, Colorado, a booming railroad town at the turn-of-the-century, the Manhattan Hotel (ca. 1901) retains integrity of fabric and detail. (Greg Cole, 1982)

CONNECTICUT

Fairfield County

Aspetuck Historic District, Roughly, Redding Rd. from jct. with Old Redding Rd. to Welles Hill Rd. and Old Redding Rd. N past Aspetuck R., Easton, 8/23/91, A, B, C, g, 91000437

BERKSHIRE NO. 7, Bridgeport Harbor, Bridgeport, 12/21/78, A, g, 78002837

Ball and Roller Bearing Company, 20–22 Maple Ave., Danbury, 8/25/89, A, B, 89001087

Barlow, Aaron, House, Umpawaug Rd. at Station Rd., Redding, 4/29/82, A, C, 82004347

Barnum Museum, 805 Main St., Bridgeport, 11/07/72, B, C, 72001300

Barnum/Palliser Historic District, Roughly bounded by Myrtle and Park Aves., Atlantic and Austin Sts. (both sides), Bridgeport, 12/16/82, B, C, 82000995

Bartlett, Daniel and Esther, House, 43 Lonetown Rd., Redding, 4/15/93, C, b, 93000290

Bassickville Historic District, 20–122 Bassick, 667–777 Howard, and 1521–1523 Fairview Aves., and 50–1380 State St., Bridgeport, 9/08/87, C, 87001511

Beth Israel Synagogue, 31 Concord St., Norwalk, 11/29/91, C, a, 91001684

Birdcraft Sanctuary, 314 Unquowa Rd., Fairfield, 6/23/82, A, B, NHL, 82004371

Bishop, Peyton Randolph, House, 135 Washington Ave., Bridgeport, 8/25/87, A, C, 87000803

Bishop, William D., Cottage Development Historic District, Cottage Pl. and Atlantic, Broad, Main and Whiting Sts., Bridgeport, 6/28/82, B, C, 82004388

Black Rock Gardens Historic District [Wartime Emergency Housing in Bridgeport MPS], Bounded by Fairfield St., Brewster St. and Nash Ln., including Rowsley and Haddon Sts., Bridgeport, 9/26/90, A, C, 90001430

Black Rock Historic District, Roughly bounded by Black Rock Harbor, Grovers Ave., Beacon and Prescott Sts., Bridgeport, 3/15/79, A, C, 79002658

Booth, Nathan B., House, 6080 Main St., Stratford, 4/17/92, C, 92000317

Boothe Homestead, Main St., Stratford, 5/01/85, C, g, 85000951

Boston Post Road Historic District, 567-728 Boston Post Rd., 1-25 Brookside Rd., and 45-70 Old Kingshighway N., Darien, 12/16/82, C, a, 82000997

Bradley-Wheeler House, 25 Avery Pl., Westport, 7/05/84, C, 84000791

Branchville Railroad Tenement, Old Main Hwy., Ridgefield, 8/12/82, A, C, 82004346

Bridgeport City Hall, 202 State St., Bridgeport, 9/19/77, A, C, 77001387

Bridgeport Downtown North Historic District [Downtown Bridgeport MRA], Roughly bounded by Congress, Water, Fairfield Ave.,

Elm, Golden Hill & Chapel Sts., Bridgeport, 11/02/87, C, 87001403

Bridgeport Downtown South Historic District [Downtown Bridgeport MRA], Roughly bounded by Elm, Cannon, Main, Gilbert, and Broad Sts., Bridgeport, 9/03/87, C, 87001402

Bronson Windmill, 3015 Bronson Rd., Fairfield, 12/29/71, C, 71000896

Brookfield Center Historic District, Long Meadow Hill Rd., Brookfield Center, 8/15/91, A, C, 91000992

Bush—Holley House, 39 Strickland Rd., Greenwich, 12/01/88, A, B, C, NHL, 88002694

Byram School, Between Sherman Ave. and Western Junior Hwy., Greenwich, 8/02/90, C, 90001110

Cain, Hugh, Fulling Mill and Elias Glover Woolen Mill Archeological Site, Address Restricted, Ridgefield vicinity, 9/19/85, D, 85002440

Church of the Holy Name [Downtown Stamford Ecclesiastical Complexes TR], 305 Washington Blvd., Stamford, 12/24/87, A, C, a, 87002131

Commodore Hull School, 130 Oak Ave., Shelton, 6/30/83, A, C, 83001251

Compo—Owenoke Historic District [Westport MPS], Roughly bounded by Gray's Cr., Compo Rd. S. and Long Island Sound, Westport, 4/19/91, A, C, 91000393

Connecticut Railway and Lighting Company Car Barn [Downtown Bridgeport MRA], 55 Congress St., Bridgeport, 12/03/87, C, 87001405

Cos Cob Power Station, Roughly bounded by Metro North RR tracks, the Mianus R. and Sound Shore Dr., Greenwich, 8/02/90, A, C, D, 90001096

Cos Cob Railroad Station, 55 Station Dr., Greenwich vicinity, 7/28/89, A, C, 89000928

Cosier—Murphy House, 67 CT 39, New Fairfield, 7/31/91, C, 91000994

Cove Island Houses, Cove Rd. and Weed Ave., Stamford, 5/22/79, A, C, b, 79002652

Curtis, Nathaniel, House, 600 Housatonic Ave., Stamford, 4/15/82, C, b, 82004342

Davenport, Deacon John, House, 129 Davenport Ridge Rd., Stamford, 4/29/82, B, C, 82004611

Davenport, Hanford, House, 353 Oenoke Ridge, New Canaan, 8/03/89, C, 89000948

Deacon's Point Historic District, Roughly bounded by Seaview Ave. and Williston, Bunnell and Deacon Sts., Bridgeport, 8/21/92, A, C, 92001019

Division Street Historic District, Roughly bounded by State St., Iranistan, Black Rock and West Aves., Bridgeport, 6/03/82, A, B, C, 82004385

Downtown Stamford Historic District, Atlantic, Main, Bank, and Bedford Sts., Stamford, 10/06/83, A, C, 83003502

Downtown Stamford Historic District (Boundary Increase), Bounded by Atlantic, Main, Bank, Bedford, Summer between Broad and Main Sts.

and Summer Pl., Stamford, 2/21/85, A, C, 85000311

ELMER S. DAILEY, Bridgeport Harbor, Bridgeport, 12/21/78, A, 78002838

Eagle's Nest, 282-284 Logan St., Bridgeport, 3/05/79, B, b, 79002630

East Bridgeport Historic District, Roughly bounded by RR tracks, Beach, Arctic, and Knowlton Sts., Bridgeport, 4/25/79, A, B, C, 79002659

East Main Street Historic District, Bounded by Walters and Nichols Sts. from 371-377, 741-747, 388-394 and to 744 East Main Sts., Bridgeport, 2/21/85, A, C, 85000306

Fairfield County Courthouse, 172 Golden Hill St., Bridgeport, 1/21/82, A, C, 82004376

Fairfield County Jail, 1106 North Ave., Bridgeport, 4/18/85, A, C, 85000841

Fairfield Historic District, Old Post Rd. from Post Rd. to Turney Rd., Fairfield, 3/24/71, A, C, 71000897

Fairfield Railroad Stations, Carter Henry Dr., Fairfield vicinity, 7/28/89, A, C, 89000926

Ferris, Samuel, House, E. Putnam and Cary Sts., Greenwich, 8/10/89, C, b, 89001086

First Baptist Church, 126 Washington Ave., Bridgeport, 2/22/90, C, a, 90000154

Fort Stamford Site, Address Restricted, Stamford vicinity, 9/10/75, A, D, 75001920

French Farm, N of Greenwich at jct. of Lake Ave. and Round Hill Rd., Greenwich vicinity, 4/03/75, C, 75001918

Gateway Village Historic District [Wartime Emergency Housing in Bridgeport MPS], Roughly bounded by Waterman St., Connecticut Ave. and Alanson Ave., Bridgeport, 9/26/90, A, C, 90001429

Georgetown Historic District, Roughly bounded by US 7, Portland Ave., CT 107, and the Norwalk River, Redding, 3/09/87, A, C, 87000343

Glover House, 50 Main St., Newtown, 2/11/82, A, C, 82004369

Godillot Place, 60, 65 Jesup Rd., Westport, 8/29/77, C, 77001396

Golden Hill Historic District [Downtown Bridgeport MRA], Roughly bounded by Congress St., Lyon Terr., Elm, and Harrison Sts., Bridgeport, 9/03/87, C, a, 87001404

Great Captain Island Lighthouse, Great Captain Island, SW of Greenwich Pt., Greenwich, 4/03/91, C, 91000351

Green Farms School [Westport MPS], Jct. of Morningside Dr. S. and Boston Post Rd., Westport, 4/19/91, C, 91000391

Greenfield Hill Historic District, Roughly bounded by Meeting House Ln., Hillside Rd., Verna Hil Rd. and Bronson Rd., Greenfield Hill, 3/11/71, B, C, a, 71000899

Greens Ledge Lighthouse [Operating Lighthouses in Connecticut MPS], Long Island Sound, S of

Fairfield County—Continued

Five Mile River and W of Norwalk Harbor, Rowayton vicinity, 5/29/90, A, C, 89001468

Greenwich Avenue Historic District, Roughly bounded by Railroad, Arch, Field Point, W. Elm, Greenwich, Putnam, Mason, Havemeyer, and Bruce, Greenwich, 8/31/89, C, 89001215

Greenwich Municipal Center Historic District, 101 Field Point Rd., 290, 299, 310 Greenwich Ave., Greenwich, 7/26/88, A, C, f, 88000579

Greenwich Town Hall, 229 Greenwich Ave., Greenwich, 5/21/87, A, B, C, 87000807

Hait, Benjamin, House, 92 Hoyclo Rd., Stamford, 11/30/78, C, 78002844

Haviland and Elizabeth Streets—Hanford Place Historic District, Roughly bounded by Haviland, Day Sts., Hanford Pl., and S. Main St., Norwalk, 5/26/88, A, C, 88000664

Hawley, Thomas, House, 514 Purdy Hill Rd., Monroe, 4/11/80, C, 80004059

Hearthstone, 18 Brushy Hill Rd., Danbury, 12/31/87, C, 87002184

Hotel Beach, 140 Fairfield Ave., Bridgeport, 12/14/78, C, 78002839

Housatonic River Railroad Bridge [Movable Railroad Bridges on the NE Corridor in Connecticut TR], AMTRAK Right-of-Way at Housatonic River, Milford-Stratford vicinity, 6/12/87, A, C, 87000842

Hoyt-Barnum House, 713 Bedford St., Stamford, 6/11/69, C, 69000199

Hyatt, Thomas, House, 11 Barlow Mountain Rd., Ridgefield, 2/16/84, C, 84000793

Ives, Charles, House, 7 Mountainville Ave., Danbury, 4/26/76, B, C, b, c, 76001968

Judson, Capt. David, House, 967 Academy Hill, Stratford, 3/20/73, C, 73001946

June, Lewis, House, 478 N. Salem Rd., Ridgefield, 2/16/84, C, 84000795

Kaatz Icehouse, N of Trumbull at 255 Whitney Ave., Trumbull vicinity, 9/19/77, A, C, 77001395

Keeler Tavern, 132 Main St., Ridgefield, 4/29/82, A, B, C, 82004345

Knap, John, House, 984 Stillwater Rd., Stamford, 3/05/79, C, 79002625

Knapp Tavern, 243 E. Putnam Ave., Greenwich, 9/15/77, B, 77001389

Lakeview Village Historic District [Wartime Emergency Housing in Bridgeport MPS], Roughly bounded by Essex St., Boston Ave., Colony St., Plymouth St. and Asylum St., Bridgeport, 9/26/90, A, C, 90001428

Lambert, David, House, 150 Danbury Rd., Wilton, 7/24/92, A, C, b, 92000908

Lattin, Nathan B., Farm, 22 Walker Hill Rd., Newtown vicinity, 5/24/90, C, 90000760

Lewis, Isaac, House, 50 Paradise Green Pl., Stratford, 11/21/91, C, 91001739

Linden Apartments, 10-12 Linden Pl., Stamford, 8/11/83, C, 83001252

Lockwood-Mathews Mansion, 295 West Ave., Norwalk, 12/30/70, C, NHL, 70000836

Locust Avenue School, Locust Ave., Danbury, 5/30/85, A, C, 85001162

Long Ridge Village Historic District, Old Long Ridge Rd. bounded by the New York State Line, Rock Rimmon Rd., and Long Ridge Rd./CT 104, Stamford, 6/02/87, A, C, 86003653

Loth, Joseph, Company Building, 25 Grand St., Norwalk, 5/17/84, A, C, 84000804

Lounsbury, Phineas Chapman, House, 316 Main St., Ridgefield, 10/03/75, B, C, 75001919

Lyon, Thomas, House, W. Putnam Ave. and Byram Rd., Greenwich, 8/24/77, A, C, b, 77001390

Main Street Bridge, Carries Main St. over the Rippowam River, Stamford, 5/21/87, A, C, 87000801

Main Street Historic District, Boughton, Elm, Ives, Keeler, Main, West and White Sts., Danbury, 11/29/83, A, B, C, 83003508

Mallett, David, Jr., House, 420 Tashua Rd., Trumbull, 2/20/86, A, C, 86000266

Maplewood School, 434 Maplewood Ave., Bridgeport, 2/21/90, A, C, 90000153

Marina Park Historic District, Marina Park, Park and Waldemere Aves., Bridgeport, 4/27/82, B, C, 82004382

Marion Castle, Terre Bonne, 1 Rogers Rd., Stamford, 7/01/82, B, C, 82004341

Marvin Tavern, 405 Danbury Rd., Wilton, 4/26/84, C, 84000806

Mather, Stephen Tyng, House, 19 Stephen Mather Rd., Darien, 10/15/66, B, NHL, 66000877

Meadowlands, 274 Middlesex Rd., Darien, 10/06/87, C, 87001408

Meeker's Hardware, 86-90 White St., Danbury, 6/09/83, A, C, 83001253

Merritt Parkway, CT 15 and right-of-way between the NY state line and the Housatonic R. bridge, Greenwich vicinity, 4/17/91, A, C, 91000410

Methodist Episcopal Church, 61 E. Putnam Ave., Greenwich, 8/25/88, C, a, 88001343

Mianus River Railroad Bridge [Movable Railroad Bridges on the NE Corridor in Connecticut TR], AMTRAK Right-of-way at Mianus River, Greenwich, 6/12/87, A, C, 87000845

Mill Cove Historic District [Westport MPS], Between Compo Mill Cove and Long Island Sound, Westport, 4/19/91, A, C, 91000392

Monroe Center Historic District, CT 110 and CT 111, Monroe, 8/19/77, A, C, a, 77001392

Nathaniel Wheeler Memorial Fountain, Park and Fairfield Aves., Bridgeport, 4/04/85, A, B, C, f, 85000706

National Hall Historic District, Riverside Ave., Wilton and Post Rds., Westport, 9/13/84, A, C, 84000812

New Mill and Depot Building, Hawthorne Woolen Mill, 350 Pemberwick Rd., Greenwich vicinity, 2/23/90, C, 90000152

New York Belting and Packing Co., 45-71 and 79-89 Glen Rd., Newtown, 6/02/82, C, D, 82004367

Nichols Farms Historic District, Center Rd., 1681–1944 Huntington Turnpike, 5–34 Priscilla Pl., and 30–172 Shelton Rd., Trumbull, 8/20/87, C, 87001392

Norfield Historic District, Roughly, jct. of Weston and Norfield Rds. NE to Hedgerow Common, Weston, 7/31/91, A, C, 91000955

Norwalk Island Lighthouse, Sheffield Island, Norwalk, 1/19/89, A, C, 88003222

Norwalk River Railroad Bridge [Movable Railroad Bridges on the NE Corridor in Connecticut TR], AMTRAK Right-of-way at Norwalk River, South Norwalk vicinity, 6/12/87, A, C, 87000844

Octagon House, 21 Spring St., Danbury, 5/07/73, C, 73001945

Octagon House, 120 Strawberry Hill Ave., Stamford, 8/17/79, C, 79002624

Ogden, David, House, 1520 Bronson Rd., Fairfield, 8/17/79, A, C, 79002651

Old Mine Park Archeological Site, Address Restricted, Trumbull vicinity, 12/13/90, A, D, 90001807

Old Town Hall, Jct. of Atlantic, Bank, and Main Sts., Stamford, 6/02/72, A, C, 72001304

Osborne, John, House, 909 King's Hwy. W, Fairfield, 2/12/87, C, 87000118

PRICILLA DAILEY, Bridgeport Harbor, Bridgeport, 12/21/78, A, 78002840

Palace and Majestic Theaters, 1315-1357 Main St., Bridgeport, 12/14/79, A, C, 79002626

Park Apartments [Wartime Emergency Housing in Bridgeport MPS], 59 Rennell St., Bridgeport, 9/26/90, A, C, 90001427

Peck Ledge Lighthouse [Operating Lighthouses in Connecticut MPS], Long Island Sound, SE of Norwalk Harbor and NE of Goose Island, Norwalk vicinity, 5/29/90, A, C, 89001472

Penfield Reef Lighthouse [Operating Lighthouses in Connecticut MPS], Long Island Sound off Shoal Point, Bridgeport vicinity, 9/27/90, A, C, 89001473

Pequonnock River Railroad Bridge [Movable Railroad Bridges on the NE Corridor in Connecticut TR], AMTRAK Right-of-way at Pequonnock River, Bridgeport, 6/12/87, A, C, 87000843

Perry, David, House, 531 Lafayette St., Bridgeport, 3/22/84, C, b, 84000814

Pike, Gustavus and Sarah T., House, 164 Fairfield Ave., Stamford, 5/24/90, C, 90000759

Pine Creek Park Bridge, N of Old Dam Rd., over Pine Cr., Fairfield, 4/08/92, C, b, 92000263

Plumb Memorial Library, 47 Wooster St., Shelton, 11/07/78, C, 78002845

Pond-Weed House, 2591 Post Rd., Darien, 10/11/78, A, C, 78002842

Putnam Hill Historic District, U.S. 1, Greenwich, 8/24/79, B, C, a, 79002657

Putnam Memorial State Park, Jct. of Rtes. 58 (Black Rock Tpke.) and 107 (Park Rd.), Redding, 12/29/70, A, B, 70000683

Railroad Avenue Industrial District, Roughly bounded by State and Cherry Sts., Fairfield and Wordin Aves., Bridgeport, 9/30/85, A, C, 85002697

Redding Center Historic District, Roughly, 4–25B Cross Hwy., including Read Cemetery, 61–100 Hill Rd., 0–15 Lonetown Rd. and 118 Sanfordtown Rd., Redding, 10/01/92, C, 92001253

Remington City Historic District [Wartime Emergency Housing in Bridgeport MPS], Roughly, Bond, Dover, and Remington Sts. and Palisade

Fairfield County—Continued

Ave., between Stewart and Tudor Sts., Bridgeport, 9/26/90, A, C, 90001426

Remington Village Historic District [Wartime Emergency Housing in Bridgeport MPS], Roughly, Willow and East Aves. between Boston and Barnum Aves., Bridgeport, 9/26/90, A, C, 90001425

Remington, Frederic, House, 154 Barry Ave., Ridgefield, 10/15/66, B, NHL, 66000880

Revonah Manor Historic District, Roughly bounded by Urban St., East Ave., Fifth, and Bedford Sts., Stamford, 7/31/86, A, C, 86002100

Rider, John, House, 43 Main St., Danbury, 11/23/77, C, 77001388

Ridgebury Congregational Church, Ridgebury Rd. and George Washington Hwy., Ridgebury, 3/01/84, C, a, 84000815

Ridgefield Center Historic District, Roughly bounded by Pound St., Fairview Ave., Prospect, Ridge, and Whipstick Rds., Ridgefield, 9/07/84, C, 84000817

Riverside Avenue Bridge, Riverside Ave. and RR tracks, Greenwich, 8/29/77, A, C, 77001391

Robinson, P., Fur Cutting Company, Oil Mill Rd., Danbury, 11/30/82, A, C, 82000998

Rock Ledge, S of Norwalk at 33, 40-42 Highland Ave., Norwalk vicinity, 8/02/77, B, C, 77001394

Rogers, John, Studio, 33 Oenoke Ridge, New Canaan, 10/15/66, B, b, NHL, 66000881

Saugatuck River Bridge, CT 136, Westport, 2/12/87, A, C, 87000126

Saugatuck River Railroad Bridge [Movable Railroad Bridges on the NE Corridor in Connecticut TR], AMTRAK Right-of-way at Saugatuck River, Westport, 6/12/87, A, C, 87000846

Seaside Institute, 299 Lafayette Ave., Bridgeport, 6/14/82, A, C, 82004374

Seaside Park, Long Island Sound, Bridgeport, 7/01/82, A, B, C, f, 82004373

Seaside Village Historic District [Wartime Emergency Housing in Bridgeport MPS], E. side of Iranistan Ave. between South St. and Burnham St., Bridgeport, 9/26/90, A, C, 90001424

Seelye, Seth, House, 189 Greenwood Ave., Bethel, 8/29/77, B, C, 77001386

Selleck, Sylvanus, Gristmill, 124 Old Mill Rd., Greenwich, 8/02/90, A, C, 90001109

Sherman Historic District, Roughly, jct. of Old Greenswood Rd. and CT 37 Center NE past jct. of CT 37 E and CT 39 N, and Sawmill Rd., Sherman, 7/31/91, A, C, 91000956

Sloan-Raymond-Fitch House, 249 Danbury Rd., Wilton, 4/29/82, C, 82004344

Sound Beach Railroad Station, 160 Sound Beach Ave., Greenwich vicinity, 7/28/89, A, C, 89000929

South End Historic District, Roughly bounded by Penn Central RR tracks, Stamford Canal, Woodland Cemetery, and Washington Blvd., Stamford, 3/19/86, A, C, 86000472

South Main and Washington Streets Historic District, 68-139 Washington St. and 2-24 S. Main St., Norwalk, 12/16/77, C, 77001393

South Main and Washington Streets Historic District (Boundary Increase), 11-15 through 54-60 S. Main St., Norwalk, 11/08/85, A, C, 85003505

Southport Historic District, Roughly bounded by Southport Harbor, RR, Old South Rd. and Rose Hill Rd., Fairfield, 3/24/71, A, C, 71000898

Southport Railroad Stations, 96 Station St. and 100 Center St., Fairfield, 7/28/89, A, C, 89000927

St. Andrew's Protestant Episcopal Church [Downtown Stamford Ecclesiastical Complexes TR (AD)], 1231 Washington Blvd., Stamford, 12/06/83, C, a, 83003510

St. Benedict's Church [Downtown Stamford Ecclesiastical Complexes TR], 1A St. Benedict's Circle, Stamford, 12/24/87, C, a, 87002130

St. John's Episcopal Church, 768 Fairfield Ave., Bridgeport, 8/02/84, C, a, 84000820

St. John's Protestant Episcopal Church [Downtown Stamford Ecclesiastical Complexes TR], 628 Main St., Stamford, 12/24/87, A, C, a, 87002128

St. Luke's Chapel [Downtown Stamford Ecclesiastical Complexes TR], 714 Pacific St., Stamford, 12/24/87, C, a, 87002129

St. Mary's Church [Downtown Stamford Ecclesiastical Complexes TR], 540 Elm St., Stamford, 12/24/87, C, a, 87002123

Stamford Harbor Lighthouse, South of breakwater, Stamford Harbor, Stamford, 4/03/91, A, C, 91000348

Starr, C. J., Barn and Carriage House, 200 Strawberry Hill Ave., Stamford, 9/14/79, C, 79002623

Sterling Block-Bishop Arcade, 993-1005 Main St., Bridgeport, 12/20/78, A, C, 78002841

Sterling Hill Historic District, Roughly bounded by Pequonnock St., Harral Ave., James St. and Washington Ave., Bridgeport, 4/02/92, A, C, b, 92000335

Sterling Homestead, 2225 Main St., Stratford, 1/01/76, B, C, 76001973

Stratfield Historic District, CT 59 and U.S. 1, Bridgeport, 6/23/80, C, a, d, 80004060

Stratford Center Historic District, Roughly bounded by E. Broadway, Ferry Blvd., Housatonic River, Connecticut Tnpke, Birdseye and Main Sts., Stratford, 12/22/83, A, C, 83003511

Stratford Point Lighthouse [Operating Lighthouses in Connecticut MPS], Stratford Point at mouth of Housatonic River, Stratford, 5/29/90, A, C, 89001476

Strickland Road Historic District, 19-47 Strickland Rd., Greenwich, 3/22/90, C, 77001625

Sturges, Jonathan, House, 449 Mill Plain Rd., Fairfield, 11/23/84, B, C, 84000247

Suburban Club, 6 Suburban Ave./580 Main St., Stamford, 8/10/89, A, C, 89001090

Tarbell, Ida, House, 320 Valley Rd., Easton, 4/19/93, B, NHL, 93001602

Tarrywile, Southern Blvd. & Mountain Rd., Danbury, 1/06/88, B, C, 87001409

Tongue Point Lighthouse [Operating Lighthouses in Connecticut MPS], W side of Bridgeport Harbor at Tongue Point, Bridgeport vicinity, 5/29/90, A, C, b, 89001478

Town Hall, 90 Post Rd. E., Westport, 5/18/82, C, 82004343

Turn-of-River Bridge, Old N. Stamford Rd. at Rippowam River, Stamford, 7/31/87, A, C, 87000798

US Post Office—Bridgeport Main, 120 Middle St., Bridgeport, 3/17/86, C, 86000453

US Post Office—Greenwich Main, 310 Greenwich Ave., Greenwich, 1/16/86, C, 86000077

US Post Office—South Norwalk Main, 16 Washington St., Norwalk, 1/21/86, C, g, 86000126

US Post Office—Stamford Main, 421 Atlantic St., Stamford, 12/12/85, C, 85003328

Umpawaug District School, Umpawaug Rd., Redding, 12/01/88, A, C, 88002695

Union Station, White St. and Patriot Dr., Danbury, 9/25/86, A, C, 86002750

Unitarian-Universalist Church [Downtown Stamford Ecclesiastical Complexes TR], 20 Forest St., Stamford, 12/24/87, C, a, 87002126

United Congregational Church, 877 Park Ave., Bridgeport, 7/19/84, C, a, 84000822

United Illuminating Company Building, 1115-1119 Broad St., Bridgeport, 2/21/85, A, C, 85000301

Weir, J. Alden, Farm (District), Nod Hill Rd. and Pelham Lane, Ridgefield, 1/05/84, B, C, d, 84000825

West Mountain Historic District, CT 102, Ridgefield vicinity, 2/23/84, C, 84000828

Wheeler, Ephraim, House, 470 Whippoorwill Ln., Stratford, 4/17/92, C, 92000318

Wilcox, Josiah, House, 354 Riversville Rd., Greenwich, 11/30/88, C, 88001344

Wilmot Apartments Historic District [Wartime Emergency Housing in Bridgeport MPS], Jct. of Connecticut and Wilmot Aves., Bridgeport, 9/26/90, A, C, 90001423

Zion Lutheran Church [Downtown Stamford Ecclesiastical Complexes TR], 132 Glenbrook Rd., Stamford, 12/24/87, C, a, 87002127

Hartford County

Academy Hall, 785 Old Main St., Rocky Hill, 10/07/77, A, C, 77001419

Allen's Cider Mill, 7 Mountain Rd., Granby, 4/28/92, A, C, b, 92000389

Allyn, Capt. Benjamin, II, House [18th and 19th Century Brick Architecture of Windsor TR (AD)], 119 Deerfield Rd., Windsor, 6/26/79, C, 79002633

Andrews, Luman, House [Colonial Houses of Southington TR], 469 Andrews St., Southington, 1/19/89, C, 88003095

Ann Street Historic District, Allyn, Ann, Asylum, Church, Hicks and Pearl Sts., Hartford, 11/28/83, A, C, 83003514

Apartment at 49-51 Spring Street [Asylum Hill MRA], 49-51 Spring St., Hartford, 3/31/83, C, 83001255

Armsmear, 80 Wethersfield Ave., Hartford, 11/13/66, B, NHL, 66000802

Hartford County—Continued

Asylum Avenue District [Asylum Hill MRA], Asylum and Farmington Aves., and Sigourney St., Hartford, 11/29/79, C, 79002672

Atwater Manufacturing Company [Historic Industrial Complexes of Southington TR], 335 Atwater St., Southington vicinity, 12/08/88, A, C, 88002678

Avon Congregational Church, Jct. of U.S. 202 and 44, Avon, 11/07/72, A, C, a, 72001342

B.P.O. Elks Lodge [Hartford Downtown MRA], 34 Prospect St., Hartford, 12/23/84, C, 84000753

Barber, Giles, House [18th and 19th Century Brick Architecture of Windsor TR], 411–413 Windsor Ave., Windsor, 9/15/88, A, C, 88001498

Barbour, Lucius, House, 130 Washington St., Hartford, 8/21/79, C, 79002629

Barnard, Henry, House, 118 Main St., Hartford, 10/15/66, B, NHL, 66000803

Barnes, Selah, House [Colonial Houses of Southington TR], 282 Prospect St., Southington, 1/19/89, C, 88003114

Barnes—Frost House [Colonial Houses of Southington TR], 1177 Marion Ave., Southington, 1/19/89, C, 88003109

Batterson Block [Hartford Downtown MRA], 26–28 High St., Hartford, 12/23/84, C, 84000758

Beach, Charles E., House, 18 Brightwood Ln., West Hartford, 8/23/90, C, 90001287

Beardsley—Mix House [Eighteenth-Century Houses of West Hartford TR], 81 Rockledge Dr., West Hartford, 9/10/86, A, C, b, 86001980

Belden, Horace, School and Central Grammar School, 933 Hopmeadow St. and 29 Massaco St., Simsbury, 3/25/93, B, C, 93000211

Beleden House, 50 Bellevue Ave., Bristol, 3/15/82, C, 82004392

Bemont, Makens, House, 307 Burnside Ave., East Hartford, 3/25/82, C, b, 82004397

Bigelow-Hartford Carpet Mills, Main and Pleasant Sts., Thompsonville, 3/10/83, A, C, 83001256

Bissell Tavern-Bissell's Stage House, 1022 Palisado Ave., Windsor, 8/23/85, B, C, 85001825

Blakeslee Forging Company [Historic Industrial Complexes of Southington TR], 100 W. Main St., Southington vicinity, 12/08/88, A, C, 88002676

Brace, Moses—Uriah Cadwell House [Eighteenth-Century Houses of West Hartford TR], 11 Flagg Rd., West Hartford, 9/10/86, A, C, 86001982

Bradley, Icabod, House [Colonial Houses of Southington TR], 537 Shuttle Meadow Rd., Southington, 7/28/89, C, 88003115

Brewer, Selden, House, 137 High St., East Hartford, 6/04/79, B, C, 79002631

Bristol Girls' Club, 47 Upson St., Bristol, 6/03/87, A, C, 87000347

Broad Brook Company, Main St., East Windsor, 5/02/85, A, C, 85000950

Brown Tavern, George Washington Tpke., Burlington, 5/05/72, C, 72001339

Buckingham Square District, Main and Buckingham St., Linden Pl., and Capitol Ave., Hartford, 6/05/77, C, 77001404

Buckingham Square Historic District (Boundary Increase), 248-250 Hudson St., Hartford, 11/30/82, C, 82000999

Building at 136-138 Collins Street [Asylum Hill MRA], 136-138 Collins St., Hartford, 11/29/79, C, 79002681

Building at 142 Collins Street [Asylum Hill MRA], 142 Collins St., Hartford, 11/29/79, C, 79002680

Building at 83-85 Sigourney Street [Asylum Hill MRA], 83-85 Sigourney St., Hartford, 11/29/79, C, 79002679

Bulkeley Bridge, I-84 over the Connecticut R., Hartford, 12/10/93, A, C, 93001347

Bull, Amos, House, 59 S. Prospect St., Hartford, 11/08/68, C, b, 68000039

Burnham, Edward L., Farm, 580 Burnham St., Manchester, 4/12/82, A, C, 82004436

Burritt Hotel, 67 W. Main St., New Britain, 7/28/83, A, C, 83001257

Burwell, Ernest R., House, 161 Grove St., Bristol, 8/18/92, C, 92001009

Bushnell Park, Bounded by Elm, Jewell, and Trinity Sts., Hartford, 10/22/70, A, B, f, 70000692

Butler, James, House [Eighteenth-Century Houses of West Hartford TR], 239 N. Main St., West Hartford, 9/10/86, A, C, 86001987

Butler-McCook Homestead, 396 Main St., Hartford, 3/11/71, B, C, 71000907

Buttolph-Williams House, 249 Broad St., Wethersfield, 11/24/68, C, NHL, 68000048

Capen-Clark Historic District, Capen, Clark, Elmer, Barbour, Martin, and Main Sts., Hartford, 4/27/82, C, 82004402

Carter, John, House [Colonial Houses of Southington TR], 1096 West St., Southington, 1/19/89, C, b, 88003189

Case, Benomi, House [18th and 19th Century Brick Architecture of Windsor TR], 436 Rainbow Rd., Windsor, 9/15/88, A, C, 88001497

Central Avenue—Center Cemetery Historic District [East Hartford MPS], Center Ave. from Main St. to Elm St. and Center Cemetery to the N, East Hartford, 4/19/93, A, C, d, 93000289

Chaffee, Hezekiah, House [18th and 19th Century Brick Architecture of Windsor TR (AD)], Meadow Lane, off Palisado Green, Windsor, 7/31/72, C, 72001336

Chapman, Taylor, House [18th and 19th Century Brick Architecture of Windsor TR], 407 Palisado Ave., Windsor, 9/15/88, A, C, 88001492

Charter Oak Bank Building, 114-124 Asylum St., Hartford, 10/11/78, C, 78002873

Charter Oak Place, 7-40 Charter Oak Pl., Hartford, 1/20/78, A, C, 78002884

Charter Oak Place (Boundary Increase), 1-3 Charter Oak Pl., Hartford, 5/12/82, C, b, 82004403

Cheney Brothers Historic District, Bounded by Hartford Rd., Laurel, Spruce, and Lampfield Sts., Manchester, 6/02/78, A, NHL, 78002885

Cheney Building, 942 Main St., Hartford, 10/06/70, A, C, 78002852

Children's Village of the Hartford Orphan Asylum, 1680 Albany Ave., Hartford, 6/28/82, A, C, 82004404

Christ Church, 955 Main St., Hartford, 12/29/83, B, C, a, 83003558

Church of the Good Shepherd and Parish House, 155 Wyllys St., Hartford, 2/20/75, A, C, a, 75001925

City Hall-Monument District, W. Main St. and Central Park, New Britain, 2/28/73, A, C, f, 73001957

Clark Brothers Factory No. 1 [Historic Industrial Complexes of Southington TR], 1331 S. Main St., Southington vicinity, 12/08/88, A, C, 88002679

Clark Brothers Factory No. 2 [Historic Industrial Complexes of Southington TR], 409 Canal St., Southington vicinity, 12/08/88, A, C, 88002680

Clark, Avery, House [Colonial Houses of Southington TR], 1460 Meriden Ave., Southington, 1/19/89, C, 88003110

Clay Hill Historic District, Roughly bounded by Main, Mather, Garden, and Walnut Sts., Hartford, 6/16/83, A, C, 83001258

Clay Hill Historic District (Boundary Increase), 8 Florence St., Hartford, 2/16/84, C, 84000833

Collins and Townley Streets District [Asylum Hill MRA], Collins and Townley Sts., Hartford, 11/29/79, C, 79002676

Collinsville Historic District, CT 179, Collinsville, 6/23/76, A, C, 76001994

Colt Industrial District, Roughly bounded by Wawarme, Wethersfield, Hendricxsen, Van Dyke Aves., and Stonington, Masseek, and Sequassen Sts., Hartford, 6/08/76, A, B, C, 76001987

Colt, James B., House, 154 Wethersfield Ave., Hartford, 4/14/75, C, 75001926

Colton, Benjamin, House [Eighteenth-Century Houses of West Hartford TR], 25 Sedgewick Rd., West Hartford, 9/10/86, A, C, 86001988

Congress Street, Both sides of Congress St. from Wyllys to Morris Sts., Hartford, 10/06/75, C, 75001927

Congress Street Historic District (Boundary Increase), 54, 56 and 58 Maple Ave., Hartford, 7/24/92, C, 92000903

Connecticut State Capitol, Capitol Ave., Hartford, 12/30/70, A, NHL, 70000834

Connecticut State Library and Supreme Court Building, 231 Capitol Ave., Hartford, 6/04/81, A, C, 81000535

Connecticut Statehouse, Main St. at Central Row, Hartford, 10/15/66, A, C, NHL, 66000878

Copper Ledges and Chimney Crest, Along Founders Dr. between Bradley and Woodland Sts., Bristol, 8/21/92, C, 92001010

Cossitt, Frederick H., Library, 388 N. Granby Rd., Granby, 6/22/88, B, C, 88000708

Cowles, Capt. Josiah, House [Colonial Houses of Southington TR], 184 Marion Ave., Southington, 1/19/89, C, 88003102

Cowles, Gen. George, House, 130 Main St., Farmington, 5/11/82, B, C, 82004400

Curtisville Historic District, Roughly, Pratt St. from Naubuc Ave. to W of Main St., also Parker Terr., Parker Terr. Extd. and adjacent parts of Naubuc, Glastonbury, 12/14/92, A, C, 92001638

Hartford County—Continued

Darling, Robert and Julia, House, 720 Hopmeadow St., Simsbury, 1/03/91, C, 90002117

Day House, 77 Forest St., Hartford, 4/16/71, A, C, 71000909

Day, Calvin, House, 105 Spring St., Hartford, 12/18/78, C, 78002872

Day-Taylor House, 81 Wethersfield Ave., Hartford, 4/14/75, C, 75001930

Deane, Silas, House, 203 Main St., Wethersfield, 10/06/70, B, C, NHL, 70000835

Dillon Building, 69-71 Pratt St., Hartford, 2/11/82, C, 82004407

Drake Hill Road Bridge, Drake Hill Rd. at Farmington River, Simsbury, 7/19/84, C, 84000999

East Granby Historic District, Church and East Sts., Nicholson and Rainbow Rds., N. Main, School and S. Main Sts., East Granby, 8/25/88, A, C, a, b, d, 88001318

East Weatogue Historic District, Roughly, properties on East Weatogue St. from just N of Riverside Dr. to Hartford Rd., and Folly Farm property to S, Simsbury, 7/19/90, A, C, 90001107

East Windsor Hill Historic District, Roughly bounded by the Scantic River, John Fitch Blvd., Sullivan Ave., and the Connecticut River, South Windsor, 5/30/86, A, C, a, 86001208

Elizabeth Park, Asylum Ave., West Hartford, 3/10/83, C, 83001259

Ellsworth, Horace H., House [18th and 19th Century Brick Architecture of Windsor TR], 316 Palisado Ave., Windsor, 9/15/88, A, C, 88001489

Ellsworth, Oliver, Homestead, 778 Palisado Ave., Windsor, 10/06/70, A, B, C, NHL, 70000707

Elm Street Historic District, 71-166 Capitol Ave., 55-97 Elm St., 20-30 Trinity St., Hartford, 6/28/84, A, C, 84001003

Elmore Houses, 78 and 87 Long Hill Rd., South Windsor, 8/23/85, A, C, 85001832

Enfield Canal, Along Connecticut River from Windsor Locks N to Thompsonville, Windsor Locks vicinity, 4/22/76, A, C, 76001998

Enfield Historic District, 1106-1492 Enfield St., Enfield, 8/10/79, C, 79002664

Enfield Shakers Historic District, Shaker, Taylor and Cybulski Rds., Enfield, 5/21/79, A, C, a, 79002663

Enfield Town Meetinghouse, Enfield St. at South Rd., Enfield, 9/10/74, C, b, 74002050

Engine Company 1 Fire Station [Firehouses of Hartford MPS], 197 Main St. and 36 John St., Hartford, 3/02/89, A, C, 89000025

Engine Company 15 Fire Station [Firehouses of Hartford MPS], 8 Fairfield Ave., Hartford, 3/02/89, A, C, 89000023

Engine Company 16 Fire Station [Firehouses of Hartford MPS] 636 Blue Hills Ave., Hartford, 3/02/89, A, C, 89000021

Engine Company 2 Fire Station [Firehouses of Hartford MPS], 1515 Main St., Hartford, 3/02/89, A, C, 89000022

Engine Company 6 Fire Station [Firehouses of Hartford MPS], 34 Huyshope Ave., Hartford, 3/02/89, A, C, 89000020

Engine Company 9 Fire Station [Firehouses of Hartford MPS], 655 New Britain Ave., Hartford, 3/02/89, A, C, 89000024

Eno Memorial Hall, 754 Hopmeadow St., Simsbury, 4/02/93, B, C, 93000210

Eno, Amos, House, Off U. S. 202 on Hopmeadow Rd., Simsbury, 4/03/75, B, 75001935

Evans, Ebenezer, House [Colonial Houses of Southington TR], 17 Long Bottom Rd., Southington, 1/19/89, C, 88003101

Farmington Canal-New Haven and Northampton Canal, Roughly from Suffield in Hartford Cty. to New Haven in New Haven Cty., Suffield, 9/12/85, A, C, D, 85002664

Farmington Historic District, Porter and Mountain Rds., Main and Garden Sts., Hatter's and Hillstead Lanes, and Farmington Ave., Farmington, 3/17/72, A, C, a, 72001331

Farmington River Railroad Bridge, Spans Farmington River and Pleasant St. W of Palisado Ave., Windsor, 8/25/72, A, C, 72001334

Farnsworth, Samuel, House [Eighteenth-Century Houses of West Hartford TR], 537 Mountain Rd., West Hartford, 9/10/86, A, C, 86001990

Federal Hill Historic District, Roughly bounded by Summer, Maple, Woodland, Goodwin, and High Sts., Bristol, 8/28/86, A, C, 86001989

First Church Parsonage [18th and 19th Century Brick Architecture of Windsor TR], 160 Palisado Ave., Windsor, 9/15/88, A, C, 88001488

First Church of Christ, 75 Main St., Farmington, 5/15/75, A, C, a, NHL, 75002056

First Church of Christ and the Ancient Burying Ground, 60 Gold St., Hartford, 12/05/72, A, C, a, d, 72001324

First Congregational Church of East Hartford and Parsonage, 829-837 Main St., East Hartford, 3/25/82, A, C, a, 82004398

First National Bank Building [Hartford Downtown MRA], 50 State St., Hartford, 12/23/84, C, 84000766

Fitch, John, School, 156 Bloomfield Ave., Windsor, 12/02/86, C, 86003326

Footguard Hall [Hartford Downtown MRA], Footguard and High Sts., Hartford, 12/23/84, A, C, 84000771

Forestville Passenger Station, 171 Central St., Bristol, 4/19/78, A, C, 78002862

Former Fire Station [18th and 19th Century Brick Architecture of Windsor TR], 14 Maple Ave., Windsor, 9/15/88, A, C, 88001485

Fourth Congregational Church, Albany Ave. and Vine St., Hartford, 4/12/82, A, C, a, 82004409

Frog Hollow, Roughly bounded by Park River, Capitol Ave., Oak, Washington, and Madison Sts. and Park Ter., Hartford, 4/11/79, A, C, 79002635

Frog Hollow Historic District (Boundary Increase), Bounded by Park Terr., Hillside Ave., Hamilton and Summit Sts., Hartford, 3/01/84, C, 84001005

Frost, Levi B., House, 1089 Marion Ave., Southington, 11/20/87, C, 87002037

Fuller, John, House, 463 Halliday Ave., Suffield vicinity, 3/15/82, A, C, 82004439

Garvan—Carroll Historic District [East Hartford MPS], Roughly bounded by S. Prospect, Chapel and Main Sts. and I-84, East Hartford, 8/26/91, A, C, 91001049

Gillett, Asa, House [Eighteenth-Century Houses of West Hartford TR], 202 S. Main St., West Hartford, 9/10/86, A, C, 86001992

Gillette, Francis, House, 545 Bloomfield Ave., Bloomfield, 3/25/82, B, C, 82004391

Gilman-Hayden House, 1871 Main St., East Hartford, 8/16/84, B, C, 84001007

Glastonbury Historic District, Roughly Main St. from Hebron Ave. to Talcott Rd., Glastonbury, 8/02/84, C, 84001011

Goodman, Timothy, House [Eighteenth-Century Houses of West Hartford TR], 567 Quaker Ln. S, West Hartford, 9/10/86, A, C, 86001993

Goodwin Block, 219-257 Asylum St., 5-17 Hayes St., 210-228 Pearl St., Hartford, 3/26/76, A, C, 76001990

Gothic Cottage, 1425 Mapleton Ave., Suffield, 2/25/82, C, 82004441

Grace Church Rectory [18th and 19th Century Brick Architecture of Windsor TR], 301 Broad St., Windsor, 9/15/88, A, C, a, 88001477

Granby Center Historic District, 3–8 E. Granby Rd., 2 Park Pl., and 207–265 Salmon Brook St. S, Granby, 10/17/85, C, 85003149

Grannis, Stephen, House [Colonial Houses of Southington TR], 1193 West St., Southington, 1/19/89, C, 88003119

Grant, Ebenezer, House, 1653 Main St., East Windsor Hill, 9/19/77, C, b, 77001408

Gridley-Parsons-Staples Homestead, 1554 Farmington Ave., Farmington, 7/30/81, C, 81000537

Hale, Dr. Elizur, House, 3181 Hebron Ave., Glastonbury, 11/13/89, C, 89001088

Hart's Corner Historic District, 247 Monce Rd. and 102 and 105 Stafford Rd., Burlington, 7/08/87, A, C, 87000351

Hart, Timothy, House [Colonial Houses of Southington TR], 521 Flanders Rd., Southington, 1/19/89, C, 88003100

Hartford & New Haven Railroad Depot [18th and 19th Century Brick Architecture of Windsor TR], Central St., Windsor, 9/15/88, A, C, 88001479

Hartford & New Haven Railroad—Freight Depot [18th and 19th Century Brick Architecture of Windsor TR], 40 Central St., Windsor, 9/15/88, A, C, 88001505

Hartford Club [Hartford Downtown MRA], 46 Prospect St., Hartford, 12/23/84, C, 84000779

Hartford Golf Club Historic District, Roughly bounded by Simsbury Rd. and Bloomfield Ave., Northmoor Rd., Albany Ave., and Mohegan Dr., West Hartford, 6/26/86, A, C, 86001370

Hartford Seminary Foundation, 55 Elizabeth St. and 72-120 Sherman St., Hartford, 6/22/82, A, C, a, 82004411

Hartford Union Station, Union Pl., Hartford, 11/25/75, A, C, 75001932

Harvey, William H., House [18th and 19th Century Brick Architecture of Windsor TR], 1173 Windsor Ave., Windsor, 9/15/88, A, C, 88001503

Hartford County—Continued

Hastings Hill Historic District, 987-1308 Hill St., 1242 Spruce St. and 1085-1162 Russell Ave., Suffield vicinity, 9/14/79, A, B, C, a, g, 79002669

Hathaways Store [18th and 19th Century Brick Architecture of Windsor TR], 32 East St., Windsor, 9/15/88, A, C, 88001482

Hatheway House, 55 S. Main St., Suffield, 8/06/75, B, C, 75001934

Hayden, Capt. Nathaniel, House [18th and 19th Century Brick Architecture of Windsor TR], 128 Hayden Station Rd., Windsor, 9/15/88, A, C, 88001483

Hayes, Samuel II, House, 67 Barndoor Hills Rd., Granby, 4/27/92, C, 92000390

Hazardville Historic District, CT 190 and CT 192, Hazardville and vicinity, 2/19/80, A, C, D, a, d, 80004061

Heublein Tower, Talcott Mountain State Park, Simsbury, 6/30/83, B, C, 83001260

Hill—Stead, 35 Mountain Rd., Farmington, 7/17/91, C, g, NHL, 91002056

Hitchcock-Schwarzmann Mill, N of Burlington at Foote and Vineyard Rds., Burlington vicinity, 9/13/77, A, C, 77001409

Holcomb, Judah, House, 257 N. Granby Rd., Granby, 6/16/88, C, 88000755

Holcomb, Nathaniel, III, House, 45 Bushy Hill Rd., Granby, 4/29/82, B, C, a, 82004486

Hollister, John, House, 14 Tryon St., Glastonbury, 11/07/72, C, 72001329

Holmes, Francis H., House, 349 Rocky Hill Ave., New Britain, 6/28/84, B, C, 84001014

Hooker, Henry, House, 111 High Rd., Kensington, 11/29/78, B, C, 78002867

Hooker, John and Isabella, House [Asylum Hill MRA], 140 Hawthorn St., Hartford, 11/29/79, C, 79002678

Hooker, Sarah Whitman, House, 1237 New Britain Ave., West Hartford, 11/01/79, A, C, D, 79002627

Hosmer, Daniel, House [Eighteenth-Century Houses of West Hartford TR], 253 N. Main St., West Hartford, 9/10/86, A, C, 86001985

House at 1010 Shuttle Meadow Road [Colonial Houses of Southington TR], 1010 Shuttle Meadow Rd., Southington, 1/19/89, C, 88003116

House at 111 Maple Avenue [18th and 19th Century Brick Architecture of Windsor TR], 111 Maple Ave., Windsor, 9/15/88, A, C, 88001486

House at 130 Hayden Station Road [18th and 19th Century Brick Architecture of Windsor TR], 130 Hayden Station Rd., Windsor, 9/15/88, A, C, 88001484

House at 140 and 144 Retreat Avenue, 140 and 144 Retreat Ave., Hartford, 2/25/82, C, 82004412

House at 36 Forest Street [Asylum Hill MRA], 36 Forest St., Hartford, 2/24/83, C, 83001262

House at 44 Court Street [18th and 19th Century Brick Architecture of Windsor TR], 44 Court St., Windsor, 9/15/88, A, C, 88001480

House at 590 West Street [Colonial Houses of Southington TR], 590 West St., Southington, 1/19/89, C, 88003118

House at 736 Palisado Avenue [18th and 19th Century Brick Architecture of Windsor TR], 736 Palisado Ave., Windsor, 9/15/88, A, C, 88001494

House at 847 Main Street, North [Eighteenth-Century Houses of West Hartford TR], 847 Main St. N, West Hartford, 9/10/86, A, C, 86001996

Humphrey, John, House, 115 E. Weatogue St., Simsbury vicinity, 11/15/90, C, 90001755

Hurwood Company [Historic Industrial Complexes of Southington TR], 379 Summer St., Southington vicinity, 12/08/88, A, C, 88002681

Hyde-St. John House, 25 Charter Oak Ave., Hartford, 10/06/77, C, 77001422

Imlay and Laurel Streets District [Asylum Hill MRA], Imlay, Laurel and Sigourney Sts., Hartford, 11/29/79, C, 79002675

Isham-Terry House, 211 High St., Hartford, 2/11/82, C, 82004413

James Pratt Funeral Service [Asylum Hill MRA], 69 Farmington Ave., Hartford, 11/29/79, C, 79002677

Jefferson-Seymour District, Cedar, Wadsworth, Seymour and Jefferson Sts., Hartford, 5/04/79, C, 79002661

Jerome, William I, House, 367 Jerome Ave., Bristol, 6/02/87, A, C, 87000792

Judd and Root Building [Hartford Downtown MRA], 175–189 Allyn St. and 5–23 High St., Hartford, 12/23/84, C, 84000784

Kellogg, Gen. Martin, House, 679 Willard Ave., Newington, 10/01/87, C, 87001770

Kelsey, Enoch, House, 1702 Main St., Newington, 6/28/82, A, C, b, 82004437

Kelsey, Ezekiel, House, 429 Beckley Rd., Berlin, 9/16/77, C, 77001410

Keney Tower, Main and Ely Sts., Hartford, 3/30/78, C, f, 78002871

Kimberly Mansion, 1625 Main St., Glastonbury, 9/17/74, B, NHL, 74002178

King's Field House, 827 North St., Suffield vicinity, 3/11/82, C, 82004440

King, Alexander, House, 232 S. Main St., Suffield vicinity, 4/26/76, C, 76001993

Lake Compounce Carousel, W of Southington on Lake Ave., Southington vicinity, 12/12/78, A, C, 78002865

Laurel and Marshall Streets District [Asylum Hill MRA], Laurel, Marshall, and Case Sts., and Farmington Ave., Hartford, 11/29/79, C, 79002673

Lewis Street Block, 1-33, 24-36 Lewis St., 8-28 Trumbull St., Hartford, 1/30/76, C, 76001991

Lewis—Zukowski House, 1095 S. Grand St., Suffield, 2/21/90, A, C, 90000147

Lighthouse Archeological Site (5-37), Address Restricted, Barkhamsted, 4/25/91, D, d, 91000445

Linke, William L., House [Asylum Hill MRA], 174 Sigourney St., Hartford, 2/24/83, C, 83001262

Little Hollywood Historic District, Farmington Ave., Owen, Frederick and Denison Sts., Hartford, 4/29/82, A, C, 82004423

Loomis, Capt. James, House [18th and 19th Century Brick Architecture of Windsor TR], 881 Windsor Ave., Windsor, 9/15/88, A, C, 88001499

Loomis, Col. James, House [18th and 19th Century Brick Architecture of Windsor TR], 208–210 Broad St., Windsor, 9/15/88, A, C, 88001476

Loomis, George G., House [18th and 19th Century Brick Architecture of Windsor TR], 1003 Windsor Ave., Windsor, 9/15/88, A, C, 88001500

Loomis, Gordon, House [18th and 19th Century Brick Architecture of Windsor TR], 1021 Windsor Ave., Windsor, 9/15/88, A, C, 88001501

Loomis, Ira, Jr., House [18th and 19th Century Brick Architecture of Windsor TR], 1053 Windsor Ave., Windsor, 9/15/88, A, C, 88001502

Lyman House, 22 Woodland St., Hartford, 10/31/75, C, 75001938

Magill, Henry, House [18th and 19th Century Brick Architecture of Windsor TR], 390 Palisado Ave., Windsor, 9/15/88, A, C, 88001491

Main Street Historic District No. 2 [Hartford Downtown MRA], W. Main, N. Central Row, E. Prospect Sts., and N. Atheneum Sq., Hartford, 12/23/84, A, C, g, 84001272

Marion Historic District, Along Marion Ave. and Meriden—Waterbury Tnpk., Southington, 12/21/88, C, a, 88001423

Marlborough Congregational Church, 35 S. Main St., Marlborough, 12/10/93, A, C, a, 93001346

Marlborough House, 226 Grove St., Bristol, 9/02/93, C, 93000906

Marlborough Tavern, Off CT 66, Marlborough, 12/06/78, A, C, b, 78002866

Massacoe Forest Pavilion [Connecticut State Park and Forest Depression-Era Federal Work Relief Programs Structures TR], Off Old Farms Rd., Stratton Brook State Park, Simsbury, 9/04/86, A, C, 86001731

Mather Homestead, 2 Mahl Ave., Hartford, 4/29/82, A, C, a, g, 82004426

Memorial Hall, Jct. of S. Main and Elm Sts., Windsor Locks, 6/02/87, A, C, f, 87000802

Meriden Avenue—Oakland Road Historic District, Roughly Oakland Rd. between Meriden and Berlin Aves., and Meriden Ave. between Oakland Rd. and Delhunty Dr., Southington, 5/25/88, A, C, 88000580

Mills, Elijah, House [18th and 19th Century Brick Architecture of Windsor TR (AD)], 45 Deerfield Rd., Windsor, 8/23/85, C, 85001829

Mills, Oliver W., House [18th and 19th Century Brick Architecture of Windsor TR (AD)], 148 Deerfield Rd., Windsor, 2/19/82, A, C, 82004443

Mills, Timothy Dwight, House [18th and 19th Century Brick Architecture of Windsor TR], 184 Deerfield Rd., Windsor, 9/15/88, A, C, 88001481

Moore, Deacon John, House, 37 Elm St., Windsor, 7/29/77, B, C, 77001416

Moore, Edward and Ann, House [18th and 19th Century Brick Architecture of Windsor TR], 464 Broad St., Windsor, 9/15/88, A, C, 88001478

Morley, Edward W., House, 26 Westland Ave., West Hartford, 5/15/75, B, NHL, 75002057

Mount St. Joseph Academy, 235 Fern St., West Hartford, 12/22/83, A, C, a, 83003561

Municipal Building, 550 Main St., Hartford, 4/27/81, A, C, 81000536

Murphy, Patrick, House [18th and 19th Century Brick Architecture of Windsor TR], 345 Palisado Ave., Windsor, 9/15/88, A, C, 88001490

Myers and Gross Building [Asylum Hill MRA], 2 Fraser Pl., Hartford, 3/31/83, C, 83001263

Hartford County—Continued

New Britain Opera House, 466-468 Main St., New Britain, 10/07/77, A, C, 77001421

New Haven District Campground, Off CT 177, Plainville vicinity, 5/19/80, A, C, a, 80004065

Newington Junction North Historic District [Newington Junction MRA], 55–108 Willard Ave., Newington, 6/02/87, C, 86003465

Newington Junction Railroad Depot [Newington Junction MRA], 160 Willard and 200 Francis Aves., Newington, 12/22/86, A, C, 86003478

Newington Junction South Historic District [Newington Junction MRA], 268–319 Willard Ave., Newington, 6/02/87, C, 86003462

Newington Junction West Historic District [Newington Junction MRA], 175 and 181–183 Willard Ave. and 269–303 W. Hill Rd., Newington, 6/02/87, C, 86003464

Nook Farm and Woodland Street District [Asylum Hill MRA], Woodland, Gillett, and Forest Sts., and Farmington Ave., Hartford, 11/29/79, C, 79002674

Northam Memorial Chapel and Gallup Memorial Gateway, 453 Fairfield Ave., Hartford, 6/29/82, C, a, 82004428

Norton, Charles H., House, 132 Redstone Hill, Plainville, 5/11/76, B, NHL, 76002139

Old Farm Schoolhouse, Jct. of Park Ave. and School St., Bloomfield, 10/18/72, A, C, b, 72001340

Old Newgate Prison, Newgate Rd., East Granby, 10/15/70, A, NHL, 70000839

Old Wethersfield Historic District, Bounded by Hartford, railroad tracks, I-91, and Rocky Hill, Wethersfield, 12/29/70, A, C, 70000719

Palisado Avenue Historic District, Palisado Ave. between the Farmington River and Bissell Ferry Rd., Windsor, 8/25/87, A, C, 87000799

Parkside Historic District, 176-230 Wethersfield Ave., Hartford, 5/31/84, C, 84001048

Payne, Daniel, House [18th and 19th Century Brick Architecture of Windsor TR], 27 Park Ave., Windsor, 9/15/88, A, C, 88001495

Peck, Stow & Wilcox Factory [Historic Industrial Complexes of Southington TR], 217 Center St., Southington, 12/08/88, A, C, 88002682

Pequabuck Bridge, Meadow Rd. at Pequabuck River, Farmington, 7/19/84, A, C, 84001049

Perkins-Clark House, 49 Woodland St., Hartford, 12/14/78, C, 78002870

Phelps, Capt. Elisha, House, 800 Hopmeadow St., Simsbury, 9/22/72, C, 72001345

Phelps, Eli, House [18th and 19th Century Brick Architecture of Windsor TR], 18 Marshall Phelps Rd., Windsor, 9/15/88, A, C, 88001487

Phelps, Ezekiel, House, 38 Holcomb St., East Granby, 2/25/82, C, 82004396

Pine Grove Historic District, CT 167, Avon, 2/11/80, A, C, 80004066

Pinney, David, House and Barn, 58 West St., Windsor Locks, 7/25/77, A, C, 77001415

Pitkin Glassworks Ruin, Address Restricted, Manchester vicinity, 4/09/79, A, D, 79002628

Plantsville Historic District, Roughly bounded by Prospect St., Summer St., Quinnipiac River, Grove St., S. Main St., W. Main St., and West St., Southington, 12/01/88, C, 88002673

Polish National Home, 60 Charter Oak Ave., Hartford, 10/20/83, A, C, 83003566

Pomeroy, Arthur G., House, 490 Ann St., Hartford, 2/04/82, A, C, 82004429

Porter, Dr. J., House [Colonial Houses of Southington TR], 391 Belleview Ave., Southington, 1/19/89, C, 88003096

Pratt Street Historic District, 31-101 and 32-110 Pratt St.; 196-260 Trumbell St., Hartford, 3/10/83, A, C, 83001264

Prospect Avenue Historic District, Roughly bounded by Albany Ave., N. Branch Park River, Elizabeth & Fern Sts., Prospect & Asylum Aves. & Sycamore Rd., Hartford, 8/29/85, A, C, 85001918

Pultz & Walkley Company [Historic Industrial Complexes of Southington TR], 120 W. Main St., Southington vicinity, 12/08/88, A, C, 88002677

Revolutionary War Campsite, Address Restricted, West Hartford vicinity, 4/24/86, A, D, 86000853

Robbins, John, House, 262 Old Main St., Rocky Hill, 9/20/88, C, 88001526

Rockwell Park, Dutton Ave. and Jacobs St., Bristol, 5/21/87, A, B, C, 87000788

Rocky Hill Congregational Church, 805-817 Old Main St., Rocky Hill, 5/07/82, C, a, 82004438

Root, Jonathan, House [Colonial Houses of Southington TR], 140–142 N. Main St., Southington, 1/19/89, C, 88003113

Rowe and Weed Houses, 208 Salmon Brook St., Granby, 1/18/78, C, b, 78002860

Royal Typewriter Company Building, 150 New Park Ave., Hartford, 2/23/89, A, C, g, 84003898

Saint Anthony Hall, 340 Summit St., Hartford, 5/09/85, A, C, 85001017

Second Church of Christ, 307 Main St., Hartford, 1/09/78, A, C, a, 78002836

Seymour, Elisha, Jr., House [Eighteenth-Century Houses of West Hartford TR], 410 and 412 Park Rd., West Hartford, 9/10/86, A, C, 86001997

Shade Swamp Shelter [Connecticut State Park and Forest Depression-Era Federal Work Relief Programs Structures TR], US 6 E of New Britain Ave., Farmington, 9/04/86, A, C, 86001746

Shelton, William, House [18th and 19th Century Brick Architecture of Windsor TR], 40 Pleasant St., Windsor, 9/15/88, A, C, 88001496

Sigourney Square District, Sargeant, Ashley and May Sts., Hartford, 1/16/79, A, C, 79002660

Sigourney Square Historic District (Boundary Increase), 216-232 Garden St., Hartford, 12/21/83, C, 83003568

Simeon North Factory Site, Address Restricted, Berlin vicinity, 8/18/90, A, B, D, 90001158

Simpson, Dr. Frank T., House, 27 Keney Terr., Hartford, 12/02/93, A, B, C, 93001246

Simsbury Bank and Trust Company Building, 760–762 Hopmeadow St., Simsbury, 11/20/86, A, C, 86003323

Simsbury Railroad Depot, Railroad Ave. at Station St., Simsbury, 3/26/76, A, C, 76001997

Simsbury Townhouse, 695 Hopmeadow St., Simsbury, 4/02/93, C, b, 93000209

Skelton, Dr. Henry, House [Colonial Houses of Southington TR], 889 S. Main St., Southington, 1/19/89, C, 88003117

Smith, H. D., Company Building [Historic Industrial Complexes of Southington TR (AD)], 24 West St., Plantsville, 9/19/77, A, C, 77001420

South Congregational Church, 90 Main St., New Britain, 4/06/90, A, C, a, 89000930

South Glastonbury Historic District, High, Hopewell, Main and Water Sts., Glastonbury, 11/23/84, A, C, 84000250

Southington Center Historic District, Roughly N. Main St. N from Vermont Ave., and Berlin St. from Main St. to Academy Ln., Southington, 5/08/89, C, 88002961

Southington Public Library, 239 Main St., Southington, 2/09/89, C, 89000015

Southwest District School, 430 Simsbury Rd., Bloomfield, 7/24/92, A, C, 92000904

Spanish House, The, 46 Fernwood Rd., West Hartford, 6/14/79, C, 79002632

Spencer House [Asylum Hill MRA], 1039 Asylum Ave., Hartford, 2/24/83, C, 83001265

St. John's Episcopal Church, 92 Main St., Warehouse Point, 4/27/82, A, C, a, b, 82004442

St. John's Episcopal Church, 1160 Main St., East Hartford, 11/28/83, A, C, a, 83003567

St. Mary's Parochial School, Beaver St. S of Broad St., New Britain, 4/03/91, A, C, 91000364

St. Paul's Methodist Episcopal Church, 1886-1906 Park St., Hartford, 8/02/84, C, a, 84001051

Stackpole, Moore, and Tryon Building, 105-115 Asylum St., Hartford, 10/19/78, C, 78002869

Stafford Hollow Historic District, Roughly parts of Leonard, Murphy, Old Monson, Orcuttville, & Patten Rds., Stafford, 10/15/87, A, C, a, 87002032

Stanley—Woodruff—Allen House [Eighteenth-Century Houses of West Hartford TR], 37 Buena Vista Rd., West Hartford, 9/10/86, A, C, 86002000

Stanley-Whitman House, 37 High St., Farmington, 10/15/66, C, NHL, 66000882

Steele, Allyn, House [Eighteenth-Century Houses of West Hartford TR], 114 N. Main St., West Hartford, 9/10/86, A, C, 86002022

Stone Bridge [Hartford Downtown MRA], 500 Main St., Hartford, 3/28/85, C, 85000793

Stony Hill School [18th and 19th Century Brick Architecture of Windsor TR], 1195 Windsor Ave., Windsor, 9/15/88, A, C, 88001504

Stowe, Harriet Beecher, House, 73 Forest St., Hartford, 10/06/70, B, 70000710

Sts. Cyril and Methodius Church, 63 Governor St., Hartford, 6/30/83, A, C, a, 83001254

Suffield Historic District, Runs along N. and S. Main St., Suffield, 9/25/79, C, 79003750

Sweetland, Sophia, House [18th and 19th Century Brick Architecture of Windsor TR], 458 Palisado Ave., Windsor, 9/15/88, A, C, 88001493

Tariffville Historic District, Roughly bounded by Winthrop St., Main St., Mountain Rd., Laurel Hill Rd. and Elm St., Simsbury, 4/02/93, C, 93000173

Hartford County—Continued

Temple Beth Israel, 21 Charter Oak Ave., Hartford, 12/01/78, A, C, a, 78002868

Terry's Plain Historic District, Roughly bounded by Pharos, Quarry and Terry's Plain Rds. and the Farmington R., Simsbury, 12/10/93, A, C, 93001417

Terry-Hayden House, 125 Middle St., Bristol, 3/25/82, A, C, 82004393

Treadway, Townsend G., House, 100 Oakland St., Bristol, 12/19/91, C, 91001871

Treadwell House, George Washington Tpke., Burlington, 4/27/82, B, C, 82004395

Tunxis Forest Headquarters House [Connecticut State Park and Forest Depression-Era Federal Work Relief Programs Structures TR], W side of Pell Rd. .2 mi. N of Town Rd., Hartland, 9/04/86, A, C, 86001759

Tunxis Forest Ski Cabin [Connecticut State Park and Forest Depression-Era Federal Work Relief Programs Structures TR], W end of Balance Rock Rd., Hartland, 9/05/86, A, C, g, 86001761

Tunxis Hose Firehouse, Lovely St. and Farmington Ave., Unionville, 7/28/83, A, C, 83001266

Twain, Mark, House, 351 Farmington Ave., Hartford, 10/15/66, B, C, NHL, 66000884

U. S. Post Office and Federal Building, 135-149 High St., Hartford, 10/19/81, A, C, 81000623

US Post Office—Manchester Main, 479 Main St. at Center St., Manchester, 1/21/86, C, 86000127

Union Baptist Church, 1913 and 1921 Main St., Hartford, 8/15/79, B, C, a, 79002634

Upper Albany Historic District, Roughly bounded by Holcomb St., Vine St., Homestead Ave., and Woodland and Ridgefield Sts., Hartford, 9/29/86, A, C, 86003383

Viets' Tavern, Newgate Rd., East Granby, 2/23/72, A, C, 72001338

Wadsworth Atheneum, 25 Atheneum Sq., Hartford, 10/06/70, A, C, 70000709

Walnut Hill District, Irregular pattern roughly bounded by Winthrup, Arch, and Lake Sts., and Walnut Hill Park, New Britain, 9/02/75, C, 75001936

Walnut Hill Park, W. Main St., New Britain, 11/30/82, C, 82001000

Washington School, High and Carmody Sts., New Britain, 7/19/84, A, C, 84001053

Washington Street School, 461 Washington St., Hartford, 2/19/82, B, C, 82004431

Webb, Joseph, House, 211 Main St., Wethersfield, 10/15/66, A, B, C, NHL, 66000885

Webster Memorial Building, 36 Trumbull St., Hartford, 4/12/82, A, C, 82004433

Webster, Horace, Farmhouse, S of Southington at 577 South End Rd., Southington vicinity, 8/24/77, C, 77001417

Webster, Noah, Birthplace, 227 S. Main St., West Hartford, 10/15/66, B, c, NHL, 66000886

Webster, Noah, Memorial Library, 7 N. Main St., West Hartford, 7/30/81, A, C, 81000534

Welles, Gideon, House, 37 Hebron Ave., Glastonbury, 10/06/70, B, C, b, 70000697

Welles-Shipman-Ward House, 972 Main St., South Glastonbury, 9/19/77, C, 77001418

Wells, John, Jr., House [Eighteenth-Century Houses of West Hartford TR], 505 Mountain Rd., West Hartford, 9/10/86, A, C, 86002025

West End North Historic District, Roughly bounded by Farmington Ave., Lorraine, Elizabeth, and Highland Sts., Hartford, 7/25/85, A, C, 85001618

West End South Historic District, Roughly bounded by Farmington Ave., Whitney and S. Whitney Sts., West Blvd. and Prospect Ave., Hartford and West Hartford, 4/11/85, C, 85000763

West Granby Historic District, Broad Hill, Hartland, W. Granby and Simsbury Rds. and Day St. S., Granby, 5/01/92, A, C, 92000385

West Street School, 1432 West St., Southington, 12/01/88, A, C, 88002689

Wethersfield Avenue Car Barn, 331 Wethersfield Ave., Hartford, 11/28/83, A, C, 83003569

Whiting Homestead [Eighteenth-Century Houses of West Hartford TR (AD)], 291 N. Main St., West Hartford, 8/03/87, C, 87001291

Whitman House [Eighteenth-Century Houses of West Hartford TR], 208 N. Main St., West Hartford, 9/10/86, A, C, 86002028

Wiard, John, House, CT 4, Burlington vicinity, 3/25/82, A, C, 82004394

Widows' Home, 1846-1860 N. Main St., Hartford, 3/10/83, A, C, 83001267

Wightman, Rev. John, House [Colonial Houses of Southington TR], 1024 Mount Vernon Rd., Southington, 1/19/89, C, 88003111

Wightman, Valentine, House [Colonial Houses of Southington TR], 1112 Mount Vernon Rd., Southington, 1/19/89, C, 88003112

Willard Homestead [Newington Junction MRA], 372 Willard Ave., Newington, 12/22/86, C, 86003461

Williams, J. B., Co. Historic District, Hubbard, Williams, and Willieb Sts., Glastonbury, 4/07/83, A, B, C, 83001268

Windsor Avenue Congregational Church, 2030 Main St., Hartford, 4/03/93, A, C, a, 93000174

Windsor Farms Historic District, Roughly bounded by Strong Rd., US 5, I-291, and the Connecticut River, South Windsor, 4/11/86, A, C, a, 86000723

Windsor Locks Passenger Station, Main St., Windsor Locks, 9/02/75, A, C, 75001937

Woodruff House [Colonial Houses of Southington TR], 377 Berlin St., Southington, 1/19/89, C, 88003097

Woodruff, Capt. Samuel, House, 23 Old State Rd., Southington, 5/05/89, C, 89000014

Woodruff, Ezekiel, House [Colonial Houses of Southington TR], 1152 East St., Southington, 1/19/89, C, 88003099

Woodruff, Jotham, House [Colonial Houses of Southington TR], 137–139 Woodruff St., Southington, 1/19/89, C, 88003120

Woodruff, Urbana, House [Colonial Houses of Southington TR], 1096 East St., Southington, 1/19/89, C, 88003098

Worthington Ridge Historic District, Roughly Worthington Ridge from Mill St. to Sunset Ln., Berlin, 7/13/89, A, C, 89000925

Litchfield County

Alldis, James, House, 355 Prospect St., Torrington, 4/29/82, C, 82004480

American Legion Forest CCC Shelter [Connecticut State Park and Forest Depression-Era Federal Work Relief Programs Structures TR], W side of West River Rd., American Legion State Forest, Barkhamsted, 9/04/86, A, C, 86001725

Bacon, Jabez, House, Hollow Rd. near jct. with U.S. 6, Woodbury, 4/16/71, B, C, 71000904

Beardsley, Capt. Philo, House, SE of Kent on Beardsley Rd., Kent vicinity, 7/03/79, C, 79002616

Beaver Meadow Complex Prehistoric Archeological District, Address Restricted, Barkhamsted vicinity, 9/21/88, D, 88000858

Beckley Furnace, SE of Canaan on Lower Rd., Canaan vicinity, 2/14/78, A, D, 78002847

Bellamy, Joseph, House, N. Main and West Sts., Bethlehem, 4/12/82, B, C, 82004444

Bethlehem Green Historic District, Parts of N. Main St., S. Main St., East St., West Rd., and Munger Lane, Bethlehem, 12/16/82, C, a, 82001001

Bissell, Henry B., House, 202 Maple St., Litchfield, 9/07/90, C, 90001288

Boardman's Bridge, Boardman Rd. at Housatonic River, NW of New Milford, New Milford vicinity, 5/13/76, A, C, 76001983

Braman Camp [Taylor, Alfredo S. G., TR], Doolittle Lake, Norfolk, 8/02/82, C, 82004451

Brooks, Hervey, Pottery Shop and Kiln Site, Address Restricted, Goshen vicinity, 12/10/93, A, D, 93001362

Bull's Bridge, About 3 mi. SW of Kent on Bull's Bridge Rd, over Housatonic River, Kent, 4/26/72, A, C, 72001314

Bull, Capt. William, Tavern, CT 202, Litchfield vicinity, 6/30/83, C, b, 83001269

Camp, Moses, House, 682 Main St., Winsted, 5/10/84, B, C, 84001060

Canaan Village Historic District, Roughly bounded by W. Main, Bragg & Orchard Sts. & Granite Ave., North Canaan, 12/13/90, A, C, 90001800

Cannondale Historic District, Roughly bounded by Cannon, Danbury and Seeley Rds., Wilton, 11/12/92, A, C, a, b, d, 92001531

Catlin, J. Howard, House, 14 Knife Shop Rd., Litchfield, 8/06/93, B, C, 93000672

Chapin, Philip, House, 1 Church St., New Hartford, 8/29/77, A, C, 77001399

Childs, Starling, Camp [Taylor, Alfredo S. G., TR], Doolittle Lake, Norfolk, 8/02/82, C, 82004463

Coffing, John C., House, US 44 W of Lime Rock Rd., Salisbury, 12/18/90, B, C, 90001922

Colebrook Center Historic District, Roughly, jct. of Rockwell, Colebrook, Schoolhouse and

Litchfield County—Continued

Smith Hill Rds. and CT 183, Colebrook, 7/26/91, C, 91000953

Colebrook Store, CT 183, Colebrook, 4/26/76, A, C, 76001980

Cornwall Bridge Railroad Station, Jct. of Poppleswamp Brook Rd. and Kent Rd., Cornwall, 4/26/72, A, 72001313

Cream Hill Agricultural School, NE of West Cornwall off CT 128 on Cream Hill Rd., West Cornwall vicinity, 3/26/76, A, C, 76001986

Cream Hill Shelter [Connecticut State Park and Forest Depression-Era Federal Work Relief Programs Structures TR], Wickwire Rd., Sharon, 9/04/86, A, C, 86001727

Downtown Torrington Historic District, Roughly bounded by Church and Alvord Sts., Center Cemetery, Willow St., E. Main St., Litchfield St., and Prospect St., Torrington, 12/22/88, A, C, 88002978

East Plymouth Historic District, E. Plymouth and Marsh Rd., Plymouth, 2/21/85, A, C, a, d, 85000312

Falls Village District, CT 126, Canaan, 6/14/79, A, C, 79002622

Farnum House [Taylor, Alfredo S. G., TR], Litchfield Rd., Norfolk, 8/02/82, C, 82004449

Flanders Historic District, U.S. 7, Cobble Rd., Cobble Lane, and Studio Hill Rd., Kent, 4/13/79, C, 79002618

Forbes, Samuel, Homestead, 89 Lower Rd., North Canaan Township, East Canaan vicinity, 11/25/92, B, C, 92001578

Fyler—Hotchkiss Estate, 192 Main St., Torrington, 2/12/87, B, C, 87000129

Gay, Ebenezer, House, Main St., Sharon, 7/09/79, B, C, 79002619

Gilbert Clock Factory, Wallens St., Winchester, 12/13/84, A, C, 84000494

Gillette's Grist Mill, E of Torrington on Maple Hollow Rd., Torrington vicinity, 8/29/77, A, D, 77001403

Glebe House, Hollow Rd., Woodbury, 3/11/71, A, C, a, 71000902

Goshen Historic District, CT 63 and 4, and Gifford Rd., Goshen, 12/27/82, A, C, a, 82000996

Gould House [Taylor, Alfredo S. G., TR], Golf Dr., Norfolk, 8/02/82, C, 82004452

Gov. Smith Homestead, South Main St., Sharon, 3/25/82, B, C, 82004475

Halpine, J. S., Tobacco Warehouse, West and Mill Sts., New Milford, 12/16/82, A, C, 82001002

Haystack Mountain Tower, 43 North St., Norfolk, 12/02/93, B, C, 93001244

Hillside [Taylor, Alfredo S. G., TR], Litchfield Rd., Norfolk, 8/02/82, C, 82004454

Holabird House, Kellog Rd., corner of Rte. 126, Canaan, 6/28/82, C, 82004445

Hose and Hook and Ladder Truck Building, Main St., Thomaston, 1/04/82, A, C, 82004479

Housatonic Railroad Station, Railroad St., New Milford, 3/01/84, A, C, 84001062

Kent Iron Furnace, N of Kent off U.S. 7, Kent vicinity, 10/05/77, A, D, 77001401

Lawrence, Isaac, House, Elm St., Canaan, 3/10/83, A, C, 83001270

Lime Rock Historic District, Roughly White Hollow, Elm, Lime Rock, Norton Hill and Furnace Rds., Salisbury, 7/05/84, A, C, 84001064

Litchfield Historic District, Roughly both sides of North and South Sts. between Gallows Lane and Prospect St., Litchfield, 11/24/68, C, NHL, 68000050

Litchfield Historic District, CT 25 and CT 63, Litchfield, 11/29/78, A, C, a, 78003456

Lover's Leap Bridge, S of New Milford on Pumpkin Hill Rd., New Milford vicinity, 5/13/76, A, C, 76001982

Low House [Taylor, Alfredo S. G., TR], Highfield Rd., Norfolk, 2/17/84, C, 84001067

Mead Camp [Taylor, Alfredo S. G., TR], Doolittle Lake, Norfolk, 8/02/82, C, 82004455

Merritt Beach & Son Building, 30 Bridge St., New Milford, 4/28/92, A, C, 92000403

Merryall Union Evangelical Society Chapel, Chapel Hill Rd., New Milford, 6/05/86, C, a, 86001240

Merwinsville Hotel, E of Gaylordsville on Brown's Forge Rd., Gaylordsville vicinity, 8/29/77, A, C, 77001398

Milton Center Historic District, Roughly bounded by Milton, Shearshop, Headquarters, Sawmill, and Blue Swamp Rds., Milton, 12/23/86, A, C, D, 86003754

Moseley House-Farm [Taylor, Alfredo S. G., TR], Greenwoods Rd., Norfolk, 2/17/84, C, 84001077

Moss Hill [Taylor, Alfredo S. G., TR], Litchfield Rd., Norfolk, 8/02/82, C, 82004457

Mount Tom Tower, Off US 202 SE of Woodville, Mount Tom State Park, Towns of Morris, Litchfield and Washington, Woodville vicinity, 12/02/93, A, C, 93001247

Mulville House [Taylor, Alfredo S. G., TR], Mountain Rd., Norfolk, 2/17/84, C, 84001079

Music Mountain, Music Mountain Rd., Canaan, 12/18/87, A, C, 87001909

New Milford Center Historic District, Bennett and Elm Sts., Center Cemetery, East, S. Main, Mill, and Railroad Sts., New Milford, 6/13/86, A, C, 86001255

New Preston Hill Historic District, New Preston Hill, Findley and Gunn Hill Rds., Washington, 8/26/85, A, C, a, 85001931

Noble House [Taylor, Alfredo S. G., TR], Highfield Rd., Norfolk, 2/17/84, C, 84001083

Noble, John Glover, House, Address Restricted, New Milford vicinity, 8/29/77, C, 77001402

Norfolk Country Club House [Taylor, Alfredo S. G., TR], Golf Dr., Norfolk, 8/02/82, C, 82004458

Norfolk Downs Shelter [Taylor, Alfredo S. G., TR], Gold Rd., Norfolk, 2/22/84, C, 84001085

Norfolk Historic District, US 44 and CT 272, Norfolk, 10/15/79, B, C, 79003749

Old Riverton Inn, 436 E. River Rd., Barkhamsted, 7/24/92, A, 92000906

Paugnut Forest Administration Building [Connecticut State Park and Forest Depression-Era Federal Work Relief Programs Structures TR], 385 Burr Mountain Rd., Torrington, 9/05/86, A, C, g, 86001736

Peoples Forest Museum [Connecticut State Park and Forest Depression-Era Federal Work Relief Programs Structures TR], Greenwood Rd., Peoples State Forest, Barkhamsted, 9/04/86, A, C, 86001737

Phelps Farms Historic District, CT 183, Colebrook vicinity, 8/18/83, A, C, 83001249

Phelps, Arah, Inn, Jct. of Prock Hill Rd. and CT 183, North Colebrook, 8/05/71, A, 71000905

Rectory and Church of the Immaculate Conception [Taylor, Alfredo S. G., TR], North St., Norfolk, 8/02/82, C, a, 82004459

Red Mountain Shelter [Connecticut State Park and Forest Depression-Era Federal Work Relief Programs Structures TR], N side of CT 4 adjacent to Appalachian Trail, Cornwall, 9/04/86, A, C, 86001740

Reeve, Tapping, House and Law School, South St., Litchfield, 10/15/66, B, NHL, 66000879

Rockwell House [Taylor, Alfredo S. G., TR], Laurel Way, W., Norfolk, 8/02/82, C, 82004460

Rockwell, Solomon, House, 226 Prospect St., Winsted, 7/15/77, C, 77001500

Roxbury Center, CT 67, Weller's Bridge Rd., South and Church Sts., Roxbury, 7/28/83, A, B, C, a, 83001271

Roxbury Iron Mine and Furnace Complex, Address Restricted, Roxbury vicinity, 6/24/79, A, D, 79002621

Rumsey Hall, 12 Bolton Hill Rd., Cornwall, 5/10/90, C, 90000762

Sanford, Frederick S., House, Hat Shop Hill, Bridgewater, 1/19/89, C, 88003230

Schoverling, Carl F., Tobacco Warehouse, 1 Wellsville Ave., New Milford, 4/12/82, A, C, 82004446

Scoville Memorial Library, Main St., Salisbury, 4/29/82, A, C, 82004473

Scoville Powerhouse, Twin Lakes and Beaver Dam Rds., Salisbury, 2/16/84, C, 84001087

Sedgwick, Maj. Gen. John, House, 52 Hautboy Hill Rd., Cornwall vicinity, 4/08/92, B, C, 92000262

Sharon Historic District, Roughly, Main St. from Low Rd. to jct. with Mitchelltown, Amenia Union and W. Woods Rds., Sharon, 4/15/93, A, C, a, 93000257

Sharon Valley Historic District, Jct. of Sharon Valley and Sharon Station Rds., Sharon, 9/09/82, A, C, D, 82004478

Shepard, John, House [Taylor, Alfredo S. G., TR], Shepard Park Rd., Norfolk, 8/02/82, C, 82004462

Skilton Road Bridge, Skilton Rd. over the Nonewaug R., Watertown, 12/10/91, A, C, 91001744

Skinner, Jason, House, 21 Wintergreen Circle, Harwinton, 6/19/85, C, 85001331

South Canaan Congregational Church, CT 63 and Barnes Rd., Canaan, 3/16/83, C, a, 83001272

South School, 362 S. Main St., Torrington, 3/27/86, A, C, 86000522

Sports Building [Taylor, Alfredo S. G., TR], Windrow Rd., Norfolk, 2/22/84, C, 84001088

Stoeckel, Robbins, House [Taylor, Alfredo S. G., TR], Litchfield Rd., Norfolk, 8/02/82, C, 82004465

Litchfield County—Continued

Sun Terrace, SW of New Hartford on CT 219, New Hartford vicinity, 12/20/78, C, g, 78002849

Tamarack Lodge Bungalow, S of Norfolk off CT 272 at Dennis Hill Park, Norfolk vicinity, 9/16/77, C, 77001499

Thomaston Opera House, Main St., Thomaston, 4/26/72, A, C, 72001319

Thumb, Tom, House [Taylor, Alfredo S. G., TR], Windrow Rd., Norfolk, 2/22/84, C, 84001094

Topsmead, 25 and 46 Chase Rd., Litchfield, 11/19/93, C, 93001243

Torringford Street Historic District, Torringford St. from Main St. N to W. Hill Rd., Torrington, 7/31/91, C, 91000991

Torrington Fire Department Headquarters, 117 Water St., Torrington, 12/31/87, C, 87002185

Town Hall and District School No. 6, 12 South St., Morris, 11/30/87, C, b, 87002109

Trinity Church, Milton Rd., Milton, 4/23/76, C, a, 76001981

Trinity Church, Main St., Thomaston, 8/01/84, C, a, 84001097

Union Church/St. Paul's Church, Riverton Rd., Riverton, 2/21/85, A, C, a, d, 85000307

Union Depot, U.S. 44, North Canaan, 4/26/72, A, C, 72001317

United Bank Building, 19-21 Main St., New Milford, 4/12/82, A, C, 82004447

Villa Friuli, 58 High St., Torrington, 4/11/91, A, C, 91000349

Warner Theatre, 68-82 Main St., Torrington, 2/16/84, A, C, 84001098

Warren Congregational Church, 4 Sackett Hill Rd., Warren, 11/29/91, A, C, a, 91001743

Warrenton Woolen Mill, 839 Main St., Torrington, 2/12/87, A, C, 87000115

Welch, David, House, Potash and Milton Rds., Milton, 2/16/84, A, B, C, 84001103

West Cornwall Bridge, CT 128 at Housatonic River, West Cornwall, 12/30/75, C, 75001923

West End Commercial District, N side of Main St. between Union and Elm Sts., Winsted, 8/03/90, A, C, 90001148

West Goshen Historic District, Roughly bounded by CT 4, Beach, Mill and Milton Sts., and Thompson Rd., Goshen, 10/23/87, A, C, D, 87000982

Wildman, E. A., & Co. Tobacco Warehouse, 34 Bridge St., New Milford, 10/20/88, A, C, b, e, g, 88000731

Wilton Center Historic District, Roughly, area around jct. of Lovers Ln. and Belden Hill and Ridgefield Rds., Wilton, 8/19/92, A, C, a, b, 92001003

Winchester Soldiers' Monument, Crown St., Winchester, 1/26/84, A, C, 84001105

Winsted Green Historic District, U.S. 44 and CT 8, Winsted, 8/16/77, A, C, 77001501

Winsted Green National Register Historic District (Boundary Increase), 86 Main St., Winsted, 4/29/82, C, 82004482

Winsted Hosiery Mill, Whiting at Holabird St., Winsted, 2/21/85, A, C, 85000308

Wolcott, Oliver, House, South St., Litchfield, 11/11/71, B, NHL, 71001011

Woodbury Historic District No. 1, Both sides of Main St. (U.S. 6) for 2 mi., radiating rds., Woodbury, 3/11/71, A, C, 71000908

Woodbury Historic District No. 2, Both sides of Main St. from Woodbury-Southbury town line to Middle Quarter, Woodbury, 2/23/72, A, C, 72001326

World War I Memorial [Taylor, Alfredo S. G., TR], Greenwoods Rd. West and North Sts., Norfolk, 2/17/84, C, f, 84001106

Middlesex County

Alsop House, 301 High St., Middletown, 10/06/70, A, C, 70000686

BOC Site [Lower Connecticut River Valley Woodland Period Archaeological TR], Address Restricted, Haddam vicinity, 10/15/87, D, 87001218

Belltown Historic District, Roughly Main St. between W. High St. and CT 16, and portions of cross Sts. W. High, Barton Hill-Summit, and Skinner, East Hampton, 10/28/85, A, C, 85003543

Black Horse Tavern, SE of Old Saybrook at 175 N. Cove Rd., Old Saybrook vicinity, 12/01/78, A, C, 78002851

Bridge No. 1603 [Connecticut State Park and Forest Depression-Era Federal Work Relief Programs Structures TR], Devil's Hopyard Rd. (Rt. 434) over unnamed brook, Devil's Hopyard SP, Millington vicinity, 7/29/93, A, C, 93000641

Bridge No. 1604 [Connecticut State Park and Forest Depression-Era Federal Work Relief Programs Structures TR], Devil's Hopyard Rd. (Rt. 434) over Muddy Brook, Devil's Hopyard SP, Millington vicinity, 7/29/93, A, C, 93000642

Bridge No. 1605 [Connecticut State Park and Forest Depression-Era Federal Work Relief Programs Structures TR], Devil's Hopyard Rd. (Rt. 434) over unnamed brook, Devil's Hopyard SP, Millington vicinity, 7/29/93, A, C, 93000643

Broad Street Historic District, Roughly bounded by High, Washington, Broad and Church Sts., Middletown, 8/25/88, A, C, a, b, 88001319

Bushnell, Benjamin, Farm, 52 Ingham Hill Rd., Essex, 5/10/90, C, 90000761

Bushnell, Elisha, House, 1445 Boston Post Rd., Old Saybrook, 11/29/78, C, 78002850

CHRISTEEN (oyster sloop), Essex Harbor, Essex, 12/04/91, A, D, NHL, 91002060

Centerbrook Congregational Church, Main St., Essex, 2/12/87, C, a, 87000113

Church of the Holy Trinity and Rectory, 381 Main St. and 144 Broad St., Middletown, 8/14/79, A, C, a, 79002615

Coite-Hubbard House, 269 High St., Middletown, 12/20/78, C, 78002846

Comstock's Bridge, SE of East Hampton off CT 16, East Hampton vicinity, 1/01/76, C, 76001978

Comstock-Cheney Hall, Main and Summit Sts., Ivoryton, 4/15/82, A, C, g, 82003769

Connecticut General Hospital for the Insane, Silver St. E. of Eastern Dr., Middletown, 8/29/85, A, B, C, 85001920

DORIS (Sailing yacht), Connecticut River off River Rd., Deep River, 5/31/84, A, C, 84001108

Daniels, Charles, House, 43 Liberty St., Chester, 2/19/88, C, b, 88000094

Day, Amasa, House, Plains Rd., Moodus, 9/22/72, C, 72001315

Deep River Town Hall, CT 80 and CT 9A, Deep River, 1/01/76, A, C, 76001977

Doane's Sawmill/Deep River Manufacturing Company, Horse Hill and Winthrop Rds., Westbrook and Deep River, 2/21/85, A, C, 85000313

Dudley, Jedidiah, House, Springbrook Rd., Old Saybrook, 4/12/82, B, C, 82004339

East Haddam Historic District, CT 149, Broom, Norwich, Creamery, Lumberyard, and Landing Hill Rds., East Haddam, 4/29/83, A, B, C, 83001273

Eliot, Samuel, House, 500 Main St., Old Saybrook, 11/09/72, C, 72001316

Goodspeed Opera House, Norwich Rd., East Haddam, 7/30/71, A, C, 71000901

Haddam Center Historic District, Roughly 2.5 mi. along Walkley Rd. and CT 154/Saybrook Rd., Haddam, 2/09/89, A, C, 89000012

Hadlyme North Historic District, Roughly bounded by CT 82, Town St., Banning Rd., and Old Town St., East Haddam vicinity, 12/08/88, C, a, 88002686

Hart, Gen. William, House, 350 Main St., Old Saybrook, 11/09/72, C, a, 72001318

Hazelton, James, House, 23 Hayden Hill Rd., Haddam, 11/16/88, C, 88001468

Highland Historic District, Atkins St. and Country Club Rd., Middletown, 6/28/82, A, C, 82003770

Hill's Academy, 22 Prospect St., Essex, 8/23/85, A, C, 85001831

Hubbard, Nehemiah, House, Laurel Grove Rd. and Wadsworth St., Middletown, 5/11/82, B, C, 82003771

Indian Hill Avenue Historic District, Main St. and Indian Hill Ave. to river, Portland, 5/26/83, A, C, D, 83001274

Lay-Pritchett House, N of Westbrook on CT 145, Westbrook vicinity, 10/11/78, C, 78002854

Lee, Daniel and Mary, House, Pepperidge Rd. E of Jobs Pond Rd., Portland, 4/03/91, C, 91000365

Lyman, David, II, House, 5 Lyman Rd., Middlefield, 2/06/86, B, C, 86000149

Lyman, Thomas, House, Middlefield Rd., Durham, 11/20/75, C, 75001921

Lynde Point Lighthouse [Operating Lighthouses in Connecticut MPS], SE terminus of Sequassen Ave., Old Saybrook, 5/29/90, A, C, 89001469

Main Street Historic District, Roughly Main St. between College and Hartford Ave., Middletown, 6/30/83, A, C, a, 83001275

Main Street Historic District, Roughly bounded by Nooks Hill Rd., Prospect Hill Rd., Wall and West Sts. and New Ln., and Stevens Ln. and Main St., Cromwell, 10/24/85, A, C, 85003389

Middlesex County—Continued

Main Street Historic District, Roughly Maple Ave. and Main St. between Talcott Ln. and Higganum Rd., Durham, 9/04/86, A, C, 86002837

Metro South Historic District, Main and College Sts., Middletown, 1/24/80, A, C, a, b, 80004064

Middle Haddam Historic District, Moodus and Long Hill Rds., Middle Haddam, 2/03/84, A, C, D, 84001112

Middletown Alms House, 53 Warwick St., Middletown, 4/29/82, A, C, 82003772

Middletown South Green Historic District, Union Park area, on S. Main, Crescent, Pleasant, and Church Sts., Middletown, 8/12/75, C, a, 75001922

Middletown Upper Houses Historic District, CT 99, Cromwell, 7/27/79, A, C, D, 79002620

Oak Lodge [Connecticut State Park and Forest Depression-Era Federal Work Relief Programs Structures TR], W side of Schreeder Pond, Chatfield Hollow State Park, Killingworth, 9/04/86, A, C, 86001734

Old Middletown High School, Pearl and Court Sts., Middletown, 8/23/85, A, C, 85001826

Old Saybrook South Green, Old Boston Post Rd., Pennywise Lane, Main St., Old Saybrook, 9/03/76, A, C, 76001984

Old Town Hall, On the green between Liberty St. and Goose Hill Rd., Chester, 2/23/72, A, C, a, 72001310

Oriole Rockshelter [Lower Connecticut River Valley Woodland Period Archaeological TR], Address Restricted, East Haddam vicinity, 10/15/87, D, 87001222

Parker House, 680 Middlesex Tpke., Old Saybrook vicinity, 11/29/78, C, 78002853

Pledger, Jacob, House, 717 Newfield St., Middletown, 3/15/82, A, C, 82003773

Plumb House, W of Middletown at 872 Westfield St., Middletown vicinity, 12/01/78, C, 78002848

Pratt House, 19 West Ave., Essex, 8/23/85, B, C, 85001824

Pratt, Dr. Ambrose, House, Pratt St., Chester, 11/09/72, C, b, 72001311

Pratt, Humphrey, Tavern, 287 Main St., Old Saybrook, 11/07/72, C, 72001320

Pratt, Read and Company Factory Complex, Main St. between Bridge and Spring Sts. and 5 Bridge St., Deep River, 8/30/84, A, C, 84001117

Rapallo Viaduct, Flat Brook and former Air Line RR right-of-way, East Hampton, 8/21/86, A, C, D, 86002728

Roaring Brook I Site [Lower Connecticut River Valley Woodland Period Archaeological TR], Address Restricted, East Haddam vicinity, 7/31/87, D, 87001220

Roaring Brook II Site [Lower Connecticut River Valley Woodland Period Archaeological TR], Address Restricted, East Haddam vicinity, 7/31/87, D, 87001221

Russell Company Upper Mill, 475 E. Main St., Middletown, 2/06/86, A, B, C, 86000150

Russell House, Corner of Washington and High Sts., Middletown, 10/06/70, C, a, 70000688

Russell, Edward Augustus, House, 318 High St., Middletown, 4/29/82, B, C, 82004336

Sage-Kirby House, 93 Shunpike Rd., Cromwell, 4/29/82, A, C, 82003767

Saint Luke's Home for Destitute and Aged Women, 135 Pearl St., Middletown, 4/29/82, A, C, 82004337

Sanseer Mill, 215 E. Main St., Middletown, 7/31/86, B, C, 86002101

Saybrook Breakwater Lighthouse [Operating Lighthouses in Connecticut MPS], S terminus of Saybrook Jetty at mouth of Connecticut River, Old Saybrook, 5/29/90, A, C, 89001474

Seventh Sister, 67 River Rd., East Haddam, 7/31/86, B, C, 86002103

Starr Mill, Jct. of Middlefield St. and Beverly Heights, Middletown, 12/14/93, C, 93001379

Starr Mill Road Bridge, Starr Mill Rd. across the Cochinaug R., Middletown, 12/10/93, A, C, 93001344

Steamboat Dock Site, Main St., Essex, 4/01/82, A, C, b, 82003768

Stevens, William, House, 131 Cow Hill Rd., Clinton, 5/30/85, C, 85001163

Town Farms Inn, Spring St. at River Rd., Middletown, 5/04/79, A, C, 79002614

Tully, William, House, 135 N. Cove Rd., Old Saybrook, 3/15/82, A, B, C, 82004340

U.S. Post Office, 291 Main St., Middletown, 4/12/82, C, 82004338

Ward, William, Jr., House, 137 Powder Hill Rd., Middlefield, 2/19/88, C, 88000109

Warner House, 307 Town St., East Haddam, 2/19/87, C, 87000174

Warner, Jonathan, House, 47 Kings Hwy., Chester, 12/19/78, B, C, 78002855

Washington Street Historic District, Roughly bounded by Washington and Main Sts., Washington Terrace and Vine St., Middletown, 5/09/85, C, 85001018

Wetmore, Seth, House, CT 66 and Camp Rd., Middletown, 9/10/70, C, 70000689

Whittlesey, Ambrose, House, 14 Main St., Old Saybrook, 8/23/85, B, C, 85001830

Whittlesey, John, Jr., House, 40 Ferry Rd., Old Saybrook, 10/26/84, C, 84002644

Wilcox, Crittenden Mill, 234–315 S. Main St., Pameacha, and Highlands Aves., Middletown, 12/03/86, A, B, C, D, 86003349

Williams and Stancliff Octagon Houses, 26 and 28 Marlborough St., Portland, 4/22/76, C, 76001985

Woodrow Wilson High School, Hunting Hill Ave. and Russell St., Middletown, 8/06/86, A, C, 86002270

New Haven County

Abbott, George S., Building, 235-247 N. Main St., Waterbury, 6/14/82, C, 82004359

Acadian House, Union St., Guilford, 9/05/75, A, C, 75001928

Allis-Bushnell House, 853 Boston Post Rd., Madison, 2/25/82, B, C, c, 82004352

American Mills Web Shop, 114-152 Orange Ave., West Haven, 3/10/83, A, C, 83001276

Andrews, Moses, House, 424 W. Main St., Meriden, 12/01/78, C, 78002859

Ansonia Library, 53 South Cliff St., Ansonia, 8/23/85, A, B, C, 85001828

Atwater, George, House, 1845 State St., Hamden, 1/17/92, C, 91001921

Atwater—Linton House, 1804 State St., Hamden, 1/17/92, B, C, 91001923

Baldwin, George, House, W of North Branford at 530 Foxon Rd., North Branford vicinity, 9/15/77, C, 77001411

Baldwin, Timothy, House [Colonial Houses of Branford TR], 186 Damascus Rd., Branford, 12/01/88, A, C, 88002633

Baldwin, Zaccheus, House [Colonial Houses of Branford TR], 154 Damascus Rd., Branford, 12/01/88, A, C, 88002631

Bank Street Historic District, 207-231 Bank St., Waterbury, 7/28/83, A, C, 83001277

Barker, John, House, 898 Clintonville Rd., Wallingford, 8/03/74, C, 74002051

Beach, Samuel, House [Colonial Houses of Branford TR], 94 E. Main St., Branford, 12/01/88, A, C, 88002634

Beaver Hills Historic District, Roughly bounded by Crescent St., Goffe Terr., and Boulevard, New Haven, 7/31/86, A, C, 86002108

Benedict-Miller House, 32 Hillside Ave., Waterbury, 6/12/81, C, 81000616

Bishop School, 178 Bishop St., Waterbury, 11/30/82, A, 82001003

Blackman, Elisha, Building, 176 York St., New Haven, 12/20/78, A, C, 78002863

Blackstone House [Colonial Houses of Branford TR], 37 First Ave., Branford, 12/01/88, A, C, 88002639

Bradley, Timothy, House [Colonial Houses of Branford TR], 12 Bradley St., Branford, 12/01/88, A, C, 88002630

Branford Center Historic District, Roughly bounded by US I, Branford River on the East and South, Monroe, and Kirkham Sts., Branford, 5/06/87, A, C, 87000636

Branford Electric Railway Historic District, 17 River St. to Court St., Branford, 6/03/83, A, C, 83001278

Branford Point Historic District, Roughly along Harbor St. N from Curve St. to Branford Point, also Maple St. E. from Reynolds St. to Harbor St., Branford, 9/15/88, C, f, 88001583

Bronson, Aaron, House, 846 Southford Rd., Southbury, 7/29/93, C, 93000656

Bronson, Josiah, House, Breakneck Hill Rd., Middlebury, 2/25/82, A, C, 82004356

Buckingham House, 61 North St., Milford, 7/25/77, C, 77001406

Bullet Hill School, Main St. and Seymour Rd., Southbury, 2/23/72, C, 72001346

Chapel Street Historic District, Roughly bounded by Park, Chapel, Temple, George, and Crown Sts., New Haven, 4/05/84, A, C, 84001123

Cheshire Historic District, Roughly bounded by Main St., Highland Ave., Wallingford Rd., S.

New Haven County—Continued

Main, Cornwall, and Spring Sts., Cheshire, 8/29/86, C, 86002793

Chittenden, Russell Henry, House, 83 Trumbull St., New Haven, 5/15/75, B, NHL, 75001944

Colony Street—West Main Street Historic District, 1–62 Colony, 55 Grove, 1–119 and 82–110 W. Main Sts., Meriden, 9/04/87, C, 87001387

Connecticut Agricultural Experiment Station, 123 Huntington St., New Haven, 10/15/66, A, NHL, 66000805

Connecticut Hall, Yale University, Bounded by High, Chapel, Elm, and College Sts., New Haven, 10/15/66, A, C, NHL, 66000806

Cook, John, House, 35 Elm St., New Haven, 11/03/83, A, B, C, 83003576

Curtis Memorial Library, 175 E. Main St., Meriden, 4/27/81, A, C, 81000618

Curtiss, Reuben, House, 1770 Bucks Hill Rd., Southbury, 7/29/93, C, 93000658

Dana, James Dwight, House, 24 Hillhouse Ave., New Haven, 10/15/66, B, C, NHL, 66000874

Darling, Thomas, House and Tavern, E of Woodbridge at 1907 Litchfield Tpke., Woodbridge vicinity, 1/17/79, A, C, 79002639

Dickerman II, Jonathan, House, 105 Mt. Carmel Ave., Hamden, 4/15/82, B, C, b, 82004351

Downtown Seymour Historic District, Roughly bounded by the Naugatuck River, Main, Wakeley, and DeForest Sts., Seymour, 8/25/83, A, B, C, 83001279

Downtown Waterbury Historic District, Roughly bounded by Main, Meadow, and Elm Sts., Waterbury, 8/03/83, A, C, 83001280

Dudleytown Historic District, Roughly, Clapboard Hill Rd. from Tanner Marsh Rd. to Murray Ln., East River Rd. SE to Trailwood Dr., and Duck Hole Rd., Guilford, 8/09/91, A, C, 91000951

Dwight Street Historic District, Roughly bounded by Park, N. Frontage, Scranton, Sherman, and Elm Sts., New Haven, 9/08/83, A, C, a, 83001281

Edgerton, 840 Whitney Ave., New Haven, 9/19/88, C, 88001469

Edgewood Park Historic District, Roughly bounded by Whalley Ave. and Elm St., Sherman Ave. and Boulevard, Edgewood and Derby, and Yale Aves., New Haven, 9/09/86, A, C, 86001991

Eells-Stow House, 34 High St., Milford, 6/17/77, C, 77001407

Eliot, Jared, House, 88 Old Chaffinch Island Rd., Guilford, 11/14/85, B, 85002792

Elton Hotel, 16-30 W. Main St., Waterbury, 6/30/83, A, C, 83001282

Falkner's Island Lighthouse [Operating Lighthouses in Connecticut MPS], Long Island Sound, 5 mi. S of Guilford, Guilford vicinity, 5/29/90, A, C, 89001467

Farmington Canal Lock, 487 N. Brooksvale Rd., Cheshire, 2/16/73, A, C, 73001949

Farmington Canal Lock No. 13, Brooksvale Ave., Hamden vicinity, 5/06/82, A, C, 82004350

First Congregational Church of Cheshire, 111 Church Dr., Cheshire, 2/16/73, C, a, 73001950

First Congregational Church of East Haven, 251 Main St., East Haven, 3/25/82, A, C, a, 82004349

Five Mile Point Lighthouse, Lighthouse Point Park, New Haven, 8/01/90, A, C, 90001108

Fort Nathan Hale, S end of Woodward Ave., New Haven, 10/28/70, A, C, D, 70000711

Fourth District School, Old Post Rd., North Branford, 8/29/85, A, C, b, 85001917

Frisbie, Edward, Homestead, 240 Stony Creek Rd., Branford, 5/16/85, A, C, 85001058

Frisbie, Edward, House [Colonial Houses of Branford TR], 699 E. Main St., Branford, 12/01/88, C, 88002638

Fulton, Lewis, Memorial Park, Roughly bounded by Cook, Pine, Fern and Charlotte Sts., Waterbury, 12/27/90, C, 90001951

Goffe Street Special School for Colored Children, 106 Goffe St., New Haven, 8/17/79, A, C, 79002643

Goffe, Solomon, House, 677 N. Colony St., Meriden, 1/16/79, C, 79002645

Griswold House, Boston St., Guilford, 10/10/75, C, 75001929

Guilford Historic Town Center, Bounded by West River, I-95, East Creek and Long Island Sound, Guilford, 7/06/76, C, a, 76001988

Hall—Benedict Drug Company Building, 763–767 Orange St., New Haven, 6/05/86, A, C, 86001205

Hamden Bank & Trust Building, 1 Circular Ave., Hamden, 3/01/90, A, C, 90000148

Harrison, Thomas, House [Colonial Houses of Branford TR], 23 N. Harbor St., Branford, 12/01/88, A, C, 88002644

Hibbard, Enoch, House and Grannis, George, House, 41 Church St. and 33 Church St., Waterbury, 4/09/79, C, 79002640

Hillhouse Avenue Historic District, Bounded by Sachem, Temple, Trumbull, and Prospect Sts., Whitney and Hillhouse Aves. & RR tracks, New Haven, 9/13/85, B, C, 85002507

Hillside Historic District, Roughly bounded by Woodlawn Terr., W. Main, and Willow, Waterbury, 8/20/87, C, 87001384

Hoadley, Isaac, House [Colonial Houses of Branford TR], 9 Totoket Rd., Branford, 12/01/88, A, C, 88002647

Hoadley, John, House [Colonial Houses of Branford TR], 213 Leete's Island Rd., Branford, 12/01/88, A, C, 88002674

Hoadley, Orrin, House [Colonial Houses of Branford TR], 15 Sunset Hill Rd., Branford, 12/01/88, A, C, 88002646

Home Woolen Company, Main St., Beacon Falls vicinity, 11/29/84, A, C, 84000410

Hotchkiss, David, House, Waterbury Rd., Prospect, 5/01/81, C, 81000617

House at 161 Damascus Road [Colonial Houses of Branford TR], 161 Damascus Rd., Branford, 12/01/88, A, C, 88002632

House at 29 Flat Rock Road [Colonial Houses of Branford TR], 29 Flat Rock Rd., Branford, 12/01/88, A, C, 88002640

Howard Avenue Historic District, Properties along Howard Ave. between I-95 and Cassius St., New Haven, 9/12/85, C, 85002308

Howd, Eliphalet, House [Colonial Houses of Branford TR], 675 E. Main St., Branford, 12/01/88, A, C, 88002637

Howd—Linsley House, 1795 Middletown Ave., North Branford, 12/10/86, C, 86003382

Howe, John I., House, 213 Caroline St., Derby, 2/06/89, B, C, 88003229

Humphreys, Gen. David, House, 37 Elm St., Ansonia, 3/17/72, B, C, 72001321

Hurd, William, House, 327 Hulls Hill Rd., Southbury, 7/29/93, C, b, 93000659

Hurley Road Historic District, 6 and 17 Hurley Rd., Southbury, 7/29/93, C, 93000662

Hyland-Wildman House, Boston St., Guilford, 3/26/76, C, 76001989

Imperial Granum—Joseph Parker Buildings, 47 and 49–51 Elm St., New Haven, 3/06/86, A, C, 86000409

Johnson, Alphonso, House, 1 Gilbert Ave., Hamden, 1/17/92, C, 91001922

Jones, Theophilus, House, 40 Jones Rd., Wallingford, 1/30/92, A, B, C, b, 91001981

Kendrick, John, House, 119 W. Main St., Waterbury, 4/12/82, B, C, 82004360

Kraus Corset Factory, Roosevelt Dr. and Third St., Derby, 2/12/87, A, C, 87000128

Leete, Pelatiah, House, SW of Guilford off CT 146, Guilford vicinity, 10/01/74, C, 74002048

Lighthouse Point Carousel, Lighthouse Point Park, Lighthouse Ave., New Haven, 12/15/83, A, C, 83003578

Lincoln Theatre, 1 Lincoln St., New Haven, 3/01/84, A, B, C, 84001134

Little Pootatuck Brook Archeological Site, Address Restricted, Southbury, 6/28/90, D, a, 90000980

Madison Green Historic District, 446-589 Boston Post Rd. and structures surrounding the green, Madison, 6/28/82, A, C, a, 82004353

Mansfield, Richard, House, 35 Jewett St., Ansonia, 3/11/71, B, C, b, 71000906

Marsh, Othniel C., House, 360 Prospect St., New Haven, 10/15/66, B, NHL, 66000875

Matthews and Willard Factory, 16 Cherry Ave., Waterbury, 1/14/88, A, C, 87002419

Meeting House Hill Historic District, Roughly bounded by Long Hill, Great Hill, and Ledge Hill Rds., Guilford, 12/14/87, A, C, a, 87002132

Meigs—Bishop House, 45 Wall St., Madison, 6/16/88, C, 88000745

Mendel, Lafayette B., House, 18 Trumbull St., New Haven, 1/07/76, B, NHL, 76002138

Meriden Curtain Fixture Company Factory, 122 Charles St., Meriden, 12/04/86, A, C, 86003290

Middlebury Center Historic District, Roughly bounded by Library Rd., North and South Sts. and Whittemore Rd., Middlebury, 5/09/85, A, C, 85001019

Milford Point Hotel, Milford Point Rd., Milford, 1/22/88, A, 87002417

Morris House, 325 Lighthouse Rd., New Haven, 12/04/72, C, 72001341

Mount Carmel Congregational Church and Parish House, 3280 and 3284 Whitney Ave., 195 Sherman Ave., Hamden, 12/27/91, C, a, 91001847

New Haven County—Continued

Murray, Jonathan, House, 76 Scotland Rd., Madison, 4/12/82, C, 82004354

New Haven City Hall, 161 Church St., New Haven, 9/09/75, C, 75001940

New Haven Green Historic District, Bounded by Chapel, College, Elm, and Church Sts., New Haven, 12/30/70, C, a, NHL, 70000838

New Haven Jewish Home for the Aged, 169 Davenport Ave., New Haven, 6/19/79, A, C, 79002641

New Haven Railroad Station, Union Ave., New Haven, 9/03/75, A, C, 75001941

Nicoll, Caroline, House, 27 Elm St., New Haven, 1/14/83, A, C, 83001283

Ninth Square Historic District, Roughly bounded by Church, State, George, and Court Sts., New Haven, 5/03/84, A, C, 84001135

Norton House [Colonial Houses of Branford TR], 200 Pine Orchard Rd., Branford, 12/01/88, A, C, b, 88002645

Old West Haven High School, 278 Main St., West Haven, 10/24/85, C, 85003368

Orange Center Historic District, Roughly Orange Center Rd. from Orange Cemetery to Nan Dr., Orange, 8/10/89, C, 89001089

Orange Street Historic District, Roughly bounded by Whitney Ave., State, Eagle & Trumbull Sts., New Haven, 9/12/85, A, C, 85002314

Osbornedale, 500 Hawthorne Ave., Derby, 6/13/86, B, C, 86001256

Overlook Historic District, Roughly bounded by Hecla St., Farmington and Columbia Blvd., Cables Ave. and Clowes Terr., Lincoln and Fiske Sts., Waterbury, 6/07/88, A, C, a, 88000662

Oyster Point Historic District, Rougly bounded by I-95, S. Water St., Howard Ave., Sea St., and Greenwich Ave., New Haven, 8/10/89, A, C, 89001085

Palace Theater, 86-110 E. Main St., Waterbury, 6/30/83, A, C, 83001284

Palmer, Hezekiah, House [Colonial Houses of Branford TR], 340–408 Leete's Island Rd., Branford, 12/01/88, A, C, 88002641

Palmer, Isaac, House [Colonial Houses of Branford TR], 736–756 Main St., Branford, 12/01/88, A, C, 88002643

Parsons, Samuel, House, 180 S. Main St., Wallingford, 4/12/82, C, 82004358

Pines Bridge Historic District, 3–17 Bishop St., 70–99 Old Broadway, 2–10 Philip Pl., 9–56 State St., North Haven, 5/27/88, A, C, b, 88000577

Pinto, William, House, 275 Orange St., New Haven, 9/12/85, B, C, 85002316

Pistol Factory Dwelling, 1322 Whitney Ave., Hamden, 12/27/91, A, B, C, b, 91001846

Pitkin, Elisha, House, 173 High Woods Dr., Guilford, 4/06/79, B, C, b, 79002646

Plaster House, 117 Plaster House Rd., Southbury, 7/29/93, C, 93000660

Plymouth Congregational Church, 1469 Chapel St., New Haven, 7/28/83, C, a, 83001250

Prospect Hill Historic District, Off CT 10, New Haven, 11/02/79, B, C, g, 79002670

Quaker Farms Historic District, 467–511 Quaker Farms Rd., Oxford, 8/09/91, C, a, 91000993

Quinnipiac Brewery, 19-23 River St., New Haven, 7/15/83, A, C, 83001285

Quinnipiac River Historic District, Roughly bounded by Quinnipiac Ave., Lexington, Chapel, Ferry, Pine, Front, and Lombard Sts., New Haven, 6/28/84, A, C, 84001139

Raynham, 709 Townsend Ave., New Haven, 7/11/80, C, 80004062

Red Bridge, Near Oregon Rd. over the Quinnipiac R., Meriden, 12/10/93, A, C, 93001345

Richardson, Nathaniel, House, NE of Middlebury on Kelly Rd., Middlebury vicinity, 9/19/77, C, 77001405

Rising Sun Tavern, Old Tavern Lane, North Haven, 8/21/79, A, C, 79002638

River Park Historic District, Roughly bounded by Boston Post Rd., Cherry St. and Amtrak, and High St., Milford, 8/14/86, A, C, 86002648

River Street Historic District, Roughly bounded by Chapel St., Blatchley Ave., New Haven Harbor, and James St., New Haven, 1/26/89, A, C, 88003213

Riverside Cemetery, Riverside St., from Sunnyside to Summit Sts., Waterbury, 9/20/88, C, d, 88001525

Rogers, John, House [Colonial Houses of Branford TR], 690 Leete's Island Rd., Branford, 12/01/88, A, C, 88002642

Route 146 Historic District, Rt. 146 between Flat Rock Rd. and West River bridge, Branford, 4/05/90, A, C, 90000569

Russian Village Historic District, Roughly Kiev Dr. and Russian Village Rd. between US 6 and the Pomperaug River, Southbury, 12/08/88, A, C, 88002687

Sabbathday House, 19 Union St., Guilford, 10/10/75, A, C, a, 75001931

Salem School, 124 Meadow St., Naugatuck, 11/03/83, A, C, 83003582

Sanford Road Historic District, 480 and 487 Sanford Rd., Southbury, 7/29/93, A, B, C, g, 93000657

Sanford-Humphreys House, 61-63 West St., Seymour, 5/11/82, B, C, 82004357

Seymour High School and Annex, 100 Bank St., Seymour, 11/17/83, A, C, 83003583

Shelley House, 248 Boston Post Rd., Madison, 2/09/89, C, 89000017

Simpson, Samuel, House, 216 N. Main St., Wallingford, 6/18/86, B, C, 86001334

Sleeping Giant Tower [Connecticut State Park and Forest Depression-Era Federal Work Relief Programs Structures TR], 200 Mt. Carmel Ave. at Mt. Carmel summit, Sleeping Giant State Park, Hamden, 9/04/86, A, C, 86001754

South Britain Historic District, E. Flat Hill, Hawkins, Library, and Middle Rds., and 497–864 S. Britain Rd., Southbury, 2/12/87, C, 87000125

Southbury Historic District No. 1, Main St. from Woodbury Town Line to Old Waterbury Rd., Southbury, 3/11/71, B, C, 71000917

Southbury Training School, 1484 S. Britain Rd., Southbury, 5/01/92, A, C, 92000368

Southwest District School, 155 Nichols Rd., Wolcott, 4/02/82, A, C, 82004363

Southwest Ledge Lighthouse [Operating Lighthouses in Connecticut MPS], SW end of east breakwater at entrance to New Haven Harbor, New Haven vicinity, 5/29/90, A, C, 89001475

St. Peter's Episcopal Church, 61, 71, 81 River St., Milford, 8/21/79, C, a, 79002644

Stapleton Building, 751 N. Main St., Waterbury, 1/14/88, A, C, 87002421

State Park Supply Yard [Connecticut State Park and Forest Depression-Era Federal Work Relief Programs Structures TR], 51 Mill Rd., Madison, 9/04/86, A, C, 86001757

Sterling Opera House, NW corner of 4th and Elizabeth Sts., Derby, 11/08/68, A, 68000040

Stick Style House at Stony Creek, 34 Prospect Hill, Branford, 12/27/72, C, 72001322

Stony Creek—Thimble Islands Historic District, Roughly Thimble Islands Rd. between Rt. 146 and Long Island Sound and the Thimble Islands, Branford, 12/16/88, A, C, 88002844

Stratford Shoal Lighthouse [Operating Lighthouses in Connecticut MPS], SW end of east breakwater at entrance to New Haven Harbor, New Haven vicinity, 5/29/90, A, C, 89001477

Swain-Harrison House, 124 W. Main St., Branford, 10/10/75, B, C, 75001924

Taylor Memorial Library, 5 Broad St., Milford, 8/21/79, C, 79002642

Todd, Orrin, House, 3369 Whitney Ave., Hamden, 12/26/91, A, C, b, 91001845

Tranquility Farm, W of Middlebury on CT 64, Middlebury vicinity, 9/23/82, A, B, C, 82004355

Trowbridge Square Historic District, Roughly bounded by Columbus & Howard Aves., New Haven, 9/12/85, B, C, 85002311

Tuttle, Bronson B., House, 380 Church St., Naugatuck, 11/29/90, C, 90001803

Tyler, John, House [Colonial Houses of Branford TR], 242–250 E. Main St., Branford, 12/01/88, A, C, 88002635

Tyler, Solomon, House [Colonial Houses of Branford TR], 260–268 E. Main St., Branford, 12/01/88, A, C, 88002636

US Post Office—Ansonia Main, 237 Main St., Ansonia, 12/12/85, C, 85003327

US Post Office—Meriden Main, 39 N. Colony St., Meriden, 1/21/86, C, 86000129

US Post Office—Milford Main, 6 W. River St., Milford, 9/25/86, C, 86002959

US Post Office—Naugatuck Main, Church and Cedar Sts., Naugatuck, 1/21/86, C, 86000130

Union School, 174 Center St., West Haven, 11/13/87, A, C, 87001899

Upper Main Street Historic District, 36-100, 85-117 Main St., Ansonia, 12/02/82, A, C, 82001004

Upper State Street Historic District, Roughly State St. from Bradley St. to Mill River St., New Haven, 9/07/84, A, C, 84001143

Wallingford Center Historic District, Roughly, Main St. from Ward St. to Church St., Wallingford, 12/02/93, A, C, 93001242

Wallingford Railroad Station, 51 Quinnipiac St. (37 Hall Ave.), Wallingford, 11/19/93, C, 93001245

New Haven County—Continued

Waterbury Brass Mill, Idlewood Ave. in Hamilton Park, Waterbury, 9/05/75, D, 75001943

Waterbury Clock Company, N. Elm, Cherry Sts. and Cherry Ave., Waterbury, 11/30/82, A, C, 82001005

Waterbury Municipal Center Complex, 195, 235, 236 Grand St; 7, 35, 43 Field St., Waterbury, 10/10/78, A, B, C, 78002882

Waterbury Union Station, 389 Meadow St., Waterbury, 3/08/78, A, C, 78002881

Webster School, Easton Ave. at Aetna St., Waterbury, 6/14/82, A, C, 82004365

Welch Training School, 495 Congress Ave., New Haven, 4/21/83, A, C, 83001286

Wheeler, Adin, House and Theodore F. Wheeler Wheelwright Shop, 125 Quaker Farms Rd., Southbury, 7/29/93, A, C, 93000661

Wheeler-Beecher House, 562 Amity Rd., Bethany vicinity, 7/15/77, C, 77001400

Whitfield, Henry, House, Old Whitfield St., Guilford, 11/27/72, C, 72001327

Whitney Avenue Historic District, Roughly bounded by Burns St., Livingston St., Cold Spring St., Orange St., Bradley St., and Whitney Ave., New Haven, 2/02/89, A, C, 88003209

Whitney, Eli, Gun Factory, 915-940 Whitney Ave., Hamden, 8/13/74, D, 74002049

Wilby High School, 260 Grove St., Waterbury, 6/14/82, A, C, 82004366

Williams, Warham, House, Old Post Rd. and CT 17 and 22, Northford, 3/11/71, B, C, 71000915

Winchester Repeating Arms Company Historic District, Roughly bounded by Sherman Pkwy., Ivy St., Mansfield St., Admiral St., and Sachem St., New Haven, 1/28/88, A, C, a, b, 87002552

Wood, Harcourt, Memorial Library, 313 Elizabeth St., Derby, 1/04/82, A, C, 82004348

Wooster Square Historic District, Roughly bounded by Columbus, Wooster Sq., Chapel St., and Court St., New Haven, 8/05/71, C, 71000914

Yale Bowl, SW of intersection of Chapel St. and Yale Ave., New Haven, 2/27/87, A, NHL, 87000756

New London County

American Thermos Bottle Company Laurel Hill Plant, 11 Thermos Ave., Norwich, 7/17/89, A, C, g, 88003091

Applewood Farm, 528 Colonel Ledyard Hwy., Ledyard, 10/15/87, A, C, 87001765

Ashlawn, 1 Potash Hill Rd., Sprague, 6/04/79, C, 79002649

Avery Homestead [Ledyard MPS], 20 Avery Hill Rd., Ledyard Township, Ledyard vicinity, 12/14/92, A, C, 92001641

Avery House [Connecticut State Park and Forest Depression-Era Federal Work Relief Programs Structures TR], NE corner of Park and Roode Rds., Griswold, 9/04/86, C, 86001726

Avery, Thomas, House, Society Rd., East Lyme, 8/22/79, A, C, D, 79002637

Backus, Nathaniel, House, 44 Rockwell St., Norwich, 10/06/70, B, C, 70000715

Bacon Academy, S. Main St., Colchester, 4/27/82, A, C, 82004364

Baltic Historic District, Roughly bounded by Fifth Ave., River, High, Main, W. Main, and the Shetucket River, Sprague, 8/03/87, A, C, 87001247

Barns, Acors, House, 68 Federal St., New London, 4/22/76, B, C, 76001992

Bean Hill Historic District, Huntington and Vergason Aves., Sylvia Lane and W. Town St., Norwich, 12/08/82, A, B, C, 82001006

Bennett Rockshelter [Lower Connecticut River Valley Woodland Period Archaeological TR], Address Restricted, Old Lyme vicinity, 7/31/87, D, 87001223

Bill, Gurdon, Store, 15 Church Hill Rd., Ledyard, 4/12/82, A, C, a, 82004368

Blackledge River Railroad Bridge, Former Air Line RR right-of-way and the Blackledge River, Colchester, 7/31/86, A, C, 86002109

Bozrah Congregational Church and Parsonage, 17 and 23 Bozrah St., Bozrah, 7/26/91, A, C, a, 91000952

Bradford-Huntington House, 16 Huntington Lane, Norwichtown, 10/06/70, B, C, 70000720

Branford House, Shennecosset and Eastern Point Rds., Groton, 1/23/84, C, 84001158

Bridge No. 1860 [Connecticut State Park and Forest Depression-Era Federal Work Relief Programs Structures TR], Massapeag Side Rd. (Rt. 433) over Shantok Brook, Fort Shantok SP, Montville, 7/29/93, A, C, 93000644

Broad Street School, 100 Broad St., Norwich, 1/19/84, A, C, 84001162

Buckingham, William A., House, 307 Main St., Norwich, 4/29/82, B, 82004379

Bulkeley School, Huntington St., New London, 8/13/81, A, C, 81000613

CHARLES W. MORGAN, Mystic Seaport, Mystic, 11/13/66, A, NHL, 66000804

Carpenter House, 55 E. Town St., Norwichtown, 10/14/70, B, C, 70000721

Carpenter, Joseph, Silversmith Shop, 71 E. Town St., Norwichtown, 10/06/70, A, B, 70000722

Carroll Building, 9-15 Main St., and 14-20 Water St., Norwich, 11/14/82, A, C, 82001007

Champion, Henry, House, Weschester Rd., Colchester, 10/10/72, C, 72001323

Chapman, David, Farmstead [Ledyard MPS], 128 Stoddards Wharf Rd., Ledyard Township, Ledyard vicinity, 12/14/92, A, C, 92001642

Charlton, Capt. Richard, House, 12 Mediterranean Lane, Norwichtown, 10/15/70, C, 70000723

Chelsea Parade Historic District, Roughly bounded by Crescent, Broad, Grove, McKinley, Perkins, Slater, Buckingham, Maple Grove, Washington, and Lincoln, Norwich, 5/12/89, A, C, 88003215

Civic Institutions Historic District, 156-158, 171, 173-175 Garfield Ave., 179 Colman St., 32 Wald Ave., New London, 4/16/90, A, C, 90000602

Clark Homestead, S of Lebanon on Madley Rd., Lebanon vicinity, 12/01/78, C, 78002875

Clark, Andrew, House, Ross Hill Rd., Lisbon, 6/28/79, C, 79002636

Cogswell, Edward, House, 1429 Hopeville Rd., Griswold, 12/15/93, C, 93001378

Coit Street Historic District, Roughly bounded by Coit St., Washington, Tilley St., Bank St., and Reed St., New London, 2/19/88, A, C, b, 88000068

Converse House and Barn, 185 Washington St., Norwich, 10/06/70, C, 70000716

Cooper Site [Lower Connecticut River Valley Woodland Period Archaeological TR], Address Restricted, Lyme vicinity, 10/15/87, D, 87001224

Deshon-Allyn House, 613 Williams St., New London, 10/28/70, A, C, 70000700

Downtown New London Historic District, Roughly bounded by Captain's Walk, Bank, Tilley and Washington Sts., New London, 4/13/79, A, C, 79002665

Downtown New London Historic District (Boundary Increase), Along Huntington, Washington and Jay Sts.; SW corner of Meridan and Gov. Winthrop Blvd.; along Bank and Sparyard Sts., New London, 2/18/88, A, C, b, 88000070

Downtown Norwich Historic District, Roughly bounded by Union Sq., Park, Main and Shetland sts., and Washington Sq., Norwich, 4/04/85, A, B, C, 85000707

East District School, 365 Washington St., Norwich, 10/28/70, A, B, C, 70000717

Eolia—Harkness Estate, Great Neck Rd., Waterford, 11/20/86, A, B, C, 86003331

Fanning, Capt. Thomas, Farmstead [Ledyard MPS], 1004 Shewville Rd., Ledyard Township, Ledyard vicinity, 12/14/92, A, C, 92001643

Fish, Abel H., House, Buckley Hill and Rathbun Hill Rds., Salem, 3/02/82, C, 82004381

Fort Griswold, Bounded by Baker Ave., Smith St., Park Ave., Monument Ave., and Thames River, Groton, 10/06/70, A, 70000694

Fort Shantok, Address Restricted, Montville vicinity, 3/20/86, A, B, C, D, NHL, 86000469

Fort Trumbull, Fort Neck, New London, 9/22/72, A, C, 72001333

Gales Ferry Historic District No. 1 [Ledyard MPS], Jct. of Hurlbutt Rd. and Riverside Pl., Ledyard Township, Gales Ferry, 12/14/92, A, C, b, 92001639

Gorton, William, Farm, 14 West Lane, East Lyme, 4/05/84, A, C, 84001166

Griswold, Florence, House and Museum, 96 Lyme St., Old Lyme, 4/19/93, B, C, NHL, 93001604

Groton Bank Historic District, Roughly bounded by the Thames River, Broad, Cottage, and Latham Sts., Groton, 3/24/83, A, C, a, 83001287

Hamburg Bridge Historic District, Joshuatown Rd. and Old Hamburg Rd., Lyme, 3/10/83, A, C, 83001288

Hamburg Cove Site [Lower Connecticut River Valley Woodland Period Archaeological TR], Address Restricted, Lyme vicinity, 10/15/87, D, 87001225

Harris, Jonathan Newton, House, 130 Broad St., New London, 4/27/82, B, C, a, 82004375

New London County—Continued

Hayward House, 9 Hayward Ave., Colchester, 10/18/72, B, C, 72001325

Hempstead Historic District, Roughly bounded by Franklin St., Jay St., and Mountain Ave., New London, 7/31/86, A, C, 86002112

Hempstead, Joshua, House, 11 Hempstead St., New London, 10/15/70, A, C, 70000701

Hempsted, Nathaniel, House, Corner of Jay, Hempstead, Coit, and Truman Sts., New London, 12/02/70, A, C, 70000702

Huntington Street Baptist Church, 29 Huntington St., New London, 4/12/82, A, C, a, 82004377

Huntington, Col. Joshua, House, 11 Huntington Lane, Norwich, 2/23/72, B, C, 72001343

Huntington, Gen. Jedidiah, House, 23 E. Town St., Norwichtown, 10/06/70, B, C, 70000724

Huntington, Gov. Samuel, House, 34 E. Town St., Norwichtown, 10/06/70, B, 70000725

Jordan Village Historic District, Jct. of North Rd. and Avery Ln. with Rope Ferry Rd., Waterford, 8/23/90, A, C, a, 90001289

L. A. DUNTON, Mystic Seaport Museum, Mystic, 11/04/93, A, C, e, NHL, 93001612

Lamb Homestead, 47 Lambtown Rd., Ledyard, 9/03/91, A, C, 91001175

Lathrop, Dr. Daniel, School, 69 E. Town St., Norwichtown, 12/29/70, A, 70000726

Lathrop, Dr. Joshua, House, 377 Washington St., Norwichtown, 12/29/70, B, C, 70000727

Lathrop-Mathewson-Ross House, Ross Hill Rd., Lisbon, 4/15/82, C, 82004370

Laurel Hill Historic District, Roughly bounded by Spruce St., Rogers and River Aves., and Talman St., Norwich, 10/26/87, A, C, 87000516

Lebanon Green Historic District, CT 87 and W. Town St., Lebanon, 6/04/79, A, B, C, 79002666

Lee, Thomas, House, CT 156 and Giant's Neck Rd., East Lyme, 10/06/70, C, 70000693

Leffingwell Inn, 348 Washington St., Norwichtown, 12/29/70, B, C, 70000728

Lester, Nathan, House, Vinegar Hill Rd., Ledyard, 6/30/72, C, 72001328

Lieutenant River III Site [Lower Connecticut River Valley Woodland Period Archaeological TR], Address Restricted, Old Lyme vicinity, 7/31/87, D, 87001227

Lieutenant River IV Site [Lower Connecticut River Valley Woodland Period Archaeological TR], Address Restricted, Old Lyme vicinity, 7/31/87, D, 87001228

Lieutenant River No. 2 [Lower Connecticut River Valley Woodland Period Archaeological TR], Address Restricted, Old Lyme vicinity, 7/31/87, D, 87001226

Little Plain Historic District, Both sides of Union, Broadway, and Huntington Pl. in irregular pattern, Norwich, 10/15/70, A, C, 70000718

Little Plain Historic District (Boundary Increase), 120–156 Broadway and 10–88 Union St., Norwich, 1/12/87, A, C, 86003541

Long Society Meetinghouse, E of Norwich off CT 165 on Long Society Rd., Norwich vicinity, 4/22/76, A, C, a, d, 76001996

Lord Cove Site [Lower Connecticut River Valley Woodland Period Archaeological TR], Address Restricted, Lyme vicinity, 10/15/87, D, 87001229

Lyman Viaduct, Dickinson Creek and former Air Line RR right-of-way, Colchester, 8/21/86, A, C, D, 86002729

Main Sawmill, Iron St., Ledyard, 4/26/72, A, C, 72001332

Mashantucket Pequot Reservation, Address Restricted, Ledyard vicinity, 6/11/86, D, d, NHL, 86001323

Mechanic Street Historic District, Roughly bounded by W. Broad St., Pawcatuck River, Cedar St., and Courtland St., Stonington, 6/07/88, A, C, a, 88000653

Miner, Samuel, House, N of North Stonington off CT 2 on Hewitt Rd., North Stonington vicinity, 6/18/76, C, 76001995

Montauk Avenue Historic District, Roughly bounded by Ocean, Willets and Riverview Aves. and Faire Harbor, New London, 12/18/90, A, C, 90001910

Monte Cristo Cottage, 325 Pequot Ave., New London, 7/17/71, B, NHL, 71001010

Mystic Bridge Historic District, U.S. 1 and CT 27, Mystic, 8/31/79, A, C, b, g, 79002671

Mystic River Historic District, U.S. 1 and CT 215, West Mystic, 8/24/79, A, C, 79002728

Natcon Site [Lower Connecticut River Valley Woodland Period Archaeological TR], Address Restricted, Old Lyme vicinity, 7/31/87, D, 87001230

New London County Courthouse, 70 Hunting St., New London, 10/15/70, A, C, 70000705

New London Customhouse, 150 Bank St., New London, 10/15/70, C, 70000706

New London Harbor Lighthouse [Operating Lighthouses in Connecticut MPS], Lower Pequot Ave., New London, 5/29/90, A, C, 89001470

New London Ledge Lighthouse [Operating Lighthouses in Connecticut MPS], Entrance to New London Harbor, E side of Main Channel, New London vicinity, 5/29/90, A, C, 89001471

New London Public Library, 63 Huntington St., New London, 10/15/70, C, 70000712

New London Railroad Station, State St., New London, 6/28/71, A, C, 71000913

Noank Historic District, CT 215, Noank, 8/10/79, A, C, 79002656

North Stonington Village Historic District, CT 2, Main St., Wyassup, Babcock, Caswell, and Rocky Hollow Rds., North Stonington, 3/17/83, A, C, a, 83001289

Norwich Hospital District, CT 12, Norwich-Preston, 1/22/88, A, C, 87002424

Norwich Town Hall, Union St. and Broadway, Norwich, 12/22/83, A, C, 83003589

Norwichtown Historic District, Roughly bounded by Huntington Ln., Scotland Rd., and Washington, Town and E. Town Sts., Norwich, 1/17/73, C, 73001951

Noyes, William, Farmstead [Ledyard MPS], 340 Gallup Hill Rd., Ledyard Township, Ledyard vicinity, 12/14/92, A, C, 92001644

Old Lyme Historic District, Lyme St. from Shore Rd. to Sill Lane, Old Boston Post Rd. from Sill Lane to Rose Lane, Old Lyme, 10/14/71, A, C, 71000916

Peck Tavern, 1 Still Lane, Old Lyme, 4/12/82, A, C, 82004380

Pequot Fort, Address Restricted, Groton vicinity, 1/19/90, A, D, 89002294

Pequotsepos Manor, Pequotsepos Rd., Mystic, 6/15/79, B, C, 79002650

Perkins—Rockwell House, 42 Rockwell St., Norwich, 10/17/85, B, C, 85003144

Plant, Morton Freeman, Hunting Lodge, 56 Stone Ranch Rd., East Lyme, 12/12/88, A, C, 88002691

Post Hill Historic District, Roughly bounded by Broad, Center, Vauxhall, Berkeley, Fremont and Walker Sts., New London, 8/05/93, A, B, C, c, d, 93000812

Preston City Historic District, Amos and Old Shetucket Rds., Northwest Corner Rd., and CT 164, Preston, 7/31/87, A, C, 87000452

Prospect Street Historic District, Roughly bounded by Bulkeley Pl., Huntington, Federal, and Hempstead Sts., New London, 7/31/86, A, C, 86002114

Randall, John, House, SE of North Stonington on CT 2, North Stonington vicinity, 12/01/78, C, 78002877

Raymond-Bradford Homestead, Raymond Hill Rd., Montville vicinity, 4/16/82, B, C, 82004372

River Road Stone Arch Railroad Bridge, River Rd. and former Air Line RR right-of-way, Colchester, 8/21/86, A, C, 86002727

Rocky Neck Pavilion [Connecticut State Park and Forest Depression-Era Federal Work Relief Programs Structures TR], Lands End Point, Rocky Neck State Park, East Lyme, 9/04/86, A, C, 86001745

SABINO (steamer), Mystic Seaport Museum, Mystic, 10/05/92, A, C, NHL, 92001887

Salem Historic District, CT 85, Salem, 9/22/80, B, C, a, b, 80004063

Selden Island Site [Lower Connecticut River Valley Woodland Period Archaeological TR], Address Restricted, Lyme vicinity, 10/15/87, D, 87001231

Shaw Mansion, 11 Blinman St., New London, 12/29/70, A, B, C, 70000713

Smith, Jabez, House, North Rd., Groton, 5/15/81, B, C, 81000615

Smith, Samuel, House, 82 Plants Dam Rd., East Lyme, 6/04/79, C, b, 79002668

Stanton, Robert, House, Green Haven Rd., Stonington, 6/04/79, A, C, 79002648

Stoddard, Capt. Mark, Farmstead [Ledyard MPS], 24 Vinegar Hill Rd., Ledyard Township, Gales Ferry vicinity, 12/14/92, A, C, 92001640

Stonington Harbor Lighthouse, 7 Water St., Stonington, 1/01/76, A, C, 76002000

Stonington High School, Church St., Stonington, 8/17/78, A, C, 78002880

Taftville, N of Norwich at CT 93 and CT 97, Norwich vicinity, 12/01/78, A, C, 78002878

Telephone Exchange Building, 23 Union St., Norwich, 11/28/83, A, C, 83003590

New London County—Continued

Thames Shipyard, Farnsworth St., New London, 4/17/75, A, C, 75001939

Tiffany, Simon, House, Darling Rd., Salem, 6/30/83, C, 83001290

Trumbull, John, Birthplace, The Common, Lebanon, 10/15/66, B, C, b, c, NHL, 66000883

Turner, Dr. Philip, House, 29 W. Town St., Norwichtown, 10/15/70, B, C, 70000729

U.S.S. NAUTILUS (submarine), Naval Submarine Base, Groton, 5/16/79, A, C, g, NHL, 79002653

US Post Office—New London Main, 27 Masonic St., New London, 1/21/86, C, 86000124

US Post Office—Norwich Main, 340 Main St., Norwich, 7/17/86, C, 86002271

United States Housing Corporation Historic District, Roughly bounded by Colman, Fuller, and W. Pleasant Sts., and Jefferson Ave., New London, 4/16/90, A, C, 90000603

Waldo, Edward, House, S of Scotland on Waldo Rd., Scotland vicinity, 11/21/78, C, 78002879

War Office, W. Town St., Lebanon, 10/06/70, A, b, 70000695

Whale Oil Row, 105-119 Huntington St., New London, 12/29/70, A, C, 70000714

Wheeler Block, 40 Norwich Ave., Colchester, 4/16/93, A, C, 93000312

Whitehall Mansion, Off CT 27, Stonington, 4/12/79, C, b, 79002647

Williams Memorial Institute, 110 Broad St., New London, 1/30/78, A, C, 78002876

Williams Memorial Park Historic District, Roughly bounded by Hempstead & Broad Sts., Williams Memorial Pkwy., & Mercer, New London, 12/03/87, A, C, 87002057

Williams, William, House, Jct. of CT 87 and 207, Lebanon, 11/11/71, B, NHL, 71001012

Wilson, John, House, 11 Ashland St., Jewett, 8/23/85, B, C, b, 85001827

Winthrop Mill, Mill St., New London, 11/30/82, A, B, C, 82001008

Woodward, Ashbel, House, 387 CT 32, Franklin, 4/08/92, A, C, 92000264

Woodworth, Nathan A., House, 28 Channing St., New London, 6/01/82, A, C, 82004378

Yantic Falls Historic District, Yantic St., Norwich, 6/28/72, A, 72001344

Yeomans, Edward, House, E of Groton on Brook St., Groton vicinity, 12/22/78, A, C, 78002874

Tolland County

Brigham's Tavern, 12 Boston Tpke., Coventry, 3/25/82, C, 82004383

Cady, John, House, 484 Mile Hill Rd., Tolland, 4/12/82, C, 82004390

Capron-Phillips House, 1129 Main St., Coventry, 4/27/82, C, 82004384

Columbia Green Historic District, Along CT 87 at jct. with CT 66, Columbia, 12/06/90, A, C, g, 90001759

Cone, Jared, House, 25 Hebron Rd., Bolton, 2/21/90, C, 90000155

Coventry Glass Factory Historic District, US 44 and N. River Rd., Coventry, 8/27/87, A, C, D, 87000806

Ellington Center Historic District, Roughly, Maple St. from Berr Ave. to just W of the High School and Main St. from Jobs Hill Rd. to East Green, Ellington, 11/15/90, C, 90001754

Florence Mill, 121 W. Main St., Rockville, 7/18/78, A, C, 78002858

Gurleyville Historic District, N of Mansfield Center off CT 195 at jct. of Gurleyville and Chaffeeville Rds., Mansfield Center vicinity, 12/30/75, B, C, D, 75001933

Hale, Nathan, Homestead, South St., Coventry, 10/22/70, C, 70000698

Hebron Center Historic District, Church, Gilead, Main, Wall and West Sts. and Marjorie Cir., Hebron, 7/30/93, A, C, 93000649

Mansfield Center Cemetery, Jct. of Storrs and Cemetery Rds., Mansfield, 7/24/92, A, C, d, 92000905

Mansfield Center Historic District, Storrs Rd., Mansfield, 2/23/72, C, 72001337

Mansfield Hollow Historic District, 86-127 Mansfield Hollow Rd., Mansfield, 5/21/79, A, C, 79002667

Mansfield Training School and Hospital, Jct. of CT 32 & CT 44, Mansfield, 12/22/87, A, C, 87001513

Minterburn Mill, 215 E. Main St., Vernon, 2/16/84, A, C, 84001171

Old Rockville High School and East School, School and Park Sts., Rockville, 4/27/81, A, C, 81000614

Parker-Hutchinson Farm, Parker Bridge Rd., Coventry, 4/29/82, A, 82004386

Post, Augustus, House, 4 Main St., Hebron, 6/28/82, A, C, 82004387

Rockville Historic District, Roughly bounded by Snipsic St., Davis Ave., West and South Sts., Rockville, 9/13/84, A, C, 84001173

Saxony Mill, 66 West St., Rockville, 11/10/83, A, C, 83003592

Somers Historic District, Main and Battle Sts., Bugbee Lane, and Springfield Rd., Somers, 9/23/82, A, C, 82004389

South Coventry Historic District, Roughly, Main St. and adjacent streets from Armstrong Rd. to Lake St. and Lake from High St. to Main, Coventry, 5/06/91, C, 91000482

Sprague, Elias, House, 2187 South St., Coventry, 11/02/87, C, 87001910

Strong House, 2382 South St., Coventry, 1/15/88, A, B, C, 87001906

Talcottville Historic District, 13–44 Elm Hill Rd. and 11–132 Main St., Vernon, 1/05/89, A, B, C, 88002959

Union Green Historic District, Roughly, area N of jct. of Buckley Hwy. and Cemetery Rd. to jct. of Kinney Hollow and Town Hall Rds., Union, 7/19/90, A, C, 90001099

University of Connecticut Historic District—Connecticut Agricultural School, Roughly CT 195/Storrs Rd. at Eagleville Rd., Mansfield, 1/31/89, A, C, 88003202

White's Tavern, 131 US 6, Andover, 7/26/91, A, C, 91000947

Williams, Eleazer, House, Storrs Rd. (Rte. 195), Mansfield Center, 3/11/71, B, C, a, 71000910

Willington Common Historic District, Properties around Willington Common and E on Tolland Tnpk. pt Old Farms Rd., Willington, 12/18/90, C, 90001911

Windham County

Abington Congregational Church, CT 97, Abington, 9/19/77, C, a, 77001413

Ashford Academy, Fitts Rd., Ashford, 12/29/88, A, C, 88002649

Bosworth, Benjamin, House, John Perry Rd., Eastford, 2/17/78, C, 78002857

Bowen, Henry C., House, CT 169, Woodstock, 8/24/77, B, C, NHL, 77001414

Bowen, Mathew, Homestead, Plaine Hill Rd., Woodstock, 9/10/87, A, C, 87000859

Brayton Grist Mill, US 44, Pomfret, 6/13/86, A, 86001257

Brooklyn Green Historic District, CT 169, 205, and 6, Wolf Den, Brown, Prince Hill, and Hyde Rds., Brooklyn, 9/23/82, A, B, C, a, f, 82004401

Bush Hill Historic District, Parts of Bush Hill Rd., CT 169, and Wolf Den Rd., Brooklyn, 2/10/87, A, C, 87000012

Central Village Historic District, Roughly, School, Main and Water Sts., and Putnam Rd. N to Plainfield High School, Plainfield, 8/09/91, A, C, 91000949

Chandler, Capt. Seth, House, 55 Converse St., East Woodstock, 12/15/93, C, 93001380

Chaplin Historic District, Chaplin St., Chaplin, 10/11/78, A, C, 78002856

Church Farm, 396 Mansfield Rd., Ashford, 11/17/88, A, C, 88002650

Clark, Capt. John, House, Rte. 169, S of Canterbury, Canterbury, 10/06/70, C, 70000699

Crandall, Prudence, House, Jct. of CT 14 and 169, Canterbury, 10/22/70, A, B, C, NHL, 70000696

Daniel's Village Archeological Site, Address Restricted, Killingly vicinity, 3/30/78, A, C, D, 78002861

Danielson Main Street Historic District, Main St. from Water St. to Spring St., Killingly, 4/08/92, A, C, 92000265

Dayville Historic District, Main and Pleasant Sts., Killingly, 8/25/88, A, C, a, 88001422

Elliottville Lower Mill, Peep Toad Rd., East Killingly vicinity, 4/15/82, A, C, 82004406

First Congregational Church of Plainfield, CT 12, Plainfield, 7/31/86, A, C, a, 86002116

Hampton Hill Historic District, Main St., Old Route 6, Cedar Swamp Rd., Hampton, 9/23/82, B, C, 82004408

Hunt, Dr. Chester, Office, Windham Center Rd., Windham Center, 10/06/70, A, b, 70000708

Huntington, Samuel, Birthplace, CT 14, 2 mi. W of CT 97, Scotland, 11/11/71, B, c, NHL, 71001009

Israel Putnam School, School and Oak Sts., Putnam, 12/13/84, A, C, 84000788

Windham County—Continued

Jillson, William, Stone House, 561 Main St., Willimantic, 8/05/71, B, C, 71000912

Killingly High School, Old, 185 Broad St., Killingly, 3/26/92, A, C, 92000266

Main Street Historic District, 21-65 Church St., 667-1009 Main St., 24-28 N. St., and 20-22 Walnut St., Willimantic, 6/28/82, A, C, a, 82004410

Main Street Historic District (Boundary Increase), 32, 50 and 54 North St., Windham, 7/29/92, A, C, 92000902

Natchaug Forest Lumber Shed [Connecticut State Park and Forest Depression-Era Federal Work Relief Programs Structures TR], Kingsbury Rd., Natchaug State Forest, Eastford, 9/04/86, C, 86001732

Nichols, George Pickering, House, 42 Thompson Rd., Thompson, 7/31/91, C, 91000990

North Grosvenordale Mill Historic Disrict, Riverside Dr. (CT 12), Buckley Hill Rd., Floral Ave., Market La., and Marshall, Central, River, and Holmes Sts., Thompson, 4/16/93, A, C, 93000288

Packerville Bridge, Packerville Rd. over Mill Brook, Plainfield, 11/27/92, C, 92001565

Plainfield Street Historic District, Roughly, Norwich Rd. from Railroad Ave. to Academy Hill Rd., Plainfield, 4/11/91, A, C, a, 91000350

Plainfield Woolen Company Mill, Main St., Plainfield, 8/29/85, A, C, 85001919

Pomfret Town House, Town House Rd., Pomfret, 1/19/89, A, C, 88003221

Putnam Farm, Spaulding Rd., Brooklyn vicinity, 3/11/82, B, C, 82004399

Putnam High School, 126 Church St., Putnam, 12/10/93, A, C, 93001343

Putnam, Israel, Wolf Den, Off Wolf Den Rd., Pomfret, 5/02/85, A, B, 85000949

Quinebaug Mill-Quebec Square Historic District, Roughly bounded by Quinebaug River, Quebec Square, Elm & S. Main Sts., Brookland-Killingly, 8/29/85, A, C, 85001921

Ramsdell, Hezekiah S., Farm, Ramsdell Rd., Thompson, 8/23/90, A, D, 90000442

Sterling Hill Historic District, Green Ln. and CT 14A, Sterling, 2/06/86, A, C, 86000152

Sumner—Carpenter House, 333 Old Colony Rd., Eastford, 12/26/91, C, 91001854

Taylor's Corner, Rt. 171, Woodstock, 1/19/89, C, 88003220

Thompson Hill Historic District, Chase & Quaddick Rds., CT 193 & CT 200, Thompson, 12/31/87, C, 87002186

Trinity Church, Church St., Brooklyn, 10/15/70, B, C, a, 70000703

Unitarian Meetinghouse, Jct. of CT 169 and 6, Brooklyn, 11/09/72, A, C, a, 72001335

Wauregan Historic District, Roughly bounded by CT 12, CT 205, Third St., Quinebaug River, and Chestnut St., Plainfield, 8/24/79, A, C, a, 79003789

Wheeler, Jonathan, House, N. Society Rd., Canterbury, 2/11/82, C, 82004405

Willimantic Armory, Pleasant St., Windham, 9/12/85, A, C, 85002310

Willimantic Footbridge, Railroad St., Willimantic, 4/19/79, A, C, 79002654

Willimantic Freight House and Office, Bridge St., Willimantic, 6/14/82, A, C, 82004414

Windham Center Historic District, CT 14 and CT 203, Windham, 6/04/79, B, C, 79002655

Witter House, Chaplin St., Chaplin, 10/06/70, C, 70000704

Woodstock Academy Classroom Building, Academy Rd., Woodstock, 2/16/84, A, C, 84001176

Wylie School, Jct. of Ekonk Hill and Wylie School Rds., Voluntown, 12/19/91, A, C, 91001742

The Thompson Public Library (ca. 1902), part of the Thompson Hill Historic District in Windom County, Connecticut, stands as the only Tudor Revival building in a district of notable Greek Revival, Italianate, Queen Anne, and Colonial Revival residences, churches, and public buildings. (Gregory Andrew, 1986)

DELAWARE

Kent County

Allee House, Off DE 9 on Dutch Neck Rd., Dutch Neck Crossroads vicinity, 3/24/71, C, 71000220

Archeological Site K-875 (7K-D-37/C) [St. Jones Neck MRA], Address Restricted, Kitts Hummock vicinity, 5/22/79, D, 79003223

Archeological Site K-873 (7K-D-35/A, B and D) [St. Jones Neck MRA], Address Restricted, Magnolia vicinity, 5/22/79, D, 79003228

Archeological Site K-876 (7K-D-38/C) [St. Jones Neck MRA], Address Restricted, Kitts Hummock vicinity, 5/22/79, D, 79003222

Archeological Site K-880 (7K-D-42/F) [St. Jones Neck MRA], Address Restricted, Magnolia vicinity, 5/22/79, D, 79003225

Archeological Site K-891 (7K-D-45/A and B) [St. Jones Neck MRA], Address Restricted, Magnolia vicinity, 5/22/79, D, 79003226

Archeological Site K-913 (7K-D-47/C, D and E) [St. Jones Neck MRA], Address Restricted, Kitts Hummock vicinity, 5/22/79, D, 79003229

Archeological Site K-914 (7K-D-48/F and G) [St. Jones Neck MRA], Address Restricted, Kitts Hummock vicinity, 5/22/79, D, 79003221

Archeological Site K-915 (7K-D-86/C) [St. Jones Neck MRA], Address Restricted, Kitts Hummock vicinity, 5/22/79, D, 79003224

Archeological Site K-916 (7K-D-49/C) [St. Jones Neck MRA], Address Restricted, Kitts Hummock vicinity, 5/22/79, D, 79003230

Archeological Site K-920 (7K-D-52/A and C) [St. Jones Neck MRA], Address Restricted, Kitts Hummock vicinity, 5/22/79, D, 79003227

Archeological Site No. 7K F 4 and 23, Address Restricted, Milford vicinity, 6/03/82, D, 82002320

Arnold, George, House [Kenton Hundred MRA], DE 42, Kenton vicinity, 6/27/83, A, C, 83001360

Aspendale, 1 mi. W of Kenton on DE 300, Kenton vicinity, 4/15/70, C, NHL, 70000170

Attix, Thomas, House [Kenton Hundred MRA], DE 140, Kenton vicinity, 6/27/83, C, 83001361

Bank House, 119 N. Walnut St., Milford, 7/31/78, A, C, 78000890

Bannister Hall and Baynard House, S of Smyrna off DE 300, Smyrna vicinity, 4/11/73, A, C, 73000503

Barratt Hall, S of Frederica off DE 372, Frederica vicinity, 4/13/73, B, C, 73000492

Barratt's Chapel, N of Frederica on U.S. 113, Frederica vicinity, 10/10/72, A, C, a, 72000281

Belmont Hall, 1 mi. S of Smyrna on U.S. 13, Smyrna vicinity, 12/16/71, B, C, 71000223

Betz, J. F., House [Kenton Hundred MRA], DE 6, Kenton vicinity, 8/29/83, C, 83001362

Blackiston, Benjamin, House [Kenton Hundred MRA], Off DE 6, Kenton vicinity, 6/27/83, C, 83001363

Bonwell House, 4 mi. W of Frederica on DE 380, Frederica vicinity, 3/20/73, A, 73000493

Bradford-Loockerman House, 419 S. State St., Dover, 11/31/72, C, 72000277

Brecknock, 0.5 mi. N of Camden off U.S. 13, Camden vicinity, 12/24/74, A, C, 74000596

Bullen, John, House, 214 S. State St., Dover, 4/14/75, A, C, 75000542

Burrows, W. D., House [Kenton Hundred MRA], DE 42, Kenton vicinity, 6/27/83, C, 83001364

Byfield Historic District [St. Jones Neck MRA], Address Restricted, Kitts Humock vicinity, 5/22/79, D, 79003232

Byrd's AME Church, Smyrna Ave., Clayton, 10/19/82, A, C, a, 82001023

Camden Friends Meetinghouse, Commerce St., Camden, 4/03/73, A, a, 73000485

Camden Historic District, Both sides of Camden-Wyoming Ave. and Main St., Camden, 9/17/74, A, C, 74000595

Carey Farm Site, Address Restricted, Dover vicinity, 10/20/77, D, 77000384

Cherbourg Round Barn, SW of Little Creek off DE 9, Little Creek vicinity, 12/22/78, C, 78000888

Cheyney Clow's Rebellion, Scene of, W of Kenton on DE 300, Kenton vicinity, 1/14/74, A, 74000598

Christ Church, S. State and Water Sts., Dover, 12/04/72, A, B, a, 72001500

Christ Church, 3rd and Church Sts., Milford, 5/08/73, A, a, 73000502

Clark-Pratt House [Kenton Hundred MRA], Main St., Kenton vicinity, 6/27/83, C, 83001365

Clayton Railroad Station, Bassett St., Clayton, 11/06/86, A, C, 86003066

Coombe Historic District, W of Felton on DE 12 and SR 281, Felton vicinity, 4/08/82, C, 82002313

Cooper House, DE 300, Kenton, 3/20/73, A, C, 73000495

Coursey, Thomas B., House, Co. Rd. 388 N of Coursey Pond, Felton vicinity, 7/23/90, B, C, 90001069

Cow Marsh Old School Baptist Church, NE of Sandtown on DE 10, Sandtown vicinity, 6/24/76, A, C, a, 76000571

Cummins, David J., House, E of Smyrna, Smyrna vicinity, 10/06/83, C, 83003504

Cummins, Timothy, House, E of Smyrna, Smyrna vicinity, 10/06/83, C, 83003505

Davis, Thomas, House [Kenton Hundred MRA], DE 6, Kenton vicinity, 2/29/83, C, 83001366

Delaware Boundary Markers, State boundary lines between DE-MD/DE-PA, Not Applicable, 2/18/75, A, C, f, 75002101

Delaware State Museum Buildings, 316 S. Governors Ave., Dover, 2/01/72, A, a, 72000278

Denny, T. H., House [Kenton Hundred MRA], DE 42, Kenton vicinity, 6/27/83, C, 83001367

Dickinson, John, House, 5 mi. SE of Dover and 3 mi. E of U.S. 13 on Kitts Hummock Rd., Dover vicinity, 10/15/66, B, C, NHL, 66000258

Dill Farm Site, Address Restricted, Sandtown vicinity, 10/02/78, D, 78000893

Dover Green Historic District, Bounded by Governors Ave., North, South, and East Sts., Dover, 5/05/77, A, C, 77000383

Downs, N. C., House [Kenton Hundred MRA], SR 1412, Kenton vicinity, 6/27/83, C, 83001368

Duck Creek Village, DE 65, between Duck Creek and Green's Branch, Smyrna vicinity, 2/01/72, A, C, b, 72000282

Eden Hill, W end of Water St., Dover, 5/08/73, B, 73000487

Felton Historic District, Roughly bounded by North, Walnut, Main, and Niles Sts., Felton, 1/26/88, C, a, 87002433

Felton Railroad Station, E. Railroad Ave., Felton, 7/13/81, A, C, 81000191

Fennimore Store [Leipsic and Little Creek MRA], Main, Lombard, and Front Sts., Leipsic, 5/24/82, A, 82002314

Fourteen Foot Bank Light, On Fourteen Foot Bank in Delaware Bay, 12 mi. E of Bowers, Bowers vicinity, 3/27/89, A, C, 89000286

Frederica Historic District, Market, Front, and David Sts., Frederica, 11/09/77, A, C, 77000385

George Farmhouse, E of Smyrna off DE 6, Smyrna vicinity, 10/19/82, C, 82001862

Golden Mine, W of Milford on DE 443, Milford vicinity, 8/24/78, C, 78000891

Governor's House, Kings Hwy., Dover, 12/05/72, C, 72000279

Great Geneva, 3 mi. S of Dover on DE 356, Dover vicinity, 3/26/73, B, C, 73000489

Green Mansion House [Kenton Hundred MRA], Main St., Kenton vicinity, 6/27/83, A, C, 83001369

Greenwold, 625 S. State St., Dover, 3/20/73, C, 73000488

Griffith's Chapel, Jct. of SR 442 and 443, Williamsville, 10/29/83, A, C, a, c, 83001370

Hill, Robert, House [Kenton Hundred MRA], DE 6, Kenton vicinity, 8/29/83, C, 83001371

Hoffecker-Lockwood House [Kenton Hundred MRA], DE 6, Kenton vicinity, 6/27/83, C, 83001372

Hudson, Alfred L., House [Kenton Hundred MRA], DE 90, Kenton vicinity, 6/27/83, C, 83001373

Hughes Early Man Sites, Address Restricted, Felton vicinity, 7/24/79, D, 79000623

Hughes-Willis Site, Address Restricted, Dover vicinity, 11/21/78, D, 78000887

Island Field Site, Address Restricted, South Bowers vicinity, 2/01/72, D, 72000283

Ivy Dale Farm, S of Smyrna off DE 9, Smyrna vicinity, 4/24/73, B, 73000504

Jones, Enoch, House, SW of Clayton off DE 300, Clayton vicinity, 6/19/73, C, 73000486

KATHERINE M. LEE (Schooner) [Leipsic and Little Creek MRA], Fox's Dock at Front and Lombard Sts., Leipsic, 4/25/83, A, C, g, 83001375

Kent County—Continued

Kenton Historic District [Kenton Hundred MRA], Commerce St., Kenton vicinity, 8/29/83, A, C, 83001396

Kenton Post Office [Kenton Hundred MRA], Main St., Kenton vicinity, 6/27/83, A, C, 83001376

Lamb, Thomas, Farm [Kenton Hundred MRA], DE 130, Kenton vicinity, 8/29/83, C, 83001374

Lamb, Thomas, House [Kenton Hundred MRA], DE 129 and DE 130, Kenton vicinity, 8/29/83, C, 83001385

Laws, Alexander, House [Leipsic and Little Creek MRA], Front and Walnut Sts., Leipsic, 4/25/83, C, 83001377

Lewis Family Tenant Agricultural Complex, CR 227, Wyoming vicinity, 8/13/86, A, C, 86001506

Lewis, Jefferson, House [Kenton Hundred MRA], DE 42, Kenton vicinity, 6/27/83, B, C, 83001349

Lindale, John B., House, 24 Walnut St., Magnolia, 5/08/73, B, C, 73002231

Little Creek Hundred Rural Historic District, DE 9, Little Creek vicinity, 11/07/84, A, C, 84000286

Little Creek Methodist Church [Leipsic and Little Creek MRA], Main St., Little Creek, 5/24/82, C, a, 82002316

Lofland, Peter, House [Milford MRA], 417 N. Walnut St., Milford, 4/22/82, C, 82002321

Logan School House K-834 [St. Jones Neck MRA], Rte. 68, Kitts Hummock vicinity, 5/22/79, A, 79003231

Loockerman Hall, Delaware State College campus, Dover, 6/21/71, C, 71000218

Lowber, Matthew, House, E of Main St. (U.S. 113A), Magnolia, 4/16/71, C, b, 71000221

Lower St. Jones Neck Historic District [St. Jones Neck MRA], Address Restricted, Kitts Hummock vicinity, 5/22/79, B, D, 79003233

MAGGIE S. MYERS (schooner) [Leipsic and Little Creek MRA], Killen's Dock at Front and Lombard Sts., Leipsic, 4/25/83, A, C, g, 83001378

Macomb Farm, Long Point Rd. off DE 8, Dover, 12/02/74, B, 74000597

McClary House [Leipsic and Little Creek MRA], Main and McClary Sts., Leipsic, 4/25/83, C, 83001353

McColley, James, House [Milford MRA], 414 NW Front St., Milford, 1/07/83, B, C, 83001354

McDaniel, Delaplane, House [Kenton Hundred MRA], DE 92, Kenton vicinity, 6/27/83, C, 83001379

Mifflin-Marim Agricultural Complex, DE 9, Dover vicinity, 11/07/84, C, 84000269

Milford New Century Club [Milford MRA], 6 S. Church Ave., Milford, 4/22/82, A, C, 82002322

Mill House [Milford MRA], 414 NW Front St., Milford, 1/07/83, C, 83001380

Moore House, 511 W. Mt. Vernon St., Smyrna vicinity, 10/19/82, C, 82001022

Mordington, S of Frederica on Canterbury Rd., Frederica vicinity, 4/13/73, C, 73000494

North Milford Historic District [Milford MRA], Roughly bounded by Mispillion River, Silver Lake, N. Walnut and NW 3rd Sts., Milford, 1/07/83, A, C, g, 83001357

Octagonal Schoolhouse, E of Cowgill, Cowgill's Corner vicinity, 3/24/71, A, C, 71000217

Old Fire House [Milford MRA], Church Ave., Milford, 1/07/83, A, 83001381

Old Statehouse, The Green, Dover, 2/24/71, A, C, 71000219

Old Stone Tavern [Leipsic and Little Creek MRA (AD)], Main St., Little Creek, 7/02/73, C, 73000499

Palmer Home, 115 American Ave., Dover, 9/13/88, A, C, 88001443

Peterson and Mustard's Hermitage Farm, E of Smyrna off DE 325, Smyrna vicinity, 10/26/82, A, C, 82001027

Poinsett House [Kenton Hundred MRA], DE 6, Kenton vicinity, 6/27/83, C, 83001350

Port Mahon Lighthouse, NE of Little Creek, Little Creek vicinity, 10/25/79, A, 79000624

Rawley House [Leipsic and Little Creek MRA], Main St., Leipsic, 4/25/83, C, 83001352

Raymond Neck Historic District, N of Leipsic between Leipsic River and CR 85, Leipsic vicinity, 11/08/82, A, B, C, 82001026

Reed House [Leipsic and Little Creek MRA], Lombard St., Leipsic, 4/25/83, C, 83001351

Reed, Jehu, House, U.S. 113 and DE 8, Little Heaven, 6/04/73, A, C, 73000500

Ruth Mansion House [Leipsic and Little Creek MRA (AD)], Main St., Leipsic, 4/11/73, C, 73000496

Saxton United Methodist Church, Jct. of Main and Church Sts., Bowers, 7/23/90, C, a, b, 90001070

Short's Landing Hotel Complex, NE of Smyrna, Smyrna vicinity, 10/17/83, A, C, 83003506

Sipple House [Leipsic and Little Creek MRA], Denny and Front Sts., Leipsic, 5/24/82, C, 82002315

Smyrna Historic District [African—American Resources in Delaware MPS (AD)], DE 6 and U.S. 13, Smyrna, 5/23/80, A, C, 80000930

Snowland, DE 42, Leipsic, 3/20/73, B, C, 73000497

Somerville, 1 mi. E of Kenton on DE 42, Kenton vicinity, 12/31/74, B, 74000599

Stevens, William, House [Kenton Hundred MRA], DE 6, Kenton vicinity, 8/29/83, C, 83001406

Stubbs, Elizabeth, House [Leipsic and Little Creek MRA], Main St., Little Creek, 5/24/82, C, 82002317

Sutton, Thomas, House, DE 79, with Woodland Beach Wildlife Area, Woodland Beach vicinity, 4/11/73, A, C, 73000505

Tharp House, E of Farmington on U.S. 13, Farmington vicinity, 3/20/73, B, C, 73000491

Thorne, Parson, Mansion, 501 N.W. Front St., Milford, 6/21/71, C, 71000222

Town Point, Kitts Hummock Rd., Dover, 12/05/72, C, 72000280

Truitt, Gov. George, House, SW of Magnolia on Rte. 388, Magnolia vicinity, 12/12/78, B, C, 78000889

Tyn Head Court, E of Dover on S. Little Creek Rd., Dover vicinity, 3/01/73, B, C, 73000490

Victorian Dover Historic District, Roughly bounded by Silver Lake, St. Jones River, North and Queen Sts., Dover, 7/16/79, A, C, 79000622

Vogl House, W of Masten, Masten's Corner vicinity, 11/07/76, C, 76000570

Voshell, John M., House, E of Smyrna, Smyrna vicinity, 10/06/83, C, 83003507

Walnut Farm, Roosa Rd., Milford, 11/10/82, B, C, 82001025

Watson, Gov. William T., Mansion [Milford MRA], 600 N. Walnut St., Milford, 4/22/82, C, 82002323

Wheel of Fortune, S of Leipsic off DE 9, Leipsic vicinity, 4/11/73, B, 73000498

Wilkerson, J. H., & Son Brickworks, Off SR 409, Milford, 7/12/78, A, D, 78000892

Williams, James, House [Kenton Hundred MRA], DE 42, Kenton vicinity, 6/27/83, C, 83001382

Woodlawn, SE of Smyrna on US 13, Smyrna vicinity, 10/19/82, C, 82001863

Woodley, Jonathan, House [Leipsic and Little Creek MRA], Main St., Little Creek, 5/24/82, C, 82002318

Wright-Carry House [Kenton Hundred MRA], Commerce St., Kenton vicinity, 6/27/83, C, 83001383

Wyoming Historic District, Roughly bounded by Front St., Rodney Ave., Southern Blvd., and Mechanic St., Wyoming, 2/18/87, A, C, 86003037

Wyoming Railroad Station, E. Railroad Ave., Wyoming, 12/04/80, A, C, 80000931

New Castle County

Academy of Newark, Main and Academy Sts., Newark, 5/24/76, A, 76000573

Achmester, N of Middletown on SR 429, Middletown vicinity, 12/28/79, B, C, 79000626

Aetna Hose, Hook and Ladder Company Fire Station No. 2 [Newark MRA], 31 Academy St., Newark, 5/07/82, C, 82002334

Aetna Hose, Hook and Ladder Company, Fire Station No. 1 [Newark MRA], 26 Academy St., Newark, 5/07/82, A, 82002335

Aiken's Tavern Historic District, Jct. of U.S. 40 and DE 896, Newark vicinity, 12/06/77, A, C, a, 77000388

Allen, Charles, House [White Clay Creek Hundred MRA], 855 Canoe Rd., Christina vicinity, 8/19/83, C, 83001348

Amstel House, Delaware and 4th Sts., New Castle, 5/12/77, C, 77000386

Anderson House [Newark MRA], 50 W. Park Pl., Newark, 2/24/83, A, C, 83001384

Appoquinimink Friends Meetinghouse, Main St., Odessa, 12/04/72, A, C, a, 72000288

Archmere, 3600 Philadelphia Pike, Claymont, 9/09/92, B, C, a, 92001143

Armor, James, House, 4905 Lancaster Pike, Christiana Hundred, Wilmington vicinity, 8/31/92, A, 92001141

Armstrong Lodge No. 26, A. F. & A. M. [Newport Delaware MPS], 112–114 E. Market St., Christiana Hundred, Newport, 7/14/93, A, C, 93000628

Armstrong, A., Farm [Agricultural Buildings and Complexes in Mill Creek Hundred, 1800–1840

New Castle County—Continued

TR], Old Wilmington Rd. W of Brackenville Rd., Newark vicinity, 11/13/86, A, C, 86003083

Armstrong-Walker House [Rebuilding St. Georges Hundred 1850–1880 TR], DE 71, Middletown vicinity, 9/13/85, A, C, 85002103

Ashland Bridge, S of Ashland over Red Clay Creek, Ashland vicinity, 3/20/73, A, C, 73000506

Ashton Historic District, N of Port Penn on Thormton Rd., Port Penn vicinity, 11/15/78, A, B, C, D, 78000903

Auburn Mills Historic District, W of Yorklyn on DE 82 and DE 253, Yorklyn vicinity, 1/22/80, A, C, 80000939

Augustine Beach Hotel, S of Port Penn on DE 9, Port Penn vicinity, 4/03/73, A, 73000537

Augustine Paper Mill, N. Brandywine Park Dr., Wilmington vicinity, 8/03/78, A, C, 78000909

Baily House [Newark MRA], 166 W. Main St., Newark, 5/07/82, B, C, 82002336

Bancroft and Sons Cotton Mills, Rockford Rd., Wilmington, 12/20/84, A, C, 84000439

Bank of Newark Building [Newark MRA], 102 E. Main St., Newark, 2/24/83, C, 83001345

Bartley—Tweed Farm [Agricultural Buildings and Complexes in Mill Creek Hundred, 1800–1840 TR], Foxden Rd. E of Polly Drummond Rd., Newark vicinity, 11/13/86, A, C, 86003084

Baynard Boulevard Historic District, Baynard Blvd. between 18th St. and Concord Ave., Wilmington, 7/26/79, C, 79000631

Beard, Duncan, Site, Address Restricted, Odessa vicinity, 12/18/73, D, 73000534

Beaver Valley Rock Shelter Site, Address Restricted, Wilmington vicinity, 9/01/78, D, 78000910

Bell Farmhouse [Newark MRA], 401 Nottingham Rd., Newark, 2/24/83, C, 83001344

Belleview [Rebuilding St. Georges Hundred 1850–1880 TR], Rt. 428, Middletown vicinity, 9/13/85, A, C, 85002104

Belmont Hall [Newark MRA], 302 W. Main St., Newark, 2/24/83, C, 83001386

Biddle House, S of St. Georges on U.S. 13, St. Georges vicinity, 12/08/78, C, 78000908

Biggs, Gov. Benjamin T., Farm, CR 435, Choptank Rd., Middletown vicinity, 9/11/87, A, B, C, 87001508

Bloomfield [Red Lion Hundred MRA], US 13, St. Georges vicinity, 4/08/82, B, C, 82002354

Blue Hen Farm [Newark MRA], 505 Stamford Dr., Newark, 2/24/83, C, 83001346

Brandywine Manufacturers Sunday School, N of Wilmington on Hagley Rd., Wilmington vicinity, 4/13/72, A, B, C, 72000291

Brandywine Park, Roughly bounded by Augustine, 18th, and Market Sts. and Lovering Ave., Wilmington, 12/22/76, A, C, 76000574

Brandywine Park and Kentmere Parkway (Boundary Increase), Roughly bounded by Kentmere Pkwy., Augustine Cutoff, Lovering Ave., 18th and Market Sts., Wilmington, 7/23/81, A, C, 81000192

Brandywine Powder Mills District, DE 141 and Brandywine River, Wilmington vicinity, 5/03/84, A, C, 84000819

Brandywine Village Historic District, Roughly bounded by Brandywine Creek, Tatnall, 22nd, Gordon Sts. , Vandever Ave., Mabel St., and 14th St. bridge, Wilmington, 2/24/71, A, C, D, a, 71000229

Brandywine Village Historic District (Boundary Increase), Along 16th St. between Market St. bridge and 14th St. bridge, Brandywine, 10/21/76, A, C, 76002296

Braunstein's Building [Market Street MRA], 704–706 N. Market St., Wilmington, 12/19/85, C, 85003190

Breck's Mill Area, Breck's Lane and Creek Rd., Wilmington, 11/05/71, B, C, 71000230

Breck's Mill Area—Henry Clay Village Historic District (Boundary Increase), Rising Sun La. and Kennett Pike, Wilmington vicinity, 1/25/88, A, C, 87000663

Breck's Mill Area—Henry Clay Village Historic District (Boundary Decrease), Roughly bounded by Mill Rd., Henry Clay Rd., Breck's Lane and Michigan Rd., Wilmington vicinity, 1/25/88, B, C, 87000683

Brindley Farm, W of Wilmington at Barley Mill Rd. and Kennett Pike, Wilmington vicinity, 9/28/76, A, B, C, 76000575

Brook Ramble [Dwellings of the Rural Elite in Central Delaware MPS], Jct. of Co. Rds. 458 and 459, Appoquinimink Hundred, Townsend vicinity, 9/11/92, A, C, 92001137

Broom, Jacob, House, 1 mi. NW of Wilmington, Montchanin, 12/02/74, B, NHL, 74000602

Brown, Dr. John A., House, 4 7th Ave., Wilmington, 4/24/79, A, C, 79000632

Buena Vista, N of St. Georges on U.S. 13, St. Georges vicinity, 4/16/71, B, C, 71000228

Building at 140 W. Main Street [Newark MRA], 140 Main St., Newark, 5/07/82, C, 82002337

Building at 28–34 1/2 Academy Street [Newark MRA], 28–34 1/2 Academy St., Newark, 5/07/82, C, 82002338

Building at 34 Choate Street [Newark MRA], 34 Choate St., Newark, 2/24/83, C, 83001387

Carpenter-Lippincott House [Centreville MRA], 5620 Kennett Pike, Centreville, 4/13/83, C, 83001388

Casperson, W., House [Red Lion Hundred MRA], Kirkwood Rd., St. Georges vicinity, 4/08/82, C, 82002355

Center Meeting and Schoolhouse, Center Meeting Rd., Centerville, 12/16/71, C, a, d, 71000224

Centreville Historic District [Centreville MRA], Kenneth Pike and Owls Nest/Twaddell Mill Rd., Centreville, 4/13/83, A, C, 83001338

Chambers House [Newark MRA], S. College Ave., Newark, 2/24/83, C, 83001389

Chambers House, Hopkins and Creek Rds., Newark vicinity, 11/29/88, C, 88003132

Chandler, Joseph, House [Centreville MRA], 5826 Kennett Pike, Centreville, 4/13/83, C, 83001390

Chelsea [Red Lion Hundred MRA], DE 9, Delaware City vicinity, 4/08/82, A, C, 82002325

Choptank [Rebuilding St. Georges Hundred 1850–1880 TR], Rt. 435, Middletown, 9/13/85, A, C, 85002108

Choptank-Upon-The-Hill [Rebuilding St. Georges Hundred 1850–1880 TR], Rt. 435, Middletown, 11/19/85, A, C, 85003528

Christiana Historic District, Jct. of DE 7 and 273, Christiana, 12/16/74, A, C, 74000600

Church Street Historic District, Bounded by Eighth, Locust, Seventh, and Church Sts., Wilmington, 6/12/87, C, 87000944

Clearfield Farm, SR 485, 1.5 mi. N of Smyrna Landing, Smyrna vicinity, 3/20/73, B, C, 73000540

Cleaver House [Rebuilding St. Georges Hundred 1850–1880 TR], Off Biddle's Corner Rd., Port Penn vicinity, 9/13/85, A, C, 85002116

Cloud, Abner, House, 14 Ravine Rd., Brandywine Hundred, Wilmington vicinity, 8/31/92, C, 92001144

Clyde Farm Site, Address Restricted, Stanton vicinity, 7/29/77, D, 77000391

Cochran Grange, W of Middletown on DE 4, Middletown vicinity, 4/03/73, B, C, 73000514

Coffee Run Mission Site, SE of Hockessin off DE 48, Hockessin vicinity, 4/11/73, A, B, a, 73000509

Collison House [Newport Delaware MPS], 21 N. Walnut St., Christiana Hundred, Newport, 7/14/93, C, 93000635

Continental Army Encampment Site, Lovering Ave. near Broom St., Wilmington, 12/18/73, A, 73000547

Cooch's Bridge Historic District, N of Newark off DE 896, Newark vicinity, 4/11/73, A, 73000528

Cool Spring Park Historic District, Bounded by Park Pl., Jackson, Van Buren, and 10th Sts., Wilmington, 12/27/83, A, C, 83003513

Corbit-Sharp House, SW corner of Main and 2nd Sts., Odessa, 12/24/67, C, NHL, 67000004

Cornucopia, CR 433, Bethel Rd., Middletown vicinity, 9/08/87, A, C, 87001517

Correll's Farm and Lawn Supply [Red Lion Hundred MRA], DE 71, Kirkwood, 4/08/82, A, C, 82002327

Crosby and Hill Building [Market Street MRA], 605 N. Market St., Wilmington, 1/30/85, C, 85000148

Curtis Mansion [Newark MRA], W. Main St., Newark, 5/07/82, C, 82002339

Curtis Paper Mill Workers' Houses [Newark MRA], Curtis Lane, Newark, 5/07/82, A, C, 82002340

Darley House, Darley Rd. and Philadelphia Pike (U.S. 13), Claymont, 7/02/73, B, 73000508

Dean, Joseph, & Son Woolen Mill, Race and Deandale Sts., Newark, 5/22/78, A, C, 78000901

Deer Park Farm [Newark MRA], 48 W. Park Pl., Newark, 2/24/83, B, C, 83001347

Deer Park Hotel [Newark MRA], 108 W. Main St., Newark, 5/07/82, A, 82002341

Delaware Avenue Historic District, Delaware Ave. from N. Harrison to N. Broom Sts. (both sides), Wilmington, 9/13/76, C, 76000576

Delaware Avenue Historic District (Boundary Increase), Roughly bounded by Shallcross Ave.,

New Castle County—Continued

Harrison St., Pennsylvania Ave., and Rodney St., Wilmington, 5/12/87, A, B, C, 87000034

Delaware City Historic District, Roughly bounded by the Delaware River, Dragon Creek, DE 9, and the Delaware and Chesapeake Canals, Delaware City, 12/15/83, A, C, 83003515

Delmarva Power and Light Building [Market Street MRA], 600 N. Market St., Wilmington, 1/30/85, C, 85000149

Dilworth House, Off DE 9, Port Penn vicinity, 11/27/73, C, 73000538

Dingee, Jacob, House, 105 E. 7th St., Wilmington, 10/16/70, C, 70000171

Dingee, Obadiah, House, 107 E. 7th St., Wilmington, 10/21/70, A, C, 70000172

Dixon, S. P., Farm [Agricultural Buildings and Complexes in Mill Creek Hundred, 1800–1840 TR], Wooddale and Brackenville Rds., Newark vicinity, 11/13/86, A, C, 86003085

Dragon Run Farm [Red Lion Hundred MRA], McCoy Rd., Kirkwood, 4/08/82, C, 82002328

Dupont, P. S., High School, Thirty-fourth St. between N. Monroe and N. Franklin Sts., Wilmington, 10/23/86, A, C, 86002917

East Brandywine Historic District, Roughly Bounded by Sixteenth St., Brandywine Creek, Twelfth St., and US 13, Wilmington, 12/19/85, A, C, a, 85003220

Eastburn, Davis, Farm [Agricultural Buildings and Complexes in Mill Creek Hundred, 1800–1840 TR], Corner Ketch Rd. SE of Wilmington-Landenberg Rd., Newark vicinity, 11/13/86, A, C, 86003087

Eastburn, J., Barn [Agricultural Buildings and Complexes in Mill Creek Hundred, 1800–1840 TR], Pleasant Hill Rd. SW of Corner Ketch Rd., Newark vicinity, 11/13/86, C, 86003088

Eastburn—Jeanes Lime Kilns Historic District, N of Newark on Limestone Rd., Newark vicinity, 4/28/77, A, 77000389

Eastern Lock of the Chesapeake and Delaware Canal, Battery Park, Delaware City, 4/21/75, A, C, 75000543

Eighth Street Park Historic District, Roughly bounded by 6th, 10th, Harrison, and Broom Sts., Wilmington, 8/04/83, A, B, C, 83001334

Eighth Street Park Historic District (Boundary Increase), Broom and 10th Sts., Wilmington, 5/03/84, C, 84000841

Eleutherian Mills, N of Wilmington on DE 141 at Brandywine Creek Bridge, Wilmington vicinity, 11/13/66, A, B, NHL, 66000259

Eliason, A., House [Rebuilding St. Georges Hundred 1850–1880 TR], Rt. 896, Mt. Pleasant vicinity, 9/13/85, A, C, 85002110

Elm Grange [Rebuilding St. Georges Hundred 1850–1880 TR], US 13, Odessa vicinity, 9/13/85, A, C, 85002120

England House and Mill, 81 Red Mill Rd., Newark vicinity, 2/23/72, C, 72001597

Evans, George, House [Newark MRA], 5 W. Main St., Newark, 5/07/82, C, 82002342

Evans, John, House [Newark MRA], W. Main St. and N. College Ave., Newark, 2/24/83, A, 83001392

Exchange Building [Newark MRA], 154–158 E. Main St., Newark, 5/07/82, A, C, 82002343

Fairview [Red Lion Hundred MRA], US 13, Delaware City vicinity, 4/08/82, C, 82002326

Fairview, SE of Odessa, Odessa vicinity, 5/03/84, C, 84000835

Fairview [Rebuilding St. Georges Hundred 1850–1880 TR], Rt. 412, Odessa vicinity, 11/19/85, A, C, 85003523

Fairview, CR 433, Bethel Church Rd., Middletown vicinity, 9/08/87, A, C, 87001494

Fell Historic District, Faulkland Rd. and New Fell's Lane, Wilmington vicinity, 6/16/83, A, B, C, 83001335

Ferguson, Robert, House, E of Newark at 636 Chestnut Hill Rd., Newark vicinity, 7/22/79, C, D, 79000628

Ferris, Zachariah, House, 414 W. 2nd St., Wilmington, 10/19/70, A, C, b, 70000173

Fields Heirs [Rebuilding St. Georges Hundred 1850–1880 TR], Off DE 71, Middletown, 9/13/85, A, C, 85002109

Fisher, Andrew, House, 725 Art Lane, Newark, 5/08/73, A, 73000525

Fleming House, NE of Smyrna on DE 9, Smyrna vicinity, 1/31/80, A, C, 80000934

Fort Christina, E. 7th St. and the Christina River, Fort Christina State Park, Wilmington, 10/15/66, A, NHL, 66000260

Fort Delaware on Pea Patch Island, Pea Patch Island in the Delaware River, Delaware City vicinity, 12/16/71, A, C, 71000226

Friends Meetinghouse, 4th and West Sts., Wilmington, 11/07/76, A, C, a, 76000577

Galloway—Walker House [Newport Delaware MPS], 107 John St., Christiana Hundred, Newport, 7/14/93, C, 93000633

Garrett Snuff Mill, Jct. DE 82 and Yorklyn Rd., Yorklyn, 5/22/78, A, C, 78000913

Garrett Snuff Mills Historic District, DE 82 and Yorklyn Rd., Yorklyn, 1/24/80, A, C, 80004486

Glebe House, DE 9, New Castle, 4/03/73, C, a, 73000521

Glynrich, Mill Rd. and Race St., Wilmington vicinity, 11/01/79, C, 79000633

Gordon, J. M., House [Rebuilding St. Georges Hundred 1850–1880 TR], Rt. 44, Odessa vicinity, 9/13/85, A, C, 85002121

Govatos'/McVey Building [Market Street MRA], 800 N. Market St., Wilmington, 1/30/85, B, C, 85000150

Grace United Methodist Church, 9th and West Sts., Wilmington, 11/12/83, A, a, c, 83001393

Granite Mansion [Newark MRA], 292 W. Main St., Newark, 2/24/83, C, 83001394

Graves Mill Historic District, E of Yorklyn on Way Rd., Yorklyn vicinity, 12/19/79, A, C, 79000640

Gray, Charles, Printing Shop [Market Street MRA], 11 E. 8th St., Wilmington, 1/30/85, C, 85000151

Green Mansion [Newark MRA], 94-96 E. Main St., Newark, 2/24/83, C, 83001395

Green Meadow [Dwellings of the Rural Elite in Central Delaware MPS], Thomas Landing Rd.

(DE 440), Appoquinimink Hundred, Odessa vicinity, 9/11/92, A, C, 92001132

Greenbank Historic Area, Greenbank Mill Rd., N of jct. of DE 41 and DE 2, Marshallton, 7/02/73, A, B, e, 73000513

Greenbank Historic Area (Boundary Increase), Greenbank Mill Road, N. of jct. of DE 41 and DE 2, Marshallton vicinity, 7/24/79, A, B, 79003441

Greenlawn, N. Broad St., Middletown, 4/24/73, C, 73000515

Hale-Byrnes House, Corner of DE 7 and 4, Stanton vicinity, 6/02/72, A, B, C, a, 72000290

Hanson, B. F., House, W of Middletown, Middletown vicinity, 4/27/82, B, C, 82002332

Harlan and Hollingsworth Office Building, West St., Wilmington, 4/26/79, A, C, 79000634

Hart House, E of Taylors Bridge on DE 453, Taylors Bridge vicinity, 3/20/73, A, C, 73000544

Hazel Glen, W of Port Penn on DE 420, Port Penn vicinity, 11/20/78, A, C, 78000904

Head of Christiana United Presbyterian Church [White Clay Creek Hundred MRA], 1100 Church Rd., Newark, 8/19/83, C, a, 83001343

Hedgelawn, 1.2 mi. W of Middletown on DE 4, Middletown vicinity, 4/03/73, A, C, g, 73000516

Hell Island Site, Address Restricted, Odessa vicinity, 4/13/77, D, 77000390

Hermitage, The, On DE 273, New Castle, 3/01/73, B, C, 73000522

Hersey—Duncan House, 2116 Duncan Rd., Mill Creek Hundred, Wilmington vicinity, 11/15/90, A, C, 90001714

Hicklen, William, House, Address Restricted, Talleyville vicinity, 10/06/83, C, 83003519

Higgins, S., Farm [Rebuilding St. Georges Hundred 1850–1880 TR], Rt. 423, Odessa vicinity, 9/13/85, A, C, 85002122

Hill Island Farm [Dwellings of the Rural Elite in Central Delaware MPS], 3379 Dupont Pkwy. (US 13), Appoquinimink Hundred, Odessa vicinity, 9/11/92, A, C, 92001139

Hockessin Friends Meetinghouse, DE 275 and 254 at Meetinghouse Rd., Hockessin, 3/20/73, C, a, 73000510

Holton, S., Farm [Rebuilding St. Georges Hundred 1850–1880 TR], Rt. 435, Middletown vicinity, 9/13/85, A, C, 85002105

Holy Trinity, 7th and Church Sts., Wilmington, 10/15/66, A, C, a, NHL, 66000261

Howard High School, 13th and Poplar Sts., Wilmington, 2/21/85, A, C, 85000309

Huguenot House, W of Taylors Bridge on DE 9, Taylors Bridge vicinity, 3/20/73, C, 73000545

Idalia Manor [Rebuilding St. Georges Hundred 1850–1880 TR], Rt. 13, Mt. Pleasant vicinity, 9/13/85, A, C, 85002118

Ivyside Farm, 1301 Naaman's Rd., Claymont, 1/04/82, C, 82002324

Johnson Home Farm [Dwellings of the Rural Elite in Central Delaware MPS], Co. Rd. 453 E of jct. with DE 9, Blackbird Hundred, Taylor's Bridge vicinity, 9/11/92, C, 92001133

Justis, Thomas, House, 1001 Milltown Rd., Mill Creek Hundred, Wilmington vicinity, 9/23/93, C, 93000989

New Castle County—Continued

Keil, Max, Building [Market Street MRA], 712 N. Market St., Wilmington, 1/30/85, C, g, 85000152

Keil, Max, Building [Market Street MRA], 700 N. Market St., Wilmington, 1/30/85, C, g, 85000153

Kerr, Andrew, House [White Clay Creek Hundred MRA], 812 Elkton Rd., Newark, 8/19/83, A, C, 83001342

Killgore Hall [Newport Delaware MPS], 101 N. James St., Christiana Hundred, Newport, 7/14/93, A, C, 93000630

Killgore, Joseph, House [Newport Delaware MPS], 107 N. James St., Christiana Hundred, Newport, 7/14/93, C, 93000627

Kingswood Methodist Episcopal Church, Fourteenth and Claymont Sts., Wilmington, 2/09/89, A, C, a, 89000008

La Grange, Near jct. of U.S. 40 and DE 896, Glasgow, 7/10/74, B, C, 74000601

Laurel, 619 Shipley Rd., Wilmington, 12/04/74, C, g, 74000603

Lesley-Travers Mansion, 112 W. 6th St., New Castle, 4/03/73, C, 73000523

Lewden, John, House, 107 E. Main St., Christiana, 9/24/79, A, C, 79003104

Linden Hill [Red Lion Hundred MRA], US 13, St. Georges vicinity, 4/08/82, A, B, C, 82002356

Lindsay, J., Barn [Agricultural Buildings and Complexes in Mill Creek Hundred, 1800–1840 TR], Middleton Rd. near Mermaid-Stoney Batter Rd., Newark vicinity, 11/13/86, A, C, 86003089

Lindsey, Samuel, House [White Clay Creek Hundred MRA], New London Rd., McClellandville vicinity, 8/19/83, C, 83001397

Liston House, E of Taylors Bridge on DE 453, Taylors Bridge vicinity, 3/26/73, A, C, 73000546

Liston Ranger Rear Light Station, W of Port Penn on DE 2, Port Penn vicinity, 11/15/78, A, C, b, 78000905

Lobdell Estate, Minquadale Home, U.S. 13, Wilmington vicinity, 6/04/73, B, C, 73000548

Logan House, 1701 Delaware Ave., Wilmington, 4/02/80, A, C, 80000935

Lombardy Hall, U.S. 202, Wilmington, 12/05/72, B, C, NHL, 72000292

Lore, Charles B., Elementary School, Fourth St. and Woodlawn Ave., Wilmington, 6/16/83, A, C, 83001337

Louviers, 10 Black Gates Rd., Wilmington, 12/13/71, B, C, 71000231

Lower Louviers and Chicken Alley, N of Wilmington on Black Gates Rd., Wilmington vicinity, 2/01/72, B, C, 72000293

Lower Market Street Historic District, Market St., Wilmington, 5/15/80, A, C, 80000936

Lower Market Street Historic District (Boundary Increase), Bounded by 4th, 5th, King and Shipley Sts., Wilmington, 2/21/85, A, C, 85000314

Lum's Mill House, Lums Pond State Park on DE 71, Kirkwood vicinity, 5/22/73, B, C, 73000511

MacDonough, Comdr. Thomas, House, N of Odessa on U.S. 13, Odessa vicinity, 12/12/78, A, B, 78000902

Main Office of the New Castle Leather Company, Eleventh and Poplar Sts., Wilmington, 12/19/85, A, C, 85003191

Maple Grove Farm [Rebuilding St. Georges Hundred 1850–1880 TR], Rt. 299, Middletown vicinity, 9/13/85, A, C, 85002106

Maples, W of Middletown on Bunker Hill Rd., Middletown vicinity, 2/17/78, C, 78000895

Marcus Hook Range Rear Light, Light House Rd., Wilmington vicinity, 3/27/89, A, C, 89000287

Marshallton United Methodist Church, 1105 Stanton Rd., Marshallton, 2/18/87, C, a, 86002945

Mason, J., Farm [Agricultural Buildings and Complexes in Mill Creek Hundred, 1800–1840 TR], DE 82 S of Way Rd., Newark vicinity, 11/13/86, A, C, 86003091

Masonic Hall and Grand Theater, 818 N. Market St., Wilmington, 12/11/72, A, C, 72000294

McCormack, J., Farm [Agricultural Buildings and Complexes in Mill Creek Hundred, 1800–1840 TR], Newport Gap Turnpike N of Mill Creek Rd., Newark vicinity, 11/13/86, A, C, 86003093

McCoy House, Kirkwood and McCoy Rds., Kirkwood vicinity, 4/24/73, A, C, 73000512

McDaniel, J., Farm [Agricultural Buildings and Complexes in Mill Creek Hundred, 1800–1840 TR], Paper Mill Rd. E of Pike Creek Rd., Newark vicinity, 11/13/86, A, C, 86003094

McIntyre, J., Farm [Agricultural Buildings and Complexes in Mill Creek Hundred, 1800–1840 TR], Limestone Rd. N of Valley Rd., Newark vicinity, 11/13/86, A, C, 86003098

McLane, Louis, House, 606 Market St., Wilmington, 4/24/73, B, 73000549

McWhorter House [Rebuilding St. Georges Hundred 1850–1880 TR], Rt. 412, Odessa vicinity, 9/13/85, A, C, 85002123

Meeteer House, 801 Kirkwood Hwy., Mill Creek Hundred, Newark vicinity, 9/02/93, C, 93000888

Memorial Hall [Newark MRA], University of Delaware campus, Newark, 5/07/82, C, 82002344

Mermaid Tavern, NE of Newark on DE 7, Newark vicinity, 12/18/73, A, 73000529

Meteer Store House [Newark MRA], 325 Paper Mill Rd., Newark, 2/24/83, A, C, 83001398

Middletown Academy, 218 N. Broad St., Middletown, 12/05/72, A, C, 72000284

Middletown Historic District, Roughly bounded by Redding, Scott, Lockwood, and Catherine Sts., Middletown, 10/04/78, A, C, b, 78000896

Mill Creek Friends Meetinghouse, 6 mi. N of Newark on Landenburg Rd., Newark vicinity, 4/03/73, A, C, a, 73000530

Misty Vale [Rebuilding St. Georges Hundred 1850–1880 TR], Rt. 423, Odessa vicinity, 9/13/85, A, C, 85002111

Mondamon Farm [Rebuilding St. Georges Hundred 1850–1880 TR], Rt. 2, Odessa vicinity, 11/19/85, A, C, 85003524

Montchanin Historic District, DE 100, Montchanin, 6/09/78, A, C, 78000900

Monterey, N of Odessa on Bayview Rd., Odessa vicinity, 12/05/80, A, C, 80000933

Montgomery House, 2900 Old Limestone Rd., Wilmington vicinity, 7/28/88, C, 88001160

Morgan, William, Farm [Agricultural Buildings and Complexes in Mill Creek Hundred, 1800–1840 TR], Wilmington-Landenberg Rd. N of Corner Ketch Rd., Newark vicinity, 11/13/86, A, C, 86003099

Morrow, James, House [White Clay Creek Hundred MRA], 1210 Ogletown Rd., Newark, 8/19/83, C, 83001399

Mount Cuba Historic District, SR 261 and DE 82, Mount Cuba, 12/19/79, A, C, 79000627

Mount Lebanon Methodist Episcopal Church, 850 Mount Lebanon Rd., Wilmington, 5/03/84, A, C, a, d, 84000845

Mount Pleasant [Dwellings of the Rural Elite in Central Delaware MPS], Sunnyside Rd. (Rt. 90), Duck Creek Hundred, Smyrna vicinity, 9/11/92, A, C, 92001134

Mt. Airy School No. 27 [Centreville MRA], 5925 Kennett Pike, Centreville, 4/13/83, C, 83001400

Naaman's Creek School, Jct. of Philadelphia Pike and Darley Rd., Brandywine Creek, Claymont, 11/15/90, A, C, 90001715

Naudain, Arnold S., House, S of Middletown on DE 71, Middletown vicinity, 4/24/73, C, a, 73000517

Nelson, John B., House, W of Port Penn off U.S. 13, Port Penn vicinity, 12/08/78, C, 78000906

New Castle Historic District, Bounded by Harmony St., The Strand, 3rd St., and Delaware St., New Castle, 12/24/67, C, NHL, 67000003

New Castle Historic District, Roughly bounded by the Delaware River, Broad Dike, 4th, 6th, 7th, and Penn Sts., New Castle, 11/08/84, A, C, a, 84000312

New Castle Ice Piers, Delaware River, New Castle vicinity, 2/04/82, A, C, 82002333

New Castle Leather Raw Stock Warehouse, 14th and Poplar Sts., Wilmington, 6/16/83, A, C, g, 83001401

New Castle and Frenchtown Railroad Right-of-Way, Off U.S. 40 between Porter, DE, and Frenchtown, MD, Porter vicinity, 9/01/76, A, C, 76002290

New Century Club, 1014 Delaware Ave., Wilmington, 6/16/83, A, C, 83001336

Newark Opera House [Newark MRA], 95 E. Main St., Newark, 5/07/82, C, 82002345

Newark Passenger Station [Newark MRA], S. College Ave. and Amtrak Conrail RR, Newark, 5/07/82, A, C, 82002346

Newport National Bank [Newport Delaware MPS], 100 E. Market St., Christiana Hundred, Newport, 7/14/93, A, C, 93000634

Noxontown, S of Middletown off DE 896, Middletown vicinity, 7/02/73, A, C, 73000518

Odessa Historic District [African—American Resources in Delaware MPS (AD)], Bounded roughly by Appoquinimink Creek on SE, High St. on NE, 4th St. on NW, and Main St. on SW, Odessa, 6/21/71, A, C, b, 71000227

Odessa Historic District (Boundary Increase), Roughly Main and High Sts. between Appoquinimink River and DE 4, Odessa, 8/09/84, A, C, 84000846

New Castle County—Continued

Okolona [Rebuilding St. Georges Hundred 1850–1880 TR], Rt. 429, Middletown vicinity, 11/19/85, A, C, 85003527

Old Asbury Methodist Church, Walnut and 3rd Sts., Wilmington, 11/07/76, A, C, a, 76000578

Old Brick Store, NE of Smyrna off U.S. 13, Smyrna vicinity, 8/14/73, A, 73000541

Old Cann Mansion House [Red Lion Hundred MRA], DE 71, Kirkwood vicinity, 4/08/82, A, C, 82002329

Old College Historic District, Main and College Sts. on University of Delaware campus, Newark, 6/04/73, A, C, 73000526

Old Courthouse, Delaware St., between 2nd and 3rd Sts., New Castle, 11/28/72, A, C, NHL, 72000285

Old Customshouse, 6th and King Sts., Wilmington, 11/21/74, C, 74000604

Old Drawyers Church, U.S. 13, Odessa, 2/06/73, C, a, 73000533

Old First Presbyterian Church of Wilmington, West St. on Brandywine Park Dr., Wilmington, 4/13/72, A, C, a, b, 72000295

Old First Presbyterian Church [Newark MRA], W. Main St., Newark, 5/07/82, C, a, 82002347

Old Ford Dairy [Rebuilding St. Georges Hundred 1850–1880 TR], US 13, Odessa vicinity, 9/13/85, A, C, 85002112

Old Ford Dairy (Boundary Increase) [Rebuilding St. Georges Hundred 1850–1880 TR], US 13, Odessa vicinity, 12/11/86, A, C, 86003486

Old Fort Church [White Clay Creek Hundred MRA], Old Baltimore Pike, Christiana, 8/19/83, A, C, a, g, 83001402

Old Newark Comprehensive School [Newark MRA], 83 E. Main St., Newark, 5/07/82, A, 82002348

Old Post Ofice [Red Lion Hundred MRA], Kirkwood and St. Georges Rd., Kirkwood, 4/08/82, C, 82002330

Old St. Anne's Church, S of Middletown off DE 71, Middletown vicinity, 3/07/73, A, C, a, 73000519

Old St. Paul's Methodist Episcopal Church, High St., Odessa, 5/13/82, A, C, a, 82002353

Old Town Hall, 512 Market St., Wilmington, 12/31/74, A, C, 74000605

Old Town Hall Commercial Historic District [Market Street MRA], Roughly bounded by 5th, N. King, 6th, and Shipley Sts., Wilmington, 1/30/85, A, C, 85000154

Old Union Methodist Church, 0.2 mi. N of Blackbird Crossroads on U.S. 13, Blackbird Crossroads, 1/18/73, C, a, d, 73000507

Ott's Chapel, CR 397, Newark vicinity, 8/13/86, A, B, C, a, 86001555

Pharo House, Odessa and Silver Lake Rds., Middletown vicinity, 8/09/84, C, 84000850

Philips-Thompson Buildings, 200-206 E. 4th St., Wilmington, 4/16/80, A, C, 80000937

Phillips, Thomas, Mill Complex [White Clay Creek Hundred MRA], 708 and 712 Nottingham Rd., Newark, 8/19/83, A, 83001403

Pierson, T., Farm [Agricultural Buildings and Complexes in Mill Creek Hundred, 1800–1840 TR], Southwood Rd., Newark vicinity, 11/13/86, A, C, 86003101

Point Farm [Red Lion Hundred MRA], US 301 South, Kirkwood vicinity, 4/08/82, A, C, 82002331

Poplar Hall, 3176 Denny Rd., Newark vicinity, 1/26/88, A, C, 87002434

Port Penn Historic District, DE 9, Port Penn, 11/20/78, A, C, D, 78000907

Postles House, 1007 N. Broom St., Wilmington, 11/12/82, C, 82001028

Public School No. 111-C, DE 7, Christiana, 10/18/79, A, B, C, 79000625

Public School No. 19, 801 S. Harrison St., Wilmington, 12/20/84, A, C, 84000453

Public School No. 29, Valley Rd. and Old Lancaster Pike, Hockessin, 5/22/78, A, g, 78000894

Pyle, Howard, Studios, 1305 and 1307 N. Franklin St., Wilmington, 3/08/78, B, C, 78000911

Pyle, Joshua, House and Wagon Barn, 2603 Foulk Rd., Brandywine Hundred, Wilmington vicinity, 9/13/93, C, 93000887

Quaker Hill Historic District, Roughly bounded by Tatnall, Jefferson, 2nd and 7th Sts., Wilmington, 9/06/79, A, C, 79000635

Quaker Hill Historic District (Boundary Increase), Roughly bounded by Eighth, Catawba and Washington, Sixth and Seventh, and Wollaston Sts., Wilmington, 12/19/85, B, C, a, 85003221

Reading, Philip, Tannery, 201 E. Main St., Yiddletown, 4/26/78, A, C, D, 78000897

Red Clay Creek Presbyterian Church, Mill Creek and McKennan's Church Rds., Newport, 4/11/73, C, a, 73000532

Reedy Island Range Rear Light, Jct. of DE 9 and Rd. 453, Taylor's Bridge vicinity, 3/27/89, A, C, 89000288

Retirement Farm [Rebuilding St. Georges Hundred 1850–1880 TR], US 13, Odessa vicinity, 9/13/85, A, C, 85002113

Reynold's Candy Company Building [Market Street MRA], 703 N. Market St., Wilmington, 1/30/85, C, 85000155

Rhodes Pharmacy [Newark MRA], 36 E. Main St., Newark, 2/24/83, A, C, 83001404

Riverdale [Rebuilding St. Georges Hundred 1850–1880 TR], Off Bay View and Silver Run Rds., Odessa vicinity, 11/19/85, A, C, 85003525

Robinson House, Naaman's Corner, Claymont, 6/21/71, A, B, 71000225

Rockford Park, Roughly bounded by Red Oak and Rockford Rds., Church and Rising Sun Lanes, and the Brandywine River, Wilmington, 9/20/78, B, C, 78000912

Rockland Historic District, Town of Rockland and its environs along Rockland Rd. and Brandywine Creek, Rockland vicinity, 2/01/72, A, C, 72000289

Rockwood, 610 Shipley Rd., Wilmington, 7/12/76, B, C, 76000579

Rodney Court, 1100 Pennsylvania Ave., Wilmington, 4/02/80, C, 80000938

Rosedale [Rebuilding St. Georges Hundred 1850–1880 TR], Rt. 437, Middletown vicinity, 9/13/85, A, C, 85002107

Rotheram Mill House, 318 Harmony Rd., Newark, 1/04/72, C, 72000287

Rumsey Farm, W of Middletown on DE4, Middletown vicinity, 3/30/78, A, C, 78000898

STATE OF PENNSYLVANIA (steamboat), Christina River, Wilmington, 4/20/79, A, C, 79000637

Savin—Wilson House [Dwellings of the Rural Elite in Central Delaware MPS], Co. Rd. 326, between DE 12 and Co. Rd. 83, Duck Creek Hundred, Smyrna vicinity, 9/11/92, A, C, 92001135

Schagrin, Charles, Building [Market Street MRA], 608 N. Market St., Wilmington, 1/30/85, C, 85000156

Schoonover, Frank E., Studios, 1616 Rodney St., Wilmington, 4/20/79, B, C, 79000636

Shallcross, Sereck, House, W of Odessa off U.S. 13, Odessa vicinity, 4/03/73, A, C, 73000535

Shipley Run Historic District, Roughly bounded by Adams, 11th, Jefferson, and 7th Sts., Wilmington, 8/09/84, C, 84000854

Springer Farm [Agricultural Buildings and Complexes in Mill Creek Hundred, 1800–1840 TR], Limestone Rd., Newark vicinity, 11/13/86, A, C, 86003103

Springer, Charles, Tavern, 4921 Lancaster Pike, Christiana Hundred, Wilmington vicinity, 9/11/92, A, C, 92001142

St. Anthony's Roman Catholic Church, W. Ninth and N. DuPont Sts., Wilmington, 5/03/84, A, C, a, 84000851

St. Georges Cemetery Caretaker's House [Red Lion Hundred MRA], Kirkwood and St. Georges Rd., St. Georges vicinity, 4/08/82, C, 82002357

St. Georges Presbyterian Church, Main St., St. Georges, 11/07/84, C, a, 84000263

St. Hedwig's Roman Catholic Church, Linden and S. Harrison Sts., Wilmington, 11/12/82, A, C, a, 82001024

St. James Church, W of Stanton on St. James Church Rd., Stanton vicinity, 5/08/73, C, a, 73000543

St. John the Baptist Roman Catholic Church [Newark MRA], 200 E. Main St, Newark, 5/07/82, C, a, 82002349

St. Joseph's Church, 15 W. Cochran St., Middletown, 2/17/78, C, a, 78000899

St. Joseph's on the Brandywine, 10 Barley Mill Rd., Greenville, 11/07/76, B, a, 76000572

St. Mary of the Immaculate Conception Church, 6th and Pine Sts., Wilmington, 12/12/76, A, B, C, a, 76000580

St. Mary's School, 502 Pine St., Wilmington, 1/05/83, A, B, C, 83001339

St. Thomas Episcopal Church [Newark MRA], 21 Elkton Rd., Newark, 5/07/82, C, a, 82002350

Starl House [Red Lion Hundred MRA], US 13, St. Georges vicinity, 4/08/82, C, 82002358

Starr House, 1310 King St., Wilmington, 3/24/71, B, C, 71000232

State Theater [Newark MRA], 39 E. Main St., Newark, 2/24/83, A, C, 83001405

New Castle County—Continued

Steel, James, House [White Clay Creek Hundred MRA], 1016 W. Church St., Newark, 8/19/83, B, C, 83001341

Stewart, James, House, CR 401, Glascow vicinity, 6/11/86, A, C, 86001314

Stewart, James, Jr., House [White Clay Creek Hundred MRA], Whitten Rd., Christina vicinity, 8/19/83, C, 83001340

Stinson, J., Farm [Agricultural Buildings and Complexes in Mill Creek Hundred, 1800–1840 TR], 750 Corner Ketch Rd., Newark vicinity, 11/13/86, A, C, b, 86003080

Stonum, 9th and Washington Sts., New Castle, 11/07/73, B, NHL, 73000524

Strand Millas and Rock Spring, Between Rockland and Montchanin off DE 100, Montchanin vicinity, 7/16/73, A, C, 73000520

Sutton House, Broad and Delaware Sts., St. Georges, 4/24/73, B, 73000542

Swanwyck, 65 Landers Lane, New Castle vicinity, 3/17/77, C, 77000387

Talley, William, House, 1813 Foulk Rd., Wilmington, 2/21/85, A, C, 85000310

Tatnall, Joseph, House [Newport Delaware MPS], S. James St., W side, near Christiana Cr., Christiana Hundred, Newport, 7/14/93, A, C, 93000631

Thomas, David W., House [Dwellings of the Rural Elite in Central Delaware MPS], 326 Thomas Landing Rd., Appoquinimink Hundred, Odessa vicinity, 9/11/92, A, C, 92001136

Townsend Historic District, Roughly bounded by Gray, Ginn and South, Lattamus and Main Sts., and Commerce St. and Cannery Ln. and Railroad Ave., Townsend, 5/08/86, A, C, 86001029

Townsend, Henry, Building [Market Street MRA], 709 N. Market St., Wilmington, 1/30/85, C, 85000157

Trinity Episcopal Church, 1108 N. Adams St., Wilmington, 8/16/84, C, a, 84000855

U.S. Post Office, Courthouse, and Customhouse, 11th and Market Sts., Wilmington, 6/14/79, A, C, g, 79000638

Vail, A. M., House [Rebuilding St. Georges Hundred 1850–1880 TR], Rt. 299, Odessa, 9/13/85, A, C, 85002117

Vandegrift, J., House [Rebuilding St. Georges Hundred 1850–1880 TR], Rt. 44, Odessa vicinity, 9/13/85, A, C, 85002114

Vandyke—Heath House [Dwellings of the Rural Elite in Central Delaware MPS], 385 Green Spring—Vandyke Rd. (Co. Rd. 47), Appoquinimink Hundred, Townsend vicinity, 9/11/92, A, C, 92001130

Vansant, John C., House, 110 Possum Hollow Rd., Newark vicinity, 2/16/89, A, C, 89000007

Vernacular Frame House [Red Lion Hundred MRA], Delaware St., St. Georges, 4/08/82, C, 82002359

Village of Arden, 6 mi. N of Wilmington between Marsh Rd., Naaman's Creek, and Ardentown, Wilmington vicinity, 2/06/73, A, B, C, 73000550

Walker's Mill and Walker's Bank, N of Wilmington on E bank of Brandywine Creek at Rising Sun Lane Bridge, Wilmington vicinity, 2/01/72, A, C, 72000296

Walker, R., Barn [Agricultural Buildings and Complexes in Mill Creek Hundred, 1800–1840 TR], Near corner of Skyline and Foxcroft Drs., Newark vicinity, 11/13/86, C, 86003082

Walnut Lane, E of Newark at 4133 Ogletown Rd., Newark vicinity, 7/22/79, C, 79000629

Wawaset Park Historic District, Bounded by Pennsylvania Ave., Woodlawn Ave., Seventh St., and Greenhill Ave., Wilmington, 1/03/86, A, C, 86000008

Weldin, Lewis, House [Newport Delaware MPS], 7–9 W. Market St., Christiana Hundred, Newport, 7/14/93, A, C, 93000632

Welsh Tract Baptist Church, Welsh Tract Rd., Newark, 3/01/73, B, C, a, 73000527

Wesley M.E. Church [White Clay Creek Hundred MRA], DE 896, McClellandville, 8/19/83, C, a, 83001407

Weston [Rebuilding St. Georges Hundred 1850–1880 TR], Off DE 71, Middletown vicinity, 11/19/85, A, C, 85003526

White Clay Creek Presbyterian Church, 2 mi. NE of Newark on DE 2, Newark vicinity, 3/20/73, C, a, 73000531

White Hall, 130 Michael Ln., Bear vicinity, 7/12/90, A, C, 90001072

Williams House, 1.2 mi. NW of Odessa on Marl Pit Rd., Odessa vicinity, 6/04/73, A, C, 73000536

Williams, J. K., House [Rebuilding St. Georges Hundred 1850–1880 TR], DE 4, Odessa vicinity, 9/13/85, A, C, 85002115

Wilmington Amtrak Station, Front and French Sts., Wilmington, 11/21/76, A, C, 76000581

Wilmington Savings Fund Society [Market Street MRA], 838 N. Market St., Wilmington, 1/30/85, C, 85000158

Wilmington Trust Company Bank [Newark MRA], 82 E. Main St., Newark, 5/07/82, C, 82002351

Wilmington and Western Railroad, DE 41, Hockessin and vicinity, 9/08/80, A, C, b, 80000932

Wilson, Edward R., House [Newark MRA], 521 S. College Ave, Newark, 4/25/83, C, 83001408

Windsor [Dwellings of the Rural Elite in Central Delaware MPS], 1060 Dutch Neck Rd., St. Georges Hundred, Port Penn vicinity, 9/11/92, A, C, 92001131

Winterthur Museum and Gardens, 6 mi. NW of Wilmington on DE 52, Wilmington vicinity, 2/24/71, A, C, 71000233

Woman's Club of Newport [Newport Delaware MPS], 15 N. Augustine St., Christiana Hundred, Newport, 7/14/93, A, C, 93000629

Wooddale Bridge, Over Red Clay Creek off DE 48, Wooddale, 4/11/73, A, 73000552

Wooddale Historic District, NW of Newport on Wooddale Rd, Newport vicinity, 8/24/79, A, D, 79000630

Woodside [Rebuilding St. Georges Hundred 1850–1880 TR], Rt. 435, Mt. Pleasant vicinity, 9/13/85, A, C, 85002119

Woodstock, 102 Middleboro Rd., Wilmington, 9/07/73, A, C, 73000551

Woodward Houses, 701–703 West St., Wilmington, 4/20/79, B, C, 79000639

Woolworth, F. W., Company Building [Market Street MRA], 839 N. Market St., Wilmington, 1/02/87, C, 86003755

Wright House [Newark MRA], 47 Kent Way, Newark, 5/07/82, B, C, 82002352

Young, William, House, E of Rockland on SR 228, Rockland vicinity, 10/29/82, A, C, 82001029

Sussex County

Abbott's Mill, SW of Milford, Milford vicinity, 8/25/72, A, 72000300

Abbott's Mill (Boundary Increase), Rd. 620 W of DE 36, Milford vicinity, 5/17/79, A, C, 79003788

All Saints' Episcopal Church, 18 Olive Ave., Lewes and Rehoboth Hundred, Rehoboth Beach, 8/02/91, C, a, 91000910

Avery's Rest Site, Address Restricted, Rehoboth Beach vicinity, 12/15/78, D, 78000924

Bethel Historic District, 0.4 mi. W of Laurel, Bethel, 2/10/75, A, C, 75000544

Blackwater Presbyterian Church, W of Clarksville on DE 54, Clarksville vicinity, 7/09/76, A, C, a, 76000583

Brick Hotel, The Circle, Georgetown, 11/13/79, A, C, 79000644

Bridgeville Public Library, 210 Market St., Bridgeville, 7/23/90, A, 90001065

Building at 200–202A High Street [Seaford Commercial Buildings TR], 200–202A High St., Seaford, 2/18/87, C, 86002981

Building at 218 High Street [Seaford Commercial Buildings TR], 218 High St., Seaford, 2/18/87, C, 86002983

Building at High and Cannon Streets [Seaford Commercial Buildings TR], SE corner of High and Cannon Sts., Seaford, 2/18/87, C, 86002985

Burton Hardware Store, High St. and Spring Alley, Seaford, 4/20/78, C, 78000927

Cannon's Ferry, Across the Nanticoke River, Woodland, 7/02/73, A, B, 73000561

Cape Henlopen Archeological District, Address Restricted, Lewes vicinity, 11/21/78, D, 78000920

Carey's Camp Meeting Ground, W of Millsboro off DE 24, Millsboro vicinity, 3/14/73, A, a, 73000557

Carlisle House [Milford MRA], 205 S. Front St., Milford, 4/22/82, B, C, 82002364

Chandler, Capt. Ebe, House, Main and Reed Sts., Frankford, 9/20/79, C, 79000643

Chipman Potato House [Sweet Potato Houses of Sussex County MPS], Jct. of DE 465 and DE 465A, Laurel vicinity, 11/15/90, A, C, 90001691

Chipman's Mill, E of Laurel on SR 465, Laurel vicinity, 5/22/78, A, 78000918

Coleman House, 422 Kings Hwy., Lewes, 4/11/77, C, 77000392

Collins Potato House [Sweet Potato Houses of Sussex County MPS], Jct. of DE 509 and DE 510A, Laurel vicinity, 11/15/90, A, C, 90001692

Sussex County—Continued

Cool Spring Presbyterian Church, W of Lewes on SR 247, Lewes vicinity, 8/31/82, A, C, a, 82002363

Cox, J. W., Dry Goods Store [Seaford Commercial Buildings TR], 214 High St., Seaford, 2/18/87, C, 86002982

Davis, Robert, Farmhouse [Nanticoke Indian Community TR], S of Rt. 24, Millsboro vicinity, 4/26/79, A, 79003309

Dawson, Dr., House [Milford MRA], 200 SE Front St., Milford, 1/07/83, C, 83001355

De Vries Palisade, Address Restricted, Lewes vicinity, 2/23/72, A, D, 72000299

Deep Creek Furnace Site, Address Restricted, Middleford vicinity, 10/20/77, A, D, 77000396

Delaware Breakwater and Lewes Harbor, E of Lewes at Cape Henlopen, Lewes vicinity, 12/12/76, A, C, 76000586

Dickerson Potato House [Sweet Potato Houses of Sussex County MPS], Jct. of DE 494 and DE 498, Delmar vicinity, 11/15/90, A, C, 90001693

Dodd Homestead, W of Rehoboth Beach on DE 1, Rehoboth Beach vicinity, 8/26/82, A, C, 82002367

Draper House [Milford MRA], 200 Lakeview Ave., Milford, 4/22/82, C, 82002365

Draper-Adkins House, 204 Federal St., Milton, 4/11/73, C, 73000558

Egglinton Hall [Milford MRA], 700 SE 2nd St., Milford, 1/07/83, B, C, 83001359

Ellendale State Forest Picnic Facility, US 113, 1/2 mi. S of DE 16, Georgetown Hundred, Ellendale vicinity, 7/22/91, C, 91000913

Eratt House, W of Bridgeville on DE 572, Bridgeville vicinity, 10/29/83, A, 83001409

Faucett, Peter S., House, W. Laurel St., Georgetown, 9/05/85, C, 85002006

Fenwick Island Lighthouse Station, Off DE 54, Fenwick Island, 8/13/79, A, C, 79000642

First Broiler House, University of Delaware Experimental Station, Georgetown, 7/03/74, A, B, e, 74000607

First National Bank of Seaford [Seaford Commercial Buildings TR], 118 Pine St., Seaford, 2/18/87, C, 86002972

Fisher Homestead, W of Lewes, Lewes vicinity, 12/11/80, C, 80000941

Fisher's Paradise, 624 Pilottown Rd., Lewes, 12/04/72, A, B, C, 72000298

Georgetown Coal Gasification Plant, N. Railroad Ave., Georgetown, 9/30/85, A, C, 85002696

Grier House [Milford MRA], 301 Lakeview Ave., Milford, 1/07/83, C, 83001410

Gyles, Stella Pepper, House, SW of Georgetown, Georgetown vicinity, 11/13/79, C, 79000645

Hall, Col. David, House, 107 King's Hwy., Lewes, 4/26/76, A, B, C, 76000585

Harmon School [Nanticoke Indian Community TR], S of jct. of Rt. 24 and CR 297, Millsboro vicinity, 4/26/79, A, 79003314

Harmon, Isaac, Farmhouse [Nanticoke Indian Community TR], CR 312A, Millsboro vicinity, 4/26/79, A, 79003315

Harmony Church [Nanticoke Indian Community TR], Rt. 24, E of CR 313, Millsboro vicinity, 4/26/79, A, a, 79003308

Hazzard House, 327 Union St., Milton, 7/02/73, B, 73000559

Hearn Potato House [Sweet Potato Houses of Sussex County MPS], .6 mi. N of jct. of DE 74 and DE 62, Laurel vicinity, 11/15/90, A, C, 90001694

Hearn and Rawlins Mill, N of Seaford on U.S. 13A, Seaford vicinity, 5/22/78, A, 78000928

Highball Signal, City park, near Penn-Central RR., Delmar, 7/02/73, A, 73000553

Hitch, E. L., Potato House [Sweet Potato Houses of Sussex County MPS], Jct. of DE 460 and DE 489, Laurel vicinity, 11/15/90, A, C, 90001695

Hitchens, Ames, Chicken Farm [Nanticoke Indian Community TR], N of Rt. 24, Millsboro vicinity, 4/26/79, A, 79003311

Hopkins' Covered Bridge Farm, N side Rd. 262, E of jct. with Rd. 286, Lewes and Rehoboth Hundred, Lewes vicinity, 8/02/91, A, C, 91000912

Indian Mission Church [Nanticoke Indian Community TR], Jct. of Rt. 5 and CR 48, Millsboro vicinity, 4/26/79, A, a, 79003307

Indian Mission School [Nanticoke Indian Community TR], Rt. 24 between CR 312A and 313A, Millsboro vicinity, 4/26/79, A, g, 79003312

Indian River Archeological Complex, Address Restricted, Millsboro vicinity, 12/15/78, D, 78000922

Indian River Life Saving Service Station, N of Bethany Beach on DE 14, Bethany Beach vicinity, 9/29/76, A, 76000582

Johnson School [Nanticoke Indian Community TR], Rt. 24 between CR 309 and 310, Millsboro vicinity, 4/26/79, A, 79003313

Judge's House and Law Office, 100 and 104 W. Market St, Georgetown, 11/13/79, A, C, 79000646

Laurel Historic District, West St. to Rossakatum Creek to Tenth St., Laurel, 7/27/88, A, a, b, d, 88001056

Lawrence, N of Seaford on U.S. 13A, Seaford vicinity, 5/22/78, C, 78000929

Lewes Historic District [African—American Resources in Delaware MPS (AD)], Ship-carpenter, Front, Savannah, 2nd, 3rd, and 4th Sts., Lewes, 9/19/77, A, C, D, a, 77000393

Lewes Historic District (Boundary Increase) [African—American Resources in Delaware MPS (AD)], Roughly bounded by Front St., Savannah Rd., McFee St. and the Penn Central RR tracks, Lewes and Rehobeth Hundred, Lewes, 9/11/92, A, C, b, 92000462

Lewes Presbyterian Church, 100 Kings Highway, Lewes, 10/05/77, C, D, a, 77000394

Lightship WLV 539, Lewes—Rehoboth Canal between Shipcarpenter and Mulberry Sts., Lewes, 2/16/89, A, b, 89000006

Marsh, Peter, House, 10 Dodd's Lane, Rehoboth Beach vicinity, 11/23/77, C, 77000397

Maston House, 3 mi. N of Seaford on Seaford-Atlanta Rd., Seaford vicinity, 3/31/75, C, 75000545

Maull House, 542 Pilottown Rd., Lewes, 11/20/70, C, D, 70000175

Maull, Thomas, House (Boundary Increase), 542 Pilottown Rd., Lewes, 4/26/78, D, 78003453

Melson House, N of Atlanta on SR 30, Atlanta vicinity, 3/08/78, C, 78000914

Messick, Dr. John W., House and Office, 144 E. Market St., Georgetown, 9/09/87, C, 87001499

Milford Railroad Station [Milford MRA], DE 36, Milford, 1/07/83, A, 83001356

Milford Shipyard Area Historic District [Milford MRA], Roughly bounded by Mispillion River, Franklin, Front and Marshall Sts., Milford, 1/07/83, A, C, 83001411

Milton Historic District, DE 5, Milton, 6/25/82, A, C, 82002366

Mispillion Lighthouse and Beacon Tower, NE end of CR 203, Milford vicinity, 2/18/87, C, 86002919

Moore Potato House [Sweet Potato Houses of Sussex County MPS], SE of jct. of DE 72 and DE 463, Laurel vicinity, 11/15/90, A, C, 90001696

National Harbor of Refuge and Delaware Breakwater Harbor Historic District, Mouth of Delaware Bay at Cape Henlopen, Lewes, 3/27/89, A, 89000289

Norwood House, SW of Lewes on DE 9, Lewes vicinity, 10/25/82, A, C, 82001030

Old Bridgeville Fire House, 102 William St., Bridgeville, 8/09/84, A, C, 84000856

Old Christ Church, SE of Laurel at jct. of SR 465 and 465A, Laurel vicinity, 4/13/72, C, a, 72000297

Old Sussex County Courthouse, S. Bedford St., Georgetown, 3/24/71, A, b, 71000236

Pagan Creek Dike, Pagan Creek near New Rd., Lewes, 6/18/73, A, C, 73000555

Pepper, Carlton, David, Farm, S of Georgetown on SR 469, Georgetown vicinity, 9/24/79, A, C, 79000647

Perry-Shockley House, 219 Washington St., Millsboro, 9/05/85, C, 85002008

Phillips Potato House [Sweet Potato Houses of Sussex County MPS], SW of jct. of DE 492 and DE 492A, Laurel vicinity, 11/15/90, A, C, 90001697

Pine Grove Furnace Site, Address Restricted, Concord vicinity, 1/26/78, A, D, 78000917

Ponder, Gov. James, House, 416 Federal St., Milton, 5/24/73, B, C, 73000560

Poplar Thicket, Address Restricted, Bethany Beach vicinity, 12/29/78, D, 78003177

Portsville Lighthouse, N side of CR 493, Portsville, 9/08/87, C, 87001514

Prince George's Chapel, E of Dagsboro on DE 26, Dagsboro vicinity, 3/24/71, C, a, 71000235

Ralph Potato House [Sweet Potato Houses of Sussex County MPS], SE of jct. of DE 493 and DE 494, Laurel vicinity, 11/15/90, A, C, 90001698

Redden Forest Lodge, Forester's House, and Stable, Redden State Forest, Georgetown vicinity, 11/25/80, A, C, 80000940

Richards Historic District, County Rd. 34, Greenwood vicinity, 12/15/83, A, C, 83003522

Richards House-Linden Hall, E of Bridgeville on US 13, Bridgeville vicinity, 8/26/82, C, 82002360

Richards Mansion, N. Bedford St. and the Circle, Georgetown, 7/26/79, A, C, 79000648

Sussex County—Continued

Rider Potato House [Sweet Potato Houses of Sussex County MPS], SE of jct. of DE 506 and DE 505, Laurel vicinity, 11/15/90, A, C, 90001699

Robinson, Jesse, House, High St., Seaford, 8/26/82, B, C, 82002368

Ross, Gov. William H., House, N of Seaford on Market St., Seaford vicinity, 10/28/77, B, C, 77000399

Russell, William, House, 410 Pilot Town Rd., Lewes, 4/18/77, B, C, 77000395

Scott's Store, NW of Bridgeville on DE 404, Bridgeville vicinity, 10/29/83, C, 83001412

Seaford Station Complex, Nanticoke River at Delaware Railroad Bridge, Seaford, 6/15/78, A, C, 78000930

Short Homestead, W of Georgetown at DE 526 and DE 529, Georgetown vicinity, 4/01/82, C, 82002361

Sipple, Thomas, House, N. Bedford & New Sts., Georgetown, 9/05/85, C, 85002007

South Milford Historic District [Milford MRA], Roughly bounded by Mispillion River, Maple Ave., Church and Washington Sts., Milford, 1/07/83, A, C, 83001358

Spring Banke, NE of Clarksville on DE 26 and Irons Lane, Clarksville vicinity, 4/30/76, A, C, 76000584

Spring Garden, NE of Laurel on Delaware Ave., Laurel vicinity, 8/26/82, A, B, C, 82002362

St. George's Chapel, 9 mi. SW of Lewes on DE 5, Lewes vicinity, 11/30/73, A, a, 73000556

St. John's Methodist Church, Springfield Crossroads, jct. of SR 30 and Co. Rd. 47, Georgetown vicinity, 7/12/90, C, a, 90001071

St. Luke's Protestant Episcopal Church, Front St., Seaford, 10/28/77, C, a, d, 77000400

St. Paul's Episcopal Church, E. Pine St, Georgetown, 11/13/79, A, C, a, 79000649

Stanley Potato House [Sweet Potato Houses of Sussex County MPS], N of jct. of DE 68 and DE 451, Laurel vicinity, 11/15/90, A, C, 90001700

Sudler House, N. Main St., Bridgeville, 12/31/74, A, C, 74000606

Sussex County Courthouse and the Circle, The Circle, Georgetown, 6/04/73, A, C, g, 73000554

Sussex National Bank of Seaford [Seaford Commercial Buildings TR], 130 High St., Seaford, 2/18/87, C, 86002977

Teddy's Tavern, E side Du Pont Blvd., 0.6 mi. N of jct. with DE 16, Cedar Creek Hundred, Ellendale vicinity, 7/22/91, A, C, 91000911

Thompson's Loss and Gain Site, Address Restricted, Rehoboth Beach vicinity, 9/13/78, D, 78000925

Thompsons Island Site, Address Restricted, Rehoboth Beach vicinity, 11/15/78, D, 78000926

Townsend Site, Address Restricted, Lewes vicinity, 9/01/78, D, 78000919

Trinity Methodist Episcopal Church, NW of Bridgeville on DE 31, Bridgeville vicinity, 5/05/78, A, C, a, 78000916

Warren's Mill, NW of Millsboro on DE 326, Millsboro vicinity, 9/13/78, A, C, 78000923

Warrington Site, Address Restricted, Rehoboth Beach vicinity, 10/20/77, D, 77000398

West Potato House [Sweet Potato Houses of Sussex County MPS], US 13 N of jct. with DE 454A, Delmar vicinity, 11/15/90, A, C, 90001701

Wilgus Site, Address Restricted, Bethany Beach vicinity, 3/30/78, D, 78000915

Wolfe's Neck Site, Address Restricted, Lewes vicinity, 11/21/78, D, 78000921

Wright Potato House [Sweet Potato Houses of Sussex County MPS], SW of jct. of DE 24 and DE 510, Laurel vicinity, 11/15/90, A, C, 90001702

Wright, Gardiner, Mansion, 228 S. Front St, Georgetown, 11/15/79, C, 79000650

Wright, Warren T., Farmhouse Site [Nanticoke Indian Community TR], Address Restricted, Millsboro vicinity, 4/26/79, A, D, 79003310

In 1886, engineers employed the pneumatic caisson method to construct the Fourteen Foot Bank Light's foundation and assure stability on the sandy bottom of Delaware Bay, the first example of that technique in American lighthouse construction. (Stephen G. Del Sordo, 1988)

DISTRICT OF COLUMBIA

District of Columbia State Equivalent

2000 Block Of Eye Street, NW, South side of 2000 block of Eye St., NW., Washington, 8/09/77, C, 77001496

Adams Memorial, Webster St. and Rock Creek Church Rd., NW., Washington, 3/16/72, C, f, 72001420

Adas Israel Synagogue, 3rd and G Sts., NW., Washington, 3/24/69, A, a, 69000288

Administration Building, Carnegie Institute of Washington, 1530 P St., NW., Washington, 10/15/66, B, C, NHL, 66000959

Alden, Babcock, Calvert Apartments, 2620 13th St., NW., Washington, 5/25/90, A, C, 90000737

American Federation of Labor Building, 901 Massachusetts Ave., NW., Washington, 9/13/74, A, NHL, 74002154

American Institute of Pharmacy Building, 2215 Constitution Ave., NW., Washington, 8/18/77, A, C, g, 77001497

American National Red Cross, 17th and D Sts., NW, Washington, 10/15/66, A, NHL, 66000853

American Peace Society, 734 Jackson Pl., NW., Washington, 9/13/74, A, NHL, 74002155

American Revolution Statuary, Public buildings and various parks within DC, Washington, 7/14/78, A, B, g, NPS, 78000256

American Security and Trust Company, 15th and Pennsylvania Ave., NW., Washington, 7/16/73, A, C, 73002070

Anacostia Historic District, Roughly bounded by Good Hope Rd., 16th St., Mapleview, Washington, 10/11/78, A, C, 78003050

Anderson, Larz, House, 2118 Massachusetts Ave., NW., Washington, 4/07/71, A, C, 71000993

Arlington Memorial Bridge, Spans Potomac River, Washington, 4/04/80, C, NPS, 80000346

Army Medical Museum, Armed Forces Institute of Pathology Building, Walter Reed Army Medical Center, 13th St. and Fern Pl., Washington, 10/15/66, A, NHL, 66000854

Arts Club of Washington, 2017 I St., NW., Washington, 3/24/69, B, C, NHL, 69000289

Arts and Industries Building, 900 Jefferson Dr., SW., Washington, 11/11/71, C, NHL, 71000994

Asbury United Methodist Church, Eleventh and K Sts. NW, Washington, 11/01/86, A, a, 86003029

Ashburton House, 1525 H St., NW., Washington, 11/07/73, A, a, NHL, 73002071

Auditor's Building Complex, 14th St. and Independence Ave., Washington, 4/27/78, A, C, 78003051

Bachelor Apartment House, 1737 H St., NW., Washington, 12/08/78, A, C, 78003052

Baker, Newton D., House, 3017 N St., NW, Washington, 12/08/76, B, NHL, 76002126

Banneker Recreation Center, 2500 Georgia Ave. NW, Washington, 4/28/86, A, C, 86000876

Battleground National Cemetery, 6625 Georgia Ave., NW., Washington, 10/15/66, A, d, NPS, 66000032

Bayly, Mountjoy, House, 122 Maryland Ave., NE, Washington, 7/20/73, B, C, g, NHL, 73002072

Beale, Joseph, House, 2301 Massachusetts Ave., NW., Washington, 5/08/73, C, 73002073

Belmont, Perry, House, 1618 New Hampshire Ave., NW., Washington, 5/08/73, C, 73002074

Blagden Alley—Naylor Court Historic District, Bounded by O, 9th, M, & 10th Sts. NW., Washington, 11/16/90, A, C, 90001734

Blair House, 1651 Pennsylvania Ave., NW, Washington, 10/15/66, A, NHL, 66000963

Bond Building, 1404 New York Ave., NW, Washington, 9/15/83, C, 83001415

Boulder Bridge and Ross Drive Bridge, Rock Creek Park, Washington, 3/20/80, C, NPS, 80000348

Bowen, Anthony, YMCA, 1816 12th St. NW, Washington, 10/03/83, A, 83003523

Brodhead—Bell—Morton Mansion, 1500 Rhode Island Ave., NW, Washington, 10/14/87, A, C, 87001769

Brooks Mansion, 901 Newton St., NE., Washington, 7/17/75, A, C, a, 75002045

Bruce, Blanche K., House, 909 M St., NW, Washington, 5/15/75, B, NHL, 75002046

Buildings at 1000 Block of Seventh Street, and 649-651 New York Avenue NW, 1005-1035 7th St., and 649-651 New York Ave. NW, Washington, 2/02/84, C, 84000861

Buildings at 1644-1666 Park Road NW, 1644-1666 Park Rd. NW, Washington, 11/06/86, C, 86003019

Bunche, Ralph, House, 1510 Jackson St., NE., Washington, 9/30/93, B, C, g, 93001013

Cady, Lucinda, House, 7064 Eastern Ave., NW., Washington, 5/28/75, C, 75002047

Canadian Embassy, 1746 Massachusetts Ave., NW., Washington, 4/03/73, C, 73002076

Capitol Hill Historic District, Roughly bounded by Virginia Ave., SE., S. Capitol St., F St. NE., and 4th Sts. SE & NE., Washington, 8/27/76, A, C, 76002127

Cardozo, Francis L., Senior High School, Jct. of 13th and Clifton Sts., NW., Washington, 9/30/93, A, C, g, 93001015

Carlton Hotel, 923 16th St., NW., Washington, 6/28/90, C, 90000911

Carnegie Endowment for International Peace, 700 Jackson Pl., NW, Washington, 9/13/74, B, NHL, 74002156

Cary, Mary Ann Shadd, House, 1421 W. St., NW, Washington, 12/08/76, B, NHL, 76002128

Castle Gatehouse, Washington Aqueduct, Near jct. of Reservoir Rd. and MacArthur Blvd., NW., Washington, 3/13/75, C, 75002048

Causeway, The, 3029 Klingle Rd., NW., Washington, 6/28/90, B, C, g, 90000910

Central Public Library, Mount Vernon Sq., 8th and K Sts., NW., Washington, 12/03/69, A, C, 69000290

Chapel Hall, Gallaudet College, Florida Ave. and 7th St., NE., Washington, 10/15/66, A, C, NHL, 66000856

Chase's Theater and Riggs Building, 1426 G St. NW. and 615–627 15th St. NW., Washington, 9/07/78, A, C, 78003053

Chesapeake and Ohio Canal National Historical Park, Bordering the Potomac River from Georgetown, D.C. to Cumberland, Maryland, Washington, 10/15/66, A, C, NPS, 66000036

Chesapeake and Potomac Telephone Company, Old Main Building, 722 Twelfth St., NW, Washington, 6/13/88, A, C, 88000652

Chesapeake and Potomac Telephone Company Building, 730 Twelfth St., NW, Washington, 8/05/88, A, C, 88001112

Christ Church, 620 G St., SE., Washington, 5/25/69, A, C, a, 69000291

Christ Church, 3116 O St., NW., Washington, 3/16/72, A, C, a, 72001421

Church of the Ascension, 1215 Massachusetts Ave. NW, Washington, 1/19/84, A, C, a, 84000863

Church of the Epiphany, 1317 G St., NW., Washington, 9/10/71, A, C, a, 71000996

City Hall, 4th and E Sts., NW, Washington, 10/15/66, A, B, e, NHL, 66000857

City Tavern, 3206 M St., NW., Washington, 1/17/92, A, C, 91001489

Civil War Fort Sites, Civil War Forts from Battery Kemble, NW to Fort Gremble, SW, Washington, 7/15/74, A, NPS, 74000274

Civil War Fort Sites (Boundary Increase), S of Washington on Rosier Bluff, N of Washington off George Washington Parkway, Washington vicinity, 9/13/78, A, NPS, 78003439

Civil War Monuments in Washington, DC, Various parks within the original boundaries of city, Washington, 9/20/78, A, B, NPS, 78000257

Cleveland Park Historic District, Roughly bounded by Tilden St., Connecticut Ave., Klingle Rd., and Wisconsin Ave., Washington, 4/27/87, C, g, 87000628

Cloverdale, 2600 and 2608 Tilden St. NW., Washington, 8/09/90, C, 90001115

Codman-Davis House, 2145 Decatur Pl., NW, Washington, 10/11/79, B, C, 79003100

Commandant's Office, Washington Navy Yard, Montgomery Sq. and Dahlgren Ave., SE., Washington, 8/14/73, A, C, 73002077

Commercial National Bank, 1405 G St., NW., Washington, 10/11/91, C, 91001488

Concordia German Evangelical Church and Rectory, 20th and G Sts., NW., Washington, 12/14/78, A, C, a, 78003055

Conduit Road Schoolhouse, 4954 MacArthur Blvd., NW., Washington, 11/30/73, A, C, NPS, 73000220

District of Columbia State Equivalent— Continued

Congressional Cemetery, 1801 E St., SE., Washington, 6/23/69, A, d, 69000292

Constitution Hall, 311 Eighteenth St., NW., Washington, 9/16/85, A, C, NHL, 85002724

Corcoran Gallery of Art, 17th St. at New York Ave., NW., Washington, 5/06/71, A, B, C, NHL, 71000997

Corcoran Hall, 721 21st St., NW., Washington, 4/12/91, A, C, 90001545

Cosmos Club, 2121 Massachusetts Ave., NW., Washington, 4/03/73, A, C, 73002079

Coues, Elliott, House, 1726 N St., NW, Washington, 5/15/75, B, NHL, 75002049

Customhouse and Post Office, 1221 31st St., NW., Washington, 9/10/71, C, 71001006

Decatur House, 748 Jackson Pl., NW., Washington, 10/15/66, B, C, NHL, 66000858

District Building, SE corner of 14th and E Sts., NW., Washington, 3/16/72, C, 72001422

Douglass, Frederick, National Historic Site, 1411 W St., SE., Washington, 10/15/66, B, NPS, 66000033

Dumbarton Bridge, Q St. over Rock Creek Park, NW., Washington, 7/16/73, A, C, 73002080

Dumbarton Oaks Park and Montrose Park, R St. NW, Washington, 5/28/67, C, NPS, 67000028

Duncanson-Cranch House, 468–470 N St., NW., Washington, 7/26/73, A, C, 73002081

Dupont Circle Historic District, Roughly bounded by Florida and Rhode Island Aves., T, 17th, 21st, and 22nd Sts., Washington, 7/21/78, A, C, 78003056

Dupont Circle Historic District (Boundary Increase), Roughly bounded by Florida Ave., 16th, 22nd, and T Sts., Rhode Island Ave. and N St., Washington, 2/06/85, A, C, 85000238

East Capitol Street Carbarn, 1400 E. Capitol St., NE., Washington, 2/05/74, A, C, 74002158

East and West Potomac Parks, Bounded by Constitution Ave., 17th St., Independence Ave., Washington Channel, Potomac River, and Rock Creek Park, Washington, 11/30/73, C, NPS, 73000217

Eastern Market, 7th and C Sts., SE., Washington, 5/27/71, A, C, 71000998

Eight Hundred Block of F St. NW, 800–818 F St. and 527 9th St., NW., Washington, 4/02/74, A, C, 74002159

Eighteen Hundred Block Park Road, NW., 1801–1869 Park Rd., NW., Washington, 11/15/78, A, C, 78003057

Embassy Building No. 10, 3149 Sixteenth St. NW, Washington, 11/06/86, B, C, 86003023

Embassy Gulf Service Station, 2200 P St., NW., Washington, 9/30/93, C, 93001014

Evans—Tibbs House, 1910 Vermont Ave. NW, Washington, 9/08/87, B, g, 86003025

Evermay, 1623 28th St., NW., Washington, 4/03/73, A, C, 73002083

Executive Office Building, Pennsylvania Ave. and 17th St., NW, Washington, 6/04/69, A, C, NHL, 69000293

Foggy Bottom Historic District, Bounded by New Hampshire Ave., Twenty-fourth, Twenty-sixth, H, and K Sts., NW, Washington, 10/14/87, A, C, 87001269

Folger Shakespeare Library, 201 E. Capitol St., SE., Washington, 6/23/69, A, C, g, 69000294

Ford's Theatre National Historic Site, 10th St., NW., between E and F Sts., Washington, 10/15/66, B, NPS, 66000034

Forrest-Marbury House, 3350 M St., NW., Washington, 7/02/73, A, C, 73002084

Franciscan Monastery and Memorial Church of the Holy Land, 1400 Quincy St., NE., Washington, 1/17/92, A, C, a, 91001943

Franklin School, 13th and K Sts., NW., Washington, 4/11/73, A, C, 73002085

Fraser Mansion, 1701 20th St., NW., Washington, 8/19/75, C, 75002054

Freer Gallery Of Art, 12th St. and Jefferson Dr., SW., Washington, 6/23/69, C, g, 69000295

Friendship House, 619 D St., SE., or 630 South Carolina Ave., SE., Washington, 1/18/73, C, 73002086

Fuller House, 2317 Ashmead Pl., NW, Washington, 2/21/85, C, 85000302

Gallaudet College Historic District, Florida Ave. and 7th St., NE., Washington, 9/10/74, A, C, 74002160

Gallinger Municipal Hospital Psychopathic Ward, Reservation 13, 19th St. and Massachusetts Ave., SE, Washington, 2/27/89, A, C, 89000074

General Federation of Women's Clubs Headquarters, 1734 N St., NW., Washington, 12/04/91, A, NHL, 91002057

General Post Office, E and F Sts. between 7th and 8th Sts., NW, Washington, 3/24/69, A, C, NHL, 69000311

Georgetown Academy for Young Ladies, 1524 35th St., NW., Washington, 3/29/91, A, B, C, 90002146

Georgetown Historic District, Roughly bounded by Whitehaven St., Rock Creek Park, Potomac River, and Georgetown University campus, Washington, 5/28/67, A, C, NHL, 67000025

Georgetown Market, 3276 M St., NW., Washington, 5/06/71, A, C, 71001000

Georgetown University Astronomical Observatory, Georgetown University, Washington, 7/02/73, A, C, a, 73002087

Glenwood Cemetery Mortuary Chapel, 2219 Lincoln Rd., NE, Washington, 1/09/89, C, a, 88003064

Godey Lime Kilns, Rock Creek and Potomac Pkwy. at 27th and L Sts., NW., Washington, 11/02/73, A, NPS, 73000221

Gompers, Samuel, House, 2122 1st St., NW, Washington, 9/23/74, B, NHL, 74002161

Grace Protestant Episcopal Church, 1041 Wisconsin Ave., NW., Washington, 5/06/71, A, C, a, 71001001

Grace Reformed Church, Sunday School and Parish House, 1405 15th St., NW., Washington, 4/18/91, C, a, 91000396

Grimke, Charlotte Forten, House 1608 R St., NW., Washington, 5/11/76, B, NHL, 76002129

Halcyon House, 3400 Prospect St., NW., Washington, 3/31/71, B, C, 71001002

Haw, John Stoddert, House, 2808 N St., NW., Washington, 7/16/73, A, C, 73002089

Healy Building, Georgetown University, Georgetown University campus, junction of O and Thirty-seventh Sts., Washington, 5/27/71, A, C, a, NHL, 71001003

Heurich, Christian, Mansion, 1307 New Hampshire Ave., NW., Washington, 6/23/69, A, C, 69000296

Hibbs, W. B., and Company Building, 725 Fifteenth St., NW., Washington, 3/19/91, C, 90002150

Highlands, The, 3825 Wisconsin Ave., NW., Washington, 3/16/72, A, C, 72001423

Holt House, Adams Mill Rd. in the National Zoological Park, Washington, 4/24/73, C, 73002090

House at 2437 Fifteenth Street, NW, 2437 Fifteenth St., NW, Washington, 3/16/88, B, C, 88000171

Howard Theatre, 620 T St., NW., Washington, 2/15/74, A, 74002162

Howard, Gen. Oliver Otis, House, 607 Howard Pl., Washington, 2/12/74, A, B, NHL, 74002163

Hughes, Charles Evans, House, 2223 R St., NW, Washington, 11/28/72, B, g, NHL, 72001424

Indonesian Embassy, 2020 Massachusetts Ave., NW., Washington, 1/18/73, C, 73002091

Ingleside, 1818 Newton St. NW, Washington, 1/08/87, C, a, 86002936

Interior Department Offices, Eighteenth and F Sts. NW, Washington, 11/23/86, A, C, g, 86003160

Japanese Embassy, 2520 Massachusetts Ave., NW., Washington, 2/20/73, A, C, g, 73002092

Kalorama Triangle Historic District, Roughly bounded by Connecticut Ave., Columbia Rd., and Calvert St., Washington, 5/04/87, C, 87000627

Kenilworth Aquatic Gardens, Kenilworth Ave. and Douglas St. NE., Washington, 8/25/78, B, C, g, NPS, 78000258

Lafayette Square Historic District, Roughly between 15th and 17th Sts. and H St. and State and Treasury Places, exclusive of the White House and its grounds, Washington, 8/29/70, A, C, NHL, NPS, 70000833

Langston Golf Course Historic District, Roughly, Anacostia Park N of Benning Rd., Washington, 10/15/91, A, NPS, 91001525

Langston Terrace Dwellings, N from Benning Rd. to H St., NE, Washington, 11/12/87, A, C, 87001851

Lansburgh, Julius, Furniture Co., Inc., 909 F St., NW., Washington, 5/08/74, A, C, 74002164

Law, Thomas, House, 1252 6th St., SW., Washington, 8/14/73, A, C, 73002093

LeDroit Park Historic District, Bounded roughly by Florida and Rhode Island Aves., 2nd and Elm Sts., Howard University, Washington, 2/25/74, A, C, 74002165

Lenthall Houses, 606-610 21St., NW, Washington, 3/16/72, B, C, 72001425

Lewis, Edward Simon, House, 456 N St., NW., Washington, 7/23/73, C, 73002094

Lincoln Memorial, West Potomac Park, Washington, 10/15/66, B, C, f, NPS, 66000030

District of Columbia State Equivalent—Continued

Lincoln Theatre, 1215 U St. NW, Washington, 10/27/93, A, C, g, 93001129

Lindens, The, 2401 Kalorama Rd., NW., Washington, 6/04/69, A, C, b, 69000297

Lisner Auditorium, 730 21st St., NW., Washington, 10/25/90, A, C, 90001548

Lockkeeper's House, C & O Canal Extension, SW corner of 17th St. and Constitution Ave., NW., Washington, 11/30/73, A, C, NPS, 73000218

Logan Circle Historic District, Jct. of Rhode Island and Vermont Aves., Washington, 6/30/72, C, 72001426

Lothrop Mansion, 2001 Connecticut Ave., Washington, 12/20/88, B, C, 88001346

Luther Place Memorial Church, 1226 Vermont Ave., NW. (Thomas Circle), Washington, 7/16/73, A, C, a, 73002096

Lyndon Baines Johnson Memorial Grove On The Potomac, Potomac Park, Washington, 12/28/73, B, C, f, g, NPS, 73002097

M Street High School, 128 M St. NW, Washington, 10/23/86, A, 86002924

Macfeely, Gen. Robert, House, 2015 I St., NW., Washington, 9/15/89, B, C, 89001214

Main Gate, Washington Navy Yard, 8th and M Sts., SE., Washington, 8/14/73, C, 73002098

Mansion at 2401 15th St., NW., 2401 15th St., NW., Washington, 1/28/91, C, 90002147

Mary McLeod Bethune Council House National Historic Site, 1318 Vermont Ave., NW, Washington, 10/15/82, NPS, 82005389

Masonic Temple, 801 Thirteenth St., NW, Washington, 2/18/87, A, C, 86002920

Massachusetts Avenue Historic District, Both sides of Massachusetts Ave. between 17th St. and Observatory Circle, NW, Washington, 10/22/74, A, C, 74002166

Mayfair Mansions Apartments, 3819 Jay St., NE., Washington, 11/01/89, A, g, 89001735

Mayflower Hotel, 1127 Connecticut Ave. NW, Washington, 11/14/83, A, C, 83003527

McCormick Apartments, 1785 Massachusetts Ave., NW, Washington, 4/03/73, B, C, g, NHL, 73002100

McLachlen Building, 1001 G St. NW, Washington, 11/06/86, A, C, 86003042

Meeting House of the Friends Meeting of Washington, 2111 Florida Ave., NW., Washington, 9/06/90, A, B, C, a, 90001294

Memorial Continental Hall, 17th St., between C and D Sts., NW, Washington, 11/28/72, A, g, NHL, 72001427

Meridian Hill Park, Bounded by 16th, Euclid, 15th, and W Sts., NW., Washington, 10/25/74, C, g, NPS, 74000273

Meridian House, 1630 Crescent Pl., NW., Washington, 5/08/73, C, 73002101

Meridian Mansions, 2400 16th St. NW, Washington, 7/28/83, A, B, C, f, 83001417

Metropolitan African Methodist Episcopal Church, 1518 M St., NW., Washington, 7/26/73, A, C, a, 73002102

Miner Normal School, 2565 Georgia Ave., NW., Washington, 10/11/91, A, C, 91001490

Moran Building, 501-509 G St., NW, Washington, 9/26/83, C, 83001413

Morrison and Clark Houses, 1013-1015 L St., NW., Washington, 3/19/91, A, C, g, 90002149

Mount Pleasant Historic District, Roughly bounded by Sixteenth & Harvard Sts., Rock Creek Church Rd., & Adams Mill Rd., Washington, 10/05/87, C, 87001726

Mount Vernon Memorial Highway, Washington St. and George Washington Memorial Pkwy., Washington, 5/18/81, A, C, NPS, 81000079

Mount Zion Cemetery, 27th and Q Sts., NW., Washington, 8/06/75, A, d, 75002050

Mount Zion United Methodist Church, 1334 29th St., NW., Washington, 7/24/75, A, C, a, 75002051

National Academy of Sciences, 2101 Constitution Ave., NW., Washington, 3/15/74, A, C, 74002168

National Archives, Constitution Ave. between 7th and 9th Sts., NW., Washington, 5/27/71, C, g, 71001004

National Bank of Washington, Washington Branch, 301 7th St., N.W., Washington, 5/08/74, A, C, 74002169

National Cathedral, The, Wisconsin and Massachusetts Ave., NW., Washington, 5/03/74, A, C, a, 74002170

National Mall, Between Independence and Constitution Aves. from the U.S. Capitol to the Washington Monument, Washington, 10/15/66, C, NPS, 66000031

National Metropolitan Bank Building, 613 15th St., NW., Washington, 9/13/78, A, C, 78003059

National Portrait Gallery, F and G Sts. between 7th and 9th Sts., NW., Washington, 10/15/66, A, C, NHL, 66000902

National Saving And Trust Company, New York Ave. and 15th St., NW., Washington, 3/16/72, A, C, 72001428

National Union Building, 918 F St., NW, Washington, 9/21/90, B, C, 90001375

National War College, P St., within Fort Lesley J. McNair, Washington, 11/28/72, A, NHL, 72001535

National Zoological Park, 3000 block of Connecticut Ave., NW., Washington, 4/11/73, A, C, 73002104

Northumberland Apartments, 2039 New Hampshire Ave., NW, Washington, 3/25/80, A, C, 80004304

Oak Hill Cemetery Chapel, R St. at 29th St., NW., Washington, 3/16/72, C, a, 72001429

Octagon, The, 1799 New York Ave., NW, Washington, 10/15/66, A, B, C, NHL, 66000863

Old Engine Company No. 6, 438 Massachusetts Ave., NW., Washington, 9/05/75, C, 75002052

Old Naval Hospital, 921 Pennsylvania Ave., SE., Washington, 5/03/74, A, C, 74002171

Old Naval Observatory, 23rd and E Sts., NW, Washington, 10/15/66, A, NHL, 66000864

Old Post Office and Clock Tower, Pennsylvania Ave. at 12th St., NW., Washington, 4/11/73, A, C, 73002105

Old Stone House, 3051 M St., NW., Washington, 11/30/73, A, C, NPS, 73000219

Old Woodley Park Historic District, Roughly bounded by Rock Creek Park, 24th St., 29th St., Woodley Rd. and Cathedral Ave., NW., Washington, 6/15/90, A, C, 90000856

Owens, Isaac, House, 2806 N St., NW., Washington, 6/19/73, C, 73002107

PHILADELPHIA (gundelo), 14th St. and Constitution Ave., NW, Washington, 10/15/66, A, D, NHL, 66000852

Page, Thomas Nelson, House, 1759 R St., NW., Washington, 9/05/75, B, C, 75002053

Pan American Union, 17th St. between C St. and Constitution Ave., NW., Washington, 6/04/69, A, C, 69000298

Park Tower, 2440 Sixteenth St., NW., Washington, 10/30/89, C, 89001744

Pennsylvania Avenue National Historic Site, Pennsylvania Ave. from Capitol Hill to the White House, Washington, 10/15/66, A, C, NPS, 66000865

Pension Building, 4th and 5th Sts. between F and G Sts., NW, Washington, 3/24/69, A, C, f, NHL, 69000312

Perkins, Frances, House, 2326 California St., NW., Washington, 7/17/91, A, B, NHL, 91002048

Phillips, Duncan, House, 1600-1614 21st St., NW., Washington, 8/14/73, C, 73002108

Pierce Mill, Rock Creek Park, NW corner of Tilden St. and Beach Dr., NW, Washington, 3/24/69, A, NPS, 69000014

Pierce Springhouse and Barn, 2400 Block of Tilden St. and Beach Dr., NW, Washington, 10/25/73, A, NPS, 73000222

Pierce Still House, 2400 Tilden St., NW., Washington, 9/06/90, A, C, 90001295

Pierce-Klingle Mansion, 3545 Williamsburg Lane, NW, Washington, 10/10/73, A, C, NPS, 73000223

Pink Palace, 2600 16th St., NW., Washington, 8/05/91, B, C, 91000916

Plymouth, The, 1236 Eleventh St. NW, Washington, 6/02/86, C, 86001242

Potomac Boat Club, 3530 Water St., NW., Washington, 6/27/91, A, C, 91000786

Potomac Palisades Site, Address Restricted, Washington vicinity, 4/15/82, D, NPS, 82001714

President's House, Gallaudet College, 7th St. and Florida Ave., NE., Washington, 2/15/74, A, C, 74002172

President's Office, George Washington University, 2003 G St., NW. and 700 20th St., NW., Washington, 9/13/91, A, C, 90001544

President's Park South, Constitution Ave., Washington, 5/06/80, C, NPS, 80000347

Prince Hall Masonic Temple, 1000 U St., NW, Washington, 9/15/83, A, C, 83001418

Prospect House, 3508 Prospect St., NW., Washington, 3/16/72, A, C, 72001430

Quality Hill, 3425 Prospect St., NW., Washington, 3/16/72, C, 72001431

Quarters A, Washington Navy Yard, E of Main Gate and S of M St., SE., in the Navy Yard, Washington, 8/14/73, A, C, 73002111

Quarters B, Washington Navy Yard, Charles Morris Ave., SE., Washington, 8/14/73, A, C, 73002112

District of Columbia State Equivalent—Continued

Renwick Museum, NE corner, 17th St. and Pennsylvania Ave., NW, Washington, 3/24/69, C, NHL, 69000300

Rhodes' Tavern, 601–603 15th St. and 1431 F St., NW., Washington, 3/24/69, A, C, 69000301

Richards, Zalmon, House, 1301 Corcoran St., NW, Washington, 10/15/66, B, NHL, 66000866

Riggs National Bank, 1503–1505 Pennsylvania Ave., NW., Washington, 7/16/73, A, C, 73002113

Riggs National Bank, Washington Loan And Trust Company Branch, SW corner of 9th and F Sts., NW., Washington, 5/06/71, A, C, 71001005

Riggs—Tompkins Building, 1403–1405 and 1413 Park Rd. NW and 3300, 3306–3316, 3328, and 3336 Fourteenth St. NW, Washington, 1/05/87, A, C, 86002915

Ringgold-Carroll House, 1801 F St., NW., Washington, 7/26/73, B, C, 73002114

Rock Creek Church Yard and Cemetery, Webster St. and Rock Creek Church Rd., NW., Washington, 8/12/77, A, C, D, a, d, 77001498

Rock Creek Park Historic District, Roughly, Rock Creek Park from Klingle Rd. to Montgomery County line, Washington, 10/23/91, A, B, C, b, NPS, 91001524

Rosedale, 3501 Newark St., NW., Washington, 5/08/73, C, 73002115

Schneider Triangle, Bounded by Washington Circle, New Hampshire Ave. NW, K, 22nd, and L Sts. NW, Washington, 12/13/82, C, 82001031

Sewall-Belmont House National Historic Site, 144 Constitution Ave., NE., Washington, 6/16/72, B, C, NHL, NPS, 72001432

Sheridan—Kalorama Historic District, Roughly bounded by Rock Creek Park, Connecticut Ave., NW., Florida Ave., NW., 22nd St., NW., and P St., NW., Washington, 10/30/89, A, B, C, g, 89001743

Sixteenth Street Historic District, 16th St. between Scott Cir. and Florida Ave. NW, Washington, 8/25/78, A, C, 78003060

Smithsonian Building, Jefferson Dr. at 10th St., SW, Washington, 10/15/66, A, C, NHL, 66000867

Southern Aid Society—Dunbar Theater Building, 1901–1903 Seventh St. NW, Washington, 11/06/86, A, C, 86003071

Springland, 3550 Tilden St. NW., Washington, 8/09/90, B, C, 90001114

St. Aloysius Catholic Church, N. Capitol and I Sts., NW., Washington, 7/26/73, C, a, 73002116

St. Elizabeths Hospital, 2700 Martin Luther King Jr., Ave., SE., Washington, 4/26/79, A, B, C, NHL, 79003101

St. John's Church, 16th and H Sts., NW, Washington, 10/15/66, A, C, a, NHL, 66000868

St. Luke's Episcopal Church, 15th and Church Sts., NW, Washington, 5/11/76, B, a, NHL, 76002131

St. Mark's Church, 3rd and A Sts., SE., Washington, 5/08/73, C, a, 73002117

St. Mary's Episcopal Church, 730 23rd St., NW., Washington, 4/02/73, C, a, 73002118

St. Matthew's Cathedral And Rectory, 1725–1739 Rhode Island Ave., NW., Washington, 1/24/74, A, C, a, 74002173

St. Paul's Episcopal Church, Rock Creek Church Rd. and Webster St., NW., Washington, 3/16/72, A, C, a, e, 72001433

Steedman—Ray House, 1925 F St., NW, Washington, 9/21/90, A, C, 90001376

Stockton Hall, 720 20th St., NW., Washington, 9/13/91, A, C, 90001546

Strivers' Section Historic District, Roughly bounded by New Hampshire and Florida Aves., 17th and 18th Sts. along T, U, and Willard Sts. NW, Washington, 2/06/85, A, C, 85000239

Strong, Hattie M., Residence Hall, 620 21st St., NW., Washington, 4/12/91, A, C, 90001547

Sulgrave Club, 1801 Massachusetts Ave., NW., Washington, 12/05/72, C, 72001434

Sumner, Charles, School, 17th and M Sts., NW, Washington, 12/20/79, A, C, 79003150

Sun Building, 1317 F St., NW., Washington, 3/27/85, A, C, 85000650

Takoma Park Historic District, Roughly bounded by DC/MD boundary, 7th, Piney Branch, Aspen, and Fern Sts., Washington, 6/30/83, A, C, a, 83001416

Tenth Precinct Station House, 750 Park Rd. NW, Washington, 11/10/86, A, C, 86003063

Terrell, Mary Church, House, 326 T St., NW, Washington, 5/15/75, B, NHL, 75002055

Theodore Roosevelt Island National Memorial, S of Key Bridge in the Potomac River, Washington, 10/15/66, A, C, f, NPS, 66000869

Thomas Jefferson Memorial, S bank of the Tidal Basin, Washington, 10/15/66, B, C, f, g, NPS, 66000029

Thomas, Alma, House, 1530 Fifteenth St. NW, Washington, 7/28/87, B, g, 86002923

Tivoli Theater, 3301-3325 14th St. NW, Washington, 4/10/85, A, B, C, 85000716

Trades Hall of National Training School for Women and Girls, 601 50th St., NE., Washington, 7/17/91, A, B, a, NHL, 91002049

True Reformer Building, 1200 U St., NW, Washington, 1/09/89, A, C, 88003063

Tucker House and Myers House, 2310–2320 S St., NW., Washington, 8/14/73, C, 73002119

Tudor Place, 1644 31st St., NW, Washington, 10/15/66, A, C, NHL, 66000871

Twin Oaks, 3225 Woodley Rd., Washington, 2/05/86, B, C, 86000153

U.S. Capitol Gatehouses And Gateposts, 7th, 15th, and 17th Sts., and Constitution Ave., NW., Washington, 11/30/73, C, b, NPS, 73002120

U.S. Court Of Military Appeals, 450 E St., NW., Washington, 1/21/74, C, 74002174

U.S. Department of Agriculture Administration Building, 12th St. and Jefferson Dr., SW., Washington, 1/24/74, C, g, 74002175

U.S. Department of the Treasury, 1500 Pennsylvania Ave., NW, Washington, 11/11/71, C, NHL, 71001007

U.S. Marine Corps Barracks and Commandant's House, 8th and I Sts., SE, Washington, 12/27/72, A, B, C, NHL, 72001435

U.S. National Arboretum, 24th and R Sts., NE., Washington, 4/11/73, C, g, 73002122

U.S. Soldiers' and Airmen's Home, Rock Creek Church Rd., NW, Washington, 2/11/74, A, NHL, 74002176

US Chamber of Commerce Building, 1615 H St., NW., Washington, 5/13/92, A, C, 92000499

US Department of the Interior Building, Eighteenth and C Sts. NW, Washington, 11/10/86, A, C, g, 86002898

USS SEQUOIA (yacht), Hains Point, Washington, 12/23/87, A, g, NHL, 87002594

Underwood, Oscar W., House, 2000 G St., NW, Washington, 12/08/76, A, B, g, NHL, 76002132

Union Station, Intersection of Massachusetts and Louisiana Aves. and 1st St., NE., Washington, 3/24/69, A, 69000302

Union Station Plaza and Columbus Fountain, 1st St., Massachusetts and Louisiana Aves., NE, Washington, 4/09/80, C, NPS, 80004523

Union Trust Building, 740 15th St. NW, Washington, 1/19/84, A, C, 84000867

United Brick Corporation Brick Complex, 2801 New York Ave., NE., Washington, 10/03/78, A, g, 78003061

Van Ness Mausoleum, Oak Hill Cemetary, 3001 R St. NW, Washington, 12/17/82, C, b, 82001032

Vigilant Firehouse, 1066 Wisconsin Ave., NW., Washington, 5/06/71, A, C, 71001008

Volta Bureau, 1537 35th St., NW, Washington, 11/28/72, B, NHL, 72001436

Walsh Stable, 1511 (rear) Twenty-second St. NW, Washington, 11/06/86, A, B, C, 86002932

Warder-Totten House, 2633 16th St., NW., Washington, 4/14/72, C, a, b, 72001437

Wardman Park Annex and Arcade, 2600 Woodley Rd. NW, Washington, 1/31/84, A, C, 84000869

Wardman Row, 1416-1440 R St. NW, Washington, 7/27/84, C, 84000871

Washington Aqueduct, 5900 MacArthur Blvd., NW, Washington, 9/08/73, A, C, NHL, 73002123

Washington Canoe Club, 3700 K St., NW., Washington, 3/19/91, A, C, NPS, 90002151

Washington Club, 15 Dupont Circle, NW., Washington, 12/05/72, C, 72001438

Washington Monument, The Mall, between 14th and 17th Sts., NW., Washington, 10/15/66, A, B, C, f, NPS, 66000035

Washington Navy Yard, 8th and M Sts., SE, Washington, 6/19/73, A, C, NHL, 73002124

Watterston House, 224 2nd St., SE., Washington, 1/17/92, B, C, 91001942

Wetzel, Margaret, House, 714 21st St., NW., Washington, 10/25/90, A, C, 90001542

Wetzell—Archbold Farmstead, 4437 Reservoir Rd., NW., Washington, 4/19/91, C, 91000395

Wheat Row, 1315, 1317, 1319, and 1321 4th St., SW., Washington, 7/23/73, A, C, 73002125

Wheatley, Phillis, YWCA 901 Rhode Island Ave. NW, Washington, 10/06/83, A, 83003532

White, David, House, 1459 Girard St., NW, Washington, 1/07/76, B, NHL, 76002133

White—Meyer House, 1624 Crescent Pl., NW, Washington, 1/20/88, C, 87002293

Whitelaw Hotel, 1839 13th St. NW, Washington D.C., 7/14/93, A, B, C, g, 93000595

District of Columbia State Equivalent—Continued

Whittemore House, 1526 New Hampshire Ave., NW., Washington, 7/16/73, B, C, 73002126

Willard Hotel, 1401–1409 Pennsylvania Ave., NW., Washington, 2/15/74, A, C, 74002177

Wilson, Woodrow, House, 2340 S St., NW, Washington, 10/15/66, B, NHL, 66000873

Winder Building, 604 17th St., NW., Washington, 3/24/69, A, 69000303

Windsor Lodge, 2139–2141 Wyoming Ave., NW, Washington, 12/08/76, B, NHL, 76002134

Woodhull, Maxwell, House, 2033 G St., NW., Washington, 4/12/91, A, B, C, 90001543

Woodson, Carter G., House, 1538 9th St., NW, Washington, 5/11/76, B, NHL, 76002135

Woodward, Robert Simpson, House, 1513 16th St., NW, Washington, 1/07/76, B, NHL, 76002136

Wyoming Apartments, 2022 Columbia Rd., NW, Washington, 9/27/83, A, C, 83001414

Springland, a circa 1845 vernacular brick house typical of rural residences built outside the fledgling City of Washington in the early-19th century, was home to religious philosopher James Macbride Sterret from 1891 to 1923. (Kathleen Sinclair Wood, 1989)

FLORIDA

Alachua County

Anderson Hall, W. University Ave., Gainesville, 6/27/79, A, C, 79000652

Bailey, Maj. James B., House, 1121 N.W. 6th St., Gainesville, 12/05/72, C, 72000301

Baird Hardware Company Warehouse, 619 S. Main St., Gainesville, 11/25/85, A, 85003053

Boulware Spring Waterworks, 3400 SE 15th St., Gainesville, 6/20/85, A, C, 85001255

Bryan Hall, W. University Ave. and 13th St., Gainesville, 6/27/79, A, C, 79000653

Buckman Hall, N.W. 17th St., Gainesville, 1/11/74, A, C, 74000609

Dixie Hotel, Hotel Kelley, 408 W. University Ave., Gainesville, 8/16/82, A, B, C, g, 82002369

Epworth Hall, 419 NE 1st St., Gainesville, 7/25/73, A, C, a, 73000562

Evinston Community Store and Post Office, Co. Rd. 225, N of jct. with Co. Rd. SE. 10, Evinston, 5/05/89, A, C, b, 89000321

Flint Hall, W. University Ave., Gainesville, 6/27/79, A, C, 79000654

Floyd Hall, University of Florida campus, Gainesville, 6/27/79, A, C, 79000655

High Springs Historic District, Roughly bounded by NW. 14th St., NW. 6th Ave., SE. 7th St. and SW. 5th Ave., High Springs, 10/31/91, A, C, 91001540

Hotel Thomas, Bounded by N.E. 2nd and 5th Sts. and N.E. 6th and 7th Aves., Gainesville, 7/16/73, C, g, 73000563

Kanapaha, 8500 FL 24, Gainesville vicinity, 5/02/86, A, C, 86000915

Library East, Murphree Way, Gainesville, 6/27/79, A, C, g, 79000656

Matheson House, 528 S.E. 1st Ave., Gainesville, 6/04/73, C, 73000564

McKenzie, Mary Phifer, House, 617 E. University Ave., Gainesville, 4/26/82, C, 82002370

Melrose Historic District, Roughly bounded by Seminole Ridge Rd., Grove St., South St., Quail St., and Melrose Bay, Melrose, 1/12/90, A, C, 89002305

Micanopy Historic District, Roughly Cholokka Blvd. from US 441 to Ocala St. then Smith St. W to Okehumkee St., Micanopy, 1/28/83, A, C, D, 83003512

Neilson House, FL 325, Windsor, 6/04/73, C, 73000566

Newberry Historic District, Roughly bounded by NW Second Ave., NW Second St., Lucile St., & NW Ninth St., Newberry, 12/24/87, A, C, 87002150

Newell Hall, Stadium Rd., Gainesville, 6/27/79, A, C, 79000657

Newnansville Town Site, Address Restricted, Alachua vicinity, 12/04/74, A, B, C, D, 74000608

Northeast Gainesville Residential District, Roughly bounded by 1st, and 9th Sts., 10th and E. University Aves., Gainesville, 2/12/80, A, C, 80000942

Peabody Hall, University of Florida campus, Gainesville, 6/27/79, A, C, 79000658

Pleasant Street Historic District, Roughly bounded by NW. 8th Ave., NW. 1st St., NW. 2nd Ave., and NW. 6th St., Gainesville, 4/20/89, A, C, 89000323

Rawlings, Marjorie Kinnan, House, FL 325, S of Cross Creek, Cross Creek, 9/29/70, A, C, g, 70000176

Rochelle School, Off FL 234, Rochelle, 4/02/73, A, C, 73000565

Rolfs Hall, Buckman Dr., University of Florida, Gainesville, 9/11/86, A, C, 86002411

Southeast Gainesville Residential District, Roughly bounded by E. University Ave., S.E. Ninth St., S.E. Fifth Ave., and Sweetwater Branch, Gainesville, 1/14/88, C, b, 87002435

Star Garage, 119 S.E. First Ave., Gainesville, 12/17/85, A, 85003197

Thomas Hall, Fletcher Dr. on University of Florida campus, Gainesville, 10/01/74, A, 74000610

U.S. Post Office, 25 SE. 2nd Pl., Gainesville, 7/10/79, C, 79000659

University of Florida Campus Historic District, Bounded by W. University Ave., US 441/SW. 13th St., Stadium Rd., and North-South Dr., Gainesville, 4/20/89, A, C, 89000322

WRUF Radio Station, Old, Museum Rd. and Newell Dr., Gainesville, 9/21/89, A, C, 89001479

Women's Gymnasium, East-West Rd., Gainesville, 6/27/79, A, C, 79000660

Yonge, P. K., Laboratory School, Old, SW. 13th St. on University of Florida campus, Gainesville, 1/26/90, A, C, 89002302

Baker County

Burnsed Blockhouse, N of Sanderson off Jacksonville Rd., Sanderson vicinity, 5/07/73, C, 73000567

Old Baker County Courthouse, 14 W. McIver St., Macclenny, 8/21/86, C, 86001729

Olustee Battlefield, 2 mi. E of Olustee on U.S. 90 in Osceola National Forest, Olustee vicinity, 8/12/70, A, 70000177

Bay County

McKenzie, Robert L., House, 17 E. Third Ct., Panama City, 8/21/86, B, 86001728

Bradford County

Call Street Historic District, Bounded by Jefferson, Cherry, Madison, and Temple Sts., Starke, 12/12/85, A, C, 85003329

Old Bradford County Courthouse, 209 W. Call St., Starke, 12/27/74, A, C, 74000611

Brevard County

Aladdin Theater, 300 Brevard Ave., Cocoa, 10/17/91, A, C, 91001541

Barton Avenue Residential District [Rockledge MPS], 11–59 Barton Ave., Rockledge, 8/21/92, A, C, 92001046

Cape Canaveral Air Force Station, Launch Pads 5, 6, 13, 14, 19, 26, 34 and Mission Control Center, Cocoa vicinity, 4/16/84, A, C, g, NHL, 84003872

Community Chapel of Melbourne Beach, 501 Ocean Ave., Melbourne Beach, 5/14/92, A, a, 92000505

Florida Power and Light Company Ice Plant, 1604 S. Harbor City Blvd., Melbourne, 11/17/82, A, 82001033

Launch Complex 39, Kennedy Space Center, Titusville vicinity, 5/24/73, A, C, g, 73000568

Melbourne Beach Pier, Ocean Ave. and Riverside Dr., Melbourne Beach, 4/12/84, A, B, C, 84000829

Old Haulover Canal, Address Restricted, Merrit Island vicinity, 12/19/78, A, NPS, 78000262

Porcher House, 434 Delannoy Ave., Cocoa, 1/06/86, B, C, 86000023

Pritchard House [Titusville MPS], 424 S. Washington Ave., Titusville, 1/12/90, C, 89002167

Robbins, Judge George, House [Titusville MPS], 703 Indian River Ave., Titusville, 1/12/90, C, 89002168

Rockledge Drive Residential District [Rockledge MPS], 15–23 Rockledge Ave., 219–1361 Rockledge Dr. and 1-11 Orange Ave., Rockledge, 8/21/92, A, C, 92001045

Spell House [Titusville MPS], 1200 Riverside Dr., Titusville, 1/12/90, C, 89002166

St. Gabriel's Episcopal Church, 414 Palm Ave., Titusville, 12/05/72, C, a, 72000302

St. Joseph's Catholic Church, Miller St., NE, Palm Bay, 12/03/87, A, C, a, 87000816

St. Luke's Episcopal Church and Cemetery, Old, 5555 N. Tropical Trail, Courteney, 6/15/90, A, C, a, 90000848

Titusville Commercial District [Titusville MPS], Roughly bounded by Julia St., Hopkins Ave., Main St., and Indian River Ave., Titusville, 1/10/90, A, C, 89002164

Valencia Subdivision Residential District [Rockledge MPS], 14–140 Valencia Rd., 825–827 Osceola Dr. and 24–28 Orange Ave., Rockledge, 8/21/92, C, 92001047

Wager House [Titusville MPS], 621 Indian River Ave., Titusville, 1/10/90, A, C, 89002165

Whaley, Marion S., Citrus Packing House, 2275 US 1, Rockledge, 4/08/93, A, C, 93000286

Brevard County—Continued

Windover Archeological Site (8BR246), Address Restricted, Titusville vicinity, 4/20/87, A, D, NHL, 87000810

Broward County

Bonnet House, 900 Birch Rd., Ft. Lauderdale, 7/05/84, B, C, 84000832

Cap's Place, 2980 NE. 31st Ave., Lighthouse Point, 8/10/90, A, C, 90001227

Davie School, 6650 Griffin Rd., Davie, 3/29/88, A, C, 88000223

Deerfield School, 651 NE. 1st St., Deerfield Beach, 4/16/90, A, C, 90000319

Dillard High School, Old, 1001 NW. Fourth St., Ft. Lauderdale, 2/20/91, A, g, 91000107

Hillsboro Inlet Light Station, Off I-95 at Hillsboro Inlet, Pompano Beach, 2/16/74, C, 79000661

Lock No. 1, North New River Canal, S of Plantation on FL 84, Plantation vicinity, 2/17/78, A, 78000932

New River Inn, 229 S.W. 2nd Ave., Fort Lauderdale, 6/19/72, A, C, 72000303

Oakland Park Elementary School, 936 N.E. Thirty-third St., Oakland Park, 6/09/88, A, C, 88000714

Sample Estate, 3161 N. Dixie Hwy., Pompano Beach, 3/01/84, A, C, 84000834

Seaboard Air Line Railway Station, Old, 1300 W. Hillsboro Blvd., Deerfield Beach, 4/05/90, A, C, 90000597

Stranahan House, 335 S.E. 6th Ave., Fort Lauderdale, 10/02/73, B, 73000569

U.S. Car. No. 1, 3398 SW. 9th Ave., Fort Lauderdale, 8/24/77, A, B, g, NHL, 77000401

Young, Joseph Wesley, House, 1055 Hollywood Blvd., Hollywood, 8/10/89, A, B, C, 89001076

Calhoun County

Cayson Mound and Village Site, Address Restricted, Blountstown vicinity, 3/15/76, D, 76000587

Old Calhoun County Courthouse, 314 E. Central Ave., Blountstown, 10/16/80, C, 80000943

Charlotte County

Big Mound Key—Boggess Ridge Archeological District, Address Restricted, Placida vicinity, 12/03/90, D, 90001764

Charlotte High School [Punta Gorda MPS], 1250 Cooper St., Punta Gorda, 12/12/90, A, 90001796

First National Bank of Punta Gorda, Old [Punta Gorda MPS], 133 W. Marion Ave., Punta Gorda, 3/14/91, A, 91000280

Freeman, A. C., House, 639 E. Hargreaves Ave., Punta Gorda, 1/07/87, B, C, b, 86003648

Icing Station at Bull Bay [Fish Cabins of Charlotte Harbor MPS], Off Bull Key in Bull Bay, Placida vicinity, 4/11/91, A, C, b, 91000399

Punta Gorda Atlantic Coast Line Depot [Punta Gorda MPS], 1009 Taylor Rd., Punta Gorda, 12/12/90, A, C, 90001797

Punta Gorda Ice Plant [Punta Gorda MPS], 408 Tamiami Trail, Punta Gorda, 12/12/90, A, 90001798

Punta Gorda Residential District [Punta Gorda MPS], Roughly bounded by W. Retta Esplanade, Berry St., West Virginia Ave. and Taylor St., Punta Gorda, 1/07/91, A, C, 90002103

Punta Gorda Woman's Club [Punta Gorda MPS], 118 Sullivan St., Punta Gorda, 4/05/91, A, C, 91000382

Smith, H. W., Building [Punta Gorda MPS], 121 E. Marion Ave., Punta Gorda, 7/25/91, A, C, 91000894

Villa Bianca, 2330 Shore Dr., Punta Gorda, 11/28/90, C, 90001760

West Coast Fish Company Residential Cabin at Bull Bay [Fish Cabins of Charlotte Harbor MPS], Bull Bay N of Bull Key, Placida vicinity, 4/11/91, A, C, b, 91000401

Willis Fish Cabin at Bull Bay [Fish Cabins of Charlotte Harbor MPS], Bull Bay N of Bull Key, Placida vicinity, 4/11/91, A, C, 91000400

Citrus County

Citrus County Courthouse, Old, 1 Courthouse Sq., Inverness, 4/17/92, A, C, 92000340

Crystal River Indian Mounds, 2 mi. NW of Crystal River on U.S. 19-98, Crystal River vicinity, 9/29/70, D, NHL, 70000178

Floral City Historic District, Roughly, Orange Ave. from S. Old Floral City Rd. to S. Annie Terr. and S. Aroostook Way from Orange to Lake Tsala Apopka, Floral City, 12/01/93, A, 93001357

Fort Cooper, Address Restricted, Inverness vicinity, 6/13/72, A, D, 72000304

Mullet Key, Address Restricted, Crystal River vicinity, 7/03/86, D, 86001409

Yulee Sugar Mill Ruins, FL 490 W of U.S. 19, Homosassa, 8/12/70, A, 70000179

Clay County

Bubba Midden (8CL84), Address Restricted, Fleming Island vicinity, 3/02/90, D, 90000159

Budington, Frosard W., House [Middleburg MPS], 3916 Main St., Middleburg, 3/09/90, C, 90000317

Chalker, George A., House [Middleburg MPS], 2160 Wharf St., Middleburg, 3/09/90, C, 90000315

Clark—Chalker House, 3891 Main St., Middleburg, 10/05/88, A, 88001701

Clay County Courthouse, Brabantio Ave., Green Cove Springs, 6/20/75, A, C, 75000546

Frisbee, George Randolph, Jr., House [Middleburg MPS], 2125 Palmetto St., Middleburg, 3/09/90, C, 90000316

Green Cove Springs Historic District, Roughly bounded by Bay St., CSX RR tracks, Center St., Orange Ave., St. Elmo St. and the St. Johns R., Green Cove Springs, 3/28/91, A, C, 91000281

Haskell—Long House [Middleburg MPS], 3858 Main St., Middleburg, 3/09/90, C, 90000314

Methodist Episcopal Church at Black Creek [Middleburg MPS], 3925 Main St., Middleburg, 3/09/90, A, C, a, d, 90000318

Middleburg Historic District [Middleburg MPS], 3881–3895 Main St. and 2145 Wharf St., Middleburg, 3/09/90, A, C, b, 90000313

Princess Mound (8CL85), Address Restricted, Green Cove Springs vicinity, 3/02/90, D, 90000311

St. Margaret's Episcopal Church, Old Church Rd., Hibernia, 6/04/73, A, C, a, b, 73000570

St. Mary's Church, St. Johns Ave., Green Cove Springs, 2/17/78, A, C, a, 78000933

Collier County

Burns Lake Site (8CR259), Address Restricted, Ochopee vicinity, 5/27/86, D, NPS, 86001192

Halfway Creek Site, Address Restricted, Carnestown vicinity, 8/15/80, D, NPS, 80000365

Hinson Mounds, Address Restricted, Miles City vicinity, 12/29/78, D, NPS, 78000345

Keewaydin Club, N end of Key Island, Naples vicinity, 12/22/87, A, C, 87001979

Naples Historic District, Roughly bounded by Ninth Ave. S, Third St., Thirteenth Ave. S, and Gulf of Mexico, Naples, 12/17/87, A, C, 87002179

Ostl, C. J., Site, Address Restricted, Ochopee vicinity, 12/15/78, D, NPS, 78003380

Palm Cottage, 137 12th Ave., S., Naples, 5/24/82, A, B, C, 82002371

Platt Island, Address Restricted, Miles City vicinity, 12/14/78, D, NPS, 78000934

Plaza Site (8CR303), Address Restricted, Ochopee vicinity, 5/28/86, D, NPS, 86001196

Seaboard Coast Line Railroad Depot, 1051 5th Ave., South, Naples, 9/10/74, A, C, g, 74000613

Smallwood, Ted, Store, FL 29 in Everglades National Park, Chokoloskee Island, 7/24/74, A, 74000612

Sugar Pot Site, Address Restricted, Ochopee vicinity, 12/15/78, D, NPS, 78000264

Turner River Site, Address Restricted, Ochopee vicinity, 12/14/78, D, NPS, 78000263

Columbia County

Columbia County High School [Lake City MPS], 528 W. Duval St., Lake City, 11/15/93, A, 93001154

Duncan, Horace, House [Lake City MPS], 202 W. Duval St., Lake City, 11/15/93, C, 93001155

Fort White Public School Historic District, E. Dorch at N. Bryant St., Fort White, 12/01/89, A, 89002061

Columbia County—Continued

Henderson, T. G., House, 207 S. Marion St., Lake City, 7/24/73, C, 73000571

Hotel Blanche, 212 N. Marion St., Lake City, 1/18/90, A, C, 89002320

Lake Isabella Historic Residential District [Lake City MPS], Roughly bounded by East, Duval and Columbia Sts., Baya Ave., Church St. and Lake Isabella, Lake City, 11/15/93, A, 93001156

Dade County

Adams, Carl G., House [Country Club Estates TR], 31 Hunting Lodge Ct., Miami Springs, 11/01/85, C, 85003464

Algonquin Apartments [Downtown Miami MRA], 1819–1825 Biscayne Blvd., Miami, 1/04/89, A, C, 88002985

Allen, Hervey, Study, 8251 S.W. 52nd Ave., South Miami, 5/07/74, A, B, g, 74002256

Anderson, William, General Merchandise Store, 15700 SW. 232nd St., SW., Goulds vicinity, 10/18/77, A, C, 77000402

Arch Creek Historic and Archeological Site, Address Restricted, North Miami, 7/15/86, A, D, 86001700

Atlantic Gas Station [Downtown Miami MRA], 668 N.W. 5th St., Miami, 12/29/88, A, C, 88003060

Baird House [Opa-Locka TR], 401 Dunad Ave., Opa-Locka, 8/17/87, A, C, 87001313

Bay Shore Historic District, Roughly bounded by NE. 55th St., Biscayne Blvd., NE. 60th St. and Biscayne Bay, Miami, 10/02/92, A, C, 92001323

Beth Jacob Social Hall and Congregation, 301 and 311 Washington Ave., Miami Beach, 10/16/80, A, a, g, 80000946

Brickell Mausoleum [Downtown Miami MRA], 501 Brickell Ave., Miami, 1/04/89, A, f, 88002977

Building at 10108 Northeast 1st Avenue [Miami Shores TR], 10108 NE. 1st Ave., Miami Shores, 11/14/88, A, C, 88002111

Building at 107 Northeast 96th Street [Miami Shores TR], 107 NE. 96th St., Miami Shores, 11/14/88, A, C, 88002094

Building at 121 Northeast 100th Street [Miami Shores TR], 121 NE. 100th St., Miami Shores, 11/14/88, A, C, 88002107

Building at 1291 Northeast 102nd Street [Miami Shores TR], 1291 NE. 102nd St., Miami Shores, 11/14/88, A, C, 88002110

Building at 145 Northeast 95th Street [Miami Shores TR], 145 NE. 95th St., Miami Shores, 11/14/88, A, C, 88002093

Building at 253 Northeast 99th Street [Miami Shores TR], 253 NE. 99th St., Miami Shores, 11/14/88, A, C, 88002103

Building at 257 Northeast 91st Street [Miami Shores TR], 257 NE. 91st St., Miami Shores, 11/14/88, A, C, 88002086

Building at 262 Northeast 96th Street [Miami Shores TR], 262 NE. 96th St., Miami Shores, 11/14/88, A, C, 88002095

Building at 273 Northeast 98th Street [Miami Shores TR], 273 NE. 98th St., Miami Shores, 11/14/88, A, C, 88002101

Building at 276 Northeast 98th Street [Miami Shores TR], 276 NE. 98th St., Miami Shores, 11/14/88, A, C, 88002102

Building at 284 Northeast 96th Street [Miami Shores TR], 284 NE. 96th St., Miami Shores, 11/14/88, A, C, 88002096

Building at 287 Northeast 96th Street [Miami Shores TR], 287 NE. 96th St., Miami Shores, 11/14/88, A, C, 88002097

Building at 310 Northeast 99th Street [Miami Shores TR], 310 NE. 99th St., Miami Shores, 11/14/88, A, C, 88002105

Building at 353 Northest 91st Street [Miami Shores TR], 353 NE. 91st St., Miami Shores, 11/14/88, A, C, 88002087

Building at 357 Northeast 92nd Street [Miami Shores TR], 357 NE. 92nd St., Miami Shores, 11/14/88, A, C, 88002088

Building at 361 Northeast 97th Street [Miami Shores TR], 361 NE. 97th St., Miami Shores, 11/14/88, A, C, 88002100

Building at 384 Northeast 94th Street [Miami Shores TR], 384 NE. 94th St., Miami Shores, 11/14/88, A, C, 88002091

Building at 389 Northeast 99th Street [Miami Shores TR], 389 NE. 99th St., Miami Shores, 11/14/88, A, C, 88002106

Building at 431 Northeast 94th Street [Miami Shores TR], 431 NE. 94th St., Miami Shores, 11/14/88, A, C, 88002092

Building at 477 Northeast 92nd Street [Miami Shores TR], 477 NE. 92nd St., Miami Shores, 11/14/88, A, C, 88002089

Building at 540 Northeast 96th Street [Miami Shores TR], 540 NE. 96th St., Miami Shores, 11/14/88, A, C, 88002098

Building at 553 Northeast 101st Street [Miami Shores TR], 553 NE. 101st St., Miami Shores, 11/14/88, A, C, 88002108

Building at 561 Northeast 101st Street [Miami Shores TR], 561 NE. 101st St., Miami Shores, 11/14/88, A, C, 88002109

Building at 577 Northeast 96th Street [Miami Shores TR], 577 NE. 96th St., Miami Shores, 11/14/88, A, C, 88002099

Cape Florida Lighthouse, SE tip of Key Biscayne off U.S. 1, Cape Florida, 9/29/70, A, C, 70000180

Central Baptist Church [Downtown Miami MRA], 500 N.E. 1st Ave., Miami, 1/04/89, A, C, a, 88002988

City National Bank Building [Downtown Miami MRA], 121 S.E. 1st St., Miami, 1/04/89, A, C, 88002975

City of Miami Cemetery [Downtown Miami MRA], 1800 N.E. 2nd Ave., Miami, 1/04/89, A, B, C, d, 88002966

Clune Building [Country Club Estates TR], 45 Curtiss Pkwy., Miami Springs, 11/01/85, C, 85003467

Congress Building, 111 Northeast 2nd Ave., Miami, 3/14/85, A, C, 85000553

Coral Gables City Hall, 405 Biltmore Way, Coral Gables, 7/24/74, C, g, 74000616

Coral Gables Congregational Church, 3010 DeSoto Blvd., Coral Gables, 10/10/78, A, B, C, a, 78000937

Coral Gables Elementary School, 105 Minorca Ave., Coral Gables, 6/30/88, A, C, 88000750

Coral Gables House, 907 Coral Way, Coral Gables, 4/13/73, A, B, C, 73000573

Coral Gables Police and Fire Station, 2325 Salzedo St., Coral Gables, 11/06/84, C, g, 84000354

Coral Gables Woman's Club, 1001 E. Ponce de Leon Blvd., Coral Gables, 3/27/90, A, C, 90000423

Cravero House [Opa-Locka TR], 1011 Sharar Ave., Opa-Locka, 8/17/87, A, C, 87001315

Crouse House [Opa-Locka TR], 1156 Peri St., Opa-Locka, 8/17/87, A, C, 87001316

Curtiss, Lua, House I [Country Club Estates TR], 85 Deer Run, Miami Springs, 11/01/85, C, 85003465

Curtiss, Lua, House II [Country Club Estates TR], 150 Hunting Lodge, Miami Springs, 11/01/85, C, 85003466

Dade County Courthouse [Downtown Miami MRA], 73 W. Flagler St., Miami, 1/04/89, A, C, 88002983

Deering, Charles, Estate, S.W. One Hundred Sixty-seventh St. and Old Cutler Rd., Cutler, 3/11/86, A, C, D, 86000325

Dorsey, D. A., House [Downtown Miami MRA], 250 N.W. 9th St., Miami, 1/04/89, B, b, 88002966

Douglas Entrance, Jct. of Douglas Rd. and 8th St. SW., Coral Gables, 9/22/72, C, g, 72000305

DuPont, Alfred I., Building [Downtown Miami MRA], 169 E. Flagler St., Miami, 1/04/89, A, C, g, 88002984

El Jardin, 3747 Main Hwy., Coconut Grove, 8/30/74, C, 74000614

Entrance to Central Miami, W of Red Rd. between S.W. 34th and S.W. 35th Sts., Coral Gables, 1/19/89, A, B, C, 88003199

Etheredge House [Opa-Locka TR], 915 Sharar Ave., Opa-Locka, 8/17/87, A, C, 87001317

Fire Station No. 2 [Downtown Miami MRA], 1401 N. Miami Ave., Miami, 1/04/89, A, C, 88002971

Fire Station No. 4, 1000 S. Miami Ave., Miami, 3/08/84, A, C, 84000836

First Coconut Grove School, 3429 Devon Rd., Coconut Grove, 1/21/75, A, C, b, 75000547

Florida East Coast Railway Locomotive #153, 12400 SW 152nd St., Miami, 2/21/85, A, 85000303

Florida Pioneer Museum, 0.5 mi. S of Lucy St. on FL 27 (Krome Ave.), Florida City, 8/14/73, A, C, b, 73000574

Freedom Tower, 600 Biscayne Blvd, Miami, 9/10/79, A, C, 79000665

Gesu Church, 118 N.E. 2nd St., Miami, 7/18/74, A, C, a, 74000617

Grand Concourse Apartments, 421 Grand Concourse, Miami Shores, 12/02/85, C, 85003060

Greater Bethel AME Church [Downtown Miami MRA], 245 N.W. 8th St., Miami, 4/17/92, C, a, 88002987

Greenwald, I. and E., Steam Engine No. 1058, 3898 Shipping Ave., Miami, 3/12/87, A, C, b, 87002197

Dade County—Continued

Griffiths House [Opa-Locka TR], 826 Superior St., Opa-Locka, 8/17/87, A, C, 87001318

Hahn Building [Downtown Miami MRA], 140 N.E. 1st Ave., Miami, 1/04/89, C, 88002989

Haislip House [Opa-Locka TR], 1141 Jann Ave., Opa-Locka, 8/17/87, A, C, 87001319

Halissee Hall, 1700 N.W. 10th Ave., Miami, 10/01/74, A, B, C, 74000618

Helm Stores and Apartments [Opa-Locka TR], 1217 Sharazad Blvd., Opa-Locka, 8/17/87, A, C, 87001321

Helms House [Opa-Locka TR], 721 Sharar Ave., Opa-Locka, 8/17/87, A, C, 87001320

Hequembourg House [Country Club Estates TR], 851 Hunting Lodge, Miami Springs, 11/01/85, C, 85003468

Hialeah Park Race Track, E. 4th Ave., Hialeah, 3/05/79, A, C, g, 79000664

Higgins Duplex [Opa-Locka TR], 1210-1212 Sesame St., Opa-Locka, 8/17/87, A, C, 87001322

Homestead Public School-Neva King Cooper School, 520 N.W. First St., Homestead, 12/04/85, A, 85003112

Huntington Building [Downtown Miami MRA], 168 S.E. 1st St., Miami, 1/04/89, A, C, 88002976

Hurt, Harry, Building [Opa-Locka TR], 490 Ali-Baba Ave., Opa-Locka, 3/22/82, B, C, 82004795

Ingraham Building [Downtown Miami MRA], 25 S.E. 2nd Ave., Miami, 1/04/89, A, C, 88002958

J & S Building [Downtown Miami MRA], 221–233 N.W. 9th St., Miami, 1/04/89, A, C, 88002967

Jackson, Dr. James M., Office, 190 S.E. 12th Ter., Miami, 2/24/75, A, B, C, b, 75000550

Kampong, Address Restricted, Coconut Grove vicinity, 3/01/84, A, B, C, 84000837

Kentucky Home [Downtown Miami MRA], 1221 and 1227 N.E. 1st Ave., Miami, 1/04/89, C, 88002969

King Trunk Factory and Showroom [Opa-Locka TR], 951 Superior St., Opa-Locka, 8/17/87, A, C, 87001323

Long House [Opa-Locka TR], 613 Sharar Ave., Opa-Locka, 8/17/87, A, C, 87001324

Lyric Theater [Downtown Miami MRA], 819 N.W. 2nd Ave., Miami, 1/04/89, A, C, 88002965

Martina Apartments [Downtown Miami MRA], 1023 S. Miami Ave., Miami, 1/04/89, A, C, 88002981

Meyer—Kiser Building [Downtown Miami MRA], 139 N.E. 1st Building, Miami, 1/04/89, A, C, 88002991

Miami Beach Architectural District, Roughly bounded by Atlantic Ocean, Miami Beach Blvd., Alton Rd. and Collins Canal, Miami Beach, 5/14/79, A, C, g, 79000667

Miami City Hospital, Building No. 1, 1611 NW 12th Ave., Miami, 12/31/79, A, b, 79000664

Miami Edison Senior High School, 6101 N.W. Second Ave., Miami, 6/05/86, A, C, 86001212

Miami Women's Club, 1737 N. Bayshore Dr., Miami, 12/27/74, A, C, g, 74002257

Miami-Biltmore Hotel, 1210 Anastasia Ave., Coral Gables, 9/27/72, A, C, 72000306

Millard-McCarty House [Country Club Estates TR], 424 Hunting Lodge, Miami Springs, 4/22/86, C, 86000872

Mount Zion Baptist Church [Downtown Miami MRA], 301 N.W. 9th St., Miami, 12/29/88, A, B, C, a, 88003059

Munroe, Ralph M., House, 3485 Main Hwy., Miami, 4/11/73, B, C, 73000575

Offshore Reefs Archeological District, Address Restricted, Homestead vicinity, 8/24/84, D, NPS, 84000838

Old Spanish Monastery, 16711 W. Dixie Hwy., North Miami Beach, 11/09/72, C, a, b, e, 72000307

Old US Post Office and Courthouse [Downtown Miami MRA], 100–118 N.E. 1st Ave., Miami, 1/04/89, A, C, 88002962

Olympia Theater and Office Building, 174 E. Flagler St., Miami, 3/08/84, A, C, 84000839

Opa-Locka Company Administration Building [Opa-Locka TR], 777 Sharazad Blvd., Opa-Locka, 3/22/82, B, C, 82004796

Opa-Locka Railroad Station [Opa-Locka TR], 490 Ali Baba Ave., Opa-Locka, 6/25/87, B, C, 87000998

Opa-locka Bank [Opa-Locka TR (AD)], 940 Caliph St., Opa-locka, 5/19/83, A, C, a, 83001420

Osceola Apartment Hotel [Country Club Estates TR], 200 Azure Way, Miami Springs, 11/01/85, C, 85003469

Palm Cottage [Downtown Miami MRA], 60 S.E. 4th St., Miami, 1/04/89, A, B, b, 88002957

Pan American Seaplane Base and Terminal Building, 3500 Pan American Dr., Coconut Grove, 2/20/75, A, g, 75000548

Plymouth Congregational Church, 3429 Devon Rd., Coconut Grove, 7/23/74, A, C, a, 74000615

Priscilla Apartments [Downtown Miami MRA], 318–320 N.E. 19th St. and 1845 Biscayne Blvd., Miami, 1/04/89, C, 88002986

Ransom School "Pagoda", 3575 Main Hwy., Coconut Grove, 7/25/73, A, C, 73000572

Rock Gate, 28655 S. Federal Hwy., Homestead vicinity, 5/10/84, C, 84000840

Root Building [Opa-Locka TR], 111 Perviz Ave., Opa-Locka, 8/17/87, A, C, 87001326

S & S Sandwich Shop [Downtown Miami MRA], 1757 N.E. 2nd St., Miami, 1/04/89, C, 88002994

Security Building [Downtown Miami MRA], 117 N.E. 1st Ave., Miami, 1/04/89, A, C, 88002990

Shoreland Arcade [Downtown Miami MRA], 120 N.E. 1st St., Miami, 1/04/89, A, C, 88002992

Silver Palm Schoolhouse, Silver Palm Dr. and Newton Rd., Goulds vicinity, 7/02/87, A, 87000581

South River Drive Historic District, 428, 438 SW First St., 437 SW Second St., 104, 109, 118 SW South River Dr., Miami, 8/10/87, A, C, 87000671

Southside School [Downtown Miami MRA], 45 S.W. 13th St., Miami, 1/04/89, A, C, 88002980

St. John's Baptist Church [Downtown Miami MRA], 1328 N.W. 3rd Ave., Miami, 4/17/92, C, a, 88002970

Taber Duplex [Opa-Locka TR], 1214–1216 Sesame St., Opa-Locka, 8/17/87, A, C, 87001327

Tinsman House [Opa-Locka TR], 1110 Peri St., Opa-Locka, 8/17/87, A, C, 87001328

Tooker House [Opa-Locka TR], 811 Dunad Ave., Opa-Locka, 8/17/87, A, C, 87001329

Trinity Episcopal Cathedral, 464 NE 16th St., Miami, 10/10/80, C, a, 80000945

US Post Office and Courthouse, 300 NE 1st Ave., Miami, 10/14/83, C, 83003518

Venetian Causeway, NE. 15th St. and Dade Blvd., Miami, 7/13/89, A, 89000852

Venetian Pool, 2701 De Soto Blvd., Coral Gables, 8/20/81, A, B, C, 81000193

Vizcaya, 3251 S. Miami Ave., Miami, 9/29/70, A, B, C, 70000181

Vizcaya (Boundary Increase), Roughly bounded by S. Dixie Hwy., SW 32nd Rd., and S. Miami Ave., Miami, 11/15/78, A, C, 78003193

Walgreen Drug Store [Downtown Miami MRA], 200 E. Flagler St., Miami, 1/04/89, A, C, 88002982

Warner, J. W., House, 111 SW 5th Ave., Miami, 6/01/83, A, C, 83001419

Wheeler House [Opa-Locka TR], 1035 Dunad Ave., Opa-Locka, 8/17/87, A, C, 87001330

Women's Club of Coconut Grove, 2985 S. Bayshore Dr., Coconut Grove, 3/26/75, A, C, 75000549

De Soto County

Arcadia Historic District, Roughly bounded by Lee and Miles Aves., Imogene, Cypress, Pine, and Magnolia Sts., Arcadia, 5/10/84, A, C, 84000842

Dixie County

Garden Patch Archeological Site (8Di4), Address Restricted, Horseshoe Beach vicinity, 4/25/91, D, d, 91000454

Duval County

310 West Church Street Apartments, 420 N. Julia St., Jacksonville, 4/07/83, A, C, 83001421

Avondale Historic District, Roughly bounded by Roosevelt Blvd., Belvedere Ave., Seminole Rd., St. Johns River, and Talbot Ave., Jacksonville, 7/06/89, A, B, C, 89000494

Bethel Baptist Institutional Church, 1058 Hogan St., Jacksonville, 4/06/78, A, C, a, 78000938

Brewster Hospital, 915 W. Monroe St., Jacksonville, 5/13/76, A, 76000588

Broward, Napoleon Bonaparte, House, 9953 Hecksher Dr., Jacksonville, 12/27/72, B, C, 72000308

Buckman and Ulmer Building [Downtown Jacksonville MPS], 29–33 W. Monroe St., Jacksonville, 12/30/92, C, 92001694

Carling Hotel, 33 W. Adams St., Jacksonville, 2/28/91, A, C, 91000225

Duval County—Continued

Casa Marina Hotel, 12 Sixth Ave., N., Jacksonville Beach, 9/02/93, A, C, 93000893

Catherine Street Fire Station, 14 Catherine St., Jacksonville, 6/13/72, C, 72000309

Centennial Hall—Edward Waters College, 1658 Kings Rd., Jacksonville, 5/04/76, A, C, 76000589

Church of the Immaculate Conception [Downtown Jacksonville MPS], 121 E. Duval St., Jacksonville, 12/30/92, C, a, 92001695

Dyal-Upchurch Building, 4 E. Bay St., Jacksonville, 4/17/80, C, 80000947

El Modelo Block, 513 W. Bay St., Jacksonville, 10/16/80, A, C, 80000948

Epping Forest, Christopher Point, off San Jose Blvd., Jacksonville, 5/09/73, B, C, 73000576

Florida Baptist Building, 218 W. Church St., Jacksonville, 1/12/84, A, C, a, 84000844

Florida Theater, 128-134 E. Forsyth St., Jacksonville, 11/04/82, A, 82001034

Fort Caroline National Memorial, 10 mi. E of Jacksonville, Jacksonville vicinity, 10/15/66, A, b, e, NPS, 66000061

Grand Site, Address Restricted, Jacksonville vicinity, 6/20/75, D, 75000551

Groover—Stewart Drug Company Building [Downtown Jacksonville MPS], 25 N. Market St., Jacksonville, 12/30/92, A, C, 92001696

House at 3325 Via de la Reiva [San Jose Estates TR], 3325 Via de la Reiva, Jacksonville, 4/10/85, A, C, 85000739

House at 3335 Via de la Reina [San Jose Estates TR], 3335 Via de la Reina, Jacksonville, 4/10/85, A, C, 85000740

House at 3500 Via de la Reina [San Jose Estates TR], 3500 Via de la Reina, Jacksonville, 4/10/85, A, C, 85000741

House at 3609 Via de la Reina [San Jose Estates TR], 3609 Via de la Reina, Jacksonville, 4/10/85, A, C, 85000742

House at 3685 Via de la Reina [San Jose Estates TR], 3685 Via de la Reina, Jacksonville, 4/10/85, A, C, 85000743

House at 3703 Via de la Reina [San Jose Estates TR], 3703 Via de la Reina, Jacksonville, 4/10/85, A, C, 85000744

House at 3764 Ponce de Leon Avenue [San Jose Estates TR], 3764 Ponce de Leon Ave., Jacksonville, 4/10/85, A, C, 85000745

House at 7144 Madrid Avenue [San Jose Estates TR], 7144 Madrid Ave., Jacksonville, 4/10/85, A, C, 85000746

House at 7207 Ventura Avenue [San Jose Estates TR], 7207 Ventura Ave., Jacksonville, 4/10/85, A, C, 85000747

House at 7217 Ventura Avenue [San Jose Estates TR], 7217 Ventura Ave., Jacksonville, 4/10/85, A, C, 85000748

House at 7227 San Pedro [San Jose Estates TR], 7227 San Pedro Rd., Jacksonville, 4/10/85, A, C, 85000749

House at 7245 San Jose Boulevard [San Jose Estates TR], 7245 San Jose Blvd., Jacksonville, 4/10/85, A, C, 85000750

House at 7246 San Carlos [San Jose Estates TR], 7246 San Carlos, Jacksonville, 4/10/85, A, C, 85000751

House at 7246 St. Augustine Road [San Jose Estates TR], 7246 St. Augustine Rd., Jacksonville, 4/10/85, A, C, 85000752

House at 7249 San Pedro [San Jose Estates TR], 7249 San Pedro Rd., Jacksonville, 4/10/85, A, C, 85000753

House at 7288 San Jose Boulevard [San Jose Estates TR], 7288 San Jose Blvd., Jacksonville, 4/10/85, A, C, 85000754

House at 7306 St. Augustine Road [San Jose Estates TR], 7306 St. Augustine Rd., Jacksonville, 4/10/85, A, C, 85000755

House at 7317 San Jose Boulevard [San Jose Estates TR], 7317 San Jose Blvd., Jacksonville, 4/10/85, A, C, 85000756

House at 7330 Ventura Avenue [San Jose Estates TR], 7330 Ventura Ave., Jacksonville, 4/10/85, A, C, 85000757

House at 7356 San Jose Boulevard [San Jose Estates TR], 7356 San Jose Blvd., Jacksonville, 4/10/85, A, C, 85000758

House at 7400 San Jose Boulevard [San Jose Estates TR], 7400 San Jose Blvd., Jacksonville, 4/10/85, A, C, 85000759

Jacksonville Terminal Complex, 1000 W. Bay St., Jacksonville, 10/22/76, A, C, 76000590

Kingsley Plantation, Northern tip of Fort George Island at Fort George Inlet, Jacksonville vicinity, 9/29/70, A, B, C, D, 70000182

Klutho, Henry John, House, 28–30 W. 9th St., Jacksonville, 12/19/78, B, C, b, 78000939

Lane-Towers House, 3730 Richmond St., Jacksonville, 11/10/82, C, 82001035

Little Theatre, 2032 San Marco Blvd., Jacksonville, 7/12/91, A, C, 91000895

Masonic Temple, 410 Broad St., Jacksonville, 9/22/80, A, C, 80000949

Mission of San Juan del Puerto Archeological Site, Address Restricted, Jacksonville vicinity, 3/25/86, A, B, D, a, 86000595

Morocco Temple, 219 Newnan St, Jacksonville, 11/29/79, A, C, 79000668

Mount Zion AME Church [Downtown Jacksonville MPS], 201 E. Beaver St., Jacksonville, 12/30/92, A, C, a, 92001697

Old Jacksonville Free Public Library, 101 E. Adams St., Jacksonville, 1/22/87, A, C, 86003679

Old St. Luke's Hospital, 314 N. Palmetto St., Jacksonville, 7/24/72, A, C, 72000310

Plaza Hotel [Downtown Jacksonville MPS], 353 E. Forsyth St., Jacksonville, 12/30/92, A, C, 92001698

Porter, Thomas V., House, 510 Julia St., Jacksonville, 5/13/76, C, a, b, 76000592

Red Bank Plantation, 1230 Greenridge Rd., Jacksonville, 10/18/72, C, 72000311

Riverside Baptist Church, 2650 Park St., Jacksonville, 9/22/72, A, C, a, 72000312

Riverside Historic District, Roughly bounded by Seaboard Coastline RR, Riverside and Memorial Pks., St. Johns River and Seminole, Jacksonville, 3/22/85, A, C, 85000689

Sammis, John S., House, 207 Noble Circle West, Jacksonville, 7/10/79, B, 79000669

San Jose Administration Building [San Jose Estates TR], 7423 San Jose Blvd., Jacksonville, 4/10/85, A, C, a, 85000760

San Jose Country Club [San Jose Estates TR], 7529 San Jose Blvd., Jacksonville, 4/10/85, A, C, 85000761

San Jose Estates Gatehouse [San Jose Estates TR], 1873 Christopher Point Rd., North, Jacksonville, 12/20/88, A, C, 88002808

San Jose Hotel [San Jose Estates TR], 7400 San Jose Boulevard, Jacksonville, 4/10/85, A, C, 85000762

South Atlantic Investment Corporation Building [Downtown Jacksonville MPS], 35–39 W. Monroe St., Jacksonville, 12/30/92, C, 92001699

Springfield Historic District, Roughly bounded by Twelfth, Clark, and First Sts., Hogans Creek and Boulevard, Jacksonville, 1/22/87, A, B, C, 86003640

St. Andrew's Episcopal Church, 317 Florida Ave., Jacksonville, 5/04/76, C, a, 76000593

St. James Building, 117 W. Duval St., Jacksonville, 5/03/76, C, 76000594

St. John's Lighthouse, U.S. Naval Station, Mayport, 6/03/76, A, C, 76002237

Stanton, Edmin M., School, 521 W. Ashley St., Jacksonville, 9/29/83, A, B, C, 83001446

Title & Trust Company of Florida Building, 200 E. Forsyth St., Jacksonville, 2/23/90, A, C, 90000312

Village Store, 4216, 4212, 4208 Oxford Ave., 2906 and 2902 Corinthian Ave., Jacksonville, 9/29/88, A, C, 88001700

Woman's Club of Jacksonville, 861 Riverside Ave., Jacksonville, 11/03/92, A, C, g, 92001505

Yellow Bluff Fort, 1 mi. S of FL 105 on New Berlin Rd., Jacksonville vicinity, 9/29/70, A, 70000183

Young Men's Hebrew Association, 712 W. Duval St., Jacksonville, 10/29/92, A, a, 92001486

Escambia County

Alger—Sullivan Lumber Company Residential Historic District, Roughly bounded by Pinewood Ave., Front St., Jefferson Ave., Church St., and Mayo St., Century, 9/28/89, A, 89001586

American National Bank Building, 226 S. Palafox St., Pensacola, 11/17/78, A, C, 78000940

Crystal Ice Company Building, 2024 N. Davis St., Pensacola, 9/29/83, A, C, g, 83001445

Dorr, Clara Barkley, House, 311 S. Adams St., Pensacola, 7/24/74, C, 74000619

Edmunds, John, Apartment House, 2007 E. Gadsden St., Pensacola, 9/29/83, A, C, 83001444

Fort Barrancas Historical District, U.S. Naval Air Station, Pensacola, 10/15/66, A, C, NHL, NPS, 66000263

Fort George Site, La Rua at Palafox Sts., Pensacola, 7/08/74, A, 74000620

Fort Pickens, FL 399, W of Pensacola Beach, Pensacola Beach vicinity, 5/31/72, A, NPS, 72000096

Escambia County—Continued

Jones, Charles William, House, 302 N. Barcelona St., Pensacola, 12/20/77, B, 77000403

King—Hooton House, 512–514 N. Seventh Ave., Pensacola, 8/23/91, A, C, 91001090

L & N Marine Terminal Building, Commendencia Street Wharf, Pensacola, 8/14/72, A, C, b, 72000315

Lavalle House, 203 E. Church St., Pensacola, 3/11/71, C, b, 71000237

Louisville and Nashville Passenger Station and Express Building, 239 N. Alcaniz St., Pensacola, 6/11/79, A, C, 79000670

North Hill Preservation District, Roughly bounded by Blount, Palafox, Wright, Belmont, Reus, and DeVilliers Sts., Pensacola, 5/09/83, A, C, D, a, 83001422

Old Christ Church, 405 S. Adams St., Pensacola, 5/03/74, A, C, a, 74000621

Pensacola Historic District, Address Unknown, Pensacola, 9/29/70, A, C, 70000184

Pensacola Hospital, N. 12th Ave., Pensacola, 2/16/82, A, C, 82002373

Pensacola Lighthouse and Keeper's Quarters, Pensacola Naval Air Station, Pensacola, 7/15/74, A, 74000622

Pensacola Naval Air Station Historic District, Pensacola Naval Air Station, Pensacola, 12/08/76, A, NHL, 76000595

Perdido Key Historic District, S of Warrington, Warrington vicinity, 3/10/80, A, C, g, NPS, 80000404

Plaza Ferdinand VII, Palafox St. between Government and Zaragossa Sts., Pensacola, 10/15/66, A, f, NHL, 66000264

Saenger Theatre, 118 S. Palafox St., Pensacola, 7/19/76, A, C, 76000596

St. Joseph's Church Buildings, 140 W. Government St., Pensacola, 7/10/79, A, C, a, 79000671

St. Michael's Creole Benevolent Association Hall, 416 E. Government St., Pensacola, 5/03/74, A, C, 74000623

Thiesen Building, 40 S. Palafox St., Pensacola, 12/13/79, A, C, 79000672

Flagler County

Bulow Plantation Ruins, Address Restricted, Bunnell vicinity, 9/29/70, A, D, 70000185

Bunnell State Bank Building, Old, 101–107 N. Bay St., Bunnell, 6/25/92, A, C, 92000824

Marine Studios, CT A1A, Box 122, Marineland vicinity, 4/14/86, A, C, g, 86000831

Franklin County

Apalachicola Historic District, Roughly bounded by Apalachicola River, Apalachicola Bay, 17th and Jefferson Sts., Apalachicola, 11/21/80, A, C, 80000951

Cape St. George Light, S point of Little St. George Island, Little St. George Island, 9/10/74, C, 74000625

Crooked River Lighthouse, SW of Carrabelle off U.S. 319, Carrabelle vicinity, 12/01/78, A, 78000941

Fort Gadsden Historic Memorial, 6 mi. SW of Sumatra, Sumatra vicinity, 2/23/72, A, NHL, 72000318

GOVERNOR STONE (schooner), Apalachicola Harbor, Apalachicola, 12/04/91, A, C, NHL, 91002063

Pierce Site, Address Restricted, Apalachicola vicinity, 1/11/74, D, 74000624

Porter's Bar Site, Address Restricted, Eastpoint vicinity, 1/23/75, D, 75000553

Raney, David G., House, SW corner of Market St. and Ave. F, Apalachicola, 9/22/72, C, 72000316

Trinity Episcopal Church, Ave. D and 6th St. (Gorrie Sq.), Apalachicola, 6/30/72, A, C, a, 72000317

Yent Mound, Address Restricted, St. Teresa vicinity, 5/24/73, D, 73000577

Gadsden County

Davis, Joshua, House, 2.5 mi. NW of Mt. Pleasant on U.S. 90, Mt. Pleasant vicinity, 5/21/75, A, C, 75000554

Gregory, Willoughby, House, Hwy. 274 and Krausland Rd., Quincy, 12/16/83, A, C, 83003520

Love, E. C., House, 219 N. Jackson St., Quincy, 12/30/74, C, 74000626

McFarlin, John Lee, House, 305 E. King St., Quincy, 12/27/74, B, C, 74000627

Old Philadelphia Presbyterian Church, 5 mi. N of Quincy off FL 65, Quincy vicinity, 2/24/75, A, C, a, 75000557

Quincy Historic District, Roughly bounded by Sharon, Clark, Stewart, and Corry Sts., Quincy, 11/09/78, A, C, 78000942

Quincy Library, 303 N. Adams St., Quincy, 9/09/74, A, C, 74000628

Quincy Woman's Club, 300 N. Calhoun St., Quincy, 3/10/75, A, C, 75000555

Shelfer, E. B., House, 205 N. Madison St., Quincy, 4/04/75, C, 75000556

Stockton-Curry House, 121 N. Duval St., Quincy, 12/31/74, C, 74000629

U.S. Arsenal—Officers Quarters, Florida State Hospital, U.S. 90, Chattahoochee, 7/02/73, A, C, 73000578

White, Judge P. W., House, 212 N. Madison St., Quincy, 12/05/72, A, C, a, 72000319

Hamilton County

Old Hamilton County Jail, 501 NE 1st Ave., Jasper, 7/07/83, A, C, 83001423

United Methodist Church, Central Ave. and 5th St., Jasper, 9/29/78, C, a, 78000943

Hardee County

Carlton, Albert, Estate, 302 E. Bay St., Wauchula, 10/03/91, A, 91000893

Payne's Creek Massacre—Fort Chokonikla Site, Address Restricted, Bowling Green vicinity, 11/21/78, A, D, 78000944

Hendry County

Clewiston Inn, US 27 W of jct. with FL 832, Clewiston, 2/21/91, A, C, 91000106

Hendry County Courthouse, Old, Jct. of Bridge St. and Hickpochee Ave., LaBelle, 11/08/90, A, C, 90001744

Highlands County

Avon Park Historic District, Main St. from S. Delaney Ave. to US 27, Avon Park, 3/22/90, A, C, 90000486

Central Station [Sebring MPS], 301 N. Mango St., Sebring, 8/14/89, C, 89001009

Haines, Elizabeth, House [Sebring MPS], 605 Summit Dr., Sebring, 10/14/93, C, 93001119

Hainz, Edward, House [Sebring MPS], 155 W. Center Ave., Sebring, 8/14/89, C, 89001010

Harder Hall [Sebring MPS], 3300 Golfview Dr., Sebring, 6/20/90, C, 90000341

Highlands County Courthouse [Sebring MPS], 430 S. Commerce Ave., Sebring, 8/14/89, A, C, 89001013

Lake Placid A. C. L. Railroad Depot, Old, 19 Park Ave. W., Lake Placid, 1/04/93, A, 92001733

Seaboard Air Line Depot, Old—Sebring [Sebring MPS], E. Center Ave., Sebring, 3/16/90, A, C, 90000425

Sebring Downtown Historic District [Sebring MPS], Circle Dr. and Ridgewood Dr. from Mango St. to Magnolia Ave., Sebring, 3/16/90, A, C, 90000424

Sebring, H. Orvel, House [Sebring MPS], 483 S. Lake View Dr., Sebring, 8/14/89, C, 89001012

Vinson, Paul L., House [Sebring MPS], 309 N. Lake View Dr., Sebring, 8/14/89, C, 89001011

Hillsborough County

Anderson-Frank House, 341 Plant Ave., Tampa, 4/22/82, C, 82002375

Bay Isle Commercial Building [Mediterranean Revival Style Buildings of Davis Islands MPS], 238 E. Davis Blvd., Tampa, 8/03/89, C, 89000971

Centro Asturiano, 1913 Nebraska Ave., Tampa, 7/24/74, A, C, 74000631

Circulo Cubano de Tampa, 10th Ave. and 14th St., Tampa, 11/15/72, C, 72000320

Cockroach Key, Address Restricted, Ruskin vicinity, 12/04/73, D, 73000579

Curtis, William E., House, 808 E. Curtis St., Tampa, 8/27/87, B, C, 87001424

Hillsborough County—Continued

Downtown Plant City Commercial District, Bounded by Baker and Wheeler Sts. and the Seaboard Coast Line RR tracks, Plant City, 6/08/93, A, C, 93000478

Egmont Key, W of Tampa at entrance to Tampa Bay, Tampa vicinity, 12/11/78, A, 78000946

El Centro Espanol de Tampa, 1526–1536 E. Seventh Ave., Tampa, 6/03/88, A, NHL, 88001823

El Centro Espanol of West Tampa, 2306 N. Howard St., Tampa, 7/30/74, A, B, C, 74000632

El Pasaje, 14th St. and Palm Ave., Tampa, 11/15/72, A, C, 72000321

Episcopal House of Prayer, 2708 Central Ave., Tampa, 2/21/91, A, C, a, 91000105

Federal Building, U.S. Courthouse, Downtown Postal Station, 601 Florida Ave., Tampa, 6/07/74, A, C, 74000633

Fort Foster, 9 mi. S of Zephyrhills, Zephyrhills vicinity, 6/13/72, A, D, 72000324

Hillsboro State Bank Building, 121 N. Collins St., Plant City, 8/01/84, A, C, 84000868

House at 100 West Davis Boulevard [Mediterranean Revival Style Buildings of Davis Islands MPS], 100 W. Davis Blvd., Tampa, 8/03/89, C, 89000972

House at 116 West Davis Boulevard [Mediterranean Revival Style Buildings of Davis Islands MPS], 116 W. Davis Blvd., Tampa, 8/03/89, C, 89000973

House at 124 Baltic Circle [Mediterranean Revival Style Buildings of Davis Islands MPS], 124 Baltic Cir., Tampa, 8/03/89, C, 89000957

House at 125 Baltic Circle [Mediterranean Revival Style Buildings of Davis Islands MPS], 125 Baltic Cir., Tampa, 8/03/89, C, 89000958

House at 131 West Davis Boulevard [Mediterranean Revival Style Buildings of Davis Islands MPS], 131 W. Davis Blvd., Tampa, 1/08/90, C, 89002161

House at 132 Baltic Circle [Mediterranean Revival Style Buildings of Davis Islands MPS], 132 Baltic Cir., Tampa, 8/03/89, C, 89000959

House at 161 Bosporous Avenue [Mediterranean Revival Style Buildings of Davis Islands MPS], 161 Bosporous Ave., Tampa, 8/03/89, C, 89000963

House at 190 Bosporous Avenue [Mediterranean Revival Style Buildings of Davis Islands MPS], 190 Bosporous Ave., Tampa, 8/03/89, C, 89000964

House at 200 Corsica Avenue [Mediterranean Revival Style Buildings of Davis Islands MPS], 200 Corsica Ave., Tampa, 8/03/89, C, 89000967

House at 202 Blanca Avenue [Mediterranean Revival Style Buildings of Davis Islands MPS], 202 Blanca Ave., Tampa, 8/03/89, C, 89000960

House at 220 Blanca Avenue [Mediterranean Revival Style Buildings of Davis Islands MPS], 220 Blanca Ave., Tampa, 8/03/89, C, 89000961

House at 301 Caspian Street [Mediterranean Revival Style Buildings of Davis Islands MPS], 301 Caspian St., Tampa, 8/03/89, C, 89000965

House at 36 Aegean Avenue [Mediterranean Revival Style Buildings of Davis Islands MPS], 36 Aegean Ave., Tampa, 11/13/89, C, 89001964

House at 36 Columbia Drive [Mediterranean Revival Style Buildings of Davis Islands MPS], 36 Columbia Dr., Tampa, 8/03/89, C, 89000966

House at 418 Blanca Avenue [Mediterranean Revival Style Buildings of Davis Islands MPS], 418 Blanca Ave., Tampa, 8/03/89, C, 89000962

House at 53 Aegean Avenue [Mediterranean Revival Style Buildings of Davis Islands MPS], 53 Aegean Ave., Tampa, 8/03/89, C, 89000955

House at 59 Aegean Avenue [Mediterranean Revival Style Buildings of Davis Islands MPS], 59 Aegean Ave., Tampa, 8/03/89, C, 89000956

House at 84 Adalia Avenue [Mediterranean Revival Style Buildings of Davis Islands MPS], 84 Adalia Ave., Tampa, 8/03/89, C, 89000953

House at 97 Adriatic Avenue [Mediterranean Revival Style Buildings of Davis Islands MPS], 97 Adriatic Ave., Tampa, 8/03/89, C, 89000954

Hutchinson House, 304 Plant Ave., Tampa, 11/01/77, C, 77000404

Hyde Park Historic Districts, Roughly bounded by Hillsborough River and Bay, Howard Ave., and Kennedy Blvd., Tampa, 3/04/85, A, C, 85000454

Johnson-Wolff House, 6823 S. DeSoto St., Tampa, 7/24/74, A, C, 74000634

Kress, S.H., and Co. Building, 811 N. Franklin St., Tampa, 4/07/83, A, C, 83001424

LeClaire Apartments, 3013–3015 San Carlos, Tampa, 11/16/88, C, 88001697

Leiman House, 716 S. Newport St., Tampa, 9/09/74, B, C, 74000635

Masonic Temple No. 25, 508 E. Kennedy Blvd., Tampa, 9/11/86, A, C, 86002415

Miller, George McA., House, 508 Tamiami Trail, Ruskin, 7/23/74, A, C, 74000630

Moseley Homestead, 1820 W. Brandon Blvd., Brandon, 1/31/85, B, C, 85000159

North Plant City Residential District, Bounded by Herring, Wheeler, Tever and Palmer Sts., Plant City, 5/27/93, C, 93000436

Old School House, Lafayette St., University of Tampa campus, Tampa, 12/04/74, A, C, b, 74000636

Palace of Florence Apartments [Mediterranean Revival Style Buildings of Davis Islands MPS], 45 E. Davis Blvd., Tampa, 8/03/89, C, 89000969

Palmerin Hotel [Mediterranean Revival Style Buildings of Davis Islands MPS], 115 E. Davis Blvd., Tampa, 8/03/89, C, 89000970

Plant City High School, N. Collins St., Plant City, 2/04/81, A, 81000194

Plant City Union Depot, E. North Drane St., Plant City, 4/14/75, A, 75000558

Seminole Heights Residential District, Roughly bounded by Osborne, Florida, Hanna, and Cherokee Aves., Tampa, 8/05/93, A, C, 93000751

Spanish Apartments [Mediterranean Revival Style Buildings of Davis Islands MPS], 16 E. Davis Blvd., Tampa, 8/03/89, C, 89000968

Stovall House, 4621 Bayshore Blvd., Tampa, 9/04/74, B, C, 74000637

Taliaferro, T. C., House, 305 S. Hyde Park, Tampa, 10/01/74, C, 74000638

Tampa Bay Hotel, 401 W. Kennedy Blvd., Tampa, 12/05/72, A, B, C, NHL, 72000322

Tampa City Hall, 315 John F. Kennedy Blvd., E., Tampa, 10/01/74, C, 74000639

Tampa Free Public Library, Old, 102 E. Seventh Ave., Tampa, 5/16/91, A, C, 91000618

Tampa Theater and Office Building, 711 Franklin St., Tampa, 1/03/78, A, C, 78000945

Tampania House, 4611 N. A St., Tampa, 9/12/85, C, 85002178

Union Railroad Station, 601 N. Nebraska St., Tampa, 6/05/74, A, C, 74000640

Upper Tampa Bay Archeological District, Address Restricted, Tampa vicinity, 12/10/85, D, 85003330

West Tampa Historic District, Roughly bounded by Cypress and Ivy Sts., Fremont and Habana Aves., Tampa, 10/18/83, A, C, 83003539

Ybor City Historic District, Roughly bounded by 6th Ave., 13th St., 10th Ave. and 22nd St., E. Broadway between 13th and 22nd Sts., Tampa, 8/28/74, A, B, C, NHL, 74000641

Ybor Factory Building, 7th Ave. between 13th and 14th Sts., Tampa, 11/15/72, A, B, 72000323

Indian River County

Lawson, Bamma Vickers, House, 1133 US 1, Sebastian, 7/26/90, A, 90001116

Old Palmetto Hotel, 1889 Old Dixie Hwy., Vero Beach, 11/13/91, A, 91001650

Pelican Island National Wildlife Refuge, E of Sebastian in the Indian River, Sebastian vicinity, 10/15/66, A, NHL, 66000265

Spanish Fleet Survivors and Salvors Camp Site, Address Restricted, Sebastian vicinity, 8/12/70, A, D, 70000186

Vero Beach Community Building, Old, 2146 14th Ave., Vero Beach, 1/19/93, A, C, g, 92001746

Vero Railroad Station, 2336 Fourteenth St., Vero Beach, 1/06/87, A, C, b, 86003560

Vero Theatre, 2036 14th Ave., Vero Beach, 4/28/92, A, C, 92000421

Jackson County

Ely-Criglar House, 242 W. Lafayette St., Marianna, 12/27/72, C, 72000326

Erwin House, Fort Rd. E of FL 71, Greenwood, 6/05/74, C, 74000642

Great Oaks, S of jct. of FL 69 and 71, Greenwood, 12/05/72, C, 72000325

Pender's Store, Near jct. of FL 71 and FL 69, Greenwood, 5/03/74, A, 74000643

Russ, Joseph W., Jr., House, 310 W. Lafayette St., Marianna, 7/18/83, A, C, 83001425

Waddells Mill Pond Site, Address Restricted, Marianna vicinity, 12/15/72, D, 72000327

West, Theophilus, House, 403 Putnam St., Marianna, 12/26/72, C, 72000328

Jefferson County

Denham-Lacy House, 555 Palmer Mill Rd., Monticello, 5/06/82, C, 82002376

Dennis—Coxetter House, Jct. of SR 158 and 59, Lloyd, 10/20/88, A, 88002025

Lloyd Historic District, Roughly, Main St. N of Bond St. and Bond E of Main, Lloyd, 9/05/91, A, C, D, 91001374

Lloyd Railroad Depot, Near jct. of FL 59 and Lester Lawrence Rd., Lloyd, 12/02/74, A, C, 74000645

Lloyd-Bond House, Bond St., Lloyd, 11/01/84, A, B, 84000198

Lyndhurst Plantation, 15 mi. NE of Monticello off Ashville Rd., Monticello vicinity, 4/02/73, A, C, 73000582

May, Asa, House, N of jct. off U.S. 19 and 27, Capps, 12/15/72, C, 72000329

Monticello Historic District, Irregular pattern along Madison, Jefferson, Dogwood, and Washington Sts., Monticello, 8/19/77, A, C, 77000405

Palmer House, Palmer Mill Rd. and S. Jefferson St., Monticello, 11/21/78, C, 78000947

Palmer—Perkins House (Boundary Increase), Walnut St., Monticello, 3/18/86, A, C, d, 86000466

Palmer-Perkins House, 625 W. Palmer Mill Rd., Monticello, 7/10/79, C, 79000674

Perkins Opera House, Washington St. and Courthouse Sq., Monticello, 9/14/72, A, 72000330

San Joseph de Ocuya Site, Address Restricted, Lloyd vicinity, 5/07/73, A, D, 73000580

San Juan De Aspalaga Site, Address Restricted, Tallahassee vicinity, 5/07/73, A, C, D, 73000581

San Miguel de Asile Mission Site, Address Restricted, Lamont vicinity, 12/17/74, D, d, 74000644

Turnbull-Ritter House, NW of Lamont off U.S. 19, Lamont vicinity, 7/18/79, A, C, 79000673

Wirick-Simmons House, Jefferson and Pearl Sts., Monticello, 6/30/72, C, 72000331

Lake County

Bowers Bluff Middens Archeological District, Address Restricted, Astor vicinity, 2/01/80, D, 80000952

Clermont Woman's Club, 655 Broome St., Clermont, 1/07/93, A, 92001747

Clifford House, 536 N. Bay St., Eustis, 4/04/75, B, C, 75000559

Donnelly House, Donnelly Ave., Mount Dora, 4/04/75, C, 75000560

Holy Trinity Episcopal Church, Spring Lake Rd., Fruitland Park, 12/27/74, A, C, a, 74000646

Howey House, Citrus St., Howey in the Hills, 1/27/83, B, C, 83001426

Kimball Island Midden Archeological Site, Address Restricted, Astor vicinity, 12/11/79, D, 79000675

Lakeside Inn, 100 N. Alexander St., Mount Dora, 3/19/87, A, C, 87000481

Mote—Morris House, 1021 N. Main St., Leesburg, 12/27/74, C, 74000647

Mount Dora A. C. L. Railroad Station, Old, 341 Alexander St., Mount Dora, 3/05/92, A, 92000099

Pendleton, William Kimbrough, House, 1208 Chesterfield Rd., Eustis, 1/13/83, A, C, 83001427

Woman's Club of Eustis, 227 N. Center St., Eustis, 8/05/91, A, C, 91001006

Lee County

Alderman House, 2572 First St., Fort Myers, 12/01/88, C, 88002690

Boca Grande Lighthouse, S of Boca Grande on Gasparilla Island, Boca Grande vicinity, 2/28/80, A, 80000953

Buckingham School, Buckingham and Cemetery Rds., Buckingham, 2/17/89, A, C, 89000011

Charlotte Harbor and Northern Railway Depot, Park and 4th Sts., Boca Grande, 12/13/79, A, 79000676

Demere Key, Address Restricted, Pine Island vicinity, 6/13/72, D, 72000332

Dunbar, Paul Lawrence, School, 1857 High St., Fort Myers, 2/24/92, A, 92000025

Edison, Thomas, Winter Estate, 2350 McGregor Blvd., Fort Myers, 8/12/91, A, B, C, 91001044

Fish Cabin at White Rock Shoals [Fish Cabins of Charlotte Harbor MPS], W. of Pine Island, Pine Island Sound, St. James City vicinity, 4/11/91, A, 91000398

Ford, Henry, Estate, 2400 McGregor Blvd., Fort Myers, 9/08/88, B, C, 88001822

Fort Myers Downtown Commercial District, Roughly bounded by Bay and Lee Sts., Anderson Ave. and Monroe St., Fort Myers, 1/26/90, A, C, 89002325

Hendrickson Fish Cabin at Captiva Rocks [Fish Cabins of Charlotte Harbor MPS], W of Little Wood Key, Pine Island Sound, Bokeelia vicinity, 4/11/91, A, 91000402

Ice House at Captiva Rocks [Fish Cabins of Charlotte Harbor MPS], SW of Little Wood Key, Pine Island Sound, Bokeelia vicinity, 4/11/91, A, 91000407

Ice House at Point Blanco [Fish Cabins of Charlotte Harbor MPS], SE of Point Blanco Island, Pine Island Sound, Bokeelia vicinity, 4/11/91, A, 91000408

Jewett-Thompson House, 1141 Wales Dr., Fort Meyers, 9/29/88, C, 88001708

Josslyn Island Site, Address Restricted, Pineland vicinity, 12/14/78, D, 78000948

Journey's End, Beachfront at 18th St., Boca Grande, 3/14/85, A, b, 85000554

Koreshan Unity Settlement Historic District, U.S. 41 at Estero River, Estero, 5/04/76, A, B, C, 76000599

Larsen Fish Cabin at Captiva Rocks [Fish Cabins of Charlotte Harbor MPS], W of Little Wood Key, Pine Island Sound, Bokeelia vicinity, 4/11/91, A, 91000404

Lee County Courthouse, 2120 Main St., Fort Myers, 3/16/89, A, C, 89000196

Leneer Fish Cabin at Captiva Rocks [Fish Cabins of Charlotte Harbor MPS], W of Little Wood Key, Pine Island Sound, Bokeelia vicinity, 4/11/91, A, 91000403

Mound Key, Address Restricted, Fort Myers Beach vicinity, 8/12/70, D, 70000187

Murphy—Burroughs House, 2505 1st St., Fort Myers, 8/01/84, C, 84000898

Norton Fish Cabin at Captiva Rocks [Fish Cabins of Charlotte Harbor MPS], W of Little Wood Key, Pine Island Sound, Bokeelia vicinity, 4/11/91, A, 91000405

Pineland Site, Address Restricted, Pineland vicinity, 11/27/73, D, 73000583

Punta Gorda Fish Company Ice House, N shore of entrance to Safety Harbor, North Captiva Island, 4/20/89, A, C, 89000320

Sanibel Lighthouse and Keeper's Quarters, Point Ybel on Sanibel Island, Sanibel, 10/01/74, A, 74000648

Whidden Fish Cabin at Captiva Rocks [Fish Cabins of Charlotte Harbor MPS], W of Little Wood Key, Pine Island Sound, Bokeelia vicinity, 4/11/91, A, 91000406

Leon County

Bellevue, SW of Tallahassee off FL 371, Tallahassee vicinity, 3/11/71, A, C, b, 71000238

Bradley's Country Store Complex, Moccasin Gap Rd., Tallahassee, 4/12/84, A, B, C, 84000902

Brevard, Caroline, Grammar School, 727 S. Calhoun St., Tallahassee, 12/17/87, A, C, 87002151

Brokaw-McDougall House, 329 N. Meridian Rd., Tallahassee, 7/24/72, C, 72000333

Calhoun Street Historic District, U.S. 90 and FL 61, Tallahassee vicinity, 10/24/79, A, C, 79000677

Carnegie Library, Florida Agricultural and Mechanical University campus, Tallahassee, 11/17/78, A, B, C, 78000949

Cascades Park, Bounded roughly by Apalachee Pkwy., Bloxham, Suwanee, Munroe, and Meridian Sts., and state property line, Tallahassee, 5/12/71, A, 71000239

Coles, Flavius C., Farmhouse, 411 Oakland Ave., Tallahassee, 1/07/92, A, C, 91001911

Columns, The, 100 N. Duval St., Tallahassee, 5/21/75, A, C, b, 75000561

Covington House, 328 Cortez St., Tallahassee, 9/07/89, A, B, C, 89001386

Escambe, Address Restricted, Tallahassee vicinity, 5/14/71, A, D, 71000240

Exchange Bank Building, 201 S. Monroe, Tallahassee, 11/29/84, B, C, 84000262

First Presbyterian Church, 102 N. Adams St., Tallahassee, 9/09/74, A, C, a, 74000649

Florida State Capitol, S. Monroe St., Tallahassee, 5/07/73, A, C, 73000584

Gallie's Hall and Buildings, Off FL 61, Tallahassee, 10/20/80, C, 80000954

Goodwood, 1500 Miccosukee Rd., Tallahassee, 6/30/72, C, 72000334

Leon County—Continued

Grove, The, Adams St. and 1st Ave., Tallahassee, 6/13/72, A, B, C, 72000335

Lake Jackson Mounds, Address Restricted, Tallahassee vicinity, 5/06/71, D, NHL, 71000241

Leon High School, 550 E. Tennessee St., Tallahassee, 9/21/93, A, C, 93000982

Lewis House, N of Tallahassee at 3117 Okeeheepkee Rd., Tallahassee vicintiy, 2/14/79, C, g, 79000679

Los Robles Gate, Thomasville and Meridian Rds., Tallahassee, 9/21/89, A, C, 89001480

Magnolia Heights Historic District, 701-1005 E. Park Ave., and Cadiz St., Tallahassee, 6/29/84, C, 84000906

Martin, Gov. John W., House, 1001 Governor's Dr., Tallahassee, 1/06/86, B, C, 86000024

Natural Bridge Battlefield, E of Woodville off U.S. 319, Woodville vicinity, 9/29/70, A, 70000188

Old City Waterworks, E. Gaines and S. Gadsden Sts., Tallahassee, 1/31/79, C, 79000680

Park Avenue Historic District, Park Ave. and Call St., Tallahassee, 10/24/79, A, C, 79000681

Pisgah United Methodist Church, N of Tallahassee, SE of FL 151, Tallahassee vicinity, 5/03/74, A, C, a, 74000650

Riley, John Gilmore, House, 419 E. Jefferson St., Tallahassee, 8/01/78, A, B, 78000950

San Luis de Apalache, 2 mi. W of Tallahassee, Tallahassee vicinity, 10/15/66, D, NHL, 66000266

San Pedro y San Pablo de Patale, 6 mi. E of Tallahassee, Tallahassee vicinity, 6/26/72, C, D, 72000336

St. John's Episcopal Church, 211 N. Monroe St., Tallahassee, 8/10/78, A, C, a, 78000951

Tall Timbers Plantation, Co. Rd. 12, 3 mi. W of US 319, Tallahassee vicinity, 4/07/89, A, B, C, 89000240

Tallahassee Historic District Zones I And II, Calhoun St. between Georgia and Tennessee Sts. and E. Park Ave. between Gadsden and Calhoun Sts., Tallahassee, 10/26/72, A, C, 72000337

Union Bank, Apalachee Pkwy. and Calhoun St., Tallahassee, 2/24/71, A, C, b, 71000242

Walker, David S., Library, 209 E. Park Ave., Tallahassee, 6/22/76, A, B, C, 76000600

Woman's Club of Tallahassee, 1513 Cristobal Dr., Tallahassee, 11/18/87, A, C, 87002046

Levy County

Cedar Keys Historic and Archaeological District, Address Restricted, Cedar Key vicinity, 10/03/89, A, C, D, a, d, 88001449

Island Hotel, 224 2nd St., Cedar Key, 11/23/84, A, B, C, 84000252

Liberty County

Hare, Otis, Archeological Site (8LI172), Address Restricted, Blountstown vicinity, 7/26/89, D, 89000862

Torreya State Park, 13 mi. NE of Bristol, Bristol vicinity, 8/14/72, A, C, b, 72000338

Yon Mound and Village Site, Address Restricted, Bristol vicinity, 12/15/78, D, 78000952

Madison County

Bishop—Andrews Hotel, 109 Redding St., Greenville, 6/28/90, A, C, 90001002

Dial-Goza House, 105 N.E. Marion St., Madison, 7/24/73, C, 73000585

First Baptist Church, Pickney and Orange Sts., Madison, 11/14/78, C, a, b, 78000953

Wardlaw-Smith House, 103 N. Washington St., Madison, 6/30/72, A, C, 72000339

Manatee County

Braden Castle Park Historic District, Roughly bounded by the Manatee and Braden Rivers, Ponce DeLeon St. and Pelot Ave., Bradenton, 5/09/83, A, C, 83001428

Bradenton Carnegie Library, 1405 Fourth Ave. W, Bradenton, 4/09/87, A, C, 87000616

DeSoto National Memorial, 5 mi. W of Bradenton, Bradenton vicinity, 10/15/66, A, B, f, NPS, 66000078

Gamble, Robert, House, On U.S. 301, Ellenton, 8/12/70, A, C, 70000189

Madira Bickel Mounds, Address Restricted, Terra Ceia Island vicinity, 8/12/70, D, 70000190

Manatee County Courthouse, Manatee Ave. and 15th St., Bradenton, 6/29/76, A, b, 76000601

Palmetto Historic District, Roughly bounded by Twenty-first Ave., Seventh St., Fifth Ave., and the Manatee River, Palmetto, 11/06/86, A, C, 86003166

Seagate, 6565 N. Tamiami Trail, Sarasota vicinity, 1/21/83, C, 83001429

Whitfield Estates—Broughton Street Historic District, 7207, 7211, 7215, 7219 and 7316 Broughton St., Sarasota, 10/29/93, C, 93001159

Woman's Club of Palmetto, 910 Sixth St. W, Palmetto, 3/06/86, A, C, 86000380

Marion County

Ayer, Alfred, House [Early Residences of Rural Marion County MPS], US Alt. 27/441 W of Oklawaha, Oklawaha vicinity, 7/13/93, A, C, 93000590

Ayer, Thomas R., House [Early Residences of Marion County MPS], 11885 SE. 128th Pl., Oklawaha, 7/13/93, A, C, 93000588

Bullock, Gen. Robert, House [Early Residences of Rural Marion County MPS], Jct. of SE. 119th Ct. and SE. 128 Pl., Oklawaha, 7/13/93, A, B, C, 93000589

Coca-Cola Bottling Plant, 939 N. Magnolia Ave., Ocala, 5/04/79, C, g, 79000682

Dunnellon Boomtown Historic District, Roughly bounded by McKinney Ave., Illinois St., Pennsylvania Ave., and Cedar St., Dunnellon, 12/08/88, A, 88002807

Josselyn, James Riley, House [Early Residences of Rural Marion County MPS], 13845 Alt. US 27, East Lake Weir, 7/13/93, A, C, 93000591

Lake Weir Yacht Club, New York Ave., Eastlake Weir, 4/22/93, A, 93000319

Marion Hotel, 108 N. Magnolia Ave., Ocala, 10/16/80, A, C, 80000955

McIntosh Historic District, Roughly bounded by RR Right-of-Way, 10th St., Aves. C and H, McIntosh, 11/18/83, A, B, C, 83003550

Mount Zion A.M.E. Church, 623 S. Magnolia Ave., Ocala, 12/17/79, A, a, 79000683

Ocala Historic District, Roughly bounded by Broadway, SE 8th St., Silver Springs Pl., SE 3rd, 13th, and Watula Aves., Ocala, 1/12/84, A, C, 84000912

Orange Springs Methodist Episcopal Church and Cemetery, SR 315 and Church St., Orange Springs, 12/22/88, A, a, d, 88002805

Ritz Apartment, The, 1205 E. Silver Springs Blvd., Ocala, 8/21/86, C, 86001722

Smith, E. C., House, 507 NE. 8th Ave., Ocala, 5/24/90, C, 90000806

Townsend, James W., House, Main and Spring Sts., Orange Springs, 10/17/88, B, C, 88001849

Tuscawilla Park Historic District, NE Fourth St., Sanchez Ave., Second St., Tuscawilla Ave., and Watula St., Ocala, 3/30/88, A, C, a, 87002015

Martin County

House of Refuge at Gilbert's Bar, Hutchinson Island between Negro and Bessie Coves, Stuart vicinity, 5/03/74, A, 74000651

Lyric Theatre, 59 SW. Flagler Ave., Stuart, 11/12/93, A, C, 93001204

Monroe County

AFRICAN QUEEN, 99701 Overseas Hwy., Key Largo, 2/18/92, A, b, g, 91001771

Adderley, George, House, 5550 Overseas Hwy., Marathon, 9/10/92, A, C, 92001243

Armory, The, 600 White St., Key West, 3/11/71, A, C, 71000243

Bat Tower-Sugarloaf Key, 1 mi. NW of U.S. 1 on Perky Key, Sugarloaf Key, 5/13/82, A, B, C, 82002377

Carysfort Lighthouse, Key Largo National Marine Sanctuary, Key Largo vicinity, 10/31/84, A, C, 84000199

Fort Jefferson National Monument, 68 mi. W of Key West, in Gulf of Mexico, Dry Tortugas Islands, 11/10/70, A, C, NPS, 70000069

Fort Zachary Taylor, U.S. Naval Station, Key West, 3/11/71, A, C, NHL, 71000244

Gato, Eduardo H., House, 1209 Virginia St., Key West, 4/11/73, B, C, b, 73000586

Monroe County—Continued

HA. 19 (Japanese Midget Submarine), NAS Key West, Key West, 6/30/89, A, g, NHL, 89001428

Hemingway, Ernest, House, 907 Whitehead St., Key West, 11/24/68, B, g, NHL, 68000023

Indian Key, Address Restricted, Lower Matecumbe Key vicinity, 6/19/72, A, C, D, 72000342

John Pennekamp Coral Reef State Park and Reserve, U.S. 1, Key Largo vicinity, 4/14/72, D, g, 72000340

Key West Historic District, Bounded approximately by White, Angela, Windsor, Passover, Thomas and Whitehead Sts., and the Gulf of Mexico, Key West, 3/11/71, A, C, g, 71000245

Key West Historic District (Boundary Increase), Roughly bounded by Emma, Whitehead, White, and South Sts., Mallory Square, and the Atlantic Ocean, Key West, 2/24/83, A, C, a, 83001430

Little White House, Naval Station, Key West, 2/12/74, B, C, g, 74000652

Martello Gallery-Key West Art and Historical Museum, S. Roosevelt Blvd., Key West, 6/19/72, A, C, 72000341

Old Post Office and Customshouse, Front St., Key West, 9/20/73, C, 73000587

Overseas Highway and Railway Bridges, Bridges on U.S. 1 between Long and Conch Key, Knight and Little Duck Key, and Bahia Honda and Spanish Key, Florida Keys, 8/13/79, A, C, g, 79000684

Pigeon Key Historic District, Off US 1 at mile marker 45, Pigeon Key, 3/16/90, A, C, 90000443

Porter, Dr. Joseph Y., House, 429 Caroline St., Key West, 6/04/73, C, 73000588

Rock Mound Archeological Site, Address Restricted, Key Largo vicinity, 7/01/75, D, 75000562

SAN JOSE Shipwreck Site, Address Restricted, Plantation Key vicinity, 3/18/75, D, 75002123

Sand Key Lighthouse, 7 mi. SW of Key West on Sand Key, Key West vicinity, 4/11/73, A, C, 73000589

U.S. Coast Guard Headquarters, Key West Station, NW corner Front St. and Whitehead St., Key West, 10/15/73, A, C, 73000590

US Naval Station, Roughly bounded by Whitehead, Eaton, and Caroline Sts., Key West, 5/08/84, A, C, 84000915

WESTERN UNION (schooner), Pier A, Truman Annex, Key West, 5/16/84, A, C, 84000930

West Martello Tower, Monroe County Beach between Reynolds and White Sts., Key West, 6/24/76, A, C, 76000602

Nassau County

Bailey House, 7th and Ash Sts., Fernandina Beach, 6/04/73, C, 73000591

Fairbanks House, 227 S. 7th St., Fernandina Beach, 6/04/73, C, 73000592

Fernandina Beach Historic District, Roughly bounded by N. 9th St., Broome, Ash, S. 5th St.,

Date, and S. 8th St., Fernandina Beach, 7/20/73, A, C, 73000593

Fernandina Beach Historic District (Boundary Increase), Roughly bounded by Sixth, Broome, N. Third, & Escambia Sts.; Seventh & Date Sts., and Ash, Fernandina Beach, 4/20/87, A, C, 87000195

Fort Clinch, 3 mi. N of Fernandina Beach on FL AIA, Fernandina Beach vicinity, 2/23/72, A, C, 72000343

Merrick-Simmons House, 102 S. 10th St., Fernandina Beach, 1/13/83, B, C, 83001431

Original Town of Fernandina Historic Site, Roughly bounded by Towngate St., City Cemetery, Nassau, Marine, and Ladies Sts., Fernandina Beach, 1/29/90, A, C, D, 86003685

Palmer, John Denham, House, 1305 Atlantic Ave., Fernandina Beach, 7/03/86, B, C, 86001453

Tabby House, 7th and Ash Sts., Fernandina Beach, 6/04/73, C, 73000594

Okaloosa County

Fort Walton Mound, Address Restricted, Fort Walton Beach vicinity, 10/15/66, D, NHL, 66000268

Gulfview Hotel Historic District, 12 Miracle Strip Pkway, SE., Fort Walton Beach, 10/22/92, A, C, 92001402

Okeechobee County

Freedman-Raulerson House, 600 S. Parrot Ave., Okeechobee, 4/11/85, B, C, b, g, 85000764

Okeechobee Battlefield, 4 mi. SE of Okeechobee on U.S. 441, Okeechobee vicinity, 10/15/66, A, NHL, 66000269

Orange County

Apopka Seaboard Air Line Railway Depot, 36 E. Station St., Apopka, 3/15/93, A, C, 93000134

Brewer, Edward Hill, House, 240 Trismen Terrace, Winter Park, 4/22/82, A, C, g, 82002378

Bridges, J.J., House, 704 S. Kuhl Ave., Orlando, 1/26/84, C, 84000932

Carroll Building, 407–409 S. Park Ave., Apopka, 3/04/93, A, C, 93000135

Comstock-Harris House, 724 Bonita Dr., Winter Park, 1/13/83, C, 83001432

First Church of Christ Scientist, 24 N. Rosalind Ave., Orlando, 6/03/80, C, a, 80000956

Huttig, John N., Estate, 435 Peachtree Rd., Orlando, 1/21/93, A, C, 91001776

Lake Eola Heights Historic District, Roughly bounded by Hillcrest St., N. Hyer Ave., Ridgewood St. and N. Magnolia Ave., Orlando, 1/16/92, C, 91001912

Maitland Art Center, 231 W. Packwood Ave., Maitland, 11/17/82, A, C, 82001036

Mitchill—Tibbetts House, 21 E. Orange St., Apopka, 11/07/91, A, 91001661

Old Orlando Railroad Depot, Depot Pl. and W. Church St., Orlando, 4/22/76, A, C, 76000604

Phillips, Dr. P., House, 135 Lucerne Circle, NE., Orlando, 7/10/79, B, C, 79000685

Rogers Building, 37-39 S. Magnolia Ave., Orlando, 7/07/83, B, C, 83001433

Ryan & Company Lumber Yard, 215 E. Fifth St., Apopka, 2/25/93, A, 93000074

Tinker Building, 16–18 W. Pine St., Orlando, 7/17/80, B, 80000957

Twin Mounds Archeological District, Address Restricted, Sorrento vicinity, 1/19/92, D, 91001957

Waite—Davis House, 5 S. Central Ave., Apopka, 8/02/90, A, B, 90001127

Waterhouse, William H., House, 820 S. Lake Lily Dr., Maitland, 2/02/83, A, C, 83001434

Withers—Maguire House, 16 E. Oakland Ave., Ocoee, 4/02/87, A, B, C, 87000579

Osceola County

Osceola County Courthouse, Bounded by Emmett, Bryan, Rose, and Vernon Sts., Kissimmee, 8/16/77, A, C, 77000406

Palm Beach County

Administration Buildings, Dixie Hwy. & Camino Real, Boca Raton, 6/27/85, C, 85001372

Aiken, Fred C., House, 801 Hibiscus St., Boca Raton, 9/24/92, A, B, C, 92001271

Big Mound City, Address Restricted, Canal Point vicinity, 5/24/73, D, 73000596

Bingham-Blossom House, 1250 S. Ocean Blvd., Palm Beach, 12/05/72, C, 72000344

Boca Raton Old City Hall, 71 N. Federal Hwy., Boca Raton, 10/16/80, C, 80000958

Boynton Woman's Club, 1010 S. Federal Hwy., Boynton Beach, 4/26/79, A, C, 79000686

Breakers Hotel Complex, S. County Rd., Palm Beach, 8/14/73, A, C, g, 73000598

Brelsford House, 1 Lake Trail, Palm Beach, 5/03/74, C, 74000653

Dixie Court Hotel, 301 N. Dixie Hwy., West Palm Beach, 8/21/86, A, C, 86001723

Flagler, Henry Morrison, House, Whitehall Way, Palm Beach, 12/05/72, B, C, 72000345

Florida East Coast Railway Passenger Station, Off FL 808, Boca Raton, 10/24/80, C, 80000959

Gulf Stream Hotel, 1 Lake Ave., Lake Worth, 1/11/83, A, C, 83001435

Hibiscus Apartments, 619 Hibiscus St., West Palm Beach, 5/10/84, C, 84000935

Jupiter Inlet Historic and Archeological Site, Address Restricted, Jupiter vicinity, 11/05/85, B, D, 85003486

Jupiter Inlet Lighthouse, Jct. of Loxahatchee River and Jupiter Sound, Jupiter, 10/15/73, A, 73000597

Kelsey City City Hall, 535 Park Ave., Lake Park, 9/03/81, C, 81000195

Lake Worth City Hall, Old, 414 Lake Ave., Lake Worth, 5/18/89, A, C, 89000432

Palm Beach County—Continued

Mar-A-Lago National Historic Landmark, 1100 S. Ocean Blvd., Palm Beach, 12/23/80, A, C, NHL, 80000961

Mickens House, 801 4th St., West Palm Beach, 4/11/85, B, 85000769

Northwest Historic District, Roughly bounded by Tamarind Ave., Eleventh St., Rosemary Ave. and Third St., West Palm Beach, 1/22/92, A, 91002005

Norton House, 253 Barcelona Rd., West Palm Beach, 7/26/90, C, 90001106

Old Palm Beach Junior College Building, 813 Gardenia Ave., West Palm Beach, 5/30/91, A, C, g, 91000601

Palm Beach Daily News Building, 204 Brazilian Ave., Palm Beach, 12/24/85, A, B, C, 85003121

Palm Beach Winter Club, U.S. 1, North Palm Beach, 8/01/80, B, C, 80000960

Paramount Theatre Building, 145 N. County Rd., Palm Beach, 12/12/73, A, C, g, 73000599

Seaboard Airline Railroad Station, 1525 W. Atlantic Ave., Delray Beach, 9/04/86, A, C, 86002172

Seaboard Coastline Railroad Passenger Station, Tamarind Ave. at Datura St., West Palm Beach, 6/19/73, A, C, g, 73000600

Sundy, John and Elizabeth Shaw, House, 106 S. Swinton Ave., Delray Beach, 1/16/92, B, C, 91001910

US Post Office, 95 N. County Rd., Palm Beach, 7/21/83, C, g, 83001436

Via Mizner, 337–339 Worth Ave., Palm Beach, 4/01/93, A, B, C, 93000256

Vineta Hotel, 363 Cocoanut Row, Palm Beach, 8/21/86, C, 86001724

Warden, William Gray, House, 112 Seminole Ave., Palm Beach, 8/01/84, C, 84000940

West Palm Beach National Guard Armory, Old, 1703 S. Lake Ave., West Palm Beach, 6/11/92, A, 92000142

Pinellas County

Alexander Hotel, 535 Central Ave., St. Petersburg, 11/01/84, C, 84000200

Andrews Memorial Chapel, Buena Vista and San Mateo, Dunedin, 7/31/72, C, a, b, 72000346

Arcade Hotel, 210 Pinellas Ave., Tarpon Springs, 1/12/84, A, C, 84000943

Arfaras, N. G., Sponge Packing House, 26 W. Park St., Tarpon Springs, 4/10/91, A, 91000412

Bay Pines Site (8Pi64), Address Restricted, Bay Pines vicinity, 2/23/83, D, 83001443

Belleview-Biltmore Hotel, Off FL 697, Clearwater, 12/26/79, A, B, C, 79000687

Boone House, 601 Fifth Ave. N, St. Petersburg, 7/03/86, B, C, 86001457

Casa Coe da Sol, 510 Park St., St. Petersburg, 7/17/80, C, g, 80000963

Casa De Muchas Flores, 1446 Park St. N., St. Petersburg, 1/31/85, C, 85000160

Central High School, 2501–5th Ave. N., St. Petersburg, 8/01/84, A, C, 84000946

Cleveland Street Post Office, 650 Cleveland St., Clearwater, 8/07/80, C, g, 80000962

DUCHESS (Sponge Hooking Boat) [Tarpon Springs Sponge Boats MPS], Tarpon Springs Sponge Docks at Dodecanese Blvd., Tarpon Springs, 8/02/90, A, C, 90001133

Dennis Hotel, 326 First Ave. N, St. Petersburg, 4/17/86, A, C, 86000804

Don Ce Sar Hotel, 3400 Gulf Blvd., St. Petersburg Beach, 4/03/75, C, g, 75000563

Douglas, J. O., House, 209 Scotland St, Dunedin, 11/29/79, B, C, 79000691

Ducros, Louis, House, 1324 S. Fort Harrison St., Clearwater, 7/02/79, B, 79000688

First Methodist Church of St. Petersburg, 212 Third St., N, St. Petersburg, 9/13/90, C, a, 90001433

Fort Desoto Batteries, 8 mi. S of St. Petersburg on Mullet Key, St. Petersburg vicinity, 12/02/77, A, 77000407

GEORGE N. CRETEKOS (Sponge Diving Boat) [Tarpon Springs Sponge Boats MPS], Tarpon Springs Sponge Docks at Dodecanese Blvd., Tarpon Springs, 8/03/90, A, C, g, 90001135

Harbor Oaks Residential District, Roughly bounded by Druid Rd., S. Fort Harrison Ave., Lotus Path, & Clearwater Harbor, Clearwater, 3/15/88, A, C, 87002133

Ingleside, 333 S. Bayshore Blvd., Safety Harbor, 4/28/92, A, 92000405

Johnson, Louis, Building, 161 First St., SW, Largo, 12/03/87, B, C, 87001632

Meres, E. R., Sponge Packing House, 106 Read St., Tarpon Springs, 4/10/91, A, 91000411

N.K. SYMI (Sponge Diving Boat) [Tarpon Springs Sponge Boats MPS], Tarpon Springs Sponge Docks at Dodecanese Blvd., Tarpon Springs, 8/02/90, A, C, 90001132

Pass-a-Grille Historic District, Roughly bounded by 12th Ave., Gulf Blvd., 4th Ave., and Gulf Ave., St. Petersburg Beach, 10/19/89, A, 89001734

Pinellas County Courthouse, Old, 315 Court St., Clearwater, 6/25/92, A, C, 92000828

Potter House, 577 Second St. S, St. Petersburg, 6/13/86, B, C, 86001258

Roebling, Donald, Estate, 700 Orange Ave., Clearwater, 12/19/79, B, C, g, 79000689

ST. NICHOLAS III (Sponge Diving Boat) [Tarpon Springs Sponge Boats MPS], Tarpon Springs Sponge Docks at Dodecanese Blvd., Tarpon Springs, 8/03/90, A, C, g, 90001136

ST. NICHOLAS VI (Sponge Diving Boat) [Tarpon Springs Sponge Boats MPS], Tarpon Springs Sponge Docks at Dodecanese Blvd., Tarpon Springs, 8/03/90, A, C, g, 90001134

Safety Harbor Site, Address Restricted, Safety Harbor vicinity, 10/15/66, D, NHL, 66000270

Safford House, Parken Pl., Tarpon Springs, 10/16/74, C, 74000654

Snell Arcade, 405 Central Ave., St. Petersburg, 11/04/82, C, 82001037

South Ward School, 610 S. Fort Harrison Ave., Clearwater, 6/18/79, A, C, 79000690

St. Petersburg Lawn Bowling Club, 536 4th Ave., N., St. Petersburg, 7/09/80, A, 80004602

St. Petersburg Public Library, 280 Fifth St. N, St. Petersburg, 6/13/86, A, C, 86001259

Studebaker Building, 600 Fourth St. South, St. Petersburg, 7/05/85, A, C, 85001485

Tarpon Springs City Hall, Old, 101 S. Pinellas Ave., Tarpon Springs, 8/10/90, A, C, g, 90001117

Tarpon Springs High School, Old, 324 E. Pine St., Tarpon Springs, 10/11/90, A, C, 90001538

Tarpon Springs Historic District, Roughly bounded by Read St., Hibiscus St., Orange St., Levis Ave., Lemon St. and Spring Bayou, Tarpon Springs, 12/06/90, A, C, g, 90001762

U.S. Post Office, SW corner of 1st Ave. N. and 4th St. N., St. Petersburg, 4/04/75, C, 75000564

Veillard House, 262 N. 4th Ave., St. Petersburg, 10/29/82, C, b, 82001038

Vinoy Park Hotel, 501 Beach Dr., St. Petersburg, 9/11/78, C, 78000955

Weeden Island Site, Address Restricted, St. Petersburg vicinity, 6/13/72, D, 72000347

Williams, John C., House, 444 5th Ave. S., St. Petersburg, 4/24/75, B, C, 75000565

Polk County

Atlantic Coast Line Railroad Depot [Lake Wales MPS], 325 S. Scenic Hwy., Lake Wales, 8/31/90, A, C, 90001277

Bartow Downtown Commercial District [Bartow MPS], Roughly bounded by Davidson and Summerlin Sts. and Broadway and Florida Aves., Bartow, 5/18/93, A, C, 93000393

Beacon Hill—Alta Vista Residential District, Roughly bounded by S. Florida Ave., W. Beacon Rd., W. Belvedere St. and Cherokee Trail, Lakeland, 3/04/93, C, 93000130

Bok Mountain Lake Sanctuary and Singing Tower, 3 mi. N of Lake Wales, Lake Wales vicinity, 8/21/72, A, B, C, NHL, 72000350

Bullard, B. K., House [Lake Wales MPS], 644 S. Lakeshore Blvd., Lake Wales, 8/31/90, A, B, C, 90001272

Casa De Josefina, 2 mi. SE of Lake Wales off U.S. 27, Lake Wales vicinity, 6/10/75, A, B, C, 75000567

Chalet Suzanne, 3800 Chalet Suzanne Dr., Lake Wales vicinity, 7/24/90, A, C, 90001085

Christ Church, 526 N. Oak, Fort Meade, 5/06/76, A, C, a, 76000605

Church of the Holy Spirit [Lake Wales MPS], 1099 Hesperides Rd., Lake Wales, 8/31/90, C, 90001271

Dixie Walesbilt Hotel [Lake Wales MPS], 115 N. First St., Lake Wales, 8/31/90, A, C, 90001273

East Lake Morton Residential District, Roughly bounded by Orange St., Ingraham Ave., Palmetto St., Lake Morton Dr. and Massachusetts Ave., Lakeland, 7/09/93, A, C, 93000621

El Retiro, Mountain Lake off FL 17, Lake Wales vicinity, 12/12/85, C, 85003331

First Baptist Church [Lake Wales MPS], 338 E. Central Ave., Lake Wales, 8/31/90, C, a, 90001275

Polk County—Continued

Florida Southern College Architectural District, McDonald and Johnson Aves., Lakeland, 6/11/75, C, a, g, 75000568

Holland, Benjamin Franklin, House, 590 E. Stanford St., Bartow, 4/03/75, B, C, 75000566

Johnson, C. L., House, 315 E. Sessoms Ave., Lake Wales, 9/21/89, B, C, 89001481

Lake Mirror Promenade, Between Lemon St. and Lake Mirror Dr., Lakeland, 1/27/83, A, C, 83001437

Lake Wales City Hall [Lake Wales MPS], 152 E. Central Ave., Lake Wales, 8/31/90, A, C, 90001274

Lake Wales Commercial Historic District [Lake Wales MPS], Roughly bounded by Scenic Hwy., Central Ave., Market St., and Orange Ave., Lake Wales, 5/10/90, A, C, 90000732

Lakeland High School, Old, 400 N. Florida Ave., Lakeland, 9/30/93, A, C, 93001027

Mountain Lake Colony House, E of FL 17, on N shore of Mountain Lake, Lake Wales vicinity, 2/22/91, A, C, 91000113

Mountain Lake Estates Historic District, US 27A N of Lake Wales, Lake Wales vicinity, 8/26/93, A, C, 93000871

Northeast Bartow Residential District [Bartow MPS], Roughly bounded by Jackson and First Aves. and by Church and Boulevard Sts., Bartow, 5/18/93, C, 93000392

Polk County Courthouse, Old, 100 E. Main St., Bartow, 8/07/89, A, C, 89001055

Polk Theatre and Office Building, 121 S. Florida Ave., Lakeland, 5/27/93, A, C, 93000446

South Bartow Residential District [Bartow MPS], Roughly bounded by Floral and First Aves. and Main and Vine Sts., Bartow, 5/18/93, C, 93000394

South Florida Military College, 1100 S. Broadway, Bartow, 7/24/72, A, 72000349

South Lake Morton Historic District, Bounded by Lake Morton Dr. and Palmetto St., Ingraham and Johnson Aves., McDonald and Balmar Sts., and Tennessee Ave., Lakeland, 11/20/85, A, C, 85002900

Swearingen, John J., House, 690 E. Church St., Bartow, 5/13/82, B, C, 82002379

Tillman, G. V., House [Lake Wales MPS], 301 E. Sessoms Ave., Lake Wales, 8/31/90, A, B, C, 90001276

Putnam County

Bronson-Mulholland House, Madison between 1st and 2nd Sts., Palatka, 12/27/72, B, C, 72000351

Hubbard House, 600 N. Park St. in Hubbard Park, Crescent City, 8/14/73, C, 73000601

Melrose Woman's Club, Pine St., Melrose, 4/06/78, A, 78000956

Mount Royal, Address Restricted, Welaka vicinity, 5/07/73, D, 73000603

Old A.C.L. Union Depot, 200 N. Twelfth St., Palatka, 2/25/88, A, 88000162

Palatka North Historic District, Roughly bounded by St. John's River, Bronson, N. 1st, N. 5th, and Main Sts., Palatka, 11/17/83, A, C, 83003552

Palatka South Historic District, Roughly bounded by St. John's River, Oak, S. 9th, and Morris Sts., Palatka, 11/17/83, A, C, 83003553

St. Marks Episcopal Church, 2nd and Main Sts., Palatka, 5/09/73, A, a, 73000602

Santa Rosa County

Arcadia Sawmill and Arcadia Cotton Mill, Address Restricted, Milton vicinity, 8/03/87, A, D, 87001300

Bagdad Village Historic District, Roughly bounded by Main, Water, & Oak Sts., Cobb & Woodville Rds., Cemetery, Pooley, & School Sts., Bagdad, 12/08/87, A, C, g, 87001991

Bethune Blackwater Schooner, Address Restricted, Milton vicinity, 8/08/91, A, C, D, 91000948

Louisville and Nashville Depot, 206 Henry St., Milton, 10/29/82, A, C, 82001041

Milton Historic District, US 90 at Blackwater River bounded by Berryhill, Willing, Hill, Canal, Margaret, & Susan Sts., Milton, 11/12/87, A, C, 87001944

Mt. Pilgrim African Baptist Church, Jct. of Alice and Clara Sts., Milton, 5/29/92, A, C, a, 92000634

Ollinger-Cobb House, 302 Pine St., Milton, 1/11/83, A, C, 83001440

St. Mary's Episcopal Church and Rectory, 300-301 Oak St., Milton, 5/06/82, C, a, 82002380

Thomas Creek Archeological District, Address Restricted, Chamuckla vicinity, 11/04/85, D, 85003482

Sarasota County

Armada Road Multi-Family District [Venice MPS], Roughly bounded by Granada Ave., Harbor Dr. S., Armada Rd. S., and Park Blvd. S., Venice, 12/18/89, A, C, 89002049

Atlantic Coast Line Passenger Depot [Sarasota MRA], 1 S. School Ave., Sarasota, 3/22/84, A, C, 84000957

Bacheller—Brewer Model Home Estate, 1903 Lincoln Dr., Sarasota, 2/10/92, A, C, 91002034

Bacon and Tomlin, Inc. [Sarasota MRA], 201 S. Palm Ave., Sarasota, 3/22/84, C, 84003829

Bay Haven School [Sarasota MRA], 2901 W. Tamiami Circle, Sarasota, 4/23/84, C, 84003832

Blalock House [Venice MPS], 241 S. Harbor Dr., Venice, 4/12/89, A, C, 89000235

Burns Court Historic District [Sarasota MRA], 400-446 Burns Court and 418, 426, and 446 S. Pineapple Ave., Sarasota, 3/22/84, A, B, C, 84003830

Burns Realty Company—Karl Bickel House [Sarasota MRA], 101 N. Tamiami Trail, Sarasota, 3/05/87, B, C, 87000196

Caples'-Ringlings' Estates Historic District, Roughly bounded by Sarasota Bay, US 41, Parkview and N. Shore Ave., Sarasota, 12/15/82, B, C, 82001039

City Waterworks [Sarasota MRA], 1015 N. Orange Ave., Sarasota, 4/23/84, C, 84003831

DeCanizares, F.A., House [Sarasota MRA], 1215 N. Palm Ave., Sarasota, 3/22/84, C, 84003833

DeMarcay Hotel [Sarasota MRA], 27 S. Palm Ave., Sarasota, 3/22/84, C, 84003834

Eagle Point Historic District, 759 N. Tamiami Trail, Venice vicinity, 10/03/91, A, D, 91001448

Earle House, 4521 Bayshore Rd., Sarasota, 9/02/93, C, 93000908

Edgewood Historic District [Venice MPS], Roughly bounded by School St., Myrtle Ave., Venice-By-Way, and Groveland Ave., Venice, 12/18/89, A, C, 89002048

Edwards Theatre [Sarasota MRA], 57 N. Pineapple Ave., Sarasota, 3/22/84, A, B, C, 84003835

El Patio Apartments, 500 N. Audubon Pl., Sarasota, 5/06/93, A, C, 93000390

El Vernona Apartments-Broadway Apartments [Sarasota MRA], 1133 4th St., Sarasota, 3/22/84, B, C, 84003836

El Vernona Hotel—John Ringling Hotel [Sarasota MRA], 111 N. Tamiami Trail, Sarasota, 3/05/87, C, 87000197

Field Estate, Field Rd. and Camino Real, Sarasota vicinity, 6/05/86, A, C, 86001238

Frances-Carlton Apartments [Sarasota MRA], 1221-1227 N. Palm Ave., Sarasota, 3/22/84, C, 84003837

Halton, Dr. Joseph, House [Sarasota MRA], 308 Cocoanut Ave., Sarasota, 3/22/84, B, C, 84003838

Hotel Venice, 200 N. Nassau St., Venice, 2/06/84, C, 84000961

House at 710 Armada Road South [Venice MPS], 710 Armada Rd. S., Venice, 8/17/89, A, C, 89001073

Keith, Edson, Estate, 5500 S. Tamiami Trail, Sarasota vicinity, 3/14/91, A, C, 91000282

Kress, S.H., Building [Sarasota MRA], 1442 Main St., Sarasota, 3/22/84, C, 84003839

Lemon Bay Woman's Club, 51 N. Maple St., Englewood, 8/11/88, A, 88001150

Levillain—Letton House [Venice MPS], 229 S. Harbor Dr., Venice, 4/12/89, A, C, 89000234

Little Salt Springs, Off U.S. 41, North Port Charlotte vicinity, 7/10/79, D, 79000692

Miakka School House, Miakka and Wilson Rds., Miakka vicinity, 7/03/86, A, C, 86001458

Osprey Archeological and Historic Site, Address Restricted, Osprey vicinity, 4/16/75, C, D, 75000569

Purdy, Capt. W. F., House [Sarasota MRA], 3315 Bayshore Rd., Sarasota, 3/22/84, C, 84003840

Reagin, L.D., House [Sarasota MRA], 1213 N. Palm Ave., Sarasota, 10/25/84, B, C, 84000111

Roth Cigar Factory [Sarasota MRA], 30 Mira Mar Court, Sarasota, 3/22/84, A, C, 84003841

Sarasota County Courthouse [Sarasota MRA], 2000 Main St., Sarasota, 3/22/84, A, C, 84003842

Sarasota Herald Building [Sarasota MRA], 539 S. Orange Ave., Sarasota, 3/22/84, A, C, 84003843

Sarasota County—Continued

Sarasota High School [Sarasota MRA], 1001 S. Tamiami Trail, Sarasota, 3/22/84, C, 84003844

Sarasota Times Building [Sarasota MRA], 1214-1216–1st St., Sarasota, 3/22/84, A, C, 84003845

Sarasota Woman's Club [Sarasota MRA], 1241 N. Palm Ave., Sarasota, 1/18/85, A, C, 85000087

South Side School [Sarasota MRA], 1901 Webber St., Sarasota, 9/14/84, C, 84003846

U.S. Post Office-Federal Building [Sarasota MRA], 111 S. Orange Ave., Sarasota, 3/22/84, C, 84003847

Venezia Park Historic District [Venice MPS], Roughly bounded by Palermo St., Sorrento St., S. Harbor Dr., and Salerno St., Venice, 12/18/89, A, C, 89002047

Venice Depot [Venice MPS], 303 E. Venice Ave., Venice, 8/17/89, A, C, 89001072

Warm Mineral Springs, 12 mi. SE of Venice on U.S. 41, Venice vicinity, 11/28/77, D, 77000408

Whitfield, J. G., Estate, 2704 Bayshore Dr., Sarasota, 9/12/85, C, 85002177

William, H.B., House [Sarasota MRA], 1509 S. Orange Ave., Sarasota, 3/22/84, C, 84003848

Wilson, Dr. C. B., House [Sarasota MRA], 235 S. Orange Ave., Sarasota, 3/22/84, B, C, 84003849

Seminole County

Bradlee-McIntyre House, 130 W. Warren Ave., Longwood, 3/28/91, C, 72000352

Longwood Historic District, Roughly bounded by W. Pine Ave., S. Milwee St., Palmetto Ave. and Co. Rd. 427, Longwood, 10/05/90, A, B, C, 90001480

Longwood Hotel, Old Dixie Highway, Longwood, 5/10/84, A, C, 84000963

Old Fernald—Laughton Memorial Hospital, 500 S. Oak Ave., Sanford, 5/21/87, A, 87000805

Sanford Commercial District, Parts of 1st, 2nd, and Commercial Sts., between Palmetto and Oak Sts., Sanford, 6/15/76, A, C, 76000606

Sanford Grammar School, 7th and Myrtle Sts., Sanford, 11/23/84, A, C, 84000253

Sanford Residential Historic District, Roughly bounded by Sanford Ave., 14th St., Elm Ave., and 3rd St., Sanford, 12/15/89, A, C, 89002119

St. James A. M. E. Church, 819 Cypress Ave., Sanford, 4/24/92, A, C, a, 92000352

St. Johns County

Abbott Tract Historic District, Roughly bounded by Matanza's Bay, Pine, San Marco, and Shenandoah Aves., St. Augustine, 7/21/83, A, C, D, 83001438

Alcazar Hotel, 79 King St., St. Augustine, 2/24/71, C, 71001013

Avero House, 39 St. George St., St. Augustine, 6/13/72, A, C, a, 72001459

Bridge of Lions, King St., St. Augustine, 11/19/82, A, C, 82001040

Castillo de San Marcos National Monument, 1 Castillo Dr., St. Augustine, 10/15/66, A, NPS, 66000062

Cathedral of St. Augustine, Cathedral St. between Charlotte and St. George Sts., St. Augustine, 4/15/70, A, a, NHL, 70000844

Fish Island Site, Address Restricted, St. Augustine vicinity, 6/13/72, D, 72001460

Fort Matanzas National Monument, 15 mi. S of St. Augustine, St. Augustine vicinity, 10/15/66, A, C, NPS, 66000098

Gonzalez-Alvarez House, 14 St. Francis St., St. Augustine, 4/15/70, C, NHL, 70000845

Grace United Methodist Church, 8 Carrera St., St. Augustine, 11/29/79, B, C, a, 79003132

Hotel Ponce De Leon [Y], Bounded by King, Valencia, Sevilla, and Cordova Sts.; See Also:St. Augustine Historic District, St. Augustine, 5/06/75, A, B, C, 75002067

Lincolnville Historic District, Bounded by Cedar, Riberia, Cerro and Washington Sts. and DeSoto Pl., St. Augustine, 11/29/91, A, C, g, 91000979

Lindsley House, 214 St. George St., St. Augustine, 9/10/71, C, 71001014

Llambias House, 31 St. Francis St., St. Augustine, 4/15/70, C, NHL, 70000846

Lopez, Xavier, House, 93 1/2 King St., St. Augustine, 7/01/93, C, b, 93000579

Markland, 102 King St., St. Augustine, 12/06/78, B, C, 78003080

Model Land Company Historic District, Roughly bounded by Ponce de Leon Blvd., King, Cordova, and Orange Sts., St. Augustine, 8/02/83, A, C, 83001439

O'Reilly House, 131 Aviles St., St. Augustine, 10/15/74, A, C, a, 74002192

Old St. Johns County Jail, 167 San Marco Ave., St. Augustine, 8/27/87, A, B, C, 87001427

Rodriguez-Avero-Sanchez House, 52 St. George St., St. Augustine, 4/16/71, C, 71001015

Sanchez Powder House Site, Marine St., St. Augustine, 4/14/72, A, 72001461

Shell Bluff Landing (8SJ32), Address Restricted, Ponte Vedra Beach vicinity, 4/25/91, D, 91000455

Solla—Carcaba Cigar Factory, 88 Riberia St., St. Augustine, 5/06/93, A, C, 93000374

Spanish Coquina Quarries, Florida AIA, Anastasia State Park, St. Augustine Beach, 2/23/72, A, C, 72001462

St. Augustine Alligator Farm Historic District, 999 Anastasia Blvd., St. Augustine, 9/10/92, A, 92001232

St. Augustine Lighthouse and Keeper's Quarters, Old Beach Rd., St. Augustine, 3/19/81, A, C, 81000668

St. Augustine Town Plan Historic District, Roughly bounded by Grove Ave., the Matanzas River, and South and Washington Sts., St. Augustine, 4/15/70, A, C, a, NHL, 70000847

Villa Zorayda, 83 King St., St. Augustine, 9/23/93, A, C, 93001002

Ximenez-Fatio House, 20 Aviles St., St. Augustine, 7/25/73, A, C, 73002135

St. Lucie County

Casa Caprona, 2605 St. Lucie Blvd., Ft. Pierce, 6/02/84, C, 84000955

Cresthaven, 239 S. Indian River Dr., Ft. Pierce, 4/11/85, B, C, 85000770

Fort Pierce Site, South Indian River Dr., Fort Pierce, 1/11/74, A, 74002181

Hammond, Captain, House, 5775 Citrus Ave., White City, 2/23/90, C, b, 90000310

Hurston, Zora Neale, House, 1734 School Ct., Fort Pierce, 12/04/91, B, g, NHL, 91002047

St. Lucie High School, 1100 Delaware Ave., Fort Pierce, 1/26/84, A, C, 84000956

St. Lucie Village Historic District, 2505–3305 N. Indian River Dr., St. Lucie Village, 12/01/89, A, 89002062

Sumter County

Dade Battlefield Historic Memorial, 1 mi. W of Bushnell off U.S. 301, Bushnell vicinity, 4/14/72, A, NHL, 72000353

Suwannee County

Blackwell, Bishop B., House, 110 Parshley St., Live Oak, 2/28/85, B, C, b, 85000360

Hull-Hawkins House, 10 mi. S of Live Oak on FL 49, Live Oak vicinity, 5/07/73, C, 73000604

Old Live Oak City Hall, 212 N. Ohio Ave., Live Oak, 4/24/86, A, C, 86000862

Union Depot and Atlantic Coast Line Freight Station, 200 blk. of N. Ohio Ave., Live Oak, 4/24/86, A, b, 86000860

Taylor County

Perry Post Office, Old, 201 E. Green St., Perry, 5/11/89, A, C, 89000404

Taylor County Jail, Old, 400 blk. N. Washington St., Perry, 5/11/89, A, B, C, 89000414

Union County

Townsend Building, 410 W. Main St., Lake Butler, 10/08/92, A, C, 92001359

Volusia County

Abbey, The, 426 S. Beach St., Daytona Beach, 4/09/87, A, B, 87000615

All Saint's Episcopal Church, Corner of DeBary Ave. NE. and Clark St., Enterprise, 5/03/74, A, C, a, 74000656

Anderson, John, Lodge [Historic Winter Residences of Ormond Beach, 1878–1925 MPS], 71

Volusia County—Continued

Orchard Ln., Ormond Beach, 9/06/89, A, B, C, 88001717

Anderson-Price Memorial Library Building, 42 N. Beach St., Ormond Beach, 1/26/84, A, C, 84000967

Barberville Central High School, 1776 Lightfoot Ln., Barberville, 2/03/93, A, C, 92001838

Bethune, Mary McLeod, Home, Bethune-Cookman College campus, Daytona Beach, 12/02/74, B, g, NHL, 74000655

Blodgett, Delos A., House, 404 Ridgewood Ave., Daytona Beach, 8/02/93, C, b, 93000724

Casements Annex [Historic Winter Residences of Ormond Beach, 1878–1925 MPS], 127 Riverside Dr., Ormond Beach, 10/06/88, A, 88001720

Casements, The, 15 E. Granada Ave., Ormond Beach, 6/30/72, B, C, 72001536

DeBary Hall, DeBary Mansion State Park, DeBary, 7/24/72, C, 72000354

DeLand Hall, Stetson University Campus, DeLand, 1/27/83, B, C, 83001441

DeLand Memorial Hospital, Old, Stone St., DeLand, 11/27/89, A, C, 89002030

Dix House [Historic Winter Residences of Ormond Beach, 1878–1925 MPS], 178 N. Beach St., Ormond Beach, 9/06/89, A, 88001721

Donnelly, Bartholomew J., House, 801 N. Peninsula Dr., Daytona Beach, 8/02/93, C, 93000726

Downtown DeLand Historic District, Roughly bounded by Florida & Rich Aves., Woodland Blvd., & Howry Ave., DeLand, 12/23/87, A, B, C, 87001796

Dunlawton Plantation—Sugar Mill Ruins, W of Port Orange off Nova Rd., Port Orange vicinity, 8/28/73, A, C, 73000606

El Pino Parque Historic District, 1412–1604 N. Halifax Dr., Daytona, 4/26/93, C, 93000318

El Real Retiro, 636 N. Riverside Dr. & 647 Faulkner St., New Smyrna Beach, 11/10/87, A, B, C, 87001557

Gamble Place Historic District, 1819 Taylor Rd., Port Orange, 9/29/93, A, C, 93000563

Hammocks, The [Historic Winter Residences of Ormond Beach, 1878–1925 MPS], 311 John Anderson Hwy., Ormond Beach, 9/05/89, B, C, 88001719

Holly Hill Municipal Building, 1065 Ridgewood Ave., Holly Hill, 4/08/93, A, C, 93000285

Kling, Amos, House, 220–222 Magnolia Ave., Daytona Beach, 12/02/93, A, B, 93001353

Kress, S.H., and Co. Building, 140 S. Beach St., Daytona Beach, 7/07/83, C, 83001442

Lake Helen Historic District [Lake Helen MPS], Roughly bounded by W. New York, Lakeview, Park and Euclid Aves., Lake Helen, 9/16/93, A, C, 93000981

Lippincott Mansion, 150 S. Beach St., Ormond Beach, 2/21/85, C, 85000304

Merchants Bank Building, 252 S. Beach St., Daytona Beach, 1/06/86, A, C, 86000025

New Smyrna Beach Historic District, Roughly bounded by Riverside Dr., US 1, Ronnoc Ln., and Smith St., New Smyrna Beach, 4/26/90, A, C, 90000714

New Smyrna Sugar Mill Ruins, 1 mi. W of New Smyrna Beach, New Smyrna Beach vicinity, 8/12/70, A, C, 70000192

Nocoroco, 2 mi. N of Ormond Beach, Ormond Beach vicinity, 5/07/73, D, 73000605

Olds Hall, 340 S. Ridgewood Ave., Daytona Beach, 9/23/93, A, C, 93001003

Ormond Hotel, 15 E. Granada Blvd., Ormond Beach, 11/24/80, A, 80000964

Ponce De Leon Inlet Lighthouse, U.S. Coast Guard Reservation, Ponce de Leon Inlet vicinity, 9/22/72, C, 72000355

Porches, The [Historic Winter Residences of Ormond Beach, 1878–1925 MPS], 176 S. Beach St., Ormond Beach, 10/06/88, A, C, 88001715

Rogers House, 436 N. Beach St., Daytona Beach, 9/11/86, B, b, 86002407

Ross Hammock Site, Address Restricted, Oak Hill vicinity, 2/05/81, A, D, NPS, 81000083

Rowallan [Historic Winter Residences of Ormond Beach, 1878–1925 MPS], 253 John Anderson Hwy., Ormond Beach, 10/06/88, A, 88001724

South Beach Street Historic District, Roughly bounded by Volusia Ave., S. Beach St., South St., and US 1, Daytona Beach, 9/15/88, A, C, 88001597

Southern Cassadaga Spiritualist Camp Historic District, Roughly bounded by Cassadaga Rd. and Marion, Stevens, Lake and Chauncey Sts., Cassadaga, 3/14/91, A, 91000249

Spruce Creek Mound Complex, Address Restricted, Port Orange vicinity, 12/03/90, D, 90001761

Stetson University Campus Historic District, Roughly bounded by Michigan Ave., N. Florida Ave., W. University Ave. and a line S from N. Hayden Ave., DeLand, 3/14/91, A, C, 91000244

Stetson, John B., House, 1031 Camphor Lane, DeLand, 11/21/78, B, C, 78000957

Stevens, Ann, House [Lake Helen MPS], 201 E. Kicklighter Rd., Lake Helen, 8/18/93, B, C, 93000734

Strawn Historic Agricultural District [Citrus Industry Resources of Theodore Strawn, Inc., MPS], Bounded by Broderick and Retta Sts. and by Central and Dundee Aves., DeLeon Springs, 9/13/93, A, 93000929

Strawn Historic Citrus Packing House District [Citrus Industry Resources of Theodore Strawn, Inc., MPS], 5707 Lake Winona Rd., DeLeon Springs, 9/13/93, A, 93000931

Strawn Historic Sawmill District [Citrus Industry Resources of Theodore Strawn, Inc., MPS], 5710 Lake Winona Rd., DeLeon Springs, 9/13/93, A, 93000930

Talahloka [Historic Winter Residences of Ormond Beach, 1878–1925 MPS], 19 Orchard Ln., Ormond Beach, 9/06/89, A, B, C, 88001716

Thurman, Howard, House, 614 Whitehall St., Daytona Beach, 2/23/90, A, B, 90000100

Turtle Mound, Address Restricted, New Smyrna Beach vicinity, 9/29/70, D, 70000193

US Post Office, 220 N. Beach St., Daytona Beach, 6/30/88, C, 88000974

West DeLand Residential District, Roughly bounded by University, Florida, New York and Orange Aves., DeLand, 11/20/92, C, 92001617

White Hall, 640 Second Ave., Daytona Beach, 7/15/92, A, C, 92000849

Woman's Club of New Smyrna, 403 Magnolia St., New Smyrna Beach, 5/11/89, A, C, 89000410

Young, S. Cornelia, Memorial Library, 302 Vermont Ave., Daytona, 6/25/92, A, C, 92000823

Wakulla County

Bird Hammock, Address Restricted, Wakulla Beach vicinity, 12/15/72, D, 72000357

Fort San Marcos de Apalache, 18 mi. S of Tallahassee, St. Marks, 11/13/66, A, D, NHL, 66000271

Old Wakulla County Courthouse, Church St., Crawfordville, 5/03/76, C, b, 76000607

Sopchoppy High School Gymnasium, Old, Jct. of Second Ave. and Summer St., Sopchoppy, 6/01/90, A, C, 90000849

St. Marks Lighthouse, N side of Apalache Bay at terminus of FL 59, St. Marks National Wildlife Refuge, 7/31/72, A, 72000356

Wakulla Springs Archeological and Historic District, 1 Spring Dr., Wakulla Springs vicinity, 1/25/93, A, B, C, D, 92001760

Walton County

Biddle, Perry L., House [DeFuniak Springs MPS], 203 Scribner Ave., DeFuniak Springs, 8/28/92, A, C, 92001049

Chautauqua Hall of Brotherhood, Circle Dr., DeFuniak Springs, 8/07/72, A, 72000358

DeFuniak Springs Historic District [DeFuniak Springs MPS], Roughly bounded by Nelson and Park Aves. and 2nd and 12th Sts., DeFuniak Springs, 8/28/92, A, C, 92001048

Sun Bright, 606 Live Oak Ave., DeFuniak Springs, 5/07/79, B, C, 79000693

Washington County

Moss Hill Church, Vernon-Greenhead Rd., Vernon vicinity, 11/07/83, A, C, a, d, 83003554

South Third Street Historic District, S. Third St. between Wells Ave. and South Blvd., Chipley, 2/21/89, A, 89000045

GEORGIA

Appling County

Appling County Courthouse [Georgia County Courthouses TR], Courthouse Sq., Baxley, 9/18/80, A, C, 80000965

Citizens Banking Company, 112-116 N. Main St., Baxley, 5/02/85, A, C, 85000932

Deen, C. W., House, 413 N. Main St., Baxley, 9/30/82, C, 82002381

Atkinson County

Atkinson County Courthouse [Georgia County Courthouses TR], Austin at Main St., Pearson, 9/18/80, A, C, 80000966

McCranie's Turpentine Still, W of Willacoochee on U.S. 82, Willacoochee vicinity, 6/28/76, A, g, 76000608

Bacon County

Alma Depot, Dixon and 11th Sts., Alma, 4/07/83, A, C, 83000182

Bacon County Courthouse [Georgia County Courthouses TR], Main St., Alma, 9/18/80, A, C, 80000967

Rabinowitz Building, 203–205 W. Eleventh St., Alma, 6/27/87, A, C, 87001238

Baker County

Baker County Courthouse [Georgia County Courthouses TR], Courthouse Sq., Newton, 9/18/80, A, C, 80004443

Pine Bloom Plantation, Tarva Rd./Co. Rt. 122, 0.75 mi. S of Baker/Dougherty county line, Newton vicinity, 2/09/90, A, B, C, 90000105

Tarver Plantation, Tarva Rd./Co. Rt. 122, N of Newton, Newton vicinity, 11/27/89, A, C, d, 89002037

Baldwin County

Andalusia, NW of Milledgeville on U.S. 441, Milledgeville vicinity, 2/08/80, B, g, 80000968

Atkinson Hall, Georgia College, Georgia College campus, Milledgeville, 1/20/72, A, C, 72000359

Barrowville, E of Milledgeville on GA 22/24, Milledgeville vicinity, 12/14/78, B, C, 78000958

Boykin, Maj. Francis, House, 10 mi. (16 km) SE of Milledgeville off GA 24, Milledgeville vicinity, 11/14/78, C, 78000959

Central Building, State Lunatic Asylum, Broad St., Milledgeville, 7/20/78, A, C, 78000960

Devereux—Coleman House, 167 Kenan Dr., Milledgeville, 4/08/93, C, b, 93000214

Milledgeville Historic District, Bounded by Irwin, Thomas, and Warren Sts. and Fishing Creek, Milledgeville, 6/28/72, A, C, 72000360

Old Governor's Mansion, 120 S. Clark St., Milledgeville, 5/13/70, C, NHL, 70000194

Old State Capitol, Greene St., Milledgeville, 5/13/70, A, C, e, 70000195

Old State Prison Building, 3 mi. (4.8 km) W of Milledgeville on GA 22, Milledgeville vicinity, 5/08/79, A, C, 79000694

Rockwell, Samuel, House, 165 Allen Memorial Dr., Milledgeville vicinity, 4/19/78, C, 78000961

Roe-Harper House, Off US 441, Milledgeville vicinity, 3/06/86, C, b, 77000437

Rutherford, John, House, 550 Allen Memorial Dr., Milledgeville vicinity, 3/21/78, C, b, 78000962

Storehouse, State Lunatic Asylum, Broad St. and Lawrence Rd., Milledgeville vicinity, 6/15/78, A, C, 78000963

Thalian Hall, Allen Memorial and Ivey Drs., Milledgeville vicinity, 3/21/78, A, B, C, 78000964

Westover, 151 Meriwether Rd. NW, Milledge vicinity, 2/12/87, C, D, d, 87000094

Woodville, 3 mi. (4.8 km) S of Milledgeville on GA 243, Milledgeville vicinity, 6/22/79, B, C, 79000695

Banks County

Banks County Courthouse [Georgia County Courthouses TR], Off U.S. 441, Homer, 9/18/80, A, C, 80000969

Banks County Jail, Silver Shoals Rd., Homer, 7/26/82, A, C, 82002382

Gillsville Historic District, GA 52, Gillsville, 8/30/85, A, B, C, 85001933

Hebron Church, Cemetery, and Academy, CR 3, Commerce vicinity, 9/12/85, A, B, C, a, d, 85002176

Homer Historic District, Along Main St. and Silver Shoals Rd., Homer, 12/03/85, A, C, 85003110

Homer Historic District (Boundary Increase), Off US 41 on E end of existing district adjacent to southern boundary, Homer, 5/14/93, C, 93000422

Kesler Covered Bridge, 10 mi. N of Homer on County Line Rd. over Middle Fork Broad River, Homer vicinity, 6/18/75, A, C, 75000571

Maysville Historic District, Along E. Main, W. Main and Homer Sts., Maysville, 9/12/85, A, B, C, a, d, 85002203

New Salem Covered Bridge, 6 mi. N of Commerce on SR S992 over Grove Creek, Commerce vicinity, 6/10/75, A, C, 75000570

Barrow County

Athens—Candler—Church Street Historic District, Roughly Candler St. between Melrose and Woodlawn Sts., Church St., and Athens St. between Horton and Center Sts., Winder, 4/17/86, A, C, 86000799

Barrow County Courthouse [Georgia County Courthouses TR], Courthouse Sq., Winder, 9/18/80, A, C, 80000970

Broad Street Commercial Historic District, Broad and Athens Sts., Winder, 7/26/84, A, C, 84000884

Jackson Street Commercial Historic District, Roughly bounded by Jackson, Athens, Candler, and Broad Sts., Winder, 7/26/84, A, C, 84000885

Jackson-Johns House, 116 Candler St., Winder, 4/18/85, B, C, 85000847

Kilgore Mill Covered Bridge and Mill Site, 3.5 mi. SW of Bethlehem across Apalachee River-/county line, Bethlehem vicinity, 4/14/75, A, C, 75000572

Manning Gin Farm, Jct. of Manning Gin and McElhannon Rds., Bethlehem vicinity, 5/08/91, A, C, 91000541

North Broad Street Residential Historic District, Roughly bounded by Woodlawn Ave., Center, Broad, and Stephens Sts., Winder, 7/26/84, C, 84000888

Rockwell Universalist Church, GA 53 & Rockwell Church Rd., Winder vicinity, 5/02/85, A, C, a, 85000933

Russell Homeplace Historic District, US 29, Russell, 9/07/84, B, C, g, 84000890

Winder Depot, Broad and Porter Sts., Winder, 5/08/79, A, C, 79000696

Bartow County

Adairsville Historic District, Roughly Main St. bounded by King & Elm Sts., & city limits on S & W, Adairsville, 12/04/87, A, C, 87002043

Bartow County Courthouse [Georgia County Courthouses TR], Courthouse Sq., Cartersville, 9/18/80, A, C, 80000971

Cassville Post Office, 1813 Cassville Rd. (Old Dixie Hwy.), Cassville, 8/31/92, A, C, 92001129

Etowah Mounds, N bank of Etowah River, Cartersville vicinity, 10/15/66, D, NHL, 66000272

Etowah Valley District, Address Restricted, Carterville vicinity, 6/30/75, A, C, D, 75000573

Felton, Rebecca Latimer, House, N of Cartersville off U.S. 411, Cartersville vicinity, 1/31/79, B, C, 79000697

First Presbyterian Church, 183 W. Main St., Cartersville, 8/29/91, C, a, 91001157

Grand Theater, 2 Wall St., Cartersville, 6/28/84, A, C, 84000893

Bartow County—Continued

Jones, Sam, Memorial United Methodist Church, 100 W. Church St., Cartersville, 9/05/85, A, C, a, 85001972

Noble Hill School, Gaddis Rd., Cassville vicinity, 7/02/87, A, C, 87001103

Old Bartow County Courthouse [Georgia County Courthouses TR], 4 E. Church St., Cartersville, 9/18/80, A, C, 80000972

Pine Log Methodist Church, Campground, and Cemetery, GA 140, W of US 411, Rydal vicinity, 9/09/88, A, C, a, d, 86002176

Roselawn, 244 Cherokee Ave., Cartersville, 1/12/73, B, C, a, 73000607

Valley View, Euharlee Rd., SW of Cartersville, Carterville vicinity, 5/08/74, C, 74000657

Ben Hill County

Ben Hill County Courthouse [Georgia County Courthouses TR], E. Central Ave., Fitzgerald, 9/18/80, A, C, 80000973

Ben Hill County Jail [County Jails of Ben Hill, Berrien, Brooks, and Turner Counties TR; Georgia County Courthouses TR], Pine St., Fitzgerald, 8/26/82, A, C, 82002383

Fitzgerald Commercial Historic District, Roughly bounded by Ocmulgee, Thomas, Magnolia and Lee Sts., Ben Hill, 4/28/92, A, C, 92000383

Holtzendorf Apartments, 105 W. Pine St., Fitzgerald, 1/12/88, C, 87001905

South Main—South Lee Streets Historic District, Roughly bounded by Magnolia St., S. Main St., Roanoke Dr., and S. Lee St., Fitzgerald, 4/13/89, A, C, a, 89000294

Berrien County

Berrien County Courthouse, Town Square, Nashville, 12/09/77, A, C, 77000409

Berrien County Jail [County Jails of Ben Hill, Berrien, Brooks, and Turner Counties TR; Georgia County Courthouses TR], N. Jefferson St., Nashville, 8/26/82, A, C, 82002384

Bibb County

Anderson, Capt. R. J., House, 1730 West End Ave., Macon, 5/27/71, C, 71000246

Anderson, Judge Clifford, House, 642 Orange St., Macon, 7/14/71, B, C, 71000247

Baber, Ambrose, House, 577–587 Walnut St., Macon, 8/14/73, B, C, 73000608

Burke, Thomas C., House, 1085 Georgia Ave., Macon, 6/21/71, B, C, 71000248

Cannonball House, 856 Mulberry St., Macon, 5/27/71, A, C, 71000249

Central City Park Bandstand, Central City Park, Macon, 3/16/72, A, C, 72000361

Cherokee Heights District, Pio Nono, Napier, Inverness, and Suwanee Aves., Macon, 7/08/82, A, C, 82002385

Christ Episcopal Church, 538–566 Walnut St., Macon, 7/14/71, C, a, 71000250

Collins—Odom—Strickland House, 1495 2nd St., Macon, 1/22/79, A, C, 79000698

Cowles House, 988 Bond St., Macon, 6/21/71, B, C, 71000251

Cowles, Jerry, Cottage, 4569 Rivoli Dr., Macon, 6/21/71, B, C, b, 71000252

Dasher-Stevens House, 904 Orange Ter., Macon, 10/18/72, A, C, 72000362

Davis-Guttenberger-Rankin House, 134 Buford Pl., Macon, 11/30/73, B, C, b, 73000609

Domingos House, 1261 Jefferson Ter., Macon, 6/21/71, B, C, 71000253

East Macon Historic District, Roughly bounded by Emery Hwy., Coliseum Dr., and Clinton, Fletcher and Fairview Sts., Macon, 4/01/93, A, C, 93000281

Emerson-Holmes Building, 566 Mulberry St., Macon, 6/21/71, A, C, 71000254

Findlay, Robert, House, 785 2nd St., Macon, 1/20/72, B, C, 72000363

First Presbyterian Church, 690 Mulberry St., Macon, 9/14/72, A, C, a, 72000364

Fort Hawkins Archeological Site, Address Restricted, Macon vicinity, 11/23/77, A, D, 77000410

Fort Hill Historic District, Roughly bounded by Emery Hwy., Second St. Ext., Mitchell and Morrow Sts. and Schaeffer Pl., Macon, 4/16/93, A, C, 93000313

Goodall House, 618 Orange St., Macon, 5/27/71, A, C, 71000255

Grand Opera House, 651 Mulberry St., Macon, 6/22/70, A, C, 70000196

Green-Poe House, 841–845 Poplar St., Macon, 7/14/71, B, C, 71000256

Hatcher-Groover-Schwartz House, 1144–1146 Georgia Ave., Macon, 6/21/71, B, C, 71000257

Holt-Peeler-Snow House, 1129 Georgia Ave., Macon, 6/21/71, B, C, 71000258

Johnston-Hay House, 934 Georgia Ave., Macon, 5/27/71, C, NHL, 71000259

Lanier, Sidney, Cottage, 935 High St., Macon, 1/31/72, C, 72000365

Lassiter House, 315 College St., Macon, 4/11/72, B, C, 72000366

Lee, W. G., Alumni House, 1270 Ash (Coleman) St., Macon, 7/14/71, B, C, 71000260

Macon Historic District, Roughly bounded by Riverside Dr., Broadway, Elm, and I-75, Macon, 12/31/74, A, C, 74000658

Macon Railroad Industrial District, Roughly bounded by Fifth, Sixth, and Seventh Sts., Central of Georgia, Southern, and Seaboard RR tracks, Macon, 6/12/87, A, C, 87000977

McCrary, DeWitt, House, 320 Hydrolia St., Macon, 3/22/74, A, C, 74000659

Mechanics Engine House No. 4, 950 Third St., Macon, 9/13/90, A, C, 90001434

Mercer University Administration Building, Coleman Ave., Macon, 8/26/71, A, C, 71000261

Militia Headquarters Building, 552–564 Mulberry St., Macon, 4/11/72, A, C, 72000367

Monroe Street Apartments, 641–661 Monroe St., Macon, 3/16/72, A, C, 72000368

Municipal Auditorium, 415–435 1st St., Macon, 6/21/71, A, C, g, 71000262

Munroe-Dunlap-Snow House, 920 High St., Macon, 7/14/71, A, C, 71000263

Munroe-Goolsby House, 159 Rogers Ave., Macon, 1/20/72, A, C, 72000369

Napier, Leroy, House, 2215 Napier Ave., Macon, 5/27/71, B, C, b, 71000264

North Highlands Historic District, Roughly bounded by Nottingham Dr., Boulevard and Clinton Rd., Macon, 11/22/93, A, C, 93000297

Ocmulgee National Monument, 1207 Emory Hwy., E of Macon, Macon, 10/15/66, A, C, D, NPS, 66000099

Old Macon Library, 652–662 Mulberry St., Macon, 11/26/73, A, C, 73000610

Old U.S. Post Office and Federal Building, 475 Mulberry St., Macon, 1/20/72, C, 72000370

Pleasant Hill Historic District, Roughly bounded by Sheridan Ave. and Schofield St., Madison, Jefferson and Ferguson, and Galliard Sts., Macon, 5/22/86, A, C, a, 86001130

Railroad Overpass at Ocmulgee, Off GA 49, Macon, 12/18/79, A, C, 79000699

Raines-Carmichael House, 1183 Georgia Ave., Macon, 6/21/71, C, NHL, 71000265

Randolph-Whittle House, 1231 Jefferson Ter., Macon, 2/01/72, B, C, b, 72000371

Riverside Cemetery, 1301 Riverside Dr., Macon, 4/28/83, C, D, c, d, 83000183

Rogers, Rock, House, 337 College St., Macon, 1/20/72, B, C, 72000372

Rose Hill Cemetery, Riverside Dr., Macon, 10/09/73, A, C, d, 73000611

Shirley Hills Historic District, Roughly Senate Pl., Parkview Dr., Curry Dr., Briarcliff Rd., Nottingham Dr., and the Ocmulgee River, Macon, 8/17/89, A, C, g, 89001093

Slate House, 931–945 Walnut St., Macon, 1/21/74, A, C, 74000660

Small House, 156 Rogers Ave., Macon, 5/27/71, C, b, 71000266

Solomon-Curd House, 770 Mulberry St., Macon, 5/27/71, C, 71000267

Solomon-Smith-Martin House, 2619 Vineville Ave., Macon, 7/14/71, C, 71000268

St. Joseph's Catholic Church, 812 Poplar St., Macon, 7/14/71, A, C, a, 71000269

Tindall Heights Historic District, Roughly bounded by Broadway, Eisenhower Pkwy., Felton and Nussbaum Aves., Central of Georgia RR tracks and Oglethorpe St, Macon, 7/01/93, A, C, 93000587

Villa Albicini, 150 Tucker Rd., Macon, 5/16/74, C, 74000661

Vineville Historic District, GA 247 and U.S. 41, Macon, 11/21/80, A, C, 80000974

Willingham-Hill-O'Neal Cottage, 535 College St., Macon, 7/14/71, B, C, 71000270

Bleckley County

Bleckley County Courthouse [Georgia County Courthouses TR], Courthouse Sq., Cochran, 9/18/80, A, C, 80000975

Hillcrest, 706 Beech St., Cochran, 4/21/83, C, 83000184

Brantley County

Mumford, Sylvester, House, Off U.S. 84, Waynesville vicinity, 6/28/82, A, C, 82002386

Brooks County

Brooks County Courthouse [Georgia County Courthouses TR], Courthouse Sq., Quitman, 9/18/80, A, C, 80000976

Brooks County Jail [County Jails of Ben Hill, Berrien, Brooks, and Turner Counties TR; Georgia County Courthouses TR], 200 S. Madison St., Quitman, 8/26/82, A, C, 82002387

Eudora Plantation, 3.5 mi. S of Quitman off GA 33, Quitman vicinity, 12/16/74, C, 74000662

Quitman Historic District, US 84, Quitman, 7/08/82, A, C, 82002388

Turner, Henry Gray, House and Grounds, 1000 Old Madison Rd., Quitman, 1/08/80, B, C, 80000977

Bryan County

Fort McAllister, 10 mi. E of Richmond Hill via GA 67, Richmond Hill vicinity, 5/13/70, A, C, 70000197

Glen Echo, 2 mi. (3.2 km) E of Ellabelle on GA 204, Ellabelle vicinity, 1/09/78, A, C, 78000965

Kilkenny, E of Richmond Hill on Kilkenny Rd., Richmond Hill vicinity, 2/14/79, A, C, 79000700

Old Fort Argyle Site, Address Restricted, Savannah vicinity, 3/31/75, A, D, 75000574

Richmond Hill Plantation, E of Richmond Hill on Ford Neck Rd., Richmond Hill vicinity, 1/30/78, B, C, g, 78000966

Seven Mile Bend, Address Restricted, Richmond Hill vicinity, 4/11/72, D, 72000373

Strathy Hall, SE of Richmond Hill, Richmond Hill vicinity, 1/21/79, A, C, 79000701

Bulloch County

Akins, Sol, Farm, Old Register Rd. off US 301, 1.2 mi. S of Statesboro, Statesboro vicinity, 3/22/90, A, C, 90000487

Brannen, James Alonzo, House [Downtown Statesboro MPS], 112 S. Main St./US 301, Statesboro, 9/06/89, B, C, 89001154

Bulloch County Courthouse [Georgia County Courthouses TR], Courthouse Sq., Statesboro, 9/18/80, A, C, 80000978

East Main Street Commercial Historic District [Downtown Statesboro MPS], Roughly E. Main St./US 301 between Siebald and Oak Sts., Statesboro, 9/06/89, A, C, 89001155

East Vine Street Warehouse and Depot District [Downtown Statesboro MPS], Roughly bounded by E. Vine St., Central of Georgia Railroad tracks, and Cherry St., Statesboro, 9/06/89, A, C, 89001156

Holland, Dr. Madison Monroe, House [Downtown Statesboro MPS], 27 S. Main St./US 301, Statesboro, 9/06/89, A, C, 89001157

Jaeckel Hotel, 50 E. Main St., Statesboro, 6/17/82, A, C, 82002389

McDougald, John A., House, 121 S. Main St., Statesboro, 6/21/82, B, C, 82002390

Nevil, Dr. John C., House, US 301 S of Register, Register vicinity, 8/10/89, A, C, 89001105

North College Street Residential Historic District [Downtown Statesboro MPS], Roughly N. College St. from Northside Dr. to Elm St., Statesboro, 9/06/89, C, 89001158

North Main Street Commercial Historic District [Downtown Statesboro MPS], Roughly N. Main St. between Courtland and W. Main Sts., Statesboro, 9/06/89, A, C, 89001159

Olliff, William W., Farm, New Hope Rd., Register vicinity, 12/04/87, B, C, 87002113

Raines, William G., House, 106 S. Main St., Statesboro, 8/31/87, B, C, 87000942

South Main Street Historic District [Downtown Statesboro MPS], Roughly S. Main St. between W. Main and Vine Sts., Statesboro, 9/06/89, A, C, 89001160

South Main Street Residential Historic District [Downtown Statesboro MPS], Roughly College Ln., Southern Railway right-of-way, Walnut, Mikell, and S. Main Sts., Statesboro, 9/06/89, C, 89001161

Statesboro City Hall and Fire Station [Downtown Statesboro MPS], Siebald and Courtland Sts., Statesboro, 9/06/89, A, C, 89001162

Stewart Stores, Jct. of Railroad and Grady Sts., Portal, 5/20/93, A, B, C, 93000430

Stewart, Dr. James A., House, Grady St., Portal, 5/27/93, A, B, C, 93000439

US Post Office—Statesboro [Downtown Statesboro MPS], 26 S. Main St./US 301, Statesboro, 9/06/89, A, C, 89001163

West Main Street Commercial Historic District [Downtown Statesboro MPS], Roughly W. Main St. between Walnut and N. and S. Main Sts., Statesboro, 9/06/89, A, C, 89001164

Burke County

Burke County Courthouse [Georgia County Courthouses TR], Courthouse Sq., Waynesboro, 9/18/80, A, C, 80000980

Hopeful Baptist Church, Winter Rd. E of jct. with Blythe Rd., Keysville vicinity, 1/11/93, A, C, a, 92001734

Jones, John James, House, 525 Jones Ave., Waynesboro, 2/15/80, B, C, 80000981

Sapp Plantation, NW of Sardis on GA 24, Sardis vicinity, 2/08/80, A, C, 80000979

Waynesboro Commercial Historic District, E. 6th, E. 7th, E. 8th, S. Liberty and Myrick Sts., Waynesboro, 6/10/93, A, C, 93000496

Butts County

Butts County Courthouse [Georgia County Courthouses TR], Courthouse Sq., Jackson, 9/18/80, A, C, 80000982

Carmichael, J. R., House, 149 McConough Rd., Jackson, 7/13/77, B, C, 77000411

Indian Springs Hotel, GA 42, Indian Springs, 5/07/73, A, C, D, 73000612

Calhoun County

Arlington Methodist Episcopal Church, South, Pioneer Rd. at Dogwood Dr., Arlington, 4/05/90, C, a, 90000572

Camden County

Camden County Courthouse [Georgia County Courthouses TR], 4th and Camden Aves., Woodbine, 9/18/80, A, C, 80000983

Crooked River Site (9CAM118), Address Restricted, St. Marys vicinity, 12/23/85, D, 85003179

Duck House [Cumberland Island National Seashore MRA], Cumberland Island, St. Marys vicinity, 2/13/84, C, NPS, 84000938

Dungeness Historic District [Cumberland Island National Seashore MRA], Address Restricted, St. Marys vicinity, 2/13/84, A, C, D, NPS, 84000920

High Point-Half Moon Bluff Historic District, NE of St. Marys on Cumberland Island, St. Marys vicinity, 12/22/78, A, D, a, NPS, 78000265

Little Cumberland Island Lighthouse, N end of Little Cumberland Island, St. Marys vicinity, 8/28/89, A, C, 89001407

Main Road [Cumberland Island National Seashore MRA], Cumberland Island, St. Marys vicinity, 2/13/84, A, NPS, 84000941

McIntosh, John Houstoun, Sugarhouse, Ga. Spur 40, 6 mi. N of St. Marys, St. Marys, 4/02/92, A, D, 92000167

Orange Hall, 311 Osborne St., St. Marys, 5/07/73, C, 73000613

Plum Orchard Historic District [Cumberland Island National Seashore MRA], Address Restricted, St. Marys vicinity, 11/23/84, C, D, NPS, 84000258

Rayfield Archeological District [Cumberland Island National Seashore MRA], Address Restricted, St. Marys vicinity, 2/13/84, D, NPS, 84000924

Camden County—Continued

St. Marys Historic District, Roughly bounded by Waterfront Rd., Norris, Alexander, and Oak Grove Cemetery, St. Marys, 5/13/76, A, C, 76000609

Stafford Plantation Historic District [Cumberland Island National Seashore MRA], Address Restricted, St. Marys vicinity, 11/23/84, A, C, D, NPS, 84000265

Table Point Archeological District [Cumberland Island National Seashore MRA], Address Restricted, St. Marys vicinity, 11/23/84, D, NPS, 84000260

Candler County

Candler County Courthouse [Georgia County Courthouses TR], Courthouse Sq., Metter, 9/18/80, A, C, 80000984

South Metter Residential Historic District, S. Kennedy, S. Roundtree, S. Lewis, and S. Leroy, Metter, 3/15/88, A, C, g, 87001429

Carroll County

Bonner-Sharp-Gunn House, West Georgia College campus, Carrollton, 5/13/70, A, C, b, 70000198

Burns Quarry, Address Restricted, Carrollton vicinity, 8/29/77, A, D, 77001539

Carroll County Courthouse [Georgia County Courthouses TR], Newnan and Dixie Sts., Carrollton, 9/18/80, A, C, 80000985

Dorough Round Barn and Farm, N of Hickory Level on Villa Rica Rd., Hickory Level vicinity, 1/20/80, A, C, 80000986

Lovvorn, Dr. James L., House, 113 E. College St., Bowdon, 5/19/88, B, C, 88000595

McDaniel—Huie Place, 1238 SR 166 W., Bowdon vicinity, 5/24/90, A, C, 90000803

South Carrollton Residential Historic District, Roughly bounded by RR tracks, Harmon and West Aves., Bradley, Mill and Garrett Sts., Tillman and Hill Drs., Carrollton, 6/28/84, A, C, 84000947

U.S. Post Office, 402 Newnan St., Carrollton, 4/18/83, A, C, 83000185

Catoosa County

Chickamauga and Chattanooga National Military Park, S of Chattanooga on U.S. 27, Fort Oglethorpe, 10/15/66, A, f, g, NPS, 66000274

Fort Oglethorpe Historic District, U.S. 27, Fort Oglethorpe, 4/20/79, A, B, C, g, 79000702

Ringgold Commercial Historic District, Nashville St. between Tennessee and Depot Sts., Ringgold, 1/30/92, A, C, 91002001

Ringgold Depot, U.S. 41, Ringgold, 11/30/78, A, C, 78000968

Stone Church, E of Ringgold off U.S. 76, Ringgold vicinity, 11/29/79, A, C, a, 79000703

Whitman-Anderson House, 309 Tennessee St., Ringgold, 10/05/77, A, C, 77000412

Charlton County

Charlton County Courthouse [Georgia County Courthouses TR], Off GA 40, Folkston, 9/18/80, A, C, 80000987

Hopkins, John M., Cabin, SW of Folkston, off GA 121/23, Folkston vicinity, 3/04/83, A, B, C, 83000186

Chatham County

Ardsley Park-Chatham Crescent Historic District, Roughly bounded by Ardsley Pk., Chatham Crescent, Bull St., Baldwin Pk. and Ardmore, Savannah, 8/15/85, A, B, C, 85001787

Bethesda Home for Boys, S of Savannah at Ferguson Ave. and Bethesda Rd., Savannah vicinity, 9/12/73, A, g, 73000614

CSS GEORGIA (ironclad), Address Restricted, Savannah vicinity, 2/10/87, A, D, 86003746

Central of Georgia Depot and Trainshed, W. Broad and Liberty Sts., Savannah, 12/08/76, A, C, NHL, 76000610

Central of Georgia Railroad: Savannah Shops and Terminal Facilities, W. Broad St. and Railroad Ave., Savannah, 6/02/78, A, C, NHL, 78000970

Central of Georgia Railway Company Shop Property, Between W. Jones St. and Louisville Rd., Savannah, 3/05/70, A, C, NHL, 70000199

Charity Hospital, 644 W. 36th St., Savannah, 5/02/85, A, C, 85000934

Davenport, Isaiah, House, 324 E. State St., Savannah, 9/22/72, C, 72000374

Drouillard—Maupas House, 2422 Abercorn St., Savannah, 5/13/91, C, 91000558

Federal Building and U.S. Courthouse, Wright Sq., Savannah, 6/07/74, C, 74000663

First Bryan Baptist Church, 575 W. Bryan St., Savannah, 5/22/78, A, C, a, 78000971

Fort Jackson, Islands Expwy., Savannah, 2/18/70, A, C, 70000200

Fort Pulaski National Monument, 17 mi. W of Savannah, Cockspur Island, Savannah vicinity, 10/15/66, A, C, NPS, 66000064

Fort Screven Historic District, Tilton, Butler, Van Horn, Railroad and Alger Aves., and Pulaski Rd., Tybee Island, 5/25/82, A, B, C, g, 82002393

Green-Meldrim House, Macon and Bull Sts., Savannah, 1/21/74, B, C, a, NHL, 74000664

Hill Hall at Savannah State College, Savannah State College campus, Savannah vicinity, 4/23/81, A, C, 81000197

Hodgson, W. B., Hall, 501 Whitaker St., Savannah, 3/25/77, A, C, 77000413

Isle of Hope Historic District, Roughly bounded by Skidaway River, Parkersburg Rd., Island, Cornus, and Noble Glen Drs., Savannah vicinity, 9/02/84, A, C, 84003850

Isle of Hope Historic District, Roughly bounded by Skidaway River, Parkersburg Rd., Island, Cornus, and Noble Glen Drs., Savannah vicinity, 9/07/84, A, C, 84003874

Laurel Grove-North Cemetery, W. Anderson St., Savannah, 8/04/83, A, C, d, f, g, 83000187

Laurel Grove-South Cemetery, 37th St., Savannah, 9/06/78, A, d, 78000972

Lebanon Plantation, SW of Savannah, Savannah vicinity, 11/29/79, A, C, D, 79000704

Low, Juliette Gordon, Birthplace, 10 Oglethorpe Ave., E., Savannah, 10/15/66, B, C, c, NHL, 66000276

Massie Common School House, 207 E. Gordon St., Savannah, 4/13/77, A, C, 77000414

Mulberry Grove Site, Address Restricted, Port Wentworth vicinity, 7/17/75, A, B, D, 75000575

Nicholsonville Baptist Church, White Bluff Rd., Nicholsonville, 5/22/78, A, C, a, 78000969

Owens-Thomas House, 124 Abercorn St., Savannah, 5/11/76, C, NHL, 76000611

Savannah Historic District, Bounded by E. Broad, Gwinnett, and W. Broad Sts. and the Savannah River, Savannah, 11/13/66, C, NHL, 66000277

Savannah Victorian Historic District, Roughly bounded by Gwinnett, Price, Anderson, and Montgomery Sts., Savannah, 12/11/74, A, C, 74000665

Savannah Victorian Historic District (Boundary Increase), Bounded by Gwinnett, Anderson and 31st Sts., Savannah, 5/20/82, A, C, 82002392

Scarbrough, William, House, 41 W. Broad St., Savannah, 6/22/70, B, C, NHL, 70000201

Slotin Building, 101 W. Broad St., Savannah, 3/24/83, A, C, 83000188

St. Bartholomew's Church, Cheves Rd., Burroughs, 6/17/82, A, C, a, 82002391

St. Philip AME Church, 613 W. Broad St., Savannah, 8/02/84, A, C, a, 84000959

Sturges, Oliver, House, 27 Abercorn St., Savannah, 7/14/71, A, C, 71000271

Telfair Academy, 121 Barnard St., Savannah, 5/11/76, A, C, NHL, 76000612

Two Pierpont Circle, 2 Pierpont Cir., Savannah, 4/04/90, C, 90000492

U.S. Customhouse, 1–3 E. Bay St., Savannah, 5/29/74, A, C, 74000666

Wild Heron, 15 mi. SW of Savannah off U.S. 17, Savannah vicinity, 12/16/77, A, C, 77000415

Wormsloe Plantation, Isle of Hope and Long Island, Savannah vicinity, 4/26/73, A, C, 73000615

Chattahoochee County

Chatahoochee County Jail, Mt. Olive and Boyd Sts., Cusseta, 3/13/86, A, C, 86000368

Riverside, 100 Vibbert Ave., Fort Benning, 5/27/71, A, C, a, 71000272

Chattooga County

Camp Juliette Low, GA 157, Cloudland vicinity, 9/01/87, A, B, C, 87001431

Chattooga County—Continued

Chattooga County Courthouse [Georgia County Courthouses TR], Courthouse Sq., Summerville, 9/18/80, A, C, 80000988

Georgia Site No. 9 CG 43, Address Restricted, Summerville vicinity, 12/20/87, D, 87002112

Penn Place, Penn Bridge Rd., Trion vicinity, 9/29/88, A, C, 88001828

Summerville Depot, 120 E. Washington Ave., Summerville, 1/29/92, A, C, 91002037

Cherokee County

Canton Commercial Historic District, Roughly bounded by Main, Church, Archer, and Marietta Sts., Canton, 1/12/84, A, C, 84000962

Cherokee County Courthouse [Georgia County Courthouses TR], 100 North St., Canton, 5/28/81, A, C, 81000198

Crescent Farm, GA 5, SE of GA 140, Canton, 11/27/89, A, C, 89002032

Roberts, Alfred W., House, GA 372, Ball Ground, 9/11/85, B, C, 85002313

Clarke County

Athens Factory, Baldwin and Williams Sts., Athens, 7/31/80, A, C, D, 80000989

Athens Warehouse Historic District, Roughly bounded by Hancock and Thomas Sts., and the RR tracks, Athens, 10/20/88, A, C, 88002021

Bishop House, Jackson St., University of Georgia campus, Athens, 3/16/72, C, 72000375

Bloomfield Street Historic District, Roughly bounded by Bloomfield and Peabody Sts., U of G campus, Rutherford St and Milledge Ave., Athens, 4/18/85, A, B, C, 85000850

Boulevard Historic District, Roughly bounded by the Seaboard Coastline RR tracks, Pulaski St., Prince Ave., and Hiawassee St., Athens, 4/18/85, A, C, 85000851

Camak House, 279 Meigs St., Athens, 7/07/75, B, C, 75000576

Carnegie Library Building, 1401 Prince Ave., Athens, 11/11/75, C, 75000577

Chase, Albon, House, 185 N. Hull St., Athens, 8/19/74, B, C, 74002255

Chestnut Grove School, 610 Epps Bridge Rd., Athens vicinity, 6/28/84, A, C, 84003873

Church-Waddel-Brumby House, 280 E. Dougherty St., Athens, 2/20/75, A, B, C, b, 75000578

Clarke County Jail, Courthouse Sq., Athens, 5/29/80, A, C, 80000990

Cobb, T. R. R., House, 194 Prince Ave., Athens, 6/30/75, B, C, a, 75000579

Cobb-Treanor House, 1234 S. Lumpkin St., Athens, 5/08/79, A, C, 79000705

Cobbham Historic District, Roughly bounded by Prince Ave., Hill, Reese, and Pope Sts., Athens, 8/24/78, A, C, 78000973

Crane, Ross, House, 247 Pulaski St., Athens, 6/18/79, C, 79000706

Dearing Street Historic District, Roughly bounded by Broad and Baxter Sts., Milledge Ave., and includes both sides of Finley St. and Henderson Ave., Athens, 9/05/75, A, C, 75000580

Dearing, Albin P., House, 338 S. Milledge Ave., Athens, 5/08/79, A, C, 79000707

Downtown Athens Historic District, Roughly bounded by Hancock Ave., Foundry, Mitchell, Athens, 8/10/78, A, C, 78000974

Downtown Athens Historic District (Boundary Increase), Roughly bounded by Hancock Ave., Foundry, Mitchell, Broad, and Lumpkin sts., Athens, 5/31/84, C, 84000965

First African Methodist Episcopal Church, 521 N. Hull St., Athens, 3/10/80, C, a, 80000991

Franklin House, 464–480 E. Broad St., Athens, 12/11/74, A, C, 74000667

Garden Club of Georgia Museum-Headquarters House, Founder's Memorial Garden, Lumpkin St., University of Georgia campus, Athens, 4/26/72, A, C, 72000376

Grady, Henry W., House, 634 Prince Ave., Athens, 5/11/76, B, NHL, 76000613

Hamilton, Dr. James S., House, 150 S. Milledge Ave., Athens, 4/24/79, B, C, 79000708

Lucy Cobb Institute Campus, 200 N. Milledge Ave., University of Georgia campus, Athens, 3/16/72, A, C, a, 72000377

Lumpkin, Gov. Wilson, House, Cedar St., University of Georgia campus, Athens, 3/16/72, C, 72000378

Lumpkin, Joseph Henry, House, 248 Prince Ave., Athens, 6/27/75, B, C, b, 75000581

Milledge Avenue Historic District, Milledge Ave. from Broad St. to Five Points, Athens, 4/18/85, A, C, 85000852

Milledge Circle Historic District, Milledge Park, Lumpkin St., Milledge Circle and Milledge Ave., Athens, 4/18/85, A, C, 85000859

Morton Building, 199 W. Washington St., Athens, 10/22/79, A, C, 79000709

Oglethorpe Avenue Historic District, Oglethorpe Ave., Athens, 11/05/87, A, C, 87001360

Old North Campus, University of Georgia, Bounded by Broad, Lumpkin, and Jackson Sts., Athens, 3/16/72, A, C, 72000379

Parr, Calvin W., House, 277 Bloomfield St., Athens, 9/09/82, C, 82002394

Parrott Insurance Building, 283 E. Broad St., Athens, 10/07/77, A, C, 77000416

President's House, 570 Prince Ave., Athens, 3/16/72, B, C, 72000380

Reese Street Historic District, Roughly bounded by Meigs, Finley, Broad, & Harris Sts., Athens, 11/10/87, A, C, 87001990

Sledge, James A., House, 749 Cobb St., Athens, 2/12/74, C, 74000668

Sorrells, R. P., House, 220 Prince Ave., Athens, 1/22/92, C, 91002003

Thomas-Carithers House, 530 S. Milledge Ave., Athens, 5/08/79, B, C, 79000710

Upson House, 1022 Prince Ave., Athens, 11/15/73, C, 73000616

Ware-Lyndon House, 293 Hoyt St., Athens, 3/15/76, A, 76000614

West Hancock Avenue Historic District, Roughly bounded by Hill, Franklin, Broad Sts. and the Plaza, Athens, 8/08/88, A, C, a, 88000227

White Hall, Whitehall and Simonton Bridge Rds., Whitehall, 6/18/79, A, C, 79000711

Wilkins House, 387 S. Milledge Ave., Athens, 5/19/70, B, C, 70000202

Woodlawn Historic District, Woodlawn Ave., Athens, 10/23/87, A, C, 87001390

Young Women's Christian Association Complex, 345–347 W. Hancock St., Athens, 5/12/87, A, C, b, 87000696

Clay County

Clay County Courthouse [Georgia County Courthouses TR], Off GA 37, Fort Gaines, 9/18/80, A, C, 80000992

Dill House, 102 S. Washington St., Fort Gaines, 5/06/75, A, C, 75000582

Fort Gaines Cemetery Site, S of SR 37, W of Chattahoochee River, Fort Gaines vicinity, 12/16/74, D, d, 74000669

Fort Gaines Historic District, Roughly bounded by Chattahoochee River, GA 37, GA 39, College, Commerce and Jefferson Sts., Fort Gaines, 5/17/84, A, C, a, 84000970

Toney-Standley House, NW of Fort Gaines off GA 39, Fort Gaines vicinity, 9/17/74, A, C, b, 74000670

Clayton County

Crawford-Dorsey House and Cemetery, Freeman and McDonough Rds., Lovejoy vicinity, 7/05/84, A, C, d, 84000972

Jonesboro Historic District, GA 54 and 3, Jonesboro, 1/20/72, A, B, C, d, g, 72000381

Orkin Early Quartz Site, Address Restricted, Fayetteville vicinity, 12/04/74, D, 74000671

Rex Mill, Rex Rd., Rex, 3/07/79, A, C, 79000712

Stately Oaks, Jodeco Rd., Jonesboro, 3/16/72, B, C, b, 72000382

Clinch County

Clinch County Courthouse [Georgia County Courthouses TR], U.S. 84, Homerville, 9/18/80, A, C, 80000993

Clinch County Jail, Court Sq., Homerville, 1/11/80, C, 80000994

Cobb County

Big Shanty Village Historic District [Kennesaw MRA], Park Ave., Whitfield Pl., Main, Harris, Lewis, and Cherokee Sts., Kennesaw, 3/20/80, A, C, 80000995

Cobb County—Continued

Braswell-Carnes House, 2430 Burnt Hickory Rd., NW, Marietta, 3/01/84, C, 84000974

Brumby, Arnoldus, House, 472 Powder Springs St., Marietta, 8/29/77, A, C, 77000417

Camp McDonald [Kennesaw MRA], Off U.S. 41, Kennesaw, 3/20/80, A, 80000996

Carmichael, J. H., Farm and General Store, SE of Smyrna at 501 Log Cabin Rd., Smyrna vicinity, 6/30/80, A, C, D, 80001002

Causey, Israel, House, 5909 Maxham Rd., Austell, 8/13/75, A, C, 75000584

Cheney, Andrew J., House, SW of Marietta at Powder Springs and Bankstone Rds., Marietta vicinity, 7/22/79, A, C, 79000713

Cherokee Street Historic District [Kennesaw MRA], Cherokee St., Kennesaw, 3/20/80, A, C, 80000997

Church Street—Cherokee Street Historic District, Roughly bounded by Margaret Ave. and Chicopee Dr., DeSoto Ave., Montgomery and Brumby, and Campbell Hill Sts., Marietta, 12/03/85, A, B, C, 85003059

Clarkdale Historic District, Powder Springs-Austell Rd., Clarkdale, 12/23/87, A, C, 87002134

General, The, Big Shanty Museum of Cherokee St., Kennesaw, 6/19/73, A, 73000617

Gibson, John S., Farmhouse [Kennesaw MRA], 3370 Cherokee St., Kennesaw, 3/20/80, A, C, 80000998

Gilgal Church Battle Site, 9 mi. W of Marietta on Sandtown Rd., Marietta vicinity, 1/23/75, A, 75000585

Glover—McLeod—Garrison House, 250 Garrison Rd., SE, Marietta, 3/25/77, C, 77000418

Johnston's Line, SE of Mableton off U.S. 78 at Chattachooche River, Mableton vicinity, 7/05/73, A, 73000618

Kennesaw Mountain National Battlefield Park, 2 mi. W of Marietta, Marietta vicinity, 10/15/66, A, C, NPS, 66000063

Mable, Robert, House and Cemetery, 5239 Floyd Rd., Mableton, 9/01/88, C, 87001345

McAdoo, William Gibbs, House, SW of Marietta on GA 5, Marietta vicinity, 11/17/78, A, C, 78000975

Midway Presbyterian Church and Cemetery, 4635 Dallas Hwy./GA 120 SW, Powder Springs, 12/29/86, A, C, a, d, 86003526

North Main Street Historic District [Kennesaw MRA], N. Main St., Kennesaw, 3/20/80, A, C, 80000999

Northwest Marietta Historic District, Roughly bounded by RR tracks, NW along Kennesaw Ave., McDonald St., and Whitlock Ave., Marietta, 6/11/75, A, C, 75000586

Rice, John W., Summer Cottage, 254 Concord Rd., Smyrna, 4/08/83, C, 83000189

Ruff's Mill and Concord Covered Bridge, 10 Concord Rd., SW, Smyrna, 11/24/80, A, C, D, 80001001

Sope Creek Ruins, Address Restricted, Marietta vicinity, 4/27/73, A, D, 73000619

Summers Street Historic District [Kennesaw MRA], Summers St., Kennesaw, 3/20/80, A, C, 80001000

Washington Avenue Historic District, Roughly bounded by Lawrence St., Rigsby St., Washington Ave., and Haynes St., Marietta, 8/10/89, A, C, 89001102

Whitlock Avenue Historic District, Roughly bounded by McCord St., Oakmont St., Whitlock Ave., Powder Springs Rd., Trammel St., Maxwell Ave., and Hazel St., Marietta, 9/14/89, A, C, 89001218

Zion Baptist Church, 149 Haynes St., Marietta, 7/11/90, A, C, a, 90001026

Coffee County

Downtown Douglas Historic District, Roughly bounded by Jackson St., Pearl Ave., Cherry St. and the Georgia—Florida RR tracks, Douglas, 9/09/93, A, C, 93000941

Gaskin Avenue Historic District, Roughly bounded by Madison Ave., Wilson St., Pearl Ave., Gordon St., McDonald Ave., Atlantic Coastline RR and Coffee Ave, Douglas, 10/21/93, A, C, 93001138

Pope, Lonnie A., House, Jackson St. and Central of Georgia RR tracks, Douglas, 6/17/82, C, b, 82002395

Union Banking Company Building, 102 Peterson Ave., Douglas, 12/10/82, C, 82000144

Colquitt County

Ashburn, W. W., House, 609 1st Ave., Moultrie, 7/15/82, A, B, C, 82002396

Carnegie Library of Moultrie, 39 N. Main St., Moultrie, 7/15/82, A, C, 82002397

Coleman, James W., House, GA 33, Moultrie vicinity, 12/22/83, B, C, 83003555

Colquitt County Courthouse [Georgia County Courthouses TR], Courthouse Sq., Moultrie, 9/18/80, A, C, 80001003

Colquitt County Jail, 126 1st Ave., SE, Moultrie, 10/10/80, A, C, 80001004

Moultrie High School, 7th Ave., Moultrie, 6/17/82, A, C, 82002398

Tucker, Henry Crawford, Log House and Farmstead, Off GA 37, Moultrie vicinity, 7/26/82, A, B, C, D, 82002399

Columbia County

Columbia County Courthouse [Georgia County Courthouses TR], GA 47, Appling, 9/18/80, A, C, 80001005

Kiokee Baptist Church, Kiokee Rd., Appling, 12/08/78, A, C, a, 78000976

Stallings Island, Address Restricted, Augusta vicinity, 10/15/66, D, NHL, 66000279

Woodville, Address Restricted, Winfield vicinity, 5/10/79, A, C, D, 79000714

Cook County

SOWEGA Building, 100 S. Hutchinson Ave., Adel, 3/29/90, A, C, 90000546

Coweta County

Brannon, W. A., Store—Moreland Knitting Mills, Main St., Moreland, 12/12/85, A, C, 85003332

Cole Town District, Roughly bounded by Washington, Thompson, and Davis Sts., and Hooligan Alley, Newnan, 9/30/82, A, C, D, 82002400

Coweta County Courthouse [Georgia County Courthouses TR], Courthouse Sq., Newnan, 9/18/80, A, C, 80001006

Crowder, William Leonard, Home Place, 1615 Handy Rd., Newnan vicinity, 3/17/86, A, C, 86000455

Goodwyn—Bailey House, 2295 Old Poplar Rd., Newnan, 10/29/92, A, C, 92001520

Gordon-Banks House, S of Newnan on U.S. 29, Newnan vicinity, 1/20/72, C, b, 72000383

Grantville Historic District, Bounded by US 29, LaGrange St., W. Grantville Rd. and the city cemetery, Grantville, 6/14/91, A, C, a, d, 91000772

Greenville Street-LaGrange Street Historic District, LaGrange, Ninnons, Greenville, Powell, Reese, Powell and Buchanan Sts., Newnan, 4/28/83, A, C, 83000190

Hollberg Hotel, Seavy and Barnes Sts., Senoia, 3/10/80, A, B, C, 80001007

Newnan Commercial Historic District, Roughly bounded by Lee, Perry, Salbide, Lagrange, W. Spring, Brown, Madison, and Jefferson, Newnan, 3/20/90, A, C, a, 90000432

Northwest Newnan Residential Historic District, Roughly bounded by RR tracks, Jefferson, Cavender, Duncan, and Browns Sts., Newnan, 5/28/82, A, C, g, 82002401

Platinum Point Historic District, Along Jackson St., 1/2 mi. N of downtown Newnan, Newnan, 7/12/90, A, C, 90000997

Senoia Historic District, Roughly bounded by Couch St., CSX Railroad tracks, GA 16, and Pylant St., Senoia, 3/17/89, A, C, a, 89000149

Sims, George R., House, 1851 Collinsworth Rd., Palmetto vicinity, 9/27/90, C, 90001435

Willcoxon—Arnold House, One Bullsboro Dr., Newnan, 5/20/91, B, C, 91000559

Crawford County

Crawford County Courthouse [Georgia County Courthouses TR], U.S. 80, Knoxville, 9/18/80, A, C, 80001008

Crawford County Jail, GA 42, Knoxville, 5/18/89, A, C, 89000418

Crawford County—Continued

Roberta Historic District, Roughly bounded by E. Cruselle St., Kirby St., Agency St., and Mather St., Roberta, 5/19/89, A, C, a, 89000365

Crisp County

Cannon Site, Address Restricted, Cordele vicinity, 9/05/75, D, 75000587

Cordele Commercial Historic District, Roughly bounded by Sixth Ave., Sixth St., Ninth Ave., and Fourteenth St., Cordele, 7/06/89, A, C, 89000803

US Post Office—Cordele, 102-104 6th St., Cordele, 6/29/84, C, 84000977

Dade County

Dade County Courthouse [Georgia County Courthouses TR], Courthouse Sq., Trenton, 9/18/80, A, C, 80001009

Dawson County

Dawson County Courthouse [Georgia County Courthouses TR], Courthouse Sq., Dawsonville, 9/18/80, A, C, 80001010

Dawson Couty Jail [County Jails of the Georgia Mountains Area TR], HW 53, Dawsonville, 9/13/85, A, C, 85002083

De Kalb County

Avondale Estates Historic District, Roughly bounded by Avondale Rd., Lakeshore Dr., Kingstone, Clarendon, and Fairchild Dr., also Lake Avondale, Avondale Estates, 12/08/86, A, C, 86003669

Briarcliff, 1260 Briarcliff Rd., NE, Atlanta, 8/04/88, A, B, C, 88001167

Callanwolde, 980 Briarcliff Rd., NE, Atlanta, 4/23/73, C, 73002137

Cameron Court District, E of Atlanta at Braircliff Rd., Atlanta vicinity, 9/30/82, C, 82004662

Candler Park Historic District, Roughly bounded by Moreland, DeKalb, McLendon, and Harold Aves., Mathews St., and Clifton Terr., Atlanta, 9/08/83, A, C, 83000191

DeKalb Avenue-Clifton Road Archeological Site, Address Restricted, Atlanta vicinity, 12/14/78, D, 78003094

Druid Hills Historic District, U.S. 29, Atlanta vicinity, 10/25/79, C, g, 79000715

Druid Hills Parks and Parkways, Both sides of Ponce de Leon Ave. between Briarcliff Rd. and the Seaboard Coast Line RR tracks, Atlanta and vicinity, 4/11/75, A, C, a, 75002070

Emory University District, N. Decatur Rd., Atlanta, 11/20/75, A, C, a, g, 75002071

Gay, Mary, House, 524 Marshall St., Decatur, 5/06/75, A, B, C, 75002072

Gentry, William T., House, 132 E. Lake Dr., SE, Atlanta, 5/02/85, A, B, C, 85000935

Hampton, Cora Beck, Schoolhouse and House, 213 Hillyer Pl., Decatur, 4/16/92, A, C, 92000366

Lee, Agnes, Chapter House of the United Daughters of the Confederacy, 120 Avery St., Decatur, 7/25/85, A, C, 85001621

Old DeKalb County Courthouse, Court Sq., Decatur, 8/26/71, C, 71001016

Pythagoras Lodge No. 41, Free and Accepted Masons, 136 E. Ponce de Leon Ave., Decatur, 8/19/82, A, C, 82004664

Scottish Rite Hospital for Crippled Children, 321 W. Hill St., Decatur, 6/17/82, A, C, 82004665

Seminary, The, 6886 Main St., Lithonia, 11/15/78, A, B, C, 78003097

Smith-Benning House, 520 Oakdale Rd., NE, Atlanta, 6/28/82, B, C, 82004663

Soapstone Ridge, Address Restricted, Atlanta vicinity, 5/07/73, D, 73002138

Steele-Cobb House, 2632 Fox Hills Dr., Decatur, 6/17/82, C, 82004666

Swanton House, 720 Swanton Way, Decatur, 8/30/78, A, B, C, b, 78000977

Decatur County

Bainbridge Commercial Historic District, Roughly bounded by Water, Clark, Troupe, West, Broughton, & Crawford Sts., Bainbridge, 11/06/87, A, C, 87001908

Bainbridge Residential Historic District, Roughly bounded by Calhoun, Scott, Evans, College, & Washington Sts., Bainbridge, 11/05/87, A, C, 87001907

Brinson Family Historic District, Bainbridge, Wainhurst and Leon Sts., Brinson, 10/02/86, C, a, 86002677

Callahan, J. W., House, 200 Evans St., Bainbridge, 12/12/76, B, C, 76000616

Curry Hill Plantation, 6 mi. E of Bainbridge on U.S. 84, Bainbridge vicinity, 1/29/73, A, B, C, a, 73000620

Decatur County Courthouse [Georgia County Courthouses TR], West and Water Sts., Bainbridge, 9/18/80, A, C, 80001011

Dodge County

Dodge County Courthouse [Georgia County Courthouses TR], Courthouse Sq., Eastman, 9/18/80, A, C, 80001012

Dooly County

Dooly County Courthouse [Georgia County Courthouses TR], GA 27, Vienna, 9/18/80, A, C, 80001013

Stovall-George-Woodward House, 305 Union St., Vienna, 4/27/79, B, C, 79000716

Dougherty County

Albany District Pecan Growers' Exchange, 211-213 Roosevelt Ave., Albany, 5/10/84, A, 84000979

Albany Housefurnishing Company, 226 W. Broad Ave., Albany, 6/17/82, A, C, 82002402

Albany Railroad Depot Historic District, E. Roosevelt Ave., Albany, 5/20/82, A, C, 82002403

Bridge House, 112 N. Front St., Albany, 11/19/74, A, C, 74000672

Carnegie Library of Albany, 215 N. Jackson St., Albany, 7/15/82, A, C, 82002404

Davis, John A., House, 514 Pine Ave., Albany, 10/16/80, B, C, 80001014

Davis-Exchange Bank Building, 100-102 N. Washington St., Albany, 2/23/84, A, C, 84000981

Farkas, Samuel, House, 328 W. Broad Ave., Albany, 11/09/77, B, C, 77000419

Municipal Auditorium, 301 Pine Ave., Albany, 6/25/74, A, C, 74000673

New Albany Hotel, 245 Pine St., Albany, 6/17/82, A, C, 82002405

Old St. Teresa's Catholic Church, 313 Residence Ave., Albany, 4/01/75, A, C, a, 75000589

Rosenberg Brothers Department Store, 126 N. Washington St., Albany, 8/19/82, A, C, 82002406

Smith, W. E., House, 516 Flint Ave., Albany, 8/30/77, C, 77000420

St. Nicholas Hotel, 141 Flint Ave., 300–310 Washington St., Albany, 12/19/91, A, C, 91001851

Tift Park, Bounded by N. Jefferson St., 5th Ave., 7th Ave. and Palmyra Rd., Dougherty, 11/15/93, A, C, g, 93001179

U.S. Post Office and Courthouse, 337 Broad Ave., Albany, 6/22/79, A, C, 79003105

Union Depot, Roosevelt Ave. and N. Front St., Albany, 2/13/75, A, 75000590

Douglas County

Douglasville Commercial Historic District, Roughly bounded by Broad St., Adair St., Church St., and Club Dr., Douglasville, 7/24/89, A, C, 89000850

Roberts, Col. William T., House, 8652 Campbellton St., Douglasville, 3/02/89, B, C, 89000153

Sweet Water Manufacturing Site, Address Restricted, Atlanta vicinity, 11/23/77, A, D, 77000421

Early County

Coheelee Creek Covered Bridge, 2 mi. N of Hilton on Old River Rd., Hilton vicinity, 5/13/76, A, C, 76000617

Early County—Continued

Early County Courthouse [Georgia County Courthouses TR], Courthouse Sq., Blakely, 9/18/80, A, C, 80001015

Harrell, Jane Donalson, House, SR 1975 off U.S. 84, Jakin, 6/17/82, A, C, 82002407

Kolomoki Mounds, 8 mi. N of Blakely on U.S. 27, Kolomoki Mounds State Park, Blakely vicinity, 10/15/66, D, NHL, 66000280

Echols County

Statenville Consolidated School, GA 94, Statenville, 6/01/88, A, C, g, 88000606

Effingham County

Ebenezer Townsite and Jerusalem Lutheran Church, E of Springfield on GA 275 at Savannah River, Springfield vicinity, 12/04/74, A, a, 74000674

Effingham County Courthouse [Georgia County Courthouses TR], SR 21, Springfield, 9/18/80, A, C, 80001016

Guyton Historic District, Bounded by city limits on the E, S, and W, and Alexander Ave., on the N, Guyton, 9/30/82, A, C, 82002408

New Hope AME Church, Alexander St., Guyton, 3/13/86, A, C, a, 86000364

Reiser—Zoller Farm, GA 119, 4 mi. N of Springfield, Springfield vicinity, 3/02/89, A, C, 89000152

Elbert County

Alexander-Cleveland House, 3.5 mi. NE of Ruckersville, Ruckersville vicinity, 9/15/77, C, 77000423

Allen, William, House, 9 mi. E of Elberton on SR 6, Elberton, 6/05/75, C, 75000591

Banks, Ralph, Place, N of Elberton off GA 77, Elberton vicinity, 5/22/78, B, C, 78000978

Chandler, Asa, House, 1003 Old Petersburg Rd., Elberton, 6/22/82, A, B, C, 82002409

Dove Creek Baptist Church, GA 72, Elberton, 7/09/87, A, C, a, b, 87001154

Elbert County Courthouse [Georgia County Courthouses TR], Courthouse Sq., Elberton, 9/18/80, A, C, 80001017

Elberton Commercial Historic District, Church, Elbert, Oliver, and McIntosh Sts., and Public Sq., Elberton, 5/20/82, A, C, 82002410

Elberton Depot, N. Oliver and Deadwyler Sts., Elberton, 9/11/86, C, 86002399

Elberton Residential Historic District, Roughly bounded by Elbert, Oliver, Adams, Thomas, Edwards, and Heard Sts., Elberton, 8/11/82, A, C, 82002411

Gaines, Ralph, House, N of Elberton on GA 368, Elberton vicinity, 10/05/77, B, 77000422

Rucker House, GA 985, Ruckersville, 6/23/78, B, C, c, 78000979

Emanuel County

Coleman, James, House, 323 N. Main St., Swainsboro, 4/28/92, C, 92000384

Davis, Josiah, House, S of Canoochee on GA 192, Canoochee vicinity, 10/05/82, A, C, 82000145

Durden, Albert Neal, House, Co. Rd. 360, Emanuel vicinity, 4/20/90, C, 90000561

Evans County

Daniel, Dr. James W., House, 102 N. Newton St., Claxton, 4/07/83, B, C, 83000192

DeLoach, George W., House, S. Railroad Ave., and Strickland St., Hagan, 6/28/82, B, C, 82002412

Evans County Courthouse [Georgia County Courthouses TR], Courthouse Sq., Claxton, 9/18/80, A, C, 80001018

Green, Mitchell J., Plantation, NE of Claxton off U.S. 301 and GA 169, Claxton vicinity, 4/09/80, A, C, 80001019

Fannin County

Blue Ridge Depot, Depot St., Blue Ridge, 7/15/82, A, C, 82002413

Fayette County

Fayette County Courthouse [Georgia County Courthouses TR], GA 85, Fayetteville, 9/18/80, A, C, 80001020

King, Tandy, House, Address Restricted, Fayetteville vicinity, 7/20/78, A, D, d, 78000980

Floyd County

Battey, Dr. Robert, House, 725 E. 2nd Ave., Rome, 6/17/82, B, C, b, 82002414

Berry Schools, N of Rome on U.S. 27, Rome vicinity, 7/21/78, A, B, C, a, g, 78000981

Between the Rivers Historic District, Roughly bounded by the Etowah and Oostanaula Rivers, and 7th Ave., Rome, 6/09/83, A, C, g, 83000193

Between the Rivers Historic District (Boundary Increase), 107 W. Fourth St., Rome, 1/10/89, A, C, 88003124

Carroll, John M., House [Cave Spring MRA], Park St., Cave Spring, 6/19/80, C, c, 80001021

Carroll-Harper House [Cave Spring MRA], Cedartown St., Cave Spring, 6/19/80, A, C, 80001023

Carroll-Richardson Grist Mill [Cave Spring MRA], Mill St., Cave Spring, 6/19/80, A, C, 80001025

Cave Spring Commerical Historic District [Cave Spring MRA], Alabama, Rome and Cedartown Rds., Broad and Padlock Sts., Cave Spring, 6/19/80, A, C, 80001028

Cave Spring Female Academy [Cave Spring MRA], Rome St., Cave Spring, 6/19/80, A, C, 80001030

Cave Spring High School [Cave Spring MRA], Rome St., Cave Spring, 6/19/80, A, C, 80001032

Cave Spring Railroad Station [Cave Spring MRA], Alabama St., Cave Spring, 6/19/80, A, C, 80001034

Cave Spring Residential Historic District [Cave Spring MRA], U.S. 411 and GA 100, Cave Spring, 6/19/80, A, C, 80001035

Chieftains, 80 Chatillon Rd., Rome, 4/07/71, B, C, NHL, 71000273

Chubb Methodist Episcopal Church, Chubbtown Rd., Cave Spring vicinity, 5/04/90, A, C, a, 90000728

Conner, Wesley O., House [Cave Spring MRA], Cedartown St., Cave Spring, 6/19/80, C, 80001037

Cowdry, William D., Plantation [Cave Spring MRA], Rome Rd., Cave Spring, 6/19/80, A, C, 80001039

East Rome Historic District, Roughly bounded by Walnut Ave., McCall Blvd., E. 8th and 10th Sts., Rome, 7/25/85, A, C, 85001637

Fannin, Oliver P., House [Cave Spring MRA], Cedartown St., Cave Spring, 6/19/80, C, 80001041

Floyd County Courthouse [Georgia County Courthouses TR], 5th Ave., and Tribune St., Rome, 9/18/80, A, C, 80001067

Ford, Joseph, House [Cave Spring MRA], Love and Alabama Sts., Cave Spring, 6/19/80, A, C, 80001043

Georgia School for the Deaf Historic District [Cave Spring MRA], Padlock St., Cave Spring, 6/19/80, A, C, 80001045

Lower Avenue A Historic District, Avenue A between N. 5th St. and Turner-McCall Blvd., Rome, 9/01/83, A, C, 83000194

Mann, John T., House [Cave Spring MRA], Rivers St., Cave Spring, 6/19/80, C, 80001047

Mayo's Bar Lock and Dam, On the Coosa River, 8 mi. SW of Rome, Rome vicinity, 11/16/89, A, C, D, 89002020

McKinney, Dr. W. T., House [Cave Spring MRA], Cedartown St., Cave Spring, 6/19/80, C, 80001049

Mt. Aventine Historic District, Address Restricted, Rome, 8/18/83, A, C, 83000195

Myrtle Hill Cemetery, Bounded by S. Broad, and Myrtle Sts., Pennington, and Branham Aves., Rome, 9/01/83, A, C, d, g, 83000196

Oakdene Place, Roughly bounded by the Etowah River, Queen, and E. 6th Sts., Rome, 8/04/83, A, C, 83000197

Old Brick Mill, Park St. at Silver Cr., Lindale, 9/09/93, A, C, 93000936

Rivers Farm [Cave Spring MRA], Rome St., Cave Spring, 6/19/80, A, C, 80001051

Robbins, Samuel W., House [Cave Spring MRA], Rome St., Cave Spring, 6/19/80, A, C, 80001053

Floyd County—Continued

Rolator Park Historic District [Cave Spring MRA], Off U.S. 411, Cave Spring, 6/19/80, A, C, 80001055

Rome Clock Tower, Off GA 101, Rome, 2/08/80, A, C, 80001068

Roving House [Cave Spring MRA], Rome St., Cave Spring, 6/19/80, C, 80001057

Simmons House [Cave Spring MRA], Cedartown St., Cave Spring, 6/19/80, A, C, 80001059

Simmons, William S., Plantation [Cave Spring MRA], Alabama St., Cave Spring, 6/19/80, A, C, 80001061

South Broad Street Historic District, S. Broad St. and Etowah Terrace, Rome, 8/18/83, A, C, 83004182

Thankful Baptist Church, 935 Spiderwebb Dr., Rome, 9/05/85, A, B, C, a, 85001973

U.S. Post Office and Courthouse, W. 4th Ave. and E. 1st St., Rome, 5/06/75, C, 75000592

Upper Avenue A Historic District, Roughly bounded by Oostanaula River, Turner-McCall Blvd., Avenue B and W. 11th St., Rome, 9/01/83, A, C, 83000198

Watts, George T., House [Cave Spring MRA], Love St., Cave Spring, 6/19/80, C, 80001063

Wharton-Trout House [Cave Spring MRA], Rome St., Cave Spring, 6/19/80, A, C, 80001065

Forsyth County

Pool's Mill Covered Bridge, NW of Cummings off GA 369 on Pool's Mill Rd., Cumming vicinity, 4/01/75, A, C, 75000593

Franklin County

Adams House [Lavonia MRA], Hartwell Rd., Lavonia, 9/01/83, A, C, 83000199

Beasley House [Lavonia MRA], 75 Grogan St., Lavonia, 9/01/83, C, 83000200

Bond—Baker—Carter House, Address Restricted, Royston vicinity, 9/11/86, B, C, a, 86002403

Burton House [Lavonia MRA], Augusta Rd., Lavonia, 9/01/83, C, 83000201

Cannon-McDaniel House [Lavonia MRA], 126 West Ave., Lavonia, 9/01/83, C, 83000202

Canon Commercial Historic District, Depot St. between Bond Ave. & Broad St., Canon, 8/01/85, A, B, C, 85001681

Cason House [Lavonia MRA], 60 Grogan St., Lavonia, 9/01/83, C, 83000203

Cheek House [Lavonia MRA], 38 Hartwell Rd., Lavonia, 9/01/83, C, 83000204

Crawford-Shirley House [Lavonia MRA], 100 Augusta Rd., Lavonia, 9/01/83, A, C, 83000205

Cromer's Mill Covered Bridge, 8 mi. S of Carnesville at Nails Creek, Carnesville vicinity, 8/17/76, A, C, 76000619

Fisher House [Lavonia MRA], 221 Hartwell Rd., Lavonia, 9/01/83, C, 83000206

Franklin County Courthouse [Georgia County Courthouses TR], Courthouse Sq., Carnesville, 9/18/80, A, C, 80001069

Historic Churches of Canon Historic District, Broad St. at Canon Ave., Canon, 8/01/85, A, C, a, 85001680

Jones Street Residential Historic District [Lavonia MRA], Jones, Baker, and Old Carnesville Rd., Lavonia, 9/01/83, A, C, 83000207

Keese House [Lavonia MRA], 4 Burgess St., Lavonia, 9/01/83, A, C, 83000208

Kidd House [Lavonia MRA], 222 Hartwell Rd., Lavonia, 9/01/83, A, C, 83000209

Killingsworth Farm [Lavonia MRA], Hartwell Rd., Lavonia, 9/01/83, A, C, 83000210

Lavonia Carnegie Library [Lavonia MRA], Hartwell Rd., Lavonia, 9/01/83, A, C, 83000211

Lavonia Commercial Historic District [Lavonia MRA], Jones, Augusta, Vickery, Grogan, Bowman Sts., Lavonia, 9/01/83, A, C, 83000212

Lavonia Cotton Mill [Lavonia MRA], Main St., Lavonia, 9/01/83, C, 83000213

Lavonia Roller Mill [Lavonia MRA], E. Main St., Lavonia, 9/01/83, A, C, 83000214

McMurray House [Lavonia MRA], Hartwell Rd., Lavonia, 9/01/83, C, 83000215

Pure Oil Service Station [Lavonia MRA], 56 West Ave., Lavonia, 9/01/83, A, C, g, 83000216

Queen House [Lavonia MRA], Hartwell Rd., Lavonia, 9/01/83, C, 83000217

Royston Commercial Historic District, Along Church and Railroad Sts., Royston, 9/05/85, A, B, C, 85001969

Southern Cotton Oil Co. [Lavonia MRA], W. Main St., Lavonia, 9/01/83, A, C, 83000218

Stevenson House and Brickyard [Lavonia MRA], Hartwell Rd., Lavonia, 9/01/83, A, C, 83000219

Stovall Homeplace [Lavonia MRA], 114 West Ave., Lavonia, 9/01/83, A, C, 83000220

Stovall-Purcell House [Lavonia MRA], 110 West Ave., Lavonia, 9/01/83, A, C, 83000221

Vandiver House [Lavonia MRA], Main St., Lavonia, 9/01/83, A, C, 83000222

Vickery House [Lavonia MRA], Grogan St., Lavonia, 9/01/83, C, 83000223

Vickery Street Historic District [Lavonia MRA], Vickery St., Lavonia, 9/01/83, A, C, 83000224

West Avenue-Roberts Street Residential Historic District [Lavonia MRA], Between Mason and Jones Sts., Lavonia, 9/01/83, A, C, 83000225

Yow House [Lavonia MRA], 109 Hartwell Rd., Lavonia, 9/01/83, C, 83000226

Fulton County

705 Piedmont Avenue Apartments, 705 Piedmont Ave., Atlanta, 12/19/91, C, 91001853

Academy of Medicine, 875 W. Peachtree St., NE, Atlanta, 4/30/80, A, C, g, 80001070

Ansley Park Historic District, Ansley Park and environs, Atlanta, 4/20/79, A, C, 79000717

Arnold, Thomas P., House, 518 S. Main St., Palmetto, 5/10/84, A, C, 84001074

Atkins Park District, St. Augustine St., St. Charles, and St. Louis Pls. between N. Highland Ave. and Briarcliff Rd., Atlanta, 8/30/82, A, C, 82004619

Atlanta Biltmore Hotel and Biltmore Apartments, 817 W. Peachtree St., Atlanta, 1/20/80, A, C, 80001071

Atlanta Buggy Company and Ware—Hatcher Bros. Furniture Company, 530–544 Means St., Atlanta, 8/21/92, A, C, 92001070

Atlanta City Hall, 68 Mitchell St. SW, Atlanta, 7/13/83, C, 83000227

Atlanta Stockade, 760 Glenwood Ave., Atlanta, 6/25/87, A, C, 87000948

Atlanta University Center District, Roughly bounded by transit right-of-way, Northside Dr., Walnut, Fair, Roach, W. End Dr., Euralee and Chestnut Sts., Atlanta, 7/12/76, A, C, a, 76000621

Atlanta Waterworks Hemphill Avenue Station, 1210 Hemphill Ave., NW., Atlanta, 3/29/78, C, 78000982

Atlanta Women's Club, 1150 Peachtree St., NE., Atlanta, 1/31/79, A, C, 79000718

Atlanta and West Point Railroad Freight Depot, 215 Decatur St., Atlanta, 3/26/76, A, C, 76000620

Ballard, Levi, House, U.S. 29 and GA 154, Palmetto, 10/22/80, A, C, D, 80001080

Baltimore Block, 5, 7, 9, 11, 13, 15, 17, 19 Baltimore Pl., Atlanta, 6/03/76, A, C, 76000622

Barrington Hall, 60 Marietta St., Roswell, 12/09/71, C, 71000275

Bass Furniture Building, 142–150 Mitchell St., Atlanta, 1/08/79, A, C, 79000719

Beavers, John F., House, NW of Fairburn off GA 92, Fairburn vicinity, 3/29/84, B, C, 84001075

Briarcliff Hotel, 1050 Ponce de Leon Ave., Atlanta, 9/09/82, A, B, C, 82002415

Brittain, Dr. Marion Luther, Sr., House, 1109 W. Peachtree St., Atlanta, 9/23/93, A, B, C, 93000999

Brookhaven Historic District, E of Peachtree-Dunwoody and N and E of Peachtree Rds., Atlanta, 1/24/86, A, C, g, 86000134

Brookwood Hills Historic District, Off U.S. 19 and GA 9, Atlanta, 12/21/79, A, C, g, 79003776

Bulloch Hall, Bulloch Ave., Roswell, 5/27/71, A, C, 71000276

Burns Cottage, 988 Alloway Pl., SE, Atlanta, 12/01/83, A, C, 83003572

Butler Street Colored Methodist Episcopal Church, 23 Butler St., SE, Atlanta, 5/09/83, C, a, 83000228

Cabbagetown District, Bounded by Boulevard, Pearl St., Memorial Dr., and railroad tracks, Atlanta, 1/01/76, A, C, 76000623

Campbell County Courthouse, E. Broad and Cole Sts., Fairburn, 3/26/76, A, C, 76000634

Candler Building, 127 Peachtree St., NE, Atlanta, 8/24/77, C, 77000424

Canton Apartments [West Paces Ferry Road MRA], 2846–2840 Peachtree Rd., Atlanta, 12/08/80, A, C, 80004456

Capital City Club, 7 Harris St., NW, Atlanta, 9/15/77, A, C, 77000425

Castleberry Hill Historic District, Roughly bounded by Nelson St., Southern & Central of

Fulton County—Continued

Georgia RR, McDaniel, Peters & Walker Sts., Atlanta, 8/08/85, A, C, 85001742

Central Presbyterian Church, 201 Washington St. SW, Atlanta, 3/13/86, A, C, a, 86000366

Church of the Sacred Heart of Jesus, 335 Ivy St., NE, Atlanta, 5/13/76, A, C, a, 76000625

Citizen's and Southern Bank Building, 35 Broad St., Atlanta, 8/18/77, C, 77000426

Cyclorama of the Battle of Atlanta, Cherokee Ave., Grant Park, Atlanta, 12/09/71, A, C, g, 71000274

Degive's Grand Opera House, 157 Peachtree St., NE, Atlanta, 6/17/77, A, C, 77000427

Dixie Coca-Cola Bottling Company Plant, 125 Edgewood Ave., Atlanta, 7/20/77, A, a, NHL, 77000428

East Point Industrial District, Roughly bounded by Martin and Taylor Sts. Norman Berry Dr. and RR tracks, East Point, 9/05/85, A, B, C, 85001971

English-American Building, 74 Peachtree St., Atlanta, 3/26/76, A, C, 76000626

Fairburn Commercial Historic District, Roughly along W. Broad St. and RR tracks between Smith and Dood Sts., Fairburn, 10/20/88, A, C, 88002015

Fairlie-Poplar Historic District, Roughly bounded by Peachtree, Luckie, Cone, and Marietta Sts., Atlanta, 9/09/82, A, C, 82002416

Farlinger, 343 Peachtree St., NE, Atlanta, 9/30/82, A, C, 82002417

Fire Station No. 11, 30 North Ave., Atlanta, 2/12/80, A, C, 80001073

First Congregational Church, 105 Courtland St., NE, Atlanta, 1/19/79, A, C, a, 79000720

Ford Motor Company Assembly Plant, 699 Ponce de Leon Ave., Atlanta, 5/10/84, A, C, 84001080

Forscom Command Sergeant Major's Quarters, Bldg. 532, Fort McPherson, 2/25/75, A, 75000595

Fox Theatre, 600 Peachtree St., Atlanta, 5/17/74, A, C, g, NHL, 74002230

Fox Theatre Historic District, Peachtree St. and Ponce de Leon Ave., Atlanta, 10/07/78, A, C, 78003178

Fulton County Courthouse [Georgia County Courthouses TR], 160 Pryor St., SW, Atlanta, 9/18/80, A, C, 80001074

Garden Hills Historic District, Roughly bounded by Delmont and Brentwood and N. Hills Drs., Piemont, E. Wesley, and Peachtree Rds., Atlanta, 8/17/87, A, C, g, 87001362

Garrison Apartments, 1325–1327 Peachtree St., NE, Atlanta, 1/29/79, C, 79000721

Georgia Institute of Technology Historic District, 225 North Ave., Atlanta, 8/25/78, A, C, 78000983

Georgia State Capitol, Capitol Sq., Atlanta, 12/09/71, A, C, NHL, 71001099

Gilbert, Jeremiah S., House, 2238 Perkerson Rd., SW, Atlanta, 4/17/80, C, 80001075

Glenridge Hall, 6615 Glenridge Dr., Atlanta, 6/17/82, C, 82002418

Grady Hospital, 36 Butler St., SE, Atlanta, 8/13/81, A, C, 81000652

Grant Park Historic District, Roughly bounded by Glenwood and Atlanta Aves., Kelly and Eloise Sts., Atlanta, 7/20/79, A, B, C, D, 79000722

Grant Park North, Roughly bounded by Woodward Ave., Boulevard, I-20, and Hill St., Atlanta, 3/17/86, A, C, 86000462

Grant, W. D., Building, 44 Broad St., NW, Atlanta, 1/08/79, B, C, 79003318

Habersham Memorial Hall, 15th St., W of jct. with Piedmont Ave., Atlanta, 6/07/74, C, 74000676

Harris, Joel Chandler, House, 1050 Gordon St., SW, Atlanta, 10/15/66, B, NHL, 66000281

Healey Building, 57 Forsyth St., Atlanta, 8/12/77, C, 77000429

Home Park School, 1031 State St., NW., Atlanta, 7/26/89, A, C, 89000851

Hotel Row Historic District, 205–235 Mitchell St., Atlanta, 7/20/89, A, C, 89000802

Howell, Mrs. George Arthur, Jr., House [West Paces Ferry Road MPS], 400 W. Paces Ferry Rd. NW., Atlanta, 1/11/91, C, 90002101

Hurt Building, 45 Edgewood Ave., NE, Atlanta, 4/13/77, C, 77000431

Imperial Hotel, 355 Peachtree St., Atlanta, 3/31/83, A, C, 83000229

Inman Park, Roughly bounded by I-485, DeKalb and Lake Aves., Atlanta, 7/23/73, A, B, C, 73000621

Inman Park—Moreland Historic District, Roughly bounded by N. Highland, Seminole and Euclid, DeKalb, and Degress and Nashita Aves., Atlanta, 6/05/86, A, C, 86001209

King, Martin Luther, Jr., Historic District, Bounded roughly by Irwin, Randolph, Edgewood, Jackson, and Auburn Aves., Atlanta, 5/02/74, B, C, a, c, g, NHL, 74000677

King, Martin Luther, Jr., National Historic Site and Preservation District, Roughly bounded by Courtland, Randolph, Chamberlain Sts. and Irwin Ave., Atlanta, 10/10/80, A, B, NPS, 80000435

Kriegshaber, Victor H., House, 292 Moreland Ave., NE, Atlanta, 1/08/79, B, C, 79000723

Long, Crawford W., Memorial Hospital, 35 Linden Ave., NE, Atlanta, 9/01/88, A, C, 88001465

Nicolson, William P., House, 821 Piedmont Ave., Atlanta, 3/25/77, A, B, C, 77000432

North Avenue Presbyterian Church, 607 Peachtree Ave., NE, Atlanta, 11/17/78, A, C, a, 78000984

Oakland Cemetery, 248 Oakland Ave., SE, Atlanta, 4/28/76, A, C, d, 76000627

Odd Fellows Building and Auditorium, 228–250 Auburn Ave., NE, Atlanta, 5/02/75, A, B, C, 75000594

Omega Chapter of the Chi Phi Fraternity, 720 Fowler St., NW, Atlanta, 6/17/82, A, C, 82002419

Peachtree Christian Church, 1580 Peachtree St. NW, Atlanta, 5/17/84, A, C, a, 84001082

Peachtree Heights Park [West Paces Ferry Road MRA], Peachtree, Habersham, and Wesley Rds., Andrews Dr., and Peachtree Battle Ave., Atlanta, 12/08/80, A, C, 80004457

Peachtree Highlands Historic District, Roughly bounded by Highland Dr., Martina Dr., E. Pace Ferry, and Piedmont Rds., Atlanta, 6/05/86, A, C, 86001252

Peachtree Southern Railway Station, 1688 Peachtree St., NW, Atlanta, 9/14/76, A, C, 76000628

Peters, Edward C., House, 179 Ponce de Leon Ave., Atlanta, 1/20/72, A, C, 72000384

Piedmont Park, Bounded by 10th St., Southern Rwy. and Piedmont Rd., Atlanta, 5/13/76, C, 76000629

Pitts, Thomas H., House and Dairy, 3105 Cascade Rd., SW, Atlanta, 6/27/79, A, C, 79000724

Raoul, William G., House, 848 Peachtree St., Atlanta, 12/15/86, C, 86003298

Retail Credit Company Home Office Building, 90 Fairlie St., SW, Atlanta, 1/08/80, A, B, C, 80001076

Rhodes Memorial Hall, 1516 Peachtree St., Atlanta, 3/01/74, B, C, 74000678

Rhodes-Haverty Building, 134 Peachtree St., NW, Atlanta, 1/19/79, A, C, 79000725

Rock Spring Presbyterian Church, 1824 Piedmont Ave. NE., Atlanta, 5/24/90, A, C, a, 90000804

Rose, Rufus M., House, 537 Peachtree St., Atlanta, 9/20/77, B, C, 77000433

Roswell Historic District, Roughly bounded by Big Creek, King and Dam Sts., SW along New Marietta Hwy., Roswell, 5/02/74, A, C, d, 74000682

Sciple, Charles E., House, 1112 Peachtree St., Atlanta, 3/01/84, C, 84001084

Shrine of the Immaculate Conception, 48 Hunter St., SW, Atlanta, 12/12/76, A, C, a, 76000630

Smith, Tullie, House, 3099 Andrews Dr., NW, Atlanta, 11/20/70, A, C, b, 70000204

Southern Bell Telephone Company Building, 51 Ivy St., NE, Atlanta, 12/01/78, A, C, 78000985

Southern Belting Company Building, 236 Forsyth St., SW, Atlanta, 8/10/88, A, C, 88001174

St. Andrews Apartments, 1041 W. Peachtree St., Atlanta, 6/13/86, C, 86001260

St. Mark Methodist Church, 781 Peachtree St., Atlanta, 11/02/87, C, a, 87001911

Staff Row and Old Post Area—Fort McPherson, NE corner of Fort McPherson, Atlanta, 11/05/74, A, C, 74000679

Stewart Avenue Methodist Episcopal Church South, 867 Stewart Ave., SW, Atlanta, 3/02/89, C, a, 89000154

Stone Hall, Atlanta University, Morris-Brown College campus, Atlanta, 12/02/74, A, NHL, 74000680

Swan House, 3099 Andrews Dr., NW., Atlanta, 9/13/77, C, g, 77000434

Sweet Auburn Historic District, Auburn Ave., Atlanta, 12/08/76, A, NHL, 76000631

Techwood Homes Historic District, Roughly bounded by North Ave., Parker, Williams, and Lovejoy Sts., Atlanta, 6/29/76, A, C, g, 76000632

Temple, The, 1589 Peachtree St., Atlanta, 9/09/82, A, C, a, g, 82002420

Texas, The, Cyclorama Bldg., Grant Park, Atlanta, 6/19/73, A, 73002234

Thornton, Albert E., House [West Paces Ferry Road MRA], 105 W. Paces Ferry Rd., Atlanta, 12/08/80, C, g, 80004458

Thorton Building, 10 Pryor St. (10 Park Place South), Atlanta, 2/23/84, A, C, 84001107

Fulton County—Continued

Tompkins, Henry B., House, 125 W. Wesley Rd., NW., Atlanta, 12/12/76, C, 76000633

Trygveson [West Paces Ferry Road MRA], 3418 Pinestream Rd., NW., Atlanta, 12/08/80, C, 80004241

Tyree Building, 679 Durant Pl., NE, Atlanta, 7/15/82, C, 82002421

U.S. Post Office and Courthouse, 76 Forsyth St., Atlanta, 5/02/74, C, 74000681

Underground Atlanta Historic District, Roughly bounded by Martin Luther King, Jr., Dr., Central Ave., Wall and Peachtree Sts., Atlanta, 7/24/80, A, C, 80001077

Van Winkle, E., Gin and Machine Works, Foster St., Atlanta, 9/10/79, A, C, 79000726

Villa Lamar [West Paces Ferry Road MRA], 801 West Paces Ferry Rd., Atlanta, 6/08/88, C, 88001152

Washington, Booker T., High School, 45 Whitehouse Dr. SW, Atlanta, 3/18/86, A, C, g, 86000437

Western and Atlantic Railroad Zero Milepost, Central Ave. between Wall St. and Railroad Ave., Atlanta, 9/19/77, A, 77000435

Wilson, Judge William, House, 501 Fairburn Rd., SW, Atlanta, 2/15/80, A, C, 80001078

Witham, Stuart, House, 2922 Andrews Dr., NW, Atlanta, 12/22/78, C, 78000986

Yonge Street School, 89 Yonge St., Atlanta, 1/24/80, A, 80001079

Gilmer County

Gilmer County Courthouse [Georgia County Courthouses TR], Courthouse Sq., Ellijay, 9/18/80, A, C, g, 80001081

Glascock County

Glascock County Courthouse [Georgia County Courthouses TR], Main St., Gibson, 9/18/80, A, C, 80001082

Glynn County

Brunswick Old Town, Address Restricted, Brunswick vicinity, 12/02/74, A, D, 74000683

Brunswick Old Town Historic District, Roughly bounded by 1st, Bay, New Bay, H and Cochran Sts., Brunswick, 4/26/79, A, C, 79000727

Faith Chapel, Old Plantation Rd., Jekyll Island, 7/14/71, C, a, 71000277

Fort Frederica National Monument, 12 mi. N of Brunswick, Brunswick vicinity, 10/15/66, A, NPS, 66000065

Hamilton Plantation Slave Cabins, Address Restricted, St. Simons Island vicinity, 6/30/88, A, C, D, 88000968

Hofwyl-Broadfield Plantation, N of Brunswick on U.S. 17, Brunswick vicinity, 7/12/76, A, C, 76000635

Horton-duBignon House, Brewery Ruins, duBignon Cemetery, Riverview Dr., Jekyll Island, 9/28/71, A, C, d, 71000278

Jekyll Island Club, Between Riverview Dr. and Old Village Blvd., Jekyll Island, 1/20/72, A, C, NHL, 72000385

Rockefeller Cottage, 331 Riverview Dr., Jekyll Island, 7/14/71, A, C, 71000279

St. Simons Lighthouse and Lighthouse Keepers' Building, 600 Beachview Dr., St. Simons Island, 4/13/72, A, C, D, 72000386

Gordon County

Calhoun Depot, Between Court and Oothcalooga Sts., Calhoun, 8/26/82, A, C, 82002422

Freeman-Hurt House, S of Oakman on U.S. 411, Oakman vicinity, 1/01/76, A, C, D, 76000636

New Echota, NE of Calhoun on GA 225, Calhoun vicinity, 5/13/70, A, NHL, 70000869

Grady County

Sasser Farm, Sasser Farm Rd. S of Cairo, Cairo vicinity, 9/08/83, A, C, 83000230

Susina Plantation, W of Beachton on Meridian Rd., Beachton vicinity, 8/12/70, C, 70000205

Greene County

Baber, Dr. Calvin M., House [Greensboro MRA], Penfield Rd., Greensboro, 12/17/87, B, C, 87001439

Church of the Redeemer [Greensboro MRA], Jct. of Main and North Sts., Greensboro, 9/09/87, A, C, a, 87001440

Copeland Site (9GE18), Address Restricted, Greensboro vicinity, 5/19/89, D, 89000373

Greene County Courthouse [Georgia County Courthouses TR], GA 12, Greensboro, 9/18/80, A, C, 80001083

Greensboro Commercial Historic District [Greensboro MRA], Broad and Main Sts., Greensboro, 11/06/87, A, C, 87001438

Greensboro Depot [Greensboro MRA], West St., Greensboro, 9/09/87, A, C, 87001441

Jefferson Hall, GA 12, Union Point vicinity, 8/10/89, A, C, 89001100

King—Knowles—Gheesling House [Greensboro MRA], North St., Greensboro, 9/09/87, B, C, 87001442

Leila, Mary, Cotton Mill and Village [Greensboro MRA], Roughly bounded by Cherry and Buffalo Sts. and Richland Ave., GA RR, Spring and Mill, and Mapple Sts., Greensboro, 9/09/87, A, C, 87001443

Moore—Crutchfield Place, GA 15, SE of Siloam, Siloam, 4/12/90, A, C, 90000549

North Street—East Street Historic District [Greensboro MRA], North, East, Greene, and Walnut Sts., Greensboro, 9/09/87, A, C, 87001444

Penfield Historic District, 7 mi. N of Greensboro on GA 5925, Greensboro vicinity, 1/20/76, A, C, b, d, 76000637

Poullain, Phillip, House [Greensboro MRA], Penfield Rd., Greensboro, 9/09/87, C, 87001448

Printup, Peter W., Plantation, GA 44, Union Point vicinity, 9/05/85, A, B, C, 85001977

South Street—Broad Street—Main Street—Laurel Street Historic District [Greensboro MRA], South, Broad, Main, and Laurel Sts., Greensboro, 9/09/87, A, C, 87001450

South Walnut Street Historic District [Greensboro MRA], S. Walnut, E. South, and E. Broad Sts., Greensboro, 9/09/87, A, C, 87001449

Springfield Baptist Church [Greensboro MRA], Canaan Circle, Greensboro, 9/09/87, A, C, a, 87001451

Union Manufacturing Company, 500 Sibley Ave., Union Point, 2/24/89, A, C, 89000026

Union Point Historic District, Roughly bounded by Lamb Ave., Washington Rd., Old Crawfordville Rd. and Hendry St., Union Point, 1/07/91, A, C, a, d, 90002100

Gwinnett County

Allen, Bona, House, 395 Main St., Buford, 9/01/83, A, B, C, 83000231

Allen, John Quincy, House, 345 E. Main St., Buford, 1/12/84, B, C, 84001109

Craig, Robert, Plantation, 1504 Five Forks Trickum Rd., Lawrenceville vicinity, 6/08/90, A, C, d, 90000805

Gwinnett County Courthouse [Georgia County Courthouses TR], Courthouse Sq., Lawrenceville, 9/18/80, A, C, 80001084

Hudson—Nash House and Cemetery, 3490 Five Forks Trickum Rd., Lilburn, 1/04/90, A, C, d, 89002264

Mechanicsville School, 3rd St. and Florida Ave., Norcross vicinity, 10/16/80, A, C, 80001085

Norcross Historic District, Off U.S. 23, Norcross, 11/21/80, A, C, 80001086

Old Seminary Building, Perry St., Lawrenceville, 12/29/70, A, C, 70000206

Parks—Strickland Archeological Complex, Address Restricted, Dacula vicinity, 12/08/89, D, 89002034

Terrell, William, Homeplace, E of Lawrenceville off US 29, Lawrenceville vicinity, 8/26/82, A, C, D, 82002423

Ware, Clarence R., House, 293 N. Perry St., Lawrenceville, 6/17/82, B, C, 82002424

Winn, Elisha, House, N of Dacula at 908 Dacula Rd., Dacula vicinity, 12/18/79, A, C, e, 79000728

Wynne, Thomas, House, N of Lilburn on U.S. 29, Lilburn vicinity, 7/08/77, A, C, 77000436

Habersham County

Acoa, Mathis Rd., Hollywood vicinity, 6/22/82, A, C, D, 82002446

Asbury, Henry, House [Clarkesville MRA], 211 E. Waters St., Clarkesville, 8/18/82, A, C, 82002425

Baron-York Building [Clarkesville MRA], 714 N. Washington St., Clarkesville, 8/18/82, A, C, 82002426

Chenocetah Fire Tower, Chenocetah Mountain, Cornelia vicinity, 6/11/84, A, C, g, 84001110

Church Furniture Store [Clarkesville MRA], N. Washington St., Clarkesville, 8/18/82, A, C, 82002427

Church, Cornelius, House [Clarkesville MRA], 304 N. Washington St., Clarkesville, 8/18/82, B, C, 82002428

Clarkesville Garage [Clarkesville MRA], 304 N. Washington St., Clarkesville, 8/18/82, A, C, 82002429

Cornelia Community House, U.S. 123 at LaVista Lane, Cornelia, 6/21/82, A, C, g, 82002445

Daes Chapel Methodist Church [Clarkesville MRA], N. Washington St., Clarkesville, 8/18/82, A, a, b, 82002430

Demorest Commercial Historic District, Georgia St. and Central Ave., Demorest, 10/16/89, A, C, 89001713

Furr-Lambert House [Clarkesville MRA], 223 Grant St., Clarkesville, 8/18/82, A, C, 82002431

Glen-Ella Springs Hotel, SW of Tallulah Falls on Co. Rd. 218, Turnerville vicinity, 1/04/90, A, C, 89002270

Grace Church [Clarkesville MRA], Wilson and Greene Sts., Clarkesville, 2/15/80, A, C, a, 80001087

Griggs-Erwin House [Clarkesville MRA], Bridge St., Clarkesville, 8/18/82, C, 82002432

Haywood English Family Log House, GA 115 W of jct. with Habersham Rd., Clarkesville vicinity, 12/19/91, C, b, 91001852

Hill, A. P., House [Clarkesville MRA], N. Washington St., Clarkesville, 8/18/82, C, 82002433

Irvin General Merchandise Store, Irvin St., Cornelia, 7/26/84, A, C, 84001113

Jackson Building [Clarkesville MRA], 710 N. Washington St., Clarkesville, 8/18/82, A, C, 82002434

Jackson Pharmacy [Clarkesville MRA], 712 N. Washington St., Clarkesville, 8/18/82, A, C, 82002435

Lewis, J. A., House [Clarkesville MRA], N. Washington St., Clarkesville, 8/18/82, B, C, 82002436

Market Building [Clarkesville MRA], N. Washington St., Clarkesville, 8/18/82, A, C, g, 82002437

Mauldin House [Clarkesville MRA], 102 E. Water St., Clarkesville, 8/18/82, A, C, b, 82002438

McMillan, Robert, House [Clarkesville MRA], Allen Lane, Clarkesville, 8/18/82, B, C, 82002439

McMillan-Garrison House [Clarkesville MRA], 403 S. Washington St., Clarkesville, 8/18/82, C, 82002440

Porter-York House [Clarkesville MRA], Bridge St., Clarkesville, 8/18/82, B, C, 82002441

Reeves Building [Clarkesville MRA], N. Washington St., Clarkesville, 8/18/82, A, C, g, 82002442

South Washington Street Historic District [Clarkesville MRA], S. Washington St. between Laurel Dr. and Spring St., Clarkesville, 8/18/82, C, 82002443

Tallulah Falls School, Jct. of US 441 and Tallulah School Rd., Tallulah Falls, 1/30/92, A, C, 91002026

Washington-Jefferson Street Historic District [Clarkesville MRA], Washington, Jefferson, and Wilson Sts. between Green St. and Laurel Dr., Clarkesville, 8/18/82, C, 82002444

Woodlands and Blythewood, 3 mi. N of Clarkesville off U.S. 441, Clarkesville vicinity, 12/30/75, C, 75002121

Hall County

Bowman-Pirkle House, NE of Buford off U.S. 23 on Friendship Rd., Buford, 8/14/73, C, 73000623

Brenau College District, Academy, Prior, Washington and Boulevard Sts., Gainesville, 8/24/78, A, C, 78000987

Candler Street School, Candler St., Gainesville, 9/30/82, A, C, 82002447

Chicopee Mill and Village Historic District, Roughly bounded by Fourth & Fifth Sts., North, K, 8th, H, G & F Aves. on US 23, Gainesville, 7/25/85, A, C, 85001638

Clermont Residential Historic District, Main, Harris, Martin, and Railroad Sts., Clermont, 9/05/85, B, C, 85001970

Dixie Hunt Hotel, 209 Spring St., SW, Gainesville, 5/16/85, A, C, g, 85001057

Federal Building and Courthouse, 126 Washington St., Gainesville, 1/24/74, C, 74000684

Flowery Branch Commercial Historic District, Main St. & Railroad Ave., Flowery Branch, 8/30/85, A, C, 85001932

Green Street District, Both sides of Green St. from Green Street Pl. to Glenwood Rd., Gainesville, 8/15/75, A, C, 75000596

Green Street-Brenau Historic District, Green, Candler, Park, Brenau, Boulevard & Prior Sts., Green St. Circle, City Park and much of Brenau College Campus, Gainesville, 9/05/85, A, B, C, 85001974

Hall County Jail [County Jails of the Georgia Mountains Area TR], Bradford St., Gainesville, 9/13/85, A, C, 85002084

Head's Mill, Whitehall Rd., E of jct. with US 23, Lula vicinity, 1/12/90, A, C, 89002301

Jackson Building, 112 Washington St. NE, Gainesville, 8/01/85, A, B, C, 85001677

Logan Building, 119 E. Washington St., Gainesville, 1/04/90, C, 89002266

Lula Residential Historic District, Cobb, Carter, Chattahoochee and Toombs Sts., Lula, 9/11/85, B, C, a, 85002244

Tanner's Mill, S of Gainesville on SR 3, Gainsville vicinity, 9/10/79, A, C, D, 79000729

Hancock County

Camilla-Zack Community Center District, Rte. 1, Mayfield vicinity, 12/02/74, A, C, g, 74000685

Cheely-Coleman House, S of Jewell off GA 123 at Ogeechee River, Jewell vicinity, 10/29/76, C, 76000638

Glen Mary, Linton Rd., S of Sparta, Sparta vicinity, 5/08/74, C, 74000687

Jackson, John S., Plantation House and Outbuildings, Off GA 16, White Plains vicinity, 6/28/84, C, 84001116

Jewell Historic District, GA 248 and GA 16, Jewell, 5/14/79, A, C, D, 79003106

Linton Historic District, Town of Linton and its environs, Linton and vicinity, 6/18/75, A, C, a, 75000597

Pearson—Boyer Plantation, Pearson Chapel Rd., Sparta vicinity, 4/12/93, A, C, 93000236

Rockby, NE of Sparta off GA 16, Sparta vicinity, 7/12/78, A, B, 78000988

Shivers-Simpson House, N of Jewell on Mayfield Rd., Jewell vicinity, 6/22/70, B, C, 70000207

Sparta Historic District, Roughly bounded by Hamilton, Elm, W, and Burwell Sts., Sparta, 4/16/74, A, C, 74000686

Haralson County

Haralson County Courthouse [Georgia County Courthouses TR (AD)], Courthouse Sq., Buchanan, 6/07/74, A, C, 74000688

Harris County

Chipley—Pine Mountain Town Hall, McDougal Ave., Pine Mountain, 4/17/86, A, C, 86000796

Hamilton Baptist Church and Pastorium, State Highway 116 and Clay St., Hamilton, 8/19/82, A, C, a, 82002448

Harris County Courthouse [Georgia County Courthouses TR], Courthouse Sq., Hamilton, 9/18/80, A, C, 80001089

White Hall, Off U.S. 29, West Point, 8/19/74, C, 74000689

Hart County

Adams—Matheson House [Hartwell MRA], 116 Athens St., Hartwell, 9/11/86, B, C, 86002003

Benson Street—Forest Avenue Residential Historic District [Hartwell MRA], Roughly along Benson St. from Forest Ave. to Adams St. and along Forest Ave. from Railroad St. to Garrison Rd., Hartwell, 9/11/86, A, B, C, 86002004

Best, Allie M., House [Hartwell MRA], 122 Athens St., Hartwell, 9/11/86, A, B, C, 86002005

Bowersville Historic District, E. and W. Main St., Bowersville, 9/05/85, A, B, C, 85001975

Chandler—Linder House [Hartwell MRA], Johnson St., Hartwell, 9/11/86, B, C, 86002006

Hart County—Continued

Fortson, H. E., House [Hartwell MRA], 221 Richardson St., Hartwell, 9/11/86, B, C, 86002007

Franklin Light and Power Company Steam Generating Station [Hartwell MRA], Leard St. at RR track, Hartwell, 9/11/86, C, 86002009

Franklin Street—College Avenue Residential Historic District [Hartwell MRA], Roughly bounded by Johnson, Maple, Franklin and First, and Carter Sts., Hartwell, 9/11/86, C, g, 86002011

Gulley—Vickery—Blackwell House [Hartwell MRA], 115 Franklin St., Hartwell, 9/11/86, A, C, 86002014

Hart County Jail [County Jails of the Georgia Mountains Area TR; Hartwell MRA (AD)], Johnson St., Hartwell, 9/13/85, A, C, 85002085

Hartwell City School [Hartwell MRA], College Ave., Hartwell, 9/11/86, A, C, g, 86002016

Hartwell Commercial Historic District [Hartwell MRA], Roughly bounded by Franklin St., Forest Ave., Railroad St., and Jackson and Carolina Sts., Hartwell, 9/11/86, A, C, 86002019

Hartwell Methodist Episcopal Church, South [Hartwell MRA], Howell St., Hartwell, 9/11/86, A, C, a, 86002021

Horton—Vickery House [Hartwell MRA], 101 Vickery St., Hartwell, 9/11/86, C, 86002024

Jones, Pearl J., House [Hartwell MRA], 401 Athens St., Hartwell, 9/11/86, C, 86002027

Kendrick—Matheson House [Hartwell MRA], 212 Athens St., Hartwell, 9/11/86, B, C, 86002029

Kidd, Charles I., House [Hartwell MRA], 304 W. Howell St., Hartwell, 9/11/86, B, C, 86002032

Linder, Roscoe Conklin, House [Hartwell MRA], 118 Athens St., Hartwell, 9/11/86, C, 86002033

McCurry—Kidd House [Hartwell MRA], 602 W. Howell St., Hartwell, 9/11/86, B, C, 86002035

McMullan—Vickery Farm [Hartwell MRA], 602 Forest Ave., Hartwell, 9/11/86, A, B, C, 86002037

Meredith, Dr. Owen, House [Hartwell MRA], 605 Benson St., Hartwell, 9/11/86, C, 86002040

Morrison, Jackson, House [Hartwell MRA], 439 Rome St., Hartwell, 9/11/86, A, B, C, 86002046

Patterson—Turner Homeplace, Smith—McGee Bridge Rd., Hartwell vicinity, 7/26/90, C, 90001126

Pure Oil Service Station [Hartwell MRA], Howell St. at Jackson St., Hartwell, 9/11/86, A, C, 86002047

Satterfield, Emory Edward, House [Hartwell MRA], 504 W. Howell St., Hartwell, 9/11/86, B, C, 86002049

Saul, Meyer, House [Hartwell MRA], 304 W. Johnson St., Hartwell, 9/11/86, B, C, 86002043

Skelton, Alexander Stephens, House [Hartwell MRA], 214 Athens St., Hartwell, 9/11/86, C, 86002050

Teasley, Ralph, House [Hartwell MRA], 421 W. Howell St., Hartwell, 9/11/86, B, C, 86002053

Teasley, Thomas William, House [Hartwell MRA], 417 W. Howell St., Hartwell, 9/11/86, B, C, 86002055

Teasley—Holland House [Hartwell MRA], 416 W. Howell St., Hartwell, 9/11/86, B, C, 86002052

Temple, John Roland, House [Hartwell MRA], 129 Athens St., Hartwell, 9/11/86, B, C, 86002059

Temple—Skelton House [Hartwell MRA], 201 Athens St., Hartwell, 9/11/86, B, C, 86002057

Underwood, John, House [Hartwell MRA], 825 S. Jackson St., Hartwell, 9/11/86, B, C, 86002062

Witham Cotton Mills Village Historic District [Hartwell MRA], Along Liberty Circle, Jackson, and Webb Sts., Hartwell, 9/11/86, A, C, 86002064

Heard County

Heard County Jail, Court Sq. and Shady Lane, Franklin, 1/27/81, A, C, 81000199

Ware, John M., Sr., House, Address Restricted, Corinth vicinity, 11/03/80, A, B, C, D, 80001090

Henry County

Brown House, 71 Macon St., McDonough, 8/01/91, A, C, 91000908

Crawford-Talmadge House, NW of Hampton at U.S. 19/41 and Talmadge Rd., Hampton vicinity, 4/01/80, B, C, 80001091

Globe Hotel, 20 Jonesboro St., McDonough, 9/05/85, A, C, b, 85001980

Griffin, Smith, House, Off Wynn Dr. NE of GA 20, Hampton vicinity, 12/19/85, B, C, 85003225

Hampton Depot, E. Main St., Hampton, 9/10/79, A, C, 79000730

Henry County Courthouse [Georgia County Courthouses TR], Courthouse Sq., McDonough, 9/18/80, A, C, 80001092

Locust Grove Institute Academic Building, 3644 GA 42, Locust Grove, 9/04/86, A, C, a, 86002179

Walden-Turner House, GA 42 and Ward St., Stockbridge, 4/09/80, C, 80001093

Houston County

Davis-Felton Plantation, NW of Henderson on Felton Rd., Henderson vicinity, 11/13/79, A, C, D, 79000731

Log Dogtrot House, 0.5 mi. E of jct. of GA 247 and Story St., Kathleen vicinity, 5/30/91, C, 91000681

Irwin County

Davis, Jefferson, Capture Site, N of Irwinville, Irwinville vicinity, 4/01/80, A, f, 80001094

Irwin County Courthouse [Georgia County Courthouses TR], 2nd St., Ocilla, 9/18/80, A, C, 80001095

Jackson County

Commerce Commercial Historic District, Roughly bounded by Line, State, Cherry, Sycamore and Broad Sts., Commerce, 1/19/89, A, C, a, 88003226

Hardman, Governor L. G., House, 208 Elm St., Commerce, 6/16/88, B, C, 88000749

Hillcrest-Allen Clinic and Hospital, GA 53 & Peachtree Rd., Hoschton, 5/02/85, A, B, C, 85000936

Holder Plantation, Jct. of Possum Creek Rd. and US 129, Jefferson vicinity, 9/05/90, C, 90001408

Jackson County Courthouse [Georgia County Courthouses TR], GA 1, Jefferson, 9/18/80, A, C, 80001096

Shankle, Seaborn M., House, 125 Cherry St, Commerce, 11/29/79, B, C, 79000732

Shields—Etheridge Farm, Jct. of GA 319 and Co. Rd. 125, approximately 5 mi. SW of Jefferson, Jackson vicinity, 6/25/92, A, C, 92000814

Jasper County

Hitchcock-Roberts House, N. Warren St., Monticello, 2/14/79, A, 79000733

Jasper County Courthouse [Georgia County Courthouses TR], Courthouse Sq., Monticello, 9/18/80, A, C, 80001097

Jordan-Bellew House, Madison Hwy., Pompano, 1/20/78, A, C, 78000990

Monticello High School, College St., Monticello, 12/14/78, A, C, 78000989

Jeff Davis County

Jeff Davis County Courthouse [Georgia County Courthouses TR], Courthouse Sq., Hazelburst, 9/18/80, A, C, 80001098

Jefferson County

Cunningham-Coleman House, SE of Wadley, Wadley vicinity, 9/07/84, A, C, 84001119

Jefferson County Courthouse [Georgia County Courthouses TR], Courthouse Sq., Louisville, 9/18/80, A, C, 80001099

Old Market, U.S. 1 and GA 24, Louisville, 2/17/78, A, 78000991

Jenkins County

Birdsville Plantation, NW of Millen, Millen vicinity, 4/07/71, C, 71000280

Camp Lawton, Address Restricted, Millen vicinity, 3/24/78, A, C, D, 78000992

Jenkins County Courthouse [Georgia County Courthouses TR], Courthouse Sq., Millen, 9/18/80, A, C, 80001100

Johnson County

Grice Inn, E. Elm St., Wrightsville, 7/20/78, A, C, 78000993

Johnson County Courthouse [Georgia County Courthouses TR], Courthouse Sq., Wrightsville, 9/18/80, A, C, 80001101

Jones County

Cabaniss-Hanberry House, NE of Bradley on Transquilla Rd., Bradley vicinity, 1/01/76, A, C, 76000639

Cabiness-Hunt House, SE of Round Oak off GA 11, Round Oak vicinity, 5/02/75, A, C, 75000598

Jarrell Plantation, 6 mi. E of East Juliette off Dames Ferry Rd., East Juliette vicinity, 5/09/73, A, 73000624

Jones County Courthouse [Georgia County Courthouses TR], GA 49, Gray, 9/18/80, A, C, 80001102

Old Clinton Historic District, Runs along US 129 and SR 11, Clinton, 9/12/74, A, C, 74000690

Lamar County

Barnesville Depot, Plaza Way and Main St., Barnesville, 4/30/86, C, 86000916

Carnegie Library of Barnesville, Library St., Barnesville, 2/03/87, A, C, 86003684

Lamar County Courthouse [Georgia County Courthouses TR], Thomaston St., Barnesville, 9/18/80, A, C, g, 80001103

Lanier County

Lanier County Auditorium and Grammar School, E. Church Ave., Lakeland, 4/10/86, A, C, 86000743

Laurens County

Carnegie Library, Jct. of Bellevue, Academy, and Jackson Sts., Dublin, 5/30/75, A, C, 75000599

Fish Trap Cut, Address Restricted, Dublin vicinity, 10/01/74, D, 74000691

Sanders Hill, S of Montrose off I-16/GA 404, Montrose vicinity, 5/28/75, A, C, 75000600

Lee County

Lee County Courthouse [Georgia County Courthouses TR], Courthouse Sq., Leesburg, 9/18/80, A, C, 80001104

Liberty County

Bacon-Fraser House, 208 E. Court St., Hinesville, 4/18/85, A, C, 85000848

Cassel's Store, Off U.S. 82, McIntosh, 8/05/83, A, C, 83000232

Dorchester Academy Boys' Dormitory, GA 38/US 82, Midway vicinity, 6/23/86, A, C, g, 86001371

Flemington Presbyterian Church, Off Old Sunbury Rd., Flemington, 6/17/82, A, C, a, d, 82002449

Fort Morris, Address Restricted, Midway vicinity, 5/13/70, D, 70000208

Liberty County Courthouse [Georgia County Courthouses TR], Courthouse Sq., Hinesville, 9/18/80, A, C, 80001105

Liberty County Jail, 302 S. Main St., Hineville, 8/18/92, A, C, 92001036

Midway Historic District, Jct. U.S. 17 and GA 38, Midway, 3/01/73, A, C, a, 73000625

St. Catherine's Island, 10 mi. off the GA coast between St. Catherines Sound and Sapelo Sound, South Newport vicinity, 12/16/69, A, B, D, a, NHL, 69000332

Woodmanston Site, SW of Riceboro off Barrington Rd., Riceboro vicinity, 6/18/73, B, 73000626

Lincoln County

Amity School [Lincoln County MPS], Clay Hill Rd. W of jct. with GA 43, Lincolnton vicinity, 9/21/93, A, C, 93000933

Chennault House, NE of Danburg at jct. of GA 44 and GA 79, Danburg vicinity, 10/14/76, A, C, 76000640

Double Branches Historic District [Lincoln County MPS], Double Branches Rd. SE of jct. with main GA 220, Lincolnton vicinity, 9/21/93, A, C, 93000934

Lamar-Blanchard House, N. Washington and Ward Sts., Lincolnton, 9/30/82, A, C, 82002450

Lincoln County Courthouse [Georgia County Courthouses TR], Courthouse Sq., Lincolnton, 9/18/80, A, C, 80001106

Lincolnton Historic District [Lincoln County MPS], Roughly, along Washington, Peachtree, Goshen and Elm Sts., Lincoln, 9/21/93, A, C, 93000932

Lincolnton Presbyterian Church and Cemetery, N. Washington St., Lincolnton, 8/26/82, A, a, d, 82002451

Matthews House, NE of Danburg on GA 79, Danburg vicinity, 10/14/76, A, C, 76000641

Woodlawn Historic District [Lincoln County MPS], Jct. of Salem Church and Woodlawn—Amity Rds., Lincolnton vicinity, 9/21/93, A, C, 93000935

Long County

Long County Courthouse [Georgia County Courthouses TR], GA 99, Ludowici, 9/18/80, A, C, 80001107

Ludowici Well Pavilion, McQueen St., Ludowici, 9/07/84, A, C, 84001153

Walthourville Presbyterian Church, Allenhurst Antioch Rd., Walthourville, 8/06/87, C, a, 87001357

Lowndes County

Barber-Pittman House, 416 N. Ashley St., Valdosta, 2/12/80, B, C, 80001108

Carnegie Library of Valdosta, 305 W. Central Ave., Valdosta, 1/12/84, A, C, 84001120

Converse-Dalton House, 305 N. Patterson St., Valdosta, 4/28/83, C, 83000233

Crescent, The, 904 N. Paterson St., Valdosta, 1/08/80, B, C, 80001109

Crestwood, 502 Eager Rd., Valdosta, 1/12/84, A, B, C, 84001147

Dasher High School, 900 S. Troup St., Valdosta, 4/18/85, A, C, 85000849

Fairview Historic District, W. Central, Floyd, River, Varnedoe, and Wells Sts., Valdosta, 6/28/84, C, 84001149

First Presbyterian Church, 313 N. Patterson St., Valdosta, 11/02/87, C, a, 87001912

Lowndes County Courthouse [Georgia County Courthouses TR], Central and Ashley Sta., Valdosta, 9/18/80, A, C, 80001110

North Patterson Street Historic District, 1003-1111 N. Patterson St., Valdosta, 6/28/84, C, 84001151

Valdosta Commercial Historic District, Roughly bounded by Savannah Ave., Lee, Toombs, and Valley Sts., Valdosta, 9/15/83, A, C, 83000234

Lumpkin County

Calhoun Mine, 3 mi. S of Dahlonega off GA 60, Dahlonega vicinity, 11/07/73, A, NHL, 73002292

Dahlonega Commercial Historic District, Chestates, Park, and Main Sts., Dahlonega, 4/07/83, A, C, 83000235

Dahlonega Consolidated Gold Mine, NE of Dahlonega, Dahlonega vicinity, 2/27/80, A, D, 80001111

Dahlonega Courthouse Gold Museum, U.S. 19, Dahlonega, 8/26/71, A, C, 71001100

Fields Place-Vickery House, W. Main St. and Vickery Dr., Dahlonega, 12/14/78, B, C, 78000994

Lumpkin County Jail [County Jails of the Georgia Mountains Area TR], Clarksville St., Dahlonega, 9/13/85, A, C, 85002086

Price Memorial Hall, College Ave., Dahlonega, 1/20/72, A, C, 72000387

Seven Oaks, 403 S. Park St., Dahlonega, 7/15/82, B, C, 82002452

Macon County

Alma Fruit Farm [Marshallville and Vicinity MRA], GA 49W, Marshallville vicinity, 11/25/80, A, C, 80004446

Macon County—Continued

Andersonville National Historic Site, 1 mi. E of Andersonville on GA 49, Andersonville vicinity, 10/16/70, A, d, NPS, 70000070

Billy Place [Marshallville and Vicinity MRA], Rt. 1, Marshallville vicinity, 11/25/80, A, C, 80004444

DeVaughn-Lewis House, 510 S. Dooly St., Montezuma, 5/02/85, B, C, 85000937

East Main Street Residential District [Marshallville and Vicinity MRA], E. Main St., Marshallville, 11/25/80, C, 80004454

Felton, William Hamilton, House [Marshallville and Vicinity MRA], McCaskill St., Marshallville, 11/25/80, A, C, 80004447

Knob, Wilkes, Plantation [Marshallville and Vicinity MRA], Rt. 1, Marshallville vicinity, 11/25/80, B, C, 80004451

Lamson-Richardson School [Marshallville and Vicinity MRA], Railroad St., Marshallville, 5/18/81, A, C, 81000697

Macon County Courthouse [Georgia County Courthouses TR], Courthouse Sq., Oglethorpe, 9/18/80, A, C, 80001113

Marshallville Commercial District [Marshallville and Vicinity MRA], Main St., Marshallville, 11/25/80, A, C, 80004452

Massee Lane [Marshallville and Vicinity MRA], Rt. 1, Marshallville vicinity, 11/25/80, A, C, 80004450

Montezuma Depot, S. Dooly St., Montezuma, 6/12/80, A, C, 80001112

Thronateeska [Marshallville and Vicinity MRA], Rt. 1, Marshallville vicinity, 11/25/80, A, C, 80004445

West Main Street Residential District [Marshallville and Vicinity MRA], W. Main St., Marshallville, 11/25/80, A, C, d, 80004453

Willow Lake [Marshallville and Vicinity MRA], Rt. 1, Marshallville vicinity, 11/25/80, B, C, 80004449

Madison County

Colbert Historic District, Roughly bounded by 4th and 5th Sts., 4th and 8th Aves., Colbert, 5/31/84, A, C, 84001154

Long, Crawford W., Childhood Home, Old Ila Rd., Danielsville, 12/06/77, B, C, 77000438

Madison County Courthouse [Georgia County Courthouses TR], Courthouse Sq., Danielsville, 9/18/80, A, C, 80001114

Marion County

Champion-McGarrah Plantation, Off GA 30, Friendship vicinity, 6/28/84, A, C, 84001156

Fort Perry, Address Restricted, Buena Vista vicinity, 7/30/75, A, D, 75000601

Marion County Courthouse [Georgia County Courthouses TR], Courthouse Sq., Buena Vista, 9/18/80, A, C, 80001115

Old Marion County Courthouse [Georgia County Courthouses TR], GA 137, Tazewell, 9/18/80, A, C, 80001116

Shiloh-Marion Baptist Church and Cemetery, GA 41, Buena Vista vicinity, 5/17/84, C, a, d, 84001159

McDuffie County

Bowdre-Rees-Knox House, SW of Thomson on Old Wrightsboro Rd., Thomas vicinity, 1/19/79, A, C, 79003109

Carr, Thomas, District, N of Thomason near jct. of GA 150 and I-20, Thomson vicinity, 12/06/75, B, C, 75002059

Hardaway, James L., House, Old Mesena Rd. W of Thomson, Thomson vicinity, 9/16/93, A, C, 93000942

Hickory Hill, Hickory Hill Dr. and Lee St., Thomson, 11/15/79, B, C, D, b, c, 79003110

McNeill House, 220 Lee St., Thomson, 11/27/92, C, 92001637

Old Rock House, NW of Thomson on Old Rock House Rd., Thomson vicinity, 12/29/70, A, C, 70000841

Sweetwater Inn, Off GA 17 on Old Milledgeville Rd., Thompson vicinity, 5/02/85, A, C, 85000938

Thomson Commercial Historic District, Roughly bounded by Journal St., Greenway St., Railroad St., Hendricks St., and Church St., Thomson, 6/09/89, A, C, 89000413

Usry House, 211 Milledge St., Thomson, 10/01/74, A, C, 74002182

Watson, Thomas E., House, 310 Lumpkin St., Thomson, 5/11/76, B, NHL, 76002144

McIntosh County

D'Antignac House, Address Restricted, Crescent vicinity, 12/16/77, A, C, 77001503

Fort Barrington, NW of Cox, Cox vicinity, 9/27/72, A, D, 72001447

Fort King George, E of U.S. 17, Darien vicinity, 12/09/71, A, D, 71001101

Ridge, The, Old Shell Rd. GA 99, Ridgeville, 4/18/85, A, C, 85000863

Vernon Square-Columbus Square Historic District, Roughly bounded by Market, Trumbull, Rittenhouse and Ft. King George Dr., Darien, 3/14/85, A, C, 85000581

Meriwether County

Champinole, GA Spur 109, 4 mi. NE of Greenville, Greenville vicinity, 10/22/92, A, C, 92001400

Clarkland Farms, La Grange Rd., Greenville vicinity, 7/12/74, C, 74000693

Greenville Historic District, Bounded by Gresham, Gaston, Woodbury, Talbotton, Baldwin, Bottom, Martin, Terrell, LaGrange, and Newnan St., Greenville, 3/16/90, A, C, 90000433

Harman-Watson-Matthews House, SW of Greenville on Odessadale/Durand Rd., Greenville vicinity, 5/09/73, C, 73000628

Hill, Burwell O., House, La Grange St., Greenville, 6/17/82, B, C, 82002453

Hill, Hiram Warner, House, LaGrange St., Greenville, 4/07/83, B, C, 83000236

Jones-Florence Plantation, Off GA 109, Odessadale, 3/29/84, A, B, C, 84001163

Mark Hall, SW of Greenville off GA 18, Greenville vicinity, 5/07/73, C, b, 73000629

Meriwether County Courthouse, Court Sq., Greenville, 5/07/73, A, C, 73000630

Meriwether County Jail, Gresham St. and GA 27 A, Greenville, 5/07/73, C, 73000631

Oakland, GA 41, Warm Springs vicinity, 6/28/82, A, C, 82002455

Phillips, William D., Log Cabin, GA 54, Hogansville vicinity, 6/28/82, A, C, 82002454

Red Oak Creek Covered Bridge, N of Woodbury on Huel Brown Rd., Woodbury, 5/07/73, A, C, 73000632

Render Family Homestead, GA 18, Greenville, 3/01/84, B, C, d, 84001167

Twin Oaks, GA 100, Greenville, 8/26/80, B, C, D, 80001117

Warm Springs Historic District, S of GA 194 and W of GA 85W, Warm Springs, 7/30/74, A, B, g, NHL, 74000694

White Oak Creek Covered Bridge, SE of Alvaton on Covered Bridge Rd., Alvaton vicinity, 6/19/73, A, C, 73000627

Miller County

Colquitt Town Square Historic District, Cuthbert, 1st, College, and Main Sts., Colquitt, 3/31/83, A, C, 83000237

Mitchell County

Bacon Family Homestead, W. Durham St. and Albany Bainbridge Stage Rd., Baconton vicinity, 11/25/83, A, B, C, D, 83003591

Baconton Commercial Historic District [Baconton MRA], E. Walton and E. Durham Sts., N. Railroad and S. Railroad Aves., and GA 3, Baconton vicinity, 12/01/83, A, C, 83003603

Camilla Commercial Historic District, Roughly bounded by Broad, S. Scott and N. Scott Sts., Camilla, 4/18/85, A, C, 85000862

Jackson, George W., House [Baconton MRA], 102 S. Jackson St., Baconton vicinity, 12/01/83, B, C, D, 83003595

McRee, James Price, House, 181 E. Broad St., Camilla, 12/11/79, B, C, 79000734

Mount Enon Church and Cemetery, Old Stage Coach Rd., Baconton vicinity, 12/22/83, C, a, d, 83003596

Mitchell County—Continued

Pelham Commercial Historic District, Roughly bounded by RR tracks, Church, Blythe, Jackson Sts. & Hand Ave., Pelham, 3/24/83, A, C, 83000238

South Railroad Historic District [Baconton MRA], S. Railroad Ave., GA 3, and Seaboard Coast Line RR tracks, Baconton vicinity, 12/01/83, A, C, 83003597

Walton Street-Church Street Historic District [Baconton MRA], Walton and Church Sts., Baconton vicinity, 12/01/83, A, C, a, 83003602

Monroe County

Culloden Historic District, Hickory Grove Rd., Main, College and Orange Sts., Culloden, 3/13/80, A, C, D, 80001119

Forsyth Commercial Historic District, Main, Lee, Johnston, Adams, Jackson, Kimball, and Harris Sts., Forsyth, 1/13/83, A, C, 83000239

Front Circle, Tift College, Tift College Dr., Forsyth, 2/08/80, A, C, 80001120

Great Hill Place, W of Bolingbroke off GA 41, Bolingbroke vicinity, 7/24/73, B, C, 73000633

Hil'ardin/Sharp-Hardin-Wright House, 212 S. Lee St., Forsyth, 6/22/79, B, C, 79000735

Monroe County Courthouse [Georgia County Courthouses TR], Courthouse Sq., Forsyth, 9/18/80, A, C, 80001121

Montpelier Female Institute, W of Macon, Macon vicinity, 10/10/75, A, C, 75000602

Montgomery County

Montgomery County Courthouse [Georgia County Courthouses TR], Courthouse Sq., Mounty Vernon, 9/18/80, A, C, 80001122

Morgan County

Bennett, Nathan, House, Dixie Ave., Madison, 11/13/74, A, C, 74000695

Bonar Hall, Dixie Ave., Madison, 1/20/72, A, C, 72000388

Cedar Lane Farm, N of Madison off GA 83, Madison vicinity, 2/24/71, A, C, 71000281

Madison Historic District, Roughly bounded on both sides by U.S. 441, Madison, 10/29/74, A, C, 74000696

Madison Historic District (Boundary Increase), Roughly Main St., Old Post Rd., Academy St., Dixie St., and Washington St., Madison, 1/08/90, A, C, 89002159

O'Flaherty, John, House, 1000 Oconee Rd., Buckhead, 8/29/91, C, 91001155

Zachry-Kingston House, 6030 Bethany Rd., Buckhead vicinity, 5/18/87, C, 87000796

Murray County

Carter's Quarters, Old US 411 9 mi. S of Chatsworth, Chatsworth vicinity, 3/17/86, A, B, C, 86000460

Fort Mountain, U.S. 76, Chatsworth vicinity, 11/23/77, D, 77001587

Murray County Courthouse [Georgia County Courthouses TR], Courthouse Sq., Chatsworth, 9/18/80, A, C, 80001123

Vann House, Jct. of U.S. 76 and GA 225, Spring Place, 10/28/69, A, B, C, 69000044

Wright Hotel, 201 E. Market St., Chatsworth, 6/17/82, A, C, 82002456

Muscogee County

Adams Cotton Gin Building, 6601 Hamilton Rd., Columbus, 5/17/84, A, C, 84001205

Berry, George O., House [Columbus MRA], 912 2nd Ave., Columbus, 9/29/80, A, C, 80001124

Broad Street Methodist Episcopal Church South [Columbus MRA], 1323–1325 Broadway, Columbus, 12/02/80, C, a, 80001125

Building at 1007 Broadway [Columbus MRA], 1007 Broadway, Columbus, 9/29/80, A, C, 80001130

Building at 1009 Broadway [Columbus MRA], 1009 Broadway, Columbus, 9/29/80, A, C, 80001131

Building at 1400 Third Avenue [Columbus MRA], 1400 Third Ave., Columbus, 9/29/80, A, C, 80001132

Building at 1429 Second Avenue [Columbus MRA], 1429 Second Ave., Columbus, 9/29/80, A, C, 80001133

Building at 1519 3rd Avenue [Columbus MRA], 1519 3rd Ave., Columbus, 12/02/80, A, C, 80001126

Building at 1520 Second Avenue [Columbus MRA], 1520 Second Ave., Columbus, 9/29/80, A, C, 80001134

Building at 1524 Second Avenue [Columbus MRA], 1524 Second Ave., Columbus, 9/29/80, A, C, 80001135

Building at 1531 3rd Avenue [Columbus MRA], 1531 3rd Ave., Columbus, 12/02/80, C, 80001127

Building at 1606 Third Avenue [Columbus MRA], 1606 Third Ave., Columbus, 9/29/80, A, C, 80001136

Building at 1612 3rd Avenue [Columbus MRA], 1612 3rd Ave., Columbus, 12/02/80, A, C, 80001128

Building at 1617 Third Avenue [Columbus MRA], 1617 Third Ave., Columbus, 9/29/80, A, C, 80001137

Building at 1619 Third Avenue [Columbus MRA], 1619 Third Ave., Columbus, 9/29/80, A, C, 80001138

Building at 1625 Third Avenue [Columbus MRA], 1625 Third Ave., Columbus, 9/29/80, A, C, 80001139

Building at 215 Ninth Street [Columbus MRA], 215 Ninth St., Columbus, 9/29/80, A, C, 80001140

Building at 221 Ninth Street [Columbus MRA], 221 Ninth St., Columbus, 9/29/80, A, C, 80001141

Building at 303 11th St. [Columbus MRA], 303 11th St., Columbus, 12/02/80, C, 80001129

Building at 920 Ninth Avenue [Columbus MRA], 920 Ninth Ave., Columbus, 9/29/80, A, C, 80001142

Building at 921 Fifth Avenue [Columbus MRA], 921 Fifth Ave., Columbus, 9/29/80, A, C, 80001143

Building at 944 Second Avenue [Columbus MRA], 944 Second Ave., Columbus, 9/29/80, A, C, 80001144

Bullard-Hart House, 1408 3rd Ave., Columbus, 7/28/77, A, B, C, 77000439

Bush-Philips Hardware Co. [Columbus MRA], 1025 Broadway, Columbus, 12/02/80, C, 80001145

Butts, Thomas V., House [Columbus MRA], 1214 3rd Ave., Columbus, 9/29/80, A, C, 80001146

C.S.S. MUSCOGEE AND CHATTAHOOCHEE (gunboats), 4th St. W of U.S. 27, Columbus, 5/13/70, A, 70000212

Cargill, Walter Hurt [Columbus MRA], 1415 3rd Ave., Columbus, 9/29/80, A, C, 80001147

Carter and Bradley, Cotton Factors and Warehouseman [Columbus MRA], 1001–1037 Front Ave., Columbus, 12/02/80, A, C, 80001148

Cedars, The, 2039 13th St., Columbus, 11/23/71, A, C, 71000282

Central of Georgia Railroad Terminal [Columbus MRA], 1200 6th Ave., Columbus, 9/29/80, A, C, 80001149

Central of Georgia Railroad Terminal [Columbus MRA], 700 12th St., Columbus, 12/02/80, A, C, 80001150

Church Square [Columbus MRA], Roughly bounded by 2nd and 3rd Aves., 11th and 12th Sts., Columbus, 12/02/80, C, a, 80001151

Church of the Holy Family [Columbus MRA], 320 12th St., Columbus, 9/29/80, A, C, a, 80001152

City Fire Department [Columbus MRA], 1338 and 1340 Broadway, Columbus, 9/29/80, A, C, 80001153

Cole-Hatcher-Hampton Wholesale Grocers [Columbus MRA], 22 W. 10 St., Columbus, 9/29/80, A, C, 80001154

Colored Cemetery [Columbus MRA], 10th Ave., Columbus, 9/29/80, A, C, d, 80001155

Columbian Lodge No. 7 Free and Accepted Masons [Columbus MRA], 101 12th St., Columbus, 9/29/80, A, C, 80001156

Columbus High School [Columbus MRA], 320 11th St., Columbus, 9/29/80, A, C, 80001157

Columbus Historic District, Roughly bounded by 9th and 4th sts., 4th Ave., and the Chattahoochee River, Columbus, 7/29/69, A, C, 69000045

Columbus Historic District (Boundary Increase), Bounded by Ninth and Fourth Sts., Chattahoochee River and Fourth Ave., Columbus, 10/21/88, A, C, 88002048

Muscogee County—Continued

Columbus Historic Riverfront Industrial District, Columbus River from 8th St. N. to 38th St., Columbus, 6/02/78, A, C, NHL, 78000995

Columbus Investment Company Building [Columbus MRA], 21 12th St., Columbus, 9/29/80, A, C, 80001158

Columbus Ironworks, 901 Front Ave., Columbus, 7/29/69, A, 69000046

Columbus Stockade [Columbus MRA], 622 10th St., Columbus, 12/02/80, C, 80001159

Cooke, Wm. L., House [Columbus MRA], 1523 3rd Ave., Columbus, 12/02/80, C, 80001210

Curtis, Walter W. House [Columbus MRA], 1427 2nd Ave., Columbus, 9/29/80, A, C, 80001160

Davis, John T., House [Columbus MRA], 1526 3rd Ave., Columbus, 9/29/80, A, C, 80001161

Denson, William H., House [Columbus MRA], 930 5th Ave., Columbus, 9/29/80, A, C, 80001162

Depot Business Buildings [Columbus MRA], 519, 521 and 523 E. 12th St., Columbus, 9/29/80, A, C, 80001163

Dinglewood, 1429 Dinglewood St., Columbus, 2/01/72, A, C, 72000389

Dismukes, Robert E., Sr., House, 1617 Summit Dr., Columbus, 1/08/79, A, C, 79000736

Elisha P. Dismukes House [Columbus MRA], 1515 3rd Ave., Columbus, 12/02/80, B, C, 80001164

First African Baptist Church [Columbus MRA], 901 5th Ave., Columbus, 9/29/80, A, C, a, 80001165

First African Baptist Church Parsonage [Columbus MRA], 911 5th Ave., Columbus, 9/29/80, A, C, a, 80001166

First National Bank, 1048 Broadway, Columbus, 11/01/74, A, C, 74000697

First Presbyterian Church [Columbus MRA], 1100 1st Ave., Columbus, 9/29/80, A, C, a, 80001167

Fletcher, John T., House [Columbus MRA], 311 11th St., Columbus, 9/29/80, A, C, 80001168

Fontaine Building [Columbus MRA], 13 W. 11th St., Columbus, 9/29/80, A, C, 80001169

Frank Brothers [Columbus MRA], 18 W. 10th St., Columbus, 12/02/80, C, 80001170

Gann's Pharmacy [Columbus MRA], 1611 2nd Ave., Columbus, 9/29/80, A, D, 80001171

Garrett-Bullock House [Columbus MRA], 1402 2nd Ave., Columbus, 9/29/80, A, C, 80001172

Girard Colored Mission [Columbus MRA], 1002 6th Ave., Columbus, 9/29/80, A, C, a, 80001173

Goetchius-Wellborn House, 405 Broadway, Columbus, 7/29/69, A, 69000047

Golden Brothers, Founders and Machinsts [Columbus MRA], 600 12th St., Columbus, 9/29/80, A, C, 80001174

Harrison-Gibson House [Columbus MRA], 309 11th St., Columbus, 9/29/80, A, C, 80001175

Highland Hall, 1504 17th St., Columbus, 4/01/80, A, C, 80004459

Hilton, 2505 Macon Rd., Columbus, 1/20/72, A, C, 72000390

Hofflin & Greentree Building [Columbus MRA], 1128–1130 Broadway, Columbus, 9/30/82, C, 82002457

Hunt, William P., House [Columbus MRA], 1527 2nd Ave., Columbus, 9/29/80, A, C, 80001177

Illges House, 1428 2nd Ave., Columbus, 6/19/73, A, C, 73000634

Illges, John Paul, House [Columbus MRA], 1425 3rd Ave., Columbus, 9/29/80, A, C, 80001178

Isaac Maund House [Columbus MRA], 1608 3rd Ave., Columbus, 12/02/80, A, C, 80001179

Joseph House, 828 Broadway, Columbus, 7/29/69, C, 69000048

Kress [Columbus MRA], 1117 Broadway, Columbus, 9/29/80, A, C, 80001180

Lafkowitz, Abraham, House [Columbus MRA], 934 5th Ave., Columbus, 9/29/80, A, C, 80001181

Lecroy, John, House [Columbus MRA], 1640 3rd Ave., Columbus, 9/29/80, A, C, 80001182

Ledger-Enquirer Building [Columbus MRA], 17 W. 12th St., Columbus, 12/02/80, C, 80001183

Liberty Theater, 821 8th Ave., Columbus, 5/22/84, A, 84001208

Lion House, 1316 3rd Ave., Columbus, 1/20/72, A, C, 72000391

McArdle House [Columbus MRA], 927 3rd Ave., Columbus, 9/29/80, A, C, 80001184

McGehee-Woodall House, 1534 2nd Ave., Columbus, 1/20/72, A, C, 72000392

McSorley, Patrick J., House [Columbus MRA], 1500 2nd Ave., Columbus, 9/29/80, A, C, 80001185

Methodist Tabernacle [Columbus MRA], 1605 3rd Ave., Columbus, 9/29/80, A, C, a, 80001186

Mischke, Charles, House [Columbus MRA], 1638 3rd Ave., Columbus, 9/29/80, A, C, 80001187

Mott House, Front Ave., Columbus, 12/03/74, A, C, 74000698

Octagon House, 527 1st Ave., Columbus, 7/29/69, C, e, NHL, 69000049

Old City Cemetery [Columbus MRA], Linwood Blvd., Columbus, 9/29/80, A, C, d, 80001188

Old Dawson Place, 1420 Wynnton Rd., Columbus, 1/08/79, A, C, 79000737

Peabody-Warner House, 1445 2nd Ave., Columbus, 12/29/70, B, 70000213

Pearce, George A., House [Columbus MRA], 1519 2nd Ave., Columbus, 9/29/80, A, C, 80001189

Pemberton House, 11 7th St., Columbus, 9/28/71, B, b, 71000283

Phillips, George, House [Columbus MRA], 1406 3rd Ave., Columbus, 9/29/80, A, C, 80001190

Pond, George, House [Columbus MRA], 922 2nd Ave., Columbus, 9/29/80, A, C, 80001191

Pou, Joseph F., Jr., House [Columbus MRA], 1528 2nd Ave., Columbus, 9/29/80, A, C, 80001192

Power and Baird, Wholesale Dry Goods and Notions [Columbus MRA], 1107 Broadway, Columbus, 12/02/80, C, 80001193

Price, William, House [Columbus MRA], 1620 3rd Ave., Columbus, 9/29/80, A, C, 80001194

Rainey, Gertrude Ma Pridgett, House, 805 5th Ave., Columbus, 11/18/92, B, 92001530

Rankin House, 1440 2nd Ave., Columbus, 3/16/72, B, C, 72000393

Rankin Square, Bounded by Broadway, 1st Ave., 10th and 11th Sts., Columbus, 10/07/77, A, C, 77000440

Ridgewood, Jenkins Rd., Upatoi, 4/02/80, A, C, D, 80001215

Roberts, John Spencer, House [Columbus MRA], 927 5th Ave., Columbus, 9/29/80, A, C, 80001195

Rosenberg, Max, House [Columbus MRA], 1011 3rd Ave., Columbus, 9/29/80, A, C, 80001196

Rothschild's, David, Wholesale Dry Goods [Columbus MRA], 1029 Broadway, Columbus, 9/29/80, A, C, 80001197

Rothschild, David, House [Columbus MRA], 1220 3rd Ave., Columbus, 9/29/80, A, C, 80001198

Secondary Industrial School, 1112 29th St., Columbus, 4/09/80, A, C, 80001199

Sixteenth Street School [Columbus MRA], 1532 3rd Ave., Columbus, 9/29/80, A, C, 80001200

Spencer, William Henry, House, 745 4th Ave., Columbus, 5/23/78, B, C, 78000996

Springer Opera House, 105 10th St., Columbus, 12/29/70, A, NHL, 70000214

St. Christoper's Normal and Industrial Parish School [Columbus MRA], 900 5th Ave., Columbus, 9/29/80, A, C, a, 80001201

St. Elmo, 2810 St. Elmo Dr., Columbus, 4/07/71, A, C, 71000284

St. John Chapel [Columbus MRA], 1516 5th Ave., Columbus, 9/29/80, A, C, a, 80001202

Stewart, John, House [Columbus MRA], 1618 3rd Ave., Columbus, 9/29/80, A, C, 80001203

Swift-Kyle House, 303 12th St., Columbus, 4/11/73, A, C, b, 73000635

Triangle Building [Columbus MRA], 1330 Broadway, Columbus, 9/29/80, C, 80001204

Trinity Episcopal Church [Columbus MRA], 1130 1st Ave., Columbus, 9/29/80, A, C, a, 80001205

Turner, Charles E., House [Columbus MRA], 909 3rd Ave., Columbus, 9/29/80, A, C, 80001206

U.S. Post Office and Courthouse [Columbus MRA], 120 12th St., Columbus, 9/29/80, D, g, 80001207

W. Jacob Burrus House [Columbus MRA], 307 11th St., Columbus, 12/02/80, C, 80001208

Walker-Peters-Langdon House, 716 Broadway, Columbus, 7/29/69, C, 69000050

Walton, James A., House [Columbus MRA], 1523 2nd Ave., Columbus, 9/29/80, A, C, 80001209

Waverly Terrace, Roughly bounded by Hamilton Rd., Peabody Ave., 27th and 30th Sts., Columbus, 12/01/83, A, C, 83003598

Wells-Bagley House, 22 6th St., Columbus, 7/29/69, C, 69000051

Wolfson Printing and Paper Co. [Columbus MRA], 24 W. 10th St., Columbus, 12/02/80, C, 80001211

Woodruff, Ernest, House [Columbus MRA], 1414 2nd Ave., Columbus, 9/29/80, A, 80001212

Woodruff, Henry Lindsay, House [Columbus MRA], 1535 3rd Ave., Columbus, 12/02/80, B, C, 80001176

Woodruff, Henry Lindsay, Second House [Columbus MRA], 1420 2nd Ave., Columbus, 9/29/80, A, C, 80001213

Muscogee County—Continued

Woolfolk, John W., House, 1615 12th St., Columbus, 1/22/79, A, C, 79000738

Wynn House, 1240 Wynnton Rd., Columbus, 2/01/72, A, B, C, 72000394

Wynnton Academy, 2303 Wynnton Rd., Columbus, 4/11/72, A, 72000395

Wynnwood, 1846 Buena Vista Rd., Columbus, 1/20/72, A, C, 72000396

Y.M.C.A. [Columbus MRA], 124 11th St., Columbus, 9/29/80, A, C, 80001214

Newton County

Floyd Street Historic District, Floyd St. from Elm to W of Sockwell St., Covington, 12/04/74, A, C, 74000699

Newton County Courthouse [Georgia County Courthouses TR], Courthouse Sq., Covington, 9/18/80, A, C, 80001216

Orna Villa, 1008 N. Emory St., Oxford, 1/29/73, A, C, 73000636

Oxford Historic District, College and residential district centered around Wesley St., Oxford, 6/05/75, A, C, a, 75000603

Oconee County

Eagle Tavern, U.S. 129, Watkinsville, 5/13/70, A, C, 70000215

Farmers and Citizens Supply Company Block, US 129, Watkinsville, 7/02/87, A, C, 87001104

South Main Street Historic District, S. Main St. and Harden Hill Rd., Watkinsville, 3/26/79, A, C, a, 79000739

Oglethorpe County

Amis-Elder House, W of Crawford on Elder Rd., Crawford vicinity, 8/02/78, C, 78000997

Bridges, J. L., Home Place, N of Lexington on GA 22, Lexington vicinity, 1/31/78, C, 78000999

Crawford Depot, U.S. 78, Crawford, 5/27/77, A, C, 77000441

Faust Houses and Outbuildings, NE of Lexington off GA 77, Lexington vicinity, 2/12/80, A, C, 80001217

Howard's Covered Bridge, 3 mi. SE of Smithsonia on SR S2164 over Big Clouds Creek, Smithsonia vicinity, 7/01/75, A, C, 75000604

Langston-Daniel House, 5 mi. (8 km) W of Crawford on U.S. 78, Crawford vicinity, 1/31/78, A, C, 78000998

Lexington Historic District, U.S. 78, Lexington, 4/13/77, A, C, 77000442

Philomath Historic District, GA 22, Philomath, 7/06/79, A, C, D, a, 79000740

Smith-Harris House, CR 207, Vesta, 7/25/85, A, B, C, d, 85001620

Smithonia, Address Restricted, Comer vicinity, 6/21/84, A, C, 84001213

Watson Mill Covered Bridge and Mill Historic District, Along S. Fork Broad R., Watson Mill State Park, Comer vicinity, 9/05/91, A, C, D, 91001147

Paulding County

Paulding County Courthouse [Georgia County Courthouses TR], Courthouse Sq., Dallas, 9/18/80, A, C, 80001218

Pickett's Mill Battlefield Site, NE of Dallas off GA 92, Dallas vicinity, 4/26/73, A, 73000637

Peach County

Everett, James A., House, 220 Northwoods Dr., Fort Valley, 12/10/92, C, b, 92001674

Peach County Courthouse [Georgia County Courthouses TR], Off GA 49, Fort Valley, 9/18/80, A, C, g, 80001219

Strother's Farm [Marshallville and Vicinity MRA], Rt. 3, Fort Valley vicinity, 11/25/80, C, g, 80004448

Pickens County

Pickens County Jail, N. Main St., Jasper, 1/12/84, C, 84001218

Tate House, E of Tate on Hwy. 53, Tate vicinity, 5/17/74, A, C, 74000700

Pierce County

Pierce County Courthouse [Georgia County Courthouses TR], Main St., Blackshear, 9/18/80, A, C, 80001220

Pierce County Jail, Taylor St., Blackshear, 5/28/80, A, C, 80001221

Pike County

Pike County Courthouse [Georgia County Courthouses TR], Courthouse Sq., Zebulon, 9/18/80, A, C, 80001222

Strickland, R. F., Company, Railroad and McLendon Sts., Concord, 8/26/82, A, C, 82002458

Polk County

Cedartown Commercial Historic District, Roughly bounded by East Ave. and S. Philpot, Gibson and College Sts., Cedartown, 12/24/92, A, C, 92001715

Hawkes Children's Library, N. College St., Cedartown, 11/24/80, A, C, 80001223

Pulaski County

Hawkinsville City Hall-Auditorium, Lumpkin and Broad Sts., Hawkinsville, 3/01/73, A, C, 73000638

Merritt—Ragan House, 316 Merritt St., Hawkinsville, 8/29/91, C, 91001156

Pulaski County Courthouse [Georgia County Courthouses TR], Courthouse Sq., Hawkinsville, 9/18/80, A, C, a, 80001224

Taylor Hall, Kibbe St., Hawkinsville, 11/17/78, A, B, C, 78001000

Putnam County

Eatonton Historic District, Most of town centered around courthouse and city hall, Eatonton, 6/13/75, A, C, a, 75000605

Gatewood House, 6 mi. NE of Eatonton off GA 44, Eatonton vicinity, 6/20/75, A, C, 75000606

Rock Eagle Site, Address Restricted, Eatonton vicinity, 5/23/78, A, D, 78001001

Singleton House, SW of Eatonton off GA 16, Eatonton vicinity, 10/01/74, A, C, 74000701

Tompkins Inn, N of Eatonton on U.S. 441, Eatonton vicinity, 10/05/78, A, C, 78001002

Turnwold, SE of Eatonton on Old Phoenix Rd., Eatonton vicinity, 3/10/80, A, C, 80001225

Woodland, NE of Eatonton on Harmony Rd., Eatonton vicinity, 1/29/79, C, 79000741

Quitman County

Quitman County Jail, Main St., Georgetown, 8/13/81, A, C, 81000200

Rabun County

Hambidge Center Historic District, W of Dillard on Betty's Creek Rd., Dillard vicinity, 10/05/82, A, B, C, g, 82000146

Hoojah Branch Site (9RA34), Address Restricted, Dillard vicinity, 1/24/87, D, 86003667

Tallulah Falls Depot, US 441, Tallulah Falls, 5/31/88, A, C, 88000607

York House, N of Mountain City off US 23/441, Mountain City vicinity, 9/09/82, A, C, 82002459

Randolph County

Cuthbert Historic District, Centered around U.S. 82 and U.S. 27, Cuthbert, 6/10/75, A, C, 75000607

Henderson, Fletcher, House, 1016 Andrew St., Cuthbert, 6/17/82, A, B, 82002460

Shellman Historic District, Roughly bounded by Dean, Church, Mary Lou, Ward, Pecan and Pine Sts., Shellman, 8/29/85, A, B, C, a, d, 85001935

Richmond County

Academy of Richmond County, 540 Telfair St., Augusta, 4/11/73, A, C, 73000639

Augusta Canal Industrial District, Along the west bank of the Savannah River from the Richmond-Columbia county line to 10th and Fenwick Sts., Augusta, 5/27/71, A, C, NHL, 71000285

Augusta Cotton Exchange Building, Reynolds St., Augusta, 7/20/78, A, C, 78001003

Benet, Stephen Vincent, House, 2500 Walton Way, Augusta, 11/11/71, B, NHL, 71000286

Brahe House, 456 Telfair St., Augusta, 4/11/73, A, C, 73000640

Broad Street Historic District, Broad St. between 5th and 13th Sts., Augusta, 4/28/80, A, C, 80001226

College Hill, 2216 Wrightsboro Rd., Augusta vicinity, 11/11/71, B, NHL, 71000287

Darling, Joseph, House, 3066 Dennis Rd., Martinez vicinity, 4/18/91, C, 91000479

Engine Company Number One, 452 Ellis St., Augusta, 5/25/88, A, C, 88000565

First Baptist Church of Augusta, Greene and 8th Sts., Augusta, 3/23/72, C, a, 72000397

FitzSimons-Hampton House, GA 28, Augusta, 10/29/76, B, C, 76000645

Fruitlands, 2604 Washington Rd., Augusta, 5/25/79, A, C, g, 79000742

Gertrude Herbert Art Institute, 506 Telfair St., Augusta, 3/20/73, B, C, 73000641

Gould-Weed House, 828 Milledge Rd., Augusta, 7/16/79, B, C, 79000743

Greene Street Historic District, Greene St., Augusta, 12/03/80, C, 80001227

Harris-Pearson-Walker House, 1822 Broad St., Augusta, 10/28/69, A, C, 69000052

Harrisburg—West End Historic District, Roughly bounded by 15th St., Walton Way, Heard Ave., Milledge Rd., and the Augusta Canal, Augusta, 6/07/90, A, C, 90000802

Lamar Building, 753 Broad St., Augusta, 4/24/79, A, C, 79000744

Laney-Walker North Historic District, Bounded by D'Antignac, 7th, Twiggs, Phillips and Harrison Sts., Walton Way and Laney-Walker Blvd., Augusta, 9/05/85, A, B, C, a, 85001976

Meadow Garden, 1230 Nelson St., Augusta, 7/19/76, B, NHL, 76000646

Old Medical College Building, Telfair and 6th Sts., Augusta, 3/16/72, A, C, 72000398

Old Richmond County Courthouse, 432 Telfair St., Augusta, 12/22/78, A, C, 78001004

Pinched Gut Historic District, Roughly bounded by Gordon Hwy., E. Boundary, Reynolds and Gwinnett Sts., Augusta, 3/06/80, A, C, 80001228

Reid-Jones-Carpenter House, 2249 Walton Way, Augusta, 11/13/79, B, C, 79000745

Sacred Heart Catholic Church, Greene and 13th Sts., Augusta, 3/16/72, A, C, a, 72000399

Seclusaval and Windsor Spring, Jct. of Windsor Spring and Tobacco Rds., Hepzibah, 10/11/88, A, C, 87001331

Springfield Baptist Church, 112 12th St., Augusta, 6/17/82, A, C, a, b, 82002461

Springfield Baptist Church (Boundary Increase), 114 Twelfth St., Augusta, 7/05/90, A, C, a, d, 90000979

St. Paul's Episcopal Church, 6th and Reynolds Sts., Augusta, 4/11/73, A, C, a, d, e, 73000642

Summerville Historic District, Roughly bounded by Milledge Lane, Wrightsboro Rd., Highland and Heard Aves., Cumming and Henry Sts., Augusta, 5/22/80, A, B, C, 80001229

Wilson, Woodrow, Boyhood Home, 419 7th St., Augusta, 2/28/79, B, C, 79000746

Rockdale County

Conyers Commercial Historic District, Roughly bounded by N. Main St., Warehouse St., GA RR, and Center St., Conyers, 5/24/88, A, C, g, 88000581

Conyers Residential Historic District, NW of the central business district, roughly along Main St., Milstead Ave., and Railroad St., Conyers, 7/05/90, A, C, 90000947

Dial Mill, NE of Conyers off GA 138, Conyers vicinity, 4/06/78, A, C, 78001005

Rockdale County Jail, 967 Milstead Ave., Conyers, 8/26/82, C, 82002462

Schley County

Schley County Courthouse [Georgia County Courthouses TR], GA 26, Ellaville, 9/18/80, A, C, 80001230

Screven County

Goodall, Seaborn, House, N of Sylvania at jct. of U.S. 301 and GA 24, Sylvania vicinity, 10/17/77, A, C, 77000443

Lines, Samuel Shepard, House, NE of Sylvania, Sylvania, 7/14/83, A, C, 83000240

Seminole County

Seminole County Courthouse [Georgia County Courthouses TR], Courthouse Sq., Donaldsonville, 9/18/80, A, C, 80001231

Southeastern Holiness Institute, 102 Hospital Circle, Donalsonville, 6/21/82, A, C, 82002463

Spalding County

Bailey-Tebault House, 633 Meriwether St., Griffin, 3/20/73, A, C, 73002146

Double Cabins, NE of Griffin on GA 16, Griffin vicinity, 3/07/73, A, C, 73002147

Griffin Commercial Historic District, Roughly bounded by Central Alley, Sixth, Taylor and Eighth Sts., Griffin, 11/16/88, A, C, 88002310

Hawkes Library, 210 S. 6th St., Griffin, 3/20/73, B, C, 73002140

Hill-Kurtz House, 570 S. Hill St., Griffin, 3/20/73, A, C, 73002141

Hunt House, 232 S. 8th St., Griffin, 3/26/73, A, C, 73002142

Mills House, 406 N. Hill St., Griffin, 10/18/72, A, C, 72001468

Mills House and Smokehouse, S of Griffin at 1590 Carver Rd., Griffin vicinity, 1/20/80, B, C, 80004308

Old Gaissert Homeplace, NE of Williamson on GA 362, Williamson vicinity, 6/04/73, A, C, 73002145

Old Medical College Historical Area, 223–233 E. Broadway St., Griffin, 12/15/72, A, C, 72001469

Pritchard-Moore-Goodrich House, 441 N. Hill St., Griffin, 3/07/73, B, C, 73002143

Sam Bailey Building, E. Poplar and 4th Sts., Griffin, 3/20/73, A, C, 73002144

Stephens County

Riverside, N of Toccoa on GA 3, Toccoa vicinity, 9/21/82, A, C, D, 82002465

Schaefer-Marks House, 316 E. Doyle St., Toccoa, 12/12/76, C, 76000647

Simmons, James B., House, 130 W. Tugalo St., Toccoa, 4/07/83, A, C, 83000241

Stephens County Courthouse [Georgia County Courthouses TR], Courthouse Sq., Toccoa, 9/18/80, A, C, 80001232

Traveler's Rest, E of Toccoa on U.S. 123, Toccoa vicinity, 10/15/66, A, C, NHL, 66000283

Walters-Davis House, 429 E. Tugalo St., Toccoa, 6/17/82, B, C, 82002464

Stewart County

Armstrong House [Lumpkin Georgia MRA], Broad St., Lumpkin, 6/29/82, A, C, 82002466

Bedingfield Inn, Cotton St., Lumpkin, 5/07/73, B, C, 73000643

Bush-Usher House [Lumpkin Georgia MRA], E. Main St., Lumpkin, 6/29/82, C, 82002467

Dr. Miller's Office [Lumpkin Georgia MRA], E. Main St., Lumpkin, 6/29/82, B, C, b, 82002468

East Main Street Residential Historic District [Lumpkin Georgia MRA], E. Main St., Lumpkin, 6/29/82, A, C, 82002469

Grier, Dr. R. L., House [Lumpkin Georgia MRA], Broad St., Lumpkin, 6/29/82, B, C, 82002470

Harrell, George Y., House [Lumpkin Georgia MRA], Broad St., Lumpkin, 6/29/82, B, C, 82002471

Irwin, Jared, House [Lumpkin Georgia MRA], E. Main St., Lumpkin, 6/29/82, A, C, 82002472

Louvale Church Row Historic District, US 27, Louvale, 4/11/86, A, C, a, 86000747

Stewart County—Continued

Lumpkin Commercial Historic District [Lumpkin Georgia MRA], Main, Broad, Cotton, and Mulberry Sts., Lumpkin, 6/29/82, A, C, 82002473
Mathis House [Lumpkin Georgia MRA], E. Main St., Lumpkin, 6/29/82, C, 82002474
Miller, Dr. Thomas B., House, 97 Nicholson St., Richland, 3/02/88, B, C, 87001900
Old Chattahoochee County Courthouse [Georgia County Courthouses TR], SW of Lumpkin, Lumpkin vicinity, 9/18/80, A, C, b, 80001233
Pigtail Alley Historic District [Lumpkin Georgia MRA], Old Chestnut Rd., Lumpkin, 6/29/82, A, C, 82002475
Prothro, Nathaniel, Plantation, Old Americus Rd., Richland vicinity, 5/02/85, A, B, C, D, 85000939
Richland Historic District, Roughly bounded by Ponder, Harmony, Broad and Olemen, and Wali Sts., Richland, 5/05/86, A, C, 86001021
Rockwell, Stoddard, House [Lumpkin Georgia MRA], Rockwell St., Lumpkin, 6/29/82, A, C, 82002476
Roods Landing Site, S of Omaha at confluence of Rood Creek and the Chattahoochee River, Omaha vicinity, 8/19/75, D, 75000609
Second Methodist Church [Lumpkin Georgia MRA], Mulberry St., Lumpkin, 6/29/82, A, C, a, b, 82002477
Singer-Moye Archeological Site, Address Restricted, Lumpkin vicinity, 8/01/75, D, 75000608
Smith-Alston House, 405 Ponder St., Richland, 6/20/80, B, C, 80001235
Stewart County Courthouse [Georgia County Courthouses TR], Courthouse Sq., Lumpkin, 9/18/80, A, C, 80001234
Tucker, John A., House [Lumpkin Georgia MRA], Florence St., Lumpkin, 6/29/82, B, C, 82002478
Uptown Residential Historic District [Lumpkin Georgia MRA], Broad and Main Sts., Lumpkin, 6/29/82, A, C, a, 82002479
Usher House [Lumpkin Georgia MRA], Florence St., Lumpkin, 6/29/82, A, C, b, 82002480
West Hill, S of Lumpkin on U.S. 27, Lumpkin vicinity, 9/18/78, A, C, 78001006

Sumter County

Americus Historic District, Irregular pattern along Lee St. with extensions to Dudley St., railroad tracks, Rees Park, and Glessner St., Americus, 1/01/76, A, C, 76000648
Americus Historic District (Boundary Increase), E. Church St. and Oak Grove Cemetery, Americus, 9/03/79, C, d, 79003319
Guerry-Mitchell House, 723 McGarrah St., Americus, 6/16/83, C, 83000242
Liberty Hall, SE of Americus on S. Lee St., Americus vicinity, 11/25/80, A, C, 80001236
McBain, Newman, House, S of Americus on U.S. 19, Americus vicinity, 2/08/80, C, 80001237
Plains Historic District, Roughly bounded by Buena Vista Rd., Hospital, Clark, Main,

Thomas, Paschal, and Bond Sts., Plains, 6/28/84, A, C, 84001220
Webb Family Farm, US 19, Sumter, 9/05/85, A, B, C, 85001968

Talbot County

Bailey, Frederick A., House, U.S. 80, Talbotton, 9/04/80, A, C, 80001238
Carreker, Newton P., House, Jackson St., Talbotton, 8/26/80, B, C, 80001239
LeVert Historic District, Roughly bounded by Washington Ave., railroad tracks, Madison and Smith Sts., Talbotton, 1/11/76, A, C, 76000649
Mathews, John Frank, Plantation, US 80 at George Smith Rd., Prattsburg, 12/04/86, A, C, D, 86003456
Shelton, David, House, George W. Towns Ave., Talbotton, 9/17/80, A, C, 80001240
Talbot County Courthouse [Georgia County Courthouses TR], Courthouse Sq., Talbotton, 9/18/80, A, C, 80001241
Towns, George W. B., House, GA 208, Talbotton, 5/07/73, B, C, 73000644
Weeks-Kimbrough House, Washington Ave., Talbotton, 12/27/79, C, 79000747
Zion Episcopal Church, S of Talbotton on U.S. 80, Talbotton vicinity, 5/08/74, A, C, a, 74000702

Taliaferro County

Colonsay Plantation, ENE of Crawfordville off SR 908, Crawfordville vicinity, 11/21/74, A, C, 74000703
Liberty Hall, Alexander H. Stephens Memorial State Park, Crawfordville, 5/13/70, B, NHL, 70000216
Taliaferro County Courthouse [Georgia County Courthouses TR], GA 12, Crawfordville, 9/18/80, A, C, 80001242

Tattnall County

Alexander Hotel, 204 W. Brazell St., Reidsville, 6/17/82, A, C, 82002481

Taylor County

Ricks, Ferdinand A., House, S. Collins and E. Calhoun Sts., Reynolds, 6/17/82, B, C, 82002482

Telfair County

South Georgia College Administration Building, College St., McRae, 10/16/80, A, C, 80001243

Terrell County

Bronwood Calaboose, GA 118, Bronwood, 6/22/82, A, C, 82002483
Dawson Woman's Clubhouse, 311 6th Ave., Dawson, 6/17/82, A, C, 82002484
Sasser Commercial Historic District, Address Restricted, Sasser, 8/18/83, A, C, 83000243
Terrell County Courthouse [Georgia County Courthouses TR], E. Lee St., Dawson, 9/18/80, A, C, 80001244

Thomas County

Anderson, D. B., and Company Building, E. Railroad and Brayton Sts., Ochlocknee, 8/19/82, A, C, 82002485
Bethany Congregational Church, 112 Lester St., Thomasville, 3/07/85, A, C, a, 85000453
Beutell, Joe M., House, 101 Montrose Dr., Thomasville, 8/29/91, C, 91001158
Birdwood, Millpond Rd. and Pinetree Blvd., Thomasville, 5/02/86, C, 86000917
Box Hall Plantation, Lower Cairo Rd. at Pinetree Blvd., Thomasville, 11/16/89, A, C, 89002015
Brandon, Dr. David, House, 329 N. Broad St., Thomasville, 9/04/70, C, 70000217
Bryan, Hardy, House, 312 N. Broad St., Thomasville, 8/12/70, C, 70000218
Burch-Mitchell House, 737 Remington Ave., Thomasville, 9/04/70, C, b, 70000220
Church of the Good Shepherd, 511–519 Oak St., Thomasville, 2/05/87, A, C, a, 86003581
Dawson Street Residential Historic District, Roughly bounded by North Blvd., Madison, Jackson, and Hansell Sts., Thomasville, 9/07/84, A, C, 84001251
East End Historic District, Roughly bounded by Metcalf, Loomis, Colton, and Blackshear Sts., Thomasville, 9/07/84, C, 84001254
East Side School, 120 N. Hansell St., Thomasville, 12/16/77, A, C, 77000444
Fletcherville Historic District, Roughly bounded by Siexas, Wright, S. College and W. Jackson St., Thomasville, 4/18/85, A, B, C, 85000861
Gordon Avenue Apartments, 424 Gordon Ave., Thomasville, 3/24/83, C, 83000244
Gordon Avenue Historic District, Gordon Ave., Thomasville, 4/18/85, A, B, C, 85000860
Greenwood Plantation, GA 84, Thomasville, 5/13/76, A, B, C, 76000650
Hansell, Augustine, House, 429 S. Hansell St., Thomasville, 6/22/70, C, 70000221
Lapham-Patterson House, 626 N. Dawson St., Thomasville, 8/12/70, C, NHL, 70000868
Melrose and Sinkola Plantations, SW of Thomasville on US 13, Thomasville vicinity, 1/04/90, A, C, 89002275
Metcalfe Historic District, Roughly bounded by Magnolia, Hancock, Louis and Williams Sts., Metcalf, 9/20/78, A, C, 78001007
Millpond Plantation, S of Thomasville on Pine Tree Blvd., Thomasville vicinity, 12/12/76, A, B, C, 76000651

Thomas County—Continued

Paradise Park Historic District, Roughly bounded by Metcalf Ave., Colton, Broad, and Loomis Sts., Thomasville, 9/07/84, A, C, 84001256

Park Front, 711 S. Hansell St., Thomasville, 8/12/70, C, 70000222

Pebble Hill Plantation, US 319, 4 mi. SW of Thomasville, Thomasville vicinity, 2/23/90, A, C, 90000146

Ponder, Ephraim, House, 324 N. Dawson St., Thomasville, 8/12/70, C, 70000223

Thomas County Courthouse, N. Broad St., Thomasville, 6/22/70, C, 70000224

Thomasville Commercial Historic District, Roughly N. Stevens, N. Madison, N. Broad, Remington, Jackson, and Jefferson Sts., Thomasville, 9/07/84, A, C, 84001258

Thomasville Depot, 420 W. Jackson St./US 319, Thomasville, 5/19/88, A, C, 88000609

Tockwotton-Love Place Historic District, Roughly bounded by McLean Ave., Hansell, Jackson, and Seward Sts., Thomasville, 9/07/84, A, C, 84001260

Wright House, 415 Fletcher St., Thomasville, 8/12/70, C, 70000225

Tift County

Tift County Courthouse [Georgia County Courthouses TR], Courthouse Sq., Tifton, 9/18/80, A, C, 80001245

Tifton Commercial Historic District, Roughly bounded by Second and Third Sts., Love, and Central Aves., Tifton, 3/04/86, A, C, g, 86000382

Toombs County

Brazell, Crawford W., House, 607 Jackson St., Vidalia, 6/17/82, B, C, 82002486

Citizens Bank of Vidalia, 117 SE. Main St., Vidalia, 1/22/92, A, C, 91002004

Lyons Woman's Club House, East Liberty St., Lyons, 5/02/85, A, C, 85000940

McLemore-Sharpe Farmstead, SW of Vidalia on GA 130, Vidalia vicinity, 8/19/82, A, C, D, 82002487

Peterson—Wilbanks House, 404 Jackson St., Vidalia, 3/22/90, C, 90000491

Smith, Jim, House, Rt. 3/Toombs County Rd. 18, Lyons vicinity, 8/31/89, C, b, 89001213

Towns County

Towns County Jail [County Jails of the Georgia Mountains Area TR], Courthouse Square, Hiawassee, 9/13/85, A, C, 85002087

Young Harris College Historic District, Young Harris College Campus, Appleby Dr., Young Harris, 8/22/83, A, B, C, 83000245

Treutlen County

Treutlen County Courthouse [Georgia County Courthouses TR], Courthouse Sq., Soperton, 9/18/80, A, C, 80001246

Troup County

Bellevue, 204 Ben Hill St., La Grange, 11/07/72, C, NHL, 72000400

Broad Street Historic District, Roughly bounded by McLendon Circle, Gordon St., Vernon Rd., and Wavely Way, La Grange, 1/12/84, A, C, 84001264

College Home/Smith Hall, LaGrange College campus, La Grange, 8/26/82, A, C, 82002488

Ferrell-Holder House, 1402 Vernon Rd., La Grange, 8/14/79, C, 79000748

Hawkes Children's Library of West Point, 100 W. 8th St., West Point, 12/28/90, A, C, 90001990

Heard-Dallis House, 206 Broad St., La Grange, 3/04/75, B, C, 75000611

Jarrell, H. Frank, House, 605 Hill St., LaGrange, 10/22/92, C, 92001399

Liberty Hill, NW of La Grange on Liberty Hill Rd., La Grange vicinity, 2/24/75, A, C, 75000612

Long Cane Historic District, N of West Point on U.S. 29, West Point vicinity, 5/24/76, A, C, 76000653

Mays-Boddie House, GA 109, Mountville vicinity, 6/28/82, A, C, D, 82002489

McFarland-Render House, 612 Hines St., La Grange, 11/29/78, B, C, 78001008

Nutwood, N of Big Springs Rd. near Newsom Cemetery, La Grange vicinity, 5/08/74, C, 74000704

Phillips—Sims House, GA 54, Hogansville, 4/17/86, A, B, C, 86000791

Potts Brothers Store, Gabbettville Rd, La Grange vicinity, 3/31/83, C, 83000246

Reid-Glanton House, E of La Grange at jct. of GA 109 and Pattillo Rd., La Grange vicinity, 6/20/72, A, C, 72000401

Rutledge House, S of LaGrange on Bartley Rd., La Grange vicinity, 8/24/77, C, 77000445

Strickland House, NW of La Grange on Glenn Rd., La Grange, 12/12/76, C, 76000652

Van Boddie, Nathan, House, W. of Mountville on GA 109, Mountville vicinity, 8/29/77, C, 77000446

Vernon Road Historic District, Vernon Rd. from Jenkins St. to Forrest Ave. incl. Ferrel Dr., Broad and Carter Sts., La Grange, 1/12/84, A, C, 84001266

Turner County

Ashburn Commercial Historic District, Roughly, Main St. between Murray and Monroe Aves., Ashburn, 8/18/92, A, C, 92001042

Ashburn Heights—Hudson-College Avenue Historic District, Roughly bounded by McLendon,

Phillips, Monnie, Hudson and College Aves., Ashburn, 10/22/92, A, C, 92001411

Shingler Heights Historic District, N. Main St. (US 41) between Murray and Hill Aves., Ashburn, 11/12/92, A, B, C, 92001571

Turner County Courthouse [Georgia County Courthouses TR], Courthouse Sq., Ashburn, 9/18/80, A, C, 80001247

Turner County Jail [County Jails of Ben Hill, Berrien, Brooks, and Turner Counties TR], 200 College St., Ashburn, 8/26/82, A, C, 82002490

Twiggs County

Chapman, John, Plantation, SE of Jeffersonville on GA 96, Jeffersonville vicinity, 8/11/82, A, B, C, D, 82002491

Myrick's Mill, NE of Fitzpatrick on SR 378, Fitzpatrick vicinity, 12/06/75, A, 75000613

Richland Baptist Church, Richland Rd., Jeffersonville, 6/22/82, A, C, a, 82002492

Twiggs County Courthouse [Georgia County Courthouses TR], Courthouse Sq., Jeffersonville, 9/18/80, A, C, 80001248

Wimberly Plantation, Jeffersonville Rd., GA 96, Jeffersonville vicinity, 6/17/82, A, B, C, D, 82002493

Union County

Old Union County Courthouse [Georgia County Courthouses TR], Courthouse Sq., Blairsville, 9/18/80, A, C, 80001249

Union County Jail [County Jails of the Georgia Mountains Area TR], Blue Ridge Rd., Blairsville, 9/13/85, A, C, 85002088

Walasi-Yi Inn, S of Blairsville on U.S. 129, Blairsville vicinity, 1/12/79, A, C, g, 79000749

Upson County

Auchumpkee Creek Covered Bridge, 10 mi. SE of Thomaston off U.S. 19 on Allen Rd., Thomaston vicinity, 4/01/75, A, C, 75000614

Harp, W. A., House, 206 Barnesville St., Thomaston, 4/19/90, C, 90000636

Rose Hill Mill and House, NW of Thomaston on Thompson Lane and Hanna Mill Rd., Thomaston vicinity, 3/10/80, A, C, 80001250

Upson County County Courthouse [Georgia County Courthouses TR], Courthouse Sq., Thomaston, 9/18/80, A, C, 80001251

Walker County

Ashland Farm, SW of Rossville off GA 193, Rossville vicinity, 10/18/73, C, 73000646

Cavender's Store, Jct. of GA 201 and GA 136, SW corner, Villanow, 3/20/92, A, C, 92000143

Walker County—Continued

Chattooga Academy, 306 N. Main St., LaFayette, 2/15/80, A, C, 80001253

Chickamauga and Chattanooga National Military Park, S of Chattanooga on U.S. 27, Wildwood, 10/15/66, A, f, g, NPS, 66000274

Gordon-Lee House, 217 Cove Rd., Chickamauga, 3/22/76, A, C, b, 76000654

Lane House, Address Restricted, Kensington vicinity, 12/12/76, C, 76000655

Lee and Gordon Mill, Red Belt Rd., Chickamauga, 2/08/80, A, C, D, 80001252

Lookout Mountain Fairyland Club, 1201 Fleetwood Dr., Lookout Mountain, 6/21/90, A, C, 90000991

Miller Brothers Farm, GA 912, Kensington, 8/06/87, C, 87001332

Ross, John, House, Lake Ave. and Spring St., Rossville, 11/07/73, B, b, NHL, 73000647

US Post Office—Rossville Main, 301 Chickamauga Ave., Rossville, 8/06/86, A, C, 86002272

Walker County Courthouse [Georgia County Courthouses TR], Duke St., LaFayette, 9/18/80, A, C, 80001254

Walton County

Bank of Jersey, Main St., Jersey, 3/07/84, A, C, 84001269

Boss, A.J., House [Monroe MRA], 324 Edwards St., Monroe, 12/28/83, C, 83003609

Brodnax, Samuel H., House, GA 81, Walnut Grove, 6/17/82, B, C, 82002496

Casulon Plantation, E of Good Hope off GA 186, Good Hope vicinity, 10/10/75, A, C, 75000615

Chick, Tom, House [Monroe MRA], 1102 E. Church St., Monroe, 12/28/83, C, 83003610

Davis-Edwards House, 238 N. Broad St., Monroe, 8/14/73, A, C, 73000648

East Church Street Historic District [Monroe MRA], E. Church St. and S. Madison Ave., Monroe, 12/28/83, A, C, 83003612

East Marable Street Historic District [Monroe MRA], E. Marable St., Monroe, 12/28/83, A, C, 83003613

Harris, William, Family Farmstead, GA 11, Campton, 6/22/82, A, C, D, 82002494

Jones, Walter, Rock House, 4435 GA 186 NE, Good Hope vicinity, 11/04/93, C, 93001190

McDaniel Street Historic District [Monroe MRA], S. Broad and McDaniel Sts., Monroe, 12/28/83, A, B, C, 83003614

McDaniel-Tichenor House, 319 McDaniel St., Monroe, 2/08/80, B, C, 80001255

Monland Place Historic District [Monroe MRA], Alvoca St. and Blvd., Monroe, 12/28/83, A, C, 83003616

Monroe City Hall [Monroe MRA], 227 S. Broad St., Monroe, 12/28/83, A, C, g, 83003618

Monroe Commercial Historic District [Monroe MRA], Spring and Broad Sts., Monroe, 12/28/83, A, C, 83003619

Monroe and Walton Mills Historic District [Monroe MRA], S. Broad St., S. Madison Ave., and Georgia RR line, Monroe, 12/28/83, A, C, 83003617

North Broad Street Historic District [Monroe MRA], N. Broad and Walton Sts., Monroe, 12/28/83, C, 83003623

Social Circle Historic District, GA 11 and GA 229, Social Circle, 3/27/80, A, C, 80001257

South Broad Street Historic District [Monroe MRA], S. Broad St., Monroe, 12/28/83, A, B, C, 83003620

South Madison Avenue-Pannell Road Historic District [Monroe MRA], S. Madison Ave. and Pannell Rd., Monroe, 12/28/83, A, C, 83003621

Upshaw, James Berrien, House, US 78/GA 11, Between, 3/06/86, B, C, 86000414

Walton County Courthouse [Georgia County Courthouses TR], Courthouse Sq., Monroe, 9/18/80, A, C, 80001256

Walton County Jail [Monroe MRA], 203 Milledge Ave., Monroe, 12/28/83, A, C, 83003624

Walton Hotel, Broad and Court Sts., Monroe, 7/15/82, A, C, 82002495

Williamson House [Monroe MRA], 925 E. Church St., Monroe, 12/28/83, C, 83003625

Ware County

Downtown Waycross Historic District, Roughly bounded by the Seaboard Coast Line RR tracks and Albany, Isabella, Remshart and Nicholls Sts., Waycross, 3/20/92, A, C, 92000125

Phoenix Hotel, 201–222 Pendleton St., Waycross, 4/17/86, A, C, 86000802

U.S. Post Office and Courthouse, 605 Elizabeth St., Waycross, 2/01/80, C, 80001258

Waycross Historic District, Roughly bounded by Plant Ave., Williams, Lee, Chandler, and Stephen Sts., Waycross, 6/29/76, C, 76000656

Warren County

Roberts-McGregor House, Depot St., Warrenton, 8/14/79, B, C, 79000750

Warren County Courthouse [Georgia County Courthouses TR], Courthouse Sq., Warrenton, 9/18/80, A, C, 80001259

Washington County

Church-Smith-Harris Street Historic District, E. Church, S. Smith, and S. Harris Sts., Sandersville, 12/31/87, A, C, a, 87001268

City Cemetery, W. Church, Cemetery, and Haynes Sts., Sandersville, 8/03/87, C, D, d, 87001296

Elder, Thomas Jefferson, High and Industrial School, 316 Hall St., Sandersville, 5/12/81, A, C, 81000202

Francis Plantation, SE of Davisboro on SR 2189, Davisboro vicinity, 7/03/75, A, C, b, 75000616

North Harris Street Historic District, Roughly bounded by First Ave., Washington Ave., E. McCarty St., N. Harris St., Malone St., and Warthen St., Sandersville, 7/20/89, A, C, 89000801

Washington County Courthouse [Georgia County Courthouses TR], Courthouse Sq., Sandersville, 9/18/80, A, C, 80001260

Wayne County

Carter, Leonard, House, 311 S. Wayne St., Jesup, 8/31/89, C, 89001212

Trowell, John W. C., House, 256 E. Cherry St., Jesup, 9/16/93, C, 93000944

Wayne County Courthouse [Georgia County Courthouses TR], Courthouse Sq., Jesup, 9/18/80, A, C, 80001261

Webster County

Webster County Courthouse [Georgia County Courthouses TR], Courthouse Sq., Preston, 9/18/80, A, C, 80001262

Wheeler County

Wheeler County Courthouse [Georgia County Courthouses TR], Pearl St., Alamo, 9/18/80, A, C, 80001263

Woodland, GA 19, Lumber City vicinity, 6/21/84, C, 84001301

White County

Harshaw-Stovall House, GA 255, Sautee vicinity, 6/28/84, C, 84001302

Nacoochee Valley, GA 17, GA 75 and GA 255, Nacoochee and Sautee, 5/22/80, A, C, D, g, 80001264

Old White County Courthouse, On GA 115, Cleveland, 10/28/70, A, C, 70000226

Sautee Valley Historic District, GA 255 and Lynch Mountain Rd., Sautee, 8/20/86, A, C, D, 86002742

Stovall, John, House, Stovall Rd. S of jct. with GA 255, White vicinity, 6/14/91, C, 91000784

White County Jail [County Jails of the Georgia Mountains Area TR], Main St., Cleveland, 9/13/85, A, C, 85002089

Whitfield County

Berry, Thomas A., House, 506 Hawthorne St., Dalton, 4/05/84, C, 84001303

Blunt, Ainsworth E., House, 506 S. Thornton Ave., Dalton, 7/09/80, A, C, 80004460

Crown Mill Historic District, U.S. 41, Dalton, 5/30/79, A, C, 79000751

Whitfield County—Continued

Dalton Commercial Historic District, Roughly bounded by Hamilton, Pentz, Waugh and Morris Sts., Dalton, 12/05/88, A, C, 88001831

Martin, William C., House, 101 S. Selvidge St., Dalton, 7/15/82, A, C, 82002497

Prater's Mill, N of Dalton on GA 2, Dalton vicinity, 4/25/78, A, C, 78001010

Thornton Avenue—Murray Hill Historic District, Roughly bounded by Crawford St., Thornton Ave., W. Franklin St., Valley Dr., Emory St. and West Hill Cemetery, Whitfield, 6/04/92, A, C, 92000669

Western and Atlantic Depot, Depot St., W end of King St., Dalton, 4/06/78, A, C, 78001009

Wilcox County

Wilcox County Courthouse [Georgia County Courthouses TR], U.S. 280 and U.S. 129, Abbeville, 9/18/80, A, C, 80001265

Wilkes County

Anderson House, GA 44, Danburg, 9/29/76, A, C, 76000657

Arnold-Callaway Plantation, NW of Washington on U.S. 78, Washington vicinity, 4/11/72, A, C, 72000402

Campbell-Jordan House, 208 Liberty St., Washington, 7/14/71, A, C, 71000288

Cedars, The, 210 Sims St., Washington, 4/11/72, A, C, 72000403

Daniel, James and Cunningham, House, S of Rayle on Bartram Trace Rd., Rayle vicinity, 11/24/80, A, C, 80001266

East Robert Toombs Historic District, East Robert Toombs Ave. between Alexander Ave. and Grove St., Washington, 4/11/72, A, C, 72000404

Fitzpatrick Hotel, 18 W. Public Square, Washington, 12/17/82, A, C, 82000147

Gilbert-Alexander House, 116 Alexander Dr., Washington, 4/11/72, A, C, 72000405

Gilmer, Thomas M., House, 5 mi. (8 km) W of Washington on U.S. 78, Washington vicinity, 11/02/77, A, C, 77001540

Holly Court, 301 S. Alexander St., Washington, 4/11/72, A, C, 72000406

Kettle Creek Battlefield, 9 mi. SW of Washington off Tyrone Rd., Washington vicinity, 6/26/75, A, 75000617

Mary Willis Library, E. Liberty and S. Jefferson Sts., Washington, 4/11/72, A, C, 72000407

North Washington District, Bounded by Jefferson and Court Sts., Poplar Dr., and U.S. 78, Washington, 3/07/73, A, C, a, 73000649

Old Jail, 103 Court St., Washington, 6/05/74, A, C, 74000706

Peacewood, 120 Tignall Rd., Washington, 4/11/72, A, C, 72000408

Pharr-Callaway-Sethness House, N of Tignall on GA 2193, Tignall vicinity, 3/26/76, A, C, 76000659

Poplar Corner, 210 W. Liberty St., Washington, 4/11/72, A, C, 72000409

Toombs, Robert, House, 216 E. Robert Toombs Ave., Washington, 4/11/72, B, C, NHL, 72000410

Tupper-Barnett House, 101 W. Robert Toombs Ave., Washington, 4/11/72, C, NHL, 72000411

Washington Commercial Historic District, Roughly bounded by Court St., Jefferson St., Robert Toombs Ave., and Allison St., Washington, 3/06/86, A, C, 86000412

Washington Presbyterian Church, 206 E. Robert Toombs Ave., Washington, 4/11/72, A, C, a, 72000412

Washington-Wilkes Historical Museum, 308 E. Robert Toombs Ave., Washington, 5/13/70, A, C, 70000227

West Robert Toombs District, W. Robert Toombs Ave. between Allison St. and Rte. 44 and Lexington Ave., Washington, 3/01/73, A, B, C, 73000650

Wilkes County Courthouse [Georgia County Courthouses TR], Court St., Washington, 9/18/80, A, C, 80001267

Willis-Sale-Stennett House, N of Danburg off GA 79 on SR 1445, Danburg vicinity, 10/14/76, A, C, 76000658

Wilkinson County

Elam-Camp House, 216 Jackson St., Gordon, 6/17/82, A, C, 82002498

Worth County

Possum Poke, US 82, Poulan, 8/26/82, A, B, C, g, 82002499

Sylvester Commercial Historic District, Bounded by E. Kelly, N. Main, E. Front, and N. Isabella Sts., Sylvester, 7/09/87, A, C, 87001153

Worth County Courthouse [Georgia County Courthouses TR], Courthouse Sq., Sylvester, 9/18/80, A, C, 80001268

Worth County Local Building, 118 N. Isabella St., Sylvester, 8/21/80, A, C, 80001269

Booker T. Washington High School (ca. 1924), the first public high school built for African Americans in Atlanta, provided a scholastic and vocational education to several prominent graduates, including Dr. Martin Luther King, Jr., Judge Romae T. Powell, Urban League director Lyndon Wade, and educator Lucile Palmer Perrino. (James R. Lockhart, 1985)

GUAM

Guam County

Achugao Bay Site, Address Restricted, Umatac vicinity, 8/19/75, D, 75001912

Agaga, Address Restricted, Umatac vicinity, 6/11/75, D, 75002155

Agana Historic District [Agana Houses TR], Roughly bounded by 2nd S., 3rd S., and 9th W., Santa Cruz and Legaspi Sts., Agana, 2/08/85, C, 85000495

Agana Spanish Bridge, Aspenall St. and Rte. 1, Agana, 9/06/74, A, C, 74002300

Agana-Hagatna Pillbox [Japanese Coastal Defense Fortifications on Guam TR], W shore of Paseo de Susana, Agana, 3/04/91, A, C, g, 88001880

Agana/Hagatna Cliffline Fortifications [Japanese Coastal Defense Fortifications on Guam TR], Address Restricted, Agana vicinity, 3/04/91, A, C, g, 88001877

Agat Invasion Beach, Coastline NW of Agat from Toocha Beach S to Bangi, Agat vicinity, 3/04/75, A, g, NPS, 75001913

Aratama Maru, Talofofo Bay, Talofofo, 6/02/88, A, g, 88000612

As Sombreru Pillbox III [Japanese Coastal Defense Fortifications on Guam TR], W of Matapang Park, Tumon, 3/04/91, A, C, g, 88001887

As Sombreru Pillbox I [Japanese Coastal Defense Fortifications on Guam TR], Address Restricted, Tumon vicinity, 3/04/91, A, C, g, 88001883

As Sombreru Pillbox II [Japanese Coastal Defense Fortifications on Guam TR], S shore of Tumon Beach in Tumon Bay, Tumon, 3/04/91, A, C, g, 88001864

Asan Invasion Beach, N edge of Asan, Asan, 2/14/79, A, g, NPS, 79002617

Asan Ridge Battle Area, Between Asan and Nimitz Hill, Asan, 7/18/75, A, g, NPS, 75001916

Asmaile Point, Address Restricted, Merizo vicinity, 11/07/78, D, 78003413

Asquiroga Cave, Address Restricted, Talofofo vicinity, 5/06/76, D, 76002277

Ayulang Pillbox [Japanese Coastal Defense Fortifications on Guam TR], Address Restricted, Agana vicinity, 3/04/91, A, C, g, 88001889

Cable Station Ruins, 6 mi. N of Agat, Agat vicinity, 9/06/79, A, 79003742

Cetti Bay, 1.1 mi. NNW of Umatac Village, Umatac vicinity, 11/21/74, D, 74002036

Cook, Merlyn G., School, GU 4, Merizo, 11/29/79, A, C, g, 79003743

Creto Site, Address Restricted, Umatac vicinity, 11/07/78, D, 78003414

Dungcas Beach Defense Guns, On Agana Bay off Rte. 1, Tamuning, 12/22/76, A, C, g, 76001965

Fafai Beach Site, Address Restricted, Tamuning vicinity, 11/19/74, D, 74002316

Faha Massacre Site, Off Rt. 4, S of Pigua R., Merizo vicinity, 8/27/91, A, g, 91001091

Fort Nuestra Senora de la Soledad, S of Umatac off Rte. 40, Umatac vicinity, 10/18/74, A, 74002042

Fort San Jose, NW of Umatac on Rte. 2, Umatac vicinity, 5/01/74, A, 74002041

Fort Santa Agueda, Rte. 7, Agana, 8/30/74, A, 74002301

Fort Santo Angel, NW corner of Umatac Bay, Umatac, 8/30/74, A, 74002043

Fouha Bay, Address Restricted, Umatac vicinity, 11/21/74, D, 74002040

Gadao's Cave, Address Restricted, Inarajan vicinity, 11/19/74, D, 74002309

Garapan Mount Pillbox [Japanese Coastal Defense Fortifications on Guam TR], Address Restricted, Talofofo vicinity, 3/04/91, A, C, g, 88001888

Gongna Beach Gun Emplacement [Japanese Coastal Defense Fortifications on Guam TR], E. San Vitores Dr., Tumon, 3/04/91, A, C, g, 88001897

Gongna Beach Gun Mount [Japanese Coastal Defense Fortifications on Guam TR], E. San Vitores Dr., Tumon vicinity, 3/04/91, A, C, g, 88001898

Gongna Beach Mount Pillbox [Japanese Coastal Defense Fortifications on Guam TR], E. San Vitores Dr., Tumon vicinity, 3/04/91, A, C, g, 88001894

Guam Institute, Off Rte. 1, Agana, 10/06/77, A, C, g, 77001568

Hanum Site, Address Restricted, Yigo vicinity, 11/07/78, D, 78003416

Haputo Beach Site, Address Restricted, Finegayan vicinity, 11/20/74, D, 74002308

Hill 40, 0.2 mi. SW of Agat off Rte. 2, Agat vicinity, 3/04/75, A, g, 75001910

Ilik River Fortification I [Japanese Coastal Defense Fortifications on Guam TR], Address Restricted, Yona vicinity, 3/04/91, A, C, g, 88001869

Ilik River Fortification II [Japanese Coastal Defense Fortifications on Guam TR], Shore of Ylig Point, Yona, 3/04/91, A, C, g, 88001871

Inalahan Pillbox [Japanese Coastal Defense Fortifications on Guam TR], Rt. 4, Inarajan vicinity, 3/04/91, A, C, g, 88001890

Inarajan Ridge, Address Restricted, Inarajan vicinity, 12/04/74, D, 74002310

Inarajan Village, Rte. 4, Inarajan, 11/07/77, C, g, 77001569

Ipao Pillbox I [Japanese Coastal Defense Fortifications on Guam TR], W of Tumon on Ypao Point, Tumon, 3/04/91, A, C, g, 88001863

Ipao Pillbox II [Japanese Coastal Defense Fortifications on Guam TR], Address Restricted, Tumon vicinity, 3/04/91, A, C, g, 88001873

Ipao Pillbox III [Japanese Coastal Defense Fortifications on Guam TR], Address Restricted, Tumon vicinity, 3/04/91, A, C, g, 88001874

Jinapsan Site, Address Restricted, Yigo vicinity, 12/27/74, D, 74002317

Light Model Tank No. 95, SW of Yona on Cross Island Rd., Yona vicinity, 12/19/79, A, g, 79003107

Machagden Point, Address Restricted, Umatac vicinity, 11/07/78, D, 78003415

Malessu' Pillbox [Japanese Coastal Defense Fortifications on Guam TR], Talona Beach on Cocos Lagoon, Merizo, 3/04/91, A, C, g, 88001872

Malolos Site, Address Restricted, Inarajan vicinity, 4/08/80, D, 80004242

Mana Pillbox [Japanese Coastal Defense Fortifications on Guam TR], S shore of As Anite Cove, Talofofo, 3/04/91, A, C, g, 88001886

Mataguac Hill Command Post, Off IR 1, Yigo vicinity, 6/10/75, A, g, 75002122

Matala' Pillbox [Japanese Coastal Defense Fortifications on Guam TR], Address Restricted, Talofofo vicinity, 3/04/91, A, C, g, 88001867

Matgue River Valley Battle Area, 0.6 mi. SW of Asan off Marine Dr., Asan, 4/03/75, A, g, NPS, 75001917

Memorial Beach Park, Rte. 1, Asan, 8/07/74, A, g, 74002039

Merizo Bell Tower, Off IR 4, Merizo, 5/29/75, C, 75002152

Merizo Conbento, IR 4, Merizo, 9/17/74, C, a, 74002315

Mesa House [Agana Houses TR], Maxwell St., Agana, 2/08/85, C, 85000408

Mochom, Address Restricted, Mangilao vicinity, 12/04/74, D, 74002314

Mount Tenjo Fortifications, NE of Santa Rita, Santa Rita vicinity, 3/13/79, A, 79003745

Naton Headland Fortification I [Japanese Coastal Defense Fortifications on Guam TR], Address Restricted, Tumon vicinity, 3/04/91, A, C, g, 88001884

Naton Headland Fortification II [Japanese Coastal Defense Fortifications on Guam TR], Address Restricted, Tumon vicinity, 3/04/91, A, C, g, 88001885

Nomna Bay Site, Address Restricted, Inarajan vicinity, 12/27/74, D, 74002311

North Inarajan Site, Address Restricted, Inarajan vicinity, 2/21/75, D, 75002151

Oka Fortification [Japanese Coastal Defense Fortifications on Guam TR], Address Restricted, Tamuning vicinity, 3/04/91, A, C, g, 88001882

Orote Field, 5 mi. N on Orote Peninsula, Agat vicinity, 6/18/75, A, g, 75002149

Orote Historical Complex, Address Restricted, Apra Harbor vicinity, 10/23/79, A, D, 79003744

Pagat Site, Address Restricted, Yigo vicinity, 3/13/74, D, 74002318

Pagu' Pillbox I [Japanese Coastal Defense Fortifications on Guam TR], Shore of Pago Bay, Chalan Pago, 3/04/91, A, C, g, 88001878

Guam County—Continued

Pagu' Pillbox II [Japanese Coastal Defense Fortifications on Guam TR], Shore of Pago Bay, Chalan Pago, 3/04/91, A, C, g, 88001879

Piti Coastal Defense Guns, E of jct. of IR 1 and 11, Piti, 6/18/75, A, g, NPS, 75001909

Plaza de Espana, Saylor St., Agana, 5/01/74, A, C, 74002302

SMS CORMORAN, Apra Harbor, Piti vicinity, 4/04/75, A, 75002156

San Dionisio Church Ruins, Rte. 2, Umatac, 8/30/74, A, 74002037

San Vitores Martyrdom Site, 0.7 mi. S of Bijia Point off Rte. 4, Tamuning, 10/31/75, A, 75002154

Sanvitores Beach Japanese Fortification [Japanese Coastal Defense Fortifications on Guam TR], E. San Vitores Dr., Tumon vicinity, 3/04/91, A, C, g, 88001891

Sella Bay Site, Address Restricted, Umatac vicinity, 11/08/74, C, D, 74002038

South Finegayan Latte Stone Park, 74 Golden Shower Lane, Finegayan, 9/05/75, D, 75002150

South Pulantat Site, Address Restricted, Yona vicinity, 3/26/79, D, 79003747

South Talofofo Site, Address Restricted, Talofofo vicinity, 2/24/75, D, 75002153

Spanish Dikes, NE of Agana Springs, Agana vicinity, 11/19/74, A, 74002303

TOKAI MARU, Apra Harbor, Naval Station, 7/14/88, A, g, 88000967

Taelayag Spanish Bridge, W of Rte. 2, Agat, 10/10/74, C, 74002304

Taleyfac Spanish Bridge, Off Rte. 2, Agat, 9/10/74, A, 74002305

Talofofo River Valley Site, Address Restricted, Inarajan vicinity, 12/27/74, D, 74002312

Talofofo-Talu'fofu' Pillbox [Japanese Coastal Defense Fortifications on Guam TR], S shore of Ylig river, Talofofo, 3/04/91, A, C, g, 88001876

Taogam Archeological Settlement, Address Restricted, Mangilao vicinity, 4/15/80, D, 80004243

Tinta Massacre Site, Espinosa Ave., Merizo vicinity, 11/26/91, A, g, 91001720

Tokcha' Pillbox [Japanese Coastal Defense Fortifications on Guam TR], Toghca Point shoreline, Ipan, 3/04/91, A, C, g, 88001875

Tomhum Cliffline Fortification III [Japanese Coastal Defense Fortifications on Guam TR], Address Restricted, Tumon vicinity, 3/04/91, A, C, g, 88001868

Tomhum Cliffline Fortification I [Japanese Coastal Defense Fortifications on Guam TR], E. San Vitores Dr., Tumon vicinity, 3/04/91, A, C, g, 88001895

Tomhum Cliffline Fortification II [Japanese Coastal Defense Fortifications on Guam TR], San Vitores Dr., Tumon vicinity, 3/04/91, A, C, g, 88001896

Tomhum Pillbox I [Japanese Coastal Defense Fortifications on Guam TR], E. San Vitores Dr., Tumon, 3/04/91, A, C, g, 88001893

Tomhum Pillbox II [Japanese Coastal Defense Fortifications on Guam TR], W shore of Naton Beach on Tumon Bay, Tumon, 3/04/91, A, C, g, 88001866

Tomhum Pillbox III [Japanese Coastal Defense Fortifications on Guam TR], E of Matapang Park on Tumon Bay, Tumon, 3/04/91, A, C, b, g, 88001865

Tonhum Fortification I [Japanese Coastal Defense Fortifications on Guam TR], Address Restricted, Tumon vicinity, 3/04/91, A, C, g, 88001870

Toves House [Agana Houses TR], Marine Dr., Anigua, 2/08/85, C, g, 85000410

Umatac-Umatak Pillbox [Japanese Coastal Defense Fortifications on Guam TR], Address Restricted, Umatac vicinity, 3/04/91, A, C, g, 88001881

Ungacta House [Agana Houses TR], 334 Hernan Cortez, Agana, 2/08/85, C, g, 85000409

Uruno Beach Site, Address Restricted, Dededo vicinity, 12/27/74, D, 74002306

Uruno Site, Address Restricted, Dededo vicinity, 12/27/74, D, 74002307

War in the Pacific National Historical Park, Marine Dr., Agana, 8/18/78, A, f, g, NPS, 78003198

West Atate, Address Restricted, Inarajan vicinity, 12/04/74, D, 74002313

West Bona Site, Address Restricted, Santa Rita vicinity, 3/26/79, D, 79003746

Yokoi's Cave, Address Restricted, Talofofo vicinity, 1/16/80, A, g, 80004244

Ypao Beach Archeological Site, Address Restricted, Tamuning vicinity, 5/24/84, D, 84000889

Native Chamorros adapted their diets and their processes of food preparation when ovens like the Inapsan Spanish Oven (ca. 1873) were introduced during the Spanish occupation of Guam. (John Salas, 1987)

HAWAII

Hawaii County

1790 Footprints, 9.1 mi. SW of park headquarters on Hwy. 11, then foot trail to SE for 1 mi., Hawaii Volcanoes National Park, 8/07/74, A, D, NPS, 74000351

Ahole Holua Complex, S of Milolii on Ahole Bay, Milolii vicinity, 11/26/73, D, 73000655

Ahua A Umi Heiau, Address Restricted, North Kona vicinity, 8/13/74, A, B, D, NPS, 74000343

Ainapo Trail, Hawaii Volcanoes National Park, Mauna Loa vicinity, 8/30/74, A, C, D, NPS, 74000290

Ala Loa, Off HI 19 from Kiholo Bay to Kalahuipaua'a, South Kohala, 6/05/87, A, 87001127

Bobcat Trail Habitation Cave (50-10-30-5004), Address Restricted, Pohakuluoa vicinity, 5/15/86, D, 86001086

Bond District, SE of Kapaau off HI 27, Kapaau vicinity, 3/30/78, B, C, a, 78001016

Brown, Francis E. Ii, House, Keawaiki Bay, Kamuela vicinity, 8/21/86, B, C, 86001616

Chee Ying Society, HI 24, Honokaa, 7/20/78, A, C, a, d, 78001014

District Courthouse and Police Station, 141 Kalakaua St., Hilo, 9/04/79, A, g, 79000752

Greenwell Store, HI 11, Kealakekua, 5/22/78, B, C, 78001017

Hale Halawai O Holualoa, Alii Dr., Kailua-Kona, 6/05/87, A, C, a, d, 87000794

Hata, S., Building, 318 Kamehameha Ave., Hilo, 8/27/91, A, B, C, 91001087

Heiau in Kukuipahu, Address Restricted, Hawi vicinity, 4/24/73, D, a, 73000652

Honokohau Settlement, Address Restricted, Kailua-Kona vicinity, 10/15/66, D, NHL, 66000287

Hulihee Palace, Alii Dr., Kailua-Kona, 5/25/73, B, C, 73000653

Imiola Church, NE of Waimea on HI 19, Waimea, 8/28/75, B, C, a, 75000618

Kahaluu Historic District, Address Restricted, Holualoa vicinity, 12/27/74, D, a, 74000713

Kahikolu Church, SE of Napoopoo, Napoopoo vicinity, 11/15/82, A, C, a, 82000148

Kalaoa Permanent House Site 10, 205, Near Kalihi Pt., Natural Energy Laboratory of Hawaii, Kailua-Kona vicinity, 11/21/92, C, D, 92001552

Kaloko-Honokohau National Historical Park, Hawaii Island, Kailua-Konna, Island of Hawaii, 11/10/78, D, NPS, 78003148

Kamakahonu, Residence Of King Kamehameha I, On NW edge of Kailua Bay, N and W of Kailua Wharf, Kailua-Kona, 10/15/66, B, D, NHL, 66000288

Kamehameha Hall, 1162 Kalanianaole Ave., Hilo, 5/20/93, A, C, 93000426

Kamehameha III's Birthplace, Off Alii Dr., Keauhou, 7/24/78, B, a, c, f, 78001018

Kamoa Point Complex, Address Restricted, Kailua-Kona vicinity, 7/14/83, A, C, D, 83000247

Kealakekua Bay Historical District, SW of Captain Cook off HI 11, Captain Cook vicinity, 12/12/73, A, B, D, a, 73000651

Keauhou Holua Slide, E of HI 18, Keauhou, 10/15/66, D, NHL, 66000290

Kii Petroglyphs, Address Restricted, Waiohinu vicinity, 7/12/84, D, 84000919

Kilauea Crater, SW of Hilo in Hawaii Volcanoes National Park, Hilo vicinity, 7/24/74, A, D, g, NPS, 74000291

Kohala District Courthouse, Government Rd., Kapaau, 8/31/79, A, C, 79000754

Kuamo'o Burials, Address Restricted, Kailua-Kona vicinity, 8/13/74, A, B, D, a, d, 74000714

Lapakahi Complex, Address Restricted, Mahukona vicinity, 7/02/73, D, a, 73000654

Lyman, Rev. D. B., House, 276 Haili St., Hilo, 3/24/78, B, C, a, b, 78001012

Mahana Archeological District (50HA10230), Address Restricted, Na'Alehu vicinity, 10/14/86, D, 86002802

Manuka Bay Petroglyphs, Address Restricted, Waiohinu vicinity, 9/19/73, D, 73000656

Mauna Kea Adz Quarry, Address Restricted, Hilo vicinity, 10/15/66, A, D, NHL, 66000285

Mokuaikaua Church, Off HI 11, Kailua-Kona, 10/03/78, A, C, a, 78001015

Mookini Heiau, Northern tip of Hawaii, 1 mi. W of Upolu Point Airport, Hawi vicinity, 10/15/66, A, C, a, NHL, 66000284

Old Volcano House No. 42, SW of Hilo on HI 11 in Hawaii Volcanoes National Park, Hilo vicinity, 7/24/74, A, C, b, NPS, 74000293

Palace Theater, 38 Haili St., Hilo, 5/11/93, A, C, 93000376

Pu'uhonua O Honaunau National Historical Park, 20 mi. S of Kailua-Kona, Kailua-Kona, Island of Hawaii vicinity, 10/15/66, D, NPS, 66000104

Pu'ukohola Heiau National Historic Site, N end of Hawaii off HI 26, about 1 mi. SE of Kawaihae, Kawaihae, Island of Hawaii vicinity, 10/15/66, C, D, NHL, NPS, 66000105

Pua'a-2 Agricultural Fields Archeological District (50HA10229), Address Restricted, Holualoa vicinity, 10/14/86, D, a, 86002804

Puako Petroglyph Archeological District, Address Restricted, Puako vicinity, 4/08/83, D, 83000248

Puna-Ka'u Historic District, Hawaii Volcanoes National Park, Pahala vicinity, 7/01/74, A, D, NPS, 74000294

Shipman, W. H., House, 141 Kalulani St., Hilo, 6/23/78, B, C, 78001013

South Point Complex, Address Restricted, Naalehu vicinity, 10/15/66, D, NHL, 66000291

St. Benedict's Catholic Church, Off HI 11, Honaunau, 5/31/79, B, C, a, d, 79000753

Tong Wo Society Building, HI 27, Halawa, 6/09/78, A, C, a, 78001011

U.S. Post Office and Office Building, Kinoole and Waianuenue Sts., Hilo, 10/01/74, C, 74000708

Volcano Block Building, 27–37 Wianuenue Ave., Hilo, 1/07/93, A, C, 92001748

Whitney Seismograph Vault No. 29, SW of Hilo on HI 11 in Hawaii Volcanoes National Park, Hilo vicinity, 7/24/74, A, NPS, 74000292

Wilkes Campsite, W of Hilo at Mauna Loa Volcano in Hawaii Volcanoes National Park, Hilo vicinity, 7/24/74, A, B, D, NPS, 74000295

Honolulu County

Alexander and Baldwin Building, 822 Bishop St., Honolulu, 9/07/79, A, C, 79000755

Aliiolani Hale, King St., Honolulu, 2/02/72, A, C, f, 72000414

Aloha Tower, Pier 9, Honolulu Harbor, Honolulu, 5/13/76, A, C, g, 76000660

Battery Hasebrouck [Artillery District of Honolulu TR], Ft. Kamehameha, Honolulu, 6/05/84, A, C, 84000925

Battery Hawkins [Artillery District of Honolulu TR], 440 Nelson Ave., Honolulu, 6/05/84, A, C, 84000928

Battery Hawkins Annex [Artillery District of Honolulu TR], Ft. Kamehameha, Honolulu, 6/05/84, A, C, 84000948

Battery Jackson [Artillery District of Honolulu TR], Ft. Kamehameha, Honolulu, 6/05/84, A, C, 84000954

Battery Randolph [Artillery District of Honolulu TR], 32 Kalia Rd., Honolulu, 6/05/84, A, C, 84000971

Battery Selfridge [Artillery District of Honolulu TR], Ft. Kamehameha, Honolulu, 6/05/84, A, C, 84000975

Bellows Field Archeological Area, Address Restricted, Waimanalo vicinity, 8/14/73, D, 73002278

Bishop, Bernice P., Museum, 1355 Kalihi St., Honolulu, 7/26/82, A, B, C, f, 82002500

Brewer, C., Building, 827 Fort St., Honolulu, 4/02/80, A, C, 80001272

Burial Platform, Address Restricted, Kahuku vicinity, 8/14/73, D, a, c, 73000670

Burningham, Thomas Alexander, House, 2849 Pali Hwy., Honolulu, 10/13/93, C, 93001029

CINCPAC Headquarters, Pearl Harbor Naval Base, Pearl Harbor, 5/28/87, A, g, NHL, 87001295

Canavarro, Georges de S., House, 2756 Rooke Ave., Honolulu, 5/28/80, C, a, 80001274

Case, Lloyd, House [Honolulu Tudor—French Norman Cottages TR], 3581 Woodlawn Dr., Honolulu, 6/05/87, C, 86002829

Central Fire Station [Fire Stations of Oahu TR], 104 S. Beretania St., Honolulu, 12/02/80, A, C, g, 80001273

Chinatown Historic District, Bounded roughly by Beretania St. on NE, Nuuanu Stream on N, Nu-

Honolulu County—Continued

uanu Ave. on SE, and Honolulu Harbor, Honolulu, 1/17/73, A, C, 73000658

Church of the Crossroads, 1212 University Ave., Honolulu, 11/20/92, A, C, a, 92001551

Coke, James L., House, 3649 Nuuanu Pali Dr., Honolulu, 8/20/86, B, C, 86001618

Cook, Grace, House, 2365 Oahu Ave., Honolulu, 10/24/83, C, 83003556

Cooke, Charles Montague, Jr., House, 2859 Manoa Rd., Honolulu, 10/31/85, B, C, 85003402

Cooke, Clarence H., House, 3860 Old Pali Rd., Honolulu, 8/20/86, C, 86001619

Cooper, Bartlett, House [Honolulu Tudor—French Norman Cottages TR], 4850 Kahala Ave., Honolulu, 6/05/87, C, 86002833

Dickey, C. W., House, 3030 Kalakaua Ave., Honolulu, 11/01/84, C, 84000201

Dillingham Transportation Building, 735 Bishop St., Honolulu, 9/07/79, A, C, 79000756

Dole, James D., Homestead, Waipahu Cultural Garden, Waipahu, 6/23/78, B, b, 78001024

Duhrsen, Carl H., House [Honolulu Tudor—French Norman Cottages TR], 3029 Felix St., Honolulu, 6/05/87, C, 86002834

Eyman, Jessie—Judson, Wilma, House, 3114 Paty Dr., Honolulu, 8/20/86, C, 86001621

FALLS OF CLYDE, Pier 7, Honolulu Harbor, Honolulu, 7/02/73, A, B, C, NHL, 73000659

Faus, Dr. Robert, House [Honolulu Tudor—French Norman Cottages TR], 2311 Ferdinand Ave., Honolulu, 6/05/87, C, 86002828

Fort Ruger Historic District, Diamond Head Rd., Honolulu, 7/14/83, A, C, 83000249

Foster Botanic Garden, 50 N. Vineyard Blvd., Honolulu, 5/13/93, A, B, C, 93000377

Guild, John, House, 2001 Vancouver Dr., Honolulu, 8/01/80, C, 80001275

Hawaii Capital Historic District, Beretania, Richards, King, Queen, Punchbowl, and Kawaiahao Sts., Honolulu, 12/01/78, A, B, C, a, b, c, f, g, 78001020

Hawaii Theatre, 1130 Bethel St., Honolulu, 11/14/78, A, C, 78001021

Heeia Fishpond, Address Restricted, Kaneohe vicinity, 1/17/73, D, 73000671

Henriques, Edgar and Lucy, House, 20 Old Pali Pl., Honolulu, 11/01/84, A, C, 84000202

Hickam Field, SE of Pearl Harbor Naval Base, Honolulu vicinity, 9/16/85, A, g, NHL, 85002725

Hocking, Alfred, House, 1302 Nehoa St., Honolulu, 11/15/84, C, 84000246

Honolulu Academy of Arts, 900 S. Beretania St., Honolulu, 3/25/72, B, C, g, 72000415

House at 3023 Kalakaua Avenue [Honolulu Tudor—French Norman Cottages TR], 3023 Kalakaua Ave., Honolulu, 6/05/87, C, 86002820

House at 3023A Kalakaua Avenue [Honolulu Tudor—French Norman Cottages TR], 3023A Kalakaua Ave., Honolulu, 6/05/87, C, 86002821

House at 3023B Kalakaua Avenue [Honolulu Tudor—French Norman Cottages TR], 3023B Kalakaua Ave., Honolulu, 6/05/87, C, 86002822

House at 3027 Kalakaua Avenue [Honolulu Tudor—French Norman Cottages TR], 3027 Kalakaua Ave., Honolulu, 6/05/87, C, 86002826

House at 3033 Kalakaua Avenue [Honolulu Tudor—French Norman Cottages TR], 3033 Kalakaua Ave., Honolulu, 6/05/87, C, 86002827

House at 3033B Kalakaua Avenue [Honolulu Tudor—French Norman Cottages TR], 3033B Kalakaua Ave., Honolulu, 6/05/87, C, 86002825

House at 4109 Black Point Road [Honolulu Tudor—French Norman Cottages TR], 4109 Black Point Rd., Honolulu, 6/05/87, C, 86002836

Huilua Fishpond, In Kahana Bay, 13 mi. N of Kaneohe on HI 83 adjacent to Kahana Bay State Park, Kaneohe vicinity, 10/15/66, D, NHL, 66000295

Iolani Palace, 364 S. King St., Honolulu, 10/15/66, A, NHL, 66000293

Kahaluu Fish Pond, NW of Laenani St. off Kamehameha Hwy., Kahaluu, 3/14/73, D, 73000668

Kahaluu Taro Lo'i, W of western end of Hui Kelu St., Kahaluu, 3/14/73, A, C, 73000669

Kahuku Habitation Area, Address Restricted, Kahuku vicinity, 9/11/72, D, 72000424

Kaimuki Fire Station [Fire Stations of Oahu TR], 971 Koko Head Ave., Honolulu, 12/02/80, A, C, 80001276

Kakaako Fire Station [Fire Stations of Oahu TR], 620 South St., Honolulu, 12/02/80, A, C, 80001277

Kakaako Pumping Station, 653 Ala Moana Blvd., Honolulu, 10/04/78, A, C, 78001022

Kalihi Fire Station [Fire Stations of Oahu TR], 1742 N. King St., Honolulu, 12/02/80, A, C, 80001278

Kamehameha V Post Office, Corner of Merchant and Bethel Sts., Honolulu, 5/05/72, C, 72000416

Kanehoe Naval Air Station, Area between First St. and Kanehoe Bay, Kailua vicinity, 5/28/87, A, g, NHL, 87001299

Kanehoe Ranch Building, Castle jct., Kailua vicinity, 6/05/87, A, C, g, 87001150

Kaniakapupu, Address Restricted, Nu'Uanu vicinity, 10/15/86, D, a, 86002805

Kapapa Island Complex, Address Restricted, Kapapa Island vicinity, 8/21/72, D, a, 72000430

Kapuaiwa Building, 426 Queen St., Honolulu, 7/02/73, A, C, 73000660

Kawaewae Heiau, Address Restricted, Kaneohe vicinity, 8/21/72, D, a, 72000427

Kawaiahao Church and Mission Houses, 957 Punchbowl St., 553 S. King St., Honolulu, 10/15/66, A, a, NHL, 66000294

Kawailoa Ryusenji Temple, N of Haleiwa at 179-A Kawailoa Dr., Haleiwa vicinity, 11/21/78, A, C, a, 78001019

Kea'au Talus Sites Archeological District, Address Restricted, Wai'anae vicinity, 5/04/87, C, D, 86002808

Keaiwa Heiau, Aeia Heights Dr., Aiea, 11/09/72, A, 72000413

Kelly, John and Kate, House, 4117 Blackpoint Rd., Honolulu, 8/27/91, B, C, 91001085

Kualoa Ahupua'a Historical District, Kamehameha Hwy., Kaneohe vicinity, 10/16/74, A, a, 74000718

Kukaniloko Birthstones, NW of Wahiawa off HI 80, Wahiawa vicinity, 4/11/73, A, a, 73000674

Kukuipilau Heiau, Address Restricted, Kailua vicinity, 11/16/84, D, 84000254

Kupopolo Heiau, Address Restricted, Haleiwa vicinity, 6/04/73, D, 73000657

Leleahina Heiau, S of Haiku Plantation Dr., Kaneohe, 3/20/73, C, a, d, 73000672

Lihiwai, 51 Kepola Pl., Honolulu, 7/26/82, B, C, 82002501

Lihiwai (Boundary Increase), 41C Kepola Pl., Honolulu, 6/05/87, B, C, 87000793

Linekona School, Victoria and Beretania Sts., Honolulu, 5/28/80, A, C, 80001279

Linn, R. N., House, 2013 Kakela Dr., Honolulu, 8/20/86, C, 86001622

Lishman Building, Makiki Park, Keeaumoku St., Honolulu, 9/13/78, B, C, 78001023

MALIA (Hawaiian canoe), Jct. of Kapiolani Blvd. and McCully St., SE corner, Honolulu, 12/17/93, A, C, 93001385

Makiki Fire Station [Fire Stations of Oahu TR], 1202 Wilder Ave., Honolulu, 12/02/80, A, C, 80001280

Marigold Building, 97-837 Waipahu St., Waipahu, 8/18/83, A, C, 83000250

McKinley High School, 1039 S. King St., Honolulu, 8/11/80, B, C, g, 80001281

Mendonca, J. P., House, 1942 Judd Hillside Rd., Honolulu, 10/07/86, C, 86002798

Merchant Street Historic District, Roughly along Merchant St. from Nuuana Ave. to Fort St., Honolulu, 6/19/73, C, 73000661

Moana Hotel, 2365 Kalakaua Ave., Honolulu, 8/07/72, A, C, 72000417

Mokapu Burial Area, Address Restricted, Kaneohe vicinity, 11/15/72, D, a, 72000428

Molii Fishpond, SE of Kamehameha Hwy. between Kualoa and Johnson Rds., Kaneohe vicinity, 12/05/72, D, 72000429

National Memorial Cemetery of the Pacific, 2177 Puowaina Dr., Honolulu, 1/11/76, A, d, g, 76002276

Necker Island Archeological District, Address Restricted, Kauai vicinity, 6/13/88, A, C, D, a, 88000641

Nihoa Island Archeological District, Address Restricted, Kauai vicinity, 6/13/88, A, C, D, a, 88000640

Nuuanu Petroglyph Complex, Restricted Address, Honolulu vicinity, 3/14/73, B, D, 73000662

Oahu Railway and Land Company Right-of-Way, Barbers Point, Nanakuli vicinity, 12/01/75, A, B, C, 75000621

Oakley, George D., House, 2110 Kakela Pl., Honolulu, 11/15/84, C, 84000249

Ohrt, Frederick, House [Honolulu Tudor—French Norman Cottages TR], 2958 Pali Hwy., Honolulu, 6/05/87, C, 86002835

Okiokilepe Pond, 0.3 mi. NW of Iroquois Point at Pearl Harbor entrance, Pearl Harbor, 3/14/73, D, 73000673

Honolulu County—Continued

Opana Radar Site, Off Kamehameha Hwy. S of Kawela Bay, Kawela, 9/19/91, A, 91001379

Our Lady of Peace Cathedral, 1183 Fort St., Honolulu, 8/07/72, A, C, a, 72000418

Pahukini Heiau, SW of Kapaa Quarry, Kailua vicinity, 9/11/72, A, a, 72000426

Palama Fire Station [Fire Stations of Oahu TR (AD)], 879 N. King St., Honolulu, 4/21/76, C, 76000661

Palm Circle Historic District, Roughly bounded by Carter Dr., Richardson and Funston Rds., A and B Sts., Honolulu, 10/26/84, A, C, g, NHL, 84000104

Pearl Harbor, U.S. Naval Base, 3 mi. S of Pearl City on HI 73, Pearl City vicinity, 10/15/66, A, C, g, NHL, 66000940

Podmore, Joseph W., Building, 202-206 Merchant St., Honolulu, 3/24/83, A, C, 83000251

Pohaku ka luahine, Address Restricted, Kanehoe vicinity, 7/23/73, D, a, 73002273

Punahou School Campus, 1601 Punahou St., Honolulu, 8/07/72, A, B, C, a, 72000419

Puu o Mahuka Heiau, 4 mi. NE of Haleiwa on HI 83, overlooking Waimea Bay, Haleiwa vicinity, 10/15/66, A, D, a, NHL, 66000292

Queen Emma's Summer Home, 2913 Pali Hwy., Honolulu, 8/07/72, B, C, 72000420

Royal Brewery, 553 S. Queen St., Honolulu, 11/29/72, A, C, 72000421

Royal Mausoleum, 2261 Nuuanu Ave., Honolulu, 8/07/72, B, C, a, 72000422

Shadinger, J. Alvin, House [Honolulu Tudor—French Norman Cottages TR], 4584 Kahala Ave., Honolulu, 6/05/87, C, 86002832

Simpson, Charles A., House [Honolulu Tudor—French Norman Cottages TR], 4354 Kahala Ave., Honolulu, 6/05/87, C, 86002831

Sinclair, Dr. Archibald Neil, House, 2726 Hillside Ave., Honolulu, 10/13/83, B, C, 83003557

Small Heiau, 1 mi. S of Kaaawa off Kaaawa Valley Rd., Kaaawa vicinity, 3/14/73, C, a, 73000667

St. Andrew's Cathedral, Beretania St. (Queen Emma Sq.), Honolulu, 7/02/73, A, C, a, 73000663

Tavares, Frank, House [Honolulu Tudor—French Norman Cottages TR], 2826 Coconut Ave., Honolulu, 6/05/87, C, 86002830

Thomas Square, Bounded by King, S. Beretania, and Victoria Sts. and Ward Ave., Honolulu, 4/25/72, B, 72000423

U.S. Coast Guard Diamond Head Lighthouse, 3399 Diamond Head Rd., Honolulu, 10/31/80, A, 80001282

U.S. Coast Guard Makapuu Point Light, SE of Waimanalo off Kalanianaole Hwy., Waimanalo vicinity, 12/07/77, A, 77000447

U.S. Immigration Office, 595 Ala Moana Blvd., Honolulu, 8/14/73, A, C, g, 73000664

U.S. Post Office, Customhouse, and Courthouse, 335 Merchant St., Honolulu, 1/27/75, C, 75000620

U.S.S. ARIZONA Memorial, 3 mi. S of Pearl City on HI 73, Pearl City vicinity, 10/15/66, A, g, NPS, 66000944

USS ARIZONA Wreck, Off Ford Island, Pearl Harbor, Honolulu, 5/05/89, A, B, D, g, NHL, 89001083

USS BOWFIN, 11 Arizona Memorial Dr., Honolulu, 11/16/82, A, g, NHL, 82000149

USS UTAH Wreck, Off Ford Island, Pearl Harbor, Honolulu, 5/05/89, A, B, D, g, NHL, 89001084

Ukanipo Heiau, Address Restricted, Makaha vicinity, 8/13/82, D, a, NHL, 82002502

Ulu Po Heiau, Address Restricted, Kailua vicinity, 11/09/72, D, a, 72000425

Van Tassel, Ernest Shelton, House, 3280 Round Top Dr., Honolulu, 12/16/81, B, C, 81000203

Waialua Agricultural Company Engine No. 6, Off HI 78, Lualualei, 8/19/74, A, B, C, 74000719

Waialua Fire Station [Fire Stations of Oahu TR], 66–420 Haleiwa Rd., Haleiwa, 12/02/80, A, C, g, 80001270

Waialua School, 66–505 Haleiwa Rd., Haleiwa, 8/11/80, A, B, C, 80001271

Waianae District, Address Restricted, Waianae vicinity, 1/21/74, D, a, 74000720

Waikane Taro Flats, 1 mi. NW of Waikane in Upper Waikane Valley, Waikane vicinity, 4/11/73, D, a, 73000675

Wakamiya Inari Shrine, Waipahu Cultural Garden, Waipahu vicinity, 1/08/80, A, C, a, b, 80001285

Walker, H. Alexander, Residence, 2616 Pali Hwy., Honolulu, 4/24/73, C, 73000665

War Memorial Natatorium, Kalakaua Ave., Honolulu, 8/11/80, A, C, 80001283

Washington Place, Beretania and Miller Sts., Honolulu, 6/18/73, B, C, 73000666

Wheeler Field, Area around Wright Ave. and the flight line, Schofield Barracks vicinity, 5/28/87, A, g, NHL, 87001297

Young, Alexander, Building, Bishop St., Honolulu, 8/05/80, A, B, C, 80001284

Kauai County

Bishop National Bank of Hawaii, HI 50, Waimea, 11/29/78, A, g, 78001026

Camp Sloggett, SW of HI 550, Kokee vicinity, 8/05/93, A, C, 93000773

Cook Landing Site, 2 mi. SW of HI 50, Waimea, 10/15/66, B, NHL, 66000298

Gay, Charles, House, Gay Rd., Waimea, 11/01/84, C, 84000203

Grove Farm, On HI 501, about 1 mi. SE of Lihue, Lihue, 6/25/74, B, C, 74000722

Grove Farm (Boundary Increase), On HI 501, about 1 mi. SE of Lihue, Lihue vicinity, 12/08/78, A, C, 78003436

Grove Farm Company Locomotives, Off HI 50, Puhi, 1/19/79, A, 79000761

Gulick-Rowell House, Missionary Row, Waimea, 4/15/78, B, C, a, 78001027

Haena Archeological Complex, Address Restricted, Hanalei vicinity, 11/16/84, D, 84000257

Hanalei Elementary School, Kuhio Hwy., Hanalei, 3/14/90, A, C, b, 90000344

Hanalei Pier, Hanalei Bay, Hanalei, 9/13/79, A, C, 79000757

Hanapepe Town Lot No. 18, Hanapepe Rd. W of jct. with Ko Rd., Hanapepe, 10/13/93, A, C, 93001033

Haraguchi Rice Mill, Ohiki Rd., Hanalei, 8/25/83, A, C, g, 83000252

Kikiaola, Waimea Rd., Waimea, 11/16/84, C, D, 84000270

Kilauea Plantation Head Bookkeeper's House [Kilauea Plantation Stone Buildings MPS], 2421 Kolo Rd., Kilauea, 8/05/93, C, 93000774

Kilauea Plantation Head Luna's House [Kilauea Plantation Stone Buildings MPS], 2457 Kolo Rd., Kilauea, 8/05/93, C, 93000775

Kilauea Plantation Manager's House [Kilauea Plantation Stone Buildings MPS], 4591 Kauwa Rd., Kilauea, 8/05/93, C, 93000777

Kilauea Point Lighthouse, N of Kilauea, Kilauea vicinity, 10/18/79, A, B, 79000759

Kilauea School, Kolo Rd., Kilauea, 8/18/83, A, C, g, 83000254

Kong Lung Store [Kilauea Plantation Stone Buildings MPS], W. side of Lighthouse Rd., about .5 mi N. of HI 56., Kilauea, 8/05/93, A, C, 93000776

Kukui Heiau, Address Restricted, Wailua vicinity, 5/18/87, C, D, a, 86002746

Lihue Civic Center Historic District, Off HI 50, Lihue, 12/17/81, A, C, g, 81000204

Lihue Hongwanji Mission, N of Lihue at HI 56, Lihue vicinity, 3/21/78, A, B, C, a, 78001025

Menehune Fishpond, S of Lihue on Huleia River, Lihue vicinity, 3/14/73, D, 73000677

Na Pali Coast Archeological District, Address Restricted, Hanalei vicinity, 11/16/84, D, 84000266

Old Sugar Mill of Koloa, Maluhia and Koloa Rds., Koloa, 10/15/66, A, NHL, 66000296

Opaekaa Road Bridge, Opaekaa Rd., Kapaa vicinity, 3/28/83, A, C, 83000253

Russian Fort, On HI 50, 200 yds. SW of the bridge over the Waimea River, Waimea vicinity, 10/15/66, A, NHL, 66000299

Seto Building, Kuhio Hwy., Kapaa, 9/04/79, B, C, 79000758

US Post Office—Lihue, 4441 Rice St., Lihue, 11/28/89, A, C, 89002011

Wailua Complex of Heiaus, E coast of Kauai at mouth of Wailua River, Lihue District, Wailua vicinity, 10/15/66, D, NHL, 66000297

Waioli Mission District, Off HI 56, Hanalei, 10/03/73, A, B, C, a, 73000676

Wilcox, Albert Spencer, Beach House, Weke Rd., Hanalei, 7/30/93, A, B, C, 93000725

Wilcox, Albert Spencer, Building, 4420 Rice St., Lihue, 5/31/79, A, 79000760

Maui County

Archeological Site (T-10) 50-60-04-702, Address Restricted, Kawela vicinity, 11/03/82, D, 82000152

Maui County—Continued

Archeological Site (T-108) 50-60-03-713, Address Restricted, Kawela vicinity, 11/05/82, D, 82000163

Archeological Site (T-111-116; T-182) 50-60-04-710, Address Restricted, Kawela vicinity, 11/05/82, D, 82000164

Archeological Site (T-12) 50-60-04-704, Address Restricted, Kawela vicinity, 11/04/82, C, D, 82000153

Archeological Site (T-125-6; T-181) 50-60-03-714, Address Restricted, Kawela vicinity, 11/05/82, D, 82000165

Archeological Site (T-134) 5060-03-718, Address Restricted, Kawela vicinity, 11/05/82, D, 82000166

Archeological Site (T-135-6) 50-60-03-719, Address Restricted, Kawela vicinity, 11/05/82, D, 82000167

Archeological Site (T-155, -158) 50-60-03-721, Address Restricted, Kawela vicinity, 11/05/82, D, 82000168

Archeological Site (T-165-6) 50-60-03-727, Address Restricted, Kawela vicinity, 11/05/82, D, 82000169

Archeological Site (T-19) 50-60-04-705, Address Restricted, Kawela vicinity, 11/04/82, D, 82000154

Archeological Site (T-5, T-122, T-178) 50-60-04-142, Address Restricted, Kawela vicinity, 11/03/82, A, C, D, 82000150

Archeological Site (T-57) 50-60-03-720, Address Restricted, Kawela vicinity, 11/04/82, C, D, 82000157

Archeological Site (T-6 complex) 50-60-04-700, Address Restricted ., Kawela vicinity, 11/03/82, D, 82000151

Archeological Site (T-76) 50-60-03-724, Address Restricted, Kawela vicinity, 11/04/82, D, 82000158

Archeological Site (T-78) 50-60-03-723, Address Restricted, Kawela vicinity, 11/04/82, D, 82000170

Archeological Site (T-79) 50-60-03-726, Address Restricted, Kawela vicinity, 11/04/82, D, 82000159

Archeological Site (T-81, -100, -101, -105, -142) 50-60-03-717, Address Restricted, Kawela vicinity, 11/04/82, A, C, D, 82000160

Archeological Site (T-88) 50-60-04-707, Address Restricted, Kawela vicinity, 11/04/82, D, 82000161

Archeological Site (T-92) 50-60-04-708, Address Restricted, Kawela vicinity, 11/05/82, D, 82000162

Archeological Site 50-60-04-140, Address Restricted, Kawela vicinity, 11/03/82, A, C, D, 82000155

Archeological Site 50-60-04-144, Address Restricted, Kawela vicinity, 11/03/82, D, 82000156

Chee Kung Tong Society Building [Chinese Tong Houses of Maui Island TR], 2151 Vineyard St., Wailuku, 11/15/82, A, C, 82000171

Crater Historic District, Address Restricted, Kahului vicinity, 11/01/74, D, NPS, 74000289

Haiku Mill, Haiku Rd., Haiku, 2/06/86, A, 86000189

Hale Pa'i, Lahainaluna High School, Lahainaluna, 5/13/76, A, B, a, 76000662

Halekii-Pihana Heiau, Hea Pl. off Kuhio Pl. from Waiehu Beach Rd., Wailuku, 11/25/85, A, B, D, 85002972

Hana District Police Station and Courthouse, Uakea Rd., Hana, 8/27/91, A, C, 91001086

Hardy House, 808 Makawao Ave., Makawao, 11/08/84, C, 84002640

Hokukano-Ualapue Complex, On HI 45, Ualapue vicinity, 10/15/66, D, NHL, 66000304

Holy Ghost Catholic Church, Lower Kula Rd., Kula, 8/18/83, A, C, g, 83000255

Honokalani Village, Address Restricted, Hana vicinity, 11/25/85, A, C, a, 85003333

Kaahumanu Church, S. High St., Wailuku, 5/12/75, C, a, d, 75000622

Kaho'olawe Island Archeological District, Address Restricted, Kaho'olawe vicinity, 3/18/81, D, a, 81000205

Kalaupapa National Historical Park, Molokai Island, Kalaupapa, 1/07/76, A, B, C, D, a, NHL, NPS, 76002145

Kamehameha V Wall, Archeological Site (T-20 and T-42-3) 50-60-04-706, Address Restricted, Kawela vicinity, 11/05/82, A, D, 82000174

Kaunolu Village Site, Address Restricted, Lanai City vicinity, 10/15/66, D, NHL, 66000303

Ket Hing Society Building [Chinese Tong Houses of Maui Island TR], Cross Rd., Keokea, 11/15/82, A, C, 82000172

Lahaina Historic District, W side of Maui on HI 30, Lahaina, 10/15/66, A, C, a, NHL, 66000302

Loaloa Heiau, SE coast of Maui, on HI 31, about 0.25 mi. N of Kaupo, Kaupo vicinity, 10/15/66, A, B, C, D, a, NHL, 66000301

Makawao Union Church, Baldwin Ave., Paia vicinity, 12/17/85, C, a, 85003227

Maui Jinsha Mission, 472 Lipo St., Wailuku, 11/21/78, A, C, a, b, 78001028

Meyer, R. W., Sugar Mill, HI 47, Kalae, 9/04/79, B, C, 79000762

Old Bailey House, Iao Valley Rd., Wailuku, 3/20/73, A, C, a, 73000678

Piilanihale Heiau, 4 mi. N of Hana, at the mouth of Honomaele Gulch near Kalahu Point, Hana vicinity, 10/15/66, A, C, a, NHL, 66000300

Pu'upehe Platform (50La19), Address Restricted, Lana'i, 10/06/86, D, a, 86002745

Southwest Moloka'i Archeological District, Address Restricted, Maunaloa vicinity, 10/15/86, A, D, a, 86002811

U.S. Coast Guard Molokai Light, N of Kalaupapa, Kalaupapa, 3/25/82, A, NPS, 82001724

Wailuku Civic Center Historic District, S. High St. between Wells and Kaohu Sts., Wailuku, 8/20/86, A, C, 86001624

Wananalua Congregational Church, Hana Hwy. and Haouli St., Hana, 11/23/88, A, C, a, 88002533

Wo Hing Society Building [Chinese Tong Houses of Maui Island TR], 848 Front St., Lahaina, 11/15/82, A, C, 82000173

The human stick figures carved into this ancient lava flow are part an extensive prehistoric petroglyph field on the island of Hawai'i. (M.J. Tomonari-Tuggle, 1982)

IDAHO

Ada County

Abbs, Walter, House [Tourtellotte and Hummel Architecture TR], 915 Fort St., Boise, 11/17/82, C, 82000175

Ada Odd Fellows Temple [Tourtellotte and Hummel Architecture TR], 109-115 1/2 N. 9th St., Boise, 11/17/82, C, 82000176

Ada Theater, 700 Main St., Boise, 11/21/74, C, g, 74000724

Aiken's Hotel, 99 E. State St., Eagle, 10/29/82, A, C, 82000177

Alexander House, 304 State St., Boise, 8/07/72, B, C, 72000431

Alexanders, 9th and Main Sts., Boise, 11/20/78, A, 78001029

Allsup, Marion, House [Tourtellotte and Hummel Architecture TR], 1601 N. 10th, Boise, 11/17/82, C, 82000178

Artesian Water Co. Pumphouse and Wells, Off ID 21, Boise, 7/26/79, A, 79000763

Assay Office, 210 Main St., Boise, 10/15/66, A, C, NHL, 66000305

Barber Dam and Lumber Mill, E of Boise, Boise vicinity, 11/21/78, A, D, 78001037

Beck, Albert, House [Tourtellotte and Hummel Architecture TR], 1101 Fort St., Boise, 11/17/82, C, 82000179

Boise Capitol Area District, Roughly bounded by 6th and Bannock, N. 8th, 8th, State, 5th Ana Jefferson Sts., Boise, 5/12/76, A, C, a, g, 76000663

Boise City National Bank, 8th and Idaho Sts., Boise, 11/28/78, C, 78001030

Boise High School Campus [Tourtellotte and Hummel Architecture TR], Washington St. between 9th and 11th Sts., Boise, 11/17/82, C, g, 82000180

Boise Historic District, 5th and 6th Sts., both sides of Idaho and Main Sts., Boise, 11/09/77, A, C, 77000448

Boise Junior College Administration Building [Tourtellotte and Hummel Architecture TR], Boise State University campus, Boise, 11/17/82, A, C, g, 82000181

Boise Junior High School [Tourtellotte and Hummel Architecture TR], 1105 N. 13th St., Boise, 11/17/82, C, g, 82000186

Bown, Joseph, House, 2020 E. Victory Rd., Boise vicinity, 6/18/79, A, C, 79000768

Brunzell House [Tourtellotte and Hummel Architecture TR], 916 Franklin St., Boise, 11/17/82, C, 82000182

Bryant, H. H., Garage [Tourtellotte and Hummel Architecture TR], 11th and Front Sts., Boise, 11/17/82, C, g, 82000184

Burnett, H. C., House [Tourtellotte and Hummel Architecture TR], 124 W. Bannock St., Boise, 11/17/82, C, 82000183

Capitol Boulevard Memorial Bridge, Capitol Blvd. over the Boise R., Boise, 11/05/90, A, C, 90001717

Carnegie Public Library, 815 Washington St., Boise, 11/21/74, C, 74000725

Cavanah, C. C., House [Tourtellotte and Hummel Architecture TR], 107 E. Idaho St., Boise, 11/17/82, C, 82000185

Chinese Odd Fellows Building [Tourtellotte and Hummel Architecture TR], 610-612 Front St., Boise, 11/17/82, C, 82000187

Christ Chapel, Broadway at Campus Dr., Boise, 7/17/74, A, B, C, a, b, 74000726

Christian Church, 9th and Franklin Sts., Boise, 2/17/78, C, a, 78001031

Coffin, Henry, House [Tourtellotte and Hummel Architecture TR], 1403 Franklin St., Boise, 11/17/82, C, 82000188

Cole School and Gymnasium [Boise Public Schools TR], 7145 Fairview Ave., Boise, 11/08/82, A, C, g, 82000189

Collister School [Boise Public Schools TR], 4426 Catalpa Dr., Boise, 11/08/82, A, C, 82000190

Congregation Beth Israel Synagogue, 1102 State St., Boise, 11/03/72, A, C, a, 72000432

Daly, John, House [Tourtellotte and Hummel Architecture TR], 1015 W. Hays St., Boise, 11/17/82, C, 82000191

Davies, Dr. James, House [Tourtellotte and Hummel Architecture TR], 1107 W. Washington St., Boise, 11/17/82, C, 82000192

Davis, R. K., House [Tourtellotte and Hummel Architecture TR], 1016 Franklin St., Boise, 11/17/82, C, 82000193

Diversion Dam and Deer Flat Embankments, SE of Boise on Boise River, Boise vicinity, 3/15/76, A, C, 76000666

Dry Creek Rockshelter, Address Restricted, Boise vicinity, 11/22/91, D, 91001719

Dunbar, William, House [Tourtellotte and Hummel Architecture TR], 1500 W. Hays St., Boise, 11/17/82, C, g, 82000195

Dunton, Minnie Preist, House [Tourtellotte and Hummel Architecture TR], 906 Hays St., Boise, 11/17/82, C, 82000194

Eagle Adventist Schoolhouse, NW of Eagle, Eagle vicinity, 8/18/80, A, a, 80001288

Echevarria, Pedro, House [Tourtellotte and Hummel Architecture TR], 5605 State St., Boise, 11/17/82, C, 82000196

Eichelberger Apartments [Tourtellotte and Hummel Architecture TR], 612-24 N. 9th St., Boise, 11/17/82, C, 82000197

Elks Temple, 310 Jefferson St., Boise, 2/17/78, C, 78001032

Fleharty, Alva, House [Tourtellotte and Hummel Architecture TR], 907 Hays St., Boise, 11/17/82, C, 82000198

Fort Boise, About 1.5 mi. NE of State Capitol, Boise, 11/09/72, A, C, 72000433

Fort Street Historic District, Roughly bounded by Fort, State, 6th, and 16th Sts., Boise, 11/12/82, C, a, g, 82000199

Franklin School [Boise Public Schools TR], 5007 Franklin Rd., Boise, 11/08/82, A, C, 82000200

Friedline Apartments, 1312-1326 State St., Boise, 10/29/82, C, 82000201

Fritchman, H. K., House [Tourtellotte and Hummel Architecture TR], 1207 W. Hays St., Boise, 11/17/82, C, 82000202

Funsten, Bishop, House [Tourtellotte and Hummel Architecture TR], 2420 Old Penitentiary Rd., Boise, 1/03/83, C, a, b, 83000256

GAR Hall, 714 W. State St., Boise, 1/21/74, A, C, 74000727

Gakey, J. H., House [Tourtellotte and Hummel Architecture TR], 1402 Franklin St., Boise, 11/17/82, C, 82000203

Garfield School [Boise Public Schools TR], 1914 Broadway Ave., Boise, 11/08/82, A, C, 82000204

Goreczky, Anton, House, 1601 N. Seventh St., Boise, 3/20/86, C, 86000438

Green, John, Mausoleum [Tourtellotte and Hummel Architecture TR], Morris Hill Cemetery, Boise, 11/17/82, C, c, 82000205

Guernsey Dairy Milk Depot [Tourtellotte and Hummel Architecture TR], 2419 State St., Boise, 11/17/82, C, g, 82000206

Guffey Butte—Black Butte Archeological District, Address Restricted, Grandview vicinity, 10/10/78, D, 78001038

Haines, John, House [Tourtellotte and Hummel Architecture TR], 919 W. Hays St., Boise, 11/17/82, C, 82000207

Harrison Boulevard Historic District, An irregular pattern along Harrison Blvd., Boise, 2/29/80, A, C, 80001286

Hays, Samuel, House [Tourtellotte and Hummel Architecture TR], 612 Franklin St., Boise, 11/17/82, C, c, 82000208

Hopffgarten House, 1115 W. Boise Ave., Boise, 8/30/79, B, C, 79000764

Hottes, Fred, House [Tourtellotte and Hummel Architecture TR], 509 W. Hays St., Boise, 11/17/82, C, 82000209

Hunt, E. F., House [Tourtellotte and Hummel Architecture TR], 49 E. State, Meridian, 11/17/82, C, 82000210

Hyde Park Historic District, Both sides of N. 13th St. between Alturas and Brumback Sts., Boise, 10/29/82, C, 82000211

Idaho Building, Bannock and 8th Sts., Boise, 12/08/78, C, 78001033

Idanha Hotel, 10th and Main Sts., Boise, 7/09/74, C, 74000728

Immanuel Evangelical Lutheran Church, 707 W. Fort St., Boise, 6/17/76, C, a, 76000664

Immanuel Methodist Episcopal Church [Tourtellotte and Hummel Architecture TR], 1406 Eastman, Boise, 11/17/82, C, a, 82000212

Ada County—Continued

Jackson, Orville, House [Tourtellotte and Hummel Architecture TR], 127 S. Eagle Rd., Eagle, 11/17/82, C, 82000213

Jacobs, Cyrus, House, 607 Grove St., Boise, 11/27/72, B, C, 72000434

Jefferson, W. E., House [Tourtellotte and Hummel Architecture TR], 1117 N. 8th St., Boise, 11/17/82, C, 82000214

Johnson, J. M., House [Tourtellotte and Hummel Architecture TR], 1002 Franklin, Boise, 11/17/82, C, 82000215

Jones, T. J., Apartments [Tourtellotte and Hummel Architecture TR], 10th St. and Fort, Boise, 11/17/82, C, 82000216

Kieldson Double House [Tourtellotte and Hummel Architecture TR], 413-415 Jefferson St., Boise, 11/17/82, C, 82000217

Kinney, Joseph, Mausoleum [Tourtellotte and Hummel Architecture TR], Morris Hill Cemetery, Boise, 11/17/82, C, c, 82000218

Logan, Thomas E., House, 602 N. Julia Davis Dr., Boise, 9/22/71, B, b, 71000289

Longfellow School [Boise Public Schools TR], 1511 N. 9th St., Boise, 11/08/82, A, C, 82000219

Lowell School [Boise Public Schools TR], 1507 N. 22nd St., Boise, 11/08/82, A, C, 82000220

Lower Main Street Commercial Historic District, Main St. between 10th and 12th Sts., Boise, 11/28/80, A, C, 80001290

MacMillan Chapel, W of Boise, Boise vicinity, 9/07/84, A, C, a, 84000989

Marks, M. J., House [Tourtellotte and Hummel Architecture TR], 1001 Hays St., Boise, 11/17/82, C, 82000221

McCarthy, Judge Charles P., House, 1415 Fort St., Boise, 8/30/79, B, C, 79000765

McElroy, H. E., House [Tourtellotte and Hummel Architecture TR], 924 W. Fort St., Boise, 11/17/82, C, 82000222

Meridian Exchange Bank [Tourtellotte and Hummel Architecture TR], 109 E. 2nd St., Meridian, 11/17/82, A, C, 82000223

Mickle, Willis, House [Tourtellotte and Hummel Architecture TR], 1415 N. 8th St., Boise, 11/17/82, C, 82000224

Mitchell Hotel [Tourtellotte and Hummel Architecture TR], 10th and Front Sts., Boise, 11/17/82, C, 82000225

Moore-Cunningham House, 1109 Warm Springs Ave., Boise, 4/29/77, A, B, C, 77000449

Morris Hill Cemetery Mausoleum [Tourtellotte and Hummel Architecture TR], Morris Hill Cemetery, Boise, 11/17/82, C, c, g, 82000226

Murphy, Daniel F., House, 1608 N. 9th St., Boise, 5/17/82, B, C, 82002504

Neal, Halbert F. and Grace, House, 101 W. Pine St., Meridian, 10/19/82, A, C, 82000227

Neal, W. Scott, House [Tourtellotte and Hummel Architecture TR], 215 E. Jefferson, Boise, 11/17/82, C, 82000228

Neitzel, H. R., House [Tourtellotte and Hummel Architecture TR], 705 N. 9th St., Boise, 11/17/82, C, 82000229

Nixon, Axel, House [Tourtellotte and Hummel Architecture TR], 815 N. Hays St., Boise, 11/17/82, C, 82000230

O'Farrell, John A., House, 420 W. Franklin St, Boise, 9/04/79, C, 79000766

Old Idaho State Penitentiary, 2200 Warm Springs Ave., Boise, 7/17/74, A, C, 74000729

Oregon Trail, 2 mi. SE of Boise and continuing SE for 8 mi., Boise vicinity, 10/18/72, A, 72000435

Parker, John, House [Tourtellotte and Hummel Architecture TR], 713 Franklin St., Boise, 11/17/82, C, 82000231

Paynton, Charles, House [Tourtellotte and Hummel Architecture TR], 1213 N. 8th St., Boise, 11/17/82, C, 82000232

Pierce Park School [Boise Public Schools TR], 5015 Pierce Park Lane, Boise, 11/08/82, A, C, 82000233

Pierce-Borah House [Tourtellotte and Hummel Architecture TR], W of Garden City off US 26, Garden City vicinity, 1/03/83, C, b, 83000257

Regan, John, American Legion Hall [Tourtellotte and Hummel Architecture TR], 401 W. Idaho St., Boise, 11/17/82, C, g, 82000234

Reiger, Fred, Houses [Tourtellotte and Hummel Architecture TR], 214 and 216-18 E. Jefferson St., Boise, 11/17/82, C, 82000235

Roosevelt School [Boise Public Schools TR], 908 E. Jefferson St., Boise, 11/08/82, A, C, 82000236

Rosedale Odd Fellows Temple [Tourtellotte and Hummel Architecture TR], 1755 Broadway, Boise, 11/17/82, C, 82000237

Rossi, Mrs. A. F., House [Tourtellotte and Hummel Architecture TR], 1711 Boise Ave., Boise, 11/17/82, C, 82000238

Schmelzel, H. A., House [Tourtellotte and Hummel Architecture TR], 615 W. Hays St., Boise, 11/17/82, C, 82000239

Schreiber, Adolph, House [Tourtellotte and Hummel Architecture TR], 524 W. Franklin St., Boise, 11/17/82, C, 82000240

Short, O. F., House, W of Eagle on ID 44, Eagle vicinity, 5/23/80, B, C, 80001289

Sidenfaden, William, House [Tourtellotte and Hummel Architecture TR], 906 Franklin St., Boise, 11/17/82, C, 82000241

Simpson, W. A., House [Tourtellotte and Hummel Architecture TR], 1004 N. 10 St., Boise, 11/17/82, C, 82000242

Smith, Nathan, House [Tourtellotte and Hummel Architecture TR], Broadway and Targhee, Boise, 1/03/83, C, 83000258

South Boise Fire Station [Tourtellotte and Hummel Architecture TR], 1011 Williams St., Boise, 11/17/82, C, 82000243

South Eighth Street Historic District, Roughly bounded by 8th, 9th, Miller, and Broad Sts., Boise, 12/12/77, A, C, 77000450

St Paul Missionary Baptist Church, 124 Broadway Ave., Boise, 10/29/82, C, a, 82000247

St. Alphonsus' Hospital Nurses' Home and Heating Plant/Laundry [Tourtellotte and Hummel Architecture TR], N. 4th St. between Washington and State Sts., Boise, 11/17/82, C, a, g, 82000244

St. John's Cathedral [Tourtellotte and Hummel Architecture TR (AD)], 8th and Hays Sts., Boise, 5/24/78, C, a, 78001035

St. John's Cathedral Block [Tourtellotte and Hummel Architecture TR], 8th and Hays, 9th and Fort Sts., Boise, 11/17/82, A, C, a, g, 82000245

St. Mary's Catholic Church [Tourtellotte and Hummel Architecture TR], State and 26th Sts., Boise, 11/17/82, C, a, g, 82000246

State Street Historic District, Jefferson, 2nd and 3rd Sts., Boise, 12/15/78, B, C, 78001036

Stephan, Louis, House [Tourtellotte and Hummel Architecture TR], 1709 N. 18th St., Boise, 11/17/82, C, 82000248

Swan Falls Dam and Power Plant, E of Murphy at Snake River, Murphy vicinity, 7/06/76, A, C, 76000667

Tourtellotte, John, Building [Tourtellotte and Hummel Architecture TR], 210-222 N. 10th St., Boise, 11/17/82, C, 82000249

Tuttle, Bishop Daniel S., House, 512 N. 8th St., Boise, 12/04/80, C, a, 80001291

Union Block and Montandon Buildings, 8th and Idaho Sts., Boise, 3/07/79, C, 79000767

Union Pacific Mainline Depot, 1701 Eastover Ter., Boise, 8/07/74, A, C, g, 74000730

Ustick School, 2971 Mumbarto St., Boise, 10/29/82, A, C, 82000250

Villeneuve, Charles and Martha, House, 7575 Moon Valley Rd., Eagle, 11/13/90, A, C, 90001731

Wallace, J. N., House [Tourtellotte and Hummel Architecture TR], 1202 Franklin St., Boise, 11/17/82, C, 82000251

Warm Springs Avenue Historic District, Warm Springs Ave., Boise, 9/22/80, C, 80001287

Waymire, C. H., Building [Tourtellotte and Hummel Architecture TR], 1521 N. 13th St., Boise, 11/17/82, C, 82000252

Welch, Edward, House [Tourtellotte and Hummel Architecture TR], 1321 E. Jefferson St., Boise, 11/17/82, C, 82000253

Wellman Apartments [Tourtellotte and Hummel Architecture TR], 5th and Franklin Sts., Boise, 11/17/82, C, 82000254

West Warm Springs Historic District, Warm Springs Ave., Main, 1st, 2nd, and Idaho Sts., Boise, 12/12/77, C, 77000451

Whitney School [Boise Public Schools TR], 1609 S. Owyhee St., Boise, 11/08/82, A, C, g, 82000255

Wolters Double Houses [Tourtellotte and Hummel Architecture TR], 712-16, 720-22 N. 8th St., Boise, 11/17/82, C, 82000256

Zurcher Apartments [Tourtellotte and Hummel Architecture TR], 102 S. 17th St., Boise, 11/17/82, C, 82000257

Adams County

Adams County Courthouse [County Courthouses in Idaho MPS], Michigan St., Council, 9/22/87, A, C, 87001599

Adams County—Continued

Council Ranger Station, Jct. of US 95 and Whiteley Ave., Council, 11/19/92, A, C, 92000689

Heigho, Col. E. M., House, ID 55, New Meadows, 5/22/78, B, C, 78001041

Hells Canyon Archeological District, Address Restricted, Cuprum vicinity, 8/10/84, A, D, 84000984

Huntley, A. O., Barn, W of Cuprum, Cuprum vicinity, 11/14/78, C, 78001040

Meadows Schoolhouse, ID 55, New Meadows, 10/30/79, C, 79000769

Pacific and Idaho Northern Railroad Depot, U.S. 95, New Meadows, 4/19/78, A, C, 78001042

Bannock County

A. F. R. Building, 501 N. Main St., Pocatello, 11/15/90, A, C, 90001737

Brady Memorial Chapel, Mountain View Cemetery, Pocatello, 5/01/79, B, C, c, 79000772

Church of the Assumption, 528 N. 5th Ave., Pocatello, 5/01/79, A, C, a, 79000773

Fort Hall, 11 mi. W of Fort Hall, Fort Hall Indian Reservation, Fort Hall vicinity, 10/15/66, A, D, NHL, 66000306

Harkness, H. O., Stable Building, 111 S. Railroad St., McCammon, 2/01/80, A, C, 80001293

Hood, John, House, 554 S. 7th Ave., Pocatello, 12/14/78, B, C, 78001043

Hyde, William A., House, 429 N. 7th St., Pocatello, 6/23/83, C, 83000259

Idaho State University Administration Building, 919 S. 8th St., Bldg. No. 10, Idaho State University, Pocatello, 9/23/93, C, 93000994

Idaho State University Neighborhood Historic District, Roughly bounded by 6th, 9th, Carter, and Center Sts., Pocatello, 9/07/84, A, C, 84001008

McCammon State Bank Building, Center and 3rd Sts., McCammon, 7/09/79, A, C, 79000771

Pocatello Carnegie Library, 105 S. Garfield Ave., Pocatello, 7/02/73, C, 73000679

Pocatello Federal Building, Arthur Ave. and Lewis St., Pocatello, 10/05/77, C, 77000452

Pocatello Historic District, Roughly bounded by RR tracks, W. Fremont, W. Bonneville and Garfield Sts., Pocatello, 6/03/82, A, C, 82002505

Quinn Apartments, 580 W. Clark St., Pocatello, 1/11/85, A, C, 85000057

Rice-Packard House, 454 N. Hayes Ave., Pocatello, 9/12/85, C, 85002159

Riverside Inn, 112 Portneuf Ave., Lava Hot Springs, 8/29/79, A, C, 79000770

St. Joseph's Catholic Church, 455 N. Hayes, Pocatello, 8/29/78, C, a, 78001044

Standrod House, 648 N. Garfield Ave., Pocatello, 1/18/73, B, C, 73000680

Sullivan-Kinney House, 441 S. Garfield, Pocatello, 11/09/77, C, 77000453

Trinity Episcopal Church, 248 N. Arthur St., Pocatello, 2/17/78, C, a, 78001045

Whitestone Hotel, 2nd Ave. and Main St., Lava Hot Springs, 4/07/80, C, 80001292

Woolley Apartments, 303 N. Hayes Ave., Pocatello, 10/31/85, C, 85003425

Bear Lake County

Allred, Ezra, Bungalow [Paris MRA], 93 Center St., Paris, 11/18/82, C, 82000258

Allred, Ezra, Cottage [Paris MRA], 159 Main St., Paris, 11/18/82, C, 82000259

Ashley, Dr. George, House [Paris MRA], 40 W. 2nd, North, Paris, 11/18/82, C, 82000261

Ashley, George, Sr., House [Paris MRA], W. 2nd, North, Paris, 11/18/82, C, 82000260

Athay, Sam, House [Paris MRA], 20 W. 2nd North, Paris, 11/18/82, C, 82004939

Bagley, John A., House, 155 N. 5th St., Montpelier, 1/20/78, B, C, 78001046

Bear Lake County Courthouse, U.S. 89, Paris, 10/07/77, C, 77000454

Bear Lake Market [Paris MRA], N. Main St., Paris, 11/18/82, A, C, 82000262

Bear Lake Stake Tabernacle, Main St., Paris, 12/08/72, C, a, 72000436

Beck Barns and Automobile Storage [Paris MRA], Center St., Paris, 11/18/82, C, 82000263

Bishop West Barn [Paris MRA], W. 2nd St., Paris, 11/18/82, C, 82000264

Browning Block [Paris MRA], Main and Center Sts., Paris, 11/18/82, A, C, 82000265

Budge Cottage [Paris MRA], Center St., Paris, 11/18/82, C, 82000266

Budge, Alfred, House [Paris MRA], N. 1st, West at W. 1st, North, Paris, 11/18/82, A, C, 82000267

Budge, Julia, House [Paris MRA], 57 W. 1st, North, Paris, 11/18/82, C, 82000268

Budge, Taft, Bungalow [Paris MRA], 86 Center St., Paris, 4/13/83, C, 83000260

Clayton, Russell, Bungalow [Paris MRA], 147 E. Center St., Paris, 4/13/83, C, 83000261

Cole House [Paris MRA], SW of Paris, Paris vicinity, 11/18/82, C, 82000269

Collings, James, Jr., House [Paris MRA], S of Paris on US 89, Paris vicinity, 11/18/82, C, 82001888

Cook, Joseph, House [Paris MRA], 63 W. 2nd, South, Paris, 11/18/82, C, 82000270

Davis, E. F., House [Paris MRA], 10 W. 2nd, North, Paris, 11/18/82, C, 82000271

Grimmett, John, Jr., House and Outbuildings [Paris MRA], 135 W. 2nd, North, Paris, 4/13/83, A, C, 83000262

Grimmett, Orson, Bungalow [Paris MRA], 28 W. 2nd, North, Paris, 4/13/83, C, 83000263

Grunder Cabin and Outbuildings [Paris MRA], E. 1st, North, Paris, 11/18/82, C, 82000272

Hoffman Barn [Paris MRA], N. 2nd, East, Paris, 11/18/82, C, 82000273

Hoge, Walter, House [Paris MRA], Center and N. 1st, East, Paris, 11/18/82, C, 82000274

Hotel Paris [Paris MRA], 7 Main St., Paris, 11/18/82, C, 82000275

Hulme, Amos, Barn [Paris MRA], N. 1st, East, Paris, 11/18/82, C, 82000276

Innes, Kate, House [Paris MRA], 100 E. 2nd, South, Paris, 4/13/83, C, 83000264

Innes, Thomas, House [Paris MRA], 42 W. 1st St., South, Paris, 11/18/82, C, 82000277

Jaussi Bungalow [Paris MRA], 170 E. 2nd, North, Paris, 11/18/82, C, 82000278

Keller House and Derick [Paris MRA], E. 1st, North, Paris, 11/18/82, C, 82001889

Kelsey, Robert, Bungalow [Paris MRA], 24 E. 2nd, South, Paris, 4/13/83, C, 83000265

LDS Seminary [Paris MRA], Tabernacle Block, Paris, 11/18/82, A, C, a, 82000279

LDS Stake Office Building [Paris MRA], S. Main St., Paris, 11/18/82, A, C, a, 82000280

Latham Bungalow [Paris MRA], 152 S. 1st, East, Paris, 4/13/83, C, 83000266

Law, Oren, House and Outbuildings [Paris MRA], 592 Main St., Paris, 11/18/82, C, 82000281

Lewis Barn [Paris MRA], W. 2nd, North, Paris, 11/18/82, C, 82000282

Lewis Bungalow [Paris MRA], W. 2nd, North, Paris, 4/13/83, C, 83000267

Lewis, Fred, Cottage [Paris MRA], W. 2nd, North, Paris, 4/13/83, C, 83000268

Linvall, J. L., House and Outbuilding [Paris MRA], E. 2nd, South, Paris, 11/18/82, C, 82000283

Linvall, Robb, House [Paris MRA], Paris Canyon Rd., Paris, 11/18/82, C, 82000284

Low, Morris, Bungalow [Paris MRA], 48 W. Center St., Paris, 11/18/82, C, 82000285

Montpelier Historic District, Washington Ave. and 6th St., Montpelier, 11/16/78, C, a, g, 78001047

Montpelier Odd Fellows Hall, 843 Washington St., Montpelier, 4/15/78, C, 78001048

Nelson, Wilhelmina, House and Cabins, U.S. 89, St. Charles, 5/03/76, A, C, 76000668

Nye, James, House [Paris MRA], E. 1st, South, Paris, 4/13/83, C, 83000269

Old LDS Tithing/Paris Post Building [Paris MRA], Main St., Paris, 11/18/82, A, C, a, 82000286

Paris Cemetery [Paris MRA], Off US 89, Paris, 11/18/82, A, C, a, d, 82000287

Paris Lumber Company Building [Paris MRA], Main St., Paris, 11/18/82, A, C, 82000288

Paris Photo Studio [Paris MRA], W. Center St., Paris, 11/18/82, C, 82000289

Paris Public School [Paris MRA], Main and 1st Sts., North, Paris, 11/18/82, C, 82000290

Pendrey Drug Store Building [Paris MRA], Main and Center Sts., Paris, 11/18/82, C, 82000291

Pendrey, Arthur, Cottage [Paris MRA], 193 Main St., Paris, 11/18/82, C, 82004938

Pendrey, Joe and Zina, Bungalow [Paris MRA], N. Main St., Paris, 4/13/83, C, 83000270

Poulson, Jim, House [Paris MRA], 146 E. 1st, North, Paris, 11/18/82, C, 82000292

Preston Bungalow [Paris MRA], W. Center St., Paris, 4/13/83, C, 83000271

Price, Dan, House [Paris MRA], W. 1st, North and N. 1st, West, Paris, 11/18/82, C, 82000293

Price, Fred, Bungalow [Paris MRA], N. 1st, West, Paris, 4/13/83, C, 83000272

Price, Herber, Bungalow [Paris MRA], 60 W. 1st, North, Paris, 4/13/83, C, 83000273

Price, Joe, House [Paris MRA], W. 1st, North, Paris, 11/18/82, C, 82000294

Bear Lake County—Continued

Price, Robert, House [Paris MRA], N. 1st, West at W. 1st, North, Paris, 11/18/82, C, 82000295

Ream, William and Nora, House, Dingle Rd. S of Ream Crockett Canal, Dingle vicinity, 4/26/91, A, C, 91000460

Rich, Joseph, Barn [Paris MRA], W. 2nd South, Paris, 11/18/82, C, 82004940

Rich, Landon, House [Paris MRA], W. 1st, South, Paris, 11/18/82, C, 82000297

Rich, William L., House [Paris MRA], 34 W. 2nd, South, Paris, 11/18/82, C, 82000298

Rich-Grandy Cabin [Paris MRA], E. 2nd, South, Paris, 11/18/82, C, 82000296

Rogers, Franklin, Bungalow [Paris MRA], 55 E. Center St., Paris, 11/18/82, C, 82000299

Rogers, Frederick, House [Paris MRA], W. 2nd, North, Paris, 11/18/82, C, 82000300

Sheidigger, John, House and Outbuildings [Paris MRA], S of Paris on US 89, Paris vicinity, 11/18/82, C, 82000303

Shepherd Bungalow [Paris MRA], 55 W. 1st, North, Paris, 4/13/83, C, 83000274

Shepherd Hardware [Paris MRA], Main St., Paris, 11/18/82, C, 82000304

Shepherd, Earl, Bungalow [Paris MRA], 104 Center St., Paris, 11/18/82, C, 82000301

Shepherd, J. R., House [Paris MRA], 58 W. Center St., Paris, 11/18/82, C, 82000305

Shepherd, Les and Hazel, Bungalow [Paris MRA], 185 Main St., Paris, 11/18/82, C, 82000306

Shepherd, Ted, Cottage [Paris MRA], N. 1st, West, Paris, 11/18/82, C, 82000302

Sleight, Thomas, Cabin [Paris MRA], Main St., Paris, 11/18/82, C, b, 82000307

Smedley, Thomas, House [Paris MRA], E. 1st St., North, Paris, 11/18/82, C, 82000308

Spencer, George, House [Paris MRA], Center St. and N. 1st, East, Paris, 11/18/82, C, 82000309

Stoker, Henry, House and Outbuildings [Paris MRA], 192 S. 2nd, East, Paris, 11/18/82, C, 82000310

Stucki, J. U., House and Outbuildings [Paris MRA], S. 1st, West, Paris, 4/13/83, A, C, 83000275

Sutton, John, House [Paris MRA], 140 Main St., Paris, 11/18/82, C, 82000311

Taylor's Candy Factory [Paris MRA], Main St., Paris, 4/13/83, C, b, 83000276

Taylor, Arthur, House [Paris MRA], W. 2nd, North, Paris, 11/18/82, C, 82000312

Telephone Company Bungalow [Paris MRA], Center St., Paris, 11/18/82, C, 82000313

Tueller, Jacob, Jr., House [Paris MRA], 75 S. 1st, East, Paris, 11/18/82, C, 82000314

Tueller, Jacob, Sr., House [Paris MRA], 165 E. 1st, South, Paris, 11/18/82, C, 82000315

Wallentine Farmstead [Paris MRA], NW of Paris, Paris vicinity, 11/18/82, C, 82000316

Weilermann, Gus, House [Paris MRA], SW of Paris, Paris vicinity, 11/18/82, C, 82000317

Wives of Charles C. Rich Historic District [Paris MRA], S. 1st, West, Paris, 11/18/82, A, C, 82000318

Benewah County

Benewah County Courthouse [County Courthouses in Idaho MPS], College Ave. and Seventh St., St. Maries, 9/22/87, A, C, 87001580

Coeur d'Alene Mission of the Sacred Heart, Off U.S. 95, Desmet, 4/21/75, A, a, 75000623

Kootenai Inn, 130 N. 9th St., St. Maries, 11/16/79, C, 79000774

St. Maries 1910 Fire Memorial [North Idaho 1910 Fire Sites TR], St. Maries Cemetery, St. Maries, 9/20/84, A, d, f, 84001010

Bingham County

Blackfoot I.O.O.F. Hall, 57 Bridge St., Blackfoot, 5/15/79, C, 79000775

Blackfoot LDS Tabernacle, 120 S. Shilling St., Blackfoot, 9/19/77, C, a, 77000456

Blackfoot Railway Depot, Main St., NW, Blackfoot, 11/20/74, A, C, 74000731

Fort Hall Site, 16 mi. N of Fort Hall, Fort Hall vicinity, 11/21/74, A, D, 74000732

Idaho Republican Building, 167 W. Bridge St., Blackfoot, 10/16/79, A, C, 79000776

Jones, J. W., Building [Tourtellotte and Hummel Architecture TR], 104 Main St., NE, Blackfoot, 11/17/82, C, 82000319

North Shilling Historic District, N. Shilling Ave., Blackfoot, 8/29/79, A, C, 79000777

Nuart Theater, 195 N. Broadway, Blackfoot, 10/19/78, A, C, g, 78001049

Ross Fork Episcopal Church [Tourtellotte and Hummel Architecture TR], Mission Rd., Fort Hall, 1/03/83, C, a, 83000277

Ross Fork Oregon Short Lines Railroad Depot, Agency Rd., Fort Hall, 9/07/84, C, b, 84001019

Shilling Avenue Historic District, Shilling Ave. between E. Idaho and Bingham Sts. and Bridge and Judicial Sts. to Stout Ave., Blackfoot, 8/18/83, A, B, C, 83000278

St. Paul's Episcopal Church, 72 N. Shilling Ave., Blackfoot, 5/15/79, A, C, a, 79000778

Standrod Bank, 59 and 75 Main St., NW, Blackfoot, 8/30/79, A, C, 79000779

US Post Office—Blackfoot Main [US Post Offices in Idaho 1900–1941 MPS], 165 W. Pacific, Blackfoot, 3/16/89, A, C, 89000128

Blaine County

Bald Mountain Hot Springs [Tourtellotte and Hummel Architecture TR], Main and 1st St., Ketchum, 11/17/82, C, 82000320

Bellevue Historic District, Roughly bounded by U.S. 93, Cedar, 4th, and Oak Sts., Bellevue, 6/16/82, C, 82002506

Blaine County Courthouse, 1st and Croy Sts., Hailey, 2/17/78, A, C, 78001050

Emmanuel Episcopal Church, 101 2nd Ave., S., Hailey, 10/05/77, C, a, 77000457

Fish Creek Dam, NE of Carey, Carey vicinity, 12/29/78, A, C, 78003437

Fox, J. C., Building, S. Main St., Hailey, 3/31/83, C, 83000279

Miller, Henry, House, S of Bellevue off U.S. 93, Bellevue vicinity, 5/30/75, C, b, 75000624

Pound, Homer, House, 314 2nd Ave., S., Hailey, 12/28/78, B, C, c, 78001051

Proctor Mountain Ski Lift, Trail Creek, Sun Valley, 1/20/80, A, C, g, 80001294

Sawtooth City, Address Restricted, Sun Valley vicinity, 4/04/75, D, 75000625

St. Charles of the Valley Catholic Church and Rectory [Tourtellotte and Hummel Architecture TR], Pine and S. 1st Sts., Hailey, 11/17/82, C, a, 82000321

Watt, W. H., Building, 120 N. Main St., Hailey, 3/31/83, C, 83000281

Werthheimer Building, 101 S. Main St., Hailey, 9/12/85, B, C, 85002160

Boise County

Arrowrock Dam, About 10 mi. E of Boise on U.S. Forest Service Roads, Boise vicinity, 11/09/72, A, C, 72000437

Greenhow and Rumsey Store Building, Main Ave., Ketchum, 8/18/83, C, 83000280

Idaho City, Bounded by city limits, Idaho City, 6/27/75, A, C, 75000626

Placerville Historic District, Roughly bounded by townsite limits, Placerville, 9/07/84, A, C, 84001029

Bonner County

Bernd, W. A., Building, 307–311 N. 1st. Ave., Sandpoint, 8/18/83, C, 83000282

Dover Church, Washington between Third and Fourth, Dover, 8/08/89, A, a, 86002153

Hotel Charbonneau, 207 Wisconsin St., Priest River vicinity, 11/19/91, A, 91001718

Nesbitt, Amanda, House, 602 N. 4th Ave., Sandpoint, 7/15/82, C, 82002508

Sandpoint Burlington Northern Railway Station, Cedar St. at Sand Creek, Sandpoint, 7/05/73, A, C, 73000682

Sandpoint Community Hall, 204 S. First Ave., Sandpoint, 9/11/86, C, 86002148

Sandpoint Historic District, Roughly 1st and 2nd Aves., Main and Cedar Sts., Sandpoint, 9/07/84, A, C, 84001100

Vinther and Nelson Cabin, Eight Mile Island, Coolin vicinity, 7/21/82, C, g, 82002507

Bonneville County

Beckman, Andrew and Johanna M., Farm [New Sweden and Riverview Farmsteads and Institutional Buildings MPS], US 20 0.5 mi. W of jct.

Bonneville County—Continued

with New Sweden Rd., Idaho vicinity, 11/06/92, A, C, 92001414

Beckman, Oscar and Christina, Farmstead [New Sweden and Riverview Farmsteads and Institutional Buildings MPS], SW corner of jct. of New Sweden—Shelley Rd. and US 20, Idaho Falls vicinity, 11/19/91, A, C, 91001713

Bonneville County Courthouse, Capital Ave. and C St., Idaho Falls, 7/10/79, A, C, 79000781

Bonneville Hotel [Idaho Falls Downtown MRA], 400 Blk W. C St., Idaho Falls, 8/30/84, C, 84001032

Douglas-Farr Building [Idaho Falls Downtown MRA], 493 N. Capital Ave., Idaho Falls, 8/30/84, C, 84001035

Eagle Rock Ferry, N of Idaho Falls on Snake River, Idaho Falls vicinity, 6/07/74, A, 74000734

Farmers and Merchants Bank Building [Idaho Falls Downtown MRA], 383 W. A St., Idaho Falls, 8/30/84, C, 84001037

First Presbyterian Church, 325 Elm St., Idaho Falls, 3/29/78, C, a, 78001052

Hasbrouck Building [Idaho Falls Downtown MRA], 362 Park Ave., Idaho Falls, 8/30/84, C, 84001039

Hotel Idaho [Idaho Falls Downtown MRA], 482 W. C St., Idaho Falls, 8/30/84, C, 84001042

I.O.O.F. Building [Idaho Falls Downtown MRA], 393 N. Park Ave., Idaho Falls, 8/30/84, C, 84001090

Idaho Falls City Building [Idaho Falls Downtown MRA], 303 W. C St., Idaho Falls, 8/30/84, C, 84001092

Idaho Falls Public Library [Idaho Falls Downtown MRA], Elm and Eastern Sts., Idaho Falls, 8/30/84, C, 84001093

Iona Meetinghouse, In Iona, Iona, 5/07/73, C, a, 73000681

Kress Building [Idaho Falls Downtown MRA], 451 N. Park Ave., Idaho Falls, 8/30/84, C, 84001095

Montgomery Ward Building [Idaho Falls Downtown MRA], 504 Shoup Ave., Idaho Falls, 8/30/84, C, 84001096

New Sweden School [New Sweden and Riverview Farmsteads and Institutional Buildings MPS], SW corner of jct. of New Sweden School Rd. and Mill Rd., Idaho Falls vicinity, 11/19/91, A, C, 91001714

Ridge Avenue Historic District, Roughly bounded by N. Eastern Ave., Birch St., S. Blvd., Ash St., W. Placer Ave. and Pine St., Idaho Falls, 5/20/93, A, C, 93000388

Rocky Mountain Bell Telephone Company Building [Idaho Falls Downtown MRA], 246 W. Broadway Ave., Idaho Falls, 8/30/84, A, C, 84001099

Salt River Hydroelectric Powerplant, End of Co. Rd. 12-104, .7 mi W of US 89, Etna, vicinity, 12/02/93, A, 93000889

Sealander, Carl S. and Lizzie, Farmstead [New Sweden and Riverview Farmsteads and Institutional Buildings MPS], W end St. John Rd., Idaho Falls, 5/05/92, A, C, 92000414

Shane Building [Idaho Falls Downtown MRA], 381 N. Shoup Ave., Idaho Falls, 8/30/84, C, 84001101

Shelton L.D.S. Ward Chapel, SW of Ririe on Shelton Rd, Ririe vicinity, 8/30/79, C, a, 79000783

Trinity Methodist Church, 237 N. Water Ave., Idaho Falls, 12/16/77, C, a, 77000458

U.S. Post Office, 581 Park Ave., Idaho Falls, 5/31/79, A, C, 79000782

Underwood Hotel [Idaho Falls Downtown MRA], 343-349 W. C Street, Idaho Falls, 8/30/84, C, 84001102

Wasden Site (Owl Cave), Address Restricted, Idaho Falls vicinity, 5/24/76, D, NHL, 76000669

Boundary County

Boundary County Courthouse [County Courthouses in Idaho MPS], Kootenai St., Bonners Ferry, 9/27/87, A, C, g, 87001581

Fry's Trading Post, Off US 95, Bonners Ferry, 9/07/84, A, 84001104

Harvey Mountain Quarry, Address Restricted, Bonners Ferry vicinity, 6/23/78, D, 78001053

North Side School [Public School Buildings in Idaho MPS], 218 W. Commanche, Bonners Ferry, 5/05/92, A, C, 92000417

Snyder Guard Station Historical District, S of Eastport on Forest Service Rd. 211, Eastport vicinity, 8/19/83, A, C, g, 83000283

US Post Office—Bonners Ferry Main [US Post Offices in Idaho 1900–1941 MPS], 215 First, Bonners Ferry, 3/16/89, A, C, 89000129

Butte County

Experimental Breeder Reactor No. 1, National Reactor Testing Station, Arco vicinity, 10/15/66, A, g, NHL, 66000307

Goodale's Cutoff, S of Arco off U.S. 20, Arco vicinity, 5/01/74, A, NPS, 74000735

Camas County

Skillern, John, House, NW of Fairfield, Fairfield vicinity, 5/14/84, A, C, 84001111

Canyon County

Beale, F. F., House, 1802 Cleveland Blvd., Caldwell, 5/14/93, B, 93000386

Blatchley Hall, College of Idaho campus, Caldwell, 3/08/78, A, B, C, 78001055

Caldwell Carnegie Library, 1101 Cleveland Blvd., Caldwell, 6/18/79, A, C, 79000784

Caldwell Historic District, Roughly bounded by Railroad and Arthur Sts., 7th and 9th Aves., Caldwell, 7/19/82, A, C, 82002509

Caldwell Odd Fellow Home for the Aged [Tourtellotte and Hummel Architecture TR], N. 14th Ave., Caldwell, 11/17/82, C, 82000322

Dewey, E. H., Stores [Tourtellotte and Hummel Architecture TR], 1013-15 1st. St., S., Nampa, 11/17/82, C, 82000323

Farmers and Merchants Bank, 101 11th Ave., S., Nampa, 5/13/76, A, C, 76000670

Fort Boise and Riverside Ferry Sites, NW of Parma on Snake River, Parma vicinity, 12/24/74, A, 74000736

Horse Barn, NE of Nampa at Idaho State School and Hospital, Nampa vicinity, 10/11/78, A, C, 78001057

Idaho State Sanitarium Administration Building [Tourtellotte and Hummel Architecture TR], NE of Nampa on 11th Ave., N., Nampa vicinity, 11/17/82, C, 82000324

Little, Thomas K., House, 703 E. Belmont St., Caldwell, 8/18/80, B, C, 80001295

Map Rock Petroglyphs Historic District, Address Restricted, Givens Springs vicinity, 11/15/82, C, D, 82000325

Middleton Substation, SR 44, Middleton, 5/07/73, A, C, 73000683

Nampa American Legion Chateau [Tourtellotte and Hummel Architecture TR], 1508 2nd St., S., Nampa, 11/17/82, C, 82000326

Nampa City Hall, 203 12th Ave., S., Nampa, 5/09/85, A, C, 85000967

Nampa Department Store [Tourtellotte and Hummel Architecture TR], 1st St., S. and 13th Ave., Nampa, 11/17/82, C, 82000327

Nampa Depot, 12th Ave. and Front St., Nampa, 11/03/72, C, 72000438

Nampa First Methodist Episcopal Church [Tourtellotte and Hummel Architecture TR], 12th Ave., S. and 4th St., Nampa, 11/17/82, C, a, g, 82000328

Nampa Historic District, 1200 and 1300 blocks S. 1st St., Nampa, 8/18/83, C, 83000284

Nampa Presbyterian Church [Tourtellotte and Hummel Architecture TR], 2nd St. and 15th Ave., S., Nampa, 11/17/82, C, a, 82000330

Nampa and Meridian Irrigation District Office [Tourtellotte and Hummel Architecture TR], 1503 1st St., S., Nampa, 11/17/82, C, 82000329

North Caldwell Historic District, 9th, Albany and Belmont Sts., Caldwell, 9/05/79, A, B, C, a, 79000785

Peckham Barn, N of Wilder on US 95, Wilder vicinity, 10/07/82, A, C, 82000389

Rice, John C., House, 1520 Cleveland Blvd., Caldwell, 5/27/80, B, C, a, 80001296

Roswell Grade School [Tourtellotte and Hummel Architecture TR], ID 18 and Stephan Lane, Roswell, 11/17/82, A, C, 82000331

Sacred Hearts of Jesus and Mary Church [Tourtellotte and Hummel Architecture TR], 608 7th St., Parma, 11/17/82, C, 82000334

St. Mary's Catholic Church [Tourtellotte and Hummel Architecture TR], 616 Dearborn, Caldwell, 11/17/82, C, g, 82000332

St. Paul's Rectory and Sisters' House [Tourtellotte and Hummel Architecture TR], 810 15th Ave., S., Nampa, 11/17/82, C, a, 82000333

Canyon County—Continued

Sterry Hall, College of Idaho campus, Caldwell, 3/08/78, A, C, 78001056

Steunenberg, A. K., House [Tourtellotte and Hummel Architecture TR], 409 N. Kimball, Caldwell, 11/17/82, C, 82000335

Stewart, A. H., House, 3rd St. and Bates Ave., Parma, 10/25/79, C, 79000786

Strahorn, Carrie Adell, Memorial Library, College of Idaho, Caldwell, 4/15/82, C, 82002510

US Post Office—Caldwell Main [US Post Offices in Idaho 1900–1941 MPS], 823 Arthur St., Caldwell, 3/16/89, A, C, 89000131

US Post Office—Nampa Main [US Post Offices in Idaho 1900–1941 MPS], 123 11th Ave. South, Nampa, 3/16/89, A, C, 89000132

Wiley, Orton H., House, 524 E. Dewey, Nampa, 9/11/86, A, a, 86002163

Caribou County

Caribou County Courthouse [County Courthouses in Idaho MPS], 159 S. Main, Soda Springs, 9/22/87, A, C, 87001582

Chesterfield Historic District, Town of Chesterfield, Chesterfield, 12/04/80, A, C, 80001297

Enders Hotel, 76 S. Main St., Soda Springs, 5/14/93, A, C, 93000384

Hopkins, William, House, E. Hooper Ave., Soda Springs, 1/08/79, C, 79000787

Lander Road, NE of Soda Springs in Caribou National Forest S of ID 34, Soda Springs vicinity, 4/24/75, A, 75000627

Largilliere, Edgar Walter Sr., House, 30 West Second South St., Soda Springs, 12/23/91, B, C, 91001870

Soda Springs City Hall, 109 S. Main St., Soda Springs, 5/14/93, A, C, 93000385

Cassia County

Albion Methodist Church, 102 North St., Albion, 9/04/86, C, a, 86002161

Albion Normal School Campus, Off ID 77, Albion, 11/28/80, A, C, 80001298

Cassia County Courthouse [County Courthouses in Idaho MPS], Fifteenth St. and Overland Ave., Burley, 9/27/87, A, C, g, 87001583

City of Rocks, City of Rocks State Park, Almo vicinity, 10/15/66, A, NHL, 66000308

Granite Pass, SW of Burley, less than 0.5 mi. N of UT boundary, Burley vicinity, 6/28/72, A, 72000439

Oakley Historic District, Main St. and Wilson Ave., Oakley, 11/28/80, A, C, 80001299

Swanger Hall, Albion State Normal School campus, Albion, 9/20/78, A, C, 78001058

Clark County

Birch Creek Rock Shelters, Address Restricted, Blue Dome vicinity, 12/02/74, D, 74000737

Camas Meadow Camp and Battle Sites, E of Kilgore, Kilgore vicinity, 4/11/89, A, NHL, 89001081

Spencer Rock House, Off US 91 at Huntley Canyon, Spencer, 11/30/89, A, C, 89001991

St. James' Episcopal Mission Church, Reynolds St. (Old Co. Hwy. 91), Dubois, 5/14/93, C, a, 93000387

Clearwater County

Brown's Creek CCC Camp Barracks, 105 1st St., E., Weippe, 7/05/84, A, C, 84001114

Lolo Trail, Parallel to U.S. 12 on ridges of Bitterroot Mountains, from Lolo Pass to Weippe, Lolo Hot Springs vicinity, 10/15/66, A, B, NHL, NPS, 66000309

Moore Gulch Chinese Mining Site (10-CW-159), Address Restricted, Pierce vicinity, 1/27/83, A, D, 83000285

Nez Perce National Historical Park, Area 90 mi. S and 150 mi. E of Spalding, Spalding vicinity, 10/15/66, A, B, C, NPS, 66000310

Orofino Historic District, 2nd, Dewey, Main, Johnson, and 6th Sts., Orofino, 10/29/82, A, C, 82000384

Pierce Courthouse, ID 11, Pierce, 11/03/72, A, NPS, 72000100

US Post Office—Orofino Main [US Post Offices in Idaho 1900–1941 MPS], 320 Michigan Ave., Orofino, 3/16/89, A, C, g, 89000133

Weippe Prairie, S of Weippe and ID 11, Weippe vicinity, 10/15/66, A, NHL, NPS, 66000311

Custer County

Bayhorse, S of Challis off U.S. 93, Challis vicinity, 3/15/76, A, C, 76000671

Board-and-Batten Commercial Building [Challis MRA], Main Ave., Challis, 12/03/80, C, 80001300

Building at 247 Pleasant Avenue [Challis MRA], 247 Pleasant Ave., Challis, 12/03/80, C, 80001301

Buster Meat Market [Challis MRA], Main Ave., Challis, 12/03/80, C, 80004551

Bux's Place [Challis MRA], 321 Main Ave., Challis, 12/03/80, C, 80001302

Challis Archeological Spring District, Address Restricted, Challis vicinity, 2/12/81, D, 81000206

Challis Bison Jump Site, Address Restricted, Challis vicinity, 9/05/75, D, 75000628

Challis Brewery Historic District, Challis Creek Rd., Challis, 2/05/80, A, C, 80001303

Challis Cold Storage [Challis MRA], Main Ave., Challis, 12/03/80, C, 80001304

Challis High School [Challis MRA], Main Ave., Challis, 12/03/80, C, 80001305

Chivers, Bill, House [Challis MRA], 3rd St., Challis, 12/03/80, C, 80001306

Chivers, Thomas, Cellar [Challis MRA], Challis Creek Rd., Challis, 12/03/80, C, 80001307

Chivers, Thomas, House [Challis MRA], Challis Creek Rd., Challis, 12/03/80, C, 80001308

Custer County Jail [Challis MRA], Main Ave., Challis, 12/03/80, C, 80001309

Custer Historic District, Address Restricted, Custer, 2/03/81, C, 81000207

Day, Ivan W., House, Boise Meridian, Stanley vicinity, 4/09/86, A, C, 86000754

East Fork Lookout, Address Restricted, Clayton vicinity, 9/27/76, D, 76000672

False-Front Commercial Building [Challis MRA], Main Ave., Challis, 12/03/80, C, 80001310

Hosford, Emmett, House [Challis MRA], 3rd St., Challis, 12/03/80, C, 80001311

I.O.O.F. Hall [Challis MRA], Main Ave., Challis, 12/03/80, C, 80001312

Mackay Episcopal Church [Tourtellotte and Hummel Architecture TR], Park Ave. and College, Mackay, 11/17/82, C, a, 82000336

Mackay Methodist Episcopal Church, Custer St. and Park Ave., Mackay, 9/07/84, A, C, a, 84001118

McKendrick House [Challis MRA], 4th St., Challis, 12/03/80, C, 80001313

Old Challis Historic District [Challis MRA], Bounded by Valley and Pleasant Aves., 2nd and 3rd Sts., Challis, 12/03/80, C, 80001314

Peck, Bill, House [Challis MRA], 16 Main Ave., Challis, 12/03/80, C, 80001315

Penwell House [Challis MRA], North Ave., Challis, 12/03/80, C, 80001316

Redfish Archeological District, Address Restricted, Stanley vicinity, 12/29/83, D, 83003574

Rowles, Donaldson, House [Challis MRA], North Ave., Challis, 12/03/80, C, 80001317

Smith, Henry, House [Challis MRA], 5th St., Challis, 12/03/80, C, 80001318

Stanley Ranger Station, S of Stanley on US 93, Stanley vicinity, 12/15/82, A, C, 82001885

Stone Building [Challis MRA], 3rd St., Challis, 12/03/80, C, 80001319

Stone and Log Building [Challis MRA], Pleasant Ave., Challis, 12/03/80, C, 80001320

Twin Peaks Sports [Challis MRA], Main Ave., Challis, 12/03/80, C, 80001321

Wilkinson, Clyde, House [Challis MRA], 9th St., Challis, 12/03/80, C, 80001322

Elmore County

Ake, F. P., Building [Tourtellotte and Hummel Architecture TR], 106-72 Main St., Mountain Home, 11/17/82, C, 82000337

Amustutz Apartments, 320 S. Ada St., Glenns Ferry, 9/23/82, A, C, 82002511

Anchustegui, Pedro, Pelota Court, W. 2nd, North, Mountain Home, 1/30/78, A, 78001060

Atlanta Dam and Power Plant, W of Atlanta on Boise River, Atlanta vicinity, 10/05/77, C, 77000459

Atlanta Historic District, Quartz Creek, Pine and Main Sts., Atlanta, 4/06/78, C, 78001059

Elmore County Courthouse [County Courthouses in Idaho MPS], 150 S. Fourth E, Mountain Home, 9/22/87, A, C, 87001584

Elmore County—Continued

Father Lobell House [Tourtellotte and Hummel Architecture TR], 125 4th St., East, Mountain Home, 11/17/82, C, a, 82000338

Glenns Ferry School, Cleveland St., Glenns Ferry, 9/07/84, A, C, 84001122

Gorby Opera Theater [Tourtellotte and Hummel Architecture TR], Idaho St., Glenns Ferry, 11/17/82, C, 82000339

McGinnis, J. S., Building [Tourtellotte and Hummel Architecture TR], 1st and Commercial Sts., Glenns Ferry, 11/17/82, C, 82000340

Mountain Home Baptist Church [Tourtellotte and Hummel Architecture TR], 265 N. 4th, East, Mountain Home, 11/17/82, C, a, 82000341

Mountain Home Carnegie Library, 180 S. 33rd St., East, Mountain Home, 7/24/78, A, C, 78001061

Mountain Home High School [Public School Buildings in Idaho MPS], 550 E. Jackson, Mountain Home, 8/08/91, A, C, 91000988

Mountain Home Hotel, 195 N. 2nd, West, Mountain Home, 10/29/82, C, 82000385

O'Neill Brothers Building [Tourtellotte and Hummel Architecture TR], Idaho St., Glenns Ferry, 11/17/82, C, 82000342

Our Lady of Limerick Catholic Church [Tourtellotte and Hummel Architecture TR], 113 W. Arthur, Glenns Ferry, 11/17/82, C, a, 82000343

South Boise Historic Mining District, In Boise and Sawtooth National Forests, Rocky Bar and vicinity, 12/30/75, A, 75000629

St. James Episcopal Church, 305 N. 3rd, East, Mountain Home, 10/05/77, C, a, 77000460

Turner Hotel, 140-170 E. Jackson St., Mountain Home, 9/07/84, C, 84001124

Franklin County

Bear River Battleground, NW of Preston off U.S. 91, Preston vicinity, 3/14/73, A, NHL, 73000685

Cowley, Matthias, House, 110 S. 1st St., E., Preston, 7/19/76, C, 76000673

Franklin City Hall, 128 E. Main St., Franklin, 11/19/91, A, C, 91001716

Franklin Co-operative Mercantile Institution, 113 E. Main St., Franklin, 11/19/91, A, C, 91001717

Franklin County Courthouse [County Courthouses in Idaho MPS], 39 W. Oneida, Preston, 9/27/87, A, C, g, 87001585

Hatch, L. H., House, In Franklin, Franklin, 5/07/73, C, 73000684

Oneida Stake Academy, NW corner of 2nd, S. and 2nd, E. Sts., Preston, 5/21/75, A, C, a, 75000630

US Post Office—Preston Main [US Post Offices in Idaho 1900–1941 MPS], 55 E. Oneida St., Preston, 3/16/89, A, C, g, 89000135

Weston Canyon Rock Shelter, Address Restricted, Weston vicinity, 7/25/74, D, 74000738

Fremont County

Bishop Mountain Lookout, Forest Rd. 80120, Island Park vicinity, 5/23/86, A, C, g, 86001184

Fremont County Courthouse, 151 W. 1st St., N., St. Anthony, 1/08/79, A, C, 79000789

Idaho State Industrial School Women's Dormitory [Tourtellotte and Hummel Architecture TR], W of St. Anthony on N. Parker Hwy., St. Anthony vicinity, 11/17/82, C, 82000344

Sack, Johnny, Cabin, Island Park, Big Springs, 4/19/79, C, g, 79000788

US Post Office—St. Anthony Main [US Post Offices in Idaho 1900–1941 MPS], 48 W. First North, St. Anthony, 3/16/89, A, C, 89000136

Gem County

Bliss, F. T., House [Tourtellotte and Hummel Architecture TR], E. 2nd and McKinley Sts, Emmett, 11/17/82, C, 82000345

Catholic Church of the Sacred Heart [Early Churches of Emmett TR], 1st St., Emmett, 12/03/80, A, C, a, 80001323

Emmett Presbyterian Church [Early Churches of Emmett TR], 2nd St., Emmett, 12/03/80, A, C, a, 80001324

First Baptist Church of Emmett [Early Churches of Emmett TR], 1st St., Emmett, 12/03/80, A, C, a, 80001325

Gem County Courthouse [Tourtellotte and Hummel Architecture TR], Main St. and McKinley Ave., Emmett, 11/17/82, C, g, 82000347

Methodist Episcopal Church [Early Churches of Emmett TR], 1st St. and Washington Ave., Emmett, 12/03/80, A, C, a, 80001326

Ola School [Public School Buildings in Idaho MPS], 5 Ola School Rd., Ola, 5/05/92, A, C, 92000415

St. Mary's Episcopal Church [Early Churches of Emmett TR], 1st St., Emmett, 12/03/80, A, C, a, 80001327

Gooding County

Citizens State Bank, 3rd Ave. and Main St., Gooding, 5/07/80, C, 80001328

Gooding College Campus [Tourtellotte and Hummel Architecture TR], ID 26, Gooding, 3/18/83, A, C, a, g, 83000286

Hagerman State Bank, Limited, 100 S. State St., Hagerman, 8/11/89, A, C, 89001000

Kelly's Hotel, 112 Main, Gooding, 9/12/85, A, C, 85002155

Mays, James Henry and Ida Owen, House, Along N bank of Snake R., 1.2 mi. W of Niagara Springs, Wendell vicinity, 3/09/93, B, 92001412

Priestly's Hydraulic Ram, 6 mi. S of Hagerman at Thousand Springs, Hagerman vicinity, 2/13/75, A, C, 75000632

Roberts, Morris, Store, Off U.S. 30, Hagerman, 7/17/78, A, C, 78001062

Teater, Archie, Studio, SE of Bliss, Bliss vicinity, 9/13/84, B, C, g, 84001132

Thompson Mortuary Chapel [Tourtellotte and Hummel Architecture TR], 737 Main St., Gooding, 11/17/82, C, a, g, 82000348

Trinity Episcopal Church [Tourtellotte and Hummel Architecture TR], 7th and Idaho Sts., Gooding, 11/17/82, C, a, 82000349

West Point Grade School [Tourtellotte and Hummel Architecture TR], Off I-86, Wendell vicinity, 11/17/82, C, g, 82000350

Idaho County

Ah Toy Garden [Chinese Sites in the Warren Mining District MPS], Along China Cr. near jct. with S. Fork Salmon R., Payette NF, Warren vicinity, 6/27/90, A, e, 90000893

Aitken Barn, SW of Riggins on US 95, Riggins vicinity, 8/09/82, C, 82002512

Bemis, Polly, House, Accessible on Salmon River via boat, Riggins vicinity, 3/04/88, A, C, 87002152

Burgdorf, About 15 mi. W of Warrens, Warrens vicinity, 4/14/72, A, 72000441

Celadon Slope Garden [Chinese Sites in the Warren Mining District MPS], Along China Cr. near jct. with S. Fork Salmon R., Payette NF, Warren vicinity, 6/27/90, A, 90000891

Chi-Sandra Garden [Chinese Sites in the Warren Mining District MPS], Along China Cr. near jct. with S. Fork Salmon R., Payette NF, Warren vicinity, 6/27/90, A, 90000892

Fenn Ranger Station, Selway Rd. 223 near Johnson Cr., Nez Perce NF, Kooskia, 6/18/90, A, C, 90000931

First Presbyterian Church, SE of Kamiah on U.S. 12, Kamiah vicinity, 5/13/76, C, a, 76000674

Foster, Blacky, House, Along Salmon R. W of Shoup, Bitterroot NF, Shoup vicinity, 4/10/92, A, C, 92000307

Lochsa Historical Ranger Station, Address Restricted, Kooskia vicinity, 6/09/78, A, C, g, 78001065

Lower Salmon River Archeological District, Address Restricted, Cottonwood vicinity, 9/04/86, A, C, D, 86002170

McBeth, Sue, Cabin, SE of Kamiah on U.S. 12, Kamiah vicinity, 6/03/76, A, C, a, 76000675

Meinert Ranch Cabin, 1.8 mi. SW of Red River Hot Springs on Red River-Beargrass Rd. No. 234, Elk City vicinity, 9/23/87, A, B, C, 87001561

Moore, Jim, Place, Salmon River Canyon, Dixie vicinity, 3/29/78, A, 78001063

Moose Creek Administrative Site, E side of Moose Cr. S of Whistling Pig Cr., Nez Perce NF, Grangeville vicinity, 6/25/90, A, C, 90000932

Old China Trail [Chinese Sites in the Warren Mining District MPS], Along China Cr. near jct. with S. Fork Salmon R., Payette NF, Warren vicinity, 6/27/90, A, 90000894

St. Gertrude's Convent and Chapel, W of Cottonwood, Cottonwood vicinity, 6/18/79, A, C, a, 79000790

State Bank of Kooskia, 1 S. Main St., Kooskia, 5/22/78, C, 78001067

White Bird Battlefield, N of White Bird off U.S. 95, White Bird vicinity, 7/18/74, A, NPS, 74000332

Idaho County—Continued

White Bird Grade, NE of White Bird, White Bird vicinity, 7/30/74, A, C, 74000740

Jefferson County

Hotel Patrie, U.S. 91, Roberts, 11/07/78, A, C, 78001068

Jefferson County Courthouse [County Courthouses in Idaho MPS], 134 N. Clark, Rigby, 9/27/87, A, C, g, 87001586

Scott, Josiah, House, SW of Annis, Annis vicinity, 11/08/82, C, 82000387

Jerome County

Allton Building [Lava Rock Structures in South Central Idaho TR], 160 E. Main St., Jerome vicinity, 9/08/83, C, 83002299

Barnes, Tom, Barn [Lava Rock Structures in South Central Idaho TR], E of Jerome, Jerome vicinity, 9/08/83, C, 83002317

Bethune-Ayres House [Lava Rock Structures in South Central Idaho TR], E of Jerome, Jerome vicinity, 9/08/83, C, 83002318

Blessing, Carl, Outbuildings [Lava Rock Structures in South Central Idaho TR], NW of Jerome, Jerome vicinity, 9/08/83, C, 83002319

Bothwell, James, Water Tank House [Lava Rock Structures in South Central Idaho TR], N of Jerome, Jerome vicinity, 9/08/83, C, 83002320

Bower, Charles, House [Lava Rock Structures in South Central Idaho TR], N of Jerome, Jerome vicinity, 9/08/83, C, 83002321

Brick, Frank J., House [Lava Rock Structures in South Central Idaho TR], 300 N. Fillmore St., Jerome vicinity, 9/08/83, C, 83002322

Caldron Linn, 2 mi. E of Murtaugh, Murtaugh vicinity, 6/27/72, A, 72000442

Callen, Dick, House [Lava Rock Structures in South Central Idaho TR], S of Jerome, Jerome vicinity, 9/08/83, C, 83002323

Canyonside School [Lava Rock Structures in South Central Idaho TR], S of Jerome, Jerome vicinity, 10/14/83, A, C, 83003579

Cook, William H., Water Tank House [Lava Rock Structures in South Central Idaho TR], SE of Jerome, Jerome vicinity, 9/08/83, C, 83004211

Cooke, E. V., House [Lava Rock Structures in South Central Idaho TR], NE of Jerome, Jerome vicinity, 9/08/83, C, 83002324

Daniels, O. J., House [Lava Rock Structures in South Central Idaho TR], S of Jerome, Jerome vicinity, 9/08/83, C, 83002325

Doughty, George V., House and Garage [Lava Rock Structures in South Central Idaho TR], NE of Jerome, Jerome vicinity, 9/15/83, C, 83002326

Epperson, George, House [Lava Rock Structures in South Central Idaho TR], SE of Jerome, Jerome vicinity, 9/08/83, C, 83002354

Erdman, G. H., House [Lava Rock Structures in South Central Idaho TR], W of Jerome, Jerome vicinity, 9/08/83, C, 83002353

Falls City School House [Lava Rock Structures in South Central Idaho TR], SE of Jerome, Jerome vicinity, 9/08/83, C, 83002352

Fry, Merrit, Farm [Lava Rock Structures in South Central Idaho TR], W of Jerome, Jerome vicinity, 9/08/83, C, 83002351

Gleason, F. C. House [Lava Rock Structures in South Central Idaho TR], 209 E. Ave. A, Jerome vicinity, 9/08/83, C, 83002350

Goff, Hugh and Susie, House [Lava Rock Structures in South Central Idaho TR], NE of Jerome, Jerome vicinity, 9/08/83, C, 83002349

Graves, Lulu, Farm [Lava Rock Structures in South Central Idaho TR], NW of Jerome, Jerome vicinity, 9/08/83, C, 83002348

Gregg, Edward M., Farm [Lava Rock Structures in South Central Idaho TR], SE of Jerome, Jerome vicinity, 9/08/83, C, 83002347

Havens, Bert and Fay, House [Lava Rock Structures in South Central Idaho TR], N of Hazelton, Hazelton vicinity, 9/08/83, C, 83002346

Hazelton Presbyterian Church, 310 Park Ave., Hazelton, 4/26/91, A, C, a, 91000459

Huer Well House/Water Tank [Lava Rock Structures in South Central Idaho TR], NE of Jerome, Jerome vicinity, 9/08/83, C, 83002345

Jerome City Pump House [Lava Rock Structures in South Central Idaho TR], 600 Block of E. B St., Jerome vicinity, 9/08/83, C, 83002344

Jerome Cooperative Creamery [Lava Rock Structures in South Central Idaho TR], 313 S. Birch St., Jerome vicinity, 9/08/83, C, 83002338

Jerome County Courthouse [County Courthouses in Idaho MPS], N. Lincoln, Jerome, 9/28/87, A, C, g, 87001600

Jerome First Baptist Church [Lava Rock Structures in South Central Idaho TR], 1st Ave., E., Jerome vicinity, 9/08/83, C, a, 83002339

Jerome National Bank, 100 E. Main St., Jerome, 1/09/78, C, 78001069

Johnson, Edgar, House [Lava Rock Structures in South Central Idaho TR], S of Jerome, Jerome vicinity, 9/08/83, C, 83002340

Keating, Clarence, House [Lava Rock Structures in South Central Idaho TR], NE of Jerome, Jerome vicinity, 9/08/83, C, 83002341

Kehrer, Thomas J., House [Lava Rock Structures in South Central Idaho TR], N of Jerome, Jerome vicinity, 9/08/83, C, 83002342

Kelley, Marion and Julia, House [Lava Rock Structures in South Central Idaho TR], 450 4th St., E., Hazelton vicinity, 9/08/83, C, 83002343

Laughlin, Ben, Water Tank House-Garage [Lava Rock Structures in South Central Idaho TR], E of Jerome, Jerome vicinity, 9/08/83, C, 83002337

Lawshe, George, Well House [Lava Rock Structures in South Central Idaho TR], SE of Jerome, Jerome vicinity, 9/08/83, C, 83002336

Lee, J. O., House [Lava Rock Structures in South Central Idaho TR], 5th Ave., E., Jerome vicinity, 9/08/83, C, 83002335

Lee, J.O., Honey House [Lava Rock Structures in South Central Idaho TR], 5th Ave., E., Jerome vicinity, 9/08/83, C, 83002334

Mandl, Joseph, House [Lava Rock Structures in South Central Idaho TR], 800 N. Fillmore St., Jerome vicinity, 9/08/83, C, 83002333

Minidoka Relocation Center, Hunt Rd., Hunt, 7/10/79, A, g, 79000791

Newman, J. W. and Rachel, House and Bunkhouse [Lava Rock Structures in South Central Idaho TR], E of Jerome, Jerome vicinity, 9/08/83, C, 83002332

North Side Canal Company Slaughter House [Lava Rock Structures in South Central Idaho TR], NE of Jerome, Jerome vicinity, 9/08/83, C, 83002331

Osborne, Jessie, House [Rock Lava Structures in South Central Idaho TR], W of Jerome, Jerome vicinity, 9/08/83, C, 83002329

Quay, Greer and Jennie, House [Lava Rock Structures in South Central Idaho TR], NE of Jerome, Jerome vicinity, 9/08/83, C, 83002330

Ricketts, Julian T., House [Lava Rock Structures in South Central Idaho TR], SE of Jerome, Jerome vicinity, 9/08/83, C, 83002328

Schmerschall, John F., House [Lava Rock Structures in South Central Idaho TR], 248 E. Ave. A, Jerome vicinity, 9/08/83, C, 83002327

Shepard, L. Fay, House [Lava Rock Structures in South Central Idaho TR], S of Hazelton, Hazelton vicinity, 9/08/83, C, 83002300

Shoshone Falls Power Plant Caretaker's House [Lava Rock Structures in South Central Idaho TR], SE of Jerome, Jerome vicinity, 9/08/83, C, 83002301

Silbaugh, W. H., House [Lava Rock Structures in South Central Idaho TR], W of Jerome, Jerome vicinity, 9/08/83, C, 83002302

Spencer, Edward S., House and Garage and the Fred Nelson Barn [Lava Rock Structures in South Central Idaho TR], N of Jerome, Jerome vicinity, 9/08/83, C, g, 83002303

Stevens, Arnold, House [Lava Rock Structures in South Central Idaho TR], W of Jerome, Jerome vicinity, 9/08/83, C, 83002304

Stickel, John, House [Lava Rock Structures in South Central Idaho TR], W of Jerome, Jerome vicinity, 9/08/83, C, 83002305

Sugarloaf School [Lava Rock Structures in South Central Idaho TR], E of Jerome, Jerome vicinity, 9/08/83, C, 83002306

Thomason Rice Barn [Lava Rock Structures in South Central Idaho TR], E of Jerome, Jerome vicinity, 9/08/83, C, 83002307

Tooley, Don, House [Lava Rock Structures in South Central Idaho TR], NE of Jerome, Jerome vicinity, 9/08/83, C, 83002308

Van Hook, Jay, Potato Cellar [Lava Rock Structures in South Central Idaho TR], S of Jerome, Jerome vicinity, 9/08/83, C, 83002309

Van Wagener, Jacob B., Barn [Lava Rock Structures in South Central Idaho TR], SE of Jerome, Jerome vicinity, 9/08/83, C, 83002310

Van Wagener, Jacob B., Caretaker's House [Lava Rock Structures in South Central Idaho TR], SE

Jerome County—Continued

of Jerome, Jerome vicinity, 9/08/83, C, 83002311

Veazie, William T. and Clara H., House [Lava Rock Structures in South Central Idaho TR], SW of Jerome, Jerome vicinity, 9/08/83, C, 83002312

Vineyard, Charles C., House [Lava Rock Structures in South Central Idaho TR], SW of Eden, Eden vicinity, 9/08/83, C, 83002313

Vipham, Thomas, House [Lava Rock Structures in South Central Idaho TR], 313 E. Ave. D, Jerome vicinity, 9/08/83, C, 83002314

Webster, Archie, House [Lava Rock Structures in South Central Idaho TR], West Ave. and W. Ave. B, Jerome vicinity, 9/08/83, C, 83002316

Weigle, William, House and Water Tank [Lava Rock Structures in South Central Idaho TR], NW of Jerome, Jerome vicinity, 9/08/83, C, 83002315

Wilson Butte Cave, Address Restricted, Hunt vicinity, 11/21/74, D, 74000741

Kootenai County

Bayview School II [Kootenai County Rural Schools TR], Careywood Rd., Bayview, 9/12/85, A, C, 85002090

Bellgrove School II [Kootenai County Rural Schools TR], Hamaker Rd., Rockford Bay vicinity, 9/12/85, A, C, 85002091

Cataldo Mission, Off U.S. 10, Cataldo, 10/15/66, A, C, D, a, NHL, 66000312

Cave Lake School [Kootenai County Rural Schools TR], ID 3, Medimont vicinity, 9/12/85, A, C, 85002092

Cedar Mountain School [Kootenai County Rural Schools TR], Parks and Lewellyn Creek Rd., Athol vicinity, 9/12/85, A, C, b, 85002093

Clark House, On Hayden Lake, Clarksville, 12/12/78, C, 78001070

Coeur d'Alene City Hall, 5th and Sherman Sts., Coeur d'Alene, 8/03/79, C, 79000792

Coeur d'Alene Federal Building, 4th and Lakeside, Coeur d'Alene, 12/16/77, C, g, 77000461

Coeur d'Alene Masonic Temple, 525 Sherman Ave., Coeur d'Alene, 5/22/78, C, 78001071

Cougar Gulch School III [Kootenai County Rural Schools TR], Cougar Gulch Rd., Post Falls vicinity, 9/12/85, A, C, 85002094

Davey, Harvey M., House, 315 Wallace Ave., Coeur d'Alene, 5/23/85, C, 85001126

East Hayden Lake School II [Kootenai County Rural Schools TR], Hayden Lake Rd., Camp Mivoden vicinity, 9/12/85, A, C, 85002095

Finch, John A., Caretaker's House, 2160 Finch Rd., Hayden Lake, 9/14/87, A, B, C, 87001562

First United Methodist Church, 618 Wallace Ave., Coeur d'Alene, 6/18/79, C, a, 79000793

Fort Sherman Buildings, North Idaho Junior College campus, Coeur d'Alene, 10/25/79, A, a, 79000794

Gray, John P. and Stella, House, 521 S. Thirteenth St., Coeur d'Alene, 3/31/88, B, C, 88000272

Indian Springs School II [Kootenai County Rural Schools TR], ID 3, Medimont vicinity, 9/12/85, A, C, 85002096

Inland Empire Electric Railway Substation, Mullan Rd. and Northwest Blvd., Coeur d'Alene, 6/27/75, A, 75000633

Kootenai County Courthouse, 501 Government Way, Coeur d'Alene, 12/23/77, C, 77000462

Lane School II [Kootenai County Rural Schools TR], Lanz Rd., Lane, 9/12/85, A, C, 85002097

McGuires School [Kootenai County Rural Schools TR], Corbin Rd. and Old Hwy. 10, McGuire, 9/12/85, A, C, 85002098

Mullan Road, 3 segments:1)between Aldar Creek and Cedar Creek; 2)Fourth of July Pass between I-80 and Old US 10; 3)Heyburn State Park, Coeur d'Alene vicinity, 4/05/90, A, 90000548

Pleasant View School II [Kootenai County Rural Schools TR], Pleasant View Rd., Pleasant View vicinity, 9/12/85, A, C, 85002099

Post Falls Community United Presbyterian Church, 4th and William Sts., Post Falls vicinity, 9/07/84, A, C, a, b, 84003851

Prairie School II [Kootenai County Rural Schools TR], Prairie Ave., Coeur d'Alene vicinity, 9/12/85, A, C, 85002100

Rathdrum State Bank, 1st and Mills Sts., Rathdrum, 11/08/74, C, 74000742

Roosevelt School, 1st and Wallace Sts., Coeur d'Alene, 7/30/76, C, 76000676

Rose Lake School II [Kootenai County Rural Schools TR], Queen St. and ID 3, Rose Lake, 9/12/85, A, C, 85002101

Sherman Park Addition, Bounded by Garden Ave., Hubbard St., Lakeshore Dr. and Park Dr., Coeur d'Alene, 4/27/92, C, 92000418

Spirit Lake Historic District, Maine St., Spirit Lake, 2/08/79, A, C, 79000795

St. Stanislaus Kostka Mission, McCartney and 3rd Sts., Rathdrum, 11/17/77, C, a, 77000464

St. Thomas Catholic Church, 919 Indiana Ave., Coeur d'Alene, 10/05/77, C, a, 77000463

Thunborg, Jacob and Cristina, House, Chicken Point, Hayden Lake vicinity, 9/12/85, B, C, 85002156

Treaty Rock, N of I-90, NE of Spokane R. falls, Post Falls vicinity, 4/30/92, D, 92000420

Upper Twin Lakes School [Kootenai County Rural Schools TR], Twin Lakes Rd., Silver Sands Beach vicinity, 9/12/85, A, C, 85002102

Latah County

Administration Building, University of Idaho, University of Idaho campus, Moscow, 2/14/78, A, C, 78001072

American Legion Cabin [Potlatch MRA], US Alt. 95, Potlatch, 9/11/86, C, 86002197

Bethany Memorial Chapel, Kendrick-Deary Hwy., Kendrick, 12/06/79, C, a, 79000798

Boarding House [Potlatch MRA], 850 Pine St., Potlatch, 9/11/86, A, C, 86002199

Commercial Historic District [Potlatch MRA], Roughly Pine St. between Seventh and Fifth Sts., Potlatch, 9/11/86, A, C, 86002201

Cornwall, Mason, House, 308 S. Hayes St., Moscow, 12/02/77, B, C, 77000465

Davids' Building, 3rd and Main Sts., Moscow, 12/11/79, A, C, 79000799

First Methodist Church, 322 E. 3rd St., Moscow, 10/05/78, C, a, 78001073

Fort Russell Neighborhood Historic District, Roughly bounded by Jefferson, Monroe, 2nd and D Sts., Moscow, 11/26/80, A, C, a, 80001329

Four-Room House [Potlatch MRA], 1015 Pine St., Potlatch, 9/11/86, C, 86002204

Freeze Community Church, 1 mi. W of US 95, Potlatch, 5/03/90, A, C, a, 90000679

Genesee Exchange Bank, Walnut St., Genesee, 1/08/79, A, C, 79000796

Hotel Moscow, 4th and Main Sts., Moscow, 11/30/78, A, C, 78001074

Lieuallen, Almon Asbury, House, 101 S. Almon St., Moscow, 1/03/78, B, C, 78001075

McConnell, W. J., House, 110 S. Adams St., Moscow, 11/21/74, B, C, 74000743

McConnell-McGuire Building, Main and 1st Sts., Moscow, 2/07/78, A, C, 78001076

Memorial Gymnasium, University of Idaho campus, Moscow, 10/05/77, A, C, b, 77000466

Moscow Carnegie Library, 110 S. Jefferson St., Moscow, 6/18/79, C, 79000800

Moscow High School [Public School Buildings in Idaho MPS], 410 3rd E., Moscow, 5/05/92, A, 92000416

Moscow Post Office and Courthouse, Washington and 3rd Sts., Moscow, 7/03/73, C, 73000686

Nob Hill Historic District [Potlatch MRA], Roughly bounded by Fourth, Spruce, Third, and Cedar Sts., Potlatch, 9/11/86, A, B, C, 86002206

Ridenbaugh Hall, University of Idaho campus, Moscow, 9/14/77, C, 77000467

Sigma Alpha Epsilon Fraternity House, 920 Deakin St., Moscow, 12/02/93, C, 93001335

Skattaboe Block, Main and 4th Sts., Moscow, 5/22/78, A, C, 78001077

St. Joseph's Catholic Church [Tourtellotte and Hummel Architecture TR], 1st and Cedar, Bovill, 11/17/82, C, a, b, 82000351

Terteling, Joseph A., House [Potlatch MRA], 1015 Fir St., Potlatch, 9/11/86, B, C, 86002208

Three-Room House [Potlatch MRA], 940 Cedar St., Potlatch, 9/11/86, C, 86002210

University of Idaho Gymnasium and Armory [Tourtellotte and Hummel Architecture TR], University of Idaho campus, Moscow, 1/03/83, C, 83000287

Vollmer Building, Walnut St., Genesee, 1/08/79, A, C, 79000797

Workers' Neighborhood Historic District [Potlatch MRA], Roughly Spruce St. between Eighth and Fifth, Potlatch, 9/11/86, A, C, 86002211

Lemhi County

Charcoal Kilns, Off SR 28, Leadore vicinity, 2/23/72, A, 72001577

Episcopal Church of the Redeemer, 1st, North, and Fulton Sts., Salmon, 1/12/79, C, a, 79000801

First Flag Unfurling Site, Lewis and Clark Trail, 5 mi. N of Tendoy in Bitterroot Mountains, Tendoy vicinity, 8/22/75, A, 75000635

Fort Lemhi, Address Restricted, Salmon vicinity, 2/23/72, A, D, 72000443

Geertson, Lars, House, SE of Salmon, Salmon vicinity, 4/03/80, C, 80001330

Leesburg, W of Salmon at Napias Creek in Salmon National Forest, Salmon vicinity, 4/04/75, A, 75000634

Lemhi County Courthouse, 1st St., N. and Broadway, Salmon, 2/07/78, A, C, 78001078

Lemhi Pass, 12 mi. E of Tendoy off ID 28, in Beaverhead and Salmon National Forests, Tendoy vicinity, 10/15/66, A, B, NHL, 66000313

Myers, Socrates A., House, 300 Hall St., Salmon, 12/02/77, A, C, 77000468

Odd Fellows Hall, 516 Main St., Salmon, 2/07/78, A, C, 78001079

Salmon City Hall and Library [Tourtellotte and Hummel Architecture TR], 200 Main St., Salmon, 11/17/82, C, g, 82000352

Salmon Odd Fellows Hall, 510–514 Main St., Salmon, 8/25/78, C, 78001080

Shoup Building, Center and Main Sts., Salmon, 3/31/78, B, C, 78001081

Shoup Rock Shelters, Address Restricted, Cobalt vicinity, 11/08/74, D, 74000744

Lewis County

Bridwell, James F., House, 107 Fifth St., Kamiah, 4/06/89, B, 88001446

St. Joseph's Mission, S of Culdesac off U.S. 95, Culdesac vicinity, 6/24/76, A, B, a, NPS, 76000677

State Bank of Kamiah, ID 64, Kamiah, 8/29/78, C, 78001082

Lincoln County

American Legion Hall [Lava Rock Structures in South Central Idaho TR], 107 W. A St., Shoshone vicinity, 9/08/83, C, 83002355

Anasola, Jose and Gertrude, House [Lava Rock Structures in South Central Idaho TR], 120 N. Alta St., Shoshone vicinity, 9/08/83, C, 83002356

Arambarri, Galo, Boarding House [Lava Rock Structures in South Central Idaho TR], 109 N. Greenwood St., Shoshone vicinity, 9/08/83, C, 83002357

Bate, S. A., Barn and Chicken House [Lava Rock Structures in South Central Idaho TR], SE of Dietrich, Dietrich vicinity, 9/08/83, C, 83002358

Baugh, W. H., House [Lava Rock Structures in South Central Idaho TR], E of Shoshone, Shoshone vicinity, 9/08/83, C, 83002359

Berriochoa, Ignacio, Farm [Lava Rock Structures in South Central Idaho TR], NW of Dietrich, Dietrich vicinity, 9/08/83, C, 83002360

Boussuet, Birdie, Farm [Lava Rock Structures in South Central Idaho TR], W of Richfield, Richfield vicinity, 9/08/83, C, 83002361

Byrne, Tom, House [Lava Rock Structures in South Central Idaho TR], NE of Shoshone, Shoshone vicinity, 9/08/83, C, 83002362

Custer Slaughter House [Lava Rock Structures in South Central Idaho TR], W of Shoshone, Shoshone vicinity, 9/08/83, C, 83002363

Darrah House and Water Tank House [Lava Rock Structures in South Central Idaho TR], NE of Shoshone, Shoshone vicinity, 9/08/83, C, 83002365

Darrah, Ben, Water Tank and Well House [Lava Rock Structures in South Central Idaho TR], N of Shoshone, Shoshone vicinity, 9/08/83, C, 83002364

Dill, Charles W., House [Lava Rock Structures in South Central Idaho TR], E of Shoshone, Shoshone vicinity, 9/08/83, C, 83002366

Eskelton, Alvin, Barn [Lava Rock Structures in South Central Idaho TR], NW of Richfield, Richfield vicinity, 9/08/83, C, 83002367

Gaches, George H., Cellar and Ice House [Lava Rock Structures in South Central Idaho TR], NW of Shoshone, Shoshone vicinity, 9/08/83, C, 83002368

Gooding, Thomas, Water Tank House [Lava Rock Structures in South Central Idaho TR], NW of Shoshone, Shoshone vicinity, 9/08/83, C, 83002369

Gottfried, Gehrig, Cabin [Lava Rock Structures in South Central Idaho TR], NW of Shoshone, Shoshone vicinity, 9/08/83, C, 83002370

Hunt, Daniel A., House [Lava Rock Structures in South Central Idaho TR], SW of Dietrich, Dietrich vicinity, 9/08/83, C, 83002371

J.C. Penney Company Building [Lava Rock Structures in South Central Idaho TR], 104 S. Rail St., Shoshone vicinity, 9/08/83, C, 83002372

Johnson, Louis, Barn [Lava Rock Structures in South Central Idaho TR], SW of Richfield, Richfield vicinity, 9/08/83, C, 83002373

Johnson, Louis, Water Tank House [Lava Rock Structures in South Central Idaho TR], W of Richfield, Richfield vicinity, 9/08/83, C, 83002374

Johnson, Quet, Farm [Lava Rock Structures in South Central Idaho TR], NW of Richfield, Richfield vicinity, 9/08/83, C, 83002375

Kohl, W. S., Barn [Lava Rock Structures in South Central Idaho TR], NE of Richfield, Richfield vicinity, 9/08/83, C, 83002376

Laine, James H., Barn [Lava Rock Structures in South Central Idaho TR], S of Richfield, Richfield vicinity, 9/08/83, C, 83002377

Lemmon Hardware Store [Lava Rock Structures in South Central Idaho TR], Main St. and Nez Perce Ave., Richfield vicinity, 9/08/83, C, 83002378

Murphy, W. H., House [Lava Rock Structures in South Central Idaho TR], 607 S. Greenwood St., Shoshone vicinity, 9/08/83, C, 83002379

Myers School [Lava Rock Structures in South Central Idaho TR], W of Shoshone, Shoshone vicinity, 9/08/83, C, 83002380

Newman, A. G., House [Lava Rock Structures in South Central Idaho TR], 309 E. C St., Shoshone vicinity, 9/08/83, C, 83002381

Olley, Thomas, House [Lava Rock Structures in South Central Idaho TR], 522 N. Apple St., Shoshone vicinity, 9/08/83, C, 83002382

Oughton, Jack, House [Lava Rock Structures in South Central Idaho TR], 123 N. Beverly St., Shoshone vicinity, 9/08/83, C, 83002383

Paul, Denton J., Water Tank [Lava Rock Structures in South Central Idaho TR], E of Dietrich, Dietrich vicinity, 9/08/83, C, 83002384

Phelphs, Kenneth G., Barn [Lava Rock Structures in South Central Idaho TR], W of Richfield, Richfield vicinity, 9/08/83, C, 83002385

Purdum Livery Stable [Lava Rock Structures in South Central Idaho TR], 113 N. Rail St., E., Shoshone, 9/15/83, A, C, 83002393

Richfield Pump House [Lava Rock Structures in South Central Idaho TR], SE of Richfield, Richfield vicinity, 9/08/83, C, 83002386

Ritter, William M., House [Lava Rock Structures in South Central Idaho TR], NE of Shoshone, Shoshone vicinity, 9/08/83, C, 83002387

Shoshone Historic District, Irregular pattern, includes N bank of Little Wood River and W. D St., Shoshone, 6/27/75, A, B, C, a, 75000636

Silva, Arthur D., Flume [Lava Rock Structures in South Central Idaho TR], NW of Shoshone, Shoshone vicinity, 9/08/83, C, 83002388

Silva, Arthur D., Ranch [Lava Rock Structures in South Central Idaho TR], NW of Shoshone, Shoshone vicinity, 9/08/83, C, 83002389

Silva, Arthur D., Water Tank [Lava Rock Structures in South Central Idaho TR], NW of Shoshone, Shoshone vicinity, 9/08/83, C, 83002390

Silva, Manuel, Barn [Lava Rock Structures in South Central Idaho TR], E of Shoshone, Shoshone vicinity, 9/08/83, C, 83002391

Turner, John G., House [Lava Rock Structures in South Central Idaho TR], W of Richfield, Richfield vicinity, 9/08/83, C, 83002392

Madison County

Madison County Courthouse [County Courthouses in Idaho MPS], E. Main St., Rexburg, 9/22/87, A, C, 87001587

Rexburg Stake Tabernacle, 25 N. Center St., Rexburg, 5/03/74, C, a, 74000745

Spori, Jacob, Building, 100 E. 2nd South, Rexburg, 4/20/89, A, a, 89000329

Minidoka County

Minidoka Dam and Power Plant, S of Minidoka, Minidoka vicinity, 10/29/74, A, C, 74000746

Nez Perce County

American Women's League Chapter House, 217 N. Main St., Peck, 9/04/86, A, C, 86002158

Breier Building, 631–633 Main St., Lewiston, 6/13/86, C, 86001261

First Christian Church, 7th Ave. and 7th St., Lewiston, 8/31/78, C, a, 78001083

First Lapwai Bank, 302 W. 1st St., Lapwai, 3/12/80, A, C, 80001331

First Presbyterian Church, Locust and 1st St., E., Lapwai, 3/12/80, C, 80001332

Garfield School, 2912 5th Ave., Lewiston, 4/15/82, C, 82002513

Hasotino, Address Restricted, Lewiston vicinity, 4/02/76, D, 76000678

Hatwai Village Site, Address Restricted, Lewiston vicinity, 11/08/82, A, D, 82000353

Hells Canyon Archeological District, Address Restricted, Lewiston, vicinity, 8/10/84, A, D, 84000984

Idaho Grocery Warehouse and Annex [Tourtellotte and Hummel Architecture TR], 1209 Main St., Lewiston, 11/17/82, C, 82000354

JEAN (steamboat), 3620 A Snake River Ave. in Hells Gate State Park, Lewistown, 8/08/89, A, C, 89001001

Kettenbach, Henry C., House, 1026 9th Ave., Lewiston, 2/07/78, B, C, 78001084

Lenore Site, Address Restricted, Lenore vicinity, 11/21/74, D, NPS, 74000284

Lewiston City Hall [Tourtellotte and Hummel Architecture TR], 207 3rd. St., Lewiston, 11/17/82, C, 82000355

Lewiston Depot, 13th and Main Sts., Lewiston, 5/07/73, A, C, 73000687

Lewiston Historic District, Irregular pattern between 1st and 5th Sts. and B St. and the Snake River, Lewiston, 6/05/75, A, C, 75000637

Lewiston Historic District (Boundary Increase), Roughly bounded by 1st, B, 6th, and F Sts., Lewiston, 9/07/84, A, C, 84003852

Lewiston Methodist Church, 805 6th Ave., Lewiston, 9/20/79, C, a, 79000802

Lewiston Vineyards Gates [Tourtellotte and Hummel Architecture TR], 18th Ave. and 10th, Lewiston, 4/14/83, C, 83000288

McLaren, William and Elizabeth, House, 1602 15th Ave., Lewiston, 11/06/92, A, C, 92001413

Nave Apartments, 600 block of 8th St., Lewiston, 8/03/78, C, 78001085

Nez Perce Snake River Archeological District, Address Restricted, Lewiston vicinity, 12/22/78, D, 78001086

St. Stanislaus Catholic Church, 633 5th Ave., Lewiston, 2/07/78, C, a, 78001087

Thompson, Gaylord, House, 1824 Seventeenth Ave., Lewiston, 5/04/92, A, C, 92000419

Twenty-One Ranchhouse, S of Lewiston at 7570 Waha Rd., Lewiston vicinity, 12/18/78, C, 78001088

Oneida County

Co-Op Block and J. N. Ireland Bank, Main and Bannock Sts., Malad City, 4/18/79, A, 79000804

Evans, D. L., Sr., Bungalow, 203 N. Main St, Malad City, 8/30/79, B, C, 79000805

Jones, Jedd, House, 242 N. Main St., Malad City, 5/01/79, A, C, 79000806

Malad Second Ward Tabernacle, 20 S. 100 W. St., Malad City, 7/27/79, C, a, 79000803

Oneida County Courthouse [County Courthouses in Idaho MPS], Court St., Malad, 11/27/87, A, C, g, 87001588

Samaria Historic District, Roughly bounded by Main and 3rd Sts., 1st Ave., N. and S end of 2nd St., Samaria, 6/11/79, A, C, 79003740

United Presbyterian Church, S. Main St., Malad City, 10/16/79, A, C, a, 79000807

Owyhee County

Bernard's Ferry, N of Murphy off ID 78, Murphy vicinity, 5/22/78, A, C, 78001090

Bruneau Episcopal Church [Tourtellotte and Hummel Architecture TR], Off ID 51, Bruneau, 11/17/82, C, a, 82000356

Camas and Pole Creeks Archeological District, Address Restricted, Wagon Box Basin vicinity, 5/28/86, D, 86001203

Camp Lyon Site, 1 mi. E of U.S. 95, Reynolds vicinity, 12/27/72, A, 72000444

Camp Three Forks, S of Silver City, Silver City vicinity, 12/15/72, A, 72000445

Delamar Historic District, 6 mi. W of Silver City, Silver City vicinity, 5/13/76, A, C, 76000679

Noble Horse Barn, Reynolds Cr. 12 mi. SW of Murphy, Murphy vicinity, 8/07/91, A, 91000989

Our Lady, Queen of Heaven Church, Address Restricted, Oreana, 11/28/80, C, a, 80001333

Owyhee County Courthouse [Tourtellotte and Hummel Architecture TR], ID 45, Murphy, 11/17/82, C, g, 82000357

Poison Creek Stage Station, S of Homedale off Jump Creek Rd., Homedale vicinity, 5/22/78, A, C, 78001089

Silver City Historic District, Silver City and its environs, Silver City vicinity, 5/19/72, A, 72000446

Wickahoney Post Office and Stage Station, Wickahoney Creek, Wickahoney, 5/27/82, A, C, 82002514

Payette County

Chase, David C., House, 307 9th St., N., Payette, 2/07/78, C, 78001091

Coughanour Apartment Block, 700–718 1st Ave., N., Payette, 5/23/78, C, 78001092

Jacobsen, N. A., Building [Tourtellotte and Hummel Architecture TR], N. 8th St. and 1st Ave., Payette, 11/17/82, C, 82000358

McCall District Administrative Site, Jct. of W. Lake and Mission Sts., McCall, 12/30/91, A, b, 91001892

Methodist Episcopal Church of Payette, 1st Ave., S. and 9th St., Payette, 10/05/77, C, a, 77000469

Moss, A. B., Building, 137 N. 8th St., Payette, 2/08/78, C, 78001093

New Plymouth Congregational Church [Tourtellotte and Hummel Architecture TR], Southwest Ave. between West Park and Plymouth, New Plymouth, 11/17/82, C, a, 82000359

Palumbo, J. C., Fruit Company Packing Warehouse Building [Tourtellotte and Hummel Architecture TR], 2nd Ave. and 6th St., Payette, 11/17/82, C, 82000360

Payette City Hall and Courthouse, 3rd Ave. and 8th St., Payette, 5/14/79, C, 79000808

St. James Episcopal Church, 1st Ave., N. and 10th St., Payette, 4/20/78, C, a, 78001094

US Post Office—Payette Main [US Post Offices in Idaho 1900–1941 MPS], 915 Center Ave., Payette, 3/16/89, A, C, 89000134

Whitney, Grant, House, 1015 7th Ave., N., Payette, 2/23/78, C, 78001095

Woodward Building, 23 8th St., Payette, 4/26/78, C, 78001096

Power County

American Falls East Shore Power Plants, ID 39, American Falls, 10/29/76, C, 76000680

Oneida Milling and Elevator Company Grain Elevator, Offshore in American Falls Reservoir, American Falls vicinity, 7/16/93, A, 93000380

Oregon Trail Historic District, SW of American Falls along U.S. 30N, American Falls vicinity, 3/20/73, A, 73000688

Oregon Trail Historic District (Boundary Increase), W of American Falls, American Falls vicinity, 6/07/74, A, 74002296

Power County Courthouse [County Courthouses in Idaho MPS], Bannock Ave., American Falls, 9/22/87, A, C, 87001601

Register Rock, W of American Falls on U.S. 30, American Falls vicinity, 7/24/78, A, 78001097

Shoshone County

Avery Depot [North Idaho 1910 Fire Sites TR], Chicago, Milwaukee, St. Paul, and Pacific RR track, Avery, 9/20/84, A, 84001142

Avery Ranger Station, Near St. Joseph National Forest, Avery, 6/27/74, A, C, g, 74000748

Bullion Tunnel [North Idaho 1910 Fire Sites TR], E of Avery, Avery vicinity, 9/20/84, A, 84001160

Cedar Snags [North Idaho 1910 Fire Sites TR], N of Avery, Avery vicinity, 9/20/84, A, 84001174

Feehan, John C., House, Main St., Murray, 8/27/80, C, 80001334

Grand Forks [North Idaho 1910 Fire Sites TR], E of Avery, Avery vicinity, 9/20/84, A, 84001175

Halm Creek, Bean Creek Fire [North Idaho 1910 Fire Sites TR], S of Red Ives, Red Ives vicinity, 9/20/84, A, 84001177

Magee Ranger Station, W of Pritchard, Pritchard vicinity, 2/18/81, A, C, g, 81000208

Mallard Peak Lookout, SE of Avery, Avery vicinity, 4/12/84, A, C, 84001178

Murray Courthouse, Main St., Murray, 11/14/78, C, 78001098

Shoshone County—Continued

Murray Masonic Hall, Main St. between Second and Third, Murray, 5/19/87, A, C, 87000774

Northern Pacific Railway Depot, 219 Sixth St., Wallace, 4/02/76, A, C, b, 76000681

Pine Creek Baptist Church [Tourtellotte and Hummel Architecture TR], Main and S. 3rd Sts., Pinehurst, 11/17/82, C, a, 82000361

Pulaski, Edward, Tunnel and Placer Creek Escape Route [North Idaho 1910 Fire Sites TR], SW of Wallace, Wallace vicinity, 9/20/84, A, 84001179

Red Ives Ranger Station, SE of Avery on Forest Service Rd. 218, Avery vicinity, 9/13/86, A, C, g, 86002151

US Post Office—Kellogg Main [US Post Offices in Idaho, 1900–1941 MPS], 302 S. Division, Kellogg, 5/30/90, A, C, 89002118

US Post Office—Wallace Main [US Post Offices in Idaho 1900–1941 MPS], 403 Cedar St., Wallace, 3/16/89, A, C, 89000137

Wallace 1910 Fire Memorial [North Idaho 1910 Fire Sites TR], N of Wallace, Wallace vicinity, 9/20/84, A, d, f, 84001180

Wallace Carnegie Library, City Park, Wallace, 2/03/81, C, 81000209

Wallace Historic District, Roughly bounded by Pine, Bank, 5th and 7th Sts., Wallace, 8/10/79, C, g, 79000809

Wallace Historic District (Boundary Increase), Roughly bounded by Oak, Silver, C, Mullan, Canyon, Fir, and 1st Sts., Wallace, 9/01/83, A, C, g, 83000289

Teton County

Pierre's Hole 1832 Battle Area Site, S of Driggs, Driggs vicinity, 9/07/84, A, 84001197

Teton County Courthouse [County Courthouses in Idaho MPS], Main St., Driggs, 9/22/87, A, C, 87001589

Twin Falls County

Alvis, James, House, 1311 Pole Line Rd., Twin Falls, 5/23/80, C, 80001335

Bickel School, 607 Second Ave. E., Twin Falls, 8/17/90, A, C, 90001233

Bowlby, T. P., Barn [Buhl Dairy Barns TR], NE of Buhl, Buhl vicinity, 9/07/83, A, C, 83000293

Buhl City Hall, Broadway and Elm St., Buhl, 2/08/78, C, 78001099

Buhl IOOF Building, 1014-16 Main St., Buhl, 12/27/84, A, C, 84000482

Cedar Draw School [Public School Buildings in Idaho MPS], 4300 N. Rd. between 1900 and 2000 E., Buhl vicinity, 8/08/91, A, 91000986

Dau-Webbenhorst Barn [Buhl Dairy Barns TR], SE of Buhl, Buhl vicinity, 9/07/83, A, C, 83000295

Duquesne, Achille, House, 710 W. Midway, Filer, 9/23/93, C, 93000990

Hollister School [Public School Buildings in Idaho MPS], 2464 Salmon Ave., Hollister, 8/08/91, A, 91000984

Hotel Buhl, 1004 Main St., Buhl, 9/12/85, C, 85002158

Idaho Power Substation, Van Buren St. and Filer Ave., Twin Falls, 6/23/78, C, 78001100

Kimberly High School, 141 Center St. W., Kimberly, 8/17/90, A, 90001229

Lincoln School, 238 Seventh St., Twin Falls, 8/17/90, A, C, 90001218

Lincoln Street Electric Streetlights, 105, 120, 147, 174, 189, 210, 217, 242, 275 and 290 Lincoln St., Twin Falls, 4/27/92, A, 92000413

Maxwell, Art and Frieda, Barn [Buhl Dairy Barns TR], SE of Buhl, Buhl vicinity, 9/07/83, A, C, 83000291

McCollum, Robert, House, 708 E. Shoshone St., Twin Falls, 11/04/82, C, 82000386

Milner Dam and the Twin Falls Main Canal, Twin Falls Main Canal between Murtaugh and Milner Lakes, Murtaugh vicinity, 7/10/86, A, 86001720

Morse, Burton, House, 136 Tenth Ave. N., Twin Falls, 9/23/93, C, 93000992

Peck, D. H., House, 207 E. 8th Ave., Twin Falls, 9/23/93, C, 93000993

Pleasant Valley School [Public School Buildings in Idaho MPS], 3501 E. 3100 N., Kimberly vicinity, 8/08/91, A, 91000985

Pleasant View School [Public School Buildings in Idaho MPS], 2500 E. 3600 N., Twin Falls vicinity, 8/08/91, A, 91000987

Priebe, Walter, House, 155 7th Ave. E., Twin Falls, 9/23/93, C, 93000991

Ramona Theater, 113 Broadway, Buhl, 12/22/76, C, g, 76000682

Schick, Henry, Barn [Buhl Dairy Barns TR], SE of Buhl, Buhl vicinity, 9/07/83, A, C, 83000290

Smith, C. Harvey, House, 255 4th Ave., E., Twin Falls, 4/03/78, C, 78001101

Stricker Store and Farm, N of Rock Creek, Twin Falls, 8/30/79, A, C, 79000810

Twin Falls Bank and Trust Company Building, 102 Main Ave. S, Twin Falls, 9/04/86, A, C, 86002155

Twin Falls City Park Historic District, 2nd N., 2nd E., and Shoshone Sts., 4th and 6th Aves., Twin Falls, 3/30/78, A, C, a, g, 78001102

US Post Office—Buhl Main [US Post Offices in Idaho 1900–1941 MPS], 830 Main, Buhl, 3/16/89, A, C, g, 89000130

Valley County

Braddock Gold Mining and Milling Company Log Building and Forge Ruins, Off Pack Trail near Suicide Rock, Thunder City vicinity, 9/12/85, A, C, 85002157

Cabin Creek Ranch, Cabin Cr. at jct. with Big Cr., Payette NF, Black Butte vicinity, 6/27/90, A, D, 90000890

Elo School [Long Valley Finnish Structures TR], SE of ID 55 on Farm to Market Rd., McCall vicinity, 7/26/82, C, 82002515

Hill, Matt N., Homestead Barn [Long Valley Finnish Structures TR], SE of McCall, McCall vicinity, 11/17/82, C, 82000362

Jarvi, Thomas, Homestead [Long Valley Finnish Structures TR], E of Lake Fork on Finn Rd., Lake Fork vicinity, 11/17/82, C, b, 82000363

Johnson, John G., (Rintakangas) Homestead [Long Valley Finnish Structures TR], NE of Lake Fork off Pearson Rd., Lake Fork vicinity, 11/17/82, C, 82000364

Johnson, John S., (Sampila) Homestead [Long Valley Finnish Structures TR], NE of Lake Fork off Pearson Rd., Lake Fork vicinity, 11/17/82, C, 82000365

Korvola, John, Homestead [Long Valley Finnish Structures TR], Roseberry Rd. and Farm to Market Rd., Donnelly vicinity, 11/17/82, C, b, 82000366

Koski, Charles, Homestead [Long Valley Finnish Structures TR], SE of McCall, McCall vicinity, 11/17/82, C, 82000367

Krassel Ranger Station, Along S Fork Salmon R., 11 mi. W of Yellowpine, Payette NF, Yellowpine vicinity, 11/19/92, A, C, D, b, 92000688

Laituri, Gust, Homestead [Long Valley Finnish Structures TR], NE of Lake Fork off Pearson Rd., Lake Fork vicinity, 11/17/82, C, 82000368

Long Valley Finnish Church, SE of Lake Fork, Lake Fork vicinity, 5/27/80, A, C, a, 80001336

Mahala, Jacob and Herman, Homestead [Long Valley Finnish Structures TR], N of Donnelly, Donnelly vicinity, 11/17/82, C, 82000369

Maki, Jacob, Homestead [Long Valley Finnish Structures TR], Off ID 55, Donnelly vicinity, 11/17/82, C, b, 82001053

Ojala, Herman, Homestead [Long Valley Finnish Structures TR], NE of Lake Fork Off Pearson Rd., Lake Fork vicinity, 11/17/82, C, 82000370

Rice Meetinghouse, NE of McCall, McCall, 4/09/80, C, 80001337

Ruatsale, Matt, Homestead [Long Valley Finnish Structures TR], N of Kantola Lane, Lake Fork vicinity, 11/17/82, C, b, 82000371

Southern Idaho Timber Protective Association (SITPA) Buildings, 1001 State St., McCall, 5/02/90, A, C, 90000680

Southern Idaho Timber Protective Association (SITPA) Buildings, SR 55, Smiths Ferry, 5/02/90, A, C, 90000681

Stibnite Historic District, US Forest Rd. 412, Yellow Pine vicinity, 7/19/87, A, g, 87001186

Wargelin, Nickolai, Homestead [Long Valley Finnish Structures TR], SE of McCall, McCall vicinity, 11/17/82, C, 82000372

Washington County

Anderson-Elwell House [Tourtellotte and Hummel Architecture TR], 547 W. 1st St., Weiser, 11/17/82, C, 82000373

Baptist Church, E. Main and 8th Sts., Weiser, 10/07/77, C, a, b, 77000470

Butterfield Livestock Company House [Tourtellotte and Hummel Architecture TR], N of

Washington County—Continued

Weiser on Jenkins Creek Rd., Weiser vicinity, 11/17/82, C, 82000374

Cambridge News Office, 155 N. Superior St., Cambridge, 12/28/89, A, 89002128

Drake, Col. C. F., House, 516 E. Main St., Weiser, 1/20/78, C, 78001104

Fisher, James M., House, 598 Pioneer Rd., Weiser, 9/04/86, C, 86002146

Galloway, Thomas C., House, 1120 E. 2nd St., Weiser, 1/26/78, B, C, 78001105

Haas, Bernard, House, 377 E. Main St., Weiser, 5/22/78, C, 78001106

Haas, Herman, House [Tourtellotte and Hummel Architecture TR], 253 W. Idaho St., Weiser, 11/17/82, C, 82000375

Intermountain Institute, Paddock Ave., Weiser, 11/01/79, B, C, 79000811

Jewell Building, 15 N. Superior, Cambridge, 1/18/90, A, 89002263

Knights of Pythias Lodge Hall, 30 E. Idaho St., Weiser, 5/13/76, A, C, 76000683

Kurtz-Van Sicklin House [Tourtellotte and Hummel Architecture TR], 439 W. 3rd. St., Weiser, 11/17/82, C, 82000376

Larsen, Archie, House [Tourtellotte and Hummel Architecture TR], S of Weiser on Larsen Rd., Weiser vicinity, 11/17/82, C, 82000377

Nesbit, G. V., House [Tourtellotte and Hummel Architecture TR], 308 W. Liberty, Weiser, 11/17/82, C, 82000378

Numbers, Dr. J. R., House [Tourtellotte and Hummel Architecture TR], 240 W. Main St., Weiser, 11/17/82, C, 82000379

Salubria Lodge No. 31, 85 W. Central St., Cambridge, 3/09/90, A, 90000368

Sommer, Morris, House [Tourtellotte and Hummel Architecture TR], 548 W. 2nd St., Weiser, 11/17/82, C, 82000380

Sommercamp, Mary Elizabeth, House [Tourtellotte and Hummel Architecture TR], 411 W. 3rd St., Weiser, 11/17/82, C, 82000381

St. Agnes Catholic Church, 204 E. Liberty St., Weiser, 7/24/78, C, a, 78001107

St. Luke's Episcopal Church, E. 1st and Liberty Sts., Weiser, 7/24/78, C, a, 78001108

Varian, B. S., House [Tourtellotte and Hummel Architecture TR], 241 Main St., Weiser, 11/17/82, C, 82000382

Washington County Courthouse [County Courthouses in Idaho MPS], E. Court St., Weiser, 9/28/87, A, C, g, 87001602

Watlington, Benjamin, House, 206 W. Court St., Weiser, 4/26/91, A, C, 91000458

Weiser Post Office [Tourtellotte and Hummel Architecture TR], Main and W. 1st Sts., Weiser, 11/17/82, C, 82000383

The F. F. Beale House (ca. 1923) is locally significant as the home and music studio of Frederick Fleming Beale, a composer and music professor at the College of Idaho who made a lasting contribution to music education and appreciation in the Boise Valley. (Susan M. Stacy, 1991)

ILLINOIS

Adams County

Downtown Quincy Historic District, Roughly bounded by Hampshire, Jersey, 4th and 8th Sts., Quincy, 4/07/83, A, C, 83000298

Ebenezer Methodist Episcopal Chapel and Cemetery, NW of Golden, Golden, 6/04/84, A, C, a, 84000921

Exchange Bank, Quincy St., Golden, 2/12/87, A, 86003714

Gardner, Robert W., House, 613 Broadway St., Quincy, 6/20/79, B, 79000812

Lewis Round Barn [Round Barns in Illinois TR], NW of Clayton, Clayton vicinity, 8/16/84, C, 84000916

Morgan-Wells House, 421 Jersey St., Quincy, 11/16/77, B, C, 77000471

Newcomb, Richard F., House, 1601 Maine St., Quincy, 6/03/82, B, C, 82002516

One Thirty North Eighth Building, 130 N. 8th St., Quincy, 2/09/84, C, 84000918

Quincy East End Historic District, Roughly bounded by Hampshire, Twenty-fourth, State, and Twelfth Sts., Quincy, 11/14/85, C, 85002791

Roy, John, Site, Address Restricted, Clayton vicinity, 5/22/78, D, 78001109

South Side German Historic District, Roughly bounded by 6th, 12th, Washington, Jersey and York Sts., Quincy, 5/22/92, A, C, 92000484

State Savings Loan and Trust, 428 Maine St., Quincy, 3/23/79, B, C, 79000813

Thomas, F. D., House, 321 N. Ohio St., Camp Point, 7/28/83, C, c, 83000299

U.S. Post Office and Courthouse, 200 N. 8th St., Quincy, 12/02/77, C, 77000472

Villa de Kathrine, 532 S. 3rd, Quincy, 12/08/78, C, 78001110

Warfield, William S., House, 1624 Maine St., Quincy, 3/21/79, B, C, 79000814

Wood, Ernest M., Office and Studio, 126 N. 8th St., Quincy, 8/12/82, C, 82002517

Wood, John, Mansion, 425 S. 12th St., Quincy, 4/17/70, B, b, 70000228

Alexander County

Cairo Historic District, Roughly bounded by Park, 33rd, Sycamore, 21st, Cedar, and 4th Sts., and the Ohio River, Cairo, 1/26/79, A, B, C, g, 79000815

Chicago and Eastern Illinois Railroad Depot, Front St., Tamms, 11/06/86, A, 86003168

Dogtooth Bend Mounds and Village Site, Address Restricted, Willard vicinity, 5/23/78, D, 78001111

Magnolia Manor, 2700 Washington Ave., Cairo, 12/17/69, C, 69000053

Old Customhouse, Washington and 15th St., Cairo, 7/24/73, C, 73000689

Thebes Courthouse, Off IL 3, Thebes, 12/26/72, A, C, 72000447

Bond County

Old Main, Almira College, 315 E. College St., Greenville, 4/21/75, A, C, 75000638

Boone County

Pettit Memorial Chapel, 1100 N. Main St., Belvidere, 12/01/78, C, a, f, 78001112

Brown County

Dewitt, Benjamin, House, Address Restricted, Versailles vicinity, 7/28/83, B, C, 83000300

Mount Sterling Commercial Historic District, Roughly bounded by Brown Co. Courthouse, Alley E of Capitol, South St., and Alley W of Capitol, Mount Sterling, 5/08/87, A, C, 87000724

Bureau County

First State Bank of Manlius, N side of Maple St., Manlius, 5/12/75, C, 75000639

Greenwood Cottage, 543 E. Peru St., Princeton, 5/09/83, A, C, 83000301

Hennepin Canal Historic District, W To Moline then N to Rock Falls vic., Hennepin vicinity, 5/22/78, A, C, 78003433

Lovejoy, Owen, Homestead, Peru St. (U.S. 6), Princeton, 5/24/73, B, 73000690

Old Danish Church, SE corner of Cook and Washington Sts., Sheffield, 10/02/73, A, C, a, 73000691

Princeton Chapter House [American Woman's League Chapter Houses TR], 1007 N. Main St., Princeton, 11/28/80, A, B, C, 80001338

Red Covered Bridge, 2 mi. N of Princeton off IL 26 on Old Dad Joe Trail, Princeton vicinity, 4/23/75, A, C, 75000640

Skinner, Richard M., House, 627 E. Peru St., Princeton, 2/10/83, C, 83000302

Stevens House, 140 E. Main St., Tiskilwa, 11/05/92, C, 92001537

Calhoun County

Golden Eagle-Toppmeyer Site, Address Restricted, Brussels vicinity, 6/14/79, D, 79000816

Kamp Mound Site, Address Restricted, Kampsville vicinity, 8/24/78, D, 78001114

Klunk, Michael, Farmstead, Address Restricted, Michael vicinity, 6/23/82, C, 82002518

Schudel No. 2 Site, Address Restricted, Hamburg vicinity, 6/15/79, D, 79000817

Carroll County

Carroll County Courthouse, Courthouse Sq., Mount Carroll, 11/26/73, C, 73000692

Halderman, Nathaniel, House, 728 E. Washington St., Mount Carroll, 11/24/80, B, C, 80001339

Mark, Caroline, House, 222 E. Lincoln St., Mount Carroll, 8/11/83, A, B, C, 83000303

Mount Carroll Historic District, IL 64 and IL 78, Mount Carroll, 11/26/80, C, 80001340

Steffens, Joseph, House, Off of Elkhorn Rd., Milledgeville vicinity, 4/10/85, C, 85000771

Cass County

Cunningham, Andrew, Farm, 2.5 mi. E of Virginia off Gridley Rd., Virginia vicinity, 5/12/75, C, 75000641

Park House, 200 W. 2nd St., Beardstown, 2/10/83, C, 83000304

Champaign County

Alpha Delta Phi Fraternity House [Fraternity and Sorority Houses at the Urbana-Champaign Campus of the University of Illinois MPS], 310 E. John St., Champaign, 5/21/90, A, C, 90000752

Alpha Xi Delta Sorority Chapter House [Fraternity and Sorority Houses at the Urbana—Champaign Campus of the University of Illinois MPS], 715 W. Michigan Ave., Urbana, 8/28/89, A, C, 89001110

Altgeld Hall, University of Illinois [University of Illinois Buildings by Nathan Clifford Ricker TR (AD)], University of Illinois campus, corner of Wright and John Sts., Urbana, 4/17/70, A, C, 70000229

Beta Theta Pi Fraternity House [Fraternity and Sorority Houses at the Urbana—Champaign Campus of the University of Illinois MPS], 202 E. Daniel St., Champaign, 8/28/89, A, C, 89001108

Burnham Athenaeum, 306 W. Church St., Champaign, 6/07/78, C, 78001115

Cattle Bank, 102 E. University Ave., Champaign, 8/19/75, A, 75000642

Chemical Laboratory [University of Illinois Buildings by Nathan Clifford Ricker TR], 1305 W. Green St., Urbana, 11/19/86, A, B, C, 86003148

Chi Psi Fraternity House [Fraternity and Sorority Houses at the Urbana—Champaign Campus of the University of Illinois MPS], 912 S. Second St., Champaign, 2/22/90, A, C, 90000115

Champaign County—Continued

Delta Kappa Epsilon Fraternity House [Fraternity and Sorority Houses at the Urbana—Champaign Campus of the University of Illinois MPS], 313 E. John, Champaign, 2/22/90, A, 90000114

Delta Upsilon Fraternity House [Fraternity and Sorority Houses at the Urbana-Champaign Campus of the University of Illinois MPS], 312 E. Armory Ave., Champaign, 5/21/90, A, C, 90000749

Farm House, 1403 E. Lorado Taft Dr., Urbana, 10/31/89, B, C, 89001728

Greek Revival Cottage, 300 W. University Ave., Urbana, 10/20/77, C, b, 77000473

Griggs, Clark R., House, 505 W. Main St., Urbana, 11/30/78, B, C, 78001116

Inman Hotel, 17 E. University Ave., Champaign, 10/20/89, A, C, 89001732

Kappa Delta Rho Fraternity House [Fraternity and Sorority Houses at the Urbana-Champaign Campus of the University of Illinois MPS], 1110 S. Second St., Champaign, 5/21/90, A, C, 90000750

Kappa Sigma Fraternity House [Fraternity and Sorority Houses at the Urbana—Champaign Campus of the University of Illinois MPS], 212 E. Daniel St., Champaign, 8/28/89, A, C, 89001109

Mahomet Graded School, Main St., Mahomet, 12/02/87, A, C, 87002035

Metal Shop [University of Illinois Buildings by Nathan Clifford Ricker TR], 102 S. Burrill Ave., Urbana, 11/19/86, B, C, 86003141

Military Drill Hall and Men's Gymnasium [University of Illinois Buildings by Nathan Clifford Ricker TR], 1402–1406 W. Springfield, Urbana, 11/19/86, A, B, C, 86003144

Morrow Plots, University of Illinois, Gregory Dr. at Matthews Ave., Urbana, 5/23/68, A, NHL, 68000024

New Orpheum Theatre, 346–352 N. Neil St., Champaign, 2/28/91, A, C, 91000085

Phi Mu Sorority House [Fraternity and Sorority Houses at the Urbana-Champaign Campus of the University of Illinois MPS], 706 W. Ohio St., Urbana, 5/21/90, A, C, 90000751

Sigma Alpha Epsilon Fraternity House [Fraternity and Sorority Houses at the Urbana—Champaign Campus of the University of Illinois MPS], 211 E. Daniel St., Champaign, 2/22/90, A, C, 90000113

Stone Arch Bridge, Springfield Ave. and 2nd St., Champaign, 5/14/81, A, C, 81000210

U.S. Post Office, Randolph and Church Sts., Champaign, 8/17/76, C, 76000684

Unitarian Church of Urbana, 1209 W. Oregon St., Urbana, 5/13/91, C, a, 91000572

University of Illinois Astronomical Observatory, 901 S. Mathews Ave., Urbana, 11/06/86, A, 86003155

University of Illinois Observatory, 901 S. Mathews Ave., Urbana, 12/20/89, A, B, C, NHL, 89002466

Vriner's Confectionery, 55 Main St., Champaign, 5/09/83, A, C, 83000305

Christian County

Illinois State Bank Building, 201 N. Chestnut St., Assumption, 8/16/84, A, C, 84000923

Kitchell Park, Jct. of Ninth and Kitchell Sts., Pana, 11/05/92, A, 92001538

Taylorville Chautauqua Audtitorium, Manners Park, Taylorville, 1/21/88, A, b, 87002519

Taylorville Courthouse Square Historic District, Roughly bounded by Vine, Walnut, Adams, and Webster Sts., Taylorville, 12/02/85, A, C, 85003058

Clark County

Archer House Hotel, 717 Archer Ave., Marshall, 3/16/76, B, 76000685

Lewis, John W., House, 503 Chestnut St., Marshall, 2/26/82, B, C, 82002519

Manly-McCann House, 402 S. 4th St., Marshall, 3/05/82, A, 82002520

Millhouse Blacksmith Shop, Main and Poplar Sts., Clarksville, 5/12/87, A, 86003156

Old Stone Arch Bridge, E of Clark Center off U.S. 40, Clark Center vicinity, 11/28/78, A, C, 78001117

Old Stone Arch, National Road, Archer St., Marshall vicinity, 2/20/75, A, C, 75000643

Clay County

Paine House, Rt. 1, Box 19 A, Xenia, 11/14/85, B, 85002843

Shriver House, 117 E. 3rd. St., Flora, 5/09/83, C, 83000306

Clinton County

General Dean Suspension Bridge, E of Carlyle over the Kaskaskia River, Carlyle vicinity, 4/03/73, A, C, 73000693

Coles County

Airtight Bridge [Coles County Highway Bridges Over the Embarras River TR], NE of Charleston, Charleston vicinity, 11/30/81, A, C, 81000211

Blakeman Bridge [Coles County Highway Bridges Over the Embarras River TR], SE of Charleston, Charleston vicinity, 11/30/81, A, C, 81000212

Briggs, Alexander, House, 210 Jackson St., Charleston, 5/31/80, B, C, 80001341

Cleveland, Cincinnati, Chicago and St. Louis Railroad Station, 1632 Broadway St., Mattoon, 1/30/86, A, 86000135

Coles County Courthouse, Charleston Public Sq., Charleston, 11/28/78, A, C, 78001118

Harrison St. Bridge [Coles County Highway Bridges Over the Embarras River TR], E of

Charleston, Charleston vicinity, 11/30/81, A, C, 81000213

McFarland House, 895 Seventh St., Charleston, 11/14/91, C, 91001690

Old Main, Lincoln Ave. and 7th St., Charleston, 6/16/81, A, C, 81000214

Pemberton Hall and Gymnasium, Lincoln Ave. and 4th St., Charleston, 8/26/82, A, 82002521

Rutherford, Dr. Hiram, House and Office, 14 S. Pike St., Oakland, 6/03/82, B, C, 82002523

Stone Quarry Bridge [Coles County Highway Bridges Over the Embarras River TR], NE of Charleston, Charleston vicinity, 11/30/81, A, C, 81000215

U. S. Post Office, 1701 Charleston Ave., Mattoon, 12/06/79, C, 79000818

Unity Church, 220 Western Ave., Mattoon, 3/19/82, A, C, a, 82002522

Will Rogers Theatre and Commercial Block, 705-715 Monroe Ave., Charleston, 1/12/84, C, 84001066

Cook County

AVR 661, Calumet Harbor, Chicago, 11/19/80, A, b, g, 80001342

Abbott, Robert S., House, 4742 Martin Luther King, Jr. Dr., Chicago, 12/08/76, B, g, NHL, 76000686

Adler Planetarium, 1300 S. Lake Shore Dr., Chicago, 2/27/87, A, NHL, 87000819

Akin, Mrs. Henry F., House [Maywood MPS], 901 S. 8th Ave., Maywood, 5/22/92, C, 92000487

Alta Vista Terrace Historic District, Block bounded by W. Byron, W. Grace, N. Kenmore, and N. Seminary Sts., Chicago, 3/16/72, A, C, 72000448

Andridge Apartments [Suburban Apartment Buildings in Evanston TR], 1627-1645 Ridge Ave., 1124-1136 Church St., Evanston, 3/15/84, A, C, 84000927

Auditorium Building, Roosevelt University, 430 Michigan Ave. and Congress St., Chicago, 4/17/70, C, NHL, 70000230

Austin Historic District, Roughly bounded by W. Ohio St., N. Waller, Parkside, W. West End & N. Mayfield Aves. & W. Corcoran Pl., Chicago, 8/08/85, C, 85001741

Bach, Emil, House, 7415 N. Sheridan Rd., Chicago, 1/23/79, C, 79000821

Bahai Temple, 100 Linden Ave., Wilmette, 5/23/78, A, C, a, g, 78001140

Bailey-Michelet House, 1028 Sheridan Rd., Wilmette, 8/12/82, C, 82002533

Baker, Frank J., House, 507 Lake Ave., Wilmette, 11/08/74, C, 74000759

Balaban & Katz Uptown Theatre, 4814–4816 N. Broadway, Chicago, 11/20/86, A, C, 86003181

Balaban and Katz Chicago Theatre, 175 N. State St., Chicago, 6/06/79, A, C, 79000822

Baldwin, Hiram, House, 205 Essex Rd., Kenilworth, 7/28/83, C, 83000307

Barrington Historic District, Roughly bounded by Chicago & Northwestern RR, S. Spring and

Cook County—Continued

Grove Sts., E. Hillside and W. Coolidge, and Dundee Aves., Barrington, 5/16/86, C, 86001047

Belden Stratford Hotel, 2300 N. Lincoln Park West, Chicago, 5/11/92, C, 92000485

Belmont-Sheffield Trust and Savings Bank Building, 1001 W. Belmont Ave. and 3146 N. Sheffield Ave., Chicago, 3/01/84, A, C, 84000931

Best Brewing Company of Chicago Building, 1315–1317 W. Fletcher, Chicago, 7/30/87, A, C, 87001263

Biograph Theater Building, 2433 N. Lincoln Ave., Chicago, 5/17/84, A, 84000934

Blackstone Hotel, 80 E. Balbo Dr., Chicago, 5/08/86, A, C, 86001005

Bloom Township High School, 10th St., Dixie Hwy. and Chicago Heights St., Chicago Heights, 6/03/82, C, g, 82002527

Bohlander, Jacob, House, 316 N. 4th Ave., Maywood, 8/21/89, C, 89001113

Buena Park Historic District, Roughly bounded by Graceland Cemetery, Marine Drive, Irving Park Road, & Montrose Ave., Chicago, 7/13/84, A, C, 84000937

Building at 1101-1113 Maple Avenue [Suburban Apartment Buildings in Evanston TR], 1101-1113 Maple Ave., Evanston, 3/15/84, A, C, 84000960

Building at 1209-1217 Maple Avenue [Suburban Apartment Buildings in Evanston TR], 1209-1217 Maple Ave., Evanston, 3/15/84, A, C, 84000964

Building at 1301-1303 Judson Avenue [Suburban Apartment Buildings in Evanston TR], 1301-1303 Judson Ave., Evanston, 4/27/84, A, C, 84000968

Building at 1305-1307 Judson Avenue [Suburban Apartment Buildings in Evanston TR], 1305-1307 Judson Ave., Evanston, 4/27/84, A, C, 84000966

Building at 1316 Maple Avenue [Suburban Apartment Buildings in Evanston TR], 1316 Maple Ave., Evanston, 3/15/84, A, C, 84000969

Building at 14–16 Pearson Street, 14–16 Pearson Street, Chicago, 5/08/80, C, 80001343

Building at 1401-1407 Elmwood Avenue [Suburban Apartment Buildings in Evanston TR], 1401-1407 Elmwood Ave., Evanston, 3/15/84, A, C, 84000973

Building at 1505-1509 Oak Avenue [Suburban Apartment Buildings in Evanston TR], 1505-1509 Oak Ave., Evanston, 3/15/84, A, C, 84000976

Building at 1929-1931 Sherman Avenue [Suburban Apartment Buildings in Evanston TR], 1929-1931 Sherman Ave., Evanston, 3/15/84, A, C, 84000978

Building at 2517 Central Street [Suburban Apartment Buildings in Evanston TR], 2517 Central St., Evanston, 3/15/84, A, C, 84000980

Building at 2519 Central Street [Suburban Apartment Buildings in Evanston TR], 2519 Central St., Evanston, 3/15/84, A, C, 84000982

Building at 2523 Central Street [Suburban Apartment Buildings in Evanston TR], 2523 Central St., Evanston, 3/15/84, A, C, 84000983

Building at 257 East Delaware, 257 E. Delaware, Chicago, 6/26/87, C, 87001113

Building at 417-419 Lee Street [Suburban Apartment Buildings in Evanston TR], 417-419 Lee St., Evanston, 3/15/84, A, C, 84000942

Building at 548-606 Michigan Avenue [Suburban Apartment Buildings in Evanston TR], 548-606 Michigan Ave., Evanston, 3/15/84, A, C, 84000945

Building at 813-815 Forest Avenue [Suburban Apartment Buildings in Evanston TR], 813-815 Forest Ave., Evanston, 3/15/84, A, C, 84000950

Building at 923-925 Michigan Avenue [Suburban Apartment Buildings in Evanston TR], 923-925 Michigan Ave., Evanston, 3/15/84, A, C, 84000953

Building at 999 Michigan, 200 Lee [Suburban Apartment Buildings in Evanston TR], 999 Michigan Ave., 200 Lee St., Evanston, 3/15/84, A, C, 84000958

Buildings at 1104–1110 Seward [Suburban Apartment Buildings in Evanston TR], 1104–1110 Seward, Evanston, 9/02/86, A, C, 86001743

Buildings at 815-817 Brummel and 819-821 Brummel [Suburban Apartment Buildings in Evanston TR], 815-817, and 819-821 Brummel, Evanston, 3/15/84, A, C, 84000952

Buildings at 860–880 Lake Shore Drive, 860–880 Lake Shore Drive, Chicago, 8/28/80, C, g, 80001344

Burlingham Building, 104 W. Oak St., Chicago, 2/14/85, C, 85000264

Calumet Plant, R. R. Donnelly & Sons Company, 350 E. 22nd St., Chicago, 2/17/83, A, C, 83000308

Carson, Pirie, Scott and Company, 1 S. State St., Chicago, 4/17/70, C, NHL, 70000231

Carter, Frederick B., Jr., House, 1024 Judson Ave., Evanston, 7/30/74, A, 74000758

Castle Tower Apartments [Suburban Apartment Buildings in Evanston TR], 2212-2226 Sherman Ave., Evanston, 3/15/84, A, C, 84000985

Chapin and Gore Building, 63 E. Adams St., Chicago, 6/27/79, C, 79000823

Charnley, James, House, 1365 N. Astor St., Chicago, 4/17/70, C, NHL, 70000232

Chicago Avenue Water Tower and Pumping Station, Both sides of N. Michigan Ave. between E. Chicago and E. Pearson Sts., Chicago, 4/23/75, C, 75000644

Chicago Beach Hotel [Hyde Park Apartment Hotels TR], 5100–5110 S. Cornell Ave., Chicago, 5/14/86, A, C, 86001193

Chicago Bee Building [Black Metropolis TR], 3647–3655 S. State Ave., Chicago, 4/30/86, A, C, 86001090

Chicago Board of Trade Building, 141 W. Jackson Blvd., Chicago, 6/16/78, A, g, NHL, 78003181

Chicago Harbor Lighthouse [U.S. Coast Guard Lighthouses and Light Stations on the Great Lakes TR], N Breakwater, Chicago, 7/19/84, A, 84000986

Chicago Portage National Historic Site, S. Harlem Ave. at Chicago Sanitary and Ship Canal, Forest View, 10/15/66, A, NPS, 66000108

Chicago Public Library, Central Building, 78 E. Washington St., Chicago, 7/31/72, C, 72000449

Chicago Savings Bank Building, 7 W. Madison St., Chicago, 9/05/75, A, C, 75000645

Chicago and Northwestern Depot, 1135–1141 Wilmette Ave., Wilmette, 4/24/75, A, C, b, 75000658

Clarke, Henry B., House, 4526 S. Wabash Ave., Chicago, 5/06/71, C, a, 71000290

Clayson, George, House, 224 E. Palatine Rd., Palatine, 3/21/79, C, 79000835

Cluever, Richard, House, 601 1st Ave., Maywood, 11/17/77, C, 77000482

Coca Cola Company Building, 1322–1336 S. Wabash Ave., Chicago, 2/22/91, A, 91000114

Colonnade Court [Suburban Apartment Buildings in Evanston TR], 501-507 Main St., 904-908 Hinman Ave., Evanston, 3/15/84, A, C, 84000987

Columbus Park [Chicago Park District MPS], 500 S. Central Ave., Chicago, 5/20/91, A, C, 91000567

Compton, Arthur H., House, 5637 Woodlawn Ave., Chicago, 5/11/76, B, g, NHL, 76000687

Conway Building, 111 W. Washington St., Chicago, 2/09/84, B, C, 84000988

Cook County Criminal Court Building, 54 W. Hubbard St., Chicago, 11/13/84, A, C, 84000281

Coonley, Avery, House, 290 and 300 Scottswood Rd., 281 Bloomingbank Rd., and 336 Coonley St., Riverside, 12/30/70, C, NHL, 70000243

Crow Island School, 1112 Willow Rd., Winnetka, 10/27/89, A, B, C, g, NHL, 89001730

Dawes, Charles Gates, House, 225 Greenwood St., Evanston, 12/08/76, B, NHL, 76000706

Dawson Brothers Plant, 517-519 N. Halsted St., Chicago, 2/14/85, A, C, 85000265

De Priest, Oscar Stanton, House, 4536–4538 S. Dr. Martin Luther King, Jr. Dr., Chicago, 5/15/75, B, g, NHL, 75000646

Dearborn Station, 47 W. Polk St., Chicago, 3/26/76, A, C, 76000688

Delaware Building, 36 W. Randolph St., Chicago, 7/18/74, C, 74000749

Dewes, Francis J., House, 503 W. Wrightwood Ave., Chicago, 8/14/73, C, 73000694

Douglas Tomb State Memorial, 636 E. State St., Chicago, 5/28/76, B, C, c, f, 76000689

Drake Hotel, 140 E. Walton St., Chicago, 5/08/80, C, 80001345

Drummond, William E., House, 559 Edgewood Pl., River Forest, 3/05/70, C, 70000241

Dryden, George B., House, 1314 Ridge Ave., Evanston, 12/18/78, A, C, 78001135

Du Sable, Jean Baptiste Point, Homesite, 401 N. Michigan Ave., Chicago, 5/11/76, B, f, NHL, 76000690

Dunham, Arthur J., House, 3131 S. Wisconsin Ave., Berwyn, 2/11/82, C, 82002524

East Park Towers [Hyde Park Apartment Hotels TR], 5236–5252 S. Hyde Park Blvd., Chicago, 5/14/86, A, C, 86001197

East Ravenswood Historic District, Roughly bounded by Lawrence Ave., Clark St., Irving

Cook County—Continued

Park Rd. and Ravenswood St., Chicago, 9/03/91, A, C, 91001364

Eighth Regiment Armory [Black Metropolis TR], 3533 S. Giles Ave., Chicago, 4/30/86, A, 86001096

Emmel Building, 1357 N. Wells St., Chicago, 11/13/84, C, 84000283

Evanston Lakeshore Historic District, Roughly bounded by Northwestern University, Lake Michigan, Calvary Cemetery, and Chicago Ave., Evanston, 9/29/80, A, C, 80001353

Evanston Ridge Historic District, Roughly bounded by Main, Asbury, Ashland, Emerson, Ridge and Maple Ave., Evanston, 3/03/83, A, C, 83000309

Evanston Towers [Suburban Apartment Buildings in Evanston TR], 554-602 Sheridan Sq., Evanston, 3/15/84, A, C, 84000990

Fairbanks, Morse and Company Building, 900 S. Wabash Ave., Chicago, 11/16/88, A, 88002233

Field Museum of Natural History, E. Roosevelt Rd. at S. Lake Shore Dr., Chicago, 9/05/75, C, 75000647

Field, Marshall, Garden Apartments, 1336–1452 Sedgwick St., 1337–1453 Hudson Ave., 400–424 Evergreen St. and 401–425 Blackhawk St., Chicago, 12/17/91, A, C, 91001691

First Congregational Church of Austin, 5701 W. Midway Pl., Chicago, 11/17/77, C, a, 77000474

First Self-Sustaining Nuclear Reaction, Site of, S. Ellis Ave. between E. 56th and 57th Sts., Chicago, 10/15/66, A, B, f, g, NHL, 66000314

Fisher Building, 343 S. Dearborn St., Chicago, 3/16/76, C, 76000691

Flamingo-On-The-Lake Apartments [Hyde Park Apartment Hotels TR], 5500–5520 S. Shore Dr., Chicago, 5/14/86, A, C, 86001194

Foley, Jennie, Building, 626–628 S. Racine Ave., Chicago, 6/19/85, A, C, 85001274

Ford Airport Hanger, Glenwood-Lansing Rd. and Burnahn Ave., Lansing, 5/09/85, A, C, 85001009

Forest, The, and Annex [Suburban Apartment Buildings in Evanston TR], 901-905 Forest Ave., Evanston, 3/15/84, A, C, 84000991

Fort Dearborn Hotel, 401 S. LaSalle St., Chicago, 11/12/82, A, C, 82000390

Fountain Plaza Apartments [Suburban Apartment Buildings in Evanston TR], 830-856 Hinman Ave., Evanston, 3/15/84, A, C, 84000992

Fourth Presbyterian Church of Chicago, 126 E. Chestnut St., Chicago, 9/05/75, C, a, 75000648

Frangenheim, William, House [Maywood MPS], 410 N. 3rd Ave., Maywood, 5/22/92, C, 92000488

Frank Lloyd Wright-Prairie School of Architecture Historic District, Bounded roughly by Harlem Ave., Division, Clyde, and Lake Sts., Oak Park, 12/04/73, C, 73000699

Gage Group—Ascher, Keith, and Gage Buildings, 18–30 S. Michigan Ave., Chicago, 11/14/85, C, 85002840

Gale, Mrs. Thomas H., House, 6 Elizabeth Ct., Oak Park, 3/05/70, C, 70000239

Gale, Walter, House, 1031 W. Chicago Ave., Oak Park, 8/17/73, C, 73000700

Garfield Park [Chicago Park District MPS], 100 N. Central Park Ave., Chicago, 8/31/93, A, C, 93000837

Gauler, John, Houses, 5917–5921 N. Magnolia Ave., Chicago, 6/17/77, C, 77000475

Germania Club, 108 W. Germania Pl., Chicago, 10/22/76, A, C, 76000692

Getty Tomb, Graceland Cemetery, N. Clark St. and W. Irving Park Rd., Chicago, 2/15/74, C, c, 74000750

Gibbs, William and Caroline, House [Maywood MPS], 515 N. 3rd Ave., Maywood, 2/24/92, C, 92000048

Glessner, John J., House, 1800 S. Prairie Ave., Chicago, 4/17/70, C, NHL, 70000233

Gold Coast Historic District, Roughly bounded by North Ave., Lake Shore Dr., Clark and Oak Sts., Chicago, 1/30/78, A, B, C, g, 78001121

Grant Park [Chicago Park District MPS], Roughly, from the Chicago R. to E. McFetridge Dr. at Lake Michigan, Chicago, 7/21/93, A, C, 92001075

Greenwood, The [Suburban Apartment Buildings in Evanston TR], 425 Greenwood St., Evanston, 3/15/84, A, C, 84000993

Griffiths, John W., Mansion, 3806 S. Michigan Ave., Chicago, 3/05/82, B, C, 82002528

Groesbeck, Abraham, House, 1304 W. Washington Blvd., Chicago, 2/04/93, C, 92001841

Gross Point Village Hall, 609 Ridge Rd., Wilmette, 8/05/91, A, 91001001

Grossdale Station, 8820 1/2 Brookfield Ave., Brookfield, 6/15/82, A, C, b, 82004912

Grosse Point Lighthouse, 2535 Sheridan Rd., Evanston, 9/08/76, A, C, 76000707

Grow, Caroline, House [Maywood MPS], 603 N. 6th Ave., Maywood, 5/22/92, C, 92000489

Guyon Hotel, 4000 W. Washington Blvd., Chicago, 5/09/85, B, C, 85000966

Halsted, Ann, House, 440 Belden St., Chicago, 8/17/73, C, 73000695

Harrer Building, 8051 Lincoln Ave., Skokie, 2/17/83, A, C, 83000310

Heller, Isadore H., House, 5132 S. Woodland Ave., Chicago, 3/16/72, C, 72000450

Hermitage Apartments, 4606 N. Hermitage Ave., Chicago, 2/14/85, C, 85000266

Hillcrest Apartment [Suburban Apartment Buildings in Evanston TR], 1509-1515 Hinman Ave., Evanston, 3/15/84, A, C, 84000994

Hinman Apartments [Suburban Apartment Buildings in Evanston TR], 1629-1631 Hinman Ave., Evanston, 3/15/84, A, C, 84000995

Hitchcock, Charles, Hall, 1009 E. 57th St., Chicago, 12/30/74, C, 74000751

Hofmann Tower, 3910 Barry Point Rd., Lyons, 12/22/78, A, 78001139

Holy Trinity Russian Orthodox Cathedral and Rectory, 1117–1127 N. Leavitt, Chicago, 3/16/76, C, a, 76000693

Hotel Del Prado [Hyde Park Apartment Hotels TR], 5307 S. Hyde Park Blvd., Chicago, 5/14/86, A, C, 86001195

Hotel Windermere East [Hyde Park Apartment Hotels TR (AD)], 1642 E. 56th St., Chicago, 10/19/82, A, C, 82000391

Hull House, 800 S. Halsted St., Chicago, 10/15/66, B, b, NHL, 66000315

Humboldt Park [Chicago Park District MPS], Roughly bounded by N. Sacramento and Augusta Blvds., and N. Kedzie, North and N. California Aves. and W. Division St., Chicago, 2/20/92, A, C, 92000074

Hyde Park-Kenwood Historic District, Roughly bounded by 47th and 59th Sts., Cottage Groves and Lake Park Aves., Chicago, 2/14/79, A, B, C, g, 79000824

Hyde Park-Kenwood Historic District (Boundary Increase), 821-829 and 816-826 E. 49th St., Chicago, 8/16/84, C, 84000996

Hyde Park-Kenwood Historic District (Boundary Increase II), 825–833 and 837–849 E. Fifty-second St., Chicago, 5/16/86, A, C, 86001041

Immaculata High School, 600 W. Irving Park Rd., Chicago, 8/30/77, C, a, 77000476

Jackson Park Historic Landscape District and Midway Plaisance, Jackson and Washington Parks and Midway Plaisance roadway, Chicago, 12/15/72, C, 72001565

Jeffery—Cyril Historic District, 7146–7148, 7128–7138 Cyril Ave., 7144–7148, 7147 and 7130 S. Jeffrey Blvd., and 1966–1974 E. Seventy-first Pl., Chicago, 5/05/86, C, 86001007

Jewelers' Building, 15-19 S. Wabash Ave., Chicago, 8/07/74, C, 74000752

Jewish People's Institute, 3500 W. Douglas Blvd., Chicago, 11/15/78, A, C, a, 78001122

Judson, The [Suburban Apartment Buildings in Evanston TR], 1243-1249 Judson Ave., Evanston, 3/15/84, A, C, 84000998

Kehilath Anshe Ma'ariv Synagogue, 3301 S. Indiana Ave., Chicago, 4/26/73, C, a, 73000696

Kenilworth Club, 410 Kenilworth Ave., Kenilworth, 3/21/79, C, 79000832

Kennicott's Grove, Milwaukee and Lake Aves., Glenview, 8/13/73, B, NHL, 73000698

Kent, Sydney, House, 2944 S. Michigan Ave., Chicago, 11/17/77, B, C, a, 77000477

Kenwood Evangelical Church, 4600–4608 S. Greenwood Ave., Chicago, 5/16/91, C, a, 91000570

Kimball, William W., House, 1801 S. Prairie Ave., Chicago, 12/09/71, A, C, 71000291

King, Patrick J., House, 3234 W. Washington Blvd., Chicago, 2/10/83, B, C, 83000311

La Grange Village Historic District, U.S. 12, La Grange, 8/08/79, C, 79000834

Lake Shore Apartments [Suburban Apartment Buildings in Evanston TR], 470-498 Sheridan Rd., Evanston, 3/15/84, A, C, 84001000

Lake-Side Terrace Apartments, 7425-7427 S. Shore Dr., Chicago, 11/13/84, C, 84000289

Lakeside Press Building, 731 S. Plymouth Ct., Chicago, 6/23/76, A, C, 76000694

Lakeview Historic District, Roughly bounded by Wrightwood, Lakeview, Sheridan, Belmont, Halsted, Wellington, Racine, and George Sts., Chicago, 9/15/77, C, 77000478

Cook County—Continued

Lakeview Historic District (Boundary Increase), 701, 705, 711, 715–717, 721, 733–735, 737, and 739 Belmont Ave., 3162 and 3164 N. Orchard, and 3171 Halsted Sts., Chicago, 5/16/86, A, C, 86001042

Larson, Mads C., House [Maywood MPS], 318 S. 1st Ave., Maywood, 5/22/92, C, 92000490

Lathrop, Bryan, House, 120 E. Bellevue Pl., Chicago, 2/15/74, B, C, 74000753

Legler, Henry E., Regional Branch of the Chicago Public Library, 115 S. Pulaski Rd., Chicago, 11/06/86, A, C, 86003169

Leiter II Building, NE corner of S. State and E. Congress Sts., Chicago, 1/07/76, C, NHL, 76000695

Lemont Central Grade School, 410 McCarthy Rd., Lemont, 3/07/75, C, 75000656

Lemont Methodist Episcopal Church, 306 Lemont St., Lemont, 5/05/86, A, C, a, 86001031

Lillie, Frank R., House, 5801 Kenwood Ave., Chicago, 5/11/76, B, NHL, 76000696

Lincoln Park, South Pond Refectory, 2021 N. Stockton Dr., Chicago, 11/20/86, A, C, 86003154

Linden Avenue Terminal, 330 Linden Ave., Wilmette, 2/08/84, A, C, 84001002

Lloyd, Henry Demarest, House, 830 Sheridan Rd., Winnetka, 11/13/66, B, NHL, 66000320

Logan Square Boulevards Historic District, W. Logan Blvd., Logan Sq., N. Kedzie Blvd., Palmer Sq., and N. Humbolt Blvd., Chicago, 11/20/85, C, 85002901

Loucks, Charles N., House, 3926 N. Keeler Ave., Chicago, 2/09/84, C, 84001006

Ludington Building, 1104 S. Wabash Ave., Chicago, 5/08/80, C, 80001347

Lynch, Timothy J., House [Maywood MPS], 416 N. 4th Ave., Maywood, 2/24/92, C, 92000047

Lyons Township Hall, 53 S. LaGrange Rd., La Grange, 11/30/78, C, 78001138

Madlener, Albert F., House, 4 W. Burton St., Chicago, 10/15/70, C, 70000234

Maher, George W., House, 424 Warwick Rd., Kenilworth, 3/21/79, C, 79000833

Malden Towers, 4521 N. Malden St., Chicago, 12/08/83, C, 83003560

Mandel Brothers Warehouse Building, 3254 N. Halsted St., Chicago, 8/19/93, C, 93000841

Manhattan Building, 431 S. Dearborn St., Chicago, 3/16/76, C, 76000697

Manor House, 1021–1029 W. Bryn Mawr Ave., Chicago, 8/12/87, C, 87001290

Maple Court Apartments [Suburban Apartment Buildings in Evanston TR], 1115-1133 Maple Ave., Evanston, 3/15/84, A, C, 84001013

Marquette Building, 140 S. Dearborn St., Chicago, 8/17/73, C, NHL, 73000697

Marshall Field Company Store, 111 N. State St., Chicago, 6/02/78, A, NHL, 78001123

Marshall Field and Company Store, 1144 W. Lake St., Oak Park, 1/21/88, A, C, 87002510

Masonic Temple Building, 119–137 N. Oak Park Ave., Oak Park, 2/11/82, C, 82002532

Masonic Temple Building [Maywood MPS], 200 S. 5th Ave., Maywood, 5/22/92, C, 92000491

Mayfair Apartments [Hyde Park Apartment Hotels TR], 1650–1666 E. Fifty-sixth St., Chicago, 5/14/86, A, C, 86001198

Maywood Fire Department Building [Maywood MPS], 511 St. Charles Rd., Maywood, 5/22/92, C, 92000492

McCarthy Building, Washington and Dearborn Sts., Chicago, 6/16/76, C, 76000698

McClurg Building, 218 S. Wabash Ave., Chicago, 8/17/70, C, 70000235

Melwood Apartments [Suburban Apartment Buildings in Evanston TR], 1201-1213 Michigan Ave. and 205-207 Hamilton, Evanston, 3/15/84, A, C, 84001016

Michigan-Lee Apartments [Suburban Apartment Buildings in Evanston TR], 940-950 Michigan Ave., Evanston, 3/15/84, A, C, 84001018

Michigan-Wacker Historic District, Michigan Ave. and Wacker Dr. and environs, Chicago, 11/15/78, A, C, 78001124

Midwest Athletic Club, 6 N. Hamlin Ave., Chicago, 10/18/84, A, C, 84000138

Miller, Allan, House, 7121 S. Paxton Ave., Chicago, 8/23/91, C, 91001082

Millikan, Robert A., House, 5605 Woodlawn Ave., Chicago, 5/11/76, B, NHL, 76000699

Millward, Caroline, House [Maywood MPS], 502 N. 5th Ave., Maywood, 5/22/92, C, 92000493

Monadnock Block, 53 W. Jackson Blvd., Chicago, 11/20/70, C, 70000236

Montgomery Ward Company Complex, 619 W. Chicago Ave., Chicago, 6/02/78, A, C, g, NHL, 78001125

Morton, J. Sterling, High School East Auditorium, 2423 S. Austin Blvd., Cicero, 5/09/83, A, C, 83000312

Muller House, 500 N. Vail Ave., Arlington Heights, 3/26/79, B, 79000819

Mundelein College Skyscraper Building, 6363 N. Sheridan Rd., Chicago, 5/31/80, A, C, a, 80001348

Municipal Courts Building, 116 S. Michigan Ave., Chicago, 8/29/85, A, C, 85001912

Municipal Pier, 200 Streeter Dr., Chicago, 9/13/79, A, C, 79000825

New Masonic Building and Oriental Theater, 20 W. Randolph St., Chicago, 9/26/78, A, C, 78003401

New Michigan Hotel, 2135 S. Michigan Ave., Chicago, 12/08/83, C, 83003562

Nichols, Harry H., House [Maywood MPS], 216 S. 4th Ave., Maywood, 2/24/92, C, 92000045

Nickerson, Samuel, House, 40 E. Erie, Chicago, 11/07/76, C, 76000700

North Wells Street Historic District, 1240-1260 N. Wells St., Chicago, 5/03/84, A, C, 84001021

Northwestern Terra Cotta Company Building, 1701–1711 W. Terra Cotta Pl., Chicago, 2/08/89, A, 88003245

Notre Dame de Chicago, 1338 W. Flournoy St., Chicago, 3/07/79, C, a, 79000826

Oak Lawn School, 9526 S. Cook Ave., Oak Lawn, 11/02/90, C, 90001725

Oak Ridge Apartments [Suburban Apartment Buildings in Evanston TR], 1615-1625 Ridge Ave., Evanston, 3/15/84, A, C, 84001025

Oakton Gables [Suburban Apartment Buildings in Evanston TR], 900-910 Oakton and 439-445 Ridge, Evanston, 3/15/84, A, C, 84001024

Octagon House, 223 W. Main St., Barrington, 3/21/79, C, 79000820

Old Chicago Historical Society Building, 632 N. Dearborn St., Chicago, 11/28/78, A, C, 78001126

Old Colony Buildings, 407 S. Dearborn St., Chicago, 1/02/76, A, C, 76000701

Old Main Building, 3235 W. Foster Ave. on North Park College Campus, Chicago, 2/11/82, A, 82002529

Old Stone Gate of Chicago Union Stockyards, Exchange Ave., Chicago, 12/27/72, A, NHL, 72000451

Old Town Triangle Historic District, Roughly bounded by Armitage and North Aves., Clark and Mohawk Sts., Chicago, 11/08/84, A, C, 84000347

Oliver Building, 159 N. Dearborn St., Chicago, 12/08/83, A, C, 83003563

Orchestra Hall, 220 S. Michigan Ave., Chicago, 3/21/78, A, C, 78001127

Orth House, 42 Abbotsford Rd., Winnetka, 10/08/76, C, 76000708

Overton Hygienic Building [Black Metropolis TR], 3619–3627 S. State St., Chicago, 4/30/86, A, 86001091

Page Brothers Building, SE corner of Lake and State Sts., Chicago, 6/05/75, C, 75000649

Pattington Apartments, 660–700 Irving Park Rd., Chicago, 3/08/80, A, C, 80001349

Peoples Gas Building, 122 S. Michigan Ave., Chicago, 11/13/84, A, C, 84000293

Perkins, Dwight, House, 2319 Lincoln St., Evanston, 8/29/85, B, C, 85001908

Pickwick Theater Building, 5 S. Prospect Ave., Park Ridge, 2/24/75, A, C, g, 75000657

Pleasant Home, 217 Home Ave., Oak Park, 6/19/72, A, C, 72000454

Poinsetta Apartments [Hyde Park Apartment Hotels TR], 5528 S. Hyde Park Blvd., Chicago, 5/14/86, A, C, 86001199

Pontiac Building, 542 S. Dearborn St., Chicago, 3/16/76, C, 76000702

Prairie Avenue District, Prairie Ave. on either side of 18th St., about 1 block in, Chicago, 11/15/72, A, C, 72000452

Pulaski Park and Fieldhouse, 1419 W. Blackhawk St., Chicago, 8/13/81, C, 81000217

Pullman Historic District, Bounded by 103rd St., C.S.S. and S.B. Railroad spur tracks, 115th St. and Cottage Grove Ave., Chicago, 10/08/69, A, C, NHL, 69000054

Quinn Chapel of the A.M.E. Church, 2401 S. Wabash Ave., Chicago, 9/04/79, A, a, 79000827

Railway Exchange Building, 80 E. Jackson Blvd. and 224 S. Michigan Ave., Chicago, 6/03/82, A, B, C, 82002530

Reebie Moving and Storage Company, 2325–2333 N. Clark St., Chicago, 3/21/79, C, 79000828

Reid Murdoch Building, 325 N. LaSalle St., Chicago, 8/28/75, A, C, 75000650

Cook County—Continued

Reliance Building, 32 N. State St., Chicago, 10/15/70, C, NHL, 70000237

Ridge Boulevard Apartments [Suburban Apartment Buildings in Evanston TR], 843-849 Ridge Ave. and 1014-1020 Main St., Evanston, 3/15/84, A, C, 84001028

Ridge Grove [Suburban Apartment Buildings in Evanston TR], 1112 Grove St., Evanston, 3/15/84, A, C, 84001030

Ridge Historic District, Roughly bounded by RR tracks, 87th, Prospects, Homewood, 115th, Lothair, Hamilton, and Western Sts., Chicago, 5/28/76, A, C, 76000703

Ridge Manor [Suburban Apartment Buildings in Evanston TR], 1603-1611 Ridge Ave. and 1125 Davis St., Evanston, 3/15/84, A, C, a, c, 84001034

Ridgeland-Oak Park Historic District, Roughly bounded by Austin Blvd., Harlem, Ridgeland, and Chicago Aves., Lake and Madison Sts., Oak Park, 12/08/83, A, C, 83003564

Ridgewood, 1703–1713 Ridge Ave., Evanston, 10/04/78, C, 78001136

River Forest Historic District, Between Harlem Ave. and Des Plaines River with 2 extensions N of Chicago Ave. and 2 extensions S of Lake St., River Forest, 8/26/77, C, 77000483

Riverside Landscape Architecture District, Bounded by 26th St., Harlem and Ogden Aves., the Des Plaines River, and Forbes Rd., Riverside, 9/15/69, A, C, NHL, 69000055

Robie, Frederick C., House, 5757 S. Woodlawn Ave., Chicago, 10/15/66, C, NHL, 66000316

Robinson House [Maywood MPS], 602 N. 3rd Ave., Maywood, 2/24/92, C, 92000046

Roloson, Robert, Houses, 3213–3219 Calumet Ave., Chicago, 6/30/77, C, 77000479

Rookery Building, 209 S. LaSalle St., Chicago, 4/17/70, C, NHL, 70000238

Rookwood Apartments [Suburban Apartment Buildings in Evanston TR], 718-734 Noyes St., Evanston, 3/15/84, A, C, 84001043

Room 405, George Herbert Jones Laboratory, The University of Chicago, S. Ellis Ave. between E. 57th and 58th Sts., Chicago, 5/28/67, A, g, NHL, 67000005

Root—Badger House, Address Restricted, Kenilworth, 5/19/92, C, 92000550

Ropp-Grabill House, 4132 N. Keeler Ave., Chicago, 4/15/85, C, 85000840

Rosehill Cemetery Administration Building and Entry Gate, 5600 N. Ravenswood Ave., Chicago, 4/24/75, C, d, 75000651

Rosenwald Apartment Building, 47th St. and Michigan Ave., Chicago, 8/13/81, A, C, 81000218

Rothschild, A. M., & Company Store, 333 S. State St., Chicago, 11/27/89, C, 89002025

Roycemore School, 60 Lincoln St., Evanston, 8/03/87, C, 87001256

S/S CLIPPER, Navy Pier 600 E. Grand Ave., Chicago, 12/08/83, A, C, g, NHL, 83003570

Schoenhofen Brewery Historic District, Roughly bounded by 16th, 18th, Canal, and Clinton Sts., Chicago, 12/27/78, A, C, 78001128

Schulze Baking Company Plant, 40 E. Garfield Blvd., Chicago, 11/12/82, A, B, C, 82000393

Schweikher, Paul, House and Studio, 645 S. Meacham Rd., Schaumburg, 2/17/87, C, g, 87000098

Sears, Roebuck and Company Complex, 925 S. Homan Ave., Chicago, 6/02/78, A, NHL, 78001129

Second Presbyterian Church, 1936 S. Michigan Ave., Chicago, 12/27/74, C, a, 74000754

Shakespeare Garden, Northwestern University campus, Evanston, 11/16/88, A, C, 88002234

Shedd Park Fieldhouse, 3660 W. 23rd St., Chicago, 12/30/74, C, 74000755

Shedd, John G., Aquarium, 1200 S. Lake Shore Dr., Chicago, 2/27/87, A, NHL, 87000820

Sheffield Historic District, Bounded roughly by Fullerton, Lincoln, Larabee, Dickens, Burlin, Wisconsin, Clayburn, Lakewood, Belder, and Southport, Chicago, 1/11/76, C, 76000704

Sheffield Historic District (Boundary Increase), Montana, Altgeld Sts., and Southport Ave., Chicago, 2/17/83, C, 83000313

Sheffield Historic District (Boundary Increase II), Roughly bounded by W. Altgeld St., N. Lakewood, N. Fullerton, and N. Southport Aves., Chicago, 6/19/85, C, a, 85001333

Sheffield Historic District (Boundary Increase III), Roughly bounded by W. Wisconsin St. and Armitage Ave., N. Howe and N. Halsted Sts., N. Willow St., and N. Kenmore Ave., Chicago, 8/22/86, A, C, 86001474

Sheridan Park Historic District, Roughly bounded by Lawrence, Racine, and Montrose Aves., and Clark St., Chicago, 12/27/85, C, 85003352

Sheridan Plaza Hotel, 4601–4613 N. Sheridan Rd., Chicago, 11/21/80, A, C, 80001350

Sheridan Square Apartments [Suburban Apartment Buildings in Evanston TR], 620-638 Sheridan Sq., Evanston, 3/15/84, A, C, 84001050

Sherman Park [Chicago Park District MPS], Bounded by W. 52nd St., Racine Ave., Garfield Blvd., and Loomis St., Chicago, 5/21/90, A, C, 90000745

Shoreland Hotel [Hyde Park Apartment Hotels TR], 5450–5484 S. Shore Dr., Chicago, 5/14/86, A, C, 86001201

Singer Building, 120 S. State St., Chicago, 2/10/83, A, C, 83000314

Smith, J. P., Shoe Company Plant, 671–699 N. Sangamon Ave. and 901–921 W. Huron St., Chicago, 11/14/85, B, C, 85002842

Soffel, Albert, House [Maywood MPS], 508 N. 5th Ave., Maywood, 5/22/92, C, 92000494

Soldier Field, 425 E. 14th St., Chicago, 8/09/84, A, C, NHL, 84001052

South Dearborn Street—Printing House Row Historic District, 343, 407, 431 S. Dearborn St. and 53 W. Jackson Blvd., Chicago, 1/07/76, C, NHL, 76000705

South Loop Printing House District, Roughly bounded by Taylor, Polk, Wells, Congress and State Sts., Chicago, 3/02/78, A, C, 78001130

South Shore Beach Apartments, 7321 S. Shore Dr., Chicago, 6/09/78, C, 78001131

South Shore Country Club, 71st St. and S. Shore Dr., Chicago, 3/04/75, A, C, 75000652

St. Ignatius College, 1076 W. Roosevelt Rd., Chicago, 11/17/77, A, C, a, 77000480

St. James Catholic Church and Cemetery, 106th St. and Archer Ave., Lemont vicinity, 8/16/84, A, C, a, d, 84001047

St. Luke's Hospital Complex, 1435 S. Michigan Ave., 1400 Block S. Indiana Ave., Chicago, 11/24/82, A, C, 82000392

St. Patrick's Roman Catholic Church, 718 W. Adams St., Chicago, 7/15/77, C, a, 77000481

St. Thomas Church and Convent, 5472 S. Kimbark Ave., Chicago, 12/18/78, C, a, 78001132

Stoneleigh Manor [Suburban Apartment Buildings in Evanston TR], 904-906 Michigan Ave. and 227-229 Main St., Evanston, 3/15/84, A, C, 84001057

Story-Camp Rowhouses, 1526–1528 W. Monroe St., Chicago, 5/08/80, A, C, 80001351

Studebaker Building, 410–418 S. Michigan Ave., Chicago, 8/11/75, A, C, 75000653

Sullivan, Joseph P. O., House [Maywood MPS], 142 S. 17th Ave., Maywood, 5/22/92, C, 92000495

Sunderlage Farm Smokehouse, 1775 Vista Walk, Hoffman Estates, 2/20/90, A, C, 89001210

Swedish American Telephone Company Building, 5235–5257 N. Ravenswood, Chicago, 9/13/85, A, C, 85002286

Swedish Club of Chicago, 1258 N. LaSalle St., Chicago, 12/02/85, A, C, 85003031

Swift House, 4500 S. Michigan Ave., Chicago, 6/09/78, B, C, 78001133

Sylvan Road Bridge, Sylvan Rd., Glencoe, 6/23/78, C, 78001137

Taft, Lorado, Midway Studios, 6016 S. Ingleside Ave., Chicago, 10/15/66, B, NHL, 66000317

Teich, Curt, and Company Building, 1733–55 W. Irving Park Rd., Chicago, 3/07/90, A, 90000340

Theurer-Wrigley House, 2466 N. Lake View Ave., Chicago, 7/28/80, B, C, 80001352

Thomas, Frank, House, 210 Forest Ave., Oak Park, 9/14/72, C, 72000455

Thompkins, Jennie S., House [Maywood MPS], 503 N. 4th Ave., Maywood, 5/22/92, C, 92000496

Tree Studio Building and Annexes, 4 E. Ohio St., Chicago, 12/16/74, B, C, 74000756

Tri-Taylor Historic District, Roughly bounded by Claremont, Harrison, Oakley, Polk, Ogden, and Roosevelt Rds., Chicago, 3/03/83, A, C, 83000315

Tri-Taylor Historic District (Boundary Increase), Roughly bounded on the N by Oakley, Harrison and Claremont Sts. and on the SE by Taylor and Oakley Sts., Chicago, 2/03/88, A, C, 87002540

Tudor Manor [Suburban Apartment Buildings in Evanston TR], 524 Sheridan Sq., Evanston, 3/15/84, A, C, 84001058

Twin Tower Sanctuary, 9967 W. 144th St., Orland Park, 11/16/88, C, a, 88002235

U-505 (IX C U-Boat), Jackson Park, Chicago, 6/29/89, A, C, g, NHL, 89001231

Cook County—Continued

USS SILVERSIDES (SS 236) National Historic Landmark, S side of Navy Pier, Chicago, 10/18/72, A, g, NHL, 72001566

Unity Building, 127 N. Dearborn St., Chicago, 9/06/79, B, C, 79000829

Unity Hall [Black Metropolis TR], 3140 S. Indiana Ave., Chicago, 4/30/86, A, a, 86001092

Unity Temple, 875 Lake St., Oak Park, 4/17/70, C, a, NHL, 70000240

Uptown Broadway Building, 4703–4715 N. Broadway, Chicago, 11/06/86, C, 86003143

Victory Sculpture [Black Metropolis TR], Thirty-fifth St. at King Dr., Chicago, 4/30/86, A, 86001089

Villa Historic District, Roughly bounded by Avondale, W. Addison, N. 40th and N. Hamlin Aves., Chicago, 9/11/79, A, C, 79000830

Villa Historic District (Boundary Increase), 3948-3952 and 3949-3953 W. Waveland Ave., Chicago, 3/10/83, A, C, 83000316

Vogt, Karl, Building, 6811 Hickory St., Tinley Park, 1/21/88, C, 87002499

Wabash Avenue YMCA [Black Metropolis TR], 3763 S. Wabash Ave., Chicago, 4/30/86, A, 86001095

Waller, William, House, 1012 N. Dearborn St., Chicago, 11/21/80, A, C, 80001346

Warner, Seth, House, 631 N. Central Ave., Chicago, 6/03/82, B, C, 82002531

Warren, Edward Kirk, House and Garage, 2829 and 2831 Sheridan Pl., Evanston, 1/30/86, B, C, a, 86000136

Washington Square [Chicago Park District MPS], 901 N. Clark St., Chicago, 5/20/91, A, 91000566

Wells-Barnett, Ida B., House, 3624 S. Martin Luther King Dr., Chicago, 5/30/74, B, NHL, 74000757

West Jackson Boulevard District, Roughly bounded by Laflin, Ashland, Adams, and Van Buren Sts., Chicago, 5/19/78, C, 78001134

West Jackson Historic District (Boundary Increase), 1513 W. Adams St., Chicago, 10/19/89, C, 89001729

Western Methodist Book Concern Building, 12 W. Washington St., Chicago, 9/11/75, A, C, 75000654

Western Springs Water Tower, 914 Hillgrove Ave., Western Springs, 6/04/81, C, 81000219

Westminster [Suburban Apartment Buildings in Evanston TR], 632-640 Hinman Ave., Evanston, 3/15/84, A, C, 84001061

Wheeler—Magnus Round Barn [Round Barns of Illinois TR], 811 E. Central Rd., Arlington Heights, 8/18/92, A, C, a, 92001017

Wicker Park Historic District, Roughly bounded by Wood, Crystal and N. Caton Sts., Claremont and North Aves., Chicago, 6/20/79, C, 79000831

Wild Flower and Bird Sanctuary in Mahoney Park, Sheridan Rd., Kenilworth, 4/10/85, C, 85000772

Willard, Frances, House, 1730 Chicago Ave., Evanston, 10/15/66, B, NHL, 66000318

Williams, Dr. Daniel Hale, House, 445 E. 42nd St., Chicago, 5/15/75, B, NHL, 75000655

Winslow, William H., House And Stable, 515 Auvergne Pl., River Forest, 4/17/70, C, 70000242

Wright, Frank Lloyd, House and Studio, 428 Forest Ave. (house), 951 Chicago Ave. (studio), Oak Park, 9/14/72, B, C, NHL, 72000456

YMCA Hotel, 820–828 S. Wabash Ave., Chicago, 8/30/89, A, B, 89001202

Yondorf Block and Hall, 758 W. North Ave., Chicago, 11/13/84, A, C, 84000297

Young, Joshua P., House, 2445 High St., Blue Island, 8/12/82, B, C, 82002525

Crawford County

Fife Opera House, 123–125 S. Main St., Palestine, 1/26/90, A, 89002348

Riverton Site, Address Restricted, Palestine vicinity, 12/18/78, D, 78001141

Stoner Site, Address Restricted, Robinson vicinity, 12/18/78, D, 78001143

Swan Island Site, Address Restricted, Palestine vicinity, 12/18/78, D, 78001142

Cumberland County

Cumberland County Courthouse, Court House Sq., Toledo, 6/11/81, A, 81000220

Greenup Commercial Historic District, 122 E.—123 W. Cumberland St., 102 N.—203 S. Kentucky St., 101 N. Mill St. and 101 E.—100 W. Illinois St., Greenup, 2/21/91, A, C, 91000083

De Kalb County

Brower, Adolphus W., House, 705 DeKalb Ave., Sycamore, 2/14/79, C, 79003160

Chicago and Northwestern Depot, Sacramento and DeKalb Sts., Sycamore, 12/08/78, A, 78003101

Egyptian Theatre, 135 N. 2nd St., De Kalb, 12/01/78, A, C, g, 78003100

Ellwood Mansion, 509 N. 1st St., De Kalb, 6/13/75, B, 75002075

Elmwood Cemetery Gates, S. Cross and Charles Sts., Sycamore, 11/28/78, A, 78003102

Glidden, Joseph F., House, 917 W. Lincoln Hwy., De Kalb, 10/25/73, B, 73002159

Gurler, George H., House, 205 Pine St., De Kalb, 3/21/79, B, 79003158

Haish Memorial Library, 309 Oak St., De Kalb, 10/09/80, C, 80004319

Marsh, William W., House, 740 W. State St., Sycamore, 12/22/78, B, C, 78003103

Nisbet Homestead Farm, Suydam Rd., Earlville vicinity, 5/31/84, A, C, 84001069

Sandwich City Hall, 144 E. Railroad St., Sandwich, 12/06/79, A, C, 79003159

Sycamore Historic District, Irregular pattern along Main and Somonauk Sts., Sycamore, 5/02/78, C, a, 78003104

von KleinSmid Mansion, 218 W. Center, Sandwich, 5/09/85, C, 85000979

De Witt County

Moore, C. H., House, 219 E. Woodlawn St., Clinton, 3/23/79, B, C, 79003112

Douglas County

McCarty, John, Round Barn [Round Barns of Illinois TR], NW of Filson, Filson vicinity, 12/07/82, C, 82000394

Streibich Blacksmith Shop, 1 N. Howard St., Newman, 2/21/91, A, 91000086

Du Page County

Adams Memorial Library, 9th St., Wheaton, 6/04/81, A, C, 81000675

Ardmore Avenue Train Station, 10 W. Park Ave., Villa Park, 11/21/80, A, 80004525

Blanchard Hall, Wheaton College campus, Wheaton, 11/14/79, A, B, C, a, 79000836

Du Page County Courthouse, 200 Reber St., Wheaton, 6/07/78, A, C, 78003107

Dupage Theatre and Dupage Shoppes, 101–109 S. Main St., Lombard, 11/20/87, C, 87002047

First Church of Lombard, Maple and Main Sts., Lombard, 8/10/78, C, a, 78001144

Glen Ellyn Main Street Historic District, Main St. between Cottage Ave. and Hawthorne St., Glen Ellyn, 10/29/84, C, 84000204

Graue Mill, NW of jct. of Spring and York Rds., Oak Brook, 5/12/75, B, C, 75002077

Gregg, William L., House, 115 S. Linden, Westmont, 10/03/80, A, B, b, 80004526

Hauptgebaude, 190 Prospect St., Elmhurst, 8/13/76, A, C, a, 76002162

McAuley School District No. 27, Roosevelt Rd., West Chicago, 6/03/82, A, C, 82004890

Middaugh, Henry C., House, 66 Norfolk Ave., Clarendon Hills, 9/21/78, A, C, a, 78003105

Naperville Historic District, Roughly bounded by Juilian, Highland, Chicago, Jackson, Eagle, and 5th Sts., Naperville, 9/29/77, A, C, a, 77001516

Pine Craig, Aurora Rd. (Rte. 65), Naperville, 8/15/75, B, C, 75002076

Stacy's Tavern, Geneva Rd. and Main St., Glen Ellyn, 10/29/74, B, 74002195

Trinity Episcopal Church, 130 N. West St., Wheaton, 1/09/78, C, a, 78003108

Turner Town Hall, 132 Main St., West Chicago, 5/13/91, A, 91000573

Villa Avenue Train Station, 220 S. Villa Ave., Villa Park, 8/22/86, A, 86001480

Wayne Village Historic District, Irregular pattern along Army Trail Rd., Wayne, 12/29/78, A, a, b, 78003106

Whitney, William, House, 142 E. First St., Hinsdale, 10/19/89, B, 89001731

Edgar County

Edgar County Courthouse, Main St., Paris, 6/04/81, A, C, 81000221

France Hotel, 118 E. Court St., Paris, 8/03/87, A, C, 87001305

Paris Elks Lodge No. 812 Building, 111 E. Washington St., Paris, 8/06/87, A, C, 87001343

Pine Grove Community Club, NW of Paris, Paris vicinity, 3/30/84, A, a, 84001071

Effingham County

Effingham County Courthouse, 110 E. Jefferson St., Effingham, 9/11/85, A, C, 85002304

Wright, Dr. Charles M., House, 3 W. Jackson St., Altamont, 5/08/86, A, C, 86001018

Fayette County

First Presbyterian Church, 301 W. Main St., Vandalia, 3/24/82, A, C, a, 82002534

Forehand, Clarence, Round Barn [Round Barns of Illinois TR], W of Vandalia off IL 185, Vandalia vicinity, 12/07/82, C, 82000395

Little Brick House, 621 St. Clair St., Vandalia, 6/04/73, A, B, C, 73000701

Vandalia Statehouse, 315 W. Gallatin St., Vandalia, 1/21/74, A, 74000760

Ford County

Paxton First Schoolhouse, 406 E. Franklin St., Paxton, 1/29/80, A, a, 80001354

Paxton Water Tower and Pump House, 145 S. Market St., Paxton, 11/13/84, C, 84000302

Franklin County

Sesser Opera House, 106 W. Franklin St., Sesser, 3/12/82, A, 82002535

Fulton County

Babylon Bend Bridge [Metal Highway Bridges of Fulton County TR], SR 123, Ellisville vicinity, 10/29/80, A, C, 80001355

Bernadotte Bridge [Metal Highway Bridges of Fulton County TR], SR 2, Smithfield vicinity, 10/29/80, A, C, 80001360

Buckeye Bridge [Metal Highway Bridges of Fulton County TR], Spans Spoon River, Smithfield vicinity, 10/29/80, A, C, 80001361

Carithers Store Building, Table Grove Village Sq., W of US 136, Table Grove, 8/03/87, A, C, a, 87001262

Chicago, Burlington & Quincy Railroad Station, Along 4th Ave. between E. Elm St. and E. Chestnut St., Canton, 8/31/93, A, 93000842

Dickson Mounds, Off CR 4, Lewistown vicinity, 5/05/72, A, D, 72000457

Dilworth, Robert, House, 606 E. Fifth St., Vermont, 11/12/93, C, 93001236

Duncan Mills Bridge [Metal Highway Bridges of Fulton County TR], W of Havanna, Lewistown vicinity, 10/29/80, A, C, 80001356

Duvall—Ash Farmstead, Off IL 9, 1 mi. E and 1.2 mi. N of jct. with IL 97, Fiatt vicinity, 11/12/93, C, 93001237

Elrod Bridge [Metal Highway Bridges of Fulton County TR], Spans Spoon River SE of Smithfield, Smithfield vicinity, 10/29/80, A, C, 80001362

Indian Ford Bridge [Metal Highway Bridges of Fulton County TR], SR 20, London Mills vicinity, 10/29/80, A, C, 80001357

Larson Site, Address Restricted, Lewistown vicinity, 11/21/78, D, 78001145

London Mills Bridge [Metal Highway Bridges of Fulton County TR], SR 39, London Mills, 10/29/80, A, C, 80001358

Ogden-Fettie Site, S of Lewistown, Lewistown vicinity, 7/31/72, D, 72000458

Orendorf Site, Address Restricted, Canton vicinity, 9/13/77, D, 77000484

Orendorff, Ulysses G., House, 345 W. Elm St., Canton, 12/09/71, C, 71000292

Seville Bridge [Metal Highway Bridges of Fulton County TR], Spans Spoon River in Seville, Seville, 10/29/80, A, C, 80001359

Sheets Site, Address Restricted, Lewistown vicinity, 12/22/78, D, 78001146

Sleeth Site, Address Restricted, Liverpool vicinity, 5/17/79, D, 79000837

St. James Episcopal Church, NE corner of MacArthur and Broadway, Lewiston, 12/31/74, C, a, 74000761

Table Grove Community Church, N. Broadway and W. Liberty Sts., Table Grove, 2/09/79, B, a, 79003783

Tampico Mounds, Address Restricted, Maples Mills vicinity, 5/14/79, D, 79000838

Tartar's Ferry Bridge [Metal Highway Bridges of Fulton County TR], Spans Spoon River SW of Smithfield, Smithfield vicinity, 10/29/80, A, C, 80001363

Vermont Masonic Hall, N. Main St., Vermont, 11/16/88, A, C, 88002236

Gallatin County

Crenshaw House, Off Rt. 1, Equality, 5/29/85, A, C, 85001164

Duffy Site, Address Restricted, New Haven vicinity, 8/26/77, D, 77000485

Marshall, John, House Site, Address Restricted, Old Shawneetown vicinity, 1/21/75, B, C, 75000659

Peeples, Robert and John McKee, Houses, Main St., Old Shawneetown, 2/24/83, A, B, C, 83000317

Saline Springs, Address Restricted, Equality vicinity, 5/24/73, A, D, 73000702

State Bank, Corner of Main St. and IL 13, Old Shawneetown, 4/19/72, A, C, 72000459

Greene County

Carrollton Courthouse Square Historic District, Roughly bounded by S. Main, W. 5th, N. Main and W. 6th Sts., Carrollton, 8/01/85, A, C, 85001667

Greene County Almshouse, Twp. Rd. TR156A NE of Carrolton, Carrolton vicinity, 5/17/91, A, 91000568

Hodges House, 532 N. Main St., Carrollton, 11/03/80, B, C, 80001364

Koster Site, S of Eldred, Eldred vicinity, 6/19/72, A, D, 72000460

Mound House Site, Address Restricted, Hillview vicinity, 9/01/78, D, 78001148

Rainey, Henry T., Farm, RR 1, N side of IL 108, Carrollton vicinity, 5/12/87, B, C, 87000682

Tillery, Virginia, Round Barn [Round Barns in Illinois TR], W of Whitehall on CR 728, Whitehall vicinity, 8/26/82, A, 82002536

White Hall Foundry, 102 S. Jacksonville St., White Hall, 5/28/80, A, C, 80001365

White Hall Historic District, Roughly bounded by Bridgeport, Jacksonville, Ayers, and Main Sts., White Hall, 5/20/87, A, 86003145

White Hall Historic District (Boundary Increase), 120 S. Jacksonville St., White Hall, 2/11/93, A, 92001837

Hamilton County

Cloud State Bank, 108 N. Washington St., McLeansboro, 11/28/78, A, C, 78001149

Cloud, Aaron G., House, 164 S. Washington St., McLeansboro, 4/15/78, C, 78001150

Hancock County

Cambre House and Farm, SW of Niota, Niota vicinity, 11/13/84, A, 84000308

Carthage Courthouse Square Historic District, Roughly bounded by Main, Adams, Wabash, and Madison Sts., Carthage, 8/13/86, A, C, 86001482

Carthage Jail, Walnut and N. Fayette Sts., Carthage, 3/20/73, B, a, 73000703

Felt, Cyrus, House, 3 mi. N of Hamilton, Hamilton vicinity, 3/18/80, A, C, 80001366

LaHarpe City Hall, 207 E. Main St., LaHarpe, 11/14/91, A, 91001689

LaHarpe Historic District, 100–124 W. Main St., 100–122 and 101–129 E. Main Sts., 101–121 S. Center St., and City Pk., LaHarpe, 4/30/87, A, 87000031

Nauvoo Historic District, Nauvoo and its environs, Nauvoo, 10/15/66, A, B, a, NHL, 66000321

Hancock County—Continued

Reimbold, William J., House, 950 White St., Nauvoo, 12/02/87, A, C, 87002033

Warsaw Historic District, Roughly bounded by the Mississippi River, Marion and 11th Sts., Warsaw, 12/16/77, C, a, 77000486

Hardin County

Illinois Iron Furnace, Shawnee National Forest, Rosiclare vicinity, 3/07/73, A, C, 73000704

Orr-Herl Mound and Village Site, Address Restricted, Rosiclare vicinity, 11/21/78, D, 78001151

Rose Hotel, S. Main St., Elizabethtown, 12/26/72, A, 72000461

Henderson County

Oquawka Wagon Bridge, 2.5 mi. S of Oquawka over Henderson Creek, Oquawka vicinity, 2/24/75, A, 75000660

Phelps, Alexis, House, On Mississippi River, Oquawka, 4/28/82, B, 82002537

South Henderson Church and Cemetery, E of Gladstone, Gladstone vicinity, 10/14/76, A, C, a, d, 76000709

Henry County

Andover Chapter House [American Woman's League Chapter Houses TR], Locust St., NW, Andover, 11/28/80, A, C, 80001367

Annawan Chapter House [American Woman's League Chapter Houses TR], 206 S. Depot St., Annawan, 11/28/80, A, C, 80001368

Bishop Hill Historic District, Off US 34, Bishop Hill, 4/17/70, A, NHL, 70000244

Francis, Frederick, Woodland Palace, 2.5 mi. NE of Kewanee on IL 34, Kewanee vicinity, 4/14/75, C, g, 75000662

Galva Opera House, 334–348 Front St., Galva, 2/11/82, A, 82002538

Johnson, Olof, House, 408 NW 4th St., Galva, 2/11/82, B, C, 82002539

Lind, Jenny, Chapel, SW corner 6th and Oak Sts., Andover, 4/01/75, A, C, a, 75000661

Ryan Round Barn, 6 mi. N of Kewanee, Kewanee vicinity, 12/31/74, A, C, 74000762

South Side School, 209 S. College Ave., Geneso, 5/06/75, A, C, 75002142

Iroquois County

Old Iroquois County Courthouse, Cherry St. at 2nd St., Watseka, 6/13/75, A, C, 75000663

Jackson County

Cleiman Mound and Village Site, Address Restricted, Gorham vicinity, 10/18/77, D, 77000487

Giant City State Park Lodge and Cabins [Illinois State Parks Lodges and Cabins TR], RR #1, Makanda, 3/04/85, C, g, 85002403

Grand Tower Mining, Manufacturing and Transportation Company Site, Devil's Backbone Park, Grand Tower, 4/13/79, A, D, 79000839

Grange Hall, SR 127/13 S of Beaucoup Cr., Murphysboro vicinity, 5/04/90, A, 90000722

Hamilton, Robert W., House, 203 S. 13th St., Murphysboro, 3/05/82, C, 82002540

Mobile and Ohio Railroad Depot, 1701 Walnut St., Murphysboro, 11/13/84, A, C, 84000317

Reef House, 411 S. Poplar St., Carbondale, 11/14/85, C, 85002839

West Walnut Street Historic District, Roughly bounded by W. Elm, S. Poplar, W. Main, and S. Forest Sts., Carbondale, 5/02/75, B, C, 75000664

Woodlawn Cemetery, 405 E. Main St., Carbondale, 12/19/85, A, B, d, 85003219

Jefferson County

Appellate Court, 5th District, 14th and Main Sts., Mount Vernon, 7/02/73, A, C, 73000705

Judd, C. H., House, Ina-Belle Rive Rd., Belle vicinity, 12/08/83, C, 83003571

Jersey County

Duncan Farm, Address Restricted, Grafton vicinity, 8/24/82, D, 82002542

Elsah Historic District, N of McAdams Hwy., Elsah, 7/27/73, A, C, a, 73000706

Jersey County Courthouse, Public Sq., Jerseyville, 5/08/86, A, C, 86001008

Jerseyville Downtown Historic District, Roughly bounded by Exchange, Lafayette, Prairie and Jefferson Sts., Jerseyville, 12/29/86, A, C, 86003528

New Piasa Chautauqua Historic District, Off McAdams Pkwy., Chautauqua, 6/15/82, A, a, 82002541

Nutwood Site, Address Restricted, Nutwood vicinity, 2/09/79, D, 79003784

Pere Marquette State Park Lodge and Cabins [Illinois State Parks Lodges and Cabins TR], Box 158, Grafton, 3/04/85, C, g, 85002405

Principia College Historic District, River Rd., Elsah vicinity, 4/19/93, C, NHL, 93001605

Stone Arch Bridge, 760–800 E. Main St., Danville, 5/16/86, A, 86001087

Jo Daviess County

East Dubuque School, Montgomery Ave., East Dubuque, 11/12/82, A, C, g, 82000396

Galena Historic District, Galena and environs, Galena, 10/18/69, A, C, 69000056

Grant, Ulysses S., House, 511 Bouthillier St., Galena, 10/15/66, B, NHL, 66000322

Old Market House, Market Square-Commerce St., Galena, 7/16/73, A, C, 73000707

Old Stone Hotel, 110 W. Main St., Warren, 4/16/75, A, C, 75000665

Scales Mound Historic District, Roughly bounded by village corporate limits, Scales Mound, 9/05/90, A, C, 90001199

Washburne, Elihu Benjamin, House, 908 3rd St., Galena, 7/05/73, B, C, 73000708

Wenner, Charles, House, Rocky Rd., Galena vicinity, 8/22/84, A, C, 84001073

Kane County

Aurora College Complex, 347 S. Gladstone Ave., Aurora, 2/16/84, A, C, 84001126

Aurora Elks Lodge No. 705, 77 S. Stolp Ave., Aurora, 3/31/80, C, 80001369

Aurora Watch Factory, 603–621 LaSalle St., Aurora, 5/08/86, A, C, 86001009

Batavia Institute, 333 S. Jefferson St., Batavia, 8/13/76, A, a, 76000712

Beith, William, House, 6 Indiana St., St. Charles, 12/07/83, C, 83003575

Campana Factory, N of Batavia on N. Batavia Ave., Batavia vicinity, 4/06/79, A, C, g, 79000841

Campana Factory (Boundary Decrease), Roughly along SR 31 and Campana Rd., Batavia vicinity, 4/06/79, A, C, g, 79003760

Camptown Town Hall, W of Wasco at Town Hall Rd. and IL 64, Wasco vicinity, 11/24/80, A, 80001378

Central Geneva Historic District, Roughly bounded by Fox River, South, 6th and W. State Sts., Geneva, 9/10/79, A, C, a, 79000845

Chicago, Burlington, & Quincy Roundhouse and Locomotive Shop, Broadway and Spring Sts., Aurora, 2/16/78, C, 78001154

Chicago, Burlington, and Quincy Railroad Depot, 155 Houston St., Batavia, 6/06/79, A, C, b, 79000842

City Building, 15 N. 1st Ave., St. Charles, 3/21/79, A, C, 79000847

Copley, Col. Ira C., Mansion, 434 W. Downer Pl., Aurora, 3/29/78, B, C, 78001155

Dundee Township Historic District, Both sides of Fox River, including sections of E. Dundee, W. Dundee, and Carpentersville, Dundee and vicinity, 3/07/75, A, C, a, b, g, 75000666

Durant House, NW of St. Charles off Dean St., St. Charles vicinity, 6/18/76, A, 76000714

Dutch Mill, N of Batavia off IL 25, Batavia vicinity, 6/04/79, C, b, 79000843

Elgin Academy, 350 Park St., Elgin, 10/08/76, A, 76000713

Elgin Historic District, Roughly bounded by Villa, Center, Park, N. Liberty, and S. Channing Sts., Elgin, 5/09/83, C, a, 83000318

Elgin Milk Condensing Co./Illinois Condensing Co., Brook and Water Sts., Elgin, 2/14/85, A, B, 85000267

Kane County—Continued

Fabyan Villa, 1511 S. Batavia Ave., Geneva, 2/09/84, C, 84001128

Fire Barn 5, 533 St. Charles Rd., Elgin, 8/05/91, A, C, 91001002

First Methodist Church of Batavia, 355 1st St., Batavia, 3/19/82, A, C, a, 82002546

First Universalist Church, 55 Villa St., Elgin, 11/07/80, C, a, 80001374

Fox River House, 166 W. Galena, Aurora, 5/04/76, A, 76000710

GAR Memorial Building, 23 E. Downer Pl., Aurora, 8/23/84, A, C, 84001130

Garfield Farm and Tavern, W of St. Charles at IL 38 and Garfield Rd., St. Charles vicinity, 6/23/78, A, C, 78001156

Geneva Country Day School, 1250 South St., Geneva, 8/21/89, A, C, 89001111

Gifford-Davidson House, 363–365 Prairie St., Elgin, 5/31/80, B, C, 80001375

Graham Building, 33 S. Stolp Ave., Aurora, 3/19/82, C, 82002543

Gray-Watkins Mill, 211 N. River St., Montgomery, 12/17/79, A, 79000846

Gridley, Mrs., A. W., House, 637 N. Batavia Ave., Batavia, 2/03/93, C, 92001850

Healy Chapel, 332 W. Downer Pl., Aurora, 2/28/85, A, C, 85000361

Hotel Aurora, 2 N. Stolp Ave., Aurora, 6/03/82, A, 82002544

Hotel Baker, 100 W. Main St., St. Charles, 12/08/78, C, 78001157

Hunt House, 304 Cedar Ave., St. Charles, 11/12/82, A, B, C, 82000397

Keystone Building, 30 S. Stolp Ave., Aurora, 3/18/80, C, 80001370

Library Hall, 21 N. Washington St., Carpentersville, 8/14/73, A, B, C, 73000709

Masonic Temple, 104 S. Lincoln Ave., Aurora, 3/19/82, C, 82002545

Memorial Washington Reformed Presbyterian Church, W of Elgin on W. Highland Ave. Rd., Elgin vicinity, 11/19/80, A, C, a, 80001376

North Geneva Historic District, Roughly bounded by RR tracks, Fox River, Stevens and W. State Sts., Geneva, 3/25/82, A, C, a, 82002549

Oaklawn Farm, Army Trail and Dunham Rds., Wayne, 7/26/79, A, C, 79000848

Old Hotel, 241 Main St., Sugar Grove, 9/21/89, A, C, 89001464

Old Second National Bank, 37 S. River St., Aurora, 5/08/79, C, 79000840

Paramount Theatre, 23 E. Galena Blvd., Aurora, 3/18/80, A, C, g, 80001371

Pelton, Ora, House, 214 S. State St., Elgin, 8/12/82, C, 82002548

Smith, Ephraim, House, NE of Sugar Grove, Sugar Grove vicinity, 6/06/80, C, b, 80001377

St. Charles Municipal Building, 2 E. Main St., St. Charles, 2/21/91, C, 91000087

St. Mary's Church of Gilberts, 10 Matteson St., Gilberts, 8/18/92, C, a, 92001018

Stearns-Wadsworth House, 1 S. 570 Bliss Rd., Batavia vicinity, 3/19/82, A, C, 82002547

Stolp Island Historic District, Stolp Island, Aurora, 9/10/86, A, C, 86001487

Stolp Woolen Mill Store, 2 W. Downer Pl., Aurora, 9/01/83, A, B, 83000319

Tanner, William A., House, 304 Oak Ave., Aurora, 8/19/76, C, 76000711

Teeple Barn, NW of Elgin on Randall Rd., Elgin vicinity, 12/10/79, A, C, 79000844

United Methodist Church of Batavia, 8 N. Batavia Ave., Batavia, 7/28/83, C, a, 83000320

Weisel, Andrew, House, 312 N. 2nd Ave., St. Charles, 2/26/82, C, 82002550

West Side Historic District, Roughly bounded by W. Downer Pl., Lake St., Garfield Ave., and S. Highland St., Aurora, 8/13/86, A, C, 86001484

White, Louise, School, Washington Ave., Batavia, 11/07/80, A, C, 80001373

Wilson, Judge Isaac, House, 406 E. Wilson St., Batavia, 5/09/85, B, C, 85000978

Kankakee County

Hickox, Warren, House, 687 S. Harrison Ave., Kankakee, 1/03/78, C, 78001158

Milk, Lemuel, Carriage House, 165 N. Indiana Ave., Kankakee, 6/04/79, B, C, 79000849

Point School, 6976 N. Vincennes Trail, Grant Park vicinity, 11/05/92, A, 92001539

Riverview Historic District, Roughly bounded by River and Eagle Sts., Wildwood Ave., and the Kankakee River, Kankakee, 8/22/86, A, C, 86001488

Swannell, Charles E., House, 901 S. Chicago, Kankakee, 6/03/82, C, 82002551

Kendall County

Chicago, Burlington & Quincy Railroad Depot, 101 W. Main St., Plano, 11/12/93, A, 93001238

Evelyn Site, Address Restricted, Newark vicinity, 12/19/78, D, 78001159

Plano Hotel, 120 W. Main St., Plano, 11/12/93, A, 93001239

Reorganized Church of Jesus Christ of Latter Day Saints, 304 S. Center Ave., Plano, 11/02/90, A, B, a, 90001724

Sears, Albert H., House, 603 E. North St., Plano, 1/29/87, B, C, 86003720

Knox County

Conger, J. Newton, House, 334 N. Knox St., Oneida, 4/20/79, C, 79003111

Galesburg Historic District, Roughly bounded by Berrien, Clark, Pearl, and Sanborn Sts., Galesburg, 11/21/76, A, C, a, 76000715

Knox County Courthouse and Hall of Records, Public Sq., Main St., Knoxville, 2/13/92, A, 92000051

Knox County Jail, Public Sq., Market St., Knoxville, 2/13/92, A, 92000050

Meetinghouse of the Central Congregational Church, Central Sq., Galesburg, 9/30/76, C, a, 76000716

Old Main, Knox College, Knox College campus, Galesburg, 10/15/66, B, NHL, 66000323

Walnut Grove Farm, Knox Station Rd., 1 mi. S of Knoxville, Knoxville vicinity, 8/24/89, A, 89001114

Wolf Covered Bridge, NW of Yates City, on CR 17 over Spoon River, Yates City vicinity, 12/04/74, A, 74000763

La Salle County

Fletcher, Ruffin Drew, House, 609 E. Broadway St., Streator, 8/05/91, C, 91001000

Hossack, John, House, 210 W. Prospect St., Ottawa, 3/16/72, B, C, 72000462

Hotel Kaskaskia, 217 Marquette St., LaSalle, 11/03/88, A, C, 88002229

Knuessl Building, 215–217 W. Main, Ottawa, 5/11/92, C, 92000486

LaSalle City Building, 745 2nd St., LaSalle, 8/29/85, A, 85001909

Marseilles Hydro Plant, Commercial St., Marseilles, 5/09/89, A, D, 89000343

O'Conor, Andrew J., III, House, 637 Chapel St., Ottawa, 4/22/93, C, 93000324

Old Kaskaskia Village, Address Restricted, Ottawa vicinity, 10/15/66, D, NHL, 66000324

Ransom Water Tower, Plumb St. between Cartier and Columbus, Ransom, 11/02/90, A, 90001723

Spring Valley House—Sulfur Springs Hotel, Dee Bennett Rd., Utica, 11/20/87, A, C, 87002055

Starved Rock, 6 mi. from Ottawa on IL 71, Starved Rock State Park, Ottawa vicinity, 10/15/66, D, NHL, 66000325

Starved Rock Lodge and Cabins [Illinois State Parks Lodges and Cabins TR], Box 116, Utica, LaSalle-Peru vicinity, 5/08/85, A, C, 85002702

Washington Park Historic District, Bounded by Jackson, LaSalle, Lafayette, and Columbus Sts., Ottawa, 4/11/73, A, C, 73000710

Williams, Silas, House, 702 E. Broadway, Streator, 6/23/76, C, 76002146

Lake County

Adams, Mary W., House [Highland Park MRA], 1923 Lake Ave., Highland Park, 9/29/82, C, 82002552

Armour, J. Ogden, House, 1500 W Kennedy Rd., Lake Forest, 6/28/82, B, C, 82002578

Armour, Lester, House, Sheridan Rd., Lake Bluff, 5/03/84, C, 84001131

Beatty, Ross J., House [Highland Park MRA], 344 Ravine Dr., Highland Park, 9/29/82, B, C, 82002553

Beatty, Ross, House [Highland Park MRA], 1499 Sheridan Rd., Highland Park, 9/29/82, B, C, 82002554

Becker, A. G., Property, 405 Sheridan Rd., Highland Park, 11/15/84, C, 84000343

Lake County—Continued

Bowen, Joseph T., Country Club, 1917 N. Sheridan Rd., Waukegan, 11/30/78, A, 78003400

Braeside School [Highland Park MRA], 124 Pierce Rd., Highland Park, 9/29/82, A, C, 82002555

Campbell, Albert, House [Highland Park MRA], 434 Marshman, Highland Park, 9/29/82, C, 82002556

Catlow Theatre, 112–116 W. Main St., Barrington, 8/21/89, A, C, 89001112

Church of the St. Sava Serbian Orthodox Monastery, N of Libertyville on N. Milwaukee Ave, Libertyville vicinity, 9/06/79, C, a, 79000850

Churchill, Richard, House [Highland Park MRA], 1214 Green Bay Rd., Highland Park, 9/29/82, C, 82002557

Deerpath Inn, 255 E. Illinois Rd., Lake Forest, 5/11/92, A, C, 92000482

Dewey House, Veterans Administration Medical Center, North Chicago, 5/08/85, B, C, 85001008

Dubin, Henry, House [Highland Park MRA], 441 Cedar, Highland Park, 9/29/82, C, 82002558

Evert House [Highland Park MRA], 2687 Logan, Highland Park, 9/29/82, C, 82002559

Florsheim, Harold, House [Highland Park MRA], 650 Sheridan Rd., Highland Park, 9/29/82, B, C, 82002560

Fort Sheridan Historic District, Off IL 22, Fort Sheridan, 9/29/80, A, C, NHL, 80001379

Geyso, Mrs. Frank, Houses [Highland Park MRA], 450 and 456 Woodland Rd., Highland Park, 9/29/82, C, 82002561

Granville-Mott House [Highland Park MRA], 80 Laurel Ave., Highland Park, 9/29/82, C, 82002562

Great Lakes Naval Training Station, Bounded by Cluverius Ave., Lake Michigan, G St., and Sheridan Rd., Waukegan vicinity, 9/15/86, A, C, 86002890

Grigsby Estate, 125 Buckley Rd., Barrington Hills, 5/12/87, C, 87000649

Hazel Avenue Prospect Avenue Historic District [Highland Park MRA], St. Johns, Hazel, Dale, Forest, and Prospect Aves., Highland Park, 9/29/82, C, 82002563

Highland Park Water Tower [Highland Park MRA], N of Central Green Bay Rd., Highland Park, 9/29/82, C, 82002564

Holmes, Samuel, House [Highland Park MRA], 2693 Sheridan Rd., Highland Park, 9/29/82, C, 82002565

Humer Building [Highland Park MRA], 1894 Sheridan Rd., Highland Park, 9/29/82, C, 82002566

James, Jean Butz, Museum of the Highland Park Historical Society [Highland Park MRA], 326 Central Ave., Highland Park, 9/29/82, C, 82002567

Jensen, Jens, Summer House and Studio [Highland Park MRA], 930–950 Dean Ave., Highland Park, 6/19/91, B, C, 91000795

Judah, Noble, Estate, 111 and 211 W. Westminster St., Lake Forest, 8/03/90, C, 90001197

Lake Forest Historic District, Roughly bounded by Western, Westleigh, Lake Michigan, and N city limits, Lake Forest, 1/26/78, C, 78001161

Lamont, Robert P., House, 810 S. Ridge Rd., Lake Forest, 11/12/93, C, 93001240

Lanzl, Haerman, House [Highland Park MRA], 1635 Linden, Highland Park, 9/29/82, C, 82002568

Lewis, Lloyd, House, 153 Little St. Mary, Libertyville, 6/15/82, C, g, 82002579

Lichtstern House [Highland Park MRA], 105 S. Deere Park Dr., Highland Park, 9/29/82, C, 82002569

Linden Park Place-Belle Avenue Historic District [Highland Park MRA], Roughly bounded by Sheridan Rd., Elm Pl., Linden, Park, and Central Aves., Highland Park, 12/13/83, C, 83003580

Loeb, Ernest, House [Highland Park MRA], 1425 Waverly, Highland Park, 5/18/83, A, C, 83000321

Maple Avenue Maple Lane Historic District [Highland Park MRA], Maple Ave. and Maple Lane between St. Johns Ave. and Sheridan Rd., Highland Park, 9/29/82, C, 82002570

Millard, George Madison, House [Highland Park MRA], 1689 Lake Ave., Highland Park, 9/29/82, C, 82002571

Millard, Sylvester, House [Highland Park MRA], 1623 Sylvester Pl., Highland Park, 9/29/82, A, C, 82002572

Millburn Historic District, U.S. 45, Millburn and Grass Lake Rds., Millburn, 9/18/79, A, C, 79000851

Mineola Hotel, 91 N. Cora St., Fox Lake, 7/29/79, A, C, 79003785

Near North Historic District, Roughly bounded by Ash St., RR. tracks, Glen Flora Ave., Waukegan, 5/03/78, C, 78001162

North Shore Sanitary District Tower [Highland Park MRA], Cary Ave., Highland Park, 6/30/83, C, 83000322

Obee House [Highland Park MRA], 1642 Green Bay Rd., Highland Park, 9/29/82, C, 82002573

Pick, George, House [Highland Park MRA], 970 Sheridan Rd., Highland Park, 9/29/82, C, 82002574

Public Service Building, 344-354 N. Milwaukee Ave., Libertyville, 12/08/83, B, C, 83003581

Ragdale, 1230 N. Green Bay Rd., Lake Forest, 6/03/76, C, 76000717

Ravinia Park Historic District [Highland Park MRA], Roughly bounded by Lambert Tree Ave., Sheridan Rd., St. Johns Ave., Rambler Lane, and Ravinia Park Ave., Highland Park, 9/29/82, C, 82002575

Rosewood Park [Highland Park MRA], Roger Williams Ave., Highland Park, 9/29/82, C, 82002576

Shiloh House, 1300 Shiloh Blvd., Zion, 5/12/77, B, C, a, 77000488

Soule, C. S., House [Highland Park MRA], 304 Laurel Ave., Highland Park, 9/29/82, C, 82002577

Vine-Oakwood-Green Bay Road Historic District, Green Bay Rd., E. Vine and N. Oakwood Aves., Lake Forest, 3/28/80, A, C, 80001381

Water Tower, Building 49, Leonard Wood Ave., Fort Sheridan, 12/04/74, C, 74000764

Willits, Ward Winfield, House, 1445 Sheridan Rd., Highland Park, 11/24/80, C, 80001380

Zion Chapter House [American Woman's League Chapter Houses TR], 2715 Emmaus Ave., Zion, 11/28/80, A, C, 80001382

Lee County

Amboy Illinois Central Depot, 50 S. East Ave., Amboy, 8/18/92, A, 92001015

Brookner, Christopher, House, 222 N. Dixon Ave., Dixon, 11/13/84, C, 84000319

Illinois Central Stone Arch Railroad Bridges, W. First, W. Second, & W. Third Sts. between Monroe & College Aves., Dixon, 12/02/87, A, 87002048

Nachusa House, 215 S. Galena Ave., Dixon, 2/10/83, A, C, 83000323

Reagan's, Ronald, Boyhood Home, 816 S. Hennepin Ave., Dixon, 3/26/82, B, c, 82002580

Van Epps, William H., House, 212 S. Ottawa Ave., Dixon, 2/11/82, C, 82002581

Whitney, Col. Nathan, House, 1620 Whitney Rd., Franklin Grove vicinity, 11/02/90, C, 90001726

Livingston County

Beach, Thomas A., House, 402 E. Hickory St., Fairbury, 7/28/83, B, C, 83000324

Dwight Chicago and Alton Railroad Depot, East St., Dwight, 12/27/82, A, C, 82000398

Jones House, 314 E. Madison St., Pontiac, 5/05/78, B, C, 78001163

Livingston County Courthouse, 112 W. Madison, Pontiac, 11/19/86, A, C, 86003165

Oughton, John R., House, 101 W. South St., Dwight, 9/23/80, B, C, 80001383

Pioneer Gothic Church, 201 N. Franklin St., Dwight, 7/28/83, C, a, 83000325

Pontiac City Hall and Fire Station, 110 W. Howard St., Pontiac, 8/16/90, A, 90001200

Schultz, Raymond, Round Barn [Round Barns in Illinois TR], S of Pontiac off US 66, Pontiac vicinity, 8/26/82, A, 82002582

Logan County

Atlanta Public Library, Race and Arch Sts., Atlanta, 12/11/79, C, 79000852

Buckles, Robert, Barn [Round Barns in Illinois TR], SE of Mt. Pulaski, Mount Pulaski vicinity, 2/10/83, A, C, 83000326

Foley, Stephan A., House, 427 Tremont St., Lincoln, 5/03/84, B, C, 84001141

Hawes, J. H., Elevator, 2nd St., Atlanta, 5/17/91, A, C, 91000571

Lincoln Courthouse Square Historic District, Roughly bounded by Sangamon, Pekin, Chi-

Logan County—Continued

cago, Delaware, Broadway, and Pulaski Sts., Lincoln, 12/24/85, A, C, 85003166

Lincoln Public Library, 725 Pekin St., Lincoln, 9/12/80, A, C, 80001384

Mount Pulaski Courthouse, Public Sq., Mount Pulaski, 8/03/78, A, C, 78001164

University Hall, 300 Keokuk St., Lincoln, 4/24/73, C, 73000711

Macon County

Decatur Downtown Historic District, Merchant St. roughly bounded by North, Water, Wood, and Church Sts., Decatur, 5/09/85, A, C, 85001011

Decatur Historic District, Roughly bounded by Hayward, El Dorado, and Church, and Lincoln Park Dr., Decatur, 11/07/76, C, 76000719

Millikin, James, House, 125 N. Pine St., Decatur, 12/03/74, B, C, 74000765

Ulery, Eli, House, SE of Mount Zion on SR 60, Mount Zion vicinity, 10/01/79, B, 79000854

Macoupin County

Anderson, John C., House, 920 W. Breckenridge St., Carlinville, 11/05/92, C, 92001535

Carlinville Chapter House [American Woman's League Chapter Houses TR], 111 S. Charles St., Carlinville, 11/28/80, A, C, 80001385

Carlinville Historic District, Roughly bounded by Oak, Mulberry, Morgan, and E. city limits, Carlinville, 5/17/76, C, 76000721

Robinson, J. L., General Store, Off IL 108, Hagaman, 9/12/80, A, 80001386

Shriver Farmstead, NW of Virden, Virden vicinity, 9/29/80, A, C, 80001387

Union Miners Cemetery, 0.5 mi. N of Mount Olive city park, Mount Olive, 10/18/72, A, d, f, 72000463

Madison County

Alton Chapter House [American Woman's League Chapter Houses TR], 509 Beacon St., Alton, 11/28/80, A, C, 80001388

Alton Military Prison Site, Address Restricted, Alton vicinity, 12/31/74, D, 74000766

Berleman House, 115 S. Main St., Edwardsville, 3/27/80, C, 80001391

Bethalto Village Hall, 124 Main St., Bethalto, 12/02/87, A, 87002049

Carney, John, House, 306 E. Market St., Troy, 7/28/83, C, 83000327

Christian Hill Historic District, Roughly bounded by Broadway, Belle, 7th, Cliff, Bluff, and State Sts., Alton, 5/22/78, A, B, C, a, 78001165

Edwardsville Chapter House [American Woman's League Chapter Houses TR], 515 W. High St., Edwardsville, 11/28/80, A, C, 80001392

Godfrey, Benjamin, Memorial Chapel, Godfrey Rd., Godfrey, 5/10/79, A, C, a, 79000856

Guertler House, 101 Blair St., Alton, 7/30/74, A, C, 74000767

Haskell Playhouse, Henry St. in Haskell Park, Alton, 7/30/74, C, 74000768

Horseshoe Lake Mound and Village Site, Address Restricted, Granite City vicinity, 11/26/80, D, 80001396

Jarvis, William W., House, 317 E. Center St., Troy, 2/03/88, C, 87002514

Kuhn Station Site, Address Restricted, Edwardsville vicinity, 11/25/80, D, 80001393

LeClaire Historic District, Roughly bounded by RR tracks, Wolf St., Hadley and Madison, Edwardsville, 8/08/79, A, 79000855

Madison County Sheriff's House and Jail, 210 N. Main St., Edwardsville, 5/31/80, C, 80001394

Marine Chapter House [American Woman's League Chapter Houses TR], Silver St., Marine, 11/28/80, A, C, 80001397

Middletown Historic District, Roughly bounded by Broadway, Market, Alton, Franklin, Common, Liberty, Humboldt, and Plum Sts., Alton, 7/11/78, C, 78001166

Middletown Historic District (Boundary Increase), 3rd St. between Market and Piasa St., Alton, 9/16/82, C, 82002583

Miners Institute Building, 204 W. Main, Collinsville, 8/29/85, A, 85001913

Mitchell Archeological Site, Address Restricted, Mitchell vicinity, 2/07/78, D, 78001168

Mount Lookout, 2018 Alby St., Alton, 6/17/80, B, C, 80001389

Post House, 1516 State St., Alton, 5/28/80, B, C, 80001390

Rutherford House, 1006 Pearl St., Alton, 3/19/82, A, C, 82002584

St. Louis Street Historic District, 603-1306 St. Louis St., Edwardsville, 5/09/83, C, 83000328

Stephenson, Benjamin, House, 409 S. Buchanan St., Edwardsville, 5/31/80, B, C, 80001395

Trumbull, Lyman, House, 1105 Henry St., Alton, 5/15/75, B, NHL, 75000667

Upper Alton Historic District, Seminary St., College, Leverett, and Evergreen Aves., Alton, 5/02/78, A, C, 78001167

Weir, John, House, 715 N. Main St., Edwardsville, 5/09/83, A, C, 83000329

Yakel House and Union Brewery, 1421–1431 Pearl St., Alton, 5/11/82, A, C, 82002585

Marion County

Badollet House, 310 N. Washington St., Salem, 12/06/90, C, 90001839

Bryan, William Jennings, Boyhood Home, 408 S. Broadway, Salem, 2/18/75, B, b, 75000668

Rohrbough, Calendar, House, 3rd and Madison Sts., Kinmundy, 9/06/79, B, C, 79000857

Sentinel Building, 232 E. Broadway, Centralia, 4/15/78, C, 78001169

Marshall County

Waugh, Robert, House, 202 School St., Sparland, 10/04/78, C, 78001170

Mason County

Clear Lake Site, Address Restricted, Manito vicinity, 11/28/78, D, 78001171

Havana Water Tower, Jct. of Pearl and Main Sts., NE corner, Havana, 4/22/93, A, 93000325

Rockwell Mound, Address Restricted, Havana vicinity, 12/10/87, C, D, 87000679

Massac County

Curtis, Elijah P., House, 405 Market St., Metropolis, 6/09/78, B, C, 78001172

Fort Massac Site, SE of Metropolis on the Ohio River, Metropolis vicinity, 7/14/71, D, 71000293

Kincaid Site, Address Restricted, Brookport vicinity, 10/15/66, D, NHL, 66000326

McCartney, R. W., Music Hall, 116–120 E. Fourth St., Metropolis, 8/13/86, C, 86001490

McDonough County

Kleinkopf, Clarence, Round Barn [Round Barns in Illinois TR], N of Colchester, Colchester vicinity, 8/26/82, A, 82002586

McDonough County Courthouse, Public Sq., Macomb, 10/30/72, C, 72001448

Welling-Everly Horse Barn, Off US 136, Adair vicinity, 8/29/85, A, C, 85001911

McHenry County

Count's House, 3803 Waukegan, McHenry, 6/03/82, C, 82002587

Covell, Lucein Boneparte, House, 5805 Broadway, Richmond, 1/26/89, C, 88003246

Hibbard, Charles H., House, 413 W. Grant Hwy., Marengo, 2/14/79, C, 79003113

Memorial Hall, 10308 Main St., Richmond, 8/19/93, A, 93000839

Old McHenry County Courthouse, City Sq., Woodstock, 11/01/74, C, 74002183

Palmer, Col. Gustavius A., House, 5516 Terra Cotta Rd., Crystal Lake, 5/24/85, C, 85001127

Rogers, Orson, House, E of Marengo at 19621 E. Grant St., Marengo vicinity, 6/22/79, B, C, 79003114

Stickney, George, House, NE of Woodstock at 1904 Cherry Valley Rd., Woodstock vicinity, 5/14/79, B, C, 79003115

Terwilliger House, E of Woodstock at Mason Hill and Cherry Valley Rds., Woodstock vicinity, 5/14/79, B, C, 79003116

McHenry County—Continued

Woodstock Opera House, 119 Van Buren St., Woodstock, 7/17/74, C, 74002184

Woodstock Square Historic District, Roughly bounded by Calhoun, Throop, Cass, Main, C and NW RR Tracks, and Jefferson Sts., Woodstock, 11/12/82, C, 82000399

McLean County

Bane, Warren, Site, Address Restricted, Ellsworth vicinity, 3/19/82, D, 82002588

Benjamin, Ruben M., House, 510 E. Grove St., Bloomington, 8/30/78, B, 78003109

Benjaminville Friends Meetinghouse and Burial Ground, N of Holder, Holder vicinity, 12/13/83, A, C, a, d, 83003584

Bloomington Central Business District, Roughly bounded by Main, Center and Front Sts., Bloomington, 2/28/85, A, C, 85000363

Clover Lawn, 1000 E. Monroe Dr., Bloomington, 10/18/72, B, C, NHL, 72001479

Cook, John W., Hall, Illinois State University, US 51, Normal, 2/20/86, A, C, 86000268

Cox, George H., House, 701 E. Grove St., Bloomington, 11/14/85, C, 85002838

Davis, David, III & IV, House, 1005 E. Jefferson, Bloomington, 11/12/82, C, 82000400

Duncan Manor, SW of Towanda off IL 4, Towanda vicinity, 2/09/79, B, C, 79003164

East Grove Street District—Bloomington, 400–700 E. Grove St., Bloomington, 2/26/87, C, 86003176

Franklin Square, 300 and 400 blocks of E. Chestnut and E. Walnut Sts., 900 block of N. Prairie and N. McLean Sts., Bloomington, 1/11/76, A, C, 76002164

Gildersleeve House, 108 Broadway, Hudson, 7/28/77, A, 77001517

Hamilton, John M., House, 502 S. Clayton St., Bloomington, 9/06/78, B, 78003110

Holy Trinity Church Rectory and Convent, 704 N. Main and 106 W. Chestnut Sts., Bloomington, 12/08/83, A, C, a, 83003585

Hubbard House, 310 Broadway, Hudson, 2/01/79, B, 79003163

McLean County Courthouse and Square, Main, Washington, Center, and Jefferson Sts., Bloomington, 2/06/73, C, 73002160

Miller, George H., House, 405 W. Market St., Bloomington, 7/20/78, B, C, 78003111

Miller-Davis Law Buildings, 101–103 N. Main St. and 102–104 E. Front St., Bloomington, 4/27/79, B, 79003162

Patton, John, Log Cabin, Lexington Park District Park, Lexington, 8/01/86, A, b, e, 86002008

Scott, Matthew T., House, 227 1st Ave., Chenoa, 2/10/83, A, C, 83000331

Scott-Vrooman House, 701 E. Taylor St., Bloomington, 8/18/83, A, C, g, 83000330

Stevenson House, 1316 E. Washington St., Bloomington, 5/24/74, B, 74002196

White Place Historic District, White Pl., Clinton Blvd., and E side of Fell Ave. between Empire and Emerson Sts., Bloomington, 8/12/88, A, C, 88001230

Menard County

Lincoln's New Salem Village, S of Petersburg in New Salem State Park, Petersburg vicinity, 6/19/72, B, b, e, g, 72000464

North Sangamon United Presbyterian Church, N of Athens on SR 2, Athens vicinity, 3/23/79, C, a, 79000858

Petersburg Historic District, IL 97, Petersburg, 6/17/76, A, C, d, 76000722

Petersburg Historic District (Boundary Increase), Smoot Hotel, corner of Sixth and Douglas, Petersburg, 1/31/86, A, C, 86000138

Robinson—Bonnett Inn, Whites Crossing Rd. E of Clary Cr., Bobtown, 8/03/90, A, C, 90001198

Mercer County

Commerical House, 4th and Main St., Keithsburg, 5/09/83, A, 83000332

Keithsburg Historic District, Roughly bounded by Jackson, Fifth, Washington, and Third Sts., Keithsburg, 5/08/86, A, 86001004

Mercer County Courthouse, SE 3rd St. (IL 17), Aledo, 6/17/82, A, 82002589

Monroe County

Fountain Creek Bridge, Off IL 156, Waterloo vicinity, 12/22/78, C, 78001176

Gundlach-Grosse House, 625 N. Main St., Columbia, 12/18/78, C, 78001173

Lunsford-Pulcher Archeological Site, Address Restricted, Columbia vicinity, 7/23/73, C, D, 73000712

Maeystown Historic District, SR 7, Maeystown, 6/23/78, A, C, 78001174

Peterstown House, 275 N. Main St., Waterloo, 11/16/77, A, 77000489

Waterloo Historic District, 517 S. Main St., Waterloo, 12/01/78, C, 78001177

Montgomery County

Blackman, George, House, 904 S. Main St., Hillsboro, 11/06/86, C, 86003180

Freeman—Brewer—Sawyer House, 532 S. Main St., Hillsboro, 11/05/92, C, 92001536

Grubbs, Samuel Moody, House, 805 E. Union, Litchfield, 2/21/90, C, 90000156

Hayward-Hill House, 540 S. Main St., Hillsboro, 5/08/80, B, C, 80001399

Thomas, Lewis H., House, N. Virden Rd., Virden vicinity, 12/07/83, A, C, 83003586

Morgan County

Ayers Bank Building, 200 W. State St., Jacksonville, 11/20/86, A, 86003178

Beecher Hall, Illinois College, Illinois College campus, Jacksonville, 4/08/74, A, C, 74000769

Duncan, Joseph, House, 4 Duncan Pl., Jacksonville, 11/05/71, B, C, 71000294

Grierson, Gen. Benjamin Henry, House, 852 E. State St., Jacksonville, 11/20/80, B, 80001400

Jacksonville Historic District, Roughly bounded by Anna, Mound, Finley, Dayton, Lafayette and Church Sts., Jacksonville, 6/09/78, A, B, C, 78001178

Jacksonville Labor Temple, 228 S. Mauvaisterre St., Jacksonville, 11/13/80, A, 80004524

Morgan County Courthouse, 300 W. State St., Jacksonville, 11/19/86, A, C, 86003167

Ogle County

Barber, Bryant H. and Lucie, House, 103 N. Barber Ave., Polo, 2/10/93, C, 92001849

Barber, Henry D., House, 410 W. Mason St., Polo, 3/28/74, C, 74000770

City and Town Hall, Jct. of Fourth Ave. and Sixth St., Rochelle, 8/18/92, A, 92001006

Deere, John, House and Shop, Illinois and Clinton Sts., Grand Detour, 10/15/66, B, NHL, 66000327

Flagg Township Public Library, NE corner 7th St. at 4th Ave., Rochelle, 10/25/73, C, 73000713

Hitt, Samuel M., House, 7782 IL 64 W, Mount Morris, 11/14/85, C, 85002841

Holcomb, William H., House, 526 N. 7th St., Rochelle, 10/25/73, C, 73000714

Moats, William, Farm, Wood Rd., Ashton vicinity, 2/12/87, A, C, 86003724

Ogle County Courthouse, Courthouse Sq., Oregon, 9/10/81, C, 81000222

Pinehill, 400 Mix St., Oregon, 7/24/78, C, 78001179

Soldier's Monument, Chestnut and 2nd Sts., Byron, 2/14/85, A, f, 85000268

Stillman's Run Battle Site, Roosevelt and Spruce Sts., Stillman Valley, 12/08/83, A, f, 83003587

White Pines State Park Lodge and Cabins [Illinois State Parks Lodges and Cabins TR], RR #1, Mount Morris, 3/04/85, C, g, 85002404

Peoria County

Central National Park Building, 103 SW Adams St., Peoria, 12/18/78, C, 78003450

Christ Church of Lower Kickapoo, W of Norwood Park on Christ Church Rd., Norwood Park vicinity, 2/10/83, A, C, a, 83000333

Cumberland Presbyterian Church, 405 N. Monson St., Peoria, 3/18/80, A, C, a, 80001401

Flanagan, Judge, Residence, 942 NE Glen Oak Ave., Peoria, 9/05/75, C, 75000670

Gale, Judge Jacob, House, 403 NE Jefferson St., Peoria, 3/19/82, B, C, 82002591

Peoria County—Continued

Grand Army of the Republic Memorial Hall, 416 Hamilton Blvd., Peoria, 7/13/76, C, 76000723

Jubilee College, NW of Kickapoo on U.S. 150 and I-74, Kickapoo vicinity, 1/04/72, A, C, a, 72000465

Madison Theatre, 502 Main St., Peoria, 11/21/80, A, C, 80001402

North Side Historic District, Roughly bounded by Perry, Caroline, Madison and Fayette Sts., Peoria, 11/21/83, A, C, 83003588

Peoria City Hall, 419 Fulton St., Peoria, 2/06/73, C, 73000715

Peoria Cordage Company, Address Restricted, Peoria vicinity, 3/19/82, A, C, 82002592

Peoria Mineral Springs, 701 W. 7th Ave., Peoria, 3/05/82, A, C, 82002593

Peoria State Hospital, Ricketts Ave. and U.S. 24, Bartonville, 2/17/82, A, C, 82002590

Peoria Waterworks, Lorentz Ave., Peoria, 3/18/80, A, C, 80001403

Pere Marquette Hotel, 501 Main St., Peoria, 8/12/82, A, C, 82002594

Pettingill-Morron House, 1212 W. Moss Ave., Peoria, 4/02/76, C, 76000724

Proctor, John C., Recreation Center, 300 S. Allen St, Peoria, 9/06/79, A, C, 79000860

Rock Island Depot and Freight House, 32 Liberty St., Peoria, 12/22/78, A, C, 78001180

Wear, Washington C., House, 1 mi. S and 0.4 mi. W of jct. of IL 90 and IL 91, Princeville, 8/19/93, C, 93000838

West Bluff Historic District, Randolph, High and Moss Sts., E of Western St., Peoria, 12/17/76, B, C, 76000725

Perry County

Du Quoin State Fairgrounds [Historic Fairgrounds in Illinois MPS], US 51 N of jct. with SR 14, Du Quoin, 7/11/90, A, C, g, 90000719

Piatt County

Voorhies Castle, S of Bement, Bement vicinity, 6/20/79, C, 79000861

Pike County

Barry Historic District, U.S. 36, Barry, 3/13/79, C, 79000862

Griggsville Historic District, Irregular pattern along Corey, Stanford, Quincy and Liberty Sts., Griggsville, 1/17/79, C, 79000863

McWorter, Free Frank, Grave Site, Off US 36, 4 mi. E of Barry, Barry vicinity, 4/19/88, B, c, 87002533

Naples Mound 8, Address Restricted, Griggsville vicinity, 10/14/75, B, D, a, 75000671

Pittsfield East School, 400 E. Jefferson St., Pittsfield, 2/12/71, A, C, 71000295

Pittsfield Historic District, Roughly bounded by Washington Ct., Sycamore, Morrison and Griggsville Sts., Pittsfield, 6/04/80, C, a, 80001404

Scott, Lyman, House, U.S. 54, Summer Hill, 2/10/83, A, 83000334

Pope County

Golconda Historic District, IL 146, Golconda, 10/22/76, A, B, C, 76000726

Millstone Bluff, Address Restricted, Glendale vicinity, 10/15/73, D, 73000716

Pulaski County

Mound City Civil War Naval Hospital, Commercial Ave. and Central St., Mound City, 10/09/74, A, 74002285

Olmstead Depot, Front St. & Caledonia Ave., Olmsted, 12/15/89, A, 89002101

Putnam County

Clear Creek Meeting House, Address Restricted, McNabb vicinity, 11/05/92, A, C, a, 92001534

Condit, Cortland, House, Off IL 29, Putman, 9/16/83, A, C, 83000335

Pulsifer, Edward, House, IL 71, Hennepin, 9/04/79, B, C, 79000864

Putnam County Courthouse, 4th St., Hennepin, 3/04/75, A, C, 75000672

Randolph County

Charter Oak Schoolhouse, W of Schuline, Schuline vicinity, 10/11/78, C, 78001181

Creole House, Market St., Prairie du Rocher, 4/03/73, C, 73000717

Fort de Chartres, Terminus of IL 155, W of Prairie du Rocher, Fort Chartres, Prairie du Rocher vicinity, 10/15/66, A, NHL, 66000329

French Colonial Historic District, From Fort Chartres State Park to Kaskasia Island, Prairie du Rocher, 4/03/74, A, C, D, a, 74000772

Kolmer Site, Address Restricted, Prairie du Rocher vicinity, 5/01/74, D, 74000773

Mary's River Covered Bridge, About 4 mi. NE of Chester on IL 150, Chester vicinity, 12/31/74, A, C, 74000771

Menard, Pierre, House, Fort Kaskaskia State Park, Ellis Grove vicinity, 4/15/70, B, C, NHL, 70000245

Modoc Rock Shelter, Address Restricted, Modoc vicinity, 10/15/66, D, NHL, 66000328

Red Bud Historic District, Irregular pattern along Main and Market Sts., Red Bud, 12/29/79, B, C, 79000865

Sparta Historic District, S. St. Louis, W. 3rd and S. James Sts., Sparta, 6/03/82, C, 82002595

Richland County

Elliott Street Historic District, S. Elliott St. between Chestnut St. and South Ave., Olney, 11/26/80, A, C, a, g, 80001405

Larchmound, 1030 S. Morgan St., Olney, 1/03/80, B, 80001406

Rock Island County

Black Hawk Museum and Lodge [Illinois State Parks Lodges and Cabins TR], 1510 46th Ave., Rock Island vicinity, 3/04/85, C, g, 85002402

Black's Store, 1st Ave., Hampton, 5/28/76, A, B, 76000727

Connor House, 702 Twentieth St., Rock Island, 8/11/88, C, 88001227

Denkmann-Hauberg House, 1300 24th St., Rock Island, 12/26/72, B, C, 72000466

Fort Armstrong Hotel, 3rd Ave. and 19th St., Rock Island, 11/13/84, A, C, 84000327

Fort Armstrong Theatre, 1826 3rd Ave., Rock Island, 5/23/80, A, C, 80001407

Lincoln School, 7th Ave. and 22nd St., Rock Island, 8/29/85, A, C, 85001910

Old Main, Augustana College, 7th Ave. between 35th and 38th Sts., Rock Island, 9/11/75, A, C, a, 75000673

Potter House, 1906 7th Ave., Rock Island, 5/05/89, B, 89000364

Rock Island Arsenal, Rock Island in Mississippi River, Rock Island, 9/30/69, A, B, C, D, d, g, NHL, 69000057

Rock Island Lines Passenger Station, 3029 5th Ave., Rock Island, 6/03/82, A, 82002596

Stauduhar House, 1609 21st St., Rock Island, 3/05/82, C, 82002597

Wagner, Robert, House, 904 23rd St., Rock Island, 5/15/90, C, 90000721

Weyerhaeuser House, 3052 10th Ave., Rock Island, 9/11/75, A, B, 75000674

Saline County

Carrier Mills Archeological District, Address Restricted, Carrier Mills vicinity, 8/25/78, D, 78001184

Sangamon County

Boult, H. P., House, 1123 S. 2nd St., Springfield, 6/03/82, C, 82002598

Bressmer-Baker House, 913 6th St., Springfield, 6/29/82, C, 82002599

Brinkerhoff, George M., House, 1500 N. 5th St., Springfield, 12/18/78, C, 78001186

Sangamon County—Continued

Caldwell Farmstead, IL 4, Chatham vicinity, 8/16/84, B, C, 84001145

Camp Lincoln Commissary Building, 1301 N. MacArthur Blvd., Springfield, 11/13/84, A, C, 84000333

Central Springfield Historic District, Roughly bounded by 14th, 7th, Jefferson, and Washington Sts., Springfield, 8/29/78, A, B, C, 78001187

Central Springfield Historic District (Boundary Increase), Sixth St. from Capitol to Monroe St., Springfield, 11/19/86, A, C, 86003184

Christ Episcopal Church, 611 E. Jackson St., Springfield, 9/12/80, C, a, 80001410

Clayville Tavern, 0.5 mi. SE of Pleasant Plains on IL 125, Pleasant Plains vicinity, 5/08/73, A, C, 73000718

Dana, Susan Lawrence, House, 301 Lawrence Ave., Springfield, 7/30/74, C, NHL, 74000774

Edwards Place, 700 N. 4th St., Springfield, 12/17/69, C, 69000058

Executive Mansion, 4th and Jackson Sts., Springfield, 7/19/76, A, g, 76000728

Flagg, Cornelius, Farmstead, Tipton School Rd., 0.4 mi. W of I-55 Bus. and 0.4 mi. S of Andrew Rd., Sherman vicinity, 2/03/93, C, 92001848

Freeman, Clarkson W., House, 704 W. Monroe St., Springfield, 9/29/80, C, 80001411

Gottschalk, Fred, Grocery Store, 301 W. Edwards St., Springfield, 3/18/85, C, 85000607

Graham, Cong. James M., House, 413 S. 7th St., Springfield, 5/01/89, B, 89000342

Hickox Apartments, 4th and Cook Sts., Springfield, 11/13/84, A, C, 84000337

Hickox, Virgil, House, 518 E. Capitol Ave., Springfield, 3/05/82, B, 82002600

Iles, Elijah, House, 1825 S. 5th St., Springfield, 2/23/78, A, B, C, b, 78001188

Illinois Department of Mines and Minerals-Springfield Mine Rescue Station, 609 Princeton Ave., Springfield, 7/05/85, A, 85001481

Illinois State Capitol, Capitol Ave. and Second St., Springfield, 11/21/85, C, 85003178

Illinois State Fairgrounds [Historic Fairgrounds in Illinois MPS], Jct. of Sangamon Ave. and Peoria Rd., Springfield, 5/14/90, A, 90000720

Lewis, John L., House, 1132 W. Lawrence Ave., Springfield, 9/10/79, B, g, 79000867

Lincoln Home National Historic Site, 8th and Jackson Sts., Springfield, 8/18/71, B, NHL, NPS, 71000076

Lincoln Tomb, Oak Ridge Cemetery, Springfield, 10/15/66, B, c, f, NHL, 66000330

Lincoln, Abraham, Memorial Garden, 2301 E. Lake Dr., Springfield, 8/12/92, C, f, 92001016

Lindsay, Vachel, House, 603 S. 5th St., Springfield, 11/11/71, B, NHL, 71000297

Maid-Rite Sandwich Shop, 118 N. Pasfield St., Springfield, 8/16/84, A, 84001146

Miller, Joseph, House, Buckhart Rd., Rochester vicinity, 11/24/80, B, C, 80001408

Old State Capitol, Bounded by 5th, 6th, Adams, and Washington Sts., Springfield, 10/15/66, A, B, NHL, 66000331

Power Farmstead, Co. Rd. 9.5 North, 0.5 mi. E of Cantrall, Cantrall vicinity, 5/01/89, A, B, 89000341

Price—Prather House, Jct. of Main and Elkhart Sts., Williamsville, 5/13/91, B, C, 91000574

Price/Wheeler House, 618 S. 7th St., Springfield, 2/14/85, C, 85000269

Rippon—Kinsella House, 1317 N. Third St., Springfield, 2/27/92, C, 92000073

St. Nicholas Hotel, 400 E. Jefferson St., Springfield, 2/10/83, A, C, 83000336

Sugar Creek Covered Bridge, SE of Chatham off I-55, Chatham vicinity, 1/09/78, A, C, 78001185

Taft Farmstead, SR 3, Rochester, 11/20/80, B, 80001409

Tiger—Anderson House, CR 3 N, Springfield vicinity, 6/11/86, C, 86001316

Union Station, Madison St., Springfield, 11/27/78, A, C, 78001189

Washington Park, Bounded by Fayette Ave., Williams Blvd., Walnut St., MacArthur Blvd., S. Grand Ave. and Chatham Rd., Springfield, 5/22/92, C, 92000483

Weber, Howard K., House, 925 S. 7th St., Springfield, 10/01/79, C, 79000868

Wheeland Haven, E of Riverton on I-72, Riverton vicinity, 3/12/85, B, C, 85000557

Yates, Gov. Richard, House, 1190 Williams Blvd., Springfield, 3/01/84, C, 84001148

Schuyler County

Phoenix Opera House Block, 112-122 W. Lafayette St., Rushville, 5/09/85, A, C, 85001010

Scott County

Naples Archeological District, Address Restricted, Naples vicinity, 12/22/79, A, C, D, a, 79000869

Winchester Historic District, IL 106, Winchester, 2/14/79, A, C, a, 79000870

Shelby County

Chatauqua Auditorium, Forest Park and NE 9th St., Shelbyville, 1/30/78, A, C, 78001190

Shelbyville Historic District, Roughly bound by the railroad tracks, Will, N. 8th, and S. 6th Sts., Shelbyville, 12/22/76, A, B, C, 76000729

Tallman, Horace M., House, 816 W. Main, Shelbyville, 5/06/88, A, 88000470

Thompson Mill Covered Bridge, 0.5 mi. NE of Cowden over Kaskaskia River, Cowden vicinity, 3/13/75, A, C, 75000675

St. Clair County

Belleville Historic District, Between E, S. Belt, Illinois, and Forest Sts., Belleville, 11/07/76, C, 76002165

Cahokia Mounds, 7850 Collinsville Rd., Cahokia Mounds State Park, Collinsville vicinity, 10/15/66, D, NHL, 66000899

Church of the Holy Family, E. 1st St., Cahokia, 4/15/70, C, a, NHL, 70000851

Eads Bridge, Spanning the Mississippi River at Washington St., East St. Louis, 10/15/66, A, C, NHL, 66000946

Emerald Mound and Village Site, Address Restricted, Lebanon vicinity, 10/26/71, D, 71001026

Jarrot, Nicholas, House, 1st St., Cahokia, 11/19/74, B, C, 74002197

Knobeloch-Seibert Farm, Address Restricted, Belleville vicinity, 5/09/83, A, 83004186

Lebanon Historic District, Irregular pattern centered along St. Louis and Belleville Sts., Lebanon, 10/04/78, A, B, C, D, 78003113

Majestic Theatre, 240-246 Collinsville Ave., East St. Louis, 5/09/85, A, C, 85000977

Martin, Pierre, House, First St. at Old Rt. 3, North Dupo, 2/09/90, A, C, D, 89002350

Mermaid House Hotel, 114 E. St. Louis St., Lebanon, 12/04/75, B, C, 75002078

Old Cahokia Courthouse, Corner of W. 1st and Elm Sts., Cahokia, 11/09/72, A, C, b, e, 72001480

Pennsylvania Avenue Historic District, Pennsylvania Ave., East St. Louis, 7/27/79, B, C, 79003166

Stark County

Chicago, Burlington & Quincy Railroad Depot, Williams St., Wyoming, 4/30/87, A, 87000650

Stephenson County

Addams, John H., Homestead, 425 N. Mill St., Cedarville, 4/17/79, A, B, c, 79000871

Bruce, James, Round Barn [Round Barns in Illinois TR], S of Freeport, Freeport vicinity, 2/23/84, A, C, 84001157

Fehr, Charles, Round Barn [Round Barns in Illinois TR], NE of Orangeville, Orangeville vicinity, 2/23/84, A, C, 84001152

Harbach, Gerald, Round Barn [Round Barns in Illinois TR], US 20, Eleroy vicinity, 2/23/84, A, C, 84001155

Jensen, Chris, Round Barn [Round Barns in Illinois TR], 11723 W. Galena Rd., Lena vicinity, 2/23/84, A, C, 84001150

Kellogg's Grove, SE of Kent, Kent vicinity, 6/23/78, A, D, 78001191

Leek, Clyde, Round Barn [Round Barns in Illinois TR], N. Dakota Rd., Dakota, 2/23/84, A, C, 84001161

Otte, Dennis, Round Barn [Round Barns in Illinois TR], E of Eleroy, Eleroy vicinity, 2/23/84, A, C, 84001164

Stephenson County Courthouse, Courthouse Sq., Freeport, 1/17/74, C, 74002284

Taylor, Oscar, House, 1440 S. Carroll Ave., Freeport, 5/11/84, B, C, 84001165

Tazewell County

Allentown Union Hall, 2 mi. E of IL 121, Allentown, 8/12/88, A, 88001228

Delavan Commercial Historic District, 307, 309–324, 400, 401, 404–410, 412 and 414 Locust St., Delavan, 11/14/91, A, C, 91001687

Farm Creek Section, S side of Farm Cr., East Peoria vicinity, 2/06/92, A, B, D, 91002039

Herget, Carl, Mansion, 420 Washington St., Pekin, 8/18/92, C, 92001005

Illinois Traction System Mackinaw Depot, N. Main St., Mackinaw, 11/30/78, A, C, 78001192

Pekin Federal Building, 334 Elizabeth St., Pekin, 10/09/80, C, 80001412

Tazewell County Courthouse, Court St. between Capitol and Fourth Sts., Pekin, 11/14/85, C, 85002837

Union County

St. Paulus Evangelisch Lutherischen Gemeinde, S of Jonseboro off IL 127, Jonesboro vicinity, 11/24/80, A, C, a, 80001413

Stinson Memorial Library, 409 S. Main St., Anna, 6/09/78, C, 78001193

Ware Mounds and Village Site, Address Restricted, Ware vicinity, 10/18/77, D, 77000490

Vermilion County

Collins Archeological District, Address Restricted, Danville vicinity, 8/03/79, D, 79000872

Danville Branch, National Home for Disabled Volunteer Soldiers Historic District, 1900 and 2000 E. Main St., Danville, 1/30/92, A, C, 91001973

Danville Public Library, 307 N. Vermillion St., Danville, 11/30/78, A, C, 78003064

Fithian House, 116 N. Gilbert St., Danville, 5/01/75, A, B, C, 75002060

Holland Apartments, 324–326 N. Vermilion St., Danville, 11/16/88, C, 88002232

Hoopes-Cunningham Mansion, 424 E. Penn St., Hoopeston, 9/11/85, B, C, 85002307

Warren County

Alexis Opera House, 101–105 N. Main St., Alexis, 7/30/87, A, 87001267

Carr House, 416 E. Broadway, Monmouth, 8/11/88, C, 88001229

Colwell, E. B., and Company Department Store, 208 S. Main St. and 211 S. A St., Monmouth, 2/03/93, A, 92001851

Martin, Sarah, House, 310 E. Broadway, Monmouth, 10/09/80, A, 80001414

Patton Block Building, 88 and 90 Public Sq., Monmouth, 11/02/90, C, 90001727

Quinby, Ivory, House, 605 N. 6th St., Monmouth, 11/20/80, B, C, 80001415

Stewart, Minnie, House, 1015 E. Euclid Ave., Monmouth, 10/19/89, A, 89001733

Weir, William S., Jr., House, 402 E. Broadway, Monmouth, 8/18/92, B, C, 92001004

Washington County

Louisville and Nashville Depot, 101 E. Railroad St., Nashville, 3/01/85, A, C, 85000496

Original Springs Hotel and Bathhouse, 301 E. Walnut St., Okawville, 12/22/78, A, C, 78001194

Schlosser, Frank, Complex, W. Walnut St., Okawville, 8/15/83, A, C, 83000337

Wayne County

Mayberry Mound and Village Site, Address Restricted, Sims vicinity, 11/21/78, D, 78001195

White County

Bieker-Wilson Village Site, Address Restricted, New Haven vicinity, 11/21/78, D, 78001197

Carmi Chapter House [American Woman's League Chapter Houses TR], 604 W. Main St., Carmi, 11/28/80, A, C, 80001416

Gray, William W., House, 119 N. Court St., Grayville, 2/13/92, C, 92000049

Hubele Mounds and Village Site, Address Restricted, Maunie vicinity, 8/25/78, D, 78001196

Old Morrison Mill, Off Liberty Rd., Burnt Prairie, 7/11/84, A, 84001169

Ratcliff Inn, 214 E. Main St., Carmi, 6/04/73, B, 73000719

Robinson-Stewart House, 110 S. Main Cross St., Carmi, 8/17/73, B, C, 73000720

Williams, James Robert, House, 310 E. Main St., Carmi, 1/29/87, B, C, 86003716

Wilson Mounds and Village Site, Address Restricted, Maunie vicinity, 11/16/77, D, 77000491

Whiteside County

Albany Mounds Site, Addrss Restricted, Albany vicinity, 10/09/74, D, 74000775

Kirk, Col. Edward N., House, 1005 E. 3rd St., Sterling, 10/09/80, B, 80001417

Main Street Historic District, S. Main St., Tampico, 6/03/82, A, B, C, c, 82002602

McCune Mound and Village Site, Address Restricted, Sterling vicinity, 8/16/79, D, 79000873

Sinnissippi Site, Address Restricted, Sterling vicinity, 5/14/79, D, 79000874

Will County

Briscoe Mounds, Address Restricted, Channahon vicinity, 12/22/78, D, 78001198

Christ Episcopal Church, 75 W. Van Buren St., Joliet, 8/12/82, C, a, 82002603

Fitzpatrick House, IL 53, Lockport vicinity, 2/09/84, B, C, 84001170

Flanders House, 405 W. Main St., Plainfield, 11/14/91, A, C, 91001688

George, Ron, Round Barn [Round Barns in Illinois TR], NE of Romeoville off US 66, Romeoville vicinity, 12/07/82, C, 82000401

Henry, Jacob H., House, 20 S. Eastern Ave., Joliet, 5/14/79, C, 79000875

Illinois and Michigan Canal, 7 mi. SW of Joliet on U.S. 6, in Channahon State Park, Joliet vicinity, 10/15/66, A, C, NHL, 66000332

Joliet East Side Historic District, Roughly bounded by Washington and Union Sts., 4th and Eastern Aves., Joliet, 8/15/80, A, C, 80001418

Joliet Municipal Airport, 4000 W. Jefferson St., Joliet, 12/10/80, A, 80001419

Joliet Steel Works, 927 Collins St., Joliet, 2/28/91, A, 91000088

Joliet Township High School, 201 E. Jefferson St., Joliet, 8/12/82, A, C, 82002604

Joliet, Louis, Hotel, 22 E. Clinton St., Joliet, 2/09/90, A, 90000101

Lockport Historic District, Area between 7th and 11th Sts. and Canal and Washington Sts., Lockport, 5/12/75, A, C, 75000676

Milne, Robert, House, 535 E. 7th St., Lockport, 12/17/79, B, C, 79000876

Plainfield Halfway House, 503 Main St., Plainfield, 9/29/80, A, 80001421

Rathje, H. A., Mill, 433 W. Corning Ave., Peotone, 3/19/82, A, C, 82002605

Rubens Rialto Square Theater, 102 N. Chicago St., Joliet, 7/24/78, A, C, 78001199

Standard Oil Gasoline Station, 600 W. Lockport St., Plainfield, 11/13/84, A, C, 84000340

Stone Manor, SE of Lockport, Lockport vicinity, 11/26/80, C, 80001420

U.S. Post Office, 150 N. Scott St., Joliet, 8/20/81, C, 81000223

Union Station, 50 E. Jefferson St., Joliet, 8/01/78, A, C, 78001200

Upper Bluff Historic District, Roughly bounded by Taylor, Center and Campbell Sts. and Raynor Ave., Joliet, 6/05/91, C, 91000687

Will County Historical Society Headquarters, 803 S. State St., Lockport, 5/17/72, A, C, 72000467

Williamson County

Allen, Willis, House, 514 S. Market St., Marion, 2/11/82, B, 82002606

Goddard Chapel, Rose Hill Cemetery, IL 37 N, Marion, 11/06/86, C, a, 86003157

Winnebago County

Beattie Park Mound Group, N. Main St. between Park and Mound Aves., Rockford, 2/27/91, C, D, 91000084

Winnebago County—Continued

Chicago & North Western Railway Stone Arch Bridge, 0.6 mi. E of IL 251, 0.6 mi. W of I-90 and 0.2 mi. S of Burr Oak Rd., Roscoe vicinity, 8/19/93, A, 93000840

Coronado, 312-324 N. Main St, Rockford, 9/06/79, A, C, 79000878

East Rockford Historic District, U.S. 20 and U.S. 51, Rockford, 3/20/80, A, C, 80001422

Graham-Cinestra House, 1115 S. Main St., Rockford, 6/11/79, B, C, 79000879

Haight Village Historic District, Roughly bounded by Walnut & Kishwaukee Sts., Chicago Northwestern RR tracks & Madison St., Rockford, 11/20/87, A, C, 87002044

Herrick Cobblestone, 2127 Broadway, Rockford, 5/14/80, A, C, 80001423

Jacoby, Lysander, House, 2 Jacoby Pl., Rockford, 3/05/82, C, 82002607

Lake-Peterson House, 1313 E. State St., Rockford, 6/25/80, B, C, 80001424

Limestones, The, 118–122 S. Main, Rockford, 8/22/86, A, 86001491

Macktown Historic District, W of Rockton on Pecatonica River, Rockton vicinity, 1/05/78, A, B, C, 78001201

Roberts, William H., House, 523 Main St., Pecatonica, 9/06/79, C, 79000877

Rockton Historic District, Roughly bounded by River, Warren, Cherry, and West Sts., Rockton, 5/02/78, B, C, 78001202

Soldiers and Sailors Memorial Hall, 211–215 N. Main St., Rockford, 1/31/76, A, f, 76000731

Spafford, Amos Catlin, House, 501 N. Prospect St., Rockford, 2/20/80, B, C, 80001425

Svea Music Hall, 326 7th St., Rockford, 3/19/82, A, 82002608

Tinker Swiss Cottage, 411 Kent St., Rockford, 12/27/72, C, 72000468

Weber, Robert, Round Barn [Round Barns in Illinois TR], E of Durand, Durand vicinity, 2/23/84, A, C, 84001172

Woodford County

Benson Water Tower, Clayton St. between Front & Pleasant Sts., Benson, 11/20/87, A, 87002034

Eureka College Administration and Chapel, 300 College Ave., Eureka, 5/31/80, A, C, a, 80001426

Metamora Courthouse, 113 E. Partridge St., Metamora, 3/30/78, B, C, 78001203

Stevenson, Adlai E., I, House, 104 W. Walnut St., Metamora, 3/18/80, B, C, 80001427

The industrial buildings and spatial design of the Joliet Steel Works (initially operated from 1869 to 1932) represent the economic development of American steel companies from a diverse number of independent plants in the mid-1800s to a chain of sites owned and operated by national conglomerates prior to World War II. (Leslie Schwartz, 1990)

INDIANA

Adams County

Bowers, John S. House, 104 Marshall St., Decatur, 3/05/82, C, 82000055

Colter, Ben, Polygonal Barn [Round and Polygonal Barns of Indiana MPS], IN 101 E side, 0.6 mi. S of jct. with Piqua Rd., Pleasant Mills vicinity, 4/02/93, A, C, 93000194

Porter, Gene Stratton, Cabin, 200 E. 6th St., Geneva, 6/27/74, B, C, 74000027

Allen County

Allen County Courthouse, 715 S. Calhoun St, Fort Wayne, 5/28/76, C, 76000031

Bass, John H., Mansion, 2701 Spring St., Fort Wayne, 6/02/82, B, C, a, 82000056

Blackstone Building, 112 W. Washington, Fort Wayne, 8/24/88, C, 88001219

Cathedral of the Immaculate Conception, Jefferson and Calhoun St., Fort Wayne, 10/23/80, A, C, a, 80000048

Craigville Depot, Ryan and Edgerton Rds., New Haven vicinity, 10/10/84, C, b, 84000181

Edsall, William S., House, 305 W. Main St., Fort Wayne, 10/08/76, C, 76000032

Embassy Theater and Indiana Hotel, 121 W. Jefferson St., Fort Wayne, 9/05/75, A, C, 75000041

Engine House No. 3, 226 W. Washington Blvd., Fort Wayne, 7/27/79, A, C, 79003772

Fairfield Manor, 2301 Fairfield Ave., Fort Wayne, 6/16/83, C, 83000047

Feustel, Robert M., House, 4101 W. Taylor St., Fort Wayne, 11/07/80, B, C, 80000049

Fort Wayne City Hall, 308 E. Berry St., Fort Wayne, 6/04/73, A, C, g, 73000027

Fort Wayne Printing Company Building, 114 W. Washington St., Fort Wayne, 8/24/88, C, 88001220

Johnny Appleseed Memorial Park, Swanson Blvd. at Parnell Ave. along Old Feeder Canal, Fort Wayne, 1/17/73, B, f, 73000028

Journal-Gazette Building, 701 S. Clinton St., Fort Wayne, 12/27/82, A, C, 82000057

Keplinger, Harry A., House, 235 W. Creighton Ave., Fort Wayne, 9/01/83, A, C, 83000048

Kresge—Groth Building, 914 S. Calhoun St., Fort Wayne, 8/25/88, C, 88001223

Landing, The, Historic District, Roughly bounded by Calhoun, Harrison, Dock and Pearl Sts. and the alley between Columbia and Main Sts., Fort Wayne, 9/16/93, A, B, C, 93000953

Lindenwood Cemetery, 2324 W. Main St., Fort Wayne, 2/17/78, C, f, 78000043

Masonic Temple, 206 E. Washington Blvd., Fort Wayne, 3/14/91, A, C, 91000273

McCulloch, Hugh, House, 616 W. Superior St., Fort Wayne, 10/23/80, A, B, 80000050

Mohr, Louis, Block, 119 W. Wayne St., Fort Wayne, 8/26/88, C, 88001222

Peters, John Claus, House, 832 W. Wayne St., Fort Wayne, 9/17/80, C, 80000051

Randall Building, 616 and 618 S. Harrison St., Fort Wayne, 12/07/90, B, C, 90001786

Robinson, Horney, House, 7320 Lower Huntington Rd., Fort Wayne vicinity, 3/21/85, B, C, 85000604

Saint Paul's Evangelical Lutheran Church, 1126 S. Barr St., Fort Wayne, 3/01/82, C, a, 82000058

Schmitz Block, 926–930 S. Calhoun St., Fort Wayne, 8/26/88, C, 88001224

South Wayne Historic District, Roughly bounded by W. Wildwood Ave., S. Wayne Ave., Packard Ave. and Beaver Ave., Fort Wayne, 9/04/92, A, C, 92001146

St. Peter's Square, Roughly bounded by St. Martin, Hanna, E. Dewald and Warsaw Sts., including 518 E. Dewald St., Fort Wayne, 3/20/91, A, C, a, 91000259

Strunz, Christian G., House, 333 E. Berry St., Fort Wayne, 10/04/79, C, 79000030

Swinney, Thomas W., House, 1424 W. Jefferson St., Fort Wayne, 4/27/81, C, 81000026

Trinity Episcopal Church, 611 W. Berry St., Fort Wayne, 9/13/78, A, a, 78000044

Wells Street Bridge, Wells St. at the St. Mary's River, Fort Wayne, 9/15/88, C, 88001575

West End Historic District, Roughly bounded by Main, Webster, Jefferson, Broadway, Jones, and St. Mary's River, Fort Wayne, 11/15/84, A, C, 84000352

West, Fisher, Farm, 17935 West Rd., Huntertown vicinity, 6/06/85, C, 85001193

Williams—Woodland Park Historic District, Roughly bounded by Hoagland and Creighton Aves. and Harrison and Pontiac Sts., Fort Wayne, 3/14/91, A, C, 91000258

Bartholomew County

Bartholomew County Courthouse, 3rd and Washington Sts., Columbus, 11/15/79, A, C, g, 79000031

Columbus City Hall, 5th and Franklin Sts., Columbus, 11/15/79, A, C, g, 79000032

Columbus Historic District, Roughly bounded by the Pennsylvania RR tracks, Chestnut, 34th, Washington, and Franklin Sts., Columbus, 12/10/82, A, C, a, 82000059

Daugherty, Elnora, Farm, 5541 E. 500 South, Columbus vicinity, 6/04/92, A, C, 92000676

Hope Historic District, Roughly bounded by Haw Cr., Grand St., Walnut St. and South St., Hope, 12/19/91, A, C, a, 91001864

Marr, James, House and Farm, NE of Columbus on Marr Rd., Columbus vicinity, 10/23/80, A, C, 80000052

McEwen-Samuels-Marr House, 524 3rd St., Columbus, 5/22/78, B, 78000045

McKinley School, Seventeenth St. and Home Ave., Columbus, 8/25/88, A, C, g, 88001221

Benton County

Presbyterian Church Building, NW of Benton and Justus Sts., Oxford, 3/01/84, C, a, 84000997

Blackford County

Blackford County Courthouse, Off IN 3, Hartford City, 8/11/80, A, C, 80000053

First Presbyterian Church, 220 N. High St., Hartford City, 6/13/86, A, C, a, 86001263

Boone County

Boone County Courthouse, Courthouse Sq., Lebanon, 9/22/86, C, 86002703

Thorntown Public Library, 124 N. Market St., Thorntown, 9/22/86, A, 86002708

Town Hall (Castle Hall), 65 E. Cedar St., Zionsville, 6/09/83, A, C, 83000115

VanHuys, Andrew B., Round Barn [Round and Polygonal Barns of Indiana MPS], Address Restricted, Lebanon vicinity, 4/02/93, A, C, 93000181

Brown County

Axsom Branch Archeological Site (12BR12), Address Restricted, Nashville vicinity, 3/25/86, D, 86000525

Brown County Bridge No. 36, Hickory Hill Rd. across the N. Fork of Salt Cr., Nashville vicinity, 12/21/93, A, C, 93001430

Brown County Courthouse Historic District, Courthouse, Old Log Jail, and the Historical Society Museum Bldg., Nashville, 7/21/83, A, C, b, 83000050

Grandview Church, Grandview Ridge Rd. SE of New Bellsville, Van Buren Township, New Bellsville vicinity, 9/13/91, A, C, a, 91001160

Hendricks, Thomas A., House and Stone Head Road Marker, IN 135 and Bellsville Rd., Stone Head, 12/06/84, C, 84000450

Refuge No. 7 Archeological Site (12BR11), Address Restricted, Nashville vicinity, 3/31/86, D, 86000629

Steele, Theodore Clement, House and Studio, SW of Nashville off IN 46, Nashville vicinity, 10/02/73, B, 73000029

Brown County—Continued

Taggart, F.P., Store, Main and VanBuren Sts., Nashville, 12/22/83, A, C, 83003559

Carroll County

Adams Mill, Off CR 50 East, Cutler vicinity, 11/23/84, A, C, 84000278

Barnett-Seawright-Wilson House, 203 E. Monroe St., Delphi, 9/17/80, A, C, 80000054

Burris House and Potawatomi Spring, Towpath Rd., Lockport, 9/15/77, A, 77000018

District School No. 3, NE corner of CR 750 N and CR 100 W, Rockfield vicinity, 3/31/88, A, C, 88000374

Foreman—Case House, 312 E. Main St., Delphi, 5/24/90, C, 90000811

Niewerth Building, 124 E. Main St., Delphi, 5/24/84, C, 84001001

Raber, Fred and Minnie, Farm, IN 218 E of Co. Rd. 425 W, Camden vicinity, 9/16/92, A, C, 92001169

Thomas, Andrew, House, W Main St., Camden, 12/27/84, C, 84000485

Cass County

Barnett, Thompson, House, IN 25, Logansport vicinity, 8/14/86, C, 86001620

Ferguson House, 803 E. Broadway, Logansport, 6/30/83, C, 83000117

Jerolaman-Long House, 1004 E. Market St., Logansport, 3/28/85, C, 85000651

Kendrick-Baldwin House, 706 E. Market St., Logansport, 9/09/82, B, 82000060

Pollard-Nelson House, 7th and Market Sts., Logansport, 10/29/75, C, 75000042

Spencer Park Dentzel Carousel, Riverside Park, Logansport, 2/27/87, A, NHL, 87000838

Clark County

Downs, Thomas, House, 1045 Main St., Charlestown, 12/06/84, C, 84000490

Ferguson, Benjamin, House, 673 High St., Charlestown, 6/16/83, C, 83000118

French, Henry, House, 217 E. High St., Jeffersonville, 6/29/89, A, C, 89000772

Grisamore House, 111-113 W. Chestnut St., Jeffersonville, 5/09/83, C, 83000119

Howard Home, 1101 E. Market St., Jeffersonville, 7/05/73, A, C, 73000031

Old Clarksville Site, Address Restricted, Clarksville vicinity, 12/16/74, B, D, 74000028

Old Jeffersonville Historic District, Roughly bounded by Court Ave., Graham St., Ohio River, & I-65, Jeffersonville, 10/06/87, A, C, 87001461

Watson House, 1015 Water St., Charlestown, 9/01/83, A, C, 83000051

Clay County

Poland Presbyterian Church and Cemetery, IN 42 near Co. Rd. 56S, Poland, 12/18/90, A, C, a, 90001932

Clinton County

Clinton County Courthouse, Public Sq., Frankfort, 12/05/78, A, C, g, 78000027

Old Frankfort Stone High School, 301 E. Clinton, Frankfort, 6/04/79, A, C, 79000012

Rosenberger Building, 83 Old Main St., Colfax, 5/03/84, A, C, 84001004

Crawford County

Potts Creek Rockshelter Archeological Site (12CR110), Address Restricted, St. Croix vicinity, 2/04/87, D, 86003174

Daviess County

Carnahan, Magnus J., House, 511 E. Main St., Washington, 8/29/91, B, C, 91001167

Glendale River Archaeological Site (12 Da 86), Address Restricted, Hudsonville vicinity, 5/30/85, D, 85001165

Graham, Robert C., House, 101 W. Maple St., Washington, 3/16/83, A, C, 83000120

Prairie Creek Site, Address Restricted, Washington vicinity, 5/12/75, D, 75000013

Washington Commercial Historic District, Roughly bounded by Fourth, Hefron and Meridian Sts. and the Chessie System RR, Washington, 11/28/90, A, C, 90001780

De Kalb County

Auburn Automobile Company Administration Building, 1600 S. Wayne St., Auburn, 9/21/78, A, C, g, 78000029

Bevier, Samuel, House [Keyser Township MRA], CR 52 and CR 11, Garrett vicinity, 5/06/83, C, 83000014

Bowman, Joseph, Farmhouse [Keyser Township MRA], CR 19 and CR 40, Garrett vicinity, 5/06/83, C, 83000013

Breechbill-Davidson House [Keyser Township MRA], IN 8 and CR 7, Garrett vicinity, 5/06/83, C, 83000012

Brethren in Christ Church [Keyser Township MRA], CR 7, Garrett vicinity, 5/06/83, C, a, d, 83000011

Clark, Orin, House [Keyser Township MRA], CR 48 and CR 3, Garrett vicinity, 5/06/83, C, 83000010

Cornell, William, Homestead, SW of Auburn off IN 427, Auburn vicinity, 8/14/73, A, C, 73000015

Dekalb County Home and Barn [Keyser Township MRA], CR 40, Garrett vicinity, 5/06/83, C, 83000015

Downtown Auburn Historic District, Roughly bounded by E. and W. Fourth, N. and S. Cedar, E. Twelfth, and N. and S. Jackson Sts., Auburn, 9/10/86, A, C, 86002858

Eckhart Public Library and Park, 603 S. Jackson St., Auburn, 11/20/81, A, C, 81000009

Fountain, William, House [Keyser Township MRA], IN 8, Garrett vicinity, 5/06/83, C, 83000021

Garrett Historic District [Keyser Township MRA], Roughly bounded by Railroad, Britton, Warfield and Hamsher Sts., and 3rd Ave., Garrett vicinity, 5/06/83, A, C, 83000121

Gump House [Keyser Township MRA], IN 8, Garrett vicinity, 5/06/83, C, 83000020

Haag, J.H., House [Keyser Township MRA], CR 54, Garrett vicinity, 5/06/83, C, 83000019

Kelham, Edward, House [Keyser Township MRA], CR 48, Garrett vicinity, 5/06/83, C, 83000018

Keyser Township School 8 [Keyser Township MRA], E. Quincy St., Garrett vicinity, 5/06/83, C, 83000017

Lehmback, Charles, Farmstead [Keyser Township MRA], CR 15, Garrett vicinity, 5/06/83, C, 83000016

Mountz House, 507 E. Houston St., Garrett, 9/11/79, B, C, 79000013

Peters, Henry, House [Keyser Township MRA], 201 N. 6th St., Garrett vicinity, 5/06/83, C, 83000022

Rakestraw House [Keyser Township MRA], CR 19, Garrett vicinity, 5/06/83, C, 83000024

Shull, Henry, Farmhouse Inn [Keyser Township MRA], CR 11-A, Garrett vicinity, 5/06/83, C, 83000023

Spencerville Covered Bridge, CR 68, Spencerville, 4/02/81, C, 81000010

Wilderson, John, House [Keyser Township MRA], 1349 S. Cowen St., Garrett vicinity, 5/06/83, C, 83000025

Wiltrout, Maria and Franklin, Polygonal Barn [Round and Polygonal Barns of Indiana MPS], 0209 Co. Rd. 16, Corunna vicinity, 4/02/93, A, C, 93000183

Dearborn County

Aurora Public Library, 414 Second St., Aurora, 5/27/93, A, C, 93000474

Dearborn County Courthouse, High and Mary Sts., Lawrenceburg, 4/09/81, C, 81000008

Downtown Lawrenceburg Historic District, Roughly bounded by ConRail Tracks, Charlotte, Tate, Williams, and Elm Sts., Lawrenceburg, 3/01/84, A, C, 84001009

George Street Bridge, George, Main, and Importing Sts., Aurora, 3/01/84, A, C, 84001012

Hamline Chapel, United Methodist Church, High and Vine Sts., Lawrenceburg, 9/09/82, C, a, 82000030

Dearborn County—Continued

Hillforest (Forest Hill), 213 5th St., Aurora, 8/05/71, C, NHL, 71000005

Jennison Guard Site, Address Restricted, Lawrenceburg vicinity, 5/12/75, D, 75000014

Laughery Creek Bridge, S of Aurora W of IN 56, Aurora vicinity, 9/29/76, C, 76000018

Veraestau, 1.mi. S of Aurora on IN 56, Aurora vicinity, 4/11/73, A, B, C, 73000013

Decatur County

Bromwell Wire Works, Jct. of First and Ireland Sts., Greensburg, 6/07/90, A, C, 90000810

Decatur County Courthouse, Courthouse Sq., Greensburg, 4/27/73, A, C, g, 73000014

Knights of Pythias Building and Theatre, 215 N. Broadway, Greensburg, 3/28/78, A, 78000028

Pleak, Strauther, Round Barn [Round and Polygonal Barns of Indiana MPS], Moscow Rd., 0.2 mi. E of Co. Rd. 100W, Greensburg vicinity, 6/24/93, A, C, 93000557

Westport Covered Bridge, E. of Westport, Westport vicinity, 6/25/82, C, 82000031

Delaware County

Boyce Block, 216-224 E. Main St., Muncie, 3/01/84, A, B, C, 84001015

City Hall [Downtown Muncie MRA], 220 E. Jackson St., Muncie, 11/14/88, C, 88002114

Felt's Farm, Race St., Eaton, 8/28/75, C, 75000015

Fire Station No. 1 [Downtown Muncie MRA], 421 E. Jackson St., Muncie, 2/17/89, C, 88002126

First Baptist Church [Downtown Muncie MRA], 309 E. Adams St., Muncie, 11/14/88, C, a, 88002125

Garner, Job—Miller, Jacob W., House, Bethel Pike at CR 700 W, Bethel vicinity, 6/13/86, B, C, 86001264

Gilbert, Goldsmith C., Historic District [Downtown Muncie MRA], Roughly bounded by Wysor St., N. Madison St., E. Washington St., and Mulberry St., Muncie, 11/14/88, A, a, 88002113

Hamilton Township Schoolhouse No. 4, IN 67, Muncie vicinity, 12/27/84, C, 84000487

Hofherr, Martin, Farm, Co. Rd. 650W N of jct. with Division Rd., Yorktown vicinity, 6/04/92, A, C, 92000677

Hoover, Eli, House and Confectionary [Downtown Muncie MRA], 316 W. Main St., Muncie, 11/14/88, A, C, 88002128

Johnson, J. C., House, 322 E. Washington, Muncie, 7/15/82, B, C, 82000032

Jones, Margaret and George Riley, House, 315 E. Charles St., Muncie, 9/27/84, C, 84001017

Judson Building [Downtown Muncie MRA], 300 W. Main St., Muncie, 11/14/88, C, 88002127

Jump, Dr. Samuel Vaughn, House, SE of Muncie on IN 2, Muncie vicinity, 11/12/82, C, 82000033

Kimbrough, Emily, Historic District, Bounded by Monroe, East Washington, Hackley, and East Charles Sts., Muncie, 11/13/80, B, C, 80000032

Kimbrough, Emily, Historic District (Boundary Increase), Roughly E. Gilbert, Beacon St., E. Charles St., Madison St., Muncie, 6/29/89, A, C, 89000779

Masonic Temple, 520 E. Main St., Muncie, 9/27/84, C, 84001020

Moore-Youse-Maxon House, 122 E. Washington St., Muncie, 5/24/84, C, 84001022

Muncie Public Library, 301 E. Jackson St., Muncie, 6/17/76, A, C, 76000019

Old West End Historic District, Roughly bounded by the White River and Washington St., Liberty St., Horward St. and Orchard Pl., and Kilgore Ave., Muncie, 9/22/86, C, 86002721

Peacock Apartments [Downtown Muncie MRA], 414 S. Jefferson St., Muncie, 11/14/88, C, 88002119

Roberts Hotel, 420 S. High St., Muncie, 7/15/82, C, 82000034

Roots, Francis T., Building, 115-119 E. Charles St., Muncie, 3/21/85, A, C, 85000605

Rose, F.D., Building, 121 E. Charles St., Muncie, 3/01/84, C, 84001023

Shirk, W. W., Building [Downtown Muncie MRA], 219 E. Jackson St., Muncie, 11/14/88, A, C, 88002116

Valentine, John, House, 1101 Riverside Ave., Muncie, 1/04/83, C, 83000026

Walnut Street Historic District [Downtown Muncie MRA], Ruoughly Walnut St. from Washington to Victor Sts., Muncie, 2/17/89, A, C, 88002112

Westwood Historic District, Roughly bounded by Briar, Petty and Warwick Rd. and Riverside Ave., Muncie, 4/03/92, A, C, 92000186

Wysor Heights Historic District, Roughly bounded by Highland Ave., White River, N. Elm St. and N. Walnut St., Muncie, 11/01/88, A, C, 88001217

YWCA [Downtown Muncie MRA], 310 E. Charles St., Muncie, 2/17/89, A, C, 88002117

Dubois County

Convent Immaculate Conception Historic District, 802 E. 10th St., Ferdinand, 7/13/83, A, C, a, d, g, 83000122

Evangelische Lutherische Emanuels Kirche, Co. Rd. 445 E., 1 mi. S of IN 56, Dubois vicinity, 2/23/90, A, C, a, b, 90000329

Gramelspacher-Gutzweiler House, 11th and Main Sts., Jasper, 2/26/83, C, b, 83000027

Huntingburg Town Hall and Fire Engine House, 311 Geiger St., Huntingburg, 5/12/75, A, C, g, 75000016

Lemmon's Church and Cemetery, Portersville Rd. E of jct. with Co. Rd. 750W, Portersville vicinity, 6/04/92, A, C, a, 92000674

Opel, John, House, St. James St., Jasper vicinity, 10/04/84, C, 84000009

Shiloh Meeting House and Cemetery, SE of Ireland on 150 North Rd., Ireland vicinity, 7/29/82, A, a, d, 82000035

St. Joseph Catholic Church, 1215 N. Newton St., Jasper, 9/30/80, A, C, a, 80000033

Elkhart County

Beardsley, Albert R., House, 302 E. Beardsley Ave., Elkhart, 11/28/78, C, 78000030

Bickel, Emmanuel C., House, 614 Bower St., Elkhart, 11/14/79, B, 79000014

Bonneyville Mills, 2.5 mi. E of Bristol on CR 131, Bristol vicinity, 10/22/76, A, 76000020

Bristol—Washington Township School, 304 W. Vistula St., Bristol, 8/29/91, A, C, 91001164

Buescher Band Instrument Company Building, 225 E. Jackson Ave., Elkhart, 9/22/86, A, 86002714

Coppes, Frank and Katharine, House, 302 E. Market St., Nappanee, 11/29/90, B, C, 90001783

Downtown Nappanee Historic District, Main and Market Sts., Nappanee, 3/08/90, A, 90000324

Elkhart County Courthouse, Courthouse Sq., Goshen, 4/10/80, A, C, 80000034

Goshen Carnegie Public Library, 202 N. 5th St., Goshen, 2/17/83, C, 83000028

Goshen Historic Distriict, Bounded by Pike, RR, Cottage, Plymouth, Main, Purl, the Canal, and Second Sts., Goshen, 2/17/83, A, C, a, 83000029

Green Block, 109-115 E. Lexington, Elkhart, 7/17/80, C, 80000035

Lerner Theatre, 401 S. Main St., Elkhart, 10/02/80, A, C, 80000036

Miller, Arthur, House, 253 E. Market St., Nappanee, 4/02/92, C, 92000184

Monteith, Mark L. and Harriet E., House, 871 E. Beardsley Ave., Elkhart, 12/26/85, B, C, 85003124

Rohrer, Joseph J., Farm, 24394 Co. Rd. 40, Goshen vicinity, 2/23/90, A, C, 90000330

St. John of the Cross Episcopal Church, Rectory and Cemetery, 601 and 611 E. Vistula Rd., Bristol, 9/17/80, A, C, a, d, 80000037

Stahly—Nissley—Kuhns Farm, 1600 W. Market St., Nappanee, 11/29/90, A, C, 90001793

Violett, William N., House, 3004 S. Main St., Goshen vicinity, 9/20/84, B, C, 84001026

Young Women's Christian Association, 120 W. Lexington Ave., Elkhart, 3/21/91, A, C, 91000257

Fayette County

Canal House, 111 E. 4th St., Connersville, 7/16/73, A, C, 73000016

Elmhurst, S. of Connersville on IN 121, Connersville vicinity, 4/11/77, A, B, C, 77000014

Lowry, William, House, Kniese Rd., Bentonville vicinity, 2/11/82, C, 82000036

Ranck, Thomas, Round Barn, N of Brownsville on CR 500 N., Brownsville vicinity, 1/11/83, C, 83000030

Floyd County

Culbertson Mansion, 914 E. Main St., New Albany, 6/28/74, B, C, 74000019

Farnsley, Gabriel, House, N of Bridgeport off IN 111, Bridgeport vicinity, 9/23/82, C, 82000037

Jersey Park Farm, Off Cunningham Sarles and Borden Rds., Galena vicinity, 3/01/84, C, 84001027

Mansion Row Historic District, Main St. between State and 15th Sts. and Market St. between 7th and 11th Sts., New Albany, 5/09/83, A, C, 83000123

New Albany and Salem Railroad Station, Pearl and Oak Sts., New Albany, 1/12/84, A, C, 84001031

Scribner House, 106 E. Main St., New Albany, 11/09/77, B, 77000015

Yenowine-Nichols-Collins House, 5118 State Rd. 64, New Albany, 5/12/75, A, B, C, 75000017

Fountain County

Attica Downtown Historic District, Roughly, Perry St. between Jackson and Ferry Sts. and Main and Mill Sts. between Third and Brady Sts., Attica, 9/16/93, A, C, 93000951

Brady Street Historic District, Roughly bounded by S. Perry, E. Jackson, S. Council and E. Pike Sts., Attica, 12/07/90, A, C, 90001785

Carnegie Library of Covington, 622 S. Fifth St., Covington, 4/03/89, A, C, 89000239

Hesler, Clinton F., Farm, Co. Rd. 450 S. between 200 E. and 300 E., Veedersburg vicinity, 7/13/89, A, B, C, 89000770

Milford, Marshall M., House, 414 E. Main St., Attica, 1/26/89, C, 88003037

Old East Historic District, 400 block of E. Washington St. and the 400 and 500 blocks of E. Monroe St., Attica, 11/28/90, C, 90001784

Sewell, William C. B., House, 602 E. Washington St., Covington, 10/11/84, C, 84000027

Franklin County

Brookville Historic District, Bounded by E and W fork of Whitewater River and IN 101, Brookville, 7/25/75, A, C, 75000018

Franklin County Seminary, 412 5th St., Brookville, 3/28/74, C, 74000020

Little Cedar Grove Baptist Church, US 52 at Little Cedar Rd., Brookville vicinity, 3/22/90, A, C, a, 90000366

Metamora Historic District, Roughly bounded by US 52, Columbia St., the Whitewater Canal, Duck Cr., Mount St. and Main St., Metamora, 12/07/92, A, C, 92001646

Oldenburh Historic District, Bounded roughly by Sycamore, church land woods, Indiana, and Water Sts., and Gehring Farm, Oldenburg, 3/03/83, A, C, 83000031

Shafer, Joseph, Farm, NE of Brookville on Flinn Road, Brookville vicinity, 8/26/82, C, 82000038

Whitewater Canal Historic District, From Laurel Feeder Dam to Brookville, Metamora, 6/13/73, A, 73000272

Fulton County

Brackett, Lyman M., House, 328 W. 9th St., Rochester, 9/27/84, B, C, 84001036

Haimbaugh, John, Round Barn [Round and Polygonal Barns of Indiana MPS], Jct. of IN 25 and Co. Rd. 400N, Rochester vicinity, 4/02/93, A, C, 93000192

Leedy, Bert, Round Barn [Round and Polygonal Barns of Indiana MPS], Jct. of Co. Rd. 375N and US 31, SW side, Rochester vicinity, 4/02/93, A, C, b, 93000182

Prill School, NW of Akron, Akron vicinity, 12/10/81, A, 81000012

Smith, John W., House, 730 Pontiac St., Rochester, 7/26/79, C, 79000015

Utter—Gerig Round Barn, Near jct. of Co. Rds. 825 E. and 100 N., Akron vicinity, 12/18/90, A, C, 90001927

Gibson County

Cockrum, William M., House, 627 W. Oak St., Oakland City, 9/13/78, B, C, 78000031

Gibson County Courthouse, Town Square, Princeton, 9/27/84, C, 84001038

Haubstadt State Bank, 101 S. Main St., Haubstadt, 12/27/84, A, C, 84000489

Mussel Knoll Archeological Site (12GI11), Address Restricted, Skelton vicinity, 3/18/86, D, 86000454

Trippett—Glaze—Duncan Farm, IN 65 E of Patoka, Patoka vicinity, 5/28/93, A, C, 93000470

Weber Village Archaeological Site (12 Gi 13), Address Restricted, Skelton vicinity, 9/12/85, D, 85002131

Grant County

Cumberland Covered Bridge, CR 1000 over Mississinewa River, Matthews, 5/22/78, C, 78000032

Grant County Jail and Sheriff's Residence, 215 E. 3rd St., Marion, 11/19/90, A, C, 83004526

Patterson, J.W., House, 203 E. Washington St., Fairmount, 11/14/79, A, 79000016

Patterson, J.W., House and Office (Boundary Increase), 209 E. Washington St., Fairmount, 1/18/85, B, 85000088

Swayzee, Aaron, House, 224 N. Washington St., Marion, 6/16/83, C, 83000124

Webster, George, Jr. and Marie Daugherty, House, 926 S. Washington St., Marion, 6/17/92, A, B, NHL, 92000678

West Ward School, 210 W. North A St., Gas City, 12/19/85, C, 85003226

Wilson, J. Woodrow, House, 723 W. Fourth St., Marion, 8/11/88, B, C, 88001218

Greene County

Osborn Site, Address Restricted, Bloomfield vicinity, 5/12/75, D, 75000019

Richland—Plummer Creek Covered Bridge, Baseline Rd. over Plummer Cr., Bloomfield vicinity, 6/10/93, A, C, g, 93000466

Scotland Hotel, Jct. of Main and Jackson Sts., NE corner, Scotland, 5/27/93, A, 93000467

Hamilton County

Conner, William, House, 13400 Allisonville Rd., Fishers, 2/08/80, A, C, 80000038

Craig, William Houston, House, 1250 E. Conner St., Noblesville, 5/24/90, C, b, 90000808

Craycraft, Daniel, House, 1095 E. Conner St., Noblesville, 1/04/89, C, 88003040

Davenport-Bradfield House, 106 E. 2nd St., Sheridan, 1/18/85, B, C, 85000089

Hamilton County Courthouse Square, Bounded by Logan, 8th, 9th, and Conner Sts., Noblesville, 5/10/78, A, C, g, 78000033

Harrell, Dr. Samuel, House, 399 N. 10th St., Noblesville, 3/01/84, B, C, 84001040

Kinzer, John, House, E of Carmel on SR 234, Carmel vicinity, 9/05/75, A, C, 75000020

Newby, Micah, House, 1149 W. One Hundred Sixteenth St., Carmel vicinity, 6/20/86, B, C, 86001349

Noblesville Commercial Historic District, Roughly bounded by Clinton, 10th, Maple and 8th Sts., Noblesville, 12/19/91, A, C, 91001862

Potter's Covered Bridge, Allisonville Rd. across the White R., Noblesville vicinity, 12/19/91, A, C, 91001866

Roads Hotel, 150 E. Main St., Atlanta, 12/30/87, A, C, 87002187

Stone, Judge Earl S., House, 107 S. 8th St., Noblesville, 12/08/78, C, 78000034

Hancock County

Greenfield Courthouse Square Historic District, Roughly bounded by North, Hinchman, South and Pennsylvania Sts., Greenfield, 3/07/85, A, C, 85000455

Lilly Biological Laboratories, W of Greenfield off U.S. 40, Greenfield vicinity, 11/23/77, A, C, g, 77000016

Littleton, Frank, Round Barn [Round and Polygonal Barns of Indiana MPS], Address Restricted, Mount Comfort vicinity, 4/02/93, A, C, 93000184

Riley, James Whitcomb, House, 250 W. Main St., Greenfield, 9/28/77, B, c, 77000017

Harrison County

Corydon Battle Site, S of Corydon on IN 135, Corydon vicinity, 7/09/79, A, e, 79000017

Corydon Historic District, Corydon, Corydon, 8/28/73, A, C, 73000017

Corydon Historic District (Boundary Increase), Roughly bounded by Summit, Maple & Walnut Sts., College Ave., Chestnut, Capitol, Poplar, Water, Beaver & Mulberry Sts., Corydon, 6/27/89, A, B, C, 89000243

Kintner House Hotel, 201 S. Capital, Corydon, 1/12/87, C, 87000099

Kintner-McGrain House, 740 N. Capital Ave., Corydon, 8/03/83, C, 83000032

Kintner-Withers House, S. of Laconia on Kintner Bottoms Rd., Laconia vicinity, 11/28/80, C, 80000039

Swan's Landing Archeological Site (12HR304), Address Restricted, New Amsterdam vicinity, 4/02/87, D, 87000517

Hendricks County

Hendricks County Jail and Sheriff's Residence, 170 S. Washington St., Danville, 6/30/83, A, 83000125

Wilson-Courtney House, 10 Cartersburg Rd., Danville, 2/09/84, C, 84001044

Henry County

Grose, Gen. William, House, 614 S. 14th St., New Castle, 6/23/83, C, 83000034

Guyer Opera House, U.S. 40, Lewisville, 12/06/79, A, 79000018

Hedrick, John W., House, 506 High St., Middletown, 12/27/84, B, C, 84000491

Henry County Courthouse, Courthouse Sq., New Castle, 4/02/81, C, 81000013

Hinshaw, Elias, House, 16 W. Main St., Knightstown, 5/03/84, C, 84001045

Knightstown Academy, Cary St., Knightstown, 9/29/76, B, C, 76000022

Knightstown Historic District, Roughly bounded by Morgan, Adams, Third, and McCullum Sts., Knightstown, 5/22/86, A, C, 86001104

New Castle Archeological Site, Address Restricted, New Castle vicinity, 4/26/76, D, 76000023

New Castle Commercial Historic District, Roughly bounded by Fleming and 11 Sts., Central Ave. and the Norfolk & Western RR tracks, New Castle, 12/19/91, A, C, 91001868

Whitelock, Henry F., House and Farm, IN 38, Shirley vicinity, 12/22/83, A, C, 83003565

Howard County

Haynes, Elwood, House, 1915 S. Webster St., Kokomo, 9/20/84, B, 84001054

Hy-Red Gasoline Station, 203 E. Main St., Greentown, 9/01/83, A, C, 83000035

Kokomo City Building, 221 W. Walnut St., Kokomo, 6/04/81, C, 81000014

Learner Building, 107-111 E. Sycamore St., Kokomo, 9/20/84, A, C, 84001055

Seiberling Mansion, 1200 W. Sycamore St., Kokomo, 12/16/71, B, C, 71000006

Smith, Henry W., House, 5 mi. (8 km) W of Kokomo, Kokomo vicinity, 3/09/79, B, C, 79000019

Huntington County

Chief Richardville House and Miami Treaty Grounds, W. of Huntington on US 24 & IN 9/37, Huntington vicinity, 9/16/85, A, B, D, 85002446

German Reformed Church, 202 Etna Ave., Huntington, 4/11/85, C, a, 85000724

Hotel LaFontaine, 200 W. State St., Huntington, 2/09/84, A, C, 84001056

Huntington Courthouse Square Historic District, Roughly bounded by State, Court and Cherry Sts., Park Dr. and the alley between Warren and Guilford Sts., Huntington, 9/04/92, A, 92001163

Kline, John and Minerva, Farm, 2715 East 400 North, Huntington vicinity, 12/22/88, A, C, 88003038

Moore/Carlew Building, 400 and 410-418 N. Jefferson St., Huntington, 9/01/83, C, 83000036

Purviance, Samuel, House, 326 S. Jefferson, Huntington, 6/13/86, B, C, a, 86001266

Snider, S.C., and George McFeeley Polygonal Barn [Round and Polygonal Barns of Indiana MPS], IN 9/37 1/2 mi. S of jct. with Division Rd., Huntington vicinity, 4/02/93, A, C, 93000185

Taylor-Zent House, 715 N. Jefferson St., Huntington, 2/11/82, C, 82000041

William Street School, 521 William St., Huntington, 6/26/86, A, C, 86001390

Jackson County

Farmers Club, 105 S. Chestnut St., Seymour, 8/11/83, A, C, 83000037

First Presbyterian Church, 301 N. Walnut St., Seymour, 12/19/91, C, a, 91001867

Low Spur Archeological Site (12J87), Address Restricted, Seymour vicinity, 5/01/87, D, 87000646

Sand Hill Archeological Site 12J62, Address Restricted, Seymour vicinity, 9/07/82, D, 82004914

Wheeler, Frank, Hotel, Jct. of Second and Main Sts., Freetown, 8/29/91, C, 91001161

Jasper County

Independence Methodist Church, SE of Wheatfield, Wheatfield vicinity, 3/05/82, A, a, 82000042

Jasper County Courthouse, W. Washington St., Rensselaer, 6/16/83, C, 83000126

St. Joseph Indian Normal School, St. Joseph's College Campus off U.S. 231, Rensselaer vicinity, 6/19/73, A, 73000018

Jay County

Floral Hall, W. Votaw and Moton Sts., Portland, 9/01/83, A, C, 83000038

Grouping of Religious Buildings at Trinity, NE of Portland, Portland vicinity, 10/23/80, A, C, a, 80000040

Jay County Courthouse, U.S. 27, Portland, 5/12/81, C, 81000016

Rankin, Rebecca, Round Barn [Round and Polygonal Barns of Indiana MPS], IN 18, 1/4 mi. W of jct. with Co. Rd. 75E, Poling vicinity, 4/02/93, A, C, 93000189

Redkey Historic District, Roughly, High St. between Oak and Meridian Sts., Redkey, 9/17/92, A, C, 92001168

Jefferson County

Crowe-Garritt House, 172 Crowe St., Hanover, 11/10/80, B, 80000041

Eleutherian College, IN 250, Lancaster, 12/15/93, A, C, 93001410

Hendricks, Thomas A., Library, College Dr. (Campus Rd.), Hanover, 2/26/82, A, C, 82000043

Jefferson County Jail, Courthouse Sq., Madison, 6/18/73, C, 73000019

Madison Historic District, Madison, Madison, 5/25/73, A, C, 73000020

Oakdale School, Morgan Rd., Jefferson Proving Ground, Madison vicinity, 5/14/93, A, C, 93000432

Jennings County

Vernon Historic District, 1 mi. S of North Vernon on IN 317, North Vernon vicinity, 8/27/76, C, 76000024

Johnson County

Edinburgh Commercial Historic District, Roughly bounded by Thompson and Main Sts., the alley N of Main Cross St. and the Conrail RR tracks, Edinburgh, 6/28/91, A, C, 91000789

Franklin College Library (Shirk Hall), 600 E. Monroe St., Franklin, 10/29/75, C, 75000021

Franklin College-Old Main, 600 E. Monroe St., Franklin, 10/29/75, A, C, 75000022

Franklin Commercial Historic District, Roughly E. & W. Court St., Jefferson, Monroe, Main, Franklin, 7/13/89, A, C, 89000773

Johnson County—Continued

Greenwood Commercial Historic District, 172–332 W. Main St. and 147–211 S. Madison Ave., Greenwood, 6/14/91, A, C, 91000792

Herriott House, 696 N. Main St., Franklin, 7/15/82, A, C, 82000044

Johnson County Courthouse Square, Courthouse Sq., Franklin, 4/16/81, A, C, 81000017

Martin Place Historic District, N and S sides of Martin Pl. between Graham Ave. and Water St., 500, 498, and 450 N. Main Sts., Franklin, 6/12/87, C, 87000951

Masonic Temple, 135 N. Main St., Franklin, 12/27/91, C, 91001863

Van Nuys Farm, IN 144, Hopewell, 2/12/87, C, 87000100

Zeppenfeld, August, House, 300 W. Jefferson St., Franklin, 12/30/87, C, 87002188

Knox County

Ebner-Free House, 120 Locust, Vincennes, 3/21/85, C, b, 85000601

Fort Knox II Site, Address Restricted, Vincennes vicinity, 3/24/82, A, D, 82000045

George Rogers Clark National Historical Park, 2nd St., S of U.S. 50, Vincennes, 10/15/66, C, f, g, NPS, 66000007

Harrison, William Henry, Home, 3 W. Scott St., Vincennes, 10/15/66, B, NHL, 66000018

Kixmiller's Store, Carlise and Indianapolis Sts., Freelandville, 12/08/78, A, C, 78000035

Old Cathedral Complex, 205 Church St., Vincennes, 8/17/76, C, a, 76000025

Old State Bank, N. 2nd St., Vincennes, 10/09/74, A, C, 74000021

Pyramid Mound (12k14), Address Restricted, Vincennes vicinity, 5/12/75, D, 75000023

Territorial Capitol of Former Indiana Territory, Bounded by Harrison, 1st, Scott, and Park Sts., Vincennes, 7/02/73, A, C, b, 73000021

Vincennes Historic District, Vincennes, Vincennes, 12/31/74, A, C, 74000022

Kosciusko County

East Fort Wayne Street Historic District, 503–613 E. Fort Wayne St., Warsaw, 5/27/93, C, 93000472

Hall Farm, Jct. of 600 N and 400 W, Clunette, 9/16/92, A, C, 92001164

Kosciusko County Jail, Main and Indiana Sts., Warsaw, 12/08/78, C, 78000036

Leesburg Historic District, 100 block of E. and W. Van Buren St., Leesburg, 5/27/93, A, C, 93000465

Orr, Robert, Polygonal Barn [Round and Polygonal Barns of Indiana MPS], IN 13, 1/2 mi. N of jct. with Co. Rd. 150N, North Webster vicinity, 4/02/93, A, C, 93000190

Pierceton Historic District, N. First St. from Catholic St. to the Conrail RR tracks, Pierceton, 9/04/92, A, C, 92001147

Pound, John, Store, Jct. of Armstrong Rd. and Second St., Oswego, 6/17/92, A, C, b, 92000672

Silver Lake Historic District, 100 blocks of N. and S. Jefferson and E. and W. Main Sts., Silver Lake, 9/04/92, A, C, 92001148

Warsaw Courthouse Square Historic District, Bounded by Center, N. Lake, Main, and Indiana Sts., Warsaw, 3/01/82, A, C, 82000046

Warsaw Courthouse Square Historic District (Boundary Increase), Roughly bounded by W. Main, W. Lake, Center and S. Indiana Sts. and the alleys behind Indiana, Market, Lake and Main Sts, Warsaw, 9/21/93, A, C, 93000952

Warsaw Cut Glass Company, 505 S. Detroit St., Warsaw, 3/01/84, A, 84001059

Winona Lake Historic District, Roughly bounded by Kings Hwy., Chestnut Ave., Twelfth St. and Park Ave., Winona Lake, 12/10/93, A, B, C, a, 93001411

Zimmer, Justin, House, 2513 E. Center St., Warsaw, 12/19/91, B, C, 91001865

La Porte County

Barker, John H., Mansion, 631 Washington St., Michigan City, 10/10/75, C, 75000027

Downtown LaPorte Historic District, Roughly bounded by State, Jackson, Maple and Chicago Sts., LaPorte, 9/15/83, A, C, 83000039

MUSKEGON Shipwreck Site, Address Restricted, Michigan City vicinity, 4/26/89, A, C, D, 89000290

Michigan City East Pierhead Light Tower and Elevated Walk, E side of entrance to Michigan City Harbor, Michigan City, 2/17/88, A, C, 88000069

Michigan City Lighthouse, Washington Park, Michigan City, 11/05/74, A, C, 74000023

Morrison, Francis H., House, 1217 Michigan Ave., LaPorte, 12/06/84, C, 84000492

Orr, William, House, 4076 W. Small Rd., LaPorte vicinity, 3/22/84, C, 84001063

Pinehurst Hall, 3042 N. U.S. 35, LaPorte, 6/03/76, C, 76000027

Ridgeway, Marion, Polygonal Barn [Round and Polygonal Barns of Indiana MPS], IN 35 N of jct. with Crescent Dr., LaPorte, 5/27/93, A, C, 93000464

Smith, Everel S., House, 56 W. Jefferson St., Westville, 12/12/90, B, C, 90001794

Washington Park, Roughly bounded by Lake Michigan, Krueger St., Trail Cr., Lakeshore Dr., Heisman Harbor Rd. and Browne Basin Rd., Michigan City, 6/26/91, A, C, 91000793

Lagrange County

La Grange County Courthouse, Detroit St., La Grange, 7/17/80, A, C, 80000042

Olde Store (John O'Ferrell Store), West and 2nd Sts., Mongo, 10/29/75, A, C, 75000024

Williams, Samuel P., House, 101 South St., Howe, 8/11/80, B, C, 80000043

Yoder, Menno, Polygonal Barn [Round and Polygonal Barns of Indiana MPS], Co. Rd. 250N, 3/4 mi. W of jct. with IN 5, Shipshewana vicinity, 4/02/93, A, C, 93000191

Lake County

Buckley Homestead, 3606 Belshaw Rd., Lowell vicinity, 12/06/84, A, C, 84000503

Gary Land Company Building, 4th Ave. and Pennsylvania St., Gary, 5/08/79, A, b, 79000021

Halsted, Melvin A., House, 201 E. Main St., Lowell, 12/08/78, B, C, 78000037

Hobart Carnegie Library, 706 E. 4th St., Hobart, 7/15/82, C, 82000047

Hoosier Theater Building, 1329–1335 One Hundred-nineteenth St., Whiting, 2/18/87, A, C, 87000069

Knights of Columbus Building, 333 W. 5th Ave., Gary, 3/01/84, C, 84001065

Lake County Courthouse, Public Sq., Crown Point, 5/17/73, A, C, g, 73000073

Lake County Sheriff's House and Jail, 232 S. Main St., Crown Point, 1/04/89, A, C, 88003039

Lassen Hotel, 7808 W. 138th Pl., Cedar Lake, 7/07/81, A, a, b, 81000019

Marktown Historic District, Bounded by Pine, Riley, Dickey, and 129th Sts., East Chicago, 2/20/75, A, C, 75000025

Meyer, Joseph Ernest, House, 1370 Joliet St., Dyer, 3/01/84, B, C, 84001068

Miller Town Hall, Jct. Miller Ave., Old Hobart Rd., and Grand Blvd., Gary, 7/07/78, A, C, 78000038

Pennsylvania Railroad Station, 1001 Lillian St., Hobart, 3/01/84, A, 84001070

State Bank of Hammond Building, 5444-5446 Calumet Ave., Hammond, 9/27/84, A, C, 84001072

West Fifth Avenue Apartments Historic District, Roughly 5th Ave. from Taft to Pierce St., Gary, 5/17/84, A, C, 84001076

Whiting Memorial Community House, 1938 Clark St., Whiting, 2/08/80, A, 80000044

Wood, John, Old Mill, E of Merrillville on IN 330, Merrillville, 10/10/75, A, C, c, 75000026

Lawrence County

Bono Archaeological Site (12 Lr 194), Address Restricted, Bono vicinity, 5/30/85, D, 85001166

Indiana Limestone Company Building, 405 I St., Bedford, 12/21/93, A, C, 93001412

Mitchell Opera House, 7th and Brooks Sts., Mitchell, 4/02/81, A, 81000020

Norton, C. S., Mansion, 1415 15th St., Bedford, 6/22/76, C, 76000026

Williams Bridge, SW of Williams on CR 11, Williams vicinity, 11/09/81, C, 81000018

Madison County

Anderson Bank Building, 931 Meridan St., Anderson, 8/30/84, A, C, 84001078

Carnegie Public Library, 32 W. 10th St., Anderson, 3/21/85, A, C, 85000603

Crawford—Whitehead—Ross House, 510 W. Main St., Madison, 11/27/92, C, 92001648

Fussell, Solomon, Farm, IN 38 E of jct. with Co. Rd. 150W, Pendleton vicinity, 6/04/92, A, C, 92000675

Gruenewald House, 626 N. Main St., Anderson, 10/08/76, C, 76000028

Makepeace, George, House, 5 W. Main St., Chesterfield, 3/21/85, A, C, 85000596

Mounds State Park, 3 mi. E of Anderson on IN 32, Anderson vicinity, 1/18/73, D, 73000022

Paramount Theater Building, 1124 Meridian St., Anderson, 8/29/91, A, C, 91001165

West Central Historic District, Roughly bounded by Brown-Delaware, 10th, John, and 13th Sts., Anderson, 12/06/84, A, C, 84000515

West Eighth Street Historic District, Roughly bounded by 7th, 9th, Jackson, and Henry Sts., Anderson, 8/27/76, A, B, C, 76000029

Marion County

Administration Building, Indiana Central University, Otterbein and Hanna Ave., Indianapolis, 3/15/84, C, 84001081

Alameda [Apartments and Flats of Downtown Indianapolis TR], 37 W. St. Clair St., Indianapolis, 9/15/83, A, C, 83000052

Alexandra [Apartments and Flats of Downtown Indianapolis TR], 402-416 N. New Jersey St. and 332-336 E. Vermont St., Indianapolis, 9/15/83, A, C, 83000053

Allison Mansion, 3200 Cold Spring Rd, Indianapolis, 12/18/70, B, C, 70000006

Ambassador [Apartments and Flats of Downtown Indianapolis TR], 39 E. 9th St., Indianapolis, 9/15/83, A, C, 83000054

Anderson—Thompson House, 6551 Shelbyville Rd., Indianapolis, 3/26/87, B, C, 87000502

Apple, Christopher, House, 11663 Pendleton Pike, Oaklandon, 9/17/80, C, 80000055

Aston Inn, 6620 N. Michigan Rd., Indianapolis, 12/26/85, A, C, 85003125

Athenaeum (Das Deutsche Haus), 401 E. Michigan St., Indianapolis, 2/21/73, A, C, 73000032

Attucks, Crispus, High School, 1140 N. Martin Luther King, Jr., St., Indianapolis, 1/04/89, A, C, g, 88003043

Ayres, L. S. Annex Warehouse, Maryland St., Indianapolis, 4/23/73, C, 73000033

Baker [Apartments and Flats of Downtown Indianapolis TR], 310 N. Alabama St. and 341 Massachusetts Ave., Indianapolis, 9/15/83, A, C, 83000055

Balmoral Court, 3055 N. Meridian St., Indianapolis, 11/27/92, C, 92001647

Bals-Wocher House, 951 N. Delaware St., Indianapolis, 12/17/79, C, 79000033

Bates-Hendricks House, 1526 S. New Jersey St., Indianapolis, 4/11/77, B, C, 77000143

Benton House, 312 S. Downey Ave., Indianapolis, 3/20/73, C, 73000034

Bethel A. M. E. Church, 414 W. Vermont St., Indianapolis, 3/21/91, A, a, 91000269

Blacherne [Apartments and Flats of Downtown Indianapolis TR], 402 N. Meridian St., Indianapolis, 9/15/83, A, B, C, 83000058

Broad Ripple Park Carousel, Meridian and Thirtieth Sts., Indianapolis, 2/27/87, A, NHL, 87000839

Burton [Apartments and Flats of Downtown Indianapolis TR], 821-823 N. Pennsylvania St., Indianapolis, 9/15/83, A, C, 83000059

Buschmann, William, Block, 968–972 Fort Wayne Ave., Indianapolis, 8/26/88, B, C, 88001225

Butler Fieldhouse, Butler University campus, 49th St., and Boulevard Pl., Indianapolis, 12/22/83, A, C, g, NHL, 83003573

Byram-Middleton House, 1828 N. Illinois St., Indianapolis, 5/09/83, C, 83000127

Cathcart [Apartments and Flats of Downtown Indianapolis TR], 103 E. 9th St., Indianapolis, 9/15/83, A, C, 83000060

Central Library (Indianapolis-Marion County Public Library), 40 E. St. Clair St., Indianapolis, 8/28/75, C, 75000045

Chadwick [Apartments and Flats of Downtown Indianapolis TR], 1005 N. Pennsylvania St., Indianapolis, 9/15/83, A, C, 83000061

Chatham-Arch Historic District, Roughly bounded by I-65, College Ave., 10th, 11th, North, New Jersey, Cleveland and East Sts., Indianapolis, 3/13/80, A, C, 80000057

Christ Church Cathedral, 131 Monument Circle, Indianapolis, 7/10/73, C, a, 73000035

Christamore House, 502 N. Tremont St., Indianapolis, 3/21/85, A, 85000597

Circle Theater, 45 Monument Circle, Indianapolis, 6/16/80, A, C, 80000058

City Market, 222 E. Market St., Indianapolis, 3/27/74, A, C, 74000030

Coburn, Henry P., Public School No. 66, 604 E. Thirty-eighth St., Indianapolis, 6/13/86, A, C, 86001267

Cole Motor Car Company, 730 E. Washington St., Indianapolis, 3/03/83, A, B, 83000128

Colonial [Apartments and Flats of Downtown Indianapolis TR], 126 E. Vermont St. and 402-408 N. Delaware St., Indianapolis, 9/15/83, A, C, 83000062

Columbia Club, 121 Monument Circle, Indianapolis, 1/27/83, A, C, 83000063

Cottage Home Historic District, Dorman and St. Clair Sts., Indianapolis, 2/23/90, C, 90000328

Cotton-Ropkey House, 6360 W. 79th St., Indianapolis, 3/22/84, B, C, 84001086

Coulter Flats, 2161 N. Meridian St., Indianapolis, 5/31/90, A, C, 90000807

Crown Hill Cemetery, Boulevard Pl., W. 32nd St., and Northwestern Ave., Indianapolis, 2/28/73, C, d, 73000036

Dartmouth [Apartments and Flats of Downtown Indianapolis TR], 221 E. Michigan St., Indianapolis, 9/15/83, A, C, 83000064

Delaware Court [Apartments and Flats of Downtown Indianapolis TR], 1001-1015 N. Delaware St., Indianapolis, 9/15/83, A, C, 83000065

Delaware Flats [Apartments and Flats of Downtown Indianapolis TR], 120-128 N. Delaware St., Indianapolis, 9/15/83, A, C, 83000066

Devonshire [Apartments and Flats of Downtown Indianapolis TR], 412 N. Alabama St., Indianapolis, 9/15/83, A, C, 83000067

Emelie [Apartments and Flats of Downtown Indianapolis TR], 326-330 N. Senate Ave.and 301-303 W. Vermont St., Indianapolis, 9/15/83, A, C, 83000068

Esplanade Apartments, 3015 N. Pennsylvania St., Indianapolis, 6/16/83, C, 83000129

Fidelity Trust Building, 148 E. Market St., Indianapolis, 9/27/80, A, B, C, 80000382

Fletcher Place Historic District, Roughly bounded by RR tracks, I 65-70 East St. and Virginia Ave., Indianapolis, 2/01/82, A, B, 82000061

Fletcher, Calvin I., House, 1031 N. Pennsylvania St., Indianapolis, 3/01/84, C, 84001089

Forest Hills Historic District, Bounded by the Monon RR Tracks, Kessler Blvd., College and Northview Aves., Indianapolis, 6/30/83, A, C, g, 83000130

Fort Harrison Terminal Station, Building 616, Fort Harrison, Lawrence, 3/16/84, A, C, 84001127

General German Protestant Orphans Home, 1404 S. State St., Indianapolis, 5/17/84, A, C, 84001129

Glencoe [Apartments and Flats of Downtown Indianapolis TR], 627 N. Pennsylvania St., Indianapolis, 9/15/83, A, C, 83000069

Glossbrenner, Alfred M., Mansion, 3202 N. Meridian St., Indianapolis, 2/19/82, C, 82000062

Golden Hill Historic District, Roughly bounded by 36th St., 37th St., Governors Rd., the rear lot lines behind Golden Hill Dr., and Central Canal, Indianapolis, 8/29/91, B, C, 91001163

Graham, William H. H., House, 5432 University Ave., Indianapolis, 7/15/82, B, C, 82001857

Grover [Apartments and Flats of Downtown Indianapolis TR], 615 N. Pennsylvania St., Indianapolis, 9/15/83, A, B, C, 83000056

Hammond Block (Budnick's Trading Mart), 301 Massachusetts Ave., Indianapolis, 1/09/79, C, 79000034

Hanna-Ochler-Elder House, 3801 Madison Ave., Indianapolis, 12/01/78, C, 78000046

Harriett [Apartments and Flats of Downtown Indianapolis TR], 124-128 N. East St., Indianapolis, 9/15/83, A, C, 83000057

Harrison, Benjamin, House, 1204 N. Delaware St., Indianapolis, 10/15/66, B, NHL, 66000010

Haughville Historic District, Roughly bounded by 10th St., Belleview Pl., Walnut St. and Concord St., Indianapolis, 12/09/92, A, 92001652

Haverstick, Hiram A., Farmstead, 7845 Westfield Blvd., Indianapolis, 12/26/85, C, 85003126

Heier's Hotel, 10–18 S. New Jersey St., Indianapolis, 9/22/86, A, C, 86002704

Herron-Morton Place Historic District, Roughly bounded by Central Ave., 16th, Pennsylvania, and 22nd Sts., Indianapolis, 6/16/83, A, C, 83000131

Marion County—Continued

Hollingsworth House, 6054 Hollingsworth Rd., Indianapolis, 4/13/77, A, C, 77000019

Holy Rosary—Danish Church Historic District, Roughly bounded by Virginia Ave., I-65/70, and S. East St., Indianapolis, 3/13/86, A, a, 86000327

Horace Mann Public School No. 13, 714 E. Buchanan St., Indianapolis, 6/26/86, C, 86001389

Hotel Washington, 32 E. Washington St., Indianapolis, 7/17/80, A, C, 80000056

Independent Turnverein, 902 N. Meridan St., Indianapolis, 12/22/83, C, 83003577

Indiana Avenue Historic District, 500 blk. of Indiana Ave. between North St., Central Canal, Michigan, and West Sts., Indianapolis, 6/12/87, A, C, 87000912

Indiana Oxygen Company, 435 S. Delaware St., Indianapolis, 3/26/87, A, C, 87000545

Indiana School for the Deaf, 1200 E. 42nd St., Indianapolis, 6/27/91, A, C, 91000790

Indiana State Capitol, W. Washington St., Indianapolis, 8/28/75, A, C, g, 75000043

Indiana State Museum, 202 N. Alabama St., Indianapolis, 10/29/74, A, C, 74000029

Indiana Theatre, 134 W. Washington St., Indianapolis, 1/29/79, A, C, 79000035

Indiana World War Memorial Plaza, Bounded by St. Clair, Pennsylvania, Vermont, and Meridian Sts., Indianapolis, 9/25/89, C, f, g, 89001404

Indianapolis Motor Speedway, 4790 W. 16th St., Speedway, 3/07/75, A, C, g, NHL, 75000044

Indianapolis News Building, 30 W. Washington St., Indianapolis, 3/07/84, A, C, 84001133

Indianapolis Union Railroad Station, 39 Jackson Pl., Indianapolis, 7/19/74, A, C, 74000032

Indianapolis Union Station—Wholesale District, Roughly bounded by Capitol Ave., Maryland, Delaware and South Sts., Indianapolis, 7/14/82, A, C, 82000067

Irvington Historic District, Roughly bounded by Ellenberger Pk., Pleasant Run Creek, Arligton Ave., B & O RR tracks, and Emerson Ave., Indianapolis, 5/29/87, A, C, 87001031

Johnson-Denny House, 4456 N. Park Ave., Indianapolis, 8/24/79, A, C, b, 79000036

Jordan, Arthur, Memorial Hall, 4600 Sunset Ave., Indianapolis, 6/30/83, C, 83000134

Julian—Clark House, 115 S. Audubon Rd., Indianapolis, 6/20/86, B, C, 86001335

Kuhn, Charles, House, 340 W. Michigan St., Indianapolis, 4/13/89, C, b, 89000237

Laurel and Prospect District [Fountain Square Commercial Areas TR], 1335 to 1419 E. Prospect St., Indianapolis, 6/30/83, A, C, 83000132

Levey, Louis, Mansion, 2902 N. Meridian St., Indianapolis, 12/22/78, C, 78000047

Lockefield Garden Apartments, 900 Indiana Ave., Indianapolis, 2/28/83, A, C, g, 83000133

Lockerbie Square Historic District, Indianopolis, Indianapolis, 2/23/73, C, 73000038

Lockerbie Square Historic District Amendment (Boundary Increase), Bounded by Michigan and Davidson Sts., New York Ave., and New Jersey St., Indianapolis, 7/28/87, A, C, a, 87000734

Lodge [Apartments and Flats of Downtown Indianapolis TR], 829 N. Pennsylvania St., Indianapolis, 9/15/83, A, C, 83000073

Lombard Building, 22-28 E. Washington St., Indianapolis, 6/01/82, C, 82000068

Majestic Building, 47 S. Pennsylvania St., Indianapolis, 11/20/80, C, 80000059

Marott Hotel, 2625 N. Meridian St., Indianapolis, 6/25/82, A, C, 82000063

Marott's Shoes Building, 18-20 E. Washington St., Indianapolis, 5/09/83, C, 83000135

Martens [Apartments and Flats of Downtown Indianapolis TR], 348-356 Indiana Ave., Indianapolis, 9/15/83, A, C, 83000070

Massachusetts [Apartments and Flats of Downtown Indianapolis TR], 421-427 Massachusetts Ave., Indianapolis, 9/15/83, A, C, 83000071

Massachusetts Avenue Commercial District, Roughly bounded by one block to either side of Massachusetts Ave. from Delaware St. to I 65, Indianapolis, 12/02/82, A, C, 82000064

Mayleeno [Apartments and Flats of Downtown Indianapolis TR], 416-418 E. Vermont St., Indianapolis, 9/15/83, A, C, 83000072

McCormick Cabin Site, Off U.S. 40, Indianapolis, 5/28/81, A, 81000028

McKay [Apartments and Flats of Downtown Indianapolis TR], 611 N. Pennsylvania St., Indianapolis, 9/15/83, A, C, 83000074

Meier, George Philip, House, 3128 N. Pennsylvania St., Indianapolis, 9/23/82, C, 82000065

Merchants National Bank and Annex, 11 S. Meridian St. and 7 E. Washington St., Indianapolis, 2/19/82, A, C, 82000066

Meridian Park Historic District, Bounded by 34th St., Washington Blvd., 30th St., and Pennsylvania St., Indianapolis, 2/23/90, C, 90000326

Michigan Road Toll House, 4702 Michigan Rd., NW., Indianapolis, 8/07/74, A, 74000031

Military Park, Bounded by West, New York, and Blackford Sts. and the canal, Indianapolis, 10/28/69, A, 69000002

Minor House, 2034 N. Capitol Ave., Indianapolis, 4/07/87, A, 87000512

Moore, Thomas, House, 4200 Brookville Rd., Indianapolis, 3/15/84, A, C, 84001137

Morris-Butler House, 1204 N. Park Ave., Indianapolis, 2/20/73, C, 73000037

Morrison Block (M. O'Connor Grocery Wholesalers), 47 S. Meridian St., Indianapolis, 11/15/79, A, C, 79000038

Mt. Pisgah Lutheran Church, 701 N. Pennsylvania St., Indianapolis, 11/28/78, C, 78000048

Myrtle Fern [Apartments and Flats of Downtown Indianapolis TR], 221 E. 9th St., Indianapolis, 9/15/83, A, C, 83000080

New Augusta Historic District, Roughly E. 71st St., E. 74th St., Coffman Rd., New Augusta Rd., Indianapolis, 7/12/89, A, 89000780

Nickel Plate Road Steam Locomotive No. 587, Off 1st Ave., Beech Grove, 11/28/84, A, C, 84000313

North Meridian Street Historic District, 4000-5694 and 4001-5747 N. Meridian St., Indianapolis, 9/22/86, C, 86002695

Northside Historic District, Roughly bounded by I-65, 16th, Bellefontaine, and Pennsylvania Sts., Indianapolis, 3/24/78, A, B, C, 78000049

Northside Historic District (Boundary Increase), Pennsylvania and 16th Sts., Indianapolis, 9/27/84, A, C, 84001144

Old Pathology Building, 3000 W. Washington St. (Central State Hospital), Indianapolis, 4/25/72, A, 72000011

Oxford [Apartments and Flats of Downtown Indianapolis TR], 316 E. Vermont St., Indianapolis, 9/15/83, A, C, 83000081

Pearson Terrace, 928-940 N. Alabama St., Indianapolis, 3/01/84, A, C, 84001187

Pennsylvania [Apartments and Flats of Downtown Indianapolis TR], 919 N. Pennsylvania St., Indianapolis, 9/15/83, A, C, 83000082

Pierson-Griffiths House, 1028 N. Delaware St., Indianapolis, 5/22/78, C, 78000050

Plaza [Apartments and Flats of Downtown Indianapolis TR], 902 N. Pennsylvania St. and 36 E. 9th St., Indianapolis, 9/15/83, A, C, 83000083

Propylaeum, The (John W. Schmidt House), 1410 N. Delaware St., Indianapolis, 6/19/73, A, C, 73000039

Prosser House, 1454 E. 10th St., Indianapolis, 9/05/75, C, 75000046

Ransom Place Historic District, Roughly bounded by 10th, St. Clair, West and Camp Sts., Indianapolis, 12/10/92, A, 92001650

Reserve Loan Life Insurance Company, 429 N. Pennsylvania St., Indianapolis, 2/23/90, A, C, 90000331

Riley, James Whitcomb, House, 528 Lockerbie St., Indianapolis, 10/15/66, B, NHL, 66000799

Rink [Apartments and Flats of Downtown Indianapolis TR], 401 N. Illinois St., Indianapolis, 9/15/83, A, C, 83000075

Rink's Womens Apparel Store, 29 N. Illinois St., Indianapolis, 9/27/84, A, C, 84001188

Roberts Park Methodist Episcopal Church, 401 N. Delaware St., Indianapolis, 8/19/82, C, a, 82000069

Saint James Court, 2102–2108 N. Meridian St., Indianapolis, 2/18/87, C, 87000071

Savoy [Apartments and Flats of Downtown Indianapolis TR], 36 W. Vermont St., Indianapolis, 9/15/83, A, C, 83000076

Schnull-Rauch House, 3050 N. Meridian St., Indianapolis, 11/14/79, A, B, C, 79000037

Scottish Rite Cathedral, 650 N. Meridian St., Indianapolis, 6/06/83, C, 83000136

Selig's Dry Goods Company Building, 20 W. Washington St., Indianapolis, 5/17/84, A, C, 84001190

Seville, The, 1701 N. Illinois St., Indianapolis, 6/22/87, C, 87000976

Shelton [Apartments and Flats of Downtown Indianapolis TR], 825 N. Delaware St., Indianapolis, 9/15/83, A, C, 83000077

Shortridge High School, 3401 N. Meridian St., Indianapolis, 9/15/83, C, 83000078

Sid-Mar [Apartments and Flats of Downtown Indianapolis TR], 401-403 Massachusetts Ave., Indianapolis, 9/15/83, A, C, 83000079

Marion County—Continued

Sommer, August, House, 29 E. McCarty St., Indianapolis, 11/28/80, C, 80000060

Spink [Apartments and Flats of Downtown Indianapolis TR], 230 E. 9th St., Indianapolis, 9/15/83, A, C, 83000084

St. John's Church and Rectory, 121 S. Capitol Ave., 124 and 126 W. Georgia St., Indianapolis, 9/17/80, A, C, a, 80000061

St. Mary's Catholic Church, 317 N. New Jersey St., Indianapolis, 11/09/77, A, C, a, 77000020

State Soldiers and Sailors Monument, Monument Circle, Indianapolis, 2/23/73, C, f, 73000040

State and Prospect District [Fountain Square Commercial Areas TR], State Ave. and Prospect St., Indianapolis, 6/30/83, A, 83000137

Stewart Manor (Charles B. Sommers House), 3650 Cold Spring Rd, Indianapolis, 10/08/76, C, 76000033

Stumpf, George, House, 3225 S. Meridian St., Indianapolis, 5/14/79, C, 79000039

Sylvania [Apartments and Flats of Downtown Indianapolis TR], 801 N. Pennsylvania St. and 108 E. St. Clair St., Indianapolis, 9/15/83, A, C, 83000086

Taylor Carpet Company Building, 26 W. Washington St., Indianapolis, 3/01/84, A, C, 84001192

Test Building, 54 Monument Circle, Indianapolis, 6/16/83, C, 83000138

The Buckingham, 3101–3119 N. Meridian St., Indianapolis, 11/27/92, B, C, 92001649

Thompson, William N., House, 4343 N. Meridian St., Indianapolis, 6/01/82, A, B, 82000070

U.S. Arsenal (Arsenal Technical High School), 1500 E. Michigan St., Indianapolis, 5/19/76, A, C, g, 76000034

U.S. Courthouse and Post Office, 46 E. Ohio St., Indianapolis, 1/11/74, A, C, g, 74000033

University Park, Bounded by Vermont, Pennsylvania, New York, and Meridian Sts., Indianapolis, 9/07/89, A, C, 89001405

Vera and the Olga, 1440 and 1446 N. Illinois St., Indianapolis, 9/27/84, C, 84001196

Vienna [Apartments and Flats of Downtown Indianapolis TR], 306 E. New York St., Indianapolis, 9/15/83, A, C, 83000087

Virginia Avenue District [Fountain Square Commercial Areas TR], Roughly Virginia Ave. from Grove Ave. To Prospect and Morris Sts., Indianapolis, 6/30/83, A, 83003442

Walker, Madame C. J., Building, 617 Indiana Ave., Indianapolis, 7/17/80, A, B, C, NHL, 80000062

West Washington Street Pumping Station, 801 W. Washington St., Indianapolis, 7/17/80, A, C, 80000063

Whittier, John Greenleaf, School, No. 33, 1119 N. Sterling St., Indianapolis, 5/28/81, C, 81000029

Wil-Fra-Mar [Apartments and Flats of Downtown Indianapolis TR], 318-320 E. Vermont St., Indianapolis, 9/15/83, A, C, 83000088

Wilson [Apartments and Flats of Downtown Indianapolis TR], 643 Ft. Wayne Ave., Indianapolis, 9/15/83, A, C, 83000089

Woodruff Place, Roughly bounded by 1700-2000 E. Michigan and E. 10th Sts., Indianapolis, 7/31/72, C, 72000012

Wyndham [Apartments and Flats of Downtown Indianapolis TR], 1040 N. Delaware St., Indianapolis, 9/15/83, A, C, 83000090

YWCA Blue Triangle Residence Hall, 725 N. Pennsylvania St., Indianapolis, 9/27/88, A, C, 88001574

Marshall County

Dietrich-Bowen House, 304 N. Center St., Bremen, 11/21/78, B, C, g, 78000023

East Laporte Street Footbridge, Spans Yellow River, Plymouth, 7/23/81, C, 81000001

Marshall County Court House, 117 W. Jefferson St., Plymouth, 6/30/83, C, 83000139

Plymouth Fire Station, 220 N. Center St., Plymouth, 7/09/81, A, C, 81000002

Woodbank, 2738 East Shore Lane, Lake Maxinkuckee, Culver vicinity, 12/02/82, C, 82000022

Miami County

B-17G "Flying Fortress" No. 44-83690, Heritage Museum Foundation, off US 31, Grissom Air Force Base, 6/29/93, A, C, 93000540

Brownell Block/Senger Dry Goods Company Building, Broadway and 5th Sts., Peru, 9/01/83, A, 83000007

Cole, James Omar, House, 27 E. 3rd St., Peru, 3/01/84, B, C, 84001198

Godfroy, Francis, Cemetery, IN 124, Peru vicinity, 3/01/84, B, D, d, 84001203

Paw Paw Creek Bridge No. 52, Paw Paw Pike, Chili vicinity, 9/30/83, A, C, 83000008

Wallace Circus and American Circus Corporation Winter Quarters, 2.5 mi. SE of Peru, Peru vicinity, 2/27/87, A, NHL, 87000837

Monroe County

Abel, Elias, House, 317 N. Fairview St., Bloomington, 2/19/82, C, 82000023

Blair-Dunning House, 608 W. 3rd St., Bloomington, 2/10/83, B, 83000009

Bloomington City Hall, 122 S. Walnut St., Bloomington, 9/14/89, A, C, 89001413

Cantol Wax Company Building, 211 N. Washington St., Bloomington, 5/24/90, A, C, 90000812

Cochran-Helton-Lindley House, 405 N. Rogers St., Bloomington, 6/20/79, C, 79000010

Courthouse Square Historic District, Roughly bounded by 7th, Walnut and 4th Sts. and College Ave., Bloomington, 12/18/90, A, C, 90001931

Epsilon II Archeological Site (12MO133), Address Restricted, Bloomington vicinity, 3/25/86, D, 86000524

Honey Creek School, NE of Bloomington on Low Gap Rd., Bloomington vicinity, 9/20/78, A, 78000024

Illinois Central Railroad Freight Depot, 301 N. Morton St., Bloomington, 6/23/83, A, 83000113

Kappa V Archeological Site (12MO301), Address Restricted, Bloomington vicinity, 3/31/86, D, 86000630

Mitchell, Joseph, House, 7008 Kercham Rd., Smithville vicinity, 6/13/86, C, 86001268

Monroe Carnegie Library, 200 E. 6th St., Bloomington, 3/08/78, C, 78000025

Monroe County Courthouse, Courthouse Sq., Bloomington, 10/08/76, C, 76000012

Morgan House, 532 N Walnut St., Bloomington, 3/03/83, C, 83000140

Nichols, J.L., House and Studio, 820 N. College Ave., Bloomington, 9/27/84, C, 84001207

North Washington Street Historic District, Roughly bounded by E. 10th, E. 8th, N. Walnut and N. Lincoln Sts., Bloomington, 3/14/91, A, C, 91000271

Old Crescent, The, Indiana University Campus, Bloomington, 9/08/80, A, C, 80000028

Princess Theatre, 206 N. Walnut St., Bloomington, 6/16/83, C, 83000112

Prospect Hill Historic District, Roughly bounded by 3rd, Rogers, Smith and Jackson Sts., Bloomington, 3/14/91, C, 91000272

Seminary Square Park, College Ave. and E. 2nd St., Bloomington, 9/19/77, A, 77000012

Stout, Daniel, House, NW of Bloomington off IN 46, on Maple Grove Rd., Bloomington vicinity, 11/30/73, A, C, 73000012

Wicks Building, 116 W. Sixth St., Bloomington, 3/03/83, C, 83000141

Wylie, Andrew, House, 307 E. 2nd St., Bloomington, 4/18/77, B, C, 77000013

Montgomery County

Ashby, SW of Ladoga on CR 350E, Ladoga vicinity, 7/17/80, C, 80000029

Crawfordsville Commercial Historic District, Roughly bounded by Walnut, North and Water Sts. and Wabash Ave., Crawfordsville, 3/25/92, A, C, 92000183

Darlington Covered Bridge, Co. Rds. 500N and 500E over Sugar Cr., Darlington vicinity, 11/28/90, A, C, 90001782

Elston Grove Historic District, Roughly bounded by Green, College and Main Sts. and the Monon RR tracks, Crawfordsville, 3/25/92, B, C, 92000187

Elston, Col. Isaac C., House, 400 E. Wabash Ave., Crawfordsville, 4/15/82, C, 82000025

Fisher, William, Polygonal Barn [Round and Polygonal Barns of Indiana MPS], Co. Rd. 850N just E of jct. with Co. Rd. 800E, Bowers vicinity, 4/02/93, A, C, 93000188

Lane, Henry S., House, 212 S. Water St., Crawfordsville, 11/23/81, C, 81000003

Linden Depot, 202 N. James St., Linden, 11/28/90, A, 90001781

Montgomery County—Continued

McClelland-Layne House, 602 Cherry St., Crawfordsville vicinity, 9/12/85, C, 85002135

Montgomery County Jail and Sheriff's Residence, 225 N. Washington St., Crawfordsville, 5/01/75, A, C, 75000007

Saint John's Episcopal Church, 212 S. Green St., Crawfordsville, 3/21/85, A, C, a, b, 85000598

Schlemmer, Otto, Building, 129-131 N. Green St., Crawfordsville, 11/28/78, B, C, 78000026

Wallace, Gen. Lew, Study, Pike St. and Wallace Ave., Crawfordsville, 5/11/76, B, NHL, 76000013

Yount's Woolen Mill and Boarding House, 3729 Old SR 32 West, Crawfordsville, 1/04/89, A, C, 88003041

Morgan County

Bradford Estate, 5040 IN 67 North, Martinsville, 4/03/89, A, C, 89000236

Cross School, Voiles and Townsend Rds., Martinsville vicinity, 6/16/83, A, C, 83000142

Martinsville High School Gymnasium, 759 S. Main St., Martinsville, 7/30/81, A, C, 81000004

Martinsville Vandalia Depot, 210 N. Marion St., Martinsville, 3/14/91, A, C, 91000268

Mooresville Friends Academy Building, 244 N. Monroe St., Mooresville, 5/12/75, A, C, 75000008

Wilbur School, Wilbur Rd., Wilbur, 5/27/93, A, 93000473

Newton County

Ade, George, House, E of Brook off IN 16, Brook vicinity, 9/27/76, A, B, C, 76000014

Noble County

Ahavas Shalom Reform Temple, 503 S. Main St., Ligonier, 6/16/83, C, a, 83000143

Iddings—Gilbert—Leader—Anderson Block, 105–113 N. Main St., Kendallville, 7/21/87, A, C, 87000544

Ligonier Historic District, Roughly bounded by Conrail right-of-way, Smith, Union, College, & Grand Sts., Ligonier, 10/23/87, A, C, 87001798

Ligonier Historic District, Roughly bounded by Conrail right-of-way, Smith, Union, College, & Grand Sts., Ligonier, 10/23/87, A, C, 87002116

Noble County Courthouse, Courthouse Sq., Albion, 5/12/81, A, C, 81000005

Noble County Sheriff's House and Jail, W. Main and Oak Sts., Albion, 12/27/82, C, 82000026

Porter, Gene Stratton, Cabin, SE of Rome City off IN 9, Rome City vicinity, 6/27/74, B, C, 74000015

Stone's Trace, US 33 and IN 5, Ligonier vicinity, 5/24/84, A, C, b, 84001212

Straus, Jacob, House, 210 S. Main St., Ligonier, 6/04/79, B, C, 79000011

Orange County

Braxtan, Thomas Newby, House, 210 N. Gospel St., Paoli, 6/29/89, A, C, 89000777

Lindley, Thomas Elwood, House, Willow Creek Rd., Paoli, 9/12/85, C, 85002132

Orange County Courthouse, Public Sq., Paoli, 2/24/75, A, C, 75000009

West Baden National Bank, IN 56 N at the West Baden Springs Hotel entrance, West Baden Springs, 9/16/93, A, C, 93000950

West Baden Springs Hotel, W of IN 56, West Baden, 6/27/74, A, C, NHL, 74000016

Owen County

Allison—Robinson House, 3 N. Montgomery St., Spencer, 6/03/93, B, C, b, 93000468

Beem, David Enoch, House, 635 W. Hillside Ave., Spencer, 7/13/89, C, 89000771

CCC Recreation Building—Nature Museum [New Deal Resources in Indiana State Parks MPS], McCormick's Creek SP, W of jct. of IN 43 and IN 46, Spencer vicinity, 3/18/93, A, C, 93000176

Ennis Archaeological Site (12 OW 229), Address Restricted, Ellettsville vicinity, 5/30/85, D, 85001167

McCormick's Creek State Park Entrance and Gatehouse [New Deal Resources in Indiana State Parks MPS], McCormick's Creek SP, W of jct. of IN 43 and IN 46, Spencer vicinity, 3/18/93, A, C, 93000175

Moffett-Ralston House, 1.5 mi. NE of Patricksburg on Bixler Rd., Patricksburg vicinity, 5/12/75, B, C, 75000010

Spencer Town Hall and Fire Station, 84 S. Washington St., Spencer, 8/19/82, C, 82000027

Stone Arch Bridge over McCormick's Creek [New Deal Resources in Indiana State Parks MPS], McCormick's Creek SP, W of jct. of IN 43 and IN 46, Spencer vicinity, 3/18/93, A, C, 93000177

Parke County

Arch in the Town of Marshall, Main and Guion Sts., Marshall, 12/26/85, C, 85003127

Beeson Bridge [Parke County Covered Bridges TR], N of Marshall, Marshall vicinity, 12/22/78, A, C, 78003447

Big Rocky Fork Bridge [Parke County Covered Bridges TR], SE of Mansfield on Greencastle Rd., Mansfield vicinity, 12/22/78, A, C, 78000383

Billie Creek Bridge [Parke County Covered Bridges TR], E of Rockville off US 36, Rockville vicinity, 12/22/78, A, C, 78000384

Bowsher Ford Bridge [Parke County Covered Bridges TR], N of Rockville, Rockville vicinity, 12/22/78, A, C, 78000385

Bridgeton Bridge [Parke County Covered Bridges TR], N of Bridgeton, Bridgeton, 12/22/78, A, C, 78000386

Bridgeton Historic District, Roughly bounded by the N bank of Big Raccoon Cr., George and Clark Sts., Mill Alley and the alley E of Main St., Bridgeton, 9/04/92, A, 92001167

Catlin Bridge [Parke County Covered Bridges TR], N of Rockville off US 41, Rockville vicinity, 12/22/78, A, C, 78000387

Conley's Ford Bridge [Parke County Covered Bridges TR], E of Bridgeton, Bridgeton vicinity, 12/22/78, A, C, 78000388

Cox Ford Bridge [Parke County Covered Bridges TR], N of Rockville off US 41, Rockville vicinity, 12/22/78, A, C, 78000390

Crooks Bridge [Parke County Covered Bridges TR], N of Bridgeton, Bridgeton vicinity, 12/22/78, A, C, 78000391

Ewbank, Lancelot C., House, Parke Co. Rds. 102E between 1200N and 300E, Tangier vicinity, 9/26/88, C, 88001578

Harry Evans Bridge [Parke County Covered Bridges TR], SE of Mecca off Old Greencastle Rd., Mecca vicinity, 12/22/78, A, C, 78000392

Hill, William, Polygonal Barn [Round and Polygonal Barns of Indiana MPS], School St., Bloomingdale, 4/02/93, A, C, 93000186

Jackson Bridge [Parke County Covered Bridges TR], N of Rockville, Rockville vicinity, 12/22/78, A, C, 78000393

Jeffries Ford Bridge [Parke County Covered Bridges TR], SW of Bridgeton, Bridgeton vicinity, 12/22/78, A, C, 78000394

Leatherwood Station Bridge [Parke County Covered Bridges TR], E of Montezuma, Montezuma vicinity, 12/22/78, A, C, 78000397

Lusk Home and Mill Site, Off IN 47 in Turkey Run State Park, Marshall, 10/29/74, B, C, 74000017

Mansfield Bridge [Parke County Covered Bridges TR], Off IN 59, Mansfield, 12/22/78, A, C, 78000399

Mansfield Roller Mill [Grain Mills in Indiana MPS], Mansfield Rd. at Big Raccoon Cr., Mansfield, 12/07/90, A, 90001788

Marshall Bridge [Parke County Covered Bridges TR], N of Rockville, Rockville vicinity, 12/22/78, A, C, 78000400

McAllister Bridge [Parke County Covered Bridges TR], N of Bridgeton, Bridgeton vicinity, 12/22/78, A, C, 78000398

Mecca Bridge [Parke County Covered Bridges TR], Off US 41, Mecca, 12/22/78, A, C, 78000401

Melcher Bridge [Parke County Covered Bridges TR], E of Montezuma, Montezuma vicinity, 12/22/78, A, C, 78000402

Mill Creek Bridge [Parke County Covered Bridges TR], N of Rockville, Rockville vicinity, 12/22/78, A, C, 78000403

Narrows Bridge [Parke County Covered Bridges TR], N of Rockville Off IN 47, Rockville vicinity, 12/22/78, A, C, 78000404

Neet Bridge [Parke County Covered Bridges TR], N of Bridgeton, Bridgeton vicinity, 12/22/78, A, C, 78000405

Nevins Bridge [Parke County Covered Bridges TR], NW of Bridgeton, Bridgeton vicinity, 12/22/78, A, C, 78000406

Parke County—Continued

Phillips Bridge [Parke County Covered Bridges TR], SE of Montezuma off US 36, Montezuma vicinity, 12/22/78, A, C, 78000407

Portland Mills Bridge [Parke County Covered Bridges TR], W of Marshall off SR 47, Marshall vicinity, 12/22/78, A, C, b, 78000408

Rockville Historic District, Roughly bounded by Howard Ave. and Jefferson, High and College Sts., Rockville, 5/27/93, A, C, 93000471

Roseville Bridge [Parke County Covered Bridges TR], SE of Mecca off Old Greencastle Rd., Mecca vicinity, 12/22/78, A, C, 78000409

Rush Creek Bridge [Parke County Covered Bridges TR], N of Rockville, Rockville vicinity, 12/22/78, A, C, 78000410

Sim Smith Bridge [Parke County Covered Bridges TR], SE of Montezuma off US 36, Montezuma vicinity, 12/22/78, A, C, 78000411

State Sanitorium Bridge [Parke County Covered Bridges TR], E of Rockville off US 36, Rockville vicinity, 12/22/78, A, C, 78000412

Thorpe Ford Bridge [Parke County Covered Bridges TR], SE of Mecca on Rosedale Catlin Rd., Mecca vicinity, 12/22/78, A, C, 78000413

Wabash Township Graded School, S. Montezuma St., Mecca, 6/22/87, A, C, 87000950

West Union Bridge [Parke County Covered Bridges TR], N of Montezuma, Montezuma vicinity, 12/22/78, A, C, 78000414

Wilkins Mill Bridge [Parke County Covered Bridges TR], N of Rockville Off US 41, Rockville vicinity, 12/22/78, A, C, 78000415

York, W. H., Round Barn [Round and Polygonal Barns of Indiana MPS], Co. Rd. 249, 0.5 mi. S of Lodi, Lodi vicinity, 9/16/93, A, C, 93000949

Zacke Cox Bridge [Parke County Covered Bridges TR], SE of Mecca off US 41, Mecca vicinity, 12/22/78, A, C, 78000416

Perry County

Cannelton Cotton Mills, Bounded by Front, 4th, Washington, and Adams Sts., Cannelton, 8/22/75, A, C, NHL, 75000011

Cannelton Historic District, Roughly bounded by Richardson, Taylor, First, and Madison Sts., Cannelton, 2/12/87, A, C, 87000108

Hall of Tell City Lodge, No. 206, IOOF, 701 Main St., Tell City, 11/27/92, A, C, 92001654

Nester House, 300 Water St., Troy, 10/11/90, A, 90001486

Old Perry County Courthouse, Town Sq., Rome, 5/12/81, A, C, 81000006

Rickenbaugh House, SW of St. Croix in Hoosier National Forest, St. Croix vicinity, 4/06/84, C, 84001215

Rockhouse Cliffs Rock Shelters (12PE98; 12PE100), Address Restricted, Derby vicinity, 4/25/86, D, 86000918

St. Luke's Episcopal Church, Third and Washington Sts., Cannelton, 3/03/83, C, a, 83000144

Pike County

Palace Lodge, Center and Main Sts., Winslow, 2/23/84, A, C, 84001217

Porter County

Bailly, Joseph, Homestead, W of Porter on U.S. 20 in Indiana Dunes National Lakeshore, Porter vicinity, 10/15/66, B, C, a, d, NHL, NPS, 66000005

Beverly Shores South Shore Railroad Station, Broadway Ave. and US 12, Beverly Shores, 7/19/89, A, NPS, 89000411

Beverly Shores—Century of Progress Architectural District, 208, 210, 212, 214, and 215 Lake Front Dr., Beverly Shores, 6/30/86, A, C, b, NPS, 86001472

Coambs, Norris and Harriet, Lustron House, 411 Bowser Ave., Chesterton, 9/17/92, C, g, 92001165

Gilson, Clinton D., Barn, 522 W. 650 S, Hebron vicinity, 9/20/84, C, 84001229

Heritage Hall, Campus Mall, S. College Ave., Valparaiso, 7/12/76, A, 76000016

Immanuel Lutheran Church, 308 N. Washington St., Valparaiso, 2/19/82, C, a, 82000028

Loring, Dr. David J., Residence and Clinic, 102 Washington St., Valparaiso, 12/06/84, A, B, 84000520

Porter County Jail and Sheriff's House, 153 Franklin St., Valparaiso, 6/23/76, A, C, 76000017

Porter County Memorial Hall, 104 Indiana Ave., Valparaiso, 5/23/84, C, 84001231

Rose, David Garland, House, 156 Garfield St., Valparaiso, 7/17/80, C, b, 80000030

Valparaiso Downtown Commercial District, Roughly bounded by Jefferson, Morgan, Indiana, and Napoleon, Valparaiso, 2/23/90, A, C, 90000327

Weller House, 1200 North Rd., Chesterton vicinity, 4/22/82, C, 82000029

Posey County

Ashworth Archaeological Site (12 Po 7), Address Restricted, Hovey Lake vicinity, 9/12/85, D, 85002137

Bentel, George, House, Brewery and Granary St., New Harmony, 9/20/84, A, C, 84001224

Bozeman—Waters National Bank, 19 W. Main St., Poseyville, 10/01/87, C, 87001768

Epple, Ludwig, House, 520 Granary St., New Harmony, 6/21/84, A, C, 84001227

Gonnerman, William, House, 521 W. Second St., Mt. Vernon, 12/19/85, B, 85003192

Hagemann, Frederick and Augusta, Farm, Jct. of IN 62 and IN 69, SW corner, Mount Vernon, 3/18/93, A, C, 93000180

Hovey Lake Archaeological District, Address Restricted, Hovey Lake vicinity, 9/12/85, D, 85002130

I.O.O.F. and Barker Buildings, 402–406 Main St., Mt. Vernon, 9/12/85, A, C, 85002133

Mann Site, Address Restricted, Mt. Vernon vicinity, 10/01/74, D, 74000018

Murphy Archeological Site, Address Restricted, Mount Vernon vicinity, 5/12/75, D, 75000012

New Harmony Historic District, Main St. between Granary and Church Sts., New Harmony, 10/15/66, A, B, NHL, 66000006

Posey County Courthouse Square, 300 Main St., Mount Vernon, 1/04/89, A, C, f, 88003042

Scholle, Mattias, House, Tavern and Brewery Sts., New Harmony, 3/02/81, C, 81000007

Welborn Historic District, Roughly bounded by Ninth, Locust and 2nd Sts. and the alley between Walnut and Main Sts., Mt. Vernon, 3/25/92, A, C, 92000188

Pulaski County

Tepicon Hall [New Deal Resources in Indiana State Parks MPS], Tippecanoe River State Park, Winamac vicinity, 4/03/92, A, C, 92000189

Thompson, Dr. George W., House, 407 N. Market St., Winamac, 9/27/84, B, C, 84001233

Putnam County

Appleyard, Address Restricted, Greencastle vicinity, 2/23/90, B, 90000325

Boulders, The, 835 E. Washington St., Greencastle, 9/16/93, C, 93000948

Courthouse Square Historic District, Roughly bounded by College Ave., Walnut, Market, and Franklin Sts., Greencastle, 3/01/84, A, C, 84001237

East College of DePauw University, 300 Simpson St., Greencastle, 9/25/75, A, C, 75000047

Hirt, Alfred, House, W. Walnut Street Rd., Greencastle, 3/14/91, B, C, 91000274

McHaffie, Melville F., Farm, US 40, Stilesville vicinity, 12/22/83, A, C, 83003600

McKim Observatory, DePauw University, DePauw and Highbridge Aves., Greencastle, 12/22/78, A, C, 78000051

Nelson, F.P., House, 701 E. Seminary, Greencastle, 7/18/83, C, 83000092

O'Hair, James Edington Montgomery, House, US 231 1/2 mi. S of jct. with 500 North Rd., Brick Chapel vicinity, 1/13/92, C, 91001909

Putnamville Presbyterian Church, IN 243, Putnamville, 3/01/84, A, C, a, 84001242

Stoner, Lycurgus, House, Manhattan Rd., Greencastle vicinity, 9/12/85, C, 85002134

Van Arsdel, William C., House, 125 Wood St., Greencastle, 9/20/84, C, 84001246

Randolph County

Kerry, William, House, 501 N. Columbia St., Union City, 10/01/87, A, B, C, 87001776

Randolph County—Continued

Kirshbaum, Raphael, Building, NW corner Columbia and W. Pearl Sts., Union City, 5/24/90, A, C, 90000813

Stone, Gen. Asahel, Mansion, 201 W. Orange St., Winchester, 3/21/79, B, C, 79000040

Union City Passenger Depot, Howard St., Union City, 5/19/83, A, 83000145

Ripley County

Central House, IN 229, Napoleon, 9/23/82, A, 82000071

Conwell, Elias, House, Wilson St. and U.S. 421, Napoleon, 5/14/79, B, C, 79000041

Taylor, Fernando G., House, NE corner of Main and Tyson Sts., Versailles, 9/22/86, C, b, 86002710

Rush County

Arnold, Dr. John, Farm, W of Glenwood, Rushville vicinity, 9/14/89, A, B, C, 89001409

Durbin Hotel, 137 W. 2nd St., Rushville, 2/19/82, A, B, g, 82000072

Forsythe Covered Bridge [Kennedy, A. M., House and Covered Bridges of Rush County TR], SR 650, Rushville vicinity, 2/02/83, C, 83000094

Gowdy, John K., House, 619 N. Perkins St., Rushville, 12/10/93, B, C, 93001414

Hall-Crull Octagonal House, N of Rushville, Rushville vicinity, 5/10/84, C, 84001575

Harcourt, James F., House, Co. Rd. 500 W. at 750 S., Moscow vicinity, 9/14/89, A, C, 89001412

Kennedy, Archibald M., House [Kennedy, A. M., House and Covered Bridges of Rush County TR], SR 200, Rushville vicinity, 2/02/83, B, C, 83000095

Manche, Maurice W., Farmstead, Co. Rd. 900 W., Carthage vicinity, 9/14/89, A, C, 89001411

Melodeon Hall, 210 N. Morgan St., Rushville, 11/15/73, A, C, 73000041

Moscow Covered Bridge [Kennedy, A. M., House and Covered Bridges of Rush County TR], SR 875 and SR 625, Rushville vicinity, 2/02/83, C, 83000096

Norris Ford Covered Bridge [Kennedy, A. M., House and Covered Bridges of Rush County TR], SR 150, Rushville vicinity, 2/02/83, C, 83000097

Offutt Covered Bridge [Kennedy, A. M., House and Covered Bridges of Rush County TR], SR 550, Rushville vicinity, 2/02/83, C, 83000098

Reeves, Jabez, Farmstead, Co. Rd. 900 N., Rushville vicinity, 6/29/89, A, C, 89000776

Rush County Courthouse, Courthouse Sq., Rushville, 10/10/75, C, 75000048

Rushville Commercial Historic District, Roughly bounded by Fourth, N. Morgan, First and N. Perkins Sts., Rushville, 12/27/93, A, C, 93001416

Smith Covered Bridge [Kennedy, A. M., House and Covered Bridges of Rush County TR], SR 300, Rushville vicinity, 2/02/83, C, 83000099

Walnut Ridge Friends Meetinghouse, W of Carthage, Carthage vicinity, 3/01/84, A, a, 84001616

Washington, Booker T., School, 525 E. Seventh St., Rushville, 5/24/90, A, 90000809

Willkie, Wendell Lewis, House, 601 N. Harrison St., Rushville, 12/27/93, B, C, g, 93001415

Scott County

Scottsburg Depot, 43 S. Railroad St., Scottsburg, 8/29/91, A, 91001162

Shelby County

Cooper-Alley House, S of Waldron, Waldron vicinity, 7/07/82, C, 82000074

Hamilton, John, House, 132 W. Washington St., Shelbyville, 6/04/79, C, 79000043

Junction Railroad Depot, U.S. 52, Morristown, 11/14/79, A, C, b, 79000044

Liberty Township Schoolhouse No. 2, Jct. of IN 244 and Co. Rd. 600 E, Waldron vicinity, 9/04/92, A, C, 92001170

Rudicel, George, Polygonal Barn [Round and Polygonal Barns of Indiana MPS], Jct. of Co. Rt. 700S and Co. Rt. 400E, Waldron vicinity, 5/27/93, A, C, 93000463

Shelbyville Commercial Historic District, Roughly bounded by Broadway, Tompkins, Mechanic, and Noble Sts., Shelbyville, 8/09/84, A, C, 84001638

St. George Lutheran Church, IN 252, Edinburgh vicinity, 5/24/84, C, a, 84001627

West Side Historic District, Roughly bounded by W. Pennsylvania, N. Harrison, N. and S. Thompkins, W. Hendricks, Montgomery, & N. Conrey, Shelbyville, 2/09/90, A, C, 90000099

Spencer County

Brown-Kercheval House, 315 S. 2nd St., Rockport, 9/20/73, B, C, 73000045

Deutsch Evangelische St. Paul's Kirche, S of Santa Claus on Sante Fe Rd., Santa Claus vicinity, 9/27/84, C, a, 84001644

Jones, Col. William, House, W of Gentryville on Troy-Vincennes Rd., Gentryville vicinity, 5/12/75, B, C, 75000050

Lincoln Boyhood National Memorial, IN 162, Lincoln City, 10/15/66, A, B, C, d, e, f, g, NHL, NPS, 66000012

Sharp, Mathias, House, 319 S. 2nd. St., Rockport, 6/16/83, C, 83000148

St. Boniface Church, IN 545, Fulda, 10/23/80, C, a, 80000065

St. Joseph County

All American Bank Building [Downtown South Bend Historic MRA], 111 W. Washington, South Bend, 6/05/85, C, 85001202

Beiger House, 317 Lincolnway E., Mishawaka, 8/28/73, B, C, 73000042

Berteling Building [Downtown South Bend Historic MRA], 228 W. Colfax, South Bend, 6/05/85, C, 85001203

Blackstone-State Theater [Downtown South Bend Historic MRA], 212 S. Michigan, South Bend, 6/05/85, A, C, 85001204

Cathedral of St. James and Parish Hall [Downtown South Bend Historic MRA], 117 N. Lafayette and 115 N. Lafayette, South Bend, 6/05/85, C, a, 85001205

Central High School & Boys Vocational School [Downtown South Bend Historic MRA], 115 N. James Court, South Bend, 6/05/85, A, C, 85001206

Chapin Park Historic District, Roughly bounded by St. Joseph River, Main, Madison, Rex, Lindsey and William Sts., Leland and Portage Aves., South Bend, 2/04/82, A, C, 82000073

Chapin, Horatio, House, 601 Park Ave., South Bend, 8/11/80, C, c, 80000064

Citizens Bank [Downtown South Bend Historic MRA], 112 W. Jefferson, South Bend, 6/05/85, C, 85001207

Commercial Building [Downtown South Bend Historic MRA], 226 W. Colfax, South Bend, 6/05/85, C, 85001209

Dodge House, 415 Lincolnway E., Mishawaka, 9/08/78, B, C, 78000052

Eller-Hosford House, 722 Lincoln Way E., Mishawaka, 1/27/83, A, C, 83000101

Ellis—Schindler House, 900 Lincolnway W., Mishawaka, 12/18/90, C, b, 90001926

Farmers Security Bank [Downtown South Bend Historic MRA], 133 S. Main St., South Bend, 6/05/85, C, 85001210

Former First Presbyterian Church [Downtown South Bend Historic MRA], 101 S. Lafayette, South Bend, 6/05/85, C, a, 85001211

Hager House [Downtown South Bend Historic MRA], 415 W. Wayne, South Bend, 6/05/85, C, 85001212

Hinkle, W. R., and Co. [Downtown South Bend Historic MRA], 225 N. Lafayette, South Bend, 6/05/85, A, C, 85001213

Hoffman Hotel [Downtown South Bend Historic MRA], 120 W. LaSalle, South Bend, 6/05/85, A, C, 85001214

I & M Building [Downtown South Bend Historic MRA], 220 W. Colfax, South Bend, 6/05/85, C, 85001215

J. M. S. Building [Downtown South Bend Historic MRA], 108 N. Main, South Bend, 6/05/85, C, 85001216

Judie, James A., House, 1515 E. Jefferson Blvd., South Bend, 3/24/83, C, 83000146

Kamm and Schellinger Brewery, 100 Center St., Mishawaka, 10/11/79, A, C, 79000042

St. Joseph County—Continued

Kelley-Fredrickson House and Office Building, 233 N. Lafayette Blvd. and 314 W. LaSalle St., South Bend, 5/24/84, B, C, 84001619

Kerr, John G., Company [Downtown South Bend Historic MRA], 121 W. Colfax, South Bend, 6/05/85, C, 85001217

Knights of Columbus-Indiana Club [Downtown South Bend Historic MRA], 320 W. Jefferson, South Bend, 6/05/85, C, 85001218

Knights of Pythias Lodge [Downtown South Bend Historic MRA], 224 W. Jefferson, South Bend, 6/05/85, C, 85001219

LaSalle Annex [Downtown South Bend Historic MRA], 306 N. Michigan, South Bend, 6/05/85, A, C, 85001220

LaSalle Hotel [Downtown South Bend Historic MRA], 237 N. Michigan, South Bend, 6/05/85, A, C, 85001221

Lakeville High School, 601 N. Michigan St., Lakeville, 8/29/91, A, C, 91001166

Lawton, Chauncey N., House, 405 W. Wayne St., South Bend, 6/23/83, C, 83000116

Leeper, Samuel, Jr., House, 113 W. North Shore Dr., South Bend, 3/21/85, A, B, C, 85000600

Merrifield-Cass House, 816 E. Lincolnway, Mishawaka, 6/16/83, C, 83000147

Morey House [Downtown South Bend Historic MRA], 110–112 Franklin Pl., South Bend, 6/05/85, C, 85001222

Morey-Lampert House [Downtown South Bend Historic MRA], 322 Washington, South Bend, 6/05/85, C, 85001223

New Carlisle Historic District, Roughly bounded by Front, Arch, Chestnut and Bray Sts., New Carlisle, 12/14/92, A, C, 92001653

Northern Indiana Gas and Electric Company Building [Downtown South Bend Historic MRA], 221 N. Michigan, South Bend, 6/05/85, C, 85001225

O'Brien Electric Priming Company, 2001 W. Washington St., South Bend, 12/28/83, A, 83003756

Old Courthouse (Second St. Joseph County Courthouse), 112 S. Lafayette Blvd., South Bend, 9/04/70, A, C, b, 70000007

Oliver, Joseph D., House, 808 W. Washington Ave., South Bend, 8/28/73, B, C, 73000043

Palace Theater [Downtown South Bend Historic MRA], 211 N. Michigan, South Bend, 6/05/85, A, C, 85001226

Palais Royale Building, 113-105 W. Colfax Ave. and 201-209 N. Michigan St., South Bend, 7/21/83, A, C, 83000102

Second St. Joseph Hotel [Downtown South Bend Historic MRA], 117–119 W. Colfax, South Bend, 6/05/85, A, C, 85001227

South Bend Remedy Company [Downtown South Bend Historic MRA], 220 W. LaSalle, South Bend, 6/05/85, C, 85001228

Studebaker Clubhouse and Tree Sign, 32132 IN 2, New Carlisle, 9/18/85, A, C, g, 85002430

Summers-Longley House-Building [Downtown South Bend Historic MRA], 312–314 W. Colfax, South Bend, 6/05/85, C, 85001229

Third St. Joseph County Courthouse [Downtown South Bend Historic MRA], 105 S. Main St., South Bend, 6/05/85, A, C, 85001230

Tippecanoe Place, 620 W. Washington Ave., South Bend, 7/02/73, B, NHL, 73000044

Tower Building [Downtown South Bend Historic MRA], 216 W. Washington, South Bend, 6/05/85, C, 85001244

University of Notre Dame: Main and South Quadrangles, Off I-80/90, Notre Dame, 5/23/78, A, C, 78000053

Water Street/Darden Road Bridge, Over St. Joseph River at Darden Rd., South Bend vicinity, 3/21/85, A, C, b, 85000599

West Washington Historic District, Irregular pattern roughly bounded by Main St., Western Ave., W. LaSalle Ave., and McPherson St., South Bend, 1/17/75, A, C, 75000049

Starke County

Starke County Bridge No. 39, Jct. of Main and Water Sts., across the former Pennsylvania RR cut, Knox, 12/10/93, C, b, 93001413

Starke County Courthouse, Courthouse Sq., Knox, 11/12/86, A, C, 86003170

Steuben County

Combination Shelter [New Deal Resources in Indiana State Parks MPS], Pokagon State Park, Angola vicinity, 4/03/92, A, C, 92000190

Free Church, Old Road 1 N., Angola vicinity, 3/24/83, A, C, a, d, 83000149

Griffin, Cornish, Round Barn [Round and Polygonal Barns of Indiana MPS], 2015 SW. Fox Lake Rd., Pleasant Lake vicinity, 4/02/93, A, C, 93000187

Lords, William L., House, Clear Lake Rd., Fremont vicinity, 6/16/83, C, 83000114

Michael, Enos, House, 200 E. Toledo St., Fremont, 2/19/82, C, 82000075

Steuben County Courthouse, Public Sq., Angola, 5/12/75, A, C, 75000051

Steuben County Jail, 201 S. Wayne, Angola, 4/02/76, A, C, 76000035

Sullivan County

Daugherty-Monroe Archaeolgical Site (12SU13), Address Restricted, Graysville vicinity, 6/12/85, D, 85001246

Merom Site and Fort Azatlan, N of Merom, Merom vicinity, 5/12/75, D, d, 75000052

Sherman Building, 2–4 S. Court St., Sullivan, 9/22/86, C, 86002712

Union Christian College, 3rd and Philip Sts., Merom, 6/25/82, A, C, a, 82000076

Switzerland County

Eggleston, Edward and George Cary, House, 306 W. Main St., Vevay, 10/15/73, B, c, 73000046

Merit-Tandy Farmstead, NE of Patriot on IN 156, Patriot vicinity, 4/29/77, C, 77000021

Old Hoosier Theatre, Cheapside and Ferry Sts., Vevay, 3/01/82, A, C, 82000077

Wright, Thomas T., House, SW of Vevay on IN 56, Vevay vicinity, 12/10/80, C, 80000066

Tippecanoe County

Andrew, Jesse, House, 123 Andrew Pl., West Lafayette, 8/11/83, B, 83000103

Ball, Judge Cyrus, House, 402 S. 9th St., Lafayette, 5/03/84, B, C, 84001649

Battle Ground Historic District, Roughly bounded by Burnett Creek, Sherman Dr. and an open ridge on the SE, Battle Ground, 7/23/85, A, B, C, a, b, f, 85001639

Centennial Neighborhood District, Roughly bounded by Union, 3rd, 4th, Ferry, and 9th Sts., Lafayette, 6/16/83, A, C, a, g, 83003443

Christian, John E. and Catherine E., House, 1301 Woodland Ave., West Lafayette, 6/16/92, C, g, 92000679

Downtown Lafayette Historic District, Roughly bounded by 2nd, Ferry, 6th and South Sts., Lafayette, 11/28/80, A, C, 80000067

Ellsworth Historic District, Roughly bounded by Columbia, Norfolk & Western RR tracks, Alabama, Seventh, South and Sixth Sts., Lafayette, 12/30/86, C, 86003501

Ely, Homestead, 4106 E. 200 North, NE of Lafayette, Lafayette vicinity, 10/08/76, C, 76000036

Enterprise Hotel, 1015 Main St., Lafayette, 6/21/84, A, 84001650

Falley Home, 601 New York St., Lafayette, 7/15/82, C, 82000078

Farmers Institute, 4626 W. CR 660 S, Lafayette, 3/27/86, A, C, a, 86000609

Fort Ouiatenon, Address Restricted, Lafayette vicinity, 2/16/70, A, D, 70000008

Fowler, Moses, House, Corner of 10th and South Sts., Lafayette, 8/05/71, C, 71000009

Hershey House, E of Lafayette on East Rd., Lafayette vicinity, 11/28/78, B, C, 78000054

Indiana State Soldiers Home Historic District, N of Lafayette off IN 43, Lafayette vicinity, 1/02/74, A, C, 74000034

Marian Apartments, 615 North St., Lafayette, 6/30/83, C, 83000150

Mars Theatre, 11 N. 6th St., Lafayette, 1/26/81, A, C, 81000030

Perrin Historic District, Roughly bounded by Murdock Park, Sheridan Rd., Columbia, Main and Union Sts., Lafayette, 9/10/79, A, C, 79000045

Pierce, James, Jr., House, 4623 N., 140 W., West Lafayette, 6/17/82, C, 82000079

Potter, William, House, 915 Columbia St., Lafayette, 1/06/83, C, 83000104

Scott Street Pavilion, Columbian Park, Lafayette, 9/27/84, A, C, 84001656

Tippecanoe County—Continued

St. John's Episcopal Church, 315 N. 6th St., Lafayette, 9/20/78, C, a, 78000055

Stidham United Methodist Church, 5300 S. 175 West, Lafayette, 11/27/92, C, a, 92001651

Temple Israel, 17 S. 7th St., Lafayette, 2/19/82, C, a, 82000080

Tippecanoe Battlefield, 7 mi. NE of Lafayette on IN 225, Lafayette vicinity, 10/15/66, A, NHL, 66000013

Tippecanoe County Courthouse, Public Sq., Lafayette, 10/31/72, A, C, 72000013

Upper Main Street Historic District, Roughly bounded by Ferry St., 6th St., Columbia St., and the Norfolk and Western Railroad tracks, Lafayette, 5/24/90, A, C, 90000814

Waldron-Beck House and Carriage House, 829 N. 21st St., Lafayette, 2/09/84, C, 84001661

Ward, James H., House, 1116 Columbia St., Lafayette, 4/07/88, C, 88000385

Tipton County

Tipton County Courthouse, Public Sq., Tipton, 3/01/84, C, 84001665

Tipton County Jail and Sheriff's Home, 203 S. West St., Tipton, 5/17/84, A, C, 84001667

Union County

Union County Courthouse, Courthouse Sq., Liberty, 7/21/87, A, C, 87000103

Vanderburgh County

Albion Flats [Downtown Evansville MRA], 701 Court St., Evansville, 7/01/82, C, 82000093

Alhambra Theatorium, 50 Adams Ave., Evansville, 10/01/79, A, C, 79000047

American Trust and Savings Bank (Indiana Bank) [Downtown Evansville MRA], 524-530 Main St, Evansville, 7/01/82, C, 82000094

Angel Mounds, 8 mi. SE of Evansville, Angel Mounds State Memorial, Evansville vicinity, 10/15/66, D, a, e, NHL, 66000124

Auto Hotel Building [Downtown Evansville MRA], 111-115 SE 3rd St., Evansville, 4/06/84, A, C, 84001673

Barrett's Britz Building [Downtown Evansville MRA], 415 Main St., Evansville, 4/06/84, C, 84001679

Bayard Park Historic District, Roughly bounded by Gum, Kentucky, Blackford and Garvin Sts., Evansville, 6/27/85, C, 85001373

Bedford, William, Sr., House, 838 Washington Ave., Evansville, 11/28/78, C, 78000056

Bernardin—Johnson House, 17 Johnson Pl., Evansville, 6/27/89, B, C, 89000238

Bitterman Building, 202-204 Main St., Evansville, 9/22/80, C, 80000068

Boehne, John W., House, 1119 Lincoln Ave., Evansville, 2/17/83, B, C, 83000105

Buckingham Apartments [Downtown Evansville MRA], 314-316 SE 3rd St., Evansville, 7/01/82, C, 82000082

Building at 223 Main Street [Downtown Evansville MRA], 223 Main St., Evansville, 7/01/82, C, 82000083

Busse House [Downtown Evansville MRA], 120 SE 1st St., Evansville, 7/01/82, C, 82000084

Cadick Apartments (Plaza Building) [Downtown Evansville MRA], 118 SE 1st St., Evansville, 7/01/82, C, 82000085

Carpenter, Willard, House, 405 Carpenter St., Evansville, 2/10/78, B, C, 78000057

Central Library [Downtown Evansville MRA], 22 SE 5th St., Evansville, 7/01/82, C, 82000086

Citizens National Bank [Evansville MRA], 329 Main St., Evansville, 7/01/82, C, 82000087

Conner's Bookstore [Downtown Evansville MRA], 611-613 Main St., Evansville, 4/06/84, A, C, 84001684

Court Building (Furniture Building) [Downtown Evansville MRA], 123-125 NW 4th St., Evansville, 7/01/82, C, 82000088

Culver Historic District, Roughly bounded by Madison Ave., Riverside Dr., Emmett and Venice Sts., Evansville, 6/01/84, A, C, 84001691

Daescher Building [Downtown Evansville MRA], 12-12 1/2 SE 2nd St., Evansville, 7/01/82, C, 82000089

Eagles Home [Downtown Evansville MRA], 221 NW 5th St., Evansville, 7/01/82, C, c, 82000090

Evansville Brewing Company [Downtown Evansville MRA], 401 NW 4th St., Evansville, 7/01/82, A, 82000091

Evansville College, 1800 Lincoln Ave., Evansville, 2/03/83, A, C, 83000106

Evansville Journal News [Downtown Evansville MRA], 7-11 NW 5th St., Evansville, 7/01/82, A, C, 82000092

Evansville Municipal Market, 813 Pennsylvania St., Evansville, 12/22/83, C, 83003771

Evansville Post Office, 100 block N.W. 2nd St., Evansville, 7/02/71, C, 71000010

Fellwock Garage [Downtown Evansville MRA], 315 Court St., Evansville, 4/06/84, A, C, 84001701

Firestone Tire and Rubber Store [Downtown Evansville MRA], 900 Main St., Evansville, 4/06/84, A, C, 84001702

Former Vanderburgh County Sheriff's Residence, 4th St. between Vine and Court Sts., Evansville, 10/06/70, C, 70000009

Garvin Park, N. Main St. and Morgan Ave., Evansville, 8/29/80, A, C, 80000069

Geiger, Fred, and Sons National Biscuit Company [Downtown Evansville MRA], 401 NW 2nd St, Evansville, 7/01/82, C, 82000096

Gemcraft-Wittmer Building [Downtown Evansville MRA], 609 Main St., Evansville, 4/06/84, C, 84001704

German Bank [Downtown Evansville MRA], 301-303 Main St., Evansville, 7/01/82, C, 82000097

Greyhound Bus Terminal, 102 NW. 3rd St., Evansville, 10/01/79, A, C, g, 79000048

Harding and Miller Music Company [Downtown Evansville MRA], 518-520 Main St., Evansville, 7/01/82, C, 82000098

Helfrich, Michael D., House, 700 Helfrich Lane, Evansville, 5/24/84, B, C, 84001710

Hooker-Ensle-Pierce House, 6531 Oak Hill Rd., Evansville vicinity, 4/28/77, C, 77000022

Hose House No. 10, 119 E. Columbia St., Evansville, 2/11/82, A, C, 82000099

Hose House No. 12, 1409 First Ave., Evansville, 6/17/82, A, C, 82000100

Huber Motor Sales Building [Downtown Evansville MRA], 215-219 SE 4th St., Evansville, 4/06/84, A, C, 84001715

Igleheart, Edgar A., House, 5500 Lincoln Ave., Evansville, 12/18/90, C, 90001930

Independence Historic District, W. Franklin St. and Wabash Ave., Evansville, 2/01/82, A, C, 82000102

Indiana Bell Building [Downtown Evansville MRA], 129-133 NW 5th St., Evansville, 7/01/82, C, 82000103

Ingle Terrace [Downtown Evansville MRA], 609-619 Ingle St., Evansville, 7/01/82, C, 82000104

Koester/Patburg House, 504 Herndon Dr., Evansville, 3/03/83, A, C, 83000151

Kuebler-Artes Building [Downtown Evansville MRA], 327 Main St., Evansville, 4/06/84, C, 84002895

Kuehn, August, House [Downtown Evansville MRA], 608-610 Ingel St., Evansville, 7/01/82, C, 82000105

Leich, Charles, and Company [Downtown Evansville MRA], 420 NW 5th St., Evansville, 7/01/82, C, 82000106

Liberty Baptist Church, 701 Oak St., Evansville, 12/08/78, A, C, a, 78000058

Lincolnshire Historic District, Roughly bounded by Lincoln, Bennighof, Bellemeade, Lodge, Washington, Harlan, E. Chandler, and College, Evansville, 10/02/89, A, C, 89001426

Lockyear College [Downtown Evansville MRA], 209 NW 5th St., Evansville, 4/06/84, A, C, 84001729

Maier, Peter Augustus, House, 707 S. 6th St., Evansville, 10/29/82, B, C, 82000107

Masonic Temple [Downtown Evansville MRA], 301 Chestnut St., Evansville, 7/01/82, C, 82000108

McCurdy Building (Sears, Roebuck and Company Building), 101 NW. 4th St., Evansville, 10/01/79, A, C, 79000050

McCurdy Hotel [Downtown Evansville MRA], 101-111 SE 1st St., Evansville, 7/01/82, C, 82000109

McJohnston Chapel and Cemetery, Kansas Rd. and Erskine Lane, McCutchanville, 1/18/79, A, C, a, d, 79000051

Mead Johnson River-Rail-Truck Terminal and Warehouse, 1830 W. Ohio St., Evansville, 12/27/84, A, C, 84000495

Montgomery Ward Building [Downtown Evansville MRA], 517 Main St., Evansville, 10/06/82, A, C, 82000110

Vanderburgh County—Continued

Morris Plan (Central Union Bank) [Downtown Evansville MRA], 20 NW 4th St., Evansville, 7/01/82, C, 82000111

National City Bank [Downtown Evansville MRA], 227 Main St., Evansville, 7/01/82, A, C, 82000112

Newman, M. G., Building [Downtown Evansville MRA], 211-213 SE 4th St., Evansville, 7/01/82, C, 82000113

O'Donnell Building [Downtown Evansville MRA], 22 NW 6th St., Evansville, 7/01/82, C, 82000115

Old Bittermann Building, 200 Main St., Evansville, 9/22/80, C, 80000070

Old Fellwock Auto Company [Downtown Evansville MRA], 214 NW 4th St., Evansville, 4/06/84, A, C, 84001735

Old Hose House No. 4 [Downtown Evansville MRA], 623 Ingle St., Evansville, 7/01/82, A, 82001856

Old Vanderburgh County Courthouse, Entire block bounded by Vine, 4th, Court, and 5th Sts., Evansville, 9/04/70, A, C, 70000010

Orr Iron Company [Downtown Evansville MRA], 1100 Pennsylvania St., Evansville, 7/01/82, A, C, 82000116

Parson and Scoville Building [Downtown Evansville MRA], 915 Main St., Evansville, 7/01/82, A, 82000117

Pearl Steam Laundry [Downtown Evansville MRA], 428 Market St., Evansville, 4/06/84, A, C, 84001738

Puster, L., and Company Furniture Manufactory [Downtown Evansville MRA], 326 NW 6th St., Evansville, 7/01/82, C, c, 82000118

Reitz, John Augustus, House, 224 S.E. 1st St., Evansville, 10/15/73, C, a, 73000047

Ridgway Building, 313-315 Main St., Evansville, 1/03/80, C, 80000071

Riverside Historic District, Roughly bounded by Southlane Dr., Walnut, 3rd., and Parrett Sts., Evansville, 11/14/78, C, 78000059

Roelker, John H., House [Downtown Evansville MRA], 555 Sycamore St., Evansville, 4/06/84, B, C, 84001741

Rose Terrace [Downtown Evansville MRA], 301-313 NW 7th St., Evansville, 7/01/82, C, 82000120

Salem's Baptist Church [Downtown Evansville MRA], 728 Court St., Evansville, 7/01/82, C, a, 82000121

Schaeffer, Michael, House, 118 E. Chandler St., Evansville, 2/11/82, C, 82001854

Siegel's Department Store [Downtown Evansville MRA], 101-105 SE 4th St., Evansville, 7/04/82, A, C, 82000122

Skora Building [Downtown Evansville MRA], 101-103 NW 2nd St., Evansville, 7/01/82, A, C, 82001855

Smith, Robert, Mortuary, 118-120 Walnut St., Evansville, 9/22/80, C, 80000072

Soldiers and Sailors Memorial Coliseum, 350 Court St., Evansville, 5/10/79, A, C, 79000052

St. John's Evangelical Protestant Church [Downtown Evansville·MRA], 314 Market St., Evansville, 7/01/82, C, a, 82000123

Sunset Park Pavilion, 411 SE. Riverside Dr., Sunset Park, Evansville, 6/17/92, C, 92000673

Van Cleave Flats [Downtown Evansville MRA], 704-708 Court St., Evansville, 7/01/82, C, 82000125

Victory Theater and Hotel Sonntag [Downtown Evansville MRA], 600-614 Main St., Evansville, 7/01/82, A, C, 82000124

Wabash Valley Motor Company [Downtown Evansville MRA], 206-208 SE 8th St., Evansville, 7/01/82, A, C, 82000126

Washington Avenue Historic District, Roughly bounded by Madison and Grand Aves., E. Gum and Parret Sts., Evansville, 11/28/80, C, 80000073

Willard Library, 21 1st Ave., Evansville, 9/28/72, C, 72000014

YMCA [Downtown Evansville MRA], 203 N. W. Fifth St., Evansville, 7/01/82, C, 82000128

YWCA [Downtown Evansville MRA], 118 Vine St., Evansville, 7/01/82, A, C, 82001853

Zion Evangelical Church [Downtown Evansville MRA], 415 NW 5th St., Evansville, 7/01/82, C, a, 82000129

Vermillion County

Salem Methodist Episcopal Church, N of Clinton on IN 63, Clinton vicinity, 2/22/79, C, a, 79000022

Vigo County

Allen Chapel African Methodist Episcopal Church, 224 Crawford St., Terre Haute, 9/05/75, A, a, 75000030

Building at 23–27 S. Sixth Street [Downtown Terre Haute MRA], 23–27 S. 6th St., Terre Haute, 6/30/83, C, 83000111

Building at 510–516 Ohio Street [Downtown Terre Haute MRA], 510–516 Ohio St., Terre Haute, 6/30/83, C, 83000152

Building at 810 Wabash Avenue [Downtown Terre Haute MRA], 810 Wabash Ave., Terre Haute, 6/30/83, C, 83000153

Butternut Hill, 4430 Wabash Ave., Terre Haute, 5/27/93, C, 93000469

Carr's Hall [Downtown Terre Haute MRA], 329–333 Walnut St., Terre Haute, 6/30/83, C, 83000154

Chamber of Commerce Building [Downtown Terre Haute MRA], 329–333 Walnut St., Terre Haute, 6/30/83, C, 83000155

Citizens' Trust Company Building [Downtown Terre Haute MRA], 19–21 S. 6th St., Terre Haute, 6/30/83, C, 83000156

Collett Park, N. 7th St. and Maple Ave., Terre Haute, 12/10/81, A, 81000021

Condit House, 629 Mulberry St. on Indiana State University campus, Terre Haute, 4/02/73, C, 73000023

Debs, Eugene V., House, 451 N. 8th St., Terre Haute, 11/13/66, B, NHL, 66000008

Dresser, Paul, Birthplace, 1st and Farrington Sts., Terre Haute, 1/22/73, B, C, b, c, 73000024

Farington's Grove Historic District, Roughly bounded by Poplar, S. Seventh, Hulman, and S. Fourth Sts., Terre Haute, 2/27/86, A, B, C, 86000270

Fire Station No. 9, 1728 S. 8th St., Terre Haute, 12/16/82, A, C, 82000049

First Congregational Church [Downtown Terre Haute MRA], 630 Ohio St., Terre Haute, 6/30/83, C, a, 83000157

First National Bank [Downtown Terre Haute MRA], 509 Wabash Ave., Terra Haute, 5/07/92, C, 83004576

Foley Hall, St. Mary of the Woods College Campus, Off US 150, St. Mary-of-the-Woods, 3/21/85, A, C, a, 85000595

Highland Lawn Cemetery, 4520 Wabash Ave., Terre Haute, 11/29/90, C, d, 90001790

Hippodrome Theatre [Downtown Terre Haute MRA], 727 Ohio St., Terre Haute, 6/30/83, C, 83000110

House at 209–211 S. Ninth Street [Downtown Terre Haute MRA], 209–211 S. 9th St., Terre Haute, 6/30/83, C, 83000109

House at 823 Ohio Street [Downtown Terre Haute MRA], 823 Ohio St., Terre Haute, 6/30/83, C, 83003441

Markle House and Mill Site, 4900 Mill Dam Rd., North Terre Haute, 9/10/79, A, C, 79000023

Ohio Boulevard—Demming Park Historic District, Roughly Ohio Blvd. from 19th to Keane, Terre Haute, 9/14/89, A, C, 89001425

Sage-Robinson-Nagel House, 1411 S. 6th St., Terre Haute, 4/11/73, C, 73000025

Senour, Frank, Round Barn [Round and Polygonal Barns of Indiana MPS], 6400 E. Organ Church Rd., Blackhawk vicinity, 4/02/93, A, C, 93000193

Star Building [Downtown Terre Haute MRA], 601–603 Ohio St., Terre Haute, 6/30/83, A, 83000158

State Bank of Indiana, Branch of (Memorial Hall), 219 Ohio St., Terre Haute, 10/25/73, A, C, 73000026

Terminal Arcade [Downtown Terre Haute MRA], 822 Wabash Ave., Terre Haute, 6/30/83, C, 83000159

Terre Haute Post Office and Federal Building [Downtown Terre Haute MRA], 7th and Cherry Sts., Terre Haute, 8/13/84, C, 84003813

Vigo County Courthouse [Downtown Terre Haute MRA], Courthouse Sq., Terre Haute, 6/30/83, A, C, 83000160

Wabash Avenue East Historic District (Boundary Increase) [Downtown Terre Haute MRA], 26–34 Eighth St., Terre Haute, 9/16/92, A, C, 92001166

Wabash Avenue-East Historic District [Downtown Terre Haute MRA], Wabash Ave., 7th and 8th Sts., Terre Haute, 6/30/83, A, C, 83000040

Wabash Avenue-West Historic District [Downtown Terre Haute MRA], Wabash Ave. and 6th St., Terre Haute, 6/30/83, A, C, 83000041

Williams-Warren-Zimmerman House, 900-904 S. 4th St., Terre Haute, 10/23/80, C, b, 80000046

Wabash County

Amoss, James M., Building, 110 S. Wabash St., Wabash, 8/30/84, C, 84001742

Downtown Wabash Historic District, Roughly bounded by Hill, Wabash, Canal, and Miami Sts., Wabash, 7/18/86, A, C, 86001678

First Christian Church, 110 W. Hill St., Wabash, 6/23/83, C, a, 83000161

Honeywell Memorial Community Center, 275 W. Market St., Wabash, 7/15/83, C, g, 83000042

Lentz House (Hotel Sheller), Walnut and 2nd Sts., North Manchester, 11/14/82, A, C, b, 82000050

Manchester College Historic District, 604 College Ave., North Manchester, 12/27/90, A, a, 90001929

Noftzger-Adams House, 102 E. 3rd St., North Manchester, 11/14/79, C, 79000024

North Manchester Covered Bridge, S. Mill St. at Eel River, North Manchester, 9/30/82, C, 82000051

North Manchester Planning and Band Saw Mill (J.A. Browne Co.Mill), 705 W. Main St. (mill); (houses) 706-708 W. Grant St. and 202 N. High St., North Manchester, 3/05/82, A, C, 82000052

Roann Covered Bridge, 4th, N of Roann on SR 700W, Roann vicinity, 8/06/81, C, 81000022

Wabash Residential Historic District, Bounded roughly by the Northfolk Southern RR and Union St., Wabash and Miami Sts., Main St., Holliday St., Wabash, 4/21/88, A, C, a, 88000447

Wilson, Solomon, Building, 102 S. Wabash St., Wabash, 8/30/84, C, 84001743

Warren County

Brier, Andrew, House, Old Hwy. 41, Carbondale, 8/14/86, A, B, 86001617

Kent House and Hitchens House, 500 Main and 303 Lincoln Sts., Williamsport, 3/01/84, C, 84001719

Warrick County

Boonville Public Square Historic District, Bounded roughly by First, Sycamore, Fourth, and Walnut, Boonville, 1/23/87, A, C, g, 86002720

Ellerbusch Archeological Site (12W56), Address Restricted, Newburgh vicinity, 3/14/91, D, 91000270

Old Newburgh Presbyterian Church, N. State and W. Main Sts., Newburgh, 5/23/78, A, C, a, 78000040

Old Warrick County Jail, 124 E. Main St., Boonville, 2/14/79, C, 79000025

Original Newburgh Historic District, Roughly bounded by IN 662, Water, Monroe, Main and Middle Sts., Newburgh, 6/16/83, A, C, 83000162

Roberts-Morton House, 1.5 mi. E of Newburgh on IN 662, Newburgh vicinity, 12/16/74, B, C, 74000024

Yankeetown Archeological Site, Address Restricted, Yankeetown vicinity, 2/28/79, D, 79000026

Washington County

Beck's Mill [Grain Mills in Indiana MPS], Beck's Mill Rd. at Mill Cr., Salem, 12/07/90, A, 90001789

First Baptist Church, 201 N. High St., Salem, 3/21/85, C, a, 85000602

Hay-Morrison House, 106 S. College Ave., Salem, 10/26/71, B, C, c, 71000007

Washington County Courthouse, Public Sq., Salem, 6/16/80, A, C, 80000047

Washington County Jail and Sheriff's Residence, 106 S. Main St., Salem, 11/23/84, A, C, 84000280

Wayne County

Beechwood (Isaac Kinsey House), 2 mi. S of Milton on Sarver Rd., Milton vicinity, 2/21/75, B, C, 75000031

Bethel A.M.E. Church, 200 S. 6th St., Richmond, 9/05/75, A, C, a, 75000032

Cambridge City Historic District, Roughly bounded by Boundary, Maple, High and Fourth Sts., Cambridge City, 6/14/91, A, C, 91000787

Centerville Historic District, Bounded by the Corporation line, 3rd and South Sts., and Willow Grove Rd., Centerville, 10/26/71, A, B, C, 71000008

Coffin, Levi, House, 115 N. Main St., Fountain City, 10/15/66, B, NHL, 66000009

Conklin-Montgomery House, 302 E. Main St., Cambridge City, 2/24/75, B, C, 75000033

Earlham College Observatory, National Rd., Earlham College campus, Richmond, 10/21/75, A, C, 75000034

East Main Street—Glen Miller Park Historic District, Both sides of E. Main St. from N. Eighteenth to N. Thirtieth Sts. and Glen Miller Pk. E of Thirtieth St., Richmond, 3/27/86, A, C, 86000612

Gaar, Abram, House and Farm, 2411 Pleasant View Rd., Richmond, 2/20/75, B, C, 75000035

Gennett, Henry and Alice, House, 1829 E. Main St., Richmond, 8/11/83, A, C, 83000043

Hagerstown I.O.O.F. Hall, Main and Perry Sts., Hagerstown, 1/03/78, A, C, 78000041

Hicksite Friends Meetinghouse (Wayne County Museum), 1150 N. A St., Richmond, 10/14/75, A, C, a, 75000036

Huddleston House Tavern, The, U.S. Hwy. 40 East, Mount Auburn, 6/15/75, A, C, 75000037

Jones, Lewis, House, College Corner and Eliason Rds., Centerville vicinity, 6/07/84, C, 84001744

Lackey-Overbeck House, 520 E. Church St., Cambridge City, 5/28/76, B, C, 76000030

Leland Hotel, 900 S. A St., Richmond, 2/28/85, A, C, 85000362

Morton, Oliver P., House, 319 W. Main St., Centerville, 10/10/75, B, C, 75000038

Murray Theater, 1003 Main St., Richmond, 3/25/82, A, C, 82000053

Old Richmond Historic District, Roughly bounded by C & O Railroad, S. 11th, South A, and alley S of South E St., Richmond, 6/28/74, A, B, C, 74000025

Richmond Gas Company Building, 100 E. Main St., Richmond, 8/25/81, A, C, 81000023

Richmond Railroad Station Historic District, Roughly bounded by Norfolk & Southern RR tracks, N. Tenth St., Elm Pl., N. D St., & Ft. Wayne Ave., Richmond, 10/08/87, A, C, 87001808

Scott, Andrew F., House, 126 N. 10th St., Richmond, 10/10/75, B, C, 75000039

Smith, Samuel G., Farm, W of Richmond at 3431 Crowe Rd., Richmond vicinity, 1/14/83, C, b, 83000044

Starr Historic District, Roughly bounded by N. 16th, E and A Sts., and alley W of N. 10th St., Richmond, 6/28/74, B, C, 74000026

Starr Piano Company Warehouse and Administration Building, 300 S. 1st St., Richmond, 6/18/81, A, 81000024

Wayne County Courthouse, Bounded by 3rd, 4th, Main and S. A Sts., Richmond, 12/08/78, C, 78000042

Wells County

Bethel Methodist Episcopal Church, SE fo Bluffton, Bluffton vicinity, 3/01/84, C, a, 84001747

Grove, John A., House, 521 W. Market St., Bluffton, 12/22/83, C, 83000045

Grove, John A., House, 521 W. Market St., Bluffton, 12/22/83, C, 83003774

Stewart-Studebaker House, 420 W. Market St., Bluffton, 5/14/79, B, C, 79000027

Villa North Historic District, 706–760 and 707–731 N. Main St., Bluffton, 6/04/85, C, 85001192

Wells County Courthouse, 100 W. Market St., Bluffton, 1/15/79, A, C, 79000028

White County

Reynolds, James Culbertson, House, 417 N. Main St., Monticello, 6/17/82, C, 82000054

South Grade School Building, 565 S. Main St., Monticello, 9/12/85, A, C, 85002136

Wolcott House, 500 N. Range St., Wolcott, 10/10/75, B, C, 75000040

Whitley County

Columbia City Historic District, Roughly bounded by Jefferson, Walnut, Ellsworth, Wayne, and N.

Whitley County—Continued

Chauncy Sts., Columbia City, 6/22/87, A, B, C,
87001307
Marshall, Thomas R., House, 108 W. Jefferson St.,
Columbia City, 7/21/83, B, 83000046
Whitley County Courthouse, Van Buren and Main
Sts., Columbia City, 2/16/79, A, C, 79000029

This early twentieth-century residence with Classical Revival details is one of the distinctive homes in the Brady Street Historic District, in Attica, Indiana. (Mary Ellen Gadski, 1988)

IOWA

Adair County

Adair County Courthouse [County Courthouses in Iowa TR], Iowa Ave. and 1st St., Greenfield, 7/02/81, C, 81000224

Catalpa, SE of Greenfield, Greenfield vicinity, 11/13/74, B, g, 74000776

Chicago, Rock Island and Pacific Railroad: Stuart Passenger Station, Front St., Stuart, 2/19/80, A, 80001428

Warren Opera House Block and Hetherington Block, 156 Public Sq., Greenfield, 10/18/79, C, 79000880

Adams County

Adams County Jail, 1000 Benton Ave., Corning, 2/28/91, A, C, 91000119

Corning Opera House [Footlights in Farm Country: Iowa Opera Houses MPS], 800 Davis Ave., Corning, 9/21/93, A, 93000954

Allamakee County

Allamakee County Courthouse [County Courthouses in Iowa TR (AD)], 107 Allamakee St., Waukon, 4/11/77, A, C, 77000492

Effigy Mounds National Monument, 3 mi. N of Marquette on IA 76, Marquette vicinity, 10/15/66, D, NPS, 66000109

Fish Farm Mound Group [Prehistoric Mounds of the Quad-State Region of the Upper Mississippi River Valley MPS], Address Restricted, New Albin vicinity, 7/25/88, D, 88001131

Hager, Otto J., House, 402 Allamakee St., Waukon, 6/27/85, C, 85001383

Iron Post, N end of Main St., New Albin, 9/29/76, A, 76000732

Kerndt G., and Brothers Elevator and Warehouses, No. 11, No.12 and No. 13, Front St., Lansing, 10/18/79, A, 79000881

Kerndt, G., & Brothers Office Block, 4th and Main Sts., Lansing, 11/10/82, A, B, 82000402

Lansing Fisheries Building [Conservation Movement in Iowa MPS], Between Co. Hwy. X-52 and the Mississippi R., south Lansing, Lansing, 12/23/91, A, 91001832

Lansing Stone School, SW corner Center and 5th Sts., Lansing, 12/18/73, A, C, 73000721

Meier, Fred W., Round Barn [Iowa Round Barns: The Sixty Year Experiment TR], Off IA 9, Ludlow vicinity, 6/30/86, A, C, 86001411

Old Allamakee County Courthouse [County Courthouses in Iowa TR], 2nd St., Lansing, 2/24/83, A, C, 83000338

Old East Paint Creek Lutheran Church, N of Waterville on County A-52, Waterville vicinity, 7/07/83, A, C, a, d, 83000339

Reburn, Thomas, Polygonal Barn [Iowa Round Barns: The Sixty Year Experiment TR], Off IA 26, New Albin vicinity, 6/30/86, A, C, 86001413

Slinde Mound Group [Prehistoric Mounds of the Quad-State Region of the Upper Mississippi River Valley MPS], Address Restricted, Hanover vicinity, 11/01/89, D, 88001132

Appanoose County

Appanoose County Courthouse [County Courthouses in Iowa TR], Van Buren and N. 12th St., Centerville, 7/02/81, C, 81000225

Porter Hall, 706 Drake Ave., Centerville, 1/24/80, C, 80001429

Stratton House, 303 E. Washington St., Centerville, 9/09/75, B, C, 75000677

Sturdivant-Sawyer House, 707 Drake Ave., Centerville, 1/12/84, C, 84001202

U.S. Post Office, 100 W. Maple St., Centerville, 11/07/78, C, 78001204

Vermilion Estate, Valley Dr., Centerville, 4/26/78, A, C, 78001205

Audubon County

Audubon County Courthouse [County Courthouses in Iowa TR (AD)], Washington and Kilworth Sts., Exira, 7/26/77, A, 77000493

Bennedsen, Boldt, and Hansen Building [Ethnic Historic Settlement of Shelby and Audubon Counties MPS], Main St., Kimballton, 10/03/91, C, 91001460

Bethany Danish Evangelical Lutheran Church [Ethnic Historic Settlement of Shelby and Audubon Counties MPS], 1.5 mi. N of IA 44, 1 mi. E of Hwy. 68, Kimballton vicinity, 10/03/91, A, C, a, 91001457

Bush, John D., House [Ethnic Historic Settlement of Shelby and Audubon Counties MPS], 219 N. Kilworth, Exira, 10/03/91, C, 91001461

Hansen, Andrew P., Farmstead [Ethnic Historic Settlement of Shelby and Audubon Counties MPS], Between IA 44 and Co Rd. P58, on Little Elkhorn Cr., Brayton vicinity, 10/03/91, A, C, 91001458

Immanuel Danish Evangelical Lutheran Church [Ethnic Historic Settlement of Shelby and Audubon Counties MPS], W. Second St., E. side, Kimballton, 10/03/91, A, C, a, 91001462

Jorgensen, Hans J., Barn [Ethnic Historic Settlement of Shelby and Audubon Counties MPS], Jct. of IA 44 and Main St., Kimballton vicinity, 10/03/91, B, C, 91001452

Koch, Hans M., House [Ethnic Historic Settlement of Shelby and Audubon Counties MPS], IA 173, W. side, 0.5 mi. S of Kimballton, Kimballton vicinity, 10/03/91, A, C, 91001453

Larsen, Jens T., House [Ethnic Historic Settlement of Shelby and Audubon Counties MPS], 103 Main St., Kimballton, 10/03/91, C, 91001451

Poplar Rural District [Ethnic Historic Settlement of Shelby and Audubon Counties MPS], Roughly, area from Poplar S and W to Wolf Cr., Jacksonville vicinity, 4/09/92, A, C, 91001463

Benton County

Benton County Courthouse [County Courthouses in Iowa TR (AD)], E. 4th St., Vinton, 10/08/76, A, C, 76000733

Burlington, Cedar Rapids & Northern Passenger Station—Vinton [Advent & Development of Railroads in Iowa MPS], 612 Second Ave., Vinton, 12/06/90, A, 90001852

McQuilkin, James Greer, Round Barn [Iowa Round Barns: The Sixty Year Experiment TR], CR D56, Eagle Center vicinity, 6/30/86, A, C, 86001414

Ray, Frank G., House & Carriage House, 912 1st Ave., Vinton, 12/10/82, B, C, 82000403

Round Barn, Bruce Township Section 3 [Iowa Round Barns: The Sixty Year Experiment TR], Off US 218, Eagle Center vicinity, 6/30/86, A, C, 86001415

Round Barn, Bruce Township Section 6 [Iowa Round Barns: The Sixty Year Experiment TR], W of US 218, La Porte vicinity, 6/30/86, A, C, 86001416

Upper Stone Schoolhouse, E of Vinton, Vinton vicinity, 7/07/83, C, 83000340

Vinton Public Library [Public Library Buildings in Iowa TR], 510 2nd Ave., Vinton, 5/23/83, A, C, 83000341

Black Hawk County

Black Hawk County Soldiers Memorial Hall [Waterloo MPS], 194 W. Fifth St., Waterloo, 11/29/88, A, C, 88001322

Cedar Falls Ice House, Franklin Ave. and 1st St., Cedar Falls, 10/21/77, A, 77000494

Central Hall, University of Northern Iowa campus, Cedar Falls, 1/18/84, A, C, 84001204

Cotton Theater, 103 Main St., Cedar Falls, 7/23/93, C, 93000764

Dunsmore House, 902 Logan Ave., Waterloo, 11/17/77, C, 77000497

Fields Barn, SW of Cedar Falls, Cedar Falls vicinity, 9/19/77, B, 77000495

Fire Station No. 2 [Waterloo MPS], 716 Commercial St., Waterloo, 11/29/88, A, C, 88001321

Forrest Milling Company Oatmeal Mill, N. Main St., Cedar Falls, 6/24/80, A, 80001430

Black Hawk County—Continued

Highland Historic District, Roughly bounded by Independence Ave., Steely, Idaho, and Vine Sts., Waterloo, 9/24/84, A, C, 84001209

Hotel Russell—Lamson [Waterloo MPS], 201–215 W. Fifth St., Waterloo, 11/29/88, A, 88001324

La Porte City Station, 202 E. Main St., La Porte, 3/13/79, A, 79003781

LaPorte City Town Hall and Fire Station, 413 Chestnut, LaPorte City, 5/12/77, A, 77000496

Newell, James, Barn, N of Cedar Falls off U.S. 218, Cedar Falls vicinity, 12/12/76, B, C, 76000734

Round Barn, Washington Township [Iowa Round Barns: The Sixty Year Experiment TR], Off US 218, Janesville vicinity, 6/30/86, A, C, 86001417

Rownd, C. A., Round Barn [Iowa Round Barns: The Sixty Year Experiment TR], 5102 S. Main, Cedar Falls, 11/19/86, A, 86003193

Russell, Rensselaer, House, 520 W. 3rd St., Waterloo, 7/05/73, B, C, 73000722

Snowden House, 306 Washington St., Waterloo, 9/14/77, C, 77000498

Waterfield, William, House, 308 3rd St., S., Raymond, 10/19/78, C, 78001206

Waterloo Public Library (West Branch) [Public Library Buildings in Iowa TR], 528 W. 4th St., Waterloo, 5/23/83, C, 83000342

Waterloo Public Library—East Side Branch [Waterloo MPS], 626 Mulberry St., Waterloo, 11/29/88, A, C, 88001323

Weis, Henry, House [Waterloo MRA], 800 W. Fourth St., Waterloo, 10/30/89, A, C, 89001779

YMCA Building, 154 W. 4th St., Waterloo, 7/07/83, C, 83000343

Boone County

Boone County Courthouse [County Courthouses in Iowa TR], N. State and W. 2nd Sts., Boone, 7/02/81, C, 81000226

Boone Viaduct, W of Boone, Boone vicinity, 11/17/78, A, C, 78001207

Cassel, Carl and Ulrika Dalander, House, 415 W. 2nd St., Madrid, 4/12/82, A, B, C, 82002609

Champlin Memorial Masonic Temple [Architectural Legacy of Proudfoot & Bird in Iowa MPS], 602 Story St., Boone, 12/20/90, C, 90001853

Ericson Public Library [Public Library Buildings in Iowa TR], 702 Greene St., Boone, 5/23/83, A, C, 83000344

First National Bank [Architectural Legacy of Proudfoot and Bird in Iowa, 1882–1940 MPS], 8th and Story Sts., Boone, 6/28/89, C, 88003232

Herman, John H., House [Architectural Legacy of Proudfoot and Bird in Iowa, 1882–1940 MPS], 711 S. Story St., Boone, 6/28/89, C, 88003233

Riekenberg, J. H., House, 310 N. Tama St., Boone, 4/11/88, C, 87002017

Bremer County

Wartburg Teachers' Seminary, Wartburg College campus, Waverly, 1/20/78, A, C, a, 78001208

Waverly House, 402 W. Bremer Ave., Waverly, 12/12/76, A, C, 76000735

Buchanan County

McKenzie, Erza, Round Barn [Iowa Round Barns: The Sixty Year Experiment TR], Off IA 150, Hazleton vicinity, 6/30/86, A, C, 86001419

Munson Building, 210 2nd St., NE, Independence, 11/21/76, A, C, 76000736

Richardson-Jakway House, R.R. #1, Aurora vicinity, 6/27/85, C, 85001382

Walter, Lowell E., House [Iowa Usonian Houses by Frank Lloyd Wright, 1945-1960, MPS (AD)], Off SR W35, NW of Quasqueton, Quasqueton vicinity, 3/02/83, C, g, 83000345

Wapsipinicon Mill, 100 1st St., W., Independence, 4/21/75, A, C, 75000678

Buena Vista County

Allee, Jesse J. and Mary F., House, 20006 640 St., Newell vicinity, 3/26/92, C, 92000271

Chan-Ya-Ta Site, Address Restricted, Linn Grove vicinity, 11/21/78, D, NHL, 78001209

Chicago, Milwaukee and Pacific Railroad-Albert City Station, 212 N. 2nd St., Albert City, 10/22/76, A, b, 76000737

Harker House, 328 Lake Ave., Storm Lake, 12/06/90, C, 90001855

Illinois Central Passenger Depot—Storm Lake [Advent & Development of Railroads in Iowa, 1855-1940, MPS], S. of W. Railroad St., between Lake and Michigan Aves., Storm Lake, 9/06/90, C, 90001300

Storm Lake Public Library [Public Library Buildings in Iowa TR], E. 5th and Erie Sts., Storm Lake, 5/23/83, A, C, 83000346

Butler County

Coldwater Church of the Brethren, 100 Block N. High St., Greene, 7/13/79, C, a, 79000883

Wolf, Charles, House, 401 5th St., Parkersburg, 10/01/79, C, 79000884

Calhoun County

Calhoun County Courthouse [County Courthouses in Iowa TR], Court and 4th Sts., Rockwell City, 7/02/81, C, 81000227

Central School, 201 S. Center, Lake City, 1/03/85, C, 85000001

Chicago and North Western Office Building-/Passenger Depot—Lake City [Lake City Iowa MPS], 401 Front St., Lake City, 8/27/90, A, C, b, 90001205

Holdoegel, Perry C. and Mattie Forrest, House [Conservation Movement in Iowa MPS], 504

Eighth St., Rockwell City, 5/06/92, B, C, 91001831

Knapp, Dr. Charles, Round Barn [Iowa Round Barns: The Sixty Year Experiment TR], Off CR D26, Jolley vicinity, 12/23/86, A, C, 86003187

Lake City Community Memorial Building [Lake City Iowa MPS; Architectural Legacy of Proudfoot and Bird in Iowa MPS], 118 E. Washington St., Lake City, 8/27/90, A, C, 90001210

Lake City Public Library [Lake City Iowa MPS], 120 N. Illinois St., Lake City, 8/27/90, A, C, 90001209

Lake City Water Standpipe [Lake City Iowa MPS], 100 block of W. Washington St., Lake City, 8/27/90, A, C, 90001211

Marsh Rainbow Arch Bridge, Hwy. N37 over North Raccoon River, Lake City vicinity, 3/30/89, C, 88002529

Smith Farmhouse [Lake City Iowa MPS], Jct. of Rainbow Rd. S. and Monroe St., Lake City, 8/27/90, C, 90001206

Smith, Gen. Cass and Belle, House [Lake City Iowa MPS], 500 W. Main St., Lake City, 8/27/90, C, 90001207

Smith, Peter and Mary, House [Lake City Iowa MPS], 304 W. Main St., Lake City, 8/27/90, B, C, 90001208

Carroll County

American Express Building—Carroll [Advent & Development of Railroads in Iowa, 1855-1940, MPS], Jct of N. West and W. Fifth Sts., Carroll, 9/06/90, C, 90001299

Carnegie Library Building, 125 E. 6th St., Carroll, 11/13/76, A, C, 76000739

Chicago & Northwestern Passenger Depot and Baggage Room—Carroll [Advent & Development of Railroads in Iowa, 1855-1940, MPS], Jct. N. West and W. Fifth Sts., Carroll, 9/06/90, C, 90001302

Fobes Octagon Barn [Iowa Round Barns: The Sixty Year Experiment TR], IA 286, Lanesboro vicinity, 6/30/86, A, C, 86001420

Cass County

Griswold National Bank, Main and Cass, Griswold, 2/22/79, C, 79003695

Hitchcock, George B., House, W of Lewis, Lewis vicinity, 11/09/77, B, C, a, 77000500

Martin, S. F., House, 419 Poplar St., Atlantic, 1/12/84, C, 84001211

Cedar County

Downey Savings Bank, Front St., Downey, 7/12/76, A, C, 76000740

Floral Hall, W of Tipton on Cedar County Fair Grounds, Tipton vicinity, 11/07/76, C, 76000741

Cedar County—Continued

Gruwell and Crew General Store, 109 W. Main St., West Branch, 9/09/82, A, 82002610

Herbert Hoover National Historic Site, Off I-80, West Branch, 10/15/66, A, B, a, c, f, NPS, 66000110

Reichert, John Christian and Bertha Landrock, House, 508 E. Fourth St., Tipton, 12/19/91, C, 91001861

St. Paul's Episcopal Church and Parish Hall, 206 6th Ave., Durant, 1/03/85, C, a, 85000002

West Branch Commercial Historic District, W. Main and N. Downey Sts., West Branch, 4/07/87, A, 87000028

West Branch Commercial Historic District (Boundary Increase), N. Downey and E. and W. Main Sts., West Branch, 2/23/90, A, 90000158

Cerro Gordo County

Andrus, A. J., Duplex [Prairie School Architecture in Mason City TR], 687–691 E. State St., Mason City, 1/29/80, C, 80001431

City National Bank Building, 4 S. Federal Ave., Mason City, 9/14/72, C, 72000469

Elks-Rogers Hotel, 223 Main Ave., Clear Lake, 6/21/82, C, 82002611

Etzel, John L., House, 214 N. 3rd St., Clear Lake, 1/27/83, C, a, 83000347

Franke, C. F., House [Prairie School Architecture in Mason City TR], 320 1st St., SE, Mason City, 1/29/80, C, 80001432

Gibson, E. R., House [Prairie School Architecture in Mason City TR], 114 4th St., NW, Mason City, 1/29/80, C, 80001433

Jewell Apartments [Prairie School Architecture in Mason City TR], 404–412 1st St., NW, Mason City, 1/29/80, C, 80001434

Kirk, The, 206 N. Federal Ave., Mason City, 4/12/82, B, C, 82002613

Lippert House [Prairie School Architecture in Mason City TR], 122–124 N. Madison Ave., Mason City, 1/29/80, C, 80001435

Mason City Public Library, 208 E. State St., Mason City, 5/25/89, A, C, 89000405

Norris, F. M., House [Prairie School Architecture in Mason City TR], 108 4th St., NE, Mason City, 1/29/80, C, 80001436

Park Inn Hotel, 15 W. State St., Mason City, 9/14/72, C, 72000470

Rock Crest-Rock Glen Historic District, Off U.S. 18, Mason City, 12/28/79, A, C, 79000885

Rogers-Knutson House, 315 N. 3rd St., Clear Lake, 9/09/82, B, 82002612

Romey, George, House [Prairie School Architecture in Mason City TR], 428 1st St., SE, Mason City, 1/29/80, C, 80001437

Rule, Duncan, House, 321 2nd St., SE, Mason City, 10/16/79, C, 79000886

Rye, Chris, House [Prairie School Architecture in Mason City TR], 630 E. State St., Mason City, 1/29/80, C, 80001438

Seney, Charles, House [Prairie School Architecture in Mason City TR], 109 7th St., NW and 622 N. Washington St., Mason City, 1/29/80, C, 80001439

Shipley, C. P., House [Prairie School Architecture in Mason City TR], 114 3rd St., NW, Mason City, 1/29/80, C, 80001440

Stockman, Dr. G. C., House [Prairie School Architecture in Mason City TR], 311 1st St., SE, Mason City, 9/17/92, C, 80001441

Wagner-Mozart Music Hall, 1st NE. and Delaware Ave., Mason City, 11/16/78, A, g, 78001210

Wolf, Mier, House [Prairie School Architecture in Mason City TR], 811 N. Adams St., Mason City, 1/29/80, C, 80001442

Yelland, Curtis, House [Prairie School Architecture in Mason City TR], 37 River Heights Dr., Mason City, 1/29/80, C, 80001443

Youngblood, Tessa, House [Prairie School Architecture in Mason City TR], 36 Oak Dr., Mason City, 1/29/80, C, 80001444

Cherokee County

Bastian Site, Address Restricted, Cherokee vicinity, 7/19/76, D, 76000742

Brewster Site, Address Restricted, Cherokee vicinity, 3/21/79, D, 79000887

Cherokee Public Library [Public Library Buildings in Iowa TR], 215 S. 2nd St., Cherokee, 4/09/85, A, 85000773

Cherokee Sewer Site, Address Restricted, Cherokee vicinity, 12/24/74, D, 74000777

Illinois Central Railroad Yard—Cherokee [Advent & Development of Railroads in Iowa, 1850-1940, MPS], Roughly bounded by S. Fourth, Fifth, W. Maple, and W. Beech Sts., Cherokee, 9/06/90, A, C, 90001308

Phipps Site, Address Restricted, Cherokee vicinity, 10/15/66, D, NHL, 66000335

Chickasaw County

Chickasaw County Courthouse [County Courthouses in Iowa TR], Prospect St. at Locust Ave., New Hampton, 7/02/81, C, 81000228

Chickasaw Octagon House, Court St., Chickasaw, 7/17/79, C, 79000888

Darrow, George, Round Barn [Iowa Round Barns: The Sixty Year Experiment TR], CR T76, Alta Vista vicinity, 6/30/86, A, C, 86001421

Foley, John, House, 511 N. Locust St., New Hampton, 4/16/79, C, 79000889

Clarke County

Banta, J. V., House, 222 McLane St., Osceola, 7/14/83, C, 83000348

Brady-Bolibaugh House, 217 W. Washington, Osceola, 1/03/85, C, 85000003

Webster, Dickinson, House, 609 W. Jefferson St., Osceola, 7/20/77, A, C, 77000501

Clay County

Adams-Higgins House, 1215 N. Grand Ave., Spencer, 9/27/84, C, 84001214

Clay County Courthouse [County Courthouses in Iowa TR], W. 4th St. and 3rd Ave., W., Spencer, 7/02/81, C, 81000229

Kirchner, Philip and Anna Parrish, Log House, 4969 120th Ave., Peterson vicinity, 9/02/93, A, 93000897

Ross, Seymour, Round Barn [Iowa Round Barns: The Sixty Year Experiment TR], Off IA 374, Gillet Grove vicinity, 6/30/86, A, C, 86001422

Wanata State Park Picnic Shelter [CCC Properties in Iowa State Parks MPS], S of jct. of Co. Rd. M27 and IA 10, Peterson vicinity, 11/15/90, A, C, 90001677

Clayton County

Albertus Building, 222 Park River Dr., Guttenberg, 4/26/79, C, 79000891

American School of Wild Life Protection Historic District [Conservation Movement in Iowa MPS], McGregor Heights Rd., N of McGregor, McGregor vicinity, 12/23/91, A, 91001840

Carter House, 101 High St., SE, Elkader, 11/07/76, C, 76000744

Clayton County Courthouse [County Courthouses in Iowa TR (AD)], 111 High St., Elkader, 10/08/76, A, C, 76000745

Clayton School, 1st St., Clayton, 7/30/74, C, 74000778

Davis, Timothy, House, 405 1st St., NW, Elkader, 6/22/76, B, C, 76000746

Eckert House [Guttenberg MRA], 413 S. 1st St., Guttenberg, 9/24/84, C, 84001216

Elkader Keystone Bridge, Bridge St., Elkader, 11/07/76, C, 76000747

Elkader Opera House, 207 N. Main, Elkader, 10/08/76, A, 76000748

First Congregational Church, Washington St., Garnavillo, 3/25/77, C, a, 77000504

Front Street (River Park Drive) Historic District [Guttenberg MRA], River Park Dr. Between Lessing and Pearl Sts., Guttenberg, 9/24/84, A, C, 84001222

Fuerste House [Guttenberg MRA], 503 S. 1st St., Guttenberg, 9/24/84, C, 84001223

Guttenberg Corn Canning Co. [Guttenberg MRA], 413 N. 3rd St., Guttenberg, 9/24/84, A, C, 84001226

Guttenberg National Fish Hatchery and Aquarium Historic District [Conservation Movement in Iowa MPS], 315 S. River Park Dr., Guttenberg, 12/23/91, A, C, 91001833

Guttenberg State Bank [Guttenberg MRA], 15 Goethe St., Guttenberg, 9/24/84, C, 84001228

I.O.O.F. Hall, Centre St., Garnavillo, 6/18/79, C, 79000890

Clayton County—Continued

Kolker House [Guttenberg MRA], 110 Goethe St., Guttenberg, 9/24/84, C, 84001230

Matt-Bahls House [Guttenberg MRA], 615 S. 3rd St., Guttenberg, 9/24/84, C, 84001232

McClaine House [Guttenberg MRA], 300 S. 1st St., Guttenberg, 9/24/84, C, 84001234

Moser Stone House [Guttenberg MRA], 211 S. 1st St., Guttenberg, 9/24/84, C, 84001236

Motor Townsite, E of Elkader, Elkader vicinity, 8/02/77, A, B, 77000502

Nieland House [Guttenberg MRA], 715 S. 1st St., Guttenberg, 9/24/84, C, 84001238

Parker House [Guttenberg MRA], 1015 S. 2nd St., Guttenberg, 9/24/84, C, 84001240

Price, Rialto, House, 206 Cedar St., NW, Elkader, 11/21/76, C, 76000749

Reynolds, Joseph "Diamond Jo," Office Building and House, A and Main Sts., McGregor, 2/19/82, B, 82002614

Round Barn, Millville Township [Iowa Round Barns: The Sixty Year Experiment TR], US 52, Millville vicinity, 6/30/86, A, C, 86001423

Schmidt House, 101 Oak St., NW, Elkader, 3/25/77, C, 77000503

St. Joseph Church and Parish Hall, 330 1st St., NW, Elkader, 11/21/76, C, a, 76000750

St. Peters United Evangelical Lutheran Church, U.S. 52, Ceres, 12/12/76, C, a, 76000743

Stemmer, J. C., House, 113 Oak, NW, Elkader, 10/21/76, C, 76000751

Stone Barn [Guttenberg MRA], 12 Goethe St., Guttenberg, 9/24/84, C, 84001244

Turkey River State Preserve Archeological District [Prehistoric Mounds of the Quad-State Region of the Upper Mississippi River Valley MPS], Address Restricted, Millville vicinity, 5/30/90, C, D, 90000774

Valley Mills, E of Garnavillo, Garnavillo vicinity, 12/12/76, A, 76000752

Weber House [Guttenberg MRA], 822 S. River Park Dr., Guttenberg, 9/24/84, A, C, 84001247

Wehmer House [Guttenberg MRA], 910 S. River Park Dr., Guttenberg, 9/24/84, C, 84001249

Clinton County

Anthony, Horace, House, 1206 Anthony Pl., Camache, 5/01/91, C, 91000533

Clinton County Courthouse [County Courthouses in Iowa TR], Between 6th and 7th Aves., Clinton, 7/02/81, C, 81000230

Clinton Public Library [Public Library Buildings in Iowa TR], 306 8th Ave, S., Clinton, 5/23/83, A, C, 83000349

Curtis, George M., House, 420 S. 5th Ave., Clinton, 10/01/79, B, C, 79000892

Delmar Calaboose, Vane St., Delmar, 3/19/81, A, C, 81000231

First National Bank, 226 Fifth Ave. S, Clinton, 10/10/85, C, 85003007

Lamb, Lafayette, House, 317 7th Ave., S., Clinton, 10/18/79, B, C, 79000893

Van Allen Store, 5th Ave. and S. 2nd St., Clinton, 1/07/76, C, NHL, 76000753

Crawford County

Chamberlin, Clarence D., House, 1434 2nd Ave., S., Denison, 4/28/77, B, 77000505

Crawford County Courthouse [County Courthouses in Iowa TR], Broadway between Ave. B and Ave. C, Denison, 7/02/81, C, 81000232

Dow House, Prince St. at S city limit, Dow City, 6/14/72, B, 72000471

Dunham, Z. T., Pioneer Stock Farm, IA 37, 1 mi. NW of Dunlap, Dunlap vicinity, 8/02/93, A, 93000652

McHenry, William A., House, 1428 1st Ave., N., Denison, 11/07/76, C, 76000755

Dallas County

Dallas County Courthouse [County Courthouses in Iowa TR (AD)], Town Sq., Adel, 11/26/73, A, C, 73000723

Dallas County Courthouse (Boundary Increase) [County Courthouses in Iowa TR (AD)], Town Sq., Adel, 10/25/79, C, 79003694

Dexter Community House, 707 Dallas St., Dexter, 3/03/75, C, 75000679

McColl, Anthony M., House, 502 S. Main St., Woodward, 2/05/87, B, 87000026

Mosher Building, 1017 Railroad, Perry, 1/25/91, C, 90002192

Wilson, John, House, SW of DeSoto, DeSoto vicinity, 3/30/79, C, 79000894

Davis County

Bloomfield Square, Madison, Jefferson, Franklin and Washington Sts., Bloomfield, 11/07/76, A, C, 76000756

Davis County Courthouse [County Courthouses in Iowa TR (AD)], Bloomfield Town Sq., Bloomfield, 5/03/74, A, C, 74000779

Findley, William, House, 302 E. Franklin St., Bloomfield, 6/09/78, C, 78001213

Russell Octagon House, SW of Bloomfield off U.S. 63, Bloomfield vicinity, 10/08/76, C, 76000757

Stringtown House, E of Centerville on IA 2, Centerville vicinity, 4/16/74, A, C, 74000780

Tarrence Round Barn [Iowa Round Barns: The Sixty Year Experiment TR], Off IA 2, Bloomfield vicinity, 6/30/86, A, C, 86001424

Troy Academy, Off IA 2, Troy, 6/23/76, A, b, 76000758

Weaver, James B., House, Weaver Park Rd. (U.S. 63), Bloomfield, 5/15/75, B, NHL, 75000680

Wilson, Asa, House, 207 S. Washington, Bloomfield, 12/10/82, C, 82000404

Decatur County

Decatur County Courthouse [County Courthouses in Iowa TR], 9th St., Leon, 7/02/81, C, 81000233

Liberty Hall, Main St., Lamoni vicinity, 9/29/83, A, C, a, 83000350

McClung, J. J., House, Jct. of Main and Vine Sts., Garden Grove, 12/06/90, C, 90001856

Missouri, Iowa & Nebraska Railway Co. Depot—Weldon [Advent & Development of Railroads in Iowa MPS], N. Main St. at Decatur County line, Weldon, 12/13/91, A, 91001827

Stearns, C. S., House, Main St., Garden Grove, 11/28/78, C, 78001214

Union Church, Clark at Sycamore St., Davis City, 12/12/76, A, a, 76000759

Delaware County

Backbone State Park Historic District [Conservation Movement in Iowa MPS; CCC Properties in Iowa State Parks MPS], Jct. of Co. Rds. C57 and W69, Strawberry Point vicinity, 12/23/91, A, C, 91001842

Backbone State Park, Cabin—Bathing Area (Area A) [CCC Properties in Iowa State Parks MPS], Jct. of Co. Hwy. W69 and Co. Hwy. C54, Dundee vicinity, 11/15/90, A, C, g, 90001681

Backbone State Park, Picnicking, Hiking & Camping Area (Area B) [CCC Properties in Iowa State Parks MPS], Jct. of Co. Hwy. W69 and Co. Hwy. C54, Dundee vicinity, 11/15/90, A, C, g, 90001682

Backbone State Park, Richmond Springs (Area C) [CCC Properties in Iowa State Parks MPS], Jct. of Co. Hwy. W69 and Co. Hwy. C54, Dundee vicinity, 11/15/90, A, C, 90001683

Bay Settlement Church and Monument, SW of Delhi, Delhi vicinity, 9/13/77, A, a, d, f, 77000506

Coffin's Grove Stagecoach House, 3 mi. W of Manchester, Manchester vicinity, 2/20/75, A, C, 75000681

Delaware County Courthouse [County Courthouses in Iowa TR], Main St., Manchester, 7/02/81, C, 81000234

Hoag, J. J., House, 120 E. Union St., Manchester, 8/13/76, C, 76000760

Old Lenox College, College St., Hopkinton, 12/19/74, A, C, 74000781

Spring Branch Butter Factory Site, Address Restricted, Manchester vicinity, 6/28/74, A, D, 74000782

Suckow, Ruth, House, S. Radcliffe and 5th St., Earlville, 12/23/77, B, 77000507

Des Moines County

Baptist Church, W of Sperry off U.S. 61, Sperry vicinity, 4/18/77, A, C, a, d, 77000509

Des Moines County—Continued

Burlington Public Library, 501 N. 4th St., Burlington, 3/27/75, A, C, 75000682

Burlington and Missouri River Railroad Passenger Station, 237 S. 4th St., Burlington, 10/22/76, A, b, 76000761

Burlington, Cedar Rapids & Northern Freight House, Front and High Sts., Burlington, 1/27/83, A, 83000351

Church of St. John the Baptist, 712 Division St., Burlington, 2/26/82, A, C, a, 82002615

Crapo Park and Arboretum Historic District, Bounded by Parkway Dr., Koestner, Madison Rd., and the Mississippi River, Burlington, 6/03/76, A, C, 76000762

Darwin, Mary, House, 537 Summer St., Burlington, 1/24/80, B, 80001445

Dodge, Augustus Caesar, House, 829 N. 5th St., Burlington, 1/25/80, B, 80001446

First Congregational Church, 313 N. 4th St., Burlington, 11/21/76, B, a, 76000763

Forney, James M., House, 401 Cedar, Burlington, 9/22/86, C, 86002689

German Methodist Episcopal Church, 7th and Washington Sts., Burlington, 9/22/77, A, C, a, 77000508

Hedge Block, 401-407 Jefferson St., Burlington, 10/07/82, A, C, 82000405

Heritage Hill Historic District, Roughly bounded by Central Ave., High, 3rd, and Jefferson Sts., Burlington, 12/21/82, A, C, a, 82000406

Hotel Burlington, 206 N. Third St., Burlington, 12/31/87, A, C, 87002214

Jagger-Churchill House, 201 Spring St., Burlington, 3/05/82, C, 82002616

Snake Alley, N. 6th St., between Washington and Columbia Sts., Burlington, 9/06/74, A, C, 74000783

Snake Alley Historic District, Roughly bounded by Columbia and Washington Sts., Cobblestone Alley, and Service Dr., Burlington, 5/21/75, A, C, 75000683

Starker-Leopold Historic District, 101, 111 Clay and 110 Grand Sts., Burlington, 2/02/83, B, C, 83000352

Union Hotel, 301–311 S. Main St., Burlington, 4/22/93, A, B, C, 93000328

West Jefferson Street Historic District, Roughly the 400 to 800 blocks of W. Jefferson St., Burlington, 4/09/91, A, 91000409

Dickinson County

Clark, Gerome, House, E of Milford, Milford vicinity, 11/09/77, A, C, 77000510

Dickinson County Courthouse [County Courthouses in Iowa TR], Hill Ave., Spirit Lake, 7/02/81, C, 81000235

Gull Point State Park, Area A [CCC Properties in Iowa State Parks MPS], Off IA 86 on W Shore of W Okoboji Lake, Milford vicinity, 11/15/90, A, C, 90001661

Gull Point State Park, Area B [CCC Properties in Iowa State Parks MPS], Off IA 86 on W shore of W Okoboji Lake, Milford vicinity, 11/15/90, A, C, 90001662

Iowa Lakeside Laboratory Historic District [Conservation Movement in Iowa MPS], IA 86 about 4 mi. N-NW of jct. with US 71, Milford vicinity, 12/23/91, A, B, C, 91001830

Pikes Point State Park Shelter and Steps [CCC Properties in Iowa State Parks MPS], W of jct. of IA 9 and US 71, Spirit Lake vicinity, 11/15/90, A, C, 90001675

Pillsbury Point State Park [CCC Properties in Iowa State Parks MPS], Off US 71 W of Minnewashta Lake, Arnolds Park, 1/12/93, A, C, 90001674

Spirit Lake Massacre Log Cabin, Arnolds Park, W of Estherville on U.S. 71, Arnolds Park, 4/03/73, A, 73000724

Spirit Lake Public Library, 1801 Hill Ave., Spirit Lake, 1/24/80, C, 80001448

Templar Park, NE of Orleans on IA 276, Orleans vicinity, 8/03/77, A, C, 77000511

Trappers Bay State Park Picnic Shelter [CCC Properties in Iowa State Parks MPS], N of jct. of IA 219 and IA 9, Lake Park vicinity, 11/15/90, A, C, 90001676

Dubuque County

Allen House, 515 1st Ave., W., Dyersville, 7/10/75, C, 75000686

Andrew-Ryan House, 1375 Locust, Dubuque, 4/11/85, C, b, 85000720

Carnegie-Stout Public Library, 11th and Bluff Sts., Dubuque, 8/01/75, C, 75000684

Cathedral Historic District, Roughly bounded by a bluffline running W. of Bluff St., W. 7th, Locust and Jones Sts., Dubuque, 9/25/85, C, 85002501

Diamond Jo Boat Store and Office, Jones and Water Sts., Dubuque, 11/23/77, A, 77000512

Dubuque City Hall, 50 W. 13th St., Dubuque, 9/14/72, A, C, 72000472

Dubuque County Courthouse [County Courthouses in Iowa TR (AD)], 720 Central Ave., Dubuque, 6/23/71, C, 71000298

Dubuque County Jail, 36 E. 8th St., Dubuque, 6/27/72, A, C, NHL, 72000473

Dubuque Freight House, E. 3rd St. Extension, Dubuque, 10/11/79, A, 79003693

Dubuque Trading Post—Village of Kettle Chief Archeological District [Mines of Spain Archeological MPS], Address Restricted, Dubuque vicinity, 11/21/88, D, NHL, 88002665

Dubuque, Julien, Monument [Mines of Spain Archeological MPS], Confluence of Mississippi River and Catfish Creek in Mines of Spain State Recreation Area, Dubuque vicinity, 11/21/88, A, f, 88002662

Fenelon Place Elevator, 512 Fenelon Pl., Dubuque, 8/03/78, A, C, e, 78001215

Garland House, 1090 Langworthy Ave., Dubuque, 7/07/83, C, 83000353

German Bank, 342 Main St., Dubuque, 3/28/78, C, 78001216

Haberkorn House and Farmstead, W of Sherrill, Sherrill vicinity, 1/25/80, C, 80001449

Ham, Mathias, House, 2241 Lincoln Ave., Dubuque, 7/19/76, C, 76000764

Hancock, Charles T., House, 1105 Grove Terr., Dubuque, 4/10/86, C, 86000741

Holland, Ora, House, 1296 Mt. Pleasant St., Dubuque, 8/14/86, C, 86001613

Hollenfelz House, 1651 White St., Dubuque, 9/13/77, C, a, 77000513

Jackson Park Historic District, Roughly bounded by Seventeenth, Iowa, Tenth and Ninth, and Bluff and Montrose Sts., Dubuque, 7/31/86, C, 86002102

Johnson House and Barn, S of Dubuque, Dubuque vicinity, 11/05/74, A, C, a, 74000784

Kelley House, 274 Southern Ave., Dubuque, 1/30/78, C, 78001217

Kidder, Zephaniah, House, Main St., Epworth, 11/14/78, C, 78001218

Langworthy House, 1095 W. 3rd St., Dubuque, 10/14/75, B, C, 75000685

Lincoln School, About 4 mi. N of Farley, Farley vicinity, 7/24/75, B, 75000687

Loetscher, T. Ben, House, 160 S. Grandview Ave., Dubuque, 11/02/89, C, 89001777

McMahon House, 800 English Lane, Dubuque, 11/21/76, C, 76000765

Mines of Spain Area Rural Community Archeological District [Mines of Spain Archeological MPS], Address Restricted, Dubuque vicinity, 11/21/88, D, 88002663

Mines of Spain Lead Mining Community Archeological District [Mines of Spain Archeological MPS], Address Restricted, Dubuque vicinity, 11/21/88, D, NHL, 88002664

Mines of Spain Prehistoric District [Mines of Spain Archeological MPS], Address Restricted, Dubuque vicinity, 11/21/88, D, 88002666

Old Chapel Hall, 2050 University Ave., Dubuque, 8/05/83, A, a, 83000355

Old Main Historic District, Main St. between 1st and 4th Sts., Dubuque, 1/12/83, A, C, 83000356

Orpheum Theatre and Site, 405 Main St., Dubuque, 11/14/72, A, C, 72000474

Rath, Johann Christian Frederick, House, 1204 Mt. Loretta Ave., Dubuque, 4/11/77, C, 77000514

Redstone, 504 Bluff St., Dubuque, 12/12/76, C, 76000766

Round Barn, Dubuque Township [Iowa Round Barns: The Sixty Year Experiment TR], 2810 Cascade Rd., Dubuque, 6/30/86, A, C, 86001425

Sauser-Lane House, 101 2nd Ave., SW, Cascade, 7/14/83, C, 83000354

Shot Tower, Commercial St. and River Front, Dubuque, 11/07/76, A, 76000767

Thedinga, J. H., House, 340 W. 5th St., Dubuque, 11/07/76, B, C, 76000768

WILLIAM M. BLACK (dredge), E. 2nd St., Dubuque, 4/12/82, A, C, g, NHL, 82002618

Washington Park, Bounded by 6th, 7th, Bluff, and Locust Sts., Dubuque, 7/14/77, A, 77000515

Western Hotel, SE of Holy Cross on U.S. 52, Holy Cross vicinity, 11/07/76, C, 76000769

Emmet County

Thomsen Round Barn [Iowa Round Barns: The Sixty Year Experiment TR], Off IA 15, Armstrong vicinity, 6/30/86, A, C, 86001426

Fayette County

Chicago, Milwaukee, St. Paul and Pacific Railroad Company Depot, NE of Fayette off IA 150, Fayette vicinity, 12/28/78, A, C, b, 78001219

College Hall, 200 block of E. Clark, Fayette, 11/07/76, A, C, 76000770

Fayette County Courthouse [County Courthouses in Iowa TR], Pine St., West Union, 7/02/81, C, 81000236

Grimes Octagon Barn [Iowa Round Barns: The Sixty Year Experiment TR], Off IA 56, West Union vicinity, 6/30/86, A, C, 86001428

Hanson, Alfred, House, 403 N. Frederick Ave., Oelwein, 7/12/84, C, 84001252

Hardware Building, 223 Mill St., Wadena, 7/15/77, C, 77000516

Hotel Mealey, 102 S. Frederick Ave., Oelwein, 1/27/83, A, C, 83000357

Montauk, 1 mi. NE of Clermont on U.S. 18, Clermont vicinity, 2/21/73, B, 73000725

Nus, August, Polygonal Barn [Iowa Round Barns: The Sixty Year Experiment TR], CR C2 W, Arlington vicinity, 6/30/86, A, C, 86001427

Union Sunday School, McGregor and Larrabee Sts., Clermont, 11/05/74, A, C, a, 74000785

Floyd County

Brooks Round Barn [Iowa Round Barns: The Sixty Year Experiment TR], W of US 218, Charles City vicinity, 6/30/86, A, C, 86001429

Central Park—North Main Street Historic District, N. Main St. and N. Jackson St., Charles City, 8/10/76, C, 76000771

Cook Farm, S of Charles City on U.S. 218, Charles City vicinity, 6/18/79, C, 79000895

Dodd, A. B. C., House, 310 3rd Ave., Charles City, 5/22/78, A, C, 78001220

Hart, Charles Walter, House, 800 3rd Ave., Charles City, 1/25/80, B, C, 80001450

Marble Rock Bank, 313 Bradford St., Marble Rock, 11/10/82, A, 82000407

Miller, Alvin, House [Iowa Usonian Houses by Frank Lloyd Wright, 1945-1960, MPS (AD)], 1107 Court St., Charles City, 11/16/78, C, g, 78001221

Parr, Charles Henry, House, 100 W. Hulin St., Charles City, 1/24/80, B, 80001451

Rockford Mill, Shell Rock River at 4th and Main St., Rockford, 7/28/83, A, C, 83000358

Spotts Round Barn [Iowa Round Barns: The Sixty Year Experiment TR], IA 14, Charles City vicinity, 6/30/86, A, C, 86001430

Suspension Bridge, Over the Big Cedar River at end of Clark St., Charles City, 10/30/89, A, 89001778

Franklin County

Beeds Lake State Park, Civilian Conservation Corps Area [CCC Properties in Iowa State Parks MPS], Jct. of IA 3 and IA 134, Hampton vicinity, 11/15/90, A, C, 90001672

Boehmler, H. E., House, 105 2nd St. SE., Hampton, 12/13/91, C, 91001829

Franklin County Courthouse [County Courthouses in Iowa TR (AD)], Central Ave. and 1st St., NW, Hampton, 8/13/76, C, 76000772

Franklin County G. A. R. Soldiers' Memorial Hall, 3 Federal St. N., Hampton, 12/13/91, A, C, 91001828

Harriman, Dr. O. B., House, 26 Tenth St. NW, Hampton, 2/05/87, B, 87000011

Maysville Schoolhouse, S of Hampton, Hampton vicinity, 6/17/81, A, 81000237

Reeve Electric Association Plant, RR 1, SW of Hampton, Hampton vicinity, 4/06/90, A, 89002307

Reeve, Leander, House, SE of Hampton on IA 134, Hampton vicinity, 7/17/79, C, 79000896

Wood, Herman, Round Barn [Iowa Round Barns: The Sixty Year Experiment TR], US 65, Iowa Falls vicinity, 6/30/86, A, C, 86001431

Fremont County

Chautauqua Pavilion, IA 42, Riverton, 10/22/76, A, 76000773

Fremont County Courthouse [County Courthouses in Iowa TR], Clay St., Sidney, 7/02/81, C, 81000238

Hamburg Public Library [Public Library Buildings in Iowa TR], 1301 Main St., Hamburg, 5/23/83, A, C, 83000359

St. Patrick Church, 3rd St., Imogene, 7/07/83, A, C, a, 83000360

Todd House, Park St., Tabor, 8/15/75, A, 75000689

Greene County

Frantz Round Barn [Iowa Round Barns: The Sixty Year Experiment TR], Off US 30, Grand Junction vicinity, 6/30/86, A, C, 86001432

Gallup, George H., House, 703 S. Chestnut St., Jefferson, 7/18/85, C, 85001581

Greene County Courthouse [County Courthouses in Iowa TR (AD)], E. Lincoln Way and Chestnut Sts., Jefferson, 12/14/78, C, 78001222

Lincoln Highway Marker (1) [Lincoln Highway in Greene County MPS], Address Restricted, Jefferson, 3/29/93, A, 93000163

Lincoln Highway Marker (2) [Lincoln Highway in Greene County MPS; County Courthouses in

Iowa TR], Jct. of Lincoln Way and Chestnut Sts., Jefferson, 3/29/93, A, f, 93000164

Lincoln Highway—Buttrick's Creek Abandoned Segment [Lincoln Highway in Greene County MPS], Approximately 3.5 mi. E of Jefferson on S side of Buttrick's Cr. bridge, Jefferson vicinity, 3/29/93, A, 93000166

Lincoln Highway—Buttrick's Creek to Grand Junction Segment [Lincoln Highway in Greene County MPS], From Buttrick's Cr. E to IA 144, Grand Junction vicinity, 3/29/93, A, 93000167

Lincoln Highway—Grand Junction Segment [Lincoln Highway in Greene County MPS], Through and 1 mi. E of Grand Junction, S of Chicago & Northwestern RR tracks, Grand Junction, 3/29/93, A, 93000168

Lincoln Highway—Little Beaver Creek Bridge [Lincoln Highway in Greene County MPS], 2.5 mi. E and 1 mi. N of Grand Junction across Little Beaver Cr., Grand Junction vicinity, 3/29/93, A, 93000170

Lincoln Highway—Raccoon River Rural Segment [Lincoln Highway in Greene County MPS], Co. Rd. E53 approximately 0.1 mi. W of Jefferson City limits, going W across Raccoon R., Jefferson, 3/29/93, A, C, 93000162

Lincoln Highway—West Beaver Creek Abandoned Segment [Lincoln Highway in Greene County MPS], Approximately 1 mi. E of Grand Junction between Chicago & Northwestern RR tracks and US 30, Grand Junction vicinity, 3/29/93, A, 93000169

Lincoln Highway—West Greene County Rural Segment [Lincoln Highway in Greene County MPS], N from jct. of IA 25 and US 30, approximately 0.5 mi. N of Scranton, then W to jct. with US 30, Scranton vicinity, 3/29/93, A, 93000161

Lincoln Statue [Lincoln Highway in Greene County MPS; County Courthouses in Iowa TR], Jct. of Lincoln Way and Chestnut Sts., Jefferson, 3/29/93, A, f, 93000165

Squirrel Hollow County Park Historic District [Conservation Movement in Iowa MPS], E bank of N. Raccoon R. SE of Jefferson, Jefferson vicinity, 12/23/91, A, C, 91001835

St. Patrick's Catholic Church, Cedar, 4 mi. W of Churdan on E 19, .5 mi. N on gravel rd., Churdan vicinity, 7/10/92, C, a, 92000840

Grundy County

Grundy County Courthouse [County Courthouses in Iowa TR], Grundy Ave., Grundy Center, 7/02/81, C, 81000239

Neessen, Chris, House, 601 E. 4th, Wellsburg, 1/12/84, C, 84001253

Guthrie County

Octagon Barn, Richland Township [Iowa Round Barns: The Sixty Year Experiment TR], Off IA 141, Jamaica vicinity, 6/30/86, A, C, 86001433

Guthrie County—Continued

Panora-Linden High School, Bounded by Main, Vine, Market, and 2nd Sts., Panora, 7/23/74, C, 74000786

Springbrook State Park, Civilian Conservation Corps Area [CCC Properties in Iowa State Parks MPS], Jct. of IA 384 and Co. Hwy. F25, Guthrie Center vicinity, 11/15/90, A, C, 90001671

Hamilton County

Kendall Young Public Library [Public Library Buildings in Iowa TR], 1201 Willson Ave., Webster City, 5/23/83, C, 83000361

Oakland, William, Round Barn [Iowa Round Barns: The Sixty Year Experiment TR], Off US 68, Blairsburg vicinity, 6/30/86, A, C, 86001434

State Bank of Stratford, 801 Shakespeare St., Stratford, 7/07/83, A, C, 83000362

Webster City Post Office, 801 Willson Ave., Webster City, 7/06/82, C, 82002619

Hancock County

Hancock County Courthouse [County Courthouses in Iowa TR], State St., Garner, 7/02/81, C, 81000240

Pilot Knob State Park, Amphitheater (Area 4) [CCC Properties in Iowa State Parks MPS], S of jct. of IA 9 and IA 332, Forest City vicinity, 11/15/90, A, C, 90001688

Pilot Knob State Park, Observation Tower (Area 2) [CCC Properties in Iowa State Parks MPS], S of jct. of IA 9 and IA 332, Forest City vicinity, 11/15/90, A, C, 90001686

Pilot Knob State Park, Picnic Shelter (Area 3) [CCC Properties in Iowa State Parks MPS], S of Jct. of IA 9 and IA 332, Forest City vicinity, 11/15/90, A, C, 90001687

Pilot Knob State Park, Portals (Area 5a) [CCC Properties in Iowa State Parks MPS], S of jct. of IA 9 and IA 332, Forest City vicinity, 11/15/90, A, C, 90001689

Pilot Knob State Park, Trail Area (Area 6a—6c) [CCC Properties in Iowa State Parks MPS], S of jct. of IA 9 and IA 332, Forest City vicinity, 11/15/90, A, C, 90001690

Hardin County

Alden Public Library, 1012 Water St., Alden, 3/17/81, A, 81000241

Carnegie-Ellsworth Public Library [Public Library Buildings in Iowa TR], 520 Rocksylvania Ave., Iowa Falls, 5/23/83, A, C, 83000363

Edgewood School of Domestic Arts, 719 River St., Iowa Falls, 4/19/79, A, B, 79000897

Eldora Public Library [Public Library Buildings in Iowa TR], 1219 14th Ave., Eldora, 5/23/83, C, 83000364

Ellsworth—Jones Building [Iowa Falls MPS], 511 Washington Ave., Iowa Falls, 10/01/93, B, C, 93000959

Estes Park Band Shell [Iowa Falls MPS], Estes Park, Iowa Falls, 10/01/93, A, C, 93000960

First National Bank [Iowa Falls MPS], 601 Washington Ave., Iowa Falls, 10/01/93, C, 93000958

Hardin County Courthouse [County Courthouses in Iowa TR], Edgington Ave., Eldora, 7/02/81, C, 81000242

Honey Creek Friends' Meetinghouse, SW of New Providence, New Providence vicinity, 2/08/80, C, a, 80001452

Illinois Central Combination Depot—Ackley [Advent & Development of Railroads in Iowa, 1855-1940, MPS], N. of Railroad St., between State and Mitchell Sts., Ackley, 9/06/90, C, 90001303

Iowa Falls Union Depot [Advent & Development of Railroads in Iowa, 1855-1940, MPS], E. Rocksylvania Ave. and Depot St., Iowa Falls, 9/06/90, A, C, 90001305

McClanahan Block [Iowa Falls MPS], 613 Washington Ave., Iowa Falls, 10/01/93, C, 93000956

Metropolitan Opera House, 515 Washington St., Iowa Falls, 2/20/75, A, C, 75000690

Mills Tower Historic District [Advent & Development of Railroads in Iowa, 1855-1940, MPS], E. Rocksylvania Ave. 1/3 mi. E of Freight House, Iowa Falls, 9/06/90, A, C, 90001304

Princess—Sweet Shop [Iowa Falls MPS], 607 Washington Ave., Iowa Falls, 10/01/93, C, 93000957

Sentinel Block [Iowa Falls MPS], 702 Washington Ave., Iowa Falls, 10/01/93, C, 93000962

St. Matthew's by the Bridge Episcopal Church [Iowa Falls MPS], Jct. of Oak and Railroad Sts., Iowa Falls, 10/01/93, C, a, 93000961

W. R. C. Hall [Iowa Falls MPS], 710 Washington Ave., Iowa Falls, 10/01/93, A, C, 93000963

Harrison County

Haner, William, Polygonal Barn [Iowa Round Barns: The Sixty Year Experiment TR], CR L16, Pisgah vicinity, 6/30/86, A, C, 86001435

Harrison County Courthouse [County Courthouses in Iowa TR], 7th St., Logan, 7/02/81, C, 81000243

Harrrison County Jail, 105 S. 1st Ave., Logan, 4/14/83, C, 83004517

Old Harrison County Courthouse [County Courthouses in Iowa TR], 401 Locust, Magnolia, 2/24/83, A, C, 83000365

State Savings Bank, 312 E. 7th St., Logan, 4/18/85, C, 85000836

Wheeler, John R., Jr., House, 407 S. Third St., Dunlap, 11/04/86, C, 86003171

Henry County

Allen, G. W. S., House, 207 E. Henry St., Mount Pleasant, 4/11/85, C, 85000721

Ambler, Henry, House, 405 Broadway, Mt. Pleasant, 4/10/86, C, 86000717

Brazelton House, 401 N. Main St., Mount Pleasant, 1/27/83, C, 83000366

Brazelton House Hotel, 100 N. Main St., Mt. Pleasant, 9/22/86, A, C, 86002700

Budde—Singer Building [Mount Pleasant MPS], 110 N. Main, Mount Pleasant, 9/06/91, C, 91001112

City Hall [Mount Pleasant MPS], 220 W. Monroe, Mount Pleasant, 9/06/91, C, 91001120

First National Bank [Mount Pleasant MPS], 101 S. Jefferson, Mount Pleasant, 9/06/91, C, 91001118

Geode State Park, Civilian Conservation Corps Area [CCC Properties in Iowa State Parks MPS], Co. Rd. X23 E of Lowell, Danville vicinity, 11/15/90, A, C, g, 90001673

Harlan House Hotel, 122 N. Jefferson St., Mount Pleasant, 11/16/87, B, 87002019

Harlan-Lincoln House, 101 W. Broad St., Mount Pleasant, 5/25/73, B, 73000726

Henry County Courthouse [County Courthouses in Iowa TR], Washington St., Mount Pleasant, 7/02/81, C, 81000244

Henry County Savings Bank [Mount Pleasant MPS], 100 S. Main, Mount Pleasant, 9/06/91, C, 91001116

Holtkamp Round Barn [Iowa Round Barns: The Sixty Year Experiment TR], Off US 218, Salem vicinity, 6/30/86, A, C, 86001436

Lewelling, Henderson, House, W. Main St., Salem, 6/21/82, B, 82002620

Louisa Building [Mount Pleasant MPS], 120 S. Main, Mount Pleasant, 9/06/91, C, 91001117

Masonic Temple Theater [Mount Pleasant MPS], 115 N. Main, Mount Pleasant, 9/06/91, C, 91001119

Masters Building [Mount Pleasant MPS], 221 W. Monroe, Mount Pleasant, 9/06/91, C, 91001121

McCandless Building [Mount Pleasant MPS], 115 W. Monroe, Mount Pleasant, 9/06/91, C, 91001111

Mount Pleasant Public Library [Public Library Buildings in Iowa TR], 200 N. Main St., Mount Pleasant, 5/23/83, C, 83000367

National State Bank [Mount Pleasant MPS], 101 W. Monroe, Mount Pleasant, 9/06/91, C, 91001115

Old Main, Iowa Wesleyan College campus, Mount Pleasant, 3/26/73, C, 73000727

Pleasant Lawn School Historic District, Off IA 218, Mt. Pleasant vicinity, 3/25/87, A, b, 87000477

Timmerman—Burd Building [Mount Pleasant MPS], 118 S. Main, Mount Pleasant, 9/06/91, C, 91001113

Union Block [Mount Pleasant MPS], 109–113 W. Monroe, Mount Pleasant, 9/06/91, C, 91001110

Zuhn Building [Mount Pleasant MPS], 201 E. Monroe, Mount Pleasant, 9/06/91, C, 91001114

Howard County

Bohemian Savings Bank, Main St., Protivin, 9/13/90, A, 88002806

Howard County—Continued

Cresco Opera House, 115 W. 2nd Ave., Cresco, 8/27/81, A, 81000245

Fellows, James C., House, Main St., Riceville, 6/21/82, B, C, 82002621

Howard County Courthouse [County Courthouses in Iowa TR], Elm St., Cresco, 7/02/81, C, 81000246

Kellow House, 324 4th Ave., W., Cresco, 11/22/77, C, 77000517

Lime Springs Mill Complex, SR 157, Lime Springs, 4/11/77, A, 77000518

Polygonal Barn, New Oregon Township [Iowa Round Barns: The Sixty Year Experiment TR], Off IA 39, Cresco, 6/30/86, A, C, 86001437

South Ward School, 500 S. Elm St., Cresco, 11/10/82, C, 82000408

Humboldt County

Brown, Corydon, House, E of Dakota City off IA 3, Dakota City vicinity, 11/14/78, C, 78001223

Humboldt Free Public Library [Public Library Buildings in Iowa TR], 30 6th St., N., Humboldt, 5/23/83, C, 83000368

Ida County

Bell, Alvin Bushnell, House, 310 Quimby St., Ida Grove, 1/27/83, C, 83000369

Ida County Courthouse [County Courthouses in Iowa TR (AD)], 401 Moorehead St., Ida Grove, 3/15/74, A, C, 74000787

Moorehead Stagecoach Inn, Off U.S. 59, Ida Grove, 8/27/74, A, B, C, 74000788

Turner Hall, SE corner of Keil and 2nd Sts., Holstein, 1/22/75, A, 75000691

Warnock, Dr. Francis B., House, 201 Maple St., Battle Creek, 10/13/88, C, 88001945

Waveland Round Barn [Iowa Round Barns: The Sixty Year Experiment TR], Off US 20, Cushing vicinity, 6/30/86, A, C, 86001438

Iowa County

Amana Villages, NE Iowa County, Middle Amana vicinity, 10/15/66, A, NHL, 66000336

Baird, E. J., House, Jackson and Fremont Sts., Millersburg, 2/25/82, B, C, 82002622

Indian Fish Weir, Address Restricted, Middle Amana vicinity, 7/21/88, D, 88001122

Iowa County Courthouse [County Courthouses in Iowa TR], Court Ave., Marengo, 7/02/81, C, 81000247

Ladora Savings Bank, 811 Pacific St., Ladora, 8/03/90, C, 90001196

Lenox Township Church of the New Jersalem, S of Norway, Norway vicinity, 9/29/83, A, a, 83000370

Pilot Grove, SW of Williamsburg, Williamsburg vicinity, 11/17/77, A, d, 77000519

Plagmann Round Barn [Iowa Round Barns: The Sixty Year Experiment TR], Off IA 209, Conroy vicinity, 6/30/86, A, C, 86001440

St. Michael's Church, Cemetery, Rectory and Ancient Order of Hibernians Hall, E of Parnell on F 52, Parnell vicinity, 1/20/83, A, C, a, d, 83000371

Turner, Fred G., House, IA 149, North English vicinity, 6/27/85, C, 85001381

Jackson County

Anderson, D. H., Building, 129 S. Main St., Maquoketa, 4/10/86, C, 86000718

Anderson, D. H., House [Maquoketa MPS], 315 E. Locust, Maquoketa, 8/09/91, C, 91000964

Bassnett—Nickerson House [Limestone Architecture of Jackson County MPS], 116 S. Vermont, Maquoketa, 7/24/92, C, 92000914

Bellevue Herald Building [Limestone Architecture of Jackson County MPS], 130 S. Riverview St., Bellevue, 8/30/91, C, 91001079

Big Mill Homestead [Limestone Architecture of Jackson County MPS], Paradise Valley Rd. W of Bellevue, Bellevue vicinity, 8/30/91, C, 91001075

Building at 101 North Riverview Street [Limestone Architecture of Jackson County MPS], 101 N. Riverview St., Belleview, 8/30/91, C, 91001068

Building at 126 South Riverview Street [Limestone Architecture of Jackson County MPS], 126 S. Riverview St., Bellevue, 8/30/91, C, 91001070

Building at 130–132 North Riverview Street [Limestone Architecture of Jackson County MPS], 130–132 N. Riverview St., Bellevue, 8/30/91, C, 91001069

Building at 306 South Second Street [Limestone Architecture of Jackson County MPS], 306 S. Second St., Bellevue, 8/30/91, C, 91001071

Butterworth, Nathaniel, House [Limestone Architecture of Jackson County MPS], E side of IA 62 N of Andrew, Andrew vicinity, 7/24/92, C, 92000909

Canton School, South St., Canton, 7/24/79, C, 79000898

Central School [Limestone Architecture of Jackson County MPS], Jct. of Bellevue—Canton and Dubuque—Canton Rds., Canton vicinity, 7/24/92, C, 92000920

Cooper, George, House [Maquoketa MPS], 413 W. Platt St., Maquoketa, 8/09/91, C, 91000963

Cundill Block [Maquoketa MPS], 202 S. Main, Maquoketa, 8/09/91, A, C, 89002112

DeFries House, Barn and Carpenter Shop [Limestone Architecture of Jackson County MPS], E side of Co. Rd. (232 Ave) W of jct. with IA 62, Andrew vicinity, 7/24/92, C, 92000910

Decker House Hotel, 128 N. Main St., Maquoketa, 12/29/78, C, 78003451

Dominy, John S., House [Limestone Architecture of Jackson County MPS], 605 Pearl St., Sabula, 7/24/92, C, 92000922

Dyas Hexagonal Barn [Iowa Round Barns: The Sixty Year Experiment TR], US 52, Bellevue vicinity, 6/30/86, A, C, 86001442

Dyas, George, House [Limestone Architecture of Jackson County MPS], Co. Rd. Z-15, SW of jct. with US 52, Bellevue vicinity, 8/30/91, C, 91001077

Dyas, William, Barn [Limestone Architecture of Jackson County MPS], Co. Rd. Z-15, SW of jct. with US 52, Bellevue vicinity, 8/30/91, C, 91001078

First National Bank [Maquoketa MPS], 120 S. Main, Maquoketa, 8/09/91, A, C, 89002108

Fritz Chapel [Limestone Architecture of Jackson County MPS], Spruce Creek Rd. W of jct. with US 52, Bellevue vicinity, 8/30/91, C, a, 91001067

Gehlen House and Barn, U.S. 52, St. Donatus, 6/18/79, A, C, 79000901

Godard, Milton, House [Limestone Architecture of Jackson County MPS], S side Co. Rd. (7 St.) SW of Maquoketa, Maquoketa vicinity, 7/24/92, C, 92000915

Harris Wagon and Carriage Shop [Limestone Architecture of Jackson County MPS], Jct. of Main and Pine Sts., LaMotte, 7/24/92, C, 92000917

Hotel Hurst [Maquoketa MPS], 227 S. Main, Maquoketa, 12/27/89, A, C, 89002105

Hotel Hurst Garage [Maquoketa MPS], 219 S. Main, Maquoketa, 12/27/89, A, C, 89002109

House at 111 E. Maple Street [Maquoketa MPS], 111 E. Maple St., Maquoketa, 8/09/91, C, 91000959

House at 505 Court Street [Limestone Architecture of Jackson County MPS], 505 Court St., Bellevue, 8/30/91, C, 91001073

Hurst, A. A., House [Maquoketa MPS], 513 W. Platt St., Maquoketa, 8/09/91, C, 91000960

Hurstville Historic District, N of Maquoketa on U. S. 61, Maquoketa vicinity, 12/03/79, A, 79000900

IOOF Building [Maquoketa MPS], 103 N. Main, Maquoketa, 8/09/91, A, C, 89002110

Insane Asylum at the County Poor Farm [Limestone Architecture of Jackson County MPS], E side Co. Rd. Y61 (250th Ave.) N of Andrew, Andrew vicinity, 7/24/92, C, 92000918

Jackson County Courthouse [County Courthouses in Iowa TR], Bounded by Third, State, Fourth, and Court Sts., Bellevue, 7/02/81, A, C, 81000248

Jackson County Jail, Emmet St., Andrew, 12/12/78, A, 78001224

Johnson, Mrs. Lydia, House [Maquoketa MPS], 209 E. Locust, Maquoketa, 8/09/91, C, 91000966

Kegler Gonner Store and Post Office, 100 E. Main, Springbrook, 6/27/85, C, 85001375

Kucheman Building [Limestone Architecture of Jackson County MPS], 100 N. Second St., Bellevue, 8/30/91, C, 91001072

Lake, John, House [Maquoketa MPS], 601 W. Platt St., Maquoketa, 12/30/91, C, 91000969

Jackson County—Continued

Lubben, Henry, House, Smokehouse and Springhouse [Limestone Architecture of Jackson County MPS], W side of Co. Rd. Y34 N of Baldwin, Baldwin vicinity, 7/24/92, C, 92000919

Lyon Block [Maquoketa MPS], 112–116 N. Main, Maquoketa, 8/09/91, A, C, 89002104

Maquoketa Caves State Park Historic District [Conservation Movement in Iowa MPS; CCC Properties in Iowa State Parks MPS], Co. Rd. 428 NW of Maquoketa, Maquoketa vicinity, 12/23/91, A, C, 91001843

Maquoketa Free Public Library [Maquoketa MPS], Second and Pleasant, Maquoketa, 12/27/89, A, C, 89002102

Merrero Building [Maquoketa MPS], 111–115 S. Main, Maquoketa, 8/09/91, A, C, 89002107

Mill Rock School [Limestone Architecture of Jackson County MPS], W side of Co. Rd. (153 Ave.) S of Baldwin, Baldwin vicinity, 7/24/92, C, 92000913

Mitchell—Maskrey Mill [Maquoketa MPS], 120 E. Pleasant, Maquoketa, 8/09/91, A, C, 89002111

New Era Building [Maquoketa MPS], 115–117 E. Platt, Maquoketa, 8/09/91, A, C, 89002103

Niemann, Theodore, House and Spring House [Limestone Architecture of Jackson County MPS], Spruce Creek Rd. W of jct. with US 52, Bellevue vicinity, 8/30/91, C, 91001065

Organ, Alexander, House [Maquoketa MPS], 607 W. Summit, Maquoketa, 8/09/91, C, 91000968

Paradise Farm, W of Bellevue, Bellevue vicinity, 7/13/77, B, 77000520

Perham House [Maquoketa MPS], 213 E. Pleasant St., Maquoketa, 8/09/91, C, 91000961

Polygonal Barn, Van Buren Township [Iowa Round Barns: The Sixty Year Experiment TR], IA 64, Van Buren vicinity, 6/30/86, A, C, 86001443

Potter's, E. G., Jasper Flour Mill, South and 2nd St., Bellevue, 4/19/84, B, C, 84001257

Robb House and Spring House [Limestone Architecture of Jackson County MPS], Paradise Valley Rd. W of Bellevue, Bellevue vicinity, 8/30/91, C, 91001076

Roling, Henry, House [Limestone Architecture of Jackson County MPS], Spruce Creek Rd. W of jct. with US 52, Bellevue vicinity, 8/30/91, C, 91001066

Sanborn, C. M., Building [Maquoketa MPS], 203 S. Main, Maquoketa, 8/09/91, A, C, 89002106

Sieben, Mrs. Margaret, House [Limestone Architecture of Jackson County MPS], .3 mi. E of Co. Rd. Y34, N of Baldwin, Baldwin vicinity, 7/24/92, C, 92000916

Slye, Thomas, House [Limestone Architecture of Jackson County MPS], S side of Co. Rd. (184 St.) E of jct. with IA 62, Andrew vicinity, 7/24/92, C, 92000911

Spring Side, Jct. of US 52 and Ensign Rd., Bellevue vicinity, 12/28/90, C, 90001955

St. Lawrence Catholic Church [Limestone Architecture of Jackson County MPS], Bellevue—

Cascade Rd. (Co. Rd. D61) W of jct. with US 61, Otter Creek vicinity, 7/24/92, C, a, 92000912

St. Patrick's Church—Garryowen [Limestone Architecture of Jackson County MPS], W. Bellevue—Cascade Rd. (Co. Rd. D61) W of Garryowen, Garryowen vicinity, 7/24/92, C, a, 92000921

Swigert, W. B., House [Maquoketa MPS], 309 N. Main St., Maquoketa, 8/09/91, C, 91000965

Taubman, Henry, House [Maquoketa MPS], 303 E. Pleasant St., Maquoketa, 8/09/91, C, 91000962

Upper Paradise [Limestone Architecture of Jackson County MPS], Paradise Valley Rd. W of Bellevue, Bellevue vicinity, 8/30/91, C, 91001074

Village of St. Donatus Historic District, Jct. of US 52/Main St. and First St., St. Donatus, 11/08/89, A, C, 89001870

West Pleasant Street Historic District [Maquoketa MPS], Pleasant St. between Second and Prospect Sts., Maquoketa, 8/09/91, C, 91000970

Williams, Seneca, Mill, E of Maquoketa on IA 64, Maquoketa vicinity, 9/01/76, A, 76000774

Wilson, Anson, House, S of Marquoketa off U.S. 61, Maquoketa vicinity, 11/17/77, B, C, 77000521

Wood, Jeremiah, House, 802 River St., Sabula, 11/10/82, A, 82000409

Jasper County

Arthur, Thomas, House, 322 N. 8th Ave., E., Newton, 10/07/82, C, 82000410

Bergman, August H., House [Architectural Legacy of Proudfoot and Bird in Iowa, 1882–1940 MPS], 629 First Ave. E., Newton, 7/13/89, C, 89000856

German Evangelical Reformed Church, N of Newton, Newton vicinity, 3/07/79, C, a, d, 79000902

Hall, James Norman, House, 416 E. Howard St., Colfax, 7/12/84, B, 84003853

Jasper County Courthouse [County Courthouses in Iowa TR], 1st Ave. between W. 1rst St. & W. 2nd Sts., Newton, 7/02/81, C, 81000249

Lynnville Mill and Dam, East St., Lynnville, 11/25/77, A, 77000522

St. Stephen's Episcopal Church, 223 E. 4th St., N., Newton, 9/22/77, C, a, 77000523

Jefferson County

Architecture of Henry K. Holsman Historic Campus District, Bounded by Merrill St., IA 1, and Carter Memorial Dr., Fairfield, 10/31/83, A, C, 83003605

Ball, W. C., House, R.R. #2, Fairfield, 4/04/85, C, 85000691

Beck, James A., House, 401 E. Burlington Ave., Fairfield, 3/29/78, C, 78001225

Burnett-Montgomery House, 605 N. 3rd St., Fairfield, 1/27/83, A, C, 83000372

Clarke, James F., House, 500 S. Main St., Fairfield, 2/08/80, C, 80001453

Fairfield Public Library [Public Library Buildings in Iowa TR], Court & Washington, Fairfield, 5/23/83, A, C, 83000373

Former US Post Office Building [US Senator James F. Wilson Historic Resources MPS], 110 S. Court St., Fairfield, 1/24/91, B, 90002128

Henn Mansion, Maharishi International University Campus, Fairfield, 1/11/83, A, C, 83000374

Jefferson County Courthouse [County Courthouses in Iowa TR], Court St. between Briggs & Hempstead Aves., Fairfield, 7/02/81, C, 81000250

McElhinny House, 300 N. Court St., Fairfield, 12/19/77, C, 77000524

New Sweden Chapel, E of Fairfield off U.S. 34, Fairfield vicinity, 3/25/77, A, a, d, 77000525

Old Settlers' Association Park and Rhodham Bonnifield House, B St., Fairfield, 8/14/86, A, e, f, 86001601

Wells, George A., House, 304 S. Main St., Fairfield, 1/27/83, A, C, 83000375

Wells—Stubbs House, 508 E. Burlington Ave., Fairfield, 10/10/85, B, C, 85003000

Wilson Building [US Senator James F. Wilson Historic Resources MPS], 106–108 S. Court St., Fairfield, 1/24/91, B, 90002129

Wilson, US Senator James F., House [US Senator James F. Wilson Historic Resources MPS], 805 S. Main St., Fairfield, 1/24/91, B, 90002130

Johnson County

Berryhill, Charles, House, 414 Brown St., Iowa City, 5/31/79, C, 79000904

Billingsley-Hills House, 629 Melrose Ave., Iowa City, 1/21/83, C, 83000376

Boerner-Fry Company/Davis Hotel, 322 E. Washington St., Iowa City, 1/27/83, B, 83000377

Buresh Farm, W of Solon off IA 382, Solon vicinity, 4/29/77, A, 77000533

Carson, Thomas C., House, 906 E. College St., Iowa City, 9/09/82, B, C, 82002623

Cavanaugh-Zetek House, 704 Reno St., Iowa City, 9/16/77, C, 77000527

Chicago, Rock Island and Pacific Railroad Passenger Station, 115 Wright St., Iowa City, 12/10/82, A, C, 82000411

Close House, 538 S. Gilbert St., Iowa City, 5/31/74, C, 74000791

Close, M. T., and Company Flaxseed Warehouse, 521 S. Gilbert St., Iowa City, 7/12/84, A, 84001262

College Block Building, 125 E. College St., Iowa City, 7/23/73, C, 73000728

Congregational Church of Iowa City, 30 N. Clinton St., Iowa City, 6/18/73, C, a, 73000729

Coralville Public School, 402-404 5th St., Coralville, 1/11/74, C, 74000789

Coralville Union Ecclesiastical Church, 405 2nd Ave., Coralville, 4/11/77, A, a, 77000526

Cottage at Rock and Dubuque Streets, Rte. 4, Box 3, Solon, 1/03/85, C, 85000004

Johnson County—Continued

Czecho Slovakian Association Hall, 524 N. Johnson St., Iowa City, 11/07/76, A, 76000775

Economy Advertising Company, 119–123 N. Linn, Iowa City, 4/28/86, A, 86000875

First Johnson County Asylum, W of Iowa City, Iowa City vicinity, 8/31/78, A, 78001226

First Welsh Congregational Church, 5 mi. SW of Iowa City off IA 1, Iowa City vicinity, 4/13/77, A, a, 77000528

Ford, Arthur Hillyer, House, 228 Brown St., Iowa City, 4/10/86, C, 86000713

Franklin Printing House, 115 S. Dubuque, Iowa City, 4/10/86, A, C, 86000712

Jackson-Swisher House and Carriage House, 120 E. Fairchild St., Iowa City, 11/10/82, C, 82000412

Johnson County Courthouse [County Courthouses in Iowa TR (AD)], S. Clinton St., Iowa City, 3/27/75, A, C, 75000692

Johnson, Sylvanus, House, 2155 Prairie du Chien Rd., Iowa City, 12/06/90, C, 90001857

Kirkwood House, 1101 Kirkwood, Iowa City, 9/17/74, B, C, 74000792

Letovsky-Rohret House, 515 E. Davenport St., Iowa City, 4/12/82, B, b, 82002624

Linsay House, 935 E. College, Iowa City, 8/02/77, C, 77000529

McCollister, James, Farmstead, SE of jct. of U.S. 6 and U.S. 218, Iowa City, 10/08/76, B, C, 76000776

Miller Round Barn [Iowa Round Barns: The Sixty Year Experiment TR], CR F62, Sharon Center vicinity, 6/30/86, A, C, 86001445

Muscatine Avenue Moffitt Cottage Historic District [Small Homes of Howard F. Moffitt in Iowa City and Coralville], 1322–1330 Muscatine Ave., Iowa City, 5/04/93, C, 93000327

Nicking House, 410 E. Market St., Iowa City, 4/21/75, C, 75000693

North Presbyterian Church, 26 E. Market St., Iowa City, 8/28/73, C, a, 73000730

Oakes-Wood House, 1142 E. Court St., Iowa City, 4/14/78, B, C, g, 78001227

Old Capitol, University of Iowa campus, Iowa City, 5/31/72, A, C, NHL, 72000475

Old Post Office, 28 S. Linn St., Iowa City, 4/17/79, C, 79000905

Opera House Block, 210–212 S. Clinton St., Iowa City, 11/29/78, C, 78001228

Park House Hotel, 130 E. Jefferson St., Iowa City, 12/11/78, C, 78001229

Paul—Helen Building, 207–215 E. Washington, Iowa City, 4/10/86, C, 86000708

Pentacrest, Bounded by Clinton, Madison, Jefferson, and Washington Sts., Iowa City, 3/29/78, A, C, 78001230

Plum Grove, 1030 Carroll Ave., Iowa City, 5/07/73, B, C, 73000731

Polygonal Barn, Lincoln Township [Iowa Round Barns: The Sixty Year Experiment TR], Off US 6, West Liberty vicinity, 6/30/86, A, C, 86001452

Pratt, A. W., House, 503 Melrose Ave., Iowa City, 2/03/83, C, 83000378

Rittenmeyer, F. X., House, 630 E. Fairchild St., Iowa City, 5/31/79, C, 79000906

Roberts Octagon Barn [Iowa Round Barns: The Sixty Year Experiment TR], CR W62, Sharon Center vicinity, 6/30/86, A, C, 86001449

Rose Hill, 1415 E. Davenport St., Iowa City, 4/28/92, C, 92000425

Secrest Octagon Barn [Iowa Round Barns: The Sixty Year Experiment TR (AD)], W of Downey, Downey vicinity, 11/05/74, A, C, 74000790

Shimek, Bohumil, House [Conservation Movement in Iowa MPS], 529 Brown St., Iowa City, 12/23/91, B, 91001837

South Summit Street District, 301-818 S. Summit St., Iowa City, 10/09/73, C, 73000732

St. John's Lutheran Church, N of Kalona, Kalona vicinity, 4/05/77, A, a, 77000532

St. Mary's Church and Rectory, 220 E. Jefferson St., Iowa City, 2/08/80, C, a, 80001454

St. Mary's High School, 104 E. Jefferson St., Iowa City, 12/19/77, A, a, 77000530

Summit Apartment Building, 228 S. Summit St., Iowa City, 9/29/83, C, 83004188

Trinity Episcopal Church, 320 E. College St., Iowa City, 12/31/74, C, a, 74000793

Union Brewery, 127–131 N. Linn and 221–227 E. Market, Iowa City, 4/10/86, A, C, 86000710

Van Patten House, 9 S. Linn St., Iowa City, 1/27/83, C, a, 83000379

Vogt House, 800 N. Van Buren St., Iowa City, 7/24/78, C, 78001231

Washington Township Center High School, NE of Amish, Amish vicinity, 12/15/79, A, C, 79000903

Wentz, Jacob, House, 219 N. Gilbert St., Iowa City, 8/27/74, C, 74000794

White, H. A., General Store and House, 10 W. Cherry St., North Liberty, 1/12/84, A, C, 84001265

Windrem House, 604 Iowa Ave., Iowa City, 9/13/77, C, 77000531

Woodlawn Historic District, Irregular pattern along Woodlawn Ave., Iowa City, 3/26/79, C, 79000907

Jones County

Anamosa Public Library [Public Library Buildings in Iowa TR], 100 E. 1st St., Anamosa, 5/23/83, C, 83000380

Caulkins, Dr. Martin H., House and Office, Washington and Main Sts., Wyoming, 3/05/82, B, 82002625

Corbett's/Eby's Mill Bridge, Spans Maquoketa River, Scotch Grove Township, Scotch Grove vicinity, 4/11/85, A, 85000722

Ely's Stone Bridge, NW of Monticello at Hardscrabble Rd., Monticello vicinity, 3/07/79, C, 79000908

Farm No. 1, Iowa Men's Reformatory [Municipal, County and State Corrections Properties MPS], Co. Trunk Hwy. E28 W of Buffalo Cr., Ahnamosa vicinity, 12/18/92, A, C, 92001664

Farwell, S. S., House, 301 N. Chestnut St., Monticello, 4/27/79, C, 79000909

Green, John A., Estate, W of Anamosa off U.S. 151, Anamosa vicinity, 8/31/78, B, C, g, 78001232

Iowa Men's Reformatory Cemetery [Municipal, County and State Corrections Properties MPS], Co. Trunk Hwy. E28 W of Buffalo Cr., Anamosa vicinity, 12/18/92, C, D, d, 92001665

Iowa Men's Reformatory Historic District [Municipal, County and State Corrections Properties MPS], N. High St., Anamosa, 12/18/92, A, C, 92001667

Odd Fellows Hall, 203 W. 1st St., Monticello, 6/27/85, C, 85001377

Shaw, Col. William T. and Elizabeth C., House, 509 S. Oak St., Anamosa vicinity, 11/27/92, B, C, 92001636

State Quarry, Iowa Men's Reformatory [Municipal, County and State Corrections Properties MPS], Unnamed rd. along E side of Buffalo Cr. NW of Anamosa, Anamosa vicinity, 12/18/92, A, C, 92001666

Keokuk County

Bruce Goldfish Fisheries, E of Thornburg off IA 22, Thornburg vicinity, 9/20/82, A, 82002626

Delta Covered Bridge, S of Delta off IA 108 across North Skunk River, Delta vicinity, 11/08/74, C, 74000795

Hayesville Independent School, 231 Washington St., Hayesville, 8/03/90, A, C, 90001195

Keokuk County Courthouse [County Courthouses in Iowa TR], Main St., Sigourney, 7/02/81, C, 81000251

Lancaster School, SE of Sigourney, Sigourney vicinity, 10/04/84, C, 84000010

Saints Peter and Paul Roman Catholic Church, SE of Harper, Harper vicinity, 8/06/86, C, a, 86002277

Sigourney Public Library [Public Library Buildings in Iowa TR], 203 N. Jefferson St., Sigourney, 5/23/83, C, 83000381

What Cheer City Hall, Barnes and Washington Sts., What Cheer, 8/27/81, A, 81000252

What Cheer Opera House, 201 Barnes St., What Cheer, 6/04/73, A, 73000733

White, Theodore, House, Broadway St., South English, 7/14/83, C, 83000382

Kossuth County

Dau, William C. and Hertha, House, 315 S. Dodge St., Algona, 7/29/93, C, 93000654

Longbottom Polygonal Barn [Iowa Round Barns: The Sixty Year Experiment TR], Off IA 226, Titonka vicinity, 6/30/86, A, C, 86001456

Lu Verne City Jail [Municipal, County and State Corrections Properties MPS], 307 Third St., Lu Verne, 12/18/92, A, C, 92001662

Lee County

Albright House, 716–718 Ave. F, Fort Madison, 7/24/78, C, 78001233

Lee County—Continued

Atchison, Topeka and Santa Fe Passenger and Freight Complex Historic District [Advent & Development of Railroads in Iowa MPS], 902 Ave. H, Fort Madison, 3/05/92, C, 92000100

Beck, Chief Justice Joseph M., House, 630 Avenue E, Fort Madison, 7/21/88, A, B, 88001116

Belknap, Gen. William Worth, House, 511 N. 3rd St., Keokuk, 10/10/75, B, C, 75000694

Cattermole Memorial Library [Public Library Buildings in Iowa TR], 614 7th St., Fort Madison, 4/05/84, A, C, 84001267

Denmark Congregational Church, Academy Ave. and 4th St., Denmark, 12/02/77, A, B, a, 77000534

GEO. M. VERITY, Keokuk River Museum, Victory Park, Keokuk, 12/20/89, A, C, g, NHL, 89002459

Harrison, E. H., House, 220 N. 4th St., Keokuk, 1/12/84, C, 84001270

Hotel Iowa, 401 Main St., Keokuk, 2/05/87, C, 87000022

Iowa State Penitentiary Cellhouses Historic District [Municipal, County and State Corrections Properties MPS], Jct. of Avenue G and US 61, Fort Madison, 12/18/92, A, C, 92001663

Keokuk Lock and Dam, At Mississippi River, Keokuk, 10/19/78, A, C, 78001234

Lee County Courthouse [County Courthouses in Iowa TR (AD)], 701 Ave. F, Fort Madison, 9/30/76, A, 76000777

Miller, Justice Samuel Freeman, House, 318 N. 5th St., Keokuk, 10/10/72, B, 72000477

Old Fort Madison Site, Address Restricted, Fort Madison vicinity, 5/07/73, A, D, 73000734

Primrose Mill, Off IA 2, Primrose, 3/17/83, A, C, 83000383

Saint Barnabas Episcopal Church, Chestnut St., Montrose, 4/11/86, C, a, 86000721

Schlapp, George E., House, 639 Ave. C, Fort Madison, 2/04/82, B, C, 82002627

Sharon Cemetery Historic District, Co. Rd. J40 about 3 mi. E of Van Buren Co. line, Farmington vicinity, 1/11/91, C, d, 90002133

Sheaffer, Craig and Virginia, House, 10 High Point, Fort Madison, 4/22/93, C, 93000329

St Mary of the Assumption Church, 1031 Ave. E, Fort Madison, 2/08/80, C, a, 80001455

St. John's Episcopal Church and Parish Hall, 4th and Concert, Keokuk, 7/11/89, C, a, 89000806

St. Peter Church, 301 S. 9th St., Keokuk, 7/14/83, C, a, 83000384

U.S. Post Office and Courthouse, 25 N. 7th St., Keokuk, 1/24/74, A, C, 74000796

Weess, Frank J., House, 224–226 Morgan St., Keokuk, 5/22/78, C, 78001235

Linn County

Armstrong, Robert and Esther, House, 370 34th St., SE., Cedar Rapids, 11/16/89, C, 89002009

Ash Park Historic District [Mount Vernon MPS], 5th—7th Aves. N, between 6th and 8th Sts. NW, Mount Vernon, 9/13/93, C, b, 93000899

Averill, A. T., House, 1120 2nd Ave., SE, Cedar Rapids, 11/28/78, C, 78001236

Beach School, NW of Mount Vernon off US 30, Mount Vernon vicinity, 9/16/82, A, 82002630

Braska House, 889 2nd Ave., Marion, 3/21/79, C, 79000911

Burlington, Cedar Rapids, and Minnesota Railroad: Walker Station, Between Rowley and Washington Sts., Walker, 2/14/78, A, 78001242

C.S.P.S. Hall, 1105 3rd St., SE, Cedar Rapids, 11/29/78, A, C, 78001237

Calder Houses, 1214 and 1216 2nd Ave., SE, Cedar Rapids, 1/18/78, C, 78001238

Cedar Rapids Post Office and Public Building, 305 2nd Ave., SE, Cedar Rapids, 11/10/82, C, g, 82000413

Cornell College-Mount Vernon Historic District, Roughly bounded by RR tracks, College Blvd., N. 10th, N. 8th, and S. 3rd Aves., N. 2nd and S. 4th Sts., Mount Vernon, 7/18/80, C, a, 80001456

Douglas, George B., House, 800 2nd Ave., SE, Cedar Rapids, 9/09/82, B, C, 82002628

First Presbyterian Church of Marion, Iowa, 802 12th St., Marion, 7/24/92, C, a, 92000924

First Universalist Church of Cedar Rapids, 600 3rd Ave., SE, Cedar Rapids, 8/24/78, B, a, 78001239

Granger House, 970 10th St., Marion, 8/13/76, C, 76000781

Grant, Douglas and Charlotte, House [Iowa Usonian Houses by Frank Lloyd Wright, 1945-1960, MPS], 3400 Adel St. SE, Marion, 11/09/88, C, g, 88002145

Highwater Rock, Cedar River near 1st Ave. and 1st St., NE, Cedar Rapids, 11/17/77, A, 77000535

Hotel Roosevelt, 200 First Ave., NE, Cedar Rapids, 5/01/91, C, 91000534

Iowa Building, 221 4th Ave., SE, Cedar Rapids, 2/17/83, A, C, 83000385

King Memorial Chapel, Cornell College campus, Mount Vernon, 11/07/76, A, C, a, 76000782

Lattner Auditorium Building, 217 4th Ave., SE, Cedar Rapids, 2/17/83, A, C, 83000386

May's Island Historic District, Between 1st and 5th Aves. on May Island, Cedar Rapids, 10/19/78, A, C, g, 78001240

Mentzer, Joseph P., House, 2233 3rd Ave., Marion, 4/12/82, B, C, 82002629

Mittvatsky House, 1035 2nd St., SE, Cedar Rapids, 9/05/75, B, C, 75000695

Mount Vernon Commercial Historic District [Mount Vernon MPS], 1st St. between 2nd and 1st Aves., N., Mount Vernon, 9/13/93, C, 93000898

Odd Fellows Hall, Troy Mills Rd., Troy Mills, 10/10/85, C, 85003008

Paramount Theater Building, 121–127 3rd Ave., SE, Cedar Rapids, 8/26/76, A, C, g, 76000778

People's Savings Bank, 101 3rd Ave., SE, Cedar Rapids, 3/29/78, C, 78001241

Security Building, 2nd Ave. and 2nd St., SE, Cedar Rapids, 12/07/77, C, 77000536

Seminole Valley Farmstead, W of Cedar Rapids, Cedar Rapids, 10/08/76, A, 76000779

Sinclair, T. M., Mansion, 2160 Linden Dr., SE, Cedar Rapids, 12/12/76, C, 76000780

St. Paul Methodist Episcopal Church, 1340 3rd Ave., SE, Cedar Rapids, 6/27/85, C, a, 85001376

Stuckslager, Harrison, House, 207 N. Jackson St., Lisbon, 10/01/79, C, 79000910

Taylor-Van Note, 4600 Blairs Ferry Rd., Cedar Rapids, 10/10/85, C, 85003009

Torrance House, S of Lisbon, Lisbon vicinity, 7/07/83, C, 83000387

West, Wesley, House, Palisades Rd., Mount Vernon, 6/27/85, C, 85001380

Whittier Friends Meeting House, Jct. of Co. Rds. E34 and X20, Whittier, 7/29/93, A, C, a, 93000653

Wolff, Philip A., House and Carriage House, 1420 Seminole Ave., NW, Cedar Rapids, 10/07/82, C, 82000414

Louisa County

Bethel Church, NE of Morning Star, off US 61, Morning Star vicinity, 2/22/79, A, a, d, 79003698

Community Building, 122 E. Maple St., Columbus Junction, 8/14/73, A, C, 73000735

Florence-Council On The Iowa Site, Address Restricted, Oakville vicinity, 12/27/78, A, B, D, 78001243

Louisa County Courthouse [County Courthouses in Iowa TR], Main St., Wapello, 7/02/81, C, 81000253

Springer, Judge Francis, House, S of Columbus City, Columbus City vicinity, 1/27/83, B, C, 83000388

Toolesboro Mound Group, Address Restricted, Toolesboro vicinity, 10/15/66, D, NHL, 66000337

Lucas County

Lucas County Courthouse [County Courthouses in Iowa TR], Courthouse Sq., Chariton, 7/02/81, C, 81000254

Payne, O. E., House, 702 Auburn Ave., Chariton, 7/17/79, C, 79000912

Stephens, A. J., House, 123 Seventeenth St., Chariton, 11/16/87, C, 87002020

Lyon County

Big Sioux Prehistoric Prairie Procurement System Archaeological District [Prehistoric Hunters and Gatherers on the Northwest Iowa Plains, c. 10, 000–200 B.P., MPS], Address Restricted, Klondike vicinity, 1/17/89, D, 88001169

Blood Run Site, Address Restricted, Sioux Falls vicinity, 8/29/70, D, NHL, 70000246

Burlington, Cedar Rapids, and Northern Railroad-Rock Rapids Station, Railroad Track and Bridge, N. Story St., Rock Rapids, 11/07/76, A, 76000783

First Methodist Church, 302 S. Carroll St., Rock Rapids, 6/23/78, C, a, 78001244

Lyon County—Continued

Kruger Mill, SW of Larchwood on Sioux River, Larchwood vicinity, 11/03/75, A, 75000696

Lyon County Courthouse [County Courthouses in Iowa TR (AD)], 3rd and Story Sts., Rock Rapids, 10/01/79, C, 79000913

Melan Bridge, E of Rock Rapids in Emma Sater Park, Rock Rapids vicinity, 10/18/74, C, 74000797

Madison County

Allen, James, Stone Barn [Legacy in Stone: The Settlement Era of Madison County, Iowa TR], 2 1/2 mi. SE of Earlham, Earlham vicinity, 9/29/87, A, C, 87001658

Armstrong, George and Susan Guiberson, House [Legacy in Stone: The Settlement Era of Madison County, Iowa TR], 2 1/2 mi. N of Winterset on G4R, Winterset vicinity, 9/29/87, A, C, 87001668

Bevington, C. D. and Eliza Heath, Privy [Legacy in Stone: The Settlement Era of Madison County, Iowa TR], 805 S. Second Ave., Winterset vicinity, 9/29/87, A, C, 87001669

Bevington, C. D., House and Stone Barn, 805 S. 2nd Ave., Winterset, 12/12/76, A, C, 76000785

Cedar Covered Bridge, 1.5 mi. E of Winterset, Winterset vicinity, 8/28/76, C, b, 76000786

Church, Seymour, House [Legacy in Stone: The Settlement Era of Madison County, Iowa TR], US 169, Winterset vicinity, 9/29/87, A, C, 87001683

Cornell, W. J. and Nettie J., House, 602 W. Court Ave., Winterset, 1/11/91, C, 90002132

Craven, J. D., Women's Relief Corps Hall, South St., Macksburg, 1/19/84, A, C, 84001274

Cutler-Donahue Covered Bridge, Winterset City Park, Winterset, 10/08/76, C, b, 76000787

Drake, John and Amanda Bigler, House [Legacy in Stone: The Settlement Era of Madison County, Iowa TR], 11 mi. W of Winterset on IA 92, Winterset vicinity, 9/29/87, A, C, 87001670

Duff Barn [Legacy in Stone: The Settlement Era of Madison County, Iowa TR], 1 1/2 mi. N of Winterset on US 169, Winterset vicinity, 3/18/93, C, 87001672

Duncan, John M., House [Legacy in Stone: The Settlement Era of Madison County, Iowa TR], 1/2 mi. S of Winterset on P69, Winterset vicinity, 9/29/87, A, C, 87001673

Earlham Public School [Legacy in Stone: The Settlement Era of Madison County, Iowa TR (AD)], 809 Main St., Earlham, 6/02/82, A, C, 82002631

Early, John and Elizabeth McMurn, House [Legacy in Stone: The Settlement Era of Madison County, Iowa TR], 1 mi. S of G31 between P53 & P57, Earlham vicinity, 3/18/93, A, C, 87001653

Evans, Henry and Elizabeth Adkinson, House [Legacy in Stone: The Settlement Era of Madison County, Iowa TR], 1/2 mi. E of US 169 on CR G50, Winterset vicinity, 9/29/87, A, C, 87001674

Ford, W. T., House [Legacy in Stone: The Settlement Era of Madison County, Iowa TR], 2 1/2 mi. S of Earlham on P57, Earlham vicinity, 9/29/87, A, C, 87001654

Guiberson House [Legacy in Stone: The Settlement Era of Madison County, Iowa TR (AD)], 302 S. 4th Ave., Winterset, 7/10/79, C, 79003697

Henderson, Daniel and Nancy Swaford, House [Legacy in Stone: The Settlement Era of Madison County, Iowa TR], 8 mi. S of Earlham on P57, Earlham vicinity, 9/29/87, A, C, 87001655

Hogback Covered Bridge, 4 mi. N of Winterset, Winterset vicinity, 8/28/76, C, 76000788

Hollowell Covered Bridge, 4 mi. SE of Winterset, Winterset vicinity, 8/28/76, C, 76000789

Holmes, John S. and Elizabeth Beem, Barn [Legacy in Stone: The Settlement Era of Madison County, Iowa TR], CR G50, St. Charles vicinity, 9/29/87, A, C, 87001665

Hornback, Emily, House [Legacy in Stone: The Settlement Era of Madison County, Iowa TR], 605 N. First St., Winterset, 9/29/87, A, C, 87001687

Imes Covered Bridge, IA 251, St. Charles vicinity, 2/09/79, C, b, 76000784

Macumber, John Andrew and Sara, Ice House [Legacy in Stone: The Settlement Era of Madison County, Iowa TR], On G53 1 1/2 mi. E of jct. with P69, Winterset vicinity, 3/18/93, C, 87001675

Madison County Courthouse [County Courthouses in Iowa TR (AD)], City Sq., Winterset, 8/13/76, C, 76000790

McDonald House [Legacy in Stone: The Settlement Era of Madison County, Iowa TR], 3 1/2 mi. W of Winterset off IA 92, Winterset vicinity, 3/18/93, A, C, 87001676

McQuie, Peter and Isabelle McCulloch, Milkhouse [Legacy in Stone: The Settlement Era of Madison County, Iowa TR], SW of Earlham, Earlham vicinity, 9/29/87, A, C, 87001656

Nichols, William Anzi, House [Legacy in Stone: The Settlement Era of Madison County, Iowa TR], 1 mi. E of Winterset on IA 92, Winterset vicinity, 9/29/87, A, C, 87001677

North River Stone Schoolhouse [Legacy in Stone: The Settlement Era of Madison County, Iowa TR (AD)], N of Winterset off U.S. 169, Winterset vicinity, 4/11/77, A, 77000537

Ogburn, William, House [Legacy in Stone: The Settlement Era of Madison County, Iowa TR], 1 1/2 mi. N of East Peru, East Peru vicinity, 9/29/87, A, C, 87001660

Queen, Hogan and Martha A. Runkle, House [Legacy in Stone: The Settlement Era of Madison County, Iowa TR], 5 mi. W of St. Charles on CR G50, St. Charles vicinity, 9/29/87, A, C, 87001667

Roseman Covered Bridge, W of Winterset off IA 94, Winterset vicinity, 9/01/76, C, 76000792

Schnellbacher, John and Fredericka Meyer, House [Legacy in Stone: The Settlement Era of Madison County, Iowa TR], On G47 1 1/2 mi. E of jct. with P53, Winterset vicinity, 9/29/87, A, C, 87001678

Schoenenberger, Nicholas, House and Barn [Legacy in Stone: The Settlement Era of Madison County, Iowa TR (AD)], Off IA 169, Winterset vicinity, 7/12/84, C, 84001275

Shriver, William R. and Martha Foster, House [Legacy in Stone: The Settlement Era of Madison County, Iowa TR], 616 E. Court Ave., Winterset, 3/18/93, C, 87001689

Smith, Hiram C., House [Legacy in Stone: The Settlement Era of Madison County, Iowa TR], 6 mi. W of Winterset on IA 92, Winterset vicinity, 9/29/87, A, C, 87001684

Smith, Hiram C., Milking Shed [Legacy in Stone: The Settlement Era of Madison County, Iowa TR], 6 mi. W of Winterset on IA 92, Winterset vicinity, 9/29/87, A, C, 87001686

Sprague, Brown, and Knowlton Store [Legacy in Stone: The Settlement Era of Madison County, Iowa TR], First and Court, Winterset, 9/29/87, A, C, 87001690

St. Patrick's Church, NW of Cumming, Cumming vicinity, 12/12/78, A, a, d, 78001245

Tidrick, Miller Richard and Mary Fisher, House [Legacy in Stone: The Settlement of Madison County, Iowa TR], 122 S. Fourth Ave., Winterset, 3/18/93, A, C, 93000126

Vawter, J. G. and Elizabeth S., House [Legacy in Stone: The Settlement Era of Madison County, Iowa TR], 223 S. First St., Winterset, 9/29/87, A, C, 87001692

Wallace, Henry C., House, 422 W. Jefferson, Winterset, 1/03/85, B, 85000005

White, Munger and Company, Store [Legacy in Stone: The Settlement Era of Madison County, Iowa TR], 102 W. Court, Winterset, 9/29/87, A, C, 87001693

Wilson, Seth and Elizabeth, House [Legacy in Stone: The Settlement Era of Madison County, Iowa TR], 1 3/4 mi. E of P57 on G14, Earlham vicinity, 9/29/87, A, C, 87001659

Mahaska County

Alsop, Carroll, House [Iowa Usonian Houses by Frank Lloyd Wright, 1945-1960, MPS], 1907 A Avenue East, Oskaloosa, 11/09/88, C, g, 88002142

Forest Cemetery Entrance [Oskaloosa MPS], Jct. of N. 9th St. and J Ave. E., Oskaloosa, 12/13/91, C, d, 91001765

Gibbs, E. H., House [Oskaloosa MPS], William Penn College Campus, N. Market Extension, Oskaloosa, 12/13/91, C, 91001761

Hoffman, Phil, House [Oskaloosa MPS], 807 High Ave. E., Oskaloosa, 12/13/91, C, 91001760

Lake Keomah State Park, Bathhouse—Lodge Area (Area A) [CCC Properties in Iowa State Parks MPS], Off IA 371 S of jct. with IA 92, Oskaloosa vicinity, 11/15/90, A, C, 90001666

Lake Keomah State Park, Erosion Control Area (Area B) [CCC Properties in Iowa State Parks

Mahaska County—Continued

MPS], Off IA 371 S of jct. with IA 92, Oskaloosa vicinity, 11/15/90, A, C, 90001667

Lamberson, Jack, House [Iowa Usonian Houses by Frank Lloyd Wright, 1945-1960, MPS], 511 N. Park Ave., Oskaloosa, 11/09/88, C, g, 88002146

Lincoln School [Oskaloosa MPS], 911 B Ave. W., Oskaloosa, 12/13/91, C, 91001766

Mahaska County Courthouse [County Courthouses in Iowa TR], Market St. and 2nd Ave., Oskaloosa, 7/02/81, C, g, 81000255

McMullin, Maj. James W., House, 403 1st Ave., E., Oskaloosa, 4/11/85, C, 85000723

Nelson, Daniel, House and Barn, SR 1, Oskaloosa, 11/20/74, A, C, 74000798

Oskaloosa City Hall [Oskaloosa MPS], Jct. of S. Market St. and 2nd Ave. E., NE corner, Oskaloosa, 12/13/91, C, 91001764

Oskaloosa City Park and Band Stand, City Park, Oskaloosa, 7/28/83, A, C, 83000389

Oskaloosa City Square Commercial Historic District, Roughly bounded by A Ave. E, N. and S. Second St., Second Ave. E, and N. and S. A St., Oskaloosa, 4/10/86, C, 86000716

Oskaloosa Fire Station [Oskaloosa MPS], 109–111 2nd Ave. E., Oskaloosa, 12/13/91, C, 91001763

Oskaloosa Public Library [Public Library Buildings in Iowa TR; Oskaloosa MPS], Jct. of Market St. and 2nd Ave. W., SW corner, Oskaloosa, 12/13/91, 83004763

Paradise Block Historic District [Oskaloosa MPS], 402, 406, 408, 410, 414, 418 and 510–714 High Ave. E., Oskaloosa, 12/13/91, C, a, 91001767

Rock Island Passenger Depot, Rock Island Ave. between 1st and 2nd Sts., Oskaloosa, 10/30/89, C, 89001780

Seeberger-Loring-Kilburn House, 509 High Ave., E., Oskaloosa, 7/14/83, C, 83000390

Shoemake, John H., House, 116 2nd Ave., W., Oskaloosa, 3/22/84, C, 84001276

Smith-Johnson House, 713 High Ave., E., Oskaloosa, 11/09/77, C, 77000538

St. James Episcopal Church [Oskaloosa MPS], Jct. of 1st Ave. and S. 3rd St., SW corner, Oskaloosa, 12/13/91, C, a, 91001762

Stock Judging Pavilion, Southern Iowa Fairgrounds, Oskaloosa, 4/12/84, A, C, 84001280

Voorhees, John K., House, NW of Oskaloosa on IA 163, Oskaloosa vicinity, 3/05/82, B, C, 82002632

Marion County

Chicago, Rock Island and Pacific Passenger Depot—Pella [Advent and Development of Railroads in Iowa MPS], Jct. of Main and Oskaloosa Sts., Pella, 7/22/91, A, 91000909

Ellis, Evan F., Farmhouse, Off Hwy. 156, Bussey, 1/03/85, C, 85000006

Hays, E. R., House, 301 N. 2nd St., Knoxville, 9/27/84, C, 84001283

Marion County Courthouse [County Courthouses in Iowa TR], Main St., Knoxville, 7/02/81, C, 81000256

Pella Opera House, 611 Franklin St., Pella, 3/20/92, C, 91001080

Scholte, Dominie Henry P., House, 739 Washington St., Pella, 12/10/82, B, 82000415

Van Asch, William, House—Huibert Debooy Commercial Room, 1105, 1107, & 1109 W. Washington St., Pella, 12/02/87, C, 87002056

Van Loon, Dirk, House, 1401 University Ave., Pella, 11/17/77, A, 77000539

Van Spanckeren, B. H. and J. H. H., Row Houses, 505–507 Franklin St., Pella, 2/12/90, C, 90000004

Marshall County

Binford, Thaddeus, House, 110 N. 2nd Ave., Marshalltown, 1/12/84, C, 84001286

Dobbin Round Barn [Iowa Round Barns: The Sixty Year Experiment TR], Off CR S52, State Center vicinity, 6/30/86, A, C, 86001459

Edel, Matthew, Blacksmith Shop and House, 1st St. and 3rd Ave., Haverhill, 3/11/83, A, B, 83000391

First Church of Christ, Scientist, 412 W. Main St., Marshalltown, 12/15/79, C, 79000915

Glick—Sower House, 201 E. State St., Marshalltown, 4/22/93, C, 93000331

Marshall County Courthouse [County Courthouses in Iowa TR (AD)], Courthouse Sq., Marshalltown, 11/21/72, C, 72000478

Sunday, Robert H., House [Iowa Usonian Houses by Frank Lloyd Wright, 1945-1960, MPS], 1701 Woodfield Rd., Marshalltown, 11/09/88, C, g, 88002141

Whitehead, C. H., House, 108 N. 3rd St., Marshalltown, 1/15/79, C, 79000916

Willard, Leroy R., House, 609 W. Main St., Marshalltown, 10/22/76, C, 76000794

Mills County

Plattsmouth Bridge [Highway Bridges in Nebraska MPS], US 34 over the Missouri R., Pacific Junction, 4/15/93, C, 92000755

Pony Creek Park, N of Glenwood, Glenwood vicinity, 7/30/71, D, 71000299

Mitchell County

Cedar Valley Seminary, N. 6th and Mechanic Sts., Osage, 11/17/77, A, C, 77000541

First Lutheran Church, 212 N. Main St., St. Ansgar, 12/12/76, B, C, a, 76000795

Mitchell County Courthouse [County Courthouses in Iowa TR (AD)], 500 State St., Osage, 8/29/77, A, C, 77000542

Mitchell Powerhouse and Dam, Red Cedar River, Mitchell, 12/08/78, A, 78001246

Severson, Nels, Barn, N of Carpenter, Carpenter vicinity, 7/15/77, A, 77000540

Union Presbyterian Church, NW of Stacyville, Stacyville vicinity, 4/13/77, C, a, 77000543

Monona County

Jones Creek Watershed Historic District [Conservation Movement in Iowa MPS], Between Little Sioux and Soldier Rivers, SW of Moorhead, Moorhead vicinity, 12/23/91, A, 91001839

Monona County Courthouse [County Courthouses in Iowa TR], Iowa Ave., Onawa, 7/02/81, C, 81000257

Onawa IOOF Opera House, 1023 Tenth Ave., Onawa, 8/03/90, A, 90001194

Onawa Public Library, Iowa Ave. and 7th St., Onawa, 10/01/79, C, 79000917

Round Barn, Cooper Township [Iowa Round Barns: The Sixty Year Experiment TR], IA 141, Mapleton vicinity, 6/30/86, A, C, 86001463

Trinity Memorial Episcopal Church, 302 S. Seventh St., Mapleton, 8/10/90, C, a, 90001217

Whiting, Newell A., House, 1106 Iowa Ave., Onawa, 8/10/90, C, 90001216

Monroe County

Albia Square and Central Commercial Historic District, Roughly bounded by the alley of S. and N. Clinton, E. and W. A Ave., N. and S. 2nd St., and E. and W. 2nd Ave., Albia, 1/03/85, A, C, 85000007

Buxton Historic Townsite, Address Restricted, Lovilia vicinity, 8/09/83, A, D, 83000392

Clark Round Barn [Iowa Round Barns: The Sixty Year Experiment TR], CR T7H, Tyrone vicinity, 6/30/86, A, C, 86001465

Elbert-Bates House, 106 2nd Ave., W., Albia, 6/27/85, C, 85001379

Jenkins, Dr. George A., House, 223 S. C St., Albia, 2/05/87, C, 87000027

Monroe County Courthouse [County Courthouses in Iowa TR], Main St., Albia, 7/02/81, C, 81000258

Noble-Kendall House, 209 E. Benton Ave., Albia, 4/12/84, B, C, 84001289

Perry, T. B., House, 212 Benton Ave., W., Albia, 7/14/83, C, 83000393

Saint Patrick's Roman Catholic Church, US 34 W of Albia, Albia vicinity, 5/06/92, A, C, a, 92000426

Montgomery County

Chautauqua Park, Oak St., Red Oak, 5/19/72, A, 72000479

Hebard, Alfred, House, 700 8th St., Red Oak, 4/12/84, C, 84001290

Montgomery County Courthouse [County Courthouses in Iowa TR], Coolbaugh and 2nd Sts., Red Oak, 7/02/81, C, 81000259

Montgomery County Jail [Municipal, County and State Corrections Properties MPS], 100 W. Coolbaugh St., Red Oak, 12/18/92, A, C, 92001661

Montgomery County—Continued

Red Oak Public Library [Public Library Buildings in Iowa TR], 2nd and Washington Sts., Red Oak, 5/23/83, C, 83000394

Round Barn, Pilot Grove Township [Iowa Round Barns: The Sixty Year Experiment TR], CR H20, Sennett vicinity, 6/30/86, A, C, 86001467

Round Barn, Washington Township [Iowa Round Barns: The Sixty Year Experiment TR], US 71, Sciola vicinity, 6/30/86, A, C, 86001466

Runnels, B. F., House, SW of Red Oak, Red Oak vicinity, 6/04/79, C, 79000918

Sciola Missionary Baptist Church, US 71, Sciola, 7/18/83, A, C, a, b, 83000395

Muscatine County

Bowman Livery Stable, 219 E. Mississippi Dr., Muscatine, 6/28/74, C, 74000799

Chicago, Rock Island and Pacific Railroad—Wilton Depot, N. Railroad St., Wilton, 8/25/88, A, 88001326

Clark, Alexander, House, 203 W. 3rd St., Muscatine, 10/14/76, B, b, 76000796

Clark-Blackwell House, 206 Cherry St., Muscatine, 1/27/83, A, C, 83000396

First Presbyterian Church, 401 Iowa Ave., Muscatine, 9/14/77, C, a, 77000544

Fuller, W. Joseph, House, 1001 Mulberry Ave., Muscatine, 12/10/82, C, 82000416

McKibben, S. M., House, Walnut St. between Front and 2nd, Muscatine, 8/27/74, B, C, 74000800

Muscatine County Courthouse [County Courthouses in Iowa TR], 3rd St., Muscatine, 7/02/81, C, 81000260

Nichols, Samuel, House, E of Nichols off IA 22, Nichols vicinity, 3/31/78, B, C, 78001247

Old Jail, 411 E. 4th St., Muscatine, 7/24/74, C, 74000801

Pine Creek Gristmill, NE of Muscatine in Wildcat Den State Park, Muscatine vicinity, 12/10/79, B, 79000919

Sinnett Octagon House, N of Muscatine near IA 38, Muscatine vicinity, 7/18/74, C, 74000802

Trinity Episcopal Church, 411 E. 2nd St., Muscatine, 10/29/74, A, C, a, 74000803

Warde, J. C. B., House, 205 Cherry St., Muscatine, 4/26/79, C, 79000920

Welch Apartments, 224 Iowa Ave., Muscatine, 1/15/79, C, 79000921

Wilton Candy Kitchen, 310 Cedar St., Wilton, 1/07/93, A, C, 92001742

O Brien County

Carnegie Library, 321 10th St., Sheldon, 4/11/77, A, C, 77001504

Indian Village Site, Address Restricted, Sutherland vicinity, 10/15/66, D, NHL, 66000888

O'Brien County Courthouse [County Courthouses in Iowa TR], Fir Ave., Primghar, 7/02/81, C, 81000656

Osceola County

Osceola County Courthouse [County Courthouses in Iowa TR], 3rd Ave. and 8th St., Sibley, 7/02/81, C, 81000261

Page County

Hepburn, Col. William Peters, House, 321 W. Lincoln St., Clarinda, 6/04/73, B, NHL, 73000736

McCoy Polygonal Barn [Iowa Round Barns: The Sixty Year Experiment TR], Off US 71, Hepburn vicinity, 6/30/86, A, C, 86001469

Page County Courthouse [County Courthouses in Iowa TR], Main St., Clarinda, 7/02/81, C, 81000262

Wabash Combination Depot—Shenandoah [Advent & Development of Railroads in Iowa, 1855-1940, MPS], Jct. Ferguson Rd. and Burlington Northern Tracks, Shenandoah, 9/06/90, C, b, 90001298

Women's Christian Temperance Union Public Fountain, Clarinda and Sheridan Sts., Shenandoah, 9/27/84, A, 84001293

Palo Alto County

Emmetsburg Public Library [Public Library Buildings in Iowa TR], 10th St. on Courthouse Sq., Emmetsburg, 5/23/83, C, 83000397

Ormsby-Kelly House, 2403 W. 7th St., Emmetsburg, 7/29/77, B, g, 77000545

Plymouth County

Le Mars Public Library, 200 Central, Le Mars, 3/26/79, C, 79000922

Plymouth County Courthouse [County Courthouses in Iowa TR], E. 3rd Ave., Le Mars, 7/02/81, A, C, 81000263

St. George's Episcopal Church, 400 1st Ave., SE, Le Mars, 11/21/76, A, a, 76000797

Thoren Hall, Westmar College campus, 10th St., SE, Le Mars, 5/22/78, A, 78001248

Tonsfeldt Round Barn [Iowa Round Barns: The Sixty Year Experiment TR], Plymouth County Fairgrounds, LeMars, 11/19/86, A, 86003194

Pocahontas County

Laurens Public Library, 263 N. 3rd St., Laurens, 11/05/74, A, C, 74000804

Pocahontas County Courthouse [County Courthouses in Iowa TR], Court Sq., Pocahontas, 7/02/81, C, 81000264

Polk County

Andrews, Josiah, House [Drake University and Related Properties in Des Moines, Iowa, 1881-1918 MPS], 1128 27th St., Des Moines, 11/01/88, A, 88001338

Ashby Manor Historic District [Suburban Developments in Des Moines Between the World Wars MPS], Roughly bounded by Beaver Ave. and Ashby Park, Des Moines, 9/04/92, A, C, 92001150

Bell, Hill McClelland, House [Drake University and Related Properties in Des Moines, Iowa, 1881-1918 MPS], 1091 26th St., Des Moines, 11/01/88, A, B, 88001334

Burns United Methodist Church, 811 Crocker St., Des Moines, 6/15/77, A, a, 77000546

Case, Larnerd, House, 3111 Easton Blvd., Des Moines, 6/21/82, A, C, 82002633

Chautauqua Park Historic District [Suburban Development in Des Moines between the World Wars, 1918-1941 MPS], Roughly bounded by 16th St., Hickman Rd., and Chautauqua Pkwy., Des Moines, 3/22/90, A, C, g, 89001776

Civic Center Historic District [The City Beautiful Movement and City Planning in Des Moines, Iowa 1892-1938 MPS], Des Moines River, Center St. Dam to Scott Ave. Dam, including both banks, Des Moines, 12/07/88, A, C, 88001168

Crawford House, 2203 Grand Ave., Des Moines, 1/27/83, C, 83000398

Cummins, Albert Baird, House, 2404 Forest Dr., Des Moines, 6/30/82, B, 82002634

Darling, Jay Norwood and Genevieve Pendleton, House [Conservation Movement in Iowa MPS], 2320 Terrace Rd., Des Moines, 9/30/92, B, C, 91001838

Denny, Professor Charles O., House [Drake University and Related Properties in Des Moines, Iowa, 1881-1918 MPS], 1084 Twenty-fifth St., Des Moines, 9/08/88, A, 88001329

Des Moines Saddlery Company Building, 307-311 Court Ave., Des Moines, 6/27/85, C, 85001378

Drake University Campus Historic District [Drake University and Related Properties in Des Moines, Iowa, 1881-1918 MPS], Roughly two blks. along University Ave. near Twenty-fifth St., Des Moines, 9/08/88, A, B, 88001341

Fire Station No. 4, 1041 8th St., Des Moines, 6/27/79, C, 79000923

First Methodist Episcopal Church, 10th and Pleasant Sts., Des Moines, 4/12/84, C, a, 84001295

Fish and Game Pavilion and Aquarium [Conservation Movement in Iowa MPS; Architectural Legacy of Proudfoot & Bird in Iowa MPS], Iowa State Fairgrounds, Des Moines, 12/23/91, A, C, 91001836

Flynn Farm, Mansion, and Barn, 2600 111th St., Des Moines, 11/30/73, A, C, 73000737

Polk County—Continued

Fort Des Moines Provisional Army Officer Training School, Fort Des Moines Military Reservation, Des Moines, 5/30/74, A, NHL, 74000805

Gabriel, Rees, House, 1701 Pennsylvania Ave., Des Moines, 12/01/78, C, 78001250

Grand View College (Old Main), 1200 Grandview Ave., Des Moines, 5/23/78, C, 78001252

Hawkeye Insurance Company Building, 209 Fourth St., Des Moines, 4/28/86, A, C, 86000874

Herndon Hall, 2000 Grand Ave., Des Moines, 7/27/77, B, C, 77000547

Homestead Building, 303 Locust St., Des Moines, 3/05/82, A, B, C, 82002635

Hotel Fort Des Moines, 10th and Walnut Sts., Des Moines, 9/16/82, C, 82002636

Iowa State Capitol, Grand Ave. and E. 12th St., Des Moines, 10/21/76, A, C, 76000799

Iowa State Fair and Exposition Grounds Historic District, E. Thirtieth St. and Grand Ave., Des Moines, 9/14/87, A, C, 87000014

Iowa State Historical Building, E. 12th and Grand Ave., Des Moines, 11/14/78, C, 78001251

Iowa-Des Moines National Bank Building, 520 Walnut St., Des Moines, 7/10/79, C, g, 79000924

Johnson, Capt. Nicholas W. and Emma, House, Jct. of 21st St. and University Ave., Des Moines, 12/06/90, C, 90001854

Jordan House, 2251 Fuller Rd., West Des Moines, 12/10/73, B, 73000738

Keeler, Rev. R. W. and Fannie E., House, 1430 10th St., Des Moines, 11/04/93, C, 93001184

Kirkham, Francis M., House [Drake University and Related Properties in Des Moines, Iowa, 1881–1918 MPS], 1026 Twenty-fourth St., Des Moines, 9/08/88, A, B, 88001328

Knotts, Nellie and Thomas, House [Drake University and Related Properties in Des Moines, Iowa, 1881–1918 MPS], 1021 Twenty-sixth St., Des Moines, 9/08/88, A, 88001333

Lexington, The, 1721 Pleasant St., Des Moines, 12/12/76, C, 76000800

Lord, Richard T. C., and William V. Wilcox House [Drake University and Related Properties in Des Moines, Iowa, 1881–1918 MPS], 2416 Kingman Blvd., Des Moines, 9/08/88, A, 88001336

Mahnke House, 2707 High St., Des Moines, 10/13/83, C, 83003622

Maish House, 1623 Center St., Des Moines, 4/11/77, C, 77000548

Municipal Building, E. 1st and Locust Sts., Des Moines, 11/10/77, A, C, 77000549

Naylor House, 944 W. 9th St., Des Moines, 7/10/74, C, 74000806

Norman Apartment Building [Drake University and Related Properties in Des Moines, Iowa, 1881–1918 MPS], 3103 University Ave., Des Moines, 9/08/88, A, 88001327

Northwestern Hotel, 321 E. Walnut, Des Moines, 1/12/84, C, 84001300

Odenweller, F. F.—James P. and Nettie Morey House [Drake University and Related Properties in Des Moines, Iowa, 1881–1918 MPS], 1115 27th St., Des Moines, 11/01/88, A, 88001337

Owl's Head Historic District, Ridge Rd., Forest Dr., 28th and 29th Sts., Des Moines, 10/11/78, A, C, 78001253

Peak, George B., House, 1080 22nd St., Des Moines, 11/14/78, B, C, 78001254

Polk County Courthouse [County Courthouses in Iowa TR (AD)], 6th and Mulberry Sts., Des Moines, 4/30/79, C, 79000925

Public Library of Des Moines, Locust St., Des Moines, 7/25/77, C, 77000550

Reynolds, Anson O., House [Drake University and Related Properties in Des Moines, Iowa, 1881–1918 MPS], 1022 Twenty-sixth St., Des Moines, 9/08/88, A, 88001331

Rollins, Ralph, House, 2801 Fleur Dr., Des Moines, 11/14/78, C, 78001255

Rumely—Des Moines Drug Company Building, 110 SW. Fourth St., Des Moines, 11/16/89, A, 89002008

Saint John's Roman Catholic Church, 1915 University Ave., Des Moines, 9/08/87, C, a, 87001497

Salisbury House, 4025 Tonawanda Dr., Des Moines, 7/20/77, C, 77000551

Scott, Mary A. and Caleb D., House [Drake University and Related Properties in Des Moines, Iowa, 1881–1918 MPS], 1014 Twenty-sixth St., Des Moines, 9/08/88, A, 88001332

Scottish Rite Consistory Building, 6th Ave. and Park St., Des Moines, 9/29/83, C, 83000399

Sherman Hill Historic District, Roughly bounded by Woodland Ave., 19th, School, and 15th Sts., Des Moines, 1/25/79, A, C, 79000926

Sherman, Hoyt, Place, 1501 Woodland Ave., Des Moines, 9/19/77, A, C, 77000552

Sherman, Lampson P., House [Drake University and Related Properties in Des Moines, Iowa, 1881–1918 MPS], 1052 Twenty-sixth St., Des Moines, 9/08/88, A, 88001335

Simmons, John P., House [Drake University and Related Properties in Des Moines, Iowa, 1881–1918 MPS], 1113 27th St., Des Moines, 11/01/88, A, 88001339

Southeast Water Trough, SE 11th and Scott St., Des Moines, 10/08/76, A, 76000801

St. Ambrose Cathedral and Rectory, 607 High St., Des Moines, 3/30/79, C, a, 79000927

Stevenson, Samuel A. and Margaret, House, 2940 Cottage Grove Ave., Des Moines, 1/03/85, C, 85000008

Stoner, Thomas I., House, 1030 56th St., Des Moines, 2/12/92, C, 92000006

Stuart, Dr. Richard and Paulina, House [Drake University and Related Properties in Des Moines, Iowa, 1881–1918 MPS], 1060 Twenty-fifth St., Des Moines, 9/08/88, A, 88001330

Studio Building, 524 E. Grand Ave., Des Moines, 11/14/78, C, 78001256

Terrace Hill, 2300 Grand Ave., Des Moines, 6/14/72, B, C, 72000480

Trier, Paul J. and Ida, House [Iowa Usonian Houses by Frank Lloyd Wright, 1945-1960, MPS], 6880 N.W. Beaver Dr., Johnston, 11/09/88, C, g, 88002148

U.S. Post Office, 2nd and Walnut Sts., Des Moines, 11/19/74, A, C, 74002323

Vail, Mrs. Marian D.—Prof. Charles Noyes Kinney House [Drake University and Related Properties in Des Moines, Iowa, 1881–1918 MPS], 1318 27th St., Des Moines, 11/01/88, A, 88001340

Valley Junction-West Des Moines City Hall and Engine House, 137 5th St., West Des Moines, 2/17/83, A, 83000400

Wallace, Henry, House, 756 16th St., Des Moines, 5/14/93, B, 93000412

Warfield, Pratt and Howell Company Warehouse, 100 West Court Ave., Des Moines, 5/15/85, C, 85001056

West Chester, 3520 Grand Ave., Des Moines, 1/19/84, C, 84001304

Pottawattamie County

Beresheim, August, House, 621 3rd St., Council Bluffs, 8/13/76, C, 76000802

Carstens Farmstead, S of Shelby on IA 168, Shelby vicinity, 7/10/79, A, 79000932

Cavin, Thomas E., House, 150 Park Ave., Council Bluffs, 9/27/84, C, 84001306

Dodge, Grenville M., House, 605 S. 3rd St., Council Bluffs, 10/15/66, B, NHL, 66000338

Dodge, Ruth Anne, Memorial, Fairview Cemetery, Council Bluffs, 2/08/80, C, f, 80001457

Eckle Round Barn [Iowa Round Barns: The Sixty Year Experiment TR], Off IA 168, Shelby vicinity, 6/30/86, A, C, 86001470

German Bank Building of Walnut, Iowa, Jct. of Highland and Central Sts., Walnut, 5/01/91, C, 91000536

Graceland Cemetery Chapel, Graceland Cemetery, US 59, Avoca, 4/28/86, C, a, 86000873

Hancock Savings Bank, 311 Main St., Hancock, 1/19/83, A, 83000401

Haymarket Commercial Historic District, S. Main St., Council Bluffs, 4/11/85, C, 85000774

Hughes, Martin, House, 903 3rd St., Council Bluffs, 9/27/84, C, 84001310

Jefferis, Thomas, House, 523 6th Ave., Council Bluffs, 12/25/79, C, 79000928

Ogden House, 169 W. Broadway, Council Bluffs, 9/13/76, A, C, 76000803

Pottawattamie County Jail, 226 Pearl St., Council Bluffs, 3/16/72, A, C, 72000481

Pottawattamie County Sub Courthouse [County Courthouses in Iowa TR], Elm St., Avoca, 7/02/81, C, 81000265

Reverend Little's Young Ladies Seminary, 541 6th Ave., Council Bluffs, 2/04/82, A, C, 82002637

South Omaha Bridge [Highway Bridges in Nebraska MPS], US 275/NE 92 over the Missouri R., Council Bluffs, 6/29/92, C, 92000742

St. Peter's Church and Rectory, 1 Bluff St., Council Bluffs, 7/24/92, C, a, 92000923

State Savings Bank, 509 W. Broadway, Council Bluffs, 6/04/84, C, g, 84001312

Tulleys, Lysander, House, 151 Park Ave., Council Bluffs, 10/18/79, C, 79000929

Wickham, O. P., House, 616 S. 7th St., Council Bluffs, 6/18/79, C, 79000930

Pottawattamie County—Continued

Y.M.C.A. Building, 628 1st Ave., Council Bluffs, 6/27/79, C, 79000931

Poweshiek County

Bowers and McDonald Office Building [Grinnell MPS], 816 Commercial St., Grinnell, 12/20/90, C, 90001849

Brooklyn Hotel, 154 Front St., Brooklyn, 10/01/79, C, 79000933

Chicago, Rock Island and Pacific Railroad-Grinnell Passenger Station, Park and State Sts., Grinnell, 12/12/76, C, 76000805

Goodnow Hall, Grinnell College campus, Grinnell, 4/26/79, C, 79000934

Grinnell Herald Building [Grinnell MPS; Architectural Legacy of Proudfoot and Bird in Iowa MPS], 813 5th Ave., Grinnell, 1/17/91, A, C, 90002131

Grinnell Historic Commercial District [Grinnell MPS], Roughly bounded by Main, Broad and Commercial Sts. and 5th Ave., Grinnell, 4/09/91, A, C, 91000384

Grinnell, Levi P., House, 1002 Park St., Grinnell, 10/01/79, C, 79000935

Interior Telephone Company Building [Grinnell MPS], 815 5th Ave., Grinnell, 12/20/90, C, 90001850

Mears Hall, Grinnell College campus, Grinnell, 4/26/79, A, C, 79000936

Merchants' National Bank, NW corner 4th Ave. and Broad St., Grinnell, 1/07/76, C, g, NHL, 76000804

New Carroll House Hotel, E. Main and 5th Sts., Montezuma, 10/01/79, C, 79000938

Poweshiek County Courthouse [County Courthouses in Iowa TR], Town Sq., Montezuma, 7/02/81, C, 81000266

Raymond, P. P., House, 4th St., Malcom, 4/24/85, C, 85000873

Ricker, B. J., House, 1510 Broad St., Grinnell, 12/25/79, C, 79000937

Spaulding Manufacturing Company, 500–610 4th Ave., 827–829 Spring St., Grinnell, 12/21/78, A, 78001257

Spencer, Charles H., House, 611 6th Ave., Grinnell, 1/25/80, C, a, b, 80001458

Stewart Library, 926 Broad St., Grinnell, 11/21/76, B, C, 76000806

Ringgold County

Buck, W. J., Polygonal Barn [Iowa Round Barns: The Sixty Year Experiment TR], Off US 169, Diagonal vicinity, 6/30/86, A, C, 86001471

Middlefork Methodist Episcopal Church, S of US 169 on E side of Middle Fork, Grand R., Redding, 11/29/90, C, a, 90001801

Ringgold County Courthouse [County Courthouses in Iowa TR], Madison St., Mount Ayr, 7/02/81, C, 81000267

Ringgold County Jail, 201 E. Monroe St., Mount Ayr, 6/19/79, C, 79000939

Shay, Lee, Farmhouse, Off CR P27, Maloy vicinity, 11/06/86, C, 86003172

Sac County

Blackhawk State Park, Black Hawk Preserve (Area B) [CCC Properties in Iowa State Parks MPS], S of jct. of US 71 and Co. Hwy. M68, Lake View, 11/15/90, A, C, 90001679

Blackhawk State Park, Denison Beach Area (Area C) [CCC Properties in Iowa State Parks MPS], S of jct. of US 71 and Co. Hwy. M68, Lake View, 11/15/90, A, C, 90001680

Blackhawk State Park, Wildlife Preserve Area (Area A) [CCC Properties in Iowa State Parks MPS], S of jct. of US 71 and Co. Hwy. M68, Lake View, 11/15/90, A, C, 90001678

Lakeside Park Historic District [Conservation Movement in Iowa MPS; CCC Properties in Iowa State Parks MPS], Third St. from Lake to Park St., Lake View, 12/23/91, A, C, 91001841

Sac County Courthouse [County Courthouses in Iowa TR], Main St., Sac City, 7/02/81, C, 81000268

Scott County

Adams, Walker, House [Davenport MRA], 1009 College Ave., Davenport, 7/27/84, C, 84001313

Adler, E. P., House [Davenport MRA], 2104 Main St., Davenport, 7/07/83, B, C, 83002394

Ambrose Hall, 518 W. Locust, Davenport, 4/11/77, A, C, 77000553

American Commercial and Savings Bank [Davenport MRA], 201-209 W. 3rd St., Davenport, 7/07/83, A, 83002395

American Telegraph & Telephone Co. Bldg. [Davenport MRA], 529 Main St., Davenport, 7/07/83, C, 83002396

Argyle Flats [Davenport MRA], 732 Brady St., Davenport, 7/07/83, C, 83002397

Ball-Waterman House [Davenport MRA], 616 Kirkwood Blvd., Davenport, 7/27/84, C, 84001315

Ballard, John W., House [Davenport MRA], 205 W. 16th St., Davenport, 7/07/83, C, 83002398

Barrows, Edward S., House, 224 E. 6th St., Davenport, 11/21/76, B, C, 76000807

Beiderbecke, Leon Bismark, House, 1934 Grande Ave., Davenport, 7/13/77, B, c, 77000554

Benton, Richard, House [Davenport MRA], 2204 and 2210 W. 3rd St., Davenport, 7/07/83, C, 83002399

Berg, Henry, Building [Davenport MRA], 246 W. 3rd St., Davenport, 7/07/83, C, 83002400

Bethel AME Church [Davenport MRA], 325 W. 11th St., Davenport, 7/07/83, A, C, a, 83002401

Bettendorf, Joseph F., House, 1821 Sunset Dr., Bettendorf, 1/27/83, B, C, a, 83004212

Bettendorf-Washington School, 533 16th St., Bettendorf, 7/12/84, A, 84001317

Blackhawk Hotel [Davenport MRA], 309 Perry St., Davenport, 7/07/83, A, C, 83002402

Boyle, John R., House [Davenport MRA], 408 E. 6th St., Davenport, 7/07/83, C, 83002403

Brammer Grocery Store [Davenport MRA], 1649 W. 3rd St., Davenport, 7/07/83, C, 83002404

Bridge Avenue Historic District [Davenport MRA], Bridge Ave. from River Dr. to 9th St., Davenport, 11/28/83, C, 83003626

Brown, James, House, 424 State St., Riverdale, 3/05/82, A, C, 82002643

Brownlie, Alexander, House, 206 Pine St., Long Grove, 12/22/76, C, 76000809

Bryan, Alden, House [Davenport MRA], 2236 W. 3rd St., Davenport, 7/07/83, C, 83002405

Buchanan School [Davenport MRA], 2104 W. 6th St., Davenport, 7/07/83, A, C, 83002406

Building at 1119-1121 W. Third Street [Davenport MRA], 1119-1121 W. 3rd St., Davenport, 7/07/83, C, 83002407

Building at 202 W. Third Street [Davenport MRA], 202 W. 3rd St., Davenport, 4/05/84, C, 84001318

Building at 813-815 W. Second Street [Davenport MRA], 813-815 W. 2nd St., Davenport, 7/07/83, C, 83002408

Burdick, Anthony, House [Davenport MRA], 833 College Ave., Davenport, 7/27/84, C, 84003854

Burtis-Kimball House Hotel, 210 E. 4th St., Davenport, 4/02/79, B, C, 79003696

Busch, Diedrich, House [Davenport MRA], 2340 E. 11th St., Davenport, 7/27/84, C, 84001324

Calvary Baptist Church/First Baptist Church [Davenport MRA], 1401 Perry St., Davenport, 7/07/83, C, a, 83002409

Cameron, W. S., House [Davenport MRA], 623 Kirkwood Blvd., Davenport, 7/27/84, C, 84001325

Carr, William V., House [Davenport MRA], 1531 W. 3rd St., Davenport, 7/07/83, C, 83002410

Cawley, James, House [Davenport MRA], 1406 Esplanade, Davenport, 7/27/84, C, 84001326

Central Fire Station, 331 Scott St., Davenport, 4/22/82, A, 82002638

Central Office Building [Davenport MRA], 230 W. 3rd St., Davenport, 7/07/83, C, 83002411

Chicago, Milwaukee, St. Paul and Pacific Freight House [Davenport MRA], 102 S. Ripley St., Davenport, 11/14/85, A, 85002825

City Market [Davenport MRA], 120 W. 5th St., Davenport, 4/05/84, A, 84001329

Claussen, William, House [Davenport MRA], 2215 W. 2nd St., Davenport, 7/07/83, C, 83002412

Clifton, 1533 Clay St., Davenport, 2/21/79, C, 79000940

Clifton-Metropolitan Hotel [Davenport MRA], 130 W. River Dr., Davenport, 7/07/83, A, C, 83002413

Cody Homestead, S of McCausland, McCausland vicinity, 1/24/74, B, C, b, 74000812

Scott County—Continued

Cody Road Historic District, Irregular pattern along Cody Rd., Le Claire, 5/07/79, A, C, 79000943

College Square Historic District [Davenport MRA], Roughly bounded by Brady, Main, Harrison, 11th, and 15th Sts., Davenport, 11/18/83, A, C, a, 83003628

Collins House, 1234 E. 29th St., Davenport, 10/08/76, C, 76000808

Columbia Avenue Historic District [Davenport MRA], Roughly W. Columbia Ave., Harrison, Ripley and W. Haynes Sts., Davenport, 11/01/84, C, 84000298

Cook, Clarissa C., Library/Blue Ribbon News Bldg. [Davenport MRA], 528 Brady St., Davenport, 7/07/83, A, C, 83002415

Cook, Clarissa, Home for the Friendless [Davenport MRA], 2223 W. 1st St., Davenport, 7/07/83, A, C, 83002414

Copeland, George, House [Davenport MRA], 929 College Ave., Davenport, 7/27/84, C, 84001333

Cork Hill District [Davenport MRA], Perry, Pershing, Iowa, 11th, 12th, and 13th Sts., Davenport, 5/16/84, C, 84001334

Cottage at 1514 and 1516 W. Second Street [Davenport MRA], 1514-1516 W. 2nd St., Davenport, 7/07/83, C, 83002416

Currier House [Davenport MRA], 1421 Grand Ave., Davenport, 7/07/83, C, 83002417

Davenport City Hall, 226 W. 4th St., Davenport, 4/22/82, A, C, 82002639

Davenport Crematorium, 3902 Rockingham Rd., Davenport, 1/19/83, A, 83002418

Davenport Hose Station No. 3 [Davenport MRA], 326 E. Locust St., Davenport, 7/27/84, C, 84001336

Davenport Hotel [Davenport MRA], 324 Main St., Davenport, 7/07/83, A, C, 83002419

Davenport Village, Roughly bounded by Mississippi River, Spring, Judson, and 13th Sts., Kirkwood Blvd., and Jersey Ridge Rd., Davenport, 3/17/80, A, C, 80001459

Davenport Water Co. Pumping Station No. 2 [Davenport MRA], 1416 Ripley St., Davenport, 4/05/84, A, C, 84001338

Davison, Abner, House [Davenport MRA], 1234 E. River Dr., Davenport, 7/27/84, C, 84001341

Dawley House [Houses of Mississippi River Men TR], 127 S. 2nd St., Le Claire, 4/13/79, B, C, 79003699

Democrat Building [Davenport MRA], 407-411 Brady St., Davenport, 7/07/83, A, C, 83002420

Dessaint, Marie Clare, House [Davenport MRA], 4808 Northwest Blvd., Davenport, 11/01/84, C, 84000300

Dillon Memorial [Davenport MRA], S. Main St., Davenport, 7/07/83, C, 83002421

Dils-Downer House [Davenport MRA], 1020 E. 15th St., Davenport, 7/07/83, B, C, 83002422

Donahue Building [Davenport MRA], 114 W. 3rd St., Davenport, 7/07/83, A, C, 83002423

East 14th Street Historic District [Davenport MRA], 14th St. from Pershing to Arlington Ave., Davenport, 11/18/83, C, 83003649

Ebeling, Arthur, House [Davenport MRA], 1106 W. 15th St., Davenport, 7/27/84, B, C, 84001397

Ebeling, Henry, House [Davenport MRA], 1623 W. 6th St., Davenport, 7/27/84, C, 84001399

Edinger, Edward, House [Davenport MRA], 1018 W. 9th St., Davenport, 7/07/83, C, 83002424

Eldridge Turn—Halle, 102 W. LeClaire St., Eldridge, 2/05/87, A, b, 87000032

Eldridge, D. C., House [Davenport MRA], 1333 E. 10th St., Davenport, 7/27/84, C, 84001402

Eldridge, Theodore, House [Davenport MRA], 1404 E. 10th St., Davenport, 7/27/84, C, 84001404

Ewert, Ferdinand, Building [Davenport MRA], 1107 W. 2nd St., Davenport, 7/07/83, C, 83002425

Fennern, Henry P., House [Davenport MRA], 1332 W. 4th St., Davenport, 4/05/84, C, 84001405

Ferner, Matthais, Building [Davenport MRA], 212 Main St., Davenport, 7/07/83, C, 83002426

Ficke Block [Davenport MRA], 307-309 Harrison St., Davenport, 7/07/83, C, 83002427

Finch, Fred, House [Davenport MRA], 719 Main St., Davenport, 7/07/83, C, 83002428

First Bible Missionary Church [Davenport MRA], 2202 W. 4th St., Davenport, 7/07/83, A, a, 83002429

First Church of Christ, Scientist [Davenport MRA], 636 Kirkwood Blvd., Davenport, 7/27/84, C, a, 84001406

First National Bank Building [Davenport MRA], 201 W. 2nd St., Davenport, 7/07/83, C, 83002430

First Presbyterian Church [Davenport MRA], 316 E. Kirkwood Blvd., Davenport, 7/07/83, C, a, 83002431

Fisher, Lewis M., House [Davenport MRA], 1003 Arlington Ave., Davenport, 7/07/83, C, 83002432

Forrest Block [Davenport MRA], 401 Brady St., Davenport, 7/07/83, C, 83002433

French, Alice, House [Davenport MRA], 321 E. 10th St., Davenport, 7/07/83, B, 83002434

Frick's Tavern, 1402–1404 W. 3rd St., Davenport, 9/09/74, A, C, 74000808

Gabbert, William, House [Davenport MRA], 1210 Tremont St., Davenport, 7/07/83, C, 83002435

Gamble, James, House, 527 Wisconsin Ave., Le Claire, 3/30/79, C, 79003692

Gannon, M. V., House [Davenport MRA], 631 Farnham St., Davenport, 7/07/83, A, B, 83002436

Gaspard, D. Julius, House [Davenport MRA], 510 W. 101/2 St., Davenport, 7/07/83, C, 83002437

Germania-Miller/Standard Hotel [Davenport MRA], 712 W. 2nd St., Davenport, 7/07/83, A, C, 83002438

Gilruth Schoolhouse, 53rd and Marquette Sts., Davenport, 9/16/77, A, 77000555

Glaspell, Isaac, House [Davenport MRA], 621 LeClaire St., Davenport, 7/07/83, C, 83002439

Goering, Jacob, House [Davenport MRA], 721 Harrison St., Davenport, 7/07/83, B, C, 83002440

Goodrich, William T., House [Davenport MRA], 1156 E. 15th St., Davenport, 7/07/83, C, 83002441

Grant, W. T., Company Building [Davenport MRA], 226 W. 2nd St., Davenport, 4/07/84, C, g, 84001420

Grilk, Charles, House [Davenport MRA], 2026 Main St., Davenport, 7/27/84, C, 84001423

Guy, Finley, Building [Davenport MRA], 310 E. Locust St., Davenport, 7/27/84, C, 84001426

Hall, Israel, House [Davenport MRA], 1316 E. 10th St., Davenport, 7/27/84, C, 84001427

Hamburg Historic District [Davenport MRA], Roughly bounded by 5th., Vine, Ripley, and 9-1/2 Sts., Davenport, 11/18/83, A, C, a, 83003656

Hauschild's Hall [Davenport MRA], 1136 W. 3rd St., Davenport, 7/07/83, A, 83002442

Hebert, Louis, House [Davenport MRA], 914 Farnan St., Davenport, 7/07/83, C, 83002443

Heinz, Bonaventura, House (second) [Davenport MRA], 1130 W. 5th St., Davenport, 7/07/83, C, 83002444

Heinz, Bonaventura, House (first) [Davenport MRA], 1128 W. 5th St., Davenport, 4/05/84, C, 84001435

Henne, Robert, House [Davenport MRA], 1445 W. 3rd St., Davenport, 7/07/83, C, 83002445

Hibernia Hall [Davenport MRA], 421 Brady St., Davenport, 7/07/83, A, C, 83002446

Hiller Building, 310–314 Gaines St., Davenport, 7/24/74, C, 74000810

Hillside, 1 Prospect Dr., Davenport, 2/04/82, C, 82002640

Hoersch, John, House [Davenport MRA], 716 Vine St., Davenport, 11/01/84, C, 84000304

Hoffman Building [Davenport MRA], 510 W. 2nd St., Davenport, 7/07/83, C, 83002447

Hoffman, Samuel, Jr., House [Davenport MRA], 2108 W. 3rd St., Davenport, 7/07/83, C, 83002448

Holbrook, William, House [Davenport MRA], 804 Kirkwood Blvd., Davenport, 7/27/84, C, 84001440

Horton-Suiter House [Houses of Mississippi River Men TR], 102 N. 2nd St., Le Claire, 4/13/79, B, 79003700

Hose Station No. 1 [Davenport MRA], 117 Perry St., Davenport, 7/07/83, A, C, 83002449

Hose Station No. 6 [Davenport MRA], 1410 Marquette St., Davenport, 7/07/83, A, C, 83002450

Hose Station No. 7 [Davenport MRA], 1354 W. 4th St., Davenport, 7/07/83, C, 83002451

House at 1646 W. Second Street [Davenport MRA], 1646 W. 2nd St., Davenport, 7/07/83, C, 83002452

House at 2123 W. Second Street [Davenport MRA], 2123 W. 2nd St., Davenport, 7/07/83, C, 83002453

House at 2212 W. River Drive [Davenport MRA], 2212 W. River Dr., Davenport, 11/01/84, C, 84000309

House at 318-332 Marquette Street [Davenport MRA], 318-332 Marquette St., Davenport, 7/07/83, C, 83002454

Scott County—Continued

House at 919 Oneida Street [Davenport MRA], 919 Oneida St., Davenport, 4/05/84, C, 84001444

Iowa Reform Building [Davenport MRA], 526 W. 2nd St., Davenport, 11/18/83, A, 83003658

Iowa Soldiers' Orphans' Home, 2800 Eastern Ave., Davenport, 4/26/82, A, 82002641

Jansen, Theodore, House [Davenport MRA], 922 Myrtle St., Davenport, 7/07/83, C, 83002455

Kahl Building [Davenport MRA], 326 W. 3rd St., Davenport, 7/07/83, C, 83002456

Kahl, Henry, House [Davenport MRA], 1101 W. 9th St., Davenport, 7/07/83, B, C, 83002457

Kattenbracher House [Houses of Mississippi River Men TR], 1125 N. 2nd St., Le Claire, 4/13/79, B, 79003701

Kiene, Albert, House [Davenport MRA], 1321 W. 8th St., Davenport, 7/27/84, C, 84001450

Kimball-Stevenson House [Davenport MRA], 116 E. 6th St., Davenport, 7/07/83, C, 83002458

Klindt, George, House [Davenport MRA], 902 Marquette St., Davenport, 7/07/83, B, C, 83002459

Klindt, Henry, House [Davenport MRA], 834 Marquette St., Davenport, 7/27/84, C, 84001454

Koch Drug Store [Davenport MRA], 1501 Harrison St., Davenport, 7/27/84, C, 84001457

Koenig Building [Davenport MRA], 619 W. 2nd St., Davenport, 7/07/83, C, 83002460

Koester, Nicholas, Building [Davenport MRA], 1353 W. 3rd St., Davenport, 7/07/83, C, 83002461

Kuhnen, Nicholas J., House [Davenport MRA], 702 Perry St., Davenport, 7/07/83, B, C, 83002462

LONESTAR, Buffalo Bill Museum, LeClaire, 12/20/89, A, C, g, NHL, 89002461

LeClaire, Antoine, House, 630 E. 7th St., Davenport, 3/22/74, B, C, a, 74000809

Lend-A-Hand Club [Davenport MRA], 105 S. Main St., Davenport, 4/05/84, A, 84001459

Lerch, Gustov C., House [Davenport MRA], 2222 W. 4th St., Davenport, 7/07/83, C, 83002463

Linden Flats [Davenport MRA], 219 Scott St., Davenport, 11/28/83, C, 83003661

Lindsay, James E., House [Davenport MRA], 911 College Ave., Davenport, 7/27/84, C, 84001465

Lippincott, John, House [Davenport MRA], 2122 W. Third St., Davenport, 7/07/83, C, 83004527

Littig Brothers/Mengel & Klindt/Eagle Brewery [Davenport MRA], 1235 W. 5th St., Davenport, 7/07/83, A, 83002464

Littig, John, House [Davenport MRA], 6035 Northwest Blvd., Davenport, 11/01/84, C, 84000310

Lueschen, John, House [Davenport MRA], 1628-1632 Washington St., Davenport, 7/27/84, C, 84001468

Mallet, Joseph, House [Davenport MRA], 415 E. 10th St., Davenport, 7/07/83, C, 83002465

Martzahn, August F., House [Davenport MRA], 2303 W. 3rd St., Davenport, 7/07/83, C, 83002466

McBride-Hickey House [Davenport MRA], 701 Iowa St., Davenport, 7/07/83, C, 83002467

McCaffrey House [Houses of Mississippi River Men TR], 208 N. Cody Rd., Le Claire, 4/13/79, B, C, 79003702

McCarthy, Patrick F., House [Davenport MRA], 842 Marquette St., Davenport, 7/27/84, C, 84001471

McClellan Heights Historic Dictrict [Davenport MRA], Roughly bounded by city limits, E. River Dr., East St., Jersey Ridge and Middle Rds., Davenport, 11/01/84, C, 84000328

McHarg, Joseph S., House [Davenport MRA], 5905 Chapel Hill Rd., Davenport, 4/09/85, C, 85000775

McKinney House [Davenport MRA], 512 E. 8th St., Davenport, 7/07/83, C, 83002468

McManus House [Davenport MRA], 2320 Telegraph Rd., Davenport, 7/07/83, C, 83002469

Meadly House [Davenport MRA], 1425 W. 10th St., Davenport, 7/27/84, C, 84001476

Meiser Drug Store [Davenport MRA], 1115 W. 3rd St., Davenport, 7/07/83, C, 83002470

Middleton, Dr. George McLelland, House and Garage, 1221 Scott St., Davenport, 11/10/82, C, 82001549

Miller Building [Davenport MRA], 724 Harrison St., Davenport, 7/07/83, C, 83002471

Miller, F. H., House [Davenport MRA], 1527 Brady St., Davenport, 7/07/83, B, C, 83002472

Miller, Severin, House [Davenport MRA], 2200 Telegraph Rd., Davenport, 7/07/83, B, C, 83002473

Motie, Joseph, House [Davenport MRA], 421 E. 10th St., Davenport, 11/18/83, C, 83003668

Mueller Lumber Company [Davenport MRA], 501 W. 2nd St., Davenport, 7/07/83, C, 83002474

Murray, Thomas, House [Davenport MRA], 628 Kirkwood Blvd., Davenport, 7/27/84, C, 84001485

Nebergall "Knoll Crest" Round Barn [Iowa Round Barns: The Sixty Year Experiment TR], Telegraph Rd., Blue Grass vicinity, 6/30/86, A, B, C, 86001473

Newcome, Daniel T., Double House [Davenport MRA], 722-724 Brady St., Davenport, 7/07/83, C, 83002475

Newhall, Lucian, House [Davenport MRA], 526 Iowa St., Davenport, 7/07/83, C, 83002476

Nichols, Oscar, House [Davenport MRA], 1013 Tremont St., Davenport, 7/07/83, C, 83002477

Nighswander, Benjamin, House [Davenport MRA], 1011 Kirkwood Blvd., Davenport, 7/27/84, C, 84001487

Northwest Davenport Savings Bank [Davenport MRA], 1529 Washington St., Davenport, 7/27/84, C, 84001491

Northwest Davenport Turner Society Hall, 1602 Washington St., Davenport, 7/10/79, A, 79000941

Oak Lane Historic District [Davenport MRA], Oak Lane between High and Locust Sts., Davenport, 11/01/84, C, 84000331

Ochs Building [Davenport MRA], 214 Main St., Davenport, 7/07/83, C, 83002478

Ockershausen, Henry, House [Davenport MRA], 1024 Charlotte St., Davenport, 4/05/84, C, 84001495

Old City Hall [Davenport MRA], 514 Brady St., Davenport, 7/07/83, A, 83002479

Old Mill House [Houses of Mississippi River Men TR], 419 N. Cody Rd., Le Claire, 4/13/79, B, C, 79003703

Outing Club, 2109 Brady St., Davenport, 7/15/77, C, 77000556

Pahl, Henry, House [Davenport MRA], 1946 W. 3rd St., Davenport, 7/07/83, C, 83002480

Palmer, B. J., House [Davenport MRA], 808 Brady St., Davenport, 7/27/84, A, B, C, 84001497

Paulsen, Peter J., House [Davenport MRA], 705 Main St., Davenport, 7/07/83, C, 83002481

Paustian, Henry, House [Davenport MRA], 1226 W. 6th St., Davenport, 7/07/83, C, 83002482

Peters' Barber Shop [Davenport MRA], 1352 W. 3rd St., Davenport, 4/05/84, C, 84001498

Peters, J. C., House [Davenport MRA], 1339 W. 13th St., Davenport, 7/27/84, C, 84001500

Petersen's, J. H. C., Sons Store [Davenport MRA], 123-131 W. 2nd St., Davenport, 7/07/83, A, C, 83002483

Petersen's, J. H. C., Sons Wholesale Building [Davenport MRA], 122-124 W. River Dr., Davenport, 7/07/83, C, 83002484

Petersen, W. D., Memorial Music Pavillion [Davenport MRA], Beiderbecke Dr., Davenport, 7/07/83, C, 83002485

Peterson, Max, House, 1607 W. 12th St., Davenport, 12/25/79, C, 79000942

Picklum, Frank, House [Davenport MRA], 1340 W. 7th St., Davenport, 7/27/84, C, 84001515

Pierce School No. 13 [Davenport MRA], 2212 E. 12th St., Davenport, 7/07/83, A, C, 83002486

Plambeck, Joachim, House [Davenport MRA], 1421 W. 14th St., Davenport, 7/27/84, C, 84001516

Pohlmann, Elizabeth, House [Davenport MRA], 1403 W. 13th St., Davenport, 7/27/84, C, 84001518

Pohlmann, Henry, House [Davenport MRA], 1204 W. 13th St., Davenport, 7/27/84, C, 84001520

Potter-Williams House [Davenport MRA], 427 E. 7th St., Davenport, 4/05/84, C, 84001522

Price, Hiram/Henry Vollmer House [Davenport MRA], 723 Brady St., Davenport, 7/07/83, B, C, 83002487

Prien Building [Davenport MRA], 506-508 W. 2nd St., Davenport, 7/07/83, C, 83002488

Prospect Park Historic District [Davenport MRA], Roughly bounded by E. River Dr., Mississippi Ave., Prospect Terr., 11th and Adams St., Davenport, 11/01/84, C, 84000338

Quickel, Jacob, House [Davenport MRA], 1712 Davenport St., Davenport, 7/27/84, C, 84001524

Radcliff, Willam, House [Davenport MRA], 904 College Ave., Davenport, 7/27/84, C, 84001530

Raible, F. J., House [Davenport MRA], 1537 W. 3rd St., Davenport, 11/28/83, C, 83003683

Rambo House [Houses of Mississippi River Men TR], 430 N. Cody Rd., Le Claire, 4/13/79, B, 79003704

Scott County—Continued

Ranzow-Sander House [Davenport MRA], 2128 W. 3rd St., Davenport, 7/07/83, C, 83002489

Raphael, Jacob, Building [Davenport MRA], 628-630 Harrison St., Davenport, 7/07/83, C, 83002490

Renwick Building [Davenport MRA], 322 Brady St., Davenport, 7/07/83, C, 83002491

Renwick House [Davenport MRA], 1429 Brady St., Davenport, 7/07/83, C, 83002492

Riepe Drug Store/G. Ott Block [Davenport MRA], 403 W. 2nd St., Davenport, 7/07/83, C, 83002493

Riverview Terrace Historic District [Davenport MRA], Roughly Riverview Terr., Clay and Marquette Sts., Davenport, 11/01/84, C, 84000339

Roberts, Edward C., House [Davenport MRA], 918 E. Locust St., Davenport, 7/27/84, C, 84001533

Roslyn Flats [Davenport MRA], 739 Perry St., Davenport, 7/07/83, C, 83004375

Rowhouses at 702-712 Kirkwood Boulevard [Davenport MRA], 702-712 Kirkwood Blvd., Davenport, 7/27/84, C, 84001535

SAINTE GENEVIEVE (dredge) [Davenport MRA], Antoine LeClaire Park, off US 67, Davenport, 8/04/86, A, C, 86002232

Sacred Heart Roman Catholic Cathedral Complex [Davenport MRA], 406 and 422 E. 10th St. and 419 E. 11th St., Davenport, 4/05/84, A, C, a, 84001537

Saengerfest Halle [Davenport MRA], 1012 W. 4th St., Davenport, 7/07/83, A, 83002494

Schauder Hotel [Davenport MRA], 126 W. River Dr., Davenport, 7/07/83, C, 83002495

Schebler, Richard, House [Davenport MRA], 1217 W. 7th St., Davenport, 7/07/83, C, 83002496

Schick's Express and Transfer Co. [Davenport MRA], 118-120 W. River Dr., Davenport, 7/07/83, C, 83002497

Schmidt Block [Davenport MRA], 115 E. 3rd St., Davenport, 7/07/83, C, 83002498

Schmidt, F. Jacob, House [Davenport MRA], 2143-and 2147 W. 5th St., Davenport, 7/07/83, C, 83002499

Schricker, John C., House [Davenport MRA], 1446 Clay St., Davenport, 7/07/83, A, C, 83002500

Schricker, John, House [Davenport MRA], 5418 Chapel Hill Rd., Davenport, 4/09/85, C, 85000776

Schroeder Bros, Meat Market [Davenport MRA], 2146 W. 3rd St., Davenport, 7/07/83, C, 83002501

Scott County Jail [Davenport MRA], 428 Ripley St., Davenport, 7/07/83, A, C, 83002502

Sharon, Fred B., House [Davenport MRA], 728 Farnan St., Davenport, 7/07/83, A, C, 83002503

Shaw, E. A., House [Davenport MRA], 1102 College Ave., Davenport, 7/27/84, C, 84001561

Shields Woolen Mill [Davenport MRA], 1235 E. River Dr., Davenport, 7/07/83, A, C, 83002504

Siemer House, 632 W. 3rd St., Davenport, 11/16/77, A, C, 77000557

Simpson, Charles S., House [Davenport MRA], 1503 Farnan St., Davenport, 7/07/83, C, 83002505

Sitz, Rudolph H., Building [Davenport MRA], 2202 W. 3rd St., Davenport, 7/07/83, C, 83002506

Smith, Alvord I., House [Davenport MRA], 2318 W. 3rd St., Davenport, 7/07/83, C, 83002507

Smith, Henry H./J.H. Murphy House [Davenport MRA], 512 E. 6th St., Davenport, 7/07/83, C, 83002508

Smith, James, House [Davenport MRA], 1037 E. 18th St., Davenport, 7/27/84, C, 84001563

Smith, John, House [Houses of Mississippi River Men TR], 426 Dodge, Le Claire, 4/13/79, B, 79003705

Smith, William G., House [Davenport MRA], 1002 Bridge St., Davenport, 4/05/84, C, 84001566

Spencer, Roswell, House, Off U.S. 67, Pleasant Valley, 4/22/82, B, C, 82002642

St. Anthony's Roman Catholic Church Complex [Davenport MRA], 407 and 417 Main St., Davenport, 4/05/84, A, a, 84001538

St. John's Methodist Church [Davenport MRA], 1325-1329 Brady St., Davenport, 7/07/83, A, C, a, 83002509

St. Joseph's Catholic Church [Davenport MRA], W. 6th and Marquette Sts., Davenport, 7/07/83, A, C, a, 83002510

St. Katherine's Historic District [Davenport MRA], 901 Tremont St., Davenport, 4/05/84, A, B, C, a, 84001551

St. Luke's Hospital [Davenport MRA], 121 W. 8th St., Davenport, 7/07/83, A, 83002511

St. Mary's Academy [Davenport MRA], 1334 W. 8th St., Davenport, 7/27/84, C, a, 84001556

St. Mary's Roman Catholic Church Complex [Davenport MRA], 516, 519, 522, and 525 Fillmore Sts., Davenport, 4/05/84, A, C, a, 84001558

St. Paul's English Lutheran Church [Davenport MRA], 1402 Main St., Davenport, 7/07/83, A, C, a, 83002512

Stewart, J. W., House [Davenport MRA], 212 E. 6th St., Davenport, 7/07/83, C, 83002513

Stone House, 817 N. 2nd St., Le Claire, 7/07/83, A, C, 83002528

Stone School, W of Le Claire, Le Claire vicinity, 12/27/77, C, 77000558

Struck, Dr. Kuno, House [Davenport MRA], 1645 W. 12th St., Davenport, 7/27/84, C, 84001567

Suiter, Jacob, House [Houses of Mississippi River Men TR], 214 S. 2nd St., Le Claire, 4/13/79, B, C, 79003707

Suiter, John H., House [Houses of Mississippi River Men TR], 1220 N. 2nd St., Le Claire, 4/13/79, B, 79003706

Suiter, William, House [Houses of Mississippi River Men TR], 227 Wisconsin, Le Claire, 4/13/79, B, 79003708

Swan, George B., House [Davenport MRA], 909 Farnan St., Davenport, 7/07/83, C, 83002514

Swedish Baptist Church [Davenport MRA], 700 E. 6th St., Davenport, 7/07/83, A, a, b, 83002515

Taylor School [Davenport MRA], 1400 Warren St., Davenport, 7/07/83, A, 83002516

Templeton, I. Edward, House [Davenport MRA], 1315 Perry St., Davenport, 7/07/83, C, 83002517

Tevoet, Lambert, House [Davenport MRA], 2017 W. 2nd St., Davenport, 7/07/83, C, 83002518

Trinity Episcopal Cathedral, 121 W. 12th St., Davenport, 12/24/74, C, a, 74000811

Tromley, George, Jr., House [Houses of Mississippi River Men TR], 127 Jones St., Le Claire, 4/13/79, B, C, 79003710

Tromley, George, Sr., House [Houses of Mississippi River Men TR], 806 N. Cody Rd., Le Claire, 4/13/79, B, 79003709

Union Electric Telephone & Telegraph [Davenport MRA], 602 Harrison St., Davenport, 7/07/83, A, C, 83002519

Union Savings Bank and Trust [Davenport MRA], 229 Brady St., Davenport, 7/07/83, A, C, 83002520

Union Station and Burlington Freight House [Davenport MRA], 120 S. Harrison St., Davenport, 7/07/83, A, 83002521

Untiedt, Claus, House [Davenport MRA], 1429 W. 14th St., Davenport, 7/27/84, C, 84001577

Van Sant, Samuel, House [Houses of Mississippi River Men TR], 322 N. Cody Rd., Le Claire, 4/13/79, B, 79003711

Vander Veer Park Historic District [Davenport MRA], Roughly bounded by Temple Lane, W. Central Park Ave., Brady, High, and Harrison Sts., Davenport, 4/09/85, C, 85000784

Von Ach, Frank J., House [Davenport MRA], 1618 Davenport St., Davenport, 7/27/84, C, 84001579

Walsh Flats/Langworth Building [Davenport MRA], 320-330 W. 4th St., Davenport, 4/05/84, A, C, 84001582

Walter-Gimble House [Davenport MRA], 123 W. 6th St., Davenport, 7/07/83, C, 83002522

Warner Apartment Building [Davenport MRA], 414-416 E. 6th St., Davenport, 7/07/83, C, 83002523

Washington Flats [Davenport MRA], 1415-1431 Washington St., Davenport, 7/27/84, C, 84001584

Washington Gardens [Davenport MRA], 1301 W. 13th St., Davenport, 7/27/84, C, 84001585

Werthman Grocery [Davenport MRA], 1402 W. 7th St., Davenport, 7/27/84, C, 84001588

West Third Street Historic District [Davenport MRA], Roughly 3rd St. between Ripley and Myrtle Sts., Davenport, 11/18/83, A, C, 83003741

Westphal-Schmidt House [Davenport MRA], 432 S. Fairmount St., Davenport, 7/27/84, C, 84001591

Whitaker, Charles, House [Davenport MRA], 1530 E. 12th St., Davenport, 1/14/85, C, 85000090

Wilkinson, Thomas C., House [Davenport MRA], 118 McManus St., Davenport, 7/27/84, C, 84001592

Wolters Filling Station [Davenport MRA], 1229 Washngton St., Davenport, 7/27/84, C, 84001595

Woods, Oscar C., House [Davenport MRA], 1825 Grand Ave., Davenport, 11/01/84, C, 84000342

Worley, Philip, House [Davenport MRA], 425 Brady St., Davenport, 7/07/83, C, 83002524

Scott County—Continued

Wupperman Block/I.O.O.F. Hall [Davenport MRA], 508-512 Brady St., Davenport, 7/07/83, C, 83002525

Young, Col. Joseph, Block [Davenport MRA], 502 Brady St., Davenport, 7/07/83, C, 83002526

Zoller Bros-Independent Malting Co. [Davenport MRA], 1801 W. 3rd St., Davenport, 7/07/83, A, 83002527

Shelby County

Floral Hall, 314 4th St. on Shelby County Fairgrounds, Harlan, 4/11/85, C, 85000765

Heese, J. C., Lumber Shed [Ethnic Historic Settlement of Shelby and Audubon Counties MPS], Railway St., E. side, Earling, 10/03/91, A, C, 91001454

Larsen, Chris, House [Ethnic Historic Settlement of Shelby and Audubon Counties MPS], 4215 Main St., Elk Horn, 10/03/91, C, 91001456

Poldberg, Chris, Farmstead [Ethnic Historic Settlement of Shelby and Audubon Counties MPS], 0.5 mi. S of IA 44 on Wolf Cr., Jacksonville vicinity, 10/03/91, A, C, 91001459

Rewerts, George, House [Ethnic Historic Settlement of Shelby and Audubon Counties MPS], 306 8th Ave., Defiance, 10/03/91, C, 91001450

Saint Boniface Catholic Church District [Ethnic Historic Settlement of Shelby and Audubon Counties MPS], Three blocks N of Co. Rd. F32, Westphalia, 10/03/91, A, B, a, d, 91001449

Shelby County Courthouse [County Courthouses in Iowa TR (AD)], 7th and Court Sts., Harlan, 11/14/78, C, 78001258

St. Paul's Episcopal Church, 712 Farnham St., Harlan, 9/01/78, C, a, 78001259

Sioux County

Fleshman, Charles M. and Emma M. Fischer, House, 919 9th St., Hawarden, 1/07/93, C, 92001743

Sioux County Courthouse [County Courthouses in Iowa TR (AD)], Off IA 10, Orange City, 4/11/77, C, 77000559

Zwemer Hall, Northwestern College, 101 7th St., SW, Orange, 5/28/75, A, C, a, 75000698

Story County

Agriculture Hall, Iowa State University, Ames, 6/27/85, C, 85001374

Alumni Hall, Iowa State University campus, Ames, 11/16/78, C, 78001260

Christian Petersen Courtyard Sculptures, and Dairy Industry Building, Union Dr. and Wallace Rd., Iowa State University campus, Ames, 4/07/87, A, C, 87000020

Edwards-Swayze House, 1110 9th St., Nevada, 11/14/78, C, 78001262

Engineering Hall, Union Dr., Iowa State University campus, Ames, 1/10/83, A, C, 83000402

Grand Auditorium and Hotel Block, Broad St., Story City, 1/25/80, A, C, 80001460

Herschel—Spillman Two-Row Portable Menagerie Carousel, North Park, Story St., and Grove Ave., Story City, 6/06/86, C, 86001244

Knapp-Wilson House, Iowa State University campus, Ames, 10/15/66, A, B, NHL, 66000339

MacDonald, Gilmour B. and Edith Craig, House [Conservation Movement in Iowa MPS], 517 Ash St., Ames, 5/06/92, B, C, 91001860

Marston Water Tower, Iowa State University campus, Ames, 5/27/82, C, 82002644

Octagon Round Barn, Indian Creek Township [Iowa Round Barns: The Sixty Year Experiment TR], Off CR S14, Iowa Center vicinity, 6/30/86, A, C, 86001439

Sheldahl First Norwegian Evangelical Lutheran Church, 3rd and Willow Sts., Sheldahl, 5/11/84, A, C, a, 84001599

Silliman Memorial Library [Public Library Buildings in Iowa TR], 631 K Ave., Nevada, 5/23/83, C, 83000403

Soper's Mill Bridge, N of Ames off IA 35, Ames vicinity, 2/14/78, C, 78001261

Tama County

Brooks and Moore Bank Building, 423 2nd St., Traer, 12/03/74, B, C, 74000813

Hope Fire Company Engine House, 109 S. Broadway, Toledo, 1/27/83, A, C, 83000404

Lincoln Highway Bridge, E. 5th St., Tama, 3/30/78, A, 78001263

Round Barn, Buckingham Township [Iowa Round Barns: The Sixty Year Experiment TR], Off US 63, Buckingham vicinity, 6/30/86, A, C, 86001441

Star-Clipper-Canfield Building and Winding Stairway, 534 2nd St., Traer, 10/29/75, C, 75000699

Tama County Courthouse [County Courthouses in Iowa TR], State St., Toledo, 7/02/81, C, 81000269

Tama County Jail, Broadway and State Sts., Toledo, 8/27/81, A, 81000270

Wieting Theater, 101 S. Church St., Toledo, 4/26/79, A, C, 79000944

Young, John W., Round Barn [Iowa Round Barns: The Sixty Year Experiment TR], Off US 63, Traer vicinity, 6/30/86, A, C, 86001444

Taylor County

Bedford House, 306 Main St., Bedford, 6/14/77, B, 77000560

Bedford Public Library [Public Library Buildings in Iowa TR], Jefferson St., Bedford, 5/23/83, C, 83000405

Taylor County Courthouse [County Courthouses in Iowa TR], Court Ave., Bedford, 7/02/81, C, 81000271

Union County

Chicago, Burlington and Quincy Railroad-Creston Station, 200 W. Adams St., Creston, 8/15/73, A, C, 73000739

U. S. Post Office, Maple St., Creston, 12/08/78, C, 78001264

Van Buren County

Aunty Green Hotel, 602 Washington St., Bonaparte, 1/20/78, B, 78001265

Bentonsport, E of Keosauqua on the Des Moines River, Keosauqua vicinity, 4/25/72, A, a, 72000482

Bonaparte Historic Riverfront District, Roughly bounded by Second St., Washington St., Des Moines River, and Richard St., Bonaparte, 4/25/89, A, 89000313

Burg Wagon Works Building, 131 S. 2nd St., Farmington, 11/14/78, B, C, 78001266

Des Moines River Locks No. 5 and No. 7, At Des Moines River, Bonaparte and Keosauqua, 12/07/77, A, 77000561

Hotel Manning, River and Van Buren Sts., Keosauqua, 4/23/73, B, C, 73000740

Lacey—Keosauqua State Park, Lodge and Picnic Area (Area A) [CCC Properties in Iowa State Parks MPS], Off IA 1 on S bank of Des Moines R., Keosauqua vicinity, 11/15/90, A, C, 90001668

Lacey—Keosauqua State Park, Picnic and Custodial Group (Area B) [CCC Properties in Iowa State Parks MPS], Off IA 1 on S bank of Des Moines R., Keosauqua vicinity, 11/15/90, A, C, 90001669

Lacey—Keosauqua State Park, Bathing Area (Area C) [CCC Properties in Iowa State Parks MPS], Off IA 1 on S bank of Des Moines R., Keosauqua vicinity, 11/15/90, A, C, 90001670

Martin, Abner, House, S of Mount Zion off IA 1, Mount Zion vicinity, 4/12/84, C, 84001604

Meek's Flour Mill, 1st St., Bonaparte, 1/27/83, A, 83000406

Pearson, Franklin, House, Dodge St., Keosauqua, 5/22/78, C, 78001267

Twombley, Voltaire, Building, 803 First St., Keosauqua, 7/29/93, C, 93000655

Van Buren County Courthouse [County Courthouses in Iowa TR (AD)], 904 4th St., Keosauqua, 11/09/77, C, 77000562

Wickfield Round Barn [Iowa Round Barns: The Sixty Year Experiment TR], Off IA 2, Cantril vicinity, 6/30/86, A, C, 86001447

Wapello County

Benson Block, 109–112 N. Market, Ottumwa, 1/03/85, C, 85000009

Wapello County—Continued

Chief Wapello's Memorial Park, SE of Agency off U.S. 34, Agency vicinity, 3/27/75, A, B, d, f, 75000700

Dibble House, Burton and Gothic Sts., Eldon, 10/01/74, A, C, g, 74002291

Foster/Bell House, 205 E. 5th St., Ottumwa, 9/29/83, C, 83000407

Mars Hill, SE of Ottumwa, Ottumwa vicinity, 9/13/74, A, C, a, d, 74000814

Ottumwa Public Library, 129 N. Court St., Ottumwa, 4/27/84, C, 84001605

U.S. Post Office, Court and 4th Sts., Ottumwa, 8/13/76, C, 76000810

Wapello County Courthouse [County Courthouses in Iowa TR], Court St., Ottumwa, 7/02/81, C, 81000272

Warren County

Lake Ahquabi State Park, Bathhouse Area (Area B) [CCC Properties in Iowa State Parks MPS], 1650 118th Ave., Indianola vicinity, 11/15/90, A, C, 90001664

Lake Ahquabi State Park, Picnic Area (Area A) [CCC Properties in Iowa State Parks MPS], 1650 118th Ave., Indianola vicinity, 11/15/90, A, C, 90001663

Lake Ahquabi State Park, Refectory Area (Area C) [CCC Properties in Iowa State Parks MPS], 1650 118th Ave., Indianola vicinity, 11/15/90, A, C, 90001665

Octagon Barn, Otter Township [Iowa Round Barns: The Sixty Year Experiment TR], Off IA 205, Milo vicinity, 6/30/86, A, C, 86001448

Palmyra Methodist Episcopal Church, SW of Hartford, Palmyra, 10/01/79, C, a, 79000945

Polled Hereford Breed Origin Site, SW of Indianola, Indianola vicinity, 6/24/83, A, 83000408

Science Hall [Architectural Legacy of Proudfoot & Bird MPS], Simpson College Campus, Indianola, 5/08/91, C, 91000535

United Presbyterian Church, Summerset, U.S. 65, Scotch Ridge, 11/07/76, A, C, a, 76000811

Washington County

Blair House, E. Washington St. and S. 2nd Ave., Washington, 6/04/73, A, C, g, 73000741

Conger, Jonathan Clark, House, 903 E. Washington St., Washington, 6/28/74, B, C, 74000815

Gracehill Moravian Church and Cemetery, SW of Washington on WA 314, Washington vicinity, 8/12/77, A, a, b, 77000563

Jordan, Thomas, Polygonal Barn [Iowa Round Barns: The Sixty Year Experiment TR], Off IA 114, Wellman vicinity, 6/30/86, A, C, 86001451

Keck, Joseph, House, 504 W. Washington St., Washington, 11/28/78, C, 78001268

Kurtz House, 305 S. Ave. C, Washington, 9/22/77, C, 77000564

Smouse, Winfield, House, 321 S. Iowa Ave., Washington, 1/27/83, A, B, 83000409

St. Mary's Parish Church Buildings, St. Mary's and Washburn Sts., Riverside, 7/09/79, C, a, 79000946

Stewart, Frank, House, 603 W. Washington St., Washington, 11/16/87, C, 87002021

Washington County Courthouse [County Courthouses in Iowa TR], N. B Ave., Washington, 7/02/81, C, 81000273

Washington County Hospital, S. 4th Ave. and Clara Barton, Washington, 12/22/77, A, 77000565

Young, Alexander, Cabin, W. Madison St., between G and H Aves., Washington, 8/14/73, A, C, b, 73000742

Wayne County

Nelson Round Barn [Iowa Round Barns: The Sixty Year Experiment TR], CR J46, Allerton vicinity, 11/19/86, A, 86003189

Pleasant Hill School, 3 mi. N of Lineville on U.S. 65, Lineville vicinity, 5/28/75, A, 75000701

Tedford, W. H., House, 312 S. West St., Corydon, 3/26/79, C, 79000947

Webster County

Coffin, Lorenzo S., Burial Plot, NW of Fort Dodge on IA 7, Fort Dodge vicinity, 11/17/77, B, c, 77000566

Corpus Christi Church, 416 N. 8th St., Fort Dodge, 10/08/76, C, a, 76000812

Dolliver Memorial State Park, Entrance Area (Area A) [CCC Properties in Iowa State Parks MPS], N of IA 50 on Des Moines R., Lehigh vicinity, 11/15/90, A, C, 90001684

Dolliver Memorial State Park, Picnic, Hiking & Maintenance Area (Area B) [CCC Properties in Iowa State Parks MPS], N of IA 50 on Des Moines R., Lehigh vicinity, 11/15/90, A, C, 90001685

Illinois Central Freight House and Office Building—Fort Dodge [Advent & Development of Railroads in Iowa, 1850-1940, MPS], Jct. of 4th St. and 4th Ave., S., Fort Dodge, 9/06/90, A, C, 90001306

Illinois Central Passenger Depot—Fort Dodge [Advent & Development of Railroads in Iowa, 1850-1940, MPS], Jct. of Fourth St., and Fourth Ave., S., Fort Dodge, 9/06/90, A, C, 90001307

Oak Hill Historic District, 8th—12th Sts., 2nd and 3rd Aves., Fort Dodge, 5/05/77, C, 77000567

Vincent House, 824 3rd Ave., S., Fort Dodge, 4/23/73, B, C, 73000743

Webster County Courthouse [County Courthouses in Iowa TR], 701 Central Ave., Fort Dodge, 7/02/81, C, 81000274

Winnebago County

Forest City Public Library [Public Library Buildings in Iowa TR], E. I St. and Clark, Forest City, 4/05/84, C, 84001609

Round Barn, Norway Township [Iowa Round Barns: The Sixty Year Experiment TR], Off CR R60, Scarville vicinity, 2/27/87, A, C, 87000507

Thompson, Charles J., House, 336 N. Clark St., Forest City, 11/30/78, C, 78001271

Winnebago County Courthouse [County Courthouses in Iowa TR], J St., Forest City, 7/02/81, C, 81000275

Winneshiek County

Birdsall Lime Kiln, NE of Decorah, Decorah vicinity, 3/21/79, A, 79000948

Broadway-Phelps Park Historic District, West Broadway from Winnebago St. to Park Dr., Decorah, 11/13/76, C, 76000813

Burr Oak House/Masters Hotel, State St., Burr Oak, 1/27/83, A, B, C, 83000410

Clarksville Diner, 504 Heivly St., Decorah, 12/10/93, C, b, 93001356

Cooley-Whitney House, 305 Grove St., Decorah, 1/25/80, C, 80001461

Decorah Ice Cave, Ice Cave Rd., Decorah, 12/20/78, A, 78001269

Ellsworth-Porter House, 401 W. Broadway, Decorah, 8/06/75, C, 75000702

Frankville School, State St., Frankville, 11/14/78, C, 78001272

Freeport Bowstring Arch Bridge, Spans Upper Iowa River, Freeport vicinity, 4/19/84, C, 84001407

Horn House, NW of Decorah, Decorah vicinity, 3/25/77, B, C, 77000568

Jacobson Farm, SE of Decorah on Rt. 1, Decorah vicinity, 6/14/82, B, C, 82002645

Kinney Octagon Barn [Iowa Round Barns: The Sixty Year Experiment TR], Off US 52, Burr Oak vicinity, 11/19/86, A, C, 86003191

Koren Library, Luther College campus, Decorah, 1/12/84, A, C, 84001610

Locust School, N of Decorah, Decorah vicinity, 5/22/78, A, C, 78001270

Luther College Farm, Luther College campus, Decorah, 7/17/79, A, B, C, 79000949

Miller, Norris, House, 118 N. Mill St., Decorah, 6/08/76, C, b, 76000814

Ossian Opera House, Main St., Ossian, 6/18/79, C, 79000950

Painter-Bernatz Mill, 200 N. Mill St., Decorah, 1/11/74, A, 74000816

Steyer Bridge, Oneata Rd. off US 52, Decorah, 1/04/83, C, 83000411

Steyer Opera House, 102–104 W. Water St., Decorah, 1/24/80, C, 80001462

Taylor, Wenzil, Building, Main St., Spillville, 3/21/79, C, 79000951

Washington Prairie Methodist Church, SE of Decorah, Decorah vicinity, 1/29/80, A, a, 80001463

Woodbury County

Badgerow Building, 622 4th St., Sioux City, 3/24/82, B, C, 82002646

Benson Archeological Site (13WD50), Address Restricted, Smithland vicinity, 4/24/84, D, 84001611

Boston Block, 1005–1013 E. 4th St., Sioux City, 1/03/85, C, 85000010

Charles City College Hall, 1501 Moringside Ave., Sioux City, 1/21/83, A, 83000412

Chicago, Milwaukee, St. Paul & Pacific Combination Depot—Hornick [Advent & Development of Railroads in Iowa, 1850-1940, MPS], Main St., S. of Railway St., Hornick, 9/06/90, A, C, 90001309

Evans Block, 1126–28 4th St., Sioux City, 1/03/85, C, 85000011

Everist, H. H., House, 37 McDonald Dr., Sioux City, 9/29/83, C, 83000413

Franz, Margaretta, House, 215 Kansas St., Sioux City, 6/21/82, C, 82002647

Knapp-Spencer Warehouse, 3rd and Nebraska Sts., Sioux City, 6/21/82, A, C, 82002648

Lexington Block, 815 Fourth St., Sioux City, 4/11/86, C, a, 86000706

Martin Hotel, 410 Pierce St., Sioux City, 1/27/83, A, C, 83000414

Midland Packing Company, 2001 Leech Ave., Sioux City, 1/25/79, A, 79000952

Motor Mart Building, 520 Nebraska St., Sioux City, 4/22/93, C, 93000330

Peirce, John, House, 2901 Jackson St., Sioux City, 12/12/78, C, 78001273

SERGEANT FLOYD, Missouri River Mile Marker 730, Sioux City, 5/05/89, A, C, NHL, 89001079

Sergeant Floyd Monument, Glenn Ave. and Lewis Rd., Sioux City, 10/15/66, B, NHL, 66000340

Sioux City Baptist Church, 1301 Nebraska Ave., Sioux City, 10/22/79, C, a, 79000953

Sioux City Central High School, 1212 Nebraska St., Sioux City, 7/23/74, A, C, 74000817

Sioux City Public Library (Smith Villa Branch) [Public Library Buildings in Iowa TR], 1509 George Ave., Sioux City, 5/23/83, C, 83000415

St. Thomas Episcopal Church, 1200 Douglas St., Sioux City, 9/27/84, C, a, 84001612

Warrior Hotel, 6th and Nebraska Sts., Sioux City, 6/27/85, A, C, 85001384

Woodbury County Courthouse [County Courthouses in Iowa TR (AD)], 7th and Douglas Sts., Sioux City, 12/18/73, A, C, 73000744

Worth County

Chicago, Milwaukee, and St. Paul Railroad-Grafton Station, IA 337, Grafton, 6/23/76, A, C, 76000815

Old Worth County Courthouse [County Courthouses in Iowa TR], 921 Central Ave., Northwood, 7/02/81, C, 81000276

Rhodes Mill, Main St., Fertile, 11/24/78, A, 78001274

Worth County Courthouse [County Courthouses in Iowa TR], Central Ave. between 10th and 11th Sts., Northwood, 7/02/81, C, 81000705

Wright County

Burlington, Cedar Rapids & Northern Passenger Depot—Dows [Advent & Development of Railroads in Iowa MPS], 200 Railroad St., Dows, 1/07/93, A, C, 92001744

Burlington, Cedar Rapids and Northern Railroad Passenger Station, 302 S. Main, Clarion, 6/23/88, A, 88000926

Eagle Grove Public Library, 401 W. Broadway, Eagle Grove, 11/22/77, C, 77000569

Wright County Courthouse [County Courthouses in Iowa TR], Central Ave., Clarion, 7/02/81, C, 81000277

The Clarksville Diner (ca. 1939) in Winneshiek County, Iowa, is one of the nation's most intact examples of the Silk City Diners manufactured by the Paterson Vehicle Company of Paterson, New Jersey in the 1930s. (Cheryl Tindall, 1991)

KANSAS

Allen County

Allen County Jail, 204 N. Jefferson St., Iola, 1/25/71, A, 71000300

Funston Home, 4 mi. N of Iola on U.S. 69, Iola vicinity, 9/03/71, B, 71000301

Anderson County

Anderson County Courthouse, 4th and Oak Sts., Garnett, 4/26/72, A, C, 72000483

Shelley-Tipton House, 812 W. 4th St., Garnett, 5/06/82, C, 82002650

Spencer's Crossing Bridge [Metal Truss Bridges in Kansas 1861–1939 MPS], Over Pottawatomie Creek, NW of Greeley, Greeley vicinity, 1/04/90, A, C, 89002177

Tipton, Samuel J., House, 4 mi. SW of Harris, Harris vicinity, 1/23/75, B, C, 75000703

Atchison County

Atchison County Courthouse, SW corner of 5th and Parallel Sts., Atchison, 4/16/75, A, C, 75000704

Atchison Post Office, 621 Kansas St., Atchison, 3/16/72, C, 72000484

Benedictine College North Campus Historic Complex, 2nd and Division Sts., Atchison, 3/17/82, A, C, a, 82002651

Brown, J. P., House, 805 N. 4th St., Atchison, 4/14/75, B, C, 75000705

Earhart, Amelia, Birthplace, 223 N. Terrace, Atchison, 4/16/71, B, c, 71000302

Glancy/Pennell House, 519 N. 5th St., Atchison, 8/26/83, B, C, 83000416

Glick—Orr House, 503 N. Second St., Atchison, 2/26/92, B, 92000060

Harwi, A. J., House, 1103 Atchison St., Atchison, 5/06/75, B, C, 75000706

Hetherington, W. W., House, 805 N. 5th St., Atchison, 7/12/74, B, C, 74000818

Howard, Frank, House, 305 N. Terrace, Atchison, 10/15/84, C, 84000141

Howe, Edgar W., House, 1117 N. 3rd St., Atchison, 3/16/72, B, 72000485

McInteer Villa, 1301 Kansas St., Atchison, 3/26/75, B, C, 75000707

Mount St. Scholastica Convent, 801 S. 8th St., Atchison, 4/13/72, A, C, a, 72000486

Muchnic, H. E., House, 704 N. 4th St., Atchison, 7/12/74, C, 74000819

Pease, Robert L., House, 203 N. 2nd St., Atchison, 8/26/83, C, 83000417

Price Villa, 801 S. 8th St., Atchison, 3/16/72, C, a, 72000487

Trinity Episcopal Church, 300 S. 5th St., Atchison, 4/04/85, A, C, a, 85000692

Waggener, B. P., House, 819 N. 4th St., Atchison, 5/03/74, B, C, 74000820

Barber County

Medicine Lodge Peace Treaty Site, SE of Medicine Lodge, Medicine Lodge vicinity, 8/04/69, A, NHL, 69000059

Nation, Carry A., House, 211 W. Fowler Ave., Medicine Lodge, 3/24/71, B, NHL, 71000303

Barton County

Pawnee Rock, 0.2 mi. N of Pawnee Rock off U.S. 56, Pawnee Rock vicinity, 12/29/70, D, 70000247

US Post Office—Hoisington [Kansas Post Offices with Artwork, 1936–1942 MPS], 121 E. 2nd St., Hoisington, 10/17/89, A, C, 89001642

Walnut Creek Bridge [Metal Truss Bridges in Kansas 1861–1939 MPS], Over Walnut Creek, NW of Heizer, Heizer vicinity, 1/04/90, C, 89002178

Walnut Creek Crossing, Address Restricted, Great Bend vicinity, 4/26/72, D, 72000488

Bourbon County

Fort Scott National Historic Site, Old Fort Blvd., Fort Scott, 10/15/66, A, e, NHL, NPS, 66000106

Fort Scott Public Carnegie Library [Carnegie Libraries of Kansas TR], 201 S. National, Fort Scott, 8/18/87, A, C, 87000930

Long Shoals Bridge [Metal Truss Bridges in Kansas 1861–1939 MPS], Over Little Osage River, E of Fulton, Fulton vicinity, 1/04/90, C, 89002182

Marmaton Bridge, 1 mile NE of Fort Scott, Fort Scott vicinity, 5/11/82, A, C, 82002652

Moody Building, 15 E. 2nd St., Fort Scott, 11/09/77, A, C, 77000570

Union Block, 24 S. Main St., Fort Scott, 4/26/72, C, 72000489

Brown County

Davis Memorial, 0.1 mi. E of Hiawatha, Mt. Hope Cemetery, Hiawatha vicinity, 8/29/77, C, f, g, 77000571

Hiawatha Memorial Auditorium, 611 Utah St., Hiawatha, 9/05/85, C, 85001978

Site No. JF00-062 [Nebraska—Kansas Public Land Survey TR], 6 1/2 mi. SE of Rulo; 200 ft. W of rd. between Rulo, NE and White cloud, KS, Rulo vicinity, 6/19/87, A, 87001001

Butler County

Augusta Theater, 525 State St., Augusta, 10/31/90, C, 90001577

Beaumont St. Louis and San Francisco Railroad Water Tank, Jct. of Third and D Sts., Beaumont, 8/19/93, A, C, 93000843

El Dorado Carnegie Library [Carnegie Libraries of Kansas TR], 101 S. Star, El Dorado, 6/25/87, A, C, 87000931

James, C. N., Cabin, 305 State St., Augusta, 4/13/73, A, 73000745

Muddy Creek Bridge [Masonry Arch Bridges of Kansas TR], Off US 77, Douglass vicinity, 7/02/85, C, 85001425

Polecat Creek Bridge [Masonry Arch Bridges of Kansas TR], 5 mi. W and 2 mi. S of Douglass, Douglass vicinity, 7/02/85, C, 85001438

US Post Office—Augusta [Kansas Post Offices with Artwork, 1936–1942 MPS], 119 E. Fifth St., Augusta, 10/17/89, A, C, g, 89001632

Chase County

Cartter Building, 303 Broadway, Cottonwood Falls, 11/23/77, A, C, 77000573

Chase County Courthouse, On the square at S end of Broadway, Cottonwood Falls, 2/24/71, A, C, 71000304

Chase County National Bank, 301 Broadway, Cottonwood Falls, 11/09/77, A, C, 77000572

Clements Stone Arch Bridge, 0.5 mi. SE of Clements over the Cottonwood River, Clements vicinity, 12/12/76, A, C, 76000816

Clover Cliff Ranch House, 4 mi. SW of Elmdale off U.S. 50, Elmdale vicinity, 11/09/77, B, 77000574

Cottonwood River Bridge [Masonry Arch Bridges of Kansas TR], KS 177, N edge of Cottonwood Falls, Cottonwood Falls, 7/02/85, C, 85001422

Crocker Ranch, 1.5 mi. N of Matfield Green on KS 177, Matfield Green vicinity, 11/17/77, A, C, 77000575

Lower Fox Creek School, NW of Strong City on K-177, Strong City vicinity, 9/06/74, A, 74000822

Pioneer Bluffs Ranch Historic District, KS 177 1 mi. N of Matfield Green, Matfield Green vicinity, 9/13/90, A, B, C, 90001441

Spring Hill Farm and Stock Ranch House, 3 mi. N of Strong City on KS 177, Strong City vicinity, 4/16/71, C, 71000305

Wood House, E of Cottonwood Falls, Cottonwood Falls vicinity, 3/17/74, B, 74000821

US Post Office—Horton

US Post Office—Horton [Kansas Post Offices with Artwork, 1936–1942 MPS], 825 1st Ave. E., Horton, 10/17/89, A, C, 89001643

Chautauqua County

Cedar Creek Bridge [Rainbow Arch Marsh Arch Bridges of Kansas TR], FAS 96, Elgin vicinity, 3/10/83, C, 83000418

Otter Creek Bridge [Metal Truss Bridges in Kansas 1861–1939 MPS], FAS 95 over Otter Creek, 3.0 mi. N of Cedar Vale, Cedar Vale vicinity, 1/04/90, C, 89002189

Cherokee County

Brush Creek Bridge [Rainbow Arch Marsh Arch Bridges of Kansas TR], N of Baxter Springs, Baxter Springs vicinity, 3/10/83, C, 83000419

Columbus Public Carnegie Library [Carnegie Libraries of Kansas TR], 205 N. Kansas, Columbus, 6/25/87, A, C, 87000932

Johnston Library, 210 W. 10th St., Baxter Springs, 11/21/76, A, C, 76000817

Schermerhorn, Edgar Backus, House, 803 E. 5th St., Galena, 8/21/89, B, C, 89001146

Clark County

Bear Creek Redoubt, Address Restricted, Ashland vicinity, 3/30/78, D, 78001275

Cimarron Redoubt, Address Restricted, Ashland vicinity, 5/23/78, D, 78001276

Stockgrowers State Bank, 8th and Main Sts., Ashland, 4/26/72, A, C, 72000490

Clay County

Clay Center Carnegie Library [Carnegie Libraries of Kansas TR], 706 Sixth St., Clay Center, 6/25/87, A, C, 87000933

Clay County Courthouse, 5th and Court Sts., Clay Center, 1/29/73, C, 73000746

Cloud County

Bankers Loan and Trust Company Building, 101 E. 6th and 517 Broadway, Concordia, 11/09/77, A, C, 77000576

Brown Grand Opera House, 310 W. 6th St., Concordia, 7/26/73, A, 73000747

County Line Bowstring [Metal Truss Bridges in Kansas 1861–1939 MPS], Over West Creek, NW of Hollis, Hollis vicinity, 1/04/90, C, b, 89002192

Nazareth Convent and Academy, 13th and Washington Sts., Concordia, 1/18/73, C, a, 73000748

Pott's Ford Bridge [Metal Truss Bridges in Kansas 1861–1939 MPS], Over Solomon River, SE of Glasco, Glasco vicinity, 1/04/90, A, C, 89002173

Republican River Pegram Truss [Metal Truss Bridges in Kansas 1861–1939 MPS], Rt. 795 over the Republican River, Concordia vicinity, 1/04/90, C, 89002190

Van De Mark, Charles W., House, 504 Washington, Clyde, 7/05/85, C, 85001492

Coffey County

Burlington Carnegie Free Library [Carnegie Libraries of Kansas TR], 201 N. Third, Burlington, 6/25/87, A, C, 87000934

Miller, Cleo F., House, Jct. of Broadway and Coffey Sts., Lebo, 12/27/91, C, 91001897

Neosho River Bridge [Rainbow Arch Marsh Arch Bridges of Kansas TR], E of Hartford, Hartford vicinity, 3/10/83, C, 83000420

US Post Office—Burlington [Kansas Post Offices with Artwork, 1936–1942 MPS], 107 S. Fourth St., Burlington, 10/17/89, A, C, g, 89001634

Williamson Archeological Site, Address Restricted, Hartford vicinity, 11/19/74, D, 74000823

Comanche County

Archeological Site Number 14CM305 [Kansas Rock Art TR], Address Restricted, Unknown vicinity, 7/09/82, D, 82004864

Cowley County

Arkansas City Commercial Historic District, Summit St. and 5th Ave., Arkansas City, 10/28/83, A, C, 83003599

Arkansas City Country Club Site, Address Restricted, Arkansas City vicinity, 8/25/78, D, 78001277

Bucher Bridge [Masonry Arch Bridges of Kansas TR], Off US 77, Rock, 7/02/85, C, 85001420

Cowley County National Bank Building, 820-822 Main St., Winfield, 8/11/83, A, C, 83000421

Esch's Spur Bridge [Masonry Arch Bridges of Kansas TR], 3 mi. S and 3 mi. W of Dexter, Dexter vicinity, 7/02/85, C, 85001423

Gladstone Hotel, N. Summit St., Arkansas City vicinity, 8/11/83, A, C, 83000422

Hackney, W. P., House, 417 E. 10th St., Winfield, 3/07/73, B, C, 73000749

Magnolia Ranch, 10 mi. SE of Winfield on U.S. 77, Winfield vicinity, 3/07/73, A, C, 73000750

Old Arkansas City High School, 300 W. Central St., Arkansas City, 11/21/74, A, C, 74000824

Silver Creek Bridge [Masonry Arch Bridges of Kansas TR], E of Winfield, Winfield vicinity, 1/30/87, C, 86003270

West Dormitory—St. John's College, 1415 E. Sixth Ave., Winfield, 12/13/91, A, 91001769

Winfield Public Carnegie Library, 1001 Millington St., Winfield, 1/11/88, A, C, 87002230

Crawford County

Girard Carnegie Library [Carnegie Libraries of Kansas TR], 128 W. Prairie, Girard, 6/25/87, A, C, 87000952

Hotel Stilwell, 707 Broadway, Pittsburg, 4/30/80, A, 80001464

Hudgeon Bridge [Masonry Arch Bridges of Kansas TR], 10 mi. S and 3.2 mi. W of Girard, Girard vicinity, 7/02/85, C, 85001433

Little Walnut Creek Bowstring [Metal Truss Bridges in Kansas 1861–1939 MPS], Over Little Walnut Creek, NE of Walnut, Walnut vicinity, 1/04/90, C, 89002174

Pittsburg Public Library, 4th and Walnut Sts., Pittsburg, 11/09/77, A, C, 77000577

Wayland, Julius A., House, 721 N. Summit, Girard, 11/21/76, A, C, 76000819

Dickinson County

Abilene Union Pacific Railroad Passenger Depot, Jct. of N. Second St. and Broadway, Abilene, 9/08/92, A, C, 92001175

Abilene Union Pacific Railroad Freight Depot, 110 N. Cedar St., Abilene, 9/02/93, A, C, 93000894

Eisenhower Home, 201 SE 4th St., Abilene, 1/25/71, B, 71000306

Herington Carnegie Public Library [Carnegie Libraries of Kansas TR], 102 S. Broadway, Herington, 6/25/87, A, C, 87000953

Johntz, John, House, 214 N. Walnut, Abilene, 9/20/91, B, C, 91001437

Lander Park Carousel, 412 S. Campbell St., Abilene, 2/27/87, A, NHL, 87000813

Lebold, C. H., House, 106 N. Vine St., Abilene, 5/08/73, B, C, 73000751

Old Belle Springs Creamery and Produce Building, Court and Cottage Sts., Abilene, 4/12/82, A, 82002653

Prospect Park Farm, SE of Chapman, Chapman vicinity, 2/19/82, B, C, 82002654

Saint Patrick's Mission Church and School, NE of Chapman, Chapman vicinity, 6/26/87, B, a, 87000983

Seelye, A. B., House, 1105 N. Buckeye, Abilene, 4/25/86, B, C, 86000859

US Post Office—Herington [Kansas Post Offices with Artwork, 1936–1942 MPS], 17 E. Main St., Herington, 10/17/89, A, C, 89001641

Doniphan County

Albers, Albert, Barn [Byre and Bluff Barns of Doniphan County TR], S of Bendena, Bendena vicinity, 5/07/87, C, 86003552

Bohr, Nicholas, Barn [Byre and Bluff Barns of Doniphan County TR], SE of Troy, Troy vicinity, 5/07/87, C, 86003531

Chrystal, Herman, Barn [Byre and Bluff Barns of Doniphan County TR], W of Wathena, Wathena vicinity, 5/07/87, C, 86003538

Doniphan Archeological Site, Address Restricted, Doniphan vicinity, 3/01/74, D, 74000825

Doniphan County Courthouse, Courthouse Sq., bounded by Walnut, Liberty, Chestnut, and Main Sts., Troy, 7/15/74, A, C, 74000826

Doniphan County—Continued

Doniphan County Waddell [Metal Truss Bridges in Kansas 1861–1939 MPS], FAS 28, 1.7 mi. NE of Doniphan, Doniphan vicinity, 1/04/90, C, 89002185

Eclipse School, Off US 36 NE of Troy, Troy vicinity, 3/07/88, A, C, 88000200

Eylar, Mathew, Barn No. 1 [Byre and Bluff Barns of Doniphan County TR], S of Denton off KS 20, Denton vicinity, 5/07/87, C, 86003549

Eylar, Mathew, Barn No. 2 [Byre and Bluff Barns of Doniphan County TR], SE of Denton off KS 20, Denton vicinity, 5/07/87, C, 86003550

Fanning Archeological Site, Address Restricted, Fanning vicinity, 6/20/72, D, 72000492

Hale, John R., Barn [Byre and Bluff Barns of Doniphan County TR], KS 120, Highland vicinity, 5/07/87, C, 86003545

Hanson, George, Barn [Byre and Bluff Barns of Doniphan County TR], S of Leona, Leona vicinity, 5/07/87, C, 86003548

Harding, Benjamin, House, 308 N. 5th, Wathena, 8/29/77, B, C, 77000578

Iowa, Sac, and Fox Presbyterian Mission, 1.5 mi. E of Highland on U.S. 36 and 0.2 mi. N on KS 136, Highland vicinity, 12/02/70, A, a, 70000248

Irvin Hall, Highland Community Junior College, Highland Community Junior College campus, Highland, 2/24/71, A, C, 71000307

Kienhoff, Fred W., Barn [Byre and Bluff Barns of Doniphan County TR], W of Wathena, Wathena vicinity, 5/07/87, C, 86003537

Kinkhead, George, Barn [Byre and Bluff Barns of Doniphan County TR], Off US 36, Troy, 5/07/87, C, 86003542

Mission—Herring Barn [Byre and Bluff Barns of Doniphan County TR], US 36, Highland vicinity, 5/07/87, C, 86003535

Nuzum, Godfrey, Barn [Byre and Bluff Barns of Doniphan County TR], KS 7, Sparkes vicinity, 5/07/87, C, 86003533

Poulet House, Poplar St. between 1st and 2nd Sts., White Cloud, 9/03/71, C, 71000308

Silvers, John, Barn [Byre and Bluff Barns of Doniphan County TR], N of Wathena, Wathena vicinity, 5/07/87, C, 86003553

Site No. JF00-062 [Nebraska—Kansas Public Land Survey TR], 6 1/2 mi. SE of Rulo; 200 ft. W of rd. between Rulo, NE and White cloud, KS, Rulo, vicinity, 6/19/87, A, 87001001

Streib, John, Barn [Byre and Bluff Barns of Doniphan County TR], N of Leona, Leona vicinity, 5/07/87, C, 86003547

Symns, J. A., Barn [Byre and Bluff Barns of Doniphan County TR], KS 7, Bendena vicinity, 5/07/87, C, 86003536

White Cloud School, SW corner of 5th and Main Sts., White Cloud, 4/13/73, A, 73000752

White, T. L., Barn [Byre and Bluff Barns of Doniphan County TR], KS 7, Bendena vicinity, 5/07/87, C, 86003544

Williams, M. D. L., Barn [Byre and Bluff Barns of Doniphan County TR], 3 mi. S of KS 20, Bendena vicinity, 5/07/87, C, 86003551

Douglas County

Achning, Ralph and Cloyd, House, 846 Missouri St., Lawrence, 9/15/87, C, 87001030

Bell, George and Annie, House, 1008 Ohio St., Lawrence, 8/11/83, A, C, 83000423

Benedict House, 923 Tennessee St., Lawrence, 1/22/92, A, C, 91001978

Blood, Col. James, House, 1015 Tennessee St., Lawrence, 2/23/72, C, 72000493

Case Library, Baker University, Eighth and Grove, Baldwin City, 6/05/86, A, C, 86001232

Chicken Creek Bridge [Masonry Arch Bridges of Kansas TR], Over Chicken Creek, SE of Lone Star, Lone Star vicinity, 3/05/90, C, 90000298

Constitution Hall, Elmore St. between Woodson and 3rd Sts., Lecompton, 5/14/71, A, NHL, 71000312

Douglas County Courthouse, SE corner of Massachusetts and 11th Sts., Lawrence, 4/14/75, A, C, 75000708

Duncan, Charles, House, 933 Tennessee St., Lawrence, 6/05/86, C, 86001215

Dyche Hall, University of Kansas, 14th St. and Oread Ave., University of Kansas campus, Lawrence, 7/14/74, B, C, 74000829

Eldridge House Hotel, Seventh and Massachusetts, Lawrence, 12/01/86, A, B, C, g, 86003278

Green Hall, University of Kansas, Jayhawk Dr., Lawrence, 7/15/74, A, C, 74000830

Haskell Institute, Address Unknown, Lawrence, 10/15/66, A, NHL, 66000342

Lane University, E side of Lecompton, Lecompton, 3/24/71, A, 71000313

Ludington House, 1613 Tennessee St., Lawrence, 5/14/71, C, 71000310

Miller, Robert H., House, 1111 E. 19th St., Lawrence, 6/14/84, B, C, 84001235

Morse, Dr. Frederic D., House, 1041 Tennessee St., Lawrence, 4/18/91, B, C, 91000469

Old Castle Hall, Baker University, 513 5th St., Baldwin City, 2/24/71, A, C, a, 71000309

Old Lawrence City Hall, 1047 Massachusetts St., Lawrence, 2/24/71, C, 71000311

Old Lawrence City Library, NW corner of 9th and Vermont Sts., Lawrence, 2/18/75, A, C, 75000709

Old West Lawrence Historic District, Bounded roughly by Tennessee, 8th, Indiana, and 6th Sts., Lawrence, 2/23/72, C, 72000494

Parmenter Memorial Hall, 8th and Dearborn Sts., Baldwin City, 9/19/77, A, 77000579

Pilla, Charles, House, 615 Elm St., Eudora, 9/06/74, B, C, 74000828

Priestly House, 1505 Kentucky St., Lawrence, 3/10/88, A, C, 88000199

Riggs, Samuel A., House, 1500 Pennsylvania, Lawrence, 8/29/77, A, B, C, 77000580

Roberts, John N., House, 1307 Massachusetts St., Lawrence, 9/06/74, C, 74000831

Santa Fe Depot, 1601 High St., Baldwin City, 1/03/83, A, C, 83000424

Spooner Hall, University of Kansas, 14th St. and Oread Ave. on the University of Kansas campus, Lawrence, 7/15/74, A, C, 74000832

Stephens, Judge Nelson T., House, 340 N. Michigan St., Lawrence, 2/19/82, B, C, 82002655

Stoebener Barn, SW of Worden, Baldwin City vicinity, 1/09/89, C, 88003083

Taylor, Lucy Hobbs, Building, 809 Vermont, Lawrence, 2/19/82, B, 82002656

Usher, John Palmer, House, 1425 Tennessee St., Lawrence, 3/07/75, B, C, 75000710

Zimmerman, S. T., House, 304 Indiana St., Lawrence, 9/06/74, C, 74000833

Edwards County

Gano Grain Elevator and Scale House, Jct. of US 50 and Co. Rd 9, Kinsley vicinity, 9/21/93, A, C, 93000943

Elk County

Durbin Archeological Site, Address Restricted, Moline vicinity, 5/02/75, D, 75000711

Elk River Archeological District, Address Restricted, Elk City vicinity, 9/13/78, D, 78001279

Ellis County

Chrysler, Walter P., House, 104 W. 10th St., Ellis, 2/23/72, B, 72000495

First Presbyterian Church, 100 W. 7th St., Hays, 3/30/73, A, a, 73000753

Fort Hays, Frontier Historical Park, Hays, 1/25/71, A, b, 71000314

Grant, George, Villa, 5 mi. S and 2 mi. E of Victoria on secondary rds., Victoria vicinity, 4/26/72, B, 72000496

Phillip Hardware Store, 719 Main St., Hays, 3/16/82, A, C, 82002658

St. Fidelis Catholic Church, SE corner of St. Anthony and Delaware Sts., Victoria, 5/14/71, C, a, 71000315

Ellsworth County

Archeological Site Number 14EW14 [Kansas Rock Art TR], Address Restricted, Carneiro vicinity, 7/09/82, D, 82004861

Archeological Site Number 14EW33 [Kansas Rock Art TR], Address Restricted, Carneiro vicinity, 7/09/82, D, 82004862

Archeological Site Number 14EW405 [Kansas Rock Art TR], Address Restricted, Geneseo vicinity, 7/09/82, D, 82004863

Archeological Site Number 14EW17 [Kansas Rock Art TR], Address Restricted, Ellsworth vicinity, 7/09/82, D, 82004874

Archeological Site Number 14EW303 [Kansas Rock Art TR], Address Restricted, Ellsworth vicinity, 7/09/82, D, 82004875

Ellsworth County—Continued

Archeological Site Number 14EW401 [Kansas Rock Art TR], Address Restricted, Ellsworth vicinity, 7/09/82, D, 82004876

Archeological Site Number 14EW403 [Kansas Rock Art TR], Address Restricted, Carneiro vicinity, 7/09/82, D, 82004877

Archeological Site Number 14EW404 [Kansas Rock Art TR], Address Restricted, Ellsworth vicinity, 7/09/82, D, 82004878

Archeological Site Number 14EW406 [Kansas Rock Art TR], Address Restricted, Ellsworth vicinity, 7/09/82, D, 82004879

Fort Harker Guardhouse, NW corner of Wyoming and Ohio Sts., Kanopolis, 2/23/72, A, 72000497

Fort Harker Officers' Quarters, Ohio St. between Kansas and Colorado Sts., Kanopolis, 11/20/74, A, 74000834

Hodgden, Perry, House, 104 W. Main St., Ellsworth, 1/29/73, B, 73000754

Indian Hill Site, Address Restricted, Marquette vicinity, 12/31/74, D, 74000835

Larkin, Arthur, House, 0.25 mi. S of Ellsworth off KS 45, Ellsworth vicinity, 2/24/75, A, B, C, 75000712

Finney County

Windsor Hotel, 421 N. Main St., Garden City, 4/26/72, C, 72000498

Ford County

Dodge City Public Library, 2nd and Spruce Aves., Dodge City, 3/26/79, A, C, 79000954

Immaculate Heart of Mary Catholic Church, SE of Spearville, Windthorst, 1/05/89, A, C, a, 88003087

Lora Locke Hotel, Central and Gunsmoke Sts., Dodge City, 1/03/85, A, C, 85000012

Mueller-Schmidt House, 112 E. Vine St., Dodge City, 2/23/72, A, C, 72000499

Sacred Heart Cathedral, 903 Central Ave., Dodge City, 2/10/83, A, C, a, 83000426

Sante Fe Trail Ruts, 9 mi. W of Dodge City on U.S. 50, Dodge City vicinity, 10/15/66, A, NHL, 66000343

Franklin County

Dietrich Cabin, Ottawa City Park, Ottawa, 2/23/72, B, C, b, 72000500

Downtown Ottawa Historic District, E side of S. Main St. from No. 135 to 3rd St., Ottawa, 6/29/72, C, 72000501

Franklin County Courthouse, Main St., Ottawa, 3/17/72, C, 72000502

Jones, Tauy, House, 3 mi. NE of Ottawa on Tauy Creek, Ottawa vicinity, 6/19/72, B, 72000503

Middle Creek Tributary Bridge [Masonry Arch Bridges of Kansas TR], 5.8 mi. W of Princeton, Princeton vicinity, 7/02/85, C, 85001428

Old Santa Fe Railroad Depot, 135 W. Tecumseh St., Ottawa, 3/01/73, C, 73000755

Ottawa Library, 5th and Main Sts., Ottawa, 12/01/80, A, C, 80001465

Ransom, James H., House, 318 S. Locust St., Ottawa, 11/21/74, B, C, 74000836

Silkville, 2.5 mi. SW of Williamsburg on U.S. 50, Williamsburg vicinity, 12/15/72, A, B, C, 72000504

Tauy Creek Bridge [Metal Truss Bridges in Kansas MPS], Over Tauy Cr. N of I-35, Ottawa vicinity, 10/25/90, C, 90001567

Tauy Jones Hall, Ottawa University campus, 10th and Cedar Sts., Ottawa, 6/14/82, A, C, a, 82002659

Walnut Creek Bridge [Masonry Arch Bridges of Kansas TR], Off KS 33 1 mi. S of Wellsville, Wellsville vicinity, 7/02/85, C, 85001445

Wellsville Bank Building, 418 Main St., Wellsville, 10/24/91, A, C, 91001519

Geary County

Bartell House, 6th and Washington Sts., Junction City, 12/01/80, B, 80001466

Bogan Archeological Site, Address Restricted, Junction City vicinity, 5/17/73, D, 73000756

Conroe Bridge [Rainbow Arch Marsh Arch Bridges of Kansas TR], E of Junction City, Junction City vicinity, 3/10/83, C, 83000427

Elliott Village Site, Address Restricted, Junction City vicinity, 12/08/78, D, 78001280

First Territorial Capitol, On KS 18 in Fort Riley Military Reservation, Junction City vicinity, 12/02/70, A, 70000249

Main Post Area, Fort Riley, NE of Junction City on KS 18, Junction City vicinity, 5/01/74, A, B, f, 74000837

Old Junction City High School, Adams and 6th Sts., Junction City, 4/24/81, A, C, 81000278

Wetzel, Christian, Cabin, About 2 mi. E of Junction City at jct. of I-70 and KS 57, Junction City vicinity, 10/15/73, C, a, b, 73000757

Gove County

Grainfield Opera House, Main and 3rd Sts., Grainfield, 11/28/80, A, 80001467

Graham County

Nicodemus Historic District, U.S. 24, Nicodemus, 1/07/76, A, B, NHL, 76000820

Penokee Stone Figure, Address Restricted, Penokee vicinity, 6/23/82, D, 82002660

Grant County

Wagon Bed Springs, 12 mi. S of Ulysses on U.S. 270, Ulysses vicinity, 10/15/66, A, NHL, 66000344

Gray County

Cimarron Hotel, 203 N. Main St., Cimarron, 2/10/83, A, 83000428

Greeley County

Greeley County Courthouse, Harper and 3rd Sts., Tribune, 7/12/76, A, C, 76000821

Greenwood County

Archeological Site Number 14GR320 [Kansas Rock Art TR], Address Restricted, Falls River State Park vicinity, 7/09/82, D, 82004880

Curry Archeological Site, Address Restricted, Madison vicinity, 11/20/74, D, 74000838

Eureka Carnegie Library [Carnegie Libraries of Kansas TR], 520 N. Main, Eureka, 8/10/88, A, C, 88001170

Lone Cone Site, Address Restricted, Madison vicinity, 5/17/76, D, 76000822

Madison Atchison, Topeka and Santa Fe Railroad Depot, Jct. of Third and Boone Sts., Madison, 12/06/91, A, C, 91001774

North Branch Otter Creek Bridge [Masonry Arch Bridges of Kansas TR], 1 mi. W and 5 mi. N of Piedmont, Piedmont vicinity, 7/02/85, C, 85001426

Two Duck Site, Address Restricted, Severy vicinity, 3/26/75, D, 75000713

US Post Office—Eureka [Kansas Post Offices with Artwork, 1936–1942 MPS], 301 N. Oak St., Eureka, 10/17/89, A, C, 89001637

Verdigris River Bridge [Masonry Arch Bridges of Kansas TR], 0.5 mi. N of Madison, Madison vicinity, 7/02/85, C, 85001444

Hamilton County

Fort Aubrey Site, Address Restricted, Syracuse vicinity, 8/31/78, A, D, 78001281

Harper County

Anthony Public Carnegie Library [Carnegie Libraries of Kansas TR], 104 N. Springfield, Anthony, 6/25/87, A, C, 87000954

Anthony Theater, 220 W. Main St., Anthony, 4/18/91, C, 91000464

Harper County Courthouse, 200 N. Jennings Ave., Anthony, 11/22/78, A, C, 78001282

Harper County—Continued

Old Runnymede Church, 11th and Pine Sts., Harper, 2/06/73, B, a, b, 73000758

Thompson-Wohlschlegel Round Barn, Off US 160, S on Cty. Rd. 1485, Harper vicinity, 2/21/85, A, 85000315

US Post Office—Anthony [Kansas Post Offices with Artwork, 1936–1942 MPS], 121 W. Steadman, Anthony, 10/17/89, A, C, 89001631

Harvey County

Bethel College Administration Building, Bethel College campus, North Newton, 3/16/72, A, C, a, 72000505

Brown, Samuel A., House, 302 W. Sixth, Newton, 10/17/88, C, 88001904

Carnegie Library, 203 Main St., Newton, 5/31/74, A, 74000840

Neal, Jairus, House, 301 E. 4th St., Newton, 5/06/82, C, 82002661

Old Railroad Savings and Loan Building, 500 Main St., Newton, 5/06/82, A, C, 82002662

Santa Fe Depot, 414 N. Main, Newton, 4/11/85, A, C, 85000735

US Post Office—Halstead [Kansas Post Offices with Artwork, 1936–1942 MPS], 319 Main St., Halstead, 10/17/89, A, C, g, 89001640

Warkentin House, 211 E. 1st St., Newton, 1/12/70, B, C, a, 70000250

Warkentin Mill, 3rd and Main Sts., Newton, 1/12/70, B, C, 70000251

Warkentin, Bernhard, Homestead, N of Halstead, Halstead vicinity, 2/15/74, A, B, C, NHL, 74000839

Hodgeman County

Hackberry Creek Bridge [Masonry Arch Bridges of Kansas TR], 13 mi. W and 11 mi. N of Jetmore, Jetmore vicinity, 7/02/85, C, 85001424

Haun, T. S., House, Main St., Jetmore, 1/18/73, B, 73000759

Jackson County

Booth Site, Address Restricted, Mayetta vicinity, 10/02/92, D, 92001322

Harris Site, Address Restricted, Soldier vicinity, 6/23/78, D, 78001283

Shedd and Marshall Store, 3rd and Whiting Sts., Whiting, 11/25/77, B, C, 77000582

State Bank of Holton, 4th and Pennsylvania Ave., Holton, 11/09/77, A, C, 77000581

Jefferson County

Buck Creek School, Off US 24, 2 mi. E of Williamstown, Perry vicinity, 12/27/88, A, C, 88002830

Jefferson Old Town Bowstring Truss [Metal Truss Bridges in Kansas 1861–1939 MPS], Off US 59, Oskaloosa vicinity, 1/04/90, C, b, 89002186

Union Block, SW corner of Delaware and Jefferson Sts., Oskaloosa, 4/23/73, C, 73000760

Jewell County

First National Bank, Commercial and Jefferson Sts., Mankato, 6/16/76, A, C, 76000823

Johnson County

Lanesfield School, 18745 S. Dillie Rd., Edgerton vicinity, 10/13/88, A, 88001902

Mahaffie, J. B., House, 1100 Kansas City Rd., Olathe, 8/29/77, A, B, b, 77000583

Parker, Martin Van Buren, House, 631 W. Park, Olathe, 12/20/88, B, C, 88002829

Pickering, I. O., House, 507 W. Park St., Olathe, 12/01/80, C, 80001468

Shawnee Mission, 53rd St. at Mission Rd., Fairway, 10/15/66, A, NHL, 66000345

WPA Beach House at Gardner Lake, W shore of Gardner Lake, N of Gardner, Gardner vicinity, 6/25/92, A, C, 92000826

Kingman County

Kingman Carnegie Library [Carnegie Libraries of Kansas TR], 455 N. Main, Kingman, 6/25/87, A, C, 87000955

Kingman City Building, Main St. and C Ave., Kingman, 4/13/72, C, 72000506

Kingman County Courthouse, 120 Spruce St., Kingman, 9/11/85, A, C, 85002128

US Post Office—Kingman [Kansas Post Offices with Artwork, 1936–1942 MPS], 425 N. Main St., Kingman, 10/17/89, A, C, g, 89001645

Kiowa County

Archeological Site Number 14KW301 [Kansas Rock Art TR], Address Restricted, Coldwater vicinity, 7/09/82, D, 82004881

Archeological Site Number 14KW302 [Kansas Rock Art TR], Address Restricted, Greensburg vicinity vicinity, 7/09/82, D, 82004897

Belvidere Medicine River Bridge [Masonry Arch Bridges of Kansas TR], 0.25 miles N of Belvidere, Belvidere vicinity, 7/02/85, C, 85001418

Fromme-Birney Round Barn, SW of Mullinville, Mullinville vicinity, 7/16/87, C, 87001253

Greensburg Well, Sycamore St., Greensburg, 2/23/72, C, 72000507

Labette County

Big Hill Archeological District, Address Restricted, Dennis vicinity, 11/23/77, D, 77000584

Carnegie Library, 17th and Broadway, Parsons, 4/14/76, C, 76000824

First State Bank, SW corner of Delaware and Main Sts., Edna, 11/01/82, C, 82000417

Harmon Site, Address Restricted, Chetopa vicinity, 5/09/83, D, 83000429

Harmon Site No. 2 (14LT323), Address Restricted, Chetopa vicinity, 5/07/84, D, 84001239

Labette Creek Tributary Bridge [Masonry Arch Bridges of Kansas TR], Off US 160 2.3 mi. W of Parsons, Parsons vicinity, 7/02/85, C, 85001431

Oswego Public Carnegie Library [Carnegie Libraries of Kansas TR], 704 Fourth St., Oswego, 6/25/87, A, C, 87000956

Parsons Filled Arch Bridge [Masonry Arch Bridges of Kansas TR], Off US 160, 1 mi. E and 1.2 mi. S of Parsons, Parsons vicinity, 7/02/85, C, 85001436

Pumpkin Creek Tributary Bridge [Masonry Arch Bridges of Kansas TR], Off KS 22 2 mi. W of Mound Valley, Mound Valley vicinity, 7/02/85, C, 85001439

US Post Office—Oswego [Kansas Post Offices with Artwork, 1936–1942 MPS], 819 4th St., Oswego, 10/17/89, A, C, g, 89001648

Lane County

Pottorff Site, Address Restricted, Healy vicinity, 3/08/78, D, 78001284

Leavenworth County

AXA Building, 205 S. 5th St., Leavenworth, 3/17/72, C, 72000509

Angell, A. J., House, 714 S. Broadway, Leavenworth, 11/17/77, C, 77000586

Atchison, Topeka and Santa Fe Railroad Passenger Depot, 781 Shawnee St., Leavenworth, 6/11/86, A, C, 86001321

Brewer, David J., House, 403 5th Ave., Leavenworth, 2/23/72, B, 72000508

Burt, Nathaniel H., House, 400 Fifth Ave., Leavenworth, 10/27/87, B, C, 87001105

Carroll, Edward, House, 334 Fifth Ave., Leavenworth, 10/02/86, B, C, 86002806

Fort Leavenworth, Fort Leavenworth Military Reservation, Leavenworth, 10/15/66, A, NHL, 66000346

Harris, Senator William A., House, NW of Linwood on KS 32, Linwood vicinity, 11/05/74, B, 74000841

Harvey, Fred, House, 624 Olive St., Leavenworth, 4/26/72, B, 72000510

Hollywood Theater, 401 Delaware St., Leavenworth, 10/25/90, C, 90001575

Lansing Man Archeological Site, Address Restricted, Lansing vicinity, 3/24/71, D, 71000316

Leavenworth County—Continued

Leavenworth Public Library, 601 S. Fifth St., Leavenworth, 7/30/86, A, C, 86002010
North Esplanade Historic District, 203–515 N. Esplanade, Leavenworth, 12/12/77, C, 77000587
Old Union Depot, 201 S. Main St., Leavenworth, 3/11/82, A, C, 82002663
Powers, David W., House, 2 mi. NW of Leavenworth off U.S. 73, Leavenworth vicinity, 8/30/77, B, C, 77000588
Quarry Creek Archeological Site, Address Restricted, Leavenworth vicinity, 4/23/73, D, 73000761
Zacharias Site (14LV380), Address Restricted, Leavenworth vicinity, 1/08/87, D, 86003517

Lincoln County

Archeological Site Number 14LC306 [Kansas Rock Art TR], Address Restricted, Lincoln vicinity, 7/09/82, D, 82004882
Bullfoot Creek Bridge [Masonry Arch Bridges of Kansas TR], 4 mi. S and .9 mi. E of Vesper, Vesper vicinity, 7/02/85, C, 85001421
Danske Evangelist Lutheran Kirke, Between Trail and Timber Creeks due E of Denmark, Grant Township, Denmark vicinity, 9/12/91, A, C, a, 91001154
Lincoln Carnegie Library [Carnegie Libraries of Kansas TR], 203 S. Third, Lincoln, 6/25/87, A, C, 87000957
Lincoln County Courthouse, 3rd and Lincoln Ave., Lincoln, 7/13/76, C, 76000825
Spring Creek Tributary Bridge [Masonry Arch Bridges of Kansas TR], 8 mi. S and 5 mi. W of Lincoln, Lincoln vicinity, 7/02/85, C, 85001440

Linn County

Battle of Mine Creek Site, 2.5 mi. SW of Pleasanton off U.S. 69, Pleasanton vicinity, 12/12/73, A, 73000762
Landers Creek Bridge [Masonry Arch Bridges of Kansas TR], S edge of Goodrich, Goodrich vicinity, 7/02/85, C, 85001430
Linn County Courthouse, 4th and Main, Mound City, 7/15/74, C, 74000842
Marais des Cygnes Massacre Site, 5 mi. NE of Trading Post, Trading Post vicinity, 6/21/71, A, NHL, 71000317
Mine Creek Bridge [Rainbow Arch Marsh Arch Bridges of Kansas TR], E of Mound City, Mound City vicinity, 3/10/83, C, 83000430
Old Linn County Jail, 312 Main St., Mound City, 11/30/78, A, 78001285
Prescott School, 3rd and Main Sts., Prescott, 5/06/82, C, 82002664

Logan County

Old Logan County Courthouse, Main St., Russell Springs, 2/23/72, A, 72000511

Lyon County

Anderson Carnegie Memorial Library [Carnegie Libraries of Kansas TR], The Way College of Emporia, 1300 W. Twelfth Ave., Emporia, 6/25/87, A, C, 87000958
Finney, Warren Wesley, House, 927 State St., Emporia, 5/07/92, B, C, 92000470
Granada Theater, 809 Commercial, Emporia, 4/04/85, C, 85000693
Harris Bridge [Masonry Arch Bridges of Kansas TR], 3 mi. N and 4 mi. W of Americus, Americus vicinity, 7/02/85, C, 85001434
Harris—Borman House, 827 Mechanic, Emporia, 4/28/92, C, 92000431
Hartford Collegiate Institute, SW corner of College and Plumb Aves., Hartford, 2/23/72, A, C, a, 72000512
Howe, Richard, House, 315 E. Logan Ave., Emporia, 7/17/86, A, C, 86001701
Keebler—Stone House, 831 Constitution St., Emporia, 4/28/92, C, 92000387
Kress Building, 702 Commercial St., Emporia, 8/25/83, A, C, 83000431
Mason, Walt, House, 606 W. 12th Ave., Emporia, 4/30/92, B, C, 92000446
Old Emporia Public Library, 118 E. 6th St., Emporia, 11/02/81, A, C, 81000279
Plumb, Mrs. Preston B., House, 224 E. 6th Ave., Emporia, 10/04/84, C, 84000011
Soden's Grove Bridge [Rainbow Arch Marsh Arch Bridges of Kansas TR], KS 57/99, Emporia vicinity, 3/10/83, C, 83000432
Soden, Hallie B., House, 802 S. Commercial St., Emporia, 11/09/77, C, 77000589
White, William Allen, House, 927 Exchange St., Emporia, 5/14/71, B, C, NHL, 71000318

Marion County

Bethel School, County Rd., Lincolnville vicinity, 12/17/87, A, C, 87002114
Burns Union School, SW corner Ohio and Main Sts., Burns, 3/26/75, A, 75000714
Elgin Hotel, 3rd and Santa Fe Sts., Marion, 9/13/78, A, C, 78001286
Harvey House, 204 W. 3rd St., Florence, 8/14/73, A, 73000763
Hill Grade School, 601 E. Main, Marion, 5/28/76, A, 76000827
Lost Springs, 2.5 mi. W of Lost Springs, Lost Springs vicinity, 9/30/76, A, 76000826
Marion Archeological District, Address Restricted, Marion vicinity, 4/21/76, D, 76000829
Marion County Courthouse, 3rd and Williams Sts., Marion, 5/28/76, C, 76000828
Old Peabody Library, Division and Walnut Sts., Peabody, 7/02/73, A, b, 73000765
Peabody Township Carnegie Library [Carnegie Libraries of Kansas TR], 214 Walnut, Peabody, 6/25/87, A, C, 87000959
Pioneer Adobe House, U.S. 56 and S. Ash St., Hillsboro, 3/30/73, A, C, b, 73000764

Schroeder, J. S., Building, 111 N. Walnut St., Peabody, 12/06/91, A, C, 91001770

Marshall County

Alcove Springs, 4 mi. N of Blue Rapids, Blue Rapids vicinity, 2/23/72, A, 72000513
Barrett Schoolhouse, 4 mi. SW of Frankfort on KS 99, Frankfort vicinity, 3/14/73, A, C, 73000766
Blue Rapids Library, E side of public square, Blue Rapids, 3/17/72, A, 72000514
Frankfort School, 400 Locust St., Frankfort, 12/27/72, C, 72000515
Hutchinson, Perry, House, 1 mi. NW of Marysville on U.S. 77, Marysville vicinity, 4/13/72, B, C, 72000516
Koester Block Historic District, Between 9th, 10th, Elm and Broadway Sts., Marysville, 12/05/80, B, C, 80001469
Koester, Charles, House, 919 Broadway, Marysville, 5/12/75, B, C, 75000715
Marshall County Courthouse, 1207 Broadway, Marysville, 11/05/74, C, 74000843
Marysville Pony Express Barn, 108 S. 8th St., Marysville, 4/02/73, A, 73000767
Moore, Z. H., Store, State and Center Sts., Oketo, 6/24/76, A, 76000830
Old Frankfort City Jail, Railway Ave., Frankfort, 11/01/82, A, C, g, 82000418
Powell, Samuel, House, 108 W. Commercial St., Waterville, 12/27/72, C, 72000517
Pusch—Randell House, 1000 Elm St., Marysville, 9/22/86, B, C, 86002680
Weaver Hotel, 126 S. Kansas St., Waterville, 8/28/75, A, 75000716

McPherson County

Canton Township Carnegie Library [Carnegie Libraries of Kansas TR], 300 N. Main, Canton, 6/25/87, A, C, 87000960
Hanson, Hans, House, 211 E. 5th St., Marquette, 2/19/82, C, 82002665
McPherson County Courthouse, Maple and Kansas Aves., McPherson, 11/21/76, C, 76002264
McPherson Opera House, 221 S. Main St., McPherson, 3/16/72, C, 72001452
Paint Creek Archeological Site, Address Restricted, Lindsborg vicinity, 6/20/72, D, 72001449
Sharps Creek Archeological Site, Address Restricted, Lindsborg vicinity, 6/22/72, D, 72001450
Smoky Valley Roller Mill, Mill St., Lindsborg, 2/23/72, A, 72001451
Swedish Pavilion, Mill St., Lindsborg, 3/20/73, A, C, 73002129
US Post Office—Lindsborg [Kansas Post Offices with Artwork, 1936–1942 MPS], 125 E. Lincoln St., Lindsborg, 10/17/89, A, C, 89001646

Miami County

Asylum Bridge [Metal Truss Bridges in Kansas 1861–1939 MPS], First St. over Marais des Cygnes, Osawatomie vicinity, 1/04/90, A, C, 89002187

Brown, John, Cabin, John Brown Memorial Park, Osawatomie, 3/24/71, B, b, 71000319

Carey's Ford Bridge [Metal Truss Bridges in Kansas 1861–1939 MPS], Over Marais des Cygnes River, E of Osawatomie, Osawatomie vicinity, 1/04/90, A, C, 89002179

Creamery Bridge [Rainbow Arch Marsh Arch Bridges of Kansas TR], FAS 456, Osawatomie, 3/10/83, C, 83000434

Hillsdale Archeological District, Address Restricted, Paola vicinity, 5/12/77, D, 77000590

Jake's Branch of Middle Creek Bridge [Masonry Arch Bridges of Kansas TR], Off US 69, Louisburg vicinity, 7/02/85, C, 85001432

Miami County Courthouse, E of jct. of Miami and Silver Sts., Paola, 3/01/73, C, 73000768

Mills, William, House, 212 First St., Osawatomie, 11/20/86, B, C, 86003291

Pottawatomie Creek Bridge [Rainbow Arch Marsh Arch Bridges of Kansas TR], FAS 1604, Osawatomie vicinity, 3/10/83, C, 83000433

Mitchell County

E. W. Norris Service Station, Market and Main Sts., Glen Elder, 12/12/76, A, C, 76000832

Hart, F. H., House, 304 E. Main St., Beloit, 1/29/73, C, 73000769

Mitchell County Courthouse, Main St. and Hersey Ave., Beloit, 11/23/77, C, 77000591

Old Cawker City Library, 7th and Lake Sts., Cawker City, 3/07/73, A, C, 73000770

Perdue, C. A., House, 422 W. 8th St., Beloit, 12/12/76, B, C, 76000831

St. John the Baptist Catholic Church, 701 E. Court St., Beloit, 4/14/75, C, a, 75000717

Wisconsin Street Historic District, 700 blk. of Wisconsin St., Cawker City, 6/11/86, A, C, 86001324

Montgomery County

Archeological Site Number 14MY1320 [Kansas Rock Art TR], Address Restricted, Independence vicinity, 7/09/82, D, 82004883

Archeological Site Number 14MY1385 [Kansas Rock Art TR], Address Restricted, Liberty vicinity, 7/09/82, D, 82004884

Archeological Site Number 14MY365 [Kansas Rock Art TR], Address Restricted, Independence vicinity, 7/09/82, D, 82004885

Archeological Site Number 14MY1 [Kansas Rock Art TR], Address Restricted, Little River vicinity, 7/09/82, D, 82004886

Blakeslee Motor Company Building, 211 W. Myrtle, Independence, 8/25/89, A, C, 89001145

Booth Hotel, 201-209 W. Main St., Independence, 4/28/83, C, 83000435

Booth Theater, 119 W. Myrtle St., Independence, 10/13/88, A, B, C, 88001903

Brown, W. P., Mansion, S. Walnut and Eldridge Sts., Coffeyville, 12/12/76, B, C, 76000833

Cherryvale Carnegie Free Library [Carnegie Libraries of Kansas TR], 329 E. Main, Cherryvale, 8/18/87, A, C, 87000961

Coffeyville Carnegie Public Library Building [Carnegie Libraries of Kansas TR], 415 W. Eighth, Coffeyville, 6/25/87, A, C, 87000962

Condon National Bank, 811 Walnut St., Coffeyville, 1/12/73, C, 73000771

Dewlen-Spohnhauer Bridge [Rainbow Arch Marsh Arch Bridges of Kansas TR], Old US 160, Independence vicinity, 3/10/83, C, 83000436

Federal Building—US Post Office, 123 N. 8th, Independence, 10/19/88, C, 88002009

Independence Bowstring [Metal Truss Bridges in Kansas 1861–1939 MPS], Over the Verdigris River, N of jct. of Burns and Myrtle Sts., Independence, 1/04/90, A, C, 89002180

Independence Public Carnegie Library, 220 E. Maple, Independence, 1/11/88, A, C, 87002231

Infinity Archeological Site, Address Restricted, Independence vicinity, 3/24/71, D, 71000320

Onion Creek Bridge [Metal Truss Bridges in Kansas 1861–1939 MPS], Over Onion Creek, S of Coffeyville, Coffeyville vicinity, 1/04/90, C, 89002172

Pennsylvania Avenue Rock Creek Bridge [Masonry Arch Bridges of Kansas TR], Pennsylvania Ave. over Rock Creek, Independence, 7/02/85, C, 85001437

Terminal Building, 717 Walnut, Coffeyville, 6/14/82, A, C, 82002666

Union Implement and Hardware Building—Masonic Temple, 121-123 W. Main, Independence, 10/13/88, A, C, 88002008

Morris County

Big John Farm Limestone Bank Barn, N of US 56, E of Big John Cr., Council Grove vicinity, 10/25/90, C, 90001576

Cottage House Hotel, 25 N. Neosho, Council Grove, 8/04/88, A, 88001172

Council Grove Carnegie Library [Carnegie Libraries of Kansas TR], 303 W. Main, Council Grove, 6/25/87, A, C, 87000963

Council Grove Historic District, U.S. 56, Council Grove, 10/15/66, A, NHL, 66000347

Council Grove National Bank, 130 W. Main, Council Grove, 6/03/76, A, C, 76000834

Diamond Spring, 6 mi. W of Wilsey, Wilsey vicinity, 9/30/76, A, 76000835

Farmers and Drovers Bank, 201 W. Main St., Council Grove, 6/21/71, C, 71000321

Farmers and Drovers Bank and Indicator Building (Boundary Increase), 201 and 203 W. Main, Council Grove, 2/19/82, A, C, 82002667

Four Mile Creek Lattice [Metal Truss Bridges in Kansas 1861–1939 MPS], Over Four Mile Creek,

SE of Wilsey, Wilsey vicinity, 1/04/90, C, 89002181

Hays, Seth, House, 203 Wood St., Council Grove, 9/25/75, A, B, 75000718

Last Chance Store, 500 W. Main St., Council Grove, 6/21/71, A, 71000322

Old Kaw Mission, 500 N. Mission St., Council Grove, 3/24/71, A, a, 71000323

Simcock House, 206–208 Columbia St., Council Grove, 3/11/82, B, C, 82004888

US Post Office—Council Grove [Kansas Post Offices with Artwork, 1936–1942 MPS], 103 W. Main St., Council Grove, 10/17/89, A, C, g, 89001636

Young, William, Archeological Site, Address Restricted, Council Grove vicinity, 2/24/71, D, 71000324

Morton County

Morton County WPA Bridge [Masonry Arch Bridges of Kansas TR], 6 mi. W and 4 mi. N of Richfield, Richfield vicinity, 10/22/86, C, 86003356

Nemaha County

Old Albany Schoolhouse, 2 mi. N of Sabetha, Sabetha vicinity, 4/13/72, C, 72000518

St. Mary's Church, NE of Baileyville, Baileyville vicinity, 12/05/80, A, C, a, 80001470

US Post Office—Sabetha [Kansas Post Offices with Artwork, 1936–1942 MPS], 122 S. 9th St., Sabetha, 10/17/89, A, C, 89001650

US Post Office—Seneca [Kansas Post Offices with Artwork, 1936–1942 MPS], 607 Main St., Seneca, 10/17/89, A, C, g, 89001651

Neosho County

Austin Bridge, SE of Chanute at Neosho River, Chanute vicinity, 9/15/77, A, C, b, 77000592

Maxwell's Slough Bridge [Masonry Arch Bridges of Kansas TR], Off KS 57 .5 mi. W and 1 mi. S of St. Paul, St. Paul vicinity, 7/02/85, C, 85001429

State Steet Bridge [Masonry Arch Bridges of Kansas TR], State St. over Neosho River tributary, Erie, 7/02/85, C, 85001441

Tioga Inn, 12 E. Main St., Chanute, 2/23/90, A, C, 90000150

Ness County

Carver, George Washington, Homestead Site, 1.5 mi. S of Beeler, Beeler vicinity, 11/23/77, A, B, 77000593

Ness County Bank, Main St. and Pennsylvania Ave., Ness City, 2/23/72, C, 72000519

Ness County—Continued

Pawnee River Tributary Bridge [Masonry Arch Bridges of Kansas TR], 8 mi. S of Bazine, Bazine vicinity, 7/02/85, C, 85001446

Norton County

West Sappa Creek Lattice [Metal Truss Bridges in Kansas 1861–1939 MPS], NW of Norton over West Sappa Creek, Norton vicinity, 1/04/90, C, 89002191

Osage County

Cow-Killer Archeological Site, Address Restricted, Melvern vicinity, 6/24/75, D, 75000719
Lyndon Carnegie Library [Carnegie Libraries of Kansas TR], 127 E. Sixth, Lyndon, 6/25/87, A, C, 87000965
Osage City Santa Fe Depot, 508 Market, Osage City, 5/11/89, A, C, 89000386

Osborne County

Downs Carnegie Library [Carnegie Libraries of Kansas TR], 504 S. Morgan, Downs, 6/25/87, A, C, 87000966
Geodetic Center of the United States, 17 mi. SE of Osborne off U.S. 281 on Meade's Ranch, Osborne vicinity, 10/09/73, A, f, 73000772
Osborne Public Carnegie Library [Carnegie Libraries of Kansas TR], Third and Main, Osborne, 6/25/87, A, C, 87000967

Ottawa County

Archeological Site Number 14OT4 [Kansas Rock Art TR], Address Restricted, Minneapolis vicinity, 7/09/82, D, 82004865
Minneapolis Archeological Site, Address Restricted, Minneapolis vicinity, 6/02/72, D, 72000520

Pawnee County

Fort Larned National Historic Site, 6 mi. W of Larned on U.S. 156, Larned vicinity, 10/15/66, A, C, NHL, NPS, 66000107
Lewis Site, Address Restricted, Larned vicinity, 5/03/76, D, 76000836
Township Line Bridge [Masonry Arch Bridges of Kansas TR], Off US 156 3 mi. W of Rozel, Rozel vicinity, 7/02/85, C, 85001442

Phillips County

Jack Creek Kingpost [Metal Truss Bridges in Kansas 1861–1939 MPS], SE of Long Island, Long Island vicinity, 1/04/90, C, 89002188

Pottawatomie County

Coffey Site, Address Restricted, Olsburg vicinity, 4/11/77, D, 77000594
Old Dutch Mill, Wamego City Park, Wamego, 1/08/73, A, C, 73000773
Pottawatomie Indian Pay Station, E of city limits on Mission St., near St. Mary's College campus, St. Mary's vicinity, 4/13/72, A, 72000521
Vermillion Creek Archeological District, Address Restricted, Onaga vicinity, 3/10/75, D, 75000721
Vermillion Creek Crossing, Oregon Trail, NW of Belvue, Belvue vicinity, 3/10/75, A, C, d, 75000720
Vermillion Creek Tributary Stone Arch Bridge [Masonry Arch Bridges of Kansas TR], 5 mi. S and 1 mi. E of Onaga, Onaga vicinity, 10/22/86, C, 86003354

Pratt County

Gebhart, S. P., House, 105 N. Iuka St., Pratt, 2/12/87, B, C, 87000074
Pratt Archeological Site, Address Restricted, Pratt vicinity, 4/13/72, D, 72000522

Reno County

Fox Theater, 18 E. First, Hutchinson, 9/07/89, C, 89001391
Hutchinson Public Carnegie Library [Carnegie Libraries of Kansas TR], 427 N. Main, Hutchinson, 6/25/87, A, C, 87000968
Kansas Sugar Refining Company Mill, 600 E. 1st St., Hutchinson, 1/03/85, A, 85000013
Plevna General Store, 3rd and Main, Plevna, 12/22/88, C, 88002968
Reno County Courthouse, 206 W. First, Hutchinson, 4/13/87, C, 86003530
Terminal Station, 111 2nd Ave., E., Hutchinson, 10/13/83, A, 83003601
US Post Office—Hutchinson [Kansas Post Offices with Artwork, 1936–1942 MPS], 128 E. First St., Hutchinson, 10/17/89, A, C, g, 89001644
Wall—Ratzlaff House, 103 N. Maple, Buhler, 4/30/92, B, C, 92000443

Republic County

Pawnee Indian Village Site, On KS 266 and the Republican River, Republic vicinity, 5/14/71, D, 71000325

Riley Creek Bridge [Metal Truss Bridges in Kansas 1861–1939 MPS], Over Riley Creek, S of Belleville, Belleville vicinity, 1/04/90, C, b, 89002175
Site No. JF00-072 [Nebraska—Kansas Public Land Survey TR], Jct. of Thayer, Jefferson, Washington and Republic Co. lines, Mahaska vicinity, 6/19/87, A, 87001000
US Post Office—Belleville [Kansas Post Offices with Artwork, 1936–1942 MPS], 1119 18th St., Belleville, 10/17/89, A, C, 89001633

Rice County

Archeological Site Number 14RC11 [Kansas Rock Art TR], Address Restricted, Little River vicinity, 7/09/82, D, 82004866
Archeological Site Number 14RC10 [Kansas Rock Art TR], Address Restricted, Little River vicinity, 7/09/82, D, 82004887
Cooper Hall, N. Broadway Ave., Sterling, 5/03/74, A, C, 74000845
Malone Archeological Site, Address Restricted, Lyons vicinity, 6/26/72, D, 72000523
Saxman Site, Address Restricted, Saxman vicinity, 5/03/76, D, 76000837
Sterling Free Public Carnegie Library [Carnegie Libraries of Kansas TR], 132 N. Broadway, Sterling, 6/25/87, A, C, 87000969
Tobias-Thompson Complex, 4 mi. SE of Geneseo, Geneseo vicinity, 10/15/66, D, NHL, 66000349

Riley County

Anderson Hall, Kansas State University campus, Manhattan, 11/28/80, A, C, 80001471
Goodnow House, 2301 Claflin Rd., Manhattan, 2/24/71, B, C, 71000326
KSAC Radio Towers, Kansas State University campus, Manhattan, 8/27/83, A, 83000437
Manhattan Carnegie Library Building [Carnegie Libraries of Kansas TR], Fifth and Poyntz, Manhattan, 6/25/87, A, C, 87000970
Platt, Jeremiah, House, 2005 Claflin Rd., Manhattan, 5/20/81, B, C, 81000281
Ulrich, Robert, House, 121 N. 8th St., Manhattan, 9/20/78, B, C, 78001287
Woman's Club House, 900 Poyntz Ave., Manhattan, 11/28/80, A, C, 80001472

Rooks County

Thomas Barn, NE of Woodston, near Osborne Co. line, Woodston vicinity, 9/06/91, B, C, 91001104

Rush County

Rush County Courthouse, 715 Elm St., La Crosse, 4/13/72, A, C, 72000524

Rush County—Continued

Rush County Line Bridge [Masonry Arch Bridges of Kansas TR], 11 mi. N of Otis, Otis vicinity, 11/04/86, C, 86003355

Walnut Creek Tributary Bridge [Masonry Arch Bridges of Kansas TR], 0.5 mi. N and 2.5 mi. W of Nekoma, Nekoma vicinity, 7/02/85, C, 85001435

Russell County

Archeological Site Number 14RU5 [Kansas Rock Art TR], Address Restricted, Russell vicinity, 7/09/82, D, 82004867

Archeological Site Number 14RU10 [Kansas Rock Art TR], Address Restricted, Dorrance vicinity, 7/09/82, D, 82004868

Archeological Site Number 14RU313 [Kansas Rock Art TR], Address Restricted, Russell vicinity, 7/09/82, D, 82004869

Archeological Site Number 14RU314 [Kansas Rock Art TR], Address Restricted, Paradise vicinity, 7/09/82, D, 82004870

Archeological Site Number 14RU315 [Kansas Rock Art TR], Address Restricted, Bunker Hill vicinity, 7/09/82, D, 82004871

Archeological Site Number 14RU316 [Kansas Rock Art TR], Address Restricted, Dorrance vicinity, 7/09/82, D, 82004872

Archeological Site Number 14RU324 [Kansas Rock Art TR], Address Restricted, Russell vicinity, 7/09/82, D, 82004873

Garden of Eden, 2nd and Kansas Ave., Lucas, 4/28/77, B, C, g, 77000595

US Post Office—Russell [Kansas Post Offices with Artwork, 1936–1942 MPS], 135 W. Sixth St., Russell, 10/17/89, A, C, g, 89001649

Saline County

Brookville Grade School, Jewitt and Anderson Sts., Brookville, 11/02/82, A, C, g, 82000419

Brookville Hotel, Perry St., Brookville, 1/07/72, A, 72000525

Flanders—Lee House and Carriage House, 200 S. Seventh St., Salina, 8/20/87, B, 87001406

Fox—Watson Theater Building, 155 S. Santa Fe Ave., Salina, 8/04/88, C, 88001171

Prescott, John H., House, 211 W. Prescott Ave., Salina, 5/17/76, B, C, 76000838

Schwartz, A. J., House, 636 E. Iron St., Salina, 4/13/73, C, 73000774

US Post Office and Federal Building—Salina [Kansas Post Offices with Artwork, 1936–1942 MPS], 211 W. Iron, Salina, 7/18/89, A, C, 89000793

Whiteford (Price) Archeological Site, E of Salina, Salina vicinity, 10/15/66, D, NHL, 66000350

Scott County

El Cuartelejo, Address Restricted, Scott City vicinity, 10/15/66, D, NHL, 66000351

Sedgwick County

Administration Building, McConnell AFB, Wichita, 6/11/90, A, C, 90000908

Allen, Henry J., House, 255 N. Roosevelt St., Wichita, 3/07/73, C, 73000775

Arkansas Valley Lodge No. 21, Prince Hall Masons, 615 N. Main St., Wichita, 8/24/77, A, 77000596

Calvary Baptist Church, 601 N. Water, Wichita, 10/28/88, A, C, a, 88001905

Campbell, B. H., House, 1155 N. River Blvd., Wichita, 4/13/73, C, 73000776

Carey House, 525 E. Douglas Ave., Wichita, 4/13/72, C, 72000526

Clapp, L. W., House, 1847 Wellington Pl., Wichita, 6/14/82, B, C, 82002668

Fairmount Cottage, 1717 Fairmount Ave., Wichita, 9/05/85, C, 85001979

Hayford Buildings, 255 N. Market and 115-127 E. 2nd Sts., Wichita, 11/02/82, C, g, 82000420

Hillside Cottage, 303 Circle Dr., Wichita, 11/21/76, C, 76000839

Hypatia House, 1215 N. Broadway, Wichita, 8/23/91, C, 91001105

Kress, S. H., Company Building, 224 E. Douglas, Wichita, 6/24/85, A, C, 85001385

Lassen Hotel, Market Ave. and 1st St., Wichita, 10/04/84, A, C, 84000108

Long, Chester I., House, 3401 E. 2nd St., Wichita, 7/10/78, B, 78001289

Mack, John, Bridge [Rainbow Arch (Marsh Arch) Bridges of Kansas MPS], S. Broadway across the Big Arkansas R., Wichita, 1/22/92, A, C, 91002018

McCormick School, 855 S. Martinson, Wichita, 8/30/78, A, C, 78001288

Munger, Darius Sales, House, Sim Park, Wichita, 6/14/82, A, C, b, 82002669

North Topeka Avenue-10th Street Historic District, 1165, 1103, 1109, 1113, and 1108 N. Topeka Ave., Wichita, 2/14/83, C, 83000438

Occidental Hotel, 300 N. Main St., Wichita, 6/14/82, A, C, 82002670

Old Sedgwick County Courthouse, 504 N. Main St., Wichita, 5/14/71, A, C, 71000327

Old Wheeler-Kelly-Hagny Building, 120 S. Market St., Wichita, 3/11/82, A, C, 82002671

Orpheum Theater and Office Building, 200 N. Broadway St., Wichita, 11/28/80, A, C, 80001473

Riverside Cottage, 901 Spaulding Ave., Wichita, 2/23/89, A, B, C, 88002824

Rock Island Depot, 729 E. Douglas St., Wichita, 4/23/73, A, C, 73000777

Scottish Rite Temple, NW corner of 1st St. at Topeka, Wichita, 5/05/72, C, 72000527

Stackman Court Apartments, 1207 Franklin Ave., Wichita, 11/29/91, A, B, C, 91001741

Sternberg, William, House, 1065 N. Waco, Wichita, 5/24/89, A, C, 89000387

US Post Office and Federal Building—Wichita [Kansas Post Offices with Artwork, 1936–1942 MPS], 401 N. Market, Wichita, 7/18/89, A, C, 89000792

University Hall, Friends University, 2100 University Ave., Wichita, 2/24/71, A, C, 71000328

Wall, Judge T. B., House, 622 N. St. Francis Ave., Wichita, 8/11/83, B, C, 83000439

Wichita City Carnegie Library Building [Carnegie Libraries of Kansas TR], 220 S. Main, Wichita, 6/25/87, A, C, 87000971

Wichita City Hall, 204 S. Main St., Wichita, 5/14/71, A, C, 71000329

Wichita Wholesale Grocery Company, 619 E. William St., Wichita, 8/11/83, A, C, 83000440

Shawnee County

Anton—Woodring House, 1011 Cambridge Ave., Topeka, 8/23/91, B, C, 91001088

Blacksmith Creek Bridge [Rainbow Arch Marsh Arch Bridges of Kansas TR], W of Topeka, Topeka vicinity, 3/10/83, C, 83000441

Cedar Crest, Cedar Crest Rd., Topeka, 5/06/82, B, C, 82002672

Central Motor and Finance Corporation Building, 222 W. 7th St., Topeka, 2/19/82, A, C, 82002673

Central National Bank, 701–703 Kansas Ave., Topeka, 7/19/76, A, C, 76000841

Columbian Building, 112–114 W. 6th St., Topeka, 9/05/75, A, C, 75000722

Crawford Building, 501 Jackson St., Topeka, 8/22/75, A, B, C, 75000723

Curtis, Charles, House, 1101 Topeka Ave., Topeka, 1/25/73, B, 73000778

Davies Building, 725–727 Kansas Ave., Topeka, 9/15/77, A, C, 77000597

England Farm, 4619 SE 37th St., Topeka vicinity, 5/07/82, A, C, 82002674

Giles—Nellis House, 915 SW. Munson, Topeka, 4/28/92, C, 92000432

Hicks Block, 600 W. 6th Ave., Topeka, 11/09/77, A, C, 77000598

Jayhawk Hotel, Theater and Walk, 700 Jackson Ave., Topeka, 3/11/82, A, C, 82002675

Kansas State Capitol, Bound by 8th and 10th Aves. and Jackson and Harrison Sts., Topeka, 9/03/71, A, C, 71000330

Lyons, Horace G., House, 4831 SE 61st St., Berryton vicinity, 8/01/84, B, C, 84001241

McCauley Bridge [Masonry Arch Bridges of Kansas TR], 0.5 mi. S of Auburn, Auburn vicinity, 7/02/85, C, 85001427

Memorial Building, 120 W. 10th Ave., Topeka, 7/17/75, C, c, 75000724

Menninger Clinic Building, 3535 W. 6th Ave., Topeka, 2/13/75, B, 75000725

Old German-American State Bank, 435 Kansas Ave., Topeka, 4/30/80, A, C, 80001475

Pottawatomie Baptist Mission Building, Off W. 6th St., 0.5 mi. W of Wanamaker Rd., Topeka, 9/03/71, A, a, 71001089

Shawnee County—Continued

Pottawatomie Baptist Mission Building and Site (Boundary Increase), On Urish Rd., 0.3 mi. N of 10th St., Topeka, 2/28/73, A, a, 73000779

Potwin Place Historic District, Roughly bounded by Elmwood, Grove, Broadmoor, and Willow Sts., Topeka, 5/01/80, C, 80001476

Sage Inn, 57th St. and Douglas Rd., Dover, 10/08/76, B, 76000840

St. John's Lutheran School, 315 W. 4th St., Topeka, 1/03/85, A, C, 85000014

St. Joseph's Catholic Church, 235 Van Buren St., Topeka, 2/24/71, C, a, 71000331

Sumner Elementary School and Monroe Elementary School, 330 Western Ave. and 1515 Monroe St., Topeka, 5/04/87, A, g, NHL, 87001283

Thacher Building, 110 E. 8th St., Topeka, 3/31/75, A, C, 75000726

Thomas Arch Bridge [Masonry Arch Bridges of Kansas TR], Jct. of Wanamaker Rd. and 105th St., across the Wakarusa R., Auburn vicinity, 5/10/90, C, 90000746

Wakarusa Hotel, Main St., Wakarusa, 4/26/79, A, 79000955

Ward-Meade House, 124 N. Fillmore, Topeka, 11/12/75, A, 75000727

Washburn University Carnegie Library Building [Carnegie Libraries of Kansas TR], Off Seventeenth St. and Washburn Ave., Topeka, 6/25/87, A, C, 87000972

Woman's Club Building, 420 W. 9th St., Topeka, 2/19/82, A, C, 82002676

Woodward, Chester B., House, 1272 SW. Fillmore St., Topeka, 6/25/92, B, C, 92000817

Sheridan County

Pratt, John Fenton, Ranch, W of Studley on U.S. 24, Studley vicinity, 4/28/83, A, C, 83000442

Sherman County

Goodland City Library, 120 W. 12th St., Goodland, 9/13/85, A, C, 85002129

US Post Office—Goodland [Kansas Post Offices with Artwork, 1936–1942 MPS], 124 E. 11th St., Goodland, 10/17/89, A, C, 89001639

Veselik, John Ludwig, House, CR FAS 881, Ruleton vicinity, 10/24/85, C, 85003228

Smith County

Home on the Range Cabin, 17 mi. NW of Smith Center off KS 8, Smith Center vicinity, 3/26/73, A, 73000780

Stafford County

Comanche Archeological Site, Address Restricted, Stafford vicinity, 9/18/78, D, 78001290

Sumner County

Buresh Archeological Site, Address Restricted, Caldwell vicinity, 5/14/71, D, 71000333

Caldwell Carnegie Library, 13 N. Osage St., Caldwell, 2/24/83, A, C, 83000443

Old Oxford Mill, NE of Oxford, Oxford vicinity, 4/26/82, A, 82002677

Salter House, 220 W. Garfield St., Argonia, 9/03/71, B, 71000332

US Post Office—Caldwell [Kansas Post Offices with Artwork, 1936–1942 MPS], 14 N. Main St., Caldwell, 10/17/89, A, C, g, 89001635

Wellington Carnegie Library [Carnegie Libraries of Kansas TR], 121 W. Seventh, Wellington, 6/25/87, A, C, 87000973

Thomas County

Thomas County Courthouse, 300 N. Court, Colby, 11/21/76, A, C, 76000842

Trego County

Walsh Archeological District, Address Restricted, Collyer vicinity, 1/15/85, D, 85000091

Wabaunsee County

Beecher Bible and Rifle Church, SE corner of Chapel and Elm Sts., Wabaunsee, 2/24/71, A, C, a, 71000334

Security State Bank, Main and 2nd Sts., Eskridge, 5/06/82, A, C, 82002678

Wallace County

Goose Creek Tipi Ring Site, Address Restricted, Weskan vicinity, 11/21/78, D, 78001291

Pond Creek Station, E of Wallace on U.S. 40, Wallace, 2/23/72, A, b, 72000528

Washington County

Hollenberg Pony Express Station, 1.5 mi E of Hanover, Hanover vicinity, 10/15/66, A, NHL, 66000352

Site No. JF00-072 [Nebraska—Kansas Public Land Survey TR], Jct. of Thayer, Jefferson, Washington and Republic Co. lines, Mahaska, vicinity, 6/19/87, A, 87001000

Washington County Kingpost [Metal Truss Bridges in Kansas 1861–1939 MPS], SE of Barnes, Barnes vicinity, 1/04/90, C, 89002184

Wilson County

Brush Creek Bridge [Masonry Arch Bridges of Kansas TR], 0.5 mi. S of Coyville, Coyville vicinity, 7/02/85, C, 85001419

Flack, Dr. A. C., House, 303 N. 8th St., Fredonia, 9/21/89, C, 89001463

Gold Dust Hotel, 402 N. Seventh St., Fredonia, 11/01/91, A, C, 91001542

Norman No. 1 Oil Well Site, E. Mill St., Neodesha, 8/28/74, A, NHL, 74000846

US Post Office—Fredonia [Kansas Post Offices with Artwork, 1936–1942 MPS], 428 Madison St., Fredonia, 10/17/89, A, C, 89001638

US Post Office—Neodesha [Kansas Post Offices with Artwork, 1936–1942 MPS], 123 N. Fifth St., Neodesha, 10/17/89, A, C, 89001647

Woodson County

Stockbrands and Kemmerer Department Store, 100 E. Rutledge, Yates Center, 10/17/85, A, C, 85003146

Woodson County Courthouse, Courthouse Sq. between Main, Rutledge, State, and Butler Sts., Yates Center, 10/10/85, A, C, 85002951

Yates Center Carnegie Library [Carnegie Libraries of Kansas TR], 218 N. Main, Yates Center, 6/25/87, A, C, 87000974

Yates Center Courthouse Square Historic District, Courthouse Sq., Yates Center, 5/20/86, A, C, 86001120

Wyandotte County

Argentine Carnegie Library, Twenty-eighth St. and Metropolitan Ave., Kansas City, 4/30/86, A, C, 86000919

Fire Station No. 9, 2 S. 14th St., Kansas City, 9/05/85, C, 85001982

Gates, Judge Louis, House, 4146 Cambridge St., Kansas City, 12/01/80, C, 80001477

Grinter Place, 1420 S. 78th St., Muncie, 1/25/71, B, 71000338

Hanover Heights Neighborhood Historic District, Roughly bounded by Olathe Blvd., Frances St., 43rd Ave., and State Line Rd., Kansas City, 5/17/90, C, 90000776

Huron Building, 905 N. 7th St., Kansas City, 7/05/84, A, C, 84001243

Huron Cemetery, On Minnesota Ave., between 6th and 7th Sts., Kansas City, 9/03/71, A, d, f, 71000335

Kansas City, Kansas City Hall and Fire Headquarters, 805 and 815 N. Sixth St., Kansas City, 4/25/86, A, C, 86000857

Rosedale World War I Memorial Arch, Mt. Marty Park, near Booth and Drexel Sts., Kansas City, 8/02/77, C, f, 77000599

Sauer Castle, 945 Shawnee Dr., Kansas City, 8/02/77, A, C, 77000600

Wyandotte County—Continued

Scottish Rite Temple, 803 N. 7th St., Kansas City, 9/11/85, A, C, 85002127

Shawnee Street Overpass, NW of US 35, Kansas City, 3/08/84, C, 84001245

Soldiers and Sailors Memorial Building, 600 N. 7th St., Kansas City, 9/05/85, C, f, 85001981

St. Augustine Hall, 3301 Parallel Ave., Kansas City, 2/24/71, C, a, 71000336

Trowbridge Archeological Site, Address Restricted, Kansas City, 2/24/71, D, 71000337

Westheight Manor District, Bounded roughly by 18th and 24th Sts., Oakland and State Aves., Kansas City, 3/26/75, C, 75000729

Westheight Manor Historic District (Boundary Increase), Roughly bounded by State and Wood Aves., 18th and 25th Sts., Kansas City, 2/19/82, C, 82004620

Whitefeather Spring, 3818 Ruby Ave., Kansas City, 8/27/75, A, 75000728

Wyandotte High School, 2500 Minnesota, Kansas City, 4/30/86, A, C, 86000920

The Fromme-Birney Round Barn (ca. 1908–12) is listed in the National Register as representative of the "round" or polygonal barn type popular with Midwestern farmers in the late-19th and early-20th centuries. (Martha Hagedorn, 1987)

KENTUCKY

Adair County

Adair County Courthouse, 500 Public Sq., Columbia, 8/27/74, C, 74000847
Archeological Site 15 Ad 33, Address Restricted, Columbia vicinity, 12/08/78, D, 78001292
Archeological Site 15 Ad 36, Address Restricted, Glens Fork vicinity, 11/16/78, D, 78001295
Archeological Site 15 Ad 54, Address Restricted, Columbia vicinity, 11/16/78, D, 78001293
Field, John, House, 111 E. Fortune St., Columbia, 2/08/78, B, C, 78001294
Gaither, Dr. Nathan, House, 100 S. High St., Columbia, 3/21/79, B, C, 79000956
Trabue, Daniel, House, 299 Jamestown St., Columbia, 12/16/74, A, C, 74000848
Zion Meetinghouse and School, SE of Columbia on KY 55, Columbia vicinity, 5/13/76, A, a, 76000843

Allen County

Allen County Poor Farm, 3540 Holland Rd., Scottsville, 11/07/91, A, 91001662

Anderson County

Crossfield, R. H., House, SW of Lawrenceburg off Anderson City Rd., Lawrenceburg vicinity, 6/11/75, B, C, 75000730
Dowling House, 321 S. Main St., Lawrenceburg, 7/10/79, B, C, 79000957
Hanks, Thomas H., House, 516 E. Woodford St., Lawrenceburg, 5/14/80, B, 80001478
Kavanaugh Academy, 241 E. Woodford St., Lawrenceburg, 9/19/73, A, C, 73000781
McBrayer-Clark House, N of Lawrenceburg on KY 326, Lawrenceburg vicinity, 9/19/73, B, C, 73000782
Moore, Rev. William Dudley, House, 4 m. (6.4 km) S of Lawrenceburg, Lawrenceburg vicinity, 2/21/79, B, C, 79000958
Old Prentice Distillery, KY 513, Lawrenceburg vicinity, 3/19/87, C, 87000478
Old Wash Place, 9 mi. W of Lawrenceburg at jct. of U.S. 62 and KY 53, Lawrenceburg vicinity, 6/11/75, B, C, 75000731
Ripy, T. B., House, 320 S. Main St., Lawrenceburg, 2/20/80, B, C, 80001479

Ballard County

Ballard County Courthouse, 4th and Court Sts., Wickliffe, 2/27/80, C, 80001480
Barlow House, Jct. of Broadway and S. Fifth St., Barlow, 11/21/91, B, C, 91001663

Lovelace, Andrew, Jr., House, W of Lovelaceville off U.S. 62, Lovelaceville vicinity, 1/03/78, C, 78001296
Wickliffe Site 15 BA 4, Address Restricted, Wickliffe, 12/08/84, D, 84000789

Barren County

Belle's Tavern [Early Stone Buildings of Kentucky Outer Bluegrass and Pennyrile TR], KY 255, Park City, 1/08/87, D, 87000169
Cave City Commercial District [Barren County MRA], Broadway between 1st and 2nd Sts., Cave City, 7/20/83, A, C, 83002529
Edmunds, Charles Penn, House [Barren County MRA], E of Becton, Beckton vicinity, 5/20/83, C, 83002530
First National Bank [Barren County MRA], Main St., Glasgow, 5/20/83, C, 83002531
First Presbyterian Church [Barren County MRA], Washington and Broadway, Glasgow, 5/20/83, C, a, 83002532
Fort Williams, Between Glasgow Municipal Cemetery and U.S. 31E Bypass, Glasgow, 6/10/75, A, D, 75000732
Glasgow Central Business District, 207 W. Main—117 E. Main, 100–114 S. Green and 104 and 109 N. Race Sts., Glasgow, 2/11/93, A, 93000051
Gullian Gerig's Mill [Early Stone Buildings of Kentucky TR], Beaver Valley Rd., Glasgow vicinity, 10/05/87, C, 87002050
Hicks, William House [Barren County MRA], Jeff Hicks Rd., Austin vicinity, 5/20/83, C, 83002533
Landrum [Barren County MRA], SR 1318, Roseville vicinity, 5/20/83, C, 83002534
Martin, Benjamin, House [Barren County MRA], Berry Store Rd., Finney vicinity, 5/20/83, C, 83002535
Mayfield, John, House [Barren County MRA], SW of Glasgow, Glasgow vicinity, 5/20/83, C, 83002536
McCoy, Andrew, House [Barren County MRA], Railroad Ave., Cave City, 5/20/83, C, 83002537
Morris Building [Barren County MRA], Washington and Green Sts., Glasgow, 5/20/83, C, 83002538
North Race Street Historic District [Barren County MRA], N. Race St. between Front and Cherry Sts., Glasgow, 7/20/83, C, 83002539
Octagon Cottage [Barren County MRA], Off SR 1297, Rocky Hill vicinity, 7/20/83, C, 83002540
Old Zion Methodist Church [Barren County MRA], SR 1297, Park City vicinity, 5/20/83, C, a, 83002541
Page, William House [Barren County MRA], S of Glasgow off of KY 249, Glasgow vicinity, 5/20/83, A, C, 83002542
Quigley, G. F., and Son Grocery [Barren County MRA], Off U.S. 31E, Goodnight, 5/20/83, C, 83002544

Renfro Hotel [Barren County MRA], S. Dixie Ave., Park City, 5/20/83, C, 83002543
Settle, Franklin, House [Barren County MRA], KY 252 and KY 255, Rocky Hill, 5/20/83, C, 83002545
Site Bn-54 [Barren County MRA], Roseville Rd., Bristle Town vicinity, 5/20/83, C, 83002546
Southwest Glasgow Residential District [Barren County MRA], Green St. between Cottage and College Sts., Leslie Ave., Liberty, Brown, and Washington Sts., Glasgow, 8/30/83, C, 83002547
Third National Bank [Barren County MRA], N. Green and Main Sts., Glasgow, 5/20/83, C, 83002548
U.S. Post Office/Board of Education Building [Barren County MRA], 202 W. Washington St., Glasgow, 5/20/83, C, 83002549
White, Jesse and Simon, House [Barren County MRA], Off U.S. 31E, Lucas vicinity, 5/20/83, C, 83002550
Wigwam Village No. 2 [Barren County MRA], NW side US 31W 1.6 mi. NE of junction with KY 70, Cave City, 3/16/88, A, C, 88000180
Wood, William Johnson, House [Barren County MRA], E of Hiseville, Hiseville vicinity, 5/20/83, C, 83002551
Wooten, Joseph, House [Barren County MRA], Crabtree Rd., Tracy vicinity, 5/20/83, C, 83002552
Young, Asa E., House [Barren County MRA], Off KY 921, Tracy vicinity, 5/20/83, C, 83002553

Bath County

Bourbon Iron Works, 2.6 mi. S of Owingsville on KY 36, Owingsville vicinity, 9/01/76, A, C, 76000844
Myrtle Hill, S of Owingsville off US 64, Owingsville vicinity, 10/29/82, C, 82001550
Owings, Col. Thomas Deye, House, Main St. and Courthouse Sq., Owingsville, 1/09/78, B, C, 78001297
Owingsville Commercial District and Courthouse Square, Main and Court Sts., Owingsville, 11/20/78, A, C, 78001298
Owingsville Commercial District and Courthouse Square (Boundary Increase), 122 E. Main St., Owingsville, 8/01/85, A, C, 85001668
Springfield Presbyterian Church, S of Sharpsburg on Springfield Rd., Sharpsburg vicinity, 4/26/79, B, a, d, 79000959

Bell County

American Association, Limited, Office Building, 2215 Cumberland Ave., Middlesboro, 12/29/78, B, C, 78001299

Bell County—Continued

Cumberland Gap Historic District, E of Middlesboro, Middlesboro vicinity, 5/28/80, A, NPS, 80000366

Cumberland Gap National Historical Park, E of Middlesboro along Kentucky-Virginia state line, Middlesboro vicinity, 10/15/66, A, C, e, g, NPS, 66000353

Hensley Settlement, Cumberland Gap National Historical Park, Cubage vicinity, 1/08/80, A, C, e, NPS, 80000367

Middlesboro Downtown Commercial District, Roughly Bounded by Cumberland Ave., 19th, 20th Sts., and Edgewood Rd., Middlesboro, 1/10/83, A, C, 83002554

Mt. Moriah Baptist Church, 314 N. Main St., Middlesboro, 8/08/85, A, a, 85001747

Pineville Courthouse Square Historic District, Along Kentucky, Pine, Virginia, and Walnut Sts., Pineville, 7/19/90, A, C, 90001019

St. Mary's Episcopal Church, 131 Edgewood Rd., Middlesboro, 11/15/84, C, a, 84000341

Boone County

Allen, B. M., House [Boone County MRA], 11301 Riddles Run Rd., Union vicinity, 2/06/89, A, C, 88003290

Anderson Ferry, Off U.S. 50, Constance, 6/10/82, A, b, 82003575

Archaeological Site 15 BE 36, Address Restricted, Union vicinity, 8/18/83, D, 83002555

Aylor, A. J., House [Boone County MRA], 2162 Petersburg Rd., Hebron, 2/06/89, C, 88003275

Barger, Donald, House [Boone County MRA], 2972 Front St., Petersburg, 2/06/89, C, 88003259

Belleview Baptist Church [Boone County MRA], 6658 Fifth St., Belleview, 2/06/89, C, a, 88003248

Belleview Post Office [Boone County MRA], 6256 Main St., Belleview, 6/14/90, A, C, 88003250

Big Bone Lick State Park, Rte. 1, Union, 6/13/72, A, D, 72001585

Big Bone Methodist Church [Boone County MRA], 3435 Beaver Rd., Union vicinity, 2/06/89, C, a, 88003287

Blankenbeker, Clinton, House [Boone County MRA], 7414 US 42, Florence, 2/06/89, C, 88003302

Boone County Distillery Superintendant's House and Guest House [Boone County MRA], 3073 Front St., Petersburg, 2/06/89, A, C, 88003256

Botts House [Boone County MRA], 4752 Petersburg Rd., Burlington vicinity, 2/06/89, A, C, 88003269

Burlington Historic District, KY 18, Burlington, 6/19/79, A, C, 79000961

Calvert, B. C., House [Boone County MRA], 10246 Lower River Rd., Union vicinity, 2/06/89, C, 88003292

Carlton, Jonathan, House, Market St., Petersburg, 11/10/82, C, 82001551

Chambers, A. E., Octagonal Barn [Boone County MRA], 5009 Petersburg Rd., Petersburg vicinity, 2/07/89, A, C, 88003268

Chambers, Robert, House, 301 E. Bend Rd., Burlington, 10/10/75, B, C, 75000733

Chandler House [Boone County MRA], 167 S. Main St., Walton, 2/06/89, C, 88003305

Christian Meeting House [Boone County MRA], 6561 Tanner St., Petersburg, 2/06/89, C, a, 88003262

Clore House [Boone County MRA], 6001 Burlington Pike, Belleview vicinity, 2/06/89, C, 88003252

Clore, Jonas, House [Boone County MRA], 6256 Main St., Belleview, 2/06/89, C, 88003249

Collins, Capt. N., House District [Boone County MRA], 6255 Aurora Ferry Rd., Petersburg vicinity, 2/06/89, A, C, 88003253

Corn, Allie, House [Boone County MRA], 2807 Graves Rd., Hebron vicinity, 2/06/89, A, C, 88003271

Crouch, Dr. M. J., House [Boone County MRA], 2063 Hathaway Rd., Union vicinity, 2/06/89, C, 88003307

Delehunty, John, House [Boone County MRA], 212 Main St., Florence, 2/06/89, C, 88003300

Delph, Sam, House [Boone County MRA], 4633 Garrison Creek Rd., Petersburg vicinity, 2/06/89, A, C, 88003270

Delph, W. T., House [Boone County MRA], 6180 Rogers Ln., Burlington, 2/06/89, A, C, 88003277

Dew, Daniel, House [Boone County MRA], 2950 Third St., Petersburg, 2/06/89, C, 88003264

Dinsmore House, W of Burlington on KY 18, Burlington vicinity, 3/28/79, C, 79000962

Early House [Boone County MRA], 2970 First St., Petersburg, 2/06/89, C, 88003297

East Bend Church [Boone County MRA], 12341 Lower River Rd., Union vicinity, 2/06/89, C, a, 88003291

Edwards House [Boone County MRA], 143 S. Main St., Walton, 2/07/89, C, 88003304

Farmers Bank of Petersburg [Boone County MRA], 3010 First St., Petersburg, 2/06/89, A, C, 88003261

Flick House [Boone County MRA], 6282 Burlington Pike, Belleview, 2/06/89, C, 88003251

Florence Fire Station [Boone County MRA], Main St., Florence, 2/06/89, C, 88003301

Florence Hotel [Boone County MRA], 262 Main St., Florence, 2/06/89, A, 88003280

Fowler, Benjamin Piatt, House, N of Union on US 40, Union vicinity, 10/29/82, C, 82001552

Gaines, Benjamin R., Farm [Boone County MRA], 3895 Idlewild Rd., Burlington vicinity, 2/06/89, A, C, 88003299

Gaines, Col. Abner, House, N of Walton at 84 Old Lexington Pike, Walton vicinity, 4/10/80, B, C, 80001483

Gordon's Hall [Boone County MRA], 6561 Market St., Petersburg, 2/06/89, A, C, 88003260

Hamilton School [Boone County MRA], 4837 Beaver Rd., Union vicinity, 2/06/89, A, C, 88003308

Hebron Deposit Bank [Boone County MRA], 1871 Petersburg Rd., Hebron, 2/06/89, A, C, 88003274

Hicks, Harvey A., House [Boone County MRA], 1325 Hicks Pike, Walton vicinity, 2/06/89, C, 88003281

Hind, Samuel, House [Boone County MRA], 417 Stephenson Mill Rd., Walton vicinity, 6/14/90, A, C, b, 88003278

Hopeful Lutheran Church [Boone County MRA], 6431 Hopeful Rd., Florence vicinity, 2/06/89, A, C, a, 88003279

Horton, Agnes, House [Boone County MRA], 2901 Second St., Petersburg, 2/06/89, C, 88003263

Hudson House [Boone County MRA], 12328 Gaines Way, Walton vicinity, 2/06/89, C, 88003283

Huey, D. W., House [Boone County MRA], 7812 East Bend Rd., Burlington vicinity, 2/06/89, C, 88003294

Hughes House [Boone County MRA], 771 Chambers Rd., Walton vicinity, 2/06/89, C, 88003282

Johnson, Cave, House [Boone County MRA], 8368 River Rd., Hebron vicinity, 2/06/89, A, C, 88003273

Kirtley House [Boone County MRA], 2451 Second Creek Rd., Petersburg vicinity, 2/09/89, C, 89000013

Kirtley, Rev. Robert E., House [Boone County MRA], 8545 River Rd., Hebron vicinity, 2/06/89, C, 88003272

Lassing, Morris, House [Boone County MRA], 10515 US 42, Union vicinity, 6/14/90, A, C, 88003285

Loder House [Boone County MRA], 3028 Front St., Petersburg, 2/06/89, A, C, 88003257

Mayhugh, John Clifton, House [Boone County MRA], 113 N. Main St., Walton, 2/06/89, C, 88003303

Miller, M., House [Boone County MRA], 3805 Beaver Rd., Union vicinity, 2/06/89, A, C, 88003289

Moore, John, House, 6 mi. (9.6 km) NW of Francisville, Francisville vicinity, 3/29/78, C, 78001300

Norman, L. C., House [Boone County MRA], 1966 Mt. Zion Rd., Union, 2/06/89, C, 88003286

Parker, Richard, House [Boone County MRA], 4312 Belleview Rd., Petersburg vicinity, 2/06/89, C, 88003296

Peters House [Boone County MRA], 2973 Third St., Petersburg, 2/06/89, C, 88003298

Piatt's Landing, S of Burlington of KY 338, Burlington vicinity, 7/18/74, B, C, c, 74000849

Prospect Farm [Boone County MRA], 6279 Petersburg Rd., Petersburg vicinity, 2/06/89, A, C, 88003265

Rabbit Hash General Store [Boone County MRA], 10021 Lower River Rd., McVille vicinity, 2/06/89, A, C, 88003293

Ransom House [Boone County MRA], 1842 Messmer Rd., Crittenden vicinity, 2/06/89, A, C, 88003284

Reeves Mound, Address Restricted, Stringtown vicinity, 8/03/90, D, 90001154

Rogers Site, Address Restricted, Petersburg vicinity, 10/31/83, D, 83003647

Boone County—Continued

Rogers, James, House [Boone County MRA], 6259 Sycamore St., Belleview, 2/06/89, A, C, 88003295

Ryle's Super Market and Oddfellows Building [Boone County MRA], 6571 Tanner St., Petersburg, 2/06/89, A, C, 88003258

Souther, Abe, House [Early Stone Buildings of Kentucky Outer Bluegrass and Pennyrile TR], Off KY 237, Francisville vicinity, 1/08/87, C, 87000143

Tanner, John, House [Early Stone Buildings of Kentucky Outer Bluegrass and Pennyrile TR], KY 20, Petersburg, 1/08/87, C, 87000207

Terrill, George W., House [Boone County MRA], 6002 Petersburg Rd., Petersburg vicinity, 2/06/89, C, 88003266

Uitz, Ephraim, House [Boone County MRA], 5208 Bullitsville Rd., Burlington vicinity, 6/14/90, A, C, 88003276

Wallace House [Boone County MRA], 67 S. Main St., Walton, 2/06/89, C, 88003306

Watts House [Early Stone Buildings of Kentucky Outer Bluegrass and Pennyrile TR], Williams Rd., Bullittsville vicinity, 1/08/87, C, 87000208

Wingate—Gaines Farm District [Boone County MRA], 5225 Whitton Rd., Petersburg vicinity, 2/07/89, A, C, 88003267

Bourbon County

Airy Castle, 8 mi. NE of Paris on LaRue Rd., Paris vicinity, 11/07/76, B, C, 76000845

Aker, Jacob, Farm, 795 Bethlehem Rd., Paris vicinity, 2/11/93, C, 93000050

Allen-Alexander House, Off U.S. 68 near jct. with U.S. 460, Paris, 7/24/75, B, C, 75000735

Bayless Quarters [Early Stone Buildings of Central Kentucky TR], KY 13, North Middletown vicinity, 6/23/83, C, 83002556

Bourbon County Courthouse, Courthouse Sq., Paris, 12/31/74, C, 74000851

Buckner Site (15BB12), Address Restricted, Paris vicinity, 1/27/83, D, 83002557

Clay, Dr. Henry, House [Early Stone Buildings of Central Kentucky TR], Off KY 227, Paris vicinity, 8/22/83, A, C, 83002558

Colville Covered Bridge, 4 mi. NW of Millersburg over Hinkston Creek, Millersburg vicinity, 12/30/74, A, C, 74000850

Cooper's Run Baptist Church [Early Stone Buildings of Central Kentucky TR], Off U.S. 27, Shawhan vicinity, 6/23/83, A, C, 83002559

David, William, House, N of Shawhan on Shawhan-Ruddles Mill Pike, Shawhan vicinity, 2/25/79, B, C, 79000965

Downtown Paris Historic District, Roughly bounded by 2nd St., Pleasant St., Main St., High St., and 12th St., Paris, 12/15/89, C, 89002123

Duncan Avenue Historic District, Duncan, Stoner, Vine, and Massie Sts., Paris, 6/23/88, A, C, 88000902

Duncan Tavern, 323 High St., Paris, 4/11/73, A, C, 73000783

Eades Tavern, 421 High St., Paris, 10/02/73, B, 73000784

Eales, James, House [Early Stone Buildings of Central Kentucky TR], Off Cook Rd., Shawhan vicinity, 6/23/83, A, C, 83002560

Escondida, S of Paris on SR 4, Paris vicinity, 2/08/78, C, 78001302

Garrard, James, House [Early Stone Buildings of Central Kentucky TR], Peacock Pike, Shawhan vicinity, 6/23/83, A, C, 83002561

Grange, The, 4 mi. N of Paris on U.S. 68, Paris vicinity, 4/11/73, A, B, C, 73000786

Harrod, Ephram, House [Early Stone Buildings of Central Kentucky TR], Off U.S. 460, North Middletown vicinity, 8/22/83, A, C, 83002562

Hopkins House [Early Stone Buildings of Central Kentucky TR], KY 537, North Middletown vicinity, 6/23/83, C, 83002563

Kennedy, Joseph, House [Early Stone Buildings of Central Kentucky TR], Off SR 1940, Shawhan vicinity, 6/23/83, C, 83002564

Kennedy, Thomas, House, SE of Paris on Paris-Winchester Rd., Paris vicinity, 12/08/80, B, C, 80001484

Kiser Station, N of Paris on Peacock Rd., Paris vicinity, 12/12/77, B, C, 77000601

Loudoun Hall, S of Paris off KY 956, Paris vicinity, 8/02/78, B, C, d, 78001303

Mauck, Rudolph, House [Early Stone Buildings of Central Kentucky TR], Off SR 1893, Shawhan vicinity, 6/23/83, A, C, 83002565

McKee-Vimont Row Houses, Main St., Millersburg, 9/09/75, B, C, 75000734

McLeod Spring House [Early Stone Buildings of Central Kentucky TR], SR 1939, Paris vicinity, 6/23/83, C, 83002566

Miller's House at Ruddels Mills [Early Stone Buildings of Central Kentucky TR], SR 1940, Millersburg, 6/23/83, A, C, 83002567

Millersburg Historic District, Roughly bounded by College Ave., Miller, Second, and Trigg Sts., Millersburg, 4/10/86, A, C, 86000697

Paris Cemetery Gatehouse, U.S. 68, Paris, 11/24/78, C, 78001301

Paris Courthouse Square Historic District, Courthouse Sq. and environs, Paris, 1/25/79, A, C, 79000963

Paris Railroad Depot, Between 10th St. and Winchester Pike, Paris, 4/11/73, A, 73000785

Rodgers, Thomas, House [Early Stone Buildings of Central Kentucky TR], U.S. 460, Paris vicinity, 6/23/83, A, C, 83002568

Rymill, Elias, House [Early Stone Buildings of Central Kentucky TR], Off Brentsville Rd., Shawhan vicinity, 6/23/83, C, 83002569

Sacred Home, W of Paris on Hume-Bedford Rd., Paris vicinity, 8/09/79, C, d, 79000964

Sandusky House [Early Stone Buildings of Central Kentucky TR], Off U.S. 68, Carlisle vicinity, 6/23/83, A, C, 83002570

Shipp, Laban, House [Early Stone Buildings of Central Kentucky TR], Off SR 1940, Shawhan vicinity, 6/23/83, A, C, 83002571

Spears, Jacob, Distillery [Early Stone Buildings of Central Kentucky TR], SR 1876, Shawhan vicinity, 6/23/83, A, C, 83002573

Spears, Jacob, House [Early Stone Buildings of Central Kentucky TR], SR 1876, Shawhan vicinity, 6/23/83, A, C, 83002572

Stephens, Joseph L., House [Early Stone Buildings of Central Kentucky TR], SR 1940, Millersburg, 6/23/83, A, C, 83002574

Widow McDowell House [Early Stone Buildings of Central Kentucky TR], KY 537, Paris vicinity, 6/23/83, A, C, 83002576

Williams, Hubbard, House [Early Stone Buildings of Central Kentucky TR], Off KY 32/36, Millersburg vicinity, 6/23/83, A, C, 83002577

Wright, Capt. James, House and Cabin, 1 mi. SW of Paris on U.S. 27, Paris vicinity, 10/08/76, B, C, 76000846

Boyd County

Ashland Coal and Iron Railroad Store [Ashland MRA], 900 Front St., Ashland, 7/03/79, A, 79003553

Ashland Coal and Iron Railroad Office [Ashland MRA], 1100 Front St., Ashland, 7/03/79, A, 79003565

Bagby, Alexander, House [Ashland MRA], 1520 Lexington Ave., Ashland, 7/03/79, C, 79003561

Bath Avenue Historic District [Ashland MRA], Bath Ave. from 13th to 17th Sts., Ashland, 7/03/79, B, C, 79003552

Catlett House, 25th and Walnut Sts., Catlettsburg, 5/25/73, B, C, 73000788

Catlettsburg National Bank, 110 26th St., Catlettsburg, 5/25/73, A, C, 73000789

Crump and Field Grocery Company [Ashland MRA], 1401–1405 Greenup Ave., Ashland, 7/03/79, A, C, 79003556

Culbertson House [Ashland MRA], 1520 Chestnut Dr., Ashland, 7/03/79, B, C, 79003560

Felty, Nando, Saloon [Ashland MRA], 1500 Front St., Ashland, 7/03/79, A, C, 79003557

Fields, Timothy, House [Ashland MRA], 1520 Lexington Ave., Ashland, 7/03/79, B, C, b, 79003562

First Christian Church of Ashland [Ashland MRA], 315 17th St., Ashland, 3/22/90, C, a, 90000475

First Presbyterian Church [Ashland MRA (AD)], 1600 Winchester Ave., Ashland, 6/19/73, A, C, a, 73000787

First United Methodist Church, 2712 Louisa St., Catlettsburg, 11/19/74, A, a, g, 74000853

Henry Clay Hotel [Ashland MRA], 1736 Winchester Ave., Ashland, 8/03/84, A, C, 84001383

Hilton, Martin, House [Ashland MRA], 1314 Hilton Ct., Ashland, 7/03/79, A, B, 79003559

Indian Mounds in Central Park [Ashland MRA (AD)], Central Park, Carter Ave., Ashland, 1/21/74, D, 74000852

Paramount Theatre [Historic Resources of Ashland MRA (AD)], 1304 Winchester Ave., Ashland, 6/30/75, A, C, g, 75000736

Boyd County—Continued

Rogers, Lon, House [Ashland MRA], 2008 Lexington Ave., Ashland, 7/03/79, B, C, 79003564

Savageot, Jacob, House and Saloon [Ashland MRA], 1512 Front St., Ashland, 7/03/79, A, C, 79003558

St. James AME Church [Ashland MRA], 12th St. and Carter Ave., Ashland, 7/03/79, A, a, 79003555

Stone Serpent Mound, Address Restricted, Catlettsburg vicinity, 1/21/74, D, 74000854

US Post Office—Ashland [Ashland MRA], 1645 Winchester Ave., Ashland, 11/15/88, C, 88002617

Boyle County

Barbee, John, House [Early Stone Buildings of Central Kentucky TR], KY 34, Bryantsville vicinity, 6/23/83, A, C, 83002578

Bottom, H. P., House, NW of Perryville on Old Mackville Rd., Perryville vicinity, 1/01/76, A, C, 76000851

Boyle County Courthouse, Main and 4th Sts., Danville, 4/11/73, A, C, 73000790

Boyle, Judge John, House, N of Danville on Bellows Mill Rd., Danville vicinity, 11/25/80, B, C, 80001485

Caldwell House [Early Stone Buildings of Central Kentucky TR], Off U.S. 150, Danville vicinity, 6/23/83, A, C, 83002579

Cambus-Kenneth Estate, 3 mi. NW of Danville off U.S. 127, Danville vicinity, 11/17/77, C, 77000602

Carnegie Library [Danville MRA], Center College campus, Danville, 3/28/86, C, 86000645

Constitution Square Historic District, Bounded by Main and Walnut Sts., 1st and 2nd Sts., Danville, 4/02/76, A, B, C, f, 76000847

Crawford House, NE of Perryville off U.S. 68, Perryville vicinity, 1/01/76, B, C, 76000852

Crow, William, House [Early Stone Buildings of Central Kentucky TR], Off KY 52, Bryantsville vicinity, 6/23/83, A, C, 83002581

Crow-Barbee House [Early Stone Buildings of Central Kentucky TR], Stanford Rd. and Alta Ave., Danville, 6/23/83, A, C, 83002580

Danville Commercial District [Danville MRA], W. Main between N. Fifth and N. First, and area bounded by S. Third, W. Walnut, and S. Fourth, Danville, 3/31/86, A, C, a, 86000643

East Main Street Historic District [Danville MRA], 419–619 E. Main St., Danville, 3/31/86, C, 86000640

First Presbyterian Church [Danville MRA], W. Main between N. Fifth and N. Sixth Sts., Danville, 3/31/86, C, a, 86000638

Forest Hill, KY 34, 3 mi. NE of Danville, Danville vicinity, 10/16/89, B, C, 89001712

Harlan's Station Site, 5 mi. W of Danville on Salt River Rd., Danville vicinity, 10/21/76, A, B, C, 76000848

Harlan, Elijah, House [Early Stone Buildings of Central Kentucky TR], U.S. 150, Danville vicinity, 6/23/83, C, 83002582

Harlan-Bruce House, 5 mi. (8 km) E of Danville off KY 52, Danville vicinity, 11/14/78, B, C, 78001304

Haskins, W. H., House [Danville MRA], 420 Lexington Ave., Danville, 3/31/86, C, 86000636

Jacobs Hall, Kentucky School for the Deaf, S. 3rd St., Danville, 10/15/66, A, NHL, 66000354

Knox, Abner, Farm [Early Stone Buildings of Central Kentucky TR], U.S. 150, Danville vicinity, 6/23/83, A, C, 83002583

Lexington Avenue—Broadway Historic District [Danville MRA], W. and E. Lexington between N. Fifth and Old Wilderness Rd. and area bounded by N. Larrimore, W. Broadway, and N. Fifth, Danville, 1/12/87, C, a, 87000198

Maple Avenue District [Danville MRA], Both sides of Maple Ave. between W. Main and High, Danville, 6/16/87, C, 87001241

Marshall House [Early Stone Buildings of Central Kentucky TR], Off KY 34, Junction City vicinity, 6/23/83, C, 83002584

Mason, Peter, House, Off US 127, 3 mi. N of Danville, Danville vicinity, 11/27/91, C, 91001711

McClure-Barbee House, 304 S. 4th St., Danville, 3/07/73, C, 73000791

McDowell, Dr. Ephraim, House, 125–127 S. 2nd St., Danville, 10/15/66, B, e, NHL, 66000355

Melrose, US 127, Danville vicinity, 4/03/86, B, 86000631

Mock, Randolf, Farm [Early Stone Buildings of Central Kentucky TR], Off KY 33, Danville vicinity, 6/23/83, C, 83002585

Old Centre, Centre College, W. Walnut St., Centre College campus, Danville, 8/25/72, A, C, 72000529

Perryville Battlefield, W of Perryville on U.S. 150, Perryville vicinity, 10/15/66, A, NHL, 66000356

Perryville Historic District, Roughly bounded by Sheridan Ave., Wood, Jefferson and 5th Sts., Perryville, 10/25/73, A, C, 73000792

Pleasant Vale, Lexington Rd., Danville vicinity, 11/15/84, A, C, 84000357

Roselawn, US 127, Danville, 3/13/86, C, 86000369

Spring Hill (Thomas Lillard House), S of Danville on U.S. 150, Danville vicinity, 1/27/83, C, 83002586

Stone House on Old Stage Road [Early Stone Buildings of Central Kentucky TR], KY 34, Bryantsville vicinity, 6/23/83, C, 83002587

Thompson, William, House [Early Stone Buildings of Central Kentucky TR], Off U.S. 68, Perryville vicinity, 6/23/83, A, C, 83002588

Three Gothic Villas, NW of Danville off U.S. 127, 525 Maple Ave., and S of Danville off KY 35, Danville and vicinity, 7/20/77, B, C, 77000603

Todd-Montgomery Houses, 229, 243, 251, and 305 N. 3rd St., Danville, 3/26/76, B, C, 76000849

Trinity Episcopal Church, 320 W. Main St., Danville, 9/15/77, A, C, a, 77000604

Warehouse District [Danville MRA], Intersection of Harding and W. Walnut Sts., Danville, 3/31/86, A, C, 86000634

Waveland, 0.5 mi. S of Danville, Danville vicinity, 5/06/76, B, C, 76000850

Bracken County

Augusta College Historic Buildings, 205 Frankfort St. and 204 Bracken St., Augusta, 2/20/80, A, C, a, 80001486

Augusta Historic District [Augusta MRA], Roughly bounded by Riverside Dr., 5th, Frankfort, and Williams Sts., Augusta, 3/13/84, A, C, 84001385

Bracken County Infirmary, NE of Chatham on KY 19, Chatham vicinity, 4/16/79, A, 79000966

Brothers-O'Neil House [Augusta MRA], 308 Seminary Rd., Augusta, 5/22/84, C, 84001390

Chalfant, Mordecai, House [Early Stone Buildings of Kentucky Outer Bluegrass and Pennyrile TR], KY 8, Augusta vicinity, 1/08/87, C, 87000142

Fee, John Gregg, House, NW of Germantown, Germantown vicinity, 8/26/80, B, 80001487

Griffith's, Evan, Grocery [Augusta MRA], 415 Railroad Ave., Augusta, 5/22/84, A, C, 84001392

McKibben, Alfonso, House [Augusta MRA], 202 4th St., Augusta, 5/22/84, C, 84001394

Minor, J. R., House [Augusta MRA], 204 2nd St., Augusta, 5/22/84, C, 84001395

Rock Spring Warehouse [Early Stone Buildings of Kentucky Outer Bluegrass and Pennyrile TR], KY 8, Wellsburg, 1/08/87, C, 87000175

Snag Creek Site (15BK2), Address Restricted, Willow Grove vicinity, 11/14/85, D, 85002821

Stone House on Bracken Creek [Early Stone Buildings of Kentucky Outer Bluegrass and Pennyrile TR], Off KY 435, Augusta vicinity, 1/08/87, C, 87000199

Stroube House [Early Stone Buildings of Kentucky Outer Bluegrass and Pennyrile TR], KY 616, Augusta vicinity, 1/08/87, C, 87000140

Turtle Creek Site (15BK13), Address Restricted, Augusta vicinity, 11/14/85, D, 85002824

Walcott Covered Bridge, 3.5 mi. N of Brooksville on SR 1159 over Locust Creek, Brooksville vicinity, 6/10/75, A, C, 75000738

Water Street Historic District, River Side Dr. from property E of Frankfort St. W to include property W of Ferry St., Augusta, 9/24/75, A, B, C, D, 75000737

Weldon, James, House [Augusta MRA], 417 Railroad St., Augusta, 5/22/84, C, 84001384

Wells-Keith House [Augusta MRA], 411-413 3rd St., Augusta, 5/22/84, C, 84001398

Wine Cellar, S of Augusta on KY 1839, Augusta vicinity, 12/30/74, A, B, C, 74000855

Breathitt County

Breathitt County Jail [Jackson MRA], 1027 College St., Jackson, 2/21/86, A, C, 86000271

Crain's Wholesale and Retail Store [Jackson MRA], College and Broadway Sts., Jackson, 2/21/86, A, 86000272

Breathitt County—Continued

Jackson Commercial District [Jackson MRA], Main St. between Court W to Broadway St., Jackson, 2/21/86, A, C, 86000284

Jackson Post Office [Jackson MPS], Jct. of Hawk and Broadway, Jackson, 7/23/90, A, C, 90001087

M. E. Church, South [Jackson MRA], 1022 College St., Jackson, 2/21/86, C, a, 86000280

Stacey Hotel [Jackson MRA], Broadway and College Sts., Jackson, 2/21/86, A, 86000282

Breckinridge County

Cloverport Historic District [Cloverport MRA], Roughly bounded by 3rd, Main, Chestnut, and Lynn Sts., Cloverport, 6/21/83, A, C, a, 83002589

Falls of Rough Historic District, KY 110, Falls of Rough, 1/31/78, A, B, C, a, 78001305

Fisher Homestead [Cloverport MRA], U.S. 60, Cloverport, 6/21/83, A, C, 83002590

Holt Bottoms Archeological District, Address Restricted, Holt vicinity, 11/16/78, D, 78001306

Holt, Joseph, House and Chapel, SW of Addison on KY 144, Addison vicinity, 7/12/76, B, C, a, d, 76000853

Mattingly Petroglyphs (15BC128) [Prehistoric Rock Art Sites in Kentucky MPS], Address Restricted, Mattingly vicinity, 9/08/89, A, C, D, a, 89001172

North Fork Rough River Petroglyph (15BC130) [Prehistoric Rock Art Sites in Kentucky MPS], Address Restricted, Roff vicinity, 9/08/89, A, C, D, a, 89001174

Oglesby-Conrad [Cloverport MRA], Off U.S. 60, Cloverport, 6/21/83, A, C, 83002591

Skillman House [Cloverport MRA], Tile Plant Rd., Cloverport, 6/21/83, C, 83002592

Tar Springs Petroglyphs (15BC129) [Prehistoric Rock Art Sites in Kentucky MPS], Address Restricted, Cloverport vicinity, 9/08/89, A, C, D, a, 89001173

Bullitt County

Ashworth Rock Shelters Site, Address Restricted, Shepherdsville vicinity, 9/11/75, D, 75000739

Bank of the Commonwealth [Early Stone Buildings of Kentucky Outer Bluegrass and Pennyrile TR], Buckman St., Shepherdsville, 1/08/87, C, 87000173

Barnes, Henry J., House, 144 N. Bardstown Rd., Mt. Washington, 3/01/93, C, 93000049

Beam, T. Jeremiah, House, Big Level Rd., Clermont, 10/15/87, B, 87001854

Brooks, Solomon Neill House, NE of Shepherdsville at Hebron Lane and KY 61, Shepherdsville vicinity, 4/10/80, C, 80001488

Crist, Henry, House [Early Stone Buildings of Kentucky Outer Bluegrass and Pennyrile TR], Mar-

aman Ln. off Ky 1604, Brownington, 1/08/87, C, 87000215

Lloyd, James M., House, Jct. of US 31 E and East St., NE corner, Mt. Washington, 2/11/93, C, 93000048

Stansbury, Zack, House, 1430 Bardstown Rd., Mt. Washington vicinity, 2/11/93, C, 93000047

Butler County

Annis Mound and Village Site (15BT2; 15BT20; 15BT21), Address Restricted, Logansport vicinity, 12/21/85, A, D, g, 85003182

Baby Track Rock Petroglyphs (15BT40) [Prehistoric Rock Art Sites in Kentucky MPS], Address Restricted, Morgantown vicinity, 9/08/89, A, C, D, a, 89001175

Carlston Annis Shell Mound (15BT5) [Green River Shell Middens of Kentucky TR], Address Restricted, Schulztown vicinity, 4/01/86, D, 86000632

Carson, John, House, 205 S. Main St., Morgantown, 7/26/91, B, C, 91000922

DeWeese Shell Mound (15BT6) [Green River Shell Middens of Kentucky TR], Address Restricted, Highview vicinity, 4/01/86, D, 86000635

Ice House on Little Muddy Creek [Early Stone Buildings of Kentucky Outer Bluegrass and Pennyrile TR], US 231, Morgantown vicinity, 1/08/87, D, 87000171

Rayburn Johnson Shell Mound (15BT41) [Green River Shell Middens of Kentucky TR], Address Restricted, Prentiss vicinity, 4/01/86, D, 86000633

Read Shell Mound (15BT10) [Green River Shell Middens of Kentucky TR], Address Restricted, Monticello vicinity, 4/01/86, D, 86000647

Reedyville Petroglyphs (15BT65) [Prehistoric Rock Art Sites in Kentucky MPS], Address Restricted, Reedyville vicinity, 9/08/89, A, C, D, a, 89001176

Russell Shell Mound (15BT11) [Green River Shell Middens of Kentucky TR], Address Restricted, Logansport vicinity, 4/01/86, D, 86000637

Turkey Rock Petroglyphs (15BT64) [Prehistoric Rock Art Sites in Kentucky MPS], Address Restricted, Morgantown vicinity, 9/08/89, A, C, D, a, 89001177

U.S. Army Corps of Engineers Superintendent's House and Workmen's Office, Woodbury Park, Woodbury, 6/19/80, A, C, 80001489

Woodbury Shell Midden (15BT67) [Green River Shell Middens of Kentucky TR], Address Restricted, Woodbury vicinity, 4/01/86, D, 86000639

Caldwell County

Adsmore, 304 N. Jefferson St., Princeton, 10/25/73, B, C, 73000793

Champion-Shepherdson House, 115 E. Main St., Princeton, 12/28/78, B, C, 78003411

Fredonia Cumberland Presbyterian Church, US 641, Fredonia, 8/08/85, C, a, 85001746

Overby, L. B., House, 317 S. Jefferson St., Princeton, 3/22/90, C, 90000476

Princeton Downtown Commercial District, Roughly along Main St., E. and W. Court Sq. Sts., Princeton, 9/19/88, A, C, 88001017

Calloway County

Archeological Site 15CW64, Address Restricted, Backusburg vicinity, 7/11/85, D, 85001506

Calloway County Courthouse [Murray Kentucky MRA], Town Sq., Murray, 2/19/86, A, 86000287

Diuguid, Edwin S., House, 601 W. Main St., Murray, 5/17/76, B, C, 76000855

First Baptist Church [Murray Kentucky MRA], 203 S. Fourth St., Murray, 2/19/86, C, a, 86000289

First Christian Church [Murray Kentucky MRA], 111 N. Fifth St., Murray, 2/19/86, C, a, 86000292

Fort Heiman Site, 1.6 mi. SE of New Concord off Fort Heiman Rd., New Concord vicinity, 12/12/76, A, 76000856

Linn, Will, House, 103 N. 6th St., Murray, 12/04/80, C, b, 80001491

Main Street Historic District [Murray Kentucky MRA], 700 and 800 blks. of W. Main St., Murray, 2/19/86, C, 86000294

Murray State University Historic Buildings, 15th, 16th, and Main Sts., Murray, 8/03/78, A, 78001307

Murray State University Historic Buildings, Addition: Main Library, Murray State University Campus, Murray, 5/26/83, C, 83002593

National Hotel [Murray Kentucky MRA], N. Sixth and Main Sts., Murray, 2/19/86, A, 86000298

Old Normal School Building, Murray State University campus, Murray, 6/11/75, A, 75000740

Seclusaval, 8 mi. E of Murray on KY 614, Murray vicinity, 6/10/75, C, 75000741

US Post Office—Murray [Murray Kentucky MRA], Maple and S. Fourth St., Murray, 2/19/86, C, 86000296

Campbell County

Barth, Peter, Farm [German Settlement, Four Mile Creek Area TR], Lower Tug Fork Rd., Alexandria vicinity, 3/09/83, A, C, 83002594

Baumann House [German Settlement, Four Mile Creek Area TR], Four Mile Pike, Camp Springs, 3/09/83, A, C, 83002595

Bellevue, 335 E. 3rd St., Newport, 4/22/76, B, C, 76000857

Bellevue High School, Washington and Center Sts., Bellevue, 1/09/86, A, C, 86000026

Bishoff House [German Settlement, Four Mile Creek Area TR], Upper Eight Mile Rd., Camp Springs vicinity, 3/09/83, A, C, 83002622

Blau's Four Mile House [German Settlement, Four Mile Creek Area TR], Four Mile Pike, Camp Springs, 3/09/83, A, C, 83002596

Campbell County—Continued

Blenk House [German Settlement, Four Mile Creek Area TR], Four and Eight Mile Rd., Alexandria vicinity, 3/09/83, A, C, 83002597

Braun, John, House [German Settlement, Four Mile Creek Area TR], Eight Mile Rd., Camp Springs vicinity, 3/09/83, A, C, 83002598

Camp Spring House [German Settlement, Four Mile Creek Area TR], Four Mile Pike, Camp Springs vicinity, 3/09/83, A, C, 83002599

Campbell County Courthouse at Newport, Fourth and York Sts., Newport, 3/08/88, C, 88000181

Dayton High School, 8th and Walnut Sts., Dayton, 7/18/85, A, C, 85001579

East Newport Historic District, Roughly bounded by the C & O RR, 6th, Saratoga, and Oak Sts., Newport, 8/25/83, A, C, 83002600

Faha, John, House [German Settlement, Four Mile Creek Area TR], Lower Tug Fork Rd., Alexandria vicinity, 3/09/83, A, C, 83002601

Fairfield Avenue Historic District [Bellevue MRA], Fairfield Ave. between LaFayette Ave. and O'Fallon, Bellevue, 2/22/88, C, a, 88000100

Foote—Fister Mansion [Bellevue MRA], 801 Lincoln Rd., Bellevue, 2/24/88, A, C, 88000099

Fort Thomas Military Reservation District, Roughly bounded by Pearson, Alexander and Cochran Aves., River Rd., and S. Fort Thomas Ave., Fort Thomas, 5/15/86, A, B, C, 86001103

Gubser-Schuchter Farm [German Settlement, Four Mile Creek Area TR], Four Mile Pike Area, Camp Springs, 3/09/83, A, C, 83002602

Heiert Farm [German Settlement, Four Mile Creek Area TR], Upper Eight Mile Pike, Camp Springs vicinity, 3/09/83, A, C, 83002603

Herndon, Elijah, House, NW of California on Washington Trace Rd., California vicinity, 10/29/83, C, 83002604

Hilbert Farm [German Settlement, Four Mile Creek Area TR], Gunkel Rd., Camp Springs vicinity, 3/09/83, A, C, 83002605

Kort Grocery [German Settlement, Four Mile Creek Area TR], Four Mile Pike, Camp Springs, 3/09/83, A, C, 83002606

Kremer, Frederich, House [German Settlement, Four Mile Creek Area TR], 317 Poplar Ridge Rd., Alexandria vicinity, 3/09/83, A, C, 83002607

Kremer, Matthias, House [German Settlement, Four Mile Creek Area TR], Four and Twelve Mile Rd., Camp Springs, 3/09/83, A, 83002608

Kremer, Nicholas, House [German Settlement, Four Mile Creek Area TR], Four and Twelve Mile Pike, Alexandria vicinity, 3/09/83, A, C, 83002609

Leick House [German Settlement, Four Mile Creek Area TR], Four Mile Pike, Camp Springs, 3/09/83, A, C, 83002610

Mansion Hill Historic District, Roughly bounded by I-471, Washington Ave., 2nd and 6th Sts., Newport, 7/17/80, C, 80001493

Mansion Hill Historic District (Boundary Increase), Roughly bounded by Washington Ave., 6th, Saratoga and 3rd Sts., Newport, 8/01/85, C, 85001678

Ort-Heeb Farm [German Settlement, Four Mile Creek Area TR], Four Mile Pike, Alexandria vicinity, 3/09/83, A, C, 83002611

Posey Flats, 101–103 E. Third St., Newport, 1/29/87, C, 86003730

Reitman House [German Settlement, Four Mile Creek Area TR], Reitman Rd., Alexandria vicinity, 3/09/83, C, 83002612

Reitman's St.Joseph House [German Settlement, Four Mile Creek Area TR], Four Mile Pike, Camp Springs, 3/09/83, A, C, 83002613

Ritter, Andrew, Farm [German Settlement, Four Mile Creek Area TR], Four Mile Pike, Alexandria vicinity, 3/09/83, A, C, 83002614

Roth Farm [German Settlement, Four Mile Creek Area TR], Off Lower Eight Mile Rd., Camp Springs vicinity, 3/09/83, A, C, 83002615

Sacred Heart Church [Bellevue MRA (AD)], 337 Taylor Ave., Bellevue, 8/13/74, A, C, a, 74000856

Salem Methodist Episcopal Church and Parsonage, 810 York St., Newport, 3/27/86, A, C, a, 86000608

Sauser Farm [German Settlement, Four Mile Creek Area TR], Upper Tug Fork Rd., Alexandria vicinity, 3/09/83, A, C, 83002616

Seiter, Joseph, House, 307–309 Berry Ave., Bellevue, 4/03/86, B, 86000617

Southgate-Parker-Maddux House, 24 E. 3rd St., Newport, 8/29/77, B, C, 77000605

St John's Lutheran Cemetery [German Settlement, Four Mile Creek Area TR], Upper Tug Fork Rd., Alexandria vicinity, 3/09/83, A, C, d, 83002617

St. John the Baptist Roman Catholic Church, 641 Licking Pike, Wilders, 8/11/80, C, 80001495

St. Joseph's Catholic Church and Cemetery [German Settlement, Four Mile Creek Area TR], Four Mile Pike, Alexandria vicinity, 5/16/83, A, a, d, 83002618

St. Paul's Episcopal Church, 15 Court Pl., Newport, 11/25/80, C, a, 80001494

St. Vincent de Paul School, 117 Main St., Newport, 10/11/89, C, a, 89001598

Taylor's Daughters Historic District [Bellevue MRA], Roughly bounded by O'Fallon Ave., Locust St., Retreat St., Clark St., Chen Ave., and Fairfield Ave., Bellevue, 2/24/88, C, a, 88000101

Tiemeyer House [German Settlement, Four Mile Creek Area TR], KY 8, Melbourne vicinity, 3/09/83, A, C, 83002619

Trutschell House [German Settlement, Four Mile Creek Area TR], KY 8, Melbourne vicinity, 3/09/83, A, C, 83002620

U.S. Army Fort Thomas Mess Hall, Cochran Ave., Fort Thomas, 3/13/80, A, C, 80001492

Uebel House [German Settlement, Four Mile Creek Area TR], Upper Tug Fork Rd., Alexandria vicinity, 3/09/83, A, C, 83002621

Wiedemann, Charles, House, 1102 Park Ave., Newport, 8/18/84, A, C, 84001401

Carlisle County

Illinois Central Railroad Station and Freight Depot, Front St., Bardwell, 7/19/76, A, C, 76000860

Marshall Site (15CE27), Address Restricted, Bardwell vicinity, 11/14/85, D, 85002818

Neville-Patterson-Lamkin House, KY 80, Arlington, 6/16/76, B, C, 76000859

Turk Site (15CE6), Address Restricted, Bardwell vicinity, 11/14/85, D, 85002822

Carroll County

Baker, Paschal Todd, House, 406 Highland Ave., Carrollton, 11/25/80, C, 80001496

Butler, Gen. William O., House, Highland Ave., Carrollton, 5/28/76, B, C, 76000861

Carrollton Historic District, Roughly bounded by Main, Polk, 2nd, 7th, and both sides of Highland Ave. to 11th St., Carrollton, 11/12/82, C, 82001553

Ghent Historic District, US 42, Fishing, Ann, Main Cross, Ferry, Water, Union and Liberty Sts., Ghent, 8/25/83, A, C, 83002623

Grass Hills, 5 mi. SE of Ghent on KY 47 at I-71, Ghent vicinity, 8/22/75, B, C, 75000743

Hunter's Bottom Historic District, W of Carrollton, Carrollton vicinity, 8/11/76, A, B, C, a, d, 76000862

Masterson, Richard, House, E of jct. of U.S. 227 and U.S. 42, Carrollton, 7/01/75, B, c, 75000742

Ogburn, Henry, House [Early Stone Buildings of Kentucky Outer Bluegrass and Pennyrile TR], Off US 42, Carrollton, 1/08/87, C, 87000149

Stone House on Kentucky River [Early Stone Buildings of Kentucky Outer Bluegrass and Pennyrile TR], KY 55, Prestonville, 1/08/87, C, 87000151

Turpin House, Butler State Park off 11th St., Carrollton, 12/02/77, C, 77000606

Carter County

Carter Caves Pictograph (15CR60) [Prehistoric Rock Art Sites in Kentucky MPS], Address Restricted, Olive Hill vicinity, 9/08/89, A, C, D, a, 89001178

Kitchen, Van, House, S of Grayson off KY 7, Grayson vicinity, 5/02/74, A, C, b, 74000857

Olive Hill C & O Depot, Railroad St. S side, W of jct. with Plum St., Olive Hill, 10/29/92, A, C, 92001487

Casey County

Casey County Courthouse, Courthouse Sq., Liberty, 8/29/77, C, 77000607

Christian County

Alumni—Latham—Mooreland Historic District [Christian County MRA], Alumni Ave., Latham Ave. and Mooreland Dr., Hopkinsville, 7/22/93, C, 93000696

Beverly School [Christian County MRA], Off SR 107, Hopkinsville vicinity, 4/30/79, A, 79003624

Blue Lantern Farm [Christian County MRA], US 68, Hopkinsville vicinity, 4/30/79, C, 79003626

Boatright House [Christian County MRA], Off US 41, Hopkinsville, 4/30/79, C, 79003611

Bradshaw House [Christian County MRA], Off SR 107, Hopkinsville vicinity, 4/30/79, B, C, 79003623

Campbell House [Christian County MRA], Jct. of SR 272 and 164, Hopkinsville vicinity, 4/30/79, B, C, 79003627

Cedar Grove, E of Oak Grove off KY 115, Oak Grove vicinity, 11/17/77, B, C, 77000608

Church Hill Grange Hall [Christian County MRA], 5.5 mi. SW of Hopkinsville on Cox Mill Rd. (KY 695), Hopkinsville vicinity, 8/28/75, A, 75000744

Cox House [Christian County MRA], S of SR 272, Julien vicinity, 4/30/79, C, 79003615

Crockett, Judge Joseph, House, 317 E. 16th St., Hopkinsville, 4/03/79, B, C, 79000968

Dalton Brick Company [Christian County MRA], 2108 S. Main, Hopkinsville, 4/30/79, C, 79003606

Dalton, Monroe, House [Christian County MRA], 713 E. 7th St., Hopkinsville, 2/10/83, C, 83002624

East 7th Street Historic District [Christian County MRA], Roughly bounded by E. 7th St. from Campbell to Belmont Sts., Hopkinsville, 9/07/83, A, C, 83000561

Elk Grove Farm [Christian County MRA], Off US 41A, Hopkinsville vicinity, 4/30/79, C, 79003613

Elliott Place [Christian County MRA], N of Lafayette Rd., Lafayette vicinity, 4/30/79, C, 79003617

Fairelond [Christian County MRA], 1303 E. 7th St., Hopkinsville, 9/07/83, B, C, 83000562

Freeman Chapel C.M.E. Church [Christian County MRA], 137 S. Virginia St., Hopkinsville, 5/26/83, A, C, a, 83000563

French, Simon, House [Christian County MRA], Carter Rd., S of Barkers Mill, Hensleytown vicinity, 4/30/79, B, C, 79003622

Gary, John C., House [Christian County MRA], Gary Lane, S of SR 695, Hopkinsville vicinity, 4/30/79, B, C, 79003629

Genoa [Christian County MRA], Palmyra Rd., Howel vicinity, 4/30/79, B, C, 79003619

Glen Burnie [Christian County MRA], Bumpus Mill Rd., Hopkinsville vicinity, 4/30/79, B, C, 79003618

Grace Episcopal Church, 220 E. 6th St., Hopkinsville, 1/28/82, C, a, 82002679

Higgins, E. H., House [Christian County MRA], 1530 E. 7th St., Hopkinsville, 1/03/84, C, 84001403

Hopkinsville Commercial Historic District [Christian County MRA], Roughly bounded by L&N RR, 10th, 5th and Bethel Sts., Hopkinsville, 4/30/79, A, C, 79003633

Hopkinsville L & N Railroad Depot, 425 E. 9th St., Hopkinsville, 8/01/75, C, 75000745

Hopkinsville Residential Historic District [Christian County MRA], Roughly bounded by 14th, 20th, Main and Virginia Sts., Hopkinsville, 4/30/79, A, C, 79003631

Hopkinsville Residential Historic District (Boundary Increase) [Christian County MPS], SW corner of Main and 13th Sts., Hopkinsville, 8/15/90, C, a, 90001203

Hopkinsville Warehouse Historic District [Christian County MRA], Roughly along Harrison St. and RR tracks from 2nd to 21st Sts., Hopkinsville, 4/30/79, A, B, C, 79003632

Hopper Court [Christian County MRA], Hopper Ct., Hopkinsville, 4/30/79, B, C, 79003605

Knight, J. B., House [Christian County MRA], 1417 E. 7th St., Hopkinsville, 4/30/79, C, 79003607

Lafayette Methodist Church [Christian County MRA], Off SR 107, Lafayette, 4/30/79, C, a, 79003616

Maplewood [Christian County MRA], Off Mason Lane, Pembroke vicinity, 4/30/79, B, C, 79003625

McClellen House [Christian County MRA], SR 508, Honey Grove vicinity, 4/30/79, B, C, 79003621

McRay Site (15CH139), Address Restricted, Hopkinsville vicinity, 2/03/83, D, d, 83002625

Oakland/Henry House [Christian County MRA], SR 164, Hopkinsville vicinity, 4/30/79, B, C, 79003628

Pilot Rock Petroglyphs (15CH200) [Prehistoric Rock Art Sites in Kentucky MPS], Address Restricted, Hopkinsville vicinity, 9/08/89, A, C, D, a, 89001179

Poston House [Christian County MRA], 809 Hayes St., Hopkinsville, 4/30/79, B, 79003608

Rich Grove [Christian County MRA], Off SR 109, N of Hwy. 1027, Hopkinsville vicinity, 4/30/79, B, C, 79003610

Ritter House [Christian County MRA], Off US 41A, Hopkinsville, 4/30/79, B, C, 79003609

Smokehouse on Riverside Creek [Early Stone Buildings of Kentucky Outer Bluegrass and Pennyrile TR], Petsch Ln. off KY 272, Hopkinsville vicinity, 1/08/87, C, 87000166

Stewart, Dr. Edward S., House [Christian County MRA], US 68, Fairview, 4/30/79, B, C, 79003620

Walker, E. W., House [Christian County MRA], 1414 E. 7th St., Hopkinsville, 9/07/83, B, C, 83000564

Western Lunatic Asylum [Christian County MRA], US 68, Hopkinsville vicinity, 4/30/79, A, 79003612

Woodlawn [Christian County MRA], Off US 41A, Hopkinsville vicinity, 4/30/79, C, 79003614

Yost, Frank K., House [Christian County MRA], 1131 E. 7th St., Hopkinsville, 9/07/83, A, C, 83000565

Clark County

Antioch Christian Church [Clark County MRA], Off Muddy Creek Rd. at Four Mile Creek and Stone Branch, Winchester vicinity, 8/01/79, C, 79003566

Boot Hill Farm, Athens-Boonesboro Pike, Rt. 7, Athens vicinity, 3/01/85, A, B, g, 85000374

Brock House [Clark County MRA], Off Red River Rd., Bloomingdale vicinity, 8/01/79, C, 79003567

Brown-Proctoria Hotel, Main St. and Lexington Ave., Winchester, 7/29/77, A, C, 77000609

Bush, Capt. Robert V., House [Clark County MRA], Combs Ferry Rd., Becknerville vicinity, 8/01/79, B, C, 79003568

Bush-Dykes, W., House [Clark County MRA], US 227, Forest Grove vicinity, 8/01/79, B, C, 79003569

Bybee House [Clark County MRA], Bybee Rd., Winchester vicinity, 8/01/79, C, 79003570

Calmes, Henry W., House [Clark County MRA], US 227, Winchester vicinity, 8/01/79, B, C, 79003571

Chiles, Tarleton, House [Clark County MRA], Jones Nursery Rd., Becknerville vicinity, 8/01/79, C, 79003598

Clark County Courthouse, Main St., Winchester, 8/07/74, B, C, 74000858

Clark, Gov. James A., Mansion, Burns Ave. and Belmont St., Winchester, 6/13/74, B, C, 74000859

Clinkenbeard, William, House [Clark County MRA], Old Paris Pike, Winchester, 11/20/80, B, C, 80001497

Colby Tavern [Clark County MRA], Jct. of Colby and Becknerville Rds., Winchester vicinity, 8/01/79, C, 79003572

Couchman House [Clark County MRA], Off Old Boonesboro Rd., Winchester vicinity, 8/01/79, B, C, 79003573

Cullom, Frances, Jr., House [Clark County MRA], Muddy Creek Rd., Winchester vicinity, 8/01/79, B, C, 79003574

Elkin House [Clark County MRA], Off US 227, Winchester vicinity, 8/01/79, A, C, 79003576

Eubank, Achilles, House [Clark County MRA], Elkin Rd., Winchester vicinity, 8/01/79, B, C, 79003577

Fishback, Jesse, House [Clark County MRA], Off Combs Ferry Rd., Becknerville vicinity, 8/01/79, B, C, 79003578

Gibbs, John, House [Clark County MRA], Fox-Quisenberry Rd., Pilotview vicinity, 8/01/79, C, 79003580

Gist, David, House [Clark County MRA], Stoner Rd., Winchester vicinity, 8/01/79, B, C, 79003581

Goff, Strauder, House [Clark County MRA], Off Van Meter Rd., Winchester vicinity, 8/01/79, B, C, 79003582

Goshen Primitive Baptist Church [Clark County MRA], Goshen Rd., Winchester vicinity, 8/01/79, A, a, 79003583

Haggard, Nathaniel, House [Clark County MRA], Off New Boonesborough Rd., Winchester vicinity, 8/01/79, B, C, 79003584

Hampton, Jesse, House [Clark County MRA], Bybee Rd., Winchester vicinity, 8/01/79, C, 79003585

Clark County—Continued

Hart, Gen. Thomas, House [Clark County MRA], Ecton Rd., Winchester vicinity, 8/01/79, B, C, 79003586

Hickman, William, House, 31 W. Hickman St., Winchester, 11/24/82, A, C, 82001554

Hodgkins House [Clark County MRA], Old Boonesborough Rd., Winchester vicinity, 8/01/79, C, 79003587

Holliday, Dailey-Milton, House [Clark County MRA], Jones Nursery Rd., Becknerville vicinity, 8/01/79, C, 79003575

Hollywood Springs [Clark County MRA], Off Kiddville Rd., Kiddville vicinity, 8/01/79, C, 79003588

Indian Fort Earthworks (15CK7), Address Restricted, Goffs Corners vicinity, 11/14/85, D, 85002823

Lampton House [Clark County MRA], Muddy Creek Rd., Winchester vicinity, 8/01/79, C, 79003589

Lewis, Alpheus, House [Clark County MRA], Off Wades Mill Rd., Winchester vicinity, 8/01/79, A, B, C, 79003590

Martin House [Clark County MRA], On Lower Howard's Creek, Hootentown vicinity, 8/01/79, B, C, 79003591

Martin, Maj. John, House [Clark County MRA], Basin Springs Rd., Pine Grove vicinity, 4/29/82, B, C, 82002680

Martin-Holder-Bush-Hampton Mill [Clark County MRA], Address Restricted, Winchester vicinity, 11/20/80, D, 80001498

Mound Hill Archeological Site, Address Restricted, Winchester vicinity, 8/25/78, D, 78001308

Parrish Place [Clark County MRA], Todd-Colby Rd., Pine Grove vicinity, 8/01/79, C, 79003592

Pendleton, Col. Edmund, House [Clark County MRA], Van Meter Rd., Clintonville vicinity, 8/01/79, C, 79003593

Preston, Maj. Walter, House [Clark County MRA], Basin Springs Rd., Becknerville vicinity, 8/01/79, C, 79003594

Providence Baptist Church, 6 mi. SW of Winchester off KY 627, Winchester vicinity, 5/13/76, A, C, a, e, 76000864

Pruett, W., House [Clark County MRA], Ecton Rd., Winchester, 11/20/80, C, 80001499

Quisenberry, J., House [Clark County MRA], Quisenberry Rd., Forest Grove vicinity, 8/01/79, B, C, 79003596

Quisenberry, Joel, House [Clark County MRA], Flanagan Station Rd., Winchester vicinity, 8/01/79, C, 79003595

Redmond House [Clark County MRA], Off US 60, Winchester vicinity, 8/01/79, C, 79003597

Scobee, Robert, House [Clark County MRA], Off SR 60, Winchester, 11/20/80, B, C, 80001500

Springhill, N of Winchester on Colby Rd., Winchester vicinity, 2/17/78, B, C, 78001309

Stipp House [Clark County MRA], Van Meter Rd., Winchester, 11/20/80, C, 80001501

Taylor, F., Mill [Clark County MRA], Address Restricted, Winchester vicinity, 11/20/80, D, 80001502

Taylor, William, House [Clark County MRA], Lower Howard's Creek, Becknerville vicinity, 8/01/79, A, C, 79003600

Tebbs, Stanley F., House [Clark County MRA], Todd's Rd., Pine Grove vicinity, 8/01/79, C, 79003579

Thomson Neighborhood District, Roughly bounded by S. Main St., Moundale Ave., Boone Ave., S. Maple St. and W. Hickman St., Winchester, 1/17/92, A, 91001925

Van Meter Distillery [Clark County MRA], Van Meter Rd., Winchester vicinity, 8/01/79, B, 79003599

Vinewood, 4 mi. NE of Winchester on U.S. 60, Winchester vicinity, 8/12/77, B, C, 77000610

Wade Farmstead [Clark County MRA], Donaldson Rd., Winchester vicinity, 8/01/79, C, 79003601

Winchester Downtown Commercial District, Roughly bounded by RR tracks, KY 627, Maple and Highland Sts., Winchester, 4/28/82, A, C, 82002681

Clay County

Fish Trap Rock Petroglyphs (15CY53) [Prehistoric Rock Art Sites in Kentucky MPS], Address Restricted, Eriline vicinity, 9/08/89, A, C, D, a, 89001181

Red Bird River Petroglyph (15CY51) [Prehistoric Rock Art Sites in Kentucky MPS], Address Restricted, Eriline vicinity, 9/08/89, A, C, D, a, 89001182

Red Bird River Shelter Petroglyphs (15CY52) [Prehistoric Rock Art Sites in Kentucky MPS], Address Restricted, Eriline vicinity, 9/08/89, A, C, D, a, 89001183

Sullen Possum Site, Address Restricted, Oneida vicinity, 10/06/93, D, 93000996

Crittenden County

Fohs Hall, 143 N. Walker St., Marion, 4/29/82, A, C, 82002682

Frances School Gymnasium [New Deal Era Construction in Kentucky MRA], 100 Elementary Cir., Marion, 3/01/93, A, 93000046

Cumberland County

Marrowbone Historic District, KY 90, Marrowbone, 7/28/83, A, C, a, 83004048

Daviess County

Archeological Site 15 Da 39, Address Restricted, Maceo vicinity, 12/22/78, D, 78001310

Bogard, D. D., House, 303 E. 4th St., Owensboro, 5/22/80, C, 80001503

Breidenbach Building [Owensboro MRA], 208 W. Third St., Owensboro, 3/28/86, C, 86000660

Callas Sweet Shop [Owensboro MRA], 420 Frederica Ave., Owensboro, 3/28/86, C, 86000661

Carnegie Free Public Library (DAOB 41) [Owensboro MRA], 901 Frederica Ave., Owensboro, 8/06/86, C, 86002234

Clements, Le Vega, House [Owensboro MRA], 1500 N. Highland Ave., Owensboro, 3/28/86, C, 86000663

Davis, Howell J., House, 3301 Veach Rd., Owensboro, 8/03/90, C, 90001168

Doctors' Row Historic District [Owensboro MRA], W. Fourth St. between Frederica and Saint Ann Sts., Owensboro, 3/28/86, A, C, 86000662

Federal Building and US Post Office—Owensboro [Owensboro MRA], 5th and Frederica, Owensboro, 4/13/89, C, 89000295

Gillim House [Owensboro MRA], 517 Frederica St., Owensboro, 3/28/86, C, 86000664

Grimes, Felix, House, 1301 Leitchfield Rd., Owensboro, 6/18/75, C, 75000746

Haphazard, Pleasant Valley Rd., Owensboro, 8/22/75, B, C, 75000747

McKay-Thornberry House, S. Hampton Rd., Owensboro vicinity, 5/03/84, C, 84001408

Medley House, 1220 Frederica St., Owensboro, 2/20/80, A, C, 80001504

Mischel, George and Sons, Building [Owensboro MRA], 412 E. Second St., Owensboro, 3/28/86, C, 86000756

Monarch-Payne House [Owensboro MRA], 1432 E. Fourth St., Owensboro, 3/28/86, C, 86000757

Moore, J. Z., Historic District [Owensboro MRA], Roughly bounded by W. and E. Twelfth, Daviess, E. and W. Fourteenth, and Saint Ann Sts., Owensboro, 3/28/86, C, 86000659

Moorman House, 2731 W. Second St., Owensboro, 3/27/92, C, 92000140

Mount St. Joseph Academy, KY 56, St. Joseph, 1/25/79, B, C, a, 79000970

Odd Fellows Building [Owensboro MRA], 200–204 W. Third St., Owensboro, 3/28/86, C, 86000758

Owensboro Historic Commerical District, 2nd St. between St. Ann and Lewis Sts., Owensboro, 1/12/83, A, C, 83002626

Phillip's Court District [Owensboro MRA], Roughly bounded by Technical High School, Cruze Dr., W. Eighteenth St., and Frederica Ave., Owensboro, 3/28/86, C, 86000658

Riley, Camden, House [Owensboro MRA], 112 E. Fourth St., Owensboro, 3/28/86, C, 86000760

Smith, Maj. Hampden, House, 909 Frederica St., Owensboro, 9/28/76, A, C, 76000865

St. Joseph Church, 4th and Clay Sts., Owensboro, 11/03/83, A, C, 83003651

Sweeney, James J., House, 121 E. 5th St., Owensboro, 8/11/80, C, 80001505

Temple Adath Israel [Owensboro MRA], 429 Daviess St., Owensboro, 3/28/86, A, C, a, 86000761

Trinity Episcopal Church, 403 W. 5th St., Owensboro, 4/10/72, A, C, a, 72000530

Daviess County—Continued

Union Station, 1039 Frederica St., Owensboro, 8/01/79, A, C, 79000969

Willow Hill, Jones Rd., Owensboro vicinity, 6/09/82, C, 82004621

Yewell House [Owensboro MRA], 630 Clay St., Owensboro, 3/28/86, C, 86000762

Edmonson County

Asphalt Rock Pictographs (15ED24) [Prehistoric Rock Art Sites in Kentucky MPS], Address Restricted, Asphalt vicinity, 9/08/89, A, C, D, a, 89001185

Bransford Spring Pumphouse [Mammoth Cave National Park MPS], Mammoth Cave National Park, Mammoth Cave, 5/08/91, A, NPS, 91000493

Colossal Cavern Entrance [Mammoth Cave National Park MPS], Mammoth Cave National Park, Mammoth Cave, 5/08/91, A, NPS, 91000491

Crystal Cave District [Mammoth Cave National Park MPS], Mammoth Cave National Park, Mammoth Cave, 5/08/91, A, B, NPS, 91000500

Dismal Rock Shelter Petroglyphs (15ED15) [Prehistoric Rock Art Sites in Kentucky MPS], Address Restricted, Sweeden vicinity, 9/08/89, A, C, D, a, 89001184

Ford, William, House, S of Brownsville on U.S. 31W, Brownsville vicinity, 11/28/80, B, C, 80001506

Good Spring Baptist Church and Cemetery [Mammoth Cave National Park MPS], Mammoth Cave National Park, Mammoth Cave, 5/08/91, A, a, NPS, 91000498

Great Onyx Cave Entrance [Mammoth Cave National Park MPS], Mammoth Cave National Park, Mammoth Cave, 5/08/91, A, NPS, 91000490

Hercules and Coach No. 2, Off KY 70 in Mammoth Cave National Park, Mammoth Cave, 10/10/75, A, C, NPS, 75000160

Joppa Baptist Church and Cemetery [Mammoth Cave National Park MPS], Mammoth Cave National Park, Mammoth Cave, 5/08/91, A, a, NPS, 91000496

Maintenance Area District [Mammoth Cave National Park MPS], Mammoth Cave National Park, Mammoth Cave, 5/08/91, A, NPS, 91000501

Mammoth Cave Baptist Church and Cemetery [Mammoth Cave National Park MPS], Mammoth Cave National Park, Mammoth Cave, 5/08/91, A, a, NPS, 91000497

Mammoth Cave Historic District [Mammoth Cave National Park MPS], Mammoth Cave National Park, Mammoth Cave, 5/08/91, A, NPS, 91000503

Maple Springs Ranger Station [Mammoth Cave National Park MPS], Mammoth Cave National Park, Mammoth Cave, 5/08/91, A, g, NPS, 91000494

Mill Hole Farm, W of Park City off U.S. 31W, Park City vicinity, 5/22/78, C, D, 78001311

Old Guide Cemetery [Mammoth Cave National Park MPS], Mammoth Cave National Park, Mammoth Cave, 5/08/91, A, d, NPS, 91000499

Reed—Dorsey House, Upper Main Cross and Jefferson Sts., Brownsville, 10/16/86, C, 86002866

Residential Area District [Mammoth Cave National Park MPS], Mammoth Cave National Park, Mammoth Cave, 5/08/91, A, NPS, 91000502

Superintendent's House [Mammoth Cave National Park MPS], Mammoth Cave National Park, Mammoth Cave, 5/08/91, A, g, NPS, 91000495

Three Springs Pumphouse [Mammoth Cave National Park MPS], Mammoth Cave National Park, Mammoth Cave, 5/08/91, A, NPS, 91000492

Willis, Mathias, Store House [Early Stone Buildings of Kentucky Outer Bluegrass and Pennyrile TR], Cummins Rd., Windyville vicinity, 1/08/87, D, 87000172

Elliott County

Conley—Greene Rockshelter (15EL4), Address Restricted, Lytten vicinity, 5/08/86, D, 86001012

Estill County

Ashley Petroglyphs (15ES27) [Prehistoric Rock Art Sites in Kentucky MPS], Address Restricted, Furnace vicinity, 9/08/89, A, C, D, a, 89001186

Cottage Iron Furnace, 7 mi. NE of Irvine in Daniel Boone National Forest, Irvine vicinity, 9/20/73, A, 73000794

Red River Iron Furnace, KY 975, in Daniel Boone National Forest, Fitchburg, 5/17/74, A, D, 74000860

Riverview Hotel, Main St., Irvine, 4/03/92, A, 92000171

Sparks Indian Rock House Petroglyphs (15ES26) [Prehistoric Rock Art Sites in Kentucky MPS], Address Restricted, Lexington vicinity, 9/08/89, A, C, D, a, 89001187

Fayette County

Allen, James House, 1020 Lane Allen Rd., Lexington, 12/30/82, B, 82001564

Ashland, 2 mi. SE of Lexington on Richmond Rd., Lexington, 10/15/66, B, e, NHL, 66000357

Ashland Park Historic District, Roughly bounded by S. Hanover Ave., Richmond Rd., Woodspoint Rd., and Fontaine Rd. and E. High St., Lexington, 3/31/86, C, 86000755

Athens Historic District, Athens-Boonesboro Pike, Athens, 10/11/79, A, C, b, 79000971

Barton, Abraham, House, 200 N. Upper St., Lexington, 8/26/77, B, 77000611

Basye, T. D., House, 3501 Georgetown Rd., Lexington vicinity, 10/22/87, C, b, 87001886

Bates Log House, 5143 Spurr Rd., Lexington, 8/26/82, C, 82002683

Beck, James Burnie, House, 209 E. High St., Lexington, 8/26/82, B, C, 82002684

Bell Court Neighborhood Historic District, Roughly bounded by RR tracks, Main St., Boonesboro and Walton Aves., Lexington, 12/08/80, C, a, 80001507

Bell Place, Sayre Ave., Lexington, 2/17/78, B, C, 78001312

Bell, John, House [Early Stone Buildings of Central Kentucky TR], SR 1978, Lexington vicinity, 6/23/83, C, 83002757

Botherum, 341 Madison Pl., Lexington, 3/07/73, B, C, 73000795

Bowman Houses, W of Lexington on Bowman's Mill Rd., Lexington vicinity, 8/09/79, A, C, 79000973

Brand-Barrow House, 203 E. 4th St., Lexington, 8/11/76, A, C, 76000866

Brown, Joshua, House, 2705 Tates Creek Rd., Lexington, 12/27/79, B, C, 79000974

Buenna Hill [Innes Houses of Fayette County TR], Off Ferguson Rd., Centerville vicinity, 6/29/83, C, 83002758

Burrier, John, House [Early Stone Buildings of Central Kentucky TR], SR 1966, Lexington vicinity, 6/23/83, A, C, 83002759

Cave Place, W of Lexington, Lexington vicinity, 12/05/80, C, 80001508

Cave Spring, SE of Lexington off US 25, Lexington vicinity, 12/22/78, A, C, 78001313

Central Christian Church, 207 E. Short St., Lexington, 9/11/79, A, C, 79000975

Chandler Normal School Building and Webster Hall, 548 Georgetown St., Lexington, 12/04/80, A, C, a, 80001509

Christ Church Episcopal, Church and Market Sts., Lexington, 10/21/76, A, C, a, 76000867

Clark Hardware Company Building, 367–369 W. Short St. and 142 N. Broadway, Lexington, 7/16/79, C, 79000976

Clark, John, House, Tates Creek Pk., Lexington, 11/25/80, C, 80001510

Clay, Henry, Law Office, 176 N. Mill St., Lexington, 3/11/71, B, C, 71000340

Cleveland-Rogers House, SE of Lexington at 8151 Richmond Rd., Lexington, 8/26/80, C, 80001511

Cloud House, 3740 Versailles Rd., Lexington, 6/17/82, C, 82002685

Conant, William, House, 1701 Elkchester Rd., Lexington, 2/22/91, C, 91000123

Constitution Historic District, Roughly bounded by E. 3rd., Limestone, Walnut and Pleasant Stone Sts., Lexington, 8/30/82, B, C, a, 82002686

Corinthia [Innes Houses of Fayette County TR], Off Lemons Mill Rd., Centerville vicinity, 6/29/83, C, 83002760

DeLong Agricultural Implements Warehouse, Patterson St., Lexington, 11/25/80, A, C, 80001512

Delta, S of Lexington at 2450 Armstrong Mill Rd., Lexington vicinity, 8/10/78, A, C, 78001314

Fayette County—Continued

Downtown Commercial District, Roughly bounded by Main, Church, Walnut Sts., and Broadway, Lexington, 8/25/83, A, C, 83000559

Elam Mound Archeological Site, Address Restricted, Lexington vicinity, 10/10/75, D, 75000749

Elley Villa, 320 Linden Walk, Lexington, 1/09/78, B, C, 78001315

Elsmere Park Historic District, Off N. Broadway, between W. 6th and 7th Sts., Lexington, 4/26/76, A, C, 76000868

Episcopal Burying Ground and Chapel, 251 E. 3rd St., Lexington, 6/24/76, A, C, a, d, 76000869

Fairlawn, 6 mi. NE of Lexington on U.S. 68, Lexington vicinity, 10/14/76, B, C, 76000870

Fayette National Bank Building, 159-167 W. Main St., Lexington, 2/27/80, C, 80001513

Fayette Safety Vault and Trust Company Building, 111-113 Cheapside St., Lexington, 8/11/80, A, C, 80001514

Featherston, Edmonson and Clark Houses, 218, 226 and 232 E. Maxwell St., Lexington, 7/21/83, C, 83002761

First African Baptist Church, 264–272 E. Short St., Lexington, 4/24/86, A, C, a, 86000854

First Presbyterian Church, 174 N. Mill St., Lexington, 12/30/74, A, C, a, 74000861

Floral Hall, 847 S. Broadway, Lexington, 8/29/77, A, C, 77000612

Grant, George W., House, 519 W. 4th St., Lexington, 10/24/80, A, 80001515

Gratz Park Historic District, Bounded by 2nd and 3rd Sts., the Byway, and Bark Alley, Lexington, 3/14/73, A, C, 73000796

Grimes House and Mill Complex, Grimes Mill Rd., Lexington vicinity, 6/21/82, A, C, 82002687

Guilfoil Village Site (15FA176), Address Restricted, Athens vicinity, 12/05/85, D, 85003063

Hartland, 2230 Armstrong Mill Rd., Lexington, 4/02/87, C, 87000568

Hayes, Samuel T., House, NE of Lexington on Sulphur Well Rd., Lexington vicinity, 3/19/80, C, 80001516

Headley, George, House, 4435 Old Frankfort Pike, Lexington vicinity, 3/04/91, C, 91000122

Helm Place, SW of Lexington on Bowman Mill Rd., Lexington vicinity, 8/03/78, B, C, 78001318

Higgins Block, 145–151 W. Main St., Lexington, 8/12/77, C, 77000613

Highland Hall, 6208 Richmond Rd., Lexington, 12/16/77, C, 77000614

Hurricane Hall, N of Lexington off U.S. 25, Lexington vicinity, 4/22/76, C, 76000871

Innes House [Innes Houses of Fayette County TR], Off Lemons Mill Rd., Centerville vicinity, 6/29/83, C, 83002762

January, Thomas, House, 437 W. 2nd St., Lexington, 12/27/74, A, C, a, 74000862

Keeneland—Keeneland Racetrack, Off Versailles and Rice Rds., Lexington, 9/24/86, A, B, g, NHL, 86003487

Kennedy, Matthew, House, 216 N. Limestone St., Lexington, 6/19/73, C, 73000797

Kinkead House, 362 Walnut St., Lexington, 6/29/82, B, 82002688

Kinkead, Henry P., House, 403 Walnut St., Lexington, 7/12/84, C, 84001411

Lemon Hill, E of Lexington off U.S. 60, Lexington vicinity, 11/20/78, C, 78001319

Lemon, James, Houses, 329–331 S. Mill St., Lexington, 11/21/74, C, 74000863

Lewis Manor, NW of Lexington on Viley Rd., Lexington vicinity, 4/26/76, B, C, 76000872

Lexington Cemetery and Henry Clay Monument, 833 W. Main St., Lexington, 7/12/76, A, d, 76000873

Lexington City National Bank Building, 259-265 W. Main St., Lexington, 4/01/80, A, C, 80001517

Lexington Dry Goods Company Building, 249–251 E. Main St., Lexington, 5/31/88, A, C, 88000182

Lexington Herald Building, 121 Walnut St., Lexington, 10/29/82, C, 82001565

Lexington-Fayette County Government Building Block, 200-228 E. Main St., Lexington, 5/19/83, A, C, 83002763

Lincoln, Mary Todd, House, 574 W. Main St., Lexington, 8/12/71, A, 71000341

Loudoun House, Corner of Bryan Ave. and Castlewood Dr., Lexington, 2/06/73, C, 73000798

Mansfield, Richmond Rd., Lexington, 8/19/82, C, 82002689

Maxwell Place, Rose St., University of Kentucky, Lexington, 10/29/82, B, C, 82000472

McAdams and Morford Building, 200–210 W. Main St., Lexington, 10/25/73, A, C, 73000799

McCann, Benjamin, House, Old Richmond Pike, Lexington vicinity, 6/03/82, B, C, 82002690

McCann, Neal, House, 5364 Todds Rd., Lexington vicinity, 6/03/82, C, 82002691

McCauley, John, House, 319 Lexington Ave., Lexington, 12/04/80, A, C, a, 80001518

McConnell Springs, Address Restricted, Lexington vicinity, 1/17/76, A, D, 76000874

McConnell, James, House [Early Stone Buildings of Central Kentucky TR], Old Frankfort Pike, Lexington, 6/23/83, A, C, 83002764

McConnell, William, House [Early Stone Buildings of Central Kentucky TR], Forbes Rd., Lexington vicinity, 6/23/83, A, C, 83002765

McCracken-Wilgus House, 327 Wilgus St., Lexington, 12/22/78, A, C, 78001320

McGarvey, Dr. John, House, 362 S. Mill St., Lexington, 5/15/74, A, C, 74000864

McPheeters, Charles, House, 352 S. Mill St., Lexington, 5/15/74, C, 74000865

Mentelle Park, Mentelle Pk., Lexington, 11/27/85, C, 85002973

Miller Brothers Building, 359-361 W. Main St., Lexington, 4/02/80, A, C, 80001519

Monsieur Giron's Confectionary, 125 N. Mill St., Lexington, 12/27/74, A, C, 74000866

Moore-Redd-Frazer House, Georgetown Pike, Lexington, 10/21/76, B, C, 76000875

Morton, Will, Tavern Stand, 137 S. Limestone St., Lexington, 1/03/78, B, 78001321

Morton, William, House, 518 Limestone St., Lexington, 6/10/75, B, C, 75000750

Mt. Horeb Earthworks, Unit A, Address Restricted, Lexington vicinity, 10/10/75, D, 75000751

North Broadway-Short Street Historic District, N. Broadway and W. Short St., Lexington, 9/15/83, A, C, g, 83000560

North Limestone Commercial District, N. Limestone St. between Church and 3rd Sts., Lexington, 11/03/83, A, C, 83003652

Northeast Residential Historic District, Roughly bounded by E. Fifth St., Kleiser Ave. and Campsie Pl., E. Fourth St., and Humbard Alley, Lexington, 10/17/85, C, 85003151

Northside Historic Residential District, Roughly bounded by RR tracks, N. Limestone, W. Short and Newtown Sts., Lexington, 8/28/79, A, C, 79000977

Northside Residential Historic District (Boundary Increase), 337–371 N. Limestone, 400–465 N. Limestone, and 356 Morris St., Lexington, 5/24/82, C, 82002692

O'Neal, Lewis, Tavern [Early Stone Buildings of Central Kentucky TR], Off U.S. 60, Versailles vicinity, 6/23/83, A, C, 83002766

Odd Fellows Temple, 115-119 W. Main St., Lexington, 2/27/80, C, 80001520

Old Morrison, Transylvania College, W. 3rd St. between Upper St. and Broadway, Lexington, 10/15/66, A, e, NHL, 66000358

Opera House and Yates Bookshop Building, 141 and 145 N. Broadway, Lexington, 6/11/75, A, C, 75000752

Payne, Henry, House [Early Stone Buildings of Central Kentucky TR], Off U.S. 421, Lexington vicinity, 6/23/83, C, 83002767

Pettit's, James, Mill [Early Stone Buildings of Central Kentucky TR], KY 418, Ford vicinity, 6/23/83, A, C, 83002768

Poindexter, William, House, 359 S. Mill St., Lexington, 5/15/74, A, B, C, a, 74000867

Poplar Grove, 2088 Parkers Mill Rd., Lexington, 8/19/82, C, 82002693

Price, Pugh, House, 2245 Liberty Rd., Lexington, 9/25/79, B, C, 79000978

Price, Williamson, House, 2497 Liberty Rd., Lexington, 9/25/79, B, C, 79000979

Ramsey, Lewis, Jr., House, 3797 Old Frankfort Pike, Lexington vicinity, 3/06/91, C, 91000121

Randall Building Bogaert's Jewelry Store, 127–129 W. Main St., Lexington, 9/09/82, B, C, 82002694

Redd Road Rural Historic District, Area largely S and E of jct. of Redd Rd. and Frankfort Rd., Lexington vicinity, 2/28/91, A, C, 91000153

Ridgely House, 190 Market St., Lexington, 5/07/73, A, B, C, a, 73000800

Rogers, Joseph Hale, House, E of Lexington on Bryan Station Pike, Lexington vicinity, 11/15/79, B, C, 79000980

Rose Hill, 461 N. Limestone St., Lexington, 12/30/74, B, C, 74000868

Russel, Robert, House [Early Stone Buildings of Central Kentucky TR], Off KY 353, Centerville vicinity, 6/23/83, A, C, 83002769

Sayre Female Institute, 194 N. Limestone St., Lexington, 8/19/82, B, C, 82002695

Scott and Wilson Houses District, 324, 328, 330, 336 S. Mill St., Lexington, 12/31/74, A, C, 74000869

Fayette County—Continued

Second Presbyterian Church, 460 E. Main St., Lexington, 8/11/80, C, a, 80001522

Shady Side, 4 mi. E of Lexington on U.S. 68, Lexington vicinity, 11/07/76, B, C, 76000876

Shelby Family Houses, SE of Lexington on Richmond Rd., Shelby Lane, and Jacks Creek Pike, Lexington vicinity, 11/17/78, A, C, 78001322

Shryack, Frederick, House [Early Stone Buildings of Central Kentucky TR], Off KY 859, Clintonville vicinity, 6/23/83, C, 83002770

Smith, Mitchell Baker, Company Building, 230-232 W. Main St., Lexington, 8/26/80, C, 80001523

South Hill Historic District, Roughly bounded by S. Broadway, W. High, S. Limestone, and Pine Sts., Lexington, 6/13/78, C, 78001323

Southeast Lexington Residential and Commercial District, Roughly bounded by High St., Rose Lane, Lexington and Woodland Aves., Lexington, 8/01/84, C, 84001415

Southern Railway Passenger Depot, 701 S. Broadway, Lexington, 8/13/87, A, C, 87001364

Spring Hill Farm, 1401 Old Frankfort Pike, Lexington, 2/17/78, B, C, 78001324

Steele, Drewsilla, House, 3951 Old Frankfort Pike, Lexington vicinity, 2/22/91, C, 91000120

Stony Point, 4935 Parkers Mill Rd., Lexington, 8/07/79, B, C, 79000981

Todd, William Lytle, House, W of Lexington at 3725 Bowman Mill, Lexington vicinity, 7/17/79, C, 79000982

Trotter's Warehouse, 122–124 S. Mill St., Lexington, 6/18/76, A, 76000877

Victorian Commercial Block, Bounded by Broadway, Main, Short, and Spring Sts., Lexington, 7/21/78, A, C, 78001325

Walnut Hill Presbyterian Church, E of Lexington off U.S. 25, Lexington vicinity, 5/07/73, A, C, a, 73000801

Warfield, Dr. Walter, Building, 122-124 N. Upper St. and 140-160 W. Short St., Lexington, 8/11/80, C, 80001524

Watkins, Thomas B., House, 1008 S. Broadway, Lexington, 6/29/82, C, 82002696

Watt, Henry, House, 703 W. High St., Lexington, 12/16/77, C, 77000615

Waveland, 5 mi. S of Lexington off U.S. 27, Lexington vicinity, 8/12/71, C, 71000342

West Fayette County Rural Historic District, Roughly bounded by Rice, Van Meter, Elk Chester, Yarnallton, Leestown and Viley Rds. and US 60, Lexington vicinity, 2/28/91, A, C, d, 91000154

West High Street Historic District, N side of 100–300 blocks of W. High St., Lexington, 7/10/69, C, 69000366

Western Suburb Historic District, Irregular pattern along W. Short St. from Saunter to KY 922, Lexington, 6/18/76, A, C, 76000878

Woodland, 1 mi. E of Lexington on Squires Rd. off U.S. 421, Lexington vicinity, 8/28/75, A, C, 75000753

Woodlands Historic District, Roughly bounded by Main and High Sts., Ashland and Woodland Aves., Lexington, 8/18/83, A, C, 83002771

Woodstock, Todds Rd., Lexington, 5/12/75, C, 75000754

Woodward Heights Neighborhood Historic District, Roughly bounded by High, Merino, and Pine Sts., Lexington, 12/01/80, C, 80001525

Worley, Allen, and Foushee Houses, 355, 361, and 367 S. Broadway, Lexington, 1/20/76, C, 76000879

Fleming County

Elizaville Presbyterian Church, KY 32, Elizaville, 6/17/77, B, C, a, 77000616

First Presbyterian Church, W. Main and W. Water Sts., Flemingsburg, 8/12/77, A, C, a, 77000617

Fleming, Thomas W., House, 114 W. Water St., Flemingsburg, 3/21/79, C, 79000983

Flemingsburg Historic District, Roughly bounded by Stockwell, Hunt, East Elm, Fox Springs, Mt. Sterling, Main Cross & Rhoades, Flemingsburg, 7/05/85, A, C, 85001479

Goddard Bridge, Maddox Rd. at KY 32, Goddard, 8/22/75, C, b, 75000756

Hillsboro Covered Bridge, S of Hillsboro on KY 111, Hillsboro vicinity, 3/26/76, C, 76000881

Johnson, Ben, House, KY 161, Flemingsburg Junction vicinity, 3/01/82, C, 82002697

Magowan, Abraham, House, Maddox Pike, Flemingsburg vicinity, 6/30/83, C, 83002772

Ringos Mill Covered Bridge, 13.7 mi. S of Flemingsburg on KY 158, Flemingsburg vicinity, 3/26/76, C, 76000880

Sousley, Franklin R., Birthplace, 4 mi. SW of Elizaville on KY 170, Elizaville vicinity, 12/31/74, B, C, g, 74000870

Floyd County

Callihan, G. D., House [Prestonsburg MPS], 105 W. Graham St., Prestonsburg, 5/18/89, C, 89000389

Combs, B. F., House [Prestonsburg MPS], 41 N. Arnold Ave., Prestonsburg, 5/18/89, C, 89000390

Fitzpatrick—Harmon House [Prestonsburg MPS], 102 E. Court St., Prestonsburg, 5/18/89, A, C, 89000388

Front Street Historic District [Prestonsburg MPS], Roughly Front St. between W. Court St. and Ford St., Prestonsburg, 5/18/89, A, C, 89000398

Harkins Law Office Building [Prestonsburg MPS], 1 S. Arnold Ave., Prestonsburg, 5/18/89, A, C, 89000395

Harkins, Joseph D., House [Prestonsburg MPS], 204 N. Arnold Ave., Prestonsburg, 5/18/89, C, 89000394

May, Samuel, House, 690 Northlake Dr., Prestonsburg, 4/01/80, B, C, 80001526

May—Fitzpatrick House [Prestonsburg MPS], 39 S. Arnold Ave., Prestonsburg, 5/18/89, C, 89000392

May—Latta House [Prestonsburg MPS], 33 N. Arnold Ave., Prestonsburg, 5/18/89, C, 89000393

Methodist Episcopal Church, South [Prestonsburg MPS], S. Arnold Ave. between Ford St. and W. Graham St., Prestonsburg, 5/18/89, C, a, 89000391

Middle Creek Battlefield, 3 mi. W of Prestonsburg at jct. of KY 114 and KY 404, Prestonsburg vicinity, 3/26/92, A, B, NHL, 91001665

Town Branch Bridge [Prestonsburg MPS], Co. Rd. 1334 over Levisa Fork, Prestonsburg, 5/18/89, A, C, 89000396

US Post Office—Prestonsburg [Prestonsburg MPS], Central Ave. and E. Court St., Prestonsburg, 5/18/89, C, 89000417

West Prestonsburg Bridge [Prestonsburg MPS], Over Levisa Fork between Prestonsburg and West Prestonsburg, Prestonsburg, 5/18/89, A, C, 89000397

Wheelwright Commercial District, Main St., Wheelwright, 11/19/80, A, g, 80001527

Franklin County

Allen, Col. R. T. P., House, S of Frankfort on Johnson Rd., Frankfort vicinity, 7/10/79, C, 79000984

Archeological Site 15 FR 368, Address Restricted, Frankfort vicinity, 9/12/85, C, D, 85002370

Archeological Site 15 Fr 26, Address Restricted, Harvieland vicinity, 3/31/78, D, 78001331

Archeological Site 15 Fr 34, Address Restricted, Frankfort vicinity, 2/17/78, D, 78001326

Archeological Site 15 Fr 52, Address Restricted, Harvieland vicinity, 2/14/78, D, 78001330

Arrowhead, US 60, 0.5 mi. S of Hanley Ln., Frankfort vicinity, 9/28/89, C, 89001597

Beeches, Off U.S. 421, Frankfort, 2/09/79, A, C, 79000985

Blanton-Crutcher Farm, 5 mi. SE of Frankfort off U.S. 60, Frankfort vicinity, 10/29/75, A, C, 75000757

Corner in Celebrities Historic District, Roughly bounded by Kentucky River on S and W, St. Clair and Main Sts., Frankfort, 3/11/71, A, C, 71000343

Dills Site, Address Restricted, Frankfort vicinity, 3/21/78, D, 78001327

Frankfort Barracks District, Bounded by New, Shelby, and Coke Sts., and Woodland Ave., Frankfort, 11/20/75, A, C, 75000758

Frankfort Cemetery and Chapel, 215 E. Main St., Frankfort, 7/12/74, A, C, d, 74000872

Frankfort Commercial Historic District, Both sides of Kentucky River at Bridge St., Frankfort, 5/10/79, A, C, 79000986

Giltner-Holt House, 5 mi. (8 km) N of Frankfort, Frankfort vicinity, 5/05/78, A, C, 78001328

Glen Willis, Leestown Pike, Frankfort, 6/13/72, B, C, 72000531

Gooch House, 104 2nd St., Frankfort, 4/30/80, C, 80001528

Franklin County—Continued

Haggin Farm [Early Stone Buildings of Central Kentucky TR], SR 1685, Midway vicinity, 6/23/83, C, 83002773

Hearn, Andrew, Log House and Farm, 3 mi. SW of Jett on Hanley Lane, Jett vicinity, 8/11/76, C, 76000886

Hume, E. E., Hall, Kentucky State University campus, Frankfort, 5/26/83, A, C, 83004050

Hutcherson Site, Address Restricted, Polsgrove vicinity, 3/21/78, D, 78001332

Jackson Hall, Kentucky State University, E. Main St., Frankfort, 4/11/73, A, C, 73000802

Julian Farm, S side of US 60, Bridgeport vicinity, 5/26/88, A, C, D, d, 88000670

Kentucky Governor's Mansion, E lawn of the Capitol at end of Capital Ave., Frankfort, 2/01/72, C, 72000532

Kentucky State Arsenal, Main St. at Capital Ave., Frankfort, 4/11/73, A, C, 73000803

Kentucky State Capitol, Capitol grounds at end of Capital Ave., Frankfort, 4/13/73, A, C, 73000804

Liberty Hall, 218 Wilkinson St., Frankfort, 11/11/71, A, C, NHL, 71000344

Morehead, Gov. Charles S., House, 217 Shelby St., Frankfort, 12/30/74, B, C, 74000873

Old Governor's Mansion, 420 High St., Frankfort, 3/11/71, A, C, 71000345

Old Statehouse, On Broadway, bounded by Madison, Clinton, and Lewis Sts., Frankfort, 3/11/71, A, C, NHL, 71000346

Old Statehouse Historic District, Roughly bounded by Broadway, Blanton, St. Clair, Ann and High Sts., Frankfort, 6/19/80, C, 80001529

Old Stone Tavern [Early Stone Buildings of Central Kentucky TR], Scruggs Lane and Leestown Pike, Frankfort vicinity, 6/23/83, A, C, 83002774

Old U.S. Courthouse and Post Office, 305 Wapping St., Frankfort, 7/03/74, C, 74000874

Patterson, Charles, House [Early Stone Buildings of Central Kentucky TR], SR 1689, Frankfort vicinity, 6/23/83, A, C, 83002775

Penn-Marshall Stone House, E of Harvieland on Stoney Creek Rd. at Kentucky River, Harvieland vicinity, 6/05/75, A, C, 75000760

Risk Brothers Site, Address Restricted, Frankfort vicinity, 11/21/78, D, 78001329

Scotland, 5 mi. E of Frankfort on Versailles Rd., Frankfort vicinity, 12/12/76, B, C, 76000883

South Frankfort Neighborhood Historic District, Roughly bounded by US 60, Rockland Ct., and the Kentucky River, Frankfort, 8/19/82, B, C, 82002698

Stewart Home School, 5.5 mi. S of Frankfort on U.S. 127, Frankfort vicinity, 6/03/76, A, C, 76000884

Switzer Covered Bridge, Off Rocky Branch Rd., over North Elkhorn Creek, Switzer, 9/06/74, C, 74000875

Todd, Robert, Summer Home [Early Stone Buildings of Central Kentucky TR], U.S. 421, Frankfort vicinity, 6/23/83, B, C, 83002776

Trumbo, Andrew, Log House, E of Frankfort on Glenns Creek Rd., Frankfort vicinity, 11/17/77, B, C, 77000618

Valley Farm Ruins, Restricted Address, Frankfort vicinity, 7/24/75, B, D, 75000759

Zeigler, Rev. Jesse R., House, 509 Shelby St., Frankfort, 5/03/76, C, 76000885

Fulton County

Adams Site (15 Fu 4), Address Restricted, Hickman vicinity, 3/15/84, D, 84001421

Amburg Mounds Site (15FU15), Address Restricted, Hickman vicinity, 12/31/85, D, 85003183

Buchanan Street Historic District [Hickman, Kentucky MPS], Roughly bounded by Wellington, Obion, Buchanan, and Union Sts., Hickman, 8/03/90, C, 90000779

Carnegie Library [Hickman, Kentucky MPS], Moscow Ave. between Troy Ave. and Third St., Hickman, 8/03/90, A, C, 90000780

Carr, Ben F., Jr., House, 203 2nd St., Fulton, 7/16/79, B, b, 79000987

Fulton County Courthouse, Off KY 94, Hickman, 4/22/76, C, 76000887

Old Hickman Historic District [Hickman, Kentucky MPS], Roughly bounded by Clinton, Exchange, Obion, Moulton, and Kentucky Sts., Hickman, 8/03/90, A, C, D, 90000778

Running Slough Site (15FU67), Address Restricted, Hickman vicinity, 12/05/85, D, 85003062

Sassafras Ridge (Site 15 FU 3), Address Restricted, Hickman vicinity, 11/23/84, D, 84000285

Thomas Chapel C.M.E. Church, Moscow Ave., Hickman, 1/09/79, A, a, 79000988

White Site (15FU24), Address Restricted, Moscow vicinity, 3/21/88, D, 88000183

Whitesell, Jesse, House, W of Fulton on KY 116, Fulton vicinity, 8/29/77, C, 77000619

Gallatin County

Montz, Dr. Lucy Dupuy, House, 200 W. High St., Warsaw, 3/30/78, B, C, 78001333

Peak, Henry C., House, Sparta Pike, Warsaw, 4/10/80, C, 80001530

Turley, Benjamin F., House, 2.5 mi. (4 N nhN of Sparta on KY 35, Sparta vicinity, 3/07/79, C, d, 79000989

Warsaw Historic District, Roughly bounded by W. High, E. Franklin, Washington, Market, Main, 3rd, 4th and Cross Sts., Warsaw, 7/29/82, C, 82002699

Garrard County

Arnold, John, House [Early Stone Buildings of Central Kentucky TR], Off 1295, Paint Lick vicinity, 6/23/83, C, 83002777

Ball, Billy, House [Lancaster MRA], 209 Richmond St., Lancaster, 3/26/84, C, 84001434

Barlow House [Garrard County MRA], Danville Rd., Lancaster vicinity, 6/17/85, A, C, 85001276

Blakeman, Calvin, House [Garrard County MRA], Polly's Bend Rd., Lancaster vicinity, 6/17/85, C, 85001277

Bonta-Owsley House [Garrard County MRA], Jct. of Boone's Creek and KY 52, Lancaster vicinity, 6/17/85, C, 85001278

Boyle-Robertson-Letcher House, 106 W. Maple St., Lancaster, 4/14/75, B, 75000761

Bradley, Gov. William O., House, Lexington St., Lancaster, 11/05/74, B, C, 74000876

Bryantsville Methodist Church [Garrard County MRA], US 27, Lancaster vicinity, 6/17/85, A, C, a, 85001279

Bryantsville Post Office and Store [Garrard County MRA], Off US 27, Bryantsville, 6/17/85, A, C, 85001280

Calico & Brown General Store [Garrard County MRA], KY 52, Paint Lick, 6/17/85, A, C, 85001281

Dalton House [Garrard County MRA], KY 39, Lancaster vicinity, 6/17/85, C, 85001282

Denny Place [Lancaster MRA], 217 Lexington St., Lancaster, 3/26/84, C, 84001439

Dunn-Watkins House [Garrard County MRA], Danville Rd., Lancaster vicinity, 6/17/85, C, 85001283

Floyd, John, House, NW of Lancaster on Burdett's Knob Rd. off US 27, Lancaster vicinity, 8/28/75, C, 75000762

Garrard County Jail [Lancaster MRA], Stanford St., Lancaster, 3/26/84, A, C, 84001442

Garrard Mills [Lancaster MRA], 205 E. Buford St., Lancaster, 3/26/84, A, C, 84001447

Gulley Farm [Garrard County MRA], US 27, Lancaster vicinity, 6/17/85, C, 85001284

Hamilton House [Lancaster MRA], 107 Maple Ave., Lancaster, 3/26/84, C, 84001449

Hamilton, Roscoe, House [Garrard County MRA], Buena Vista Rd., Lancaster vicinity, 6/17/85, C, 85001285

Hemphill, J. C., House [Lancaster MRA], 211 Lexington St., Lancaster, 3/26/84, C, 84001451

Hill, Dr. Oliver Perry, House [Lancaster MRA], 106 Hill Court, Lancaster, 3/26/84, C, 84001455

Hutcherson, John, House [Early Stone Buildings of Central Kentucky TR], Off KY 39, Buckeye vicinity, 6/23/83, A, C, 83002778

Jennings-Salter House, 208 Danville St., Lancaster, 2/21/80, C, 80001531

Lancaster Cemetery [Lancaster MRA], Campbell, Crab Orchard, and Richmond Sts., Lancaster, 3/26/84, C, d, 84001458

Lancaster Commercial Historic District [Lancaster MRA], Danville, Lexington, Richmond, and Stanford Sts., Lancaster, 3/26/84, A, C, 84001461

Lane Farm [Garrard County MRA], Polly's Bend Rd., Lancaster vicinity, 6/17/85, C, 85001286

Lear, Judge V. A., House [Lancaster MRA], 222 Lexington St., Lancaster, 3/26/84, C, 84001464

Leavell, John, Quarters [Early Stone Buildings of Central Kentucky TR], Off KY 753, Bryantsville vicinity, 6/23/83, A, C, 83002779

Garrard County—Continued

Male Academy [Lancaster MRA], 108 S. Campbell St., Lancaster, 3/26/84, C, 84001467

Mason, Sue Shelby, House [Lancaster MRA], 213 Lexington St., Lancaster, 3/26/84, C, 84001470

Metcalf, Isaac, House [Garrard County MRA], Broadus Branch Rd., Lancaster vicinity, 6/17/85, A, C, 85001287

Methodist Episcopal Church [Lancaster MRA], Stanford St., Lancaster, 7/02/84, C, a, 84001473

Miller, William, Place [Garrard County MRA], Jct. of KY 52 and KY 21, Paint Lick, 6/17/85, C, 85001288

Mt. Olivet Methodist Church [Garrard County MRA], Off KY 152, Lancaster vicinity, 6/17/85, A, C, a, 85001289

Nation, Carry A., House, W of Lancaster on Fisher Ford Rd., Lancaster vicinity, 12/16/77, B, c, 77000620

Owsley, Gov. William, House, 0.5 mi. S of Lancaster on U.S. 27, Lancaster vicinity, 5/06/75, B, 75000763

Paint Lick Presbyterian Church [Garrard County MRA], KY 52, Paint Lick, 6/17/85, A, C, a, 85001290

Parke-Moore House [Garrard County MRA], US 27, Lancaster vicinity, 6/17/85, C, 85001291

Parks, William, House [Garrard County MRA], Locust Lane, Lancaster vicinity, 6/17/85, C, 85001292

Peacock House [Lancaster MRA], 215 Buford St., Lancaster, 3/26/84, C, 84001481

Peacock-Miller House [Lancaster MRA], 212 Danville St., Lancaster, 3/26/84, C, 84001482

Perkins, Lucien, Farm [Garrard County MRA], Crab Orchard Rd. 4.3 mi. S of Lancaster, Lancaster vicinity, 9/28/89, C, 85003767

Perkins-Daniel House [Garrard County MRA], Gilbert's Creek, Lancaster vicinity, 6/17/85, C, 85001293

Petrie House [Lancaster MRA], 404 Danville St., Lancaster, 3/26/84, C, 84001484

Proctor House [Early Stone Buildings of Central Kentucky TR], U.S. 27, Bryantsville vicinity, 6/23/83, A, C, 83002780

Rankin Place [Garrard County MRA], Old Danville Rd., Lancaster vicinity, 6/17/85, C, 85001294

Ray House [Garrard County MRA], Jess Ray Rd., Lancaster vicinity, 6/17/85, C, 85001295

Salter, Tom, House [Garrard County MRA], KY 39, Lancaster vicinity, 6/17/85, A, C, 85001296

Sebastian Log House [Garrard County MRA], Nina Ridge, Lancaster vicinity, 6/17/85, C, 85001297

Sharp House [Garrard County MRA], Fisher Ford Rd., Lancaster vicinity, 6/17/85, C, 85001298

Smith House [Garrard County MRA], Jct. of KY 52 & SR 1647, Paint Lick vicinity, 6/17/85, C, 85001299

Smith, James, Tanyard [Early Stone Buildings of Central Kentucky TR], Off U.S. 27, Bryantsville vicinity, 6/23/83, A, C, 83002781

Spring Garden-John Leavell [Garrard County MRA], Ballard Lane-Tanyard Branch, Bryantsville vicinity, 6/17/85, C, 85001300

Stapp Homeplace [Garrard County MRA], KY 39, Lancaster vicinity, 6/17/85, C, 85001301

Teater, Paris, House [Garrard County MRA], KY 39, Lancaster vicinity, 6/17/85, C, 85001303

Teater, William, House [Garrard County MRA], KY 39, Teatersville, 6/17/85, C, 85001302

Thomas, Kings, III, House [Early Stone Buildings of Central Kentucky TR], Off KY 39, Lancaster vicinity, 6/23/83, A, C, 83002782

Thompson, Smith, Log House [Garrard County MRA], Wolf Trail Rt. 563, Lancaster vicinity, 6/17/85, C, 85001304

Walden Place [Garrard County MRA], Sugar Creek, Lancaster vicinity, 6/17/85, A, C, 85001305

Walker House [Garrard County MRA], SR 1295, Lancaster vicinity, 6/17/85, A, C, 85001306

Wallace, Michael, House [Early Stone Buildings of Central Kentucky TR], Broadus Branch Rd., Kirksville vicinity, 6/23/83, A, C, 83002783

Wearren Place [Lancaster MRA], Stanford St., Lancaster, 3/26/84, C, 84001490

Wherritt House [Lancaster MRA], 210 Lexington St., Lancaster, 3/26/84, C, 84001494

Wilson, Paul, Place [Garrard County MRA], Off Polly's Bend Rd., Lancaster vicinity, 6/17/85, C, 85001307

Grant County

Ford Stone House, S of Elliston, Elliston vicinity, 2/27/80, C, 80001532

Sherman Tavern, S of Sherman on U.S. 25, Sherman vicinity, 2/09/79, A, C, 79000990

Graves County

Mayfield Downtown Commercial District, Roughly bounded by North, Water, 5th and 9th Sts., Mayfield, 8/16/84, A, C, 84001477

Meacham Manor, 7 mi. E of Fulton off KY 116, Fulton vicinity, 12/31/74, A, C, 74000877

U.S. Post Office, 9th St. and Broadway, Mayfield, 12/02/82, C, 82001566

Wooldridge Monuments, Maplewood Cemetery, Mayfield, 8/11/80, C, c, 80001533

Youngblood Site (15GV26), Address Restricted, Hicksville vicinity, 4/04/86, D, 86000694

Grayson County

Cedars, The, E of Leitchfield on KY 1214, Leitchfield vicinity, 5/17/76, A, C, 76000889

Court Square Historic District, Court House Square between Walnut and Market Sts., Leitchfield, 11/23/84, C, 84000288

Court Square Historic District (Boundary Increase), 106 & 104 N. Main, Leitchfield, 1/12/88, A, C, 87001917

Crow Hollow Petroglyphs (15GY65) [Prehistoric Rock Art Sites in Kentucky MPS], Address Restricted, Clarkson vicinity, 9/08/89, A, C, D, a, 89001188

Grayson Springs, S of Clarkson, Clarkson vicinity, 12/06/78, A, D, 78001334

Hunter House, 118 W. Walnut St., Leitchfield, 5/16/85, C, 85001055

Saltsman Branch Petroglyphs (15GY66) [Prehistoric Rock Art Sites in Kentucky MPS], Address Restricted, Moutardier vicinity, 9/08/89, A, C, D, a, 89001189

Saltsman Branch Shelter Petroglyphs (15GY67) [Prehistoric Rock Art Sites in Kentucky MPS], Address Restricted, Moutardier vicinity, 9/08/89, A, C, D, a, 89001190

St. Augustine Catholic Church, KY 88, Grayson Springs vicinity, 4/07/89, C, a, 89000259

Thomas, Jack, House, 108 E. Main St., Leitchfield, 4/21/76, B, C, 76000890

Walnut Grove School, Walnut Grove Rd., Caneyville vicinity, 2/02/88, A, 87002516

Green County

Allen's, James, Inn [Early Stone Buildings of Kentucky Outer Bluegrass and Pennyrile TR], 103 E. Court St., Greensburg, 1/08/87, C, 87000206

Allen, John C., House [Green County MRA], KY 61, Summersville vicinity, 4/19/85, C, 85000917

Anderson House [Green County MRA], KY 1913, Haskingsville vicinity, 8/24/84, A, C, 84001496

Barrett-Blakeman House [Green County MRA], Hodgenville Rd., Greensburg, 4/19/85, C, 85000909

Brents-Lisle House [Green County MRA], US 68, Greensburg vicinity, 8/24/84, C, 84001501

Chewning House [Green County MRA], KY 88, Donansburg, 8/24/84, C, 84001502

Christie, Christopher Columbus, House [Green County MRA], KY 1915, Haskingsville vicinity, 8/24/84, C, 84001503

Court Clerk's Office-County & Circuit [Early Stone Buildings of Kentucky Outer Bluegrass and Pennyrile TR], East Court St., Greensburg, 1/08/87, C, 87000176

Cowherd, Francis, House [Green County MRA], Off U.S. 68, Greensburg vicinity, 4/19/85, C, 85000908

Creal Store [Green County MRA], KY 61, Creal, 8/24/84, C, 84001504

Ebenezer School [Green County MRA], Off KY 61, Greensburg vicinity, 8/24/84, A, 84001505

Edwards House [Green County MRA], KY 745, Exie vicinity, 8/24/84, C, 84001507

Edwards, David, House [Green County MRA], Off KY 745, Exie vicinity, 8/24/84, C, 84001506

Elmore-Carter House [Green County MRA], KY 793, Summersville vicinity, 8/24/84, C, 84001508

Green County—Continued

Emory-Blakeman-Penick House [Green County MRA], Off KY 487, Greensburg vicinity, 8/24/84, C, 84001509

Federal House [Green County MRA], S. Main and E. Columbia, Greensburg, 4/19/85, C, 85000910

Goose Creek Foot Bridge [Green County MRA], Court and Depot Sts., Greensburg, 4/19/85, A, C, 85000911

Greensburg Academy, 101 2nd St., Greensburg, 12/12/76, A, 76000891

Greensburg Bank Building, E. Court St., Greensburg, 8/21/79, A, 79000991

Greensburg Cumberland Presbyterian Church [Green County MRA], Hodgenville Ave. and N. 1st St., Greensburg, 4/19/85, C, a, 85000912

Groves-Cabell House [Green County MRA], Off KY 61, Gresham vicinity, 8/24/84, C, 84001510

Herndon, William H., House [Green County MRA], 203 S. Main St., Greensburg, 4/19/85, C, 85000913

Hilliard, David, House [Green County MRA], Off KY 487, Greensburg vicinity, 8/24/84, C, 84001511

Hobson, William, House [Green County MRA], 102 S. Depot St., Greensburg, 4/19/85, C, 85000914

Keltner House [Green County MRA], KY 1913, Haskingsville vicinity, 8/24/84, C, 84001512

L & N Passenger Depot [Green County MRA], 103 N. Depot St., Greensburg, 8/24/84, A, C, 84001513

Lewis, Woodson, House [Green County MRA], Main St. and Hodgenville Ave., Greensburg, 4/19/85, C, 85000915

Livesay House [Green County MRA], Off KY 208, Campbellsville vicinity, 8/24/84, C, 84001514

Mears House [Green County MRA], KY 61, Greensburg vicinity, 8/24/84, C, 84001517

Montgomery House [Green County MRA], Off KY 1464, Donansburg vicinity, 8/24/84, C, 84001521

Montgomery's Mill [Green County MRA], Off KY 88, Greensburg vicinity, 8/24/84, A, 84001523

Mt. Gilead Baptist Church [Green County MRA], KY 767, Haskingsville vicinity, 8/24/84, A, C, a, 84001519

Old Courthouse, Public Sq., Greensburg, 4/10/72, A, 72000533

Philpot House [Green County MRA], KY 729, Exie vicinity, 4/19/85, C, 85000907

Sandidge House [Green County MRA], KY 88, Donansburg vicinity, 8/24/84, C, 84001525

Simpson Log House [Green County MRA], KY 1464, Webbs vicinity, 8/24/84, C, 84001526

Wallace, Napoleon, House [Green County MRA], Off KY 218, Pierce vicinity, 8/24/84, C, 84001527

Webbs Female Academy [Green County MRA], Off KY 88, Webbs, 8/24/84, A, C, 84001528

White-Penick House [Green County MRA], 106 S. Depot St., Greensburg, 4/19/85, C, 85000916

Whitlock Log Cabin [Green County MRA], US 68, Exie, 8/24/84, C, 84001529

Williams, Daniel Motley, House [Green County MRA], KY 323, Summersville vicinity, 8/24/84, A, C, 84001531

Wilson, R. H., House [Green County MRA], 402 N. Water St., Greensburg, 8/24/84, C, 84001532

Woodward House [Green County MRA], Off US 68, Greensburg vicinity, 8/24/84, C, 84001534

Greenup County

Bennett's Mill Covered Bridge, SR 2125 W of Greenup, Greenup vicinity, 3/26/76, A, C, 76000892

Front Street District [Greenup MRA], Front St., Greenup, 1/27/88, C, 87002448

Greenup Masonic Lodge [Greenup MRA], 314 Main St., Greenup, 1/27/88, C, 87002447

KY 2541 Bridge [Greenup MRA], Main St. over Little Sandy River, Greenup, 1/27/88, C, 87002446

Kouns—Hoffman House [Greenup MRA], 208 Jefferson St., Greenup, 1/27/88, B, C, 87002445

Lower Shawneetown, Address Restricted, South Portsmouth vicinity, 4/28/83, D, 83002784

Lower Shawneetown Archeological District, Address Restricted, South Portsmouth vicinity, 11/29/85, A, C, D, 85003334

McConnell House, Law Office, and Slave Quarters, W of Wurtland on U.S. 23, Wurtland vicinity, 7/30/75, A, B, C, d, 75000764

McKee House [Greenup MRA], 1023 Riverside Dr., Greenup, 1/27/88, C, 87002439

Methodist Episcopal Church South [Greenup MRA], Main St., Greenup, 1/27/88, C, a, 87002444

Oldtown Covered Bridge, S of Oldtown off KY 1, Oldtown vicinity, 3/26/76, C, 76000893

Portsmouth Earthworks, Group A, Address Restricted, South Portsmouth vicinity, 12/04/80, C, D, 80001534

South Greenup District [Greenup MRA], Roughly bounded by the C & O Railroad, Laurel St., Seaton Ave., and Washington St., Greenup, 1/27/88, C, a, 87002443

Stuart, Jesse, House, Stuarts Lane off W-Hollow Rd., Greenup vicinity, 6/01/82, B, g, 82002700

Warnock House [Greenup MRA], 404 Harrison, Greenup, 1/27/88, C, 87002442

West Main Street District [Greenup MRA], W. Main St., Greenup, 1/27/88, C, a, 87002441

Worthington House [Greenup MRA], US 23 at Academy Rd., Greenup, 1/27/88, B, C, 87002438

Hancock County

Beauchamp, Robert C., House, NW of Hawesville on U.S. 60, Hawesville vicinity, 7/06/76, B, C, 76000894

Hancock County Courthouse, Courthouse Sq., Hawesville, 6/18/75, C, 75000765

Hawesville Historic District, Main, Water, Main Cross, and Clay Sts., Hawesville, 4/12/84, A, C, 84001536

Hayden, Isaac R., House [Lewisport MRA], Pell St., Lewisport, 8/01/84, C, 84001539

Henderson, Tom, House [Lewisport MRA], 4th St., Lewisport, 8/01/84, C, 84001540

Immaculate Conception Church, Water St., Hawesville, 6/18/75, A, C, a, 75000766

Jeffry Cliff Petroglyphs (15HA114) [Prehistoric Rock Art Sites in Kentucky MPS], Address Restricted, Indian Lake vicinity, 9/08/89, A, C, D, a, 89001191

Lewisport Masonic Lodge [Lewisport MRA], 4th St., Lewisport, 8/01/84, C, 84001541

Pate, Samuel, House, E of Lewisport of KY 334, Lewisport vicinity, 12/21/78, B, C, 78001335

Patterson, Horace, House [Lewisport MRA], Market St., Lewisport, 8/01/84, C, 84001543

Pell, Joe, Building [Lewisport MRA], Pell St., Lewisport, 8/01/84, A, C, 84001544

Taylor, J. B., and Son Feed Store [Lewisport MRA], 307 4th St., Lewisport, 8/01/84, A, C, 84001546

Hardin County

Abel, Dr., House [Hardin County MRA], KY 1904 1 mi. W of KY 222, Glendale vicinity, 10/04/88, C, 88001768

Applegate—Fisher House [Hardin County MRA], 404 Elm St., West Point, 10/04/88, A, C, 88001787

Arnold, Philip, House [Hardin County MRA], 422 E. Poplar St., Elizabethtown, 10/04/88, B, 88001798

Ashe House [Hardin County MRA], KY 1868, 1 mi. W of jct. with KY 1136, Glendale vicinity, 10/04/88, C, 88001755

Bethlehem Academy Historic District [Hardin County MRA], Near jct. of KY 1357 and KY 253, St. John vicinity, 10/04/88, A, 88001813

Bland, John D., House [Hardin County MRA], KY 720, 2 mi. W of jct. with KY 84, Sonora vicinity, 10/04/88, C, 88001729

Bland, William, House [Hardin County MRA], KY 222, 2.5 mi. W of Glendale, Glendale vicinity, 10/04/88, C, 88001734

Bland—Overall House [Hardin County MRA], KY 1868, .8 mi. W of jct. of KY 1136 & KY 1868, Sonora vicinity, 10/04/88, C, 88001728

Blue Ball Church [Hardin County MRA], Blue Ball Church Rd., .6 mi. S of jct. of KY 220 & KY 1375, Howe Valley vicinity, 10/04/88, C, a, 88001727

Bond, J. Roy, House [Hardin County MRA], 317 College St., Elizabethtown, 10/04/88, C, 88001811

Brackett, Daniel, House [Hardin County MRA], KY 1391, .5 mi. S of KY 224, Upton vicinity, 10/04/88, C, 88001752

Brown Pusey House Community Center, 128 N. Maine St., Elizabethtown, 7/12/74, B, C, 74000878

Bush, William, House [Hardin County MRA], 1927 Tunnel Hill Rd., Elizabethtown, 10/04/88, B, C, 88001807

Hardin County—Continued

Carroll, Dr. Clyde, House [Hardin County MRA], Dead Man's Cave Rd., White Mills, 10/04/88, A, C, 88001764

Chenault House [Hardin County MRA], KY 1375, 1.5 mi. N of KY 84, Star Mills vicinity, 10/04/88, C, 88001781

Chestnut Grove [Hardin County MRA], KY 222, 1 mi. W of Glendale, Glendale vicinity, 10/04/88, C, 88001731

Christ Episcopal Church [Hardin County MRA], Poplar St., Elizabethtown, 10/04/88, C, a, 88001792

Ditto, Abraham, House [Hardin County MRA], 204 Elm St., West Point, 10/04/88, A, 88001789

Ditto—Prewitt House [Hardin County MRA], 306 Elm St., West Point, 10/04/88, A, 88001786

Elizabethtown Courthouse Square and Commercial District, KY 61, Elizabethtown, 3/19/80, C, 80001535

Embry Chapel Church [Hardin County MRA], 117 Mulberry St., Elizabethtown, 10/04/88, A, C, a, 88001803

First Baptist Church, 112 W. Poplar St., Elizabethtown, 12/31/74, A, 74000879

First Presbyterian Church [Hardin County MRA], 212 W. Dixie Ave., Elizabethtown, 10/04/88, C, a, 88001802

Glendale Historic District [Hardin County MRA], Main St. between County Hwy. 1136 and Railroad Ave., Glendale, 10/04/88, A, C, 88001816

Hagan House [Hardin County MRA], KY 1136 2.5 mi. W of jct. with US 31W, Elizabethtown vicinity, 10/04/88, C, 88001760

Hamilton, Hance, House [Hardin County MRA], Porter Rd., 1 mi. east of jct. with US 62, Boston vicinity, 10/04/88, C, 88001741

Hardin Springs School [Hardin County MRA], KY 84, .4 mi. E of Hardin Springs Bridge, Hardin Springs vicinity, 10/04/88, A, 88001783

Hatfield Hotel [Hardin County MRA], Dead Man's Cave Rd., White Mills, 10/04/88, A, 88001763

Haycraft Inn [Hardin County MRA], 2315 S. Wilson Rd., Radcliffe, 10/04/88, A, C, 88001742

Hazel Hill [Hardin County MRA], Gaither's Station Rd., 2 mi. S of US 62, Elizabethtown vicinity, 10/05/88, C, 88001744

Heller Hotel [Hardin County MRA], Robinson St., Cecilia, 10/04/88, A, C, 88001756

Helm Place, 1.5 mi. N of Elizabethtown on U.S. 31W, Elizabethtown vicinity, 11/09/76, B, C, 76000895

Helm, Benjamin, House [Hardin County MRA], 238 Helm Ave., Elizabethtown, 10/04/88, B, 88001801

Helm, John B., House [Hardin County MRA], 210 Helm Ave., Elizabethtown, 10/04/88, B, 88001800

Kentucky and Indiana Bank [Hardin County MRA], 309 Elm St., West Point, 10/04/88, A, 88001788

Kerrick, W. T., House [Hardin County MRA], 604 N. Main St., Elizabethtown, 10/04/88, C, 88001808

Larue-Layman House [Hardin County MRA], 115 W. Poplar St., Elizabethtown, 10/04/88, C, 88001794

Lincoln Heritage House, N of Elizabethtown on Freeman Lake, Elizabethtown vicinity, 3/26/73, C, 73000805

Maple Hill [Hardin County MRA], Maple St., Glendale, 10/04/88, C, 88001735

Maplehurst [Hardin County MRA], KY 222, 1 mi. NE of Glendale, Glendale vicinity, 10/04/88, C, 88001732

Mason, Haynes, House [Hardin County MRA], Haynes Mason Rd., .3 mi. S of KY 720, Upton vicinity, 10/04/88, C, 88001782

May, David L., House [Hardin County MRA], 201 N. Main St., Elizabethtown, 10/05/88, B, 88001805

McDougal, Stiles, House [Hardin County MRA], .3 mi. S of jct. of KY 1375 and US 62, Glendale vicinity, 10/04/88, C, 88001740

McKinney-Helm House [Hardin County MRA], 218 W. Poplar St., Elizabethtown, 10/05/88, B, 88001795

Melton House [Hardin County MRA], KY 1904 2 mi. E of KY 1375, Glendale vicinity, 10/05/88, C, 88001769

Monin, Adam, House [Hardin County MRA], Monin Rd., off Rt. 1, Glendale vicinity, 10/05/88, A, B, C, 88001745

Montgomery Avenue Historic District [Hardin County MRA], 602, 606, 608, 610, 614, 616, and 624 Montgomery Ave., Elizabethtown, 10/05/88, A, B, 88001814

Montgomery, William, House [Hardin County MRA], 414 Central Ave., Elizabethtown, 10/05/88, B, 88001806

Morrison Lodge [Hardin County MRA], 121 N. Mulberry St., Elizabethtown, 10/05/88, A, C, 88001804

Nall House [Hardin County MRA], Middle Creek Rd., .2 mi. W of Locust Grove Rd., Elizabethtown vicinity, 10/05/88, C, 88001784

Nolin Banking Company [Hardin County MRA], KY 1407, Nolin, 10/05/88, A, C, 88001749

Penniston House [Hardin County MRA], US 62, .4 mi. E of Upper Colesburg Rd., Elizabethtown vicinity, 10/05/88, C, 88001785

Phillips, Josiah, House [Hardin County MRA], Western Ave., Sonora, 10/05/88, B, 88001747

Pusey, Dr. Robert B., House [Hardin County MRA], 204 N. Mulberry St., Elizabethtown, 1/04/89, C, 88001793

Raine, John, House [Hardin County MRA], KY 84, Sonora, 10/05/88, B, C, 88001748

Rawlings, Stephen, House [Hardin County MRA], 811 N. Main St., Elizabethtown, 10/05/88, B, 88001791

Richards—Hamm House [Hardin County MRA], KY 1136 0.4 mi. W of US 31W, Glendale vicinity, 10/05/88, C, 88001766

Richards—Murray House [Hardin County MRA], Jct of KY 1136 and US 31W, Glendale vicinity, 10/05/88, C, 88001767

Richardson Hotel [Hardin County MRA], Dead Man's Cave Rd., White Mills, 10/05/88, A, 88001762

Riney, Zachariah, House [Hardin County MRA], Jct. of KY 1600 and KY 220, Rineyville, 10/05/88, B, 88001758

Robertson, Samuel, House [Hardin County MRA], 214 W. Poplar St., Elizabethtown, 10/05/88, C, 88001812

Skees, Richard, House [Hardin County MRA], Jerome Peerce Rd., off KY 1823, White Mills vicinity, 10/05/88, C, 88001780

Skees, William, House [Hardin County MRA], Off KY 1866 2 mi. N of jct. with KY 720, White Mills vicinity, 10/05/88, C, 88001757

Smith, George W., House [Hardin County MRA], KY 1904, 3 mi. S of jct. with US 62, Elizabethtown vicinity, 10/05/88, C, 88001738

Sprigg, William, House [Hardin County MRA], KY 1375, 1 mi. N of jct. with KY 84, Glendale vicinity, 1/04/89, B, 88001736

Stader Hotel [Hardin County MRA], 104 E. Main St., Vine Grove, 10/05/88, A, C, 88001751

Stark House [Hardin County MRA], .4 mi. W of jct. of KY 1868 & Gilead Church/Star Mills Rd., Glendale vicinity, 10/05/88, C, 88001725

Stuart, John, House [Hardin County MRA], St. Anthony Church Rd. 0.5 mi. E of US 31W, Glendale vicinity, 10/05/88, C, 88001765

Thomas, Samuel B., House [Hardin County MRA], 337 W. Poplar St., Elizabethtown, 10/05/88, B, 88001797

Tichenor, William, House [Hardin County MRA], Sonora—Upton Rd., 1 mi. W of Upton, Upton vicinity, 10/05/88, C, 88001753

US Bullion Depository, Fort Knox, Kentucky, Gold Vault Rd. and Bullion Blvd., Fort Knox, 2/18/88, A, g, 88000056

US Post Office—Elizabethtown [Hardin County MRA], 200 W. Dixie Ave., Elizabethtown, 10/05/88, C, 88001810

Van Meter, Jacob, House [Hardin County MRA], KY 222, .6 mi. W of Glendale, Glendale vicinity, 10/05/88, B, 88001746

Vertrees, Eliza, House [Hardin County MRA], 206 W. Poplar St., Elizabethtown, 10/05/88, C, 88001809

Vine Grove Historic District [Hardin County MRA], 104–221 W. Main St., Vine Grove, 10/05/88, A, C, 88001815

West Point Hotel [Hardin County MRA], 401 South St., West Point, 10/05/88, A, C, 88001790

White Mill [Hardin County MRA], Nolin River, White Mills, 10/05/88, A, 88001761

Wilson, William, House [Hardin County MRA], 200 Logan Ave., Elizabethtown, 10/05/88, B, C, 88001799

Wintersmith, Horatio, House [Hardin County MRA], 221 W. Poplar St., Elizabethtown, 10/05/88, C, 88001796

Young, James, House and Inn, 109 Elm St., West Point, 2/17/78, A, B, C, D, 78001336

Harlan County

Benham Historic District, KY 160, Central Ave., McKnight and Cypress Sts., Benham, 7/21/83, A, C, a, c, 83002785

Harlan County—Continued

Harlan Commercial District, Roughly bounded by Mound, Second, Clover, and Main Sts., Harlan, 3/20/86, A, C, 86000461

Pine Mountain Settlement School, E of Bledsoe on KY 510, Bledsoe vicinity, 9/06/78, A, B, 78001337

Harrison County

Archeological Site No. 15HR4, Address Restricted, Lair vicinity, 2/20/86, D, 86000269

Church of the Advent, Episcopal, 122 N. Walnut St., Cynthiana, 12/22/78, C, a, 78001339

Coleman—Desha Plantation, US 62 E, Oddville Pike, 1 mi. NE of Cynthiana, Cynthiana vicinity, 2/26/93, A, C, 93000045

Cynthiana Commercial District, Pike St. from Church to Main Sts., and Main St. from Bridge to Pleasant Sts., Cynthiana, 10/19/82, A, C, 82001567

Fraizer, Joel, House [Early Stone Buildings of Central Kentucky TR], Off KY 982, Cynthiana vicinity, 6/23/83, C, 83002786

Harrison County Courthouse, 100 Main St., Cynthiana, 12/06/74, A, C, 74000880

Haviland House [Early Stone Buildings of Central Kentucky TR], Off U.S. 62, Cynthiana vicinity, 6/23/83, C, 83002787

Hinkson, John, House [Early Stone Buildings of Central Kentucky TR], Off U.S. 27, Shawhan vicinity, 6/23/83, A, C, 83002788

Kimbrough-Hehr House, U.S. 62, Broadwell, 4/20/79, A, C, 79000992

Lafferty, William T., House, 548 E. Pike St., Cynthiana, 4/10/80, B, C, 80001538

Lair, John, House [Early Stone Buildings of Central Kentucky TR], Old Lair Rd., Shawhan vicinity, 6/23/83, A, C, 83002789

McKee, John, House [Early Stone Buildings of Central Kentucky TR], Cook Rd., Shawhan vicinity, 6/23/83, C, 83002790

McMillan, Samuel, House [Early Stone Buildings of Central Kentucky TR], Off U.S. 62, Shawhan vicinity, 6/23/83, A, C, 83002791

Monticello, Monticello Heights, Cynthiana, 12/31/74, B, C, 74000881

Poplar Hill, E of Cynthiana on KY 32, Cynthiana vicinity, 11/07/76, A, C, 76000896

Roberts, Wesley, House, 113-115 N. Main St., Cynthiana vicinity, 11/10/82, C, 82001568

Shawhan, Joseph, House [Early Stone Buildings of Central Kentucky TR], Off U.S. 27, Shawhan vicinity, 6/23/83, A, C, 83002792

Smith House [Early Stone Buildings of Central Kentucky TR], Off Lair Rd., Shawhan vicinity, 6/23/83, C, 83002793

Spur Gasoline Station, 201 E. Bridge St., Cynthiana, 4/27/87, A, C, 87000647

Stone House of Indian Creek [Early Stone Buildings of Central Kentucky TR], Off U.S. 62, Cynthiana vicinity, 6/23/83, C, 83002794

Stoney Castle, W of Berry on Lafferty Pike, Berry vicinity, 12/12/78, A, C, 78001338

Williams, John, House [Early Stone Buildings of Central Kentucky TR], Off KY 32/36, Shawhan vicinity, 6/23/83, A, C, 83002795

Hart County

Barrett, Dr. Lewis, House [Munfordville MRA], 2nd and Caldwell Sts., Munfordville, 7/24/80, B, C, 80001539

Chapline Building [Munfordville MRA], Main St., Munfordville, 7/24/80, C, 80001540

Cox, Alvey, House [Munfordville MRA], 1st and Washington Sts., Munfordville, 7/24/80, C, 80001541

Hart County Courthouse [Munfordville MRA], Town Sq., Munfordville, 7/24/80, A, 80001542

Hart County Deposit Bank and Trust Company Building [Munfordville MRA], Main St., Munfordville, 7/24/80, A, C, 80001543

Munford Inn [Munfordville MRA], 109 Washington St., Munfordville, 3/19/84, A, C, 84001615

Munfordville Baptist Church [Munfordville MRA], 313 S. 5th St., Munfordville, 7/24/80, C, a, 80001544

Munfordville Presbyterian Church and Green River Lodge No.88 [Munfordville MRA], 3rd and Washington Sts., Munfordville, 7/24/80, A, a, 80001545

Munfordville School [Munfordville MRA], 3rd and Washington Sts., Munfordville, 3/19/84, A, 84001613

Salts Cave Archeological Site, Address Restricted, Mundfordville vicinity, 5/15/79, D, NPS, 79000278

Smith, F. A., House [Munfordville MRA], 204 N. Washington St., Munfordville, 7/24/80, A, B, C, 80001546

Wood, Gen. George T., House [Munfordville MRA], 2nd and Caldwell Sts., Munfordville, 7/24/80, B, C, 80001547

Henderson County

Alves Historic District, Roughly bounded by Green, Center, S. Alvasia, Powell, S. Adams and Washington Sts., Henderson, 9/07/89, A, C, 89001151

Archeological Site KHC-3 (15HE635) [Green River Shell Middens of Kentucky TR], Address Restricted, Hebbardsville vicinity, 4/01/86, D, 86000641

Archeological Site KHC-4 (15HE580) [Green River Shell Middens of Kentucky TR], Address Restricted, Hebbardsville vicinity, 4/01/86, D, 86000642

Audubon, John James, State Park, US 41, Henderson, 3/10/88, A, C, g, 87002220

Barret House, 204 S. Elm St., Henderson, 1/05/78, B, C, 78001340

Bluff City Shell Mound (15HE160) [Green River Shell Middens of Kentucky TR], Address Restricted, Hebbardsville vicinity, 4/01/86, D, 86000644

Delano—Alves House, 536 Chestnut St., Henderson, 2/11/93, C, 93000044

Ehlen, E. L., Livery and Sale Stable, 110 First St., Henderson, 11/16/89, A, C, 89002007

Henderson Commercial District, Roughly bounded by Main, Third, Elm, and First Sts., Henderson, 11/13/89, A, C, 89001975

Henderson, Louisville and Nashville Railroad Depot, 300 Clark St., Henderson, 5/14/80, C, 80001549

James Giles Shell Midden (15HE589) [Green River Shell Middens of Kentucky TR], Address Restricted, Rumsey vicinity, 4/01/86, D, 86000646

Klee Funeral Parlor, 13–17 S. Main St., Henderson, 11/16/89, A, C, 89002006

McCallister, John E., House, 839 N. Green St., Henderson vicinity, 9/21/82, C, 82002701

North Main Street Historic District, N. Main St. from Fifth to Eighth Sts., Henderson, 3/07/90, A, C, 90000297

O'Byrne, John, House, 317 N. Main St., Henderson, 3/22/90, B, C, 90000485

South Main and South Elm Streets Historic District, Roughly bounded by Washington, Center, S. Green, Jefferson, S. Main and Water Sts., Henderson, 5/11/92, A, C, 92000500

St. Paul's Episcopal Church, 338 Center St., Henderson, 10/19/78, C, a, 78001341

Henry County

Crutcher House, Mulberry Pike, Eminence, 12/08/80, C, 80001550

Eminence Historic Commercial District, Broadway, Main and Penn Sts., Eminence, 2/09/79, A, C, 79000994

Henderson, Isham, House [Early Stone Buildings of Kentucky Outer Bluegrass and Pennyrile TR], Main Cross Rd., New Castle, 1/08/87, C, 87000156

Henry County Courthouse, Jail, and Warden's House, Courthouse Sq., New Castle, 4/11/77, C, 77000621

Hieatt, Samuel, House, N of Smithfield on Hieatt Rd., Smithfield vicinity, 10/29/82, C, 82001569

Highlands, SW of Smithfield on KY 22, Smithfield vicinity, 7/09/79, C, 79000995

Ricketts, Robert, House, N of New Castle off U.S. 421, New Castle vicinity, 7/12/78, B, C, a, 78001342

Smith, Thomas, House, 524 Cross Main St., New Castle, 2/08/78, B, C, 78001343

Thompson House, KY 22 and Old Giltner Rd., Eminence vicinity, 5/05/87, C, 87000567

Hickman County

Burcham Site (15HI15), Address Restricted, Clinton vicinity, 3/22/90, D, 90000479

Hickman County—Continued

Columbus-Belmont Civil War State Park, On U.S. 80, Columbus, 5/09/73, A, 73000806

Hickman County Courthouse, Court Sq., Clinton, 9/11/75, C, 75000767

Marvin College Boys Dormitory, 404 and 416 N. Washington St., Clinton, 1/02/76, A, a, 76000897

Hopkins County

Archeological Site 15 HK 79, Address Restricted, Nebo vicinity, 12/04/80, D, 80001552

Archeological Site 15 Hk 46 and 47, Address Restricted, White Plains vicinity, 7/28/80, D, 80001553

Archeological Site 15 Hk 8, Address Restricted, Hanson vicinity, 8/01/80, D, 80001551

Beulah Lodge [Hopkins County MPS], KY 70, .5 mi. W of jct. with KY 109, Dawson Springs vicinity, 3/08/89, A, a, 88002718

Cox, John, House [Hopkins County MPS], KY 502, .5 mi. N of Nebo, Nebo vicinity, 12/13/88, C, 88002715

Cranor School [Hopkins County MPS], Buttermilk Rd., .2 mi. SE of jct. with Hamby Rd., St. Charles vicinity, 3/08/89, A, 88002721

Dawson Springs Historic District [Hopkins County MPS], 100 blk. S. Main St., Dawson Springs, 12/13/88, A, C, 88002710

Edmiston, Bazle, House [Hopkins County MPS], KY 291, .2 mi. W of jct. with KY 109, Nebo vicinity, 12/13/88, C, 88002719

Gardiner, Dr. Thomas, House [Hopkins County MPS], 173 Sugg St., Madisonville, 12/13/88, B, 88002727

Hanson Historic District [Hopkins County MPS], Roughly Main St. from US 41 to E. Railroad St., Hanson, 12/13/88, A, C, 88002711

Harvey, John, House [Hopkins County MPS], 175 N. Seminary St., Madisonville, 12/13/88, C, 88002731

Hockersmith, L. D., House [Hopkins County MPS], 218 S. Scott St., Madisonville, 12/13/88, C, 88002729

Hotel Earlington [Hopkins County MPS], 118 E. Main St., Earlington, 12/13/88, A, 88002725

Jackson, Beckley, House [Hopkins County MPS], Rt. 1069, .2 mi. S of jct. with Jones Rd., Hanson vicinity, 3/23/89, A, 88002733

Jennings, Gabriel, House [Hopkins County MPS], KY 70, 1 mi. E of jct. with KY 291, Dawson Springs vicinity, 12/13/88, A, 88002720

Kington, W. W., House [Hopkins County MPS], 109 Crooked St., Mortons Gap, 12/13/88, B, 88002724

Lyon, Chittenden P., Jr., House, 304 Union St., Madisonville, 10/18/76, B, C, 76000898

Madisonville Commercial Historic District [Hopkins County MPS], Center and Main Sts., Madisonville, 12/13/88, A, C, 88002712

Madisonville Public Library [Hopkins County MPS], 107 S. Union St., Madisonville, 12/13/88, C, 88002728

Miller, Frederick, House [Hopkins County MPS], US 62, 2.1 mi. W of White Plains, White Plains vicinity, 12/13/88, C, 88002723

Munn's School, Princeton Rd., Madisonville vicinity, 8/30/83, A, g, 83002796

North Main Street Historic District [Hopkins County MPS], Roughly 200 and 300 blks. N. Main St., Madisonville, 12/13/88, C, 88002713

Oakmoor [Hopkins County MPS], E. Main St., Earlington, 12/13/88, C, 88002726

Porter, Bradford, House [Hopkins County MPS], US 41A, 1 mi. W of jct. with KY 630, Nebo vicinity, 12/13/88, C, 88002714

Ruby, Turner, House [Hopkins County MPS], 264 S. Union St., Madisonville, 12/13/88, C, 88002730

Salmon, Richard, House [Hopkins County MPS], KY 112, Dawson Springs vicinity, 12/13/88, B, 88002722

Slaton, James E., House [Hopkins County MPS], CH 1221, Madisonville vicinity, 12/13/88, C, 88002717

US Post Office—Madisonville [Hopkins County MPS], 56 N. Main St., Madisonville, 1/03/89, A, C, 88003196

Zion Brick Missionary Church [Hopkins County MPS], Crossroad Chapel Rd., .3 mi. N of jct. with KY 138, Hanson vicinity, 12/13/88, C, a, 88002716

Jackson County

Brushy Ridge Petroglyphs [Prehistoric Rock Art Sites in Kentucky MPS], Address Restricted, McKee vicinity, 1/02/92, A, C, D, 91001890

Daugherty Bear Track Petroglyphs (15JA160) [Prehistoric Rock Art Sites in Kentucky MPS], Address Restricted, McKee vicinity, 9/08/89, A, C, D, a, 89001192

Gay, William, Petroglyph [Prehistoric Rock Art Sites in Kentucky MPS], Address Restricted, Macedonia vicinity, 1/02/92, A, C, D, 91001889

Jefferson County

Abell House [Jefferson County MRA], 12210 Old Shelbyville Rd., Middletown, 12/05/80, B, C, 80001635

Adath Israel Cemetery, 2716 Preston St., Louisville, 6/22/82, A, C, a, d, 82002702

Adath Israel Temple, 834 S. 3rd St., Louisville, 12/31/74, A, C, a, 74000882

Adath Jeshurun Temple and School, 749-757 S. Brook St., Louisville, 1/28/82, C, a, 82002703

Allison-Barrickman House [Jefferson County MRA], Wolf Pen Branch Rd., Harrods Creek vicinity, 7/12/83, C, 83002628

Almsted Brothers Building, 425 W. Market St., Louisville, 3/01/82, C, 82002704

Anchorage Historic District [Jefferson County MRA], KY 146, Anchorage, 12/05/80, B, C, 80001554

Anchorage, The [Jefferson County MRA], 804 Evergreen Rd., Anchorage, 12/05/80, C, 80001555

Ancient and Accepted Scottish Rite Temple, 200 E. Gray St., Louisville, 4/29/82, C, 82002705

Ashbourne [Jefferson County MRA], Upper River Rd., Harrods Creek vicinity, 7/12/83, C, 83002629

Atherton Carriage House [Jefferson County MRA], 3204 Woodside Rd., Louisville, 8/16/83, C, 83002630

Avery, B. F., and Sons Industrial District [Louisville and Jefferson Co. MPS], 1721–1821 Seventh St., Louisville, 12/21/90, A, 90001837

Aydelott House [Jefferson County MRA], 6814 Bethany Lane, Valley Station, 12/05/80, C, 80001644

BELLE OF LOUISVILLE (steamer), 4th St. and River Rd., Louisville, 4/10/72, A, C, NHL, 72000535

Baker-Hawkins House, 3603 W. Market St., Louisville, 8/21/80, C, 80001593

Ballard, Rogers Clark, Memorial School [Jefferson County MRA], 4200 Lime Kiln Ln., Louisville, 12/08/83, A, C, 83003697

Bank of Middletown [Jefferson County MRA], 11615 Main St., Middletown, 7/12/83, A, C, 83002631

Bannon, Patrick, House [Jefferson County MRA], 4518 Bardstown Rd., Buechel, 12/05/80, C, 80001573

Barber-Barbour House [Jefferson County MRA], 6415 Transylvania Ave., Harrods Creek, 12/05/80, C, 80001582

Bates, Levin, House [Jefferson County MRA], 7300 Bardstown Rd., Buechel, 12/05/80, C, 80001574

Bayless House [Jefferson County MRA], 1116 Bellewood Rd., Anchorage, 12/05/80, C, 80001556

Bayly-Schroering House, 1012 S. 4th St., Louisville, 11/14/78, C, 78001345

Beech Lawn [Jefferson County MRA], 8000 Six Mile Lane, Jeffersontown, 12/05/80, C, 80001585

Beechland [Jefferson County MRA], 8500 Six Mile Lane, Jeffersontown vicinity, 7/12/83, C, 83002633

Belknap, Willam R., School, 1800 Sils Ave., Louisville, 8/12/82, C, 82002706

Belleview [Louisville and Jefferson County MRA], 6600 Upper River Rd., Harrods Creek, 4/02/92, A, C, 92000158

Bellevoir-Ormsby Village [Jefferson County MRA], Whipps Mill Rd., Lyndon, 12/05/80, C, 80001632

Bernheim Distillery Bottling Plant [West Louisville MRA], 822-828 S. 15th St., Louisville, 9/08/83, C, g, 83002634

Berry Hill [Jefferson County MRA], Dunraven Ct., Glenview vicinity, 7/12/83, C, 83002635

Beynroth House [Jefferson County MRA], 11503 Main St., Middletown, 5/31/84, C, 84001552

Bingham-Hilliard Doll House [Jefferson County MRA], 5001 Avish Lane, Harrods Creek, 12/05/80, C, 80001583

Jefferson County—Continued

Blankenbaker Station [Jefferson County MRA], 21 Poplar Hill Rd., St. Matthews, 12/05/80, C, 80001642

Board of Extension of the Methodist Episcopal Church, South [North Old Louisville MRA], 1115 S. 4th St., Louisville, 6/03/83, C, a, 83002636

Bodley, Temple, Summer House [Jefferson County MRA], Off Riva Ridge Rd. SW of Palatka Rd., Louisville, 3/29/85, B, 85002449

Bonavita-Weller House [Jefferson County MRA], 12006 Ridge Rd., Anchorage vicinity, 7/12/83, C, 83002637

Bonnycot [Jefferson County MRA], 1111 Bellewood Rd., Anchorage vicinity, 7/12/83, C, 83002638

Bosler Fireproof Garage, 423 S. 3rd St., Louisville, 8/18/83, A, C, 83002639

Bowman Field Historic District, Taylorsville Rd. and Peewee Reese Blvd., Louisville, 11/10/88, A, C, 88002616

Bradford Mills [Textile Mills of Louisville TR], 1034 E. Oak St., Louisville, 10/06/82, A, C, 82001555

Brandeis House, 310 E. Broadway, Louisville, 3/01/84, A, B, 84001553

Brandeis, Albert S., Elementary School, 1001 S. 26th St., Louisville, 12/08/80, C, 80001594

Bray Place, 2227 Bashford Manor Lane, Louisville, 8/11/80, C, 80001595

Bridges, C. A., Tobacco Warehouse [West Louisville MRA], 1719-23 W. Main St., Louisville, 9/08/83, A, C, 83002640

Broadway Temple A.M.E. Zion Church, 662 S. 13th St., Louisville, 12/08/80, C, a, 80001596

Brown Hotel Building and Theater, 675 River City Mall, Louisville, 2/17/78, B, C, 78001346

Brown Tobacco Warehouse [West Louisville MRA], 1019-25 W. Main St., Louisville, 9/08/83, A, C, 83002643

Brown, James, House [Jefferson County MRA], Browns Lane, St. Matthews vicinity, 7/12/83, C, 83002641

Brown, Theodore, House [Jefferson County MRA], Browns Lane, St. Matthews vicinity, 7/12/83, C, 83002642

Bull, William, House [Jefferson County MRA], 11918 Old Shelbyville Rd., Middletown, 12/05/80, C, 80001636

Bullock-Clifton House, 1824 Rosedale Ave., Louisville, 5/06/82, B, C, 82002707

Bush, Cornelia, House, 316 Kenwood Dr., Louisville, 5/06/82, C, 82002708

Bush, S. S., House, 230 Kenwood Hill Rd., Louisville, 4/30/79, B, C, 79000998

Butchertown Historic District, Roughly bounded by Main, Hancock, Geiger, Quincy Sts., US 42, S. Fort Beargrass Creek, and Baxter Ave., Louisville, 8/11/76, A, C, 76000900

Calvary Episcopal Church, 821 S. 4th St., Louisville, 1/18/78, C, a, 78001347

Caperton Block, 564-574 4th Ave., Louisville, 7/12/84, C, 84001554

Cardinal Hill Reservoir [Jefferson County MRA], Cardinal Hill Rd., Louisville, 12/05/80, C, g, 80001597

Carmichael House [Jefferson County MRA], Off KY 155, Fisherville vicinity, 7/12/83, C, 83002645

Cathedral of the Assumption, 443 S. 5th St., Louisville, 9/21/77, A, C, a, 77000623

Cave Hill Cemetery, 701 Baxter Ave., Louisville, 12/11/79, C, d, 79000999

Cedarbrook Farm [Louisville and Jefferson Co. MPS], 4800 Springdale Rd., Louisville vicinity, 12/21/90, A, 90001835

Central Colored School, 542 W. Kentucky St., Louisville, 9/13/76, A, B, C, 76000901

Central Kentucky Lunatic Asylum [Jefferson County MRA], Lakewood Dr., Anchorage vicinity, 7/12/83, A, C, 83002646

Chenoweth Fort-Springhouse, Avoca Rd., Middletown, 7/01/75, A, B, C, 75000779

Chenoweth House [Jefferson County MRA], 255 Chenoweth Lane, St. Matthews, 12/05/80, C, 80001643

Cherokee Triangle Area Residential District, Roughly bounded by Bardstown Rd., Sherwood Rd., Broadway, E to jct. of Grinstead Dr. and Cherokee Pkwy., Louisville, 6/30/76, C, 76000902

Chestnut Street Baptist Church, 912 W. Chestnut St., Louisville, 12/03/80, C, a, 80001598

Chestnut Street Methodist Church, 809 W. Chestnut St., Louisville, 7/16/79, C, a, 79001000

Chrisler House [Jefferson County MRA], 4508 Upper River Rd., Harrods Creek, 12/05/80, C, 80001584

Christ Church Cathedral, 421 S. 2nd St., Louisville, 8/14/73, A, C, a, 73000807

Christ the King School and Church [West Louisville MRA], 718-724 S. 44th St., Louisville, 9/08/83, C, a, 83002647

Church of Our Merciful Saviour [West Louisville MRA], 473 S. 11th St., Louisville, 9/08/83, A, C, a, 83002648

Church of the Messiah, 805 S. 4th St., Louisville, 4/21/76, A, B, C, a, 76000903

Churchill Downs, 700 Central Ave., Louisville, 11/15/78, A, C, g, NHL, 78001348

Citizens National Life Insurance Building, 100 Park Rd., Anchorage, 11/11/77, A, C, 77000622

Clifton Historic District, Roughly bounded by Brownsboro Rd., William and E. Main Sts., Frankfort and N. Ewing Aves., Louisville, 8/29/83, A, C, 83002649

Clore, James, House [Jefferson County MRA], N of Prospect off KY 329, Prospect vicinity, 11/15/84, C, 84000387

Clover Hill, 2618 Dixie Hwy., Louisville, 7/17/78, B, C, 78001349

Coldeway House [Jefferson County MRA], 12005 E. Osage Rd., Anchorage, 12/05/80, C, 80001557

College Street Presbyterian Church, 113 W. College St., Louisville, 11/29/78, A, C, a, 78001350

Columbian School [West Louisville MRA], 18th and Wilson, Louisville, 9/08/83, C, 83002650

Commodore Apartment Building, 2140 Bonnycastle Ave., Louisville, 4/29/82, C, 82002709

Cooper Memorial Church [Jefferson County MRA], 9900 Preston Hwy., Okolona, 12/05/80, C, a, 80001639

Cornwall and Brown Houses, 957 S. 4th St., Louisville, 7/19/78, B, C, 78001351

Courteney, James, House [Jefferson County MRA], 12006 Hazelwood Rd., Anchorage, 12/05/80, C, 80001558

Crescent Hill Branch Library, 2762 Frankfort Ave., Louisville, 3/10/81, C, 81000282

Crescent Hill Historic District, Roughly bounded by Brownsboro and Lexington Rds, Peterson, Zorn, and Frankfort Aves., and Crabbs Lane, Louisville, 11/12/82, C, 82001556

Crescent Hill Reservoir, Reservoir Ave., Louisville, 9/10/79, A, C, 79001001

Davis Tavern [Jefferson County MRA], 11180 Shelbyville Rd., Middletown vicinity, 7/12/83, A, C, 83002651

Diamond Fruit Farm [Jefferson County MRA], 8101 Six Mile Lane, Jeffersontown vicinity, 7/12/83, C, 83002652

Diamond Fruit Farm (Boundary Increase) [Jefferson County MRA], 8101 Six Mile Ln., Jeffersontown vicinity, 5/30/90, A, C, 90000783

Diebold, Anton, House [West Louisville MRA], 4303 W. Broadway, Louisville, 9/08/83, C, 83002653

Diebold, J. W., Jr. House [West Louisville MRA], 4119 W. Broadway, Louisville, 9/08/83, C, 83002654

District #1 [North Old Louisville MRA], S. Brook and E. Breckinbridge St., Louisville, 6/03/83, C, 83002655

District #2 [North Old Louisville MRA], W. Breckinridge St. and S. 2nd St., Louisville, 6/03/83, C, 83002656

Doerhoefer, Basil, House [West Louisville MRA], 4432 W. Broadway, Louisville, 9/08/83, C, a, 83002657

Doerhoefer, Peter C., House [West Louisville MRA], 4422 W. Broadway, Louisville, 9/08/83, C, a, 83002658

Doerhoefer-Hampton House, 2422 W. Chestnut St., Louisville, 7/16/79, B, C, 79001002

Dogwood Hill [Louisville and Jefferson County MPS], 7001 US 42, Lyndon vicinity, 2/26/93, C, 93000043

Dolfinger, J., and Company Building [Louisville and Jefferson Co. MPS], 642 S. Fourth St., Louisville, 12/21/90, C, 90001836

Drumanard (Boundary Increase) [Louisville and Jefferson County MRA], 6401 Wolf Pen Branch Rd., Louisville vicinity, 1/29/92, C, g, 88002654

Dumesnil Street ME Church [West Louisville MRA], 17th and Dumesnil Sts., Louisville, 9/08/83, C, a, 83002659

Eclipse Woolen Mill, 1044 E. Chestnut St., Louisville, 12/22/78, A, C, 78001352

Edgewood [Jefferson County MRA], 3605 Glenview Ave., Louisville, 8/16/83, C, 83002660

Eight-Mile House, N of Louisville on Shelbyville Rd., Louisville vicinity, 3/26/76, A, C, 76000904

Electric Building, 619 S. 4th Ave., Louisville, 3/14/85, C, 85000558

Jefferson County—Continued

Elks Athletic Club, 604 S. 3rd St., Louisville, 7/16/79, C, 79001003

Emerson School, 1100 Sylvia Ave., Louisville, 5/03/82, C, 82002710

Engelhard House, 1080 Baxter Ave., Louisville, 12/05/80, A, C, 80001599

Epworth Methodist Evangelical Church [South Louisville MRA], 412 M. St., Louisville, 9/06/83, C, a, 83002661

Ewing, D. H., & Sons Creamery [North Old Louisville MRA], 981 S. 3rd St., Louisville, 6/03/83, C, 83002662

Falls City Jeans and Woolen Mills [Textile Mills of Louisville TR], 1010 S. Preston St., Louisville, 10/06/82, C, 82001557

Farmington, 3033 Bardstown Rd., Louisville, 10/18/72, C, 72000536

Farnsley, David, House [Jefferson County MRA], 4816 Cane Run Rd., Louisville, 7/12/83, A, C, 83002663

Farnsley-Moremen House, W of Louisville at 10908 Lower River Rd., Louisville vicinity, 4/20/79, C, 79003117

Fifth Ward School, 743 S. 5th St., Louisville, 3/31/78, A, C, 78001353

Finzer, Nicholas, House, 1212 Hull St., Louisville, 5/09/79, B, C, 79001004

Fire Department Headquarters [Historic Firehouses of Louisville TR], 1135 W. Jefferson St., Louisville, 11/07/81, C, g, 81000283

Firehouse No. 13 [Historic Firehouses of Louisville TR], 100 N. 34th St., Louisville, 3/10/81, C, 81000284

First Christian Church, 850 S. 4th St., Louisville, 7/16/79, C, a, 79001005

First Lutheran Church, 417 E. Broadway, Louisville, 10/29/82, C, a, 82001558

First National Bank-Kentucky Title Company Building, 214 S. 5th St., Louisville, 5/19/83, C, 83002664

First Street District [North Old Louisville MRA], Roughly bounded by E. Breckinridge, E. Kentucky, and I-65, Louisville, 7/14/84, C, 84001555

Fisher House [Jefferson County MRA], Old Taylorsville Rd., Fisherville vicinity, 7/12/83, A, C, 83002667

Fishpool Plantation [Jefferson County MRA], 9710 Preston Hwy., Louisville, 7/12/83, A, C, 83002668

Fitzhugh House [Jefferson County MRA], Wolf Pen Branch Rd., Harrods Creek vicinity, 7/12/83, C, 83002665

Ford Motor Plant, 1400 Southwestern Pkwy., Louisville, 1/27/83, A, C, 83002666

Forrester House [Jefferson County MRA], 1103 Evergreen Rd., Anchorage vicinity, 4/09/84, C, 84001559

Fourth Avenue Methodist Episcopal Church, 318 W. St. Catherine St., Louisville, 7/16/79, C, a, 79001006

Frank, Henry, House [Jefferson County MRA], Madison Ave., Middletown, 12/05/80, C, 80001637

Funk, Harriet, House [Jefferson County MRA], 9316 Hurstbourne, Jeffersontown, 12/05/80, C, 80001587

Funk, James H., House [Jefferson County MRA], 9000 Taylorsville, Jeffersontown, 12/05/80, C, 80001588

Gaar-Fenton House [Jefferson County MRA], 4124 Nachand Lane, Buechel vicinity, 7/12/83, C, 83002670

Gaffney House [Jefferson County MRA], River Rd., Louisville, 12/08/83, C, 83003710

Gardencourt Historic District [Louisville and Jefferson County MPS], 1010 Alta Vista Rd., Louisville, 12/01/88, C, 88002653

Garr House [Jefferson County MRA], 2100 Evergreen Rd., Anchorage vicinity, 7/12/83, A, C, 83002669

German Bank Building, 150 S. 5th St., Louisville, 10/11/84, C, 84000029

German Evangelical Church of Christ Complex, 1236 E. Breckinridge St., Louisville, 5/21/87, A, a, 87000795

German Insurance Bank [Market and Jefferson Streets MRA (AD)], 207 W. Market St., Louisville, 3/14/85, C, 85000559

Givens Headley and Co. Tobacco Warehouse [West Louisville MRA], 1119-1121 W. Main St., Louisville, 9/08/83, A, C, 83002672

Glenview Historic District [Jefferson County MRA], Glenview Ave., Louisville, 8/16/83, A, C, 83002673

Gordon, Cornelia, House, 308 Kenwood Hill Rd., Louisville, 5/06/82, C, 82002711

Green Tree Manor Residential Historic District [Louisville and Jefferson County MRA], 107 Fenley Ave., Louisville, 11/21/91, A, 91001664

Greve, Buhrlage, and Company [West Louisville MRA], 312-316 N. 15th St., Louisville, 9/08/83, A, C, 83002674

Greve, Buhrlage, and Company [West Louisville MRA], 1501 Lytle St., Louisville, 9/08/83, A, C, 83002675

Grove, Benjamin, House [West Louisville MRA], 518 N. 26th St., Louisville, 11/15/84, B, 84000371

Gwathmey, Richard, House [Jefferson County MRA], 1205 Elm Rd., Anchorage vicinity, 7/12/83, C, 83002676

Haldeman House [Jefferson County MRA], 3609 Glenview Ave., Louisville, 12/08/83, C, 83003712

Hannah House [Jefferson County MRA], 1306 Evergreen Rd., Anchorage, 12/05/80, C, 80001559

Harrods Creek Historic District [Louisville and Jefferson County MRA], Jct. of Upper River and Wolf Pen Branch Rds., Harrods Creek, 11/22/91, C, 91001679

Hausgen House [Jefferson County MRA], 1404 Walnut Lane, Anchorage vicinity, 7/12/83, C, 83002677

Hayfield, 1809 Tyler Lane, Louisville, 8/19/80, C, 80001600

Head House, Main St., Middletown, 6/28/74, B, C, 74000885

Herr-Rudy Family Houses, 520 Old Stone Lane, 4319 and 4417 Westport Rd., 612 Rudy Lane, 726 Waterford Rd., 1823 Ballard Mill Lane, 1705

Lynn Way, Louisville vicinity, 5/19/78, B, C, 78001354

Heyburn Building, 332 W. Broadway, Louisville, 7/16/79, C, 79001007

Heywood, John H., Elementary School [South Louisville MRA], 422 Heywood Ave., Louisville, 9/06/83, C, 83002679

Highlands Historic District, Roughly bounded by Barrett Ave., Eastern Pkwy., Frenwood, Bardstown, Woodbourne, Ellerbee, and Sherwood Aves., Louisville, 2/11/83, A, C, a, 83002680

Hikes Family Houses, 4118 Taylorsville Rd., 2806 Meadow Dr., 3026 Hikes Lane, Louisville, 3/21/78, B, C, 78001355

Hikes-Hunsinger House, 2834 Hikes Lane, Louisville, 10/10/75, C, 75000769

Hillcrest [Jefferson County MRA], 11600 Owl Creek Rd., Anchorage, 12/05/80, C, 80001560

Hite, Abraham, House [Jefferson County MRA], Starlight Lane, Buechel, 12/05/80, C, 80001575

Hite-Chenoweth House [Jefferson County MRA], 4219 Starlight Lane, Buechel, 12/05/80, C, 80001576

Hite-Foree Log House, 12401 Lucas Lane, Anchorage, 7/30/76, A, B, C, 76000899

Hoke, Andrew, House [Jefferson County MRA], 2700 Llandovery Dr., Jeffersontown vicinity, 7/14/83, C, 83002681

Holy Cross Catholic Church, School and Rectory [West Louisville MRA], 31st and Broadway, Louisville, 9/08/83, C, a, 83002684

Holy Name Church Rectory, Convent and School, 2920 and 2914 S. 3rd St. and 2911 and 2921 S. 4th St., Louisville, 5/13/82, C, a, g, 82002712

Hook and Ladder Company No. 2 [Historic Firehouses of Louisville TR], 221 S. Hancock St., Louisville, 11/07/80, C, 80001601

Hook and Ladder Company No. 3 [Historic Firehouses of Louisville TR], Frankfort Ave. and Pope St., Louisville, 11/07/80, C, 80001602

Hook and Ladder Company No. 4 [Historic Firehouses of Louisville TR], 2301 Jefferson St., Louisville, 11/07/80, C, 80001603

Hook and Ladder Company No. 5 [Historic Firehouses of Louisville TR], 1824 Garland Ave., Louisville, 11/07/80, C, 80001604

Hord, Robert, House [Jefferson County MRA], US 60, Eastwood vicinity, 7/12/83, C, 83002682

Horner House [Jefferson County MRA], 3509 Woodside, Louisville, 8/16/83, C, 83002683

House of Weller, 121 W. Main St., Louisville, 9/26/79, A, C, 79001008

Howard-Gettys House, 1226 Bates Ct., Louisville, 2/08/78, C, 78001356

Humphrey—McMeekin House, 2240 Douglass Blvd., Louisville, 3/20/86, C, 86000475

Ideal Theatre [West Louisville MRA], 2315-19 W. Market St., Louisville, 9/08/83, C, 83002686

Immanuel Chapel Protestant Episcopal Church [South Louisville MRA], 410 Fairmont Ave., Louisville, 9/06/83, C, a, 83002687

Inter-Southern Insurance Building, 239-247 S. 5th St., Louisville, 3/19/80, C, 80001605

Irvin, James F., House [West Louisville MRA], 2910 Northwestern Pkwy., Louisville, 9/08/83, C, 83002688

Jefferson County—Continued

Jefferson Branch Louisville Free Public Library, 1718 W. Jefferson St., Louisville, 7/18/79, A, C, 79001009

Jefferson County Armory, 525 W. Muhammad Ali Blvd., Louisville, 3/24/80, C, 80001606

Jefferson County Courthouse, 527 W. Jefferson St., Louisville, 4/10/72, A, C, 72000537

Jefferson County Courthouse Annex, 517 Court Pl., Louisville, 4/21/80, A, C, 80001607

Jefferson County Jail, 514 W. Liberty St., Louisville, 7/16/73, C, 73000808

Jeffersontown Colored School [Jefferson County MRA], 10400 Shelby St., Jeffersontown, 3/29/85, A, 85002448

Jones Estate [Jefferson County MRA], 1905 Stonegate Rd., Anchorage, 12/05/80, C, 80001561

Jones House [Jefferson County MRA], 4998 Valley Station Rd., Valley Station, 7/12/83, C, 83002689

Judge Kirby House [Jefferson County MRA], Kirby Lane, Jeffersontown vicinity, 7/12/83, C, 83002690

KYANG Site (15JF267), Address Restricted, Louisville vicinity, 9/12/72, D, 72000539

Kaufman-Straus Building, 427–437 S. 4th St., Louisville, 2/14/78, C, 78001357

Keneseth Israel Synagogue, 232-236 W. Jacob St., Louisville, 10/29/82, C, a, 82001559

Kennedy—Hunsinger Farm [Jefferson County MRA], 4334 Taylorsville Rd., Jeffersontown vicinity, 7/12/83, C, 83002685

Kennedy—Hunsinger Farm (Boundary Increase) [Louisville and Jefferson County MPS], 4334 Taylorsville Rd., Louisville vicinity, 10/11/90, A, 90001481

Kentucky National Bank, 300 W. Main St., Louisville, 7/16/79, A, C, 79001010

Kentucky Street School [North Old Louisville MRA], 119 E. Kentucky St., Louisville, 6/03/83, C, 83002691

Kentucky Wagon Works [South Louisville MRA], 2601 S. 3rd St., Louisville, 9/06/83, C, 83002692

Knights of Pythias Temple, 928–932 W. Chestnut St., Louisville, 11/29/78, A, C, 78001358

Kosmosdale Depot [Jefferson County MRA], Off Dixie Hwy., Valley Station vicinity, 4/09/84, C, 84001562

Ladless Hill [Jefferson County MRA], 6501 Longview Lane, Louisville, 8/16/83, C, 83002693

Landward House, 1385-1387 S. 4th St., Louisville, 9/20/73, C, 73000809

Leatherman House [Jefferson County MRA], 3606 College Dr., Jeffersontown, 12/05/80, C, 80001589

Levy Brothers Building [Market and Jefferson Streets MRA (AD)], 235 W. Market St., Louisville, 3/24/78, B, C, 78001359

Lewis, Dr. John, House [Jefferson County MRA], 220 Ridgeway Ave., St. Matthews vicinity, 4/09/84, C, 84001564

Lewiston House [Jefferson County MRA], 4902 Ranchland, Valley Station, 12/05/80, C, 80001645

Limerick Historic District, Roughly bounded by Breckinridge, Oak, 5th and 7th Sts., Louisville, 9/13/78, A, B, C, 78001360

Limerick Historic District (Boundary Increase), Between Breckinridge and Oak, 5th and 8th St., Louisville, 12/23/83, A, C, 83003715

Lincliff [Jefferson County MRA], 6100 Longview Lane, Louisville, 8/16/83, C, 83002694

Little Loomhouses, 328 Kenwood Hill Rd., Louisville, 6/30/75, A, C, 75000770

Locust Avenue [Jefferson County MRA], 1814 Fern Valley Rd., Louisville, 7/12/83, C, 83002695

Locust Grove, 561 Blankenbaker Ln., Louisville vicinity, 3/11/71, B, C, NHL, 71000347

Loew's and United Artists State Theatre, 625 S. 4th St., Louisville, 3/28/78, A, C, 78001361

Long Run Baptist Church and Cemetery, Long Run Rd., Eastwood, 8/06/75, A, C, a, d, 75000768

Louisville City Hall Complex, 601, 603, 617 W. Jefferson St., Louisville, 9/01/76, A, C, 76000905

Louisville Cotton Mills [Textile Mills of Louisville TR], 1008 Goss Ave., Louisville, 10/06/82, A, C, 82001560

Louisville Free Public Library, Western Colored Branch, 604 S. 10th St., Louisville, 12/06/75, A, C, 75000771

Louisville Free Public Library, 301 W. York St., Louisville, 3/27/80, A, C, 80001608

Louisville Male High School, 911 S. Brook St., Louisville, 4/18/79, A, C, 79001011

Louisville Municipal Bridge, Pylons and Administration Building, Spans Ohio River between Louisville, KY and Jeffersonville, IN, Louisville, 3/08/84, A, C, 84001578

Louisville Trust Building, 208 S. 5th St., Louisville, 4/18/77, C, 77000624

Louisville War Memorial Auditorium, 970 S. 4th St., Louisville, 12/27/77, A, C, 77000625

Louisville Water Company Pumping Station, Zorn Ave., Louisville, 11/11/71, C, NHL, 71000348

Louisville and Nashville Railroad Office Building [West Louisville MRA], 908 W. Broadway, Louisville, 9/08/83, C, 83002696

Lowell, James Russell, Elementary School [South Louisville MRA], 4501 Crittenden Dr., Louisville, 9/06/83, C, 83002697

Lower West Market Street District, 1500-2200 W. Market St., Louisville, 11/04/82, C, 82001561

Lyndon Cottage [Louisville and Jefferson County MPS], Terminus of Hurstbourne Country Club Dr., Louisville vicinity, 5/30/90, C, 90000781

Lynnford-Lyndon Hall [Jefferson County MRA], 8222 Shelbyville Rd., Lyndon vicinity, 4/18/85, C, 85002447

MAYOR ANDREW BROADDUS, 4th St. and River Rd., Louisville, 6/30/89, A, NHL, 89001446

Madrid Building, 545 S. 3rd St., Louisville, 7/11/85, C, 85001509

Maghera Glass-Ormsby Hall [Jefferson County MRA], 8521 La Grange Rd., Lyndon, 12/05/80, A, C, 80001633

Main Street District, Expanded, 316, 320, 324 and 328 W. Main St., Louisville, 4/01/80, C, 80001609

Marders, Jefferson, House [Jefferson County MRA], 211 Madison Ave., Middletown vicinity, 7/12/83, C, 83002698

Marlow Place Bungalows District [West Louisville MRA], 3139 to 3209 W. Broadway, Louisville, 9/08/83, C, 83002699

Marmaduke Building [Louisville and Jefferson County MRA], 520 S. Fourth Ave., Louisville, 7/26/91, C, 91000921

Marshall, John, Sr., House [Jefferson County MRA], 12106 Osage Rd., Anchorage, 12/05/80, C, 80001562

Marvin, Dr. J. B., House [North Old Louisville MRA], 809 S. 4th St., Louisville, 6/03/83, C, a, 83002700

Masonic Hall [Jefferson County MRA], 15116 Old Taylorsville Rd., Fisherville vicinity, 7/12/83, A, 83002701

May, Robert, House [Jefferson County MRA], 11104 Owl Creek Lane, Anchorage vicinity, 7/12/83, C, 83002702

McClure House [Jefferson County MRA], N of Westport Rd., Lyndon vicinity, 7/28/84, C, 84001581

McFerran, J. B., School [West Louisville MRA], Cypress and Hill Sts., Louisville, 9/08/83, C, 83002703

Meek-Miller House, 3123 N. Western Pkwy., Louisville, 9/10/79, C, 79001012

Meier, William G., Warehouse [West Louisville MRA], 2100 Rowan St., Louisville, 9/08/83, A, C, 83002704

Mengel Box Company [West Louisville MRA], 1247-1299 S. 12th St., Louisville, 9/08/83, C, 83002705

Merriwether House [Jefferson County MRA], 6421 Upper River Rd., Louisville, 3/22/89, A, 87000361

Middletown Inn [Jefferson County MRA], 11705 Main St., Middletown vicinity, 4/09/84, A, 84001580

Middletown United Methodist Church [Jefferson County MRA], Madison and Main Sts., Middletown, 12/05/80, C, a, 80001638

Midlands [Jefferson County MRA], 25 Poplar Hill Rd., Louisville, 8/16/83, C, 83002706

Monon Freight Depot [West Louisville MRA], 1400 W. Main St., Louisville, 9/08/83, A, C, 83002707

Montgomery Street School, 2500-2506 Montgomery St., Louisville, 5/06/82, C, 82002713

Moore, Simeon, House [Jefferson County MRA], 17317 Taylorsville Rd., Fisherville, 12/05/80, C, 80001581

Municipal College Campus, Simmons University, 1018 S. 7th St., Louisville, 11/21/76, A, C, 76000906

Murray, Dr. John, Farm [Jefferson County MRA], Murray Hill Pike, Lyndon vicinity, 7/12/83, A, 83002708

Nash-McDonald House [Jefferson County MRA], 1306 Bellewood Rd., Anchorage, 12/05/80, C, 80001564

National Foundry and Machine Company, 1402 W. Main St., Louisville, 5/01/80, A, 80001610

Jefferson County—Continued

National Tobacco Work Branch Stemmery [West Louisville MRA], 2410-18 W. Main St., Louisville, 9/08/83, A, C, 83002709

National Tobacco Works [West Louisville MRA], 1800-10 W. Main St., Louisville, 9/08/83, A, C, 83002710

National Tobacco Works Branch Drying House [West Louisville MRA], 2400 W. Main St., Louisville, 9/08/83, A, C, 83002711

National Tobacco Works Warehouse [West Louisville MRA], 101-113 S. 24th St., Louisville, 9/08/83, A, C, 83002712

New Enterprise Tobacco Warehouse, 925 W. Main St., Louisville, 12/04/80, A, C, 80001611

Newland Log House [Jefferson County MRA], 12007 Log Cabin Lane, Anchorage vicinity, 7/12/83, A, C, 83002713

Nitta Yuma Historic District, 5028, 5040, 5044, and 5051 Nitta Yuma, Harrods Creek, 2/10/83, C, 83002714

Nock House [Jefferson County MRA], 1401 Elm Rd., Anchorage, 12/05/80, C, 80001565

Nock House (Boundary Increase) [Jefferson County MRA], 1401 Elm Rd., Anchorage, 3/22/89, A, C, 87000364

Oakdale District [South Louisville MRA], Roughly bounded by Terrace Park, Southern Pkwy., 4th and Kenton Sts., Louisville, 9/06/83, C, 83002715

Old Louisville Residential District, Irregular pattern roughly bounded by S. 7th St. on W, North-South Expwy. on E, Kentucky St. on N, and Avery St. on S, Louisville, 2/07/75, A, B, C, 75000772

Old Louisville Residential District (Boundary Increase), Roughly bounded by I-65, 7th, Kentucky, and Avery Sts., Louisville, 7/12/84, C, 84001583

Old Presbyterian Theological Seminary, 109 E. Broadway, Louisville, 3/24/78, A, C, a, 78001362

Old U.S. Customshouse and Post Office, 300 W. Liberty St., Louisville, 11/23/77, A, C, 77000626

Old U.S. Customshouse and Post Office and Fireproof Storage Company Warehouse (Boundary Increase), 300–314 W. Liberty St., Louisville, 5/31/80, C, 80001612

Olmstead Park System, Algonquin, Cherokee, Eastern, Southern, North, and South Western Pkwys., Louisville, 5/17/82, A, C, 82002715

Omer/Pound House [Jefferson County MRA], 6609 Billtown Rd., Louisville, 7/12/83, C, 83002716

Oxmoor, 7500 Shelbyville Rd., Louisville, 7/13/76, B, C, 76000907

Paget House and Heigold House Facade, 1562 Fulton St. and River Rd., Louisville, 11/17/78, C, b, 78001363

Parkland Evangelical Church [West Louisville MRA], 1102 S. 26th St., Louisville, 9/08/83, C, a, 83002717

Parkland Historic District, Roughly bounded by RR tracks, Hale Ave., S. 26th and S. 30th Sts., Louisville, 6/04/80, C, 80001613

Parkland Junior High School [West Louisville MRA], 2509 Wilson Ave., Louisville, 9/08/83, C, 83002718

Peaslee-Gaulbert Warehouse [West Louisville MRA], 1427 Lytle St., Louisville, 9/08/83, C, 83002719

Pennsylvania Run Presbyterian Church [Jefferson County MRA], Vaughn's Mill Rd., Okolona vicinity, 7/12/83, A, C, a, 83002720

Peterson Avenue Hill, Peterson Ave., Louisville, 3/24/80, A, 80001614

Peterson-Dumesnil House, 310 S. Peterson Ave., Louisville, 10/31/75, B, C, 75000773

Phoenix Hill Historic District, Roughly bounded by Main, Campbell, Jefferson, Chestnut, Broadway, Hancock, Walnut, Shelby, Market and Floyd Sts., Louisville, 1/10/83, C, 83002721

Pirtle House [Jefferson County MRA], 5803 Orion Rd., Louisville, 8/16/83, C, 83002722

Planter's Tobacco Warehouse [West Louisville MRA], 1027-1031 W. Main St., Louisville, 9/08/83, A, C, 83002723

Porter-Todd House, 929 S. 4th St., Louisville, 4/30/79, C, 79001013

Portland Historic District, Roughly bounded by Missouri Alley, Pflanz Ave., Bank, N. 33rd and N. 37th Sts., Louisville, 2/21/80, A, C, 80001615

Presbyterian Manse [Jefferson County MRA], 125 Bellewood Rd., Anchorage vicinity, 7/12/83, C, 83002724

Presentation Academy, 861 S. 4th St., Louisville, 12/22/78, B, C, 78001364

Preston-St. Catherine Street Historic District, Roughly bounded by Roland, Preston, Jackson, St. Catherine and Floyd Sts., Louisville, 5/02/85, C, 85000953

Railway Depot [Jefferson County MRA], 1500 Evergreen Rd., Anchorage, 12/05/80, A, C, 80001566

Rauchfuss Houses, 837–847 S. Brook St., Louisville, 8/12/82, C, 82002716

Reed, J. V., and Company [West Louisville MRA], 1100 W. Main St., Louisville, 9/08/83, C, 83002725

Repton, 314 Ridgedale Rd., Louisville, 5/13/82, B, C, 82002717

Republic Building, 429 W. Muhammad Ali Blvd., Louisville, 8/12/82, C, 82002718

Ridgeway, 4095 Massie Ave., Louisville, 4/11/73, C, 73000810

Rockdale [Jefferson County MRA (Tyler Settlement Rural Historic District) (AD)], 12109 Taylorsville Rd., Jeffersontown vicinity, 7/12/83, C, 83002727

Rockledge [Jefferson County MRA], 4810 Upper River Rd., Louisville, 8/16/83, C, 83002728

Ronald-Brennan House, 631 S. 5th St., Louisville, 8/11/75, C, 75000774

Roosevelt, Theodore, Elementary School, 222 N. 17th St., Louisville, 3/22/82, A, C, 82002719

Rose Hill, 1835 Hampden Ct., Louisville, 12/03/80, C, 80001616

Rossmore Apartment House, 664 River City Mall, Louisville, 11/14/78, C, 78001365

Russell Historic District, Roughly bounded by S. 15th, S. 26th, Congress and W. Broadway Sts., Louisville, 5/07/80, A, B, C, 80001617

Saint Frances of Rome School, 2105–2117 Payne St., Louisville, 3/26/87, C, a, 87000515

Saint Francis of Assisi Complex, 1960 Bardstown Rd., Louisville, 5/29/87, C, a, 87000850

Savoy Historic District [Market and Jefferson Streets MRA], 209–221 W. Jefferson St., Louisville, 6/01/88, A, B, C, 88000188

Schneikert, Valentine, House, 1234 Lexington Rd., Louisville, 4/17/86, B, C, 86000848

Schuster Building, 1500-1512 Bardstown Rd., Louisville, 3/19/80, A, C, 80001618

Sears, Roebuck and Company Store, 800 W. Broadway, Louisville, 2/18/83, C, 83002729

Second and Market Streets Historic District [Market and Jefferson Streets MRA], Address Restricted, Louisville vicinity, 3/17/88, A, C, 88000186

Seelbach Hotel, 500 S. 4th St., Louisville, 8/12/75, C, 75000775

Selema Hall, 2837 Riedling Dr., Louisville, 9/06/78, B, C, 78001366

Shady Brook Farm [Jefferson County MRA], Avish Lane, Harrods Creek, 8/16/83, C, 83002731

Shallcross [Jefferson County MRA], 11804 Ridge Rd., Anchorage, 12/05/80, C, 80001567

Shawnee Elementary School [West Louisville MRA], 4151 Herman St., Louisville, 11/02/84, C, 84000275

Shawnee High School [West Louisville MRA], 4015 Herman St., Louisville, 11/02/84, C, 84000277

Shelby Park Branch Library, 600 E. Oak St., Louisville, 12/03/80, C, 80001619

Sherley Mansion [Jefferson County MRA], 2018 Homewood Dr., Anchorage, 7/12/83, C, 83002732

Shwab House [Jefferson County MRA], 4812 Upper River Rd., Louisville, 8/16/83, C, 83002733

Simrall-Warfield House [Jefferson County MRA], 1509 Cold Spring Rd., Anchorage, 12/05/80, C, 80001568

Snapp House [Jefferson County MRA], 8300 Bardstown Rd., Buechel, 12/05/80, C, 80001577

Snead Manufacturing Building, 817 W. Market St., Louisville, 8/01/78, A, C, 78001367

Soldiers Retreat [Jefferson County MRA], Seaton Springs Pkwy, Lyndon vicinity, 7/12/83, C, 83002734

South Central Bell Company Office Building, 521 W. Chestnut St., Louisville, 12/03/80, C, 80001620

South Louisville Reformed Church [South Louisville MRA], 1060 Lynnhurst Ave., Louisville, 9/06/83, C, a, 83002735

Southern Heights-Beechmont District [South Louisville MRA], Roughly bounded by Southern Pkwy., 6th St., Ashland, and Southern Heights Aves., Louisville, 9/06/83, C, 83002736

Southern National Bank, 320 W. Main St., Louisville, 8/12/71, C, NHL, 71000349

Speed Building, 319 Guthrie Green, Louisville, 5/18/83, C, 83002737

Jefferson County—Continued

Spring Station, 3241 Trinity Rd., Louisville, 12/12/77, A, C, 77000627

St George's Roman Catholic Church, 1909 Standard Ave., Louisville, 10/29/82, A, C, a, 82001563

St. Anthony's Roman Catholic Church, Rectory, Convent, and School, 2222–233 W. Market St., Louisville, 3/01/82, C, a, 82002720

St. Elizabeth of Hungary Roman Catholic Church, 1024–1028 E. Burnett St., Louisville, 5/06/82, C, a, 82002721

St. James Roman Catholic Church, Rectory, and School, 1430 Bardstown Rd., 1826 and 1818 Edenside Ave., Louisville, 3/01/82, C, a, 82002722

St. James-Belgravia Historic District, Roughly bounded by Central Park, S. 4th, S. 6th and Hill Sts., Louisville, 12/05/72, A, B, C, 72000538

St. Lukes Church [Jefferson County MRA], 1204 Maple Lane, Anchorage, 12/05/80, C, a, 80001569

St. Patrick's Roman Catholic Church, Rectory, and School, 1301–1305 W. Market St., Louisville, 3/01/82, C, a, 82002723

St. Paul's German Evangelical Church and Parish House, 213 E. Broadway, Louisville, 2/25/82, C, a, 82002724

St. Peter's German Evangelical Church, 1231 W. Jefferson St., Louisville, 12/04/80, C, a, 80001621

St. Therese Roman Catholic Church, School, and Rectory, 1010 Schiller Ave., Louisville, 7/28/75, A, C, a, g, 75000776

St. Vincent DePaul Church, Rectory, School, St. Ursula Home and Convent, Oak and Shelby Sts., and 1214 Logan St., Louisville, 11/15/84, C, a, 84000380

St.Bonifacius Kirche Complex, 501-531 E. Liberty St., Louisville, 10/29/82, A, C, a, 82001562

Starks Building, 455 S. 4th Ave., Louisville, 7/11/85, C, 85001508

Steam Engine Company No. 10 [Historic Firehouses of Louisville TR], 1419 E. Washington, Louisville, 11/07/80, C, 80001622

Steam Engine Company No. 11 [Historic Firehouses of Louisville TR], 1122 Rogers, Louisville, 11/07/80, C, 80001623

Steam Engine Company No. 18 [Historic Firehouses of Louisville TR], 2600 S. 4th St., Louisville, 11/07/80, C, 80001624

Steam Engine Company No. 2 [Historic Firehouses of Louisville TR], 617–621 W. Jefferson St., Louisville, 11/07/80, C, 80001625

Steam Engine Company No. 20 [Historic Firehouses of Louisville TR], 1330 Bardstown Rd., Louisville, 11/07/80, C, 80001626

Steam Engine Company No. 21 [Historic Firehouses of Louisville TR], 1761 Frankfort Ave., Louisville, 11/07/80, C, 80001627

Steam Engine Company No. 22 [Historic Firehouses of Louisville TR], 37th and Broadway, Louisville, 11/07/80, C, 80001628

Steam Engine Company No. 20 [Historic Firehouses of Louisville TR], 1735 Bardstown Rd., Louisville, 11/07/80, C, 80004498

Steam Engine Company No. 3 [Historic Firehouses of Louisville TR], 802–804 E. Main St., Louisville, 11/07/80, C, 80001629

Steam Engine Company No. 4 [Historic Firehouses of Louisville TR], 1024 Logan St., Louisville, 11/07/80, C, 80001630

Steam Engine Company No. 7 [Historic Firehouses of Louisville TR], 821 S. 6th St., Louisville, 11/07/80, C, 80001631

Steam Engine Company No.4 [Historic Firehouses of Louisville TR], 1617 W. Main St., Louisville, 11/07/80, C, 80004497

Stewart's Dry Goods Company Building, 501 S. 4th Ave., Louisville, 8/12/82, A, C, 82002725

Stitzel, Arthur P., House [Jefferson County MRA], 9707 Shelbyville Rd., Louisville, 3/22/89, B, C, 87000366

Stivers, Zodia, House [Jefferson County MRA], Fern Creek, Buechel, 12/05/80, C, 80001578

Stout, Ben, House [Jefferson County MRA], 8630 Stout Rd., Jeffersontown vicinity, 7/12/83, C, 83002738

Stuart Building, 601 W. Oak St., Louisville, 3/14/85, C, 85000560

Stucky House [Jefferson County MRA], 3504 Marlin Dr., Jeffersontown, 12/05/80, C, 80001590

Sunnyside, 3020 Poppy Way, Louisville, 3/14/85, C, 85000561

Taggart House [Jefferson County MRA], 5000 Bardstown Rd., Buechel, 12/05/80, C, 80001579

Taylor, Zachary, House, 5608 Apache Rd., Louisville, 10/15/66, B, NHL, 66000359

Taylor, Zachary, National Cemetery [Jefferson County MRA], 4701 Brownsboro Rd., St. Matthews vicinity, 11/03/83, B, d, 83003733

Theater Building, 625–33 S. 4th Ave., Louisville, 8/12/82, C, 82002726

Thierman Apartments [North Old Louisville MRA], 416-420 W. Breckinridge St., Louisville, 6/03/83, C, 83002740

Third and Jefferson Streets Historic District [Market and Jefferson Streets MRA], 301–317 S. Third St. and 232–244 Jefferson St., Louisville, 3/17/88, A, C, 88000190

Third and Market Streets Historic District [Market and Jefferson Streets MRA], 201–219 S. Third St. and 224–240 W. Market St., Louisville, 3/17/88, A, C, 88000187

Thompson, James, House [Jefferson County MRA], 1400 Walmut Land, Anchorage, 12/05/80, C, 80001570

Thornburgh House [West Louisville MRA], 376 N. 26th St., Louisville, 12/08/83, C, 83003735

Three Mile Tollhouse, 2311 Frankfort Ave., Louisville, 10/01/90, A, 90001489

Tiller, F. M., House [West Louisville MRA], 4309 W. Broadway, Louisville, 9/08/83, C, 83002741

Tingley, George H., Elementary School, 1311-1317 S. Preston St., Louisville, 7/12/84, C, 84001586

Tobacco Realty Company [West Louisville MRA], 118-126 N. 10th St., Louisville, 9/08/83, A, C, 83002742

Tompkins—Buchanan House, 851 S. 4th St., Louisville, 4/27/77, B, C, 77000628

Trade Mart Building, 131 W. Main St., Louisville, 5/25/73, C, 73000811

Trigg, James, House [Jefferson County MRA], Covered Bridge Rd., Prospect, 12/05/80, C, 80001640

Tucker, Hazael, Farm (Boundary Increase) [Jefferson County MRA], 2406 Tucker Station Rd., Jeffersontown vicinity, 5/01/86, A, C, 86001046

Tucker, Hazael, House [Jefferson County MRA], 2406 Tucker Station Rd., Jeffersontown, 12/05/80, C, 80001591

Tway House [Jefferson County MRA], 1021 Watterson Trail, Jeffersontown, 12/05/80, C, 80001592

Twin Gates Carriage House [Jefferson County MRA], 11801 Osage Rd., Anchorage vicinity, 7/14/83, A, C, 83002743

Tyler Block, 319 W. Jefferson, Louisville, 10/15/73, C, 73002253

Tyler Hotel [Market and Jefferson Streets MRA], 229–245 W. Jefferson St., Louisville, 3/17/88, C, 88000189

Tyler Settlement Rural Historic District [Jefferson County MRA], Roughly bounded by Southern RR, Taylorsville Rd., and Jeffersontown City, Jeffersontown vicinity, 5/01/86, A, C, 86001045

Tyler, Moses, House [Jefferson County MRA (Tyler Settlement Rural Historic District) (AD)], 3200 Tucker Station Rd., Jeffersontown vicinity, 7/12/83, C, 83002744

Tyler-Muldoon House, 132 E. Gray St., Louisville, 7/20/77, B, C, 77000629

Tylor, Robert, Place [Jefferson County MRA (Tyler Settlement Rural Historic District) (AD)], 12603 Taylorsville Rd., Jeffersontown vicinity, 7/12/83, A, C, 83002739

U.S. Marine Hospital, 2215 Portland Ave., Louisville, 1/09/78, A, C, 78001368

Union Station, 1000 W. Broadway, Louisville, 8/11/75, A, C, 75000777

University of Louisville Belknap Campus, 2301 S. 3rd St., Louisville, 6/25/76, A, C, g, 76000908

University of Louisville School of Medicine, 101 W. Chestnut St., Louisville, 7/30/75, A, C, 75000778

Ursuline Academy and Convent, 800 E. Chestnut St., Louisville, 6/13/78, A, C, a, 78001369

Vogt, Henry, Machine Company Shop, 10th St. and Ormsby Ave., Louisville, 2/11/82, A, C, 82002727

Walker, James, House [Jefferson County MRA], 1902 Evergreen Rd., Anchorage vicinity, 7/12/83, C, 83002745

Walnut Street Theater, 416 W. Walnut St., Louisville, 9/01/78, A, C, 78001370

Warehouse A, Brown—Forman Corporation, 18th and Howard Sts., Louisville, 4/16/90, C, 89001144

Waverly Hills Tuberculosis Sanitarium Historic Buildings [Jefferson County MRA], 8101 Dixie Hwy., Louisville, 7/12/83, A, C, 83002746

Webb, John, House [Jefferson County MRA], 12200 Lucas Lane, Anchorage, 12/05/80, C, 80001571

Jefferson County—Continued

Wedekind House and Servant's Quarters [West Louisville MRA], 2630 and 2532 W. Burnett St., Louisville, 9/08/83, C, 83002747

Weissinger-Gaulbert Apartments, 709 S. 3rd St., Louisville, 12/12/77, B, C, 77000630

West Main Street Historic District, W. Main St., Louisville, 3/22/74, A, C, 74000884

West Main Street Historic District, Expanded, 600-800 blocks W. Main St., and S side of 500 block, Louisville, 3/27/80, C, 80004594

Western Junior High School [West Louisville MRA], 22nd and Main Sts., Louisville, 9/08/83, C, 83002748

Westwood Farm [Jefferson County MRA], 7800 Six Mile Lane, Jeffersontown vicinity, 7/02/83, C, 83002749

White Mills Distillery Company, 18th and Howard Sts., Louisville, 12/08/78, A, C, 78001371

Whiteside Bakery, 1400 W. Broadway St., Louisville, 4/24/79, A, C, 79001014

Widman's Saloon and Grocery, 2317–19 Frankfort Ave., Louisville, 6/13/90, A, C, 89002016

Wilhoyte House [Jefferson County MRA], Covered Bridge Rd., Prospect, 12/05/80, C, 80001641

Williams, Abraham L., L & N Guest House [Jefferson County MRA], Murphy Lane, Lyndon, 12/05/80, C, 80001634

Williams, Eustace, House [Jefferson County MRA], 11705 Owl Creek Lane, Anchorage vicinity, 7/12/83, C, 83002750

Wilson, David, House, 2215 Carolina Ave., Louisville, 3/26/87, C, 87000511

Winchester House [Jefferson County MRA], 613 Breckinridge Lane, Louisville, 7/12/83, C, 83002751

Winkworth [Jefferson County MRA], 3200 Boxhill Lane, Louisville, 8/16/83, C, 83002752

Winston's, Dr., House [Jefferson County MRA], 11906 Ridge Rd., Anchorage, 12/05/80, C, 80001572

Wolf Pen Branch Mill, E of Harrods Creek on Wolf Pen Branch Rd., Harrods Creek vicinity, 1/05/78, A, 78001344

Woodside/John T. Bate House [Jefferson County MRA], 3100 Woodside Rd., Louisville, 8/16/83, C, 83002753

Wrampelmeier Furniture Company [West Louisville MRA], 226-228 N. 15th St., Louisville, 9/08/83, A, C, 83002754

Wright and Taylor Building, 611-617 S. 4th St., Louisville, 11/15/84, C, 84000383

Y.M.C.A. Building, 227–229 W. Broadway, Louisville, 12/16/77, A, C, 77000631

Yager House [Jefferson County MRA], Aiken Rd., Anchorage vicinity, 7/12/83, C, 83002755

Yenowine, George B., House [Jefferson County MRA], 1021 Watterson Trail, Middletown, 12/28/80, A, C, 80004599

Yenowine-Kennedy House [Jefferson County MRA], 4420 Taylorsville Rd., Jeffersontown vicinity, 7/12/83, C, 83002756

Jessamine County

Asbury College Administration Building [Jessamine County MRA], KY 29, Wilmore, 7/06/85, A, C, 85001532

Ashurst, Craig, House [Jessamine County MRA], Off US 27, Nicholasville vicinity, 7/05/84, C, 84001587

Barkley House [Jessamine County MRA], US 68, Nicholasville vicinity, 7/05/84, C, 84001590

Barkley, Isaac, House [Jessamine County MRA], KY 169, Nicholasville vicinity, 7/05/84, C, 84001594

Bethel Academy Site (15JS80), Address Restricted, Wilmore vicinity, 3/15/84, D, 84001597

Bicknell House [Jessamine County MRA], KY 29, Wilmore vicinity, 7/05/84, C, 84001600

Brick House on Shun Pike [Jessamine County MRA], Off KY 1268, Nicholasville vicinity, 7/05/84, C, 84001601

Bronaugh, J. S., House [Jessamine County MRA], 103 N. 2nd St., Nicholasville, 7/05/84, C, 84001603

Brown, George I., House, 206 Linden Lane, Nicholasville, 12/02/77, B, C, 77000632

Bryan, George and Betty, House [Jessamine County MRA], US 68, Nicholasville vicinity, 7/05/84, C, 84001606

Bryant House [Jessamine County MRA], U.S. 27, Nicholasville vicinity, 7/06/85, A, C, 85001541

Burrier House [Jessamine County MRA], N of Keene, Keene vicinity, 7/13/84, C, 84001607

Butler's Tavern [Jessamine County MRA], US 27, Nicholasville vicinity, 7/05/84, C, 84001608

Chaumiere des Prairies, N of Nicholasville off U.S. 68, Nicholasville vicinity, 9/25/75, A, C, D, 75000780

Chrisman, Joseph, House [Jessamine County MRA], US 27, Nicholasville vicinity, 7/05/84, C, 84001618

Curd House [Jessamine County MRA], KY 29, Wilmore vicinity, 7/13/84, C, 84001621

Duncan, J. W., House [Jessamine County MRA], KY 169, Nicholasville vicinity, 7/05/84, C, 84001622

Dunn, Nathaniel, House, N of Nicolasville off U.S. 68, Nicolasville vicinity, 3/07/79, C, 79001015

Ebenezer Presbyterian Church [Early Stone Buildings of Central Kentucky TR], Off SR 1267, Keene vicinity, 6/23/83, C, a, 83002797

Federal House on Hickman Creek [Jessamine County MRA], W of Logana, Logana vicinity, 7/06/85, C, 85001542

Fort Bramlette, Address Restricted, Nicholasville vicinity, 6/13/75, D, 75000781

Grubb, A., House [Jessamine County MRA], KY 169, Spears, 7/05/84, C, 84001626

Hoover House [Jessamine County MRA], US 27, Nicholasville vicinity, 7/05/84, C, 84001629

Hughes House [Jessamine County MRA], KY 169, Keene vicinity, 7/05/84, C, 84001632

Hunter, John, House [Jessamine County MRA], S of Logana, Logana vicinity, 7/06/85, A, C, 85001540

January, Ephriam, House [Early Stone Buildings of Central Kentucky TR], Address Restricted, Keene vicinity, 6/23/83, A, C, 83002798

Keene Springs Hotel [Jessamine County MRA], KY 1267, Keene, 7/05/84, A, 84001636

Knight, Grant, House [Jessamine County MRA], KY 169, Nicholasville vicinity, 7/05/84, C, 84001639

Lancaster, John, House [Early Stone Buildings of Central Kentucky TR], KY 169, Keene vicinity, 6/23/83, A, C, 83002799

Locust Grove Stock Farm [Jessamine County MRA], N of Keene, Keene vicinity, 7/05/84, C, 84001642

Log House on Shun Pike [Jessamine County MRA], Off KY 1268, Nicholasville vicinity, 7/05/84, C, 84001645

Lowry, William C., House [Jessamine County MRA], Off KY 169, Nicholasville vicinity, 7/05/84, C, 84001647

Marshall-Bryan House [Jessamine County MRA], US 27, Nicholasville vicinity, 7/05/84, C, 84001653

Martin, James G., House [Jessamine County MRA], Tates Creek Rd., Nicholasville vicinity, 7/05/84, C, 84001654

McClure-Shelby House, 5 mi. (8 km) E of Nicholasville on KY 169, Nicholasville vicinity, 11/20/78, C, 78001372

McConnell-Woodson-Philips House [Jessamine County MRA], 303 S. Main St., Nicholasville, 7/05/84, C, 84001657

Morrison-Kenyon Library [Jessamine County MRA], KY 29, Wilmore, 7/06/85, C, 85001539

Mt. Pleasant Baptist Church [Jessamine County MRA], N of Keene, Keene vicinity, 7/05/84, C, a, 84001659

Nave-Brown House [Jessamine County MRA], KY 29, Nicholasville vicinity, 7/05/84, C, 84001663

Newman, Davis, House [Jessamine County MRA], W of Spears, Spears vicinity, 7/05/84, C, 84001669

Nicholasville Historic District [Jessamine County MRA], Court Row, Maple and Main Sts., Nicholasville, 7/19/84, A, C, 84001674

O'Neal, George, House [Jessamine County MRA], Off U.S. 68, Nicholasville vicinity, 7/06/85, C, 85001538

O'Neal, James, House [Jessamine County MRA], Off KY 169, Nicholasville vicinity, 7/06/85, C, 85001537

Pleasant Grove [Jessamine County MRA], N of Keene, Keene vicinity, 7/05/84, C, 84001678

Providence Church [Jessamine County MRA], US 27, Nicholasville vicinity, 7/05/84, C, a, 84001682

Roberts Chapel [Jessamine County MRA], US 27, Nicholasville vicinity, 7/05/84, C, a, 84001686

Sandy Bluff [Jessamine County MRA], Off KY 1268, Nicholasville vicinity, 7/13/84, B, C, 84001689

Scott House [Early Stone Buildings of Central Kentucky TR], U.S. 27, Little Hickman vicinity, 6/23/83, A, C, 83002800

Jessamine County—Continued

Scott, John Harvey, House [Jessamine County MRA], Off US 27, Nicholasville vicinity, 7/13/84, C, 84001692

Shady Grove [Jessamine County MRA], Off U.S. 27, Nicholasville vicinity, 7/06/85, C, 85001536

Shanklin House [Jessamine County MRA], KY 169, Nicholasville vicinity, 7/06/85, B, C, 85001535

Steele, Robert, House [Early Stone Buildings of Central Kentucky TR], Troy Rd., Keene vicinity, 6/23/83, C, 83002801

Stone House on Brooklyn Hill [Early Stone Buildings of Central Kentucky TR], Off U.S. 68, Wilmore vicinity, 6/23/83, C, 83002802

Stone House on West Hickman [Early Stone Buildings of Central Kentucky TR], SR 1980, Nicholasville vicinity, 6/23/83, A, C, 83002803

Sunnyside Farm House [Jessamine County MRA], US 27, Nicholasville vicinity, 7/05/84, C, 84001695

Taylor, Ridge, Farm [Jessamine County MRA], Off KY 595, Nicholasville vicinity, 7/06/85, A, C, 85001534

Thornwood [Jessamine County MRA], Baker Lane, Nicholasville vicinity, 7/13/84, C, 84001697

Venable-Todhunter Houses [Jessamine County MRA], Tates Creek Rd., Nicholasville vicinity, 7/05/84, C, 84001781

Woodland [Jessamine County MRA], US 27, Nicholasville vicinity, 7/05/84, C, 84001783

Young House [Jessamine County MRA], KY 29, Nicholasville vicinity, 7/13/84, C, 84001787

Young, A. M., House [Jessamine County MRA], W of Ash Grove Pike, Nicholasville vicinity, 7/06/85, C, 85001533

Johnson County

Archer House [Johnson County MRA], 170 Euclid St., Paintsville, 1/26/89, C, 88003162

Blanton Archeological Site, Address Restricted, Oil Springs vicinity, 7/30/75, D, 75000782

Bond, Jeff, House [Johnson County MRA], Rt. 172, Red Bush, 1/26/89, C, 88003174

Dameron Shelter Archeological Site, Address Restricted, Paintsville vicinity, 8/01/75, D, 75000784

Davis, Daniel, House, NW of Paintsville on U.S. 460, Paintsville vicinity, 10/09/74, B, C, 74000886

First Baptist Church [Johnson County MRA], College St., Paintsville, 1/26/89, C, a, 88003165

First Methodist Church [Johnson County MRA], Main and Church Sts., Paintsville, 1/26/89, C, a, 88003155

First National Bank Building [Johnson County MRA], Main and College Sts., Paintsville, 1/26/89, C, 88003154

Flat Gap School [Johnson County MRA], KY 689 near jct. with KY 1092, Flat Gap, 1/26/89, C, 88003187

Foster Hardware [Johnson County MRA], Main and Court Sts., Paintsville, 1/26/89, C, 88003156

Lemaster, John J. and Ellen, House [Johnson County MRA], .6 mi. NE of Low Gap on Low Gap Fork, Low Gap vicinity, 1/26/89, C, 88003177

Mayo Methodist Church [Johnson County MRA], Third St., Paintsville, 1/26/89, C, a, 88003152

Mayo, John C. C., Mansion and Office, 3rd St., Paintsville, 5/03/74, B, C, a, 74000887

Mayo, Thomas, House [Johnson County MRA], 228 Second St., Paintsville, 1/26/89, C, 88003166

McKenzie, David, Log Cabin, McKenzie Branch, Volga vicinity, 8/26/82, A, C, 82002728

Meade Memorial Gymnasium [Johnson County MRA], Jct. KY 2040 and KY 40, Williamsport, 1/26/89, C, 88003170

Mine No. 5 Store [Johnson County MRA], KY 302, Van Lear, 1/26/89, C, 88003172

Mollett, Ben, Cabin [Johnson County MRA], Off KY 40 at Pigeon Roost Fork of Greasy Creek, Williamsport vicinity, 1/26/89, C, 88003171

Mott, Lloyd Hamilton, House [Johnson County MRA], Rt. 172, Red Bush, 1/26/89, C, 88003175

Oil Springs High School Gymnasium [Johnson County MRA], KY 580 off US 40, Oil Springs, 1/26/89, C, 88003178

Oil Springs Methodist Church [Johnson County MRA], Jct. KY 580 and US 40, Oil Springs, 1/26/89, C, a, 88003179

Paintsville City Hall [Johnson County MRA], Main St. and spur of KY 40, Paintsville, 1/26/89, C, 88003158

Paintsville Country Club [Johnson County MRA], KY 1107 at Davis Branch, Paintsville, 1/26/89, C, 88003168

Paintsville High School [Johnson County MRA], Second St., Paintsville, 1/26/89, C, 88003163

Paintsville Public Library [Johnson County MRA], Second St., Paintsville, 1/26/89, C, 88003164

Patterson House [Johnson County MRA], West and Second, Paintsville, 1/26/89, C, 88003167

Rice, H. B., Insurance Building [Johnson County MRA], Court and Main Sts., Paintsville, 1/26/89, C, 88003157

Rice, Wiley, House [Johnson County MRA], KY 825 at Asa Creek, Asa, 1/26/89, C, 88003180

Salyer House [Johnson County MRA], Off KY 825 at Asa Creek, Asa, 1/26/89, C, 88003181

Salyer, Addison, House [Johnson County MRA], Off KY 825 at Middle Fork of Jenny's Creek, Paintsville vicinity, 1/26/89, C, 88003169

Sparks Shelter Archeological Site, Address Restricted, Oil Springs vicinity, 7/30/75, D, 75000783

Stafford, Francis M., House, 102 Broadway, Paintsville, 10/29/75, C, 75000785

Stambaugh Church of Christ [Johnson County MRA], KY 1559 at Frog Ornery Branch, Stambaugh, 1/26/89, C, a, 88003182

Stambaugh House [Johnson County MRA], KY 1559 at Van Hoose Branch, Stambaugh, 1/26/89, C, 88003183

Turner, Judge Jim, House [Johnson County MRA], 315 Third St., Paintsville, 1/26/89, C, 88003153

Webb House [Johnson County MRA], 139 Main St., Paintsville, 1/26/89, C, 88003160

Webb, Byrd and Leona, House [Johnson County MRA], 137 Main, Paintsville, 1/26/89, C, 88003159

Wiley, Tobe, House [Johnson County MRA], 141 Euclid St., Paintsville, 1/26/89, C, 88003161

Williams House [Johnson County MRA], Rt. 689/Elna Rd., Red Bush, 1/26/89, C, 88003173

Kenton County

Austinberg Historic District [Eastside MRA], Roughly bounded by Chesapeake & Ohio RR, Licking River floodwall, rear lot lines N side of Wallace Ave., and Madison Ave, Covington, 2/18/87, A, C, 86003483

Beard, Daniel Carter, Boyhood Home, 322 E. 3rd St., Covington, 10/15/66, B, NHL, 66000360

Beechwood Historic District [Fort Mitchell MPS], Roughly bounded by Beechwood Rd., Dixie Hwy., and Woodlawn Ave., Fort Mitchell, 12/11/89, A, C, 89001168

Cathedral Basilica of the Assumption, 1130 Madison Ave., Covington, 7/20/73, C, a, 73000812

Central Ludlow Historic District [Ludlow MRA], Roughly bounded by Glenwood, Church, Adela, and Carneal Sts., Ludlow, 11/28/84, A, C, 84000526

Covington Downtown Commercial Historic District, Roughly bounded by C & O Railroad, Robbins, Greenup and 4th Sts., Covington, 6/09/83, A, C, 83002804

Covington Downtown Commercial Historic District (Boundary Increase), Roughly bounded by Ninth, Washington, and Seventh Sts. and Madison Ave., Covington, 4/11/91, A, C, 91000457

Covington and Cincinnati Suspension Bridge, Spans Ohio River between Covington, KY and Cincinnati, OH, Covington, 5/15/75, C, NHL, 75000786

Dixie Highway Historic District, 2696, 2698, 2700, 2708, and 2712 Dixie Hwy., Lakeside Park, 2/19/88, C, 88000146

Eleventh District School, Parkway and Altamont St., Covington, 6/16/83, A, C, 83002805

Elmwood Hall, 244–246 Forrest Ave., Ludlow, 8/07/72, C, 72000541

Emery Row, 810–828 Scott Blvd., Covington, 11/14/85, C, 85002820

Emery—Price Historic District [Eastside MRA], Roughly bounded by Eighth, Greenup, and Eleventh Sts., and alley behind W side of Scott Blvd., Covington, 2/18/87, A, C, 86003484

Fort Mitchell Heights Historic District [Fort Mitchell MPS], Roughly bounded by Park Rd., Barrington Rd., Dixie Hwy., and Fortside Dr., Fort Mitchell, 9/08/89, A, C, 89001169

Hearne House, 500 Garrard St., Covington, 6/24/74, B, C, 74000888

Helentown Historic District [Eastside MRA], Roughly bounded by Eleventh and Wheeler

Kenton County—Continued

Sts., Chesapeake & Ohio RR, and Madison Blvd., Covington, 2/18/87, A, C, 86003481

Highland Cemetery Historic District [Fort Mitchell MPS], 2167 Dixie Hwy., Fort Mitchell, 10/12/89, C, d, 89001585

Holy Cross Church and School Complex—Latonia, 3600 blk. of Church St., Covington, 4/17/86, A, C, a, 86000800

House at 855-857 Oak Street [Ludlow MRA], 855-857 Oak Street, Ludlow, 11/28/84, C, 84000320

House at 859 Oak Street [Ludlow MRA], 859 Oak St., Ludlow, 11/28/84, C, 84000329

JOHN W. HUBBARD (sternwheeler), Greenup St., Covington, 5/20/82, A, C, g, 82002729

Kenney's Crossing, 1001 Highway Ave., Covington, 3/22/90, A, 90000481

Kenton County Library, 1028 Scott St., Covington, 10/31/72, C, 72000540

Kruempelman Farmhouse [Fort Mitchell MPS], 24 Ridge Rd., Fort Mitchell, 9/08/89, C, 89001171

Lewisburg Historic District, Roughly bounded by I-75 and the Covington city limits, Covington, 11/05/93, A, C, 93001165

Licking Riverside Historic District, Roughly bounded by 4th, Scott, 8th Sts., and the Licking River, Covington, 7/30/75, A, C, 75000787

Ludlow Lagoon Clubhouse [Ludlow MRA], 312 Lake St., Ludlow, 11/28/84, C, 84000348

Maxwell House [Ludlow MRA], 27 River Rd., Ludlow, 11/28/84, C, 84000350

Merry, Prettyman, House [Early Stone Buildings of Kentucky Outer Bluegrass and Pennyrile TR], Shelby St., Bromley, 1/08/87, C, 87000203

Mother Of God Roman Catholic Church, 119 W. 6th St., Covington, 7/24/73, C, a, 73000813

Mutter Gottes Historic District, Roughly bounded by Madison Ave., 4th, Harvey, and Johnson Sts., Covington, 5/29/80, C, 80004499

Mutter Gottes Historic District (Boundary Increase), Roughly bounded by Madison Ave., 4th, Harvey, and Johnson Sts., Covington, 8/18/80, C, 80004552

Odd Fellows Hall, 5th and Madison Sts., Covington, 8/11/80, C, 80001646

Ohio Riverside Historic District (Boundary Increase), Along sections of Greenup St., Court Ave., Third, and Fourth Sts., Covington, 4/09/87, A, C, 87000612

Old Fort Mitchell Historic District [Fort Mitchell MPS], Roughly bounded by Saint Johns Rd., Dixie Hwy., E. Maple Ave., and Edgewood Rd., Fort Mitchell, 9/08/89, A, C, 89001170

Patton, Robert, House, 1533 Garrand St., Covington, 3/01/84, A, B, C, 84001789

Pleasant Run Stone House I [Early Stone Buildings of Kentucky Outer Bluegrass and Pennyrile TR], Bromley Rd. off KY 8, Bromley vicinity, 1/08/87, C, 87000153

Pleasant Run Stone House II [Early Stone Buildings of Kentucky Outer Bluegrass and Pennyrile TR], Bromley Rd. off KY 8, Bromley vicinity, 1/08/87, C, 87000154

Ritte's Corner Historic District, Latonia, Roughly bounded by DeCoursey, Southern, Inez, and Winston Aves., Covington, 5/21/87, A, C, g, 87000776

Riverside Drive Historic District, Bounded by Riverside Dr., 4th St., Licking River, and the alley between Greenup and Garrard Sts., Covington, 11/23/71, C, 71000350

Seminary Square Historic District, Roughly bounded by RR tracks, Holman, 9th and 12th Sts., Covington, 5/27/80, A, C, a, 80001647

Shinkle, Amos, Summer Residence, U.S. 25, South Ft. Mitchell, 4/28/83, B, 83002806

Trinity Episcopal Church, 326 Madison Ave., Covington, 3/01/82, C, a, 82002730

Wallace Woods Area Residential Historic District, Roughly bounded by 24th St., Glenway, Wallace, and Madison Aves., Covington, 8/11/83, A, C, 83002807

West Fifteenth Street Historic District [Eastside MRA], 1445–1451 and 1501–1513 Madison Ave., 1421-1423 Neave St., and 10–32 W. Fifteenth St., Covington, 2/18/87, C, 86003485

West Side-Main Strasse Historic District, Roughly bounded by C&0 Railroad, 6th, Philadelphia, Dalton, Pike, and Robbins Sts., Covington, 11/10/83, A, C, 83003650

Knox County

Barbourville Commercial District, Roughly bounded by Daniel Boone Dr., Liberty, High and Jail Sts., Barbourville, 8/02/84, A, C, 84003885

Croley—Evans Site (15KX24), Address Restricted, Rockhold vicinity, 11/30/85, D, 85002975

East Main Street Bridge [Corbin MRA], Engineers St. and Lynn Camp, Corbin, 3/28/86, A, C, b, 86000605

Mitchell Building-First State Bank Building, 222 Knox St., Barbourville, 8/01/84, A, C, 84002751

Old Classroom Building, Union College, College St., Barbourville, 5/30/75, C, a, 75000788

Saint Camillus Academy [Corbin MRA], Center St., Corbin, 3/28/86, A, C, a, 86000607

Soldiers and Sailors Memorial Gymnasium, Union College Campus, Barbourville, 8/01/84, A, C, f, 84001794

Speed Hall, College St., Barbourville, 4/29/82, C, 82002731

Larue County

Abraham Lincoln Birthplace National Historic Site, 3 mi. S of Hodgenville, Hodgenville vicinity, 10/15/66, A, B, C, c, NPS, 66000066

Atherton, Aaron, House [Larue County MPS], US 31E S of Athertonville, Hodgenville vicinity, 1/10/91, A, C, 90001962

Beeler, Dorsey, House [Larue County MPS], Edlin Rd. E of Lyons, Hodgenville vicinity, 1/10/91, A, C, 90001963

Brown House [Larue County MPS], KY 462 W of Gleanings, Hodgenville vicinity, 1/10/91, C, 90001964

Burch, Walter, House [Larue County MPS], Spaulding Rd., Hodgenville vicinity, 1/10/91, C, 90001965

Carter, Nicholas, House [Larue County MPS], Carter Brothers Rd., Hodgenville vicinity, 1/10/91, C, 90001966

Ferrill, Edward S., House [Larue County MPS], KY 470 N of jct. with KY 61, Buffalo vicinity, 1/10/91, B, C, 90001967

Goodin, Albert, House [Larue County MPS], KY 64 NE of Tonieville, Hodgenville vicinity, 1/10/91, C, 90001968

Hodgenville Christian Church, 100 W. Main St., Hodgenville, 12/20/77, C, a, 77000633

Hodgenville Commercial Historic District, Public Sq. and N. Lincoln Blvd., Hodgenville, 11/10/88, A, C, 88002540

Hodgenville Women's Club [Larue County MPS], Public Sq., Hodgenville vicinity, 1/10/91, A, 90001969

Kirkpatrick, Joseph, Springhouse [Larue County MPS], US 31E W of jct. with Co Rd. 1832, Hodgenville vicinity, 1/10/91, B, C, 90001970

Larue County Jail [Larue County MPS], E High Ave. S of jct. with US 31E, Hodgenville vicinity, 1/10/91, A, 90001971

Lincoln Boyhood Home, US 31E, 1 mi. S of Athertonville, Athertonville vicinity, 11/16/88, A, f, 88002531

Lincoln, Abraham, Statue [Larue County MPS], Public Square, Hodgenville, 1/10/91, A, f, 90001972

Lincoln, Nancy, Inn [Larue County MPS], US 31E, Lincoln Memorial National Historic Park, Hodgenville vicinity, 1/10/91, A, f, 90001973

McClain Hotel [Larue County MPS], KY 470 S of jct. with KY 61, Buffalo vicinity, 1/10/91, A, C, 90001974

Miller, William, House [Larue County MPS], 211 W. Water St., Hodgenville vicinity, 1/10/91, C, 90001975

Miller—Blanton House [Larue County MPS], Blanton Rd. E of Athertonville, New Haven vicinity, 1/10/91, C, 90001976

Nolynn Baptist Church [Larue County MPS], KY 222 SE of jct. with McCubbin—Harned Rd., Hodgenville vicinity, 4/18/91, B, C, a, d, 90001977

Patterson, Thomas, House [Larue County MPS], KY 84 W of Mathers Mill, Hodgenville vicinity, 1/10/91, C, 90001978

Phillips, William, House [Larue County MPS], KY 84 E of jct. with Co. Rd. 1517, Hodgenville vicinity, 1/10/91, C, 90001979

Saunders—Boyd House [Larue County MPS], 118 Forrest Ave., Hodgenville vicinity, 1/10/91, C, 90001980

School No. 20 [Larue County MPS], Stack Rd., Hodgenville vicinity, 1/10/91, A, 90001981

School No. 24 [Larue County MPS], McCubbin—Harned Rd. N of jct. with KY 222, Hodgenville vicinity, 1/10/91, A, 90001982

Larue County—Continued

Smith, David H., House [Larue County MPS], 223 Greensburg Ave., Hodgenville vicinity, 1/10/91, B, C, 90001983

Thomas, R. H., House [Larue County MPS], Brooks Rd. W of jct. with KY 470, Hodegenville vicinity, 1/10/91, C, 90001984

Tonieville Store [Larue County MPS], Tonieville—Glendale Rd. N of jct. with KY 61, Hodgenville vicinity, 1/10/91, A, 90001985

Walters, Thomas, House [Larue County MPS], US 31E N of Magnolia, Hodgenville vicinity, 1/10/91, C, 90001986

Laurel County

Bennett, Sue, Memorial School Building, College St., London, 9/11/79, A, a, 79001017

Federal Building-Courthouse, Main and 3rd Sts., London, 8/19/74, A, C, g, 74000889

First Evangelical Reformed Church, KY 80, Bernstadt, 4/22/80, A, a, 80001648

Pennington Infirmary, 411 Main St., London, 6/11/87, A, B, 87000900

Poynter Building, Main St., London, 8/08/85, A, C, 85001745

Sanders, Harland, Cafe, Jct. of W. Dixie Hwy. and E. Dixie Ave., Corbin, 8/07/90, A, B, 90001169

Wildcat Battlefield Site, 13.4 mi. N of London off U.S. 25, London vicinity, 6/28/79, A, 79001018

Lawrence County

Atkins—Carter House [Louisa MRA], 314 E. Madison St., Louisa, 11/01/88, C, 88002044

Big Sandy Milling Company [Louisa MRA], Pike St. between Lock Ave. and RR tracks, Louisa, 11/01/88, A, C, 88002045

First United Methodist Church, 204 W. Main St., Louisa, 11/15/84, C, a, 84000391

Freese, Capt., House [Louisa MRA], Sycamore St. facing Big Sandy River, Louisa, 11/01/88, B, C, 88002042

Garred House, Chapel, and Burial Vault, 9 mi. S of Louisa on U.S. 23, Louisa vicinity, 10/29/75, B, C, a, d, 75000790

Louisa Commercial Historic District [Louisa MRA], E. Main and Main Cross Sts., Louisa, 11/01/88, A, C, 88002041

Louisa Residential Historic District [Louisa MRA], Roughly bounded by Perry, Lock, Madison and S. Lady Washington Sts., Louisa, 11/01/88, C, 88002040

Louisa United Methodist Church [Louisa MRA], Main Cross and Madison Sts., Louisa, 11/01/88, C, a, 88002043

Vinson, Fred M., Birthplace, E. Madison and Vinson Blvd., Louisa, 9/04/74, B, c, 74000890

Yatesville Covered Bridge, S of Fallsburg over Blaine Creek off KY 3, Fallsburg vicinity, 3/26/76, C, 76000910

Lee County

Bear Track Petroglyphs (15LE112) [Prehistoric Rock Art Sites in Kentucky MPS], Address Restricted, Mount Olive vicinity, 9/08/89, A, C, D, a, 89001194

Big Sinking Creek Turtle Rock Petroglyphs [Prehistoric Rock Art Sites in Kentucky MPS], Address Restricted, Mt. Olive vicinity, 1/02/92, A, C, D, 91001888

Old Landing Petroglyphs (15LE113) [Prehistoric Rock Art Sites in Kentucky MPS], Address Restricted, Old Landing vicinity, 9/08/89, A, C, D, a, 89001195

Perdue Petroglyphs (15LE111) [Prehistoric Rock Art Sites in Kentucky MPS], Address Restricted, Fixer vicinity, 9/08/89, A, C, D, a, 89001193

St. Thomas Episcopal Church, Hill St., Beattyville, 4/21/76, A, C, a, 76000911

Leslie County

Frontier Nursing Service, Hospital Hill, off Hickory St., Hyden, 1/11/91, B, 90002126

McIntosh, Roderick, Farm, S of Dry Hill—McIntosh Rd. on confluence of McIntosh and Cutshin Crs., Dryhill vicinity, 11/07/91, A, C, 91001666

Shell, John, Cabin, S of Chappell on SR 2005, Chappell vicinity, 11/12/75, A, C, 75000791

Wendover, S of Hyden off KY 80, Hyden vicinity, 10/21/75, A, B, g, NHL, 75000792

Wooton Presbyterian Center, KY 80, Wooton, 5/24/79, A, a, 79001019

Lewis County

Cabin Creek Covered Bridge, 4.5 mi. NW of Tollesboro on KY 984, Tollesboro vicinity, 3/26/76, A, 76000912

Ohio River Lock and Dam No. 31 Grounds and Buildings, Rt. 1, Box 18, Kirkville vicinity, 5/12/87, A, 87000479

Stone Cellar on Cabin Creek [Early Stone Buildings of Kentucky Outer Bluegrass and Pennyrile TR], Cabin Creek Rd., Tollesboro vicinity, 1/08/87, C, 87000168

Lincoln County

Alcorn, James W., House, 409 Danville Ave., Stanford, 4/22/80, B, C, 80001649

Arcadia, S of Shelby City on U.S. 127, Shelby City vicinity, 5/04/76, C, 76000913

Baughman's Mill and Stanford Railroad Depot, Depot and Mill Sts., Stanford, 3/29/78, A, 78001373

Baughman, John, House, S of Stanford on KY 1247, Stanford vicinity, 12/22/78, C, 78001374

Briggs, Samuel and Mary Logan, House, 315 W. Main St., Stanford, 8/28/75, A, a, 75000794

Helm-Engleman House, N of Hubble on Engleman Lane, Hubble vicinity, 1/27/83, C, 83002808

Hoffman House [Early Stone Buildings of Central Kentucky TR], U.S. 27, Lancaster, 6/23/83, C, 83002809

Huston, Nathan, House [Early Stone Buildings of Central Kentucky TR], KY 78, Hustonville, 6/23/83, A, C, 83002810

Lincoln County Courthouse, Main and Lancaster Sts., Stanford, 4/22/76, C, 76000915

Logan, John, House, E of Stanford at jct. of U.S. 150 and Goshen Rd. (KY 642), Stanford vicinity, 6/11/75, B, C, 75000795

McCormack Church, 4 mi. W of Stanford on SR 1194, Stanford vicinity, 3/16/76, A, C, a, 76000916

Montgomery, Dr. Thomas, House, Somerset St., Stanford, 11/17/78, B, C, 78001375

Pence, Adam, House, S of Stanford on KY 1247, Stanford vicinity, 12/22/78, C, 78001376

Stanford Commercial District, Main St. from Somerset St. to Third St., Stanford, 11/17/86, A, C, 86003173

Swope-Dudderar House and Mill Site, E of Stanford on Goshen Rd., Stanford vicinity, 4/16/79, A, 79001020

Traveler's Rest, S of Shelby City off KY 300, Shelby City vicinity, 5/03/76, A, C, b, c, 76000914

Walnut Meadows, SE of Stanford on U.S. 150, Stanford vicinity, 12/22/78, C, 78001377

Whitley, William, House State Shrine, 2 mi. W of Crab Orchard off U.S. 150, Crab Orchard vicinity, 4/11/73, A, C, 73000814

Withers, Horace, House, KY 590 (Hubble Rd.), Stanford vicinity, 12/30/87, C, 87002189

Livingston County

Gower House, Water St., Smithland, 5/24/73, A, C, 73000815

Lawson, Thomas, House, Wabash Ave., Grand Rivers, 7/12/78, B, C, 78001378

Olive, Richard, House, Court St., Smithland, 4/29/82, C, 82002732

Logan County

Brodnax—Conn House, 3288 Conn Rd., Adairville vicinity, 10/23/92, B, C, 92001339

Davidson, G. W., House and Bank, Main St., Auburn, 10/29/82, A, C, 82001570

Forst, William, House, 4th and Winter Sts., Russellville, 7/19/73, A, C, 73000816

Long-Briggs House, Cornelius Ave., Russellville, 11/27/78, B, 78001379

Longview Farm House, Bores Rd., Adairville vicinity, 3/19/92, C, 92000170

McCutchen Meadows, Off U.S. 68, Auburn vicinity, 11/23/84, C, 84000292

McGready, Rev. James, House, W of Russellville off U.S. 68, Russellville vicinity, 4/21/76, A, B, C, a, 76000918

Logan County—Continued

Page Site (15LO1), Address Restricted, Lewisburg vicinity, 11/14/85, D, 85002819

Pleasant Run Methodist Church, SE of Russellville on KY 663, Russellville vicinity, 10/29/82, A, C, a, 82001571

Red River Presbyterian Meetinghouse Site and Cemetery, NE of Adairville off KY 663, Adairville vicinity, 6/18/76, A, a, d, 76000917

Russellville Historic District, Roughly bounded by 2nd, 9th, Caldwell, and Nashville Sts., Russellville, 7/14/76, A, C, 76000919

Savage Cave Archeological Site, Address Restricted, Adairville vicinity, 4/03/70, D, 70000252

Sawyer, David, House [Early Stone Buildings of Kentucky Outer Bluegrass and Pennyrile TR], Off KY 103, Chandler's Chapel vicinity, 1/08/87, C, 87000214

South Union Shaker Center House and Preservatory, U.S. 68, South Union, 6/28/74, A, C, a, 74000891

South Union Shakertown Historic District, KY 73 at Louisville and Nashville RR tracks, and jct. of U.S. 68, South Union and vicinity, 4/03/75, A, C, a, 75000796

Watkins Site (15L012), Address Restricted, South Union vicinity, 12/05/85, D, 85003065

Lyon County

Kelly's Suwanee Furnace Office, Address Restricted, Kuttawa vicinity, 8/26/71, B, D, 71000351

MAMIE S. BARRETT (towboat), Eddy Creek Marina, Eddyville, 4/28/83, A, 83002811

Old Eddyville Historic District, Off KY 730, Eddyville, 4/30/81, A, C, 81000285

Whalen Site (125-Ly-48), Address Restricted, Kuttawa vicinity, 1/27/83, D, 83002812

Madison County

Archeological Site 15 Ma 24, Address Restricted, Round Hill vicinity, 8/18/80, D, 80001651

Archeological Site No. 15MA25, Address Restricted, Bighill vicinity, 4/28/83, A, D, 83002816

Arlington [Richmond MRA], Lexington Rd., Richmond, 10/13/83, B, C, 83003778

Blair Park [Richmond MRA], 108 Rosedale St., Richmond, 10/13/83, B, C, 83003779

Blythewood [Madison County MRA], Jct. of Peytontown and Duncanon Rds., Richmond vicinity, 2/08/89, C, 88003330

Bogie Circle, Address Restricted, Ruthton vicinity, 3/28/83, D, 83002814

Bogie Houses and Mill Site, 8 mi. W of Richmond on Silver Creek, Richmond vicinity, 8/13/76, B, C, 76000920

Breck, Judge Daniel, House, 312 Lancaster Ave., Richmond, 11/07/76, B, C, 76000921

Bronston Place [Richmond MRA], Woodland Ave., Richmond, 10/13/83, C, 83003781

Burnawood [Richmond MRA], Burnam Ct., Richmond, 1/03/84, B, C, 84001801

Campbell House [Madison County MRA], KY 52 near Paint Lick, Paint Lick vicinity, 2/08/89, C, 88003334

Cane Springs Primitive Baptist Church, N of College Hill, College Hill vicinity, 12/22/78, B, a, 78001381

Chenault House [Madison County MRA], N of Richmond off I-75, Richmond vicinity, 2/08/89, C, 88003339

Clay, Brutus and Pattie Field, House [Madison County MRA], Lexington Rd. W of Richmond, Richmond vicinity, 6/13/90, C, 88003341

Cobb, Whitney, House [Madison County MRA], KY 388, Richmond vicinity, 2/08/89, C, 88003312

Cornelison Pottery, KY 52, Bybee, 7/24/78, B, 78001380

Covington House [Madison County MRA], SW of Richmond on KY 595, Richmond vicinity, 2/08/89, C, 88003329

Downtown Richmond Historic District, Main St. and Courthouse Sq., Richmond, 9/30/76, A, C, a, 76000922

Dozier—Guess House [Madison County MRA], KY 388, Red House Rd., Richmond vicinity, 5/01/89, C, 88003343

Duncannon, S of Richmond on John Parrish Lane, Richmond vicinity, 9/17/80, C, 80001650

Eastern Kentucky University Historic District [Richmond MRA], Lancaster, Crabbe Sts. and University Dr., Richmond, 1/03/84, A, C, 84001804

Elk Garden [Madison County MRA], S of Kirksville off KY 595, Kirksville vicinity, 2/08/89, B, 88003326

Farmers Bank of Kirksville [Madison County MRA], Near jct. of KY 595 and CR 1295, Kirksville, 6/13/90, C, 88003324

Griggs House [Madison County MRA], N of Waco, Waco vicinity, 2/08/89, C, 88003316

Hagan House [Madison County MRA], Hagans Mill Rd., Richmond vicinity, 2/08/89, C, 88003337

Hakins—Stone—Hagan—Curtis House [Madison County MRA], 1875 Curtis Pike, Kirksville vicinity, 2/08/89, C, 88003327

Hawkins, Nathan, House [Early Stone Buildings of Central Kentucky TR], Curtis Rd., Kirksville vicinity, 6/23/83, A, C, 83002815

Holloway, William, House [Richmond MRA], Hillsdale St., Richmond, 10/13/83, C, 83003783

Homelands [Madison County MRA], NW of Richmond on US 25, Richmond vicinity, 2/08/89, C, 88003332

Irvinton, 319 Lancaster Ave., Richmond, 5/06/75, B, C, 75000798

Jones, Merritt, Tavern, 1 mi. S of Big Hill on U.S. 421, Big Hill vicinity, 4/02/73, A, B, C, 73000817

Karr House [Madison County MRA], Lost Fork Rd., Richmond vicinity, 2/08/89, C, 88003313

Kirksville Christian Church [Madison County MRA], KY 595, Kirksville, 2/08/89, C, a, 88003325

Lincoln Hall, Berea College campus, Berea, 12/02/74, A, NHL, 74000892

Louisville and Nashville Railroad Passenger Depot, Broadway at Adams St., Berea, 8/22/75, A, C, 75000797

Madison County Courthouse, Main St. between N. 1st and N. 2nd Sts., Richmond, 5/12/75, A, C, 75000800

Mason House [Madison County MRA], S of Richmond off Meneleus Pike, Richmond vicinity, 2/08/89, C, 88003320

Miller, William M., House, S of Richmond, Richmond vicinity, 7/16/79, B, C, 79003602

Moberly House [Madison County MRA], 0.3 mi. N of Old KY 52, Moberly vicinity, 2/08/89, C, 88003315

Moberly, John, House [Early Stone Buildings of Central Kentucky TR], Gum Bottom Rd., Moberly vicinity, 6/23/83, A, C, 83002817

Morrison House [Madison County MRA], E of Kirksville off KY 595, Kirksville vicinity, 2/08/89, C, 88003340

Mt. Pleasant [Richmond MRA], 2nd and Water Sts., Richmond, 10/13/83, A, C, 83003784

Mt. Pleasant Christian Church [Madison County MRA], N of Richmond on US 25, Richmond vicinity, 2/08/89, C, a, 88003331

Mt. Zion Christian Church [Madison County MRA], US 421 S of jct. with US 25, Richmond vicinity, 2/08/89, A, C, a, 88003318

Murphy, Stephen, House [Early Stone Buildings of Central Kentucky TR], Off KY 39, Little Hickman, 6/23/83, C, 83002818

Newland, Isaac, House [Early Stone Buildings of Central Kentucky TR], Off U.S. 25, Richmond vicinity, 6/23/83, A, C, 83002819

Noland Mound (15-Ma-14), Address Restricted, Richmond vicinity, 1/27/83, D, 83002820

Old Central University, University Dr. on Eastern Kentucky University campus, Richmond, 6/19/73, A, C, 73000818

Richmond Cemetery [Richmond MRA], E. Main St., Richmond, 10/13/83, C, d, 83003785

Rolling Meadows [Madison County MRA], KY 595 N of Round Hill, Round Hill vicinity, 2/08/89, C, 88003321

Shearer Store [Madison County MRA], KY 1936 at Union City, Richmond vicinity, 6/13/90, C, 88003314

Simmons House [Madison County MRA], Arbuckle Lane off CR 1295, Richmond vicinity, 2/08/89, C, 88003323

Squire Turner House [Richmond MRA], 302 N. 2nd St., Richmond, 10/13/83, B, 83003786

Stephenson House [Madison County MRA], N of Round Hill on KY 595, Round Hill vicinity, 2/08/89, C, 88003322

Tates Creek Baptist Church [Madison County MRA], KY 627/Boonesborough Rd., Richmond vicinity, 2/08/89, C, a, 88003333

Taylor House [Richmond MRA], 216 Water St., Richmond, 10/13/83, C, 83003787

Madison County—Continued

Taylor House [Madison County MRA], N of Baldwin, Baldwin vicinity, 2/08/89, C, 88003336

Tevis House [Madison County MRA], KY 627/Boonesborough Rd., Richmond vicinity, 2/08/89, C, 88003335

Turner House [Madison County MRA], SE of Richmond on Curtis Pike, Richmond vicinity, 2/08/89, C, 88003338

Turner—Fitzpatrick House [Madison County MRA], Off Mule Shed Rd., Richmond vicinity, 2/08/89, C, 88003328

Viney Fork Baptist Church [Madison County MRA], Jct. of CR 499 and 374, Speedwell vicinity, 2/08/89, C, a, 88003317

Walker House [Richmond MRA], 315 Lancaster Ave., Richmond, 10/13/83, B, C, 83003789

Walker, William, House [Madison County MRA], Duncannon Rd., Richmond vicinity, 2/08/89, C, 88003319

West Richmond Historic District [Richmond MRA], Roughly W. Main St. between Church and Norwood Sts., Richmond, 1/12/84, C, 84001815

Whitehall, 7 mi. N of Richmond on Clay Lane off U.S. 25, Richmond vicinity, 3/11/71, B, C, 71000352

Magoffin County

Gardner, Judge D. W., House, KY 7, Salyersville, 3/28/79, B, C, 79001021

Marion County

Burks' Distillery, E of Loretto off KY 49 and 52, Loretto vicinity, 12/31/74, A, C, NHL, 74000893

Lebanon Historic Commercial District, Main St. roughly between Proctor Knott and Spalding Aves., Lebanon, 11/10/87, C, 87000857

Lebanon National Cemetery, 1 mi. SW of Lebanon off KY 208, Lebanon vicinity, 6/05/75, A, C, d, 75000801

Loretto Motherhouse, Off KY 152, Nerinx, 4/02/80, A, B, a, d, 80001653

Spalding, Leonard A., House, 307 E. Main St., Lebanon, 4/03/91, C, 91000367

St. Mary's College Historic District, S of St. Mary, St. Mary vicinity, 4/10/80, A, C, a, 80001654

Marshall County

Archeological Site No. 15 Ml 109, Address Restricted, Benton vicinity, 1/27/83, D, 83002813

Lemon, James R., House, 1309 Main St., Benton, 8/28/75, B, 75000802

Oak Hill, 26 Aspen St., Calvert City, 12/31/74, B, 74000894

Stilley House, 925 Birch St., Benton, 9/04/86, B, 86002195

Martin County

Himler, Martin, House, W of jct. of KY 40 and KY 2031, Beauty, 11/21/91, A, B, 91001667

Mason County

Armstrong Row, 207-227 W. 2nd St., Maysville, 3/01/84, A, C, 84001818

Bracken Baptist Church, CR 1235, Minerva, 4/28/83, A, C, a, 83002821

Courthouse Square and Mechanics' Row Historic District, W. 3rd St. between Market and Sutton Sts., Maysville, 5/12/75, A, C, a, 75000803

Cox-Hord House, 128 E. 3rd St., Maysville, 7/14/78, B, C, g, 78001382

Forman, Tom, House [Early Stone Buildings of Kentucky Outer Bluegrass and Pennyrile TR], Off US 62, Washington vicinity, 1/08/87, D, 87000170

Fox Farm, Address Restricted, Mays Lick vicinity, 5/09/83, D, 83002822

Gillespie Site (15MS50), Address Restricted, Mays Lick vicinity, 12/21/85, D, 85003180

Lee House, Front and Sutton Sts., Maysville, 12/20/77, B, C, 77000634

Lee's Creek Covered Bridge, S of Dover on Tuckahoe Rd. off KY 8, Dover vicinity, 3/26/76, A, C, 76000923

Mays Lick Consolidated School, U.S. 68 and KY 324, Mays Lick, 4/29/82, A, 82002733

Maysville Downtown Historic District, Roughly bounded by McDonald Pkwy., Front, Wall, Limestone and 3rd Sts., Maysville, 3/01/82, A, C, a, g, 82002734

Maysville-Aberdeen Bridge, Spans Ohio River between Maysville, KY, and Aberdeen, OH, Maysville, 6/30/83, A, C, 83002823

Moran, Ben, House [Early Stone Buildings of Kentucky Outer Bluegrass and Pennyrile TR], Intersection of KY 8 and KY 10, Moranburg vicinity, 1/08/87, C, 87000161

Newdigate-Reed House, W of Maysville at jct. of old KY 68 and U.S. 62, Maysville vicinity, 10/10/75, B, g, 75000804

Old Library Building, 221 Sutton St., Maysville, 8/30/74, A, C, 74000895

Pelham, Charles, House [Early Stone Buildings of Kentucky Outer Bluegrass and Pennyrile TR], Taylor Mill Rd., Orangeburg vicinity, 1/08/87, A, C, 87000148

Phillips' Folly, 227 Sutton St., Maysville, 8/10/78, B, C, 78001383

Poague House [Early Stone Buildings of Kentucky Outer Bluegrass and Pennyrile TR], Parker Ln., Mays Lick vicinity, 1/08/87, C, 87000210

Point Au View, 721 Hillcrest Rd., Maysville, 1/04/85, B, C, 85000015

Pyles Site (15MS28), Address Restricted, Mays Lick vicinity, 4/05/84, D, 84001821

Rust House, S of Maysville on KY 11, Maysville vicinity, 2/23/78, C, 78001384

Spring House at Flat Fork [Early Stone Buildings of Kentucky TR], KY 161, Flat Fork vicinity, 10/06/87, C, 87002051

Springhouse in Mays Lick [Early Stone Buildings of Kentucky TR], Off KY 324, Mays Lick, 10/06/87, C, 87002052

Stone Barn on Lee's Creek [Early Stone Buildings of Kentucky Outer Bluegrass and Pennyrile TR], US 68, Mays Lick vicinity, 1/08/87, C, 87000200

Valley Pike Covered Bridge, W of Maysville off KY 8, Maysville vicinity, 3/26/76, A, 76000924

Van Meter Site, Address Restricted, Mays Lick vicinity, 12/05/85, D, 85003040

Washington Historic District, Roughly bounded by Hoppe St., Bartlett Lane, and city limits on E & W, Washington, 1/21/70, A, C, a, 70000253

Washington Historic District (Boundary Increase), Extending N & S along U.S. 62 & 68, Washington, 5/28/76, A, C, D, d, 76002274

Washington Opera House, 116 W. 2nd St., Maysville, 6/11/75, A, C, 75000805

West Fourth Street District, 24, 29, 31, 32, 33 W. 4th St., Maysville, 11/07/74, B, C, 74000896

Woodlawn, S of Maysville on KY 11, Maysville vicinity, 11/24/78, C, 78001385

McCracken County

Anderson, Artelia, Hall, 1400 H.C. Mathis Dr., Paducah, 5/26/83, A, B, 83002824

Anderson-Smith House, Lone Oak Rd., Paducah, 3/01/84, C, 84001824

Angles, The, Alben W. Barkley Dr. near 40th St., Paducah, 7/19/76, B, C, 76002147

Archeological Site 15McN51, Address Restricted, Paducah vicinity, 7/11/85, D, 85001513

Grace Episcopal Church, 820 Broadway, Paducah, 3/16/76, A, C, a, 76002148

Hotel Irvin Cobb, Broadway and 6th St., Paducah, 8/24/78, B, C, g, 78003065

Jefferson Street-Fountain Avenue Residential District, Jefferson and Madison Sts., Broadway, Fountain Ave., and Harahan Blvd., Paducah, 7/14/82, B, C, 82002735

Lincoln School, S. Eighth St., between Ohio and Tennessee Sts., Paducah, 6/23/88, A, 88000895

Lower Town Neighborhood District, Roughly bounded by Park Ave., Jefferson, 5th and 9th Sts., Paducah, 3/15/82, B, C, 82002736

Market House, S. 2nd St. between Broadway and Kentucky Ave., Paducah, 6/19/73, A, C, 73002255

Nashville, Chattanooga, and St. Louis Railway Office and Freight House, 300 S. 3rd St., Paducah, 7/17/79, A, 79003118

Paducah Downtown Commercial District, Roughly bounded by 7th, 1st, Clark and Monroe Sts., Paducah, 4/20/82, A, C, g, 82002737

Paducah Downtown Commercial District (Boundary Increase), Roughly bounded by 1st, Clark, Seventh and Monroe Sts., Paducah, 5/02/85, A, 85000952

McCracken County—Continued

Paducah Market House District, 2nd St. between Broadway and Kentucky Ave., Paducah, 4/03/78, A, C, 78003066

People's First National Bank and Trust Company Building, 300 Broadway, Paducah, 8/11/80, A, C, 80001655

Saint Mary Academy Complex, Bounded by Fourth, Fifth, Monroe, and Jefferson Sts., Paducah, 3/17/87, A, C, a, g, 87000449

St. Francis DeSales Roman Catholic Church, 116 S. 6th St., Paducah, 4/16/79, A, C, a, 79003119

Yeiser, Mayor David A., House, 533 Madison St., Paducah, 3/07/73, B, C, 73002130

McCreary County

Stearns Administrative and Commercial District, Old US 27, Stearns, 11/16/88, A, 88002528

McLean County

Archaeological Site 15 McL 18, Address Restricted, Livermore vicinity, 3/15/82, D, 82002738

Archeological Site No. 15McL16 [Green River Shell Middens of Kentucky TR], Address Restricted, Rumsey vicinity, 4/01/86, D, 86000648

Archeological Site No. 15McL17 [Green River Shell Middens of Kentucky TR], Address Restricted, Livermore vicinity, 4/01/86, D, 86000649

Austin Site (15McL15) [Green River Shell Middens of Kentucky TR], Address Restricted, Calhoun vicinity, 4/01/86, D, 86000650

Butterfield Site (15McL7) [Green River Shell Middens of Kentucky TR], Address Restricted, Livermore vicinity, 4/01/86, D, 86000651

Crowe Shell Midden (15McL109) [Green River Shell Middens of Kentucky TR], Address Restricted, Kirtley vicinity, 4/01/86, D, 86000652

Ford, R. D., Shell Midden (15McL2) [Green River Shell Middens of Kentucky TR], Address Restricted, Ashbyburg vicinity, 4/01/86, D, 86000653

Griffith-Franklin House, 207 W. 2nd St., Calhoun, 7/07/75, B, 75002061

Meade County

Brandenburg Commercial District, Main St., Brandenburg, 3/27/86, A, C, 86000523

Brandenburg Methodist Episcopal Church [Brandenburg MRA], 215 Broadway, Brandenburg, 8/14/84, C, a, 84001828

Clarkson House, Clarkson Rd., Flaherty vicinity, 5/24/83, C, 83002825

Doe Run Creek Historic District, SE of Brandenburg off KY 448, Brandenburg vicinity, 12/19/78, A, C, 78001386

Doe Run Mill [Early Stone Buildings of Kentucky TR], SR 1638 on Doe Run Creek, Brandenburg vicinity, 10/06/87, D, 87002053

Goff-Baskett House [Brandenburg MRA], 550 Lawrence St., Brandenburg, 8/14/84, C, 84001832

Jones-Willis House [Brandenburg MRA], 321 Main St., Brandenburg, 8/14/84, C, 84001835

Meade County Clerk Office-Rankin House [Brandenburg MRA], 205 Lafayette St., Brandenburg, 8/14/84, A, C, 84001836

Meade County Jail [Brandenburg MRA], 125 Main St., Brandenburg, 8/14/84, A, C, 84001837

Payneville Petroglyphs (15MD308) [Prehistoric Rock Art Sites in Kentucky MPS], Address Restricted, Payneville vicinity, 9/08/89, A, C, D, a, 89001196

Richardson House [Brandenburg MRA], 547 Lawrence St., Brandenburg, 8/14/84, C, 84001838

St. Theresa Roman Catholic Church, 3 mi. NW of Rhodelia on KY 144, Rhodelia vicinity, 11/17/77, A, C, a, 77000635

Yeakel, Edward, House [Brandenburg MRA], 116 Decatur St., Brandenburg, 8/14/84, C, 84001839

Menifee County

Archeological Site 15MF355, Address Restricted, Frenchburg vicinity, 7/11/85, D, 85001505

Frenchburg School Campus, U.S. 460, Frenchburg, 12/22/78, A, a, g, 78001387

Skidmore Petroglyphs [Prehistoric Rock Art Sites in Kentucky MPS], Address Restricted, Fagan vicinity, 1/02/92, A, C, D, 91001887

Spratt's Petroglyphs (15MF353) [Prehistoric Rock Art Sites in Kentucky MPS], Address Restricted, Frenchburg vicinity, 9/08/89, A, C, D, a, 89001197

Webb, W. S., Memorial Rock Shelter, Address Restricted, Frenchburg vicinity, 1/09/79, D, 79001022

Mercer County

Adams House [Mercer County MRA], Van Arsdell Pike, Salvisa vicinity, 2/08/89, C, 88003357

Archeological Site 15ME15, Address Restricted, Harrodsburg vicinity, 7/11/85, D, 85001507

Aspen Hall [Mercer County MRA], 558 Aspen Hall Dr., Harrodsburg, 2/08/89, C, 88003372

Baldin House [Mercer County MRA], S of Ebeneezer on Ebeneezer Rd., Ebeneezer vicinity, 2/08/89, C, 88003349

Beaumont Avenue Residential District [Mercer County MRA], 338–538 Beaumont Ave., Harrodsburg, 2/08/89, C, 88003359

Boise House [Mercer County MRA], Bohon Rd. E of Salt River, Harrodsburg vicinity, 2/08/89, C, 88003356

Bonta House [Mercer County MRA], NE of Danville on US 127, Danville vicinity, 2/08/89, C, 88003354

Bowman, Col. John, House [Mercer County MRA], Kennedy Bridge Rd., Harrodsburg vicinity, 2/08/89, C, 88003353

Burford Hill [Mercer County MRA], Greenville St., Harrodsburg, 2/08/89, C, 88003367

Burris House [Mercer County MRA], S of Kirkwood Rd., Salvisa vicinity, 2/08/89, C, 88003362

Burrus, Nathaniel, House, 955 Vanarsdall Rd., Harrodsburg vicinity, 8/01/84, C, 84001840

Burton, Ambrose, House, Unity Rd., Harrodsburg vicinity, 8/11/83, A, C, 83002826

Cardwellton, 103 E. Broadway, Harrodsburg, 11/17/77, B, C, 77000636

Clay Hill, 433 Beaumont Ave., Harrodsburg, 11/07/76, B, C, 76000925

College Street Historic District, College St. from North Lane to Factory St., Harrodsburg, 2/09/79, C, 79001023

Cunningham House [Mercer County MRA], W of RR tracks in Bondville, Salvisa vicinity, 2/09/89, C, 88003361

Curry, Daniel, House [Mercer County MRA], 414 N. Main St., Harrodsburg, 2/09/89, C, 88003383

Daniel, Benjamin, House, NE of Harrodsburg off KY 68, Harrodsburg, 8/02/83, C, 83002827

Daughters' College, 638 Beaumont Dr., Harrodsburg, 4/02/80, B, 80001656

Doricham, 409 N. College St., Harrodsburg, 10/22/76, B, C, 76000926

Dunn, Peter, House [Mercer County MRA], S of McAfee off Old US 127, McAfee vicinity, 2/09/89, C, 88003358

Dutch Reformed Church, 3 mi. SW of Harrodsburg on Dry Branch Rd., Harrodsburg vicinity, 2/16/73, A, C, a, d, 73000819

Elms, The [Mercer County MRA], 354 E. Lexington, Harrodsburg, 2/09/89, C, 88003370

Fairview, 2408 Lexington Rd., Harrodsburg vicinity, 8/01/84, C, 84001883

Greek Revival Houses of Mercer County: Lynnwood, Walnut Hall, Glenworth, N and E of Harrodsburg off US 127, Harrodsburg vicinity, 3/30/78, B, C, 78001388

Greystone [Mercer County MRA], 618 Beaumont Ave., Harrodsburg, 2/09/89, C, 88003382

Gritton, Floyd, House [Mercer County MRA], Bondville Rd. W of Salt River, Salvisa vicinity, 2/09/89, C, 88003363

Harrodsburg Commercial District, Roughly bounded by Lexington, Greenville, and Chiles Sts., Moreland and Beaumont Aves., Harrodsburg, 4/03/80, A, C, a, 80001657

Honeysuckle Hill, 712 Beaumont Ave., Harrodsburg, 8/11/83, C, 83002828

Jones, Moses, House, N of Harrodsburg on Oregon Rd., Harrodsburg vicinity, 2/09/79, B, C, 79001024

Matheny—Taylor House [Mercer County MRA], Poplar and College Sts., Harrodsburg, 2/09/89, C, 88003378

McAfee Farm Historic District [Mercer County MRA], S of McAfee on Old Louisville Rd., McAfee vicinity, 2/09/89, A, C, 88003360

McAfee, George, House [Early Stone Buildings of Central Kentucky TR], Off SR 1160, Cornishville vicinity, 6/23/83, A, C, 83002829

Mercer County—Continued

McAfee, James, House [Early Stone Buildings of Central Kentucky TR], Talmage Rd, Harrodsburg vicinity, 6/23/83, A, C, 83002830

McGee House [Mercer County MRA], Jackson Rd., Harrodsburg vicinity, 2/09/89, A, 88003364

McGee, John, House [Early Stone Buildings of Central Kentucky TR], Jackson Rd., Cornishville vicinity, 6/23/83, A, C, 83002831

Mercer County Jailer's Residence [Mercer County MRA], 320 S. Chiles St., Harrodsburg, 2/09/89, C, 88003375

Millwood, S of Salvisa off U.S. 127, Salvisa vicinity, 7/06/76, B, C, 76000928

Moreland House [Mercer County MRA], Off US 68, Harrodsburg, 2/09/89, C, 88003371

Morgan Row, 222, 230, 232 S. Chiles St., Harrodsburg, 2/16/73, A, C, 73000820

Morgan, Joseph, House [Mercer County MRA], Moberly Rd., Harrodsburg vicinity, 4/18/90, C, 88003365

New Providence Presbyterian Church, 3 mi. S of Salvisa on U.S. 127, Salvisa vicinity, 10/10/75, C, a, 75000806

Passmore, Benjamin, Hotel [Mercer County MRA], N. Main St. and Broadway, Harrodsburg, 6/18/90, A, 88003374

Passmore, Benjamin, House [Mercer County MRA], 111 W. Broadway, Harrodsburg, 2/08/89, C, 88003376

Passmore, George, House [Mercer County MRA], Poplar and Greenville Sts., Harrodsburg, 2/09/89, C, 88003379

Pioneer Memorial State Park [Mercer County MRA], College Ave. between Lexington and Poplars Sts., Harrodsburg, 2/09/89, A, e, f, 88003377

Price, Dr. A. D., House [Mercer County MRA], 115 W. Poplar St., Harrodsburg, 2/09/89, C, 88003373

Roach—Ison House [Mercer County MRA], NE of Harrodsburg off US 68, Harrodsburg vicinity, 2/09/89, C, 88003352

Shaker West Lot Farm [Early Stone Buildings of Central Kentucky TR], Off U.S. 68, Harrodsburg vicinity, 6/23/83, C, 83002832

Shakertown at Pleasant Hill Historic District, On U.S. 68, Shakertown and vicinity, 11/11/71, A, C, a, NHL, 71000353

Shawnee Springs, 4 mi. NE of Harrodsburg on Curry Rd., Harrodsburg vicinity, 7/19/76, B, C, d, 76000927

Smith—Williams House [Mercer County MRA], S of Cane Run Pike, Burgin vicinity, 2/09/89, C, 88003355

St. Peters AME Church [Mercer County MRA], Lexington St. and US 127, Harrodsburg, 2/09/89, C, a, 88003381

St. Philips Episcopal Church, Short and Chiles Sts., Harrodsburg, 1/31/78, C, a, 78001389

Stone Quarters on Burgin Road [Early Stone Buildings of Central Kentucky TR], KY 152, Harrodsburg vicinity, 6/23/83, A, B, C, 83002833

Sutfield House [Mercer County MRA], 304 N. Main St., Harrodsburg, 2/09/89, C, 88003368

Sutfield-Thompson House, 362 N. Main, Harrodsburg, 9/13/77, C, 77000637

Taylor, Capt. Samuel, House, NE of Harrodsburg on Chatham Pike, Harrodsburg vicinity, 4/13/77, B, C, 77000638

Tobin House [Mercer County MRA], 1450 Curry Pike, Harrodsburg vicinity, 2/09/89, C, 88003350

US Post Office—Harrodsburg [Mercer County MRA], 105 N. Main St., Harrodsburg, 3/01/89, C, 89000019

Wildwood [Mercer County MRA], 388 Curry Pike, Harrodsburg vicinity, 2/09/89, C, 88003356

Williams House [Mercer County MRA], Warwick Rd., Harrodsburg vicinity, 6/18/90, A, C, 88003351

Woods, Archibald, House, 129 N. East St., Harrodsburg vicinity, 10/29/83, C, 83002834

Metcalfe County

Stockton—Ray House, Off jct. of US 68/KY 80 and Cumberland Pkwy., Edmonton vicinity, 4/13/92, C, 92000289

Monroe County

Evans, Thomas P., House, 701 N. Main St., Tompkinsville, 10/29/92, C, 92001488

Mount Vernon A.M.E. Church, N of Gamaliel on KY 100, Gamaliel vicinity, 11/17/77, A, a, 77000639

Old Mulkey Meetinghouse, S of Tompkinsville on KY 1446, Tompkinsville vicinity, 5/07/73, A, C, a, d, 73000821

Montgomery County

Bondurant House [Early Stone Buildings of Central Kentucky TR], Off U.S. 60, Mount Sterling vicinity, 6/23/83, A, C, 83002835

Chesapeake and Ohio Railroad Passenger and Baggage Depots [Mount Sterling MPS], N of C & O RR tracks between S. Maysville and S. Bank Sts., Mount Sterling, 4/23/91, A, C, 91000431

Chiles, William, House [Mount Sterling MPS], Off Richmond Rd. S of US 60, Mount Sterling, 4/23/91, C, 91000430

Church of the Ascension, High and Broadway Sts., Mount Sterling, 7/10/79, C, a, 79001025

East Mount Sterling Historic District [Mount Sterling MPS], Roughly, Harrison Ave. and N. Queen St. between E High St. and alley N of Strother St., Mount Sterling, 4/23/91, C, 91000433

Fitzpatrick, W. T., House [Mount Sterling MPS], Apperson Heights E of S. Bank St., Mount Sterling, 4/23/91, B, C, 91000429

Gaitskill Mound Archeological Site, Address Restricted, Mount Sterling vicinity, 10/21/75, D, 75000807

Hicks, Miss Emma, Bungalow [Mount Sterling MPS], 10 White Ave., Mount Sterling, 4/23/91, C, 91000428

KEAS Tabernacle Christian Methodist Episcopal Church, 101 S. Queen St., Mount Sterling, 5/26/83, A, C, 83002836

Machpelah Cemetery [Mount Sterling MPS], E. Main St. at eastern city limits, Mount Sterling, 4/23/91, C, d, 91000427

Methodist Episcopal Church South [Mount Sterling MPS], Jct. of E. Main and N. Wilson Sts., Mount Sterling, 4/23/91, C, a, 91000426

Monarch Milling Company [Mount Sterling MPS], Jct. of S. Maysville and E. Locust, Mount Sterling, 4/23/91, A, 91000425

Morgan, Ralph, Stone House, E of Mount Sterling on Harper's Ridge Rd., Mount Sterling vicinity, 4/10/80, A, C, 80001658

Mount Sterling Commercial District, U.S. 60 and KY 11, Mount Sterling, 10/03/80, C, 80001659

Northwest Residential District, Roughly AR 1991, N. Maysville St., W. Main St., Samuels Ave., High St., Antwerp Ave., Holt, Sycamore, and Sterling, Mt. Sterling, 9/14/89, A, C, 89001422

Smith, Enoch, House, SR 1, Mount Sterling, 8/19/80, B, C, 80001660

Morgan County

Burchwell, Ray, Archeological Site, Address Restricted, Redbush vicinity, 7/30/75, D, 75000808

Ferguson, Gar, Site, Address Restricted, Redbush vicinity, 7/24/75, D, 75000809

Hill, Ray, Archeological Site, Address Restricted, Redbush vicinity, 7/30/75, D, 75000810

Lonnie Hill Site, Address Restricted, Redbush vicinity, 8/22/75, D, 75000811

Morgan County Courthouse, Main St., West Liberty, 7/19/76, A, C, 76000929

Patoker Archeological Site, Address Restricted, Relief vicinity, 7/30/75, D, 75000812

Sherman Archeological Site, Address Restricted, Relief vicinity, 7/30/75, D, 75000813

Muhlenberg County

Baker Site (15MU12) [Green River Shell Middens of Kentucky TR], Address Restricted, Skilesville vicinity, 4/01/86, D, 86000654

Greenville City Hall [Greenville Kentucky MRA], Court Street, Greenville, 8/26/85, C, g, 85001906

Greenville Commercial Historic District [Greenville Kentucky MRA], 100 blks. of N. Main and E. Main Cross Sts., Greenville, 8/15/85, A, C, 85001903

Martin House [Greenville Kentucky MRA], 144 E. Main Cross St., Greenville, 8/15/85, B, C, 85001900

Muhlenberg County Courthouse, Courthouse Sq., Greenville, 12/22/78, A, C, 78001390

Muhlenberg County—Continued

North Main Street Historic District [Greenville Kentucky MRA], 100 and 200 blks. of N. Main St., Greenville, 8/15/85, C, a, 85001904

Old Muhlenberg County Jail [Greenville Kentucky MRA], Court Row, Greenville, 8/15/85, C, 85001901

Rice Tobacco Factory [Greenville Kentucky MRA], 112 N. Cherry St., Greenville, 8/15/85, A, 85001902

Short, George, House [Greenville Kentucky MRA (AD)], 121 N. Main St., Greenville, 9/15/80, C, 80001661

South Cherry Street Historic District [Greenville Kentucky MRA], Roughly bounded by S. Cherry, Hopkinsville, W. Main Cross and N. Cherry Sts., Greenville, 8/15/85, C, a, 85001905

Thomas, Robert, House, 516 Broad St., Central City, 12/06/90, B, C, 90001833

Nelson County

Archeological Site 15 Ne 3, Address Restricted, Lenore vicinity, 9/27/79, D, 79001027

Bardstown Historic District, Roughly bounded by 1st, 3rd, and 5th Sts. Muir Ave., and RR track, Bardstown, 2/17/83, C, 83002837

Beechwold, 500 E. Stephen Foster St., Bardstown, 11/29/84, C, 84000355

Bloomfield Historic District, Central Bloomfield, including parts of Hill, Main, Perry and Depots Sts. and Fairfield, Springfield and Taylorsville Rds, Bloomfield, 3/18/91, A, C, a, d, 91000234

Bruntwood, 714 N. 3rd St., Bardstown, 9/09/75, C, 75000814

Cobblestone Path, E end of Flaget Ave., NE to Broadway, Bardstown, 11/16/89, A, 89002018

Cottage Grove Historic District, 1015 Old Bloomfield Pike, Bardstown, 4/18/91, B, C, 91000390

Culpeper, N side of Springfield Rd./US 150, Bardstown vicinity, 5/26/88, A, C, 88000674

Duncan, Henry, House, Taylorsville Rd. N of Maple Grove Cemetery, Bloomfield, 12/06/90, C, 90001843

Edgewood, 310 S. 5th St., Bardstown, 7/30/75, B, 75000815

Howard Brothers' Store, General Delivery, Howardstown, 10/16/86, A, C, b, 86002861

Johnson, Ben, House, 1003 N. 3rd St., Bardstown, 7/16/79, B, 79001026

Kelley, John S., House, 306 S. Fifth St., Bardstown, 3/06/92, C, 91001103

L & N Steam Locomotive No. 152, Jct. of Depot and First Sts., New Haven, 12/30/74, A, C, 74000883

Mattingly House [Early Stone Buildings of Kentucky Outer Bluegrass and Pennyrile TR], Off US 150, Bardstown vicinity, 1/08/87, C, 87000201

Merrifield, Samuel B., House, N of Bloomfield on KY 55, Bloomfield vicinity, 4/01/80, C, 80001662

My Old Kentucky Home, U.S. 150, Stephen Foster St., Bardstown, 3/11/71, B, C, 71000354

Nelson County Jail [Early Stone Buildings of Kentucky Outer Bluegrass and Pennyrile TR], 111 W. Stephen Foster, Bardstown, 1/08/87, C, 87000178

New Sherwood Hotel, 138 S. Main St., New Haven, 3/26/92, A, C, 92000291

Old L & N Station [Early Stone Buildings of Kentucky TR], US 150, Bardstown, 7/12/90, C, 87002613

Old Talbott Tavern, Court Sq., Bardstown, 10/30/73, A, C, 73000822

Samuels, T. W., Distillery Historic District, Jct. of KY 523 and Corman RR tracks, Deatsville, 11/01/88, A, C, g, 88002047

Sisters of Charity of Nazareth Historic District, N of Bardstown off US 31E, Bardstown vicinity, 3/15/84, A, C, a, 84001425

Spalding Hall, St. Joseph's College, N. 5th St., Bardstown, 5/07/73, A, C, 73000823

St. Joseph Cathedral and College Complex, W. Stephen Foster Ave., Bardstown, 6/03/76, A, C, 76000930

St. Joseph Proto Cathedral, W. Stephen Foster Ave., Bardstown, 1/09/74, A, C, a, 74000897

St. Thomas Roman Catholic Church and Howard-Flaget House, 3 mi. S of Bardstown off U.S. 31E, Bardstown vicinity, 7/12/76, A, C, a, 76000931

Stone House on Buffalo Creek, Off SR 1330, Bardstown vicinity, 8/18/83, A, C, 83002838

Stone, John, House, US 62, Bloomfield vicinity, 7/12/84, A, C, 84001885

Wickland, 0.5 mi. E of Bardstown on U.S. 62, Bardstown, 2/16/73, B, C, 73000824

Nicholas County

Carlisle Historic District, Roughly Second, Broadway, North, Archdeacon, Trueman, Chestnut, Walnut, Market, Elm, W. Main, and School Dr., Carlisle, 10/26/89, A, 89001599

Carlisle, Louisville and Nashville Passenger Depot, Market and Locust Sts., Carlisle, 5/18/79, A, 79001028

Dinsmore House, 210 S. Elm St., Carlisle, 10/11/89, C, 89001602

Dorsey, Thomas A., Farmhouse, 416 High St., Carlisle, 9/28/89, B, 89001603

Ellis, James, Stone Tavern, U.S. 68, Ellisville, 3/16/76, A, C, 76000932

Forest Retreat Farm and Tavern, NW of Carlisle at jct. of U.S. 68 and KY 32, Carlisle vicinity, 10/02/73, A, B, C, 73000825

Kennedy, Thomas, House, Eastern Ave. at E. Main St., Carlisle, 9/28/89, C, 89001601

Mathers, William, House, KY 36, Carlisle, 10/12/89, A, C, a, 89001600

Riggs, Erasmus, House [Early Stone Buildings of Central Kentucky TR], Off KY 13, Carlisle vicinity, 6/23/83, A, C, 83002839

Stone Barn on Brushy Creek [Early Stone Buildings of Central Kentucky TR], U.S. 68, Carlisle vicinity, 6/23/83, A, C, 83002840

Thompson, John Henry, House [Early Stone Buildings of Central Kentucky TR], Off KY 32/36, Millersburg vicinity, 6/23/83, C, 83002841

Ohio County

Archeological Site KHC-6 (15OH97) [Green River Shell Middens of Kentucky TR], Address Restricted, Kirtley vicinity, 4/01/86, D, 86000655

Barnard, J. T., Shell Midden (KHC-1) [Green River Shell Middens of Kentucky TR], Address Restricted, Central City vicinity, 4/01/86, D, 86000669

Bowles Site (15OH13) [Green River Shell Middens of Kentucky TR], Address Restricted, Rochester vicinity, 4/01/86, D, 86000656

Chiggerville Site (15OH1) [Green River Shell Middens of Kentucky TR], Address Restricted, Knightsburg vicinity, 4/01/86, D, 86000665

Downtown Hartford Historic District, Roughly 100 and 200 blks. Main St. and Courthouse Sq., Hartford, 12/12/88, A, C, 88002760

Hartford Seminary, 224 E. Center St., Hartford, 6/19/73, A, C, 73000826

Hill, Samuel E., House, 519 E. Union St., Hartford, 5/27/80, B, 80001663

Indian Knoll, Address Restricted, Paradise vicinity, 10/15/66, D, NHL, 66000362

Jackson Bluff Site (15OH12) [Green River Shell Middens of Kentucky TR], Address Restricted, Rockport vicinity, 4/01/86, D, 86000666

Jimtown Site (15OH19) [Green River Shell Middens of Kentucky TR], Address Restricted, Kirtley vicinity, 4/01/86, D, 86000667

Louisville, Henderson, and St. Louis Railroad Depot, SE side Walnut St., 200' N of jct. with KY 54, Fordsville, 7/26/91, A, 91000923

Old Town Historic District, Roughly bounded by E. Union, Clay, E. Washington and Liberty Sts., Hartford, 11/15/88, A, C, 88002535

Pendleton House, 403 E. Union St., Hartford, 5/17/73, B, C, 73000827

Smallhous Shell Mound (15OH10) [Green River Shell Middens of Kentucky TR], Address Restricted, Smallhous vicinity, 4/01/86, D, 86000668

Wallace, Charles, House, Address Restricted, Hartford vicinity, 3/15/84, A, C, 84001890

Oldham County

Ashwood Avenue Historic District [Pewee Valley MPS], Roughly Ash Ave. from La Grange Rd. to Elm Ave., Pewee Valley, 8/07/89, A, C, 89000951

Bate, John Leslie, House [Early Stone Buildings of Kentucky Outer Bluegrass and Pennyrile TR], E of Buckeye Ln. off KY 42, Goshen vicinity, 1/08/87, C, 87000144

Bondurant—Hustin House [Peewee Valley MPS], 104 Castlewood Dr., Peewee Valley, 11/27/89, A, C, 89001989

Building at 301 La Grange Road [Peewee Valley MPS], 301 La Grange Rd., Peewee Valley, 11/27/89, A, C, 89001980

Carpenter-Smith House, Covered Bridge Rd., Crestwood vicinity, 2/25/82, C, 82002739

Oldham County—Continued

Central Avenue Historic District [Pewee Valley MPS], Roughly Central Ave. from Peace Ln. to Mt. Mercy Dr., Pewee Valley, 8/07/89, A, B, C, 89000950

Central La Grange Historic District, Primarily along Washington, Main, and Jefferson Sts., Kentucky Ave., and First through Sixth Aves., La Grange, 9/08/88, A, C, a, 88001316

Clore, Albert E., House, 6400 Clore Lane, Crestwood, 5/26/83, C, 83002842

Ellis, Joseph H., House [Peewee Valley MPS], 320 Maple Ave., Peewee Valley, 11/27/89, A, C, 89001988

Forrester—Duvall House [Peewee Valley MPS], 115 Old Forest Rd., Peewee Valley, 11/27/89, A, C, 89001987

Griffith, D. W., House, 206 N. 4th St., La Grange, 6/03/76, B, 76000935

Harrods Creek Baptist Church and Rev. William Kellar House, NW of Crestwood on Old Brownsboro Rd., Crestwood vicinity, 9/08/76, A, C, a, 76000934

Hermitage, The, Off U.S. 42, Goshen vicinity, 12/02/82, C, 82001572

Ingram, William, House, 6800 Shrader Lane, Buckner vicinity, 8/18/83, C, 83002843

Kellar, Abraham, House, W of Brownsboro off KY 329, Brownsboro vicinity, 7/09/79, C, 79001029

Locke-Mount House, S of Goshen off U.S. 42, Goshen vicinity, 11/24/82, C, 82001573

Locust, The, LaGrange Rd. off KY 146, Pewee Valley, 7/30/75, B, C, 75000817

McMahan House, 203 Washington St., La Grange, 5/13/82, C, 82002741

McMakin, William, House [Early Stone Buildings of Kentucky Outer Bluegrass and Pennyrile TR], Off KY 1817, Brownsboro vicinity, 1/08/87, C, 87000211

Miller, George, House [Peewee Valley MPS], 331 Central Ave., Peewee Valley, 11/27/89, A, C, 89001986

Peebles, Dr. Thomas C., House [Peewee Valley MPS], 114 Maple Ave., Peewee Valley, 11/27/89, A, C, 89001985

Peewee Valley Confederate Cemetery [Peewee Valley MPS], Maple Ave., SE of jct. with Old Floydsburg Rd., Peewee Valley vicinity, 11/27/89, A, d, 89001984

Ritter, John, House [Early Stone Buildings of Kentucky Outer Bluegrass and Pennyrile TR], Old Floydsburg Rd. off KY 1408, Floydsburg, 1/08/87, C, 87000159

Russell Court, Roughly bounded by Madison St., Chestnut St., E. Jefferson St., and Maple St., La Grange, 11/10/88, A, C, 88002612

Saint James' Episcopal Church, 401 Old LaGrange Rd., Pewee Valley vicinity, 12/05/85, C, a, 85003072

Sale, Reuben, House, 3700 Smith Lane, La Grange, 11/24/82, C, 82001574

Smith, William Alexander, House [Peewee Valley MPS], 108 Mt. Mercy Dr., Peewee Valley, 11/27/89, A, B, C, 89001982

Spring Hill, S of Ballardsville off KY 53, Ballardsville vicinity, 4/02/80, B, C, 80001664

St. Aloysius Church [Peewee Valley MPS], 202 Mt. Mercy Dr., Peewee Valley, 11/27/89, A, C, a, 89001983

Tanglewood [Peewee Valley MPS], 417 La Grange Rd., Peewee Valley, 11/27/89, A, C, 89001981

Taylor, Phillip R., House, Shuler Lane, Louisville vicinity, 5/24/83, C, 83002844

Tuliphurst [Peewee Valley MPS], 115 La Grange Rd., Peewee Valley, 11/27/89, A, B, C, 89001979

Van Horn—Ross House [Peewee Valley MPS], 138 Rosswoods Dr., Peewee Valley, 11/27/89, A, C, 89001978

Wesley Methodist Church [Early Stone Buildings of Kentucky Outer Bluegrass and Pennyrile TR], Haunz Ln., Anchorage vicinity, 1/08/87, A, C, 87000179

Woolfolk, William, House [Early Stone Buildings of Kentucky Outer Bluegrass and Pennyrile TR], Off US 42, La Grange vicinity, 1/08/87, C, 87000202

Yager House, SE of Goshen on Covered Bridge Rd., Goshen vicinity, 6/17/82, C, 82002740

Yewell-Snyder House, 6206 N. Hitt Lane, Brownsboro vicinity, 11/03/83, C, 83003802

Owen County

Central Owenton Historic District [Owenton MRA], Roughly Bryan, Madison, Seminary, and Thomas Sts., Owenton, 9/04/84, A, 84001893

Cox, L. O., House [Owenton MRA], 311 N. Main St., Owenton, 9/04/84, C, 84001895

Ford House [Owenton MRA], 311 S. Main St., Owenton, 9/04/84, C, 84001897

Highfield, 303 N. Adams St., Owenton, 11/17/77, C, 77000640

Hunter, Jacob, House [Early Stone Buildings of Kentucky Outer Bluegrass and Pennyrile TR], Off KY 325 near Big South Fork of KY River, New Liberty vicinity, 1/08/87, A, D, 87000204

Linsey, William, House [Owenton MRA], 220 W. Seminary St., Owenton, 9/04/84, C, 84001900

McKay House [Owenton MRA], 105 E. Adair St., Owenton, 9/04/84, C, 84001902

North Main-North Adams Historic District [Owenton MRA], N. Main, N. Adams, Bryan, and North Sts., Owenton, 9/04/84, C, 84001905

Owen County Courthouse and Jail, N. Thomas and N. Madison Sts., Owenton, 5/06/76, A, C, 76000937

Settle, E. E., House [Owenton MRA], 403-405 N. Adams St., Owenton, 9/04/84, C, 84001910

Owsley County

Moyers Buildings, S. Court St., Booneville, 10/29/82, A, C, 82001575

Pendleton County

Aluck, Dolph, Smokehouse [Early Stone Buildings of Kentucky Outer Bluegrass and Pennyrile TR], Milford Rd., Falmouth vicinity, 1/08/87, C, 87000162

Applegate, Leslie T., House [Falmouth MRA], 410 Maple St., Falmouth, 3/04/83, C, 83002845

Bishop House [Falmouth MRA], 200 4th St., Falmouth, 3/04/83, C, 83002846

Central Falmouth Historic District [Falmouth MRA], Roughly bounded by Shelby, 2nd, Montjoy, and Main Sts., Falmouth, 3/04/83, A, C, 83002847

Charity's House [Falmouth MRA], 108 Montjoy St., Falmouth, 3/04/83, A, C, 83002848

Chipman House [Falmouth MRA], 901 Shelby St., Falmouth, 3/04/83, C, 83002849

Colvin, Henry, House [Early Stone Buildings of Kentucky Outer Bluegrass and Pennyrile TR], Colvin Bend Rd., Kentucky vicinity, 1/08/87, C, 87000145

Fryer House, NE of Butler on U.S. 27, Butler vicinity, 10/08/76, A, B, C, 76000938

House at 206 Park Street [Falmouth MRA], 206 Park St., Falmouth, 3/04/83, A, C, 83002850

Hughes, Elzey, House [Falmouth MRA], 308 2nd St., Falmouth, 3/04/83, C, 83002851

Immaculate Conception Catholic Church and Cemetery, Stepstone Rd., Peach Grove vicinity, 1/28/87, C, a, d, 86003729

Jameson, George W., House [Falmouth MRA], 306 Park St., Falmouth, 3/04/83, C, 83002852

Kellum House [Falmouth MRA], 714 Shelby St., Falmouth, 3/04/83, C, 83002853

McBride House [Falmouth MRA], 401 Main St., Falmouth, 3/04/83, C, 83002854

Oldham Plantation [Falmouth MRA], KY 159, Falmouth, 3/04/83, A, C, 83002855

Pendleton House [Falmouth MRA], 506 W. Shelby St., Falmouth, 3/04/83, A, C, 83002856

Reed, Frederick, House [Falmouth MRA], 405 Broad St., Falmouth, 3/04/83, A, 83002857

Seaman Sisters' House [Falmouth MRA], 706 Shelby St., Falmouth, 3/04/83, C, 83002858

Sheehan House [Falmouth MRA], 206 N. Maple St., Falmouth, 3/04/83, C, 83002859

Southgate House [Falmouth MRA], 106 Montjoy St., Falmouth, 3/04/83, C, 83002860

Watson Store [Falmouth MRA], 504 W. Shelby St., Falmouth, 3/04/83, A, C, 83002861

Perry County

Buckhorn Presbyterian Church and the Greer Gymnasium, Off KY 28, Buckhorn, 6/27/75, A, C, a, g, 75000818

Pike County

Chesapeake and Ohio Passenger Depot [Pikeville MRA], Hellier Ave., Pikeville, 4/23/87, A, 87000618

Pike County—Continued

College Street Historic District [Pikeville MRA], Roughly College St. from Elm St. to Huffman Ave., Pikeville, 9/20/84, C, 84001913

Commercial Historic District [Pikeville MRA], Main St. and Division Ave., Pikeville, 9/20/84, A, C, 84001916

Greer, R. T., and Company [Pikeville MRA], Auxier St., Pikeville, 9/20/84, A, 84001918

Hatfield-McCoy Feud Historic District, Multiple locations in Pike county, Pikeville and vicinity, 8/05/76, A, B, c, d, 76000939

Huffman Avenue Historic District [Pikeville MRA], Huffman Ave. and Main St., Pikeville, 4/26/84, B, C, a, 84001927

Odd Fellows Building [Pikeville MRA], 333 2nd St., Pikeville, 4/26/84, A, 84001929

Pauley Bridge, Across the Levisa Fork, Big Sandy R. from Pauley to US 23/460, Pikeville, 3/26/92, C, 92000290

Pikeville College Academy Building, College St., Pikeville, 2/16/73, A, C, 73000828

Scott Avenue Historic District [Pikeville MRA], Scott Ave., 6th and 7th Sts., Pikeville, 9/20/84, C, 84001931

Third Street Historic District [Pikeville MRA], 3rd St. and Scott Ave., Pikeville, 9/20/84, C, 84001933

York House [Pikeville MRA], Main St., Pikeville, 4/26/84, C, 84001935

York Mansion [Pikeville MRA], 209 Elm St., Pikeville, 4/26/84, C, 84001937

Powell County

Amburgy Hollow Petroglyphs [Prehistoric Rock Art Sites in Kentucky MPS], Address Restricted, Nada vicinity, 1/02/92, A, C, D, 91001885

Anderson Site, Address Restricted, Stanton vicinity, 8/14/75, D, 75000820

Branham Ridge Petroglyphs (15PO158) [Prehistoric Rock Art Sites in Kentucky MPS], Address Restricted, Vaughn's Mill vicinity, 1/02/92, A, C, D, a, 89001198

Clay City National Bank Building, 6th Ave., Clay City, 7/13/76, A, B, C, 76000940

Haystack Rock Shelter, Address Restricted, Stanton vicinity, 8/14/75, D, 75000821

High Rock Petroglyphs (15PO25) [Prehistoric Rock Art Sites in Kentucky MPS], Address Restricted, Nada vicinity, 9/08/89, A, C, D, a, 89001201

Martin Fork Petroglyphs [Prehistoric Rock Art Sites in Kentucky MPS], Address Restricted, Nada vicinity, 1/02/92, A, C, D, 91001886

Martin Site, Address Restricted, Stanton vicinity, 8/14/75, D, 75000822

McKinney Bluff Petroglyphs (15PO107) [Prehistoric Rock Art Sites in Kentucky MPS], Address Restricted, Nada vicinity, 9/08/89, A, C, D, a, 89001199

Nada Tunnel 1 Petroglyphs [Prehistoric Rock Art Sites of Kentucky MPS], Address Restricted, Nada vicinity, 4/20/92, A, C, D, 92000342

Nada Tunnel 2 [Prehistoric Rock Art Sites in Kentucky MPS], Address Restricted, Nada vicinity, 1/02/92, A, C, D, 91001883

Seldon Skidmore Site, Address Restricted, Stanton vicinity, 8/14/75, D, 75000823

Shepherd Site, Address Restricted, Slade vicinity, 8/13/75, D, 75000819

State Rock Petroglyph Site (15PO106) [Prehistoric Rock Art Sites in Kentucky MPS], Address Restricted, Furnace vicinity, 9/08/89, A, C, D, a, 89001200

White's Rockshelter Petroglyphs [Prehistoric Rock Art Sites in Kentucky MPS], Address Restricted, Knowlton vicinity, 1/02/92, A, C, D, 91001884

Pulaski County

Battle of Mill Springs Historic Areas, Roughly, three discontiguous areas, one S of Nancy, one in Mill Springs and one to the N across the Cumberland R., Nancy vicinity, 2/18/93, A, 93000001

Beatty-Newell House [Pulaski County MRA], Off KY 90, Bronston, 8/16/85, C, 85001834

Boland House [Pulaski County MRA], Lakeshore Dr., Burnside, 8/14/84, C, 84001939

Buck-Mercer House [Pulaski County MRA], Waynesburg Rd., Somerset vicinity, 8/14/84, C, 84001941

Burnside Historic District [Pulaski County MRA], Lakeshore Dr. and French Ave., Burnside, 8/14/84, C, 84001944

Burnside Lodge [Pulaski County MRA], Off US 27, Burnside, 8/14/84, C, 84001946

Burnside Methodist Church [Pulaski County MRA], Off U.S. 27, Burnside, 8/16/85, C, a, 85001836

City Hall [Pulaski County MRA], 400 E. Mt. Vernon St., Somerset, 8/14/84, C, 84001949

Crawford House [Pulaski County MRA], 121 Maple St., Somerset, 8/14/84, C, 84001952

Crawford, A. Jackson, Building, 207 S. Main St., Somerset, 8/18/80, B, 80001665

Dabney Post Office [Pulaski County MRA], KY 39, Dabney, 8/14/84, C, 84001954

Evans House [Pulaski County MRA], KY 461, Shopville vicinity, 8/16/85, C, 85001837

Fox, William, House, 206 W. Columbia St., Somerset, 7/31/78, B, 78001391

Harvey's Hill Historic District [Pulaski County MRA], 401-527 N. Main St., and 402-526 N. Main St., Somerset, 8/14/84, C, 84001958

Hotel Beecher [Pulaski County MRA], 203 S. Main St., Somerset, 8/14/84, A, C, 84001960

James-Hansford House [Pulaski County MRA], On KY 80, Shopville, 8/16/85, C, 85001838

James-Owens House [Pulaski County MRA], Off KY 80, Shopville, 8/16/85, C, 85001839

Morrow House [Pulaski County MRA], 208 E. Oak St., Somerset, 8/14/84, B, 84001962

North Main Street Historic District [Pulaski County MRA], N. Main and Columbia Sts., Somerset, 8/14/84, C, 84001964

Parker House [Pulaski County MRA], 206 N. Vine St., Somerset, 8/14/84, C, 84001970

Payne House [Pulaski County MRA], Off SR 1247, Eubank, 8/16/85, C, 85001840

Payne Mill [Pulaski County MRA], Off SR 1247, Eubank, 8/14/84, A, 84001968

Perkins, Dr. John Milton, House, 109 N. Main St., Somerset, 8/10/78, C, 78001392

Robinson Mill [Pulaski County MRA], S. Main St., Somerset, 8/14/84, A, C, 84001971

Scott, Dill, House [Pulaski County MRA], 200 N. Main St., Somerset, 8/14/84, C, 84001972

Smith House [Pulaski County MRA], 200 N. College St., Somerset, 8/14/84, B, C, 84001974

Smith, Beecher, House [Pulaski County MRA], 405 College St., Somerset, 8/14/84, C, 84001973

Somerset City School and Carnegie Library, 300 College St., Somerset, 7/07/78, A, C, 78001393

Somerset Downtown Commercial District, 108–236 and 201–223 E. Mt. Vernon St., Somerset, 8/27/82, C, 82002742

South Courthouse Square Historic District [Pulaski County MRA], Public Sq., Zachary Way, W. Mt. Vernon, S. Main, and S. Maple Sts., Somerset, 8/14/84, A, C, 84001975

US Post Office—Bronston [Pulaski County MRA], KY 790, Bronston, 8/16/85, C, 85001835

Waddle-Prather House [Pulaski County MRA], 311 N. College St., Somerset, 8/14/84, C, 84001976

West Columbia Street District [Pulaski County MRA], 201-303 W. Columbia St., Somerset, 8/14/84, C, 84001977

Withers House [Pulaski County MRA], 116 Maple St., Somerset, 8/14/84, C, 84001978

Robertson County

Johnson Creek Covered Bridge, NE of Mount Olivet on SR 1029, Mount Olivet vicinity, 9/27/76, A, C, 76000941

Metcalf, Thomas, House [Early Stone Buildings of Kentucky Outer Bluegrass and Pennyrile TR], Off US 62, Mt. Olivet vicinity, 1/08/87, B, C, 87000187

Robertson County Courthouse, Court St., Mount Olivet, 2/14/78, C, 78001394

Rockcastle County

Hiatt, Bennett, Log House, U.S. 25, Renfro Valley vicinity, 11/15/84, A, C, 84000394

Mount Vernon Commercial District, Main St. from Church to Richmond Sts., Mount Vernon, 11/10/83, A, C, 83003815

Rowan County

Rowan County Courthouse, Main St., Morehead, 7/21/83, A, C, 83002862

Scott County

Allenhurst, Cane Run Pike W of Georgetown, Georgetown vicinity, 4/02/73, B, C, 73000829

Audubon, SW of Georgetown off U.S. 62, on Moore's Mill Pike, Georgetown vicinity, 12/04/73, C, 73000830

Blackburn, Julius, House, W of Georgetown off U.S. 460, Georgetown vicinity, 4/14/77, C, 77000641

Bradford, Alexander, House, Main St. at Locust Fork Pike, Stamping Ground, 6/27/74, B, C, 74000905

Bradford, Fielding, House, N of Georgetown off U.S. 25 on Long Lick Pike, Georgetown vicinity, 12/04/73, B, C, 73000831

Bradley, John W., House, SW of Georgetown off U.S. 62, Georgetown vicinity, 11/05/74, B, C, 74000898

Branham House, 208 S. Broadway, Georgetown, 4/02/73, C, 73000832

Branham, Richard, House [Early Stone Buildings of Central Kentucky TR], Prate Rd., Midway vicinity, 6/23/83, A, C, 83002863

Briscoe, James, Quarters [Early Stone Buildings of Central Kentucky TR], Off U.S. 25, Delaplain vicinity, 6/23/83, A, C, 83002864

Brooking, Vivion Upshaw, House, W of Georgetown off Stamping Ground Pike (KY 227), Georgetown vicinity, 5/28/75, C, 75000824

Buford-Duke House, SE of Georgetown off U.S. 75, Georgetown vicinity, 6/19/73, B, C, 73000833

Burgess, Joseph Fields, House, Off US 25 and SW corner of SR 608, Sadieville vicinity, 11/29/84, C, 84000368

Campbell, William, House, Off U.S. 227, Stamping Ground vicinity, 11/29/84, C, 84000415

Cantrill House, 324 E. Jackson St., Georgetown, 4/02/73, A, C, 73000834

Cardome, 0.5 mi. N of Georgetown on U.S. 25, Georgetown vicinity, 3/13/75, B, C, 75000825

Choctaw Indian Academy, 4.5 mi. W of Georgetown off U.S. 227, Georgetown vicinity, 3/07/73, A, a, 73000835

Coppage, Rhodin, Spring House [Early Stone Buildings of Central Kentucky TR], Off U.S. 25, Georgetown vicinity, 6/23/83, A, C, 83002865

Craig, Newton, House and Penitentiary Buildings Complex, US 460, Georgetown vicinity, 7/19/84, B, C, 84001980

Craig-Johnson Mill Dam and Mill Sites, Address Restricted, Great Crossing vicinity, 6/10/75, A, C, 75000828

Dry Run Site, Address Restricted, Georgetown vicinity, 12/05/85, D, 85003041

Edge Hill Farm, 1661 Payne's Depot Pike, Georgetown vicinity, 3/01/84, B, C, 84001983

Elkwood, NW of Georgetown, Georgetown vicinity, 1/20/78, B, C, 78001395

Elmwood, NE of Georgetown off U.S. 227 and 460, Georgetown vicinity, 11/19/74, C, 74000899

Emison, Ash, Quarters [Early Stone Buildings of Central Kentucky TR], Off U.S. 25, Delaplain vicinity, 6/23/83, A, C, 83002866

First African Baptist Church and Parsonage, 209-211 W. Jefferson St., Georgetown, 3/01/84, A, C, a, 84001985

Flournoy, Matthew, House [Early Stone Buildings of Central Kentucky TR], Off Crumbough Pike, Centerville vicinity, 6/23/83, A, C, 83002867

Flournoy-Nutter House, E of Georgetown off KY 922, Georgetown vicinity, 7/28/77, C, 77000642

Gaines, James, House, S of Georgetown on Yarnallton Pike, Georgetown vicinity, 11/07/76, B, C, 76000942

Garth School, 501 S. Hamilton St., Georgetown, 11/16/88, A, 88002187

Garth, John M., House, SE of Georgetown off I-75, Georgetown vicinity, 11/20/74, C, 74000900

Georgetown College Historic Buildings, E. Jackson St., Georgetown, 8/08/79, A, C, a, 79001030

Georgetown East Main Street Residential District, Irregular pattern along Main St. between Warrendale Ave. and Mulberry St., Georgetown, 6/07/78, A, B, C, 78001396

Giddings Hall, Georgetown College, Giddings Dr. between Jackson and College Sts., Georgetown, 2/06/73, A, C, a, 73000836

Griffith House [Payne's Depot MRA], S of I-64 on Moore's Mill Pike, Midway vicinity, 8/29/79, C, 79003545

Halley Place [Payne's Depot MRA], US 62, Georgetown vicinity, 8/28/79, C, 79003546

Henry, Matthew, House [Early Stone Buildings of Central Kentucky TR], KY 922, Centerville vicinity, 6/23/83, A, C, 83002868

Herndon, Dr. H. C., House, W of Georgetown on KY 227, Georgetown vicinity, 4/10/80, C, 80001666

Holy Trinity Episcopal Church, S. Broadway and W. Clinton Sts., Georgetown, 10/30/73, A, C, a, 73000837

Johnson, George W., Slave Quarters and Smokehouse, SW of Georgetown off Ironworks Rd., Georgetown vicinity, 11/19/74, B, C, 74000901

Johnson, James, Quarters [Early Stone Buildings of Central Kentucky TR], Off KY 227, Georgetown vicinity, 10/11/83, C, 83003818

Johnson, Leonidas, House, 7 mi. NW of Georgetown on U.S. 227, Georgetown vicinity, 10/08/76, C, 76000943

Johnson-Pence House, W of Georgetown off U.S. 460, Georgetown vicinity, 11/20/78, B, C, 78001397

Johnston-Jacobs House, 205 N. Hamilton St., Georgetown, 10/02/73, C, 73000838

Lane's Run Historic District, Old Oxford Rd., US 62 and US 460, Georgetown vicinity, 1/12/84, A, C, 84001986

Leatherer-Lemon House, Lemon's Mill Pike, 0.5 mi. W of Newtown Pike, Georgetown vicinity, 7/20/77, B, C, 77000643

Lindsay, James-Trotter, William, House [Payne's Depot MRA], US 62, Georgetown vicinity, 8/28/79, A, C, 79003550

Longview, About 4 mi. W of Georgetown off U.S. 460, Georgetown vicinity, 10/25/73, B, C, 73000839

Main Street Commercial District, Both sides of E. Main St. from Mulberry to Broadway, S side from Elley Alley to Broadway, Georgetown, 2/24/75, A, C, 75000826

Main Street Historic Commercial District (Boundary Increase), N. Hamilton, Court Alley, N. Broadway, S. Broadway, W. Main and Court Sts., Georgetown, 4/15/82, C, 82002743

McFarland House, 510 Fountain Ave., Georgetown, 10/15/73, A, C, 73000840

Miller's Run Historic District, Roughly bounded by Old Oxford Pike, KY 922, U.S. 460 and Miller's Run, Oxford, 11/15/78, A, C, 78001398

Miller, John Andrew, House, 3 mi. E of Georgetown off U.S. 460, Georgetown vicinity, 11/09/77, B, C, 77000644

Nuckols, Lewis, House [Payne's Depot MRA], US 421, Georgetown vicinity, 8/28/79, B, C, 79003547

Osburn House, 4 mi. N of Georgetown on U.S. 25, Georgetown vicinity, 4/11/73, B, C, 73000841

Oxford Historic District, NE of Georgetown at U.S. 62 and KY 922, Georgetown vicinity, 9/11/79, C, 79001031

Patterson, Joseph, Quarters [Early Stone Buildings of Central Kentucky TR], Off U.S. 421, Midway vicinity, 6/23/83, A, C, 83002869

Payne, Asa, House [Payne's Depot MRA], US 62, Georgetown vicinity, 8/28/79, B, C, 79003548

Payne, Gen. John, House, 1.5 mi. W of Georgetown on U.S. 460, Georgetown vicinity, 3/03/75, B, C, 75000827

Payne-Desha House, Kelly Ave., Georgetown, 12/02/74, B, 74000902

Prewitt, Levi, House, S of Georgetown off I-64, Georgetown vicinity, 11/01/74, C, 74000903

Royal Spring Park, Between Clinton and Jefferson Sts. W of Water, Broadway, and Georgetown Sts., Georgetown, 4/02/73, A, 73000842

Sanders, Robert, House, 2 mi. S of Georgetown on U.S. 25, Georgetown vicinity, 10/15/73, B, C, 73000843

Scott County Courthouse, E. Main and Broadway, Georgetown, 9/28/72, A, C, 72000542

Showalter House, 316 N. Hamilton St., Georgetown, 4/02/73, C, 73000844

Shropshire House, 355 E. Main St., Georgetown, 4/02/73, B, C, a, 73000845

Smith, Dr. William Addison, House, 1589 Newton Pike, Georgetown vicinity, 11/29/84, C, 84000363

Smith, Nelson and Clifton Rodes, House, NE of Georgetown off Leesburg Pike, Georgetown vicinity, 10/03/73, B, C, 73000846

South Broadway Neighborhood District, Roughly, Georgetown Cemetery, S. Broadway N to College St. and S. Hamilton St. from Clayton Ave. to College, Georgetown, 12/19/91, A, 91001856

St. Francis Mission at White Sulphur, 7 mi. W of Georgetown on U.S. 460, Georgetown vicinity, 4/11/73, A, C, a, 73000847

Stevenson, Henry, House [Payne's Depot MRA], US 62, Georgetown vicinity, 8/28/79, A, C, 79003549

Stone-Grant House, E of Georgetown on E. Main St. extended, Georgetown vicinity, 1/11/74, B, C, a, 74000904

Scott County—Continued

Suggett, John, House [Early Stone Buildings of Central Kentucky TR], U.S. 460, Georgetown vicinity, 6/23/83, A, C, 83002870

Suggett, William, Agricultural and Industrial District, SW of jct. of Cane Run Rd. and US 460, Georgetown, 11/16/88, A, B, C, D, 88002182

Thomsons Mill Warehouse [Early Stone Buildings of Central Kentucky TR], Off U.S. 460, Georgetown vicinity, 6/23/83, A, C, 83002871

Ward Hall, 1.5 mi. W of Georgetown on U.S. 460, Georgetown vicinity, 4/02/73, C, 73000848

Ward Hall (Boundary Increase), 1782 Frankfort Pike, Georgetown vicinity, 8/23/85, B, C, 85001841

Weisenberger Mills and Related Buildings, Off US 421, Midway vicinity, 8/16/84, A, C, 84001987

West Main Street Historic District, 217–600 W. Main St., Georgetown, 11/05/85, A, B, C, 85003491

Whitaker, Charles, House [Early Stone Buildings of Central Kentucky TR], Off Old Oxford Rd., Georgetown vicinity, 6/23/83, A, C, 83002872

Williams, Merritt, House [Payne's Depot MRA], Moore's Mill Pike at Can Run Pike, Midway vicinity, 2/28/79, B, C, 79003551

Shelby County

Allen Dale Farm, Off US 60, Shelbyville vicinity, 11/17/83, A, C, 83003821

Allen, J. B., House [Shelby County MRA], KY 53, .5 mi. N of Chestnut Grove, Chestnut Grove vicinity, 12/27/88, C, 88002867

Ballard, William H., House [Shelby County MRA], KY 53, .5 mi. E of McMakin Rd., Shelbyville vicinity, 12/27/88, C, 88002936

Bank of Simpsonville [Shelby County MRA], Third and Railroad Sts., Simpsonville, 12/27/88, A, C, 88002878

Basket Farm [Shelby County MRA], KY 395, 1 mi. S of KY 1779, Clay Village vicinity, 12/27/88, A, C, 88002848

Bayne House [Shelbyville MRA], 37 Main St., Shelbyville, 9/28/84, C, 84001989

Bethel AME Church [Shelbyville MRA], 414 Henry Clay St., Shelbyville, 9/28/84, A, C, a, 84001990

Bethel Church [Shelby County MRA], US 60, 1 mi. W of Clay Village, Clay Village vicinity, 12/27/88, C, a, d, 88002907

Bird Octagonal Mule Barn [Shelby County MRA], KY 43, 3 mi. S of Cropper, Cropper vicinity, 12/27/88, A, 88002858

Bird's Nest [Shelby County MRA], KY 43, 3 mi. S of Cropper, Cropper vicinity, 12/27/88, C, 88002859

Bird, Philomen, House [Shelby County MRA], KY1005/Vigo Rd., E of Beards Rd., Bagdad vicinity, 12/27/88, C, 88002917

Blades, William, House [Shelby County MRA], KY 1005, .5 mi. W of KY 395, Bagdad vicinity, 12/27/88, C, 88002924

Bland Farm [Shelby County MRA], Vigo Rd., 1 mi. W of Rt. 1005, Bagdad vicinity, 12/27/88, A, C, 88002882

Blaydes House [Shelby County MRA], Blaydes Ln., 1 mi. N of KY 1779, Bagdad vicinity, 12/27/88, C, 88002852

Booker, Samuel, House [Shelby County MRA], Clore—Jackson Rd., 1.5 mi. W of KY 55, Chestnut Grove vicinity, 12/27/88, C, 88002868

Booker—Giltner House [Shelby County MRA], KY 322, 1.5 mi. S of Henry County line, Chestnut Grove vicinity, 12/27/88, C, 88002870

Brown, Cameron, Farm [Shelby County MRA], KY 55 at Clear Creek, Shelbyville vicinity, 12/27/88, A, 88002914

Brown, John C., House [Shelby County MRA], KY 43, .5 mi. N of KY 12, Mulberry vicinity, 12/27/88, C, 88002856

Bryan House [Shelby County MRA], US 60, .5 mi. W of Simpsonville, Simpsonville vicinity, 12/27/88, C, 88002880

Building at Jct. of KY 395 and 1779 [Shelby County MRA], KY 395 and 1779, Bagdad vicinity, 12/27/88, A, 88002885

Burton House [Shelby County MRA], Burks Branch Rd., 1 mi. S of Fox Run Rd., Chestnut Grove vicinity, 12/27/88, C, 88002896

Burton, David, House [Shelby County MRA], Burks Branch Rd., 3 mi. N of Shelbyville, Shelbyville vicinity, 12/27/88, C, 88002866

Caldwell House [Shelby County MRA], US 60 at KY 53, Shelbyville vicinity, 12/27/88, C, 88002939

Calloway House [Shelby County MRA], Clear Creek Rd., 2 mi. S of Henry County line, Eminence vicinity, 12/27/88, C, 88002886

Carnegie Public Library [Shelbyville MRA], 8th and Washington Sts., Shelbyville, 6/12/85, C, 85001253

Carpenter House [Shelby County MRA], KY 148, 1 mi. S of Clark Station, Clark Station vicinity, 12/27/88, A, C, 88002928

Carriss's Feed Store [Shelby County MRA], KY 55 and KY 44, Southville, 12/27/88, A, 88002897

Carriss's Store [Shelby County MRA], KY 714 and KY 53, Southville, 12/27/88, A, 88002898

Chiles—Bailey House [Shelby County MRA], KY 395, .5 mi. N of Benson Pike, Bagdad vicinity, 12/27/88, C, 88002923

Church of the Annunciation [Shelbyville MRA], 105 Main St., Shelbyville, 9/28/84, C, a, 84002011

Clay, Henry, School [Shelby County MRA], US 60, Clay Village, 12/27/88, A, C, 88002944

Coca-Cola Plant [Shelby County MRA], US 60 at Clear Creek, Shelbyville vicinity, 12/27/88, A, C, 88002925

Collins House [Shelby County MRA], KY 362, .5 mi. W of Webb Rd., Todds Point vicinity, 12/27/88, C, 88002876

Courtney House [Shelby County MRA], S end of Popes Corner Rd., Finchville vicinity, 12/27/88, C, 88002933

Crockett, John Edward, House [Shelby County MRA], Logan Rd., .5 mi. S of KY 12, Mulberry vicinity, 12/27/88, C, 88002851

Cross Keys Tavern Kitchen and Quarters [Early Stone Buildings of Kentucky Outer Bluegrass and Pennyrile TR], US 60, Shelbyville vicinity, 1/08/87, C, 87000205

Dale, John, House [Shelby County MRA], Webb Rd., 1.5 mi. N of US 60, Simpsonville vicinity, 12/27/88, C, 88002877

Davis, E. M., Farm [Shelby County MRA], KY 43/Christiansburg Pike, .75 mi. E of KY 55, Shelbyville vicinity, 12/27/88, A, 88002919

Dependency on Mulberry Creek [Early Stone Buildings of Kentucky Outer Bluegrass and Pennyrile TR], Off KY 1871, Shelbyville vicinity, 1/08/87, C, 87000167

Duvall, Marene, House [Shelby County MRA], Simpsonville—Buck Creek Rd. at Bullskin Creek, Finchville vicinity, 12/27/88, C, 88002905

East Shelbyville District [Shelbyville MRA], Roughly E. 3rd St. from Washington to Bradshaw St., Shelbyville, 6/12/85, B, C, c, 85001252

Ellis, Samuel, House [Shelby County MRA], KY 53, 2 mi. W of KY 322, Chestnut Grove vicinity, 12/27/88, C, 88002872

Figg, Bushrod, House [Shelby County MRA], Zaring Mill Rd., .7 mi. NW of KY 148, Olive Branch vicinity, 12/27/88, C, 88002915

Fry, Froman, Farm [Shelby County MRA], KY 714, 1.5 mi. E of Southville, Southville vicinity, 12/27/88, A, C, 88002952

Fry, L. C., Farm [Shelby County MRA], KY 53, N of Harrington Mill Rd., Shelbyville vicinity, 12/27/88, A, C, 88002884

Frye, C. E., Farm [Shelby County MRA], KY 714 and Rockbridge Rd., Southville vicinity, 12/27/88, A, C, 88002883

Fullenwider House [Shelby County MRA], Anderson Ln., 1 mi. W of Hebron Rd., Todds Point vicinity, 12/27/88, C, 88002874

Fullenwielder, Peter, House [Early Stone Buildings of Kentucky Outer Bluegrass and Pennyrile TR], Off Aikens-Anderson Ln. W of Hebron-Scotts Station Rd., Shelbyville vicinity, 1/08/87, C, 87000180

Glass, S. D., House [Shelby County MRA], KY 55, .5 mi. N of Fox Run Rd., Shelbyville vicinity, 12/27/88, C, 88002887

Goodman, J. W., House [Shelby County MRA], KY 55, 1 mi. N of KY 43, Shelbyville vicinity, 12/27/88, C, 88002864

Graham House [Shelby County MRA], KY 1779, 1.5 mi. W of KY 395, Clay Village vicinity, 12/27/88, C, 88002849

Grasslands, 4 mi. W of Finchville, Finchville vicinity, 8/12/77, C, 77000645

Gray House [Shelby County MRA], Zaring Mill Rd., .3 mi. S of Locust Grove Rd., Shelbyville vicinity, 12/27/88, A, C, 88002913

Grove Hill Cemetery Chapel [Shelby County MRA], S of Shelbyville at Clear Creek, Shelbyville vicinity, 12/27/88, C, a, 88002922

Hansbrough, John G. and William, House [Shelby County MRA], Burks Branch Rd., 1.5 mi. N of Shelbyville, Shelbyville vicinity, 12/27/88, C, 88002865

Shelby County—Continued

Harbison House [Shelby County MRA], Harrington Mill Pike, 1.5 mi. W of KY 53, Scotts Station vicinity, 12/27/88, C, 88002875

Harbison House [Shelby County MRA], Zaring Mill Rd., .25 mi. S of I-64, Shelbyville vicinity, 12/27/88, C, 88002931

Hedden House [Shelby County MRA], KY 637 and Ditto Rd., Harrisonville vicinity, 12/27/88, C, 88002846

Helmwood Hall, KY 55 at Moody Pike, Shelbyville vicinity, 3/20/86, C, 86000463

Hornsby Bridge [Shelby County MRA], Clore—Jackson Rd. over Fox Run, .5 mi. W of KY 55, Eminence vicinity, 12/27/88, A, C, 88002906

Hornsby, John A., House [Shelby County MRA], Clore—Jackson Rd., .5 mi. W of KY 55, Eminence vicinity, 12/27/88, C, 88002869

Hornsby, John A., House (Boundary Increase) [Shelby County MRA], Clore—Jackson Rd., Eminence vicinity, 1/27/89, A, B, C, 88003195

Huss, M. W., House [Shelby County MRA], US 60, .5 mi. E of Clay Village, Clay Village vicinity, 12/27/88, C, 88002946

Jackson, Eli, House [Shelby County MRA], KY 55 near jct. with Clore—Jackson Rd., Eminence vicinity, 12/27/88, C, 88002891

Johnston House [Shelby County MRA], KY 714 and KY 1790, Clay Village vicinity, 12/27/88, A, C, 88002890

King, M. J., House [Shelby County MRA], Bellview—Clear Creek Rd., .3 mi. W of Bellview Rd., Shelbyville vicinity, 12/27/88, C, 88002916

Knight-Stout House, 1 mi. N of Finchville on KY 55, Finchville vicinity, 8/19/75, B, 75000829

Lincoln Institute Complex [Shelby County MRA], US 60 W of Simpsonville, Simpsonville vicinity, 12/27/88, A, C, 88002926

Logan House [Shelby County MRA], Brunerstown Rd. at Bullskin Creek, Finchville vicinity, 12/27/88, C, 88002929

Long, D. T., House [Shelby County MRA], US 60 and Joyes Station Rd., Scotts Station vicinity, 12/27/88, C, 88002902

Martin House [Shelby County MRA], KY 53, 1 mi. S of Rockbridge Rd., Shelbyville vicinity, 12/27/88, C, 88002937

McMicken House [Shelby County MRA], KY 53, 2.5 mi. W of KY 322, Chestnut Grove vicinity, 12/27/88, C, 88002871

Middleton, Henri, House [Shelby County MRA], Old US 60, .75 mi. E of Peytona, Peytona vicinity, 12/27/88, C, 88002847

Money Farm [Shelby County MRA], Finchville Rd., .6 mi. S of Brunerstown Rd., Finchville vicinity, 12/27/88, A, C, 88002910

Montgomery House [Shelby County MRA], Buzzard Roost Rd., 1.5 mi. S of US 60, Clay Village vicinity, 12/27/88, C, 88002948

Morris, Dr. William, Office and House [Shelby County MRA], KY 53, Southville, 12/27/88, A, 88002909

Moxley Farm [Shelby County MRA], Zaring Mill Rd. S of I-64, Shelbyville vicinity, 12/27/88, C, 88002932

Muir House [Shelby County MRA], Montana St. at Clear Creek, Shelbyville vicinity, 12/27/88, C, 88002899

Nash, Dr., House [Shelby County MRA], US 60, Clay Village, 12/27/88, C, 88002903

Neal—Hamblen House [Shelby County MRA], Hinkle Ln., 2 mi. W of KY 53, Chestnut Grove vicinity, 12/27/88, C, 88002873

Newton House [Shelby County MRA], US 60, Clay Village, 12/27/88, C, 88002943

Old Stone Inn, E of Simpsonville on U.S. 60, Simpsonville vicinity, 10/08/76, C, 76000944

Olive Branch Methodist Episcopal Church [Shelby County MRA], Zaring Mill Rd. and KY 148, Finchville vicinity, 12/27/88, C, a, 88002895

Owen, Brackett, House [Shelby County MRA], Hooper Station Rd., .25 mi. E of KY 53, Shelbyville vicinity, 12/27/88, A, 88002940

Payne House [Shelby County MRA], KY 44/53, 1.5 mi. N of Mount Eden, Mount Eden vicinity, 12/27/88, C, 88002954

Pemberton Farm [Shelby County MRA], Finchville—Clark Station Rd., .5 mi. E of KY 148, Clark vicinity, 12/27/88, A, C, 88002908

Pickett, James A., House [Shelby County MRA], KY 55, .75 mi. S of KY 148, Finchville vicinity, 12/27/88, C, 88002930

Pugh House [Shelby County MRA], KY 44, 1 mi. W of KY 53, Southville vicinity, 12/27/88, C, 88002935

Radcliffe—Duvall Farm [Shelby County MRA], Finchville—Buck Creek Rd., .5 mi. S of Brunerstown Rd., Finchville vicinity, 12/27/88, A, 88002920

Ramsey House [Shelby County MRA], KY 148, 1.5 mi. W of KY 44, Southville vicinity, 12/27/88, C, 88002934

Redmon House [Shelby County MRA], KY 395, 2 mi. N of Bagdad, Bagdad vicinity, 12/27/88, C, 88002853

Rice House [Shelby County MRA], US 60, .5 mi. N of Clay Village, Clay Village vicinity, 12/27/88, C, 88002945

Robertson House [Shelby County MRA], Buzzard Roost Rd., 1.5 mi. E of Hemp Ridge, Hemp Ridge vicinity, 12/27/88, C, 88002949

Rockbridge Church [Shelby County MRA], KY 714 and Rockbridge Rd., Hemp Ridge vicinity, 12/27/88, C, a, 88002951

Rodgers House [Shelby County MRA], Zaring Mill Rd., 1.5 mi. S of Popes Corner Rd., Shelbyville vicinity, 12/27/88, C, 88002918

Royalty—Smith Farm [Shelby County MRA], Burks Branch Rd. N of Clear Creek, Shelbyville vicinity, 12/27/88, A, 88002901

Saffell Funeral Home [Shelbyville MRA], 4th and Clay Sts., Shelbyville, 9/28/84, C, 84002012

Salem Baptist Church [Shelby County MRA], KY 44/53, .5 mi. S of Southville, Southville vicinity, 12/27/88, C, a, 88002953

Science Hill School, Washington St., Shelbyville, 9/18/75, A, 75000831

Seventh Street Historic District [Shelbyville MRA], Main and 7th Sts., Shelbyville, 6/12/85, A, C, a, 85001254

Shady Rest [Shelby County MRA], US 60, .5 mi. E of Clay Village, Clay Village vicinity, 12/27/88, A, C, 88002947

Shelby Academy, KY 55 and KY 148, Finchville, 9/18/75, B, C, 75000830

Shelby County Courthouse and Main Street Commercial District, Roughly bounded by Washington, Clay, 4th and 6th Sts., Shelbyville, 3/21/78, A, C, 78001399

Shelby County Courthouse and Main Street Commercial District (Boundary Increase) [Shelbyville MRA], 6th St. from Washington to Main St., Shelbyville, 4/12/85, C, 85000864

Shelbyville L & N Railroad Depot, 220 N. 7th St., Shelbyville, 6/20/75, A, C, b, 75000832

Shropshire Farm [Shelby County MRA], KY 714/Hemp Ridge Rd., 1 mi. S of I-64, Hemp Ridge vicinity, 12/27/88, A, 88002911

Simpsonville Christian Church [Shelby County MRA], US 60, Simpsonville, 12/27/88, C, a, 88002881

Simpsonville Methodist Church [Shelby County MRA], First St., Simpsonville, 12/27/88, C, a, 88002879

Sleadd, William, Farm [Shelby County MRA], KY 1790, .5 mi. E of Hooper, Hooper vicinity, 12/27/88, A, C, 88002941

Snook House [Shelby County MRA], KY 12 and KY 43, Mulberry vicinity, 12/27/88, C, 88002855

Snook, Van B., House [Shelby County MRA], Mulberry—Eminence Pike, 1 mi. N of Stoney Point Rd., Cropper vicinity, 12/27/88, C, 88002863

St. John United Methodist Church [Shelbyville MRA], College St., Shelbyville, 9/28/84, A, C, a, 84002016

Stapleton Farm [Shelby County MRA], KY 1005/Vigo Rd., .5 mi. E of Logan Rd., Bagdad vicinity, 12/27/88, A, 88002912

Stewart, G. W., House [Shelby County MRA], KY 55, Shelbyville vicinity, 12/27/88, C, 88002888

Stone House on Clear Creek [Early Stone Buildings of Kentucky Outer Bluegrass and Pennyrile TR], Off KY 55 W of Bellview Rd., Shelbyville vicinity, 1/08/87, C, 87000141

Sturgeon-Gregg House, US 60, Simpsonville, 11/29/84, C, 84000418

Swindler House [Shelby County MRA], Mulberry—Eminence Pike, .5 mi. N of Stoney Point Rd., Cropper vicinity, 12/27/88, C, 88002862

Tevis Cottage [Shelbyville MRA], 607 Washington St., Shelbyville, 9/28/84, A, C, 84002018

Thomas House [Shelby County MRA], KY 43, .25 mi. E of Mulberry—Eminence Pike, Mulberry vicinity, 12/27/88, C, 88002857

Thomas, William J., House [Shelby County MRA], Off KY 12, near jct. with KY 43, Mulberry vicinity, 12/27/88, C, 88002860

Threlkeld, Thomas, House, Benson Pike, Shelbyville vicinity, 5/14/84, C, 84002021

Tindall House [Shelby County MRA], US 60, Clay Village, 12/27/88, C, 88002904

Shelby County—Continued

Todd, Charles and Letitia Shelby, House, 5 mi. N of Shelbyville on KY 55, Shelbyville vicinity, 6/05/75, B, C, 75000833

Undulata, S of Shelbyville on Old Zaring Mill Rd., Shelbyville vicinity, 6/22/80, B, C, 80004519

Vanatta House [Shelby County MRA], US 60, Clay Village, 12/27/88, C, 88002942

Venable—Chase House [Shelby County MRA], KY 43, 2.5 mi. NE of Shelbyville, Shelbyville vicinity, 12/27/88, C, 88002861

Waddy Bank Building, KY 395, Waddy, 2/14/78, A, 78001400

Waddy Historic District [Shelby County MRA], Roughly KY 395/Main St. S of the Southern Railroad tracks, Waddy, 12/27/88, A, 88002921

Ware, Charles, House [Shelby County MRA], Pea Ridge Rd., .5 mi. W of KY 395, Harrisonville vicinity, 12/27/88, C, 88002845

Ware, Shelby D., House [Shelby County MRA], KY 714, .5 mi. S of Hemp Ridge, Hemp Ridge vicinity, 12/27/88, C, 88002950

Washburn, Benjamin, House, Bellevue Pike, 8 mi. N of Shelbyville, Shelbyville vicinity, 8/12/77, B, C, 77000646

Weakley, Thomas, House [Shelby County MRA], KY 1779 and Beard Rd., Clay Village vicinity, 12/27/88, C, 88002850

Weissinger Mule Barn [Shelby County MRA], KY 53, .25 mi. S of I-64, Shelbyville vicinity, 12/27/88, A, 88002938

West Shelbyville District [Shelbyville MRA], Roughly Main from Adair to 8th, Magnolia to Linden, 7th, 8th, 9th, 10th, and Bland Sts., Shelbyville, 6/12/85, C, 85001273

White House [Shelby County MRA], Cropper Rd., .75 mi. S of Christianburg, Christianburg vicinity, 12/27/88, C, 88002854

Wickland [Shelbyville MRA], 169 Kentucky St., Shelbyville, 9/28/84, C, 84002023

Wise House [Shelby County MRA], KY 44/53, .5 mi. N of Mount Eden, Mount Eden vicinity, 12/27/88, C, 88002955

Wright House [Shelby County MRA], KY 1848, 1.5 mi. S of Simpsonville, Simpsonville vicinity, 12/27/88, C, 88002927

Young, Whitney M., Jr., Birthplace, SW of Simpsonville off U.S. 60, Simpsonville vicinity, 10/18/72, B, c, NHL, 72000543

Simpson County

Duncan House, 301 N. Main St., Franklin, 10/29/82, C, 82001576

Franklin Downtown Commercial District, Roughly Main and College Sts. between Washington and Madison Sts., Franklin, 2/17/83, A, C, 83002873

Franklin Downtown Commercial District (Boundary Increase), 200 S. Main and 207 S. College Sts., Franklin, 8/18/83, A, C, 83002874

Goodnight House, 201 S. Main St., Franklin, 8/12/77, B, C, 77000647

Octagon Hall, SE of Franklin on KY 31W, Franklin vicinity, 4/10/80, C, 80001667

Simpson County Courthouse, KY 73, Franklin, 3/18/80, C, 80001668

Sinking Creek Cave System, Address Restricted, Franklin vicinity, 4/28/83, D, 83002875

Spencer County

All Saints Church, E. side of Jefferson St. between Park Alley and Red Row Alley, Taylorsville, 4/02/92, A, C, a, 92000302

Beechland, 2.5 mi. N of Taylorsville, Taylorsville vicinity, 11/07/76, B, C, 76000945

Bourne-Anderson House, 0.5 mi. N of Taylorsville on KY 55, Taylorsville vicinity, 12/02/77, A, C, 77000648

Minor Chapel A. M. E. Church, E. side of Jefferson St. between Red Row Alley and Reasor St., Taylorsville, 4/02/92, A, a, 92000300

Ross, L.W., House, N. side of KY 44 E of Taylorsville, Taylorsville vicinity, 4/02/92, C, 92000299

Shelburne, Perry, House, W side of Railroad St., N of Red Row Alley, Taylorsville, 4/02/92, A, 92000297

Shelburne—Cox House, 501 Main St., Taylorsville, 4/02/92, A, C, 92000298

Stone House on Plum Creek [Early Stone Buildings of Kentucky Outer Bluegrass and Pennyrile TR], Intersection of KY 1060 and KY 1319, Whitfield vicinity, 1/08/87, C, 87000213

Taylorsville Historic District, Roughly, the 200 and 300 blocks of Main and Garrard Sts., Taylorsville, 4/02/92, A, 92000296

Van Dyke House [Early Stone Buildings of Kentucky Outer Bluegrass and Pennyrile TR], Buck Henry Foster Ln., Rivals vicinity, 1/08/87, C, 87000181

Taylor County

Campbellsville Historic Commercial District, Roughly bounded by Columbia Ave., Broadway, 1st, Hotchkiss Sts., Central Ave. (both sides), and RR tracks, Campbellsville, 2/10/83, A, C, 83002876

Chandler, John, House [Early Stone Buildings of Kentucky Outer Bluegrass and Pennyrile TR], Off KY 210, Campbellsville vicinity, 1/08/87, C, 87000184

Clay Hill, 5 mi. N of Campbellsville on KY 55, Campbellsville vicinity, 10/10/75, C, 75000835

Cowherd, Jonathan, Jr., House, W of Campbellsville off KY 70, Campbellsville vicinity, 4/11/77, B, C, 77000649

Hiestand, Jacob, House, W of Campbellsville off KY 210, Campbellsville vicinity, 2/10/83, A, 83002877

Merchant's Hotel, 102 E. Main St., Campbellsville, 11/25/80, A, C, 80001669

Taylor County Clerk's Office, Courthouse Sq., Campbellsville, 12/20/77, A, 77000650

Todd County

Allensville Historic District, KY 102/Main St., Allensville, 11/14/88, A, C, 88002611

Bethel Baptist Church, U.S. 68, Fairview, 11/17/77, C, a, 77000651

Davis, Jefferson, Monument, On KY 115 near jct. with U.S. 68, Fairview, 5/09/73, B, C, 73000849

Edwards Hall, S side of Goebel Ave., Elkton, 1/11/74, B, C, 74000906

Elkton Commercial Historic District, Jct. of N., S., E., and W. Main Sts., Elkton, 11/13/89, A, C, 89001976

Gray, John, Springhouse [Early Stone Buildings of Kentucky Outer Bluegrass and Pennyrile TR], US 68, Elkton, 1/08/87, A, C, 87000146

Hadden Site (15TO1), Address Restricted, Elkton vicinity, 12/19/85, D, 85003218

Idlewild, SE of Trenton on U.S. 41, Trenton vicinity, 4/10/80, B, C, 80001670

McReynolds House, S. Main St., Elkton, 10/22/76, B, 76000946

Milliken Memorial Community House, 208 W. Main St., Elkton, 12/06/90, A, 90001834

Reeves, W. L., House, KY 102, Elkton vicinity, 2/02/84, A, C, 84002024

Todd County Courthouse, Public Sq., Elkton, 8/22/75, C, 75000836

Trigg County

Brick Inn, Off KY 80, Canton, 4/10/80, B, C, 80001672

Cadiz Downtown Historic District, Roughly Main St. from Scott to Franklin Sts., Cadiz, 11/14/88, A, B, C, 88002606

Cadiz Main Street Residential District, Main St., between Line St. and Scott St., Cadiz, 5/16/89, A, C, 89000384

Cadiz Masonic Lodge No. 121 F. and A.M., Jefferson and Monroe Sts., Cadiz, 4/17/79, A, 79001032

Center Furnace, Address Restricted, Golden Pond vicinity, 5/12/77, A, D, 77000652

Dawson, Thomas, House, S of Cadiz, Cadiz vicinity, 12/01/80, A, C, 80001671

McCaughan, John, House [Early Stone Buildings of Kentucky Outer Bluegrass and Pennyrile TR], KY 276, Cadiz vicinity, 1/08/87, C, 87000212

Trimble County

Bates House [Trimble County MRA], New Hope Rd., Bedford vicinity, 4/09/84, C, 84002026

Callis General Store and Post Office [Trimble County MRA], New Hope Rd., Bedford vicinity, 7/21/83, C, 83002878

Coleman, House [Trimble County MRA], Main St., Bedford, 7/21/83, C, 83002880

Trimble County—Continued

Coleman, William L., House [Trimble County MRA], Sulphur-Bedford Rd., Bedford vicinity, 7/21/83, C, 83002879

Ginn's Furniture Store [Trimble County MRA], Main St., Milton, 7/21/83, A, C, 83002881

Hancock House [Trimble County MRA], Main St., Bedford, 4/09/84, C, 84002029

House Tm-B-7 [Trimble County MRA], Main St., Bedford, 4/09/84, C, 84002033

House Tm-M-27 [Trimble County MRA], KY 36, Milton, 4/09/84, C, 84002035

House Tm-M-28 [Trimble County MRA], KY 36, Milton, 4/09/84, C, 84002036

House at Moffett Cemetery Road [Trimble County MRA], Moffett Cemetery Rd., Milton vicinity, 7/21/83, A, C, 83002882

House on KY 1492 [Trimble County MRA], KY 1492, Milton vicinity, 4/09/84, C, 84002031

Humphrey Place [Trimble County MRA], N of Bedford on US 421, Bedford vicinity, 7/21/83, C, 83002883

Logan, W. W., House [Trimble County MRA], Sulpher-Bedford Pike, Bedford vicinity, 4/09/84, C, 84002052

Milton Masonic Lodge and County General Store [Trimble County MRA], Main St., Milton, 7/21/83, A, C, 83002884

Moreland School [Trimble County MRA], Cooper's Bottom Rd., Milton vicinity, 4/09/84, A, C, 84002053

Neal House [Trimble County MRA], US 421, Milton vicinity, 4/09/84, C, 84002054

Old Kentucky Tavern [Trimble County MRA], US 42, Bedford vicinity, 7/21/83, A, C, 83002885

Page [Trimble County MRA], Cooper's Bottom Rd., Milton vicinity, 4/10/84, C, 84002056

Page-Bell House [Trimble County MRA], Cooper's Bottom Rd., Milton vicinity, 7/21/83, C, 83002886

Peak House [Trimble County MRA], Spring and West Sts., Bedford, 4/09/84, C, 84002057

Preston House [Trimble County MRA], Rodgers Rd., Milton vicinity, 7/21/83, C, 83002887

Rowlett House [Trimble County MRA], KY 625, Milton vicinity, 4/09/84, C, 84002058

Rowlett's Grocery [Trimble County MRA], Main St., Milton, 7/21/83, A, C, 83002888

Third Street Historic District [Trimble County MRA], 3rd St. at US 421, Milton, 4/10/84, C, 84002059

Trimble County Jail [Trimble County MRA], Main St., Bedford, 4/09/84, A, C, 84002061

Trout House [Trimble County MRA], KY 625, Milton vicinity, 7/21/83, C, 83002889

Yeager General Store [Trimble County MRA], Barebone Rd., Wise's Landing, 7/21/83, A, C, 83004528

Union County

Hughes, Daniel H., House, 213 W. O'Bannon St., Morganfield, 5/27/80, C, 80001673

Morganfield Commercial District, Main, Court, and Morgan Sts., Morganfield, 7/19/84, C, 84002063

Proctor, George N., House, KY 1180 E of jct. with Proctor Rd., Waverly vicinity, 10/01/90, C, 90001488

Union County Courthouse, Main St., Morganfield, 11/17/78, C, 78001401

Warren County

Allen, Carter, House [Warren County MRA], Off SR 31W, Smiths Grove vicinity, 12/18/79, C, 79003541

Allen, Thomas, House [Warren County MRA], SR 31W, Smiths Grove vicinity, 12/18/79, C, 79003542

Barren River L & N Railroad Bridge [Warren County MRA], Spans Barren River, Bowling Green, 11/26/80, A, 80001674

Blakeley, W. H., House [Warren County MRA], 1162 College St., Bowling Green, 12/18/79, C, 79003514

Bryant, Garnett, House [Warren County MRA], Sunnyside Rd., Oakland vicinity, 12/18/79, B, C, 79003503

Burnett, Aubrey, House [Warren County MRA], Aubrey Burnett St., Oakland, 12/18/79, C, 79003506

Campbell, David C., House [Warren County MRA], Beech Bend Rd., Plum Springs vicinity, 12/18/79, C, 79003497

Cecilia Memorial Christian Church [Warren County MRA], 716 College St., Bowling Green, 12/18/79, A, C, a, 79003515

Cherry Hall [Warren County MRA; Davis, Brinton B., Buildings on the Western Kentucky University campus TR], College St., Western Kentucky University campus, Bowling Green, 12/18/79, C, g, 79003496

College Hill District [Warren County MRA], Roughly bounded by College and Chestnut Sts., 11th and 15th Aves., Bowling Green, 12/18/79, C, a, 79003509

College Street Bridge [Warren County MRA], Spans Barren River, Bowling Green, 11/26/80, A, 80001684

Cooke, Peyton , House [Warren County MRA], Off SR 31W, Oakland vicinity, 12/18/79, C, 79003504

Curd-Moss House [Warren County MRA], Off SR 68, Bowling Green, 11/26/80, C, 80001685

Davidson, A. C., House [Warren County MRA], W of Leayou Rd., Bowling Green, 11/26/80, C, 80001686

Downtown Commercial District [Warren County MRA], Roughly bounded by Adams and State Sts., 8th and 10th Aves., Bowling Green, 12/18/79, A, C, 79003510

Drakes Creek Baptist Church [Warren County MRA], Cemetery Rd., Bowling Green, 12/18/79, C, a, 79003516

Dunklau Site (15WA374; 15WA380), Address Restricted, Hadley vicinity, 12/05/85, D, 85003066

Ennis, Willis, House [Warren County MRA], Beech Bend Rd., Plum Springs vicinity, 12/18/79, C, 79003498

Everhardt, W. H., House [Warren County MRA], 1223 College St., Bowling Green, 12/18/79, C, 79003522

Ewing, James F., House [Warren County MRA], Cemetery Rd., Bowling Green, 12/18/79, C, 79003523

Fairview Methodist Church [Warren County MRA], SR 526, Oakland vicinity, 12/18/79, C, g, 79003505

First Colored Baptist Church [Warren County MRA], 340 State St., Bowling Green, 12/18/79, A, C, g, 79003524

Ford, John Jackson, House [Warren County MRA], Off SR 31W, Smiths Grove vicinity, 12/18/79, C, 79003543

Fort C.F. Smith [Warren County MRA], E Main St., Bowling Green, 12/05/84, A, C, 84000847

Fort Lytle [Warren County MRA], Western Kentucky University, Bowling Green, 12/05/84, A, C, 84000848

Fort Webb [Warren County MRA], Country Club Dr., Bowling Green, 12/05/84, A, C, 84000849

Gossom, William, House [Warren County MRA], SR 31W, Plum Springs vicinity, 12/18/79, C, 79003499

Grider House [Warren County MRA], 1320 Park St., Bowling Green, 12/18/79, C, 79003525

Grider, Tobias, House [Warren County MRA], 864A Fairview Ave., Bowling Green, 12/18/79, C, 79003526

Hall House [Warren County MRA], 104 W. Main St., Bowling Green, 12/18/79, C, 79003527

Hays, James, House [Warren County MRA], US 68 and SR 259, Hays, 12/18/79, A, C, 79003517

Health Buildings-Gymnasium [Warren County MRA; Davis, Brinton B., Buildings on the Western Kentucky University campus TR], Normal Dr., Western Kentucky University campus, Bowling Green, 12/18/79, C, g, 79001034

Heating Plant [Warren County MRA; Davis, Brinton B., Buildings on the Western Kentucky University campus TR], Dogwood Dr., Western Kentucky University campus, Bowling Green, 12/18/79, C, 79001035

Hines House [Warren County MRA], 1103 Adams St., Bowling Green, 12/18/79, C, 79003518

Home Economics Building [Warren County MRA; Davis, Brinton B., Buildings on the Western Kentucky University campus TR], State St., Western Kentucky University campus, Bowling Green, 12/18/79, C, 79001036

Houchens, Elouise B., Center for Women [Warren County MRA], 1115 Adams St., Bowling Green vicinity, 12/18/79, C, 79003532

Industrial Arts Building [Warren County MRA; Davis, Brinton B., Buildings on the Western Kentucky University campus TR], State St., Western Kentucky University campus, Bowling Green, 12/18/79, C, 79001037

Ironwood [Warren County MRA], Old Richardsville Rd., Bowling Green vicinity, 7/02/73, B, C, 73000857

Warren County—Continued

Joggers, J. C., House [Warren County MRA], E of Pondsville, Pondsville vicinity, 12/18/79, C, 79003502

Kelley, James, House [Warren County MRA], SR 68, Bowling Green vicinity, 12/18/79, C, 79003533

Kentucky Building [Warren County MRA; Davis, Brinton B., Buildings on the Western Kentucky University campus TR], Russellville Rd., Western Kentucky University campus, Bowling Green, 12/18/79, C, g, 79001038

Kinlock [Warren County MRA], 1.5 mi. N of Bowling Green, Bowling Green vicinity, 12/18/79, A, C, 79003778

Kirby, Jesse, Springhouse [Early Stone Buildings of Kentucky Outer Bluegrass and Pennyrile TR], Off US 231 on Love Howell Rd., Bowling Green vicinity, 1/08/87, A, C, 87000147

Lost River Archeological Cave, Address Restricted, Bowling Green vicinity, 6/18/75, A, D, 75000839

Louisville and Nashville Railroad Station [Warren County MRA], Kentucky St., Bowling Green, 12/18/79, C, 79003519

Magnolia Street Historic District, Magnolia St. between Broadway and Tenth St., Bowling Green, 11/16/89, C, 89002017

Merritt-Hardin House [Warren County MRA], SR 31W, Bowling Green vicinity, 12/18/79, C, 79003534

Middleton, Jesse, House [Warren County MRA], Tuckertown Rd., Oakland vicinity, 12/18/79, C, 79003507

Moore, Maria, House [Warren County MRA (AD)], 801 State St., Bowling Green, 6/20/72, C, 72000545

Mount Olivet Cumberland Presbyterian Church [Warren County MRA], SR 526, Bowling Green, 12/18/79, C, a, 79003529

Murrell, Samuel, House [Warren County MRA (AD)], 8 mi. NE of Bowling Green on U.S. 31W, Bowling Green vicinity, 3/26/76, B, C, 76000957

Neale, William P., House [Warren County MRA], N of Woodburn, Woodburn vicinity, 11/26/80, C, 80001688

Newton-Kemp Houses [Warren County MRA], 804–806 Chestnut St., Bowling Green, 12/18/79, C, 79003530

Nine Hearths [Warren County MRA], 1244 Park St., Bowling Green, 12/18/79, B, C, 79003531

Old Log Church [Warren County MRA], W of Riverside, Riverside vicinity, 12/18/79, C, a, 79003520

Polk House [Warren County MRA], Ring Rd., Woodburn, 12/18/79, C, 79001045

President's Home [Warren County MRA; Davis, Brinton B., Buildings on the Western Kentucky University campus TR], State St., Western Kentucky University campus, Bowling Green, 12/18/79, C, g, 79001039

Rauscher House, 818 Adams St., Bowling Green, 7/12/78, A, C, 78001409

Richardsville Road Bridge [Warren County MRA], Spans Barren River, Bowling Green, 11/26/80, A, C, 80004496

Riverview [Warren County MRA], Hobson Grove Park at end of Main St., Bowling Green, 2/23/72, B, C, 72000546

Robb, Dr. William, House [Warren County MRA], Market St., Woodburn, 12/18/79, B, C, 79001046

Seeley, Edward B., House [Warren County MRA], Beech Bend Rd., Plum Springs vicinity, 12/18/79, B, C, 79003500

Shobe, Moses, House [Warren County MRA], SR 31W, Smiths Grove vicinity, 12/18/79, C, 79003521

Sloss, John, House [Warren County MRA], Old Springfield Rd., Bowling Green vicinity, 12/18/79, C, 79003536

Smiths Grove Baptist Church [Warren County MRA], Main and 5th Sts., Smiths Grove, 12/18/79, C, a, 79003538

Smiths Grove District [Warren County MRA], 1st and Main Sts., Smiths Grove, 12/18/79, C, 79003512

Smiths Grove Historic District (Boundary Increase) [Warren County MRA], NW corner of Second and Main Sts., Smiths Grove, 5/20/87, A, 87000480

Smiths Grove Presbyterian Church [Warren County MRA], College and 2nd Sts., Smiths Grove, 12/18/79, C, a, 79003539

Snell, Perry, Hall [Warren County MRA; Davis, Brinton B., Buildings on the Western Kentucky University campus TR], State St., Western Kentucky University campus, Bowling Green, 12/18/79, C, 79001040

St. James Apartments [Warren County MRA], 1133 Chestnut St., Bowling Green, 8/02/84, A, C, 84002064

St. Joseph Roman Catholic Church, 430 Church St., Bowling Green, 7/03/75, C, a, 75000840

St. Joseph's District [Warren County MRA], Roughly bounded by Gilbert and Potter Sts., Church and Brown's Lock Aves., Bowling Green, 11/26/80, A, C, 80001687

Stadium [Warren County MRA; Davis, Brinton B., Buildings on the Western Kentucky University campus TR], Russellville Rd., Western Kentucky University campus, Bowling Green, 12/18/79, C, 79001041

Sterrett House [Warren County MRA], SR 526, Plum Springs vicinity, 12/18/79, C, 79003501

Underwood-Jones House [Warren County MRA (AD)], 506 State St., Bowling Green, 7/07/78, C, 78001410

Upper East Main Street District [Warren County MRA], E. Main and Elm Sts., Bowling Green, 12/18/79, C, 79003511

Van Meter Hall [Warren County MRA; Davis, Brinton B., Buildings on the Western Kentucky University campus TR], 15th St., Western Kentucky University campus, Bowling Green, 12/18/79, C, 79001042

Walnut Lawn [Warren County MRA], W of Bowling Green on Morgantown Rd., Bowling Green vicinity, 10/20/83, B, C, 83003881

Wardlaw, Andrew James, House [Warren County MRA], Off SR 31W, Oakland vicinity, 12/18/79, C, 79003508

Warren County Courthouse, 429 E. 10th St., Bowling Green, 8/02/77, A, C, 77000657

West Hall [Warren County MRA; Davis, Brinton B., Buildings on the Western Kentucky University campus TR], Virginia Garrett Ave., Western Kentucky University campus, Bowling Green, 12/18/79, C, 79001043

Wilson, Gordon, Hall [Warren County MRA; Davis, Brinton B., Buildings on the Western Kentucky University campus TR], 15th St., Western Kentucky University campus, Bowling Green, 12/18/79, C, 79001044

Wright, J. L., House [Warren County MRA], 1st St., Smiths Grove, 12/18/79, C, 79003540

Young's Ferry House [Warren County MRA], Ferry Rd., Bowling Green vicinity, 12/18/79, B, C, 79003537

Washington County

Barber, John R., House [Washington County MRA], W of Springfield on US 150, Springfield vicinity, 2/10/89, C, 88003423

Beech Fork Bridge, Mackville Road [Washington County MRA], E of Springfield on KY 152, Springfield vicinity, 2/10/89, C, 88003429

Beechfork Presbyterian Church [Washington County MRA], N of Springfield off KY 555, Springfield vicinity, 2/10/89, C, a, 88003406

Berry, Richard, Jr., House [Washington County MRA], N of Springfield on Hwy. 438, Springfield vicinity, 2/10/89, C, 88003400

Blackwell, William, House [Washington County MRA], 138 Lebanon Hill, Springfield, 2/10/89, C, 88003391

Caldwell, William, Kitchen [Early Stone Buildings of Kentucky TR], Off KY 55 on Spaulding Lane, Springfield vicinity, 10/06/87, C, 87002054

Cartwright Creek Bridge [Washington County MRA], W of Springfield on Booker Rd., Springfield vicinity, 2/10/89, C, 88003425

Clements House [Washington County MRA], W of Springfield on US 150, Springfield vicinity, 2/10/89, C, 88003401

Cocanougher House [Washington County MRA], Off US 150, Mackville vicinity, 2/10/89, C, 88003413

Conner, George, House [Washington County MRA], Off US 150, Fredericktown, 2/10/89, C, 88003402

Covington Institute Teachers' Residence, 333 E. Main St., Springfield, 1/27/83, A, C, 83002890

Cusick, Ed, House [Washington County MRA], W of Springfield on Bearwallow Rd., Springfield vicinity, 2/10/89, C, 88003426

Doe Run Trestle [Washington County MRA], W of Springfield off US 150, Springfield vicinity, 2/10/89, C, 88003418

Duncan House [Washington County MRA], 206 Lincoln Park Rd., Springfield, 2/10/89, C, 88003393

Washington County—Continued

Edelen House [Washington County MRA], Hwy. 1183, Springfield vicinity, 2/10/89, C, 88003433

Elmwood, KY 55, Springfield, 12/20/77, A, C, 77000658

Farmer's Bank of Mackville [Washington County MRA], KY 152, Mackville, 2/10/89, A, C, 88003431

Fields' House [Washington County MRA], Hwy. 1183, Springfield vicinity, 2/10/89, C, 88003422

Glenn Cottage Tract [Washington County MRA], KY 55, Maud vicinity, 2/10/89, C, 88003416

Gregory—Barlow Place [Washington County MRA], S of Mooresville off KY 55, Mooresville vicinity, 2/10/89, C, 88003398

Grundy Houses, N of Springfield off KY 55, Springfield vicinity, 1/17/78, A, C, 78001411

Hamilton Farm, US 150 0.7 mi. W of Parker's Branch crossing, Springfield vicinity, 7/22/93, A, C, 93000695

Hamilton, Thomas H., House [Washington County MRA], W of Springfield on US 150, Springfield vicinity, 2/10/89, C, 88003403

Holy Rosary Church [Washington County MRA], Hwy. 1183, Springfield vicinity, 2/10/89, C, a, 88003409

Johnson's Chapel AME Church [Washington County MRA], E. High St., Springfield, 2/10/89, A, C, a, 88003396

Kendrick—Croake House [Washington County MRA], Hog Run, Booker Station, Maud vicinity, 2/10/89, C, 88003417

Kendrick—Tucker—Barber House [Washington County MRA], Off US 150, Mooresville vicinity, 2/10/89, C, 88003421

Lincoln, Mordecai, House, 5.9 mi. N of Springfield on KY 528, Springfield, 8/21/72, B, C, 72000547

Litsey, John, House [Washington County MRA], N of Springfield off KY 438, Springfield vicinity, 2/10/89, C, 88003404

Long Lick Creek Bridge [Washington County MRA], Hardesty-Polin Rd. over Long Lick Creek, Willisburg vicinity, 2/10/89, C, 88003414

Lyddan, Pat, House [Washington County MRA], S of Mooresville on KY 55, Mooresville vicinity, 2/10/89, C, 88003420

Mayes, Archibald Scott, House [Washington County MRA], E of Springfield off US 150, Springfield vicinity, 2/10/89, C, 88003405

McChord, William C., House, 202 Lincoln Park Rd., Springfield, 12/11/78, B, C, 78001412

McElroy, T. I., House [Washington County MRA], E of Springfield on US 150, Springfield vicinity, 2/10/89, C, 88003397

McElroy, Wilson, House [Washington County MRA], 321 E. High St., Springfield, 2/10/89, C, 88003392

Mount Zion Covered Bridge, N of Mooresville on KY 458, Mooresville vicinity, 3/26/76, A, C, 76000958

Parrot House [Washington County MRA], E of Springfield on KY 152, Springfield vicinity, 2/10/89, C, 88003412

Pile, Benjamin, House [Washington County MRA], Off KY 55, Springfield vicinity, 2/10/89, C, 88003407

Pope, John, House, 207 Walnut St., Springfield, 5/13/76, B, C, 76000959

Ray—Wakefield House [Washington County MRA], Off KY 55, Maud vicinity, 2/10/89, C, 88003415

Road Run School [Washington County MRA], W of Springfield off KY 152, Springfield vicinity, 2/10/89, A, C, 88003424

Round Stone Smokehouse [Early Stone Buildings of Kentucky Outer Bluegrass and Pennyrile TR], US 150, Fredericktown vicinity, 1/08/87, C, 87000164

Simms—Edelen House [Washington County MRA], SE of Springfield, Springfield vicinity, 2/10/89, C, 88003427

Simms—Mattingly House [Washington County MRA], E of Springfield off KY 152, Springfield vicinity, 2/10/89, C, 88003428

Simmstown [Washington County MRA], S of Springfield on Rineltown-Simmstown Rd., Springfield vicinity, 2/10/89, C, 88003408

Smith, Levi J., House [Washington County MRA], W of Springfield on US 150, Springfield vicinity, 2/10/89, C, 88003411

Springfield Baptist Church [Washington County MRA], Lincoln Park Rd., Springfield, 2/10/89, C, a, 88003394

Springfield Graded School [Washington County MRA], Mackville and Perry Rds., Springfield, 2/10/89, C, 88003389

Springfield Historic Commercial District [Washington County MRA], Roughly bounded by McCord, Walnut, Ballard and Doctor Sts., Springfield, 2/10/89, A, C, 88003434

St. Catherine of Sienna Convent [Washington County MRA], W of Springfield on US 150, Springfield vicinity, 2/10/89, C, a, 88003395

St. Dominic's Catholic Church [Washington County MRA], Main St., Springfield, 2/10/89, C, a, 88003388

St. Rose Roman Catholic Church Complex, W of Springfield off U.S. 150, Springfield vicinity, 2/14/78, A, a, 78001413

Tatham Springs [Washington County MRA], N of Willisburg on Hwy. 1796, Willisburg vicinity, 2/10/89, A, 88003399

Thomas, John, House [Washington County MRA], S of Mooresville on KY 55, Mooresville vicinity, 2/10/89, C, 88003419

Thompson, Dr., House [Washington County MRA], E of Springfield on Mackville Rd., Springfield vicinity, 2/10/89, C, 88003430

Turner, S. F., and Company Steam Flouring and Grist Mill [Washington County MRA], 400 W. Main St., Springfield, 2/10/89, C, 88003390

Walnut Street Historic District [Washington County MRA], 200–600 blocks of Walnut St., Springfield, 2/10/89, C, g, 88003435

Walton Manor Cottage, 2 mi. W of Springfield on KY 150, Springfield, 8/24/77, B, 77000659

Washington County Courthouse, Public Sq., Main at Lincoln Park Rd., Springfield, 7/25/77, A, C, 77000660

Williams, Thomas H., House [Washington County MRA], Hardesty Rd., Springfield vicinity, 2/10/89, C, 88003410

Willisburg Central Bank and Post Office [Washington County MRA], KY 53, Willisburg, 2/10/89, A, C, 88003432

Wayne County

Adkins—Hurt Mill, Off KY 167, Mount Pisgah, 5/06/77, A, C, 77000662

Hotel Breeding, 201–211 N. Main St., Monticello, 8/25/88, A, B, C, 88001315

Mill Springs Mill, Off KY 90, Mill Springs, 4/11/73, A, C, 73000858

Monticello Historic Commercial District, Main and Columbus Sts., Monticello, 10/29/82, A, C, 82001577

West-Metcalfe House, 1.75 mi. S of Mill Springs off KY 90, Mill Springs vicinity, 11/17/77, A, C, 77000661

Webster County

McMullin—Warren House, 301 W. Main St., Sebree, 3/08/88, C, 88000185

Providence Commercial Historic District, 100–200 blks. on E. and W. Main and N. and S. Broadway, Providence, 3/01/93, A, 93000042

Webster County Courthouse, Courthouse Square, Dixon, 8/08/91, A, 91000924

Whitley County

Bowman Site (15WH14), Address Restricted, Lot vicinity, 11/30/85, D, 85002974

Carnegie Library [Corbin MRA], E. Center St., Corbin, 3/28/86, A, 86000603

Corbin Bank Building [Corbin MRA], 101 Center St., Corbin, 3/28/86, C, 86000604

First Christian Church [Corbin MRA], S. Kentucky and W. First St., Corbin, 3/28/86, C, a, 86000693

Gatliff, Dr. Ancil, House, S. 5th St., Williamsburg, 8/11/80, B, C, 80001689

Gatliff, J. B., House, 10th and Main Sts., Williamsburg, 12/16/77, C, 77000663

Gordon Hill Road Historic District [Corbin MRA], 309–501 Gordon Hill Rd., Corbin, 3/28/86, C, 86000692

Louisville and Nashville Railroad Depot, Lynn Ave., Corbin, 6/15/78, A, 78001414

Mershon Building [Corbin MRA], E. Center St., Corbin, 3/28/86, A, C, 86000606

Wolfe County

Hazel Green Academy Historic Buildings, KY 191, Hazel Green, 7/18/79, A, a, 79001047

Hurst, William L., Law Office, N. Washington St., Campton, 8/26/93, C, 93000697

Wolfe County—Continued

Trinity Rockhouses, Address Restricted, Slade vicinity, 8/14/75, D, 75000841

Woodford County

Airy Mount [Cohen Mural Houses TR], SW of Versailles off U.S. 62, Versailles vicinity, 11/15/78, A, B, C, 78001417

Alexander Plantation House [Early Stone Buildings of Central Kentucky TR], Off Old Frankford Pike, Midway vicinity, 6/23/83, A, C, 83002891

Allen, John, House [Early Stone Buildings of Central Kentucky TR], Off KY 169, Keene vicinity, 6/23/83, A, C, 83002892

Archeological Site 15Wd61, Address Restricted, Nonesuch vicinity, 6/02/82, D, 82004853

Arnold-Wooldridge House, S of Versailles, Versailles vicinity, 5/29/79, A, C, 79001048

Big Spring Church, 121 Rose Hill St., Versailles, 5/06/75, A, C, a, 75000842

Black, Charles, Farm [Pisgah Area of Woodford County MPS], Faywood Rd., Versailles vicinity, 2/10/89, A, C, 88003347

Blackburn, Edward M., House, Spring Station Rd., Midway vicinity, 12/05/85, C, 85003073

Buck Pond [Pisgah Area of Woodford County MPS], Paynes Mill Rd., Versailles vicinity, 2/10/89, A, B, C, 88003344

Calmes, Marquis, Tomb [Pisgah Area of Woodford County MPS], Paynes Mill Rd., Versailles vicinity, 2/10/89, B, C, c, d, 88003346

Carter House, 110 Morgan St., Versailles, 5/02/75, B, C, 75000843

Downtown Versailles Historic District, Both sides of Main St. between Rose Hill Ave. and Green St., Versailles, 9/02/75, C, 75000844

DuPuy, Joel, House [Early Stone Buildings of Central Kentucky TR], Griers Creek Rd., Tyrone vicinity, 6/23/83, A, C, 83002893

Edgewood, 1 mi. E of Versailles on U.S. 60, Versailles vicinity, 5/28/76, A, C, 76000960

Edwards, Thomas, House and Quarters [Early Stone Buildings of Central Kentucky TR], SR 1659, Tyrone vicinity, 6/23/83, C, 83002894

Garrett, William, House [Early Stone Buildings of Central Kentucky TR], Off KY 169, Keene vicinity, 6/23/83, A, C, 83002895

Graham, John, House, SE of Midway on Weisenberger Mill Rd., Midway vicinity, 11/14/78, C, 78001416

Guyn's Mill Historic District, Mundy's Landing and Pauls Mill Rds., Troy vicinity, 8/29/83, A, C, 83002897

Guyn, Robert, Jr., House [Early Stone Buildings of Central Kentucky TR], S of Troy on KY 33, Troy vicinity, 8/25/83, A, C, 83002896

Hammon, Ezra, House [Early Stone Buildings of Central Kentucky TR], Off KY 33, Keene vicinity, 8/22/83, A, C, 83002898

Harris, A. T., House [Pisgah Area of Woodford County MPS], Big Sink Pike, Versailles vicinity, 2/10/89, C, 88003345

Hogan Quarters [Early Stone Buildings of Central Kentucky TR], Off KY 33, Keene vicinity, 8/22/83, A, C, 83002899

Humphries Estate Quarters [Early Stone Buildings of Central Kentucky TR], SR 1967, Versailles vicinity, 6/23/83, C, 83002900

Jennings, Dr. William, House, S of Pinckard on KY 169, Pinckard vicinity, 1/12/83, C, 83002901

Jouett, Capt. Jack, House, 5 mi. SW of Versailles off KY 1964, Versailles vicinity, 6/13/72, B, C, 72000548

Lyne, Thomas, House, S of Versailles on Smith Lane, Versailles vicinity, 11/28/80, C, 80001691

Margaret Hall, 117 Elm St., Versailles, 8/03/87, A, C, 87001304

McCrackin Distillery and Mill [Early Stone Buildings of Central Kentucky TR], SR 1659, Tyrone vicinity, 6/23/83, A, C, 83002903

McCrackin, Cyrus, House and Quarters [Early Stone Buildings of Central Kentucky TR], Off Steele Rd., Tyrone vicinity, 8/22/83, A, C, 83002902

Midway Historic District, U.S. 62, Midway, 11/17/78, A, C, a, 78001415

Miller's House at Mortonsville Mill [Early Stone Buildings of Central Kentucky TR], SR 1965, Salvisa vicinity, 6/23/83, C, 83002904

Moore, George F., Place [Early Stone Buildings of Central Kentucky TR], Off U.S. 62, Versailles vicinity, 6/23/83, C, 83002905

Morgan Street Historic District, Morgan St., Versailles, 5/08/80, C, 80001692

Moss Side, SW of Versailles on McCowans Ferry Pike, Versailles vicinity, 1/08/79, A, C, 79001049

Mt. Pisgah Presbyterian Church [Early Stone Buildings of Central Kentucky TR], Off U.S. 60, Versailles vicinity, 8/22/83, A, C, 83002906

Muldrow, Andrew, Quarters [Early Stone Buildings of Central Kentucky TR], Griers Creek Rd., Tyrone vicinity, 6/23/83, A, C, 83002907

Munday's Landing, Munday's Landing Rd., S of Versailles on Kentucky River, Versailles vicinity, 9/05/75, A, C, 75000845

Offutt-Cole Tavern, N of Versailles on U.S. 62, Versailles vicinity, 11/23/77, A, C, 77000664

Paul Family Complex, W of Troy on Paul's Mill Rd., Troy vicinity, 9/23/80, A, C, 80001690

Payne, Lewis, House, Lansing Lane, Midway vicinity, 4/29/82, C, 82002750

Pinkerton Hall, 650 East St., Midway, 11/20/74, A, C, 74000919

Pisgah Rural Historic District [Pisgah Area of Woodford County MPS], Area NE of Versailles roughly bounded by S. Elkhorn Creek, US 60, and Big Sink Rd., Versailles vicinity, 2/10/89, A, C, D, a, d, 88003348

Pleasant Lawn [Cohen Mural Houses TR], N of Versailles off U.S. 62 at Bonita, Versailles vicinity, 11/15/78, C, 78001418

Robertson Place [Early Stone Buildings of Central Kentucky TR], Clifton and Steele Rds., Tyrone vicinity, 6/23/83, C, 83002908

Rose Hill Historic District, Base Hill Ave., Versailles, 12/17/82, C, 82001578

Scearce House, McCracken Pike, Versailles, 4/09/87, C, 87000602

Shipp House, Address Restricted, Midway vicinity, 6/30/83, C, D, 83002909

South Main Street Historic District, 298–321 S. Main St., Versailles, 7/02/87, A, C, 87001106

Stone House at Fisher's Mill [Early Stone Buildings of Central Kentucky TR], Off U.S. 421, Midway vicinity, 6/23/83, C, 83002912

Stone House on Beale's Run [Early Stone Buildings of Central Kentucky TR], Off SR 1685, Midway vicinity, 6/23/83, C, 83002910

Stone House on Clifton Pike [Early Stone Buildings of Central Kentucky TR], SR 1964, Tyrone vicinity, 6/23/83, A, C, 83002911

Stone House on Steele's Grant [Early Stone Buildings of Central Kentucky TR], Off SR 1964, Tyrone vicinity, 6/23/83, C, 83002575

Stone House on Tanner's Creek [Early Stone Buildings of Central Kentucky TR], Carpenter Pike, Salvisa vicinity, 6/23/83, C, 83002913

Thomas, Solomon, House [Early Stone Buildings of Central Kentucky TR], Craigs Creek Rd., Salvisa vicinity, 6/23/83, A, C, 83002914

W.B. Spring House [Early Stone Buildings of Central Kentucky TR], Off U.S. 62, Versailles vicinity, 6/23/83, C, 83002915

Welcome Hall, 4 mi. W of Versailles off Clifton Rd., Versailles vicinity, 10/10/75, C, 75000846

Wilson, Benjamin, House [Early Stone Buildings of Central Kentucky TR], Off U.S. 62, Versailles vicinity, 6/23/83, A, C, 83002916

Wyndehurst [Cohen Mural Houses TR], 5 mi. (8 km) SW of Versailles off SR 1964, Versailles vicinity, 11/15/78, B, C, 78001419

LOUISIANA

Acadia Parish

Colorado Southern Railroad Depot, N. Ave. G and E. Front St., Crowley, 3/26/80, A, C, 80001693
Crowley Historic District, LA 13 and U.S. 90, Crowley, 3/12/82, A, C, a, b, 82002751

Allen Parish

Allen Parish Courthouse, 5th St., Oberlin, 6/03/81, A, C, 81000287
Elizabeth Hospital Building, Mimosa Dr., Elizabeth, 1/18/85, A, 85000092
Genius Brothers Building, Jct. of 8th St. and 4th Ave., Kinder, 6/27/90, A, 90000909

Ascension Parish

Ashland, 2 mi. (3.2km) S of Geismar on LA 75, Geismar vicinity, 5/04/79, B, C, 79001050
Bocage, LA 942 S of Marchandville, Darrow vicinity, 6/20/91, C, 91000705
Donaldsonville Historic District, Roughly bounded by Bayou LaFourche, the Mississippi River levee, Jackson Ave., Marchand Dr., and Monroe and Church Sts., Donaldsonville, 1/19/84, A, C, 84001248
Evan Hall Slave Cabins, W of Donaldsonville, Donaldsonville vicinity, 9/20/83, A, C, 83000484
Helvetia Dependency [Louisiana's French Creole Architecture MPS], LA 942, Darrow vicinity, 6/04/92, C, b, 92000570
Hermitage, 1.75 mi. E of Darrow on LA 942, Darrow vicinity, 4/13/73, C, 73000859
Houmas, The, W of Burnside off LA 22 and LA 44, Burnside vicinity, 9/27/80, A, C, 80001694
Kraemer House, Off US 61, Prairieville, 8/02/84, C, 84001250
Landry Tomb, Ascension Catholic Church Cemetery, St. Vincent and Claiborne Sts., Donaldsonville, 8/11/82, C, d, 82002752
Lemann Store, 314 Mississippi St., Donaldsonville, 8/11/82, C, 82002753
Mulberry Grove, LA 405, 7 mi. ENE of jct. with LA 1, White Castle vicinity, 10/14/93, C, 93001118
Palo Alto Dependency [Louisiana's French Creole Architecture MPS], LA 944, Donaldsonville vicinity, 6/04/92, C, b, 92000579
Palo Alto Plantation, W of Donaldsonville on LA 1, Donaldsonville vicinity, 4/13/77, A, B, C, 77000665
Rome House, LA 1 at Delany Ln., Smoke Bend, 3/08/90, C, b, 90000323
St. Emma, S of Donaldsonville, Donaldsonville vicinity, 6/30/80, A, B, C, 80001695
St. Joseph's School, LA 22 and 44, Burnside, 11/17/88, A, a, b, 88002651

Tezcuco, S. of Burnside on River Rd., Burnside vicinity, 3/03/83, C, 83000485
Warren, Robert Penn, House, 16381 Old Jefferson Hwy., Prairieville, 1/07/93, B, 92001732

Assumption Parish

Christ Episcopal Church and Cemetery, LA 1 between Courthouse St. and LA 1008, Napoleonville, 5/02/77, A, B, C, a, d, 77000666
Church of the Assumption of the Blessed Virgin Mary, LA 308, Plattenville, 5/08/79, C, a, 79001051
Madewood, E of Napoleonville on LA 308, Napoleonville vicinity, 10/30/73, C, NHL, 73000860
St. Elizabeth Catholic Church, LA 402, Paincourtville, 3/24/83, C, a, 83000486
St. Philomene Catholic Church and Rectory, LA 1, Labadieville, 9/27/83, C, a, 83000487

Avoyelles Parish

Bailey Theatre, Oak St., Bunkie, 7/26/79, A, C, 79001052
Bayou Rouge Baptist Church, Church and College Sts., Evergreen, 12/03/80, C, a, 80001696
Bordelon, Alfred H., House, 511 N. Washington, Marksville, 11/06/86, C, 86003133
Bordelon, Hypolite, House, LA 1, Marksville, 10/16/80, C, b, 80001698
Bordelonville Floodgate, Camber Rd. and LA 451, on the Bayou des Glaises levee, Bordelonville vicinity, 3/14/91, A, 91000277
Calliham Plantation House, Old Hwy 1, Hamburg, 7/22/82, C, 82002754
Clarendon Plantation House, LA 29, Evergreen vicinity, 5/09/85, C, 85000970
Des Fosse, Dr. Jules Charles, House, L'Eglise St., Mansura, 4/23/76, C, 76000961
Epps, Edwin, House, US 71, Bunkie, 4/12/84, A, b, 84001255
Frithland, LA 29, Bunkie vicinity, 5/09/85, C, 85000969
Joffrion House, 605 N. Monroe, Marksville, 8/11/82, C, 82002755
Lacour's Fish and Ice Company Building, LA 1, Simmesport, 9/08/83, A, 83000488
Lemoine, Thomas A., House, LA 451, Moreauville, 7/18/85, C, 85001588
Lemoine, Thomas A., House, LA 451, Hamburg, 7/18/85, C, b, 85001589
Lone Pine, Off LA 361, Evergreen vicinity, 10/28/82, C, 82000430
Marksville Commercial Historic District, Roughly Bounded by Monroe, Washington, N. Ogden, and Bontempt Sts., Marksville, 3/16/83, A, C, 83000489

Marksville Prehistoric Indian Site, Marksville Prehistoric Indian Park State Monument, Marksville vicinity, 10/15/66, D, NHL, 66000372
Oak Hall, LA 29, Bunkie vicinity, 11/06/86, C, 86003134
Oakwold Plantation House, W of Evergreen off LA 29, Evergreen vicinity, 7/23/80, C, 80001697
Roy, Dr. Thomas A., Sr., House, L'Eglise St., Mansura, 5/09/85, C, 85000971
Sarto Bridge, Off LA 451 over Bayou Des Glaises, Big Bend, 11/21/89, C, 89002027
St. Mary's Assumption Church, Front St., Cottonport, 5/01/89, C, a, 89000330
St. Paul Lutheran Church, LA 107, N of Mansura, Mansura vicinity, 3/01/90, A, a, 90000353
Texas and Pacific Railroad Depot, Jct. of W. Main and Oak Sts., Bunkie, 3/22/91, A, 91000345

Beauregard Parish

Beauregard Parish Courthouse, 1st St., DeRidder, 9/22/83, C, 83000490
Beauregard Parish Jail, Courthouse Sq., DeRidder, 12/17/81, C, 81000711
Burks House, Jct. of Railroad Ave. and Main St., Merryville, 9/08/87, C, b, 87001512
DeRidder Commercial Historic District, Roughly bounded by the RR line, Second, Stewart, and Port Sts., DeRidder, 8/09/83, A, C, 83000491
DeRidder USO Building, Jct. of Pine and 7th Sts., DeRidder, 2/25/92, A, g, 92000037
Dry Creek High School Building, LA 113, Dry Creek, 1/28/88, C, a, 87002572
First United Methodist Church, Jct. of Pine and N. Port Sts., DeRidder, 11/21/91, C, a, 91001659

Bienville Parish

Colbert House [Antebellum Greek Revival Buildings of Mount Lebanon TR], LA 517, Gibsland vicinity, 2/01/80, C, 80001699
Dog Trot [Antebellum Greek Revival Buildings of Mount Lebanon TR], LA 517, Gibsland vicinity, 2/01/80, A, C, 80001700
Down House [Antebellum Greek Revival Buildings of Mount Lebanon TR], LA 154, Gibsland vicinity, 2/01/80, C, 80001701
Hill, The, 700 Line St., Arcadia, 10/27/88, C, 88002055
Jones House [Antebellum Greek Revival Buildings of Mount Lebanon TR], LA 154, Gibsland vicinity, 2/01/80, B, C, 80001702
Mount Lebanon Baptist Church [Antebellum Greek Revival Buildings of Mount Lebanon TR], LA 154, Gibsland vicinity, 2/01/80, A, C, a, 80001703

Bienville Parish—Continued

Stage Coach Inn [Antebellum Greek Revival Buildings of Mount Lebanon TR], LA 517, Gibsland vicinity, 2/01/80, A, C, 80001704

Sylvan Retreat, 610 N. 3rd St, Gibsland, 12/06/79, C, b, e, 79001053

Thurmond House [Antebellum Greek Revival Buildings of Mount Lebanon TR], LA 154, Gibsland vicinity, 2/01/80, C, 80001705

Vicksburg, Shreveport, and Pacific Railroad Depot, LA 151, Arcadia, 2/29/88, A, 87001516

Wayside Inn [Antebellum Greek Revival Buildings of Mount Lebanon TR], LA 154, Gibsland vicinity, 2/01/80, B, C, 80001706

Bossier Parish

Barksdale Field Historic District, Jct. of US 71 and West Gate Dr., Bossier City, 4/13/92, C, 92000332

Cashpoint Plantation House, N of Elm Grove off LA 71, Elm Grove vicinity, 8/11/82, C, b, 82002757

Hughes House, 13 mi. NE of Benton on LA 160, Benton vicinity, 5/24/76, A, C, 76000962

Caddo Parish

Antioch Baptist Church, 1057 Texas Ave., Shreveport, 11/01/82, C, a, 82000431

Byrd, C. E., High School, 3201 Line Ave., Shreveport, 6/10/91, C, 91000704

Caspiana House, Louisiana State University campus, Shreveport, 12/10/81, C, b, 81000288

Central Fire Station, 801 Crockett St., Shreveport, 5/28/91, C, 91000625

Central High School, 1627 Weinstock St., Shreveport, 5/16/91, A, 91000606

Central Railroad Station, 1025 Marshall St., Shreveport, 5/28/91, A, 91000622

Davidson House, 654 Wichita Ave., Shreveport, 12/22/83, C, 83003604

Dodd College President's Home, 601 Ockley Dr., Shreveport, 7/22/82, B, C, 82002758

Fairfield Historic District, Fairfield Ave. and adjacent Sts. roughly bounded by Olive and Dalzell Sts., Line Ave., and Kings Hwy., Shreveport, 2/19/87, C, 87000190

Flesch House, 415 Sherwood Rd., Shreveport, 6/10/91, C, 91000703

Flournoy—Wise House, 9152 Bois d'Arc Ln., Greenwood, 3/16/90, C, 90000435

Forest Home, Jct. Johns Rd. and Johns Gin Rd., Four Forks vicinity, 10/30/89, C, 89001873

Highland Historic District, Roughly bounded by Vine, Gilbert, and Topeka Sts., and Irving Pl., Shreveport, 2/19/87, C, 87000192

Holy Trinity Catholic Church, 315 Marshall St., Shreveport, 9/27/84, C, a, 84001261

Jefferson Hotel, 907 Louisiana Ave., Shreveport, 7/27/89, A, 89000977

Kings Highway Christian Church, 806 Kings Hwy., Shreveport, 8/07/89, C, a, 89001042

Lewis House, 675 Jordan St., Shreveport, 7/27/79, A, 79001054

Lindsay, Col. Robert H., House, 2803 Woodlawn Ave., Shreveport, 7/16/73, A, B, b, 73000861

Line Avenue School, 1800 Line Ave., Shreveport, 6/03/81, C, 81000289

Long, Huey P., House, 2403 Laurel St., Shreveport, 6/10/91, B, 91000701

Long, Huey P., House, 305 Forest Ave., Shreveport, 8/15/91, B, 91001060

Louisiana State Exhibit Building, 3015 Greenwood Rd., Shreveport, 2/20/91, C, 91000071

Masonic Temple, 1805 Creswell St., Shreveport, 6/10/91, C, 91000702

Oakland Cemetery, Bounded by Milam, Christian, Sprague, and Baker Sts., Shreveport, 7/13/77, A, B, C, d, 77000667

Old Commercial National Bank Building, 509 Market St., Shreveport, 3/11/82, A, C, 82002759

Scottish Rite Cathedral, 725 Cotton St., Shreveport, 11/06/86, C, 86003132

Shreveport Commercial Historic District, Roughly bounded by Commerce, Crockett, Common and Travis Sts., Shreveport, 3/11/82, C, a, 82002760

Shreveport Municipal Building, 724 McNeil St., Shreveport, 5/05/82, C, 82002761

Shreveport Municipal Memorial Auditorium, 705 Grand Ave., Shreveport, 5/28/91, C, 91000624

Shreveport Water Works Company, Pump Station, Off LA 3036, Shreveport, 5/09/80, A, C, NHL, 80001707

Shreveport Woman's Department Club Building, 802 Margaret Pl., Shreveport, 7/18/85, A, C, 85001590

South Highlands Fire Station, 763 Oneonta, Shreveport, 5/28/91, C, 91000626

Sprague Street Houses, 1100-1118 Sprague St., Shreveport, 10/03/83, C, 83003606

St. Mark's Episcopal Church, 875 Cotton St., Shreveport, 6/11/91, C, a, 91000700

St. Paul's Bottoms, Roughly bounded by Western and Pierre Aves., Alston, Christian, Oakland, and Snow Sts., Shreveport, 10/11/84, C, 84000033

Steere, A. C., Elementary School, 4009 Youree Dr., Shreveport, 2/20/91, C, 91000074

Strand Theatre, 630 Crockett, Shreveport, 5/26/77, A, B, C, 77000668

Tally's Bank, 525 Spring St., Shreveport, 7/14/76, A, C, 76000963

Taylor Wholesale Grocers and Cotton Factors Warehouse—Lee Hardware Building, 719, 723, and 729 Edwards St., Shreveport, 2/13/86, A, 86000251

Texas Avenue Buildings, 824–864 Texas Ave., Shreveport, 5/25/79, C, g, 79001055

Thrasher House, 8515 Youree Dr., Pioneer Heritage Center, LA State University, Shreveport, 9/10/87, C, b, 87001565

Trees City Office and Bank Building, 207 Land Ave., Oil City, 8/13/86, A, b, 86001492

Trosper House, 304 Magnolia St., Greenwood, 5/14/87, C, 87000728

U.S. Post Office and Courthouse, Marshall and Texas Sts., Shreveport, 9/12/74, A, C, 74000920

Wile House, 626 Wilder Pl., Shreveport, 8/05/91, C, 91001007

Wray-Dickinson Building, 308 Market St., Shreveport, 3/24/83, C, 83000492

YMCA, Downtown Branch, 400 McNeill St., Shreveport, 5/28/91, C, 91000621

Calcasieu Parish

All Saints Episcopal Church, Hall and Harrison Sts., DeQuincy, 9/20/83, C, a, b, 83000493

Arcade Theater, 822 Ryan St., Lake Charles, 7/07/78, A, C, 78001420

Calcasieu Marine Bank, 840 Ryan St., Lake Charles, 3/11/91, C, 91000221

Calcasieu Parish Courthouse, Ryan St. at Kirby St., Lake Charles, 11/02/89, A, C, 89001938

Charleston Hotel, Ryan and Broad Sts., Lake Charles, 5/27/82, A, C, 82002762

Episcopal Church of the Good Shepherd, 715 Kirkman St., Lake Charles, 12/22/83, C, a, 83003607

Jackson House, Off LA 27, DeQuincy vicinity, 2/13/86, C, b, 86000252

Kansas City Southern Depot, Lake Charles Ave., DeQuincy, 9/22/83, C, 83000494

Lake Charles City Hall, Old, Ryan St. at Kirby St., Lake Charles, 10/30/89, A, C, 89001872

Lake Charles Historic District, Roughly bounded by Iris, Hodges, Lawrence, Kirkman, S. Division and Louisiana, Lake Charles, 3/16/90, A, C, 90000434

Lyons House, 1335 Horridge St., Vinton, 4/27/82, C, g, 82002763

McNeese State University Auditorium, Ryan St. S of Sale St., Lake Charles, 5/05/89, C, 89000381

Waters Pierce Oil Company Stable Building, 1019 Lakeshore Dr., Lake Charles, 9/29/80, A, 80001708

Caldwell Parish

Breston Plantation House, N of Columbia, Columbia vicinity, 11/22/80, C, 80001709

First United Methodist Church, LA 165 and Church St., Columbia, 8/12/82, C, a, 82002764

Martin House, Jct. of Martin Ln. and US 165, 2 mi. N of Columbia, Columbia vicinity, 8/12/93, C, 93000832

Oasis, The, Main St./LA 845, Clarks, 7/31/89, A, 89000976

Shepis Building, Main St., Columbia, 1/16/86, C, 86000069

Synope Plantation House, N of Columbia off US 165, Columbia vicinity, 10/05/82, C, 82000432

Cameron Parish

Sabine Pass Lighthouse, Lighthouse Bayou, Cameron vicinity, 12/17/81, C, 81000290

Catahoula Parish

Battleground Plantation, 4 mi. (6.4 km) N of Sicily Island, Sicily Island vicinity, 5/14/79, A, B, C, 79001056
Catahoula Parish Courthouse, LA 124, Harrisonburg, 10/27/88, C, 88002056
Ferry Place, Address Restricted, Sicily Island vicinity, 8/29/80, A, B, D, 80001711
Green-Lovelace House, N of Sicily Island off LA 15, Sicily Island vicinity, 4/05/83, C, 83000495
Hardin House, LA 913 N of jct. with LA 8, Sicily Island vicinity, 11/08/90, C, 90001740
Kirby House, Spencer and Pearl Sts., Trinity, 1/21/88, C, 87002498
Marengo Plantation House, US 84, 6 mi. W of Jonesville, Jonesville vicinity, 12/14/87, C, 87002135
Sargent House, Catahoula St., Harrisonburg, 12/03/80, C, 80001710
Spring Ridge Baptist Church, Sherwood Rd., near jct. with LA 559 and LA 124, Enterprise vicinity, 10/07/93, C, a, 93001037
Wildwood, Off LA 15, Sicily Island vicinity, 10/30/89, C, 89001874

Claiborne Parish

Arizona Methodist Church, LA 806, Arizona, 12/22/83, C, a, 83003608
Burnham, J. W., House, Off US 79, Haynesville vicinity, 1/22/87, C, 86003671
Capers-McKenzie House, N. 5th St., Homer, 6/30/83, C, 83000496
Claiborne Parish Courthouse, Courthouse Sq., Homer, 10/07/81, C, 81000291
Homer Historic District, Roughly bounded by N. Second, E. Main, S. Third, and W. Main Sts., Homer, 8/28/86, C, 86001994
Killgore House, Jct. of LA 2 and LA 518, Lisbon, 5/14/87, C, 87000731
Monk House, Claiborne Parish Rt. 39 and LA 9, Homer vicinity, 8/23/91, C, 91001081
Todd, Dr. John W., House, 306 Pine St., Homer, 1/22/87, C, b, 86003683
Tulip Methodist Church, Off LA 518, Marsalis vicinity, 8/13/87, C, a, 87001367
Wasson, Alberry, Homeplace, 1-1/2 mi. S of Summerfield, Summerfield vicinity, 6/25/82, C, b, 82002766

Concordia Parish

Campbell, Sheriff Eugene P., House, 2 Concordia Ave., Vidalia, 4/13/79, A, C, 79001058
Canebrake, NE of Ferriday on LA 901, Ferriday vicinity, 8/29/82, A, b, 82002767
Frogmore, U.S. 84, Ferriday vicinity, 5/31/80, C, 80001712
Lisburn Plantation House, SE of Ferriday, Ferriday vicinity, 7/26/79, C, b, 79001057

Roseland, 500 Fisherman Dr., Ferriday vicinity, 10/10/85, C, b, 85003002
Tacony Plantation House, Off U.S. 84, Vidalia, 4/19/79, A, B, 79001059

De Soto Parish

Allen House, Smyrna Rd. and LA 5, Keachi vicinity, 7/28/88, C, b, 88001154
Bank of Grand Cane, US 171, Grand Cane, 2/11/88, C, 88000105
Buena Vista, Red Bluff Rd., Stonewall vicinity, 1/19/89, C, 88003197
DeSoto Parish Courthouse, Jct. of Adams and Texas Sts., Mansfield, 1/22/87, C, 86003677
Grand Cane United Methodist Church, US 171 S of LA 3015, Grand Cane, 1/28/92, C, a, 91002024
Guy House, Off LA 513, 5 mi. S of Mansfield, Mansfield vicinity, 2/11/88, C, 88000103
International Boundary Marker, SE of Deadwood off SR 31 at LA State line, Logansport vicinity, 4/13/77, A, 77001463
Kansas City Southern Depot, Polk St. on Kansas City Southern railroad tracks, Mansfield, 1/19/89, A, 88003198
Keachi Baptist Church, LA 172, Keachi, 10/20/88, C, a, 88002039
Keachi Presbyterian Church, LA 5, Keachi, 6/30/88, C, a, 88000981
Keachi Store, Jct. of LA 5 and 789, Keachi, 10/20/88, C, 88002036
Keachi United Methodist Church, LA 5, Keachi, 7/14/88, C, 88001046
Land's End Plantation, 7 mi. SE of Stonewall on Red Bluff Rd., Stonewall vicinity, 4/26/72, B, C, 72001453
Liberty Lodge No. 123, F & A M, LA 5 and 172, Keachi, 1/13/89, C, 88003136
Mansfield Battle Park, 4 mi. SE of Mansfield on LA 175, Mansfield vicinity, 4/13/73, A, 73002131
Mansfield Historic District, Texas and Adams Sts. at Courthouse Sq., Mansfield, 10/27/88, C, 88002067
Mundy-McFarland House, 200 Welsh St., Mansfield, 12/06/79, C, 79003120
Myrtle Hill Plantation House, SE of Gloster off LA 5, Gloster vicinity, 12/04/74, C, 74002185
Oaks, The, LA 172, Keachi vicinity, 1/19/89, C, 88003203
Prude House, LA 5, Keachi vicinity, 7/14/88, C, b, 88001048
Roseneath, LA 5, Gloster vicinity, 1/13/89, C, 88003137
Scott, Thomas, House, LA 5, 4 mi. E of Gloster, Gloster vicinity, 11/06/86, C, 86003131
Spell House, LA 5, Keachi vicinity, 7/14/88, C, 88001047
Stribling House, US 84, Mansfield, 5/11/89, C, 89000403
Swearingen House, LA 5, Keachi, 11/17/88, C, 88002658
U. S. Post Office, 104 Jefferson St., Mansfield, 1/12/83, C, 83000497

Wood Park, S of Mansfield off LA 175, Mansfield vicinity, 1/21/83, C, 83000498

East Baton Rouge Parish

Audubon Plantation House, 21371 Hoo Shoo Too Rd., Baton Rouge vicinity, 5/14/87, C, 87000729
Baker Presbyterian Church, 3015 Groom Rd., Baker, 3/01/90, C, a, 90000346
Barthel Pigeonnier, 2161 Nicholson Dr., Baton Rouge, 7/13/83, C, b, 83000499
Baton Rouge High School, 2825 Government St., Baton Rouge, 11/06/86, C, 86003130
Baton Rouge Junior High School, 1100 Laurel St., Baton Rouge, 9/27/84, C, 84001271
Baton Rouge Waterworks Company Standpipe, 131 Lafayette St., Baton Rouge, 12/04/73, A, C, 73002242
Beauregard Town Historic District, LA 73, Baton Rouge, 10/14/80, C, a, 80001713
Beauregard Town Historic District (Boundary Increase), Front St., Baton Rouge, 4/14/83, C, 83000500
Beauregard Town Historic District (Boundary Increase), Mayflower St., Baton Rouge, 10/11/83, A, C, 83003611
Belisle Building, 344 and 350 Third St., Baton Rouge, 10/19/93, C, 93001104
Capital City Press Building, 340 Florida, Baton Rouge, 10/16/86, C, 86002870
Central Fire Station, 427 Laurel St., Baton Rouge, 4/05/84, C, 84001277
Cushman House, 1606 Main St., Baker, 2/20/91, C, 91000072
Fairhaven Plantation House, 18630 Samuel Rd., Zachary vicinity, 2/11/88, C, 88000102
Florence Coffee House, 130 Main St., Baton Rouge, 1/20/80, C, 80001714
French House, The, Louisiana State University Campus, Baton Rouge, 1/13/82, A, C, g, 82002768
Hart House, Iowa St., Baton Rouge, 8/01/80, B, c, 80001715
Heidelberg Hotel, 201 Lafayette St., Baton Rouge, 5/20/82, A, B, C, 82002769
Kleinpeter House, Perkins Rd., Baton Rouge vicinity, 8/13/86, C, b, 86001494
Lee Site (16 EBR 51), Address Restricted, Baton Rouge vicinity, 12/27/84, D, 84000792
Leland College, W of Baker off LA 19, Baker vicinity, 11/10/82, A, 82000433
Les Chenes Verts [Louisiana's French Creole Architecture MPS], Jct. Highland Rd. and Jean Lafitte Ave., Baton Rouge, 1/21/93, C, 92001831
Longwood, 10417 River Rd., Baton Rouge, 7/07/83, C, 83000501
Louisiana State Capitol Building and Gardens, Capitol Dr., Baton Rouge, 6/09/78, A, B, C, g, NHL, 78001421
Louisiana State University, Baton Rouge, Highland Rd., Baton Rouge, 9/15/88, C, 88001586
Magnolia Cemetery, Bounded by Main, 19th, Florida, and 22nd Sts., Baton Rouge, 1/31/85, A, d, 85000161

East Baton Rouge Parish—Continued

Magnolia Mound Plantation House, 2161 Nichol-son Dr., Baton Rouge, 9/07/72, C, 72000549

Magnolia Mound Plantation Dependency, 2530 Vermont St., Baton Rouge, 8/09/77, C, 77000669

Main Street Historic District, 442–660 Main St., Baton Rouge, 11/07/85, C, 85002785

Manship House, 2250 Kleinert Ave., Baton Rouge, 11/21/80, B, C, c, 80001716

McKinley High School, 1500 East Blvd., Baton Rouge, 11/16/81, A, 81000292

Mount Hope Plantation House, 8151 Highland Rd., Baton Rouge, 12/03/80, C, 80001717

Old Louisiana Governor's Mansion, 502 North Blvd., Baton Rouge, 7/24/75, B, C, g, 75000847

Old Louisiana State Capitol, North Blvd. and St. Philip St., Baton Rouge, 1/12/73, A, C, NHL, 73000862

Old Post Office, 355 North Blvd., Baton Rouge, 6/09/80, A, C, 80001718

Ory House [Louisiana's French Creole Architecture MPS], Jct. of Highland Rd. and Jean Lafitte Ave., Baton Rouge, 1/21/93, C, b, 92001818

Pentagon Barracks, North Riverside Mall, Baton Rouge, 7/26/73, A, 73000863

Petitpierre—Kleinpeter, Joseph, House, 5544 Highland Rd., Baton Rouge, 1/23/86, C, b, 86000111

Planter's Cabin, 7815 Highland Rd., Baton Rouge, 8/23/84, C, 84001279

Potts House, 831 North St., Baton Rouge, 9/14/72, C, 72000550

Powder Magazine, State Capitol Dr., Baton Rouge, 6/04/73, A, D, 73000864

Reiley-Reeves House, 810 Park Blvd., Baton Rouge, 5/24/79, C, 79001060

Roseland Terrace Historic District, Bounded by Government, 18th, Myrtle, and 22nd Sts., Baton Rouge, 3/11/82, C, 82002770

Roumain Building, 343 Riverside Mall, Baton Rouge, 4/11/85, C, 85000727

Santa Maria Plantation House, S of Baton Rouge on Perkins Rd., Baton Rouge vicinity, 12/29/78, C, 78003448

Southern University Archives Building, Southern University campus, Scotlandville, 6/11/81, A, C, 81000294

Spanish Town, Bounded by State Capitol Dr., 5th, 9th and North Sts., Baton Rouge, 8/31/78, C, 78001422

St. James Episcopal Church, 208 N. 4th St., Baton Rouge, 5/05/78, C, a, 78001423

St. Joseph Cathedral, Main and Fourth Sts., Baton Rouge, 3/22/90, C, a, 90000502

Stewart-Dougherty House, 741 North St., Baton Rouge, 3/28/73, A, C, 73000865

Tessier Buildings, 342, 346, and 348 Lafayette St., Baton Rouge, 3/16/78, B, C, 78001424

U.S.S. KIDD, Mississippi River near Government St. and River Rd., Baton Rouge, 8/09/83, A, C, g, NHL, 83000502

Warden's House—Old Louisiana State Penitentiary, 701-705 Laurel St., Baton Rouge, 12/02/74, C, 74000921

Zachary Railroad Depot, 4434 W. Central Ave., Zachary, 12/28/83, A, 83003615

East Carroll Parish

Arlington Plantation [Lake Providence MRA], 214 Arlington, Lake Providence, 10/03/80, B, C, 80004476

Buckmeadow Plantation House, NW of Lake Providence off LA 2, Lake Providence vicinity, 9/15/83, C, 83000503

Byerley House, Jct. of Lake and Ingram Sts., Lake Providence, 11/13/91, C, b, 91001681

Fischer House [Lake Providence MRA (AD)], 15 Lake St., Lake Providence, 1/11/80, C, 80001726

Lake Providence Historic District [Lake Providence MRA (AD)], Lake, Levee, and Scarborough Sts, Lake Providence, 12/06/79, A, C, 79001063

Lake Providence Residential Street Historic District [Lake Providence MRA], Lake and Davis Sts., Lake Providence, 10/03/80, C, 80004477

Nelson House [Lake Providence MRA], 407 Davis St., Lake Providence, 10/03/80, C, 80001727

Old Courthouse Square [Lake Providence MRA], 1st and Hoad Sts., Lake Providence, 10/03/80, A, C, 80001728

East Feliciana Parish

Asphodel Plantation and Cemetery, S of Jackson on LA 74, Jackson vicinity, 11/15/72, C, 72000552

Avondale Plantation Home, E of Clinton off LA 10, Clinton vicinity, 12/17/82, C, 82000434

Boatner House, Plank and Taylor Rds., Clinton, 5/31/80, C, 80001719

Brame-Bennett House, 227 S. Baton Rouge St., Clinton, 5/22/73, C, 73000866

Centenary College, College St., Jackson, 4/19/79, A, C, 79001062

Center Building of East Louisiana State Hospital, E of Jackson on LA 10, Jackson vicinity, 8/01/80, A, C, 80001721

Courthouse and Lawyers' Row, Liberty, St. Helena, Bank, and Woodville Sts., Clinton, 5/30/74, C, NHL, 74002249

East Feliciana Parish Courthouse, Public Sq., Clinton, 6/04/73, A, C, 73002232

Fairview Plantation House, 8338 LA 963, Ethel vicinity, 8/12/93, C, 93000821

Hope Terrace, Church and Silliman Sts., Clinton, 8/13/86, C, 86001493

Jackson Historic District, Roughly bounded by Institute Dr., LA 314, Horton and Race Sts., Jackson, 12/04/80, A, C, 80001722

Lane Plantation House, 7684 Lane Ln., Ethel vicinity, 4/22/93, C, 93000322

Linwood, 7.3 mi. S of Jackson, Jackson vicinity, 6/09/80, B, C, 80001723

Marston House, Bank St., Clinton, 6/29/72, B, C, 72000551

Oakland Plantation House, W of Gurley, Gurley vicinity, 10/03/80, C, b, 80001720

Port Hudson, Port Hudson and environs along US 61, Port Hudson vicinity, 5/30/74, A, NHL, 74002349

Richland Plantation, SW of Norwood on LA 442, Norwood vicinity, 3/28/79, C, 79001064

Shades, The, NE of Jackson, Jackson vicinity, 11/06/80, C, 80001724

Silliman Institute, Bank St., Clinton, 4/18/83, C, 83000504

St. Andrew's Episcopal Church, Church and St. Andrew's Sts., Clinton, 6/21/84, C, a, 84001282

Thompson House, E of Jackson, Jackson vicinity, 9/29/80, C, 80001725

Wall House, Woodville St., Clinton, 5/31/84, C, 84001285

Wildwood Plantation House, LA 68, near US 61, Jackson vicinity, 6/30/88, C, 88000977

Woodside, St. Helena St., Clinton, 10/04/84, C, 84000012

Evangeline Parish

Dardeau Building, 224 W. Main, Ville Platte, 6/01/82, A, C, 82002771

LaTour, Alexis, House, 247 E. Main, Ville Platte, 9/14/87, C, 87001492

Franklin Parish

Baskin High School Building, LA 857, Baskin, 10/07/81, A, C, 81000295

Chennault House, LA 15 S. of Gilbert, Gilbert vicinity, 6/23/83, B, g, 83000505

Grayson House, SE of Fort Necessity on LA 562, Fort Necessity vicinity, 10/27/82, C, 82000435

Jackson House, 703 Jackson St., Winnsboro, 9/21/82, C, 82002773

Jackson Street Historic District, Jackson St., Winnsboro, 10/05/82, C, 82000436

Winnsboro Commercial Historic District, Prairie St., Winnsboro, 7/09/82, A, C, 82002774

Grant Parish

Ethridge House, 401 Louise St., Colfax, 8/07/89, C, b, 89001043

Kateland, N of Boyce off LA 8, Boyce vicinity, 4/12/84, C, 84001288

McNeely House, 3rd, 4th and Main Sts., Colfax, 3/31/83, A, C, 83000506

Roberts, Earl, House, 253 Second St., Colfax, 4/20/89, C, 89000328

Iberia Parish

Alice, LA 87, Jeanerette vicinity, 6/14/84, C, b, 84001291

Iberia Parish—Continued

Bayside, LA 87, Jeanerette vicinity, 1/29/87, C, 86003747

Broussard, Amant, House, 1400 E. Main St., New Iberia, 6/09/80, C, b, 80001729

Conrad Rice Mill, 307 Ann St., New Iberia, 11/10/82, A, C, 82000437

Darby Plantation, N of Iberia on Darby Lane, New Iberia vicinity, 3/26/73, A, C, 73000868

East Main Street Historic District, East Main, Lee, Ann and Phillip Sts., New Iberia, 7/28/83, A, C, 83000507

Enterprise Plantation, 2 mi. W of Jeanerette in Patoutville community, Jeanerette vicinity, 3/17/75, A, C, 75000848

Episcopal Church of the Epiphany, 303 W. Main St., New Iberia, 4/29/77, A, C, a, 77000670

First United Methodist Church, 119 Jefferson St., New Iberia, 11/16/89, C, a, 89002002

Jefferson, Joseph, House, On Jefferson Island, Jefferson Island, 6/04/73, B, C, g, 73000867

Lamperez, Santiago, House, 203 Front St., New Iberia, 10/17/85, C, 85003147

Magnolias, The, 115 Jefferson St., New Iberia, 12/06/79, A, C, b, 79001065

Mintmere, 1400 E. Main St., New Iberia, 6/06/80, C, 80001730

Olivier Store, LA 83, Lydia, 10/25/82, C, 82000438

Pascal Building, 223 E. Main St., New Iberia, 11/21/85, C, 85003054

Romero, Andrew, House, 310 Marie St., New Iberia, 10/30/89, C, 89001855

Shadows-on-the-Teche, E. Main St., New Iberia, 10/05/72, C, NHL, 72000553

Southern Pacific Railroad Depot, 402 W. Washington, New Iberia, 11/30/87, A, 87002082

Steamboat House, 623 E. Main St., New Iberia, 7/27/79, B, C, 79001066

Iberville Parish

Bayou Plaquemine Lock, U.S. Government Reservation at confluence of Bayou Plaquemine and the Mississippi River, Plaquemine, 5/19/72, A, C, 72000554

Carville Historic District, 5445 Point Clair Rd., Carville, 11/18/92, A, C, 92001529

Church of the Nativity, Laurel St., Rosedale, 8/11/82, C, a, 82002775

Desobry Building, Court and Marshall Sts., Plaquemine, 11/06/86, C, 86003128

Gay, Andrew H., House, 1010 McDuffie St., Plaquemine, 7/18/85, C, 85001582

Homestead Plantation Complex, LA 3066, 3 mi. SW of Plaquemine, Plaquemine vicinity, 11/06/86, C, b, 86003129

Iberville Parish Courthouse, 209 Main St., Plaquemine, 5/31/80, A, C, 80001732

Live Oaks Plantation, LA 77 N, Rosedale, 11/20/74, C, a, 74000924

Nottoway Plantation House, NW of White Castle, White Castle vicinity, 6/06/80, A, C, 80001733

Plaquemine High School, 600 Plaquemine St., Plaquemine, 2/13/92, C, 92000041

Plaquemine Historic District, Roughly Church St., Court St., Railroad Ave., and Main St., Plaquemine, 10/30/89, C, d, 89001791

Schexnayder House, 1681 Pecan Dr., Iberville, 1/19/89, C, b, 88003224

St. Basil's Academy, 311 Church St., Plaquemine, 10/05/82, C, 82000439

St. Gabriel Roman Catholic Church, S of St. Gabriel off LA 75, St. Gabriel vicinity, 11/27/72, A, C, a, b, 72000555

St. Louis Plantation, 1 mi. S of Plaquemine on LA 405, Plaquemine vicinity, 12/03/75, A, B, C, 75000849

Tally-Ho Plantation House, River Rd., Bayou Goula, 1/20/80, B, C, 80001731

Jackson Parish

Brooklyn Church and Cemetery, SE of Chatham off LA 4, Chatham vicinity, 8/02/84, C, a, d, 84001294

Hickory Springs Methodist Episcopal Church, Off LA 499 near Bear Creek, Chatham vicinity, 5/05/89, C, a, 89000382

Simms-Ellis House, LA 148, Clay vicinity, 7/07/83, C, 83000508

Wilder House, Shell and Pine Sts., Chatham, 7/13/83, A, C, 83000509

Jefferson Parish

Barataria Unit of Jean Lafitte Historical Park Historic District, Roughly bounded by Bayou Coquilles, Bayou des Familles, Bayou Barataria, Bayou Villars, and Lake Salvador, Barataria vicinity, 10/15/66, A, D, NPS, 66000966

Camp Parapet Powder Magazine, Arlington St., E of Causeway Blvd., Metairie, 5/24/77, A, 77000671

Crockett, David, Fire Hall and Pumper, 205 Lafayette St., Gretna, 1/27/83, A, C, 83000510

Felix-Block Building, 303 Williams Blvd., Kenner, 7/18/85, C, 85001587

Fort Livingston, W tip of Grande Terre Island, Grand Isle vicinity, 8/30/74, A, B, C, 74000925

Gretna Historic District, Roughly bounded by First, Amelia and Ninth Sts., Gulf Dr., Fourth, and Huey P. Long Ave., Gretna, 5/02/85, C, 85000954

Harahan Elementary School, 6723 Jefferson Hwy, Harahan, 4/14/83, C, 83000511

Kenner Town Hall, 1903 Short St., Kenner, 1/23/86, A, 86000112

Magnolia Lane Plantation House, LA 541 at Nine Mile Pt., Westwego vicinity, 2/13/86, C, 86000253

Old Jefferson Parish Courthouse, 200 Huey P. Long Ave., Gretna, 1/21/83, C, 83000512

St. Joseph Church-Convent of the Most Holy Sacrament Complex, Lavousier and 7th Sts., Gretna, 4/15/83, C, 83000513

Jefferson Davis Parish

Angelus, 1114 N. Cutting, Jennings, 4/16/93, C, 93000296

Derouen House, 214 W. Plaquemine, Jennings, 8/05/91, C, 91001021

Funk House, 523 Cary Ave., Jennings, 4/01/93, C, 93000267

Ilgenhurst, 402 W. Nezpique, Jennings, 4/01/93, C, 93000273

Jaenke, F. R., House, 114 Davies Ave., Jennings, 4/16/93, C, 93000301

Jennings Carnegie Public Library, 303 Cary Ave., Jennings, 1/08/82, C, 82002776

Jennings Post Office, 118 W. Plaquemine St., Jennings, 5/20/82, C, 82002777

Mahaffey, T. C., House, 802 Cary, Jennings, 4/08/93, C, 93000292

Sunny Meade, 819 Cary Ave., Jennings, 4/18/85, C, 85000837

Twitchell House, 803 Cary Ave., Jennings, 4/01/93, C, 93000268

La Salle Parish

Good Pine Lumber Company Building, W. Bradford St., Good Pine, 10/26/82, A, 82000440

White Sulphur Springs, SW of Jena on LA 8, Jena vicinity, 12/17/82, A, 82000441

Lafayette Parish

Alesia [Broussard MRA], 108 N. Morgan St., Broussard, 3/14/83, C, 83000514

Billeaud House [Broussard MRA], 303 W. Main St., Broussard, 3/14/83, C, 83000515

Billeaud, Martial, Jr., House [Broussard MRA], 118 N. Morgan St., Broussard, 3/14/83, C, 83000516

Broussard, Valsin, House [Broussard MRA], 408 W. Main St., Broussard, 3/14/83, A, C, 83000517

Comeaux House [Broussard MRA], 406 Second St., Broussard, 3/14/83, C, 83000518

Daigle House, 1022 S. Washington St., Lafayette, 6/14/84, C, 84001298

Ducrest Building [Broussard MRA], 101 W. Main St., Broussard, 3/14/83, C, 83000519

Dupleix House, 106 Lafayette St., Youngsville, 10/04/84, C, 84000013

Elrose, 217 W. University Ave., Lafayette, 6/14/84, C, 84001305

First United Methodist Church, 703 Lee Ave., Lafayette, 6/21/84, C, a, 84001307

Gordon Hotel, 108-110 E. Vermilion St., Lafayette, 6/25/82, A, C, 82002778

Holy Rosary Institute, 421 Carmel Ave., Lafayette, 12/03/80, A, a, 80001734

Hope Lodge #145, 116 E. Vermilion St., Lafayette, 1/21/83, C, 83000520

Janin Store [Broussard MRA], 121 N. Morgan St., Broussard, 3/14/83, C, 83000521

Lafayette Parish—Continued

Lafayette Elementary School, 1301 W. University Ave., Lafayette, 6/14/84, C, 84001308

Lafayette Hardware Store, 121 W. Vermilion St., Lafayette, 6/14/84, C, 84001309

Latiolais, Alexandre, House, 900 E. Butcher Switch Rd., Lafayette, 5/09/85, C, 85000972

Main Street Historic District [Broussard MRA], 203-302 E. Main St., Broussard, 3/14/83, C, 83000522

Martin, Sidney, House, 310 Sidney Martin Rd., Lafayette, 11/08/84, C, 84000351

Mouton, Alexandre, House, 1122 Lafayette St., Lafayette, 6/18/75, A, B, C, 75000850

Mouton, Charles H., House, 338 N. Sterling St., Lafayette, 6/09/80, C, 80001735

Old Guaranty Bank Building, 500 Jefferson St., Lafayette, 7/12/84, C, 84001311

Old Lafayette City Hall, 217 W. Main St., Lafayette, 6/10/75, A, 75000851

Roy, J. Arthur, House, 1204 Johnston St., Lafayette, 6/14/84, C, 84001314

Roy-LeBlanc House [Broussard MRA], 105 St. Pierre St., Broussard, 3/14/83, C, 83000523

Salles House and Office, 512 and 514 S. Buchanan St., Lafayette, 7/19/84, C, 84001316

St. Cecilia School [Broussard MRA], 302 W. Main St., Broussard, 3/14/83, C, 83000524

St. John's Cathedral, St. John St., Lafayette, 7/27/79, B, C, a, 79001067

St. Julien House [Broussard MRA], 203 E. Second St., Broussard, 3/14/83, C, 83000525

Sterling Grove Historic District, Roughly bounded by Evangeline Thwy., E. Simcoe, Chopin, and N. Sterling Sts., Lafayette, 7/26/84, C, 84001320

Vermilion Inn, 1304 Pinhook Rd., Lafayette, 7/13/83, C, 83000526

Lafourche Parish

Acadia Plantation, Address Restricted, Thibodaux vicinity, 5/29/87, C, D, 87000849

Bank of Lafourche Building [Thibodaux MRA], 206 Green St., Thibodaux, 3/05/86, C, 86000425

Bouverans Plantation House, LA 1, Lockport vicinity, 7/21/83, C, 83000527

Breaux House [Thibodaux MRA], 401 Patriot, Thibodaux, 3/05/86, C, 86000426

Building at 108 Green Street [Thibodaux MRA], 108 Green St., Thibodaux, 3/05/86, A, C, 86000424

Chanticleer Gift Shop [Thibodaux MRA], 103 W. Third, Thibodaux, 4/29/86, C, 86000877

Chatchie Plantation House, E of Thibodaux on LA 308, Thibodaux vicinity, 10/25/82, C, 82000442

Citizens Bank of Lafourche [Thibodaux MRA], 413 W. Fourth St., Thibodaux, 3/05/86, C, 86000427

Dansereau House, 506 St. Philip St., Thibodaux, 11/21/78, C, 78001425

Grand Theatre [Thibodaux MRA], 401 Green St., Thibodaux, 3/05/86, C, 86000428

Lafourche Parish Courthouse, 200 Green St, Thibodaux, 8/21/79, A, C, 79001068

Lamartina Building [Thibodaux MRA], 700–704 W. Third, Thibodaux, 3/05/86, C, 86000429

Laurel Valley Sugar Plantation, NE of Thibodaux off LA 308, Thibodaux vicinity, 3/24/78, A, C, 78001426

McCulla House [Thibodaux MRA], 422 E. First, Thibodaux, 3/05/86, C, 86000430

Peltier House [Thibodaux MRA], 403 Canal Blvd., Thibodaux, 4/29/86, C, 86000878

Percy—Lobdell Building [Thibodaux MRA], 314 Saint Mary St., Thibodaux, 3/05/86, A, C, 86000431

Rienzi Plantation House, LA 308, Thibodaux, 5/31/80, C, 80001736

Riviere Building [Thibodaux MRA], 405 W. Third, Thibodaux, 3/05/86, C, 86000432

Riviere House [Thibodaux MRA], 208 Canal Blvd., Thibodaux, 3/05/86, C, 86000433

Robichaux House [Thibodaux MRA], 322 E. Second St., Thibodaux, 3/05/86, C, 86000434

Saint Joseph's Co-Cathedral and Rectory [Thibodaux MRA], 721 Canal Blvd., Thibodaux, 3/05/86, C, a, 86000435

St. John's Episcopal Church and Cemetery, 702 Jackson St., Thibodaux, 9/13/77, A, C, a, d, 77000672

Thibodaux, Jean Baptiste, House, W of Raceland on LA 308, Raceland vicinity, 11/02/82, C, 82000443

Toups, Zephirin, Sr., House [Louisiana's French Creole Architecture MPS], 1045 Bayou Blue By-Pass Rd., Thibodaux vicinity, 8/12/93, C, 93000820

White, Edward Douglass, House, 5 mi. N of Thibodaux on LA 1, Thibodaux vicinity, 12/08/76, B, NHL, 76000964

Lincoln Parish

Autrey House, 1 mi. W of Dubach on LA 152, Dubach vicinity, 10/20/80, A, C, 80001737

Calhoun Farmhouse, NE of Ruston on LA 821, Ruston vicinity, 5/03/82, C, 82002780

Dixie Theatre, 206 N. Vienna St., Ruston, 10/14/93, A, 93001105

Dubach, Fred B., House, LA 151, Dubach, 9/08/83, B, C, 83000528

Federal Building, Vienna and Mississippi Sts., Ruston, 10/09/74, A, C, 74000926

First Presbyterian Church, 212 N. Bonner St., Ruston, 1/12/84, C, a, 84001323

James, T. L., House, 504 N. Vienna St., Ruston, 10/18/84, C, 84000142

Kidd-Davis House, 609 N. Vienna St., Ruston, 3/29/84, C, 84001330

Lewis House, 210 E. Alabama Ave., Ruston, 10/20/88, C, 88002035

Meadows House, 508 N. Bonner St., Ruston, 10/08/92, C, 92001338

Ruston Central Fire Station, 200 E. Mississippi Ave., Ruston, 10/08/92, A, 92001340

Ruston High School, 900 Bearcat Dr., Ruston, 10/08/92, C, 92001335

Ruston P. O. W. Camp Buildings, LA 150, Ruston vicinity, 12/13/91, A, g, 91001825

Ruston State Bank, 107 N. Trenton St., Ruston, 11/02/90, C, 90001730

Townsend House, 410 N. Bonner St., Ruston, 6/25/82, A, b, 82002779

Vicksburg, Shreveport and Pacific Depot, 101 E. Railroad Ave., Ruston, 10/08/92, A, 92001337

Walnut Creek Baptist Church, NW of Simsboro off I-20, Simsboro vicinity, 10/04/84, C, a, 84000014

Livingston Parish

Carter Plantation, SW of Springfield on SR 1038, Springfield vicinity, 2/23/79, A, C, 79001069

Decareaux House [Louisiana's French Creole Architecture MPS], 16021 LA 16, French Settlement, 5/14/92, C, 92000507

Denham Springs City Hall, 115 Mattie St., Denham Springs, 4/16/93, A, 93000304

Guitreau House [Louisiana's French Creole Architecture MPS], 16825 LA 16, French Settlement, 5/14/92, C, 92000508

Livingston Parish Courthouse, Old, Second and Mulberry Sts., Springfield, 8/07/89, A, C, 89001040

Lobell, Adam, House [Louisiana's French Creole Architecture MPS], 15715 LA 16, French Settlement, 5/14/92, C, 92000509

Macedonia Baptist Church, N of Holden, Holden vicinity, 6/06/80, C, a, 80001738

St. Margaret Catholic Church, Jct. of LA 43 and I-12, Albany vicinity, 1/28/92, A, a, 91002025

Madison Parish

Bloom's Arcade, 102 Depot St., Tallulah, 1/19/89, C, 88003214

Crescent Plantation, S of Tallulah off LA 602, Tallulah vicinity, 10/18/84, C, 84000144

Hermione Plantation House, Parish Rd. 3030, Tallulah, 11/17/88, C, 88002652

Kell House, 502 N. Mulberry St., Tallulah, 6/23/88, C, 88000900

Madison Parish Courthouse, Jct. of US 80 and US 65, Tallulah, 2/21/89, C, 89000044

Mississippi River Bridge [Historic Bridges of Mississippi TR], Spans Mississippi River on Old US 80, Delta, 2/14/89, A, C, 88002423

Montrose Plantation House, SE of Tallulah on LA 603, Tallulah vicinity, 10/05/82, C, 82000444

Scottland Plantation House, 903 Bayou Dr., Tallulah, 11/02/82, C, 82000445

Shirley Field, Off US 80, Tallulah vicinity, 2/14/85, A, 85000270

Tallulah Book Club Building, 515 Dabney St., Tallulah, 11/07/91, A, 91001660

Tallulah Men's Club Building, 108 N. Cedar St., Tallulah, 11/07/91, C, 91001658

Thompson, Francis, Site (16 MA 112), Address Restricted, Delhi vicinity, 10/08/91, D, 91001464

Morehouse Parish

Cedars Plantation, 3 mi. W of Oak Ridge on SR 5503, Oak Ridge vicinity, 5/19/76, A, C, 76000965

Christ Episcoal Church, 206 S. Locust, Bastrop, 7/22/82, C, a, 82002781

Excelsior, LA 133, Oak Ridge, 9/07/89, C, 89001387

Rose Theatre, US 165, Bastrop, 9/08/87, A, 87001474

Natchitoches Parish

Badin-Roque House, S of Natchez, Natchez vicinity, 6/06/80, A, C, 80001739

Caspiana Plantation Store, 1300 Texas St., Natchitoches, 6/05/92, A, b, 92000583

Cedar Bend Plantation, LA 119, Natchez vicinity, 7/14/88, C, 88001049

Cherokee Plantation, SE of Natchitoches on Cane River Rd., Natchitoches vicinity, 8/14/73, A, C, 73000869

Chopin, Kate, House, Main St. (LA 1), Cloutierville, 4/19/93, B, NHL, 93001601

City Hotel, Jct. of LA 120 and Rains Ave., Marthaville, 4/22/93, A, 93000317

Cloutier, Alexis, House, Main St., Cloutierville, 12/31/74, A, B, 74000927

Jones House [Louisiana's French Creole Architecture MPS], LA 484 along Cane R. Lake, Melrose vicinity, 9/09/93, C, 93000937

Keegan House, 225 Williams Ave., Natchitoches, 3/01/90, C, 90000342

Los Adaes, NE of Robeline off LA 6, Robeline vicinity, 6/07/78, A, D, NHL, 78001427

Los Adaes (Boundary Increase), 1/2 mi. N of LA 6 N of Robeline, Robeline vicinity, 11/04/93, A, D, NHL, 93001622

Magnolia Plantation, N of Derry on LA 119, Derry vicinity, 3/07/79, A, C, 79001071

Maison De Marie Therese, 1 mi. NW of Bermuda, Bermuda vicinity, 12/06/79, A, C, 79001070

Melrose Plantation, LA 119 off LA 493, Melrose, 6/13/72, A, C, NHL, 72000556

Narcisse Prudhomme Plantation, SE of Natchitoches on Cane River Rd., Natchitoches vicinity, 7/13/76, C, 76000966

Natchitoches Historic District, Roughly bounded by 2nd, 4th, Jefferson, and Parie Sts. and Williams and College Aves., Natchitoches, 6/05/74, A, C, NHL, 74000928

Natchitoches Historic District (Boundary Increase), Address unknown at this time, Natchitoches, 11/25/80, C, NHL, 80001740

Normal Hill Historic District, Northwestern State University campus, Natchitoches, 1/15/80, A, C, g, 80001741

Oaklawn Plantation, E of Natchez on LA 494, Natchez vicinity, 3/28/79, C, 79001072

President's Home, Northwestern State University, College Ave., Natchitoches, 7/19/84, C, 84001332

Prud'homme, Jean Pierre Emmanuel, Plantation, SE of Natchez on LA 19, Natchez vicinity, 8/29/79, A, C, 79001073

Robeline Methodist Church, Texas St., LA 6, Robeline, 2/11/88, C, a, 88000113

Texas and Pacific Railroad Depot, Sixth St., Natchitoches, 5/14/87, C, 87000732

Women's Gymnasium, Northwestern State University, College Ave., Natchitoches, 6/21/84, C, 84001335

Orleans Parish

Aldrich-Genella House, 4801 St. Charles Ave., New Orleans, 10/08/80, C, b, 80001742

Algiers Point, Bounded by Mississippi River, Slidell St., and Atlantic Ave., New Orleans, 8/01/78, A, C, 78001428

Bank of Louisiana, 334 Royal St., New Orleans, 6/19/73, A, C, 73000870

Big Oak-Little Oak Islands, Address Restricted, New Orleans vicinity, 7/14/71, A, D, NHL, 71000357

Bullitt-Longenecker House, 3627 Carondelet St., New Orleans, 10/01/81, C, b, 81000296

Bywater Historic District, Roughly bounded by the N. Claiborne Ave. and Urquhart St., Kentucky St., Mississippi River, and Montegut and Press Sts., New Orleans, 1/23/86, C, 86000113

Cabildo, The, 701 Chartres St., New Orleans, 10/15/66, A, C, NHL, 66000373

Cable, George Washington, House, 1313 8th St., New Orleans, 10/15/66, B, NHL, 66000374

Canal Station, 2819 Canal St., New Orleans, 2/04/93, A, C, 92001873

Carrollton Historic District, Roughly bounded by Lowerline St., Mississippi River, Monticello Ave., & Earhart Blvd., New Orleans, 11/02/87, C, 87001893

Central City Historic District, Roughly bounded by Pontchartrain Expwy., Louisiana, St. Charles and Claiborne Aves., New Orleans, 7/09/82, C, 82002783

Confederate Memorial Hall, 929 Camp St., New Orleans, 6/11/75, A, C, 75000852

Congo Square, Jct. of Rampart and St. Peter Sts., New Orleans, 1/28/93, A, 92001763

Criminal Courts Building, 2700 Tulane Ave., New Orleans, 1/12/84, A, C, 84001337

DELTA QUEEN (Steamboat), 30 Robin St. Wharf, New Orleans, 6/15/70, A, C, b, g, NHL, 70000495

DELUGE, Mississippi River N of Canal St. Algiers Ferry, New Orleans, 6/30/89, A, C, NHL, 89001427

Dillard, James H., House, 571 Audubon St., New Orleans, 12/02/74, B, NHL, 74000929

Esplanade Ridge Historic District, U.S. 90, New Orleans, 6/30/80, A, C, d, 80001743

Factors Row and Thiberge Buildings, 401-405 Carondelet and 802-830 Perdido St., New Orleans, 4/04/83, C, 83000529

Faubourg Marigny, Roughly bounded by Mississippi River, Esplanade Ave., Marias St., and

Montegut St., New Orleans, 12/31/74, A, B, C, 74000930

Federal Fibre Mills Building, 1101 S. Peters St., New Orleans, 3/24/83, C, 83004190

Flint—Goodridge Hospital of Dillard University, Louisiana Ave. and LaSalle St., New Orleans, 1/13/89, A, 88003139

Fort Macomb, E of New Orleans at Chef Menteur Pass on U.S. 90, New Orleans vicinity, 10/11/78, C, 78001429

Fort Pike, N of New Orleans off U.S. 90 E, New Orleans vicinity, 8/14/72, C, 72000557

Fort St. John, Bayou St. John off Robert E. Lee Blvd., New Orleans, 2/11/83, A, 83000530

French Market-Old Vegetable Market, 1000 Decatur St., New Orleans, 3/29/72, A, C, D, 72000558

Gallier Hall, 545 St. Charles Ave., New Orleans, 5/30/74, A, C, NHL, 74002250

Gallier House, 1132 Royal St., New Orleans, 2/15/74, C, NHL, 74000932

Garden District, Bounded by Carondelet, Josephine, and Magazine Sts., and Louisiana Ave., New Orleans, 6/21/71, C, NHL, 71000358

Genella, Mary Louise Kennedy, House, 5022-5028 Prytania St., New Orleans, 11/10/82, C, 82000446

General Laundry Building, 2512 St. Peter St., New Orleans, 12/27/74, C, 74000933

Girod, Nicholas, House, 500 Chartres St., New Orleans, 4/15/70, C, NHL, 70000254

Grant-Black House, 3932 St. Charles Ave., New Orleans, 7/26/79, C, 79001074

Greenville Hall, 7214 St. Charles Ave., New Orleans, 8/29/77, A, C, 77000673

Hart House, 2108 Palmer Ave., New Orleans, 6/07/84, C, 84001339

Hennen Building, 203 Carondelet, New Orleans, 7/31/86, C, 86002104

Hermann-Grima House, 818–820 St. Louis St., New Orleans, 8/19/71, C, NHL, 71000359

Hernsheim, Simon, House, 3811 St. Charles Ave., New Orleans, 6/24/82, C, 82002784

Holy Cross Historic District, Roughly bounded by Burgundy and Dauphine Sts., Delery St., the Mississippi River, and the Industrial Canal, New Orleans, 7/31/86, C, 86002105

Howard Memorial Library, 615 Orleans Ave., New Orleans, 3/22/91, C, 91000343

Irish Channel Area Architectural District, Roughly bounded by Jackson Ave., Aline and Magazine Sts., and the Mississippi River, New Orleans, 9/29/76, A, C, 76000967

Isaacs—Williams Mansion, 5120 St. Charles Ave., New Orleans, 10/21/76, A, C, 76000968

Jackson Barracks, 6400 St. Claude Ave., New Orleans, 11/07/76, A, C, 76000969

Jackson Square, Bounded by Decatur, St. Peter, St. Ann, and Chartres Sts., New Orleans, 10/15/66, A, NHL, 66000375

Julia Street Row, 602–646 Julia St., New Orleans, 3/28/77, C, 77000674

Jung Hotel, 1500 Canal St., New Orleans, 9/27/82, C, 82002785

Lafayette Cemetery No. 1, 1400 Washington Ave., New Orleans, 2/01/72, B, C, d, 72000559

Orleans Parish—Continued

Lafitte's Blacksmith Shop, 941 Bourbon St., New Orleans, 4/15/70, C, NHL, 70000255

LeBeuf Plantation House, 101 Carmick, US Naval Support Activity, New Orleans, 7/29/93, C, 93000694

LeCarpentier-Beauregard-Keyes House, 1113 Chartres St., New Orleans, 11/20/75, A, B, C, 75000853

Lee, Robert E., Monument, Lee Cir. (900–1000 blocks St. Charles Ave.), New Orleans, 3/19/91, A, f, 91000254

Leeds Iron Foundry, 923 Tchoupitoulas St., New Orleans, 1/11/76, A, C, 76000970

Long, Huey P., Mansion, 14 Audubon Blvd., New Orleans, 6/09/80, A, B, C, 80001744

Longue Vue House and Gardens, 7 Bamboo Rd., New Orleans, 9/20/91, C, 91001419

Louisiana State Bank Building, 403–409 Royal St., New Orleans, 5/04/83, C, NHL, 83004387

Lowe-Forman House, 5301 Camp St., New Orleans, 6/29/82, C, 82002786

Lower Central Business District, Roughly bounded by Canal, Tchoupitoulas, Poydras, O'Keefe, Common and S. Saratoga, New Orleans, 6/24/91, C, 91000825

Lower Garden District, Roughly bounded by St. Charles Ave., Jackson St., Mississippi River, Annunciation, and Race Sts., New Orleans, 9/07/72, A, C, 72000560

Lower Garden District (Boundary Increase), Roughly, S side of St. Charles Ave. between US 90 and Josephine St. and two parcels on S side of Annunciation St., New Orleans, 7/26/90, A, C, 90001128

Macheca Building, 828 Canal St., New Orleans, 1/06/83, C, 83000531

Madame John's Legacy, 632 Dumaine St., New Orleans, 4/15/70, C, NHL, 70000256

McDonogh School No. 6, 4849 Chestnut St., New Orleans, 10/05/82, C, 82000447

Merieult House, 533 Royal St., New Orleans, 5/05/72, A, C, 72000561

Metairie Cemetery, Jct. of I-10 and Metairie Rd., New Orleans, 12/06/91, C, d, 91001780

Mid-City Historic District, Roughly bounded by Derbigny St., Conti St., City Park Ave. and I-10, New Orleans, 12/10/93, C, 93001394

Napoleon Street Branch Library, Napoleon St., New Orleans, 1/12/79, A, 79001075

National American Bank Building, 200 Carondelet, New Orleans, 5/15/86, C, 86001048

New Canal Lighthouse, West End Blvd. and Lakeshore Dr., New Orleans, 12/30/85, C, 85003186

New Orleans City Park Carousel and Pavilion, City Park, off City Park Ave., New Orleans, 2/13/86, A, b, 86000254

New Orleans Cotton Exchange Building, 231 Carondelet St., New Orleans, 12/22/77, A, B, NHL, 77000675

Newberger House, 1640 Palmer Ave., New Orleans, 9/27/84, C, 84001340

Odd Fellows Rest Cemetery, Canal St. and City Park Ave., New Orleans, 5/23/80, A, C, d, 80001745

Old Handleman Building, 1824-1832 Dryades St., New Orleans, 6/11/80, C, 80001746

Old Meat Market-Old Meat Market, 800 Decatur St., New Orleans, 3/29/72, A, C, 72000562

Old Ursuline Convent, 1114 Chartres St., New Orleans, 10/15/66, A, C, NHL, 66000376

Orpheum Theatre, 125–129 University Pl., New Orleans, 8/11/82, A, C, 82002787

Park View Guest House, 7004 St. Charles Ave., New Orleans, 11/05/82, A, C, 82000448

Perseverance Hall, 901 St. Claude Ave., New Orleans, 10/02/73, A, 73000871

Pessou House, 6018 Benjamin St., New Orleans, 6/15/82, C, 82002788

Pitot House, 1440 Moss St., New Orleans, 9/28/71, A, C, b, 71000360

Pontalba Buildings, 500 St. Ann St. and 500 St. Peter St., New Orleans, 5/30/74, C, NHL, 74000934

Presbytere, The, 751 Chartres St., New Orleans, 4/15/70, C, a, NHL, 70000257

Rabassa, Jean Louis, House, 1125 St. Ann St., New Orleans, 2/15/74, C, 74000935

Rice House, 3643 Camp St., New Orleans, 8/24/78, A, C, 78001430

Saenger Theatre, 1111 Canal St., New Orleans, 11/25/77, A, C, 77000676

Saenger Theatre (Boundary Increase), 1101-1111 Canal St., New Orleans, 4/01/85, C, 85000794

Saux, Jean Marie, Building, 900 City Park Ave., New Orleans, 1/12/83, A, 83000532

Sincer, Louis, House, 1061 Camp St., New Orleans, 7/12/78, C, 78001431

Sommerville-Kearney House, 1401 Delachaise St., New Orleans, 12/29/78, C, 78003449

St. Alphonsus Church, 2029 Constance St., New Orleans, 5/22/73, A, C, a, 73000872

St. Charles Streetcar Line, St. Charles Ave. route from downtown to Carrollton, New Orleans, 5/23/73, A, 73000873

St. James AME Church, 222 N. Roman St., New Orleans, 10/26/82, C, a, 82000449

St. Louis Cemetery No. 1, Bounded by Basin, St. Louis, Conti, and Treme Sts., New Orleans, 7/30/75, A, C, d, 75000855

St. Louis Cemetery No. 2, Bounded by Claiborne, Robertson, St. Louis, and Iberville St., New Orleans, 7/30/75, A, C, d, 75000856

St. Mary's Assumption Church, 2030 Constance St., New Orleans, 8/12/71, A, C, a, NHL, 71000361

St. Patrick's Church, 724 Camp St., New Orleans, 5/30/74, C, a, NHL, 74000936

St. Peter A.M.E. Church, 1201 Cadiz St., New Orleans, 3/21/79, A, C, a, 79001077

St. Vincent De Paul Roman Catholic Church, 3051 Dauphine, New Orleans, 4/13/76, A, a, 76000971

Tewell House, 1503 Valence St., New Orleans, 11/21/78, C, 78001432

Tulane University of Louisiana, St. Charles Ave., S. Claiborne, Broadway, and Calhoun Sts., New Orleans, 3/24/78, A, C, g, 78001433

Turner's Hall, 606 O'Keefe St., New Orleans, 11/02/82, C, 82000450

Turpin-Kofler-Buja House, 2319 Magazine St., New Orleans, 5/08/73, C, 73000874

U.S. Court of Appeals—Fifth Circuit, 600 Camp St., New Orleans, 2/15/74, A, C, 74000937

U.S. Customhouse, 423 Canal St., New Orleans, 7/17/74, A, C, NHL, 74000938

U.S. Mint, New Orleans Branch, 420 Esplanade Ave., New Orleans, 3/30/73, A, C, NHL, 73000875

USS CABOT (CVL-28), Foot of Jackson St., New Orleans, 6/21/90, A, B, C, g, NHL, 90000334

Upper Central Business District, Roughly bounded by O'Keefe, Poydras, Convention Center Blvd., and the Expressway (B.R. 90), New Orleans, 8/10/90, A, C, 90001231

Upper Central Business District (Boundary Increase), Jct. of Howard and St. Charles Aves. and along O'Keefe Ave. and Poydras St., New Orleans, 8/12/93, A, C, 93000831

Uptown New Orleans Historic District, Roughly bounded by Louisiana, Claiborne, Lowerline and the Mississippi River, New Orleans, 7/03/85, C, 85001417

Vieux Carre Historic District, Bounded by the Mississippi River, Rampart and Canal Sts., and Esplanade Ave., New Orleans, 10/15/66, A, C, NHL, 66000377

Walker House, 1912 Saint Charles Ave., New Orleans, 5/15/86, C, 86001057

Whitney National Bank (Poydras Branch), Poydras and Camp Sts., New Orleans, 1/18/85, C, 85000093

Ouachita Parish

Allen-Barringer House, SW of West Monroe off Elkins Rd., West Monroe vicinity, 5/03/82, C, b, 82002790

Block, J. S., Building, 101 N. Grand St., Monroe, 9/30/80, C, 80001747

Boscobel Cottage, Cordell Lane, Bosco, 5/07/79, A, C, 79001078

Bright—Lamkin—Easterling House, 918 Jackson St., Monroe, 5/15/86, C, 86001063

Cooley, G. B., House, 1011 S. Grand St., Monroe, 5/15/86, C, 86001060

Downtown Monroe Historic District, Roughly bounded by Desiard, Jackson, Telemaque, and S. Grand Sts., Monroe, 9/04/86, C, 86002202

Garrett, Isaiah, Law Office, 520 S. Grand St., Monroe, 7/12/76, A, C, 76000972

Hall, Gov. Luther, House, 1515 Jackson St., Monroe, 5/07/79, B, C, 79001079

Logtown Plantation, S of Monroe, Monroe vicinity, 10/16/80, B, C, 80001748

Lower Pargoud, 2111 S. Grand St., Monroe, 10/04/84, C, 84000015

Masur House, 901 N. 3rd St., Monroe, 7/22/82, C, 82002789

Mulberry Grove, 1133 S. Grand St., Monroe, 7/07/78, C, 78001434

Ouachita Parish—Continued

Neville High School, 600 Forsythe Ave., Monroe, 5/09/85, C, 85000973

Ouachita Parish High School, 500 S. Grand St., Monroe, 4/09/81, C, 81000297

Rawls Cabin, 223 Charlie Rawls Rd., West Monroe vicinity, 8/09/91, C, 91001047

St. James United Methodist Church, 916 Adams St., Monroe, 10/29/92, C, a, 92001519

Whitehall Plantation House, Buckhorn Bend Rd., Monroe vicinity, 9/08/87, C, b, 87001475

Plaquemines Parish

Fort De La Boulaye Site, Address Restricted, Phoenix vicinity, 10/15/66, D, NHL, 66000378

Fort Jackson, 2.5 mi. SE of Triumph on LA 23, W bank of Mississippi River, Triumph vicinity, 10/15/66, A, NHL, 66000379

Fort St. Philip, 2.5 mi. SE of Triumph on LA 23 on the E bank of the Mississippi River, Triumph vicinity, 10/15/66, A, NHL, 66000380

Harlem Plantation House, W of Pointe a la Hache on LA 39, Pointe a la Hache vicinity, 10/26/82, C, 82000451

Mary Plantation House, LA 39, Braithwaite vicinity, 7/13/83, C, 83000533

Pointe Coupee Parish

Austerlitz [Louisiana's French Creole Architecture MPS], LA 1 SE of jct. with LA 78, Oscar vicinity, 4/22/91, C, 91000416

Bergeron, Valmont, House [Louisiana's French Creole Architecture MPS], LA 414, Jarreau vicinity, 5/14/92, C, 92000512

Bonnie Glen, SW of New Roads on LA 1, New Roads vicinity, 1/11/80, C, 80001749

El Dorado Plantation House, Bayou Maringouin, LA 77, Livonia vicinity, 3/24/82, C, 82002791

Glynnwood, LA 416, Glynn, 11/02/82, A, C, 82000452

LaCour, Ovide, Store, LA 419, LaCour, 7/27/79, C, 79001080

Labatut [Louisiana's French Creole Architecture MPS], Jct. of LA 420 and LA 10, New Roads vicinity, 8/15/91, C, 91001056

Lakeside, LA 419, Batchelor vicinity, 3/29/84, C, 84001346

LeBeau House and Kitchen, LA 414, Jarreau vicinity, 5/09/85, C, 85000974

LeJeune House, 507 E. Main St., New Roads, 11/28/78, C, 78001435

Major, Albin, House [Louisiana's French Creole Architecture MPS], 1304 False River Rd. (LA 1), New Roads, 4/22/91, C, 91000415

North Bend [Louisiana's French Creole Architecture MPS], LA 1 W of jct. with LA 416, E of Oscar, Oscar vicinity, 10/08/92, C, 92001336

Old Hickory, SE of LaCour, LaCour vicinity, 6/15/79, C, 79001081

Parlange Plantation House, Jct. of LA 1 and 78, Mix vicinity, 4/15/70, C, NHL, 70000258

Pleasant View Plantation House, LA 1, Oscar, 4/05/84, C, 84001347

Pointe Coupee Parish Courthouse, Main St., New Roads, 10/07/81, C, 81000710

Pointe Coupee Parish Museum, 6 mi. SW of New Roads on LA 1, New Roads vicinity, 9/30/80, C, 80001750

Riche, Fannie, House [Louisiana's French Creole Architecture MPS], LA 420 near jct. with LA 10, New Roads vicinity, 4/22/91, C, 91000413

Riverlake, LA 1, Oscar vicinity, 4/13/83, C, 83000534

Saizon House [Louisiana's French Creole Architecture MPS], LA 414 E of jct. with LA 413, Jarreau vicinity, 4/22/91, C, 91000417

St. Francis Chapel, NW of New Roads on LA 10, New Roads vicinity, 5/25/79, A, C, b, 79001082

St. Stephen's Episcopal Church, N of Innis off LA 418, Innis vicinity, 4/24/74, A, C, a, 74000939

White Hall Plantation House, E of Simmesport on LA 418, Simmesport vicinity, 5/26/77, A, B, C, 77000677

Wickliffe [Louisiana's French Creole Architecture MPS], LA 415 E of Patin Duke Slough, New Roads vicinity, 4/22/91, C, 91000414

Rapides Parish

Alexander State Forest Headquarters Building, Alexander State Forest, Woodworth, 5/21/87, A, 87000771

Alexandria Hall—Louisiana College, Louisiana College, Pineville, 5/15/86, C, 86001059

Alexandria Public Library, Old, 503 Washington St., Alexandria, 1/19/89, C, 88003225

Bailey's Dam Site, Red River S of U.S. 71, Alexandria, 6/29/76, A, C, 76000973

Bayouside, N of McNutt off LA 121, McNutt vicinity, 3/26/80, C, 80001757

Bennett Plantation House and Store, E of Alexandria on U.S. 71, Alexandria vicinity, 5/14/79, A, C, 79001083

Bentley Hotel, 801 3rd St., Alexandria, 11/15/79, C, 79001084

Blanchard House, W of Boyce on Bayou Jean de Jean, Boyce vicinity, 7/22/82, B, 82002793

Bland House, 330 Saint James St., Alexandria, 10/17/85, C, 85003148

Bolton High School, 2101 Vance Ave., Alexandria, 1/09/84, C, 84001349

Bolton, James Wade, House, 1330 Main St., Alexandria, 11/15/79, B, C, 79001085

Bontemps, Arna Wendell, House, 1327 Third St., Alexandria, 9/13/93, B, b, 93000886

Britt Place, E of Glenmora on Lake Cocodrie Rd., Glenmora vicinity, 11/21/80, B, 80001756

Central Louisiana State Hospital Dairy Barn, US 165, Pineville, 5/15/86, C, 86001078

China Grove [Neo-Classical Architecture of Bayou Rapides TR], Hwy 496, Gardner vicinity, 12/05/84, C, 84000553

Commercial Building, 3rd and Johnston Sts., Alexandria, 11/29/78, A, C, 78001436

Conerly House [Neo-Classical Architecture of Bayou Rapides TR], Off US 71, Alexandria vicinity, 12/05/84, C, 84000534

Cook House, 222 Florence Ave., Alexandria, 11/15/79, C, 79001086

Cottingham House, 1403 College Dr., Pineville, 9/08/87, C, 87001477

Crowell Sawmill Historic District, 11789 US 165 S, Long Leaf, 2/11/93, A, 93000036

Eden [Neo-Classical Architecture of Bayou Rapides TR], Off Hwy 121, Gardner vicinity, 12/05/84, C, 84000554

First Methodist Church, 630 Jackson St., Alexandria, 6/06/80, C, a, 80001751

Fort Buhlow, Off U.S. 165, Pineville, 6/01/81, A, 81000299

Fort Randolph, Off U.S. 165, Pineville, 6/01/81, A, 81000300

Geneva [Neo-Classical Architecture of Bayou Rapides TR], Hwy 496, Alexandria vicinity, 12/05/84, C, 84000539

Hemenway Furniture Co. Building, 3rd and Jackson Sts., Alexandria, 10/04/83, C, 83003632

Hirsch, Mayer, House, 1216 Jackson St., Alexandria, 7/26/79, C, 79001087

Hope [Neo-Classical Architecture of Bayou Rapides TR], Off Hwy 121 and Mill Race Rd., Gardner, 12/13/84, C, 84003856

Hopson House [Neo-Classical Architecture of Bayou Rapides TR], Brown's Bend Rd., Alexandria vicinity, 12/05/84, C, 84000549

Inglewood Plantation Historic District, Off US 71, Alexandria vicinity, 1/14/88, A, 87002449

Island Home [Neo-Classical Architecture of Bayou Rapides TR], Across Bayou Rapides off Hwy 121, Gardner vicinity, 12/05/84, C, 84000557

Jones, Wade H., Sr., House, Meeker Rd., Meeker, 8/27/87, C, 87001428

Kent Plantation House, W of Alexandria on Bayou Rapides at Virginia Ave., Alexandria vicinity, 8/05/71, C, b, 71000362

Lecompte High School, 1610 Charter St., Lecompte, 9/22/92, C, 92001251

Longview [Neo-Classical Architecture of Bayou Rapides TR], Across Bayou Rapides from Hwy 121 near intersection with Hwy 1200, Gardner vicinity, 12/05/84, C, 84000559

Loyd Hall Plantation, NW of Cheneyville on Loyd Bridge Rd., Cheneyville vicinity, 4/29/77, C, 77000678

Masonic Building, Fourth and Johnston Sts., Alexandria, 1/16/86, C, 86000079

Masonic Home for Children, 5800 Masonic Dr., Alexandria, 11/20/87, C, 87002038

McNutt Rural Historic District, Belgard Bend Rd. and LA 121, McNutt, 9/15/88, A, 88001595

Meeker Sugar Refinery, US 71, Meeker, 11/16/87, A, 87002023

Old LSU Site, N of Pineville at 2500 Shreveport Hwy, Pineville vicinity, 8/14/73, A, 73000876

Overton, Senator John H., House, 1128 8th St., Alexandria, 7/18/85, C, 85001584

Rapides Parish—Continued

Oxland [Neo-Classical Architecture of Bayou Rapides TR], Hwy 1202, Alexandria vicinity, 12/05/84, C, 84000551

Rapides Bank and Trust Company Building, 933 Main St., Alexandria, 5/15/80, C, 80001752

Rapides Cemetery, Hardtner and Main Sts., Pineville, 6/15/79, A, d, 79001088

Rapides Lumber Company Sawmill Manager's House, Jct. of US 165 and Castor Plunge Rd., Woodworth, 11/26/90, A, 90001753

Rapides Opera House, 1125 3rd St., Alexandria, 6/11/81, A, C, 81000298

Rosalie Plantation Sugar Mill, S of Alexandria off U.S. 71, Alexandria vicinity, 1/02/76, A, C, 76000974

Rose Cottage, Azalea St., Pineville, 9/15/83, C, 83000535

St. Francis Xavier Cathedral, 626 4th St., Alexandria, 12/03/80, C, a, 80001753

St. Francis Xavier Cathedral Complex (Boundary Increase), 626 4th St., Alexandria, 3/29/84, C, a, 84001353

St. John Baptist Church, Off LA 456, Lecompte vicinity, 6/25/82, C, 82002794

Tioga Commissary, Tioga Rd., Tioga, 10/16/86, A, 86002880

Trinity Episcopal Church, Bayou Rapides, Cheneyville vicinity, 10/16/80, C, 80001754

Veterans Administration Medical Center, US 167/71, Alexandria, 9/29/86, A, C, 86003116

Walker, Morgan, House, 2400 Horseshoe Dr., Alexandria, 1/22/87, C, 86003682

Walnut Grove, E of Cheneyville, Cheneyville vicinity, 11/21/80, C, 80001755

Welcek Farmstead, LA 107, Kolin, 7/18/85, A, 85001586

Red River Parish

Coushatta Bank Building, 103 Carroll St., Coushatta, 9/08/83, C, 83000536

Planter's Hotel, Carroll St., Coushatta, 12/03/80, A, 80001758

Richland Parish

Mangham State Bank Building, Main and Horace Sts., Mangham, 5/09/85, C, 85000975

Poplar Chapel AME Church, LA 135, Rayville vicinity, 6/02/89, C, a, b, 89000475

Rayville High School, 109 Madeline St., Rayville, 10/29/92, C, 92001491

Rhymes, Nonnie Roark, Memorial Library, 206 S. Louisa St., Rayville, 11/02/90, A, 90001736

Vickers House, LA 15, Alto, 5/15/86, C, 86001056

Sabine Parish

Fisher Historic District, Roughly bounded by 4 L Dr., 3rd Ave., S. 2nd and North Sts., Fisher, 7/27/79, A, C, 79001089

Fort Jesup, 7 mi. NE of Many on LA 6, Fort Jesup State Monument, Many vicinity, 10/15/66, A, e, NHL, 66000381

Kansas City Southern Depot, Zwolle, Spanish and Port Arthur Sts., Zwolle, 8/07/89, A, 89001041

Stoker House, NE of Many, Many vicinity, 6/23/76, A, C, 76000975

St. Bernard Parish

Chalmette Unit of Jean Lafitte National Historical Park Historic District, 6 mi. S of New Orleans, New Orleans vicinity, 10/15/66, A, C, D, d, e, f, NPS, 66000889

Chandeleur Light, Breton National Wildlife Refuge, New Orleans vicinity, 6/25/86, A, C, 86001404

Fort Proctor, N of Shell Beach on Lake Borgne, Shell Beach vicinity, 9/20/78, A, C, 78003067

Magnolia Mound, Address Restricted, St. Bernard vicinity, 5/22/78, D, 78003068

Sebastopol Plantation House, LA 46, St. Bernard vicinity, 8/13/86, C, 86001495

St. Charles Parish

Destrehan Plantation, River Rd. (LA 48), Destrehan, 3/20/73, A, C, 73002132

Dorvin House, SR 18 NW of Hahnville, Hahnville vicinity, 5/24/90, C, b, 90000799

Homeplace Plantation House, LA 18, 0.5 mi. S of Hahnville, Hahnville vicinity, 4/15/70, C, NHL, 70000842

Kenner and Kugler Cemeteries Archeological District, Address Restricted, Norco vicinity, 10/16/87, A, D, a, d, 87001762

LaBranche Plantation Dependency, SW of Kenner off LA 48, Kenner vicinity, 10/18/84, C, 84000145

Ormond Plantation House, Jct. of LA 48 and Oak Ave., Destrehan, 11/08/90, C, 90001748

St. Helena Parish

Greensburg Land Office, Courthouse Sq., Greensburg, 10/07/80, A, C, 80004249

Old St. Helena Parish Jail, Off LA 10, Greensburg, 10/07/80, C, 80004478

St. James Parish

Bay Tree [Louisiana's French Creole Architecture MPS], 3785 LA 18, Vacherie vicinity, 11/21/91, C, 91001738

Colomb House, NW of Convent on River Rd., Convent vicinity, 8/07/80, C, 80004250

Desire Plantation House, LA 644, Vacherie vicinity, 5/15/86, A, 86001054

Graugnard Farms Plantation House [Louisiana's French Creole Architecture MPS], 5825 LA 18, St. James vicinity, 5/14/92, C, b, 92000510

Laura Plantation [Louisiana's French Creole Architecture MPS], 2247 LA 18, Vacherie vicinity, 2/03/93, A, C, 92001842

Little Texas [Louisiana's French Creole Architecture MPS], 2834 LA 44, Paulina vicinity, 5/14/92, C, b, 92000511

Longview, LA 44, Lutcher, 9/21/83, C, b, 83000537

Lutcher United Methodist Church, 2347 Texas St., Lutcher, 2/13/92, C, a, 92000042

Manresa House of Retreats/Jefferson College, LA 44, Convent vicinity, 1/31/85, C, a, 85000162

OLIVE JEANETTE, Main St., Lutcher, 10/03/91, A, b, 91001421

Oak Alley Plantation, 2.5 mi. N of Vacherie, Vacherie vicinity, 12/02/74, A, C, NHL, 74002187

Poche', Judge Felix, Plantation House, River Rd., Convent, 12/03/80, B, C, b, 80004251

St. Michael's Church Historic District, LA 44, Convent, 11/15/79, C, a, b, 79003121

St. John The Baptist Parish

Bacas House, SR 18 E of Evergreen Plantation, Edgard vicinity, 5/17/90, C, 90000786

Bayou Jasmine Archeological Site, Address Restricted, LaPlace vicinity, 7/12/76, D, 76002149

Dugas House, LA 18, Edgard vicinity, 8/31/89, C, b, 89001211

Emilie Plantation House, LA 44, Garyville, 1/13/89, C, 88003135

Evergreen Plantation, LA 18 SE of Fiftymile Pt., Wallace vicinity, 9/25/91, A, C, NHL, 91001386

Garyville Historic District, Roughly bounded by Main, Bluebird, West, Azalea, Cypress, St. Francis, and N. Railroad Sts., Garyville, 4/20/90, A, 89001711

Montegut Plantation House, 402 E. Fifth St., LaPlace, 1/21/88, C, 87002505

San Francisco Plantation House, 3 mi. W of Reserve on LA 44, Reserve vicinity, 5/30/74, C, NHL, 74002186

Whitney Plantation Historic District [Louisiana's French Creole Architecture MPS], LA 18 E of Wallace, Wallace vicinity, 11/24/92, A, C, D, 92001566

St. Landry Parish

Academy of the Sacred Heart, NE of Grand Coteau, Grand Coteau vicinity, 2/18/75, A, B, C, a, 75002079

Arlington Plantation House, N of Washington off LA 103, Washington vicinity, 8/11/82, C, 82004676

Burleigh House, Burleigh Lane, Grand Coteau, 8/11/82, A, 82004673

Chretien Point Plantation, 2 mi. SW of Sunset on Blue Spring Rd., Sunset vicinity, 5/26/77, A, C, 77001519

St. Landry Parish—Continued

Dupre, Jacques, House, Off US 167, N of Opelousas, Opelousas vicinity, 4/12/90, C, 90000543

Fontenot, Alexandre, fils, House, S of Grand Prairie off LA 103, Grand Praire vicinity, 10/22/82, C, 82000453

Frozard Plantation House, S of Grand Coteau off LA 93, Grand Coteau vicinity, 8/12/82, C, 82004674

Grand Coteau Historic District, LA 93, Grand Coteau, 11/25/80, A, C, a, 80004320

Homeplace, N of Washington on LA 182, Washington vicinity, 10/08/80, C, 80004321

LaLanne, Dominique, House and Store, SW corner of Bridge and Dejean Sts., Washington, 8/03/76, C, 76002166

Labyche-Estorge House, 427 N. Market St., Opelousas, 10/05/82, C, 82000454

Lamorandier-Prudhomme-Jackson House, Off US 167, Opelousas vicinity, 12/22/83, C, 83003635

Lewis, John, House [Louisiana's French Creole Architecture MPS], Address Restricted, Opelousas vicinity, 4/22/91, C, 91000418

Liberty Theatre, 200 W. Park Ave., Eunice, 2/19/87, A, 87000177

MacLand Plantation House, 3.4 mi N of Washington on LA 10, Washington vicinity, 10/08/80, C, 80004322

Midland Branch Railroad Depot, 1st and North Sts., Eunice, 9/27/83, A, b, 83000538

Moundville Plantation House, 2.5 mi. NW of Washington off LA 103, Washington vicinity, 12/12/76, A, C, 76002167

Mouton House, 261 N. Liberty St., Opelousas, 8/09/91, C, 91001045

Old Federal Building, 162 S. Court St., Opelousas, 12/28/82, C, 82000455

Opelousas City Hall, Jct. of Market and Bellevue Sts., Courthouse Sq., Opelousas, 9/08/87, C, 87001470

Opelousas Historic District, Roughly bounded by Bellevue, Court St., Landry St., and Market St., Opelousas, 6/02/89, C, 89000477

Poiret Place, NW of Opelousas off LA 167, Opelousas vicinity, 4/07/83, C, 83000539

Prudhomme, Michel, House, 1152 Prudhomme Circle, Opelousas, 5/24/77, C, 77001518

Ray Homestead, 378 W. Bellevue St., Opelousas, 11/28/90, C, 90001758

St. Landry Catholic Church, 900 N. Union St., Opelousas, 5/03/82, C, a, 82004675

St. Landry Lumber Company, 215 N. Railroad Ave., Opelousas, 8/07/89, A, 89001044

Starvation Point, N of Washington off LA 10/132, Washington vicinity, 5/15/80, C, 80004323

Venus House [Louisiana's French Creole Architecture MPS], Jct. of US 190 and Academy St., Opelousas, 4/22/91, C, b, 91000419

Washington Historic District, LA 182, Washington, 11/15/78, A, 78003114

White's Chapel United Methodist Church, S of Bunkie off LA 29, Bunkie vicinity, 4/05/83, C, a, 83000540

St. Martin Parish

Acadian House, LA 31 within Longfellow Evangeline State Park, St. Martinville, 3/30/73, C, NHL, 73002133

Fontenette-Durand Maison Dimanche, LA 94, Breaux Bridge vicinity, 4/19/84, C, 84001356

Old Castillo Hotel, 220 Port St., St. Martinville, 7/24/79, A, 79003122

Olivier Pigeonnier, SW of Breaux Bridge off LA 94, Breaux Bridge vicinity, 3/14/83, C, 83000541

Patin House, 219 W. Bridge St., Breaux Bridge, 11/13/91, C, 91001680

Pellerin-Chauffe House, S of Breaux Bridge on LA 347, Breaux Bridge vicinity, 4/05/84, C, 84001358

Penne, Henri, House, W of Breaux Bridge, Breaux Bridge vicinity, 6/09/80, C, b, 80004252

Ransonet House, 431 E. Bridge St., Breaux Bridge, 5/10/90, C, 90000748

Sandoz House, W of St. Martinville on LA 96, St. Martinville vicinity, 10/29/82, C, 82000456

St. Martin Parish Courthouse, S. Main St., St. Martinville, 11/19/81, A, C, 81000658

St. Martin of Tours Catholic Church, 133 S. Main St., St. Martinville, 4/10/72, C, a, 72001454

St. Martinville Historic District, LA 96 and LA 31, St. Martinville, 1/27/83, A, C, 83000542

U.S. Post Office, Main and Port Sts., St. Martinville, 4/05/72, B, C, D, 72001455

St. Mary Parish

Arlington Plantation House, 56 E. Main St., Franklin, 10/05/82, C, 82000457

Atkinson Memorial Presbyterian Church, 214 Fourth St., Morgan City, 3/19/91, C, a, b, 91000248

Birg House, Off LA 182, Baldwin vicinity, 6/24/82, C, 82004837

Bittersweet, 301 Main St., Franklin, 10/28/80, C, 80004324

Calumet Plantation House, W of Patterson on LA 182, Patterson vicinity, 10/18/84, B, C, 84002859

Cary, Joshua B., House, US 90 and LA 317, Centerville, 8/11/82, C, 82004677

Darby House, 102 Main St., Baldwin, 8/11/82, C, 82004678

Dixie Plantation House, LA 182, 1 mi. SE of Franklin, Franklin vicinity, 5/29/87, B, 87000851

Franklin Historic District, US 90, Franklin, 12/29/82, A, C, 82000458

Grevemberg House, Sterling Rd., Franklin, 6/06/80, C, 80004325

Hanson Lumber Company Office, 10400 LA 182, Garden City, 10/07/93, A, 93001034

Hanson Lumber Company Owner's House, 10407 LA 182, Garden City, 10/07/93, A, 93001035

Heaton House, N of Baldwin on Charenton Rd., Baldwin vicinity, 10/30/80, C, b, 80004328

Idlewild, S of Patterson on LA 182, Patterson vicinity, 11/02/82, C, 82000459

Morgan City City Hall and Courthouse, Corner of Everett and First Sts., Morgan City, 4/09/81, A, C, 81000676

Morgan City Historic District, Roughly bounded by Greenwood St., Arkansas St., Railroad Ave., and Front St., Morgan City, 1/09/86, C, 86000060

Oaklawn Manor, 5 Mi. NE of Franklin on Irish Bend Rd., Franklin vicinity, 3/30/73, A, B, C, 73002162

Smith House, 909 2nd St., Franklin, 6/06/80, C, 80004326

Southwest Reef Lighthouse, Jct. of Bellevue Front and Canton Sts., Berwick, 9/12/91, C, b, 91001152

St. Mary's Episcopal Church, 805 1st St., Franklin, 11/21/80, B, C, a, 80004327

Tillandsia, 202 Charenton Rd., Baldwin, 8/11/82, B, C, 82004679

US Post Office, 1st and Everett Sts., Morgan City, 12/17/82, C, 82000460

St. Tammany Parish

Abita Springs Historic District, LA 435, LA 36 and LA 59, Abita Springs, 3/12/82, A, C, a, g, 82004622

Abita Springs Pavilion, NW end of Main St., Abita Springs, 8/19/75, A, C, 75002062

Christ Episcopal Church, 120 N. New Hampshire St., Covington, 4/17/80, C, a, 80004253

Dendinger House, 206 Covington St., Madisonville, 9/22/92, C, 92001252

Division of St. John Historic District, US 190 and LA 21, Covington, 12/06/82, A, C, 82000461

Flagstaff, 1815 Lakeshore Dr., Mandeville, 9/15/83, C, 83000543

Frederick House, 238 Vermont St., Covington, 8/11/82, A, B, C, 82004624

Lacombe School, Jct. of St. Mary and 14th Sts., Lacombe, 11/08/90, A, 90001742

Longbranch Annex, LA 36 and Gordon St., Abita Springs, 7/21/83, A, 83000544

Longbranch Hotel Complex, Rangeline Rd., Abita Springs, 6/24/82, A, C, 82004623

Madisonville Bank, 400 Cedar St., Madisonville, 12/28/83, C, 83003636

Madisonville Town Hall, 203 Cedar, Madisonville, 11/08/90, A, 90001741

McCaleb House, 906 Main St., Madisonville, 6/07/90, C, 90000874

Moore House, 1717 Lakeshore Dr., Mandeville, 4/20/83, C, 83000545

Morel-Nott House, Lakefront Dr., Mandeville, 6/06/80, C, b, 80004254

Rankin House, 61467 Jacques Lemieux Blvd., Mandeville vicinity, 3/19/91, A, C, 91000253

Salmen, Albert, House, 213 Cleveland Ave., Slidell, 1/21/93, C, 92001822

Salmen, Fritz, House, 127 Cleveland Ave., Slidell, 11/21/91, B, 91001722

Sunnybrook, N of Covington on LA 21, Covington vicinity, 8/29/79, C, 79003123

Tchefuncte River Range Rear Light, N side of Lake Pontchartrain, Madisonville vicinity, 7/14/86, C, 86001684

Tangipahoa Parish

Arcola Presbyterian Church, Church St., Arcola, 10/22/82, C, a, 82000462

Blythewood, 205 Elm St., Amite, 6/25/82, C, 82002795

Camp Moore, Off LA 440, Tangipahoa vicinity, 8/21/79, A, 79001092

Carter House, S of Hammond on Happywoods Rd., Hammond vicinity, 8/11/82, B, 82002796

Episcopal Church of the Incarnation, 111 E. Olive St., Amite, 10/08/80, C, a, 80001759

Epney, Off LA 445, Amite vicinity, 6/21/84, C, 84001362

Grace Memorial Episcopal Church, 100 W. Church St., Hammond, 2/23/73, A, C, a, 73000877

Green Shutters, Franklin St., Tangipahoa, 8/11/82, C, 82002797

Greenlawn, 200 E. Chestnut St., Amite, 5/31/80, C, 80001760

Hammond Historic District, Roughly bounded by Magnolia, Robert, Cherry, and Morris Sts., Hammond, 2/12/80, A, C, 80001761

Independence Historic District, Roughly bounded by LA 40, 5th St., Anzalone, and E. and W. Railroad Aves., Independence, 10/05/82, A, C, 82000463

June House, 408 E. Coleman Ave., Hammond, 3/31/83, C, 83000546

Kent, Charles Adolph, Sr., House, 701 Ave. E, Kentwood, 10/10/85, B, 85003098

Loranger Methodist Church, Allman Ave. and Magnolia Blvd., Loranger, 10/05/82, A, 82000464

McGehee Hall, Southeastern Louisiana State University, Southeastern Louisiana University, Hammond, 1/18/85, C, 85000094

McGehee House, 1106 S. Holly St., Hammond, 11/02/82, C, 82000465

Mount's Villa, Off LA 22, Ponchatoula vicinity, 1/31/85, C, 85000163

Nichols House, 2 mi. W. of Ponchatoula on LA 22, Ponchatoula vicinity, 5/31/80, C, 80001762

Oaks Hotel, SW Railroad Ave., Hammond, 12/09/79, A, 79001090

Pass Machac Light, W end of Lake Pontchartrain, Ponchatoula vicinity, 7/09/86, C, 86001554

Ponchatoula Commercial Historic District, Roughly bounded by 5th, 7th, Hickory and Oak Sts., Ponchatoula, 10/05/82, A, C, 82000466

Reed Farmstead Log Dependencies, LA 445, Husser vicinity, 1/21/93, C, 92001821

Stevenson House, 113 S. Pine, Hammond, 11/17/82, C, 82000467

Tangipahoa Parish Training School Dormitory, Off LA 38, Kentwood, 7/27/79, A, 79001091

Zemurray Gardens Lodge Complex, LA 40, Loranger vicinity, 10/03/83, C, 83003637

Zemurray Gardens Lodge Complex (Boundary Increase), LA 40, Loranger vicinity, 7/18/85, C, d, 85001605

Tensas Parish

Burn, The, N of Waterproof off LA 65, Waterproof vicinity, 8/11/82, C, 82002798

Lakewood, N of St. Joseph on LA 606, St. Joseph vicinity, 3/24/83, C, 83000547

Moro Plantation House, W of Waterproof off LA 566, Waterproof vicinity, 10/05/82, C, 82000468

Myrtle Grove Plantation, LA 568, Waterproof, 5/10/79, C, 79001094

St. Joseph Historic District, Roughly bounded by Panola Ave., Front, Hickory, 4th, and Pauline Sts., St. Joseph, 12/10/80, A, C, 80001763

Tensas Parish Courthouse, Courthouse Sq., St. Joseph, 3/30/79, A, C, 79001093

Winter Quarters, 6 mi. (9.6 km) SE of Newellton on LA 608, Newellton vicinity, 11/21/78, B, C, 78001437

Terrebonne Parish

Ardoyne Plantation House, NW of Houma on LA 311, Houma vicinity, 11/01/82, C, 82000469

Armitage, LA 20 and Colonial Dr., Schriever vicinity, 4/12/84, C, b, 84001366

Ducros Plantation House, LA 20, Thibodaux vicinity, 11/07/85, C, 85002759

Gibson Methodist Episcopal Church, S. Bayou Black Dr., Gibson, 5/08/86, C, a, 86001032

Houma Historic District, Roughly bounded by E. Park Ave., Main, Canal, Lafayette, Academy, High, Roussell and Barrow Sts., Houma, 12/08/83, A, 83003640

Magnolia, LA 311, Schriever vicinity, 8/04/83, C, 83000548

Montegut School, 1137 LA 55, Montegut, 10/07/93, A, 93001036

Orange Grove Plantation House, W of Houma on U.S. 90, Houma vicinity, 3/26/80, C, 80001764

Smith, Clifford Percival, House, 501 E. Park Ave., Houma, 4/20/89, C, 89000327

Southdown Plantation, 1 mi. SW of Houma on LA 311, Houma vicinity, 1/18/74, A, B, 74002188

St. George Plantation House, LA 24, Schriever, 10/05/82, C, 82000470

St. Matthew's Episcopal Church, 243 Barrow St., Houma, 5/01/89, C, a, 89000331

Wesley House, 1210 E. Main St., Houma, 8/11/82, C, 82002799

Union Parish

Edgewood, 1 mi. W of Farmerville on Bernice Hwy., Farmerville vicinity, 10/08/80, C, 80001765

Hopkins House, Hopkins Lane, Marion, 3/14/83, C, 83000549

Stein, Daniel, House, 208 W. Bayou, Farmerville, 6/23/88, C, 88000899

Vermilion Parish

A La Bonne Veillee, NE of Abbeville, Abbeville vicinity, 10/25/84, C, b, 84000079

Abbeville Commercial Historic District, Roughly bounded by Concord, State, Lafayette, and Jefferson Sts., Abbeville, 5/21/87, C, 87000767

Abbeville Residential Historic District, Roughly bounded by W. Oak, W. State, and Cherry Sts., and the Vermilion River, Abbeville, 9/08/87, C, 87001500

Bank of Gueydan, 214 Main St., Gueydan, 5/10/90, C, 90000747

LeBlanc House, N of Erath on LA 339, Erath vicinity, 4/15/82, C, 82002800

Narrows Plantation House, Off Hwy. 717 on S. Shore of Lake Arthur, Lake Arthur vicinity, 5/09/85, C, 85000976

Perry House, Orange Dr., Perry, 11/16/87, C, 87002025

St. Mary Magdalen Church, Rectory, and Cemetery, Pere Megret and Main St., Abbeville, 2/11/88, C, a, d, 88000116

Vernon Parish

Fullerton Mill and Town, Address Restricted, Fullerton vicinity, 10/24/86, A, D, 86003353

Holly Grove Methodist Church, SW of Anacoco, Anacoco vicinity, 10/08/80, A, C, a, 80001766

Kansas City Southern Depot, Louisiana Ave. and 3rd St., Leesville, 10/25/84, A, 84000080

Vernon Parish Courthouse, 201 S. 3rd St., Leesville, 9/22/83, C, 83000550

Wingate House, 800 S. 8th St., Leesville, 9/26/83, C, 83000551

Washington Parish

Babington, Robert H., House, 608 Main St., Franklinton, 12/06/79, A, C, 79001097

Bogalusa City Hall, 214 Arkans Hall Ave., Bogalusa, 7/26/79, A, C, 79001095

Bogalusa Railroad Station, 400 Austin St., Bogalusa, 5/01/80, A, 80001767

Knight Cabin, Washington Parish Fairgrounds, Franklinton, 1/23/79, A, C, b, 79001098

Magee, Nehemiah, House, SW of Mt. Hermon, Mt. Hermon vicinity, 8/12/82, A, C, 82002802

Magee, Robert D., House, W of Angie off SR 438, Angie vicinity, 8/11/82, C, b, 82002801

Sullivan House, 223 S. Border Dr., Bogalusa, 7/27/79, A, C, 79001096

Sylvest House, Washington Parish Fairgrounds, Franklinton, 1/23/79, A, C, b, 79001099

US Post Office, 305 Avenue B, Bogalusa, 1/27/83, C, 83000552

Webster Parish

Bank of Minden, 605 Main St., Minden, 2/11/88, C, 88000104

Bank of Webster, 704 Main St., Minden, 9/16/87, C, 87001468

Webster Parish—Continued

Drake House, 1202 Broadway, Minden, 7/18/85, C, 85001585

Germantown, Off U.S. 79, Minden, 3/12/79, A, 79001100

Hodges House, W of Cotton Valley off LA 7 and 160, Cotton Valley vicinity, 1/12/83, C, 83000553

McDonald House, 328 Lewisville Rd., Minden, 8/13/86, C, 86001496

Minden Historic District, Roughly, Broadway, East/West St. and Lewisville Rd. bordering Academy Park and adjacent parts of Elm St. and Fort St., Minden, 11/05/92, C, 92001527

O'Bier House, Webster Parish Hwy. 114, N of Minden, Minden vicinity, 11/27/92, C, b, 92001633

Webster Parish Library Building, 521 East-West St., Minden, 12/10/80, C, 80001768

West Baton Rouge Parish

Aillet House [Louisiana's French Creole Architecture MPS], 845 N. Jefferson Ave., Port Allen, 8/09/91, C, b, 91001046

Bank of Addis, 7843 Ray Rivet St., Addis, 2/13/92, A, 92000038

Hebert House [Louisiana's French Creole Architecture MPS], 919 E. Main St., Brusly, 10/07/93, C, b, 93001032

Monte Vista Plantation House, N of Port Allen, Port Allen vicinity, 6/09/80, B, C, 80001769

Poplar Grove Plantation House, 3142 N. River Rd., Port Allen vicinity, 12/14/87, C, b, 87002136

Port Allen High School, 610 Rosedale St., Port Allen, 4/20/89, C, 89000326

West Carroll Parish

Poverty Point, 12 mi. N of Delhi on Bayou Macon, Delhi vicinity, 10/15/66, D, NHL, 66000382

West Feliciana Parish

3 V Tourist Court, 111 E. Commerce St., St. Francisville, 1/21/93, A, 92001832

Afton Villa Gardens, N of St. Francisville on U.S. 61, St. Francisville vicinity, 2/24/83, C, 83000554

Bloodhound Site, Address Restricted, Angola vicinity, 5/02/83, A, D, 83000555

Catalpa, US 61, St. Francisville vicinity, 7/12/84, C, 84001367

Cottage Plantation, 6 mi. N of St. Francisville on U.S. 61, St. Francisville vicinity, 3/17/75, A, C, 75000857

Grace Episcopal Church, 510 Ferdinand St., St. Francisville, 3/28/79, C, a, 79001102

Greenwood Plantation, N of St. Francisville on U.S. 61, St. Francisville vicinity, 4/17/79, A, C, 79001103

Hazelwood Plantation, SE of Laurel Hill on Hazelwood Rd., Laurel Hill vicinity, 7/31/78, C, 78001438

Highland, NW of St. Francisville, off Highland Rd., St. Francisville vicinity, 8/23/83, B, C, 83000556

Laurel Hill, NE of St. Francisville, St. Francisville vicinity, 6/06/80, C, 80001770

Live Oak, 1.3 mi. S of Weyanoke, Weyanoke vicinity, 3/11/77, C, 77000680

Myrtles Plantation, U.S. 61, St. Francisville, 9/06/78, A, C, 78001439

Oak Grove Plantation Dependencies, US 61 S of jct. with LA 421, St. Francisville vicinity, 2/13/92, C, 92000036

Oakley Plantation House, 4.5 mi. E of St. Francisville in Audubon Memorial State Park, St. Francisville vicinity, 1/25/73, A, C, 73000878

Oaks, The, U.S. 61, Hardwood, 8/20/79, C, 79001101

Propinquity, Royal and Johnson Sts., St. Francisville, 3/26/73, A, 73000879

Rosale Plantation, N of St. Francisville off U.S. 61, St. Francisville vicinity, 12/08/80, A, B, C, 80001771

Rosale Plantation (Boundary Increase), N of St. Francisville on U.S. 61, St. Francisville vicinity, 6/16/83, A, C, b, 83000557

Rosebank Plantation House, SE of Weyanoke off LA 66, Weyanoke vicinity, 4/13/73, A, C, 73000880

Solitude Plantation House, NW of St. Francisville on Tunica Rd., St. Francisville vicinity, 1/27/83, C, 83000558

St. Francisville Historic District, Royal and Prosperity Sts., St. Francisville, 4/02/80, A, C, 80001772

St. Francisville Historic District (Boundary Increase), Ferdinand and Sewell Sts., St. Francisville, 10/01/82, A, C, 82000471

St. John's Episcopal Church, Old Laurel Hill Rd., Laurel Hill, 10/04/84, C, a, d, 84000016

St. Mary's Episcopal Church, NW of Weyanoke on LA 66, Weyanoke vicinity, 9/29/80, C, a, 80001774

Trudeau Landing, Address Restricted, Tunica vicinity, 6/17/77, D, 77000679

Wakefield, U.S. 61, Wakefield, 6/06/80, C, 80001773

Weyanoke, Sligo Rd., 5 mi. N of jct. with LA 66, Weyanoke vicinity, 11/15/90, C, 90001750

Winn Parish

Long, George Parker, House, 1401 Maple St., Winnfield, 8/11/82, C, 82002803

St. Maurice Plantation, Off LA 477, St. Maurice, 4/03/79, C, 79001104

Winnfield Hotel, 302 E. Main St., Winnfield, 6/11/80, A, C, 80001775

MAINE

Androscoggin County

All Soul's Chapel, S of Mechanic Falls on ME 26 at Poland Spring, Mechanic Falls vicinity, 11/17/77, A, C, a, 77000060

Androscoggin County Courthouse and Jail, 2 Turner St., Auburn, 12/29/83, A, C, 83003633

Atkinson Building, 220 Lisbon St., Lewiston, 2/02/83, C, 83000444

Auburn Public Library, 49 Spring St., Auburn, 3/22/84, C, 84001357

Barker Mill, 143 Mill St., Auburn, 5/08/79, A, C, 79000123

Bergin Block [Lewiston Commercial District MRA], 330 Lisbon St., Lewiston, 4/25/86, A, C, 86002278

Big Ram Site [Androscoggin River Drainage Prehistoric Sites MPS], Address Restricted, Ram Island vicinity, 11/14/92, D, 92001515

Bradford House, 54-56 Pine St., Lewiston, 12/22/78, C, 78000154

Briggs, William, Homestead, 1470 Turner St., Auburn, 3/20/86, A, C, 86000477

C. Varney Site [Androscoggin River Drainage Prehistoric Sites MPS], Address Restricted, Keens Mills vicinity, 11/14/92, D, 92001514

Cape Site [Androscoggin River Drainage Prehistoric Sites MPS], Address Restricted, West Leeds vicinity, 11/14/92, D, 92001511

Clifford, John D., House, 14–16 Ware St., Lewiston, 12/30/87, C, 87002190

College Block—Lisbon Block [Lewiston Commercial District MRA], 248–274 Lisbon St., Lewiston, 4/25/86, C, 86002279

Continental Mill Housing, 66-82 Oxford St., Lewiston, 7/10/79, A, 79000124

Cowan Mill, Island Mill St., Lewiston, 8/01/85, B, C, 85001656

Cushman Tavern, NE of Lisbon on ME 9, Lisbon vicinity, 10/09/79, A, 79000125

Cushman, Charles L., House, 8 Cushman Pl., Auburn, 6/16/80, B, C, 80000210

Day, Holman, House, 2 Goff St., Auburn, 1/20/78, B, C, 78000155

Dingley, Frank L., House, 291 Court St., Auburn, 4/23/80, B, C, 80000211

Dominican Block, 141-145 Lincoln St., Lewiston, 1/15/80, A, C, 80000212

Elms, Elm St., Mechanic Falls, 3/21/85, A, C, 85000610

Engine House, Court and Spring Sts., Auburn, 5/22/78, C, 78000156

Farwell Mill, ME 196, Lisbon, 6/20/85, A, 85001260

First Callahan Building [Lewiston Commercial District MRA], 276 Lisbon St., Lewiston, 4/25/86, C, 86002280

First McGillicuddy Block [Lewiston Commercial District MRA], 133 Lisbon St., Lewiston, 4/25/86, C, 86002281

First National Bank [Lewiston Commercial District MRA], 157–163 Main St., Lewiston, 4/25/86, C, 86002282

First Universalist Church, Elm and Pleasant Sts., Auburn, 5/07/79, C, a, 79000126

Foss, Horatio G., House, 19 Elm St., Auburn, 11/21/76, B, C, 76000084

Free Baptist Church, Riverside Dr., Auburn, 7/13/89, C, a, 89000843

Frye, Sen. William P., House, 453-461 Main St., Lewiston, 10/08/76, B, C, 76000189

Garcelon, A. A., House, 223 Main St., Auburn, 6/13/86, C, 86001269

Gilead Railroad Station, Former, Off NE end of Twin Rd., Auburn vicinity, 3/26/92, C, 92000272

Grand Trunk Railroad Station, Lincoln St., Lewiston vicinity, 6/04/79, A, 79000127

Hallowell Historic District, The hillside of Hallowell, Hallowell, 10/28/70, A, C, a, 70000076

Hathorn Hall, Bates College, Bates College campus, Lewiston, 8/25/70, A, 70000071

Healey Asylum, 81 Ash St., Lewiston, 10/01/79, A, C, 79000128

Holland, Captain, House, 142 College St., Lewiston, 3/21/85, B, C, 85000609

Holland-Drew House, 377 Main St., Lewiston, 12/22/78, B, C, 78000324

Irish Site [Androscoggin River Drainage Prehistoric Sites MPS], Address Restricted, East Auburn vicinity, 11/14/92, D, 92001517

Jordan School, 35 Wood St., Lewiston, 3/22/84, A, C, 84001355

Jordan, Charles A., House, 63 Academy St., Auburn, 7/15/74, C, 74000147

Kora Temple, 11 Sabattus St., Lewiston, 9/11/75, C, 75000088

Lamoreau Site, Address Restricted, Auburn vicinity, 7/13/89, D, 89000837

Lewiston City Hall, Pine and Park Sts., Lewiston, 10/21/76, C, 76000085

Lewiston Public Library, Park and Pine Sts., Lewiston, 1/31/78, A, C, 78000157

Lewiston Trust and Safe Deposit Company [Lewiston Commercial District MRA], 46 Lisbon St., Lewiston, 4/25/86, C, 86002283

Little, Edward, House, 217 Main St., Auburn, 5/12/76, A, B, C, 76000086

Livermore, Deacon Elijah, House, 6 mi. S of Livermore Falls on Hillman's Ferry Rd., Livermore Falls vicinity, 2/24/75, B, C, 75000089

Lord Block [Lewiston Commercial District MRA], 379 Lisbon St., Lewiston, 4/25/86, C, 86002284

Lord, James C., House, 497 Main St., Lewiston, 7/21/78, C, 78000158

Lower Lisbon Street Historic District, Lisbon St. between Cedar and Chestnut, Lewiston, 5/21/85, A, C, 85001128

Lyceum Hall [Lewiston Commercial District MRA], 49 Lisbon St., Lewiston, 4/25/86, C, 86002285

Main Street Historic District, Roughly bounded by Drummond, Main, Elm, and High Sts., Auburn, 4/21/89, A, B, C, 89000255

Maine State Building, Poland Spring, Poland, 7/18/74, C, b, 74000148

Maine Supply Company Building [Lewiston Commercial District MRA], 415–417 Lisbon St., Lewiston, 4/25/86, C, 86002286

Manufacturer's National Bank [Lewiston Commercial District MRA], 145 Lisbon St., Lewiston, 4/25/86, C, 86002287

Marcotte Nursing Home, 100 Campus Ave., Lewiston, 12/26/85, A, 85003128

Martel, Dr. Louis J., House, 122-124 Bartlett St., Lewiston, 1/04/83, B, C, 83000445

Moyer Site [Androscoggin River Drainage Prehistoric Sites MPS], Address Restricted, Keens Mills vicinity, 11/14/92, D, 92001518

Munroe, Horace, House, 123 Pleasant St., Auburn, 11/10/80, C, 80000213

Nelson Family Farm, End of Shackley Hill Rd., .8 mi. N of jct. with ME 108, Livermore vicinity, 12/17/92, A, C, 92001707

Norlands, The, Norlands Rd., Livermore, 12/30/69, A, C, 69000004

Oak Street School, Oak St., Lewiston, 10/08/76, C, 76000190

Odd Fellows Block [Lewiston Commercial District MRA], 182–190 Lisbon St., Lewiston, 4/25/86, C, 86002288

Osgood Building [Lewiston Commercial District MRA], 129 Lisbon St., Lewiston, 4/25/86, C, 86002289

Osgood, Nathaniel, House, ME 136, Durham, 3/21/85, C, 85000608

Pilsbury Block, 200-210 Lisbon St., Lewiston, 4/14/83, C, 83000446

Poland Railroad Station, Harris Hill & Plain Rds., Poland, 7/04/80, C, 80004600

Poland Spring Bottling Plant and Spring House, Ricker Rd., Poland, 3/22/84, A, C, 84001354

Quartz Scraper Site [Androscoggin River Drainage Prehistoric Sites MPS], Address Restricted, Keens Mills vicinity, 11/14/92, D, 92001508

Roak Block, 144-170 Main St., Auburn, 1/28/82, A, C, g, 82000738

Robinson, William A., House, 11 Forest Ave., Auburn, 4/03/93, C, 93000204

Saint Mary's General Hospital, 45 Golder St., Lewiston, 12/30/87, A, C, 87002191

Savings Bank Block, 215 Lisbon St., Lewiston, 1/20/78, A, C, 78000323

Seaverns, George, House, 8 High St., Mechanic Falls, 9/12/85, C, 85002180

Second Callahan Block [Lewiston Commercial District MRA], 282 Lisbon St., Lewiston, 4/25/86, C, 86002290

Shiloh Temple, S of Lisbon Falls on S bank of Androscoggin River, Lisbon Falls vicinity, 5/12/75, A, B, a, 75000203

Androscoggin County—Continued

St. Cyril and St. Methodius Church, Main and High Sts., Lisbon Falls, 5/26/77, A, a, 77000061

St. Joseph's Catholic Church, 253 Main St., Lewiston, 7/13/89, C, a, 89000845

Sts. Peter and Paul Church, 27 Bartlett St., Lewiston, 7/14/83, C, a, 83000447

Trinity Episcopal Church, Bates and Spruce Sts., Lewiston, 3/30/78, C, a, 78000159

Turner Town House, ME 117, Turner, 7/09/79, A, C, 79000129

US Post Office—Lewiston Main, 49 Ash St., Lewiston, 5/02/86, C, 86000879

Union Block [Lewiston Commercial District MRA], 21–29 Lisbon St., Lewiston, 4/25/86, C, 86002291

Webster Rubber Company Plant, Greene St., Sabattus, 10/16/89, A, 89001701

Wedgewood, Dr. Milton, House, 101 Pine St., Lewiston, 1/10/86, C, 86000071

Wilson I Site [Androscoggin River Drainage Prehistoric Sites MPS], Address Restricted, East Auburn vicinity, 11/14/92, D, 92001512

Wood Island Site [Androscoggin River Drainage Prehistoric Sites MPS], Address Restricted, Keens Mills vicinity, 11/14/92, D, 92001516

Worumbo Mill, On the bank of the Androscoggin River, Lisbon Falls, 10/15/73, A, 73000235

Aroostook County

Acadian Historic Buildings, N of Van Buren on U.S. 1, Van Buren vicinity, 12/13/77, A, C, b, 77000062

Acadian Landing Site, E of Madawaska on the St. John River off U.S. 1, Madawaska vicinity, 9/20/73, A, 73000098

Amazeen House, 15 Weeks St., Houlton, 9/11/86, C, 86002470

Aroostook County Courthouse and Jail, Court St., Houlton, 1/26/90, A, C, 89002340

Big Black Site, Address Restricted, Eagle Lake vicinity, 9/09/75, D, 75000090

Bridgewater Town Hall and Jail, Rt. 1, Bridgewater, 1/26/90, A, C, 89002339

Cary Library, 107 Main St., Houlton, 6/25/87, C, 87000929

Church of the Advent, Church St. 1 block S of jct. with ME 229, Limestone, 6/21/91, C, a, b, 91000767

Clase, Nicholas P., House, Capitol Hill Rd., New Sweden, 10/16/89, C, 89001699

Cleveland, Edward L., House, 87 Court St., Houlton, 6/12/87, C, 87000939

Elmbrook Farm Barn, Parson's Rd., Presque Isle, 1/10/86, A, C, 86000072

First National Bank of Houlton, Market Sq., Houlton, 9/20/73, C, 73000099

Fort Fairfield Public Library [Maine Public Libraries MPS], Main St., Fort Fairfield, 1/05/89, A, C, 88003021

Fort Kent, About 0.75 mi. SW of Fort Kent off ME 11, Fort Kent vicinity, 12/01/69, A, NHL, 69000005

Fort Kent Railroad Station, Jct. Main and Market Sts., Fort Kent, 4/21/89, A, C, 89000249

Governor Brann School, US 1 E side, 1.25 mi. S of jct. with Madore Rd., Van Buren vicinity, 12/23/93, A, C, 93001432

Island Falls Opera House, Patten Rd. and Sewall St., Island Falls, 7/19/84, A, 84001359

Larsson—Noak Historic District, Station Rd. NE of New Sweden, New Sweden vicinity, 7/26/89, A, C, g, 89000847

Leavitt, A. B., House, ME 158, Sherman, 6/20/86, C, 86001336

Mansur, Walter P., House, 10 Water St., Houlton, 2/09/90, C, a, 89002342

Market Square Historic District, Market Sq., Main, Water and Court Sts., Houlton, 6/22/80, A, C, 80000214

McElwain House, 2 Main St., Caribou, 4/12/82, B, C, 82000739

Michaud, Fortunat O., House, 231 Main St., Van Buren, 1/26/90, C, 89002343

Oakfield Station, Station St., Oakfield, 6/25/87, A, C, b, 87000928

Our Lady of Mount Carmel Catholic Church, U.S. 1, Grand Isle, 10/15/73, A, C, a, 73000100

Presque Isle National Bank, 422 Main St., Presque Isle, 7/31/86, A, C, 86002106

Putnam, Blackhawk, Tavern, 22 North St., Houlton, 1/30/76, A, C, 76000087

Reed, Philo, House, 38 Main St., Fort Fairfield, 4/04/86, B, C, 86000673

Roosevelt School, ME 161 S side, .1 mi. E of private rd. 861, St. John, 12/17/92, A, C, 92001706

Sewall, William, House, Main St., Island Falls, 4/12/82, B, 82000740

Smith Bridge, Lowery Rd. at jct. with Foxcroft Rd., across the Meduxnekeag R., Houlton vicinity, 4/02/93, C, 93000202

St. David Catholic Church, E of Madawaska on U.S. 1, Madawaska vicinity, 10/02/73, A, C, a, 73000101

Timmerhuset, Jemtland Rd., New Sweden vicinity, 8/23/73, A, C, 73000102

US Post Office—Presque Isle Main, 23 Second St., Presque Isle, 5/09/86, C, 86001034

Unitarian Church of Houlton, Military St., Houlton, 6/25/87, C, a, 87000945

Violette House, 464 Main St., Van Buren, 5/17/76, C, 76000088

Watson Settlement Bridge, 2 mi. SE of Littleton over Meduxnekeag River, Littleton vicinity, 2/16/70, A, C, 70000039

White Memorial Building, 109 Main St., Houlton, 1/15/80, A, C, 80000376

Wilder, Benjamin C., House, Main St., Washburn, 6/12/87, C, 87000946

Cumberland County

Academy Building, Gorham Campus of University of Maine at Portland-Gorham, Gorham, 1/18/73, A, C, 73000111

Art Gallery, Gorham campus of University of Maine at Portland-Gorham, Gorham, 12/27/72, C, 72000071

Auburn-Harpswell Association Historic District, ME 123, South Harpswell, 3/21/85, A, 85000615

Back Cove, Roughly Baxter Blvd. along Back Cove from Baxter to Veranda Sts., Portland, 10/16/89, C, 89001706

Bailey Island Cobwork Bridge, On ME 24 connecting Bailey and Orrs Islands, Harpswell vicinity, 4/28/75, A, C, g, 75000093

Barrows-Scribner Mill, SE of Harrison on Scribner's Mill Rd., Harrison vicinity, 3/26/76, A, 76000090

Baxter House, South St., Gorham, 6/27/79, A, C, b, 79000135

Baxter Summer Home, Mackworth Island, Falmouth, 12/26/85, B, C, 85003155

Beckett's Castle, off ME 77, Cape Elizabeth, 12/31/74, A, C, 74000156

Blanchard, Capt. S. C., House, 46 Main St., Yarmouth, 5/07/79, C, 79000136

Boody, Henry, House, Maine St., Brunswick, 2/24/75, C, 75000094

Brown, C. A., Cottage, 9 Delano Park, Cape Elizabeth, 7/30/74, C, 74000157

Brown, Harrison B., House, 400 Danforth St., Portland, 6/23/80, B, 80000227

Brown, J. B., Memorial Block, Congress and Casco Sts., Portland, 5/23/78, C, 78000167

Burnell Tavern, ME 113, West Baldwin, 12/29/83, A, C, 83003638

Butler, A. B., House, 4 Walker St., Portland, 5/08/74, C, 74000158

Camp Hammond, 74 Main St., Yarmouth, 2/01/79, C, 79000137

Cathedral of the Immaculate Conception, Cumberland Ave. & Congress Sts., Portland, 6/20/85, A, C, a, 85001257

Central Parish Church, 146 Main St., Yarmouth, 6/23/88, C, a, 88000892

Chapman, Leonard Bond, House, 90 Capisic St., Portland, 4/23/80, B, C, 80000228

Chestnut Street Methodist Church, 11-19 Chestnut St., Portland, 10/20/77, C, a, 77000063

Clapp, Charles Q., Block, Congress Sq., Portland, 1/31/78, C, 78000168

Clapp, Charles Q., House, 97 Spring St., Portland, 2/23/72, A, C, 72000072

Cleaves, Benjamin, House, S. High St., Bridgton, 4/20/88, C, 88000390

Cumberland Mills Historic District, Both sides of Presumpscot River between railroad tracks and Warren Ave., Westbrook, 5/02/74, A, B, C, 74000316

Cumberland and Oxford Canal, From Sabago Lake Basin to Conant St., Standish, 11/01/74, A, C, 74000317

Davis, Dalton Holmes, Memorial Library [Maine Public Libraries MPS], Main St., Bridgton, 1/05/89, A, C, 88003020

Deering Oaks, Roughly bounded by I-295, Forest St., Park Ave., and Deering Ave., Portland, 10/16/89, C, 89001708

Deering Street Historic District, Congress, Deering, Mellen, and State Sts., Portland, 1/27/83, A, C, 83000448

Deertrees Theatre, Deertrees Rd., Harrison vicinity, 1/05/89, A, C, 88003002

Cumberland County—Continued

Dow, Gen. Neal, House, 714 Congress St., Portland, 4/11/73, B, NHL, 73000236

Dunlap, John, House, 4 Oak St., Brunswick, 6/14/79, C, 79000138

Dunstan Methodist Episcopal Church, US 1, Scarborough, 7/13/89, C, a, 89000839

Dyer, Nathaniel, House, 168 York St., Portland, 4/15/87, C, 86003534

Eagle Island, S of Harpswell on Eagle Island, Harpswell vicinity, 11/23/71, A, B, 71000069

East Harpswell Free Will Baptist Church, Cundys Harbor Rd., East Harpswell, 6/23/88, A, C, a, 88000888

Eastern Cemetery, Congress St., corner Mountford St., Portland, 12/12/73, B, C, d, 73000112

Eastern Promenade, Roughly bounded by Eastern Promenade and Casco Bay, Portland, 10/16/89, C, 89001707

Evergreen Cemetery, Off W side of Stevens Ave., N of jct. with Brighton Ave., Portland, 6/18/92, A, C, d, 92000791

Falmouth House, 340 Gray Rd., North Falmouth vicinity, 9/01/76, A, b, 76000091

Farnsworth House, SR 17, North Bridgton, 11/14/80, C, 80000229

Federal Street Historic District, Roughly bounded by Mason, Maine, College, and Federal Sts., Brunswick, 10/29/76, A, C, 76000092

Fifth Maine Regiment Community Center, Seashore Ave., Peaks Island, Portland, 1/05/78, B, C, f, 78000169

First Baptist Church, 353 Congress St., Portland, 1/31/78, C, a, 78000170

First Parish Church, 207 Maine St., Brunswick, 12/02/69, C, a, 69000008

First Parish Church, 425 Congress St., Portland, 1/12/73, B, C, a, 73000113

First Parish Meetinghouse, Oak Hill Rd., Standish, 3/27/75, A, C, a, 75000204

Fort Gorges, E of Portland on Hog Island, Portland Harbor, Portland vicinity, 8/28/73, A, C, 73000114

Fort McKinley Historic District, Great Diamond Island, Portland, 3/21/85, A, C, 85000611

Freeport Main Street Historic District, Main St., Freeport, 11/16/77, A, C, 77000064

Friends Meetinghouse, Quaker Ridge, Casco vicinity, 9/09/75, A, C, a, 75000095

Goold House, 280 Windham Center Rd., Windham vicinity, 8/10/90, B, 89000251

Gorham Campus Historic District, College Ave., Gorham, 5/05/78, A, C, 78000171

Gorham Historic District, Roughly bounded by College, Church, Cross, State and Maple Sts., including School St. from State to N of Church, Gorham, 10/02/92, A, C, 92001298

Gothic House, The, 387 Spring St., Portland, 12/31/74, C, 72001539

Grand Trunk Railroad Station, ME 115, Yarmouth, 7/10/79, C, 79000139

Green Memorial A.M.E. Zion Church, 46 Sheridan St., Portland, 1/17/73, A, a, 73000115

Greenough, Byron, Block, Free and Middle Sts., Portland, 3/10/77, A, C, 77000065

Griffin House, 200 High St., Portland, 7/19/84, C, 84001360

Halfway Rock Light Station [Light Stations of Maine MPS], Casco Bay off Bailey Island, South Harpswell vicinity, 3/14/88, A, C, 88000150

Hall's Tavern, W of Falmouth at 377 Gray Rd., Falmouth vicinity, 3/30/78, A, C, b, 78000172

Hamblen Block, 188-194 Danforth St., Portland, 7/21/83, C, 83000449

Hamblen Development Historic District, 188–208 Danforth St., Portland, 6/18/92, A, C, 92000802

Harpswell Meetinghouse, Harpswell Center on ME 123, 9 mi. S of Brunswick, Brunswick vicinity, 11/24/68, C, a, NHL, 68000014

Harraseeket Historic District, Roughly both sides of the Harraseeket River, including South Freeport, Porters Landing, and Mast Landing, Freeport, 6/28/74, A, C, 74000160

Harris, Nathan, House, 425 Main St., Westbrook, 10/14/93, C, 93001116

Hawthorne, Nathaniel, Boyhood Home, Hawthorne and Raymond Cape Rds., South Casco, 12/02/69, B, b, 69000030

Homer, Winslow, Studio, Winslow Homer Rd., Prout's Neck, Scarborough, 10/15/66, B, NHL, 66000092

How Houses, Danforth and Pleasant Sts., Portland, 1/20/80, C, 80000377

How, Daniel, House, 23 Danforth St., Portland, 4/24/73, C, 73000265

Hunniwell, Richard, House, W of Scarborough at Winnock's Neck and Old County Rds., Scarborough vicinity, 5/12/76, A, b, 76000093

Ingraham, Joseph Holt, House, 51 State St., Portland, 7/16/73, C, 73000116

Kellogg, Elijah, Church, ME 123, Harpswell, 6/27/79, B, C, a, 79000140

Kellogg, Elijah, House, N of North Harpswell on ME 123, Harpswell vicinity, 4/28/75, B, 75000096

Lancaster Block, 474 Congress St., Portland, 9/29/82, A, C, 82000745

Leighton, Adam P., House, 261 Western Promenade, Portland, 9/29/82, B, C, 82000746

Lightship No. 112, NANTUCKET, Southern Maine Vocational Technical Institute Pier, South Portland, 12/20/89, A, C, g, NHL, 89002464

Lincoln Park, Bounded by Pearl, Franklin, Market, and Federal Sts., Portland, 10/16/89, C, 89001709

Lincoln Street Historic District, Lincoln St. between Main and Union Sts., Brunswick, 12/12/76, C, 76000094

Longfellow, Henry Wadsworth, Monument, SE corner of State and Congress Sts., Portland, 4/05/90, C, f, 90000580

Longfellow, Stephen, House, Longfellow Rd., Gorham vicinity, 3/22/84, A, 84001365

Maine Archeological Site No. 9-16, Address Restricted, Portland, 5/07/79, D, 79000141

Maine Central Railroad General Office Building, 222–224 St. John St., Portland, 1/07/88, A, C, 87002192

Maine Eye and Ear Infirmary, 794–800 Congress St., Portland, 9/25/86, B, C, 86002469

Maine Historical Society, 485 Congress St., Portland, 11/17/80, A, 80000230

Maine Publicity Bureau Building, 3 St. John St., Portland, 1/26/90, A, C, 89002344

Mallett Hall, Rt. 9, E side, N of Dyer Rd., Pownal Center, 10/16/91, A, C, 91001511

Mallett, E. B., Office Building, Mill St., Freeport, 2/19/82, B, C, 82000747

Manning, Richard, House, Raymond Cape Rd., W side, 0.3 mi. S of US 302, South Casco, 7/29/93, B, C, 93000639

Manor House, U.S. 302, Naples, 7/12/78, A, C, 78000173

Maplewood Farm, River Rd. SE of jct. with Webber Rd., South Windham vicinity, 12/13/91, A, B, C, 91001813

Marine Hospital, 331 Veranda St., Portland, 8/21/74, A, C, 74000161

Mariner's Church, 368-374 Fore St., Portland, 4/23/73, A, C, 73000117

Marrett, Daniel, House, On ME 25, Standish, 2/15/74, A, C, 74000314

Masonic Temple, 415 Congress St., Portland, 2/11/82, C, 82000748

Massachusetts Hall, Bowdoin College, Bowdoin College campus, Brunswick, 7/27/71, A, 71000042

McLellan House, School St., Gorham, 12/05/72, C, 72000073

McLellan-Sweat Mansion, 111 High St., Portland, 3/05/70, C, NHL, 70000073

Mechanics' Hall, 519 Congress St., Portland, 10/03/73, C, 73000118

Merriconegan Farm, ME 123, Harpswell, 6/15/79, B, C, 79000269

Merrill, Capt. Reuben, House, 97 W. Main St., Yarmouth, 7/12/74, A, C, 74000313

Minott, William, House, 45 Park St., Portland, 7/10/79, C, 79000142

Mitchell House, 40 Main St., Yarmouth, 1/20/78, B, C, 78000325

Morse-Libby Mansion, 109 Danforth St., Portland, 5/19/70, C, NHL, 70000074

New Gloucester Historic District, Both sides of ME 33 and ME 231, New Gloucester, 11/13/74, B, C, 74000162

North School, 248-264 Congress Street, Portland, 4/12/82, A, 82000749

North Yarmouth Academy, On ME 115, Yarmouth, 3/04/75, A, C, 75000097

North Yarmouth and Freeport Baptist Meetinghouse, Hillside St., Yarmouth, 11/20/78, A, C, a, 78000174

Nutting Homestead, The, S of Otisfield off ME 121, Otisfield vicinity, 12/03/74, A, C, 74000163

Paine Neighborhood Historic District, ME 113, Standish, 4/11/85, A, d, 85000731

Park Street Row, 88-114 Park St., Portland, 2/23/72, A, C, 72000074

Peabody—Fitch House, Off Ingalls Rd., South Bridgton vicinity, 4/07/89, A, C, 89000254

Pennellville Historic District, Roughly bounded by Pennellville Rd., Middle Bay Cove, and Pennell Way, Brunswick, 10/10/85, A, C, 85002923

Cumberland County—Continued

Perley, Sam, Farm, Perley Rd., Naples, 7/10/79, A, C, 79000143

Perry, William F., House, 6 Main Hill, Bridgton, 9/25/75, B, C, 75000098

Pettengill House and Farm, S of Bow St., Freeport, 10/06/70, A, C, 70000041

Portland Breakwater Light, NE end of Portland Breakwater in Portland Harbor, South Portland, 6/19/73, A, C, 73000238

Portland City Hall, 389 Congress St., Portland, 5/07/73, C, 73000119

Portland City Hospital, Brighton Ave., Portland, 3/21/85, A, C, 85000612

Portland Club, 156 State St., Portland, 1/25/73, B, C, 73000120

Portland Headlight, Portland Head off Shore Rd., Cape Elizabeth, 4/24/73, A, C, 73000121

Portland High School, 284 Cumberland Ave., Portland, 11/23/84, A, C, 84003879

Portland Observatory, 138 Congress St., Portland, 4/24/73, A, C, 73000122

Portland Railroad Company Substation, US 1, West Scarborough, 3/22/91, A, 91000320

Portland Stove Foundry, 57 Kennebec St., Portland, 11/18/74, A, 74000164

Portland Waterfront, Waterfront Area, Portland, 5/02/74, A, C, 74000353

Portland Waterfront Historic District (Boundary Increase), 79-85 and 295-309 Commercial and 3 Center Sts., Portland, 12/23/84, A, C, 84000497

Pote, Capt. Greenfield, House, Wolf Neck Rd., Freeport, 10/06/70, C, b, 70000042

Purington, Elisha, House, 71 Mast Rd., Falmouth, 2/14/85, B, C, 85000271

Rackleff Building, 127, 129, 131, 133 Middle St., Portland, 5/09/73, A, C, 73000123

Ram Island Ledge Light Station [Light Stations of Maine MPS], Ram Island Ledge, Portland Harbor, Cape Elizabeth vicinity, 3/14/88, A, C, 88000157

Randall, Jacob, House, Lawrence Rd., Pownal, 3/02/79, A, C, 79000144

Reed, Thomas Brackett, House, 30-32 Deering St., Portland, 5/07/73, B, NHL, 73000239

Richardson House, 11 Lincoln St., Brunswick, 5/16/74, B, C, 74000165

Richmond's Island Archeological Site, Address Restricted, Cape Elizabeth vicinity, 11/02/78, A, D, 78000175

Russwurm, John B., House, 238 Ocean Ave., Portland, 7/21/83, B, 83000450

Seavey—Robinson House, 580 Ocean St., South Portland, 9/11/86, C, 86002468

Shaker Village, ME 26, Sabbathday Lake and vicinity, 9/13/74, A, a, NHL, 74000318

Skelton, Thomas, House, 124 U.S. 1, Falmouth, 5/07/73, C, b, 73000124

Smith, F.O.J., Tomb, Stevens Ave. in Evergreen Cemetery, Portland, 12/31/74, B, C, b, d, 74000166

Smith, Parson, House, SE of South Windham on River Rd., South Windham vicinity, 7/16/73, A, C, 73000237

Songo Lock, S of Naples off ME 114, Naples vicinity, 2/16/70, A, C, 70000093

South Bridgton Congregational Church, Fosterville Rd., South Bridgton, 6/25/87, C, a, 87000947

South Street Historic District, South St. between Green and Morrill, Gorham, 4/20/88, A, C, 88000398

Sparrow House, 35 Arlington St., Portland, 10/29/82, C, 82000421

Spring Point Ledge Light Station [Light Stations of Maine MPS], Spring Point Ledge, Portland Harbor, South Portland, 1/21/88, A, C, 87002279

Spring Street Historic District, Roughly bounded by Forest, Oak, Danforth, Brackett and Pine Sts., Portland, 4/03/70, B, C, 70000043

Spurwink Congregational Church, Spurwink Ave., Cape Elizabeth, 5/19/70, A, a, 70000044

St. Lawrence Church, 76 Congress St., Portland, 10/01/79, A, C, a, 79000145

St. Paul's Church and Rectory, 279 Congress St., Portland, 12/22/78, C, a, 78000176

St. Paul's Episcopal Church, 27 Pleasant St., Brunswick, 1/31/78, C, a, 78000177

Standish Corner Historic District, Jct. of ME 25/113 and ME 35, Standish, 10/14/93, A, C, 93001117

State Reform School Historic District, Westbrook St., South Portland, 4/11/85, A, C, 85000730

Stevens, John Calvin, House, 52 Bowdoin St., Portland, 7/16/73, C, 73000125

Stimson Memorial Hall, ME 26 E side, .5 mi. N of jct. with US 202, Gray, 10/02/92, A, C, 92001296

Stone House, Burnham Rd., Bridgton, 7/19/84, A, C, 84001361

Stowe, Harriet Beecher, House, 63 Federal St., Brunswick, 10/15/66, B, NHL, 66000091

Stroudwater Historic District, Residental area at confluence of Stroudwater and Fore Rivers, Portland, 2/16/73, A, C, 73000126

Tate House, 1270 Westbrook St., Stroudwater, 1/12/70, A, NHL, 70000072

Thompson Block, 117, 119, 121, 123 and 125 Middle St., Portland, 2/28/73, C, 73000127

Two Lights, Off ME 77, Cape Elizabeth, 12/27/74, A, 74000167

U.S. Courthouse, 156 Federal St., Portland, 2/12/74, A, C, 74000168

U.S. Customhouse, 312 Fore St., Portland, 5/17/73, C, 73000128

US Post Office—Portland Main, 125 Forest Ave., Portland, 5/09/86, C, 86001011

Union Church, ME 123, North Harpswell, 6/28/88, C, a, 88000889

Union Hotel, Cundy's Harbor Rd., Cundy's Harbor vicinity, 9/12/85, A, 85002179

Universalist Meeting House, ME 231, Intervale, New Gloucester vicinity, 6/23/88, C, a, 88000887

Vallee Family House, 36 Monroe Ave., Westbrook, 10/13/88, B, 88001853

Valley Lodge, Saddleback Mountain Rd., Steep Falls vicinity, 9/19/77, A, C, 77000138

Wadsworth-Longfellow House, 487 Congress St., Portland, 10/15/66, B, NHL, 66000090

Wales and Hamblen Store, 134 Main St., Bridgton, 6/14/90, C, 90000924

Walker Memorial Hall, Lower Ridge Rd., Bridgton vicinity, 12/29/83, A, C, a, 83003639

Walker Memorial Library, 800 Main St., Westbrook, 11/10/80, A, C, 80000231

Warren Block, Main St., Westbrook, 11/05/74, B, C, 74000315

Watkins House and Cabins, Jct. of Raymond Cape Rd. and US 302, South Casco, 7/02/92, A, C, b, 92000792

Westbrook College Historic District, 716 Stevens Ave., Portland, 9/15/77, A, C, 77000066

Westbrook High School, 765 Main St., Westbrook, 11/27/79, C, 79000146

Western Promenade, Roughly Western Promenade from Maine Medical Center to Valley St., Portland, 10/16/89, C, 89001710

Western Promenade Historic District, Roughly bounded by Western Promenade and Bramhall, Brackett, Emery, and Danforth Sts., Portland, 2/16/84, C, a, 84001363

Williston-West Church and Parish House, 32 Thomas St., Portland, 6/22/80, A, C, a, 80000232

Winn Road School, Winn Rd., Cumberland Center vicinity, 3/22/84, C, 84001364

Woodman Building, 133-141 Middle St., Portland, 2/23/72, A, C, 72000075

Franklin County

Abbott, Jacob, House, ME 27, Farmington, 11/26/73, B, C, 73000103

Arnold Trail to Quebec, Along the Kennebec River, through Wayman and Flagstaff Lakes along the Dead River and Chain of Ponds to Quebec Canada, Coburn Gore vicinity, 10/01/69, A, B, 69000018

Bass Boarding House, Canal St., Wilton, 4/07/88, A, 88000396

Blanchard, Ora, House, Main St., Stratton, 1/15/80, B, C, 80000215

Cutler Memorial Library, Academy and High Sts., Farmington, 11/02/73, A, C, 73000104

First Congregational Church, United Church of Christ, Main St., Farmington, 7/25/74, C, a, 74000149

Franklin County Courthouse, Main and Anson Sts., Farmington, 10/06/83, C, 83003641

Free Will Baptist Meetinghouse, Main St., Farmington, 8/28/73, A, C, a, 73000264

Goodspeed Memorial Library [Maine Public Libraries MPS], 104 Main St., Wilton, 1/05/89, A, C, 88003019

Greenacre, 17 Court St., Farmington, 10/29/82, A, C, 82000422

Greenwood, Chester, House, ME 27, Farmington, 7/12/78, B, C, 78000160

Holmes-Crafts Homestead, Old N. Jay Rd. on ME 4, North Jay, 4/26/73, A, C, 73000105

Hutchins, Frank, House, High St., Kingfield, 12/29/86, C, 86003532

Jay-Niles Memorial Library, US 4, North Jay, 3/13/87, C, 87000414

Franklin County—Continued

Little Red Schoolhouse, S of West Farmington on Wilton Rd., West Farmington vicinity, 2/23/72, A, b, 72000070

Maine Woods Office, Main St., Phillips, 11/10/80, A, C, a, 80000216

McCleary Farm, S. Strong Rd., Strong vicinity, 4/07/89, A, C, 89000253

Merrill Hall, Maine and Academy Sts., Farmington, 1/23/80, C, 80000217

New Sharon Congregational Church, ME 134, New Sharon, 6/20/85, C, a, 85001261

Nordica Homestead, N of Farmington on Holly Rd. off ME 27, Farmington vicinity, 12/23/69, B, c, 69000006

North Jay Grange Store, ME 17, North Jay, 10/23/74, A, 74000150

Norton, William F., House, 1 Stanley Ave., Kingfield, 7/08/82, C, 82000741

Old Union Meetinghouse, U.S. 2, Farmington, 10/30/73, A, C, a, 73000106

Oquossoc Log Church, ME 4, Rangeley vicinity, 7/19/84, C, a, 84001368

Pennell Institute, Lewiston Rd., Gray, 7/12/82, A, C, 82000750

Porter-Bell-Brackley Estate, Lower Main St., Strong, 11/10/80, C, 80000218

Ramsdell, Hiram, House, High and Perham Sts., Farmington, 12/04/73, C, 73000107

Rangeley Trust Company Building, Main St., Rangeley, 7/13/89, A, B, C, 89000846

Rangley Public Library, Lake St., Rangely, 7/12/78, A, 78000161

Temple Intervale School, Temple Intervale, Temple, 2/08/85, A, 85000240

Thompson's Bridge, Over Thompson's Cr. off N. side of ME 43 at Franklin—Somerset Co. line, Allen's Mills vicinity, 3/22/91, A, C, 91000321

Tufts House, SE of Farmington on U.S. 2, Farmington vicinity, 5/08/79, A, C, 79000130

Union Church, Main and Pleasant Sts., Phillips, 7/13/89, C, a, 89000844

Upper Dallas School, Saddleback Rd., Dallas Plantation, 2/09/90, A, C, 89002345

Winter, Amos G., House, Winter's Hill off ME 27, Kingfield, 5/03/76, A, C, 76000191

Hancock County

Abbe, Robert, Museum of Stone Antiquities, S of Bar Harbor off ME 3, Bar Harbor vicinity, 1/19/83, C, 83000451

BOWDOIN (schooner), Maine Maritime Academy, Castine, 2/12/80, A, B, g, NHL, 80000411

Baker Island Light Station [Light Stations of Maine MPS], Baker Island, Acadia National Park, Islesford vicinity, 3/14/88, A, C, NPS, 88000046

Barncastle, South St., Blue Hill, 11/10/80, C, 80000219

Bass Harbor Head Light Station [Light Stations of Maine MPS], Bass Harbor Head, Bass Harbor vicinity, 1/21/88, A, C, 87002273

Bear Island Light Station [Light Stations of Maine MPS], Bear Island, Acadia National Park, Northeast Harbor vicinity, 3/14/88, A, C, NPS, 88000043

Black Mansion, W. Main St. (ME 172), Ellsworth, 12/23/69, C, 69000026

Blue Hill Historic District, ME 15, ME 172, ME 176, and ME 177, Blue Hill, 12/08/80, A, C, 80000220

Brick School House, School House Hill, Aurora, 4/23/80, A, C, 80000221

Brooklin IOOF Hall, SR 175, Brooklin, 1/26/90, C, 89002341

Buck Memorial Library, Maine St., Bucksport, 12/30/87, C, 87002193

Bucksport Railroad Station, Main St., Bucksport, 4/28/75, C, 75000091

Burnt Coat Harbor Light Station [Light Stations of Maine MPS], Hockamock Head, Swans Island vicinity, 1/21/88, A, C, 87002272

Carriage Paths, Bridges and Gatehouses, Acadia National Park and vicinity, Acadia National Park vicinity, 11/14/79, A, B, C, NPS, 79000131

Castine Historic District, Roughly bounded by Bagaduce and Penobscot Rivers, and Wadsworth Cove Rd., Castine, 2/23/73, A, C, 73000240

Cate House, Corner of Court and Pleasant Sts., Castine, 1/26/70, A, C, 70000040

Claremont Hotel, Claremont Rd, Southwest Harbor, 3/29/78, A, C, 78000162

Criterion Theatre, 35 Cottage St., Bar Harbor, 4/23/80, A, 80000222

Dix Family Stable, Rt. 102A, Bass Harbor, 4/05/90, C, b, 90000578

Duck Cove School, ME 46, E side, at jct. with Stubbs Brook Rd., Bucksport vicinity, 7/15/93, A, C, 93000640

Duck Cove Library, Miliken Rd., East Blue Hill, 4/05/90, A, C, 90000577

Eastbrook Baptist Church and Eastbrook Town House, ME 200, Eastbrook, 12/18/78, C, a, 78000163

Eegonos, 145 Eden St., Bar Harbor, 1/15/80, C, 80000223

Egg Rock Light Station [Light Stations of Maine MPS], Egg Rock, in Frenchman Bay, Winter Harbor vicinity, 1/21/88, A, C, 87002270

Ellsworth City Hall, City Hall Plaza, Ellsworth, 1/10/86, C, 86000073

Ellsworth Congregational Church, State St., Ellsworth, 4/23/73, C, a, 73000108

Ellsworth Power House and Dam, Union River, Ellsworth, 6/20/85, A, C, 85001262

Elm Street Congregational Church and Parish House, Jct. of Elm and Franklin Sts., Bucksport, 6/14/90, C, a, 90000925

Emery, James, House, Main St., Bucksport, 8/13/74, C, 74000151

Fernald Point Prehistoric Site, Address Restricted, Southwest Harbor vicinity, 7/21/78, D, NPS, 78000164

First Baptist Church, Off ME 172, Sedgwick, 4/24/73, C, a, 73000109

Flye Point 2, Address Restricted, Brooklin vicinity, 4/15/85, D, 85000842

Fort George, Wadsworth St. off Battle Ave., Castine, 12/30/69, A, 69000007

Gavin Watson Site, Address Restricted, Sullivan vicinity, 3/18/87, D, 87000415

Gilman, Daniel Coit, Summer Home, Off Huntington Rd., Northeast Harbor, 10/15/66, A, NHL, 66000093

Goddard Site, Address Restricted, Brooklin vicinity, 5/07/79, D, 79000132

Granite Store, U.S. 1, Sullivan, 12/16/74, A, C, 74000152

Great Duck Island Light Station [Light Stations of Maine MPS], Southern tip of Great Duck Island, Frenchboro vicinity, 3/14/88, A, C, 88000159

Haskell, Squire Ignatius, House, ME 172A, Deer Isle, 2/03/78, A, C, 78000165

Heywood, Phineas, House, 343 Maine St., Bucksport, 1/07/88, C, 87002194

Highseas, S of Bar Harbor on Schooner Head Rd., Bar Harbor vicinity, 11/30/78, A, C, 78000326

Hinckley, Ward, House, Address Restricted, Blue Hill, 12/16/74, C, 74000153

Islesford Historical Museum and Blue Ducks Ships Store, Little Cranberry Island, Islesford, 9/30/80, A, NPS, 80000224

Jesup Memorial Library [Maine Public Libraries MPS], 34 Mt. Desert St., Bar Harbor, 4/01/91, A, C, 91000323

Jonathan Fisher Memorial, SW of Blue Hill on ME 15 (Outer Main St.), Blue Hill vicinity, 12/30/69, A, 69000031

Jordon, Col. Meltiah, House, State St., Ellsworth, 8/13/74, C, 74000154

Kane, John Innes, Cottage, Off SE end of Hancock St., Bar Harbor, 3/26/92, C, 92000275

Lucerne Inn, Bar Harbor Rd., Rte 1A, Dedham vicinity, 6/16/82, A, C, b, 82000742

Mount Desert Light Station [Light Stations of Maine MPS], Mount Desert Rock, Frenchboro vicinity, 3/14/88, A, C, 88000155

Nannau, Lower Main St., Bar Harbor, 11/08/84, B, C, 84000322

Off-the-Neck Historic District, ME 166, Castine, 9/25/86, A, C, 86002442

Old Hancock County Buildings, Cross St., Ellsworth, 11/23/77, A, C, 77000161

Olmsted, Frederick Law, Summer Home, SW of Sunset on Deer Isle, Sunset vicinity, 11/07/76, B, C, 76000089

Pentagoet Archeological District, Address Restricted, Castine, 4/12/93, D, a, NHL, 93000603

Perkins, John, House, Perkins St., Castine, 12/30/69, C, b, e, 69000019

Peters, John, House, Off ME 176, Blue Hill, 10/06/83, B, C, 83003642

Pond Island Archeological District, Address Restricted, Deer Isle vicinity, 1/28/79, D, 79000133

Powers, Peter, House, ME 15 and Sunshine Rd., Deer Isle, 4/23/80, C, 80000225

Prospect Harbor Light Station [Light Stations of Maine MPS], Prospect Harbor Pt., Prospect Harbor vicinity, 3/14/88, A, C, 88000151

Prouty, Jed, Tavern and Inn, 52–54 Main St., Bucksport, 1/10/86, C, 86000074

Pumpkin Island Light Station [Light Stations of Maine MPS], Pumpkin Island, Eggemoggin Reach, Sargentville vicinity, 2/01/88, A, C, 87002537

Hancock County—Continued

Raventhorp, Greening Island, Southwest Harbor vicinity, 1/07/88, C, 87002195

Redwood, Barberry Lane, Bar Harbor, 4/03/78, A, C, 78000166

Reverie Cove, Harbor Lane, Bar Harbor, 2/19/82, A, C, 82000743

Robertson Quarry Galamander, ME 182 E side, NE of jct. with Old Rd., West Franklin, 10/02/92, A, C, b, 92001292

Saint Jude's Episcopal Church, ME 3, Seal Harbor, 7/24/86, C, a, b, 86001905

Seal Harbor Congregational Church, ME 3, Seal Harbor, 2/14/85, C, a, 85000272

Sellers, Salome, House, S of Deer Isle on ME 172, Deer Isle vicinity, 1/27/83, C, 83004189

Soderholtz, Eric E., Cottage, Off W side of WA 186, .5 mi. S of US 1, West Gouldsboro, 6/18/92, B, C, 92000793

Somesville Historic District, Somes Harbor and its environs, Mount Desert, 1/08/75, A, C, 75000092

Sproul's Cafe, 128 Main St., Bar Harbor, 2/04/82, A, 82000744

Stanwood Homestead, 1 mi. S of Ellsworth on ME 3, Ellsworth, 6/19/73, B, 73000110

Stonington Opera House, NW corner of Main St. and Russ Hill Rd., Stonington, 10/16/91, A, C, 91001509

Topside, N bank of Walker Pond off ME 176, Brooksville, 8/13/75, C, 75000229

Turrets, The, Eden St., Bar Harbor, 12/24/74, A, C, 74000155

US Post Office—Bar Harbor Main, Cottage St., Bar Harbor, 5/02/86, C, 86000880

Von Mach Site (ME 151/02), Address Restricted, Brooksville vicinity, 1/17/89, B, D, 88000901

Waldo-Hancock Bridge, US 1, Verona, 6/20/85, A, C, 85001267

West Gouldsboro Union Church, SR 186 between Jones Cove and Jones Pond, West Gouldsboro, 6/14/90, C, a, 90000926

West Gouldsboro Village Library [Maine Public Libraries MPS], ME 186, E side, between Jones Cove and Jones Pond, West Gouldsboro, 10/23/91, A, C, 91001512

West Street Historic District, West St. between Billings Ave. and Eden St., Bar Harbor, 5/06/80, A, C, 80000226

White, E. B., House, ME 175, Brooklin, 9/22/86, B, C, g, 86002467

Whiting, Samuel Kidder, House, 214 Main St, Ellsworth, 7/14/83, C, 83000453

Wilson Hall, Franklin St., Bucksport, 4/27/83, A, C, 83000452

Winter Harbor Light Station [Light Stations of Maine MPS], Mark Island, Winter Harbor, Winter Harbor vicinity, 2/01/88, A, C, 87002538

Kennebec County

Adams, D. V., Co.—Bussell and Weston [Augusta Central Business District MRA], 190 Water St., Augusta, 5/02/86, C, 86001690

Alls Souls Church, 70 State St., Augusta, 1/31/78, C, a, 78000178

Bailey, Charles M., Library, Bowdoin St., Winthrop, 6/20/85, A, 85001264

Bailey, Moses, House, ME 135, Winthrop Center vicinity, 11/08/84, B, C, 84000325

Bangs, Algernon, House, 16 E. Chestnut St., Augusta, 2/19/82, B, C, 82000751

Beck, Klir, House, W of Mt. Vernon off ME 41, Mt. Vernon vicinity, 11/23/77, B, C, 77000067

Blaine, James G., House, Capitol and State Sts., Augusta, 10/15/66, B, NHL, 66000024

Blossom House, Main St., Monmouth, 4/07/89, C, 89000250

Brick School, S of Winslow on Cushman Rd., Winslow vicinity, 4/18/77, A, C, 77000068

Brown Memorial Library, Downtown Clinton, Clinton, 4/28/75, A, C, 75000099

Capitol Park, Roughly bounded by Capitol St., Kennebec River, Union St., and State St., Augusta, 4/07/89, C, 89000252

Chandler Store, ME 27, Belgrade, 6/20/85, A, C, 85001263

China Village Historic District, ME 9, China, 11/23/77, A, C, 77000069

Christ Episcopal Church, 1 Dresden Ave., Gardiner, 7/24/73, C, a, 73000129

Cobbossee Lighthouse, Ladies Delight Island, Winthrop, 1/12/84, A, 84001369

Cobbosseecontee Dam Site, Address Restricted, Manchester vicinity, 6/03/76, D, 76000219

Cony High School, Cony Circle at Cony and Stone Sts., Augusta, 9/29/88, A, C, 88001841

Cony, Gov. Samuel, House, 71 Stone St., Augusta, 4/11/85, B, C, 85000732

Crosby Street Historic District, Crosby St. and Crosby Ln., Augusta, 9/11/86, A, C, 86002438

Cumston Hall, Main St., Monmouth, 8/14/73, C, 73000130

Cushnoc (ME 021.02), Address Restricted, Augusta vicinity, 10/27/89, A, C, D, a, NHL, 89001703

Davis, John, House, ME 9, Chelsea, 7/14/83, C, 83000454

Dinsmore Grain Company Mill, W of Palermo on ME 3, Palermo vicinity, 11/03/79, A, 79000147

Doughty Block [Augusta Central Business District MRA], 265 Water St., Augusta, 5/02/86, C, 86001691

Dutton—Small House, Bog Rd. W of Taber Hill Rd., Vassalboro vicinity, 12/18/90, C, 90001907

East Vassalboro Grist and Saw Mill, ME 32, East Vassalboro, 1/28/82, A, b, 82000752

Ellis, Dr. J. W., House, 62 State St., Augusta, 8/15/79, C, 79000148

Elm Hill Farm, Litchfield Rd., Hallowell, 8/25/70, B, 70000045

First Baptist Church, Park and Elm Sts., Waterville, 11/07/76, A, C, a, 76000095

Fort Halifax, On U.S. 201 at Winslow, Winslow, 11/24/68, C, NHL, 68000015

Fort Western, Bowman St., Augusta, 12/02/69, A, NHL, 69000009

Fuller-Weston House, 11 Summer St., Augusta, 3/22/84, B, a, 84001374

Gannett, Guy P., House, 184 State St., Augusta, 4/28/83, A, C, 83000455

Gardiner Historic District, Water St., Gardiner, 5/06/80, A, C, 80000233

Gardiner Railroad Station, 51 Maine Ave., Gardiner, 10/29/82, C, 82000423

Governor's House, Off ME 17, Togus, 2/23/74, A, NHL, 74000319

Grant, Peter, House, 10 Grant St., Farmingdale, 5/17/76, A, C, 76000096

Hill, Gov. John F., Mansion, 136 State St., Augusta, 11/21/77, B, C, 77000070

Jones, Abel, House [Rufus Jones TR], Off ME 202, China vicinity, 8/04/83, B, 83000456

Jones, Eli and Sybil, House, Dirigo Corner, South China vicinity, 3/22/84, B, 84001376

Journal Building [Augusta Central Business District MRA], 325–331 Water St., Augusta, 5/02/86, C, 86001692

Kennebec Arsenal, Arsenal St., Augusta, 8/25/70, A, 70000046

Kennebec County Courthouse, 95 State St., Augusta, 7/25/74, C, 74000169

Kent's Hill School Historic District, ME 17, Kent's Hill, 4/26/79, A, C, g, 79000149

Kresge Building [Augusta Central Business District MRA], 241–249 Water St., Augusta, 5/02/86, C, 86001693

Leach, Philip, House, Hussey Hill Rd., Vassalboro vicinity, 10/20/83, C, 83003644

Lee, Jesse, Church, ME 17 and Plains Rd., Readfield vicinity, 7/19/84, C, a, b, 84001378

Libby—Hill Block [Augusta Central Business District MRA], 227–233 Water St., Augusta, 5/02/86, C, 86001694

Lithgow Library, Winthrop St., Augusta, 7/24/74, C, 74000170

Lombard, Alvin O., House, 65 Elm St., Waterville, 2/19/82, B, C, 82000753

Lund, Jon, Site, Address Restricted, Winthrop vicinity, 11/21/80, D, 80000234

Maine Archeological Survey Site 53.36, Address Restricted, Winslow vicinity, 12/27/90, D, 90001901

Maine Insane Hospital, Hospital St., Augusta, 7/19/82, A, C, 82000754

Maine State House, Capitol St., Augusta, 4/24/73, A, C, 73000266

Masonic Hall [Augusta Central Business District MRA], 313–321 Water St., Augusta, 5/02/86, C, 86001695

Memorial Hall, Church St., Oakland, 11/23/77, A, C, 77000071

Mill Agent's House, ME 32, North Vassalboro, 10/06/83, A, C, 83003645

Morrill, Lot, House, 113 Winthrop St., Augusta, 7/18/74, B, C, 74000171

Noble Block [Augusta Central Business District MRA], 186 Water St., Augusta, 5/02/86, C, 86001696

Oaklands, S end of Dresden St., Gardiner, 7/27/73, C, 73000131

Old Post Office, Water St., Augusta, 7/18/74, C, 74000172

Pendle Hill [Rufus Jones TR], Off ME 202, China vicinity, 8/04/83, A, B, g, 83000457

Kennebec County—Continued

Pittston Congregational Church, Jct. ME 27 and ME 194, Pittston, 1/31/78, C, 78000179

Pond Meeting House [Rufus Jones TR], On ME 202, China vicinity, 8/04/83, A, B, 83000458

Powers House, S of Sidney on ME 104, Sidney vicinity, 10/01/79, A, C, 79000150

Pressey House, 287 Summer St., Oakland, 9/15/77, C, 77000072

Professional Building, 177 and 179 Main St., Waterville, 2/19/82, C, 82000755

Quimby, Dr. Samuel, House, North Rd. E of jct. with Church Rd., Mount Vernon vicinity, 12/18/90, C, b, 90001903

Readfield Union Meeting House, Church Rd., Readfield, 7/08/82, A, C, a, 82000756

Redington House, 64 Silver St., Waterville, 7/21/78, A, C, 78000180

Reed, G. W., Travellers Home, Address Restricted, Benton vicinity, 2/11/82, A, 82000757

Richards, Laura, House, 3 Dennis St., Gardiner, 6/14/79, B, g, 79000151

River Meetinghouse, U.S. 201, Vasalboro, 9/19/77, A, C, a, 77000073

Robinson, Edward Arlington, House, 67 Lincoln Ave., Gardiner, 11/11/71, B, NHL, 71000070

Row House, 106-114 2nd St., Hallowell, 7/01/70, C, 70000047

Shrewsbury Round Barn, 109 Benton Ave., Winslow, 2/19/82, A, C, 82000758

Shurtleff, Jonas R., House, Augusta Rd., Winslow, 12/30/74, C, 74000173

South China Meeting House [Rufus Jones TR], S. China Village, China vicinity, 8/04/83, A, B, g, 83000459

South Parish Congregational Church and Parish House, Church St., Augusta, 6/22/80, C, a, 80000235

St. Mark's Episcopal Church, 9 Summer St., Augusta, 7/19/84, C, a, 84001379

St. Mary's Church, 39 Western Ave., Augusta, 6/12/87, C, a, 87000943

Sturgis and Haskell Building [Augusta Central Business District MRA], 180–182 Water St., Augusta, 5/02/86, C, 86001697

Tappan-Viles House, 154 State St., Augusta, 2/11/82, C, 82000759

Two Cent Bridge, Spans the Kennebec River at Temple St., Waterville-Winslow, 9/20/73, A, C, 73000132

Universalist-Unitarian Church, Silver and Elm Sts., Waterville, 2/17/78, C, a, 78000181

Vaughan Homestead, Middle St. off Litchfield Rd., Hallowell, 10/06/70, A, B, C, 70000091

Vickery Building, 261 Water St., Augusta, 3/22/84, B, C, 84001380

Vienna Town House, ME 41, Vienna, 10/29/82, C, 82000424

Waterville Opera House and City Hall, Castonguay Sq., Waterville, 1/01/76, A, 76000097

Waterville Post Office, Main and Elm St., Waterville, 4/18/77, C, 77000074

Wayne Town House, ME 133, Wayne, 1/01/76, A, 76000098

Whitehouse Block [Augusta Central Business District MRA], 188 Water St., Augusta, 5/02/86, C, 86001698

Williams Block [Augusta Central Business District MRA], 183–187 Water St., Augusta, 5/02/86, C, 86001699

Williams, John, House, Church St., Mount Vernon, 12/06/84, C, 84000531

Wing Family Cemetery, Pond Rd., E side, N of jct. with ME 133, Wayne vicinity, 10/16/91, C, 91001514

Knox County

AMERICAN EAGLE (schooner), Rockland Harbor, Rockland, 12/04/91, A, C, g, NHL, 91002064

Alden, Ebenezer, House, Off ME 131, Union, 4/28/75, C, 75000100

Allen's Island, Address Restricted, St. George vicinity, 12/15/83, D, 83003646

American Boathouse, Atlantic Ave., Camden, 2/19/82, A, 82000761

Amesbury, Joe, Place [Prehistoric Sites in North Haven TR], Address Restricted, North Haven vicinity, 3/11/82, D, 82000760

Bortz-Lewis Site [Prehistoric Sites in North Haven TR], Address Restricted, North Haven vicinity, 3/11/82, D, 82000762

Browns Head Light Station, Browns Head, Vinalhaven, 1/27/83, A, C, 83000460

Bull Rock [Prehistoric Sites in North Haven TR], Address Restricted, North Haven vicinity, 3/11/82, D, 82000763

Burton, Benjamin, Garrison Site, Address Restricted, Cushing vicinity, 9/09/83, A, C, D, 83000461

Cabot I Site [Prehistoric Sites in North Haven TR], Address Restricted, North Haven vicinity, 3/11/82, D, 82000764

Camden Opera House Block, Off US 1, Camden, 12/29/86, C, 86003539

Camden Yacht Club, Bay View St., Camden, 1/11/80, A, C, 80000378

Chestnut Street Historic District, Chestnut St. from Elm to Beacon Ave. including parts of Penobscot, Pleasant and Wood Sts., and Dillingham Pt., Camden, 3/22/91, A, C, 91000325

Conway House, Conway Rd., Camden, 12/23/69, A, C, 69000010

Crocker Site [Prehistoric Sites in North Haven TR], Address Restricted, North Haven vicinity, 3/11/82, D, 82000765

Crockett, Knott, House, 750 Main St., Rockland, 10/14/93, B, C, 93001112

Curtis Island Light, 3.8 mi. from Camden Harbor in Penobscot Bay, Camden, 5/17/73, A, C, 73000263

Farnsworth Homestead, 21 Elm St., Rockland, 5/25/73, C, 73000241

GRACE BAILEY (two-masted schooner), Camden Harbor, Camden, 10/01/90, A, C, NHL, 90001466

Georges River Canal, Upper Falls, Georges River in Warren to Union town line, extending to

Quantabacook Pond in Searsmont, Warren vicinity, 3/05/70, A, 70000048

Goose Rocks Light Station [Light Stations of Maine MPS], East Entrance, Fox Islands Thorofare, North Haven vicinity, 1/21/88, A, C, 87002267

Heron Neck Light Station [Light Stations of Maine MPS], Heron Neck, Greens Island, Vinalhaven vicinity, 1/21/88, A, C, 87002266

High Street Historic District, Roughly High St. between Main St. and Sherman Point Rd., Camden, 1/05/89, A, C, 88001843

ISAAC H. EVANS (schooner), Rockland Harbor, Rockland, 12/04/91, A, C, g, NHL, 91002061

Indian Island Light Station [Light Stations of Maine MPS], Indian Island, Rockport Harbor, Rockport vicinity, 3/23/88, A, C, 87002539

Isle Au Haut Light Station [Light Stations of Maine MPS], Robinson Point, Isle Au Haut vicinity, 1/21/88, A, C, 87002265

J. & E. RIGGIN (schooner), Rockland Harbor, Rockland, 12/04/91, A, C, g, NHL, 91002062

King, Thomas, Inscription, Address Restricted, Cushing vicinity, 5/07/79, A, 79000152

Knox County Courthouse, 62 Union St., Rockland, 4/18/77, C, 77000075

LEWIS R. FRENCH (schooner), North End Shipyard, Rockland, 12/04/91, A, C, NHL, 82005263

Lermond Mill, Union Village, Union, 12/27/84, A, 84000499

MERCANTILE (schooner), Camden Harbor, Camden, 12/04/91, A, C, NHL, 82005265

MERCANTILE (two-masted schooner), Camden Harbor, Camden, 10/01/90, A, C, 90001470

Main Street Historic District, Main St. from Limerock to Winter Sts., Rockland, 6/07/78, A, C, 78000182

Marshall Point Light Station [Light Stations of Maine MPS], Marshall Point, Port Clyde Harbor, Port Clyde vicinity, 3/23/88, A, C, 87002262

Matinicus Rock Light Station [Light Stations of Maine MPS], Matinicus Rock, Matinicus Island vicinity, 3/14/88, A, C, 88000149

Mequnticook Golf Club, 212 Calderwood Ln., Rockport, 7/22/93, A, C, 93000636

Mosquito Island House, S of St. George on Mosquito Island, St.George vicinity, 9/29/83, C, 83000462

Mullen's Cove [Prehistoric Sites in North Haven TR], Address Restricted, North Haven vicinity, 3/30/84, D, 84001382

Murch Family House, Calderwood Neck SE side, 2 mi. NE of North Haven Rd., Vinalhaven vicinity, 3/25/93, A, C, 93000205

Norumbega, High St., Camden, 7/12/74, B, C, 74000174

Norumbega Carriage House, High St., Camden, 2/19/82, C, 82000766

Owls Head Light Station, NE of Owls Head on W. Penobscot Bay, Owls Head vicinity, 1/18/78, A, 78000183

Rankin Block, 600-610 Main St., Rockland, 11/07/78, A, C, 78000184

Rockland Breakwater Lighthouse, Rockland Harbor, Rockland, 3/20/81, A, C, 81000067

Knox County—Continued

Rockland Public Library, Union St., Rockland, 7/10/79, C, 79000153

Rockland Railroad Station, Union St., Rockland, 2/07/78, A, C, 78000327

Rockland Residential Historic District, Roughly bounded by Granite, Union, Masonic, Broad, Limerock, and Broadway Sts., Rockland, 4/15/87, C, 86003513

Rockland Turntable and Engine House, Park St. W of Rockland RR Station, Rockland, 6/24/93, A, 90001953

Rockport Historic District, Irregular pattern along Pascal Ave. from Russell, Union, and Winter Sts. on N to School St. on S., Rockport, 5/28/76, A, C, 76000099

Rockport Historic Kiln Area, On W side of mouth of Goose River at confluence with Rockport Harbor, Rockport, 1/26/70, A, 70000090

STEPHEN TABER (schooner), Camden Harbor, Camden, 7/30/84, A, C, g, NHL, 84001386

SURPRISE (schooner), Camden Harbor, Camden, 6/14/91, C, 91000771

Saddleback Ledge Light Station [Light Stations of Maine MPS], Saddleback Ledge, Isle Au Haut Bay, Vinalhaven vicinity, 3/14/88, A, C, 88000158

Sail Loft, Off ME 131, Tenants Harbor, 10/28/77, A, 77000076

Security Trust Building, Elm and Main Sts., Rockland, 1/20/78, C, 78000185

Spite House, Deadman's Point, Rockport, 8/13/74, C, b, 74000175

Star of Hope Lodge, Maine St., Vinalhaven, 2/19/82, C, 82000767

TIMBERWIND (Schooner), Rockport Harbor, Rockport, 3/26/92, C, 92000274

Thomaston Historic District, Runs through Blue Star Memorial Hwy. between Wadsworth St. and ME 131, Thomaston, 5/02/74, B, C, 74000176

Thorndike, George, House, ME 73, South Thomaston, 1/11/83, C, 83000463

Tillson Farm Barn, Warrenton Rd. SE of jct. with Commercial St., Glen Cove vicinity, 12/18/90, C, 90001902

Tillson, Gen. Davis, House, 157 Talbot Ave., Rockland, 1/11/83, C, 83000464

Turner Farm II [Prehistoric Sites in North Haven TR], Address Restricted, North Haven vicinity, 3/11/82, D, 82000768

Turner Farm Site [Prehistoric Sites in North Haven TR (AD)], Address Restricted, North Haven vicinity, 3/26/76, D, 76000100

US Post Office—Camden Main, Chestnut St., Camden, 9/25/86, C, 86002960

Union Church of Vinalhaven, E. Main St., Vinalhaven, 7/19/84, C, a, 84001388

Vinalhaven Galamander, The, Bandstand Park, Vinalhaven, 7/01/70, A, e, 70000049

Vinalhaven Public Library [Maine Public Libraries MPS], Carver St., Vinalhaven, 1/05/89, A, C, 88003014

WENDAMEEN (Yacht), Camden Harbor, Camden, 3/26/92, C, 92000273

Wharf House, SE of jct. of Main and Smith Sts., North Haven, 10/16/91, C, 91001508

Whitehead Lifesaving Station, S side Whitehead Island, Sprucehead vicinity, 10/12/88, A, C, 88001839

Whitehead Light Station [Light Stations of Maine MPS], E side of Whitehead Island, Tenants Harbor vicinity, 3/14/88, A, C, 88000154

Lincoln County

Alna Meetinghouse, ME 218, Alna Center, 5/19/70, A, C, a, 70000079

Alna School, Alna Center, Alna, 4/28/75, A, C, 75000101

Archeological Site 16.175 [Boothbay Region Prehistoric Sites TR], Address Restricted, Boothbay vicinity, 6/29/84, D, 84001462

Archeological Site 16.198 [Boothbay Region Prehistoric Sites TR], Address Restricted, Boothbay vicinity, 6/29/84, D, 84001460

Archeological Site 16.20 [Boothbay Region Prehistoric Sites TR], Address Restricted, Boothbay vicinity, 6/29/84, D, 84001456

Archeological Site 16.21 [Boothbay Region Prehistoric Sites TR], Address Restricted, Boothbay vicinity, 6/29/84, D, 84001452

Archeological Site 16.37 Area I and II [Boothbay Region Prehistoric Sites TR], Address Restricted, Boothbay vicinity, 6/29/84, D, 84001428

Archeological Site 16.38 [Boothbay Region Prehistoric Sites TR], Address Restricted, Boothbay vicinity, 6/29/84, D, 84001448

Archeological Site 16.47 [Boothbay Region Prehistoric Sites TR], Address Restricted, Boothbay vicinity, 6/29/84, D, 84001445

Archeological Site 16.68 [Boothbay Region Prehistoric Sites TR], Address Restricted, Boothbay vicinity, 6/29/84, D, 84001436

Archeological Site 16.73 [Boothbay Region Prehistoric Sites TR], Address Restricted, Boothbay vicinity, 5/29/84, D, 84001431

Archeological Site 16.8 [Boothbay Region Prehistoric Sites TR], Address Restricted, Boothbay vicinity, 6/29/84, D, 84001433

Archeological Site 26.27 [Boothbay Region Prehistoric Sites TR], Address Restricted, Boothbay vicinity, 6/29/84, D, 84001430

Auld—McCobb House, Oak St., Boothbay Harbor, 6/28/88, C, 88000883

Boothbay Harbor Memorial Library, ME 27, Boothbay Harbor, 4/18/77, A, C, f, 77000077

Bowman-Carney House, Off ME 197, Dresden, 4/07/71, A, B, C, 71000071

Bridge Academy, ME 127 and ME 197, Dresden, 1/09/87, B, C, 86003540

Burnt Island Light Station, S of Boothbay Harbor on Brunt Island, Boothbay Harbor vicinity, 11/23/77, A, 77000139

CORA F. CRESSEY, Keene Narrows, Bremen, 4/18/90, A, C, 90000586

Chapman-Hall House, Main and Vine Sts., Damariscotta, 5/19/70, A, C, 70000077

Coffin, Stephen, House, Main St., Damariscotta, 4/15/87, C, 86003519

Congregational Church of Edgecomb, Cross Point Rd., North Edgecomb, 6/12/87, C, a, 87000923

Cottrill, Matthew, House, Main St. (U.S. 1), Damariscotta, 5/02/74, B, C, 74000177

Damariscotta Baptist Church, King's Square, Damariscotta, 6/20/85, A, C, a, 85001265

Damariscotta Oyster Shell Heaps, Address Restricted, Damariscotta vicinity, 12/30/69, D, 69000027

Damariscove Island Archeological Site, Address Restricted, Boothbay vicinity, 5/22/78, A, D, 78000186

Damariscove Lifesaving Station, Damariscove Island, Boothbay vicinity, 6/25/87, A, C, 87000924

Dodge Point Site, Address Restricted, Newcastle vicinity, 3/22/91, D, 91000319

Dresden Brick School House, ME 128, Dresden, 6/13/86, A, C, 86001273

Fort Edgecomb, On Davis Island in the Sheepscot River, Edgecomb, 10/01/69, A, 69000020

Fort Edgecomb (Boundary Increase), Address Restricted, Edgecomb vicinity, 12/22/91, D, 91001814

Fort William Henry, NW of Pemaquid Beach, Pemaquid Beach vicinity, 12/01/69, A, D, e, f, 69000021

German Church and Cemetery, 1 mi. S of Waldoboro Village on ME 32, Waldoboro vicinity, 5/19/70, A, C, a, b, d, 70000050

Glidden-Austin Block, Jct. of U.S. 1 and ME 215, Newcastle, 4/28/75, A, C, 75000102

HESPER and LUTHER LITTLE, Wiscasset waterfront off Water St., Wiscasset, 4/18/90, A, C, D, 90000589

Harrington Meetinghouse, NW of Pemaquid on Old Harrington Rd., Pemaquid vicinity, 5/19/70, A, b, 70000051

Head Tide Historic District, Both sides of Sheepscot River, Alna, 11/19/74, A, B, C, a, c, 74000320

Hendricks Head Light Station [Light Stations of Maine MPS], Hendricks Head, Southport Island, West Southport vicinity, 11/20/87, A, C, 87002024

Hilton, Anne, Site, Address Restricted, Newcastle vicinity, 7/13/89, D, 89000838

Huston House, Bristol Rd., Damariscotta, 2/08/85, C, 85000241

Hutchins House, 77 Main St., Waldoboro, 2/19/82, C, 82000769

Influence, The, Monhegan Island, Monhegan, 12/29/83, A, C, 83003655

Jackson, Dr. F. W., House, ME 32, Jefferson, 11/10/80, C, 80000236

Kavanaugh, Gov. Edward, House, ME 213 (Damariscotta Mills), Newcastle, 5/03/74, B, C, 74000178

Kent, Rockwell, Cottage and Studio, Off N side of Horn Hill Rd., Monhegen Island, Monhegen Plantation, 4/08/92, B, 92000278

Knight-Corey House, Corey Lane, Boothbay, 3/13/80, C, 80000237

Lincoln County—Continued

Lithgow House, Blinn Hill Rd., Dresden, 12/26/85, B, C, 85003156

Ludwig, Godfrey, House, ME 32, Waldoboro vicinity, 9/22/80, A, C, 80000238

Main Street Historic District, Main St., Damariscotta, 8/10/79, A, C, g, 79000154

Means, Emily, House, Birch Island, South Bristol, 2/08/85, A, C, 85000242

Monhegan Island Lighthouse and Quarters, Monhegan Island, Monhegan Island, 5/07/80, A, 80000239

Moore, John, House, SW of Edgecomb on Cross Point Rd., Edgecomb vicinity, 7/10/79, A, C, 79000155

Nahanada Village Site, , Bristol vicinity, 7/22/80, D, 80000240

Nickels-Sortwell House, NE corner of Main and Federal Sts., Wiscasset, 12/30/70, C, NHL, 70000078

Parsons, Josiah K., Homestead, Greenleaf Cove Rd., Wiscasset vicinity, 2/04/82, B, C, 82000770

Parsons, Stephen, House, SW of Edgecomb on Parsons Creek, Edgecomb vicinity, 10/06/83, B, C, 83003648

Pemaquid Point Light, Pemaquid Point, Bristol, 4/16/85, A, 85000843

Pemaquid Restoration and Museum, N of Pemaquid Beach at Pemaquid Point, Pemaquid Beach vicinity, 12/02/69, A, D, NHL, 69000022

Pownalborough Courthouse, Cedar Grove Rd., Dresden, 1/12/70, A, B, 70000052

Ram Island Light Station [Light Stations of Maine MPS], Ram Island, Boothbay Harbor, Boothbay Harbor vicinity, 1/21/88, A, C, 87002280

Red Brick School, Warren St., Wiscasset, 10/06/70, A, 70000089

Scott, Capt. George, House, Federal St., Wiscasset, 2/23/72, B, C, 72000104

Second Congregational Church, River St., Newcastle, 5/07/79, C, a, 79000156

Sheepscot Historic District, W of New Castle, New Castle vicinity, 6/23/78, A, C, D, 78000424

Smith, Asa, Homestead, ME 218, Alna, 8/11/83, C, 83000465

Sproul Homestead, N of South Bristol on ME 129, South Bristol vicinity, 3/21/78, A, C, b, 78000188

Squire Tarbox House, ME 144, Westport, 4/11/85, B, C, b, 85000725

St. Andrew's Church, Glidden St., Newcastle, 10/08/76, C, a, 76000101

St. Denis Catholic Church, W of North Whitefield on ME 218, North Whitefield vicinity, 10/29/76, A, a, d, 76000102

St. John's Anglican Church and Parsonage Site, Address Restricted, Dresden vicinity, 11/21/78, D, d, 78000187

St. John's Episcopal Church, S side of ME 27 at jct. with Blinn Hill Rd., Dresden Mills, 6/14/91, C, a, 91000769

St. Patrick's Catholic Church, Academy Rd., Newcastle, 4/23/73, A, C, a, 73000133

Taylor Site 16.65 [Boothbay Region Prehistoric Sites TR], Address Restricted, Boothbay vicinity, 6/29/84, D, 84001441

Tenants Harbor Light Station [Light Stations of Maine MPS], Southern Island, Tenants Harbor vicinity, 11/20/87, A, C, 87002026

Thompson Icehouse, ME 129, South Bristol, 12/31/74, A, 74000179

U.S. Customhouse (Old Customhouse) and Post Office, Water St., Wiscasset, 8/25/70, C, 70000053

U.S. Customhouse and Post Office, Main St., Waldoboro, 1/18/74, A, C, 74000180

Waldo Theatre, Main St., Waldoboro, 9/11/86, C, 86002434

Waldoborough Town Pound, Washington Rd., Waldoboro, 5/28/76, A, 76000103

Walpole Meetinghouse, N of Walpole on Meeting House Rd., Walpole vicinity, 11/07/76, C, a, 76000104

Weston, Daniel, Homestead, W of Medomak on ME 32, Medomak vicinity, 10/01/79, A, C, 79000157

Wetherill Site, Address Restricted, Waldoboro vicinity, 12/17/92, D, 92001709

Wiscasset Historic District, Roughly Parker, Dresden, Bradford, Main, and Federal Sts., Wiscasset, 1/12/73, A, C, d, 73000242

Wiscasset Jail and Museum, ME 218, Wiscasset, 1/26/70, A, C, 70000054

Oxford County

Andover Public Library, Church St., Andover, 1/27/81, A, C, a, 81000103

Barrows-Steadman Homestead, 134 Main St., Fryeburg, 4/12/82, B, C, 82000771

Bennett Bridge, 1.5 mi. S of Wilsons Mills off ME 16, over Magallow River, Wilson Mills vicinity, 2/16/70, A, C, 70000055

Brickett Place, US 113, Stow, 7/28/82, A, C, 82000772

Broad Street Historic District, Broad St. and the Common, Bethel, 12/28/77, A, C, 77000078

Broad Street Historic District (Boundary Increase), Along Church and Park Sts., Bethel, 2/09/90, A, C, 89002346

Chase, Squire, House, 151 Main St., Fryeburg, 5/07/79, A, C, 79000158

Church of the New Jerusalem, 4 Oxford St., Fryeburg, 6/13/86, C, a, 86001274

Deacon Hutchins House, NW of Rumford on ME 5, Rumford vicinity, 7/10/79, B, C, 79000159

District No. 1 Schoolhouse, 98 Main St., Fryeburg, 7/19/84, A, 84001466

Eastman Hill Rural Historic District, Eastman Hill Rd., E of Center Lovell, Center Lovell vicinity, 6/08/93, A, C, 93000477

Fryeburg Registry of Deeds, 96 Main St., Fryeburg, 12/30/87, A, C, 87002196

Fryeburg Town House, Former, ME 5 E side, .1 mi. N of jct. with Woodlawn Ave., Fryeburg Center, 10/02/92, A, 92001295

Gehring Clinic, Off ME 5, Bethel, 8/02/76, A, B, 76000105

Hall, Enoch, House, Bean Rd. W side, 0.5 mi. SE of jct. with ME 117, Buckfield vicinity, 12/23/93, C, 93001431

Hemlock Bridge, NE of Fryeburg Center, over the Old Course Saco River, Fryeburg Center vicinity, 2/16/70, A, C, 70000056

Hershey Plow Company Building, Hill St. near Stony Brook, South Paris, 6/14/90, A, 90000922

Hubbard—Cotton Store, SR 5/113 across Saco R. from jct. with SR 117, Hiram, 6/14/90, C, 90000923

Irish, J. & O., Store, ME 140, Hartford, 12/29/83, A, C, 83003666

Lovejoy Bridge, Over Ellis River, South Andover, 2/16/70, A, 70000057

Lovell Village Church, Church St., Lovell, 6/20/86, A, C, a, 86001337

Lower Sunday River School, SW of Newry on Sunday River Rd., Newry vicinity, 5/23/78, A, 78000189

Main Street Historic District, Main Street from Portland St. to about Swans Falls Rd., Fryeburg, 3/22/91, A, C, 91000324

Mann, Arthur L., Memorial Library [Maine Public Libraries MPS], Main St., West Paris, 1/05/89, A, C, 88003016

Mason, Dr. Moses, House, Broad St., Bethel, 10/17/72, B, C, 72000110

McWain—Hall House, McWain Hill Rd., Waterford vicinity, 3/25/87, C, 87000416

Mechanic Institute [Rumford Commercial MRA], 44-56 Congress St., Rumford, 5/13/80, A, C, 80000241

Merrill-Poor House, NE of Andover on ME 120, Andover vicinity, 5/17/76, A, C, 76000106

Municipal Building [Rumford Commercial MRA], Congress St., Rumford, 5/13/80, A, C, 80000242

North Waterford Congregational Church, Off ME 35, North Waterford, 6/13/86, A, C, a, 86001275

Norway Historic District, Roughly bounded by Pearl St., Danforth St. and Greenleaf Ave., Pennesseewassee Stream, and Main and Whitman Sts., Norway, 7/21/88, A, C, b, 88000391

Osgood Family House, Main St., Fryeburg, 4/05/90, C, 90000576

Paris Hill Historic District, Main St. and Hannibal Hamlin Dr. E to Mt. Mica and Christian Ridge Rds., Paris Hill, 6/19/73, A, C, d, 73000243

Paris Public Library [Maine Public Libraries MPS], 3 Main St., South Paris, 1/05/89, A, C, 88003015

Parsons, Marion, House, 90 Main St., Fryeburg, 1/23/87, B, c, g, 86002432

Peabody Tavern, E of Gilead on U.S. 2, Gilead vicinity, 12/13/76, A, C, 76000107

Porter Old Meetinghouse, N of Porter off ME 25, Porter vicinity, 4/02/73, A, C, a, 73000267

Porter-Parsonfield Bridge, 0.5 mi. S of Porter over the Ossipee River, Porter vicinity, 2/16/70, A, 70000058

Robinson-Parsons Farm, Town Farm Brook Rd., Paris, 2/04/82, A, C, 82000773

Rumford Falls I—IV Site [Androscoggin River Drainage Prehistoric Sites MPS], Address Re-

Oxford County—Continued

stricted, South Rumford vicinity, 11/14/92, D, 92001513

Rumford Falls Power Company Building [Rumford Commercial MRA], 59 Congress St., Rumford, 5/13/80, A, C, 80000243

Rumford Falls V Site [Androscoggin River Drainage Prehistoric Sites MPS], Address Restricted, South Rumford vicinity, 11/14/92, D, 92001509

Rumford Point Congregational Church, ME 5 and US 2 jct., Rumford, 6/20/85, C, a, 85001259

Rumford Public Library [Maine Public Libraries MPS], Rumford Ave., Rumford, 1/05/89, A, C, 88003023

Sargent, Levi, House, Otisfield Gore Rd., Otisfield vicinity, 3/13/87, C, 87000419

Stone, Elisha F., House, Gothic St., South Paris, 4/28/83, C, 83000466

Strathglass Building [Rumford Commercial MRA], 33 Hartford St., Rumford, 5/13/80, A, C, 80000244

Strathglass Park District, Bounded by Lincoln Ave., Hancock St., Maine Ave., and York St., Rumford, 10/18/74, A, C, 74000181

Sturtevant Hall, ME 119, Hebron, 9/19/77, A, C, 77000079

Sunday River Bridge, W of Newry, over Sunday River, Newry vicinity, 2/16/70, A, C, 70000059

Town of Rumford Site [Androscoggin River Drainage Prehistoric Sites MPS], Address Restricted, Rumford vicinity, 11/14/92, D, 92001507

Union Church, Off ME 140, Buckfield, 6/22/80, C, 80000245

Vail Site, Address Restricted, Parkertown vicinity, 1/23/80, D, 80000246

Vail Site 81.1 (Boundary Increase), Address Restricted, Parkerton vicinity, 1/11/84, D, 84001474

Wadsworth Hall, S of Hiram, Hiram vicinity, 1/21/74, A, B, C, 74000182

Warren, David, House, Off ME 140, Hartford, 4/28/83, C, 83000467

Waterford Historic District, ME 35 and ME 37, Waterford, 4/24/80, C, 80000247

Watson, John, House, 1 mi. NW of Hiram off ME 117, Hiram vicinity, 12/31/74, A, C, 74000183

Wiley, Benjamin, House, SE of North Fryeburg on Fish St., North Fryeburg vicinity, 11/10/80, B, C, 80000248

Penobscot County

Abbott Memorial Library, ME 7, Dexter, 11/20/78, C, 78000190

Adams-Pickering Block, Corner of Main and Middle Sts., Bangor, 5/02/74, A, C, 74000184

All Souls Congregational Church, 10 Broadway, Bangor, 6/18/92, C, a, 92000790

Bangor Children's Home, 218 Ohio St., Bangor, 9/09/75, A, C, 75000103

Bangor Fire Engine House No. 6, 284 Center St., Bangor, 4/07/88, C, 88000394

Bangor House, 174 Main St., Bangor, 2/23/72, A, C, 72000076

Bangor Mental Health Institute, 656 State St., Bangor, 7/16/87, A, C, 87000420

Bangor Standpipe, Jackson St, Bangor, 8/30/74, C, 74000185

Bangor Theological Seminary Historic District, Union St., Bangor, 8/02/77, A, C, a, 77000080

Blake House, 107 Court St., Bangor, 10/31/72, C, 72000077

Bodwell Water Power Company Plant, E side of Penobscot River at Bridge St., Milford, 9/29/88, A, C, 88001842

Broadway Historic District, Bounded by Garland, Essex, State, Park and Center Sts., Bangor, 5/07/73, A, C, 73000244

Bryant, Charles G., Double House, 16–18 Division St., Bangor, 6/20/86, C, 86001338

Bussey, Louis I., School, U.S. 202, Dixmont, 11/07/76, A, C, 76000108

Colburn, William, House, 91 Bennoch Rd., Orono, 6/19/73, A, C, 73000134

Congregational Church of Medway, Off ME 11, Medway, 11/21/77, C, 77000081

Connors House, 277 State St., Bangor, 10/06/83, C, 83003669

Corinth Village, 3.5 mi. W of East Corinth, East Corinth vicinity, 6/04/73, A, 73000135

Cushman, Abial, Store, Main St. E of ME 168, Lee, 12/18/90, C, 90001906

Dexter Grist Mill, ME 7, Dexter, 10/10/75, A, C, 75000104

Dexter Universalist Church, Church St., Dexter, 6/20/85, C, a, 85001258

Dixmont Corner Church, US 202, Dixmont, 7/21/83, C, a, 83000468

Eddington Bend (Site 74-8), Address Restricted, Eddington vicinity, 9/28/88, D, 88000937

Farrar, Samuel, House, 123 Court St., Bangor, 5/23/74, C, a, 74000186

Garland Grange Hall, Off ME 94, Garland, 5/12/75, A, C, 75000105

Godfrey-Kellogg House, 212 Kenduskeag Ave., Bangor, 6/18/73, C, 73000136

Grand Army Memorial Home, 159 Union St., Bangor, 10/31/72, A, C, 72000105

Great Fire of 1911 Historic District, Harlow, Center, Park, State, York, and Central Sts., Bangor, 6/14/84, A, C, 84001479

Hamlin, Hannibal, House, 15 5th St., Bangor, 10/09/79, B, C, 79000160

Hammond Street Congregation Church, Hammond and High Sts., Bangor, 7/08/82, C, a, 82000774

Hampden Academy, Alt. U.S. 1, Hampden, 9/11/75, A, C, 75000106

Hampden Congregational Church, Main Rd. N, Hampden, 6/25/87, C, a, 87000921

Hexagon Barn, Spring and Railroad Sts., Newport, 1/24/80, C, 80000412

Hirundo Site, Address Restricted, Old Town vicinity, 9/11/75, D, 75000107

Jenkins, Charles W., House, 67 Pine St., Bangor, 9/18/90, C, b, 90001469

Jonas Cutting-Edward Kent House, 48-50 Penobscot St., Bangor, 4/02/73, A, C, 73000137

Kingman, Romanzo, House, Main St., Kingman, 2/19/82, A, C, 82000775

Kinsley, Martin, House, Main Rd., Hampden Highlands, 4/14/83, B, C, 83000469

Knowlton, Jabez, Store, W of Newburgh on ME 9, Newburgh vicinity, 1/18/78, A, C, 78000191

Low, Joseph W., House, 51 Highland St., Bangor, 12/04/73, A, C, 73000138

Maine Archeological Survey Site, Address Restricted, Indian Island vicinity, 1/26/84, D, 84001486

Maine Experiment Station Barn, University of Maine campus, Orono, 9/18/90, A, b, 90001468

Mallett Hall, ME 6 N side, 0.1 mi. E of jct. with ME 168, Lee, 10/29/93, A, 93001115

Milford Congregational Church, Main and Perry Sts., Milford, 7/13/89, C, a, 89000841

Morse & Co. Office Building, Harlow St., Bangor, 4/02/73, A, 73000139

Morse Bridge, Valley Ave., over Kenduskeag Stream, Bangor, 2/16/70, A, C, b, 70000060

Mount Hope Cemetery District, U.S. 2, Bangor, 12/04/74, A, C, d, 74000187

Old Fire Engine House, N. Main St., Orono, 9/12/85, C, 85002181

Old Tavern, ME 188 and Old Dam Rd., Burlington, 4/04/86, A, C, 86000674

Orono Main Street Historic District, Main St. from Maplewood Ave. to Pine St., Orono, 12/07/77, A, C, 77000082

Penobscot Expedition Site, Address Restricted, Bangor-Brewer vicinity, 4/23/73, D, 73000140

Penobscot Salmon Club and Pool, N. Main St., North Brewer vicinity, 9/15/76, A, 76000109

Robyville Bridge, Over Kenduskeag Stream, Robyville, 2/16/70, A, C, 70000061

Sargent, Daniel House, 613 S. Main St., Brewer, 10/29/82, A, C, 82000425

Smith, George W., Homestead, Main St., Mattawamkeag, 1/15/80, C, 80000249

Smith, Zebulon, House, 55 Summer St., Bangor, 1/21/74, C, 74000189

Springfield Congregational Church, ME 6, Springfield, 12/22/78, C, a, 78000193

St. Anne's Church and Mission Site, On Indian Island off ME 43, Old Town, 11/26/73, A, C, a, 73000141

St. James Episcopal Church, Centre St., Old Town, 11/19/74, C, a, 74000188

St. John's Catholic Church, York St., Bangor, 4/02/73, A, C, a, 73000142

Stetson Union Church, ME 222, Stetson, 7/15/81, C, a, 81000068

Stewart Free Library, ME 11/43, Corinna, 7/30/74, B, C, 74000190

Symphony House, 166 Union St., Bangor, 10/26/72, C, 72000078

Treat, Nathaniel, House, 114 Main St., Orono, 9/20/73, B, C, 73000143

US Post Office—Old Town Main, Center St., Old Town, 9/25/86, C, 86002958

US Post Office—Orono Main, Forest and Bennoch Sts., Orono, 5/02/86, C, 86000881

University of Maine at Orono Historic District, Munson, Sebec, and Schoodic Rds., Orono, 7/12/78, A, C, 78000194

Penobscot County—Continued

Veazie, Jones P., House, 88 Fountain St., Bangor, 6/23/88, C, 88000890

Wardwell—Trickey Double House, 97–99 Ohio St., Bangor, 6/18/92, C, 92000795

Washburn, Gov. Israel, House, 120 Main St., Orono, 1/12/73, B, C, 73000144

West Market Square Historic District, W. Market Sq., Bangor, 12/27/79, A, C, 79000161

Wheelwright Block, 34 Hammond St., Bangor, 7/18/74, A, C, 74000191

Whitney Park Historic District, Roughly bounded by 8th, Union, Pond and Hayford Sts., Bangor, 10/13/88, A, C, b, 88001844

Williams, Gen. John, House, 62 High St., Bangor, 12/22/78, A, C, 78000195

Young Site, , Hudson vicinity, 3/26/76, D, 76000110

Zions Hill, 37 Zions Hill, Dexter, 10/16/89, C, 89001705

Piscataquis County

Ambajejus Boom House, About 11 mi. NW of Millinocket and Ambajejus Lake, Millinocket vicinity, 4/02/73, A, 73000145

Archeological Site No. 133.7, Address Restricted, Chesuncook vicinity, 4/25/86, D, 86000858

Archeological Site No. 133.8, Address Restricted, Chesuncook vicinity, 4/25/86, D, 86000861

Brockway Site (ME 90.3), Address Restricted, Milo vicinity, 7/27/87, D, 87001152

Brown House, High St., Brownville, 2/14/85, A, 85000273

Burgess House, Off ME 11, Sebec, 5/03/78, A, C, 78000196

Carleton, Robert, House, N. Main St., Sangerville, 12/06/75, C, 75000108

Chandler—Parsons Blacksmith Shop, Dawes Rd., Dover-Foxcroft vicinity, 10/16/89, A, 89001702

Chesuncook Village, NW Shore, Chesuncook Lake, Chesuncook, 4/11/73, A, C, b, d, 73000262

Guilford Memorial Library, Library and Water Sts., Guilford, 7/31/86, C, 86002107

Hudson, H., Law Office, Hudson Ave., Guilford, 10/09/79, A, C, 79000162

KATAHDIN (Lake Boat), Moosehead Lake, Greenville, 9/13/78, A, 78003435

Katahdin Ironworks, NW of Brownville Junction at Silver Lake, Brownville Junction vicinity, 12/23/69, A, e, 69000011

Little Schoodic Stream Archeological Site (107-4), Address Restricted, Medford vicinity, 4/20/89, D, 89000256

Milo Public Library [Maine Public Libraries MPS], 4 Pleasant St., Milo, 1/05/89, A, C, 88003017

Munsungan-Chase Lake Thoroughfare Archeological District, , Millinocket Lake vicinity, 9/06/79, D, 79000163

Sangerville Town Hall, Main St., Sangerville, 3/22/91, A, C, 91000322

Sebec—Piscataquis River Confluence Prehistoric Archeological District, Address Restricted, Milo vicinity, 12/24/86, D, 86003482

Straw House, Golda Ct., Guilford, 2/19/82, A, C, 82000776

Swedish Lutheran Church, Wilkins and Hebron Sts., Monson, 7/19/84, A, C, a, 84001489

Tramway Historic District, NE of Greenville, Greenville vicinity, 5/07/79, A, C, 79000164

Wiley, James Sullivan, House, Main St., Dover-Foxcroft, 11/21/76, B, C, 76000111

Willard Brook Quarry, Address Restricted, Chisuncook vicinity, 9/26/86, D, 86002182

Sagadahoc County

Bath Historic District, Roughly bounded by High, Beacon, and Court Sts., U.S. 1 and Kennebec River, Bath, 5/17/73, A, C, 73000261

Carr, Robert P., House, Main St., Bowdoinham, 12/18/90, B, C, 90001904

Clarke and Lake Company Archeological Site, Address Restricted, Bath vicinity, 11/21/78, D, 78000329

Cold Spring Farm, Off Fiddler's Reach Rd., Phippsburg, 2/14/85, C, 85000274

Coombs, Viola, House, Main St., Bowdoinham, 12/13/91, C, 91001816

Cornish House, Main St., Bowdoinham, 1/15/80, C, 80000250

Crooker, W. D., House, 71 South St., Bath, 7/10/79, A, C, 79000165

Days Ferry Historic District, N of Bath along ME 128, Bath vicinity, 2/20/75, A, C, 75000109

Donnell, William T., House, 279 Washington St., Bath, 7/13/89, B, 89000840

Doubling Point Light Station [Light Stations of Maine MPS], W side of Arrowsic Island, Bath vicinity, 1/21/88, A, C, b, 87002271

Fort Baldwin Historic Site, Sabino Hill, Phippsburg, 8/03/79, A, C, g, 79000166

Fort Popham Memorial, N of Popham on Hunnewell Point, Popham Beach vicinity, 10/01/69, A, C, f, 69000012

Grey Havens Inn, Reid Park Rd., Georgetown, 3/21/85, C, 85000614

Hathorn, Lt. Richard, House, ME 127, Woolwich, 2/26/80, C, 80000251

Hunter Site, Address Restricted, Topsham vicinity, 1/26/84, D, 84001493

Hyde Mansion, 616 High St., Bath, 11/21/78, B, C, 78000197

Ingraham, Charles H., Cottage, Off ME 209, Phippsburg vicinity, 12/29/86, C, 86003512

Kennebec River Light Station [Light Stations of Maine MPS], Fiddler Reach, Arrowsic Island, Bath vicinity, 1/21/88, A, C, 87002263

King, Gov. William, House, Whiskeag Rd., Bath, 5/24/76, B, C, 76000112

McCobb-Hill-Minott House, Parker Head Rd., Phippsburg, 11/23/77, A, C, 77000083

Merritt, Captain, House, 619 High St., Bath, 2/08/85, B, C, 85000243

Peacock Tavern, US 201, Richmond, 4/04/86, C, 86000675

Pejepscot Paper Company, Off U.S. 201 at Androscoggin River, Topsham, 9/17/74, A, C, 74000192

Pejepscot Site, Address Restricted, Pejepscot vicinity, 6/12/87, D, 87000922

Percy and Small Shipyard, 451 Washington St., Bath, 7/27/71, A, 71000043

Perkins Island Light Station [Light Stations of Maine MPS], Perkins Island, Georgetown vicinity, 1/21/88, A, C, 87002282

Popham Colony Site, Address Restricted, Popham Beach vicinity, 2/16/70, D, 70000063

Purinton Family Farm, 65 Elm St., Topsham, 7/13/89, A, D, b, 89000842

Reed, Robert, House, ME 128 and Chop Point Rd., Woolrich, 2/11/82, A, C, 82000777

Richmond Historic District, Roughly bounded by South, High, Kimbal Sts., and the Kennebec River, Richmond, 11/12/73, A, C, 73000146

Riggs, Benjamin, House, Robinhood Rd., Georgetown vicinity, 12/22/88, C, 88003008

Riggs—Zorach House, Off Robinhood Rd., Georgetown vicinity, 12/30/88, B, g, 88003007

SEQUIN (tugboat), Bath Marine Museum, Bath, 12/02/69, A, 69000013

Sequin Island Light Station, S of Georgetown, Georgetown vicinity, 3/08/77, A, 77000084

Southard Block, 25 Front St., Richmond, 2/23/72, A, B, C, 72000079

Squirrel Point Light Station [Light Stations of Maine MPS], Squirrel Point, Arrowsic Island, Phippsburg vicinity, 1/21/88, A, C, 87002281

Stone Schoolhouse, S of Georgetown on Bay Point Rd., Georgetown vicinity, 8/12/77, A, C, 77000085

Topsham Fairgrounds Grandstand, Off N side of Elm St., E of jct. with Fair Cir., Topsham, 3/26/92, A, C, 92000277

Topsham Historic District, Elm, Main, and Green Sts., Topsham, 1/09/78, C, 78000198

U.S. Customhouse and Post Office, 25 Front St., Bath, 10/06/70, C, 70000064

Winter Street Chruch, Corner of Washington and Winter Sts., Bath, 7/27/71, C, a, 71000044

Woolwich Town House, NE of Bath at Old Stage and Dana Mills Rds., Bath vicinity, 2/17/78, A, C, 78000199

Somerset County

Bailey Farm Windmill, ME 16, North Anson vicinity, 6/28/88, C, 88000885

Bigelow—Page House, 20 High St., Skowhegan, 4/20/88, C, 88000395

Bingham Free Meetinghouse, S. Main St. (U.S. 201), Bingham, 6/03/76, A, C, 76000113

Bloomfield Academy, Main St., Skowhegan, 2/19/82, A, C, 82000778

Caratunk Falls Archeological District, Address Restricted, Solon vicinity, 5/30/86, D, 86001200

Coburn, Gov. Abner, House, Main St., Skowhegan, 7/30/74, B, C, 74000193

Somerset County—Continued

Concord Haven, ME 16 E side, 1.7 mi. N of jct. with Berry Rd., Embden vicinity, 10/02/92, B, C, 92001297

Connor-Bovie House, 22 Summit Street, Fairfield, 1/18/74, B, C, 74000321

Cotton—Smith House, 42 High St., Fairfield, 6/18/92, C, 92000794

Douglas, C. F., House, ME 8, Norridgewock, 12/18/78, C, 78000200

Eaton School, Jct. of Main St. and Mercer Rd., Norridgewock, 6/23/88, A, C, 88000884

Embden Town House, Cross Town Rd., Embden vicinity, 10/16/89, A, 89001704

Evergreens, The, , , 2/08/82, D, 82000779

First Baptist Church, Former, W side of Main St., S of ME 104, Skowhegan, 6/21/91, C, a, 91000770

Founders Hall, S. Main St., Pittsfield, 10/09/79, A, C, 79000167

Gerald, Amos, House, 107 Main St., Fairfield, 6/24/80, C, 80000252

Gould House, 31 Elm St., Skowhegan, 2/19/82, B, C, 82001886

Hinckley Good Will Home Historic District, US 201, Hinckley, 1/09/87, B, C, 87000232

History House, 40 Elm St., Skowhegan, 12/29/83, C, 83003677

Hodgdon Site, Address Restricted, Embden vicinity, 4/23/80, C, D, 80000253

Ingalls House, Off U.S. 2, Mercer, 6/05/75, C, 75000110

Lakewood Theater, NE of Madison in town of Lakewood on bank of Lake Wesserunsett, Madison vicinity, 6/18/75, A, 75000111

Lawrence Library, Fairfield off U.S. 201, Fairfield, 12/31/74, C, 74000322

Madison Public Library [Maine Public Libraries MPS], Old Point Ave., Madison, 1/05/89, A, C, 88003022

May, Sophie, House, Sophie May Lane, Norridgewock, 10/08/76, B, C, 76000114

New Portland Wire Bridge, Wire Bridge Rd., over the Carrabasssett River, New Portland vicinity, 1/12/70, C, 70000065

Norridgewock Archeological District, Address Restricted, Madison, 4/12/93, D, NHL, 93000606

Norridgewock Free Public Library, Sophie May Lane, Norridgewock, 2/04/82, A, C, 82000780

Old Point and Sebastian Rale Monument, S of Madison off Alt. US 201, Madison vicinity, 4/02/73, A, B, 73000147

Pittsfield Public Library, Main St., Pittsfield, 1/04/83, C, 83000471

Pittsfield Railroad Station, Central St., Pittsfield, 1/23/80, A, C, 80000254

Pittsfield Universalist Church, N. Main and Easy Sts., Pittsfield, 7/14/83, C, a, 83000472

Quincy Building, S of Hinckley, Hinckley vicinity, 10/04/78, A, C, 78000330

Skowhegan Fire Station, Island Ave., Skowhegan, 10/20/83, C, 83003679

Skowhegan Free Public Library, Elm St., Skowhegan, 4/14/83, A, C, 83000473

Skowhegan Historic District, Madison Ave., Water and Russell Sts., Showhegan, 2/19/82, A, C, 82000781

Somerset Academy, Academy St., Athens, 7/19/84, A, C, 84001499

Somerset County Courthouse, Court St., Skowhegan, 11/08/84, A, 84000332

South Solon Meetinghouse, 5 mi. SE of Solon, Solon vicinity, 6/16/80, C, a, 80000255

Spaulding House, Main St., Norridgewock, 12/18/78, C, 78000201

Steward—Emery House, Main St., .25 mi. N of jct. with ME 16, North Anson, 12/17/92, C, 92001705

Temples Historic District, Madison Ave., North Anson, 5/12/83, C, 83000474

Weston Homestead, N of Madison on Weston Ave., Madison vicinity, 11/23/77, A, C, 77000086

Weston, Samuel, Homestead, S of Skowhegan on U.S. 201, Skowhegan vicinity, 11/10/80, B, C, 80000256

Waldo County

Archeological Site No. 29-64, Address Restricted, Islesboro vicinity, 2/22/82, C, D, 82000782

Belfast Commercial Historic District, Main St. between Church and Cross Sts., Belfast, 4/04/80, A, C, 80000257

Belfast Historic District, Roughly bounded by High, Grove and Elm, Congress, Main and Market and Imrose, Belfast, 8/21/86, A, C, 86002733

Belfast Historic District (Boundary Increase), 59–63 Anderson St., Belfast, 4/02/93, A, C, 93000195

Belfast National Bank, Main and Beaver Sts., Belfast, 4/23/73, A, C, 73000148

Black Horse Tavern, Searsport Ave., Belfast, 2/11/82, A, 82000783

Carver Memorial Library [Maine Public Libraries MPS], Jct. of Union and Mortland Sts., NE corner, Searsport, 10/14/93, A, C, 93001113

Chase, Hezekiah, House, U.S. 202, Unity, 1/31/78, B, C, 78000202

Christ Church, Off W side of Main Rd., S of Dark Harbor, Dark Harbor vicinity, 3/26/92, C, 92000276

Church Street Historic District, Irregular pattern along Church St. from High to Franklin Sts., Belfast, 11/28/78, C, 78000331

Cobe Estate, N of Northport on Bluff Rd., Northport vicinity, 10/20/83, C, 83003684

Drexel Estate, The Bluff, Islesboro, 3/21/85, B, C, 85000613

East Main Street Historic District, US 1 between Black Rd. and Navy St., Searsport, 12/13/91, A, B, C, 91001815

First Church of Belfast, Church St., Belfast, 11/07/76, C, a, 76000115

Fort Knox State Park, U.S. 1 near Prospect, Prospect vicinity, 10/01/69, A, C, NHL, 69000023

Fort Point Light Station [Light Stations of Maine MPS], Fort Point Rd., Stockton Springs vicinity, 3/23/88, A, C, 87002269

Fort Pownall Memorial, SE of Stockton Springs on Fort Point, Stockton Springs vicinity, 10/28/69, A, D, 69000028

Free Will Baptist Church and Cemetery, Church Rd., North Islesboro vicinity, 9/27/88, C, a, d, 88000891

Greer's Corner School, SE corner of Back Belmont and Greer's Corner Rd., Belmont Corner vicinity, 10/16/91, A, 91001513

Grindle Point Light Station, Ferry Rd., Islesboro, 3/13/87, A, C, b, 87000427

Hayford Block, 47 Church St., Belfast, 8/29/77, A, C, 77000087

Hichborn, Nathan G., House, Church St., Stockton Springs, 4/07/88, B, C, 88000392

Islesboro Free Library [Maine Public Libraries MPS], Main Rd., Islesboro, 1/05/89, A, C, 88003018

Lincolnville Center Meeting House, ME 173, Lincolnville Center, 7/21/83, C, a, 83000475

Masonic Temple, High St. (U.S. 1), Belfast, 4/26/73, A, C, 73000246

McGilvery, Capt. John, House, E. Main St., Searsport, 12/29/83, B, C, 83003685

McGilvery, Capt. William, House, E. Main St., Searsport, 12/29/83, B, C, 83003686

Mortland Family Farm, E side Mortland Rd. N of Searsport, Searsport vicinity, 10/24/91, A, C, 91001510

Mount Waldo Granite Works, Address Restricted, Frankfort vicinity, 3/15/74, A, 74000194

Nichols, Capt. John P., House, US 1, Searsport, 1/04/83, C, 83000476

Old Post Office, Main St. (ME-173), Liberty, 6/19/73, A, 73000149

Penobscot Marine Museum, Church St., Searsport, 7/01/70, A, 70000088

Philler Cottage, Main Rd., Dark Harbor, Islesboro, 4/11/85, A, C, 85000726

Primrose Hill Historic District, High and Anderson Sts., Belfast, 10/03/73, A, C, 73000150

Privateer Brigantine DEFENCE Shipwreck Site, Address Restricted, Stockton Springs vicinity, 3/18/75, D, 75000205

Searsport Historic District, Main St., Searsport, 7/27/79, A, C, 79000168

Stockton Springs Community Church, ME 3 and US 1, Stockton Springs, 6/20/85, C, a, 85001266

Tiffany, George S., Cottage, Off Main Rd., Dark Harbor, 10/16/89, C, 89001700

Union Hall, 3 Reservoir St., Searsport, 3/20/86, C, 86000478

Union School, Mt. Ephraim Rd. E side, 0.2 mi. N of jct. with US 1, Searsport, 3/25/93, A, C, 93000203

White, James P., House, 1 Church St., Belfast, 4/24/73, B, C, 73000245

Winterport Congregational Church, Alt. U.S. 1, Winterport, 4/24/73, A, C, a, 73000151

Winterport Historic District, Irregular pattern along Main, Elm, Cushing, Lebanon, Commercial, Dean, and Water Sts., Winterport, 10/03/75, A, C, a, 75000112

Washington County

"The Rim" and Site of Fort Foster, S of East Machias of U.S. 1, East Machias vicinity, 7/23/73, A, 73000155

Washington County—Continued

Archibald—Adams House, ME 193, Cherryfield, 3/13/87, C, 87000429

Atkinson-Koskinen Site 45.13, Address Restricted, Steuben vicinity, 11/23/84, D, 84000282

Best, Charles, House, County Rd., West Pembroke, 3/02/82, B, c, 82000784

Boynton Street Historic District, 13-26 Boynton St., Eastport, 7/19/84, C, 84001542

Brewer, Henrietta, House, US 1, Robbinston, 10/06/83, C, 83003688

Brewer, John N.M., House, US 1, Robbinston, 10/06/83, C, 83003690

Bucknam House, Maine St., Columbia Falls, 4/28/75, C, 75000113

Bucknam, Samuel, House, U.S. 1, Columbia Falls, 10/19/78, C, 78000203

Burnham Tavern, Main St., Machias, 4/11/73, A, C, 73000152

Calais Historic District, Church, Main and North Sts., Calais, 12/20/78, A, C, 78000204

Campbell, Col, Samuel, House, U.S. 1, Cherryfield, 2/04/82, C, 82000785

Campbell, David W., House, Main St., Cherryfield, 7/19/84, C, 84001545

Campbell, Frank, House, US 1, Cherryfield, 10/29/82, C, 82000426

Campbell, Gen. Alexander, House, Campbell Hill, Cherryfield, 4/13/77, B, 77000088

Central Congregational Church, Middle St., Eastport, 6/23/76, C, a, 76000116

Centre Street Congregational Church, Centre St., Machias, 5/12/75, C, 75000114

Cherryfield Academy, Main St., Cherryfield, 2/19/82, A, C, 82000786

Cherryfield Historic District, Roughly bounded by Church, Main, Park, New and High Sts., as well as River Rd. properties from US 1 to Driscoll Island, Cherryfield, 10/01/90, A, B, C, 90001467

Dennysville Historic District, The Lane, Main and King Sts., Dennysville, 10/29/82, C, 82000427

East Machias Historic District, High, Water, and Bridge Sts., East Machias, 4/11/73, A, C, a, 73000153

Eastport Historic District, Water St., Eastport, 6/01/82, A, C, 82000787

First Congregational Church, Calais Ave., Calais, 7/12/78, C, a, 78000205

Fort O'Brien, S of Machiasport on secondary rd., Machiasport vicinity, 10/01/69, A, 69000024

Fort Sullivan, Moose Island; barracks, 74 Washington St., Eastport, 1/26/70, A, 70000081

Fowler, Jeremiah, House, 35 School St., Lubec, 12/29/83, A, C, 83003693

Gates House, ME 92, Machiasport, 4/28/75, A, C, 75000115

Gilmore House, 316 Main St., Calais, 6/14/79, C, 79000380

Hamilton, Thomas, House, 78 South St., Calais, 2/04/82, C, 82000788

Holmes Cottage, 241 Main St., Calais, 4/04/88, C, 87001855

Holmes, Dr. Job, House, 247 Main St., Calais, 4/05/90, C, 90000579

Indian River Baptist Church, ME 187, Indian River, Addison vicinity, 6/23/88, C, a, 88000893

Jellison, Theodore, House, River Rd., Calais, 11/23/84, C, 84000274

Libby Island Light Station, S of Machiasport on Lilly Island, Machiasport vicinity, 6/18/76, A, 76000117

Liberty Hall, ME 92, Machiasport, 11/23/77, A, C, 77000089

Lincoln House, U.S. 1, Dennysville, 3/29/78, B, C, 78000206

Lion, The (locomotive), University of Maine at Machias, Machias, 12/15/76, A, 76000118

Little River Light Station [Light Stations of Maine MPS], Little River Island, Cutler vicinity, 3/14/88, A, C, 88000156

Lubec Channel Light Station [Light Stations of Maine MPS], Lubec Channel, Lubec vicinity, 3/14/88, A, C, 88000152

Machias Post Office and Customhouse, Main and Center Sts., Machias, 11/23/77, C, 77000090

Machias Railroad Station, 27 E. Main St., Machias, 10/02/92, A, C, 92001293

Mansion House, The, N of Kobbinston on U.S. 1, Robbinston vicinity, 5/22/73, A, B, C, 73000154

McCurdy Smokehouse, Water St., E side, at jct. with School St., Lubec, 7/15/93, A, C, 93000638

McGlashan—Nickerson House, St. Croix Dr. near Pettegrove Pt., Red Beach, 6/14/90, C, 90000920

Narraguagus Light Station [Light Stations of Maine MPS], E side of Pond Island, Milbridge vicinity, 11/20/87, A, C, 87002022

Nash, William M., House, River Rd., Cherryfield, 1/04/83, C, 83000477

Patten Building, Main St., Cherryfield, 12/22/78, A, C, 78000207

Perry, Clark, House, Court St., Machias, 10/09/79, C, 79000169

Petit Manan Light Station, Petit Manan Island, Milbridge vicinity, 10/30/87, A, C, 87001879

Porter Memorial Library, Court St., Machias, 1/20/78, B, C, 78000208

Reversing Falls Site [Cobscook Area Coastal Prehistoric Sites MPS], Address Restricted, Pembroke vicinity, 6/27/90, D, 90000907

Ruggles House, Main Street, Columbia Falls, 1/26/70, B, C, 70000080

St. Anne's Episcopal Church, Church St., Calais, 7/08/82, C, a, 82000789

St. Croix Island International Historic Site, On the international boundary in the St. Croix River, St. Croix Junction vicinity, 10/15/66, A, B, D, f, NPS, 66000932

Talbot, James R., House, US 1, East Machias, 1/04/83, C, 83000478

Todd House, 11 Capens Ave., Eastport, 4/23/80, A, C, 80000258

Union Hall, Near Jct. of US 1 and ME 169, Danforth, 6/25/87, A, C, 87000938

Washburn, George, House, 318 Main St., Calais, 2/11/82, C, 82000790

Washington County Courthouse, Court St., Machias, 11/07/76, A, C, 76000119

Washington County Jail, Court St., Machias, 4/07/88, C, 88000393

West Quoddy Head Light Station, SE of Lubec on West Quoddy Head, Lubec vicinity, 7/04/80, A, 80004601

West Quoddy Lifesaving Station [Lifesaving Stations of Maine MPS], N side W. Quoddy Head, Lubec vicinity, 4/20/90, A, 90000581

Whitlocks Mill Light Station [Light Stations of Maine MPS], S bank of St. Croix River, Calais vicinity, 1/21/88, A, C, 87002276

Whitneyville Congregational Church, Main St., Whitneyville, 6/26/79, C, a, 79000170

Young, Daniel, House, 34 Main St., Lubec, 3/22/84, C, 84001547

York County

Alfred Historic District, Kennebunk, and Saco Rds., Alfred, 4/28/83, A, C, 83000479

Austin-Hennessey Homestead [Wells Township Cape Cod Houses TR], Brunt Mill Rd., Wells vicinity, 12/27/79, A, C, 79000171

Barrell Homestead, W of York Corner on Beech Ridge Rd., York Corner vicinity, 12/12/76, B, C, 76000195

Berwick Academy, Academy St., South Berwick, 3/29/78, A, C, 78000336

Biddeford City Hall, 205 Main St., Biddeford, 4/24/73, A, C, 73000156

Blazo-Leavitt House, ME 160, Parsonsfield, 2/19/82, C, 82000791

Boon Island Light Station [Light Stations of Maine MPS], Boon Island, York vicinity, 3/14/88, A, C, 88000153

Bourne Mansion, 8 Bourne St., Kennebunk, 1/24/80, C, 80000381

Bray House, Pepperell Rd., Kittery Point, 10/09/79, A, C, 79000271

Breckinridge, Isabella, House, Off U.S. 1, York vicinity, 4/28/83, C, 83000480

Brewster, Royal, House, Buxton Lower Corner, Buxton, 6/05/75, B, C, 75000116

Buxton Powder House, ME 22, Buxton Center, 1/02/76, A, 76000120

Cape Arundel Summer Colony Historic District, Roughly bounded by Chick's Creek, Ocean Ave., S. Main St., Endcliff Rd., and Walkers Point, Kennebunkport, 8/16/84, A, C, 84001549

Cape Neddick Light Station, Cape Neddick, York, 4/16/85, A, 85000844

Chase, Capt. Josiah E., Octagon House, Chase's Mill Rd., East Limington vicinity, 3/25/87, C, 87000431

Clock Farm, ME 9 and Goose Rocks Rd., Kennebunkport vicinity, 2/19/82, C, 82000792

Conant—Sawyer Cottage, 14 Kendall Rd., York Beach, 3/26/92, A, C, b, 92000279

Conway Junction Railroad Turntable Site, Fife Ln. and Rt. 236, South Berwick vicinity, 1/05/89, A, 88003001

Deering, J. G., House, 371 Main St., Saco, 2/17/82, A, C, 82000793

Dennett Garrison, 100 Dennett Rd., Kittery, 12/22/78, C, 78000334

York County—Continued

Dorfield Farm [Wells Township Cape Cod Houses TR], Harrisecket Rd., Wells vicinity, 12/27/79, A, C, 79000172

Dudley Block, 28-34 Water St., Biddeford, 11/12/82, A, B, C, 82000428

Early Post Office [Wells Township Cape Cod Houses TR], Bragdon's Crossing, Wells, 12/27/79, A, C, 79000173

Eaton House [Wells Township Cape Cod Houses TR], Sanford Rd., North Berwick vicinity, 12/27/79, A, C, 79000174

Elden's Store, ME 22, Buxton, 4/28/83, C, 83000481

Elder Grey Meetinghouse, N of North Waterboro, North Waterboro vicinity, 10/09/79, A, C, a, 79000175

Emery Homestead, 1 and 3 Lebanon St., Sanford, 6/22/80, A, C, 80000379

Emery House [Wells Township Cape Cod Houses TR], Sanford Rd., Highpine, 12/27/79, A, C, 79000176

First Baptist Church, West side, Jct. of West Rd. and Federal St., Waterboro vicinity, 6/28/88, C, a, 88000886

First Congregational Church and Parsonage, Pepperrell Rd., Kittery Point, 12/18/78, A, C, a, b, 78000333

First Congregational Church of Buxton, ME 112, Buxton, 6/22/80, B, C, a, 80000259

First Congregational Church, Former, SW corner of Rt. 1 and Barker's Ln., Wells, 6/21/91, C, a, 91000768

First Parish Congregational Church, 12 Beach St., Saco, 6/14/90, C, a, 90000921

First Parish Meetinghouse, Old Pool Rd., Biddeford, 10/26/72, B, C, 72000080

Flagg, James Montgomery, House, St. Martin's Lane, Biddeford, 4/23/80, B, 80000260

Fletcher's Neck Lifesaving Station, Ocean Ave., Biddeford Pool, 11/01/74, A, C, 74000195

Fogg, William, Library [Maine Public Libraries MPS], Old Rd., Eliot vicinity, 12/21/91, A, C, 91001817

Fort McClary, Off ME 103 near Fort McClary State Park, Kittery Point vicinity, 10/01/69, A, 69000025

Foss, Levi, House, ME 35, Goodwins Mills, 3/22/84, C, 84001550

Frost Garrison and House, Frost's Hill, Eliot vicinity, 6/27/71, A, C, 71000045

Gerrish Warehouse, Pepperrell Cove off ME 103, Kittery, 5/26/77, A, B, C, 77000140

Goat Island Light Station [Light Stations of Maine MPS], Goat Island, Cape Porpoise Harbor, Cape Porpoise vicinity, 3/23/88, A, C, 87002268

Goodale-Bourne Farm [Wells Township Cape Cod Houses TR], N. Village Rd., Ogunquit, 12/27/79, A, C, 79000177

Goodale-Stevens Farm [Wells Township Cape Cod Houses TR], N. Village Rd., Ogunquit, 12/27/79, A, C, 79000178

Goodall, Thomas, House, 232 Main St., Sanford, 4/28/75, B, C, 75000207

Grant Family House, 72 Grant Rd., Saco vicinity, 6/21/90, C, 90000927

Graves, Abbott, House, Ocean Ave., Kennebunkport, 4/23/80, C, 80000261

Grist Mill Bridge, Little River Rd. across the Little R., Lebanon vicinity, 12/27/90, C, 90001905

Hamilton, Jonathan, House, Vaughan's Lane and Old South Rd., South Berwick, 12/30/70, C, NHL, 70000082

Hancock, John, Warehouse, Lindsay Rd., York, 12/02/69, A, 69000029

Hatch House [Wells Township Cape Cod Houses TR], Sanford Rd., North Berwick vicinity, 12/27/79, A, C, 79000179

Hawkes Pharmacy, 7 Main St., York Beach, 10/14/93, C, 93001111

Hedden Site, Address Restricted, Kennebunk vicinity, 10/16/91, D, 91001515

Higgin, Kate Douglas, House, E of Hollis Center on Salmon Falls Rd., Wollis Center vicinity, 9/16/77, B, C, 77000142

Hobbs, Thomas, Jr., House, Wells St., North Berwick, 2/11/82, A, C, 82000794

Holmes, Sen. John, House, U.S. 202, Alfred, 4/24/75, B, C, 75000117

Howels, William Dean, House, Pepperrell Rd., Kittery Point, 10/25/79, B, 79000270

Hurd, Mary R., House, Elm St., North Berwick, 9/11/79, B, C, 79000180

Hussey Plow Company Building, Dyer St., North Berwick, 12/19/79, A, b, 79000181

Isles of Shoals, 6.5 mi. SE of Kittery, Kittery vicinity, 5/16/74, A, C, 74000325

Jacobs Houses and Store, 9-17 Elm St., Saco, 3/02/82, A, C, 82000795

Jewett, Sarah Orne, House, ME 4 and 236, South Berwick, 6/04/73, B, C, NHL, 73000248

Jewett-Eastman House, 37 Portland St., South Berwick, 12/29/83, C, 83003700

Kennebunk Historic District, Both sides of ME 35 from Kennebunk River to U.S. 1, radiating streets at intersection, Kennebunk, 6/05/74, A, C, 74000324

Kennebunk River Club, Ocean Ave., Kennebunkport, 9/09/75, A, C, 75002169

Kennebunkport Historic District, Bounded roughly by South, Maine, North, and Lock Sts., and the Kennebunkport River, Kennebunkport, 5/06/76, A, C, 76000121

Lady Pepperrell House, ME 103, Kittery Point, 10/15/66, C, NHL, 66000094

Laudholm Farm, Laudholm Farm Rd., Wells vicinity, 10/20/83, A, C, 83003702

Laudholm Farm (Boundary Increase), Laudholm Farm Rd., Wells, 10/30/87, A, C, 87000570

Libby-MacArthur House, ME 11, Limington, 4/20/88, C, 88000397

Limerick Upper Village Historic District, ME 5, Limerick, 4/05/84, A, a, 84001557

Limington Academy, ME 117, Limington, 6/23/80, A, C, 80000380

Littlefield Homestead [Wells Township Cape Cod Houses TR], Chick's Crossing Rd., Wells vicinity, 12/27/79, A, C, 79000182

Littlefield Tavern [Wells Township Cape Cod Houses TR], 9B Charles Chase L. Rd., North Berwick vicinity, 12/27/79, A, C, 79000186

Littlefield-Chase Farmstead [Wells Township Cape Cod Houses TR], Rt. 9 N. Berwock Rd., North Berwick vicinity, 12/27/79, A, C, 79000183

Littlefield-Dustin Farm [Wells Township Cape Cod Houses TR], Dodge Rd., North Berwick vicinity, 12/27/79, A, C, 79000184

Littlefield-Keeping House [Wells Township Cape Cod Houses TR], Rt. 9B Charles Chase L. Rd., North Berwick vicinity, 12/27/79, A, C, 79000185

Lord Farm [Wells Township Cape Cod Houses TR], Laudholm Rd., Wells, 12/27/79, A, C, 79000187

Lord Mansion, 20 Summer St., Kennebunk, 4/02/73, A, C, 73000158

Lord, Capt. Nathaniel, Mansion, Pleasant and Green Sts., Kennebunkport, 9/20/73, C, 73000157

Lord—Dane House, Federal St. W side, 2 mi. N of jct. with US 202, Alfred vicinity, 12/17/92, C, 92001708

Maine Trolley Cars, Seashore Trolley Museum, Kennebunkport vicinity, 11/14/80, A, 80000262

McIntire Garrison House, On ME 91 about 5 mi. W of York, York vicinity, 11/24/68, C, NHL, 68000017

Mill House [Wells Township Cape Cod Houses TR], Post Rd., Ogunquit vicinity, 12/27/79, A, C, 79000188

Moody Homestead, Ridge Rd., York, 4/28/75, C, 75000209

Morison, Capt. James, House, SE of Parsonsfield on South Rd., Parsonsfield vicinity, 7/12/78, B, C, 78000335

Morrell House, N of N. Berwick on Bauneg Beg Pond Rd., North Berwick vicinity, 9/29/76, C, 76000194

Newfield (Willowbrook) Historic District, Elm St., Newfield, 2/14/85, A, C, 85000275

North Berwick Woolen Mill, Canal St., North Berwick, 7/21/83, A, C, 83000482

Ocean Park Historic Buildings, Temple Ave., Ocean Park, 3/02/82, A, C, a, 82000796

Odd Fellows-Rebekah Hall, High St., Cornish, 12/29/83, A, C, 83003704

Ogunquit Memorial Library, Shore Rd., Ogunquit, 12/29/83, C, 83003706

Old Grist Mill, Little River Rd., East Lebanon, 6/05/75, A, 75000118

Old Schoolhouse, York St. (on the Village Green), York, 4/02/73, A, C, b, 73000247

Old York Gaol, 4 Lindsey Rd., York, 11/24/68, C, NHL, 68000016

Parsonsfield Seminary, ME 160, Parsonsfield, 6/20/86, A, C, 86001339

Pebbledene, 99 Freeman St., York Beach, 10/14/93, C, 93001110

Pepperrell, William, House, On ME 103, Kittery Point, 8/14/73, B, C, 73000159

Perkins Tide Mill, Mill Lane, Kennebunkport, 9/07/73, A, C, 73000160

York County—Continued

Perkins, Charles, House [Wells Township Cape Cod Houses TR], Scotch Hill, Ogunquit, 12/27/79, A, C, 79000189

Portsmouth Company Cotton Mills: Counting House, ME 4 at Salmon Falls River, South Berwick, 10/10/75, A, C, 75000208

Portsmouth Naval Shipyard, Seavey Island, Kittery, 11/17/77, A, C, 77000141

Prescott, J. L., House, High St., North Berwick, 6/20/85, C, 85001268

Rice Public Library, 8 Wentworth St., Kittery, 10/01/79, C, 79000190

Rose, Robert, Tavern, Off Long Sands Rd., York, 10/10/75, A, B, C, 75000206

Saco City Hall, 300 Main St., Saco, 10/09/79, A, C, 79000192

Saco High School (old), Spring St., Saco, 7/14/83, C, 83000483

Salmon Falls (East) Historic District, Portions of ME 117 and Simpson Rd., Buxton, 10/15/87, C, 87001859

Salmon Falls (West) Historic District, Salmon Falls Rd. and portion of US 202, Hollis vicinity, 10/30/87, B, C, 87001858

Seavey, A. B., House, 90 Temple St., Saco, 3/31/78, C, 78000332

Sedgley, John, Homestead, N of York Corner on Chases Pond Rd., York Corner vicinity, 1/02/76, C, 76000192

Smith, James, Homestead, ME 35, Kennebunk, 2/04/82, A, C, 82001887

St. Joseph's School, Birch St., Biddleford, 12/29/83, A, C, a, 83003708

Staples Inn, 8 Portland Ave., Old Orchard Beach, 6/26/87, A, 86002422

Sunnycroft, Locust Hill, Limerick, 11/08/84, C, 84000335

Tarr, John, House, 29 Ferry Lane, Biddleford, 4/23/80, C, 80000263

Temple, The, Temple Ave. in Ocean Park, Old Orchard Beach, 4/28/75, A, C, 75000119

Thacher-Goodale House, 121 North St., Saco, 11/21/76, B, C, 76000193

U.S. Customhouse, Main St., Kennebunkport, 1/18/74, A, C, 74000323

U.S. Post Office, 35 Washington St., Biddleford, 5/07/73, A, C, 73000161

US Post Office—Sanford Main, 28 School St., Sanford, 5/02/86, C, 86000882

Wells Baptist Church Parsonage [Wells Township Cape Cod Houses TR], ME 9A, Wells vicinity, 12/27/79, A, C, a, 79000191

Wells Homestead [Wells Township Cape Cod Houses TR], Sanford Rd., Wells, 12/27/79, A, C, 79000193

West Lebanon Historic District, Irregular pattern along W. Lebanon, Rochester, Milton, Shapleigh and Meeting House Rds., West Lebanon, 6/05/75, C, 75000210

Whaleback Light Station [Light Stations of Maine MPS], Portsmouth Harbor, Kittery Point vicinity, 3/23/88, A, C, 87002278

Winn House [Wells Township Cape Cod Houses TR], King's Hwy., Ogunquit, 12/27/79, A, C, 79000194

Wood Island Light Station [Light Stations of Maine MPS], E side of Wood Island, Biddleford Pool vicinity, 1/21/88, A, C, 87002274

York Cliffs Historic District, Agamenticus Ave., York, 7/26/84, C, 84001560

York Historic District, Roughly U.S. 1, U.S. 1A, ME 103 and Woodbridge Rd., York, 7/16/73, A, C, 73000249

The Charles Berry House (ca. 1899) in the Rockland Residential Historic District is one of a collection of turn-of-the-century homes executed in Queen Anne and Revival styles by local architects. (R. Reed, 1986)

MARSHALL ISLANDS

Kwajalein Municipality

Kwajalein Island Battlefield, Kwajalein Missile Range, Kwajalein Atoll, 2/04/85, A, g, NHL, 85001757

Roi-Namur Battlefield, Kwajalein Missile Range, Kwajalein Atoll, 2/04/85, A, g, NHL, 85001758

Likiep Municipality

Debrum House, Likiep Island, Likiep Atoll, 9/30/76, A, C, 76002160

Majuro Municipality

Marshall Islands War Memorial Park, Kalap Island, Majuro Atoll, 9/30/76, A, g, 76002194

In 1944, U.S. Army troops captured Kwajalein Island, Marshall Islands, one of the first Japanese territories to fall in World War II. Designated a National Historic Landmark in 1985, the battlefield includes this monument commemorating a fallen comrade of the Seventh Infantry Division. (E.N. Thompson, 1983)

MARYLAND

Allegany County

16 Altamont Terrace, NE corner of Altamont Ter. and Union St., Cumberland, 7/07/75, A, C, 75000858

200–208 Decatur Street, 200, 202, 204, 206, 208 Decatur St., Cumberland, 7/07/75, C, 75000859

African Methodist Episcopal Church, Decatur and Frederick Sts., Cumberland, 4/20/79, A, C, a, 79001105

B'er Chayim Temple, Union and S. Centre Sts, Cumberland, 11/15/79, A, C, a, 79001106

Barton Village Site, Address Restricted, Cumberland vicinity, 5/12/75, D, 75000860

Bell Tower Building, Bedford and Liberty Sts., Cumberland, 2/20/73, A, C, 73000881

Big Bottom Farm, Hazen Rd., Cumberland vicinity, 6/07/84, C, 84001319

Borden Mines Superintendent's House, MD 36, Frostburg vicinity, 3/22/84, A, B, C, 84001322

Breakneck Road Historic District, W of Flintstone, Flintstone vicinity, 5/29/80, A, C, 80001777

Butler, Wright, House, 205 Columbia St., Cumberland, 1/31/78, C, 78001440

Canada Hose Company Building, 400–402 N. Mechanic St., Cumberland, 9/21/79, C, 79003257

Chesapeake and Ohio Canal National Historical Park, Bordering the Potomac River from Georgetown, D.C. to Cumberland, Maryland, Oldtown, 10/15/66, A, C, NPS, 66000036

City Hall, N. Center St. between Frederick and Bedford Sts., Cumberland, 2/27/73, A, C, 73000882

Cresap, Michael, House, Main St. at Green Spring Rd., Oldtown, 4/14/72, B, C, 72000563

Downtown Cumberland Historic District, Roughly bounded by Mechanic, Bedford, George, and Harrison Sts., Cumberland, 8/04/83, A, C, 83002917

First Baptist Church, 212 Bedford St., Cumberland, 11/10/80, A, C, a, 80001776

Frostburg Historic District, Western RR, Mt. Pleasant Terr., Main, Frost, Water, Broadway, Bealls, and Fairview Sts., Frostburg, 9/08/83, A, C, 83002918

Haley, Francis, House, 634 Maryland Ave., Cumberland, 7/08/82, B, C, 82002804

Hocking House, 144 E. Main St., Frostburg, 12/02/82, C, 82001579

Inns on the National Road, E and W of Cumberland on U.S. 40 from Flintstone to Grantsville (also in Garrett County), Cumberland vicinity, 12/22/76, A, 76000976

Koon, Thomas, House, 221 Baltimore Ave., Cumberland, 7/08/82, B, C, 82002805

La Vale Tollgate House, US 40, La Vale, 1/25/71, A, C, 71000363

Lonaconing Furnace, E. Main St., Lonaconing, 6/19/73, A, C, 73000886

Lonaconing Historic District, MD 36, MD 657, and Douglas Ave., Church, E. Main and Railroad Sts., Lonaconing, 9/15/83, A, C, 83002919

Mount Savage Historic District, Roughly bounded by Foundry Row, Jennings Run, New School Rd., Yellow Row, Cherry St., and Columbia Ave., Mount Savage, 9/08/83, A, 83004213

Old National Pike Milestones, MD 44 and 165, US 40, Alternate US 40, and Scenic US 40, Bellegrove vicinity, 11/27/75, A, 75002107

Phoenix Mill Farm, NE of Cumberland off MD 220, Cumberland vicinity, 8/12/77, A, C, 77000681

Public Safety Building, Frederick and Liberty Sts., Cumberland, 4/13/73, A, C, 73000883

Shaw Mansion, Laurel Run Rd., Barton, 6/19/85, C, a, 85001345

Shawnee Old Fields Village Site, Address Restricted, Oldtown vicinity, 5/12/75, B, D, NPS, 75000150

Town Clock Church, 312 Bedford St., Cumberland, 8/06/79, A, B, C, a, 79001107

Truog, George, House, 230 Baltimore Ave., Cumberland, 9/11/86, B, C, 86002382

Union Grove Schoolhouse, NE of Cumberland on Mason Rd., Cumberland vicinity, 7/24/79, A, 79001108

Washington Street Historic District, Washington St. from Wills Creek to mid 600 block, including Prospect Square, Cumberland, 2/06/73, A, C, 73000884

Waverly Street Bridge, Waverly St. at Georges Creek, Westernport, 9/07/84, C, 84001327

Western Maryland Railroad Right-of-Way, Milepost 126 to Milepost 160, Milepost 126 to Milepost 160, North Branch vicinity, 7/23/81, A, C, NPS, 81000078

Western Maryland Railway Station, Canal St., Cumberland, 6/19/73, A, 73000885

Anne Arundel County

Abington Farm, 1761 Severn Chapel Rd., Millersville vicinity, 9/13/84, C, 84001328

Aisquith Farm E Archeological Site [Prehistoric Human Adaptation to the Coastal Plain Environment of Anne Arundel County MPS], Address Restricted, Riva vicinity, 11/08/91, D, 91001601

All Hallows' Church, Jct. of MD 2, All Hallows' Church Rd., and South River Club Rd., Davidsonville vicinity, 5/15/69, A, C, a, 69000060

Anne Arundel County Free School, 1298 Lavall Dr., Gambrills, 6/16/83, A, 83002920

Artisan's House, 43 Pinckney St., Annapolis, 11/29/72, A, C, 72000564

Arundel Cove Archaeological Site, Address Restricted, Baltimore vicinity, 7/21/83, D, 83002921

Beck Northeast Site (18AN65), Address Restricted, Davidsonville vicinity, 1/02/86, D, 86000003

Belvoir, 0.5 mi. E of Crownsville on MD 178, Crownsville vicinity, 11/19/71, B, C, 71000366

Benson-Hammond House, Poplar Ave., Linthicum Heights vicinity, 4/05/90, C, 90000595

Brice House, 42 East St., Annapolis, 4/15/70, C, NHL, 70000259

Bunker Hill, MD 178 and Millersville Rd., Millersville vicinity, 10/11/84, B, C, 84000034

Burrages End, Nutwell Rd. off MD 2, Lothian vicinity, 4/11/73, C, 73000897

CHESAPEAKE BAY BROGAN MUSTANG, Dock St., Annapolis, 4/02/80, A, 80001778

Callahan, John, House, 164 Conduit St., Annapolis, 10/02/73, A, C, b, 73000888

Cedar Park, N of Galesville off Cumberstone Rd., Galesville vicinity, 5/15/69, A, B, C, a, 69000061

Chase-Lloyd House, 22 Maryland Ave., Annapolis, 4/15/70, C, NHL, 70000260

Childs Residence, 1003 Cecil Ave., Millersville, 3/06/86, A, B, C, 86000416

Christ Church, Owensville Rd. (MD 255), Owensville, 6/18/73, C, a, 73000898

Colonial Annapolis Historic District, District boundaries approximate city boundaries surveyed in 1695, Annapolis, 10/15/66, A, C, NHL, 66000383

Colonial Annapolis Historic District (Boundary Increase), Roughly bounded by Spa Creek, Southgate Ave., Hanover and West Sts., Annapolis, 9/29/84, A, C, 84003875

Creagh, Patrick, House, 160 Prince George St., Annapolis, 1/29/73, C, 73000889

Cross Roads Church, 911 Old General's Highway, Millersville vicinity, 2/10/83, C, b, 83002922

Davidsonville Historic District, Along MD 214 E to jct. with Davidsonville Rd., Davidsonville, 3/27/92, C, 92000141

Douglass Summer House, 3200 Wayman Ave., Highland Beach, 2/20/92, A, 92000069

Elkridge Site, Address Restricted, Elkridge vicinity, 5/22/78, D, 78001441

Evergreen, Sudley Rd., off MD 255, Owensville vicinity, 5/15/69, A, C, a, 69000066

Fort Nonsense, Address Restricted, Annapolis vicinity, 10/28/84, A, C, D, 84000408

Grassland, MD 32, Annapolis Junction vicinity, 9/13/84, A, C, 84001331

Gresham, 784 Mayo Rd., Edgewater, 9/07/84, B, 84001342

HELIANTHUS III (yacht), Hilton Inn dock, Annapolis, 8/09/84, C, 84001343

Hammond-Harwood House, Maryland Ave. and King George St., Annapolis, 10/15/66, C, NHL, 66000384

Hancock's Resolution, E of Pasadena on Bayside Beach Rd., Pasadena, 10/10/75, A, C, 75000865

Holly Hill, SE of Friendship off MD 631, Friendship, 10/26/71, A, C, a, 71000367

House by the "Town Gates", 63 West St., Annapolis, 6/19/73, C, 73000890

Iglehart, MD 178, Iglehart, 3/07/73, C, 73000896

Anne Arundel County—Continued

Indian Range, 1012 Mt. Airy Rd., Davidsonville, 2/13/86, C, 86000255

Katcef Archeological Site [Prehistoric Human Adaptation to the Coastal Plain Environment of Anne Arundel County MPS], Address Restricted, Crofton vicinity, 11/08/91, D, 91001600

Larkin's Hill Farm, Off MD 2 on Mill Swamp Rd., Harwood vicinity, 5/15/69, A, C, 69000062

Larkin's Hundred, NE of Harwood on Mill Swamp Rd., Harwood vicinity, 5/15/69, A, C, a, 69000063

Linthicum Walks, 2295 Davidsonville Rd., Crofton vicinity, 8/09/84, C, d, 84001344

London Town Publik House, NE of Woodland Beach at the end of Londontown Rd., Woodland Beach vicinity, 4/15/70, C, NHL, 70000262

Magothy Quartzite Quarry Archeological Site [Prehistoric Human Adaptation to the Coastal Plain Environment of Anne Arundel County MPS], Address Restricted, Pasadena vicinity, 11/08/91, D, 91001599

Martins Pond Site, Address Restricted, Annapolis vicinity, 6/05/75, D, 75000862

Mary's Mount, NE of Harwood off Mill Swamp Rd., Harwood vicinity, 5/15/69, C, 69000064

Maryland Statehouse, State Circle, Annapolis, 10/15/66, A, NHL, 66000385

Mount Airy, Mount Airy Rd. off MD 424, Davidsonville, 4/13/73, A, C, 73000894

Mt. Moriah African Methodist Episcopal Church, 84 Franklin St., Annapolis, 1/25/73, A, C, a, 73000891

Norman's Retreat, 5325 Muddy Creek Rd., Galesville vicinity, 9/07/84, C, 84001345

OLIVER'S GIFT (log canoe) [Chesapeake Bay Sailing Log Canoe Fleet TR], 3473 Ranger Rd., Davidsonville vicinity, 9/18/85, A, C, g, 85002247

Obligation, 1.8 mi. N of Harwood off MD 2, Harwood vicinity, 5/15/69, C, 69000065

Old City Hall and Engine House, 211–213 Main St., Annapolis, 1/29/73, A, C, 73000892

Old Colony Cove Site, Address Restricted, Rose Haven vicinity, 11/21/78, D, 78001442

Owens, James, Farm, 5682 Greenock Rd., Bristol vicinity, 9/21/87, A, C, 87001566

Paca House and Garden, 186 Prince George St., Annapolis, 11/11/71, B, C, NHL, 71000364

Peggy Stewart House, 207 Hanover St., Annapolis, 11/07/73, B, NHL, 73000887

Pinkney-Callahan House, 5 St. John's St., Annapolis, 11/12/71, C, b, 71000365

Rising Sun Inn, 1090 Generals' Hwy., Millersville vicinity, 9/12/85, C, 85002199

Rosehill, 2403 Bell Branch Rd., Gambrills vicinity, 5/29/87, C, 87000852

Sandy Point Farmhouse, Sandy Point State Park, Sandy Point, 2/11/72, A, C, 72000566

Scott, Upton, House, 4 Shipwright St., Annapolis, 6/05/75, B, C, 75000863

South River Club, W of South River on South River Club Rd., South River vicinity, 5/15/69, A, C, 69000067

St. James Church, 3 mi. E of Bristol on MD 2, Bristol vicinity, 5/07/72, B, C, a, 72000565

St. Paul's Chapel, MD 178, Crownsville, 3/20/73, A, C, a, 73000893

Stanton Center, 92 W. Washington St., Annapolis, 12/01/83, A, C, 83003627

Sudley, N of Deale off MD 468 on Old Sudley Rd., Deale vicinity, 6/18/73, B, C, a, 73000895

Summer Hill, E of Davidsonville off MD 214, Davidsonville vicinity, 7/25/74, C, 74000940

Sunnyfields, 825 Hammonds Lane, Linthicum Heights, 8/11/83, C, 83002923

Thomas Point Shoals Light Station, Kent Island, Chesapeake Bay, Annapolis, 2/20/75, A, C, 75000864

Tracy's Landing Tobacco House No. 2, Off MD 2, Tracy's Landing vicinity, 11/30/82, C, 82001580

Tulip Hill, About 2.5 mi. W of Galesville on Owensville Rd., Galesville vicinity, 4/15/70, C, NHL, 70000261

Turkey Hill, 106 W. Maple Rd., Linthicum Heights, 7/24/79, B, C, 79001109

Twin Oaks, 421 Twin Oaks Rd., Linthicum Heights, 3/21/86, B, C, 86000670

U.S. Coast Guard Yard Curtis Bay, Off MD 173, Baltimore vicinity, 8/05/83, A, C, g, 83002924

U.S. Naval Academy, Maryland Ave. and Hanover St., Annapolis, 10/15/66, A, C, NHL, 66000386

Whitehall, Off St. Margaret's Rd., Annapolis, 10/15/66, C, NHL, 66000387

Baltimore County

Auburn House, Osler Dr. between Towsontown Blvd. and Stevenson Lane, Towson, 3/17/75, C, 75000869

Ballestone Mansion, E of Essex on Back River Neck Rd. in Rocky Point Park, Essex vicinity, 6/18/75, C, 75000866

Baltimore County Courthouse, Washington Ave. between Pennsylvania and Chesapeake Aves., Towson, 10/27/72, C, 72000569

Bare Hills House, N of Baltimore at 6222 Falls Rd., Baltimore vicinity, 8/06/80, B, C, 80001793

Brooklandville House, S of Brooklandville at Falls and Hillside Rds., Brooklandville vicinity, 11/23/77, A, C, 77000682

Brooklandwood, Falls Rd., Brooklandville, 2/11/72, B, C, 72000567

Caves Valley Historic District, Caves and Garrison Forest Rds., and Park Heights Ave., Owings Mills vicinity, 10/20/88, A, C, 88001859

Choate House, 9600 Liberty, Randallstown vicinity, 7/20/89, C, 89000807

Cloisters, The, W of Lutherville at 10440 Falls Rd., Lutherville vicinity, 8/07/79, A, C, g, 79001115

Corbett Historic District, 1615–1827 Corbett Rd. & 16200–16225 Corbett Village Ln., Monkton vicinity, 9/12/85, A, C, 85002245

Dundalk Historic District, Roughly bounded by Liberty Pkwy., Dunman, Willow Spring and Sunship Rds., Chesapeake and Patapsco Aves., Dundalk, 12/08/83, A, C, 83003630

Eagle's Nest, Jarrettsville Pike, Phoenix, 7/25/74, C, 74000942

Ellicott's Mills Historic District, Both sides of MD 144, S of Patapsco River Bridge, Oella vicinity, 11/19/76, B, 76000980

Fort Garrison, S of Stevenson at Garrison Farms Ct., Stevenson vicinity, 1/25/71, A, C, 71000368

Glencoe, 1314 Glencoe Rd., Glencoe, 5/09/83, A, C, 83002942

Glyndon Historic District, Town of Glyndon and its environs along MD 128, Glyndon and vicinity, 9/20/73, A, C, a, 73000902

Green Spring Valley Historic District, MD 25 and MD 140, Stevenson and vicinity, 10/03/80, A, C, 80001797

Half-Way House, 1.3 mi. S. of Parkton at 18200 York Rd., Parkton vicinity, 9/08/80, A, 80001795

Half-Way House (Boundary Increase), York Rd. and Weisburg Rd., Parkton vicinity, 7/12/89, A, 89000809

Hampton National Historic Site, Hampton Lane, N off I-495, Towson, 10/15/66, A, B, C, NPS, 66000389

Hill House, 19301 York Rd., Parkton, 3/06/86, C, 86000415

Hilton, 800 S. Rolling Rd., Catonsville, 10/31/80, C, 80001794

Hull Memorial Christian Church, 101 Clyde Ave., Lansdowne, 9/15/77, A, a, f, 77000684

Jericho Covered Bridge, E of Kingsville on Franklinville Rd., Kingsville vicinity, 9/13/78, A, C, 78001444

Jericho Farm, 12230 Jericho Rd., Kingsville vicinity, 9/07/84, A, C, 84001352

Lake Roland Historic District, Robert E. Lee Memorial Park, Baltimore (Independent City) vicinity, 10/15/92, A, C, 92001285

Long Green Valley Historic District, Glen Arm, Baldwin Mill, Manor, and Hartford Rds. areas, Baldwin, 12/30/82, A, C, 82001589

Lorraine Park Cemetery Gate Lodge, 5608 Dogwood Rd., Woodlawn vicinity, 7/25/85, A, C, 85001613

Lutherville Historic District, Roughly bounded by I 695, York and Ridgely Rds., and Lutherville Dr., Lutherville, 11/09/72, A, C, 72000568

Meadows, The, 302 Meadows Ln., Owings Mill, 3/23/88, B, 88000203

Mettam Memorial Baptist Church, Old Court Rd. between Sudbrook and Reisterstown Rds., Pikesville, 4/24/75, A, a, 75000867

Montrose Mansion and Chapel, 13700 Hanover Rd., Reisterstown, 3/19/90, C, a, 90000354

Mount de Sales Academy, 700 Academy Rd., Catonsville, 5/30/86, A, C, a, 86001187

Mt. Gilboa Chapel, Oella and Westchester Aves., Oella, 10/21/76, B, C, a, 76000978

My Lady's Manor, MD 138, Monkton and vicinity, 4/15/78, A, C, 78001445

Oella Historic District, Oella Ave., Glen Rd., Hollow Rd., Oella, 11/07/76, A, 76000979

Old Catonsville High School, 20 Winters Ln., Catonsville, 9/10/87, A, 87001568

Old Salem Church and Cemetery, Ingleside Ave. and Calverton St., Catonsville, 12/13/77, A, C, a, 77000683

Baltimore County—Continued

Owings Upper Mill, Bonita Ave. and Reisterstown Rd., Owings Mills, 9/13/78, A, 78001446

Parkton Hotel, York Rd., Parkton, 12/08/83, A, C, 83003634

Patterson Viaduct Ruins, S of Catonsville at Patapsco River, Catonsville vicinity, 6/03/76, A, C, 76002221

Perry Hall, N of Perry Hall on Perry Hall Rd., Perry Hall vicinity, 4/23/80, B, C, 80001796

Pikesville Armory [Maryland National Guard Armories TR], 610 Reisterstown Rd., Pikesville, 9/25/85, A, C, 85002674

Plinlimmon Farm, 9401 Lyons Mill Rd., Owings Mills vicinity, 5/19/83, C, 83002943

Prospect Hill, NE of Long Green on Kane's Rd., Long Green vicinity, 7/26/73, A, C, 73000903

Ravenshurst, 12915 Dulaney Valley Rd., Glen Arm vicinity, 8/14/78, B, C, 78001443

Reisterstown Historic District, U.S. 140 and MD 30, Reisterstown, 11/15/79, A, C, 79001118

Rockland, 10214 Falls Rd., Brooklandville vicinity, 2/02/83, B, C, 83002944

Rockland Historic District, Both sides of Falls Rd. (MD 25) at jct. of Old Court Rd. (MD 133), Brooklandville, 4/11/73, A, C, 73000899

Sheppard and Enoch Pratt Hospital and Gatehouse, Charles St., Towson, 11/11/71, C, NHL, 71000369

St. Charles College Historic District, 711 Maiden Choice Lane, Catonsville, 9/30/83, A, C, a, 83002945

St. Charles College Historic District (Boundary Increase), 711 Maiden Choice La., Catonsville, 12/29/87, A, a, 87002181

St. James Church, SE of Monkton off Manor Rd., Monkton vicinity, 9/12/74, A, C, a, 74000941

St. John's Church, 7538 Bellona Ave., Ruxton, 3/15/82, A, C, a, 82002807

St. Mary's Episcopal Church/Woodlawn, 5610 Dogwood Rd., Woodlawn vicinity, 3/14/85, C, a, 85000583

St. Michael's Church, Academy Lane and Reisterstown Rd., Reisterstown, 10/22/79, A, C, a, 79003273

St. Thomas Church, St. Thomas Lane and Garrison Forest Rd., Owings Mills, 5/24/79, C, a, 79001117

Stone Hall, N of Cockeysville off MD 25 on Cuba Rd., Cockeysville vicinity, 7/26/73, A, C, 73000900

Sudbrook Park, S of Pikesville off U.S. 40 on Greenwood Rd., Pikesville vicinity, 6/19/73, C, 73000904

Summit, 10 Stanley Dr., Catonsville, 7/24/79, B, C, 79001114

The Wilderness, 2 Thistle Rd., Catonsville vicinity, 9/12/85, B, C, 85002173

Thomas Viaduct, Baltimore & Ohio Railroad, Over the Patapsco River between Relay and Elkridge, Relay, 10/15/66, A, C, NHL, 66000388

Todd Farmhouse, 9000 Old North Point Rd. (MD 20), Fort Howard, 10/18/73, A, C, d, 73000901

Towson Academy [Maryland National Guard Armories TR], Washington St. & Chesapeake Ave., Towson, 9/25/85, A, C, 85002675

Tyrconnell, 120 Woodbrook Lane, Baltimore vicinity, 3/14/85, C, 85000582

Villa Anneslie, 529 Dunkirk Rd., Towson, 12/13/77, A, C, 77000685

Wester Ogle, 8948-8950 Reisterstown Rd., Pikesville vicinity, 1/11/85, C, 85000058

Western Run-Belfast Road Historic District, NW of Lutherville, Lutherville, 1/23/79, C, b, 79001116

Worthington Valley Historic District, Bounded by Falls and Shawan Rds., Tufton and Worthington Aves., and the Baltimore Gas and Electric Right-of-Way, Glyndon vicinity, 12/12/76, A, C, 76000977

Baltimore Independent City

Alcott, Louisa May, School, 2702 Keyworth Ave., Baltimore (Independent City), 3/29/90, A, 90000544

American Brewery, 1701 N. Gay St., Baltimore (Independent City), 5/09/73, A, 73002179

BALTIMORE (tug), 1415 Key Hwy., Baltimore (Independent City), 11/04/93, A, C, NHL, 93001613

BANCROFT (motor vessel), Fell's Point, Baltimore (Independent City), 3/27/80, A, 80001780

Bachrach, David, House, 2406–2408 Linden Ave., Baltimore (Independent City), 9/05/85, B, 85001947

Baltimore City College, 530 N. Howard St., Baltimore (Independent City), 8/11/83, B, C, 83002925

Baltimore City Hall, 100 N. Holliday St., Baltimore (Independent City), 5/08/73, A, C, 73002180

Baltimore College of Dental Surgery, 429–433 N. Eutaw St., Baltimore (Independent City), 5/08/87, A, C, 87000697

Baltimore Equitable Society, 21 N. Eutaw St., Baltimore (Independent City), 10/06/77, A, C, 77001528

Baltimore General Dispensary, 500 W. Fayette St., Baltimore (Independent City), 3/18/80, A, 80001779

Baltimore Hebrew Congregation Synagogue, 1901 Madison Ave., Baltimore (Independent City), 11/07/76, A, C, a, 76002181

Baltimore and Ohio Transportation Museum and Mount Clare Station, Pratt and Poppleton Sts., Baltimore (Independent City), 10/15/66, A, NHL, 66000906

Bankard-Gunther Mansion, 2102 E. Baltimore St., Baltimore (Independent City), 8/06/80, B, C, 80001781

Barre Circle Historic District, Roughly bounded by Scott, Ramsey, Boyd, and Harbor City-Blvdd.-S. Fremont Sts., Baltimore (Independent City), 1/10/83, A, C, 83002926

Battle Monument, Calvert St. between Fayette and Lexington Sts., Baltimore (Independent City), 6/04/73, C, f, 73002181

Belvedere Hotel, 1 E. Chase St., Baltimore (Independent City), 8/29/77, A, C, 77001529

Benson Building, 4 E. Franklin St., Baltimore (Independent City), 3/26/80, A, C, 80001782

Bolton Hill Historic District, Roughly bounded by North Ave., Eutaw Pl., and the Pennsylvania RR tracks, Baltimore (Independent City), 9/17/71, B, C, 71001031

Brewers Exchange, 20 Park Ave., Baltimore (Independent City), 3/28/85, A, C, 85000652

Brick Hill, Seneca St., Oakington St., Parkden Ave., Baltimore (Independent City), 7/01/88, A, g, 88000743

Brown's Arcade, 322-328 N. Charles St., Baltimore (Independent City), 1/17/83, A, C, 83002927

Brown, Alex, Building, 135 E. Baltimore St., Baltimore (Independent City), 12/02/82, A, C, g, 82001581

Buildings at 10, 12, 14, and 16 East Chase Street, 10, 12, 14, and 16 E. Chase St., Baltimore (Independent City), 3/10/80, C, 80001783

Buildings at 1601-1830 St. Paul Street and 12-20 E. Lafayette Street, 1601-1830 St. Paul St., and 12-20 E Lafayette St., Baltimore (Independent City), 12/27/84, A, C, 84000502

Business and Government Historic District, Roughly bounded by Saratoga St., City Blvd., Water, Lombard, & Charles St., Baltimore (Independent City), 11/25/87, A, C, g, 87002065

Butchers Hill Historic District, Roughly Bounded by Patterson Park Ave., Fayette, Pratt, Chapel, Washington, and Chester Sts., Baltimore (Independent City), 12/28/82, A, C, a, 82001582

CHESAPEAKE (lightship), Inner Harbor, Baltimore (Independent City), 8/01/80, A, C, b, g, NHL, NPS, 80000349

Canton Historic District, Eastern Ave., Waterfront, Conklin and Chester Sts., Baltimore (Independent City), 1/29/80, A, C, 80001784

Canton House, 300 Water St., Baltimore (Independent City), 12/13/78, A, C, 78003140

Carroll Mansion, 800 E. Lombard St., Baltimore (Independent City), 5/25/73, B, C, 73002182

Carrollton Viaduct, Gwynn's Falls near Carroll Park, Baltimore (Independent City), 11/11/71, A, C, NHL, 71001032

Cathedral Hill Historic District, Roughly bounded by Hamilton, Saint Paul, Charles, Saratoga and Cathedral Sts., Baltimore (Independent City), 4/27/87, A, C, a, g, 87000622

Chamber of Commerce Building, 17 Commerce St., Baltimore (Independent City), 2/02/83, A, C, 83002929

Charlcote House, 15 Charlcote Pl., Baltimore (Independent City), 10/17/88, C, 88001858

Charles Village-Abell Historic District, Roughly bounded by University Pkwy., Guilford Ave., and 25th, Mace, Charles, and Barclay Sts., Baltimore (Independent City), 12/15/83, A, B, C, 83003629

Chizuk Amuno Synagogue, 27–35 Lloyd St., Baltimore (Independent City), 4/19/78, A, C, a, 78003141

Clifton Park Valve House, 2801 Harford Rd., Baltimore (Independent City), 2/18/71, C, 71001034

Clifton School, 2670 Kennedy Ave., Baltimore (Independent City), 12/16/82, A, 82001583

Baltimore Independent City—Continued

Continental Trust Company Building, 1 S. Calvert St., Baltimore (Independent City), 2/03/83, A, 83002930

Cummins Memorial Church, 1210 W. Lanvale St., Baltimore (Independent City), 10/31/79, A, B, C, a, 79003215

Cylburn House and Park District, 4915 Green Spring Ave., Baltimore (Independent City), 5/04/72, C, 72001493

Davidge Hall, University of Maryland, 522 W. Lombard St., Baltimore (Independent City), 4/24/74, A, C, 74002212

Dickeyville Historic District, Both sides of Forest Park Ave. in Gwynn's Falls area, Baltimore (Independent City), 7/12/72, A, C, 72001494

Dorguth Memorial United Methodist Church, Scott and Carroll St., Baltimore (Independent City), 8/14/79, A, C, a, 79003216

Douglass Place, 516-524 S. Dallas St., Baltimore (Independent City), 9/15/83, B, 83004214

Douglass, Frederick, High School, 1601 N. Calhoun St., Baltimore (Independent City), 5/18/89, A, g, 89000412

Druid Hill Park Historic District, Druid Hill Park, Baltimore (Independent City), 5/22/73, A, C, 73002183

Eastern Female High School, 249 Aisquith St., Baltimore (Independent City), 9/10/71, A, B, C, 71001035

Emerson Bromo-Seltzer Tower, 312–318 Lombard St., Baltimore (Independent City), 6/04/73, B, C, 73002184

Engine House No. 6, 416 N. Gay St., Baltimore (Independent City), 6/18/73, A, C, 73002185

Erlanger Buildings, 519-531 W. Pratt St., Baltimore (Independent City), 3/10/80, A, C, 80001785

Eutaw-Madison Apartment House Historic District, 2502 and 2525 Eutaw Pl., and 2601 Madison Ave., Baltimore (Independent City), 5/12/83, A, C, 83002931

Evergreen House, 4545 N. Charles St., Baltimore (Independent City), 1/17/83, A, C, g, 83002932

Evergreen on the Falls, 3300 Falls Rd., Baltimore (Independent City), 7/30/75, B, C, 75002095

Federal Hill Historic District, Bounded by Baltimore Harbor, Hughes, Hanover, and Cross Sts., Baltimore (Independent City), 4/17/70, A, C, 70000859

Federal Reserve Bank of Richmond, Baltimore Branch, 114 E. Lexington St., Baltimore (Independent City), 1/27/83, C, 83002933

Fells Point Historic District, Bounded on the N by Aliceanna St., on the E by Wolfe St., on the S by the Harbor, and on the W by Dallas St., Baltimore (Independent City), 3/28/69, A, C, 69000319

Fells Point Historic District (Boundary Increase), Roughly bounded by Cough St., Chester St. and Fells Pt., N.W. Harbor, and Wills and Dallas and Edens Sts., Baltimore (Independent City), 7/14/86, A, C, 86003777

Fifth Regiment Armory [Maryland National Guard Armories TR], 210–247 W. Hoffman St., Baltimore (Independent City), 9/25/85, A, C, 85002671

First Church of Christ, Scientist, 102 W. University Pky., Baltimore (Independent City), 12/27/82, C, a, 82001584

First Presbyterian Church and Manse, 200–210 W. Madison St., Baltimore (Independent City), 6/18/73, C, a, 73002186

First Unitarian Church, 2–12 W. Franklin St., Baltimore (Independent City), 2/11/72, C, a, NHL, 72001495

Flag House, 844 E. Pratt St., Baltimore (Independent City), 12/03/69, A, NHL, 69000320

Fort McHenry National Monument and Historic Shrine, Locust Point, at E end of Fort Ave., Baltimore (Independent City), 10/15/66, A, C, NPS, 66000907

Franklin Square Historic District, Bounded by Mulberry, N. Carey, W. Baltimore, and Monroe Sts., Baltimore (Independent City), 12/10/82, A, C, 82001585

Franklin Street Presbyterian Church and Parsonage, 100 W. Franklin St. (church), 504 Cathedral St. (parsonage), Baltimore (Independent City), 11/05/71, A, C, a, 71001036

Gallagher Mansion and Outbuilding, 431-435 Notre Dame Lane, Baltimore (Independent City), 9/15/83, B, C, 83002934

Gandy Belting Company Building, 726-734 W. Pratt St., Baltimore (Independent City), 10/25/84, A, 84000085

Garrett Building, 233-239 Redwood St., Baltimore (Independent City), 12/16/82, B, C, 82001586

Gompers School, 1701 East North Ave., Baltimore (Independent City), 6/20/85, A, C, 85001272

Green Mount Cemetery, Bounded by North and Greenmount Aves., Ensor and Hoffman Sts., Baltimore (Independent City), 4/02/80, C, d, 80001786

Heiser, Rosenfeld, and Strauss Buildings, 32-42 S. Paca St., Baltimore (Independent City), 3/10/80, A, C, 80001787

Homewood, N. Charles and 34th Sts., Baltimore (Independent City), 9/10/71, B, C, NHL, 71001033

Hooper, James E., House, 100 E. 23rd St., Baltimore (Independent City), 3/15/82, A, B, C, 82004746

House at 9 North Front Street, 9 N. Front St., Baltimore (Independent City), 6/14/79, B, C, 79003217

Howard Street Tunnel, Beneath Howard St. from Mt. Royal Station to Camden Station, Baltimore (Independent City), 7/02/73, A, C, 73002187

Hutzler Brothers Palace Building, 210-218 N. Howard St., Baltimore (Independent City), 6/07/84, A, C, 84001348

Industrial Building, 501 E. Preston St., Baltimore (Independent City), 3/10/80, A, C, 80001788

Johns Hopkins Hospital Complex, 601 N. Broadway, Baltimore (Independent City), 2/24/75, A, C, 75002094

Kernan, James Lawrence, Hospital, Windsor Mill Rd. and Forest Park Ave., Baltimore (Independent City), 9/24/79, A, B, C, 79003275

Krug Iron Works, 415 W. Saratoga St., Baltimore (Independent City), 4/29/82, A, 82004747

Leadenhall Street Baptist Church, 1021–1023 Leadenhall St., Baltimore (Independent City), 3/16/79, A, C, a, 79003218

Little Montgomery Street Historic District, West Montgomery and Leadenhall Sts., Baltimore (Independent City), 4/15/82, A, C, 82004748

Lloyd Street Synagogue, 11 Lloyd St., Baltimore (Independent City), 4/19/78, A, C, a, 78003142

Loft Historic District North, Roughly bounded by Paca, Redwood, Eutaw, and Lombard Sts., Baltimore (Independent City), 1/03/85, A, C, 85000016

Loft Historic District South, Along 500 Blk. W. Pratt St. bounded by Green St. and 100 Blk. S. Paca St., Baltimore (Independent City), 1/03/85, A, C, 85000017

Lombard Street Bridge, Over Gwynns Falls off Wetheredsville Rd., Baltimore (Independent City), 9/27/72, A, C, b, 75002093

Londontown Manufacturing Company, Inc., 3600 Clipper Mill Rd., Baltimore (Independent City), 1/12/73, A, 73002188

Lord Baltimore Hotel, 20 West St., Baltimore (Independent City), 12/02/82, A, C, 82001587

Lovely Lane Methodist Church, 2200 St. Paul St., Baltimore (Independent City), 5/25/73, A, B, C, a, 73002189

Lyric Theatre, 124 W. Mt. Royal Ave., Baltimore (Independent City), 1/23/86, A, C, 86000131

Madison Avenue Methodist Episcopal Church, 1327 Madison Ave., Baltimore (Independent City), 9/04/92, C, a, 92001153

McCollum, Elmer V., House, 2301 Monticello Rd., Baltimore (Independent City), 1/07/76, B, g, NHL, 76002182

McKim's School, 1120 E. Baltimore St., Baltimore (Independent City), 3/30/73, A, C, 73002190

Mencken, H. L., House, 1524 Hollins Rd., Baltimore (Independent City), 7/28/83, B, g, NHL, 83004384

Mercantile Trust and Deposit Company, 202 E. Redwood St., Baltimore (Independent City), 3/17/83, A, C, 83002935

Mother Seton House, 600 N. Paca St., Baltimore (Independent City), 6/13/72, B, C, a, 72001496

Mount Clare, Carroll Park, Baltimore (Independent City), 4/15/70, C, NHL, 70000860

Mount Royal Station, 1400 Cathedral St., Baltimore (Independent City), 6/18/73, A, C, NHL, 73002191

Mount Vernon Place Historic District, Mount Vernon Pl. and Washington Pl., Baltimore (Independent City), 11/11/71, C, f, NHL, 71001037

Mount Vernon Place United Methodist Church and Asbury House, 2–10 E. Mount Vernon Place, Baltimore (Independent City), 9/17/71, C, a, 71001038

Mount Washington Mill, 1330–1340 Smith Avenue, Baltimore (Independent City), 5/04/90, A, 90000727

NOBSKA (steamship), Inner harbor, Baltimore (Independent City), 5/02/74, A, C, b, 74002216

Null House, 1037 Hillen St., Baltimore (Independent City), 1/27/83, C, b, 83002936

Baltimore Independent City—Continued

Odd Fellows Hall, 300 Cathedral St., Baltimore (Independent City), 3/25/80, A, C, 80001789

Old Goucher College Buildings, Roughly bounded by 24th, N. Calvert, and 23rd Sts., and Maryland Ave., Baltimore (Independent City), 8/25/78, A, C, 78003143

Old Pine Street Station, 214 N. Pine St., Baltimore (Independent City), 1/03/85, A, C, 85000018

Old Roman Catholic Cathedral, 401 Cathedral St., Baltimore (Independent City), 10/01/69, A, C, a, NHL, 69000330

Old Town Friends' Meetinghouse, 1201 E. Fayette St., Baltimore (Independent City), 3/30/73, A, C, a, 73002192

Orchard Street United Methodist Church, 510 Orchard St., Baltimore (Independent City), 11/12/75, A, C, a, 75002096

Otterbein Church, 112 W. Conway St., Baltimore (Independent City), 10/28/69, A, B, C, a, 69000324

Paca Street Firehouse, 106 N. Paca St., Baltimore (Independent City), 10/28/83, A, B, C, 83003631

Pascault Row, 651–665 W. Lexington St., Baltimore (Independent City), 1/29/73, B, C, 73002193

Peale's Baltimore Museum, 225 N. Holliday St., Baltimore (Independent City), 10/15/66, A, NHL, 66000915

Pennsylvania Station, 1525 N. Charles St., Baltimore (Independent City), 9/12/75, A, C, 75002097

Perkins Square Gazebo, George St. and Myrtle Ave., Baltimore (Independent City), 7/28/83, A, C, 83002937

Poe, Edgar Allan, House, 203 Amity St., Baltimore (Independent City), 11/11/71, B, NHL, 71001043

Poole and Hunt Company Buildings, 3500 Clipper Rd., Baltimore (Independent City), 7/02/73, A, B, C, 73002194

Poppleton Fire Station, 756-760 W. Baltimore St., Baltimore (Independent City), 9/08/83, A, C, 83002938

Pratt Street Power Plant, 601 E. Pratt St., Baltimore (Independent City), 4/09/87, A, C, 87000564

President Street Station, Jct. of President and Fleet Sts., Baltimore (Independent City), 9/10/92, A, 92001229

Public School No. 109, N. Broadway and Ashland Ave., Baltimore (Independent City), 9/25/79, A, C, 79001110

Public School No. 111, N. Carrollton Ave. and Riggs Rd., Baltimore (Independent City), 9/25/79, A, C, 79003219

Public School No. 25, S. Bond St., Baltimore (Independent City), 9/25/79, A, C, 79001111

Public School No. 37, E. Biddle St. and N. Patterson Park Ave., Baltimore (Independent City), 9/25/79, A, C, 79001112

Public School No. 99, E. North Ave. and N. Washington St., Baltimore (Independent City), 9/25/79, A, C, 79001113

Remsen, Ira, House, 214 Monument St., Baltimore (Independent City), 5/15/75, B, NHL, 75002102

Ridgely's Delight Historic District, Roughly bounded by S. Fremont Ave., W. Pratt, Conway and Russell Sts., Baltimore (Independent City), 6/06/80, A, C, 80001790

Rieman Block, 617-631 W. Lexington St., Baltimore (Independent City), 6/07/84, A, C, 84001350

Roland Park Historic District, Irregular pattern between Belvedere Ave., Falls Rd., 39th St., and Stoney Run, Baltimore (Independent City), 12/23/74, A, C, 74002213

Rowhouses at 303-327 East North Avenue, 303-327 E. North Ave., Baltimore (Independent City), 9/13/84, C, 84001351

Rowland, Henry August, House, 915 Cathedral St., Baltimore (Independent City), 5/15/75, B, NHL, 75002098

School No. 27 (Commodore John Rodgers Elementary School), 2031 E. Fayette St., Baltimore (Independent City), 3/21/86, A, C, 86000613

Schuler, Hans, Studio and Residence, 5 East Lafayette Ave., Baltimore (Independent City), 9/27/85, B, C, 85002510

Schwartze Mansion, 4206 Euclid Ave., Baltimore (Independent City), 9/12/85, A, B, C, 85002174

Senator Theatre, 5904–5906 York Rd., Baltimore (Independent City), 8/24/89, C, 89001153

Seton Hill Historic District, Bounded by Pennsylvania Ave., Franklin, Eutaw, McCulloh, and Orchard Sts., Baltimore (Independent City), 7/30/75, A, C, a, 75002099

Seven-Foot Knoll Lighthouse, Pier 5, Inner Harbor, Baltimore (Independent City), 8/22/89, C, b, 89001096

Sharp Street Memorial United Methodist Church and Community House, 508–516 Dolphin St. & 1206–1210 Etting St., Baltimore (Independent City), 7/21/82, A, C, a, 82004749

Shot Tower, SE corner of Fayette and Front Sts., Baltimore (Independent City), 10/01/69, C, NHL, 69000373

Sonneborn Building, 110 S. Paca St., Baltimore (Independent City), 10/29/82, A, C, 82001588

St. Alphonsus' Church, Rectory, Convent and Halle, 112–116, 125–127 W. Saratoga St., Baltimore (Independent City), 5/23/73, A, C, a, 73002195

St. James the Less Roman Catholic Church, Aisquith St. at Eager St., Baltimore (Independent City), 3/15/82, C, a, 82004750

St. John the Evangelical Roman Catholic Church, 901 E. Eager St., Baltimore (Independent City), 3/15/82, C, a, 82004751

St. John's Protestant Episcopal Church, 3009 Greenmount Ave., Baltimore (Independent City), 3/27/74, A, C, a, 74002214

St. Leo's Church, 221 S. Exeter St., Baltimore (Independent City), 7/28/83, A, C, a, 83002939

St. Luke's Church, 217 N. Carey St., Baltimore (Independent City), 3/30/73, A, C, a, 73002196

St. Mary's Seminary Chapel, 600 N. Paca St., Baltimore (Independent City), 11/11/71, A, C, a, NHL, 71001046

St. Michael's Church Complex, 1900–1920 E. Lombard St., Baltimore (Independent City), 5/17/89, A, a, 89000383

St. Paul's Cemetery, Redwood St. and Martin Luther King Blvd., Baltimore (Independent City), 6/30/88, A, C, d, 88000746

St. Paul's Church Rectory, 24 W. Saratoga St., Baltimore (Independent City), 3/20/73, A, C, a, 73002197

St. Paul's Protestant Episcopal Church, 233 N. Charles St., Baltimore (Independent City), 3/30/73, C, a, 73002198

St. Peter the Apostle Church and Buildings, 11 and 13 S. Poppleton St. and 848 Hollins St., Baltimore (Independent City), 10/14/76, A, C, a, 76002184

St. Vincent De Paul Roman Catholic Church, 120 N. Front St., Baltimore (Independent City), 2/12/74, A, C, a, 74002215

Swiss Steam Laundry Building, 100–102 N. Greene St., Baltimore (Independent City), 6/20/85, A, C, 85001271

Taylor's Chapel, 6001 Hillen Rd., Mount Pleasant Park, Baltimore (Independent City), 7/28/83, C, a, 83002940

Terminal Warehouse, 211 E. Pleasant St., Baltimore (Independent City), 11/14/78, A, C, 78003144

Tivoli, 1301 Woodbourne Ave., Baltimore (Independent City), 10/09/80, B, C, 80001791

U.S. Custom House, 40 S. Gay St., Baltimore (Independent City), 2/15/74, A, C, 74002217

U.S. Post Office and Courthouse, 111 N. Calvert St., Baltimore (Independent City), 3/25/77, C, g, 77001530

U.S.S. CONSTELLATION, Pier 1, Pratt St., Baltimore (Independent City), 10/15/66, A, NHL, 66000918

USCGC TANEY (WHEC-37), 1101 Key Hwy., Baltimore (Independent City), 6/07/88, A, g, NHL, 88001826

USS TORSK (submarine), Pier IV, Pratt St., Baltimore (Independent City), 1/14/86, A, g, NHL, 86000090

Union Square-Hollins Market Historic District, Roughly bounded by Fulton, Fayette, Pratt and Schroeder Sts., Baltimore (Independent City), 9/15/83, A, C, 83002941

Walters Bath No. 2, 900 Washington Blvd., Baltimore (Independent City), 6/19/79, A, 79003220

Weiskittel-Roehle Burial Vault, Section P, Loudon Park Cemetery, Baltimore (Independent City), 5/19/76, A, C, d, 76002185

Welch, William H., House, 935 St. Paul St., Baltimore (Independent City), 1/07/76, B, NHL, 76002186

Westminster Presbyterian Church and Cemetery, 509 W. Fayette St., Baltimore (Independent City), 9/17/74, A, C, a, d, 74002218

Wilkens-Robins Building, 308–312 W. Pratt St., Baltimore (Independent City), 12/03/80, A, C, 80001792

Woman's Industrial Exchange, 333 N. Charles St., Baltimore (Independent City), 12/19/78, A, C, 78003145

Baltimore Independent City—Continued

Young Men's and Young Women's Hebrew Association Building, 305–311 W. Monument St., Baltimore (Independent City), 11/14/85, A, C, 85002836

Calvert County

All Saints' Church, 3.4 mi. E of Lower Marlboro on MD 416, Lower Marlboro vicinity, 3/14/73, A, C, a, 73000908

Cedar Hill, 2 mi. W of Barstow on Buena Vista Rd., Barstow vicinity, 5/22/73, C, 73000905

Chesapeake Beach Railway Station, 8005 Bayside Rd., Chesapeake Beach, 9/11/80, A, 80001798

Christ Church, SW of Port Republic on Broome Island Rd., Port Republic vicinity, 11/12/75, A, C, a, 75000871

Cornehill, Emmanuel Church Rd., Parran, 10/31/72, C, 72000572

Cove Point Lighthouse, Off MD 497, Cove Point, 4/11/73, A, 73000907

Drum Point Lighthouse, W shore of Back Creek, Calvert County Marine Museum, Solomons Island, 4/11/73, A, 73000910

Grahame House, NE of SR 262 and 523, Lower Marlboro, 4/26/72, B, C, 72000571

La Veille, W of Mutual on Ben La Veille Rd. off MD 264, Mutual vicinity, 9/20/73, C, 73000909

Lore, J. C., Oyster House, MD 2, Solomons, 3/22/84, A, C, 84003869

Maidstone, Chesapeake Beach Rd., Owings, 6/21/71, C, 71000370

Middleham Chapel, 1 mi. SE of Lusby on U.S. 4, Lusby vicinity, 2/20/75, A, C, a, 75000870

Morgan Hill Farm, Sollers Rd., W of Lusby, Lusby vicinity, 4/03/76, C, 76000981

Patterson's Archeological District, Address Restricted, Wallville vicinity, 4/12/82, D, 82002808

Preston-on-the-Patuxent, N of Johnstown off Sollers Mill Rd., Johnstown vicinity, 10/09/74, C, 74000943

TENNISON, WM. B. (Chesapeake Bay Bugeye), Calvert Marine Museum, Solomons, 3/27/80, A, 80001799

Taney Place, S of Adelina on MD 508, Adeline vicinity, 9/22/72, B, C, c, 72000570

Willow Glenn, NW of Barstow on Barstow Rd., Barstow vicinity, 7/02/73, A, C, 73000906

Caroline County

Athol, Melville Rd. near Trunk Line Rd., Henderson vicinity, 6/09/89, C, 89000485

Castle Hall, 8 mi. N of Goldsboro on MD 311, Goldsboro, 12/04/75, B, C, 75000872

Daffin House, 3 mi. S of Hillsboro on Deep Branch Rd., Hillsboro vicinity, 10/21/75, A, C, 75000873

Denton Armory [Maryland National Guard Armories TR], Maple Ave. & Randolph St., Denton, 9/25/85, A, C, g, 85002665

Denton Historic District, Roughly bounded by 1st, 10th, Gay, High, Franklin and Sunnyside Sts., Denton, 12/01/83, A, C, 83003738

Exeter, N of Federalsburg on MD 630, Federalsburg vicinity, 1/03/78, C, 78001448

Leonard House, Main St., Greensboro, 11/14/88, C, a, 88001444

Neck Meetinghouse and Yard, MD 404, West Denton, 10/22/76, A, d, 76000982

Oak Lawn, 2.8 mi. N of Ridgely on MD 312, Ridgely vicinity, 5/28/75, B, C, 75000875

Potter Hall, Martin Lane, Williston, 11/30/82, A, C, 82001590

Schoolhouse, Denton, 104 S. 2nd St., Denton, 4/19/78, A, C, 78001447

St. Paul's Episcopal Church, S of MD 404, Hillsboro, 5/12/75, B, C, a, 75000874

Willow Grove, MD 457 off MD 213, Greensboro vicinity, 6/13/72, B, C, 72000573

Carroll County

Antrim, S of Taneytown on Uniontown Rd., Taneytown vicinity, 9/16/77, C, 77000686

Arter, Solomon, House, 4029 Geeting Rd., Union Mills vicinity, 9/10/87, A, C, 87001569

Avalon, MD 31, New Windsor vicinity, 9/03/87, C, 87001407

Avondale, 2.5 mi. SW of Westminster on MD 31, Westminster vicinity, 10/10/75, B, C, 75000877

Branton Manor, 2819 Old Liberty Rd., Sykesville vicinity, 8/18/78, C, 78001450

Brown, Moses, House, SE of Eldersburg at 7604 Ridge Rd., Eldersburg vicinity, 12/11/80, A, C, 80001800

Carroll County Almshouse and Farm, 500 S. Center St., Westminster vicinity, 12/04/75, A, C, 75000878

Chambers, Whitakker, Farm, E. Saw Mill Rd., Westminster, 5/17/88, B, g, NHL, 88001824

Erb, Christopher, House, 3333 Flickinger Rd., Silver Run vicinity, 6/19/85, A, C, 85001269

Farm Content, on Old New Winsor Rd. off MD 31, Westminster vicinity, 6/20/75, B, C, 75000879

Friendship Valley Farm, S of Westminster at 950 Gist Rd., Westminster vicinity, 9/16/77, B, C, 77000688

Frizzell, Andrew P., House and Farm Complex, 3801 Salem Bottom Rd., Westminster, 9/11/86, C, 86002391

Hard Lodging, 1 mi. (1.6 km) E of Union Bridge on Ladiesburg Rd., Union Bridge vicinity, 6/09/78, C, 78001451

Hoffman, Isaac, House, 364 Shamer Lane, Houcksville vicinity, 7/25/85, A, C, 85001612

Hopewell, Pearre and Clemsonville Rds., Union Bridge vicinity, 12/08/80, B, C, 80001803

Linwood Historic District, McKinstry's Mill Rd., Linwood, 9/27/80, A, C, D, 80001801

Meadow Brook Farm, 1006 Taneytown Pike, Westminster vicinity, 7/25/85, B, C, 85001622

Mount Airy Historic District, Roughly Main, Church, Maple, Park, Hill, and Warfield Sts., Mount Airy, 9/13/84, A, C, 84001589

Pipe Creek Friends Meetinghouse, Quaker Hill Rd., Union Bridge, 11/07/76, A, C, a, 76000983

Rockland Farm, 201 Rockland Rd., Westminster vicinity, 8/21/86, A, C, 86001730

Royer, Christian, House, N of Westminster on Fridinger Mill Rd., Westminster vicinity, 11/07/79, B, C, a, 79001119

Rudisel, Ludwick, Tannery House, 65 Frederick St., Taneytown, 11/10/80, C, 80001802

Springfield Presbyterian Church, 7300 Spout Hill Rd., Sykesville, 7/31/86, A, C, a, 86002110

Sykesville Historic District, Main St., eld, Norwood & Mellor Aves., Sykesville, 9/25/85, A, C, 85002498

Taneytown Historic District, MD 140 and 194, Taneytown, 10/09/86, A, C, 86002850

Terra Rubra, 1 mi. (1.6 km) S of Keysville, Keysville vicinity, 7/24/78, B, C, c, f, 78001449

Trevanion, 3 mi. NW of Uniontown on Trevanion Rd., Uniontown vicinity, 9/15/77, B, C, 77000687

Union Bridge Station, Main St., Union Bridge, 11/07/76, A, C, 76000984

Union Mills Homestead Historic District, Jct. of U.S. 140 and Deep Run Rd., Westminster, 1/25/71, B, C, 71000371

Uniontown Academy, Uniontown Rd., Uniontown, 8/14/73, A, C, 73000911

Uniontown Historic District, Uniontown and Trevanion Rds., Uniontown, 1/03/86, A, C, 86000059

Weaver-Fox House, 3411 Main St. (Uniontown Rd.), Uniontown, 11/20/75, B, C, 75000876

Wesley Chapel Methodist Episcopal Church, Liberty and Johnsville Rds., Eldersburg vicinity, 3/22/84, A, C, a, 84001593

Western Maryland College Historic District, W. Main and College Sts., Westminster, 3/26/76, A, 76000985

Westminster Historic District, MD 32 and MD 97, Westminster, 8/06/80, A, C, 80001804

Wilson's Inheritance, 4400 Green Valley Rd., Union Bridge vicinity, 6/19/85, A, C, 85001270

Cecil County

Bohemia Farm, 1 mi. S of Bohemia River off U.S. 213, Earleville, 4/11/73, B, C, 73000912

Brown, Jeremiah, House and Mill Site, 1416 Telegraph Rd., Rising Sun vicinity, 11/02/87, A, C, 87001391

Brown, Mercer, House, 1270 England Creamery Rd., Rising Sun vicinity, 5/29/87, C, 87000815

Bumpstead Archeological Site [Delaware Chalcedony Complex TR], Address Restricted, Elkton vicinity, 12/16/83, D, 83003745

Charlestown Historic District, Bounded by Tasker and Ogle Sts., Louisa Lane, and the North East River, Charlestown, 4/14/75, A, C, 75000880

Churchman, John, House, 115 Churchman Ln., Calvert vicinity, 9/11/86, B, C, a, 86002337

Cecil County—Continued

Colora Meetinghouse, N of Colora on Lipencott Rd., Colora vicinity, 8/22/77, A, C, a, 77000689

ELF, THE (yacht), Sassafrass River, Fredericktown, 3/26/80, A, 80001807

East Nottingham Friends Meetinghouse, E of Rising Sun at jct. of MD 272 and MD 273, Rising Sun vicinity, 8/19/77, C, a, d, 77000691

Elk Landing, Landing Lane, Elkton vicinity, 9/07/84, C, 84001596

Elkton Armory [Maryland National Guard Armories TR], Railroad Ave. & Bow St., Elkton, 9/25/85, A, C, g, 85002670

England, Isaac, House, 1 mi. W of Zion on England Creamery Rd., Zion vicinity, 3/20/80, C, 80001808

Grear Prehistoric Village Site, Address Restricted, Crystal Beach vicinity, 7/30/75, D, 75000882

Great House, 284 Great House Farm Rd., St. Augustine vicinity, 6/07/84, C, 84001598

Greenfields, S of Cecilton on U.S. 213, Cecilton vicinity, 2/11/72, B, C, 72000574

Harris, Nathan and Susannah, House, 541 Rising Sun Rd., Harrisville, 3/22/84, C, 84001602

Heath Farm Camp Archeological Site [Delaware Chalcedony Complex TR], Address Restricted, Elkton vicinity, 12/16/83, D, 83003747

Heath Farm Jasper Quarry Archeological Site [Delaware Chalcedony Complex TR], Address Restricted, Elkton vicinity, 12/16/83, D, 83003753

Holly Hall, 259 S. Bridge St., Elkton, 10/08/76, B, C, 76000986

Hopewell, NW of Providence on Little Elk Creek Rd., Providence vicinity, 5/09/79, A, C, 79001120

Indian Queen Tavern and Black's Store, Market St. between Bladen and Cecil Sts., Charlestown, 2/20/75, A, C, 75000881

Iron Hill Cut Jasper Quarry Archeological Site [Delaware Chalcedony Complex TR], Address Restricted, Elkton vicinity, 12/16/83, D, 83003754

Kirk, Elisha, House, on Old Post Rd., Calvert vicinity, 7/21/82, C, 82002809

Little Elk Farm, NW of Providence on Little Elk Rd., Providence vicinity, 5/09/79, C, 79001121

McCandless Archeological Site [Delaware Chalcedony Complex TR], Address Restricted, Elkton vicinity, 12/16/83, D, 83003775

Mitchell House, 131 E. Main St., Elkton, 5/13/76, B, C, 76000987

Mitchell House, MD 213 and MD 273, Fair Hill, 4/11/80, B, C, 80001806

Mount Harmon, SW of Earlville on Grove Neck Rd., Earleville vicinity, 6/05/74, A, B, b, e, 74000945

New Castle and Frenchtown Railroad Right-of-Way, Off U.S. 40 between Porter, DE, and Frenchtown, MD, Frenchtown, vicinity, 9/01/76, A, C, 76002290

Octorara Farm, S of Conowingo, Conowingo vicinity, 5/07/80, A, C, 80001805

Old Lock Pump House, Chesapeake and Delaware Canal, U.S. 213, Chesapeake City, 10/15/66, C, NHL, 66000390

Paw Paw Building, 68 N. Main St., Port Deposit, 11/28/77, A, a, 77000690

Perry Point Mansion House and Mill, Veterans Administration Hospital grounds, Perryville, 7/02/75, A, 75000883

Port Deposit, E bank of Susquehanna River 10 mi. (16 km) S of Mason-Dixon Line, Port Deposit, 5/23/78, A, C, 78001452

Principio Furnace, Address Restricted, Perryville vicinity, 2/11/72, A, D, 72000575

Richards, Thomas, House, 3 mi. W of Rising Sun on U.S. 1, Rising Sun vicinity, 12/19/79, C, 79001122

Rock United Presbyterian Church, MD 273 at Rock Church Rd., Elkton vicinity, 12/01/83, A, C, a, 83003776

Rodgers Tavern, W. Main St., Perryville, 4/26/72, B, C, 72000576

Rose Hill, SW of Earleville on Grave Neck Rd., Earleville vicinity, 11/05/74, B, C, 74000946

Snow Hill Site, Address Restricted, Port Deposit vicinity, 4/27/84, D, 84001758

South Chesapeake City Historic District, E of U.S. 213, S of Chesapeake and Delaware Canal, Chesapeake City, 7/15/74, A, C, 74000944

St. Francis Xavier Church, 2 mi. NW of Warwick off MD 299, Warwick vicinity, 10/10/75, A, a, d, 75000884

St. Stephen's Episcopal Church, N of Earleville on MD 282, Earleville vicinity, 4/29/82, C, a, 82002810

Tome School for Boys Historic District, Bainbridge Naval Training Grounds, Port Deposit vicinity, 5/16/84, A, C, 84001760

West Nottingham Academy Historic District, Jct. of Harrisville and Firetower Rds., Colora vicinity, 7/26/90, A, C, 90001125

West Nottingham Meetinghouse, SW of Rising Sun at jct. of Cox and Cowen Rds., Rising Sun vicinity, 11/07/76, C, a, d, 76000988

Woodlands, E of Perryville on MD 7, Perryville vicinity, 9/24/79, A, B, C, a, 79003274

Charles County

Acquinsicke, Billingsley Rd. W of jct. with MD 228, Pomfret vicinity, 2/20/92, C, 92000070

Araby, SE of Mason on MD 425, Mason's Springs, 7/25/74, B, C, 74000947

Bryantown Historic District, MD 5 and County Rt. 232, Bryantown, 3/14/85, A, B, C, 85000590

Cedar Grove, S of La Plata off MD 6 W of Blossom Point Rd., La Plata vicinity, 3/02/79, B, C, 79001124

Ellerslie, W of Port Tobacco on MD 6, Port Tobacco vicinity, 9/24/79, B, C, b, e, 79003264

Exchange, The, Spring Hill-Newtown Rd., La Plata vicinity, 6/07/84, C, 84001763

Green's Inheritance, NE of Pomfret on MD 227, Pomfret vicinity, 12/16/77, A, C, 77000692

Habre-de-Venture, Rose Hill Rd., near jct. with MD 225 and 6, Port Tobacco, 10/31/72, B, C, NHL, 72001595

Johnsontown, Fairgrounds Rd. E of Penn Central RR tracks, La Plata vicinity, 5/31/91, C, 91000610

La Grange, MD 6, W of U.S. 301, La Plata, 10/22/76, B, C, 76000990

Linden, N of Port Tobacco on Mitchell Rd., Port Tobacco vicinity, 11/23/77, B, C, 77000693

Lindens, The, SR 488, Bryantown vicinity, 4/23/90, C, 90000607

Locust Grove, W of La Plata on MD 225, La Plata vicinity, 7/21/78, C, 78001454

Marshall Hall, 5 mi. N. of MD 210 and MD. 227, Bryan's Road vicinity, 5/12/76, A, C, NPS, 76000152

Maxwell Hall, E of Patuxent on Teagues Point Rd., Patuxent vicinity, 7/30/74, C, 74000949

McPherson's Purchase, MD 227, Pomfret vicinity, 1/03/85, A, C, 85000019

Mount Air, W of Faulkner off U.S. 301, Faulkner vicinity, 12/22/78, C, 78001453

Mt. Carmel Monastery, N of Port Tobacco on Mt. Carmel Rd., Port Tobacco vicinity, 12/04/73, A, a, 73000913

Oak Grove, Turkey Hill Rd., La Plata vicinity, 11/23/83, C, 83003777

Oakland, MD 5, Bryantown vicinity, 8/04/83, C, 83002946

Port Tobacco Historic District, Off MD 6, Port Tobacco, 8/04/89, A, C, D, 79003911

Retreat, MD 484/Poor House Rd. and MD 6, Port Tobacco vicinity, 6/28/88, C, 88000222

Rich Hill, NE of Bel Alton on Bel Alton-Newtown Rd., Bel Alton vicinity, 11/12/75, A, C, 75000885

Rose Hill, Rose Hill Rd., Port Tobacco, 3/30/73, B, C, 73000914

Rosemary Lawn, Fire Tower Rd., Welcome vicinity, 4/16/92, A, C, 92000380

Sarum, SE of Newport off MD 234, Newport vicinity, 8/13/74, C, 74000948

Spye Park, Padgett Road, White Plains vicinity, 10/04/90, C, 90001523

St. Catharine, E of Waldorf near jct. of MD 232 and 382, Waldorf vicinity, 10/01/74, B, 74000950

St. Mary's Roman Catholic Church, Newport, St. Mary's Church Rd., Newport vicinity, 5/30/91, C, a, d, 91000603

St. Thomas Manor, SR 427/Chapel Point Rd., Port Tobacco vicinity, 11/10/88, A, C, D, a, d, 88002050

Stagg Hall, CR 469/Chapel Point Rd., Port Tobacco, 12/29/88, C, 88003061

Thainston, Mitchell Rd., N of MD 225, La Plata vicinity, 3/28/90, A, C, 90000436

Timber Neck Farm, SE of Faulkner Rd., Faulkner vicinity, 9/06/79, A, C, D, 79001123

Truman's Place, Gallant Green Rd., Hughesville vicinity, 1/20/88, C, 87002264

Waverley, SE of Morgantown off Wayside—Morgantown Rd., Morgantown vicinity, 8/11/75, A, C, 75000886

Widow's Pleasure, Piney Church Rd., Waldorf vicinity, 4/18/91, A, 89000664

Dorchester County

Bethlehem Methodist Episcopal Church, Hoopers Neck Rd., Taylor's Island, 6/07/79, A, C, a, 79001126

Brinsfield I Site, Address Restricted, Cambridge vicinity, 5/12/75, D, 75000887

Cambridge Historic District, Wards I and III, Roughly bounded by Glasgow, Glenburn, Poplar, Race, and Gay Sts. and the Choptank River, Cambridge, 9/05/90, A, C, 90001370

Christ Episcopal Church and Cemetery, High St., Cambridge, 4/12/84, A, C, a, d, 84001767

Dale's Right, S of Cambridge on Casson Neck Rd., Cambridge vicinity, 4/03/79, C, 79001125

Dorchester County Courthouse and Jail, 206 High St., Cambridge, 12/16/82, A, C, 82001591

East New Market Historic District, MD 14 and MD 16, East New Market, 10/01/75, A, C, 75000889

Fletcher, K. B., Mill, Address Restricted, East New Market vicinity, 12/14/78, A, C, 78001456

Friendship Hall, Off MD 14, East New Market, 10/18/73, B, C, 73000915

Glasgow, 1500 Hambrooks Blvd., Cambridge, 10/08/76, C, 76000991

Glen Oak Hotel, 201 Academy St., Hurlock, 9/08/83, A, 83002947

Goldsborough House, 200 High St., Cambridge, 12/29/88, C, 88003062

Grace Episcopal Church Complex, Hooper Neck Rd., Taylor's Island, 7/24/79, A, C, a, 79001127

LaGrange, 904 LaGrange Ave., Cambridge, 1/24/80, B, C, 80001809

PATRICIA (log canoe) [Chesapeake Bay Sailing Log Canoe Fleet TR], 903 Roslyn Ave., Cambridge, 9/18/85, A, C, g, 85002246

Rehoboth, W side of Punkum Rd., Eldorado, 11/09/72, A, B, C, 72000577

Ridgeton Farm, SW of Taylor Island on Bay Shore Rd., Taylor's Island vicinity, 10/05/77, C, 77000694

Stanley Institute, S of Cambridge on MD 16, Cambridge vicinity, 9/11/75, A, 75000888

Sycamore Cottage, 417 High St., Cambridge, 3/30/88, A, C, b, 88000231

Willin Village Archeological Site, Address Restricted, Eldorado vicinity, 5/12/75, D, 75000890

Yarmouth, SE of Cambridge on Bestpitch Ferry Rd., Cambridge vicinity, 3/29/78, C, 78001455

Frederick County

Amelung House and Glassworks, 4 mi. SW of Urbana off U.S. 240, Urbana vicinity, 10/03/73, A, B, C, 73000919

Arcadia, 3.5 mi. (5.6 km) S of Frederick on MD 85, Frederick vicinity, 8/03/78, A, C, 78001458

Bennies Hill Road Bridge, SW of Middletown on Bennies Hill Rd. over Catoctin Creek, Middletown vicinity, 6/27/79, A, C, 79003265

Biggs Ford Site, Address Restricted, Frederick vicinity, 6/10/75, D, 75000894

Brunswick Historic District, Roughly bounded by Potomac River, Central, Park and 10th Aves., and C St., Brunswick, 8/29/79, A, C, 79001128

Buckeystown Historic District, MD 85, Buckeystown, 4/06/82, A, C, 82002811

Buckingham House and Industrial School Complex, Off MD 80 and MD 85, Buckeystown, 5/20/82, A, C, D, a, 82002812

Bullfrog Road Bridge, NW of Taneytown off MD 97, Taneytown vicinity, 11/21/78, A, C, 78001461

Burkittsville, MD 17 and Jefferson—Boonsboro Rd., Burkittsville, 11/20/75, A, C, 75000891

Camp Greentop Historic District [ECW Architecture in Catoctin Mountain Park MPS], Off Park Central Rd. in Catoctin Mountain Park, Thurmont vicinity, 10/11/89, A, C, NPS, 89001583

Camp Misty Mount Historic District [ECW Architecture in Catoctin Mountain Park MPS], Off Park Central Rd. in Catoctin Mountain Park, Thurmont vicinity, 10/11/89, A, C, NPS, 89001582

Catoctin Furnace Historic District, E side of U.S. 15, Catoctin Furnace, 2/11/72, A, B, C, 72000578

Crum Road Bridge, E of Walkersville at Crum Rd. and Israel's Creek, Walkersville vicinity, 12/28/78, A, C, 78001463

Cullen, Victor, Center, Old Administration Building, Victor Cullen Center Campus, Sabillasville, 8/22/90, A, 90001228

Cullen, Victor, School Power House, MD 81, Sabillasville, 1/07/87, A, 87000045

Drummine Farm, 6901 Green Valley Rd., New Market vicinity, 1/08/87, A, C, 86003543

Edgewood, N of Frederick off Poole Jones Rd., Frederick vicinity, 9/06/79, B, C, 79001129

Emmitsburg Historic District, Roughly, Main St. E of Mountain View Cemetery to Creamery Rd. and Seton Ave. adjacent to Main, Emmitsburg, 3/10/92, A, C, 92000076

Fat Oxen, N of Urbana on MD 355, Urban vicinity, 5/21/79, C, 79001133

Fourpoints Bridge, SE of Emmitsburg, Emmitsburg vicinity, 11/29/78, A, C, 78001457

Frederick Armory [Maryland National Guard Armories TR], Bentz & Second Sts., Frederick, 9/25/85, A, C, 85002672

Frederick Historic District, 2 blocks E and 3 blocks W of Market St., from South St. to 7th St., Frederick, 10/18/73, A, B, C, 73000916

Frederick Historic District (Boundary Increase), Roughly bounded by Thirteenth, East and Wisner, South and Madison Sts., W. College Terr. and Rosemont and Trail Aves., Frederick, 6/13/88, A, C, g, 88000713

Gambrill House, Monocacy National Battlefield—MD 355, Frederick vicinity, 11/18/85, B, C, NPS, 85002902

Graceham Moravian Church And Parsonage, 2 mi. E of Thurmont on MD 77, Thurmont vicinity, 5/13/76, A, a, 76000995

Guilford, S of Frederick on MD 85, Frederick vicinity, 10/14/75, A, C, 75000895

Hessian Barracks, 242 S. Market St., Frederick, 1/25/71, A, C, 71000373

Jones, Abraham, House, Main St., Libertytown, 7/24/73, B, C, 73000917

LeGore Bridge, N of Woodsboro over Monacacy River, Woodsboro vicinity, 9/18/78, A, C, 78001464

Lewis Mill Complex, 3205 Poffenberger Rd., Jefferson vicinity, 5/06/82, A, C, 82002813

Linden Grove, Solarex Ct., Frederick, 9/10/87, C, 87001570

Loats Female Orphan Asylum of Frederick City, 24 E. Church St., Frederick, 10/10/72, C, 72000580

Loys Station Covered Bridge [Covered Bridges in Frederick County TR], Old Frederick Rd. at Owen's Creek, Thurmont vicinity, 6/23/78, A, C, 78003175

Maynard, Thomas, House, 1.5 mi. NW of New London on Gas House Pike, New London vicinity, 7/18/79, C, 79001130

Monocacy National Battlefield, SE of Frederick, Frederick vicinity, 10/15/66, A, NHL, NPS, 66000908

Monocacy Site, Address Restricted, Dickerson vicinity, 7/30/75, D, NPS, 75000151

Motter, John C., House, 1005 Motter Ave., Frederick, 12/02/82, B, C, 82001592

Nallin Farm House, Fort Detrick, Frederick vicinity, 5/23/74, C, 74000951

Nallin Farm Springhouse and Bank Barn, N of Frederick, Frederick vicinity, 9/16/77, A, C, 77000695

Nelson, Henry, House, N of New Market on Gas House Pike, New Market vicinity, 12/04/80, C, 80001811

New Market Historic District, Jct. of MD 144 and Old MD 75, New Market, 12/06/75, A, C, 75000897

Nolands Ferry I Archeological Site (18FR17), Address Restricted, Tuscarora vicinity, 10/18/85, D, 85003152

Old Mill Road Bridge, W of Rocky Ridge on Old Mill Rd. over Owens Creek, Rocky Ridge vicinity, 3/07/79, A, C, 79001131

One-Million-Liter Test Sphere, N of Frederick on Fort Detrick, Frederick vicinity, 11/23/77, A, g, 77000696

Pearre-Metcalfe House, NE of Unionville off MD 31, Unionville vicinity, 7/02/79, C, 79001132

Pennterra, SE of Creagerstown off MD 550, Creagerstown vicinity, 1/30/76, C, 76000992

Poffenberger Road Bridge, S of Middletown, Middletown vicinity, 11/29/78, A, C, 78001459

Point of Rocks Railroad Station, On U.S. 15, Point of Rocks, 4/11/73, A, C, 73000918

Prospect Hall, SW of Frederick on Butterfly Lane, Frederick vicinity, 9/08/80, A, C, 80001810

Roddy Road Covered Bridge [Covered Bridges in Frederick County TR], Roddy Rd. at Owen's Creek, Thurmont vicinity, 6/23/78, A, C, 78003176

Rose Hill Manor, 1611 N. Market St., Frederick, 12/09/71, B, C, 71000374

Saleaudo, New Design Rd., N of Rt 28, Frederick vicinity, 9/24/79, B, C, 79003258

Scheifferstadt, W. 2nd and Rosemont Sts., Frederick, 7/22/74, A, C, 74000952

Frederick County—Continued

Shafer's Mill, 3018 Bennies Hill Rd., Middletown, 6/26/86, B, C, 86001372

Shoemaker III Village Site, Address Restricted, Emmitsburg vicinity, 9/05/75, D, 75000893

Shoemaker, Henry, Farmhouse, 2136 Old National Pike, Middletown vicinity, 5/11/89, A, C, 89000416

Spring Bank, 7945 Worman's Mill Rd., Frederick, 9/07/84, C, 84001772

St. Euphemia's School and Sisters' House, 5052 DePaul St., Emmitsburg, 9/13/84, C, a, 84001770

St. Joseph's College and Mother Seton Shrine, MD 806, Emmitsburg, 1/01/76, B, C, a, 76000994

St. Paul's Episcopal Church, N of Point of Rocks off U.S. 15, Point of Rocks vicinity, 1/31/78, A, C, a, 78001460

Stancioff House, Rt. 2, Urbana, 4/23/75, A, C, 75000896

Strawberry Hill, SE of Creagerstown off MD 550, Creagerstown vicinity, 1/30/76, C, 76000993

Utica Covered Bridge [Covered Bridges in Frederick County TR], Utica Rd. at Fishing Creek, Thurmont vicinity, 6/23/78, A, C, 78003174

Widrick, George, House, Ballenger Creek Pk., Frederick vicinity, 9/12/85, C, 85002172

Willard, George, House, 4804 Old Middletown Rd., Jefferson vicinity, 7/22/93, C, 93000665

Woodsboro and Frederick Turnpike Company Tollhouse, Off MD 194, Walkersville vicinity, 9/24/79, A, 79003276

Garrett County

Anderson Chapel, Swanton Hill and Pine Hill Rds., Swanton, 6/07/84, C, a, 84001775

Baltimore and Ohio Railroad Station, Oakland, Liberty St., Oakland, 2/05/74, A, C, 74000953

Bloomington Viaduct, Potomac River, S of MD 135, Bloomington, 11/21/76, A, C, 76000996

Borderside, Oakland—Westernport Rd., Bloomington, 10/29/75, B, C, 75000898

Casselman's Bridge, National Road, E of Grantsville on U.S. 40, Grantsville vicinity, 10/15/66, A, NHL, 66000391

Creedmore, 510 G St., Mountain Lake Park, 12/27/84, C, 84000505

Drane, James, House, Accident-Bittinger Rd., Accident vicinity, 1/11/85, A, C, d, 85000059

Fuller-Baker Log House, 0.5 mi. W of Grantsville on U.S. 40, Grantsville vicinity, 2/12/71, A, C, 71000375

Garrett County Courthouse, 3rd and Alder Sts., Oakland, 11/12/75, A, C, 75000899

Glamorgan, MD 135, Deer Park vicinity, 9/13/84, C, 84001778

Hoye Site, Address Restricted, Oakland vicinity, 5/12/75, D, 75000900

Kaese Mill, N of Accident, Accident vicinity, 9/13/84, A, C, 84001782

Mercy Chapel at Mill Run, Mill Run Rd., Selbysport vicinity, 9/07/84, C, a, 84001792

Meyer Site, Address Restricted, Westernport vicinity, 6/19/73, D, 73000921

Mountain Lake Park Historic District, Roughly bounded by Alleghany Dr., Oakland Ave., D and N Sts., Mountain Lake Park, 9/01/83, A, C, 83002948

Oakland Historic District, Roughly bounded by Oak, 8th, High, 3rd, Omaha, and Bartlet Sts., Oakland, 1/26/84, A, B, C, 84001798

Pennington Cottage, Deer Park Hotel Rd., Deer Park, 5/17/76, C, 76000997

Stanton's Mill, E of Grantsville on MD 40, Grantsville vicinity, 1/17/83, A, C, 83002949

Tomlinson Inn and the Little Meadows, 3 mi. E of Grantsville on U.S. 40, Grantsville vicinity, 9/20/73, A, 73000920

Harford County

Baker, James B., House, 452 W. Bel Air Ave., Aberdeen, 12/10/82, B, C, 82001593

Bel Air Armory [Maryland National Guard Armories TR], N. Main St., Bel Air, 9/25/85, A, C, 85002667

Bel Air Courthouse Historic District, Office, Courtland and Main Sts., Bel Air, 7/25/85, A, C, 85001617

Berkley School, Castleton Rd., MD 623, Darlington vicinity, 7/22/88, A, g, 88001011

Best Endeavor, 1612 Calvary Rd., Churchville vicinity, 12/28/90, C, 90001993

Bon Air, Laura Brook Rd., Fallston vicinity, 11/10/77, C, 77000697

Broad Creek Soapstone Quarries, Address Restricted, Whiteford vicinity, 5/12/75, D, 75000903

Broom's Bloom, 1616 S. Fountain Green Rd., Bel Air vicinity, 12/19/91, C, 91001778

Chestnut Ridge, 3850 W. Chapel Rd., Aberdeen vicinity, 12/01/83, A, C, 83003780

Churchville Presbyterian Church, Intersection of MD 22 and MD 136, Churchville, 8/21/86, A, C, a, 86001733

D. H. Springhouse, About 6 mi. NE of Bel Air on Sandy Hook Rd., Bel Air vicinity, 5/08/73, C, 73000923

Darlington Historic District, Main St., Shuresville Rd., Quaker Ln., Richmond Ave., and Trappe Church Rd., Darlington, 9/10/87, A, C, 87001571

Deer Creek Friends Meetinghouse, MD 161, Darlington, 4/23/80, A, C, a, 80001817

Dibb House, E of Bel Air at 1737 Churchville Rd., Bel Air vicinity, 3/18/80, C, 80001812

Fair Meadows, Creswell Rd., Creswell vicinity, 11/25/80, B, C, 80004255

Finney Houses Historic District, Glenville Rd. near jct. MD 155, Churchville vicinity, 6/16/89, C, 89000502

Gladden Farm, 3881 Rocks Station Rd., Street vicinity, 5/28/93, A, C, g, 93000444

Graham-Crocker House, 30 N. Main St., Bel Air, 3/17/80, C, 80001813

Gray Gables, 4528 Conowingo Rd., Darlington vicinity, 3/27/86, C, 86000582

Griffith House, SW of Aberdeen at 1120 Old Philadelphia Rd., Aberdeen vicinity, 11/14/78, C, 78001465

Gunpowder Meetinghouse, Magnolia Rd., Aberdeen Proving Ground, 6/05/74, A, a, 74000954

Harford Furnace Historic District, Creswell and Goat Hill Rds., Bel Air vicinity, 7/18/90, A, D, 90001020

Harford National Bank, Wall and Courtland Sts., Bel Air, 3/20/80, A, C, 80001814

Havre de Grace Historic District, Roughly bounded by Chesapeake, Bay, Susquehanna River, US 40, Stokes, Juniata and Superior Sts., Havre de Grace, 3/25/82, A, C, 82002815

Havre de Grace Lighthouse, Concord and Lafayette Sts., Havre de Grace, 4/02/76, A, 76000999

Hays House, 324 S. Kenmore Ave., Bel Air, 1/03/80, C, b, 80001815

Hays-Heighe House, 401 Thomas Run Rd., Bel Air, 2/11/72, C, 72000581

Heighe House, Jct. of Southampton and Moores Mill Rds., Bel Air vicinity, 11/01/90, B, C, g, 90001568

Hidden Valley Farm, 2916 Green Rd., Baldwin vicinity, 1/17/83, C, 83002950

Husband Flint Mill Site, Address Restricted, Kalmia vicinity, 6/18/75, D, 75000902

Jerusalem Mill Village, Jerusalem and Jericho Rds., Jerusalem, 8/20/87, A, C, 87001400

Joshua's Meadows, 300 N. Tollgate Rd., Bel Air, 12/21/82, B, C, 82001594

Ladew Topiary Gardens and House, 0.5 mi. NE of Taylor on MD 146, Taylor vicinity, 5/13/76, C, g, 76001002

Liriodendron, 501 and 502 W. Gordon St., Bel Air, 9/27/80, B, C, 80001816

Little Falls Meetinghouse, Old Fallston Rd., Fallston, 5/07/80, A, C, a, 80001818

Lower Deer Creek Valley Historic District, Roughly bounded by the Susquehanna R., MD 543 and Harmony Church and Trappe Rds., Darlington vicinity, 11/03/93, A, C, D, 93001143

McComas Institute, N of Joppa on Singer Rd., Joppa vicinity, 9/08/80, A, a, 80001819

Medical Hall Historic District, W of Churchville off MD 154, Churchville vicinity, 8/28/73, B, D, 73000926

Mill Green Historic District, Jct. of Mill Green and Prospect Rds., Street vicinity, 6/03/93, A, C, 93000445

Mount Adams, 1912 Fountain Green Rd., Bel Air vicinity, 10/27/88, B, d, 88002062

Nelson—Reardon—Kennard House, 3604 Philadelphia Rd., Abingdon, 4/15/91, C, 91000001

Norris-Stirling House, Ring Factory Rd., Bel Air vicinity, 5/30/79, A, C, 79001135

Odd Fellows Lodge, 21 Pennsylvania Ave., Bel Air, 8/22/75, C, a, 75000901

Old Joppa Site, Address Restricted, Jappatowne vicinity, 8/24/79, A, B, D, 79001136

Olney, 1001 Old Joppa Rd., Joppa, 7/09/87, B, C, 87001197

Poplar Hill, 115 Poplar Hill Rd., Aberdeen, 5/28/76, C, 76000998

Harford County—Continued

Presbury Meetinghouse, Austin and Parrish Rds., Aberdeen Proving Ground, 5/23/74, A, C, a, 74000955

Priest Neal's Mass House and Mill Site, 2618 Cool Spring Rd., Bel Air vicinity, 3/15/90, A, C, a, 90000352

Proctor House, 54 E. Gordon St., Bel Air, 3/23/90, C, 90000376

Rigbie House, SE of Berkley off MD 623, Berkley vicinity, 8/14/73, A, B, C, 73000925

Rockdale, N of Fallston at 1724 Carrs Mill Rd., Fallston vicinity, 6/30/82, B, C, 82002814

Silver Houses Historic District, S of Darlington on MD 161, Darlington vicinity, 9/07/84, C, 84001800

Sion Hill, 2026 Level Rd., Havre de Grace vicinity, 4/30/90, A, C, NHL, 90000608

Slate Ridge School, Old Pylesville Rd., Whiteford, 7/16/87, A, C, 87000657

Sophia's Dairy, SW of Aberdeen off U.S. 40, Aberdeen vicinity, 9/20/73, B, C, 73000922

Southern Terminal, Susquehanna and Tidewater Canal, N of Erie St. between Conesteo St. and the Susquehanna, Havre de Grace, 5/28/76, A, C, 76001000

St. George's Parish Vestry House, 1522 Perryman Rd., Perryman, 3/26/76, A, C, a, 76001001

St. Ignatius Church, 533 E. Jarrettsville Rd., Forest Hill, 4/16/74, A, a, 74000956

St. Mary's Church, S of Emmorton on MD 24, Emmorton, 3/30/73, A, C, a, 73000928

Streett, Col. John, House, N side of Holy Cross Rd., E of Deer Cr., Street vicinity, 7/16/90, B, C, 90001022

Thomas Run Church, NE of Bel Air off MD 136, Bel Air vicinity, 1/03/78, A, C, a, 78001466

Tudor Hall, NE of Bel Air off MD 22, Bel Air vicinity, 3/14/73, B, C, 73000924

Tudor Hall (Boundary Decrease), NE of Bel Air on Tudor Lane, Bel Air vicinity, 12/16/82, B, C, b, 82001595

Webster's Forest, 500 Asbury Rd., Churchville vicinity, 9/01/83, C, 83002951

Whitaker's Mill Historic District, 1210, 1212, and 1213 Whitaker Mill Rd., Joppa, 7/16/90, A, C, 90001021

Wildfell, NW of Darlington on U.S. 1, Darlington vicinity, 9/20/73, C, 73000927

Winsted, N of Aberdeen at 3844 W. Chapel Rd., Aberdeen vicinity, 9/19/79, B, C, 79003266

Woodside, NW of Abingdon at 400 Singer Rd, Abingdon vicinity, 11/01/79, C, 79001134

Woodview, 1236 Somerville Rd., Bel Air vicinity, 10/25/90, C, 90001574

Howard County

Barney, Commodore Joshua, House, N of Savage at 7912 Savage-Guilford Rd., Savage vicinity, 8/25/78, A, C, 78001470

Bollman Suspension and Trussed Bridge, Gorman and Savage Rds., Savage, 10/18/72, A, C, 72000582

Burleigh, Centennial Lane, Ellicott City vicinity, 11/30/82, C, 82001596

Christ Church Guilford, N of Guilford at 6800 Oakland Mills Rd., Guilford vicinity, 1/30/78, A, C, a, 78001469

Daniels Mill, Alberton Rd., Daniels, 4/11/73, A, C, a, 73000929

Doughoregan Manor, 8 mi. W of Ellicott City on Manor Lane, Ellicott City vicinity, 11/11/71, B, C, NHL, 71000376

Elkridge Furnace Complex, 5730 and 5741–5745 Furnace Ave., 5735 Race Rd., Elkridge, 6/28/90, A, C, 90000635

Ellicott City Historic District, MD 144, Ellicott City, 7/31/78, A, C, 78001467

Ellicott City Station, S of the Patapsco River Bridge, Ellicott City, 11/24/68, A, NHL, 68000025

Elmonte, N of Ellicott City at Mt. Hebron Dr. and MD 99, Ellicott City vicinity, 8/25/78, C, 78001468

Enniscorthy, 3412 Folly Quarter Rd., Ellicott City vicinity, 5/08/86, C, 86001019

Glenelg Manor, SE of Glenelg on Folly Quarter Rd., Glenelg vicinity, 2/03/83, C, 83002952

Hobson's Choice, 2921 Florence Rd., Woodbine vicinity, 9/13/84, C, 84001802

Lawn, The, 6036 Old Lawyers Hill Rd., Elkridge, 10/29/84, B, C, 84000412

Lawyers Hill Historic District, Area surrounding Lawyers Hill and Old Lawyers Hill Rds. and Elibank Dr., Elkridge vicinity, 9/23/93, A, C, 93001000

Savage Mill, SW corner of Foundry Rd. and Washington St., Savage, 4/18/74, A, 74002251

Savage Mill Historic District, N of Little Patuxent River off U.S. 1, Savage, 2/20/75, A, 75000905

Temora, 4252 Columbia Rd., Ellicott City vicinity, 4/30/76, C, 76001003

Trinity Church, 7474 Washington Blvd., Elkridge, 5/06/74, A, C, a, 74000957

Troy, I 95 & MD Rt. 176, Dorsey vicinity, 6/22/79, A, C, 79001137

Union Chapel, 1 mi. N of Glenwood on MD 97, Glenwood vicinity, 3/17/75, A, B, C, a, 75000904

Waverley, S of Marriottsville off U.S. 40, Marriottsville vicinity, 10/18/74, C, 74000958

White Hall, W of Ellicott City at 4130 Chatham Rd., Ellicott City vicinity, 8/12/77, C, 77000698

Woodlawn, 9254 Old Annapolis Rd., Columbia vicinity, 2/03/83, B, C, 83002953

Kent County

BERNICE J. (skipjack) [Chesapeake Bay Skipjack Fleet TR], Town Dock, Chestertown, 9/05/85, A, 85001946

Betterton Historic District, Roughly bounded by Sassafras River, Gut Marsh, 6th, and Ericsson Aves., Betterton, 6/07/84, A, C, 84001805

Brampton, MD 20, Chestertown vicinity, 8/04/83, C, 83002954

Carvill Hall, Great Oak Estates, 10 mi. W of Chestertown, Chestertown vicinity, 3/14/73, C, 73000930

Chestertown Armory [Maryland National Guard Armories TR], Quaker Neck Rd., Chestertown, 9/25/85, A, C, g, 85002668

Chestertown Historic District, Roughly bounded by Maple Ave., Chester River, Cannon and Cross Sts., Chestertown, 4/15/70, C, NHL, 70000263

Chestertown Historic District (Boundary Increase), Roughly bounded by Chester River, Lynchberg, and Cannon Sts., College Ave., Philosophers and Riverside Terrs., Chestertown, 9/13/84, A, C, 84001808

Chestertown Railroad Station, Cross St., Chestertown, 12/08/82, A, C, g, 82001597

Chesterville Brick House, Jct. of MD 290 and MD 447, Chesterville, 7/17/79, A, C, b, 79001139

Christ Church, Graveyard and Sexton's House, N of Worton on MD 298, Worton vicinity, 4/02/80, A, C, a, d, 80001822

Clark's Conveniency, 2 mi. S of Pomona on Quaker Neck Rd., Pomona vicinity, 9/09/75, A, C, 75000906

Denton House, 107 Water St., Chestertown, 3/11/71, B, C, 71000377

Fairlee Manor Camp House, 1.5 mi. W of Fairlee off MD 445, Fairlee vicinity, 4/11/73, C, 73000931

Godlington Manor, Wilkins Lane, Chestertown, 2/11/72, C, 72000583

Harper, George, Store, MD 292 and Main St., Still Pond, 7/09/82, B, C, 82002816

Hebron, SE of Stillpond off MD 292, Stillpond vicinity, 9/18/78, B, C, a, 78001471

Hinchingham, N of Rock Hall off MD 445, Rock Hall vicinity, 9/05/75, C, 75000907

ISLAND IMAGE (log canoe) [Chesapeake Bay Sailing Log Canoe Fleet TR], Walnut Point Rd., Chestertown vicinity, 9/18/85, A, C, 85002248

Knocks Folly, N of Kennedyville on MD 448, Kennedyville vicinity, 6/17/76, C, 76001006

Middle, East and West Halls, Washington Ave., Chestertown, 9/06/79, A, C, 79001138

Reward-Tilden's Farm, S of Chestertown, off MD 289 on Walnut Point Rd., Chestertown vicinity, 5/06/76, C, 76001004

Rich Hill, MD 299, Sassafras, 12/15/72, C, a, 72000585

Rose Hill, 2 mi. N of Chestertown on MD 213, Chestertown vicinity, 12/12/76, C, 76001005

SILVER HEEL (log canoe) [Chesapeake Bay Sailing Log Canoe Fleet TR], Quaker Neck Landing, Chestertown vicinity, 9/18/85, A, C, 85002249

Shepherd's Delight, S of Still Pond on MD 292, Still Pond vicinity, 6/17/76, C, 76001007

Shrewsbury Church, Shrewsbury Ln., Kennedyville vicinity, 6/04/86, A, C, a, 86001245

St. Paul's Church, Sandy Bottom Rd. & Ricaud's Branch-Lankford Rd., Fairlee vicinity, 6/06/80, A, C, a, 80001820

Trumpington, S of Rock Hall on MD 445, Rock Hall vicinity, 11/10/80, C, 80001821

Valley Cottage, Princess Stop St., Georgetown, 1/11/83, C, 83002955

White House Farm, MD 213 SW of jct. with MD 292, Chestertown vicinity, 3/12/92, C, 92000080

Kent County—Continued

Widehall, 101 Water St., Chestertown, 10/31/72, B, C, 72000584

Montgomery County

Annington, W of Poolesville on White's Ferry Rd., Poolesville vicinity, 12/11/78, A, C, 78001474

Beall-Dawson House, 103 W. Montgomery Ave., Rockville, 3/30/73, A, C, 73000933

Belt, J. A., Building, 227 E. Diamond Ave., Gaithersburg, 8/09/84, B, C, 84001845

Bethesda Meetinghouse, 9400 Wisconsin Ave., Bethesda, 4/18/77, A, C, a, 77000699

Bethesda Naval Hospital Tower, 8901 Wisconsin Ave., Bethesda, 3/08/77, A, C, g, 77000700

Bingham-Brewer House, 307 Great Falls Rd., Rockville, 11/24/80, C, 80001828

Brookeville Historic District, MD 97, Brookeville, 10/11/79, A, C, 79003272

Brookeville Woolen Mill and House, 1901 Brighton Dam Rd., Brookeville vicinity, 9/06/78, A, C, D, 78001472

Cabin John Aqueduct, MacArthur Blvd. over Cabin John Creek and Cabin John Pkwy., Glen Echo vicinity, 2/28/73, A, C, 73000932

Carousel at Glen Echo Park, MacArthur Blvd., Glen Echo, 7/04/80, A, NPS, 80000351

Carson, Rachel, House, 11701 Berwick Rd., Silver Spring, 12/04/91, A, B, NHL, 91002058

Chautauqua Tower, Glen Echo Park, Glen Echo, 7/04/80, A, C, NPS, 80000350

Chiswell's Inheritance, NW of Poolesville off MD 109, Poolesville vicinity, 9/10/74, C, 74000960

Clara Barton National Historic Site, 5801 Oxford Rd., Glen Echo, 10/15/66, B, NHL, NPS, 66000037

Clarksburg School, S of jct. of MD 121 and MD 355, Clarksburg, 2/20/75, A, 75000909

Clifton, 17107 New Hampshire Ave., Ednor, 6/25/74, A, C, 74000959

Clover Hill, 21310 Zion Rd., Brookeville, 7/20/82, C, 82002817

Darnall Place, E of Poolesville at 17615 White's Ferry Rd., Poolesville vicinity, 8/13/79, A, C, 79001140

Dawson Farm, 1070 and 1080 Copperstone Ct., Rockville, 1/11/85, C, 85000060

Dowden's Luck, 18511 Beallsvile Rd., Poolesville vicinity, 11/10/88, C, 88002143

Drury—Austin House, 16112 Barnesville Rd., Boyds, 3/13/86, C, 86000371

Friends Advice, 19001 Bucklodge Rd., Boyds vicinity, 10/28/92, A, B, g, 92001383

Gaithersburg B & O Railroad Station and Freight Shed, Summit and E. Diamond Aves., Gaithersburg, 10/05/78, A, C, 78001473

Gaithersburg Latitude Observatory, 100 DeSellum Ave, Gaithersburg, 7/12/85, A, g, NHL, 85001578

Garrett Park Historic District, Roughly bounded by B & O Railroad tracks, Rock Creek Park, and Flanders Ave., Garrett Park, 1/31/75, A, C, g, 75000910

Glen Echo Park Historic District, MacArthur Blvd., Glen Echo, 6/08/84, A, C, NPS, 84001850

Hanover Farm House, 19501 Darnestown Rd., Beallsville vicinity, 8/06/80, A, B, C, 80001823

Kensington Historic District, Roughly bounded by RR tracks, Kensington Pkwy., Summit Ave. Washington and Warner Sts., Kensington, 9/04/80, A, C, 80001827

Layton House, SW corner MD 108 and MD 420, Laytonsville, 9/25/75, A, C, 75000911

Milimar, 410 Randolph Rd., Silver Spring, 4/13/73, C, 73000935

Milton, 5312 Allendale Rd., Bethesda, 9/25/75, A, B, 75000908

Montgomery County Courthouse Historic District, Courthouse Sq. and S. Washington St., Rockville, 9/02/86, A, C, g, 86003352

Montrose Schoolhouse, Randolph Rd., Rockville vicinity, 1/24/83, C, 83002956

Mt. Nebo, 14510 Mt. Nebo Rd., Poolesville vicinity, 3/28/85, A, B, C, 85000653

National Park Seminary Historic District, Linden Lane near I-495, Forest Glen, 9/14/72, A, C, 72000586

Oaks II, 5815 Riggs Rd., Laytonsville vicinity, 11/30/82, C, b, 82001598

Old Chiswell Place, E of Poolesville on Cattail Rd., Poolesville vicinity, 9/09/75, A, C, 75000912

Poole, Nathan Dickerson, House, 15600 Edwards Ferry Rd., Poolesville, vicinity, 1/24/83, C, 83002957

Poolesville Historic District, Area around jcts. of MD 107, 109, and Willard Rd., Poolesville and vicinity, 5/29/75, A, C, 75000913

Ridge, The, 19000 Muncaster Rd., Derwood vicinity, 4/05/88, C, 88000267

Rockville Railroad Station, 98 Church St., Rockville, 7/18/74, A, C, 74000961

Sandy Spring Friends Meetinghouse, Meetinghouse Lane and MD 108, Sandy Spring, 9/22/72, B, C, a, 72000587

Seneca Historic District, SE of Poolesville, Poolesville vicinity, 11/15/78, A, 78001475

Seneca Quarry, Tschiffeley Mill Rd., Seneca, 4/24/73, C, NPS, 73000224

Susanna Farm, 17700 White Grounds Rd., Dawsonville vicinity, 1/27/83, C, 83002958

Takoma Park Historic District, Roughly bounded by D.C., Silver Spring, and E to jct. of Woodland and Elm Aves., Takoma Park, 7/16/76, C, 76001008

Taylor, David W., Model Basin, Bounded by MacArthur Blvd. and George Washington Memorial Pkwy., Bethesda, 10/17/85, A, C, g, 85003231

Third Addition to Rockville and Old St. Mary's Church and Cemetery, Veirs Mill and Old Baltimore Rds., Rockville, 11/20/78, A, C, a, 78001476

Thomas and Company Cannery, Jct. of W. Diamond and N. Frederick Aves., Gaithersburg, 7/05/90, A, 90001025

Valhalla, 19010 White's Ferry Rd., Poolesville vicinity, 3/15/82, C, 82002818

Walker Prehistoric Village Archeological Site, Address Restricted, Poolesville vicinity, 5/12/75, D, 75000914

Washington Aqueduct, 5900 MacArthur Blvd., NW, Great Falls, 9/08/73, A, C, NHL, 73002123

Washington Grove Historic District, MD 124, Washington Grove, 4/09/80, A, C, a, 80001829

West Montgomery Avenue Historic District, Residential area centered around W. Montgomery Ave., Rockville, 5/29/75, A, C, 75000915

Woodend, 8940 Jones Mill Rd., Chevy Chase, 3/20/80, B, C, 80001824

Wright, Robert Llewellyn, House, 7927 Deepwell Dr., Bethesda, 8/12/86, C, g, 86002621

Prince George's County

Accokeek Creek Site, Address Restricted, Accokeek vicinity, 10/15/66, D, NHL, NPS, 66000909

Ammendale Normal Institute, Jct. of Ammendale Rd. and U.S. 1, Beltsville, 4/14/75, A, C, a, 75002081

Ash Hill, 3308 Rosemary Lane, Hyattsville, 9/16/77, A, C, 77001523

Avondale Mill, 21 Avondale St., Laurel, 9/20/79, A, 79003267

Baltimore—Washington Parkway [Parkways of the National Capital Region MPS], DC border near the Anacostia R., NE to just below Jessup Rd. (MD 175), Baltimore vicinity, 5/09/91, A, C, g, NPS, 91000532

Beall's Pleasure, SE of Landover at 7250 Old Landover Rd., Landover vicinity, 5/04/79, A, B, C, b, 79003169

Belair, Tulip Grove and Belair Drives, Bowie, 9/16/77, A, C, 77001520

Belair Stables, Belair Dr., Bowie, 5/08/73, A, C, 73002163

Bellefields, S of Croom on Dudley Station Rd., Croom vicinity, 9/10/71, A, C, 71001027

Bellevue, 200 Manning Rd. E, Accokeek, 8/21/86, C, 86001738

Bostwick, 3901 48th St., Bladensburg, 8/19/75, A, C, 75002082

Bowieville, 2300 Church Rd., Upper Marlboro, 3/14/73, A, B, C, 73002167

Bowling Heights, 3610 Old Crane Hwy., Upper Marlboro vicinity, 11/30/82, C, 82001599

Brookefield of the Berrys, 12510 Molly Berry Rd., Croom vicinity, 6/25/87, C, 87001032

Buck House, Main St., Upper Marlboro, 4/20/78, A, C, 78003118

Civil War Fort Sites (Boundary Increase), S of Washington on Rosier Bluff, N of Washington off George Washington Parkway, Oxon Hill, vicinity, 9/13/78, A, NPS, 78003439

Coffren, John W., House and Store, 10007 Croom Rd., Croom, 6/02/87, B, C, 87000768

College Park Airport, E of College Park off Kenilworth Ave., College Park vicinity, 9/23/77, A, C, 77001522

Compton Bassett, 16508 Marlboro Pike, Upper Marlboro vicinity, 3/08/83, A, B, C, 83002959

Concord, 8000 Walker Mill Rd., District Heights vicinity, 5/12/82, A, C, 82004681

Content, 14518 Church St., Upper Marlboro, 9/13/78, A, C, 78003119

Prince George's County—Continued

Cottage, The, 11904 Old Marlboro Pk., Upper Marlboro vicinity, 7/13/89, B, C, 89000769

Early, William W., House, 13907 Cherry Tree Crossing Rd., Brandywine, 6/30/88, C, 88000984

Fort Washington, Fort Washington Park, Washington vicinity, 10/15/66, A, C, D, NPS, 66000965

Goodloe, Don S. S., House, 13809 Jericho Park Rd., Bowie vicinity, 10/13/88, B, 88001900

Greenbelt Historic District, Off MD 193, Greenbelt, 11/25/80, A, C, a, g, 80004331

Hamilton, James, House, 1311 Crain Hwy. North, Mitchellville, 11/10/88, C, 88002064

Harmony Hall, 10511 Livingston Rd., Oxon Hill, 6/06/80, C, NPS, 80000673

Hilleary, William, House, 4703 Annapolis Rd., Bladensburg, 7/20/78, A, C, 78003116

His Lordship's Kindness, 3.5 mi. NW of Rosaryville off Rosaryville Rd., Rosaryville vicinity, 4/15/70, C, NHL, 70000853

Hyattsville Armory, 5340 Baltimore Ave., Hyattsville, 3/27/80, A, C, 80004332

Hyattsville Historic District, Off US 1, Hyattsville, 3/25/82, C, a, 82004682

Kingston, 5415 Old Crain Hwy., Upper Marlboro, 7/21/78, A, C, 78003120

Laurel High School, 700 block of Montgomery St., Laurel, 6/27/79, A, C, 79003170

Laurel Railroad Station, E. Main St., Laurel, 3/30/73, A, C, 73002165

Market Master's House, 4006 48th St., Bladensburg, 3/29/90, A, 90000553

Melford, 5103 Crain Hwy., Mitchellville vicinity, 4/06/88, C, 88000271

Melwood Park, W of Upper Marlboro on MD 408, 0.5 mi. E of jct. with Melwood Rd., Upper Marlboro vicinity, 10/08/76, A, C, a, 76002169

Montpelier, 2.1 mi. E of Laurel on MD 197, Laurel vicinity, 4/17/70, C, NHL, 70000852

Mount Hope, 1 Cheverly Circle, Cheverly, 11/29/78, A, B, 78003180

Mount Lubentia, 603 Largo Rd., Largo, 7/09/87, C, b, 87001033

Mount Pleasant, Mt. Pleasant Rd., Upper Marlboro, 11/29/72, A, C, 72001482

Mount Rainier Historic District, Roughly bounded by Arundel St., 37th St., Bladensburg Rd. and Eastern Ave., Mount Rainier, 9/07/90, A, 90001319

Nottingham Site, Address Restricted, Upper Marlboro vicinity, 5/12/75, D, 75002083

O'Dea House, 5804 Ruatan St., Berwyn Heights, 6/04/87, A, C, 87000899

Oxon Hill Manor, 6701 Oxon Hill Rd., Oxon Hill, 6/09/78, A, B, 78003117

Piscataway Park, E of Potomac River, south of Piscataway Creek, in Prince George's and Charles Counties, Accokeek vicinity, 10/15/66, A, NPS, 66000144

Pleasant Hills, 7001 Croom Station Rd., Upper Marlboro vicinity, 8/06/80, A, C, 80004334

Pleasant Prospect, 12806 Woodmore Rd., Mitchellville, 4/30/76, A, C, 76002168

Riversdale, Riverdale Rd. between 18th and Taylor Sts., Riverdale, 4/11/73, A, C, 73002166

Saint Mary's Rectory, 16305 Saint Mary's Church Rd., Aquasco, 9/10/87, C, a, 87001572

Smith, Harry, House, 4707 Oliver St., Riverdale, 5/04/93, A, 93000342

Snow Hill, S of Laurel off MD 197, Laurel vicinity, 8/13/74, B, C, 74002200

Spacecraft Magnetic Test Facility, Goddard Space Flight Center, Greenbelt, 10/03/85, A, C, g, NHL, 85002811

St. Ignatius Church, 2317 Brinkley Rd., Oxon Hill, 6/27/74, A, C, a, 74002201

St. John's Church, 9801 Livingston Rd., Oxon Hill, 4/08/74, A, C, a, 74002202

St. Matthew's Church, Addison Rd. and 62nd Pl., Seat Pleasant, 4/10/72, A, C, a, 72001481

St. Paul's Parish Church, SE of Brandywine off MD 381, Brandywine vicinity, 9/15/77, A, C, a, 77001521

Sunnyside, 16005 Dr. Bowen Rd., Aquasco, 5/29/87, B, C, 87000840

Surratt House, 9110 Brandywine Rd., Clinton, 3/30/73, A, 73002164

Traband, John H., House, 14204 Marlboro Pike, Upper Marlboro, 3/22/84, C, 84001856

US Post Office—Hyattsville Main, 4325 Gallatin St., Hyattsville, 7/24/86, C, 86001906

Villa DeSales, 22410 Aquasco Rd., Aquasco, 7/14/88, C, 88001063

Washington, George, House, Baltimore Ave. at Upshur St., Bladensburg, 8/07/74, A, C, 74002198

Waverly, 8901 Duvall Rd., Croom vicinity, 6/02/87, C, 87000800

Williams Plains, MD 3, White Marsh Recreational Park, Bowie, 11/28/80, C, 80004329

Woodstock, 8706 SE Crain Hwy., Upper Marlboro vicinity, 9/21/87, C, 87001573

Woodyard Archeological Site, Address Restricted, Clinton vicinity, 12/19/74, A, B, D, 74002199

Wyoming, S of Clinton on Thrift Rd., Clinton vicinity, 1/24/80, A, C, 80004330

Queen Anne's County

Bachelor's Hope, MD 18, Centreville vicinity, 5/03/84, C, 84001855

Bishopton, Pinder Hill Rd., Church Hill vicinity, 9/12/85, C, 85002194

Bloomingdale, Bloomingdale Rd. and U.S. 50, Queenstown, 10/18/72, B, C, 72001457

Bowlingly, Off MD 18, Queenstown, 8/21/72, A, C, 72001458

Captain's Houses, Corsica St., Centreville, 11/17/80, A, C, 80001830

Centreville Armory [Maryland National Guard Armories TR], S. Commerce St., Centreville, 9/25/85, A, C, g, 85002666

Chester Hall, 1 mi. SE of Chestertown on SR 213, Chestertown vicinity, 1/18/80, C, 80001831

Christ Church, MD 18, Stevensville, 7/24/79, A, C, a, 79003268

Content, MD 305 near Tanyard Rd., Centreville vicinity, 2/13/86, C, 86000256

Cray House, Cockey's Lane, Stevensville, 5/09/83, C, 83002960

Dudley's Chapel, SW of Sudlersville off MD 300, Sudlersville vicinity, 11/15/79, A, C, a, 79003124

Embert, John, Farm, SE of Millington on Baxter Rd., .6 mi. E of Peters Comer Rd., Millington vicinity, 6/22/80, C, 80001832

Hawkins Pharsalia, MD 304, Ruthsburg vicinity, 12/20/84, C, 84000458

Kennersley, Clabber Hill Rd., Church Hill vicinity, 5/19/83, B, C, 83002961

Lansdowne, MD 305, Centreville vicinity, 6/07/84, C, 84001858

Lexon, Corsica Neck Rd. SW of Earle Cove, Centreville vicinity, 5/04/90, C, 90000726

MYSTERY (log canoe) [Chesapeake Bay Sailing Log Canoe Fleet TR], Round Top Rd., Kingstown vicinity, 9/18/85, A, C, 85002250

Ozmon, Capt. John H., Store, Centreville Wharf, Centreville, 2/14/85, A, C, 85000277

Readbourne, 5.4 mi. NW of Centreville, Centreville vicinity, 4/11/73, A, C, 73002134

Reed's Creek Farm, W of Centreville on Wright's Neck Rd. off MD 18, Centreville vicinity, 7/07/75, A, C, 75002106

St. Andrew's Episcopal Chapel, Church St. and Maple Ave., Sudlersville, 9/07/84, C, a, 84001853

St. Luke's Church, Jct. of MD 213 and MD 19, Church Hill, 11/23/77, A, C, a, 77001505

St. Peter's Church, SE of Queenstown on U.S. 50, Queenstown vicinity, 3/10/80, A, C, a, 80001833

Stevensville Bank, Love Point Rd., Stevensville, 1/03/85, A, C, 85000020

Stevensville Historic District, MD 18 and Love Point Rd., Stevensville, 9/11/86, A, C, 86002333

Thomas House, 1.8 mi. NE of Ruthsburg on MD 304, Ruthsburg vicinity, 5/13/76, C, 76002150

Wilton, N of Wye Mills on MD 213, Wye Mills vicinity, 12/12/77, A, C, 77001506

Wye Mill, MD 662, Wye Mills, 4/09/85, A, 85000717

Somerset County

Academy Grove Historic District, MD 361, Upper Fairmount vicinity, 5/03/84, C, 84001863

Adams Farm, Princess Anne—Westover Rd., Princess Anne vicinity, 11/10/88, C, 88002140

All Saints Church at Monie, Venton Rd. NW of jct. with Deal Island Rd., Venton vicinity, 8/03/90, C, a, 90001167

Arlington, MD 361, Westover vicinity, 5/21/92, C, 92000588

Beauchamp House, Old Westover-Marion Rd., Westover vicinity, 8/09/84, C, 84003855

Beckford, Beckford Ave., Princess Anne, 8/13/74, A, C, 74000963

Beverly, S of Princess Anne on U.S. 13, Princess Anne vicinity, 3/30/73, B, C, 73000937

Brentwood Farm, Allen Rd., Allen vicinity, 9/04/86, C, 86002174

Somerset County—Continued

CLARENCE CROCKETT [Chesapeake Bay Skipjack Fleet TR], Lower Thorofare, Wenona, 5/16/85, A, 85001079

Caldicott, SW of US 13, Rehobeth vicinity, 12/22/83, B, C, 83003796

Cannon, Burton, House, 1 mi. N of Cokesbury on Dublin Rd., Cokesbury vicinity, 4/03/75, C, 75000916

Catalpa Farm, Old Princess Anne—Westover Rd., Princess Anne vicinity, 11/10/88, C, 88002049

Cedar Hill, E. side of Sign Post Rd. at Back Cr., Westover vicinity, 3/14/91, C, 91000255

Costen, William, House, Courthouse Hill Rd., Wellington vicinity, 3/28/85, C, 85000654

Coventry Parish Ruins, Off MD 667, Rehobeth vicinity, 8/09/84, A, C, a, 84001869

Crisfield Armory [Maryland National Guard Armories TR], Main St. Extended, Crisfield, 9/25/85, A, C, g, 85002669

Crisfield Historic District, Roughly bounded by Chesapeake Ave., Maryland Ave., 4th and Cove Sts., including area between Asbury Ave. and E. Main St., Crisfield, 7/09/90, A, C, 90001018

F. C. LEWIS, JR [Chesapeake Bay Skipjack Fleet TR], Lower Thorofare, Wenona, 5/16/85, A, 85001080

FANNIE L. DAUGHERTY [Chesapeake Bay Skipjack Fleet TR], Lower Thorofare, Wenona, 5/16/85, A, 85001081

Grace Episcopal Church, Mt. Vernon Rd. N of jct. with Ridge Rd., Mt. Vernon vicinity, 11/01/90, C, a, 90001565

HOWARD [Chesapeake Bay Skipjack Fleet TR], Lower Thorofare, Wenona, 5/16/85, A, 85001082

Harrington, NW of Princess Anne off MD 362, Princess Anne vicinity, 9/11/75, A, C, 75000918

Hayman, Jeptha, House, Westover—Marion Rd. S of jct. with Charles Barnes Rd., Kingston vicinity, 12/27/90, C, 90001939

Hayward's Lott, 1.75 mi. NW of Pocomoke City on Hayward Rd., Pocomoke City vicinity, 5/13/76, C, 76001009

IDA MAY [Chesapeake Bay Skipjack Fleet TR], Upper thorofare, Chance, 5/16/85, A, 85001077

ISLAND BELLE, Ewell, Smith Island, 3/16/79, A, 79001141

Kingston Hall, W side of MD 667, 0.5 mi. from Kingston, Kingston, 12/31/74, B, C, 74000962

Lankford House, MD 667, Marion vicinity, 8/09/84, C, 84001870

Liberty Hall, S of Westover off MD 361, Westover vicinity, 12/27/76, C, 76001012

Maddox, George, Farm, River Rd., Manokin vicinity, 9/17/85, A, C, 85002410

Make Peace, 1.5 mi. SE of Crisfield on Johnson's Creek Rd., Crisfield vicinity, 11/20/75, C, 75000917

Manokin Historic District, SW of Princess Anne at Manokin River, Princess Anne vicinity, 6/29/76, A, C, 76001010

Manokin Presbyterian Church, N. Somerset Ave., Princess Anne, 11/21/76, A, C, a, 76001011

Nelson Homestead, Cash Corner & Hopewell-Bedsworth Rds., Crisfield vicinity, 9/12/85, C, 85002175

Panther's Den, Drawbridge Rd., Ventor, 3/22/84, C, 84001872

Pomfret Plantation, MD 667, Marion vicinity, 9/07/84, C, d, 84001874

Princess Anne Historic District, Off MD 413, Princess Anne, 10/14/80, A, C, 80001834

Rehobeth Presbyterian Church, S of Rehobeth off MD 667, Rehobeth, 11/05/74, A, C, a, 74000964

Reward, SE of Shelltown on Williams Point Rd., Shelltown vicinity, 8/13/74, C, 74000965

Rock Creek Methodist Episcopal Church, Deal Island Rd. NE of Scotts Cove, Chance, 11/02/90, C, a, 90001718

SEA GULL [Chesapeake Bay Skipjack Fleet TR], Lower thorofare, Deal Island, 5/16/85, A, 85001078

SUSAN MAY [Chesapeake Bay Skipjack Fleet TR], Lower Thorofare, Wenona, 5/16/85, A, 85001083

Salisbury Plantation, SW of Westover off MD 361, Westover vicinity, 6/20/75, C, 75000919

Schoolridge Farm, MD 361, Upper Fairmount vicinity, 9/07/84, C, d, 84001876

Smith, William S., House, S side of Oriole Rd. E of jct. with Crab Island Rd., Oriole, 7/09/91, C, 91000891

Somerset Academy, Address Restricted, Princess Anne vicinity, 9/11/86, D, 86002356

St. John's Methodist Episcopal Church and Joshua Thomas Chapel, Deal Island Rd. N of jct. with Tangier Rd., Deal Island, 11/01/90, A, C, a, 90001550

St. Mark's Episcopal Church, Jct. of Westover—Marion and Charles Barnes Rds., Kingston vicinity, 10/25/90, C, a, b, 90001569

St. Paul's Protestant Episcopal Church, Near jct. of Farm Market Rd. and St. Pauls Church Rd., Tulls Corner vicinity, 8/03/90, C, a, 90001153

St. Peter's Methodist Episcopal Church, Jct. of Old Crisfield—Marion Rd. and Heart's Ease Rd., Hopewell vicinity, 11/02/90, C, a, 90001721

Sudler's Conclusion, NW of Manokin off MD 361, Manokin vicinity, 8/28/73, A, C, 73000936

THOMAS W. CLYDE [Chesapeake Bay Skipjack Fleet TR], Lower Thorofare, Wenona, 5/16/85, A, 85001084

Tawes, Capt. Leonard, House, Somerset Ave., Crisfield, 4/05/90, C, 90000598

Teackle Mansion, Mansion St., Princess Anne, 10/26/71, B, C, 71000378

Tudor Hall, SE of Upper Fairmount off MD 36, Upper Fairmount vicinity, 12/19/74, A, C, 74000966

Upper Fairmount Historic District, Both sides of MD 361, Upper Fairmount, 9/13/93, A, C, 93000900

Waddy House, Perryhawkin Rd., Princess Anne vicinity, 11/03/88, C, 88002221

Waterloo, Mt. Vernon Rd., Princess Anne vicinity, 2/13/86, C, 86000257

Waters' River, Hood Rd., Manokin vicinity, 8/09/84, C, 84001882

White Hall, Cooley Rd., Princess Anne vicinity, 6/07/84, C, 84003868

Williams' Conquest, Charles Cannon Rd., Marion Station vicinity, 5/03/84, C, 84001886

St. Mary's County

Bachelor's Hope, Off MD 238, Chaptico, 11/07/72, C, 72001483

Bard's Field, 1.2 mi. W of Ridge off Curleys Rd., Ridge vicinity, 11/07/76, C, 76002172

Cecil's Mill Historic District, N of Great Mills on Indian Bridge Rd., Great Mills vicinity, 1/30/78, A, C, 78003121

Charlotte Hall Historic District, S of Hughesville at jct. of MD 5 and 6, Hughesville vicinity, 5/02/75, A, C, 75002085

Cross Manor, Cross Manor Rd., St. Inigoes vicinity, 10/06/88, B, C, 88001705

Deep Falls, 1 mi. SE of Chaptico on N side of MD 234, Chaptico vicinity, 5/12/75, A, C, 75002084

MARY W.SOMERS (Chesapeake Bay skipjack), SE of St. Marys City at St. Inigoe's Creek, St. Marys City vicinity, 10/08/76, A, 76002173

Mattapany-Sewall Archeological Site, Address Restricted, Lexington Park vicinity, 2/01/85, A, B, D, 85000164

Mulberry Fields, About 4.5 mi. SE of Beauvue off MD 244, Beauvue vicinity, 3/14/73, A, C, 73002169

Ocean Hall, Bushwood Rd. off MD 239 at Bushwood Wharf, Bushwood vicinity, 10/25/73, C, 73002170

Piney Point Coast Guard Light Station, W of Piney Point on MD 498, Piney Point vicinity, 6/16/76, A, 76002171

Porto Bello, MD 244 E of Drayden, Drayden, 4/26/72, A, C, 72001486

Resurrection Manor, 4.5 mi. SE of Hollywood, Hollywood vicinity, 4/15/70, C, NHL, 70000855

River View, The, SE of Oakley on Burch Rd. on Canoe Neck Creek, Oakley vicinity, 5/04/76, B, C, 76002170

Sandgates On Cat Creek, E of Oakville on MD 472, 1/2 mi. from Patuxent River, Oakville vicinity, 11/14/78, A, C, 78003179

Sotterley, E of jct. of MD 245 and Vista Rd., Hollywood vicinity, 11/09/72, A, C, 72001487

St. Andrew's Church, 5 mi. E of Leonardtown on St. Andrew's Church Rd., Leonardtown vicinity, 3/14/73, A, C, a, 73002171

St. Clement's Island Historic District, S of Colton Point on the Potomac River, Colton vicinity, 4/10/72, A, 72001484

St. Francis Xavier Church and Newtown Manor House, S of Compton on MD 243, Compton, 11/09/72, A, C, a, 72001485

St. George's Protestant Episcopal Church, W of Valley Lee, off MD 249 on MD 244, Valley Lee vicinity, 10/03/73, C, a, d, 73002173

St. Ignatius Roman Catholic Church, W of St. Inigoes on Villa Rd., St. Inigoes vicinity, 11/03/75, A, a, 75002086

St. Mary's County—Continued

St. Marys City Historic District, Address Restricted, St. Marys City vicinity, 8/04/69, A, C, D, NHL, 69000310

St. Richard's Manor, Millstone Landing Rd., Lexington Park vicinity, 3/28/85, C, 85000655

Tudor Hall, Tudor Hall Rd., Leonardtown, 4/26/73, A, C, 73002172

West St. Mary's Manor, About 1 mi. E of Drayden on the St. Mary's River, Drayden vicinity, 4/15/70, C, NHL, 70000854

Woodlawn, S of St. Marys on MD 252, W of MD Rt. 5, St. Marys, 4/02/80, C, 80004335

Talbot County

All Saints' Church, MD 662, Easton vicinity, 5/27/83, C, 83002962

Anchorage, The, NW of Easton off MD 370, Easton vicinity, 7/30/74, B, C, 74000968

BILLIE P. HALL (log canoe) [Chesapeake Bay Sailing Log Canoe Fleet TR], Evergreen Rd., Oxford vicinity, 9/18/85, A, C, 85002251

Barnaby House, 212 N. Morris St., Oxford, 11/24/92, C, 92001228

CLAUDE W. SOMERS [Chesapeake Bay Skipjack Fleet TR], Old Ferry Terminal, Washington St., Clairborne, 5/16/85, A, 85001085

Cannonball House, 200 Mulberry St., St. Michaels, 12/03/80, A, C, 80001839

Clay's Hope, Bellevue Rd, Bellevue, 10/31/79, A, C, 79001142

Compton, W of Trappe on Howell Point Rd., Trappe vicinity, 7/25/74, B, C, 74000970

Crooked Intention, W of MD 33, St. Michaels, 7/24/74, B, C, 74000969

Doncaster Town Site, Address Restricted, Easton vicinity, 9/05/75, D, 75000920

E.C. COLLIER [Chesapeake Bay Skipjack Fleet TR], Gibsontown Rd., Tilghman, 5/16/85, A, 85001087

EDMEE S. (log canoe) [Chesapeake Bay Sailing Log Canoe Fleet TR], Mill St., St. Michaels, 9/18/85, A, C, 85002258

EDNA E. LOCKWOOD (Chesapeake Bay bugeye), Navy Pt., foot of Mill St., St. Michaels, 2/13/86, A, C, 86000258

ELSWORTH [Chesapeake Bay Skipjack Fleet TR], Gibsontown Rd., Tilghman, 5/16/85, A, 85001088

Easton Historic District, MD 565, MD 328 and MD 331, Easton, 9/17/80, A, C, 80001835

FLYING CLOUD (log canoe) [Chesapeake Bay Sailing Log Canoe Fleet TR], Magee Rd., Wittman vicinity, 9/18/85, A, C, 85002263

HILDA M. WILLING [Chesapeake Bay Skipjack Fleet TR], Gibsontown Rd., Tilghman, 5/16/85, A, 85001089

Hope House, NW of Easton, NE of Voit Rd., .8 mi. NW of bridge at Tunis Mill, Easton vicinity, 11/01/79, A, C, 79001143

ISLAND BIRD (log canoe) [Chesapeake Bay Sailing Log Canoe Fleet TR], Miles River Yacht Club, St. Michaels vicinity, 9/18/85, A, C, 85002254

ISLAND BLOSSOM (log canoe) [Chesapeake Bay Sailing Log Canoe Fleet TR], Miles River Yacht Club, St. Michaels vicinity, 9/18/85, A, C, 85002255

ISLAND LARK (log canoe) [Chesapeake Bay Sailing Log Canoe Fleet TR], Carpenter St., St. Michaels, 9/18/85, A, C, 85002259

JAY DEE (log canoe) [Chesapeake Bay Sailing Log Canoe Fleet TR], Miles River Yacht Club, St. Michaels vicinity, 9/18/85, A, C, 85002256

Jena, E of Oxford off MD 333, Oxford vicinity, 8/06/80, C, 80001838

KATHRYN [Chesapeake Bay Skipjack Fleet TR], Gibsontown Rd., Tilghman, 5/16/85, A, 85001090

MAGGIE LEE [Chesapeake Bay Skipjack Fleet TR], Gibsontown Rd., Tilghman, 5/16/85, A, 85001091

MAGIC (log canoe) [Chesapeake Bay Sailing Log Canoe Fleet TR], St. Michaels Marina, St. Michaels, 9/18/85, A, C, 85002260

MINNIE V [Chesapeake Bay Skipjack Fleet TR], Gibsontown Rd., Tilghman, 5/16/85, A, 85001092

Myrtle Grove, Goldsborough Neck Rd., Easton, 8/13/74, B, C, 74000967

NELLIE L. BYRD [Chesapeake Bay Skipjack Fleet TR], Gibsontown Rd., Tilghman, 5/16/85, A, 85001093

NODDY (log canoe) [Chesapeake Bay Sailing Log Canoe Fleet TR], Deepwater Point Rd., St. Michaels vicinity, 9/18/85, A, C, 85002257

Old Bloomfield, W of Easton on Bloomfield Rd., Easton vicinity, 12/03/80, A, C, 80001836

Old Inn, The, Talbot and Mulberry Sts., St. Michaels, 3/25/80, A, C, 80001840

Old Wye Church, Queenstown-Easton Rd., Wye Mills, 8/09/84, C, a, 84001888

Orem's Delight, S of Bellevue off Ferry Neck Rd., on Benoni Point Rd., Bellevue vicinity, 4/04/78, C, 78001477

Otwell, Otwell Rd., Oxford vicinity, 3/15/82, C, 82002819

PERSISTENCE (log canoe) [Chesapeake Bay Sailing Log Canoe Fleet TR], St. Michaels Marina, St. Michaels, 9/18/85, A, C, 85002261

RALPH T. WEBSTER [Chesapeake Bay Skipjack Fleet TR], Gibsontown Rd., Tilghman, 5/16/85, A, 85001094

REBECCA T. RUARK [Chesapeake Bay Skipjack Fleet TR], Gibsontown Rd., Tilghman, 5/16/85, A, 85001095

RELIANCE (Chesapeake Bay skipjack), Knapps Narrows off MD 33, Tilghman, 7/30/76, A, 76001013

ROVER (log canoe) [Chesapeake Bay Sailing Log Canoe Fleet TR], St. Michaels Marina, St. Michaels, 9/18/85, A, C, 85002262

RUBY G. FORD [Chesapeake Bay Skipjack Fleet TR], Gibsontown Rd., Tilghman, 5/16/85, A, 85001096

Rock Clift, SE of Matthews off MD 328, Matthews vicinity, 7/30/80, A, C, 80001837

S. C. DOBSON (log canoe) [Chesapeake Bay Sailing Log Canoe Fleet TR], Peach Blossom Rd., Oxford vicinity, 9/18/85, A, C, 85002252

SANDY (log canoe) [Chesapeake Bay Sailing Log Canoe Fleet TR], Sherwood Rd., Sherwood, 9/18/85, A, C, 85002253

SIGSBEE [Chesapeake Bay Skipjack Fleet TR], Knapps Narrows, Tilghman, 5/16/85, A, 85001097

STANLEY NORMAN [Chesapeake Bay Skipjack Fleet TR], Edgar Cove, St. Michaels, 5/16/85, A, 85001086

Saint Michaels Mill, 100 Chew Ave., St. Michaels, 7/15/82, A, C, 82002820

Sharps Island Light, SW of Tilghman Island, Tilghman Island vicinity, 7/22/82, A, 82002821

Sherwood Manor, 4 mi. N of St. Michaels on MD 451, St. Michaels vicinity, 4/05/77, B, C, 77000701

St. John's Chapel of St. Michael's Parish, 3 mi. W of Easton on MD 370, Easton vicinity, 3/30/73, A, C, a, 73000938

St. Michaels Historic District, Roughly bounded by North Ave., Mill St., the Miles River, Seymour, Baltimore & Eastern RR tracks, and Glory Ave., St. Michaels, 9/11/86, A, C, 86002427

Troth's Fortune, 3.25 mi. E of Easton on MD 331, Easton vicinity, 4/24/75, B, C, 75000921

VIRGINIA W [Chesapeake Bay Skipjack Fleet TR], Knapps Narrows, Tilghman, 5/16/85, A, 85001098

Victorian Corn Cribs, 6.8 mi. E of St. Michaels off MD 33, St. Michaels vicinity, 1/11/76, A, C, b, 76002289

Wilderness, The, SW of Trappe on Island Neck Rd., Trappe vicinity, 7/25/74, B, C, 74000971

Wye House, 7 mi. NW of Easton on Miles Neck River, Easton vicinity, 4/15/70, C, NHL, 70000264

Wye Town Farm House, NW of Easton on Bruff's Island Rd., Easton vicinity, 12/16/82, C, 82001600

Washington County

Antietam Furnace Complex Archeological Site, Address Restricted, Hagerstown vicinity, 8/25/83, A, C, D, 83002963

Antietam Hall, 525 Indian Lane, Hagerstown, 9/24/79, C, 79003269

Antietam Iron Furnace Site and Antietam Village, Confluence of Antietam Creek and Potomac River, Antietam vicinity, 6/26/75, A, NPS, 75000149

Antietam National Battlefield, N of Sharpsburg off MD 45, Sharpsburg, 10/15/66, A, d, NPS, 66000038

B & O Bridge, NW of Keedysville over Antietam Creek, Keedysville vicinity, 11/23/77, A, C, 77000704

B & O Railroad Potomac River Crossing, At confluence of the Shenandoah and Potomac Rivers, Harpers Ferry vicinity, 2/14/78, A, C, g, 78001484

Washington County—Continued

Baker Farm, N of Keedysville off MD Rt. 34, Keedysville vicinity, 10/19/78, A, C, 78001485

Bell-Varner House, SE of Leitersburg on Unger Rd., Leitersburg vicinity, 9/24/79, C, 79003271

Bowman House, 323 N. Main St., Boonsboro, 4/29/77, B, C, 77000702

Brightwood, N of Hagerstown off MD 6, 2 mi. N of Paramont, Hagerstown vicinity, 7/30/74, A, C, 74000973

Chapline, William, House, 109 W. Main St., Sharpsburg, 10/08/76, A, B, C, 76001020

Colonial Theatre, 12–14 S. Potomac St., Hagerstown, 8/02/78, A, C, a, 78001478

Ditto Knolls, E of Hagerstown on Landis Rd., Hagerstown vicinity, 7/12/76, A, C, 76001014

Dorsey-Palmer House, N of Hagerstown on MD 60, Hagerstown vicinity, 4/15/78, A, C, 78001479

Doub Farm, N of Keedysville, Keedysville vicinity, 11/15/78, A, C, 78001486

Doub's Mill Historic District, SW of Beaver Creek on Beaver Creek Rd., Beaver Creek vicinity, 10/01/79, A, C, 79003270

Elliot-Bester House, 205–207 S. Potomac St., Hagerstown, 5/02/75, B, C, 75000924

Fort Frederick State Park, SE of Big Pool near jct. of MD 56 and 44, Big Pool vicinity, 11/07/73, A, C, e, NHL, 73000939

Geeting Farm, S of Keedysville at Geeting and Dog Rds., Keedysville vicinity, 11/25/77, C, 77000705

Hager House, 19 Key St., Hagerstown, 11/05/74, A, C, 74000974

Hagerstown Armory [Maryland National Guard Armories TR], 328 N. Potomac St., Hagerstown, 9/25/85, A, C, 85002673

Hagerstown Charity School, 102 E. Washington St., Hagerstown, 12/16/82, A, C, 82001601

Hagerstown City Park Historic District, Roughly bounded by W. Howard St., Guilford Ave., Memorial, S. Walnut St., and the Norfolk & Western RR tracks, Hagerstown, 7/05/90, A, C, 90001017

Hagerstown Commercial Core Historic District, Potomac, Washington, Franklin, Antietam, Summit and Jonathan Sts., Hagerstown, 1/17/83, A, C, 83002964

Harpers Ferry National Historical Park, At confluence of Shenandoah and Potomac rivers, Harpers Ferry, 10/15/66, A, B, C, D, b, e, NPS, 66000041

Hitt's Mill and Houses, W of Keedysville off MD 34, Keedysville vicinity, 4/12/79, A, C, 79001147

Hogmire-Berryman Farm, N of Spielman off MD 63, Spielman vicinity, 3/28/80, A, C, 80001842

Houses At 16–22 East Lee Street, 16–22 E. Lee St., Hagerstown, 11/25/77, A, C, 77000703

Huckleberry Hall, Charles Mill Rd. W of jct. with MD 64, Leitersburg vicinity, 12/28/90, C, 90001994

Ingram-Schipper Farm, N of Boonsboro, Boonsboro vicinity, 9/24/79, C, 79003259

John Brown's Headquarters, Chestnut Grove Rd., Samples Manor, 11/07/73, B, NHL, 73000941

Keedy House, NW of Boonsboro off U.S. 40A on Barnes Rd., Boonsboro vicinity, 7/25/74, A, C, 74000972

Lehman's Mill Historic District, Lehman's Mill Rd. between Marsh Pike and Marsh Run, Hagerstown vicinity, 1/04/91, A, C, 90001945

Long Meadows, N of Hagerstown on Marsh Pike, Hagerstown vicinity, 9/01/78, A, C, 78001480

Magnolia Plantation, NW of Knoxville off Sandy Hook Rd., Knoxville vicinity, 6/18/75, C, 75000926

Mannheim, San Mar Rd., Sanmar, 9/25/79, A, C, 79003260

Maples, The, 2 mi. SW of Smithsburg on MD 66, Smithsburg vicinity, 2/24/75, C, 75000927

Maryland Theatre, 21–23 S. Potomac St., Hagerstown, 11/13/76, A, C, 76001015

McCauley, Henry, Farm, E of Hagerstown on Mt. Aetna Rd., Hagerstown vicinity, 6/29/76, A, C, 76001016

Mount Airy, MD 34, Sharpsburg vicinity, 7/10/86, A, B, C, 86001550

Oak Hill Historic District, Roughly bounded by W. Irvin, Potomac, and Prospect Aves. and Forest Dr., Hagerstown, 9/18/87, A, C, g, 87001574

Old Forge Farm, E of Hagerstown, Hagerstown vicinity, 11/07/79, A, C, 79001145

Old Washington County Library, 21 Summit Ave., Hagerstown, 10/02/78, C, b, 78001481

Paradise Manor, N of Hagerstown at 2550 Paradise Dr., Hagerstown vicinity, 3/31/78, A, C, 78001482

Potomac—Broadway Historic District, Roughly, Potomac St. & Oak Hill Ave. from Franklin St. to Maple Ave. & North Ave. & Broadway from Park Pl. to Mulberry, Hagerstown, 12/12/90, A, C, 90001804

Price-Miller House, 131–135 W. Washington St., Hagerstown, 5/24/76, B, C, 76001018

Rockland Farm, 728 Antietam Dr., Hagerstown vicinity, 7/21/78, C, 78001483

Rohrer House, E of Hagerstown, Hagerstown vicinity, 11/07/79, A, C, 79001146

Rose Hill, 0.5 mi. S of Williamsport on MD 63, Williamsport vicinity, 4/11/73, C, 73000942

Search Well, SE of Burtner on Manor Church Rd., Burtner vicinity, 1/17/83, C, 83002965

Snively Farm, N of Eakles Mills on Mt. Briar Rd., Eakles Mills vicinity, 9/24/79, A, C, 79001144

South Prospect Street Historic District, 18–278 S. Prospect St., Hagerstown, 10/01/79, A, C, 79003261

Sprechers Mill House, NE of Williamsport on Hopewell Rd., Williamsport vicinity, 1/05/78, A, C, 78001487

Springfield Farm, S of U.S. 11, Williamsport, 7/30/74, B, 74000977

Tammany, NE of Williamsport off US 11, Williamsport vicinity, 9/24/79, A, C, 79003262

Trovinger Mill, 3 mi. E of Hagerstown on Trovinger Mill Rd. and Antietam Creek, Hagerstown vicinity, 4/21/75, A, 75000925

Valentia, S of Hagerstown on Poffenberger Rd. off MD 65, Hagerstown vicinity, 6/27/74, A, C, 74000975

Washington County Courthouse, W. Washington St. and Summit Ave., Hagerstown, 12/24/74, C, 74000976

Washington Monument, Washington Monument State Park, Boonsboro vicinity, 11/03/72, A, C, e, 72000588

Western Maryland Railroad Right-of-Way, Milepost 126 to Milepost 160, Milepost 126 to Milepost 160, Woodmont, vicinity, 7/23/81, A, C, NPS, 81000078

Western Maryland Railway Station, Burhans Blvd., Hagerstown, 4/22/76, A, C, 76001019

Western Maryland Railway Steam Locomotive No. 202, City Park, Hagerstown, 6/07/84, A, 84001884

Willows, The, SW of Cavetown on MD 66, Cavetown vicinity, 2/23/73, A, C, 73000940

Wilson's Bridge, U.S. 40, Hagerstown vicinity, 3/15/82, A, C, 82002822

Wilson-Miller Farm, SE of Sharpsburg, Sharpsburg vicinity, 5/23/80, A, C, 80001841

Wicomico County

Bennett's Adventure, 3 mi. W of Allen on Clifford Cooper Rd., Allen vicinity, 11/20/75, C, 75000928

Bounds Lott, 4 mi. (6.4 km) W of Allen, Allen vicinity, 11/14/78, C, 78001488

Gillis-Grier House, 401 N. Division St., Salisbury, 10/31/72, C, 72000589

Jackson, Sen. William P., House, 514 Camden Ave., Salisbury, 9/28/76, B, C, a, 76001022

Long Hill, Wetipquin Ferry Rd, Wetipquin vicinity, 12/31/74, B, C, 74000978

Pemberton Hall, Pemberton Rd., Salisbury, 2/18/71, B, C, 71000379

Perry-Cooper House, 200 E. William St., Salisbury, 11/17/77, B, C, 77000706

Poplar Hill Mansion, 117 Elizabeth St., Salisbury, 10/07/71, C, 71000380

Spring Hill Church, 1 mi. NE of Hebron at jct. of U.S. 50 and MD 347, Hebron vicinity, 10/22/76, A, C, a, 76001021

St. Bartholomew's Episcopal Church, Green Hill Church Rd., Quantico, 6/05/75, A, C, a, 75000929

St. Giles, SW of Hebron on MD 347, Hebron vicinity, 12/20/82, C, 82001602

Western Fields, Porter Mill Rd., Hebron vicinity, 6/12/87, C, 87000641

Whitehaven Historic District, Whitehaven Rd., Church and River Sts., Cinder and Locust Lanes, Whitehaven, 1/09/80, A, C, 80001843

Yellow Brick House, MD 352, .4 mi. E of MD 349, Bilvalve vicinity, 5/22/78, C, 78001489

Worcester County

All Hallows Episcopal Church, 101 N. Church St., Snow Hill, 8/06/79, C, a, 79001148

Worcester County—Continued

Berlin Commercial District, Main, Broad, Williams, Bay, Pitts and Commerce Sts., Berlin, 4/17/80, C, 80001844

Beverly, 4.5 mi. SW of Pocomoke City off Cedarhall Rd., Pocomoke City vicinity, 10/29/75, C, 75000933

Buckingham Archeological Site, Address Restricted, Berlin vicinity, 2/24/75, D, 75000930

Burley Manor, 3 S. Main St., Berlin, 7/07/74, C, 74000979

Caleb's Discovery, 2 mi. W of Berlin on U.S. 50, Berlin vicinity, 5/27/75, C, 75000931

Costen House, 206 Market St., Pocomoke, 12/06/75, B, C, 75000934

Genesar, SE of Berlin on MD 611 off U.S. 50, Berlin vicinity, 9/17/71, C, 71000381

Henry's Grove, MD 611, Berlin vicinity, 9/13/84, C, 84001891

Merry Sherwood, 8909 Worcester Hwy., Berlin vicinity, 9/20/91, C, 91001420

Nassawango Iron Furnace Site, NW of Snow Hill off MD 12 on Old Furnace Rd., Snow Hill vicinity, 10/31/75, A, 75000935

Nun's Green, S of Snow Hill on Cherrix Rd., Snow Hill vicinity, 9/20/79, C, 79003263

Sandy Point Site, Address Restricted, Ocean City vicinity, 4/28/75, D, 75000932

St. Martins Church, 1 mi. S of Showell at jct. of U.S. 113 and MD 589, Showell vicinity, 4/13/77, C, a, 77000707

The Chesapeake Bay Skipjack Fleet is the last commercial sailing fleet in the nation. Crews of 35 skipjacks, including the Talbot County, Maryland, based KATHYRN (built 1901), continue to dredge for oysters as their predecessors have since the 1890s. (M.C. Wootton, 1983)

MASSACHUSETTS

Barnstable County

Adams—Crocker—Fish House [Barnstable MRA], 449 Willow St., Barnstable, 3/13/87, C, b, 87000219

Ahearn House and Summer House, Pamet Point Rd., Wellfleet, 11/21/84, C, NPS, 84000575

Ames, Josiah A., House [Barnstable MRA], 145 Bridge St., Barnstable, 9/18/87, A, C, 87000300

Ancient Burying Ground [Barnstable MRA], Phinney's Ln., Barnstable, 3/13/87, A, C, d, 87000283

Atwood, Thomas, House, NW of Wellfleet on Boundbrook Island, Wellfleet vicinity, 7/30/76, C, NPS, 76000154

Baker, Benjamin, Jr., House [Barnstable MRA], 1579 Hyannis Rd., Barnstable, 11/10/87, A, C, 87000352

Baker, Capt. Seth, Jr., House [Barnstable MRA], 35 Main St., Barnstable, 9/18/87, A, C, 87000299

Baker, Nathaniel, House [Barnstable MRA], 1606 Hyannis Rd., Barnstable, 3/13/87, B, C, 87000229

Barnstable County Courthouse, Main St., Barnstable, 6/11/81, A, C, 81000104

Baxter Mill, MA 28, West Yarmouth, 8/27/81, A, 81000120

Baxter, Capt. Rodney J., House [Barnstable MRA], South and Pearl Sts., Barnstable, 3/13/87, B, C, 87000273

Baxter, Capt. Sylvester, House [Barnstable MRA], 156 Main St., Barnstable, 3/13/87, B, C, 87000313

Baxter, Charles L., House [Barnstable MRA], 77 Main St., Barnstable, 3/13/87, C, 87000315

Baxter, Shubael, House [Barnstable MRA], 9 E. Bay Rd., Barnstable, 9/18/87, C, 87000304

Beacon, The [Lighthouses of Massachusetts TR], Nauset Beach, Eastham, 6/15/87, A, C, b, NPS, 87001527

Bearse, Capt. Allen H., House [Barnstable MRA], 48 Camp St., Barnstable, 3/13/87, B, C, 87000264

Bearse, Capt. Oliver, House [Barnstable MRA], 31 Pearl St., Barnstable, 3/13/87, C, 87000276

Berry, Captain James, House, 37 Main St., Harwich, 9/26/86, B, C, 86001837

Blish—Garret House [Barnstable MRA], 350 Plum St., Barnstable, 3/13/87, A, C, 87000327

Brandeis, Louis, House, Neck Lane, off Cedar St., 8 mi. SW of Stage Harbor Rd. intersection, Chatham, 11/28/72, B, NHL, 72000148

Bray, Thomas, Farm, 280 Weir Rd., Yarmouth, 9/15/88, A, C, 88001455

Brick Block, Main St. and Chatham Bars Rd., Chatham, 4/13/79, A, C, 79000323

Briggs, George I., House, Sandwich Rd., Bourne, 9/10/81, B, C, 81000119

Building at 237–239 Main Street [Barnstable MRA], 237–239 Main St., Barnstable, 3/13/87, A, C, 87000293

Building at 600 Main Street [Barnstable MRA], 600 Main St., Barnstable, 3/13/87, A, C, 87000286

Building at 606 Main Street [Barnstable MRA], 606 Main St., Barnstable, 3/13/87, A, C, 87000287

Building at 614 Main Street [Barnstable MRA], 614 Main St., Barnstable, 3/13/87, A, C, 87000285

Campbell, Collen C., House [Barnstable MRA], 599 Main St., Barnstable, 3/13/87, A, C, 87000297

Canary—Hartnett House [Barnstable MRA], 113 Winter St., Barnstable, 3/13/87, A, C, 87000260

Center Methodist Church, 356 Commercial St., Provincetown, 10/31/75, A, C, a, 75000247

Centerville Historic District [Barnstable MRA], Main St., Barnstable, 11/10/87, A, C, a, 87002587

Chase, Lemuel B., House [Barnstable MRA], 340 Scudder Ave., Barnstable, 3/13/87, C, 87000267

Chatham Light Station [Lighthouses of Massachusetts TR], Main St., Chatham, 6/15/87, A, C, 87001501

Chatham Railroad Depot, 153 Depot Rd., Chatham, 11/27/78, A, C, 78000422

Chatham Windmill, Chase Park, Shattuck Pl., Chatham, 11/30/78, A, 78000421

Cleveland Ledge Light Station [Lighthouses of Massachusetts TR], Cape Cod Canal, Bourne vicinity, 6/15/87, A, C, g, 87001462

Codman, Col. Charles, Estate [Barnstable MRA], 43 Ocean View Ave., Barnstable, 3/13/87, A, C, 87000321

Cotuit Historic District [Barnstable MRA], Main St., Lowell & Ocean View Aves. bounded by Osterville Harbor, Nantucket Sound, & Popponessett Bay, Barnstable, 11/10/87, A, C, 87000317

Craigville Historic District [Barnstable MRA], Centerville Harbor, Nantucket Sound, Red Lily Pond, and Lake Elizabeth, Barnstable, 11/10/87, A, C, a, 87000275

Crocker, Benomi and Barnabas, House [Barnstable MRA], 325 Willow St., Barnstable, 3/13/87, A, B, C, 87000216

Crocker, Capt. Alexander, House [Barnstable MRA], 358 Sea St., Barnstable, 3/13/87, B, C, 87000274

Crocker, Ebenezer, Jr., House [Barnstable MRA], 49 Putnam Ave., Barnstable, 11/10/87, A, C, 87000323

Crocker, Lot, House [Barnstable MRA], 284 Gosnold St., Barnstable, 3/13/87, A, B, C, 87000263

Crosby House [Barnstable MRA], 33 Pine St., Barnstable, 3/13/87, C, 87000272

Crosby, Daniel, House [Barnstable MRA], 18 Bay St., Barnstable, 9/18/87, C, 87000306

Crowell-Bourne Farm, W. Falmouth Hwy., West Falmouth, 4/23/80, A, C, 80000501

Dennis, Josiah, House, Nobscusset Rd. at Whig St., Dennis, 2/15/74, B, a, 74000360

Dillingham House, W of Brewster off MA 6A, Brewster vicinity, 4/30/76, A, C, 76000225

Eldredge Public Library, 564 Main St., Chatham, 4/28/92, A, C, 92000430

First Universalist Chruch, 236 Commercial St., Provincetown, 2/23/72, C, a, 72000122

French Cable Hut, E of N. Eastham at jct. of Cable Rd. and Ocean View Dr., North Eastham vicinity, 4/22/76, A, NPS, 76000153

French Cable Station, SE corner of Cove Rd. and MA 28, Orleans, 4/11/72, A, 72000121

Fuller House [Barnstable MRA], Parker Rd., Barnstable, 3/13/87, A, C, 87000325

Gifford Farm [Barnstable MRA], 261 Cotuit Rd., Barnstable, 3/13/87, A, C, 87000245

Gleason, Dr. Edward Francis, House [Barnstable MRA], 88 Lewis Bay Rd., Barnstable, 9/18/87, A, C, 87000262

Goodspeed House [Barnstable MRA], 271 River Rd., Barnstable, 3/13/87, A, B, C, 87000235

Gray, Capt. Thomas, House [Barnstable MRA], 14 Main St., Barnstable, 3/13/87, C, 87000280

Half Way House, Andrew Harding La., Chatham, 7/21/78, A, 78000423

Hallett, Capt. William, House [Barnstable MRA], 570 Main St., Barnstable, 9/18/87, A, C, 87000296

Hallett, Seth, House [Barnstable MRA], 110 Main St., Barnstable, 9/18/87, C, 87000298

Harlow Homestead [Barnstable MRA], 391 Main St., Barnstable, 9/18/87, C, 87000324

Harwich Historic District, Irregular pattern on both sides of Main St., W to Forest St. and E to jct. of Rte. 39 and Chatham Rd., Harwich, 2/24/75, A, C, a, 75000245

Hawley, Gideon, House [Barnstable MRA], 4766 Falmouth Rd., Barnstable, 3/13/87, A, B, a, b, 87000312

Hawthorne Class Studio, Off Miller Hill Rd., Provincetown, 7/21/78, B, b, 78000434

Higgins, Jedediah, House, Higgins Hollow Rd., North Truro vicinity, 11/21/84, C, NPS, 84000550

Highland House, Off U.S. 6 on Cape Cod National Seashore, Truro, 6/05/75, A, C, NPS, 75000157

Highland Light Station [Lighthouses of Massachusetts TR], Off SR 6, Truro, 6/15/87, A, C, 87001463

Hinckley Homestead [Barnstable MRA], 1740 S. County Rd., Barnstable, 9/18/87, A, C, 87000248

Hinckley, Capt. Joseph, House [Barnstable MRA], 142 Old Stage Rd., Barnstable, 3/13/87, A, C, 87000249

Hinckley, Nymphus, House [Barnstable MRA], 38 Bay St., Barnstable, 3/13/87, C, 87000250

Hinckley, S. Alexander, House [Barnstable MRA], 151 Pine St., Barnstable, 9/18/87, C, 87000279

Hyannis Port Historic District [Barnstable MRA], Roughly bounded by Massachusetts Ave. & Edgehill Rd., Hyannis Ave., Hyannis Harbor, and

Barnstable County—Continued

Scudder Ave., Barnstable, 11/10/87, A, B, C, 87000259

Hyannis Road Historic District [Barnstable MRA], Bounded by Old King's Hwy., Bow Ln., Cape Cod Branch RR tracks, and Hyannis Rd., Barnstable, 3/13/87, A, B, C, 87000231

Isham, Herman, House [Barnstable MRA], 1322 Main St., Barnstable, 3/13/87, C, 87000295

Jenkins, John, Homestead [Barnstable MRA], Church St., Barnstable, 3/13/87, A, B, C, 87000318

Jenkins, Joseph, House [Barnstable MRA], 310 Pine St., Barnstable, 3/13/87, A, B, C, 87000322

Jenkins—Whelden Farmstead [Barnstable MRA], 221 Pine St., Barnstable, 3/13/87, A, B, C, 87000320

Kennedy Compound, Irving and Marchant Aves., Hyannis Port, 11/28/72, B, g, NHL, 72001302

Liberty Hall [Barnstable MRA], Main St., Barnstable, 3/13/87, A, C, 87000246

Lincoln House Club [Barnstable MRA], 135 Bridge St., Barnstable, 3/13/87, A, C, 87000301

Long Point Light Station [Lighthouses of Massachusetts TR], Herring Cove Beach, Provincetown, 9/28/87, A, C, 87002039

Lovell, Capt. George, House [Barnstable MRA], 8 E. Bay Rd., Barnstable, 11/10/87, C, 87000290

Lovell, Nehemiah, House [Barnstable MRA], 691 Main St., Barnstable, 9/18/87, C, 87000291

Marconi Wireless Station Site, 1 mi. NE of Cape Cod National Seashore, South Wellfleet, 5/02/75, A, B, C, NPS, 75000158

Marston, William, House [Barnstable MRA], 71 Cotuit Rd., Barnstable, 3/13/87, B, C, 87000234

Marstons Mills Hearse House and Cemetery [Barnstable MRA], MA 149, Barnstable, 3/13/87, A, C, d, 87000302

Merrill Estate [Barnstable MRA], 1874 S. County Rd., Barnstable, 9/18/87, C, 87000268

Methodist Church [Barnstable MRA], Main St., Barnstable, 3/13/87, A, C, a, b, 87000247

Mill Way Historic District [Barnstable MRA], Mill Way Rd., Barnstable, 11/10/87, A, C, 87000271

Monomoy Point Lighthouse [Lighthouses of Massachusetts TR (AD)], Monomoy Island, Chatham vicinity, 11/01/79, A, C, 79000324

Municipal Group Historic District [Barnstable MRA], Roughly bounded by Main, Municipal Bldgs., South, and Pearl Sts., Barnstable, 11/10/87, A, C, 87000288

Nauset Archeological District, Address Restricted, Eastham, 4/19/93, D, NHL, NPS, 93000607

Nauset Beach Light [Lighthouses of Massachusetts TR], Nauset Beach, Eastham, 6/15/87, A, C, b, 87001484

Newcomb, John, House, Address Restricted, Wellfleet vicinity, 9/15/88, A, C, 88001457

Nickerson Mansion, 2871 Main St., Brewster, 2/20/86, B, C, 86000300

Nobska Point Light Station [Lighthouses of Massachusetts TR], Nobska Rd., Falmouth, 6/15/87, A, C, 87001483

Northside Historic District, US 6A between Barnstable-Yarmouth town line & White Brock, Yarmouth, 11/24/87, A, C, 87001777

Nye, Benjamin, Homestead, 85 Old County Rd., Sandwich, 1/06/92, A, C, 91001899

Old Harbor U.S. Life Saving Station, NE of Chatham on Nauset Beach, Chatham vicinity, 8/18/75, A, C, NPS, 75000159

Old Higgins Farm Windmill, Off Old King's Highway, Brewster, 6/10/75, A, b, 75000240

Old Jail, Route 6A, Barnstable, 7/02/71, A, C, b, 71000078

Old King's Highway Historic District [Barnstable MRA], Old King's Highway between Sandwich town line on the West to Yarmouth town line on the East, Barnstable, 3/12/87, A, C, 87000314

Osterville Baptist Church [Barnstable MRA], Main St., Barnstable, 9/18/87, A, C, a, 87000292

Penniman, Edward, House and Barn, S of Eastham at Fort Hill and Governor Prence Rds., Eastham vicinity, 5/28/76, B, C, NPS, 76000155

Phinney, William and Jane, House [Barnstable MRA], 555 Phinney's Ln., Barnstable, 3/13/87, A, C, 87000284

Pleasant—School Street Historic District [Barnstable MRA], Roughly bounded by Main, School, South, and Pleasant Sts., Barnstable, 11/10/87, A, C, 87000257

Pond Hill School, US 6, Wellfleet, 3/23/89, A, C, 89000222

Port Royal House, 606 Main St., Chatham, 4/15/82, A, C, 82004943

Provincetown Historic District, Roughly bounded by US 6, W end of Commercial St., Provincetown Harbor, and SE end of Commerical St., Provincetown, 8/30/89, A, C, b, 89001148

Provincetown Public Library, 330 Commercial St., Provincetown, 4/21/75, C, 75000248

Race Point Light Station [Lighthouses of Massachusetts TR], Race Point Beach, Provincetown, 6/15/87, A, C, NPS, 87001482

Rhodehouse, Nelson, House [Barnstable MRA], 131 Main St., Barnstable, 3/13/87, C, 87000308

Richardson, John, House [Barnstable MRA], 242 Phinney's Ln., Barnstable, 9/18/87, A, C, 87000281

Robbins, Joseph, House [Barnstable MRA], 12 Bay St., Barnstable, 11/10/87, A, C, 87000289

Round House [Barnstable MRA], 971 W. Main St., Barnstable, 3/13/87, C, 87000282

Rowell House, Gull Pond Rd., Wellfleet, 9/01/88, A, C, 88001458

Sampson's Folly—Josiah Sampson House [Barnstable MRA], 40 Old King's Rd., Barnstable, 9/18/87, C, 87000326

Sandy Neck Cultural Resources District [Barnstable MRA], Address Restricted, Barnstable, 11/10/87, A, B, C, D, g, 87000305

Santuit Historic District [Barnstable MRA], MA 28, Barnstable, 11/10/87, A, C, 87000319

Santuit Post Office [Barnstable MRA], Main St., Barnstable, 11/10/87, C, 87000309

Smith, Matthias, House [Barnstable MRA], 375 Cedar St., Barnstable, 3/13/87, C, 87000240

Smith, Samuel, Tavern Site, Address Restricted, Wellfleet vicinity, 11/11/77, A, C, D, NPS, 77000108

South Harwich Methodist Church, 270 Chatham Rd., Harwich, 8/21/86, A, C, a, 86001887

South Yarmouth/Bass River Historic District, Roughly Main St. from Pine to South St., River St. from Main to Bass R. Pkwy., and Willow St. from River to South St., Yarmouth, 5/29/90, A, C, a, d, 90000787

Taylor—Bray Farm, Jct. of Bray Farm Rd. N. and Nottingham Rd., Yarmouth, 9/29/93, A, C, 92000287

Three Sisters of Nauset (Twin Lights) [Lighthouses of Massachusetts TR], Off Cable Rd., Eastham, 6/15/87, A, C, b, 87001502

Town Boundary Marker [Barnstable MRA], Race Ln. at Sandwich town line, Barnstable, 9/18/87, A, 87000269

Town Hall Square Historic District, Roughly bounded by Main, Grove, Water Sts., and Tupper Rd. from Beale Ave. to MA 6A, Sandwich, 10/31/75, A, C, a, 75001914

Town Line Boundary Marker [Barnstable MRA], Great Hill Rd., Barnstable, 9/18/87, A, 87000242

Town Line Boundary Marker [Barnstable MRA], 410 High St., Barnstable, 9/18/87, A, 87000243

U.S. Customshouse, Cobbs Hill, MA 6A, Barnstable, 11/12/75, A, C, 75000239

US Post Office—Provincetown Main, 217 Commercial St., Provincetown, 10/19/87, A, C, 87001772

Weeks, Barzillai, House [Barnstable MRA], 313 High St., Barnstable, 3/13/87, A, B, C, 87000241

Wellfleet Center Historic District, Roughly bounded by Cross St., Holbrook Ave., Main, E. Main and School Sts., and Duck Creek, Wellfleet, 8/21/89, A, C, a, b, 89001147

West Barnstable Village—Meetinghouse Way Historic District [Barnstable MRA], Meetinghouse Way from County Rd. to Meetinghouse, Barnstable, 11/10/87, A, B, C, a, 87000255

West Schoolhouse, Nobscusset Road at Whig St., Dennis, 4/24/75, C, b, 75000262

Whitman, Josiah B., House [Barnstable MRA], 210 Maple St., Barnstable, 3/13/87, C, 87000236

Wianno Club, Seaview Ave., Osterville, 3/02/79, A, C, 79000325

Wianno Historic District [Barnstable MRA], Roughly E. Bay Rd., Wianno and Sea View Aves. between Nantucket Sound and Crystal Lake, Barnstable, 11/10/87, A, C, 87000316

Wing Fort House, Spring Hill Rd., East Sandwich, 6/03/76, A, C, 76000227

Wing's Neck Light [Lighthouses of Massachusetts TR], Wing's Neck Rd., Bourne, 6/15/87, A, C, b, 87001503

Wood End Light Lookout Station [Lighthouses of Massachusetts TR], Long Pt., Provincetown, 6/15/87, A, C, 87001504

Woods Hole School, 24 School St., Falmouth, 10/21/82, A, C, 82000473

Yarmouth Camp Ground Historic District, South of mid-Cape Hwy, (Rt. 6) and roughly bounded by County Ave., Willow St., Wood Rd., and

Barnstable County—Continued

Camp Ground Pond, Yarmouth/Barnstable, 8/28/90, A, C, a, 90001244

Berkshire County

Allen Hotel, Wendell Ave., Pittsfield, 9/01/83, A, C, 83000566

Allen, William Russell, House, 359 East St., Pittsfield, 5/07/80, C, 80000427

Anthony House, 67 East Rd., Adams, 1/03/85, A, B, C, c, 85000021

Armory Block, 39–45 Park St., Adams, 4/01/82, B, C, 82004944

Armstrong House [North Adams MRA], 60 Brooklyn St., North Adams, 10/25/85, A, C, 85003394

Arnold Print Works [North Adams MRA], 87 Marshall St., North Adams, 10/25/85, A, 85003379

Ashley, Col. John, House, W of Ashley Falls on Cooper Hill Rd., Sheffield vicinity, 2/10/75, B, C, b, 75001915

Ashley, Col. John, House (Boundary Increase), W of Ashley Halls on Cooper Hill Rd., Sheffield vicinity, 8/11/75, B, 75002172

Barrett, P. J., Block, 70–76 Park St., Adams, 4/01/82, A, C, 82004945

Beaver Mill, Beaver St., North Adams, 5/11/73, A, B, C, 73000292

Becket Center Historic District, MA 8, Hamilton and YMCA Rds., Becket, 8/11/82, A, C, D, a, 82004952

Berkshie Mill No. 1, Hoosac St., Adams, 4/01/82, A, 82004946

Berkshire Life Insurance Company Building, 5–7 North St., Pittsfield, 2/27/86, A, C, 86000276

Bidwell, Rev. Adonijah, House, Royal Hemlocks and Art School Rds., Monterey, 8/26/82, A, B, C, D, 82004954

Blackinton Historic District [North Adams MRA], Roughly Massachusetts Ave. between Ashton and Doanes Aves. and Church Hill and Boston & Maine RR, North Adams, 10/25/85, A, B, C, 85003384

Boardman, The [North Adams MRA], 39–53 Montana St., North Adams, 10/25/85, C, 85003403

Brewer, Capt. John, House, Main Rd., Monterey, 3/29/84, B, C, 84002083

Browne, Charles, House [North Adams MRA], 932 S. Church St., North Adams, 10/25/85, A, B, C, 85003413

Chesterwood, 2 mi. W of Stockbridge, Stockbridge vicinity, 10/15/66, B, NHL, 66000652

Church Street Historic District [North Adams MRA (AD)], Roughly E. Main St. from Church to Pleasant St., and Church St. from Summer St. to Elmwood Ave., North Adams, 3/10/83, A, C, 83000567

Church Street—Caddy Hill Historic District (Boundary Increase) [North Adams MRA], Roughly bounded by E. Main and Holbrook Sts., Wall and Meadow Sts., Elmwood Ave., and Perry, South, and Ashland Sts., North Adams, 10/25/85, A, B, C, 85003376

Church on the Hill, Main St., Lenox, 9/30/82, A, B, C, a, 82001894

Citizens Hall, Off U.S. 90, Interlaken, 6/19/72, C, 72000126

Clark—Eames House [Washington MRA], Middlefield Rd., Washington, 9/12/86, C, 86002139

Crane and Company, Off Main St., Dalton, 7/01/83, A, NHL, 83004376

Crowley House [North Adams MRA], 365 W. Main St., North Adams, 10/25/85, C, 85003414

Dalton Grange Hall No. 23, South St. and Grange Hall Rd., Dalton, 11/10/83, A, C, 83003924

Du Bois, William E.B., Boyhood Homesite, MA 23, Great Barrington, 5/11/76, B, NHL, 76000947

Dwight-Henderson House, Main St., Great Barrington, 3/26/76, B, C, 76000237

Eames, Philip, House [Washington MRA], Stone House Rd., Washington, 9/12/86, C, 86002140

Eaton, Crane & Pike Company Factory, 75 S. Church St., Pittsfield, 8/03/90, A, C, 90001166

Elm Court, Stockbridge St., Lenox, 12/30/85, A, B, C, 85003184

Five Corners Historic District, Jct. of Cold Spring, Green River, New Ashford, Hancock and Sloan Rds. and surrounding area, Williamstown, 1/07/93, A, C, 92001717

Freeman's Grove Historic District [North Adams MRA], Roughly bounded by Liberty St., Eagle St., Bracewell Ave., and Houghton St., North Adams, 10/25/85, A, C, 85003388

Freight Yard Historic District, W of the Hadley Overpass and SW of the Hoosac River, North Adams, 6/13/72, A, 72000131

Glendale Power House, MA 183, Stockbridge, 6/24/82, A, C, 82004957

Goodwood, Summit Rd., Richmond, 4/15/82, C, 82004955

Hall's Tavern, 3 North St., Cheshire, 3/10/83, A, C, 83000568

Hancock Shaker Village, 5 mi. S of Pittsfield on U.S. 20, Hancock Tpke., Hancock vicinity, 11/24/68, A, NHL, 68000037

Hancock Town Hall, MA 43, Hancock, 9/26/75, A, C, 73001956

Hathaway Tenement [North Adams MRA], 311–321 River St., North Adams, 10/25/85, A, C, 85003415

Hoosac Street School, 20 Hoosac St., Adams, 2/10/88, A, C, 87002547

Hoosac Tunnel, From North Adams on the W to the Deerfield River on the E, North Adams, 11/02/73, A, 73000294

Hyde House, 144 W. Park St., Lee, 11/21/76, B, C, 76000239

Johnson Manufacturing Company [North Adams MRA], 65 Brown St., North Adams, 10/25/85, A, C, 85003418

Johnson School [North Adams MRA], School St., North Adams, 10/25/85, A, C, 85003416

Jones Block, 49–53 Park St., Adams, 4/01/82, A, C, 82004947

Lenox Academy, 75 Main St., Lenox, 9/30/82, A, C, 82001895

Lenox Library, 18 Main St., Lenox, 4/03/73, C, 73000291

Lenox Railroad Station, Housatonic St. and Willow Creek Rd., Lenox, 6/16/89, A, C, 89000225

Lower Historic District [Washington MRA], Washington Mountain Rd., Washington, 9/12/86, A, C, 86002141

Maplewood Hotel, 328-330 Maple St., Holyoke, 11/10/83, A, B, C, 83003925

Mausert Block, 19–27 Park St., Adams, 4/01/82, C, 82004948

Melville, Herman, House, Holmes Rd., Pittsfield, 10/15/66, B, NHL, 66000126

Merrell Tavern, MA 102, South Lee, 2/23/72, A, B, C, 72000136

Mill Village Historic District, Cole Ave., Mill, Arnold, and Elm Sts., Williamstown, 10/06/83, A, C, 83003926

Mission House, Main St., Stockbridge, 11/24/68, C, b, e, NHL, 68000038

Mohawk Trail, Along the bank of the Cold River, Florida and Savoy vicinity, 4/03/73, A, 73000283

Monument Mills, Park and Front Sts., Great Barrington, 11/29/83, A, B, C, 83003927

Monument Square—Eagle Street Historic District, Monument Square and environs, at E end of Main St., North Adams, 6/19/72, A, C, a, b, f, 72000132

Monument Square—Eagle Street Historic District (Boundary Increase) [North Adams MRA], Roughly bounded by Holden, Center, and Union Sts., East Middle School, Summer, and Main Sts., North Adams, 8/25/88, A, C, 85003623

Morewood School, S. Mountain Rd., Pittsfield, 5/31/84, A, C, 84002084

Mount, The, S of Lenox on U.S. 7, Lenox vicinity, 11/11/71, B, NHL, 71000900

Naumkeag, Prospect St., Stockbridge, 11/03/75, B, C, 75000264

New Boston Inn, Jct. of MA 8 and MA 57, Sandisfield, 9/01/88, A, C, 88001459

New Marlborough Village, MA 57, New Marlborough, Monterey and Southfield Rds., New Marlborough, 9/30/82, A, C, 82001896

Nichols—Sterner House, Swamp Rd., Richmond, 9/17/87, C, 87001997

Norad Mill [North Adams MRA], 60 Roberts Dr., North Adams, 10/25/85, A, B, C, 85003417

Normal School Historic District [North Adams MRA], Roughly Church and Blackinton Sts., North Adams, 10/25/85, A, C, 85003391

North Becket Village Historic District, Main, High, and Pleasant Sts., Becket, 7/26/88, A, C, a, 88000229

North Egremont Historic District, Roughly bounded by Shun Toll Rd., Rt. 71, Hillsdale Rd., and Mill Rd., Egremont, 1/20/89, A, C, 88003126

Old Central Fire Station, 66 Allen St., Pittsfield, 11/02/77, C, 77000177

Old Central High School, 1st St., Pittsfield, 8/06/80, C, 80000428

Old Covered Bridge, Covered Bridge Lane, Sheffield, 11/24/78, C, 78000445

Old Curtisville Historic District, N of Stockbridge on MA 183, Stockbridge vicinity, 10/29/76, A, C, a, b, 76000250

Old Town Hall, 32 East St., corner of Allen St., Pittsfield, 4/26/72, A, 72001299

Berkshire County—Continued

Osborn, Benjamin, House, West St., E on private Rd., Mt. Washington, 10/01/87, A, C, a, 87001758

Park Square Historic District, At jct. of North, South, East, and West Sts., Pittsfield, 7/24/75, A, C, a, 75001911

Park Square Historic District (Boundary Increase), Roughly bounded by E. Housatonic, South, North and Fenn Sts. and Wendell Ave., Pittsfield, 12/23/91, A, C, a, 91001826

Park Street Firehouse, 47 Park St., Adams, 1/28/82, A, C, 82004949

Pettibone Farm, Old Cheshire Rd. N of jct. with Nobodys Rd., Lanesborough, 1/04/91, A, C, 90001944

Phillips Woolen Mill, 71 Grove St., Adams, 9/30/82, A, C, 82001897

Pittsfield & North Adams Passenger Station and Baggage & Express House, 10 Pleasant St., Adams, 4/01/82, A, C, 82004950

Providence Court, 379 East St., Pittsfield, 11/20/87, A, C, 87001107

Quaker Meetinghouse, Maple Street Cemetery, Adams, 8/17/76, C, a, 76000236

Renfrew Mill No. 2, 217 Columbia St., Adams, 10/14/82, A, C, 82000474

Rising Paper Mill, N of Great Barrington on MA 183 at Risingdale, Great Barrington vicinity, 8/11/75, A, C, 75000253

Rock Ridge, Tyringham Rd., Monterey, 9/16/83, A, C, 83000569

Sage, Philemon, House, MA 183, Sandisfield, 8/31/82, A, C, 82001898

Saint Andrew's Chapel [Washington MRA], Washington Mountain Rd., Washington, 9/12/86, C, a, 86002142

Searles Castle, Main St., Great Barrington, 4/15/82, B, C, 82004953

Shadow Brook Farm Historic District, Lenox West Rd., MA 183 near Bucks Ln., Stockbridge, 3/10/88, A, C, 88000202

Sheffield Center Historic District, Roughly US 7/Main St. from Miller Ave. to Salisbury Rd., Sheffield, 12/01/89, A, C, b, 89002060

Sheffield Plain Historic District, Roughly 1/2 mi. of US 7, S from Cook Rd., Sheffield, 6/23/88, A, C, d, 88000881

Shepard, Thomas, House, East Hill Rd., New Marlborough, 5/31/84, A, B, C, 84002085

Sherman, Eber, Farm, 1010 State Rd., North Adams, 10/06/83, A, C, 83003929

Sherman, William B., Farm [North Adams MRA], 1072 State Rd., North Adams, 10/25/85, C, 85003419

Sibley—Corcoran House [Washington MRA], Valley Rd., Washington, 9/12/86, A, C, 86002143

Simmons Block, 86–90 Park St., Adams, 4/01/82, C, 82004951

Simond, Col. Benjamin, House, 643 Simonds Rd., Williamstown, 9/01/83, A, B, C, 83000570

Society of the Congregational Church of Great Barrington, 241 and 251 Main St., Great Barrington, 8/20/92, A, C, a, 92000999

South Center School House [Washington MRA], Washington Mountain Rd., Washington, 9/12/86, A, C, 86002144

South Egremont Village Historic District, MA 23-41, Buttonball Lane, Sheffield, and Pinecrest Hill Rds., South Egremont, 5/31/84, A, C, 84002086

South Mountain Concert Hall, New South Mountain Rd., Pittsfield vicinity, 8/14/73, A, 73001943

St. Joseph's School, Eagle St., North Adams, 12/22/83, A, C, 83003928

St. Luke's Episcopal Church, U.S. 7, Lanesborough, 2/23/72, C, a, 72000127

Stafford Hill Memorial, Stafford Hill Rd., Cheshire, 2/14/86, B, c, f, 86000260

Stockbridge Casino, E. Main St. at Yale Hill Rd., Stockbridge, 8/27/76, A, C, b, 76000249

Summer Street Historic District, Crandall, Center, East, Liberty, Orchard and Summer Sts., Adams, 9/05/85, A, B, C, 85002009

Sykes House [North Adams MRA], 521 W. Main St., North Adams, 10/25/85, A, C, 85003420

Tyringham Shaker Settlement Historic District, Jerusalem Rd., Tyringham, 10/15/87, A, C, D, a, 87001785

US Post Office—Great Barrington Main, 222 Main St., Great Barrington, 1/10/86, C, 86000163

US Post Office—Williamstown Main, 63 Spring St., Williamstown, 7/17/86, C, 86002243

Upper Historic District [Washington MRA], Roughly between Branch and Frost Rds. on Washington Mountain Rd., Washington, 9/02/87, A, C, 86002145

Ventfort Hall, 120 and 148 Walker St. and 55 Kemble St., Lenox, 3/05/93, A, C, 93000055

Villa Virginia, Ice Glen Rd., Stockbridge, 11/29/83, C, 83003930

Wells House [North Adams MRA], 568 W. Main St., North Adams, 10/25/85, B, C, 85003393

Westover—Bacon—Potts Farm, MA 41, S of jct. with MA 23, Egremont, 7/27/90, A, C, 90000157

Wheatleigh, W. Hawthorne Rd., Stockbridge vicinity, 4/06/82, C, 82004956

Windsor Print Works, 121 Union St., North Adams, 5/17/73, A, C, 73000296

Wollison-Shipton Building, 142-156 North St., Pittsfield, 9/30/82, C, 82001899

Bristol County

Academy Building, S. Main St., Fall River, 7/02/73, A, C, 73000277

Acushnet Heights Historic District, Roughly bounded by Summer, Weld, Purchase, Pope, County, and Robeson, New Bedford, 12/01/89, A, C, 89002035

Algonquin Printing Co. [Fall River MRA], Bay St., Fall River, 2/16/83, A, C, 83000615

Allen, Elisha, House [Rehoboth MRA], 108 Homestead Rd., Rehoboth, 6/06/83, C, 83000616

American Printing Co. and Metacomet Mill [Fall River MRA], Anawan St., Fall River, 2/16/83, A, C, 83000617

Anawan Club Clubhouse and Caretaker's House [Rehoboth MRA], 13 Gorham St., Rehoboth, 6/06/83, A, C, 83000618

Anawan Rock [Rehoboth MRA], Anawan St., Rehoboth, 6/06/83, A, 83000619

Angle Tree Stone, W of North Attleborough off High St., North Attleborough vicinity, 1/01/76, A, 76000228

Anthony, David M., House [Fall River MRA], 368 N. Main St., Fall River, 2/16/83, C, 83000620

Anthony, David M., House [Swansea MRA], 98 Bay Point Ave., Swansea, 2/16/90, A, C, 90000059

Anthony, Harold H., House [Swansea MRA], 132 Bay Point Ave., Swansea, 2/12/90, A, C, 90000058

Apponegansett Meeting House, Russells Mills Rd. E of Fresh River Valley Rd., Dartmouth, 3/14/91, A, C, a, d, 91000241

Ashley House [Fall River MRA], 3159 Main St., Fall River, 2/16/83, A, C, 83000621

Atwood, Charles R., House [Taunton MRA], 30 Dean St., Taunton, 7/05/84, B, C, 84002087

Baker House [Rehoboth MRA], 191 Hornbine St., Rehoboth, 6/06/83, C, 83000622

Bark Street School [Swansea MRA], Stevens Rd. at Bark St., Swansea, 2/16/90, C, 90000062

Barnard Mills [Fall River MRA], 641-657 Quarry St., Fall River, 2/16/83, A, C, 83000623

Barneyville Historic District [Swansea MRA], Old Providence and Barneyville Rds., Swansea, 2/16/90, A, C, 90000052

Barnum School [Taunton MRA], Barnum St., Taunton, 7/05/84, A, C, 84002088

Bartlett, J.C., House [Taunton MRA], 12 Walnut St., Taunton, 7/05/84, C, 84002089

Bassett, C.J.H., House [Taunton MRA], 20 Chestnut St., Taunton, 7/05/84, A, C, 84002091

Bay Road, 416-535 Bay Rd. (Foundry St. to the Norton town line), Easton, 5/05/72, A, C, 72000118

Beattie, W.C., House [Taunton MRA], 289 W. Brittania St., Taunton, 7/05/84, C, 84002092

Belmont Club/John Young House [Fall River MRA], 34 Franklin St., Fall River, 2/16/83, C, 83000624

Bend of the Lane [Swansea MRA], 181 Cedar Ave., Swansea, 2/12/90, A, C, 90000057

Blackinton Houses and Park, N. Main St., Attleboro, 4/20/79, B, C, 79000326

Bliss, Abiah, House [Rehoboth MRA], 154 Agricultural Ave., Rehoboth, 6/06/83, C, 83000625

Bliss, Daniel, Homestead [Rehoboth MRA], 76 Homestead Ave., Rehoboth, 6/06/83, A, C, 83000626

Blossom, Barnabus, House [Fall River MRA], 244 Grove St., Fall River, 2/16/83, C, 83000627

Boguslavsky Triple-Deckers [Fall River MRA], 53-87 Albion St., Fall River, 2/16/83, C, 83000628

Borden Flats Light Station [Lighthouses of Massachusetts TR], Taunton River, Fall River, 6/15/87, A, C, 87001528

Borden, A.J., Building [Fall River MRA], 91-111 S. Main St., Fall River, 2/16/83, A, C, 83000629

Bristol County—Continued

Borden, Ariadne J. and Mary A., House [Fall River MRA], 92 Globe St., Fall River, 2/16/83, C, 83000630

Borden, N. B., School [Fall River MRA], 43 Morgan St., Fall River, 2/16/83, A, C, 83000631

Borden-Winslow House [Fall River MRA], 3063 N. Main St., Fall River, 2/16/83, C, 83000632

Border City Mill No. 2 [Fall River MPS], One Weaver St., Fall River, 6/28/90, A, C, 90000999

Bowen, Nathan, House [Rehoboth MRA], 26 Kelton St., Rehoboth, 6/06/83, C, 83000633

Bramble Hill [Rehoboth MRA], 32 Moulton St., Rehoboth, 6/06/83, C, 83000634

Brayton Methodist Episcopal Church [Fall River MRA], 264 Griffin St., Fall River, 2/16/83, A, C, a, 83000635

Briggs Tavern [Rehoboth MRA], 2 Anawan St., Rehoboth, 6/06/83, C, 83000636

Brightman, Hathaway, House [Fall River MRA], 205 Crescent St., Fall River, 2/16/83, C, 83000637

Bristol County Courthouse Complex, 9, 11, 15 Court St., Taunton, 3/28/78, A, C, 78000427

Bristol County Superior Court [Fall River MRA], 441 N. Main St., Fall River, 2/16/83, C, 83000638

Brow's Tavern [Taunton MRA], 211 Tremont St., Taunton, 7/05/84, A, C, 84002094

Brown House [Rehoboth MRA], 384 Tremont St., Rehoboth, 6/06/83, C, 83000639

Brown, John, IV, House [Swansea MRA], 703 Pearse Rd., Swansea, 2/16/90, A, C, 90000064

Brownell, Henry G., House [Taunton MRA], 119 High St., Taunton, 7/05/84, C, 84002095

Buffington, Deacon John, House [Swansea MRA], 262 Cedar Ave., Swansea, 2/16/90, C, 90000056

Buildings at 80 and 88 W. Brittania St. [Taunton MRA], 80 and 88 W. Brittania St., Taunton, 7/05/84, C, 84002097

Butler Flats Light Station [Lighthouses of Massachusetts TR], New Bedford Channel, New Bedford, 6/15/87, A, C, 87001530

Cadman—White—Handy House, 202 Hixbridge Rd., Westport, 7/16/92, A, C, 92000831

Canedy, Squire William B., House [Fall River MRA], 2634 N. Main St., Fall River, 2/16/83, C, 83000640

Capron House, 42 North Ave., Attleboro, 7/21/78, A, C, 78000426

Capron, George, House [Taunton MRA], 6 N. Pleasant St., Taunton, 7/05/84, C, 84002099

Carney, Sgt. William H., House, 128 Mill St., New Bedford, 4/21/75, B, 75000243

Carpenter Bridge [Rehoboth MRA], Carpenter St., Rehoboth, 6/06/83, C, 83000641

Carpenter Homestead, 80 Walnut St., Seekonk/Rehoboth, Seekonk, 9/17/93, A, C, 93000902

Carpenter House [Rehoboth MRA], 89 Carpenter St., Rehoboth, 6/06/83, C, 83000642

Carpenter, Christopher, House [Rehoboth MRA], 60 Carpenter St., Rehoboth, 6/06/83, C, 83000643

Carpenter, Col. Thomas, III, House [Rehoboth MRA], 77 Bay State Rd., Rehoboth, 6/06/83, C, b, c, 83000644

Cataract Engine Company No. 3 [Fall River MRA], 116 Rock St., Fall River, 2/16/83, C, 83000645

Central Congregational Church [Fall River MRA], 100 Rock St., Fall River, 2/16/83, C, a, 83000646

Central Fire Station [Taunton MRA], Leonard and School Sts., Taunton, 7/05/84, A, C, 84002101

Central New Bedford Historic District, Roughly bounded by Acushnet Ave., School, Middle and 6th Sts., New Bedford, 4/24/80, A, C, 80000430

Chace Mills [Fall River MRA], Lewiston and Salem Sts., Fall River, 2/16/83, C, 83000648

Chace, A. B., Rowhouses [Fall River MRA], 655-685 Middle St., Fall River, 2/16/83, C, 83000647

Charlton Mill [Fall River MRA], 109 Howe St., Fall River, 2/16/83, A, C, 83000650

Chase's, Oliver, Thread Mill [Fall River MRA], 505 Bay St., Fall River, 2/16/83, A, C, 83000649

Chase-Hyde Farm [Fall River MRA], 1281-1291 New Boston Rd., Fall River, 2/16/83, A, C, 83000651

Children's Home [Fall River MRA], 427 Robeson St., Fall River, 2/16/83, A, C, 83000652

Church Green, U.S. 44 and MA 140, Taunton, 12/16/77, A, C, a, 77000168

Church of Christ, Swansea [Swansea MRA], G. A. R. Hwy./US 6 at Maple Ave., Swansea, 2/16/90, A, C, a, 90000075

Church of the Ascension [Fall River MRA], 160 Rock St., Fall River, 2/16/83, A, C, a, 83000653

Clarke, Pitt, House, 42 Mansfield Ave., Norton, 7/13/76, A, C, 76000230

Colby, Samuel, House [Taunton MRA], 74 Winthrop St., Taunton, 7/05/84, A, C, 84002103

Cole, Benjamin, House [Swansea MRA], 412 Old Warren Rd., Swansea, 2/16/90, A, C, 90000066

Collins, William, House [Fall River MRA], 3775 N. Main St., Fall River, 2/16/83, C, 83000654

Colony Historic District [Swansea MRA], Gardner's Neck and Mattapoisett Rds. at Mt. Hope Bay, Swansea, 2/16/90, A, C, 90000079

Connell, William M., School [Fall River MRA], 650 Plymouth Ave., Fall River, 2/16/83, A, C, 83000655

Corky Row Historic District [Fall River MRA], Roughly bounded by Plymouth Ave. I195 and 2nd St., Fall River, 6/23/83, A, C, 83000656

Cornell Mills [Fall River MRA], Alden St., Fall River, 2/16/83, A, C, 83000657

Coughlin School [Fall River MRA], 1975 Pleasant St., Fall River, 2/16/83, A, C, 83000658

County Street Historic District, Roughly bounded by Acushnet, Page, Middle, and Bedford Sts. (both sides), New Bedford, 8/11/76, A, C, 76000229

Crescent Mill [Fall River MRA], 30 Front St., Fall River, 2/16/83, A, C, 83000659

Cuffe, Paul, Farm, 1504 Drift Rd., Westport, 5/30/74, B, NHL, 74000394

Cushing, Caleb, House and Farm [Rehoboth MRA], 186 Pine St., Rehoboth, 6/06/83, C, 83000660

Davol School [Fall River MRA], 112 Flint St., Fall River, 2/16/83, A, C, 83000661

Davol, William C., Jr., House [Fall River MRA], 252 High St., Fall River, 2/16/83, C, 83004286

Dawson Building, 1851 Purchase St., New Bedford, 9/30/82, A, C, 82001900

Dean, Abiezar, House [Taunton MRA], 57 Summer St., Taunton, 7/05/84, C, 84002104

Dean, George, House [Taunton MRA], 135 Winthrop St., Taunton, 7/05/84, C, 84002105

Dean, Jonathan, House [Taunton MRA], 175 Dean St., Taunton, 7/05/84, A, C, 84002106

Dean, Lloyd, House [Taunton MRA], 164 Dean St., Taunton, 7/05/84, A, C, 84002107

Dean, Theodore, House [Taunton MRA], 26 Dean St., Taunton, 7/05/84, A, B, C, 84002108

Dean-Barstow House [Taunton MRA], 275 William St., Taunton, 7/05/84, A, B, C, 84002109

Dean-Hartshorn House [Taunton MRA], 68 Dean St., Taunton, 7/05/84, A, C, 84002111

Dighton Rock, Across the Taunton River from Dighton in Dighton Rock State Park, Dighton vicinity, 7/01/80, D, b, 80000438

Donaghy, Thomas, School, 68 South St., New Bedford, 3/02/89, A, C, 89000041

Downtown Fall River Historic District [Fall River MRA], N. and S. Main, Bedford, Granite, Bank, Franklin, and Elm Sts., Fall River, 2/16/83, A, C, 83000662

Drown, Nathaniel, House [Rehoboth MRA], 116 Summer St., Rehoboth, 6/06/83, C, 83000663

Durfee Mills [Fall River MRA], 359-479 Pleasant St., Fall River, 2/16/83, A, C, 83000664

Durfee, B.M.C., High School, 289 Rock St., Fall River, 6/11/81, A, C, f, 81000109

ERNESTINA (schooner), Steamship Wharf, New Bedford, 1/03/85, A, C, NHL, 85000022

Earle, John M., House [Fall River MRA], 352 Durfee St., Fall River, 2/16/83, C, 83000665

East Attleborough Academy, 28 Sanford St., Attleboro, 4/04/85, A, C, b, 85000694

East Taunton Fire Station [Taunton MRA], Middleboro Ave., Taunton, 7/05/84, A, C, 84002112

Eldridge House [Taunton MRA], 172 County St., Taunton, 7/05/84, C, 84002114

Elm Cottage/Blanding Farm [Rehoboth MRA], 103 Broad St., Rehoboth, 6/06/83, C, 83000666

Fairbanks-Williams House [Taunton MRA], 19 Elm St., Taunton, 7/05/84, A, C, 84002116

Fairhaven High School, Huttleston Ave., Fairhaven, 1/22/81, C, 81000121

Fairhaven Town Hall, Center St., Fairhaven, 1/22/81, A, C, 81000122

Fall River Bleachery [Fall River MRA], Jefferson St., Fall River, 2/16/83, A, C, 83000667

Fall River Waterworks, Bedford St., Fall River, 12/07/81, A, C, 81000714

Field, Albert, Tack Company [Taunton MRA], 19 Spring St., Taunton, 7/05/84, A, C, 84002117

Fire Barn, Commonwealth Ave., North Attleborough, 1/28/82, A, C, 82004960

Fire Station No. 4, 79 S. 6th St., New Bedford, 7/24/75, A, 75000250

First Baptist Church, 149 William St., New Bedford, 4/21/75, C, a, 75000251

Bristol County—Continued

First Baptist Church [Fall River MRA], 200-228 N. Main St., Fall River, 2/16/83, A, C, 83000668

First Baptist Church and Society [Swansea MRA], Baptist St., Swansea, 2/16/90, A, C, a, d, 90000060

First Parsonage for Second East Parish Church, 41 S. Main St., Attleboro, 4/02/80, C, a, 80000429

Flint Mills [Fall River MRA], Alden St., Fall River, 2/16/83, A, C, 83000669

Fort Phoenix, S of U.S. 6 in Fort Phoenix Park, Fairhaven, 11/09/72, A, 72000120

Fort Taber District, Wharf Rd. within Fort Rodman Military Reservation, New Bedford, 2/08/73, A, 73001954

Foster Spinning Co. [Fall River MRA], Cover St., Fall River, 2/16/83, A, C, 83000670

Fuller-Dauphin Estate [Taunton MRA], 145 School St., Taunton, 7/05/84, A, C, 84002118

Furnace Village Historic District, MA 106/123, Easton, 10/06/83, A, C, D, 83003938

Gardner, Francis L., House [Swansea MRA], 1129 Gardner's Neck Rd., Swansea, 2/16/90, A, C, 90000077

Gardner, Joseph, House [Swansea MRA], 1205 Gardner's Neck Rd., Swansea, 2/16/90, A, C, 90000076

Gardner, Preserved, House [Swansea MRA], 90 Milford Rd., Swansea, 2/16/90, A, C, 90000061

Gardner, Samuel, House [Swansea MRA], 1035 Gardner's Neck Rd., Swansea, 2/16/90, A, C, 90000068

Globe Yarn Mills [Fall River MRA], Globe St., Fall River, 2/16/83, A, C, 83000671

Godfrey, Gen. George, House [Taunton MRA], 125 County St., Taunton, 7/05/84, A, B, C, 84002119

Godfrey, Richard, House [Taunton MRA], 62 County St., Taunton, 7/05/84, A, C, 84002121

Goff Farm [Rehoboth MRA], 158 Perryville Rd., Rehoboth, 6/06/83, C, 83000672

Goff Homestead [Rehoboth MRA], 40 Maple Lane, Rehoboth, 6/06/83, C, 83000673

Greany Building [Fall River MRA], 1270-1288 Pleasant St., Fall River, 2/16/83, A, C, 83000674

H.H. Richardson Historic District of North Easton, Main St., Elm St., & railway right-of-way off Oliver St., North Easton, 12/23/87, C, f, NHL, 87002598

Hargraves Mill No. 1 [Fall River MRA], Quarry St., Fall River, 2/16/83, A, C, 83000675

Harris Street Bridge [Taunton MRA], Spans Taunton River at Dean and Harris Sts., Taunton, 7/05/84, A, C, 84002123

Haskins, Sarah A., House [Taunton MRA], 18 Harrison St., Taunton, 7/05/84, C, 84002124

Hathaway, James D., House [Fall River MRA], 311 Pine St., Fall River, 2/16/83, C, 83000676

Hebronville Mill Historic District, Knight Ave., Read and Phillip Sts., Attleboro, 5/17/84, A, C, a, 84002126

Higgins-Hodgeman House [Taunton MRA], 19 Cedar St., Taunton, 7/05/84, A, C, 84002128

Highlands Historic District [Fall River MRA], Roughly bounded by June, Cherry, and Weetamae Sts., Lincoln, Highland, President, N. Main, and Hood Aves., Fall River, 2/16/83, A, C, 83000677

Hill School, 4 Middle St., South Dartmouth, 4/11/80, A, C, 80000432

Hixville Village Historic District, Jct. of Old Fall River, Hixville and N. Hixville Rds., Dartmouth, 6/17/91, A, C, a, d, 91000698

Hodges House [Taunton MRA], 41 Worcester St., Taunton, 7/05/84, C, 84002130

Hooper House [Swansea MRA], 306 Hortonville Rd., Swansea, 8/08/90, A, C, 90000074

Hopewell Mills District [Taunton MRA], Bay St. and Albro Ave., Taunton, 7/05/84, A, C, 84002133

Hopewell School [Taunton MRA], Monroe St., Taunton, 7/05/84, A, C, 84003859

Hornbine Baptist Church [Rehoboth MRA], 141 Hornbine Rd., Rehoboth, 6/06/83, C, a, 83000678

Hornbine School [Rehoboth MRA], 144 Hornbine Road, Rehoboth, 6/06/83, A, C, 83000679

Horton, Welcome, Farm [Rehoboth MRA], 122 Martin St., Rehoboth, 6/06/83, C, 83000680

Hortonville Historic District [Swansea MRA], Locust St. from Oak St. to Hortonville Rd., Swansea, 2/16/90, A, C, 90000051

Hotel Waverly, 1162–1166 Acushnet Ave., New Bedford, 1/26/90, A, C, 89002326

House at 108-112 Quarry Street [Fall River MRA], 108-112 Quarry St., Fall River, 2/16/83, C, 83000683

House at 197 Hornbine Road [Rehoboth MRA], 197 Hornbine Rd., Rehoboth, 6/06/83, C, 83000681

House at 30 Kelton Street [Rehoboth MRA], 30 Kelton St., Rehoboth, 6/06/83, C, 83000682

Ingalls-Wheeler-Horton Homestead Site [Rehoboth MRA], 214 Chestnut St., Rehoboth, 6/06/83, C, 83000684

Jesus Marie Convent [Fall River MRA], 138 St. Joseph's St., Fall River, 2/16/83, A, C, a, 83000685

Johnson, J. V., House [Swansea MRA], 36 Riverview Ave., Swansea, 8/08/90, A, C, 90000069

Kennedy Park [Fall River MRA], Bounded by S. Main St., Bradford Ave., Middle, and Bay Sts., Fall River, 2/16/83, A, C, g, 83000686

Kilmer Street Fire Station [Taunton MRA], Oak and Kilmer Sts., Taunton, 7/05/84, A, C, 84002138

King Airfield Hanger [Taunton MRA], Middleboro Ave., Taunton, 7/05/84, A, 84002141

King Philip Mills [Fall River MRA], Kilburn St., Fall River, 2/16/83, A, C, 83000687

Kingsley House [Rehoboth MRA], 96 Davis St., Rehoboth, 6/06/83, C, 83000688

Knapp, Job, House [Taunton MRA], 81 Shores St., Taunton, 7/05/84, A, C, 84002150

Knapp, Seth, Jr. House [Rehoboth MRA], 82 Water St., Rehoboth, 6/06/83, C, 83000689

Lafayette-Durfee House, 94 Cherry St., Fall River, 4/15/82, B, b, 82004959

Lawrence, William, House [Taunton MRA], 101 Somerset Ave., Taunton, 7/10/85, C, 85001531

Leonard School [Taunton MRA], W. Brittania St., Taunton, 7/05/84, A, C, 84002155

Leonard, James, House [Taunton MRA], 3 Warren St., Taunton, 7/05/84, A, C, 84002152

Lightship No. 114, State Pier, New Bedford, 5/30/90, A, C, g, 90000777

Lincoln, Ambrose, Jr., House [Taunton MRA], 1916 Bay St., Taunton, 7/05/84, C, 84002157

Lincoln, Asa, House [Taunton MRA], 171 Shores St., Taunton, 7/05/84, C, 84002159

Lincoln, Gen. Thomas, House [Taunton MRA], 104 Field St., Taunton, 7/05/84, A, B, C, 84002162

Lindsey, William, House [Fall River MRA], 373 N. Main St., Fall River, 2/16/83, A, C, 83000690

Long Plain Friends Meetinghouse, 1341 N. Main St., Acushnet, 6/26/86, A, C, a, 86001374

Lord-Baylies-Bennett House [Taunton MRA], 66 Winthrop St., Taunton, 7/05/84, C, 84002165

Lothrop Memorial Building-G.A.R. Hall [Taunton MRA], Washington and Governor Sts., Taunton, 7/05/84, A, C, a, 84002168

Lothrop, H.B., Store [Taunton MRA], 210 Weir St., Taunton, 7/05/84, A, C, 84002166

Lower Highlands Historic District [Fall River MRA], Roughly bounded by Cherry, Main, Winter, and Bank Sts., Fall River, 1/10/84, A, C, 84002171

Luther House [Swansea MRA], 177 Market St., Swansea, 8/08/90, C, 90000073

Luther Store, W of Swansea at 160 Old Warren Rd., Swansea vicinity, 5/22/78, A, C, 78000438

Luther's Corner [Swansea MRA], Old Warren and Pierce Rds., Swansea, 2/16/90, A, C, 90000054

Luther, William, House [Swansea MRA], 79 Old Warren Rd., Swansea, 2/16/90, A, C, 90000067

Macomber, Calvin T., House [Taunton MRA], 312 W. Brittania St., Taunton, 7/05/84, C, 84002174

Makepeace, D. E., Company, 46 Pine St., Attleboro, 7/18/85, A, C, 85001577

Manley, William M., House [Fall River MRA], 610 Cherry St., Fall River, 6/26/86, A, C, 86001401

Martin Farm [Rehoboth MRA], 121 Martin St., Rehoboth, 6/06/83, C, 83000691

Martin House, 940 Court St., Seekonk, 5/02/74, B, C, 74000365

Martin House and Farm, 22 Stoney Hill Rd., North Swansea, 10/02/78, A, C, 78000437

Marvel, Theodore L., House [Taunton MRA], 188 Berkley St., Taunton, 7/05/84, C, 84002176

Mason, N. S., House [Taunton MRA], 58 Tremont St., Taunton, 7/05/84, C, 84002178

Mason, William P., House [Swansea MRA], 5 Mason St., Swansea, 8/08/90, A, C, 90000121

Massasoit Fire House No. 5 [Fall River MRA], 83 Freedom St., Fall River, 2/16/83, C, 83000692

McKinstrey House [Taunton MRA], 115 High St., Taunton, 7/05/84, C, a, 84002181

Mechanics Mill [Fall River MRA], 1082 Dawol St., Fall River, 2/16/83, A, C, 83000693

Merrill's Wharf Historic District, MacArthur Dr., New Bedford, 11/11/77, A, C, 77000167

Millicent Library, 45 Center St., Fairhaven, 5/15/86, A, B, C, 86001051

Morse House [Taunton MRA], 6 Pleasant St., Taunton, 7/05/84, C, 84002185

Bristol County—Continued

Morse, Henry, House [Taunton MRA], 32 Cedar St., Taunton, 7/05/84, C, 84002183

Narragansett Mills [Fall River MRA], 1567 N. Main St., Fall River, 2/16/83, A, C, 83000694

Neck of Land Cemetery [Taunton MRA], Summer St., Taunton, 7/10/85, C, d, 85001530

New Bedford Historic District, Bounded by Front St. on E, Elm St. on N, Acushnet Ave. on W, and Commercial St. on S, New Bedford, 11/13/66, A, NHL, 66000773

North Attleborough Town Center Historic District, Roughly N. and S. Washington St. between Fisher and Bank Sts., North Attleborough, 12/20/85, A, C, 85003168

North Burial Ground [Fall River MRA], N. Main St. between Brightman and Cory Sts., Fall River, 2/16/83, A, d, 83000695

North Christian Congregational Church [Fall River MRA], 3538 N. Main St., Fall River, 2/16/83, A, C, a, 83000696

North Easton Historic District, Section of town N of and including both sides of Main-Lincoln St., Easton, 11/03/72, A, C, 72000119

North Easton Railroad Station, Off Oliver St. on railroad right-of-way, North Easton, 4/11/72, A, C, 72000125

North Taunton Baptist Church [Taunton MRA], 1940 Bay St., Taunton, 7/05/84, A, C, a, 84002188

Northbound and Southbound Stations, 1 and 3 Mill St., Attleboro, 1/05/89, A, C, 88003128

Norton Center Historic District, MA 123, Norton, 12/23/77, A, C, a, 77000170

Norton House [Swansea MRA], 61 Old Providence Rd., Swansea, 2/16/90, A, C, 90000078

Notre Dame School [Fall River MRA], 34 St. Joseph's St., Fall River, 2/16/83, C, a, 83000697

Oak Grove Cemetery [Fall River MRA], 765 Prospect St., Fall River, 2/16/83, A, 83000698

Old Bay Road, From Easton Town Line to Taunton Town Line, Norton, 11/08/74, A, 74000362

Old Colony Iron Works-Nesmasket Mills Complex [Taunton MRA], Old Colony Ave., Taunton, 7/05/84, A, C, 84002190

Old Colony Railroad Station [Taunton MRA], 40 Dean St., Taunton, 7/05/84, A, C, 84002192

Old Third District Courthouse, 2nd and William Sts., New Bedford, 9/28/71, A, C, 71000083

Old Town Historic District, SE of jct. of I-295 and Washington St., North Attleborough, 5/30/91, A, C, a, 91000599

Old Weir Stove Company [Taunton MRA], W. Water St., Taunton, 7/05/84, A, C, 84002194

Osborn House, 456 Rock St., Fall River, 4/04/80, A, C, 80000431

Osborn Street School [Fall River MRA], 160 Osborn St., Fall River, 2/16/83, A, C, 83000699

PT BOAT 796 (torpedo boat), Battleship Cove, Fall River, 1/14/86, A, g, NHL, 86000092

Padanaram Village Historic District, Elm, Water, Middle, High, Pleasant, Prospect, Hill, School, Fremont, and Bridge Sts., Dartmouth, 9/05/85, A, C, a, 85002010

Palmer Island Light Station [Lighthouses of Massachusetts TR (AD)], New Bedford Harbor, New Bedford, 3/26/80, A, C, 80000433

Paull, Alfred, House [Taunton MRA], 467 Weir St., Taunton, 7/05/84, C, 84002196

Peck-Bowen House [Rehoboth MRA], 330 Fairview Ave., Rehoboth, 6/06/83, C, 83000700

Perry, James, House [Rehoboth MRA], 121 Perryville Rd., Rehoboth, 6/06/83, C, 83000701

Picard, Israel, House [Fall River MRA], 690 County St., Fall River, 2/16/83, C, 83000702

Pierce, Capt, Mial, Farm [Rehoboth MRA], 177 Hornbine Rd., Rehoboth, 6/06/83, A, C, 83000703

Pilgrim Congregational Church [Taunton MRA], 45 Broadway, Taunton, 7/05/84, A, C, a, 84002199

Pilgrim Mills [Fall River MRA], 847 Pleasant St., Fall River, 2/16/83, A, C, 83000704

Pine Street School [Fall River MRA], 880 Pine St., Fall River, 2/16/83, C, 83000705

Pocasset Firehouse No. 7 [Fall River MRA], 1058 Pleasant St., Fall River, 2/16/83, C, 83000706

Qheguechan Club [Fall River MRA], 306 N. Main St., Fall River, 2/16/83, C, 83000708

Queguechan Valley Mills Historic District [Fall River MRA], Queguechan, Jefferson, and Stevens Sts. between I-195 and Denver St., Fall River, 2/16/83, A, C, 83000709

Read, Nathan, House [Fall River MRA], 506 N. Main St., Fall River, 2/16/83, C, 83000710

Reed and Barton Complex [Taunton MRA], W. Brittania and Danforth Sts., Taunton, 7/05/84, A, C, 84002207

Rehoboth Village Historic District [Rehoboth MRA], Bay State Rd. and Locust Ave., Rehoboth, 6/06/83, A, B, C, 83000707

Robinson, Capt. Joel, House, 111 Rocklawn Ave., Attleboro, 11/20/78, B, C, 78000428

Ruggles Park [Fall River MRA], Bounded by Seabury, Robeson, Pine, and Locust Sts., Fall River, 2/16/83, A, C, 83000711

Russells Mills Village Historic District, Russells Mills, Rock O' Dundee, Slades Corner, Horseneck and Fisher Rds., Dartmouth, 9/05/85, A, B, C, D, a, 85002011

Sacred Heart School [Fall River MRA], 90 Linden St., Fall River, 3/09/87, A, C, a, 87000371

Sadler, Herbert A., House, 574 Newport Ave., Attleboro, 10/21/82, B, C, 82000489

Sagamore Mill No. 2 [Fall River MRA], 1822 N. Main St., Fall River, 2/16/83, A, C, 83000712

Sagamore Mills No. 1 and No. 3 [Fall River MRA], Ace St., Fall River, 2/16/83, A, C, 83000713

Sanford Spinning Co. [Fall River MRA], Globe Mills Ave., Fall River, 2/16/83, A, C, 83000714

Santo Christo Church [Fall River MRA], 240 Columbia St., Fall River, 2/16/83, A, C, a, 83000715

Sawin, Ezekiel, House, 44 William St., Fairhaven, 6/15/79, B, C, 79000327

School Street School [Taunton MRA], School and Fruit Sts., Taunton, 7/05/84, A, C, 84002214

Seaconnett Mills [Fall River MRA], E. Warren St., Fall River, 2/16/83, A, C, 83000716

Short's Tavern [Swansea MRA], 282 Market St., Swansea, 2/16/90, A, C, 90000072

Simcock House [Swansea MRA], 1074 Sharps Lot Rd., Swansea, 2/16/90, C, 90000063

Smith, Bradford, Building, 1927-1941 Purchase St., New Bedford, 5/17/84, A, C, 84002216

Smith, John Mace, House [Fall River MRA], 399 N. Main St., Fall River, 2/16/83, C, 83000717

Smuggler's House [Swansea MRA], 361 Pearse Rd., Swansea, 2/16/90, A, C, 90000065

South Swansea Union Church [Swansea MRA], Gardner's Neck Rd., Swansea, 2/16/90, A, C, a, 90000055

St. Anne's Church and Parish Complex [Fall River MRA], 780 S. Main St., Fall River, 2/16/83, A, C, a, 83000719

St. Joseph's Church [Fall River MRA], 1355 N. Main St., Fall River, 2/16/83, A, C, a, 83000720

St. Joseph's Orphanage [Fall River MRA], 56 St. Joseph's St., Fall River, 2/16/83, A, C, a, 83000721

St. Louis Church [Fall River MRA], 440 Bradford Ave., Fall River, 2/16/83, A, C, a, 83000722

St. Mary's Cathedral and Rectory [Fall River MRA], 407 Spring St., Fall River, 2/16/83, A, C, a, 83000723

St. Mary's Complex [Taunton MRA], Broadway and Washington St., Taunton, 7/05/84, A, C, a, 84002211

St. Patrick's Church [Fall River MRA], 1588 S. Main St., Fall River, 2/16/83, A, C, a, 83000724

St. Thomas Epsicopal Church [Taunton MRA], 115 High St., Taunton, 7/05/84, A, C, a, 84002213

Stafford Mills [Fall River MRA], County St., Fall River, 2/16/83, A, C, 83000718

Staples, Sylvanus N., House [Taunton MRA], 21 Second St., Taunton, 7/05/84, A, C, 84002217

Stone House [Taunton MRA], 15-17 Plain St., Taunton, 7/05/84, C, 84002219

Swansea Village Historic District [Swansea MRA], Roughly Main St. from Gardners Neck Rd. to Stephens Rd., and Ledge Rd., Swansea, 2/16/90, A, C, 90000053

Sweet, Albert, House [Taunton MRA], 179 Highland St., Taunton, 7/05/84, C, 84002221

Taunton Alms House [Taunton MRA], Norton Ave., Taunton, 7/05/84, C, 84002223

Taunton Green Historic District [Taunton MRA], Broadway, Taunton Green, Main and Court Sts., Taunton, 3/01/85, A, C, 85000547

Taunton Public Library [Taunton MRA], Pleasant St., Taunton, 7/05/84, A, C, 84002225

Thomas, H.P., House [Taunton MRA], 322 Somerset Ave., Taunton, 7/05/84, C, 84002228

Thompson Street School, 58 Crapo St., New Bedford, 1/26/90, A, C, 89002329

Times and Olympia Buildings, 908-912 and 880-898 Purchase St., New Bedford, 7/07/83, A, C, 83000725

Tisdale-Morse House [Taunton MRA], 17 Fayette Pl., Taunton, 7/05/84, C, 84002231

Torpedo Boat PT-617, Battleship Cove, Falls River, 12/20/89, A, C, g, NHL, 89002465

Truesdale Hospital [Fall River MRA], 1820 Highland Ave., Fall River, 4/15/86, A, B, C, 86000801

Tucker Farm Historic District, 1178 Tucker Rd., Dartmouth, 8/25/88, A, C, 88000705

Bristol County—Continued

U.S. Customhouse, SW corner of 2nd and Williams Sts., New Bedford, 12/30/70, C, NHL, 70000735

U.S.S. JOSEPH P. KENNEDY JR. (DD-850) [Fall River MRA (AD)], Battleship Cove, Fall River, 9/30/76, A, f, g, NHL, 76000231

U.S.S. LIONFISH [Fall River MRA], Battleship Cove, Fall River, 9/30/76, A, g, 76000232

U.S.S. MASSACHUSETTS [Fall River MRA], Battleship Cove, Fall River, 9/30/76, A, g, 76000233

US Post Office—Attleboro Main, 75 Park St., Attleboro, 10/19/87, A, C, 87001767

US Post Office—Taunton Main, 37 Taunton Green, Taunton, 10/19/87, A, C, 86003476

USS LIONFISH (SS0298) National Historic Landmark, Battleship Cove, Fall River, 9/30/76, A, g, NHL, 76002270

USS MASSACHUSETTS (BB-59) National Historic Landmark, Battleship Cove, Fall River, 9/30/76, A, g, NHL, 76002269

Union Congregational Church [Taunton MRA], W. Brittania and Rockland Sts., Taunton, 7/05/84, A, C, a, 84002232

Union Mills [Fall River MRA], Pleasant St., Fall River, 2/16/83, A, C, 83000726

Union Mission Chapel-Historical Hall [Taunton MRA], Cedar St., Taunton, 7/05/84, A, C, a, 84002235

Union Street Railway Carbarn, Repair Shop, 1959 Purchase St., New Bedford, 10/02/78, A, 78000431

Unitarian Society, The, 309 N. Main St., Fall River, 5/13/82, A, C, a, b, 82004958

Valentine-French House [Fall River MRA], 5105 N. Main St., Fall River, 2/16/83, C, 83000727

Viall, Samuel, House [Rehoboth MRA], 85 Carpenter St., Rehoboth, 6/06/83, C, 83000728

Vickery, Capt. David, House [Taunton MRA], 33 Plain St., Taunton, 7/05/84, A, C, 84002254

Vickery-Baylies House [Taunton MRA], 56 Summer St., Taunton, 7/05/84, A, C, 84002252

Walkden Farm [Swansea MRA], 495 Marvel St., Swansea, 2/16/90, A, C, 90000071

Walker School [Taunton MRA], Berkley St., Taunton, 7/05/84, A, C, 84002257

Walker, Peter, House [Taunton MRA], 1679 Somerset Ave., Taunton, 7/05/84, C, 84002256

Wampanoag Mills [Fall River MRA], Queguechan St., Fall River, 2/16/83, A, C, 83000729

Washburn, Samuel, House [Taunton MRA], 68 Winthrop St., Taunton, 7/05/84, C, 84002258

Washington School [Taunton MRA], 40 Vernon St., Taunton, 7/05/84, A, C, 84002261

Weir Engine House [Taunton MRA], 530 Weir St., Taunton, 7/05/84, C, 84002263

Westport Point Historic District, Roughly, Main St. from Charles St. to W. Branch, Westport R., including Cape Bial and Valentine Lns., Westport, 6/25/92, A, C, 92000815

Westville Congregational Church [Taunton MRA], Winthrop and N. Walker Sts., Taunton, 7/05/84, A, C, a, 84002266

Wheeler, Aaron, House [Rehoboth MRA], 371 Fairview Ave., Rehoboth, 6/06/83, C, 83000730

Wheeler-Ingalls House [Rehoboth MRA], 51 Summer St., Rehoboth, 7/05/83, C, 83000731

White, William L., Jr., House [Taunton MRA], 242 Winthrop St., Taunton, 7/05/84, C, 84002268

Whittenton Fire and Police Station [Taunton MRA], Bay St., Taunton, 7/05/84, A, C, 84002271

Whittenton Mills Complex [Taunton MRA], Mill River and Whittenton St., Taunton, 7/05/84, A, C, 84002275

Williams, Abiathar King, House [Taunton MRA], 43 Ingell St., Taunton, 7/05/84, C, 84002278

Williams, Enoch, House [Taunton MRA], 616 Middleboro Ave., Taunton, 7/05/84, A, C, 84002280

Williams, Francis D., House [Taunton MRA], 3 Plain St., Taunton, 7/05/84, C, 84002282

Williams, N.S., House [Taunton MRA], 1150 Middleboro Ave., Taunton, 7/05/84, C, 84002285

Willis, Joseph, House [Taunton MRA], 28 Worchester St., Taunton, 7/05/84, A, C, 84002286

Winslow Congregational Church [Taunton MRA], 61 Winthrop St., Taunton, 7/05/84, A, C, a, 84002288

Winslow, Luther, Jr., House [Fall River MRA], 5225 N. Main St., Fall River, 2/16/83, C, 83000732

Winthrop Street Baptist Church [Taunton MRA], 58 Winthrop St., Taunton, 7/05/84, A, C, a, 84002291

Woman's Club of Fall River [Fall River MRA], 1542 Walnut St., Fall River, 2/16/83, A, C, 83000733

Woodcock—Hatch—Maxcy House Historic District, 362 N. Washington St., North Attleborough, 7/12/90, A, C, d, 90001081

Woodward, William, House [Taunton MRA], 117 Arlington St., Taunton, 7/10/85, A, C, 85001529

Dukes County

Cape Poge Light [Lighthouses of Massachusetts TR], Chappaquiddick Island, Edgartown, 9/28/87, A, C, b, 87002040

East Chop Light [Lighthouses of Massachusetts TR], Lighthouse Rd., Oak Bluffs, 6/15/87, A, C, 87001480

Edgartown Harbor Light [Lighthouses of Massachusetts TR], Off N. Water St., Edgartown, 6/15/87, A, C, b, 87001465

Edgartown Village Historic District, Bounded by Water St. (North and South) and Pease's Point Way(North and South), Edgartown, 12/09/83, A, C, 83003967

Flying Horses, 33 Oak Bluffs Ave., Oak Bluffs, 8/27/79, A, b, NHL, 79000342

Gay Head Light [Lighthouses of Massachusetts TR], Lighthouse Rd., Gay Head, 6/15/87, A, C, 87001464

Martha's Vineyard Campground, Roughly bounded by Cottage Park, Quequechan, Clinton, Dukes, County, Siloam, Lake, and Central Aves., Oak Bluffs, 12/14/78, A, C, a, 78000439

Old Mill, Edgartown-West Tisbury Rd., West Tisbury, 3/29/84, A, B, C, 84002303

Ritter House, Beach St., Vineyard Haven, 12/06/77, C, 77000169

Tarpaulin Cove Light [Lighthouses of Massachusetts TR], Naushon Island, Gosnold, 6/15/87, A, C, 87001505

Tucker, Dr. Harrison A., Cottage, 42 Ocean Ave., Oak Bluffs, 10/22/90, B, C, 90000678

Union Chapel, Bounded by Circuit, Kennebec, and Narragansett Aves. and Grove St., Oak Bluffs, 6/07/90, A, C, a, 90000677

West Chop Light Station [Lighthouses of Massachusetts TR], W. Chop Rd., Tisbury, 6/15/87, A, C, 87001506

William Street Historic District, Williams St. from Wood Lawn Ave. to 24 Williams St., Tisbury, 1/27/83, A, C, 83000571

Essex County

ADVENTURE (schooner), State Fish Pier, Gloucester Inner Harbor, Gloucester, 12/11/89, A, C, g, 89002054

Abbot Hall, Washington Sq., Marblehead, 9/06/74, C, 74000374

Abbot Tavern [Town of Andover MRA], 70 Elm St., Andover, 6/10/82, A, C, 82004810

Abbot, Asa and Sylvester, House [Town of Andover MRA], 15-17 Andover Rd., Andover, 6/10/82, C, 82004833

Abbot, Benjamin, House, 9 Andover St., Andover, 2/24/75, B, C, 75000242

Abbot, J. T., House [Town of Andover MRA], 34 Essex St., Andover, 6/10/82, C, 82004814

Abbot—Stinson House [First Period Buildings of Eastern Massachusetts TR], 6 Stinson Rd., Andover, 3/09/90, C, 90000190

Abbot-Baker House [Town of Andover MRA], 5 Argilla Rd., Andover, 6/10/82, C, 82004811

Abbot-Battles House [Town of Andover MRA], 31 Lowell St., Andover, 6/10/82, C, 82001905

Academy Hill Historic District [Town of Andover MRA], MA 28, Andover, 10/07/82, A, B, C, b, d, 82000475

Adams, Abraham, House [First Period Buildings of Eastern Massachusetts TR], 8 Pearson Dr., Newbury, 3/09/90, C, 90000245

Adams—Clarke House [First Period Buildings of Eastern Massachusetts TR], 93 W. Main St., Georgetown, 3/09/90, C, 90000211

American Woolen Mill Housing District, 300-328 Market St., Lawrence, 4/08/82, A, C, 82001990

Amesbury and Salisbury Mills Village Historic District, Market Sq. roughly bounded by Boardman, Water, Main and Pond Sts., Amesbury, 5/16/85, A, C, 85001121

Andover National Bank [Town of Andover MRA], 23 Main St., Andover, 6/10/82, A, C, 82001907

Andover Town Hall [Town of Andover MRA], 20 Main St., Andover, 6/10/82, A, C, 82004961

Andover Village Industrial District [Town of Andover MRA], MA 28, Andover, 10/07/82, A, C, 82000476

Essex County—Continued

Annisquam Bridge, Address Restricted, Gloucester, 6/23/83, A, C, 83000572

Annisquam Harbor Light Station [Lighthouses of Massachusetts TR], Wigwam Pt., Gloucester, 6/15/87, A, C, 87001526

Arden [Town of Andover MRA], 276 N. Main St., Andover, 6/10/82, A, B, C, 82004812

Arlington Mills Historic District, Broadway between Manchester, Stafford and Chase Sts., Lawrence and Methuen, 1/03/85, A, C, 85000023

Arlington-Basswood Historic District, Roughly bounded by Lawrence, Alder, Arlington, and Juniper Sts., Lawrence, 11/13/84, A, C, 84000406

Bailey House [Central Village, Ipswich, Massachusetts MRA], 40 Market St., Ipswich, 9/17/80, C, 80000457

Bailey, Timothy P., House [Town of Andover MRA], 210 Chandler Rd., Andover, 6/10/82, A, C, 82004828

Baker's Island Light Station [Lighthouses of Massachusetts TR (AD)], E of Salem on Baker's Island, Salem, 11/21/76, A, 76000289

Balch, John, House, 448 Cabot St., Beverly, 2/23/73, B, C, e, 73000275

Ballardvale District [Town of Andover MRA], Off I-93, Andover, 10/07/82, A, C, 82000477

Barker, Stephen, House [Methuen MRA], 165 Haverhill St., Methuen, 1/20/84, C, 84002307

Barnard Block [Town of Andover MRA], 10-16 Main St., Andover, 6/10/82, A, C, 82004803

Barnard, Parson, House, 179 Osgood St., North Andover, 9/06/74, A, C, a, 74000918

Beauport, Eastern Point Blvd., Gloucester vicinity, 4/26/76, B, C, 76000246

Beverly Center Business District, Roughly bounded by Chapman, Central, Brown, Dane, and Essex Sts., Beverly, 7/05/84, A, C, 84002313

Beverly Grammar School [First Period Buildings of Eastern Massachusetts TR], 50 Essex St., Beverly, 3/09/90, C, D, b, 90000198

Blanchard—Upton House [First Period Buildings of Eastern Massachusetts TR], 62 Osgood St., Andover, 3/09/90, C, 90000192

Boardman House, Howard St., Saugus, 10/15/66, C, NHL, 66000131

Boardman, John, House [First Period Buildings of Eastern Massachusetts TR], 6 Lawrence Rd., Boxford, 3/09/90, C, D, b, 90000361

Bowditch, Nathaniel, House, North St., Salem, 10/15/66, B, b, NHL, 66000135

Bowker Place [Downtown Salem MRA], 144-156 Essex St., Salem, 7/29/83, A, C, 83000573

Boxford Village Historic District, Middleton and Topsfield Rds. and Main and Elm Sts., Boxford, 4/11/73, C, 73000279

Bradford Common Historic District, S. Main St., Haverhill, 9/14/77, A, C, 77000179

Bradlee School [Town of Andover MRA], 147 Andover St., Andover, 6/10/82, C, 82004829

Brown House [First Period Buildings of Eastern Massachusetts TR], 76 Bridge St., Hamilton, 3/09/90, C, 90000223

Brown Square House, 11 Brown Sq., Newburyport, 3/07/75, A, C, 75000284

Brown's Manor [Central Village, Ipswich, Massachusetts MRA], 115 High St., Ipswich, 9/17/80, C, 80000459

Brown, Austin, House [First Period Buildings of Eastern Massachusetts TR], 1028 Bay Rd., Hamilton, 3/09/90, C, 90000222

Buildings at 24–30 Summer St., 24–30 Summer St., Lawrence, 12/05/85, C, 85003067

Burnham, David, House, Pond St., Essex, 7/30/83, C, 83000574

Burnham, James, House [First Period Buildings of Eastern Massachusetts TR], 37 Heartbreak Rd., Ipswich, 3/09/90, C, D, 90000236

Burnham-Patch House [Central Village, Ipswich, Massachusetts MRA], 1 Turkey Shore Rd., Ipswich, 9/17/80, A, B, C, 80000452

Buswell, J.E., House [Methuen MRA], 535-537 Prospect St., Methuen, 1/20/84, C, 84002317

Cable, Benjamin Stickney, Memorial Hospital, Jct. of SR 1A and SR 133, Ipswich, 5/10/90, A, C, 90000683

Cabot, Capt. John, House, 117 Cabot St., Beverly, 4/16/75, A, C, 75000246

Caldwell Block [Central Village, Ipswich, Massachusetts MRA], S. Main St., Ipswich, 7/07/83, A, C, 83003434

Calef, Dr. John, House [Central Village, Ipswich, Massachusetts MRA], 7 Poplar St., Ipswich, 9/17/80, B, C, 80000447

Capen, Parson, House, Howlett St., Topsfield, 10/15/66, C, NHL, 66000139

Carlton—Frie—Tucker House [First Period Buildings of Eastern Massachusetts TR], 140 Mill Rd., North Andover, 3/09/90, C, 90000251

Castle Hill, E of Ipswich on Argilla Rd., Ipswich vicinity, 12/02/77, B, C, 77000183

Central Gloucester Historic District, Roughly bounded by Middle, Main, Center, Hancock, Short, Prospect and Pleasant Sts., Gloucester, 7/08/82, A, B, C, a, 82001881

Central Square Historic District, Central Sq., Monroe, Union, and Willow Sts., Lynn, 12/10/85, A, C, 85003335

Central Street District [Town of Andover MRA], Irregular Pattern along Central St., Andover, 10/07/82, A, B, C, a, 82004478

Chandler-Bigsby-Abbot House [Town of Andover MRA], 88 Lowell St., Andover, 6/10/82, A, C, 82004830

Chandler-Hidden House [Town of Andover MRA], 17 Hidden Rd., Andover, 6/10/82, C, 82004832

Chaplin-Clarke House, 109 Haverhill St., Rowley, 5/10/79, A, C, 79000343

Charter Street Historic District, Bounded by Liberty, Derby, Central, and Charter Sts., Salem, 3/10/75, A, C, 75000294

Chase, Samuel, House [First Period Buildings of Eastern Massachusetts TR], 154 Main St., West Newbury, 3/09/90, C, D, 90000273

Chestnut Street District, Bounded roughly by Broad, Flint, Federal, and Summer Sts., Salem, 8/28/73, A, C, 73000312

Chestnut Street District (Boundary Increase), Roughly bounded by Bridge, Lynn, Beckford, and River Sts., Salem, 10/04/78, A, C, 78000468

Chickering House [Town of Andover MRA], 28 Essex St., Andover, 6/10/82, C, 82004831

Choate Bridge, MA 133/1A over the Ipswich River (S. Main St.), Ipswich, 8/21/72, A, C, 72000137

Choate, Rufus, House, 14 Lynde St., Salem, 11/12/82, B, C, 82000481

City Hall, 93 Washington St., Salem, 4/03/73, A, C, 73000316

Claflin-Richards House, 132 Main St., Wenham, 4/03/73, A, C, a, 73000853

Cochran, Jehiel, House [Town of Andover MRA], 63 Burnham Rd., Andover, 6/10/82, C, 82004827

Cogswell's Grant, 60 Spring St., Essex, 4/19/90, A, B, C, 90000666

Coker, Benjamin, House [First Period Buildings of Eastern Massachusetts TR], 172 State St., Newburyport, 3/09/90, C, b, 90000247

Conant, Exercise, House [First Period Buildings of Eastern Massachusetts TR], 634 Cabot St., Beverly, 3/09/90, C, 90000199

Corning, Samuel, House [First Period Buildings of Eastern Massachusetts TR], 87 Hull St., Beverly, 3/09/90, C, 90000196

Crombie Street District [Downtown Salem MRA], 7-15 and 16-18 Crombie St., and 13 Barton St., Salem, 9/16/83, C, 83000575

Cushing, Caleb, House, 98 High St., Newburyport, 11/07/73, B, NHL, 73000327

Daddy Frye's Hill Cemetery [Methuen MRA], East and Arlington Sts., Methuen, 1/20/84, A, d, 84002320

Dalton House, 95 State St., Newburyport, 3/29/78, B, C, 78000464

Dascomb House [Town of Andover MRA], 125 Dascomb Rd., Andover, 6/10/82, C, 82004826

Davis, Ephraim, House [First Period Buildings of Eastern Massachusetts TR], Merrimack Rd., N of jct. with Amesbury Line Rd., Haverhill, 3/09/90, C, 90000228

Davis—Freeman House [First Period Buildings of Eastern Massachusetts TR], 302 Essex St., Gloucester, 3/09/90, C, 90000214

Derby Summerhouse, Magna Estate, Ingersoll St., Danvers, 11/24/68, C, b, NHL, 68000020

Derby Waterfront District, Derby St. from Herbert St. to Block House Sq., waterfront sts. between Kosciusko and Blaney Sts., Salem, 5/17/76, A, C, 76000297

Derby Wharf Light Station [Lighthouses of Massachusetts TR], Derby Wharf, Salem, 6/15/87, A, C, NPS, 87001466

Dickinson—Pillsbury—Witham House [First Period Buildings of Eastern Massachusetts TR], 170 Jewett St., Georgetown, 3/09/90, C, D, 90000210

Dodge Building, 19-23 Pleasant St., Newburyport, 8/26/82, A, C, 82001878

Dolan, Terence, House [Methuen MRA], 478 Prospect St., Methuen, 1/20/84, C, 84002323

Essex County—Continued

Double-arch Sandstone Bridge [Methuen MRA], Hampshire Rd., Methuen, 6/20/84, C, 84002326

Downtown Lawrence Historic District, Roughly bounded by MA 110, Methuen, Lawrence and Jackson Sts., Lawrence, 11/01/79, A, C, 79000329

Downtown Salem District [Downtown Salem MRA], Roughly bounded by Church, Central, New Derby, and Washington Sts., Salem, 10/18/83, A, C, 83003969

Dustin House [First Period Buildings of Eastern Massachusetts TR], 665 Hilldale Ave., Haverhill, 3/09/90, C, 90000227

Dyke—Wheeler House [First Period Buildings of Eastern Massachusetts TR], 144 Wheeler St., Gloucester, 3/09/90, C, 90000215

East End Historic District [Central Village, Ipswich, Massachusetts MRA], East St., Ipswich, 9/17/80, A, C, 80000461

Eastern Point Light Station [Lighthouses of Massachusetts TR], Eastern Pt., Gloucester, 9/30/87, A, B, C, 87002027

Emerson House [Methuen MRA], 58 Ayers Village Rd., Methuen, 1/20/84, C, 84002351

Emerson House [First Period Buildings of Eastern Massachusetts TR], 5–9 Pentucket St., Haverhill, 3/09/90, C, b, 90000229

Emerson, Capt. Oliver, Homestead [Methuen MRA], 133 North St., Methuen, 1/20/84, B, C, 84002347

Emmons, G.B., House [Methuen MRA], 283 Broadway, Methuen, 1/20/84, C, 84002353

English High School, Essex and James Sts., Lynn, 9/11/86, A, C, 86002508

Essex Company Machine Shop, Union St., Lawrence, 11/09/72, A, C, 72000138

Essex Company Offices and Yard, 6 Essex St., Lawrence, 4/26/79, A, C, 79000330

Essex County Court Buildings, 32 Federal St., Salem, 5/17/76, A, C, 76000299

Essex Insitiue Historic District, 134-132, 128, 126 Essex St. and 13 Washington Sq. W., Salem, 6/22/72, A, C, b, 72000147

Estey Tavern, Central and Maple Sts. at MA 114, Middleton, 10/12/89, A, C, 89001587

Fabens Building, 312-314 Union St., Lynn, 2/25/82, A, C, 82001879

Federal Street District [Downtown Salem MRA], Roughly bounded by Bridge, Washington, Federal, and Summer Sts., Salem, 9/16/83, C, 83000576

Felton, Nathaniel, Houses, 43 Felton St. (Jr.) and 47 Felton St. (Sr.), Peabody, 4/01/82, A, C, b, 82001882

First Baptist Church [Methuen MRA], 253 Lawrence St., Methuen, 1/20/84, C, a, 84002365

First Church Congregational, Pleasant and Stevens Sts., Methuen, 12/01/78, C, a, 78000461

First Religious Society Church and Parish Hall, 26 Pleasant St., Newburyport, 4/02/76, C, a, 76000278

First Unitarian Church, 7 Park St., Peabody, 9/18/89, C, a, 88001091

First Universalist Church [Downtown Salem MRA], 6 Rust St., Salem, 7/29/83, C, a, 83000577

Fish Flake Hill Historic District, N and S sides of Front St. from Cabot to Bartlett Sts., Beverly, 10/26/71, A, C, 71000082

Fish Flake Hill Historic District (Boundary Increase), Roughly bounded by Cabot, Bartlett, and Water Sts., Beverly, 6/26/86, A, C, 86001375

Flint Farm [Town of Andover MRA], 85 Osgood St., Andover, 6/10/82, C, 82004825

Follansbee House [Town of Andover MRA], 459 Lowell St., Andover, 6/10/82, C, 82004485

Fort Pickering, Winter Island, Salem, 2/08/73, A, C, 73000320

Fort Sewall, Fort Sewall Promontory, Marblehead, 4/14/75, A, 75001908

Foster, Gen. Gideon, House, 35 Washington St., Peabody, 6/23/76, B, C, b, 76000287

Foster, Phineas, House [First Period Buildings of Eastern Massachusetts TR], 15 Old Topsfield Rd., Boxford, 3/09/90, C, D, 90000193

Foster, Stephen, House [First Period Buildings of Eastern Massachusetts TR], 109 North St., Topsfield, 3/09/90, C, 90000262

Foster, William, House [First Period Buildings of Eastern Massachusetts TR], 96 Central St., Andover, 3/09/90, C, D, 90000191

Fowler House, 166 High St., Danversport, 9/17/74, A, C, 74000367

Fowler, Rea Putnam, House [First Period Buildings of Eastern Massachusetts TR], 4 Elerton Pl., Danvers, 3/09/90, C, 90000202

Fox Hill School, 81 Water St., Danvers, 2/10/88, A, C, 87002554

French—Andrews House [First Period Buildings of Eastern Massachusetts TR], 86 Howlett Rd., Topsfield, 3/09/90, C, 90000263

Friend, James, House [First Period Buildings of Eastern Massachusetts TR], 114 Cedar St., Wenham, 3/09/90, C, b, 90000268

Front Street Block, West End, 55-71 Main St., Gloucester, 5/08/74, A, C, 74000369

Frye, Nathan, House [Town of Andover MRA], 166 N. Main St., Andover, 6/10/82, B, C, 82004824

Frye, Samuel, House [First Period Buildings of Eastern Massachusetts TR], 920 Turnpike St., North Andover, 3/09/90, C, 90000252

Fuller, Joseph, House [First Period Buildings of Eastern Massachusetts TR], 161 Essex St., Middleton, 3/09/90, C, 90000244

Fuller, Lieut. Thomas, House [First Period Buildings of Eastern Massachusetts TR], Old S. Main St. between Mt. Vernon and Boston Sts., Middleton, 3/09/90, C, D, 90000242

G.A.R. Hall and Museum, 58 Andrew St., Lynn, 5/07/79, A, C, 79000331

Gardiner-Pingree House, 128 Essex St., Salem, 12/30/70, C, NHL, 70000541

Gedney and Cox Houses, 21 High St., Salem, 10/01/74, C, 74000389

Gerry, Elbridge, House, 44 Washington St., Marblehead, 7/02/73, A, B, c, 73000304

Giddings, George, House and Barn [First Period Buildings of Eastern Massachusetts TR], 66 Choate St., Essex, 3/09/90, C, D, 90000206

Giddings—Burnham House [First Period Buildings of Eastern Massachusetts TR], 37 Argilla Rd., Ipswich, 3/09/90, C, 90000233

Gleason Building, 349-351 Essex St., Lawrence, 4/15/82, A, C, 82001880

Gloucester City Hall, Dale Ave., Gloucester, 5/08/73, A, C, 73000297

Glover, Gen. John, House, 11 Glover St., Marblehead, 11/28/72, B, NHL, 72001101

Goodale, Isaac, House [First Period Buildings of Eastern Massachusetts TR], 141 Argilla Rd., Ipswich, 3/09/90, C, b, 90000232

Gott House [First Period Buildings of Eastern Massachusetts TR], Gott Ave. at Gott Ln., Rockport, 3/09/90, C, 90000255

Gould, Capt. Joseph, House [First Period Buildings of Eastern Massachusetts TR], 129 Washington St., Topsfield, 3/09/90, C, 90000259

Gould, Zaccheus, House [First Period Buildings of Eastern Massachusetts TR], 73 Prospect St., Topsfield, 3/09/90, C, 90000261

Grace Episcopal Church, Common and Jackson Sts., Lawrence, 11/07/76, A, C, a, 76001966

Granite Keystone Bridge, Granite St., Rockport, 8/27/81, A, C, 81000117

Grant, Benjamin, House [Central Village, Ipswich, Massachusetts MRA], 47 County St., Ipswich, 9/17/80, A, C, 80000449

Gray, David, House [Town of Andover MRA], 232 Salem St., Andover, 6/10/82, C, 82004823

Great Stone Dam, Merrimack River & MA 28, Lawrence, 4/13/77, C, 77000184

Hale, Reverend John, House, 39 Hale St., Beverly, 10/09/74, A, B, 74000364

Hale-Boynton House, Middle St., Newbury, 4/14/83, B, C, 83000578

Hamilton Hall, 9 Cambridge St., Salem, 12/30/70, C, NHL, 70000543

Hamilton Historic District, 540-700 and 563-641 Bay Rd., Hamilton, 4/13/73, A, C, 73000300

Hammond Castle, 80 Hesperus Ave., Gloucester, 5/08/73, B, C, 73000298

Harding, Sarah H., House [Town of Andover MRA], 6-8 Harding St., Andover, 6/10/82, C, 82004822

Hardy, Joseph, House [First Period Buildings of Eastern Massachusetts TR], 93 King St., Groveland, 3/09/90, C, 90000219

Hardy, Urias, House [Methuen MRA], 50 Brown St., Methuen, 1/20/84, C, 84002367

Harnden Farm [Town of Andover MRA], 261 Salem St., Andover, 6/10/82, C, 82004821

Harraden, Edward, House [First Period Buildings of Eastern Massachusetts TR], 12–14 Leonard St., Gloucester, 3/09/90, C, D, 90000212

Harris Farm [First Period Buildings of Eastern Massachusetts TR], 3 Manataug Trail, Marblehead, 3/09/90, C, 90000241

Hart House [First Period Buildings of Eastern Massachusetts TR], 172 Chestnut St., Lynnfield, 3/09/90, C, D, 90000239

Haskell, William, House [First Period Buildings of Eastern Massachusetts TR], 11 Lincoln St., Gloucester, 3/09/90, C, D, 90000217

Essex County—Continued

Hastings—Morse House [First Period Buildings of Eastern Massachusetts TR], 595 E. Broadway, Haverhill, 3/14/91, C, 90000225

Hazen—Kimball—Aldrich House [First Period Buildings of Eastern Massachusetts TR], 225 E. Main St., Georgetown, 3/09/90, C, 90000209

Hazen—Spiller House [First Period Buildings of Eastern Massachusetts TR], 8 Groveland St., Haverhill, 3/09/90, C, 90000226

Heard-Lakeman House [Central Village, Ipswich, Massachusetts MRA], 2 Turkey Shore Rd., Ipswich, 9/17/80, C, 80000441

Henfield House [First Period Buildings of Eastern Massachusetts TR], 300 Main St., Lynnfield, 3/04/91, C, D, 90000240

Herrick, Ella Proctor, House [First Period Buildings of Eastern Massachusetts TR], 189 Concord St., Gloucester, 3/09/90, C, 90000213

Hickey—Osborne Block, 38–60 Main St., Peabody, 9/19/85, A, C, b, 85002416

High Service Water Tower and Reservoir, Off MA 110, Lawrence, 11/20/78, A, C, 78000450

High Street Historic District [Central Village, Ipswich, Massachusetts MRA], High St., Ipswich, 9/17/80, A, C, d, 80000454

Holmes, Oliver Wendell, House, 868 Hale St., Beverly, 11/28/72, B, NHL, 72001301

Holt Farm [Town of Andover MRA], 89 Prospect Rd., Andover, 6/10/82, C, 82004819

Holt-Cummings-Davis House [Town of Andover MRA], 67 Salem St., Andover, 6/10/82, C, 82004820

Holyoke-French House, Elm St. and Topsfield Rd., Boxford, 4/26/72, A, C, 72000123

Hooper, Robert "King", Mansion, 8 Hooper St., Marblehead, 5/12/76, A, B, C, 76000264

Hopkinson, George, House [First Period Buildings of Eastern Massachusetts TR], 362 Main St., Groveland, 3/09/90, C, D, 90000220

Hose House No. 2, 30 Rantoul St., Beverly, 7/03/86, A, C, 86001461

Hospital Point Light Station [Lighthouses of Massachusetts TR], Bayview Ave., Beverly, 9/28/87, A, C, 87002031

House 15–19 Park Street [Methuen MRA], 15–19 Park St., Methuen, 1/20/84, A, C, 84002388

House at 10 Park Street [Methuen MRA], 10 Park St., Methuen, 1/20/84, C, 84002385

House at 113–115 Center Street [Methuen MRA], 113–115 Center St., Methuen, 1/20/84, C, 84002381

House at 13 Annis Street [Methuen MRA], 13 Annis St., Methuen, 1/20/84, A, C, 84002387

House at 136 Hampstead Street [Methuen MRA], 136 Hampstead St., Methuen, 6/20/84, C, 84002377

House at 23 East Street [Methuen MRA], 23 East St., Methuen, 1/20/84, C, 84002382

House at 262–264 Pelham Street [Methuen MRA], 262–264 Pelham St., Methuen, 1/20/84, C, 84002390

House at 306 Broadway [Methuen MRA], 306 Broadway, Methuen, 1/20/84, A, C, 84002379

House at 4 Birch Avenue [Methuen MRA], 4 Birch Ave., Methuen, 1/20/84, C, 84002374

House at 491 Prospect Street [Methuen MRA], 491 Prospect St., Methuen, 1/20/84, A, C, 84002396

House at 50 Pelham Street [Methuen MRA], 50 Pelham St., Methuen, 1/20/84, A, C, 84002392

House at 526 Prospect Street [Methuen MRA], 526 Prospect St., Methuen, 1/20/84, C, 84002394

House at 9 Park Street [Methuen MRA], 9 Park St., Methuen, 1/20/84, C, 84002384

House at 922 Dale Street [First Period Buildings of Eastern Massachusetts TR], 922 Dale St., North Andover, 3/09/90, C, D, 90000248

House of Seven Gables Historic District, Turner, Derby, and Hardy Sts., Salem, 5/08/73, A, B, C, b, c, 73000323

House on Labor-in-Vain Road [First Period Buildings of Eastern Massachusetts TR], Labor in Vain Rd., Ipswich, 3/09/90, C, D, 90000234

Howe Barn [First Period Buildings of Eastern Massachusetts TR], 403 Linebrook Rd., Ipswich, 3/09/90, C, b, 90000230

Howe Village Historic District, NE of Boxford on MA 97, Boxford vicinity, 4/03/73, B, C, 73000282

Humphreys, Sir John, House [First Period Buildings of Eastern Massachusetts TR], 99 Paradise Rd., Swampscott, 3/09/90, C, D, b, 90000258

Intervale Factory, 402 River St., Haverhill, 6/30/88, A, C, 88000958

Jackson Terrace Historic District, 43-59 Jackson St., Jackson Court, Jackson Terr., and 58-62 Newberry St., Lawrence, 11/13/84, A, C, 84000414

Jenkins, Benjamin, House [Town of Andover MRA], 362 Salem St., Andover, 6/10/82, A, C, 82004818

Johnson House [Methuen MRA], 8 Ditson Pl., Methuen, 1/20/84, C, 84002398

Johnson, Capt. Timothy, House [First Period Buildings of Eastern Massachusetts TR], 18–20 Stevens St., North Andover, 3/09/90, C, D, 90000249

Kimball, Solomon, House [First Period Buildings of Eastern Massachusetts TR], 26 Maple St., Wenham, 3/09/90, C, D, 90000264

Kittredge Mansion, 56 Academy Rd., North Andover, 12/12/76, B, C, 76000282

Kunhardt, George, Estate, 1518 Great Pond Rd., North Andover vicinity, 4/22/76, A, B, C, a, 76000284

Lake, Stanley, House [First Period Buildings of Eastern Massachusetts TR], 95 River Rd., Topsfield, 3/09/90, C, 90000260

Lambert, Thomas, House [First Period Buildings of Eastern Massachusetts TR], 142 Main St., Rowley, 3/09/90, C, 90000256

Lane, Fitz Hugh, House, Harbor side of Rogers St., Gloucester, 7/01/70, B, C, 70000837

Larch Farm [First Period Buildings of Eastern Massachusetts TR], 38 Larch Rd., Wenham, 3/09/90, C, 90000266

Lawrence Street Cemetery [Methuen MRA], Lawrence St., Methuen, 1/20/84, C, d, 84002399

Lee, Jeremiah, House, Washington St., Marblehead, 10/15/66, C, NHL, 66000766

Lincolnshire, The [Town of Andover MRA], 22 Hidden Rd. and 28 Hidden Way, Andover, 6/10/82, B, C, 82004804

Livermore, William, House [First Period Buildings of Eastern Massachusetts TR], 271 Essex St., Beverly, 3/09/90, C, D, 90000197

Lodge, Henry Cabot, House, 5 Cliff St., Nahant, 12/08/76, B, NHL, 76001971

Lovejoy, Charles, House, 64 Broad St., Lynn, 11/28/78, B, C, 78000454

Low, Thomas, House [First Period Buildings of Eastern Massachusetts TR], 36 Heartbreak Rd., Ipswich, 3/09/90, C, D, 90000237

Lowell's Boat Shop, 459 Main St., Amesbury, 6/09/88, A, B, C, NHL, 88000706

Lynn Bank Block, 21–29 Exchange St., Lynn, 8/26/82, A, C, 82004964

Lynn Common Historic District, Roughly, N. and S. Common St. from Market Sq. to City Hall, Lynn, 4/10/92, A, C, 92000247

Lynn Masonic Hall, 64-68 Market St., Lynn, 8/21/79, A, C, 79000333

Lynn Public Library, 5 N. Common St., Lynn, 8/21/79, A, C, 79000334

Lynn Realty Company Building No. 2, 672-680 Washington St., Lynn, 3/31/83, A, C, 83000579

Lynn, Armory, 36 S. Common St., Lynn, 9/07/79, C, 79000332

Machine Shop Village District, Roughly bounded by Main, Pleasant, Clarendon, Water, 2nd Sts., and B&M Railroad, North Andover, 10/14/82, A, C, 82000482

Main Street-Locke [Town of Andover MRA], Main Street-Locke Street District, Andover, 10/07/82, A, C, 82000479

Manchester Village Historic District, Roughly Friend, School, North, Washington, Sea, Union, Central, Bennett, Bridge Sts., and Ashland Ave., Manchester, 1/08/90, A, C, 89002156

Manning House [Town of Andover MRA], 37 Porter Rd., Andover, 6/10/82, C, 82004817

Marblehead Historic District, Roughly bounded by Marblehead Harbor, Waldron Court, Essex, Elm, Pond, and Norman Sts., Marblehead, 1/10/84, A, B, C, 84002402

Marblehead Light [Lighthouses of Massachusetts TR], Marblehead Neck, Marblehead, 6/15/87, A, C, 87001479

March, Samuel, House [First Period Buildings of Eastern Massachusetts TR], 444 Main St., West Newbury, 3/09/90, C, 90000272

Market Square Historic District, Market Sq. and properties fronting on State, Merrimac, Liberty, and Water Sts., Newburyport, 2/25/71, A, C, 71000088

Mechanics Block Historic District, 107-139 Garden St. and 6-38 Orchard St., Lawrence, 4/03/73, A, C, 73001942

Mechanics Block Historic District (Boundary Increase), 38-52 Union St., Lawrence, 5/23/78, A, C, 78000451

Meetinghouse Common District, Summer, S. Common, and Main Sts., Lynnfield, 11/21/76, A, C, a, 76000260

Essex County—Continued

Meetinghouse Green Historic District [Central Village, Ipswich, Massachusetts MRA], N. Main St., Ipswich, 9/17/80, A, C, 80000464

Memorial Hall Library [Town of Andover MRA], 2 N. Main St., Andover, 6/10/82, A, C, b, f, 82004805

Merrifield House [Central Village, Ipswich, Massachusetts MRA], 7 Woods Lane, Ipswich, 9/17/80, C, 80000469

Methuen Memorial Music Hall, 192 Broadway, Methuen, 12/14/78, B, C, 78000462

Methuen Water Works [Methuen MRA], Cross St., Methuen, 1/20/84, C, 84002403

Monroe, Bessie, House [Downtown Salem MRA], 7 Ash St., Salem, 7/29/83, C, 83000580

Moore—Hill House, 82 Franklin St., Peabody, 6/09/88, A, C, 88000704

Morse, Moses, House [Methuen MRA], 311 Pelham St., Methuen, 1/20/84, C, 84002404

Morse, Timothy, House [First Period Buildings of Eastern Massachusetts TR], 628 Main St., West Newbury, 3/09/90, C, D, 90000271

Mowers' Block, 7 Willow St. and 67-83 Blake St., Lynn, 2/25/82, A, C, 82001991

Murray, William, House [First Period Buildings of Eastern Massachusetts TR], 39 Essex St., Salem, 3/09/90, C, D, 90000257

Musgrove Block [Town of Andover MRA], 2 Main St., Andover, 6/10/82, C, 82004816

Nahant Civic Historic District, 332 and 334 Nahant Rd. and 15 Pleasant St., Nahant, 9/03/91, A, C, 91001174

Nevins Memorial Library [Methuen MRA], 305 Broadway, Methuen, 1/20/84, C, 84002407

Nevins, Henry C., Home for Aged and Incurables [Methuen MRA], 110 Broadway, Methuen, 1/20/84, C, 84002406

New Hampshire, The, SE of Manchester off Graves Island, Manchester vicinity, 10/29/76, A, C, 76000261

Newbury Historic District, Irregular pattern along High Rd., Green and Hanover Sts., Newbury, 5/24/76, A, C, 76000275

Newburyport Harbor Front Range Light [Lighthouses of Massachusetts TR], Merrimac River Coast Guard Station, Newburyport, 6/15/87, A, C, b, 87001486

Newburyport Harbor Light [Lighthouses of Massachusetts TR], Northern Blvd., Newburyport, 6/15/87, A, C, 87001485

Newburyport Harbor Rear Range Light [Lighthouses of Massachusetts TR], Water St. near Merrimac River, Newburyport, 6/15/87, A, C, 87000887

Newburyport Historic District, Roughly bounded by Merrimack River, Plummer Ave., Marlboro, Plummer, State, and High Sts., Newburyport, 8/02/84, A, B, C, D, 84002411

Newell Farm, 243 Main St., West Newbury, 7/21/78, A, C, 78001406

Newhall, Lucian, House, 281 Ocean St., Lynn, 7/18/85, B, C, 85001576

Newman—Fiske—Dodge House [First Period Buildings of Eastern Massachusetts TR], 162 Cherry St., Wenham, 3/09/90, C, 90000267

North Andover Center Historic District, Roughly bounded by Osgood, Pleasant, Stevens, Johnson, and Andover Sts. and Wood Lane, North Andover, 3/05/79, A, C, 79000336

North Canal, Parallel to Canal St., Lawrence, 7/29/75, A, C, 75000278

North Canal Historic District, Roughly bounded by Merrimack and Spicket Rivers, North, Canal, and Broadway, Lawrence, 11/13/84, A, C, 84000417

Noyes, James, House [First Period Buildings of Eastern Massachusetts TR], 7 Parker Rd., Newbury, 3/09/90, C, D, 90000246

Oak Grove Cemetery, Bounded by Derby, Washington, and Grove Sts., and Maplewood Ave., Gloucester, 4/03/75, A, d, 75000263

Odd Fellows' Hall, 188-194 Cabot St., Beverly, 11/20/78, A, C, 78001408

Old Castle, N of Rockport on MA 127, Rockport vicinity, 9/01/78, A, C, 78000466

Old Farm [First Period Buildings of Eastern Massachusetts TR], 9 Maple St., Wenham, 3/09/90, C, 90000265

Old Garrison House [First Period Buildings of Eastern Massachusetts TR], 188 Granite St., Rockport, 3/04/91, C, 90000254

Old Post Office Building, 360 Washington St., Lynn, 9/14/81, A, C, 81000118

Old Public Library, 190 Hampshire St., Lawrence, 11/28/78, A, C, 78000452

Old Town Farm [Methuen MRA], 430 Pelham St., Methuen, 1/20/84, A, C, 84002413

Old Town Hall Historic District, Derby Sq. and 215-231 Essex, 121-145 Washington, and 6-34 Front Sts., Salem, 12/04/72, A, C, 72000149

Old Town House, Town House Sq., Marblehead, 8/13/76, A, 76000265

Orlando [Town of Andover MRA], 260 N. Main St., Andover, 6/10/82, B, C, 82004815

Osborne, Prince, House [First Period Buildings of Eastern Massachusetts TR], 273 Maple St., Danvers, 3/09/90, C, b, 90000203

Osgood Farm [Town of Andover MRA], 116 Osgood St., Andover, 6/10/82, C, 82004806

Osgood, Col. John, House [First Period Buildings of Eastern Massachusetts TR], 547 Osgood St., North Andover, 3/09/90, C, b, 90000250

Osgood, Samuel, House, 440 Osgood St., North Andover, 12/30/74, A, B, C, c, 74000380

Our Lady of Good Voyage Church, 136–144 Prospect St. and 2–4 Taylor St., Gloucester, 5/10/90, A, C, a, 90000706

Paine—Dodge House [First Period Buildings of Eastern Massachusetts TR], 49 Jeffrey's Neck Rd., Ipswich, 3/09/90, C, 90000231

Park Lodge [Methuen MRA], 257 Lawrence St., Methuen, 1/20/84, C, 84002414

Patch, Emeline, House [First Period Buildings of Eastern Massachusetts TR], 918 Bay Rd., Hamilton, 3/09/90, C, D, b, 90000221

Peabody Central Fire Station, 41 Lowell St., Peabody, 4/11/79, C, 79000344

Peabody City Hall, 24 Lowell St., Peabody, 7/27/72, A, C, 72000142

Peabody Civic Center Historic District, Chestnut, Church, Foster, Franklin, and Lowell Sts., Peabody, 11/25/80, A, C, a, 80000477

Peabody Institute Library, Main St., Peabody, 6/04/73, C, 73000311

Peabody Museum of Salem, 161 Essex St., Salem, 10/15/66, A, NHL, 66000783

Peabody School, 170 Salem St., Haverhill, 10/23/86, C, 86002900

Peabody, George, House, 205 Washington St., Peabody, 7/06/88, A, B, C, c, 88000911

Peabody, John P., House [Downtown Salem MRA], 15 Summer St., Salem, 7/29/83, A, C, 83000581

Pearson, Abiel, House [Town of Andover MRA], 33 High St., Andover, 6/10/82, C, 82004807

Peirce-Nichols House, 80 Federal St., Salem, 11/24/68, C, NHL, 68000041

Perkins, John, House [First Period Buildings of Eastern Massachusetts TR], 75 Arbor St., Wenham, 3/09/90, C, D, 90000269

Perkins, Joseph, House [Methuen MRA], 297 Howe St., Methuen, 1/20/84, C, 84002416

Perrin, William, House [Town of Andover MRA], 464 River Rd., Andover, 6/10/82, C, 82004799

Pillsbury-French House [Town of Andover MRA], 103 Dascomb Rd., Andover, 6/10/82, C, 82004800

Platts-Bradstreet House, Main St., Rowley, 9/27/80, A, C, 80000645

Pleasant-High Historic District [Methuen MRA], Roughly bounded by Broadway, High, Vine, Charles, and Pleasant Sts., Methuen, 6/20/84, C, 84002417

Primrose Street Schoolhouse, 71 Primrose St., Haverhill, 6/23/83, A, C, 83000582

Proctor, John, House [First Period Buildings of Eastern Massachusetts TR], 348 Lowell St., Peabody, 3/09/90, C, D, 90000253

Punchard, Benjamin House [Town of Andover MRA], 8 High St., Andover, 6/10/82, B, C, 82004801

Puritan House, 3 Washington St. and 2 Main St., Gloucester, 5/28/76, C, 76000244

Putnam, Deacon Edward, Jr., House [First Period Buildings of Eastern Massachusetts TR], 4 Gregory St., Middleton, 3/09/90, C, 90000243

Putnam, Gen. Israel, House, 431 Maple St., Danvers, 4/30/76, A, B, C, c, 76000235

Putnam, James, Jr., House [First Period Buildings of Eastern Massachusetts TR], 42 Summer St., Danvers, 3/09/90, C, 90000205

Rea-Proctor Homestead, 180 Conant Farm, Danvers, 6/02/82, A, B, C, D, 82001915

Rockport Downtown Main Street Historic District, Portions of Main, Cleaves, Jewett, and School Sts., Rockport, 5/28/76, A, C, a, 76000288

Rocks Village Historic District, NE of Haverhill at Merrimack River, Haverhill vicinity, 12/12/76, B, C, 76001967

Rocky Hill Meetinghouse and Parsonage, Portsmouth Rd. and Elm St., Amesbury, 4/11/72, A, C, a, 72000115

Essex County—Continued

Rogers-Downing House [Town of Andover MRA], 269 Highland Rd., Andover, 6/10/82, C, 82004802

Ross Tavern [First Period Buildings of Eastern Massachusetts TR], 52 Jeffrey's Neck Rd., Ipswich, 3/09/90, C, b, 90000235

Russell House [Town of Andover MRA], 28 Rocky Hill Rd., Andover, 6/10/82, C, 82004808

Rust, Nathaniel, Mansion [Central Village, Ipswich, Massachusetts MRA], 83 County St., Ipswich, 9/17/80, C, 80000440

Salem Common Historic District, Bounded roughly by St. Peter's, Bridge, and Derby Sts. and Collins Cove, Salem, 5/12/76, A, C, 76000303

Salem Landry [Downtown Salem MRA], 55 Lafayette St., Salem, 7/29/83, A, C, 83000583

Salem Maritime National Historic Site, Derby St., Salem, 10/15/66, A, C, NPS, 66000048

Salem Village Historic District, Irregular pattern along Centre, Hobart, Ingersoll, and Collins Sts., as far N as Brentwood Circle, and S to Mello Pkwy., Danvers, 1/31/75, A, C, 75000252

Saugus Iron Works National Historic Site, Off U.S. 1, Saugus, 10/15/66, A, C, e, NHL, NPS, 66000047

Saugus Town Hall, Central St., Saugus, 6/20/85, A, C, 85001332

Sawyer House [First Period Buildings of Eastern Massachusetts TR], 21 Endicott Rd., Boxford, 3/09/90, C, D, 90000194

School Street School, 40 School St., Haverhill, 10/23/86, A, C, 86002922

Searles High School [Methuen MRA], 41 Pleasant St., Methuen, 1/20/84, A, C, 84002431

Second O'Shea Building, 9-13 Peabody Sq., Peabody, 3/27/80, A, C, 80004237

Sewall-Scripture House, 40 King St., Rockport, 9/30/82, A, C, 82001902

Shawsheen Village Historic District, MA 133, Andover, 2/09/79, A, C, 79000328

Shepard Block [Downtown Salem MRA], 298-304 Essex St., Salem, 7/29/83, C, 83000584

Simpson, James E., House [Methuen MRA], 606 Prospect St., Methuen, 1/20/84, C, 84002432

Smith House [First Period Buildings of Eastern Massachusetts TR], 142 Argilla Rd., Ipswich, 3/09/90, C, D, 90000238

Smith, Hazadiah, House [First Period Buildings of Eastern Massachusetts TR], 337 Cabot St., Beverly, 3/09/90, C, D, 90000200

South Green Historic District [Central Village, Ipswich, Massachusetts MRA], MA 1A, Ipswich, 9/17/80, A, B, C, 80000471

Southwick House, 151 Lowell St., Peabody, 11/29/83, A, C, 83003974

Spencer-Pierce-Little House, Little's Lane, Newbury, 11/24/68, C, NHL, 68000043

Spicket Falls Historic District [Methuen MRA], Roughly bounded by Spicket River, Railroad, Pelham, Hampshire, Broadway and Osgood Sts., Methuen, 6/20/84, A, C, 84002435

Spofford-Barnes House, Kelsey Rd., Boxford, 9/06/74, C, 74000366

Sprague House, 59 Endicott St., Danvers, 7/02/87, C, 87001108

St. Michael's Church, 26 Pleasant St., Marblehead, 6/18/73, A, C, a, 73000305

St. Stephen's Memorial Church, 74 S. Common St., Lynn, 9/07/79, A, C, a, 79000335

Stacy, George O., House, 107 Atlantic Rd., Gloucester, 7/08/82, A, B, C, 82004963

State Lunatic Hospital at Danvers, 450 Maple St., Danvers, 1/26/84, A, C, 84002436

Stevens, Abiel, House, 280 Salem St., North Andover, 6/23/83, A, C, 83000585

Story Grammar School, 140 Elm St., Marblehead, 3/13/86, A, C, 86000378

Story, Joseph, House, 26 Winter St., Salem, 11/07/73, B, NHL, 73001952

Straightsmouth Island Light [Lighthouses of Massachusetts TR], Straightsmouth Island, Rockport, 6/15/87, A, C, 87001487

Superior Courthouse and Bartlett Mall, Bounded by High, Pond, Auburn, and Greenleaf Sts., Newburyport, 4/30/76, A, C, 76000280

Sutton Block, 76–78 Main St., Peabody, 9/05/85, A, C, 85002012

Swampscott Fish House, Humphrey St., Swampscott, 5/16/85, A, C, 85001120

Swan, Asie, House [Methuen MRA], 669 Prospect St., Methuen, 1/20/84, A, C, b, 84002437

Tapley Building, 206 Broad St., Lynn, 3/31/83, A, C, 83000586

Ten Pound Island Light [Lighthouses of Massachusetts TR], Gloucester Harbor, Gloucester, 8/04/88, A, C, 88001179

Tenny Castle Gatehouse [Methuen MRA], 37 Pleasant St., Methuen, 1/20/84, C, 84002438

Third Railroad Station [Town of Andover MRA], 100 School St., Andover, 6/10/82, A, C, 82004809

Thomson, Elihu, House, 33 Elmwood Ave., Swampscott, 1/07/76, B, NHL, 76002002

Thorndike, Capt. John, House [First Period Buildings of Eastern Massachusetts TR], 184 Hale St., Beverly, 3/09/90, C, 90000195

Titcomb, Benaiah, House [First Period Buildings of Eastern Massachusetts TR], 189 John Wise Ave., Essex, 3/09/90, C, b, 90000208

Tufts, Rev. John, House [First Period Buildings of Eastern Massachusetts TR], 750 Main St., West Newbury, 3/09/90, C, 90000270

Turner Hill, 315 Topsfield Rd., Ipswich, 11/26/82, C, a, 82000483

Turnpike House [Methuen MRA], 314 Broadway, Methuen, 1/20/84, C, 84002439

Twin Lights Historic District [Lighthouses of Massachusetts TR (AD)], 1 mi. E of Rockport on Thatcher's Island, Rockport vicinity, 10/07/71, A, C, 71000355

US Customhouse, 25 Water St., Newburyport, 2/25/71, A, C, 71000089

US Post Office—Beverly Main, 161 Rantoul St., Beverly, 6/04/86, C, 86001210

US Post Office—Lynn Main, 51 Willow St., Lynn, 6/20/86, A, C, 86001342

US Post Office—Newburyport Main, 61 Pleasant St., Newburyport, 6/18/86, C, 86001341

US Post Office—Salem Main, 2 Margin St., Salem, 6/04/86, C, 86001211

United Shoe Machinery Corporation Clubhouse, 134 McKay St., Beverly, 11/26/82, A, C, 82000484

Vamp Building, 3-15 Liberty Square, Lynn, 3/31/83, A, C, 83000587

Wade House [Central Village, Ipswich, Massachusetts MRA], 5 Woods Lane, Ipswich, 9/17/80, C, 80000467

Waldo, George A., House [Methuen MRA], 233 Lawrence St., Methuen, 1/20/84, C, 84002441

Walnut Grove Cemetery [Methuen MRA], Grove and Railroads Sts., Methuen, 1/20/84, A, C, d, 84002444

Ward, John, House, 132 Essex St., Salem, 11/24/68, C, b, NHL, 68000045

Ward, Joshua, House, 148 Washington St., Salem, 2/08/78, A, C, 78000481

Ward, Richard, House [Town of Andover MRA], 71 Lowell St., Andover, 6/10/82, C, 82004962

Washington Street Historic District, Washington, Main, Holton and Sewall Sts., Peabody, 9/12/85, A, C, 85002380

Washington Street Shoe District, Washington, Wingate, Emerson Sts. Railroad and Washington Sqs., Haverhill, 10/14/76, A, C, 76000257

Wenham Historic District, Both sides of Main St. between Beverly and Hamilton city lines, Wenham, 4/13/73, A, C, 73000852

Wesley Methodist Church [Downtown Salem MRA], 8 North St., Salem, 7/29/83, C, a, 83000588

West Cogswell House [Downtown Salem MRA], 5-9 Summer St., Salem, 7/29/83, A, C, 83000589

West Parish Center District [Town of Andover MRA], MA 133, Andover, 10/07/82, A, C, a, 82000480

Whipple, John, House, 53 S. Main St., Ipswich, 10/15/66, C, b, NHL, 66000791

White—Ellery House [First Period Buildings of Eastern Massachusetts TR], 244 Washington St., Gloucester, 3/09/90, C, b, 90000216

White—Preston House [First Period Buildings of Eastern Massachusetts TR], 592 Maple St., Danvers, 3/09/90, D, 90000204

Whittemore House [First Period Buildings of Eastern Massachusetts TR], 179 Washington St., Gloucester, 3/09/90, C, D, 90000218

Whittier, John Greenleaf, House, 86 Friend St., Amesbury, 10/15/66, B, NHL, 66000792

Wilson, Shoreborne, House [Central Village, Ipswich, Massachusetts MRA], 4 S. Main St., Ipswich, 9/17/80, A, C, 80000456

Woodberry—Quarrels House [First Period Buildings of Eastern Massachusetts TR], 180 Bridge St., Hamilton, 3/09/90, C, 90000224

Woodbridge, Thomas March, House, 48 Bridge St., Salem, 3/31/75, C, 75000304

Woodbury, Peter, House [First Period Buildings of Eastern Massachusetts TR], 82 Dodge St., Beverly, 3/09/90, C, D, 90000201

Woodridge House [Town of Andover MRA], 293 Salem St., Andover, 6/10/82, C, 82004813

Essex County—Continued

YMCA [Downtown Salem MRA], 284-296 Essex St., Salem, 7/29/83, A, C, 83000590

Franklin County

Alexander, Simeon, Jr. House, Millers Falls Rd. S of Pine Meadow Rd., Northfield, 5/28/91, A, C, 91000598

Ashfield Plain Historic District, Roughly, along Main and South Sts. and adjacent parts of Buckland and Norton Hill Rds., Ashfield, 9/20/91, A, C, 91001373

Bernardston Congregational Unitarian Church, Jct. of Church and Depot Sts., Bernardston, 3/18/93, A, C, a, b, 93000128

Burkeville Covered Bridge, Main Poland Rd. over South River, Conway, 9/09/88, A, C, 88001456

Charlemont Village Historic District, MA 2 (Main St.) between South & Harmont Sts., Charlemont, 2/10/88, A, C, 87001880

Dedic Site, Address Restricted, South Deerfield vicinity, 7/16/80, D, 80000504

East Hawley Center Historic District, East Hawley, Plainfield, Buckland and Ashfield Rds., Hawley, 7/24/92, A, C, d, 92000951

East Main—High Street Historic District, Roughly bounded by Church, High, E. Main and Franklin Sts., Greenfield, 3/16/89, A, C, a, b, 88002011

Garden Theater Block, 353-367 Main St., Greenfield, 9/01/83, C, 83000591

Griswold, Maj. Joseph, House, Upper St., Buckland, 2/23/72, B, C, 72000130

King Philip's Hill, Address Restricted, Northfield vicinity, 12/16/81, A, 81000106

Leavitt-Hovey House, 402 Main St., Greenfield, 12/22/83, A, C, 83003977

Main Street Historic District, Main St. between Chapman and Hope Sts., also along Bank Row, Greenfield, 10/13/88, A, C, 88001908

New Salem Common Historic District, S. Main St., New Salem, 4/12/78, C, a, d, 78000443

Newton Street School, Shelburne Rd., Greenfield, 10/27/88, A, C, 88001907

Northfield Main Street Historic District, Full length of Main St. from Millers Brook to Pauchaug Brook, Northfield, 7/08/82, A, C, 82004965

Odd Fellow's Hall, 1-5 State St., Buckland, 5/10/79, A, 79000345

Old Deerfield Village Historic District, W of US 5, bounded by Mill Village Rd., "The Street", Broughton's Pond Rd., and Pogues Hole Rd., Deerfield, 10/15/66, A, NHL, 66000774

Orange Center Historic District, Roughly N. and S. Main St. from Prospect St. to River St., Orange, 4/27/89, A, C, 89000057

Riverside Archeological District, Address Restricted, Greenfield vicinity, 7/09/75, A, D, 75000256

Shelburne Falls Historic District, Bridge and State Sts., Shelburne, 1/28/88, A, C, a, 87002548

Smith, Arthur A., Covered Bridge, W of Colrain on Lyonsville Rd., Colrain vicinity, 2/03/83, A, C, b, 83000592

Turner Falls Historic District, Roughly bounded by Connectict River, Power Canal, 9th and L St., Turner Falls, 5/02/82, A, B, C, D, 82004966

US Post Office—Greenfield Main, 442 Main St., Greenfield, 12/20/85, C, 85003224

Weldon Hotel, 54 High St., Greenfield, 8/06/80, A, C, 80000503

Wendell Town Common Historic District, Jct. of Depot, Lock's Village, Montague and Morse Village Rds., Wendell, 5/21/92, A, C, a, b, d, 92000580

Whitaker-Clary House, Elm St., New Salem, 6/18/75, C, 75000257

Hampden County

1767 Milestones, Between Boston and Springfield along Old Post Rd., Springfield, 4/07/71, A, 71000084

Academy Historic District, Mountain Rd., Main and Faculty Sts., Wilbraham, 4/20/79, A, C, a, 79000351

Ames Hill/Crescent Hill District, Bounded by sections of Central, Maple, Mill, and Pine Sts., Crescent Hill, Ames Hill Drive, and Maple Ct., Springfield, 5/01/74, B, C, 74000368

Ames Manufacturing Company, 5-7 Springfield St., Chicopee, 6/23/83, A, C, 83000734

Apremont Triangle Historic District [Downtown Springfield MRA], Jct. Pearl, Hillman, Bridge, and Chestnut, Springfield, 5/27/83, A, C, 83000735

Bangs Block [Downtown Springfield MRA], 1119 Main St., Springfield, 2/24/83, A, C, 83000736

Baystate Corset Block [Downtown Springfield MRA], 395-405 Dwight St. and 99 Taylor St., Springfield, 2/24/83, C, 83000737

Bellamy, Edward, House, 91-93 Church St., Chicopee Falls, 11/11/71, B, NHL, 71000091

Belle and Franklin Streets Historic District, 77–103 Belle St. and 240–298 Franklin St., Springfield, 3/02/89, A, C, 89000039

Bicycle Club Building [Downtown Springfield MRA], 264-270 Worthington St., Springfield, 2/24/83, A, C, 83000738

Burbach Block [Downtown Springfield MRA], 1113-1115 Main St., Springfield, 2/24/83, A, C, 83000739

Burgess, Thornton W., House, 789 Main St., Hampden, 4/21/83, B, C, g, 83000740

Burt, Elijah, House, 201 Chestnut St., East Longmeadow, 4/26/76, C, 76000240

Caledonia Building, 185-193 High St., Holyoke, 7/03/79, A, C, a, 79000346

Carlton House Block [Downtown Springfield MRA], 9-13 Hampden St., Springfield, 2/24/83, A, C, 83000741

Chapin National Bank Building [Downtown Springfield MRA], 1675-1677 Main St., Springfield, 2/24/83, A, C, 83000742

Chester Center Historic District, Skyline Trail at intersection of Bromley and Lyman Rds., Chester, 2/25/88, A, C, a, 88000161

Chester Factory Village Historic District, Roughly bounded by Middlefield Rd., River, Main, and Maple Sts., US 20, and Williams St., Chester, 3/16/89, A, C, 89000145

City Hall, Market Sq., Chicopee, 7/30/74, A, C, 74002052

Colonial Block [Downtown Springfield MRA], 1139-55 Main St., Springfield, 2/24/83, A, C, 83000743

Court Square Historic District, Bounded by Main, State, Broadway, Pynchon Sts. and City HallPl., Springfield, 5/02/74, A, C, 74000370

Cutler and Porter Block [Downtown Springfield MRA], 109 Lyman St., Springfield, 2/24/83, A, C, 83000744

Day, Josiah, House, 70 Park St., West Springfield, 4/16/75, C, 75000265

Downtown Springfield Railroad District [Downtown Springfield MRA], Roughly bounded by Lyman, Main, Murray, and Spring Sts., Springfield, 5/27/83, A, C, 83000745

Driscoll's Block [Downtown Springfield MRA], 211-13 Worthington St., Springfield, 2/24/83, C, 83000746

Dwight Manufacturing Company Housing District, Front, Depot, Dwight, Exchange, Chestnut Sts., Chicopee, 6/03/77, A, 77000173

Ethel Apartment House, 70 Patton St., Springfield, 3/06/87, A, C, 87000353

First Church of Christ, Congregational, 50 Elm St., Springfield, 2/01/72, A, C, a, 72000135

First Congregational Church of East Longmeadow, 7 Somers Rd., East Longmeadow, 1/03/78, A, a, b, 78000444

First Congregational Church of Blandford, North St., Blandford, 10/24/85, C, a, 85003371

Fitzgerald's Stearns Square Block [Downtown Springfield MRA], 300-308 Bridge St., Springfield, 2/24/83, B, C, 83000747

Forest Park Heights Historic District, Off MA 21, Springfield, 8/31/82, A, C, 82004942

French Congregational Church [Downtown Springfield MRA], 33-37 Bliss St., Springfield, 2/24/83, C, a, 83004288

Fuller Block [Downtown Springfield MRA], 1531-1545 Main St., Springfield, 2/24/83, A, C, 83000748

Granville Center Historic District, Main Rd., Granville, 11/05/91, A, C, 91001587

Granville Village Historic District, Roughly, area around jct. of Maple St. and Main and Granby Rds., including part of Water St., Granville, 11/05/91, A, C, 91001588

Guenther & Handel's Block [Downtown Springfield MRA], 7–9 Stockbridge St., Springfield, 2/24/83, A, C, 83000749

Gunn and Hubbard Blocks, 463-477 State St., Springfield, 12/03/80, A, C, 80000474

Hadley Falls Company Housing District, Center, N. Canal, Grover, and Lyman Sts., Holyoke, 11/09/72, A, C, 72000133

Hampden County Courthouse, Elm St., Springfield, 2/01/72, C, 72000134

Hampden County—Continued

Hampden Savings Bank [Downtown Springfield MRA], 1665 Main St., Springfield, 2/24/83, A, 83000750

Haynes Hotel Waters Building [Downtown Springfield MRA], 1386-1402 Main St., Springfield, 2/24/83, A, C, 83000751

Henking Hotel and Cafe [Downtown Springfield MRA], 15-21 Lyman St., Springfield, 2/24/83, A, C, 83000752

Hiberian Block [Downtown Springfield MRA], 345-349 Worthington St., Springfield, 2/24/83, A, 83000753

Holyoke Canal System, Front and South St. and CT River, Holyoke, 12/03/80, A, C, 80000473

Holyoke City Hall, 536 Dwight St., Holyoke, 12/06/75, C, 75000259

Kennedy-Worthington Blocks, 1585-1623 Main St. and 166-190 Worthington St., Springfield, 6/14/79, A, B, C, 79000347

Landlord Fowler Tavern, 171 Main St., Westfield, 8/11/82, A, C, 82001914

Laurel Hall, 72–74 Patton St., Springfield, 3/06/87, A, C, 87000355

Leonard, Capt. Charles, House, 663 Main St., Agawam, 3/10/75, C, 75000273

Longmeadow Historic District, Roughly Longmeadow St. from Birdie Rd. to Wheelmeadow Brook, Longmeadow, 11/12/82, A, C, 82000490

Ludlow Center Historic District, Along Center, Church and Booth Sts., Ludlow, 10/21/88, A, C, a, d, 88001999

Maple-Union Corners, 77, 83, 76-78, 80-84 Maple St., Springfield, 4/26/76, C, 76000243

Maplewood Hotel, 328-330 Maple St., Holyoke, 11/10/83, B, C, 83003980

Masonic Temple, 339-341 State St., Springfield, 11/10/83, A, C, 83003979

McIntosh Building [Downtown Springfield MRA], 158-64 Chestnut St., Springfield, 2/24/83, C, 83000754

McKinney Building [Downtown Springfield MRA], 1121-27 Main St., Springfield, 2/24/83, A, C, 83000755

McKnight District, Roughly bounded by Penn Central, State St., the Armory, and includes both sides of Campus Pl., and Dartmouth St., Springfield, 4/26/76, A, C, 76000255

McKnight District (Boundary Increase), Roughly bounded by New England RR, Pease, and Sherman and Harvard Sts, and Saint James Ave., Florida, and Bay Sts., Springfield, 9/26/86, A, B, C, 86002466

Memorial Square District, Main and Plainfield Sts., Springfield, 8/29/77, B, C, a, 77000180

Memorial Town Hall, Main St., Monson, 5/17/84, A, B, C, 84002449

Mills—Hale—Owen Blocks, 959–991 Main St., Springfield, 10/31/85, A, C, 85003424

Mills-Stebbins Villa, 3 Crescent Hill, Springfield, 10/15/73, B, C, 73000299

Milton-Bradley Company [Downtown Springfield MRA], Park, Cross, and Willow Sts., Springfield, 2/24/83, A, C, g, 83000756

Morgan Block [Downtown Springfield MRA], 313-333 Bridge St., Springfield, 5/27/83, A, C, 83000757

Myrtle Street School, 64 Myrtle St., Springfield, 1/03/85, A, C, 85000024

Norcross, William, House, 14 Cushman St., Monson, 3/29/84, A, C, 84002450

North High Street Historic District, High St. between Dwight and Lyman Sts., Holyoke, 6/26/86, A, C, 86001376

North High Street Historic District (Boundary Increase), 233–411 High St., Holyoke, 12/24/92, A, C, 92001725

Octagon House, 28 King St., Westfield, 4/01/82, B, C, 82004967

Olmsted-Hixon-Albion Block [Downtown Springfield MRA], 1645-1659 Main St., Springfield, 2/24/83, A, C, 83000758

Page, Thomas D., House, 105 East St., Chicopee, 10/25/88, B, C, 87001782

Patton Building [Downtown Springfield MRA], 15-19 Hampden St., Springfield, 2/24/83, A, C, 83000760

Patton and Loomis Block [Downtown Springfield MRA], 1628-40 Main St., Springfield, 2/24/83, A, C, 83000759

Polish National Home, 136-144 Cabot St., Chicopee, 11/14/80, A, 80000475

Produce Exchange Building [Downtown Springfield MRA], 194-206 Chestnut and 115-125 Lyman St., Springfield, 2/24/83, A, 83000761

Purchase—Ferre House, 1289 Main St., Agawam, 11/29/90, A, C, 90001805

Quadrangle-Mattoon Street Historic District, Bounded by Chestnut St. to the W, State St. to the S, and includes properties on Mattoon, Salem, Edwards and Elliot Sts., Springfield, 5/08/74, A, C, a, g, 74000371

Radding Building [Downtown Springfield MRA], 143-147 State St., Springfield, 2/24/83, A, C, 83000762

Republican Block, 1365 Main St., Springfield, 1/26/78, A, B, C, 78000447

Sanderson, Julia, Theater, 1676-1708 Main St., Springfield, 5/10/79, A, C, 79000348

Smith Carriage Company District [Downtown Springfield MRA], Bounded by Main, Peabody, Willow, and Park Sts., Springfield, 2/24/83, A, 83000763

Smith's Building [Downtown Springfield MRA], 201-207 Worthington St., Springfield, 2/24/83, A, C, 83000764

South Congregational Church, 45 Maple St., Springfield, 4/30/76, B, C, a, 76000245

South Main Street School, 11 Acushnet Ave., Springfield, 1/03/85, A, C, 85000025

Springfield Armory, Armory Sq., Springfield, 10/15/66, A, NHL, NPS, 66000898

Springfield District Court [Downtown Springfield MRA], 1600 E. Columbus Ave., Springfield, 2/24/83, A, C, 83000765

Springfield Fire & Marine Insurance Co. [Downtown Springfield MRA], 195 State St., Springfield, 2/24/83, A, C, 83000766

Springfield Steam Power Company Block [Downtown Springfield MRA], 51-59 Taylor St., Springfield, 2/24/83, A, C, 83000767

Springfield Street Historic District, Roughly bounded by Springfield St., Gaylord St. and Fairview Ave., Chicopee, 1/25/91, A, C, a, d, 90002217

St. Joseph's Church [Downtown Springfield MRA], Howard St. and E. Columbus Ave., Springfield, 2/24/83, A, C, a, 83002999

Stacy Building [Downtown Springfield MRA], 41-43 Taylor St., Springfield, 5/27/83, C, 83000768

State Armory, 29 Howard St., Springfield, 5/03/76, C, 76000254

State Normal Training School, Washington St., Westfield, 7/07/83, A, C, 83000769

Stearns Building [Downtown Springfield MRA], 289-309 Bridge St., Springfield, 2/24/83, A, C, 83000770

Swetland-Pease House, SE of East Longmeadow at 191 Pease Rd., East Longmeadow vicinity, 4/09/80, C, 80000505

Trinity Block [Downtown Springfield MRA], 266-84 Bridge St., Springfield, 2/24/83, A, C, 83000771

US Post Office—Holyoke Main, 650 Dwight St., Holyoke, 1/21/86, C, 86000122

US Post Office—Palmer Main, Park and Central Sts., Palmer, 12/12/85, C, 85003336

Union Station, Depot St., Palmer, 6/09/88, A, C, 88000715

Union Trust Company Building, 1351 Main St., Springfield, 1/09/78, A, C, 78000448

United Electric Co. Building [Downtown Springfield MRA], 73 State St., Springfield, 2/24/83, A, C, 83000772

United States Whip Company Complex, 24 Main St., Westfield, 11/29/83, A, B, C, 83003983

Upper Worthington Historic District, Worthington, Federal, Summit and Armory Sts., Springfield, 3/31/83, A, C, 83000773

Upper Worthington Historic District (Boundary Increase), 443–472 Taylor St., Springfield, 3/05/92, A, C, 92000075

Valentine School, Grape and Elm Sts., Chicopee, 9/16/83, C, 83000774

Van Deusen, H. M., Whip Company, 42 Arnold St., Westfield, 2/18/87, A, B, C, 87000037

W C A Boarding House [Downtown Springfield MRA], 19 Bliss St., Springfield, 2/24/83, A, C, 83000776

Walker Building [Downtown Springfield MRA], 1228-1244 Main St., Springfield, 2/24/83, A, C, 83000775

Wason-Springfield Steam Power Blocks, 27-43 Lyman St. and 26-50 Taylor St., Springfield, 6/19/79, A, C, 79000349

Water Shops Armory, 1 Allen St., Springfield, 12/03/80, A, C, 80000476

Wells Block [Downtown Springfield MRA], 250-264 Worthington St., Springfield, 2/24/83, A, C, 83000777

West Granville Historic District, Roughly, Main Rd. from W of Beach Hill Rd. to South Ln. No. 2, Granville, 11/05/91, A, C, 91001589

Hampden County—Continued

Westfield Municipal Building, 59 Court St., Westfield, 3/08/78, A, C, 78000449

Westfield Whip Manufacturing Company, 360 Elm St., Westfield, 10/17/85, A, C, 85003233

Whitcomb Warehouse [Downtown Springfield MRA], 32-34 Hampden St., Springfield, 2/24/83, A, C, 83004291

Willy's Overland Block [Downtown Springfield MRA], 151-157 Chestnut and 10-20 Winter Sts., Springfield, 2/24/83, A, C, 83000778

Winchester Square Historic District, U.S. 20, Springfield, 5/10/79, A, 79000350

Wistariahurst, 238 Cabot St., Holyoke, 4/23/73, B, C, b, 73000295

Worthy Hotel [Downtown Springfield MRA], 1571 Main St., Springfield, 2/24/83, A, C, 83000779

Hampshire County

Amherst Central Business District, 1–79 Main St., 13–31 N. Pleasant St., 1–79 S. Pleasant St., 1–18 Boltwood Ave., Amherst, 12/27/91, A, C, 91001859

Baird House, 38 Shays St., Amherst, 1/03/85, C, g, 85000026

Belchertown Center Historic District, Main, Maple, Walnut, Park, and Jabish Sts., Belchertown, 6/02/82, A, B, C, a, 82001913

Bryant, William Cullen, Homestead, 2 mi. from Cummington on side rd., Cummington vicinity, 10/15/66, B, NHL, 66000136

Building at 8–22 Graves Avenue, 8–22 Graves Ave., Northampton, 11/07/85, A, C, 85002784

Church Street Historic District, Church St. between Park Ave. and Highland St., Ware, 5/23/86, A, B, C, 86001246

Conkey-Stevens House, 664 Main St., Amherst, 5/10/79, B, C, 79000352

Coolidge, Calvin, House, 19-21 Massasoit St., Northampton, 12/12/76, B, 76000262

Cushman Village Historic District, Roughly bounded by E. Leverett Rd. and Pine, Henry, Bridge and State Sts., Amherst, 11/05/92, A, C, b, 92001553

Dickinson Historic District, Kellogg Ave., Main, Gray, and Lessey Sts., Amherst, 8/16/77, B, C, 77000182

Dickinson, Emily, House, 280 Main St., Amherst, 10/15/66, B, NHL, 66000363

East Village Historic District, Main, N. and S. East Sts., Amherst, 7/06/86, A, C, 86001408

Fort Hill Historic District, Roughly South St. from Lyman to Monroe, Northampton, 4/07/89, C, 88000910

Grove Hill Mansion, Florence Rd. and Front St., Northampton, 8/11/82, B, C, 82001910

Hadley Center Historic District, Middle and Russell Sts., Hadley, 12/02/77, B, C, a, 77000185

Haydenville Historic District, Main and High Sts., and Kingsley Ave., Williamsburg, 3/26/76, A, B, C, 76000273

Hockanum Rural Historic District, Area surrounding Hockanum Rd., from Hockanum Cemetery to the NE corner of Skinner State Park, Hadley, 12/30/93, A, C, 93001474

Hollis, Thomas, Historic District, Washington St. from Winter to Highland Sts., Holliston, 10/30/89, A, C, 89001786

Main Street Historic District, Main St. between Northampton and Center Sts., Easthampton, 3/17/86, A, C, 86000451

Manse, The, 54 Prospect St., Northampton, 10/14/76, C, 76000263

Middlefield-Becket Stone Arch Railroad Bridge District, Middlefield vicinity, Middlefield vicinity, 4/11/80, A, C, 80000502

Mountain Rest, Spruce Corner Rd., Goshen, 11/10/83, A, C, 83003984

North Amherst Center Historic District, 1184–1136 N. Pleasant St., 1–39 Pine St., 11–13 Meadow St., Amherst vicinity, 12/13/91, A, C, 91001824

North Hadley Historic District, Roughly, area along River Dr.from Stockwell Rd. to Stockbridge St., including French, Meadow and Mt. Warner Sts., Hadley, 12/30/93, A, C, 93001475

Northampton Downtown Historic District, Roughly bounded by Hampton, Pearl, Strong, Bedford, Elm, MA 66, and railroad tracks, Northampton, 5/17/76, A, C, a, 76000270

Northampton Downtown Historic District (Boundary Increase), East of RR Tracks including 2–10 Bridge and 1–30 Market Sts., Northampton, 7/03/85, A, C, 85001464

Old Mill Site Historic District, 48 and 50 Prospect St., Hatfield, 6/02/82, A, C, 82001911

Otis Company Mill· No. 1, E. Main St., Ware, 5/02/82, A, C, 82001909

Pelham Town Hall Historic District, Amherst Rd. at the corner of Daniel Shays Hwy., Pelham, 11/23/71, A, B, C, a, b, d, 71000085

Porter-Phelps-Huntington House, 130 River Dr., Hadley, 3/26/73, A, B, C, 73000303

Prospect—Gaylord Historic District, Roughly, Prospect St. from Northampton Rd. to Hallock St. and Gaylord and Amity Sts. W from Prospect toward Lincoln Ave., Amherst, 2/04/93, A, C, a, 93000007

Smith Alumnae Gymnasium, Smith College campus Green St., Northampton, 4/30/76, A, C, b, 76000259

South Hadley Canal Historic District, Address Restricted, South Hadley vicinity, 3/11/92, A, C, D, 92000077

Southampton Center Historic District, Roughly, High St. from Fomer Rd. to Maple St., College Hwy. from Clark St. to East St. and East from College to Clark, Southampton, 4/04/91, A, C, 91000363

Strong House, 67 Amity St., Amherst, 7/05/84, B, C, 84002457

US Post Office—Easthampton Main, 19 Union St., Easthampton, 4/01/86, C, 86000714

US Post Office—South Hadley Main, 1 Hadley St., South Hadley, 5/28/86, C, g, 86001188

Walker-Collis House, 1 Stadler St., Belchertown, 9/30/82, B, C, 82001903

Ware Center Historic District, MA 9 and Greenwich Plains Rd., Ware, 5/08/86, A, C, 86001013

Ware Millyard Historic District, Roughly bounded by South St., the Ware River, Upper Dam Complex, Park St., Otis Ave. and Church St., Ware, 11/21/86, A, C, g, 86003508

Ware Town Hall, Main and West Sts., Ware, 6/26/86, A, C, 86001403

Ware—Hardwick Covered Bridge, Old Gilbertville Rd. and Bridge St., Ware, 5/08/86, C, 86001006

Williamsburg Center Historic District, MA 9, Williamsburg, 6/22/80, A, C, 80000506

Woodbridge Street Historic District, 3 and 7 Silver St., 25-82 Woodbridge St., South Hadley, 11/14/83, A, C, 83003987

Middlesex County

1790 House, 827 Main St., Woburn, 10/09/74, C, a, 74000381

Abbot, Edwin, House, 1 Follen St., Cambridge, 5/10/79, C, 79000354

Aborn, John, House [Cambridge MRA], 41 Orchard St., Cambridge, 4/13/82, C, 82001883

Ace Art Company [Reading MRA], 24 Gould St., Reading, 2/01/85, A, B, C, 85000497

Acton Centre Historic District, Main St., Wood and Woodbur Lanes, Newton, Concord, and Nagog Hill Rds., Acton, 3/10/83, A, C, 83000780

Adams, Amos, House [Newton MRA], 37 Park Ave., Newton, 9/04/86, C, 86001767

Adams, Charles—Woodbury Locke House [Somerville MPS], 178 Central St., Somerville, 9/18/89, A, B, C, 89001240

Adams, Seth, House [Newton MRA], 72 Jewett St., Newton, 9/04/86, B, 86001768

Adams—Magoun House [Somerville MPS], 438 Broadway, Somerville, 9/18/89, A, C, 89001239

Agudas Achim Anshei Sfard Synagogue [Newton MRA], 168 Adams St., Newton, 2/16/90, A, C, a, 90000035

Albree-Hall-Lawrence House, 353 Lawrence Rd., Medford, 4/30/76, A, C, 76000256

Allen House, 57 Rolfe St., Lowell, 8/11/82, B, C, 82001992

Allen, Abel, House, S of Weston at 1 Chestnut St., Weston vicinity, 1/09/78, B, C, 78000465

Allen, Nathaniel Topliff, Homestead, 25 Webster St., Newton, 1/09/78, A, B, C, 78000457

Allyn House [Arlington MRA], 94 Oakland Ave., Arlington, 9/27/85, C, 85002680

Almshouse [Cambridge MRA], 41 Orchard St., Cambridge, 4/13/82, A, C, a, 82001908

Almshouse [Stoneham MRA], 136 Elm St., Stoneham, 4/13/84, A, C, 84002464

American Net and Twine Company Factory [Cambridge MRA], 155 2nd St., Cambridge, 4/01/82, A, C, 82001906

American Waltham Watch Company Historic District [Waltham MRA], 185–241 Crescent St., Waltham, 9/28/89, A, C, 89001501

American Watch Tool Company [Waltham MRA], 169 Elm St., Waltham, 9/28/89, A, C, 89001574

Middlesex County—Continued

Andrews, Joseph, House [Waltham MRA], 258 Linden St., Waltham, 9/28/89, C, b, 89001554

Angier, John B., House, 129 High St., Medford, 4/23/75, C, 75000267

Arlington Center Historic District [Arlington MRA (AD)], Bounded by Massachusetts Ave. and Academy, Pleasant and Maple Sts., Arlington, 7/18/74, C, 74000361

Arlington Center Historic District (Boundary Increase) [Arlington MRA], Roughly bounded by Jason St., Massachusetts Ave., Pleasant and Gray Sts., Arlington, 9/27/85, A, C, a, 85002691

Arlington Coal & Lumber [Arlington MRA], 41 Park Ave., Arlington, 4/18/85, C, 85001020

Arlington Gaslight Company [Arlington MRA], Grove St. Town Yard, Arlington, 4/18/85, A, C, 85001021

Arlington Pumping Station [Arlington MRA], Brattle Court off Brattle St., Arlington, 4/18/85, A, C, 85001022

Arlington Reservoir [Arlington MRA], Park Circle, Arlington, 9/27/85, C, 85002676

Ash Street Historic District [Cambridge MRA], Ash St. and Ash St. Place between Brattle and Mount Auburn Sts., Cambridge, 4/13/82, C, g, 82001916

Ashland Dam and Spillway [Water Supply System of Metropolitan Boston MPS], N end of Ashland Reservoir in Ashland State Park, Ashland, 1/18/90, A, C, 89002289

Assington [Sherborn MRA], 172 Forest St., Sherborn, 1/03/86, A, C, 86000490

Athenaeum Press [Cambridge MRA], 215 1st St., Cambridge, 4/13/82, A, C, 82001917

Atwood, Ephraim, House [Cambridge MRA], 110 Hancock St., Cambridge, 6/30/83, C, 83000781

Auburndale Congregational Church [Newton MRA], 64 Hancock St., Newton, 9/04/86, A, C, a, 86001769

Austin Hall, Harvard University campus, Cambridge, 4/19/72, C, 72000128

Avon Hill Historic District [Cambridge MRA], Washington and Walnut Aves. and Agassiz, Humboldt, Arlington and Lancaster Sts., Cambridge, 6/30/83, C, 83000782

Ayer, Albert, House [Winchester MRA], 8 Brooks St., Winchester, 7/05/89, B, C, 89000635

Ayer, Thomas, House [Winchester MRA], 8 Grove St., Winchester, 7/05/89, A, C, 89000630

B and B Chemical Company [Cambridge MRA], 780 Memorial Dr., Cambridge, 4/13/82, C, g, 82001918

Bacon, Clifton, House [Somerville MPS], 27 Chester St., Somerville, 9/18/89, C, 89001244

Bacon, Robert, House [Winchester MRA], 6 Mystic Valley Pkwy., Winchester, 7/05/89, B, C, 89000611

Bacon, Stephen, House [First Period Buildings of Eastern Massachusetts TR], 105 N. Main St., Natick, 3/09/90, C, 90000174

Bacon-Gleason-Blodgett Homestead, 118 Wilson Rd., Bedford vicinity, 4/14/77, B, C, 77000166

Badger, Rev. Stephen, House, 87 Eliot St., Natick, 4/01/80, A, B, C, 80000647

Baker, Charles, House [Waltham MRA], 107 Adams St., Waltham, 9/28/89, A, C, 89001484

Baker, Charles, Property [Waltham MRA], 119–121 Adams St., Waltham, 9/28/89, A, C, 89001485

Baker, Kenelum, House [Winchester MRA], 4 Norwood St., Winchester, 7/05/89, C, 89000632

Baldwin, Loammi, Mansion, 2 Alfred St., Woburn, 10/07/71, B, C, b, 71000090

Baldwin, Maria, House, 196 Prospect St., Cambridge, 5/11/76, B, NHL, 76000272

Bancroft, Joseph, House [Reading MRA], 101 Lowell St., Reading, 7/19/84, C, 84002467

Bancroft, Samuel, House [Reading MRA], 232 West St., Reading, 7/19/84, B, C, 84002471

Bancroft, Wendell, House [Reading MRA], 20 Washington St., Reading, 7/19/84, B, C, 84002477

Banks, E. Sybbill, House [Waltham MRA], 27 Appleton St., Waltham, 9/28/89, C, 89001488

Baptist Society Meeting House [Arlington MRA], 3–5 Brattle St., Arlington, 4/18/85, A, C, a, b, 85001023

Barnes, James B., House [Cambridge MRA], 200 Monsignor O'Brien Hwy., Cambridge, 4/13/82, C, 82001919

Barnes, Walter S. and Melissa E., House [Somerville MPS], 140 Highland Ave., Somerville, 3/08/90, C, 89001266

Barrett, Col. James, Farm, 448 Barrett's Mill Rd., Concord, 11/15/73, A, B, C, 73000290

Bartlett—Hawkes Farm [Newton MRA], 15 Winnetaska Rd., Newton, 9/04/86, C, 86001770

Bassett, Edwin, House [Reading MRA], 115 Prescott St., Reading, 7/19/84, B, C, 84002482

Bassett, Maria, House [Arlington MRA], 8 College Ave., Arlington, 9/27/85, C, 85002681

Batchelder House [Reading MRA], 607 Pearl St., Reading, 7/19/84, B, C, 84002501

Batchelder, Alden, House [Reading MRA], 797 Main St., Reading, 7/19/84, B, C, 84002491

Batchelder, George, House [Reading MRA], 127-129 Franklin St., Reading, 7/19/84, C, 84002496

Batchelder, Nathaniel, House [Reading MRA], 71 Franklin St., Reading, 7/19/84, A, C, 84002503

Battell House [Reading MRA], 293 Haverhill St., Reading, 7/19/84, B, C, 84002504

Bayley House [Newton MRA], 16 Fairmont Ave., Newton, 9/04/86, C, 86001771

Beacon Street Tomb [Wakefield MRA], Beacon St., Wakefield, 7/06/89, A, C, 89000714

Beard, Benjamin, House [Reading MRA], 251 Ash St., Reading, 7/19/84, B, C, 84002505

Beard, Josiah, House [Waltham MRA], 70 School St., Waltham, 9/28/89, A, C, 89001529

Beard, Padilla, House [Stoneham MRA], 18 Maple St., Stoneham, 4/13/84, B, 84002507

Bedford Center Historic District, Irregular pattern along Great Rd. from Bacon to Concord and North Rds., Bedford, 11/17/77, A, C, 77000165

Beebe Estate, 235 W. Foster St., Melrose, 5/20/81, B, C, 81000116

Beebe Homestead [Wakefield MRA], 142 Main St., Wakefield, 7/06/89, A, C, 89000667

Bemis Mill [Newton MRA], 1–3 Bridge St., Newton, 9/04/86, A, C, 86001773

Bennink—Douglas Cottages [Cambridge MRA], 35–51 Walker St., Cambridge, 5/19/86, A, C, 86001272

Berkeley Street Historic District [Cambridge MRA], Berkeley St., Cambridge, 4/13/82, C, 82001920

Berkeley Street Historic District (Boundary Increase) [Cambridge MRA], 1–8 Berkeley Pl., Cambridge, 5/19/86, B, C, 86001265

Bertram Hall at Radcliffe College [Cambridge MRA], 53 Shepard St., Cambridge, 5/19/86, A, C, 86001270

Beth Eden Baptist Church [Waltham MRA], 82 Maple St., Waltham, 9/28/89, A, C, a, 89001544

Beth Israel Synagogue [Cambridge MRA], 238 Columbia St., Cambridge, 4/13/82, A, a, 82001921

Bickford, John, House [First Period Buildings of Eastern Massachusetts TR], 235 Elm St., North Reading, 3/09/90, C, D, 90000177

Bigelow Block, NE Corner of Forest and Salem Sts., Medford, 2/24/75, C, 75000268

Bigelow Street Historic District [Cambridge MRA], Bigelow St., Cambridge, 4/13/82, C, 82001922

Bigelow, Dr. Henry Jacob, House, 742 Dedham St., Newton, 1/01/76, A, B, 76000266

Bigelow, Henry, House [Newton MRA], 15 Bigelow Terr., Newton, 9/04/86, B, b, 86001774

Billerica Mills Historic District, Roughly bounded by Concord River, Treble Cove Terr., Kohlrausch Ave., Indian Rd., Holt Ruggles, and Rogers Sts., Billerica, 11/10/83, A, C, 83003996

Billerica Town Common District, Bounded by Cummings St., Concord Rd., and Boston Rd., Billerica, 8/14/73, A, C, a, 73000280

Billings, Frederick, House [Cambridge MRA], 45 Orchard St., Cambridge, 4/13/82, C, 82001923

Birkhoff, George D., House, 22 Craigie, Cambridge, 5/15/75, B, NHL, 75000295

Blodgett, William, House [Newton MRA], 645 Centre St., Newton, 9/04/86, C, 86001776

Boardman, E., House [Wakefield MRA], 34 Salem St., Wakefield, 7/06/89, C, 89000686

Bogle—Walker House, 55 and 62 Goodman's Rd., Sudbury, 8/27/92, A, C, 92001044

Boit, Elizabeth, House [Wakefield MRA], 127 Chestnut St., Wakefield, 7/06/89, C, 89000720

Boston Edison Power Station [Newton MRA], 374 Homer St., Newton, 2/16/90, A, C, 90000023

Boston Manufacturing Company, 144 Moody St., Waltham, 12/22/77, A, C, NHL, 77001412

Boston Manufacturing Company Housing [Waltham MRA], 380–410 River St., Waltham, 9/28/89, A, C, 89001534

Boston Manufacturing Company Housing [Waltham MRA], 153–165 River St., Waltham, 9/28/89, A, C, 89001535

Boston Post Road Historic District, Both sides of the Boston Post Rd. from Plain Rd. to Stony Brook, Weston, 2/11/83, A, C, 83000783

Boston and Maine Railroad Depot [Reading MRA], Lincoln St., Reading, 7/19/84, A, C, 84002509

Middlesex County—Continued

Boston and Maine Railroad Depot [Stoneham MRA], 36 Pine St., Stoneham, 4/13/84, A, C, 84002510

Bottle House Block [Cambridge MRA], 204-214 3rd St., Cambridge, 4/13/82, A, C, 82001924

Bottume, John, House [Stoneham MRA], 4 Woodland Rd., Stoneham, 4/13/84, C, 84002513

Bow Street Historic District, Bow St., Somerville, 3/26/76, C, a, 76000274

Bowers, Jonathan, House, 58 Wannalancit St., Lowell, 6/18/76, B, C, 76000253

Bowser Gazebo [Reading MRA], 25 Linden St., Reading, 7/19/84, B, C, 84002514

Brabrook, E. H., House [Cambridge MRA], 42–44 Avon St., Cambridge, 5/19/86, C, 86001276

Brackett House [Reading MRA], 276 Summer Ave., Reading, 7/19/84, C, 84002515

Brackett House [Newton MRA], 621 Centre St., Newton, 9/04/86, C, 86001777

Brackett, Edward A., House [Winchester MRA], 290 Highland Ave., Winchester, 7/05/89, C, 89000626

Brackett, S. E., House [Somerville MPS], 63 Columbus Ave., Somerville, 9/18/89, A, C, 89001252

Bradbury, William F., House [Cambridge MRA], 369 Harvard St., Cambridge, 6/30/83, A, C, 83000784

Braddock, Edward, House [Winchester MRA], 112 Highland Ave., Winchester, 7/05/89, A, C, 89000651

Brae-Burn Historic District [Newton MRA], Brae Burn and Windmere Rds., Newton, 2/16/90, A, C, 90000009

Brande House [Reading MRA], 54 Woburn St., Reading, 7/29/84, B, C, 84002516

Brattle Hall [Cambridge MRA], 40 Brattle St., Cambridge, 4/13/82, A, 82001925

Brattle, William, House, 42 Brattle St., Cambridge, 5/08/73, A, C, 73000286

Brewer, Moses, House [First Period Buildings of Eastern Massachusetts TR], 88 Concord Rd., Sudbury, 3/09/90, C, b, 90000184

Bridgman, Percy, House, 10 Buckingham Pl., Cambridge, 5/15/75, B, NHL, 75000298

Brigham House [Waltham MRA], 235 Main St., Waltham, 9/28/89, A, C, 89001551

Brine, George, House [Winchester MRA], 219 Washington St., Winchester, 7/05/89, A, C, 89000638

Broadway Winter Hill Congregational Church [Somerville MPS], 404 Broadway, Somerville, 9/18/89, A, C, a, 89001238

Brooks, Charles, House, 309 High St., Medford, 6/18/75, B, C, 75000269

Brooks, Daniel, House, Brooks Rd. E., Lincoln vicinity, 10/25/73, B, C, 73000293

Brooks, Francis, House [Reading MRA], 78-80 Prescott St., Reading, 7/19/84, B, C, 84002524

Brooks, James H., House [Somerville MPS], 61 Columbus Ave., Somerville, 9/18/89, A, C, 89001251

Brooks, Jonathan, House, 2 Woburn St., Medford, 6/26/75, A, B, C, 75000270

Brooks, Luther, House [Cambridge MRA], 34 Kirkland St., Cambridge, 9/12/86, C, 86002068

Brooks, Shepherd, Estate, 275 Grove St., Medford, 4/21/75, A, C, 75000271

Brown, C.H., Cottage [Stoneham MRA], 34 Wright St., Stoneham, 4/13/84, A, C, 84002525

Brown, Col. Roger, House, 1694 Main St., Concord, 1/27/83, A, C, 83000785

Brown—Maynard House, 84 Tenth St., Lowell, 7/02/86, A, C, 86001460

Brown—Stow House [First Period Buildings of Eastern Massachusetts TR], 172 Harvard Rd., Stow, 3/09/90, C, D, 90000182

Browne, Abraham, House [First Period Buildings of Eastern Massachusetts TR], 562 Main St., Watertown, 3/09/90, C, D, 90000186

Bruner, Mayall, House [Newton MRA], 36 Magnolia Ave., Newton, 2/16/90, A, C, 90000040

Bryant, William, Octagon House [Stoneham MRA], Spring and Washington Sts., Stoneham, 4/13/84, C, 84002526

Buck, Charles, House [Stoneham MRA], 68 Pleasant St., Stoneham, 4/13/84, B, C, 84002527

Buck, Ephraim, House [First Period Buildings of Eastern Massachusetts TR], 216 Wildwood St., Wilmington, 3/09/90, D, 90000189

Buckingham, John, House [Newton MRA], 33–35 Waban St., Newton, 9/04/86, A, C, 86001778

Buckman Tavern, Hancock St., on the E side of Lexington Green, Lexington, 10/15/66, A, NHL, 66000137

Building at 1–6 Walnut Terrace [Newton MRA], 1–6 Walnut Terr., Newton, 9/04/86, A, C, 86001779

Building at 10 Follen Street [Cambridge MRA], 10 Follen St., Cambridge, 4/13/82, C, 82001926

Building at 102-104 Inman Street [Cambridge MRA], 102-104 Inman St., Cambridge, 6/30/83, C, 83000790

Building at 104-106 Hancock Street [Cambridge MRA], 104-106 Hancock St., Cambridge, 6/30/83, C, 83000789

Building at 106-108 Inman St [Cambridge MRA], 106-108 Inman St., Cambridge, 4/13/82, C, 82001927

Building at 1707-1709 Cambridge Street [Cambridge MRA], 1707-1709 Cambridge St., Cambridge, 6/30/83, C, 83000787

Building at 1715-1717 Cambridge Street [Cambridge MRA], 1715-1717 Cambridge St., Cambridge, 6/30/83, C, 83000788

Building at 202–204 Charles Street [Waltham MRA], 202–204 Charles St., Waltham, 9/28/89, A, C, 89001493

Building at 259 Mount Auburn Street [Cambridge MRA], 259 Mt. Auburn St., Cambridge, 6/30/83, C, 83000786

Building at 38–48 Richardson Avenue [Wakefield MRA], 38–48 Richardson Ave., Wakefield, 7/06/89, C, 89000709

Building at 42 Edward J. Lopez Avenue [Cambridge MRA], 42 Edward J. Lopez Ave., Cambridge, 4/13/82, C, b, 82001928

Buildings at 110-112 Inman St. [Cambridge MRA], 110-112 Inman St., Cambridge, 4/13/82, C, 82001929

Buildings at 15-17 Lee St. [Cambridge MRA], 15-17 Lee St., Cambridge, 4/13/82, C, 82001930

Buildings at 35–37 Richardson Avenue [Wakefield MRA], 35–37 Richardson Ave., Wakefield, 7/06/89, C, 89000710

Bullard, Isaac, House [First Period Buildings of Eastern Massachusetts TR], 77 Ashland St., Holliston, 3/09/90, C, 90000171

Bullen—Stratton—Cozzen House [Sherborn MRA], 52 Brush Hill Rd., Sherborn, 1/03/86, A, C, 86000496

Buswell, Clara, House [Stoneham MRA], 481 Main St., Stoneham, 4/13/84, C, 84002528

Butterfield-Whittemore House, 54 Massachusetts Ave., Arlington, 3/30/78, A, C, 78000429

Buttrick, Francis, House [Waltham MRA], 44 Harvard St., Waltham, 9/28/89, A, C, 89001566

Buttrick, Francis, Library [Waltham MRA], 741 Main St., Waltham, 9/28/89, A, C, 89001547

Byam, Charles, House [Waltham MRA], 337 Crescent St., Waltham, 9/28/89, A, C, 89001576

Call-Bartlett House [Arlington MRA], 216 Pleasant St., Arlington, 4/18/85, B, C, 85001024

Calvary Methodist Church, 300 Massachusetts Ave., Arlington, 6/23/83, A, C, a, 83003433

Cambidge Common Historic District Amendment [Cambridge MRA], Massachusetts Ave. and Garden, Waterhouse, Cambridge, and Peabody Sts., Cambridge, 6/30/83, A, C, 83004293

Cambridge Common Historic District, Garden, Waterhouse, Cambridge, and Peabody Sts., and Massachusetts Ave., Cambridge, 4/13/73, A, C, a, c, 73000281

Cambridge Common Historic District (Boundary Increase and Decrease) [Cambridge MRA], Roughly NW of Waterhouse St. on Concord Ave. between Garden and Follen Sts., Cambridge, 1/26/87, A, C, a, 87000499

Cambridge Public Library [Cambridge MRA], 449 Broadway St., Cambridge, 4/13/82, A, B, C, 82001931

Capitol Theater Building [Arlington MRA], 202–208 Massachusetts Ave., Arlington, 4/18/85, C, 85001025

Capron, Charles, House [Uxbridge MRA], 2 Capron St., Uxbridge, 10/07/83, B, C, 83004111

Carpenter Center for the Visual Arts, 19 Prescott St., Cambridge, 4/20/78, C, g, 78000435

Carr, Martin W., School, 25 Atherton St., Somerville, 7/05/84, A, C, 84002530

Carr—Jeeves House [Winchester MRA], 57 Lake St., Winchester, 8/02/89, A, C, 89000639

Carroll-Hartshorn House [Reading MRA], 572 Haverhill St., Reading, 7/19/84, A, C, 84002532

Carter Mansion [Reading MRA], 89 Woburn St., Reading, 7/19/84, B, C, 84002535

Castle, The, 415 South St., Waltham, 4/09/79, A, C, 79000359

Cedar Swamp Archeological District, Address Restricted, Hopkinton vicinity, 5/23/88, D, 88000587

Center Depot [Wakefield MRA], 57 Water St., Wakefield, 7/06/89, A, C, 89000693

Middlesex County—Continued

Central Congregational Church [Newton MRA], 218 Walnut St., Newton, 9/04/86, C, a, 86001781

Central Library [Somerville MPS], 79 Highland Ave., Somerville, 9/18/89, A, C, 89001274

Central Square Historic District [Waltham MRA], Roughly bounded by Church, Carter, Moody, Main and Lexington Sts., Waltham, 9/28/89, A, C, 89001526

Central Square Historic District [Stoneham MRA], Roughly bounded by Main, Central, Church, Winter and Common Sts., Stoneham, 1/17/90, A, C, 89002277

Central Square Historic District [Cambridge MRA], Roughly Massachusetts Ave. from Clinton St. to Main St., Cambridge, 3/02/90, A, C, 90000128

Chamberlain, Samuel, House [Stoneham MRA], 3 Winthrop St., Stoneham, 4/13/84, B, C, 84002536

Chandler, Gen. Samuel, House, 8 Goodwin Rd., Lexington, 4/13/77, C, 77000176

Chapel of St. Anne [Arlington MRA], Claremont Ave., Arlington, 4/18/85, C, a, 85001026

Charles River Basin Historic District, Both banks of Charles River from Eliot Bridge to Charles River Dam, Cambridge, 12/22/78, A, C, g, 78000436

Charles Street Workers' Housing Historic District [Waltham MRA], 128–144 Charles St., Waltham, 9/28/89, A, C, 89001503

Chelmsford Center Historic District, MA 4, MA 110 and MA 27, Chelmsford, 2/20/80, C, a, 80000646

Chelmsford Glass Works' Long House, 139-141 Baldwin St., Lowell, 1/25/73, A, C, 73000302

Chestnut Hill, The [Newton MRA], 219 Commonwealth Ave., Newton, 9/04/86, C, 86001782

Child, Francis J., House [Cambridge MRA], 67 Kirkland St., Cambridge, 6/30/83, C, 83000791

Childs, Mayor Edwin O., House [Newton MRA], 340 California St., Newton, 2/16/90, B, C, 90000039

Childs, Webster, House [Winchester MRA], 16A Ginn St., Winchester, 7/05/89, A, C, 89000644

Christ Church, Garden St., Cambridge, 10/15/66, C, a, NHL, 66000140

Christ Episcopal Church [Waltham MRA], 750 Main St., Waltham, 9/28/89, A, C, a, 89001546

Church of the New Jerusalem [Cambridge MRA], 50 Quincy St., Cambridge, 6/30/83, C, a, 83000792

Church, William L., House [Newton MRA], 145 Warren St., Newton, 2/21/90, A, C, 90000112

Church—Lafayette Streets Historic District [Wakefield MRA], Roughly Church St. from Lafayette St. to North Ave., Wakefield, 7/06/89, A, C, 89000757

City Hall Historic District, Roughly area between Broadway and French Sts., Colburn St. and both sides of Kirk St., Lowell, 4/21/75, A, C, NPS, 75000156

City Hall Historic District [Cambridge MRA], Massachusetts Ave., Bigelow and Temple Sts., Inman and Richard Allen Dr., Cambridge, 4/13/82, C, a, b, 82001932

City Hall Historic District (Boundary Increase), 165 Market St., Lowell, 10/13/88, A, C, 88001906

City Stable and Garage [Newton MRA], 74 Elliot St., Newton, 2/16/90, A, C, 90000022

Claflin School, 110-112 Washington Park, Newton, 8/16/84, A, C, 84002543

Claflin, Adams, House [Newton MRA], 156 Grant Ave., Newton, 9/04/86, B, C, 86001783

Clark House [Newton MRA], 379 Central St., Newton, 9/04/86, B, C, a, 86001785

Clark Houses, 74 and 76 W. Central St., Natick, 2/17/78, B, C, 78000453

Clark—Northrup House [Sherborn MRA], 93 Maple St., Sherborn, 1/03/86, C, 86000497

Cleale, Joseph, House [Sherborn MRA], 147 Western Ave., Sherborn, 1/03/86, C, 86000498

Cliff, Z. E., House [Somerville MPS], 29 Powderhouse Terr., Somerville, 9/18/89, C, 89001280

Clough, Benjamin F., House [Waltham MRA], 42–44 Prospect St., Waltham, 9/28/89, A, C, 89001536

Cloverden [Cambridge MRA], 29 Fallen St., Cambridge, 6/30/83, A, C, 83000793

Cogan, Bernard, House [Stoneham MRA], 10 Flint St., Stoneham, 4/13/84, A, C, 84002546

Cogan, James, House [Stoneham MRA], 48 Elm St., Stoneham, 4/13/84, A, C, 84002550

Coggin, Gilman, House [Reading MRA], 123 Prescott St., Reading, 7/19/84, B, C, 84002551

Colburn, Gilbert, House [Waltham MRA], 110–112 Crescent St., Waltham, 9/28/89, A, C, 89001578

Colburn, Sara Foster, House [Cambridge MRA], 7 Dana St., Cambridge, 4/13/82, C, 82004968

Colby Hall, 141 Herrick Rd., Newton Centre, 1/30/78, A, C, a, 78000459

Cole House [Winchester MRA], 12 Mason St., Winchester, 7/05/89, C, 89000646

Collins, Frederick, House [Newton MRA], 1734 Beacon St., Newton, 9/04/86, C, 86001786

Colonial Beacon Gas Station [Stoneham MRA], 474 Main St., Stoneham, 4/13/84, A, C, 84002554

Commanding Officer's Quarters, Watertown Arsenal, 443 Arsenal St., Watertown, 10/07/76, A, C, 76000279

Common Burying Ground at Sandy Bank, Green St., Malden, 8/27/81, A, C, d, 81000108

Common District [Wakefield MRA], Roughly bounded by Lake Quannapowitt, Main St., Common St., Church St., and Lake Ave., Wakefield, 3/02/90, C, a, 89000754

Common Historic District [Reading MRA], Roughly bounded by Main, Highland, and Federal Sts., Reading, 2/01/85, A, C, a, d, 85000548

Commonwealth Avenue Historic District [Newton MRA], Roughly Commonwealth Ave. from Walnut St. to Waban Hill Rd., Newton, 2/16/90, A, C, 90000012

Company F State Armory [Waltham MRA], Curtis and Sharon Sts., Waltham, 9/28/89, C, 89001571

Concord Monument Square-Lexington Road Historic District, MA 2A, Concord, 9/13/77, A, B, C, 77000172

Concord Square Historic District, Park, Concord, and Kendall Sts., and Union Ave., Farmington, 3/10/83, A, C, 83000794

Conventual Church of St. Mary and St. John [Cambridge MRA], 980 Memorial Dr., Cambridge, 4/13/82, C, a, g, 82001933

Converse Memorial Building, 36 Salem St., Malden, 9/05/85, B, C, NHL, 85002014

Cook, Asa M., House [Reading MRA], 81 Prospect St., Reading, 7/19/84, B, C, 84002555

Cook, Thomas, House [Somerville MPS], 21 College Hill Rd., Somerville, 9/18/89, C, b, 89001250

Cook, William, House [Cambridge MRA], 71 Appleton St., Cambridge, 4/13/82, C, 82001934

Coolidge, Josiah, House [Cambridge MRA], 24 Coolidge Hill Rd., Cambridge, 6/30/83, C, 83000795

Cooper—Davenport Tavern Wing [Somerville MPS], 81 Eustis St., Somerville, 9/18/89, C, b, 89001257

Cooper-Frost-Austin House, 21 Linnaean St., Cambridge, 9/22/72, C, 72000124

Cotting, John, House, 74 Main St., Marlborough, 8/16/84, A, C, 84002556

Cowdrey, George, House [Stoneham MRA], 42 High St., Stoneham, 4/13/84, B, C, 84002557

Cowdry, Jonas, House [Wakefield MRA], 61 Prospect St., Wakefield, 7/06/89, C, 89000739

Cowdry, Nathaniel, House [Wakefield MRA], 71 Prospect St., Wakefield, 7/06/89, C, 89000738

Craigie Arms [Cambridge MRA], 2–6 University Rd., 122 Mt. Auburn, and 6 Bennett Sts., Cambridge, 7/10/86, A, C, 86001575

Crimmins, Thomas A., House [Newton MRA], 19 Dartmouth St., Newton, 2/16/90, A, C, 90000021

Crowell, C. C., House [Somerville MPS], 85 Benton Rd., Somerville, 9/18/89, C, 89001236

Crystal Lake and Pleasant Street Historic District [Newton MRA], Roughly bounded by Sudbury Aqueduct, Pleasant Ave., Lake Ave., and Crystal St. and Webster Ct., Newton, 9/04/86, A, C, 86001735

Cuming, Dr. John, House, W of Concord at Barretts Mill Rd. and Reformatory Circle, Concord vicinity, 11/11/77, B, 77000175

Curtis, Allen Crocker, House—Pillar House [Newton MRA], 26 Quinobequin Rd., Newton, 9/04/86, B, C, 86001787

Curtis, Paul, House, 114 South St., Medford, 5/06/75, B, C, 75000272

Curtis, William, House [Newton MRA], 2330 Washington St., Newton, 9/04/86, B, C, 86001788

Cushman House [Arlington MRA], 104 Bartlett Ave., Arlington, 4/18/85, C, 85001027

Cutter, Ephraim, House, 4 Water St., Arlington, 3/29/78, B, C, b, 78000430

Cutter, Jefferson, House [Arlington MRA], 1 Whittemore Park, Arlington, 1/23/92, C, 85001028

Cutter, Second, A. P., House [Arlington MRA], 89 Summer St., Arlington, 4/18/85, C, 85001029

Daly, Reginald A., House, 23 Hawthorn St., Cambridge, 1/07/76, B, NHL, 76000305

Middlesex County—Continued

Damon House [Arlington MRA], 275 Broadway, Arlington, 4/18/85, C, 85001030

Damon Mill, 9 Pond Lane, Concord, 5/25/79, A, C, 79000360

Damon, Joseph, House [Reading MRA], 178 South St., Reading, 7/19/84, A, C, 84002559

Damon, Washington, House [Reading MRA], 38 Salem St., Reading, 7/19/84, C, 84002560

Dana—Palmer House [Cambridge MRA], 12–16 Quincy St., Cambridge, 5/19/86, C, b, 86001682

Daniels, Blake, Cottage [Stoneham MRA], 111-113 Elm St., Stoneham, 4/13/84, A, C, 84002562

Daniels, Charles A., School, Daniels St., Malden, 1/06/87, A, C, 86003562

Davis, Isaac, Trail, Running E-W between towns of Acton and Concord, Acton, 4/11/72, A, 72001347

Davis, Seth, House [Newton MRA], 32 Eden Ave., Newton, 9/04/86, B, C, 86001960

Davis, William Morris, House, 17 Francis St., Cambridge, 1/07/76, B, NHL, 76000306

Day Estate Historic District [Newton MRA], Commonwealth Ave. and Dartmouth St., Newton, 2/16/90, A, C, 90000008

Day, Anna, House [Cambridge MRA], 139 Cushing St., Cambridge, 4/13/82, C, 82001935

DeRochmont House [Winchester MRA], 2–4 Rangeley Rd., Winchester, 7/05/89, A, C, 89000642

DeRosay—McNamee House [Cambridge MRA], 50 Mt. Vernon St., Cambridge, 3/02/90, A, C, 90000142

Dean, Silas, House [Stoneham MRA], 8 Pine St., Stoneham, 4/13/84, B, 84002565

Deane-Williams House [Cambridge MRA], 21-23 Fayette St., Cambridge, 4/13/82, C, 82001936

Dewey Place [Reading MRA], 176 Summer Ave., Reading, 7/19/84, B, C, 84002567

Dike—Orne House [Winchester MRA], 257 Forest St., Winchester, 7/05/89, C, 89000621

Divinity Hall [Cambridge MRA], 12 Divinity Ave., Cambridge, 9/12/86, A, C, 86002071

Dodge, Edward, House [Cambridge MRA], 70 Sparks St., Cambridge, 4/13/82, C, 82001937

Dow Block [Stoneham MRA], Central Square, Stoneham, 4/13/84, A, C, 84002570

Dow, Lenoir, House [Waltham MRA], 215 Adams St., Waltham, 9/28/89, A, C, 89001487

Downer Rowhouses (Adams Street) [Somerville MPS], 55 Adams St., Somerville, 9/18/89, C, 89001225

Downer Rowhouses (Central Street) [Somerville MPS], 192–200 Central St., Somerville, 9/18/89, C, 89001241

Dowse, Rev. Edmund, House [Sherborn MRA], 25 Farm Rd., Sherborn, 1/03/86, A, B, C, a, 86000499

Dunbar—Stearns House [Waltham MRA], 209 Linden St., Waltham, 3/09/90, C, b, 89001517

Dunvegan, The [Cambridge MRA], 1654 Massachusetts Ave., Cambridge, 5/19/86, A, C, 86001279

Dupee Estate [Newton MRA], 400 Beacon St., Newton, 9/04/86, C, a, 86001790

Durant, Capt. Edward, House, 286 Waverly Ave., Newton, 5/13/76, B, C, 76000267

Durgin House [Reading MRA], 66 Prospect St., Reading, 7/19/84, C, 84002574

Durgin, E. A., House [Stoneham MRA], 113 Summer St., Stoneham, 4/13/84, B, C, 84002572

Dwight, Edmund, House [Winchester MRA], 5 Cambridge St., Winchester, 7/05/89, A, C, 89000633

East Cambridge Historic District [Cambridge MRA], Roughly bounded by Cambridge, Hurley and 5th Sts., Cambridge, 6/30/83, A, C, 83000797

East Cambridge Savings Bank [Cambridge MRA], 292 Cambridge St., Cambridge, 4/13/82, C, 82001938

East Main Street Historic District [Waltham MRA], Roughly E. Main St. from Townsend St. to Chamberlain Ter., Waltham, 9/28/89, A, C, 89001498

East Parish Burying Ground, Centre and Cotton Sts., Newton, 11/23/83, A, B, C, d, 83004010

Eastern Middlesex County Second District Court [Waltham MRA], 38 Linden St., Waltham, 9/28/89, A, C, 89001516

Eaton-Prescott House [Reading MRA], 284 Summer Ave., Reading, 7/19/84, C, 84002597

Echo Bridge, Spans Charles River, Newton, 4/09/80, A, C, 80000638

Eddy, George W., House [Newton MRA], 85 Bigelow Rd., Newton, 2/16/90, A, C, 90000038

Edward's Plain—Dowse's Corner Historic District [Sherborn MRA], N. Main St. between Eliot and Everett Sts., Sherborn, 1/03/86, A, B, C, 86000492

Elder, Samuel, House [Winchester MRA], 38 Rangeley Rd., Winchester, 7/05/89, A, C, 89000643

Eliot Hall at Radcliffe College [Cambridge MRA], 51 Shepard St., Cambridge, 5/19/86, A, C, 86001280

Elliott, Charles D., House [Newton MRA], 7 Colman St., Newton, 9/04/86, C, 86001792

Elliott, Luther, House [Reading MRA], 309 Haven St., Reading, 7/19/84, B, C, 84002598

Ellis, Asa, House [Cambridge MRA], 158 Auburn St., Cambridge, 6/30/83, C, 83000798

Ellis, Moses, House, 283 Pleasant St., Framingham, 11/29/83, C, 83004022

Elmwood, 33 Elmwood Ave., Cambridge, 10/15/66, B, C, NHL, 66000364

Emerson, Ralph Waldo, House, Lexington Rd. and Cambridge Tpke., Concord, 10/15/66, B, NHL, 66000365

Emerson—Franklin Poole House [Wakefield MRA], 23 Salem St., Wakefield, 7/06/89, C, 89000685

Eminence, The [Newton MRA], 122 Islington Rd., Newton, 9/04/86, C, 86001793

Estabrook, Rufus, House [Newton MRA], 33 Woodland Rd., Newton, 9/04/86, A, C, 86001795

Evangelical Baptist Church [Newton MRA], 23 Chapel St., Newton, 9/04/86, C, a, 86001796

Everett Avenue—Sheffield Road Historic District [Winchester MRA], Roughly bounded by Bacon St., Mystic Valley Pkwy., Mystic Lake, Niles Ln., Everett Ave., Sheffield Rd., and Church St., Winchester, 7/05/89, A, C, 89000661

Exchange Hall, Quimby Sq. on School St., Acton, 6/13/86, A, C, 86001327

Farlow Hill Historic District [Newton MRA], Roughly bounded by Shornecliffe Rd., Franklin St., Chamberlain Rd., Huntington Rd., and Farlow Rd., Newton, 2/21/90, A, C, 90000110

Farlow and Kendrick Parks Historic District [Newton MRA (AD)], Roughly bounded by Franklin, Park, Church, Center and Wesley Sts. and Maple Ave., Newton, 7/08/82, C, a, 82002745

Farlow and Kendrick Parks Historic District (Boundary Increase) [Newton MRA], 223, 226, 234, 237, 242, 243, 248, and 256 Park St., Newton, 9/04/86, A, C, 86001739

Farmer, Kimball, House [Arlington MRA], 1173 Massachusetts Ave., Arlington, 4/18/85, C, 85001031

Farquhar, Samuel, House [Newton MRA], 7 Channing St., Newton, 9/04/86, C, 86001798

Farrier, Amasa, Boardinghouse [Stoneham MRA], 280 Main St., Stoneham, 4/13/84, A, C, 84002601

Farrier, Amasa, House [Stoneham MRA], 55 Central St., Stoneham, 4/13/84, B, C, 84002605

Farwell, R.H., House [Cambridge MRA], 2222-2224 Massachusetts Ave., Cambridge, 4/13/82, A, C, 82001939

Faulkner Homestead, High St., Acton, 12/16/71, B, C, 71000080

Fay, Issac, House [Cambridge MRA], 123 Antrim St., Cambridge, 6/30/83, C, 83000799

Fenno, John A., House [Newton MRA], 171 Lowell Ave., Newton, 9/04/86, C, 86001800

Fernald, George P., House, 12 Rock Hill St., Medford, 4/30/76, C, 76000258

Fessenden, Reginald A., House, 45 Waban Hill Rd., Newton, 1/07/76, B, NHL, 76000950

First Baptist Church, Magazine and River Sts., Cambridge, 4/14/75, C, a, 75000249

First Baptist Church, 1013 Worcester Rd., Framingham, 4/09/80, C, a, 80000642

First Baptist Church [Stoneham MRA], 461 Main St., Stoneham, 4/13/84, C, a, 84002607

First Baptist Church in Newton, 848 Beacon St., Newton, 4/15/82, A, C, a, 82002746

First Congregational Church [Stoneham MRA], Main and Church Sts., Stoneham, 4/13/84, A, C, a, 84002609

First Congregational Church [Waltham MRA], 730 Main St., Waltham, 9/28/89, A, C, a, 89001548

First Congregational Church in Woburn, 322 Main St., Woburn, 1/06/92, A, C, a, 91001898

First Parish Church [Waltham MRA], 87 School St., Waltham, 9/28/89, A, C, a, 89001507

First Parish Church Parsonage [Arlington MRA], 232–234 Pleasant St., Arlington, 4/18/85, C, a, 85001032

First Unitarian Church [Stoneham MRA], Central and Common Sts., Stoneham, 4/13/84, A, C, a, 84002612

Middlesex County—Continued

First Unitarian Church [Newton MRA], 1326 Washington St., Newton, 9/04/86, C, a, 86001802

First Unitarian Church [Somerville MPS], 130 Highland Ave., Somerville, 9/18/89, A, C, a, 89001264

First Universalist Church [Somerville MPS], 125 Highland St., Somerville, 9/18/89, A, C, a, 89001262

Firth—Glengarry Historic District [Winchester MRA], Roughly bounded by Pine St., Grassmere Ave., Dix St., and Wildwood St., Winchester, 7/05/89, C, 89000662

Fisher, Henry N., House [Waltham MRA], 120 Crescent St., Waltham, 9/28/89, A, B, C, 89001577

Fiske House, 1 Billerica Rd., Chelmsford Center, 12/09/77, C, 77000171

Fiske, Elijah, House [Waltham MRA], 457 Lincoln St., Waltham, 9/28/89, B, 89001514

Flagg, Frederick, House [Waltham MRA], 65 Fairmont Ave., Waltham, 9/28/89, C, 89001573

Flagg—Coburn House, 722 E. Merrimack St., Lowell, 5/15/86, C, 86001052

Flanley's Block [Wakefield MRA], 349–353 Main St., Wakefield, 7/06/89, C, 89000729

Fleming, Thomas, House [Sherborn MRA], 18 Maple St., Sherborn, 1/03/86, A, C, 86000500

Flentje, Ernst, House [Cambridge MRA], 129 Magazine St., Cambridge, 6/30/83, C, 83000800

Fletcher, Henry, House, 224 Concord Rd., Westford, 9/30/93, A, C, 93000010

Fletcher, Jonathan, House, 283 High St., Medford, 6/23/75, C, 75000274

Fogg Art Museum [Cambridge MRA], 26–32 Quincy St., Cambridge, 5/19/86, A, C, 86001282

Foley, Michael, Cottage [Stoneham MRA], 14 Emerson St., Stoneham, 4/13/84, A, 84002614

Follen Community Church, 755 Massachusetts Ave., Lexington, 4/30/76, A, C, a, 76000242

Follen Street Historic District [Cambridge MRA], 1–44 and 5–29 Follen St., Cambridge, 5/19/86, A, C, 86001681

Fort Devens Historic District, Roughly bounded by El Caney St., Antietam St., Sherman Ave., MacArthur Ave. and Buena Vista St., Ayer, 6/10/93, A, C, 93000437

Fort Washington, 95 Waverly St., Cambridge, 4/03/73, A, C, f, 73000284

Foster, Alexander, House [Somerville MPS], 45 Laurel St., Somerville, 9/18/89, C, 89001270

Foster, Samuel, House [First Period Buildings of Eastern Massachusetts TR], 288 Grove St., Reading, 3/09/90, C, D, 90000178

Foster, Walter K., House [Stoneham MRA], 57 Central St., Stoneham, 4/13/84, B, C, 84002616

Fowle, Edmund, House, 26-28 Marshall St., Watertown, 11/11/77, A, C, b, 77000189

Fowle-Reed-Wyman House, 64 Old Mystic St., Arlington, 4/14/75, C, 75000244

Fox, Warren, Building, 190–196 Middlesex St., Lowell, 10/12/89, A, C, 89001609

Framingham Centre Common Historic District, Roughly centered on Framingham Centre Common, between MA 9 and I-90, Framingham, 10/25/90, A, C, a, b, d, 90001564

Framingham Railroad Station, 417 Waverly St., Framingham, 1/17/75, A, C, 75000258

Framingham Reservoir No. 1 Dam and Gatehouse [Water Supply System of Metropolitan Boston MPS], E end of Framingham Reservoir No. 1, off Winter St. N of Long Ave., Framingham, 1/18/90, A, C, 89002291

Framingham Reservoir No. 2 Dam and Gatehouse [Water Supply System of Metropolitan Boston MPS], Between Framingham Reservoirs Nos. 1 and 2, W of jct. of Winter and Fountain Sts., Framingham, 1/18/90, A, C, 89002290

Framingham Reservoir No. 3 Dam and Gatehouse [Water Supply System of Metropolitan Boston MPS], SE end of Framingham Reservoir No. 3, off MA 9/30, Framingham, 1/18/90, A, C, 89002261

French, Daniel, School [Waltham MRA], 38–40 Common St., Waltham, 9/28/89, A, C, 89001581

Fresh Pond Hotel [Cambridge MRA], 234 Lakeview Ave., Cambridge, 4/13/82, A, b, 82001940

Frost, David, House [Cambridge MRA], 26 Gray St., Cambridge, 6/30/83, A, C, 83000801

Frost, Elizabeth, Tenanthouse [Cambridge MRA], 35 Bowdoin St., Cambridge, 6/30/83, C, 83000802

Frost, Robert, House [Cambridge MRA], 29-35 Brewster St., Cambridge, 4/13/82, B, g, 82001941

Frost, Walter, House [Cambridge MRA], 10 Frost St., Cambridge, 4/13/82, A, C, b, 82001942

Fuller, Capt. Edward, Farm [Newton MRA], 59–71 North St., Newton, 9/04/86, B, C, 86001804

Fuller, Enoch, House [Stoneham MRA], 72 Pine St., Stoneham, 4/13/84, C, 84002619

Fuller, Margaret, House, 71 Cherry St., Cambridge, 7/02/71, B, NHL, 71000686

Fuller, William Griffin, House [Stoneham MRA], 32 Franklin St., Stoneham, 4/13/84, B, C, 84002621

Fuller—Bemis House [Waltham MRA], 41–43 Cherry St., Waltham, 3/09/90, C, 89001495

Gale, George, House [Cambridge MRA], 14–16 Clinton St., Cambridge, 2/10/88, A, C, 87002543

Gale—Banks House [Waltham MRA], 935 Main St., Waltham, 3/09/90, C, 89001545

Gane, Henry, House [Newton MRA], 121 Adena Rd., Newton, 9/04/86, C, 86001806

Gardner, Addington, House [First Period Buildings of Eastern Massachusetts TR], 128 Hollis St., Sherborn, 3/09/90, C, 90000179

Gardner, Edward, House [Winchester MRA], 89 Cambridge St., Winchester, 7/05/89, A, C, 89000605

Gardner, O. W., House [Winchester MRA], 5 Myrtle St., Winchester, 7/05/89, C, b, 89000791

Gardner, Patience and Sarah, House [Winchester MRA], 103–105 Cambridge St., Winchester, 7/05/89, A, C, 89000608

Garfield Street Historic District [Cambridge MRA], Garfield St. between Massachusetts Ave.

and Oxford St., Cambridge, 6/30/83, C, 83000803

Gaut, Samuel, House [Somerville MPS], 137 Highland Ave., Somerville, 9/18/89, C, 89001265

Gibbs, Paul, House, 1147 Edmands Rd., Framingham vicinity, 3/10/83, C, 83000804

Gibbs, William, House [Waltham MRA], 14 Liberty St., Waltham, 9/28/89, A, C, 89001561

Gilbrae Inn [Waltham MRA], 403 River St., Waltham, 9/28/89, A, C, 89001550

Gill, Charles, House [Stoneham MRA], 76 Pleasant St., Stoneham, 4/13/84, A, C, 84002623

Gilmore, Onslow, House [Stoneham MRA], 477 Main St., Stoneham, 4/13/84, C, 84002625

Ginn Carriage House [Winchester MRA], 24 Ginn Rd., Winchester, 7/05/89, C, 89000655

Ginn Gardener's House [Winchester MRA], 22 Ginn Rd., Winchester, 7/05/89, C, 89000654

Golden Ball Tavern, 662 Boston Post Rd., Weston, 9/28/72, A, C, 72000141

Goodale Homestead, 100 Chestnut St., Hudson, 1/21/75, B, C, b, 75000260

Goodbar, Lafayette, House [Newton MRA], 614 Walnut St., Newton, 2/16/90, A, C, 90000044

Goodwin, Captain—James Custis House [Wakefield MRA], 1 Elm St., Wakefield, 3/02/90, C, 89000744

Gore Place, 52 Gore St., Waltham, 12/30/70, C, NHL, 70000542

Gould, Samuel, House [Wakefield MRA], 48 Meriam St., Wakefield, 7/06/89, C, 89000704

Goulding, Eleazer, House [Sherborn MRA], 137 Western Ave., Sherborn, 1/03/86, C, 86000501

Grace Episcopal Church, 160 High St., Medford, 11/03/72, C, a, 72000139

Grandview, The [Somerville MPS], 82 Munroe St., Somerville, 9/18/89, A, C, 89001275

Grange, The, Codman Rd., Lincoln, 4/18/74, A, B, C, 74000373

Grange, The, (Boundary Increase), Codman Rd., Lincoln, 5/28/76, A, C, 76001969

Gray Cliff Historic District [Newton MRA], 35, 39, 43, 53, 54, 64, 65, and 70 Gray Cliff Rd., Newton, 9/04/86, C, 86001741

Gray Cliff Historic District (Boundary Increase) [Newton MRA], The Ledges and Bishopsgate Rds., Newton, 2/16/90, A, C, 90000011

Gray Gardens East and West Historic District [Cambridge MRA], 1–37 Gray Gardens E, 3–24 Gray Gardens W, 91 Garden and 60 Raymond Sts., Cambridge, 5/19/86, A, C, 86001283

Gray, Asa, House, 88 Garden St., Cambridge, 10/15/66, B, b, NHL, 66000655

Greek Orthodox Church, 735 Massachusetts Ave., Arlington, 6/23/83, A, C, a, 83000805

Greek Revival Cottage [Cambridge MRA], 59 Rice St., Cambridge, 4/13/82, C, 82001943

Green House [First Period Buildings of Eastern Massachusetts TR], 391 Vernon St., Wakefield, 3/09/90, C, b, 90000185

Green, Capt. William, House [Wakefield MRA], 391 Vernon St., Wakefield, 7/06/89, C, b, 89000672

Green, Deacon Daniel, House [Wakefield MRA], 747 Main St., Wakefield, 7/06/89, C, 89000706

Middlesex County—Continued

Green, Jonathan, House [Stoneham MRA], 63 Perkins St., Stoneham, 4/13/84, B, C, 84002627

Greenwood Union Church [Wakefield MRA], Main and Oak, Wakefield, 7/06/89, C, a, 89000697

Groton Inn, Main St., Groton, 8/03/76, A, C, 76000241

Grove Hill Cemetery [Waltham MRA], 290 Main St., Waltham, 9/28/89, A, C, d, 89001549

Grover, Henry, House [Winchester MRA], 223–225 Cambridge St., Winchester, 7/05/89, A, 89000641

Gunderson, Jos., House [Newton MRA], 983 Centre St., Newton, 9/04/86, C, 86001808

Hagar—Smith—Livermore—Sanderson House [Waltham MRA], 51 Sanders Ln., Waltham, 9/28/89, A, C, 89001532

Hager—Mead House [Waltham MRA], 411 Main St., Waltham, 9/28/89, A, C, 89001572

Hall Tavern [Cambridge MRA], 20 Gray Gardens West St., Cambridge, 6/30/83, C, b, 83000806

Hall, Edward, House [Arlington MRA], 187 Pleasant St., Arlington, 4/18/85, C, 85001033

Hall, Henry C., House [Waltham MRA], 107 Crescent St., Waltham, 9/28/89, A, C, 89001579

Hall, Isaac, House, 43 High St., Medford, 4/16/75, B, C, 75000275

Hall, Stephen, House [Reading MRA], 64 Minot St., Reading, 7/19/84, C, 84002630

Hammond House [First Period Buildings of Eastern Massachusetts TR], 9 Old Orchard Rd., Newton, 3/09/90, C, D, 90000175

Hammond, E. C., House [Newton MRA], 35 Groveland St., Newton, 2/16/90, C, 90000046

Hammond, Ephraim, House [Waltham MRA], 265 Beaver St., Waltham, 9/28/89, A, C, b, 89001490

Hammond, Jonathan, House [Waltham MRA], 311 Beaver St., Waltham, 9/28/89, A, C, 89001491

Hancock School, 33 Forest St., Lexington, 8/22/75, C, 75000261

Hancock-Clarke House, 35 Hancock St., Lexington, 7/17/71, B, b, NHL, 71000895

Hapgood House [First Period Buildings of Eastern Massachusetts TR], 76 Treaty Elm Ln., Stow, 3/09/90, C, 90000180

Hapgood, Richard, House [Cambridge MRA], 382–392 Harvard St., Cambridge, 5/19/86, A, C, 86001284

Harbach, John, House [Newton MRA], 303 Ward St., Newton, 9/04/86, C, 86001809

Harding House—Walker Missionary Home [Newton MRA], 161–163 Grove St., Newton, 9/04/86, B, C, 86001810

Hardy, Nahum, House [Waltham MRA], 724 Lexington St., Waltham, 9/28/89, C, 89001562

Harnden Tavern, 430 Salem St., Wilmington, 4/08/75, B, C, 75000293

Harnden-Browne House [Reading MRA], 60-62 Salem St., Reading, 2/01/85, C, 85000498

Harriman, Henry I., House [Newton MRA], 825 Centre St., Newton, 2/16/90, A, C, 90000028

Harrington Block [Waltham MRA], 376–390 Moody St., Waltham, 9/28/89, A, C, 89001543

Harrington House, 555 Wellesley St., Weston, 6/22/76, A, C, 76000281

Harrington, Samuel, House [Waltham MRA], 475 South St., Waltham, 9/28/89, A, C, 89001508

Harrison, C. Lewis, House [Newton MRA], 14 Eliot Memorial Rd., Newton, 2/16/90, C, 90000045

Hartshorn, Timothy, House [Reading MRA], 379 Haverhill St., Reading, 7/19/84, B, C, 84002633

Hartwell House [Reading MRA], 121 Willow St., Reading, 7/19/84, C, 84002635

Harvard Houses Historic District [Cambridge MRA], Roughly bounded by Mt. Auburn & Grant & Cowperwaite Sts., Banks St. & Putman Ave., the Memorial River, & Boyleston St., Cambridge, 9/12/86, A, C, 86002073

Harvard Lampoon Building, 44 Bow St., Cambridge, 3/30/78, A, C, 78000440

Harvard Square Historic District [Cambridge MRA], Massachusetts Ave., Boylston and Brattle Sts., Cambridge, 4/13/82, C, 82001944

Harvard Square Historic District (Boundary Increase) [Cambridge MRA], Roughly bounded by Harvard & Massachusetts Aves., Mt. Auburn, Winthrop, Bennett, Story & Church Sts., Cambridge, 7/28/88, A, C, 86003654

Harvard Square Subway Kiosk, Massachusetts Ave. and Boylston St., Cambridge, 1/30/78, A, C, 78000441

Harvard Street Historic District [Cambridge MRA], Harvard St. Between Ellery and Hancock Sts., Cambridge, 4/13/82, C, 82001945

Harvard Union [Cambridge MRA], Quincy and Harvard Sts., Cambridge, 1/26/87, C, 87000500

Harvard Yard Historic District [Cambridge MRA], Roughly bounded by underpass, Broadway & Quincy Sts., Massachusetts Ave., & Peabody St., Cambridge, 12/14/87, A, C, 87002137

Haskell, Charles, House [Newton MRA], 27 Sargent St., Newton, 9/04/86, C, 86001812

Hastings Square Historic District [Cambridge MRA], Roughly bounded by Rockingham, Henry, Chestnut and Brookline Sts., Cambridge, 4/13/82, C, 82001946

Hastings, Oliver, House, 101 Brattle St., Cambridge, 12/30/70, C, NHL, 70000681

Hasty Pudding Club, 12 Holyoke St., Cambridge, 1/09/78, A, 78000442

Hatch, Horace, House [Winchester MRA], 26 Grove St., Winchester, 7/05/89, C, b, 89000612

Haven, Wilbur Fiske, House, 339 Pleasant St., Malden, 12/17/92, A, C, 92001659

Haverhill Street Milestone [Reading MRA], Haverhill St., Reading, 2/01/85, A, f, 85000499

Hawkins, Lorenzo D., House [Stoneham MRA], 1 Cedar St., Stoneham, 4/13/84, B, C, 84002639

Hayward, Fred R., House [Newton MRA], 1547 Centre St., Newton, 2/16/90, A, C, 90000025

Henderson Carriage Repository [Cambridge MRA], 2067-2089 Massachusetts Ave., Cambridge, 4/13/82, A, 82001947

Hibbard, Benjamin, Residence [Stoneham MRA], 5-7 Gerry St., Stoneham, 4/13/84, C, 84002642

Higginson, Col. Thomas Wentworth, House [Cambridge MRA], 29 Buckingham St., Cambridge, 4/13/82, B, C, 82001948

Highland Hose House [Arlington MRA], 1007 Massachusetts Ave., Arlington, 4/18/85, A, C, 85001034

Highland School [Reading MRA], 64 Middlesex Ave., Reading, 7/19/84, C, 84002643

Highland, The [Somerville MPS], 66 Highland St., Somerville, 9/18/89, A, C, 89001260

Hildreth, Jonathan, House, 8 Barrett's Mill Rd., Concord, 4/03/91, A, C, 91000362

Hill, Aaron, House [Cambridge MRA], 17 Brown St., Cambridge, 6/30/83, C, 83000807

Hill, Abraham, House [First Period Buildings of Eastern Massachusetts TR], 388 Pleasant St., Belmont, 3/09/90, C, 90000164

Hill, Addison, House [Arlington MRA], 83 Appleton St., Arlington, 9/27/85, C, 85002682

Hill, Deacon Samuel, House [First Period Buildings of Eastern Massachusetts TR], 33 Riverhurst Rd., Billerica, 3/09/90, C, 90000165

Hill, Rev. Thomas, House [Waltham MRA], 132 Church St., Waltham, 9/28/89, B, C, a, 89001528

Hill, Sidney A., House [Stoneham MRA], 31 Chestnut St., Stoneham, 4/13/84, A, C, 84002645

Hillside Avenue Historic District, Property on both sides of Hillside and Grand View Aves., Medford, 4/21/75, C, 75000276

Hoar Tavern, NE of Lincoln on MA 2, Lincoln, 7/23/73, A, C, 73000301

Hobbs Brook Basin Gate House [Waltham MRA], Off Winter St. at mouth of Hobbs Brook, Waltham, 9/28/89, A, C, 89001524

Hobbs, Isaac, House, 87 North Ave., Weston, 6/01/82, B, C, 82002747

Holbrook, Charles, House [Sherborn MRA], 137 S. Main St., Sherborn, 1/03/86, A, C, 86000502

Holbrook, Richard, Houses [Waltham MRA], 29–31 Heard St., Waltham, 9/28/89, A, C, 89001565

Hollander Blocks [Somerville MPS], Walnut St. and Pleasant Ave., Somerville, 9/18/89, A, C, 89001296

Holmes, Joseph, House [Cambridge MRA], 144 Coolidge Hill St., Cambridge, 6/30/83, C, 83000808

Holy Trinity Greek Orthodox Church, Lewis St., Lowell, 4/13/77, A, C, a, 77000181

Homer-Lovell House [Cambridge MRA], 11 Forest St., Cambridge, 12/22/83, C, 83004030

Hooper-Eliot House [Cambridge MRA], 25 Reservoir Rd., Cambridge, 6/30/83, A, C, 83000809

Hooper-Lee Nichols House, 159 Brattle St., Cambridge, 6/15/79, B, C, 79000355

Hopestill Bent Tavern [First Period Buildings of Eastern Massachusetts TR], 252 Old Connecticut Path, Wayland, 3/09/90, C, b, 90000188

Hopewell, Frank B., House [Newton MRA], 301 Waverley Ave., Newton, 2/16/90, A, C, 90000034

Hopkins, Elisha, House [Somerville MPS], 237 School St., Somerville, 9/18/89, C, 89001284

Hopkinton Dam and Spillway [Water Supply System of Metropolitan Boston MPS], E end of Hopkinton Reservoir in Hopkinton State Park, Ashland, 1/18/90, A, C, 89002288

Middlesex County—Continued

Hopkinton Supply Co. Building, 26-28 Main St., Hopkinton, 3/10/83, C, 83000810

Hornblower, Edward, House and Barn [Arlington MRA], 200 Pleasant St., Arlington, 4/18/85, A, C, b, 85001035

Hosmer, Joseph, House [First Period Buildings of Eastern Massachusetts TR], 572 Main St., Concord, 3/09/90, C, D, 90000170

Houghton Memorial Building, 4 Rogers St., Littleton, 3/18/91, A, C, 91000242

House at 1 Morrison Avenue [Wakefield MRA], 1 Morrison Ave., Wakefield, 7/06/89, C, 89000722

House at 1 Woodcrest Drive [Wakefield MRA], 1 Woodcrest Dr., Wakefield, 7/06/89, A, C, 89000673

House at 10 Arlington Street [Somerville MPS], 10 Arlington St., Somerville, 9/18/89, C, 89001230

House at 1008 Beacon Street [Newton MRA], 1008 Beacon St., Newton, 9/04/86, C, 86001813

House at 102 Staniford Street [Newton MRA], 102 Staniford St., Newton, 9/04/86, A, 86001814

House at 107 Waban Hill Road [Newton MRA], 107 Waban Hill Rd., Newton, 9/04/86, C, 86001815

House at 107 William Street [Stoneham MRA], 107 William St., Stoneham, 4/13/84, C, 84002660

House at 11 Beach Street [Reading MRA], 11 Beach St., Reading, 7/19/84, B, C, 84002659

House at 11 Wave Avenue [Wakefield MRA], 11 Wave Ave., Wakefield, 7/06/89, C, 89000678

House at 113 Salem Street [Wakefield MRA], 113 Salem St., Wakefield, 7/06/89, A, C, 89000688

House at 114 Marble Street [Stoneham MRA], 114 Marble St., Stoneham, 4/13/84, C, 84002661

House at 115–117 Jewett Street [Newton MRA], 115–117 Jewett St., Newton, 9/04/86, C, 86001816

House at 1177 Main Street [Reading MRA], 1177 Main St., Reading, 7/19/84, C, 84002668

House at 118 Greenwood Street [Wakefield MRA], 118 Greenwood St., Wakefield, 7/06/89, C, 89000702

House at 12 West Water Street [Wakefield MRA], 12 W. Water St., Wakefield, 7/06/89, C, 89000708

House at 129 High Street [Reading MRA], 129 High St., Reading, 7/19/84, C, 84002664

House at 13 Sheffield Road [Wakefield MRA], 13 Sheffield Rd., Wakefield, 7/06/89, C, 89000734

House at 14 Chestnut Street [Somerville MPS], 14 Chestnut St., Somerville, 9/18/89, A, C, 89001245

House at 15 Chestnut Street [Wakefield MRA], 15 Chestnut St., Wakefield, 7/06/89, C, 89000726

House at 15 Davis Avenue [Newton MRA], 15 Davis Ave., Newton, 9/04/86, C, 86001817

House at 15 Lawrence Avenue [Wakefield MRA], 15 Lawrence Ave., Wakefield, 7/06/89, C, 89000682

House at 15 Wave Avenue [Wakefield MRA], 15 Wave Ave., Wakefield, 7/06/89, C, 89000679

House at 152 Suffolk Road [Newton MRA], 152 Suffolk Rd., Newton, 9/04/86, C, 86001818

House at 16 Mineral Street [Reading MRA], 16 Mineral St., Reading, 7/19/84, C, 84002677

House at 16–18 Preston Road [Somerville MPS], 16–18 Preston Rd., Somerville, 9/18/89, C, 89001279

House at 170 Otis Street [Newton MRA], 170 Otis St., Newton, 9/04/86, B, C, 86001819

House at 173–175 Ward Street [Newton MRA], 173–175 Ward St., Newton, 9/04/86, C, 86001820

House at 18 Park Street [Wakefield MRA], 18 Park St., Wakefield, 7/06/89, C, 89000690

House at 18A and 20 Aborn Street [Wakefield MRA], 18A and 20 Aborn St., Wakefield, 7/06/89, C, 89000676

House at 19 Tremont Street [Stoneham MRA], 19 Tremont St., Stoneham, 4/13/84, A, 84002671

House at 19–21 Salem Street [Wakefield MRA], 19–21 Salem St., Wakefield, 7/06/89, C, 89000684

House at 190 Main Street [Wakefield MRA], 190 Main St., Wakefield, 7/06/89, C, 89000666

House at 193 Vernon Street [Wakefield MRA], 193 Vernon St., Wakefield, 7/06/89, C, 89000674

House at 196 Main Street [Wakefield MRA], 196 Main St., Wakefield, 7/06/89, C, 89000668

House at 197 Morrison Avenue [Somerville MPS], 197 Morrison Ave., Somerville, 9/18/89, C, 89001273

House at 199 Summer Avenue [Reading MRA], 199 Summer Ave., Reading, 7/19/84, B, C, 84002667

House at 2 Nichols Street [Wakefield MRA], 2 Nichols St., Wakefield, 7/06/89, C, 89000740

House at 20 Hancock Road [Wakefield MRA], 20 Hancock Rd., Wakefield, 7/06/89, C, b, 89000671

House at 20 Lawrence Street [Wakefield MRA], 20 Lawrence St., Wakefield, 7/06/89, C, 89000680

House at 20 Morrison Road [Wakefield MRA], 20 Morrison Rd., Wakefield, 7/06/89, C, 89000724

House at 203 Islington Road [Newton MRA], 203 Islington Rd., Newton, 9/04/86, B, C, 86001821

House at 206 West Street [Reading MRA], 206 West St., Reading, 7/19/84, A, C, 84002680

House at 21 Chestnut Street [Wakefield MRA], 21 Chestnut St., Wakefield, 7/06/89, C, 89000727

House at 21 Dartmouth Street [Somerville MPS], 21 Dartmouth St., Somerville, 9/18/89, A, C, 89001255

House at 215 Brookline Street [Newton MRA], 215 Brookline St., Newton, 9/04/86, B, C, 86001822

House at 22 Parker Road [Wakefield MRA], 22 Parker Rd., Wakefield, 7/06/89, C, 89000735

House at 2212 Commonwealth Avenue [Newton MRA], 2212 Commonwealth Ave., Newton, 9/04/86, C, 86001823

House at 23 Avon Street [Wakefield MRA], 23 Avon St., Wakefield, 7/06/89, C, 89000730

House at 23 Lawrence Street [Wakefield MRA], 23 Lawrence St., Wakefield, 7/06/89, C, 89000681

House at 230 Melrose Street [Newton MRA], 230 Melrose St., Newton, 9/04/86, C, 86001961

House at 230 Winchester Street [Newton MRA], 230 Winchester St., Newton, 9/04/86, C, 86001825

House at 242 Summer Avenue [Reading MRA], 242 Summer Ave., Reading, 7/19/84, C, 84002681

House at 25 Avon Street [Wakefield MRA], 25 Avon St., Wakefield, 7/06/89, C, 89000731

House at 25 Clyde Street [Somerville MRA], 25 Clyde St., Somerville, 9/18/89, A, C, 89001247

House at 26 Center Avenue [Reading MRA], 26 Center Ave., Reading, 7/19/84, B, C, 84002679

House at 26 Francis Avenue [Wakefield MRA], 26 Francis Ave., Wakefield, 7/06/89, C, 89000701

House at 269 Green Street [Stoneham MRA], 269 Green St., Stoneham, 4/13/84, C, 84002682

House at 28 Cordis Street [Wakefield MRA], 28 Cordis St., Wakefield, 7/06/89, C, 89000675

House at 28 Wiley Street [Wakefield MRA], 28 Wiley St., Wakefield, 7/06/89, C, 89000695

House at 29 Mt. Vernon Street [Somerville MPS], 29 Mt. Vernon St., Somerville, 9/18/89, C, 89001302

House at 3 Davis Avenue [Newton MRA], 3 Davis Ave., Newton, 9/04/86, C, 86001826

House at 30 Sheffield Road [Wakefield MRA], 30 Sheffield Rd., Wakefield, 7/06/89, C, 89000733

House at 307 Lexington Street [Newton MRA], 307 Lexington St., Newton, 9/04/86, C, 86001827

House at 309 Waltham Street [Newton MRA], 309 Waltham St., Newton, 9/04/86, C, 86001828

House at 31 Woodbine Street [Newton MRA], 31 Woodbine St., Newton, 9/04/86, A, C, 86001829

House at 32 Morrison Road [Wakefield MRA], 32 Morrison Rd., Wakefield, 7/06/89, A, C, 89000723

House at 322 Haven Street [Reading MRA], 322 Haven St., Reading, 7/19/84, B, C, 84002686

House at 343 Highland Avenue [Somerville MPS], 343 Highland Ave., Somerville, 9/18/89, A, C, 89001267

House at 35 Temple Street [Somerville MPS], 35 Temple St., Somerville, 9/18/89, C, b, 89001288

House at 38 Salem Street [Wakefield MRA], 38 Salem St., Wakefield, 7/06/89, C, 89000687

House at 380 Albion Street [Wakefield MRA], 380 Albion St., Wakefield, 7/06/89, C, 89000711

House at 39 Converse Street [Wakefield MRA], 39 Converse St., Wakefield, 7/06/89, C, 89000718

House at 391 Williams Street [Stoneham MRA], 391 Williams St., Stoneham, 4/13/84, C, 84002688

House at 40 Crescent Street [Wakefield MRA], 40 Crescent St., Wakefield, 7/06/89, C, 89000691

House at 41 Middlesex Road [Newton MRA], 41 Middlesex Rd., Newton, 9/04/86, C, 86001830

House at 42 Hopkins Street [Wakefield MRA], 42 Hopkins St., Wakefield, 7/06/89, C, 89000732

House at 42 Salem Street [Reading MRA], 42 Salem St., Reading, 7/19/84, B, C, 84002649

House at 42 Vinal Avenue [Somerville MPS], 42 Vinal Ave., Somerville, 9/18/89, C, 89001290

House at 44 Temple Street [Reading MRA], 44 Temple St., Reading, 7/19/84, B, C, 84002650

Middlesex County—Continued

House at 45 Claremont Avenue [Arlington MRA], 45 Claremont Ave., Arlington, 4/18/85, C, 85001036

House at 47 Sargent Street [Newton MRA], 47 Sargent St., Newton, 9/04/86, C, 86001831

House at 483 Summer Avenue [Reading MRA], 483 Summer Ave., Reading, 7/19/84, B, C, 84002652

House at 49 Vinal Avenue [Somerville MPS], 49 Vinal Ave., Somerville, 9/18/89, A, C, 89001292

House at 5 Bennett Street [Wakefield MRA], 5 Bennett St., Wakefield, 7/06/89, C, 89000698

House at 5 Prospect Hill [Somerville MPS], 5 Prospect Hill, Somerville, 9/18/89, C, 89001281

House at 5 Willow Court [Arlington MRA], 5 Willow Court, Arlington, 4/18/85, C, b, 85001038

House at 5–7 Winter Street [Arlington MRA], 5–7 Winter St., Arlington, 4/18/85, A, C, 85001037

House at 509 North Avenue [Wakefield MRA], 509 North Ave., Wakefield, 7/06/89, C, b, 89000746

House at 511 Watertown Street [Newton MRA], 511 Watertown St., Newton, 9/04/86, C, 86001832

House at 52 Oak Street [Wakefield MRA], 52 Oak St., Wakefield, 7/06/89, C, 89000700

House at 54 Spring Street [Wakefield MRA], 54 Spring St., Wakefield, 7/06/89, A, C, 89000703

House at 556 Lowell Street [Wakefield MRA], 556 Lowell St., Wakefield, 7/06/89, C, 89000670

House at 57 Woburn Street [Reading MRA], 57 Woburn St., Reading, 7/19/84, B, C, 84002657

House at 6 Adams Street [Wakefield MRA], 6 Adams St., Wakefield, 7/06/89, C, 89000721

House at 6 Kent Court [Somerville MPS], 6 Kent Ct., Somerville, 9/18/89, C, b, 89001269

House at 6 S. Marble Street [Stoneham MRA], 6 S. Marble St., Stoneham, 4/13/84, A, 84002690

House at 60 William Street [Newton MRA], 60 William St., Newton, 9/04/86, C, 86001833

House at 68 Maple Street [Newton MRA], 68 Maple St., Newton, 9/04/86, C, 86001963

House at 7 Salem Street [Wakefield MRA], 7 Salem St., Wakefield, 7/06/89, C, 89000683

House at 729 Dedham Street [Newton MRA], 729 Dedham St., Newton, 9/04/86, C, 86001835

House at 72R Dane Street [Somerville MPS], 72R Dane St., Somerville, 9/18/89, C, 89001254

House at 77 Howard Street [Reading MRA], 77 Howard St., Reading, 7/19/84, C, 84002675

House at 79-81 Salem Street [Reading MRA], 79-81 Salem St., Reading, 7/19/84, C, 84002676

House at 8 Park Street [Wakefield MRA], 8 Park St., Wakefield, 7/06/89, C, 89000689

House at 81 Pearl Street [Somerville MPS], 81 Pearl St., Somerville, 9/18/89, A, C, 89001277

House at 81–83 Gardner Street [Newton MRA], 81–83 Gardner St., Newton, 9/04/86, C, 86001836

House at 88 Prospect Street [Wakefield MRA], 88 Prospect St., Wakefield, 7/06/89, C, 89000737

House at 9 White Avenue [Wakefield MRA], 9 White Ave., Wakefield, 7/06/89, C, 89000677

House at 90 Prospect Street [Wakefield MRA], 90 Prospect St., Wakefield, 7/06/89, C, 89000736

House at 95 Chestnut Street [Wakefield MRA], 95 Chestnut St., Wakefield, 7/06/89, C, 89000725

Houses at 28–36 Beacon Street [Somerville MPS], 28–36 Beacon St., Somerville, 9/18/89, A, C, 89001232

Hovey—Winn House [Winchester MRA], 384 Main St., Winchester, 7/05/89, C, 89000616

Howe Building, 208 Middlesex St., Lowell, 10/12/89, A, C, 89001608

Howe House [Cambridge MRA], 6 Appleton St., Cambridge, 6/30/83, C, 83000811

Howells, William Dean, House [Cambridge MRA], 37 Concord Ave., Cambridge, 4/13/82, B, C, 82001949

Howes, C. G., Dry Cleaning—Carley Real Estate [Newton MRA], 1173 Washington St., Newton, 2/16/90, C, 90000031

Hoyt, Benjamin, House [Cambridge MRA], 134 Otis St., Cambridge, 4/13/82, C, 82001953

Hoyt-Shedd Estate, 386-396 Andover St., 569-579 E. Merrimack St., Lowell, 5/17/84, A, B, C, 84002697

Hubbard Park Historic District [Cambridge MRA], Hubbard Park, Mercer Circle and Sparks Sts., Cambridge, 4/13/82, B, C, 82001950

Hutchins, Oliver, House, 79 Elm St., Chelmsford, 9/05/85, A, C, 85002013

Hutchinson—Blood House [Winchester MRA], 394–396 Main St., Winchester, 7/05/89, C, 89000615

Hyde Avenue Historic District [Newton MRA], 36, 42, 52, 59, and 62 Hyde Ave., Newton, 12/23/86, C, 86001742

Hyde House [Newton MRA], 27 George St., Newton, 9/04/86, B, 86001838

Hyde, Eleazer, House [Newton MRA], 401 Woodward St., Newton, 9/04/86, A, C, 86001839

Hyde, Gershom, House [Newton MRA], 29 Greenwood St., Newton, 9/04/86, C, 86001840

Inman Square Historic District [Cambridge MRA], Hampshire, Cambridge, and Inman Sts., Cambridge, 4/13/82, C, 82001951

Ireland, Samuel, House [Somerville MPS], 117 Washington, Somerville, 9/18/89, C, 89001299

Irving Square Historic District, Irving Square, Waverly, South, Columbia, Irving, Gordon and Hollis Sts., Framingham, 11/30/82, A, C, 82000491

Item Building [Wakefield MRA], 26 Albion St., Wakefield, 7/06/89, A, C, 89000712

Jackson Homestead, 527 Washington St., Newton, 6/04/73, B, C, 73000306

Jackson House [Newton MRA], 125 Jackson St., Newton, 9/04/86, A, C, 86001841

Jackson, Samuel, Jr., House [Newton MRA], 137 Washington St., Newton, 9/04/86, C, 86001843

Jaquith, Abraham, House [First Period Buildings of Eastern Massachusetts TR], 161 Concord Rd., Billerica, 3/14/91, C, 90000166

Jarvis, The [Cambridge MRA], 27 Everett St., Cambridge, 5/19/86, C, 86001308

Jenison, Robert, House, N of Natick off I 90, Natick vicinity, 9/06/78, B, C, 78000456

Jenkins, Franklin B., House [Stoneham MRA], 2 Middle St., Stoneham, 4/13/84, A, B, C, 84002699

Jenkins, Franklin B., House [Stoneham MRA], 35 Chestnut St., Stoneham, 4/13/84, A, B, C, 84002702

Jennison, Joshua, House [Newton MRA], 11 Thornton St., Newton, 9/04/86, C, 86001844

John Eliot Historic District, Eliot, Pleasant, and Auburn Sts., Natick, 6/23/83, A, B, C, D, d, 83000812

Johnson, Edwin C., House [Waltham MRA], 177 Weston St./8 Caldwell St., Waltham, 9/28/89, A, C, 89001522

Johnson, Newell D., House [Waltham MRA], 428 Lexington St., Waltham, 9/28/89, C, 89001564

Johnson—Thompson House [Winchester MRA], 201 Ridge St., Winchester, 7/05/89, A, C, 89000604

Jones Tavern, 128 Main St., Acton, 6/13/86, A, B, C, 86001333

Jones, John, House [Stoneham MRA], 1 Winthrop St., Stoneham, 4/13/84, C, 84002708

Jones, Marshall W., House [Winchester MRA], 326 Highland Ave., Winchester, 7/05/89, C, 89000649

Jones, Thomas W., House [Stoneham MRA], 34 Warren St., Stoneham, 4/13/84, B, C, 84002716

Jones, William R., House [Cambridge MRA], 307 Harvard St., Cambridge, 6/30/83, A, C, 83000813

Jordan, Dr. Charles, House [Wakefield MRA], 9 Jordan Ave., Wakefield, 7/06/89, C, 89000716

Judkins, Amos, House [Newton MRA], 8 Central Ave., Newton, 9/04/86, C, 86001846

Keene, Walter, House [Stoneham MRA], 28 High St., Stoneham, 4/13/84, B, C, 84002719

Kemp Barn [Reading MRA], 186 Summer Ave., Reading, 7/19/84, A, C, 84002721

Kemp Place [Reading MRA], 186 Summer Ave., Reading, 7/19/84, A, C, 84002723

Kendall, Deacon Thomas, House [Wakefield MRA], One Prospect St., Wakefield, 7/06/89, C, 89000742

Kennedy, F. A., Steam Bakery, 129 Franklin St., Cambridge, 1/04/90, A, C, 89002285

Kenney, David, House [Stoneham MRA], 67 Summer St., Stoneham, 4/13/84, A, 84002725

Kensington Park Historic District [Arlington MRA], Roughly bounded by Kensington Park, Brantwood and Kensington Rds., Arlington, 9/27/85, A, C, 85002679

Kessler, William F., House [Newton MRA], 211 Highland St., Newton, 2/16/90, A, C, 90000048

Keyes, Amos, House [Somerville MPS], 12 Adams St., Somerville, 9/18/89, C, b, 89001224

Kidder-Sargent-McCrehan House [Cambridge MRA], 146 Rindge Ave., Cambridge, 4/13/82, C, 82001952

Kimball, W.W., House [Arlington MRA], 13 Winter St., Arlington, 4/18/85, A, C, 85001039

King House [Newton MRA], 328 Brookline St., Newton, 9/04/86, A, B, C, 86001847

Kingsbury House [Newton MRA], 137 Suffolk St., Newton, 9/04/86, B, C, b, 86001848

Kingsley, Chester, House [Cambridge MRA], 10 Chester St., Cambridge, 4/13/82, C, 82001954

Middlesex County—Continued

Kirkland Place Historic District [Cambridge MRA], Kirkland Pl., Cambridge, 5/19/86, C, 86001683

Kistler House [Newton MRA], 945 Beacon St., Newton, 9/04/86, C, 86001849

Knight, R. A.—Eugene Lacount House [Somerville MPS], 34 Day St., Somerville, 9/18/89, C, 89001256

Lake Cochituate Dam [Water Supply System of Metropolitan Boston MPS], NW side of Lake Cochituate, Framingham, 1/18/90, A, C, 89002250

Lakeside Cemetery Chapel [Wakefield MRA], North Ave., Wakefield, 7/06/89, C, a, 89000745

Lamson, Newton, House [Stoneham MRA], 33 Chestnut St., Stoneham, 4/13/84, A, C, 84002727

Lamson, Rufus, House [Cambridge MRA], 72-74 Hampshire St., Cambridge, 4/13/82, C, 82001955

Lane, David, House, 147 North Rd., Bedford, 4/02/80, B, C, 80000644

Lane, Job, House, 295 North St., Bedford, 5/08/73, A, C, 73000278

Langmaid Building [Somerville MPS], 48–52 Highland Ave., Somerville, 9/18/89, A, C, 89001259

Langmaid Terrace [Somerville MPS], 359–365 Broadway, Somerville, 9/18/89, A, C, 89001237

Larches, The [Cambridge MRA], 22 Larch Rd., Cambridge, 4/13/82, C, b, 82001956

Larrabee's Brick Block, 500-504 Main St., Melrose, 3/29/84, A, B, C, 84002729

Lasell Neighborhood Historic District [Newton MRA], Roughly bounded by Woodland and Studio Rds., Aspen and Seminary Aves., and Grove St., Newton, 9/04/86, A, C, 86001744

Lawrence Light Guard Armory, 90 High St., Medford, 3/10/75, A, B, C, 75000277

Lawrence, Phineas, House, 257 Trapelo Rd., Waltham, 8/20/87, A, B, C, 87001397

Lawton Place Historic District [Waltham MRA], Lawton Pl. between Amory Rd. and Jackson St., Waltham, 9/28/89, A, C, b, 89001504

Lechmere Point Corporation Houses [Cambridge MRA], 45-51 Gore St. and 25 3rd St., Cambridge, 4/13/82, A, C, 82001957

Leland, Deacon William, House [Sherborn MRA], 27 Hollis St., Sherborn, 1/03/86, A, C, 86000503

Lewis House [Reading MRA], 276 Woburn St., Reading, 7/19/84, C, b, 84002741

Lewis, Charles D., House [Sherborn MRA], 81 Hunting Ln., Sherborn, 1/03/86, A, C, 86000504

Lexington Green, Massachusetts and Hancock Sts., Lexington, 10/15/66, A, f, NHL, 66000767

Libby, Nelson F., House [Waltham MRA], 147–149 Weston St., Waltham, 9/28/89, C, 89001521

Lincoln Center Historic District, Bedford, Lincoln, Old Lexington, Sandy Pond, Trapelo & Weston Rds., Lincoln, 7/18/85, A, B, C, a, 85001604

Linden Street Bridge [Waltham MRA], Boston & Maine Railroad over Linden St., Waltham, 9/28/89, A, C, 89001515

Little, Arthur D., Inc., Building, Memorial Dr., Cambridge, 12/08/76, A, B, NHL, 76001970

Littlefield—Roberts House [Cambridge MRA], 16 Prescott St., Cambridge, 9/12/86, C, 86002070

Locke School [Arlington MRA], 88 Parke Ave., Arlington, 9/27/85, C, 85002684

Locke, Asa, House [Winchester MRA], 68 High St., Winchester, 7/05/89, A, C, 89000631

Locke, Capt. Benjamin, House, 21 Appleton St., Arlington, 7/21/78, B, 78000432

Locke, Capt. Josiah, House, 195 High St., Winchester, 3/02/79, C, 79000356

Locke, Lt. Benjamin, Store [Arlington MRA], 11–13 Lowell St., Arlington, 4/18/85, A, C, 85001068

Locke-Baldwin-Kinsley House [Stoneham MRA], 45 Green St., Stoneham, 4/13/84, A, C, 84002742

Lockhardt, Charles H., House [Somerville MPS], 88 College Ave., Somerville, 9/18/89, C, 89001249

Longfellow National Historic Site, 105 Brattle St., Cambridge, 10/15/66, A, B, C, NHL, NPS, 66000049

Lord's Castle [Waltham MRA], 211 Hammond St., Waltham, 9/28/89, C, 89001567

Loring, George, House [Somerville MPS], 76 Highland Ave., Somerville, 9/18/89, A, C, 89001263

Lovejoy, A. L., House [Somerville MPS], 30 Warren Ave., Somerville, 9/18/89, A, C, 89001297

Lovell Block [Cambridge MRA], 1853 Massachusetts Ave., Cambridge, 6/30/83, C, 83000814

Lovering, Joseph, House [Cambridge MRA], 38 Kirkland St., Cambridge, 9/12/86, B, C, 86002076

Lowell Locks and Canals Historic District, Between Middlesex St. and the Merrimack River, Lowell, 8/13/76, A, C, NHL, NPS, 76001972

Lowell National Historical Park, Merrimack St., Lowell, 6/05/78, A, C, NPS, 78003149

Lowell School [Cambridge MRA], 25 Lowell St., Cambridge, 4/13/82, A, C, 82001958

Lowell, The [Cambridge MRA], 33 Lexington Ave., Cambridge, 6/30/83, C, 83000815

Luke, Arthur F., House [Newton MRA], 221 Prince St., Newton, 2/16/90, A, C, 90000042

Lyman Street Historic District [Waltham MRA], Roughly Lyman St. from Church to Main Sts., Waltham, 9/28/89, A, C, b, 89001505

Lynnwood [Wakefield MRA], 5 Linden Ave., Wakefield, 7/06/89, A, C, 89000705

Lyon, T.U., House [Stoneham MRA], 9 Warren St., Stoneham, 4/13/84, C, 84002743

Mann, James H., House [Winchester MRA], 23 Hancock St., Winchester, 7/05/89, A, C, 89000624

Manning Manse, 56 Chelmsford Rd., Billerica, 8/11/82, A, B, C, 82001912

Manning, Charles, House [Reading MRA], 145 Salem St., Reading, 7/19/84, B, C, 84002744

Manning, Jacob, House [Reading MRA], 140 High St., Reading, 7/19/84, B, C, 84002745

Manning, Joseph K., House, 35–37 Forest St., Medford, 4/07/89, C, 88000712

Maple Avenue Historic District [Cambridge MRA], Maple Ave. between Marie Ave. and Broadway, Cambridge, 6/30/83, C, 83000816

Martin, Aaron, House [Waltham MRA], 786 Moody St., Waltham, 9/28/89, A, C, 89001540

Martin, Aaron, Houses [Waltham MRA], 188–194 Adams St., Waltham, 9/28/89, A, C, 89001486

Mason, John, House [Winchester MRA], 8–10 Hillside Ave., Winchester, 7/05/89, A, C, 89000634

Mason, John, House [First Period Buildings of Eastern Massachusetts TR], 1303 Massachusetts Ave., Lexington, 3/09/90, C, 90000172

Mason, Josiah, Jr., House [Cambridge MRA], 11 Market St., Cambridge, 4/13/82, C, 82001959

Mason, W. A., House [Cambridge MRA], 87 Raymond St., Cambridge, 6/30/83, B, 83000817

Masonic Block [Reading MRA], 600-622 Main St., Reading, 9/19/84, A, C, 84002746

Massachusetts Hall, Harvard University, Harvard University Yard, Cambridge, 10/15/66, A, NHL, 66000769

Massachusetts State Armory [Wakefield MRA], Main St., Wakefield, 7/06/89, C, 89000707

Maxwell, Louis N., House [Winchester MRA], 16 Herrick St., Winchester, 7/05/89, C, 89000650

McCune Site, Address Restricted, Lincoln vicinity, 1/23/86, D, 86000115

McGill, John H., House, 56 Vernon St., Medford, 4/09/80, A, C, 80000640

McLean, Isaac, House [Cambridge MRA], 2218 Massachusetts Ave., Cambridge, 4/13/82, C, 82001960

Mead, Alpheus, House [Cambridge MRA], 2200 Massachusetts Ave., Cambridge, 4/13/82, C, 82001961

Medford Pipe Bridge [Water Supply System of Metropolitan Boston MPS], Over the Mystic River, between S. Court St. and Mystic Ave., Medford, 1/18/90, C, 89002253

Meeting House of the Second Parish in Woburn [First Period Buildings of Eastern Massachusetts TR], 12 Lexington St., Burlington, 3/09/90, C, a, 90000167

Melrose Public Library, 63 W. Emerson St., Melrose, 6/23/88, A, C, 88000909

Melrose Town Center Historic District, Main St., Melrose, 4/01/82, A, C, a, 82002744

Melvin, Isaac, House [Cambridge MRA], 19 Centre St., Cambridge, 4/13/82, C, 82001962

Memorial Drive Apartments Historic District [Cambridge MRA], 983–984, 985–986, 987–989, and 992–993 Memorial Dr., Cambridge, 5/19/86, C, 86001310

Memorial Hall, Harvard University, Cambridge and Quincy Sts., Harvard University campus, Cambridge, 12/30/70, C, f, NHL, 70000685

Merriam, Galen, House [Newton MRA], 102 Highland St., Newton, 9/04/86, C, 86001850

Merrimack—Middle Streets Historic District (Boundary Increase), Merrimack, Middle, Prescott, Central and Market Sts., Lowell, 7/15/88, A, C, 88000971

Metropolitan District Commission Pumping House [Stoneham MRA], Woodland Rd., Stoneham, 4/13/84, A, C, 84002747

Middlesex Canal, Running SE between towns of Lowell and Woburn, Woburn, 8/21/72, A, C, 72000117

Middlesex County—Continued

Middlesex Fells Reservoirs Historic District [Water Supply System of Metropolitan Boston MPS], Roughly bounded by Pond St., Woodland Rd., I-93, and MA 28, Stoneham, 1/18/90, A, C, 89002249

Milestone [Arlington MRA], Appleton St. and Paul Revere Rd., Arlington, 9/27/85, A, b, 85002683

Millard-Souther-Green House [Stoneham MRA], 218 Green St., Stoneham, 4/13/84, C, 84002752

Minute Man National Historical Park, From Concord to Lexington on MA 2A, Concord vicinity, 10/15/66, A, C, f, NPS, 66000935

Mitchell, Amy B., House [Winchester MRA], 237 Highland Ave., Winchester, 7/05/89, C, 89000653

Monadnock Road Historic District [Newton MRA], Roughly Monadnock Rd., Wachusett Rd., Hudson St., Tudor Rd., Beacon St., and Hobart Rd., Newton, 2/16/90, A, C, 90000019

Montrose, The [Cambridge MRA], 1648 Massachusetts Ave., Cambridge, 5/19/86, A, C, 86001311

Moody Street Fire Station [Waltham MRA], 533 Moody St., Waltham, 9/28/89, A, C, 89001541

Moody Street Historic District [Waltham MRA], Moody and Crescent Sts., Waltham, 3/09/90, A, C, 89001502

Moore House [Winchester MRA], 85 Walnut St., Winchester, 7/05/89, A, C, 89000620

Morse, Daniel, III, House [Sherborn MRA], 210 Farm Rd., Sherborn, 1/03/86, A, C, 86000505

Morse—Barber House [Sherborn MRA], 46 Forest St., Sherborn, 1/03/86, A, C, 86000493

Morse—Tay—Leland—Hawes House [Sherborn MRA], 266 Western Ave., Sherborn, 1/03/86, A, C, 86000506

Morton Road Historic District [Newton MRA], Morton Rd. at Morton St., Newton, 2/16/90, A, C, 90000010

Mossman, Col. Adelbert, House, 76 Park St., Hudson, 9/30/82, B, C, 82001904

Mount Auburn Cemetery, 580 Mount Auburn St., Cambridge, 4/21/75, C, d, 75000254

Mount Auburn Cemetery Reception House [Cambridge MRA], 583 Mt. Auburn St., Cambridge, 6/30/83, A, C, 83000818

Mount Feake Cemetery [Waltham MRA], 203 Prospect St., Waltham, 9/28/89, A, C, d, 89001497

Mount Pleasant [Newton MRA], 15 Bracebridge Rd., Newton, 9/04/86, B, C, 86001851

Mt. Prospect School for Boys [Waltham MRA], 90 Worcester Ln., Waltham, 3/09/90, A, C, 89001525

Mt. Vernon Street Historic District [Somerville MPS], 8–24 Mt. Vernon St., Somerville, 9/18/89, A, C, 89001223

Munroe, Robert, House [Somerville MPS], 37 Walnut St., Somerville, 9/18/89, C, 89001294

Murray, Robert, House [Waltham MRA], 85 Crescent St., Waltham, 9/28/89, C, 89001580

Mystic Dam [Water Supply System of Metropolitan Boston MPS], Between Lower and Upper Mystic Lakes, Winchester, 1/18/90, C, 89002282

Mystic Gatehouse [Water Supply System of Metropolitan Boston MPS], E of Edgewater Pl. on SE end of Upper Mystic Lake, Winchester, 1/18/90, A, C, 89002284

Mystic Pumping Station [Water Supply System of Metropolitan Boston MPS], Alewife Brook Pkwy., Somerville, 1/18/90, C, 89002255

Mystic Water Works [Somerville MPS], Alewife Brook Pkwy. and Capen St., Somerville, 9/18/89, C, 89001227

Natick Center Historic District, North Ave., Main, Central, and Summer Sts., Natick, 12/16/77, A, C, a, 77000186

Needham Street Bridge [Newton MRA], Needham St. at Charles River, Newton, 9/04/86, C, 86001852

Newman, Andrew, House [Cambridge MRA], 23 Fairmont St., Cambridge, 4/13/82, C, 82001963

Newton Centre Branch Library [Newton MRA], 1294 Centre St., Newton, 2/16/90, A, C, 90000024

Newton City Hall and War Memorial [Newton MRA], 1000 Commonwealth Ave., Newton, 2/16/90, A, C, 90000020

Newton Cottage Hospital Historic District [Newton MRA], 2014 Washington St., Newton, 2/21/90, A, C, 90000108

Newton Highlands Historic District [Newton MRA], Roughly bounded by Lincoln and Hartford Sts., Erie Ave., and Woodward St., Newton, 9/04/86, A, B, C, 86001747

Newton Highlands Historic District (Boundary Increase) [Newton MRA], Roughly Lincoln St., Hartford St., Erie Ave., and Woodward St., Newton, 2/16/90, A, C, 90000013

Newton Lower Falls Historic District [Newton MRA], Roughly bounded by Hagar, Grove, Washington, and Concord Sts., Newton, 9/04/86, A, C, 86001748

Newton Street Bridge [Waltham MRA], Newton St. at River St. over the Charles River, Waltham, 9/28/89, A, C, 89001539

Newton Street Railway Carbarn [Newton MRA], 1121 Washington St., Newton, 9/04/86, A, C, 86001855

Newton Theological Institution Historic District [Newton MRA], Roughly bounded by Braeland Ave., Ripley St. and Langley Rd., Bowdoin School Access Rd., and Cypress St., Newton, 9/04/86, A, C, 86001749

Newton Upper Falls Historic District [Newton MRA], Roughly bounded by Boylston, Elliot, and Oak Sts., and the Charles River, Newton, 9/04/86, A, B, C, 86001750

Newtonville Historic District [Newton MRA], Roughly bounded by Highland Ave., Walnut Mill St., Otis St., and Lowell Ave., Newton, 9/04/86, A, C, 86001753

Newtonville Historic District (Boundary Increase) [Newton MRA], Roughly Highland and Lowell Aves., Otis St., and Birch Hill Rd., and Walnut St. from Newtonville to Washington, Newton, 2/16/90, A, C, 90000014

Nichols House [Newton MRA], 140 Sargent St., Newton, 9/04/86, C, 86001857

Nichols, Daniel, Homestead [Reading MRA], 434 Haverhill St., Reading, 7/19/84, A, C, 84002753

Nichols, James, House [Reading MRA], 273 Pearl St., Reading, 7/19/84, A, C, 84002755

Nichols, Jerry, Tavern [Reading MRA], 51 Mill St., Reading, 7/19/84, B, C, 84002757

Nichols, John F., House [Somerville MPS], 17 Summit St., Somerville, 9/18/89, C, 89001285

Nichols, Richard, House [Reading MRA], 483 Franklin St., Reading, 7/19/84, C, 84002760

Niles, Louville V., House [Somerville MPS], 97 Munroe St., Somerville, 9/18/89, C, 89001276

Niles, Louville, House [Somerville MPS], 45 Walnut St., Somerville, 9/18/89, A, C, 89001295

Nobility Hill Historic District [Stoneham MRA], Roughly bounded by Chestnut and Maple Sts. and Cedar Ave., Stoneham, 2/09/90, A, C, 89002328

Norfolk Street Historic District [Cambridge MRA], Norfolk St. between Suffolk and Austin Sts., Cambridge, 4/13/82, C, 82001964

North Avenue Congregational Church [Cambridge MRA], 183 Massachusetts Ave., Cambridge, 6/30/83, A, C, 83000819

North Lexington Street Historic District [Waltham MRA], 508–536 N. Lexington St., Waltham, 9/28/89, A, C, 89001500

Noyes, Charles W., House [Newton MRA], 271 Chestnut St., Newton, 2/16/90, A, C, 90000030

Noyes, J.A., House [Cambridge MRA], 1 Highland St., Cambridge, 4/13/82, C, 82001965

Noyes—Parris House [First Period Buildings of Eastern Massachusetts TR], 204 Old Connecticut Path, Wayland, 3/09/90, C, 90000187

O'Hara Waltham Dial Company [Waltham MRA], 74 Rumford Ave., Waltham, 9/28/89, A, C, 89001533

Oak Knoll [Winchester MRA], 39 Oak Knoll, Winchester, 7/05/89, B, C, 89000648

Oakes, Edward, House, 5 Sylvia Rd., Medford, 4/09/80, C, b, 80000639

Octagon House [Reading MRA], 97 Pleasant St., Reading, 7/19/84, B, C, 84002762

Odd Fellows Building, 442 Main St., Malden, 12/22/88, C, 87002564

Odd Fellows Hall [Cambridge MRA], 536 Massachusetts Ave., Cambridge, 4/13/82, A, C, 82001967

Oddfellows Building [Stoneham MRA], Central Square, Stoneham, 4/13/84, A, C, 84002765

Olcott, John E., House [Waltham MRA], 35–37 Central St., Waltham, 9/28/89, C, 89001492

Old Burying Ground [Stoneham MRA], Pleasant and William Sts., Stoneham, 4/13/84, A, d, 84002766

Old Cambridge Baptist Church [Cambridge MRA], 398 Harvard St., Cambridge, 4/13/82, C, a, b, 82001968

Old Cambridge Historic District [Cambridge MRA], Irregular pattern along Brattle St., Cambridge, 6/30/83, A, C, g, 83000821

Old Cambridgport Historic District [Cambridge MRA], Cherry, Harvard and Washington Sts., Cambridge, 6/30/83, A, C, 83000820

Middlesex County—Continued

Old Cemetery [Somerville MPS], Somerville Ave. and School St., Somerville, 9/18/89, A, C, d, 89001301

Old Chelmsford Garrison House Complex, 105 Garrison Rd., Chelmsford, 5/08/73, C, 73000289

Old Chestnut Hill Historic District [Newton MRA], Along Hammond St. and Chestnut Hill Rd. roughly bounded by Beacon St. and Essex Rd., and Suffolk Rd., Newton, 9/04/86, C, 86001756

Old Chestnut Hill Historic District (Boundary Increase) [Newton MRA], Roughly Chestnut Hill, Essex, and Gate House; Middlesex, Hammond, and Longwood; and Suffolk and Old Orchard, Newton, 2/16/90, A, C, a, 90000007

Old Harvard Yard, Massachusetts Ave. and Cambridge St., Cambridge, 2/06/73, A, C, 73000287

Old Hose House [Reading MRA], 1249 Main St., Reading, 7/19/84, A, C, 84002769

Old Manse, Monument St., Concord, 10/15/66, B, NHL, 66000775

Old Medford High School, 22-24 Forest St., Medford, 10/06/83, A, C, 83004068

Old Schwamb Mill, 17 Mill Lane and 29 Lowell St., Arlington, 10/07/71, A, 71000081

Old Shephard Farm [Newton MRA], 1832 Washington St., Newton, 9/04/86, B, C, b, 86001859

Old Ship Street Historic District, Both sides of Pleasant St. from Riverside Ave. to Park St., Medford, 4/14/75, A, C, 75000279

Old Town Bridge, N of Weyland on MA 27, Weyland vicinity, 5/02/75, A, C, 75000292

Opposition House [Cambridge MRA], 2-4 Hancock Pl., Cambridge, 4/13/82, A, B, C, b, 82001969

Orchard House, Lexington Rd., Concord, 10/15/66, B, NHL, 66000781

Orne, Sarah, House [Cambridge MRA], 10 Coolidge Hill Rd., Cambridge, 6/30/83, C, 83000822

Orvis Road Historic District [Arlington MRA], Roughly bounded by Massachsetts Ave., Freeman, Randolph and Newcomb Sts. on Orvis Rd., Arlington, 9/27/85, A, C, 85002677

Otis—Wyman House [Somerville MPS], 67 Thurston St., Somerville, 9/18/89, A, C, 89001289

Our Lady Help of Christians Historic District [Newton MRA], Adams and Washington Sts., Newton, 9/04/86, A, C, a, 86001758

Oxford, The [Waltham MRA], 4 Adams St., Waltham, 9/28/89, A, C, 89001483

Page, Christopher, House [First Period Buildings of Eastern Massachusetts TR], 50 Old Billerica Rd., Bedford, 3/09/90, C, 90000163

Page, H. P., House [Newton MRA], 110 Jewett St., Newton, 9/04/86, C, 86001860

Page, Nathaniel, House, 89 Page Rd., Bedford, 3/29/78, A, C, b, 78000433

Paine, Robert Treat, Jr., House, 577 Beaver St., Waltham, 10/07/75, B, C, b, NHL, 75000291

Park Street Railroad Station, 20 Magoun Ave., Medford, 4/21/75, A, C, 75000280

Parker House [Reading MRA], 52 Salem St., Reading, 7/19/84, C, 84002774

Parker House [Reading MRA], 316 Haven St., Reading, 7/19/84, C, 84002778

Parker House [Winchester MRA], 180 Mystic Valley Pkwy., Winchester, 7/05/89, C, 89000628

Parker Tavern [Reading MRA (AD)], 103 Washington St., Reading, 8/19/75, A, B, C, 75000286

Parker, Capt. Nathaniel, Red House [Reading MRA], 77-83 Ash St., Reading, 7/19/84, B, C, 84002772

Parker, Edmund, Jr., House [Winchester MRA], 287 Cambridge St., Winchester, 7/05/89, A, C, 89000610

Parker, Harrison, Sr., House [Winchester MRA], 60 Lloyd St., Winchester, 7/05/89, B, C, b, 89000627

Parker, James, House, R.R. 1, Box 30 Center Rd., Shirley, 2/25/88, A, C, 88000163

Parker, Joseph, House [Reading MRA], 107 Grove St., Reading, 7/19/84, C, 84002781

Parker, Samuel, House [Reading MRA], 132 West St., Reading, 7/19/84, B, C, 84002783

Parker, Stillman, House [Reading MRA], 484 Summer Ave., Reading, 7/19/84, B, C, 84002785

Parker, William, House [Reading MRA], 55 Walnut St., Reading, 7/19/84, B, C, a, 84002791

Parker—Burnett House [Somerville MPS], 48 Vinal Ave., Somerville, 9/18/89, A, C, 89001291

Parkman Tavern, S of Concord at 20 Powder Mill Rd., Concord vicinity, 6/19/79, A, C, 79000358

Parsonage, The, 16 Pleasant St., Natick, 11/11/71, B, a, NHL, 71000903

Parsons, Edward, House [Newton MRA], 56 Cedar St., Newton, 9/04/86, C, 86001862

Peabody Court Apartments [Cambridge MRA], 41–43 Linnaean St., Cambridge, 5/19/86, C, 86001312

Peabody—Williams House [Newton MRA], 7 Norman Rd., Newton, 9/04/86, C, 86001863

Peck, John M., House [Waltham MRA], 27 Liberty St., Waltham, 9/28/89, A, C, 89001559

Peirce School, 88 Chestnut St., Newton, 12/06/79, A, C, 79000357

Pest House, 153 Fairhaven Rd., Concord, 4/18/77, A, 77000174

Pierce Farm Historic District [Arlington MRA], Roughly bounded by Claremont and Oakland Aves., Arlington, 9/27/85, A, C, 85002678

Pierce House [Reading MRA], 128 Salem St., Reading, 7/19/84, B, C, 84002794

Pierce Organ Pipe Factory [Reading MRA], 10-12 Pierce St., Reading, 7/19/84, B, C, 84002795

Pierce, F. Lincoln, Houses [Newton MRA], 231–237 Mill St., Newton, 2/16/90, A, C, 90000041

Piety Corner Historic District [Waltham MRA], Roughly Bacon and Lexington Sts., Waltham, 3/09/90, A, C, a, 89001499

Pine Ridge Road—Plainfield Street Historic District [Newton MRA], Roughly Pine Ridge Rd., Upland Rd., Plainfield St., and Chestnut St., Newton, 2/16/90, A, C, 90000015

Pleasant Street Congregational Church, 75 Pleasant St., Arlington, 6/23/83, A, C, a, 83000823

Pleasant Street Historic District, Irregular Pattern along Pleasant St., Belmont, 6/12/79, A, C, 79000353

Pleasant Street School, Pleasant St., Ayer, 1/23/86, A, C, 86000094

Plummer Memorial Library [Newton MRA], 375 Auburn St., Newton, 2/16/90, A, C, 90000036

Porcellian Club [Cambridge MRA], 1320-24 Massachusetts Ave., Cambridge, 6/30/83, A, C, 83000824

Potter Estate [Newton MRA], 65–71 Walnut Pk., Newton, 12/23/86, C, 86001864

Potter—O'Brian House [Waltham MRA], 206 Newton St., Waltham, 9/28/89, A, C, 89001538

Powder House Park, Powder House Circle, Somerville, 4/21/75, A, C, 75000287

Pratt House [Reading MRA], 456 Haverhill St., Reading, 7/19/84, C, 84002797

Pratt, Dexter, House, 54 Brattle St., Cambridge, 5/08/73, A, C, 73000288

Pratt, Miles, House, 106 Mt. Auburn St., Watertown, 5/09/85, B, C, 85000980

Pratt, Stillman, House [Reading MRA], 472 Summer Ave., Reading, 7/19/84, C, 84002799

Prentiss, William, House [Arlington MRA], 252 Gray St., Arlington, 9/27/85, C, 85002685

Prentiss-Payson House [Arlington MRA], 224–226 Pleasant St., Arlington, 4/18/85, C, 85001040

Prescott Estate [Newton MRA], 770 Centre St., Newton, 9/04/86, C, 86001866

Prescott, Gustavus G., House [Somerville MPS], 65–67 Perkins St., Somerville, 9/18/89, C, 89001278

Pressey—Eustis House [Winchester MRA], 14 Stevens St., Winchester, 7/05/89, C, 89000623

Proctor, John, House, 218 Concord Rd., Westford, 2/04/93, A, C, 93000011

Proctor, William, House [Arlington MRA], 390 Massachusetts Ave., Arlington, 4/18/85, C, 85001041

Prospect Congregational Church [Cambridge MRA], 99 Prospect St., Cambridge, 4/13/82, C, a, 82001970

Prospect House [Waltham MRA], 11 Hammond St., Waltham, 9/28/89, A, C, 89001568

Putnam Street Historic District [Newton MRA], Roughly bounded by Winthrop, Putnam, Temple, and Shaw Sts., Newton, 9/04/86, A, C, 86001760

Putnam, Rev. Daniel, House [First Period Buildings of Eastern Massachusetts TR], 27 Bow St., North Reading, 3/09/90, C, 90000176

Railroad Hotel [Newton MRA], 1273–1279 Washington St., Newton, 9/04/86, A, C, 86001868

Rawson Estate [Newton MRA], 41 Vernon St., Newton, 9/04/86, C, 86001869

Rawson, Warren, Building [Arlington MRA], 68–74 Franklin St., Arlington, 9/27/85, A, C, 85002686

Rawson, Warren, House [Arlington MRA], 37–49 Park St., Arlington, 4/18/85, A, C, 85001042

Read, Cheney, House [Cambridge MRA], 135 Western Ave., Cambridge, 4/13/82, C, 82001971

Reading Municipal Building [Reading MRA], 49 Pleasant St., Reading, 7/19/84, C, 84002810

Reading Municipal Light and Power Station [Reading MRA], 226 Ash St., Reading, 7/19/84, A, C, 84002811

Middlesex County—Continued

Reading Standpipe [Reading MRA], Auburn and Beacon Sts., Reading, 2/01/85, C, 85000549

Reardon, Edmund, House [Cambridge MRA], 195 Erie St., Cambridge, 4/13/82, C, 82001972

Red Top, 90 Somerset St., Belmont, 11/11/71, B, NHL, 71000911

Remick, Joseph, House [Winchester MRA], 84 Cambridge St./4 Swan Rd., Winchester, 7/05/89, C, 89000656

Reversible Collar Company Building [Cambridge MRA], 25–27 Mt. Auburn & 10–12 Arrow Sts., Cambridge, 9/27/85, A, C, 85002663

Rice, Capt. Peter, House, 377 Elm St., Marlborough, 4/09/80, A, C, 80000641

Richards, James Lorin, House [Newton MRA], 47 Kirkstall and 22 Oakwood Rds., Newton, 9/04/86, C, 86001871

Richards, Theodore W., House, 15 Follen St., Cambridge, 1/07/76, B, NHL, 76001999

Richardson, Dr. S. O., House [Wakefield MRA], 694 Main St., Wakefield, 7/06/89, C, b, 89000696

Richardson, Zachariah, House [Winchester MRA], 597 Washington St., Winchester, 7/05/89, A, C, b, 89000618

Riley, Charles, House [Newton MRA], 93 Bellevue St., Newton, 9/04/86, A, C, 86001872

River Street Firehouse [Cambridge MRA], 176 River St., Cambridge, 4/13/82, C, 82001973

Riverside Concrete Company—Lamont's Market [Newton MRA], 2 Charles St., Newton, 2/16/90, C, 90000029

Robbins, George, House [First Period Buildings of Eastern Massachusetts TR], 523 Curve St., Carlisle, 3/09/90, C, D, 90000168

Robbins, Royal E., School [Waltham MRA], 58 Chestnut St., Waltham, 9/28/89, A, C, 89001496

Roberts House [Reading MRA], 59 Prospect St., Reading, 7/19/84, C, 84002815

Robindreau, Alfred E., House [Arlington MRA], 28 Lafayette St., Arlington, 4/18/85, C, 85001043

Robinson House [Arlington MRA], 19 Winter St., Arlington, 4/18/85, A, C, 85001044

Robinson-Lewis-G. F. Fessenden House [Arlington MRA], 40 Westminster Ave., Arlington, 4/18/85, C, 85001045

Rowhouses at 256-274 Haven Street [Reading MRA], 256-274 Haven St., Reading, 7/19/84, B, C, 84002817

Royall, Isaac, House, 15 George St., Medford, 10/15/66, C, NHL, 66000786

Rumford, Count, Birthplace, 90 Elm St., Woburn, 5/15/75, B, c, NHL, 75001942

Russell Common [Arlington MRA], 2–10 Park Terrace, Arlington, 4/18/85, A, C, 85001046

Russell, Arthur H., House [Winchester MRA], 10 Mt. Pleasant St., Winchester, 7/05/89, C, 89000652

Russell, Charles, House [Winchester MRA], 993 Main St., Winchester, 7/05/89, B, C, 89000617

Russell, Jason House, 7 Jason St., Arlington, 10/09/74, A, C, 74000363

Russell, Philemon, House [Somerville MPS], 25 Russell St., Somerville, 9/18/89, C, 89001282

Russell, Susan, House [Somerville MPS], 58 Sycamore St., Somerville, 9/18/89, C, 89001286

Sabbath Day House, 20 Andover Rd., Billerica, 8/14/73, A, 73000285

Sacco—Pettee Machine Shops [Newton MRA], 156 Oak St., Newton, 12/23/86, A, C, 86001964

Saco-Lowell Shops Housing Historic District [Newton MRA], Oak, William, Butts, and Saco Sts., Newton, 2/16/90, A, C, 90000016

Sacred Heart Church, Rectory, School and Convent [Cambridge MRA], 6th and Thorndike Sts., Cambridge, 4/13/82, A, C, a, 82001974

Saint John's Episcopal Church, Maynard Rd. and Church St., Framingham, 1/12/90, A, C, a, 89002300

Salem Street Burying Ground, Medford Sq., Medford, 8/27/81, C, d, 81000115

Salem-Auburn Streets Historic District [Cambridge MRA], Salem and Auburn Sts., Cambridge, 4/13/82, C, 82001975

Salisbury, Jonas, House [Newton MRA], 62 Walnut Pk., Newton, 9/04/86, C, 86001875

Salisbury, Jonas, House [Newton MRA], 85 Langley Rd., Newton, 9/04/86, C, 86001876

Sanborn House, 15 High St., Winchester, 12/14/81, B, C, 81000286

Sanborn, Rev. Peter, House [Reading MRA], 55 Lowell St., Reading, 7/19/84, C, 84002819

Sanderson House and Munroe Tavern, 1314 and 1332 Massachusetts Ave., Lexington, 4/26/76, A, 76000248

Sanderson, John, House [Waltham MRA], 562 Lexington St., Waltham, 9/28/89, A, C, 89001563

Sanderson, Nathan, I, House [Waltham MRA], 107 Lincoln St., Waltham, 9/28/89, A, C, 89001556

Sanderson, Nathan, II, House [Waltham MRA], 111 Lincoln St., Waltham, 9/28/89, C, b, 89001513

Sanderson—Clark Farmhouse [Waltham MRA], 75 Lincoln/26 Lincoln Ter., Waltham, 9/28/89, A, C, 89001557

Sands, Hiram, House, 22 Putnam Ave., Cambridge, 4/30/76, A, C, 76000238

Sands, Ivory, House [Cambridge MRA], 145 Elm St., Cambridge, 4/13/82, B, C, 82001976

Sanger, Asa, House [Sherborn MRA], 70 Washington St., Sherborn, 1/03/86, C, 86000507

Sanger, Richard, III, House [Sherborn MRA], 60 Washington St., Sherborn, 1/03/86, A, B, C, 86000508

Saunders, William, House [Cambridge MRA], 6 Prentiss St., Cambridge, 6/30/83, C, b, 83000825

Sawin—Bullen—Bullard House [Sherborn MRA], 60 Brush Hill Rd., Sherborn, 1/03/86, A, C, 86000509

Sawyer, C. A., House (Second) [Newton MRA], 221 Prince St., Newton, 2/16/90, A, C, 90000043

Saxonville Historic District, Roughly, along Elm, Danforth, Central, Water and Concord Sts., Framingham, 8/20/92, A, C, 92000992

Schuebeler, Charles, House [Somerville MPS], 384 Washington St., Somerville, 9/18/89, C, 89001298

Sears Tower—Harvard Observatory [Cambridge MRA], 60 Garden St., Cambridge, 2/26/87, C, 86002075

Second Cambridge Savings Bank Building [Cambridge MRA], 11-21 Dunster St., Cambridge, 6/30/83, C, 83000826

Second Church of Newton [Newton MRA], 60 Highland St., Newton, 2/16/90, A, C, a, 90000049

Second Waterhouse House [Cambridge MRA], 9 Follen St., Cambridge, 6/30/83, C, 83000827

Sever Hall, Harvard University, Harvard Yard, Cambridge, 12/30/70, C, NHL, 70000732

Sewall—Ware House [Sherborn MRA], 100 S. Main St., Sherborn, 1/03/86, A, C, 86000494

Shady Hill Historic District [Cambridge MRA], Roughly bounded by Museum, Beacon and Holden, and Kirkland Sts., and Francis Ave., Cambridge, 5/19/86, A, B, C, 86001680

Sharon House [Winchester MRA], 403 Main St., Winchester, 7/05/89, A, 89000613

Shattuck, Ralph W., House [Arlington MRA], 274–276 Broadway, Arlington, 9/27/85, B, C, 85002687

Shaw, Thomas Mott, Estate, 317 Garfield Rd., Concord, 11/20/87, A, C, 87001395

Sherborn Center Historic District [Sherborn MRA], Roughly bounded by Zion's Ln., Conrail RR tracks, Farm and Sawin Sts., and Washington and N. Main Sts., Sherborn, 1/03/86, A, B, C, a, 86000495

Sherburne, Warren E., House, 11 Percy Rd., Lexington, 12/02/77, C, 77000178

Shirley Center Historic District, Brown, Center, Horsepond, Parker and Whitney Rds., Shirley, 9/01/88, A, C, a, b, d, f, 88001454

Shirley Shaker Village, S of Shirley on Harvard Rd., Shirley vicinity, 5/24/76, A, C, a, 76000271

Shirley Village Historic District, Roughly bounded by Center, Harvard, Leominster and Shaker Rds., Shirley, 1/23/92, A, C, 91001958

Shoe Shop-Doucette Ten Footer [Stoneham MRA], 36 William St., Stoneham, 4/13/84, A, C, 84002821

Simonds Tavern, 331 Bedford St., Lexington, 10/14/76, A, 76000251

Simonds, William, House [Winchester MRA], 420 Main St., Winchester, 7/05/89, A, C, 89000640

Simpson House [Newton MRA], 57 Hunnewell Ave., Newton, 9/04/86, C, 86001880

Simpson, Dr. Thomas, House [Wakefield MRA], 114 Main St., Wakefield, 7/06/89, C, 89000665

Skillings Estate House [Winchester MRA], 37 Rangeley Rd., Winchester, 7/05/89, A, C, 89000645

Slowey, Patrick, House [Cambridge MRA], 73 Bolton St., Cambridge, 4/13/82, C, 82001977

Smith Shoe Shop [Reading MRA], 273 Haverhill St., Reading, 2/01/85, A, C, 85000550

Smith, Curtis S., House [Newton MRA], 56 Fairmont Ave., Newton, 9/04/86, C, 86001881

Smith, Marshall, House [Waltham MRA], 26 Liberty St., Waltham, 9/28/89, A, C, 89001560

Smith, Perez, House [Waltham MRA], 46 Lincoln St., Waltham, 9/28/89, A, C, 89001558

Middlesex County—Continued

Smith—Peterson House [Newton MRA], 32 Farlow Rd., Newton, 9/04/86, C, 86001882

Snow, Lemuel, Jr., House [Somerville MPS], 81 Benton Rd., Somerville, 9/18/89, C, 89001234

Somerville High School [Somerville MPS], 93 Highland St., Somerville, 9/18/89, A, C, 89001261

Somerville Journal Building [Somerville MPS], 8–10 Walnut St., Somerville, 9/18/89, A, C, 89001300

Somerville Theatre [Somerville MRA], 55 Davis Sq., Somerville, 1/26/90, A, C, 89002330

Soule, Lawrence, House [Cambridge MRA], 11 Russell St., Cambridge, 4/13/82, C, 82001978

South Common Historic District, Roughly bounded by Summer, Gorham, Horndike, and Highland Sts., Lowell, 8/10/82, A, C, a, 82001993

South Reading Academy [Wakefield MRA], 7 Foster St., Wakefield, 7/06/89, C, b, 89000713

South School [Stoneham MRA], 9-11 Gerry St., Stoneham, 4/13/84, A, C, 84002828

Souther, John, House [Newton MRA], 43 Fairmont St., Newton, 9/04/86, C, 86001883

Spaulding, Zeb, House [First Period Buildings of Eastern Massachusetts TR], 1044 Lowell Rd., Carlisle, 3/09/90, C, 90000169

Spot Pond Archeological District [Stoneham MRA], Address Restricted, Stoneham vicinity, 7/24/92, A, D, 92000925

Spring Hill Historic District [Somerville MPS], Roughly bounded by Summer, Central, Atherton, and Spring, Somerville, 9/18/89, A, C, 89001222

St. Charles Borromeo Church [Waltham MRA], Hall and Cushing Sts., Waltham, 9/28/89, A, C, a, 89001569

St. James Episcopal Church [Cambridge MRA], 1991 Massachusetts Ave., Cambridge, 6/30/83, A, C, a, 83000828

St. John's Roman Catholic Church [Cambridge MRA], 2270 Massachusetts Ave., Cambridge, 6/30/83, C, a, 83000829

St. Joseph's School [Wakefield MRA], Gould St., Wakefield, 7/06/89, C, a, 89000749

St. Mary's Catholic Church [Winchester MRA], 159 Washington St., Winchester, 7/05/89, A, C, a, 89000625

St. Mary's Church and Cemetery, 258 Concord St., Newton, 4/16/80, C, a, d, 80000637

St. Mary's Roman Catholic Church Complex [Waltham MRA], 133 School St., Waltham, 9/28/89, A, C, a, 89001527

St. Patrick's Church, 284 Suffolk St., Lowell, 1/03/85, A, C, a, 85000027

Stanley, Leonard W., House [Waltham MRA], 23–25 Taylor St., Waltham, 9/28/89, C, 89001509

Stanstead, The [Cambridge MRA], 19 Ware St., Cambridge, 5/19/86, A, C, 86001313

Stanton, Jacob, House [Winchester MRA], 21 Washington St., Winchester, 7/05/89, B, C, b, 89000614

Staples—Crafts—Wiswall Farm [Newton MRA], 1615 Beacon St., Newton, 9/04/86, A, B, 86001884

Stark Building [Waltham MRA], 416–424 Moody St., Waltham, 9/28/89, A, C, 89001542

Stark, Robert M., House [Waltham MRA], 176 Main St., Waltham, 9/28/89, A, C, 89001552

Stearns, Amos, House [Waltham MRA], 1079 Trapelo Rd., Waltham, 9/28/89, A, C, 89001518

Steele, John, House [Stoneham MRA], 2-4 Montvale St., Stoneham, 4/13/84, A, 84002829

Sterling, Ella Mahalla Cutter, House [Arlington MRA], 93 Summer St., Arlington, 4/18/85, C, 85001047

Stewart, Frank H., House [Newton MRA], 41 Montvale Rd., Newton, 2/21/90, A, C, 90000111

Stewart, Henry, House [Waltham MRA], 294 Linden St., Waltham, 9/28/89, A, C, 89001553

Stickney—Shepard House [Cambridge MRA], 11–13 Remington St., Cambridge, 5/19/86, C, 86001315

Stimpson, William, House [Wakefield MRA], 22 Prospect St., Wakefield, 7/06/89, C, 89000741

Stone Building, 735 Massachusetts Ave., Lexington, 4/30/76, A, C, 76000252

Stone, Joseph L., House [Newton MRA], 77–85 Temple St., Newton, 9/04/86, C, 86001889

Stoneham Firestation [Stoneham MRA], Central and Emerson Sts., Stoneham, 4/13/84, C, 84002831

Stoneham Public Library [Stoneham MRA], Main and Maple Sts., Stoneham, 4/13/84, B, C, 84002832

Stoughton, Mary Fisk, House, 90 Brattle St., Cambridge, 6/29/89, C, NHL, 89001246

Stratton, Edward B., House [Newton MRA], 25 Kenmore St., Newton, 2/16/90, A, C, 90000050

Strong's Block [Newton MRA], 1637-1651 Beacon St., Newton, 9/04/86, C, 86001891

Sudbury Aqueduct Linear District [Water Supply System of Metropolitan Boston MPS], Along Sudbury Aqueduct from Farm Pond at Waverly St. to Chestnut Hill Reservoir, Framingham, 1/18/90, A, C, 89002293

Sudbury Center Historic District, Concord and Old Sudbury Rds., Sudbury, 7/14/76, A, C, 76000277

Sudbury Dam Historic District [Water Supply System of Metropolitan Boston MPS], SE end of Sudbury Reservoir off MA 30, Sudbury, 1/18/90, A, C, 89002265

Sullivan, Edward, House [Winchester MRA], 9 Kendall St., Winchester, 7/05/89, A, C, 89000636

Sumner and Gibbs Streets Historic District [Newton MRA], Roughly Sumner St. between Willow St. and Cotswold Terr. and 184 Gibbs St., Newton, 9/04/86, C, 86001762

Swadkins, Thomas, House [Arlington MRA], 160 Westminster Ave., Arlington, 4/18/85, C, 85001048

Swan, Henry, House [Arlington MRA], 418 Massachusetts Ave., Arlington, 9/27/85, C, 85002688

Swasey, James, House [Waltham MRA], 30 Common St., Waltham, 9/28/89, A, C, 89001530

Sweetser, Daniel, House [Wakefield MRA], 458 Lowell St., Wakefield, 7/06/89, A, C, 89000669

Sweetser, Michael, House [Wakefield MRA], 15 Nahant St., Wakefield, 7/06/89, C, b, 89000699

Symmes, Deacon John, House [Winchester MRA], 212–214 Main St., Winchester, 7/05/89, A, C, 89000606

Symmes, Marshall, House [Winchester MRA], 230 Main St., Winchester, 7/05/89, A, C, 89000607

Symmes, Marshall, Tenant House [Winchester MRA], 233 Main St., Winchester, 7/05/89, A, 89000637

Symmes, Stephen, Jr., House [Arlington MRA], 215 Crosby St., Arlington, 4/18/85, C, 85001049

Symonds, Thomas, House [Reading MRA], 320 Haverhill St., Reading, 7/19/84, C, 84002833

Tay, Jesse, House [Stoneham MRA], 51 Elm St., Stoneham, 4/13/84, A, C, 84002834

Taylor Square Firehouse [Cambridge MRA], 113 Garden St., Cambridge, 4/13/82, C, 82001979

Taylor-Dallin House [Arlington MRA], 69 Oakland Ave., Arlington, 9/27/85, B, g, 85002689

Temple Building, 149 Main St., Marlborough, 3/10/83, A, C, 83000830

Temple Israel Cemetery [Wakefield MRA], North Ave., Wakefield, 7/06/89, A, d, 89000753

Temple, Joseph, House [Reading MRA], 42 Chute St., Reading, 7/19/84, B, C, 84002835

Temple, Mark, House [Reading MRA], 141 Sumner Ave., Reading, 7/19/84, C, 84002838

Tenney Homestead [First Period Buildings of Eastern Massachusetts TR], 156 Taylor Rd., Stow, 3/09/90, C, D, 90000181

Thaxter, Celia, House [Newton MRA], 524 California St., Newton, 9/04/86, B, C, 86001892

Thayer House [Newton MRA], 17 Channing St., Newton, 9/04/86, C, 86001893

Thompson, Abijah, House [Winchester MRA], 81 Walnut St., Winchester, 7/05/89, A, C, 89000619

Thoreau-Alcott House, 255 Main St., Concord, 7/12/76, B, 76000247

Tilton, D. Horace, House [Wakefield MRA], 379 Albion St., Wakefield, 7/06/89, C, 89000715

Towle, Loren, Estate [Newton MRA], 785 Centre St., Newton, 2/16/90, C, 90000026

Train, Samuel, House, 342 Winter St., Weston vicinity, 12/12/76, B, C, 76000286

Treadwell—Sparks House [Cambridge MRA], 21 Kirkland St., Cambridge, 9/12/86, B, C, b, 86002078

Trowbridge—Badger House [Winchester MRA], 12 Prospect St., Winchester, 7/05/89, C, 89000647

Tufts, Peter and Oliver, House [Somerville MPS], 78 Sycamore St., Somerville, 9/18/89, A, C, b, 89001287

Tufts, Peter, House, 350 Riverside Ave., Medford, 11/24/68, C, NHL, 68000044

Turnbull, R.P., House [Stoneham MRA], 6 Pine St., Stoneham, 4/13/84, C, 84002839

Twitchell, Joseph, House [Sherborn MRA], 32 Pleasant St., Sherborn, 1/03/86, C, 86000510

Tyler Park Historic District, Roughly bounded by Princeton, Foster, and Pine Sts., Lowell, 8/17/89, A, C, 89001056

Tyler, Frank J., House [Waltham MRA], 238 Linden St., Waltham, 9/28/89, A, C, 89001555

Middlesex County—Continued

Tyng, Col. Jonathan, House, 80 Tyng Rd., Tyngsboro vicinity, 8/19/77, A, B, C, a, c, 77000188

US Post Office, 50 Kearny Sq., Lowell, 3/10/86, C, 86000373

US Post Office—Arlington Main, 10 Court St., Arlington, 6/18/86, A, C, 86001351

US Post Office—Central Square, 770 Massachusetts Ave., Cambridge, 6/18/86, C, 86001343

US Post Office—Lexington Main, 1661 Massachusetts Ave., Lexington, 6/26/86, C, g, 86001377

US Post Office—Medford Main, 20 Forest St., Medford, 6/18/86, A, C, 86001346

US Post Office—Somerville Main, 237 Washington St., Somerville, 5/30/86, C, 86001247

US Post Office—Wakefield Main, 321 Main St., Wakefield, 10/19/87, A, C, 86003439

US Post Office—Waltham Main, 774 Main St., Waltham, 5/30/86, C, 86001248

US Post Office—Winchester Main, 48 Waterfield Rd., Winchester, 10/19/87, A, C, 87001773

US Post Office—Woburn Center Station, 2 Abbott St., Woburn, 10/19/87, A, C, 86003436

Union Railway Car Barn [Cambridge MRA], 613-621 Cambridge St., Cambridge, 4/13/82, A, 82001980

Union Station, 20 Commonwealth Ave., Concord, 3/02/89, A, C, 89000143

Union Street Historic District [Newton MRA], Roughly Union St. between Langley Rd. and Herrick St., and 17-31 Herrick St., Newton, 9/04/86, A, C, 86001763

Unitarian Universalist Church and Parsonage, 141 and 147 High St., Medford, 4/21/75, B, C, a, 75000281

United States Watch Company [Waltham MRA], 256 Charles St., Waltham, 9/28/89, A, C, 89001494

University Hall, Harvard University, Harvard Yard, Cambridge, 12/30/70, C, NHL, 70000736

University Museum [Cambridge MRA], 11-25 Divinity Ave., Cambridge, 9/12/86, A, B, 86002081

Upham, Phineas, House [First Period Buildings of Eastern Massachusetts TR], 255 Upham St., Melrose, 3/09/90, C, D, 90000173

Upper Magazine Street Historic District [Cambridge MRA], Cottage, Magazine, William and Perry Sts., Cambridge, 4/13/82, C, a, 82001981

Urban Rowhouse [Cambridge MRA], 40-48 Pearl St., Cambridge, 4/13/82, A, C, 82001982

Urban Rowhouse [Cambridge MRA], 30-38 Pearl St., Cambridge, 4/13/82, A, C, 82001983

Urban Rowhouse [Cambridge MRA], 26-32 River St., Cambridge, 6/30/83, C, 83000831

Vale, The, Lyman and Beaver Sts., Waltham, 12/30/70, C, NHL, 70000737

Valentine Soap Workers Cottage [Cambridge MRA], 5-7 Cottage St., Cambridge, 6/30/83, A, C, 83000832

Valentine Soap Workers Cottage [Cambridge MRA], 101 Pearl St., Cambridge, 6/30/83, A, C, 83000833

Varnum Building, 401-405 Bridge St., Lowell, 12/19/88, A, C, 88002752

Vaughn, H. G., House [Sherborn MRA], 5 Sparhawk Rd., Sherborn, 1/03/86, A, C, 86000511

Vinal, Albert, House [Cambridge MRA], 325 Harvard St., Cambridge, 6/30/83, C, 83000834

Vinton, Alfred, House [Winchester MRA], 417 Main St., Winchester, 7/05/89, A, C, 89000629

Waban Branch Library [Newton MRA], 1608 Beacon St., Newton, 2/16/90, A, C, 90000037

Wade, John, House, 253 High St., Medford, 6/18/75, B, C, 75000282

Wade, Jonathan, House, 13 Bradlee Rd., Medford, 4/21/75, A, C, 75000283

Waitt Brick Block, 422-424 Main St., Malden, 11/12/82, A, C, 82000492

Wakefield Park [Wakefield MRA], Roughly Park Ave. between Summit Ave. and Chestnut St., Wakefield, 3/02/90, A, C, 89000755

Wakefield Rattan Co. [Wakefield MRA], 134 Water St., Wakefield, 7/06/89, A, C, 89000692

Wakefield Trust Company [Wakefield MRA], 371 Main St., Wakefield, 7/06/89, C, 89000728

Wakefield Upper Depot [Wakefield MRA], 27-29 Tuttle St., Wakefield, 7/06/89, A, C, 89000719

Walcott—Whitney House [First Period Buildings of Eastern Massachusetts TR], 137 Tuttle Ln., Stow, 3/09/90, C, 90000183

Walden Pond, 1.5 mi. S of Concord, Concord vicinity, 10/15/66, B, NHL, 66000790

Walker Home for Missionary Children [Newton MRA], 161-63, 165, 167 Grove Sts., 136, 138, 144 Hancock St., Newton, 6/04/92, A, C, 90000047

Walnut Street School [Reading MRA], 55 Hopkins St., Reading, 7/19/84, A, C, 84002841

Waltham Gas Light Company [Waltham MRA], 2 Cooper St., Waltham, 9/28/89, A, C, 89001506

Waltham Gas and Electric Company Generating Plant [Waltham MRA], 96 Pine St., Waltham, 9/28/89, A, C, 89001537

Waltham High School [Waltham MRA], 55 School St., Waltham, 9/28/89, A, C, 89001531

Waltham Water Works Shop [Waltham MRA], 92 Felton St., Waltham, 9/28/89, A, C, 89001570

Wamesit Canal-Whipple Mill Industrial Complex, 576 Lawrence St., Lowell, 8/11/82, A, B, C, 82001994

Ward, Ephraim, House [Newton MRA], 121 Ward St., Newton, 9/04/86, B, C, 86001894

Ware Hall [Cambridge MRA], 383 Harvard St., Cambridge, 6/30/83, A, C, 83000835

Ware Paper Mill, 2276 Washington St., Newton, 5/22/78, A, 78000458

Ware's Tavern [Sherborn MRA], 113 S. Main St., Sherborn, 1/03/86, A, C, 86000512

Warren Block, 155 Main St., Marlborough, 3/10/83, A, C, 83000836

Warren, Dr. Samuel, House, 432 Cherry St., Newton, 1/03/85, A, C, b, 85000028

Warren, H. M., School [Wakefield MRA], 30 Converse St., Wakefield, 7/06/89, A, C, 89000750

Warren, H., House [Somerville MPS], 205 School St., Somerville, 9/18/89, C, 89001283

Warren, Langford H., House [Cambridge MRA], 6 Garden Terr., Cambridge, 5/19/86, C, 86001317

Warren, Levi, Jr., High School [Newton MRA], 1600 Washington St., Newton, 2/16/90, A, C, 90000032

Warren, Nathan, House [Waltham MRA], 50 Weston St., Waltham, 3/09/90, C, 89001520

Washington Square Historic District, Roughly bounded by Merrimack, Park, Andover, Oak, Harrison, and Willow Sts., Lowell, 8/11/82, A, B, C, 82001995

Watson, Abraham, House [Cambridge MRA], 181-183 Sherman St., Cambridge, 4/13/82, A, B, C, b, 82001984

Wayland Center Historic District, Irregular pattern along both sides of U.S. 20 and MA 27, Wayland, 9/06/74, A, B, C, 74000378

Wayside Inn [Arlington MRA], 393 Massachusetts Ave., Arlington, 9/27/85, A, C, 85002690

Wayside Inn Historic District, Old Boston Post Rd., Sudbury, 4/23/73, B, C, b, e, 73000307

Wayside, The, 455 Lexington Rd., Concord, 7/11/80, A, B, C, NHL, NPS, 80000356

Webster Park Historic District [Newton MRA], Along Webster Pk. and Webster St. between Westwood St. and Oak Ave., Newton, 9/04/86, A, C, 86001764

Wedgemere Historic District [Winchester MRA], Roughly bounded by Foxcroft, Fletcher, Church, and Cambridge, Winchester, 7/05/89, A, C, 89000659

Weeks Junior High School, 7 Hereward Rd., Newton, 10/23/84, A, C, 84000105

Wellington Farm Historic District, 487-500 Wellesley St., Weston, 4/14/88, A, C, 88000426

Wellington, Benjamin, House [Waltham MRA], 56 Whittier St., Waltham, 9/28/89, A, C, 89001523

Wellington, William, House [Waltham MRA], 785 Trapelo Rd., Waltham, 9/28/89, A, C, 89001512

Wellington—Castner House [Waltham MRA], 685 Trapelo Rd., Waltham, 9/28/89, A, C, 89001511

Wells, Charles, House [Reading MRA], 99 Prescott St., Reading, 7/19/84, C, 84002842

West Newton Hill Historic District [Newton MRA], Roughly bounded by Highland Ave., Lenox, Hampshire, and Chestnut Sts., Newton, 9/04/86, A, C, 86001766

West Newton Village Center Historic District [Newton MRA], Roughly Washington St. from Putnam to Davis Ct., Newton, 2/16/90, A, C, 90000017

West Schoolhouse, Shawsheen Ave. at Aldrich Rd., Wilmington, 2/21/90, A, C, 90000144

West Somerville Branch Library [Somerville MPS], 40 College Ave., Somerville, 9/18/89, A, C, 89001248

West Ward School [Wakefield MRA], 39 Prospect St., Wakefield, 7/06/89, A, C, 89000748

Weston Aqueduct Linear District [Water Supply System of Metropolitan Boston MPS], Along Weston Aqueduct from Sudbury Reservoir to Weston Reservoir, Weston, 1/18/90, A, C, 89002274

Weston, Ephraim, House [Reading MRA], 224 West St., Reading, 7/19/84, B, C, 84002845

Weston, Jabez, House [Reading MRA], 86 West St., Reading, 7/19/84, C, 84002846

Middlesex County—Continued

Wetherbee House [Waltham MRA], 357 Crescent St., Waltham, 9/28/89, A, C, 89001575

Wheat, Samuel, House [Newton MRA], 399 Waltham St., Newton, 9/04/86, B, C, 86001895

Wheeler-Merriam House, 477 Virginia Rd., Concord, 11/26/82, A, C, 82000493

White, S. B., House [Winchester MRA], 8 Stevens St., Winchester, 7/05/89, C, 89000622

White, Warren, House [Waltham MRA], 192 Warren St., Waltham, 9/28/89, C, 89001519

Whitney—Farrington—Cook House [Waltham MRA], 385 Trapelo Rd., Waltham, 9/28/89, A, C, 89001510

Whittemore House [Arlington MRA], 267 Broadway, Arlington, 4/18/85, C, 85001050

Whittemore's Tavern [Newton MRA], 473 Auburn St., Newton, 9/04/86, A, C, 86001896

Wildwood Cemetery [Winchester MRA], Palmer and Wildwood Sts., Winchester, 7/05/89, C, d, 89000658

Wiley, Caleb, House [Stoneham MRA], 125 North St., Stoneham, 4/13/84, C, 84002848

Williams, Charles, House [Somerville MPS], 108 Cross St., Somerville, 9/18/89, A, C, 89001253

Williams, Charles, Jr., House [Somerville MPS], 1 Arlington St., Somerville, 9/18/89, A, C, 89001228

Williams, F. G., House [Somerville MPS], 37 Albion St., Somerville, 9/18/89, C, 89001226

Williams, Micah, House [Stoneham MRA], 342 William St., Stoneham, 4/13/84, C, 84002851

Williams-Linscott House [Stoneham MRA], 357 William St., Stoneham, 4/13/84, C, 84002853

Willis, Stillman, House [Cambridge MRA], 1 Potter Park, Cambridge, 4/13/82, C, b, 82001985

Wilmington Centre Village Historic District, Roughly, Middlesex Dr. and Church St. from Adams St. to Wildwood Cemetery, Wilmington, 4/08/92, A, C, 92000246

Winchester Center Historic District, Roughly bounded by Mt. Vernon and Washington Sts., Waterfield Rd., Church and Main Sts., Winchester, 11/21/86, A, C, 86002943

Winchester Savings Bank, 26 Mt. Vernon St., Winchester, 6/19/79, A, C, 79000361

Winchester Town Hall, 71 Mount Vernon St., Winchester, 3/31/83, A, C, 83000837

Windsor Road Historic District [Newton MRA], Windsor and Kent Rds., Newton, 2/16/90, A, C, 90000018

Winn Farm [Arlington MRA], 57 Summer St., Arlington, 4/18/85, C, 85001051

Winn, Suell, House [Wakefield MRA], 72–74 Elm St., Wakefield, 7/06/89, C, 89000743

Winship, Charles, House [Wakefield MRA], 13 Mansion Rd., Wakefield, 7/06/89, A, C, 89000717

Winslow-Haskell Mansion, 53 Vista Ave., Newton, 10/25/79, B, C, 79000362

Winter Street Historic District [Cambridge MRA], Winter St., Cambridge, 4/13/82, C, b, 82001986

Wisteria Lodge [Reading MRA], 146 Summer Ave., Reading, 7/19/84, C, 84002857

Withey, S. B., House [Cambridge MRA], 10 Appian Way, Cambridge, 5/19/86, C, 86001318

Woburn Public Library, Pleasant St., Woburn, 11/13/76, B, C, NHL, 76000290

Woburn Street Historic District [Reading MRA], Woburn St. from Temple St. to Summer Ave., Reading, 2/01/85, C, 85000551

Wood, Charles, House [Stoneham MRA], 34 Chestnut St., Stoneham, 4/13/84, C, 84002860

Wood, J. A., House [Cambridge MRA], 3 Sacramento St., Cambridge, 5/19/86, C, b, 86001319

Woodland Farm—Leland House [Sherborn MRA], 104 Woodland St., Sherborn, 1/03/86, C, 86000513

Woodland, Newton Highlands, and Newton Centre Railroad Stations, and Baggage and Express Building, 1897 Washington St., 18 Station Ave., 80 and 50 Union St., Newton, 6/03/76, A, C, 76002137

Woods End Road Historic District, 68 Baker Bridge Rd., 1, 5, 9, and 10 Woods End Rd., Lincoln, 7/08/88, B, C, g, 88000956

Woodville School [Wakefield MRA], Farm Rd., Wakefield, 7/06/89, C, 89000694

Woodward Homestead [Wakefield MRA], 17 Main St., Wakefield, 7/06/89, C, 89000747

Woodward, John, House [Newton MRA], 50 Fairlee Rd., Newton, 9/04/86, A, C, 86001897

Woodward, Rev. Samuel, House, 19 Concord Rd., Weston, 10/08/76, A, B, C, a, 76000283

Worcester House, 658 Andover St., Lowell, 12/22/83, A, C, 83004091

Working Boys Home [Newton MRA], 333 Nahanton St., Newton, 9/04/86, C, 86001898

Worthen, Daniel, House [Somerville MPS], 8 Mt. Pleasant St., Somerville, 9/18/89, A, C, 89001272

Wright House [Somerville MPS], 54 Vinal Ave., Somerville, 9/18/89, C, 89001293

Wright's Tavern, Lexington Rd. opposite the Burying Ground, Concord, 10/15/66, A, NHL, 66000793

Wright, Elisha, Homestead [Stoneham MRA], 170 Franklin St., Stoneham, 4/13/84, A, C, 84002863

Wright, Philemon/Asa Locke Farm, 78 Ridge St., Winchester, 3/10/83, A, C, 83000838

Wyatt, George, House [Somerville MPS], 33 Beacon St., Somerville, 9/18/89, A, C, 89001233

Wyeth Brickyard Superintendent's House [Cambridge MRA], 336 Rindge Ave., Cambridge, 4/13/82, A, C, 82001987

Wyeth, John, House [Cambridge MRA], 56 Aberdeen Ave., Cambridge, 4/13/82, C, b, 82001988

Wyeth-Smith House [Cambridge MRA], 152 Vassal Lane, Cambridge, 4/13/82, C, b, 82001989

Wyman, Francis, House, Francis Wyman St., Burlington, 3/17/75, C, 75000255

Wyman, George, House [Winchester MRA], 195 Cambridge St., Winchester, 7/05/89, A, C, 89000609

Yale Avenue Historic District [Wakefield MRA], 16–25 Yale Ave., Wakefield, 7/06/89, A, C, 89000756

cummings, e.e., House [Cambridge MRA], 104 Irving St., Cambridge, 6/30/83, B, 83000796

Nantucket County

Brant Point Light Station [Lighthouses of Massachusetts TR], Brant Pt., Nantucket, 9/28/87, A, C, 87002029

Coffin, Jethro, House, Sunset Hill, Nantucket, 11/24/68, C, NHL, 68000019

Nantucket Historic District, Nantucket Island, Nantucket, 11/13/66, A, C, NHL, 66000772

Sankaty Head Light [Lighthouses of Massachusetts TR], Sankaty Head, Nantucket Island, Nantucket, 10/15/87, A, C, 87002028

Norfolk County

Adams Academy, 8 Adams St., Quincy, 9/06/74, C, 74000379

Adams Building, 1342-1368 Hancock St.; 1-9 Temple St., Quincy, 6/23/83, A, C, 83000593

Adams National Historic Site, 135 Adams St., Quincy, 10/15/66, A, B, C, NPS, 66000051

Adams, John Quincy, Birthplace, 141 Franklin St., Quincy, 10/15/66, B, c, NHL, NPS, 66000128

Adams, John, Birthplace, 133 Franklin St., Quincy, 10/15/66, B, c, NHL, NPS, 66000129

Adams, John, School, 16 Church St., Weymouth, 12/05/85, A, C, 85003068

Alden, Arthur, House [Quincy MRA], 24 Whitney Rd., Quincy, 9/20/89, A, C, 89001382

Ames Schoolhouse, 450 Washington St., Dedham, 3/31/83, A, C, 83004284

Anderson, Larz, Park Historic District [Brookline MRA], Bounded by Goddard and Avon Sts., Brookline, 10/17/85, A, B, C, 85003245

Arcade Building [Brookline MRA], 314–320A Harvard St., Brookline, 10/17/85, A, C, 85003247

Bainbridge, Randolph, House [Quincy MRA], 133 Grandview Ave., Quincy, 9/20/89, A, C, 89001340

Barker, George A., House [Quincy MRA], 74 Greenleaf St., Quincy, 9/20/89, A, C, 89001345

Barker, Henry F., House [Quincy MRA], 103 Greenleaf St., Quincy, 9/20/89, A, C, 89001346

Barnes House [Quincy MRA], 183 Pine St., Quincy, 9/20/89, C, 89001362

Barnicoat, S. H., Monuments [Quincy MRA], 114 Columbia St., Quincy, 9/20/89, A, C, 89001325

Bateman, William R., House [Quincy MRA], 148 Monroe Rd., Quincy, 9/20/89, A, C, 89001359

Baxter Street Historic District [Quincy MRA], Roughly 19–34 Baxter St., Quincy, 9/20/89, A, C, 89001309

Baxter—King House [Quincy MRA], 270 Adams St., Quincy, 11/13/89, A, C, 89001953

Beacon Street Historic District [Brookline MRA], Roughly on Beacon St. from Saint Mary's to Ayr Rd., Brookline, 10/17/85, A, B, C, 85003322

Beaconsfield Terraces Historic District [Brookline MRA], 11–25, 33–43, and 44–55 Garrison Rd. and 316–326, 332–344, and 350–366 Tappan St., Brookline, 10/17/85, A, C, 85003248

Belcher, Jonathan, House, 360 N. Main St., Randolph, 4/30/76, B, C, 76000291

Norfolk County—Continued

Belcher-Rowe House, 26 Governor Belcher Lane, Milton, 4/01/82, B, C, 82002748

Bethany Congregational Church [Quincy MRA], 8 Spear St., Quincy, 9/20/89, C, a, 89001374

Blue Hills Headquarters [Blue Hills and Neponset River Reservations MRA], Hillside St., Milton, 9/25/80, A, C, 80000654

Bowditch, William Ingersoll, House [Brookline MRA], 9 Toxteth St., Brookline, 10/17/85, A, B, C, 85003249

Boyden, Seth, House, 135 Oak St., Foxboro, 11/10/83, C, 83004092

Brandegee Estate [Brookline MRA], 280 Newton St., Brookline, 10/17/85, C, 85003244

Brookline Town Green Historic District, Chestnut Pl., Fairmont, Dudley, Boyston, Walnut and Warren Sts., Hedge, Codman, and Kennard Rds., Brookline, 6/22/80, A, B, C, D, a, d, 80000650

Brookline Village Commercial District, Irregular Pattern along Washington St., Brookline, 5/22/79, A, C, 79000364

Brookwood Farm [Blue Hills and Neponset River Reservations MRA], off Hillside Ave., Milton, 9/25/80, A, 80000655

Brown—Hodgkinson House [Quincy MRA], 42 Bicknell St., Quincy, 9/20/89, A, 89001319

Building at 1–7 Moscow Street [Quincy MRA], 1–7 Moscow St., Quincy, 9/20/89, A, C, 89001360

Building at 30–34 Station Street [Brookline MRA], 30–34 Station St., Brookline, 10/17/85, C, 85003250

Building at 51 Hunt Street [Quincy MRA], 51 Hunt St., Quincy, 9/20/89, C, 89001355

Burgess, Charles H., House [Quincy MRA], 17 Whitney Rd., Quincy, 9/20/89, A, C, 89001381

Burgess, Frank, House [Quincy MRA], 355 Highland Ave., Quincy, 9/20/89, B, C, 89001354

Burgin, Clarence, House [Quincy MRA], 95 President's Ln., Quincy, 9/20/89, A, C, 89001364

Cabot, Lewis, Estate [Brookline MRA], 514 Warren St., Brookline, 10/17/85, C, a, 85003251

Candler Cottage [Brookline MRA], 447 Washington St., Brookline, 10/17/85, C, 85003252

Canton Viaduct, Neponset and Walpole Sts., Canton, 9/20/84, A, C, 84002870

Carpenter, Ezra, House, 168 South St., Foxborough, 1/03/85, A, C, 85000029

Cary, Otis, House, 242 South St., Foxboro, 3/13/86, B, C, 86000379

Central Fire Station [Quincy MRA], 26 Quincy Ave., Quincy, 9/20/89, A, C, 89001371

Central Square Historic District, Roughly, Broad St. from Middle to Putnam Sts. and Middle from Charles to Center Sts., Weymouth, 2/13/92, A, C, 92000040

Chestnut Hill Historic Distric [Brookline MRA], Roughly bounded by Middlesex Rd., Reservoir Ln., Denny Rd., Boylston St. and Dunster Rd., Brookline, 10/17/85, A, C, 85003253

Chickatawbut Observation Tower [Blue Hills and Neponset River Reservations MRA], Chickatawbut Rd., Quincy, 9/25/80, A, g, 80000652

Child, Isaac, House [Brookline MRA], 209 Newton St., Brookline, 10/17/85, C, 85003254

Christ Church [Quincy MRA], 14 Quincy St., Quincy, 9/20/89, C, a, 89001369

Christ Church Burial Ground [Quincy MRA], 54–60 School St., Quincy, 9/20/89, A, c, 89001372

Clapp, Lucius, Memorial, 6 Park St., Stoughton, 8/18/92, A, C, 92000998

Cobb's Tavern, 41 Bay Rd., Sharon, 8/07/74, A, 74000383

Coddington School [Quincy MRA], 26–44 Coddington St., Quincy, 9/20/89, A, C, 89001323

Comfort Station [Blue Hills and Neponset River Reservations MRA], Blue Hill Ave., Milton, 9/25/80, A, C, 80000658

Corey, Timothy, House No. 1 [Brookline MRA], 808 Washington St., Brookline, 10/17/85, A, B, C, 85003255

Corey, Timothy, House No. 2 [Brookline MRA], 786–788 Washington St., Brookline, 10/17/85, C, 85003256

Cottage Farm Historic District, Roughly bounded by Amory, Dummer, Lenox, Brookline and Beacon Sts., Brookline, 3/29/78, B, C, a, 78000455

Cranch School, 270 Whitwell St., Quincy, 7/05/84, A, C, 84002872

Crane, Frank W., House [Quincy MRA], 11 Avon Way, Quincy, 9/20/89, A, C, 89001312

Crane, Thomas, Public Library, 40 Washington St., Quincy, 10/18/72, C, NHL, 72000143

Curtis, Noah, House [Quincy MRA], 313 Franklin St., Quincy, 9/20/89, A, C, 89001335

Curtis, Thomas, House [Quincy MRA], 279 Franklin St., Quincy, 9/20/89, A, C, b, 89001334

Cypress—Emerson Historic District [Brookline MRA], Roughly bounded by Waverly, Emerson, and Cypress Sts., Brookline, 10/17/85, A, C, 85003257

Davis, Dr. Frank, House [Quincy MRA], 25 Elm St., Quincy, 9/20/89, A, C, 89001330

Davis, Robert S., House [Brookline MRA], 50 Stanton Rd., Brookline, 10/17/85, C, 85003259

Davis, Thomas Aspinwall, House [Brookline MRA], 29 Linden Pl., Brookline, 10/17/85, A, B, C, b, 85003260

Day, Fred Holland, House, 93 Day St., Norwood, 4/18/77, B, C, 77000191

Dean Junior College Historic District, Dean Junior College campus, Franklin, 4/23/75, B, C, 75000285

Devotion, Edward, House, 347 Harvard St., Brookline, 2/14/78, C, 78002835

Dicey, Russell M., House [Quincy MRA], 56 Pope St., Quincy, 9/20/89, A, C, 89001363

Dogget, Solon, House [Quincy MRA], 50 Union St., Quincy, 9/20/89, C, 89001379

Dorothy Q Apartments [Quincy MRA], 36 Butler Rd., Quincy, 9/20/89, A, C, 89001322

Douglass, Alfred, House [Brookline MRA], 157 Clyde St., Brookline, 10/17/85, A, C, 85003261

Dutch House, The [Brookline MRA], 20 Netherlands Rd., Brookline, 1/24/86, A, C, b, 86000093

Eaton-Moulton Mill, 37 Walnut St., Wellesley, 5/16/76, A, 76000294

Eliot Memorial Bridge [Blue Hills and Neponset River Reservations MRA], Milton, Milton, 9/25/80, A, B, f, 80000662

Elks Building [Quincy MRA], 1218–1222 Hancock St., Quincy, 9/20/89, A, C, 89001348

Elliot, Gen. Simon, House [Brookline MRA], 61 Heath St., Brookline, 10/17/85, C, 85003262

Elm Bank, Bounded by the Charles River to the W, N, and E, and the carriage path to the S, off 900 Washington St., Dover, 7/10/87, A, B, C, 86003565

Emmett Cottage [Brookline MRA], 217 Freeman St., Brookline, 10/17/85, C, 85003263

Fairbanks House, Eastern Ave. and East St., Dedham, 10/15/66, C, NHL, 66000367

Faxon House [Quincy MRA], 310 Adams St., Quincy, 9/20/89, C, 89001310

Fernwood [Brookline MRA], 155 Clyde St., Brookline, 10/17/85, C, a, 85003264

Fire Station No. 7 [Brookline MRA], 665 Washington St., Brookline, 10/17/85, A, C, 85003265

First Baptist Church of Wollaston [Quincy MRA], 187 Warren Ave., Quincy, 9/20/89, A, C, a, 89001380

First Parish Unitarian Church, North St., Medfield, 4/18/74, A, C, a, b, 74000376

Fisher Hill Historic District [Brookline MRA], Roughly bounded by Clinton and Sumner Rds., Boylston St. and Chestnut Hill Ave., Brookline, 10/17/85, A, C, 85003266

Fisher Hill Reservoir and Gatehouse [Water Supply System of Metropolitan Boston MPS], Fisher Rd. between Hyslop and Channing Rds., Brookline, 1/18/90, A, C, 89002254

Fogg Building, 100-110 Pleasant St. and 6-10 Columbian St., Weymouth, 3/10/83, A, C, 83000594

Fogg Library, 1 Columbian St., Weymouth, 6/11/81, C, f, 81000113

Forbes Hill Standpipe [Water Supply System of Metropolitan Boston MPS], Reservoir Rd., Quincy, 1/18/90, C, 89002252

Forbes, Capt. Robert B., House, 215 Adams St., Milton, 11/13/66, A, B, C, NHL, 66000651

Fore River Club House [Quincy MRA], Follett and Beechwood Sts., Quincy, 9/20/89, A, C, 89001333

Foxboro Grange Hall, 11-15 Bird St., Foxboro, 4/21/83, A, C, 83000595

Francis, Dr. Tappan Eustis, House [Brookline MRA], 35 Davis Ave., Brookline, 10/17/85, C, 85003267

Fuller, Amos, House, 220 Nehoiden St., Needham, 3/31/83, C, 83000596

Fuller, Peter, Building [Brookline MRA], 808 Commonwealth Ave., Brookline, 10/17/85, A, C, 85003269

Fuller, Robert, House, 3 Burrill Ln., Needham, 9/08/87, C, b, 87001476

Gills Farm Archeological District, Address Restricted, Randolph, 10/24/83, D, 83004093

Glover House [Quincy MRA], 249 E. Squantum St., Quincy, 9/20/89, A, C, 89001328

Goddard, John, House [Brookline MRA], 235 Goddard Ave., Brookline, 10/17/85, A, B, C, 85003270

Norfolk County—Continued

Graffam Development Historic District [Brookline MRA], Roughly bounded by Abbottsford Rd., Babcock St., Manchester, and Naples Rds., Brookline, 10/17/85, A, B, C, 85003271

Granite Trust Company [Quincy MRA], 1400 Hancock St., Quincy, 9/20/89, C, 89001351

Great Blue Hill Observation Tower [Blue Hills and Neponset River Reservations MRA], Milton, Milton, 9/25/80, A, 80000661

Great Blue Hill Weather Observatory [Blue Hills and Neponset River Reservations MRA], Milton, Milton, 9/25/80, A, B, C, NHL, 80000665

Green Hill Historic District [Brookline MRA], Roughly Warren St., Sargent Rd., and Cottage St., Brookline, 10/17/85, A, B, C, 85003272

Green Hill Site [Blue Hills and Neponset River Reservations MRA], Address Restricted, Canton vicinity, 9/25/80, D, 80000651

Grover, Emery, Building, 1330 Highland Ave., Needham, 8/20/87, A, C, 87001393

Halloran, John, House [Quincy MRA], 99 E. Squantum St., Quincy, 9/20/89, C, 89001327

Hancock Cemetery, Hancock St. in Quincy Sq., Quincy, 1/28/82, A, C, d, 82004421

Hardwick House [Quincy MRA], 59–61 Spear St., Quincy, 9/20/89, A, C, 89001376

Harris, John, House and Farm [Brookline MRA], 284 Newton St., Brookline, 10/17/85, A, 85003246

Heath, Charles, House [Brookline MRA], 12 Heath Hill, Brookline, 10/17/85, C, 85003273

Heath, Ebenezer, House [Brookline MRA], 30 Heath St., Brookline, 10/17/85, C, 85003274

Holbrook, Dr. Amos, House, 203 Adams St., Milton, 2/13/75, B, C, 75000289

Holyhood Cemetery [Brookline MRA], Heath St., Brookline, 10/17/85, C, d, 85003275

Hotel Adelaide [Brookline MRA], 13–21 High St., Brookline, 10/17/85, A, C, 85003276

Hotel Kempsford [Brookline MRA], 72 Walnut St., Brookline, 10/17/85, C, 85003277

House at 105 Marion Street [Brookline MRA], 105 Marion St., Brookline, 10/17/85, C, 85003278

House at 105 President's Lane [Quincy MRA], 105 President's Ln., Quincy, 9/20/89, A, C, 89001365

House at 12 Linden Street [Brookline MRA], 12 Linden St., Brookline, 10/17/85, A, C, 85003279

House at 12 Vernon Street [Brookline MRA], 12 Vernon St., Brookline, 10/17/85, C, 85003280

House at 12–16 Corey Road [Brookline MRA], 12–16 Corey Rd., Brookline, 10/17/85, A, C, 85003281

House at 15 Gilmore Street [Quincy MRA], 15 Gilmore St., Quincy, 9/20/89, A, C, 89001336

House at 155 Reservoir [Brookline MRA], 155 Reservoir Rd., Brookline, 10/17/85, C, b, 85003282

House at 156 Mason Terrace [Brookline MRA], 156 Mason Terr., Brookline, 10/17/85, C, 85003283

House at 19 Linden Street [Brookline MRA], 19 Linden St., Brookline, 10/17/85, A, C, 85003284

House at 20 Sterling Street [Quincy MRA], 20 Sterling St., Quincy, 9/20/89, A, C, 89001377

House at 23–25 Prout Street [Quincy MRA], 23–25 Prout St., Quincy, 9/20/89, A, C, 89001367

House at 25 High School Avenue [Quincy MRA], 25 High School Ave., Quincy, 9/20/89, C, 89001352

House at 25 Stanton Road [Brookline MRA], 25 Stanton Rd., Brookline, 10/17/85, C, 85003285

House at 32 Bayview Avenue [Quincy MRA], 32 Bayview Ave., Quincy, 9/20/89, A, C, 89001314

House at 38–40 Webster Place [Brookline MRA], 38–40 Webster Pl., Brookline, 10/17/85, C, 85003286

House at 4 Perry Street [Brookline MRA], 4 Perry St., Brookline, 10/17/85, A, C, b, 85003287

House at 44 Linden Street [Brookline MRA], 44 Linden St., Brookline, 10/17/85, C, 85003288

House at 44 Stanton Road [Brookline MRA], 44 Stanton Rd., Brookline, 10/17/85, C, b, 85003289

House at 5 Lincoln Road [Brookline MRA], 5 Lincoln Rd., Brookline, 10/17/85, C, 85003290

House at 53 Linden Street [Brookline MRA], 53 Linden St., Brookline, 10/17/85, A, C, 85003291

House at 83 Penniman Place [Brookline MRA], 83 Penniman Pl., Brookline, 10/17/85, C, b, 85003292

House at 89 Rawson Road and 86 Colburne Crescent [Brookline MRA], 89 Rawson Rd. and 86 Colburne Crescent, Brookline, 10/17/85, C, 85003302

House at 9 Linden Street [Brookline MRA], 9 Linden St., Brookline, 10/17/85, A, B, C, b, 85003293

House at 92 Willard Street [Quincy MRA], 92 Willard St., Quincy, 9/20/89, C, 89001383

House at 94 Grandview Avenue [Quincy MRA], 94 Grandview Ave., Quincy, 9/20/89, A, C, 89001339

Houses at 76–96 Harvard Avenue [Brookline MRA], 76–96 Harvard Ave., Brookline, 10/17/85, A, C, 85003294

Hunnewell Estates Historic District, Washington St. and Pond Rd., Wellesley, 4/14/88, A, C, b, 88000438

Hutchinson's, Gov. Thomas, Ha-ha, 100, 122 Randolph Ave., Milton, 2/13/75, B, C, 75000290

Intermediate Building, 324 Washington St., Wellesley Hills, 8/27/81, A, C, 81000112

Jackson, Thaddeus, House [Brookline MRA], 15 Alberta Rd., Brookline, 10/17/85, A, C, 85003295

Jefferson School, 200 Middle St., Weymouth, 5/12/81, A, C, 81000114

Jewell, David L., House [Quincy MRA], 48 Grandview Ave., Quincy, 9/20/89, A, C, 89001338

John Fitzgerald Kennedy National Historic Site, 83 Beals St., Brookline, 5/26/67, B, c, NHL, NPS, 67000001

Kilsyth Terrace [Brookline MRA], 15–27 Kilsyth Rd., Brookline, 10/17/85, A, C, 85003296

Kingsbury—Whitaker House, 53 Glendoon St., Needham, 7/12/90, A, B, C, 90001080

Lennon, Edward J., House [Quincy MRA], 53 Taber St., Quincy, 9/20/89, A, C, 89001378

Lewis, Deacon Willard, House, 33 West St., Walpole, 10/29/75, B, 75000297

Lewis, Joshua, House, 178 South St., Needham, 4/01/82, B, 82002749

Linden Park [Brookline MRA], Linden Pl. and Linden St., Brookline, 10/17/85, A, 85003297

Linden Square [Brookline MRA], Linden Pl., Brookline, 10/17/85, A, 85003298

Longwood Historic District, Roughly bounded by Chapel, St. Marys, Monmouth, and Kent Sts., Brookline, 9/13/78, B, C, a, 78000460

Lothrop, Caleb, House, 14 Summer St., Cohasset, 5/03/76, B, C, 76000269

Lynch—O'Gorman House [Brookline MRA], 41 Mason Terr., Brookline, 10/17/85, C, b, 85003299

Lyon's Turning Mill [Blue Hills and Neponset River Reservations MRA], Address Restricted, Quincy vicinity, 9/25/80, A, D, 80000656

Marsh, Charles, House [Quincy MRA], 248 President's Ln., Quincy, 9/20/89, C, 89001366

Marsh, Edwin W., House [Quincy MRA], 17 Marsh St., Quincy, 9/20/89, C, 89001356

Masonic Temple [Quincy MRA], 1156 Hancock St., Quincy, 11/13/89, A, C, 89001952

Massachuetts Hornfels-Braintree Slate Quarry [Blue Hills and Neponset River Reservations MRA], Address Restricted, Milton vicinity, 9/25/80, A, D, 80000653

Massachusetts Fields School, Rawson Rd. and Beach St., Quincy, 11/13/90, A, C, 88000960

McIntire, Herman, House [Quincy MRA], 55 Dixwell Ave., Quincy, 9/20/89, A, C, 89001326

McIntosh Corner Historic District, Roughly Great Plain and Central Aves., Needham, 1/05/89, A, C, 88003127

Memorial Hall, 22 South St., Foxboro, 4/21/83, C, f, 83000597

Metropolitan District Commission Stable [Blue Hills and Neponset River Reservations MRA], Hillside St., Milton, 9/25/80, A, C, 80000663

Milestone [Brookline MRA], Boylston St., Brookline, 10/17/85, A, b, 85003300

Milestone [Brookline MRA], Harvard St., Brookline, 10/17/85, A, b, 85003301

Miller, Edward, House [Quincy MRA], 36 Miller Stile Rd., Quincy, 3/08/90, C, 89001358

Mills, Davis, House, 945 Central Ave., Needham, 4/01/82, B, C, 82004418

Milton Centre Historic District, Canton Ave. between Readsdale Rd. and Thacher and Highland Sts., Milton, 4/28/88, A, C, a, b, f, 88000428

Minot, George R., House, 71 Sears Rd., Brookline, 1/07/76, B, NHL, 76001976

Morse, Amos, House, 77 North St., Foxboro, 1/09/86, A, C, 86000027

Moswetuset Hummock, Squantum St., near jct. with Morrissey Rd., Quincy, 7/01/70, A, D, f, 70000094

Munroe Building [Quincy MRA], 1227–1259 Hancock St., Quincy, 9/20/89, A, C, 89001349

Murphy, William, House [Brookline MRA], 97 Sewall Ave., Brookline, 10/17/85, B, C, 85003303

Norfolk County—Continued

Needham Town Hall Historic District, Great Plain Ave. between Highland Ave. and Chapel St., Needham, 11/15/90, A, C, 90001756

Nelson, John R., House [Quincy MRA], 4 Brunswick St., Quincy, 9/20/89, A, C, 89001321

New England Telephone Building [Quincy MRA], 10 Merrymount Rd., Quincy, 9/20/89, A, C, 89001357

Newcomb Place [Quincy MRA], 109 Putnam St., Quincy, 9/20/89, C, 89001368

Nightengale House [Quincy MRA], 24 Quincy St., Quincy, 9/20/89, C, 89001370

Nightengale, Solomon, House [Quincy MRA], 429 Granite St., Quincy, 9/20/89, A, C, 89001342

Norfolk County Courthouse, 650 High St., Dedham, 11/28/72, A, NHL, 72001312

Norfolk Grange Hall, 28 Rockwood Rd., Norfold, 5/25/89, A, C, 89000438

Nowland, J. Martin, House [Quincy MRA], 31 Edgemere Rd., Quincy, 9/20/89, A, C, 89001329

Old Barn [Blue Hills and Neponset River Reservations MRA], Off Hillside St., Milton, 9/25/80, A, C, 80000660

Old South Union Church, 25 Columbian St., Weymouth, 4/01/82, C, a, 82004422

Olmsted Park System, Encompassing the Back Bay Fens, Muddy River, Olmsted (Leverett Park), Jamaica Park, Arborway, and Franklin Park, Brookline, 12/08/71, A, C, f, 71000086

Olmsted, Frederick Law, House, 99 Warren St., Brookline, 10/15/66, B, NHL, NPS, 66000780

Orrock, Rev. John, House [Brookline MRA], 68 Winchester St., Brookline, 10/17/85, B, C, b, 85003304

Paine Estate [Brookline MRA], 325 Heath St., Brookline, 10/17/85, A, C, 85003305

Partridge, John, House, 315 Exchange St., Millis, 10/15/74, C, b, 74000377

Paul's Bridge, Neponset Valley Pkwy., over the Neponset River, Milton, 12/11/72, A, C, 72000140

Peak House, 347 Main St., Medfield, 9/05/75, B, C, 75000288

Perkins Estate [Brookline MRA], 450 Warren St., Brookline, 10/17/85, A, B, C, 85003306

Pettengill, C. F., House [Quincy MRA], 53 Revere Rd., Quincy, 11/13/89, C, 89001951

Pill Hill Historic District, Roughly bounded by Boylston St., Pond Ave., Acron, Oakland and Highland Rds., Brookline, 12/16/77, A, B, C, a, 77000187

Pinkham House [Quincy MRA], 79 Winthrop Ave., Quincy, 9/20/89, A, C, 89001384

Plimpton—Winter House, 127 South St., Wrentham, 12/05/85, B, C, 85003071

Ponkapoag Camp of Appalachian Mountain Club [Blue Hills and Neponset River Reservations MRA], Randolph, Randolph, 9/25/80, A, 80000657

Pratt, Capt. Josiah, House, 141 East St., Foxboro, 4/21/83, A, C, 83000598

Pratt—Faxon House [Quincy MRA], 75 Faxon Ln., Quincy, 9/20/89, C, 89001331

Quincy Electric Light and Power Company Station [Quincy MRA], 76 Field St., Quincy, 9/20/89, A, 89001332

Quincy Granite Railway, Bunker Hill Lane, Quincy, 10/15/73, A, C, 73000309

Quincy Granite Railway Incline, Mullin Ave., Quincy, 6/19/73, A, f, 73000310

Quincy Homestead, 34 Butler St., Quincy, 7/01/70, B, C, 70000095

Quincy Police Station [Quincy MRA], 442 Southern Artery, Quincy, 3/08/90, A, C, 89001373

Quincy Savings Bank [Quincy MRA], 1370 Hancock St., Quincy, 9/20/89, A, C, 89001350

Quincy School, 94 Newbury Ave., Quincy, 6/23/83, A, C, 83000599

Quincy Town Hall, 1305 Hancock St., Quincy, 1/11/80, A, C, 80000649

Quincy Water Company Pumping Station [Quincy MRA], 106 Penn St., Quincy, 9/20/89, A, 89001361

Quincy, Josiah, House, 20 Muirhead St., Quincy, 5/28/76, B, C, 76000285

Rabbit Hill Historic District, Roughly bounded by Highland, Main, Franklin, and Milford Sts., Medway, 4/01/88, A, C, a, 88000224

Record, Jonathan Dexter, House [Quincy MRA], 39–41 Grandview Ave., Quincy, 9/20/89, A, C, 89001337

Red Brick School, 2 Lincoln St., Franklin, 1/01/76, A, 76000276

Redman Farm House [Blue Hills and Neponset River Reservations MRA], Corner of Washington St. and Homans La., Canton, 9/25/80, A, C, 80000664

Reed, Timothy, House [Quincy MRA], 284 Adams St., Quincy, 9/20/89, A, C, 89001311

Refreshment Pavillion [Blue Hills and Neponset River Reservations MRA], Hillside St., Milton, 9/25/80, A, 80000659

Reservoir Park [Brookline MRA], Boylston St., Brookline, 10/17/85, A, 85003307

Richards, Alfred H., House [Quincy MRA], 354 Highland Ave., Quincy, 9/20/89, A, C, 89001353

Richmond Court, 1209-1217 Beacon St., Brookline, 7/18/85, C, 85001575

Ritchie Building [Brookline MRA], 112 Cypress St., Brookline, 10/17/85, A, B, 85003308

Roebuck Tavern, 21 Dedham St., Wrentham, 5/17/84, A, B, C, 84002878

Roughwood [Brookline MRA], 400 Heath St., Brookline, 10/17/85, A, C, 85003309

Saint Aidan's Church and Rectory [Brookline MRA], 207 Freeman and 158 Pleasant Sts., Brookline, 10/17/85, A, C, a, 85003310

Saint Mary of the Assumption Church, Rectory, School and Convent [Brookline MRA], 67 Harvard St. and 3 and 5 Linden Pl., Brookline, 10/17/85, A, B, C, a, 85003311

Saint Paul's Church, Chapel, and Parish House [Brookline MRA], 15 and 27 Saint Paul St. and 104 Aspinwall Ave., Brookline, 10/17/85, A, C, a, 85003312

Saint Paul's Rectory [Brookline MRA], 130 Aspinwall Ave., Brookline, 10/17/85, A, C, 85003313

Salem Lutheran Church [Quincy MRA], 199 Granite St., Quincy, 9/20/89, A, C, a, 89001341

Sargent's Pond [Brookline MRA], Sargent Rd., Brookline, 10/17/85, C, 85003314

Scott's Woods Historic District, Hillside St. between Randolph Ave. and MDC Blue Hills Reservation, Milton, 11/05/92, A, C, b, e, 92001528

Second Unitarian Church [Brookline MRA], 11 Charles St., Brookline, 10/17/85, A, C, a, g, 85003315

Sharon Historic District, Both sides of N. Main St. from Post Office Sq. to School St., Sharon, 8/22/75, A, C, a, 75000296

Sidelinger, George A., House [Quincy MRA], 19 Avon Way, Quincy, 9/20/89, A, C, 89001313

Smith, James, House, 706 Great Plain Ave., Needham, 8/21/86, C, 86001845

South Junior High School [Quincy MRA], 444 Granite St., Quincy, 9/20/89, A, C, 89001343

Spear, Seth, Homestead [Quincy MRA], 47–49 Spear St., Quincy, 9/20/89, C, 89001375

Spurr, Eliphalet, House [Brookline MRA], 103 Walnut St., Brookline, 10/17/85, B, C, 85003316

St. Mark's Methodist Church, 90 Park St., Brookline, 12/17/76, C, a, 76000268

Standish, James H., House [Brookline MRA], 54 Francis St., Brookline, 10/17/85, C, 85003317

Stoneholm, 188 Ames St., Sharon, 4/02/80, B, C, 80000648

Stoughton Railroad Station, 53 Wyman St., Stoughton, 1/21/74, A, C, 74000384

Stoughtonham Furnace Site, Address Restricted, Sharon vicinity, 8/16/84, A, D, 84002881

Strathmore Road Historic District [Brookline MRA], Strathmore Rd. and Clinton Path, Brookline, 10/17/85, A, C, 85003318

Suffolk Resolves House, 1370 Canton Ave., Milton, 7/23/73, A, b, 73000308

Thayer Public Library, 2 John F. Kennedy Memorial Dr., Braintree, 7/21/78, A, C, 78000446

Thayer, Gen. Sylvanus, House, 786 Washington St., Braintree, 12/03/74, B, C, c, 74000372

Tolman-Gay House, 1196 Central Ave., Needham, 6/01/82, A, B, C, 82004419

Toussaint, Winand, House [Brookline MRA], 203 Aspinwall Ave., Brookline, 10/17/85, B, C, 85003319

Town Stable [Brookline MRA], 237 Cypress St., Brookline, 10/17/85, A, C, 85003320

Townsend House, 980 Central Ave., Needham, 4/01/82, B, C, 82004420

Tuckerman, William F., House [Brookline MRA], 63 Harvard Ave., Brookline, 10/17/85, C, 85003321

Turner, Stephen, House, N of Norfolk at 187 Seekonk St., Norfolk vicinity, 5/10/79, B, C, 79002682

Twitchell, Ginery, House [Brookline MRA], 17 Kent St., Brookline, 10/17/85, B, C, 85003240

US Post Office—Milton Main, 499 Adams St., Milton, 5/30/86, B, C, 86001213

US Post Office—Quincy Main, 47 Washington St., Quincy, 5/23/86, C, 86001217

US Post Office—Weymouth Landing, 103 Washington St., Weymouth, 5/27/86, A, C, g, 86001186

Norfolk County—Continued

United First Parish Church (Unitarian) of Quincy, 1266 Hancock St., Quincy, 12/30/70, C, a, NHL, NPS, 70000734

Walnut Hills Cemetery [Brookline MRA], Grove St. and Allandale Rd., Brookline, 10/17/85, A, C, d, 85003241

Walpole Town Hall, Main St., Walpole, 10/08/81, A, C, 81000619

Warelands, N of Norfolk at 103 Boardman St., Norfolk vicinity, 11/10/77, A, B, C, 77000190

Washington School, 8 School St., Weymouth, 6/05/86, C, 86001218

Wellesley Farms Railroad Station, Croton St. extension, Wellesley, 2/14/86, A, C, 86000259

Wellesley Town Hall, 525 Washington St., Wellesley, 4/30/76, A, C, 76000295

Weymouth Civic District, 75 Middle St., Weymouth, 3/27/92, A, C, 92000146

White Place Historic District [Brookline MRA], White Pl. between Washington St. and Davis Path, Brookline, 10/17/85, A, C, 85003243

White, Benjamin, House [Brookline MRA], 203 Heath St., Brookline, 10/17/85, A, B, C, b, 85003242

White, Charles E., House [Quincy MRA], 101 Billings Rd., Quincy, 9/20/89, A, C, 89001320

Whitney, Israel, House, 963 Central Ave., Needham, 2/25/88, B, C, 88000160

Winfield House [Quincy MRA], 853 Hancock St., Quincy, 9/20/89, C, 89001347

Winthrop, John, Jr., Iron Furnace Site, Address Restricted, Quincy vicinity, 9/20/77, A, D, 77000192

Wollaston Branch, Thomas Crane Public Library [Quincy MRA], 41 Beale St., Quincy, 9/20/89, A, C, 89001316

Wollaston Fire Station [Quincy MRA], 111 Beale St., Quincy, 9/20/89, A, C, 89001317

Wollaston Theatre [Quincy MRA], 14 Beale St., Quincy, 9/20/89, A, C, 89001315

Wollaston Unitarian Church [Quincy MRA], 155 Beale St., Quincy, 9/20/89, A, C, a, 89001318

Woodward Institute [Quincy MRA], 1098 Hancock St., Quincy, 11/13/89, A, C, 89001954

Plymouth County

Alden, John, House, 105 Alden St., Duxbury, 12/14/78, C, D, 78000476

Bartlett-Russell-Hedge House, 32 Court St., Plymouth, 4/30/76, B, C, 76001614

Bird Island Light [Lighthouses of Massachusetts TR], Sippican Harbor, Marion, 9/28/87, A, C, 87002030

Bradford, Capt. Gamaliel, House, W of Duxbury at 942 Tremont St., Duxbury vicinity, 2/17/78, B, C, 78001402

Bradford, Capt. Gershom, House, W of Duxbury at 931 Tremont St., Duxbury vicinity, 2/08/78, B, C, 78001403

Bradford, Captain Daniel, House, 251 Harrison St., Duxbury, 2/20/86, A, B, C, 86000301

Bradford-Union Street Historic District, Bradford, Union, Emerald, Water Cure, and Freedom Sts., Plymouth, 11/10/83, A, C, 83004094

Brockton City Hall, 45 School St., Brockton, 3/26/76, A, C, 76000296

Brockton Edison Electric Illuminating Company Power Station, 70 School St., Brockton, 9/17/87, A, C, 87000874

Bryant-Cushing House, 768 Main St., Norwell, 3/26/76, C, 76001613

Central Fire Station, 40 Pleasant St., Brockton, 7/25/77, A, C, 77000193

Chubbuck, Thomas, Jr., House, 1191 Main St., Hingham, 8/07/92, C, 92000954

Clifford-Warren House, E of Plymouth at 3 Clifford Rd., Plymouth vicinity, 4/08/80, A, B, C, 80000666

Cole's Hill, Carver St., Plymouth, 10/15/66, A, d, f, NHL, 66000142

Curtis Building, 105-109 Main St., Brockton, 4/15/82, B, C, 82004424

Cushing Homestead, W of Cohasset on MA 128, Hingham vicinity, 6/04/73, C, 73000326

Dean, Dr. Edgar Everett, House, 81 Green St., Brockton, 5/05/78, B, C, 78000471

First Parish Church, SW of Duxbury at Tremont and Depot Sts., Duxbury vicinity, 7/21/78, C, a, 78001404

Forest Avenue School, Concord Ave., Brockton, 7/15/82, A, C, b, 82004425

Franklin Block, 1102–1110 Main St., Brockton, 2/21/89, A, C, 89000042

Goldthwaite Block, 99-103 Main St., Brockton, 4/15/82, B, C, 82004427

Graves Light Station [Lighthouses of Massachusetts TR], N of Hull in the Massachusetts Bay, Hull vicinity, 9/28/87, A, C, 87002041

Harlow Old Fort House, 119 Sandwich St., Plymouth, 12/27/74, B, C, 74001762

Harlow, Sgt. William, Family Homestead, 8 Winter St., Plymouth, 4/15/82, C, 82004434

Hillside, 230 Summer St., Plymouth, 9/18/75, A, C, 75001626

Howard Block, 93–97 Main St., Brockton, 4/15/82, A, C, 82004969

Howland, Jabez, House, 33 Sandwich St., Plymouth, 10/09/74, B, C, 74002032

James, Capt. Benjamin, House, 301 Driftway, Scituate, 11/29/83, A, C, 83004095

King Caesar House, King Caesar Rd., Duxbury, 3/29/78, B, C, 78000477

Kingman, Gardner J., House, 309 Main St., Brockton, 7/25/77, B, C, 77000196

Lawson Tower, Off First Parish Rd., Scituate Center, 9/28/76, A, B, C, 76001963

Lincoln Historic District, Roughly, North & South Sts. from West to Water Sts., Main St. S to Garrison Rd., & Lincoln St. & Fearing Rd. N to Miles, Hingham, 1/07/91, A, C, a, b, d, 90001728

Lincoln, Gen. Benjamin, House, 181 North St., Hingham, 11/28/72, B, NHL, 72001303

Lower Union Street Historic District, Union St. from Water St. to Market St., Rockland, 4/07/89, A, C, 89000219

Lyman Block, 83-91 Main St., Brockton, 4/15/82, B, C, 82004430

Middleborough Waterworks, E. Grove St. at Nesmasket River and Wareham St. at Barden Hill Rd., Middleborough, 3/02/90, A, C, 90000129

Minot's Ledge Light [Lighthouses of Massachusetts TR], Minot's Ledge, Scituate, 6/15/87, A, C, 87001489

National Monument to the Forefathers, Allerton St., Plymouth, 8/30/74, C, f, 74002033

Ned Point Light [Lighthouses of Massachusetts TR], Ned Point Rd., Mattpoisett, 6/15/87, A, C, 87001488

North Abington Depot, Railroad St., North Abington, 5/13/76, A, C, 76001612

Norwell Village Area Historic District, MA 123, Norwell, 6/02/82, A, C, 82004432

Old County Courthouse, Leyden and Market Sts., Plymouth, 2/23/72, A, 72001297

Old Post Office Building, Crescent St., Brockton, 3/08/78, A, C, 78000474

Old Ship Meetinghouse, Main St., Hingham, 10/15/66, C, a, NHL, 66000777

Old Shipbuilder's Historic District, Both sides of Washington St. from Rowder Ave. to N of South Duxbury, Duxbury, 8/21/86, A, C, 86001899

Packard, Moses, House, 647 Main St., Brockton, 2/17/78, B, C, 78000475

Parting Ways Archeological District, Address Restricted, Plymouth vicinity, 3/19/79, D, 79000367

Phoenix Building, 315–321 Union St., Rockland, 4/07/89, A, C, 89000220

Pierce, Peter, Store, N. Main and Jackson Sts., Middleboro, 4/30/76, B, C, 76001611

Pilgrim Hall, 75 Court St., Plymouth, 4/11/72, C, 72001298

Plymouth Antiquarian House, 126 Water St., Plymouth, 12/27/74, B, C, b, 74002034

Plymouth Light Station [Lighthouses of Massachusetts TR (AD)], SE of Duxbury at Gurnet Point, Duxbury vicinity, 3/08/77, A, 77000655

Plymouth Post Office Building, 5 Main St., Plymouth, 10/23/86, C, 86002926

Plymouth Rock, Water St., Plymouth, 7/01/70, A, C, b, f, g, 70000680

Plymouth Village Historic District, Roughly bounded by Water, Main and Brewster Sts., Plymouth, 6/02/82, A, B, C, D, 82004435

Point Allerton Lifesaving Station, Nantasket Ave., Hull, 6/11/81, A, B, 81000110

Rockland Almshouse, 198 Spring St., Rockland, 4/28/83, A, C, g, 83000600

Rockland High School, 394 Union St., Rockland, 3/23/89, A, C, 89000217

Rockland Memorial Library, 382 Union St., Rockland, 3/23/89, A, C, 89000221

Rockland Trust Company, 288 Union St., Rockland, 4/07/89, A, C, 89000218

Scituate Light [Lighthouses of Massachusetts TR], Cedar Pt., Scituate, 6/15/87, A, C, 87001490

Snow Fountain and Clock, N. Main and E. Main Sts., Brockton, 7/25/77, B, C, 77000197

South Street Historic District, Roughly South St. from Main St. to Warren Ave., Brockton, 10/06/83, A, C, a, 83004096

Sparrow, Richard, House, 42 Summer St., Plymouth, 10/09/74, C, 74002035

Plymouth County—Continued

Standish, Alexander, House, 341 Standish St., Duxbury vicinity, 7/12/78, A, 78001407

Stetson House, Hanover St., Hanover, 9/07/79, A, C, 79000366

Tack Factory, The, SW of Norwell at 49 Tiffany Rd., Norwell vicinity, 12/03/80, A, 80000472

Telegraph Hill, Address Restricted, Hull, 7/12/76, A, D, 76000953

Third Meetinghouse, 1 Fairhaven Rd., Mattapoisett, 1/02/76, C, a, 76000956

Thomas—Webster Estate, 238 Webster St., Marshfield, 4/05/93, B, C, 93000206

Thumb, Tom, House, 351 Plymouth St., Middleborough, 4/16/93, B, C, 93000298

Tobey Homestead, Main St. and Sandwich Rd., Wareham, 6/05/86, B, C, 86001219

Town Hall, Bedford St., Lakeville, 10/22/76, A, C, 76000955

Tremont Nail Factory District, 21 Elm St., Wareham, 10/22/76, C, 76001964

US Post Office-Middleborough Main, 90 Center St., Middleborough, 10/19/87, A, C, 87001774

Wampanoag Royal Cemetery, Address Restricted, Middleboro vicinity, 11/11/75, D, d, 75001625

Wampanucket Site, Address Restricted, Middleboro vicinity, 6/04/73, D, d, 73001596

Washburn, C.P., Grain Mill, Central and Cambridge Sts., Middleboro, 4/08/80, A, C, 80000667

Webster, Daniel, Law Office and Library, Careswell and Webster Sts., Marshfield, 5/30/74, B, b, NHL, 74002053

Suffolk County

Abbotsford, 300 Walnut Ave., Boston, 9/16/87, C, 87000885

Adams-Nervine Asylum, 990-1020 Centre St., Boston, 6/01/82, A, C, 82004456

African Meetinghouse, 8 Smith St., Boston, 10/07/71, A, C, a, NHL, NPS, 71000087

All Saints' Church, 211 Ashmont St., Boston, 6/16/80, C, a, 80000678

Ames Building, 1 Court St., Boston, 4/26/74, C, 74000382

Appleton, Nathan, Residence, 39-40 Beacon St., Boston, 12/22/77, B, NHL, 77001541

Arlington Street Church, Arlington and Boylston Sts., Boston, 5/04/73, A, C, a, 73000313

Armory of the First Corps of Cadets, 97-105 Arlington St. and 130 Columbus Ave., Boston, 5/22/73, A, C, 73000314

Arnold Arboretum, 22 Divinity Ave., Boston, 10/15/66, B, NHL, 66000127

Austin, Francis B., House, 58 High St., Boston, 10/21/88, C, 87001478

Back Bay Historic District, Roughly bounded by the Charles River, Arlington, Providence, Boylston and Newbury Sts., and Charlesgate East, Boston, 8/14/73, A, C, D, a, 73001948

Baker, Sarah J., School, 33 Perrin St., Boston, 7/07/83, A, C, 83004285

Beach-Knapp District [Boston Theatre MRA], Roughly bounded by Harrison Ave., Washington, Kneeland, and Beach Sts., Boston, 12/09/80, A, C, 80000462

Beacon Hill Historic District, Bounded by Beacon St., the Charles River Embankment, and Pinckney, Revere, and Hancock Sts., Boston, 10/15/66, B, C, NHL, 66000130

Bedford Building, 89-103 Bedford St., Boston, 8/21/79, C, 79000368

Bellevue Standpipe [Water Supply System of Metropolitan Boston MPS], On Bellevue Hill at Washington St. and Roxbury Pkwy., Boston, 1/18/90, C, 89002251

Bellingham Square Historic District, Roughly bounded by Broadway, Shawmut, Chestnut, and Shurtleff Sts., Chelsea, 1/03/85, A, B, C, 85000030

Bellingham-Cary House, 34 Parker St., Chelsea, 9/06/74, B, C, 74000908

Berger Factory, 37 Williams St., Boston, 4/09/80, A, C, 80000677

Bigelow School, 350 W. 4th St., Boston, 2/21/85, C, 85000316

Blackstone Block Historic District, Area bound by Union, Hanover, Blackstone, and North Sts., Boston, 5/26/73, A, C, 73000315

Blake, James, House, 735 Columbia Rd., Boston, 5/01/74, C, b, 74002350

Boston African American National Historic Site, Museum of Afro American History, Dudley Station, Box 5, Boston, 10/10/80, A, C, a, f, NPS, 80004396

Boston Athenaeum, 10 1/2 Beacon St., Boston, 10/15/66, A, NHL, 66000132

Boston Common, Beacon, Park, Tremont, Boylston, and Charles St., Boston, 2/27/87, A, NHL, 87000760

Boston Common and Public Garden, Beacon, Park, Tremont, Boylston, and Arlington Sts., Boston, 7/12/72, A, C, 72000144

Boston Edison Electric Illuminating Company [Boston Theatre MRA], 25-39 Boylston St., Boston, 12/09/80, A, C, 80000453

Boston Harbor Islands Archeological District, Address Restricted, Boston vicinity, 12/21/85, D, 85003323

Boston Light [Lighthouses of Massachusetts TR (AD)], Little Brewster Island, Boston Harbor, Boston, 10/15/66, A, C, NHL, 66000133

Boston National Historical Park, Inner harbor at mouth of Charles River, Boston, 10/26/74, A, C, a, f, NPS, 74002222

Boston Naval Shipyard, E of Chelsea St., Charlestown, Boston, 11/15/66, A, C, D, g, NHL, NPS, 66000134

Boston Public Garden, Beacon, Charles, Boylston, and Arlington Sts., Boston, 2/27/87, A, NHL, 87000761

Boston Public Library, Copley Sq., Boston, 5/06/73, A, C, g, NHL, 73000317

Boston Young Men's Christian Union [Boston Theatre MRA], 48 Boylston St., Boston, 12/09/80, A, C, 80000451

Bowditch School, 80–82 Greene St., Boston, 8/03/90, A, C, 90001145

Boylston Building [Boston Theatre MRA], 2-22 Boylston St., Boston, 12/09/80, A, C, 80000450

Brook Farm, 670 Baker St., Boston, 10/15/66, A, B, d, NHL, 66000141

Building at 138–142 Portland Street, 138–142 Portland St., Boston, 9/05/85, A, C, 85002015

Bulfinch Triangle Historic District, Roughly bounded by Canal, Market, Merrimac, and Causeway Sts., Boston, 2/27/86, A, C, 86000274

Bunker Hill Monument, Breed's Hill, Boston, 10/15/66, A, f, NHL, NPS, 66000138

Bunker Hill School, 65 Baldwin St., Boston, 10/15/87, A, C, 87001771

Calf Pasture Pumping Station Complex, 435 Mount Vernon St., Boston, 8/02/90, A, C, 90001095

Charles Playhouse, 74-78 Warenton St., Boston, 6/16/80, A, C, a, 80000676

Charles Street African Methodist Episcopal Church, 551 Warren St., Boston, 9/01/83, A, C, a, g, 83000601

Chelsea Square Historic District, Broadway, Medford, Tremont, Winnisimmett, Cross, Park and Beacon Sts., Chelsea, 4/08/82, A, C, 82004461

Chestnut Hill Reservoir Historic District [Water Supply System of Metropolitan Boston MPS], Beacon St. and Commonwealth Ave., Boston, 1/18/90, A, C, 89002271

Christ Church, 1220 River Rd., Boston, 1/30/86, C, a, 86000140

Church of Christ, 265 Beech St., Revere, 11/13/84, C, a, 84000430

Clapp Houses, 199 and 195 Boston St., Boston, 5/02/74, B, C, b, 74000911

Codman Building, 55 Kilby St., Boston, 10/19/83, C, 83004097

Codman Square District, Norfolk, Talbot, Epping, Lithgow, Centre, and Moultrie Sts., Boston, 6/23/83, A, C, 83000602

Congregation Agudath Shalom, 145 Walnut St., Chelsea, 4/16/93, A, C, a, 93000283

Congress Street Fire Station, 344 Congress St., Boston, 9/03/87, A, C, 87001396

Copp's Hill Burial Ground, Charter, Snowhill, and Hull Sts., Boston, 4/18/74, A, C, d, 74000385

Copp's Hill Terrace, Between Commercial and Charter Sts. W of Jackson Place, Boston, 4/19/90, A, C, 90000631

Crowninshield House, 164 Marlborough St., Boston, 2/23/72, C, 72000145

Customhouse District, Between J.F.K. Expwy. and Kirby St. and S. Market and High Sts., Boston, 5/11/73, A, C, 73000321

Cyclorama Building, 543-547 Tremont St., Boston, 4/13/73, A, C, 73000318

Dill Building [Boston Theatre MRA], 11-25 Stuart St., Boston, 12/09/80, A, C, 80000448

Dillaway School, 16-20 Kenilworth St., Boston, 4/09/80, A, C, 80001683

Dimock Community Health Center Complex, 41 and 55 Dimock St., Boston, 2/21/85, A, B, C, NHL, 85000317

District 13 Police Station, 28 Seaverns Ave., Boston, 2/10/88, C, 87002549

Suffolk County—Continued

Dorchester Heights National Historic Site, South Boston, Boston, 10/15/66, A, B, C, f, NPS, 66000050

Dorchester North Burying Ground, Stroughton St. and Columbia Rd., Boston, 4/18/74, A, C, d, 74000915

Dorchester Pottery Works, 101-105 Victory Rd., Boston, 2/21/85, A, C, D, 85000318

Dorchester-Milton Lower Mills Industrial District, Both sides of Neponset River, Boston, 4/02/80, A, C, 80000675

Downtown Chelsea Residential Historic District, Roughly bounded by Shurtleff, Marginal, and Division Sts. and Bellingham Sq., Chelsea, 6/22/88, A, C, 88000718

Dudley Station Historic District, Washington, Warren, and Dudley Sts., Boston, 12/05/85, A, C, 85003074

Eliot Burying Ground, Eustis and Washington Sts., Boston, 6/25/74, A, C, d, 74000388

Eliot Hall, 7A Eliot St., Boston, 7/15/88, A, C, 88000959

Engine House No. 34, 444 Western Ave., Boston, 10/24/85, A, C, 85003375

Ether Dome, Massachusetts General Hospital, Fruit St., Boston, 10/15/66, A, NHL, 66000366

Faneuil Hall, Dock Sq., Boston, 10/15/66, A, C, NHL, NPS, 66000368

Fenway Studios Building, 30 Ipswich St., Boston, 9/13/78, C, 78000473

Fenway-Boylston Street District, Fenway, Boylston, Westland, and Hemenway Sts., Boston, 9/04/84, C, 84002875

Fields Corner Municipal Building, 1 Arcadia St., 195 Adams St., Boston, 11/12/81, A, C, 81000620

Filene's Department Store, 426 Washington St., Boston, 7/24/86, A, C, 86001909

First Baptist Church, Commonwealth Ave. and Clarendon St., Boston, 2/23/72, C, a, 72000146

First Church of Jamaica Plain, 6 Eliot St., Boston, 7/15/88, A, C, a, d, 88000955

Fort Independence, Castle Island, Boston, 10/15/70, A, 70000921

Fort Warren, Georges Island, Boston Harbor, Boston vicinity, 8/29/70, A, C, NHL, 70000540

Fulton-Commercial Streets District, Fulton, Commercial, Mercantile, Lewis, and Richmond Sts., Boston, 3/21/73, A, C, 73000319

Gardner, Isabella Stewart, Museum, 280 The Fenway, Boston, 1/27/83, A, B, C, 83000603

Garrison, William Lloyd, House, 125 Highland St., Boston, 10/15/66, B, NHL, 66000653

Garrison, William Lloyd, School, 20 Hutchings St., Boston, 4/16/80, A, C, 80000674

Goodwin, Ozias, House, 7 Jackson Ave., Boston, 6/23/88, A, C, 88000908

Greek Orthodox Cathedral of New England, 520 Parker St., Boston, 6/30/88, A, C, a, 88000957

Haffenreffer Brewery, Germania St., Boston, 5/02/82, A, C, 82004453

Hale, Edward Everett, House, 12 Morley St., Boston, 3/21/79, B, C, b, 73000325

Harding, Chester, House, 16 Beacon St., Boston, 10/15/66, B, NHL, 66000764

Harriswood Crescent, 60–88 Harold St., Boston, 3/13/86, A, C, 86000375

Harvard Avenue Fire Station, 16 Harvard Ave., Boston, 3/31/83, C, 83000605

Harvard Stadium, 60 N. Harvard St., Boston, 2/27/87, A, C, NHL, 87000757

Hayden Building [Boston Theatre MRA], 681-683 Washington St., Boston, 12/09/80, A, C, 80000446

Headquarters House, 55 Beacon St., Boston, 10/15/66, B, NHL, 66000765

Hoosac Stores 1 & 2-Hoosac Stores 3, 25 and 115 Water St., Charlestown, 8/14/85, A, C, NPS, 85002339

House at 17 Cranston Street, 17 Cranston St., Boston, 11/20/87, C, 87001398

Howe, Samuel Gridley and Julia Ward, House, 13 Chestnut St., Boston, 9/13/74, B, C, NHL, 74002044

Hoxie, Timothy, House, 135 Hillside St., Boston, 11/20/87, C, b, 87001399

International Trust Company Building, 39-47 Milk St., Boston, 9/10/79, A, C, 79000369

John Eliot Square District, John Eliot Sq., Boston, 4/23/73, A, C, a, 73000854

Kimball, C. Henry, House, 295 Washington St., Chelsea, 4/15/82, B, C, 82004464

King's Chapel, Tremont and School Sts., Boston, 5/02/74, C, a, NHL, 74002045

Kittredge, Alvah, House, 12 Linwood St., Boston, 5/08/73, B, C, b, 73000855

LUNA (tugboat), NDC Pier, Charles River, Boston, 10/06/83, A, C, g, NHL, 83004099

Lawrence Model Lodging Houses, 79, 89, 99 and 109 E. Canton St., Boston, 9/22/83, A, C, 83000606

Leather District, Roughly bounded by Atlantic Ave., Kneeland, Lincoln, and Essex Sts., Boston, 12/21/83, A, C, 83004098

Liberty Tree District [Boston Theatre MRA], Roughly bounded by Harrison Ave., Washington, Essex and Beach Sts., Boston, 12/09/80, A, C, 80000460

Locke—Ober Restaurant, 3–4 Winter Pl., Boston, 7/24/86, A, C, 86001911

Long Island Head Light [Lighthouses of Massachusetts TR], Long Island, Boston, 6/15/87, A, C, 87001481

Long Wharf and Customhouse Block, Foot of State St., Boston, 11/13/66, A, NHL, 66000768

Loring, Harrison, House, 789 E. Broadway St., Boston, 9/01/83, A, C, 83000604

Loring-Greenough House, 12 South St., Boston, 4/26/72, A, B, C, 72000544

Massachusetts General Hospital, Fruit Street, Boston, 12/30/70, A, C, NHL, 70000682

Massachusetts Historical Society Building, 1154 Boylston St., Boston, 10/15/66, A, NHL, 66000770

Massachusetts School of Art, 364 Brookline Ave., Boston, 8/03/89, A, C, 89000974

Massachusetts Statehouse, Beacon Hill, Boston, 10/15/66, C, NHL, 66000771

McKay, Donald, House, 78-80 White St., Boston, 6/02/82, B, C, 82004450

Metropolitan Theatre [Boston Theatre MRA], 252-272 Tremont St., Boston, 12/09/80, A, C, 80000445

Mission Hill Triangle Historic District, Roughly bounded by Smith St., Worthington St., Tremont St., and Huntington Ave., Boston, 11/06/89, A, C, 89001747

Monument Square Historic District, Monument Sq., Boston, 6/02/87, A, B, C, 87001128

Monument Square Historic District, Roughly bounded by Jamaicaway, Pond, Centre and Eliot Sts., Boston, 10/11/90, A, C, 90001536

Moreland Street Historic District, Roughly bounded by Kearsarge, Blue Hill Aves., Warren, Waverly, and Winthrop Sts., Boston, 3/29/84, A, B, C, 84002890

Mount Pleasant Historic District, Roughly bounded by Forest St. and Mount Pleasant Ave., Boston, 2/09/89, A, C, 89000004

Naval Hospital Boston Historic District, 1 Broadway, Chelsea, 8/14/73, A, 73000851

Nell, William C., House, 3 Smith Ct., Boston, 5/11/76, B, NHL, 76001979

New England Conservatory of Music, 290 Huntington Ave., Boston, 5/14/80, A, C, 80000672

New Riding Club, 52 Hemenway St., Boston, 8/20/87, A, C, 87001394

Newspaper Row, 322-328 Washington St., 5-23 Milk St., and 11 Hawley St., Boston, 7/07/83, A, C, 83000607

Oak Square School, 35 Nonantum St., Boston, 11/10/80, C, 80000465

Old City Hall, School and Providence Sts., Boston, 12/30/70, C, NHL, 70000687

Old Corner Bookstore, NW corner of Washington and School Sts., Boston, 4/11/73, A, C, 73000322

Old North Church, 193 Salem St., Boston, 10/15/66, A, C, a, NHL, NPS, 66000776

Old South Church in Boston, 645 Boylston St., Boston, 12/30/70, C, a, NHL, 70000690

Old South Meetinghouse, Milk and Washington Sts., Boston, 10/15/66, A, C, a, NHL, NPS, 66000778

Old Statehouse, Washington and State Sts., Boston, 10/15/66, A, C, NHL, NPS, 66000779

Old West Church, 131 Cambridge St., Boston, 12/30/70, C, a, NHL, 70000691

Otis, (First) Harrison Gray, House, 141 Cambridge St., Boston, 12/30/70, C, NHL, 70000539

Otis, (Second) Harrison Gray, House, 85 Mt. Vernon St., Boston, 7/27/73, C, 73001955

Park Street District, Tremont, Park, and Beacon Sts., Boston, 5/01/74, A, C, a, d, 74000390

Parkman, Francis, House, 50 Chestnut St., Boston, 10/15/66, B, NHL, 66000782

Phipps Street Burying Ground, Phipps St., Boston, 5/14/74, A, B, C, d, f, 74000907

Piano Row District [Boston Theatre MRA], Boston Common, Park Sq., Boylston Pl. and Tremont St., Boston, 12/09/80, A, C, 80000458

Pierce House, 24 Oakton Ave., Boston, 4/26/74, B, C, 74000917

Pierce-Hichborn House, 29 North Sq., Boston, 11/24/68, C, NHL, 68000042

Suffolk County—Continued

Quincy Market, S. Market St., Boston, 11/13/66, A, C, NHL, 66000784

Revere, Paul, House, 19 North Sq., Boston, 10/15/66, B, C, NHL, NPS, 66000785

Richards, Ellen H. Swallow, House, 32 Eliot St., Jamaica Plain, 3/31/92, A, B, NHL, 92001874

Richardson Block, 113-151 Pearl and 109-119 High Sts., Boston, 8/09/86, A, C, 86001504

Ronan, Mary, T., School, 154 Bradstreet Ave., Revere, 12/10/82, A, C, 82000485

Roslindale Congregational Church, 25 Cummins Hwy., at jct. with Summer Ave., Roslindale, 7/26/91, A, C, a, 91000925

Roughan Hall, 15-18 City Sq., Boston, 4/15/82, A, C, 82004448

Roxbury High Fort, Beech Glen St. at Fort Ave., Boston, 4/23/73, C, f, 73000856

Roxbury Highlands Historic District, Roughly bounded by Dudley St., Washington St., and Columbus Ave., Boston, 2/22/89, A, C, 89000147

Roxbury Presbyterian Church, 328 Warren St., Boston, 3/15/91, A, C, a, 89002125

Russia Wharf Buildings, 518-540 Atlantic Ave., 270 Congress St. and 276-290 Congress St., Boston, 12/02/80, C, 80000463

Saint Augustine Chapel and Cemetery, Dorchester St. between W. Sixth and Tudor Sts., Boston, 9/18/87, A, B, C, a, d, 87001495

Sears Roebuck and Company Mail Order Store, 309 Park Dr. and 201 Brookline Ave., Boston, 1/15/91, A, C, 90001992

Sears' Crescent and Sears' Block, 38-68 and 70-72 Cornhill, Boston, 8/09/86, A, C, 86001486

Sears, David, House, 42 Beacon St., Boston, 12/30/70, C, NHL, 70000731

Second Brazer Building, 25-29 State St., Boston, 7/24/86, C, 86001913

Shirley-Eustis House, 31-37 Shirley St., Roxbury, 10/15/66, C, b, NHL, 66000787

Shubert, Sam S., Theatre [Boston Theatre MRA], 263-265 Tremont St., Boston, 12/09/80, A, C, 80000444

South End District, South Bay area between Huntington and Harrison Aves., Boston, 5/08/73, C, a, g, 73000324

South Station Headhouse, Atlantic Ave. and Summer St., Boston, 2/13/75, A, C, 75000299

St. Joseph's Roman Catholic Church Complex, Bounded by Circuit, Regent, Hulbert, and Fenwick Sts., Boston, 12/28/89, A, C, a, 89002169

St. Paul's Church, 136 Tremont St., Boston, 12/30/70, C, a, NHL, 70000730

St. Stephen's Church, Hanover St. between Clark and Harris Sts., Boston, 4/14/75, A, C, a, 75000300

Stearns, R. H., House, 140 Tremont St., Boston, 6/16/80, A, C, 80000671

Suffolk County Courthouse, Pemberton Sq., Boston, 5/08/74, C, 74000391

Suffolk County Jail, 215 Charles St., Boston, 4/23/80, A, C, 80000670

Sumner Hill Historic District, Roughly bounded by Seaverns Ave., Everett St., Carolina Ave., & Newbern St., Boston, 10/22/87, A, C, 87001889

Sumner, Charles, House, 20 Hancock St., Boston, 11/07/73, B, NHL, 73001953

Symphony and Horticultural Halls, Massachusetts and Huntington Aves., Boston, 5/30/75, C, 75000301

Temple Place Historic District, 11-55, 26-58 Temple Pl., Boston, 7/26/88, A, C, 88000427

Textile District, Roughly, Essex St. from Phillips Sq. to Columbia St. and Chauncy St. from Phillips Sq. to Rowe Pl., Boston, 11/29/90, A, C, 90001757

Town Hill District, Bounded roughly by Rutherford Ave. and Main and Warren Sts., Boston, 5/11/73, A, C, 73000850

Tremont Street Subway, Beneath Tremont, Boylston, and Washington Sts., Boston, 10/15/66, A, NHL, 66000788

Trinity Church, Copley Sq., Boston, 7/01/70, C, a, NHL, 70000733

Trinity Neighborhood House, 406 Meridian St., Boston, 4/14/92, A, C, 92000356

Trinity Rectory, Clarendon and Newbury Sts., Boston, 2/23/72, B, C, a, 72000150

Trotter, William Monroe, House, 97 Sawyer Ave., Dorchester, 5/11/76, B, NHL, 76002003

U.S.S. CONSTITUTION, Boston Naval Shipyard, Boston, 10/15/66, A, NHL, 66000789

US Post Office Garage, 135 A St., South Boston, 6/26/86, C, g, 86001378

USS CASSIN YOUNG (destroyer), Charlestown Navy Yard, Boston, 1/14/86, A, g, NHL, 86000084

Union Wharf, 295-353 Commercial St., Boston, 6/22/80, A, C, 80000669

United Shoe Machinery Corporation Building, 138-164 Federal St., Boston, 8/19/80, A, C, 80000668

Upham's Corner Market, 600 Columbia Rd., Boston, 10/11/90, A, C, 90001537

Vermont Building, 6-12 Thacher St., Boston, 11/13/84, A, C, 84000421

Washington Street Theatre District, 511-559 Washington St., Boston, 3/19/79, A, C, 79000370

West Street District [Boston Theatre MRA], West St., Boston, 12/09/80, A, C, 80000455

Westerly Burial Ground, Centre St., West Roxbury, 11/20/87, A, C, d, 87001401

Wigglesworth Building, 89-83 Franklin St., Boston, 10/21/82, A, C, 82000486

Wilbur Theatre [Boston Theatre MRA], 244-250 Tremont St., Boston, 12/09/80, A, C, 80000443

Winthrop Building, 7 Water St., Boston, 4/18/74, C, 74000392

Winthrop, Deane, House [First Period Buildings of Eastern Massachusetts TR], 40 Shirley St., Winthrop, 3/09/90, C, 90000162

Wirth, Jacob, Buildings [Boston Theatre MRA], 31-39 Stuart St., Boston, 12/09/80, A, C, 80000442

Youth's Companion Building, 209 Columbus Ave., Boston, 5/02/74, A, C, 74000393

Worcester County

Abbott Street School [Worcester MRA], 36 Abbott St., Worcester, 3/05/80, C, 80000595

Academie Brochu [Southbridge MRA], 29 Pine St., Southbridge, 6/22/89, A, C, 89000568

Adams, Benjamin, House [Uxbridge MRA], 81 N. Main St., Uxbridge, 10/07/83, B, C, 83004101

Adams, Elwood, Store [Worcester MRA], 156 Main St., Worcester, 3/05/80, A, 80000584

Adriatic Mills [Worcester MRA], 3-35 Armory St., Worcester, 3/05/80, A, B, C, 80000483

Ahern, Catherine, Three-Decker [Worcester MRA; Worcester Three-Deckers TR], 215 Cambridge St., Worcester, 2/09/90, A, C, 89002392

Albee, E., House [Uxbridge MRA], Highland St., Uxbridge, 10/07/83, C, 83004102

Alden, William E., House [Southbridge MRA], 428 Hamilton St., Southbridge, 6/22/89, A, C, 89000562

Alden—Delahanty Block [Southbridge MRA], 858 Main St., Southbridge, 6/22/89, A, C, 89000572

Aldrich, Daniel, Cottage and Sawmill [Uxbridge MRA], Aldrich St., Uxbridge, 10/07/83, A, C, 83004103

Aldrich, J., House [Uxbridge MRA], Aldrich St., Uxbridge, 1/20/84, C, 84002896

Aldrich, S., House [Uxbridge MRA], Aldrich St., Uxbridge, 10/07/83, C, 83004104

Aldrich, W., House [Uxbridge MRA], Henry St., Uxbridge, 10/07/83, C, 83004105

Alexander, Arad, House [Worcester MRA], 53 Waverly St., Worcester, 3/05/80, C, 80000544

Allen, Charles, House [Worcester MRA], 65 Elm St., Worcester, 3/05/80, B, C, 80000579

American Antiquarian Society, 185 Salisbury St., Worcester, 11/24/68, A, NHL, 68000018

Ammidown—Harding Farmhouse [Southbridge MRA], 83 Lebanon Hill Rd., Southbridge, 6/22/89, A, C, 89000552

Anderson, Ludwig, Three-Decker [Worcester MRA; Worcester Three-Deckers TR], 4 Fairbanks St., Worcester, 2/09/90, A, C, 89002355

Armsby Block [Worcester MRA], 144-148 Main St., Worcester, 3/05/80, C, 80000598

Ash Street School [Worcester MRA], Ash St., Worcester, 3/05/80, A, C, 80000542

Ashland Mill Tenement [Southbridge MRA], 141-145 Ashland Ave., Southbridge, 6/22/89, A, C, 89000545

Ashworth and Jones Factory [Worcester MRA], 1511 Main St., Worcester, 3/05/80, A, C, 80000489

Atherton Bridge, Bolton Rd., Lancaster, 9/19/79, A, C, 79000377

Aurora Hotel [Worcester MRA], 652-660 Main St., Worcester, 4/28/88, A, C, 88000429

Ayer Main Street Historic District, Main St. roughly between Park and Columbia Sts., Ayer, 3/16/89, A, C, 88000193

Babcock Block [Worcester MRA], 600 Main St., Worcester, 3/05/80, C, 80000611

Worcester County—Continued

Bacon—Morse Historic District [Southbridge MRA], N. Woodstock Rd. at Tipton Rock Rd., Southbridge vicinity, 6/22/89, A, C, d, 89000602

Baker, Peter, Three-Decker [Worcester MRA; Worcester Three-Deckers TR], 90 Vernon St., Worcester, 2/09/90, A, C, 89002445

Baldwinville Village Historic District, Roughly Elm and S. Main Sts. between Pleasant St. and Mt. View, Templeton, 2/27/86, A, B, C, a, 86000273

Bancroft Hotel [Worcester MRA], 50 Franklin St., Worcester, 3/05/80, A, C, 80000614

Bancroft Tower [Worcester MRA], Bancroft Tower Rd., Worcester, 3/05/80, C, 80000524

Bank Building [Uxbridge MRA], 40-44 S. Main St., Uxbridge, 10/07/83, C, 83004106

Bannister, Emory, House [Worcester MRA], 3 Harvard St., Worcester, 3/05/80, C, 80000569

Barker, Richard, Octagon House [Worcester MRA], 312 Plantation St., Worcester, 3/05/80, C, 80000592

Barlin Acres, 284 School St., Boylston, 11/26/82, A, C, 82000487

Barre Common District, Bounded roughly by South, Exchange, Main, Pleasant, Broad, School and Grove Sts., Barre, 5/04/76, C, a, 76000298

Barton, Clara, Homestead, 3 mi. W of Oxford on Clara Barton Rd., Oxford, 9/22/77, B, 77000202

Battelle, Marion, Three-Decker [Worcester MRA; Worcester Three-Deckers TR], 13 Preston St., Worcester, 2/09/90, A, C, 89002429

Beacon Street Firehouse [Worcester MRA], 108 Beacon St., Worcester, 3/05/80, A, C, 80000538

Beaver Street Historic District [Worcester MRA; Worcester Three-Deckers TR], 31–39 Beaver St., Worcester, 2/09/90, A, C, 89002377

Beechwood [Southbridge MRA], 495 Main St., Southbridge, 6/22/89, A, C, 89000527

Bentley, George, House [Worcester MRA], 9 Earle St., Worcester, 3/05/80, A, C, 80000560

Bigelow Carpet Company Woolen Mills, Main St., Clinton, 10/06/83, A, C, 83004107

Bigelow Carpet Mill, Union and High Sts., Clinton, 12/22/78, A, B, C, 78000467

Bigelow Tavern Historic District, 60, 64 and 65 Worcester St., West Boylston, 9/24/92, A, C, 92000043

Black Tavern, Dudley Center Rd., Dudley, 5/09/85, A, C, 85000981

Blackstone Canal, E of MA 122 between Northbridge and Uxbridge, Northbridge and vicinity, 2/06/73, A, 73000328

Bliss Building [Worcester MRA], 26 Old Lincoln St., Worcester, 3/05/80, A, C, 80000497

Blodgett, Lydia, Three-Decker [Worcester MRA; Worcester Three-Deckers TR], 167 Eastern Ave., Worcester, 2/09/90, A, C, 89002417

Bloomingdale Firehouse [Worcester MRA], 676 Franklin St., Worcester, 3/05/80, A, C, 80000593

Bloomingdale School [Worcester MRA], 327 Plantation St., Worcester, 3/05/80, C, 80000562

Borden-Pond House [Worcester MRA], 40 Laurel St., Worcester, 3/05/80, A, C, 80000590

Bostrom, Eric, Three-Decker [Worcester MRA; Worcester Three-Deckers TR], 152 Eastern Ave., Worcester, 2/09/90, A, C, 89002414

Bousquet, Henry, Three-Decker [Worcester MRA; Worcester Three-Deckers TR], 8/10 Fairmont Ave., Worcester, 2/09/90, A, C, 89002360

Bowers School, 411 Water St., Clinton, 11/10/83, A, C, 83004108

Boyer, Alexis, House [Southbridge MRA], 306 Hamilton, Southbridge, 6/22/89, A, C, 89000560

Boynton and Windsor [Worcester MRA], 718 and 720 Main St., Worcester, 3/05/80, C, 80000540

Brightside Apartments [Worcester MRA], 2 King St., Worcester, 3/05/80, A, C, 80000635

Brookfield Common Historic District, Roughly Howard, Sherman, Prouty, W. Main, Main, and Upper River Sts., Brookfield, 2/23/90, A, C, 90000161

Brooks, John, House [Worcester MRA], 12 Nelson Pl., Worcester, 3/05/80, A, C, 80000516

Brown, E., House [Uxbridge MRA], 3 Sutton St., Uxbridge, 10/07/83, C, 83004109

Building at 25–27 River Street [Southbridge MRA], 25–27 River St., Southbridge, 6/22/89, C, 89000574

Building at 29–31 River Street [Southbridge MRA], 29-31 River St., Southbridge, 6/22/89, A, C, 89000575

Building at 38–42 Worcester Street [Southbridge MRA], 38–42 Worcester St., Southbridge, 6/22/89, A, C, 89000589

Building at 52 Main Street [Southbridge MRA], 52 Main St., Southbridge, 6/22/89, A, C, 89000583

Butler Block [Uxbridge MRA], 210 Linwood St., Uxbridge, 10/07/83, C, 83004110

Calvinistic Congregational Church, 820 Main St., Fitchburg, 6/15/79, C, a, 79000371

Cambridge Street Firehouse [Worcester MRA], 534 Cambridge St., Worcester, 3/05/80, A, C, 80000487

Cambridge Street School [Worcester MRA], 510 Cambridge St., Worcester, 3/05/80, A, C, 80000484

Camp Atwater, Shore Rd., North Brookfield, 4/15/82, A, D, 82004477

Carlson, Eric, Three-Decker [Worcester MRA; Worcester Three-Deckers TR], 154 Eastern Ave., Worcester, 2/09/90, A, C, 89002415

Carpenter, George, House [Uxbridge MRA], 67 S. Main St., Uxbridge, 10/07/83, C, 83004112

Castle Street Row [Worcester MRA], 4-18 Castle St., Worcester, 3/05/80, A, C, 80000625

Cathedral of St. Paul [Worcester MRA], 38 Chatham St., Worcester, 3/05/80, C, a, 80000604

Center Village District, Irregular pattern along Main St., Lancaster, 9/15/77, C, a, 77000198

Central Mills Historic District [Southbridge MRA], Roughly bounded by Quinebaug River, North St., and Central St., Southbridge, 6/22/89, A, C, 89000595

Central Woolen Mills District [Uxbridge MRA], Mendon and Cross Sts., Uxbridge, 1/20/84, A, B, C, 84002905

Centre Village Historic District, Along Main St., Southbridge, 9/07/79, C, g, 79000379

Chadwick-Brittan House [Worcester MRA], 309 Lincoln St., Worcester, 3/05/80, C, 80000518

Chamberlain, Charles, House [Worcester MRA], 373 Pleasant St., Worcester, 3/05/80, C, 80000596

Chamberlain—Bordeau House [Southbridge MRA], 718 Main St., Southbridge, 6/22/89, A, C, 89000569

Chamberlain-Flagg House [Worcester MRA], 2 Brookshire Dr., Worcester, 3/05/80, A, C, 80000519

Chapin Block [Southbridge MRA], 208–222 Hamilton, Southbridge, 6/22/89, A, C, 89000558

Chapin, A., House [Uxbridge MRA], 26 Pleasant St., Uxbridge, 10/07/83, C, 83004113

Cheney, Alpha M., House [Southbridge MRA], 61 Chestnut St., Southbridge, 6/22/89, A, C, 89000526

Cheney, J. M., Rental House [Southbridge MRA], 32 Edwards St., Southbridge, 6/22/89, A, C, 89000564

Chestnut Hill Meetinghouse, Chestnut and Thayer Sts., Millville vicinity, 11/13/84, A, C, a, 84000434

Clark University [Worcester MRA], Clark University Campus, Worcester, 3/05/80, A, B, C, 80000547

Clarke—Glover Farmhouse [Southbridge MRA], 201 South St., Southbridge, 6/22/89, A, C, 89000536

Cliff Cottage [Southbridge MRA], 787 Mill St., Southbridge, 6/22/89, A, C, 89000570

Cluett Peabody & Company, 123 First St., Leominster, 6/08/89, A, C, 89000439

Cobb, George, House [Worcester MRA], 24 William St., Worcester, 3/05/80, C, 80000571

Cole, E. Merritt, House [Southbridge MRA], 386 Main St., Southbridge, 6/22/89, A, C, 89000576

Colton's Block [Worcester MRA], 588 Main St., Worcester, 3/05/80, C, 80000610

Comins—Wall House [Southbridge MRA], 42 Hamilton St., Southbridge, 6/22/89, A, C, 89000555

Congregational Church [Southbridge MRA], 61 Elm St., Southbridge, 6/22/89, A, C, a, 89000591

Cook, A. E., House [Uxbridge MRA], Aldrich St., Uxbridge, 10/07/83, C, 83004115

Copeland, Samuel, House [Worcester MRA], 31 Harvard St., Worcester, 3/05/80, A, C, 80000563

Crabtree, Thomas, Three-Decker [Worcester MRA; Worcester Three-Deckers TR], 22 Haynes St., Worcester, 2/09/90, A, C, 89002383

Crawford, Elias, House [Worcester MRA], 3 Norwood St., Worcester, 3/05/80, C, 80000552

Crompton Loom Works [Worcester MRA], 132-142 Green St., Worcester, 3/05/80, A, B, C, 80000541

Crystal Street Historic District [Worcester MRA; Worcester Three-Deckers TR], 30–34 Crystal St., Worcester, 2/09/90, A, C, 89002379

Cummings, E. B., House [Southbridge MRA], 52 Marcy St., Southbridge, 6/22/89, A, C, 89000566

Dani and Soldani Cabinet Makers and Wood Workers Factory [Southbridge MRA], 484

Worcester County—Continued

Worcester St., Southbridge, 6/22/89, A, C, 89000529

Daniels, Frederick, House [Worcester MRA], 148 Lincoln St., Worcester, 3/05/80, B, C, 80000526

Dartmouth Street School [Worcester MRA], 13 Dartmouth St., Worcester, 3/05/80, A, C, 80000546

Davis, Isaac, House [Worcester MRA], 1 Oak St., Worcester, 3/05/80, B, C, 80000578

Davis, Joseph, House [Worcester MRA], 41 Elm St., Worcester, 3/05/80, B, C, 80000574

Davis, Rodney, Three-Decker [Worcester MRA; Worcester Three-Deckers TR], 62 Catharine St., Worcester, 2/09/90, A, C, 89002398

Davis, Wesley, Three-Decker [Worcester MRA; Worcester Three-Deckers TR], 7 Albert St., Worcester, 2/09/90, A, C, 89002386

Dean, Mary, Three-Decker [Worcester MRA; Worcester Three-Deckers TR], 130 Belmont St., Worcester, 2/09/90, A, C, 89002390

Deane, Francis, Cottage [Uxbridge MRA], 58 N. Main St., Uxbridge, 10/07/83, C, 83004116

Delsignore, Louis, Three-Decker [Worcester MRA; Worcester Three-Deckers TR], 12 Imperial Rd., Worcester, 2/09/90, A, C, 89002396

Dennison School House [Southbridge MRA], Dennison Ln., Southbridge, 6/22/89, A, C, 89000551

Dewey Francis, House [Worcester MRA], 71 Elm St., Worcester, 3/05/80, C, 80000580

District Five Schoolhouse, School St. between Boyden and 1st Sts., Webster, 6/05/91, A, C, 91000697

Dodge, Helen, Three-Decker [Worcester MRA; Worcester Three-Deckers TR], 570 Pleasant St., Worcester, 2/09/90, A, C, 89002427

Doran, Thomas F., Three-Decker [Worcester MRA; Worcester Three-Deckers TR], 27 John St., Worcester, 2/09/90, A, C, 89002406

Dowley-Taylor House [Worcester MRA], 770 Main St., Worcester, 3/05/80, A, C, b, 80000627

Downing Street School [Worcester MRA], 92 Downing St., Worcester, 3/05/80, C, 80000621

Downtown Clinton Historic District, Roughly bounded by Union and Prospects Sts. on High and Church Sts., Clinton, 2/21/85, A, C, 85000319

Dresser, Sylvester, House [Southbridge MRA], 29 Summer St., Southbridge, 6/22/89, A, C, 89000523

Drew, Elvira, Three-Decker [Worcester MRA; Worcester Three-Deckers TR], 42 Abbott St., Worcester, 2/09/90, A, C, 89002384

Duck Mill, 60 Duck Mill Rd., Fitchburg, 5/09/85, A, C, 85000982

Duke, Philip, Three-Decker [Worcester MRA; Worcester Three-Deckers TR], 7 Maxwell St., Worcester, 2/09/90, A, C, 89002425

Dunbar—Vinton House [Southbridge MRA], Hook and Hamilton Sts., Southbridge, 6/22/89, C, 89000573

Durfee, Henry E., Farmhouse [Southbridge MRA], 281 Eastford Rd., Southbridge, 6/22/89, A, C, 89000547

Dworman, David, Three-Decker [Worcester MRA; Worcester Three-Deckers TR], 159 Providence St., Worcester, 2/09/90, A, C, 89002430

East Worcester School-Norcross Factory [Worcester MRA], 10 E. Worcester St., Worcester, 3/05/80, A, C, 80000618

Eddy Block, 119-131 Main St. and 4 Davis St., Webster, 12/03/80, A, C, 80000470

Elizabeth Street School [Worcester MRA], 31 Elizabeth St., Worcester, 3/05/80, C, 80000589

Elm Hill Farm Historic District, E Main St. E of jct. with Brookfield Rd., Brookfield, 5/16/91, A, C, 91000600

Elm Park [Worcester MRA], Elm Park, Worcester, 7/01/70, A, C, 70000096

Elm Street Fire House [Southbridge MRA], 24 Elm St., Southbridge, 6/22/89, A, C, 89000530

Elm Street Fire Station, 58 Elm St., Gardner, 4/02/80, A, C, 80001677

Elm Street Historic District [Worcester MRA; Worcester Three-Deckers TR], 132–148 Elm St., Worcester, 2/09/90, A, C, 89002374

Emmanuel Baptist [Worcester MRA], 717 Main St., Worcester, 3/05/80, C, a, 80000536

English High School [Worcester MRA], 20 Irving St., Worcester, 3/05/80, C, 80000601

Enterprise Building [Worcester MRA], 540 Main St., Worcester, 3/05/80, C, 80000608

Erikson, Knut, Three-Decker [Worcester MRA; Worcester Three-Deckers TR], 19 Stanton St., Worcester, 2/09/90, A, C, 89002438

Euclid Avenue—Montrose Street Historic District [Worcester MRA; Worcester Three-Deckers TR], Along Euclid Ave. and Montrose St., between Vernon St. and Perry Ave., Worcester, 2/09/90, A, C, 89002357

Evangelical Free Church [Southbridge MRA], Hamilton St., Southbridge, 6/22/89, A, C, a, 89000561

Fairlawn [Worcester MRA], 189 May St., Worcester, 3/05/80, A, B, 80000594

Farnum Block [Uxbridge MRA], 2-6 N. Main St., Uxbridge, 10/07/83, A, C, 83004117

Farnum, Coronet John, House, Mendon St., Uxbridge, 5/07/80, A, C, 80001682

Farnum, Moses, House [Uxbridge MRA], MA 146, Uxbridge, 10/07/83, B, C, 83004118

Farnum, R., House [Uxbridge MRA], 20 Oak St., Uxbridge, 10/07/83, C, 83004119

Farnum, William and Mary, House [Uxbridge MRA], Albee Rd., Uxbridge, 1/20/84, C, 84002914

Fay Club, 658 Main St., Fitchburg, 1/31/78, B, C, 78000470

Fay Street Historic District [Worcester MRA; Worcester Three-Deckers TR], 4–6 Fay St., Worcester, 2/09/90, A, C, 89002372

Felton Street School, 20 Felton St., Hudson, 2/27/86, A, C, 86000275

First Church of Christ, Lancaster, Facing the Common, Lancaster, 12/30/70, C, a, NHL, 70000897

First Methodist Church, 75 Walnut St., Clinton, 11/02/90, A, C, a, 90001720

First Minister's House, 186 Elm St., Gardner, 11/14/79, C, 79000372

Fisher, Nathan, House, E of Shrewsbury on MA 9, Westborough vicinity, 3/25/80, A, C, 80001679

Fitch, C.H., House [Worcester MRA], 15 Oread St., Worcester, 3/05/80, B, C, 80000631

Flagg, Amos, House [Worcester MRA], 246 Burncoat St., Worcester, 3/05/80, C, 80000515

Flagg, Benjamin, House [Worcester MRA], 136 Plantation St., Worcester, 3/05/80, A, B, C, 80000620

Flagg, Levi, Three-Decker [Worcester MRA; Worcester Three-Deckers TR], 79 Florence St., Worcester, 2/09/90, A, C, 89002362

Fontaine, George, Three-Decker [Worcester MRA; Worcester Three-Deckers TR], 141 Vernon St., Worcester, 2/09/90, A, C, 89002447

Forbes, William Trowbridge, House [Worcester MRA], 23 Trowbridge Rd., Worcester, 3/05/80, B, C, 80000636

Forest Hill Cottage [Worcester MRA], 22 Windsor St., Worcester, 3/05/80, A, C, 80000529

Founder's Hall, Atlantic Union College Campus, Lancaster, 4/14/80, A, C, a, 80001678

Freegrace Marble Farm Historic District, 80 Burbank Rd., Sutton, 11/13/89, A, C, 89001967

Freeland Street School [Worcester MRA], 12 Freeland St., Worcester, 3/05/80, A, C, 80000482

Friberg, Andrew, Three-Decker [Worcester MRA; Worcester Three-Deckers TR], 26 Ames St., Worcester, 2/09/90, A, C, 89002387

Friends Meetinghouse, S of Uxbridge on MA 146, Uxbridge vicinity, 1/24/74, A, C, a, d, e, 74000395

Fruitlands, Prospect Hill, Harvard, 3/19/74, B, NHL, 74001761

G.A.R. Hall, 55 Pearl St., Worcester, 3/13/75, C, 75000303

Gabriel, George, House [Worcester MRA], 31 Lenox St., Worcester, 3/05/80, C, 80000523

Gale, George, House [Worcester MRA], 15 Elizabeth St., Worcester, 3/05/80, A, C, 80000561

Garbose Building, 3 Pleasant St., Gardner, 4/12/83, A, C, 83000609

Gardner News Building, 309 Central St., Gardner, 11/14/79, A, C, 79000373

Gay Farm, S of Petersham off Nichewaug Rd., Petersham vicinity, 9/22/77, B, C, 77000201

Giguere, Thomas, Three-Decker [Worcester MRA; Worcester Three-Deckers TR], 18 Fairhaven Rd., Worcester, 2/09/90, A, C, 89002356

Gilbertville Historic District, Roughly Main, Church, High, North, Broad and Bridge Sts., Hardwick, 12/26/91, A, C, 91001848

Gillon Block, 189 Main St., Milford, 10/21/82, A, C, 82000488

Gleason, James, Cottage [Southbridge MRA], 31 Sayles St., Southbridge, 6/22/89, A, C, b, 89000533

Globe Village Fire House [Southbridge MRA], West St. at Main St., Southbridge, 6/22/89, A, C, 89000540

Glover Street Historic District [Southbridge MRA], Glover St. between High and Poplar Sts., Southbridge, 6/22/89, A, C, 89000601

Worcester County—Continued

Goddard House [Worcester MRA], 12 Catherine St., Worcester, 3/05/80, B, C, 80000555

Goddard Rocket Launching Site, Ninth fairway, Pakachoag Golf Course, Pakachoag Rd., Auburn vicinity, 11/13/66, A, f, NHL, 66000654

Goddard, Harry, House [Worcester MRA], 190 Salisbury St., Worcester, 3/05/80, A, C, 80000525

Gough, John B., House, 215 Main St., Boylston, 3/19/74, B, NHL, 74001763

Goulding, Henry, House [Worcester MRA], 26 Harvard St., Worcester, 3/05/80, B, C, 80000564

Goulding, W.H., House [Worcester MRA], 4 Dix St., Worcester, 3/05/80, C, 80000566

Grafton Common Historic District, Roughly Worcester, Oak, Millbury, Church, South, Upton, and North Sts., Grafton, 6/22/88, A, C, a, f, 88000707

Grafton Inn, 25 Central Sq., Grafton, 6/16/80, A, C, 80001675

Grafton Street School [Worcester MRA], 311 Grafton St., Worcester, 3/05/80, A, C, 80000545

Granite Store [Uxbridge MRA], 112-116 Hecla St., Uxbridge, 10/07/83, A, C, 83004120

Green Hill Park Shelter [Worcester MRA], Green Hill Parkway, Worcester, 3/05/80, C, 80000522

Greendale Branch Library [Worcester MRA], 470 W. Boylston St., Worcester, 3/05/80, A, C, 80000511

Greendale Village Improvement Society Building [Worcester MRA], 480 W. Boylston St., Worcester, 11/07/76, A, 76000949

Gullberg, Evert, Three-Decker [Worcester MRA; Worcester Three-Deckers TR], 18 Ashton St., Worcester, 2/09/90, A, C, 89002388

Hadley, Gilbert, Three-Decker [Worcester MRA; Worcester Three-Deckers TR], 31 Russell St., Worcester, 2/09/90, A, C, 89002433

Hall, Charles A., Three-Decker [Worcester MRA; Worcester Three-Deckers TR], 68 Mason St., Worcester, 2/09/90, A, C, 89002423

Hall, S.A., House [Uxbridge MRA], 133 N. Main St., Uxbridge, 10/07/83, C, 83004121

Hamilton Mill Brick House [Southbridge MRA], 16 High St., Southbridge, 6/22/89, A, C, 89000542

Hamilton Mill—West Street Factory Housing [Southbridge MRA], 45 West St., Southbridge, 6/22/89, A, C, 89000541

Hamilton Millwright—Agent's House [Southbridge MRA], 757–761 Main St., Southbridge, 6/22/89, A, C, 89000543

Hamilton Woolen Company Historic District [Southbridge MRA], Roughly bounded by McKinstry Brook, Quinebaug River, and Mill St., Southbridge, 6/22/89, A, C, 89000594

Hammond Heights [Worcester MRA], Properties along Germain, Haviland, Highland, and Westland Sts. and Institute Rd., Worcester, 3/05/80, C, 80000531

Hammond Organ Factory [Worcester MRA], 9 May St., Worcester, 3/05/80, A, C, 80000632

Harding-Winter Street Manufacturing District [Worcester MRA], 28-88 Winter St., Worcester, 3/05/80, A, C, 80000543

Hardwick Village Historic District, Petersham, Barre, Greenwich, Ruggles Hill and Gilbertville Rds., Hardwick, 12/19/91, A, C, 91001849

Harrington, Theodore, House [Southbridge MRA], 77 Hamilton St., Southbridge, 6/22/89, A, C, 89000557

Harris-Merrick House [Worcester MRA], 41 Fruit St., Worcester, 3/05/80, A, C, 80000602

Hartwell, George H., House [Southbridge MRA], 105 Hamilton St., Southbridge, 6/22/89, A, C, 89000556

Hartwell, Samuel C., House [Southbridge MRA], 79 Elm St., Southbridge, 6/22/89, A, C, a, 89000592

Harvard Shaker Village Historic District, Roughly Shaker Rd., S. Shaker Rd., and Maple Ln., Harvard, 10/30/89, A, C, D, a, 89001871

Hastins, John, Cottage [Worcester MRA], 31 William St., Worcester, 3/05/80, C, 80000572

Hayward Mill, Jct. of North and Cook Sts., on the Mumford R., Douglas, 6/17/91, A, C, 91000695

Hayward, William, House [Uxbridge MRA], 77 N. Main St., Uxbridge, 10/07/83, B, C, 83004122

Heywood, Levi, Memorial Library Building, 28 Pearl St., Gardner, 12/06/79, B, C, f, 79000374

Heywood-Wakefield Company Complex, 206 Central St., Gardner, 9/15/83, A, C, 83000610

Higgins Armory Museum [Worcester MRA], 100 Barber Ave., Worcester, 3/05/80, A, C, 80000514

Higgins, Aldus Chapin, House [Worcester MRA], 1 John Wing Rd., Worcester, 3/05/80, C, 80000496

High—School Streets Historic District [Southbridge MRA], High St. at School St., Southbridge, 6/22/89, A, C, 89000600

Hirst, Samuel, Three-Decker [Worcester MRA; Worcester Three-Deckers TR], 90 Lovell St., Worcester, 2/09/90, A, C, 89002420

Hobbs, Marcus, House [Worcester MRA], 16 William St., Worcester, 3/05/80, A, C, 80000582

Hodgson, William, Two-Family House [Southbridge MRA], 103–105 Sayles St., Southbridge, 6/22/89, A, C, 89000578

Hogg, William, House [Worcester MRA], 54 Elm St., Worcester, 3/05/80, B, C, 80000576

Holbrook, Sylvanus, House [Uxbridge MRA], Albee Rd., Uxbridge, 10/07/83, C, 83004123

Holden Center Historic District, Main, Maple, Highland, and Reservoir Sts., Holden, 12/22/77, A, C, a, b, d, 77000194

Holland—Towne House, SR 32, Petersham, 8/13/90, B, C, 89002327

Holy Cross College [Worcester MRA], Holy Cross College Campus, Worcester, 3/05/80, A, 80000491

Holy Name of Jesus Complex [Worcester MRA], Illinois St., Worcester, 6/09/88, A, C, a, 88000721

Houghton Street Historic District [Worcester MRA; Worcester Three-Deckers TR], Houghton St. between Palm and Dorchester Sts., Worcester, 2/09/90, A, C, 89002371

House at 18 Walnut Street [Southbridge MRA], 18 Walnut St., Southbridge, 6/22/89, A, C, 89000580

House at 3 Dean Street [Southbridge MRA], 3 Dean St., Southbridge, 6/22/89, A, C, b, 89000587

House at 34 Benefit Street [Southbridge MRA], 34 Benefit St., Southbridge, 6/22/89, A, C, 89000585

House at 59–63 Crystal Street [Southbridge MRA], 59–63 Crystal St., Southbridge, 6/22/89, A, C, 89000584

House at 64 Main Street [Southbridge MRA], 64 Main St., Southbridge, 6/22/89, A, C, 89000582

House at 70–72 Main Street [Southbridge MRA], 70–72 Main St., Southbridge, 6/22/89, A, C, 89000581

House at 91 Coombs Street [Southbridge MRA], 91 Coombs St., Southbridge, 6/22/89, A, C, 89000525

Hudson House, NE of Oxford on Hudson Rd., Oxford vicinity, 2/08/78, A, C, 78000480

Huguenot Fort, Fort Hill Rd., Oxford, 4/27/88, A, C, D, 88000424

Hunt, Daniel, Three-Decker [Worcester MRA; Worcester Three-Deckers TR], 9 Wyman St., Worcester, 2/09/90, A, C, 89002451

Hunt, David, Three-Decker [Worcester MRA; Worcester Three-Deckers TR], 26 Louise St., Worcester, 2/09/90, A, C, 89002412

I00F Building [Worcester MRA], 674 Main St., Worcester, 3/05/80, A, C, 80000535

Indian Hill-North Village [Worcester MRA], properties along Ararat St. and Delaval, Heroult, Marconi, Watt, and Westinghouse Rds., Worcester, 3/05/80, A, 80000510

Ingleside Avenue Historic District [Worcester MRA; Worcester Three-Deckers TR], 218–220 and 226–228 Ingleside Ave., Worcester, 2/09/90, A, C, 89002369

Ingraham, Harry B., Three-Decker [Worcester MRA; Worcester Three-Deckers TR], 19 Freeland St., Worcester, 2/09/90, A, C, 89002363

Institutional District [Worcester MRA], Properties on Lincoln and Wheaton Squares and on Salisbury and Tuckerman Sts., Worcester, 3/05/80, A, C, a, 80000554

Ironstone Mill Housing and Cellar Hole [Uxbridge MRA], Ironstone St., Uxbridge, 10/07/83, A, C, 83004124

Jenckes, E. N., Store, Main St., Douglas, 1/28/88, A, C, 87002558

Johnson, Edwin, Three-Decker [Worcester MRA; Worcester Three-Deckers TR], 183 Austin St., Worcester, 2/09/90, A, C, 89002389

Johnson, John and Edward, Three-Decker [Worcester MRA; Worcester Three-Deckers TR], 31 Louise St., Worcester, 2/09/90, A, C, 89002416

Johnson, John, Three-Decker [Worcester MRA; Worcester Three-Deckers TR], 140 Eastern Ave., Worcester, 2/09/90, A, C, 89002408

Johnson, Paul, Three-Decker [Worcester MRA; Worcester Three-Deckers TR], 7 Stanton St., Worcester, 2/09/90, A, C, 89002437

Worcester County—Continued

Judson—Litchfield House [Southbridge MRA], 313 South St., Southbridge, 6/22/89, A, C, 89000539

Judson-Taft House [Uxbridge MRA], 30 Pleasant St., Uxbridge, 10/07/83, C, 83004125

Junction Shop and Herman Street District [Worcester MRA], Properties on Jackson, Herman, and Beacon Sts., Worcester, 3/05/80, A, C, 80000533

Kaller, Erick, Three-Decker [Worcester MRA; Worcester Three-Deckers TR], 146 Eastern Ave., Worcester, 2/09/90, A, C, 89002411

Kaller, Erick, Three-Decker [Worcester MRA; Worcester Three-Deckers TR], 148 Eastern Ave., Worcester, 2/09/90, A, C, 89002413

Katz and Leavitt Apartment House [Worcester MRA], 53 Elm St., Worcester, 3/05/80, C, 80000575

Kensely, J., House [Uxbridge MRA], Chestnut St., Uxbridge, 10/07/83, C, 83004126

Kinney, A., House [Southbridge MRA], 42 Edwards St., Southbridge, 6/22/89, A, C, 89000565

Knollwood [Worcester MRA], 425 Salisbury St., Worcester, 3/05/80, C, 80000520

Knowles, Lucius, House [Worcester MRA], 838 Main St., Worcester, 3/05/80, B, C, 80000628

Knowlton Hat Factory, 134 Main St., Upton, 6/01/82, A, B, C, 82004467

LaCroix—Mosher House [Southbridge MRA], 56 Everett St., Southbridge, 6/22/89, A, C, 89000524

LaRochelle, Napoleon, Two-Family House [Southbridge MRA], 30 Pine St., Southbridge, 6/22/89, A, C, 89000567

Lake Street Fire Station, 2 Lake St., Gardner, 3/25/80, C, 80001676

Lancaster Industrial School for Girls, SE of Lancaster on Old Common Rd., Lancaster vicinity, 10/08/76, A, C, a, b, 76000301

Lane, Anthony, House, NE of Lancaster on Seven Bridge Rd., Lancaster vicinity, 11/07/76, C, 76000300

Larchmont [Worcester MRA], 36 Butler St., Worcester, 3/05/80, A, B, C, 80000492

Larson, Swan, Three-Decker [Worcester MRA; Worcester Three-Deckers TR], 12 Summerhill Ave., Worcester, 2/09/90, A, C, 89002443

Legg, John, House [Worcester MRA], 5 Claremont St., Worcester, 3/05/80, B, C, 80000623

Levenson, Morris, Three-Decker [Worcester MRA; Worcester Three-Deckers TR], 38 Plantation St., Worcester, 2/09/90, A, C, 89002446

Liberty Farm [Worcester MRA], 116 Mower St., Worcester, 9/13/74, B, NHL, 74002046

Lincoln Estate-Elm Park Historic District [Worcester MRA], Properties along Cedar, Fruit, Oak, Sever, West, and William Sts., Worcester, 3/05/80, A, C, 80000570

Lincoln, Gov. Levi, House [Worcester MRA], 4 Avalon Pl., Worcester, 3/05/80, B, C, 80000573

Linwood Historic District, Roughly Linwood Ave., Maple Ct., and Pine Ct., Northbridge, 6/16/89, A, B, C, 88002753

Lothrop, Joseph, House, E of Shrewsbury at 208 Turnpike Rd., Shrewsbury vicinity, 3/27/80, A, C, 80001680

Lower Pleasant Street District [Worcester MRA], 418-426 Main St. and 9-49 Pleasant St., Worcester, 3/05/80, C, 80000613

Lumb, Thomas, Three-Decker [Worcester MRA; Worcester Three-Deckers TR], 80 Dewey St., Worcester, 2/09/90, A, C, 89002403

Lumb, Thomas, Three-Decker [Worcester MRA; Worcester Three-Deckers TR], 44 Winfield St., Worcester, 2/09/90, A, C, 89002448

Lundberg, Charles, Three-Decker [Worcester MRA; Worcester Three-Deckers TR], 67 Catharine St., Worcester, 2/09/90, A, C, 89002399

Lunenburg Historic District, Leominster Rd., Highland St., Oak and Massachusetts Aves., Main St., and Lancaster Ave., Lunenburg, 8/24/88, A, B, C, a, 87001060

Magnuson, Charles, Three-Decker [Worcester MRA; Worcester Three-Deckers TR], 56/58 Olga Ave., Worcester, 2/09/90, A, C, 89002434

Main Street Historic District, 175-299 and 228-274 Main St., Webster, 4/06/82, A, C, 82004484

Malvern Road School [Worcester MRA], Malvern Rd. and Southbridge St., Worcester, 10/04/84, A, C, 84000096

Maple Street Historic District [Southbridge MRA], Maple St., Southbridge, 6/22/89, A, C, 89000597

Maples Cottage, E of Shrewsbury on Oak St., Westborough vicinity, 3/25/80, A, C, 80001681

Marble, Jerome, House [Worcester MRA], 23 Harvard St., Worcester, 3/05/80, C, 80000567

Marcy, Mrs. R., House [Southbridge MRA], 64 South St., Southbridge, 6/22/89, C, 89000535

Mark, John, Three-Decker [Worcester MRA; Worcester Three-Deckers TR], 24 Sigel St., Worcester, 2/09/90, A, C, 89002435

Marlborough Brook Filter Beds [Water Supply System of Metropolitan Boston MPS], Framingham Rd., Marlborough, 1/18/90, A, C, 89002286

Marsh, Alexander, House [Worcester MRA], 57 Elm St., Worcester, 3/05/80, B, C, 80000583

Masonic Temple [Worcester MRA], Ionic Ave., Worcester, 3/05/80, C, 80000537

Massachusetts Avenue Historic District [Worcester MRA], Between Salisbury St. and Drury Lane, Worcester, 12/16/71, A, C, b, 71000356

Massad, Anthony, Three-Decker [Worcester MRA; Worcester Three-Deckers TR], 14 Harlow St., Worcester, 2/09/90, A, C, 89002380

Matthews Fulling Mill Site, Address Restricted, North Brookfield vicinity, 11/12/75, A, B, D, 75000302

May Street Historic District [Worcester MRA], Properties from 29 to 46 May St., Worcester, 3/05/80, C, 80000622

McCafferty, Elizabeth, Three-Decker [Worcester MRA; Worcester Three-Deckers TR], 45 Canterbury St., Worcester, 2/09/90, A, C, 89002395

McCarron, Andrew, Three-Decker [Worcester MRA; Worcester Three-Deckers TR], 3 Pitt St., Worcester, 2/09/90, A, C, 89002442

McDermott, John B., Three-Decker [Worcester MRA; Worcester Three-Deckers TR], 21 Freeland St., Worcester, 2/09/90, A, C, 89002366

McFarland, William, House [Worcester MRA], 525 Salisbury St., Worcester, 3/05/80, C, 80000517

McGrath, Patrick, Three-Decker [Worcester MRA; Worcester Three-Deckers TR], 50 Dorchester St., Worcester, 2/09/90, A, C, 89002407

McGuinness, Patrick, Three-Decker [Worcester MRA; Worcester Three-Deckers TR], 25 Suffield St., Worcester, 2/09/90, A, C, 89002439

McKinstry, William, Farmhouse [Southbridge MRA], 361 Pleasant St., Southbridge, 6/22/89, A, C, 89000571

McKinstry, William, Jr., House [Southbridge MRA], 915 W. Main St., Southbridge, 6/22/89, A, C, 89000528

McPartland, Frank, Three-Decker [Worcester MRA; Worcester Three-Deckers TR], 61 Paine St., Worcester, 2/09/90, A, C, 89002436

McPartland, James, Three-Decker [Worcester MRA; Worcester Three-Deckers TR], 17 Pond St., Worcester, 2/09/90, A, C, 89002428

Mechanics Hall, 321 Main St., Worcester, 11/09/72, A, C, 72000152

Mechanics' Hall District [Worcester MRA], Properties between 282 and 343 Main St., Worcester, 3/05/80, A, B, C, 80000577

Memorial Hall, School St., Milford, 5/09/85, C, f, 85000983

Merrill Double House [Worcester MRA], 18-20 West St., Worcester, 3/05/80, C, 80000581

Miles, Charles, House [Worcester MRA], 131 Lincoln St., Worcester, 3/05/80, C, 80000527

Milford Town Hall, 52 Main St., Milford, 9/22/77, C, 77000200

Mission Chapel [Worcester MRA], 205 Summer St., Worcester, 3/05/80, A, C, a, 80000616

Montvale [Worcester MRA], Properties along Monadnock, Sagamore, Waconah, and Whitman Rds., and Salisbury St., Worcester, 3/05/80, C, 80000521

Monument Park Historic District, Monument Park and environs N of Main St., Fitchburg, 5/16/78, A, C, a, 78000478

Monument Square Historic District, Main and Water Sts., and Grove Ave., Leominster, 7/08/82, A, C, 82004474

Moore, Jesse, House [Worcester MRA], 25 Catherine St., Worcester, 3/05/80, C, 80000557

Morse, H., House [Southbridge MRA], 230 South St., Southbridge, 6/22/89, A, C, 89000538

Munroe, Sarah, Three-Decker [Worcester MRA; Worcester Three-Deckers TR], 11 Rodney St., Worcester, 2/09/90, A, C, 89002432

Murdock School, Murdock Ave., Winchendon, 1/28/88, A, C, 87002562

Murphy, Patrick, Three-Decker [Worcester MRA; Worcester Three-Deckers TR], 31 Jefferson St., Worcester, 2/09/90, A, C, 89002404

Nelson, Christina, Three-Decker [Worcester MRA; Worcester Three-Deckers TR], 45 Butler St., Worcester, 2/09/90, A, C, 89002391

New York, New Haven & Hartford Passenger Depot [Southbridge MRA], Depot St., Southbridge, 6/22/89, A, C, 89000554

Newton, Charles, House [Worcester MRA], 24 Brattle St., Worcester, 3/05/80, C, 80000508

Worcester County—Continued

No. 4 Schoolhouse, Farrington Rd., Barre, 6/22/88, A, C, 88000711

Norcross Brothers Houses [Worcester MRA], 16, 18 Claremont St., Worcester, 3/05/80, B, C, 80000624

North Uxbridge School [Uxbridge MRA], 87 E. Hartford Ave., Uxbridge, 10/07/83, C, 83004127

North Village Historic District, N. Main St., Lancaster, 11/23/77, C, 77000199

North Worcester Aid Society [Worcester MRA], 58 Holden St., Worcester, 3/05/80, A, C, 80000512

Northborough Town Hall, NE corner of W. Main and Blake St., Northborough, 2/23/72, C, 72000151

Northside Village Historic District, Stafford St., Northside and Cemetery Rds., Charlton, 10/05/77, B, C, 77000195

Notre Dame Catholic Church [Southbridge MRA], Main St. at Marcy St., Southbridge, 6/22/89, A, C, a, 89000563

O'Brien, Richard, Three-Decker [Worcester MRA; Worcester Three-Deckers TR], 43 Suffolk St., Worcester, 2/09/90, A, C, 89002441

O'Connor, James, Three-Decker [Worcester MRA; Worcester Three-Deckers TR], 23 Endicott St., Worcester, 2/09/90, A, C, 89002419

O'Connor, James—John Trybowski Three-Decker [Worcester MRA; Worcester Three-Deckers TR], 21 Canton St., Worcester, 2/09/90, A, C, 89002393

Oakes, J. J., House [Southbridge MRA], 14 South St., Southbridge, 6/22/89, A, C, 89000534

Odd Fellows' Home [Worcester MRA], 40 Randolph Rd., Worcester, 3/05/80, A, C, 80000513

Old Centre Historic District, Roughly Old County and Baldwinsville Rds., Hale St., and Teel Rd., Winchendon, 9/18/87, A, C, 87000901

Old State Mutual Building [Worcester MRA], 240 Main St., Worcester, 3/05/80, A, C, 80000585

Old Stone Church, Off MA 140, West Boylston, 4/13/73, A, a, 73000329

Old Town Hall, 1307 Main St., Athol, 6/17/87, A, C, a, 87000876

Oxford-Crown Extension District [Worcester MRA], Properties along Ashland, Austin, Chatham, Congress, Crown, and Pleasant Sts., Worcester, 3/05/80, A, C, 80000605

Oxford-Crown Historic District [Worcester MRA], Roughly bounded by Chatham, Congress, Crown, Pleasant, Oxford Sts. and Oxford Pl., Worcester, 5/06/76, C, a, 76000954

Paine, Timothy, House [Worcester MRA], 140 Lincoln St., Worcester, 4/30/76, B, C, 76000948

Park Building [Worcester MRA], 507 Main St., Worcester, 3/05/80, A, C, 80000607

Partridge, Jabez, Homestead, 81 Partridge Rd., Gardner, 12/06/79, B, C, 79000375

Pequoig Hotel, Main St., Athol, 11/17/78, A, C, 78000469

Perry Avenue Historic District [Worcester MRA; Worcester Three-Deckers TR], 49–55 Perry Ave., Worcester, 2/09/90, A, C, 89002367

Petersham Common Historic District, MA 32/122, Petersham, 5/11/82, A, C, a, e, 82004481

Petterson, Lars—Adolph Carlson Three-Decker [Worcester MRA; Worcester Three-Deckers TR], 76 Fairhaven Rd., Worcester, 2/09/90, A, C, 89002358

Petterson, Lars—Fred Gurney Three-Decker [Worcester MRA; Worcester Three-Deckers TR], 2 Harlow St., Worcester, 2/09/90, A, C, 89002368

Petterson, Lars—Silas Archer Three-Decker [Worcester MRA; Worcester Three-Deckers TR], 80 Fairhaven Rd., Worcester, 2/09/90, A, C, 89002359

Petterson, Lars—James Reidy Three-Decker [Worcester MRA; Worcester Three-Deckers TR], 4 Harlow St., Worcester, 2/09/90, A, C, 89002376

Phillips, E. M., House [Southbridge MRA], 35 Dresser St., Southbridge, 6/22/89, A, C, 89000532

Pilgrim Congregational Church [Worcester MRA], 909 Main St., Worcester, 3/05/80, C, a, 80000551

Pleasant Street Firehouse [Worcester MRA], 408 Pleasant St., Worcester, 3/05/80, C, 80000597

Plimpton, Simon, Farmhouse [Southbridge MRA], 561 South St., Southbridge, 6/22/89, A, C, 89000550

Ponakin Bridge, N of Lancaster on Ponakin Rd., Lancaster vicinity, 9/10/79, A, C, 79000378

Prentiss, Addison, House [Worcester MRA], 3 Channing Way, Worcester, 3/05/80, A, B, C, 80000558

Prescott Town House, MA 32, Petersham, 2/21/89, A, B, C, b, 89000043

Prospect Heights Historic District, Roughly bounded by Prospect Heights, Prospect, and Water Sts., Milford, 9/05/90, A, C, 90001344

Providence Street Firehouse [Worcester MRA], 98 Providence St., Worcester, 3/05/80, C, 80000553

Providence Street Historic District [Worcester MRA; Worcester Three-Deckers TR], 127–145 Providence St., Worcester, 2/09/90, A, C, 89002381

Provost, Arthur, Three-Decker [Worcester MRA; Worcester Three-Deckers TR], 30 Thorne St., Worcester, 2/09/90, A, C, 89002444

Putnam, Gen. Rufus, House, 344 Main St., Rutland, 11/28/72, B, NHL, 72001330

Putnam, Otis, House [Worcester MRA], 25 Harvard St., Worcester, 3/05/80, C, 80000565

Quinepoxet River Bridge [Water Supply System of Metropolitan Boston MPS], Thomas St. over the Quinepoxet River at the Wachusett Reservoir, West Boylston, 4/08/90, A, C, 89002292

Quinsigamond Branch Library [Worcester MRA], 812 Millbury St., Worcester, 3/05/80, A, C, 80000494

Quinsigamond Firehouse [Worcester MRA], 837 Millbury St., Worcester, 3/05/80, A, C, 80000495

Raymond, Tilley, House [Worcester MRA], 12 George St., Worcester, 3/05/80, A, C, 80000568

Reed, Frank, Three-Decker [Worcester MRA; Worcester Three-Deckers TR], 913/915 Main St., Worcester, 2/09/90, A, C, 89002422

Rice, Ezra, House [Worcester MRA], 1133 W. Boylston St., Worcester, 3/05/80, C, 80000507

Richard, Stephen, House [Southbridge MRA], 239–241 Elm St., Southbridge, 6/22/89, A, C, 89000522

Richardson, Dexter, House [Uxbridge MRA], South St., Uxbridge, 10/07/83, C, 83004128

Richardson, Joseph, House [Uxbridge MRA], Chockalog St., Uxbridge, 10/07/83, B, C, 83004129

Richmond, Willard, Apartment Block [Worcester MRA], 43 Austin St., Worcester, 11/07/85, A, C, 85002783

Rider Tavern, NE of Charlton on Stafford St., off U.S. 90, Charlton vicinity, 5/19/76, B, C, 76000292

Ridyard, Albert, Three-Decker [Worcester MRA; Worcester Three-Deckers TR], 5 Mount Pleasant St., Worcester, 2/09/90, A, C, 89002431

Ridyard, B. E., Three-Decker [Worcester MRA; Worcester Three-Deckers TR], 29 Dewey St., Worcester, 2/09/90, A, C, 89002402

Riordan, John, Three-Decker [Worcester MRA; Worcester Three-Deckers TR], 8 Dix St., Worcester, 2/09/90, A, C, 89002405

Rivulet Mill Complex [Uxbridge MRA], 60 Rivulet St., Uxbridge, 10/07/83, A, C, 83004130

Rock Castle School, Prospect St., Webster, 6/07/89, A, C, 89000437

Rockdale Common Housing District, 4-20 McBride, 46-58 Plantation, and 37-42 Taft Sts., Northbridge, 3/31/83, A, C, 83000611

Rogers House, 28 Boyden Rd., Holden, 6/01/82, A, C, D, 82004471

Rogerson's Village Historic District, N and S sides of Hartford Ave., North Uxbridge, 11/23/71, A, C, 71000092

Royalston Common Historic District, Main St., Frye Hill Rd., and Athol Rd., Royalston, 12/12/76, A, C, a, 76000304

Roynane, Catharine, Three-Decker [Worcester MRA; Worcester Three-Deckers TR], 18 Ingalls St., Worcester, 2/09/90, A, C, 89002397

Ruggles, Draper, House [Worcester MRA], 21 Catherine St., Worcester, 3/05/80, B, C, b, 80000556

Russell, The [Worcester MRA], 49 Austin St., Worcester, 11/07/85, A, C, 85002782

Sacred Heart Church Historic District [Southbridge MRA], Charlton St., Southbridge, 6/22/89, A, C, a, 89000598

Salisbury Factory Building [Worcester MRA], 25 Union St., Worcester, 3/05/80, A, 80000587

Salisbury Factory Building [Worcester MRA], 49-51 Union St., Worcester, 3/05/80, A, 80000588

Salisbury House [Worcester MRA], 61 Harvard St., Worcester, 6/10/75, B, C, b, 75000837

Salisbury Mansion and Store [Worcester MRA], 30, 40 Highland St., Worcester, 5/30/75, B, C, b, 75000838

Sayles, Richard, House [Uxbridge MRA], 80 Mendon St., Uxbridge, 10/07/83, C, 83004131

Worcester County—Continued

Schofield, James, House [Worcester MRA], 3 Mt. Pleasant St., Worcester, 3/05/80, B, C, 80000634

Shaarai Torah Synagogue [Worcester MRA], 32 Providence St., Worcester, 5/07/90, A, C, a, 90000729

Shattuck, Moody, House [Worcester MRA], 768 Main St., Worcester, 3/05/80, A, C, 80000626

Shea, Bridget, Three-Decker [Worcester MRA; Worcester Three-Deckers TR], 21 Jefferson St., Worcester, 2/09/90, A, C, 89002400

Shrewsbury Historic District, Church Rd., Main, Prospect, Boylston, and Grafton Sts., Shrewsbury, 10/08/76, A, C, a, b, d, 76000309

Shumway Block, 112-116 Main St., Webster, 12/03/80, A, C, 80000468

Simpson, Clara, Three-Decker [Worcester MRA; Worcester Three-Deckers TR], 69 Piedmont St., Worcester, 2/09/90, A, C, 89002440

Slater Building [Worcester MRA], 390 Main St., Worcester, 3/05/80, C, 80000609

Smith, Ellen M., Three-Decker [Worcester MRA; Worcester Three-Deckers TR], 22 Kilby St., Worcester, 2/09/90, A, C, 89002409

Smith, Elliot, House [Worcester MRA], 839 Main St., Worcester, 3/05/80, A, C, 80000629

Smith, F.W., Silver Company, 60 Chestnut St., Gardner, 11/14/79, A, C, 79000376

Smith—Lyon Farmhouse [Southbridge MRA], 400 N. Woodstock Rd., Southbridge, 6/22/89, C, 89000546

Smith-Thaxter-Merrifield House [Worcester MRA], 158 Holden St., Worcester, 3/05/80, C, 80000509

Soho Cottage [Worcester MRA], 21 Windsor St., Worcester, 3/05/80, C, 80000528

South Lancaster Engine House, 283 S. Main St., South Lancaster, 10/22/76, A, 76000307

South Unitarian [Worcester MRA], 888 Main St., Worcester, 3/05/80, C, a, 80000550

South Worcester Branch Library [Worcester MRA], 705 Southbridge St., Worcester, 3/05/80, C, 80000486

Southbridge Town Hall, 41 Elm St., Southbridge, 11/20/87, A, C, 87001378

Southbridge-Sargent Manufacturing District [Worcester MRA], Southbridge, Sargent, and Gold Sts., Worcester, 3/05/80, A, C, 80000534

Southwick, Elisha, House [Uxbridge MRA], Chockalog St., Uxbridge, 10/07/83, C, 83004132

Southwick, Israel, House [Uxbridge MRA], 70 Mendon St., Uxbridge, 10/07/83, B, C, 83004133

Spaulding Block, 141-143 Main St., Webster, 12/03/80, A, C, 80000466

Spencer Town Center Historic District, Main between High and North Sts., Spencer, 6/26/86, A, B, C, a, 86001399

Spurr, John, House, Main St., Charlton, 4/26/76, B, C, 76000293

St. George's Greek Orthodox Church [Southbridge MRA], 55 North St., Southbridge, 6/22/89, A, C, a, 89000579

St. John's Catholic Church [Worcester MRA], 40 Temple St., Worcester, 3/05/80, A, C, a, 80000619

St. Marks [Worcester MRA], Freeland St., Worcester, 3/05/80, C, a, 80000481

St. Matthews [Worcester MRA], 693 Southbridge St., Worcester, 3/05/80, C, a, 80000485

St. Peter's Roman Catholic Church—St. Mary's School [Southbridge MRA], Hamilton and Pine Sts., Southbridge, 6/22/89, A, C, a, 89000559

St. Peters Catholic Church [Worcester MRA], 935 Main St., Worcester, 3/05/80, C, a, 80000548

Stark, Edward, House [Worcester MRA], 21 Oread St., Worcester, 3/05/80, C, 80000633

Stearns Tavern [Worcester MRA], 651 Park Ave., Worcester, 3/05/80, C, 80000479

Sterling Center Historic District, Roughly bounded by Meetinghouse Hill and Main, Maple and Kendall Hill, Boulding, Worcester and Princeton, Sterling, 4/14/88, A, C, a, d, f, 88000425

Stevens' Building [Worcester MRA], 24-44 Southbridge St., Worcester, 3/05/80, B, C, 80000615

Stevens, Daniel, House [Worcester MRA], 7 Sycamore St., Worcester, 3/05/80, C, 80000532

Stoliker, Edna, Three-Decker [Worcester MRA; Worcester Three-Deckers TR], 41 Plantation St., Worcester, 2/09/90, A, C, 89002449

Stone, Edward, Three-Decker [Worcester MRA; Worcester Three-Deckers TR], 8 Wyman St., Worcester, 2/09/90, A, C, 89002450

Stone, Joseph, House, 35 Stone St., Auburn, 1/09/86, B, C, 86000028

Stone, Lorenzo R., House [Southbridge MRA], 218 South St., Southbridge, 6/22/89, A, C, 89000537

Sturbridge Common Historic District, Main St. between Hall Rd. and I-86, Sturbridge, 11/09/77, A, C, a, 77000656

Sturtevant, Leonard, House [Worcester MRA], 84 Mulberry St., Worcester, 3/05/80, A, C, 80000591

Sumner, George, House [Southbridge MRA], 32 Paige Hill Rd., Southbridge, 6/22/89, A, C, 89000577

Swift, D. Wheeler, House [Worcester MRA], 22 Oak Ave., Worcester, 3/05/80, B, C, 80000559

Taft Brothers Block [Uxbridge MRA], 2-8 S. Main St., Uxbridge, 10/07/83, C, 83004137

Taft, Aaron, House [Uxbridge MRA], Hazel St., Uxbridge, 10/07/83, A, C, 83004134

Taft, Bazaleel, Jr., House and Law Office [Uxbridge MRA], 147 S. Main St., Uxbridge, 10/07/83, B, C, 83004135

Taft, George, House [Uxbridge MRA], Richardson St., Uxbridge, 10/07/83, C, 83004138

Taft, Hon. Bazaleel, House [Uxbridge MRA], S. Main St., Uxbridge, 10/07/83, B, C, 83004136

Taft, Moses, House [Uxbridge MRA], 66 S. Main St., Uxbridge, 10/07/83, B, C, 83004139

Taft, Samuel, House [Uxbridge MRA], Sutton St., Uxbridge, 10/07/83, C, 83004140

Taft, Zadock, House [Uxbridge MRA], 112 S. Main St., Uxbridge, 10/07/83, C, 83004148

Tantiusques Reservation, Leadmine Rd., Sturbridge, 10/06/83, A, 83004141

Tapin, Eugene, House [Southbridge MRA], 215 Lebanon Hill Rd., Southbridge, 6/22/89, A, C, 89000549

Templeton Common Historic District, Athol, Gardner, Hubbardston, Dudley, Wellington, and South Rds., Templeton, 7/07/83, A, C, 83000608

Thayer, Nathaniel, Estate, 438 S. Main St., Lancaster, 7/06/76, A, B, C, 76000302

Thom Block, 83-89 Main St., Milford, 6/23/83, A, C, 83003435

Thompson School, Prospect St., Webster, 6/07/89, A, C, 89000436

Thomson, C.R., House and Barn [Uxbridge MRA], Chockalog St., Uxbridge, 10/07/83, C, 83004142

Tiffany—Leonard House [Southbridge MRA], 25 Elm St., Southbridge, 6/22/89, A, C, 89000590

Tower, Horatio, House [Worcester MRA], 71 Pleasant St., Worcester, 3/05/80, C, 80000600

Troupes, John, Three-Decker [Worcester MRA; Worcester Three-Deckers TR], 25 Canton St., Worcester, 2/09/90, A, C, 89002394

Twinehurst American Optical Company Neighborhood [Southbridge MRA], Winchurst St., Southbridge, 6/22/89, A, C, 89000593

US Post Office—Whitinsville Main, 58 Church St., Northbridge, 10/15/87, A, C, g, 86003433

US Post Office-Millbury Main, 119 Elm St., Millbury, 10/15/87, A, C, g, 87001764

Union Congregational Church [Worcester MRA], 5 Chestnut St., Worcester, 3/05/80, C, a, 80000599

Union Station [Worcester MRA], Washington Sq., Worcester, 3/05/80, A, C, 80000617

Upper Chapin Street Historic District [Southbridge MRA], Chapin St. at Forest Ave., Southbridge, 6/22/89, C, 89000599

Upsala Street School [Worcester MRA], 36 Upsala St., Worcester, 3/05/80, A, C, 80000493

Uxbridge Common District [Uxbridge MRA], Main, Court, and Douglas Sts., Uxbridge, 1/20/84, A, B, C, a, 84002920

Uxbridge Passenger Depot [Uxbridge MRA], 28 S. Main St., Uxbridge, 10/07/83, A, C, 83004143

Uxbridge Town Hall [Uxbridge MRA], 45 S. Main St., Uxbridge, 10/07/83, A, C, 83004144

Vendome, The, and the St. Ives [Worcester MRA], 17–19 and 21–23 Chandler St., Worcester, 2/09/90, A, C, 89002331

View Street Historic District [Worcester MRA; Worcester Three-Deckers TR], 7–17 and 8–16 View Street, Worcester, 2/09/90, A, C, 89002361

Vinton—Boardman Farmhouse [Southbridge MRA], 93 Torrey Rd., Southbridge, 6/22/89, A, C, 89000586

Vinton—Torrey House [Southbridge MRA], 5 Torrey Rd., Southbridge, 6/22/89, A, C, 89000588

WCIS Bank [Worcester MRA], 365 Main St., Worcester, 3/05/80, A, C, 80000606

Wachusett Aqueduct Linear District [Water Supply System of Metropolitan Boston MPS], Along Wachusett Aqueduct from Wachusett Reservoir to Sudbury Reservoir, Clinton, 1/18/90, A, C, 89002276

Wachusett Dam Historic District [Water Supply System of Metropolitan Boston MPS], N end of

Worcester County—Continued

Wachusett Reservoir at Lancaster Millpond, Clinton, 1/18/90, A, C, 89002269

Wachusett Shirt Company, 97-100 Water St., Leominster, 7/08/82, A, C, 82004476

Waldo Street Police Station [Worcester MRA], Waldo St., Worcester, 3/05/80, C, 80000586

Ward Street School-Millbury Street [Worcester MRA], 389 Millbury St., Worcester, 3/05/80, A, C, 80000488

Ward, Gen. Artemas, Homestead, Main St., opposite Dean Park, Shrewsbury, 5/04/76, B, C, 76000308

Washburn and Moen North Works District [Worcester MRA], Properties on Grove St., Worcester, 3/05/80, A, 80000439

Waters Farm, 53 Waters Rd., Sutton, 4/04/85, A, C, D, 85000695

Waters, Asa, Mansion, 123 Elm St., Millbury, 2/14/78, B, C, 78000479

Waucantuck Mill Complex [Uxbridge MRA], Mendon and Patrick Henry Sts., Uxbridge, 1/20/84, A, C, 84002921

Webster Street Firehouse [Worcester MRA], 40 Webster St., Worcester, 3/05/80, C, 80000480

Wellington Piano Case Company Building, 54 Green St., Leominster, 5/31/84, A, C, 84002922

Wellington Street Apartment House District [Worcester MRA], Properties along Jacques Ave., and Wellington and Irving Sts., Worcester, 3/05/80, C, 80000539

Wells, George B. and Ruth D., House [Southbridge MRA], Durfee Rd., Southbridge, 6/22/89, A, C, 89000548

Wells, H. C., Double House [Southbridge MRA], 28–30 Dresser St., Southbridge, 6/22/89, A, C, 89000531

Wells, John M., House [Southbridge MRA], 491 Eastford Rd., Southbridge, 6/22/89, A, C, 89000553

Wescott, John, Three-Decker [Worcester MRA; Worcester Three-Deckers TR], 454 Pleasant St., Worcester, 2/09/90, A, C, 89002426

Wesson, Franklin, House [Worcester MRA], 8 Claremont St., Worcester, 3/05/80, B, C, 80000603

West Brookfield Center Historic District, Roughly Central and Cottage Sts. from Sherman St. to Lake St. and W., N. and S. Main Sts. from Chapman Ave. to Maple St., West Brookfield, 6/28/90, A, C, 90000885

West Gardner Square Historic District, Roughly bounded by City Hall Ave., Pleasant, Connors, Parker, and Central Sts., and Providence & Worcester RR tracks., Gardner, 12/30/85, A, C, g, 85003185

West Main Street Historic District, Roughly bounded by Milk, Main, Blake, and Fay Sts., Westborough, 6/16/87, A, C, a, 87000884

West Main Street Historic District (Boundary Increase), 83–118 W. Main St., Westborough, 12/06/90, A, C, 90001851

Westminster Village-Academy Hill Historic District, Bacon, Adams, Main, Dawley, Academy Hill, Leominster, and Pleasant Sts., Westminster, 6/23/83, A, C, 83000612

Wheeler, Albert H., House [Southbridge MRA], 219 South St., Southbridge, 6/22/89, A, C, 89000544

Wheelockville District [Uxbridge MRA], Mendon and Henry Sts., Uxbridge, 1/20/84, A, C, 84002923

Whipple, A., House [Uxbridge MRA], Sutton St., Uxbridge, 10/07/83, C, 83004146

Whitcomb House, 51 Harvard St., Worcester, 11/09/77, B, C, 77000653

Whitcomb Mansion [Worcester MRA], 51 Harvard St., Worcester, 3/05/80, B, C, 80000499

Whitinsville Historic District, Church, East, Fletcher, Hill, Woodland, Lake, and Water Sts., Castle Hill Rs., and Linwood Ave., Northbridge, 4/07/83, A, C, 83000613

Whitney & Company, 142 Water St., Leominster, 6/08/89, A, C, 89000440

Whitney, F. A., Carriage Company Complex Historic District, Off 124 Water St., Leominster, 6/23/88, A, C, 88000716

Whittall Mills [Worcester MRA], properties off Brussels St., Worcester, 3/05/80, A, 80000490

Wight, Oliver, House, Main St., Sturbridge, 6/01/82, C, 82004483

Willard House and Clock Museum, 11 Willard St., Grafton, 6/01/82, B, C, 82004470

Williams, N., House [Uxbridge MRA], Rawson St., Uxbridge, 10/07/83, C, 83004147

Windsor Court Historic District [Southbridge MRA], Windsor Ct. at North St., Southbridge, 6/22/89, A, C, 89000596

Wood, Ahijah, House, 174 Worcester Rd., Westminster, 9/17/87, A, C, 87000374

Wood, Ezra-Levi Warner Place, 165 Depot Rd., Westminster, 7/07/83, B, C, b, e, 83000614

Wood, Nathan, House, 164 Worcester Rd., Westminster, 9/16/87, A, C, 87000375

Woodford Street Historic District [Worcester MRA; Worcester Three-Deckers TR], 35–39 and 38–40 Woodford St., Worcester, 2/09/90, A, C, 89002365

Woodland Street Firehouse [Worcester MRA], 36 Woodland St., Worcester, 3/05/80, A, C, 80000630

Woodland Street Historic District [Worcester MRA], Properties along Hawthorne, Loudon, Norwood, and Woodland Sts., Worcester, 3/05/80, A, C, 80000549

Worcester Academy [Worcester MRA], Worcester Academy Campus, Worcester, 3/05/80, A, C, 80000478

Worcester Asylum and related buildings [Worcester MRA], 305 Belmont St., Worcester, 3/05/80, A, C, 80000530

Worcester City Hall and Common [Worcester MRA], 455 Main St., Worcester, 3/29/78, A, C, 78001405

Worcester Corset Company Factory [Worcester MRA], 30 Wyman St., Worcester, 10/04/84, A, C, 84000097

Worcester Five Cents Savings Bank, 316 Main St., Worcester, 9/13/78, A, C, 78000472

Worcester Market Building [Worcester MRA], 831 Main St., Worcester, 3/05/80, A, C, 80000612

Zemaitis, Anthony, Three-Decker [Worcester MRA; Worcester Three-Deckers TR], 35 Dartmouth St., Worcester, 2/09/90, A, C, 89002401

MICHIGAN

Alcona County

Sturgeon Point Light Station [U.S. Coast Guard Lighthouses and Light Stations on the Great Lakes TR], Point Rd., Harrisville vicinity, 7/19/84, A, C, 84001370

Alger County

Au Sable Light Station, W of Grand Marais, Grand Marais vicinity, 5/23/78, A, C, NPS, 78000374

Bay Furnace, NW of Christmas off MI 28 in Hiawatha National Forest, Christmas vicinity, 9/31/71, A, 71000382

Grand Island Harbor Rear Range Light, SR M-28 W of Powell Pt., Christmas vicinity, 6/26/90, A, C, 90000906

Grand Island North Light Station, Grand Island, Munising vicinity, 9/12/85, A, 85002149

Lobb House, 203 W. Onota St., Munising, 10/08/76, A, B, C, 76001023

Mikulich General Store, Jct. of Co. Rts. 1 and 44, Limestone Township, Traunik, 7/15/93, A, B, C, 93000428

Paulson House, S of AuTrain on USFS Rd. 2278 in Hiawatha National Forest, AuTrain vicinity, 11/09/72, A, 72000590

Schoolcraft Furnace Site, NE of Munising off MI 94, Munising vicinity, 12/28/77, A, NPS, 77000151

Allegan County

All Saints' Episcopal Church, 252 Grand St., Saugatuck, 12/27/84, C, a, 84000511

Born, Edward D., House [Allegan MRA], 158 Hill St., Allegan, 3/12/87, B, 87000237

Born, Engelbert B., House [Allegan MRA], 128 Hill St., Allegan, 3/12/87, B, C, 87000238

Brown, William H., House [Allegan MRA], 800 Ely St., Allegan, 7/08/87, C, 87000239

DeLefebvre, Cherry, House [Plainwell MPS], 115 W. Chart St., Plainwell, 11/01/91, C, 91001548

Downtown Allegan Historic District [Allegan MRA], Roughly bounded by Trowbridge, Locust, Hubbard, Brady, and Water Sts., Allegan, 3/12/87, A, C, 87000251

Eesley, J. F., Milling Co. Flour Mill—Elevator [Plainwell MPS], 717 E. Bridge St., Plainwell, 11/01/91, A, b, 91001547

Franks, Henry, House [Allegan MRA], 535 Ely St., Allegan, 3/12/87, C, b, 87000252

Griswold Civic Center Historic District [Allegan MRA], Roughly bounded by Hubbard, Walnut, and Trowbridge Sts., Allegan, 3/12/87, A, C, b, 87000253

Hacklander Site, Address Restricted, Douglas vicinity, 7/27/73, D, 73002150

Island Historic District [Plainwell MPS], Roughly bounded by Hill St., Anderson St., the mill race, Park St., Bannister St. and the Kalamazoo R., Plainwell, 11/01/91, A, B, C, 91001546

Lilly, Augustus, House [Allegan MRA], 132 Cora St., Allegan, 3/12/87, C, 87000254

Marshall Street Historic District [Allegan MRA], 231-237, 335-705, 232-630 Marshall St., Allegan, 3/12/87, C, 87000256

Messenger, William C., House [Allegan MRA], 310 River St., Allegan, 3/12/87, B, C, 87000258

Oakwood Cemetery Chapel [Allegan MRA], Arbor St., Allegan, 3/12/87, C, 87000261

Old Wing Mission, 5298 E. One hundred Forty-seventh Ave., Fillmore, 8/13/86, A, a, 86001551

Pritchard's Outlook Historic District [Allegan MRA], Roughly bounded by Park Dr., Walnut, Crescent, and Davis Sts., Allegan, 7/08/87, B, C, a, 87000265

Second Street Bridge, 2nd St., Allegan, 6/11/80, A, C, 80001845

Sherwood, James Noble, House, 768 Riverview Dr., Plainwell, 12/27/84, C, 84000507

Stedman, Sarah Lowe, House [Allegan MRA], 632 Grand St., Allegan, 3/12/87, C, 87000266

Sutton, Warner P., House, 736 Pleasant St., Saugatuck, 1/22/92, B, 91001999

West Bridge Street Historic District [Plainwell MPS], 320, 414–550 and 321–563 W. Bridge St., Plainwell, 11/01/91, B, C, 91001549

Alpena County

Alpena County Courthouse, 720 Chisholm Ave., Alpena, 12/08/83, C, g, 83003643

Thunder Bay Island Light Station [U.S. Coast Guard Lighthouses and Light Stations on the Great Lakes TR], Thunder Bay Island, Alpena vicinity, 7/19/84, A, C, 84001371

Antrim County

Antrim County Courthouse, S. Cayuga St., Bellaire, 3/10/80, A, C, 80001846

Elk Rapids Township Hall, River St., Elk Rapids, 9/22/77, A, 77000709

Holtz Site, Address Restricted, Bellaire vicinity, 6/19/73, D, 73002151

Hughes House, 109 Elm St., Elk Rapids, 5/06/76, A, C, 76001024

Richardi, Henry, House, 402 N. Bridge St., Bellaire, 1/18/78, B, C, 78001491

Arenac County

Michigan Central Railroad Standish Depot, 107 N. Main St., Standish, 2/28/91, C, 91000215

Second Arenac County Courthouse, Central Ave., Omer, 4/15/82, A, C, 82002823

Baraga County

Assinins, U.S. 41, Assinins, 5/19/72, A, a, d, 72000591

Avon Township Hall, Park Rd., Skanee, 7/30/81, A, C, 81000302

Hanka, Herman and Anna, Farm, NE of Pelkie, Pelkie vicinity, 7/19/84, A, C, 84001372

Hebard-Ford Summer House, NE of L'Anse, L'Anse vicinity, 5/05/82, A, C, 82002824

Kewawenon Mission, Peter Marksman Rd., Zeba, 4/10/80, A, C, a, 80001847

Sand Point Site, Address Restricted, Baraga vicinity, 6/19/73, D, 73002152

Barry County

Barry County Courthouse Complex, 220 W. State St., Hastings, 8/03/81, A, C, 81000303

Carveth, John, House, 614 W. Main St., Middleville, 8/21/92, C, 92001076

Dwight, Austin H., and Frankie A., Summer House, 11456 Marsh Rd., Shelbyville, 3/28/85, B, C, 85000656

Shriner—Ketcham House, 327 Shriner St., Hastings, 3/17/87, B, 87000186

Striker, Daniel, House, 321 S. Jefferson St., Hastings, 1/13/72, C, 72000592

Bay County

Bay City Downtown Historic District, Roughly bounded by Saginaw River, Second and Adam Sts. and Center Ave., Bay City, 9/12/85, A, C, 85002338

Bay County Building, 515 Center Ave., Bay City, 3/25/82, A, C, g, 82002825

Center Avenue Neighborhood Residential District, Roughly bounded by Green and N. Madison Aves., 5th and 6th Sts., Bay City, 4/22/82, A, C, 82002826

City Hall, 301 Washington St., Bay City, 7/18/75, A, C, 75000936

Clements, James, Airport Administration Building, 614 S. River Rd., Bay City, 11/22/82, A, B, C, 82000494

Fletcher Site, Address Restricted, Bay City vicinity, 4/16/71, D, 71001018

Mercy Hospital and Elizabeth McDowell Bialy Memorial House, 15th and Water Sts., Bay City, 4/22/80, A, a, 80001848

Midland Street Commercial District, Roughly bounded by John, Vermont, Catherine and Litchfield Sts., Bay City, 4/22/82, A, C, 82002827

Bay County—Continued

Pere Marquette Railroad Depot, Bay City Station, 919 Boutell Pl., Bay City, 4/15/82, A, C, 82002828

Sage Library, 100 E. Midland St., Bay City, 12/31/79, A, B, C, 79001149

Saginaw River Light Station [U.S. Coast Guard Lighthouses and Light Stations on the Great Lakes TR], Coast Guard St., Bay City, 7/19/84, A, C, 84001373

Tromble House, Veterans Memorial Park, Bay City, 1/25/73, A, 73000943

Benzie County

CITY OF MILWAUKEE, Marine Terminal Railyard, E. slip, Elberta, 12/14/90, A, C, NHL, 90002221

Mills Community House, 891 Michigan Ave., Benzonia, 8/21/72, A, a, 72000593

Platte River Campground, E bank of Platte R. in Sleeping Bear Dunes National Seashore, Empire vicinity, 4/27/90, D, NPS, 90000605

Point Betsie Light Station [U.S. Coast Guard Lighthouses and Light Stations on the Great Lakes TR], Point Betsie, Frankfort, 7/19/84, A, C, 84001375

Berrien County

Berrien Springs Courthouse, Corner of Union and Cass Sts., Berrien Springs, 2/16/70, A, C, 70000265

Chapin, Henry A., House, 508 E. Main St., Niles, 7/30/81, B, C, 81000304

Fort St. Joseph Site, Address Restricted, Niles vicinity, 5/24/73, A, D, a, 73000944

Lardner, Ring, House, 519 Bond St., Niles, 3/16/72, B, C, 72000595

Moccasin Bluff Site, Address Restricted, Buchanan vicinity, 4/13/77, D, 77000710

Ninth District Lighthouse Depot, 128 N. Pier, St. Joseph, 12/02/93, A, C, 93001348

Old Berrien County Courthoue Complex, Roughly bounded by Cass, Kimmel, Madison and Union Sts., Berrien Springs, 4/29/82, A, C, b, 82004941

Old US Post Office, 322 E. Main St., Niles, 9/12/85, A, C, 85002152

Paine Bank, 1008 Oak St., Niles, 5/08/73, A, C, b, 73000945

Sandburg House, Address Restricted, Harbert vicinity, 4/14/72, B, 72001470

Shiloh House, Britain Rd., Benton Harbor, 9/29/72, A, a, 72000594

Union Meat Market, 14 S. Elm St., Three Oaks, 9/22/72, A, C, 72000596

Warren Featherbone Company Office Building, 3 N. Elm St., Three Oaks, 1/23/86, A, B, C, 86000117

Branch County

Coldwater Downtown Historic District, W. Chicago St. from Division to Clay Sts., Coldwater, 7/26/90, A, C, 90001124

Doll, Benedict, House, 665 W. Chicago St., Coldwater, 8/20/90, B, C, 90001238

East Chicago Street Historic District, Chicago St. from Wright St. to Division St. including parks, Coldwater, 5/12/75, A, C, 75000937

East Chicago Street Historic District (Boundary Increase I), Roughly, Pearl St. between Hudson and Lincoln Sts., Coldwater, 8/06/90, C, 90001129

East Chicago Street Historic District (Boundary Increase II), Roughly, Church St. from Jefferson to Daugherty Sts., Hull St. from Morse St. to Park Pl., and Park from Church to Hull, Coldwater, 8/06/90, C, 90001130

First Presbyterian Church, 52 Marshall St., Coldwater, 7/31/86, C, a, 86002111

Fisk, Abram C., House, 867 E. Chicago Rd., Coldwater, 1/12/90, B, C, 89002306

Lanphere—Pratt House, 90 Division St., Coldwater, 8/20/90, B, C, 90001237

Marshall Street Historic District, Roughly bounded by Taylor, Hull, N. Hudson, Montgomery and Clay Sts., Coldwater, 8/09/90, B, C, 90001123

South Monroe Street Historic District, 89–175 and 90–146 S. Monroe St. and 17 Park Ave., Coldwater, 7/26/90, A, C, 90001121

West Pearl Street Historic District, 155–225 and 160–208 W. Pearl St., Coldwater, 7/26/90, B, C, 90001122

Wing House, 27 S. Jefferson St., Coldwater, 2/24/75, C, 75000938

Calhoun County

Arnold, Adam C., Block, 12–14 E. State St., Battle Creek, 3/24/83, B, C, 83000839

Battle Creek City Hall, 103 E. Michigan Ave., Battle Creek, 4/05/84, A, C, 84001377

Battle Creek Post Office, 67 E. Michigan St., Battle Creek, 8/21/72, C, 72000597

Brooks, Harold C., House, 310 N. Kalamazoo Ave., Marshall, 7/08/70, C, 70000266

Brooks, Harold C., House (Boundary Increase), 310 N. Kalamazoo Ave., Marshall, 4/18/84, C, 84001422

Capitol Hill School, 603 Washington St., Marshall, 3/16/72, A, C, 72000598

Cortright-Van Patten Mill, 109 Byron St., Homer, 8/31/79, A, C, 79001150

Emporium, 154–156 W. Michigan Ave., Marshall, 8/09/79, A, C, 79001151

Federal Center, 74 N. Washington St., Battle Creek, 7/30/74, B, 74000980

Gardner House, 509 S. Superior St., Albion, 5/06/71, C, 71000383

Governor's Mansion, 621 S. Marshall Ave., Marshall, 1/08/75, B, C, 75000939

Honolulu House, 107 N. Kalamazoo St., Marshall, 7/08/70, C, 70000267

Joy House, 224 N. Kalamazoo Ave., Marshall, 4/19/72, B, C, 72000599

Kellogg, W.K., House, 256 W. Van Buren St., Battle Creek, 4/18/85, B, C, 85000838

Marshall Michigan Historic Landmark District, Roughly bounded by Plum St., East Dr., Forest St. and Hanover St., Marshall, 7/17/91, C, NHL, 91002053

Masonic Temple Building, 115 E. Green St., Marshall, 9/29/88, C, 88001836

National House, 102 S. Parkview, Marshall, 1/03/78, A, 78001493

Oakhill, 410 N. Eagle St., Marshall, 12/31/74, C, 74000981

Penn Central Railway Station, W. Van Buren, Battle Creek, 4/16/71, A, C, 71000384

Pine Creek Potawatomi Reservation, 1 mi. W of Athens, Athens vicinity, 3/30/73, A, 73000946

Prindle, William, Livery Stable, 323 W. Michigan Ave., Marshall, 8/19/82, A, C, 82002829

Robertson, Eugene P., House, 412 S. Clinton St., Albion, 2/08/88, C, 88000028

Stonehall, 303 N. Kalamazoo St., Marshall, 6/28/72, C, 72000600

Stow—Hasbrouck House, 18600 16 Mile Rd., Convis Township, Marshall vicinity, 12/02/93, C, 93001361

Wagner's Block, 143 W. Michigan Ave., Marshall, 10/07/71, B, C, 71000385

Wright-Brooks House, 122 N. High St., Marshall, 3/16/72, C, 72000601

Cass County

Mason District Number 5 Schoolhouse, 17049 US 12, Edwardsburg, 9/12/85, A, C, 85002153

Michigan Central Railroad Dowagiac Depot, 200 Depot Dr., Dowagiac, 12/02/93, C, 93001349

Newton, George, House, 20689 Marcellus Hwy., Marcellus vicinity, 5/12/82, B, C, 82002830

Smith's Chapel, Redfield Rd. between Brush & Fir Rds., Niles vicinity, 12/31/87, A, C, a, 87002224

Charlevoix County

Beaver Island Light Station, S of St. James on Beaver Island, St. James vicinity, 12/29/78, A, 78001495

Charlevoix City Park Site, Address Restricted, Charlevoix, 3/16/72, D, 72000602

Garden Island Indian Cemetery, Address Restricted, Charlevoix vicinity, 2/17/78, D, d, g, 78001494

Greensky Hill Mission, E of Charlevoix at jct. of U.S. 31 and CR 630, Charlevoix vicinity, 3/16/72, B, a, 72000603

Horton Bay General Store, 05115 Boyne City Rd., Bay Township, Horton Bay, 9/23/91, A, B, C, 91001411

Mormon Print Shop, Main and Forest Sts., St. James, 1/25/71, B, a, 71000386

Charlevoix County—Continued

Mt. McSauba Site, Address Restricted, Charlevoix vicinity, 9/29/76, D, 76001025

O'Neill Site, Address Restricted, Charlevoix vicinity, 5/27/71, D, 71001019

Pewangoing Quarry, Address Restricted, Norwood Township vicinity, 6/20/72, A, D, 72001471

Pi-wan-go-ning Prehistoric District, Address Restricted, Norwood vicinity, 10/03/73, D, 73002153

Pine River Site, Address Restricted, Charlevoix vicinity, 11/15/72, D, 72001472

Protar, Feodar, Cabin, SW of St. James, on Beaver Island, St. James vicinity, 3/16/72, B, 72000604

Wolverine Hotel, 300 Water St., Boyne City, 2/13/86, C, 86000261

Wood Site, Address Restricted, Charlevoix vicinity, 5/19/76, D, 76001026

Cheboygan County

Campbell Farm Site, Address Restricted, Campbell vicinity, 1/31/78, A, D, 78001496

Cheboygan County Courthouse, 229 Court St., Cheboygan, 5/08/86, A, B, C, b, 86001010

Faunce-McMichael Farm, 11126 SR M-68, Burt Lake vicinity, 5/31/90, A, B, C, 90000801

Mackinac Point Lighthouse, Michilimackinac State Park, Mackinac City, 10/01/69, A, 69000068

Newton-Allaire House, 337 Dresser St., Cheboygan, 2/10/83, B, C, 83000840

Stimpson, Forrest J., House, 516 N. Huron Blvd., Mackinaw City, 5/12/80, B, C, 80001849

Chippewa County

Central Methodist Episcopal Church, 111 E. Spruce St., Sault Ste. Marie, 12/27/84, C, a, 84000537

Chippewa County Courthouse, Court St., Sault Ste. Marie, 9/13/84, A, C, 84001381

Church of Our Saviour, Friend of Children, Payment Settlement and Sugar Island, Sault Ste. Marie, 7/08/82, B, C, a, 82002831

Church, Philetus S., House, North Shore Rd., Sugar Island, 11/24/82, C, 82000495

Elmwood, 705 E. Portage Ave., Sault Ste. Marie, 2/25/74, B, C, b, 74000982

Federal Building, 209 E. Portage Ave., Sault Ste. Marie, 9/09/77, C, 77000711

First United Presbyterian Church, 309 Lyon St., Sault Ste. Marie, 12/27/84, C, a, 84000538

Fort Drummond, W end of Drummond Island, Drummond Island, 10/01/69, A, 69000069

Johnston, John, House, 415 Park Pl., Sault Ste. Marie, 7/08/70, B, 70000268

Naomikong Point Site, Address Restricted, Bay Mills Township, 4/16/71, D, 71001020

New Fort Brady, Lake Superior State College campus, Sault Ste. Marie, 1/13/72, A, 72000605

Old Fort Brady, Bounded by the C.O.E. Service Plaza on the N, Portage St. on the S, Brady St. on the E, and Bingham St. on the W, Sault Ste. Marie, 3/11/71, A, 71000387

Point Iroquois Light Station, 6 mi. NW of Brimley in the Hiawatha National Forest, Brimley vicinity, 5/30/75, A, 75000940

S.S. VALLEY CAMP, Old Union Carbide Dock, Sault Ste. Marie, 2/01/72, A, 72000606

St. Mary's Falls Canal, Portage St., Sault Ste. Marie, 11/13/66, A, NHL, 66000394

St. Mary's Pro-Cathedral, 320 E. Portage Ave., Sault Ste. Marie, 12/27/84, A, C, a, 84000540

Whitefish Point Lighthouse, 5 mi. NE of Shelldrake on Whitefish Rd., Shelldrake vicinity, 2/28/73, A, 73000947

Clare County

Hitchcock, George and Martha, House, 205 E. Michigan St., Farwell, 6/21/82, A, B, C, 82002832

Clinton County

East Ward School, 106 N. Traver St., St. Johns, 5/12/80, A, C, 80001850

Main Street Building, United Church of Ovid, 222 Main St., Ovid, 1/13/72, A, C, a, b, 72000607

Union School, 205 W. Baldwin St., St. Johns, 5/15/80, C, 80001851

Delta County

Carnegie Public Library, 201 S. 7th St., Escanaba, 7/25/77, A, C, 77000712

Fayette, On a peninsula in Big Bay de Noc, on MI 149 in Fayette State Park, Fayette, 2/16/70, A, 70000269

Peninsula Point Lighthouse, 6.5 mi. SE of Escanaba in Hiawatha National Forest, Escanaba vicinity, 4/28/75, A, 75000941

Spider Cave, Address Restricted, Fayette vicinity, 4/16/71, D, 71001021

St. Martin Island Light Station [U.S. Coast Guard Lighthouses and Light Stations on the Great Lakes TR], St. Martin Island, Fairport vicinity, 7/19/84, A, C, 84001387

Summer Island Site, Address Restricted, Summer Island, 9/03/71, D, 71000388

Winter Site, Address Restricted, Garden vicinity, 5/19/76, D, 76001027

Dickinson County

Chapin Mine Steam Pump Engine, Kent St., Iron Mountain, 7/09/81, A, C, b, 81000305

Ardis Furnace, Aragon and Antoine Sts., Iron Mountain, 6/29/72, B, 72000608

Dickinson County Courthouse and Jail, 700 S. Stephenson Ave., Iron Mountain, 5/15/80, A, C, 80001852

Immaculate Conception Church, 500 E. Blaine St., Iron Mountain, 4/05/90, A, C, a, 90000562

Eaton County

9622nd Army Air Corps Reserve Recovery Unit—Civil Air Patrol Quonset Huts, 16601 Airport Rd., Lansing, 8/16/91, A, C, g, 91001017

Bellevue Mill, W bank of Battle Creek on Riverside St., Bellevue, 3/04/75, A, 75000942

Eaton County Courthouse, W. Lawrence Ave. at Cochran and Bostwick Sts., Charlotte, 4/02/71, C, 71000389

Eaton County Courthouse Complex (Boundary Increase), 100 W. Lawrence, 120 N. Bostwick, Charlotte, 8/02/93, A, C, 93000712

First Congregational Church, 341 S. Main St., Vermontville, 9/03/71, A, C, a, 71000390

First Congregational Church, 106 S. Bostwick St., Charlotte, 8/26/93, C, a, 93000872

Grand Ledge Chair Company Plant, 101 Perry St., Grand Ledge, 11/03/87, A, C, 87001377

Hance House, 217 Yale St., Olivet, 8/21/72, C, 72000609

Reynolds, Isaac N., House, 123 N. East St., Eaton Rapids, 7/18/74, C, 74000983

River Ledge Historic District, Jefferson, Scott, and Lincoln Sts. between Franklin and Maple Sts., Grand Ledge, 9/24/87, A, C, 87001576

Sunfield Grand Army of the Republic Post No. 283 Hall, 115 Main St., Sunfield, 10/29/92, A, 92001502

Vermontville Chapel and Academy, N. Main St., Vermontville, 8/07/72, A, C, a, b, 72000610

Vermontville Opera House, 120 E. First St., 219 S. Main St., Vermontville, 7/14/93, A, C, 93000620

Emmet County

Allen, J. B., House [Petoskey MRA], 822 Grove St., Petoskey, 9/10/86, C, 86001973

Bartram, Isaac, House [Petoskey MRA], 508 Wachtel Ave., Petoskey, 9/10/86, C, 86001975

Bay View, NE of Petoskey on US 31, Petoskey vicinity, 3/16/72, A, C, a, NHL, 72000613

Blackbird, Chief Andrew J., House, 368 E. Main St., Harbor Springs, 4/14/72, B, 72000611

Carmichael, W. S., House [Petoskey MRA], 301 Jackson St., Petoskey, 9/10/86, C, 86001977

Chesapeake & Ohio Railway Station, Pioneer Park, W. Lake St., Petoskey, 10/15/70, C, 70000270

Debenham, I. N., House [Petoskey MRA], 1101 Emmet St., Petoskey, 9/10/86, C, 86001979

East Mitchell Street Historic District [Petoskey MRA], Roughly bounded by Rose, Kalamazoo, State, Howard, Michigan, and Division, Petoskey, 11/12/86, C, 86001983

Emmet County—Continued

Fochtman, Gerhard, House [Petoskey MRA], 1004 Waukazoo Ave., Petoskey, 9/10/86, C, 86001998

Fort Michilimackinac, Near Mackinac Bridge at the terminus of U.S. 31, Mackinaw City, 10/15/66, A, NHL, 66000395

Fourth Ward Polling Place [Petoskey MRA], 209 Washington St., Petoskey, 9/10/86, C, 86002001

Fryman, Meyer, House [Petoskey MRA], 211 Michigan St., Petoskey, 9/10/86, C, 86002002

Grace Methodist Episcopal Church [Petoskey MRA], 625 Connable St., Petoskey, 9/10/86, C, a, 86002012

Hemingway, Ernest, Cottage, Between N shore of Walloon Lake and Lake Grove Rd., Walloon Lake, 11/24/68, B, NHL, 68000026

Hobbins, Bert and John, House [Petoskey MRA], 1024 Emmet St., Petoskey, 9/10/86, C, 86002013

Hosman and Wheeler Meat Market [Petoskey MRA], 621 Ingalls Ave., Petoskey, 9/10/86, C, 86002015

Kabler, John, House [Petoskey MRA], 415 Jackson St., Petoskey, 9/10/86, C, 86002017

Lesher, Frank, House [Petoskey MRA], 122 Sheridan St., Petoskey, 9/10/86, C, 86002018

Malin, A., House [Petoskey MRA], 54 Bridge St., Petoskey, 9/10/86, C, 86002020

Markle, George and Eugene, House [Petoskey MRA], 701 Kalamazoo St., Petoskey, 9/10/86, C, 86002023

McManus, George, House [Petoskey MRA], 121 State St., Petoskey, 9/10/86, C, 86002026

Meyers, Elias, House [Petoskey MRA], 912 Baxter St., Petoskey, 9/10/86, C, 86002030

Miller, Jacob, House [Petoskey MRA], 307 Jackson St., Petoskey, 9/10/86, C, 86002031

Mineral Well Park [Petoskey MRA], W. Lake St., Petoskey, 3/25/87, A, 86002036

Nyman, John, House [Petoskey MRA], 915 Emmet St., Petoskey, 9/10/86, C, 86002039

Olin, G. W., House [Petoskey MRA], 610 Kalamazoo St., Petoskey, 9/10/86, C, 86002042

Pennington, Sarah, House [Petoskey MRA], 719 Maple St., Petoskey, 9/10/86, C, 86002045

Petoskey Downtown Historic District [Petoskey MRA], Roughly bounded by Rose, Division, Michigan, and Petoskey, Petoskey, 11/12/86, A, C, 86002048

Petoskey Grocery Company Building [Petoskey MRA], 616 Petoskey St., Petoskey, 9/10/86, C, 86002051

Petoskey Public Works Utility Building [Petoskey MRA], 106 W. Lake St., Petoskey, 9/13/86, C, g, 86002056

Ponshewaing Point Site, Address Restricted, Ponshewaing vicinity, 5/05/72, D, 72001473

Rehkopf, Phillip, House [Petoskey MRA], 918 Howard St., Petoskey, 9/10/86, C, 86002069

Schantz, George, House and Store [Petoskey MRA], 534 Wachtel Ave., Petoskey, 9/10/86, C, 86002072

Schapler, Frank, House [Petoskey MRA], 106 E. Lake St., Petoskey, 9/10/86, C, 86002074

Seventh Day Adventist Church [Petoskey MRA], 224 Michigan St., Petoskey, 9/10/86, C, a, 86002077

Shafer's Grocery and Residence [Petoskey MRA], 1018 Emmet St., Petoskey, 9/10/86, C, 86002079

Shay Complex, Main and Judd Sts., Harbor Springs, 11/07/72, B, C, 72000612

Skillagalee Light Station [U.S. Coast Guard Lighthouses and Light Stations on the Great Lakes TR], SW of Waugoshance Island, Cross Village vicinity, 7/19/84, A, C, 84001389

St. Francis Solanus Mission, W. Lake St., Petoskey, 3/16/72, A, a, 72000614

Stout House [Petoskey MRA], 606 Grove St., Petoskey, 9/10/86, C, 86002080

Trinity Evangelical Church [Petoskey MRA], 219 State St., Petoskey, 9/10/86, C, 86002082

VanZolenburg, Jacob, House [Petoskey MRA], 209 State St., Petoskey, 9/10/86, C, 86002083

Waugoshance Light Station [U.S. Coast Guard Lighthouses and Light Stations on the Great Lakes TR], NW of Waugoshance Island, Waugoshance Island vicinity, 8/04/83, A, C, 83000841

Wells, J. M., House [Petoskey MRA], 203 W. Lake St., Petoskey, 9/10/86, C, 86002084

West Mitchell Street Bridge [Petoskey MRA], W. Mitchell St. at Bear River, Petoskey, 9/10/86, A, 86002085

White Shoal Light Station [U.S. Coast Guard Lighthouses and Light Stations on the Great Lakes TR], NW of Waugashance Island, Mackinaw City vicinity, 7/19/84, A, C, 84001391

Wycamp Creek Site, Address Restricted, Levering vicinity, 3/11/71, D, 71001022

Zion Evangelical Lutheran Church [Petoskey MRA], 610 Petoskey St., Petoskey, 9/10/86, C, a, 86002086

Genesee County

Aitkan, Robert, Farm House [Genesee County MRA], 1110 Linden Rd., Flint, 11/26/82, B, C, 82000496

Applewood, 1400 E. Kearsley St., Flint, 4/16/79, B, 79001152

Atlas Grange Hall [Genesee County MRA], 8530 Perry Rd., Atlas, 11/26/82, C, 82000497

Bangs, Benjamin, House [Genesee County MRA], 819 S. Leroy St., Fenton, 11/26/82, B, C, 82000498

Barn at 4277 Irish Road [Genesee County MRA], 4277 Irish Rd., Davison, 11/26/82, C, 82000499

Bird/Boyd Farm House [Genesee County MRA], 14215 Bird Rd., Byron, 11/26/82, A, C, 82000500

Bloss, Frank D., and Sons Farm House [Genesee County MRA], 8380 Reid Rd., Swartz Creek, 11/26/82, C, 82000501

Bridge Street-Broad Street Historic District [Genesee County MRA], 3 Central blocks of Broad St., 2 blocks Bridge St., Linden, 11/26/82, A, C, 82000502

Buck, Jesse H., Farm House [Genesee County MRA], 6095 Baldwin Rd., Swartz Creek, 11/26/82, C, 82000503

Capitol Theatre Building, 140 E. 2nd St., Flint, 1/31/85, A, C, 85000165

Carmer, William, House [Genesee County MRA], 10448 Washburn Rd., Ortonville, 11/26/82, C, 82000504

Church, Volney-Carlos B. Shotwell House [Genesee County MRA], 812 S. Adelaide St., Fenton, 11/26/82, C, 82000505

Civic Park Historic District, Roughly bounded by Welch and Brownell Blvds., Trumbull Ave., Dupont and Dartmouth Sts., Flint, 9/07/79, A, C, 79001153

Clio Depot [Genesee County MRA], 300-308 W. Vienna Rd., Clio, 6/20/83, A, 83000842

Colwell, David B., House [Genesee County MRA], 901 S. Leroy St., Fenton, 11/26/82, C, 82000506

Dibbleville-Fentonville Historic District [Genesee County MRA], Roughly bounded by Shiawassee, Riggs, Holly and George Sts., Fenton, 11/26/82, A, B, C, 82000507

Durant-Dort Carriage Company Office, 315 W. Water St., Flint, 9/02/75, B, NHL, 75000943

Elks Lodge Building, 142 W. 2nd St., Flint, 10/04/78, A, B, C, 78001497

Fenton Railroad Depot [Genesee County MRA], 207 Silver Lake Rd., Fenton, 6/20/83, A, C, 83000843

Fenton Seminary [Genesee County MRA], 309 High St., Fenton, 11/26/82, A, C, 82000508

First Baptist Church of Grand Blanc [Genesee County MRA], 6101 S. Saginaw St., Grand Blanc, 6/20/83, A, C, 83000844

Flint Brewing Company, 2001 S. Saginaw St., Flint, 4/10/80, A, C, a, 80001854

Genesee Avenue-Walker Street Historic District [Genesee County MRA], Roughly bounded by Washington, Elm, Lord Sts., and RR Tracks, Gaines, 6/20/83, A, C, 83000845

Genesee County Courthouse and Jail, 920 S. Saginaw St., Flint, 5/24/90, A, C, 90000798

Gilbert, Horace/Morgan and Enos Miller House [Genesee County MRA], 5023 Holland Dr., Swartz Creek, 11/26/82, C, 82000509

Green, Alanson, Farm House [Genesee County MRA], 11226 Green Rd., Goodrich, 11/26/82, C, 82000510

Hegel Road Historic District [Genesee County MRA], Hegel Rd. between Seneca and the Goodrich Millpond, Goodrich, 11/26/82, A, B, C, 82000511

Hinckley, Col. J., House [Genesee County MRA], 210 High St., Fenton, 11/26/82, B, C, 82000512

House at 10410 Stanley Road [Genesee County MRA], 10410 Stanley Rd., Flushing, 11/26/82, C, 82000514

House at 1339 Cummings Road [Genesee County MRA], 1339 Cummings Rd., Davison, 11/26/82, C, 82000515

House at 4305 South Linden Road [Genesee County MRA], 4305 S. Linden Rd., Flint, 11/26/82, C, 82000516

House at 4344 Frances Road [Genesee County MRA], 4344 Frances Rd., Clio, 11/26/82, C, 82000517

Genesee County—Continued

House at 5556 Flushing Road [Genesee County MRA], 5556 Flushing Rd., Flushing, 11/26/82, C, 82000518

House at 6112 Carpenter Road [Genesee County MRA], 6112 Carpenter Rd., Flint, 11/26/82, C, 82000513

House at 7066 Lobdell Road [Genesee County MRA], 7066 Lobdell Rd., Linden, 11/26/82, C, 82000519

Industrial Mutual Association Auditorium, 815 E. 2nd Ave., Flint, 7/28/83, A, C, 83000849

Industrial Savings Bank Building, 432 N. Saginaw St., Flint, 4/19/84, A, B, C, 84001393

Jennings, H.N., House [Genesee County MRA], 800 S. East St., Fenton, 11/26/82, B, C, 82000520

Johnson, Abner C., House, 625 East St., Flint, 2/19/87, C, 87000183

Knight, Morris A., House, 1105 Church ST., Flint, 7/29/82, B, C, 82004680

Linden Mill, Tickner St., Linden, 8/21/72, A, 72000615

Main Street Historic District [Genesee County MRA], Main St. from Maple to 628 Main St., Flushing, 6/20/83, A, C, 83000846

Mauk & Hammer/Houghton Elevator [Genesee County MRA], 315 W. Vienna St., Clio, 11/26/82, A, C, 82000521

McAra, John, House [Genesee County MRA], 2157 Irish Rd., Davison, 11/26/82, C, 82000522

McCaslin, William Henry and Lucinda, Farm House [Genesee County MRA], 15237 McCaslin Lake Rd., Linden, 11/26/82, B, C, 82000523

McClew, Alexander, Farm House [Genesee County MRA], 7115 Farrand Rd., Millington, 11/26/82, C, 82000524

Middlesworth, Isaac R., Farm House [Genesee County MRA], 11355 Rolston Rd., Byron, 11/26/82, C, 82000525

Murray, James H., House [Genesee County MRA], 7232 Silver Lake Rd., Linden, 11/26/82, A, B, C, 82000526

O'Sullivan, Daniel, House/Halfway House [Genesee County MRA], 5035 Flushing Rd., Flushing, 11/26/82, B, C, 82000527

Parker and Dunstan Hardware/Dr. E. D. Lewis Building [Genesee County MRA], 129–133 W. Main St., Otisville, 11/26/82, C, 82000528

Paterson, William A., Factory Complex, 126 E. 3rd St., Flint, 2/16/84, A, 84001396

Superintendent's Cottage, Michigan School for the Deaf campus, Flint, 7/07/75, A, C, 75000944

Swayze, E. S., Drugstore/Otisville Mason Lodge No. 401 [Genesee County MRA], 106 Main St., Otisville, 11/26/82, C, 82000529

Thayer, H. Elmer, House [Genesee County MRA], G-3202 Court St., Flint, 11/26/82, C, 82000530

Tinker, Harry C., House [Genesee County MRA], 12030 Lewis Rd., Clio, 11/26/82, A, C, 82000531

Trump, Edwin, House [Genesee County MRA], 801 S. East St., Fenton, 11/26/82, C, 82000532

Van Buskirk, John, Farm House [Genesee County MRA], 7348 Coldwater Rd., Davison, 6/20/83, B, C, 83000847

Vermont House and Fenton Grain Elevator, 302 and 234 N. Leroy St., Fenton, 5/15/80, A, 80001853

West Vienna United Methodist Church [Genesee County MRA], 5461 Wilson Rd., Clio, 6/20/83, C, 83000848

Whaley, Robert J., House, 624 E. Kearsley St., Flint, 5/15/80, B, C, 80001855

Gogebic County

Chicago and Northwestern Railroad Depot, Between Suffolk and Lowell Sts., Ironwood, 1/14/85, A, C, 85000095

Copper Peak, N. Black River Valley Pkwy., Ironwood, 1/04/73, A, C, 73000948

Curry, Solomon S., House, 631 E. McLeod Ave., Ironwood, 4/22/82, B, C, 82002833

Gogebic County Courthouse, Moore St., Bessemer, 5/08/81, A, C, 81000306

Ironwood City Hall, McLeod Ave. and Norfolk St., Ironwood, 11/28/80, A, C, 80001856

Ironwood Theatre Complex, Aurora St., Ironwood, 1/11/85, A, C, 85000061

Memorial Building, McLeod Ave. and Marquette St., Ironwood, 11/10/80, A, C, 80001857

Grand Traverse County

Boardman Neighborhood Historic District, Roughly bounded State and Webster Sts., and Railroad and Boardman Aves., Traverse City, 10/03/78, A, C, 78001498

Central Neighborhood Historic District, Roughly bounded by 5th, Locust, Union, 9th, and Division Sts., Traverse City, 12/11/79, B, C, 79001154

City Opera House, 106–112 Front St., Traverse City, 9/07/72, A, C, 72000616

Fife Lake—Union District No. 1 Schoolhouse, 5020 Fife Lake Rd., Fife Lake vicinity, 8/27/87, C, 87001433

Hannah, Perry, House, 305 6th St., Traverse City, 3/16/72, B, C, 72000617

Hedden Hall, 18599 Old Mission Rd., Traverse City vicinity, 4/15/82, A, C, 82002834

Northern Michigan Asylum, Bounded by C & O RR tracks, Division and 11th Sts., Elmwood Ave., Orange and Red Drs., Traverse City, 10/03/78, A, C, 78001499

Skegemog Point Site, Address Restricted, Williamsburg vicinity, 3/24/72, D, 72001474

Gratiot County

Brown Site (20GR21), Address Restricted, Alma vicinity, 9/19/85, D, 85002411

Conservation Park Site (20GR33), Address Restricted, Alma, 9/30/85, D, 85002695

Gratiot County Courthouse, Center St., Ithaca, 1/31/76, A, C, 76002291

Holiday Park Site (20GR91), Address Restricted, Alma vicinity, 12/06/85, D, 85003519

MacLachlan, Dr. Charles H., Sanitarium and House, 6482 Pingree Rd., Elwell, 11/22/82, A, C, 82000533

Hillsdale County

Grace Episcopal Church, 360 E. Chicago St., Jonesville, 5/06/71, A, C, a, 71000391

Grosvenor, E. O., House, 211 Maumee St., Jonesville, 12/06/77, B, C, 77000713

Hillsdale County Courthouse, Howell St, Hillsdale, 8/11/82, A, C, 82002835

Kirby, William R., Sr., House, 377 State Rd., Hillsdale vicinity, 7/20/82, A, C, 82002836

McCourtie, W. H. L., Estate, Jct. of US 12 and Jackson Rd., Somerset Center, 1/24/92, B, C, 91001984

Treadwell, William, House, 446 N. Meridian Rd., Hudson, 12/31/74, C, 74000984

Houghton County

Big Traverse Bay Historic District, E of Lake Linden at mouth of Traverse River, Lake Linden vicinity, 11/20/75, A, g, 75000946

Bosch, Joseph, Building, 302 Calumet Ave., Lake Linden, 4/22/82, A, C, 82002839

Calumet Downtown Historic District, 5th and 6th Sts. between Scott and Pine Sts., Calumet, 6/25/74, A, C, 74000986

Calumet Fire Station, 6th St., Calumet, 11/05/74, A, C, 74000987

Calumet Historic District, Area W of MI 26 S of Calumet Lake to Osceola, Calumet, 3/28/89, A, C, NHL, 89001097

Calumet Theatre, 340 6th St., Calumet, 8/05/71, A, 71000392

Calumet and Hecla Industrial District, Roughly bounded by Hecla and Torch Lake RR tracks, Calumet Ave., Mine and Depot Sts., Calumet, 6/28/74, A, 74000985

College Club House and Gymnasium, 1416 College Ave., Houghton, 5/15/80, A, C, 80001861

Douglass House, Sheldon Ave. and Isle Royale St., Houghton, 5/13/82, A, C, 82002837

East Hancock Neighborhood Historic District, Roughly bounded by Front, Dunston and Vivian Sts., Mason and Cooper Aves., Hancock, 6/23/80, A, C, 80001859

First Congregational Church, 1st St. and M 26, Lake Linden, 11/17/80, A, C, a, 80001863

Hancock Town Hall and Fire Hall, 399 Quincy St., Hancock, 6/01/81, A, C, 81000307

Houghton County Courthouse, 401 E. Houghton St., Houghton, 5/12/75, A, C, 75000945

Jacobsville Finnish Lutheran Church, W of Jacobsville, Jacobsville vicinity, 10/08/76, A, C, a, 76001028

Houghton County—Continued

Kaleva Temple, Trimountain Ave., South Range, 3/19/82, A, C, 82002840

Lake Linden Village Hall and Fire Station, 401 Calumet Ave., Lake Linden, 10/26/81, A, C, 81000308

Lieblein House, 525 Quincy St., Hancock, 4/03/80, B, C, 80001860

Michels, John J., House, 1121 E. Houghton Ave., Houghton, 8/05/91, B, 91001018

Old Main, Suomi College, Quincy St., Suomi College campus, Hancock, 1/13/72, A, 72000618

Painesdale, Area encompassing Painesdale streets and the Champion Mine, Painesdale, 7/16/93, A, C, D, 93000623

Quincy Mine No. 2 Shaft Hoist House, Off U.S. 41, Hancock vicinity, 2/16/70, A, C, 70000271

Quincy Mining Company Historic District, Area N from Portage Lake to Quincy Hill and along US 41, Hancock vicinity, 2/10/89, A, C, NHL, 89001095

Quincy Street Historic District, 100, 200, and 300 blks. of Quincy St. and 416 Tezcuco St., Hancock, 10/13/88, A, C, 88000143

Redridge Steel and Log Dams, N of Co. Rt. 557 at Salmon Trout R., Stanton Township, Redridge, 4/02/92, C, 92000166

Saint Ignatius Loyola Church, 703 E. Houghton Ave., Houghton, 8/03/87, A, C, a, 87001261

Shelden Avenue Historic District, Shelden, Lake, & Montezuma Aves., Houghton, 12/30/87, A, C, 87002154

Shelden, Ransom B., House, 1304 College Ave., Houghton, 6/18/80, B, C, 80001862

Shelden-Dee Block, Shelden Ave. and Isle Royale St., Houghton, 4/22/82, A, C, 82002838

South Range Community Building, Trimountain Ave., South Range, 4/09/81, A, C, g, 81000310

Huron County

Bay Port Historic Commercial Fishing District, Off MI 25, Bay Port, 9/22/77, A, 77000714

First Methodist Episcopal Church [Port Hope MPS], 4451 Second St., Port Hope, 11/20/87, C, a, 87001963

Grice, James and Jane, House, 865 N. Huron Ave., Harbor Beach, 11/12/82, C, 82000534

Grindstone City Historic District, On U.S. 25, Grindstone City, 9/03/71, A, 71000393

Harbor Beach Lighthouse [U.S. Coast Guard Lighthouses and Light Stations on the Great Lakes TR], Breakwater Entrance, Harbor Beach, 8/04/83, A, C, 83000850

Herman House [Port Hope MPS], 4405 Main St., Port Hope, 11/20/87, A, 87001974

Indian Mission, 590 E. Bay St., Sebewaing, 9/22/72, A, a, 72000620

Learned, Charles G., House, 8544 Lake St., Port Austin, 5/31/84, A, B, C, 84001400

Leuty, Isaac, House [Port Hope MPS], 7955 School St., Port Hope, 11/20/87, C, 87001975

Masonic Temple [Port Hope MPS], 4425 Main St., Port Hope, 11/20/87, A, C, 87001962

Melligan Store-Agriculture Hall [Port Hope MPS], 4432 Main St., Port Hope, 1/04/88, C, 87001965

Murphy, Frank, Birthplace, 142 S. Huron St., Harbor Beach, 9/22/71, B, c, 71000394

Pointe Aux Barques Lighthouse, E of Huron City on Light House Rd., Huron City vicinity, 3/20/73, A, 73000949

Schlichtling Building [Port Hope MPS], 4443 Main St., Port Hope, 11/20/87, C, 87001973

Sleeper, Albert E., House, 302 W. Huron St. (MI 53), Bad Axe, 2/01/72, B, 72000619

St. John's Lutheran Church [Port Hope MPS], 4527 Second St., Port Hope, 11/20/87, A, C, a, 87001964

Stafford House [Port Hope MPS (AD)], 4467 Main St., Port Hope, 1/25/73, B, C, 73000950

Stafford, Frederick H. and Elizabeth, House [Port Hope MPS], 4489 Main St., Port Hope, 11/20/87, B, C, 87001976

Stafford, W. R., Flour Mill and Elevator [Port Hope MPS], 4310 Huron St., Port Hope, 11/20/87, A, 87001961

Stafford, W. R., Planing Mill Site [Port Hope MPS], Huron St., Port Hope, 11/20/87, A, 87001960

Stafford, W. R., Saw Mill Site [Port Hope MPS], Huron St., Port Hope, 11/20/87, A, 87001959

Stafford, W. R., Worker's House [Port Hope MPS], 8022 Cedar St., Port Hope, 11/20/87, C, 87001978

Winsor and Snover Bank Building, 8648 Lake St., Port Austin, 3/19/87, B, C, 87000482

Ingham County

Brown-Price House, 1003 N. Washington Ave., Lansing, 3/22/84, C, 84001429

Central Methodist Episcopal Church [Downtown Lansing MRA], 215 N. Capitol Ave., Lansing, 9/17/80, C, a, 80001864

Central School, 325 W. Grand River Ave., East Lansing, 4/10/86, A, C, 86000709

Courthouse Square Historic District [Mason Michigan Historic MRA], Bounded by Park, E. Columbia, Rodgers and South, Mason, 6/06/85, A, B, C, 85001243

Dodge Mansion, 106 E. North St., Lansing, 9/14/72, C, a, 72000621

Emery Houses [Lansing Downtown MRA], 320–322 and 326–328 W. Ottawa, Lansing, 12/10/93, B, C, 93001409

Eustace Hall, Michigan State University campus, East Lansing, 9/03/71, A, B, 71000395

Federal Building [Downtown Lansing MRA], 315 W. Allegan St., Lansing, 9/17/80, C, g, 80001865

First Baptist Church [Downtown Lansing MRA], 227 N. Capitol Ave., Lansing, 9/17/80, C, a, 80001866

Franklin Avenue Presbyterian Church, 108 W. Grand River Ave., Lansing, 5/27/88, C, a, 88000564

Grand Trunk Western Rail Station/Lansing Depot, 1203 S. Washington Ave., Lansing, 7/03/80, A, C, 80004605

Ingham County Courthouse, Jefferson and Ash Sts., Mason, 12/13/71, A, 71000397

Knapp, J.W., Company Building [Downtown Lansing MRA], 300 S. Washington Ave., Lansing, 5/21/83, C, g, 83000851

Lansing Woman's Club Building [Downtown Lansing MRA], 118 W. Ottawa St., Lansing, 9/17/80, A, C, a, 80001867

Maple Grove Cemetery [Mason Michigan Historic MRA], W. Columbia St., Mason, 6/06/85, C, d, 85001237

Masonic Temple Building [Downtown Lansing MRA], 217 S. Capitol Ave., Lansing, 9/17/80, C, 80001868

Merrylees-Post House [Mason Michigan Historic MRA], 519 W. Ash St., Mason, 6/06/85, C, 85001238

Michigan Central Railroad Mason Depot [Mason Michigan Historic MRA], 111 N. Mason St., Mason, 6/06/85, A, C, 85001239

Michigan Millers Mutual Fire Insurance Company Building [Downtown Lansing MRA], 120-122 W. Ottawa St., Lansing, 9/17/80, C, 80001869

Michigan State Capitol [Downtown Lansing MRA (AD)], Capitol and Michigan Aves., Lansing, 1/25/71, A, C, NHL, 71000396

Moon, Darius B., House, 216 Huron St., Lansing, 11/30/82, C, b, 82000535

Moores, J.H., Memorial Natatorium, 2700 Moores River Dr., Lansing, 1/14/85, C, 85000096

Mutual Building [Downtown Lansing MRA], 208 N. Capitol Ave., Lansing, 9/17/80, A, C, 80001870

Nice, Philip, House [Mason Michigan Historic MRA], 321 Center St., Mason, 6/06/85, B, C, 85001240

North Lansing Historic Commercial District, E. Grand River Ave. and Turner St., Lansing, 4/30/76, A, C, 76001029

Raynor, John, House [Mason Michigan Historic MRA], 725 E. Ash St., Mason, 6/06/85, A, C, 85001241

Smith-Turner House, 326 W. Grand River Ave., Lansing, 7/11/80, A, B, 80004604

St. Katherine's Chapel, 4650 Meridian Rd., E of East Lansing, East Lansing vicinity, 7/08/70, C, a, 70000272

St. Mary Cathedral, 229 Seymour St., Lansing, 11/02/90, A, C, a, 90001716

State Office Building, 316 S. Walnut St., Lansing, 5/17/84, A, C, 84001432

Stockbridge Town Hall, 101 S. Clinton St., Stockbridge, 3/10/80, C, 80001872

Strand Theatre and Arcade [Downtown Lansing MRA], 211-219 S. Washington Ave., Lansing, 9/17/80, A, C, 80001871

Westside Neighborhood Historic District [Mason Michigan Historic MRA], Roughly bounded by W. Maple, W. Ash, Lansing and McRoberts Sts., Mason, 6/06/85, B, C, 85001242

Ionia County

Belding, Alvah N., Memorial Library, 302 E. Main St., Belding, 5/21/93, A, B, C, 93000427

Ionia County—Continued

Blanchard, John C., House, 253 E. Main St., Ionia, 7/24/74, C, 74002346

Hall-Fowler Memorial Library, 126 E. Main St., Ionia, 5/06/71, C, 71000398

Ionia County Courthouse, E. Main St., Ionia, 8/09/79, A, C, 79001155

Ionia Downtown Commercial Historic District, Roughly W. Main and Washington Sts., from Dexter to Library Sts., Ionia, 9/13/84, A, C, 84001437

Ionia Historic District, Roughly bounded by Summit, Pleasant, Jefferson and Main Sts., Ionia, 9/13/84, A, C, 84001443

Lovell-Webber House, 111 E. Main St., Ionia, 7/30/74, C, 74000988

Muir Church of Christ, 138 Garden St., Muir, 2/17/83, C, a, 83000852

Portland First Congregational Church, 421 E. Bridge St., Portland, 12/27/84, A, C, a, b, 84000542

Richardson Silk Mill, 101 Front St., Belding, 9/26/85, A, C, 85002496

Sessions Schoolhouse, Riverside Dr., Ionia vicinity, 2/11/85, C, 85000278

VanderHeyden, William H., House, 926 W. Main St., Ionia, 12/28/90, B, C, 90001959

Iosco County

Alabaster Historic District, Bounded by Lake Huron, Gypsum, Keystone, and Rempert Rds., Alabaster, 12/16/77, A, g, 77000715

Tawas Point Light Station [U.S. Coast Guard Lighthouses and Light Stations on the Great Lakes TR], Tawas Point Rd., East Tawas, 7/19/84, A, C, 84001453

Iron County

Alpha Public Buildings Historic Complex [Iron County MRA], 404 Main St., Alpha, 12/22/83, A, C, 83003659

Amasa Historic Business District [Iron County MRA], 100, 200, and 300 block of Pine St., Amasa, 12/22/83, A, C, 83003660

Beechwood Store [Iron County MRA], 215 Beechwood Rd., Iron River, 12/22/83, A, 83003662

Bethany Lutheran Church [Iron County MRA], 184 Beechwood Rd., Iron River, 12/22/83, A, C, a, 83003664

Bowers, Joseph, House [Iron County MRA], 318 Hemlock Ave., Amasa, 12/22/83, C, 83003665

Byers, Isaac W., House [Iron County MRA], 5 N. 8th Ave., Iron River, 12/22/83, B, 83003667

Caspian Community Center [Iron County MRA], 404 Brady Ave., Caspian, 12/22/83, A, 83003671

Caspian Mine Headframe [Iron County MRA], N of Caspian Rd., Caspian, 12/22/83, A, 83003672

Cloverland Hotel [Iron County MRA], 423 3rd St., Iron River, 12/22/83, C, 83003673

Cole, Frank W., House [Iron County MRA], 121 3rd St., Crystal Falls, 12/22/83, C, 83003674

Cooks Run Trout Feeding Station [Iron County MRA], 180 Cooks Run Rd., Stambaugh, 12/22/83, A, C, 83003675

Courthouse Residential Historic District [Iron County MRA], Roughly bounded by Crystal and Michigan Aves., Iron and 5th Sts., Crystal Falls, 12/29/83, A, B, C, a, b, c, 83003676

Crystal Falls Dam and Power Plant [Iron County MRA], Pine St., Crystal Falls, 12/22/83, A, C, 83003678

Crystal Inn [Iron County MRA], 400 Superior Ave., Crystal Falls, 12/22/83, A, C, 83003680

Diele, Ernest, House [Iron County MRA], 213 Marquette Ave., Crystal Falls, 12/22/83, C, 83003682

Dober Mining Company House [Iron County MRA], 1 19th St., Caspian, 12/22/83, A, C, 83003681

Ericson, Rudolf, House [Iron County MRA], 626 W. Boyington St., Iron River, 12/22/83, B, 83003687

Falls Location Historic District [Iron County MRA], At Paint River, Crystal Falls, 12/22/83, A, 83003689

Finnish and Swedish Mercantile Association Building [Iron County MRA], 336 Superior Ave., Crystal Falls, 12/22/83, A, a, 83003691

First National Bank Building [Iron County MRA], 303 Main St., Alpha, 12/22/83, A, C, 83003692

Fisher, Nelson E., House-High Banks [Iron County MRA], US 2, Iron River, 12/22/83, B, C, 83003694

Frailing, Henry H., House [Iron County MRA], 19 W. Cuyuga St., Iron River, 12/22/83, B, C, 83003696

Haggerty, Dennis J., House [Iron County MRA], 7 N. 7th Ave., Iron River, 12/22/83, B, C, 83003699

Hamilton, George, House [Iron County MRA], 504 Seldon Rd., Stambaugh, 12/22/83, C, 83003703

Hane, Gottfried, House [Iron County MRA], 703 W. Cayuga St., Iron River, 12/22/83, C, 83003701

Hanna, M.A., Company Michigan District Superintendent's House [Iron County MRA], 506 Selden Rd., Stambaugh, 12/22/83, A, C, 83003705

Hanson, John W., House [Iron County MRA], 601 Roosevelt Ave., Stambaugh, 12/22/83, C, 83003707

Harris, Joseph, House [Iron County MRA], 615 Washington Ave., Stambaugh, 12/22/83, C, 83003709

Harte, H.W., Block-Chrystal Falls Village Hall [Iron County MRA], 414-418 Superior Ave., Crystal Falls, 12/22/83, A, C, b, 83003698

Hasselstrom, John, House [Iron County MRA], 400 Crystal Ave., Crystal Falls, 12/22/83, C, 83003723

Hiawatha Mine Number One Complex [Iron County MRA], W of Selden Rd., Stambaugh, 12/22/83, A, 83003711

Holmes, Nels A., Farmstead [Iron County MRA], Off MI 189, Stambaugh, 12/22/83, A, 83003713

House at 902 Selden Road [Iron County MRA], 902 Selden Rd., Stambaugh, 12/22/83, A, C, 83003714

Huse, Frank C., House [Iron County MRA], 408 5th St., Crystal Falls, 12/22/83, C, 83003724

Iron County Courthouse, W end of Superior Ave., Crystal Falls, 2/24/75, C, 75000948

Iron County Fair Exhibition Hall [Iron County MRA], Franklin St., Iron River, 12/22/83, A, C, 83003716

Iron River Creamery [Iron County MRA], 5 W. Cayuga St., Iron River, 12/22/83, A, C, 83003717

Iron River Town Hall [Iron County MRA], 106 W. Genesee St., Iron River, 12/22/83, A, C, 83003718

Italian Society Duke of Abruzzi Hall [Iron County MRA], E of McGillis Ave. between Morgan and Sawyer Sts., Caspian, 12/22/83, A, 83003719

Jacobson, Jacob, House [Iron County MRA], 327 Maple Ave., Amasa, 12/22/83, C, 83003720

James Mine Historic District [Iron County MRA], Mineral Ave. and Mower St., Mineral Hills, 12/22/83, A, 83003721

Joseph, Joseph, House [Iron County MRA], 105 N. 8th Ave., Iron River, 12/22/83, C, 83003722

Levine, Louis, House [Iron County MRA], 502 Selden Rd., Stambaugh, 12/22/83, C, 83003725

Lincoln School [Iron County MRA], NW of Madison St. and 2nd Ave., Iron River, 12/22/83, C, 83003726

MacKinnon, Alexander, House [Iron County MRA], 134 Cayuga St., Iron River, 12/22/83, B, 83003727

MacKinnon, Donald C., House [Iron County MRA], 411 N. 9th St., Iron River, 12/22/83, B, C, b, 83003728

Mansfield Mine Location Historic District [Iron County MRA], Stream Rd., Mansfield, 12/22/83, A, C, 83003731

McLean, John S., House [Iron County MRA], 230 4th St., Stambaugh, 12/22/83, B, C, 83003729

McQuown, Lafayette, House [Iron County MRA], 411 Adams St., Stambaugh, 12/22/83, C, 83003730

Moss, William, House [Iron County MRA], 528 W. Genesee St., Iron River, 12/22/83, C, 83003734

Munro-M.A. Hanna Mining Company Office Building [Iron County MRA], 702 N. 4th St., Iron River, 12/22/83, A, 83003736

Murphy, Timothy, House [Iron County MRA], 17 N. 4th St., Crystal Falls, 12/22/83, C, 83003737

Park City Historic District [Iron County MRA], Park City and DNR Rds., Amasa, 12/22/83, A, C, 83003739

Parks, John H., Company-Wills Hardware Building [Iron County MRA], 319 Superior Ave., Crystal Falls, 12/22/83, A, C, 83003740

Rau, Herman, House [Iron County MRA], 309 Marquette Ave., Crystal Falls, 12/22/83, C, 83003742

Ross, David M., House [Iron County MRA], 120 S. 4th St., Crystal Falls, 12/22/83, C, 83003743

Royce, Steven, House [Iron County MRA], 920 Forest Pkwy., Crystal Falls, 12/22/83, A, 83003744

Russell, William, House [Iron County MRA], 209 Michigan Ave., Crystal Falls, 12/22/83, B, C, 83003746

Iron County—Continued

Scalcucci's Grocery [Iron County MRA], 2102 River Ave., Iron River, 12/22/83, A, 83003748

Soderman, John, Farmhouse [Iron County MRA], North 6th St., Crystal Falls, 12/22/83, A, 83003749

Spies Boardinghouse [Iron County MRA], 700 Grant St., Mineral Hills, 12/22/83, A, C, 83003750

St. Mary's Assumption Catholic Church [Iron County MRA], 105 5th Ave., Iron River, 12/22/83, A, C, a, 83003759

Stolberg, Charles, House [Iron County MRA], 411 3rd St., Stambaugh, 12/22/83, C, 83003751

Sturgeon, Robert H., House [Iron County MRA], 112 Cayuga St., Iron River, 12/22/83, B, 83003752

Swanson, John, House [Iron County MRA], 226 4th St., Stambaugh, 12/22/83, C, 83003761

Triangle Ranch Headquarters Historic District [Iron County MRA], N of Amasa, Amasa vicinity, 12/29/83, A, 83003762

Tully, William J., House [Iron County MRA], 419 W. Cayuga St., Iron River, 12/22/83, B, C, 83003764

Van Ornum's Addition Historic District [Iron County MRA], 927, 937, 941, 947, and 953 4th St., Iron River, 12/22/83, B, C, g, 83003770

Van Platen-Fox Lumber Camp Historic Complex [Iron County MRA], 281 University Rd., Stambaugh, 12/22/83, A, 83003766

Van Wagner, Harvey, House [Iron County MRA], 103 N. 7th Ave., Iron River, 12/22/83, C, 83003767

Wall-Seppanen House [Iron County MRA], 21 N. 7th Ave., Iron River, 12/22/83, B, C, 83003768

Windsor, Joseph, House [Iron County MRA], 629 W. Genesee St., Iron River, 12/22/83, C, 83003769

Isabella County

Doughty House, 301 Chippewa St., Mount Pleasant, 10/29/74, A, C, 74000989

Michigan Condensed Milk Factory, 320 W. Broadway St., Mount Pleasant, 4/07/83, A, 83000853

St. John's Episcopal Church, 206 W. Maple St., Mount Pleasant, 4/22/82, B, C, a, 82002842

Jackson County

Clark-Stringham Site, Address Restricted, Jackson vicinity, 6/19/73, D, 73002154

Collins Manufacturing—Jackson Automobile Company Complex, 2301 E. Michigan Ave., Jackson, 7/09/93, A, C, 93000622

Grass Lake Public School, 661 E. Michigan Ave., Grass Lake, 5/31/84, A, C, g, 84001693

Jackson District Library, 244 W. Michigan St., Jackson, 3/10/80, A, C, 80001873

Jameson, James M., Farm, E. of Springport at 10220 N. Parma Rd., Springport vicinity, 7/15/80, C, 80001875

Mann House, 205 Hanover St., Concord, 10/15/70, A, C, 70000273

Michigan State Prison, Armory Court and Cooper St., Jackson, 8/10/79, A, C, 79001156

Michigan Theater, 124 N. Mechanic St., Jackson, 5/08/80, A, C, 80001874

Richard, Hugh H., House, 505 Wildwood Ave., Jackson, 12/02/93, B, C, 93001352

Sharp, Ella, House, 3225 4th St., Jackson, 8/25/72, A, C, 72000622

Siebold Farm/Ruehle (Realy) Farm, 9998 Waterloo-Munith Rd., Waterloo Township, 3/30/73, A, C, 73000952

Stone Post Office, Rear of 125 N. Jackson St., Jackson, 3/16/72, C, 72000623

Wilcox, Andrew, House, 231 E. High St., Jackson, 12/14/87, C, 87002138

Kalamazoo County

Appeldorn, Peter B., House [Kalamazoo MRA], 532 Village St., Kalamazoo, 5/27/83, C, 83000854

Bronson Park Historic District [Kalamazoo MRA], Roughly bounded by S. Rose, S. Park, W. Lovell, and W. Michigan Aves., Kalamazoo, 5/27/83, A, C, 83000855

Brown, Isaac, House [Kalamazoo MRA], 427 S. Burdick St., Kalamazoo, 5/27/83, C, 83000856

Delano, William S., House, N of Kalamazoo at 555 W. E Ave., Kalamazoo vicinity, 8/09/79, A, C, 79001157

Desenberg Building, 251 E. Michigan Ave., Kalamazoo, 8/13/79, C, 79001158

East Hall, Oakland Dr., Kalamazoo, 2/23/78, A, C, 78001501

Engine House No. 3 [Kalamazoo MRA], 607 Charlotte Ave., Kalamazoo, 5/27/83, A, C, 83000857

Gibbs, John, House [Kalamazoo MRA], 3403 Parkview Ave., Kalamazoo, 5/27/83, A, C, 83000858

Gilbert, Henry, House [Kalamazoo MRA], 415 W. Lovell, Kalamazoo, 5/27/83, B, C, g, 83000859

Haymarket Historic District [Kalamazoo MRA], Michigan Ave. between Portage St. and Grand Rapids & Indiana RR, Kalamazoo, 5/27/83, A, C, 83000860

Illinois Envelope Co. Building [Kalamazoo MRA], 400 Bryant St., Kalamazoo, 5/27/83, A, 83000861

Kalamazoo State Hospital Water Tower, Oakland Dr., Kalamazoo, 3/16/72, C, 72000624

Kendall, Silas W., House, 7540 W. Michigan Ave., Oshtemo Township, Kalamazoo vicinity, 12/28/90, C, 90001958

Ladies Library Association Building, 333 S. Park St., Kalamazoo, 7/08/70, A, C, 70000274

Lawrence and Chapin Building [Kalamazoo MRA], 201 N. Rose St., Kalamazoo, 5/27/83, A, C, 83000862

Lilienfeld, David, House [Kalamazoo MRA], 447 W. South St., Kalamazoo, 1/23/86, C, 86000119

Marlborough, The [Kalamazoo MRA], 471 W. South St., Kalamazoo, 5/27/83, C, 83000863

Masonic Temple Building, 309 N. Rose St., Kalamazoo, 5/12/80, A, C, 80001876

Michigan Central Depot, 459 N. Burdick St., Kalamazoo, 6/11/75, A, C, 75000949

Montague, Henry, House [Kalamazoo MRA], 814 Oakland Dr., Kalamazoo, 5/27/83, B, C, 83000864

Oaklands, The [Kalamazoo MRA], 1815 W. Michigan Ave., Kalamazoo, 5/27/83, C, 83000865

Old Central High School [Kalamazoo MRA], 714 S. Westnedge Ave., Kalamazoo, 8/16/83, C, 83000866

Old Fire House No. 4 [Kalamazoo MRA], 526 N. Burdick St., Kalamazoo, 5/27/83, A, C, 83000867

Portage Street Fire Station, 1249 Portage St., Kalamazoo, 9/12/85, A, 85002150

Prentice, Alonzo T., House [Kalamazoo MRA], 839 W. Lovell St., Kalamazoo, 5/27/83, C, 83000868

Roberts, Martin W., House [Kalamazoo MRA], 703 Wheaton Ave., Kalamazoo, 5/27/83, C, 83000869

Rose Place Historic District [Kalamazoo MRA], Rose Pl., Kalamazoo, 5/27/83, A, C, 83000870

Shaffer, Enoch, House [Kalamazoo MRA], 1437 Douglas Ave., Kalamazoo, 5/27/83, C, 83000871

South Street Historic District, South St. between Oakland Dr. and Westnedge Ave., Kalamazoo, 8/28/79, B, C, 79001159

State Hospital Gatehouse [Kalamazoo MRA], 1006 Oakland Dr., Kalamazoo, 5/27/83, C, 83000872

Stevens, Andrew J., House [Kalamazoo MRA], 4024 Oakland Dr., Kalamazoo, 5/27/83, C, 83000873

Stuart Neighborhood/Henderson Park Historic District [Kalamazoo MRA], Roughly bounded by Michigan Central RR, Douglas, Forbes, W. Main, North, Elm Sts., Kalamazoo and Grand Ave., Kalamazoo, 5/27/83, A, C, d, 83000874

Stuart, Charles E., House, 427 Stuart Ave., Kalamazoo, 3/16/72, B, C, 72000625

Thomas, Dr. Nathan M., House, 613 E. Cass St., Schoolcraft, 4/22/82, B, b, 82002843

Vine Area Historic District [Kalamazoo MRA], Roughly bounded by S. Rose, S. Westnedge, W. Walnut, and Ranney Sts., Kalamazoo, 8/16/83, C, 83000875

Welsh, William L., Terrace [Kalamazoo MRA], 101-105 W. Dutton St., Kalamazoo, 5/27/83, C, 83000876

Western State Normal School Historic District [Kalamazoo MRA], Roughly bounded by Stadium Dr., Oliver St., and Davis St., Kalamazoo, 8/10/90, A, C, 90001230

Kent County

Ada Covered Bridge, Across the Thornapple River, Ada vicinity, 2/16/70, A, 70000275

Kent County—Continued

Aldrich Building, 98 Monroe Center, NW, Grand Rapids, 11/12/82, C, 82000536

Blodgett, John W., Estate, 250 Plymouth Rd., SE, East Grand Rapids, 7/28/83, A, C, 83000877

Fallasburg Covered Bridge, Covered Bridge Rd., Lowell vicinity, 3/16/72, A, C, 72000627

Fine Arts Building, 220 Lyon St., NW, Grand Rapids, 11/12/82, A, C, 82000537

First (Park) Congregational Church, 10 E. Park Pl., NE, Grand Rapids, 11/12/82, A, C, a, 82000538

Goodspeed Brothers Building, 188 Monroe St., NW, Grand Rapids, 4/17/80, B, C, 80001877

Graham House, 323–325 Main St., Lowell, 1/13/72, C, 72000626

Grand Rapids Savings Bank Building, 60 Monroe Center, NW, Grand Rapids, 12/28/90, A, C, 90001956

Heartside Historic District, Division, Commerce, and Ionia Aves., Fulton, Weston, Oakes, and Cherry Sts., Grand Rapids, 3/02/82, A, C, 82002844

Heritage Hill Historic District, Bounded by Michigan Ave. on the N, Pleasant St. on the S, Union Ave. on the E, and Clarendon Pl. and Jefferson Ave. W, Grand Rapids, 3/11/71, C, 71000399

Ladies' Literary Club, 61 Sheldon St., SE., Grand Rapids, 10/26/71, A, C, 71000400

Ledyard Block Historic District, 123-145 Ottawa Ave., and 104-124 Monroe Center, NW, Grand Rapids, 9/08/83, A, C, 83000878

Loraine Building, 124 E. Fulton St., Grand Rapids, 11/24/82, C, 82000539

Michigan Trust Company Building, 40 Pearl St., NW, Grand Rapids, 2/24/83, C, 83000879

Mt. Mercy Academy and Convent, 1425 Bridge St., NW, Grand Rapids, 8/05/93, A, 93000769

Norton Mound Group, Address Restricted, Grand Rapids vicinity, 10/15/66, D, NHL, 66000396

Paddock, Augustus, House, 1033 Lake Dr., SE, Grand Rapids, 9/12/85, B, C, 85002154

Pike, Abram W., House, 230 Fulton St., E., Grand Rapids, 7/08/70, C, 70000276

Rood Building, Address Restricted, Grand Rapids vicinity, 3/04/88, C, 88000142

Sixth Street Bridge, Spans Grand River between Newberry and 6th St., Grand Rapids, 8/13/76, A, C, 76001030

St. Cecilia Society Building, 24–30 Ransom Ave., NE, Grand Rapids, 12/09/71, A, C, 71000401

Third Reformed Church, 1009 Hermitage St., SE, Grand Rapids, 4/22/82, C, a, 82002845

Thornapple River Drive Bridge, Thornapple River Dr. over Thornapple River, Cascade Township, 4/18/90, A, C, 90000570

Turner House, 731 Front St., NW, Grand Rapids, 7/08/70, C, 70000277

U.S. Post Office, Ionia and Pearl Sts., Grand Rapids, 7/10/74, C, 74000990

Villa Maria, 1315 Walker NW, Grand Rapids, 3/27/87, A, a, 86003373

Keweenaw County

ALGOMA [Shipwrecks of Isle Royale National Park TR], Address Restricted, Isle Royale National Park vicinity, 6/14/84, C, D, NPS, 84001699

AMERICA [Shipwrecks of Isle Royale National Park TR], Address Restricted, Isle Royale National Park vicinity, 6/14/84, A, D, NPS, 84001708

CHESTER A. CONGDON [Shipwrecks of Isle Royale National Park TR], Address Restricted, Isle Royale National Park vicinity, 6/14/84, A, C, D, NPS, 84001716

CUMBERLAND [Shipwrecks of Isle Royale National Park TR], Address Restricted, Isle Royale National Park vicinity, 6/14/84, C, D, NPS, 84001732

Central Mine Historic District, U.S. 41, Central, 6/28/74, A, C, 74000991

Central Mine Methodist Church, About 1 mi. N of U.S. 41, Central, 10/15/70, A, a, 70000278

EMPEROR [Shipwrecks of Isle Royale National Park TR], Address Restricted, Isle Royale National Park vicinity, 6/14/84, A, C, D, NPS, 84001748

Eagle Harbor Light Station [U.S. Coast Guard Lighthouses and Light Stations on the Great Lakes TR], Eagle Harbor, Eagle Harbor, 7/19/84, A, C, 84001745

Eagle Harbor Schoolhouse, Block 10, Eagle Harbor, 9/22/72, B, 72000628

Eagle River Historic District, Roughly Front, 2nd, 3rd, 4th, 5th, and Main Sts., Eagle River, 9/13/84, A, C, 84001746

Edisen Fishery, Rock Harbor, Isle Royale National Park, 3/08/77, A, C, g, NPS, 77000152

Fort Wilkins, Fort Wilkins State Park, Copper Harbor, 7/08/70, A, 70000279

GEORGE M. COX [Shipwrecks of Isle Royale National Park TR], Address Restricted, Isle Royale National Park vicinity, 6/14/84, A, C, D, NPS, 84001749

GLENLYON [Shipwrecks of Isle Royale National Park TR], Address Restricted, Isle Royale National Park vicinity, 6/14/84, A, C, D, NPS, 84001750

Gull Rock Light Station [U.S. Coast Guard Lighthouses and Light Stations on the Great Lakes TR], Gull Rock, Copper Harbor vicinity, 7/19/84, A, C, 84001751

HENRY CHISHOLM [Shipwrecks of Isle Royale National Park TR], Address Restricted, Isle Royale National Park vicinity, 6/14/84, A, C, D, NPS, 84001752

Holy Redeemer Church, Off U.S. 41, Eagle Harbor, 3/16/72, A, a, 72000629

Isle Royale Light Station [U.S. Coast Guard Lighthouses and Light Stations on the Great Lakes TR], Managerie Island, Isle Royale vicinity, 8/04/83, A, C, 83000880

KAMLOOPS [Shipwrecks of Isle Royale National Park TR], Address Restricted, Isle Royale National Park vicinity, 6/14/84, A, C, D, NPS, 84001769

Keweenaw Mountain Lodge and Golf Course Complex, SW of Copper Harbor on U.S. 41, Copper Harbor vicinity, 6/18/80, A, C, g, 80001878

MONARCH [Shipwrecks of Isle Royale National Park TR], Address Restricted, Isle Royale National Park vicinity, 6/14/84, A, C, D, NPS, 84001779

Manitou Island Light Station [U.S. Coast Guard Lighthouses and Light Stations on the Great Lakes TR], Manitou Island, Copper Harbor vicinity, 7/19/84, A, C, 84001773

Minong Mine Historic District, Address Restricted, Isle Royale National Park vicinity, 11/11/77, A, D, NPS, 77000153

Rock Harbor Lighthouse, Rock Harbor, Isle Royale National Park, 3/08/77, A, C, NPS, 77000154

Rock of Ages Light Station [U.S. Coast Guard Lighthouses and Light Stations on the Great Lakes TR], SW of Isle Royale, Isle Royale vicinity, 8/04/83, A, C, 83000881

Lake County

Idlewild Historic District, U.S. 10, Idlewild, 6/07/79, A, 79001160

Marlborough Historic District, James Rd., Marlborough vicinity, 9/07/72, A, 72000630

Lapeer County

Armstrong, Joseph, House [Lapeer MRA], 707 Monroe St., Lapeer, 7/26/85, B, C, 85001625

Currier House, 231 E. St. Clair St., Almont, 6/10/75, C, 75000950

Day, John W., House, 4985 Dryden Rd., Dryden vicinity, 12/17/87, C, 87002153

Detroit-Bay City Railroad Company Columbiaville Depot, 4643 1st St.., Columbiaville, 4/05/84, A, B, C, 84001785

Druden Community Country Club—General Squier Historic Park Complex, 4725 S. Mill Rd., Dryden, 6/05/86, B, b, 86001220

Dutton, James B., House [Lapeer MRA], 605 Calhoun St., Lapeer, 7/26/85, A, B, C, a, 85001626

Fairweather, James F.—Lamb, Jacob C., House, 540 S. Almont Ave., Imlay City, 9/26/85, A, B, C, 85002494

Hadley Flour and Feed Mill, 3633 Hadley Rd., Hadley Township, 9/25/86, A, 86002770

Hart, Rodney G., House [Lapeer MRA], 326 W. Park St., Lapeer, 7/26/85, B, C, 85001627

Hevener, John and Julia, House [Lapeer MRA], 1444 W. Genesee, Lapeer, 7/26/85, B, C, 85001628

Lapeer County Courthouse, Courthouse Sq., Nepessing St., Lapeer, 9/03/71, A, C, 71000402

Lee, John and Rosetta, House [Lapeer MRA], 823 Calhoun St., Lapeer, 7/26/85, B, C, a, 85001629

Metamora Crossroads Historic District, Oak and High Sts., Metamora, 7/19/84, A, C, 84001790

Palmer, Charles, House, 240 N. Main St., Imlay City, 6/12/87, B, C, 87000916

Perry, Warren, House [Lapeer MRA], 892 Saginaw St., Lapeer, 7/26/85, B, C, 85001630

Lapeer County—Continued

Piety Hill Historic District [Lapeer MRA], Roughly bounded by Park, Calhoun, Nepressing, Cramton & Main, Lapeer, 7/26/85, A, C, a, 85001631

Pioneer State Bank No. 36, 4046 Huron St., North Branch, 4/22/82, A, C, 82002846

Tomlinson, Samuel J., House [Lapeer MRA], 841 Calhoun St., Lapeer, 7/26/85, B, C, 85001632

Tuttle, Columbus, House [Lapeer MRA], 610 N. Main St., Lapeer, 7/26/85, B, C, 85001633

Van Dyke, Peter, House [Lapeer MRA], 1091 Pine St., Lapeer, 7/26/85, B, C, 85001634

Watson, William H. and Sabrina, House [Lapeer MRA], 507 Cedar St., Lapeer, 7/26/85, B, C, 85001635

West Saint Clair Street Historic District, 124–328 W. Saint Clair St., Almont, 5/08/86, B, C, 86000998

White, Jay, House [Lapeer MRA], 1109 W. Genesee St., Lapeer, 7/26/85, B, C, 85001636

Younge Site, Address Restricted, Goodland vicinity, 10/29/76, D, 76002161

Leelanau County

Bingham District No. 5 Schoolhouse, Jct. of Co. Rds. 618 and 633, Bingham Township, Bingham, 7/31/91, A, 91000353

Glen Haven Village Historic District, MI 209, Glen Haven, 6/24/83, A, B, C, b, NPS, 83000882

Grand Traverse Light Station [U.S. Coast Guard Lighthouses and Light Stations on the Great Lakes TR], Leelanau Peninsula, Northport, 7/19/84, A, C, 84001799

Grove Hill New Mission Church, On MI 22, Omena, 6/29/72, A, B, a, 72000631

Hutzler's Barn, W of Leland on South Manitou Island, Leland vicinity, 1/03/78, A, C, NPS, 78000375

Hutzler, George Conrad, Farm, S. Manitou Island, Sleeping Bear Dunes National Seashore, Glen Haven vicinity, 5/03/91, A, NPS, 91000466

Leland Historic District, Roughly bounded by the park, Main St., Ave. A, and the harbor, Leland, 11/20/75, A, 75000951

Saint Joseph's Catholic Church, 5899 Co. Rd. 669, Cleveland Township, Glen Arbor vicinity, 1/22/92, A, C, a, 91001997

Sleeping Bear Inn, MI 209, Glen Haven, 9/06/79, A, NPS, 79000284

Sleeping Bear Point Life Saving Station, N of Glen Haven, Glen Haven vicinity, 4/26/79, A, C, b, NPS, 79000285

South Manitou Island Lighthouse Complex and Life Saving Station Historical District, Sandy Point, South Manitou Island, 10/28/83, A, a, NPS, 83003782

Lenawee County

Adrian Engine House No. 1, 126 E. Church St., Adrian, 8/21/89, A, C, 89000789

Adrian Public Library, 110 E. Church St., Adrian, 12/06/77, A, C, 77000719

Adrian Union Hall-Croswell Opera House, Address Restricted, Adrian, 4/18/85, A, C, 85000839

Brookside Cemetery [Tecumseh MRA], N. Union St., Tecumseh, 8/13/86, C, d, 86001559

Carpenter, David, House, 424 W. Adrian St., Blissfield, 11/20/79, B, C, 79001163

Catlin, Dr. Samuel, House [Tecumseh MRA], 213 E. Chicago Blvd., Tecumseh, 8/13/86, C, 86001563

Civil War Memorial, Monument Park, Adrian, 6/29/72, A, C, b, f, 72000632

Clark Memorial Hall, 120-124 S. Winter St., Adrian, 1/14/85, A, C, 85000097

Croswell, Gov. Charles, House, 228 N. Broad St., Adrian, 3/16/72, B, 72000633

Dennis and State Streets Historic District, Roughly bounded by Union, Dennis and State Sts., and New York Central RR, Adrian, 4/14/75, C, 75002170

Dennis and State Streets Historic District (Boundary Increase), SE corner of Dennis and State Streets, Adrian, 7/26/79, C, 79003780

Downtown Adrian Commercial Historic District, Roughly bounded by Toledo, N. Broad, E. Church and W. Maumee Sts., and S. Winter St. and the Raisin River, Adrian, 4/17/86, A, C, 86000803

Evans, Musgrove, House, 409–411 E. Logan St., Tecumseh, 3/16/72, B, C, b, 72000634

First Presbyterian Church of Blissfield, 306 Franklin St., Blissfield, 9/03/71, C, a, b, 71000403

Goodrich, Heman R., House, 428 Church St. S., Hudson, 1/22/92, C, 91001996

Hall, Dr. Leonard, House, 334 W. Main St., Hudson, 10/02/78, A, C, 78001503

Hall, Joseph E., House [Tecumseh MRA], 210 S. Oneida St., Tecumseh, 8/13/86, C, 86001566

Hayden, William, House [Tecumseh MRA], 108 W. Pottawatamie, Tecumseh, 8/13/86, A, B, 86001568

Hudson Downtown Historic District, W. Main St. between Howard and Market Sts., and Church St. between Seward and Railroad Sts., Hudson, 12/24/74, A, C, 74000992

Kempf, George J., House [Tecumseh MRA], 212 E. Kilbuck, Tecumseh, 8/13/86, C, 86001570

Lenawee County Courthouse, 309 N. Main St., Adrian, 2/28/91, C, 91000212

Pennington, John-Ford, Henry, House, 8281 Clinton Macon Rd., Macon, 12/31/74, A, C, 74000993

Raisin Valley Friends Meetinghouse, 3552 N. Adrian Hwy., Adrian vicinity, 4/28/82, A, B, C, a, d, 82002847

Saint Elizabeth's Church [Tecumseh MRA], 302 E. Chicago Blvd., Tecumseh, 8/13/86, A, C, a, 86001572

Sparks, G. P., House [Tecumseh MRA], 509 E. Logan St., Tecumseh, 8/13/86, C, 86001571

St. John's Lutheran Church, 121 S. Locust St., Adrian, 12/27/84, A, C, a, 84000544

St. Mary of Good Counsel Catholic Church, 320 Division St., Adrian, 2/24/83, C, a, 83000883

Tecumseh Downtown Historic District, E. and W. Chicago Blvd. and S. Evans St., Tecumseh, 4/17/86, A, C, 86000805

Tecumseh Historic District, W. Chicago Blvd. and Union St., Tecumseh, 9/13/84, C, 84001796

Tecumseh Historic District (Boundary Increase) [Tecumseh MRA], 704–710 W. Chicago Blvd., Tecumseh, 5/18/90, B, C, 86001560

Temple, Samuel W., House [Tecumseh MRA], 115 W. Shawnee St., Tecumseh, 8/13/86, B, C, 86001561

Thompson, Gamaliel, House, 101 Summit St., Hudson, 4/03/75, C, 75000952

Walker Tavern, 11710 US 12, Cambridge Junction, 1/25/71, A, 71000404

Wheeler, Nathaniel S., House, N of Onsted at 7075 M-50, Onsted vicinity, 2/24/75, C, 75000953

Livingston County

Ann Arbor Railway Station, 126 Wetmore St., Howell, 5/06/71, A, C, 71000405

Bingham House, 13270 Silver Lake Rd., Brighton, 10/18/72, A, C, 72000635

Howell Downtown Historic District, Roughly bounded by Clinton, Barnard, Sibley, and Chestnut Sts., Howell, 2/27/87, A, C, 86003363

Livingston County Courthouse, Grand River Ave., Howell, 8/13/76, C, 76001031

Olds, Alonzo W., House, 10084 Rushton Rd., Rushton vicinity, 5/05/72, C, 72000636

Western House, 500 W. Main St., Brighton, 4/17/86, A, C, 86000806

Westphal, August, Farmstead, 6430 Brighton Rd., Brighton vicinity, 9/12/85, A, C, 85002151

Luce County

Luce County Sheriff's House and Jail, 411 W. Harrie St., Newberry, 4/27/82, C, 82002848

Mackinac County

Chambers, John, House, 90 North State St., St. Ignace, 4/22/82, B, C, 82002849

Fort Mackinac, Huron Rd., Mackinac Island, 7/08/70, A, 70000280

Geary, Mathew, House, Market St., Mackinac Island, 5/06/71, A, 71000407

Grand Hotel, Grand Ave., Mackinac Island, 5/05/72, A, C, NHL, 72000637

Gros Cap Archaeological District, Address Restricted, Moran Township vicinity, 10/29/82, A, D, 82000540

Gros Cap Cemetery, SE of Gros Cap on U.S. 2, Gros Cap vicinity, 4/16/71, A, d, 71000406

Indian Dormitory, Huron St., Mackinac Island, 11/05/71, A, 71000408

Juntunen Site, Address Restricted, Pointe Aux Pins vicinity, 3/21/78, D, 78001504

Mackinac County—Continued

Lasanen Site, Address Restricted, St. Ignace vicinity, 5/06/71, D, 71000412

Mackinac Island, NE across the Straits of Mackinac from Mackinaw City, Mackinac Island, 10/15/66, A, a, NHL, 66000397

Marquette Street Archaeological District, Address Restricted, St. Ignace, 10/29/82, A, B, D, 82000541

Mission Church, Huron St., Mackinac Island, 1/25/71, A, a, 71000409

Mission House, Huron St., Mackinac Island, 4/16/71, A, a, 71000410

Round Island Lighthouse, S of Mackinac Island in Hiawatha National Forest, Mackinac Island vicinity, 8/21/74, A, 74000994

Scott Point Site, Address Restricted, Gould City vicinity, 7/30/76, D, 76001032

St. Helena Island Light Station, St. Helena Island, Lake Michigan, St. Ignace vicinity, 4/27/88, A, 88000442

St. Ignace Mission, State and Marquette Sts., Marquette Park, St. Ignace, 10/15/66, A, B, a, d, NHL, 66000398

Stuart, Robert, House, Market St., Mackinac Island, 4/16/71, A, 71000411

Macomb County

Clinton-Kalamazoo Canal, Runs between Utica and Yates, Yates vicinity, 3/24/72, A, 72000638

First Congregational Church, 69619 Parker, Richmond, 12/06/75, C, 75000954

Ford, Edsel and Eleanor, House, 1100 Lakeshore Dr., St. Clair Shores, 7/24/79, B, C, 79001164

Grand Trunk Western Railroad, Mount Clemens Station, 198 Grand St., Mount Clemens, 10/26/81, B, C, 81000311

Holcombe Site, Address Restricted, Warren, 4/16/71, D, 71001023

Romeo Historic District, Roughly bounded by the corporate lines of the city, Romeo, 7/08/70, A, C, 70000281

Upton, William, House, 40433 Utica Rd., Sterling Heights, 7/31/86, C, 86002113

Washington Octagon House, 57000 Van Dyke St., Washington, 9/03/71, C, 71000413

Manistee County

First Congregational Church, 412 S. 4th St., Manistee, 6/25/74, A, B, C, a, 74000995

Makinen, John J., Bottle House, 14551 Wuoksi Ave., Kaleva, 7/09/87, C, g, 87000423

Manistee Central Business District, Roughly bonded by Maple, Washington, Water and River Sts., Manistee, 5/07/82, A, C, 82002851

Manistee County Courthouse Fountain, Onekama Village Park, Onekama, 2/08/88, C, b, 88000065

Manistee North Pier, W end of Fifth Ave., Manistee, 5/17/90, A, 90000718

Our Saviour's Evangelical Lutheran Church, 300 Walnut St., Manistee, 8/21/72, A, C, a, 72000639

Portage Point Inn Complex, 8513 S. Portage Point Dr., Onekama vicinity, 10/08/85, A, C, 85003001

Ramsdell Theatre, 101 Maple St., Manistee, 1/13/72, A, 72000640

Marquette County

Arch and Ridge Streets Historic District, Arch and Ridge Sts. from Front St. to Lake Superior, Marquette, 6/18/80, B, C, 80001879

Big Bay Point Light Station, 3 Lighthouse Rd., Big Bay vicinity, 10/12/88, A, C, 88001837

Call House, 450 E. Ridge St., Marquette, 1/13/72, C, 72000641

Cliffs Shaft Mine, Euclid St. between Lakeshore Dr. and Spruce St., Ishpeming, 7/17/92, A, C, 92000832

Cohodas, Sam, Lodge, Off US 41 at E end of Lake Michigamme, Michigamme Township, Champion vicinity, 4/04/91, B, C, 91000331

Granite Island Light Station [U.S. Coast Guard Lighthouses and Light Stations on the Great Lakes TR], 12 mi. N of Marquette on Granite Island, Marquette vicinity, 8/04/83, A, C, 83000884

Granot Loma, Co. Rd. 550 on Lake Superior shore N of Thoneys Pt., Powell Township, Marquette vicinity, 4/04/91, B, C, 91000330

Harlow Block, 100 W. Washington St., Marquette, 3/24/83, A, C, 83000885

Huron Islands Lighthouse, NW of Big Bay in Lake Superior, Big Bay vicinity, 9/02/75, A, 75000955

Ishpeming Municipal Building, 100 E. Division St., Ishpeming, 7/09/81, A, C, 81000312

Jackson Iron Company Site, N of Negaunee limits off SR 492, Negaunee vicinity, 5/30/75, A, C, 75000957

Jackson Mine, W of Negaunee, Negaunee vicinity, 9/03/71, A, 71000414

Longyear Hall of Pedagogy-Northern Michigan University, Presque Isle Ave., Marquette, 4/03/80, C, 80001880

Marquette City Hall, 204 Washington St., Marquette, 4/11/75, A, C, 75000956

Marquette County Courthouse, 400 S. 3rd St., Marquette, 3/29/78, A, C, 78001506

Marquette Harbor Light Station [U.S. Coast Guard Lighthouses and Light Stations on the Great Lakes TR], Marquette Harbor, Marquette, 7/19/84, A, C, 84001803

Mather Inn, 107 Canda St., Ishpeming, 12/20/78, B, C, g, 78001505

Savings Bank Building, 125 W. Washington St., Marquette, 9/13/78, B, C, 78001507

Stannard Rock Lighthouse, Off Keweenaw Peninsula, Lake Superior, 3/30/73, A, C, 73000953

State House of Correction and Branch Prison, Off U.S. 41 and MI 28, Marquette, 11/23/77, A, C, 77000720

Upper Peninsula Brewing Company Building, Meeske St. and U.S. 41, Marquette, 5/15/80, B, C, 80001881

Mason County

Big Sable Point LIght Station [U.S. Coast Guard Lighthouses and Light Stations on the Great Lakes TR], Big Sable Point, Mason, 8/04/83, A, C, 83004296

Mason County Courthouse, 300 E. Ludington Ave., Ludington, 5/19/88, C, 88000602

Not-A-Pe-Ka-Gon Site, Address Restricted, Mason County vicinity, 7/27/73, D, 73002155

Mecosta County

Fairman Building, 102–106 S. Michigan Ave., Big Rapids, 2/12/87, B, C, 87000072

Nisbett Building, 101 S. Michigan Ave., Big Rapids, 12/04/86, A, C, 86003452

Menominee County

ALVIN CLARK (schooner), Mystery Ship Seaport, Lake Michigan, Menominee vicinity, 5/16/74, A, 74000996

Chicago, Milwaukee, St. Paul and Pacific Railroad Station, 219 West Fourth Ave., Menominee, 4/22/82, A, 82002852

First Street Historic District, Roughly bounded by N side of 10th Ave., 4th Ave., 2nd St., and Green Bay Shoreline, Menominee, 12/31/74, A, C, 74000997

Menominee County Courthouse, 10th Ave. between 8th and 10th Sts., Menominee, 3/07/75, A, C, 75000958

R. J. HACKETT (steamer) Shipwreck Site, Address Restricted, Green Bay vicinity, 5/21/92, A, C, D, 92000464

Riverside Site, Address Restricted, Menominee vicinity, 3/24/78, D, 78001508

Wisconsin Land and Lumber Company Office Building, N5551 River St., Meyer Township, Hermansville, 7/26/91, A, C, 91000901

Midland County

Ball, Howard, House [Residential Architecture of Alden B. Dow in Midland 1933–1938 MPS], 1411 W. St. Andrews, Midland, 12/04/89, C, 89001432

Bradley House, Corner of Cook Rd. and Main St., Midland, 7/31/72, C, b, 72000642

Cavanagh, Joseph A., House [Residential Architecture of Alden B. Dow in Midland 1933–1938 MPS], 415 W. Main, Midland, 12/04/89, C, 89001434

Conner, Donald L., House [Residential Architecture of Alden B. Dow in Midland 1933–1938 MPS], 2705 Manor, Midland, 12/04/89, C, 89001439

Diehl, Oscar C., House [Residential Architecture of Alden B. Dow in Midland 1933–1938 MPS], 919 E. Park, Midland, 12/04/89, C, 89001436

Midland County—Continued

Dow, Alden B., House and Studio, 315 Post St., Midland, 6/29/89, C, g, NHL, 89001167

Dow, Herbert H., House, 1038 W. Main St., Midland, 5/11/76, B, NHL, 76001033

Greene, George, House [Residential Architecture of Alden B. Dow in Midland 1933–1938 MPS], 115 W. Sugnet, Midland, 12/04/89, C, 89001441

Hanson, Alden, House [Residential Architecture of Alden B. Dow in Midland 1933–1938 MPS], 1605 W. St. Andrews, Midland, 12/04/89, C, 89001443

Heath, Sheldon, House [Residential Architecture of Alden B. Dow in Midland 1933–1938 MPS], 1505 W. St. Andrews, Midland, 12/04/89, C, 89001438

Lewis, F. W., House [Residential Architecture of Alden B. Dow in Midland 1933–1938 MPS], 2913 Manor, Midland, 12/04/89, C, 89001435

MacCallum, Charles, House [Residential Architecture of Alden B. Dow in Midland 1933–1938 MPS], 1227 W. Sugnet, Midland, 12/04/89, C, 89001442

Midland County Courthouse, 301 W. Main St., Midland, 3/13/86, A, B, C, 86000381

Oxbow Archeological District, Address Restricted, Eastern Midland County vicinity, 6/19/73, D, 73002156

Pardee, James T., House [Residential Architecture of Alden B. Dow in Midland 1933–1938 MPS], 812 W. Main St., Midland, 12/04/89, C, 89001431

Stein, Earl, House [Residential Architecture of Alden B. Dow in Midland 1933–1938 MPS], 209 Revere, Midland, 12/04/89, C, 89001437

Whitman, John S., House [Residential Architecture of Alden B. Dow in Midland 1933–1938 MPS], 2407 Manor, Midland, 12/04/89, C, 89001440

Missaukee County

Aetna Earthworks, Address Restricted, Missaukee County vicinity, 3/30/73, D, 73002157

Boven Earthwork, Address Restricted, Lake City vicinity, 8/14/73, D, 73002293

Monroe County

Detroit River Light Station [U.S. Coast Guard Lighthouses and Light Stations on the Great Lakes TR], Lake Erie, Rockwood vicinity, 8/04/83, A, C, 83000886

Dundee Historic District, Roughly bounded by Main, Monroe, and Toledo Sts., River Raisin, Riley, Tecumseh, and Ypsilanti Sts., Dundee, 8/20/90, A, C, 90001239

East Elm-North Macomb Street Historic District [City of Monroe MRA], Roughly bounded by River Raisin, Lorain, Monroe and Macomb Sts., Monroe, 5/06/82, A, C, 82002853

Loranger, Edward, House, 7211 S. Stony Creek Rd., Monroe vicinity, 5/31/84, C, 84001807

McClelland, Gov. Robert, House, 47 E. Elm St., Monroe, 9/03/71, C, 71000415

Navarre-Anderson Trading Post, W of Monroe at N. Custer (MI 130) and Raisinville Rds., Monroe vicinity, 7/31/72, A, C, b, 72000645

Nims, Rudolph, House, 206 W. Noble Ave., Monroe, 10/18/72, C, 72000644

North Maumee Bay Archeological District, Address Restricted, Erie vicinity, 12/05/80, D, 80001882

Old Village Historic District [City of Monroe MRA], MI 50 and MI 125, Monroe, 5/06/82, A, C, 82002854

River Raisin Battlefield Site (20MR227), Address Restricted, Monroe vicinity, 12/10/82, A, D, 82000542

Sawyer House, 320 E. Front St., Monroe, 11/23/77, B, C, 77000721

St. Mary's Church Complex Historic District [City of Monroe MRA], Elm Ave. and MI 125, Monroe, 5/06/82, A, C, a, 82002855

Weis Manufacturing Company, Union and 7th Sts., Monroe, 10/26/81, A, C, 81000313

Montcalm County

Gilbert, Giles, House, 306 N. Camburn St., Stanton, 2/12/87, B, C, 87000137

Winter Inn, 100 N. Lafayette St., Greenville, 4/17/80, A, C, 80001883

Muskegon County

Amazon Hosiery Mill, 530–550 W. Western Ave., Muskegon, 4/15/82, A, 82002857

Hackley, Charles H., House, 484 W. Webster Ave., Muskegon, 7/08/70, C, 70000282

Hovey, Horatio N., House, 318 Houston Ave., Muskegon, 9/08/83, A, B, C, 83000887

Hume House, 472 W. Webster Ave., Muskegon, 1/13/72, B, C, 72000646

Muskegon Historic District, Bounded roughly by Clay, Muskegon, 2nd, and 6th Sts., Muskegon, 9/27/72, A, B, C, 72000647

Muskegon YMCA Building, 297 W. Clay Ave., Muskegon, 8/11/82, A, C, 82002858

Spring Creek Site, Address Restricted, Unknown vicinity, 6/20/72, D, 72001475

U.S.S. SILVERSIDES, Naval Reserve Center, Fulton and Bluff Sts., Muskegon, 10/18/72, A, g, 72000453

Newaygo County

Croton Hydroelectric Plant, Croton Dam Rd., Croton, 8/16/79, A, C, 79001165

Toft Lake Village Site, Address Restricted, Croton vicinity, 6/20/72, D, 72001476

Oakland County

Affleck, Gregor S. and Elizabeth B., House, 1925 N. Woodward Ave., Bloomfield Hills, 10/03/85, C, g, 85003005

Andrews—Leggett House, 722 Farr St., Commerce vicinity, 6/12/87, C, 87000949

Botsford Inn, 28000 Grand River Ave., Farmington, 9/19/79, A, C, b, 79003274

Brooks Farm, 3521 Big Beaver Rd., Troy, 3/16/72, A, C, 72001594

Casa del Rey Apartments, 111 Oneida Rd., Pontiac, 6/29/89, C, 89000787

Caswell House, 60 W. Wattles Rd., Troy, 1/13/72, C, b, 72000650

Central School, 101 E. Pike St., Pontiac, 2/16/84, A, C, 84001809

Clarkston Village Historic District, MI 15, Clarkston Village, 5/15/80, A, C, 80001884

Cranbrook, Lone Pine Rd., Bloomfield Hills, 3/07/73, A, B, C, g, NHL, 73000954

Detroit Zoological Park, 8450 W. Ten Mile Rd., Huntington Woods/Royal Oak, 8/24/90, A, C, 90001226

Downtown Holly Commercial District, Roughly bounded by Mapple St., S. Broad St., Grand Trunk RR, and First St., Holly, 4/25/86, A, C, 86000866

Eagle Theater, 11-15 S. Saginaw St., Pontiac, 2/16/84, A, C, 84001810

Eastern Michigan Asylum Historic District, 140 Elizabeth Lake Rd., Pontiac, 3/20/81, A, C, 81000315

Everts, Caleb, House, 8880 Hickory Ridge Rd., Davisburg vicinity, 10/14/80, A, C, 80001886

Fairgrove Avenue Historic District, Along Fairgrove Ave. between N. Saginaw and Edison Sts., Pontiac, 1/31/85, C, 85000166

Farmington Historic District, Grand River Ave. and Shiawassee Ave. from Warner St. to jct., Farmington, 6/18/76, A, B, a, 76001034

Foote, Dr. Henry K., House, 213 W. Huron St., Milford, 1/11/85, B, C, 85000062

Franklin Boulevard Historic District, Roughly bounded by Grand Trunk Western RR, Orchard Lake Ave., Miller and W. Huron Sts., Pontiac, 8/11/83, C, 83000888

Franklin Historic District, Roughly bounded by Fourteen Mile Rd., the Franklin River, Romany Wy., and Franklin Rd., Franklin, 2/10/69, C, 69000070

Grand Trunk Western Railroad Birmingham Depot, 245 S. Eton St., Birmingham, 9/12/85, A, C, 85002148

Grinnell Brothers Music House, 27 S. Saginaw St., Pontiac, 4/19/84, A, C, 84001812

Highland United Methodist Church, 205 W. Livingston Rd., Highland, 7/09/81, A, C, a, 81000314

Hirst Hotel, 110 Battle Alley, Holly, 2/08/80, A, C, 80001887

Howard, Horatio N., House, 403 N. Saginaw, Pontiac, 12/27/84, B, C, 84000545

Hunter, John W., House, 556 W. Maple Rd., Birmingham, 1/13/72, C, b, 72000648

Oakland County—Continued

Meadow Brook Farms, 480 S. Adams Rd., Rochester vicinity, 4/17/79, A, C, 79001166

Milford Rural Agricultural School, 630 Hickory St., Milford, 1/22/92, A, 91001995

Modern Housing Corporation Addition Historic District, Roughly bounded by Montcalm St., Perry St., Joslyn Ave., Gage St., Glenwood, and Nelson St., Pontiac, 6/09/89, A, C, 89000490

Myrick-Palmer House, 223 W. Huron St., Pontiac, 7/08/70, C, 70000283

Oak Hill Cemetery, 216 University Dr., Pontiac, 6/20/89, A, B, C, d, 89000493

Orchard Lake Schools Historic District, Indian Trail, Orchard Lake, 3/19/82, B, C, 82002859

Ortonville Mill, 366 Mill St., Ortonville, 4/16/71, A, 71000416

Pleasant Ridge Historic District, Roughly bounded by Willington Rd., Woodward Ave., Ferndale and Ridge Rd., Pleasant Ridge, 8/11/92, A, C, 92000165

Pontiac Commercial Historic District, 1-29 N. Saginaw St., 5-29 W. Lawrence St., and 10-18 W. Pike St., Pontiac, 2/16/84, A, C, 84001817

Pontiac Commercial Historic District (Boundary Increase), Roughly E. Huron St. and S. Saginaw St. within loop of Wide Track Dr., Pontiac, 6/23/89, C, 89000491

Rowe House, 2360 Lone Tree Rd., NW of Milford, Milford vicinity, 12/06/75, C, 75000959

Sashabaw Presbyterian Church, NE of Clarkston at 5331 Maybee Rd., Clarkston vicinity, 10/09/80, C, a, 80001885

St. Vincent DePaul Catholic Church, Convent, and School, 150 E. Wide Track Dr., Pontiac, 6/09/89, B, C, a, 89000492

Stony Creek Village Historic District, NE of Rochester on Washington Rd., Rochester vicinity, 6/26/72, C, 72000649

Torrey, Charles, House, 1141 Foxwood Ct., Bloomfield Township, Birmingham vicinity, 5/21/92, C, 92000585

Waterford Village Historic District, Dubay and Pontiff Sts., Steffeus, Andersonville and Airport Rds., Waterford, 8/10/79, C, 79001167

Wisner House, 405 Oakland Ave., Pontiac, 7/08/70, B, C, 70000284

Yerkes, Joseph D., House, 42580 Eight Mile Rd., Novi, 1/26/84, A, B, C, 84001822

Yerkes, Robert, House, 535 E. Base Line Rd., Northville, 11/30/73, C, 73000955

Oceana County

Dumaw Creek Site, Address Restricted, Pentwater vicinity, 11/15/72, D, 72001477

Gay, Jared H., House, Rt. 2, 128th Ave., Crystal Valley, 1/26/89, A, B, 88003235

Green Quarry Site, Address Restricted, Mears vicinity, 11/09/72, D, 72001478

Little Sable Point Light Station [U.S. Coast Guard Lighthouses and Light Stations on the Great Lakes TR], Little Sable Point, Golden Township, 7/19/84, A, C, 84001827

Mears, Charles, Silver Lake Boardinghouse, Corner of Lighthouse and Silver Lake Channel Rds., Mears vicinity, 7/31/86, B, 86002115

Ontonagon County

Ontonagon County Courthouse, 601 Trap St., Ontonagon, 11/14/80, A, 80001888

Ontonagon Lighthouse, Off MI 64, Ontonagon, 10/07/75, A, C, b, 75000960

Oscoda County

Oscoda County Courthouse, Morence St., Mio, 8/25/72, A, C, 72000651

Ottawa County

Battle Point Site, Address Restricted, NW Ottawa County, 8/14/73, D, 73000956

Bilz, Aloys, House, 107 S. Division St., Spring Lake, 12/14/87, B, C, 87002139

Cappon, Isaac, House, 228 W. 9th St., Holland, 1/26/84, A, C, 84001478

Ferry, Edward P., House, 514 Lafayette St., Grand Haven, 3/19/82, B, C, 82002860

Gold, Egbert H., Estate, 1116 Hazel Ave., Holland, 12/27/84, A, C, 84000548

Grand Rapids, Grand Haven and Muskegon Railway Depot, 363 W. Main St., Coopersville, 2/06/73, A, 73002294

Holland Downtown Historic District, Roughly, Eighth St. from just E of College Ave. to River Ave. and River Ave. from Ninth St. to just N of Eighth St., Holland, 10/04/90, A, C, 90001534

Holland Harbor Lighthouse, South Pier, Holland Harbor, Holland vicinity, 7/20/78, A, C, 78001509

Holland Historic District, 11th, 12th, 13th Sts., and Washington, Maple, and Pine Aves., Holland, 5/12/83, A, C, a, 83000889

Holland Historic District (Boundary Increase), Roughly bounded by River Ave., Pine Ave., 16th St., 14th St., Columbia Ave., 13th St., Central Ave., and 10th St., Holland, 8/10/90, B, C, 90001234

Holland Old City Hall and Fire Station, 108 E. 8th St., Holland, 1/11/85, A, C, 85000063

Spoonville Site, Address Restricted, Crockery vicinity, 3/30/73, D, 73002158

Third Reformed Church of Holland, 110 W. 12th St., Holland, 4/16/71, A, C, a, 71000418

Van Raalte, Benjamin, House, 1076 Sixteenth St., Holland, 12/04/89, A, 89000790

Presque Isle County

BARNEY, F. T., Shipwreck, Address Restricted, Rogers City vicinity, 8/19/91, A, C, D, 91001016

Forty Mile Point Light Station [U.S. Coast Guard Lighthouses and Light Stations on the Great Lakes TR], Presque Isle County Park, Alpena vicinity, 7/19/84, A, C, 84001830

Old Presque Isle Lighthouse, Off SR 405, Presque Isle, 4/11/73, A, 73000957

Presque Isle County Courthouse, State and Maple Sts., Onaway, 4/03/80, A, B, C, 80001889

Presque Isle Light Station [U.S. Coast Guard Lighthouses and Light Stations on the Great Lakes TR], Presque Isle, Presque Isle Township, 8/04/83, A, C, 83000890

Radka—Bradley House, 176 W. Michigan Ave., Rogers City, 8/05/91, B, 91001019

Saginaw County

Bearinger Building [Center Saginaw MRA], 124 N. Franklin, Saginaw, 7/09/82, A, B, C, 82002861

Brockway, Abel, House [Center Saginaw MRA], 1631 Brockway, Saginaw, 7/09/82, A, B, C, 82002862

Bugai Site (20SA215), Address Restricted, Bridgeport vicinity, 10/29/82, D, 82000543

Castle Station, S. Jefferson at Federal St., Saginaw, 1/13/72, C, 72000652

Central Warehouse [Center Saginaw MRA], 1800 N. Michigan, Saginaw, 7/09/82, B, C, 82002864

Cushway, Benjamin, House [Center Saginaw MRA], 1404 S. Fayette, Saginaw, 7/09/82, A, B, b, 82002865

Davis Carriage House [Center Saginaw MRA], 519 N. Fayette, Saginaw, 7/09/82, A, B, C, 82002863

East Genesee Historic Business District [Center Saginaw MRA], Bounded by Federal, Weadock, 2nd and Jones Sts., Saginaw, 7/09/82, C, 82002866

East Saginaw Historic Business District [Center Saginaw MRA], Roughly bounded by Federal, N. Water, N. Washington and N. Franklin Sts., Saginaw, 7/09/82, A, B, C, 82002867

Fosters Site (20SA74), Address Restricted, Fosters vicinity, 10/29/82, D, 82000544

Grove, The [Center Saginaw MRA], S. Washington, Saginaw, 7/09/82, A, B, C, a, 82002868

House at 1514 N. Michigan Street [Center Saginaw MRA], 1514 N. Michigan St., Saginaw, 7/09/82, C, 82002869

Mahoney Site (20SA193), Address Restricted, St. Charles vicinity, 10/29/82, D, 82000545

Michigan Bell Building [Center Saginaw MRA], 309 S. Washington, Saginaw, 7/09/82, C, 82002870

Morseville Bridge, Burt Rd. at Flint River, Taymouth Township, 4/05/90, C, 90000573

North Jefferson Avenue Historic District [Center Saginaw MRA], Carroll and Jefferson Aves., Saginaw, 7/09/82, B, C, 82002871

North Michigan Avenue Historic District [Center Saginaw MRA], Roughly bounded by Monroe, Fayette, N. Hamilton and W. Remington Sts., Saginaw, 7/09/82, B, C, 82002872

Passolt House, 1105 S. Jefferson Ave., Saginaw, 10/18/72, A, C, 72000653

Saginaw County—Continued

Peters, Charles, Sr., House [Center Saginaw MRA], 130 N. 6th, Saginaw, 7/09/82, A, B, C, 82002873

Sackett, Russell, House [Center Saginaw MRA], 1604 Ct., Saginaw, 7/09/82, A, C, 82002874

Saginaw Central City Expansion District [Center Saginaw MRA], Off MI 13, Saginaw, 7/09/82, A, C, 82002875

Saginaw Central City Historic Residential District, Roughly bounded by Federal Ave., S. Baum St., Park and Hoyt Aves., Saginaw, 2/01/79, A, C, 79001168

Saginaw City Historic Business District [Center Saginaw MRA], Roughly bounded by Saginaw River, S. Michigan, Cleveland and Van Buren Aves., Saginaw, 7/09/82, A, B, C, 82002876

Schmidt Site, Address Restricted, Bridgeport vicinity, 7/27/73, D, 73000958

Schultz Site (20SA2) Green Point Site (20SA1), Address Restricted, Spaulding Township vicinity, 12/08/78, D, 78002843

South Jefferson Avenue Historic District [Center Saginaw MRA], Off MI 13, Saginaw, 7/09/82, A, B, C, 82002877

South Michigan Avenue Historic District [Center Saginaw MRA], Roughly bounded by Fayette, Lyon, Lee and S. Hamilton Sts., Saginaw, 7/09/82, A, B, 82002878

St. John's Episcopal Church [Center Saginaw MRA], 509 Hancock, Saginaw, 7/09/82, A, C, a, 82002879

Wenzel House [Center Saginaw MRA], 1203 S. Fayette, Saginaw, 7/09/82, C, 82002880

West Side Historic Residential District [Center Saginaw MRA], Roughly bounded by Mason, Madison, Harrison and Lyon Sts., Saginaw, 7/09/82, A, B, C, 82002881

Wright, Ammi and William, House [Center Saginaw MRA], 207 Garden Lane, Saginaw, 7/09/82, A, B, C, 82002882

Sanilac County

Divine, John, Law Office/Moore Public Library, 7239 Huron Ave., Lexington, 1/31/85, A, C, 85000167

Fead, John L., House, 5349 Washington St., Lexington, 10/05/78, B, C, 78001510

Loop, Joseph M., House, 228 S. Ridge, Port Sanilac, 11/09/72, A, 72000654

Moore, Charles H./Sleeper, Albert E., House, 7277 Simons St., Lexington, 1/11/85, A, B, C, 85000064

Nims, William Reuben, House, 7156 Huron Ave., Lexington, 4/11/85, B, C, 85000719

Port Sanilac Light Station [U.S. Coast Guard Lighthouses and Light Stations on the Great Lakes TR], Lake St., Port Sanilac, 7/19/84, A, C, 84001842

SPORT (tug) Shipwreck Site, Address Restricted, Lexington vicinity, 10/29/92, A, C, D, 92001503

Sanilac Petroglyphs, Address Restricted, Minden City vicinity, 1/25/71, A, 71001024

Schoolcraft County

Ekdahl-Goudreau Site, Address Restricted, Restricted, 11/16/78, D, 78003099

Manistique Pumping Station, Deer St., Manistique, 10/26/81, A, C, 81000316

Seul Choix Pointe Light Station [U.S. Coast Guard Lighthouses and Light Stations on the Great Lakes TR], County Rd. 431, Manistique vicinity, 7/19/84, A, C, 84001846

Shiawassee County

Ayres, Nathan, House [Owosso MRA], 604 N. Water St., Owosso, 11/04/80, C, 80001891

Byron Historic Commercial District, Roughly Saginaw St. from Maple to Water Sts., Byron, 9/13/84, A, C, 84001848

Calkins, Charles H., House, 127 E. 1st St., Perry, 3/29/78, A, B, 78001511

Christian, Leigh, House [Owosso MRA], 622 N. Ball St., Owosso, 11/04/80, C, 80001892

Christian-Ellis House [Owosso MRA], 600 N. Water St., Owosso, 11/04/80, C, 80001893

Comstock, Elias, Cabin [Owosso MRA], Curwood Castle Dr., and John St., Owosso, 11/04/80, A, B, b, 80001894

Curwood Castle, 224 John St., Owosso, 9/03/71, A, B, g, 71000420

Duff Building [Owosso MRA], 118 W. Exchange St, Owosso, 1/31/85, A, B, C, 85000168

Frieseke, Frederick, Birthplace and Boyhood Home [Owosso MRA], 654 N. Water St., Owosso, 11/04/80, B, c, 80001895

Frieseke, Julius, House, 529 Corunna Ave., Owosso, 4/05/90, B, 90000574

Gould, Amos, House [Owosso MRA], 115 W. King St., Owosso, 11/04/80, B, 80001896

Gould, Daniel, House [Owosso MRA], 509 E. Main St., Owosso, 11/04/80, B, C, 80001897

Gould, Ebenezer, House [Owosso MRA], 603 W. Main St., Owosso, 11/04/80, A, B, 80001898

Grand Trunk Railway Station, 200 Railroad St., Durand, 5/06/71, A, C, 71000419

Grow Block [Owosso MRA], 120-122 W. Exchange St., Owosso, 1/31/85, A, B, C, 85000169

Horton, William, Farmhouse, 1647 W. Miller Rd., Morrice vicinity, 4/10/86, A, C, 86000711

House at 314 W. King St. [Owosso MRA], 314 W. King St., Owosso, 11/04/80, C, 80001899

Ingersoll, John N., House, 570 W. Corunna Ave., Corunna, 5/09/80, B, C, 80001890

Jacobs, Eugene, House [Owosso MRA], 220 W. King St., Owosso, 11/04/80, C, 80004553

Martin Road Bridge, Martin Rd. across the Shiawassee R., Caledonia Township, Corunna vicinity, 7/12/91, C, 91000876

Mason Street Historic residential District [Owosso MRA], Roughly bounded by Laverock Alley,

Dewey, Hickory and Exchange Sts., Owosso, 11/04/80, C, 80001900

McCormick, Colin, House [Owosso MRA], 222 E. Exchange St., Owosso, 11/04/80, C, 80001901

Michigan Avenue-Genessee Street Historic Residential District [Owosso MRA], Roughly bounded by Michigan Ave.; Shiawassee, Cass and Clinton Sts., Owosso, 11/04/80, A, C, 80001902

Miner, Selden, House [Owosso MRA], 418 W. King St., Owosso, 11/04/80, B, 80001903

Old Miller Hospital [Owosso MRA], 121 Michigan Ave., Owosso, 11/04/80, A, 80001904

Oliver Street Historic District [Owosso MRA], Oliver St. between 3rd and Oak Sts., Williams and Goodhue Sts., Owosso, 11/04/80, B, C, 80001905

Opdyke, Sylvester, House [Owosso MRA], 655 N. Pine St., Owosso, 11/04/80, C, 80001906

Palmer, Albert, House [Owosso MRA], 528 530 River St., Owosso, 11/04/80, B, 80001907

Pardee, George, House [Owosso MRA], 603 N. Ball St., Owosso, 11/04/80, C, 80001908

Perrigo, George, House [Owosso MRA], 213 N. Cedar St., Owosso, 11/04/80, B, 80001909

Shiawassee County Courthouse, Shiawassee St., Corunna, 11/12/82, A, C, 82000546

Todd, Edwin, House [Owosso MRA], 520 N. Adam St., Owosso, 11/04/80, B, C, 80001910

West Town Historic Commercial and Industrial District [Owosso MRA], Main St., Owosso, 11/04/80, A, C, 80001911

Williams, Alfred, House [Owosso MRA], 611 N. Ball St., Owosso, 11/04/80, B, b, 80001912

Williams, Benjamin, House [Owosso MRA], 628 N. Ball St., Owosso, 11/04/80, B, 80001913

Williams—Cole House, 6810 Newburg Rd., Durand vicinity, 12/04/86, C, 86003418

Woodard, Lee, and Sons Building [Owosso MRA], 306 S. Elm St., Owosso, 11/04/80, A, 80001914

Woodard, Lyman, Company Workers' Housing [Owosso MRA], 601 Clinton St., Owosso, 11/04/80, A, 80001916

Woodard, Lyman, Furniture and Casket Company Building [Owosso MRA], 216–222 Elm St., Owosso, 11/04/80, A, C, 80001915

St. Clair County

Davidson, Wilbur F., House, 1707 Military St., Port Huron, 10/05/72, B, C, 72001306

Federal Building, 526 Water St., Port Huron, 8/07/74, A, C, 74002047

Fort Gratiot, Address Restricted, Port Huron vicinity, 4/14/80, A, D, 80004069

Fort Gratiot Lighthouse, Omar and Garfield Sts., Port Huron, 7/30/76, A, B, 76001975

Grand Trunk Western Railroad Depot, 520 State St., Port Huron, 4/13/77, A, B, 77001397

HURON (lightship), Pine Grove Park on St. Clair River, Port Huron, 7/12/76, A, C, g, NHL, 76001974

St. Clair County—Continued

Harrington Hotel, 1026 Military Street, Port Huron, 4/22/82, A, C, 82004468

Ladies of the Maccabees Building, 901 Huron Ave., Port Huron, 4/22/82, A, C, 82004469

Marine City City Hall, 300 Broadway St., Marine City, 1/11/82, A, C, 82004466

McColl, James, House, 205 S. Main St., Yale, 1/31/85, B, C, 85000170

St. Clair Flats South Channel Range Lights, 0.6 mi. W of southern tip of Harsens Island, Algonac vicinity, 5/24/90, A, 90000853

St. Clair River Tunnel, St. Clair River between Port Huron, Michigan and Sarnia, Ontario, Port Huron, 10/15/70, A, C, NHL, 70000684

Ward-Holland House, 433 N. Main St., Marine City, 1/13/72, B, C, 72001305

St. Joseph County

Art Gallery Building, 156 S. Washington St., Constantine, 5/09/80, C, 80004070

Barry, Gov. John S., House, 280 N. Washington St., Constantine, 3/16/72, B, 72001308

Constantine Historic Commercial District, Washington St. between Second and Water & Water St. between White Pigeon and 125 W. Water, Constantine, 9/17/85, A, C, 85002444

Downtown Three Rivers Commercial Historic District, N. Main St., Michigan and Portage Aves., Three Rivers, 4/29/82, A, C, 82004472

Farrand Hall, 451 Farrand Rd., Colon, 8/25/72, C, 72001307

Marantette House, Simpson Rd., Mendon, 4/11/73, A, C, D, 73001947

Nottawa Stone School, E of Nottawa at Jct. of Sturgis and Filmore Rds., Nottawa vicinity, 1/13/72, A, C, 72001309

Silliman, Arthur, House, 116 S. Main St., Three Rivers, 11/20/79, A, B, 79002662

St. Joseph County Courthouse, 125 W. Main St., Centreville, 9/16/93, A, C, 93000984

US 12 St. Joseph River Bridge, US 12 over the St. Joseph R., Mottville Township, Mottville, 4/05/91, A, C, 91000388

US Government Land Office Building, Old, 113 W. Chicago Rd., White Pigeon, 2/07/89, A, 88003234

Tuscola County

Burtis, R. C., House, 2163 S. Ringle Rd., Vassar, 6/26/75, C, 75000962

Hotel Columbia, 194 E. Huron Ave., Vassar, 1/22/92, A, B, C, 91001998

Hotel Montague, 200 S. State St., Caro, 7/09/91, A, C, 91000875

McKinley School, 510 Butler St., Vassar, 3/24/72, C, 72000655

North, Townsend, House, 325 N. Main, Vassar, 4/13/77, B, C, 77000723

Randall House, 5927 Treasurer Rd., Mayville, 11/07/76, C, 76001035

Smith House, 113–115 Prospect St., Vassar, 3/16/72, B, C, 72000656

Trinity Episcopal Church, 106 Joy St., Caro, 5/12/75, A, C, a, 75000961

Watrous General Store, 4607 W. Caro Rd., Watrousville, 10/01/74, A, 74000998

Van Buren County

Bailey, Liberty Hyde, Birthplace, 903 Bailey Ave., South Haven, 4/18/83, B, c, 83000892

Paw Paw City Hall, E. Michigan Ave., Paw Paw, 8/21/72, A, C, b, 72000657

Van Buren County Courthouse Complex, Paw Paw St., Paw Paw, 8/09/79, A, C, 79001169

Washtenaw County

Anderson, William, House, 2301 Packard Rd., Ann Arbor, 8/19/82, C, a, 82002884

Ann Arbor Central Fire Station, Corner of 5th Ave. and Huron St., Ann Arbor, 1/13/72, A, 72000658

Annin, Joseph, House [Saline MRA], 218 Monroe St., Saline, 10/10/85, C, 85002952

Bell—Spalding House, 2117 Washtenaw Ave., Ann Arbor, 12/28/90, C, 90001957

Bennett, Henry, House, 312 S. Division St., Ann Arbor, 3/01/73, A, B, 73000959

Brinkerhoff-Becker House, 601 W. Forest Ave., Ypsilanti, 7/08/82, C, 82002890

Church, Zalmon, House [Saline MRA], 113 N. Ann Arbor, Saline, 10/10/85, C, 85002966

Davenport, William H., House, 300 E. Michigan Ave., Saline, 3/03/75, C, 75000964

Detroit Observatory, Observatory and Ann Sts., Ann Arbor, 9/20/73, A, B, C, 73000960

Dixboro United Methodist Church, 5221 Church St., Dixboro, 3/16/72, A, C, a, 72000665

Earl, Thomas, House, 415 N. Main St., Ann Arbor, 6/25/92, C, 91002000

East Michigan Avenue Historic District [Saline MRA], 300–321 E. Michigan Ave., 99–103 Maple St., and 217, 300 and 302 E. Henry, Saline, 10/10/85, A, C, 85002953

Eastern Michigan University Historic District, Cross St., Washtenaw and Forest Aves., Ypsilanti, 10/04/84, A, C, 84000017

First National Bank Building, 201 S. Main St., Ann Arbor, 11/24/82, A, C, 82000547

Forbes, Jortin, House [Saline MRA], 211 N. Ann Arbor St., Saline, 10/10/85, C, 85002954

Fountain-Bessac House, 102 W. Main St., Manchester, 9/29/88, C, 88001833

Friend—Hack House, 775 County St., Milan, 4/25/91, B, C, 91000441

Frieze, Henry S., House, 1547 Washtenaw Ave., Ann Arbor, 11/15/72, B, C, 72000659

Germania Building Complex, 119-123 W. Washington St. and 209-211 Ashley St., Ann Arbor, 3/10/83, A, C, 83000893

Goodyear Block, 138 E. Main St., Manchester, 8/05/93, C, 93000770

Gordon Hall, 8347 Island Lake Rd., Dexter, 11/09/72, B, C, 72000664

Guthard, Charles, House [Saline MRA], 211 E. Michigan Ave., Saline, 10/10/85, B, C, 85002955

Harris Hall, 617 East Huron St., Ann Arbor, 4/22/82, A, C, a, 82002885

Hoffstetter, Jacob, House, 322 E. Washington St., Ann Arbor, 3/19/82, C, 82002886

Ladies' Literary Club Building, 218 N. Washington St., Ypsilanti, 3/16/72, C, 72000666

Litchfield, James, House, 3512 Central St., Dexter, 12/27/84, C, 84000567

Lutz, George R., House [Saline MRA], 103 W. Henry St., Saline, 10/10/85, C, 85002956

Main Street Post Office, 220 N. Main St., Ann Arbor, 5/22/78, C, 78001512

Methodist Episcopal Church Parsonage, 322 E. Washington St., Ann Arbor, 3/18/82, B, C, a, 82002887

Michigan Central Railroad Depot, 401 Depot St., Ann Arbor, 3/10/75, C, 75000963

Michigan Central Railroad Chelsea Depot, 150 Jackson St., Chelsea, 6/12/87, A, C, 87000915

Michigan Theater Building, 521-109 E. LIberty St., Ann Arbor, 11/28/80, A, C, 80001917

Miller—Walker House [Saline MRA], 117 McKay St., Saline, 10/10/85, C, a, 85002957

Newberry Hall, 434 S. State St., Ann Arbor, 3/24/72, A, C, a, 72000660

Nickels Arcade, 326–330 S. State St., Ann Arbor, 7/09/87, A, C, 87001180

North Ann Arbor Street Historic District [Saline MRA], 301, 303, and 305–327 N. Ann Arbor St., Saline, 10/10/85, A, C, 85002958

Northern Brewery, 1327 Jones Dr, Ann Arbor, 11/20/79, A, C, 79001170

Oakwood Cemetery Mausoleum [Saline MRA], Off Monroe St., Saline, 10/10/85, C, a, d, 85003047

Old West Side Historic District, Bounded roughly by 7th, Main, and Huron Sts., Pauline Blvd., and Crest Ave., Ann Arbor, 4/14/72, A, B, C, 72000661

Parker Mill Complex, E of Ann Arbor at Geddes and Dixboro Rds., Ann Arbor vicinity, 8/04/82, A, C, 82002888

Pease Auditorium, College Pl., Ypsilanti, 10/04/84, A, C, 84000018

President's House, University Of Michigan, 815 S. University, University of Michigan campus, Ann Arbor, 10/15/70, A, C, 70000285

Salem Methodist Episcopal Church and Salem Walker Cemetery, 7150 Angle Rd., Salem Township, Salem, 8/18/92, C, a, 92001054

Saline First Presbyterian Church [Saline MRA], 143 E. Michigan Ave., Saline, 10/10/85, A, C, a, 85002960

St. Patrick's Parish Complex, Northfield Church and Whitmore Lake Rds., Ann Arbor, 4/23/82, A, C, a, d, 82002889

Starkweather Religious Center, 901 W. Forest, Ypsilanti, 4/13/77, A, C, a, 77000724

Sturm, Louis, House [Saline MRA], 100 Russell, Saline, 10/10/85, C, 85002961

Washtenaw County—Continued

Ticknor, Dr. Benajah, House, 2781 Packard Rd., Ann Arbor, 11/21/72, C, 72000662

Union Block [Saline MRA], 100–110 E. Michigan Ave., Saline, 10/10/85, A, C, 85002962

Unitarian Universalist Church, 100 N. State St., Ann Arbor, 10/04/78, A, C, a, 78001513

University Of Michigan Central Campus Historic District, University of Michigan campus, Ann Arbor, 6/15/78, A, C, 78001514

Van Duzer, Samuel D., House [Saline MRA], 205 S. Ann Arbor St., Saline, 10/10/85, C, 85002963

Wallace Block—Old Saline Village Hall [Saline MRA], 101–113 S. Ann Arbor St., Saline, 10/10/85, A, C, 85002964

Watson, Henry R., House [Saline MRA], 7215 N. Ann Arbor-Saline Rd., Saline, 10/10/85, A, C, 85002965

Weinmann Block, 219-223 E. Washington St., Ann Arbor, 9/08/83, A, C, 83000891

White, Orrin, House, 2940 Fuller Rd., Ann Arbor, 4/16/71, C, 71000421

Wilson, Judge Robert S., House, 126 N. Division St., Ann Arbor, 3/16/72, C, 72000663

Ypsilanti Historic District, Irregular pattern along Huron River with boundaries extending to Forest Ave., Grove, Buffalo, and Hamilton Sts., Ypsilanti, 4/11/78, A, B, C, 78001515

Ypsilanti Historic District (Boundary Increase), Roughly Michigan, Summit, W. Cross, W. Forest, and Ballard; S. Adams and Woodward; Forest, Grove, Cross, and River, Ypsilanti, 1/05/89, A, B, C, 88003055

Ypsilanti Water Works Stand Pipe, Summit and Cross Sts., Ypsilanti, 10/26/81, A, C, 81000318

Wayne County

Academy of the Sacred Heart, 171 Lake Shore Dr., Grosse Pointe Farms, 6/25/87, A, C, a, 87001061

Alden Park Towers [East Jefferson Avenue Residential TR], 8100 E. Jefferson Ave., Detroit, 10/09/85, C, 85002933

Alger, Russell A., Jr., House, 32 Lake Shore Dr., Grosse Pointe Farms, 7/08/82, C, 82002917

Arden Park-East Boston Historic District, Arden Park & E. Boston Aves. between Woodward and Oakland Aves., Detroit, 4/29/82, C, 82002891

Assumption of the Blessed Virgin Mary Church Complex, 13770 Gratiot Ave., Detroit, 8/05/91, C, a, 91001020

Bagley Memorial Fountain, Woodward and Monroe Aves., Detroit, 11/05/71, B, C, b, f, 71000422

Bagley, John N., House [East Jefferson Avenue Residential TR], 2921 E. Jefferson Ave., Detroit, 10/09/85, C, 85002934

Baker, Henry W., House, 233 S. Main St., Plymouth, 4/22/82, B, C, 82002922

Belcrest Hotel, 5440 Cass Ave., Detroit, 5/31/84, A, C, 84001851

Belle Isle, Detroit River, Detroit, 2/25/74, A, C, 74000999

Boston-Edison Historic District, Roughly bounded by Edison St., Woodward and Linwood Aves. and Glynn Ct., Detroit, 9/05/75, C, 75000965

Boydell, William C., House, 4614 Cass Ave, Detroit, 3/19/82, B, C, 82002892

Breitmeyer-Tobin Building, 1308 Broadway St., Detroit, 3/10/80, A, C, 80001918

COLUMBIA (steamer), 661 Civic Center Dr., Detroit, 11/02/79, A, C, NHL, 79001171

Campau, Joseph, House [East Jefferson Avenue Residential TR], 2910 E. Jefferson Ave., Detroit, 10/09/85, A, C, 85002935

Cary Building, 229 Gratiot Ave., Detroit, 11/25/83, A, C, 83003670

Cass Avenue Methodist Episcopal Church, 3901 Cass Ave., Detroit, 12/10/82, A, C, a, 82000548

Cass Motor Sales [University—Cultural Center Phase I MRA], 5800 Cass Ave., Detroit, 4/29/86, A, C, 86001039

Cathedral Church of St. Paul Complex [Religious Structures of Woodward Ave. TR], 4800 Woodward Ave., Detroit, 8/03/82, C, a, 82002893

Cathedral of the Most Blessed Sacrament [Religious Structures of Woodward Ave. TR], 9844-9854 Woodward Ave., Detroit, 8/03/82, C, a, 82002894

Central United Methodist Church [Religious Structures of Woodward Ave. TR], Woodward Ave. E. Adams St., Detroit, 8/03/82, C, a, 82002895

Central Woodward Christian Church [Religious Structures of Woodward Ave. TR], 9000 Woodward Ave., Detroit, 8/03/82, C, a, 82002896

Century Building and Little Theatre, 58–62 E. Columbia, Detroit, 5/09/85, A, C, 85000993

Chapoton, Alexander, House, 511 Beaubien St., Detroit, 3/10/80, C, 80001919

Chateau Frontenac Apartments [East Jefferson Avenue Residential TR], 10410 E. Jefferson Ave., Detroit, 2/28/91, C, 91000213

Chatsworth Apartments [University—Cultural Center Phase II MRA], 630 Merrick, Detroit, 5/01/86, A, C, 86001001

Chene, Alexander, House [East Jefferson Avenue Residential TR], 2681 E. Jefferson Ave., Detroit, 10/09/85, A, C, 85002936

Christ Church Chapel, 61 Grosse Pointe Rd., Grosse Pointe Farms, 9/10/93, C, a, g, 93000424

Christ Church, Detroit, 960 E. Jefferson Ave., Detroit, 3/11/71, C, a, 71000423

Commandant's Quarters, 21950 Michigan Ave., Dearborn, 10/15/70, A, C, 70000286

Corktown Historic District, Roughly bounded by Lodge Freeway, Porter, Trumbull, Bagley, Rosa Parks Blvd., and Michigan Ave., Detroit, 7/31/78, A, C, 78001517

Coronado Apartments, 3751-73 Second Ave., Detroit, 4/22/82, C, 82002897

Croul-Palms House, 1394 E. Jefferson Ave., Detroit, 12/20/83, B, C, 83003790

Cultural Center Historic District, 5200, 5201 Woodward Ave., and 100 Farnsworth Ave., Detroit, 11/21/83, A, C, g, 83003791

Curtiss, Charles G., Sr., House, 168 S. Union St., Plymouth, 12/02/93, C, 93001350

Dearborn Inn and Colonial Homes, 20301 Oakwood Blvd., Dearborn, 12/10/82, B, C, 82000549

Detroit Cornice and Slate Company Building, 733 St. Antoine St. at E. Lafayette St., Detroit, 12/16/74, A, C, 74001000

Detroit Masonic Temple, 500 Temple Ave., Detroit, 11/28/80, A, C, 80001920

Dunbar Hospital, 580 Frederick St., Detroit, 6/19/79, A, C, 79001172

East Ferry Avenue Historic District, E. Ferry Ave., Detroit, 3/10/80, C, 80001921

East River Road Historic District, E. River Rd., Grosse Ile, 8/13/74, C, 74001003

Eastern Market Historic District, Bounded by Gratiot Ave., Riopelle, Rivard, and Division Sts., Detroit, 11/29/78, A, 78001518

Eastside Historic Cemetery District, Bounded by Elmwood and Mt. Elliot Aves., Lafayette and Waterloo Sts., Detroit, 12/02/82, A, C, d, 82000550

Eighth Precinct Police Station, 4150 Grand River, Detroit, 12/31/74, C, 74001001

El Tovar Apartments, 210 E. Grand Blvd., Detroit, 2/28/91, C, 91000214

Elwood Bar, 2100 Woodward, Detroit, 5/15/85, C, g, 85001074

Engine House No. 11, 2737 Gratiot Ave., Detroit, 1/09/78, A, 78001519

Everitt, Orson, House, 39040 W. Seven Mile Rd., Livonia, 10/14/80, C, 80001933

Fair Lane, 4901 Evergreen Rd., Dearborn, 11/13/66, B, NHL, 66000399

Farwell Building, 1249 Griswold St., Detroit, 4/30/76, C, 76001037

First Baptist Church of Detroit [Religious Structures of Woodward Ave. TR], 8601 Woodward Ave., Detroit, 8/03/82, C, a, 82002898

First Congregational Church, 33 E. Forest St., Detroit, 6/04/79, C, a, 79001173

First Presbyterian Church, 2930 Woodward Ave., Detroit, 12/19/79, A, C, a, 79001174

First Unitarian Church of Detroit [Religious Structures of Woodward Ave. TR], 2870 Woodward Ave., Detroit, 8/03/82, C, a, 82002899

First United Methodist Church [Religious Structures of Woodward Ave. TR], 16300 Woodward Ave., Highland Park, 8/03/82, C, a, 82002918

Fisher and New Center Buildings, 7430 2nd Ave. and 3011 W. Grand Blvd., Detroit, 10/14/80, A, C, NHL, 80001922

Ford River Rouge Complex, 3001 Miller Rd., Dearborn, 6/02/78, A, B, C, NHL, 78001516

Ford, Henry, Square House, 29835 Beechwood Ave., Garden City, 11/25/80, B, b, 80001932

Fort Shelby Hotel, 525 W. Lafayette St., Detroit, 11/25/83, A, C, 83003695

Fort Street Presbyterian Church, 631 W. Fort St., Detroit, 9/03/71, C, a, 71000424

Fort Wayne, 6053 W. Jefferson Ave., Detroit, 5/06/71, A, C, 71000425

Fox Theater Building, 2111 Woodward Ave., Detroit, 2/14/85, A, C, NHL, 85000280

Freer, Charles Lang, House, 71 E. Ferry Ave., Detroit, 4/16/71, A, B, C, 71000426

GAR Building, 1942 Grand River Ave., Detroit, 2/13/86, A, C, 86000262

Wayne County—Continued

Garden Court Apartments [East Jefferson Avenue Residential TR], 2900 E. Jefferson Ave., Detroit, 10/09/85, C, 85002937

Garfield, James A., School, 840 Waterman St., Detroit, 1/26/84, A, C, 84001857

General Motors Building, 3044 W. Grand Blvd., Detroit, 6/02/78, A, NHL, 78001520

George, Edwin S., Building, 4612 Woodward Ave., Detroit, 7/22/93, A, B, C, 93000651

Gethsemane Evangelical Lutheran Church, 4461 Twenty-Eighth St., Detroit, 4/22/82, A, C, a, 82002900

Ginsburg, Bernard, House, 236 Adelaide, Detroit, 8/19/91, B, C, 91001015

Globe Tobacco Building, 407 E. Fort St., Detroit, 11/13/84, A, C, 84000442

Grace Evangelical Lutheran Church [Religious Structures of Woodward Ave. TR], 12375 Woodward Ave., Highland Park, 8/03/82, C, a, 82002919

Grand Circus Park Historic District, Roughly bounded by Clifford, John R. and Adams Sts., Detroit, 2/28/83, A, C, 83000894

Grand Riviera Theater, 9222 Grand River Ave., Detroit, 4/22/82, A, C, 82002901

Greektown Historic District, Monroe Ave., between Brush and St. Antoine Sts., Detroit, 5/06/82, A, C, 82002902

Greenfield Village and Henry Ford Museum, Bounded by Michigan Ave. on the N, Village Rd. on the S, Southfield Expwy. on the E, and Oakland Blvd. on the W, Dearborn, 10/20/69, A, b, NHL, 69000071

Greenmead Farms, 38125 Base Line Rd., Livonia, 3/24/72, A, C, 72000672

Griswold Building, 1214 Griswold St., Detroit, 6/09/80, C, 80001923

Grosse Pointe High School, 11 Grosse Pointe Blvd., Grosse Pointe Farms, 5/20/93, A, C, 93000429

Grosse Pointe Memorial Church, 16 Lake Shore Dr., Grosse Pointe Farms, 12/06/93, C, a, 93001351

Guardian Building, 500 Griswold St., Detroit, 6/29/89, C, NHL, 89001165

Harmonie Club, The, 267 E. Grand River Ave., Detroit, 9/04/80, A, C, 80001924

Harvey, John, House, 97 Winder, Detroit, 4/03/91, B, C, 91000354

Hecker, Col. Frank J., House, 5510 Woodward Ave., Detroit, 9/03/71, C, 71000427

Hibbard Apartment Building [East Jefferson Avenue Residential TR], 8905 E. Jefferson Ave., Detroit, 10/09/85, C, 85002938

Highland Heights—Stevens' Subdivision Historic District, Bounded by Woodward Ave., the alley S of E. Buena Vista Ave., Oakland Ave., and the alley S of Massachusetts Ave., Highland Park, 2/08/88, C, 88000050

Highland Park General Hospital, 357 Glendale Ave., Highland Park, 10/31/85, A, 85003400

Highland Park Plant, Ford Motor Company, 15050 Woodward Ave., Highland Park, 2/06/73, A, C, NHL, 73000961

Highland Park Presbyterian Church [Religious Structures of Woodward Ave. TR], 14 Cortland St., Highland Park, 8/03/82, C, a, 82002920

Hudson-Evans House, 79 Alfred St., Detroit, 3/05/75, B, C, 75000966

Hunter House, 3985 Trumbull Ave., Detroit, 12/31/74, C, 74001002

Hurlbut Memorial Gate, E. Jefferson at Cadillac Blvd., Detroit, 3/27/75, C, 75000967

Indian Village Historic District, Bounded by Mack, Burns, Jefferson, and Seminole Aves., Detroit, 3/24/72, C, 72000667

Jefferson Hall [East Jefferson Avenue Residential TR], 1405 E. Jefferson Ave., Detroit, 10/09/85, C, 85002939

Kahn, Albert, House, 208 Mack Ave., Detroit, 10/18/72, C, 72000668

Kean, The [East Jefferson Avenue Residential TR], 8925 E. Jefferson Ave., Detroit, 10/09/85, C, 85002940

King, L. B. and Co. Building, 1274 Library, Detroit, 6/12/87, A, C, 87000927

Kresge, S. S., World Headquarters, 2727 2nd Ave., Detroit, 12/19/79, A, C, 79001175

Lawyers Building, 137 Cadillac Sq., Detroit, 4/22/82, A, B, C, 82002903

Lee Plaza Hotel, 2240 W. Grand Blvd., Detroit, 11/05/81, C, 81000319

Lincoln Motor Company Plant, 6200 W. Warren Ave., Detroit, 6/02/78, A, B, NHL, 78001521

MacNichol, George P., House, 2610 Biddle Ave., Wyandotte, 5/24/84, B, C, 84001859

Maccabees Building, 5057 Woodward Ave., Detroit, 7/07/83, A, C, 83003436

Manchester Apartments [East Jefferson Avenue Residential TR], 2016 E. Jefferson Ave., Detroit, 10/09/85, C, 85002941

Mariners' Church, 170 E. Jefferson Ave., Detroit, 3/11/71, A, C, a, b, 71000428

Marx House, 2630 Biddle Ave., Wyandotte, 8/13/76, B, C, 76001043

McAdow, Perry, House, 4605 Cass Ave., Detroit, 7/03/80, C, a, 80004405

Medbury's—Grove Lawn Subdivisions Historic District, Roughly bounded by Hamilton Ave., the alley S of Louise Ave., Woodward Ave., and the alley S of Puritan Ave., Highland Park, 2/08/88, C, 88000049

Merchants Building, 206 E. Grand River Blvd., Detroit, 11/25/83, B, C, 83003732

Metropolitan United Methodist Church [Religious Structures of Woodward Ave. TR], 8000 Woodward Ave., Detroit, 8/03/82, C, a, 82002904

Michigan Soldiers' and Sailors' Monument, Woodward Ave. at Campus Martius, Detroit, 5/31/84, C, 84001862

Michigan State Fair Riding Coliseum, Dairy Cattle Building, and Agricultural Building, Michigan State Fairgrounds, Detroit, 6/06/80, A, C, 80001925

Monroe Avenue Commercial Buildings, 16–118 Monroe Ave., Detroit, 2/13/75, A, C, 75000968

Moross House, 1460 E. Jefferson Ave., Detroit, 1/13/72, C, 72000669

Norris, Philetus W., House, 17815 Mt. Elliott Ave., Detroit, 1/28/92, B, 91001982

North Woodward Congregational Church [Religious Structures of Woodward Ave. TR], 8715 Woodward Ave., Detroit, 8/03/82, C, a, 82002905

Northville Historic District, Bounded roughly by Cady, Rogers, and Randolph Sts., Northville, 7/31/72, C, 72000673

Orchestra Hall, 3711 Woodward Ave., Detroit, 4/16/71, A, 71000429

Palmer Park Apartment Building Historic District, Roughly bounded by Pontchartrain Blvd., McNichols Rd. and Covington Dr., Detroit, 5/21/83, A, C, 83000895

Palmer Park Boulevard Apartments District, 1981, 2003 and 2025 W. McNichols Rd., Highland Park, 1/22/92, A, C, 91001983

Palmer Woods Historic District, Roughly bounded by Seven Mile Rd., Woodward Ave., and Strathcona Dr., Detroit, 8/11/83, C, g, 83000896

Palms, Francis, Building & State Theater, 2111 Woodward Ave., Detroit, 11/24/82, A, C, 82000551

Palms, Francis, Building and State Theater, 2111 Woodward Ave., Detroit, 10/25/84, A, C, 84000112

Palms, The [East Jefferson Avenue Residential TR], 1001 E. Jefferson Ave., Detroit, 10/09/85, C, 85002942

Parke-Davis Research Laboratory, Joseph Campau St. at Detroit River, Detroit, 5/11/76, A, NHL, 76001039

Parke-Davis and Company Pharmaceutical Company Plant, Bounded by Joseph Campau Ave., Wight St., and McDougal Ave., Detroit, 9/16/85, A, C, g, 85002445

Parker, Arthur M., House [East Jefferson Avenue Residential TR], 8115 E. Jefferson Ave., Detroit, 10/09/85, C, 85002943

Parker, Thomas A., House, 975 E. Jefferson Ave., Detroit, 11/12/82, C, 82000552

Pasadena Apartments [East Jefferson Avenue Residential TR], 2170 E. Jefferson Ave., Detroit, 10/09/85, C, 85002944

Penn Central Station, 2405 W. Vernor St., Detroit, 4/16/75, A, C, 75000969

Pewabic Pottery, 10125 E. Jefferson Ave., Detroit, 9/03/71, A, B, NHL, 71000430

Players, The, 3321 E. Jefferson Ave., Detroit, 6/12/87, A, C, 87000920

Ponchartrain Apartments [East Jefferson Avenue Residential TR], 1350 E. Jefferson Ave., Detroit, 10/09/85, A, C, 85002945

Randolph Street Commercial Buildings Historic District, 1208–1244 Randolph St., Detroit, 7/08/80, A, C, 80004404

Redford Theatre Building, 17354 Lahser Ave., Detroit, 1/31/85, A, C, 85000171

STE. CLAIRE (steamer), 661 Civic Center Dr., Detroit, 11/02/79, A, C, NHL, 79001177

Wayne County—Continued

Sacred Heart Roman Catholic Church, Convent and Rectory, 1000 Eliot St., Detroit, 6/06/80, A, C, a, 80001926

Sacred Heart Seminary, 2701 W. Chicago Blvd., Detroit, 12/02/82, A, C, a, 82000553

Saint Andrew's Memorial Episcopal Church [University—Cultural Center Phase II MRA], 5105 Anthony Wayne Dr., Detroit, 5/15/86, A, C, a, 86001003

Saint Joseph Roman Catholic Parish Complex (Boundary Increase), 1828 Jay St., Detroit, 1/28/92, A, C, a, 91002013

Saints Peter And Paul Church, 629 E. Jefferson Ave., Detroit, 9/03/71, C, a, 71000431

Sante Fe Apartments [University—Cultural Center Phase II MRA], 681 Merrick, Detroit, 5/01/86, A, C, 86000996

Scarab Club, 217 Farnsworth Ave, Detroit, 11/20/79, C, 79001176

Second Baptist Church Of Detroit, 441 Monroe St., Detroit, 3/19/75, A, a, 75000970

Sibley House, 976 Jefferson Ave., Detroit, 4/16/71, C, a, 71000432

Sibley, Frederic M., Lumber Company Office Building, 6460 Kercheval Ave., Detroit, 4/04/91, A, C, b, 91000329

Smith, Samuel L., House [University—Cultural Center Phase I MRA], 5035 Woodward, Detroit, 4/29/86, B, C, 86001038

Somerset Apartments [East Jefferson Avenue Residential TR], 1523 E. Jefferson Ave., Detroit, 10/09/85, C, 85002946

Sprague, Thomas S., House [University—Cultural Center Phase I MRA], 80 W. Palmer, Detroit, 4/29/86, A, C, 86001037

St. Albertus Roman Catholic Church, 4231 St. Aubin St., Detroit, 1/18/78, A, C, a, 78001522

St. Bonaventure Monastery, 1740 Mt. Elliot Ave, Detroit, 12/02/82, A, C, a, 82000554

St. Boniface Roman Catholic Church, 2356 Vermont Ave., Detroit, 6/09/89, A, C, a, 89000487

St. Catherine of Siena Roman Catholic Parish Complex, 4151 Seminole, Detroit, 4/05/91, C, a, 91000389

St. Charles Borromeo Roman Catholic Parish Complex, Baldwin Ave. at St. Paul Ave., Detroit, 6/09/89, A, C, a, 89000488

St. Florian Historic District, Roughly bounded by Joseph Campau Ave., Holbrook Ave., Dequindre, Norwalk, Lumpkin, and Yemans Sts., Hamtramck, 9/13/84, A, C, a, 84001865

St. James Episcopal Church, 25150 E. River Rd., Grosse Ile, 11/19/71, A, C, a, 71000434

St. John's Episcopal Church [Religious Structures of Woodward Ave. TR], Woodward Ave. at E. Fisher Freeway, Detroit, 8/03/82, C, a, 82002906

St. John's-St. Luke's Evangelical Church, 2120 Russell St., Detroit, 4/22/82, A, C, a, 82002907

St. Josaphat's Roman Catholic Church Complex, 715 E. Canfield Ave., Detroit, 12/08/82, A, C, a, 82000555

St. Joseph's Episcopal Church [Religious Structures of Woodward Ave. TR], 5930 Woodward Ave., Detroit, 8/03/82, C, a, 82002908

St. Joseph's Episcopal Church [Religious Structures of Woodward Ave. TR], 8850 Woodward Ave., Detroit, 8/03/82, C, a, 82002909

St. Joseph's Roman Catholic Church, 1828 Jay St., Detroit, 12/08/72, A, C, a, 72000670

St. Stanislaus Bishop and Martyr Roman Catholic Parish Complex, 5818 Dubois St., Detroit, 7/14/89, A, C, a, 89000788

St. Theresa of Avila Roman Catholic Parish Complex, 8666 Quincy Ave., Detroit, 7/14/89, A, C, a, 89000786

St. Thomas the Apostle Catholic Church and Rectory, 8363–8383 Townsend Ave., Detroit, 6/29/89, C, a, 89000785

State Savings Bank, 151 W. Fort St., Detroit, 3/19/82, A, C, 82002910

Ste. Anne Roman Catholic Church Complex, Howard and Ste. Anne Sts., Detroit, 6/03/76, A, C, a, 76001040

Stearns, Frederick K., House [East Jefferson Avenue Residential TR], 8109 E. Jefferson Ave., Detroit, 10/09/85, B, C, 85002947

Stearns, Frederick, Building, 6533 E. Jefferson Ave., Detroit, 10/14/80, A, B, C, 80001927

Strasburg, Herman, House [University—Cultural Center Phase I MRA], 5415 Cass, Detroit, 4/29/86, A, C, 86001036

Stratton, William B. and Mary Chase, House, 938 Three Mile Dr., Grosse Pointe Park, 5/24/84, B, C, 84001867

Sweet, Ossian H., House, 2905 Garland, Detroit, 4/04/85, A, 85000696

Sweetest Heart Of Mary Roman Catholic Church, 4440 Russell St., Detroit, 1/31/78, A, C, a, 78001523

Taylor, Elisha, House, 59 Alfred St., Detroit, 3/05/75, C, 75000971

Temple Beth-El [Religious Structures of Woodward Ave. TR], 3424 Woodward Ave., Detroit, 8/03/82, C, a, 82002911

Temple Beth-El [Religious Structures of Woodward Ave. TR], 8801 Woodward Ave., Detroit, 8/03/82, C, a, 82002912

The Clay School, 453 Martin Luther King, Jr., Blvd., Detroit, 7/08/82, A, C, 82002913

Third Precinct Police Station, 2200 Hunt St., Detroit, 2/29/80, A, C, 80001928

Thompson Home, 4756 Cass Ave., Detroit, 6/03/76, A, C, 76001041

Tiger Stadium, 2121 Trumbull Ave., Detroit, 2/06/89, A, C, 88003236

Trinity Episcopal Church, 1519 Myrtle St., Detroit, 5/22/80, B, C, a, 80001929

Trinity Evangelical Lutheran Church Complex, 1345 Gratiot Ave., Detroit, 2/10/83, A, C, a, 83000897

Trinity United Methodist Church [Religious Structures of Woodward Ave. TR], 13100 Woodward Ave., Highland Park, 8/03/82, C, a, 82002921

Trombly, Charles, House, 553 E. Jefferson Ave., Detroit, 8/13/79, C, 79001178

Trowbridge, Charles, House, 1380 E. Jefferson Ave., Detroit, 5/28/76, B, 76001042

Vanity Ballroom Building, 1024 Newport St., Detroit, 11/12/82, A, C, 82000556

Verona Apartments [University—Cultural Center Phase I MRA], 92 W. Ferry, Detroit, 4/29/86, A, C, 86001040

Vinton Building, 600 Woodward Ave, Detroit, 2/17/83, A, C, 83000898

Virginia Park Historic District, Both sides of Virgia Park From Woodward Ave. to John Lodge Service Dr., Detroit, 12/02/82, A, C, 82000557

Walker, Franklin H., House [East Jefferson Avenue Residential TR], 2730 E. Jefferson Ave., Detroit, 10/09/85, C, 85002948

Washington Boulevard Historic District, Washington Blvd., State and Clifford Sts., Detroit, 7/15/82, A, C, 82002914

Wayne County Courthouse, 600 Randolph St., Detroit, 2/24/75, A, C, 75000972

Wayne State University Buildings, 4735–4841 Cass Ave., Detroit, 6/23/78, A, C, 78001524

Wells, William H., House [East Jefferson Avenue Residential TR], 2931 E. Jefferson Ave., Detroit, 10/09/85, C, 85002949

West Canfield Historic District, Canfield Ave. between 2nd and 3rd Sts., Detroit, 5/27/71, C, 71000433

West Village District, Roughly bounded by Jefferson, Kercheval, Parker and Seyburn Aves., Detroit, 10/14/80, C, 80001930

Whitney, David, House, 4421 Woodward Ave., Detroit, 8/21/72, A, C, 72000671

Whittier Hotel [East Jefferson Avenue Residential TR], 415 Burns Dr., Detroit, 10/09/85, C, a, 85002950

Wilson Barn, NE corner of Middlebelt and W. Chicago Rds., Livonia, 12/12/73, A, 73000962

Wilson Theatre, 350 Madison Ave., Detroit, 8/09/77, A, C, g, 77000725

Women's City Club, 2110 Park Ave, Detroit, 11/20/79, A, C, 79001179

Woodbridge Neighborhood Historic District, Bounded by Trumbull, Calumet, Gibson, Grand River, 12th W. Warren and Wabashg Sts., RR Tracks, and Edsel Ford Expwy., Detroit, 3/06/80, C, 80001931

Woodward Ave. Presbyterian Church [Religious Structures of Woodward Ave. TR], 8501 Woodward Ave., Detroit, 8/03/82, C, a, 82002916

Woodward East Historic District, Bounded by Alfred, Edmund, Watson, and Brush and John R Sts., Detroit, 1/21/75, C, 75000973

Wexford County

Cobbs, Frank J., House, 407 E. Chapin St., Cadillac, 3/31/88, B, C, 88000376

Elks Temple Building, 122 S. Mitchell St., Cadillac, 9/29/88, C, 88001835

Mitchell, Charles T., House, 118 N. Shelby St., Cadillac, 12/01/86, B, 86003369

Old Cadillac City Hall, 201 Mitchell St., Cadillac, 6/26/86, C, 86001380

Shay Locomotive, Cass St., Cadillac, 10/26/81, B, C, 81000321

MICRONESIAN STATES

Kosrae Freely Associated State

Leluh Ruins, Address Restricted, Lelu Island vicinity, 8/16/83, D, 83004524

Ponape Freely Associated State

Catholic Belltower, Catholic Mission, Kolonia (Ponape), 11/25/80, C, a, 80004399

Chief Agriculturist House, Kolonia, Kolonia (Ponape), 9/30/76, C, 76002200

German Cemetery, Kolonia, Kolonia (Ponape), 9/30/76, A, d, 76002201

Japanese Hydro-electric Power Plant, Kolonia, Kolonia (Ponape), 9/30/76, A, C, 76002204

Japanese Shrine, Kolonia, Kolonia (Ponape), 9/30/76, A, a, 76002205

Japenese Artillery Road and Pohndolap Area, Sokehs, Sokehs (Ponape), 9/30/76, A, g, 76002202

Japenese Elementary School for Ponapean Children, Kolonia, Kolonia (Ponape), 9/30/76, A, 76002203

Nan Madol, E side of Temwen Island, Temwen Island, 12/19/74, A, C, D, NHL, 74002226

Sokehs Mass Grave Site, Kolonia, Kolonia (Ponape), 9/30/76, A, 76002206

Spanish Wall, Litkin Kel, Kolonia (Ponape), 12/19/74, A, 74002227

Truk Freely Associated State

Fauba Archaelogical Site, Address Restricted, Tol Island vicinity, 3/21/78, D, 78003152

Japanese Army Headquarters, Roro, Dublon Island (Truk), 9/30/76, A, g, 76002208

Japanese Lighthouse, Allei Island, Puluwat Atoll (Truk), 8/16/83, A, C, g, 83004523

St. Xavier Academy, Winipis, Moen Island (Truk), 9/30/76, C, 76002209

Tonnachau Mountain, Iras, Moen Island (Truk), 9/30/76, A, 76002210

Tonotan Guns and Caves, Nantaku, Moen Island (Truk), 9/30/76, A, C, 76002211

Truk Lagoon Underwater Fleet, Truk Atoll, Truk Lagoon, Truk, 9/30/76, A, g, NHL, 76002267

Wiichen Men's Meetinghouse, Peniesene, Moen Island (Truk), 9/30/76, A, D, 76002213

Yap Freely Associated State

Bechiel Village Historic District, Address Restricted, Yap vicinity, 8/16/83, A, C, D, e, g, 83004522

O'Keefe's Island, Near Colonia, Colonia (Yap) vicinity, 9/30/76, A, 76002216

Rull Men's Meetinghouse, Rull, Balebat (Yap), 9/30/76, A, C, a, 76002214

Spanish Fort, Colonia, Colonia (Yap), 9/30/76, A, C, 76002215

The Bechiel Village Historic District is known as one of the earliest prehistoric occupation sites in Yap, Micronesia, and is considered sacred by the Yapese. (Michael Roberts, 1983)

MINNESOTA

Aitkin County

Aitkin Carnegie Library [Aitkin County MRA], 121 2nd St., NW, Aitkin, 4/16/82, A, C, 82002924

Aitkin County Courthouse and Jail [Aitkin County MRA], 209 and 217 2nd St., NW, Aitkin, 4/16/82, C, 82002923

Arthyde Stone House [Aitkin County MRA], CR 27, McGrath vicinity, 4/16/82, A, 82002930

Bethelhem Lutheran Church [Aitkin County MRA], Off Co. Hwy. 12, Aitkin vicinity, 4/16/82, A, a, 82002928

Casey, Patrick, House [Aitkin County MRA], 4th St. SE and 2nd Ave., Aitkin, 4/16/82, B, C, 82002925

Malmo Mounds and Village Site, Address Restricted, McGrath vicinity, 4/03/75, D, 75000974

National Woodenware Company Superintendent's Residence [Aitkin County MRA], SW Elm St. and Ione Ave., Hill City, 4/16/82, A, 82002929

Northern Pacific Depot [Aitkin County MRA], 20 Pacific St., SW, Aitkin, 4/16/82, A, 82002926

Potter/Casey Company Building [Aitkin County MRA], E. Minnesota Ave. between 1st and 2nd Sts., NW, Aitkin, 4/16/82, A, 82002927

Savanna Portage, Off Co. Hwy. 5 in Savanna Portage State Park, McGregor vicinity, 4/23/73, A, 73000963

Anoka County

Anoka Post Office, 300 E. Main St., Anoka, 12/31/79, C, 79001180

Anoka-Champlin Mississippi River Bridge, U.S. 52, Anoka, 12/31/79, A, C, 79001181

Avery, Carlos, Game Farm [Federal Relief Construction in Minnesota MPS], 5463 W. Broadway, Columbus Township, Ham Lake vicinity, 8/09/91, A, 91000977

Banfill Tavern, 6666 E. River Rd., Fridley, 12/12/76, C, 76001044

Colonial Hall and Masonic Lodge No. 30, 1900 3rd Ave., S., Anoka, 12/31/79, B, C, 79001182

Crescent Grange Hall No. 512, W of Martin Lake on Type Lake Rd., East Bethel vicinity, 12/26/79, A, C, 79001190

District School No. 28, 14100 St. Francis Blvd., NW, Anoka vicinity, 12/27/79, A, C, 79001188

Jackson Hotel, 214 Jackson St., Anoka, 12/08/78, A, 78001525

Kelsey, Porter, House, 14853 N. 7th Ave., Andover, 12/26/79, B, C, 79001186

Kline Sanatarium, 1500 S. Ferry St., Anoka vicinity, 12/26/79, A, C, 79001187

Leathers, H. G., House, 22957 Rum River Blvd., St. Francis, 12/26/79, B, C, b, 79001192

Richardson Barn, 22814 Sunrise Rd., NE, East Bethel vicinity, 12/26/79, C, 79001191

Riverside Hotel, 3631 Bridge St., St. Francis, 12/26/79, A, 79001193

Shaw-Hammons House, 302 Fremont St., Anoka, 12/26/79, A, C, 79001183

Sparre Barn, 20071 Nowthen Blvd., Ramsey vicinity, 1/10/80, A, C, 80001935

Swedish Evangelical Lutheran Church, 2200 Swedish Dr., NE, Ham Lake, 12/26/79, A, C, a, 79001189

Ticknor, Heman L., House, 1625 3rd Ave., S., Anoka, 12/27/79, B, C, 79001184

Windego Park Auditorium/Open Air Theater, Between S. Ferry St. and Rum River, Anoka, 1/08/80, A, C, 80001934

Woodbury House, 1632 S. Ferry St., Anoka, 12/26/79, B, C, 79001185

Becker County

Detroit Lakes Carnegie Library, 1000 Washington Ave., Detroit Lakes, 3/16/76, C, 76001045

Northern Pacific Passenger Depot, Off US 10, Detroit Lakes, 12/20/88, A, 88002833

Sargent, Homer E., House, 1036 Lake Ave., Detroit Lakes, 12/22/88, A, C, 88003005

St. Benedict's Mission School, Co. Hwy. 133, Ogema vicinity, 8/24/82, A, a, 82002931

Beltrami County

Beltrami County Courthouse, Beltrami Ave. and Sixth St., Bemidji, 5/26/88, A, C, 88000665

Bemidji Carnegie Library, 426 Bemidji Ave., Bemidji, 11/25/80, A, C, 80001936

Bunyan, Paul, and Babe the Blue Ox, Third St. and Bemidji Ave., Bemidji, 3/10/88, A, 88000204

District School No. 132, CR 500, Pinewood vicinity, 10/27/88, C, 88002083

Great Northern Depot, Minnesota Ave., Bemidji, 5/26/88, A, 88000673

Lake Bemidji State Park CCC/NYA/Rustic Style Historic Resources [Minnesota State Park CCC/WPA/Rustic Style MPS], Off Co. Hwy. 20 NE of Bemidji, Bemidji vicinity, 10/25/89, A, C, 89001674

Nymore Bridge [Reinforced-Concrete Highway Bridges in Minnesota MPS], First St. over Mississippi River, Bemidji, 11/06/89, C, 89001849

Park, David, House, 1501 Birchmont Dr., Bemidji, 5/16/88, C, 88000566

Rabideau CCC Camp, Off Co. Hwy. 39 in Chippewa National Forest, Blackduck vicinity, 6/16/76, A, g, 76001046

Saum Schools, Co. Hwy. 23, Kelliher vicinity, 3/27/80, A, b, 80001937

Benton County

Church of Sts. Peter and Paul—Catholic [Benton County MRA], State St., Gilman, 4/06/82, A, C, a, 82002932

Cota Round Barns [Benton County MRA], Co. Hwy. 48, St. Cloud vicinity, 4/06/82, A, C, 82002936

Esselman Brothers General Store [Benton County MRA], Co. Hwys. 1 and 13, Rice vicinity, 4/06/82, A, C, 82002933

Posch Site, Address Restricted, Rice vicinity, 10/02/73, D, 73000964

Robinson, Leonard, House [Benton County MRA], 202 2nd Ave., S., Sauk Rapids, 4/06/82, B, 82002935

Ronneby Charcoal Kiln [Benton County MRA], Off MN 23, Ronneby vicinity, 4/06/82, A, 82002934

Big Stone County

Big Stone County Courthouse, 20 2nd St., SE, Ortonville, 8/15/85, A, C, 85001764

Chicago, Milwaukee, St. Paul and Pacific Depot, Main and Center Sts., Clinton, 7/31/86, A, 86002118

Columbian Hotel, 305 2nd St., NW, Ortonville, 8/15/85, A, C, 85001766

District School No. 13, CR 25, Correll vicinity, 8/15/85, A, C, 85001772

Odessa Jail, Main and Second Sts., Odessa, 7/24/86, A, 86001916

Ortonville Commercial Historic District, Second St., Madison and Monroe Aves., between Jefferson and Jackson Aves., Ortonville, 8/15/85, A, C, 85001765

Ortonville Free Library, 412 2nd St., NW, Ortonville, 8/15/85, A, C, 85001767

Shannon Hotel, Studdart Ave. and 2nd St., Graceville, 8/15/85, A, C, 85001773

Blue Earth County

Blue Earth County Courthouse [Blue Earth County MRA], Courthouse Sq., Mankato, 7/28/80, A, C, 80001940

Brandrup, J. R., House [Blue Earth County MRA], 704 Byron, Mankato, 7/28/80, B, C, 80001941

Chapman, Charles, House [Blue Earth County MRA], 418 McCauley, Mankato vicinity, 7/28/80, B, 80001942

Cray, Lorin, House [Blue Earth County MRA], 603 S. 2nd St., Mankato, 7/28/80, B, C, 80001943

Eberhart, Adolph O., House [Blue Earth County MRA], 228 Clark St., Mankato, 7/28/80, B, 80001944

Blue Earth County—Continued

Federal Courthouse and Post Office, 401 S. 2nd St., Mankato, 6/17/80, C, 80001945

First Baptist Church [Blue Earth County MRA], U.S. 169, Lake Crystal vicinity, 7/28/80, A, C, a, 80001938

First National Bank of Mankato [Blue Earth County MRA (AD)], 229 S. Front St., Mankato, 7/30/74, C, 74001004

First Presbyterian Church [Blue Earth County MRA], Hickory and S. Broad Sts., Mankato, 7/28/80, C, a, 80001946

Gail, James P., Farmhouse [Blue Earth County MRA], Off U.S. 169, Lake Crystal vicinity, 7/28/80, A, C, 80001939

Hubbard, Renesselaer D., House [Blue Earth County MRA (AD)], 606 S. Broad St., Mankato, 6/07/76, B, C, b, 76001047

Irving, William, House [Blue Earth County MRA], 320 Park Lane, Mankato, 7/28/80, B, C, 80001947

Jones-Roberts Farmstead [Blue Earth County MRA], MN 68, Lake Crystal vicinity, 7/28/80, A, C, 80001949

Kennedy Bridge [Iron and Steel Bridges in Minnesota MPS], Twp. Rd. 167 over LeSueur River, Mankato vicinity, 11/06/89, A, C, 89001832

Kern Bridge [Blue Earth County MRA], Twp. Rd. over LeSueur River, Skyline vicinity, 7/28/80, C, 80001950

Main Street Commercial Buildings [Blue Earth County MRA], Main St., Mapleton, 7/28/80, A, C, 80001957

Mankato Holstein Farm Barn [Blue Earth County MRA], Co. Hwy. 5, Mankato vicinity, 7/28/80, A, 80001951

Mankato Public Library and Reading Room [Blue Earth County MRA], 120 S. Broad, Mankato, 7/28/80, A, C, 80001952

Mankato Union Depot [Blue Earth County MRA], 112 Pike St., Mankato, 7/28/80, A, 80001956

Marsh Concrete Rainbow Arch Bridge [Blue Earth County MRA], CR 101 over Little Cottonwood River, Courtland vicinity, 7/28/80, C, 80001953

Minneopa State Park WPA/Rustic Style Historic Resources [Minnesota State Park CCC/WPA-/Rustic Style MPS], Off US 169 W of Mankato, Mankato vicinity, 10/25/89, A, C, g, 89001663

North Front Street Commercial District [Blue Earth County MRA], 301-415 N. Front St., Mankato, 7/28/80, A, C, 80001954

Old Main, Mankato State Teachers College, 5th St., S. and Jackson St., Mankato, 6/02/83, A, C, 83000899

Seppman Mill [Blue Earth County MRA (AD)], MN 68 in Minneopa State Park, Sky Line vicinity, 8/26/71, A, C, 71000435

Sterling Congregational Church [Blue Earth County MRA], CR 151, Amboy vicinity, 7/28/80, A, a, b, 80001958

Troendle, Lucas, House [Blue Earth County MRA], 2nd and Silver Sts., Mapleton, 7/28/80, B, C, 80001959

Zieglers Ford Bridge [Iron and Steel Bridges in Minnesota MPS], Twp. Rd. 96 over Big Cobb River, Good Thunder vicinity, 11/06/89, C, 89001830

Brown County

Bendixon-Schmid House [Brown County MRA], 123 N. Marshall St., Springfield, 12/31/79, B, C, 79001218

Bjorneberg Garage [Brown County MRA], Broadway St., Hanska, 12/31/79, A, 79001197

Boesch, Hummel, and Maltzahn Block [Brown County MRA], 6-12 N. Minnesota St., New Ulm, 12/31/79, A, C, 79001201

Chicago and North Western Railroad Depot [Brown County MRA], S. Valley St., New Ulm, 12/31/79, A, C, 79001202

Chicago and North Western Depot, Oak St. NW., Sleepy Eye, 6/25/92, A, 92000822

Fesenmaier, Bernard, House [Brown County MRA], 426 N. State St., New Ulm, 12/31/79, C, 79001203

Flandrau State Park CCC/WPA/Rustic Style Historic Resources [Minnesota State Park CCC/WPA/Rustic Style MPS], Off Co. Hwy. 13 SE of New Ulm, New Ulm vicinity, 10/25/89, A, C, g, 89001658

Gag, Wanda, Childhood Home [Brown County MRA], 226 N. Washington St., New Ulm, 12/31/79, A, B, 79001204

Grand Hotel, 210 N. Minnesota St., New Ulm, 6/21/90, A, C, 90000986

Hermann Monument, Hermann Heights Park, New Ulm, 10/02/73, A, C, 73000965

Kiesling, Frederick W., House, 220 N. Minnesota St., New Ulm, 2/23/72, A, 72000674

Kreitinger Garage [Brown County MRA], 1 N. Cass St., Springfield, 12/31/79, A, 79001219

Lampert Lumber Company Line Yard [Brown County MRA], Center St., New Ulm vicinity, 12/31/79, A, 79001196

Liberal Union Hall [Brown County MRA], Broadway and Main Sts., Hanska, 12/31/79, A, a, 79001198

Lind, Gov. John, House, 622 Center St., New Ulm, 12/31/74, B, C, 74001005

Melges Bakery, 213 S. Minnesota St., New Ulm, 6/28/74, A, 74001006

New Ulm Armory [Brown County MRA], 205 N. Broadway St., New Ulm, 12/31/79, A, 79001205

New Ulm Oil Company Service Station [Brown County MRA], Broadway and 5th Sts., New Ulm, 12/31/79, A, 79001206

New Ulm Post Office, Center St. and Broadway, New Ulm, 4/28/70, A, C, 70000287

Nora Free Christian Church, MN 257, Hanska vicinity, 8/04/88, A, B, a, d, 88001176

Ochs, Adolph C., House [Brown County MRA], 303 N. Marshall St., Springfield, 12/31/79, B, C, 79001220

Old Main, Dr. Martin Luther College [Brown County MRA], College Hts., New Ulm, 12/31/79, A, C, 79001208

Schell, August, Brewing Company, 20th South St., New Ulm, 12/27/74, A, C, 74001007

Schell, Otto, House [Brown County MRA], Point Lookout, New Ulm, 12/31/79, A, C, 79001210

Shady Lane Stock Farm [Brown County MRA], US 14, Springfield vicinity, 12/31/79, A, 79001221

Sleepy Eye Milling Company, Jct. of Fourth and Oak Sts., NE., Sleepy Eye, 2/08/91, A, 91000038

Smith, W. W., House [Brown County MRA], 101 Linden St., SW, Sleepy Eye, 12/31/79, A, C, 79001211

South Broadway Historic District [Brown County MRA], 200-238 S. Broadway, New Ulm, 12/31/79, B, C, 79001212

South German Street Historic District [Brown County MRA], 110-312 S. German St., New Ulm, 12/31/79, B, C, 79001217

St. Michael's School and Convent [Brown County MRA], 500 N. State St., New Ulm, 12/31/79, A, C, a, 79001213

Synsteby Site, Address Restricted, Hanska vicinity, 5/12/75, A, D, 75000976

Thormodson Barn [Brown County MRA], Off MN 257, Hanska vicinity, 12/31/79, A, 79001199

Turner Hall [Brown County MRA], State and 1st South Sts., New Ulm, 12/31/79, A, e, 79001215

Winona and St. Peter Freight Depot [Brown County MRA], Oak St., NE, Sleepy Eye, 12/31/79, A, 79001216

Carlton County

Carlton County Courthouse, 3rd St. and Walnut Ave., Carlton, 8/29/85, A, C, 85001926

Church of Sts. Joseph and Mary—Catholic, Mission Rd., Cloquet vicinity, 3/29/84, A, C, a, 84001409

Cloquet City Hall, Ave. B and Arch St., Cloquet, 9/11/85, A, C, 85002312

Cloquet-Northern Office Building, Ave. C and Arch St., Cloquet, 8/29/85, A, 85001925

Cooke, Jay, State Park CCC/Rustic Style Historic District [Minnesota State Park CCC/WPA/Rustic Style MPS], Off MN 210 E of Carlton, Thomson Township, Carlton vicinity, 6/11/92, A, C, g, NHL, 89001665

Cooke, Jay, State Park CCC/WPA/Rustic Style Picnic Grounds [Minnesota State Park CCC/WPA-/Rustic Style MPS], Off MN 210 SE of Forbay Lake, Thomson Township, Carlton vicinity, 6/11/92, A, C, 92000640

Cooke, Jay, State Park CCC/WPA/Rustic Style Service Yard [Minnesota State Park CCC/WPA-/Rustic Style MPS], Off MN 210 E of Forbay Lake, Thomson Township, Carlton vicinity, 6/11/92, A, C, 92000642

Grand Portage of the St. Louis River, W of Duluth in Jay Cooke State Park off MN 210, Duluth vicinity, 5/24/73, A, 73000966

Lindholm Oil Company Service Station, 202 Cloquet Ave., Cloquet vicinity, 9/11/85, C, g, 85002202

Northeastern Hotel, 115 St. Louis Ave., Cloquet, 11/08/84, A, 84000218

Carlton County—Continued

Park Place Historic District, 1, 512, 520, and 528 Park Pl., Cloquet, 8/29/85, A, C, 85001924

Shaw Memorial Library, 406 Cloquet Ave., Cloquet, 8/29/85, A, C, 85001927

Carver County

Amblard, Emile, Guest House [Carver County MRA], 32-36 N. Vine St., Waconia, 1/04/80, A, C, 80001982

Brinkhaus Saloon Livery Barn [Carver County MRA], 112 W. 4th St., Chaska, 1/04/80, A, 80001962

Carver Historic District [Carver County MRA], Roughly bounded by Lime, 1st, Walnut and 6th Sts., Carver, 1/04/80, A, C, 80001960

Church of St. Hubertus—Catholic, Great Plains Blvd., and W. 78th St., Chanhassen, 3/19/82, A, a, 82002937

Coney Island of the West, Lake Waconia off MN 5, Waconia, 8/11/76, A, 76001048

DuToit, Frederick E., House [Carver County MRA], 121 Hickory St., Chaska, 1/04/80, B, 80001965

Eder-Baer House [Carver County MRA], 105 Elm St., Chaska, 1/04/80, C, 80001966

Greiner, Frederick, House [Carver County MRA], 319 E. 3rd St., Chaska, 1/04/80, B, C, 80001967

Grimm, Wendelin, Farmstead, Off Co. Hwy. 11 in Carver Park Reserve, Victoria vicinity, 12/30/74, A, B, 74001008

Guettler, Philip, House [Carver County MRA], Adams and Mill Sts., Cologne, 1/04/80, A, 80001963

Hebeisen, Jacob, Hardware Store [Carver County MRA], Railroad and Maria Sts., Hamburg, 1/04/80, A, 80001975

Hebeisen, Jacob, House [Carver County MRA], Off Co. Hwy. 50, Hamburg, 1/04/80, C, 80001976

Herald Block [Carver County MRA], 123 W. 2nd St., Chaska, 1/04/80, A, 80001968

King Oscar's Settlement [Carver County MRA], Co. Hwy. 40, Carver vicinity, 1/04/80, A, a, 80001974

Knotz, John, House [Carver County MRA], Paul and Mill Sts., Cologne, 1/04/80, B, 80001970

Kusske and Hahn Saloon [Carver County MRA], Co. Hwy. 23, Mayer vicinity, 1/04/80, A, C, 80001977

Laketown Moravian Brethren's Church [Carver County MRA], Co. Hwy. 11, Victoria, 1/04/80, A, C, a, 80001981

Lewis, E. H., House [Carver County MRA], 321 W. 2nd St., Chaska, 1/04/80, B, C, 80001971

Maiser, Charles, House [Carver County MRA], 16 W. Main St., Waconia, 1/04/80, A, C, 80001983

Mock Cigar Factory and House [Carver County MRA], 48 W. Main St., Waconia, 1/04/80, A, C, 80001984

Mohrbacher, Paul, House [Carver County MRA], Paul St., Cologne, 1/04/80, B, C, 80001972

Norwood Methodist Episcopal Church [Carver County MRA], Hill and Union Sts., Norwood, 1/04/80, A, C, a, 80001978

Peterson, Andrew, Farmstead, NE of Waconia on MN 5, Waconia vicinity, 10/11/79, B, 79003713

Schimmelpfennig, Johann, Farmstead [Carver County MRA], Off US 212, Young America vicinity, 1/04/80, A, 80001980

Simons Building and Livery Barn [Carver County MRA], 123 W. 3rd St., Chaska, 1/04/80, A, C, 80001964

Waconia City Hall, 9 W. 1st St., Waconia, 5/09/83, A, C, 83000900

Walnut Street Historic District [Carver County MRA], Roughly around Walnut, 2nd, Chestnut and 6th Sts., Chaska, 1/04/80, A, 80001973

West Main Street Houses [Carver County MRA], 417, 429, and 453 W. Main St., Waconia, 1/04/80, C, 80001986

West Union [Carver County MRA], Co. Hwy. 50, Cologne vicinity, 1/04/80, A, a, d, 80001987

Winter Saloon [Carver County MRA], Elm and Hazel Sts., Norwood, 1/04/80, A, C, 80001979

Young America City Hall [Carver County MRA], 102 2nd Ave., S., Young America, 1/04/80, A, C, 80001988

Zoar Moravian Church [Carver County MRA], Co. Hwy. 10, Chaska vicinity, 1/04/80, A, C, a, 80001985

Cass County

Battle Point (21CA12), 6 mi. W of Co. Hwy. 8 on Leech Lake, Battleground SF, Cass Lake vicinity, 8/17/90, A, C, D, 90001144

Chase Hotel, 329 Cleveland Ave., Walker, 6/04/80, A, 80001994

Chippewa Agency Historic District, Address Restricted, Pillager vicinity, 5/22/73, D, 73000967

Crow Wing State Park, Off MN 371, Pillager vicinity, 7/28/70, D, 70000288

Great Northern Railway Company Bridge, SW of Cass Lake off MN 371, Cass Lake vicinity, 10/14/80, C, 80001990

Gull Lake Mounds Site, Address Restricted, Pillager vicinity, 5/07/73, D, 73000968

Hole-in-the-Day House Site, Address Restricted, Pillager vicinity, 6/19/73, D, 73000969

Neils, Julius, House, N. 3rd St., Cass Lake, 6/20/80, B, 80001991

Old Backus, Address Restricted, Backus vicinity, 12/24/74, D, 74001009

Rice Lake Hut Rings, Address Restricted, Pillager vicinity, 8/14/73, D, 73000970

Sherwood Forest Lodge Complex, Co. Hwy. 77, Lake Shore, 6/16/80, C, b, g, 80001992

Soo Line Depot, Off Main St., Remer, 5/23/80, C, 80001993

Supervisor's Office Headquarters, Ash Ave., Cass Lake, 1/31/76, A, C, 76001049

Winnibigoshish Resort, U.S. 2, Bena, 5/23/80, C, g, 80001989

Chippewa County

Budd, Charles H., House, 219 N. 3rd St., Montevideo, 9/19/77, B, 77000726

Chicago, Milwaukee and St. Paul Depot, S. First St. at Park Ave., Montevideo, 10/27/88, A, 88002079

Chippewa County Bank, N. 1st St. and Lincoln Ave., Montevideo, 9/19/77, A, C, 77000727

Gippe, Henry, Farmstead, U.S. 59, Watson vicinity, 9/25/85, C, 85002558

Lac qui Parle Mission Site, Address Restricted, Montevideo vicinity, 3/14/73, D, a, 73000971

Montevideo Carnegie Library, 125 N. 3rd St., Montevideo, 8/26/82, A, C, 82002938

Swensson, Olof, Farmstead, Co. Hwys. 15 and 6, Granite Falls vicinity, 12/30/74, B, C, a, 74001010

Weaver, Julian A., House, 837 Minnesota Ave., Granite Falls, 6/20/86, B, C, 86001344

Chisago County

Anderson, Gustaf, House [Chisago County MRA], 13045 Lake Blvd., Lindstrom, 7/21/80, B, C, 80002000

Angel's Hill Historic District [Chisago County MRA (AD)], Roughly bounded by Military Rd., Mill, Mulberry and Government Sts., Taylors Falls, 4/11/72, C, a, 72000675

Archeological Site No. 21CH23, Address Restricted, Taylors Falls vicinity, 1/16/89, D, NPS, 88003129

Carlson, J. C., House [Chisago County MRA], Bremer and 6th Sts., Rush City, 7/21/80, B, C, 80002004

Center City Historic District [Chisago County MRA], Summit Ave., Center City, 7/21/80, A, C, a, 80001996

Daubney, John, House [Chisago County MRA], Oak and River Sts., Taylors Falls, 7/21/80, B, C, 80002008

Diffenbacher, Aaron, Farmhouse [Chisago County MRA], Co. Hwy. 5, Rush City, 7/21/80, A, C, 80002007

Franconia Historic District, Roughly Cornelian, Summer and Henry Sts., Taylors Falls, 6/17/80, A, NPS, 80000406

Grant House [Chisago County MRA], 4th St. and Bremer, Rush City, 7/21/80, A, 80002005

Interstate State Park CCC/WPA/Rustic Style Campground [Minnesota State Park CCC/WPA-/Rustic Style MPS], Off US 8 SW of Taylors Falls, Shafer Township, Taylors Falls vicinity, 6/11/92, A, C, 92000638

Interstate State Park WPA/Rustic Style Historic District [Minnesota State Park CCC/WPA/Rustic Style MPS], Off US 8, Taylors Falls vicinity, 6/11/92, A, C, g, 89001664

Larson, Frank A., House [Chisago County MRA], Newell Ave., Lindstrom, 7/21/80, A, C, 80002001

Moody Barn [Chisago County MRA], Co. Hwy. 24, Chisago City vicinity, 7/21/80, A, 80001998

Chisago County—Continued

Munch, Paul, House [Chisago County MRA (AD)], Summer St., Taylors Falls vicinity, 5/04/76, C, 76001050

Munch-Roos House [Chisago County MRA (AD)], 360 Bench St., Taylors Falls, 11/20/70, C, 70000289

Point Douglas to Superior Military Road: Deer Creek Section [Minnesota Military Roads MPS], Off Co. Hwy. 16, St. Croix Wild River State Park, Amador Twp., Taylors Falls vicinity, 2/07/91, A, 90002200

Sayer House [Chisago County MRA], Co. Hwys. 30 and 9, Harris, 7/21/80, A, C, 80002002

Taylors Falls Public Library [Chisago County MRA (AD)], 417 Bench St., Taylors Falls, 10/15/70, A, C, 70000290

Victor, Charles A., House [Chisago County MRA], 3495 Park St., Lindstrom, 7/21/80, B, 80002003

Clay County

Barnesville City Hall and Jail [Clay County MRA], Front and Main Sts., Barnesville, 5/07/80, A, 80002009

Bergquist, John, House [Clay County MRA], 719 10th Ave., N., Moorhead, 5/07/80, B, 80002014

Bernhardson, Bernard, House [Clay County MRA], CR 59, Comstock vicinity, 5/07/80, B, 80002011

Buffalo River State Park WPA/Rustic Style Historic Resources [Minnesota State Park CCC/WPA-/Rustic Style MPS], Off US 10, E of Glyndon, Glyndon vicinity, 10/25/89, A, C, g, 89001671

Burnham Building [Clay County MRA], 420 Main Ave., Moorhead, 5/07/80, B, C, 80002013

Comstock Public School [Clay County MRA], Main St., Comstock, 5/07/80, C, 80002012

Comstock, Solomon Gilman, House [Clay County MRA (AD)], 5th Ave. and 8th St., S., Moorhead, 12/30/74, B, C, 74001011

Fairmont Creamery Company, 801 2nd Ave., N., Moorhead, 2/10/83, A, 83000901

Federal Courthouse and Post Office [Clay County MRA], 521 Main Ave., Moorhead, 5/07/80, A, C, 80002015

Huntoon, Lew A., House [Clay County MRA], 709 8th St., S., Moorhead, 5/07/80, C, 80002016

Krabbenhoft, Wulf C., Farmstead [Clay County MRA], CR 69, Sabin vicinity, 5/07/80, A, b, 80002021

Main Building, Concordia College [Clay County MRA], S. 8th St., Moorhead, 5/07/80, C, 80002017

Olness, John, House [Clay County MRA], US 75, Georgetown vicinity, 5/07/80, B, C, 80002018

Park Elementary School, 121 6th Ave. South, Moorhead, 12/22/88, A, 88003013

Patterson-Hernandez House [Clay County MRA], 1st Ave. and Elm St., Barnesville, 5/07/80, C, 80002010

Probstfield, Randolph M., House [Clay County MRA], Co. Hwy 96, Moorhead vicinity, 5/07/80, B, 80002019

St. John the Divine Episcopal Church [Clay County MRA], 120 S. 8th St., Moorhead, 5/07/80, C, a, 80002020

Clearwater County

Gran Evangelical Lutheran Church, CR 92 and CH 20, Bagley vicinity, 5/19/88, A, a, 88000593

Itasca Bison Site, Address Restricted, Park Rapids vicinity, 12/29/70, D, 70000912

Itasca State Park [Minnesota State Park CCC/WPA/Rustic Style MPS], 21 mi. N of Park Rapids off U.S. 71, Park Rapids vicinity, 5/07/73, A, B, C, D, 73000972

Lower Rice Lake Site, Address Restricted, Bagley vicinity, 12/18/78, A, D, 78001527

Upper Rice Lake Site, Address Restricted, Shevlin vicinity, 12/19/78, D, 78001526

Cook County

Bally Blacksmith Shop, Broadway and First Sts., Grand Marais, 8/13/86, A, 86001548

Church of St. Francis Xavier—Catholic, US 61, Grand Marais vicinity, 7/31/86, A, a, 86002119

Clearwater Lodge, Off CR 66, Grand Marais vicinity, 12/02/85, A, 85003032

Cook County Courthouse, 5th Ave. W. and 2nd St., Grand Marais, 5/09/83, C, 83000902

Fowl Lake Site, Address Restricted, Hovland vicinity, 12/30/74, D, 74001013

Grand Portage National Monument, Off US 61, Grand Marais vicinity, 10/15/66, A, NPS, 66000111

Height of Land, Between North and South Lake in Superior National Forest, Grand Marais vicinity, 10/18/74, A, 74001012

Lightkeeper's House, 12 S. Broadway, Grand Marais, 11/28/78, A, 78001528

Naniboujou Club Lodge, E of Grand Morals on US 61, Grand Marais vicinity, 10/21/82, A, C, 82000558

Schroeder Lumber Company Bunkhouse, US 61, Schroeder vicinity, 7/31/86, A, 86002120

Scott, Jim, Fishhouse, US 61 at Fifth Ave., Grand Marais, 10/23/86, A, 86002904

Cottonwood County

Bargen, Isaac, House, 1215 Mountain Lake Rd., Mountain Lake, 6/13/86, B, g, 86001285

Chicago, St. Paul, Minneapolis, and Omaha Depot, Fourth St. at First Ave., Westbrook, 6/13/86, A, 86001286

Cottonwood County Courthouse, 10th St., Windom, 4/18/77, C, 77000728

Jeffers Petroglyphs Site, Off Co. Hwy. 2, Jeffers vicinity, 10/15/70, D, 70000291

Mountain Lake Site, Address Restricted, Mountain Lake vicinity, 6/04/73, D, 73000973

Crow Wing County

Brainerd Public Library, 206 N. 7th St., Brainerd, 5/23/80, A, C, 80002022

Brainerd Water Tower, Washington at 6th St., Brainerd, 7/17/74, C, 74001014

Broach, H. H., House, Pequot Blvd., Pequot Lakes, 5/23/80, C, 80002037

Crow Wing County Courthouse and Jail, Laurel St., Brainerd, 5/23/80, A, C, 80002023

Elevated Metal Water Tank [Cuyuna Iron Range Municipally-Owned Elevated Metal Water Tanks TR], 1st Ave., Crosby, 10/22/80, A, C, 80002027

Elevated Metal Water Tank [Cuyuna Iron Range Municipally-Owned Elevated Metal Water Tanks TR], North St., Cuyuna, 10/22/80, A, C, 80002028

Elevated Metal Water Tank [Cuyuna Iron Range Municipally-Owned Elevated Metal Water Tanks TR], 211 Maple St., Deerwood, 10/22/80, A, C, 80002029

Elevated Metal Water Tank [Cuyuna Iron Range Municipally-Owned Elevated Metal Water Tanks TR], 7th St., Ironton, 10/22/80, A, C, 80002030

Elevated Metal Water Tank [Cuyuna Iron Range Municipally-Owned Elevated Metal Water Tanks TR], In Trommald, Trommald, 10/22/80, A, C, 80002038

Fawcett, Wilford H., House, Off Co. Hwy. 4, Breezy Point, 5/23/80, B, C, 80002036

Fort Flatmouth Mounds, Address Restricted, Crosslake vicinity, 8/14/73, D, 73000975

Gordon-Schaust Site, Address Restricted, Cross Lake vicinity, 12/23/74, D, 74001015

Grand View Lodge, Off Co. Hwy. 77, Nisswa, 5/23/80, A, C, 80002034

Hemstead, Werner, House, 303 N. 4th St., Brainerd, 5/23/80, B, C, 80002024

Ironton Sintering Plant Complex, Co. Hwy. 30, Crosby, 9/11/80, A, C, 80002031

Minnesota and International Railroad Freight House and Shelter Shed, Co. Hwy. 30, Nissawa vicinity, 5/27/80, A, b, 80002033

Minnewawa Lodge, Co. Hwy. 13, Nisswa, 8/11/80, A, 80002035

Northern Pacific Railroad Shops Historic District, Roughly bounded by the Burlington Northern Railroad tracks, Laurel and 13th Sts., Brainerd, 1/03/89, A, C, 88003024

Parker Building, 222-224 S. 7th St., Brainerd, 5/23/80, A, C, 80002025

Red River Trail: Crow Wing Section [Minnesota Red River Trails MPS], Off Co. Hwy. 27, Crow Wing State Park, Ft. Ripley Twp., Baxter vicinity, 2/06/91, A, 90002201

Sebre Lake Site (21-CW-55), Address Restricted, Fort Ripley vicinity, 11/16/84, D, 84000445

Soo Line Depot, 1st St., N. and 1st Ave., E., Crosby, 11/25/80, A, 80002026

Spina Hotel, Curtis Ave. and 4th St., Ironton, 5/23/80, A, C, 80002032

St. Columba Mission Site, Address Restricted, Nissawa vicinity, 12/18/73, D, a, 73000974

Crow Wing County—Continued

Upper Hay Lake Mound District, Address Restricted, Jenkins vicinity, 1/21/74, D, 74001016

Dakota County

Akin, Daniel F., House, NW of Farmington at 19185 Akin Rd., Farmington vicinity, 12/31/79, B, C, 79001223

Church of St Mary's—Catholic, 8433 239th St., E., New Trier, 12/31/79, A, a, 79001233

Church of the Advent, 412 Oak St., Farmington, 12/31/79, A, C, a, 79001225

Dakota County Courthouse, Vermillion St. between 3rd and 4th Sts., Hastings, 7/21/78, C, 78003069

District School No. 72, 321st St. and Cornell Ave., Northfield vicinity, 12/31/79, A, C, 79001236

East Second Street Commercial Historic District, E. 2nd St. between Ramsey and Vermillion Sts., Hastings, 7/31/78, A, C, 78003070

Eckert, Ignatius, House, 724 Ashland St., Hastings, 7/21/78, C, b, 78003071

Exchange Bank Building, 344 3rd St., Farmington, 12/31/79, A, 79001226

Fasbender Clinic Building, 801 Pine St., Hastings, 12/31/79, C, g, 79001228

Fort Snelling, Bounded by Minnehaha Park, the Mississippi River, the airport and Bloomington Rd., St. Paul vicinity, 10/15/66, A, NHL, 66000401

Fort Snelling-Mendota Bridge, MN 55 over Mississippi River, Mendota, 12/01/78, A, C, 78001534

Freeman, Reuben, House, 9091 Inver Grove Trail, Inver Grove Heights, 12/31/79, C, 79001231

Good Templars Hall, 9965 124th St., E., Hastings vicinity, 12/31/79, A, 79001234

Hastings Foundry-Star Iron Works, 707 E. 1st St., Hastings, 12/31/79, A, 79001229

Hastings Methodist Episcopal Church, 8th and Vermillion Sts., Hastings, 6/07/78, C, a, b, 78001531

Howes, Byron, House, 718 Vermillion St., Hastings, 6/15/78, B, C, 78001529

Latto, Rudolph, House, 620 Ramsey St., Hastings, 5/23/78, C, 78001530

Le Duc, William G., House, 1629 Vermillion St., Hastings, 6/22/70, B, C, 70000292

MacDonald-Todd House, 309 W. 7th St., Hastings, 12/31/79, B, b, 79001230

Mendota Historic District, Roughly bounded by government lot 2, I-55, Sibley Hwy., D St., and Minnesota River, Mendota, 6/22/70, A, B, a, 70000293

Minneapolis St. Paul Rochester & Dubuque Electric Traction Company Depot, Co. Hwy. 5 at 155th St., Burnsville, 12/31/79, A, 79001222

Oberhoffer, Emil J., House, 17045 Judicial Rd., W., Lakeville, 12/31/79, B, C, 79001232

Serbian Home, 404 3rd Ave. S., South St. Paul, 3/26/92, A, 92000257

Sibley, Henry H., House, Willow St., Mendota, 1/20/72, B, C, 72000676

Stockyards Exchange, 200 N. Concord St., South St. Paul, 3/07/79, A, C, 79001235

Thompson-Fasbender House, 649 W. 3d St., Hastings, 5/22/78, C, 78001532

VanDyke-Libby House, 612 Vermillion St., Hastings, 10/02/78, C, 78001533

Wentworth, George W., House, 1575 Oakdale Ave., West St. Paul, 12/31/79, B, C, 79001237

West Second Street Residential Historic District, W. 2nd St. between Forest and Spring Sts., Hastings, 7/31/78, C, 78003072

Dodge County

Carlson, Ole, House [Dodge County MRA], Hwy. 15, Kasson vicinity, 4/16/82, B, C, 82002944

Eureka Hotel [Dodge County MRA], 3rd Ave. at 1st, SW, Kasson, 4/16/82, A, 82002941

Holtermann, Andrew, House [Dodge County MRA], SR 30, S side, Hayfield vicinity, 4/16/82, A, C, 82002940

Kasson Municipal Building [Dodge County MRA], 12 W. Main, Kasson, 4/16/82, A, C, 82002942

Kasson Water Tower, 4th Ave., NW, Kasson, 6/03/76, C, 76001051

Leuthold, Jacob, Jr., House [Dodge County MRA], 108 2nd Ave., NW, Kasson, 4/16/82, B, C, 82002943

Mantorville Historic District, Both sides of MN 57 and 5th St., Mantorville, 6/28/74, A, B, C, a, 74001017

Mantorville and Red Wing Stage Road—Mantorville Section [Overland Staging Industry in Minnesota MPS], N side of 5th St., E of jct. with MN 57, Mantorville, 8/30/91, A, 91001062

Nelson, Perry, House [Dodge County MRA], Co. Hwy. 22, West Concord vicinity, 4/16/82, B, C, 82002939

Wasioja Historic District, Co. Hwy. 16, Mantorville vicinity, 3/13/75, A, C, a, 75000977

Douglas County

Alexandria Public Library, 7th Ave. W. and Fillmore St., Alexandria, 8/23/85, A, C, 85001817

Alexandria Residential Historic District, Roughly bounded by Cedar and Douglas Sts. and Lincoln and Twelfth Aves., Alexandria, 1/11/91, A, C, 90002120

Brandon Auditorium and Fire Hall, Holmes Ave., Brandon, 8/29/85, A, C, 85001928

Cowing, Thomas F., House, 316 Jefferson St., Alexandria, 8/23/85, A, B, C, 85001821

Douglas County Courthouse, 320 7th Ave., W., Alexandria, 8/23/85, A, C, 85001816

Great Northern Passenger Depot, N. Broadway & Agnes Blvd., Alexandria, 8/15/85, A, C, 85001760

Johnson, John B., House, U.S. 52, Osakis, 12/09/77, C, b, 77000730

Lake Carlos State Park WPA/Rustic Style Historic District [Minnesota State Park CCC/WPA/Rustic Style MPS], Off MN 29 at NW end of Lake Carlos, Carlos vicinity, 7/02/92, A, C, 89001654

Lake Carlos State Park WPA/Rustic Style Group Camp [Minnesota State Park CCC/WPA/Rustic Style MPS], Off MN 29 on NE shore of Lake Carlos, Carlos Township, Carlos vicinity, 7/02/92, A, C, 92000776

Nelson, Knute, House, 1219 S. Nokomis St., Alexandria, 4/13/77, B, b, 77000729

Tonn, August, Farmstead, CR 65, Carlos vicinity, 9/25/85, A, C, 85002485

U.S. Post Office—Alexandria, 625 Broadway St., Alexandria, 4/16/79, A, C, 79001238

Ward, Noah P., House, 422 7th Ave., W., Alexandria, 8/23/85, B, C, 85001822

Faribault County

Bullis, Adams H., House [Faribault County MRA], Address Restricted, Delavan vicinity, 5/23/80, B, C, 80004259

Center Creek Archeological District, Address Restricted, Winnebago vicinity, 9/15/76, D, 76001052

Chicago, Milwaukee, St. Paul and Pacific Depot and Lunchroom [Faribault County MRA], 89-100 1st St., NW, Walters, 5/23/80, A, 80004263

Church of the Good Shepherd—Episcopal [Faribault County MRA], Moore and 8th Sts., Blue Earth, 5/23/80, C, a, 80004257

District School No. 40 [Faribault County MRA], MN 109, Wells vicinity, 5/23/80, A, b, 80004264

Dunn, Andrew C., House [Faribault County MRA], 133 S. Main St., Winnebago, 5/23/80, B, C, 80004265

Faribault County Courthouse [Faribault County MRA (AD)], N. Main and 2nd Sts., Blue Earth, 4/11/77, C, 77000731

First National Bank [Faribault County MRA], Main St. and Cleveland Ave., Winnebago, 5/23/80, A, C, 80004266

Kremer, Peter, House [Faribault County MRA], Main and 4th Sts., Minnesota Lake, 5/23/80, B, C, 80004260

Leland, Muret N., House [Faribault County MRA], 410 2nd Ave., SW, Wells, 5/23/80, B, C, 80004261

Memorial Library, Sixth St. and Ramsey Ave., Blue Earth, 12/20/88, A, C, 88002835

Wakefield, James B., House [Faribault County MRA], 405 E. 6th St., Blue Earth, 5/23/80, B, 80004258

Walters Jail [Faribault County MRA], 3rd and Main Sts., Walters, 5/23/80, A, 80004262

Fillmore County

Allis Barn [Fillmore County MRA], County Hwy. 17, Lanesboro vicinity, 4/27/82, A, 82005038

Bartlett, Francis H., House, Gold and Pearl Sts., Wykoff, 5/24/84, A, C, 84001410

Fillmore County—Continued

Bridge No. L4770 [Minnesota Masonry-Arch Highway Bridges MPS], Twp. Rd. 213 over Mahoney Creek, Fountain vicinity, 11/06/89, C, 89001827

Chatfield Public Library [Fillmore County MRA], Main St., Chatfield, 4/27/82, A, C, 82005033

Dayton, Daniel, House [Overland Staging Industry in Minnesota MPS], Off Co. Hwy. 17, Harmony vicinity, 12/06/77, A, B, C, 77000732

Dickson, Samuel Thompson, House, 225 3rd St., SW, Chatfield, 8/15/85, B, 85001755

Fillmore County Jail and Carriage House, Houston and Preston Sts., Preston, 3/05/82, A, C, 82002947

Forestville Townsite—Meighan Store, Co. Hwy. 12, Preston vicinity, 4/13/73, B, C, 73000976

Haven, George H., House [Fillmore County MRA], 132 Winona St., Chatfield, 11/19/82, C, 82000559

Lanesboro Historic District [Fillmore County MRA], Roughly Kirkwood, Coffee and Parkway Sts., Lanesboro, 9/09/82, A, C, 82002946

Lenora Methodist Episcopal Church [Fillmore County MRA], Co. Hwys. 23 and 24, Canton vicinity, 11/19/82, A, a, 82001892

Lovell, Ellen, M., House [Fillmore County MRA], 218 Winona St., Chatfield, 11/19/82, C, 82001893

Norway Township Stone House [Fillmore County MRA], County Hwy. 10, Rushford vicinity, 4/27/82, A, C, 82005034

Parsons Block and Hall [Fillmore County MRA], 112 S. Broadway, Spring Valley, 11/19/82, A, C, 82000560

Pietenpol, Bernard H., Workshop and Garage [Fillmore County MRA], Co. Hwy. 5, Spring Valley vicinity, 4/27/82, B, 82002949

Preston Brewery [Fillmore County MRA], Bluff St., Preston, 4/27/82, A, 82005035

Quickstad Farm Implement Company [Fillmore County MRA], Mill St., Peterson, 4/27/82, A, C, 82005036

Rushford City Mill [Fillmore County MRA], 301 Winona St., Rushford, 4/27/82, A, 82002806

Rushford Wagon and Carriage Company [Fillmore County MRA], Elm St., Rushford, 4/27/82, A, 82002948

Scanlan, Michael, House [Fillmore County MRA], 708 Parkway S., Lanesboro, 4/27/82, A, C, 82005037

Southern Minnesota Depot, Elm St. and Pickle Alley, Rushford, 6/20/86, A, 86001363

Spring Valley Carnegie Library [Fillmore County MRA], 201 S. Broadway, Spring Valley, 4/27/82, A, C, 82002951

Spring Valley Mausoleum [Fillmore County MRA], Spring Valley Cemetery, Spring Valley, 4/27/82, A, 82004911

Spring Valley Methodist Episcopal Church, 221 W. Courtland St., Spring Valley, 5/12/75, C, a, 75000979

Steffens, Ephraim, House [Fillmore County MRA], 404 N. Broadway, Spring Valley, 4/27/82, B, C, 82002952

Strong, William, House [Fillmore County MRA], 508 N. Huron Ave., Spring Valley, 4/27/82, B, C, 82002953

Strong, William, House [Fillmore County MRA], County Hwy. 12, Preston vicinity, 4/27/82, A, C, 82005040

Tunnel Mill, Off Co. Hwy. 1, Spring Valley vicinity, 5/12/75, A, 75000978

Walker and Valentine House [Fillmore County MRA], 504 High St., Rushford, 4/27/82, B, C, 82005039

Freeborn County

Albert Lea City Hall, 212 N. Broadway Ave., Albert Lea, 5/17/84, A, 84001412

Albert Lea Commercial Historic District, N. Broadway Ave. between Water and E. Main Sts., Albert Lea, 7/16/87, A, C, 87001214

Chicago, Milwaukee, St. Paul and Pacific Railroad Depot, 606 S. Broadway, Albert Lea, 2/04/82, A, 82002954

Clarks Grove Cooperative Creamery, Main St. E and Independence Ave., Clarks Grove, 3/20/86, A, C, 86000480

Lodge Zare Zapadu No. 44, CH 30, Hayward vicinity, 3/20/86, A, 86000479

Niebuhr, John, Farmhouse, Off Co. Hwy. 2, Conger vicinity, 3/20/86, B, C, 86000439

Paine, H. A., House, 609 W. Fountain St., Albert Lea, 3/20/86, C, 86000481

Wedge, Dr. Albert C., House, 216 W. Fountain St., Albert Lea, 6/13/86, B, C, 86001332

Goodhue County

Barn Bluff, Jct. of US 61 and US 63, Red Wing, 8/03/90, A, 90001165

Bartron Site, Address Restricted, Red Wing vicinity, 10/15/70, D, 70000294

Baslington, George, Farmhouse [Rural Goodhue County MRA], Off US 52, Pine Island vicinity, 2/12/80, A, C, 80002050

Bridge No. 12 [Iron and Steel Bridges in Minnesota MPS], Twp. Rd. 43 over Bullard Creek, Red Wing vicinity, 11/06/89, A, C, 89001837

Bringghold, Jacob, House [Rural Goodhue County MRA], 314 2nd St., SW, Pine Island, 2/12/80, B, C, 80002051

Cannon Falls School [Rural Goodhue County MRA], 115 W. Minnesota St., Cannon Falls, 2/12/80, A, C, 80002039

Carlson, G. A., Lime Kiln, E. 5th St., Red Wing, 9/27/76, A, C, 76001053

Chicago Great Western Depot, W. Main and Fulton Sts., Red Wing, 6/04/80, A, 80002056

Church of the Redeemer—Episcopal [Rural Goodhue County MRA], 123 N. 3rd St., Cannon Falls, 2/12/80, A, C, a, 80002040

Cross of Christ Lutheran Church [Rural Goodhue County MRA], MN 61, Red Wing vicinity, 2/12/80, A, C, a, 80002057

Dammon Round Barn [Rural Goodhue County MRA], MN 61, Red Wing vicinity, 2/12/80, A, 80002058

District No. 20 School [Rural Goodhue County MRA], MN 58, Red Wing vicinity, 2/12/80, A, 80002059

Ellsworth Hotel Livery Stable [Rural Goodhue County MRA], 4th St., Cannon Falls, 2/12/80, A, 80002043

Firemen's Hall [Rural Goodhue County MRA], 206 W. Mill St., Cannon Falls, 2/12/80, A, C, 80002041

First Congregational Church of Zumbrota [Rural Goodhue County MRA], 455 East Ave., Zumbrota, 2/12/80, A, C, a, 80002065

Fort Sweeney Site, Address Restricted, Red Wing vicinity, 8/05/70, D, 70000295

Fryk, E. J., Barn [Rural Goodhue County MRA], Off MN 61, Red Wing vicinity, 2/12/80, A, 80002060

Gellett, Capt. Charles, House [Rural Goodhue County MRA], 311 N. 6th St., Cannon Falls, 2/12/80, B, C, 80002042

Gladstone Building, 309 Bush St., Red Wing, 11/14/79, C, 79001239

Gunderson, Martin T., House [Rural Goodhue County MRA (AD)], 107 2nd St., Kenyon, 6/10/75, B, C, 75000980

Hall, Dr. Orrin I., House [Rural Goodhue County MRA], 206 W. 3rd St., Zumbrota, 2/12/80, B, C, 80002066

Hauge Lutheran Church [Rural Goodhue County MRA], Off MN 60, Kenyon vicinity, 2/12/80, A, a, 80002048

Hewitt, Dr. Charles, Laboratory, 216 Dakota St., Red Wing, 11/15/79, B, 79001240

Holden Lutheran Church Parsonage [Rural Goodhue County MRA], Co. Hwy. 60, Kenyon vicinity, 2/12/80, A, B, C, a, 80002049

Hoyt, E. S., House, 300 Hill St., Red Wing, 6/05/75, C, 75000981

Immanuel Lutheran Church [Rural Goodhue County MRA], Off MN 58, Red Wing vicinity, 2/12/80, A, C, a, 80002061

Kappel Wagon Works, 221 W. 3rd St., Red Wing, 11/14/79, A, C, 79001241

Kenyon Opera House [Rural Goodhue County MRA], Main St., Kenyon, 2/12/80, A, C, 80002047

Keystone Building, 409 Main St., Red Wing, 11/14/79, A, C, 79001242

Lawther, James L., House, 927 W. 3rd St., Red Wing, 5/21/75, B, C, 75000982

Mendota to Wabasha Military Road: Cannon River Section [Minnesota Military Roads MPS], Cannon Bottom Rd., Red Wing, 2/07/91, A, 90002199

Miller, Harrison, Farmhouse [Rural Goodhue County MRA (AD)], MN 19, Cannon Falls vicinity, 5/22/78, C, 78001535

Miller, John, Farmhouse [Rural Goodhue County MRA], Co. Hwy. 1, Cannon Falls vicinity, 2/12/80, A, B, C, 80002062

Minnesota State Training School, E. 7th St., Red Wing, 6/04/73, A, C, 73000979

Goodhue County—Continued

Minnesota Stoneware Company, 1997 W. Main St., Red Wing, 12/26/79, A, 79001243

Nelson, Julia B., House, 219 5th St., Red Wing, 11/15/79, B, 79001244

Old Frontenac Historic District [Rural Goodhue County MRA (AD)], Roughly bounded by Winona Dr., Burr Oak St., Lake and Westervelt Aves., Red Wing vicinity, 6/04/73, A, B, C, 73000978

Opera Block House [Rural Goodhue County MRA], Main St., Pine Island, 2/12/80, A, C, 80002052

Oxford Mill Ruin [Rural Goodhue County MRA], W of Hwy. 52, Cannon Falls vicinity, 2/12/80, A, 80002044

Pine Island City Hall and Fire Station [Rural Goodhue County MRA], Main and 3rd Sts., Pine Island, 2/12/80, A, C, 80002053

Pratt-Tabor House, 706 W. 4th St., Red Wing, 11/14/79, C, 79001245

Red Wing City Hall, W. 4th St., Red Wing, 11/14/79, A, C, 79001246

Red Wing Iron Works, 401 Levee St., Red Wing, 11/14/79, A, 79001247

Red Wing Mall Historic District, Along East and West Aves. and Broadway between 6th St. and the levee, Red Wing, 1/08/80, A, C, a, 80002063

Red Wing Residential Historic District, Roughly bounded by W. 5th, W. Main, Cedar and Dakota Sts., Red Wing, 4/15/82, C, 82002955

Roscoe Butter and Cheese Factory [Rural Goodhue County MRA], Co. Hwy. 11, Pine Island vicinity, 2/12/80, A, 80002054

Roscoe Store [Rural Goodhue County MRA], Co. Hwy. 11, Pine Island vicinity, 2/12/80, A, 80002055

Sheldon, T. B., Memorial Auditorium, 443 W. 3rd St., Red Wing, 6/03/76, A, 76001054

Sheldon, Theodore B., House, 805 W. 4th St., Red Wing, 6/07/76, B, 76001055

St. James Hotel, Bush and Main Sts., Red Wing, 9/15/77, A, C, 77000733

St. James Hotel and Buildings (Boundary Increase), Bush and Main Sts., Red Wing, 1/08/82, A, C, 82002956

Third Street Bridge [Iron and Steel Bridges in Minnesota MPS], Third St. over Cannon River, Cannon Falls, 11/06/89, C, 89001836

Tower View, W of Red Wing on U.S. 61, Red Wing vicinity, 4/13/77, A, C, 77000734

Towne-Akenson House, 1121 W. 3rd St., Red Wing, 11/15/79, C, 79001248

Vasa Historic District [Rural Goodhue County MRA (AD)], Off MN 19, Red Wing vicinity, 5/30/75, A, C, a, 75000983

Wallauer, Fred, Farmhouse [Rural Goodhue County MRA], MN 58, Red Wing vicinity, 2/12/80, A, C, 80004593

Yale Hardware Store [Rural Goodhue County MRA], 139 N. 4th St., Cannon Falls, 2/12/80, A, C, 80002045

Yale, Darwin E., House [Rural Goodhue County MRA], 421 N. 6th St., Cannon Falls, 2/12/80, B, C, 80002046

Zumbrota Covered Bridge [Rural Goodhue County MRA (AD)], Zumbrota Covered Bridge Park off MN 58, over Zumbro River, Zumbrota, 2/20/75, A, b, 75000984

Grant County

Fort Pomme de Terre Site, Address Restricted, Ashby vicinity, 5/23/74, A, 74001018

Grant County Courthouse, 2nd St. and Central Ave., Elbow Lake, 9/05/85, A, C, 85001945

Roosevelt Hall, Hawkins Ave., Barrett, 8/23/85, A, C, 85001819

Hennepin County

Advance Thresher/Emerson-Newton Implement Company, 700–704 S. 3rd St., Minneapolis, 9/20/77, C, 77000736

Ames-Florida House, 8131 Bridge St., Rockford, 10/16/79, B, C, 79003714

Architects and Engineers Building, 1200 2nd Ave., S., Minneapolis, 2/23/84, A, C, 84001414

Baird, George W., House, 4400 W. 50th St., Edina, 3/27/80, B, C, 80002067

Bardwell-Ferrant House, 2500 Portland Ave., S., Minneapolis, 8/09/84, C, b, 84001416

Bartholomew, Riley Lucas, House, 6901 Lyndale Ave., S., Richfield, 11/28/78, B, 78001545

Basilica of St. Mary—Catholic, Hennepin Ave. at 16th St., Minneapolis, 3/26/75, A, C, a, 75000985

Bennett-McBride House, 3116 3rd Ave., S., Minneapolis, 9/19/77, C, 77000737

Bremer, Fredrika, Intermediate School, 1214 Lowry Ave., N., Minneapolis, 1/31/78, A, C, 78001536

Burwell, Charles H., House, Co. Hwy. 5 and McGinty Rd., Minnetonka, 5/02/74, A, C, 74001025

Butler Brothers Company, 100 N. 6th St., Minneapolis, 3/11/71, C, 71000437

Cahill School, Eden Ave. and MN 100, Edina, 10/09/70, A, C, b, 70000297

Cappelen Memorial Bridge, Franklin Ave. and Mississippi River, Minneapolis, 11/28/78, A, C, 78001537

Carpenter, Elbert L., House, 314 Clifton Ave., Minneapolis, 9/13/77, B, C, 77000738

Carpenter, Eugene J., House, 300 Clifton Ave., Minneapolis, 9/13/77, B, C, 77001566

Cedar Avenue Bridge [Reinforced-Concrete Highway Bridges in Minnesota MPS], Tenth Ave. over Mississippi River, Minneapolis, 11/06/89, A, C, 89001845

Chadwick, Loren L., Cottages, 2617 W. 40th St., Minneapolis, 2/09/84, A, C, 84001417

Chamber of Commerce Building, 400 4th St., S., Minneapolis, 11/23/77, A, C, 77000741

Chicago, Milwaukee, St. Paul and Pacific Depot, W. 37th St. and Brunswick Ave., St. Louis Park, 11/25/69, A, b, 69000072

Chicago, Milwaukee, St. Paul and Pacific Depot, Freight House and Train Shed, 201 3rd Ave., S., Minneapolis, 11/28/78, A, C, 78001542

Church of St. Stephen (Catholic), 2201 Clinton Ave. S., Minneapolis, 8/15/91, C, a, 91001058

Coe, Amos B., House, 1700 S. 3rd Ave., Minneapolis, 1/12/84, C, 84001418

Como-Harriet Streetcar Line and Trolley, 42nd St., W. and Queen Ave., S., Minneapolis, 10/17/77, A, 77000739

Country Club Historic District, Roughly bounded by 45th St., Arden Ave., 50th St., and Browndale Ave., Edina, 4/26/82, C, 82002958

Crane Island Historic District, Crane Island in Lake Minnetonka, Minnetrista, 8/05/91, A, 91001005

Cummins, John R., Farmhouse, 13600 Pioneer Trail, Eden Prairie, 9/02/82, C, 82002957

Cutter, B. O., House, 400 10th Ave., SE, Minneapolis, 1/30/76, C, 76001058

Dania Hall, Corner of 5th St. and Cedar Ave., Minneapolis, 12/27/74, A, C, 74001020

Excelsior Fruit Growers Association Building, 450 3rd St., Excelsior, 1/04/82, A, 82002959

Excelsior Public School, 261 School Ave., Excelsior, 11/13/80, A, C, 80002068

Farmers and Mechanics Savings Bank, 115 S. 4th St., Minneapolis, 1/12/84, C, 84001419

Fire Station No. 19, 2001 University Ave., SE, Minneapolis, 1/14/82, B, C, 82002960

First Church of Christ Scientist, 614–620 E. Fifteenth St., Minneapolis, 6/20/86, A, C, a, 86001340

First Congregational Church, 500 8th Ave., SE, Minneapolis, 1/15/79, A, C, a, 79001249

Fisk, Woodbury, House, 424 5th St., SE, Minneapolis, 10/06/83, C, 83003654

Flour Exchange Building, 310 4th Ave., S., Minneapolis, 8/29/77, C, 77000740

Foshay Tower, 821 Marquette Ave., Minneapolis, 9/20/78, C, 78001538

Fowler Methodist Episcopal Church, 2011 Dupont Ave., S., Minneapolis, 1/30/76, A, C, a, 76001062

Gethsemane Episcopal Church, 901-905 4th Ave., S., Minneapolis, 3/08/84, A, C, a, 84001424

Gideon, Peter, Farmhouse, 24590 Glen Rd., Shorewood, 9/17/74, B, 74001019

Gluek, John G. and Minnie, House and Carriage House, 2447 Bryant Ave. S., Minneapolis, 2/09/90, C, 90000103

Great Northern Railroad Depot, 402 E. Lake St., Wayzata, 7/07/81, A, C, 81000322

Grimes, Jonathan Taylor, House, 4200 W. 44th St., Edina, 3/16/76, B, C, 76001056

Healy Block Residential Historic District, 3101–3145 2nd Ave. S. and 3116–3124 3rd Ave. S., Minneapolis, 5/27/93, A, 93000417

Hennepin County Library, 4915 N. 42nd Ave., Robbinsdale, 10/02/78, A, 78001546

Hewitt, Edwin H., House, 126 E. Franklin Ave., Minneapolis, 4/06/78, B, C, 78001539

Hinkle-Murphy House, 619 10th St., S., Minneapolis, 9/20/84, C, 84001438

Hennepin County—Continued

Interlachen Bridge [Reinforced-Concrete Highway Bridges in Minnesota MPS], William Beery Dr. over Minnesota Transportation Museum street railway track in William Beery Park, Minneapolis, 11/06/89, C, 89001840

Jones, Harry W., House, 5101 Nicollet Ave., Minneapolis, 6/07/76, B, C, 76001060

Lakewood Cemetery Memorial Chapel, 3600 Hennepin Ave., Minneapolis, 10/20/83, C, 83003657

Legg, Harry F., House, 1601 Park Ave., S., Minneapolis, 6/03/76, C, 76001061

Little Sisters of the Poor Home for the Aged, 215 Broadway Ave., NE, Minneapolis, 9/21/78, A, C, a, 78001540

Lohmar, John, House, 1514 Dupont Ave., N., Minneapolis, 4/18/77, C, 77000742

Lumber Exchange Building, 425 Hennepin Ave., 10 S. 5th St., Minneapolis, 5/19/83, A, C, 83000903

Martin, Charles J., House, 1300 Mount Curve Ave., Minneapolis, 4/26/78, C, 78001541

Masonic Temple, 528 Hennepin Ave., Minneapolis, 9/05/75, C, 75000987

Maternity Hospital, 300 Queen Ave., N., Minneapolis, 3/27/80, B, 80002069

Milwaukee Avenue Historic District, Milwaukee Ave. from Franklin Ave. to 24th St., Minneapolis, 5/02/74, A, C, 74001021

Minneapolis Armory, 500–530 6th St., S., Minneapolis, 9/26/85, C, 85002491

Minneapolis Brewing Company, Jct. of Marshall St. and 13th Ave. NE., Minneapolis, 6/21/90, A, C, 90000988

Minneapolis City Hall-Hennepin County Courthose, 400 S. 4th Ave., Minneapolis, 12/04/74, C, 74001022

Minneapolis Public Library, North Branch, 1834 Everson Ave., N., Minneapolis, 12/07/77, A, C, 77000743

Minneapolis Warehouse Historic District, Roughly bounded by River St., 1st Ave. N., 6th St. N., 2nd Ave. N., 5th St. N., 5th Ave. N., 3rd St. N., & 10th Ave. N., Minneapolis, 11/03/89, A, C, 89001937

Minnehaha Grange Hall, Eden Ave. at Hwy. 100, Edina, 10/09/70, A, C, b, 70000914

Minnehaha Historic District, Roughly Hiawatha and Minnehaha Aves., and Godfrey Rd., Minneapolis, 11/25/69, A, B, C, b, e, 69000369

Minnesota Soldiers' Home Historic District, Roughly bounded by Minehaha Ave., Mississippi River, and Godfrey Pkwy., Minneapolis, 3/02/89, A, C, 89000076

Moline, Milburn and Stoddard Company, 250 3rd Ave., N., Minneapolis, 2/20/75, C, 75000986

New Main—Augsburg Seminary, 731 21st Ave., S., Minneapolis, 10/06/83, A, C, a, 83003653

Newell, George R., House, 1818 LaSalle Ave., Minneapolis, 9/15/77, B, C, 77000744

Northwestern Knitting Company Factory, 718 Glenwood Ave., Minneapolis, 6/03/83, A, 83000904

Ogden Apartment Hotel, 66–68 S. 12th St., Minneapolis, 1/13/92, A, 91001956

Olson, Floyd B., House, 1914 W. 49th St., Minneapolis, 12/31/74, B, g, 74001023

Owre, Dr. Oscar, House, 2625 Newton Ave., S., Minneapolis, 3/08/84, B, C, 84001446

Parker, Charles and Grace, House, 4829 Colfax Ave. S., Minneapolis, 6/11/92, C, 92000699

Peavey-Haglin Experimental Concrete Grain Elevator, Jct. MN 7 and MN 100, St. Louis Park, 12/19/78, C, NHL, 78001547

Pillsbury A Mill, Main St. and 3rd Ave., SE, Minneapolis, 11/13/66, A, NHL, 66000402

Pittsburgh Plate Glass Company Building, 616 S. 3rd St., Minneapolis, 9/13/77, C, 77000745

Pond, Gideon H., House, 401 E. 104th St., Bloomington, 7/16/70, B, C, a, 70000296

Purcell, William Gray, House, 2328 Lake Pl., Minneapolis, 10/29/74, B, C, 74001024

Queene Avenue Bridge [Reinforced-Concrete Highway Bridges in Minnesota MPS], W. Lake Harriet Blvd. over Minnesota Transportation Museum street railway track, Minneapolis, 11/06/89, C, 89001847

Smith, H. Alden, House, 1405 Harmon Pl., Minneapolis, 3/16/76, C, 76001063

Smith, Lena O., House, 3905 5th Ave. S., Minneapolis, 9/26/91, B, 91001472

St. Anthony Falls Historic District, Around Mississippi River between Plymouth and S. 10th Aves., Minneapolis, 3/11/71, A, C, D, 71000438

Station 28 Minneapolis Fire Department, 2724 W. 43rd St., Minneapolis, 11/12/93, A, 93001235

Stevens Square Historic District, Roughly bounded by E. 17th St., 3rd Ave. S., Franklin and 1st Aves. S., Minneapolis, 7/01/93, A, 93000594

Stewart Memorial Presbyterian Church, 116 E. 32nd St., Minneapolis, 11/28/78, C, a, 78001543

Swinford Townhouses and Apartments, 1213–1221, 1225 Hawthorne Ave., Minneapolis, 10/25/90, C, 90001552

Turnblad, Swan, House, 2600 Park Ave., Minneapolis, 8/26/71, B, C, 71000436

University of Minnesota Old Campus Historic District, University Ave. and 15th Ave., Minneapolis, 8/23/84, A, C, 84001463

Van Cleve, Horatio P., House, 603 5th St., SE, Minneapolis, 3/16/76, B, C, 76001064

Washburn A Mill Complex, 1st St., S. at Portland Ave., Minneapolis, 5/04/83, A, NHL, 83004388

Washburn Park Water Tower, 401 Prospect Ave., Minneapolis, 10/06/83, A, C, 83003663

Washburn-Fair Oaks Mansion District, 1st and 2nd Aves., 22 St., and Stevens Ave., Minneapolis, 2/17/78, B, C, 78001544

Wesley Methodist Episcopal Church, 101 E. Grant St., Minneapolis, 2/09/84, A, C, a, 84001469

White Castle Building No. 8, 3252 Lyndale Ave. S, Minneapolis, 10/16/86, A, C, b, 86002868

Willey, Malcolm, House, 255 Bedford St., SE, Minneapolis, 2/23/84, C, g, 84001472

Wyer—Pearce House, 201 Mill St., Excelsior, 4/18/77, C, 77000735

Houston County

Bridge No. L4013 [Minnesota Masonry-Arch Highway Bridges MPS], Twp. Rd. 126 over Riceford Cr., Spring Grove vicinity, 7/05/90, C, 90000976

Bunge, Christian, Jr., Store [Houston County MRA], Iowa Ave. at Main St., Eitzen, 4/06/82, A, 82002964

Cameron, Daniel, House [Houston County MRA], 429–435 S. 7th St., La Crescent, 4/06/82, A, B, C, 82002968

Church of the Holy Comforter—Episcopal, Main St., Brownsville, 6/02/70, A, C, a, 70000298

Eitzen Stone Barn [Houston County MRA], S of Eitzen, Eitzen vicinity, 4/06/82, A, C, 82002965

Houston County Courthouse and Jail [Houston County MRA], Courthouse Sq., Caledonia, 3/18/83, A, C, 83000905

Johnson Mill [Houston County MRA], CR 5 and 23, Eitzen vicinity, 4/06/82, A, 82002966

Portland Prairie Methodist Episcopal Church [Houston County MRA], Off MN 76, Eitzen vicinity, 4/06/82, A, C, a, 82002967

Schech Mill, Off CR 10 in Beaver Creek Valley State Park, Caledonia vicinity, 1/31/78, A, C, 78001548

Sprague, David R. and Ellsworth A., Houses [Houston County MRA], 204 and 224 W. Main St., Caledonia, 4/06/82, B, 82002962

Williams, Spafford, Hotel [Houston County MRA], E. Main at N. Marshall, Caledonia, 4/06/82, A, C, 82002963

Hubbard County

Hubbard County Courthouse, Court St., Park Rapids, 3/08/84, A, C, 84001475

Moser, Louis J., House, Off CR 90, Nevis vicinity, 4/17/79, A, C, 79001250

Park Rapids Jail, 205 W. Second St., Park Rapids, 10/27/88, A, 88002053

Shell River Prehistoric Village and Mound District, Address Restricted, Park Rapids vicinity, 6/19/73, D, 73000980

Isanti County

District School No. 1 [Isanti County MRA], Off Co. Hwy. 7, Isanti vicinity, 7/24/80, A, 80002078

Erickson, Edward, Farmstead [Isanti County MRA], Co. Hwy. 56 and MN 65, Isanti vicinity, 7/24/80, A, B, C, 80002071

Farmers Cooperative Mercantile Company of West Stanford [Isanti County MRA], Co. Hwy. 7, Isanti vicinity, 7/24/80, A, 80002079

Isanti County Courthouse [Isanti County MRA], 237 2nd Ave., SW, Cambridge, 7/24/80, A, 80002074

Linden Barn [Isanti County MRA], Co. Hwy. 19, Isanti vicinity, 7/24/80, A, 80002075

Olson, Oscar, House [Isanti County MRA], 309 Beechwood, Braham, 7/24/80, B, C, 80002073

Isanti County—Continued

St. John's Lutheran Church [Isanti County MRA], Co. Hwy. 5, Isanti vicinity, 7/24/80, A, C, a, 80002072

Svenska Mission Kyrka I Sodre Maple Ridge [Isanti County MRA], Co. Hwy. 1, Brahm vicinity, 7/24/80, A, C, a, 80002077

West Riverside School [Isanti County MRA], Co. Hwy. 14, Cambridge vicinity, 7/24/80, A, C, 80002076

Itasca County

Bovey Village Hall [Federal Relief Construction in Minnesota MPS], 402 2nd St., Bovey, 8/15/91, A, C, 91001059

Canisteo District General Office Building [Itasca County MRA; Oliver Iron Mining Company Buildings TR], 200 Cole Ave., Coleraine, 4/22/82, A, 82002970

Central School, N. Pokegama and 4th St., Grand Rapids, 8/16/77, A, C, 77000746

Church of the Good Shepherd, Off U.S. 169, Coleraine, 8/11/80, A, C, a, 80002081

Coleraine Carnegie Library, Clemson and Cole Aves., S., Coleraine, 7/17/80, A, C, 80002080

Coleraine City Hall, 302 Roosevelt Ave., Coleraine, 6/18/92, A, C, 92000800

Coleraine Methodist Episcopal Church [Itasca County MRA], NW Gayley and Cole Aves., Coleraine, 4/22/82, A, C, a, 82002971

General Superintendent's House [Itasca County MRA; Oliver Iron Mining Company Buildings TR], Cole Ave., Coleraine, 4/22/82, A, 82002972

Gran, Frank, Farmstead [Itasca County MRA], Co. Hwy. 10, La Prairie vicinity, 4/22/82, A, 82002969

Hartley Sugar Camp [Itasca County MRA], Off Co. Hwy. 10, Bovey vicinity, 4/22/82, A, 82002973

Hill Annex Mine, Off US 169, Calumet vicinity, 8/01/86, A, 86002126

Itasca Lumber Company Superintendent's House [Itasca County MRA], 506 5th St., SE, Deer River, 4/22/82, A, 82002976

Old Cut Foot Sioux Ranger Station, MN 46 in Chippewa National Forest, Squaw Lake vicinity, 8/07/74, A, 74001026

Oliver Boarding House [Itasca County MRA; Oliver Iron Mining Company Buildings TR], Jessie St., Marble, 4/22/82, A, 82002977

Scenic State Park CCC/Rustic Style Service Yard [Minnesota State Park CCC/WPA/Rustic Style MPS], Off Co. Hwy. 7, Scenic State Park, Bigfork vicinity, 6/08/92, A, C, b, 92000595

Scenic State Park CCC/WPA/Rustic Style Historic Resources [Minnesota State Park CCC/WPA-/Rustic Style MPS], Off Co. Hwy. 7 E of Bigfork, Bigfork vicinity, 6/08/92, A, C, 89001670

Turtle Oracle Mound, Address Restricted, Squaw Lake vicinity, 8/27/74, D, 74001027

White Oak Point Site, Address Restricted, Zemple vicinity, 10/18/72, D, 72000677

Winnibigoshish Lake Dam, Co. Hwy. 9 at Mississippi River, Inger vicinity, 5/11/82, A, C, 82004629

Jackson County

Church of the Sacred Heart (Catholic), 9th St. and 4th Ave., Heron Lake, 3/20/89, A, C, a, 89000157

District School No. 92, Co. Hwy. 9, Jackson vicinity, 10/27/88, C, 88002082

Jackson Commercial Historic District, Second St. between Sheridan & White Sts., Jackson, 12/17/87, A, B, C, 87002155

Jackson County Courthouse, Bounded by Sherman, W. Ashley, 4th and 5th Sts., Jackson, 4/13/77, A, C, 77000747

Moore, George M., Farmstead, Off Co. Hwy. 4, Jackson vicinity, 1/07/87, C, 86003604

Robertson Park Site, Address Restricted, Jackson vicinity, 8/01/80, D, 80002082

Kanabec County

Ann River Logging Company Farm [Kanabec County MRA], MN 23, Mora vicinity, 8/18/80, A, 80002085

Coin School [Kanabec County MRA], Co. Hwys. 4 and 16, Mora vicinity, 8/18/80, A, 80002086

Kanabec County Courthouse, Maple and Vine Sts., Mora, 4/11/77, A, C, 77000748

Knife Lake Prehistoric District, Address Restricted, Mora vicinity, 1/21/74, A, D, 74001028

Ogilvie Watertower [Kanabec County MRA], Anderson St., Ogilvie, 8/18/80, A, C, 80002087

Williams, C. E., House [Kanabec County MRA], 206 E. Maple Ave., Mora, 8/18/80, B, C, 80002083

Zetterberg Company [Kanabec County MRA], 630 E. Forest St., Mora, 8/18/80, A, 80002084

Kandiyohi County

Bosch, John, Farmstead, CR 4, Lake Lillian vicinity, 4/23/87, A, B, 87000620

Broman, Andreas, Johanna, Anna and Frank E., Farmstead, Off Co. Rd. 8 between Swan Lake and Kasota Lake, Kandiyohi Township, Kandiyohi vicinity, 2/28/91, A, 91000098

District School No. 55, Co. Hwy. 13, Willmar vicinity, 4/16/87, A, 87000619

Endreson, Lars and Guri, House, Off Co. Hwy. 5, Willmar vicinity, 7/24/86, A, 86001920

Hotel Atwater, 322 Atlantic Ave., Atwater, 6/13/86, A, 86001330

Larson, A., & Co. Building, 539 W. Pacific Ave., Willmar, 3/02/89, A, C, 89000156

Sibley State Park CCC/Rustic Style Historic District [Minnesota State Park CCC/WPA/Rustic Style MPS], Off US 71 W of New London, New London vicinity, 1/22/92, A, C, 89001673

Spicer, John M., House, 515 Seventh St. NW, Willmar, 8/13/86, B, 86001545

Spicer, John M., Summer House and Farm, 600 S. Lake Ave., Spicer vicinity, 8/06/86, A, 86002292

Willmar Auditorium [Federal Relief Construction in Minnesota MPS], 311 6th St. SW., Willmar, 8/09/91, A, C, 91000976

Willmar Hospital Farm for Inebriates Historic District, Off US 71, Willmar, 8/13/86, A, C, 86001535

Kittson County

Lake Bronson Site, Address Restricted, Lake Bronson vicinity, 5/22/78, D, 78001549

Lake Bronson State Park WPA/Rustic Style Historic Resources [Minnesota State Park CCC/WPA/Rustic Style MPS], Off Co. Hwy. 28 E of Lake Bronson, Lake Bronson vicinity, 10/25/89, A, C, g, 89001659

St. Nicholas Orthodox Church, Co. Hwy. 4, Lancaster vicinity, 3/08/84, A, a, 84001480

Koochiching County

Finsted's Auto Marine Shop, Sand Bay between Oak Ave. and Spruce St., Ranier, 1/27/83, A, 83000906

Gold Mine Sites, Off MN 11 in Voyageurs National Park, Island View vicinity, 5/06/77, A, NPS, 77000155

Koochiching County Courthouse, 4th St. and 8th Ave., International Falls, 9/15/77, A, C, 77000749

Laurel Mounds, Address Restricted, International Falls vicinity, 1/20/72, D, 72000678

Little American Mine, Off Mn 11 in Voyageurs National Park, Island View vicinity, 4/16/75, A, NPS, 75000226

McKinstry Mounds and Village Site, Address Restricted, International Falls vicinity, 12/18/78, D, 78001550

Nett Lake Petroglyphs Site, Address Restricted, Orr vicinity, 12/30/74, A, D, 74001029

Scenic Hotel, Main and 3rd Sts., Northome, 1/27/83, A, 83000907

Sts. Peter and Paul Russian Orthodox Church, MN 65, Bramble vicinity, 1/27/83, A, a, 83000908

White, Francis, Homestead, N of Littlefork off US 71, Littlefork vicinity, 1/27/83, A, 83000909

Lac Qui Parle County

Camp Release State Monument, About 2 mi. SW of Montevideo off U.S. 212, Montevideo vicinity, 3/14/73, A, 73000981

Commercial Bank Building, Off US 212, Dawson, 1/28/82, B, C, 82002978

Dawson Carnegie Library, 677 Pine St., Dawson, 8/15/85, A, C, 85001770

Hotel Lac qui Parle, 202 6th Ave., Madison, 12/06/90, A, 90001820

Lac Qui Parle County—Continued

Lac qui Parle County Courthouse, 600 6th St., Madison, 8/15/85, A, C, 85001759

Lac qui Parle State Park WPA/Rustic Style Historic District [Minnesota State Park CCC/WPA-/Rustic Style MPS], Off Co. Hwy. 33 at SE end of Lac qui Parle, Lac qui Parle Township, Montevideo vicinity, 8/19/91, A, C, 91001055

Louisburg School, First St. at Third Ave., Louisburg, 6/20/86, A, C, 86001348

Madison Carnegie Library, 401 6th Ave., Madison, 8/23/85, A, C, 85001823

Madison City Hall, 404 6th Ave., Madison, 8/23/85, A, C, 85001820

Yellow Bank Church Campground Bridge [Iron and Steel Bridges in Minnesota MPS], Twp. Rd. 76 over Yellow Bank River, Odessa vicinity, 11/06/89, C, 89001831

Lake County

Duluth and Iron Range Railroad Company Depot, 6th St. off South Ave., Two Harbors, 2/24/83, A, 83000910

Dwan, John, Office Building, 201 Waterfront Dr., Two Harbors, 6/11/92, A, b, 92000700

EDNA G (tugboat), Home port at S end of Poplar St. in Agate Bay, Two Harbors vicinity, 6/05/75, A, 75002144

Gooseberry Falls State Park CCC/WPA/Rustic Style Historic Resources [Minnesota State Park CCC/WPA/Rustic Style MPS], Off US 61 NE of Two Harbors, Two Harbors vicinity, 10/25/89, A, C, g, 89001672

Lake County Courthouse and Sheriff's Residence, 3rd Ave. at 6th St., Two Harbors, 2/24/83, A, C, 83000912

Larsmont School, Co. Hwy. 61, Two Harbors vicinity, 6/18/92, A, 92000799

MADEIRA (Schooner—Barge) Shipwreck [Minnesota's Lake Superior Shipwrecks MPS], Address Restricted, Beaver Bay vicinity, 7/23/92, A, C, 92000843

Mattson, Edward and Lisa, House and Fish House, Off US 61, at Beaver Bay shore near Wieland Island, East Beaver Bay, 8/09/90, A, 90001152

ONOKO (Bulk Freight Steamer) Shipwreck [Minnesota's Lake Superior Shipwrecks MPS], Address Restricted, Knife River vicinity, 7/23/92, A, C, D, 92000845

SAMUEL P. ELY Shipwreck, Address Restricted, Two Harbors vicinity, 6/18/92, A, C, D, 92000694

Split Rock Lighthouse, About 20 mi. NE of Two Harbors on U.S. 61, Two Harbors vicinity, 6/23/69, A, C, 69000073

Tettegouche Camp Historic District, Off County Hwy. 4, Silver Bay vicinity, 1/17/89, A, C, 88003084

Two Harbors Carnegie Library, Fourth Ave. and Waterfront Dr., Two Harbors, 7/31/86, C, 86002121

Two Harbors Light Station [U.S. Coast Guard Lighthouses and Light Stations on the Great Lakes TR], Agate and Burlington Bays, Two Harbors, 7/19/84, A, C, 84001483

Lake Of The Woods County

Fort St. Charles Archeological Site, Address Restricted, Angle Inlet vicinity, 4/08/83, D, 83000911

Northwest Point, Between Bear and Harrison Creeks, Angle Inlet vicinity, 2/23/73, A, 73000982

Spooner Public School, 1st St., N. and 8th Ave., E., Baudette, 2/11/83, A, 83000913

Le Sueur County

Andrews, John R., House, Co. Hwy. 19, Kasota vicinity, 10/10/78, B, 78003123

Bridge No. 4846 (1) [Le Sueur County MRA], Co. Hwy. 102 over MN 22, Kasota vicinity, 2/17/81, C, b, 81000681

Cosgrove, Carson H., House [Le Sueur County MRA], 228 S. 2nd, Le Sueur, 3/15/82, B, C, 82004694

Dehn, Arthur, House [Le Sueur County MRA], Herbert St., Waterville, 11/19/82, A, g, 82000561

Elysian Public School [Le Sueur County MRA], 4th and Frank Sts., Elysian, 2/17/81, C, b, 81000677

First National Bank [Le Sueur County MRA], 112 E. Main, New Prague, 3/15/82, C, 82004703

Geldner Sawmill, Co. Hwy. 13, Cleveland vicinity, 6/11/75, A, b, 75000991

German Evangelical Salem Church [Le Sueur County MRA], CR 156, Le Sueur vicinity, 3/15/82, A, C, a, 82004696

Hilltop Hall [Le Sueur County MRA], 206 N. 1st St., Montgomery, 3/15/82, A, 82004701

Hotel Broz [Le Sueur County MRA], 212 W. Main, New Prague, 3/15/82, A, 82004704

Kasota Township Hall [Le Sueur County MRA], Hill and Rice Sts., Kasota, 2/17/81, A, 81000679

Kasota Village Hall [Le Sueur County MRA], Cherry and Webster Sts., Kasota, 2/17/81, A, C, 81000680

Le Sueur County Courthouse and Jail [Le Sueur County MRA], 88 S. Park Ave. and 130 S. Park Ave., Le Center, 2/17/81, A, C, 81000682

Mayo, Dr. William W., House, 118 N. Main St., Le Sueur, 11/25/69, A, B, 69000074

Methodist Episcopal Church [Le Sueur County MRA; Ottawa Stone Buildings TR], Liberty and Whittier St., Ottawa, 3/15/82, C, a, 82004697

Needham-Hayes House [Le Sueur County MRA], Off Railroad St., Le Sueur vicinity, 3/15/82, B, C, 82004698

Ottawa Township Hall [Le Sueur County MRA; Ottawa Stone Buildings TR], Buchanan and Bryant Sts., Ottawa, 3/15/82, C, 82004705

Patten, David, Farmhouse [Le Sueur County MRA; Ottawa Stone Buildings TR], Liberty St., Ottawa, 3/15/82, C, 82004706

Rinshed, John, House [Le Sueur County MRA; Ottawa Stone Buildings TR], Sumner and Whittier Sts., Ottawa, 3/15/82, C, 82004707

Schwartz, Charles, House and Barn [Le Sueur County MRA; Ottawa Stone Buildings TR], Off Co. Hwy. 23, Ottawa, 3/15/82, C, 82004708

Smith-Cosgrove House [Le Sueur County MRA], 228 S. Main St., Le Sueur, 3/15/82, B, C, 82004700

Taylor, George W., House, 103 S. 2nd St., Le Sueur, 9/05/75, B, C, 75000992

Trinity Chapel—Episcopal [Le Sueur County MRA; Ottawa Stone Buildings TR], Sumner and Exchange Sts., Ottawa, 3/15/82, C, a, 82004695

Union Hotel [Le Sueur County MRA], 201 Paquin St., E., Waterville, 3/15/82, A, 82004709

Westerman Lumber Office and House [Le Sueur County MRA], 201 S. 1st St., Montgomery, 3/15/82, B, 82004702

Lincoln County

Danebod, Danebod Ct., Tyler, 6/30/75, A, C, b, 75000993

Drammen Farmers' Club [Lincoln County MRA], Co. Hwy. 13, Lake Benton vicinity, 12/01/80, A, 80004539

Lake Benton Opera House, Benton St. between Fremont and Center Sts., Lake Benton, 3/25/77, A, 77000753

Lake Benton Opera House and Kimball Building (Boundary Increase), Benton St., Lake Benton, 4/22/82, A, 82002979

Lincoln County Courthouse and Jail [Lincoln County MRA], Rotherwood St., Ivanhoe, 12/01/80, A, C, 80004541

Lincoln County Fairgrounds [Lincoln County MRA], Strong and Marsh Sts., Tyler, 12/12/80, A, b, g, 80002088

Osbeck, Ernst, House [Lincoln County MRA], 106 S. Fremont St., Lake Benton, 12/02/80, B, C, b, 80004540

Tyler Public School [Lincoln County MRA], Strong St., Tyler, 12/01/80, C, 80002089

Lyon County

Anderson, J. S., House [Lyon County MRA], 402 E. 2nd St., Minneota, 3/15/82, C, 82002984

Anderson, O. G., & Co. Store [Lyon County MRA], Jefferson St., Minneota, 3/15/82, A, C, 82002985

Camden State Park CCC/WPA/Rustic Style Historic District [Minnesota State Park CCC/WPA-/Rustic Style MPS], Off MN 23 SW of Lynd, Lynd vicinity, 4/19/91, A, C, 89001669

First National Bank [Lyon County MRA], 101 3rd St., Tracy, 3/15/82, A, C, 82002987

Gieske, William F., House [Lyon County MRA], 601 W. Lyon, Marshall, 3/15/82, B, C, 82002982

Lyon County—Continued

Kiel & Morgan Hotel/Lyon County Courthouse [Lyon County MRA], Off Co. Hwy. 5, Lynd vicinity, 3/15/82, A, 82002981

Masonic Temple Delta Lodge No. 119 [Lyon County MRA], 325 W. Main, Marshall, 3/15/82, C, 82002983

Norseth, Martin, House [Lyon County MRA], 86 E. Main, Cottonwood, 3/15/82, B, C, 82002980

St. Paul's Evangelical Lutheran Church & Parsonage [Lyon County MRA], 412–414 E. Lyon St., Minneota, 3/15/82, A, a, 82002986

Mahnomen County

Mahnomen City Hall, 104 W. Madison Ave., Mahnomen, 12/22/88, A, C, 88003011

Mahnomen County Courthouse, Main St. at Washington Ave., Mahnomen, 2/16/84, A, C, 84001488

Mahnomen County Fairgrounds Historic District, Jct. MN 200 and Co. Hwy. 137, Mahnomen vicinity, 3/02/89, A, C, 89000077

Marshall County

Larson Mill, CR 39 in Old Mill State Park, Argyle vicinity, 6/04/73, A, b, 73000983

Old Mill State Park WPA/Rustic Style Historic Resources [Minnesota State Park CCC/WPA/Rustic Style MPS], Off Co. Hwy. 39 E of Argyle, Argyle vicinity, 10/25/89, A, C, g, 89001667

Martin County

Fairmont Opera House, Downtown Plaza and Blue Earth Ave., Fairmont, 7/02/80, C, 80004530

First Church of Christ Scientist, 222 Blue Earth Ave., E., Fairmont, 5/19/88, A, C, a, 88000594

Martin County Courthouse, Lake Ave. and 2nd St., Fairmont, 9/22/77, C, 77000755

Sherburn Commercial Historic District, Main St. N between Front and Second Sts., Sherburn, 8/03/87, A, C, 87001303

Wohlheter, George, House, 320 Woodland Ave., Fairmont, 6/20/75, C, 75000994

McLeod County

Goodnow, Merton S., House, 446 S. Main St., Hutchinson, 8/15/85, C, 85001771

Hutchinson Carnegie Library, Main St., Hutchinson, 12/12/77, A, C, 77001507

McLeod County Courthouse, 830 11th St., E., Glencoe, 8/23/84, A, C, 84001620

Winsted City Hall, 181 1st St., N., Winsted, 8/19/82, A, C, 82002988

Meeker County

Ames, Henry, House, MN 24, Litchfield vicinity, 8/09/84, B, 84001623

Brightwood Beach Cottage, S. Ripley Dr., Litchfield vicinity, 5/22/78, A, C, 78001551

Grand Army of the Republic Hall, 370 N. Marshall St., Litchfield, 5/21/75, A, C, 75000995

Litchfield Opera House, 126 N. Marshall Ave., Litchfield, 10/04/84, A, 84000019

Trinity Episcopal Church, 400 N. Sibley Ave., Litchfield, 6/20/75, C, a, 75000996

Mille Lacs County

Cooper Site, Address Restricted, Onamia vicinity, 9/22/70, D, 70000299

Dunn, Robert C., House, 708 S. 4th St., Princeton, 8/29/85, B, C, 85001922

Gile, Ephraim C., House, 311 8th Ave., S., Princeton, 8/29/85, C, 85001907

Great Northern Depot, 1st St. and MN 95, Princeton, 11/23/77, A, 77000757

Kathio Site, Address Restricted, Vineland and vicinity vicinity, 10/15/66, D, NHL, 66000403

Milaca Municipal Hall, 145 Central Ave, S., Milaca, 9/11/85, A, C, g, 85002201

Mille Lacs County Courthouse, 5th Ave., SE and 2nd St., SE, Milaca, 3/25/77, A, C, 77000756

Onamia Municipal Hall, Main and Birch Sts., Onamia, 9/10/85, A, C, 85002333

Petaga Point, Address Restricted, Onamia vicinity, 9/22/70, D, 70000300

Saw Mill Site, Address Restricted, Onamia vicinity, 9/22/70, D, 70000301

Vineland Bay Site, Address Restricted, Vineland vicinity, 9/22/70, D, 70000302

Morrison County

Ayer Mission Site, Address Restricted, Little Falls vicinity, 6/18/73, B, 73000984

Belle Prairie Village Site, Address Restricted, Little Falls vicinity, 8/14/73, A, 73000985

Burton—Rosenmeier House, 606 First St. SE, Little Falls, 3/13/86, B, C, 86000328

Church of Our Savior—Episcopal, 113 4th St., NE, Little Falls, 7/17/80, C, a, 80002090

Clough Township Hall, CR 206, Randall vicinity, 9/05/85, C, 85001985

Fort Duquesne (21-MO-20), Address Restricted, Little Falls vicinity, 11/15/84, D, 84000452

Fort Ripley, Address Restricted, Little Falls vicinity, 9/10/71, A, D, 71000439

Lindbergh, Charles A., House and Park, SW of Little Falls on SR 52, Little Falls vicinity, 11/20/70, B, NHL, 70000303

Lindbergh, Charles A., State Park WPA/Rustic Style Historic Resources [Minnesota State Park CCC/WPA/Rustic Style MPS], Off Co. Hwy. 52, S of Little Falls, Little Falls vicinity, 10/25/89, A, C, 89001655

Little Falls Carnegie Library, 108 3rd St., NE, Little Falls, 11/03/80, A, C, 80002091

Morrison County Courthouse, Broadway and 2nd Sts., Little Falls, 12/05/78, C, 78001552

Northern Pacific Railway Depot, 200 1st St., NW, Little Falls, 9/05/85, A, C, 85001987

Pelkey Lake Site, Address Restricted, Little Falls vicinity, 10/02/73, D, 73000986

Pike's, Zebulon, 1805–1806 Wintering Quarters, Address Restricted, Little Falls vicinity, 7/11/88, A, D, 88000538

Pine Tree Lumber Company Office Building, 735 1st St., NE, Little Falls, 9/05/85, A, B, 85001991

Rice Lake Prehistoric District, Address Restricted, Little Falls vicinity, 10/02/73, D, 73000987

St. Joseph's Church—Catholic, Main St., Pierz, 9/05/85, A, C, a, 85001998

Swan River Village Site, Address Restricted, Little Falls vicinity, 10/02/73, D, 73000988

Warren, William, Two Rivers House Site and McDougall, Peter, Farmstead, CR 231, Royalton vicinity, 12/07/74, A, B, C, 74001031

Weyerhaeuser, Charles A., and Musser, Richard Drew, Houses, Highland Ave., Little Falls, 9/05/85, A, 85001990

White, Almond A., House, Cleveland and Beaulieu Sts., Motley, 3/13/86, C, 86000330

Mower County

Booth Post No. 130—Grand Army of the Republic Hall, S. Main St. between First and Second Sts., Grand Meadow, 6/13/86, A, C, 86001278

Cook-Hormel House, 208 4th Ave., NW, Austin, 8/19/82, B, C, 82002989

Exchange State Bank, NW corner of Main and 1st Sts., Grand Meadow, 6/10/75, C, 75000997

First National Bank of Adams, 322 Main St., Adams, 3/20/86, B, C, 86000442

First State Bank of LeRoy, Main St. and Broadway, LeRoy, 3/20/86, C, 86000445

Freund Store, Co. Hwy. 7, Adams vicinity, 4/24/86, A, 86000867

LeRoy Public Library, Luella St. and Broadway, LeRoy, 3/20/86, A, C, 86000447

Paramount Theater, 125 Fourth Ave. NE, Austin, 10/23/86, C, 86002906

Wright, Arthur W., House, 300 Fourth Ave. NW, Austin, 3/20/86, C, 86000441

Murray County

Avoca Public School, Cole Ave. and 2nd St., Avoca, 10/16/79, A, 79003715

Chicago, Milwaukee, St. Paul, and Pacific Depot, St. Paul and Front Sts., Fulda, 10/16/79, A, 79003716

Chicago, St. Paul, Minneapolis, and Omaha Turntable, Co. Hwy. 38, Currie, 12/12/77, A, C, 77000758

Dinehart-Holt House [Murray County MRA], 2812 Linden Ave., Slayton, 12/07/82, C, 82000562

Murray County—Continued

First National Bank [Murray County MRA], 115 N. St. Paul Ave., Fulda, 12/07/82, C, 82000563

Lake Shetak State Park WPA/Rustic Style Group Camp [Minnesota State Park CCC/WPA/Rustic Style MPS], Off Co. Hwy. 37 on Lake Shetek, Murray and Shetek Townships, Currie vicinity, 7/02/92, A, C, 92000777

Nicollet County

Center Building—Minnesota Hospital for The Insane, Freeman Dr., St. Peter, 7/31/86, A, C, 86002117

Church of the Holy Communion—Episcopal, 116 N. Minnesota Ave., St. Peter, 5/19/83, A, C, 83000914

Cox, E. St. Julien, House, 500 N. Washington Ave., St. Peter, 11/20/70, B, C, b, 70000305

Donahower, Frederick A., House, 720 S. Minnesota Ave., St. Peter, 5/19/83, A, C, 83000915

Fort Ridgely, SR 4, Fairfax, 12/02/70, A, D, e, 70000304

Fort Ridgely State Park CCC/Rustic Style Historic Resources [Minnesota State Park CCC/WPA-/Rustic Style MPS], Off Co. Hwy. 30 NW of New Ulm, New Ulm vicinity, 10/25/89, A, C, 89001668

Harkin, Alexander, Store, Co. Hwy. 21, New Ulm vicinity, 6/04/73, B, 73000989

Johnson, John A., House, 418 N. 3rd St., St. Peter, 5/19/83, A, 83000916

Nicollet County Bank, 224 S. Minnesota Ave., St. Peter, 5/19/83, A, C, 83000917

Nicollet House Hotel, Minnesota Ave. at Park Row, St. Peter, 5/12/75, A, 75000998

Norseland General Store, Co. Hwy. 3, St. Peter vicinity, 5/19/83, A, 83000918

North Mankato Public School, 442 Belgrade Ave., North Mankato, 1/27/83, A, C, 83000919

Old Main—Gustavus Adolphus College, Gustavus Adolphus College campus, St. Peter, 5/12/76, A, C, 76001065

St. Peter Carnegie Library, 429 S. Minnesota Ave., St. Peter, 5/19/83, A, 83000920

St. Peter Central School, 300 S. 5th St., St. Peter, 10/29/80, A, C, 80002092

Stewart, William E., House, 733 Range St., North Mankato, 11/08/84, A, 84000223

Swift, Henry A., House, 820 S. Minnesota Ave., St. Peter, 5/19/83, A, 83000921

Traverse des Sioux, 2 mi. N of St. Peter off U.S. 169, St. Peter vicinity, 3/20/73, A, D, 73000990

Union Presbyterian Church, 311 W. Locust St., St. Peter, 5/19/83, C, a, 83000922

Nobles County

Adrian State Bank [Nobles County MRA], Main St. and 2nd Ave., Adrian, 5/15/80, A, C, 80002093

Church of St. Adrian—Catholic [Nobles County MRA], Main and Church Sts., Adrian, 5/15/80, C, a, 80002094

Citizens' National Bank, 326 10th St., Worthington, 3/18/82, A, C, 82002990

Hotel Thompson, 300-310 10th St., Worthington, 2/16/84, A, 84001625

Kilbride, Dr. E. A., Clinic [Nobles County MRA (AD)], 701 11th St., Worthington, 11/23/77, A, g, 77000760

Siemer Silo and Barn [Nobles County MRA], Co. Hwy. 19, Ellsworth vicinity, 5/15/80, A, g, 80002095

Sioux City and St. Paul Railroad Section House [Nobles County MRA], Spencer and 1st Sts., Dundee, 5/15/80, A, 80002096

Slade Hotel [Nobles County MRA (AD)], 2nd and Main Sts., Adrian, 6/30/75, A, C, 75000999

Norman County

Canning Site (21NR9), Address Restricted, Hendrum vicinity, 6/19/86, A, D, 86001358

Congregational Church of Ada, E. 2nd Ave. and 1st St., Ada, 11/08/84, C, a, 84000236

Norman County Courthouse, 3rd Ave., E. and 1st St., E., Ada, 5/09/83, A, C, 83000923

Olmsted County

Avalon Hotel, 301 N. Broadway, Rochester, 3/19/82, A, 82002992

Bush, John G., House, Center St., Dover, 7/02/80, B, C, 80004531

Chateau Dodge Theatre, 15 1st St., SW, Rochester, 7/17/80, A, C, 80002098

Coan House, 118 W. 5th St., Eyota, 7/02/80, C, 80004532

Eyota Farmers Cooperative Creamery Association, 222 Washington Ave., S., Eyota, 7/02/80, A, C, 80004533

Frank's Ford Bridge, CR 121 over S. Branch of Zumbro River, Oronoco vicinity, 7/08/80, A, C, 80004534

Krause, Christoph, Farmstead, Co. Hwy. 30, Dover vicinity, 10/10/80, C, 80002097

Mayo Clinic Buildings, 110 and 115 2nd Ave., Rochester, 8/04/69, A, NHL, 69000075

Mayo, Dr. William J., House, 701 4th St., SW, Rochester, 3/26/75, A, B, C, g, 75001001

Mayowood Historic District, Co. Hwy. 125, Rochester, 9/22/70, B, C, g, 70000306

Oronoco School, Co. Hwy. 18, Oronoco, 7/02/80, A, C, 80004536

Pierce House, 426 2nd Ave., SW, Rochester, 7/21/80, A, b, 80002101

Pill Hill Residential Historic District, Roughly bounded by 3rd and 9th Sts. and 7th and 10th Aves. SW, Rochester, 11/29/90, A, C, 85003768

Pleasant Grove Masonic Lodge, Off Co. Hwy. 1, Stewartville vicinity, 10/10/80, A, 80002102

Plummer, Henry S., House, 1091 Plummer Lane, Rochester, 5/21/75, B, C, 75001002

Rochester Armory, 121 N. Broadway, Rochester, 12/02/80, A, C, 80004268

Rochester Public Library, 226 2nd St., SW, Rochester, 7/02/80, C, g, 80004537

St. Mary's Hospital Dairy Farmstead, E of Rochester on Co. Hwy. 104, Rochester vicinity, 7/02/80, A, 80004538

Stopple, George, Farmstead, Co. Hwys. 25 and 122, Rochester vicinity, 5/12/75, A, C, 75001000

Toogood Barns, 16th St. SW of U.S. 63, Rochester, 6/26/75, B, C, 75001003

White, Milo, House, 122 Burr Oak St., Chatfield, 3/19/82, B, C, 82002991

Whiting, Timothy A., House, 225 1st Ave., NW, Rochester, 12/04/80, B, C, b, 80004269

Otter Tail County

Barnard Mortuary, 119 N. Union Ave., Fergus Falls, 8/13/86, C, 86001538

Blyberg, O. A. E., House, 22 5th Ave., SW, Pelican Rapids, 2/16/84, B, C, 84001631

Clement, C. C., House, 608 N. Burlington Ave., Fergus Falls, 8/13/86, C, 86001485

District School No. 182 [Federal Relief Construction in Minnesota MPS], Off Co. Hwy. 35, Sverdrup Township, Underwood vicinity, 8/09/91, C, 91000978

Elizabeth Village Hall and Jail, Broadway Ave., Elizabeth, 2/16/84, A, C, 84001634

Fergus Falls City Hall, 112 W. Washington Ave., Fergus Falls, 5/10/84, A, C, 84001635

Fergus Falls State Hospital Complex, MN 297, Fergus Falls, 6/26/86, C, 86001386

Hotel Kaddatz, 111-113 W. Lincoln Ave., Fergus Falls, 2/24/83, A, C, 83000924

Maplewood Site, Address Restricted, Pelican Rapids vicinity, 12/18/78, D, 78001555

Mason, John W., House, 205 W. Vernon Ave., Fergus Falls, 8/13/86, B, 86001533

Morrison Mounds, Address Restricted, Battle Lake vicinity, 6/04/73, D, 73000991

Orwell Site, Address Restricted, Fergus Falls vicinity, 12/04/74, D, 74001032

Otter Tail County Courthouse, Court St. at Junius Ave., Fergus Falls, 5/10/84, A, C, 84001637

Park Region Luther College, 715 W. Vernon Ave., Fergus Falls, 11/08/84, C, a, 84000241

Perham Village Hall and Fire Station, 153 E. Main, Perham, 7/31/86, A, C, 86002122

Phelps Mill, Co. Hwy. 45, Underwood vicinity, 2/24/75, A, B, 75002145

Phelps Mill Historic District, Co. Hwy. 45, Underwood vicinity, 5/10/84, A, 84001640

River Inn, 133 Mill St., South, Fergus Falls, 12/20/88, A, C, 88002831

Wright, C. J., House, 831 Mount Faith Ave., E., Fergus Falls, 11/30/78, C, 78001554

Pennington County

Red River Trail: Goose Lake Swamp Section [Minnesota Red River Trails MPS], Off Co. Hwy. 10,

Pennington County—Continued

S of Goose Lake Swamp, Polk Centre Twp., St. Hilaire vicinity, 2/06/91, A, 90002202

Thief River Falls Public Library, 102 N. Main Ave., Thief River Falls, 10/06/83, C, 83003763

Pine County

Bethlehem Lutheran Church [Pine County MRA], Kirke Alle, Askov, 8/18/80, A, C, a, 80002103

Cloverton School [Pine County MRA], CR 32, Askov vicinity, 8/18/80, A, 80002104

District School No. 74, Co. Hwy. 22 N of Co. Hwy. 30, Danforth Township, Sandstone vicinity, 6/25/92, A, 92000820

Doboszenski, John, Farmstead [Pine County MRA], Off Co. Hwy. 43, Willow River vicinity, 8/18/80, A, 80002105

Hinckley Fire Relief House [Pine County MRA], Court Ave. and 6th St., Sandstone, 8/18/80, A, 80002112

Hultgren, Louis, House and Sand Pit [Pine County MRA], MN 23, Kerrick, 8/18/80, A, B, 80002108

Kettle River Sandstone Company Quarry, N of MN 123 on W bank of Kettle R., Sandstone Twp., Sandstone, 7/18/91, A, 91000877

Kilstofte, Peter P., Farmstead [Pine County MRA], Co. Hwy. 33, Askov, 8/18/80, A, B, C, 80002109

Minneapolis Trust Company Commercial Building [Pine County MRA], Main and 4th Sts., Sandstone, 8/18/80, A, B, 80002113

Northern Pacific Depot, Old U.S. 61 and 1st St., SE, Hinckley, 5/07/73, A, e, 73000992

Northern Pacific Depot [Pine County MRA], Front St. at Finland Ave., Finlayson, 8/18/80, A, 80002107

Northwest Company Post, On the Snake River, W of Pine City, Pine City vicinity, 8/07/72, A, C, e, g, 72000679

Oldenburg, John A., House, MN 18, Finlayson, 12/13/78, B, C, 78001556

Partridge Township Hall [Pine County MRA], Kobmagergade, Askov, 8/18/80, A, b, 80002110

Pine City Naval Militia Armory [Pine County MRA], 1st Ave., Pine City, 8/18/80, A, g, 80002111

Red Clover Land Company Demonstration Farm [Pine County MRA], Off CR 32, Askov vicinity, 8/18/80, A, 80002106

Sandstone School, Commercial Ave. between 5th and 6th Sts., Sandstone, 2/07/79, C, 79001251

Schwyzer, Arnold, Summer House and Farmstead [Pine County MRA], CR 17, Sandstone vicinity, 8/18/80, A, 80002114

Stumne Mounds, Address Restricted, Pine City vicinity, 6/20/72, D, 72000680

Willow River Rutabaga Warehouse and Processing Plant, Off Co. Hwy. 61, Willow River, 6/21/90, A, 90000935

Pipestone County

Bauman Hall [Pipestone County MRA], 201 W. Wall St., Jasper, 3/03/80, A, b, 80002116

Calumet Hotel [Pipestone County MRA (AD)], 104 S. Hiawatha, Pipestone, 3/16/76, A, C, 76001066

Gerber Hospital and Garage [Pipestone County MRA], 120 E. Wall St., Jasper, 3/03/80, C, 80002119

Ihlen Mercantile Company [Pipestone County MRA], Holman St. and Sherman Ave., Ihlen, 3/03/80, C, 80002115

Pipestone Commercial Historic District [Pipestone County MRA (AD)], Along Main St. between 2nd Ave. N.W./S.W. and 2nd Ave. N.E./S.E., Pipestone, 5/02/77, C, 77000761

Pipestone County Courthouse [Pipestone County MRA], 3rd St., Pipestone, 3/03/80, C, 80002121

Pipestone Indian School Superintendent's House, Off N. Hiawatha Ave., Pipestone, 4/05/93, A, 93000232

Pipestone National Monument [Pipestone County MRA (AD)], Off Hiawatha Ave., Pipestone vicinity, 10/15/66, C, D, NPS, 66000112

Pipestone Public Library [Pipestone County MRA], 3rd St., SE and S. Hiawatha Ave., Pipestone, 3/03/80, A, C, 80002122

Pipestone Water Tower [Pipestone County MRA], 2nd St., NE, Pipestone, 3/03/80, C, 80002123

Rock Island Depot [Pipestone County MRA], 400 N. Hiawatha Ave., Pipestone, 3/03/80, A, 80002124

Rowe, John, House [Pipestone County MRA], 200 E. 2nd St., Jasper, 3/03/80, C, 80002118

Stordahl Building [Pipestone County MRA], 119 W. Wall St., Jasper, 3/03/80, A, C, 80002120

Polk County

Church of St. Peter—Catholic, Off US 2, Crookston vicinity, 8/19/82, C, a, 82002994

Crookston Carnegie Public Library, N. Ash St. at 2nd Ave., Crookston, 5/10/84, C, 84001646

Crookston Commercial Historic District, Roughly Main St. and Broadway between Fletcher and W. 2nd St., Crookston, 11/23/84, A, C, 84002709

Davis, E. C., House, 406 Grant St., Crookston, 5/10/84, B, C, 84001648

Hamm Brewing Company Beer Depot, 401 DeMers Ave., East Grand Forks, 9/20/84, A, 84001651

Pope County

Fremad Association Building [Pope County MRA], 2–22 S. Franklin, Glenwood, 4/01/82, A, C, 82002995

Glenwood Public Library [Pope County MRA], 108 1st Ave., Glenwood, 4/01/82, A, C, 82002996

Iverson, Urjans, House, Off MN 104, Sedan vicinity, 2/11/82, A, a, 82003001

Minnewaska Hospital [Pope County MRA], Wollan and 5th Sts., Starbuck, 4/01/82, B, 82003002

Northern Pacific Depot, Off Washington Ave., Villard, 10/06/83, A, 83003760

Pennie, Daniel, House [Pope County MRA], Co. Hwy. 27, Villard vicinity, 4/01/82, A, C, 82003003

Pope County Courthouse [Pope County MRA], E. Minnesota St., Glenwood, 4/01/82, A, C, 82002997

Sunset Beach Hotel, Co. Hwy. 17, Glenwood vicinity, 2/11/82, A, 82002998

Terrace Historic District [Pope County MRA], Off MN 104, Sedan vicinity, 4/01/82, A, 82002999

Terrace Mill Historic District [Pope County MRA], Off MN 104, Sedan vicinity, 7/17/79, A, C, 79001252

Ramsey County

Arlington Hills Library [Carnegie Libraries of St. Paul TR], 1105 Greenbrier St., St. Paul, 2/10/84, A, C, 84001660

Armstrong, John M., House, 233-235 W. 5th St., St. Paul, 1/27/83, C, 83000925

Assumption School, 68 Exchange St., St. Paul, 3/26/75, A, C, a, 75001005

Beebe, Dr. Ward, House, 2022 Summit Ave., St. Paul, 8/29/77, C, 77000762

Blair Flats, 165 Western Ave., St. Paul, 7/18/75, B, C, 75001006

Bridges No. L-5853 and 92247 [Reinforced-Concrete Highway Bridges in Minnesota MPS], Lexington Ave. in Como Park, St. Paul, 11/06/89, C, 89001842

Brunson, Benjamin, House, 485 Kenny Rd., St. Paul, 5/12/75, B, C, 75001007

Burbank-Livingston-Griggs House, 432 Summit Ave., St. Paul, 10/15/70, C, 70000307

Butler, Pierce and Walter, House, 1345-1347 Summit Ave., St. Paul, 4/22/82, B, C, 82004625

C.S.P.S. Hall, 381–383 Michigan St., St. Paul, 2/17/77, A, 77000763

Central Presbyterian Church, 500 Cedar St., St. Paul, 2/10/83, C, 83000926

Church of St. Agnes—Catholic, 548 Lafond Ave., St. Paul, 11/19/80, A, C, a, 80002125

Church of St. Bernard—Catholic, 197 W. Geranium Ave., St. Paul, 2/24/83, B, C, a, 83000927

Church of St. Casimir—Catholic, 937 E. Jessamine Ave., St. Paul, 3/31/83, A, C, a, 83000939

Church of the Assumption—Catholic, 51 W. 9th St., St. Paul, 2/10/75, A, C, a, 75001008

Cobb, Cyrus B., House, 2199 1st St., White Bear Lake, 4/14/83, C, 83000928

Colorado Street Bridge [Minnesota Masonry-Arch Highway Bridges MPS], E side of S. Wabasha St. near Terrace Park, St. Paul, 7/05/90, C, 90000977

Como Park Conservatory, Como Park, St. Paul, 11/19/74, A, C, 74001033

Dahl, William, House, 136 13th St., St. Paul, 8/29/78, B, C, 78001557

Ramsey County—Continued

Davern, William and Catherine, Farm House, 1173 S. Davern St., St. Paul, 10/06/83, C, 83003765

Derham Hall and Our Lady of Victory Chapel, College of St. Catherine, 2004 Randolph Ave., St. Paul, 10/31/85, A, C, a, 85003423

Finch, Vanslyck and McConville Dry Goods Company Building, 366 Wacouta St., St. Paul, 2/01/82, A, C, 82004626

First Baptist Church of St. Paul, 499 Wacouta St., St. Paul, 2/24/83, A, C, a, 83000929

First National Bank of White Bear, 4744 Washington Ave., White Bear Lake, 2/24/83, A, C, 83000930

Fitzgerald, F. Scott, House, 599 Summit Ave., St. Paul, 11/11/71, B, NHL, 71000440

Fitzpatrick Building, 465–467 N. Wabasha St., St. Paul, 7/19/90, C, 90001113

Foss House, 321 Silver Lake Rd., New Brighton, 5/19/83, A, C, 83000931

Germania Bank Building, 6 W. 5th St., St. Paul, 12/06/77, C, 77000764

Gibbs, Heman, Farmstead, 2097 Larpentuer Ave., Falcon Heights, 4/23/75, A, b, 75001009

Giesen-Hauser House, 827 Mound St., St. Paul, 5/19/83, A, C, 83000932

Hall, S. Edward, House, 996 Iglehart Ave., St. Paul, 4/16/91, B, 91000440

Harriet Island Pavilion, 75 Water St., St. Paul, 7/10/92, C, 92000821

Highland Park Tower, 1570 Highland Pkwy., St. Paul, 7/17/86, C, 86001670

Hill, James J., House, 240 Summit Ave., St. Paul, 10/15/66, B, a, NHL, 66000405

Hinkel, Jacob, House, 531 Brainerd Ave., St. Paul, 1/03/78, C, 78001558

Historic Hill District, Irregular pattern from Pleasant and Grand Aves. to Holly and Marshall Aves., from Lexington Pkwy. to 4th and Pleasant, St. Paul, 8/13/76, C, a, 76001067

Hobe, E. H., House-Solheim, 5590 W. Bald Eagle Blvd., White Bear Lake, 5/19/83, B, C, g, 83000933

Holman Field Administration Building, 644 Bayfield St., St. Paul, 8/15/91, A, C, 91001004

Intercity Bridge [Reinforced-Concrete Highway Bridges in Minnesota MPS], Ford Pkwy. over Mississippi River, St. Paul, 11/06/89, C, 89001838

Irvine Park Historic District, Roughly bounded by Irvine Park, W. 7th, Walnut, and Sherman, St. Paul, 11/27/73, B, C, a, b, 73000993

Irvine, Horace Hills, House, 1006 Summit Ave., St. Paul, 12/16/74, A, C, 74001034

Kellogg, Frank B., House, 633 Fairmount Ave., St. Paul, 11/06/74, B, C, NHL, 74001035

Krank Manufacturing Company, 1855 W. University Ave., St. Paul, 2/24/83, A, C, 83000934

Lauer Flats, 226 Western Ave., St. Paul, 6/05/75, C, 75001010

Lee, Olaf, House, 955 N. Jessie St., St. Paul, 2/16/84, C, 84001670

Lowertown Historic Distruct, Roughly bound by Kellogg Blvd., Broadway, 7th and Jackson Sts., St. Paul, 2/21/83, A, C, 83000935

Luckert, David, House, 480 Iglehart St., St. Paul, 5/12/75, B, C, 75001011

Manhattan Building, 360 N. Robert St., St. Paul, 6/22/88, A, B, C, 88001128

McGill, Andrew R., House, 2203 Scudder Ave., St. Paul, 12/31/74, B, C, 74001037

Mendota Road Bridge [Minnesota Masonry-Arch Highway Bridges MPS], Water St. over Pickerel Lake Outlet, St. Paul, 11/06/89, C, 89001825

Merchants National Bank, 366–368 Jackson St., St. Paul, 12/19/74, A, B, C, 74001036

Mickey's Diner, 36 W. 9th St., St. Paul, 2/24/83, C, 83000936

Minnesota Boat Club Boathouse on Raspberry Island, 1 S. Wabasha St., St. Paul, 2/04/82, A, 82004627

Minnesota Historical Society Building, 690 Cedar St., St. Paul, 3/20/73, A, C, 73000994

Minnesota State Capitol, Aurora Between Cedar and Park Sts., St. Paul, 2/23/72, B, C, 72000681

Muench, Adolf, House, 653 E. 5th St., St. Paul, 5/12/75, B, C, 75001012

Northern Pacific Railway Company Como Shops Historic District, Energy Park Dr. and Bandanna Blvd., St. Paul, 3/31/83, A, C, 83000937

Norway Lutheran Church, 2375 Como Ave., W., St. Paul, 5/12/75, A, C, a, b, e, 75001013

Noyes, Charles P., Cottage, 4735 Lake Ave., White Bear Lake, 12/12/76, C, 76001070

Old Federal Courts Building, 109 W. 5th St., St. Paul, 3/24/69, C, 69000076

Old Main, Macalester College, 1600 Grand Ave., St. Paul, 8/16/77, A, C, 77000765

Pilgrim Baptist Church, 732 W. Central Ave., St. Paul, 4/16/91, A, B, a, 91000438

Pioneer and Endicott Buildings, 4th and Robert Sts., St. Paul, 7/10/74, A, C, 74001038

Ramsey County Poor Farm Barn, 2020 White Bear Ave., St. Paul, 9/22/77, A, 77000766

Ramsey, Alexander, House, 265 S. Exchange St., St. Paul, 11/25/69, B, C, 69000077

Ramsey, Justus, Stone House, 252 W. 7th St., St. Paul, 5/06/75, C, 75001014

Rau/Strong House, 2 George St., St. Paul, 6/18/75, C, 75001015

Riverview Branch Library [Carnegie Libraries of St. Paul TR], 1 E. George St., St. Paul, 2/10/84, A, C, 84001672

Robert Street Bridge [Reinforced-Concrete Highway Bridges in Minnesota MPS], Robert St. over Mississippi River, St. Paul, 11/06/89, C, 89001846

Rochat-Louise-Sauerwein Block, 261–277 W. 7th St., St. Paul, 11/19/80, A, C, 80002126

Salvation Army Women's Home and Hospital, 1471 W. Como Ave., St. Paul, 2/10/83, A, C, 83000938

Schneider, Charles W., House, 1750 E. Ames Pl., St. Paul, 2/16/84, C, 84001677

Schornstein Grocery and Saloon, 707 E. Wilson Ave. and 223 N. Bates Ave., St. Paul, 8/21/84, C, 84001681

Seventh Street Improvement Arches [Minnesota Masonry-Arch Highway Bridges MPS], E. 7th St. over Burlington Northern right-of-way, St. Paul vicinity, 11/06/89, C, 89001828

Spangenberg, Frederick, House, 375 Mt. Curve Blvd., St. Paul, 6/22/76, C, 76001068

St. Agatha's Conservatory of Music and Arts, 26 E. Exchange St., St. Paul, 5/25/89, A, a, 89000443

St. Anthony Park Branch Library [Carnegie Libraries of St. Paul TR], 2245 W. Como Ave., St. Paul, 2/10/84, A, C, 84001675

St. Joseph's Academy, 355 Marshall Ave., St. Paul, 6/05/75, A, C, a, 75001016

St. Matthew's School, 7 W. Robie St., St. Paul, 11/08/84, C, a, 84000243

St. Paul Cathedral—Catholic, Summit Ave. at Shelby Ave., St. Paul, 6/28/74, A, C, a, 74001039

St. Paul City Hall and Ramsey County Courthouse, 15 W. Kellogg Blvd., St. Paul, 2/11/83, A, C, 83000940

St. Paul Public/James J. Hill Reference Library, 80–90 W. 4th St., St. Paul, 9/11/75, A, C, 75001017

St. Paul Union Depot, 214 E. 4th St., St. Paul, 12/18/74, A, B, C, 74001040

St. Paul Women's City Club, 305 St. Peter St., St. Paul, 3/19/82, C, 82004628

St. Paul, Minneapolis, & Manitoba Railway Company Shops Historic District, Jackson St. and Pennsylvania Ave., St. Paul, 12/21/87, A, B, C, 86003564

Triune Masonic Temple, 1898 Iglehart Ave., St. Paul, 11/13/80, A, C, 80002127

United Church Seminary, 2481 Como Ave., St. Paul, 10/31/85, A, C, a, 85003437

University Hall-Old Main, Hamline University, 1536 Hewitt Ave., St. Paul, 9/22/77, C, 77000767

Vienna and Earl Apartment Buildings, 682-688 Holly Ave., St. Paul, 4/10/84, C, 84001685

Wabasha Street Bridge [Iron and Steel Bridges in Minnesota MPS], Wabasha St. over Mississippi River, St. Paul, 11/06/89, C, 89001834

Walsh Building, 189–191 E. 7th St., St. Paul, 5/25/89, C, 89000444

West Summit Avenue Historic District, Summit Ave. between Lexington Pkwy. and Mississippi R. Blvd., St. Paul, 5/04/93, A, C, 93000332

Woodland Park District, Roughly bounded by Marshall and Selby Aves., Arundel and Dale Sts., St. Paul, 5/12/78, C, 78001559

Yoerg, Anthony, Sr., House, 215 W. Isabel St., St. Paul, 5/25/89, B, C, 89000442

Red Lake County

Red Lake County Courthouse, Main Ave., Red Lake Falls, 5/09/83, A, C, 83000941

Redwood County

Anderson, J. A., House [Redwood County MRA], 402 4th Ave., Lamberton, 8/11/80, C, 80002132

Redwood County—Continued

Bank of Redwood Falls Building [Redwood County MRA], 2nd St., Redwood Falls, 8/11/80, A, C, 80002141

Birch Coulee School, Off Co. Hwy. 2, S of Morton, Morton vicinity, 4/12/90, A, 90000554

Chicago and North Western Railroad Depot [Redwood County MRA], 1st St., Lucan, 8/11/80, A, b, 80002135

Chollar, H. D., House [Redwood County MRA], 4th and Minnesota Sts., Redwood Falls, 8/11/80, A, C, 80002142

City Blacksmith Shop [Redwood County MRA], Douglas St. and 2nd Ave., Lamberton, 8/11/80, A, 80002133

Clements State Bank Building [Redwood County MRA], 1st and Pine Sts., Clements, 8/11/80, 80002130

Commercial Hotel [Redwood County MRA], Front and Main Sts., Wabasso, 8/11/80, A, 80002146

Delhi Coronet Band Hall, 3rd St., Delhi, 5/17/84, A, 84001687

District School No. 8 [Redwood County MRA], CR 70, Clements vicinity, 8/11/80, A, 80002131

Gilfillan [Redwood County MRA], MN 67, Redwood Falls vicinity, 8/11/80, A, B, 80002143

Gimmestad Land and Loan Office [Redwood County MRA], Main St., Belview, 8/11/80, A, 80002128

Honnor-Hosken House [Redwood County MRA], North and Main Sts., North Redwood, 8/11/80, B, 80002138

Lower Sioux Agency, Address Restricted, Morton vicinity, 9/22/70, A, 70000308

Milroy Block [Redwood County MRA], Euclid Ave. and Cherry St., Milroy, 8/11/80, A, 80002136

Milroy State Bank Building [Redwood County MRA], Superior St. and Euclid Ave., Milroy, 8/11/80, A, 80002137

Minneapolis and St. Louis Railroad Depot [Redwood County MRA], Off Main St., Belview, 8/11/80, A, b, 80002129

Odeon Theater, Main St., Belview, 8/30/74, A, C, 74001041

Ramsey Park Swayback Bridge [Redwood County MRA], Ramsey Park, Redwood Falls, 8/11/80, C, g, 80002144

Redwood Falls Carnegie Library [Redwood County MRA], 334 S. Jefferson St., Redwood Falls, 8/11/80, A, 80002139

Revere Fire Hall [Redwood County MRA], 2nd St., Revere, 8/11/80, C, 80002145

Scenic City Cooperative Oil Company [Redwood County MRA], 2nd and Mill Sts., Redwood Falls, 8/11/80, A, 80002140

St. Cornelia's Episcopal Church, Off Co. Hwy. 2, Morton vicinity, 10/11/79, A, C, a, 79003717

Renville County

Birch Coulee, Off Co. Hwys. 18 and 2, Morton vicinity, 6/04/73, A, 73000995

Brown, Joseph, House Ruins, CR 15, Sacred Heart vicinity, 8/03/86, A, 86002838

Minneapolis and St. Louis Depot, Park St. and Second Ave. S, Fairfax, 7/24/86, A, 86001921

Renville County Courthouse and Jail, DePue Ave. E and Fifth St. S, Olivia, 6/13/86, A, C, 86001281

Rudi, Lars, House, CR 15, Sacred Heart vicinity, 7/24/86, B, 86001924

Rice County

Administration Building—Girls' Dormitory, Minnesota School for the Deaf, MN 299, Faribault, 11/06/86, C, 86003095

All Saints Church—Episcopal [Rice County MRA], Washington and 5th Sts., Northfield, 4/06/82, A, C, a, 82003027

Allen, W. Roby, Oral Home School, 525 5th St. NE., Faribault, 7/12/90, A, B, 90001091

Archibald Mill, Railway St., Dundas, 10/08/76, A, B, 76001071

Archibald, Edward T., House, Hamilton and 2nd Sts., Dundas, 6/17/76, B, 76001072

Ault Store [Rice County MRA], 2nd St., Dundas, 4/06/82, A, 82003004

Baker, Laura, School, 211 Oak St., Northfield, 3/29/78, B, C, 78001560

Batchelder's Block, 120 Central Ave. N., Faribault, 7/12/90, A, C, 90001089

Berry, Frank A., and Elizabeth, House [Architecture of Olof Hanson MPS], 319 3rd St. NW, Faribault, 8/09/90, C, 90001172

Blind Department Building and Dow Hall, State School for the Blind, 400 6th Ave. SE., Faribault, 7/25/90, A, b, 90001092

Bonde Farmhouse [Rice County MRA], CR 27 and MI Hwy. 246, Nerstrand vicinity, 4/06/82, B, C, 82003023

Buck, Cassius, House [Rice County MRA], 124 1st Ave., SW, Faribault, 4/06/82, B, C, 82003007

Buckham, Thomas Scott, Memorial Library [Rice County MRA], Central Ave. and Division St., Faribault, 4/06/82, A, C, 82003008

Carufel, Louis, and E. LaRose, House, 425 3rd St. SW, Faribault, 8/03/90, C, 90001160

Cathedral of Our Merciful Saviour, 515 2nd Ave., NW, Faribault, 8/10/79, A, C, a, 79001253

Cathedral of Our Merciful Saviour and Guild House (Boundary Increase), 515 2nd Ave., NW, Faribault, 2/19/82, A, B, C, a, 82003009

Chapel of the Good Sheperd, At Shattuck School, Faribault, 4/04/75, A, C, a, 75001018

Church of St. Patrick—Catholic [Rice County MRA], MN 21, Faribault vicinity, 4/06/82, A, a, 82003032

Church of the Annunciation—Catholic [Rice County MRA], Co. Hwy. 46, Northfield vicinity, 4/06/82, A, C, a, 82003033

Church of the Holy Cross—Episcopal [Rice County MRA], 2nd St., Dundas, 4/06/82, A, C, a, 82003005

Cole, Gordon, and Kate D. Turner, House, 111 2nd St. NW, Faribault, 8/03/90, C, 90001150

Congregational Church of Faribault, 227 3rd St., NW, Faribault, 5/12/77, A, C, a, 77000768

Cottrell, John N. and Elizabeth Taylor Clinton, House, 127 1st St. NW, Faribault, 8/03/90, C, 90001163

Dobbin, Reverend James, House, 1800 14th St. NE., Faribault, 7/23/90, C, 90001090

Drake, Edwin S., Farmhouse [Rice County MRA], Co. Hwy. 22, Northfield vicinity, 4/06/82, A, B, C, 82003028

Dump Road Bridge [Iron and Steel Bridges in Minnesota MPS], Twp. Rd. 45 over Straight River, Faribault vicinity, 11/06/89, A, C, 89001835

Episcopal Rectory [Architecture of Olof Hanson MPS], 112 6th St. NW, Faribault, 8/09/90, C, 90001171

Faribault City Hall [Rice County MRA], 208 1st Ave., NW, Faribault, 4/06/82, A, C, 82003010

Faribault Historic Commercial District [Rice County MRA], Central Ave, 2nd and 3rd Sts., Faribault, 4/06/82, A, C, 82003011

Faribault Viaduct [Reinforced-Concrete Highway Bridges in Minnesota MPS], Division St. over Straight River, Faribault, 11/06/89, A, C, 89001848

Faribault Water Works [Rice County MRA], 7th St., NW, Faribault, 4/06/82, A, g, 82003012

Faribault, Alexander, House, 12 1st Ave., NE, Faribault, 9/22/70, B, C, 70000309

Farmer Seed and Nursery Company [Rice County MRA], 818 4th St., NW, Faribault, 4/06/82, A, 82003013

Goodsell Observatory—Carlton College, Off 1st St., E., Northfield, 5/12/75, A, B, C, 75001025

Holman, M. P., House, 107 3rd Ave. NW, Faribault, 8/03/90, C, 90001162

Hospital, State School for the Feeble Minded [Rice County MRA], Off 6th Ave., SE, Faribault, 4/06/82, A, B, 82003014

Hutchinson, John, House [Rice County MRA], 305 2nd St., NW, Faribault, 4/06/82, B, C, 82003015

Johnston Hall—Seabury Divinity School, 1st and State Sts., SE, Faribault, 3/21/75, A, B, C, 75001022

Lieb, Vincent and Elizabeth, House, 201 4th Ave. SW., Faribault, 7/23/90, C, 90001093

Lonsdale Public School, 3rd Ave., SW, Lonsdale, 8/30/79, A, C, 79001254

Lord, Drew H., House [Rice County MRA], 201 E. 3rd, Northfield, 4/06/82, B, C, 82003029

Martin, Wiliam, House [Rice County MRA], Bridge and 1st Sts., Dundas, 4/06/82, A, C, 82003006

McCall, Cormack, House, 817 Ravine St. NE, Faribault, 8/03/90, B, C, 90001149

McCall, Thomas, House, 102 4th Ave. SW, Faribault, 8/03/90, B, C, 90001159

McCarthy, Timothy J., Building, 24 3rd St. NW, Faribault, 8/03/90, C, 90001161

McMahon, Thomas Bridget Shanahan, House, 603 Division St., E., Faribault, 7/19/90, C, 90001112

Nerstrand City Hall [Rice County MRA], Main St., Nerstrand, 4/06/82, A, 82003024

Rice County—Continued

Northfield Historic District, Roughly bounded by Water, Division, 3rd and 5th Sts., Northfield, 6/11/79, A, C, 79003125

Noyes Hall, State School for the Deaf, Off 6th Ave., NE, Faribault, 5/12/75, A, C, 75001020

Noyes, Jonathon L. and Elizabeth H. Wadsworth, House [Architecture of Olof Hanson MPS], 105 1st Ave. NW, Faribault, 8/09/90, C, 90001170

Nutting, John C., House [Rice County MRA (AD)], 217 Union St., Northfield, 10/15/70, C, 70000310

Old Main, St. Olaf College, St. Olaf College campus, Northfield, 6/03/76, A, C, a, 76001073

Osmund Osmundson House [Rice County MRA], E. Nerstrand, N. Main Sts., Nerstrand, 4/06/82, B, 82003025

Pfeiffer, John Gottlieb, House, 931 3rd Ave. NW, Faribault, 8/03/90, B, C, 90001151

Phelps Library, Shattuck School, Off Shumway Ave., Faribault, 4/04/75, A, B, C, 75001021

Rice County Courthouse and Jail [Rice County MRA], 3rd St. and 2nd Ave., NW, Faribault, 4/06/82, A, C, g, 82003016

Rock Island Depot [Rice County MRA], 3rd St. and 1st Ave., NE, Faribault, 4/06/82, A, C, 82003017

Rolvaag, O. E., House, 311 Manitou St., Northfield, 8/04/69, B, NHL, 69000078

Sciver Block Building, Bridge Sq. and Division St., Northfield, 5/05/78, A, 78001561

Scoville Memorial Library—Carlton College [Rice County MRA], 1st St., E. and College St., Northfield, 4/06/82, A, C, 82003030

Shattuck Historic District [Rice County MRA], Shumway Ave., Faribault, 4/06/82, A, C, 82003018

Shumway Hall and Morgan Refectory—Shattuck School, Off Shumway Ave., Faribault, 4/04/75, A, C, 75001023

Skinner Memorial Chapel [Rice County MRA], 1st, Winona, and College Sts., Northfield, 4/06/82, A, C, a, 82003031

St. Mary's Hall [Rice County MRA], 4th St., NE and 4th Ave. NE, Faribault, 4/06/82, A, C, 82003019

Steensland Library—St. Olaf College [Rice County MRA], Off St. Olaf Ave., Northfield, 4/06/82, A, C, 82003020

Theopold Mercantile Co. Wholesale Grocery Building [Rice County MRA], 1st Ave. and 3rd St., NE, Faribault, 4/06/82, A, 82003021

Valley Grove [Rice County MRA], CR 29 off MI Hwy. 246, Nerstrand vicinity, 4/06/82, A, C, a, 82003026

Veblen Farmstead, NE of Nerstrand off MN 246, Nerstrand vicinity, 6/30/75, B, NHL, 75001024

Weyer, Adam, Wagon Shop, 32 2nd St. NE., Faribault, 7/12/90, A, 90001088

Willis Hall—Carlton College, College St., Northfield, 6/13/75, A, C, 75001026

Wilson, Hudson, House [Rice County MRA], 104 1st Ave., NW, Faribault, 4/06/82, B, C, 82003022

Rock County

Blue Mounds State Park WPA/Rustic Style Historic Resources [Minnesota State Park CCC/WPA/Rustic Style MPS], Off US 75 N of Luverne, Luverne vicinity, 10/25/89, A, C, g, 89001657

Bridge No. 1482 [Iron and Steel Bridges in Minnesota MPS], Off US 75 S of Luverne, Schoneman Park, Luverne Township, Luverne vicinity, 6/25/92, C, b, 92000775

Bridge No. L-2162 [Reinforced-Concrete Highway Bridges in Minnesota MPS], Co. Rd. 51 over Split Rock Creek, Jasper vicinity, 11/06/89, C, 89001839

Bridge No. L-2315 [Reinforced-Concrete Highway Bridges in Minnesota MPS], Twp. Rd. 89 over Rock River, Luverne vicinity, 11/06/89, C, 89001841

Bridge No. L-2316 [Reinforced-Concrete Highway Bridges in Minnesota MPS], Twp. Rd. 89 over Rock River, Luverne vicinity, 11/06/89, C, 89001843

Bridge No. L-4646 [Reinforced-Concrete Highway Bridges in Minnesota MPS], Sixth St. over Spring Brook, Beaver Creek, 11/06/89, C, 89001844

First National Bank of Beaver Creek [Rock County MRA], 1st Ave., Beaver Creek, 3/18/80, A, C, 80002148

Gerber, J. W., House [Rock County MRA], 324 W. Main St., Luverne, 3/18/80, A, C, 80002151

Hinkly, R. B., House, 217 N. Freeman Ave., Luverne, 6/10/75, C, 75001027

Holy Trinity Church—Episcopal [Rock County MRA], N. Cedar and E. Luverne Sts., Luverne, 3/18/80, A, C, a, 80002152

Jasper Stone Company and Quarry, Off Sherman Ave., Jasper, 1/05/78, A, 78001562

Kenneth School [Rock County MRA], 230 W. 1st Ave., Kenneth, 3/18/80, A, 80002150

Kniss, Pierce J., House [Rock County MRA], 209 N. Estey St., Luverne, 3/18/80, B, C, 80002153

Luverne Carnegie Library [Rock County MRA], 205 N. Freeman Ave., Luverne, 3/18/80, A, 80002154

Maplewood Chapel [Rock County MRA], W. Warren St., Luverne, 3/18/80, C, a, 80002155

Nuffer, Jacob, Farmstead [Rock County MRA], CR 53 and 57, Hills vicinity, 3/18/80, A, C, g, 80002149

Omaha Depot [Rock County MRA], E. Fletcher St., Luverne, 3/18/80, A, 80002156

Palace Theater [Rock County MRA], Main St. and Freeman Ave., Luverne, 3/18/80, A, C, 80002157

Rock County Courthouse and Jail, Cedar St., N. and Luverne St., E., Luverne, 4/18/77, C, 77000769

Roseau County

Canadian National Depot, Main St., Warroad, 4/06/82, A, 82003034

Roseau County Courthouse, 216 Center St., W., Roseau, 8/15/85, A, 85001763

Scott County

Bisson, Abraham, House [Scott County MRA], CR 57, Jordan vicinity, 4/17/80, C, 80002164

Bridge No. L3040 [Minnesota Masonry-Arch Highway Bridges MPS], Co. Rd. 51, N of MN 19, Belle Plain vicinity, 11/06/89, C, 89001829

Church of St. Wenceslaus—Catholic, E. Main St., New Prague, 2/19/82, A, a, 82003035

Coller, Julius A., House [Scott County MRA], 434 S. Lewis St., Shakopee, 4/17/80, B, C, 80002168

Early Shakopee Houses [Scott County MRA], 411 and 419 E. 2nd Ave., Shakopee, 4/17/80, A, C, 80002169

Episcopal Church of the Transfiguration [Scott County MRA], Walnut and Church Sts., Belle Plaine, 4/17/80, C, a, 80002159

Foss and Wells House [Scott County MRA], 613 S. Broadway St., Jordan, 4/17/80, B, C, 80002161

Hooper-Bowler-Hillstrom House [Scott County MRA], Court and Cedar Sts., Belle Plaine, 4/17/80, B, C, 80002160

Jordan Brewery Ruins [Scott County MRA], S. Broadway St., Jordan, 4/17/80, A, C, 80002162

Jordan Historic District [Scott County MRA], Water St. and S. Broadway, Jordan, 4/17/80, A, C, 80002163

Kajer, Wencl, Farmstead [Scott County MRA], Co. Hwy. 2, New Market vicinity, 4/17/80, A, C, 80002166

Mudbaden Sulphur Springs Company [Scott County MRA], Co. Hwy. 63, Jordan vicinity, 4/17/80, A, 80002165

New Market Hotel and Store [Scott County MRA], Main St., New Market, 4/17/80, A, C, 80002167

Roehl—Lenzmeier House [Scott County MRA], MN 300, Shakopee vicinity, 4/17/80, B, C, 80002170

Shakopee Historic District [Scott County MRA (AD)], MN 101, Shakopee, 4/11/72, A, C, b, 72000682

St. Mary's Church of the Purification—Catholic [Scott County MRA], Co. Hwy. 13, Shakopee vicinity, 4/17/80, A, C, a, 80002173

Strunk-Nyssen House [Scott County MRA], Off U.S. 169, Shakopee vicinity, 4/17/80, B, C, 80002174

Sherburne County

Fox, Herbert M., House, US 10 NW of Becker, Becker vicinity, 4/10/80, A, C, 80002175

Kelley, Oliver H., Homestead, 2 mi. SE of Elk River on U.S. 10, Elk River vicinity, 10/15/66, B, NHL, 66000406

Minnesota State Reformatory for Men Historic District, Off MN 301, St. Cloud, 7/17/86, A, C, 86001671

Sherburne County Courthouse, 326 Lowell Ave., Elk River, 1/23/86, A, 86000120

Sibley County

Church of St. Thomas, County Hwys. 6 and 9, Henderson vicinity, 9/16/91, A, a, 88003085

Gibbon Village Hall, 1st Ave. and 12th St., Gibbon, 8/19/82, C, 82003036

Henderson Commercial Historic District, Roughly Main St. between Fifth and Sixth Sts., Henderson, 12/20/88, A, C, 88002834

Poehler, August F., House, 700 Main St., Henderson, 2/04/82, B, C, 82003037

Sibley County Courthouse and Sheriff's Residence and Jail, 400 Court St. and 319 Park Ave., Gaylord, 12/29/88, A, C, 88003071

Sibley County Courthouse—1879, 6th and Main Sts., Henderson, 7/02/79, C, 79001255

St. Louis County

Aerial Lift Bridge, Lake Ave., Duluth, 5/22/73, C, 73002174

Aho, Elias and Lisi, Historic Farmstead [Rural Finnish Log Buildings of St. Louis County, Minnesota, 1890–1930s MPS], Off Twnshp. Rd. 358, Tower vicinity, 4/09/90, A, C, 90000499

Alango School, Co. Hwys. 25 and 22, Cook vicinity, 7/17/80, A, 80004338

Anderson, Andrew G., House, 1001 E. Howard St., Hibbing, 12/04/80, B, C, 80004348

Androy Hotel, 592 E. Howard St., Hibbing, 6/13/86, A, C, 86001290

Archaeological Site No. 21SL82, Address Restricted, International Falls vicinity, 2/17/88, D, NPS, 88000067

Archeological Site 21SL141, Address Restricted, International Falls vicinity, 12/31/87, D, NPS, 87002164

Archeological Site 21SL35, Address Restricted, International Falls vicinity, 12/29/87, D, NPS, 87002165

Archeological Site 21SL55, Address Restricted, International Falls vicinity, 7/08/88, D, NPS, 88000989

Archeological Site No. 21SL73, Address Restricted, International Falls vicinity, 1/16/89, D, NPS, 88003130

B'nai Abraham Synagogue, 328 S. 5th St., Virginia, 8/18/80, A, a, 80004356

Bailey, W. T., House, 816 S. 5th Ave., Virginia, 12/04/80, B, C, 80004357

Bailey, W., House, 705 Pierce St., Eveleth, 8/27/80, C, 80004347

Bridge No. L6007 [Minnesota Masonry-Arch Highway Bridges MPS], Skyline Pkwy. over Stewart Creek, Duluth, 11/06/89, C, 89001826

Bruce Mine Headframe, Off U.S. 169, Chisholm vicinity, 11/28/78, C, 78003124

Buhl Public Library, Jones Ave. at Frantz St., Buhl, 2/10/83, A, C, 83004605

Buhl Village Hall, Jones Ave. at 4th St., Buhl, 2/10/83, A, C, 83000944

Burntside Lodge Historic District, Off Co. Hwy. 88, Ely vicinity, 6/23/88, A, C, 88000896

Butler, Emmett, House, 2530 3rd Ave., W., Hibbing, 12/04/80, B, C, 80004349

Chester Terrace, 1210–1232 E. 1st St., Duluth, 11/19/80, C, 80004341

Church of St. John the Baptist (Catholic), 309 S. 3rd Ave., Virginia, 8/27/80, A, a, 80004362

Church of the Holy Family (Catholic), 307 Adams Ave., Eveleth, 8/27/80, A, a, 80004345

Civilian Conservation Corps Camp S-52, Off US 53, Orr vicinity, 3/02/89, A, 89000158

Coates House, 817 S. 5th Ave., Virginia, 8/18/80, A, C, 80004358

Congdon, Chester and Clara, Estate, 3300 London Rd., Duluth, 8/15/91, C, 91001057

DeWitt-Seitz Building, 394 Lake Ave., S., Duluth, 9/05/85, A, C, 85001999

Delvic Building, 1st Ave. and Howard St., Hibbing, 7/17/80, A, 80004350

Duluth Central High School, Lake Ave. and 2nd St., Duluth, 11/09/72, C, 72001488

Duluth Civic Center Historic District, Fifth Ave. W and First St., Duluth, 11/06/86, A, C, 86003097

Duluth Missabe and Iron Range Depot (Endion), 1504 South St., Duluth, 4/16/75, A, C, 75002088

Duluth Public Library, 101 W. 2nd St., Duluth, 5/05/78, A, C, 78003125

Duluth South Breakwater Inner (Duluth Range Rear) Lighthouse [U.S. Coast Guard Lighthouses and Light Stations on the Great Lakes TR], S Breakwater, Duluth, 8/04/83, A, 83000945

Duluth State Normal School Historic District, E. Fifth St., Duluth, 11/08/85, A, C, 85002757

Duluth Union Depot, 5th Ave., W. and Michigan St., Duluth, 12/09/71, A, C, 71001028

Duluth, Winnipeg, and Pacific Depot, 600 Chestnut St., Virginia, 8/18/80, A, C, 80004364

East Howard Street Commercial Historic District, 101–510 E. Howard St., Hibbing, 4/01/93, A, 93000255

Endion School, 1801 E. 1st St., Duluth, 2/10/83, C, 83000946

Eveleth Manual Training Center, Roosevelt Ave., Eveleth, 8/18/80, A, C, 80004343

Eveleth Recreation Building, Garfield St. and Adams Ave., Eveleth, 11/25/80, A, 80004344

Finnish Sauna, 105 S. 1st St., Virginia, 8/26/80, A, C, 80004360

Fire House No. 1, NW corner of 1st Ave., E. and 3rd St., Duluth, 5/12/75, A, C, 75002089

Fitger Brewing Company, 600 E. Superior St., Duluth, 2/09/84, A, C, 84001690

Flint Creek Farm Historic District, MN 1, Cook vicinity, 3/02/89, A, B, 89000139

Hanka, Gregorius and Mary, Historic Farmstead [Rural Finnish Log Buildings of St. Louis County, Minnesota, 1890–1930s MPS], Off Twnshp. Rd. 6544, Tower vicinity, 4/09/90, A, C, 90000500

Hartley Building, 740 E. Superior St., Duluth, 12/15/89, C, 89002127

Height of Land Portage [Portage Trails in Minnesota MPS], Off Co. Rd. 138, Embarrass, White and Pike Townships, Embarrass vicinity, 7/23/92, A, D, 92000842

Hibbing City Hall, 21st St., E. and 4th Ave., Hibbing, 2/12/81, A, C, 81000683

Hibbing Disposal Plant [Federal Relief Construction in Minnesota MPS], 1300 E. 23rd St., Hibbing, 8/09/91, A, C, 91001022

Hibbing High School, 21st St. at 8th Ave., Hibbing, 8/11/80, A, C, 80004351

Hill, Matt and Emma, Historic Farmstead [Rural Finnish Log Buildings of St. Louis County, Minnesota, 1890–1930 MPS], Off Twnshp. Rd. 303, Tower vicinity, 4/09/90, A, C, 90000768

Hull-Rust-Mahoning Open Pit Iron Mine, 3rd Ave., E., Hibbing vicinity, 11/13/66, A, NHL, 66000904

Irving School, 101 N. 56th Ave. W., Duluth, 11/20/92, A, C, 92001611

Johnson, Otto, House, 202 3rd Ave., Mountain Iron, 11/25/80, A, B, C, 80004354

Jukola Boardinghouse, 201 N. 3rd Ave., Virginia, 3/10/82, A, C, 82004710

Kabetogama Ranger Station District [Federal Relief Construction in Minnesota MRA], SW shore of Kabetogama Lake, Voyageurs NP (VOYA), Ray vicinity, 6/18/93, A, C, NPS, 93000479

Kettle Falls Historic District, Kettle Channel in Voyageurs National Park, Island View vicinity, 7/17/78, A, C, g, NPS, 78000376

Kettle Falls Hotel, Kettle Channel in Voyageurs National Park, Island View vicinity, 1/11/76, A, C, NPS, 76000210

Kitchi Gammi Club, 831 E. Superior St., Duluth, 4/16/75, C, 75002090

LeMoine Building, Off Co. Hwy. 74, Orr vicinity, 3/02/89, A, 89000140

Lenont, Charles, House, 202 N. 5th Ave., Virginia, 8/18/80, A, C, 80004359

Lincoln School Building, 3rd Ave., Virginia, 11/28/78, C, 78003130

Longyear, E. J., First Diamond Drill Site, Off Co. Hwy. 110, Hoyt Lake, 7/20/77, A, C, 77001526

Matson, Mike and Mary, Historic Farmstead [Rural Finnish Log Buildings of St. Louis County, Minnesota, 1890–1930 MPS], Off Co. Hwy 21, Tower vicinity, 4/09/90, A, C, 90000769

Minnesota Point Lighthouse, On Minnesota Point, Duluth, 12/27/74, A, 74002206

Mitchell-Tappan House, 2145 4th Ave., Hibbing, 12/02/80, A, C, b, 80004352

Moe, Bergetta, Bakery, 716 E. Superior St., Duluth, 6/03/76, C, 76002175

Mountain Iron Mine, N of Mountain Iron, Mountain Iron vicinity, 11/24/68, A, NHL, 68000052

Munger Terrace, 405 Mesabi Ave., Duluth, 12/12/76, C, 76002176

Nelimark, Erick and Kristina, Sauna [Rural Finnish Log Buildings of St. Louis County, Minnesota, 1890–1930s MPS], Jct. Twnshp. Rds. 615 and 21, Tower vicinity, 4/09/90, A, C, 90000770

Northland, Off U.S. 2, Proctor, 7/31/78, A, 78003129

Park Hotel, 222 Adams Ave., Eveleth, 11/25/80, A, 80004346

Pioneer Mine Buildings and A Headframe, Off Pioneer Rd., Ely, 11/28/78, A, C, g, 78003127

Sacred Heart Cathedral and Cathedral School, 206 and 211 W. Fourth St., Duluth, 6/26/86, A, C, a, 86001382

St. Louis County—Continued

Saints Peter and Paul Church—Ukranian Catholic, 530 Central Ave., Chisholm, 8/27/80, A, a, 80004340

Seitaniemi, Alex, Housebarn [Rural Finnish Log Buildings of St. Louis County, Minnesota, 1890–1930s MPS], Off Twnshp. Rd. 797, Tower vicinity, 4/09/90, A, C, 90000771

Sons of Italy Hall, 704 E. Howard St., Hibbing, 11/25/80, A, 80004353

Soudan Iron Mine, Tower-Soudan State Park, Tower vicinity, 11/13/66, A, NHL, 66000905

St. Louis County 4-H Club Camp, 100 Pine Lane, Gilbert vicinity, 3/04/85, A, C, 85000456

St. Mark's African Methodist Episcopal Church, 530 N. 5th Ave. E., Duluth, 4/16/91, A, a, 91000439

St.Louis County District Courthouse, 300 S. Fifth Ave., Virginia, 6/18/92, A, C, 92000798

THOMAS WILSON (Whaleback Freighter) Shipwreck [Minnesota's Lake Superior Shipwrecks MPS], Address Restricted, Duluth vicinity, 7/23/92, A, C, 92000844

Tanner's Hospital, 204 E. Camp St., Ely, 7/28/80, A, C, 80004342

Tanttari, Waino, Field Hay Barn [Rural Finnish Log Buildings of St. Louis County, Minnesota, 1890–1930s MPS], End of Twnshp Rd. 585, Tower vicinity, 4/09/90, A, 90000773

Tower Fire Hall, Main St., Tower, 7/17/80, A, 80004355

Traphagen, Oliver G., House, 1509-1511 E. Superior St., Duluth, 4/04/75, C, 75002091

US Fisheries Station, Duluth, 6008 London Rd., Duluth, 11/28/78, A, C, 78003126

Valon Tuote Raittiusseura, 125 3rd St., N., Virginia, 8/24/79, A, 79003199

Virginia Brewery, 305 S. 7th Ave., Virginia, 8/27/80, A, C, 80004363

Virginia Recreation Building, 305 S. 1st St., Virginia, 2/04/82, A, g, 82004711

Virginia-Rainy Lake Lumber Company Manager's Residence, 402 and 404 S. 5th Ave., Virginia, 8/18/80, A, 80004361

Virginia-Rainy Lake Lumber Company Office, 731 3rd St., S., Virginia, 8/26/80, A, 80004365

WILLIAM A. IRVIN (freighter), Minnesota Slip, Duluth Harbor, Duluth, 7/13/89, A, C, 89000858

Western Bohemian Fraternal Union Hall, Co. Hwy. 29, Meadowlands vicinity, 7/31/86, A, 86002123

Wirth Building, 13 W. Superior St., Duluth, 7/25/91, C, 91000896

Stearns County

Bensen, John N., House, 402 6th Ave., S., St. Cloud, 2/11/82, B, C, 82003050

Bishop's House/Chancery Office [Stearns County MRA], 214 3rd Ave., S., St. Cloud, 4/15/82, C, a, 82003051

Borgerding, Christopher, House [Stearns County MRA], Washburn Ave., Belgrade, 4/15/82, B, C, 82003039

Carter Block, 501–511 First St. N, St. Cloud, 6/13/86, A, 86001297

Church of St. Boniface, 203 S. 5th Ave. East, Melrose, 11/12/93, A, a, 93001234

Church of St. Joseph—Catholic [Stearns County MRA; Ethnic Hamlet Churches-Stearns County Catholic Settlement Churches TR], Minnesota St. and College Ave., St. Joseph, 4/15/82, A, C, a, 82003057

Church of St. Mary Help of Christians—Catholic [Stearns County MRA; Ethnic Hamlet Churches-Stearns County Catholic Settlement Churches TR], Co. Hwy. 7, St. Augusta, 4/15/82, A, C, a, 82003049

Church of St. Stephen—Catholic [Stearns County MRA; Ethnic Hamlet Churches-Stearns County Catholic Settlement Churches TR], Co. Hwy. 7, St. Stephen, 4/15/82, A, C, a, 82003059

Church of the Immaculate Conception—Catholic [Stearns County MRA; Ethnic Hamlet Churches-Stearns County Catholic Settlement Churches TR], Co. Hwy. 9, Avon vicinity, 4/15/82, A, C, a, 82003038

Church of the Sacred Heart (Catholic), 110 3rd Ave., NE., Freeport, 7/12/91, A, a, 91000906

Clark and McCormack Quarry and House [Stearns County MRA], MN 23 at Pine St., Rockville, 4/15/82, A, 82003046

Clarke, Nehemiah P., House [Stearns County MRA], 356 3rd Ave., S., St. Cloud, 4/15/82, B, C, 82003052

Fair Haven Flour Mill, Off Co. Hwy. 7, Fairhaven vicinity, 4/14/78, A, C, 78001574

Fifth Avenue Commercial Buildings [Stearns County MRA], 14–30 5th Ave., S., St. Cloud, 4/15/82, A, C, 82003053

First National Bank [Stearns County MRA], 501 St. Germain St., St. Cloud, 4/15/82, A, C, 82003054

First State Bank [Stearns County MRA], 23 Minnesota St., W., St. Joseph, 4/15/82, C, 82003058

Foley-Brower-Bohmer House, 385 3rd Ave., S., St. Cloud, 5/05/78, B, C, 78001563

Freeport Roller Mill and Miller's House [Stearns County MRA], Mary St., Freeport, 4/15/82, A, 82003043

Gogala, Anton, Farmstead [Stearns County MRA], Co. Hwy. 39 and MN 238, St. Anthony vicinity, 4/15/82, B, C, g, 82003048

Hermanutz, Eugene, House [Stearns County MRA; Cold Spring Brewers' Houses TR], 302 N. Red River Ave., Cold Spring, 4/15/82, A, C, 82003040

Kimball Prairie Village Hall [Stearns County MRA], Main St. and Hazel, Kimball, 4/15/82, A, 82003045

Lewis, Sinclair, Boyhood Home, 812 Sinclair Lewis Ave., Sauk Centre, 5/23/68, B, NHL, 68000027

Majerus, Michael, House, 404 9th Ave., S., St. Cloud, 5/05/78, C, 78001564

Minnesota Home School for Girls Historic District, Off MN 302, Sauk Centre, 1/19/89, C, 88003090

Model School, 826 First Ave., South, St. Cloud, 12/29/88, A, 88003072

Oster, John, House [Stearns County MRA; Cold Spring Brewers' Houses TR], 201 N. Red River Ave., Cold Spring, 4/15/82, A, C, 82003041

Palmer House Hotel, 500 Sinclair Lewis Ave., Sauk Centre, 2/11/82, A, C, 82003047

Pan Motor Company Office and Sheet Metal Works, 435-437 33rd Ave., N., St. Cloud, 1/31/84, A, 84001694

Peters, Ferdinand, House [Stearns County MRA; Cold Spring Brewers' Houses TR], 214 N. Red River Ave., Cold Spring, 4/15/82, A, C, 82003042

St. Benedict's Convent and College Historic District, College Ave. and Minnesota St., St. Joseph, 3/20/89, A, C, a, 89000160

St. John's Abbey and University Historic District, Co. Hwy. 159, Avon vicinity, 3/23/79, A, C, a, g, 79001256

Stearns County Courthouse and Jail [Stearns County MRA], 1st St. and 8th Ave., N., St. Cloud, 4/15/82, A, C, 82003056

Steele County

Abbott, Ezra, House, 345 E. Broadway, Owatonna, 6/10/75, A, 75001029

Adair, Dr. John H., House, 322 E. Vine St., Owatonna, 7/03/86, C, 86001406

Administration Building—Minnesota State Public School For Dependent and Neglected Children, West Hills Circle, Owatonna, 5/12/75, A, C, 75001030

Clinton Falls Mill and Dam, Off Co. Hwy. 9, Medford vicinity, 7/03/86, A, 86001462

Kaplan Apartments, 115 W. Rose St., Owatonna, 7/03/86, A, B, 86001464

National Farmers' Bank, N. Cedar St. and E. Broadway, Owatonna, 8/26/71, A, C, NHL, 71000441

Owatonna Free Public Library, 105 N. Elm St., Owatonna, 6/07/76, A, C, 76001075

Owatonna High School, 333 E. School St., Owatonna, 7/31/86, C, 86002124

Pillsbury Academy Campus Historic District, Roughly Academy, Grove, and Main Sts., Owatonna, 1/22/87, A, C, a, 86003680

Piper, Daniel S., House, Co. Hwy. 45, Medford vicinity, 2/24/75, A, B, C, 75001028

Steele County Courthouse, 139 E. Main St., Owatonna, 11/14/78, C, 78001565

Stevens County

Alberta Teachers House, Main St., Alberta, 2/11/83, A, 83000942

Morris Carnegie Library, Nevada and 6th Sts., Morris, 1/27/83, A, C, 83000943

Morris Industrial School for Indians Dormitory, Off 4th St., Morris, 5/10/84, A, 84001696

Stanton, Lewis H., House, 907 Park St., Morris, 8/19/82, C, 82003060

Swift County

Appleton City Hall, 23 S. Miles St., Appleton, 6/17/77, A, C, 77000770

Christ Church—Episcopal, 310 13th St., N., Benson, 8/15/85, B, C, a, b, 85001761

Church of St. Bridget—Catholic, 3rd St. and Ireland Ave., DeGraff, 8/15/85, A, B, C, a, 85001768

Church of St. Francis Xavier—Catholic, 13th St., N. and Montana Ave., Benson, 8/15/85, A, C, a, 85001753

Monson Lake State Park CCC/WPA/Rustic Style Historic Resources [Minnesota State Park CCC/WPA/Rustic Style MPS], Off Co. Rd. 95 SE of Sunburg, Sunburg vicinity, 10/25/89, A, C, 89001666

Murdock, Sabin S., House, Clara Ave., Murdock, 8/15/85, B, C, 85001752

Swift County Courthouse, Idaho Ave. and 14th St., Benson, 9/19/77, A, C, 77000771

Uytendale, Christian F., Farmstead, Off Co. Hwy. 25, Benson vicinity, 9/05/85, A, C, 85001989

Todd County

Bank of Long Prairie, 262 Central Ave., Long Prairie, 9/05/85, A, C, 85001994

Church of St. Joseph—Catholic, Main St. between 7th and 8th Sts., Browerville, 9/05/85, A, C, a, 85001996

Grey Eagle Village Hall, Spruce and Woodman Sts., Grey Eagle, 9/05/85, A, C, 85001992

Hotel Reichert, 20 3rd St., N., Long Prairie, 9/05/85, A, 85001995

Kahlert Mercantile Store, Main St., Browerville, 9/05/85, A, 85001997

Saint Cloud and Red River Valley Stage Road—Kandota Section [Overland Staging Industry in Minnesota MPS], Off Co. Hwy. 92 SE of West Union, Kandota Township, West Union vicinity, 8/30/91, A, 91001061

Todd County Courthouse, Sheriff's House and Jail, 215 1st Ave., S., Long Prairie, 9/05/85, A, C, 85001986

Traverse County

Browns Valley Carnegie Public Library, Broadway Ave. and 2nd St., Browns Valley, 8/15/85, A, C, 85001762

Chicago, Milwaukee, and St. Paul Depot, Broadway Ave. and Front St., Wheaton, 8/23/85, A, C, 85001818

Fort Wadsworth Agency and Scout Headquarters Building, Broadway and Dakota Aves., Browns Valley, 7/17/86, B, C, b, 86001672

Larson's Hunters Resort, Co. Hwy. 76, Wheaton vicinity, 8/15/85, A, C, 85001774

Wabasha County

Bear Valley Grange Hall, Co. Hwy. 3, Zumbro Falls vicinity, 1/05/89, A, 88003089

Campbell, William H. and Alma Downer, House [Red Brick Houses in Wabasha, Minnesota, Associated with Merchant-Tradesmen MPS], 211 W. Second St., Wabasha, 5/15/89, C, 89000367

Ginthner, Lorenz and Lugerde, House [Red Brick Houses in Wabasha, Minnesota, Associated with Merchant-Tradesmen MPS], 130 W. Third St., Wabasha, 5/15/89, C, 89000368

Grace Memorial Episcopal Church, 205 E. 3rd St., Wabasha, 2/04/82, A, C, a, 82003062

Hurd House—Anderson Hotel, 333 W. Main St., Wabasha, 9/18/78, B, 78001566

Lake City City Hall, 205 W. Center St., Lake City, 6/16/81, A, C, 81000325

Lake City and Rochester Stage Road—Mount Pleasant Section [Overland Staging Industry in Minnesota MPS], Off US 63 SW of Lake City, Mount Pleasant Township, Lake City vicinity, 8/30/91, A, 91001063

Lake Zumbro Hydroelectric Generating Plant [Minnesota Hydroelectric Generating Facilities MPS], Off Co. Hwy. 21 at N end of Lake Zumbro, Mazeppa Township, Mazeppa vicinity, 3/14/91, C, 91000243

Rahilly, Patrick H., House, 3 mi. W of Lake City on Co. Hwy. 15, Lake City vicinity, 2/13/75, B, C, 75001032

Rahilly, Patrick H., House (Boundary Increase), Co. Hwy. 15, W of Lake City, Lake City vicinity, 3/02/79, C, 79003766

Reads Landing School, Third St. and First Ave., Reads Landing, 1/19/89, A, C, 88003217

Schmidt, Clara and Julius, House [Red Brick Houses in Wabasha, Minnesota, Associated with Merchant-Tradesmen MPS], 418 E. Second St., Wabasha, 5/15/89, C, 89000370

Schwedes, Henry S. and Magdalena, House [Red Brick Houses in Wabasha, Minnesota, Associated with Merchant-Tradesmen MPS], 230 E. Main St., Wabasha, 5/15/89, C, 89000371

Stout, James C. and Agnes M., House, 310 S. Oak St., Lake City, 1/13/89, C, 88003138

Swedish Evangelical Lutheran Church, Bridge St., Millville, 1/19/89, A, a, 88003086

Wabasha Commercial Historic District, Roughly along Main St. between Bridge and Bailey Aves., Wabasha, 4/15/82, A, 82003063

Wabasha County Poor House, Hiawatha Dr., Wabasha, 8/26/82, A, 82003064

Weaver Mercantile Building, U.S. 61 and MN 74, Minneiska vicinity, 9/21/78, A, C, 78001567

Williamson-Russell-Rahilly House, 304 Oak St., Lake City, 3/08/84, C, 84001709

Zumbro Parkway Bridge [Minnesota Masonry-Arch Highway Bridges MPS], Co. Rd. 68 over Zumbro River, Zumbro Falls vicinity, 11/06/89, C, 89001824

Wadena County

Blueberry Lake Village Site, Address Restricted, Menahga vicinity, 10/02/73, D, 73000996

Commercial Hotel, Jefferson St. South, Wadena, 12/22/88, A, 88003010

Northern Pacific Passenger Depot, Off 1st St. Southwest, Wadena, 1/03/89, A, 88003012

Old Wadena Historic District, Address Restricted, Staples vicinity, 10/09/73, D, 73000997

Peterson-Biddick Seed and Feed Company, 102 SE Aldrich Ave., Wadena, 1/30/89, A, C, 88003227

Reaume's Trading Post, Address Restricted, Wadena vicinity, 12/24/74, D, 74001042

Wadena Fire and City Hall, 10 SE Bryant Ave., Wadena, 1/19/89, A, 88003228

Waseca County

Armstrong, W. J., Company Wholesale Grocers, 202 2nd St., SW, Waseca, 8/19/82, A, 82003067

Aughenbaugh, John W., House, 831 3rd Ave., NE, Waseca, 8/24/82, B, C, 82003068

Janesville Free Public Library, 102 W. 2nd St., Janesville, 8/19/82, A, C, 82003065

Seha Sorghum Mill, Co. Hwy. 5, Janesville vicinity, 6/04/79, A, B, C, g, 79003718

Vista Lutheran Church, N of New Richland off MN 13, New Richland vicinity, 11/08/82, A, 82000565

Ward, Roscoe P., House, 804 E. Elm Ave., Waseca, 8/19/82, B, C, 82003069

Waseca County Courthouse, 307 N. State St., Waseca, 9/02/82, A, C, 82003070

Wolf, William R., House, 522 2nd Ave., NE, Waseca, 8/24/82, B, C, 82003071

Washington County

Bolles, Erastus, House [Washington County MRA; Valley Creek Residences TR], 1741 Stagecoach Trail, Afton vicinity, 4/20/82, C, 82003072

Chicago, Milwaukee and St. Paul Freight House [Washington County MRA (AD)], 233–335 Water St., Stillwater, 7/13/77, A, C, 77000773

Chyphers, John T., House [Washington County MRA (AD)], 661 Quinnell Ave., N., Lakeland, 9/10/71, C, 71000442

Copas, John, House [Washington County MRA (AD)], N of Marine on St. Croix on MN 95, Marine on St. Croix vicinity, 7/21/80, B, C, NPS, 80002176

Cushing Hotel, 3291 St. Croix Trail Ave., S., Afton, 1/17/85, A, 85000098

Erickson, Johannes, House [Washington County MRA (AD)], Co. Hwy. 3, Scandia vicinity, 6/17/76, A, C, b, 76001078

Furber, John P., House [Washington County MRA], 7310 Lamar Ave., Cottage Grove, 4/20/82, A, 82003074

Gilbert, Newington, House [Washington County MRA; Valley Creek Residences TR], 1678 Stagecoach Trail, Afton vicinity, 4/20/82, C, 82003073

Grey Cloud Lime Kiln [Washington County MRA (AD)], 10398 Grey Cloud Island Trail, Cottage Grove, 12/18/78, A, C, 78001568

Washington County—Continued

Hay Lake School [Washington County MRA (AD)], Co. Hwy. 3, Marine on St. Croix vicinity, 7/01/70, A, C, 70000312

Hersey, Roscoe, House [Washington County MRA (AD)], 416 S. 4th St., Stillwater, 2/19/82, B, C, 82003084

Jackson, Mitchell, Farmhouse [Washington County MRA (AD)], 16376 7th St. Lane, S., Lakeland, 2/19/82, B, C, 82003075

Jenks, Capt. Austin, House [Washington County MRA], 504 S. 5th St., Stillwater, 4/20/82, B, C, 82003085

Lammers, Albert, House [Washington County MRA], 1306 S. 3rd St., Stillwater, 4/20/82, B, C, 82003076

Marine Mill Site [Washington County MRA (AD)], Mill Reservation, Block 47, Marine on St. Croix, 1/26/70, A, 70000311

Marine on St. Croix Historic District [Washington County MRA (AD)], Roughly bounded by the St. Croix River, RR tracks, and Kennedy and Spruce Sts., Marine on St. Croix, 6/28/74, A, B, C, 74001043

McKusick, Ivory, House [Washington County MRA], 504 N. 2nd St., Stillwater, 4/20/82, B, C, 82003077

Minnesota Territorial-State Prison Warden's House [Washington County MRA (AD)], 602 N. Main St., Stillwater, 12/17/74, A, C, 74001044

Mower, John and Martin, House and Arcola Mill Site [Washington County MRA (AD)], Arcola Tr., Stillwater vicinity, 6/17/80, A, C, NPS, 80000407

Nelson School [Washington County MRA (AD)], 1018 S. 1st St, Stillwater, 10/25/79, A, C, 79001257

Oliver, Capt. John, House [Washington County MRA (AD)], 1544 Rivercrest Rd., Lakeland, 12/16/77, B, C, 77000772

Pest House [Washington County MRA (AD)], N of Stillwater at 9033 Fairy Falls Rd., Stillwater vicinity, 6/17/80, A, NPS, 80000408

Point Douglas-St. Louis River Road Bridge [Washington County MRA (AD)], Off Co. Hwy. 5, Stillwater vicinity, 2/24/75, A, C, 75001033

Sauntry, William, House and Recreation Hall [Washington County MRA], 626 N. 4th St. and 625 N. 5th St., Stillwater, 4/20/82, B, C, 82003080

Schilling Archeological District [Washington County MRA (AD)], Address Restricted, Cottage Grove vicinity, 12/22/78, D, 78001569

Severance, Cordenio, House [Washington County MRA (AD)], 6940 Keats Ave., S., Cottage Grove vicinity, 6/03/76, B, C, 76001077

Sheffield, Benjamin B., House [Washington County MRA (AD)], N of Stillwater at 4 Croixside Rd., Stillwater vicinity, 6/03/80, A, C, NPS, 80002177

Soo Line High Bridge [Washington County MRA (AD)], Address Restricted, Stillwater, vicinity, 8/22/77, A, C, NPS, 77000056

Spangenberg, Charles, Farmstead [Washington County MRA (AD)], SE of Woodbury at 9431 Dale Rd., Woodbury, 12/05/78, B, 78001570

St. Croix Boom Company House and Barn [Washington County MRA (AD)], NE of Stillwater at 9666 N. St. Croix Trail, Stillwater vicinity, 6/03/80, A, NHL, NPS, 80000409

St. Croix Boom Site [Washington County MRA (AD)], 3 mi. N of Stillwater on St. Croix River, Stillwater vicinity, 11/13/66, A, NHL, 66000407

St. Croix Lumber Mills—Stillwater Manufacturing Company [Washington County MRA], 318 N. Main, Stillwater, 4/20/82, B, 82003081

St. Croix River Access Site, Address Restricted, Stillwater vicinity, 8/23/84, D, 84001712

State Prison Historic District, 5500 Pickett Ave., Bayport, 7/10/86, C, 86001574

Stillwater Bridge, MN 36/WI 64 over St. Croix River, Stillwater, 5/25/89, C, 89000445

Stillwater Commercial Historic District, Vicinity of Main, 2nd and Chestnut Sts., Stillwater, 3/26/92, A, C, 92000288

Stussi, Henry, House [Washington County MRA], 9097 Mendel Rd., Stillwater, 4/20/82, B, C, 82003082

Territorial-State Prison [Washington County MRA], Main and Laurel Sts., Stillwater, 4/20/82, A, 82003079

Washington County Courthouse [Washington County MRA (AD)], W. Pine St. at S. 3rd St., Stillwater, 8/26/71, A, C, 71000443

Webster, Mortimer, House [Washington County MRA], 435 S. Broadway, Stillwater, 4/20/82, B, C, 82003083

Watonwan County

Flanders' Block, 30 W. Main St., Madelia, 3/08/84, A, 84001714

Nelson and Albin Cooperative Mercantile Association Store, Co. Hwy. 6, LaSalle vicinity, 1/07/87, A, 86003599

Voss, Alfred R., Farmstead, Co. Hwy. 14, St. James vicinity, 10/27/88, B, C, 88002054

Watonwan County Courthouse, Seventh St., S. and Second Ave., S., St. James, 1/07/87, A, C; 86003591

Wilkin County

Femco Farm No. 2 [Wilkin County MRA], CR 153, Kent vicinity, 7/17/80, B, 80002184

Peet, David N., Farmstead [Wilkin County MRA], CR 32, Wolverton vicinity, 7/17/80, B, 80002187

Stiklestad United Lutheran Church [Wilkin County MRA], CR 17, Doran vicinity, 7/17/80, A, C, a, 80002183

Tenney Fire Hall [Wilkin County MRA], Concord Ave., Tenney, 7/17/80, A, b, 80002186

Wilkin County Courthouse [Wilkin County MRA], 316 S. 5th, Breckenridge, 7/17/80, A, C, 80002182

Wolverton Public School [Wilkin County MRA], N. 1st St., Wolverton, 7/17/80, A, 80002188

Winona County

Anger's Block, 116–120 Walnut St., Winona, 1/31/78, C, 78001571

Bridge No. L1409 [Minnesota Masonry-Arch Highway Bridges MPS], Twp. Rd. 62 over Garvin Brook, Winona vicinity, 7/05/90, C, 90000978

Bunnell, Willard, House, Homer and Matilde Sts., Winona vicinity, 4/23/73, B, C, 73000998

Choate Deparment Store, 51 E. 3rd St., Winona, 6/03/76, B, 76001079

Church of St. Stanislaus—Catholic, 601 E. 4th St., Winona, 11/08/84, C, a, 84000251

Church of the Holy Trinity—Catholic, Off Rollingstone Rd., Rollingstone, 8/09/84, A, C, a, 84001721

East Second Street Commercial Historic District, 66–78 Center, 54–78 E. Second and 67–71 Lafayette Sts., Winona, 1/25/91, A, C, 90002198

Ellsworth, Benjamin, House, US 14, Utica, 8/09/84, B, C, 84001718

Gallagher, Dr. J. W. S., House, 451 W. Broadway St., Winona, 11/08/84, C, 84000245

Grain and Lumber Exchange Building, 51 E. 4th St., Winona, 12/02/77, C, 77000774

Hemmelberg, William, House, Co. Hwys. 26 and 37, Elba vicinity, 10/23/86, A, 86002916

Hodgins, Abner F., House, 275 Harriet St., Winona, 11/08/84, B, C, 84000248

Huff-Lamberton House, 207 Huff St., Winona, 12/12/76, C, a, 76001080

Kirch/Latch Building, 114–122 E. 2nd St., Winona, 5/21/75, A, C, 75001036

Marnach, Nicholas, House, Off Co. Hwy. 26 in Whitewater Wildlife Management Area, Elba vicinity, 1/30/78, A, C, 78003406

Merchants National Bank, 102 E. 3rd St., Winona, 10/16/74, A, C, 74001045

Pickwick Mill, Co. Hwy. 7, Winona vicinity, 9/22/70, A, B, C, 70000314

Schlitz Hotel, 129 W. 3rd St., Winona, 8/26/82, A, C, 82003087

St. Charles City Bakery, 501 Whitewater Ave., St. Charles, 8/09/84, A, 84001723

Sugar Loaf, SW of jct. of US 61 and MN 43, Winona, 8/03/90, A, 90001164

Sugar Loaf Brewery, Lake Blvd. and Sugar Loaf Rd., Winona, 3/31/78, B, 78001572

Trinity Episcopal Church, 805 St. Charles Ave., St. Charles, 8/09/84, C, a, 84001726

Trinity Episcopal Church, E. Main St. and Broadway, Stockton, 8/09/84, A, C, a, 84001727

Watkins, Paul, House, 175 E. Wabasha St., Winona, 11/08/84, B, C, 84000255

Whitewater Avenue Commercial Historic District, 900-1012 Whitewater Ave., St. Charles, 8/09/84, C, 84001736

Whitewater State Park CCC/WPA/Rustic Style Historic Resources [Minnesota State Park CCC/WPA/Rustic Style MPS], Off MN 74, SW of Elba, Elba vicinity, 10/25/89, A, C, g, 89001661

Winona County—Continued

Winona County Courthouse, Washington St. between 3rd and 4th Sts., Winona, 12/02/70, A, C, 70000313

Winona Free Public Library, 151 W. 5th St., Winona, 7/29/77, A, C, 77000775

Winona Hotel, 151 Johnson St., Winona, 3/31/83, A, C, 83000947

Winona Savings Bank Building, 204 Main St., Winona, 9/15/77, A, C, 77000776

Winona and St. Peter Engine House, 75 Gould St., Winona, 1/12/84, A, 84001730

Winona and St. Peter Railroad Freight House, Front and Center Sts., Winona, 1/26/84, A, 84001733

Wright County

Akerlund, August, Photographic Studio, 390 Broadway Ave., Cokato, 4/11/77, B, 77000777

Albertville Roller Mill [Wright County MRA], 5790 Main Ave., NE, Albertville, 12/11/79, A, 79001258

Church of St. Michael—Catholic [Wright County MRA], Central Ave. and Main St., St. Michael, 12/11/79, C, a, 79001279

Clearwater Masonic Lodge-Grand Army of the Republic Hall [Wright County MRA], Oak and Main Sts., Clearwater, 12/11/79, A, C, 79001259

Cokaton P.R.S. Onnen Tovio Raittiusseura, Co. Hwy. 3 and CR 100, Cokato vicinity, 12/12/76, A, a, 76001081

Delano Village Hall [Wright County MRA], 127 River St., Delano, 12/11/79, A, C, 79001264

Eagle Newspaper Office [Wright County MRA], 300 Railroad Ave., Delano, 12/11/79, A, 79001265

First Congregational Church of Clearwater [Wright County MRA], Bluff and Elm Sts., Clearwater, 12/11/79, A, C, a, 79001260

Franklin Township School No. 48 [Wright County MRA], U.S. 12, Delano vicinity, 12/11/79, A, C, 79001267

Hanaford, David, Farmstead [Wright County MRA], Off Co. Hwy. 106, Monticello vicinity, 12/11/79, A, B, 79001273

Hanover Bridge [Wright County MRA], Off Co. Hwy. 19 over Crow River, Hanover, 12/11/79, A, C, 79001268

Hawkins, Dr. E. P., Clinic, Hospital and House [Wright County MRA], Buffalo St., Montrose, 12/11/79, B, 79001277

Howard Lake City Hall [Wright County MRA], 737, 739 and 741 6th St., Howard Lake, 12/11/79, A, C, 79001269

Marsh Octagon Barn [Wright County MRA], Off Co. Hwy. 14, Rockford vicinity, 12/11/79, A, C, 79001278

Marysville Swedesburg Lutheran Church [Wright County MRA], Co. Hwy. 9, Waverly vicinity, 12/11/79, C, a, 79001270

Mealey, Tobias G., House, Territorial Rd., Monticello, 12/12/76, B, 76001082

Middleville Township Hall [Wright County MRA], CR 6, Howard Lake vicinity, 12/11/79, A, 79001271

Nicherson-Tarbox House, Shed and Barn [Wright County MRA], 514 E. Broadway, Monticello, 12/11/79, C, 79001274

Rand, Rufus, Summer House and Carriage Barn [Wright County MRA], Washington St., Monticello, 12/11/79, A, B, C, 79001275

Simpson Methodist Episcopal Church [Wright County MRA], 4th and Linn Sts., Monticello, 12/11/79, A, a, 79001276

St. Mark's Episcopal Chapel [Wright County MRA], Off MN 24, Annandale vicinity, 12/11/79, A, C, a, 79001272

Thayer Hotel, 60 Elm St., W., Annandale, 8/24/78, A, 78001573

Webster, William W., House [Wright County MRA], Spring and Linn Sts., Clearwater, 12/11/79, B, C, 79001261

Weldele, Simon, House [Wright County MRA], 309 River St., Delano, 12/11/79, C, 79001266

Yellow Medicine County

Canby Commercial Historic District, Roughly 1st and 2nd Sts. and St. Olaf Ave., Canby, 11/25/80, A, 80002189

Lund, John G., House, 101 W. 4th St., Canby, 10/02/78, B, C, 78001575

Lundring Service Station, 201 First St. E, Canby, 6/20/86, C, 86001356

Swede Prairie Progressive Farmers' Club, Co. Hwy. 9, Clarkfield vicinity, 6/13/86, A, 86001331

Upper Sioux Agency, Address Restricted, Granite Falls vicinity, 10/15/70, A, C, D, 70000315

Volstead, Andrew John, House, 163 9th Ave., Granite Falls, 12/30/74, B, NHL, 74001046

These revitalized commercial buildings are part of the Minneapolis Warehouse Historic District, which developed in the late 19th and early 20th centuries as Minneapolis became a midwestern hub for flour milling, production of agricultural machinery, and wholesale distribution of goods including lumber, flour, wheat, dry goods, and groceries. (Rolf T. Anderson, 1985)

MISSISSIPPI

Adams County

Ailes, William, House, 657 S. Canal St., Natchez, 3/12/80, C, 80002190

Airlie, 9 Elm St., Natchez, 10/29/82, C, 82000566

Anna Site, Address Restricted, Natchez vicinity, 9/14/93, D, NHL, 93001606

Arlington, Main St., Natchez, 12/12/73, C, NHL, 73000999

Assembly Hall, Assembly and Main Sts., Washington, 4/19/78, A, C, 78001587

Auburn, Duncan Park, Natchez, 5/30/74, C, NHL, 74001047

Baynton, John, House, 821 Main St., Natchez, 10/16/74, C, 74001048

Bedford Plantation, NE of Natchez off U.S. 61, Natchez vicinity, 11/16/78, C, 78001576

Beechland, S. of Natchez off US 61, Natchez vicinity, 11/04/82, C, 82000567

Belvidere, 70 Homochitto St., Natchez, 4/08/80, C, b, 80002191

Brandon Hall, NE of Washington on U.S. 61, Washington vicinity, 6/12/80, C, 80002198

Brandon, Gerard, IV, House, 708 N Union St., Natchez, 3/19/82, C, 82003094

Briars, SW of Natchez, Natchez vicinity, 8/24/77, C, 77000778

Brumfield High School, 100 St. Catherine St., Natchez, 10/21/93, A, C, 93001139

Buie House, NE of Natchez, Natchez vicinity, 7/13/83, C, b, 83000948

Burn, The, 307 Oak St., Natchez, 7/03/79, C, 79001280

Carmel Presbyterian Church, Carmel Church Rd., Natchez vicinity, 10/31/85, C, a, 85003441

Cedar Grove, SE of Natchez, Natchez vicinity, 3/19/82, C, 82003088

Cemetery Bluff District, Cemetery Rd., Natchez, 10/24/80, A, C, d, 80002192

Cherry Grove Plantation, S of Natchez off Kingston Rd., Natchez vicinity, 3/31/83, A, C, 83000949

China Grove Plantation, S of Natchez, Natchez vicinity, 4/07/82, A, C, 82003089

Cliffs Plantation, S of Natchez, Natchez vicinity, 9/18/80, C, 80002193

Clifton Heights Historic Distruct, Roughly bounded by Ridge and Mulberry Alley, Natchez Bluff, Park Ave., and Maple St., Natchez, 11/12/82, C, 82000568

Commercial Bank and Banker's House, 206 Main St. and 107 Canal St., Natchez, 5/30/74, C, NHL, 74002252

Cottage Gardens, 816 Myrtle Ave., Natchez, 7/05/79, B, C, 79001281

D'Evereux, D'Evereaux Dr., Natchez, 1/13/72, C, 72000683

Dicks, John, House, 802 N. Union St., Natchez, 3/25/82, C, 82003090

Dixon Building, 514 Main St., Natchez, 5/30/79, C, 79001282

Dubs, Dr. Charles H., Townhouse, 311 N. Pearl St., Natchez, 5/05/78, B, C, 78001577

Dunleith, 84 Homochitto St., Natchez, 9/14/72, B, C, NHL, 72000684

Edgewood, N of Natchez on MS 554, Natchez vicinity, 3/30/79, C, 79001283

Elgin, S of Natchez off U.S. 61, Natchez vicinity, 1/19/79, B, C, 79001284

Elizabeth Female Academy Site (No. 101-3X), E of Natchez on U.S. 84/98, Natchez vicinity, 5/06/77, A, f, NPS, 77000109

Elms Court, 42 John R. Junkin Dr., Natchez, 12/02/77, B, C, 77000780

Elms, The, 215 S. Pine St., Natchez, 11/07/76, B, C, 76001083

Emerald Mound Site (22AD504), Address Restricted, Stanton vicinity, 11/18/88, D, NHL, NPS, 88002618

Eola Hotel, Main and Pearl Sts., Natchez, 1/11/79, A, C, 79001285

Fair Oaks, S of Natchez on U.S. 61, Natchez vicinity, 11/13/76, A, C, 76001084

First Presbyterian Church of Natchez, 117 S. Pearl St., Natchez, 12/22/78, C, a, 78001578

Fort Dearborn Site, N of Washington off U.S. 61, Washington vicinity, 9/17/74, A, 74001054

Foster's Mound, NE of Natchez off US 61, Natchez vicinity, 9/02/82, C, 82003091

Glen Aubin, Off US 61, Natchez vicinity, 8/29/85, A, C, 85001930

Glen Mary Plantation and Tenant House, Foster Mound Rd., Natchez vicinity, 7/06/79, C, D, 79003380

Glenburnie, 551 John R. Junkin Dr., Natchez, 12/19/78, C, 78001579

Glencannon, Jct. of Providence Rd. and Gov. Fleet Rd., Natchez, 2/08/90, C, 89002322

Gloucester, S of Natchez on Lower Woodville Rd., Natchez vicinity, 11/07/76, B, C, d, 76001085

Grand Village of the Natchez Indians, 3 mi. SE of Natchez, Natchez vicinity, 10/15/66, D, NHL, 66000408

Hawthorne Place, Lower Woodville Rd., Natchez, 7/03/79, C, 79001286

Henderson-Britton House, 215 S. Pearl St., Natchez, 6/09/78, C, 78001580

Hillside, Hutchins Landing Rd., Natchez vicinity, 9/15/87, C, 87000617

Hope Farm, 147 Homochitto St., Natchez, 8/22/75, B, C, 75001037

House on Ellicott's Hill, N. Canal and Jefferson Sts., Natchez, 5/30/74, C, NHL, 74001050

Institute Hall, 111 S. Pearl ST., Natchez, 6/20/79, A, C, 79001287

Jefferson College, North St., Washington, 8/25/70, A, C, 70000316

Johnson, William, House, 210 State St., Natchez, 6/16/76, B, 76001086

Keyhole House, 1016 Main St., Natchez, 3/25/82, C, 82003092

King's Tavern, 611 Jefferson St., Natchez, 5/06/71, A, C, 71000444

Kingston Methodist Church, SE of Natchez, Natchez vicinity, 5/13/82, C, a, 82003093

Koontz House, 303 S. Rankin St., Natchez, 3/29/79, A, B, C, 79001288

Lansdowne, N of Natchez on Pine Ridge Rd., Natchez vicinity, 7/24/78, A, C, 78001581

Laurel Hill Plantation, S of Natchez off US 61, Natchez vicinity, 10/26/82, C, a, 82000569

Linden, 1 Linden Pl., Natchez, 9/01/78, B, C, 78001582

Lisle-Shields Town House, 701 N. Union St., Natchez, 3/29/79, B, C, 79001289

Longwood, 1.5 mi. SE of Natchez, Natchez vicinity, 12/16/69, C, NHL, 69000079

Magnolia Hill, SE of Natchez, Natchez vicinity, 3/30/79, C, 79001290

Manse, The, 307 S. Rankin St., Natchez, 3/07/79, C, a, 79001291

Mazique Archeological Site, Address Restricted, Natchez vicinity, 10/23/91, D, 91001529

Meadvilla, Address Restricted, Washington, 11/17/82, C, 82000570

Melrose, Melrose Ave., Natchez, 5/30/74, C, NHL, 74002253

Mercer House, 118 S. Wall St., Natchez, 8/09/79, C, 79001292

Mistletoe, NE of Natchez on MS 554, Natchez vicinity, 10/10/73, C, 73001000

Monmouth, E. Franklin St. and Melrose Ave., Natchez, 4/26/73, B, C, NHL, 73001001

Monteigne, Liberty Rd., Natchez, 12/11/74, B, 74001052

Montpellier, SE of Natchez on MS 551, Natchez vicinity, 12/18/79, C, 79001293

Mount Olive, NE of Natchez, Natchez vicinity, 11/28/80, C, 80002194

Mount Repose, N of Natchez on MS 555, Natchez vicinity, 6/19/79, C, 79001294

Murphy, Patrick, House, 21 Irvine Lane, Natchez, 4/09/80, C, 80002195

Myrtle Bank, 408 N. Pearl St., Natchez, 12/22/78, C, 78001583

Natchez On-Top-of-the-Hill Historic District, US 61, US 84 and US 98, Natchez, 9/17/79, A, C, 79003381

Natchez Bluffs and Under-the-Hill Historic District, Bounded by S. Canal St., Broadway, and Mississippi River, Natchez, 4/11/72, A, C, 72000685

Neibert-Fisk House, 310 N. Wall St., Natchez, 1/22/79, B, C, 79001295

Oakland, 9 Oakhurst Dr., Natchez, 10/21/76, A, C, 76001087

Oakland, Lower Woodville Rd., Natchez vicinity, 6/29/89, A, C, 89000781

Oakwood, Off Kingston Rd., Natchez vicinity, 5/09/85, C, 85000968

Adams County—Continued

Pine Ridge Church, NE of Natchez at Pine Ridge Rd. and MS 554, Natchez vicinity, 12/13/79, B, C, a, 79001296

Pleasant Hill, 310 Pearl St., Natchez, 3/28/79, C, b, 79001297

Prentiss Club, Pearl and Jefferson Sts., Natchez, 4/17/79, C, 79001298

Ravenna, 601 S. Union St., Natchez, 11/04/82, C, 82004975

Ravennaside, 601 S. Union St., Natchez, 7/05/79, B, C, 79001299

Richmond, Government Fleet Rd., Natchez, 11/16/78, B, C, 78001584

Roos House, 208 Linton Ave, Natchez, 11/08/79, B, C, 79001300

Rosalie, 100 Orleans St., Natchez, 8/16/77, A, C, NHL, 77000781

Routhland, 92 Winchester Rd., Natchez, 8/22/77, B, C, 77000782

Saragossa, S of Natchez on Saragossa Rd., Natchez vicinity, 11/24/80, C, 80002196

Selma Plantation House, 467 Selma Rd., Natchez, 6/15/89, C, 89000207

Shadyside, 107 Shadyside St., Natchez, 3/29/79, B, C, 79001301

Smart-Griffin House, 180 St. Catherine St., Natchez, 5/18/79, C, 79001302

Smith-Buntura-Evans House, 107 Broadway St., Natchez, 3/29/78, B, C, 78001585

Smithland, 1 mi. S of Kingston-Hutchins Rd., Natchez vicinity, 4/02/87, C, 87000575

Stanton Hall, High St. between Pearl and Commerce Sts., Natchez, 5/30/74, C, NHL, 74002254

Texada Tavern, 222 S. Wall St., Natchez, 4/17/79, B, C, 79001303

Tillman House, 506 High St., Natchez, 4/17/79, C, 79001304

Traveller's Rest, Address Restricted, Natchez vicinity, 5/03/84, C, 84002110

Upriver Residential District, Roughly bounded by Pine, Monroe, Elm-Bishop, and Ridge-Maple Sts., Natchez, 12/01/83, A, C, 83004371

Van Court Town House, 510 Washington St., Natchez, 7/09/80, C, 80004474

Warren-Erwin House, Palestine Rd., Washington vicinity, 3/19/82, C, b, 82003095

Washington Methodist Church, Main and Church Sts., Washington, 9/04/86, A, C, a, 86002168

Weymouth Hall, 1 Cemetery Rd., Natchez, 3/12/80, C, 80002197

White Cottage, 71 Homochitto St., Natchez, 10/13/83, C, 83003937

Winchester House, 816 Main St., Natchez, 1/31/79, B, C, 79001305

Woodstock, Carmel Church Rd., 12 mi. SE of Natchez, Natchez vicinity, 6/29/89, C, 89000782

Alcorn County

Battery Williams, Fulton Dr. at Southern Railroad, Corinth, 4/11/77, A, 77000783

Battle of Corinth, Confederate Assault Position, Shiloh Rd., Corinth, 4/30/76, A, 76001088

Coliseum Theatre, 404 Taylor St., Corinth, 8/21/80, C, 80002199

Dilworth, Thomas F., House, W off Hwy. 45, S of Biggersville, Biggersville vicinity, 9/15/88, C, 88001463

Downtown Corinth Historic District, Roughly bounded by Wick, Jackson, Foote and Webster Sts., Corinth, 1/28/93, A, C, 92001792

Federal Siege Trench, N of Corinth off U.S. 45, Corinth vicinity, 11/13/76, A, 76001089

Fort Robinette, Robinette St., Corinth, 4/11/72, A, c, f, 72000686

Jacinto Courthouse, Rte. 1, Rienzi, 11/25/69, C, 69000080

Midtown Corinth Historic District, Roughly bounded by Cass, Bunch, Washington, Main, Filmore, Linden, Douglas and Cruise Sts., Corinth, 12/23/93, C, 93001433

Moores Creek Site, Address Restricted, Rienzi vicinity, 7/07/75, D, 75001039

Siege and Battle of Corinth, Various locations in and around the town of Corinth, Corinth vicinity, 5/06/91, NHL, 91001050

Steele, L. C., House, 515 Fourth St., Corinth, 7/16/92, C, 92000855

US Post Office, Old, 515 Fillmore St., Corinth, 1/29/92, C, 91002038

Union Battery F, Battle of Corinth, Rabbitt Ranch Rd., Corinth vicinity, 9/10/87, A, 87001577

Veranda House, 711 Jackson St., Corinth, 8/22/75, A, B, C, 75001038

Amite County

Amite County Courthouse, Main St., Liberty, 4/09/74, C, g, 74001055

Amite Female Seminary, MS 569, Liberty, 4/17/80, C, a, 80002200

Batchelor, Thomas, House, 5 mi. E of Liberty of Olio Rd., Liberty vicinity, 3/27/75, B, C, 75001040

Bethany Institute, E of Centreville on MS 48, Centreville vicinity, 8/03/78, A, 78001588

Butler, Decatur N., House, Off MS 567, Liberty vicinity, 5/01/84, C, 84002113

Felder-Richmond House, Off I-55, Magnolia vicinity, 7/12/84, C, 84002115

Lea, Hampton, House, Lea Rd., Magnolia vicinity, 7/12/84, C, 84002120

Liberty Presbyterian Church, North Church St., Liberty, 5/16/85, C, a, 85001075

McGehee House, SE of Zion Hill, Liberty vicinity, 11/25/83, C, 83003939

Pinewood, S of Liberty off Greensburg Rd., Liberty vicinity, 7/05/84, C, 84002122

Sturdivant Fishweir, Address Restricted, Rosetta vicinity, 4/14/78, D, 78001589

Sunnyslope, NE of Centreville, Centreville vicinity, 3/22/82, C, 82003096

Talbert-Cassels House, Off MS 574, Gloster vicinity, 3/01/84, C, 84002125

Webb, George, House, E of Old Zion Hill Rd., Liberty vicinity, 11/17/83, C, 83003940

Wilkinson, Winston, House, N of Liberty on MS 567, Liberty vicinity, 4/17/80, C, 80002201

Attala County

Anderson, Col. Chap, House [Johnson, Andrew, Architecture in North Mississippi TR], 402 N. Jackson St., Kosciusko, 2/26/87, C, 87000233

Brown, David L., House, 200 E. Washington St., Kosciusko, 12/02/77, C, 77000784

Coffey, Col. J. K., House, E of Sallis off MS 12, Sallis vicinity, 2/08/79, B, C, 79001306

First Presbyterian Church, Old, Jct. of Huntington and Washington Sts., Kosciusko, 7/10/92, C, a, 92000846

Jackson—Browne House, 107 N. Wells St., Kosciusko, 2/05/87, C, 87000038

Jackson-Niles House, 121 N. Wells St., Kosciusko, 9/27/84, C, 84002127

Johnson—Sullivant House, 709 S. Wells St., Kosciusko, 6/26/86, C, 86001385

Lucas, John Copeland, House, 500 N. Huntington St., Kosciusko, 6/24/93, C, 93000573

Niles, Judge Henry C., House, 305 N. Huntington St., Kosciusko, 5/06/93, C, 93000383

Old Natchez Trace (212-3K 213-3K), NE of Kosciusko, Kosciusko vicinity, 11/07/76, A, NPS, 76000203

Shrock House, Shrock Rd., Goodman vicinity, 12/10/85, C, 85003520

Benton County

Davis' Mills Battle Site, Off MS 7, Michigan City, 10/02/73, A, 73001002

Bolivar County

Alligator Mounds, Address Restricted, Alligator vicinity, 7/24/74, D, 74001056

Donelson House, 2.5 mi. SW of Duncan, Duncan vicinity, 8/13/76, B, C, 76001091

Grace Episcopal Church, 203 Main St., Rosedale, 12/11/80, C, a, 80002202

Hollywood, S of Benoit on MS 448, Benoit vicinity, 4/01/75, C, 75001041

Montgomery, I. T., House, W. Main St., Mount Bayou, 5/11/76, B, NHL, 76001092

U.S. Post Office [Mississippi Post Offices 1931-1941 TR], 301 S. Sharpe Avenue, Cleveland, 4/07/81, A, C, 81000326

Calhoun County

West Mound, Address Restricted, Slate Springs vicinity, 12/02/92, D, 92001626

Carroll County

Carrollton Historic District, MS 35, Carrollton, 11/27/78, A, C, 78001590

Cotesworth, N of North Carrollton on Old Grenada Rd., North Carrollton vicinity, 6/09/78, B, C, 78001592

George, James Z., Law Office, Washington St. between Lexington and Green Sts., Carrollton, 1/13/72, B, 72000687

Malmaison Site, Address Restricted, Carrollton vicinity, 8/25/70, B, D, d, 70000317

Merrill's Store, Jackson and Lexington Sts., Carrollton, 1/13/72, A, 72000688

Rowland Site, Address Restricted, Greenwood vicinity, 6/23/78, D, 78001591

Teoc Creek Site, Address Restricted, Avalon vicinity, 5/06/71, D, 71000445

Chickasaw County

Bynum Mound and Village Site (22CS501), Address Restricted, Houston vicinity, 7/16/89, D, NPS, 89000783

Elliott-Donaldson House, 109 Church St., Okolona, 9/15/80, C, 80002203

Houston Carnegie Library, Madison and Huddleston Sts., Houston, 12/22/78, A, C, 78001593

Judge Bates House, S. Monroe St., Houston, 5/06/82, C, 82003097

Merchants and Farmers Bank Building, 423 Main St., Okolona, 5/14/87, C, 87000733

Owl Creek Site, Address Restricted, Old Houlka vicinity, 8/01/75, D, 75001042

Choctaw County

Drane, Col. James, House, Natchez Trace Pkwy, French Camp, 7/21/83, C, b, 83000950

Janet's Mound, Address Restricted, French Camp vicinity, 1/11/91, D, 90002125

Old Natchez Trace (230-3H), S of Mathiston, Mathiston vicinity, 11/07/76, A, NPS, 76000159

Claiborne County

Alcorn State University Historic District, Alcorn State University campus, Lorman, 5/20/82, A, B, C, 82003098

Bayou Pierre Site, Address Restricted, Port Gibson vicinity, 6/23/78, D, 78001596

Bethel Presbyterian Church, N of Alcorn on MS 552, Alcorn vicinity, 11/28/78, A, C, a, 78001594

Buena Vista Cotton Gin, NE of Port Gibson, Port Gibson vicinity, 12/27/74, A, 74001059

Building at 801 Chinquepin Street [Port Gibson MRA], 801 Chinquepin St., Port Gibson, 7/22/79, C, b, 79003420

Canemount, N of Alcorn off MS 552, Alcorn vicinity, 12/02/82, C, 82000572

Catholic Cemetery [Port Gibson MRA; Historic Cemeteries in Port Gibson TR], 700 Coffee St., Port Gibson, 7/22/79, A, a, d, 79003425

Catledge Archeological Site, Address Restricted, Alcorn vicinity, 7/15/74, D, 74001058

Centers Creek Mound, Address Restricted, Russum vicinity, 8/14/73, D, 73001003

Chamberlain-Hunt Academy Historic District [Port Gibson MRA], Roughly bounded by US 61, city limits, Woodstock St., and SR 547, Port Gibson, 7/22/79, C, 79003411

Claremont [Port Gibson MRA], 366 Claremont Dr., Port Gibson, 7/22/79, B, C, 79003418

Collins [Port Gibson MRA], Greenwood St. Extension, Port Gibson, 7/22/79, B, C, 79003419

Drake Hill Historic District [Port Gibson MRA], Drake Hill Rd., Port Gibson, 7/22/79, B, C, 79003412

Golden West Cemetery [Port Gibson MRA; Historic Cemeteries in Port Gibson TR], Rodney Rd., Port Gibson, 7/22/79, A, d, 79003417

Grand Gulf Military State Park, 6 mi. W of Port Gibson, Port Gibson vicinity, 4/11/72, A, 72000689

Idlewild [Port Gibson MRA], 310 Idlewild Dr., Port Gibson, 7/22/79, C, 79003416

Jewish Cemetery [Port Gibson MRA; Historic Cemeteries in Port Gibson TR], 900 Marginal St., Port Gibson, 7/22/79, A, C, a, d, 79003415

Market Street-Suburb Ste. Mary Historic District [Port Gibson MRA], Roughly bounded by Orange, Marginal, Greenwood, and Market Sts., Port Gibson, 7/22/79, A, C, 79003410

McGregor [Port Gibson MRA], SR 547, Port Gibson, 7/22/79, C, 79003424

Nelson, John, Site, Address Restricted, Willows vicinity, 6/13/74, D, 74001060

Oakland Chapel, Alcorn State University campus, Alcorn, 12/27/74, A, C, a, NHL, 74001057

Old Brickyard Place [Port Gibson MRA], Anthony St., Port Gibson, 7/22/79, A, C, 79003423

Old Depot Restaraunt and Lounge [Port Gibson MRA], 1202 Market St., Port Gibson, 7/22/79, A, 79003421

Old Natchez Trace (132-3T), NE of Port Gibson, Port Gibson vicinity, 11/07/76, A, NPS, 76000161

Owens Creek Bridge [Historic Bridges of Mississippi TR], Spans Owen Creek on Old CR, Utica vicinity, 11/16/88, A, C, 88002398

Port Gibson Battlefield, 4 mi. W of Port Gibson, Port Gibson vicinity, 11/03/72, A, 72000690

Port Gibson Oil Works Mill Building [Port Gibson MRA], Anthony St., Port Gibson, 7/22/79, A, 79003422

Sacred Heart Roman Catholic Church, Grand Gulf Military Monument Park, Port Gibson vicinity, 11/23/87, C, a, b, 73002241

Smithfield Site, Address Restricted, Bruinsburg vicinity, 6/09/78, D, 78001595

Van Dorn House [Port Gibson MRA], Van Dorn Dr., Port Gibson, 6/21/71, B, C, 71000446

Widow's Creek Bridge [Historic Bridges of Mississippi TR], Spans Widow's Creek on CR, Port Gibson vicinity, 11/16/88, A, C, 88002409

Windsor Ruins, 12 mi. SW of Port Gibson on MS 552, Port Gibson vicinity, 11/23/71, A, 71000447

Windsor Site, Address Restricted, Port Gibson vicinity, 2/07/79, D, 79003126

Wintergreen Cemetery [Port Gibson MRA; Historic Cemeteries in Port Gibson TR], E. Greenwood St., Port Gibson, 7/22/79, C, d, 79003414

Clarke County

Adams-Taylor-McRae House [Clarke County Antebellum Houses TR], E of Pachuta, Elwood Community, 5/22/80, C, 80002207

Asher's Cabin [Clarke County Antebellum Houses TR], SR 513, Stonewall, 5/22/80, B, C, 80002234

Barbour-Estes House [Clarke County Antebellum Houses TR], River Rd., Enterprise, 5/22/80, C, 80002209

Bradshaw-Booth House [Clarke County Antebellum Houses TR], Stonewall St., Enterprise, 5/22/80, C, 80002210

Brown-Wilson House [Clarke County Antebellum Houses TR], SR 11, Enterprise, 5/22/80, C, 80002211

Carmichael House [Clarke County Antebellum Houses TR], S of DeSoto on Gulf, Mobile and Ohio RR tracks, DeSoto, 5/22/80, C, 80002204

Compton-Short House [Clarke County Antebellum Houses TR], Tuscaboma St., Enterprise, 5/22/80, A, C, 80002212

Cook-Sellers House [Clarke County Antebellum Houses TR], E. Station St., DeSoto, 5/22/80, A, 80002205

Covington House [Clarke County Antebellum Houses TR], NE of DeSoto, DeSoto vicinity, 5/22/80, B, C, 80002206

Davis House [Clarke County Antebellum Houses TR], River Rd., Enterprise, 5/22/80, A, C, a, 80002213

Dearman House [Clarke County Antebellum Houses TR], Bridge St. and River Rd., Enterprise, 5/22/80, C, 80002214

Enterprise Bridge [Historic Bridges of Mississippi TR], Spans Chickasawhay River on Bridge St., Enterprise, 11/16/88, A, C, 88002402

Ford-Williams House [Clarke County Antebellum Houses TR], SR 514, Energy vicinity, 5/22/80, C, 80002208

Forestdale Plantation [Clarke County Antebellum Houses TR], Address unknown at this time, Pachuta, 5/22/80, A, 80002229

Hand House [Clarke County Antebellum Houses TR], North St., Shubuta, 5/22/80, A, C, 80002231

Highway 11 Bridge over Chunky River [Historic Bridges of Mississippi TR], Spans Chunky River on US 11, Enterprise vicinity, 11/16/88, A, C, 88002400

Hunter-Frost House [Clarke County Antebellum Houses TR], River Rd., Enterprise, 5/22/80, A, C, 80002215

Lee-Mitts House [Clarke County Antebellum Houses TR], Stonewall St., Enterprise, 5/22/80, B, C, 80002216

Clarke County—Continued

McCrory-Deas-Buckley House [Clarke County Antebellum Houses TR], Bridge St., Enterprise, 5/22/80, C, 80002217

McNeill-McGee House [Clarke County Antebellum Houses TR], NE of Lake Bounds, Lake Bounds, 5/22/80, A, C, 80002226

Methodist Parsonage House [Clarke County Antebellum Houses TR], A St., Enterprise, 5/22/80, C, a, 80002219

Overseer's House and Outbuildings of Lang Plantation [Clarke County Antebellum Houses TR], Address unknown at this time, Langsdale, 5/22/80, A, C, 80002227

Pilgrim's Rest [Clarke County Antebellum Houses TR], Tuscaboma St., Enterprise, 5/22/80, C, 80002220

Prairie Place [Clarke County Antebellum Houses TR], Address unknown at this time, Langsdale, 5/22/80, A, C, 80002228

Price-Patton-Pettis House [Clarke County Antebellum Houses TR], North and 2nd Sts., Shubuta, 5/22/80, A, 80002232

Riverside Plantation [Clarke County Antebellum Houses TR], SR 11, Enterprise, 5/22/80, A, C, 80002221

Shubuta Bridge [Historic Bridges of Mississippi TR], Spans Chickasawhay River on CR E of Shubuta, Shubuta vicinity, 11/16/88, A, C, 88002490

Smith-McClain-Buckley House [Clarke County Antebellum Houses TR], Stonewall St., Enterprise, 5/22/80, B, C, 80002222

Stephenson-Allen House [Clarke County Antebellum Houses TR], Bridge St., Enterprise, 5/22/80, A, C, 80002223

Sumrall-Albritton House [Clarke County Antebellum Houses TR], SR 45, Shubuta, 5/22/80, A, 80002233

Trotter-Byrd House [Clarke County Antebellum Houses TR], 419 E. Franklin St., Quitman, 5/22/80, B, C, 80002230

Ward House [Clarke County Antebellum Houses TR], 3 mi N of Enterprise, Enterprise vicinity, 5/22/80, A, C, 80002224

Woolverton-Boyd House [Clarke County Antebellum Houses TR], Off SR 513, Enterprise, 5/22/80, C, 80002225

Clay County

Anderson, Dewitt, House [West Point MPS], 104 W. Broad St., West Point, 8/31/90, C, 90001279

Brandtown Gin Historic District [Clay County MPS], MS 47 at Brandtown, W of Prairie, Prairie vicinity, 11/15/91, A, 91001634

Brogan Mound and Village Site Discontiguous District, Address Restricted, West Point vicinity, 5/24/91, D, 91000607

Colbert and Barton Townsites, Address Restricted, West Point vicinity, 6/20/77, A, D, 77000785

Commerce Street Historic District [West Point MPS], 508–731 Commerce St., West Point, 8/31/90, C, 90001283

Cooper, Robert L., House [Clay County MPS], Mhoon Valley Rd., W of West Point, West Point vicinity, 11/15/91, C, 91001635

Court Street Historic District, Court Street between Travis and E. Broad Streets, West Point, 8/12/82, C, 82004835

East Main Street Historic District [West Point MPS], 510–1030 E. Main St., West Point, 8/31/90, C, 90001282

Holmes, Mary, Junior College Historic District [Clay County MPS], MS 50 W of jct. with MS 45W, West Point, 11/15/91, A, 91001637

Jordan, Charles R., House [Clay County MPS], Tibbee—Columbus Rd. S of New Hope Church, West Point vicinity, 11/15/91, C, 91001636

Jordan, Moses, House [West Point MPS], 940 E. Broad St., West Point, 8/31/90, C, b, 90001278

Mathews, Nathan, House and Mathews Cotton Gin [Clay County MPS], Mathews Gin Rd. N of Union Staff Church, West Point vicinity, 11/15/91, A, 91001638

Montpelier Historic District [Clay County MPS], Jct. of MS 389 and MS 46, Montpelier, 11/15/91, A, 91001639

Pheba Historic District [Clay County MPS], Pheba St. No. 2, just W of MS 389, Pheba, 11/15/91, A, 91001640

Powell—Vail House [Clay County MPS], E side of Vail Rd., 1.2 mi. N of MS 50, Pheba vicinity, 11/15/91, C, 91001641

South Division Street Historic District [West Point MPS], 447–646 S. Division St., West Point, 8/31/90, C, 90001281

Tibbee Bridge [Historic Bridges of Mississippi TR], Spans Tibbee Creek on Old Tibbee Rd., West Point vicinity, 11/16/88, A, C, 88002411

Tibbee School [Clay County MPS], Tibbee—Columbus Rd., at Tibbee, West Point vicinity, 11/15/91, A, 91001642

Town of Palo Alto, Address Restricted, Palo Alto vicinity, 8/20/87, D, 87000473

Turnage House [Clay County MPS], Turnage Rd. NE of Palestine Church, Montpelier vicinity, 11/15/91, C, 91001643

Una Consolidated School [Clay County MPS], Una—Prairie Rd. E of Pleasant Grove Church, Prairie vicinity, 11/15/91, A, 91001644

Waverley, 10 mi. E of West Point, West Point vicinity, 9/20/73, B, C, NHL, 73001004

Waverly Bridge [Historic Bridges of Mississippi TR], Spans Tombigbee River on Columbus and Greenville RR, Waverly vicinity, 3/20/89, A, C, 88002412

West Clay County Agricultural School [Clay County MPS], Between Pheba Sts. Nos. 7 and 8, S of MS 50, Pheba, 11/15/91, A, 91001645

West Point Central City Historic District, MS 50, West Point, 6/01/82, A, C, 82003099

West Point School Historic District [West Point MPS], Roughly bounded by E. Westbrook, Calhoun, Travis and East Sts., West Point, 8/31/90, C, 90001280

Coahoma County

Barner Site (22CO542), Address Restricted, Clarksdale vicinity, 3/08/84, D, 84002129

Carson Mounds, Address Restricted, Clarksdale vicinity, 4/19/79, A, D, 79003382

Davis, Rufus, Site, Address Restricted, Clarksdale vicinity, 6/15/78, C, 78001597

Dickerson Site (22CO502), Address Restricted, Friars Point vicinity, 9/11/86, D, 86002323

Humber Site, Address Restricted, Farrel vicinity, 5/12/75, A, D, d, 75001043

Oliver Site, Address Restricted, Clarksdale vicinity, 12/30/74, D, d, 74001061

Parchman Place Site, Address Restricted, Coahoma vicinity, 5/17/73, D, 73001005

Salomon (Salmon) Site, Address Restricted, Coahoma vicinity, 3/08/84, D, 84002134

Spendthrift Site (22CO520), Address Restricted, Mattson vicinity, 9/11/86, D, 86002330

Sunflower Landing, Address Restricted, Rena Lara vicinity, 10/02/91, D, 91001422

Wilsford, Address Restricted, Lula vicinity, 12/30/74, D, 74001062

Yazoo Pass Levee, Near Moon Lake on MS 1, Moon Lake vicinity, 6/19/73, A, 73001006

Copiah County

Ailes House, Rhymes Rd. near jct. with MS 27, Crystal Springs vicinity, 4/09/91, C, 91000420

Alford-Little House, S of Georgetown off MS 27, Georgetown vicinity, 10/19/82, C, 82000573

Cherry Grove, Old Hwy. 51 N of jct. with MS 27, Crystal Springs vicinity, 8/10/90, C, d, 90001224

Cook House, 222 Extension St., Hazlehurst, 12/08/83, C, 83003941

Covington, Robert L., House, 240 S. Extension St., Hazlehurst, 3/01/84, C, 84002139

Ellis, Isaac Newton, House, 258 S. Extension St., Hazlehurst, 11/02/87, C, 87001914

Gallman Historic District, Roughly US 51 and Church St., Gallman, 3/31/86, A, C, 86000832

Gatesville Bridge [Historic Bridges of Mississippi TR], Spans Pearl River on CR E of Gatesville, Gatesville vicinity, 11/16/88, A, C, 88002482

Hargrave House, MS 28 14 mi. W of Hazlehurst, Hazlehurst vicinity, 4/05/93, C, c, 91001465

Homochitto River Bridge [Historic Bridges of Mississippi TR], Spans Homochitto River on CR, Hazlehurst vicinity, 11/16/88, A, C, 88002491

Little, Dr. William, House, 1022 Collier St., Wesson, 3/04/93, C, 93000143

Mount Hope, Off Rt. 2 across from Mt. Hope Cemetery, Hazlehurst vicinity, 3/21/85, A, C, 85000616

Old Wesson Public School Building, Off U.S. 51, Wesson, 10/16/80, A, C, 80002235

Parsons, C. H., House, 208 W. Georgetown St., Crystal Springs, 9/07/84, C, 84002140

Rockport Bridge [Historic Bridges of Mississippi TR], Spans Pearl River on CR S of Georgetown, Georgetown vicinity, 11/16/88, A, C, 88002414

Copiah County—Continued

US Post Office—Crystal Springs [Mississippi Post Offices TR], 224 E. Marion St., Crystal Springs, 3/18/93, A, C, 80004887

US Post Office—Hazlehurst [Mississippi Post Offices TR], 130 Caldwell Dr., Hazlehurst, 3/18/93, A, C, 80004886

Welch, Jenkins H., House, 1/2 mi. N of MS 28 on Dentville Rd., Hazlehurst vicinity, 6/30/88, C, 88000972

Willing, Col. William James, House, 272 S. Jackson St., Crystal Springs, 7/10/92, A, B, 92000835

Covington County

Covington County Courthouse, Dogwood Ave., Collins, 12/31/91, C, 91001894

De Soto County

Labauve, Felix, House, 235 Magnolia Dr., Hernando, 3/29/78, B, C, 78003074

Miller Plantation House, Miller Rd., Olive Branch vicinity, 7/15/82, C, 82004630

Forrest County

Building 6981, Camp Shelby, Camp Shelby, Hattiesburg vicinity, 6/11/92, A, 92000698

Hattiesburg Historic Neighborhood District, Roughly bounded by RR tracks, Katie Ave., Frederick and Hardy Sts., Hattiesburg, 9/17/80, B, C, 80002236

Hub City Historic District, U.S. 49 and U.S. 11, Hattiesburg, 8/29/80, A, C, 80002237

North Main Street Historic District, Roughly bounded by Jackson St., Gordon's Cr., South, North, Providence and Red Sts. and the Illinois Central RR tracks, Hattiesburg, 4/16/93, C, 93000307

Oaks Historic District, Roughly bounded by Hardy, Second, Railroad and 11th Aves., Hattiesburg, 3/04/93, C, 93000136

Old Hattiesburg High School, 846 Main St., Hattiesburg, 5/29/87, C, 87000817

Saenger Theatre, Forrest and Front Sts., Hattiesburg, 5/29/79, A, C, 79001307

Tall Pines, S of Hattiesburg on Memorial Dr., Hattiesburg vicinity, 10/16/80, B, 80002238

U.S. District Courthouse, S corner of Pine and Forrest Sts., Hattiesburg, 9/18/73, C, 73001007

U.S. Post Office [Mississippi Post Offices 1931-1941 TR], 115 W. Pine St., Hattiesburg, 4/21/83, C, g, 83000951

Franklin County

Beam, Charles Walton, House, Jct. of Bogue Chitto-Meadville Rd. and Upper Meadville-Summit Rd., 7 mi. S of McCall Creek, McCall Creek vicinity, 3/21/90, C, 90000437

Ediceton Bridge [Historic Bridges of Mississippi TR], Spans Homochitto River on CR, Ediceton vicinity, 11/16/88, A, C, 88002404

Franklin County Courthouse, Courthouse Sq., Meadville, 12/17/81, C, 81000327

George County

Bilbo Basin Shell Deposit Site, Address Restricted, Lucedale vicinity, 2/25/92, D, 92000039

Greene County

Leaf River Bridge [Historic Bridges of Mississippi TR], Spans Leaf River N of McClain on CR, McClain vicinity, 11/16/88, A, C, 88002478

Grenada County

Confederate Earthworks, W of Grenada off MS 8, Grenada vicinity, 7/02/73, A, 73001008

Evergreen Plantation, 4 mi. N of Grenada on Hardy Rd., Grenada vicinity, 10/18/77, B, C, 77000786

Grenada Bank, 223 1st St., Grenada, 11/28/78, A, C, 78001598

Grenada Masonic Temple [Grenada MRA], 210 S. Main St., Grenada, 1/20/88, C, 87002307

Illinois Central Depot [Grenada MRA], 643 First St., Grenada, 4/07/88, A, 87002308

Lee-Dubard House [Grenada MRA], 317 Third St., Grenada, 1/20/88, C, 87002312

Margin St. Historic District [Grenada MRA], Margin St. & part of Line St. between Commerce and Green Sts., Grenada, 4/07/88, C, a, 87002338

Odd Fellows and Confederate Cemetery [Grenada MRA], Corner of Cemetery and Commerce Sts., Grenada, 1/20/88, C, d, 87002341

Providence Cemetery, Rt. 4, Providence Rd. E of Grenada, Grenada vicinity, 10/02/91, A, d, 91001423

South Main Historic District [Grenada MRA], S. Main St., Grenada, 1/20/88, C, a, 87002345

US Post Office—Grenada, 178 S. Main St., Grenada, 1/09/85, C, 85000117

Walthall, Sen. Edward C., House [Grenada MRA], 73 College Blvd., Grenada, 1/20/88, B, 87002349

Wild Wings Mounds (22Gr713), Address Restricted, Holcomb vicinity, 12/14/88, D, 88002704

Hancock County

Beach Boulevard Historic District [Bay St. Louis MRA], Roughly bounded by Beach Blvd., Necaise Ave., Seminary Dr., 2nd and 3rd Sts., Bay St. Louis, 11/25/80, A, C, a, d, 80002239

Building at 242 St. Charles Street [Bay St. Louis MRA], 242 St. Charles St., Bay St. Louis, 11/25/80, C, 80002240

Claiborne Site (22Ha501), Address Restricted, Pearlington vicinity, 11/12/82, D, 82000574

Glen Oak—Kimbrough House [Bay St. Louis MRA], 806 N. Beach Blvd., Bay St. Louis, 11/21/86, C, 86003271

Jackson Landing Site, Address Restricted, Pearlington vicinity, 7/27/73, D, 73001009

Main Street Historic District [Bay St. Louis MRA], Main St., Bay St. Louis, 11/25/80, C, 80002241

Nugent Site (22HA592), Address Restricted, Kiln vicinity, 4/13/88, D, 88000307

Rocket Propulsion Test Complex, National Space Technology Laboratories (NSTL), Bay St. Louis, 10/03/85, A, C, g, NHL, 85002805

SJ Mound (22HA594), Address Restricted, Pearlington vicinity, 4/13/88, D, 88000304

Sycamore Street Historic District [Bay St. Louis MRA], Sycamore St., Bay St. Louis, 11/25/80, A, C, 80002242

Taylor House [Bay St. Louis MRA], 808 N. Beach Blvd., Bay St. Louis, 11/21/86, C, 86003273

Taylor School [Bay St. Louis MRA], 116 Leonard St., Bay St. Louis, 1/15/87, A, C, 87000209

Three Sisters Shell Midden (22-Ha-596), Address Restricted, Pearlington vicinity, 7/28/88, D, 88001138

Up the Tree Shell Midden (22HA595), Address Restricted, Pearlington vicinity, 4/13/88, D, 88000306

Washington Street Historic District [Bay St. Louis MRA], Washington St., Bay St. Louis, 11/25/80, A, C, g, 80002243

Webb School/Gulf Coast Community Action Agency [Bay St. Louis MRA], 300 Third St., Bay St. Louis, 11/21/86, A, C, 86003554

Williams Site (22-Ha-585), Address Restricted, Pearlington vicinity, 7/28/88, D, 88001137

Harrison County

Bailey House [Biloxi MRA], 1333 E. Beach Blvd., Biloxi, 5/18/84, C, a, 84002160

Barq, E., Pop Factory [Biloxi MRA], 224 Keller Ave., Biloxi, 5/18/84, A, C, 84002164

Bass, Raymond, Site (22HR636), Address Restricted, Biloxi, 2/26/87, D, 87000230

Beauvoir, 200 W. Beach Blvd., Biloxi, 9/03/71, B, NHL, 71000448

Biloxi Garden Center, 410 E. Bayview Ave., Biloxi, 1/18/73, B, C, 73001011

Biloxi Lighthouse, On U.S. 90 at Porter Ave., Biloxi, 10/03/73, A, 73001012

Biloxi's Tivoli Hotel [Biloxi MRA], 863 E. Beach Dr., Biloxi, 5/18/84, C, 84002167

Bond House [Biloxi MRA], 925 W. Howard Ave., Biloxi, 5/18/84, C, a, 84002169

Brielmaier House [Biloxi MRA], 436 Main St., Biloxi, 5/18/84, C, 84002170

Brunet-Fourchy House [Biloxi MRA], 138 Magnolia St. Mall, Biloxi, 5/18/84, C, 84002173

Harrison County—Continued

Church of the Redeemer [Biloxi MRA], Bellman St., Biloxi, 5/18/84, C, a, 84002177

Clemens House [Biloxi MRA], 120 W. Water St., Biloxi, 5/18/84, C, 84002180

Dantzler, G. B., House, 1238 E. Beach Blvd., Gulfport, 12/01/89, C, 89002051

Fisherman's Cottage [Biloxi MRA], 138 Lameuse St., Biloxi, 3/09/90, C, b, 84002182

Fort Massachusetts, S of Gulfport on Ship Island, in Gulf Islands National Seashore, Gulfport vicinity, 6/21/71, A, C, NPS, 71000067

French Warehouse Site, Gulf Islands National Seashore, Ocean Springs vicinity, 12/13/91, D, NPS, 91001768

Gillis House, 513 E. Beach Blvd., Biloxi, 7/07/78, C, b, 78001599

Gulf Coast Center for the Arts [Biloxi MRA], 138 Lameuse St., Biloxi, 5/18/84, C, 84002187

Harbor Square Historic District, Roughly bounded by L & N Railroad, 23rd Ave., 13th St. and 27th Ave., Gulfport, 8/13/85, A, C, 85001788

Hermann House [Biloxi MRA], 523 E. Beach Blvd., Biloxi, 5/18/84, C, 84002189

Hewes Building, 2505 14th St., Gulfport, 10/07/82, A, C, 82000575

House at 121 W. Water Street [Biloxi MRA], 121 W. Water St., Biloxi, 5/18/84, C, 84002191

House at 407 East Howard Avenue, 407 E. Howard Ave., Biloxi, 7/17/86, C, 86001673

Magnolia Hotel, 137 Magnolia St., Biloxi, 3/14/73, A, C, 73001013

Milner House, 720 E. Beach Blvd., Gulfport, 7/31/72, B, C, 72000692

Nativity BVM Cathedral [Biloxi MRA], W. Howard Ave. and Fayard St., Biloxi, 5/18/84, C, a, 84002193

Peoples Bank of Biloxi [Biloxi MRA], 318 Lameuse St., Biloxi, 5/18/84, C, 84002195

Quarles, W. J., House and Cottage, 120 and 122 E. Railroad St., Long Beach, 10/16/80, B, 80002244

Redding House [Biloxi MRA], 126 W. Jackson St., Biloxi, 5/18/84, C, 84002197

Reed, Pleasant, House, 928 Elmer St., Biloxi, 1/11/79, A, C, 79001308

Saenger Theater [Biloxi MRA], 416 Reynoir St., Biloxi, 5/18/84, C, 84002200

Scenic Drive Historic District, Scenic Dr., Pass Christian, 5/07/79, A, C, 79001309

Scherer House [Biloxi MRA], 206 W. Water St., Biloxi, 5/18/84, C, 84002201

Seashore Campground School [Biloxi MRA], Leggett Dr. and Chalmers St., Biloxi, 5/18/84, C, a, 84002204

Suter House [Biloxi MRA], 165 Suter Pl., Biloxi, 5/18/84, C, 84002205

Swetman, Glenn, House [Biloxi MRA], 2770 Wilkes Ave., Biloxi, 5/18/84, C, 84002206

Toledano-Philbrick-Tullis House, 947 E. Beach Blvd., Biloxi, 11/05/76, A, C, 76001095

U.S. Post Office, Courthouse, and Customhouse, 216 Lameuse St., Biloxi, 1/30/78, A, C, 78001600

US Post Office and Customhouse, 2421 13th St., Gulfport, 3/19/84, C, 84002209

West Beach Historic District [Biloxi MRA], Roughly U.S. 90 between Rosell and Chalmers Ave., Biloxi, 5/18/84, C, d, 84002210

West Central Historic District [Biloxi MRA], Roughly bounded by U.S. 90, Hopkins Blvd., Howard and Benachi Aves., Biloxi, 5/18/84, C, 84002212

Hinds County

Armour Company Smokehouse and Distribution Plant, 320 W. Pearl St., Jackson, 11/25/83, A, 83003956

Ayer Hall, 1400 Lynch St. on Jackson State University campus, Jackson, 7/14/77, A, 77000788

Bailey Hill Civil War Earthworks, Off U.S. 51, Jackson, 5/06/75, A, 75001044

Belhaven Heights Historic District, Bellevue Place, N. Jefferson, Madison, and Morningside Sts., Jackson, 11/25/83, C, 83003958

Berry Mound and Village Archeological Site, Address Restricted, Terry vicinity, 11/25/69, D, 69000088

Big Black River Battlefield, On both banks of the Big Black River between Smith's Station and Bovina, Smith's Station vicinity, 11/23/71, A, B, 71000451

Boteler, Lillian, House [Raymond and Vicinity MRA], 214 Port Gibson Rd., Raymond, 7/15/86, C, 86001703

Byram Bridge [Swinging Suspension Bridges TR], Old Byram and Florence Rd., Bryam, 5/23/79, A, C, 79003427

Capitol Green, Bounded on the N by Amite St., on the S by Pearl St., on the W by State St., on the E by the Gulf, Mobile and Ohio RR, Jackson, 11/25/69, A, 69000083

Cates, John F., House, MS 22, Brownsville vicinity, 5/16/85, A, C, 85001076

Cedars, The, 405 E. College St., Clinton, 1/04/77, C, 77000787

Central Fire Station, S. President St., Jackson, 10/30/75, A, 75001045

Champion Hill Battlefield, 4 mi. SW of Bolton, Bolton vicinity, 10/07/71, A, NHL, 71000450

City Hall, 203 S. President St., Jackson, 11/25/69, A, C, 69000084

City Mound (22Hi672), Address Restricted, Jackson, 12/01/88, D, 88002703

Dupree House, W of Raymond on Dupree Rd., Raymond vicinity, 1/31/79, C, 79001314

Dupree Mound and Village Archeological Site, Address Restricted, Edwards vicinity, 11/25/69, D, 69000082

Dupree—Ratliff House [Raymond and Vicinity MRA], 101 Dupree St., Raymond, 7/15/86, C, 86001704

Edwards Hotel, Capitol and Mill Sts., Jackson, 11/07/76, C, 76001096

Farish Street Neighborhood Historic District, Roughly bounded by Amite, Mill, Fortification and Lamar Sts., Jackson, 3/13/80, A, B, C, g, 80002245

Farish Street Neighborhood Historic District (Boundary Increase), Roughly bounded by Amite, Lamar, Mill and Fortifications Sts., Jackson, 9/18/80, B, C, g, 80004542

Floyd Mound, Address Restricted, Bovina vicinity, 11/25/69, D, 69000081

Fountainhead, 306 Glen Way, Jackson, 11/28/80, C, g, 80002246

Futch, James M., House, Dry Grove Rd. 1 1/2 mi. S of jct. with MS 18, Raymond vicinity, 3/12/92, C, 92000144

Galloway—Williams House, 427 E. Fortification St., Jackson, 10/10/85, C, 85003100

Gibbs—Von Seutter House [Raymond and Vicinity MRA], S side of Dupree St., Raymond, 7/15/86, C, 86001705

Green, Garner Wynn, House, 647 N. State St., Jackson, 10/31/85, B, C, 85003440

Greenwood Cemetery, Bounded by West, Davis, Lamar and George Sts., Jackson, 12/20/84, A, C, d, 84000474

Hinds County Courthouse [Raymond and Vicinity MRA], E. Main and N. Oak Sts., Raymond, 7/15/86, A, C, 86001706

Hinds County Courthouse, Pascagoula St., Jackson, 7/31/86, C, 86002125

Illinois Central Railroad Depot [Raymond and Vicinity MRA], E. Main and Railroad Sts., Raymond, 7/15/86, A, C, 86001707

Jones, Dudley, House, 115 Railroad Ave., Terry, 8/02/84, C, 84002218

Keith Press Building [Raymond and Vicinity MRA], 234 Town Sq., Raymond, 7/15/86, C, 86001708

Lewis, A. J., House, S. Magnolia and Lewis Sts., Edwards, 8/04/83, B, C, 83000952

Lewis, Ervin, House, 5461 Old Byram Rd., Byram, 12/01/89, C, 89002052

Magnolia Vale, Off MS 18, Raymond vicinity, 11/17/83, C, 83003960

Main Hall [Raymond and Vicinity MRA], NW of Cain Hall, Raymond, 7/15/86, A, 86001709

Manship House, 412 E. Fortification St., Jackson, 10/18/72, B, C, 72000693

Manship House (Boundary Increase), 412 E. Fortification, Jackson, 7/17/80, A, 80004543

McNair Plantation, SE of Raymond on MS 18, Raymond vicinity, 5/03/82, C, 82003101

Merrill-Maley House, 739 N. State St., Jackson, 4/29/82, C, 82003100

Millsaps-Buie House, 628 N. State St., Jackson, 6/19/73, B, 73001014

Mississippi Federation of Women's Clubs, 2407 N. State St., Jackson, 6/30/88, A, C, 88000975

Mississippi Governor's Mansion, 316 E. Capitol St., Jackson, 11/25/69, A, B, C, g, 69000085

Mississippi State Capitol, Fronting Mississippi St., between N. President and N. West Sts., Jackson, 11/25/69, A, C, 69000086

Morris, Joseph Henry, House, 305 N. State St., Jackson, 8/11/83, C, 83000953

Oaks, The, 823 N. Jefferson St., Jackson, 5/25/73, B, 73001015

Hinds County—Continued

Old State Capitol, 100 N. State St., Jackson, 11/25/69, A, B, C, NHL, 69000087

Peyton House, N of Raymond on Clinton Rd., Raymond vicinity, 10/03/73, A, C, 73001016

Phoenix Hall—Johnson-Harper House [Raymond and Vicinity MRA], 527 E. Palestine St., Raymond, 7/15/86, C, 86001710

Pocahontas Mound A, Address Restricted, Pocahontas vicinity, 11/25/69, D, 69000365

Pocahontas Mound B, Address Restricted, Pocahontas vicinity, 4/11/72, D, 72000694

Porter Family Homestead [Raymond and Vicinity MRA], Off MS 18, Raymond vicinity, 7/15/86, C, 86001702

Raymond Battlefield Site, 2.5 mi. SW of Raymond on MS 18, Raymond vicinity, 1/13/72, A, B, 72000695

Robertson, Smith, Elementary School, 528 Bloom St., Jackson, 12/13/78, A, C, g, 78001601

Saint Mark's Episcopal Church [Raymond and Vicinity MRA], W. Main and N. Oak Sts., Raymond, 7/15/86, A, C, 86001712

Shelton House [Raymond and Vicinity MRA], 561 W. Main St., Raymond, 7/15/86, C, 86001711

Sims House, 513 N. State St., Jackson, 3/31/83, C, 83000954

Smith Park Architectural District, Irregular pattern along N. West and N. Congress Sts. between Captiol St. and State Capitol, Jackson, 4/23/76, C, a, g, 76001097

Smith Park Architectural District (Boundary Increase), 225 E. Capitol St., Jackson, 10/29/93, C, 93001152

Spengler's Corner, 101 N. State St., Jackson, 10/20/77, A, B, 77000789

Spengler's Corner Historic District, E. Capitol, N. State and N. President Sts, Jackson, 11/15/79, A, C, 79001311

Sub Rosa, S of Pocahontas on U.S. 49, Pocahontas vicinity, 4/28/75, C, 75001046

Virden-Patton House, 512 N. State St., Jackson, 12/16/83, C, 83003962

Warren-Guild-Simmons House, 734 Fairview St., Jackson, 1/11/79, C, 79001312

West Capitol Street Historic District, Roughly bounded by RR tracks, Amite, Roach and Pearl Sts., Jackson, 3/13/80, A, C, g, 80002248

Williams, Alex, House, 937 N. Lamar St., Jackson, 7/03/79, C, 79001313

Wilson, Woodrow, Bridge [Historic Bridges of Mississippi TR], Spans Pearl River on Silas Brown St., Jackson, 11/16/88, A, C, 88002485

Wolfe House, 401 Claiborne, Terry, 6/22/89, C, 89000762

Holmes County

Clark, Mollie, House, 2221 Yazoo St., Pickens, 9/15/80, C, 80002249

Clifton Plantation House, Off MS 12, Howard vicinity, 10/03/85, A, C, 85002721

Cowsert, Joe, Place Site (22HO507), Address Restricted, Goodman vicinity, 2/27/87, D, 87000227

Eureka Masonic College, On MS 17, Richland, 11/10/70, A, B, 70000318

French Site (22HO565), Address Restricted, Cruger vicinity, 11/06/86, D, 86002328

Lee, Frances, Mound Group (22HO654), Address Restricted, Tchula vicinity, 4/06/88, D, 88000236

Old Hoover Place Site (22HO502), Address Restricted, Pickens vicinity, 3/01/87, D, 87000132

Oswego Site (22HO658), Address Restricted, Tchula vicinity, 4/06/88, D, 88000235

Providence Mound (22HO609), Address Restricted, Lexington vicinity, 3/01/87, D, 87000136

Tye House, 2440 N. 1st St., Pickens, 12/18/79, C, 79001315

West Historic District, Roughly bounded by Emory St., Anderson Ave. and Cross Sts. and the Illinois Central Gulf RR tracks, West, 9/14/93, A, 93000646

Humphreys County

Belzoni Mound (22HU500), Address Restricted, Belzoni vicinity, 4/13/88, D, 88000305

Jaketown Site, Address Restricted, Belzoni vicinity, 6/19/73, D, d, NHL, 73001017

Midnight Mound Site (22HU509), Address Restricted, Midnight vicinity, 4/25/86, D, 86000870

Slate Archeological Site, Address Restricted, Lake City vicinity, 7/08/82, D, 82003102

Issaquena County

Aden Site (22Is509;22M3), Address Restricted, Valley Park vicinity, 12/14/88, D, 88002698

Mayersville Archeological Site, Address Restricted, Mayersville vicinity, 4/29/80, D, 80002250

Itawamba County

Pharr Mounds, Address Restricted, Kirkville vicinity, 2/23/78, D, NPS, 78000346

Jackson County

Applestreet Site (22Ja530), Address Restricted, Gautier, 9/12/85, D, 85002200

Bertuccini House and Barbershop [Ocean Springs MRA], 619–619A Washington Ave., Ocean Springs, 6/09/87, A, C, 87000598

Bodden, Capt. Willie, House [Pascagoula MPS], 4002 Pine St., Pascagoula, 12/20/91, C, 91001783

Brash, Anna C., House [Pascagoula MPS], 802 Buena Vista St., Pascagoula, 12/20/91, C, 91001784

Carter—Callaway House [Ocean Springs MRA], 916 State St., Ocean Springs, 4/20/87, C, 87000596

Clark, Clare T., House [Pascagoula MPS], 1709 Beach Blvd., Pascagoula, 12/20/91, C, 91001785

Clinton, Capt. F. L., House [Pascagoula MPS], 903 Tucker St., Pascagoula, 12/20/91, C, 91001786

Cochran—Cassanova House [Ocean Springs MRA], 9000 Robinson St., Ocean Springs, 4/20/87, C, 87000595

Colle Company Housing [Pascagoula MPS], 3611 Frederic St., Pascagoula, 12/20/91, C, 91001788

Colle, Capt. Herman H. Sr., House [Pascagoula MPS], 410 Live Oak St., Pascagoula, 12/20/91, A, B, C, 91001787

Cottage by the Sea Tavern [Pascagoula MPS], 1205 Beach Blvd., Pascagoula, 12/20/91, A, B, 91001789

Cudabac—Gantt House, 4836 Main St., Moss Point, 7/24/90, C, 90001082

Dantzler, A. F., House, 5005 Griffin St., Moss Point, 3/26/87, C, 87000504

DeGroote Folk House, NE of Hurley off MS 613, Hurley vicinity, 5/04/82, C, b, 82003103

DeJean House [Pascagoula MPS], 3603 Frederic St., Pascagoula, 2/25/93, C, 93000082

Farnsworth, R. A., Summer House [Pascagoula MPS], 901 Beach Blvd., Pascagoula, 12/20/91, C, 91001790

Ford, Mayor Ebb, House [Pascagoula MPS], 3434 Pascagoula St., Pascagoula, 12/20/91, C, 91001791

Frentz, George, House [Pascagoula MPS], 503 Morgan St., Pascagoula, 12/20/91, B, C, 91001792

Front Street Historic District, 2810, 2816, 2905, 2914, 2916 Front St., Pascagoula, 5/17/84, C, 84002224

Gautier, Adam, House [Pascagoula MPS], 4418 Cedar St., Pascagoula, 12/20/91, A, C, 91001793

Gautier, Eugene, House [Pascagoula MPS], 3803 Willow St., Pascagoula, 12/20/91, C, 91001794

Gautier, Walter, House [Pascagoula MPS], 3012 Canty St., Pascagoula, 12/20/91, B, C, 91001795

Graveline Mound Site (22JK503), Address Restricted, Gautier vicinity, 7/02/87, D, 87001109

Griffin House, 100 Griffin St., Moss Point, 7/07/83, C, 83000955

Halstead Place [Ocean Springs MRA], E. Beach Dr., Ocean Springs, 4/20/87, A, 87000594

Hansen—Dickey House [Ocean Springs MRA], 108 Shearwater Dr., Ocean Springs, 4/20/87, C, 87000593

Herrick, Lemuel D., House [Pascagoula MPS], 2503 Pascagoula St., Pascagoula, 12/20/91, B, C, 91001796

House at 1112 Bowen Avenue [Ocean Springs MRA], 1112 Bowen Ave., Ocean Springs, 4/20/87, C, 87000600

House at 1410 Bowen Avenue [Ocean Springs MRA], 1410 Bowen Ave., Ocean Springs, 4/20/87, C, 87000599

Jackson County—Continued

Hughes, William, House [Pascagoula MPS], 2425 Pascagoula St., Pascagoula, 10/21/93, C, 93001137

Hull, Edgar W., House [Pascagoula MPS], 2903 Beach Blvd., Pascagoula, 12/20/91, C, 91001797

Indian Springs Historic District [Ocean Springs MRA], Iberville St., Church St., and Washington Ave. N, Ocean Springs, 4/20/87, C, 87000587

Keys, Thomas Isaac, House [Ocean Springs MRA], 1017 DeSoto Ave., Ocean Springs, 4/20/87, B, 87000592

Kinne, Georgia P., House [Pascagoula MPS], 1101 Beach Blvd., Pascagoula, 12/20/91, C, 91001798

Krebs, Agnes V., House [Pascagoula MPS], 803 Buena Vista St., Pascagoula, 12/20/91, C, 91001799

Krebs, James, House [Pascagoula MPS], 4702 River Rd., Pascagoula, 12/20/91, C, 91001800

Krebsville Historic District [Pascagoula MPS], 803, 809, 811 Kell Ave, 611, 703, 706, 707, 710, 802 Mill Rd., 4011, 4013, 4205, 4215 Pine St., Pascagoula, 12/20/91, C, 91001801

Levin, Leonard, House [Pascagoula MPS], 1403 Washington Ave., Pascagoula, 12/20/91, C, 91001802

Lewis, Col. Alfred E., House [Anderson, Walter, MPS (AD)], 1901 Watersedge Dr., Gautier vicinity, 10/16/80, B, C, b, g, 80002251

Louisville and Nashville Railroad Depot, Railroad Ave., Pascagoula, 8/27/74, A, 74001063

Louisville and Nashville Railroad Depot at Ocean Springs, 1000 Washington Ave., Ocean Springs, 12/31/79, A, C, 79001316

Lover's Lane Historic District [Ocean Springs MRA], Lover's Ln., Ocean Springs, 6/09/87, C, 87000584

Marble Springs Historic District [Ocean Springs MRA], Along Iberville Ave., between Washington Ave. N and Sunset Ave., Ocean Springs, 4/20/87, C, 87000586

Nelson Tenement [Pascagoula MPS], 3615 Pine St., Pascagoula, 12/20/91, C, 91001804

Nelson, John C., House [Pascagoula MPS], 2434 Pascagoula St., Pascagoula, 12/20/91, C, 91001803

O'Keefe—Clark Boarding House [Ocean Springs MRA], 2122 Government St., Ocean Springs, 4/20/87, A, C, b, 87000591

Ocean Springs Community Center [Anderson, Walter, MPS], Washington Ave., Ocean Springs, 8/24/89, C, g, 89001092

Old Farmers and Merchants State Bank [Ocean Springs MRA], 998 Washington Ave., Ocean Springs, 4/20/87, C, 87000590

Old Ocean Springs High School [Ocean Springs MRA], Magnolia and Government St., Ocean Springs, 8/02/90, C, 87000589

Old Ocean Springs Historic District [Ocean Springs MRA], Roughly bounded by Porter and Dewey Aves., Front Beach Dr., Martin Ave., Cleveland St., & Rayburn Ave., Ocean Springs, 10/07/87, C, 87000597

Old Spanish Fort, 200 Fort St., Pascagoula, 9/03/71, C, 71000452

Olsen, Lena, House [Pascagoula MPS], 706 Buena Vista St., Pascagoula, 12/20/91, C, 91001805

Pascagoula Central Fire Station No. 1, 623 Delmas Ave., Pascagoula, 12/08/78, A, 78001604

Pascagoula Street Railroad and Power Company [Pascagoula MPS], 3708 Pascagoula St., Pascagoula, 12/20/91, A, C, 91001806

Randall's Tavern [Pascagoula MPS], 919 Beach Blvd., Pascagoula, 12/20/91, A, 91001807

Round Island Lighthouse, SW corner of Round Island, Pascagoula vicinity, 10/09/86, C, 86002815

Saint John's Episcopal Church [Ocean Springs MRA], NW corner of Rayburn and Porter Ave., Ocean Springs, 4/20/87, C, a, 87000588

Shearwater Historic District [Anderson, Walter, MPS], Shearwater Dr., Ocean Springs, 8/24/89, B, C, g, 87000585

St. Mary's By the River, 3855 River Rd., Moss Point, 5/02/91, C, a, 91000542

Sullivan—Charnley Historic District [Ocean Springs MRA], Shearwater Dr. and Holcomb Blvd., Ocean Springs, 4/20/87, B, C, 87000583

Tabor, Dr. Joseph A., House [Pascagoula MPS], 520 Live Oak St., Pascagoula, 12/20/91, B, C, 91001808

Thompson, George, House [Pascagoula MPS], 523 Orange St., Pascagoula, 12/20/91, C, 91001809

Vancleave Cottage [Ocean Springs MRA], 1302 Government St., Ocean Springs, 4/20/87, C, 87000582

Westphal, Laura, House [Pascagoula MPS], 711 Krebs St., Pascagoula, 12/20/91, C, 91001810

Jasper County

Archeological Site No. 22-Js-572, Address Restricted, Bay Springs vicinity, 11/10/93, D, 93001150

Jefferson County

Blantonia Plantation House, 3 mi. E of Red Lick on unmarked rd. off MS 552, Lorman vicinity, 3/04/93, C, 93000145

Cedar Grove Place, MS 553, Church Hill, 3/28/79, B, C, g, 79001317

China Grove, W of Lorman off U.S. 61, Lorman vicinity, 4/03/80, C, d, 80002254

Christ Church, MS 553, Church Hill, 5/06/77, A, C, a, 77000790

Coon Box Fork Bridge [Swinging Suspension Bridges TR], Coon Box Rd., Coon Box, 5/23/79, A, C, 79003429

Hughes—Clark House, 221 Poindexter St., Fayette, 8/03/87, C, 87001260

Laurietta, S of Fayette off MS 33, Fayette vicinity, 11/24/80, C, 80002253

Mud Island Creek Complex (22JE508 and 22JE513), Address Restricted, Lorman vicinity, 6/29/89, D, NPS, 89000447

Oak Grove, MS 553, Church Hill, 2/22/79, C, 79001318

Old Hill Place Bridge [Swinging Suspension Bridges TR], Hill Rd., Fayette vicinity, 5/23/79, A, C, 79003430

Pecan Grove, N of Church Hill off MS 551, Church Hill vicinity, 3/13/80, C, 80002252

Richland, Off MS 553, Church Hill vicinity, 7/05/84, C, 84002227

Rodney Center Historic District, NW of Lorman, Lorman vicinity, 8/29/80, A, B, C, D, a, 80002255

Rodney Presbyterian Church, W of Alcorn in village of Rodney, Alcorn vicinity, 2/06/73, A, C, a, 73001018

Rosswood, E of Lorman on MS 552, Lorman vicinity, 12/08/78, C, 78001606

Springfield Plantation, 8 mi. W of Fayette off MS 553, Fayette vicinity, 11/23/71, B, C, 71000454

Union Church Presbyterian Church, MS 550, Union Church, 7/18/79, B, a, d, 79001322

Woodland Plantation, S of Church Hill on MS 553, Church Hill vicinity, 11/27/78, B, C, 78001605

Wyolah Plantation, Off MS 553, Church Hill vicinity, 5/30/85, C, 85001168

Youngblood Bridge [Swinging Suspension Bridges TR], Youngblood Rd., Union Church vicinity, 5/23/79, A, C, 79003428

Jefferson Davis County

1907 House, E of Prentiss on Fort Stephens Rd., Prentiss vicinity, 2/14/79, A, C, b, 79001321

Jones County

Deason, Amos, House, 410 N. Deason St., Ellisville, 7/05/84, C, 84002229

Laurel Central Historic District, Roughly bounded by Tenth and Thirteenth Sts., First Ave., Seventh and Fifth Sts., and Eighth Ave., Laurel, 9/04/87, A, C, 86001908

Rogers, Newell, House, 706 N. Sixth Ave., Laurel, 4/20/87, C, 87000604

Kemper County

Oliver House, 1 mi. SW of Moscow off MS 493, Moscow vicinity, 10/31/85, C, 85003439

Lafayette County

Ammadelle, 637 N. Lamar St., Oxford, 5/30/74, C, NHL, 74001064

Barnard Observatory, University of Mississippi campus, Oxford, 12/08/78, C, 78001607

College Church, College Hill Rd, College Hill, 11/13/79, A, C, a, d, 79001324

Lafayette County—Continued

Faulkner, William, House, Old Taylor Rd., Oxford, 5/23/68, B, g, NHL, 68000028

Isom Place, 1003 Jefferson Ave., Oxford, 4/02/80, B, 80002256

Lafayette County Courthouse, Courthouse Sq., Oxford, 9/23/77, A, C, 77000791

Lamar, Lucius Quintus Cincinnatus, House, 616 N. 14th St., Oxford, 5/15/75, B, NHL, 75001048

Oxford Courthouse Square Historic District, S. Lamar Blvd., Jackson and Van Buren Aves., Oxford, 4/02/80, A, B, C, 80002257

Sand Spring Presbyterian Church, Jct. of Co. Rts. 354 and 399 in Orwood, NW of Water Valley, Water Valley vicinity, 2/25/93, C, 93000083

St. Peter's Episcopal Church, 113 S. 9th St., Oxford, 7/24/75, A, C, a, 75001049

Lamar County

U.S. Post Office [Mississippi Post Offices 1931-1941 TR], 104 Heber Ladner Dr., Lumberton, 4/07/81, A, C, g, 81000328

Lauderdale County

Beth Israel Cemetery [Meridian MRA], 19th St. and 5th Ave., Meridian, 3/22/89, C, d, 89000169

Cahn-Crawford House [Meridian MRA], 1200 22nd Ave., Meridian, 12/18/79, B, C, 79003384

Carnegie Branch Library [Meridian MRA], 2721 13th St., Meridian, 12/18/79, A, 79003385

Causeyville Historic District, Meridian-Causeyville Rd., Causeyville, 1/02/86, A, 86000058

Coosha, Address Restricted, Lizelia vicinity, 11/21/78, D, 78001608

Dabney-Green House [Meridian MRA], 1017 22nd Ave., Meridian, 12/18/79, C, 79003386

Dement Printing Company [Meridian MRA], 2002 6th St., Meridian, 12/18/79, A, 79003387

Dial House [Meridian MRA], 1003 30th Ave., Meridian, 12/18/79, B, C, 79003388

East End Historic District [Meridian MRA], Roughly bounded by Eighteenth St., Eleventh Ave., Fourteenth St., Fourteenth Ave., Fifth St., and Seventeenth Ave., Meridian, 8/21/87, A, C, 87000470

Elson-Dudley House [Meridian MRA], 1101 29th Ave., Meridian, 12/18/79, C, 79003390

First Presbyterian Church of Meridian [Meridian MRA], 911 23rd Ave., Meridian, 12/18/79, C, a, 79003391

Grand Opera House [Meridian MRA (AD)], 2208 5th St., Meridian, 12/27/72, A, C, 72000696

Gulf, Mobile & Ohio Freight Depot [Meridian MRA], 20 22nd Ave., Meridian, 12/18/79, A, C, 79003392

Highland Park, Roughly bounded by 15th and 19th Sts., 37th and 47th Aves., Meridian, 2/28/79, A, C, 79001325

Highland Park Dentzel Carousel and Shelter Building, Highland Park, Meridian, 2/27/87, A, b, NHL, 87000863

Highlands Historic District [Meridian MRA], Roughly bounded by Fifteenth St., Thirty-fourth Ave., Fifth St., Nineteenth St., and Thirty-sixth Ave., Meridian, 8/21/87, C, 87000467

Lamar Hotel [Meridian MRA], 410 21st St., Meridian, 12/18/79, C, 79003393

Loeb, Alex, Building [Meridian MRA], 2115 5th St., Meridian, 12/18/79, A, 79003394

Masonic Temple [Meridian MRA], 1220 26th Ave., Meridian, 12/18/79, A, 79003395

McLemore Cemetery [Meridian MRA], 601 16th Ave., Meridian, 12/18/79, A, d, 79003396

Meridian Baptist Seminary, 16th St. and 31st Ave., Meridian, 1/08/79, A, 79001326

Meridian Depot District [Meridian MRA], Roughly bounded by 18th and 19th Aves., 5th St., and Gulf Mobile & Ohio RR, Meridian, 12/18/79, A, B, 79003731

Meridian Museum of Art [Meridian MRA], 628 25th Ave., Meridian, 12/18/79, A, 79003397

Meridian Urban Center Historic District [Meridian MRA], Roughly bounded by 21st and 25th Aves., 6th St., Gulf Mobile & Ohio RR, Meridian, 12/18/79, A, C, g, 79003732

Meridian Waterworks Pumping Station and Clear Water Basin [Meridian MRA], B St. and 17th Ave., Meridian, 7/26/89, A, C, 89000931

Merrehope, 905 31st Ave., Meridian, 12/09/71, C, 71000455

Merrehope Historic District [Meridian MRA], Roughly bounded by Thirty-third Ave., Thirtieth Ave., Fourteenth St., Twenty-fifth Ave. and Eighth St., Meridian, 9/19/88, A, C, a, 88000973

Mid-Town Historic District [Meridian MRA], Roughly bounded by Twenty-third Ave., Fifteenth St., Twenty-eighth Ave., and Twenty-second St., Meridian, 8/21/87, C, 87000463

Municipal Building [Meridian MRA], 601 24th Ave., Meridian, 12/18/79, C, 79003399

Niolon Building [Meridian MRA], 718 23rd Ave., Meridian, 12/18/79, A, 79003400

Pigford Building [Meridian MRA], 818 22nd Ave., Meridian, 12/18/79, A, 79003401

Poplar Springs Road Historic District [Meridian MRA], Roughly bounded by Twenty-ninth St., Twenty-third Ave., Twenty-second St., and Twenty-ninth Ave., Meridian, 8/21/87, A, C, 87000461

Porter-Crawford House [Meridian MRA], 1208 22nd Ave., Meridian, 12/18/79, C, 79003402

St. Patrick Catholic Church [Meridian MRA], 2614 Davis St., Meridian, 12/18/79, B, C, a, 79003403

Standard Drug Company [Meridian MRA], 601 25th Ave., Meridian, 12/07/89, A, 89002050

Stevenson Primary School [Meridian MRA], 1015 25th Ave., Meridian, 12/18/79, C, 79003405

Stuckey's Bridge [Historic Bridges of Mississippi TR], Spans Chunky River on CR, Meridian vicinity, 11/16/88, A, C, 88002415

Suttle Building [Meridian MRA], 801 22nd Ave., Meridian, 12/18/79, A, 79003406

Temple Theater [Meridian MRA], 2318 8th St., Meridian, 12/18/79, A, 79003407

Threefoot Building [Meridian MRA], 601 22nd Ave., Meridian, 12/18/79, C, 79003408

US Post Office and Courthouse, 2100 9th St., Meridian, 5/17/84, C, 84002236

US Sugar Crop Field Station, Jct. of Sonny Montgomery Industrial Pkwy. and Peavy Dr., Meridian vicinity, 1/11/91, A, 90002124

Union Hotel [Meridian MRA], 2000 Front St., Meridian, 12/18/79, A, 79003409

Wechsler School, 1415 30th Ave., Meridian, 7/15/91, A, 91000880

West End Historic District [Meridian MRA], Roughly bounded by Seventh St., Twenty-eighth Ave., Shearer's Branch, and Fifth St., Meridian, 8/21/87, A, C, 87000459

Lawrence County

Armstrong-Lee House [Lawrence County Folk and Vernacular TR], MS 43, Monticello vicinity, 9/29/80, B, C, 80002262

Bahala Creek Bridge [Historic Bridges of Mississippi TR], Spans Bahala Creek on CR SW of Oma, Oma vicinity, 11/16/88, A, C, 88002417

Boyd-Cothern House [Lawrence County Folk and Vernacular TR], W of Jayess, Jayess vicinity, 9/29/80, C, 80002258

Buckley House [Lawrence County Folk and Vernacular TR], W of New Hebron, New Hebron vicinity, 9/29/80, A, C, 80002267

Bush House [Lawrence County Folk and Vernacular TR], E of New Hebron on MS 42, New Hebron, 9/29/80, C, 80002268

Cannon House [Lawrence County Folk and Vernacular TR], MS 43, Monticello vicinity, 9/29/80, C, 80002263

Crane-Mason House [Lawrence County Folk and Vernacular TR], SW of Monticello, Monticello vicinity, 9/29/80, C, 80002264

Douglas House [Lawrence County Folk and Vernacular TR], E of Sontag, Sontag vicinity, 9/29/80, C, 80002275

Fox House [Lawrence County Folk and Vernacular TR], NE of Wanilla, Wanilla vicinity, 9/29/80, B, C, 80002277

George Mound (22LW591), Address Restricted, Oma vicinity, 3/01/87, D, 87000138

Gunnell House [Lawrence County Folk and Vernacular TR], W of Topeka, Jayess vicinity, 9/29/80, C, 80002259

Hilliard House [Lawrence County Folk and Vernacular TR], NE of Wanilla, Wanilla vicinity, 9/29/80, C, 80002278

Johnson-White House [Lawrence County Folk and Vernacular TR], E of Sontag, Sontag vicinity, 9/29/80, C, 80002276

Knapp-Stephens House [Lawrence County Folk and Vernacular TR], SW of New Hebron, New Hebron vicinity, 9/29/80, C, 80002269

Lawrence County Courthouse, N. side Broad St. between Jefferson and Washington Sts., Monticello, 3/04/93, C, 93000146

Longino House, Caswell St., Monticello, 8/21/72, A, B, 72000697

Lawrence County—Continued

Lowe—Steen Site (22LW511), Address Restricted, Monticello vicinity, 3/01/87, D, 87000134

Mill Creek Site, S of Monticello, Monticello vicinity, 6/09/78, D, 78001609

Monticello Consolidated School, 125 E. Broad St., Monticello, 7/09/91, C, 91000879

Newsom-Lane House [Lawrence County Folk and Vernacular TR], MS 43, New Hebron vicinity, 9/29/80, A, C, 80002270

Newsom-Smith House [Lawrence County Folk and Vernacular TR], MS 43, New Hebron vicinity, 9/29/80, C, 80002271

Price-Stephens House [Lawrence County Folk and Vernacular TR], MS 43, New Hebron vicinity, 9/29/80, C, 80002272

Robbins House [Lawrence County Folk and Vernacular TR], E of Topeka, Jayess vicinity, 9/29/80, A, C, 80002260

Rogers House [Lawrence County Folk and Vernacular TR], S of Silver Creek, Silver Creek vicinity, 9/29/80, B, C, 80002274

Smith, A. L., House [Lawrence County Folk and Vernacular TR], N of Monticello on MS 27, Monticello vicinity, 9/29/80, B, C, 80002265

Stringer House [Lawrence County Folk and Vernacular TR], SW of New Hebron, New Hebron vicinity, 9/29/80, C, 80002273

Tynes House [Lawrence County Folk and Vernacular TR], E of Topeka, Jayess vicinity, 9/29/80, C, 80002261

Wilson House [Lawrence County Folk and Vernacular TR], SW of Monticello, Monticello vicinity, 9/29/80, C, 80002266

Leake County

Jordan House, E. Franklin St., Carthage, 11/30/82, C, 82000576

Robinson Road (190-191-3M), SW of Kosciusko, Kosciusko vicinity, 11/07/76, A, NPS, 76000158

Steep Mound Site (22LK26), Address Restricted, Carthage vicinity, 1/14/87, D, 86003634

U.S. Post Office [Mississippi Post Offices 1931-1941 TR], 201 N. Pearl St., Carthage, 4/21/83, C, g, 83000956

Lee County

Brices Cross Roads National Battlefield Site, 6 mi. W of Baldwyn on MS 370, Baldwyn vicinity, 10/15/66, A, NPS, 66000067

Burrow, Barlow, House, 157 N. 2nd St., Saltillo, 3/01/84, C, 84002251

First Methodist Church, 412 W. Main St., Tupelo, 3/15/90, C, a, 90000348

Goodlett, R. F., House [Tupelo MPS], 219 Broadway, Tupelo, 4/03/92, C, b, 92000162

Lee County Courthouse [Tupelo MPS], Court St. between Spring and Broadway, Tupelo, 4/03/92, C, 92000161

Mill Village Historic District [Tupelo MPS], Roughly bounded by the Illinois Central RR and St. Louis—San Francisco RR tracks, Chestnut and Green Sts., Tupelo, 4/03/92, A, 92000159

Mutt-Thomason Site, Address Restricted, Tupelo vicinity, 8/31/78, D, 78001611

North Broadway Historic District, 300 blk. of N. Broadway St., Tupelo, 10/31/85, C, 85003438

North Church Primary School [Tupelo MPS], Jct. of Church and Jackson Sts., SW corner, Tupelo, 4/03/92, C, 92000164

Old Superintendent's House, Tupelo Fish Hatchery, 111 Elizabeth St., Tupelo, 7/14/92, C, 92000837

Peoples Bank and Trust Company, 211 Main St., Tupelo, 8/24/78, A, C, 78001610

South Church Street Historic District [Tupelo MPS], 602–713 S. Church St., Tupelo, 4/03/92, C, 92000160

Spight, F. L., House [Tupelo MPS], 363 N. Broadway, Tupelo, 4/03/92, C, 92000163

Tupelo National Battlefield, On MS 6 about 1 mi. W of its jct. with U.S. 45, Tupelo, 10/15/66, A, f, NPS, 66000068

Leflore County

Black Site, Address Restricted, Greenwood vicinity, 11/21/78, D, 78001612

Black Site, Address Restricted, Sidon vicinity, 1/11/91, D, 90002107

Boulevard Subdivision Historic District [Greenwood MRA], Roughly bounded by Jeff Davis Ave., Poplar St., President Ave., and Grand Boulevard, Greenwood, 3/02/86, C, 86000521

Building at 308 Lamar Street [Greenwood MRA], 308 Lamar St., Greenwood, 11/04/85, C, 85003456

Building at 312 George Street [Greenwood MRA], 312 George St., Greenwood, 11/04/85, C, 85003454

Building at 710 South Boulevard [Greenwood MRA], 710 South Blvd., Greenwood, 11/04/85, C, 85003455

Central Commercial and Railroad Historic District [Greenwood MRA], Roughly bounded by Washington St., Main and Lamar Sts. and Ave. F, Wardaman and Johnson Sts., and Cotton and Fulton Sts., Greenwood, 11/04/85, A, C, 85003463

Cotton Row Historic District, Cotton, Front, Fulton, Howard, Main, and Market Sts., Greenwood, 5/15/80, A, C, 80002279

Falls Site (22LF507), Address Restricted, Minter City vicinity, 5/01/86, D, 86000922

First Methodist Church of Greenwood [Greenwood MRA], 310 W. Washington St., Greenwood, 11/04/85, C, a, 85003457

Fort Leflore, N of Greenwood off MS 7, Greenwood vicinity, 4/04/79, A, 79001327

Fort Pemberton Site, W of Greenwood off US 49E, Greenwood vicinity, 6/19/73, A, 73001020

Four Corners Historic District, Washington and Henderson Sts., Greenwood, 2/14/85, C, a, 85000282

Greenwood High School [Greenwood MRA], 400 Cotton St., Greenwood, 11/04/85, C, 85003458

Keesler Bridge [Historic Bridges of Mississippi TR], Spans Yazoo River at Fulton St., Greenwood, 11/16/88, A, C, 88002489

Lane's Chapel Site, Address Restricted, Money vicinity, 5/04/76, D, 76001099

Marclare, River Rd., Greenwood, 11/25/80, C, 80002280

McLean Site (22LF513), Address Restricted, Itta Bena vicinity, 4/06/88, D, 88000230

Murphey Site, Address Restricted, Itta Bena vicinity, 11/10/93, D, 93001151

Neill Archeological Site, Address Restricted, Whaley vicinity, 4/26/76, D, 76001100

Provine House, 319 Grand Blvd., Greenwood, 4/08/80, C, 80002281

Rebecca Site, Address Restricted, Sidon vicinity, 1/11/91, D, 90002105

River Road and Western Downtown Residential Historic District [Greenwood MRA], Roughly bounded by River Rd., Dewey and Gillespie, Washington and Johnson, and First Sts., Greenwood, 3/02/86, C, 86000519

Rosemary—Humphreys House [Greenwood MRA], 1440 Grand Blvd., Greenwood, 11/04/85, C, 85003459

STAR OF THE WEST, W of Greenwood on Tallahatchie River, Greenwood vicinity, 5/21/75, A, 75001050

Southworth House [Greenwood MRA], 1108 Mississippi Ave., Greenwood, 11/04/85, C, 85003460

Sweethome Mound, Address Restricted, Wakeland vicinity, 6/09/78, D, 78001613

Wesley Memorial Methodist Episcopal [Greenwood MRA], 800 Howard St., Greenwood, 11/04/85, A, C, a, 85003461

Whaley Archeological Site, Address Restricted, Whaley vicinity, 3/15/76, D, 76001101

Whittington, W. M., House, 401 E. Market St., Greenwood, 7/19/84, B, C, 84002255

Williams Landing and Eastern Downtown Residential Historic District [Greenwood MRA], Roughly bounded by Front, McLemore and Lamar, Market, and George Sts., Greenwood, 3/02/86, A, C, 86000520

Wright House [Greenwood MRA], 414 Fulton Ave., Greenwood, 11/04/85, B, C, 85003462

Lincoln County

Brookhaven City Hall, Whitworth Ave., Brookhaven, 6/16/83, A, C, 83000957

Building at 306 South Jackson Street, 306 South Jackson Street, Brookhaven, 4/17/80, C, 80002282

Inez Hotel, 104 E. Monticello St., Brookhaven, 10/21/88, C, 88002038

Scherck, R. T., House, 417 S. Whitworth Ave., Brookhaven, 4/14/92, C, 92000353

Lincoln County—Continued

US Post Office, 201 W. Cherokee St., Brookhaven, 10/28/83, C, 83003963

Union Station, S. Whitworth Ave., Brookhaven, 8/21/80, A, 80002283

Lowndes County

Bethel Presbyterian Church, 12 mi. off US 45, Columbus vicinity, 12/19/86, C, a, 86003126

Brownrigg-Harris-Kennebrew House, 515 9th St. N., Columbus, 5/22/78, C, 78001614

Butler Mound and Village Site, Address Restricted, Columbus vicinity, 12/08/78, D, 78001615

Cedars, The, 1311 Military Rd., Columbus, 3/29/79, A, C, 79001328

Columbus Bridge [Historic Bridges of Mississippi TR], Spans Tombigbee River on Old US 82, Columbus, 11/16/88, A, C, 88002396

Columbus Central Commercial Historic District, U.S. 82 and U.S. 45, Columbus, 4/23/80, A, C, a, 80002284

Cox-Uithoven House, N of Columbus on Old Aberdeen Rd., Columbus vicinity, 5/08/80, A, C, 80002285

Ervin, William E., House, Armstrong Rd./Rt. 4, SE of Columbus, Columbus vicinity, 12/01/89, C, b, d, 89002053

Factory Hill-Frog Bottom-Burns Bottom Historic District, Roughly bounded by 2nd and 6th Aves., 2nd and 5th Sts., Columbus, 9/02/80, A, C, 80002286

Friendship Cemetery, 1300 4th St., Columbus, 7/23/80, A, d, 80002287

Gatchell, Kenneth, House, 1411 College St., Columbus, 3/21/78, C, 78001616

Harris-Banks House, 122 7th Ave. S., Columbus, 11/16/78, C, 78001617

Hickory Sticks, 1206 N. 7th St., Columbus, 4/29/77, B, C, 77000792

James Creek No. 1 Site, Address Restricted, Columbus vicinity, 5/23/78, D, 78001618

Jones—Banks—Leigh House, 824 Seventh St. N, Columbus, 10/31/85, C, 85003445

Lee, S. D., House, 314 N. 7th St., Columbus, 5/06/71, B, C, 71000456

Lindamood Building of Palmer Home for Children, 912 11th Ave. S., Columbus, 6/24/93, C, 93000574

MacKay Mound, Address Restricted, Columbus vicinity, 8/25/78, D, 78001619

McLaran, Charles, House, 514 2nd St., S., Columbus, 12/12/76, C, 76001102

Motley Slough Bridge [Historic Bridges of Mississippi TR], Spans Motley Slough on Shaeffer's Chapel Rd., Columbus vicinity, 11/16/88, A, C, 88002405

Old Fort House, 510 Seventh St. N, Columbus, 10/31/85, C, 85003444

Plymouth, Address Restricted, Columbus vicinity, 4/22/80, A, D, 80002288

Snowdoun, 906 3rd Ave. N., Columbus, 10/19/78, C, 78001620

South Columbus Historic District, U.S. 82, Columbus, 6/08/82, A, C, 82003104

Sykes-Leigh House, 719–7th St. North, Columbus, 3/14/85, C, 85000555

Symons House, 304 4th Ave. S, Columbus, 3/28/79, C, 79001329

U.S. Post Office [Mississippi Post Offices 1931-1941 TR], 524 Main St., Columbus, 4/21/83, C, g, 83000958

Weaver Place, 216 3rd Ave. S., Columbus, 11/16/78, C, 78001621

Madison County

Boddie, John W., House, Tougaloo College campus, Tougaloo, 5/13/82, A, C, 82003106

Boyd Mounds Site (22MD512), Address Restricted, Ridgeland vicinity, 7/14/89, D, NPS, 89000784

Canton Courthouse Square Historic District, Center, Liberty, Peace and Union Streets, Canton, 8/30/82, A, C, 82004895

Canton Courthouse Square Historic District (Boundary Increase), W. Peace St., Canton, 6/29/89, A, 89000778

Chapel of the Cross, 6 mi. NW of jct. of MS 463 and I-55, Mannsdale, 6/13/72, A, C, a, d, 72000698

Curran, John, House [Madison MRA], Main St., Madison, 3/02/86, C, 86000516

Doak's Stand Treaty Site, Address Restricted, Canton vicinity, 1/30/78, A, D, 78003196

Dorroh Street Historic District [Madison MRA], 103, 105, and 115 Dorroh St., Madison, 3/02/86, C, 86000514

Farr Mercantile Co.—R. B. Price Mercantile Co. [Madison MRA], Main and Railroad, Madison, 3/02/86, C, 86000517

Kirkpatrick Dental Office, 229 E. Center St., Canton, 7/09/91, C, b, 91000878

Madison County Jail, 234 E. Fulton St., Canton, 3/28/79, A, C, 79001330

Madison—Ridgeland Public School [Madison MRA], Montgomery St., Madison, 3/02/86, C, 86000518

Montgomery House, Main St., Madison, 9/07/84, C, 84002260

Old Natchez Trace (170-30), E of Ridgeland, Ridgeland vicinity, 11/07/76, A, NPS, 76000160

Puckshunubbee-Haley Site, Address Restricted, Madison vicinity, 5/09/84, B, D, 84002264

Strawberry Fields Site (22Md644), Address Restricted, Canton vicinity, 12/22/88, D, 88002707

Strawberry Patch—McKay House [Madison MRA], Old Canton Rd., Madison, 3/02/86, C, 86000515

Tilda Bogue, Address Restricted, Canton vicinity, 12/09/83, C, b, 83003965

White Perch Paradise Site (22MD641), Address Restricted, Goshen Springs vicinity, 2/27/87, D, 87000226

Marion County

Ford House, S of Sandy Hook on Old Columbia-Covington Rd., Sandy Hook vicinity, 6/21/71, A, B, 71000457

Keys Hill Historic District, Broad St., Columbia, 6/14/82, B, C, 82004836

U.S. Post Office [Mississippi Post Offices 1931-1941 TR], 815 Main St., Columbia, 4/07/81, A, C, 81000329

Marshall County

Byhalia United Methodist Church [Johnson, Andrew, Architecture in North Mississippi TR], College Ave., Byhalia, 4/09/84, C, a, 84002276

Chalmers Institute [Holly Springs MRA], W. Chulahoma Ave., Holly Springs, 6/28/82, A, 82003107

Civil War Earthworks at Tallahatchie Crossing, Off MS 7, Abbeville vicinity, 8/14/73, A, 73001021

Confederate Armory Site, N of Holly Springs, Holly Springs vicinity, 4/11/72, A, 72000699

Depot-Compress Historic District [Holly Springs MRA], Bounded by RR tracks, Chesterman St., College and Van Dorn Aves., Holly Springs, 4/20/83, A, C, 83000959

East Holly Springs Historic District [Holly Springs MRA], Bounded by Compress, Chesterman, Randolph, and Spring Sts. and Salem, Van Dorn Aves., Holly Springs, 4/20/83, A, C, 83000960

Hillcrest Cemetery [Holly Springs MRA], Center St., Holly Springs, 6/28/82, C, d, 82003108

Holly Springs Courthouse Square Historic District, US 78, Holly Springs, 1/20/80, A, C, 80004550

Mississippi Industrial College Historic District, Memphis St., Holly Springs, 1/20/80, A, C, 80002290

Myers-Hicks Place, MS 309, Byhalia vicinity, 3/07/83, C, 83000961

North Memphis Street Historic District [Holly Springs MRA], Bounded by N. Memphis St., Falconer, Salem, and Park Aves. and the Anderson Chapel, Holly Springs, 4/20/83, A, C, 83000962

Oakview [Holly Springs MRA], Rust College Campus, Rust Ave., Holly Springs, 6/28/82, A, 82003110

Old Water and Electric Light Plant [Holly Springs MRA], 140 E. Falconer Ave., Holly Springs, 6/28/82, A, 82003111

Southwest Holly Springs Historic District [Holly Springs MRA], Bounded by S. Center, S. Memphis, and Craft Sts., Marbury Ct., Ghulahoma, Gholson, Elder and Mason Aves., Holly Springs, 4/20/83, A, C, 83000963

Summer Trees, NE of Red Banks on Mayhome Rd., Red Banks vicinity, 1/19/79, C, 79001331

Monroe County

Aberdeen City Hall [Aberdeen MRA], 125 W. Commerce St., Aberdeen, 2/22/88, C, 88000126

Monroe County—Continued

Adams—French House [Aberdeen MRA], N. Meridian and Marshall Sts., Aberdeen, 2/22/88, C, 88000125

Baker Mound, Address Restricted, Aberdeen vicinity, 7/17/80, D, 80002291

Building at 133 East Commerce Street [Aberdeen MRA; Commercial Buildings of Aberdeen TR], 133 E. Commerce St., Aberdeen, 2/22/88, A, C, 88000136

Buildings at 110–122 East Commerce Street [Aberdeen MRA; Commercial Buildings of Aberdeen TR], 110–122 E. Commerce St., Aberdeen, 2/22/88, A, C, 88000138

Buildings at NW Corner of Commerce and Meridian Streets [Aberdeen MRA; Commercial Buildings of Aberdeen TR], 100–104 W. Commerce St. and 107 N. Meridian St., Aberdeen, 2/22/88, A, C, 88000135

Cotton Gin Port Site, Address Restricted, Amory vicinity, 10/18/72, A, D, 72000700

Crawford Site, Address Restricted, Aberdeen vicinity, 11/28/80, D, 80002292

Davis, Reuben, House, 803 W. Commerce St., Aberdeen, 11/16/78, B, C, 78001622

Day, C. C., House [Aberdeen MRA], 517 S. Meridian St., Aberdeen, 2/22/88, C, 88000123

Dunklin, William A., House [Aberdeen MRA], 301 High St., Aberdeen, 2/22/88, C, 88000122

Harmon Subdivision Historic District [Aberdeen MRA], 933–939 and 943 W. Commerce St., Aberdeen, 4/22/88, C, 88000121

Hester-Standifer Creek Site, Address Restricted, Amory vicinity, 6/05/75, D, 75001051

Holliday, John, House [Aberdeen MRA], 609 S. Meridian St., Aberdeen, 2/22/88, C, 88000120

Inzer Site, Address Restricted, Amory vicinity, 7/05/73, D, 73001022

Johnson—Butler House [Aberdeen MRA], 210 High St., Aberdeen, 2/22/88, C, 88000119

Lawson Site, Address Restricted, Amory vicinity, 7/07/75, D, 75001052

Lenoir Plantation House, Off US 45 Alt., 3 mi. S of jct. with NM 382, Prairie vicinity, 4/28/92, C, 91001893

Mobile and Ohio Railroad Depot, 612 W. Commerce St., Aberdeen, 12/08/83, A, 83003966

Monroe County Courthouse, Courthouse Sq., Aberdeen, 12/22/78, A, C, 78001623

Monroe County Jail, Off MS 8, Athens, 7/14/78, A, 78001624

Mound Cemetery Site, Address Restricted, Amory vicinity, 10/14/75, D, 75001053

North Aberdeen Historic District [Aberdeen MRA], Roughly bounded by Meridian, Marshall, Long, and Commerce Sts., Aberdeen, 4/22/88, C, 88000131

Old Homestead [Aberdeen MRA], 503 W. Commerce, Aberdeen, 2/22/88, C, 88000124

Rogers, Francis M., House [Aberdeen MRA], High and Hickory Sts., Aberdeen, 11/03/88, C, 88002222

South Central Aberdeen Historic District [Aberdeen MRA], Roughly bounded by Locust,

Washington, Franklin, and High Sts., Aberdeen, 4/22/88, A, C, 88000134

Thompson, James Young, House, Old Cotton Gin Rd., 1/4 mi. N of US 278, Amory vicinity, 8/16/90, C, 90001223

U.S. Courthouse and Post Office, 201 W. Commerce St., Aberdeen, 9/29/76, A, C, 76001104

US Post Office—Amory [Mississippi Post Offices 1931-1941 TR], 215 First Ave., Amory, 4/11/88, A, C, g, 88000691

Watkins, W. W., House [Aberdeen MRA], 600 W. Commerce St., Aberdeen, 4/05/91, C, 91000387

West Commerce Street Historic District [Aberdeen MRA], 721–919 and 730–900 W. Commerce St., Aberdeen, 4/19/88, C, 88000128

Word Mound, Address Restricted, Aberdeen vicinity, 7/17/80, D, 80002293

Montgomery County

Purnell, James C., House, 504 Summit St., Winona, 7/12/90, B, C, 90001077

U.S. Post Office [Mississippi Post Offices 1931-1941 TR], 306 Summit St., Winona, 4/07/81, A, C, g, 81000330

Wisteria Hotel, Central Ave., Winona, 12/18/79, A, C, 79001332

Neshoba County

Nanih Waiya Cave Mound, Address Restricted, Philadelphia vicinity, 5/07/73, D, 73001023

Neshoba County Fair Historic District, NW of Neshoba on MS 21, Neshoba vicinity, 4/22/80, A, 80002294

Philadelphia Historic District, Holland and Poplar Aves., Jefferson, Watkins and Welsh Sts., Philadelphia, 3/04/83, A, C, 83000964

Newton County

Alabama and Vicksburg Railroad Depot, S. Main St., Newton, 7/12/90, A, 90001076

Lavelle Site, Address Restricted, Enterprise vicinity, 6/09/78, D, 78001625

Newton West Church Historic District, W. Church St., Newton, 1/20/80, C, 80002295

Noxubee County

Central Shuqualak Historic District, Off MS 39, Shuqualak, 8/26/80, A, C, 80002297

Dancing Rabbit Creek Treaty Site, Address Restricted, Macon vicinity, 4/03/73, A, D, 73001024

Flora House, Line St., Shuqualak, 12/02/82, C, 82000577

Goodwin-Harrison House, 213 N. Jefferson St., Macon, 11/28/80, C, 80002296

Maudwin, 101 Washington St., Macon, 8/29/85, C, 85001929

McGeehee—Ames House, Magnolia Dr. S of jct. with US 45, Macon vicinity, 7/10/92, C, 92000853

Old Noxubee County Jail, 209 Monroe St., Macon, 1/08/79, C, 79001333

Old Noxubee County Jail of 1870, 503 S. Washington St., Macon, 1/03/91, A, 90002102

Running Water Creek Bridge [Historic Bridges of Mississippi TR], Spans Running Water Creek on CR, Shuqualak vicinity, 11/16/88, A, C, 88002487

Salem School, Old, 3.4 mi. W of Macon on SR 14, Macon vicinity, 1/26/90, A, 89002323

Yates-Flora House, 100 N. Wayne St., Macon, 12/02/82, C, 82000578

Oktibbeha County

Bardwell House, 309 Blackjack Rd., Starkville, 7/16/92, C, 92000890

Bell House, 1280 MS 25 S, Starkville, 10/29/92, C, 92001480

Carroll, Thomas Battle, House, 304 S. Jackson St., Starkville, 5/01/91, C, 91000531

Cedars, The, Old W. Point Rd., Starkville, 10/10/85, B, C, 85003003

Gay, C. E., House, 110 E. Gillespie St., Starkville, 1/03/91, C, 90002108

Gillespie—Jackson House, SE corner MS 12 and MS 25, Starkville, 11/06/86, C, 86003127

Greensboro Street Historic District, Greensboro St., Starkville, 6/14/82, B, C, 82003112

Herman Mound and Village Site, Address Restricted, Starkville vicinity, 3/17/93, D, 93000137

Hotel Chester, 217-223 E. Main St., Starkville, 1/18/85, A, C, 85000099

Lampkin-Owens House, 117 N. Montgomery St., Starkville, 11/24/80, C, 80002298

Lyon's Bluff Site, Address Restricted, Starkville vicinity, 4/22/76, D, 76001105

Magruder-Newsom House, 306 S. Jackson St., Starkville, 8/30/84, C, 84002284

Montgomery Hall, Mississippi State University campus, Starkville vicinity, 3/26/75, A, C, 75001054

Nash Street Historic District, 525 University Dr. and 101–117 N. Nash St., Starkville, 6/24/93, A, C, 93000572

Odd Fellows Cemetery, Jct. of US 82 and Henderson St., Starkville, 7/24/90, A, d, 90001064

Overstreet School Historic District, Roughly bounded by Hogan, Montgomery, Gillespie, Jackson, Wood and Washington Sts. and the Illinois Central RR tracks, Starkville, 10/23/92, A, C, 92001398

Stone, John M., Cotton Mill, Gillespie St., Starkville, 4/29/75, A, 75001055

Textile Building, S of Starkville on Mississippi State University campus, Starkville vicinity, 5/12/75, A, C, 75001056

Walker—Critz House, 414 Chapin St., Starkville, 3/22/89, C, 89000171

Panola County

Ballentine-Bryant House [Johnson, Andrew, Architecture in North Mississippi TR], 506 Butler St., Sardis, 4/09/84, C, 84002287

Ballentine-Seay House [Johnson, Andrew, Architecture in North Mississippi TR], Pocahontas St., Sardis, 4/09/84, C, 84002289

Batesville Mounds (22Pa500), Address Restricted, Batesville vicinity, 12/14/88, D, 88002702

Craig-Seay House [Johnson, Andrew, Architecture in North Mississippi TR], Craig St., Como, 4/09/84, C, 84002292

Crenshaw House [Johnson, Andrew, Architecture in North Mississippi TR], MS 310, Crenshaw, 4/09/84, C, 84002295

Fredonia Church, 6 mi. (9.6 km) E of Como on Old Union Rd., Como vicinity, 3/30/78, A, C, a, d, 78001626

Fredrickson No. 2 (22-Pa-821), Address Restricted, Batesville vicinity, 7/28/88, D, 88001139

Hall-Henderson House [Johnson, Andrew, Architecture in North Mississippi TR], Sycamore St., Sardis, 4/09/84, C, 84002298

Hall-Roberson House [Johnson, Andrew, Architecture in North Mississippi TR], 510 S. Main St., Sardis, 4/09/84, C, 84002300

Holly Grove Site, Address Restricted, Sledge vicinity, 10/21/76, D, 76001106

Holy Innocents' Episcopal Church, Jct. of Main & Craig St., Como, 11/05/87, C, a, 87001936

Hufft House [Johnson, Andrew, Architecture in North Mississippi TR], 117 Pocahontas St., Sardis, 4/09/84, C, 84002302

Hunt Mound (22Pa980), Address Restricted, Pope vicinity, 12/14/88, D, 88002701

Johnson-Tate Cottage [Johnson, Andrew, Architecture in North Mississippi TR], Stonewall St., Sardis, 4/09/84, C, 84002305

Kyle, John Curtis, House [Johnson, Andrew, Architecture in North Mississippi TR], 109 McLaurin St., Sardis, 4/09/84, C, 84002309

Kyle, Judge John William, Law Office, 147 S. Main St., Sardis, 7/24/80, B, C, 80002299

Lee House [Johnson, Andrew, Architecture in North Mississippi TR], 201 Booth St., Batesville, 4/09/84, C, 84002312

Popular Price Store [Johnson, Andrew, Architecture in North Mississippi TR], Railroad St., Como, 4/09/84, C, 84002316

Short's Hill, 203 Childress St., Sardis, 10/16/80, C, 80002300

Tait-Taylor House [Johnson, Andrew, Architecture in North Mississippi TR], Oak Ave., Como, 4/09/84, C, 84002319

Taylor-Falls House [Johnson, Andrew, Architecture in North Mississippi TR], Pointer Ave., Como, 4/09/84, C, 84002321

Taylor-Mansker House [Johnson, Andrew, Architecture in North Mississippi TR], Railroad St., Como, 4/09/84, C, 84002327

Taylor-Wall-Yancy House [Johnson, Andrew, Architecture in North Mississippi TR], 114 Sycamore St., Sardis, 4/09/84, C, 84002334

Walton-Howry House [Johnson, Andrew, Architecture in North Mississippi TR], 308 S. Main St., Sardis, 4/09/84, C, 84002339

Wardlaw-Swango House [Johnson, Andrew, Architecture in North Mississippi TR], Railroad St., Como, 4/09/84, C, 84002341

Well, The, E of Sardis on Sardis-Union Rd., Sardis vicinity, 12/17/82, C, d, 82000579

Pearl River County

Tiger Hammock Site 22 PR 594, Address Restricted, Picayune vicinity, 8/01/85, D, 85001679

Perry County

Old Augusta Historic Site, Address Restricted, New Augusta vicinity, 4/24/79, A, D, 79001334

Pike County

Annex, The [Magnolia MRA], 225 Magnolia St., Magnolia, 10/11/84, A, C, 84000036

Bank of Summit, 811 Robb St., Summit, 7/07/83, C, 83000965

Berryhill House [Magnolia MRA], 265 W. Railroad Ave., Magnolia, 10/11/84, C, 84000038

Brentwood, 601 Delaware Ave., McComb, 3/09/89, C, 89000170

Buie Building [Magnolia MRA], 110 E. Railroad Ave., Magnolia, 10/11/84, C, 84000040

Carraway House [Magnolia MRA], 420 N. Clark St., Magnolia, 10/11/84, C, 84000041

Chadwick, George, House [Magnolia MRA], 560 N. Cherry St., Magnolia, 10/11/84, C, 84000043

Depot [Magnolia MRA], 101 E. Railroad Ave., Magnolia, 10/11/84, A, C, 84000045

Everette-Gottig-Bilbo House [Magnolia MRA], 109 E. Myrtle St., Magnolia, 10/11/84, A, C, 84000046

Holmes House [Magnolia MRA], 405 N. Cherry St., Magnolia, 10/11/84, C, 84000048

Kramertown-Railroad Historic District, S. Railroad Blvd., McComb, 3/13/80, A, C, 80002301

Lanier House [Magnolia MRA], 400 N. Clark St., Magnolia, 10/11/84, C, 84000049

Lieb-Rawls House [Magnolia MRA], 303 Magnolia St., Magnolia, 10/11/84, C, 84000051

Magnolia Manor, 3rd and Amite Sts., Osyka, 9/09/83, C, 83000966

Mullendore House [Magnolia MRA], 515 N. Cherry St., Magnolia, 10/11/84, C, 84000052

Myrtle Street Historic District [Magnolia MRA], W. Myrtle St. between N. Clark and N. Prewitt Sts., Magnolia, 10/11/84, C, a, 84000054

Norwood-TWL Building [Magnolia MRA], 131 W. Railroad Ave., Magnolia, 10/11/84, C, 84000055

Simmons House [Magnolia MRA], 489 Prewitt St., Magnolia, 10/11/84, C, 84000057

Southtown Historic District [Magnolia MRA], Roughly bounded by Minnehaha Creek, Illi-

nois Central RR, Bay, Laurel, and Prewitt Sts., Magnolia, 10/11/84, C, 84000059

Stogner House [Magnolia MRA], 550 N. Cherry St., Magnolia, 10/11/84, C, 84000068

Tanglewood, Co. Rd. 468, 1 mi. N of MS 48, Magnolia vicinity, 8/23/91, C, 91001102

US Post Office—Magnolia [Mississippi Post Offices TR], 205 Magnolia St., Magnolia, 3/18/93, A, C, 80004885

White-Alford House, 845 White Blvd., McComb, 4/21/83, C, 83000967

Pontotoc County

Lochinvar, MS 15 S of Pontotoc, Pontotoc vicinity, 3/13/86, B, C, 86000331

Pontotoc Historic District, Roughly, along Main and Liberty Sts. between Reynolds and 8th Sts., Pontotoc, 10/29/93, C, 93001164

Treaty of Pontotoc Site, Address Restricted, Pontotoc vicinity, 7/27/73, A, D, 73001025

Quitman County

Denton Site, Address Restricted, Denton vicinity, 2/02/79, D, 79001335

Norman Site, Address Restricted, Lambert vicinity, 5/02/75, D, 75001057

Posey Site (22QU500), Address Restricted, Marks vicinity, 9/11/86, D, 86002326

Shady Grove Site (22QU525), Address Restricted, Marks vicinity, 9/11/86, D, a, 86002316

Rankin County

Armstrong Site (22RA576), Address Restricted, Goshen Springs vicinity, 2/02/87, D, 86003686

Hebron Academy, S of Brandon on MS 18, Brandon vicinity, 5/05/78, A, C, 78001627

Misterfeldt Home Place, 1101 Old Hwy. 49S, Richland, 12/18/86, A, C, 86003496

Stevens-Buchanan House, 505 College St., Brandon, 5/05/78, B, C, 78001628

Turcotte House, SE of Brandon on MS 17, Brandon vicinity, 6/04/87, C, 86002869

Scott County

Lake Railroad Station, Brook St., Lake, 7/19/84, A, C, b, 84002346

US Post Office—Forest [Mississippi Post Offices TR], 119 Second St., Forest, 3/18/93, A, C, 80004884

Sharkey County

Cary Site (22Sh507), Address Restricted, Cary, 12/14/88, D, 88002705

Sharkey County—Continued

Leist A Site (22Sh520;22N1), Address Restricted, Rolling Fork vicinity, 12/14/88, D, 88002700

Rolling Fork Mounds, SW of Rolling Fork, Rolling Fork vicinity, 10/18/74, A, 74001065

Savory Site (22-Sh-518), Address Restricted, Holly Bluff vicinity, 7/28/88, D, 88001141

Spanish Fort Site (22SH500), Address Restricted, Holly Bluff vicinity, 4/06/88, D, 88000234

Simpson County

Lewis, L'Dora, Mound (22SI512), Address Restricted, Pearl vicinity, 3/01/87, D, 87000133

Simpson County Courthouse, Courthouse Square, Mendenhall, 8/29/85, A, C, 85001898

Smith County

Taylorsville Signal Office and Watkins General Store, 326 Eureka St., Taylorsville, 11/06/86, A, C, b, 86003056

Stone County

McHenry, George Austin, House, McHenry Ave. and Fifth St., McHenry, 11/03/88, B, 88002223

Sunflower County

Woodburn Bridge [Historic Bridges of Mississippi TR], Spans Big Sunflower River on CR SE of Indianola, Indianola vicinity, 11/16/88, A, C, 88002492

Tallahatchie County

Allison Mound (22Tl1024), Address Restricted, Webb vicinity, 12/14/88, D, 88002708

Buford Site (22Tl501), Address Restricted, Sumner vicinity, 10/15/86, D, 86002797

Dell Bullion Mound (22Tl998), Address Restricted, Grenada vicinity, 12/14/88, D, 88002706

Jacks Site, Address Restricted, Philipp vicinity, 3/24/78, D, 78001630

Lamb-Fish Bridge, E of Charleston, Charleston, 5/17/82, A, C, 82004631

Murphey-Jennings House, 307 Walnut St., Sumner, 3/25/82, B, C, 82004632

Spivey Site, Address Restricted, Crowder vicinity, 12/06/78, D, 78001629

Tate County

Hickahala Creek Bridge [Historic Bridges of Mississippi TR], Spans Hickahala Creek on CR, Senatobia vicinity, 11/16/88, A, C, 88002479

Tippah County

Blue Mountain College Historic District, MS 15, Blue Mountain, 5/23/79, A, C, a, 79003383

Tishomingo County

Bear Creek Mound and Village Site (22Ts500), Address Restricted, Tishomingo vicinity, 12/22/88, D, NPS, 88002825

Central Iuka Historic District [Iuka MPS], Roughly, Fulton and Main Sts. from Eastport St. to Southern Railway tracks and Front St. from Pearl to Fulton Sts., Iuka, 11/01/91, A, 91001577

Church of Our Savior [Iuka MPS], E. Eastport St. between Main and Fulton Sts., Iuka, 8/09/91, C, a, 91000929

Coman, J. M., House [Iuka MPS], 202 E. Quitman St., Iuka, 8/09/91, A, b, 91000930

Davis, James S., House [Iuka MPS], 102 E. Meigg St., Iuka, 8/09/91, A, C, b, 91000931

Doan, James H., House [Iuka MPS], 203 W. Quitman St., Iuka, 8/09/91, A, C, 91000932

Edwards, R. D., House [Iuka MPS], 603 Indian Creek Rd., Iuka, 8/09/91, C, 91000933

Hammerly, G. P., House [Iuka MPS], 102 E. Quitman St., Iuka, 8/09/91, A, C, 91000934

Jourdan, J. C., House [Iuka MPS], 305 W. Eastport St., Iuka, 8/09/91, C, 91000935

Merrill—Newhardt House [Iuka MPS], 508 W. Quitman St., Iuka, 8/09/91, A, C, 91000936

Old Tishomingo County Courthouse, NE corner of Quitman and Liberty Sts., Iuka, 4/11/73, C, 73001026

Reid House [Iuka MPS], 702 W. Eastport St., Iuka, 8/09/91, A, C, 91000937

Stone—Reid House [Iuka MPS], 503 W. Eastport St., Iuka, 8/09/91, A, C, 91000938

Tunica County

Beaverdam Site, Address Restricted, Evansville vicinity, 8/31/78, D, 78001631

Canon Site (22-Tu-523), Address Restricted, Crenshaw vicinity, 1/07/87, D, 86003635

Dundee Site (22TU501), Address Restricted, Dundee vicinity, 1/07/87, D, 86003655

Evansville Mounds (22TU502), Address Restricted, Evansville vicinity, 1/07/87, D, 86003632

Hollywood Site, Address Restricted, Tunica vicinity, 5/19/72, D, 72000701

Johnson Cemetery Site (22TU516), Address Restricted, Hollywood vicinity, 1/07/87, D, a, 86003633

Owens Site (22TU512), Address Restricted, Evansville vicinity, 1/07/87, D, 86003657

Union County

Ingomar Mound, Address Restricted, Ingomar vicinity, 6/09/78, D, 78001632

Union County Courthouse, Bankhead St. between Court and Camp Aves., New Albany, 8/10/90, C, 90001222

Walthall County

China Grove Methodist Church, MS 585, Tylertown vicinity, 7/05/84, C, a, 84002350

Collins, George H., House, 615 Union Rd., Tylertown, 3/16/92, A, B, C, 92000102

Warren County

1300 Grove Street House, 1300 Grove Street, Vicksburg, 11/29/83, C, 83003976

Anchuca, 1010 1st E. St., Vicksburg, 3/22/82, C, 82003113

Balfour House, 1002 Crawford St., Vicksburg, 10/26/71, A, C, 71000458

Beck House, 1101 South St., Vicksburg, 3/29/79, B, C, 79001336

Belle Fleur, 1123 South St., Vicksburg, 5/07/92, C, 92000469

Bethel African Methodist Episcopal Church [Vicksburg MPS], 805 Monroe St., Vicksburg, 7/30/92, C, a, 92000858

Beulah Cemetery [Vicksburg MPS], Jct. of Openwood St. and Old Jackson Rd., Vicksburg, 10/23/92, A, d, 92001404

Biedenharn Candy Company Building, 1107–1109 Washington St., Vicksburg, 12/02/77, B, 77000793

Big Black River Railroad Bridge [Historic Bridges of Mississippi TR], Spans Big Black River E of Bovina, Bovina vicinity, 11/16/88, A, C, 88002418

Blum House [Vicksburg MPS], 1420 Cherry St., Vicksburg, 7/30/92, C, 92000859

Bobb House, 1503 Harrison St., Vicksburg, 1/08/79, B, C, 79001337

Bonham, Isaac, House, 601 Klein St., Vicksburg, 5/26/77, C, 77000794

Cedar Grove, 2200 Oak St., Vicksburg, 7/19/76, B, C, 76001107

Chickasaw Bayou Battlefield, N of Vicksburg on U.S. 61, Vicksburg vicinity, 4/24/73, A, 73001028

Church of the Holy Trinity, South and Monroe Sts., Vicksburg, 5/22/78, A, C, a, g, 78001633

Confederate Avenue Brick Arch Bridge [Historic Bridges of Mississippi TR], Confederate Ave., Vicksburg, 11/16/88, A, C, 88002421

Confederate Avenue Steel Arch Bridge [Historic Bridges of Mississippi TR], Spans Jackson Rd.

Warren County—Continued

in Vicksburg National Military Park, Vicksburg, 9/05/90, A, C, NPS, 88002483

Craig-Flowers House, 2011 Cherry St., Vicksburg, 8/02/84, C, 84002352

Davis-Mitchell House, 901 Crawford St., Vicksburg, 6/01/82, C, 82003114

Fairground Street Bridge [Historic Bridges of Mississippi TR], Spans ICG RR yard on Fairground St., Vicksburg, 11/16/88, A, C, 88002420

Federal Fortifications Along Bear Creek, SW of Youngton, Youngton vicinity, 8/30/74, A, 74001066

Feld House, 2108 Cherry St., Vicksburg, 8/02/82, C, 82003115

Fitz-Hugh Hall, 1322 Chambers St., Vicksburg, 11/06/86, C, 86003030

Flowerree, Col. Charles C., House, 2309 Pearl St., Vicksburg, 5/29/75, B, C, 75001058

Fonsylvania, Fisher Ferry Rd., S of Vicksburg, Vicksburg vicinity, 9/07/84, A, C, 84002355

Galleries, The, 2421 Marshall St., Vicksburg, 4/17/80, C, 80002303

Green, Duff, House, 806 Locust St., Vicksburg, 1/11/79, B, C, 79001338

Grove Street Houses, 1117 and 1121 Grove St., Vicksburg, 5/08/80, C, 80002304

Guider House, 1115 Grove St., Vicksburg, 5/08/80, C, 80002305

Harding, P. M., House, 1402 Chambers St., Vicksburg, 7/17/86, C, 86001674

Hotel Vicksburg, 801 Clay St., Vicksburg, 6/04/79, A, C, 79001339

Hullum-Mallett-Brewer House, Redbone Rd., Redbone vicinity, 7/05/84, C, 84002358

Johnson, Fannie Willis, House, 2430 Drummond St., Vicksburg, 4/08/88, B, C, 88000241

Knox, Dr. Isaac Cecil, House, 2823 Confederate Ave., Vicksburg, 9/18/90, C, 90001478

Lane, John, House, 905 Crawford St., Vicksburg, 5/06/82, C, 82003116

Luckett Compound, 1116-1122 Crawford St, Vicksburg, 7/28/83, C, g, 83000968

Magnolias, The, 1617 Monroe St., Vicksburg, 2/26/87, C, 87000217

Magruder-Morrissey House, 1117 Cherry St., Vicksburg, 5/24/84, C, 84002361

Main Street Historic District [5], 1st, East, Adams, Main and Openwoods Sts., Vicksburg, 4/16/79, C, 79001340

Main Street Historic District (Boundary Increase), Roughly bounded by Adams St., Main St., Cherry St., and First East St., Vicksburg, 1/05/89, C, 88003088

McDermott House, 1100 South St., Vicksburg, 7/12/84, C, 84002359

McNutt House, NW corner of Monroe and E. 1st Sts., Vicksburg, 5/29/75, B, 75001059

Mississippi River Bridge [Historic Bridges of Mississippi TR], Spans Mississippi River on Old US 80, Vicksburg, 2/14/89, A, C, 88002423

Old Courthouse, Warren County, Court Sq., Vicksburg, 5/23/68, A, C, NHL, 68000029

Pemberton's Headquarters, 1018 Crawford St., Vicksburg, 7/23/70, A, B, C, NHL, 70000319

Planters Hall, 822 Main St., Vicksburg, 6/21/71, A, C, 71000459

Planters Hall (Boundary Increase), 822 Main St., Vicksburg, 10/21/88, A, C, 88002068

Rose, Adolph, Building [Vicksburg MPS], 717 Clay St., Vicksburg, 11/12/92, C, 92001567

Shlenker House, 2212 Cherry St., Vicksburg, 11/17/83, C, 83003975

Snyder's Bluff, Address Restricted, Redwood vicinity, 2/06/73, A, D, 73001027

South Vicksburg Public School No. 200, 900 Speed St., Vicksburg, 3/20/86, A, C, 86000482

St. Francis Xavier Convent, 1021 Crawford St., Vicksburg, 4/18/77, A, C, a, 77000796

U.S.S. CAIRO, Ingalls Shipyard, Pascagoula, 9/03/71, A, NPS, 71000068

Uptown Vicksburg Historic District [Vicksburg MPS], Roughly bounded by Locust, South, Washington and Clay Sts., Vicksburg, 8/19/93, C, 93000850

Vicksburg National Military Park, N and E of Vicksburg, Vicksburg vicinity, 10/15/66, A, B, f, NPS, 66000100

Vicksburg Public Library, Old [Vicksburg MPS], 819 South St., Vicksburg, 7/30/92, C, 92000857

Vicksburg Siege Cave, Near Vicksburg City Cemetery, Vicksburg, 3/14/73, A, 73001029

Walnut Hills, 1214 Adams St., Vicksburg, 3/19/82, C, 82003117

Yazoo And Mississippi Valley Depot, 500 Grove St., Vicksburg, 11/13/79, A, C, 79001341

Yokena Presbyterian Church, S of Vicksburg on US 61, Vicksburg vicinity, 9/07/84, C, a, 84002442

Young-Bradfield House, 913 Crawford St., Vicksburg, 5/06/82, C, 82003118

Washington County

Arcola Mounds, Address Restricted, Arcola vicinity, 1/03/91, D, 90002118

Bank of Washington, 120 S. Poplar St., Greenville, 7/16/87, C, 87001209

Belmont, Jct. of MS 1 and 438, Wayside, 4/11/72, C, 72000702

Finlay House, 137 N. Poplar St., Greenville, 4/27/82, A, b, 82003119

First National Bank of Greenville, Main and S. Poplar Sts., Greenville, 1/30/78, A, C, 78003195

Griffen-Spragins House, SW of Greenville off US 82, Greenville vicinity, 4/05/84, A, C, 84002445

Hollyknowe, SE of jct. of US 82 and CR 299, Leland vicinity, 10/10/85, C, 85003004

Leavenworth-Wasson-Carroll House, 623 S. Washington Ave., Greenville, 7/23/80, B, C, g, 80002306

Linden, N of Glen Allan jct. of SR 97 and 69, Glen Allan vicinity, 11/12/82, C, 82000581

Mount Holly, NW of Foote off MS 1, Foote vicinity, 8/14/73, A, C, g, 73001030

Old Delta Democrat Times Building, 201–203 Main St., Greenville, 3/25/82, B, g, 82003120

U.S. Post Office [Mississippi Post Offices 1931-1941 TR], 204 N. Broad St., Leland, 4/21/83, C, g, 83000969

Ward, Junius R., House, Old Hwy. 1, Erwin, 4/28/75, B, C, 75001060

Washington Avenue-Main Street Historic District, Roughly bounded by RR tracks, Yerger, Arnold Ave., and Cherry St., Greenville, 5/03/84, C, 84002446

Wetherbee House, 509 Washington Ave., Greenville, 10/28/77, B, C, 77000797

Winterville Site, Address Restricted, Greenville vicinity, 8/17/73, D, NHL, 73001031

Wayne County

Waynesboro Bridge [Historic Bridges of Mississippi TR], Spans Chickasawhay River on Old US 84, Waynesboro vicinity, 11/16/88, A, C, 88002494

Yellow Creek Bridge [Historic Bridges of Mississippi TR], Spans Yellow Creek on CR NW of Waynesboro, Waynesboro vicinity, 11/16/88, A, C, 88002493

Webster County

Wood Home for Boys, Horton St., Mathiston, 4/05/84, A, 84002448

Wilkinson County

Anderson Mound, Address Restricted, Woodville vicinity, 5/01/86, D, 86000921

Branch Banking House, Bank St., Woodville, 3/30/78, A, C, 78001635

Desert Plantation, E of Pinckneyville-Woodville Rd., Woodville vicinity, 4/01/87, C, 87000543

Forest Home Plantation, SW of Centreville, Centreville vicinity, 3/19/82, C, 82003121

Fort Adams Site, S of Fort Adams, Fort Adams vicinity, 1/11/74, A, 74001067

Hampton Hall, MS 61, Woodville, 10/24/80, C, 80002307

Holly Grove, MS 33, 4 mi. S of MS 24, Centreville vicinity, 10/21/88, C, d, 88002037

Office and Banking House of West Feliciana Railroad, Depot St., Woodville, 10/28/77, A, C, 77000798

Pleasant Hill, E of Woodville on MS 24, Woodville vicinity, 11/17/82, C, b, 82000582

Rosemont, E of Woodville on MS 24, Woodville vicinity, 12/30/74, B, C, 74001068

Salisbury Plantation, Off Woodville Rd., Woodville, 6/16/83, C, 83000970

Smith Creek Site, Address Restricted, Fort Adams vicinity, 6/13/78, D, 78001634

Woodville Historic District, Roughly bounded by Prentiss, 2nd, College, Siglo, and Water Sts., Woodville, 9/30/82, C, 82003122

Wilkinson County—Continued

Woodville Historic District (Boundary Increase), 546 Depot St. and 559 Third St., Woodville, 10/21/93, C, 93001200

Winston County

Nanih Waiya Mound And Village, Address Restricted, Fearns Springs vicinity, 3/28/73, D, 73001032

Old Robinson Road, 16.6 mi. NE of Louisville in Noxubee National Wildlife Refuge, Louisville vicinity, 4/03/75, A, 75001061

Yalobusha County

US Post Office—Water Valley, 2322 Main St., Water Valley, 4/18/85, C, 85000845

Yazoo County

Casey Jones Wreck Site, 1 mi. N of Vaughan, Vaughan vicinity, 4/03/73, B, 73001033

Deasonville Archeological Site, Address Restricted, Deasonville vicinity, 4/29/93, A, D, 93000299

Fairview Landing (22Yz561), Address Restricted, Holly Bluff vicinity, 12/14/88, D, 88002699

Hart, Big John, House, Castle Chapel Rd., SE of Yazoo City, Yazoo City vicinity, 7/01/93, C, b, 93000580

Holly Bluff Site, Address Restricted, Holly Bluff vicinity, 10/15/66, D, NHL, 66000412

Home Place, 2 mi. E of MS 433, S side of Midway to Ebeneezer Rd., Benton vicinity, 9/26/88, C, d, 88001584

Oakes, Augustus J., House, 308 Monroe St., Yazoo City, 4/08/93, B, 93000207

Ricks Memorial Library, 310 N. Main St., Yazoo City, 9/18/75, A, C, 75001062

Shellwood Site (22YZ600), Address Restricted, Lake City vicinity, 4/25/86, D, 86000869

Yazoo City Town Center Historic District, Irregular pattern along Main, Madison and Broadway Sts., Yazoo City, 4/16/79, A, C, 79001342

The Lowe-Steen Site is one of two large prehistoric platform mounds in south-central Mississippi that may yield information about the social structure and religious customs of native inhabitants from 1250–1500 A.D. (James Lauro, 1985)

MISSOURI

Adair County

Adair County Courthouse, Washington St., Kirksville, 8/11/78, A, C, 78001636

Bear Creek Baptist Church, N of Kirksville off US 63, Kirksville vicinity, 3/29/84, A, C, a, d, 84002132

Cabins Historic District, S of Novinger off MO 6, Novinger vicinity, 7/17/79, A, C, D, b, d, 79001344

Dockery Hotel, Elson & McPherson Sts., Kirksville, 2/10/83, C, 83000971

Grim Building, 113–115 E. Washington St., Kirksville, 6/27/79, C, 79001343

Harris, Capt. Thomas C., House, 1308 N. Franklin St., Kirksville, 10/15/73, A, C, 73001034

St. Mary's Church, On MO 11, Adair, 12/16/74, A, C, a, d, 74001069

Thousand Hills State Park Petroglyphs Archeological Site, W of Kirksville, Kirksville vicinity, 1/23/70, C, D, 70000320

Andrew County

Andrew County Courthouse, 4th and Main Sts., Savannah, 9/11/80, C, 80002308

Atchison County

Atchison County Memorial Building, 417 S. Main St., Rock Port, 12/22/87, A, C, f, 87001578

Brownville Bridge [Highway Bridges in Nebraska MPS], US 136 over the Missouri R., Phelps City, 6/17/93, C, 93000536

Dopf, John Dickinson, Mansion, 407 Cass St., Rock Port, 2/08/84, C, 84003858

Gibbs Site, Address Restricted, Watson vicinity, 2/23/72, D, 72000703

Mule Barn Theatre, 10th and Park Sts., Tarkio, 10/15/70, B, C, 70000321

St. Oswald's Protestant Episcopal Church, MO EE S of jct. with MO 46, Skidmore vicinity, 1/13/92, C, a, 91001959

Walnut Inn, 224 Main St., Tarkio, 4/12/82, A, C, 82003124

Audrain County

Ross House, 501 S. Muldrow St., Mexico, 7/26/78, B, C, 78001637

Barry County

Camp Smokey/Company 1713 Historic District [ECW Architecture in Missouri State Parks 1933-1942 TR], Off Park Rd., Cassville vicinity, 2/26/85, A, C, 85000513

Courdin, David W., House, 2.4 mi. SE of Monett, Monett vicinity, 11/05/71, A, C, 71000460

Natural Bridge Archeological Site, Address Restricted, Cassville vicinity, 5/05/72, D, 72000704

Roaring River State Park Bath House [ECW Architecture in Missouri State Parks 1933-1942 TR], Off Park Rd., Cassville vicinity, 3/04/85, A, C, g, 85000500

Roaring River State Park Dam/Spillway [ECW Architecture in Missouri State Parks 1933-1942 TR], Off Park Rd., Cassville vicinity, 2/28/85, A, C, 85000518

Roaring River State Park Deer Leap Trail [ECW Architecture in Missouri State Parks 1933-1942 TR], Off Park Rd., Cassville vicinity, 2/26/85, A, C, g, 85000519

Roaring River State Park Hotel [ECW Architecture in Missouri State Parks 1933-1942 TR], Off Park Rd., Cassville vicinity, 3/04/85, A, C, g, 85000501

Roaring River State Park Honeymoon Cabin [ECW Architecture in Missouri State Parks 1933-1942 TR], Off Park Rd., Cassville vicinity, 2/26/85, A, C, g, 85000520

Roaring River State Park Shelter Kitchen No. 2 and Rest Room [ECW Architecture in Missouri State Parks 1933-1942 TR], Off Park Rd., Cassville vicinity, 2/26/85, A, C, 85000521

Tom Town Historic District, Off Co. Rd. VV, S of Pleasant Ridge, Pleasant Ridge vicinity, 12/15/89, A, 89002126

Waldensian Church and Cemetery of Stone Prairie, Rt. 2, Monett vicinity, 1/18/85, A, a, d, 85000100

Barton County

Truman, Harry, Birthplace Memorial, N corner, 11th St. and Truman Ave., Lamar, 6/23/69, B, c, 69000089

Benton County

Rodgers Shelter Archeological Site, Address Restricted, Fristoe vicinity, 6/23/69, D, 69000090

Boone County

Bond's Chapel Methodist Episcopal Church, MO A, 2.5 mi. NE of Hartsburg, Hartsburg vicinity, 9/09/93, C, a, 93000940

Boone, John W., House [Social Institutions of Columbia's Black Community TR], 4th St. between E. Broadway and Walnut, Columbia, 9/04/80, A, 80002309

Chance, Albert Bishop, House and Gardens, 319 E. Sneed St., Centralia, 7/03/79, B, C, 79001345

Chatol, 543 S. Jefferson St., Centralia, 4/20/79, B, C, g, 79001346

Columbia National Guard Armory, 701 E. Ash St., Columbia, 3/25/93, A, C, 93000197

Conley, Sanford F., House, 602 Sanford Pl., Columbia, 12/18/73, C, 73001035

Douglass, Fred, School [Social Institutions of Columbia's Black Community TR], 310 N. Providence Rd., Columbia, 9/04/80, A, 80002310

First Christian Church, 101 N. Tenth St., Columbia, 10/29/91, C, a, 91001590

Francis Quadrangle Historic District, Bounded by Conley Ave. and Elm, 6th, and 9th Sts., Columbia, 12/18/73, A, C, g, 73001036

Gordon Tract Archeological Site, Address Restricted, Columbia vicinity, 3/16/72, D, 72000705

Gordon, David, House and Collins Log Cabin, 2100 E. Broadway, Columbia, 8/29/83, A, C, b, 83000972

Greenwood, 3005 Mexico Gravel Rd., Columbia, 1/15/79, B, C, 79001347

Guitar, David, House, 2815 Oakland Gravel Rd., Columbia, 9/09/93, C, 93000939

Maplewood, Nifong Blvd. and Ponderosa Dr., Columbia, 4/13/79, A, C, 79001348

Missouri State Teachers Association, 407 S. 6th St., Columbia, 9/04/80, A, C, 80002311

Missouri Theater, 201-215 S. 9th St., Columbia, 6/06/79, A, C, 79001349

Missouri United Methodist Church, 204 S. 9th St., Columbia, 9/04/80, A, C, a, 80002312

Missouri, Kansas, and Texas Railroad Depot, 402 E. Broadway, Columbia, 1/29/79, A, C, 79001350

Pierce Pennant Motor Hotel, 1406 Old US 40W, Columbia, 9/02/82, A, C, 82003125

Rocheport, MO 240, Rocheport, 10/08/76, A, C, 76001108

Sanborn Field and Soil Erosion Plots, University of Missouri campus, Columbia, 10/15/66, A, NHL, 66000413

Second Baptist Church [Social Institutions of Columbia's Black Community TR], 4th St. and Broadway, Columbia, 9/04/80, A, a, 80002313

Second Christian Church [Social Institutions of Columbia's Black Community TR], 401 N. 5th, Columbia, 9/04/80, A, a, 80002314

Senior Hall, Stephens College campus, Columbia, 8/02/77, C, 77000799

St. Paul A.M.E. Church [Social Institutions of Columbia's Black Community TR], 15th and Park Sts., Columbia, 9/04/80, A, a, 80002315

Tiger Hotel, 23 S. 8th St., Columbia, 2/29/80, A, C, 80002316

Wabash Railroad Station and Freight House, 126 N. 10th St., Columbia, 10/11/79, A, C, 79001351

Buchanan County

Buchanan County Courthouse and Jail, Courthouse Sq., St. Joseph, 8/21/72, A, C, 72001563

Buchanan County Courthouse (Boundary Decrease), Courthouse Sq., St. Joseph, 8/02/78, A, C, 78003397

Central—North Commercial Historic District [St. Joseph MPS], Roughly bounded by N. 4th, Main, Francis and Robidoux Sts., St. Joseph, 3/08/91, A, C, 91000125

Christian Sachau Saloon [Frederick Avenue MRA], 1615 Frederick Ave., St. Joseph, 10/25/85, A, C, 85003358

City Hose Company No. 9 [Frederick Avenue MRA], 2217 Frederick Ave., St. Joseph, 10/25/85, C, 85003357

Corby-Forsee Building, 5th and Felix Sts., St. Joseph, 3/27/80, A, C, 80002317

Eckel, Edmond Jacques, House, 515 N. 4th St., St. Joseph, 1/31/80, C, 80002318

Fenton, Enoch Madison, House, SE of Rushville, Rushville vicinity, 4/12/82, B, C, 82003126

Geiger, Dr. Jacob, House—Maud Wyeth Painter House [Frederick Avenue MRA], 2501 Frederick Ave., St. Joseph, 3/12/86, B, C, 86000826

German-American Bank Building, 624 Felix St., St. Joseph, 11/24/78, C, 78001638

Hall Street Historic District, Roughly bounded by Isadore, Corby, 6th and 9th Sts., St. Joseph, 7/17/79, B, C, 79001352

James, Jesse, House, 12th St. and Mitchell Ave., St. Joseph, 9/04/80, A, B, b, 80002319

Kelley and Browne Flats [St. Joseph MPS], 1208–1216 Frederick Ave., St. Joseph, 8/03/89, A, C, 89000991

King's Hill Archeological Site, Address Restricted, St. Joseph vicinity, 4/16/69, D, 69000091

Maple Grove, 2100 N. 11th St., St. Joseph, 10/16/74, B, C, 74001070

Miller, Issac, House, 3003 Ashland Ave., St. Joseph, 9/17/80, B, C, 80002320

Miller-Porter-Lacy House, 2912 Frederick Blvd., St. Joseph, 9/09/82, B, C, 82003127

Missouri Theater and Missouri Theater Building, 112-128 S. 8th St. and 713-721 Edmond St., St. Joseph, 10/11/79, A, C, 79001353

Missouri Valley Trust Company Historic District, Felix and 4th Sts., St. Joseph, 3/04/75, A, C, 75001063

Museum Hill Historic District [St. Joseph MPS], Roughly bounded by 9th, Francis, 12th, Jules, 15th and Messanie Sts., St. Joseph, 3/08/91, A, C, 91000112

Patee, John, House, 12th and Penn Sts., St. Joseph, 10/15/66, A, NHL, 66000414

Pleasant Ridge School, R.F.D. #4, St. Joseph vicinity, 5/02/85, A, C, 85000941

Pony Express Stables, 914 Penn St., St. Joseph, 4/03/70, A, 70000322

Richardson, John D., Dry Goods Company, 300 N. 3rd St., St. Joseph, 4/12/82, A, C, 82003128

Robidoux Hill Historic District [St. Joseph MPS], Roughly bounded by Franklin St., Robidoux

St., Fourth St., Louis St., and Fifth St., St. Joseph, 8/03/89, A, C, 89000992

Robidoux Row, 219-225 E. Poulin St., St. Joseph, 3/07/73, B, 73001037

Robidoux School, 201 S. 10th St., St. Joseph, 8/11/83, A, C, 83000973

South Fourth Street Commercial Historic District [St. Joseph MPS], Roughly bounded by S. 3rd, S. 5th, Charles and Messanie Sts., St. Joseph, 3/08/91, A, C, 91000124

St. Joseph City Hall [Frederick Avenue MRA], Frederick Ave. at Eleventh St., St. Joseph, 10/25/85, A, C, 85003356

St. Joseph Public Library, 10th and Felix Sts., St. Joseph, 9/20/82, A, C, 82003129

Sugar Lake State Park Open Shelter [ECW Architecture in Missouri State Parks 1933-1942 TR], Off MO 138, Rushville vicinity, 2/28/85, A, C, 85000522

Thompson-Brown-Sandusky House, 207 E. Cliff St., St. Joseph, 2/10/83, C, 83004297

Virginia Flats [St. Joseph MPS], 516–518 and 520–528 N. 10th St., St. Joseph, 5/21/92, A, C, 92000586

Vosteen-Hauck House, 913 N. 2nd St., St. Joseph, 9/23/82, B, C, 82003130

Wholesale Row, Bounded by Jules, 3rd, 4th, and Francis Sts., St. Joseph, 9/19/77, A, C, 77000800

Wyeth Flats [Frederick Avenue MRA], 1015–1031 Faraon St., St. Joseph, 10/25/85, B, 85003355

Butler County

Hargrove Pivot Bridge, Carries CR 159 over the Black River, Poplar Bluff vicinity, 10/15/85, C, 85003234

Koehler Fortified Archeological Site, Address Restricted, Naylor vicinity, 12/18/70, D, 70000323

Little Black River Archeological District, Address Restricted, Naylor vicinity, 4/21/75, D, 75001064

Wilborn-Steinberg Site, Address Restricted, Neelyville vicinity, 11/09/72, D, 72000706

Caldwell County

Caldwell County Courthouse, Main St., Kingston, 1/13/72, C, 72000707

Far West, 5.5 mi. W of Kingston via CR D and H, Kingston vicinity, 9/22/70, A, a, 70000324

Callaway County

Cote Sans Dessein Archeological Site, Address Restricted, Tebetts vicinity, 5/27/71, A, D, 71000462

Hockaday, John Augustus, House, 105 Hockaday Ave., Fulton, 9/17/80, A, B, C, 80002321

Mealy Mounds Archeological Site, Address Restricted, Mokane vicinity, 1/25/71, D, 71000461

Research Cave, Address Restricted, Portland vicinity, 10/15/66, D, NHL, 66000415

Westminster College Gymnasium, Westminster College campus, Fulton, 5/23/68, B, g, NHL, 68000030

Westminster College Historic District, Off Westminster Ave., Fulton, 4/12/82, A, C, a, 82004633

Willing, Dr. George M., House, 211 Jefferson St., Fulton, 10/03/80, A, B, C, 80002322

Winston Churchill Memorial, 7th St. and Westminster Ave., Fulton, 3/16/72, B, C, a, b, e, f, g, 72000708

Camden County

Camp Hawthorne Central Area District [ECW Architecture in Missouri State Parks 1933-1942 TR], NE of Camdenton in State Park, Camdenton vicinity, 2/28/85, A, C, g, 85000526

Camp Pin Oak Historic District [ECW Architecture in Missouri State Parks 1933-1942 TR], NE of Camdenton in State Park, Camdenton vicinity, 6/27/85, A, C, g, 85001477

Lake of the Ozarks Recreational Demonstration Area Barn/Garage in Kaiser Area [ECW Architecture in Missouri State Parks 1933-1942 TR], NE of Camdenton in State Park, Camdenton vicinity, 2/28/85, A, C, g, 85000523

Lake of the Ozarks Recreational Demonstration Area Rising Sun Shelter [ECW Architecture in Missouri State Parks 1933-1942 TR], NE of Camdenton in State Park, Camdenton vicinity, 2/26/85, A, C, g, 85000524

Lake of the Ozarks Recreational Demonstration Area Shelter at McCubbin Point [ECW Architecture in Missouri State Parks 1933-1942 TR], NE of Camdenton in State Park, Camdenton vicinity, 2/26/85, A, C, g, 85000525

Lake of the Ozarks State Park Camp Clover Point Recreation Hall [ECW Architecture in Missouri State Parks 1933-1942 TR], NE of Camdenton in State Park, Camdenton vicinity, 3/04/85, A, C, g, 85000502

Lake of the Ozarks State Park Camp Rising Sun Recreation Hall [ECW Architecture in Missouri State Parks 1933-1942 TR], NE of Camdenton in State Park, Camdenton vicinity, 3/04/85, A, C, g, 85000503

Pin Oak Hollow Bridge [ECW Architecture in Missouri State Parks 1933-1942 TR], Lake of the Ozarks State Park, Pin Oak Hollow, 9/13/85, A, C, 85002737

Cape Girardeau County

Bennett-Tobler-Pace-Oliver House, 224 E. Adams, Jackson, 4/18/85, B, C, 85000853

Burfordville Covered Bridge, E edge of Burfordville on CR HH, Burfordville vicinity, 5/19/70, A, C, 70000325

Burfordville Mill, Off MO 34, Burfordville, 5/27/71, A, 71000463

Glenn House, 325 S. Spanish St., Cape Girardeau, 10/11/79, B, C, 79001354

Cape Girardeau County—Continued

Hanover Lutheran Church, 2949 Perryville Rd., Cape Girardeau, 9/14/87, C, a, 87001575

McKendree Chapel, Off I-55, Jackson vicinity, 4/13/87, A, C, a, 87000811

Oliver-Leming House, 740 North St., Cape Girardeau, 9/12/80, B, C, 80002323

Reynolds, James, House, 623 N. Main St., Cape Girardeau, 10/13/83, B, C, 83003942

St. Vincent De Paul Catholic Church, 131 South Main St., Cape Girardeau, 4/12/82, C, a, 82003131

Thilenius, Col, George C., House, 100 Longview Pl., Cape Girardeau, 4/14/83, A, C, 83000974

Trail of Tears State Park Archeological Site, Address Restricted, Oriole vicinity, 12/02/70, D, 70000326

Carroll County

Carroll County Sheriff's Quarters and Jail, 101 W. Washington St., Carrollton, 10/11/79, B, C, 79001355

U.S. Post Office, 101 N. Folger St., Carrollton, 5/12/77, C, 77001570

Wilcoxson and Company Bank, 1 W. Washington Ave., Carrollton, 1/21/83, A, C, 83000975

Wright II Archeological Site, Address Restricted, Miami Station vicinity, 5/27/71, D, 71000464

Carter County

Bedell, Mrs. Louis, House [Missouri Lumber and Mining Company MRA], 3rd and Maple Sts., Grandin, 10/14/80, A, 80002324

Big Spring Historic District, E of Van Buren on MO 103, Van Buren vicinity, 3/17/81, A, C, g, NPS, 81000101

Boyer, Earl, House [Missouri Lumber and Mining Company MRA], 5th St., Grandin, 10/14/80, A, 80002325

Chubb Hollow Site, Address Restricted, Van Buren vicinity, 1/18/90, D, NPS, 89002272

Gibson, J. W., House [Missouri Lumber and Mining Company MRA], 6th and Pine Sts., Grandin, 10/14/80, A, 80002326

Gooseneck Site, Address Restricted, Poplar Bluff vicinity, 10/02/90, D, NPS, 90001473

Greensfelder, Delia, House [Missouri Lumber and Mining Company MRA], 4th and N. Cherry Sts., Grandin, 10/14/80, A, 80002327

Herrington, Loretta, House [Missouri Lumber and Mining Company MRA], 5th St., Grandin, 10/14/80, A, 80002328

Hinton, James, House [Missouri Lumber and Mining Company MRA], Walnut St., Grandin, 10/14/80, A, 80002329

Jacobson, Nettie, House [Missouri Lumber and Mining Company MRA], 6th and Oak Sts., Grandin, 10/14/80, A, 80002330

Kelley, Isaac, Site (23CT111 and 23CT1), Address Restricted, Hunter vicinity, 2/04/88, D, NPS, 87002531

Kitterman, Nola, House [Missouri Lumber and Mining Company MRA], 6th St., Grandin, 10/14/80, A, 80002331

Knapp, Wallace, House [Missouri Lumber and Mining Company MRA], 6th and S. Elm Sts., Grandin, 10/14/80, A, 80002332

Lawhorn, Buford, House [Missouri Lumber and Mining Company MRA], 6th St., Grandin, 10/14/80, A, 80002333

Lewis, Iva, House [Missouri Lumber and Mining Company MRA], 6th St., Grandin, 10/14/80, A, 80002334

Masonic Lodge [Missouri Lumber and Mining Company MRA], 5th and S. Elm Sts., Grandin, 10/14/80, A, 80002335

Mays, Terry, House [Missouri Lumber and Mining Company MRA], 6th and S. Plum St., Grandin, 10/14/80, A, 80002336

McNew, Thornton, House [Missouri Lumber and Mining Company MRA], 6th and Spruce Sts., Grandin, 10/14/80, A, 80002337

Mill Pond [Missouri Lumber and Mining Company MRA], Off MO 21, Grandin, 10/14/80, A, 80002338

Nance, Della, House [Missouri Lumber and Mining Company MRA], 6th St., Grandin, 10/14/80, A, 80002339

Owens, Hazel, House [Missouri Lumber and Mining Company MRA], 5th St., Grandin, 10/14/80, A, 80002340

Phillips Bay Mill (23CT235), Address Restricted, Eastwood vicinity, 2/03/88, D, NPS, 87002536

Phillips, Ernie, House [Missouri Lumber and Mining Company MRA], 3rd and N. Cherry Sts., Grandin, 10/14/80, A, 80002341

Powers, Alvis, House [Missouri Lumber and Mining Company MRA], Walnut St., Grandin, 10/14/80, A, 80002342

Shoat, Hazel, House [Missouri Lumber and Mining Company MRA], 5th St., Grandin, 10/14/80, A, 80002343

Sixth Street Historic District [Missouri Lumber and Mining Company MRA], 6th St., Grandin, 10/14/80, A, 80002344

Smith, James, House [Missouri Lumber and Mining Company MRA], 6th St., Grandin, 10/14/80, A, 80002345

Smith, Lawrence, House [Missouri Lumber and Mining Company MRA], 3rd St., Grandin, 10/14/80, A, 80002346

Smith, William F., House [Missouri Lumber and Mining Company MRA], 6th St., Grandin, 10/14/80, A, 80002347

Tucker, Lee, House [Missouri Lumber and Mining Company MRA], 3rd St., Grandin, 10/14/80, A, 80002348

Cass County

Brown, Robert A., House, N of Harrisonville off Alt. U.S. 71, Harrisonville vicinity, 6/15/70, C, 70000327

O'Bannon Homestead, NE of Garden City off MO NN, Garden City vicinity, 7/03/79, C, 79001356

St. Peter's Episcopal Church, 400 W. Wall St., Harrisonville, 9/09/82, C, a, g, 82003132

Cedar County

Caplinger Mills Historic District, Jct. of Washington Ave. and the Sac R., Caplinger Mills, 9/02/93, A, C, 93000903

Montgomery Archeological Site, Address Restricted, Stockton vicinity, 9/21/78, D, 78001639

Chariton County

First Presbyterian Church, Hill and East Sts., Keytesville, 11/23/77, C, a, 77000802

Locust Hill, E of Brunswick on SR Y, Brunswick vicinity, 1/10/80, C, 80002349

Redding-Hill House, 100 W. North St., Keytesville, 7/29/69, C, 69000092

Christian County

Southwest Missouri Prehistoric Rock Shelter and Cave Sites Discontiguous Archeological District [Prehistoric Rock Shelter and Cave Sites in Southwestern Missouri MPS], Address Restricted, Chadwick vicinity, 10/24/91, D, 91002046

Clark County

Boulware Mound Group Archeological Site, Address Restricted, Canton vicinity, 1/21/70, D, 70000328

Clark County Courthouse, 101 E. Court St., Kahoka, 9/08/83, A, C, g, 83000976

Hiller, Col. Hiram M., House, 520 N. Washington, Kahoka, 7/21/86, B, 86001927

Montgomery Opera House, 201–209 W. Commercial St., Kahoka, 10/20/88, A, C, 88002018

Sickles Tavern, NW of Wayland on MO B, Wayland vicinity, 10/22/79, C, 79001357

Clay County

Aker Cemetery, NE of Smithville off MO W, Smithville vicinity, 11/13/74, A, d, 74001071

Antioch Christian Church, 4805 NE Antioch Rd., Kansas City, 4/02/79, A, C, a, b, 79001358

Clay County Savings Association Building [Liberty MPS], 104 E. Franklin St., Liberty, 12/28/92, A, C, 92001675

Claybrook House, NE of Kearney, Kearney vicinity, 12/21/81, B, C, 81000332

Clinton House, 404 S. Leonard St., Liberty, 11/22/78, C, 78001641

Clay County—Continued

Compton, Dr. James, House, 5410 NE Oak Ridge Rd., Kansas City, 7/10/79, B, C, 79003677

Elms Hotel, Regent and Elms Blvd., Excelsior Springs, 3/29/85, A, C, 85000648

Hall of Waters, 201 E. Broadway, Excelsior Springs, 6/09/83, A, C, g, 83000977

Hughes, Frank, Memorial Library [Liberty MPS], 210 E. Franklin St., Liberty, 12/28/92, A, C, 92001676

IOOF Liberty Lodge No. 49 [Liberty MPS], 16–18 E. Franklin St., Liberty, 12/28/92, A, C, 92001677

James Brothers' House and Farm, 2.25 mi. E of Kearney, Kearney vicinity, 3/16/72, B, 72000709

James Brothers' House and Farm (Boundary Increase), NE of Kearney, Kearney vicinity, 9/27/78, B, 78003417

Jewell Hall, Jewell St. between Kansas and Mississippi Sts., Liberty, 9/06/78, A, C, a, 78001642

Major Hotel [Liberty MPS], 112 E. Franklin St., Liberty, 12/28/92, A, C, 92001678

Miller Building [Liberty MPS], 2 E. Franklin St., Liberty, 12/28/92, A, C, 92001679

Nebo Hill Archeological Site, Address Restricted, Liberty vicinity, 3/04/71, D, 71000465

Odd Fellows Home District, MO 291, Liberty, 9/15/87, A, C, 87001595

South Liberty Courthouse Square Historic District [Liberty MPS], 2 S. Main St., 10 E. Kansas St., 1–17 E. Kansas St., Liberty, 12/28/92, A, C, 92001680

Watkins Mill, 6 mi. NW of Excelsior, Excelsior vicinity, 11/13/66, A, NHL, 66000416

West Liberty Courthouse Square Historic District [Liberty MPS], 12–16 N. Main St., Liberty, 12/28/92, A, C, 92001681

Woodneath, 8900 NE Flintlock Rd., Kansas City, 2/17/78, B, C, 78001640

Cole County

Cole County Courthouse and Jail-Sheriff's House, Monroe and E. High Sts., Jefferson City, 4/03/73, A, C, 73001038

Cole County Historical Society Building, 109 Madison St., Jefferson City, 5/21/69, B, C, 69000093

Dulle Farmstead Historic District, 1101 Hwy. 54 W., Jefferson City, 12/30/93, A, C, 93001468

Gay Archeological Site, Address Restricted, Osage City vicinity, 1/25/71, D, 71000466

Ivy Terrace, 500 E. Capitol Ave., Jefferson City, 3/16/90, C, 90000426

Jefferson City Community Center, 608 E. Dunklin St., Jefferson City, 5/14/92, A, g, 92000503

Lincoln Univ. Hilltop Campus Historic District, 820 Chestnut St., Jefferson City, 4/28/83, A, g, 83000978

Lohman's Landing Building, W corner of Jefferson and Water Sts., Jefferson City, 2/25/69, A, 69000094

Missouri Governor's Mansion, 100 Madison St., Jefferson City, 5/21/69, B, C, 69000095

Missouri State Capitol Building and Grounds, High St. between Broadway and Jefferson Sts., Jefferson City, 6/23/69, A, C, 69000096

Missouri State Capitol Historic District, Bounded roughly by Adams, McCarthy, Mulberry Sts. and the Missouri River, Jefferson City, 6/18/76, A, C, 76001109

Missouri State Penitentiary Warden's House, 700 E. Capitol Ave., Jefferson City, 10/24/91, A, C, 91001518

Villa Panorama, 1310 Swifts Hwy., Jefferson City, 1/03/85, A, B, C, 85000031

Cooper County

Andrews—Wing House [Boonville Missouri MRA], 733 Main St., Boonville, 3/16/90, C, 82005304

Beckett, William S. and Mary, House [Boonville MRA], 821 Third St., Boonville, 3/16/90, C, 82005288

Blakey, Albert Gallatin, House [Boonville Missouri MRA], 226 W. Spring St., Boonville, 3/16/90, C, 82005289

Boller House, 223 E. Spring St., Boonville, 8/02/77, A, C, 77000803

Cobblestone Street [Boonville Missouri MRA], 100 Main St., Boonville, 3/16/90, A, 82005293

Dauwalter, John S., House [Boonville Missouri MRA], 817 Seventh St., Boonville, 3/16/90, C, 82005296

Dick-Kobel Homestead, W of Jamestown, Jamestown vicinity, 9/09/82, A, C, 82003133

Diggs, Duke and Mary, House [Boonville, Missouri MRA], 1217 Rural St., Boonville, 3/16/90, C, 82005297

Fessler—Secongost House [Boonville Missouri MRA], 119 W. Morgan St., Boonville, 3/16/90, C, 82005335

Gantner, Andrew, House [Boonville Missouri MRA], 1308 Sixth St., Boonville, 3/16/90, C, 82005303

Hamilton—Brown Shoe Company Building [Boonville Missouri MRA], First St., Boonville, 3/16/90, A, 82005305

Harley Park Archeological Site, Address Restricted, Boonville vicinity, 10/15/70, D, 70000329

Historic District A [Boonville Missouri MRA], Vine and 2nd Sts., Boonville, 1/24/83, A, C, 83000979

Historic District B [Boonville Missouri MRA], 4th and E. Spring Sts., Boonville, 1/24/83, A, C, 83000980

Historic District C [Boonville Missouri MRA], E. High and 4th Sts, Boonville, 1/24/83, A, C, 83000981

Historic District D [Boonville Missouri MRA], High and Main Sts., Boonville, 1/24/83, A, C, 83000982

Historic District E [Boonville Missouri MRA], High, Spring and Morgan Sts., Boonville, 1/24/83, A, C, 83000983

Historic District F [Boonville Missouri MRA], Extends North and South along 6th and 7th Sts., Boonville, 1/24/83, A, C, g, 83000984

Historic District H [Boonville Missouri MRA], SE corner of E. Morgan St. and Reformatory Dr., Boonville, 1/24/83, A, C, g, 83000985

Imhoff Archeological Site, Address Restricted, Blackwater vicinity, 8/07/72, D, 72000710

Johnson, Juliet Trigg, House [Boonville Missouri MRA], 1304 Main St., Boonville, 3/16/90, C, 82005327

Johnson, Wilbur T. and Rhoda Stephens, House [Boonville Missouri MRA], 821 Main, Boonville, 3/16/90, C, 82005322

Lyric Theater, NE corner of Main and Vine Sts., Boonville, 5/21/69, A, C, 69000097

Meierhoffer House [Boonville Missouri MRA], 120 E. High St., Boonville, 3/16/90, C, 82005317

Meierhoffer Sand Company Office Building [Boonville Missouri MRA], 201 Second St., Boonville, 3/16/90, C, 82005318

Mellor Village and Mounds Archeological District, Address Restricted, Lamine vicinity, 5/21/69, D, 69000098

Mellor Village and Mounds Archeological District (Boundary Increase), Address Restricted, Lamine vicinity, 8/07/74, B, D, c, 74002282

Missouri, Kansas and Texas Railroad Depot [Boonville Missouri MRA], 320 First St., Boonville, 3/16/90, A, C, 82005312

Morton—Myer House [Boonville Missouri MRA], 1000 Eleventh St., Boonville, 3/16/90, C, 82005316

Mount Nebo Baptist Church, MO 135/E, Pilot Grove, 5/23/86, A, C, a, 86001111

Nelson, Thomas, House [Boonville Missouri MRA], 700 Tenth St., Boonville, 3/16/90, A, C, 82005302

New Lebanon Cumberland Presbyterian Church and School, MO A, New Lebanon, 7/09/79, A, C, a, 79001359

Pigott, Josephine Trigg, House [Boonville Missouri MRA], 1307 Sixth St., Boonville, 3/16/90, C, 82005328

Pleasant Green, 8 mi. SW of Pilot Grove on U.S. 135, Pilot Grove vicinity, 7/29/77, B, C, 77000804

Prairie View, E of Pleasant Green off MO 135, Pleasant Green vicinity, 9/20/82, B, C, 82003134

Ravenswood, NW of Bunceton on MO 5, Bunceton vicinity, 2/24/75, A, C, 75001065

Roeschel-Toennes-Oswald Property [Boonville Missouri MRA], 515 W. Spring, Boonville, 7/07/83, A, C, 83000986

St. Matthew's Chapel A.M.E. Church [Boonville Missouri MRA], 309 Spruce St., Boonville, 3/16/90, A, a, 82005324

Summer Public School [Boonville Missouri MRA], 321 Spruce St., Boonville, 3/16/90, A, 82005331

Wooldridge Archeological Site, Address Restricted, Wooldridge vicinity, 12/02/70, D, 70000330

Crawford County

Big Bend Rural School, MO 19, Steelville vicinity, 12/12/78, A, 78001643

Crawford County—Continued

Harney, Maj. Gen. William S., Summer Home, 332 S. Mansion Ave., Sullivan, 4/19/84, B, C, 84002144

Scotia Iron Furnace Stack, 6.3 mi. SE of Leasburg on CR H, Leasburg vicinity, 5/21/69, A, 69000099

Dade County

Dilday Mill, SE of South Greenfield on Turnback Creek, South Greenfield vicinity, 8/26/77, A, 77000805

Dallas County

Bennett Spring State Park Shelter House and Water Gauge Station [ECW Architecture in Missouri State Parks 1933-1942 TR], Off MO A64, Bennett Spring, 2/28/85, A, C, g, 85000527

Daviess County

Daviess County Courthouse, Public Sq., Gallatin, 11/14/80, C, 80002350

Daviess County Rotary Jail and Sheriff's Residence, 310 W. Jackson, Gallatin, 2/23/90, C, 90000131

Ray, A., Taylor House, 212 W. Van Buren St., Gallatin, 4/12/82, B, C, 82003135

De Kalb County

Dalton-Uphoff House, N of Stewartsville, Stewartsville vicinity, 4/12/82, B, C, 82004634

Riggs, Absolom, House, SR 1, Weatherby vicinity, 4/12/82, B, C, 82004635

Dent County

Dam and Spillway in the Hatchery Area at Montauk State Park [ECW Architecture in Missouri State Parks 1933-1942 TR], Off MO 119, Salem vicinity, 2/26/85, A, C, 85000528

Dent County Courthouse, Main and 4th Sts., Salem, 2/23/72, C, 72000711

Montauk State Park Open Shelter [ECW Architecture in Missouri State Parks 1933-1942 TR], Off MO 119, Salem vicinity, 2/28/85, A, C, 85000529

Nichols Farm District, W of Co. Rd. V, N of Current River, Cedar Grove vicinity, 12/27/89, A, C, NPS, 89002129

Old Mill at Montauk State Park [ECW Architecture in Missouri State Parks 1933-1942 TR], Off MO 119, Salem vicinity, 6/27/85, A, 85001478

Young, W. A., House, CR 513, Salem vicinity, 3/30/89, C, 88000147

Dunklin County

Campbell Commercial Historic District, Roughly bounded by Magnolia St., Martin Ave., Locust St. and the St. Louis & Southwest RR tracks, Campbell, 10/08/91, A, C, 91001482

Kennett Archeological Site, Address Restricted, Kennett vicinity, 2/17/78, D, 78001644

Kennett City Hall and Masonic Lodge, 122 College St., Kennett, 9/17/81, A, 81000333

Langdon Site, Address Restricted, Harnersville vicinity, 1/11/74, D, 74001072

Owens, Given, House, Off MO 53, Campbell vicinity, 3/29/83, C, 83000987

Franklin County

AME Church of New Haven, 225 Selma St., New Haven, 8/18/92, A, a, 92001002

Bethel Church, MO T 2 mi. W of Labadie, Labadie vicinity, 2/03/93, C, a, 92001867

Caldwell Farm, S of Washington on Bieker Rd., Washington vicinity, 10/20/80, A, C, 80002351

Downtown Washington Historic District, Roughly W. Front St. from Stafford St. to Market St. and Elm St. from W. Front St. to Fourth St., Washington, 10/05/89, A, C, 89001465

Grauer, Gustav, Farm, N of Pacific, Pacific vicinity, 9/06/84, A, C, 84002142

Meramec State Park Beach Area Historic District [ECW Architecture in Missouri State Parks TR], MO 185 at the Meramec R., Sullivan vicinity, 12/06/91, A, C, 91001772

Meramec State Park Lookout House/Observation Tower [ECW Architecture in Missouri State Parks 1933-1942 TR], E of Sullivan off MO 185, Sullivan vicinity, 2/28/85, A, C, 85000530

Meramec State Park Pump House [ECW Architecture in Missouri State Parks 1933-1942 TR], E of Sullivan off MO 185, Sullivan vicinity, 2/28/85, A, C, 85000531

Meramec State Park Shelter House [ECW Architecture in Missouri State Parks 1933-1942 TR], E of Sullivan off MO 185, Sullivan vicinity, 2/26/85, A, C, 85000532

Moselle Iron Furnace Stack, 1 mi. SE of Moselle, Moselle vicinity, 5/21/69, A, 69000100

North, James, House, MO T, Labadie, 4/05/84, A, C, 84002534

Panhorst Feed Store, 465 St. Clair St., St. Clair, 7/05/90, C, 90001023

Pelster, Wilhelm, House-Barn, S of New Haven, New Haven vicinity, 12/05/78, A, B, C, 78001645

Schwarzer, Franz, House, 2 Walnut St., Washington, 7/17/78, B, C, 78001646

Schwegmann, John F., House, 438 W. Front St., Washington, 3/22/84, B, C, 84002538

Tavern Cave, Address Restricted, St. Albans vicinity, 6/15/70, A, D, 70000331

Thias, Henry C., House, 304 Elm St., Washington, 9/20/84, A, C, 84002539

Tibbe Historic District, Bounded by Front, Market, Main, Lafayette, Second, Oak, Fifth, Cedar,

Main, and Olive, Washington, 3/22/90, C, 90000501

Gasconade County

Hermann Historic District, Roughly bounded by E. Wharf, Mozart, E. 5th, and Gellert Sts., Hermann, 2/01/72, A, C, 72000712

Kotthoff-Weeks Farm Complex, Off SR J, Hermann vicinity, 3/28/83, A, C, 83000988

Old Stone Hill Historic District, Bounded roughly by W. 12th, Goethe and Jefferson Sts., and Iron Rd., Hermann, 5/21/69, A, C, 69000102

Peenie Petroglyph Archeological Site, Address Restricted, Bem vicinity, 7/29/69, D, 69000101

Poeschel, William, House, W. Tenth St. approximately 2 mi. W of Hermann city limits, Hermann vicinity, 6/21/90, A, B, C, 90000982

Ruskaup House, W of Drake on U.S. 50, Drake vicinity, 3/29/83, A, C, 83000989

Shobe-Morrison House, W of Morrison off MO 100, Morrison vicinity, 2/10/83, B, C, 83000990

Vallet-Danuser House, E of Hermann on MO 100, Hermann vicinity, 9/23/82, A, B, C, 82003136

Gentry County

Albany Carnegie Public Library, 101 W. Clay St., Albany, 2/23/90, A, C, 90000130

Gentry County Courthouse, Public Sq., Albany, 9/18/80, A, C, 80002352

Greene County

Abou Ben Adhem Shrine Mosque, 601 E. St. Louis, Springfield, 9/09/82, A, C, 82003137

Anderson, Elijah Teague, House, 406 N. Pine St., Republic, 11/14/80, C, 80002353

Bentley House, 603 E. Calhoun St., Springfield, 11/14/80, B, C, 80002354

Boegel and Hine Flour Mill—Wommack Mill, E side of N. Main St., S of intersection with MO 125, Fair Grove, 11/06/86, A, 86003140

Boone, Nathan, House, 1.75 mi. N of Ash Grove on Hwy. V, Ash Grove vicinity, 10/01/69, A, C, 69000103

Christ Episcopal Church, Address Restricted, Springfield vicinity, 3/26/87, C, a, 87000514

Commercial Street Historic District, Commercial St., Springfield, 5/24/83, A, C, 83000991

Day House, 614 South St., Springfield, 11/07/76, B, C, 76001110

Gillioz Theater, 325 Park Central E., Springfield, 7/09/91, A, C, 91000887

Keet-McElhany House, 435 E. Walnut St., Springfield, 3/22/84, B, C, 84002545

Landers Theater, 311 E. Walnut, Springfield, 8/12/77, A, C, 77000806

Mid-Town Historic District, Roughly bounded by Pacific, Clay, Pythian, Summit, Calhoun, Wash-

Greene County—Continued

ington, Central, Benton, Division, and Jefferson, Springfield, 7/13/89, A, C, 89000938

Old Calabosse, 409 W. McDaniel St., Springfield, 11/14/80, A, C, 80002355

Pearson Creek Archeological District, Address Restricted, Springfield vicinity, 10/11/78, A, D, 78001647

Stone Chapel, Benton and Central Sts, Springfield, 10/21/82, A, C, 82000583

U.S. Customhouse and Post Office, 830 Boonville Ave., Springfield, 6/27/79, A, C, 79001360

Walnut Street Historic District, Roughly bounded by McDaniel, Walnut and Elm Sts. and Sherman Pkwy., Springfield, 3/21/85, C, 85000623

Wilson's Creek National Battlefield, SW of Springfield on MO 174, Springfield vicinity, 10/15/66, A, NPS, 66000113

Grundy County

Crowder State Park Vehicle Bridge [ECW Architecture in Missouri State Parks 1933-1942 TR], MO 128, Trenton vicinity, 3/04/85, A, C, g, 85000505

Norris, Jewett, Library, 1331 Main St., Trenton, 9/07/84, A, B, C, f, 84002549

St. Philip's Episcopal Church, 141 E. 9th St., Trenton, 7/17/79, A, C, a, 79001361

Harrison County

Hamilton House, 1228 W. Main, Bethany, 4/11/85, B, C, 85000733

Slatten House, MO 4, Bethany vicinity, 7/09/84, A, C, 84002553

Henry County

Anheuser—Busch Brewing Association Building, 203 W. Franklin St., Clinton, 8/09/91, A, C, 91001030

Dorman, Judge Jerubial Gideon, House, 302 W. Franklin St., Clinton, 2/10/83, B, C, 83000992

Williams, C. C., House, 303 W. Franklin St., Clinton, 10/21/82, C, 82000584

Hickory County

Williams, John Siddle, House, Off U.S. 54, Hermitage, 9/27/80, B, C, 80002356

Holt County

Carroll Stagecoach Inn, E of Oregon, Oregon vicinity, 8/18/83, B, C, 83000993

Chicago, Burlington and Quincy Depot, S. State St., Mound City, 12/12/78, A, 78001648

City Hall, MO 111, Forest City, 6/27/79, A, C, 79001362

Rulo Bridge [Highway Bridges in Nebraska MPS], US 159 over the Missouri R., Fortescue, 1/04/93, C, 92000718

Howard County

Boonslick State Park, 1 mi. N of Boonsboro on MO 87, 2 mi. SW on MO 187, Boonsboro vicinity, 12/30/69, A, B, 69000104

Cedar Grove, W of Franklin, Franklin vicinity, 7/19/82, B, C, 82003140

Central Methodist College Campus Historic District, Roughly bounded by Mulberry, Elm, Church and MO 5, Fayette, 9/15/80, A, C, a, g, 80002357

Coleman Hall, 502 N. Linn, Fayette, 6/11/86, A, C, 86001326

Finks-Harvey Plantation, W of Roanoke, Roanoke vicinity, 12/11/78, B, C, 78001649

Glasgow Commercial Historic District, 501–623 First St., 100–195 Market St., 603 Second St., Glasgow, 1/16/92, A, C, 91001915

Glasgow Presbyterian Church, Commerce and 4th Sts., Glasgow, 9/09/82, A, C, a, 82003141

Glasgow Public Library, NW corner Market and 4th Sts., Glasgow, 5/21/69, A, C, 69000106

Greenwood, MO 5, Fayette vicinity, 3/29/83, C, 83000994

Harris-Chilton-Ruble House, 108 N. Missouri Ave., New Franklin, 9/04/80, B, C, 80002359

Inglewood, 701 Randolph St., Glasgow, 6/21/90, C, 90000981

Jackson, Prior, Homeplace, S of Fayette on MO DD, Fayette vicinity, 3/10/80, B, C, g, 80002358

Morrison, Alfred W., House, 1 mi. SW of Fayette on MO 5, Fayette vicinity, 4/16/69, B, C, 69000105

Oakwood, 1 Leonard Ave., Fayette, 9/23/82, B, C, 82003138

Rivercene, R.F.D. 1, New Franklin, 2/16/73, B, C, 73001039

St. Mary's Episcopal Church, 104 W. Davis St., Fayette, 9/09/82, A, C, a, b, 82003139

Wright, Dr. Uriel S., Office, 120 Church St., Fayette, 12/22/87, C, 87001727

Iron County

Fort Davidson, On MO 21, S of jct. with Rte. V in Clark National Forest, Pilot Knob vicinity, 2/26/70, A, 70000332

Immanuel Evangelical Lutheran Church, Palmer and Zeigler Sts., Pilot Knob, 1/22/79, A, a, 79001364

Iron County Courthouse Buildings, Courthouse Sq. and 220 S. Shepherd St., Ironton, 6/27/79, A, C, 79001363

St. Paul's Episcopal Church, NW corner of Knob and Reynolds Sts., Ironton, 5/21/69, A, C, a, 69000107

Jackson County

18th and Vine Historic District [18th and Vine Area of Kansas City MPS], Roughly bounded by 18th St., Woodland Ave., 19th St. and The Paseo, Kansas City, 9/09/91, A, 84004142

Ambassador Hotel Historic District, 3527, 3600 Broadway and 435, 441 Knickerbocker Pl., Kansas City, 2/17/83, C, 83000995

Attucks School [18th and Vine Area of Kansas City MPS], 1815 Woodland Ave., Kansas City, 9/09/91, A, 91001150

Bellerive Hotel, 214 E. Armour Blvd., Kansas City, 2/28/80, C, 80002361

Benton, Thomas Hart, House and Studio, 3616 Belleview St., Kansas City, 11/21/80, B, g, 80002362

Beth Shalom Synagogue, 3400 The Paseo, Kansas City, 9/09/82, A, C, a, 82003142

Bingham-Waggoner House and Estate, 313 W. Pacific Ave., Independence, 5/22/80, A, B, 80002360

Bixby, Walter E., House, 6505 State Line Rd., Kansas City, 11/21/78, B, C, g, 78001651

Boley Building, 1130 Walnut St., Kansas City, 3/09/71, C, 71000467

Bonfils Building, 1200 Grand Ave., Kansas City, 3/22/84, B, C, 84002568

Bryant Building, 1102 Grand Ave., Kansas City, 4/24/89, C, 89000312

Bryant, Dr. John S. Jr. and Harriet Smart, House, 519 S. Main St., Independence, 5/21/92, A, C, 92000582

Bunker Building, 820 Baltimore Ave., Kansas City, 9/05/75, A, C, 75001067

Byram's Ford Historic District, 63rd St. and Manchester Trafficway at Big Blue River, Kansas City, 10/16/89, A, 89001629

Cave Spring, 7100 Blue Ridge Extension, Kansas City, 8/10/78, A, 78001652

Chappell, Philip E., House, 1836 Pendleton Ave., Kansas City, 8/03/90, C, 90001157

Chicago Apartments, 1110–1112 E. Armour Blvd., Kansas City, 9/11/80, C, 80002363

City Bank Building, 1801 Grand Ave., Kansas City, 2/17/83, A, C, 83000996

Coates House Hotel, 1005 Broadway, Kansas City, 2/23/72, A, C, 72000715

Coca-Cola Building, 2101–2111 Grand Ave., Kansas City, 8/18/88, C, 88001300

Continental Hotel [Hotels in Downtown Kansas City TR], 106 W. 11th St., Kansas City, 8/08/83, A, C, 83000997

Corrigan, Bernard, House, 1200 W. 55th St., Kansas City, 1/18/78, B, C, 78001653

Corrigan, Thos., Building, 1828 Walnut St., Kansas City, 9/16/82, B, C, 82003143

Curtiss, Louis, Studio Building, 1116–1120 McGee St., Kansas City, 6/19/72, B, C, 72000716

Jackson County—Continued

Disney, Walt, House, and Garage, 3028 Bellefontaine Ave., Kansas City, 5/22/78, B, 78001654

District I [Armour Boulevard MRA], Armour Blvd. between Broadway and Baltimore Aves., Kansas City, 7/28/83, A, C, 83000998

District I [Hotels in Downtown Kansas City TR], Roughly bounded by Baltimore Ave., W. 12th, W. 13th, and Wyandotte Sts., Kansas City, 8/08/83, A, C, 83001000

District II [Armour Boulevard MRA], Armour Blvd. between Warwick and Kenwood Aves., Kansas City, 7/28/83, A, C, 83001001

District III [Armour Boulevard MRA], Armour Blvd. between Charlotte St. and The Paseo, Kansas City, 7/28/83, A, C, 83000999

Dorson Apartment Building, 912–918 Benton Blvd., Kansas City, 5/05/87, C, 87000906

Elmwood Cemetery, 4900 Truman Rd., Kansas City, 7/28/83, A, C, d, 83001002

Fire Department Headquarters; Fire station #2, 1020 Central Ave., Kansas City, 9/02/82, A, C, 82003144

Firestone Building, 2001 Grand Ave., Kansas City, 1/03/86, A, C, 86000004

Floyd, Jacobs, House [Residential Structures by Mary Rockwell Hook TR], 5050 Sunset Dr., Kansas City, 9/08/83, C, 83001003

Fort Osage, N edge of Sibley on the Missouri River, Sibley, 10/15/66, A, D, e, NHL, 66000418

Fort Osage Archeological District, Address Restricted, Sibley vicinity, 3/17/72, A, D, d, 72000720

Four Gates Farm [Residential Structures in Kansas City by Mary Rockwell Hook TR], 13001 Little Blue Rd., Kansas City, 7/15/91, 83004871

Fowler, Henry T., House [Armour Boulevard MRA], 3 E. Armour Blvd., Kansas City, 7/28/83, C, 83001004

Gate City National Bank, 1111 Grand Ave., Kansas City, 9/02/82, C, 82003145

German Evangelical Pastors' Home Historic District, 1808–1812 W. Walnut and 300–311 19th Terrace, Blue Springs, 10/13/88, A, a, 88001856

Gloyd Building, 921 Walnut, Kansas City, 7/25/85, C, 85001610

Grand Avenue Temple and Grand Avenue Temple Building, 205 E. 9th St. & 903 Grand Ave., Kansas City, 5/08/85, A, C, a, 85001006

Gumbel Building, 801 Walnut St., Kansas City, 1/22/79, C, 79001367

Harris, Col. John, House, 4000 Baltimore Ave., Kansas City, 10/18/72, A, C, b, 72000717

Harry S Truman National Historic Site, 219 N. Delaware St., Independence, 5/31/85, B, g, NPS, 85001248

Henderson, Dr. Generous, House, 1016 The Paseo, Kansas City, 2/26/79, C, 79001368

Hook, Mary Rockwell, House [Residential Structures by Mary Rockwell Hook TR], 4940 Summit St., Kansas City, 9/08/83, C, 83001005

Hotel Phillips, 106 W. 12th St., Kansas City, 6/04/79, C, g, 79001369

House at 5011 Sunset Drive [Residential Structures by Mary Rockwell Hook TR], 5011 Sunset Dr., Kansas City, 9/08/83, C, 83001006

House at 54 E. 53rd Terrace [Residential Structures by Mary Rockwell Hook TR], 54 E. 53rd Terr., Kansas City, 9/08/83, C, 83001007

Howe, Frank M., Residence, 1707 Jefferson St., Kansas City, 4/18/85, C, 85000854

Hyde Park Historic District, Roughly bounded by Armour and Harrison Blvds., 39th St. and Gillham Rd., Kansas City, 11/21/80, C, 80002364

Ivanhoe Masonic Temple, 2301 E. Linwood Blvd. and 3201 Park Ave., Kansas City, 5/02/85, A, C, 85000942

Jackson County Courthouse, Bounded by Lexington and Maple Aves. and Liberty and Main Sts., Independence, 10/18/72, A, B, C, 72000713

Jackson County Jail and Marshal's House, 217 N. Main St., Independence, 6/15/70, A, C, 70000333

Janssen Place Historic District, Janssen Pl., Kansas City, 11/07/76, C, 76001111

Jenkins Music Company Building, 1217–1223 Walnut St., Kansas City, 3/02/79, A, B, C, g, 79001370

Jensen-Salsbery Laboratories, 520 W. 21st St., Kansas City, 7/16/85, A, C, 85001574

Kansas City Athenaeum, 900 E. Linwood Blvd., Kansas City, 10/11/79, B, C, 79001371

Kansas City Live Stock Exchange, 1600 Genessee St., Kansas City, 4/05/84, A, 84002571

Kansas City Masonic Temple, 903 Harrison St., Kansas City, 11/14/80, A, C, 80002365

Kansas City Public Library, 500 E. 9th St., Kansas City, 5/23/77, A, B, C, 77000807

Kelly's Westport Inn, Westport Rd. and Pennsylvania Ave., Kansas City, 9/07/72, A, B, 72000718

Kritser House, 115 E. Walnut, Independence, 4/10/85, C, 85000734

Land Bank Building, 15 W. 10th St., Kansas City, 1/18/85, A, C, 85000101

Lewis—Webb House, 302 W. Mill, Independence, 2/06/86, B, C, 86000154

Loew's Midland Theater-Midland Building, 1232–1234 Main St. and 1221–1233 Baltimore Ave., Kansas City, 9/28/77, A, C, 77000808

Long, R. A., House, 3218 Gladstone Blvd., Kansas City, 11/14/80, C, 80002366

Longview Farm, 11700 and 850 S.W. Longview Rd., Lee's Summit, 10/24/85, A, B, C, a, 85003378

Loose, Jacob, House [Armour Boulevard MRA], 101 E. Armour Blvd., Kansas City, 7/28/83, C, 83001008

Loretto Academy, 1111 W. 39th St., Kansas City, 7/28/83, A, C, 83001009

Love, Emily Rockwell, House [Residential Structures by Mary Rockwell Hook TR], 5029 Sunset Dr., Kansas City, 9/08/83, C, 83001010

Majors, Alexander, House, 8145 State Line Rd., Kansas City, 4/03/70, B, C, 70000335

McConahay Building, 1121–1131 E. 31st St., Kansas City, 5/22/78, B, C, 78001655

McIntire, Levi, House [Armour Boulevard MRA], 710 E. Armour Blvd., Kansas City, 7/28/83, C, 83001011

Meyer, August, House, 4415 Warwick Blvd., Kansas City, 9/09/82, A, B, C, 82003146

Mineral Hall, 4340 Oak St., Kansas City, 7/12/76, B, C, 76001112

Minor, Charles, House, 314 N. Spring St., Independence, 3/22/84, B, C, 84002573

Missouri Pacific Depot, 600 S. Grand, Independence, 1/22/79, A, B, C, g, 79001365

Mutual Musicians' Foundation Building, 1823 Highland Ave., Kansas City, 2/07/79, A, g, NHL, 79001372

Myers, George J., House [Armour Boulevard MRA], 633 E. Armour Blvd., Kansas City, 7/28/83, C, 83001012

New York Life Building, 20 W. 9th St., Kansas City, 7/08/70, A, C, 70000336

Newbern Hotel, 525 E. Armour Blvd., Kansas City, 9/23/80, C, 80002367

Newcomer's, D. W., Sons Funeral Home, 1331 Brush Creek, Kansas City, 8/09/83, A, C, 83001013

Old New England Building, 112 W. 9th St., Kansas City, 10/25/73, A, C, 73001040

Old Town Historic District, Roughly bounded by Independence Ave., 2nd, Delaware and Walnut Sts., Kansas City, 6/07/78, A, B, C, 78001656

Ostertag, Robert, House [Residential Structures by Mary Rockwell Hook TR], 5030 Summit St., Kansas City, 9/08/83, C, 83001014

Overfelt-Campbell-Johnston House, 305 S. Pleasant St., Independence, 9/05/75, C, 75001066

Palace Clothing Company Building, 1126-1128 Grand Ave., Kansas City, 1/18/85, A, C, 85000102

Paseo YMCA [18th and Vine Area of Kansas City MPS], 1824 The Paseo, Kansas City, 9/09/91, A, 91001151

Peck, George B., Dry Goods Company Building, 1044 Main St., Kansas City, 4/30/80, A, C, 80002368

Peppard, Joseph Grear, House, 1704 Jefferson St., Kansas City, 3/26/85, A, C, 85000649

Pink House [Residential Structures by Mary Rockwell Hook TR], 5012 Summit St., Kansas City, 9/08/83, C, 83001015

President Hotel [Hotels in Downtown Kansas City TR], 1327-1335 Baltimore Ave., Kansas City, 8/08/83, A, C, 83001016

Professional Building, 1101–1107 Grand Ave., Kansas City, 7/17/79, A, C, 79001373

Quality Hill, Roughly bounded by Broadway, 10th, 14th, and Jefferson Sts., Kansas City, 7/07/78, A, B, C, a, 78001657

Reff, William D., House [Armour Boulevard MRA], 3500 Charlotte St., Kansas City, 7/28/83, C, 83001017

Rice-Tremonti House, 8801 E. 66th St., Raytown, 3/02/79, A, e, 79001376

Rockhill Neighborhood, Both sides of 47th St. from Locust St. (S. Pierce St.) to both sides of Harrison St. (N to Brush Creek Blvd.), Kansas City, 7/21/75, A, C, 75001068

Rockwell, Bertrand, House [Residential Structures by Mary Rockwell Hook TR], 1004 W. 52nd St., Kansas City, 9/08/83, C, 83001018

Jackson County—Continued

Row House Building, 1–7 E. 34th St. and 3401 Main St., Kansas City, 5/22/78, C, 78001658

Row House Buildings (Boundry Increase), 9-23 E. 34th St., Kansas City, 1/15/85, C, 85000103

Sacred Heart Church, School and Rectory, 2540–2544 Madison Ave. and 910 W. 26th St., Kansas City, 11/14/78, A, C, a, 78001659

Saint Paul's Episcopal Church, Fifth and S. Green Sts., Lee's Summit, 10/03/85, A, C, a, 85002720

Santa Fe Place Historic District, Roughly bounded by Twenty-seventh St., Indiana Ave., Thirtieth St., and Prospect Ave., Kansas City, 5/30/86, A, C, 86001204

Savoy Hotel and Grill, 219 W. 9th St. and 9th and Central Sts., Kansas City, 12/30/74, A, C, 74001073

Scarritt Building and Arcade, Corner of 19th and Grand Sts. and 819 Walnut St., Kansas City, 3/09/71, C, 71000468

Scarritt, Edward Lucky, House, 3500 Gladstone Blvd., Kansas City, 5/23/77, B, C, 77000809

Scarritt, Rev. Nathan, House, 4038 Central St., Kansas City, 5/08/78, B, C, 78001660

Scarritt, William Chick, House, 3240 Norledge Ave., Kansas City, 3/21/78, B, C, 78001661

Shelley, William Francis, House, 3601 Baltimore Ave., Kansas City, 3/17/78, C, 78001662

Simpson-Yeomans-Country Side Historic District, Roughly bounded by 51st Terr., Wornall Rd., Wyandotte and 54th Sts., Kansas City, 9/06/84, C, 84002576

Sophian Plaza, 4618 Warwick Blvd., Kansas City, 7/05/83, C, 83001019

South Side Historic District, Roughly bounded by 38th, 40th, Walnut, and Baltimore Sts., Kansas City, 6/09/83, A, C, 83001020

St. Mary's Episcopal Church, 1307 Holmes St., Kansas City, 11/07/78, C, a, 78001663

Standard Theatre, 300 W. 12th St., Kansas City, 6/05/74, A, C, 74001074

Stine and McClure Undertaking Company Building, 924–926 Oak St., Kansas City, 7/19/90, C, 90001105

Temple Block Building, 531 Walnut, Kansas City, 6/19/85, A, C, 85001344

Temple Site, Lexington Ave. and River Blvd., Independence, 9/22/70, A, a, 70000334

Tocoma, The, 3835 Main St., Kansas City, 11/24/79, C, 79003782

Toll, Alfred, House [Armour Boulevard MRA], 3502 Warwick Blvd., Kansas City, 7/28/83, A, 83001022

Trinity Episcopal Church, 409 N. Liberty St., Independence, 4/27/79, A, B, C, a, 79001366

Truman, Harry S, Historic District, N. Delaware St. area, Independence, 11/11/71, B, NHL, 71001066

Union Station, Pershing Rd. and Main St., Kansas City, 2/01/72, A, C, 72000719

Unity School of Christianity Historic District, Jct. US 50 and Colborn Rd., Unity Village, 4/12/89, C, a, 89000246

Uptown Building and Theatre, 3700–3712 Broadway, Kansas City, 6/27/79, A, C, 79001374

Vaile, Harvey M., Mansion, 1500 N. Liberty St., Independence, 10/01/69, C, 69000108

Van Noy, Ira C. and Charles S., Houses, 6700 and 6800 Elmwood, Kansas City, 7/08/87, C, 87000505

Volker, William, House, 3717 Bell St., Kansas City, 5/20/93, B, g, 93000408

WILLIAM S. MITCHELL (dredge), Army Corps of Engineer Harbor, Kansas City, 10/09/85, A, C, 85003102

Waldo Water Tower, 75th St. and Holmes Rd., Tower Park, Kansas City, 4/18/77, C, f, 77000810

Ward, Seth E., Homestead, 1032 W. 55th St., Kansas City, 2/17/78, A, B, C, 78001664

Warner, Maj. William, House, 1021 Pennsylvania Ave., Kansas City, 5/23/77, B, C, 77000811

Webster School, 1644 Wyandotte St., Kansas City, 9/02/82, A, C, 82003147

West 9th Street-Baltimore Avenue Historic District, Roughly bounded by Main, 8th, 10th and Central Sts., Kansas City, 11/07/76, A, C, 76001113

West Eleventh Street Historic District, Central and W. 11th Sts., Kansas City, 9/09/82, A, C, a, 82003148

Westminister Congregational Church, 3600 Walnut St., Kansas City, 2/28/80, C, a, 80002369

Wholesale District, Roughly bounded by 6th, Wyandotte, 8th, May, 11th and Washington Sts., Kansas City, 10/25/79, A, C, 79001375

Woodson—Sawyer House, 1604 W. Lexington, Independence, 3/20/86, B, C, 86000457

Wornall House, 146 W. 61st St., Kansas City, 5/21/69, A, C, 69000109

Young, Solomon, Farm, 12121 and 12301 Blue Ridge Extension, Grandview, 5/05/78, B, C, NHL, 78001650

Jasper County

Carthage Courthouse Square Historic District, Roughly bounded by E. Central Ave., S. Maple, Lincoln, and W. 5th Sts., Carthage, 5/15/80, A, C, 80002370

Carthage South Historic District [City of Carthage MRA], City limits of Carthage, Carthage, 5/06/82, C, 82004915

Cassill Place Historic District [City of Carthage MRA], W. Central, Carthage, 1/02/86, C, 86000005

Elks Club Lodge #501, 318–320 W. 4th St., Joplin, 6/03/85, A, C, 85001188

Fox Theater, 415 S. Main St., Joplin, 7/30/90, A, C, 90001100

Jasper County Courthouse, Courthouse Sq., Carthage, 2/08/73, A, 73001041

Joplin Carnegie Library, 9th and Wall Sts., Joplin, 7/10/79, C, 79001377

Joplin Connor Hotel, 324 Main St., Joplin, 2/28/73, A, C, 73001042

Joplin Union Depot, Broadway and Main Sts., Joplin, 3/14/73, C, 73001043

Middle West Hotel, 1 S. Main St., Webb City, 9/16/82, A, 82003149

Newman Brothers Building, 602–608 S. Main St., Joplin, 7/23/90, A, C, 90001101

Phelps Country Estate [City of Carthage MRA], SR 1, Carthage vicinity, 8/29/83, C, 83001023

Rains Brothers Building, 906–908 S. Main St., Joplin, 7/19/90, C, 90001102

Scottish Rite Cathedral, 505 Byers Ave., Joplin, 6/21/90, A, C, 90000989

St. Peter the Apostle Catholic Church and Rectory, 812 Pearl St., Joplin, 6/28/91, C, a, 91000851

Jefferson County

Beaumont-Tyson Quarry District, Address Restricted, Times Beach vicinity, 10/10/74, D, 74001079

Boemler Archeological District, Address Restricted, Byrnes Mill vicinity, 10/01/74, D, 74001075

Boland Archeological District, Address Restricted, Times Beach vicinity, 10/01/74, D, 74001080

Fletcher, Thomas C., House, Elm between 1st and 2nd Sts., Hillsboro, 11/19/74, B, C, 74001076

Greystone-Meissner, Gustave, House, NE of Pevely off U.S. 61, Pevely vicinity, 12/31/74, A, B, C, 74001078

Kimmswick Bone Bed, Address Restricted, Imperial vicinity, 11/05/80, A, D, g, 80002371

Leight, Valentine, General Store, 4566 Main St., House Springs, 8/18/92, A, C, 92001014

Moder Archeological District, Address Restricted, House Springs vicinity, 10/16/74, D, 74001077

Sandy Creek Covered Bridge, 5 mi. N of Hillsboro off U.S. 21, Hillsboro vicinity, 7/08/70, A, C, 70000337

Windsor Harbor Road Bridge, Windsor Harbor Rd. at Rock Creek, Kimmswick, 9/08/83, C, b, 83001024

Johnson County

Camp Shawnee Historic District [ECW Architecture in Missouri State Parks 1933-1942 TR], SW of Knob Noster, Knob Noster, 3/04/85, A, C, g, 85000506

Chilhowee Historic District, Roughly Walnut and Main Sts., Chilhowee, 6/02/88, A, C, 88000650

Johnson County Courthouse, Old Public Sq., Warrensburg, 6/15/70, C, 70000338

Montserrat Recreation Demonstration Area Bridge [ECW Architecture in Missouri State Parks 1933-1942 TR], MO 132, Knob Noster, 3/04/85, A, C, g, 85000507

Montserrat Recreation Demonstration Area Dam and Spillway [ECW Architecture in Missouri State Parks 1933-1942 TR], SW of Knob Noster, Knob Noster, 3/04/85, A, C, g, 85000508

Montserrat Recreation Demonstration Area Entrance Portal [ECW Architecture in Missouri

Johnson County—Continued

State Parks 1933-1942 TR], Off MO 132, Knob Noster, 3/04/85, A, C, g, 85000509

Montserrat Recreational Demonstration Area Rock Bath House [ECW Architecture in Missouri State Parks 1933-1942 TR], SW of Knob Noster, Knob Noster, 3/04/85, A, C, g, 85000510

Montserrat Recreational Demonstration Area Warehouse #2 and Workshop [ECW Architecture in Missouri State Parks 1933-1942 TR], Off MO 132, Knob Noster, 3/04/85, A, C, g, 85000511

Laclede County

Bennett Spring State Park Hatchery-Lodge Area Historic District [ECW Architecture in Missouri State Parks 1933-1942 TR], MO A64, Bennett Spring, 3/04/85, A, C, g, 85000504

Laclede County Jail, Adams and 3rd Sts., Lebanon, 3/27/80, A, 80002372

Ploger-Moneymaker Place, 291 Harwood Ave., Lebanon, 9/23/82, B, C, 82003150

Wallace House, 230 Harwood Ave., Lebanon, 3/22/84, A, B, C, 84002579

Lafayette County

Anderson House and Lexington Battlefield, Roughly bounded by 10th, 15th, Utah and Wood Sts., and Missouri Pacific RR, Lexington, 6/04/69, A, 69000110

Cheatham, John E., House [Lexington MRA], 739 MO 13, Lexington, 7/08/93, C, 93000550

Chicago and Alton Railroad Depot at Higginsville, 2109 Main St., Higginsville, 3/25/87, A, C, 87000451

Commerical Community Historic District [Lexington MRA], Roughly bounded by 8th, 13th, South, Broadway, and Main Sts., Lexington, 8/04/83, C, 83001025

Confederate Chapel, Cemetery and Cottage, N of Higginsville, Higginsville vicinity, 12/16/81, A, a, b, d, 81000335

Cumberland Presbyterian Church, 112 S. 13th St., Lexington, 11/14/78, C, a, 78001665

Eneberg, John F., House [Lexington MRA], 157 N. 10th St., Lexington, 7/08/93, C, 93000551

Graves, Alexander and Elizabeth Aull, House [Lexington MRA], 2326 Aull Ln., Lexington, 7/08/93, C, 93000552

Hicklin Hearthstone, E of Lexington on US 24, Lexington vicinity, 12/28/82, A, C, 82000585

Highland Avenue Historic District [Lexington MRA], Roughly bounded by Highland Ave. from Rock to Bluff Sts., Lexington, 8/04/83, C, 83001026

Houx-Hoefer-Rehkop House, 1900 Walnut St., Higginsville, 3/29/83, A, C, 83001027

John, David, House [Lexington MRA], 103 S. 23rd St., Lexington, 7/08/93, C, 93000553

Johnson, George, House [Lexington MRA], 102 S. 30th St., Lexington, 7/08/93, C, 93000554

Lafayette County Courthouse, Public Sq., Lexington, 9/22/70, C, 70000339

Linwood Lawn, SE of Lexington off U.S. 24, Lexington vicinity, 4/23/73, C, 73001044

Old Neighborhoods Historic District [Lexington MRA], Roughly bounded by 13th, 22nd, South Sts., Forest and Washington Aves., Lexington, 8/04/83, C, 83001028

Spratt—Allen—Aull House [Lexington MRA], 2321 Aull Ln., Lexington, 7/08/93, C, 93000555

Tevis, D. W. B. and Julia Waddell, House [Lexington MRA], 505 S. 13th St., Lexington, 7/08/93, C, 93000556

Waddell House, 1704 South St., Lexington, 10/11/79, B, 79001378

Wentworth Military Academy, Washington Ave. and 18th St., Lexington, 11/24/80, A, C, 80002373

Lawrence County

Lawrence County Courthouse, City Sq., Mount Vernon, 9/23/80, C, 80002374

Old Spanish Fort Archeological Site, Address Restricted, Mount Vernon vicinity, 1/25/71, D, 71000469

Lewis County

Henderson Hall, College Hill, Canton, 10/02/78, A, C, 78001666

Lincoln School, MO B, Canton, 2/10/83, A, 83001029

Quincy, Missouri, and Pacific Railroad Station, Off MO 16, Lewistown, 5/07/79, A, b, 79001379

Lincoln County

Camp Sherwood Forest Historic District [ECW Architecture in Missouri State Parks 1933-1942 TR], SW of Elsberry in Cuivre State Park, Elsberry vicinity, 3/04/85, A, C, g, 85000512

Cuivre River State Park Administrative Area Historic District [ECW Architecture in Missouri State Parks 1933-1942 TR], SW of Elsberry in Cuivre State Park, Elsberry vicinity, 3/04/85, A, C, g, 85000514

Old Rock House, 2nd and Mill Sts., Moscow Mills, 10/18/72, C, 72000721

Linn County

Locust Creek Covered Bridge, 3 mi. W of Laclede off U.S. 36, Laclede vicinity, 5/19/70, C, 70000340

Pershing, Gen. John J., Boyhood Home, State and Worlow Sts., Laclede, 5/21/69, B, NHL, 69000111

Livingston County

Grace Episcopal Church and Building, 421 Elm St., Chillicothe, 9/17/80, C, a, 80002375

Macon County

Blees Military Academy, U.S. 63, Macon, 10/11/79, B, C, 79001380

Dent, Lester and Norma, House, 225 N. Church St., La Plata, 5/18/90, B, g, 90000763

Doneghy, John T. and Mary M., House, 301 N. Owensby St., La Plata, 3/22/90, C, 90000488

Gilbreath-McLorn House, 225 N. Owenby, La Plata, 11/16/78, B, C, 78001667

Macon County Courthouse and Annex, Courthouse Sq., Macon, 12/08/78, A, C, 78001668

Wardell House, 1 Wardell Rd., Macon, 3/12/86, B, C, 86000333

Marion County

Barkley, Levi, House, W of Hannibal, Hannibal vicinity, 3/02/84, B, C, 84002583

Broadway District [Hannibal Central Business District MRA], Roughly bounded by S. Main, Broadway, and S. Third Sts., Hannibal, 8/01/86, A, C, 86002128

Buildings at 207–209 South Main St. [Hannibal Central Business District MRA], 207–209 S. Main St., Hannibal, 8/01/86, A, C, 86002129

Central Park Historic District, Roughly bounded b 4th, 7th, North and Lyon Sts., Hannibal, 10/07/82, A, C, 82000586

Davidson Building [Hannibal Central Business District MRA], 106 S. Main St., Hannibal, 8/01/86, C, 86002130

Digel Block [Hannibal Central Business District MRA], 218–222 S. Main St., Hannibal, 8/01/86, A, C, 86002131

Dryden-Louthan House, 402 E. Ross St., Palmyra, 1/18/85, C, 85000104

Ebert-Dulany House, 1000 Center St., Hannibal, 2/17/83, A, C, 83001030

Eighth and Center Streets Baptist Church, 722 Center St., Hannibal, 9/04/80, C, a, 80002376

Elliott's, Robert, Wholesale Grocery [Hannibal Central Business District MRA], 116–120 S. Third St., Hannibal, 8/01/86, A, C, 86002132

Federal Building, 600 Broadway, Hannibal, 10/15/80, B, C, 80002377

Gardner House, 421 Hamilton and Main Sts., Palmyra, 3/04/71, A, 71000470

Green Double House [Hannibal Central Business District MRA], 113–115 S. Third St., Hannibal, 8/01/86, C, 86002133

Hafner Grocery Warehouse [Hannibal Central Business District MRA], 101 E. Church St., Hannibal, 8/01/86, C, 86002134

Hannibal Lime Company Office, 623 Collier St., Hannibal, 9/06/84, A, 84002585

Marion County—Continued

Hannibal Old Police Station and Jail, 4th and Church Sts., Hannibal, 7/17/79, C, 79001381

Hendren Farm, Rt. 2, Hannibal vicinity, 8/22/84, A, C, 84002587

Hock Building [Hannibal Central Business District MRA], 312 Center St., Hannibal, 12/02/86, A, 86003588

Holmes-Dakin Building [Hannibal Central Business District MRA], 120–122 S. Main St., Hannibal, 8/01/86, A, C, 86002135

Horr, Benjamin, House [Hannibal Central Business District MRA], 308 Center St., Hannibal, 12/02/86, A, B, 86003587

Mark Twain Historic District, Bird, Main, and Hill Sts., Hannibal, 1/04/78, A, B, C, 78003398

Mark Twain Hotel [Hannibal Central Business District MRA], 200 S. Main St., Hannibal, 8/01/86, A, C, 86002136

Masterson, Robert, House, NW of Hannibal, Hannibal vicinity, 4/05/84, A, C, 84002591

North Main Street Historic District [Hannibal Central Business District MRA], Roughly bounded by Bird, N. Main, and Hill Sts., Hannibal, 8/01/86, A, B, C, 86002137

Osterhout Mound Park, Wauneta Pl., Hannibal, 4/11/73, D, 73001045

Rockcliffe Mansion, 1000 Bird St., Hannibal, 9/18/80, B, C, 80002378

Sharkey Mound Group, Address Restricted, Hannibal vicinity, 12/18/73, D, 73001046

Sowers, Peter J., House, 221 Home St., Palmyra, 1/18/85, B, C, 85000105

Speigle House, 406 S. Dickerson, Palmyra, 2/14/85, C, 85000283

Standard Printing Company [Hannibal Central Business District MRA], 301 N. Third St., Hannibal, 8/01/86, A, C, 86002138

Twain, Mark, Boyhood Home, 206–208 Hill St., Hannibal, 10/15/66, B, NHL, 66000419

Walker-Woodward-Schaffer House, 1425 S. Main St., Palmyra, 2/16/84, B, C, c, 84002592

Wilson, Ephraim J., Farm Complex, E of Palmyra off MO 168, Palmyra vicinity, 12/28/82, A, C, 82000587

Miller County

Boeckman Bridge, SE of St. Elizabeth over Big Tavern Creek, St. Elizabeth vicinity, 3/19/79, C, 79001382

Iberia Academy and Junior College, SR 17 and SR 42, Iberia, 9/04/80, A, 80002379

Lake of the Ozarks State Park Highway 134 Historic District [ECW Architecture in Missouri State Parks 1933-1942 TR], W of Brumley along MO 134, Brumley vicinity, 2/26/85, A, C, g, 85000533

Olean Railroad Depot, Main St. E of jct. with California St., Olean, 12/23/93, A, C, 93001452

Mississippi County

Beckwith's Fort Archeological Site, Address Restricted, Wolf Island vicinity, 7/29/69, D, 69000113

Crosno Fortified Village Archeological Site, Address Restricted, Crosno vicinity, 5/21/69, D, 69000112

Hearnes Site, Address Retricted, Charleston vicinity, 11/26/73, D, 73001047

Hess Archeological Site, Address Restricted, East Prairie vicinity, 7/12/74, D, 74001081

Hoecake Village Archeological Site, Address Restricted, East Prairie vicinity, 1/13/72, D, 72000723

Missouri Pacific Depot, E of intersecting branches of Missouri Pacific RR., Charleston, 11/30/72, C, 72000722

Moore House, 403 N. Main St., Charleston, 9/18/80, B, C, 80002380

Mueller Archeological Site, Address Restricted, East Prairie vicinity, 8/13/74, D, 74001082

O'Bryan Ridge Archeological District, Address Restricted, Wyatt vicinity, 11/09/72, D, 72000724

Swank, Jacob, House, 0.2 mi. W of Charleston on U.S. 60 and 62, Charleston vicinity, 4/13/73, B, C, 73001048

Moniteau County

Bruce, Louis, Farmstead Historic District, MO V N of jct. with MO A, at Rock Enon Cr., Russellville vicinity, 1/07/92, A, C, 91001916

Geiger Archeological Site, Address Restricted, Sandy Hook vicinity, 7/29/69, D, 69000114

Gray-Wood Buildings, 401-407 N. High St., California, 1/19/84, B, C, 84002594

Maclay Mansion, 209 W. Howard St., Tipton, 2/26/79, A, C, 79001383

Moniteau County Courthouse Square, Public Sq., California, 10/15/70, C, 70000341

Old Barnhill Building, 301 N. High St., California, 4/12/82, C, 82003151

Old California City Hall and Fire Station, 101 N. High St., California, 4/12/82, C, 82003152

Monroe County

Crigler Mound Group Archeological Site, Address Restricted, Florida vicinity, 5/21/69, D, 69000115

Holliday Petroglyphs, Address Restricted, Holliday vicinity, 1/11/74, D, 74001083

Mark Twain State Park Picnic Shelter at Buzzard's Roost [ECW Architecture in Missouri State Parks 1933-1942 TR], Off MO 107, Santa Fe vicinity, 3/04/85, A, C, g, 85000515

Paris Male Academy, 411 E. Monroe St., Paris, 7/19/90, A, C, 90001103

Twain, Mark, Birthplace Cabin, Mark Twain State Park, 2.5 mi. S of Florida on MO 107, Florida vicinity, 5/21/69, B, b, c, 69000116

Union Covered Bridge, 6 mi. W of Paris on Elk Fork of the Salt River, Paris vicinity, 6/15/70, C, 70000342

Violette, Merritt, House, Off MO 107, Florida, 9/08/83, B, C, b, g, 83001031

Montgomery County

Graham Cave, 0.5 mi. N of Mineola, Mineola vicinity, 10/15/66, D, NHL, 66000420

High Hill School, Off U.S. 40, High Hill, 11/14/80, A, C, a, 80002381

Mount Horeb Baptist Church, W of Mineola, Mineola vicinity, 9/27/80, A, C, a, 80002382

Pinnacle Lake Rock Shelter, Address Restricted, Big Spring vicinity, 7/29/69, A, 69000117

Shrine of Our Lady of Sorrows, SR P, Starkenburg, 9/09/82, A, C, a, b, 82003153

Morgan County

Martin Hotel, 118 N. Monroe St., Versailles, 9/06/78, A, 78001669

Morgan County Courthouse, Courthouse Sq., Versailles, 1/10/80, A, C, 80002383

Old St. Patrick's Church, S of Gravois Mills on SR 0, Gravois Mills vicinity, 3/02/79, A, C, a, 79001384

Ratcliff, Jesse, House, NE of Barnett, Barnett vicinity, 4/12/82, B, C, 82003154

New Madrid County

Double Bridges Archeological Site, Address Restricted, Portageville vicinity, 7/25/74, D, 74001085

Hurricane Ridge Site, Address Restricted, Catron vicinity, 11/09/72, D, 72000725

King II Archeological Site, Address Restricted, Howardville vicinity, 6/26/75, D, 75001070

La Plant Archeological Site, Address Restricted, La Forge vicinity, 7/25/74, D, 74001084

Lilbourn Fortified Village Archeological Site, Address Restricted, Lilbourn vicinity, 7/29/69, D, 69000118

Portwood Village and Mound, Address Restricted, Portageville vicinity, 11/25/77, D, 77000812

Sikeston Fortified Village Archeological Site, Address Restricted, Sikeston vicinity, 2/12/71, D, 71000471

St. Johns-Laplant IV Archeological District, Address Restricted, Bayouville vicinity, 8/28/75, D, 75001069

Newton County

George Washington Carver National Monument, 3 mi. S of Monument, Diamond vicinity, 10/15/66, B, c, NPS, 66000114

Jolly Mill, SW of Pierce City, Pierce City vicinity, 10/13/83, A, C, 83004021

Neosho Commercial Historic District [Neosho MPS], Along sections of Main, Spring, Washington and Wood Sts., Neosho, 8/12/93, A, C, 93000722

Ritchey, Mathew H., House, Mill St., Newtonia, 12/05/78, A, B, C, 78003399

Nodaway County

Big Pump, 903 S. Main St., Maryville, 9/18/80, A, g, 80002384

Burns, Caleb, House, 422 W. 2nd St., Maryville, 11/17/80, A, C, 80002385

Frank House, 307 E. 7th St., Maryville, 9/08/83, C, 83001032

Gaunt, Thomas, House, 703 College Ave., Maryville, 4/19/79, B, C, 79001385

Nodaway County Courthouse, 3rd and Main Sts., Maryville, 10/11/79, A, C, 79001386

Possum Walk Hotel, N of Burlington Junction, Burlington Junction vicinity, 3/29/83, C, 83001033

Simpson's College, 515 E. Jackson St., Graham, 1/30/78, A, b, 78001670

Oregon County

Pigman Mound Archeological Site, Address Restricted, Riverton vicinity, 3/04/71, D, 71000472

Osage County

Bonnots Mill Historic District, Roughly Old Mill Rd., Riverside Dr., Highwater Rd., Iris Ave., Wildwood Ln., Hwy. A and Main, Short and Church Hill Sts., Bonnots Mill, 1/21/93, A, C, 92001738

Dauphine Hotel, Off MO A, Bonnot's Mill, 11/14/80, A, B, C, 80002386

Sacred Heart Catholic Church and Parsonage, SR U, Rich Fountain, 9/09/82, B, C, a, 82003155

St. Joseph Church, Main St., Westphalia, 4/11/72, A, C, a, 72000726

Pemiscot County

Campbell Archeological Site, Address Restricted, Cooter vicinity, 7/24/74, D, 74001086

Caruthersville Water Tower, W. 3rd St., Caruthersville, 9/09/82, A, 82003156

Delta Center Mound, Address Restricted, Portageville vicinity, 7/24/74, D, 74001087

Denton Mound and Village Archeological Site, Address Restricted, Denton vicinity, 7/29/69, D, 69000120

Murphy Mound Archeological Site, Address Restricted, Caruthersville vicinity, 5/21/69, D, 69000119

Wallace, J. M., Archeological Site, Address Restricted, Wardell vicinity, 12/02/70, D, d, 70000343

Perry County

Bergt, Christian A., Farm, E of Frohna, Frohna vicinity, 1/10/80, A, B, C, a, 80002387

Concordia Log Cabin College, Main St., Altenburg, 11/21/78, A, a, b, 78001671

Doerr-Brown House, 17 E. St. Joseph St., Perryville, 11/14/80, B, C, 80002388

Shelby-Nicholson-Schindler House, 701 W. St. Joseph St., Perryville, 7/24/74, B, C, 74001088

Tower Rock, 1 mi. S of Wittenburg in Mississippi River, Wittenburg vicinity, 2/26/70, A, a, 70000344

Pettis County

Bois d'Arc Cooperative Dairy Farm Historic District [Osage Farms Resettlement Properties in Pettis County MPS], MO J near jct. with Bois d'Arc Rd., Hughesville vicinity, 9/27/91, A, C, g, 91001407

Harris House, 705 W. 6th St., Sedalia, 7/10/79, A, C, 79001387

Hillview Cooperative Dairy Farm Historic District [Osage Farms Resettlement Properties in Pettis County MPS], Jct. of MO T and Hillview Rd., Hughesville vicinity, 9/27/91, A, C, g, 91001399

Hotel Bothwell, 103 E. Fourth St., Sedalia, 9/08/89, A, C, 89001406

Missouri State Fairgrounds Historic District, Roughly bounded by US 65, Co. Rd. Y, Clarendon Rd. and the Missouri—Kansas—Texas RR tracks, Sedalia, 6/28/91, A, C, 91000853

Missouri, Kansas and Texas Railroad Depot, 600 E. 3rd St., Sedalia, 3/28/79, C, 79001388

Missouri/Sedalia Trust Company, 322 S. Ohio St., Sedalia, 3/29/83, A, C, 83001034

Osage Farms Type 315:13 Government Farmhouse [Osage Farms Resettlement Properties in Pettis County MPS], MO J near jct. with Miller Chapel Rd., Hughesville vicinity, 9/27/91, C, b, g, 91001406

Osage Farms Unit No. 1 Historic District [Osage Farms Resettlement Properties in Pettis County MPS], MO D near jct. with Moon Rd., Hughesville vicinity, 9/27/91, A, C, g, 91001408

Osage Farms Unit No. 25 Historic District [Osage Farms Resettlement Properties in Pettis County MPS], Houston Rd. near jct. with Montgomery Rd., Hughesville vicinity, 9/27/91, A, C, g, 91001405

Osage Farms Unit No. 26 Historic District [Osage Farms Resettlement Properties in Pettis County

MPS], MO D near jct. with High Point Rd., Hughesville vicinity, 9/27/91, A, C, g, 91001409

Osage Farms Unit No. 30 Historic District [Osage Farms Resettlement Properties in Pettis County MPS], Durley Rd. near jct. with MO D, Hughesville vicinity, 9/27/91, A, C, g, 91001401

Osage Farms Unit No. 31 [Osage Farms Resettlement Properties in Pettis County MPS], Durley Rd. near jct. with MO D, Hughesville vicinity, 9/27/91, A, C, g, 91001402

Osage Farms Unit No. 41 [Osage Farms Resettlement Properties in Pettis County MPS], Hill View Rd. near jct. with McCubbin Rd., Houstonia vicinity, 9/27/91, A, C, g, 91001403

Osage Farms Unit No. 43 Historic District [Osage Farms Resettlement Properties in Pettis County MPS], MO J near jct. with Lowry Rd., Hughesville vicinity, 9/27/91, A, C, g, 91001410

Osage Farms Units No. 5 and No. 6 Historic District [Osage Farms Resettlement Properties in Pettis County MPS], Range Line Rd. near jct. with Trickum Rd., Houstonia vicinity, 9/27/91, A, C, g, 91001404

Osage Farms Units No. 8 and No. 9 Historic District [Osage Farms Resettlement Properties in Pettis County MPS], MO D near jct. with MO T, Houstonia vicinity, 9/27/91, A, C, g, 91001400

Sedalia Public Library, 311 W. 3rd St., Sedalia, 1/10/80, A, C, 80002389

Thomson, Gen. David, House, S of Hughesville on SR H, Hughesville vicinity, 10/04/82, C, 82000588

Phelps County

Gourd Creek Cave Archeological Site, Address Restricted, Newburg vicinity, 7/29/69, D, 69000121

Maramec Iron Works District, 7 mi. S of St. James on MO 8, St. James vicinity, 4/16/69, A, 69000122

Ozark Iron Furnace Stack, 2 mi. W of Newburg, Newburg vicinity, 6/15/70, A, 70000345

Phelps County Courthouse, Jct. of Third and Main Sts., Rolla, 1/07/93, A, 92001745

Phelps County Jail, Park St. between Second and Third Sts., Rolla, 5/10/90, A, 90000766

St. James Chapel, Church and Meramec Sts., St. James, 7/28/83, A, a, 83001035

Verkamp Shelter, Address Restricted, St. James vicinity, 7/30/74, D, 74001089

Pike County

Bacon, Charles, House, 819 Kentucky St., Louisiana, 7/19/90, C, 90001104

Clark, James Beauchamp, House, 204 E. Champ Clark Dr., Bowling Green, 12/08/76, B, NHL, 76001114

Clarksville Historic District [Clarksville MPS], Roughly bounded by Lewis, Front, Virginia and 3rd Sts., Clarksville, 5/09/91, A, C, 91000489

Pike County—Continued

Clifford-Wyrick House, 105 S. 2nd St., Clarksville, 7/09/84, B, C, 84002600

Georgia Street Historic District, Roughly Georgia St. between Main and Seventh Sts., Louisiana, 5/06/87, C, 87000653

Griffith—McCune Farmstead Historic District, MO WW E of jct. with MO D, Eolia vicinity, 8/18/92, A, C, 92001001

Luce-Dyer House, 220 N. 3rd St., Louisiana, 9/23/82, A, C, 82003157

Meloan, Cummins & Co., General Store, Jct. of Middle and Water Sts., NW corner, Paynesville, 6/24/93, A, C, 93000571

Northern Methodist Episcopal Church of Clarksville [Clarksville MPS], 309 Smith St., Clarksville, 5/09/91, C, 91000487

St. John's Episcopal Church, 0.25 mi. N of Eolia on CR D, 0.25 mi. E on CR H, Eolia vicinity, 7/08/70, C, a, 70000346

Stark, Gov. Lloyd Crow, House and Carriage House, 1401 Georgia St., Louisiana, 12/21/87, B, C, 87002142

Turner—Pharr House [Clarksville MPS], 101 N. Fourth St., Clarksville, 5/09/91, A, C, 91000488

Platte County

Babcock Site, Address Restricted, Waldron vicinity, 11/15/73, D, 73001049

Deister Archeological Site, Address Restricted, Kansas City vicinity, 1/21/70, D, 70000347

Krause, Frederick, Mansion, 3rd and Harrel Ferrel Dr., Platte City, 5/22/78, C, 78001672

Mackay Building, Park College, Parkville, 4/06/79, A, C, a, 79001389

McCormick Distillery, MO JJ, Weston vicinity, 4/16/74, A, 74001090

Platte County Courthouse, 3rd and Main Sts., Platte City, 1/17/79, C, 79001390

Renner Village Archeological Site, Address Restricted, Riverside vicinity, 4/16/69, D, 69000123

Scott, Charles Smith, Memorial Observatory, 8700 River Park Dr., Parkville, 5/29/92, A, C, 92000625

Sugar Creek Site, Address Restricted, Weston vicinity, 12/12/73, D, 73001050

Waddell "A" Truss Bridge, English Landing Park, over Rush Cr., Parkville, 1/25/91, C, b, 90002173

Washington Chapel C.M.E. Church, 1137 West St., Parkville, 8/31/92, A, C, a, 92001055

Weston Historic District, Roughly bounded by Summit, Rock, Market and Ashley, Weston, 8/21/72, A, C, 72000727

Pulaski County

Decker Cave Archeological Site, Address Restricted, Buckhorn vicinity, 2/12/71, D, 71000473

Manes, Calloway, Homestead, NW of Richland, Richland vicinity, 6/06/80, B, a, 80002390

Old Stagecoach Stop, Linn St., Courthouse Sq., Waynesville, 11/24/80, A, 80002391

Pulaski County Courthouse, Courthouse Sq., Waynesville, 7/17/79, C, 79001391

Ralls County

Brown, James B., House, 2400 Carrs Lane, Hannibal, 1/26/84, C, 84002603

Garth, John, House, S of Hannibal off U.S. 61, Hannibal vicinity, 7/11/77, C, 77000813

Ralls County Courthouse and Jail-Sheriff's House, Courthouse Sq., New London, 9/14/72, A, C, 72000728

St. Paul Catholic Church, W of Center off SR EE, Center vicinity, 5/31/79, A, C, a, 79001392

St. Peter's Catholic Church, SW of Rensselaer on SR 2, Rensselaer vicinity, 11/14/80, A, C, a, 80002392

Randolph County

Burkholder—O'Keefe House, 605 S. Fifth St., Moberly, 9/25/89, C, 89001414

Mitchell Petroglyph Archeological Site, Address Restricted, Cairo vicinity, 6/23/69, D, 69000124

Ray County

Dougherty Auditorium, 203 W. Main St., Richmond, 9/16/82, A, C, 82003158

New Hope Primitive Baptist Church, SW of Richmond on Old Orrick Rd., Richmond vicinity, 11/14/80, C, a, 80002393

Ray County Courthouse, Off MO 10 and MO 13, Richmond, 10/11/79, C, 79001393

Ray County Poor Farm, W. Royale St., Richmond, 7/10/79, A, C, 79001394

Watkins House, 302 S. Camden St., Richmond, 2/10/83, C, 83001036

Ripley County

B-9 Structure Archeological Site, Address Restricted, Grandin vicinity, 10/07/75, D, 75001072

Barrett, Randolph Columbus, House, 209 Plum St., Doniphan, 11/07/76, B, C, 76001115

Mule Camp Site, Address Restricted, Fairdealing vicinity, 11/11/75, D, 75001071

Price Site, Address Restricted, Currentview vicinity, 4/03/78, D, 78001674

Ripley County Courthouse, Courthouse Circle, Doniphan, 11/07/76, B, C, 76001116

Ripley County Jail, Sheriff's Office and Sheriff's Residence, Courthouse Cir., Doniphan, 4/05/91, A, 91000386

Saline County

Arrow Rock, Arrow Rock State Park, Arrow Rock, 10/15/66, A, NHL, 66000422

Arrow Rock State Historic Site Bridge [ECW Architecture in Missouri State Parks 1933-1942 TR], SE of Arrow Rock, Arrow Rock vicinity, 3/04/85, A, C, g, 85000516

Arrow Rock State Historic Site Grave Shelter [ECW Architecture in Missouri State Parks 1933-1942 TR], SE of Arrow Rock, Arrow Rock vicinity, 2/27/85, A, C, 85000534

Arrow Rock State Historic Site Lookout Shelter [ECW Architecture in Missouri State Parks 1933-1942 TR], E of Arrow Rock, Arrow Rock vicinity, 2/27/85, A, C, g, 85000535

Arrow Rock State Historic Site Open Shelter [ECW Architecture in Missouri State Parks 1933-1942 TR], SE of Arrow Rock, Arrow Rock vicinity, 2/28/85, A, C, g, 85000536

Arrow Rock Tavern, Main St., Arrow Rock, 2/23/72, A, 72000729

Baity Hall, Missouri Valley College, 500 E. College, Marshall, 6/25/86, A, C, a, 86001396

Bingham, George Caleb, House, 1st and High Sts. in Arrow Rock State Park, Arrow Rock, 10/15/66, B, NHL, 66000423

Blosser, Henry, House, E of Malta Bend off U.S. 65, Malta Bend vicinity, 12/29/78, B, C, 78001675

Buckner House, 125 N. Brunswick Ave., Marshall, 4/19/84, C, 84002581

Chicago and Alton Depot, Sebree St., Marshall, 6/27/79, A, C, 79001395

First Christian Church, 400 Bridge St., Sweet Springs, 9/12/80, A, C, a, 80002394

First Presbyterian Church, 212 E. North St., Marshall, 9/20/77, C, a, 77000814

Fisher-Gabbert Archeological Site, Address Restricted, Miami vicinity, 3/16/72, D, 72000730

Free Will Baptist Church of Pennytown, Off MO UU 8 mi. SE of Marshall, Marshall vicinity, 4/19/88, A, a, 88000388

Gumbo Point Archeological Site, Address Restricted, Grand Pass vicinity, 8/25/69, D, 69000125

Guthrey Archeological Site, Address Restricted, Miami vicinity, 12/02/70, D, 70000349

Neff Tavern Smokehouse, NE of Napton off MO 41, Napton vicinity, 11/30/78, A, B, 78001676

Old Fort, Address Restricted, Miami vicinity, 1/13/72, D, 72000731

Plattner Archeological Site, Address Restricted, Malta Bend vicinity, 3/04/71, D, 71000474

Saline County Courthouse, Courthouse Sq., Marshall, 8/24/77, A, C, 77000815

Sappington, William B., House, 3 mi. SW of Arrow Rock on CR TT, Arrow Rock vicinity, 1/21/70, B, C, 70000348

Utz Site, Restricted Address, Marshall vicinity, 10/15/66, D, NHL, 66000424

Van Meter State Park Combination Building [ECW Architecture in Missouri State Parks 1933-1942 TR], Van Meter State Park, Marshall vicinity, 2/27/85, A, C, 85000537

Saline County—Continued

Van Meter State Park Shelter Building [ECW Architecture in Missouri State Parks 1933-1942 TR], Van Meter State Park, Marshall vicinity, 2/28/85, A, C, 85000538

Schuyler County

Downing Railroad Depot, City Park, Downing, 3/29/83, A, C, b, 83001037
Hall, William P., House, U.S. 136, W of Schuyler County Courthouse, Lancaster, 4/01/75, B, g, 75001073

Scotland County

Downing House, 311 S. Main St., Memphis, 6/27/79, B, C, 79001396

Scott County

Brown, E. L., Village and Mound Archeological Site, Address Restricted, Diehlstadt vicinity, 2/12/71, D, 71000475
Marshall Hotel, 103 E. Malone Ave., Sikeston, 3/22/84, A, B, C, 84002715
Sandy Woods Settlement Archeological Site, Address Restricted, Diehlstadt vicinity, 3/04/71, D, 71000476

Shannon County

Akers Ferry Archeological District, Address Restricted, Rector vicinity, 10/25/90, D, NPS, 90001541
Alley Spring Roller Mill, W of Eminence off MO 106, Eminence vicinity, 12/08/81, A, NPS, 81000336
Chilton-Williams Farm Complex, E of Eminence off MO 106, Eminence vicinity, 9/02/81, A, C, NPS, 81000696
Culpepper—Pummil Site (23SH14/55), Address Restricted, Alley Spring vicinity, 2/03/88, D, NPS, 87002500
Klepzig, Walter, Mill and Farm, Along Rocky Creek in Ozark National Scenic Riverway, Eminence vicinity, 2/13/90, A, C, NPS, 90000001
Old Eminence Site (23SH104), Address Restricted, Round Spring vicinity, 2/09/88, D, NPS, 87002534
Owl's Bend Site (23SH10), Address Restricted, Eminence vicinity, 5/12/88, D, NPS, 87002530
Pulltite Site (23SH94), Address Restricted, Eminence vicinity, 2/04/88, D, NPS, 87002532
Reed Log House, Along Current R. S of Powder Mill Ferry, Ozark National Scenic Riverways, Eminence vicinity, 4/29/91, A, C, NPS, 91000456

Rhinehart Ranch, NW of Eminence, Eminence vicinity, 11/14/80, A, C, 80002395
Round Spring Archeological District, Address Restricted, Eminence vicinity, 1/25/93, D, NPS, 92001749
Shawnee Creek Site, Address Restricted, Eminence vicinity, 4/27/90, D, NPS, 90000604
Two Rivers Site, Address Restricted, Eminence vicinity, 1/23/93, D, NPS, 92001750

Shelby County

Benjamin House, 322 S. Shelby St., Shelbina, 6/27/72, C, 72000732
Bethel Historic District, Roughly bounded by Liberty, King, 1st, and 4th Sts., Bethel, 11/10/70, A, B, a, 70000350
Elim, 1.5 mi. E of Bethel, Bethel vicinity, 5/27/71, B, a, 71000477
Hebron, 0.8 mi. (1.3 km) NW of Bethel, Bethel vicinity, 1/31/78, A, C, a, 78001677

St. Charles County

African Church, 554 Madison St., St. Charles, 11/21/80, A, C, a, 80004366
Boone, Daniel, House, Hwy. F, Defiance, 4/11/73, B, C, 73002175
First Missouri State Capitol Buildings, 208–216 S. Main St., St. Charles, 4/16/69, A, 69000313
Frenchtown Historic District, Roughly bounded by N. Fifth, Clark and French Sts. and the Missouri R., St. Charles, 3/14/91, A, B, C, a, 91000216
Hays, Daniel Boone, House, SW of Defiance off Hwy. F, Defiance vicinity, 4/23/73, B, C, 73002176
Lindenwood Hall, Lindenwood Colleges campus, St. Charles, 11/29/78, A, C, 78003131
Marten-Becker House, 837 First Capitol Dr., St. Charles, 10/11/79, C, 79003200
Newbill-McElhiney House, 625 S. Main St., St. Charles, 4/11/72, C, 72001489
Old City Hall, Central Ave. and Main St., St. Charles, 11/14/80, A, C, 80004367
St. Charles Historic District, Roughly bounded by the Missouri River and Madison, Chauncey, and 2nd Sts., St. Charles, 9/22/70, A, C, 70000856
St. Charles Historic District (Boundary Increase), 1000 S. Main St., St. Charles, 6/04/87, C, 87000903
St. Charles Historic District (Boundary Increase II), Bounded by Madison, Second, Jefferson and the alley behind the 100 block of S. Main St., St. Charles, 5/01/91, C, 91000504
St. Charles Odd Fellows Hall, 117 S. Main, St. Charles, 4/13/87, C, 87000569
St. Paul's Church, SR D, New Melle, 9/09/82, A, B, C, a, 82004713
Staudinger—Grumke House—Store, 5503 Locust St., Augusta, 5/28/92, C, 92000504

Stone Row, 314-330 S. Main St., St. Charles, 7/29/69, C, 69000314
Stumberg, Dr. John H., House, 100 S. 3rd St., St. Charles, 7/12/78, B, C, 78003132
Watson, Samuel Stewart, House, 205 S. Duchesne Dr., St. Charles, 9/23/82, B, C, 82004714
Wentzville Tobacco Company Factory, 406 Elm St., Wentzville, 7/05/90, A, 90001024
Wolf-Ruebeling House, MO 94, Defiance vicinity, 3/29/83, A, C, 83001038

St. Francois County

Bonne Terre Depot, Oak St., Bonne Terre, 4/05/84, A, C, 84002606
Bonne Terre Mine, MO 47, Bonne Terre, 9/09/74, A, 74002281
St. Joe Lead Company Administration Building, Elm St., Bonne Terre, 4/05/84, A, C, 84002611

St. Louis County

Archambault House [St. Ferdinand City MRA (AD)], 603 rue St. Denis, Florissant, 5/13/76, B, C, 76002178
Assumption Greek Orthodox Church, 6900 Delmar Blvd., University City, 9/23/80, C, a, 80004389
Aubuchon, August, House [St. Ferdinand City MRA], 1002 St. Louis, Florissant, 9/12/79, C, 79003648
Aubuchon, Baptiste G., House [St. Ferdinand City MRA (AD)], 450 rue St. Jacques, Florissant, 5/06/76, A, C, 76002179
B'Nai Amoona Synogogue, 524 Trinity Ave., University City, 4/22/84, C, a, g, 84002698
Barretts Tunnels, 3015 Barrett Station Rd., Kirksville, 12/08/78, A, C, 78003138
Barteau House [St. Ferdinand City MRA], 305 N. Costello, Florissant, 9/12/79, C, g, 79003649
Barton House [St. Ferdinand City MRA], 680 St. Catherine, Florissant, 9/12/79, C, 79003650
Bassett, Dr. Samuel A., Office and Residence, 1200 S. Big Bend Blvd., Richmond Heights, 2/03/93, C, 92001866
Benoist, Louis Auguste, House, 7802 Genesta St., Affton, 6/23/69, C, 69000317
Bissell, Gen. Daniel, House, 10225 Bellefontaine Rd., Bellefontaine Neighbors, 11/28/78, B, C, a, 78003135
Bockwrath-Wiese House, St. Ferdinand Park, Florissant, 2/02/79, C, 79003676
Bonhomme Creek Archeological District, Address Restricted, Chesterfield vicinity, 11/21/74, D, 74002207
Bouas House [St. Ferdinand City MRA], 1290 St. Joseph, Florissant, 9/12/79, C, 79003651
Brentmoor Park, Brentmoor and Forest Ridge District, Big Bend and Wydown Blvds., Clayton, 9/23/82, A, B, C, 82004716
Busch's Grove, 9160 Clayton Rd., Ladue, 9/09/82, A, 82004721

St. Louis County—Continued

Carrswold Historic District, 1–26 Carrswold Dr., Clayton, 9/09/82, A, C, 82004889

Casa Alvarez [St. Ferdinand City MRA (AD)], 289 rue St. Denis, Florissant, 6/18/76, A, C, 76002180

Central Webster Historic District, Roughly bounded by E. and S. Cedar, Plant and W. Maple Aves., E. and W. Jackson Rd., and Gray Ave., Webster Groves, 6/11/86, A, C, 86001329

Church Street Commercial District, 2-100 Church St., Ferguson, 8/23/84, A, C, 84002701

Coral Court Motel, 7755 Watson Rd., Marlborough, 4/25/89, A, C, g, 89000311

Cori House, 1080 N. Berry Rd., Glendale, 10/02/86, B, C, 86002799

Crescent Quarry Archeological Site, Address Restricted, Crescent vicinity, 2/12/71, D, 71001030

Des Peres Presbyterian Church, Geyer Rd., Frontenac, 4/14/78, B, C, a, d, 78003137

Donaldson Court Apartments, 601-615 Westgate Ave., University City, 10/13/83, C, 83004032

Douglas House [St. Ferdinand City MRA], 801 St. Francois, Florissant, 9/12/79, C, 79003652

Dr. Edmund A. Babler Memorial State Park Historic District [ECW Architecture in Missouri State Parks 1933-1942 TR], NW of Grover, Grover vicinity, 2/27/85, A, C, g, 85000539

Ferguson School Central School, 201 Wesley Ave., Ferguson, 9/07/84, A, 84002706

Ferguson, Charles W., House, 15-17 W. Lockwood Ave., Webster Groves, 9/18/84, C, 84002704

Goldbeck House [St. Ferdinand City MRA], 1061 St. Louis, Florissant, 9/12/79, C, 79003653

Gorlock Building, 101-113 W. Lockwood Ave., Webster Groves, 11/08/84, A, C, 84000256

Grace Episcopal Church, Taylor and Argonne Sts., Kirkwood, 4/12/82, C, a, 82004720

Haarstick-Whittemore Houses, 6420 and 6440 Forsyth Blvd., Clayton, 9/20/82, B, C, 82004717

Hanley, Martin Franklin, House, 7600 Westmoreland Ave., Clayton, 5/27/71, C, 71001029

Hanson House [St. Ferdinand City MRA], 704 Ste. Catherine, Florissant, 9/12/79, C, 79003654

Hawken House, 1155 S. Rock Hill Rd., Webster Groves, 2/16/70, C, 70000858

Hubecky House [St. Ferdinand City MRA], 197 Lafayette, Florissant, 9/12/79, C, 79003674

Hunt, Wilson Price, House, 7717 Natural Bridge Rd., Normandy, 9/23/80, C, 80004386

Jarville, 1723 Mason Rd., St. Louis vicinity, 2/16/84, B, C, 84002634

Jefferson Barracks Historic District, 10 mi. S of St. Louis on the Missouri River, St. Louis vicinity, 2/01/72, A, 72001492

Kirkwood Missouri Pacific Depot, W. Argonne Dr. at Kirkwood Rd., Kirkwood, 7/05/85, A, C, 85001476

Koch, Robert, Hospital, 4101 Koch Rd., Oakville vicinity, 10/31/84, A, C, g, 84000206

Kramer House [St. Ferdinand City MRA], 520 Ste. Catherine, Florissant, 9/12/79, C, 79003675

Kuehn House [St. Ferdinand City MRA], 410 S. Harrison, Florissant, 9/12/79, C, 79003655

Lance House [St. Ferdinand City MRA], 508 St. Antoine, Florissant, 9/12/79, C, 79003656

Laramie, Marcus, House [St. Ferdinand City MRA], 929 St. Denis, Florissant, 9/12/79, C, 79003657

Larimore, Wilson, House, 11510 Larimore Rd., Bellefontiane Neighbors, 2/10/89, A, C, 88003244

Link, Theodore, Historic Buildings, 7100, 7104 and 7108 Delmar Blvd., University City, 9/11/80, B, C, 80004390

Long, William, Log House, 9385 Pardee Rd., Crestwood, 12/05/78, B, C, 78003136

Lyceum, The, 920 Manchester Rd., Manchester, 4/03/79, A, C, 79003206

Manchester Methodist Episcopal Church, 129 Woods Mill Rd., Manchester, 2/10/83, C, a, d, 83001053

Marshall Place Historic District, Marshall Pl., Webster Groves, 6/17/82, A, C, 82004726

McGarry House, 6965 Pershing Ave., University City, 4/12/82, A, C, 82004724

McPherson-Holland House, 115 Edwin Ave., Glendale, 9/16/82, C, 82004719

Meyer House [St. Ferdinand City MRA], 915 N. Lafayette, Florissant, 9/12/79, C, 79003658

Moellring, Frank, House [St. Ferdinand City MRA], 1002 Boone, Florissant, 9/12/79, B, 79003659

Moller House [St. Ferdinand City MRA], 300 Washington, Florissant, 9/12/79, C, 79003660

Mudd's Grove, 302 W. Argonne Dr., Kirkwood, 4/05/84, B, C, 84002710

Myers, John B., House, 180 Dunn Rd., Florissant, 12/13/74, A, C, 74002210

Myers, John B., House and Barn (Boundary Increase), 108 Dunn Rd., Florissant, 9/19/77, A, C, 77001563

Narrow Gauge Railroad Station [St. Ferdinand City MRA], 1060 St. Catherine, Florissant, 9/12/79, A, b, 79003661

Nicolay House [St. Ferdinand City MRA], 549 N. St. Jacques, Florissant, 9/12/79, C, 79003662

Old Stone Church, Conway Rd. at White Rd., Chesterfield, 4/13/73, C, a, 73002274

Pappas, Theodore, A., House, 865 Masonridge Rd., St. Louis vicinity, 2/14/79, A, C, g, 79003208

Parkview Historic District, Roughly bounded by Delmar Ave., Skinker, Millbrook Blvds., and Mellville Ave., University City, 3/14/86, A, C, 86000788

Payne-Gentry House, 4211 Fee Fee Rd., Bridgeton, 4/17/79, A, C, 79003202

Peters House [St. Ferdinand City MRA], 903 rue St. Francois, Florissant, 9/12/79, C, 79003664

Pine Lawn Carriage House, 6292-94 Stillwell Dr., Pine Lawn, 2/16/84, A, C, 84002666

Plant, Samuel, House, 800 Cella Rd., Ladue, 4/19/84, A, C, 84002711

Price School, Price School Lane, Ladue, 2/14/85, C, 85000285

Reeb House [St. Ferdinand City MRA], 446 St. Charles, Florissant, 9/12/79, C, 79003665

Rickelman House [St. Ferdinand City MRA], 680 Washington, Florissant, 9/12/79, C, 79003666

Ripple, Otto, Agency [St. Ferdinand City MRA], 755 rue St. Francois, Florissant, 9/12/79, C, 79003663

Rock House, Edgewood Children's Center, 330 N. Gore, Webster Groves, 9/09/82, A, 82004727

Sappington, Joseph, House, SW of Affton at 10734 Clearwater Drive, Affton vicinity, 10/14/82, C, 82000589

Sappington, Thomas J., House, 1015 S. Sappington Rd., Crestwood, 6/28/74, A, C, 74002209

Sappington, Zephaniah, House, S of Crestwood at 11145 Gravois Rd., Crestwood vicinity, 9/18/80, A, C, 80004384

Schmidt House [St. Ferdinand City MRA], 359 St. Jean, Florissant, 9/12/79, C, 79003667

Schoonover House [St. Ferdinand City MRA], 983 St. Antoine, Florissant, 9/12/79, C, 79003668

Seed, Miles A., Carriage House, 2456 Hord Ave., rear, Jennings, 3/25/87, C, 87000455

Seven Gables Building, 18–26 N. Meramec, Clayton, 7/16/85, A, C, 85001564

Shanley Building, 7800 Maryland Ave., Clayton, 9/20/82, C, g, 82004718

Sioux Passage Park Archeological Site, Address Restricted, Florissant vicinity, 7/24/74, D, 74002211

Smith House [St. Ferdinand City MRA], 310 Florissant Rd., Florissant, 9/12/79, C, 79003669

St. Ferdinand Central Historic District [St. Ferdinand City MRA], Roughly bounded by rue St. Francois, rue St. Ferdinand, and rue St. Denis, and Lafayette St., Florissant, 9/12/79, A, C, a, 79003647

St. Ferdinand's Shrine Historic District [St. Ferdinand City MRA], Between Cold Water and Fountain Creeks, Florissant, 9/12/79, A, C, a, 79003759

St. Stanislaus Seminary, 700 Howdershell Rd., Florissant, 9/22/72, A, C, a, 72001491

St. Vincent's Hospital, 7301 St. Charles Rock Rd., Normandy, 4/12/82, A, C, 82004722

Stroer House [St. Ferdinand City MRA], 700 Aubuchon, Florissant, 9/12/79, C, 79003670

Sutter-Meyer House, 6826 Chamberlain Court, University City, 4/12/82, A, C, 82004725

Taille de Noyer, 1 rue Taille de Noyer, Florissant, 1/10/80, A, b, 80004385

Tebeau House [St. Ferdinand City MRA], 250 St. Catherine, Florissant, 9/12/79, C, 79003671

Tebeau, Marvin, House [St. Ferdinand City MRA], 449 St. Joseph, Florissant, 9/12/79, C, 79003672

Thornhill, Olive Street Rd. in Faust County Park, Chesterfield, 7/18/74, B, C, 74002208

Tuxedo Park Station, 643 Glen Rd., Webster Groves, 3/22/84, A, C, 84002713

University City Education District, 7400 and 7401 Balson Ave., and 951 N. Hanley Rd., University City, 1/31/85, A, C, g, 85000172

University City Plaza, Roughly bounded by Delmar Blvd., Trinity, Harvard, and Kingsland Aves., University City, 3/07/75, B, C, 75002092

University Heights Subdivision Number One, Roughly bounded by Delmar Blvd., Yale, Dartmouth and Harvard Aves., University City, 9/23/80, A, C, 80004391

St. Louis County—Continued

Utz-Tesson House, 615 Utz Lane, Hazelwood, 1/22/73, C, 73002178

Webster College-Eden Theological Seminary Collegiate District, 470 and 475 E. Lockwood Ave., Webster Groves, 12/28/82, A, C, a, 82000590

White Haven, 9060 Whitehaven Dr., Grantwood Village vicinity, 4/04/79, B, C, NHL, 79003205

Williams Creek Archeological District, Address Restricted, St. Louis vicinity, 11/23/77, A, D, 77001527

Withington House [St. Ferdinand City MRA], 502 St. Marie, Florissant, 9/12/79, C, 79003673

Wydown—Forsyth District, Roughly bounded by Forsyth, Skinker Blvd., Fauquier and Wydown Terrace Dr., and University Ln., Clayton, 5/23/88, B, C, 88000628

St. Louis Independent City

Advertising Building, 1627-1629 Locust St., St. Louis (Independent City), 1/18/85, A, C, 85000106

Ambassador Theater Building, 411 N. 7th St., St. Louis (Independent City), 3/29/83, C, 83001039

American Theater, 416 N. 9th St., St. Louis (Independent City), 3/18/85, C, 85000617

Anheuser-Busch Brewery, 721 Pestalozzi St., St. Louis (Independent City), 11/13/66, A, NHL, 66000945

Aubert Place, Fountain Ave. between Walton Ave. and Kings Hwy., St. Louis (Independent City), 9/30/82, A, C, a, 82004730

B'nai El Temple, 3666 Flad Ave., St. Louis (Independent City), 7/21/83, A, C, 83001042

Barr Branch Library Historic District, 2500–2630 Lafayette Ave., St. Louis (Independent City), 9/02/82, A, C, 82004731

Beaumont Medical Building, 3714-26 Washington Ave., St. Louis (Independent City), 1/19/84, A, B, C, 84002615

Beethoven Conservatory, 2301 Locust St., St. Louis (Independent City), 3/02/89, B, C, 89000075

Benton Park District, Bounded by Gravois Ave., I-55, S. Broadway, and Jefferson St., St.Y Louis (Independent City), 12/30/85, A, C, a, 85003232

Bissel Street Water Tower, Jct. of Bissell St. and Blair Ave., St. Louis (Independent City), 6/05/70, A, C, 70000906

Blackwell-Wielandy Building, 1601-09 Locust St., St. Louis (Independent City), 7/21/83, A, C, 83001040

Blair, Frank P., School, 2707 Rauschenbach Ave., St. Louis (Independent City), 2/10/83, A, C, 83001041

Blind Girls' Home, 5235 Page Blvd., St. Louis (Independent City), 8/23/84, A, C, 84002617

Brown Shoe Company's Homes-Take Factory, 1201 Russell Blvd., St. Louis (Independent City), 10/20/80, B, C, 80004503

Brown, A. D., Building, 1136 Washington Ave., St. Louis (Independent City), 3/28/80, B, C, 80004502

Building at 1300 Washington Avenue, 1300–1310 Washington Ave., St. Louis (Independent City), 9/02/82, A, C, 82004732

Buildings at 2327-31 and 2333-35 Rutger Street, 2327-31 and 2333-35 Rutger St., St. Louis (Independent City), 1/19/84, C, 84002620

Butler House, 4484 W. Pine Blvd., St. Louis (Independent City), 9/02/82, B, C, 82004733

Campbell, Robert G., House, 1508 Locust St., St. Louis (Independent City), 4/21/77, A, B, C, 77001560

Carlin-Rathgeber House [Carondelet, East of Broadway, St. Louis MRA], 122 Davis St., St. Louis (Independent City), 5/29/80, B, C, 80004554

Chatillon-DeMenil House, 3352 DeMenil Pl., St. Louis (Independent City), 6/09/78, B, C, 78001673

Chemical Building, 721 Olive St., St. Louis (Independent City), 3/19/82, C, 82004734

Chopin, Kate, House, 4232 McPherson Ave., St. Louis (Independent City), 2/14/86, B, 86000209

Chouteau Apartments/Parkway Dwellings, 4937-4943 Laclede Ave., St. Louis (Independent City), 2/10/83, C, 83001043

Christ Church Cathedral, 1210 Locust St., St. Louis (Independent City), 3/07/90, C, a, 90000345

Clemens House—Columbia Brewery District, Roughly bounded by Maiden Lane, Cass Ave., 21st, Helen, and Howard Sts., St. Louis (Independent City), 7/19/84, A, C, 84002622

Clemens House—Columbia Brewery District (Boundary Increase), Roughly bounded by St. Louis Ave., N. Florissant Ave., Maiden Ln., and N. Twenty-first and N. Twentyieth Sts., St. Louis (Independent City), 7/22/86, A, C, a, 86001929

Compton Hill Water Tower, Resevoir Park, Grant and Russell Blvds. and Lafayette Ave., St. Louis (Independent City), 9/29/72, A, C, 72001555

Convent of the Sisters of St. Joseph Carondelet, 6400 Minnesota Ave., St. Louis (Independent City), 2/28/80, A, C, a, 80004505

Crittenden Historic District, 3401 Arsenal, 3400 and 3500 blocks of Crittenden, St. Louis (Independent City), 7/07/83, A, C, 83001044

Cupples, Samuel, House, 3673 W. Pine Blvd., St. Louis (Independent City), 10/21/76, B, C, 76002260

DePaul Hospital, 2415 N. Kingshighway Blvd., St. Louis (Independent City), 3/29/83, A, C, 83001045

Delmar Loop-Parkview Gardens Historic District, Roughly bounded by Kingsland Ave., North Dr., Delmar Blvd., and Eastgate, St. Louis (Independent City), 2/16/84, A, C, 84002624

Des Peres School, 6307 Michigan Ave., St. Louis (Independent City), 9/02/82, B, C, 82004735

Dolman Row, 1424-1434 Dolman St., St. Louis (Independent City), 1/19/84, C, 84002629

Dorris Motor Car Company, 4100 Laclede, St. Louis (Independent City), 5/01/86, A, B, C, 86000883

Eads Bridge, Spanning the Mississippi River at Washington St., St. Louis (Independent City), 10/15/66, A, C, NHL, 66000946

Eliot School [St. Louis Public Schools of William B. Ittner MPS], 4242 Grove, St. Louis (Independent City), 9/02/92, C, 92001092

Emerson Electric Company Building, 2012–2018 Washington Ave., St. Louis (Independent City), 11/06/86, C, 86003138

Emerson, Ralph Waldo, School [St. Louis Public Schools of William B. Ittner MPS], 5415 Page Blvd., St. Louis (Independent City), 9/02/92, C, 92001145

Erlanger, Joseph, House, 5127 Waterman Blvd., St. Louis (Independent City), 12/08/76, B, NHL, 76002234

Fashion Square Building, 1307 Washington Ave., St. Louis (Independent City), 10/09/85, C, 85003105

Field, Eugene, House, 634 S. Broadway, St. Louis (Independent City), 8/19/75, A, B, C, 75002137

Field, Eugene, School [St. Louis Public Schools of William B. Ittner MPS], 4466 Olive, St. Louis (Independent City), 9/02/92, C, 92001093

Forest Park Headquarters Building, 115 Union, Forest Park, St. Louis, 6/11/86, C, 86001300

Forest Park Hotel, 4910 W. Pine Blvd., St. Louis (Independent City), 3/22/84, C, 84002632

Fox Theater, 527 N. Grand Blvd., St. Louis (Independent City), 10/08/76, A, C, g, 76002261

Frisco Building, 906 Olive St., St. Louis (Independent City), 3/29/83, A, C, 83001046

Fullerton's Westminster Place, Westminster Pl., St. Louis (Independent City), 4/10/80, A, C, 80004506

Fulton Bag Company Building, 612–618 S. Seventh St., St. Louis (Independent City), 9/05/91, C, 91001372

GOLDENROD, 400 N. Wharf St., St. Louis (Independent City), 12/24/67, A, NHL, 67000029

Gateway Arch, Memorial Dr. between Poplar St. & Eads bridges, St. Louis (Independent City), 5/28/87, A, C, f, g, NHL, NPS, 87001423

Goodfellow—Julian Concrete Block District, Roughly bounded by Julian Ave., Blackstone, & Goodfellow Blvd., St. Louis (Independent City), 8/13/87, C, 87001389

Grand Avenue Water Tower, Jct. of E. Grand Ave. and 20th St., St. Louis (Independent City), 6/15/70, C, 70000908

Hadley-Dean Glass Company, 701–705 N. 11th St., St. Louis (Independent City), 8/01/79, A, B, C, 79003634

Hager, C., and Sons Hinge Co., 139 Victor St., St. Louis (Independent City), 2/26/87, A, g, 87000508

Hargadine-McKittrick Dry Goods Building, 911 Washington Ave., St. Louis (Independent City), 3/19/82, A, C, 82004728

Hickory Street District, Bounded roughly by Lasalle, Missouri, Rutger, and Jefferson Sts., and along Hickory St., St. Louis (Independent City), 1/18/85, C, 85000107

Holy Corners Historic District, Both sides of Kings Highway between and including Westminster Pl. and Washington Ave., St. Louis (Independent City), 12/29/75, A, C, a, g, 75002138

St. Louis Independent City—Continued

Holy Cross Parish District, 8115 Church Rd., St. Louis (Independent City), 3/27/80, A, B, C, a, 80004507

Hotel Statler, 822 Washington Ave., St. Louis (Independent City), 3/19/82, C, 82004729

Immaculate Conception School, 2912 Lafayette, St. Louis (Independent City), 5/08/85, C, 85000995

Jackson School [St. Louis Public Schools of William B. Ittner MPS], 1632 Hogan St., St. Louis (Independent City), 9/02/92, C, 92001094

Jefferson National Expansion Memorial National Historic Site, Mississippi River between Washington and Poplar Sts., St. Louis (Independent City), 10/15/66, A, C, a, g, NHL, NPS, 66000941

Joplin, Scott, House, 2658 Delmar Blvd., St. Louis (Independent City), 12/08/76, B, NHL, 76002235

Laclede's Landing, Roughly bounded by Washington, N. 3rd, Dr. Martin Luther King Dr., and the Mississippi River, St. Louis (Independent City), 8/25/76, A, C, 76002262

Lafayette Square Historic District, Roughly bounded by Hickory and 18th Sts., Jefferson and Lafayette Aves., St. Louis (Independent City), 6/28/72, A, C, 72001557

Lafayette Square Historic District (Boundary Increase), Roughly bounded by Chouteau Ave., Dolman, Lafayette Ave., and S. Eighteenth St. and Vail Pl. and McKay Pl., St. Louis (Independent City), 7/24/86, C, 86002127

Lambert Building, 2101-2107 Locust St., St. Louis (Independent City), 2/24/83, A, C, 83001047

Lambert-Deacon-Hull Printing Company Building, 2100 Locust St., St. Louis (Independent City), 10/20/80, C, 80004508

Lambskin Temple, 1054 S. Kingshighway Blvd., St. Louis (Independent City), 8/12/87, C, 87001361

Lennox Hotel, 823-827 Washington Ave., St. Louis (Independent City), 9/06/84, A, C, 84002647

Leonardo, 4166 Lindell Blvd., St. Louis (Independent City), 8/11/83, C, 83001048

Lesan—Gould Building, 1320–1324 Washington Ave., St. Louis (Independent City), 11/06/86, C, 86003137

Lewis Place Historic District, Lewis Pl., St. Louis (Independent City), 9/15/80, A, C, 80004509

Liggett & Myers Tobacco Co. Building, 1900-1912 Pine St., St. Louis (Independent City), 2/10/83, A, C, 83001049

Liggett and Myers (Rice-Stix) Building, 1000 Washington Ave., St. Louis (Independent City), 2/16/84, A, C, 84002648

Lincoln Trust Building, 706 Chestnut St., St. Louis (Independent City), 3/19/82, A, C, 82004736

Lindell Real Estate Company Buidling, 1015 Washington Ave., St. Louis (Independent City), 3/19/82, A, C, 82004737

Lister Building, 4500 Olive St., St. Louis (Independent City), 2/10/83, A, C, 83004298

Loretto Academy, Address Restricted, St. Louis (Independent City) vicinity, 3/05/92, A, C, a, 92000079

Louise Apartments, 3900 Lindell Blvd. and Vandeventer Ave., St. Louis (Independent City), 8/23/84, C, 84002651

Majestic Hotel, 1017-23 Pine St. and 200-10 N. 11th St., St. Louis (Independent City), 1/26/84, A, C, 84002653

Mann, Horace, School [St. Louis Public Schools of William B. Ittner MPS], 4047 Juniata, St. Louis (Independent City), 9/02/92, C, 92001095

Marquette Hotel, 1734 Washington Ave., St. Louis (Independent City), 9/26/85, A, C, 85002557

May Company Department Store Building, 509-23 Washington Ave., St. Louis (Independent City), 6/23/83, A, C, 83001050

Mayfair Hotel, 806 St. Charles Ave., St. Louis (Independent City), 9/17/79, C, 79003638

McKinley Fox District, Roughly bounded by 18th St., I-44, Jefferson and Gravois Aves., St. Louis (Independent City), 9/07/84, A, C, 84002655

Midtown Historic District, Lendell and Grand Blvds., St. Louis (Independent City), 7/07/78, C, a, 78003392

Missouri Botanical Gardens, 2345 Tower Grove Ave., St. Louis (Independent City), 11/19/71, A, C, NHL, 71001065

Mount Pleasant School, 4528 Nebraska Ave., St. Louis (Independent City), 5/02/85, C, 85000943

Mullanphy Historic District, N. 14th St. between Mullanphy and Howard and N. 13th between Howard and Tyler, St. Louis (Independent City), 2/14/83, C, 83001051

Murphy-Blair District, Roughly bounded by I-70, Florissant Ave., Chambers and Branch Sts., St. Louis (Independent City), 1/26/84, A, C, 84002658

Negro Masonic Hall, 3615–3619 Dr. Martin Luther King Blvd., St. Louis (Independent City), 4/15/93, A, 93000262

Neighborhood Gardens Apartments, 1205 N. Seventh St., St. Louis (Independent City), 1/31/86, A, C, 86000143

Oakherst Place Concrete Block District, Roughly bounded by Julian, Oakley, Plymouth and Oakherst, St. Louis (Independent City), 5/05/87, C, 87000642

Old Laclede Gas and Light Company Building, Central Ave. and Main St., St. Louis (Independent City), 11/26/80, C, 80004392

Olive Street Terra Cotta District, 600–622 Olive St., St. Louis (Independent City), 1/02/86, C, 86000006

Olympia, The, 3863 W. Pine and 200 N. Vandeventer, St. Louis (Independent City), 8/01/86, C, 86002088

Otzenberger House [Carondelet, East of Broadway, St. Louis MRA], 7827 Reilly St., St. Louis (Independent City), 5/29/80, A, C, 80004515

PRESIDENT, 500 N. Leonor K. Sullivan Blvd., St. Louis (Independent City), 12/20/89, A, C, g, NHL, 89002460

Page Boulevard Police Station, Page and Union Blvds., St. Louis (Independent City), 9/11/80, A, C, 80004504

Peters Shoe Company Building, 1232-36 Washington Ave., St. Louis (Independent City), 1/26/84, A, C, 84002663

Phillips, Homer G., Hospital, 26101 Whittier St., St. Louis (Independent City), 9/23/82, A, C, g, 82004738

Plaza Hotel Complex, 307 N. Leonard, 3301-3321 Olive, 3300-3322 & 3339 Lindell, 3322-3334 Locust & 308-310 Channing, St. Louis (Independent City), 5/07/85, A, C, 85001007

Portland and Westmoreland Places, NE corner of Forest Park, St. Louis (Independent City), 2/12/74, A, C, g, 74002276

Principia Page-Park YMCA Gymnasium, 5569 Minerva Ave., St. Louis (Independent City), 9/02/82, A, B, C, a, 82004739

Quinn Chapel AME Church, 227 Bowen St., St. Louis (Independent City), 10/16/74, A, C, a, 74002277

Robert, Johnson and Rand-International Shoe Company Complex, Mississippi and Hickory Sts., St. Louis (Independent City), 8/23/84, A, C, 84002670

Rock Spring School [St. Louis Public Schools of William B. Ittner MPS], 3974 Sarpy Ave., St. Louis (Independent City), 9/02/92, C, 92001097

S.S. Cyril and Methodius Historic District, I-70, St. Louis (Independent City), 6/28/82, A, B, C, a, 82004740

Saint Matthew's Parish Complex, Sarah and Kennerly, St. Louis (Independent City), 8/06/86, C, a, 86002236

Sanitol Building, 4252–4264 Laclede Ave., St. Louis (Independent City), 10/21/85, A, C, 85003362

Schlichtig House [Carondelet, East of Broadway, St. Louis MRA], 8402 Vulcan St., St. Louis (Independent City), 5/29/80, A, B, C, 80004516

Schmitt, Anton, House, 8000–04 Alaska, St. Louis (Independent City), 4/30/92, C, 92000445

Schollmeyer Building, 1976-1982 Arsenal St., St. Louis (Independent City), 9/28/84, C, 84002683

Scruggs-Vandervoort-Barney Warehouse, 917 Locust St., St. Louis (Independent City), 2/21/85, A, C, 85000320

Second Presbyterian Church, 4501 Westminster Pl., St. Louis (Independent City), 9/11/75, A, C, a, 75002140

Seventh District Police Station, 2800 S. Grand Ave., St. Louis (Independent City), 3/22/84, A, C, 84002685

Shaw Avenue Place, Roughly bounded by De Tanty St., S. Spring, Shaw and S. Grand Aves., St. Louis (Independent City), 4/12/82, B, C, 82004741

Shelley House, 4600 Labadie Ave., St. Louis (Independent City), 4/18/88, A, g, NHL, 88000437

Silk Exchange Building, 501-511 N. Tucker Blvd., St. Louis (Independent City), 9/02/82, A, C, 82004742

Soulard Neighborhood Historic District, Roughly bounded by 7th Blvd., Soulard, Lynch and 12th Sts., St. Louis (Independent City), 12/26/72, A, C, a, g, 72001559

Soulard-Page District [LaSalle Park MRA], Roughly bounded by Soulard, 8th, 12th, and LaSalle Sts., St. Louis (Independent City), 8/19/83, A, C, a, 83004515

St. Louis Independent City—Continued

Speck District [LaSalle Park MRA], Roughly bounded by S. 11th, Park, Rutger, and S. 12th Sts., St. Louis (Independent City), 8/15/83, A, C, 83004516

St. Augustine's Roman Catholic Church, 3114 Lismore, St. Louis (Independent City), 10/02/86, C, a, 86002819

St. Francis de Sales Church, 2653 Ohio St., St. Louis (Independent City), 11/02/78, A, C, a, 78003393

St. John Nepomuk Parish Historic District [LaSalle Park MRA], 11th and 12th Sts. between Carroll St. and Lafayette Ave., St. Louis (Independent City), 6/19/72, A, a, e, 72001558

St. Joseph's Roman Catholic Church, 1220 N. 11th St., St. Louis (Independent City), 5/19/78, A, C, a, 78003396

St. Liborius Church and Buildings, 1835 N. 18th St., St. Louis (Independent City), 10/11/79, A, C, a, 79003637

St. Louis Air Force Station, 2nd and Arsenal Sts., St. Louis (Independent City), 1/17/75, A, B, C, 75002139

St. Louis Post-Dispatch Printing Building, 1111 Olive St., St. Louis (Independent City), 8/29/84, C, g, 84002672

St. Louis Union Station, 18th and Market Sts., St. Louis (Independent City), 6/15/70, A, C, NHL, 70000888

St. Mary of Victories Church, 744 S. 3rd St., St. Louis (Independent City), 8/28/80, A, C, a, 80004510

St. Stanislaus Kostka Church, 1413 N. 20th St., St. Louis (Independent City), 7/10/79, A, C, a, 79003635

Steins Street District [Carondelet, East of Broadway, St. Louis MRA], Steins St., St. Louis (Independent City), 5/29/80, A, C, 80004514

Steins, Jacob, House [Carondelet, East of Broadway, St. Louis MRA], 7600 Reilly St., St. Louis (Independent City), 5/29/80, A, C, 80004517

Stockton, Robert Henry, House, 3508 Samuel Shepard Dr., St. Louis (Independent City), 8/10/88, C, 88001177

Stone Houses, 200–204 Stein St., St. Louis (Independent City), 3/27/80, A, C, 80004511

Strassberger's Conservatory, 2302–2306 S. Grand St., St. Louis (Independent City), 3/27/80, B, C, 80004512

Sugar Loaf Mound, Address Restricted, St. Louis (Independent City) vicinity, 2/17/84, D, 84002689

Sumner, Charles, High School, 4248 W. Cottage Ave., St. Louis (Independent City), 4/19/88, A, C, 88000469

Tiffany Neighborhood District, Roughly bounded by 39th St., Park, Grand, and Lafayette Aves., St. Louis (Independent City), 2/10/83, A, C, 83001052

Tiffany Neighborhood District (Boundary Increase-Decrease)-Dundee Place), Roughly bounded by Park Ave., S. Grand Blvd., Lafayette, Vandeventer, Towergrove, and Folsome

Aves., St. Louis (Independent City), 2/26/87, A, C, 87000124

Tiffany Neighborhood Historic District (Boundary Increase), West side 39th St. between Park & Lafayette Aves., St. Louis (Independent City), 7/26/85, A, C, 85001643

Tower Grove Park, Bounded by Magnolia Ave. on N, Grand Blvd. on E, Arsenal St. on S, and Kings Highway Blvd. on W, St. Louis (Independent City), 3/17/72, C, NHL, 72001556

U.S. Customhouse and Post Office, 8th and Olive Sts., St. Louis (Independent City), 11/22/68, A, C, NHL, 68000053

USS INAUGURAL (fleet minesweeper), 300 N. Wharf St., St. Louis, 1/14/86, A, g, NHL, 86000091

Union Market, Broadway and Lucas Ave., St. Louis (Independent City), 1/16/84, A, C, 84002692

Union Station Post Office Annex, 329 S. 18th St., St. Louis (Independent City), 9/26/85, A, C, 85002488

Union Trust Company Building, 705 Oliver St., St. Louis (Independent City), 6/17/82, C, 82004743

Unitarian Church of the Messiah, Locust and Garrison Sts., St. Louis (Independent City), 9/22/80, A, B, C, a, 80004513

Vesper-Buick Auto Company Building, 3900–3912 W. Pine, St.Louis (Independent City), 10/02/86, C, 86002814

Wainwright Building, 709 Chestnut St., St. Louis (Independent City), 5/23/68, C, NHL, 68000054

Wainwright Tomb, Bellefontaine Cemetery, 4947 W. Florissant Ave., St. Louis (Independent City), 6/15/70, A, C, c, f, 70000907

Washington Avenue Historic District, Roughly bounded by Delmar, Tucker, St. Charles, N. Fifteenth, Olive, N. Eighteenth, Washington Ave., and Lucas St., St. Louis (Independent City), 2/12/87, A, C, 86003733

Washington Avenue: East of Tucker District, Roughly bounded by Lucas, N. Ninth, St. Charles, Locust, and Tucker Blvd., St. Louis (Independent City), 3/24/87, A, C, g, 87000458

Washington University Hilltop Campus Historic District, Roughly bounded by Big Bend, Forsyth, Skinker, and Millbrook Blvds., St. Louis (Independent City), 1/12/79, A, B, C, g, NHL, 79003636

West Cabanne Place Historic District, Central Ave. and Main St., St. Louis (Independent City), 11/21/80, A, C, 80004393

Wiltshire and Versailles Historic Buildings, 724 and 709 Skinker Blvd., St. Louis (Independent City), 9/29/82, C, 82004744

Winkelmeyer Building, 11th and Walnut Sts., St. Louis (Independent City), 7/11/85, C, 85001500

Winston Churchill Apartments, 5475 Cabanne, St. Louis (Independent City), 4/04/85, C, 85000697

Wyman, Edward, School [St. Louis Public Schools of William B. Ittner MPS], 1547 S. Teresa, St. Louis (Independent City), 9/02/92, C, 92001096

YWCA, Phyllis Weatley Branch, 2709 Locust St., St. Louis (Independent City), 7/24/84, A, C, 84002694

Zeiss Houses [Carondelet, East of Broadway, St. Louis MRA], 7707–7713 Vulcan St., St. Louis (Independent City), 5/29/80, C, 80004518

Ste. Genevieve County

Bolduc, Louis, House, 123 S. Main St., Ste. Genevieve, 4/16/69, B, C, NHL, 69000305

Common Field Archeological Site, Address Restricted, Ste. Genevieve vicinity, 7/29/69, D, 69000306

Guibourd, Jacques Dubreuil, House, NW corner of 4th and Merchant Sts., Ste. Genevieve, 5/21/69, C, 69000307

Kreilich Archeological Site, Address Restricted, Ste. Genevieve vicinity, 5/21/69, D, 69000308

Ste. Genevieve Historic District, Address unknown at this time, Ste. Genevieve, 10/15/66, A, C, NHL, 66000892

Stoddard County

Mingo National Wildlife Refuge Archeology District, Address Restricted, Puxico vicinity, 5/12/75, D, 75001074

Rich Wood Archeological Site, Address Restricted, Bernie vicinity, 1/25/71, D, 71000478

Stoddard County Courthouse, Praire and Court Sts., Bloomfield, 9/18/84, A, C, 84002718

Stone County

Morrill, Levi, Post, SE of Reeds Spring, Reeds Spring vicinity, 4/03/79, A, B, 79001397

Stone County Courthouse, Public Sq., Galena, 11/14/80, A, C, 80002396

Y Bridge, Jct. of MO 43 and 13, across the James R., Galena, 5/23/91, A, C, 91000591

Sullivan County

Camp Ground Church and Cemetary, W of Milan, Milan vicinity, 9/23/85, A, a, d, 85002483

Quincy, Omaha and Kansas City Railroad Office Building, 117 N. Water St., Milan, 1/07/92, A, C, 91001917

Taney County

Bonniebrook Homestead, US 65, Walnut Shade vicinity, 4/20/84, B, d, f, 84002720

Branson City Park Historic District [Taneycomo Lakefront Tourism Resources of Branson MPS], Jct. of St. Limas and Oklahoma Sts., Branson, 8/31/93, A, C, 93000874

Downing Street Historic District, Downing St. between 3rd and 4th Sts., Hollister, 12/29/78, A, C, a, 78001678

Taney County—Continued

Ross, John, House, MO 76, Branson vicinity, 7/21/83, A, C, 83001054

Sammy Lane Resort Historic District [Taneycomo Lakefront Tourism Resources of Branson MPS], 320 E. Main St., Branson, 8/31/93, A, C, 93000875

Swan Creek Bridge, N of Forsyth, Forsyth vicinity, 9/08/83, C, b, 83001055

Texas County

Bates-Geers House, E of Plata on Slabtown Rd., Plato vicinity, 9/23/82, B, C, 82003159

White Rock Bluffs Archeological Pictograph Site, Address Restricted, Buckyrus vicinity, 5/21/69, C, D, 69000126

Vernon County

Brown Archeological Site, Address Restricted, Fair Haven vicinity, 2/12/71, D, 71000480

Carrington Osage Village Site, Address Restricted, Nevada vicinity, 10/15/66, D, NHL, 66000425

Coal Pit Archeological Site, Address Restricted, Arthur vicinity, 2/12/71, D, 71000479

Halleys Bluff Site, Address Restricted, Shell City vicinity, 7/24/74, D, 74001091

Vernon County Jail, Sheriff's House and Office, 229 N. Main St., Nevada, 8/16/77, A, C, 77000816

Warren County

Borgmann Mill, 5 mi. E of Marthasville on CR D, Marthasville vicinity, 11/10/70, A, 70000351

Callaway, Flanders, House, 1 mi. S of Marthasville off MO 94, Marthasville vicinity, 7/29/69, A, C, 69000127

Schowengerdt, Ernst, House, 308 E. Boone's Lick Rd., Warrenton, 10/03/80, B, C, 80002397

Warren County Courthouse and Circuit Court Building, Main St., Warrenton, 3/17/72, A, C, 72000733

Washington County

Caledonia Historic District, Roughly bounded by Patrick, College, and Alexander Sts., and MO 21, Caledonia, 10/27/86, A, B, C, a, 86003389

Cresswell Petroglyph Archeological Site, Address Restricted, Fertile vicinity, 2/12/71, C, D, 71000482

Cresswell, George, Furnace, MO F, Potosi vicinity, 5/23/88, A, C, 88000613

Land Archeological Site, Address Restricted, Caledonia vicinity, 5/05/72, D, 72000734

Lost Creek Pictograph Archeological Site, Address Restricted, Caledonia vicinity, 1/25/71, D, 71000481

Susan Cave (23WA190), Address Restricted, Shirley vicinity, 7/08/89, D, 89000758

Washington State Park CCC Historic District [ECW Architecture in Missouri State Parks 1933-1942 TR], Roughly bounded by MO 102 and MO 104, Potosi vicinity, 3/04/85, A, C, g, 85000517

Washington State Park Petroglyph Archeological Site, Address Restricted, Fertile vicinity, 4/03/70, D, 70000352

Wayne County

Old Greenville (23WE637), Address Restricted, Greenville vicinity, 2/17/90, D, d, 90000005

Sam A. Baker State Park Historic District [ECW Architecture in Missouri State Parks 1933-1942 TR], St. Francis Mountains bounded roughly around Cedar Creek, Big Creek and Mudlick Canyon off MO 143, Patterson vicinity, 2/27/85, A, C, g, 85000540

Webster County

Love, Col. Thomas C., House, Off Rt. 1, Seymour vicinity, 1/18/85, B, C, 85000108

Worth County

Worth Count Courthouse, Public Sq., Grant City, 1/20/83, C, 83001056

Wright County

Administration Building, Missouri State Fruit Experiment Station, N of Mountain Grove off MO 60, Mountain Grove vicinity, 1/12/79, A, C, 79001398

Kelton House, MO 38 and Church St., Hartville, 10/02/83, C, 86002803

Mountain Grove Bandstand, Main and Second Sts., Mountain Grove, 1/19/89, A, C, 88003218

Wilder, Laura Ingalls, House, 1 mi. E of Mansfield on U.S. Business 60, Mansfield vicinity, 5/19/70, B, NHL, 70000353

The Coral Court Motel in St. Louis County is "both an outstanding example . . . of Streamline Moderne architecture and perhaps the premier surviving example in the country" of early 1940s roadside motel development. (Esley Hamilton, 1988)

MONTANA

Beaverhead County

Bannack Historic District, 22 mi. from Dillon off MT 278, Dillon vicinity, 10/15/66, A, NHL, 66000426

Barrett Hospital, Chapman and S. Atlantic Sts., Dillon, 1/18/85, A, C, 85000109

Barrett, Martin, House, 733 S. Pacific, Dillon, 1/28/87, B, C, 86003675

Big Hole National Battlefield, 12 mi. W of Wisdom, Wisdom vicinity, 10/15/66, A, NPS, 66000427

Birch Creek CCC Camp, N of Dillon on US FS Rd. 98, Dillon vicinity, 12/07/82, A, C, g, 82000591

Dillon City Library, 121 S. Idaho St., Dillon, 11/14/78, A, C, 78001679

Hotel Metlen, 5 S. Railroad Ave., Dillon, 12/13/83, A, C, 83003978

Lamarche Game Trap, Address Restricted, Dillon vicinity, 9/28/76, D, 76001117

Montana State Normal School, 710 S. Atlantic St., Dillon, 8/27/80, A, C, 80002398

Oregon Short Line Passenger Depot, S. Montana St., Dillon, 4/19/90, A, C, 90000628

Sheep Creek Wickiup Cave, Address Restricted, Lima vicinity, 9/23/81, D, 81000338

US Post Office—Dillon Main [US Post Offices in Montana, 1900–1941, TR], 117 S. Idaho St., Dillon, 3/14/86, A, C, a, 86000683

Big Horn County

Baldwin House [Lodge Grass MRA], 25 Third Ave., Lodge Grass, 8/03/87, A, C, 87001270

Battle of the Rosebud Site, 6 mi. S of Kirby, Kirby vicinity, 8/21/72, A, 72000735

Bighorn Ditch Headgate, W of Fort Smith at mouth of Bighorn Canyon, Fort Smith, 12/12/76, A, C, NPS, 76000174

Boyum, John, House [Hardin MPS], 225 W. Sixth St., Hardin, 4/11/91, C, 91000371

Burke, Thomas H., House [Hardin MPS], 604 N. Cody, Hardin, 4/11/91, C, 91000368

Cammock's Hotel [Lodge Grass MRA], 28 N. Main St., Lodge Grass, 8/30/87, A, C, 87001271

Camp Four, 11 mi. NE of Fort Smith on Fort Smith—Hardin Co. Rd., Fort Smith vicinity, 1/21/92, A, B, 91001940

Chief Plenty Coups Memorial, 1 mi. W of Pryor off MT 416, Pryor vicinity, 10/06/70, A, D, 70000354

Chivers Memorial Church [Lodge Grass MRA], E of Chicago Burlington RR tracks, W side of US 87, Lodge Grass, 8/03/87, A, B, a, 87001272

Commercial District [Hardin MRA], Roughly bounded by 4th, Crook, Burlington Northern RR, 1st and Crow Sts., Hardin, 8/14/85, A, C, 85001845

Custer Battlefield National Monument, 15 mi. S of Hardin, Hardin vicinity, 10/15/66, A, B, d, f, NPS, 66000428

Drew, J. W., Grain Elevator [Lodge Grass MRA], E side of Main St., Lodge Grass, 8/03/87, C, 87001274

Ebeling, William, House [Hardin MPS], 704 N. Crow Ave., Hardin, 4/11/91, C, 91000370

Eder, Charles S., House [Hardin MPS], 416 W. Third St., Hardin, 4/11/91, B, C, 91000374

First Baptist Church [Hardin MPS], 524 N. Custer Ave., Hardin, 4/11/91, C, a, 91000369

Fort C. F. Smith Historic District, E of Fort Smith in Bighorn Canyon National Recreation Area, Fort Smith vicinity, 10/10/75, A, NPS, 75000163

Haverfield Hospital [Hardin MPS], 520 W. Third St., Hardin, 4/11/91, A, B, C, b, 91000376

Kopriva, Francis, House [Hardin MPS], 416 Crawford Ave., Hardin, 4/11/91, C, 91000377

Lee Homestead, NE of Decker, Decker vicinity, 7/08/81, A, B, 81000659

Lodge Grass City Jail [Lodge Grass MRA], Alley S of Third Ave., Lodge Grass, 8/03/87, A, 87001276

Lodge Grass Merchandise Company Store [Lodge Grass MRA], First Ave., Lodge Grass, 8/03/87, A, B, C, 87001275

OW Ranch, Roughly 15 mi. S of Birney on Hanging Woman Cr., Birney vicinity, 12/15/92, A, C, 92001321

Pease's, George, Second Store [Lodge Grass MRA], 8 N. Main St., Lodge Grass, 8/03/87, A, B, 87001278

Ping, J. J., House [Hardin MPS], 119 W. Sixth St., Hardin, 4/11/91, B, C, 91000373

Reno Apartments [Hardin MPS], 719 N. Custer Ave., Hardin, 4/11/91, A, C, 91000378

Residential District [Hardin MRA], Roughly bounded by 5th, 4th, Crow and Cody, Hardin, 8/14/85, A, C, 85001846

Ryan's, John, House [Lodge Grass MRA], 15 N. Helen St., Lodge Grass, 8/03/87, B, 87001277

Sharp's, Jay, Store [Lodge Grass MRA], 18 Helen St., Lodge Grass, 8/03/87, B, C, 87001279

Simmonsen's House [Lodge Grass MRA], 4 S. George St., Lodge Grass, 8/03/87, C, 87001273

St. Joseph Catholic Church [Hardin MPS], 710 N. Custer Ave., Hardin, 4/11/91, C, a, 91000379

St. Xavier Mission Church and Rectory, On Big Horn River in the Crow Indian Reservation, St. Xavier, 8/17/90, A, a, b, 90001214

Stevens, Dominic, House [Lodge Grass MRA], 10 W. Hester Ave., Lodge Grass, 8/03/87, A, C, 87001280

Sullivan Rooming House [Hardin MPS], 217 W. Sixth St., Hardin, 4/11/91, C, 91000372

Sullivan, James J., House [Hardin MPS], 220 W. Third St., Hardin, 4/11/91, C, 91000380

Trytten, J. M., House [Lodge Grass MRA], George St., Lodge Grass, 8/03/87, C, 87001281

Tupper, J. S., House [Hardin MPS], 502 N. Cody, Hardin, 4/11/91, C, 91000381

Blaine County

Chief Joseph Battleground of the Bear's Paw, About 15 mi. S of Chinook, T 30N R 19E, Sections 1 and 12, Chinook vicinity, 10/06/70, A, B, NHL, 70000355

Lohman Block, 239-225 Indiana St., Chinook, 3/19/80, B, C, 80002399

Broadwater County

McCormick's Livery and Feed Stable Sign, W of Townsend, Townsend vicinity, 7/08/81, A, 81000339

Rankin Ranch, 2 1/2 mi. NE of the Helena-Diamond City Rd., Avalanche Gulch, 5/11/76, B, g, NHL, 76001119

State Bank of Townsend, 400 Broadway, Townsend, 1/13/92, A, C, 91001941

Carbon County

Bad Pass Trail, E of Warren along Big Horn River in Bighorn Canyon National Recreation Area, Warren vicinity, 10/29/75, A, D, NPS, 75000215

Baker and Lovering Store [Joliet Montana MRA], Main St., Joliet, 5/02/86, A, C, 86000885

Baldwin Building [Fromberg MPS], Jct. of W. River St. and Harley Ave., Fromberg, 1/28/93, A, C, 92001777

Benson, Dr. Theodore J., House [Fromberg MPS], 10 N. Montana, Fromberg, 1/28/93, A, B, 92001780

Blewett, John, House [Fromberg MPS], 2411 E. River St., Fromberg, 1/28/93, A, B, C, 92001789

Bridger Coal Company House [Bridger MRA], 307 W. Broadway, Bridger, 9/15/87, C, b, 87001215

Bridger Opera House [Bridger MRA], E. Broadway, Bridger, 9/15/87, A, C, 87001217

Brooder, Frank, House [Fromberg MPS], 303 North St., Fromberg, 1/28/93, A, C, 92001787

Calvary Episcopal Church, 9 N. Villard Ave., Red Lodge, 10/23/86, C, a, 86002928

Camp Senia Historic District, Custer National Forest, Red Lodge vicinity, 4/14/88, A, B, C, 88000441

Cedarvale, Present town of Hillsboro and its environs in Bighorn Canyon National Recreation Area, Hillsboro vicinity, 8/19/75, B, NPS, 75000161

Corey House [Bridger MRA], 106 N. E St., Bridger, 7/21/87, C, 87001219

Demijohn Flat Archeological District, Address Restricted, Bridger vicinity, 11/20/74, D, 74001092

Carbon County—Continued

Ewing-Snell Ranch, S of Dryhead, Dryhead vicinity, 5/12/77, A, NPS, 77000114

Fire Hall [Joliet Montana MRA], Main St., Joliet, 5/02/86, A, C, b, 86000884

Forsman House [Bridger MRA], 406 E. Carbon Ave., Bridger, 7/21/87, C, 87001233

Fromberg Concrete Arch Bridge [Fromberg MPS], River St. over the Clarks Fork of the Yellowstone R., Fromberg, 1/28/93, C, 92001790

Fromberg High School [Fromberg MPS], Kids Ct., Fromberg, 1/28/93, A, C, 92001788

Fromberg Methodist—Episcopal Church [Fromberg MPS], Jct. of N. Montana Ave. and School St., Fromberg, 1/28/93, A, C, 92001781

Fromberg Opera House [Fromberg MPS], Jct. of Harley Ave. and C St., Fromberg, 1/28/93, A, 92001779

Gebo Cemetery, Co Rd. linking Gebo and Fromberg, Fromberg vicinity, 4/08/93, A, d, 93000291

Gebo, Henry, House [Bridger MRA], E of Bridger, Bridger, 7/21/87, C, 87001234

Gibson, John, House [Fromberg MPS], 219 W. River St., Fromberg, 1/28/93, B, C, 92001785

Glidden House [Bridger MRA], 112 N. E St., Bridger, 7/21/87, C, 87001236

Glidden Mercantile [Bridger MRA], 102 N. Main, Bridger, 9/15/87, A, B, C, 87001237

Greenblatt, Samuel, House [Fromberg MPS], 215 W. River St., Fromberg, 1/28/93, A, B, C, 92001784

Heatherington Boarding House [Bridger MRA], 209 E. Broadway, Bridger, 9/15/87, A, 87001240

Hi Bug Historic District, Roughly bounded by W. Third St., N. Villard Ave., W. Eighth St., and N. Word Ave., Red Lodge, 7/23/86, A, C, 86001932

Hough, Raymond, House [Bridger MRA], 312 S. Second, Bridger, 9/15/87, B, C, 87001242

House on Railroad Avenue [Joliet Montana MRA], Railroad Ave., Joliet, 5/02/86, C, 86000889

IOOF Hall and Fromberg Co-operative Mercantile Building [Fromberg MPS], 123 W. River St., Fromberg, 1/28/93, A, C, 92001778

Joliet Bridge [Joliet Montana MRA], Carries Main St. over Rock Creek, Joliet vicinity, 5/02/86, A, 86000888

Joliet High School [Joliet Montana MRA], Main St., Joliet, 5/02/86, A, 86000887

Joliet Residential Historic District [Joliet Montana MRA], Roughly bounded by Northern Pacific RR and US 12, State St., Carbon Ave., and Second St., Joliet, 5/02/86, A, C, a, 86000892

Lockhart, Caroline, Ranch, Davis Creek, 70 mi. S of Hardin, Dead Hill, 11/03/89, B, C, NPS, 89000155

Marcus, Dr. Carl, House [Bridger MRA], 210 S. Second, Bridger, 9/15/87, C, 87001243

McCall, Tracy, House [Fromberg MPS], 110 N. Montana Ave., Fromberg, 1/28/93, A, C, 92001782

Methodist Episcopal Church and Parsonage [Bridger MRA], 220 W. Broadway, Bridger, 9/15/87, A, C, a, 87001244

Northern Pacific Railroad Depot—Fromberg [Fromberg MPS], Jct. of US 310 and River St., Fromberg, 1/28/93, A, C, b, 92001776

Nutting Rental [Bridger MRA], Carbon Ave., Bridger, 9/15/87, A, 87001245

Petroglyph Canyon, Address Restricted, Warren vicinity, 11/20/75, C, D, 75001079

Pretty Creek Archeological Site, Address Restricted, Hardin vicinity, 1/17/75, D, NPS, 75000162

Rahrer, Francis, House [Fromberg MPS], 309 School St., Fromberg, 1/28/93, C, 92001786

Red Lodge Commercial Historic District, Roughly Broadway from 8th to 13th Sts., Red Lodge, 4/14/83, C, g, 83001057

Red Lodge Commercial Historic District (Boundary Increase), Roughly Broadway from 8th to 13th Sts., Red Lodge, 5/31/84, A, C, 84002456

Red Lodge Commercial Historic District (Boundary Increase), S. Broadway between Eighth and Fifteenth Sts., Red Lodge, 8/28/86, C, 86001904

Rock Creek State Bank [Joliet Montana MRA], Main St., Joliet, 5/02/86, A, C, 86000890

Smith, T. W., House [Joliet Montana MRA], Front St., Joliet, 5/02/86, A, C, 86000886

Southern Hotel [Joliet Montana MRA], Main St., Joliet, 5/02/86, A, C, 86000891

Suydam, Hester E., Boarding House [Fromberg MPS], 209 W. River St., Fromberg, 1/28/93, A, C, 92001783

Warila Boarding House and Sauna, 20 N. Haggin, Red Lodge, 10/24/85, A, C, 85003382

Wool Warehouse [Bridger MRA], E. Bridger, Bridger, 7/21/87, A, 87001246

Cascade County

Adam's, J. C., Stone Barn, NE of Sun River off U.S. 81, Sun River vicinity, 1/12/79, A, B, C, 79001399

Arvon Block, 114–116 First Ave. S., Great Falls, 9/26/91, A, C, 91001446

Belt Jail, Castner St., Belt, 3/10/80, A, 80002400

Burlingame School [Korpivaara MPS], Address Restricted, Belt vicinity, 6/01/92, A, C, a, 92000575

Cascade County Courthouse, 415 2nd Ave., N., Great Falls, 4/16/80, C, 80002401

Chicago, Milwaukee and St. Paul Passenger Depot, River Dr., N, Great Falls, 10/13/88, A, C, 88001119

Collins, Timothy Edwards, Mansion, 1003–1017 2nd Ave., NW, Great Falls, 8/27/80, C, 80002402

Crocker—Jarvi Homestead [Korpivaara MPS], Address Restricted, Belt vicinity, 6/01/92, A, C, 92000572

Ford, Lee M., House, 401 4th Ave. N., Great Falls, 8/10/90, C, 90001215

Fort Shaw Historic District and Cemetery, 1 mi. NW of Town of Fort Shaw, Fort Shaw vicinity, 1/11/85, A, C, d, 85000065

Great Falls Central High School, 1400 1st Ave., N., Great Falls, 9/01/76, B, C, 76001120

Great Falls Northside Residential Historic District, 200–900 blocks 4th Ave. N., 100–900 blocks 3rd

Ave. N. and 500–900 blocks 2nd Ave. N., Great Falls, 4/01/91, A, B, C, 91000355

Great Falls Portage, SE of Great Falls at jct. of U.S. 87, 89, and 91, Great Falls vicinity, 10/15/66, A, NHL, 66000429

Great Falls Railroad Historic District, Park and River Drs., 100–400 blks. 2nd St. S., 100–200 blks. 1st and 2nd Aves. S. and 100–300 blks. 3rd St. S., Great Falls, 2/19/93, A, B, C, 93000038

Heikkila—Mattila Homestead [Korpivaara MPS], Address Restricted, Belt vicinity, 6/01/92, A, C, 92000573

Kraftenberg Homestead [Korpivaara MPS], Address Restricted, Belt vicinity, 6/01/92, A, C, 92000574

Lewis—Nevala Homestead [Korpivaara MPS], Address Restricted, Belt vicinity, 6/01/92, A, C, 92000576

Margaret Block, 413-415 Central Ave., Great Falls, 8/02/84, B, C, 84002447

Mullan Road, N of Great Falls in Benton Lake National Wildlife Refuge, Great Falls vicinity, 3/13/75, A, 75001080

Northern Montana State Fairground Historic District, 3rd St., NW, Great Falls, 1/13/89, A, C, 88003143

Randall, Harry E., House, 1003 Fourth Ave. N, Great Falls, 3/27/86, C, 86000583

Roberts Building, 520–526 Central Ave., Great Falls, 9/12/85, B, 85002165

Russell, Charles M., House and Studio, 1217–1219 4th Ave., N., Great Falls, 10/15/66, B, NHL, 66000430

St. Peter's Mission Church and Cemetery, W of Cascade, Cascade vicinity, 8/03/84, A, C, a, 84002452

Stone Homestead [Korpivaara MPS], Address Restricted, Belt vicinity, 6/01/92, A, C, 92000577

US Post Office and Courthouse—Great Falls [US Post Offices in Montana, 1900–1941, TR], 215 First Ave. N, Great Falls, 3/14/86, A, C, 86000681

Ulm Pishkun, Address Restricted, Ulm vicinity, 12/17/74, D, 74001093

Ursuline Academy, 2300 Central Ave., Great Falls, 9/26/91, A, C, a, 91001447

Vaughn, Robert, Homestead, Vaughn Cemetery Rd. (Cascade County Rd.), Vaughn vicinity, 6/14/82, A, B, 82003160

Wargelin—Warila Homestead [Korpivaara MPS], Address Restricted, Belt vicinity, 6/01/92, A, C, b, g, 92000578

Chouteau County

Baker, I. G., House, 1604 Front St., Fort Benton, 11/20/80, B, 80002403

Chouteau County Courthouse, 1308 Franklin St., Fort Benton, 9/29/80, A, C, 80002404

Citadel Rock, E of Fort Benton, Fort Benton vicinity, 11/13/74, A, B, 74001095

Fort Benton, Fort Benton, Fort Benton, 10/15/66, A, C, NHL, 66000431

Fort Benton Bridge, Spans Missouri River, Fort Benton, 8/06/80, A, C, 80002406

Chouteau County—Continued

Fort Benton Engine House, Front and 15th Sts., Fort Benton, 11/20/80, A, 80002407

Grand Union Hotel, 14th and Front Sts., Fort Benton, 1/02/76, A, C, 76001121

Judith Landing Historic District, Address Restricted, Winifred vicinity, 12/06/75, A, B, C, D, a, b, 75001081

Lewis and Clark Camp at Slaughter River, 40 mi. S of Big Sandy River on Missouri River, Big Sandy vicinity, 12/16/74, A, 74001094

Lonetree, S of Geraldine, Geraldine vicinity, 9/11/80, A, 80002410

Masonic Building, 1418 Front St., Fort Benton, 10/14/80, A, C, 80002408

St. Paul's Episcopal Church, 14th and Chouteau Sts., Fort Benton, 9/29/80, A, C, a, 80002409

Teton River Crossing on the Whoop-Up Trail [Whoop-Up Trail of Northcentral Montana MPS], Address Restricted, Carter vicinity, 4/15/93, A, 93000275

Custer County

Carriage House Historic District, Roughly bounded by Main, N. 9th, Palmer, N. 10th, Orr and N. 13th Sts. and Montana Ave., Miles City, 6/07/91, A, C, 91000720

East Main Street Residential Historic District, 1600–2315 E. Main St., Miles City, 1/10/90, A, B, C, 89002171

Fort Keogh, 2.5 mi. (4 km) SW of Miles City, Miles City vicinity, 3/08/78, A, C, 78001680

Harmon, William, House, 1005 Palmer, Miles City, 9/25/86, B, C, 86002747

Main Street Historic District, Roughly Main St. from Prairie Ave. to Fourth St., Miles City, 7/21/89, A, C, a, b, g, 89000808

Miles City Steam Laundry, 800 Bridge St., Miles City, 7/05/79, B, 79001400

Miles City Waterworks Building and Pumping Plant Park, W of Miles City on Pumping Plant Rd., Miles City vicinity, 9/26/79, C, 79003723

Miles, George M., House, 28 S. Lake St., Miles City, 2/17/82, B, C, 82003161

Mountain States Telephone and Telegraph Company, 908 Main St., Miles City, 7/21/88, A, C, 88001118

Olive Hotel, 501 Main St., Miles City, 10/13/88, A, C, 88001117

US Post Office—Miles City Main [US Post Offices in Montana, 1900–1941, TR], 106 N. Seventh St., Miles City, 3/14/86, A, C, 86000686

Ursuline Convent of the Sacred Heart, 1411 Leighton Blvd., Miles City, 3/05/92, A, C, a, 92000115

Dawson County

Bell Street Bridge [Glendive MRA], W. Bell St., Glendive, 2/03/88, A, C, 87002517

Blackstock Residence [Glendive MRA], 217 W. Towne, Glendive, 2/03/88, C, 87002515

First Methodist Episcopal Church and Parsonage [Glendive MRA], 209 N. Kendrick, Glendive, 2/03/88, C, a, 87002513

Glendive City Water Filtration Plant [Glendive MRA], 420 W. Bell St., Glendive, 2/03/88, A, 87002512

Glendive Heat, Light and Power Company Power Plant [Glendive MRA], Clough St., Glendive, 2/03/88, A, g, 87002511

Hagen Site, Address Restricted, Glendive vicinity, 10/15/66, D, NHL, 66000432

Krug, Charles, House, 103 N. Douglas St., Glendive, 6/03/76, B, C, 76001122

McCone Residence [Glendive MRA], 218 W. Towne, Glendive, 2/03/88, B, 87002509

Merrill Avenue Historic District [Glendive MRA], W side of Merrill Ave. between S. Douglas St. and W. Clement St., E side of Merrill Ave. between W. Towne and W. Clement, Glendive, 2/03/88, A, B, C, 87002508

Northern Pacific Railroad Settling Tanks [Glendive MRA], Towne and Clough Sts., Glendive, 2/03/88, A, b, 87002507

Sacred Heart Church [Glendive MRA], 316 W. Benham, Glendive, 2/03/88, C, a, 87002504

US Post Office [Glendive MRA], 221 N. Kendrick, Glendive, 2/03/88, A, C, 87002503

Deer Lodge County

Anaconda Copper Mining Company Smoke Stack, Anaconda Copper Smelter, Anaconda, 4/09/87, A, C, 87000607

Ancient Order of Hibernians Hall, 321–323 E. Commercial, Anaconda, 8/10/79, A, C, 79003721

Barich Block, 416-420 E. Park St., Anaconda, 1/19/83, A, C, 83001058

Butte, Anaconda and Pacific Railway Historic District, Right-of-way begins in Butte and travels to Anaconda, generally along course of Silver Bow Creek, Anaconda, 10/13/88, A, B, C, 88001111

City Hall, 401 E. Commercial, Anaconda, 8/10/79, C, 79003722

Club Moderne, 811 E. Park, Anaconda, 8/14/86, C, g, 86001498

Davidson Building, 301-303 E. Park St., Anaconda, 1/19/83, A, C, 83001059

Deer Lodge County Courthouse, U.S. 10, Anaconda, 12/29/78, C, 78001681

Hearst Free Library, Main and 4th Sts., Anaconda, 6/04/73, C, 73001051

St. Mark's Episcopal Church, 601 Main St., Anaconda, 12/29/78, A, a, 78001682

US Post Office—Anaconda Main [US Post Offices in Montana, 1900–1941, TR], 218 Main St., Anaconda, 3/14/86, A, C, 86000677

Washoe Theater, 305 Main St., Anaconda, 4/30/82, A, C, 82003162

Fergus County

Anderson House [Stone Buildings in Lewistown MPS], 1015 W. Watson, Lewistown, 1/27/93, C, 92001770

Ayers House [Lewistown MRA], 316 Eighth Ave. S, Lewistown, 1/10/86, C, 86000061

Bright House [Stone Buildings in Lewistown MPS], 707 W. Boulevard, Lewistown, 1/27/93, C, 92001766

Clark-Cardwell House [Lewistown MRA], 523 W. Watson, Lewistown, 1/10/86, C, 86000063

Culver Studio, 212 5th Ave., Lewistown, 8/11/80, B, 80002412

Fergus County High School [Lewistown MRA], 412 6th Ave., S., Lewistown, 6/27/85, C, 85001409

Fergus County Improvement Corporation Dormitory, 216 7th St., S., Lewistown, 2/01/80, A, C, 80002413

First Presbyterian Church [Lewistown MRA], 215 Fifth Ave. S, Lewistown, 1/10/86, C, a, 86000065

House at 301 Eighth Avenue, South [Lewistown MRA], 301 Eighth Ave. S, Lewistown, 1/10/86, C, 86000066

House at 324 W. Corcoran [Stone Buildings in Lewistown MPS], 324 W. Corcoran, Lewistown, 1/27/93, C, 92001773

House at 618 West Janeaux [Lewistown MRA], 618 W. Janeaux, Lewistown, 1/10/86, C, 86000062

House at 805 W. Watson [Stone Buildings in Lewistown MPS], 805 W. Watson, Lewistown, 1/27/93, C, 92001767

House at 809 W. Watson [Stone Buildings in Lewistown MPS], 809 W. Watson, Lewistown, 1/27/93, C, 92001768

House at 813 W. Watson [Stone Buildings in Lewistown MPS], 813 W. Watson, Lewistown, 1/27/93, C, 92001769

Huntoon Residence [Lewistown MRA], 722 W. Water, Lewistown, 6/27/85, C, 85001408

Judith Place Historic District, Roughly bounded by Main St., the alley between Hawthorne andRidgelawn Sts., Washington St., and Oullette St., Lewistown, 5/04/88, A, C, 88000465

Lewis House [Stone Buildings in Lewistown MPS], 702 W. Boulevard, Lewistown, 1/27/93, C, 92001765

Lewistown Carnegie Library, 701 W. Main St., Lewistown, 8/11/80, A, C, 80002411

Lewistown Central Business Historic District [Lewistown MRA], Roughly bounded by Washington St., 1st Ave., Janeaux St., and 8th Ave., Lewistown, 6/27/85, A, C, 85001405

Lewistown Courthouse Historic District [Lewistown MRA], Roughly bounded by Washington St., 6th Ave., Main and Broadway Sts., Lewistown, 6/27/85, A, C, 85001406

Lewistown Mercantile Company [Lewistown MRA], 220 E. Main, Lewistown, 2/03/86, A, C, 86000064

Lewistown Silk Stocking District [Lewistown MRA], Roughly bounded by 2nd Ave., Boule-

Fergus County—Continued

vard and Washington Sts. and 3rd Ave., Lewistown, 6/27/85, A, C, 85001407

Masonic Temple, 322 W. Broadway St., Lewistown, 7/03/79, A, C, 79001401

Mill House [Stone Buildings in Lewistown MPS], MT 466 4.5 mi. SE of Lewistown, along Spring Cr., Lewistown vicinity, 1/27/93, A, C, 92001764

N-Bar Ranch, 15 mi. SW of Grass Range, Grass Range vicinity, 7/09/91, A, 91000881

Rocky Point, 30 mi. S of Landusky in Charles M. Russell National Wildlife, Landusky vicinity, 5/21/75, A, 75001082

Schroeder Hospital [Stone Buildings in Lewistown MPS], 502 Fifth Ave. S., Lewistown, 1/27/93, C, 92001771

St. James Episcopal Church and Parish House, 502 W. Montana St., Lewistown, 11/16/78, A, C, a, 78001683

St. Joseph's Hospital, U.S. 87, Lewistown, 9/13/78, A, C, b, 78001684

St. Leo's Catholic Church, 124 W. Broadway, Lewistown, 5/06/82, A, C, a, 82003163

US Post Office and Federal Building—Lewistown [US Post Offices in Montana, 1900–1941, TR], 204 Third Ave. N, Lewistown, 3/14/86, A, C, 86000684

Flathead County

Adair, W. L., General Mercantile Historic District, On Polebridge Loop Rd. 1/4 mi. E of its intersection with N. Fork Rd., Polebridge, 2/06/86, A, B, 86000155

Apgar Fire Lookout [Glacier National Park MRA], Near Lake McDonald, West Glacier vicinity, 12/16/86, A, C, NPS, 86003695

Belly River Ranger Station Historic District [Glacier National Park MRA], Head of Belly River Valley, West Glacier vicinity, 2/14/86, A, C, NPS, 86000329

Belton Chalets, U.S. 2, West Glacier, 11/15/78, A, C, 78001685

Bowman Lake Patrol Cabin [Glacier National Park MRA], Lower end of Bowman Lake 1/2 mi. E of Bowman Lake Ranger Station, West Glacier vicinity, 2/14/86, A, C, NPS, 86000340

Bull Head Lodge and Studio, Off Going-to-the-Sun-Rd., Apgar, 2/06/84, B, 84002465

Conrad, Charles E., Mansion, 313 6th Ave., E., Kalispell, 2/20/75, B, C, 75001083

Cornelius Hedges Elementary School, 827 4th Ave. East, Kalispell, 6/29/89, C, 89000765

Dean, A. J., House, 244 Woodland Ave., Kalispell, 8/11/80, C, b, 80002415

East Glacier Ranger Station Historic District [Glacier National Park MRA], 3/4 mi. N of East Glacier Park on MT 49, West Glacier vicinity, 12/16/86, A, C, NPS, 86003696

Fielding Snowshoe Patrol Cabin [Glacier National Park MRA], Off US 2, West Glacier, 2/14/86, A, NPS, 86000341

Ford Creek Patrol Cabin [Glacier National Park MRA], Rt. 7, West Glacier vicinity, 2/14/86, A, C, NPS, 86000342

Granite Park Chalet, Glacier National Park, West Glacier vicinity, 6/27/83, C, NHL, NPS, 83001060

Great Northern Railway Buildings, Glacier National Park, Glacier National Park, 5/28/87, A, C, NHL, NPS, 87001453

Gunsight Pass Shelter [Glacier National Park MRA], Jct. of Gunsight Pass Trail and the Continental Divide, West Glacier vicinity, 2/14/86, A, C, NPS, 86000344

Heaven's Peak Fire Lookout [Glacier National Park MRA], Mount Cannon, West Glacier vicinity, 12/19/86, A, C, g, NPS, 86003688

Heller Building, 140 Main St., Kalispell, 3/22/91, A, C, 91000332

Hornet Lookout, Hornet Mountain, Flathead National Forest vicinity, 8/19/83, A, C, 83001061

Huckleberry Fire Outlook [Glacier National Park MRA], Summit of Huckleberry Mt., West Glacier vicinity, 2/14/86, A, C, NPS, 86000346

Izaak Walton Inn, Off US 2 adjacent to RR in Essex, Essex, 10/18/85, A, g, 85003235

Keith, Harry C., House, 538 Fifth Ave. E, Kalispell, 7/16/87, C, 87001198

Kintla Lake Ranger Station [Glacier National Park MRA], S shore of Kintla Lake, West Glacier vicinity, 2/14/86, A, C, NPS, 86000332

Kishenehn Ranger Station Historic District [Glacier National Park MRA], 3 mi. S of Canadian-US border near the intersection of the N fork of the Flathead River and Kishenehn Creek, West Glacier vicinity, 2/14/86, A, C, NPS, 86000335

Lake McDonald Lodge, Off Going to the Sun Rd., West Glacier, 5/28/87, C, NHL, NPS, 87001447

Lewis Glacier Hotel, N of West Glacier, West Glacier vicinity, 5/22/78, A, C, g, NPS, 78000280

Logan Creek Patrol Cabin [Glacier National Park MRA], E side of Going-to-the-Sun Hwy. at Logan Creek crossing, West Glacier vicinity, 2/14/86, A, C, NPS, 86000348

Logging Creek Ranger Station Historic District [Glacier National Park MRA], Glacier Rt. 7 near Logging Creek, West Glacier vicinity, 12/16/86, A, C, NPS, 86003697

Loneman Fire Lookout [Glacier National Park MRA], Access via Loneman Mountain Trail, West Glacier vicinity, 2/14/86, A, C, NPS, 86000353

Lower Logging Lake Snowshoe Cabin [Glacier National Park MRA], Near foot of Logging Lake, West Glacier vicinity, 12/16/86, A, C, NPS, 86003692

Lower Nyack Snowshoe Cabin [Glacier National Park MRA], W side of Nyack Creek Trail, West Glacier vicinity, 2/14/86, A, C, NPS, 86000356

Lower Park Creek Patrol Cabin [Glacier National Park MRA], E side of Park Creek Trail past crossing of Fielding-Coal Creek Trail, West Glacier vicinity, 12/16/86, A, C, NPS, 86003701

McCarthy Homestead Cabin [Glacier National Park MRA], On the N fork of the Flathead River, West Glacier vicinity, 12/16/86, A, NPS, 86003691

McCarthy, Margaret, Homestead [Settlement on the North Fork of the Flathead River, Glacier National Park TR], Glacier National Park, Big Prairie vicinity, 7/21/88, A, NPS, 88001095

Miller, J. K., Homestead [Settlement on the North Fork of the Flathead River, Glacier National Park TR], Glacier National Park, Big Prairie vicinity, 7/21/88, A, C, NPS, 88001092

Mount Brown Fire Lookout [Glacier National Park MRA], Off Rt. 1 near Snyder Lake, West Glacier vicinity, 12/16/86, A, C, NPS, 86003693

Numa Ridge Fire Lookout [Glacier National Park MRA], Near Bowman Lake, West Glacier vicinity, 2/14/86, A, C, NPS, 86000357

Nyack Ranger Station Barn and Fire Cache [Glacier National Park MRA], Nyack Ranger Station, West Glacier vicinity, 2/14/86, C, NPS, 86000359

Pass Creek Snowshoe Cabin [Glacier National Park MRA], Confluence of Waterton River and Pass Creek, West Glacier vicinity, 12/19/86, A, C, g, NPS, 86003689

Polebridge Ranger Station Historic District [Glacier National Park MRA], Near the NE end of Henshaw Bridge on Rte. 7, West Glacier vicinity, 2/14/86, A, C, NPS, 86000337

Ptarmigan Tunnel [Glacier National Park MRA], N of Ptarmigan Lake, West Glacier vicinity, 2/14/86, A, C, NPS, 86000360

Quartz Lake Patrol Cabin [Glacier National Park MRA], Foot of Quartz Lake, West Glacier vicinity, 2/14/86, A, C, NPS, 86000361

Raftery, William, Homestead [Settlement on the North Fork of the Flathead River, Glacier National Park TR], Glacier National Park, Big Prairie vicinity, 7/21/88, A, NPS, 88001099

Ringleberg, Cornelius, House, 1028 Third Ave. W, Kalispell, 1/22/87, C, 86003673

Saint Mary Ranger Station [Glacier National Park MRA], E end of Upper Saint Mary Lake, West Glacier vicinity, 2/14/86, A, C, NPS, 86000367

Scalplock Mountain Fire Lookout [Glacier National Park MRA], Accessible by trail connecting to Boundary Trail near Walton Ranger Station, West Glacier vicinity, 2/14/86, A, C, NPS, 86000363

Schoenberger, Anton, Homestead [Settlement on the North Fork of the Flathead River, Glacier National Park TR], Glacier National Park, Big Prairie vicinity, 7/21/88, A, NPS, 88001094

Schoenberger, Charlie, Homestead [Settlement on the North Fork of the Flathead River, Glacier National Park TR], Glacier National Park, Big Prairie vicinity, 7/21/88, A, B, C, NPS, 88001093

Sherburne Ranger Station Historic District [Glacier National Park MRA], Glacier Rt. 3 near Glacier Entrance, West Glacier vicinity, 12/16/86, A, C, NPS, 86003698

Skyland Camp—Bowman Lake Ranger Station [Glacier National Park MRA], SW shore of Bowman Lake, West Glacier vicinity, 2/14/86, A, C, NPS, 86000365

Slide Lake-Otatso Creek Patrol Cabin and Woodshed [Glacier National Park MRA], N side of Otatso Creek, West Glacier vicinity, 2/14/86, A, NPS, 86000370

Flathead County—Continued

Sperry Chalets, E of West Glacier, West Glacier vicinity, 8/02/77, A, C, NHL, NPS, 77000115

St. Richard's Church, 505 W. 4th Ave., Columbia Falls, 3/19/80, A, C, a, 80002414

Stillwater Ranger Station Historic District, U.S. 93, Olney vicinity, 7/08/81, A, 81000340

Swiftcurrent Fire Lookout [Glacier National Park MRA], Near the Continental Garden Wall in vicinity of Swiftcurrent Mountain, West Glacier vicinity, 12/16/86, A, C, NPS, 86003694

Swiftcurrent Ranger Station Historic District [Glacier National Park MRA], Off Rt. 3 near Swiftcurrent Lake, West Glacier vicinity, 12/19/86, A, C, g, NPS, 86003690

Taylor, Ray E., House, 900 S. Baker Ave., Whitefish, 8/10/90, C, 90001204

Two Medicine General Store [Glacier National Park MRA], E shore of Two Medicine Lake, West Glacier vicinity, 2/14/86, A, C, NHL, NPS, 86000372

Upper Kintla Lake Patrol Cabin [Glacier National Park MRA], Head of Kintla Lake, West Glacier vicinity, 2/14/86, A, C, NPS, 86000374

Upper Lake McDonald Ranger Station Historic District [Glacier National Park MRA], N shore Lake McDonald, West Glacier vicinity, 12/16/86, A, C, NPS, 86003699

Upper Logging Lake Snowshoe Cabin [Glacier National Park MRA], Near head of Logging Lake, West Glacier vicinity, 2/14/86, A, C, NPS, 86000376

Upper Nyack Snowshoe Cabin [Glacier National Park MRA], N side of Nyack Creek, West Glacier vicinity, 2/14/86, A, C, NPS, 86000377

Upper Park Creek Patrol Cabin [Glacier National Park MRA], Jct. of Park Creek and Two Medicine Pass Trails, West Glacier vicinity, 12/16/86, A, C, NPS, 86003702

Walsh's, Johnnie, Guest Lodge [Settlement on the North Fork of the Flathead River, Glacier National Park TR], Glacier National Park, Big Prairie vicinity, 7/21/88, C, b, NPS, 88001096

Walsh, Johnnie, Homestead [Settlement on the North Fork of the Flathead River, Glacier National Park TR], Glacier National Park, Big Prairie vicinity, 7/21/88, A, NPS, 88001098

Walton Ranger Station Historic District [Glacier National Park MRA], US 2 near Essex, West Glacier vicinity, 12/16/86, A, C, NPS, 86003700

Gallatin County

Anderson School [One Room Schoolhouses of Gallatin County TR], E of Gallatin Gateway, Gallatin Gateway vicinity, 7/21/81, A, C, 81000354

Barnett, R. T., and Company Building, 13 E. Main St., Bozeman, 12/01/80, A, C, 80002416

Beall Park Community Center [Bozeman MRA], 409 N. Bozeman, Bozeman, 10/23/87, C, 87001807

Belgrade City Hall and Jail, Broadway at Northern Pacific Blvd., Belgrade, 10/25/82, A, C, 82000592

Blackmore Apartments, 120 S. Black St., Bozeman, 7/07/83, A, C, 83001062

Bohart House [Bozeman MRA], 510 N. Church, Bozeman, 10/23/87, C, 87001810

Bon Ton Historic District [Bozeman MRA], Roughly bounded by Olive St., Willson Ave., Cleveland St., & Fourth Ave., Bozeman, 10/23/87, A, C, 87001816

Bozeman Armory [Bozeman MRA], 24 W. Mendenhall, Bozeman, 10/22/87, A, C, g, 87001800

Bozeman Brewery Historic District [Bozeman MRA], 700–800 N. Wallace Ave., Bozeman, 10/23/87, A, C, 87001844

Bozeman Carnegie Library, 35 N. Bozeman Ave., Bozeman, 2/02/79, A, C, 79001402

Bozeman National Fish Hatchery, 4050 Bridger Canyon Rd., Bozeman, 1/06/83, A, C, 83001063

Bozeman Sheet Metal Works [Bozeman MRA], 26 S. Grand, Bozeman, 10/23/87, C, 87001836

Bozeman YMCA [Bozeman MRA], 6 W. Babcock, Bozeman, 10/23/87, A, C, 87001819

Brandenburg House [Bozeman MRA], 122 W. Lamme, Bozeman, 10/23/87, C, 87001804

Bridger Arms Apartments [Bozeman MRA], 103–111 S. Fourth Ave., Bozeman, 10/23/87, A, C, 87001799

Busch House [Bozeman MRA], 224 N. Church, Bozeman, 10/23/87, C, 87001805

Buttelman Ranch [Willow Creek Area MPS], Address Restricted, Willow Creek vicinity, 4/19/93, A, B, C, 93000309

Colburn House [Bozeman MRA], 607 W. Lamme, Bozeman, 10/23/87, C, 87001813

Cooper Park Historic District [Bozeman MRA], 200–700 blks. S. Fifth, Sixth, Seventh, Eighth, & Cross Sts., Bozeman, 10/23/87, A, C, 87001845

Cottonwood School [One Room Schoolhouses of Gallatin County TR], SE of Gallatin Gateway, Gallatin Gateway vicinity, 7/21/81, A, C, 81000356

Crail Ranch Buildings, Meadow Village, Gallatin Gateway vicinity, 4/15/82, A, C, 82003167

Dokken—Nelson Funeral Home [Bozeman MRA], 113 S. Willson, Bozeman, 12/21/87, C, 87001833

Dry Creek School [One Room Schoolhouses of Gallatin County TR], E of Manhattan, Manhattan vicinity, 7/21/81, A, C, 81000360

Eagle's Store [West Yellowstone MRA], 3 Canyon St., West Yellowstone, 11/06/86, C, 86002957

Emerson School [Bozeman MRA], 111 S. Grand Ave., Bozeman, 8/10/90, A, C, 90001212

First Baptist Church [Bozeman MRA], 120 S. Grand, Bozeman, 10/23/87, A, C, a, 87001803

First Presbyterian Church [Bozeman MRA], 26 W. Babcock, Bozeman, 12/21/87, A, C, a, 87001820

Fisher, Burr, House, 712 S. Willson Ave., Bozeman, 3/28/85, C, 85000643

Gallatin County Courthouse [Bozeman MRA], 301 W. Main, Bozeman, 12/21/87, A, C, 87001794

Gallatin County High School [Bozeman MRA], 404 W. Main, Bozeman, 1/22/88, A, C, 87002309

Gallatin County Jail, 317 W. Main St., Bozeman, 1/19/83, A, C, 83001064

Gallatin Gateway Inn, U.S. 191, Gallatin Gateway, 1/24/80, A, C, 80002417

Gallatin Valley Seed Company [Bozeman MRA], 209 S. Wallace, Bozeman, 10/23/87, A, 87001830

Gifford House [Bozeman MRA], 112 S. Grand, Bozeman, 10/23/87, C, a, 87001802

Graf Building [Bozeman MRA], 219–221 W. Arthur, Bozeman, 10/22/87, C, g, 87001811

Green Ranch [Willow Creek Area MPS], Address Restricted, Willow Creek vicinity, 4/19/93, A, B, C, 93000310

Green, Jesse R., Homestead, 6 mi. NE of Trident, Trident vicinity, 1/21/92, A, 91001939

Hamill Apartments [Bozeman MRA], 427 E. Main, Bozeman, 10/23/87, C, 87001817

Hamill House [Bozeman MRA], 205 S. Church, Bozeman, 10/23/87, B, C, 87001814

Harris House [Bozeman MRA], 502 W. Mendenhall, Bozeman, 1/22/88, C, 87002310

Hines House [Bozeman MRA], 420 W. College, Bozeman, 1/22/88, C, 87002311

Holy Rosary Church Rectory [Bozeman MRA], 220 W. Main, Bozeman, 10/23/87, C, a, 87001801

Hotel Baxter, 105 W. Main St., Bozeman, 4/19/84, A, C, 84002469

House at 22 West Lamme [Bozeman MRA], 22 W. Lamme, Bozeman, 10/23/87, C, 87001806

House at 714 North Tracy [Bozeman MRA], 714 N. Tracy, Bozeman, 1/22/88, C, b, 87002315

House at 818 South Eighth [Bozeman MRA], 818 S. Eighth, Bozeman, 1/22/88, C, 87002318

Johnson House [Bozeman MRA], 506 N. Bozeman, Bozeman, 1/22/88, C, 87002321

Kennedy Building [West Yellowstone MRA], 127 Yellowstone Ave., West Yellowstone, 5/13/83, A, C, 83001065

Ketterer, Emil, House, 35 N. Grand Ave., Bozeman, 3/31/83, B, C, 83001066

Kolble House [Bozeman MRA], 716 S. Black, Bozeman, 10/23/87, C, 87001812

Lindley Place Historic District [Bozeman MRA], 200–300 Lindley Pl., Bozeman, 10/23/87, A, C, 87001842

Litening Gas [Bozeman MRA], 424 E. Main, Bozeman, 10/22/87, C, g, 87001843

Little Bear School [One Room Schoolhouses of Gallatin County TR], Bear Creek Rd., Gallatin Gateway, 4/15/82, A, C, 82003168

Lower Bridger School [One Room Schoolhouses of Gallatin County TR], E of Bozeman, Bozeman vicinity, 7/21/81, A, C, 81000347

Lower Willow Creek Rural Historic Landscape District [Willow Creek Area MPS], Address Restricted, Willow Creek vicinity, 4/19/93, A, C, 93000311

MISCO Grain Elevator [Bozeman MRA], 700 N. Wallace, Bozeman, 10/23/87, A, C, 87001831

Madison Buffalo Jump State Monument, 7 mi. S of Logan, Logan vicinity, 4/28/70, D, 70000356

Madison Hotel and Cafe [West Yellowstone MRA], 137 Yellowstone Ave., West Yellowstone, 5/13/83, A, C, 83001067

Gallatin County—Continued

Main Street Historic District [Bozeman MRA], 100 blk. W. Main—300 blk. E. Main, Bozeman, 12/21/87, A, C, 87001848

Malmborg School [One Room Schoolhouses of Gallatin County TR], E of Bozeman, Bozeman vicinity, 7/21/81, A, C, 81000349

Maudlow School [One Room Schoolhouses of Gallatin County TR], Milwaukee Rd., Belgrade, 8/23/82, A, C, 82003164

Methodist Episcopal Church [Bozeman MRA], 121 S. Willson, Bozeman, 10/23/87, A, C, a, 87001839

Newman House [Bozeman MRA], 216 N. Church, Bozeman, 10/23/87, C, 87001835

North Tracy Avenue Historic District [Bozeman MRA], 300–500 blks. N. Tracy Ave., Bozeman & Montana, Bozeman, 10/23/87, A, C, 87001846

Panton House [Bozeman MRA], 801 S. Seventh, Bozeman, 10/23/87, C, 87001828

Pass Creek School [One Room Schoolhouses of Gallatin County TR], NE of Belgrade, Belgrade vicinity, 7/21/81, A, C, 81000341

Peterson House [Bozeman MRA], 216 N. Wallace, Bozeman, 1/22/88, C, 87002350

Peterson Place [Willow Creek Area MPS], Address Restricted, Willow Creek vicinity, 4/19/93, A, C, 93000308

Pine Butte School [One Room Schoolhouses of Gallatin County TR], W of Bozeman, Bozeman vicinity, 7/21/81, A, C, 81000351

Quaw, Thomas, House, 5 Central Ave., Belgrade, 3/04/91, A, B, C, 91000217

Rea School [One Room Schoolhouses of Gallatin County TR], W of Bozeman, Bozeman vicinity, 7/21/81, A, C, 81000346

Reese Creek School [One Room Schoolhouses of Gallatin County TR], NE of Belgrade, Belgrade vicinity, 7/21/81, A, C, 81000342

Rouse House [Bozeman MRA], 506 E. Babcock, Bozeman, 10/23/87, B, C, 87001832

Ruby Theatre, 212 Main St., Three Forks, 4/30/82, A, 82003169

Sacajawea Hotel, 5 Main St., Three Forks, 1/24/80, A, C, b, 80002418

Sedan School [One Room Schoolhouses of Gallatin County TR], NE of Belgrade, Belgrade vicinity, 7/21/81, A, C, 81000344

South Tracy Avenue Historic District [Bozeman MRA], 802–824 S. Tracy Ave., Bozeman, 10/23/87, C, 87001847

South Tracy—South Black Historic District [Bozeman MRA], 200–600 blks. of S. Tracy & S. Black Aves., Bozeman, 12/21/87, A, C, g, 87001840

South Willson Historic District, Willson Ave. between Curtiss and Arthur Sts., Bozeman, 12/18/78, B, C, 78001687

Spanish Creek School [One Room Schoolhouses of Gallatin County TR], NW of Gallatin Gateway, Gallatin Gateway vicinity, 7/21/81, A, C, 81000358

Spieth Houses [Bozeman MRA], 204 N. Bozeman & 209 E. Lamme, Bozeman, 10/23/87, C, 87001838

Spieth and Krug Brewery, 238-246 E. Main St., Bozeman, 4/19/84, A, C, 84002473

Springhill School [One Room Schoolhouses of Gallatin County TR], NE of Belgrade, Belgrade vicinity, 7/21/81, A, C, 81000345

St. James Episcopal Church and Rectory [Bozeman MRA], 9 W. Olive, Bozeman, 10/23/87, A, C, a, 87001841

Story Motor Company [Bozeman MRA], 202 W. Main, Bozeman, 10/23/87, C, 87001837

Three Forks of the Missouri, NE of Three Forks on the Missouri River, Missouri Headwaters State Monument, Three Forks vicinity, 10/15/66, A, B, NHL, 66000433

Trident School [One Room Schoolhouses of Gallatin County TR], S of Trident, Trident, 7/21/81, A, C, 81000364

Upper Madison School [One Room Schoolhouses of Gallatin County TR], Buffalo Jump Rd., Three Forks, 1/19/83, A, C, 83001068

West Yellowstone Oregon Shortline Terminus Historic District [West Yellowstone MRA], Yellowstone Ave., West Yellowstone, 4/13/83, A, C, 83001069

Garfield County

Hornaday Camp, 10 mi. S of MT 200, Sand Springs, 3/26/91, A, B, 91000298

Glacier County

Camp Disappointment, 12 mi. NE of Browning, Browning vicinity, 10/15/66, A, NHL, 66000434

Going-to-the-Sun Road, Glacier Rt. 1, West Glacier vicinity, 6/16/83, A, C, g, NPS, 83001070

Holy Family Mission, E of Browning, Browning vicinity, 6/14/82, A, a, 82003170

Many Glacier Hotel Historic District, W of Babb, Babb vicinity, 9/29/76, A, C, NHL, NPS, 76000173

Golden Valley County

Grace Lutheran Church of Barber, W of Ryegate, Ryegate vicinity, 2/01/82, A, C, a, 82003171

Sims-Garfield Ranch, E of Ryegate, Ryegate vicinity, 8/27/80, A, C, 80002419

Granite County

Anderson Lumber Company [Philipsburg Montana MRA], Roughly bounded by Brown, First, and Holland Sts., Philipsburg, 12/03/86, A, B, 86002790

Doe, M. E., House [Philipsburg Montana MRA], Dearborn and Montgomery Sts., Philipsburg, 12/03/86, B, C, 86002788

Granite County Jail, Kearney St., Philipsburg, 8/27/80, A, C, 80002420

Miners Union Hall, E of Philipsburg in Deerlodge National Forest, Philipsburg vicinity, 12/19/74, A, C, 74001096

Philipsburg Grade School [Philipsburg Montana MRA], W of Schnepel St., Philipsburg, 12/03/86, C, 86002789

Philipsburg Historic District [Philipsburg Montana MRA], Roughly bounded by Gamma St. and Cleveland Ave., Montgomery, Madison and Duffy, and Cedar and McDonald Sts., Philipsburg, 9/30/86, A, C, 86002791

Ringeling House [Philipsburg Montana MRA], Caledonian Mining Claim, E of Doe and Morse Addition, Philipsburg, 12/03/86, A, C, 86002787

Rock Creek Guard Station (24GN165), W of Philipsburg on Hwy. 348 and the Rock Creek Rd., Philipsburg vicinity, 7/13/82, A, C, 82003172

Superintendent's House, E of Philipsburg in Deerlodge National Forest, Philipsburg vicinity, 12/17/74, A, B, 74001097

Hill County

Carnegie Public Library, 447 Fourth Ave., Havre, 7/24/86, A, C, 86001934

Clack, H. Earl, House, 532 Second Ave., Havre, 10/24/85, C, 85003385

Fort Assinniboine, County Rd. 82nd Ave. West, .5 mi. SE of US 87, Havre vicinity, 5/31/89, A, C, 89000040

Havre Residential Historic District, Rouhgly bounded by Third St., Seventh Ave., Eleventh St., Fifth Ave., Tenth St., Third Ave., Seventh St., and First Ave., Havre, 10/05/89, A, C, 89001630

Too Close For Comfort Site (24HL101), Address Restricted, Havre vicinity, 12/30/74, D, 74001098

US Post Office and Courthouse—Havre Main [US Post Offices in Montana, 1900–1941, TR], 306 Third Ave., Havre, 3/14/86, A, C, 86000682

Young—Almas House, 419 4th Ave., Havre, 10/14/80, C, 80002421

Jefferson County

Boulder Hot Springs Hotel, SE of Boulder on MT 281, Boulder vicinity, 1/12/79, A, C, 79001403

Child, W. C., Ranch, S of East Helena on SR 518, East Helena vicinity, 11/23/77, B, C, 77000819

Fraternity Hall, Main St., Elkhorn, 4/03/75, A, C, 75001084

Jefferson County Courthouse, 200 Centennial Ave., Boulder, 8/06/80, A, C, 80002422

MacHaffie Site (24JF4), Address Restricted, Montana City vicinity, 4/03/86, A, D, 86000619

Montana Deaf and Dumb Asylum, Off MT 281, Boulder, 5/10/85, A, C, 85000994

Judith Basin County

Judith River Ranger Station, Along the Middle Fork, Judith R., SW of Utica in Lewis & Clark NF, Utica vicinity, 4/10/92, A, C, 92000333

Judith Basin County—Continued

Meadowbrook Stock Farm, US 87, Hobson vicinity, 1/13/92, A, B, C, 91001938

Wood Lawn Farm, 5 mi. W of Hobson on Utica Rd. No. 239, Hobson vicinity, 1/27/93, A, C, 92001762

Lake County

Fort Connah Site, US 93, Post Creek vicinity, 4/28/82, A, C, d, 82003173

Kootenai Lodge Historic District, Sunburst Dr., Bigfork, 1/17/84, A, C, 84002476

Linderman, Frank Bird, House, Address Restricted, Lake, 2/22/84, B, C, 84002479

Polson Feed Mill, 501 Main St., Polson, 4/29/80, A, C, 80002423

St. Ignatius Mission, About 0.1 mi. SE of MT 93 in St. Ignatius, St. Ignatius, 6/19/73, A, C, a, 73001053

Swan Lake Rock House Historic District, Off MT 83, Swan Lake vicinity, 8/01/84, B, C, 84002485

Lewis and Clark County

Algeria Shrine Temple, Neill and Park Aves., Helena, 4/14/88, A, C, 88000434

Appleton House No. 13, 2200 Cannon, Helena, 10/25/82, A, C, 82000593

Cathedral of Saint Helena, 530 N. Ewing St., Helena, 4/30/80, C, a, 80004270

Eagle's Site [Archeological Resources of the Upper Missouri River Corridor MPS], Address Restricted, Helena vicinity, 10/07/93, D, 93000995

Evans, Christmas Gift, House, 404 N. Benton Ave., Helena, 4/16/80, C, 80004271

Forestvale Cemetery, 490 Forestvale Rd., Helena, 2/21/90, A, d, 90000145

Former Montana Executive Mansion, 6th Ave. and Ewing St., Helena, 4/28/70, C, 70000357

Gilman State Bank, Main St., Gilman, 12/01/83, A, C, 83003993

Hauser Mansion, 720 Madison Ave., Helena, 2/12/79, B, C, a, 79001404

Helena Historic District, Irregular pattern from Hauser Blvd. to Acropolis and between Garfield and Rodney Sts., Helena, 6/02/72, A, B, C, g, 72000737

Helena Historic District (Boundary Increase), Roughly bounded by Cruse, Neill and Park Aves. and Lawrence, Helena, 6/14/90, A, B, C, g, 90000934

Helena Historic District (Boundary Increase II), Bounded by E. Sixth, N. Davis, Broadway and N. Rodney Sts., Helena, 10/07/93, A, 93001001

Helena South-Central Historic District, Roughly bounded by Broadway, S. Davis St., city limits, and S. Warren St., Helena, 7/28/86, A, C, g, 86002274

House of the Good Shepherd Historic District, Area surrounding jct. of 9th Ave. and N. Hoback St., Helena, 12/23/93, A, C, a, 93001448

Kemna, Herman, House, 635 First St., Helena, 8/18/92, A, C, 92001056

Kleinschmidt, T. H., House, 1823 Highland Ave., Helena, 8/06/80, B, C, 80004272

Kluge House, 540 W. Main St., Helena, 4/28/70, C, 70000358

Lincoln Community Hall, MT 200, Lincoln, 1/22/87, A, C, 86003674

Lincoln Lodge, Stemple Pass Rd., Lincoln, 10/23/86, C, 86002931

Methodist-Episcopal Church of Marysville, 3rd St., Marysville, 1/05/84, C, a, 84002489

Montana State Capitol Building, Central Ave. and Main St., Helena, 2/17/81, A, C, 81000660

Murphy, John T., House, 418 N. Benton Ave., Helena, 8/01/84, A, B, 82004495

Olsen House, 516 N. Park, Helena, 3/22/91, C, 91000333

Porter Flats Apartments, 335 N. Ewing St., Helena, 1/14/93, A, C, 92001761

Silver Creek School, N of Helena on Sierra Rd., Helena vicinity, 8/11/80, A, 80004273

Silver King Ranch, Roughly 15 mi. NE of Lincoln in Helena NF, Lincoln vicinity, 3/10/92, A, C, 92000114

Silverman, Morris, House, 412 N. Rodney St., Helena, 6/14/82, B, C, 82004636

Summit Lodge, 30 mi. NW of Helena in Helena National Forest, Helena vicinity, 5/17/90, C, 90000723

Wassweiler Hotel and Bath Houses, W of Helena on U.S. 12, Helena vicinity, 8/01/78, A, C, 78001688

Western Clay Manufacturing Company, 2915 Country Club Rd., Helena, 5/09/85, A, C, 85001052

Young Women's Christian Association (Independent), 501 N. Park St., Helena, 12/27/84, A, C, 84000569

Lincoln County

Eureka Community Hall, Cliff St., Eureka, 10/18/85, A, C, g, 85003236

Madison County

Beaverhead Rock-Lewis and Clark Expedition, About 14 mi. NE of Dillon, Dillon vicinity, 2/11/70, A, 70000359

Christ Episcopal Church and Rectory, SW jct. of Poppleton and Main Sts., Sheridan, 1/22/87, C, a, 86003672

Madison County Fairgrounds, MT 41, Twin Bridges, 8/03/84, A, C, 84002500

O'Brien, William, House, 114 E. Poppleton, Sheridan, 10/23/86, C, 86002933

Pony Historic District [Pony MRA], Town of Pony, SW of Harrison, Pony, 8/04/87, A, C, 87001264

Powder House [Pony MRA], 1/2 mi. SE of Pony on Potosi Rd., Pony, 8/03/87, A, C, 87001266

Robbers Roost, 5 mi. N of Alder at MT 387A, Alder vicinity, 1/01/76, A, 76001124

Saint Mary of the Assumption, Off MT 287, Laurin, 10/24/85, C, a, 85003380

Strawberry Mine Historic District [Pony MRA], Roughly Bounded by Strawberry Ridge, Pony Rd., and Pony Creek, Pony vicinity, 8/04/87, B, C, 87001265

Virginia City Historic District, Wallace St., Virginia City, 10/15/66, A, NHL, 66000435

McCone County

Gladstone Hotel, 101 Main St., Circle, 8/28/80, A, 80004592

Meagher County

Fort Logan and Blockhouse, 17 mi. NW of White Sulphur Springs, White Sulphur Springs vicinity, 10/06/70, A, b, 70000360

Sherman, Byron R., House, 310 2nd Ave., NE, White Sulphur Springs, 9/15/77, B, C, 77000820

Mineral County

DeBorgia Schoolhouse, Thompson Falls DeBorgia Rd., DeBorgia, 12/27/79, A, 79001405

Missoula County

Apartment Building at 116 Spruce Street [Historic Resources in Missoula, 1864-1940, MPS], 116 W. Spruce St., Missoula, 4/30/90, A, C, 90000644

Atlantic Hotel [Historic Resources in Missoula, 1864-1940, MPS], 519 N. Higgins Ave., Missoula, 4/30/90, A, C, 90000652

Belmont Hotel, 430 N. Higgins Ave., Missoula, 4/20/83, A, C, 83001071

Brunswick Hotel [Historic Resources in Missoula, 1864-1940, MPS], 223 Railroad St., Missoula, 4/30/90, A, C, 90000645

Camp Paxson Boy Scout Camp (24MO77), Seeley Lake, Lolo National Forest, 3/21/86, A, C, g, 86000584

Carnegie Public Library, 335 N. Pattee St., Missoula, 4/30/82, A, C, 82003174

DeSmet Schoolhouse, 6105 Old Hwy. 10 W., Missoula, 2/28/91, A, C, 91000151

East Pine Street Historic District, Roughly bounded by E. Pine St., Madison St., E. Broadway, and Pattee St., Missoula, 7/13/89, A, B, C, 89000768

Florence Hotel [Missoula MPS], 111 N. Higgins Ave., Missoula, 6/18/92, A, C, 92000782

Flynn Farm, W of Missoula on Mullan Rd., Missoula vicinity, 3/19/80, C, 80002426

Missoula County—Continued

Forkenbrock Funeral Home, 234 E. Pine St., Missoula, 12/27/84, A, C, 84000570

Fort Fizzle Site, 5 mi. W of Lolo, Lolo vicinity, 7/21/77, A, 77000821

Fort Missoula Historic District, Reserve St. and South Ave., Missoula, 4/29/87, A, C, g, 87000865

Garden City Drug [Historic Resources in Missoula, 1864-1940, MPS], 118 N. Higgins Ave., Missoula, 4/30/90, C, 90000660

Gibson, A. J., House, 402 S. 2nd St., Missoula, 4/16/80, B, 80002427

Gleim Building [Historic Resources in Missoula, 1864-1940, MPS], 265 W. Front St., Missoula, 4/30/90, A, C, 90000653

Grand Pacific Hotel, 118 W. Alder, Missoula, 9/29/83, A, C, 83001072

Hammond Arcade [Historic Resources in Missoula, 1864-1940, MPS], 101 S. Higgins Ave., Missoula, 4/30/90, A, C, 90000646

Hellgate Lodge 383 BPOE [Historic Resources in Missoula, 1864-1940, MPS], 120 N. Pattee St., Missoula, 4/30/90, A, C, 90000661

Herzog, J. M., House, 1210 Toole Ave., Missoula, 9/12/85, C, 85002164

Higgins Block, 202 N. Higgins Ave., Missoula, 10/01/79, B, C, 79003720

Independent Telephone Company Building [Historic Resources in Missoula, 1864-1940, MPS], 207 E. Main St., Missoula, 4/30/90, A, C, 90000648

Johnston, John S., House, 412 W. Alder St., Missoula, 8/02/84, C, 84002502

Keith, John M., House, 1110 Gerald Ave., Missoula, 7/07/83, C, 83001073

Knowles Building, 200–210 S. Third St. W, Missoula, 4/09/87, B, C, 87000608

Labor Temple [Historic Resources in Missoula, 1864-1940, MPS], 208 E. Main St., Missoula, 4/30/90, A, 90000650

Laird's Lodge Historic District, N end of Lindbergh Lake at end of Lindbergh Lake Rd., Seeley Lake vicinity, 8/17/90, A, C, 90001213

Lolo Trail, Parallel to U.S. 12 on ridges of Bitterroot Mountains, from Lolo Pass to Weippe, Bitterroot Mountains, vicinity, 10/15/66, A, B, NHL, NPS, 66000309

Lucy Building [Historic Resources in Missoula, 1864-1940, MPS], 330 N. Higgins Ave., Missoula, 4/30/90, C, 90000656

Marsh and Powell Funeral Home [Historic Resources in Missoula, 1864-1940, MPS], 224 W. Spruce St., Missoula, 4/30/90, A, C, 90000655

Masonic Lodge [Historic Resources in Missoula, 1864-1940, MPS], 120–136 E. Broadway Ave., Missoula, 4/30/90, A, C, 90000649

Milwaukee Depot, 250 Station Dr., Missoula, 4/30/82, A, C, 82003175

Missoula County Courthouse, 220 W. Broadway, Missoula, 9/01/76, C, 76001125

Missoula Laundry Company [Historic Resources in Missoula, 1864-1940, MPS], 111 E. Spruce St., Missoula, 4/30/90, C, 90000651

Missoula Mercantile [Historic Resources in Missoula, 1864-1940, MPS], 114 N. Higgins Ave., Missoula, 4/30/90, A, B, C, 90000647

Missoula Southside Historic District, Roughly bounded by the Clark Fork R., S. Higgins Ave., S. 6th St. W. and Orange St., Missoula, 3/22/91, A, B, C, 91000334

Model Laundry and Apartments [Historic Resources in Missoula, 1864-1940, MPS], 131 W. Alder St., Missoula, 4/30/90, C, 90000657

Montgomery Ward [Historic Resources in Missoula, 1864-1940, MPS], 201 N. Higgins Ave., Missoula, 4/30/90, A, C, 90000659

Northern Pacific Railroad Depot, Railroad and Higgins Ave., Missoula, 3/28/85, A, C, 85000644

Palace Hotel, 147 W. Broadway, Missoula, 10/25/82, A, C, 82000594

Paxson, Edgar, House, 611 Stephens Ave., Missoula, 11/06/86, B, 86002935

Potomac School, 220 Potomac Rd., Potomac, 3/30/92, A, C, 92000244

Prescott, Clarence R., House, University of Montana, Missoula, 9/26/85, C, 85002515

Saint John the Baptist Catholic Church, Mullan Rd., Frenchtown, 3/27/86, A, C, a, 86000585

St. Francis Xavier Church, 420 W. Pine St., Missoula, 4/28/82, A, C, a, 82003176

Sterling, Fred T., House, 1310 Gerald Ave., Missoula, 7/07/83, C, 83001074

Toole, John R., House, 1005 Gerald Ave., Missoula, 4/25/83, B, C, 83004308

Traveler's Rest, 1 mi. S of Lolo near U.S. 93, Lolo vicinity, 10/15/66, A, NHL, 66000437

U.S. Forest Service Remount Depot, 2.4 mi. SW of Huson, Huson vicinity, 4/10/80, A, g, 80002425

U.S. Post Office, 200 E. Broadway St., Missoula, 11/30/79, A, 79001406

University Apartments, 400-422 Roosevelt Ave., Missoula, 3/28/85, C, 85000645

University of Montana Historic District, Roughly bounded by Arthur, Connell and Beckwith Aves. and the ridge lines of Mt. Sentinel, Missoula, 10/02/92, A, C, 92001284

Wilma Theatre, 104 S. Higgins Ave., Missoula, 12/31/79, B, C, 79001407

Zip Auto [Historic Resources in Missoula, 1864-1940, MPS], 251 W. Main St., Missoula, 4/30/90, A, C, 90000658

Musselshell County

St. Benedict's Catholic School, 524 First St., W, Roundup, 7/21/88, A, C, a, 88001120

Park County

B Street District [Livingston MRA], B St., Livingston, 9/05/79, A, C, 79001408

Commercial District [Livingston MRA], Roughly bounded by Park, C, Clark, 3rd, and Callendar Sts., Livingston, 9/05/79, A, C, 79001409

Cooke City Store, Main St., Cooke City, 3/27/86, A, C, 86000527

Detention Hospital [Livingston MRA], 325 E. Gallatin St., Livingston, 9/05/79, A, 79001410

East Side Residential District [Livingston MRA], Roughly bounded by I, Clark, E and Park Sts., Livingston, 9/05/79, A, C, 79001411

Ebert Ranch [Livingston MRA], U.S. 89, Livingston, 9/05/79, B, C, 79001412

Harvat Ranch [Livingston MRA], SE of Livingston off U.S. 89, Livingston vicinity, 9/05/79, B, C, 79001413

KPRK Radio [Livingston MRA], E of Livingston off U.S. 89, Livingston vicinity, 9/05/79, C, g, 79001414

Krohne Island House [Livingston MRA], Krohne Island, Livingston, 9/05/79, C, 79001415

Krohne Spring House [Livingston MRA], 329 S. H St., Livingston, 9/05/79, B, C, 79001416

Northeast Entrance Station, US 212, Yellowstone National Park, 5/28/87, C, NHL, NPS, 87001435

Northside School [Livingston MRA], 118 W. Chinook St., Livingston, 9/05/79, A, 79001417

Rolfson House [Livingston MRA], W of Livingston on Bozeman Rd., Livingston vicinity, 9/05/79, B, C, 79001418

Sixty-Three Ranch, Address Restricted, Livingston vicinity, 12/07/82, A, C, 82000595

Trowbridge Dairy [Livingston MRA], 207 S. M St., Livingston, 9/05/79, A, C, 79001419

US Post Office—Livingston Main [US Post Offices in Montana, 1900–1941, TR], 105 N. Second St., Livingston, 3/14/86, A, C, 86000685

Urbach Cabin [Livingston MRA], 9th St. Island, Livingston, 9/05/79, A, C, 79001420

West Side Residential District [Livingston MRA], Roughly bounded by Sacajawea Park, 7th, Park, and 3rd Sts., Livingston, 9/05/79, C, 79001421

Phillips County

Phillips County Carnegie Library, S. 1st St., Malta, 8/27/80, A, 80002428

Pondera County

Conrad City Hall, 15 4th Ave., SW, Conrad, 2/01/80, A, C, 80002429

Froggie's Stopping Place on the Whoop-Up Trail [Whoop-Up Trail of Northcentral Montana MPS], Address Restricted, Conrad vicinity, 4/15/93, A, D, 93000277

Two Medicine Fight Site, About 25 mi. SE of Browning, Browning vicinity, 10/06/70, A, 70000361

Valier Public School, 820 3rd St., Valier, 3/28/85, C, 85000646

Powell County

Bielenberg, Nick J., House, 801 Milwaukee Ave., Deer Lodge, 8/10/79, B, C, 79003719

Powell County—Continued

Coleman, William E., House, 500 Missouri Ave., Deer Lodge, 5/21/79, C, 79001422

Deer Lodge American Women's League Chapter House, 802 Missouri Ave., Deer Lodge, 6/14/82, A, C, 82003177

Fitzpatrick Ranch Historic District, NW of Avon, Avon vicinity, 7/08/81, A, B, 81000365

Grant-Kohrs Ranch National Historic Site, Edge of Deer Lodge, Deer Lodge, 8/25/72, A, C, f, NHL, NPS, 72000738

Kohrs, William K., Free Memorial Library, 5th St. and Missouri Ave., Deer Lodge, 5/07/79, A, C, 79001423

Montana Territorial and State Prison, 925 Main St., Deer Lodge, 9/03/76, A, C, 76001126

Northern Pacific Railroad Completion Site, 1883, Off I-90, Gold Creek vicinity, 8/19/83, A, 83001075

Prison Brickyard Historic District, Gravel rd. off I-90 1/4 mi. S of Deer Lodge, Deer Lodge vicinity, 4/14/88, A, 88000430

Trask Hall, 703 5th Ave., Deer Lodge, 4/30/82, A, 82003178

Prairie County

Grandey Elementary School, Off U.S. 10, Terry, 11/16/78, A, B, 78001689

Ravalli County

Allison—Reinkeh House [Hamilton MRA], 207 Adirondac St., Hamilton, 8/26/88, A, B, C, 88001280

Alta Ranger Station, S of Conner in Bitterroot National Forest, Conner vicinity, 12/19/74, A, 74001099

Bass Mansion, 216 N. College St., Stevensville, 11/14/78, B, C, 78001691

Bean, Daniel V., House [Hamilton MRA], 611 N. Second, Hamilton, 8/26/88, C, 88001288

Big Creek Lake Site, Address Restricted, Stevensville vicinity, 5/17/76, D, 76001127

Bitter Root Cooperative Creamery [Stevensville MPS], 3730 Eastside Hwy., Stevensville, 6/19/91, A, 91000726

Blood, Oliver, House [Hamilton MRA], 524 S. First St., Hamilton, 8/26/88, C, 88001279

Brooks Hotel, Off East Side Hwy., Corvallis, 11/10/80, A, C, 80002430

Buck, Charles Amos, House [Stevensville MPS], 211 Buck St., Stevensville, 6/18/91, B, C, 91000727

Buck, Fred, House [Stevensville MPS], 217 Buck St., Stevensville, 6/18/91, B, C, 91000729

Canyon Creek Laboratory of the U.S. Public Health Service, W of Hamilton city limits, Hamilton vicinity, 10/15/70, A, g, 70000362

Caple, W. T., House [Stevensville MPS], 210 Church St., Stevensville, 6/19/91, C, 91000730

Clark, Jennie, House [Stevensville MPS], 423 Pine St., Stevensville, 6/19/91, C, 91000731

Cochran, William, House [Stevensville MPS], 3713 East Side Hwy., Stevensville, 6/19/91, C, 91000732

Conway House [Hamilton MRA], 805 S. Fourth St., Hamilton, 8/26/88, C, 88001291

Cook, Calvin and Maggie, House [Stevensville MPS], 501 Main St., Stevensville, 6/19/91, C, 91000734

Cook, Wilbur, House [Stevensville MPS], 3717 East Side Hwy., Stevensville, 6/19/91, C, 91000733

Cramer, Martin, House, 326 Groff La., Stevensville vicinity, 8/03/87, C, 87001259

Daly, Marcus, Memorial Hospital, 211 S. 4th St., Hamilton, 12/15/78, A, C, g, 78001690

Drinkenberg's, F. H., First Home [Hamilton MRA], 701 N. Second, Hamilton, 8/26/88, B, C, 88001289

El Capitan Lodge, Access Rd. 1111, N shore of Lake Como, Bitterroot NF, Hamilton vicinity, 11/29/90, A, C, 90001792

Ellis, E. G., House [Hamilton MRA], 801 N. Third, Hamilton, 8/26/88, C, 88001281

Emhoff House [Stevensville MPS], 401 Church St., Stevensville, 6/19/91, C, 91000736

First Baptist Church [Stevensville MPS], 402 Church, Stevensville, 9/03/91, C, a, 91000737

First State Bank, Dowling and Emhoff Buildings [Stevensville MPS], 300–304, 306–308 Main St., Stevensville, 6/19/91, A, C, 91000738

Fisher, Joseph, House [Stevensville MPS], 103 College St., Stevensville, 6/19/91, C, 91000739

Fort Owen, About 0.5 mi. NW of Stevensville, Stevensville vicinity, 10/06/70, A, D, 70000363

Foust, Perry, House [Stevensville MPS], 401 Mission St., Stevensville, 6/19/91, C, 91000740

Foye Rental Houses [Hamilton MRA], 819 and 821 N. Fourth, Hamilton, 8/26/88, A, C, 88001292

Fulton, Charles, House [Stevensville MPS], 377 Fifth St., Stevensville, 6/19/91, C, 91000742

Gavin House [Stevensville MPS], 219 College St., Stevensville, 6/19/91, C, 91000743

Gill, Sherman, House [Hamilton MRA], 605 N. Third, Hamilton, 8/26/88, C, 88001282

Gleason Building [Stevensville MPS], 200–202 Main St., Stevensville, 6/19/91, A, C, 91000744

Goff House [Hamilton MRA], 115 N. Fifth, Hamilton, 8/26/88, C, 88001283

Gordon House [Hamilton MRA], 806 S. Fourth, Hamilton, 8/26/88, C, 88001294

Granke, Charles, House [Hamilton MRA], 406 S. Seventh St., Hamilton, 8/26/88, C, 88001278

Hamilton Commercial Historic District [Hamilton MRA], Main, N. Second, S. Second, S. Third, and State Sts., Hamilton, 9/01/88, A, C, g, 88001273

Hamilton Southside Residential Historic District [Hamilton MRA], S. First, S. Second, S. Third, S. Fourth, and S. Fifth Sts., Hamilton, 9/01/88, A, C, a, g, 88001272

Hamilton Town Hall, 175 S. 3rd St., Hamilton, 4/21/80, A, C, 80002431

Harrington, Rose, House [Stevensville MPS], 3709 East Side Hwy., Stevensville, 6/19/91, C, 91000745

Hoffman, Charles, House [Hamilton MRA], 807 S. Third, Hamilton, 8/26/88, C, 88001277

Howe, John G., House [Stevensville MPS], 215 Park Ave., Stevensville, 6/18/91, B, C, 91000746

IOOF Hall [Stevensville MPS], 217–219 Main St., Stevensville, 6/19/91, A, C, 91000747

Lagerquist, John, House [Hamilton MRA], 701 N. Fourth St., Hamilton, 8/26/88, C, 88001284

Lancaster House [Stevensville MPS], 407 Third St., Stevensville, 6/19/91, C, 91000748

Lockridge House [Stevensville MPS], 301 Mission St., Stevensville, 6/19/91, C, 91000750

Lost Horse Fireman's Cabin (24RA197), Off Lost Horse Rd. near Bear Creek Pass, Darby vicinity, 4/17/89, A, C, 88003437

May, Albert, House [Stevensville MPS], 218 Church St., Stevensville, 6/18/91, B, C, 91000751

May, Charles, House [Stevensville MPS], 109 Church St., Stevensville, 6/18/91, C, 91000753

May, George, House, 100 Park Ave., Stevensville, 10/25/82, B, C, 82000596

May, Harry, House [Stevensville MPS], 526 Third St., Stevensville, 6/18/91, B, C, 91000752

May, Louis, House [Stevensville MPS], 100 Church St., Stevensville, 6/19/91, C, 91000754

McFarlane House [Stevensville MPS], 200 College St., Stevensville, 6/19/91, C, a, 91000755

McGlauflin House [Hamilton MRA], 518 S. Eighth, Hamilton, 8/26/88, C, 88001276

McLaughlin, John, House [Stevensville MPS], 105 Main St., Stevensville, 6/19/91, B, C, 91000757

Metcalf House [Stevensville MPS], 214 Pine St., Stevensville, 6/19/91, C, 91000758

Morr, Philip and Ella, House [Stevensville MPS], 502 Buck St., Stevensville, 6/19/91, C, 91000760

Pine Apartments [Hamilton MRA], 804 S. Fourth St., Hamilton, 8/26/88, A, C, 88001295

Popham Ranch, 460 N.E. Popham Ln., Corvallis vicinity, 1/13/89, A, C, 88003141

Ravalli County Courthouse, 225 Bedford St., Hamilton, 4/20/79, A, C, 79001424

Riverside, Eastside Hwy., Hamilton, 7/16/87, C, 87001235

Rocky Mountain Laboratory Historic District [Hamilton MRA], 900 blk. of Fourth St., Hamilton, 9/01/88, A, C, g, 88001274

Sharp, John, House [Stevensville MPS], 306 College St., Stevensville, 6/19/91, B, C, 91000761

St. Mary's Church and Pharmacy, North Ave., Stevensville, 10/06/70, A, a, 70000364

Stevensville Feed Mill [Stevensville MPS], 407 Main St., Stevensville, 6/19/91, A, 91000762

Stevensville Grade School—United Methodist Church [Stevensville MPS], 216 College St., Stevensville, 6/19/91, A, C, a, 91000764

Stevensville Mercantile Company Oil Storage Building [Stevensville MPS], 300 Mission St., Stevensville, 6/19/91, A, 91000763

Stout, John, House [Hamilton MRA], 1000 S. First, Hamilton, 8/26/88, C, 88001290

Thornton Hospital [Stevensville MPS], 107 E. Third St., Stevensville, 6/19/91, A, B, C, 91000765

Ravalli County—Continued

Trosdahl, Erick, House [Hamilton MRA], 206 S. Seventh St., Hamilton, 8/26/88, C, 88001275

VFW Club [Hamilton MRA], 930 Adirondac, Hamilton, 8/26/88, A, C, 88001287

Wallin, Frank, House [Hamilton MRA], 608 N. Seventh St., Hamilton, 8/26/88, C, 88001293

Wamsley, Other C., House [Hamilton MRA], 200 N. Fifth St., Hamilton, 8/26/88, C, 88001285

Williams House [Stevensville MPS], 500 Fifth St., Stevensville, 6/19/91, C, 91000766

Williams, John and Ann, House [Stevensville MPS], 205 Church St., Stevensville, 6/19/91, C, 91000735

Young, Benjamin, House [Stevensville MPS], 523 Main St., Stevensville, 6/19/91, C, 91000741

Richland County

Peoples' Congregational Church, 203 2nd Ave., SW, Sidney, 4/30/82, A, C, a, 82003179

Roosevelt County

Fort Peck Agency, In Poplar, Poplar, 5/19/70, A, 70000365

Fort Union Trading Post National Historic Site, W of Buford, Buford, vicinity, 10/15/66, A, D, NHL, NPS, 66000103

Rosebud County

Anderson, Herman and Hannah, House [Forsyth MPS], 209 S. 7th Ave., Forsyth, 2/12/90, A, C, 90000084

Blue Front Rooming House [Forsyth MPS], 1187 Main St., Forsyth, 2/12/90, A, C, 90000085

Brotherhood of Locomotive Engineers Hall [Forsyth MPS], 262 S. 7th Ave., Forsyth, 2/12/90, A, C, 90000086

Cold Springs Ranch House, US 12 W., Forsyth vicinity, 1/26/90, A, C, 89002347

First Presbyterian Church and Manse [Forsyth MPS], 1160–1180 Cedar St., Forsyth, 2/12/90, C, a, 90000089

Forsyth Bridge [Forsyth MPS], 3rd Ave. at the Yellowstone River, Forsyth, 2/12/90, A, 90000090

Forsyth Main Street Historic District [Forsyth MPS], Roughly bounded by Cedar St., 11th Ave., Main St., and 8th St., Forsyth, 2/12/90, A, B, C, 90000081

Forsyth Residential Historic District [Forsyth MPS], Roughly bounded by Cedar St., 11th Ave., Willow St., 12th Ave., Oak St., and 14th Ave., Forsyth, 2/12/90, A, C, 90000082

Forsyth Water Pumping Station [Forsyth MPS], 3rd Ave. at the Yellowstone River, Forsyth, 2/12/90, A, C, 90000087

Marcyes, Claude O., House [Forsyth MPS], 390 S. 7th Ave., Forsyth, 2/12/90, A, B, C, 90000088

Rosebud County Courthouse, 1250 Main St., Forsyth, 4/17/86, A, C, 86000807

Rosebud County Deaconess Hospital, N. 17th Ave, Forsyth, 11/16/79, A, 79001425

Vananda Historic District, US 12, 17 mi. W of Forsyth, Forsyth vicinity, 4/19/90, A, C, 90000629

Sanders County

Ainsworth House [Thompson Falls MRA], 911 Maiden Ln., Thompson Falls, 10/07/86, C, 86002771

Bedard House [Thompson Falls MRA], 207 Spruce St., Thompson Falls, 10/07/86, C, 86002783

Bull River Guard Station, On banks of Bull R. near confluence with E. Fork Bull R., Kootenai NF, Noxon vicinity, 6/27/90, A, C, 90000990

Gem Saloon [Thompson Falls MRA], 808 Main St., Thompson Falls, 10/07/86, A, B, 86002767

Grandchamp House [Thompson Falls MRA], 1012 Preston Ave., Thompson Falls, 10/07/86, C, 86002776

Griffen House [Thompson Falls MRA], 205 Gallatin St., Thompson Falls, 10/07/86, C, 86002779

House at 112 Park Street [Thompson Falls MRA], 112 Park St., Thompson Falls, 10/07/86, C, 86002778

House at 916 Preston Avenue [Thompson Falls MRA], 916 Preston Ave., Thompson Falls, 10/07/86, C, 86002777

Hoyt House [Thompson Falls MRA], 204 Gallatin St., Thompson Falls, 10/07/86, C, 86002780

IOOF Lodge [Thompson Falls MRA], 520 Main St., Thompson Falls, 10/07/86, A, C, 86002761

Norby House [Thompson Falls MRA], 13 Pond St., Thompson Falls, 10/07/86, C, 86002775

Northern Pacific Warehouse [Thompson Falls MRA], Bounded by Preston Ave. and Main St. along Burlington Northern Right-of-Way, Thompson Falls, 10/07/86, A, 86002785

Preston House [Thompson Falls MRA], 205 Ferry St., Thompson Falls, 10/07/86, C, 86002784

Rinard House [Thompson Falls MRA], 210 Jefferson St., Thompson Falls, 10/07/86, A, 86002782

Sanders County Jail [Thompson Falls MRA], Madison and Maiden Lane, Thompson Falls, 10/07/86, A, C, 86002774

Thayer House [Thompson Falls MRA], 109 Jefferson St., Thompson Falls, 12/22/86, C, 86002781

Thompson Falls Hydroelectric Dam Historic District [Thompson Falls MRA], US ALT 10 at Clark Fork River within NW part of Thompson Falls, Thompson Falls, 10/07/86, A, C, 86002756

Tourist Hotel [Thompson Falls MRA], 101 Main St., Thompson Falls, 10/07/86, A, 86002765

Ward Hotel [Thompson Falls MRA], 919 Main St., Thompson Falls, 12/22/86, A, B, 86002769

Weber's Store [Thompson Falls MRA], 510 Main St., Thompson Falls, 10/07/86, A, 86002763

Sheridan County

Comertown Historic District [Sheridan County MPS], Roughly, entire town of Comertown, W of Westby, Westby vicinity, 10/27/93, A, 93001149

Larsen, Aage and Kristine, Homestead [Sheridan County MPS], Co. Hwy. 516 N of Dagmar, Dagmar vicinity, 10/27/93, A, C, 93001146

Outlook Depot [Sheridan County MPS], S of western edge of Marr St., S of Block 10, Outlook, 10/27/93, A, C, 93001144

Raymond Grain Elevators Historic District [Sheridan County MPS], Unnamed Co. Rd. E of MT 16, NE of Raymond, Raymond vicinity, 10/27/93, A, C, 93001148

Rocky Valley Lutheran Church [Sheridan County MPS], Jct. of Ueland St. and unnamed Co. Rd., Dooley, 10/27/93, C, 93001145

Thornwood School [Sheridan County MPS], Unnamed Co. Rd. approximately 17 mi. W of Reserve, Reserve vicinity, 10/28/93, A, C, g, 93001147

Tipi Hills, Address Restricted, Medicine Lake vicinity, 8/01/75, D, 75001085

Silver Bow County

Big Hole Pumpstation, MT 43, Divide vicinity, 9/24/80, C, 80002432

Butte Historic District, Butte city limits, Butte, 10/15/66, A, NHL, 66000438

Butte, Anaconda and Pacific Railway Historic District (Boundary Increase), Confluence of German Gulch and Silver Bow Creeks at E end of Silver Bow Canyon, Durant, 1/13/89, A, 88003149

Clark, Charles W., Mansion, 108 N. Washington St., Butte, 10/22/76, B, C, 76001128

Clark, W. A., Mansion, 219 W. Granite, Butte, 10/06/70, B, C, 70000366

Hawthorne Grade School [Suburban Schools in Butte TR], 3500 White Way, Butte, 1/25/88, A, C, 87002304

Longfellow Grade School [Suburban Schools in Butte TR], 1629 Roosevelt Ave., Butte, 1/25/88, A, C, 87002305

Madison Grade School [Suburban Schools in Butte TR], 45 E. Greenwood, Butte, 1/25/88, A, C, 87002306

Ramsay Historic District, 6.5 mi. W of Butte on I 90, Butte vicinity, 1/14/88, A, C, 87002227

Silver Bow Brewery Malt House, W of Butte off US 91, Butte vicinity, 1/19/83, A, 83001076

Silver Bow County Poor Farm Hospital, 3040 Continental Dr., Butte, 7/16/81, A, C, 81000366

U. S. Post Office, 400 N. Main St, Butte, 11/15/79, A, 79001426

Wheeler, Burton K., House, 1232 E. 2nd St., Butte, 12/08/76, B, NHL, 76001129

Stillwater County

Hovda, Oliver H., House, N. Woodward St., Absarokee, 8/16/84, B, 84002506

Jacobs, Michael, House, 4 W. First Avenue N, Columbus, 1/28/87, C, 86003676

Mountain View Cemetery, US 10 and Rapelje Rd., Columbus, 7/16/87, C, d, 87001200

Norton, W. H., House, 3rd Ave., Columbus, 10/25/82, A, B, C, 82000597

Sandstone and Cobblestone Schools, Main St., Absarokee, 1/15/87, A, C, 86002949

Stoltz House, 405 SW. First St., Park City, 4/16/91, A, C, 91000422

Sweet Grass County

Brannin Ranch, W of Melville on Sweet Grass Creek, Melville vicinity, 1/13/89, A, C, 88003142

Grand Hotel, 139 McLeod, Big Timber, 9/19/85, A, 85002424

Yellowstone Crossing, Bozeman Trail, NE of Springdale on US 10, Springdale vicinity, 12/01/78, A, 78003407

Toole County

Bethany Lutheran Church, 0.25 mi. S of Gus Blaze Rd., Oilmont vicinity, 12/14/93, A, C, a, b, 93001375

Kevin Depot, Central Ave. and 1st St., Kevin, 8/11/80, A, C, b, 80002433

Rocky Springs Segment of the Whoop-Up Trail [Whoop-Up Trail of Northcentral Montana MPS], Address Restricted, Kevin vicinity, 4/15/93, A, 93000278

US Customs Building, I-15 just S of US—Canada border, Sweetgrass, 2/28/91, A, C, 91000152

Valley County

Administration Building [Fort Peck MRA], E. Kansas Ave., Fort Peck, 8/13/86, A, C, 86002058

Employee's Hotel and Garage [Fort Peck MRA], S. Missouri Ave., Fort Peck, 8/13/86, A, C, 86002060

Fort Peck Dam [Fort Peck MRA], On the Missouri River, Fort Peck, 8/13/86, C, 86002061

Fort Peck Original Houses Historic District [Fort Peck MRA], 1101–1112 E. Kansas Ave., Fort Peck, 8/13/86, A, C, 86002067

Fort Peck Theatre, Missouri Ave., Fort Peck, 6/27/83, C, 83001077

Garage and Fire Station [Fort Peck MRA], Gasconade St., Fort Peck, 8/13/86, A, C, 86002063

Hospital [Fort Peck MRA], S. Platte St., Fort Peck, 8/13/86, A, C, 86002054

Recreation Hall [Fort Peck MRA], Missouri Ave., Fort Peck, 8/13/86, A, C, 86002066

Sargent, Charles C., House, 615 Front St., Nashua, 7/08/82, B, 82003180

US Post Office and Courthouse—Glasgow Main [US Post Offices in Montana, 1900–1941, TR], 605 Second Ave. S, Glasgow, 3/21/86, A, C, g, 86000679

Wheatland County

Graves Hotel, 106 S. Central Ave., Harlowton, 8/06/80, A, C, 80002434

Milwaukee Road Historic District, S end of Central Ave., Harlowton vicinity, 7/08/88, A, C, b, 88001024

Wibaux County

St. Peter's Catholic Church, W. Orgain Ave., Wibaux, 3/14/90, C, a, 90000356

Wibaux Commercial Historic District, Roughly bounded by W. Orgain Ave., Wibaux, E. First Ave. S., and E, Wibaux, 12/28/89, A, B, C, 89002170

Wibaux, Pierre, House, Orgain Ave., Wibaux, 9/10/71, A, B, 71000483

Yellowstone County

Antelope Stage Station, E of Broadview, Broadview vicinity, 1/19/83, A, 83001078

Billings Chamber of Commerce Building, 303 N. 27th St., Billings, 1/20/72, C, 72000739

Billings Historic District, Roughly bounded by N. 23rd and N. 25th Sts., 1st and Montana Aves., Billings, 3/13/79, A, C, 79001427

Boothill Cemetery, N of Billings, Billings vicinity, 4/17/79, B, d, 79001428

Fire House No. 2, 201 E. 30th St., Billings, 2/29/80, A, C, 80002436

Hoskins Basin Archeological District, Address Restricted, Billings vicinity, 11/20/74, D, 74001100

Masonic Temple, 2806 Third Ave. N, Billings, 4/17/86, A, C, 86000847

Moss, Preston B., House, Address Restricted, Billings, 4/30/82, C, 82003181

North, Austin, House, 622 N. 29th St., Billings, 11/23/77, B, C, 77000822

O'Donnell, I. D., House, 105 Clark Ave., Billings, 11/23/77, B, C, 77000823

Parmly Billings Memorial Library, 2822 Montana Ave., Billings, 10/26/72, A, C, 72000740

Pictograph Cave, 7 mi. SE of Billings in Indian Caves Park, Billings vicinity, 10/15/66, A, D, NHL, 66000439

Pompey's Pillar, W of Pompey, Pompey's Pillar vicinity, 10/15/66, A, NHL, 66000440

Prescott Commons, Rimrock Rd., Billings, 4/30/82, A, C, 82003182

US Post Office and Courthouse—Billings [US Post Offices in Montana, 1900–1941, TR], 2602 First Ave. N, Billings, 3/14/86, A, C, 86000678

Yegen, Christian, House, 208 S. 35th St., Billings, 10/01/79, B, C, 79003779

Yegen, Peter, House, 209 S. 35th St., Billings, 4/16/80, B, C, 80002437

N. MARIANA ISLANDS

Rota Municipality

Commissioner's Office, N of Songsong Village, Songsong (Rota) vicinity, 4/17/81, A, C, 81000663

Dugi Archeological Site, Address Restricted, Songsong (Rota) vicinity, 2/11/85, D, 85000287

Japanese Coastal Defense Gun, SE of Songsong, Songsong (Rota) vicinity, 11/02/84, C, g, 84000422

Japanese Hospital, W side of Sasanhaya Bay, Songsong (Rota) vicinity, 4/16/81, C, 81000664

Mochong, Address Restricted, Songsong (Rota) vicinity, 9/11/85, A, D, 85002301

Nanyo Kohatsu Kabushiki Kaisha Sugar Mill, SW of Songsong Village, near the harbor, Songsong (Rota) vicinity, 4/16/81, A, C, 81000665

Rectory, N end of island, Songsong (Rota) vicinity, 4/16/81, C, a, 81000666

Rota Latte Stone Quarry, Address Restricted, Songsong (Rota) vicinity, 12/23/74, D, 74002225

Saipan Municipality

Banzai Cliff, Banadero, Magpi area, San Roque (Saipan) vicinity, 8/27/76, A, g, 76002192

Campaneyan Kristo Rai, Beach Rd., Garapan (Saipan), 10/30/84, A, a, 84000207

Chalan Galaide, Address Restricted, Garapan vicinity, 10/04/87, D, g, 87001559

House of Taga, San Jose Village, San Jose (Tinian), 12/19/74, D, 74002193

Isley Field Historic District, Saipan International Airport, Chalan Kanoa (Saipan) vicinity, 6/26/81, A, g, 81000667

Japanese Hospital, Rte. 3, Garapan (Saipan), 12/19/74, A, C, g, 74002189

Japanese Lighthouse, Navy Hill, Garapan (Saipan), 12/19/74, C, g, 74002224

Landing Beaches, Aslito-Isley Field, and Marpi Point, Saipan International Airport and Beaches, Chalan Kanoa (Saipan) vicinity, 2/04/85, A, g, NHL, 85001789

Managaha Island Historic District, W of Saipan, Garapan (Saipan) vicinity, 11/05/84, A, B, D, g, 84000425

Sabanetan Toro Latte Site, Address Restricted, Garapan (Saipan) vicinity, 11/08/84, D, 84000731

Suicide Cliff, Banadero, San Roque (Saipan) vicinity, 9/30/76, A, g, 76002193

Tachognya, Address Restricted, San Jose (Saipan) vicinity, 2/13/86, A, C, D, 86000235

Unai Lagua Japanese Defense Pillbox, Unai Lagua, San Roque (Saipan) vicinity, 6/01/84, A, C, g, 84002777

Unai Obyan Latte Site, Address Restricted, Chalan Kanoa (Saipan) vicinity, 2/05/85, D, 85000244

Waherak MAIHER, Public Works Headquarters Compound, Chalan Kanoa (Saipan) vicinity, 1/31/78, A, C, g, 78003081

Tinian Municipality

Japanese Structure, Near Red 2 Beach, Tinian Village (Tinian), 4/16/81, C, 81000669

Nanyo Kohatsu Kabushiki Kaisha Administration Building, Near Red 2 Beach, Tinian Village (Tinian), 4/16/81, A, C, 81000670

Nanyo Kohatsu Kabushiki Kaisha Ice Storage Building, Near Red 2 Beach, Tinian Village (Tinian), 4/17/81, A, 81000671

Nanyo Kohatsu Kabushiki Kaisha Laboratory, Near Red 2 Beach, Tinian Village (Tinian), 4/16/81, A, C, 81000672

Tinian Landing Beaches, Ushi Point Field, Tinian Island, Address unknown at this time, Tinian Village (Tinian), 12/30/85, A, g, NHL, 85003268

The World War II Unai Lagua Japanese Defense Pillbox in the Northern Mariana Islands is uniquely constructed: faced with shortages of cement and reinforcing steel, Japanese military engineers substituted coral limestone reinforced by narrow-gauge railroad tracks. (Colt Denfeld, n.d.)

NEBRASKA

Adams County

Antioch School, Near Crooked Creek, Pauline vicinity, 9/28/88, C, 88000914

Brach, William, House, 823 N. Lincoln Ave., Hastings, 2/01/79, B, C, 79001429

Burlington Station, 1st St. and St. Joseph Ave., Hastings, 3/29/78, A, C, 78001693

Chautauqua Pavilion, Chautauqua Park, Hastings, 10/19/78, A, C, 78001692

Clarke Hotel, 233 N. Hastings Ave., Hastings, 12/07/87, C, 87002094

Farrell Block, 533–537 2nd St., and 112 Denver Ave., Hastings, 5/01/79, B, C, 79001430

McCormick Hall, Hastings College campus, Hastings, 5/12/75, A, C, 75001086

Nebraska Loan and Trust Company Building, 2nd St. and Lincoln Ave., Hastings, 5/01/79, A, C, 79001431

Nowlan-Dietrich House, 1105 N. Kansas Ave., Hastings, 4/17/79, B, 79001432

Ringland Hall, Hastings College campus, Hastings, 5/12/75, A, C, 75001087

St. Mark's Episcopal Pro-Catherdral, Jct. of Fourth & Burlington, Hastings, 11/30/87, C, a, 87002086

Stein Brothers Building, 630 W. 2nd St., Hastings, 5/01/79, A, C, 79001433

Thirty-Two Mile Station Site, Address Restricted, Hastings vicinity, 2/20/75, A, D, 75001088

Victory Building, Second at Saint Joseph Ave., Hastings, 3/31/87, C, 86003379

Antelope County

Antelope County Courthouse, 501–511 Main St., Neligh, 12/03/80, A, C, 80002438

Bridge [Highway Bridges in Nebraska MPS], Twp. Rd. over unnamed stream, 6.8 mi. NE of Royal, Royal vicinity, 6/29/92, C, 92000725

Elkhorn River Bridge [Highway Bridges in Nebraska MPS], Twp. Rd. over the Elkhorn R., 3 mi. E of Clearwater, Clearwater vicinity, 6/29/92, C, b, 92000771

Gates College Gymnasium, 509 L St., Neligh, 4/20/81, A, 81000367

Neligh Mill, 111 W. 2nd St., Neligh, 10/15/69, A, 69000128

Neligh Mill Bridge [Highway Bridges in Nebraska MPS], Elm St. over the Elkhorn R., Neligh, 6/29/92, C, 92000724

Neligh Mill Elevators (Boundary Increase), 111 W. 2nd, Neligh, 12/15/83, A, 83003982

St. Peter's Episcopal Church, 411 L St., Neligh, 12/03/80, C, a, 80002439

Verdigris Creek Bridge [Highway Bridges in Nebraska MPS], Twp. Rd. over Verdigris Cr., 1.9 mi. NE of Royal, Royal vicinity, 6/29/92, C, 92000770

Arthur County

First Arthur County Courthouse and Jail [County Courthouses of Nebraska MPS], Marshall St. between Fir and Elm Sts., Arthur, 1/10/90, A, C, 89002241

Pilgrim Holiness Church, Off NE 61, Arthur, 6/18/79, A, C, a, 79001434

Banner County

Hampton, C. C., Homestead, Address Restricted, Harrisburg vicinity, 12/13/84, A, 84000501

Boone County

St. Bonaventure Church Complex, Off NE 14, Raeville, 10/19/82, A, C, a, 82000598

US Post Office—Albion [Nebraska Post Offices Which Contain Section Artwork MPS], 310 W. Church St., Albion, 5/11/92, A, C, 92000475

Box Butte County

Box Butte County Courthouse [County Courthouses of Nebraska MPS], Box Butte Ave. between E. 5th and 6th Sts., Alliance, 1/10/90, A, C, 89002212

City of Alliance Central Park Fountain, Jct. of 10th St. and Niobrara Ave., Alliance, 11/28/90, C, 90001772

Running Water Stage Station Site, Address Restricted, Marsland vicinity, 2/20/75, D, 75001089

Boyd County

Lynch Archeological Site, Address Restricted, Lynch vicinity, 12/02/74, D, 74001101

Ponca Creek Bridge [Highway Bridges in Nebraska MPS], Co. Rd. over Ponca Cr., 3 mi. E of Lynch, Lynch vicinity, 6/29/92, C, 92000769

SS Peter & Paul Catholic School, Jct. of 2nd and Broadway Sts., SE corner, Butte, 1/07/92, A, a, 91001751

White Horse Ranch, SE of Naper between the Keya Paha and Niobrara Rivers, Naper vicinity, 7/05/90, A, 90000984

Brown County

Miller Hotel, 197 W. Third St., Long Pine, 11/27/89, A, C, 89002041

Buffalo County

Barnd, John, House, 320 E. 31st St., Kearney, 3/31/83, A, C, 83001079

Frank, George W., House, Kearney State College, Kearney, 2/23/73, B, C, 73001054

Hanson-Downing House, 723 W. 22nd St., Kearney, 12/10/80, C, 80002440

Kilgore Bridge [Highway Bridges in Nebraska MPS], NE 10 over N. Channel Platte R., 7.1 mi. SE of Kearney, Kearney vicinity, 6/29/92, C, 92000768

Meisner, George, House, Address Restricted, Shelton vicinity, 6/23/88, C, 88000903

Saint Luke's Protestant Episcopal Church, 2304 Second Ave., Kearney, 12/01/86, C, a, 86003360

Sweetwater Mill Bridge [Highway Bridges in Nebraska MPS], Co. Rd. over Mud Cr., Sweetwater, 6/29/92, C, 92000767

Thomas, Dr. A. O., House, 2222 9th Ave., Kearney, 2/28/80, B, C, 80002441

U.S. Post Office, 2401 Central Ave., Kearney, 9/17/81, C, 81000368

Burt County

Burt County Courthouse [County Courthouses of Nebraska MPS], 13th St. between M and N Sts., Tekamah, 1/10/90, A, C, 89002223

Deutsche Ev. Luth. St. Johannes Kirche, Address Restricted, Lyons vicinity, 8/02/82, A, C, a, d, 82003183

Houston, E. C., House, 319 N. Thirteenth St., Tekamah, 3/13/86, C, 86000338

Logan Creek Site, Address Restricted, Oakland vicinity, 1/26/70, D, 70000367

Spielman, H. M. S., House, 1103 I St., Tekamah, 7/17/86, B, C, 86001713

Stork, John Henry, Log House, Address Restricted, Tekamah vicinity, 5/29/80, A, C, 80002442

Tekamah City Bridge [Highway Bridges in Nebraska MPS], US 75 over Tekamah Cr., Tekamah, 6/29/92, C, 92000766

Butler County

Barcal Site, Address Restricted, Abie vicinity, 3/24/72, D, 72000741

Bellwood Archeological Site, Address Restricted, Bellwood vicinity, 8/13/74, D, 74001102

Big Blue River Bridge [Highway Bridges in Nebraska MPS], Twp. Rd. over Big Blue R., 1 mi. SE of Surprise, Surprise vicinity, 6/29/92, C, 92000708

Clear Creek Bridge [Highway Bridges in Nebraska MPS], Twp. Rd. over Clear Cr., 5.8 mi. NW of

Butler County—Continued

Bellwood, Bellwood vicinity, 6/29/92, C, b, 92000734

Fremont, Elkhorn and Missouri Valley Railroad Depot, 1st and Maple Sts., Dwight, 10/11/79, A, 79003682

Linwood Site, Address Restricted, Linwood vicinity, 3/16/72, D, 72000742

Surprise Opera House [Opera House Buildings in Nebraska 1867-1917 MPS], SE corner, intersection of Miller and River Sts., Surprise, 7/06/88, A, 88000940

Taylor, Chauncey S., House, 715 4th St., David City, 6/25/82, B, C, 82003184

Thorpe's Opera House [Opera House Buildings in Nebraska 1867-1917 MPS], 457-1/2 D St., David City, 9/28/88, A, 88000941

Upper Oak Creek Descent Ruts of the Woodbury Cutoff, Ox Bow Trail of the California Road, Roughly, 4 mi. SE of Brainard, Brainard vicinity, 11/27/92, A, 92001572

Cass County

Ashland Archeological Site, Address Restricted, Ashland vicinity, 2/10/75, D, 75001090

Bridge [Highway Bridges in Nebraska MPS], Co. Rd. over unnamed stream, 4.7 mi. SE of Louisville, Louisville vicinity, 6/29/92, C, 92000707

Cass County Courthouse [County Courthouses of Nebraska MPS], Main St. between 3rd and 4th Sts., Plattsmouth, 1/10/90, A, C, 89002248

Davis, Theodore, Site, Address Restricted, Weeping Water vicinity, 5/19/72, D, 72000743

Gibson House, 107 Clinton, Weeping Water, 3/20/86, C, 86000471

Gilmore, Walker, Site (22CC28), Address Restricted, Murray vicinity, 10/15/66, D, NHL, 66000441

Kehlbeck Farmstead, Address Restricted, Avoca vicinity, 9/26/85, A, C, 85002577

McLaughlin-Waugh-Dovey House, 414 B Ave., Plattsmouth, 10/14/80, B, C, 80002443

Naomi Institute, 3 mi. E of Murray, Murray vicinity, 3/24/77, A, 77000825

Nehawka Flint Quarries, Address Restricted, Nehawka vicinity, 1/26/70, D, 70000368

Plattsmouth Bridge [Highway Bridges in Nebraska MPS], US 34 over the Missouri R., Plattsmouth, 4/15/93, C, 92000755

Plattsmouth Main Street Historic District, Main St. bounded by Avenue A, S. and N. 3rd St., 1st Ave. and S. and N. 7th St., Plattsmouth, 9/26/85, A, C, 85002585

The Elms, Off NE 1, Elmwood, 3/24/77, B, g, 77000824

Weeping Water Historic District, Randolph and H Sts., Weeping Water, 12/08/72, A, C, a, 72000744

Cedar County

Bow Valley Mills, N of Wynot, Wynot vicinity, 11/17/78, B, C, 78003402

Cedar County Courthouse [County Courthouses of Nebraska MPS], Broadway Ave. between Centre and Franklin Sts., Hartington, 1/10/90, A, C, 89002214

City Hall and Auditorium, 101 N. Broadway, Hartington, 7/21/83, C, 83001080

Couser Barn, Address Restricted, Laurel vicinity, 7/17/86, C, 86001714

Meridian Bridge [Highway Bridges in Nebraska MPS], US 81 over the Missouri R., just S of Yankton, SD, South Yankton vicinity, 6/17/93, C, 93000537

Schulte Archeological Site, Address Restricted, St. Helena vicinity, 7/30/74, D, 74001103

St. Boniface Catholic Church Complex, Main St., Menominee, 7/21/83, A, C, a, d, 83001081

Wiseman Archeological Site, Address Restricted, Wynot vicinity, 12/02/74, D, 74001104

Zavadil, Franz, Farmstead, Address Restricted, Menominee vicinity, 1/31/85, A, C, 85000173

Chase County

Champion Mill, Mill and Second Sts., Champion, 6/23/88, A, 88000913

Chase County Courthouse [County Courthouses of Nebraska MPS], Broadway between 9th and 10th Sts., Imperial, 1/10/90, A, C, 89002222

Lovett Site, Address Restricted, Wauneta vicinity, 5/05/72, D, 72000745

Cherry County

Adamson Bridge [Highway Bridges in Nebraska MPS], NE 97 over the Niobrara R., 7.8 mi. SW of Valentine, Valentine vicinity, 6/29/92, C, 92000749

Bell Bridge [Highway Bridges in Nebraska MPS], Co. Rd. over the Niobrara R., 11.9 mi. NE of Valentine, Valentine vicinity, 6/29/92, C, 92000752

Berry State Aid Bridge [Highway Bridges in Nebraska MPS], Co. Rd. over the Niobrara R., 10 mi. NE of Valentine, Valentine vicinity, 6/29/92, C, 92000753

Borman Bridge [Highway Bridges in Nebraska MPS], Co. Rd. over the Niobrara R., 2.3 mi. SE of Valentine, Valentine vicinity, 6/29/92, C, 92000751

Brewer Bridge [Highway Bridges in Nebraska MPS], Co. Rd. over the Niobrara R., 14.7 mi. E of Valentine, Valentine vicinity, 6/29/92, C, b, 92000754

Bryan Bridge, US 20, Valentine vicinity, 6/23/88, C, 88000912

Cherry County Courthouse [County Courthouses of Nebraska MPS], 4th and Main Sts., Valentine, 1/10/90, A, 89002229

Twin Bridge [Highway Bridges in Nebraska MPS], Co. Rd. over the N. Loup R., 7.9 mi. NW of Brownlee, Brownlee vicinity, 6/29/92, C, 92000750

US Post Office—Valentine [Nebraska Post Offices Which Contain Section Artwork MPS], 348 N. Main St., Valentine, 12/13/91, A, C, 91001750

Valentine Public School, 3rd and Macomb Sts., Valentine, 6/14/84, A, C, 84002454

Walcott, F. M., House, 431 N. Hall St., Valentine, 10/07/82, B, C, 82000599

Cheyenne County

Brownson Viaduct [Highway Bridges in Nebraska MPS], NE Spur 17A over US 30 and UPRR tracks, .8 mi. NW of Brownson, Brownson vicinity, 6/29/92, C, 92000747

Deadwood Draw, NW of Sidney, Sidney vicinity, 11/12/92, A, D, 92001574

Fort Sidney Historic District, Roughly bounded by 6th and 5th Aves., Linden and Jackson, Sidney, 3/28/73, A, 73001056

Herboldsheimer, Daniel and Sarah, Ranch, NE of Potter, Potter vicinity, 4/05/90, C, 90000566

Lodgepole Opera House [Opera House Buildings in Nebraska 1867-1917 MPS], W side of Oberfelder at Front, Lodgepole, 7/07/88, A, 88000947

Sidney Carnegie Library [Carnegie Libraries in Nebraska MPS], 740 Illinois St., Sidney, 7/03/91, A, 91000838

Stevens, Wes, Site, Address Restricted, Potter vicinity, 8/28/73, D, 73001055

Water Holes Ranch, Roughly, 7.5 mi. W of Gurley, Gurley vicinity, 11/12/92, A, D, 92001575

Clay County

Clark, Isaac Newton, House, 468 Cedar St., Sutton, 12/15/83, B, C, b, 83003985

Clay County Courthouse [County Courthouses of Nebraska MPS], Fairfield St. between Alexander and Brown Aves., Clay Center, 1/10/90, A, C, 89002240

Deering Bridge [Highway Bridges in Nebraska MPS], Co. Rd. over School Cr., 2 mi. N, 2 mi. E of Sutton, Sutton vicinity, 6/29/92, C, 92000748

Saint Martin's Catholic Church, NW of DeWeese, DeWeese vicinity, 9/26/85, A, C, a, 85002574

Colfax County

Colfax County Courthouse, Off NE 15, Schuyler, 9/03/81, C, 81000369

Janecek, John, House, 805 E. 8th St., Schuyler, 7/15/82, B, C, 82003185

Oak Ballroom, Colfax St., Schuler, 2/01/83, A, C, g, 83001082

Our Lady of Perpetual Help Catholic Church & Cemetery, Address Restricted, Schuyler vicinity, 11/12/82, A, C, a, 82000600

Schuyler City Hall, 1020 A St., Schuyler, 9/03/81, C, 81000370

Colfax County—Continued

Schuyler Site, Address Restricted, Schuyler vicinity, 8/14/73, D, 73001057

US Post Office—Schuyler [Nebraska Post Offices Which Contain Section Artwork MPS], 119 E. 11th St., Schuyler, 5/11/92, A, C, 92000476

Wolfe Archeological Site, Address Restricted, Schuyler vicinity, 7/30/74, D, 74001105

Zion Presbyterian Church, 5 mi. SE of Clarkson off NE 15, Clarkson vicinity, 1/07/88, A, C, a, 87002071

Cuming County

Neihardt, John G., Study, NW corner of Washington and Grove Sts., Bancroft, 7/28/70, B, 70000369

Rattlesnake Creek Bridge [Highway Bridges in Nebraska MPS], Co. Rd. over Rattlesnake Cr., 2.8 mi. NW of Bancroft, Bancroft vicinity, 6/29/92, C, 92000743

Custer County

Arrow Hotel, 509 S. 9th Ave., Broken Bow, 9/12/85, A, C, 85002145

Custer County Courthouse and Jail, Courthouse Square, Main St., Broken Bow, 4/19/79, C, 79001435

Dowse, William R., House, Address Restricted, Comstock vicinity, 12/01/86, C, 86003365

First Custer County Courthouse [County Courthouses of Nebraska MPS], Pacific St. and Cameron Ave., Callaway, 1/10/90, A, b, 89002213

Sargent Bridge [Highway Bridges in Nebraska MPS], Dawson St. over the Middle Loup R., 1 mi. S of Sargent, Sargent vicinity, 6/29/92, C, 92000740

Security State Bank Building, 403 S. Ninth St., Broken Bow, 11/30/87, C, 87002072

Wescott, Gibbons & Bragg Store, Off NE 106, Comstock, 1/31/78, B, C, b, 78001694

Dakota County

Emmanuel Lutheran Church, 1500 Hickory St., Dakota City, 10/15/69, A, C, a, 69000129

Homer Site, Address Restricted, Homer vicinity, 8/14/73, D, 73001058

Meisch House, 213 Seventeenth St., South Sioux City, 3/13/86, C, 86000387

O'Connor, Cornelius, House, E of Homer, Homer vicinity, 11/23/77, C, 77000826

Dawes County

Army Theatre [Opera House Buildings in Nebraska 1867-1917 MPS], Fort Robinson State Park, Crawford, 7/07/88, A, 88000930

Bordeaux Trading Post, 3 mi. E of Chadron on U.S. 20, Chadron vicinity, 3/16/72, A, D, e, 72000746

Chadron Public Library, 507 Bordeaux St., Chadron, 6/21/90, A, 90000985

Co-operative Block Building, 435–445 2nd, Crawford, 9/12/85, A, C, 85002146

Crites Hall [Chadron State College Historic Buildings TR], 10th and Main Sts., Chadron, 9/08/83, A, B, C, g, 83001083

Dawes County Courthouse [County Courthouses of Nebraska MPS], S. Main St. between 4th and 5th Sts., Chadron, 7/05/90, A, C, 90000975

Fort Robinson and Red Cloud Agency, 2 mi. W of Crawford, Crawford vicinity, 10/15/66, A, NHL, 66000442

Library [Chadron State College Historic Buildings TR], 10th and Main Sts., Chadron, 9/08/83, A, C, 83001084

Miller Hall [Chadron State College Historic Buildings TR], 10th and Main Sts., Chadron, 9/08/83, A, 83001085

Sparks Hall [Chadron State College Historic Buildings TR], 10th and Main Sts., Chadron, 9/08/83, A, B, C, 83001086

US Post Office—Crawford [Nebraska Post Offices Which Contain Section Artwork MPS], 144 Main St., Crawford, 5/11/92, A, C, 92000477

Work, Edna, Hall [Chadron State College Historic Buildings TR], 10th and Main Sts., Chadron, 9/08/83, A, B, C, 83001087

Dawson County

Allen's Opera House [Opera House Buildings in Nebraska 1867-1917 MPS], 100 E. Eighth, Cozad, 9/28/88, A, 88000951

Calling, Ernest A., House, 1514 Lake Ave., Gothenburg, 10/25/79, C, 79001437

Carnegie Public Library, 1104 Lake Ave., Gothenburg, 12/19/86, A, C, 86003443

Dawson County Courthouse [County Courthouses of Nebraska MPS], Washington St. between 7th and 8th Sts., Lexington, 1/10/90, A, C, 89002236

Hendee Hotel, 220 E. 8th St., Cozad, 3/21/79, A, 79001436

Midway Stage Station, S of Gothenburg, Gothenburg vicinity, 10/15/69, A, 69000372

Olive, Ira Webster, House, 401 E. 13th St., Lexington, 11/27/89, C, 89002042

Deuel County

Deuel County Courthouse [County Courthouses of Nebraska MPS], 718 3rd St., Chappell, 1/10/90, A, C, 89002239

Phelps Hotel, NE corner of 2nd and Pine Sts., Big Springs, 10/15/70, A, 70000370

Sudman, Fred and Minnie Meyer, House, 490 Vincent Ave., Chappell, 12/06/90, C, 90001770

Dixon County

Cook Blacksmith Shop, 204 3rd St., Ponca, 12/27/74, A, 74001106

Dixon County Courthouse [County Courthouses of Nebraska MPS], 3rd and Iowa Sts., Ponca, 1/10/90, A, C, 89002247

Indian Hill Archeological District, Address Restricted, New Castle vicinity, 7/06/84, D, 84002460

Ponca Historic District, Roughly bounded by East, Court, 2nd and 3rd Sts., Ponca, 5/18/79, A, C, 79001438

Swedish Evangelical Lutheran Salem Church, Off NE 35, Wakefield, 2/01/83, A, C, 83001088

Dodge County

Barnard Park Historic District, Bounded by 4th, 8th, and Union Sts. and Platte Ave., Fremont, 7/12/90, A, 90001053

Bullock, Samuel, House, 508 W. Military Ave., Fremont, 9/12/85, C, 85002147

Dodge County Courthouse [County Courthouses of Nebraska MPS], 435 N. Park Ave., Fremont, 1/10/90, A, C, 89002208

Harder Hotel, 503 Main St., Scribner, 11/27/89, A, C, 89002046

Hooper Historic District, Main, Elk, Fulton and Myrtle Sts., Hooper, 5/08/80, A, C, 80002445

Knoell, Christopher, Farmstead, NW of Fremont, Fremont vicinity, 1/13/83, A, C, 83001089

Love-Larson Opera House [Opera House Buildings in Nebraska 1867-1917 MPS (AD)], 543-545 Broad St., Fremont, 9/10/74, A, 74001107

McDonald, J. D., House, 310 E. Military Ave., Fremont, 12/10/80, B, C, 80002444

North Bend Carnegie Library, 140 E. 8th St., North Bend, 9/03/81, A, C, 81000371

Nye House, 1643 N. Nye Ave., Fremont, 11/23/77, B, C, 77000827

Osterman and Tremaine Building, 455 N. Broad St., Fremont, 5/23/78, A, C, 78001695

Scheider's Opera House [Opera House Buildings in Nebraska 1867-1917 MPS], 104 Ash, Snyder, 9/28/88, A, 88000939

Schneider, R. B., House, 234 W. 10th St., Fremont, 7/15/82, B, C, 82003186

Uehling, Frank, Barn, Off U.S. 77, Uehling vicinity, 8/01/85, B, C, 85001666

Douglas County

Anheuser-Busch Beer Depot, 1207–1215 Jones St., Omaha, 2/01/79, A, C, 79001440

Aquila Court Building, 1615 Howard St., Omaha, 10/02/73, C, 73001059

Astro Theater, 2001 Farnam St., Omaha, 8/13/74, A, C, g, 74001108

Bank of Florence, 8502 N. 30th St., Omaha, 10/15/69, A, 69000130

Douglas County—Continued

Barton, Guy C., House, 3522 Farnam St., Omaha, 8/14/73, B, C, 73001060

Bemis Omaha Bag Company Building, 614-624 S. 11th St. and 1102-1118 Jones St., Omaha, 1/11/85, A, C, 85000066

Blackstone Hotel, 302 S. 36th St., Omaha, 1/11/85, A, C, 85000067

Bradford-Pettis House, 404 S. 39th St., Omaha, 7/21/83, A, B, C, 83001090

Brandeis, J. L., and Sons Store Building, 200 S. 16th St., Omaha, 10/20/82, A, C, 82000601

Brandeis-Millard House, 500 S. 38th St., Omaha, 11/28/80, B, C, 80002446

Burlington Headquarters Building, 1004 Farnam St., Omaha, 12/04/74, A, C, 74001109

Burlington Station, 925 S. 10th St., Omaha, 8/07/74, A, C, 74001110

Cabanne Archeological Site, Address Restricted, Omaha vicinity, 5/05/72, A, 72000749

Center School, 1730 S. 11th St., Omaha, 8/23/85, C, 85001796

Champe-Fremont 1 Archeological Site, Address Restricted, Omaha vicinity, 10/21/75, D, 75001091

City National Bank Building and Creighton Orpheum Theater [Opera House Buildings in Nebraska 1867-1917 MPS (AD)], 16th and Harney Sts., Omaha, 3/26/73, A, 73001061

Columbian School, 3819 Jones St., Omaha, 11/28/90, C, 90001769

Cornish, Joel N., House, 1404 S. 10th St., Omaha, 8/13/74, B, C, 74001111

Crook, Gen. George, House, Quarters No. 1, Fort Omaha, Omaha, 4/16/69, B, 69000131

Douglas County Courthouse, 1700 Farnam St., Omaha, 10/11/79, C, 79003683

Drake Court Apartments and the Dartmore Apartments Historic District, Jones St., Omaha, 11/10/80, C, 80002447

Eggerss—O'Flyng Building [Warehouses in Omaha MPS], 801 S. 15th St., Omaha, 12/13/91, A, C, 91001759

Father Flanagan's Boys' Home, W. Dodge Rd., Boys Town, 2/04/85, A, NHL, 85002439

Father Flanagan's House, Off U.S. 6, Boys Town, 9/06/79, B, C, 79001439

First National Bank Building, 300-312 16th St., and 1601-1605 Farnam St., Omaha, 6/25/82, A, C, 82003187

First Unitarian Church of Omaha, 3114 Harney St., Omaha, 3/27/80, C, a, 80002448

Flatiron Hotel, 1722 St. Mary's Ave., Omaha, 9/21/78, C, 78003403

Ford Hospital, 121-129 S. Twenty-fifth St., Omaha, 3/20/86, A, B, 86000444

Fort Omaha Historic District, 30th St. between Fort St. and Laurel Ave., Omaha, 3/27/74, A, D, 74001112

Garneau-Kilpatrick House, 3100 Chicago St., Omaha, 10/07/82, B, C, 82000602

Georgia Row House, 1040-1044 S. 29th St., Omaha, 11/12/82, C, 82000603

Havens-Page House, 101 N. 39th St., Omaha, 10/07/82, C, 82000604

Hill Hotel, 509 S. Sixteenth St., Omaha, 4/20/88, C, 88000377

Holy Family Church, 915 N. Eighteenth St., Omaha, 7/17/86, C, a, 86001715

Jewell Building, 2221-2225 N. 24th St., Omaha, 7/21/83, A, C, 83001091

Jobbers' Canyon Historic District, Roughly bounded by Farnum, Eighth, Jackson, and Tenth Sts., Omaha, 12/04/86, A, C, 86003408

Joslyn, George A., Mansion, 3902 Davenport St., Omaha, 8/25/72, B, C, 72000747

Kelly, George H., House, 1924 Binney St., Omaha, 7/21/83, A, C, 83001092

Kennedy Building, 1517 Jackson St., Omaha, 8/23/85, C, 85001794

Leone, Florentine, and Carpathia Apartment Buildings, 832 S. 24th St., 834 S. 24th St. and 907-911 S. 25th St., Omaha, 5/16/85, A, C, 85001073

Lincoln Highway, CR 120 between One Hundred Eightieth & One Hundred Ninety First Sts., Elkhorn vicinity, 12/01/87, A, 87002098

Main Street Bridge [Highway Bridges in Nebraska MPS], Main St. over W. Papillion Cr., Elkhorn, 6/29/92, C, 92000746

Malcolm X House Site, 3448 Pinkney St., Omaha, 3/01/84, B, 84002463

Mason School, 1012 S. Twenty-fourth St., Omaha, 3/13/86, C, 86000339

McLaughlin, Charles D., House, 507 S. 38th St., Omaha, 11/08/82, A, C, 82000605

Melrose, The, 602 N. 33rd St., Omaha, 11/29/89, C, 89002044

Mercer, Dr. Samuel D., House, 3920 Cuming St., Omaha, 6/17/76, B, C, 76001130

Military Road Segment, Jct. of 82nd and Fort Sts., Omaha, 12/10/93, A, 93001400

Monmouth Park School, 4508 N. 33rd St., Omaha, 12/15/83, C, 83003988

Nash Block, 902-912 Farnam, Omaha, 5/16/85, A, C, 85001072

Normandie Apartments, 1102 Park Ave., Omaha, 12/06/91, C, 91001758

North Presbyterian Church, 3105 N. Twenty-fourth St., Omaha, 3/20/86, C, a, 86000443

Old Market Historic District, Bounded by 13th, Farnam, 10th and Jackson, Omaha, 3/23/79, A, C, 79001441

Old People's Home, 3325 Fontenelle Blvd., Omaha, 10/21/87, A, 87001182

Omaha Bolt, Nut and Screw Building [Warehouses in Omaha MPS], 1316 Jones St., Omaha, 7/10/92, A, C, 92000816

Omaha High School, 124 N. 20th St., Omaha, 10/11/79, A, C, 79003684

Omaha National Bank Building, 17th and Farnam Sts., Omaha, 10/18/72, C, 72000748

Omaha Public Library, 1823 Harney St., Omaha, 5/22/78, A, C, 78001696

Omaha Quartermaster Depot Historic District, Roughly bounded by Hickory and 22nd Sts., Woolworth Ave., and Union Pacific RR, Omaha, 7/26/79, A, C, 79003685

Packer's National Bank Building, 4939 S. 24th St., Omaha, 5/16/85, A, C, 85001071

Park School, 1320 S. 29th St., Omaha, 11/29/89, C, 89002043

Poppleton Block, 1001 Farnam St., Omaha, 10/07/82, B, C, 82000606

Porter-Thomsen House, 3426 Lincoln Blvd., Omaha, 10/21/82, B, C, 82000607

Prague Hotel, 1402 S. Thirteenth St., Omaha, 7/09/87, A, 87001148

Redick Tower, 1504 Harney St., Omaha, 6/21/84, C, 84002470

Robinson, J. C., House, 102 E. Lincoln Ave., Waterloo, 11/28/80, B, C, 80002452

Robinson, Lizzie, House, 2864 Corby St., Omaha, 2/25/93, B, a, 93000058

Rosewater School, 3764 S. 13th St., Omaha, 5/16/85, B, C, f, 85001070

Sacred Heart Catholic Church Complex, 2218 Binney St., Omaha, 3/24/83, C, 83001093

Saddle Creek Underpass [Highway Bridges in Nebraska MPS], US 6 (Dodge St.) over Saddle Cr. Rd., Omaha, 6/29/92, C, 92000741

Saint Joseph Parish Complex, 1730 S. Sixteenth St., Omaha, 7/17/86, A, C, a, 86001716

Sanford Hotel, 1913 Farnam St., Omaha, 9/26/85, B, C, 85002556

Saunders School, 415 N. Fourty-first Ave., Omaha, 3/13/86, C, 86000336

South Omaha Bridge [Highway Bridges in Nebraska MPS], US 275/NE 92 over the Missouri R., Omaha, 6/29/92, C, 92000742

South Omaha Main Street Historic District, Roughly S. 24th St. between M and O Sts., Omaha, 2/14/89, A, C, 88002828

Specht, Christian, Building, 1110 Douglas St., Omaha, 9/19/77, A, C, 77000828

St. Cecilia's Cathedral, 701 N. 40th St., Omaha, 1/25/79, C, a, 79001442

St. John's A.M.E. Church, 2402 N. 22nd St., Omaha, 5/29/80, C, a, 80002449

St. Martin of Tours Episcopal Church, 2312 J St., Omaha, 10/21/82, C, a, 82000608

St. Matthias' Episcopal Church, 1423 S. 10th St., Omaha, 11/23/80, C, a, 80002450

St. Philomena's Cathedral and Rectory, 1335 S. 10th St., Omaha, 1/03/80, A, C, a, 80002451

Standard Oil Company Building of Nebraska, 500 S. 18th St., Omaha, 8/24/79, A, 79001443

Steiner Rowhouse No. 1, 638-642 S. 19th St., Omaha, 7/03/91, C, 91000836

Steiner Rowhouse No. 2, 1906-1910 Jones St., Omaha, 7/03/91, C, 91000837

Storz, Gottlieb, House, 3708 Farnam St., Omaha, 8/07/74, B, C, 74001113

Strehlow Terrace, 2024 and 2107 N. Sixteenth St., Omaha, 12/23/86, B, C, 86003446

The Sherman, 2501 N. Sixteenth St., Omaha, 3/13/86, C, 86000334

Trinity Cathedral, 113 N. 18th St., Omaha, 8/07/74, A, C, a, 74001114

U.S.S. HAZARD and U.S.S. MARLIN, 2500 N. 24th St., Omaha, 1/17/79, A, g, 79001444

USS HAZARD (AM-240) National Historic Landmark, 2500 N. 24th St., Omaha, 1/01/79, A, g, NHL, 79003712

Douglas County—Continued

Union Passenger Terminal, 10th and Marcy Sts., Omaha, 11/12/71, A, C, g, 71000484

Vinton School, 2120 Deer Park Blvd., Omaha, 11/29/89, C, 89002045

Webster Telephone Exchange Building, 2213 Lake St., Omaha, 12/05/77, A, C, g, 77000829

Zabriskie, Edgar, House, 3524 Hawthorne Ave., Omaha, 11/28/78, C, 78001697

Dundy County

Dundy County Courthouse [County Courthouses of Nebraska MPS], W. 7th Ave. and Chief St., Benkelman, 1/10/90, A, C, 89002237

Fillmore County

Auditorium, The [Opera House Buildings in Nebraska 1867-1917 MPS], 160 N. Ninth, Geneva, 9/28/88, A, 88000950

Belle Prairie Township Hall & Strang Town Hall—Jail, Main St., Strang, 11/29/91, A, 91001752

Big Blue River Bridge [Highway Bridges in Nebraska MPS], Co. Rd. over W. Fork of the Big Blue R., 5 mi. N, 1 mi. W of Grafton, Grafton vicinity, 6/29/92, C, 92000745

Eberhardt, Philip and Addie Ellis, Farmstead, 3 mi. N of US 6, Exeter vicinity, 3/14/91, C, 91000299

Fairmont Creamery Company Building, SE of 6th Ave. and F St., Fairmont, 12/15/83, A, C, 83003989

Fillmore County Courthouse, 9th and G Sts., Geneva, 12/12/78, A, C, 78001698

Smith, George W., House, Twelfth St. between I and J Sts., Geneva, 5/08/86, B, C, 86001022

Strang School District No. 36, Main St., Strang, 6/25/92, C, 91001753

US Post Office—Geneva [Nebraska Post Offices Which Contain Section Artwork MPS], 202 N. 9th St., Geneva, 5/11/92, A, C, 92000478

Franklin County

Dupee Music Hall, 1402 P St., Franklin, 9/26/85, A, a, 85002484

First Congregational Church, U.C.C., Off NE 31C, Naponee, 9/14/82, C, a, 82003188

Franklin Bridge [Highway Bridges in Nebraska MPS], NE 10 over the Republican R., 1 mi. S of Franklin, Franklin vicinity, 6/29/92, C, 92000764

Franklin County Courthouse [County Courthouses of Nebraska MPS], 15th Ave. between N and O Sts., Franklin, 7/05/90, A, C, 90000962

Lincoln Hotel, 519 15th Ave., Franklin, 7/06/89, A, C, 89000799

Lost Creek Archeological Site, Address Restricted, Bloomington vicinity, 5/26/83, D, 83001094

Republican River Bridge [Highway Bridges in Nebraska MPS], Co. Rd. over the Republican R., 1 mi. E and 1.5 mi. S of Riverton, Riverton vicinity, 6/29/92, C, 92000765

Frontier County

Mowry Bluff Archeological Site, Address Restricted, Cambridge vicinity, 7/12/74, D, 74001115

Red Smoke Archeological Site, Address Restricted, Stockville vicinity, 10/01/74, D, 74001116

Furnas County

Cambridge State Aid Bridge [Highway Bridges in Nebraska MPS], NE 47 over the Republican R., .6 mi. S of Cambridge, Cambridge vicinity, 6/29/92, C, 92000763

Gage County

Barneston Site, Address Restricted, Barneston vicinity, 1/21/74, D, 74001117

Beatrice Chautauqua Pavilion and Gatehouse, 6th and Grable Sts., Beatrice, 4/09/79, A, C, b, 79001445

Beatrice City Library, 220 N. 5th St., Beatrice, 7/12/76, A, C, 76001131

Big Indian Creek Bridge [Highway Bridges in Nebraska MPS], Twp. Rd. over Big Indian Cr., 3 mi. SW of Wymore, Wymore vicinity, 6/29/92, C, 92000760

Bloody Run Bridge [Highway Bridges in Nebraska MPS], Twp. Rd. over Bloody Run, 4 mi. SW of Virginia, Virginia vicinity, 6/29/92, C, 92000759

Blue Springs Site, Address Restricted, Blue Springs vicinity, 8/14/73, D, 73001063

Bridge [Highway Bridges in Nebraska MPS], Twp. Rd. over Sicily Cr., 6 mi. NW of Wymore, Wymore vicinity, 6/29/92, C, 92000761

Burlington Northern Depot, 118 Court St., Beatrice, 5/02/75, A, C, 75001092

DeWitt Flour Mills and King Iron Bridge, E of DeWitt on Big Blue River, DeWitt vicinity, 12/27/78, A, B, C, b, 78001699

Farmers State Bank, 601 Main, Adams, 6/11/92, C, 92000702

Filley, Elijah, Stone Barn, S of Filley off U.S. 136, Filley vicinity, 4/11/77, B, C, 77000830

Gage County Courthouse [County Courthouses of Nebraska MPS], 612 Grant St., Beatrice, 1/10/90, A, C, 89002226

Homestead National Monument of America, 4.5 mi. NW of Beatrice on NE 4, Beatrice vicinity, 10/15/66, A, C, NPS, 66000115

Hoyt Street Bridge [Highway Bridges in Nebraska MPS], Vacated Twp. Rd. over the Big Blue R., Beatrice, 6/29/92, C, b, 92000758

Kilpatrick, Samuel D., House, 701 N. 7th St., Beatrice, 12/20/84, A, B, C, 84000476

Lake Bridenthal House, 113 S. 9th St., Wymore, 2/24/83, A, C, 83001095

Mission Creek Bridge [Highway Bridges in Nebraska MPS], Co. Hwy. over Mission Cr., 7 mi SW of Barneston, Barneston vicinity, 6/29/92, C, 92000762

Paddock Hotel, 105 N. Sixth St., Beatrice, 11/30/87, C, 87002084

Paddock, Algernon S., House, 1401 N. 10th St., Beatrice, 3/14/73, B, C, 73001062

Garden County

Ash Hollow Cave, Address Restricted, Lewellen vicinity, 10/15/66, D, NHL, 66000445

Ash Hollow Historic District, SW of Lewellen along U.S. 26, Lewellen vicinity, 8/06/75, A, d, 75001093

Garden County Courthouse [County Courthouses of Nebraska MPS], F and Main Sts., Oshkosh, 1/10/90, A, C, 89002231

Lewellen State Aid Bridge [Highway Bridges in Nebraska MPS], Co. Rd. over the N. Platte R., 1 mi. S of Lewellen, Lewellen vicinity, 6/29/92, C, 92000756

Lisco State Aid Bridge [Highway Bridges in Nebraska MPS], Co. Rd. over the N. Platte R., .6 mi S of Lisco, Lisco vicinity, 6/29/92, C, 92000757

Garfield County

Burwell Bridge [Highway Bridges in Nebraska MPS], NE 11 over the N. Loup R., Burwell, 6/29/92, C, 92000715

Garfield County Frontier Fairgrounds, Off NE 91, Burwell vicinity, 5/09/85, A, 85001005

Gosper County

Gosper County Courthouse [County Courthouses of Nebraska MPS], 507 Smith Ave., Elwood, 7/05/90, A, C, 90000961

Grant County

Hotel DeFair, NE 2 and Main St., Hyannis, 10/29/76, B, 76001132

Greeley County

Church of the Visitation of the Blessed Virgin Mary, Off NE 56, O'Connor, 2/23/84, A, C, a, g, 84002472

Greeley County—Continued

Greeley County Courthouse [County Courthouses of Nebraska MPS], Kildare St., Greeley, 1/10/90, A, C, 89002228

Scotia Chalk Building, Off NE 22, Scotia, 10/11/79, C, 79003686

St. Michael's Catholic Church Complex, NE of Greeley Ctr., Spalding, 12/15/83, A, C, a, 83003990

Hall County

Bartenbach, H. J., House, 720 W. Division, Grand Island, 12/08/86, C, g, 86003385

Cathedral of the Nativity of the Blessed Virgin Mary, 204 S. Cedar St., Grand Island, 7/15/82, C, a, 82003189

Evangelische Lutherische Dreienigkeit Kirche, 512 E. Second St., Grand Island, 12/01/86, C, a, 86003378

Glade—Donald House, 1004 W. Division, Grand Island, 9/12/85, B, C, 85002140

Grand Island Carnegie Library, 321 W. 2nd St., Grand Island, 5/02/75, A, C, 75001094

Grand Island FCC Monitoring Station, 5 mi. W of Grand Island near NE Spur 430, Grand Island vicinity, 1/16/73, A, g, 73001064

Hall County Courthouse, 1st and Locust, Grand Island, 9/15/77, A, C, 77000831

Hamilton—Donald House, 820 W. Second St., Grand Island, 3/13/86, B, C, 86000390

Hargis, Andrew M., House, 1109 W. 2nd St., Grand Island, 6/09/78, B, C, 78001700

Hotel Yancey (The), 123 N. Locust St., Grand Island, 12/13/84, A, C, 84000504

Liederkranz, 401 W. 1st St., Grand Island, 11/30/78, A, 78001701

Nine Bridges Bridge [Highway Bridges in Nebraska MPS], Private rd. over Middle Channel of the Platte R., 3.9 mi. N of Doniphan, Doniphan vicinity, 6/29/92, C, 92000716

Roeser, Oscar, House, 721 W. Koenig St., Grand Island, 6/25/82, B, C, 82003190

Stolley Homestead Site, Stolley Park, Grand Island, 3/16/72, A, B, C, e, 72000750

Stolley, William, Homestead and Site of Fort Independence (Boundary Decrease), Area on N, S and W sides of Stolley Park, Grand Island, 3/16/72, A, C, e, 72001584

Stolley, William, Homestead and Site of Fort Independence (Boundary Increase), Area along E side of Stolley Park, Grand Island, 4/21/76, A, C, b, 76002281

Hamilton County

Hamilton County Courthouse, Courthouse Sq., Aurora, 7/29/85, A, C, 85001665

Hearn, Kathleen, Building, 10th and O Sts., Aurora, 8/01/84, B, C, 84002480

IOOF Opera House [Opera House Buildings in Nebraska 1867-1917 MPS], N. Third and B Sts., Hampton, 9/28/88, A, 88000952

Royal Highlanders Building, 1235 M St., Aurora, 9/12/85, A, C, 85002144

St. Johannes Danske Lutherske Kirke, 2170 N. T Rd., Marquette vicinity, 11/13/92, A, a, 92001570

Streeter—Peterson House, 1121 9th St., Aurora, 11/29/91, C, 91001754

Harlan County

Prairie Dog Creek Bridge [Highway Bridges in Nebraska MPS], Twp. Rd. over Prairie Dog Cr., 8.5 mi. S and 1 mi. W of Orleans, Orleans vicinity, 6/29/92, C, 92000712

Sappa Creek Bridge [Highway Bridges in Nebraska MPS], Co. Rd. over Sappa Cr., 2 mi. E of Stamford, Stamford vicinity, 6/29/92, C, b, 92000713

Turkey Creek Bridge [Highway Bridges in Nebraska MPS], Co. Rd. over Turkey Cr., 2 mi. W and 1 mi. S of Ragan, Ragan vicinity, 6/29/92, C, 92000711

Hayes County

Daniel, J. M., House, Address Restricted, Hamlet vicinity, 5/30/85, B, 85001169

Daniel, J. M., School-District #3, Address Restricted, Hamlet vicinity, 5/30/85, B, 85001170

St. John's Evangelical Lutheran German Church and Cemetery, Address Restricted, Hayes Center vicinity, 5/16/85, A, C, a, d, 85001069

Hitchcock County

Bridge [Highway Bridges in Nebraska MPS], Co. Rd. over intermittent stream, 2 mi. E of Stratton, Stratton vicinity, 6/29/92, C, 92000714

Massacre Canyon Battlefield, Address Restricted, Trenton vicinity, 7/25/74, D, 74001118

St. Paul's Methodist Protestant Church, S of Culbertson on NE 17, Culbertson vicinity, 1/25/79, C, a, 79001446

Holt County

Eagle Creek Archeological Site, Address Restricted, O'Neill vicinity, 10/01/74, D, 74001119

Golden Hotel, 406 E. Douglas St., O'Neill, 11/27/89, A, 89002040

Holt County Courthouse [County Courthouses of Nebraska MPS], N. 4th St. between E. Clay and Benton Sts., O'Neill, 7/05/90, A, C, 90000974

Old Nebraska State Bank Building, Douglas and 4th Sts., O'Neill, 10/01/74, B, 74001120

Redbird I Site, Address Restricted, Redbird vicinity, 11/21/74, D, 74001121

US Post Office—O'Neill [Nebraska Post Offices Which Contain Section Artwork MPS], 204 N. 4th St., O'Neill, 5/11/92, A, C, 92000479

Hooker County

Hooker County Courthouse [County Courthouses of Nebraska MPS], Cleveland Ave. between Railroad and 1st Sts., Mullen, 1/10/90, A, C, 89002218

Humphrey Archeological Site, Address Restricted, Mullen vicinity, 1/21/74, D, 74001122

Kelso Site, Address Restricted, Mullen vicinity, 1/21/74, D, 74001123

Howard County

Coufal Site, Address Restricted, Cotesfield vicinity, 10/15/66, D, NHL, 66000446

Howard County Courthouse [County Courthouses of Nebraska MPS], Indian St. between 6th and 7th Sts., St. Paul, 1/10/90, A, C, 89002233

Palmer Site, Address Restricted, Palmer vicinity, 10/15/66, D, NHL, 66000447

Jefferson County

Colman House, 501 Lavelle St., Diller, 6/25/82, A, C, 82003191

Diller, Anna C., Opera House [Opera House Buildings in Nebraska 1867-1917 MPS], Commercial and Hilton, Diller, 7/06/88, A, 88000932

District No. 10 School, W of Powell, Powell vicinity, 12/15/78, A, 78001702

Fairbury Public-Carnegie Library, 601 7th St., Fairbury, 9/12/85, A, C, 85002141

IOOF Temple Building, 523 E St., Fairbury, 6/15/87, C, 87000925

Jefferson County Courthouse, Courthouse Sq., Fairbury, 11/27/72, C, 72000751

People's State Bank, NE 103, Diller, 12/13/84, A, C, 84000509

Site No. JF00-072 [Nebraska—Kansas Public Land Survey TR], Jct. of Thayer, Jefferson, Washington and Republic Co. lines, Mahaska, vicinity, 6/19/87, A, 87001000

Smith, Woral C., Lime Kiln and Limestone House, 2 mi. NW of Fairbury, Fairbury vicinity, 12/03/74, B, 74001124

Steele City Historic District, Roughly bounded by Main and 2nd Sts., Gardline, and St. J. and W. RR, Steele City, 3/16/72, A, C, 72000752

Johnson County

Johnson County Courthouse [County Courthouses of Nebraska MPS], Courthouse Sq., Tecumseh, 1/10/90, A, C, 89002246

Johnson County—Continued

Keim Stone Arch Bridge [Highway Bridges in Nebraska MPS], Co. Rd. over unnamed stream, 3 mi. E and 1 mi. N of Tecumseh, Tecumseh vicinity, 6/29/92, C, 92000710

Tecumseh Historic District, Irregular pattern roughly bounded by Atchison & Nebraska RR tracks, 9th and Washington Sts., and US 136, Tecumseh, 6/20/75, A, C, 75001095

Tecumseh Opera House [Opera House Buildings in Nebraska 1867-1917 MPS], 123 S. Third, Tecumseh, 9/28/88, A, 88000929

Kearney County

Carpenter, Eddie Eugene and Harriet Cotton, Farmstead, Approximately 0.5 mi. W of Lowell, Lowell vicinity, 2/25/93, B, 93000059

Dobytown, Address Restricted, Kearney vicinity, 12/16/74, D, 74001125

Fort Kearney, 2 mi. W of Newark on NE 10, Newark vicinity, 7/02/71, D, e, f, 71000485

Kearney County Courthouse [County Courthouses of Nebraska MPS], 5th St. between Colorado and Minden Aves., Minden, 1/10/90, A, C, 89002234

Salem Swedish Methodist Episcopal Church, SW of Axtell, Axtell vicinity, 7/29/82, A, C, a, b, d, 82003192

Thorne, W. T., Building, 5th St., Minden, 9/12/85, C, 85002139

US Post Office—Minden [Nebraska Post Offices Which Contain Section Artwork MPS], 410 N. Minden St., Minden, 5/11/92, A, C, 92000471

Keith County

Beauvais' Ranche Archeological Site, Address Restricted, Brule vicinity, 2/20/75, A, D, 75001096

Brandhoefer, Leonidas A., Mansion, 10th and Spruce Sts., Ogallala, 10/03/73, A, C, 73001065

California Hill, W of Brule, Brule vicinity, 7/15/74, A, 74001126

Diamond Springs Stage Station Site, 1 mi. W of Brule exit on I-80, Brule vicinity, 10/15/70, A, 70000371

Keystone Community Church, McGinley St., Keystone, 1/01/79, A, C, a, 79001447

Roscoe State Aid Bridge [Highway Bridges in Nebraska MPS], State Link 51B over the S. Platte R., .5 mi. SE of Roscoe, Roscoe vicinity, 6/29/92, C, 92000709

US Post Office—Ogallala [Nebraska Post Offices Which Contain Section Artwork MPS], 301 N. Spruce St., Ogallala, 5/11/92, A, C, 92000481

Keya Paha County

Keya Paha County High School, Off NE 12, Springview, 12/01/86, A, 86003377

Lewis Bridge [Highway Bridges in Nebraska MPS], Co. Rd. over the Keya Paha R., 13.6 mi. NE of Springview, Springview vicinity, 6/29/92, C, 92000774

Kimball County

Fraternal Hall, 2nd and Chestnut Sts., Kimball, 2/28/83, A, C, 83001096

Stone Building, 126 S. Chestnut St., Kimball, 3/31/83, C, 83001097

Knox County

Commercial Hotel, The, 117 Main St., Verdigre, 4/05/90, A, C, 90000563

Congregational Church and Manse, Santee Indian Reservation, Santee, 3/16/72, A, C, 72000753

Episcopal Church, On the Missouri River in the Santee Indian Reservation, Santee, 3/16/72, A, C, a, 72000754

Gross State Aid Bridge [Highway Bridges in Nebraska MPS], Co. Hwy. over Verdigris Cr., 3.5 mi. N, .2 mi. W of Verdigre, Verdigre vicinity, 6/29/92, C, 92000773

Knox County Courthouse [County Courthouses of Nebraska MPS], Main St. between Brazile and Bridge Sts., Center, 7/05/90, A, 90000972

Niobrara River Bridge, Over the Niobrara R. 1.3 NW of Niobrara, Niobrara vicinity, 11/12/92, C, 92001576

Ponca Fort Site, Address Restricted, Verdel vicinity, 4/03/73, A, D, 73001066

Pospeshil Theatre [Opera House Buildings in Nebraska 1867-1917 MPS], 123 Broadway, Bloomfield, 9/28/88, A, 88000935

Rad Sladkovsky, Address Restricted, Verdigre vicinity, 6/29/82, A, C, 82003193

Z.C.B.J. Opera House [Opera House Buildings in Nebraska 1867-1917 MPS], Fourth Ave. and Main, Verdigre, 7/06/88, A, 88000946

Lancaster County

Antelope Grocery, 2406 J St., Lincoln, 3/17/88, C, 88000213

Baldwin Terrace [Nineteenth Century Terrace Houses TR], 429–443 S. 12th St., and 1134–1142 K St., Lincoln, 10/01/79, C, 79003687

Barr Terrace [Nineteenth Century Terrace Houses TR], 627–643 S. 11th, and 1044 H St., Lincoln, 10/01/79, C, 79003688

Beal Slough Bridge [Highway Bridges in Nebraska MPS], W. Pioneers Blvd. over Beal Slough, .5 mi. W of Lincoln, Lincoln vicinity, 6/29/92, C, 92000744

Beattie, James A., House, 6706 Colby St., Lincoln, 12/04/90, A, C, 90001773

Bell, Jasper Newton, House, 2212 Sheldon St., Lincoln, 6/21/84, C, 84002483

Burr Block, 1206 O St., Lincoln, 5/18/79, A, C, 79001448

Christian Record Building, 3705 S. Forty-eighth St., Lincoln, 12/01/86, A, C, a, 86003384

City Hall, 920 O St., Lincoln, 10/15/69, A, C, 69000132

College View Public Library, 3800 S. 48th St., Lincoln, 6/28/84, A, 84002486

Eddy-Taylor House, 435 N. 25th, Lincoln, 7/21/83, A, C, 83001098

Fairview, 4900 Sumner St., Lincoln, 10/15/66, B, NHL, 66000947

Ferguson, William H., House, 700 S. 16th St., Lincoln, 11/29/72, B, C, 72000755

First State Bank of Bethany, 1551 N. Cotner Blvd., Lincoln, 7/24/86, C, 86001936

Gold and Company Store Building, 1033 O St., Lincoln, 10/19/82, A, C, g, 82000609

Harris House, 1630 K St., Lincoln, 9/02/82, A, C, b, 82003194

Hayward School, 1215 N. 9th, Lincoln, 8/23/85, A, C, 85001795

Helmer-Winnett-White Flats [Nineteenth Century Terrace Houses TR], 1022–1028 K St., Lincoln, 10/01/79, B, C, 79003690

Hotel Capital, 139 N. 11th St., Lincoln, 12/05/83, A, C, 83003994

Kennard, Thomas P., House, 1627 H St., Lincoln, 4/16/69, A, C, 69000134

Lancaster Block, 6201–6205 Havelock Ave., Lincoln, 4/12/89, A, 89000245

Lewis-Syford House, 700 N. 16th St., Lincoln, 2/18/71, C, 71000486

Lincoln Army Air Field Regimental Chapel, 4601 NW. 48th St., Lincoln, 6/17/93, A, C, a, 93000535

Lincoln Liberty Life Insurance Building, 113 N. Eleventh St., Lincoln, 1/19/88, C, 87002299

Lincoln YWCA Building, 1432 N St., Lincoln, 6/21/84, A, C, 84002490

Lyman Terrace [Nineteenth Century Terrace Houses TR], 1111–1119 H St., Lincoln, 10/01/79, C, 79003689

Metropolitan Apartments, 502 S. Twelfth St, Lincoln, 1/19/88, C, 87002298

Mount Emerald and Capitol Additions Historic Residential District, Roughly bounded by A, G, 17th and 22nd Sts., Lincoln, 6/05/80, A, B, C, 80002453

Municipal Lighting and Waterworks Plant, 2901 A St., Lincoln, 7/24/86, A, C, 86001938

Nebraska State Capitol, 1445 K St., Lincoln, 10/16/70, A, C, NHL, 70000372

Nebraska Telephone Company Building, 128–130 S. 13th St., Lincoln, 11/16/78, A, C, 78001703

Nine-Mile Prairie, NW of Huskerville, Lincoln vicinity, 7/30/86, B, 86002089

Old Main, Nebraska Wesleyan University, 50th and St. Paul Sts., Lincoln, 5/21/75, A, C, 75001097

Old University Library, 11th and R Sts., Lincoln, 8/06/75, A, C, 75001098

Olive Branch Bridge [Highway Bridges in Nebraska MPS], W. Stagecoach Rd. over Olive Br., 1.7 mi. SW of Sprague, Sprague vicinity, 6/29/92, C, 92000739

Lancaster County—Continued

Peterson, Peter, Farmstead, Address Restricted, Waverly vicinity, 2/11/80, C, 80002456

Phi Delta Theta Fraternity House, 1545 R St., Lincoln, 5/28/86, C, g, 86001183

Phillips, R. O., House, 1845 D St, Lincoln, 11/29/79, C, 79001449

Pioneers Park, Jct of W. Van Dorn and Coddington Sts., Lincoln vicinity, 6/17/93, A, C, 93000538

President and Ambassador Apartments, 1330 and 1340 Lincoln Mall, Lincoln, 12/10/93, C, 93001401

Retzlaff Farmstead, Address Restricted, Walton vicinity, 5/31/79, A, C, 79001450

Rock Island Depot, 1944 O St., Lincoln, 9/03/71, A, C, 71000487

Royer-Williams House, 407 N. 26th St., Lincoln, 6/14/82, B, C, 82003195

Ryons-Alexander House, 1835 Ryons St., Lincoln, 7/08/82, B, C, 82003196

Schrader Archeological Site, Address Restricted, Roca vicinity, 1/21/74, D, 74002290

Scottish Rite Temple, 332 Centennial Mall S, Lincoln, 12/01/86, C, 86003359

South Bottoms Historic District, Roughly bounded by M and J and H and G Sts., Second and Ninth Sts., and W. B Sts., and Salt Creek, Lincoln, 7/17/86, A, C, D, 86001717

St. Charles Apartments, 4717 Baldwin Ave., Lincoln, 9/12/85, C, 85002138

State Arsenal, 17th and Court Sts., Lincoln, 9/17/81, A, 81000372

Temple of Congregation B'nai Jeshurun, 20 and South Sts., Lincoln, 6/25/82, A, C, a, 82003197

Terminal Building, 947 O St., Lincoln, 12/29/86, A, C, 86003527

Tifereth Israel Synagogue, 344 S. 18th St., Lincoln, 5/09/85, C, a, 85000958

Townsend Photography Studio, 226 S. 11th St., Lincoln, 12/20/84, B, C, 84000478

Tyler, William H., House, 808 D St., Lincoln, 4/06/78, B, C, 78001704

Veith Building, 816 P St., Lincoln, 9/18/80, C, 80002454

Watkins, Albert, House, 920 D St., Lincoln, 4/03/89, B, 89000244

Whitehall, 5903 Walker, Lincoln, 10/29/82, A, C, 82000610

Woods Brothers Building, 132 S. 13th St., Lincoln, 9/18/80, A, C, 80002455

Wyuka Cemetery, 3600 O St., Lincoln, 7/19/82, C, a, d, 82003198

Ziemer, Arthur C., House, 2030 Euclid St., Lincoln, 11/23/77, C, 77000832

Lincoln County

Fox Theatre, 301 E. 5th, North Platte, 5/09/85, A, C, 85000957

Hotel Yancey, 221 E. 5th St., North Platte, 5/09/85, A, C, 85000956

Johnston Memorial Building, Off NE 25, Wallace, 3/20/86, A, C, 86000473

Lincoln County Courthouse [County Courthouses of Nebraska MPS], Dewey St. between 3rd and 4th Sts., North Platte, 1/10/90, A, C, 89002224

O'Fallons Bluff, SE of Sutherland, Sutherland vicinity, 7/12/74, A, 74001127

Scout's Rest Ranch, NW of North Platte off U.S. 30, North Platte vicinity, 1/30/78, B, C, 78001705

Sutherland State Aid Bridge [Highway Bridges in Nebraska MPS], Co. Rd. over the N. Platte R., 4.2 mi. N of Sutherland, Sutherland vicinity, 6/29/92, C, 92000705

Loup County

Pavillion Hotel, Main St. Square, Taylor, 11/27/89, A, 89002039

Madison County

Hotel Norfolk, 108 N. Fourth St., Norfolk, 12/01/88, A, C, 88002755

St. Leonard's Catholic Church, 502–504 S. Nebraska St., Madison, 11/27/89, C, a, 89002038

U.S. Post Office and Courthouse, 125 S. 4th St., Norfolk, 10/09/74, C, 74001128

Warrick, John Wesley and Grace Shafer, House, 4th St., Meadow Grove, 11/28/90, C, 90001767

McPherson County

McPherson County Courthouse [County Courthouses of Nebraska MPS], Jct. of 6th and Anderson Sts., Tryon, 7/05/90, A, 90000970

Merrick County

Cahow Barber Shop, SW Main St., Chapman, 1/12/84, B, C, 84002493

Ellen, Martha, Auditorium [Opera House Buildings in Nebraska 1867-1917 MPS], 706 C Ave., Central City, 9/28/88, A, 88000944

Hord, Heber, House, 1505 Sixteenth St., Central City, 12/07/87, A, B, 87002096

Merrick County Courthouse [County Courthouses of Nebraska MPS], 18th St. between 15th and 16th Aves., Central City, 1/10/90, A, C, 89002211

Morris, Wright, Boyhood House, 304 D St., Central City, 10/22/80, B, 80002457

Patterson Law Office, 1517 18th St., Central City, 3/13/79, B, C, 79001451

Morrill County

Camp Clarke Bridge Site, W of Bridgeport, Bridgeport vicinity, 11/08/74, A, C, 74001129

Chimney Rock National Historic Site, 3 mi. SW of Bayard, Bayard vicinity, 10/15/66, A, D, NPS, 66000116

Courthouse and Jail House Rocks, 5 mi. S of Bridgeport, Bridgeport vicinity, 4/24/73, A, D, 73001067

Morrill County Courthouse [County Courthouses of Nebraska MPS], M St. between 5th and 6th Sts., Bridgeport, 1/10/90, A, C, 89002227

Mud Springs Pony Express Station Site, Address Restricted, Dalton vicinity, 4/24/73, A, D, 73001068

Nance County

Burkett Archeological Site, Address Restricted, Genoa vicinity, 7/12/74, D, 74001133

Cottonwood Creek Archeological Site, Address Restricted, Belgrade vicinity, 10/18/74, D, 74001130

Cunningham Archeological Site, Address Restricted, Fullerton vicinity, 2/13/75, D, 75001099

Fullerton Archeological Site, Address Restricted, Fullerton vicinity, 11/01/74, D, 74001131

Genoa Site, Address Restricted, Genoa vicinity, 10/15/70, D, 70000373

Horse Creek Pawnee Village, Address Restricted, Fullerton vicinity, 7/12/74, D, 74001132

Pawnee Mission and Burnt Village Archeological Site, Address Restricted, Genoa vicinity, 8/07/74, A, D, 74001134

U.S. Indian Industrial School, NE 22, Genoa vicinity, 5/22/78, A, D, 78001706

Wright Site, Address Restricted, Genoa vicinity, 8/14/73, D, 73001069

Nemaha County

Bennett, John W., House, Off NE 67, Brownville vicinity, 9/16/83, C, 83001099

Brownville Bridge [Highway Bridges in Nebraska MPS], US 136 over the Missouri R., Brownville, 6/17/93, C, 93000536

Brownville Historic District, Bounded by Allen, Richard, Nemaha, Nebraska, 7th, and 2nd Sts. and the Missouri River, Brownville, 5/19/70, A, B, C, 70000374

CAPTAIN MERIWETHER LEWIS (dredge), SE of Brownville, Brownville vicinity, 10/28/77, A, C, NHL, 77000833

First United Presbyterian Church of Auburn, 1322 19th St., Auburn, 7/15/82, C, a, 82003199

Majors, Thomas J., Farmstead, W of Peru at 800 Mulberry St., Peru vicinity, 6/15/78, B, 78001707

Nehama County Courthouse [County Courthouses of Nebraska MPS], 1824 N St., Auburn, 1/10/90, A, C, 89002243

New Opera House [Opera House Buildings in Nebraska 1867-1917 MPS], 921 Central Ave., Auburn, 9/28/88, A, 88000936

Reed, Wilber T., House, 1204 N St., Auburn, 3/24/80, C, 80002458

Nemaha County—Continued

St. John's Lutheran Church Complex, SW of Auburn, Auburn vicinity, 1/25/79, A, C, a, 79001452

US Post Office—Auburn [Nebraska Post Offices Which Contain Section Artwork MPS], 1320 Courthouse Ave., Auburn, 5/11/92, A, C, 92000480

Nuckolls County

Kendall, Wallace Warren and Lillian Genevieve Bradshaw, House, 412 E. Seventh St., Superior, 12/10/93, C, 93001402

Lawrence Opera House [Opera House Buildings in Nebraska 1867-1917 MPS], Second and Calvert Sts., Lawrence, 9/28/88, A, 88000933

Nuckolls County Courthouse [County Courthouses of Nebraska MPS], 150 S. Main St., Nelson, 1/10/90, A, C, 89002219

Stewart Bridge [Highway Bridges in Nebraska MPS], Co. Rd. over Big Sandy Cr., 1 mi. E and 8 mi. N of Oak, Oak vicinity, 6/29/92, C, 92000717

Otoe County

Arbor Lodge, Arbor Lodge State Park, W of Nebraska City, Nebraska City vicinity, 4/16/69, B, C, NHL, 69000135

Boscobel, N of Nebraska City on Steamwagon Rd., Nebraska City vicinity, 6/17/76, B, C, 76001133

Bridge [Highway Bridges in Nebraska MPS], Co. Rd. over unnamed stream, 4.1 mi. SW of Lorton, Lorton vicinity, 6/29/92, C, b, 92000733

Bridge [Highway Bridges in Nebraska MPS], Co. Rd. over unnamed stream, 1.5 mi. SW of Nebraska City, Nebraska City vicinity, 6/29/92, C, 92000737

Camp Creek School, Otoe County District No. 54, SE of Nebraska City on RR3, Nebraska City, 6/05/80, A, 80002459

Kregel Wind Mill Company, 1416 Central Ave., Nebraska City, 2/25/93, A, 93000061

Lee, George F., Octagon Houses, S of Nebraska City off U.S. 73, Nebraska City vicinity, 11/23/77, C, 77000834

Little Nemaha River Bridge [Highway Bridges in Nebraska MPS], Co. Rd. over the Little Nemaha R., 1.8 mi. NW of Dunbar, Dunbar vicinity, 6/29/92, C, b, 92000720

Little Nemaha River Bridge [Highway Bridges in Nebraska MPS], Co. Rd. over the Little Nemaha R., 3 mi. NW of Syracuse, Syracuse vicinity, 6/29/92, C, 92000723

Morton-James Public Library, 11th St. and 1st Corso, Nebraska City, 5/28/76, B, C, 76001134

Nebraska City Historic District, Roughly bounded by 5th Ave., 3rd, 19th, and 1st Corso Sts., Nebraska City, 10/29/76, A, C, 76001135

Otoe County Courthouse, 10th St. and Central Ave., Nebraska City, 6/18/76, C, 76001136

South 13th Street Historic District, Roughly bounded by 12th, 14th, 1st Corso, and 6th Corso Sts., Nebraska City, 10/29/76, A, B, 76001137

South Nebraska City Historic District, Roughly bounded by 4th, 11th, 1st Corso, and 4th Corso Sts., Nebraska City, 10/22/76, B, C, 76001138

St. Benedict's Catholic Church, 411 5th Rue, Nebraska City, 1/27/83, A, 83001100

U.S. Post Office, 202 S. 8th St., Nebraska City, 9/03/71, A, C, 71000488

Ware, Jasper A., House, S of Nebraska City on Steinhart Park Rd., Nebraska City vicinity, 7/16/73, C, 73001070

Wolf Creek Bridge [Highway Bridges in Nebraska MPS], Vacated Co. Rd. over Wolf Cr., 10.3 mi. NE of Dunbar, Dunbar vicinity, 6/29/92, C, b, 92000738

Wyoming Bridge [Highway Bridges in Nebraska MPS], Co. Rd. over Squaw Cr., 9.1 mi. NE of Dunbar, Dunbar vicinity, 6/29/92, C, b, 92000736

Pawnee County

Cincinnati Bridge [Highway Bridges in Nebraska MPS], Closed Co. Rd. over S. Fk. Big Nemaha R., 1 mi. S, .2 mi. E of Du Bois, Du Bois vicinity, 6/29/92, C, 92000719

Hempstead, E. F., House, 14th and H St., Pawnee City, 10/19/82, B, C, 82000611

Lloyd, Harold, Birthplace, Jct. of Pawnee and 4th Sts., NW corner, Burchard, 12/22/93, B, 93001403

Pawnee County Courthouse [County Courthouses of Nebraska MPS], 625 6th St., Pawnee City, 1/10/90, A, C, 89002232

Rad Jan Kollar cis 101 Z. C. B. J., Address Restricted, DuBois vicinity, 4/05/90, A, C, 90000567

Steinauer Opera House [Opera House Buildings in Nebraska 1867-1917 MPS], 215 Main, Steinauer, 7/07/88, A, 88000934

Table Rock Archeological Site, Address Restricted, Table Rock vicinity, 7/12/74, D, 74001135

Table Rock Opera House [Opera House Buildings in Nebraska 1867-1917 MPS], Houston St., Table Rock, 9/28/88, A, 88000931

US Post Office—Pawnee City [Nebraska Post Offices Which Contain Section Artwork MPS], 703 G St., Pawnee City, 5/11/92, A, C, 92000472

Perkins County

Perkins County Courthouse [County Courthouses of Nebraska MPS], Lincoln St. between 2nd and 3rd Sts., Grant, 7/05/90, A, C, 90000969

Phelps County

Phelps County Courthouse [County Courthouses of Nebraska MPS], 5th Ave. between East and West Aves., Holdrege, 1/10/90, A, C, 89002242

Pierce County

Athletic Park Band Shell, Jct. of Harper and Main Sts., NW corner, Plainview, 11/12/92, A, C, 92001573

Plainview Carnegie Library [Carnegie Libraries in Nebraska MPS], 102 S. Main St., Plainview, 2/25/93, A, 93000056

Willow Creek Bridge [Highway Bridges in Nebraska MPS], Co. Rd. over Willow Cr., 6.5 mi. S of Foster, Foster vicinity, 6/29/92, C, 92000706

Platte County

Columbus Loup River Bridge [Highway Bridges in Nebraska MPS], US 30 over the Loup R., Columbus, 6/29/92, C, 92000735

Evans, Dr. Carroll D. and Lorena R. North, House, 2204 14th St., Columbus, 3/14/91, C, 91000301

Feye Archeological Site, Address Restricted, Creston vicinity, 1/21/74, D, 74001136

Glur's Tavern, 2301 11th St., Columbus, 7/30/75, A, 75001100

Gottschalk, Frederick L. and L. Frederick, Houses, 2022 17th St., Columbus, 6/25/82, B, C, 82003200

Hill—Rupp Site, Address Restricted, Monroe vicinity, 9/30/85, D, 85002698

Larson, Hanna, Archeological Site, Address Restricted, Monroe vicinity, 2/20/75, D, 75001101

Monroe Congregational Church and New Hope Cemetery, Rt. 1, about 7.5 mi. NW of Monroe, E of Looking Glass Cr., Monroe vicinity, 11/28/90, C, a, d, 90001768

Platte County Courthouse [County Courthouses of Nebraska MPS], 2610 14th St., Columbus, 1/10/90, A, C, 89002217

Segelke, C., Building, 1065 17th Ave., Columbus, 6/25/82, B, C, 82004891

Snyder, H. E., House, 2522 Sixteenth St., Columbus, 7/10/86, C, 86001552

St. Michael's Catholic Church, Jct. of Third & Cedar Sts., Tarnov, 11/28/90, C, a, d, 90001766

Wurdeman-Lawson Archeological Site, Address Restricted, Creston vicinity, 7/12/74, D, 74001137

Polk County

Clarks Site, Address Restricted, Osceola vicinity, 8/14/73, D, 73001071

Mickey, Gov. John Hopwood, House, State St., Osceola, 5/12/77, B, 77000835

Polk County—Continued

Morrill, Charles H., Homestead, 0.5 mi. SE of Stromsburg on U.S. 81, Stromsburg vicinity, 6/04/73, B, C, 73001072

Polk County Courthouse [County Courthouses of Nebraska MPS], Courthouse Sq., Osceola, 1/10/90, A, C, 89002238

Wilson, Victor E., House, 518 Main St., Stromsburg, 7/07/88, B, C, 88000915

Red Willow County

Doyle Archeological Site, Address Restricted, McCook vicinity, 12/04/74, D, 74001138

McCook Public-Carnegie Library, 423 Norris Ave., McCook, 9/12/85, A, C, 85002142

Norris, Senator George William, House, 706 Norris Ave., McCook, 5/28/67, B, NHL, 67000006

Red Willow County Courthouse [County Courthouses of Nebraska MPS], NW corner Norris Ave. and E. E St., McCook, 7/05/90, A, C, 90000966

Second—Generation Norden Bombsight Vault [Significant Relic Components of US Army Air Fields in Nebraska MPS], Off US 83 NW of McCook at former McCook Army Air Base, McCook vicinity, 6/17/93, A, 93000534

Stutton, H. P., House, 602 Norris Ave., McCook, 5/22/78, C, 78001708

Richardson County

Gehling's Theatre [Opera House Buildings in Nebraska 1867-1917 MPS], 1592 Stone St., Falls City, 9/28/88, A, 88000942

Holman, John, House, 947 Nemaha St., Humboldt, 4/25/72, C, 72000756

Leary Site, Address Restricted, Rulo vicinity, 10/15/66, D, NHL, 66000449

Mount Zion Brick Church, Address Restricted, Barada vicinity, 12/01/88, C, a, d, 88002763

Richardson County Courthouse [County Courthouses of Nebraska MPS], Courthouse Sq., Falls City, 7/05/90, A, C, 90000965

Rulo Bridge [Highway Bridges in Nebraska MPS], US 159 over the Missouri R., Rulo, 1/04/93, C, 92000718

Site No. JF00-062 [Nebraska—Kansas Public Land Survey TR], 6 1/2 mi. SE of Rulo; 200 ft. W of rd. between Rulo, NE and White cloud, KS, Rulo, vicinity, 6/19/87, A, 87001001

Rock County

Carns State Aid Bridge [Highway Bridges in Nebraska MPS], Co. Rd. over the Niobrara R., 10.8 mi. NE of Bassett, Bassett vicinity, 6/29/92, C, b, 92000722

Rock County Courthouse [County Courthouses of Nebraska MPS], State St. between Caroline and Bertha Sts., Bassett, 7/05/90, A, C, 90000968

Saline County

Bickle, Jesse C., House, W of Crete off NE 33, Crete vicinity, 11/23/77, B, C, 77000838

College Hill Historic District, Roughly bounded by Juniper, 15th, Boswell and 9th Sts., Crete, 2/10/83, A, C, 83001101

Doane College Historic Buildings, Doane College campus, Crete, 8/16/77, A, C, 77000836

Freidell, William, House, 10th and Main Sts., Dorchester, 10/03/80, B, C, 80002461

Hotel Wilber, 2nd and Wilson Sts., Wilber, 9/20/78, A, C, 78001709

Johnston-Muff House, 1422 Boswell Ave., Crete, 9/19/77, B, C, 77000837

Kiddle, Richard R., House, 819 8th St., Friend, 9/12/85, C, 85002143

Mann-Zwonecek House, 524 W. 1st St., Wilber, 12/29/78, B, C, 78001710

Pisar, Frank, Farmstead, Address Restricted, Dorchester vicinity, 8/06/86, A, C, 86002275

Rademacher, Frank J., House, 1424 Grove St., Crete, 3/11/80, B, C, 80002460

Saline County Bank, E of SR 15 in downtown Western, Western, 4/05/90, C, 90000568

Saline County Courthouse [County Courthouses of Nebraska MPS], 215 S. Court, Wilber, 7/05/90, A, C, 90000967

Telocvicna Jednota Sokol, Address Restricted, Wilber vicinity, 1/18/85, A, 85000110

Trinity Memorial Episcopal Church, 14th and Juniper Sts., Crete, 9/14/79, C, a, 79001453

Warren's Opera House [Opera House Buildings in Nebraska 1867-1917 MPS], 511 Second St., Friend, 9/28/88, A, 88000945

Witt, Michael, Fachwerkbau, Address Restricted, Western vicinity, 1/14/80, B, C, b, 80002462

Z.C.B.J. Rad Tabor No. 74, R.F.D., Dorchester vicinity, 8/23/85, A, 85001798

Sarpy County

Big Papillion Creek Bridge [Highway Bridges in Nebraska MPS], 120th St. over S. Br. of Big Papillion Cr., 3.2 mi. W of La Vista, La Vista vicinity, 6/29/92, C, 92000728

Blacksmith Shop, S of Bellevue on Offutt Air Force Base, Bellevue vicinity, 5/12/78, A, 78001711

Fontanelle Bank, 2212 Main St., Bellevue, 4/16/69, C, 69000136

Fontenelle Forest Historic District, Address Restricted, Bellevue vicinity, 1/21/74, A, C, D, 74001139

Fort Crook Historic District, SW of Bellevue on Offutt Air Force Base, Bellevue vicinity, 12/12/76, A, 76001139

Hamilton, William, House, 2003 Bluff St., Bellevue, 10/15/69, B, a, 69000137

Kurz Omaha Village, Address Restricted, Papillion vicinity, 8/14/73, D, 73001073

McCarty-Lilley House, W of Bellevue on Quail Dr., Bellevue vicinity, 12/22/78, B, 78001712

Moses Merrill Mission and Oto Indian Village, Address Restricted, La Platte vicinity, 3/16/72, B, D, a, 72000757

Old Log Cabin, 1805 Hancock St., Bellevue, 10/16/70, C, b, 70000376

Presbyterian Church, 2002 Franklin St., Bellevue, 10/15/70, A, C, a, 70000377

Sarpy, Peter A., Trading Post Site, Address Restricted, Bellevue vicinity, 6/10/75, B, C, D, a, 75001102

Sautter, John, Farmhouse, 220 N. Jefferson St., Papillion, 9/30/80, B, C, b, 80002463

Third Sarpy County Courthouse [County Courthouses of Nebraska MPS], 3rd St. between Washington and Jefferson Sts., Papillion, 7/05/90, A, C, 90000964

Saunders County

Ashland Bridge [Highway Bridges in Nebraska MPS], Silver St. over Salt Cr., Ashland, 6/29/92, C, 92000721

Ashland Public Library, 207 N. 15th St., Ashland, 1/27/83, A, C, 83001102

Beetison, Israel, House, SE of Ashland, Ashland vicinity, 4/18/77, C, 77000839

Hanson, Howard, House, 12th and Linden Sts., Wahoo, 1/27/83, A, C, 83001103

Leshara Site, Address Restricted, Leshara vicinity, 3/16/72, D, 72000759

McClean Site, Address Restricted, Inglewood vicinity, 3/16/72, D, 72000758

National Bank of Ashland, 1442 Silver St., Ashland, 1/27/83, A, C, 83001104

O. K. Market, 542 N. Linden Ave., Wahoo, 7/03/91, A, C, 91000835

Pahuk, Address Restricted, Cedar Bluffs vicinity, 8/14/73, A, D, a, 73001074

Rad Plzen cis. 9 Z.C.B.J. (SD10-6), Off NE 79, Morse Bluff, 3/20/86, A, C, 86000440

Saunders County Courthouse [County Courthouses of Nebraska MPS], Chestnut between 4th and 5th Sts., Wahoo, 1/10/90, A, C, 89002220

St. Stephen's Episcopal Church, 15th and Adams Sts., Ashland, 1/25/79, C, a, 79001454

Wahoo Burlington Depot, 431 W. 3rd, Wahoo, 5/09/85, A, C, 85000955

Woodcliff Burials, Address Restricted, Inglewood vicinity, 3/07/73, D, 73001075

Yutan Site, Address Restricted, Yutan vicinity, 6/26/72, A, D, 72000760

Scotts Bluff County

Fort Mitchell Site, Address Restricted, Scottsbluff vicinity, 6/07/78, D, 78001713

Scotts Bluff County—Continued

Henry State Aid Bridges [Highway Bridges in Nebraska MPS], NE 86 over the N. Platte R., .6 mi. S of Henry, Henry vicinity, 6/29/92, C, 92000732

Interstate Canal Bridge [Highway Bridges in Nebraska MPS], Co. Rd. over Interstate Canal, 9.3 mi. N of Scottsbluff, Scottsbluff vicinity, 6/29/92, C, 92000731

Knorr—Holden Continuous Corn Plot, Scottsbluff Experiment Station, off NE 71 N of Scottsbluff, Scottsbluff vicinity, 6/11/92, A, 92000703

Marquis Opera House, 1601–1603 Broadway, Scottsbluff, 10/10/85, C, 85003103

Quivey, M. B., House, 1462 19th Ave., Mitchell, 3/24/83, A, C, 83001105

Robidoux Pass, 9 mi. W of Gering, Gering vicinity, 10/15/66, A, NHL, 66000450

Scotts Bluff County Courthouse [County Courthouses of Nebraska MPS], 10th and Q Sts., Gering, 1/10/90, A, C, 89002230

Scotts Bluff National Monument, 3 mi. W of Gering on NE 92, Gering vicinity, 10/15/66, A, NPS, 66000117

Scottsbluff Carnegie Library, 106 E. 18th St., Scottsbluff, 9/03/81, A, C, 81000373

Signal Butte, Address Restricted, Gering vicinity, 10/15/66, D, NHL, 66000452

Sorensen, Severin, House, 2345 17th St., Gering, 3/31/83, A, C, 83001106

US Post Office—Scottsbluff, 120 E. 16th St., Scottsbluff, 10/05/89, C, 89001462

Seward County

Cattle, John, Jr., House, W. Hillcrest St., Seward, 9/13/78, B, C, 78001714

Deutsche Evangelisch Lutherische Zion Kirche, SW of Staplehurst, Staplehurst vicinity, 6/25/82, C, a, 82003202

Germantown State Bank Building, Main St., Garland, 12/13/84, C, 84000512

Jones, Harry T., House, 136 N. Columbia Ave., Seward, 11/28/90, C, 90001771

Seward County Courthouse [County Courthouses of Nebraska MPS], Seward between 5th and 6th Sts., Seward, 1/10/90, A, C, 89002245

Seward County Courthouse Square Historic District, Roughly bounded by Jackson, 7th, and South Sts., Seward, 7/15/82, A, C, 82003201

States Ballroom, Off NE 415, Bee, 10/14/81, A, C, g, 81000375

Zimmerer, John and Philomena Sand, House, 316 N. Sixth St., Seward, 2/25/93, C, 93000060

Sheridan County

Antioch Potash Plants, Address Restricted, Antioch vicinity, 5/16/79, A, D, 79001455

Camp Sheridan and Spotted Tail Indian Agency, Address Restricted, Hay Springs vicinity, 11/19/74, A, D, 74001140

Colclesser Bridge [Highway Bridges in Nebraska MPS], Co. Rd. over the Niobrara R., 11 mi. S of Rushville, Rushville vicinity, 6/29/92, C, b, 92000729

Gourley's Opera House [Opera House Buildings in Nebraska 1867-1917 MPS], Second St., Rushville, 7/06/88, A, a, 88000943

Loosveldt Bridge [Highway Bridges in Nebraska MPS], Private ranch rd. over the Niobrara R., 9.1 mi. SE of Rushville, Rushville vicinity, 6/29/92, C, b, 92000730

Sheridan County Courthouse [County Courthouses of Nebraska MPS], 2nd and Sprague Sts., Rushville, 1/10/90, A, C, 89002216

Spade Ranch, NW of Ellsworth, Ellsworth vicinity, 2/28/80, A, 80002464

Sherman County

Sherman County Courthouse [County Courthouses of Nebraska MPS], 630 O St., Loup City, 1/10/90, A, C, 89002225

Sweetwater Archeological Site, Address Restricted, Sweetwater vicinity, 7/29/74, D, 74001141

Sioux County

Cook, Harold J., Homestead Cabin, 3 mi. E of Agate off NE 29 on Agate Fossil Beds National Monument, Agate vicinity, 8/24/77, A, NPS, 77000156

Hudson-Meng Bison Kill Site, Address Restricted, Crawford vicinity, 8/28/73, D, 73001076

Sioux County Courthouse [County Courthouses of Nebraska MPS], NE corner of Main and 3rd Sts., Harrison, 7/05/90, A, C, 90000963

Thayer County

Dill, Richard E., House, Off SR 76, Alexandria, 1/29/73, C, g, 73001077

US Post Office—Hebron [Nebraska Post Offices Which Contain Section Artwork MPS], 145 N. 15th St., Hebron, 5/11/92, A, C, 92000473

Thomas County

Bessey Nursery, W of Halsey off NE 2, Halsey vicinity, 5/24/78, A, C, g, 78001715

Thomas County Courthouse [County Courthouses of Nebraska MPS], 503 Main St., Thedford, 7/05/90, A, 90000971

Thurston County

Blackbird Hill, Address Restricted, Macy vicinity, 5/02/79, A, D, 79001456

First Thurston County Courthouse [County Courthouses of Nebraska MPS], 400–412 Main St., Pender, 1/10/90, A, 89002210

North Omaha Creek Bridge [Highway Bridges in Nebraska MPS], Twp. Rd. over N. Omaha Cr., 3 mi. SW of Winnebago, Winnebago vicinity, 6/29/92, C, 92000727

Picotte, Dr. Susan, Memorial Hospital, 505 Matthewson St., Walthill, 12/16/88, B, NHL, 88002762

Thurston County Courthouse [County Courthouses of Nebraska MPS], Main St. between 5th and 6th Sts., Pender, 1/10/90, A, 89002209

Valley County

Bruha, Josef, and Anna Beran, House, W of Elyria, Burwell vicinity, 4/05/90, A, C, D, 90000564

Fort Hartsuff, N of Elyria, Elyria vicinity, 3/24/78, A, C, D, 78001716

North Loup Bridge [Highway Bridges in Nebraska MPS], Co. Rd. over the N. Loup R., 1.5 mi. NE of North Loup, North Loup vicinity, 6/29/92, C, 92000704

People's Unitarian Church, 1640 N St., Ord, 6/14/84, A, C, a, 84002497

Rad Slavin cis. 112 Z. C. B. J. Hall, Address Restricted, Comstock vicinity, 11/12/92, A, C, 92001569

Schultz Site, Address Restricted, North Loup vicinity, 10/15/66, D, NHL, 66000453

Valley County Courthouse [County Courthouses of Nebraska MPS], 16th St. between L and M Sts., Ord, 1/10/90, A, C, 89002235

Washington County

Bertrand Site, DeSoto National Wildlife Refuge, Blair vicinity, 3/24/69, A, 69000138

Blair High School, Jct. of Sixteenth and Colfax Sts., Blair, 3/14/91, C, 91000300

Castetter, Abraham, House, 1815 Grant St., Blair, 6/25/82, B, C, 82003203

Congregational Church of Blair, 16th and Colfax Sts., Blair, 2/01/79, C, a, 79001457

Crowell, C. C., Jr., House, 2138 Washington St., Blair, 7/19/82, B, C, 82003204

Fontanelle Township Hall, Off NE 91, Fontanelle, 9/09/82, A, C, 82003205

Fort Atkinson, 1 mi. E of Fort Calhoun, Fort Calhoun vicinity, 10/15/66, A, D, NHL, 66000454

Trinity Seminary Building, College Dr., Blair, 7/03/80, A, C, a, 80004528

Washington County Courthouse [County Courthouses of Nebraska MPS], 16th St. between Colfax and South Sts., Blair, 1/10/90, A, C, 89002221

Wayne County

Wayne County Courthouse, 510 Pearl St., Wayne, 5/02/79, C, 79001458

Wayne County—Continued

Wightman, Dr. W. C., House, 702 Lincoln St., Wayne, 6/13/78, C, 78001717

Webster County

Auld Public Library, 537 N. Webster, Red Cloud, 12/10/93, A, C, 93001404

Bentley, Matthew R., House [Willa Cather TR], 845 N. Cedar, Red Cloud, 8/11/82, B, 82004927

Burlington Depot [Willa Cather TR], Seward St., Red Cloud, 3/05/81, B, C, b, 81000376

Cather House [Willa Cather TR (AD)], SW corner of 3rd and Cedar Sts., Red Cloud, 4/16/69, B, NHL, 69000139

Cather, George, Farmstead [Willa Cather TR], SW of Bladen, Bladen vicinity, 8/11/82, B, C, 82004917

Cather, William, Homestead Site [Willa Cather TR], NW of Red Cloud, Red Cloud vicinity, 8/11/82, B, 82004921

Chalk Cliff and Republican River [Willa Cather TR], 1 mi. S of Red Cloud, Red Cloud vicinity, 8/11/82, B, 82004919

City Pharmacy [Willa Cather TR], 410 N. Webster, Red Cloud, 2/11/82, B, 82004929

Crossroads Grave Site [Willa Cather TR], NW of Red Cloud, Red Cloud vicinity, 8/11/82, A, B, 82004920

Ducker, William, House [Willa Cather TR], 821 Franklin St., Red Cloud, 2/11/82, B, 82004930

Elm St. Historic District [Willa Cather TR], Roughly bounded by 10th & 6th Aves., Locust & Webster Sts., Red Cloud, 8/11/82, B, 82004934

Farmer's and Merchant's Bank Building [Willa Cather TR], 338 N. Webster St., Red Cloud, 3/05/81, B, C, 81000377

First Baptist Church [Willa Cather TR], 442 N. Seward St., Red Cloud, 8/12/82, B, C, a, 82003206

Garber Grove [Willa Cather TR], E of Red Cloud, Red Cloud vicinity, 8/11/82, B, 82004916

Grace Protestant Episcopal Church [Willa Cather TR], 546 N. Cedar St., Red Cloud, 2/11/82, B, a, b, 82004931

IOOF Hall and Opera House [Opera House Buildings in Nebraska 1867-1917 MPS], Main St., Bladen, 7/06/88, A, 88000953

Jackson's Reserve [Willa Cather TR], Bounded by Seward, Cedar and 3rd Sts., Red Cloud, 8/11/82, B, 82004936

Main Street Historic District [Willa Cather TR], Roughly bounded by 3rd & 5th Aves., Elm & Cedar Sts., Red Cloud, 2/11/82, B, 82004932

McKeeby, Dr. Gilbert, House [Willa Cather TR], 641 N. Cherry St., Red Cloud, 8/11/82, B, 82004937

Miner Brothers Store [Willa Cather TR], 3rd and Webster Sts., Red Cloud, 8/11/82, B, 82004924

Miner House [Willa Cather TR], 241 N. Seward, Red Cloud, 8/11/82, B, C, 82004922

Moon Block [Willa Cather TR], Webster St. bet. 4th and 5th Aves., Red Cloud, 8/11/82, B, 82004926

Opera House [Willa Cather TR], 413 N. Webster, Red Cloud, 8/11/82, B, 82004925

Pavelka Farmstead [Willa Cather TR (AD)], SE of Bladen, Bladen vicinity, 4/13/79, A, B, C, 79001459

Perkins-Wiener House [Willa Cather TR], 238 N. Seward, Red Cloud, 8/11/82, B, b, 82004923

Pike-Pawnee Village Site, Address Restricted, Guide Rock vicinity, 10/15/66, D, NHL, 66000455

Railroad Addition Historic District [Willa Cather TR], Roughly Bounded by Vine, Division, Seward, Railroad and First Sts., Red Cloud, 8/11/82, B, 82004935

Red Cloud Bridge [Highway Bridges in Nebraska MPS], NE 281 over the Republican R., 2 mi. S of Red Cloud, Red Cloud vicinity, 6/29/92, C, 92000726

Seward Street Historic District [Willa Cather TR], Roughly bounded by Walnut & Cedar Sts., Tenth & A Aves., Red Cloud, 2/11/82, B, 82004933

St. Juliana Falconieri Catholic Church [Willa Cather TR], 425 W. 3rd St., Red Cloud, 3/05/81, B, C, a, 81000378

St. Stephenie Scandinavian Evangelical Lutheran Church [Willa Cather TR], 8 mi. NW of Red Cloud, Red Cloud vicinity, 8/11/82, A, B, a, e, 82004918

Starke Round Barn, 4.5 mi. E of Red Cloud on U.S. 163, Red Cloud vicinity, 3/16/72, A, 72000761

US Post Office—Red Cloud [Nebraska Post Offices Which Contain Section Artwork MPS], 300 N. Webster, Red Cloud, 5/11/92, A, C, 92000474

Warner-Cather House [Willa Cather TR], 541 N. Seward St., Red Cloud, 8/11/82, B, 82004928

Webster County Courthouse [Willa Cather TR], 225 W. 6th St., Red Cloud, 3/05/81, A, B, C, 81000379

Willa Cather Memorial Prairie [Willa Cather TR], S of Red Cloud on U.S. Hwy. 281, Red Cloud, 8/12/82, A, B, 82003207

Wheeler County

A. T. Ranch Headquarters, Star Rt. 1, Bartlett vicinity, 5/02/90, C, 90000565

Wheeler County Courthouse, Former [County Courthouses of Nebraska MPS], Maine St. between 2nd and 3rd Sts., Bartlett, 1/10/90, A, C, 89002215

York County

Bradshaw Town Hall, Off US 34, Bradshaw, 5/31/84, A, C, 84002499

Clem's Opera House [Opera House Buildings in Nebraska 1867-1917 MPS], Main and Post Sts., Gresham, 9/28/88, A, 88000949

Jeffery, W. S., Farmstead, W of Benedict, Benedict vicinity, 7/26/82, B, C, 82003208

York Public Library, 306 E. Seventh St., York, 12/04/90, C, 90001765

York Subway [Highway Bridges in Nebraska MPS], 14th and 15th Sts. and BNRR tracks over US 81, York, 6/29/92, C, 92000772

NEVADA

Carson City Independent City

Bank Saloon, 418 S. Carson St., Carson City (Independent City), 12/10/80, A, 80004483

Brougher Mansion, 204 W. Spear St., Carson City (Independent City), 8/11/80, B, C, 80004274

Carson Brewing Company, 102 S. Division St., Carson City (Independent City), 8/18/78, A, C, 78003210

Carson City Civic Auditorium, 813 N. Carson St., Carson City (Independent city), 6/19/90, A, C, 90000912

Carson City Post Office, 401 N. Carson St., Carson City (Independent City), 2/09/79, A, C, 79003440

Carson City Public Buildings [DeLongchamps, Frederick J., Architecture TR], Carson St., Carson City (Independent City), 10/02/87, A, C, 87001625

Clemens, Orion, House, 502 N. Division St., Carson City (Independent City), 3/12/79, B, 79003439

Curry, Abraham, House, 406 N. Nevada St., Carson City (Independent City), 3/30/87, B, C, 87000501

Ferris, G. W. G., House, 311 W. 3rd St., Carson City (Independent City), 2/09/79, B, c, 79003438

Glenbrook, The, 600 N. Carson St., Carson City (Independent City), 5/01/81, A, 81000702

Governor's Mansion, 606 Mountain St., Carson City (Independent City), 10/22/76, A, C, 76002242

Kitzmeyer Furniture Factory, 319 N. Carson St., Carson City (Independent City), 6/22/87, C, 87000714

Lakeview House, U.S. 395 S of E. Lake Blvd., Carson City (Independent City), 1/05/78, A, C, 78003211

Leport-Toupin House, 503 E. Telegraph St., Carson City (Independent City), 9/16/85, B, C, 85002407

Meder, Lew M., House, 308 N. Nevada St., Carson City (Independent City), 8/02/78, C, 78003075

Nevada State Capitol, 101 N. Carson St., Carson City (Independent City), 6/10/75, A, C, 75002126

Nevada State Printing Office, 101 S. Fall St., Carson City (Independent City), 3/29/78, A, C, 78003212

Nye, Gov. James W., Mansion, 108 N. Minnesota St., Carson City (Independent City), 4/16/75, B, a, 75002128

Olcovich—Meyers House, 214 W. King St., Carson City, 7/29/93, A, C, 93000682

Ormsby-Rosser House, 304 S. Minnesota St., Carson City (Independent City), 5/17/79, A, B, C, 79003437

Raycraft Ranch, N of Carson City, on U. S. 395, Carson City (Independent City), 5/04/76, A, B, 76002243

Rinckel Mansion, 102 N. Curry St., Carson City (Independent City), 11/20/75, B, C, 75002129

Roberts, James D., House, 1217 N. Carson St., Carson City (Independent City), 1/03/78, C, 78003213

Sadler, Gov. Reinhold, House, 310 Mountain St., Carson City (Independent City), 3/02/79, B, 79003436

Second Railroad Car No. 21, 2180 S. Carson St., Carson City (Independent City), 12/01/78, A, C, 78003214

Smaill, David, House, 313 W. Ann St., Carson City (Independent City), 9/16/85, A, C, 85002408

Spence, William, House, 308 S. Thompson St., Carson City (Independent City), 7/18/85, A, C, 85001602

St. Charles-Muller's Hotel, 302-304-310 S. Carson St., Carson City (Independent City), 5/27/82, A, 82003209

St. Peter's Episcopal Church, 312 N. Division St., Carson City (Independent City), 1/03/78, A, C, a, 78003215

Stewart Indian School, S of Carson City off US 395, Carson City (Independent City), 9/18/85, A, C, g, 85002432

U.S. Mint, 600 N. Carson St., Carson City (Independent City), 9/05/75, B, C, 75002127

Virginia and Truckee RR. Engines No. 18, The Dayton; and No. 22, The Inyo, NE corner of Colorado and Carson Sts., Carson City (Independent City), 12/18/73, A, C, 73002245

Virginia and Truckee Railroad Shops, Between Stewart and Plaza St., Carson City (Independent City), 12/02/77, A, C, 77001508

Wabuska Railroad Station, S. Carson St., Carson City (Independent City), 8/30/84, A, C, 84002070

Churchill County

Carson River Diversion Dam [Newlands Reclamation TR], Carson River, Fallon vicinity, 3/25/81, A, C, 81000380

Churchill County Courthouse, 10 Williams St., Fallon, 9/23/92, A, C, 92001258

Cold Springs Pony Express Station Ruins, Address Restricted, Frenchman vicinity, 5/16/78, A, 78001718

Cold Springs Station Site, 51 mi. W of Austin on U.S. 50, Austin vicinity, 2/23/72, A, 72000762

Grimes Point, Address Restricted, Fallon vicinity, 2/23/72, D, a, 72000763

Harmon School, Jct. Kirn Rd. and Harmon Rd., Fallon vicinity, 5/23/89, A, 89000055

Humboldt Cave, S of Lovelock off U.S. 40, Lovelock vicinity, 3/15/76, D, 76001140

Lahontan Dam and Power Station [Newlands Reclamation TR], SW of Fallon, Fallon vicinity, 3/25/81, A, C, 81000381

Lovelock Cave, Address Restricted, Lovelock, 5/24/84, D, 84002073

Oats Park Grammar School, 167 E. Park St., Fallon, 5/02/90, A, C, 90000715

Sand Springs Station, Address Restricted, Fallon vicinity, 11/21/80, A, D, 80002465

Stillwater Marsh, Address Restricted, Fallon vicinity, 3/19/75, D, 75001104

Clark County

Boulder City Historic District, Roughly bounded by Nevada Hwy., Avenue L, Date, and 5th Sts., Boulder City, 8/19/83, C, g, 83001107

Boulder Dam Hotel, 1305 Arizona St., Boulder City, 7/13/82, A, g, 82003210

Brownstone Canyon Archeological District, Address Restricted, Las Vegas vicinity, 9/22/82, D, 82003212

Corn Creek Campsite, Address Restricted, Las Vegas vicinity, 3/04/75, A, C, D, 75001105

Desert Valley Museum, 31 W. Mesquite Blvd., Mesquite, 10/24/91, A, C, 91001527

Goodsprings Schoolhouse [Historic School Buildings in the Evolution of the Fifth Supervision School District MPS], San Pedro Ave. E of jct. with Esmeralda St., Goodsprings, 3/10/92, A, C, 92000121

Grapevine Canyon Petroglyphs (AZ:F:14:98 ASM), Address Restricted, Laughlin vicinity, 12/15/84, D, NPS, 84000799

Hidden Forest Cabin, About 20 mi. N of Las Vegas on Hidden Forest Rd., Las Vegas vicinity, 2/20/75, A, 75001106

Homestake Mine, Address Restricted, Searchlight vicinity, 7/17/85, A, D, NPS, 85001601

Hoover Dam [Vehicular Bridges in Arizona MPS (AD) D], E of Las Vegas on U.S. 93, Boulder City vicinity, 4/08/81, A, C, NHL, 81000382

Hunt, Parley, House, Canal St. near jct. with Virgin St., Bunkerville, 11/14/91, A, C, 91001652

Huntridge Theater, 1208 E. Charleston Blvd., Las Vegas, 7/22/93, A, C, 93000686

Kyle Ranch, Losee St. and Carey Ave., North Las Vegas, 10/06/75, A, C, 75001107

Las Vegas Grammar School, Washington and D Sts., Las Vegas, 4/02/79, A, 79001460

Las Vegas Grammar School, 400 Las Vegas Blvd. S, Las Vegas, 5/20/88, A, C, 88000549

Las Vegas High School Academic Building and Gymnasium, 315 S. Seventh St., Las Vegas, 9/24/86, A, C, 86002293

Las Vegas High School Neighborhood Historic District, Roughly bounded by E. Bridger, S. 9th, E. Gass and S. 6th Sts., Las Vegas, 1/30/91, A, C, 90002204

Las Vegas Hospital, 201 N. Eight St., Las Vegas, 10/13/87, A, C, 87001340

Las Vegas Mormon Fort, 900 Las Vegas Blvd., N., Las Vegas, 2/01/72, C, 72000764

Clark County—Continued

Las Vegas Mormon Fort (Boundary Increase), 900 Las Vegas Blvd., N, Las Vegas, 12/12/78, D, 78003379

Las Vegas Springs, Address Restricted ., Las Vegas vicinity, 12/14/78, A, D, 78001719

Leavitt, Thomas, House, 160 S. First West St., Bunkerville, 11/14/91, A, B, C, 91001653

Little Church of the West, 3960 Las Vegas Blvd. S., Las Vegas, 9/14/92, A, C, b, 92001161

Mesquite High School Gymnasium [Historic School Buildings in the Evolution of the Fifth Supervision School District MPS], 144 E. North 1st St., Mesquite, 3/10/92, C, 92000119

Mormon Well Spring, N of Las Vegas on Mormon Spring, Las Vegas vicinity, 12/24/74, A, 74001143

Moulin Rouge Hotel, 900 W. Bonanza Rd., Las Vegas, 12/22/92, A, g, 92001701

Old Boulder City Hospital, 701 Park Pl., Boulder City, 4/01/82, A, a, 82003211

Overton Gymnasium [Historic School Buildings in the Evolution of the Fifth Supervision School District MPS], N. West Thomas St. W of jct. with S. Anderson St., Overton, 3/10/92, C, 92000118

Potosi, S of Las Vegas off I-15 near Potosi Pass, Las Vegas vicinity, 11/13/74, A, 74001144

Pueblo Grande de Nevada, SE of Overton, Overton vicinity, 10/08/82, D, NPS, 82000612

Railroad Cottage Historic District [Properties Associated with the San Pedro, Los Angeles, and Salt Lake Railroad TR], 601–629 S. Casino Center, Las Vegas, 12/22/87, A, C, 87001622

Sandstone Ranch, 20 mi. SW of Las Vegas, Las Vegas vicinity, 4/02/76, A, 76001141

Sheep Mountain Range Archeological District, Address Restricted, Las Vegas vicinity, 12/31/74, D, 74001145

Sloan Petroglyph Site, Address Restricted, Las Vegas vicinity, 12/19/78, D, 78001720

Smith, Jay Dayton, House, 624 S. Sixth St., Las Vegas, 2/20/87, C, 87000077

Tim Springs Petroglyphs, Address Restricted, Indian Springs vicinity, 12/16/74, D, 74001142

Tule Springs Archeological Site, Address Restricted, Las Vegas vicinity, 4/20/79, A, D, g, 79001461

Tule Springs Ranch, 9200 Tule Springs Rd., Las Vegas, 9/23/81, A, C, g, 81000383

U.S. Post Office and Courthouse, 301 E. Stewart Ave., Las Vegas, 2/10/83, A, C, 83001108

Washington School [Historic School Buildings in the Evolution of the Fifth Supervision School District MPS], 1901 N. White St., North Las Vegas, 3/10/92, C, 92000120

Whitehead, Stephen R., House, 333 N. Seventh St., Las Vegas, 8/06/87, C, 87001341

Willow Beach Gauging Station, Lake Mead National Recreation Area, Boulder City vicinity, 3/21/86, A, C, NPS, 86000587

Douglas County

Carson Valley Hospital, 1466 U.S. 395, Gardnerville, 5/29/79, A, 79001462

Carson Valley Improvement Club Hall, 1606 Esmeralda Ave., Minden, 8/04/83, A, C, 83004184

Cavell, Dr. William Henry, House, 402 W. Robinson St., Carson City, 6/22/87, C, 86001655

Douglas County Courthouse [Architecture of Frederick J. DeLongchamps TR], 1616 Eighth St., Minden, 8/06/86, A, C, 86002266

Douglas County High School [DeLongchamps, Frederick J., Architecture TR], 1477 US 395, Gardnerville, 3/09/92, A, C, 92000117

Farmers Bank of Carson Valley [Architecture of Frederick J. DeLongchamps TR], 1597 Esmeralda Ave., Minden, 8/06/86, A, C, 86002264

Friday's Station, US 50 between Kingsbury Grade and Loop Rd., Stateline, 10/09/86, A, C, 86003259

Genoa Historic District, 7 mi. NW of Minden on NV 57, Minden vicinity, 4/16/75, A, 75001108

Home Ranch, W of Minden, Minden vicinity, 12/05/80, A, B, C, 80002466

Jensen, Arendt, House, 1431 Ezell St., Gardnerville, 3/08/89, C, 89000126

Lake Shore House, Glenbrook Rd, Glenbrook, 10/04/79, A, B, b, 79001463

Minden Butter Manufacturing Company [Architecture of Frederick J. DeLongchamps TR], 1617 Water St., Minden, 8/06/86, A, C, 86002263

Minden Flour Milling Company, 6th St. and U.S. 395, Minden, 11/14/78, A, C, 78001721

Minden Inn [Architecture of Frederick J. DeLongchamps TR], 1594 Esmeralda Ave., Minden, 8/06/86, A, C, 86002262

Minden Wool Warehouse [Architecture of Frederick J. DeLongchamps TR], 1615 Railroad Ave., Minden, 8/06/86, A, C, 86002261

Elko County

Elko County Courthouse, 571 Idaho St., Elko, 9/23/92, A, C, 92001259

Gold Creek Ranger Station, E of Mountain City, Humboldt NF, Mountain City vicinity, 9/15/92, A, C, 92001187

Ruby Valley Pony Express Station, 1515 Idaho St., Elko, 3/10/75, A, b, e, 75001110

US Post Office—Elko Main [US Post Offices in Nevada MPS], 275 Third, Elko, 2/28/90, A, C, 90000133

Esmeralda County

Goldfield Historic District, Roughly bounded by 5th St., Miner, Spring, Crystal and Elliott Aves., Goldfield, 6/14/82, A, B, C, D, 82003213

Eureka County

Eureka Historic District, Along U.S. 50, Eureka, 4/13/73, A, 73001078

Humboldt County

Applegate-Lassen Trail, Trail extends from Rye Patch NW to state line, Sulphur vicinity, 12/18/78, A, D, 78001722

Golconda School, Jct. of Morrison and Fourth Sts., Golconda, 11/14/91, A, C, 91001651

Humboldt County Courthouse, 5th and Bridge Sts., Winnemucca, 8/19/83, C, 83001109

Last Supper Cave, Address Restricted, Denio vicinity, 12/06/75, D, 75001111

Micca House, Bridge St., Paradise Valley, 6/11/75, C, 75001112

Nixon Opera House, Winnemucca Blvd. and Melarkey St., Winnemucca, 5/18/83, A, 83001110

Record, W. C., House, 146 W. 2nd St., Winnemucca, 8/27/80, C, 80002467

Silver State Flour Mill, 7 mi. E of Paradise Valley off NV 8B, Paradise Valley vicinity, 5/13/76, A, 76001142

US Post Office—Winnemucca Main [US Post Offices in Nevada MPS], 4th and Melarkey Sts., Winnemucca, 2/28/90, A, C, 90000137

Winnemucca Grammar School, 522 Lay St., Winnemucca, 11/14/91, A, C, 91001654

Lander County

Austin Historic District, In Pony Canyon at jct. of U.S. 50 and NV 8A, Austin, 11/23/71, C, 71000489

Lincoln County

Black Canyon Petroglyphs, Address Restricted, Alamo vicinity, 5/27/75, D, 75001113

Bristol Wells Town Site, 23 mi. N of Pioche off U.S. 93, Pioche vicinity, 3/24/72, A, D, 72000765

Brown's Hall-Thompson's Opera House, N. Main St., Pioche, 8/16/84, A, C, 84002074

Caliente Railroad Depot, 100 Depot Ave., Caliente, 3/05/74, A, 74001146

Lincoln County Courthouse, Lacour St., Pioche, 2/23/78, A, C, 78001724

Panaca Summit Archeological District, Address Restricted, Panaca vicinity, 3/19/90, D, 90000362

White River Narrows Archeological District, Address Restricted, Hiko vicinity, 8/01/78, D, 78001723

Lyon County

East Walker River Petroglyph Site, Address Restricted, Yerington vicinity, 7/24/80, D, 80002468

Fort Churchill, U.S. 95A, 8 mi. S of U.S. 50, Weeks vicinity, 10/15/66, A, NHL, 66000456

I.O.O.F. Building, Mason Valley, 1 S. Main St., Yerington, 8/04/83, C, 83001111

Lyon County—Continued

Lyon County Courthouse, 31 S. Main St., Yerington, 3/24/83, C, 83001112

US Post Office—Yerington Main [US Post Offices in Nevada MPS], 28 N. Main St., Yerington, 2/28/90, A, C, 90000138

Yerington Grammar School, 112 N. California St., Yerington, 8/16/84, A, C, 84002075

Mineral County

Aurora, SW of Hawthorne, Hawthorne vicinity, 7/30/74, A, 74001147

Mineral County Courthouse, 551 C St., Hawthorne, 1/29/82, A, 82003214

Nye County

Bartlett, George A., House [Tonopah MRA], McQuillan and Booker Sts., Tonopah, 5/20/82, A, B, C, 82003215

Bass Building [Tonopah MRA], 119 St. Patrick, Tonopah, 5/20/82, C, 82003216

Belmont, 46 mi. NE of Tonopah off NV 82, Tonopah vicinity, 6/13/72, A, D, 72000766

Berg, William H., House, Mariposa and Davis Sts., Round Mountain, 1/11/84, A, C, 84002076

Berlin Historic District, Off NV 23, Berlin, 11/05/71, A, 71000490

Boak, Cada C., House [Tonopah MRA], Ellis St., Tonopah, 5/20/82, A, B, 82003217

Board and Batten Cottage [Tonopah MRA], Prospect St., Tonopah, 5/20/82, C, 82003218

Board and Batten Miners Cabin [Tonopah MRA], Oddie Ave., Tonopah, 5/20/82, A, C, 82003219

Brann Boardinghouse [Tonopah MRA], Bryan St., Tonopah, 5/20/82, A, C, 82003220

Brokers Exchange [Tonopah MRA], 209–251 Brougher, Tonopah, 5/20/82, A, C, 82003221

Brown, Hugh H., House [Tonopah MRA (AD)], 129 Ellis St., Tonopah vicinity, 10/13/82, A, 82000613

Burdick, E. E., House [Tonopah MRA], 248 Prospect St., Tonopah, 5/20/82, A, C, a, 82003223

Butler, Jim, Mining Company Stone Row Houses [Tonopah MRA], 314 Everett Ave., Tonopah, 5/20/82, A, C, 82003224

Campbell and Kelly Building [Tonopah MRA (AD)], Corona and Main Sts., Tonopah vicinity, 10/13/82, A, C, 82000614

Clinton, Charles, Stone Row House [Tonopah MRA], 151 Central, Tonopah, 5/20/82, C, 82003225

Combellack Adobe Row House [Tonopah MRA], Central St., Tonopah, 5/20/82, A, C, 82003226

Curtis, Uri B., House [Tonopah MRA], 169 Booker St., Tonopah, 5/20/82, B, C, 82003227

Curtis, Uri B., House/Tasker L. Oddie House [Tonopah MRA], Ellis St., Tonopah, 5/20/82, B, C, 82003228

Dunham, Samuel C., House [Tonopah MRA], Belmont Ave., Tonopah, 5/20/82, B, C, 82003229

Frame Cottage [Tonopah MRA], 183 Prospect St., Tonopah, 5/20/82, A, C, 82003230

Gatecliff Rockshelter, SE of Austin, Austin vicinity, 4/27/79, D, 79001464

Golden, Frank, Block [Tonopah MRA], Brougher and Main Sts., Tonopah, 5/20/82, A, B, C, 82003231

Gregovich, John, House [Tonopah MRA], 101 Summit, Tonopah, 5/20/82, C, 82003232

James Wild Horse Trap, About 5 mi. E of Fish Springs, Fish Springs vicinity, 11/19/74, A, 74001148

Kendall, Zeb, House [Tonopah MRA], 159 University Ave., Tonopah, 5/20/82, C, 82003233

Masterson, Dr. J. R., House [Tonopah MRA], Ohio Ave. and 2nd St., Tonopah, 5/20/82, A, C, 82003234

McDonald, Irving, House [Tonopah MRA], 191 Booker, Tonopah, 5/20/82, B, C, 82003235

McKim, H. A., Building [Tonopah MRA], Main and Oddie Sts., Tonopah, 5/20/82, A, C, 82003236

Mizpah Hotel [Tonopah MRA (AD)], 100 Main St., Tonopah, 7/07/78, A, 78001725

Nevada-California Power Company Substation and Auxiliary Power Building [Tonopah MRA], Corner of Knapp and Cutting Sts., Tonopah, 7/26/82, A, b, 82003237

Nye County Courthouse [Tonopah MRA], McCulloch St., Tonopah, 5/20/82, A, C, g, 82003238

Nye County Mercantile Company Building [Tonopah MRA], 147 Main St., Tonopah, 5/20/82, C, 82003239

Raycraft, Arthur, House [Tonopah MRA], Booker St., Tonopah, 5/20/82, C, 82003240

Sawle, Judge W. A., House [Tonopah MRA], 155 Central St., Tonopah, 5/20/82, A, C, 82003241

Shaw, Cal, Adobe Duplex [Tonopah MRA], 129 Central, Tonopah, 5/20/82, C, 82003243

Shaw, Cal, Stone Row House [Tonopah MRA], Central St., Tonopah, 5/20/82, C, 82003242

Shields, E. R., House [Tonopah MRA], 351 St. Patrick, Tonopah, 5/20/82, A, C, 82003244

Smith, J. E., Stone Duplex [Tonopah MRA], 415 Florence, Tonopah, 7/26/82, C, 82003245

St. Marks P. E. Church [Tonopah MRA], 210 University Ave., Tonopah, 5/20/82, C, a, 82003246

State Bank and Trust Company [Tonopah MRA], 102 Brougher, Tonopah, 5/20/82, A, C, 82003247

Stone Jail Building and Row House [Tonopah MRA], Water St., Tonopah, 5/20/82, A, C, 82003248

Tonapah Liquor Company Building [Tonopah MRA], Main St., Tonopah, 5/20/82, A, C, 82003249

Tonapah Mining Company Cottage [Tonopah MRA], Queen St., Tonopah, 5/20/82, A, C, 82003250

Tonapah Mining Company House [Tonopah MRA], Queen St., Tonopah, 5/20/82, A, C, 82003251

Tonapah Public Library [Tonopah MRA], 171 Central, Tonopah, 5/20/82, A, C, 82003252

Tonapah Volunteer Firehouse and Gymnasium [Tonopah MRA], Brougher and Burro Sts., Tonopah, 5/20/82, A, C, 82003253

Tonapah-Extension Mining Company Power Building [Tonopah MRA], Main St., Tonopah, 5/20/82, A, C, 82003254

Tybo Charcoal Kilns, About 55 mi. NE of Tonopah off U.S. 6, Tonopah vicinity, 11/19/74, A, C, 74001149

US Post Office—Tonopah Main [US Post Offices in Nevada MPS], 201 Main St., Tonopah, 2/28/90, A, C, g, 90000136

Verdi Lumber Company Building [Tonopah MRA], Main St., Tonopah, 5/20/82, A, 82003255

Water Company of Tonapah Building [Tonopah MRA], Burro and Brougher Aves., Tonopah, 5/20/82, A, C, 82003256

Wieland Brewery Building [Tonopah MRA], Mineral St., Tonopah, 5/20/82, A, C, 82003257

Pershing County

Leonard Rock Shelter, Address Restricted, Lovelock vicinity, 10/15/66, D, NHL, 66000457

Marzen House, S of Lovelock, Lovelock vicinity, 8/27/81, A, C, b, 81000384

Pershing County Courthouse, 400 Main St., Lovelock, 5/13/86, A, C, 86001077

Rye Patch Archeological Sites, Address Restricted, Lovelock vicinity, 8/02/78, D, 78001726

US Post Office—Lovelock Main [US Post Offices in Nevada MPS], 390 Main St., Lovelock, 2/28/90, A, C, 90000134

Vocational—Agriculture Building, 1170 Elmhurst St., Lovelock, 10/24/91, A, C, 91001528

Storey County

Chollar Mansion, 565 S. D St., Virginia City, 8/05/93, A, B, C, b, 93000689

Derby Diversion Dam [Newlands Reclamation TR (AD)], 19 mi. (30.4 km) E of Sparks on I-80, Sparks vicinity, 4/26/78, A, C, 78001727

Lagomarsino Petroglyph Site, Address Restricted, Virginia City vicinity, 3/24/78, D, 78001728

Marlette Lake Water System, Roughly, from Marlette Lake E to NV 80, Virginia City vicinity, 9/16/92, C, 92001162

Parish House, 109 S. F St., Virginia City, 8/05/93, A, C, 93000688

Piper—Beebe House, 2 S. A St., Virginia City, 8/05/93, B, C, 93000684

Prescott, C. J., House, 12 Hickey St., Virginia City, 8/05/93, A, C, 93000687

Virginia City Historic District, Virginia City and its environs, Virginia City, 10/15/66, A, C, NHL, 66000458

Washoe County

1872 California-Nevada State Boundary Marker, NW of Verdi on CA/NV border, Verdi vicinity, 8/27/81, A, 81000387

Washoe County—Continued

20th Century Club, 335 W. First St., Reno, 4/21/83, C, 83001113

Alamo Ranchhouse, SW of Steamboat at 20205 S. Virginia St., Steamboat vicinity, 11/23/79, A, C, b, 79001466

Bell Telephone of Nevada [Architecture of Frederick J. DeLongchamps TR], 100 N. Center, Reno, 8/06/86, C, 86002260

Billinghurst, Benson Dillon, House, 729 Evans Ave., Reno, 11/08/74, A, B, C, 74001151

Bowers Mansion, 19 mi. S of Reno off U.S. 395, Reno vicinity, 1/31/76, A, C, 76001143

Burke, Charles H., House, 36 Steward St., Reno, 5/31/84, A, C, 84002077

California Building, 1000 Cowan Dr., Idlewild Park, Reno, 9/23/92, A, C, 92001257

Cliff, Walter, Ranch District, 7635 Old HW 395, Washoe Valley, 9/16/85, A, C, 85002428

Clifford House, 339 Ralston St., Reno, 3/07/83, C, 83001114

El Cortez Hotel, 239 W. 2nd St., Reno, 6/13/84, C, 84002078

First United Methodist Church, W. 1st and West Sts., Reno, 2/24/83, C, a, 83001115

Francovich House, 557 Washington St., Reno, 4/25/83, C, 83001116

Gerlach Water Tower, Main St., Gerlach, 10/29/81, C, 81000385

Giraud, Joseph, House, 442 Flint St., Reno, 4/05/84, C, 84002079

Glendale School, S. Virginia St. and Lietzke Lane, Reno, 1/30/78, C, b, 78001729

Graham, William J., House, 548 California Ave., Reno, 3/07/83, A, B, 83001117

Gray, Joseph H., House, 457 Court St., Reno, 11/20/87, C, 87001472

Hawkins House, 549 Court St., Reno, 12/17/79, C, 79001465

Humphrey House, 467 Ralston St., Reno, 3/07/83, C, 83001118

Immaculate Conception Church [DeLongchamps, Frederick J., TR], 590 Pyramid Way, Sparks, 12/23/92, A, C, a, 92001700

Lake Mansion, Adjacent to the Centennial Coliseum on U.S. 395, Reno, 6/29/72, C, b, 72000767

Levy House, 111-121 California Ave., Reno, 2/24/83, C, b, 83001119

MacKay School of Mines Building, University of Nevada, Reno campus, Reno, 4/01/82, A, C, 82003258

Mapes Hotel and Casino, 10 N. Virginia St., Reno, 5/04/84, A, C, 84002081

McCarthy-Platt House, 1000 Plumas St., Reno, 5/31/84, B, C, 84002080

McKinley Park School, Riverside Dr. and Keystone Ave., Reno, 9/16/85, A, C, 85002406

Morrill Hall, University of Nevada/Reno, University of Nevada campus, Reno, 5/01/74, A, C, 74001152

Mount Rose Elementary School, 915 Lander St., Reno, 11/25/77, A, C, 77000841

Nevada-California-Oregon Railroad Depot, 325 E. 4th St., Reno, 2/08/80, A, C, 80002469

Neveda-California-Oregon Railway Locomotive House and Machine Shop, 401 E. 4th St., Reno, 5/09/83, C, 83001120

Newlands, Senator Francis G., House, 17 Elm Ct., Reno, 10/15/66, B, NHL, 66000459

Nortonia Boarding House, 150 Ridge St., Reno, 2/24/83, C, 83001121

Odd Fellows Building, 133 N. Sierra St., Reno, 11/27/78, A, g, 78001730

Old Winters Ranch/Winters Mansion, N of Carson City, Carson City vicinity, 7/30/74, A, C, 74001150

Pincolini Hotel, 214 Lake St., Reno, 10/11/84, A, C, 84000086

Rainier Brewing Company Bottling Plant, 310 Spokane St., Reno, 3/26/80, A, C, 80002470

Reno National Bank—First Interstate Bank [Architecture of Frederick J. DeLongchamps TR], 204 N. Virginia St., Reno, 8/06/86, B, C, 86002257

Riverside Hotel [Architecture of Frederick J. DeLongchamps TR], 17 S. Virginia St., Reno, 8/06/86, A, C, 86002256

Riverside Mill Company Flourmill, 345 E. 2nd St., Reno, 8/18/82, A, 82003259

Southside School, 190 E. Liberty, Reno, 8/05/93, A, C, 93000683

Twaddle Mansion, 485 W. Fifth St., Reno, 3/07/83, C, 83001122

Tyson House, 242 W. Liberty St., Reno, 2/24/83, C, 83001123

US Post Office—Reno Main [US Post Offices in Nevada MPS], 50 S. Virginia St., Reno, 2/28/90, A, C, 90000135

University of Nevada Reno Historic District, Virginia St., Reno, 2/25/87, A, B, C, g, 87000135

Vachina Apartments—California Apartments [Architecture of Frederick J. DeLongchamps TR], 45 California Ave., Reno, 8/06/86, A, C, 86002258

Virginia Street Bridge, Spans Truckee River, Reno, 12/10/80, A, C, 80002471

Washoe County Courthouse [Architecture of Frederick J. DeLongchamps TR], 117 S. Virginia St., Reno, 8/06/86, A, C, 86002254

Washoe County Library—Sparks Branch [DeLongchamps, Frederick J., Architecture TR], 814 Victorian St., Sparks, 3/09/92, A, C, 92000116

Wingfield, George, House, 219 Court St., Reno, 7/15/82, A, B, C, 82003260

White Pine County

Capital Theater, 460 Aultman St., Ely, 8/05/93, A, C, 93000692

Central Theater, 145 W. 15th Ave., Ely, 8/05/93, A, C, 93000691

East Ely Depot, 11th St., East Ely, 4/12/84, A, C, 84002082

Ely L. D. S. Stake Tabernacle, 900 Aultman St., Ely, 7/29/93, A, C, a, 93000685

Fort Ruby, Near Hobson on W side of Ruby Lake, Hobson vicinity, 10/15/66, C, NHL, 66000460

Fort Schellbourne, 43 mi. N of Ely off U.S. 93 on NV 2, Ely vicinity, 2/23/72, A, D, 72000768

Fort Schellbourne (Boundary Increase), N of Ely off US93, Ely vicinity, 8/04/77, A, D, 77001544

Lehman Orchard and Aqueduct, Lehman Caves National Monument, Baker vicinity, 2/25/75, A, NPS, 75000181

Nevada Northern Railway East Ely Yards and Shops, 11th St. E., N terminus, Ely, 7/29/93, A, B, C, 93000693

Rhodes Cabin, Lehman Caves National Monument, Baker vicinity, 2/25/75, A, NPS, 75000180

Sunshine Locality, Address Restricted, Ely vicinity, 1/30/78, D, 78001731

Ward Charcoal Ovens, S of Ely off U.S. 6, Ely vicinity, 9/28/71, A, C, 71000491

White Pine County Courthouse, Campton St., Ely, 9/11/86, C, 86001958

NEW HAMPSHIRE

Belknap County

Alton Bay Railroad Station, NH 11, Alton, 9/22/83, A, C, 83001124

Bay Meeting House and Vestry, Upper Bay and Steele Rds., Sanbornton, 6/07/84, C, a, 84002508

Belknap—Sulloway Mill, Mill St., Laconia, 1/25/71, A, 71000046

Belmont Public Library, Main St., Belmont, 9/12/85, C, 85002191

Busiel—Seeburg Mill, Mill St., Laconia, 1/25/71, A, C, 71000047

Centre Congregational Church, Province Rd., Gilmanton, 9/08/83, C, a, 83001125

Centre Harbor Village Historic District, Main and Plymouth Sts., Centre Harbor, 9/08/83, C, 83001126

Dana Meeting House, Dana Hill Rd., New Hampton, 12/13/84, C, a, 84000516

Endicott Rock, Weirs Channel, Laconia, 5/28/80, A, B, D, f, 80000264

Evangelical Baptist Church, Veterans Sq., Laconia, 9/12/85, C, a, 85002189

First Baptist Church of Gilmanton, Province Rd./NH 107, .25 mi. N of Stage Rd., Gilmanton, 12/01/89, C, a, 89002059

First Congregational Church, Church St, W of Main St., Alton, 3/09/90, C, a, 90000386

First Free Will Baptist Church in Meredith, Winona Rd., Meredith, 12/01/86, C, a, 86003368

First Freewill Baptist Church, N of Lovelock, East Alton, 8/02/78, A, C, a, 78000209

Foss, Oscar, Memorial Library, Main St., Barnstead, 11/07/85, C, 85002770

Gale Memorial Library, 695 Main St., Laconia, 9/12/85, C, 85002185

Gilmanton Academy, Province Rd., Gilmanton, 9/08/83, A, C, 83001127

Gordon—Nash Library, Main St., New Hampton, 9/15/88, A, C, 88001437

Goss, Ossian Wilbur, Reading Room, 188 Elm St., Laconia, 9/04/86, C, 86002165

House by the Side of the Road, 61 School St., Tilton, 11/26/80, B, C, 80000265

Kimball Castle, Locke's Hill Rd., Gilford, 8/16/82, A, B, C, 82001666

Laconia District Court, Academy Sq., Laconia, 11/09/82, C, 82004990

Laconia Passenger Station, Veterans Sq., Laconia, 1/11/82, A, B, C, 82001667

Lochmere Archeological District, Address Restricted, Tilton vicinity, 11/01/82, D, 82000615

Meredith Public Library, 50 Main St., Meredith, 12/13/84, C, 84000514

Monument Square Historic District, Main, Factory, Church, and Depot Sts., Alton, 3/15/84, C, 84002512

Morrill, John J., Store, Belknap Mountain Rd., Gilford, 8/29/80, A, C, 80000266

New Hampshire Veterans' Association Historic District, N of Laconia on Lakeside Ave., Laconia vicinity, 5/22/80, A, C, D, 80000267

New Hampton Community Church, Main St., New Hampton, 3/07/85, C, a, 85000474

Sanbornton Square Historic District, Sanbornton Square, Sanbornton vicinity, 12/08/80, A, C, D, 80000417

Second Free Baptist Church, Main St., S of Church St., Alton, 3/09/90, C, a, 90000387

Tilton Downtown Historic District, Roughly Main St. between Central and Bridge Sts., Tilton, 7/07/83, A, C, 83001128

Tilton Island Park Bridge, Tilton Island Park, Tilton, 3/21/80, A, C, 80000268

Tilton, Charles E., Mansion, School St., Tilton, 8/10/82, B, C, 82004995

US Post Office—Laconia Main, 33 Church St., Laconia, 7/18/86, C, 86002252

United Baptist Church of Lakeport, 23 Park St., Laconia, 6/06/85, C, a, 85001198

Weirs, The, Address Restricted, Laconia vicinity, 5/12/75, D, 75000120

Carroll County

Abenaki Indian Shop and Camp, Intervale Crossroad, 1 mi. E of NH 16, Conway, 2/28/91, A, B, 91000218

Brewster Memorial Hall, S. Main and Union Sts., Wolfeboro, 9/08/83, C, 83001129

Brookfield Town Hall, NH 109, Brookfield, 6/06/85, A, C, 85001189

Center Sandwich Historic District, Roughly bounded by Skinner, Grove, Church, Maple and Main Sts., and Creamery Brook and Quimby Field Rds., Sandwich, 12/22/83, C, 83003997

Cook Memorial Library, Main St., Tamworth, 6/25/80, A, C, 80000269

Cotton Mountain Community Church, Stoneham Rd., Wolfeborough, 3/07/85, C, a, 85000475

District No. 2 Schoolhouse, NH 153, Wakefield, 10/03/80, A, C, 80000270

Durgin Bridge, Durgin Bridge Rd., Sandwich, 9/22/83, C, 83001130

Eagle Mountain House, Carter Notch Rd. N of jct. with NH 16A, Jackson, 12/06/90, A, C, 90001848

Eastern Slope Inn, Main St., North Conway, 8/10/82, A, C, 82004994

First Free Will Baptist Church, Granite Rd., Ossipee, 3/15/84, C, a, 84002518

Freese's Tavern, Main St., Moultonborough, 4/29/82, A, C, 82001668

Hansen's Annex, Main St., Center Sandwich, 9/22/83, C, 83001131

Jewell, Bradbury, House, Ferncroft Rd., Sandwich, 8/27/86, C, 86002792

Joy Farm, Salter Hill Rd., Silver Lake, 11/11/71, B, g, NHL, 71000048

Lord's Hill Historic District, NH 153, Effingham, 9/12/85, C, a, d, 85002162

Lower Corner Historic District, NH 109, Sandwich, 12/01/86, C, 86003380

Madison School, District No. 1, NH 113, Madison, 12/11/80, A, C, b, 80000271

Moultonborough Town House, NH 25, .3 mi. SW of NH 109, Moultonborough, 12/01/89, A, 89002057

North Conway Depot and Railroad Yard, Norcross Circle, North Conway, 8/10/79, A, C, 79003792

North Sandwich Meeting House, Quaker-Whiteface Rd., Sandwich vicinity, 6/05/86, C, a, 86001230

Russell—Colbath House, Kancamagus Hwy., Albany, 4/23/87, A, B, C, 86003416

St. John's Church, Rectory, and Parish Hall, High St., Wakefield, 6/07/84, C, a, 84002519

Swallow Boathouse, S of Moultonborough, Moultonborough vicinity, 8/26/80, A, C, 80000272

Town Hall, Maple St., Center Sandwich, 5/15/80, A, C, 80000273

Union Church, S. Main St., South Wolfeboro, 4/29/82, A, a, 82001669

Union Hotel, Main St. at Chapel St., Wakefield, 12/01/89, A, 89002055

Wakefield House, NH 153, Wakefield, 6/23/83, A, C, 83001133

Wakefield Public Library, Mountain Laurel Rd., Wakefield, 9/08/83, B, C, 83001132

Wakefield Village Historic District, Off NH 153, Wakefield, 3/15/84, C, 84002521

White Meetinghouse, S of Eaton Center on Towle Hill Rd., Eaton Center vicinity, 5/15/80, A, C, a, 80000274

Whittier Bridge, Old NH 25, Ossipee, 3/15/84, A, C, 84002558

Windermere, SW of Moultonborough on Long Island, Moultonborough vicinity, 11/14/79, A, C, 79000195

Wolfeboro Centre Community Church, NH 109, Wolfeboro Centre, 3/15/84, C, a, 84002564

Cheshire County

Acre (The) [Harrisville MRA], S of lower Harrisville village at S-curve in road to Dublin, Harrisville, 1/14/88, A, C, 86003257

Adams Farm [Harrisville MRA], Off MacVeagh Rd. near Fansnacloich, Harrisville, 1/14/88, A, C, 86003246

Adams, Dr. Daniel, House, 324 Main St., Keene, 6/08/89, C, 89000449

Adams, John, Homestead—Wellscroft [Harrisville MRA], W of Sunset Hill Rd., Harrisville, 1/14/88, A, C, 86003250

Aldworth Manor [Harrisville MRA], On hill above IP-14, N side of Chesham-Harrisville Rd., Harrisville, 1/14/88, A, B, C, a, b, 86003244

Cheshire County—Continued

Allison, Capt. Samuel, House [Dublin MRA], Keene Rd., Dublin, 12/18/83, C, 83004005

Amory Ballroom [Dublin MRA], Off Old Troy Rd., Dublin, 5/02/85, A, C, 85000921

Amory House [Dublin MRA], Off Old Troy Rd., Dublin, 12/15/83, A, C, 83004006

Amory—Appel Cottage [Dublin MRA], Off Old Troy Rd., Dublin, 5/02/85, A, C, 85000920

Appleton Farm [Dublin MRA], Hancock Rd., Dublin, 12/18/83, A, C, 83004008

Appleton—Hannaford House [Dublin MRA], Hancock Rd., Dublin, 12/15/83, A, C, 83004007

Asbury United Methodist Church, NH 63, Chesterfield, 12/21/83, A, C, a, 83004009

Ashuelot Covered Bridge, NH 119 and Bolton Rd., Ashuelot, 2/20/81, A, C, 81000069

Ballou—Newbegin House [Dublin MRA], Old Marlborough Rd., Dublin, 12/18/83, A, C, 83004011

Bancroft, Timothy, House [Harrisville MRA], N side of access road to Mosquitobush, off Tolman Pond Rd., Harrisville, 1/14/88, A, C, 86003241

Beal, Persia, House [Harrisville MRA], N side of Chesham Rd., W of IP-13, Harrisville, 1/14/88, A, C, 86003243

Beech Hill [Dublin MRA], Off New Harrisville Rd., Dublin, 12/15/83, A, C, 83004012

Beech Hill Summer Home District [Harrisville MRA], Roughly Venable, Appleton and Old Harrisville Rds., Harrisville, 1/14/88, A, C, 86003079

Bemis, Elbridge G., House [Harrisville MRA], Chesham Rd., Harrisville, 1/14/88, A, C, 86003247

Bemis, George, House [Harrisville MRA], Chesham Rd., Harrisville, 1/14/88, A, C, 86003248

Brackett House [Dublin MRA], High Ridge Rd., Dublin, 12/18/83, A, C, 83004013

Burpee Farm [Dublin MRA], Burpee Rd., Dublin, 12/18/83, A, C, 83004014

Cabot, Louis, House [Dublin MRA], Windmill Hill Rd., Dublin, 12/18/83, A, C, 83004015

Cabot, T.H., Cottage [Dublin MRA], Snow Hill Rd., Dublin, 12/15/83, A, C, 83004016

Carleton Bridge, On Carleton Rd. over South Branch Ashuelot River, East Swanzey vicinity, 6/10/75, A, C, 75000121

Cheever, George, Farm [Harrisville MRA], Intersection of Nelson and Tolman Pond Rds., Harrisville, 1/14/88, C, 86003238

Chesham Village District [Harrisville MRA], Roughly bounded by Yellow Wings, Seaver, Chesham, and Marienfield Rds., Harrisville, 12/29/86, A, B, C, 86003102

Cheshire County Courthouse, 12 Court St., Keene, 12/13/78, A, C, 78000210

Clymer House [Harrisville MRA], Off Tolman Pond Rd. at end of entry road, Harrisville, 1/14/88, C, 86003239

Colony's Block, 4–7 Central Square, Keene, 3/24/83, A, C, 83001134

Conant Public Library, Main St., Winchester, 8/27/87, C, 87001420

Cooke, Noah, House, W of Keene on Daniels Hill Rd., Keene vicinity, 4/23/73, B, C, b, 73000268

Coombs Covered Bridge, N of Winchester off NH 10, Winchester vicinity, 11/21/76, A, C, 76000122

Corey Farm [Dublin MRA], Parsons Rd., Dublin, 12/15/83, A, C, 83004017

Dinsmoor—Hale House, Main and Winchester Sts., Keene, 4/26/76, A, B, C, 76000197

Dublin Lake Historic District [Dublin MRA], Lake, E. Lake, W. Lake, and Old Harrisville Rds., Dublin, 12/18/83, A, C, 83004018

Dublin Town Hall, NH 101, Dublin, 6/25/80, C, 80000275

Dublin Village Historic District [Dublin MRA], Old Common and Harrisville Rds., and Main and Church Sts., Dublin, 12/15/83, A, C, 83004019

Eaton, Moses, Jr., House [Harrisville MRA], NH 137, Harrisville, 1/14/88, A, B, C, 86003106

Elliot Mansion, 305 Main St., Keene, 4/30/76, A, C, 76000220

Eveleth Farm [Dublin MRA], Burpee Rd., Dublin, 12/18/83, A, C, 83004020

Far Horizons [Dublin MRA], Learned Rd., Dublin, 12/15/83, C, 83004023

Farwell, Corban C., Homestead [Harrisville MRA], N side of Childs Bog Rd., Harrisville, 1/14/88, A, C, 86003253

Fasnacloich [Harrisville MRA], Four Hill Rd. N of Dublin town line, Harrisville, 1/14/88, A, B, C, 86003245

Fisk Barn [Dublin MRA], Gerry Rd., Dublin, 12/18/83, A, C, 83004024

Fiske, Catherine, Seminary For Young Ladies, 251 Main St., Keene, 5/03/76, A, C, 76000196

Foothill Farm [Dublin MRA], Old Troy Rd., Dublin, 12/15/83, C, 83004025

Frost Farm [Dublin MRA], Old Marlborough Rd., Dublin, 12/15/83, B, C, a, 83004026

Frost Farm [Dublin MRA], Korpi Rd., Dublin, 12/18/83, A, C, 83004027

Gilchrest [Harrisville MRA], NH 137, Harrisville, 1/14/88, A, C, 86003105

Gilsum Stone Arch Bridge, Surry Rd. over the Ashuelot River W of jct. NH 10, Gilsum, 8/31/89, C, 89001207

Glenchrest [Harrisville MRA], NH 137, Harrisville, 1/14/88, A, C, 86003104

Gowing, James, Farm [Dublin MRA], Page Rd., Dublin, 12/18/83, A, C, 83004028

Gowing, Joseph, Farm [Dublin MRA], Page Rd., Dublin, 12/15/83, A, C, 83004029

Grace United Methodist Church, 34 Court St., Keene, 3/07/85, C, a, 85000476

Greenwood, Isaac, House [Dublin MRA], Peterborough Rd., Dublin, 12/18/83, A, C, 83004034

Greenwood, Moses, House [Dublin MRA], Pierce and Old County Rds., Dublin, 12/15/83, A, C, 83004036

Harrisville Historic District [Harrisville MRA (AD)], Town of Harrisville and its environs, Harrisville and vicinity, 9/17/71, A, C, NHL, 71000072

Harrisville Rural District [Harrisville MRA], Roughly along Venable, Old Harrisville, New Harrisville, and Bonds Corner Rds., Harrisville, 2/18/87, A, B, C, D, g, 86003078

High Tops School, Reynolds and River Rds., Westmoreland, 12/13/84, C, 84000519

Ivanov-Rinov House [Dublin MRA], Pierce Rd., Dublin, 12/18/83, C, g, 83004038

Jaffrey Center Historic District, NW of Jaffrey on NH 124, Jaffrey vicinity, 6/11/75, A, C, a, 75000122

Jaffrey Mills, 41 Main St., Jaffrey, 8/10/82, A, C, 82004992

Jones Hall, Church St., Marlow, 6/07/84, C, a, b, 84002722

Kendall Cottage [Harrisville MRA], N side of Silver Lake Rd., Harrisville, 1/14/88, A, C, 86003251

Knollwood [Dublin MRA], Windmill Hill Rd., Dublin, 12/18/83, A, C, 83004039

Lattice Cottage [Dublin MRA], Off Old Troy Rd., Dublin, 12/15/83, A, C, 83004040

Learned Homestead [Dublin MRA], Upper Jaffrey Rd., Dublin, 12/15/83, A, C, 83004043

Learned, Amos, Farm [Dublin MRA], NH 137, Dublin, 12/15/83, A, C, 83004041

Learned, Benjamin, House [Dublin MRA], Upper Jaffrey Rd., Dublin, 12/18/83, A, C, 83004042

Markham House [Dublin MRA], Snow Hill Rd., Dublin, 12/18/83, A, C, 83004044

Marshall, Benjamin, House [Dublin MRA], Peterborough Rd., Dublin, 12/18/83, A, C, 83004046

Martin, Micajah, Farm [Dublin MRA], Old Peterborough Rd., Dublin, 12/18/83, A, C, 83004047

Mason House [Dublin MRA], Snow Hill Rd., Dublin, 12/15/83, A, C, 83004049

Mason—Watkins House, RD # 2, Surry, 3/11/82, C, 82001670

McKenna Cottage [Dublin MRA], Windmill Hill Rd., Dublin, 12/18/83, A, C, 83004051

Moore Farm and Twitchell Mill Site [Dublin MRA], Off Page Rd., Dublin, 12/18/83, A, C, 83004052

Morse, Asa, Farm [Dublin MRA], NH 101, Dublin, 12/15/83, A, 83004054

Morse, Capt. Thomas, Farm [Dublin MRA], Old Marlborough Rd., Dublin, 12/15/83, A, C, 83004055

Morse, Eli, Farm, Lake Rd., Dublin, 4/11/83, A, C, 83001135

Morse, Eli, Sawmill Foundations [Dublin MRA], Off Old Marlborough Rd., Dublin, 12/18/83, A, 83004056

Mountain View Farm [Dublin MRA], Upper Jaffrey Rd., Dublin, 12/18/83, A, C, 83004057

Needham House [Harrisville MRA], Meadow Rd., Harrisville, 1/14/88, C, 86003254

Nelson Schoolhouse, Old Sullivan Rd., Nelson, 4/23/73, A, 73000251

New Hampshire Conservatory of Music and the Arts, Central Sq., Winchester, 5/15/80, C, a, 80000276

Old Patch Place, W of Fitzwilliam on Rhododendron Rd., Fitzwilliam vicinity, 8/15/80, A, C, 80000277

Cheshire County—Continued

Park Hill Meetinghouse, Park Hill, Westmoreland, 9/08/80, C, a, b, 80000278

Parsons Studio and Casino [Dublin MRA], Parsons Rd., Dublin, 12/18/83, A, C, 83004058

Perry, Ivory, Homestead [Dublin MRA], Corner Valley and Dooe Rds., Dublin, 12/15/83, A, C, 83004061

Perry, John, Homestead [Dublin MRA], Dooe Rd., Dublin, 12/18/83, A, C, 83004063

Piper, Rufus, Homestead [Dublin MRA], Pierce Rd., Dublin, 12/15/83, C, 83004065

Piper, Solomon, Farm [Dublin MRA], Valley Rd., Dublin, 12/18/83, A, C, 83004067

Point Comfort [Harrisville MRA], S. Skatutakee Rd., Harrisville, 1/14/88, C, 86003256

Pottersville District [Harrisville MRA], Roughly intersection of Roxbury and Meadow Rds., and along Brown Rd. NE of Chesham Rd., Harrisville, 12/29/86, A, C, D, 86003096

Pumpelly Studio [Dublin MRA], Snow Hill Rd., Dublin, 12/15/83, A, C, 83004069

Raubold House [Harrisville MRA], N side of Chesham Rd. W of IP-9A, Harrisville, 1/14/88, A, 86003242

Richardson, Abijah, Sr., Homestead [Dublin MRA], Hancock Rd., Dublin, 12/18/83, A, C, 83004070

Richardson, Deacon Abijah, House [Dublin MRA], Hancock Rd., Dublin, 12/15/83, A, 83004071

Richardson, John, Homestead [Dublin MRA], Hancock Rd., Dublin, 12/18/83, A, C, 83004072

Richardson, Luke, House [Dublin MRA], Hancock Rd., Dublin, 12/15/83, C, 83004073

Richmond Community Church, Fitzwilliam Rd., Richmond, 3/24/83, C, a, 83001136

Richmond School House No. 6, NH 119, Richmond, 11/25/80, A, 80000279

Richmond Town Hall, NH 32, Richmond, 12/19/79, A, C, a, 79000273

Robbe, James, Jr., House [Dublin MRA], Old Peterborough Rd., Dublin, 12/18/83, A, C, 83004074

Sawyer Tavern, 63 Arch St., Keene, 5/15/80, C, 80000280

Sawyers Crossing Covered Bridge, N of Swanzey off NH 32, Swanzey vicinity, 11/14/78, A, C, 78000211

Second Rindge Meetinghouse, Horsesheds and Cemetery, US 202 and Rindge Common, Rindge, 10/05/79, A, C, a, d, 79003791

Silver Lake District [Harrisville MRA], Roughly along Old Nelson, Eastside, and Westside Rds., Harrisville, 12/29/86, A, C, 86003100

Silver Lake Farm [Harrisville MRA], Between Silver Lake and Seaver Rds. near intersection with Old Nelson Rd., Harrisville, 1/14/88, A, C, 86003252

Slate Covered Bridge, Off NH 10, Westport, 11/14/78, A, C, 78000212

Smith—Mason Farm [Harrisville MRA], NW of Meadow and Old Roxbury Rds. intersection, Harrisville, 1/14/88, A, C, 86003255

Spur House [Dublin MRA], Off Old Common Rd., Dublin, 12/15/83, A, C, 83004075

Stationmaster's House [Harrisville MRA], Jaquith Rd., Harrisville, 1/14/88, A, 86003108

Stone Farm [Dublin MRA], Old Marlborough Rd., Dublin, 12/18/83, A, C, 83004076

Stone—Darracott House [Dublin MRA], Old Marlborough Rd., Dublin, 12/15/83, A, C, 83004077

Stonehenge [Dublin MRA], Windmill Hill Rd., Dublin, 12/18/83, A, C, 83004079

Strong, Capt. Richard, House [Dublin MRA], Peterborough Rd., Dublin, 12/18/83, A, C, 83004080

Strong, Richard, Cottage [Dublin MRA], Off Peterborough Rd., Dublin, 12/15/83, A, C, 83004081

Strongman, Henry, House [Dublin MRA], Peterborough Rd., Dublin, 12/15/83, A, C, 83004082

Strongman, William, House [Dublin MRA], Old County Rd., Dublin, 12/18/83, A, C, 83004083

Third Fitzwilliam Meetinghouse, Village Green, Fitzwilliam, 8/26/77, A, C, a, 77000162

Todd Block, 27–31 Main St., Hinsdale, 6/14/88, A, C, 88000646

Townsend Farm [Dublin MRA], E. Harrisville Rd., Dublin, 12/15/83, C, 83004084

Townsend, Jabez, House [Harrisville MRA], E. Harrisville and Cherry Hill Rds., Harrisville, 1/14/88, A, C, 86003107

United Church of Christ in Keene, 23 Central Sq., Keene, 3/09/82, C, a, b, 82001671

Veterans' Memorial Hall, NH 32, Richmond, 9/04/86, A, B, C, a, 86002160

Wales, Mary Anne, House [Dublin MRA], Snow Hill Rd., Dublin, 12/18/83, A, C, 83004085

Walpole Academy, Main St., Walpole, 5/21/75, A, C, 75000230

Weldwood [Dublin MRA], Old Troy Rd., Dublin, 12/15/83, A, C, 83004086

West Swanzey Covered Bridge, Main St., West Swanzey, 2/29/80, A, 80000281

Wildwood Cottage [Harrisville MRA], S of access road to Mosquitobush, off Tolman Pond Rd., Harrisville, 1/14/88, A, C, 86003240

Willard Homestead [Harrisville MRA], Sunset Hill Ave., Harrisville, 1/14/88, A, C, 86003249

Winchester Town Hall, Main St., Winchester, 8/27/87, C, 87001419

Windmill Hill [Dublin MRA], Windmill Hill Rd., Dublin, 12/18/83, C, g, 83004087

Wood House [Dublin MRA], NH 101 and 137, Dublin, 12/15/83, C, 83004088

Wyman Tavern, 339 Main St., Keene, 4/03/72, A, C, 72000106

Coos County

Columbia Covered Bridge, Across Connecticut River between US 3 and VT 102, Columbia, 12/12/76, A, C, 76000123

Congregational Church, 921 Main St., Berlin, 1/04/80, A, C, a, 80000282

Crawford Depot, Off US 302, Gorham vicinity, 4/29/82, A, C, 82001672

Crawford House Artist's Studio, Address Restricted, Carroll, 9/12/85, B, C, 85002193

Garland Mill, Garland Rd., Lancaster, 11/12/82, C, 82000616

Holy Resurrection Orthodox Church, Petrograd St., Berlin, 5/16/79, A, C, a, 79000196

Mount Orne Covered Bridge, SW of Lancaster off NH 135, Lancaster vicinity, 12/12/76, A, C, 76000124

Mount Washington Hotel, Off US 302, Bretton Woods vicinity, 9/27/78, A, C, g, NHL, 78000213

Mt. Jasper Lithic Source, 1 1/2 mi. NW of confluence of Dead R. and Androscoggin R., Berlin, 5/29/92, D, 92000631

Philbrook Farm Inn, North Rd., Shelburne, 3/15/84, A, 84002804

St. Anne Church, 58 Church St., Berlin, 5/29/79, A, C, a, 79000197

Stark Covered Bridge, E of Groveton at NH 10 and Northside Rd., Groveton vicinity, 12/01/80, A, C, 80000283

Stark Union Church, NH 110, Stark, 12/08/83, C, a, 83004089

Tip-Top House, Mt. Washington State Park, Sargent's Purchase, 1/11/82, A, C, 82001673

US Post Office—Lancaster Main, 120 Main St., Lancaster, 7/17/86, C, 86002245

Weeks Estate, NH 3, Lancaster, 6/06/85, B, C, 85001190

Wilder—Holton House, 226 Main St., Lancaster, 6/11/75, A, C, a, 75000231

Grafton County

Ashland Gristmill and Dam, Main St., Ashland, 12/10/79, C, 79000317

Ashland Junior High School, 12 School St., Ashland, 4/08/83, C, 83001137

Ashland Railroad Station, 39 Depot St., Ashland, 11/10/82, A, C, 82000617

Ashland Town Hall, 10 Highland St., Ashland, 3/24/83, A, C, 83001138

Bath Covered Bridge, Off US 302, NH10, Bath, 9/01/76, A, C, 76000125

Bedell Covered Bridge, Crosses Connecticut River between Haverhill and Newbury, Haverhill, 5/28/75, A, C, 75002171

Brick Store, Main St., Bath, 11/07/85, A, C, 85002780

Burt—Cheney Farm, US 302, Bethlehem, 3/25/82, C, 82001674

Canaaan Meetinghouse, Canaan St., Canaan, 3/24/72, C, a, 72001598

Canaan Street Historic District, Canaan St., Canaan, 5/07/73, A, C, 73000163

Carr, Daniel, House, Brier Hill Rd. N side, 1.5 mi. from jct. with NH 10, Haverhill, 3/27/92, C, 92000156

Central Square Historic District, 2–27 Central Square, 1 Summer St., 1–3 N. Main St., and 2 S. Main St., Bristol, 3/24/83, A, C, 83001139

Centre Village Meeting House, NH 4A, Enfield, 6/06/85, C, a, 85001197

Grafton County—Continued

Colburn Park Historic District, N., S., E., and W. Park Sts., 3 Campbell St., 1 School St., 1 Bank St., and 9–10 Lebanon Mall, Lebanon, 1/10/86, A, C, 86000782

Dorchester Common Historic District, Roughly bounded by N. Dorchester 2 mile NW of intersection with NH 118, Dorchester, 3/07/85, C, 85000477

Dorchester Community Church, Off NH 118, Dorchester, 11/25/80, C, a, b, 80000284

Dow Academy, Dow Ave., Franconia, 8/31/82, C, 82001675

Enfield Shaker Historic District, SR 4A, Enfield, 11/07/79, A, C, D, a, 79000198

Felsengarten, SE of Bethlehem on Lewis Hill Rd., Bethlehem, 6/18/73, B, 73002296

First Free Will Baptist Church and Vestry, 13–15 N. Main St., Ashland, 4/08/83, C, a, 83001140

Frost Place, S of Franconia off NH 116 on Ridge Rd., Franconia vicinity, 11/30/76, B, 76000126

Goodall-Woods Law Office, NE of Bath on U.S. 302, Bath vicinity, 8/26/80, C, 80000285

Haverhill Corner Historic District, NH 10 from N. Piedmont to bisection of NH 25 and Court St., Haverhill, 8/27/87, C, 87001415

Haverhill—Bath Covered Bridge, NH 135, Woodsville, 4/18/77, A, C, 77000091

Hebron Village Historic District, Roughly bounded by Hebron Village Cemetery, N. and W. Shore Rds., Hobart Hill and Groton Rds., Hebron, 3/07/85, A, C, d, 85000492

Hewitt House, US 4, Enfield, 11/07/85, C, 85002778

Holderness Free Library, Junction of US 3 and NH 113, Holderness, 3/07/85, C, 85000478

Holderness Inn, Rt. 3, Holderness, 12/13/84, A, C, 84000523

Hutchins, Jeremiah, Tavern, NE of Bath on US 302, Bath vicinity, 9/07/84, A, C, 84003194

Kent, Moses, House, Address Restricted, Lyme vicinity, 6/07/84, C, 84002808

Lane, Edward H., House, 16 Cottage St., Littleton, 12/08/80, C, 80000286

Lisbon Inn, Main St., Lisbon, 12/01/80, C, 80000287

Littleton Town Building, 1 Union St., Littleton, 5/07/73, A, C, 73000164

Lovett's by Lafayette Brook, S of Franconia on Profile Rd., Franconia vicinity, 3/11/82, A, 82001676

Lyme Common Historic District, Dorchester Rd., John Tomson Way, On the Common; Pleasant and Union Sts., E. Thetford Rd., Main and Market Sts., Lyme, 9/01/88, C, a, d, 88001435

North Holderness Freewill Baptist Church—Holderness Historical Society Building, Owl Brook Rd., Holderness, 9/04/86, C, a, 86002171

Old Grafton County Courthouse, 1 Court St., Plymouth, 4/29/82, A, C, b, 82001677

Orford Street Historic District, Orford St. (NH 10) from Rt. 25A to Archertown Rd., E to include cemetery, Orford, 8/26/77, A, C, 77000163

Plymouth Historic District, Bounded by Court, Main, and Highland Sts., Plymouth, 3/14/86, A, C, 86000343

Rocks Estate, W of Bethlehem on US 302, Bethlehem vicinity, 9/07/84, B, C, 84003197

Sawyer—Medlicott House, Jct. of Bradford and River Rds., Piermont, 12/06/91, C, 91001757

St. Mark's Episcopal Church, 6–8 Highland St., Ashland, 12/13/84, C, a, 84000522

Stone Arch Underpass, Glen Rd., Lebanon, 9/12/85, C, 85002190

Swiftwater Covered Bridge, S of Bath on Valley Rd., Bath vicinity, 11/21/76, A, C, 76000127

Thayer's Hotel, 136 Main St., Littleton, 3/09/82, C, 82001678

Trinity Church, E of Plymouth on NH 175, Plymouth vicinity, 9/07/84, B, C, a, 84003203

US Post Office and Courthouse—Littleton Main, 165 Main St., Littleton, 7/17/86, C, 86002251

Webster Estate, NH 113, Holderness vicinity, 6/09/89, A, B, C, 89000448

Whipple House, 4 Pleasant St., Ashland, 12/13/78, B, C, c, 78000338

Woodsville Opera Building, 67 Central St., Woodsville, 5/15/80, C, 80000288

Hillsborough County

Abbot House, 1 Abbott Sq., Nashua, 4/17/80, C, 80000289

All Saints' Church, 51 Concord St., Peterborough, 12/01/80, C, a, 80000290

Amherst Village Historic District, NH 101 and NH 122, Amherst, 8/18/82, A, C, 82001679

Ash Street School, Bounded by Ash, Bridge, Maple, and Pearl Sts., Manchester, 5/30/75, A, C, 75000232

Athens Building, 76–96 Hanover St., Manchester, 5/30/75, A, C, 75000123

Barnes, Jonathan, House, North Rd., Hillsborough Center, 3/01/82, C, 82001680

Bedford Town Hall, 70 Bedford Center Rd., Bedford, 12/13/84, A, C, 84000530

Birchwood Inn, NH 45, Temple, 6/06/85, C, 85001194

Chase, Amos, House and Mill, NH 114 W side, 1/8 mi. S of jct. with NH 77, Weare, 3/12/92, A, 92000155

Contoocook Mills Industrial District, Between Mill St. and Contoocook River, Hillsborough, 6/10/75, A, C, D, 75000124

Contoocook Mills Industrial District (Boundary Increase), Mill St., Hillsboro, 12/12/85, A, C, 85003530

County Farm Bridge, NW of Wilton on Old County Farm Rd., Wilton vicinity, 5/14/81, C, 81000070

Cragin, Daniel, Mill, W of Wilton at Jct. of Davisville Rd. and Burton Hwy., Wilton vicinity, 3/23/82, A, B, 82001681

Currier Gallery of Art, 192 Orange St., Manchester, 12/19/79, A, C, 79000199

District A [Amoskeag Manufacturing Company Housing Districts TR], Bounded by Pleasant, State, Granite, and Bedford Sts., Manchester, 11/12/82, A, C, 82000618

District B [Amoskeag Manufacturing Company Housing Districts TR], Roughly bounded by Canal, Mechanic, Franklin, and Pleasant Sts., Manchester, 11/12/82, A, C, 82000619

District C [Amoskeag Manufacturing Company Housing Districts TR], Roughly bounded by N. Hampshire Lane, Hollis, Canal, and Bridge Sts., Manchester, 11/12/82, A, C, 82000620

District D [Amoskeag Manufacturing Company Housing Districts TR], Roughly bounded by Canal, Langdon, Elm, and W. Brook Sts., Manchester, 11/12/82, A, C, 82000621

District E [Amoskeag Manufacturing Company Housing Districts TR], 258–322 McGregor St., Manchester, 11/12/82, A, C, 82000622

Flint Estate, The, Old Keene and Old Center Rd., Antrim, 12/13/84, C, a, 84000525

Gay, Alpheus, House, 184 Myrtle St., Manchester, 3/09/82, C, 82001682

Goffstown Covered Railroad Bridge, NH 114 (Main St.) over Piscataquog River, Goffstown, 6/18/75, A, C, 75000125

Grasmere Schoolhouse #9 and Town Hall, 87 Center St., Goffstown, 9/05/90, A, C, 90001350

Greenfield Meeting House, Forest Rd., Greenfield, 12/08/83, C, a, 83004090

Hancock Village Historic District, Main St. roughly between Norway Pond La. and Old Dublin Rd., and Bennington and Norway Hill Rds., Hancock, 3/08/88, C, a, b, d, 88000178

Hancock—Greenfield Bridge, Forest Rd., Hancock vicinity, 5/05/81, A, C, g, 81000071

Harrington—Smith Block, 18–52 Hanover St., Manchester, 1/28/87, A, C, 86003367

Hill—Lassonde House, 269 Hanover St., Manchester, 12/02/85, C, 85003033

Hills House, 211 Derry Rd., Hudson, 4/08/83, C, 83001141

Hills Memorial Library, 16 Library St., Hudson, 6/07/84, C, 84002812

Hillsborough County Courthouse, 19 Temple St., Nashua, 6/06/85, A, C, 85001196

Hillsborough Railroad Bridge, Spans Contoocook River SW of NH 149, Hillsborough, 6/10/75, A, C, 75000126

Hoyt Shoe Factory, 477 Silver and 170 Lincoln Sts., Manchester, 11/07/85, A, C, 85002777

Hubbard, Thomas Russell, House, 220 Myrtle St., Manchester, 3/08/88, C, 88000177

Hunt Memorial Library, 6 Main St., Nashua, 6/28/71, C, 71000049

Kennedy Hill Farm, Kennedy Hill Rd., Goffstown, 6/07/84, C, 84002813

Killicut—Way House, 2 Old House Ln., Nashua, 12/01/89, C, 89002056

Kimball Brothers Shoe Factory, 335 Cypress St., Manchester, 11/07/85, A, C, 85002776

Lamson Farm, Lamson Rd., Mount Vernon vicinity, 2/24/81, A, C, D, g, 81000072

Lyndeborough Center Historic District, Center Rd., Lyndeborough Center, 6/07/84, A, C, a, 84002814

MacDowell Colony, W of US 202, Peterborough, 10/15/66, A, NHL, 66000026

Hillsborough County—Continued

Manchester City Hall, 908 Elm St., Manchester, 6/13/75, A, C, 75000233

McClure—Hilton House, 16 Tinker Rd., Merrimack, 12/01/89, C, 89002058

Meetinghouse, The, Monument Sq., Hollis, 3/11/82, C, 82001683

Milford Cotton and Woolen Manufacturing Company, 2 Bridge St., Milford, 8/18/82, A, 82001684

Milford Town House and Library Annex, Nashua St., Milford, 12/01/88, C, 88001436

Nashua Manufacturing Company Historic District, Factory and Pine Sts., Nashua, 9/11/87, A, B, C, g, 87001460

Nashville Historic District, Roughly bounded by Nashua River, Merrimack River, and Rt. 3, Nashua, 12/13/84, A, C, a, 84000574

New England Glassworks Site, Address Restricted, Temple vicinity, 6/10/75, A, D, 75000127

New Hampshire State Union Armory, 60 Pleasant St., Manchester, 8/10/82, A, C, 82004993

New Ipswich Center Village Historic District, Roughly bounded by Turnpike Rd., Porter Hill Rd., Main St., NH 123A, Preston Hill, Manley and King Rds., New Ipswich, 9/03/91, C, 91001173

New Ipswich Town Hall, Main St., New Ipswich, 12/13/84, C, 84000555

Old County Road South Historic District, S of Francestown off NH 186, Francestown vicinity, 5/15/80, A, C, D, 80000413

Old Post Office Block, 54–72 Hanover St., Manchester, 12/01/86, A, B, C, 86003364

Parker's Store, W of Goffstown on NH 114, Goffstown vicinity, 5/14/80, A, C, 80000414

Peabody, William, House, N. River Rd., Milford, 11/30/79, A, C, e, 79000200

Peterborough Unitarian Church, Main and Summer Sts., Peterborough, 4/23/73, A, C, a, 73000165

Pierce, Franklin, Homestead, 3 mi. W of Hillsborough on NH 31, Hillsborough vicinity, 10/15/66, B, NHL, 66000027

Sanders, G. O., House, 10 Derry St., Hudson, 2/27/86, C, 86000277

Signer's House and Matthew Thornton Cemetery, S of Merrimack on US 3, Merrimack vicinity, 12/22/78, B, C, D, d, 78000214

Smyth Tower, 718 Smyth Rd., Manchester, 7/24/78, A, B, C, 78000215

St. George's School and Convent, 12 Orange St., Manchester, 9/12/85, A, C, a, 85002192

Stark, Gen. George, House, 22 Concord St., Nashua, 11/25/80, B, C, a, 80000291

Stark, Gen. John, House, 2000 Elm St., Manchester, 6/29/73, A, B, b, 73000166

Stonyfield Farm, NW of Wilton on Foster Rd., Wilton vicinity, 8/03/83, A, C, 83001142

Straw, William Parker, House, 282 N. River Rd., Manchester, 12/08/87, B, C, 87002068

US Post Office—Peterborough Main, 23 Grove St., Peterborough, 7/17/86, C, 86002253

Varney School, 84 Varney St., Manchester, 1/11/82, A, C, 82001685

Weare Town House, NH 114, Weare, 12/02/85, C, a, 85003034

Weston Observatory, Oak Hill, Derryfield Park, Manchester, 5/28/75, A, C, 75000128

Whiting, Oliver, Homestead, Old County Farm Rd., Wilton vicinity, 3/09/82, A, C, 82001686

Whittaker, Caleb, Place, Perkins Pond Rd., Weare vicinity, 8/03/83, C, 83001143

Wilton Public and Gregg Free Library, Forest St., Wilton, 1/11/82, A, C, 82001687

Zimmerman House, 223 Heather St., Manchester, 10/18/79, C, g, 79003790

Merrimack County

2 1/2 Beacon Street, 2 1/2 Beacon St., Concord, 12/17/84, A, 84000500

Bear Brook State Park Civilian Conservation Corps (CCC) Camp Historic District, 1/2 mi. from park entrance, 160 yds. S of Allenstown—Deerfield Rd., Bear Brook State Park, Allenstown, 6/11/92, A, 92000632

Beaver Meadow Brook Archeological Site (27MR3), Address Restricted, Concord vicinity, 6/02/89, D, 89000434

Bement Covered Bridge, Center Rd., Bradford, 11/21/76, A, C, 76000128

Boscawen Academy and Much-I-Do-Hose House, King St., Boscawen, 12/08/80, A, C, 80000292

Boscawen Public Library, King St., Boscawen, 5/28/81, C, 81000073

Bradford Town Hall, W. Main St., Bradford, 11/13/80, A, C, 80000293

Canterbury Shaker Village, 4 mi. E of Canterbury on Shaker Rd., Canterbury vicinity, 6/17/75, A, C, NHL, 75000129

Center Meetinghouse, NH 103, Newbury, 12/19/79, A, C, a, 79000201

Chamberlin House, 44 Pleasant St., Concord, 8/16/82, A, C, 82001688

Concord Civic District, 107 N. Main St., 25 Capitol St., 39–45 Green St., 20–30 Park St., and 33 N. State St., Concord, 12/22/83, A, C, g, 83004203

Concord Historic District, Roughly bounded by N. State St., Horse Shoe Pond, Boston and Maine RR. tracks, Sen. Styles Bridges Hwy. and Church St., Concord, 6/11/75, A, C, 75000234

Crippen, Henry J., House, 189–191 N. Main St., Concord, 12/22/83, B, C, 83004204

Dalton Covered Bridge, Joppa Rd., Warner, 11/21/76, C, 76000221

Downing, Lewis, Jr., House, 33 Pleasant St., Concord, 9/11/87, B, C, 87001425

Eagle Hotel, 110 N. Main St., Concord, 9/20/78, A, C, 78000216

Endicott Hotel, 1–3 S. Main St., Concord, 5/29/87, A, C, 87000818

Farrington House, 30 S. Main St., Concord, 3/09/82, C, 82001858

First Congregational Church of Boscawen, King St., Boscawen, 4/19/82, A, C, a, b, 82001689

Foster, Reuben, House and Cleaves, Perley, House, 64 and 62 N. State St., Concord, 3/15/82, C, 82001690

Franklin Falls Historic District, Roughly bounded by Bow, River, School, Aylers Sts. and Winnipesaukee River, Franklin, 8/19/82, A, C, 82001691

Hall Memorial Library, Park St., Northfield, 10/04/78, C, 78000217

Harvey, Matthew, House, W side of Harvey Rd., 0.25 mi. N of jct. with Keyser St., Sutton, 9/04/92, A, C, 92001082

Henniker Town Hall, Depot Hill Rd., Henniker, 2/24/81, A, C, 81000074

Hill Center Church, Hill Center Rd., Hill vicinity, 9/12/85, C, a, 85002186

Hopkinton Railroad Covered Bridge, Off NH 103 and NH 127, Hopkinton, 1/11/80, A, C, 80000294

Howe—Quimby House, NW of Hopkinton on Sugar Hill Rd., Hopkinton vicinity, 6/27/80, C, 80000295

Leavitt Farm, 103 Old Loudon Rd., Concord, 3/11/82, A, C, 82001692

Long, William H., Memorial, Main St., Hopkinton, 7/15/77, C, f, 77000092

Loudon Town Hall, Jct. of Clough Hill and Youngs Hill Rds., Loudon, 9/05/90, A, a, 90001351

Lower Warner Meetinghouse, NH 103, Lower Warner, 5/25/89, C, a, 89000450

Memorial Arch of Tilton, Elm St., Northfield, 5/19/80, A, C, f, 80000296

Merrimack County Bank, 214 N. Main St., Concord, 2/28/80, B, C, 80000415

Merrimack County Courthouse, 163 N. Main St., Concord, 11/27/79, C, 79000202

Millville School, 2 Fiske Rd., Concord, 11/07/85, A, C, 85002781

Morrill—Lassonde House, E of King St., Boscawen, 3/15/84, B, C, 84003216

Murray Hill Summer Home District, Murray Hill Rd. roughly between Cass Mill and Lynch Rds., Hill, 3/17/88, A, b, d, 88000179

New Hampshire Savings Bank Building, 97 N. Main St., Concord, 6/14/88, A, C, 88000658

Northfield Union Church, Sondogardy Pond Rd., Northfield, 3/15/84, C, a, 84003219

Noyes, Jacob, Block, 48 Glass St., Suncook, 2/27/86, A, C, 86000278

Old Post Office, N. State St., between Capitol and Park St., Concord, 8/13/73, C, 73000269

Old Webster Meeting House, Off NH 127 on Battle St., Webster, 3/07/85, C, a, b, 85000479

Pembroke Mill, 100 Main St., Pembroke, 9/12/85, A, C, 85002188

Pierce, Franklin, House, 52 S. Main St., Concord, 10/15/79, B, C, 79000318

Pillsbury Memorial Hall, 93 Main St., Sutton, 3/04/93, A, C, 93000147

Pittsfield Center Historic District, NH 28 and NH 107, Pittsfield, 12/12/80, A, C, 80000416

Pleasant View Home, 227 Pleasant St., Concord, 9/19/84, A, C, a, 84003222

Rollins, Gov. Frank West, House, 135 N. State St., Concord, 3/15/84, B, C, a, 84003225

Rowell's Covered Bridge, Clement Hill Rd., West Hopkinton, 11/21/76, A, C, 76000129

Merrimack County—Continued

Salisbury Academy Building, Jct. of NH 127 and US 4, Salisbury, 5/30/75, A, b, 75000235

South Danbury Christian Church, US 4, Danbury, 6/06/85, C, a, 85001191

South Sutton Meeting House, 17 Meeting House Hill Rd., South Sutton, 5/27/93, C, a, 93000462

Sulphite Railroad Bridge, Off US 3 over Winnipesaukee River, Franklin, 6/11/75, A, C, 75000130

Upham—Walker House, 18 Park St., Concord, 5/15/80, A, B, C, a, 80000418

Waterloo Covered Bridge, Newmarket Rd., Waterloo, 11/21/76, A, C, 76000130

Webster Congregational Church, Off NH 127 on Long St., Webster, 3/07/85, C, a, 85000480

Webster, Daniel, Family Home, S. Main St., West Franklin, 5/30/74, B, NHL, 74000196

Whipple, Dr. Solomon M., House, Main St., New London, 9/12/85, C, 85002187

White Farm, 144 Clinton St., Concord, 5/15/81, A, B, C, 81000075

White Park, Bounded by Washington, Centre, High, Beacon, and White Sts., Concord, 11/09/82, C, 82000623

Rockingham County

Adams Memorial Building, West Broadway, Derry, 1/11/82, C, 82001875

Atkinson Academy School, Academy Ave., Atkinson, 8/26/80, A, C, 80000297

Bartlett, Josiah, House, Main St., Kingston, 11/11/71, B, NHL, 71000050

Beck, Samuel, House, The Hill, Portsmouth, 4/03/73, C, b, 73000167

Benedict House, 30 Middle St., Portsmouth, 5/11/73, A, C, 73000168

Chester Congregational Church, 4 Chester St., Chester, 6/05/86, C, a, 86001231

Chester Village Cemetery, NH 102 and NH 121, Chester, 11/29/79, A, C, D, d, 79000203

Crockett, John, House, 245 Portsmouth Ave., Stratham, 3/24/83, C, 83001144

Currier, Capt. Jonathan, House [South Hampton MRA], Hilldale Ave., South Hampton, 4/11/83, A, C, 83001145

Dame School, NH 152, Nottingham, 10/30/80, A, C, a, b, 80000298

Danville Meetinghouse, N. Main St., Danville, 4/19/82, A, C, a, 82001876

Dudley House, 14 Front St., Exeter, 6/21/71, A, C, 71000051

East Derry Historic District, Roughly bounded by Hampstead, Lane, and Cemetery Rds., East Derry, 8/10/82, A, C, a, d, 82004991

Elm Farm, 599 Main St., Danville, 1/22/88, A, C, 88000191

Exeter Waterfront Commercial Historic District, Chestnut Hill Ave., Water, Franklin, Pleasant, High and Chestnut Sts., Exeter, 12/03/80, A, C, 80000299

Exeter Waterfront Commercial Historic District (Boundary Increase), Chestnut St., Exeter, 12/29/86, A, C, 86003516

First Church, 21 Front St., Exeter, 9/10/71, A, C, a, 71000052

First Universalist Church, Main St., Kingston, 12/26/79, C, a, 79000204

Fort Constitution, Walbach St., New Castle, 7/09/73, A, D, 73000169

Franklin Block, 75 Congress St., Portsmouth, 6/07/84, A, C, 84003228

Fremont Meeting House, 464 Main St., Fremont, 5/27/93, C, 93000461

Front Street Historic District, Front St. to the jct. of Spring and Water Sts., Exeter, 7/05/73, A, C, 73000270

Frost, Robert, Homestead, 2 mi. SE of Derry, Derry vicinity, 5/23/68, B, NHL, 68000008

Gilman Garrison House, 12 Water St., Exeter, 9/27/76, A, C, 76000131

Gilman, Maj. John, House, 25 Cass St., Exeter, 6/14/88, C, 88000659

Greeley House, E of East Kingston on NH 108, East Kingston vicinity, 6/16/80, C, D, 80000300

Hampstead Meetinghouse, Emerson Ave., Hampstead, 4/10/80, C, a, 80000301

Hart, Jeremiah, House, The Hill, Portsmouth, 11/14/72, C, b, 72000081

Hart, John, House, The Hill, Portsmouth, 11/14/72, C, b, 72000082

Hart, Phoebe, House, The Hill, Portsmouth, 4/02/73, C, b, 73000170

Hart-Rice House, The Hill, Portsmouth, 8/07/72, B, C, b, 72000083

Haven—White House, 229 Pleasant St., Portsmouth, 6/06/85, C, 85001195

Highland Road Historic District [South Hampton MRA], Highland and Woodman Rds., South Hampton, 4/11/83, A, C, 83001146

Isles of Shoals, Address Restricted, Rye vicinity, 12/10/80, A, B, C, D, d, 80000419

Jackson, Richard, House, Northwest St., Portsmouth, 11/24/68, C, NHL, 68000009

Jewell Town District [South Hampton MRA], W. Whitehall Rd. and Jewell St., South Hampton, 4/11/83, A, C, 83001147

Jones, John Paul, House, Middle and State Sts., Portsmouth, 11/28/72, B, NHL, 72000084

Ladd—Gilman House, Governors Lane and Water St., Exeter, 12/02/74, B, NHL, 74002055

Lamprey, Reuben, Homestead, 416 Winnacunnet Rd., Hampton, 11/09/82, C, 82000624

Lane, Deacon Samuel and Jabez, Homestead, Portsmouth Ave., Stratham, 4/08/83, A, C, 83001148

Langdon, Gov. John, Mansion, 143 Pleasant St., Portsmouth, 12/02/74, B, NHL, 74000197

Larkin—Rice House, 180 Middle St., Portsmouth, 11/29/79, C, 79000205

Locke, Elijah, House, 5 Grove Rd., Rye, 12/19/79, A, C, 79000206

MacPheadris—Warner House, Chapel and Daniel Sts., Portsmouth, 10/15/66, C, NHL, 66000028

Margeson, Richman, Estate, Long Point Rd. near Great Bay shore, Newington, 6/21/90, A, C, 90000873

Moffatt—Ladd House, 154 Market St., Portsmouth, 11/24/68, B, C, NHL, 68000010

Moses—Kent House, 1 Pine St., Exeter, 9/12/85, C, 85002184

Neal, James, House, 74 Deer St., Portsmouth, 8/07/72, A, C, 72000112

New Hampshire Bank Building, 22–26 Market Sq., Portsmouth, 9/10/79, A, C, 79000207

Newington Center Historic District, 272–336, 305–353 Nimble Hill Rd., Newington, 11/30/87, A, C, 87002106

Newmarket Industrial and Commercial Historic District, NH 108, Newmarket, 12/01/80, A, C, 80000302

Nichols Memorial Library, Main St., Kingston, 1/28/81, C, 81000076

Northwood Congregational Church, US 4, Northwood, 11/30/79, C, 79000208

Nutter—Rymes House, 48 School St., Portsmouth, 11/03/72, A, C, 72000085

Old North Cemetery, Maplewood Ave., Portsmouth, 3/08/78, A, B, d, 78000218

Parsons Homestead, 520 Washington Rd., Rye, 12/05/80, C, 80000420

Pinkham, Daniel, House, The Hill, Portsmouth, 11/03/72, C, b, 72000086

Plaistow Carhouse, 27 Elm St., Plaistow, 12/10/80, A, C, 80000303

Porter, General, House, 32–34 Livermore St., Portsmouth, 10/11/85, A, B, C, b, 85003359

Portsmouth Athenaeum, 9 Market Sq., Portsmouth, 5/24/73, A, C, 73000171

Portsmouth Public Library, 8 Islington St., Portsmouth, 3/20/73, A, B, C, 73000172

Prescott, Benjamin Franklin, House, Prescott Rd., Epping, 12/03/87, B, C, 87002069

Raymond Boston and Maine Railroad Depot, Main St., Raymond, 5/16/79, A, C, 79000209

Rockingham Hotel, 401 State St., Portsmouth, 3/11/82, C, 82001693

Rogers, George, House, 76 Northwest St., Portsmouth, 6/07/76, A, 76000132

Rundlet—May House, 364 Middle St., Portsmouth, 6/07/76, B, C, 76000133

Sanborn Seminary, 178 Main St., Kingston, 3/15/84, C, 84003233

Sandown Depot, Boston and Maine Railroad, Depot Rd., Sandown, 9/04/86, A, C, 86002167

Sandown Old Meetinghouse, Fremont Rd., Sandown, 8/09/78, C, a, 78000219

Searles School and Chapel, Range and Searles Rds., Windham, 1/11/82, C, a, 82001694

Sewall, Edward, Garrison, 16 Epping Rd., Exeter, 1/11/80, C, 80000304

Shapley Town House, 454–456 Court St., Portsmouth, 2/28/73, A, C, 73000173

Sherburne, Henry, House, The Hill, Portsmouth, 8/07/72, C, b, 72000087

Smith's Corner Historic District [South Hampton MRA], Main Ave., South, Stagecoach, and Chase Rds., South Hampton, 4/11/83, A, C, 83001149

Smith, Simeon P., House, The Hill, Portsmouth, 11/14/72, C, b, 72000088

Rockingham County—Continued

South Meetinghouse, Marcy St. and Meeting House Hill, Portsmouth, 4/19/82, A, C, 82001695

South Parish, 292 State St., Portsmouth, 8/21/79, C, a, 79000210

Square Schoolhouse, SR 156 and Ledge Farm Rd., Nottingham, 4/17/80, A, C, 80000305

St. John's Church, 105 Chapel St., Portsmouth, 1/31/78, C, a, 78000417

Stone School, Granite St., Newmarket, 7/12/78, A, C, 78000418

Strawberry Banke Historic District, Bounded by Court and Marcy Sts. and both sides of Hancock and Washington Sts., Portsmouth, 6/20/75, A, C, 75000236

Tenney, Samuel, House, 65 High St., Exeter, 11/25/80, A, C, b, 80000306

Thornton, Matthew, House, 2 Thornton St., Derry Village, 11/11/71, B, NHL, 71000053

Town Center Historic District [South Hampton MRA], Main and Hilldale Aves. and Jewell St., South Hampton, 4/11/83, A, C, 83001150

Town House, Old Centre Rd., Deerfield, 4/17/80, C, 80000307

USS ALBACORE, Portsmouth Maritime Museum, Portsmouth, 4/11/89, A, B, C, g, NHL, 89001077

Unitarian Church, Exeter Rd., Hampton Falls vicinity, 12/13/84, C, a, 84000558

Watson Academy, Academy St., Epping, 11/09/82, A, C, 82000625

Weare, Gov. Meshech, House, Exeter Rd. (NH 88), Hampton Falls, 6/29/73, B, 73000174

Weeks House, Weeks Ave. off NH 101, Greenland, 6/20/75, C, 75000131

Wentworth, Gov. John, House, 346 Pleasant St., Portsmouth, 6/29/73, A, B, C, 73000175

Wentworth—Coolidge Mansion, 2 mi. S of Portsmouth, off US 1A, Portsmouth vicinity, 11/24/68, C, NHL, 68000011

Wentworth—Gardner House, 140 Mechanic St., Portsmouth, 11/24/68, C, NHL, 68000012

Wentworth—Gardner and Tobias Lear Houses, Mechanic and Gardner Sts., Portsmouth, 10/30/79, C, 79000319

Whidden-Ward House, The Hill, Portsmouth, 11/05/71, C, b, 71000077

Wiggin Memorial Library, Jct. of Portsmouth Ave. (NH 101) and Stratham Rd., SE corner, Stratham, 12/10/93, A, C, 93001381

Wiggin, Cornet Thomas, House, 249 Portsmouth Ave., Stratham, 3/24/83, C, 83001151

Woodman Road Historic District [South Hampton MRA], Woodman Rd., South Hampton, 4/11/83, A, C, 83001152

Young, Gen. Mason J., House, 4 Young Rd., Londonderry, 2/27/86, C, 86000281

Strafford County

Back River Farm, Bay View Rd., Dover, 6/22/84, C, 84003236

Canaan Chapel, Canaan Rd., Barrington, 3/11/82, A, C, a, 82001877

County Farm Bridge, NW of Dover on County Farm Rd., Dover vicinity, 5/21/75, A, C, 75000237

Durham Historic District, Main St. and Newmarket Rd., Durham, 5/31/80, C, 80000308

Farmington Town Pound, NW side of Pound Rd. 300 ft. north of the jct. of Ten Rod Rd., Farmington, 9/02/93, A, 93000884

First Parish Church, 218 Central Ave., Dover, 3/11/82, C, a, 82001696

First Parish Church Site-Dover Point, Dover Point Rd., Dover, 5/27/83, A, D, a, 83001153

Free Will Baptist Church, Ridge Top Road, New Durham vicinity, 11/13/80, A, C, a, 80000310

Garrison Hill Park and Tower, Abbie Sawyer Memorial Dr., Dover, 9/11/87, C, 87001413

Green Street School, 104 Green St., Somersworth, 3/07/85, A, C, 85000481

Hale, William, House, 5 Hale St., Dover, 11/18/80, C, a, 80000309

Hayes, Richard, House, 184 Gonic Rd., Rochester, 2/27/86, C, 86000283

Lehoullier Building, 161–169 Main St., Somersworth, 12/26/79, A, C, 79000211

Milton Town House, NH 16 and Town House Rd., Milton, 11/26/80, A, C, 80000311

New Durham Meetinghouse and Pound, Old Bay Rd., New Durham, 12/08/80, A, C, a, 80000312

New Durham Town Hall, Main St. and Ridge Rd., New Durham, 11/13/80, C, 80000313

Plumer—Jones Farm, N of Milton on NH 16, Milton vicinity, 3/23/79, C, 79000212

Public Market, 93 Washington St., Dover, 3/07/85, B, C, 85000541

Queensbury Mill, 1 Market St., Somersworth, 4/10/87, A, 86003362

Reade, Michael, House, 43 Main St., Dover, 2/12/80, B, C, 80000314

Religious Society of Friends Meetinghouse, 141 Central Ave., Dover, 2/29/80, A, C, a, 80000421

Rochester Commercial and Industrial District, N. Main, Wakefield, Hanson, S. Main Sts. and Central Square, Rochester, 4/08/83, A, C, 83001154

Salmon Falls Mill Historic District, Front St., Rollinsford, 2/29/80, A, C, 80000315

Sawyer Building, 4–6 Portland St., Dover, 5/23/80, A, C, 80000316

Sawyer Woolen Mills, 1 Mill St., Dover, 9/13/89, A, C, 89001208

St. Thomas Episcopal Church, 5 Hale St., Dover, 6/07/84, C, a, 84003241

Strafford County Farm, County Farm Rd., Dover, 2/25/81, A, C, 81000100

Strafford Union Academy, NH 202A and 126, Strafford, 9/22/83, A, C, a, 83001155

Sullivan, Gen. John, House, 23 New Market Rd., Durham, 11/28/72, B, NHL, 72000089

US Post Office—Dover Main, 133–137 Washington St., Dover, 7/17/86, C, 86002273

US Post Office—Somersworth Main, 2 Elm St., Somersworth, 7/17/86, C, 86002246

Wiswall Falls Mills Site, Address Restricted, Durham vicinity, 3/18/88, A, D, 88000184

Woodman Institute, 182 Central Ave., Dover, 7/24/80, A, B, C, b, 80000317

Wyatt, Samuel, House, 7 Church St., Dover, 12/02/82, A, C, 82000626

Sullivan County

Acworth Congregational Church, N end of town common, Acworth, 6/13/75, A, C, a, 75000132

Acworth Silsby Library, Intersection of Cold Pond and Lynn Hill Rds., Acworth, 12/08/83, A, C, 83004206

Backside Inn [Plank Houses of Goshen New Hampshire TR], Brook Rd., Goshen, 6/21/85, C, 85001308

Blow-Me-Down Covered Bridge, S of Plainfield off NH 12A, Plainfield vicinity, 5/19/78, A, C, 78000220

Burford House [Plank Houses of Goshen New Hampshire TR], NH 10, Goshen, 6/21/85, C, 85001309

Central Business District [Downtown Claremont and Lower Village MRA], Roughly bounded by Crescent, Broad, Pine and Franklin Sts., Claremont, 2/21/78, A, C, a, 78003454

Charlestown Main Street Historic District, Main St., Charlestown, 6/10/87, C, 87000835

Charlestown Town Hall, N of Summer St., off Main St., Charlestown, 3/15/84, C, 84003252

Chase, Salmon P., Birthplace, 8 mi. N of Claremont, Cornish Flat, 5/15/75, B, b, c, NHL, 75000133

Claremont City Hall, Tremont Sq., Claremont, 4/26/73, A, C, 73000176

Claremont Warehouse No. 34 [Downtown Claremont and Lower Village MRA], 43 River St., Claremont, 2/28/79, C, 79000320

Cold River Bridge, E of Langdon on McDermott Rd, Langdon vicinity, 5/17/73, C, 73000177

Cornish—Windsor Covered Bridge, W of Cornish City, Cornish City vicinity, 11/21/76, A, C, 76000135

Cote House [Plank Houses of Goshen New Hampshire TR], Goshen Center Rd., Goshen, 6/21/85, C, 85001310

Covit House [Plank Houses of Goshen New Hampshire TR], Goshen Center Rd., Goshen, 6/21/85, C, 85001311

Dexter, David, House, Dexter Heights, Claremont, 11/29/79, A, B, C, b, 79000213

Dingleton Hill Covered Bridge, Off NH 12A, Cornish Mills, 11/08/78, A, 78000221

Durham House [Plank Houses of Goshen New Hampshire TR], Ball Park Rd., Goshen, 6/21/85, C, 85001312

English Church, Old Church Rd., Claremont, 2/01/80, A, C, a, 80000318

Farwell School, NH 12A S of Hope Hill Cemetery, Charlestown, 12/06/90, C, 90001847

First Baptist Church of Cornish, Meriden Stage Rd. and NH 120, Cornish Flat, 2/14/78, A, C, a, b, 78000222

Garber House [Plank Houses of Goshen New Hampshire TR], Willey Hill Rd., Goshen, 6/21/85, C, 85001313

Sullivan County—Continued

Giffin House [Plank Houses of Goshen New Hampshire TR], NH 10, Goshen, 6/21/85, C, 85001314

Gunnison, Capt. John, House, E of Goshen on Goshen Center Rd., Goshen vicinity, 12/19/79, B, 79000214

Hunter Archeological Site, Address Restricted, Claremont vicinity, 6/07/76, D, 76000222

Janicke House [Plank Houses of Goshen New Hampshire TR], Goshen Center Rd., Goshen, 6/21/85, C, 85001315

Kenyon Bridge, Off NH 12A at Mill Brook and Town House Rd., Cornish City, 5/22/78, A, 78000223

Knights-Morey House [Plank Houses of Goshen New Hampshire TR], Province Rd., Goshen, 6/21/85, C, 85001316

Lear House [Plank Houses of Goshen New Hampshire TR], Province Rd., Goshen, 6/21/85, C, 85001317

Lempster Meetinghouse, Lempster St., Lempster, 9/08/80, A, C, a, b, 80000319

Little Red School House 1835 District No. 7, S of Newport on NH 10, Newport vicinity, 12/01/80, A, C, 80000320

Lower Village District [Downtown Claremont and Lower Village MRA], Along Central St. and Main St. on both sides of Sugar River, Claremont, 2/21/78, A, C, a, 78003455

Meriden Bridge, NW of Meriden, Meriden vicinity, 8/27/80, C, 80000321

Monadnock Mills, Broad, Water, Crescent Sts., and Mill Rd., Claremont, 2/15/79, A, C, 79000272

Mothers' and Daughters' Club House, Main St., Plainfield, 3/11/82, A, C, 82001697

Nettleton House, 26–30 Central St., Newport, 11/16/77, A, C, 77000164

Newport Downtown Historic District, Main St. roughly bounded by Depot, Sunapee, Central and West Sts., Newport, 6/06/85, C, 85001201

Pier Bridge, 3 mi. W of Newport on Chandler Rd. over Sugar River, Newport vicinity, 6/10/75, A, C, 75000134

Pike House [Plank Houses of Goshen New Hampshire TR], NH 10, Goshen, 6/21/85, C, 85001318

Plainfield Town Hall, NH 12A, Plainfield, 6/06/85, A, C, 85001200

Prentiss Bridge, S of Langdon off Old Cheshire Tpke., Langdon vicinity, 5/24/73, C, 73000179

Protectworth Tavern, NH 4A, Grantham vicinity, 11/25/80, A, C, 80000322

Purnell House [Plank Houses of Goshen New Hampshire TR], NH 10, Goshen, 6/21/85, C, 85001319

Reed, Isaac, House, 30–34 Main St., Newport, 7/19/78, C, 78000337

Richards Free Library, 58 N. Main St., Newport, 9/07/84, C, 84003257

Rossiter, William, House, 11 Mulberry St., Claremont, 5/25/79, B, C, 79000215

Saint-Gaudens National Historic Site, S of Plainfield off NH 12-a, Cornish vicinity, 10/15/66, B, C, NHL, NPS, 66000120

Scranton House [Plank Houses of Goshen New Hampshire TR], Brook Rd., Goshen, 6/21/85, C, 85001320

Seavey House [Plank Houses of Goshen New Hampshire TR], NH 10, Goshen, 6/21/85, C, 85001321

South Congregational Church, 58 S. Main St., Newport, 3/30/89, C, a, 89000187

Springfield Town Hall and Howard Memorial Methodist Church, Four Corners Rd. SE of New London Rd., Springfield, 6/05/86, C, a, b, 86001235

St. Gaudens, Louis, House and Studio, Dingleton Hill and Whitten Rds., Cornish, 11/15/72, A, 72000111

Stelljes House [Plank Houses of Goshen New Hampshire TR], NH 31, Goshen, 6/21/85, C, 85001322

Sullivan County Courthouse, Court Sq., Newport, 6/25/73, A, C, 73000178

Town Hall and Courthouse, 20 Main St., Newport, 2/29/80, C, 80000383

Trinity Church, W of Cornish Mills on NH 12-A, Cornish Mills vicinity, 7/31/78, A, C, a, 78000419

Unity Town Hall, Off Unity Rd. & Old NH Tnpk., Unity, 6/06/85, C, a, 85001199

Washington Common Historic District, Jct. of Half Moon Pond and Millen Pond Rds., Washington, 3/14/86, C, a, g, 86000345

Welcome Acres [Plank Houses of Goshen New Hampshire TR], NH 10, Goshen, 6/21/85, C, 85001323

Williamson House [Plank Houses of Goshen New Hampshire TR], Messer Rd., Goshen, 6/21/85, C, 85001324

Windswept Acres-Powers House [Plank Houses of Goshen New Hampshire TR], NH 31, Goshen, 6/21/85, C, 85001325

Wright's Bridge, E of Claremont on Chandler Rd. over Sugar River, Claremont vicinity, 6/10/75, A, C, 75000135

Once the largest woolen mill in New Hampshire, the Sawyer Woolen Mill in Dover grew between 1873 and 1899, leaving Greek Revival, Second Empire, and Lombard Romanesque brick buildings to testify to the prosperity of New England's textile industry at the close of the 19th century. (Christopher W. Closs, 1986)

NEW JERSEY

Atlantic County

Absecon Lighthouse, Vermont and Pacific Aves., Atlantic City, 1/25/71, A, C, 71000492

Atlantic City Convention Hall, Georgia and Mississippi Aves. and the Boardwalk, Atlantic City, 2/27/87, A, C, NHL, 87000814

Barclay Court, 9–11 S. Pennsylvania Ave., Atlantic City, 6/22/88, C, 88000725

Bay Front Historic District, Roughly bounded by Decatur Ave., Egg Harbor Bay, George Ave., and Shore Rd., Somers Point, 3/22/89, A, C, 89000227

Black, William L., House, 458 Bellevue Ave., Hammonton, 8/26/93, B, C, 93000828

Blake, Amanda, Store, 104 Main St., Port Republic, 1/15/79, A, 79001469

Church of the Ascension, 1601 Pacific Ave., Atlantic City, 7/24/86, A, C, a, 86001941

Church of the Redeemer, Jct. of 20th and Atlantic Aves., Longport, 9/10/92, A, B, C, a, 92001179

Estellville Glassworks Historic District, Roughly bounded by Estell Manor Park, Stevens Cr. and NJ 50, Estell Manor City, 11/21/91, A, D, 91001678

Head of the River Church, NJ 49, Estell Manor, 3/07/79, A, C, a, 79001467

Holmhurst Hotel, 121 S. Pennsylvania Ave., Atlantic City, 1/18/78, A, 78001732

Jacobus Evangelical Lutheran Church, Mays Landing Rd. and NJ 54, Folsom Borough, 6/09/88, A, a, 88000635

Jeffries, Capt. John, Burial Marker, Palestine Bible Church Cemetery, NJ 559, Somers Point vicinity, 6/14/84, A, 84002511

Linwood Borough School No. 1, 16 W. Poplar Ave., Linwood, 12/20/84, A, C, 84000510

Linwood Historic District, Roughly Shore Rd. from Royal Ave. to Sterling Ave., Linwood, 7/13/89, A, C, 89000800

Lucy, the Margate Elephant, Decatur and Atlantic Aves., Margate City, 8/12/71, A, C, NHL, 71000493

Madison Hotel, 123 S. Illinois Ave., Atlantic City, 12/20/84, A, C, 84000506

Marven Gardens Historic District, Bounded by Ventnor, Fredericksburg, Winchester and Brunswick Aves., Margate, 9/13/90, A, C, 90001440

Mays Landing Historic District, Jct. US 40, NJ 50; roughly bounded by Lake Lenape and Great Egg Harbor, Mays Landing, 8/23/90, A, C, 90001245

Mays Landing Presbyterian Church, Main St. and Cape May Ave., Mays Landing, 4/20/82, B, C, a, 82003261

Morton Hotel, 150 S. Virginia Ave., Atlantic City, 7/15/77, A, C, 77000843

Neutral Water Health Resort Sanitarium, Jct. of Claudius St. and London Ave., Egg Harbor City, 3/20/91, A, D, 91000267

Port Republic Historic District, Roughly bounded by Mill St., Clark's Landing Rd., Adams Ave., Port Republic—Smithville Rd. and Riverside Dr., Port Republic City, 5/16/91, A, C, 91000596

Richards, Samuel, Hotel, 106 E. Main St, Mays Landing, 8/31/79, A, C, 79001468

Risley, Jeremiah II or Edward, House, 8 Virginia Ave., Northfield, 5/31/91, A, C, 91000609

Santa Rita Apartments, 66 South Carolina Ave., Atlantic City, 6/14/91, C, 91000675

Segal Building, 1200 Atlantic Ave., Atlantic City, 2/09/84, A, C, 84002517

Shelburne Hotel, Michigan Ave. and the Boardwalk, Atlantic City, 5/19/78, A, C, 78001733

Smithville Apothecary, Off Moss Mill Rd., Smithville, 6/09/78, A, C, b, 78001734

Somers Mansion, Shore Rd. and Somers Point Circle, Somers Point, 12/18/70, C, 70000378

Stafford, John, Historic District, Roughly bounded by Atlantic Ave., Vassar Ave., Boardwalk, and Austin Ave., Ventnor, 6/09/88, A, C, g, 88000723

WEYMOUTH (schooner), Address Restricted, Hamilton Township vicinity, 4/25/85, A, C, D, 85000874

World War I Memorial, O'Donnell Pkwy., S. Albany and Ventnor Aves., Atlantic City, 8/28/81, A, C, f, 81000388

Bergen County

Achenbach House [Saddle River MRA (AD)], 184 Chestnut Ridge Rd., Saddle River, 4/18/79, C, 79001475

Ackerman House [Stone Houses of Bergen County TR; Saddle River MRA (AD)], 136 Chestnut Ridge Rd., Saddle River, 1/10/83, C, 83001449

Ackerman House [Stone Houses of Bergen County TR], 222 Doremus Ave., Ridgewood, 1/10/83, C, 83001450

Ackerman House [Stone Houses of Bergen County TR], 252 Lincoln Ave., Ridgewood, 1/10/83, C, 83001451

Ackerman, Abram, House [Stone Houses of Bergen County TR; Saddle River MRA (AD)], 199 E. Saddle River Rd., Saddle River, 1/10/83, A, C, 83001447

Ackerman, David, House [Stone Houses of Bergen County TR], 415 E. Saddle River, Ridgewood, 1/10/83, A, C, 83001448

Ackerman, Garret Augustus, House [Saddle River MRA], 212 E. Saddle River Rd., Saddle River, 8/29/86, C, 86001597

Ackerman, Garret and Maria, House [Saddle River MRA], 150 E. Saddle River Rd., Saddle River, 8/29/86, C, 86001598

Ackerman—Dewsnap House [Saddle River MRA], 176 E. Saddle River Rd., Saddle River, 8/29/86, C, 86001599

Ackerman—Smith House [Saddle River MRA], 171 E. Allendale Rd., Saddle River, 8/29/86, B, C, 86001600

Ackerman-Boyd House [Stone Houses of Bergen County TR], 1095 Franklin Lake Rd., Franklin Lakes, 1/09/83, C, 83001452

Ackerman-Dater House [Stone Houses of Bergen County TR; Saddle River MRA (AD)], 109 W. Saddle River Rd., Saddle River, 1/10/83, A, C, 83001453

Ackerman-Demarest House [Stone Houses of Bergen County TR], 745 E. Saddle River Rd., Ho-Ho-Kus, 1/10/83, C, 83001454

Ackerman-Hopper House [Stone Houses of Bergen County TR], 652 Ackerman Ave., Glen Rock, 1/09/83, A, C, 83001455

Ackerman-Van Emburgh, House [Stone Houses of Bergen County TR], 789 E. Glen Ave., Ridgewood, 1/10/83, A, C, 83001456

Ackerman-Zabriskie-Steuben House [Stone Houses of Bergen County TR], 1209 Main St., River Edge, 1/10/83, A, C, 83001457

Ackerson, John G., House [Stone Houses of Bergen County TR], 142 Pascack Rd., Park Ridge, 1/10/83, C, 83001458

Alcoa Edgewater Works, 700 River Rd., Edgewater, 8/10/78, A, C, 78001735

Anderson Outkitchen [Stone Houses of Bergen County TR], 18 E. Camden St., Hackensack, 8/08/85, A, C, 85002591

Anderson Street Station [Operating Passenger Railroad Stations TR], Anderson St., Hackensack, 6/22/84, A, C, a, 84002520

Archibald-Vroom House [Stone Houses of Bergen County TR], 160 E. Ridgewood Ave., Ridgewood, 7/24/84, A, C, 84002596

BINGHAMTON (ferryboat), 725 River Rd., Edgewater, 7/09/82, A, C, 82003262

Baldwin, David, House [Stone Houses of Bergen County TR], 60 Lake Ave., Midland Park, 1/10/83, C, 83001459

Banta, Derick, House [Stone Houses of Bergen County TR], 180 Washington Ave., Dumont, 1/09/83, C, 83001461

Banta, John, House [Stone Houses of Bergen County TR], 211 Pascack Rd., Hillsdale, 1/09/83, C, 83001462

Banta-Coe House [Stone Houses of Bergen County TR], 884 Lone Pine Lane, Teaneck, 1/10/83, A, C, 83001460

Bartholf, John, House [Stone Houses of Bergen County TR], 1122 Ramapo Valley Rd., Mahwah, 1/09/83, C, 83001463

Beauclaire-Vreeland House [Stone Houses of Bergen County TR], 88 E. Clinton Ave., Bergenfield, 1/09/83, C, 83001464

Benson, John G., House [Stone Houses of Bergen County TR], 60 Grand Ave., Englewood, 1/09/83, C, 83001465

Bergen County—Continued

Berdan, G. V. H., House [Stone Houses of Bergen County TR], 1219 River Rd., Fair Lawn, 1/09/83, C, 83001466

Berdan, Richard J., House [Stone Houses of Bergen County TR], 24-07 Fair Lawn Ave., Fair Lawn, 1/09/83, C, 83001467

Bergen County Court House Complex, Court, Main and Essex Sts., Hackensack, 1/11/83, A, C, 83001468

Blackledge-Gair House [Stone Houses of Bergen County TR], 111 Madison Ave., Cresskill, 1/09/83, C, 83001469

Blackledge-Kearney [Stone Houses of Bergen County TR], Alpine Landing, Alpine, 7/24/84, A, C, 84002537

Blanch, Capt. Thomas, House [Stone Houses of Bergen County TR], 130 Tappan Rd., Norwood, 1/10/83, C, 83001470

Blanch-Haring House [Stone Houses of Bergen County TR], 341 Lafayette Rd., Harrington Park, 1/09/83, A, C, 83001471

Blauvelt House [Stone Houses of Bergen County TR], 622 Lafayette Rd., Harrington Park, 1/09/83, A, C, 83001473

Blauvelt House [Stone Houses of Bergen County TR], 54 Tappan Rd., Norwood, 1/10/83, C, 83001474

Blauvelt House [Stone Houses of Bergen County TR], 205 Woodside Ave., Franklin Lakes, 8/08/85, A, C, 85002590

Blauvelt-Demarest House [Stone Houses of Bergen County TR], 230 Broadway, Hillsdale, 1/09/83, C, 83001472

Bogert House [Stone Houses of Bergen County TR], 4 Lynn Court, Bogota, 1/09/83, C, 83001475

Bogert House [Stone Houses of Bergen County TR], 324 County Rd., Demarest, 1/09/83, C, 83001476

Bogert, Isaac, House [Stone Houses of Bergen County TR], 640 Campgaw Rd., Mahwah, 1/10/83, C, 83001477

Brinkerhoff House [Stone Houses of Bergen County TR], 231 Hackensack Ave., Wood-Ridge, 7/24/84, A, C, 84002541

Brinkerhoff-Demarest House [Stone Houses of Bergen County TR], 493 Teaneck Rd., Teaneck, 1/10/83, C, 83001478

Cadmus House [Stone Houses of Bergen County TR], 264 Glen Rd., Woodcliff Lake, 7/24/84, A, C, 84002544

Cadmus-Folly House [Stone Houses of Bergen County TR], 19-21 Fair Lawn Ave., Fair Lawn, 1/10/83, C, 83001479

Cairns-Whitten-Blauvelt House [Stone Houses of Bergen County TR], 160 Ravine Ave., Wyckoff, 1/10/83, C, 83001480

Campbell-Christie House [Stone Houses of Bergen County TR], 1201 Main St., River Edge, 1/10/83, C, b, 83001481

Carlock, J. J., House [Saddle River MRA], 2 Chestnut Ridge Rd., Saddle River, 8/29/86, C, 86001602

Christie-Parsels House [Stone Houses of Bergen County TR], 195 Jefferson Ave., Tenafly, 1/10/83, C, 83001482

Church of the Holy Communion, Summit Ave., Norwood, 6/23/88, C, a, 88000928

Church of the Madonna, Hoefley's Lane, Fort Lee, 4/08/76, C, a, 76001145

Civil War Drill Hall and Armory, 130 Grand Ave., Leonia, 10/19/78, A, 78001737

Cole-Allaire House [Stone Houses of Bergen County TR], 112 Prospect St., Leonia, 1/10/83, C, 83001483

Concklin-Sneden House [Stone Houses of Bergen County TR], 37 Rockleigh Rd., Rockleigh, 1/10/83, A, C, 83001484

Cooper, Thunise & Richard, House, 608–610 Brookside Ave., Oradell, 9/12/85, A, C, 85002182

Crim-Tice House [Stone Houses of Bergen County TR], 16 County Rd., Woodcliff Lake, 1/10/83, C, 83001485

Cruse-Hossington House [Stone Houses of Bergen County TR], 301 Newtown Rd., Wyckoff, 1/10/83, C, 83004100

De Clark, William, House [Stone Houses of Bergen County TR], 145 Piermont Rd., Closter, 1/10/83, C, 83001488

De Gray House [Stone Houses of Bergen County TR], 650 Ewing Ave., Franklin Lakes, 1/09/83, C, 83001489

Debaun, Isaac, House [Stone Houses of Bergen County TR], 124 Rivervale Rd., Park Ridge, 1/10/83, C, 83001487

Debaun-Demarest House [Stone Houses of Bergen County TR], 56 Spring Valley Rd., River Edge, 1/10/83, A, C, 83001486

Demaree, Abram, House, Schraalenburgh and Old Hooks Rds., Closter, 11/01/79, A, C, 79001471

Demarest House [Stone Houses of Bergen County TR], 213 Ramapo Valley Rd., Oakland, 1/10/83, C, 83001491

Demarest House [Stone Houses of Bergen County TR], Main St., River Edge, 1/10/83, C, b, 83001492

Demarest House [Stone Houses of Bergen County TR], 268 Grove St., Oradell, 1/10/83, C, 83001496

Demarest, Cornelius, House [Stone Houses of Bergen County TR], 12 Rochelle Ave., Rochelle Park, 1/10/83, C, 83001495

Demarest, Daniel, House [Stone Houses of Bergen County TR], 404 Washington Ave., Dumont, 1/09/83, C, 83001499

Demarest, Jacobus, House [Stone Houses of Bergen County TR], 252 Ramapo Valley Rd., Oakland, 1/10/83, C, 83001493

Demarest, John R., House [Stone Houses of Bergen County TR], 35 County Rd., Demarest, 1/09/83, C, 83001497

Demarest, Samuel R., House [Stone Houses of Bergen County TR], 212 County Rd., Demarest, 7/24/84, A, C, 84002552

Demarest, Thomas, House [Stone Houses of Bergen County TR], 370 Grand Ave., Englewood, 1/09/83, C, 83001498

Demarest—Bloomer House, 147 River Edge Ave., New Milford, 11/07/85, C, 85002775

Demarest-Atwood House [Stone Houses of Bergen County TR], 84 Jefferson Ave., Cresskill, 7/24/84, A, C, 84002548

Demarest-Hopper House [Stone Houses of Bergen County TR], 21 Breakneck Rd., Oakland, 1/10/83, C, 83001490

Demarest-Lyle House [Stone Houses of Bergen County TR], 91 W. Clinton Ave., Tenafly, 1/10/83, C, 83001494

Demott-Westervelt House [Stone Houses of Bergen County TR], 285 Grand Ave., Englewood, 1/09/83, A, C, 83001500

DesMarest, Jacobus, House, 618 River Rd., New Milford, 2/17/78, C, 78001739

Doremus House [Stone Houses of Bergen County TR], 73 Main St., Hackensack, 7/24/84, A, C, 84002561

Draw Bridge at New Bridge, Main St. and Old New Bridge Rd. over Hackensack River, River Edge, 7/05/89, A, C, 89000775

Durie, Garret J., House [Stone Houses of Bergen County TR], 371 Schraalenburgh Rd., Haworth, 1/09/83, A, C, 83001502

Durie, Garret, House [Stone Houses of Bergen County TR], 156 Ell Rd., Hillsdale, 1/09/83, C, 83001501

Durie, John P., House [Stone Houses of Bergen County TR], 265 Schraalenburgh Rd., Haworth, 1/09/83, C, 83001503

Dutch Reformed Church at Romopock, Island Rd. at W. Ramapo Ave., Mahwah, 9/05/85, A, 85002000

Eckerson House [Stone Houses of Bergen County TR], 200 Chestnut Ridge Rd., Montvale, 1/10/83, C, 83001504

Erie Railroad Signal Tower, Waldwick Yard, NE end of Bohnert Pl., W side of RR Tracks, Waldwick, 12/23/87, A, C, 87000847

Evangelical Lutheran Church of Saddle River and Ramapough Building [Saddle River MRA], 96 E. Allendale Rd., Saddle River, 8/29/86, A, C, a, 86001603

Ferdon House [Stone Houses of Bergen County TR], 366 14th St., Norwood, 1/10/83, C, 83001505

Folly House [Stone Houses of Bergen County TR], 310 Crescent Ave., Wyckoff, 1/10/83, A, C, 83001506

Ford Motor Company Edgewater Assembly Plant, 309 River Rd., Edgewater, 9/15/83, A, C, 83001507

Foringer, Alonzo, House and Studio [Saddle River MRA], 107 and 107B E. Saddle River Rd., Saddle River, 8/29/86, B, C, 86001604

Forshee-Van Orden House [Stone Houses of Bergen County TR], 109 Summit Ave., Montvale, 7/24/84, C, 84002563

Garretson, Peter, House, 4-02 River Rd., Fair Lawn, 11/19/74, A, 74001153

Garrison, Garret, House [Stone Houses of Bergen County TR], 980 Ramapo Valley Rd., Mahwah, 1/10/83, C, 83001508

Bergen County—Continued

Haring, Abraham A., House [Stone Houses of Bergen County TR], Piermont Rd., Rockleigh, 1/10/83, A, C, 83001510

Haring, Frederick, House [Stone Houses of Bergen County TR], Old Tappan and De Wolf Rds., Old Tappan, 1/10/83, C, 83001513

Haring, Gerrit, House [Stone Houses of Bergen County TR], 224 Old Tappan Rd., Old Tappan, 1/10/83, C, 83001514

Haring, Nicholas, House [Stone Houses of Bergen County TR], Piermont Rd., Rockleigh, 1/10/83, A, C, 83001515

Haring, Teunis, House, 70 Old Tappan Rd., Old Tappan, 4/20/79, A, C, 79001473

Haring-Auryanson House [Stone Houses of Bergen County TR], 377 Piermont Rd., Closter, 8/15/83, A, C, 83001516

Haring-Blauvelt House [Stone Houses of Bergen County TR], 454 Tappan Rd., Northvale, 1/10/83, C, 83001511

Haring-Blauvelt-Demarest House [Stone Houses of Bergen County TR], 525 Rivervale Rd., River Vale, 1/10/83, C, 83001509

Haring-Corning House [Stone Houses of Bergen County TR], Rockleigh Rd., Rockleigh, 8/08/85, A, C, 85002589

Haring-DeWolf House [Stone Houses of Bergen County TR], 95 De Wolf Rd., Old Tappan, 1/10/83, C, 83001512

Haring-Vervalen House [Stone Houses of Bergen County TR], 200 Tappan Rd., Norwood, 1/10/83, C, 83001517

Hennion House [Stone Houses of Bergen County TR], 54 Pleasant Ave., Upper Saddle River, 1/10/83, C, 83001518

Hermitage, The, 335 N. Franklin Tpke., Ho-Ho-Kus, 8/29/70, C, NHL, 70000379

Hillsdale Station [Operating Passenger Railroad Stations TR], Broadway and Hillsdale Ave., Hillsdale, 6/22/84, A, C, 84002566

Holdrum, William, House [Stone Houses of Bergen County TR], 606 Prospect St., River Vale, 1/10/83, A, C, 83001519

Holdrum-Van Houten House [Stone Houses of Bergen County TR], 43 Spring Valley Rd., Montvale, 1/09/83, C, 83001520

Hopper Gristmill Site, Address Restricted, Mahwah, 3/03/83, D, 83001524

Hopper House [Stone Houses of Bergen County TR], 72 Hopper Farm Rd., Upper Saddle River, 1/10/83, A, C, 83001525

Hopper House [Stone Houses of Bergen County TR; Saddle River MRA (AD)], 45 W. Saddle River Rd., Saddle River, 7/24/84, A, C, 84002569

Hopper, Andrew H., House [Stone Houses of Bergen County TR], 762 Prospect St., Glen Rock, 1/09/83, C, 83001521

Hopper, Garret, House [Stone Houses of Bergen County TR], 470 Prospect St., Glen Rock, 1/09/83, C, 83001522

Hopper, Hendrick, House [Stone Houses of Bergen County TR], 724 Ackerman Ave., Glen Rock, 1/09/83, C, 83001526

Hopper, John, House [Stone Houses of Bergen County TR], 231 Polifly Rd., Hackensack, 1/09/83, C, 83001527

Hopper-Goetschius House [Stone Houses of Bergen County TR], 363 E. Saddle River Rd., Upper Saddle River, 1/10/83, A, C, 83001523

Hopper-Van Horn House, 398 Ramapo Valley Rd., Mahwah, 4/11/73, A, C, 73001079

Huyler, Peter, House [Stone Houses of Bergen County TR], 50 County Rd., Cresskill, 1/09/83, C, 83001528

Jefferson, Joe, Clubhouse [Saddle River MRA], 29 E. Saddle River Rd., Saddle River, 8/29/86, A, C, 86001605

Kip Homestead [Stone Houses of Bergen County TR], 12 Meadow Rd., Rutherford, 1/10/83, A, C, 83001529

Lehigh Valley Railroad Barge No. 79, 1263 River Rd., Edgewater, 4/10/89, A, C, 89000151

Lozier House and Van Riper Mill, 34 Goffle Rd. and 11 Paterson Ave., Midland Park, 10/10/75, A, 75001119

Lydecker, Garret, House [Stone Houses of Bergen County TR], 228 Grand Ave., Englewood, 1/09/83, C, 83001530

Masker House [Stone Houses of Bergen County TR], 470 Wyckoff Ave., Wyckoff, 1/10/83, A, C, 83001531

Meyerhoff, John, House [Stone Houses of Bergen County TR], 279 County Rd., Demarest, 1/09/83, C, 83001532

Midland School, 239 W. Midland Ave., Paramus, 4/07/78, A, C, b, 78001740

Myers-Masker House [Stone Houses of Bergen County TR], 179 Park Ave., Midland Park, 1/09/83, C, 83001533

Nagle, John, House [Stone Houses of Bergen County TR], 75 Harvard St., Closter, 1/09/83, C, 83001534

Naugle House [Stone Houses of Bergen County TR], 42-49 Dunkerhook Rd., Fair Lawn, 1/09/83, C, 83001536

Naugle, Henry, House [Stone Houses of Bergen County TR], 119 Hickory Lane, Closter, 1/09/83, C, 83001535

Naugle, Isaac, House [Stone Houses of Bergen County TR], 80 Hickory Lane, Closter, 1/09/83, C, 83001537

New North Reformed Low Dutch Church, E. Saddle River Rd. at Old Stone Church Rd., Upper Saddle River, 4/15/82, A, C, a, 82003263

North Church, 120 Washington Ave. and 191 Washington Ave., Dumont, 5/26/83, A, C, a, 83001538

O'Blenis House [Saddle River MRA], 220 E. Saddle River Rd., Saddle River, 8/29/86, B, C, 86001606

Oradell Station [Operating Passenger Railroad Stations TR], 400 Maple Ave., Oradell, 6/22/84, A, C, 84002575

Osborn, Garret K., House and Barn [Saddle River MRA], 88 and 90 E. Allendale Rd., Saddle River, 8/29/86, C, 86001607

Outwater, Richard, House [Stone Houses of Bergen County TR], 231 Hackensack St., East Rutherford, 1/09/83, C, 83001539

Packer House [Stone Houses of Bergen County TR], 600 Ewing Ave., Franklin Lakes, 1/09/83, C, 83001540

Palisades Interstate Park, W bank of the Hudson River, Fort Lee and vicinity, 10/15/66, A, NHL, 66000890

Paramus Reformed Church Historic District, Bounded by Franklin Tpke., NJ 17, Saddle River, S side of cemetery, and Glen Ave., Ridgewood, 2/25/75, A, C, a, d, 75001121

Park Ridge Station [Operating Passenger Railroad Stations TR], Hawthorne and Park Ave., Park Ridge, 6/22/84, A, C, 84002577

Paulison-Christie House [Stone Houses of Bergen County TR], 8 Homestead Pl., Ridgefield Park, 1/10/83, C, 83001541

Perry, Peter D., House [Stone Houses of Bergen County TR], 107 Rivervale Rd., Park Ridge, 1/10/83, C, 83001542

Post, Peter P., House [Stone Houses of Bergen County TR], 259 Pascack Rd., Woodcliff, 1/10/83, C, 83001543

Pulis, Albert, House [Stone Houses of Bergen County TR], 322 Pulis Ave., Franklin Lakes, 1/09/83, C, 83001544

Radburn, Irregular pattern between Radburn Rd. and Erie RR. tracks, Fair Lawn, 4/16/75, C, g, 75001118

Radburn-Fair Lawn Station [Operating Passenger Railroad Stations TR], Pollitt Dr., Fair Lawn, 6/22/84, A, C, 84002580

Rathbone-Zabriskie House [Stone Houses of Bergen County TR], 570 N. Maple Ave., Ridgewood, 1/10/83, C, 83001545

Reaction Motors Rocket Test Facility, 936 Dogwood Trail, Franklin Lakes, 6/06/79, A, C, g, 79001472

Reformed Dutch Church and Green, 42 Court St., Hackensack, 6/09/83, A, C, a, 83001546

Ridgewood Station [Operating Passenger Railroad Stations TR], Garber Sq., Ridgewood, 6/22/84, A, C, 84002582

River Road School, 400 Riverside Ave., Lyndhurst, 11/11/77, A, C, 77000844

Rockleigh Historic District, E of Norwood on Willow Ave., Rockleigh and Piermont Rds., Norwood vicinity, 6/29/77, A, C, 77000845

Romeyn-Oldis-Brinkerhoff House [Stone Houses of Bergen County TR], 279 Maywood Ave., Maywood, 1/10/83, C, 83001548

Romine-Van Voorhis House [Stone Houses of Bergen County TR], 306 Maywood Ave., Maywood, 1/10/83, C, 83001547 ·

Roy, Dr. E. G., House [Saddle River MRA], 229 W. Saddle River Rd., Saddle River, 8/29/86, C, 86001608

Rutherford Station [Operating Passenger Railroad Stations TR], Station Sq., Rutherford, 6/22/84, A, C, 84002584

Saddle River Center Historic District [Saddle River MRA], Along W. Saddle River Rd. at jct. of E. Allendale Rd., Saddle River, 8/29/86, A, C, 86001609

Seven Chimneys, 25 Chimney Ridge Ct., Westwood, 8/12/71, A, B, C, 71000494

Bergen County—Continued

Smith, Albert, House [Stone Houses of Bergen County TR], 289 Wycoff Ave., Waldwick, 1/10/83, A, C, 83004870

Smith, John, House [Stone Houses of Bergen County TR], 290 Forest Rd., Mahwah, 1/10/83, C, 83001549

South Church Manse, 138 W. Church St., Bergenfield, 8/24/79, A, C, a, 79001470

South Schraalenburgh Church, Prospect Ave. and W. Church St., Bergenfield, 12/06/75, A, C, a, 75001116

Stagg, John C., House [Stone Houses of Bergen County TR], 308 Sicomac Ave., Wyckoff, 1/10/83, A, C, 83001550

Stanton, Elizabeth Cady, House, 135 Highwood Ave., Tenafly, 5/15/75, B, NHL, 75001122

Steuben Estate Complex, New Bridge Rd., Main St. and Hackensack River, River Edge, 12/09/80, A, B, C, b, 80004403

Steuben House, Old New Bridge Rd., at the Hackensack River, River Edge, 12/18/70, A, C, 70000381

Stillwell—Preston House [Saddle River MRA], 9 E. Saddle River Rd., Saddle River, 8/29/86, C, 86001610

Storms House [Stone Houses of Bergen County TR], 1069 Franklin Lake Rd., Franklin Lakes, 7/24/84, A, C, 84002586

Tallman-Vanderbeck House [Stone Houses of Bergen County TR], 639 Piermont Rd., Closter, 1/09/83, C, 83001551

Tenafly Station, Off Hillside Ave., Tenafly, 1/25/79, A, C, 79001476

Terhune House [Stone Houses of Bergen County TR], 161 Godwin Ave., Wyckoff, 1/10/83, A, C, 83001552

Terhune-Gardner-Lindenmeyr House, 218 Paramus Rd., Paramus, 2/07/72, C, 72000769

Terhune-Hopper House [Stone Houses of Bergen County TR], 349 W. Saddle River Rd., Upper Saddle River, 1/10/83, C, 83001553

Terhune-Hopper House [Stone Houses of Bergen County TR], 825 E. Saddle River Rd., Ho-Ho-Kus, 1/10/83, C, 83001554

Terhune-Ranlett House [Stone Houses of Bergen County TR], 933 E. Saddle River Rd., Ho-Ho-Kus, 1/10/83, C, 83001555

U.S.S. LING, Hackensack River at 150 River St., Hackensack, 10/19/78, A, C, g, 78001736

Upper Closter-Alpine Historic District, Roughly bounded by Forest St., Old Dock Rd., School House Ln., Church St. and Closter Dock Rd., Alpine, 5/08/85, A, C, 85001013

Vaill, Edward W., House, 863 Midland Rd., Oradell, 1/18/90, C, 89001595

Van Allen House, Corner of U.S. 202 and Franklin Ave., Oakland, 7/24/73, A, 73001080

Van Blarcom—Jardine House [Stone Houses of Bergen County TR], 380 Wyckoff Ave., Wyckoff, 1/10/83, C, 83001557

Van Blarcom House [Stone Houses of Bergen County TR], 131 Godwin Ave., Wyckoff, 1/10/83, C, 83001556

Van Blarcom House [Stone Houses of Bergen County TR], 834 Franklin Lake Rd., Franklin Lakes, 7/24/84, A, C, 84002588

Van Blarcom, Albert, House [Stone Houses of Bergen County TR], 250 Crescent Ave., Wyckoff, 1/10/83, C, 83001558

Van Buskirk, Andries Thomas, House [Stone Houses of Bergen County TR; Saddle River MRA (AD)], 164 E. Saddle River Rd., Saddle River, 1/10/83, A, C, 83001559

Van Buskirk, Laurance Thomas, House [Stone Houses of Bergen County TR; Saddle River MRA (AD)], 116 E. Saddle River Rd., Saddle River, 1/10/83, A, C, 83001560

Van Buskirk-Oakley House, 467 Kinderkamack Rd., Oradell, 7/03/79, C, 79001474

Van Dien House [Stone Houses of Bergen County TR], 627 Grove St., Ridgewood, 1/10/83, C, 83001567

Van Dien, Harmon, House [Stone Houses of Bergen County TR], 449 Paramus Rd., Paramus, 1/10/83, C, 83001561

Van Gelder House [Stone Houses of Bergen County TR], 347 Godwin Avenue, Wyckoff, 1/10/83, A, C, 83001568

Van Gelder, Abraham, House [Stone Houses of Bergen County TR], 86 W. Crescent Ave., Mahwah, 1/10/83, C, 83001569

Van Gelder, David, House [Stone Houses of Bergen County TR], 37 W. Crescent Ave., Ramsey, 1/10/83, C, 83001570

Van Horn, David & Cornelius, House [Stone Houses of Bergen County TR], 11 Cedar Lane, Closter, 1/09/83, C, 83001572

Van Horn-Ackerman House [Stone Houses of Bergen County TR], 101 Wyckoff Ave., Wyckoff, 1/10/83, A, C, 83001571

Van Horn-Newcomb House [Stone Houses of Bergen County TR], 303 Tenafly Rd., Englewood, 7/24/84, A, C, 84002590

Van Houten House [Stone Houses of Bergen County TR], 778 Vee Dr., Franklin Lakes, 1/09/83, A, C, 83001576

Van Houten-Ackerman House [Stone Houses of Bergen County TR], 1150 Franklin Lake Rd., Franklin Lakes, 1/09/83, C, 83001573

Van Houten-Ackerman House [Stone Houses of Bergen County TR], 480 Sicomac Ave., Wyckoff, 1/10/83, C, 83001574

Van Houten-Hillman House [Stone Houses of Bergen County TR], 891 River Rd., Elmwood Park, 1/09/83, C, 83001575

Van Koert-Winters House [Stone Houses of Bergen County TR], 615 Franklin Ave., Franklin Lakes, 7/24/84, A, C, 84002593

Van Voorhees-Quackenbush House [Stone Houses of Bergen County TR], 421 Franklin Ave., Wyckoff, 1/10/83, C, 83001577

Van Voorhis-Quackenbush House [Stone Houses of Bergen County TR], 625 Wyckoff Ave., Wyckoff, 7/24/84, A, C, 84002578

Van Winkle House [Stone Houses of Bergen County TR], 798 Franklin Lake Rd., Franklin Lakes, 7/24/84, C, 84002595

Van Winkle-Fox House [Stone Houses of Bergen County TR], 669 Ramapo Valley Rd., Oakland, 1/10/83, C, 83001578

Van Zile House [Stone Houses of Bergen County TR], 714 Godwin Ave., Midland Park, 1/10/83, C, 83001579

Vandelinda, Adam, House [Stone Houses of Bergen County TR], 586 Teaneck Rd., Teaneck, 1/10/83, C, 83001562

Vandelinda, James, House [Stone Houses of Bergen County TR], 566 Teaneck Rd., Teaneck, 1/10/83, C, 83001563

Vanderbeck House [Stone Houses of Bergen County TR], 249 Prospect St., Ridgewood, 1/10/83, C, 83001564

Vanderbeck House [Stone Houses of Bergen County TR], 69 Vanderbeck Ave., Mahwah, 1/10/83, C, 83001565

Vanderbeck, Jacob, Jr., House [Stone Houses of Bergen County TR], 41-25 Dunderhook Rd., Fair Lawn, 1/09/83, C, 83001566

Vanderbeek House [Stone Houses of Bergen County TR], 126 Weirimus Rd., Hillsdale, 7/24/84, A, C, 84002589

Vervalen House [Stone Houses of Bergen County TR], 151 West St., Closter, 1/09/83, C, 83001580

Vreeland House, 125 Lakeview Ave., Leonia, 11/17/78, A, C, D, 78001738

Waldwick Railroad Station, Hewson Ave. and Prospect St., Waldwick, 2/23/78, A, 78001742

Wandell, B. C., House—The Cedars [Saddle River MRA], 214, 223, and 224 W. Saddle River Rd., Saddle River, 8/29/86, C, 86001612

Wandell, F. L., Estate and Ward Factory Site [Saddle River MRA], 255–261 E. Saddle River Rd., Saddle River, 11/01/90, A, C, 86001614

Ware, Dr. John Christie, Bungalow [Saddle River MRA], 246 E. Saddle River Rd., Saddle River, 8/29/86, C, 86001615

Westervelt House [Stone Houses of Bergen County TR], 81 Westervelt Ave., Tenafly, 8/15/83, A, B, C, 83001586

Westervelt, Benjamin P., House [Stone Houses of Bergen County TR], 235 County Rd., Cresskill, 1/09/83, C, 83001583

Westervelt, Caspar, House [Stone Houses of Bergen County TR], 20 Sherwood Rd., Teaneck, 1/10/83, A, C, 83001584

Westervelt, John, House [Stone Houses of Bergen County TR], 29 The Parkway, Harrington Park, 1/09/83, A, C, 83001585

Westervelt, Peter, House and Barn, 290 Grand Ave., Englewood, 3/19/75, A, C, 75001117

Westervelt-Ackerson House, 538 Island Rd., Ramsey, 7/20/77, A, C, 77000846

Westervelt-Cameron House [Stone Houses of Bergen County TR], 26 E. Glen Ave., Ridgewood, 1/10/83, A, C, 83001581

Westervelt-Lydecker House [Stone Houses of Bergen County TR], Weirmus and Old Mill Rds., Woodcliff Lake, 1/10/83, A, C, 83001582

White Tenant House [Stone Houses of Bergen County TR], 16 White's Lane, Waldwick, 1/10/83, C, 83001587

Williams, William Carlos, House, 9 Ridge Rd., Rutherford, 6/04/73, B, 73001082

Bergen County—Continued

Winkle, Jacob W., House [Stone Houses of Bergen County TR], 316 Riverside Ave., Lyndhurst, 1/10/83, C, 83001588

Winters, Aaron, House [Stone Houses of Bergen County TR], 358 Woodside Ave., Franklin Lakes, 7/24/84, A, C, 84002599

Winters-Courter House [Stone Houses of Bergen County TR], 831 Circle Ave., Franklin Lakes, 1/09/83, C, 83001589

Wortendyke Barn, 13 Pascack Rd., Park Ridge, 5/07/73, C, 73001081

Wortendyke, Frederick, House [Stone Houses of Bergen County TR], 168 Pascack Rd., Woodcliff Lake, 1/10/83, C, 83001591

Wortendyke, Frederick, House [Stone Houses of Bergen County TR], 12 Pascack Rd., Park Ridge, 1/10/83, C, 83001592

Wortendyke, Jacob, House [Stone Houses of Bergen County TR], 445 Chestnut Ridge, Woodcliff Lake, 1/10/83, C, 83001593

Wortendyke-Demund House [Stone Houses of Bergen County TR], 57 Demund Lane, Midland Park, 1/10/83, C, 83001590

Yeareance, Jeremiah J., House, 410 Riverside Ave., Lyndhurst, 4/03/86, C, 86000628

Yereance-Berry House [Stone Houses of Bergen County TR], 91 Crane Ave., Rutherford, 1/10/83, C, 83001594

Zabriskie House [Stone Houses of Bergen County TR], Franklin Turnpike & Sheridan Ave., Ho-Ho-Kus, 1/10/83, C, 83001598

Zabriskie Tenant House [Stone Houses of Bergen County TR], 273 Dunkerhook Rd., Paramus, 7/24/84, A, C, 84002602

Zabriskie, Albert J., Farmhouse, E of Ridgewood at E. 37 Ridgewood Ave., Ridgewood vicinity, 11/07/77, A, C, 77000847

Zabriskie, Garret, House [Stone Houses of Bergen County TR], 317 Massachusetts Ave., Haworth, 1/09/83, C, 83001596

Zabriskie, Henry, House [Stone Houses of Bergen County TR], 58 Schraalenburgh Rd., Haworth, 1/09/83, C, 83001597

Zabriskie, Nicholas, House [Stone Houses of Bergen County TR], 25 Chimney Ridge Rd., Washington Township, 1/10/83, C, 83001599

Zabriskie-Christie House [Stone Houses of Bergen County TR], 2 Colonial Court, Dumont, 1/09/83, C, 83001595

Zabriskie-Kipp-Cadmus House, 664 River Rd., Teaneck, 12/13/78, A, C, 78001741

Burlington County

Allen, William R., School, Jct. of Mitchell Ave. and E. Federal St., Burlington, 8/08/91, A, 90001450

Arney's Mount Friends Meetinghouse and Burial Ground, Jct. of Mount Holly-Juliustown and Pemberton-Arney's Mount Rds., Arney's Mount, 1/18/73, A, C, D, a, 73001083

Arneytown Historic District, N of Jacobstown, Jacobstown vicinity, 12/12/77, A, C, 67451850

Atsion Village, U.S. 206, Atsion, 10/22/74, A, C, 74001154

Batsto Village, 10 mi. E of Hammonton on CR 542, Batsto, 9/10/71, A, C, 71000495

Bead Wreck Site, Address Restricted, New Gretna vicinity, 10/18/88, D, 88001899

Birmingham School, Birmingham Rd., N of N. Branch, Rancocas Cr., Birmingham, 12/31/92, A, C, a, 92001683

Bishop—Irick Farmstead, 17 Pemberton Rd., Southampton Township, Vincentown vicinity, 8/04/92, A, B, C, 92000975

Bordentown Historic District, In an irregular pattern within the City limits, Bordentown, 6/14/82, A, C, 82003264

Breidenhart, 255 E. Main St., Moorestown, 12/22/77, A, C, 77000851

Burlington County Prison, High St., Mount Holly, 6/24/86, C, NHL, 86003558

Burlington Historic District, Roughly L-shaped, bounded by Delaware River and High, W. Broad, Albot, and Reed Sts., Burlington, 3/13/75, A, C, a, 75001124

Cinnaminson Avenue and Spring Garden Street Schools, Spring Garden St. between Cinnaminson and Parry Aves., Palmyra, 5/29/92, A, 92000635

Collins, Isaac, House, 201 Broad St., Burlington, 7/24/92, B, C, 92000926

Cooper, Benjamin, Farm, Address Restricted, Moorestown vicinity, 12/12/78, A, C, D, 78001744

Coopertown Meetinghouse, NW of Willingboro on Cooper St., Willingboro vicinity, 5/22/78, A, a, 78001750

Cropwell Friends Meeting House [Evesham Township MPS], 810 Cropwell Rd., Evesham Township, Cropwell, 8/14/92, C, a, 92000976

Crosswicks, Roughly bounded by Bordentown-Crosswicks and Ellisdale Rds., Crosswicks, 5/03/76, A, C, a, 76001146

Crosswicks Creek Site III, Address Restricted, Bordentown City vicinity, 11/26/90, A, D, 87001795

Eayres Plantation and Mill Site, Eayrestown—Red Lion and E. Bella Bridge Rds., Lumberton, 8/13/86, A, C, D, 86001501

Evans, William and Susan, House [Evesham Township MPS], 2 Bill's Ln., Evesham Township, Marlton vicinity, 8/14/92, A, B, C, 92000978

Evans—Cooper House [Evesham Township MPS], N. Elmwood Rd. between NJ 70 and Marlton Pike, Evesham Township, Pine Grove, 8/26/93, C, 93000868

Evens, Thomas and Mary, House [Evesham Township MPS], S. Elmwood Rd., Evesham Township, Pine Grove, 8/26/93, C, 93000867

Evesham Friends Meeting House, Moorestown-Mt. Laurel and Hainesport-Mt. Laurel Rds. (Evesboro Rd.), Mt. Laurel, 4/22/82, A, C, a, 82003268

Farmer's Hall, SE corner of Moorestown on Mt. Laurel Rd., Moorestown vicinity, 8/01/79, A, C, 79003248

Fenwick Manor, 15 Springfield Rd. (Pemberton Township), New Lisbon, 10/25/90, B, C, 90001549

French, Thomas, Jr., House, 512 Camden Ave., Moorestown, 1/09/78, C, 78001745

Green Hill Farm, Oxmead and Deacon Rds., Burlington Township, 7/08/82, A, C, 82003265

Haines, Jonathan, House, NE of Medford on Fostertown Rd., Medford vicinity, 6/16/76, A, B, C, 76001147

Hanover Furnace, Address Restricted, Brown's Mills vicinity, 3/01/74, A, D, 74001155

High Street Historic District, Roughly, High St. from Pearl St. to Federal St., Burlington, 12/15/93, A, C, 93001386

Hollinshead, Thomas, House [Evesham Township MPS], 18 W. Stow Rd., Evesham Township, Marlton vicinity, 8/14/92, C, 92000977

Holloway, James and Charles B., Farm Complex, Newbold La., Chesterfield vicinity, 7/08/82, A, C, 82003266

Hopkinson, Francis, House, 101 Farnsworth Ave. at Park Ave., Bordentown, 7/17/71, B, NHL, 71000496

Inskeep, John, Homestead [Evesham Township MPS], 70 N. Locust Rd., Evesham Township, Marlton, 8/26/93, B, C, 93000866

Irick, John, House, E of Burlington off NJ Turnpike, Burlington vicinity, 9/16/77, C, 77000849

Ivins—Conover House, N of Moorestown off U.S. 130 on Cox Rd., Moorestown vicinity, 4/29/77, C, 77000852

Jones, Benjamin, House, Pemberton-Browns Mills Rd., Pemberton vicinity, 11/30/82, A, C, 82001042

Kirby's Mill, NE of Medford at Church and Fostertown Rds., Medford vicinity, 8/12/71, A, C, 71000497

Log Cabin Lodge, Stokes and Tabernacle Rds., Medford Lakes, 4/12/82, A, C, 82003267

Moorestown Friends School and Meetinghouse, Main St. at Chester Ave., Moorestown, 7/22/88, A, C, a, 86003796

Moorestown Historic District, Roughly bounded by Maple Ave., Chestnut Ave., Main St. from Zelley Ave. to Locust St., and Mill St., Moorestown, 8/30/90, A, C, 89002295

Morris Mansion and Mill, Hanover St., Pemberton, 9/13/77, A, C, 77000855

Mount Holly Historic District, Roughly bounded by Prospect, Elm and Top-E-Toy Sts., RR tracks, Madison and Clifton Aves., Mount Holly, 2/20/73, A, C, 73001084

New St. Mary's Episcopal Church, N side of Broad St. between Talbot and Wood Sts., Burlington, 5/31/72, A, C, a, NHL, 72000770

Newbold, Barzillai, House, E of Columbus on Columbus-Georgetown Rds., Columbus vicinity, 1/26/78, A, C, 78001749

Newbold, William and Susannah, House, E of Georgetown, Georgetown vicinity, 9/29/80, A, B, C, 80002472

North Pemberton Railroad Station, Hanover St., Pemberton, 5/23/78, A, C, 78001746

Burlington County—Continued

Oakwood, W of Wrightstown on Springfield Meeting Rd., Wrightstown vicinity, 1/30/78, A, C, 78001751

Paul, Alice, Birthplace, 118 Hooten Rd., Mt. Laurel Township, 7/05/89, B, c, NHL, 89000774

Peachfield, N of Mount Holly on Burr Rd., Mount Holly vicinity, 6/19/73, C, 73001085

Pearson-How, Cooper, and Lawrence Houses, 453–459 High St., Burlington, 4/26/78, A, C, 78001743

Pemberton Historic District, Roughly bounded by Budd Ave., Budd's Run, Egbert and Cedar Rd., and Rancocas Creek and NJ Central Power and Light Co., Pemberton, 3/22/89, A, C, a, d, 88000688

Perkins House, Camden Ave. and King's Highway, Moorestown, 9/15/77, C, 77000853

Philadelphia Watch Case Company Building, Pavilion and Lafayette Aves., Riverside, 1/31/78, A, C, 78001747

Point Breeze, U.S. 206 and Park St., Bordentown, 8/10/77, A, C, D, 77000848

Providence Presbyterian Church of Bustleton, Jct. of Old York and Burlington-Bustleton Rds., Roebling vicinity, 11/18/88, C, a, 87000377

Quaker School, York and Penn Sts., Burlington, 12/31/74, B, C, 74001156

Rancocas Historic Village, Irregular pattern bounded N and W by Willingboro line, E to Springside Rd. and to S 3rd St., Rancocas, 6/05/75, A, C, a, 75001126

Recklesstown, Present town of Chesterfield along Chesterfield—Georgetown Rd. and NJ 528, Chesterfield, 8/19/75, A, a, 75001125

Roebling Historic District, Roughly bounded by Roebling Park, South St., 2nd and 8th Aves., Roland St., Alden, Norman Railroad, and Amboy Aves., Roebling, 5/22/78, A, C, 78001748

Rosebud Farm, E of Jobstown on Springfield Meetinghouse Rd., Jobstown vicinity, 8/17/79, C, 79003249

Schoolhouse, 2 mi. E of Bridgeboro on Salem Rd., Bridgeboro vicinity, 4/21/75, A, 75001123

Shamong Hotel, Main St., Chatsworth, 9/13/79, A, C, 79001477

Singleton-Lathem-Large House, NW of Chesterfield on NJ 528, Chesterfield vicinity, 3/07/79, A, C, 79001478

Smith Mansion, 12 High St., Moorestown, 10/22/76, A, C, 76001148

Smith, Thomas, House, 1645 Hainesport—Mt. Laurel Rd., Mount Laurel, 9/27/90, A, B, C, 90001437

Smithville Historic District, Off NJ 38, Smithville, 5/12/77, A, C, 77000856

Stokes, Charles, House, 600 Beverly—Rancocas Rd., Willingboro Township, Riverside vicinity, 8/12/93, B, C, 93000827

Taylor—Newbold House, Off Old York Rd. (Rt 660), Chesterfield, 11/18/88, A, C, 87001815

Town Hall, 40 E. Main St., Moorestown, 8/10/77, A, C, 77000854

Upper Springfield Meetinghouse, W of Wrightstown, Wrightstown vicinity, 8/24/79, A, D, a, 79001479

Vincentown Historic District, Roughly bounded by Mill, Church, Pleasant, Main, & Race Sts., & Red Lion Rd., Vincentown, 9/21/88, A, C, D, a, 87002107

Whitesbog Historic District, N of SR 70 and S of Fort Dix, Browns Mills vicinity, 10/27/88, A, B, C, 88002115

Wills, Jacob, House [Evesham Township MPS], Brick Rd., W of Evans Rd., Marlton, 11/01/90, C, 89002296

Camden County

American National Bank [Banks, Insurance, and Legal Buildings in Camden, New Jersey, 1873-1938 MPS], 1219 Broadway, Camden, 8/22/90, A, C, 90001256

Barclay Farm House, NE of Haddonfield near jct. of I-295 and NJ 70, Haddonfield, 1/26/78, C, 78001753

Bennett, Volney G., Lumber Company, 138 Division St. and 845 S. Second St., Camden City, 8/05/93, A, C, 93000749

Blackwood Historic District, Roughly Church St. from E. Railroad Ave. to Indiana Ave., Blackhorse Pike, and Central Ave., Blackwood, 7/27/89, A, 89000996

Bonnie's Bridge, 350 Wayland Rd., Cherry Hill, 9/13/84, A, C, 84002604

Broadway Trust Company [Banks, Insurance, and Legal Buildings in Camden, New Jersey, 1873-1938 MPS], 938–944 Broadway, Camden, 8/24/90, A, C, a, 90001284

Building at 525 Cooper Street [Banks, Insurance, and Legal Buildings in Camden, New Jersey, 1873-1938 MPS], 525 Cooper St., Camden, 8/24/90, A, C, 90001286

Burrough-Dover House, Off the Haddonfield Rd., Pennsauken, 10/25/73, A, 73001089

Camden Fire Insurance Association [Banks, Insurance, and Legal Buildings in Camden, New Jersey, 1873-1938 MPS], 428–432 Federal St., Camden, 8/22/90, A, C, 90001262

Camden Free Public Library Main Building, 616 Broadway, Camden, 10/15/92, C, 92001385

Camden Safe Deposit & Trust Company [Banks, Insurance, and Legal Buildings in Camden, New Jersey, 1873-1938 MPS], Market St. and Broadway, Camden, 8/22/90, A, C, 90001258

Centennial House, 17–19 E. Chestnut Ave., Merchantville, 5/30/91, C, 91000674

Chew-Powell House, 500–502 Good Intent Rd., Blenheim, 3/27/75, B, 75001127

Coles, Samuel, House, 1743 Old Cuthbert Rd., Cherry Hill, 6/18/73, C, 73001087

Collings—Knight Homestead, 500 Collings Ave., Collingswood, 9/10/87, B, C, 87001518

Collingswood Commercial Historic District, Roughly, Haddon Ave. between Woodlawn and Fern, including adjacent areas on Collings Ave., Collingswood, 9/13/90, A, 90001439

Collingswood Residential Historic District, Roughly, Knight Park and its bordering properties, including Park Ave. E to Dayton Ave., Collingswood, 9/13/90, A, C, 90001436

Collingswood Theatre, 843 Haddon Ave., Collingswood, 6/03/82, A, C, 82003269

Collins and Pancoast Hall, 4-8 S. Centre St., Merchantville, 2/16/84, A, C, 84002608

Cooper Grant Historic District, Point, N. Front, Linden, Penn & N. Second Sts., Camden, 1/30/89, C, a, 87002229

Cooper Library in Johnson Park, 2nd and Cooper Sts., Camden, 3/11/80, B, C, 80002473

Cooper Street Historic District, Cooper St. from 2nd to 7th Sts., Camden, 8/07/89, A, C, 89001057

Cooper, Joseph, House, Head of 7th St. in Pyne Point Park, Camden, 3/14/73, C, 73001086

Downey, James M., Building [Banks, Insurance, and Legal Buildings in Camden, New Jersey, 1873-1938 MPS], 521 Cooper St., Camden, 8/22/90, A, C, 90001261

East End Trust Company [Banks, Insurance, and Legal Buildings in Camden, New Jersey, 1873-1938 MPS], 2614–2616 Federal St., Camden, 8/22/90, A, C, 90001254

Fairview District, Roughly bounded by Newton Creek, Crescent Blvd., Mt. Ephraim Ave., Olympia and Hull Rds., Camden, 11/19/74, A, C, 74001157

Finance Building [Banks, Insurance, and Legal Buildings in Camden, New Jersey, 1873-1938 MPS], 549–559 Cooper St., Camden, 8/22/90, A, C, 90001260

First Camden National Bank & Trust [Banks, Insurance, and Legal Buildings of Camden, New Jersey, 1873-1938 MPS], Jct. of Broadway and Cooper St., Camden, 8/24/90, A, C, 90001285

Gatehouse at Colestown Cemetery, Kings Hwy. and Church Rd., Cherry Hill, 5/21/75, A, 75001128

Glover Fulling Mill Site, Address Restricted, Haddon Heights vicinity, 9/28/90, A, 90001452

Grant A.M.E. Church, 4th and Washington Sts., Chesilhurst, 10/05/77, A, a, 77000857

Greenfield Hall, 343 Kings Hwy. E, Haddonfield, 6/05/74, A, 74001158

Haddon Fortnightly Club House, 301 King's Hwy., Haddonfield, 10/26/72, A, a, 72000771

Haddonfield Historic District, Roughly bounded by Washington, Hopkins, Summit, and E. Park Aves., and Kings Hwy., Haddonfield, 7/21/82, A, C, 82003270

Hillman Hospital House, 500 3rd Ave., Glendora, 7/14/77, A, C, 77000858

Indian King Tavern, 233 Kings Hwy. E., Haddonfield, 12/18/70, A, C, 70000382

Inter-County Mortgage and Finance Company [Banks, Insurance, and Legal Buildings in Camden, New Jersey, 1873-1938 MPS], 333 Arch St., Camden, 8/22/90, A, C, 90001263

Marcouse Building [Banks, Insurance, and Legal Buildings in Camden, New Jersey, 1873-1938 MPS], 231 Market St., Camden, 8/24/90, A, C, 90001266

Camden County—Continued

Mickle, Samuel, House, 345 Kings Hwy., E., Haddonfield, 5/21/75, C, b, 75001129

Morgan, Griffith, House, 2 mi. W of Cinnaminson at confluence of Delaware River and Pennsauken Creek, Cinnaminson vicinity, 1/25/73, C, 73001088

National State Bank [Banks, Insurance, and Legal Buildings in Camden, New Jersey, 1873-1938 MPS], 123 Market St., Camden, 8/24/90, A, C, 90001267

New Jersey Safe Deposit and Trust Company [Banks, Insurance, and Legal Buildings in Camden, New Jersey, 1873-1938 MPS], Market and Third Sts., Camden, 8/24/90, A, C, 90001265

Newton Friends' Meetinghouse, 722 Cooper St., Camden, 8/12/71, A, C, a, 71000498

Newton Union Schoolhouse, Collins and Lynne Aves., Camden, 10/27/88, A, C, 88002122

Pomona Hall, Park Blvd. and Euclid Ave., Camden, 8/12/71, B, C, 71000499

Sharp, Edward, House, 200 Cooper St., Camden, 2/29/80, B, C, 80002474

Smith—Austermuhl Insurance Company [Banks, Insurance, and Legal Buildings in Camden, New Jersey, 1873-1938 MPS], NW corner of 5th and Market Sts., Camden, 8/24/90, A, C, 90001301

Solomon Wesley United Methodist Church, 291-B Davistown Rd./Asyla Rd., Blackwood, 4/10/89, A, a, 89000241

South Camden Historic District, Roughly bounded by Jackson St., S. Fourth St., Chelton Ave. and Railroad Ave., Camden, 9/28/90, A, B, C, 90001453

South Camden Trust Company [Banks, Insurance, and Legal Buildings in Camden, New Jersey, 1873-1938 MPS], Broadway at Ferry St., Camden, 8/24/90, A, C, a, 90001255

St. John's Episcopal Church and Burying Ground, Chews Landing Rd. and Old Black Horse Pk., Runnemede vicinity, 11/22/80, C, a, d, 80002475

Station Avenue Business District, Station Ave. from Seventh Ave. to White Horse Pike, Haddon Heights, 11/13/89, A, C, 89001945

Stokes—Lee House, 615–617 Lees Ave., Collingswood, 9/10/87, A, B, C, 87001519

Taylor, Dr. Henry Genet, House and Office, 305 Cooper St., Camden, 8/12/71, C, 71000500

Thackara House, 912 Eldridge Ave., West Collingswood, 9/10/87, A, C, 87001520

Victory Trust Company [Banks, Insurance, and Legal Buildings in Camden, New Jersey, 1873-1938 MPS], Broadway and Spruce St., Camden, 8/24/90, A, C, 90001257

White Horse Pike Historic District, Roughly bounded by Fourth Ave., High and Haddon Sts., E. Atlantic St., and Kings Hwy. and Green St., Haddon Heights, 10/27/88, A, C, 88002104

Whitman, George, House, 431 Stevens St., Camden, 10/11/90, B, 90001482

Whitman, Walt, House, 330 Mickle St., Camden, 10/15/66, B, NHL, 66000461

Whitman, Walt, Neighborhood, 326–332 Mickle St., Camden, 1/20/78, B, C, 78001752

Wilson Building [Banks, Insurance, and Legal Buildings in Camden, New Jersey, 1873-1938 MPS], Cooper St. and Broadway, Camden, 8/24/90, A, C, 90001259

Woodruff, A. S. and Law Buildings [Banks, Insurance, and Legal Buildings in Camden, New Jersey, 1873-1938 MPS], 328–330 Market St., Camden, 8/24/90, A, C, 90001264

Cape May County

Avalon Life Saving Station, 76 W. 15th St., Avalon, 3/02/79, A, C, 79001480

Beesley, Thomas, Sr., House, 12 Beesley's Pl., Upper Township, Beesley's Point, 12/17/92, B, C, 92001682

Calvary Baptist Church, SW of Ocean View at Seaville Rd. and NJ 9, Ocean View vicinity, 11/25/80, C, a, d, 80002477

Cape May Historic District, Cape May, Cape May, 12/29/70, A, C, NHL, 70000383

Cape May Lighthouse, On Cape May Point W of Cape May off Sunset Blvd., Cape May vicinity, 11/12/73, A, 73001090

Cold Spring Presbyterian Church, 780 Seashore Rd., Lower Township, 6/14/91, A, B, C, a, d, 91000785

Dennisville Historic District, Petersburg Rd., Main St., Church Rd., Hall Ave., Fidler and Academy Rds., and NH 47, Dennisville, 11/24/87, A, C, D, a, 87000848

Fishing Creek Schoolhouse, 2102 Bayshore Rd., Villas, 3/06/80, A, C, 80002478

Hereford Lighthouse, Central Ave., North Wildwood, 9/20/77, A, C, 77000859

Holmes, John, House, U.S. 9, Cape May Court House, 6/12/79, C, 79001481

Ludlam, Henry, House, 1336 NJ 47, Dennis Township, Dennisville vicinity, 8/12/93, C, 93000826

Marshallville Historic District, Roughly Marshallville Rd. at Co. Rt. 557, Marshallville, 11/28/89, A, 89002013

New Asbury Methodist Episcopal Meetinghouse, Shore Rd., Cape May Court House vicinity, 9/17/80, A, C, a, 80002476

Ocean City 34th Street Station [Operating Passenger Railroad Stations TR], 34th St., Ocean City, 6/22/84, A, C, 84002613

Ocean City Tenth Street Station [Operating Passenger Railroad Stations TR], Between 9th and 10th Sts., Ocean City, 6/22/84, A, C, 84002610

Old Cape May County Courthouse Building, N. Main St., Cape May, 12/22/81, A, C, 81000389

Townsend, William S., House, 96 Delsea Dr., Dennisville, 4/05/84, A, C, 84002618

Tuckahoe Station [Operating Passenger Railroad Stations TR], Railroad Ave., Tuckahoe, 6/22/84, A, C, 84002626

Woodbine Brotherhood Synagogue, 612 Washington Ave., Woodbine, 9/17/80, A, C, a, 80002479

Cumberland County

Beth Hillel Synagogue, Irving Ave., Carmel, 11/07/78, A, C, a, 78001755

Bridgeton Historic District, Roughly bounded by RR Tracks, South Ave., Lake, Commerce, Water, Belmont, Cohensey, and Penn Sts., Bridgeton, 10/29/82, A, C, 82001043

Buck, Jeremiah, House, 297 E. Commerce St., Bridgeton, 12/30/75, B, C, 75001130

Deerfield Pike Tollgate House, 89 Old Deerfield Pike, Bridgeton, 5/21/75, A, 75001131

Deerfield Presbyterian Church, NE of Seabrook, Seabrook vicinity, 9/29/80, A, C, a, 80002481

Giles, Gen. James, House, 143 W. Broad St., Bridgeton, 3/08/78, B, C, 78001754

Greenwich Historic District, Main St. from Cohansey River N to Othello, Greenwich, 1/20/72, A, C, 72000772

Hoskins, Caesar, Log Cabin, Jct. of South and Second Sts., Mauricetown, 9/10/87, A, C, D, 87001521

Maskel, Thomas, House, 2 mi. W of Greenwich on Bacon's Neck Rd., Greenwich vicinity, 6/10/75, A, 75001132

Miah Maull Shoal Lighthouse, In Delaware Bay 5 mi. SW of Egg Island Point, Delaware Bay, 2/04/91, A, C, 90002188

Millville's First Bank Building, 2nd and E. Main Sts., Millville, 11/20/80, A, C, 80002480

Old Broad Street Presbyterian Church and Cemetery, Broad and Lawrence Sts., Bridgeton, 12/02/74, A, C, a, 74001159

Old Stone Church, N of Cedarville on NJ 553, Cedarville vicinity, 5/12/77, C, a, 77000860

Potter's Tavern, 49–51 Broad St., Bridgeton, 9/10/71, A, C, 71000501

SPINDRIFT SAILING YACHT, S. of Bridgeton, Bridgeton vicinity, 4/22/82, A, B, 82003271

Seeley, Samuel W., House, 274 E. Commerce St., Bridgeton, 5/13/76, C, 76001150

Essex County

Ambrose-Ward Mansion, 132 S. Harrison St., East Orange, 9/20/82, A, C, 82003272

Ampere Station [Operating Passenger Railroad Stations TR], Ampere Plaza and Whitney Pl., East Orange, 6/22/84, A, C, 84002628

Anchorage, The [Montclair MRA], 155 Wildwood Ave., Montclair, 7/01/88, C, 86003061

Ballantine, John, House, 43 Washington St., Newark, 10/02/73, C, NHL, 73001093

Bardsley, Joseph, House [Montclair MRA], 345 Park St., Montclair, 7/01/88, C, 86003059

Belleville Avenue Congregational Church, 151 Broadway, Newark, 8/13/86, C, a, 86001505

Bethany Baptist Church, 117 W. Market St., Newark, 5/10/89, A, B, C, a, g, 88000466

Bloomfield Green Historic District, Bounded by Belleville Ave., Montgomery, Spruce, State, Liberty, and Franklin Sts., Bloomfield, 4/20/78, A, C, 78001757

Essex County—Continued

Bloomfield Station [Operating Passenger Railroad Stations TR], Washington St. and Glenwood Ave., Bloomfield, 6/22/84, A, C, 84002631

Bradner's Pharmacy [Montclair MRA], 33 Watchung Plaza, Montclair, 7/01/88, C, 86003010

Branch Brook Park, Roughly bounded by Belleville Park, Washington and Clifton Aves., 6th and Orange Sts., Newark and Belleville, 1/12/81, A, C, 81000392

Brick Church Station [Operating Passenger Railroad Stations TR], Brick Church Plaza, East Orange, 6/22/84, A, C, 84002636

Caldwell Presbyterian Church Manse, 207 Bloomfield Ave., Caldwell, 11/16/77, B, C, a, c, 77000861

Carnegie Library [Montclair MRA], Church St. at Valley Rd., Montclair, 7/01/88, C, a, 86003074

Casa Deldra [Montclair MRA], 35 Afterglow Way, Montclair, 7/01/88, C, 86003062

Catedral Evangelica Reformada, 27 Lincoln Park and Halsey St., Newark, 10/26/72, A, C, a, 72000773

Cathedral of the Sacred Heart, 89 Ridge St., Newark, 12/22/76, A, C, a, 76001151

Central Avenue Commercial Historic District, 560-654 Central Ave., East Orange, 8/26/83, A, C, 83001600

Central Presbyterian Church [Montclair MRA], 46 Park St., Montclair, 11/14/86, C, a, 86003051

Chapman, J. M., House [Montclair MRA], 10 Rockledge, Montclair, 7/01/88, C, 86002975

Clark, William, House, 346 Mount Prospect Ave., Newark, 11/10/77, B, C, 77000863

Cliffside Hose Company No. 4 [Montclair MRA], 588 Valley Rd., Montclair, 7/01/88, C, 86003077

Congregational Church [Montclair MRA], 42 S. Fullerton Ave., Montclair, 7/01/88, C, a, 86003050

Crane, Israel, House, 110 Orange Rd., Montclair, 3/14/73, B, C, b, 73001091

Dock Bridge, Spans Passaic River, Newark, 10/03/80, A, C, g, 80002484

East Orange Station [Operating Passenger Railroad Stations TR], 65 City Hall Plaza, East Orange, 6/22/84, A, C, 84002638

Eastward [Montclair MRA], 50 Lloyd Rd., Montclair, 7/01/88, C, 86002980

Edison National Historic Site, Main St. between Alden and Lakeside Sts., West Orange, 10/15/66, A, B, NPS, 66000052

Egbert Farm [Montclair MRA], 128 N. Mountain Ave., Montclair, 7/01/88, C, 86002996

Enclosure Historic District, Enclosure and Calico Lane, Nutley, 12/31/74, A, C, 74001160

Essex Club, Address Restricted, Newark, 2/22/91, A, C, 91000110

Essex County Courthouse, 470 High St., Newark, 6/26/75, C, 75001135

Essex County Jail, 21 Wilsey St., Newark, 9/03/91, C, 91001366

Essex County Park Commission Administration Building, 115 Clifton Ave., Newark, 11/11/77, A, C, 77000864

Fairfield Dutch Reformed Church, Fairfield Rd., Fairfield, 10/07/75, A, C, a, 75001134

Feigenspan Mansion, 710 High St., Newark, 10/05/77, B, C, 77000865

Fenn, Henry, House [Montclair MRA], 208 N. Mountain Ave., Montclair, 7/01/88, B, C, 86002988

First Baptist Peddie Memorial Church, Broad and Fulton Sts., Newark, 10/30/72, C, a, 72000774

First Methodist Episcopal Church [Montclair MRA], 24 N. Fullerton Ave., Montclair, 7/01/88, C, a, 86003048

First National State Bank Building, 810 Broad St., Newark, 8/10/77, C, D, 77000866

Forest Hill Historic District, Roughly bounded by Verona Ave., Mt. Prospect Ave., 2nd Ave., and Branch Brook Park, Newark, 8/03/90, B, C, 90001193

Free Public Library, Upper Montclair Branch [Montclair MRA], 185 Bellevue Ave., Montclair, 7/01/88, C, 86003076

Glen Ridge Historic District, Roughly bounded by Bay St., Essex and Midland Aves., Adams Pl., Spencer Rd., and Franklin Pl., Glen Ridge, 8/09/82, A, C, 82004784

Glen Ridge Historic District (Boundary Increase), N side roughly along Ridgewood and Forest Ave. from Bay to Gray St., S side along Hawthorne, Carteret, and Midland Ave., Glen Ridge, 11/14/88, A, C, 88002155

Glencoe, 698 Martin Luther King Blvd., Newark, 10/01/91, B, C, 91001481

Goodwillie, Frank, House [Montclair MRA], 17 Wayside Pl., Montclair, 7/01/88, C, 86003058

Grace Church, Broad and Walnut Sts., Newark, 11/02/72, A, C, a, NHL, 72000776

Griffith Building, 605-607 Broad St., Newark, 5/24/84, A, C, 84002641

Harrison, Samuel Orton, House, 153 Orton Rd., West Caldwell, 6/30/80, A, C, 80002488

Haskell's Bloomfield Villa [Montclair MRA], 84 Llewellyn Rd., Montclair, 7/01/88, C, 86003002

Home Office Building, 8–12 Park Pl., Newark, 6/17/82, A, C, 82003273

House at 147 Park Street [Montclair MRA], 147 Park St., Montclair, 7/01/88, C, 86003064

House at 18 Brunswick Road [Montclair MRA], 18 Brunswick Rd., Montclair, 7/01/88, C, 86003035

House at 21 Stonebridge Road [Montclair MRA], 21 Stonebridge Rd., Montclair, 7/01/88, C, 86003073

House at 52 Wayside Place [Montclair MRA], 52 Wayside Pl., Montclair, 7/01/88, C, 86003041

House at 53 Lloyd Road [Montclair MRA], 53 Lloyd Rd., Montclair, 7/01/88, C, 86002973

House at 67 Warren Place [Montclair MRA], 67 Warren Pl., Montclair, 7/01/88, C, 86003004

House at 68 Eagle Rock Way [Montclair MRA], 68 Eagle Rock Way, Montclair, 7/01/88, C, 86003009

House at 7 South Mountain Terrace [Montclair MRA], 7 S. Mountain Terr., Montclair, 11/15/86, C, 86003235

House at 80 Lloyd Road [Montclair MRA], 80 Lloyd Rd., Montclair, 7/01/88, C, 86003003

House at 97 Warren Place [Montclair MRA], 97 Warren Pl., Montclair, 7/01/88, C, 86003070

House of Prayer Episcopal Church and Rectory, Broad and State Sts., Newark, 10/30/72, A, B, C, a, 72000777

House that Lives, The [Montclair MRA], 83 Watchung Ave., Montclair, 7/01/88, C, 86002976

Jacobus House, 178 Grove Ave., Cedar Grove, 4/01/75, A, C, 75001133

James Street Commons Historic District, Roughly bounded by Halsey, Warren, Boyden, Bleeker, Orange, and Broad Sts., Newark, 1/09/78, A, C, 78001758

James Street Commons Historic District Addendum, 18 Washington Pl., Newark, 9/22/83, C, 83001601

Kelly, Eugene V., Carriage House, S. Orange Ave., Seton Hall University campus, South Orange, 11/10/75, B, C, 75001136

Kingsland Manor, 3 Kingsland St., Nutley, 3/24/78, A, B, C, 78001762

Krueger Mansion, 601 High St., Newark, 11/09/72, C, 72000778

Lincoln Park Historic District, Lincoln Park, Clinton Ave., and Spruce and Broad Sts., Newark, 1/05/84, C, 84002646

Llewellyn Park Historic District, Roughly bounded by Eagle Rock Ave., Main St., Pleasant Ave., and NJ 280, West Orange, 2/28/86, B, C, NPS, 86000423

Marlboro Park Historic District [Montclair MRA], Roughly along Fairfield St., Waterbury Rd., Montclair Ave., and Watchung Ave. between N. Fullerton and Grove Sts., Montclair, 7/22/88, C, 86002967

Marsellis House [Montclair MRA], 190 Cooper Ave., Montclair, 7/01/88, C, 86003031

Miller Street Historic District [Montclair MRA], Miller and Fulton Sts. between Elmwood Ave., Elm, and New Sts., Montclair, 7/01/88, C, 86002971

Miller, George A., House [Montclair MRA], 275 Claremont Ave., Montclair, 7/01/88, C, 86002979

Montclair Art Museum [Montclair MRA], 3 S. Mountain Ave., Montclair, 11/14/86, A, C, 86002984

Montclair Railroad Station, Lackawanna Plaza, Montclair, 1/08/73, A, C, 73001092

Morris Canal, Irregular line beginning at Phillipsburg and ending at Jersey City, Not Applicable, 10/01/74, A, C, 74002228

Mount Pleasant Cemetery, 375 Broadway, Newark, 10/28/88, A, C, d, 87000836

Mountain Avenue Station [Operating Passenger Railroad Stations TR], 451 Upper Mountain Ave., Upper Montclair, 6/22/84, A, C, 84002654

Mountain District [Montclair MRA], Roughly bounded by Highland, Bradford, Upper Mountain, and Claremont Aves., Montclair, 7/22/88, C, 86002970

Mountain Station [Operating Passenger Railroad Stations TR], 449 Vose Ave., South Orange, 9/29/84, A, C, 84002656

Mulford House [Montclair MRA], 207 Union St., Montclair, 7/01/88, C, 86003038

Essex County—Continued

Murphy Varnish Works, McWhorter, Vesey, and Chestnut Sts., Newark, 3/09/79, A, B, C, 79001484

Mutual Benefit Life Insurance Company, 300 Broadway and 2nd St., Newark, 11/17/83, A, C, 83004031

New Point Baptist Church, 17 E. Kinney St., Newark, 11/02/72, C, a, 72000779

Newark Broad Street Station [Operating Passenger Railroad Stations TR], Broad and University Sts., Newark, 6/22/84, A, C, 84002662

Newark City Hall, 920 Broad St., Newark, 2/17/78, A, C, 78001759

Newark Female Charitable Society, 305 Halsey St., 41–43 Hill St., Newark, 9/12/79, A, C, 79001485

Newark Metropolitan Airport Buildings, U.S. 22, Newark, 12/12/80, A, C, g, 80002485

Newark Orphan Asylum, High and Bleeker Sts., Newark College of Engineering, Newark, 6/19/73, A, C, 73001094

North Reformed Church, 510 Broad St., Newark, 10/05/72, A, a, 72000780

Oakes Estate, 240 Belleville Ave., Bloomfield, 8/06/81, B, C, 81000390

Old First Presbyterian Church, 820 Broad St., Newark, 11/02/72, A, C, a, 72000781

Orange Free Public Library, 348 Main St., Orange, 9/28/81, A, C, 81000393

Orange Station [Operating Passenger Railroad Stations TR], 73 Lincoln Ave., Orange, 6/22/84, A, C, 84002665

Pan American C.M.A. Church, 76 Prospect St., Newark, 7/31/72, A, C, a, 72000782

Passaic Machine Works—Watts, Campbell & Company, 1270 McCarter Hwy., Newark, 8/13/86, A, 86001503

Pennsylvania Station, Raymond Plaza West, Newark, 12/20/78, A, C, 78001760

Post Office Building, Upper Montclair [Montclair MRA], 242–244 Bellevue Ave., Montclair, 7/01/88, C, 86003012

Presby Memorial Iris Gardens Horticultural Center, 474 Upper Mountain Ave., Montclair, 9/17/80, A, C, 80002483

Protestant Foster Home, 272–284 Broadway, Newark, 2/13/86, A, C, 86000211

Queen of Angels Church, Belmont Ave. at Morton St., Newark, 10/26/72, A, C, a, 72000783

Reading, M. F., House [Montclair MRA], 87 Midland Ave., Montclair, 7/01/88, C, 86003006

Red Gables [Montclair MRA], 99 S. Fullerton Ave., Montclair, 7/01/88, B, C, 86002992

Reformed Dutch Church of Second River, 171 Main St., Belleville, 12/21/78, A, C, a, 78001756

Salaam Temple, 1020 Broad St., Newark, 10/05/77, A, C, g, 77000867

Schultz, Charles S. House, 30 N. Mountain Ave., Montclair, 7/22/79, C, 79001482

Second Reformed Dutch Church, 178-184 Edison Pl., Newark, 3/07/79, A, C, a, 79001486

Short Hills Park Historic District, Off NJ 24, Millburn, 9/18/80, C, 80002482

Smith, S. C., House [Montclair MRA], 40 Northview Ave., Montclair, 7/01/88, C, 86002978

South Orange Station [Operating Passenger Railroad Stations TR], 19 Sloan St., South Orange, 6/22/84, A, C, 84002669

South Orange Village Hall, S. Orange Ave. and Scotland Rd., South Orange, 5/28/76, C, 76001152

South Park Calvary United Presbyterian Church, 1035 Broad St., Newark, 12/05/72, C, a, 72000784

St. Barnabas' Episcopal Church, W. Market St. and Sussex and Roseville Aves., Newark, 10/18/72, C, a, 72000785

St. Columba's Church, Pennsylvania Ave. and Brunswick St., Newark, 10/30/72, A, C, a, 72000786

St. James' A. M. E. Church, High and Court Sts., Newark, 10/18/72, A, C, a, 72000787

St. John's Church, 22–26 Mulberry St., Newark, 10/30/72, B, C, a, 72000789

St. Joseph's Roman Catholic Church Rectory and School, W. Market St., Newark, 12/08/80, A, C, a, 80002486

St. Luke's Church [Montclair MRA], 69 S. Fullerton Ave., Montclair, 7/01/88, C, a, 86003045

St. Mark's Episcopal Church, 13 Main St., West Orange, 9/22/77, A, C, a, 77000868

St. Mary's Abbey Church, High and William Sts., Newark, 11/03/72, A, C, a, 72000790

St. Patrick's Pro Cathedral, Washington St. and Central Ave., Newark, 11/03/72, A, C, a, 72000791

St. Rocco's Roman Catholic Church, 212–216 Hunterdon St., Newark, 9/29/80, A, C, a, 80002487

St. Stephan's Church, Ferry St. and Wilson Ave., Newark, 10/05/72, A, C, a, 72000792

Stanley Theater, 985 S. Orange Ave., Newark, 8/28/86, A, C, 86001957

State Street Public School, 15 State St., Newark, 8/03/90, A, B, C, 90001201

Stone Eagles [Montclair MRA], 60 Undercliff Rd., Montclair, 7/01/88, C, 86003005

Stone House by the Stone House Brook, 219 S. Orange Ave., South Orange, 11/22/91, B, D, 87001333

Sydenham House, Old Road to Bloomfield, at Heller Pkwy., Newark, 7/29/70, A, C, 70000384

Symington House, 2 Park Place, Newark, 3/02/79, C, a, 79001487

Trinity Cathedral, Broad and Rector Sts., Newark, 11/03/72, A, C, a, 72000793

Upper Montclair Station [Operating Passenger Railroad Stations TR], 275 Bellvue Ave., Upper Montclair, 6/22/84, A, C, 84002673

Van Ness House, 236 Little Falls Rd., Fairfield vicinity, 7/29/77, B, C, 77000862

Van Reyper-Bond House, 848 Valley Rd., Montclair, 1/22/79, B, C, 79001483

Von Schmid House [Montclair MRA], 580 Park St., Montclair, 7/01/88, C, 86002974

Ward-Force House and Condit Family Cook House, 366 S. Livingston Ave., Livingston, 12/29/81, A, C, 81000391

Watchung Avenue Station [Operating Passenger Railroad Stations TR], Park St., Montclair, 6/22/84, A, C, 84002674

Wickcliffe Presbyterian Church, 111 13th Ave., Newark, 5/22/78, A, C, a, 78001761

Wight, Allyn, House [Montclair MRA], 75 Gates Ave., Montclair, 7/01/88, C, 86003007

Williams-Harrison House, 126 Eagle Rock Ave., Roseland, 3/13/79, A, C, 79001488

Gloucester County

Barnsboro Hotel, Jct. of Pitman and Sewell Rds., Barnsboro, 1/25/73, A, C, 73001095

Butler Farm, E of Swedesboro, Swedesboro vicinity, 12/01/78, A, C, 78001763

Chew, Jesse, House, 611 Mantua Blvd., Sewell, 10/18/72, C, 72000797

Clark, Benjamin, House, Glassboro Rd., Wenonah, 1/25/73, B, C, 73001099

Free Library and Reading Room—Williamstown Memorial Library, 405 S. Main St., Williamstown, 10/01/87, A, C, 87001761

Hunter—Lawrence—Jessup House, 58 N. Broad St., Woodbury, 10/18/72, B, C, 72000798

Ladd's Castle, 1337 Lafayette Ave., Colonial Manor, 10/31/72, B, C, 72000794

Moravian Church, Swedesboro-Sharptown Rd., Oliphant's Mill, 4/03/73, A, C, a, 73001097

Mullica Hill Historic District, Roughly, Main St. from Mullica Hill—Bridgeport Rd. to jct. of Commissioner's Rd. and Bridgeton Pike, Harrison Township, Mulllica Hill, 4/25/91, A, C, 91000483

Nothnagle, C. A., Log House, Swedesboro-Paulsboro Rd., Gibbstown, 4/23/76, C, 76001153

Otto, Bodo, House, SR 551 and Quaker Rd., Mickleton, 12/12/76, B, 76001154

Pitman Grove, Bounded by Holly, East, Laurel, and West Aves. (both sides), Pitman, 8/19/77, A, C, a, 77000870

Red Bank Battlefield, E bank of Delaware River and W end of Hessian Ave., National Park, 10/31/72, A, C, NHL, 72000796

Richwood Methodist Church, Elmer Rd., Richwood, 1/19/79, C, a, 79001490

Salisbury Farm, Address Restricted, Bridgeport vicinity, 3/07/79, D, 79001489

St. Peter's Episcopal Church, King's Hwy., Clarksboro, 8/10/77, A, C, a, 77000869

St. Thomas Episcopal Church, SE corner Main and Focer Sts., Glassboro, 3/03/75, C, a, 75001137

Stratton, Gov. Charles C., House, 0.5 mi. E of Swedesboro on King's Hwy., Woolwich Township, 1/29/73, A, C, 73001101

Thompson House [Woodbury MRA], 103 Penn St., Woodbury, 7/13/88, A, C, 88000996

Trinity Church, NW corner of Church St. and King's Hwy., Swedesboro, 1/29/73, A, C, a, 73001098

Whitall, James, Jr., House, 100 Grove Ave., National Park, 2/06/73, C, 73001096

Gloucester County—Continued

Whitney Mansion, Whitney Ave., Glassboro, 12/05/72, B, C, 72000795

Woodbury Friends' Meetinghouse, 120 N. Broad St., Woodbury, 2/06/73, A, C, a, 73001100

Hudson County

Assembly of Exempt Firemen Building [Hoboken Firehouses and Firemen's Monument TR], 213 Bloomfield St., Hoboken, 3/30/84, A, C, 84002678

Barrow, Dr. William, Mansion, 83 Wayne St., Jersey City, 5/02/77, C, 77000872

Bayonne Truck House No. 1, 12 W. 47th St., Bayonne, 1/02/76, A, 76001155

Buildings at 1200–1206 Washington Street, 1200–1206 Washington St., Hoboken, 3/09/87, C, 87000350

Church of the Holy Innocents, Willow Ave. and 6th St., Hoboken, 5/24/77, A, C, a, 77000871

Clark Thread Company Historic District, 900 Passaic Ave., East Newark, 6/02/78, A, NHL, 78001764

Engine Company No. 2 [Hoboken Firehouses and Firemen's Monument TR], 1313 Washington St., Hoboken, 3/30/84, A, C, 84002684

Engine Company No. 3 [Hoboken Firehouses and Firemen's Monument TR], 201 Jefferson St., Hoboken, 3/30/84, A, C, 84002687

Engine Company No. 4 [Hoboken Firehouses and Firemen's Monument TR], 212 Park Ave., Hoboken, 3/30/84, A, C, 84002691

Engine Company No. 5 [Hoboken Firehouses and Firemen's Monument TR], 412 Grand St., Hoboken, 3/30/84, A, C, 84002693

Engine Company No. 6 [Hoboken Firehouses and Firemen's Monument TR], 801 Clinton St., Hoboken, 3/30/84, A, C, 84002695

Engine House No. 3, Truck No. 2 [Hoboken Firehouses and Firemen's Monument TR], 501 Observer Hwy., Hoboken, 3/30/84, A, C, 84002700

Erie-Lackawanna Railroad Terminal at Hoboken, On the Hudson River at the foot of Hudson Pl., Hoboken, 7/24/73, A, C, 73001102

Ficken's Warehouse, 750-766 Grand St., Jersey City, 6/14/84, A, C, 84002703

Firemen's Monument [Hoboken Firehouses and Firemen's Monument TR], Church Square Pk., Hoboken, 10/30/86, A, C, f, 86003454

First Reformed Dutch Church of Bergen Neck, Avenue C and 33rd St., Bayonne, 4/22/82, A, C, a, 82003274

Grace Church Van Vorst, 268 2nd St, Jersey City, 8/01/79, A, C, a, 79001492

Great Atlantic and Pacific Tea Company Warehouse, Provost St. between 1st and Bay Sts., Jersey City, 6/02/78, A, NHL, 78001766

Hackensack Water Company Complex, 4100 Park Ave., Weehawken, 1/03/80, C, 80002491

Hamilton Park Historic District, Roughly bounded by Brunswick, Grove, 6th, and 9th Sts., Jersey City, 1/25/79, C, 79001493

Hamilton Park Historic District Extension (Boundary Increase), Jersey Ave. and 10th St., Jersey City, 12/02/82, A, C, 82001044

Harsimus Cove Historic District, Roughly bounded by Grove Dr., Bay & First Sts., Jersey Ave., Second, & Coles Sts., Jersey City, 12/09/87, A, C, 87002118

Highland Hose No. 4, 72–74 Halstead St., Kearny, 5/29/87, A, C, 87000856

Hoboken City Hall, 86-98 Washington St., Hoboken, 1/01/76, A, C, 76001156

Hoboken Land and Improvement Company Building, 1 Newark St., Hoboken, 7/03/79, A, C, 79001491

Holland Tunnel, Connecting Lower Manhattan and Jersey City, running under the Hudson R., Jersey City, 11/04/93, A, C, NHL, 93001619

Hudson County Courthouse, Newark and Baldwin Aves., Jersey City, 8/25/70, A, C, 70000385

Jefferson Trust Company, 313–315 First St., Hoboken, 2/13/86, A, C, 86000214

Jersey City Central Railroad Terminal, U.S. 78 N of Ellis Island, Jersey City, 9/12/75, A, C, 75001138

Jersey City High School, 2 Palisade Ave., Jersey City, 6/01/82, A, C, 82003275

Jersey City Medical Center, Roughly bounded by Montgomery St., Cornelison Ave., Dupont St. and Clifton Pl., and Baldwin Ave., Jersey City, 11/27/85, C, g, 85003057

KESTREL (steam yacht), S end of River Rd., West New York, 8/12/77, A, 77000873

Keuffel and Esser Manufacturing Complex, 3rd, Grand & Adams St., Hoboken, 9/12/85, C, 85002183

Labor Bank Building, 26 Journal Sq., Jersey City, 6/14/84, A, C, 84002705

Lembeck and Betz Eagle Brewing Company District, Bounded by 9th, 10th, Grove and Henderson StS., Jersey City, 6/21/84, A, C, 84002707

Monastery and Church of Saint Michael the Archangel, 2019 West St., Union, 3/06/86, A, C, a, 86000418

Old Bergen Church, Bergen and Highland Aves., Jersey City, 8/14/73, A, C, a, 73001103

Paulus Hook Historic District, Greene, Washington, Grand, Sussex, Morris, Essex, Warren and York Sts., Jersey City, 6/21/82, C, 82003276

Paulus Hook Historic District (Boundary Increase), Roughly bounded by York, Green, Essex and Henderson, Jersey City, 5/13/85, C, 85002450

Pohlmann's Hall, 154 Ogden Ave., Jersey City, 9/05/85, A, C, 85002001

St. Patrick's Parish and Buildings, Grand St., Ocean and Bramhall Aves., Jersey City, 9/17/80, A, C, a, 80002489

Statue of Liberty National Monument, Ellis Island and Liberty Island, Liberty Island, New York Harbor, Jersey City, 10/15/66, A, C, f, NPS, 66000058

Van Vorst Park Historic District, Roughly bounded by Railroad Ave., Henderson, Grand, Bright, and Monmouth Sts., Jersey City, 3/05/80, A, C, 80002490

Van Vorst Park Historic District (Boundary Increase), Roughly bounded by Railroad Ave., Henderson, Bright, Varick and Monmouth Sts., Jersey City, 10/11/84, A, C, a, 84000084

Hunterdon County

Apgar, J. K., Farmhouse, CR 512 and Guinea Hollow Rd., Califon, 11/01/79, C, 79001494

Bray-Hoffman House, On Bray's Hill Rd., Annandale, 1/25/73, B, C, 73001104

Califon Historic District, Main and Academy Sts., Califon, 10/14/76, A, 76001157

Case Farmstead, W of Pattenburg on SR 14, Pattenburg vicinity, 8/14/79, B, C, 79001496

Clover Hill Historic District, Amwell and Wertsville-Clover Hill Rds., Flemington vicinity, 9/29/80, A, a, 80002492

Dart's Mill Historic District, NE of Flemington on Rt. 523, Flemington vicinity, 4/29/82, A, C, D, 82003279

Delaware and Raritan Canal, Follows the Delaware River to Trenton, then E to New Brunswick, Lambertville vicinity, 5/11/73, A, C, 73001105

Dunham's Mill, 7 Center St., Clinton, 4/15/82, A, 82003277

Everittstown Historic District, E of Milford at int. of CR 12, CR 15 and Palmyra Rd., Milford vicinity, 8/28/80, A, C, D, 80002496

Fink-Type Truss Bridge, W of Allerton off NJ 31 over South Branch of Raritan River, Allerton vicinity, 12/24/74, C, 74001161

Flemington Historic District, Roughly bounded by NJ 12, NJ 31, N. Main, Shields, and Hopewell Aves., Flemington, 9/17/80, A, C, 80002493

Glen Gardner Pony Pratt Truss Bridge, Mill St. at Spruce Run, Glen Gardner, 9/22/77, A, C, 77000876

Green Sergeants Covered Bridge, N of Stockton off Rosemont-Sergeantsville Rd., Stockton vicinity, 11/19/74, A, C, e, 74001165

High Bridge Reformed Church, Church St. and CR 513, High Bridge, 11/21/80, A, C, a, 80002494

Kline Farmhouse, NJ 517, Oldwick vicinity, 7/11/84, A, C, 84002712

Lambertville Historic District, NJ 29 and NJ 179, Lambertville, 6/30/83, A, C, 83001602

Lambertville House, 32 Bridge St., Lambertville, 9/06/78, A, C, 78001768

Lansdown, NE of Pittstown on SR 2, Pittstown vicinity, 11/02/79, B, C, 79001497

Little York Historic District, CR 614 and Sweet Hollow Rd., Little York, 8/04/88, A, C, a, 88001207

Locktown Baptist Church, W of Stockton on Locktown-Stugeonville Rds., Stockton vicinity, 2/15/74, A, C, a, 74001166

Marshall, James W., House, 60 Bridge St., Lambertville, 12/18/70, B, C, 70000386

McKinney, David, Mill, 56 Main St., Clinton, 1/08/74, A, C, 74001162

Mechlins Corner Tavern, NW of Pittstown, Pittstown vicinity, 11/01/74, A, C, 74001164

Hunterdon County—Continued

Mount Airy Historic District, Roughly bounded by NJ 179, Rt. 605, Rt. 603, and Rt. 601, Lambertville vicinity, 11/13/89, A, C, 89001943

Mount Pleasant Historic District, CR 519 & Rick Rd., Mount Pleasant, 11/16/87, A, C, 87002012

Mount Salem Methodist Episcopal Church, CR 579, Mt. Salem vicinity, 5/19/88, C, a, 88000592

Mountainville Historic District, Guinea Hollow Rd., Saw Mill Rd., Main St., Rockaway Creek Rd. and Philhower Rd., Tewksbury Township, Mountainville, 12/07/93, A, C, 93001360

Music Hall, 23 W. Main St., Clinton, 5/07/82, A, 82003278

New Hampton Pony Pratt Truss Bridge, N of Hampton over Musconetcong River, Hampton vicinity, 7/26/77, A, C, 77000877

Old Grandin Library, 12 E. Main St., Clinton, 11/01/74, A, C, 74001163

Oldwick Historic District, Roughly along CR 517, Church, King, James, Joliet and William Sts., Oldwick, 11/14/88, A, C, 88002153

Perryville Tavern, W of Clinton at I-78 and CR 42, Clinton vicinity, 7/15/77, A, C, 77000874

Pittstown Historic District, Pittstown Rd. and adjacent portions of Race St. and Quakertown Rds., Franklin and Alexandra Townships, Pittstown, 10/11/90, A, B, C, 90001483

Potterstown Rural Historic District, Along Potterstown and Hall's Mill Rds. and I-78, Readington and Clinton Townships, Potterstown, 7/02/92, A, C, 92000806

Pottersville Village Historic District, Properties fronting on Black River, Pottersville, McCann Mill and Hacklebarney Rds. and Fairmount Rd. E and Hill St., Pottersville, 9/18/90, A, C, D, 90001475

Prallsville District, NJ 29, Prallsville, 6/27/79, A, 79001498

Pursley's Ferry Historic District, River and Church Rds., Holland vicinity, 10/08/80, A, C, D, 80002495

Quaker Meeting, Roughly bounded by Quakertown, Cherryville Rds., Quaker Ln., and Locust Grove Rd. (Franklin Township), Quakertown, 8/23/90, A, C, 90001242

Raritan-Readington South Branch Historic District, Running roughly E of Raritan River from NJ 31 to US 202, Flemington vicinity, 1/26/90, A, B, C, 89002410

Reading, John, Farmstead, NE of Flemington at 523 River Rd., Flemington vicinity, 11/21/78, A, B, C, 78001767

Readington Village Historic Village, Jct. of Readington, Hillcrest, Centerville and Brookview Rds., Readington Township, Readington, 6/24/91, A, B, C, a, 91000827

Rockhill Agricultural Historic District, N of Pittstown on SR 513, Pittstown vicinity, 4/05/84, A, 84002717

St. Thomas Episcopal Church, SW of Pittstown on Sky Manor Rd., Pittstown vicinity, 7/21/77, A, C, a, 77000878

Stanton Historic Rural District, Jct. of Stanton and Mountain Rds., between Round and Cushetunk Mtns., Stanton, 8/10/90, A, C, 90001225

Taylor's Mill Historic District, Jct. of Taylor's Mill and Rockaway Rds., Readington Township, Oldwick vicinity, 6/11/92, A, B, C, 92000636

Turner-Chew-Carhart Farm, NW of Clinton on Syckles Corner Rd., Clinton vicinity, 8/11/77, A, C, 77000875

Van Syckel Corner District, Van Syckels Corner and Norton Rds, Clinton vicinity, 11/08/79, A, C, 79001495

White House Station [Operating Passenger Railroad Stations TR], Main St., White House, 6/22/84, A, C, 84002726

Mercer County

Abbott Farm Archeological Site, Address Restricted, Trenton vicinity, 12/08/76, A, D, NHL, 76001158

Abbott, John II, House, 2200 Kuser Rd., Trenton, 6/18/76, A, C, e, 76001159

Abbott-Decou House, 58 Soloff Dr., Trenton vicinity, 7/01/76, C, D, 76001160

Adams and Sickles Building, 1 W. End Ave., Trenton, 1/31/80, C, 80002498

Anderson-Capner House, 700 Trumbull Ave., Lawrence, 4/03/73, C, 73001107

Archeological Site No. 1–18th Century Vessel (28ME196), Address Restricted, Trenton vicinity, 8/14/86, A, D, 86001508

Baker-Brearley House, E of Lawrenceville on Meadow Rd, Lawrenceville vicinity, 8/31/79, C, 79001499

Berkeley Square Historic District, Roughly bounded by W. State St., Parkside, Riverside, and Overbrook Aves., Trenton, 11/20/80, C, 80002499

Bow Hill, Jeremiah Ave. off Lalor St., Trenton, 1/25/73, C, 73001111

Clay, Henry and Bock and Company Cigar Factory, 507 Grand St., Trenton, 6/12/79, A, C, g, 79001500

Cleveland, Grover, Home, 15 Hodge Rd., Princeton, 10/15/66, B, NHL, 66000463

Dickinson, Gen. Philemon, House, 46 Colonial Ave., Trenton, 5/17/74, B, 74001172

Douglass House, Corner of Front and Montgomery Sts., Trenton, 12/18/70, B, C, b, 70000387

Drumthwacket, 344 Stockton Rd., Princeton, 6/10/75, B, C, 75001142

Einstein, Albert, House, 112 Mercer St., Princeton, 1/07/76, B, g, NHL, 76002297

Green, William, House, Off NJ 69 on Green Lane, Ewing, 12/04/73, A, C, 73001106

Harbourton Historic District, Jct. of Harbourton/Rocktown Rd. and Harbourton/Mt. Airy Rd., Harbourton, 12/31/74, C, a, 74001167

Hart, John D., House, Curlis Ave., Pennington, 10/18/72, C, 72000800

Hart-Hoch House, SW of Pennington on CR 546 and Scotch Rd., Pennington vicinity, 3/14/73, C, 73001109

Henry, Joseph, House, Princeton University campus, Princeton, 10/15/66, B, b, NHL, 66000464

Herring, Donald Grant, Estate, 52, 72 and 75 Arreton Rd., Princeton Township, Rocky Hill vicinity, 1/17/92, A, C, 91001927

Hog Island Cranes, Trenton Marine Terminal, Trenton, 6/17/80, A, C, b, 80002500

Hopewell Station [Operating Passenger Railroad Stations TR], Railroad Pl., Hopewell, 6/22/84, A, C, 84002728

House at 379 West State Street, 379 W. State St., Trenton, 1/23/80, C, 80002501

Hunt Farmstead, 197 Blackwell Rd., Rosedale vicinity, 10/28/88, A, C, 87002555

In and Out Social Club, 714–716 S. Clinton Ave., Trenton, 3/26/87, A, C, 87000513

Jugtown Historic District, Nassau and Harrison Sts., Harrison St. N, and Evelyn Pl., Princeton Borough, 1/22/87, A, C, 86003670

Kingston Mill Historic District, Roughly bounded by Herrontown, River, Princeton-Kingston Rds., and lots W of Princeton Twp., Princeton, 4/10/86, A, B, C, 86000707

Kuser, Rudolph V., Estate, 315 W. State St., Trenton, 8/24/79, C, 79001501

Lake Carnegie Historic District, Roughly bounded by Lake Carnegie shoreline from Conrail bridge at W end to dam W of Kingston at E end, Princeton, 6/28/90, A, 90001000

Lawrence Township Historic District, Lawrenceville and vicinity N, including both sides of U.S. 206, Lawrenceville, 9/14/72, A, B, C, 72000799

Lawrenceville School, Main St., Lawrenceville, 2/24/86, C, NHL, 86000158

Leigh, Ichabod, House, Pennington-Rocky Hill Rd., Hopewell, 3/04/75, C, 75001139

Mansion House, Cadwalader Park, Trenton, 2/06/73, C, 73001112

Maybury Hill, 346 Snowden Lane, Princeton, 11/11/71, B, c, NHL, 71000502

Mercer Street Friends Center, 151 Mercer St., Trenton, 8/12/71, C, a, 71000505

Mill Hill Historic District, Roughly bounded by Clay, Jackson, Front, Market, Broad, and Greenwood Sts., Trenton, 12/12/77, A, C, 77000880

Morven, 55 Stockton St., Princeton, 1/25/71, A, B, C, c, NHL, 71000503

Mott School and Second Street School, Centre and 643–645 Second Sts., Trenton, 4/15/86, A, C, 86000809

Nassau Hall, Princeton University, Princeton University campus, Princeton, 10/15/66, A, C, e, NHL, 66000465

Old Barracks, S. Willow St., Trenton, 1/25/71, A, C, NHL, 71000506

Old Eagle Tavern, 431, 433 S. Broad St., Trenton, 11/03/72, A, C, 72000801

Old Ryan Farm, Federal City Rd., Trenton, 9/10/71, A, C, 71000507

Pennington Railroad Station, Corner of Franklin and Green Ave., Pennington, 12/31/74, A, 74001170

Penns Neck Baptist Church, US 1 at Princeton—Hightstown Rd., Penns Neck, 12/28/89, B, C, a, d, 89002160

Mercer County—Continued

Pennsylvania Railroad Bridge, Spans Delaware River, Trenton, 6/06/79, A, C, 79001502

Philadelphia and Reading Railroad Freight Station, 260 N. Willow St., Trenton, 5/14/79, A, C, 79001503

Phillips, Joseph, Farm, N of Titusville on Hunter Rd., Titusville vicinity, 5/02/77, A, C, 77000879

Pleasant Valley Historic District, Centered on jct. of Pleasant Valley Rd. with Woodens Ln. and Hunter Rd., Hopewell and West Amwell Twps., Lambertville vicinity, 6/14/91, A, C, D, 91000676

President's House, Nassau St., Princeton, 7/17/71, B, NHL, 71000504

Princeton Battlefield, Princeton Battlefield State Park, Princeton, 10/15/66, A, NHL, 66000466

Princeton Battlefield Historic District (Boundary Increase), Roughly Quaker Rd. from Stockton Rd. to Stony Brook, Princeton, 10/10/89, A, NHL, 89000761

Princeton Historic District, Irregular pattern between Lytle St. and Haslet Ave. from Lovers Lane to Olden Sts., Princeton, 6/27/75, A, B, C, d, 75001143

Prospect, Princeton University campus, Princeton, 2/04/85, B, C, NHL, 85002434

Rogers, John, House, S of Princeton on S. Post Rd., Princeton vicinity, 1/31/78, C, 78001770

Sloan, Samuel, House, 238 S. Main St., Hightstown, 3/28/74, C, 74001168

Smith—Ribsam House, 45 Pine Knoll Dr., Eldridge Park vicinity, 6/09/88, A, C, 88000722

Somerset Roller Mills, NJ 29, Titusville vicinity, 11/19/74, A, C, 74001171

St. Michael's Episcopal Church, 140 N. Warren St., Trenton, 4/29/82, A, C, a, 82003280

State House District, Roughly bounded by Capitol Plaza, Willow, State and Lafayette Sts., Trenton, 8/27/76, A, C, 76001161

State House Historic District (Boundary Increase), W. State St. S side, W of New Jersey State House, Trenton, 4/02/92, A, C, 92000295

Stokely-Van Camp Industrial Complex, Lalor Street at Stokely Ave., Trenton, 3/11/83, A, 83001603

Stout, Joseph, House, Province Line Rd., Hopewell vicinity, 10/29/74, A, 74001169

Titusville Historic District, River Dr., Titusville, 3/17/83, A, C, 83001604

Trent, William, House, 539 S. Warren St., Trenton, 4/15/70, C, NHL, 70000388

Trenton Battle Monument, Warren and Broad Sts., Trenton, 5/06/77, C, f, 77000881

Trenton City Hall, 309 State St., Trenton, 1/30/78, A, C, 78001771

Trenton City/Calhoun Street Bridge, Spans Delaware River between Morrisville, PA and Trenton, NJ, Trenton, 11/20/75, A, 75001621

Trenton Jewish Community Center Bath House and Day Camp, 999 Lower Ferry Rd., Ewing, 2/23/84, C, g, 84002730

Trenton and Mercer County War Memorial—Soldiers' and Sailors' Memorial Building, W. Lafayette St., Trenton, 12/11/86, A, C, f, 86003480

Tusculum, N of Princeton on Cherry Hill Rd., Princeton vicinity, 1/05/78, B, C, 78003171

Van Cleve, Col. John, Homestead, NW of Pennington on Poor Farm Rd., Pennington vicinity, 2/16/83, A, C, 83001605

Vandyke, Jeremiah, House, Featherbed Lane, Hopewell vicinity, 3/29/78, C, 78001769

Washington Crossing State Park, Between Yardley and New Hope, on the Delaware River, Yardley, vicinity, 10/15/66, A, B, NHL, 66000650

Watson, Isaac, House, 151 Westcott St., Trenton, 1/21/74, C, 74001173

Welling, John, House, Curlis Ave. at Birch St., Pennington, 3/14/73, C, e, 73001110

West Trenton Station [Operating Passenger Railroad Stations TR], Sullivan Way, West Trenton, 6/22/84, A, C, 84004031

White, John, House, 1 mi. N of Lawrenceville on Cold Soil Rd., Lawrenceville vicinity, 1/29/73, C, 73001108

Windsor Historic District, Roughly bounded by properties along Main St. and Church St., Windsor, 4/10/92, A, a, 88001710

Woolsey, Jeremiah, House, SW of Pennington on Washington Crossing Rd., Pennington vicinity, 1/27/75, B, C, 75001140

Middlesex County

Agnew, Thomas I., House, Memorial Pkwy., New Brunswick, 5/13/82, C, 82003281

Ayers-Allen House, 16 Durham Ave., Metuchen, 9/05/85, C, 85002002

Barron Library, 582 Rahway Ave., Woodbridge, 11/11/77, A, C, 77000886

Bishop, James, House, College Ave. near Bishop St., New Brunswick, 7/12/76, B, C, 76001162

Buccleuch Mansion, 200 College Ave., Buccleuch Park, New Brunswick, 4/13/77, B, C, 77000883

Cedar Grove School, E of Old Bridge on NJ 516, Old Bridge vicinity, 10/24/76, A, 76001165

Christ Episcopal Church, 5 Paterson St., New Brunswick, 7/28/89, C, a, 89000994

Cranbury Historic District, Off U.S. 130, Cranbury, 9/18/80, A, C, D, 80002502

Demarest House, 542 George St., New Brunswick, 8/10/77, B, C, 77000884

Dutch Reformed Church, 160 Neilson St., New Brunswick, 9/27/88, A, C, a, d, 88001703

Edison, Thomas A., Memorial Tower, Christie St., Edison, 11/30/79, C, f, g, 79001505

Ensley-Mount-Buckalew House, Buckalew Ave., Jamesburg, 9/12/79, B, C, 79001507

Fitz-Randolph, Ephraim, House, 430 S. Randolphville Rd., Piscataway, 3/14/73, C, 73001114

Guest, Henry, House, 58 Livingston Ave., New Brunswick, 5/24/76, B, C, b, 76001163

Gulick House, W of Monmouth Junction on Raymond Rd., Monmouth Junction vicinity, 7/03/79, A, C, 79001509

Helme, G. W., Snuff Mill District, Irregular pattern along Main St., Helmetta, 8/15/80, A, D, 80002503

Holmes-Tallman House, NW of Jamesburg at Cranbury and Brown's Corner Rds., Jamesburg vicinity, 9/12/79, C, 79001508

Inness, George, House, 313 Convery Blvd., Perth Amboy, 10/10/79, A, B, C, 79003250

Ivy Hall, 1225 River Rd., Piscataway, 5/27/71, C, 71000510

Jarrard, Levi D., House, George St., Douglass College campus, New Brunswick, 4/22/82, B, C, 82003282

Kearney, Edward S., House, NJ 18, East Brunswick, 4/06/79, A, C, 79001504

Kearny, Lawrence, House, 63 Catalpa St., Perth Amboy, 5/28/76, B, b, 76001166

King Block, 316–324 Memorial Pkwy., New Brunswick, 5/26/88, A, 88000644

Kingston Village Historic District, Roughly NJ 27 from Raymond Rd. to Delaware & Raritan Canal, Church St., Laurel Ave., Heathcote Brook Rd., & Academy St., Kingston, 1/11/90, A, C, a, d, 89002163

Laing House of Plainfield Plantation, 1707 Woodland Ave., Edison, 10/27/88, A, 88002124

Main Post Office, 86 Bayard St., New Brunswick, 7/18/84, A, B, C, 84002731

Metlar House, 1281 River Rd., Piscataway, 3/07/73, B, C, 73001115

Milltown India Rubber Company, 40 Washington Ave., Milltown, 2/13/86, A, C, 86000216

National Musical String Company, 120 Georges Rd., New Brunswick, 4/20/82, A, C, 82003283

New Brunswick Station [Operating Passenger Railroad Stations TR], Eaton Ave. and Albany St., New Brunswick, 6/22/84, A, C, 84002732

New Jersey Hall, 73 Hamilton St., New Brunswick, 2/24/75, A, 75001144

Old Bridge Historic District, NJ 18, East Brunswick, 6/29/77, A, B, 77000882

Old Cranbury School, 23 N. Main St., Cranbury, 6/21/71, A, C, 71000508

Old Queen's, Rutgers University, New Brunswick, 5/11/76, A, C, NHL, 76001164

Old School Baptist Church and Cemetery, 64–66 Main St., South River, 1/07/92, A, C, a, d, 91001926

Onderdonk, Isaac, House, 685 River Rd., Piscataway, 10/30/73, C, 73001116

Perth Amboy City Hall and Surveyor General's Office, 260 High St., Perth Amboy, 1/21/81, A, C, 81000394

Perth Amboy Ferry Slip, Smith St., Perth Amboy, 11/28/78, A, 78001773

Perth Amboy Station [Operating Passenger Railroad Stations TR], Between Smith and Market Sts., Perth Amboy, 6/22/84, A, C, 84002735

Proprietary House, 139–151 Kearny Ave., Perth Amboy, 2/24/71, B, C, 71000509

Queen's Campus, Rutgers University, Bounded by College Ave. and George, Hamilton, and Somerset Sts., New Brunswick, 7/02/73, A, C, 73001113

Raritan Landing Archeological District, Address Restricted, Highland Park vicinity, 8/10/79, A, D, 79001506

Middlesex County—Continued

Raritan Landing Archeological District (Boundary Increase), Address Restricted, Highland Park vicinity, 2/10/84, D, 84002738

Rutgers Preparatory School, 101 Somerset St., New Brunswick, 7/18/75, A, C, 75001145

Sayre and Fisher Reading Room, Main St. and River Rd., Sayreville, 9/12/79, A, C, 79001511

Shotwell, Benjamin, House, 26 Runyon's Ln., Edison, 6/04/87, A, C, 87000875

Simpson United Methodist Church, High and Jefferson Sts., Perth Amboy, 4/06/79, A, C, a, 79001510

Smock, Matthias, House, Off River Rd. (NJ 18), Piscataway, 12/04/73, C, 73001117

St. Peter's Episcopal Church, Rector and Gordon Sts., Perth Amboy, 5/12/77, A, a, 77000885

St. Peters Church and Buildings, Main St. and DeVoe Ave., Spotswood, 10/10/79, A, C, a, 79003251

White, Joseph and Minnie, House, 243 Hazelwood Ave., Middlesex, 10/28/88, B, C, 87001763

Withington Estate, Spruce Lane, Kingstown, 9/27/84, A, C, D, 84002740

Wood Lawn, Clifton Ave. and George St., New Brunswick, 3/08/78, B, C, 78001772

Monmouth County

ALEXANDER HAMILTON (steamship), Off NJ 36, Atlantic Highlands, 3/25/77, A, C, 77000887

All Saints' Memorial Church Complex, Navesink Ave. and Locust Rd., Navesink, 2/15/74, A, C, a, d, NHL, 74001179

Allaire Village, 3 mi. SE of Farmingdale on NJ 524, Farmingdale, 1/11/74, B, C, 74001174

Allen House, Broad St. and Sycamore Ave., Shrewsbury, 5/08/74, A, C, 74001180

Allenhurst Railroad Station, Main St., Allenhurst, 9/17/80, A, C, 80002504

Allentown Historic District, N. and S. Main Sts., Allentown, 6/14/82, A, C, 82003284

Allentown Mill, 42 S. Main St., Allentown, 2/14/78, A, 78001774

Allgor-Barkalow Homestead, New Bedford Rd., Asbury Park vicinity, 6/21/84, A, C, 84002748

Asbury Park Convention Hall, Ocean Ave., Asbury Park, 3/02/79, A, C, 79001512

Audenried Cottage [Spring Lake, NJ as a Coastal Resort MPS], 21 Tuttle Ave., Spring Lake, 3/08/91, A, C, b, 91000117

Bradley Beach Station [Operating Passenger Railroad Stations TR], Between LaReine and Brimley Aves., Bradley Beach, 6/22/84, A, C, 84002749

Burrowes, Maj. John, Mansion, 94 Main St., Matawan, 9/29/72, B, C, 72000803

Christ Church, 92 Kings Hwy., Middletown, 11/12/71, A, C, a, 71000511

Church of the Presidents, 1260 Ocean Ave., Long Branch, 11/07/76, A, B, a, 76001169

Coward—Smith House, Burlington Path Rd., Upper Freehold, 7/06/89, A, B, C, 89000804

Coward-Hendrickson House, Address Restricted, Cream Ridge vicinity, 3/21/85, A, C, 85000594

Fisk Chapel, Cedar Ave., Fair Haven, 10/29/75, A, a, b, 75001146

Fort Hancock and the Sandy Hook Proving Ground Historic District, NJ 36, Fort Hancock and vicinity, 4/24/80, A, g, NHL, NPS, 80002505

Fort Hancock, U.S. Life Saving Station, N of Highlands on Sandy Hook, Highlands vicinity, 11/30/81, A, C, g, NPS, 81000080

Fortune, T. Thomas, House, 94 W. Bergen Pl., Red Bank, 12/08/76, B, NHL, 76001171

Guggenheim, Murry, House, Cedar and Norwood Aves., West Long Branch, 3/28/78, C, 78001778

Hankinson-Moreau-Covenhoven House, 150 W. Main St., Freehold, 5/01/74, A, B, C, 74001175

Holmdel Dutch Reformed Church, 41 Main St., Holmdel, 10/22/80, A, C, a, 80002506

Holmes-Hendrickson House, N of Holmdel, Holmdel vicinity, 4/26/78, A, C, b, 78001776

Holy Trinity Episcopal Church [Spring Lake, NJ as a Coastal Resort MPS], Jct. of Monmouth and Third Aves., Spring Lake, 3/08/91, A, C, a, 91000116

Horn Antenna, Off Garden State Parkway in Crawford Hill Facility, Holmdel, 12/20/89, A, B, g, NHL, 89002457

House at 364 Cedar Avenue, 364 Cedar Ave., Long Branch, 11/01/79, A, 79001514

Imlaystown Historic District, Roughly Imlaystown-Davis Station Rd., and Imlaystown-Red Valley Rd., Upper Freehold Township, 1/03/85, A, 85000032

Jersey Homesteads Historic District, All that area within the corporate boundaries of the Borough of Roosevelt, Roosevelt, 12/05/83, A, B, C, g, 83004053

Kings Highway District, Irregular pattern—both sides of Kings Highway, S and W of NJ 35, Middletown, 5/03/74, A, C, a, 74001177

Kovenhoven, N of Holmdel off NJ 34, Holmdel vicinity, 4/26/74, B, 74001176

Little Silver Station [Operating Passenger Railroad Stations TR], Sycamore and Branch Aves., Little Silver, 6/22/84, A, C, 84002754

Longstreet Farm, N of Holmdel on Longstreet Rd., Holmdel vicinity, 11/29/79, A, C, b, 79003255

MacGregor-Tallman House, 407 Monmouth Rd., West Long Branch, 9/05/85, B, C, 85002003

Maloney, Martin, Cottage [Spring Lake, NJ as a Coastal Resort MPS], 101 Morris Ave., Spring Lake, 10/26/92, C, 91000115

Manasquan Friends Meetinghouse and Burying Ground, NJ 35 at Manasquan Cir., Wall Township, Manasquan, 7/22/92, A, a, 91000902

Matawan Station [Operating Passenger Railroad Stations TR], Between Main and Atlantic Aves., Matawan, 6/22/84, A, C, 84002756

Merino Hill House and Farm, Allentown—Clarksburg Rd., CR 524, Wrightsville vicinity, 2/11/88, A, B, C, d, 87002561

Monmouth Battlefield, NW of Freehold on NJ 522, W of Rte. 9, Freehold, 10/15/66, A, NHL, 66000467

Navesink Historic District, Roughly triangular area including both sides of Monmouth Ave.

and Locust Ave. to junction with Hillside and Grand Aves., Navesink, 9/05/75, A, 75001148

Ocean Grove Camp Meeting Association District, Bounded by Fletcher Lake, NJ 71, Lake Wesley, and the Ocean, Ocean Grove, 4/12/76, A, C, a, 76001170

Old Kentuck, NW of Holmdel off NJ 34 on Pleasant Valley Rd., Holmdel vicinity, 11/06/73, B, C, 73001118

Old Mill at Tinton Falls, 1205 Sycamore Ave., Tinton Falls, 4/24/73, A, 73001119

Reckless, Anthony, Estate, 164 Broad St., Red Bank, 6/03/82, B, C, b, 82003286

Red Bank Passenger Station, Ridge and Monmouth Sts., Red Bank, 5/28/76, A, C, 76001172

Salter's Mill, Imlaystown-Davis Station Rd., Imlaystown, 9/29/80, A, C, 80002507

Sandy Hook Light, Fort Hancock Military Reservation, Sandy Hook, 10/15/66, A, NHL, 66000468

Seabright Lawn Tennis and Cricket Club, Jct. of Rumson Rd. and Tennis Court Ln., Rumson, 7/09/91, A, C, NHL, 91000883

Seabrook-Wilson House, 119 Port Monmouth Rd., Middletown, 10/29/74, B, 74001178

Shadow Lawn, Cedar and Norwood Aves., West Long Branch, 3/28/78, C, NHL, 78001780

Shrewsbury Historic District, Broad and Sycamore Sts., Shrewsbury, 7/17/78, A, C, a, 78001779

Shrewsbury Township Hall, 51 Monmouth St., Red Bank, 12/08/80, A, C, a, 80002508

St. James Memorial Church of Eatontown, 69 Broad St., Eatontown, 2/17/78, C, a, 78001775

St. John's Episcopal Church, Little Silver Point Rd., Little Silver, 12/27/90, C, a, 90001374

Steinbach-Cookman Building, Cookman Ave., Asbury Park, 7/08/82, A, C, 82003285

Tinton Falls Historic District, Irregular pattern along Tinton and Sycamore Aves., Tinton Falls, 11/10/77, B, C, D, 77000888

Twin Lights, S of NJ 36 on a promontory between the Navesink River and Sandy Hook Bay, Highlands, 12/02/70, A, C, 70000389

Union Schoolhouse, W of Red Bank on Middletown-Lincroft Rd., Red Bank vicinity, 6/23/76, A, 76001173

Upper Freehold Baptist Meeting, E of Imlaystown on Red Valley Rd., Imlaystown vicinity, 4/21/75, A, a, 75001147

Upper Meeting House of the Baptist Church of Middletown, 40 Main St., Holmdel, 12/07/90, C, a, d, 87002573

Village Inn, Water and Main Sts., Englishtown, 11/13/72, B, C, 72000802

Walker—Combs—Hartshorne Farmstead, 189 Wemrock Rd., Freehold, 10/04/90, A, C, 90001474

Walnford, S of Allentown off CR 539, Allentown vicinity, 6/29/76, A, 76001167

Wardell House, 419 Sycamore Ave., Shrewsbury, 7/24/74, A, C, 74001181

Water Witch Club Casino, Jct. of E. Twin Rd. and W. Twin Rd., Highlands, 8/13/90, A, C, 90001219

Monmouth County—Continued

Winsor Building, 400-420 Main St. and 715-131 Bangs Ave, Asbury Park, 9/13/79, C, 79001513

Wurts, George, Summer Home, 306 Eighth Ave., Asbury Park, 12/28/89, B, C, 89002162

Morris County

Acorn Hall, 68 Morris Ave., Morristown, 4/03/73, C, 73001124

Alnwick Hall, 355 Madison Ave., Morris Township, 4/11/85, B, C, 85000783

Anthony—Corwin Farm [Stone Houses and Outbuildings in Washington Township MPS], 244 W. Mill Rd., Washington Township, Long Valley vicinity, 5/01/92, C, 92000371

Baker Building, 16 W. Blackwell St. S4703, Dover, 7/01/81, A, C, 81000396

Berry, Martin, House, 581 NJ 23 at Jackson Ave., Pompton Plains, 6/19/73, A, C, 73001129

Blackwell Street Historic District, Blackwell and Sussex Sts., Dover, 5/21/82, A, C, a, 82003287

Boisaubin Manor, SE of Morristown on Treadwell Ave., Morristown vicinity, 10/22/76, B, C, 76001175

Boonton Historic District, Main, Church, Birch, Cornelia and Cedar Sts., Boonton, 9/29/80, C, 80002509

Boonton Public Library, 619 Main St., Boonton, 11/13/72, A, B, 72000804

Bower, David S., House, 427 Main St., Chatham, 11/30/82, C, 82001045

Bowers-Livingston-Osborn House, 25 Parsippany Rd., Parsippany, 6/19/73, B, C, 73001128

Bowlsby-Degelleke House, NW of Parsippany at 320 Baldwin Rd., Parsippany vicinity, 12/15/78, A, C, 78001784

Boyle/Hudspeth-Benson House, 100 Basking Ridge Rd., Millington, 2/10/75, B, C, 75001151

Carey, Lewis, Farmhouse, 208 Emmans Rd., Flanders vicinity, 7/20/77, A, C, 77000893

Cary Station, 239 Emmans Rd., Ledgewood, 9/05/85, A, B, C, D, 85002005

Cary, Stephen, House, Mountainside Rd., Mendham vicinity, 7/27/89, C, 89000995

Chester House Inn, Main St. and Hillside Rd., Chester, 7/18/74, A, C, 74001183

Condict, Dr. Lewis, House, 51 South St., Morristown, 4/03/73, B, C, 73001125

Condit, Stephen, House, NE of Parsippany on Beverwyck Rd. off U.S. 46, Parsippany vicinity, 2/15/74, A, C, 74001187

Cook, Ellis, House, 174 Mount Pleasant Ave., East Hanover, 5/12/75, B, C, 75001149

Cooper, Gen. Nathan, Mansion, W of Mendham on NJ 24, Mendham vicinity, 12/29/78, B, C, 78001781

Cooper, Nathan, Gristmill, W of Chester at Hacklebarney Rd. and NJ 24, Chester vicinity, 11/21/76, A, 76001174

Craft—Clausen House [Stone Houses and Outbuildings in Washington Township MPS], 170

Fairmont Rd., Washington Township, Long Valley vicinity, 5/01/92, C, 92000372

Craftsman Farms, Jct. of NJ 10 and Manor Ln., Parsippany, 4/10/89, A, B, C, NHL, 85003730

Cutler Homestead, 21 Cutler St., Morristown, 3/10/75, B, C, 75001152

Davenport—Demarest House [Dutch Stone Houses in Montville MPS], 140 Changebridge Rd., Montville, 1/17/92, C, 91001934

Delaware Lackawanna and Western Railroad Station, 132 Morris St., Morristown, 3/11/80, A, C, 80002514

Delaware, Lackawanna and Western Railroad Station, Myrtle Ave., Main, and Division Sts., Boonton, 7/13/77, A, C, 77000889

Delaware, Lackawanna and Western Railroad Station, N. Dickerson St., Dover, 5/23/80, A, C, 80002511

Dixon, James, Farm, NW of Boonton on Rockaway Valley Rd., Boonton vicinity, 8/29/77, A, 77000890

Dod, John, House and Tavern, 11 Highland St. and 8 Chapel Hill Rd., Lincoln Park, 8/12/77, A, 77000895

Doremus House [Dutch Stone Houses in Montville MPS], 490 Main Rd., Towaco, 10/31/72, C, 72000805

Dusenberry House, 186 Main St, Chatham, 11/01/79, A, B, a, 79001515

First Congregational Church, Hillside Rd., Chester, 8/10/77, A, C, a, 77000892

First Presbyterian Church of Hanover, W of Livingston at Mount Pleasant and Hanover Aves., Livingston vicinity, 11/10/77, A, C, a, 77000896

Flock—Stephens Farmstead [Stone Houses and Outbuildings in Washington Township MPS], 244 Flocktown Rd., Washington Township, Long Valley vicinity, 5/01/92, C, 92000373

Flocktown Schoolhouse, Flocktown and Naughright Rds., Long Valley vicinity, 11/30/82, A, C, b, 82001046

Ford, Samuel, Jr.'s, Hammock Farm, 310 Columbia Tpke., Florham Park, 12/23/74, B, 74001185

Ford-Faesch House, N of Dover at Mt. Hope Rd. and Mt. Hope Ave., Dover vicinity, 2/12/74, A, 74001184

Fordville, E of Morristown at 30 Ford Hill Rd., Morristown vicinity, 11/02/78, A, C, 78001782

Fosterfields (Boundary Increase), Jct. of Mendham and Kahdena Rds., Morris Township, Morristown, 10/09/91, A, 91000478

Fredericks House, 6 Duchess Dr., Fayson Lakes, 10/18/79, A, 79003254

Friends Meetinghouse, S of Dover at Quaker Ave. and Quaker Church Rd., off NJ 18, Dover vicinity, 6/04/73, A, C, a, b, 73001121

German Valley Historic District, NJ 24, Fairmount and Fairview Rds., Chester vicinity, 7/14/83, A, C, 83001606

Gibbons Mansion, 36 Madison Ave., Madison, 8/10/77, B, C, a, 77000897

Glanville Blacksmith Shop [Morristown MRA], 47 Bank St., Morristown, 3/25/87, C, 86003112

Glynallen, Canfield Rd., Morristown vicinity, 3/09/87, B, C, 87000354

Grimes Homestead, 45 Bloomfield Ave., Mountain Lakes, 4/01/77, B, 77000900

Hancock, Rev. John, House, Cider Mill and Cemetery, 45 Ridgedale Ave., Florham Park, 8/30/84, A, C, 84002761

Hanover Village Historic District, Area surrounding Hanover Rd. and Mount Pleasant Ave., East Hanover Township, East Hanover, 9/13/93, A, B, C, 93000901

Hartley Farms, Jct. of Spring Valley and Blue Mill Rds., Harding Twp., Morristown vicinity, 7/19/91, A, B, 91000888

Howell, Benjamin, Homestead, 709 S. Beverwyck Rd., Parsippany vicinity, 10/19/78, A, B, C, 78001786

Jackson, Joseph, House, 82 E. Main St., Rockaway Borough, 3/04/75, B, 75001155

Kemble, Peter, House, Old Camp Rd. and Mount Kemble Ave., Chatham vicinity, 8/26/80, B, b, 80002510

Lindenwold [Morristown MRA], 247 South St., Morristown, 11/13/86, C, 86003113

Little Red Schoolhouse, 203 Ridgedale Ave., Florham Park, 6/06/86, A, C, b, 73001122

Low, Effingham, House [Dutch Stone Houses in Montville MPS], 102 Hook Mountain Rd., Montville Township, Pinebrook, 1/17/92, C, 91001930

Madison Civic Commercial District, Roughly Main St., Waverly Pl., Lincoln Pl., Prospect St., Kings Rd., Green Ave., Wilmer St., and Green Village Rd., Madison, 10/18/91, A, C, 89002115

Madison Public Library and the James Building, Main St. and Green Village Rd., Madison, 2/08/80, A, C, 80002512

Madison Station [Operating Passenger Railroad Stations TR], Kings Rd., Madison, 6/22/84, A, C, 84002764

Mendham Historic District, Roughly bounded by Halstead St. and Country Ln. on W. and E. Main St., Mountain Ave., Hilltop Rd. and Prospect St., Mendham Borough, 4/18/85, A, C, 85000865

Merchiston Farm, Longview Rd., Chester, 11/13/89, B, C, 89001946

Middle Valley Historic District, Along W. Mill Rd. and Middle Valley Rd. S of Beacon Rd., Long Valley vicinity, 9/25/90, A, C, 89002353

Miller-Kingsland House, Vreeland Ave., 900 ft. W of Montville Township boundary, Boonton, 7/24/73, A, C, 73001120

Millington Station [Operating Passenger Railroad Stations TR], Long Hill Rd., Millington, 6/22/84, C, 84002767

Mills, Timothy, House, 27 Mills St., Morristown, 2/24/75, C, 75001153

Morris County Courthouse, Washington St. between Court St. and Western Ave., Morristown, 8/19/77, A, C, 77000898

Morris Plains Station [Operating Passenger Railroad Stations TR], Speedwell Ave., Morris Plains, 6/22/84, A, C, 84002780

Morristown District, Roughly bounded by the cemetery, King Pl., Madison and Colles Aves., DeHart St., and N. Park Pl., Morristown, 10/30/73, A, B, C, 73001126

Morris County—Continued

Morristown Historic District (Boundary Increase) [Morristown MRA], Irregularly bounded by Lackawanna, Franklin Pl., James, Ogden Pl., Doughty, Mt. Kemble, Western, and Speedwell, Morristown, 11/13/86, C, 86003109

Morristown National Historical Park, At jct. of U.S. 202 and NJ 24, Morristown, 10/15/66, A, B, C, D, NPS, 66000053

Mott Hollow, Roughly, Gristmill Rd. from Millbrook Ave. to Zandep Ln. and adjacent area along Millbrook, Randolph Township, Millbrook vicinity, 8/31/92, A, 92001085

Mount Arlington Historic District, Howard Blvd., Edgemere and Windemere Aves., Mount Arlington, 8/26/83, C, 83001607

Mount Freedom Presbyterian Church, Jct. of Sussex Tpk. and Church Rd., Randolph Township, Mount Freedom, 10/11/91, A, C, a, b, 91001484

Mount Kemble Home [Morristown MRA], 1 Mt. Kemble Ave., Morristown, 11/13/86, C, 86003115

Nast, Thomas, Home, MacCulloch Ave. and Miller Rd., Morristown, 10/15/66, B, NHL, 66000470

Neighbor, Jacob Wise (J. W.), House, 143 W. Mill Rd., Washington Township, Long Valley vicinity, 2/22/91, C, 91000111

Neighbor, Leonard, Farmstead [Stone Houses and Outbuildings in Washington Township MPS], 177 W. Mill Rd., Washington Township, Long Valley vicinity, 5/01/92, C, 92000374

New Vernon Historic District, Lee's Hill, Village, Mill Brook and Glen Alpin Rds., Harding, 7/08/82, A, C, 82003288

Oak Dell [Morristown MRA], Franklin St. and Madison Ave., Morristown, 11/13/86, C, 86003114

Our Lady of Mercy Chapel, 100 Whippany Rd., Whippany, 9/18/78, A, C, a, 78001785

Parlaman, Johannes, House [Dutch Stone Houses in Montville MPS], 15 Vreeland Ave., Montville, 1/17/92, C, 91001933

Parsonage of the Montville Reformed Dutch Church [Dutch Stone Houses in Montville MPS], 107 Changebridge Rd., Montville, 1/17/92, C, a, 91001931

Ralston Historic District, 1 mi. W of Mendham at NJ 24 and Roxiticus Rd., Mendham vicinity, 2/20/75, A, C, 75001150

Rarick—Kellihan House [Stone Houses and Outbuildings in Washington Township MPS], 358 Fairview Ave., Washington Township, Long Valley vicinity, 5/01/92, C, 92000375

Revere, Joseph W., House, NW of Morristown on Mendham Ave., Morristown vicinity, 9/20/73, B, C, 73001127

Riggs, Silas, House, 217 Main St., Ledgewood, 11/11/77, B, C, b, 77000894

Ringling, Alfred T., Manor, S of Oak Ridge on Berkshire Valley Rd., Oak Ridge vicinity, 6/03/76, B, 76001177

Rockaway Valley Methodist Church, NW of Boonton, Boonton vicinity, 11/11/77, A, a, d, 77000891

Sayre House, 31 Ridgedale Ave., Madison, 2/12/80, A, C, 80002513

Schooley's Mountain Historic District, Roughly along Schooley's Mt. Rd., Pleasant Grove Rd. and Flocktown Rd., Washington Twp., Schooley's Mountain, 6/14/91, A, B, C, a, 91000677

Sharpenstine Farmstead [Stone Houses and Outbuildings in Washington Township MPS], 98 E. Mill Rd., Washington Township, Long Valley vicinity, 5/01/92, C, 92000376

Slater's Mill, 96 Paterson-Hamburg Tpke., Riverdale, 6/18/75, A, 75001154

Smith, John, House, Washington Valley Rd., Morristown, 1/01/76, B, C, 76001176

Speedwell Village—The Factory, 333 Speedwell Ave., Morristown, 9/13/74, B, NHL, 74001186

Split Rock Furnace, NW of Boonton, Boonton vicinity, 11/06/74, A, 74001182

Spring Brook House [Morristown MRA], 167 James St., Morristown, 11/13/86, B, C, a, 86003111

Thompson, David, House, 56 W. Main St., Mendham, 7/24/73, B, C, 73001123

Thorne and Eddy Estates, E of Morristown on Columbia Rd., Morristown vicinity, 12/14/78, B, C, 78001783

Trimmer—Dufford Farmstead [Stone Houses and Outbuildings in Washington Township MPS], 186 W. Mill Rd., Washington Township, Long Valley vicinity, 5/01/92, C, 92000377

Tuttle House, 341 NJ 10, Whippany, 10/05/77, C, 77000901

Tuttle, David, Cooperage, 83 Gristmill Rd., Dover vicinity, 6/19/79, A, 79001516

Van Duyne, James, Farm House, 32 Waughaw Rd., Towaco vicinity, 4/15/82, A, B, d, 82003289

Van Duyne, Martin, House [Dutch Stone Houses in Montville MPS], 292 Main Rd., Montville, 1/17/92, C, 91001935

Van Duyne, Simon, House [Dutch Stone Houses in Montville MPS], 58 Maple Ave., Montville Township, Pinebrook, 1/17/92, C, 91001932

Van Duyne—Jacobus House [Dutch Stone Houses in Montville MPS], 29 Changebridge Rd., Montville, 1/17/92, C, 91001929

Washington Valley Historic District, Roughly bounded by Schoolhouse, Gaston, Sussex, Kahdena, Mendham, Tingley and Washington Valley, Morristown vicinity, 11/12/92, A, B, C, a, 92001583

Washington Valley Schoolhouse, Washington Valley Rd. and Schoolhouse Lane, Washington Valley, 10/15/73, A, 73001130

Whippany Farm, 53 E. Hanover Ave., Morristown vicinity, 9/22/77, B, C, 77000899

Ocean County

Barnegat Light Public School, 501 Central Ave., Barnegat Light, 6/07/76, A, 76001178

Barnegat Lighthouse, N end of Long Beach Island, off Broadway Ave., Barnegat Light, 1/25/71, A, C, 71000512

Beach Haven Historic District [Beach Haven MRA], Roughly bounded by Bay and Atlantic Aves., Pearl and 3rd Sts., Beach Haven, 7/14/83, C, 83001608

Birdsall, Capt. Amos , House [Old Village of Toms River MRA], 234 Washington St., Toms River, 5/13/82, B, 82003298

Brant, A.A., House [Old Village of Toms River MRA], 9 Allen St., Toms River, 5/13/82, C, 82003294

Cassville Crossroads Historic District [Cassville MRA], Jct. of CR 571 and 528, Jackson Township, 8/26/82, A, C, a, 82003291

Converse Cottage [Beach Haven MRA], 504 Atlantic Ave., Beach Haven, 7/14/83, C, 83001609

Crawford House [Old Village of Toms River MRA], 46 E. Water St., Toms River, 5/13/82, A, C, 82003295

Double Trouble Historic District, S of Beachwood off Garden State Pkwy., Beachwood vicinity, 2/23/78, A, 78001787

Falkinburg Farmstead, 28 Westcott Ave., Ocean Township, Waretown, 8/12/93, A, C, 93000829

Georgian Court, Lakewood Ave., Lakewood, 12/20/78, C, a, NHL, 78001788

Giberson, Capt. George W., House [Old Village of Toms River MRA], 54 E. Water St., Toms River, 8/12/82, B, 82004693

Hangar No. 1, Lakehurst Naval Air Station, N of Lakehurst on CR 547, Manchester Township, 5/23/68, A, NHL, 68000031

Horner House [Old Village of Toms River MRA], 44 E. Water St., Toms River, 5/13/82, A, C, 82003296

Island Heights Historic District, Roughly bounded by Toms River, Summit and River Aves., Island Heights, 7/08/82, A, C, a, 82003290

Manahawkin Baptist Church, N. Main St. (US 9) and Lehigh Ave., Manahawkin, 4/03/73, A, C, a, 73001131

Ocean County Courthouse [Old Village of Toms River MRA], Washington St., Toms River, 8/16/83, C, 83001610

Ocean County Jail [Old Village of Toms River MRA], Sheriff St., Toms River, 8/16/83, A, C, 83001611

Orient Baptist Church, NJ 88, Laurelton, 8/10/77, A, C, a, 77000902

Stewart House [Old Village of Toms River MRA], 57 E. Water St., Toms River, 5/13/82, A, 82003297

Stoutenburgh-Minturn House [Old Village of Toms River MRA], 86 E. Water St., Toms River, 5/13/82, A, B, 82003293

Strand Theatre, 400 Clifton Ave., Lakewood, 4/22/82, A, C, 82003292

U.S. Life Saving Station Station No. 14, S of Seaside Park on Island Beach State Park, Seaside Park vicinity, 1/30/78, A, C, 78001789

Williams, Dr. Edward H., House [Beach Haven MRA], 506 S. Atlantic Ave., Beach Haven, 7/14/83, C, 83001612

Passaic County

Ailsa Farms, 300 Pompton Rd., Wayne, 4/30/76, A, C, 76001181

Passaic County—Continued

Aycrigg Mansion, Main Ave. and Temple Pl., City of Passaic, 4/29/82, A, C, 82003299

Belle Vista, Valley Rd. in Garret Mountain Reservation, Paterson, 6/03/76, A, C, 76001180

Botany Worsted Mills Historic District, 80–82 and 90 Dayton Ave. and 6–32 Mattimore St., Passaic, 7/26/91, A, C, 91000928

Botto, Pietro, House, 83 Norwood St., Haledon, 7/30/74, A, NHL, 74001188

Cathedral of St. John the Baptist, Main and Grand Sts., Paterson, 12/16/77, A, C, a, 77000903

Clinton Furnace, Off NJ 23 at Clinton Reservoir, Newfoundland vicinity, 6/18/76, A, 76001179

Cooke, Frederick William, Residence, 384 Broadway, Paterson, 7/08/82, B, C, 82003302

Danforth Memorial Library, 250 Broadway, Paterson, 3/01/84, A, C, 84002782

Dey Mansion, 199 Totowa Rd., Wayne, 12/18/70, B, C, 70000392

Ferguson, John W., House, 421 12th Ave., Paterson, 5/23/80, B, C, 80002516

Great Falls of Paterson/S.U.M. Historic District, At Passaic River, Paterson, 4/17/70, A, C, NHL, 70000391

Great Falls of the Passaic and Society for Useful Manufactures Historic District (Boundary Increase), 6 Mill St., Paterson, 8/14/86, A, 86001507

Kossuth Street School, 47 Kossuth St., Haledon, 4/10/80, A, C, 80002515

Long Pond Ironworks, NE of West Milford on NJ 511, West Milford vicinity, 1/11/74, A, 74001189

Public School Number Two, Mill and Passaic Sts., Paterson, 3/08/78, A, C, 78001790

Ringwood Manor, 3 mi. E of Hewitt, Ringwood Manor State Park, Ringwood Borough, 11/13/66, A, D, NHL, 66000471

Schuyler-Colfax House, 2343 Paterson Hamburg Tpke., Wayne, 4/03/73, C, 73001133

Skylands, Ringwood State Park, Ringwood, 9/28/90, C, 90001438

Speer, Reynier, House, 612 Upper Mountain Ave., Little Falls, 7/18/85, C, 85001566

St. John's Evangelical Lutheran Church, 140 Lexington Ave., Passaic, 5/07/82, A, C, a, 82003301

St. Michael's Roman Catholic Church, 74 Cianci St., Paterson, 12/15/78, A, C, a, 78001791

St. Nicholas Roman Catholic Church, Washington, State and Ann Sts., Passaic, 5/14/79, A, C, a, 79001517

Thompson, Daniel, and Ryle, John, Houses, 8 and 9 Mill St., Paterson, 7/30/81, A, C, 81000398

U.S. Animal Quarantine Station, Clifton Ave., Clifton, 10/09/81, A, g, 81000397

Van Riper-Hopper House, 533 Berdan Ave., Wayne vicinity, 8/21/72, A, C, 72000806

Vreeland, John and Anna, House, 971 Valley Rd., Clifton, 5/13/82, A, C, 82003300

Westside Park, 114 Totowa Ave., Paterson, 3/07/73, C, 73001132

Salem County

Brick, Richard, House, NE of Salem off NJ 45 on Compromise Rd., Salem vicinity, 5/13/76, B, C, 76001183

Broadway Historic District, Broadway from Front to Yorke Sts., Salem, 3/05/92, A, C, a, d, 92000098

Dickinson House, NE of Alloway on Brickyard Rd., Alloway vicinity, 2/20/75, C, 75001156

Dunn, Zaccheus, House, S of Woodstown on East Lake Rd., Woodstown vicinity, 8/10/77, A, B, C, 77000905

Finn's Point Rear Range Light, NW of Salem at Fort Mott and Lighthouse Rds., Salem vicinity, 8/30/78, C, 78001792

Fort Mott and Finns Point National Cemetery District, NW of Salem on Fort Mott Rd., Salem vicinity, 8/31/78, A, C, d, 78001793

Fries, Philip, House, Cohansey—Daretown Rd. N of Alloway—Friesburg Rd., Alloway Twnshp., Friesburg, 9/28/90, C, 90001451

Hancock House, Rte. 49 and Front St., Lower Alloways Creek Township, 12/18/70, A, C, 70000393

Holmes, Benjamin, House, W of Salem on Fort Elfsborg-Hancock's Bridge Rd., Salem vicinity, 8/31/78, B, C, 78001794

Market Street Historic District, Irregular pattern on both sides of Market St. from Broadway to Fenwick Creek, Salem, 4/10/75, A, C, a, 75001157

Nicholson, Sarah and Samuel, House, 2 mi. S of Salem on Amwellbury Rd., Salem vicinity, 2/24/75, B, C, 75001158

Pittsgrove Presbyterian Church, Main St., Daretown, 9/19/77, A, B, C, a, 77000904

Seven Stars Tavern, N of Woodstown at jct. of Sharptown-Swedesboro and Woodstown-Auburn Rds., Woodstown vicinity, 5/17/76, A, C, 76001184

Shinn, Joseph, House, 68 N. Main St., Woodstown, 3/07/79, B, C, 79001518

Smith, David V., House, 104 S. Main St., Elmer, 5/17/76, B, C, 76001182

Ware, Joseph, House, 134 Poplar St., Hancock's Bridge vicinity, 1/26/90, A, B, C, 89002418

Somerset County

Alward Farmhouse, 40 Mt. Airy Rd., Basking Ridge, 3/13/86, B, C, 86000388

Basking Ridge Classical School, 15 W. Oak St., Basking Ridge, 7/21/76, B, a, 76001185

Bernardsville Station [Operating Passenger Railroad Stations TR], US 202, Bernardsville, 6/22/84, A, C, 84002786

Blawenburg Historic District, Georgetown—Franklin Tpk./CR 588, Great Rd./CR 601, and Mountain View Rd., Blawenburg, 12/07/90, A, C, a, b, d, 88000632

Bound Brook Station [Operating Passenger Railroad Stations TR], E. Main St., Bound Brook, 6/22/84, A, C, 84002787

Bridgepoint Historic District, N of Rocky Hill off U.S. 206, Rocky Hill vicinity, 6/10/75, A, C, 75001161

Cat Tail Brook Bridge, NW of Rocky Hill on Montgomery Rd, Rocky Hill vicinity, 8/01/79, A, 79001520

Coffee House, 214 N. Maple Ave., Basking Ridge, 11/07/77, A, 77000906

East Millstone Historic District, Amwell Rd. and Delaware & Raritan Canal, East Millstone, 3/17/83, A, C, a, d, 83001613

Elmendorf House, 1246 Millstone River Rd., Hillsborough Township, Millstone vicinity, 4/16/92, C, 92000378

Far Hills Station [Operating Passenger Railroad Stations TR], US 202, Far Hills, 6/22/84, A, C, 84002789

Franklin Corners Historic District, N of Bernardsville on Hardscrabble and Childs Rds. and U.S. 202, Bernardsville vicinity, 5/12/75, A, C, 75001159

Frelinghuysen, Gen. John, House, Somerset St. and Wyckoff Ave., Raritan, 3/04/71, C, 71000513

Gladstone Station [Operating Passenger Railroad Stations TR], Main St., Gladstone, 6/22/84, A, C, 84002792

Griggstown Historic District, Roughly Canal Rd. from Old Georgetown Rd. to Ten Mile Run, Griggstown, 8/02/84, A, C, 84002798

Huff House and Farmstead, River Rd. at S branch of Raritan River, Flagtown vicinity, 11/07/76, A, B, 76001186

Kirch—Ford House, 1 Reinman Rd., Warrenville vicinity, 10/20/88, A, C, 88002033

Lamington Historic District, Lamington, Black River, Rattlesnake Bridge, and Cowperthwaite Rds., Lamington, 6/21/84, A, C, a, 84002802

Liberty Corner Historic District, Roughly, jct. of Church St. and Valley and Lyons Rds., and area W and SW, Bernards Township, Liberty Corner, 10/11/91, A, C, 91001477

Linn, Alexander and James, Homestead, Rt. 202/Mine Brook Rd., between Sunnybranch Rd. and Lake Rd., Far Hills, 10/27/88, B, C, 88002057

Lyons Station [Operating Passenger Railroad Stations TR], Lyons Rd., Lyons, 6/22/84, A, C, 84002805

McDonald's—Kline's Mill, Address Restricted, Bedminster vicinity, 3/09/87, A, C, D, 87000410

Meadows, The, 1289 Easton Ave., Franklin, 12/04/73, A, C, 73001134

Middlebrook Encampment Site, Address Restricted, Bound Brook vicinity, 7/03/75, A, D, 75001160

Millstone Historic District, Amwell and River Rds., Millstone, 9/13/76, A, 76001188

Millstone Valley Agricultural District, S of Millstone on River Rd., Millstone vicinity, 8/10/77, A, 77000907

Mount Bethel Baptist Meetinghouse, About 2 mi. N of Martinsville off U.S. 78, Martinsville vicinity, 6/03/76, A, C, a, 76001187

Neshanic Historic District, Amwell and Zion Rds, Neshanic, 8/01/79, A, a, 79001519

Neshanic Mills, Main Rd. and Mill Lane, Neshanic, 1/09/78, A, C, 78001797

Old Dutch Parsonage, 65 Washington Pl., Somerville, 1/25/71, A, a, 71000514

Parker, John, Tavern, 2 Morristown Rd., Bernardsville, 12/14/78, A, 78001796

Somerset County—Continued

Pluckemin Village Historic District, US 206 and Burnt Mills Rd., Bedminster, 7/26/82, A, C, 82003303

Presbyterian Church in Basking Ridge, 6 E. Oak St., Basking Ridge, 12/31/74, A, C, a, 74001190

Raritan Bridge [Metal Truss Bridges in Somerset County MPS], Nevius St. over Raritan R., Bridgewater and Hillsborough Townships, Raritan, 11/12/92, C, 92001526

Raritan Station [Operating Passenger Railroad Stations TR], Anderson and Thompson Sts., Raritan, 6/22/84, A, C, 84002824

Reformed Dutch Church of Blawenburg, 424 CR 518, Blawenburg, 9/05/85, A, C, a, 85002004

Reynolds—Scherman House, 71 Hardscrabble Rd., Bernardsville, 4/29/89, A, B, C, 89000298

River Road Historic Rural District, Millstone River Rd. from Hillsborough Rd. to Van Horne Rd., Hillsborough and Montgomery Townships, Griggstown vicinity, 3/21/91, A, C, d, 91000256

Rockingham, E of Kingston on Old Rocky Hill Rd. (518), Franklin Township, 12/18/70, A, B, C, b, 70000394

Rocky Hill Historic District, Washington, Montgomery, and Princeton Aves., Rocky Hill, 7/08/82, A, C, D, 82003304

Smalley-Wormser House, W of Plainfield at 84 Mountain Ave., Plainfield vicinity, 10/19/78, B, C, 78001798

Somerset Courthouse Green, Roughly E. Main St. from Grove St. to N. Bridge St., Somerville, 9/07/89, A, C, a, 89001216

South Branch Historic District, SW of Raritan, Raritan vicinity, 12/13/77, A, C, 77000908

Stirling, Lord, Manor Site, SE of Basking Ridge at 96 Lord Stirling Rd., Basking Ridge vicinity, 5/22/78, B, D, 78001795

Van Veghten House, S of Somerville off NJ 28, Somerville vicinity, 10/10/79, A, C, 79003253

Vosseller's—Castner's—Allen's Tavern, 664 Foothill Rd., Bridgewater, 1/23/86, C, 86000133

Wallace House, 38 Washington Pl., Somerville, 12/02/70, B, C, 70000395

Washington Park Historic District, Roughly bounded by Green Brook Rd., Grove Ave., E. Front St., and Geraud Ave., North Plainfield, 4/09/87, A, C, 87000603

Sussex County

Bethany Chapel, 103 Hamburg Tpke., Hamburg, 2/29/80, A, C, a, 80002517

First Presbyterian Church of Wantage, N of Sussex on NJ 23, Sussex vicinity, 9/23/82, A, C, a, 82003305

Foster-Armstrong House, N of Branchville on River Rd., Branchville vicinity, 7/23/79, A, C, NPS, 79000235

Gunn, Cornelius, House, SW of Wallpack Center on Ridge Rd., Wallpack Center vicinity, 7/23/79, C, NPS, 79000238

Harmony Hill United Methodist Church, N of Stillwater on Fairview Lake Rd., Stillwater vicinity, 9/19/77, A, a, 77000913

High Breeze Farm, Barrett Rd. off NJ 94, Highland Lakes vicinity, 7/27/89, A, C, 89000993

Hill Memorial, 82 Main St., Newton, 7/18/85, A, C, 85001565

Lawrence Mansion, W of Hamburg on NJ 94, Hamburg vicinity, 11/02/79, B, C, 79001522

Layton, Richard, House, SW of Wallpack Center on Ridge Rd., Wallpack Center vicinity, 7/23/79, C, NPS, 79000237

Log Cabin and Farm, N of Branchville on Mattison Ave., Branchville vicinity, 8/24/77, C, 77000910

Meadowburn Farm, Address Restricted, Vernon vicinity, 8/09/93, B, C, 93000748

Merriam, Henry W., House, 131 Main St., Newton, 12/18/70, A, C, 70000396

Millville Historic and Archaeological District, Address Restricted, Millville vicinity, 1/30/84, A, D, NPS, 84002807

Minisink Archeological Site, Address Restricted, Millbrook, vicinity, 4/19/93, D, NHL, NPS, 93000608

Newton Town Plot Historic District, Roughly, Church St., Park Pl. and Spring St. from Main St. to High St. and Main and High from Church to Spring, Newton, 11/12/92, A, B, C, a, b, d, 92001521

Old Mine Road Historic District, NJ 521, Delaware, Old Mine, and River Rds., Wallpack Center vicinity, 12/03/80, A, C, NPS, 80000410

Old Monroe School House, NJ 94, Monroe, 8/12/77, A, 77000911

Peters Valley Historic District, Sandyston-Haney's Mill, Walpack, and Kuhn Rds., Wallpack Center vicinity, 2/29/80, A, C, a, NPS, 80000437

Plaster Mill, Off Main St. and Kelly Pl., Stanhope, 8/03/77, A, 77000912

Shoemaker-Houck Farm, S of Wallpack Center on Heney's Mill-Wallpack Center Rd., Wallpack Center vicinity, 7/23/79, C, NPS, 79000234

Snable, Andrew, House, NE of Wallpack Center on Sandyston-Haney's Mill Rd., Wallpack Center vicinity, 7/23/79, A, C, NPS, 79000236

Sterling Hill Mine, 30 Plant St., Ogdensburg, 9/03/91, A, 91001365

Stockholm United Methodist Church, CR 515, Stockholm, 3/26/76, A, a, 76001189

Sussex County Courthouse, High and Spring Sts., Newton, 7/23/79, A, C, 79001523

Van Bunschooten, Elias, House, NW of Sussex on NJ 23, Sussex vicinity, 11/01/74, A, a, 74001191

Wallpack Center Historic District, Wallpack Center Rd., Wallpack Center, 7/17/80, A, C, NPS, 80000354

Waterloo, 1 mi. S of Andover at Musconetcong River and CR 604, Andover vicinity, 9/13/77, A, 77000909

White Deer Plaza and Boardwalk District, White Deer Plaza, Winona Pkwy., and W. Shore Trail, Sparta, 7/11/88, A, C, 88001012

Union County

Badgley House and Site, N of Mountainside off New Providence Rd., Watchung Reservation, Mountainside vicinity, 9/27/76, C, D, b, 76001190

Belcher—Ogden Mansion—Price, Benjamin—Price—Brittan Houses District, Corner of E. Jersey and Catherine Sts., Elizabeth, 8/28/86, A, C, 86001969

Belcher-Ogden House, 1046 E. Jersey St., Elizabeth, 11/02/78, A, C, 78001799

Boxwood Hall, 1073 E. Jersey St., Elizabeth, 12/18/70, B, NHL, 70000397

Caldwell Parsonage, 909 Caldwell Ave., Union, 8/12/82, A, 82004785

Central Railroad of New Jersey, 238 North Ave., Fanwood, 7/17/80, A, C, 80002521

Crescent Area Historic District, Roughly bounded by Park, Prospect, and Carnegie Aves., 7th and Richmond Sts., Plainfield, 12/12/80, C, 80002523

De Camp, John, House, 2101 Raritan Rd., Scotch Plains, 12/04/73, C, 73001136

Drake, Nathaniel, House, 602 W. Front St., Plainfield, 6/19/73, C, 73001135

Droeschers Mill, 347 Lincoln Ave. E., Cranford, 1/08/74, C, 74001192

Elizabeth Station [Operating Passenger Railroad Stations TR], Morris Ave., and Broad St., Elizabeth, 9/29/84, A, C, 84002825

Evergreen Cemetery, 1137 N. Broad St., Hillside, 7/09/91, C, d, 91000882

Feltville Historic District, S of New Providence, New Providence vicinity, 6/06/80, A, C, D, 80002522

Firehouse No. 4, 1015 South Ave., Plainfield, 3/11/93, A, C, 93000133

First Congregation of the Presbyterian Church at Springfield, 201 Morris Ave. and 11–41 Church Mall, Springfield, 5/07/90, C, 90000668

First Presbyterian Church of Elizabeth, 14–44 Broad St., Elizabeth, 5/06/77, A, C, a, 77000914

First Presbyterian Congregation of Connecticut Farms, Stuyvesant Ave. at Chestnut St., Union, 4/03/70, A, C, a, 70000398

Fowler, Charles N., House, 518 Salem Ave., Elizabeth, 3/13/86, B, C, 86000389

Hetfield, Deacon Andrew, House, Constitution Plaza, Mountainside, 7/27/89, A, B, C, 89001004

Hillside Avenue Historic District, Hillside Ave. from Watchung Ave. to Martine Ave., Plainfield, 6/01/82, C, 82003307

Hutchings Homestead, 126 Morris Ave., Springfield vicinity, 9/16/77, A, 77000915

Liberty Hall, Morris and North Aves., Elizabeth, 11/28/72, B, NHL, 72000807

Littel-Lord Farmstead, 23 and 31 Horseshoe Rd., Berkeley Heights, 3/07/79, B, C, 79001528

Merchants' and Drovers' Tavern, 1632 St. Georges Ave., Rahway, 11/21/78, A, C, b, 78001801

Miller-Cory House, 614 Mountain Ave., Westfield, 11/03/72, B, C, 72000808

Union County—Continued

Murray Hill Station [Operating Passenger Railroad Stations TR], The Circle, Murray Hill, 6/22/84, A, C, 84002826

Netherwood Station [Operating Passenger Railroad Stations TR], Between North and South Aves., Plainfield, 6/22/84, A, C, 84002830

North Avenue Commerical District, Park, North, and Watchung Aves., Plainfield, 3/29/84, A, C, 84002836

North Avenue Commerical Historic District, Park, North, and Watchung Aves., Plainfield, 3/29/84, A, C, 84002776

Old Baptist Parsonage, 547 Park Ave., Scotch Plains, 1/18/73, C, a, 73001137

Plainfield Central Fire Headquarters, 315 Central Ave., Plainfield, 3/04/93, A, C, 93000131

Plainfield Civic District, Roughly, Watchung Ave. between E. Fifth and E. Seventh Sts., Plainfield, 6/17/93, A, C, 93000533

Plainfield Station [Operating Passenger Railroad Stations TR], North Ave., Plainfield, 6/22/84, A, C, 84002837

Rahway Theatre, 1601 Irving St., Rahway, 8/13/86, A, C, 86001509

Saint Mary's Catholic Church Complex, Liberty and W. 6th Sts., Plainfield, 4/11/85, A, C, a, 85000785

Sayre Homestead, Sayre Homestead Lane, Springfield, 8/24/79, A, C, 79001529

Scotch Plains School, Park Ave., Scotch Plains, 12/12/78, A, C, 78001802

Seventeenth Century Clark House, 593 Madison Hill Rd., Rahway vicinity, 11/19/74, A, C, 74001193

Smith, Nathaniel, House, 105 Springfield Ave., Berkeley Heights, 9/28/89, A, C, 89001584

St. John's Parsonage, 633 Pearl St., Elizabeth, 9/16/82, A, C, a, 82003306

Stage House Inn, Park Ave. and Front St., Scotch Plains, 4/15/82, A, C, 82003308

Stoneleigh Park Historic District, Roughly bounded by Westfield Ave., Shackamaxon Dr., Rahway and Dorian Rd., Westfield, 10/28/88, A, C, 88002020

The Clearing, 165 Hobart Ave., Summit, 4/09/93, C, 93000233

Townley, James, House, Morris Ave. and Green Lane, Union, 5/14/79, C, 79001530

Union County Park Commission Administration Buildings, Acme and Canton Sts., Elizabeth, 11/25/85, C, 85002976

Van Wyck Brooks Historic District, Roughly bounded by Plainfield Ave., W. Eighth St., Park Ave., W. Ninth St. and Madison Ave., and Randolph Rd., Plainfield, 12/10/85, C, 85003337

Waring, Orville, T., House, 900 Park Ave., Plainfield, 5/14/79, A, C, 79003252

Westfield Fire Headquarters, 405 North Ave., W., Westfield, 12/08/80, A, C, 80002524

Whyman House, 705 Newark Ave., Elizabeth, 4/10/86, C, a, 86000705

Woodruff House, 111–113 Conant St., Hillside, 12/11/78, A, C, 78001800

Warren County

Asbury Historic District, Roughly, NJ 643 from Maple Ave. to NJ 623 and adjacent parts of Maple, NJ 623 and Kitchen and School Sts., Asbury, 3/19/93, B, C, 93000132

Beattystown, Jct. of NJ 57 and Kings Hwy., Mansfield Twnshp., Beattystown, 9/28/90, A, C, 90001449

Belvidere Historic District, Off U.S. 46, Belvidere, 10/03/80, A, C, 80002525

Fairview Schoolhouse, E of Columbia on Dean Rd., Columbia vicinity, 8/12/77, A, C, 77000916

Great Meadows Railroad Station, Cemetery Rd., Great Meadows vicinity, 3/23/89, A, C, 89000229

Hixson-Skinner Mill Complex, Still Valley Rd., Phillipsburg vicinity, 12/02/82, A, C, 82001047

Hope District, Roughly bounded by Beaver Brook, Washington St., and Brookaloo Swamp, Hope, 7/20/73, A, C, 73001138

Hunt, George, House, SW of Alpha at 135 Warren Glen Rd., Alpha vicinity, 9/12/79, C, 79001531

Imlaydale Historic District, Imlaydale Rd. and surrounding land between NJ 31 and the Musconetcong R., Washington and Lebanon Townships, Hampton vicinity, 3/27/91, A, B, C, 91000306

Johnsonburg Historic District, NJ 519 and 661 and adjacent parts of Mott and Allamuchy Rds., Frelinghuysen Township, Johnsonburg, 10/15/92, A, C, 92001386

Miller Farmstead, NJ 57, Anderson vicinity, 9/11/89, A, C, 88002118

Mount Bethel Methodist Church, S of Vienna on Mount Bethel Rd., Vienna vicinity, 2/29/80, A, C, a, d, 80002526

Oxford Furnace, Belvidere and Washington Aves., Oxford, 7/06/77, A, 77000919

Oxford Industrial Historic District, NJ 31, Mine Hill Rd., Belvidere and Axford Aves., Oxford Township, Oxford, 8/27/92, A, B, 91001471

Roseberry, John, Homestead, 540 Warren St., Phillipsburg, 4/03/73, A, C, 73001139

Seigle Homestead, N of Finesville, Finesville vicinity, 11/07/77, C, 77000918

Shippen Manor, Belvidere Rd., Oxford, 12/20/84, A, C, D, 84000517

Warrington Stone Bridge, NE of Columbia off NJ 94, Columbia vicinity, 12/16/77, A, 77000917

Washington Railroad Station, Railroad Ave., Washington, 7/03/79, A, 79001532

Famous as a Monopoly board game property, Marven Gardens in Atlantic County, New Jersey, is historically significant as an early 20th-century affluent residential subdivision developed according to contemporary precepts of organic planning as dictated by the natural landscape. (Alfred C. Bruhin, 1989)

NEW MEXICO

Bernalillo County

Albuquerque Municipal Airport Building, Old, 2920 Yale Blvd. SE., Albuquerque, 5/05/89, A, C, 89000348

Albuquerque Veterans Administration Medical Center, 2100 Ridgecrest, SE, Albuquerque, 8/19/83, C, g, 83001614

Anaya, Gavino, House [Albuquerque North Valley MRA], 2939 Duranes Rd., NW, Albuquerque, 2/09/84, C, 84002840

Armijo, Juan Cristobal, Homestead [Albuquerque North Valley MRA], 207 Griegos Rd., NE, Albuquerque, 9/30/82, B, C, 82003309

Armijo, Salvador, House, 618 Rio Grande Blvd., NW, Albuquerque, 10/08/76, A, C, 76001191

Art Annex [New Mexico Campus Buildings Built 1906–1937 TR], NE corner of Central Ave. and Terrace St., UNM, Albuquerque, 9/22/88, A, C, 88001540

Aztec Auto Court [Route 66 Through New Mexico MPS], 3821 Central Ave. NE., Albuquerque, 11/22/93, A, C, g, 93001217

Barela, Adrian, House [Albuquerque North Valley MRA], 7618 Guadalupe Trail, NW, Albuquerque, 2/09/84, C, 84002843

Barela-Bledsoe House [Albuquerque North Valley MRA], 7017 Edith Blvd., NE, Albuquerque, 3/12/79, A, C, 79001534

Bottger, Charles A., House, 110 San Felipe, NW, Albuquerque, 3/07/83, C, 83001615

Building at 701 Roma NW, 701 Roma, NW, Albuquerque, 2/28/85, B, C, 85000375

Carlisle Gymnasium [New Mexico Campus Buildings Built 1906–1937 TR], UNM campus W of Yale Blvd., Albuquerque, 9/22/88, C, 88001541

Carnes, Chester, House [Albuquerque Downtown Neighborhoods MRA], 701 13th St., NW, Albuquerque, 12/01/80, C, 80002529

Castle Apartments, 1410 Central SW, Albuquerque, 2/13/86, C, 86000219

Chavez, Juan de Dios, House [Albuquerque North Valley MRA], 205 Griegos Rd., NW, Albuquerque, 2/09/84, C, 84002847

Chavez, Juan, House [Albuquerque North Valley MRA], 7809 4th St., NW, Albuquerque, 2/09/84, C, 84002849

Chavez, Rumaldo, House [Albuquerque North Valley MRA], 10023 Edith Blvd., NE, Albuquerque, 11/24/80, A, C, 80002530

Cottage Bakery [Route 66 Through New Mexico MPS], 2000 Central Ave. SE., Albuquerque, 11/22/93, A, C, g, 93001218

Davis House, 704 Parkland Circle, SE, Albuquerque, 11/17/80, C, 80002531

De Garcia, Tomasa Griego, House [Albuquerque North Valley MRA], 6939 Edith Blvd., NE, Albuquerque, 6/19/79, A, C, 79001535

Dietz, Robert, Farmhouse [Albuquerque North Valley MRA], 4117 Rio Grande Blvd., NW, Albuquerque, 2/09/84, C, 84002852

Eighth Street-Forrester District [Albuquerque Downtown Neighborhoods MRA], Roughly bounded by Mountain Rd., Lomas Blvd., Forrester and 7th Sts., Albuquerque, 12/01/80, C, 80002532

El Vado Auto Court [Route 66 Through New Mexico MPS], 2500 Central Ave. SW., Albuquerque, 11/22/93, A, C, g, 93001214

Eller Apartments, 113-127 8th St., SW, Albuquerque, 1/12/84, C, 84002855

Employees' New Dormitory and Club, Albuquerque Indian School Campus, Albuquerque, 7/26/82, A, C, 82003310

Estufa [New Mexico Campus Buildings Built 1906–1937 TR], SE corner of University Blvd. and Grand Ave., UNM, Albuquerque, 9/22/88, C, 88001542

Federal Building, 421 Gold Ave., SW, Albuquerque, 11/22/80, A, C, 80002533

First Methodist Episcopal Church, 3rd St. and Lead Ave., Albuquerque, 11/07/76, A, C, a, 76001192

First National Bank Building, 217-233 Central Ave., NW, Albuquerque, 2/02/79, A, C, 79003127

Foraker, C. M., Farmhouse [Albuquerque North Valley MRA], 905 Menaul Blvd., NW, Albuquerque, 2/09/84, B, C, 84002858

Fourth Ward District [Albuquerque Downtown Neighborhoods MRA], Roughly bounded by Central Ave., Lomas Blvd., 8th and 15th Sts., Albuquerque, 12/01/80, C, 80002534

Garcia, Juan Antonio, House [Albuquerque North Valley MRA], 7442 Edith Blvd., NE, Albuquerque, 9/28/82, C, 82003311

Gladding, James N., House, 643 Cedar St., NE, Albuquerque, 11/17/80, C, 80002535

Gomez, Refugio, House [Albuquerque North Valley MRA], 7604 Guadalupe Trail, NW, Albuquerque, 2/09/84, C, 84002864

Grande, Charles, House [Albuquerque North Valley MRA], 4317 Grande St., NW, Albuquerque, 2/09/84, C, 84002866

Gurule, Delfinia, House [Albuquerque Downtown Neighborhoods MRA], 306 16th St., NW, Albuquerque, 12/01/80, C, 80002536

Harwood School [Albuquerque Downtown Neighborhoods MRA], 1114 7th St., NW, Albuquerque, 12/01/80, A, C, 80002537

Hayden, A. W., House [Albuquerque Downtown Neighborhoods MRA], 609 Marble St., NW, Albuquerque, 12/01/80, C, 80002538

Hodgin Hall, University of New Mexico campus, Albuquerque Mountain, 1/30/78, A, C, 78001803

Holy Child Church, Off I-40, Tijeras, 3/08/78, A, C, a, 78001810

Hope Building, 220 Gold St., SW, Albuquerque, 8/29/80, A, C, 80002539

Hudson House, 817 Gold Ave., SW, Albuquerque, 2/24/82, C, 82003313

Huning Highlands Historic District, Bounded by Grand Ave., I-25, Iron Ave. and AT & SF RR, Albuquerque, 11/17/78, A, C, 78001804

Isleta Pueblo, U.S. 85, Isleta, 9/05/75, A, D, a, 75001162

Jones Motor Company [Route 66 Through New Mexico MPS], 3226 Central Ave. SE., Albuquerque, 11/22/93, A, C, g, 93001219

Kimo Theater, 421 Central Ave., Albuquerque, 5/02/77, A, C, 77000920

Kress, S. H., Building, 414–416 Central Ave., SW, Albuquerque, 4/19/84, A, C, 84002871

Kromer House [Albuquerque North Valley MRA], 1024 El Pueblo Rd., NW, Albuquerque, 10/04/82, A, C, 82001048

La Mesa Motel [Route 66 Through New Mexico MPS], 7407 Central Ave. NE., Albuquerque, 11/22/93, A, C, g, 93001220

LaGlorieta House [Albuquerque Downtown Neighborhoods MRA], 1801 Central Ave., NW, Albuquerque, 8/19/83, A, 83001616

Las Imagines Archeological District—Albuquerque West Mesa Escarpment, Address Restricted, Albuquerque vicinity, 11/19/86, A, D, a, 86003142

LeFeber, Charles, House [Albuquerque Downtown Neighborhoods MRA], 313 5th St., Albuquerque, 12/01/80, C, 80002540

Lembke House, 312 Laguna St., SW, Albuquerque, 11/25/80, C, g, 80002541

Leverett, William J., House, 301 Dartmouth NE, Albuquerque, 2/13/86, B, C, 86000221

Lewis, Charles W. Building, 1405–1407 2nd St., SW, Albuquerque, 7/03/79, C, 79001533

Lopez, Hilario, House [Albuquerque Downtown Neighborhoods MRA], 208 16th St., NW, Albuquerque, 12/01/80, C, 80002542

Los Candelarias Chapel-San Antonio Chapel [Albuquerque North Valley MRA], 1934 Candelaria Rd., NW, Albuquerque, 2/09/84, A, C, a, 84002844

Los Duranes Chapel [Albuquerque North Valley MRA], 2601 Indian School Rd., NW, Albuquerque, 2/09/84, C, a, 84002854

Los Griegos Historic District [Albuquerque North Valley MRA], Griegos Rd. and Rio Grande Blvd., Albuquerque, 2/09/84, A, C, 84002874

Los Poblanos Historic District [Albuquerque North Valley MRA], NM 194, Los Ranchos vicinity, 5/27/82, A, B, C, g, 82003321

Los Tomases Chapel [Albuquerque North Valley MRA], 3101 Los Tomases, NW, Albuquerque, 2/09/84, A, 84002876

Lucero y Montoya, Francisco, House [Albuquerque North Valley MRA], 9742 4th St., NW, Albuquerque, 2/09/84, C, 84002880

Maisel's Indian Trading Post [Route 66 Through New Mexico MPS], 510 Central Ave. SW., Albuquerque, 11/22/93, A, C, g, 93001215

Bernalillo County—Continued

Mann, Henry, House [Albuquerque Downtown Neighborhoods MRA], 723 14th St., NW, Albuquerque, 12/01/80, C, 80002543

McCanna-Hubbell Building, 418–424 Central, SW, Albuquerque, 5/13/82, A, C, 82003314

Menaul School Historic District [Albuquerque North Valley MRA], Roughly bounded by Broadway, Claremont, Edith, and Menaul Aves. and 301 Menaul Blvd., NE, Albuquerque, 2/14/83, A, g, 83001617

Milne, John, House, 804 Park Ave. SW, Albuquerque, 2/13/86, B, g, 86000223

Modern Auto Court [Route 66 Through New Mexico MPS], 3712 Central Ave. SE., Albuquerque, 11/22/93, A, C, g, 93001221

Monte Vista Fire Station, 3201 Centra Ave. NE, Albuqerque, 3/19/87, A, C, 87001121

Monte Vista School, 3211 Monte Vista Blvd., NE, Albuquerque, 8/12/81, A, C, 81000399

National Humane Alliance Animal Fountain, 615 Virginia Ave. SE, Albuquerque, 9/30/86, A, b, 86003120

New Mexico-Arizona Wool Warehouse, 520 1st St., NW, Albuquerque, 7/23/81, A, B, C, 81000400

Nordhaus, Robert, House [Albuquerque North Valley MRA], 6900 Rio Grande Blvd., NW, Albuquerque, 2/09/84, C, g, 84002883

O'Rielly, J. H., House, 220 9th St., NW, Albuquerque, 1/29/79, C, 79003442

Occidental Life Building, 119 3rd Ave., SW, Albuquerque, 1/30/78, A, C, 78001805

Old Armijo School, 1021 Isleta Blvd., SE, Albuquerque, 9/16/82, A, C, 82003315

Old Hilton Hotel, 125 2nd St., NW, Albuquerque, 3/02/84, A, C, g, 84002868

Old Post Office, 123 4th St., Albuquerque, 11/17/80, A, C, 80002544

Our Lady of Mt. Carmel Church [Albuquerque North Valley MRA], 7813 Edith Blvd., NE, Albuquerque, 2/09/84, A, C, a, 84002884

Our Lady of the Angels School, 320 Romero St., NW, Albuquerque, 11/29/84, A, C, a, 84000426

Pacific Desk Building, 213-215 Gold Ave., SW, Albuquerque, 9/30/80, C, 80002545

Pearce, John, House, 718 Central Ave., SW, Albuquerque, 11/22/80, C, 80002546

Piedras Marcadas Pueblo (LA 290), Address Restricted, Albuquerque vicinity, 3/02/90, A, D, 90000160

President's House [New Mexico Campus Buildings Built 1906–1937 TR], NE corner of Roma Ave. and Yale Blvd., UNM, Albuquerque, 9/22/88, C, 88001543

Rancho de Carnue Site, Address Restricted, Albuquerque vicinity, 5/04/77, A, D, 77000921

Raynolds, Sara, Hall [New Mexico Campus Buildings Built 1906–1937 TR], UNM campus on Terrace St. north of Central Ave., Albuquerque, 9/22/88, C, 88001544

Romero, Felipe, House [Albuquerque North Valley MRA], 7522 Edith Blvd., NE, Albuquerque, 2/09/84, C, 84002885

Rosenwald Building, 320 Central Ave., SW, Albuquerque, 6/29/78, A, C, 78001806

Saint Joseph 1930 Hospital, 715 Grand, NE, Albuquerque, 5/27/82, A, C, a, 82003316

San Felipe de Neri Church, Old Town Plaza, NW, Albuquerque, 10/01/69, A, C, a, 69000140

San Ignacio Church, 1300 Walter St., NE, Albuquerque, 8/21/79, A, C, a, 79001536

Santa Barbara School, 1420 Edith Blvd., NE., Albuquerque, 9/28/89, A, C, 89001590

Scholes Hall [New Mexico Campus Buildings Built 1906–1937 TR], UNM campus S of Roma Ave., Albuquerque, 9/22/88, C, 88001545

Second United Presbyterian Church, 812 Edith Blvd., NE, Albuquerque, 12/06/84, A, C, a, 84000563

Shalit, Samuel, House [Albuquerque North Valley MRA], 5209 4th St., NW, Albuquerque, 2/09/84, C, g, 84002888

Shoup Boardinghouse, 707 1st St., SW, Albuquerque, 2/17/83, A, C, 83001618

Silver Hill Historic District, Roughly bounded by Central Ave., Yale Blvd., Lead Ave., and Sycamore St., Albuquerque, 9/18/86, C, 86002414

Skinner Building, 722–724 Central Ave. and 108 8th St., SW, Albuquerque, 11/22/80, A, C, 80004485

Solar Building, 213 Truman St., NE., Albuquerque, 10/10/89, C, g, 89001589

Southwestern Brewery and Ice Company, 601 Commercial St., NE, Albuquerque, 3/30/78, A, C, 78001807

Spitz, Berthold, House [Albuquerque Downtown Neighborhoods MRA], 323 N. 10th St., Albuquerque, 12/22/77, A, B, C, 77000922

Springer Building, 121 Tijeras Ave., NE, Albuquerque, 11/18/80, A, C, 80002547

Spruce Park Historic District, Roughly bounded by University Blvd., Grand Ave., Las Lomas Rd. and Cedar St., Albuquerque, 7/06/82, A, C, g, 82003317

Superintendent's House, Atlantic & Pacific Railroad, 1023 S. 2nd St., Albuquerque, 1/20/78, A, C, 78001808

Tafoya, Domingo, House [Albuquerque North Valley MRA], 10021 Edith Blvd., NE, Alameda, 11/17/80, A, C, 80002528

Tower Courts [Route 66 Through New Mexico MPS], 2210 Central Ave. SW., Albuquerque, 11/22/93, A, C, g, 93001216

Vigil, Antonio, House, 413 Romero St., Albuquerque, 5/05/78, A, C, 78001809

Washington Apartments, 1002–1008 Central Ave., SW, Albuquerque, 2/19/82, C, 82003319

Werner-Gilchrist House, 202 Cornell, SE, Albuquerque, 8/02/82, A, C, 82003320

Zeiger, Charles, House [Albuquerque North Valley MRA], 3200 Edith Blvd., NE, Albuquerque, 4/27/84, C, 84002889

Catron County

Ake Site, Address Restricted, Datil vicinity, 4/02/76, A, D, 76001193

Bat Cave, Address Restricted, Horse Springs vicinity, 4/23/76, A, D, 76001194

Bearwallow Mountain Lookout Cabins and Shed [National Forest Fire Lookouts in the Southwestern Region TR], Bearwallow Lookout Rd., Gila National Forest, Bearwallow Park, 1/28/88, A, C, g, 87002473

Black Mountain Lookout Cabin [National Forest Fire Lookouts in the Southwestern Region TR], Gila National Forest, Black Mountain, 1/28/88, A, C, 87002474

El Caso Lookout Complex [National Forest Fire Lookouts in the Southwestern Region TR], Gila National Forest, El Caso Lake, 1/28/88, A, C, 87002476

Gila Cliff Dwellings National Monument, Address Restricted, Silver City vicinity, 10/15/66, C, D, NPS, 66000472

Mangas Mountain Lookout Complex [National Forest Fire Lookouts in the Southwestern Region TR], Mangas Mountain, Mangas vicinity, 1/28/88, A, C, 87002471

Mogollon Baldy Lookout Cabin [National Forest Fire Lookouts in the Southwestern Region TR], Gila National Forest, Mogollon Baldy Peak, 1/28/88, A, C, 87002470

Mogollon Historic District, NM 78/Bursum Rd., Mogollon, 9/10/87, A, C, g, 87001541

Mogollon Pueblo, Address Restricted, Red Hill vicinity, 5/05/78, D, 78001811

Socorro Mines Mining Company Mill, Fannie Hill, Fannie Hill and W to Fannie Hill Mill, Mogollon vicinity, 9/10/87, A, C, g, 87001567

Chaves County

CA Bar Ranch [Roswell New Mexico MRA], US 82 3 mi. W of jct. with NM 24, Mayhill vicinity, 8/29/88, A, B, 85003634

Chaves County Courthouse [County Courthouses of New Mexico TR], 400 Blk. Main St., Roswell, 2/15/89, A, C, 87000892

Diamond A Ranch [Roswell New Mexico MRA], US 380 14 mi. W of Roswell, Roswell vicinity, 8/29/88, A, B, 85003635

Downtown Roswell Historic District [Roswell New Mexico MRA], Roughly bounded by 8th St., Richardson Ave., Albuquerque St. and Missouri Ave., Roswell, 5/16/85, B, C, 85001543

Flying H Ranch [Roswell New Mexico MRA], Off US 70 between Hope and Elk Area, Roswell vicinity, 9/14/88, A, 85003633

Garrett, Patrick Floyd, House [Roswell New Mexico MRA], Bosque Rd. 3 mi. N of Roswell, Roswell vicinity, 8/29/88, A, B, 85003637

Goddard, Robert H., House [Roswell New Mexico MRA], Rt 3 E. on Mescalero Rd., Roswell, 7/15/88, A, B, g, 85003594

Massey, Louise, House [Roswell New Mexico MRA], 209 W. Alameda St., Roswell, 5/16/85, B, 85001544

Millhiser—Baker Farm [Roswell New Mexico MRA], Rt. 1 .5 mi. S of McGaffey, Roswell vicinity, 8/29/88, A, C, 85003638

Chaves County—Continued

Milne—Bush Ranch [Roswell New Mexico MRA], Rt. 1, Roswell, 8/29/88, A, 85003639

New Mexico Military Institute Historic District [Roswell New Mexico MRA], Roughly bounded by Nineteenth and N. Main Sts., College Blvd. and Kentucky Ave., Roswell, 5/07/87, A, C, 87000907

Saunders-Crosby House [Roswell New Mexico MRA], 200 E. Deming, Roswell, 5/16/85, C, 85001545

Slaughter—Hill Ranch [Roswell New Mexico MRA], 1601 E. Second St., Roswell, 8/29/88, A, B, C, 85003640

South Spring Ranch [Roswell New Mexico MRA], Rt. 2, Roswell, 4/24/89, A, B, 88003465

Urton Orchards [Roswell New Mexico MRA], Rt. 3, Roswell, 8/29/88, A, C, 85003641

White, James Phelps, House, 200 N. Lea Ave., Roswell, 7/24/78, A, C, 78001812

Cibola County

Candelaria Pueblo, Address Restricted, Grants vicinity, 3/10/83, D, 83001619

Colfax County

Catskill Charcoal Ovens, 35 mi. (56 km) W of Raton, Raton vicinity, 1/30/78, A, C, 78001813

Cimmaron Historic District, S edge of city along NM 21, Cimmaron, 4/03/73, A, C, D, 73001140

Colfax County Courthouse [County Courthouses of New Mexico TR], Third and Savage, Raton, 6/18/87, A, C, 87000882

Colfax County Courthouse in Springer [County Courthouses of New Mexico TR], 614 Maxwell Ave., Springer, 12/07/87, C, 87000883

Cowan, R. H., Livery Stable, 220 Maxwell Ave., Springer, 8/03/79, A, C, 79001538

Dawson Cemetery, Approximately 4 mi. NW of jct. of US 64 and the Dawson Rd., Dawson, 4/09/92, A, D, d, 92000249

Dorsey Mansion, About 12 mi. NE of Abbott off U.S. 56., Abbott vicinity, 9/04/70, C, 70000399

Eagle Nest Dam, 3 mi. SE of Eagle Nest off U.S. 64, Eagle Nest vicinity, 4/18/79, A, C, 79001537

Folsom Site, Address Restricted, Folsom vicinity, 10/15/66, A, D, NHL, 66000473

Maxwell—Abreu and North (Martinez) Houses [Rayado Ranch MPS], Jct. of NM 121 and Rayado Creek Rd., NW corner, Cimarron vicinity, 6/23/93, A, C, D, 93000253

Mills House, 509 1st St., Springer, 10/06/70, B, C, 70000400

Raton Downtown Historic District, Roughly bounded by Rio Grande, Clark, 1st and 3rd Sts., Raton, 10/21/77, A, C, 77000923

Raton Pass, U.S. 85-87, CO/NM border, Raton vicinity, 10/15/66, A, NHL, 66000474

Ring Place, The, Questa Ranger District, Carson National Forest, Forest Rds. 1950 and 1918A, Cimarron vicinity, 7/19/88, A, C, D, 88001054

St. John's Methodist Episcopal Church, 17 mi. (27 km) E of Raton on NM 72, Raton vicinity, 1/18/78, A, C, 78001814

Curry County

1908 Clovis City Hall and Fire Station, 308 Pile St., Clovis, 7/16/87, A, C, 87001110

Clovis Baptist Hospital, 515 Prince St., Clovis, 2/05/82, A, C, a, g, 82003322

Clovis Central Fire Station, 320 Mitchell St., Clovis, 7/02/87, A, C, 87001111

Curry County Courthouse [County Courthouses of New Mexico TR], 700 blk. of Main St., Clovis, 6/18/87, A, C, 87000881

First Methodist Church of Clovis, 622 Main St., Clovis, 7/02/87, C, a, 87001112

Hotel Clovis, 210 Main St., Clovis, 12/27/84, A, C, 84000571

Old Clovis Post Office, 4th and Mitchell Sts., Clovis, 12/27/84, A, C, 84000573

De Baca County

De Baca County Courthouse [County Courthouses of New Mexico TR], 500 blk. Ave. C, Fort Sumner, 12/07/87, C, 87000896

Fort Sumner Railroad Bridge, 2 mi. (3.2 km) W of Fort Sumner over Pecos River, Fort Sumner vicinity, 3/21/79, A, C, 79001539

Fort Sumner Ruins, Addess Restricted, Fort Sumner vicinity, 8/13/74, A, D, f, 74001194

Dona Ana County

Air Science [New Mexico Campus Buildings Built 1906–1937 TR], NE corner of N. Horseshoe and Espina Sts., NMSU, Las Cruces, 5/16/89, C, 88001546

Alameda-Depot Historic District, Includes properties centered around Pioneer Park and extending up Alameda Blvd., Las Cruces, 4/11/85, A, C, 85000786

Armijo, Nestor, House, Lohman Ave. and Church St., Las Cruces, 12/12/76, B, C, 76001195

Barela-Reynolds House, Off NM 292, Mesilla, 1/20/78, A, C, 78001815

Fort Fillmore, Address Restricted, Las Cruces vicinity, 7/30/74, A, D, 74001196

Fort Selden, 18 mi. N of Las Cruces, Las Cruces vicinity, 7/09/70, A, 70000401

Foster Hall [New Mexico Campus Buildings Built 1906–1937 TR], SE corner of S. Horseshoe and Sweet, NMSU, Las Cruces, 5/16/89, C, 88001547

Goddard Hall [New Mexico Campus Buildings Built 1906–1937 TR], S. Horseshoe between Espina and Sweet, NMSU, Las Cruces, 9/22/88, C, 88001548

Hadley—Ludwick House, 2640 El Paseo, Las Cruces, 4/03/91, A, B, C, 91000352

International Boundary Marker No. 1, U.S. and Mexico, W of El Paso off I-10, El Paso vicinity, 9/10/74, A, 74001195

La Mesilla Historic District, Roughly bounded by Calle del Norte, Calle del El Paso, Calle del Cura and Calleion Guerro, La Mesilla, 7/20/82, A, C, g, 82003323

Launch Complex 33, White Sands Missile Range, White Sands Missile Range, 10/03/85, A, g, NHL, 85003541

Mesilla Plaza, 2 mi. S of Las Cruces on NM 28, Las Cruces vicinity, 10/15/66, A, NHL, 66000475

Mesquite Street Original Townsite Historic District, Roughly bounded by E. Texas, Campo, Tornillo and E. Court, Las Cruces, 8/01/85, A, C, 85001669

Our Lady of Purication Catholic Church, Camino Real and 2nd St., Dona Ana, 6/27/85, A, C, a, 85001386

San Jose Church, 317 Josephine St., La Mesa, 1/21/93, A, C, a, 92001817

University President's House [New Mexico Campus Buildings Built 1906–1937 TR], S of University Ave. between Espina and Solano, NMSU, Las Cruces, 5/16/89, C, 88001549

Eddy County

Acord, John, House [Artificial Stone Houses of Artesia TR], W. Main St., Artesia, 3/02/84, A, C, 84002891

Atkeson, Willie D., House [Artificial Stone Houses of Artesia TR], 303 W. Grand Ave., Artesia, 3/02/84, A, C, 84002894

Baskin Building, 332 W. Main St., Artesia, 7/18/90, C, 90000599

Baskin, William, House [Artificial Stone Houses of Artesia TR], 811 W. Quay Ave., Artesia, 3/02/84, A, C, 84002898

Carlsbad Reclamation Project, N of Carlsbad, Carlsbad vicinity, 10/15/66, A, NHL, 66000476

Caverns, The, Historic District, End of NM 7, Carlsbad vicinity, 8/18/88, A, C, g, NPS, 88001173

Dam—Sitting Bull Falls Recreation Area [Public Works of the CCC in the Lincoln National Forest MPS], Sitting Bull Falls, Lincoln NF, Carlsbad vicinity, 12/23/93, A, C, 93001420

First National Bank of Eddy, 303 W. Fox St., Carlsbad, 12/12/76, A, C, 76001196

Gesler, Edward R., House [Artificial Stone Houses of Artesia TR], 411 W. Missouri Ave., Artesia, 3/02/84, A, C, 84002924

Group Picnic Shelter—Sitting Bull Falls Recreation Area [Public Works of the CCC in the Lincoln National Forest MPS], Sitting Bull Falls, Lincoln NF, Carlsbad vicinity, 12/23/93, A, C, 93001419

Hodges-Runyan-Brainard House [Artificial Stone Houses of Artesia TR], 504 W. Quay Ave., Artesia, 3/02/84, A, C, 84002925

Hodges-Sipple House [Artificial Stone Houses of Artesia TR], 804 W. Missouri Ave., Artesia, 3/02/84, A, C, 84002926

Eddy County—Continued

Lukins, F. L., House [Artificial Stone Houses of Artesia TR], 801 W. Richardson Ave., Artesia, 3/02/84, A, C, 84002928

Mauldin-Hall House [Artificial Stone Houses of Artesia TR], 501 S. Roselawn Ave., Artesia, 3/02/84, A, C, 84002930

Moore-Ward Cobblestone House, 505 W. Richardson Ave., Artesia, 2/16/84, A, C, 84002932

Painted Grotto, Address Restricted, Carlsbad vicinity, 3/08/77, D, NPS, 77000159

Picnic Shelter—Sitting Bull Falls Recreation Area [Public Works of the CCC in the Lincoln National Forest MPS], Sitting Bull Falls, Lincoln NF, Carlsbad vicinity, 12/23/93, A, C, 93001418

Rattlesnake Springs Historic District, W of US 62-180, off CR 418, Carlsbad vicinity, 7/14/88, A, C, D, g, NPS, 88001130

Robert, Sallie Chisum, House [Artificial Stone Houses of Artesia TR], 801 W. Texas St., Artesia, 3/02/84, A, B, C, 84002939

Ross, Dr. Robert M., House [Artificial Stone Houses of Artesia TR], 1002 S. Roselawn Ave., Artesia, 3/02/84, A, C, 84002936

Sipple—Ward Building, 331 W. Main St., Artesia, 10/04/91, C, 91001503

Grant County

Acklin Store [Mimbres Valley MRA], NM 90, San Lorenzo vicinity, 5/16/88, A, b, 88000502

Ailman, H. B., House, 314 W. Broadway, Silver City, 5/12/75, A, B, C, 75001163

Andazola, Trinidad, House [Mimbres Valley MRA], SE of NM 61 and S of Eby Ranch Rd., Dwyer vicinity, 5/16/88, C, 88000500

Bowden Hall [New Mexico Campus Buildings Built 1906–1937 TR], NE of Light Hall and SW of Heating Plant, WNMU, Silver City, 9/22/88, C, 88001552

Bullard Hotel, 105 S. Bullard St., Silver City, 7/11/88, A, 88000435

Burro Springs Site, Address Restricted, Tyrone vicinity, 12/31/74, C, 74001197

Chihuahua Hill Historic District, Bounded by Cooper, Spring, Bullard, and Chihuahua Sts., Silver City, 1/23/84, A, C, 84002943

Eby, Tom, Storage Building [Mimbres Valley MRA], W of NM 61 and N of Eby Ranch Rd., Dwyer vicinity, 5/16/88, C, 88000514

Fleming Hall [New Mexico Campus Buildings Built 1906–1937 TR], 10th St. NE of Bowden Hall, WNMU, Silver City, 9/22/88, C, 88001553

Graham Gymnasium [New Mexico Campus Buildings Built 1906–1937 TR], Florida St., WNMU, Silver City, 9/22/88, C, 88001554

Grijalva, Luciana B., House [Mimbres Valley MRA], E of NM 61, San Lorenzo vicinity, 5/16/88, C, 88000499

Heating Plant [New Mexico Campus Buildings Built 1906–1937 TR], 10th St. NE of Bowden Hall, WNMU, Silver City, 9/22/88, C, 88001555

Hooks—Moore Store [Mimbres Valley MRA], NM 61 and Forest Rt. 73, Mimbres, 5/16/88, A, C, b, 88000490

Huechling, Otto, House [Mimbres Valley MRA], E of NM 61, Mimbres vicinity, 5/16/88, C, 88000496

Janss Site, Address Restricted, San Lorenzo vicinity, 7/23/80, A, D, 80002550

L. C. Ranch Headquarters, Off U.S. 260, Gila, 12/06/78, A, C, 78001816

Light Hall [New Mexico Campus Buildings Built 1906–1937 TR], N side of College Ave. at B St., WNMU, Silver City, 9/22/88, C, 88001556

Mattocks Site, Address Restricted, Mimbres vicinity, 12/09/80, A, D, 80002548

Menard—Galaz House [Mimbres Valley MRA], W of NM 90, San Lorenzo vicinity, 5/16/88, A, C, 88000503

Mimbres School [Mimbres Valley MRA], E of NM 61 and Forest Rt. 73, Mimbres, 5/16/88, A, C, 88000491

NAN Ranch [Mimbres Valley MRA], E of NM 61, Dwyer vicinity, 5/16/88, A, C, 88000509

Perrault, George O., House [Mimbres Valley MRA], E of NM 61 1.7 mi. N of Mimbres Hot Springs Canyon Rd., Sherman vicinity, 5/16/88, A, C, 88000507

Pinos Altos Historic District, Roughly bounded by Gold Ave., Cherry, Main, Church, and Silver Sts., Pinos Altos, 5/21/84, A, C, a, 84002945

Portillo, Mauricio, House [Mimbres Valley MRA], E of NM 61 1 mi. S of NM 90, San Lorenzo vicinity, 5/16/88, A, C, 88000504

Redding, William, House [Mimbres Valley MRA], Off NM 61, Mimbres, 5/16/88, A, C, 88000483

Reeds Peak Lookout Tower [National Forest Fire Lookouts in the Southwestern Region TR], Squeaky Spring, Gila National Forest, Reeds Peak, 1/28/88, A, C, 87002472

Ritch Hall [New Mexico Campus Buildings Built 1906–1937 TR], 10th St. SE of Fleming Hall, WNMU, Silver City, 9/22/88, C, 88001557

San Juan Historic District [Mimbres Valley MRA], 2261–2291 NM 61, San Juan, 5/16/88, A, C, a, 88000481

San Juan Teacherage [Mimbres Valley MRA], W of NM 61 1.7 mi. N of Mimbres Hot Springs Canyon Rd., Sherman vicinity, 5/16/88, C, 88000508

San Lorenzo Historic District [Mimbres Valley MRA], Roughly Galaz St. between C and H Sts., San Lorenzo, 5/16/88, A, C, a, 88000480

Sibole, George, Store [Mimbres Valley MRA], E of NM 61, N of Forest Rt. 73, Mimbres, 5/16/88, C, 88000482

Silver City Historic District, Roughly bounded by Black, College, Hudson, and Spring Sts., Silver City, 5/23/78, A, B, C, a, 78001817

Silver City Historic District North Addition, Roughly bounded by the San Vicente Arroyo, College Ave., Chloride and 13th Sts., Silver City, 2/17/83, C, 83001620

Silver City Water Works Building, Little Walnut Rd., Silver City, 1/26/84, C, 84002950

Soliz—Baca House [Mimbres Valley MRA], SE of NM 61 and S of Eby Ranch Rd., Dwyer vicinity, 6/17/88, C, 88000518

St. Mary's Academy Historic District, 1813 N. Alabama St., Silver City, 9/15/83, A, C, a, 83001621

Torres, Antonio, House [Mimbres Valley MRA], N of NM 90 W of Mimbres River bridge, San Lorenzo vicinity, 5/16/88, C, 88000505

Trujillo, Maria J. and Juan, House [Mimbres Valley MRA], E of NM 61 and S of Eby Ranch Rd., Dwyer vicinity, 5/16/88, A, C, 88000516

Valencia, Jesus, House [Mimbres Valley MRA], E of NM 61, San Juan vicinity, 5/16/88, C, 88000506

Valencia, Ysabel, House [Mimbres Valley MRA], E of NM 61, Mimbres vicinity, 5/16/88, A, C, 88000493

Wheaton-Smith Site, Address Restricted, San Juan vicinity, 7/23/80, A, C, D, 80002549

Wood, Dr. Granville, House [Mimbres Valley MRA], E of NM 61, Mimbres vicinity, 5/16/88, A, C, 88000498

Woodrow Ruin, Address Restricted, Cliff vicinity, 7/09/70, D, 70000402

Guadalupe County

Abandoned Route 66—Cuervo to NM 156 [Route 66 Through New Mexico MPS], Cuervo SW to jct. with NM 156, Cuervo vicinity, 11/22/93, A, g, 93001206

Anton Chico de Abajo Historic District [Anton Chico Land Grant MRA], Address Restricted, Anton Chico vicinity, 9/29/86, A, D, 86002334

Casaus, Jesus M., House, 628 3rd St., Santa Rosa, 4/01/82, B, C, 82003324

Colonias de San Jose Historic District [Anton Chico Land Grant MRA], Address Restricted, Colonias vicinity, 9/29/86, A, D, 86002331

Grzelachowski, Alexander, House and Store, SW of jct. of NM 91 and NM 203, Puerto de Luna, 6/24/93, A, B, C, 93000570

Guadalupe County Courthouse in Santa Rosa [County Courthouses of New Mexico TR], NW corner S. Fourth St. and Parker Ave., Santa Rosa, 12/07/87, C, 87000890

La Placita De Abajo District [Anton Chico Land Grant MRA], Address Restricted, Colonias vicinity, 9/29/86, A, D, 86002338

Moise, Julius J., House, 400 Capitan, Santa Rosa, 12/27/84, C, 84000633

Harding County

Harding County Courthouse [County Courthouses of New Mexico TR], Pine St., Mosquero, 12/07/87, C, 87000895

Hidalgo County

Alamo Hueco Site [Animas Phase Sites in Hidalgo County MPS], Address Restricted, Animas vicinity, 1/28/93, D, 92001800

Hidalgo County—Continued

Archeological Site No. LA 54021 [Animas Phase Sites in Hidalgo County MPS], Address Restricted, Animas vicinity, 1/23/93, D, 92001802

Archeological Site No. LA 54042 [Animas Phase Sites in Hidalgo County MPS], Address Restricted, Animas vicinity, 1/23/93, D, 92001811

Archeological Site No. LA 54049 [Animas Phase Sites in Hidalgo County MPS], Address Restricted, Animas vicinity, 1/23/93, D, 92001813

Archeological Site No. LA 54050 [Animas Phase Sites in Hidalgo County MPS], Address Restricted, Animas vicinity, 1/23/93, D, 92001814

Box Canyon Site [Animas Phase Sites in Hidalgo County MPS], Address Restricted, Animas vicinity, 1/28/93, D, 92001796

Brushy Creek Ruin [Animas Phase Sites in Hidalgo County MPS], Address Restricted, Animas vicinity, 1/28/93, D, 92001815

Clanton Draw Site [Animas Phase Sites in Hidalgo County MPS], Address Restricted, Animas vicinity, 1/28/93, D, 92001795

Cloverdale Park Site [Animas Phase Sites in Hidalgo County MPS], Address Restricted, Animas vicinity, 1/28/93, D, 92001808

Culberson Ruin [Animas Phase Sites in Hidalgo County MPS], Address Restricted, Animas vicinity, 1/28/93, D, 92001799

Double Adobe Creek Site [Animas Phase Sites in Hidalgo County MPS], Address Restricted, Animas vicinity, 1/28/93, D, 92001807

Fortress—Stewart Ranch Site [Animas Phase Sites in Hidalgo County MPS], Address Restricted, Animas vicinity, 1/23/93, D, 92001803

Hidalgo County Courthouse [County Courthouses of New Mexico TR], 300 S. Shakespeare St., Lordsburg, 12/07/87, C, 87000897

Hoskins Site [Animas Phase Sites in Hidalgo County MPS], Address Restricted, Animas vicinity, 1/28/93, D, 92001804

Joyce Well Site [Animas Phase Sites in Hidalgo County MPS], Address Restricted, Animas vicinity, 1/28/93, D, 92001798

Little Site [Animas Phase Sites in Hidalgo County MPS], Address Restricted, Animas vicinity, 1/28/93, D, 92001805

Lunch Box Site [Animas Phase Sites in Hidalgo County MPS], Address Restricted, Animas vicinity, 1/28/93, D, 92001801

Metate Ruin [Animas Phase Sites in Hidalgo County MPS], Address Restricted, Animas vicinity, 1/28/93, D, 92001812

Pendleton Ruin [Animas Phase Sites in Hidalgo County MPS], Address Restricted, Animas vicinity, 1/28/93, D, 92001794

Pigpen Creek Site [Animas Phase Sites in Hidalgo County MPS], Address Restricted, Animas vicinity, 1/28/93, D, 92001806

Saddle Bronc—Battleground Site [Animas Phase Sites in Hidalgo County MPS], Address Restricted, Animas vicinity, 1/28/93, D, 92001810

Shakespeare Ghost Town, SW of Lordsburg, off NM 494, Lordsburg vicinity, 7/16/73, A, 73001141

Sycamore Well Site [Animas Phase Sites in Hidalgo County MPS], Address Restricted, Animas vicinity, 1/28/93, D, 92001797

Timberlake Ruin—Walnut Creek Site [Animas Phase Sites in Hidalgo County MPS], Address Restricted, Animas vicinity, 1/28/93, D, 92001809

Lea County

Laguna Plata Archeological District, Address Restricted, Hobbs vicinity, 9/14/89, D, 89001209

Lea County Courthouse [County Courthouses of New Mexico TR], 100 blk. Main St., Lovington, 12/07/87, C, 87000880

Lincoln County

Archeological Site LA 12151 [Prehistoric and Historic Agricultural Sites in the Lower Rio Bonito Valley TR], Address Restricted, Lincoln vicinity, 9/13/88, D, 88001507

Archeological Site LA 12153 [Prehistoric and Historic Agricultural Sites in the Lower Rio Bonito Valley TR], Address Restricted, Lincoln vicinity, 2/18/90, A, D, 88001508

Archeological Site LA 12155 [Prehistoric and Historic Agricultural Sites in the Lower Rio Bonito Valley TR], Address Restricted, Lincoln vicinity, 2/18/90, A, D, 88001509

Archeological Site LA 61201 [Prehistoric and Historic Agricultural Sites in the Lower Rio Bonito Valley TR], Address Restricted, Lincoln vicinity, 9/13/88, A, D, 88001510

Archeological Site LA 61202 [Prehistoric and Historic Agricultural Sites in the Lower Rio Bonito Valley TR], Address Restricted, Lincoln vicinity, 2/18/90, A, D, 88001511

Archeological Site LA 61204 [Prehistoric and Historic Agricultural Sites in the Lower Rio Bonito Valley TR], Address Restricted, Lincoln vicinity, 9/13/88, A, D, 88001512

Archeological Site LA 61206 [Prehistoric and Historic Agricultural Sites in the Lower Rio Bonito Valley TR], Address Restricted, Lincoln vicinity, 9/13/88, A, D, 88001513

Archeological Site LA 61208 [Prehistoric and Historic Agricultural Sites in the Lower Rio Bonito Valley TR], Address Restricted, Lincoln vicinity, 9/13/88, A, D, 88001514

Archeological Site LA 61211 [Prehistoric and Historic Agricultural Sites in the Lower Rio Bonito Valley TR], Address Restricted, Lincoln vicinity, 9/13/88, A, D, 88001515

Archeological Site LA 61210 [Prehistoric and Historic Agricultural Sites in the Lower Rio Bonito Valley TR], Address Restricted, Lincoln vicinity, 9/13/88, A, D, 88001516

Archeological Site No. AR-03-08-01-051 [Corona Phase Sites in the Jicarilla Mountains, New Mexico MPS], Address Restricted, White Oaks vicinity, 8/28/90, D, 90001251

Archeological Site No. AR-03-08-01-052 [Corona Phase Sites in the Jicarilla Mountains, New Mexico MPS], Address Restricted, White Oaks vicinity, 8/28/90, D, 90001252

El Paso And Southwestern Railway Water Supply System, S of Nogal, Nogal vicinity, 11/21/79, A, C, 79001540

Feather Cave, Address Restricted, Lincoln vicinity, 11/20/74, A, C, D, a, 74001198

Fort Stanton, 7 mi. SE of Capitan near U.S. 380, Capitan vicinity, 4/13/73, A, C, D, 73001142

Funston Site (AR-03-08-01-046) [Corona Phase Sites in the Jicarilla Mountains, New Mexico MPS], Address Restricted, White Oaks vicinity, 8/28/90, D, 90001250

Jicarilla Schoolhouse, NM 349, Lincoln National Forest, Jicarilla, 4/14/83, A, C, 83001623

Lincoln Historic District, U.S. 380, Lincoln, 10/15/66, A, NHL, 66000477

Mesa Ranger Station Site [Lincoln Phase Sites in the Sierra Blanca Region MPS], Address Restricted, Nogal vicinity, 10/22/90, D, 90001533

Monjeau Lookout [National Forest Fire Lookouts in the Southwestern Region TR], Lincoln National Forest, Villa Madonna vicinity, 1/27/88, A, C, g, 87002483

New Mexico Military Institute Summer Camp, Main Building, Carrizo Canyon, Ruidoso vicinity, 5/02/83, A, C, 83001622

Nogal Mesa Kiva Site [Lincoln Phase Sites in the Sierra Blanca Region MPS], Address Restricted, Nogal vicinity, 10/22/90, D, 90001532

Nogal Mesa Site [Lincoln Phase Sites in the Sierra Blanca Region MPS], Address Restricted, Nogal vicinity, 10/22/90, D, 90001531

Ruidoso Lookout Tower [National Forest Fire Lookouts in the Southwestern Region TR], Lincoln National Forest, Ruidoso, 1/27/88, A, C, g, 87002485

White Oaks Historic District, 12 mi. NE of Carrizozo on NM 349, White Oaks, 9/04/70, A, C, 70000403

Wizard's Roost, Address Restricted, Capitan vicinity, 8/02/82, A, D, 82004841

Los Alamos County

Bandelier CCC Historic District, Off NM 4, Bandelier National Monument, 5/28/87, A, C, g, NHL, NPS, 87001452

Chupaderos Canyon Small Structural Site [Cultural Developments on the Pajarito Plateau MPS], Address Restricted, Espanola vicinity, 11/07/90, D, 90001585

Chupaderos Mesa Village [Cultural Developments on the Pajarito Plateau MPS], Address Restricted, Espanola vicinity, 11/07/90, D, 90001583

Guaja Water/Soil Control Site [Cultural Developments on the Pajarito Plateau MPS], Address Restricted, Espanola vicinity, 11/07/90, D, 90001582

Guaje Site, Address Restricted, Los Alamos vicinity, 12/07/82, A, C, D, 82001049

Los Alamos County—Continued

Los Alamos Scientific Laboratory, Central Ave., Los Alamos, 10/15/66, A, g, NHL, 66000893

Pajarito Springs Site, Address Restricted, White Rock vicinity, 12/06/82, A, C, D, 82001050

White Rock Canyon, Address Restricted, White Rock vicinity, 5/18/90, D, 90000717

White Rock Canyon (Boundary Increase), Address Restricted, White Rock vicinity, 5/28/92, C, D, 92000501

Luna County

Deming Armory, 301 S. Silver Ave., Deming, 4/21/83, A, C, 83001624

Field, Seaman, House, 304 Silver Ave., Deming, 2/20/90, A, B, 90000102

Luna County Courthouse and Park, 700 S. Silver Ave., Deming, 10/05/77, A, C, g, 77000925

Mahoney Building, Gold and Spruce Sts., Deming, 9/30/80, C, 80002551

US Post Office—Deming Main [US Post Offices in New Mexico MPS], 201 W. Spruce St., Deming, 2/23/90, A, C, D, 90000139

Upton Site, Address Restricted, Deming vicinity, 12/09/80, A, D, 80002552

Village of Columbus and Camp Furlong, Portions of Columbus and Pancho Villa State Park, Columbus, 5/15/75, A, B, C, NHL, 75001164

McKinley County

Andrews Archeological District, Address Restricted, Prewitt vicinity, 5/17/79, D, 79003129

Archeological Site # LA 15278 (Reservoir Site; CM 100) [Chaco Mesa Pueblo III TR], Address Restricted, Pueblo Pintado vicinity, 8/02/85, D, 85001700

Archeological Site # LA 45, 780 [Chaco Mesa Pueblo III TR], Address Restricted, Pueblo Pintado vicinity, 8/02/85, D, 85001701

Archeological Site # LA 45, 781 [Chaco Mesa Pueblo III TR], Address Restricted, Pueblo Pintado vicinity, 8/02/85, D, 85001702

Archeological Site # LA 45, 782 [Chaco Mesa Pueblo III TR], Address Restricted, Pueblo Pintado vicinity, 8/02/85, D, 85001703

Archeological Site # LA 45, 784 [Chaco Mesa Pueblo III TR], Address Restricted, Pueblo Pintado vicinity, 8/02/85, D, 85001704

Archeological Site # LA 45, 785 [Chaco Mesa Pueblo III TR], Address Restricted, Pueblo Pintado vicinity, 8/02/85, D, 85001705

Archeological Site # LA 45, 786 [Chaco Mesa Pueblo III TR], Address Restricted, Pueblo Pintado vicinity, 8/02/85, D, 85001706

Archeological Site # LA 45, 789 [Chaco Mesa Pueblo III TR], Address Restricted, Pueblo Pintado vicinity, 8/02/85, D, 85001707

Archeological Site # LA 50, 000 [Chaco Mesa Pueblo III TR], Address Restricted, Pueblo Pintado vicinity, 8/02/85, D, 85001708

Archeological Site # LA 50, 001 [Chaco Mesa Pueblo III TR], Address Restricted, Pueblo Pintado vicinity, 8/02/85, D, 85001709

Archeological Site # LA 50, 013 (CM101) [Chaco Mesa Pueblo III TR], Address Restricted, Pueblo Pintado vicinity, 8/02/85, D, 85001710

Archeological Site # LA 50, 014 (CM 102) [Chaco Mesa Pueblo III TR], Address Restricted, Pueblo Pintado vicinity, 8/02/85, D, 85001711

Archeological Site # LA 50, 015 (CM 102A) [Chaco Mesa Pueblo III TR], Address Restricted, Pueblo Pintado vicinity, 8/02/85, D, 85001712

Archeological Site # LA 50, 016 (CM 103) [Chaco Mesa Pueblo III TR], Address Restricted, Pueblo Pintado vicinity, 8/02/85, D, 85001713

Archeological Site # LA 50, 017 (CM 104) [Chaco Mesa Pueblo III TR], Address Restricted, Pueblo Pintado vicinity, 8/02/85, D, 85001714

Archeological Site # LA 50, 018 [Chaco Mesa Pueblo III TR], Address Restricted, Pueblo Pintado vicinity, 8/02/85, D, 85001715

Archeological Site # LA 50, 019 (CM 105) [Chaco Mesa Pueblo III TR], Address Restricted, Pueblo Pintado vicinity, 8/02/85, D, 85001716

Archeological Site # LA 50, 020 (CM 106) [Chaco Mesa Pueblo III TR], Address Restricted, Pueblo Pintado vicinity, 8/02/85, D, 85001717

Archeological Site # LA 50, 021 [Chaco Mesa Pueblo III TR], Address Restricted, Pueblo Pintado vicinity, 8/02/85, D, 85001718

Archeological Site # LA 50, 022 (CM 107) [Chaco Mesa Pueblo III TR], Address Restricted, Pueblo Pintado vicinity, 8/02/85, D, 85001719

Archeological Site # LA 50, 023 (CM 118) [Chaco Mesa Pueblo III TR], Address Restricted, Pueblo Pintado vicinity, 8/02/85, D, 85001720

Archeological Site # LA 50, 024 (CM 108) [Chaco Mesa Pueblo III TR], Address Restricted, Pueblo Pintado vicinity, 8/02/85, D, 85001721

Archeological Site # LA 50, 025 (CM 109) [Chaco Mesa Pueblo III TR], Address Restricted, Pueblo Pintado vicinity, 8/02/85, D, 85001722

Archeological Site # LA 50, 026 (CM 108) [Chaco Mesa Pueblo III TR], Address Restricted, Pueblo Pintado vicinity, 8/02/85, D, 85001723

Archeological Site # LA 50, 027 (CM 111) [Chaco Mesa Pueblo III TR], Address Restricted, Pueblo Pintado vicinity, 8/02/85, D, 85001724

Archeological Site # LA 50, 028 (CM 112) [Chaco Mesa Pueblo III TR], Address Restricted, Pueblo Pintado vicinity, 8/02/85, D, 85001725

Archeological Site # LA 50, 030 (CM 114) [Chaco Mesa Pueblo III TR], Address Restricted, Pueblo Pintado vicinity, 8/02/85, D, 85001726

Archeological Site # LA 50, 031 (CM 115) [Chaco Mesa Pueblo III TR], Address Restricted, Pueblo Pintado vicinity, 8/02/85, D, 85001727

Archeological Site # LA 50, 033 (CM 117) [Chaco Mesa Pueblo III TR], Address Restricted, Pueblo Pintado vicinity, 8/02/85, D, 85001728

Archeological Site # LA 50, 034 [Chaco Mesa Pueblo III TR], Address Restricted, Pueblo Pintado vicinity, 8/02/85, D, 85001729

Archeological Site # LA 50, 036 [Chaco Mesa Pueblo III TR], Address Restricted, Pueblo Pintado vicinity, 8/02/85, D, 85001730

Archeological Site # LA 50, 037 [Chaco Mesa Pueblo III TR], Address Restricted, Pueblo Pintado vicinity, 8/02/85, D, 85001731

Archeological Site # LA 50, 038 [Chaco Mesa Pueblo III TR], Address Restricted, Pueblo Pintado vicinity, 8/02/85, D, 85001732

Archeological Site # LA 50, 044 [Chaco Mesa Pueblo III TR], Address Restricted, Pueblo Pintado vicinity, 8/02/85, D, 85001733

Archeological Site # LA 50, 071 (CM 148) [Chaco Mesa Pueblo III TR], Address Restricted, Pueblo Pintado vicinity, 8/02/85, D, 85001734

Archeological Site # LA 50, 072 (CM 94) [Chaco Mesa Pueblo III TR], Address Restricted, Pueblo Pintado vicinity, 8/02/85, D, 85001735

Archeological Site # LA 50, 074 (CM 181) [Chaco Mesa Pueblo III TR], Address Restricted, Pueblo Pintado vicinity, 8/02/85, D, 85001736

Archeological Site # LA 50, 077 [Chaco Mesa Pueblo III TR], Address Restricted, Pueblo Pintado vicinity, 8/02/85, D, 85001737

Archeological Site # LA 50, 080 [Chaco Mesa Pueblo III TR], Address Restricted, Pueblo Pintado vicinity, 8/02/85, D, 85001738

Archeological Site No. LA 50, 035 [Chaco Mesa Pueblo III TR], Address Restricted, Pueblo Pintado vicinity, 10/09/85, D, 85003143

Ashcroft—Merrill Historic District, Jct. of Bloomfield and McNeil Sts., Ramah, 7/27/90, A, B, C, a, 90001079

Bee Burrow Archeological District [Anasazi Sites Within the Chacoan Interaction Sphere TR], Address Restricted, Seven Lakes vicinity, 12/10/84, D, 84001296

Casa de Estrella Archeological Site [Anasazi Sites Within the Chacoan Interaction Sphere TR], Address Restricted, Crownpoint vicinity, 10/10/80, D, 80002553

Chaco Culture National Historical Park, Address Restricted, Thoreau vicinity, 10/15/66, A, C, D, NPS, 66000895

Chief Theater [Downtown Gallup MRA], 228 W. Coal Ave., Gallup, 5/16/88, A, C, 87002223

Cotton, C. N., Warehouse [Downtown Gallup MRA], 101 N. Third St., Gallup, 1/14/88, A, B, C, 87002226

Dalton Pass Archeological Site [Anasazi Sites Within the Chacoan Interaction Sphere TR], Address Restricted, Crownpoint vicinity, 10/10/80, A, C, D, 80002554

Drake Hotel [Downtown Gallup MRA], 216 E. Sixty-sixth Ave., Gallup, 1/14/88, A, C, 87002218

El Morro Theater [Downtown Gallup MRA], 205–209 W. Coal Ave., Gallup, 5/16/88, A, C, 87002221

El Rancho Hotel [Downtown Gallup MRA], 100 E. Sixty-sixth Ave., Gallup, 1/14/88, A, C, 87002222

Fort Wingate Archeological Site [Anasazi Sites Within the Chacoan Interaction Sphere TR],

McKinley County—Continued

Address Restricted, Fort Wingate vicinity, 10/10/80, D, 80002558

Fort Wingate Historic District, NM 400, Fort Wingate, 5/26/78, A, 78003076

Grand Hotel [Downtown Gallup MRA], 306 W. Coal Ave., Gallup, 5/25/88, A, C, 87002217

Greenlee Archeological Site [Anasazi Sites Within the Chacoan Interaction Sphere TR], Address Restricted, Crownpoint vicinity, 10/10/80, A, C, D, 80002555

Halona Pueblo, Zuni, Gallup vicinity, 2/10/75, A, C, D, a, 75002066

Harvey Hotel [Downtown Gallup MRA], 408 W. Coal Ave., Gallup, 5/25/88, A, C, 87002219

Haystack Archeological District [Anasazi Sites Within the Chacoan Interaction Sphere TR], Address Restricted, Crownpoint vicinity, 10/10/80, D, 80002556

Herman's, Roy T., Garage and Service Station [Route 66 Through New Mexico MPS], NM 122, 150 yds. W of I-40 exit, Thoreau, 11/22/93, A, C, g, 93001212

Lebanon Lodge No. 22 [Downtown Gallup MRA], 106 W. Aztec, Gallup, 2/14/89, A, C, 87002225

Manuelito Complex, Address Restricted, Manuelito vicinity, 10/15/66, D, NHL, 66000894

McKinley County Courthouse [County Courthouses of New Mexico TR], 205–209 W. Hill St., Gallup, 2/15/89, A, C, g, 87000879

Palace Hotel [Downtown Gallup MRA], 236 W. Sixty-sixth Ave., Gallup, 5/16/88, A, C, 87002216

Rex Hotel [Downtown Gallup MRA], 300 W. Sixty-sixth, Gallup, 1/14/88, A, C, 87002215

State Maintained Route 66—Manuelito to the Arizona Border [Route 66 Through New Mexico MPS], W side of the Manuelito grade separation SW to AZ border, Mentmore vicinity, 11/22/93, A, g, 93001209

US Post Office [Downtown Gallup MRA], 201 S. First St., Gallup, 5/25/88, A, C, 87002228

Upper Kin Klizhin Archeological Site [Anasazi Sites Within the Chacoan Interaction Sphere TR], Address Restricted, Crownpoint vicinity, 10/10/80, A, C, D, 80002557

Vogt, Evon Zartman, Ranch House, 1 mi. S of Ramah, 500 ft. E of NM 53, Ramah vicinity, 2/04/93, B, 92001819

White Cafe [Downtown Gallup MRA], 100 W. Sixth-sixth Ave., Gallup, 1/14/88, A, C, 87002212

Mora County

Cassidy Mill, SE of Cleveland off NM 3, Cleveland vicinity, 12/06/78, A, 78001818

Cassidy, Daniel, House [Upland Valleys of Western Mora County MPS], Address Restricted, Mora vicinity, 7/27/90, A, C, 90001062

Cassidy, Daniel, and Sons General Merchandise Store, NM 3, Cleveland, 8/01/79, A, C, 79001541

Fort Union National Monument, 9 mi. N of Watrous on NM 477, Watrous vicinity, 10/15/66, A, NPS, 66000044

Garcia House [Upland Valleys of Western Mora County MPS], Address Restricted, Mora vicinity, 12/24/90, A, C, 90001063

Gordon—Sanchez Mill [Upland Valleys of Western Mora County MPS], Address Restricted, Mora vicinity, 7/27/90, A, C, 90001061

La Cueva Historic District, 6 mi. SE of Mora at jct. of NM 3 and 21, Mora vicinity, 5/25/73, A, C, a, 73001144

Ledoux Rural Historic District [Upland Valleys of Western Mora County MPS], Address Restricted, Ledoux, 12/24/90, A, C, 90001057

Mora Historic District [Upland Valleys of Western Mora County MPS], Address Restricted, Mora, 12/24/90, A, C, 90001056

North Carmen Historic District [Upland Valleys of Western Mora County MPS], Address Restricted, Ledoux vicinity, 12/24/90, A, C, 90001058

Olguin, Jose, Barn—Corral Complex [Upland Valleys of Western Mora County MPS], Address Restricted, Mora vicinity, 12/24/90, A, C, 90001060

Santa Clara Hotel, 111 Railroad Ave., Wagon Mound, 5/16/91, A, C, 91000602

St. Vrain's Mill, On NM 38, Mora, 8/28/73, A, B, 73001143

Strong, J. P., Store, NM 21 and NM 120, Ocate, 7/27/79, A, B, C, 79001542

Valdez, Desiderio, House [Upland Valleys of Western Mora County MPS], Address Restricted, Cleveland vicinity, 12/24/90, A, C, 90001059

Valdez, Narciso, House, NM 120, Ocate, 7/11/80, B, C, 80004484

Wagon Mound, E of Wagon Mound on U.S. 85, Wagon Mound vicinity, 10/15/66, A, NHL, 66000478

Watrous, U.S. 85, Watrous, 10/15/66, A, NHL, 66000480

Otero County

Administration Building [New Mexico Campus Buildings Built 1906–1937 TR], 1900 N. White Sands Blvd., NMSVH, Alamogordo, 5/16/89, C, 88001564

Auditorium and Recreation Building [New Mexico Campus Buildings Built 1906–1937 TR], 1900 N. White Sands Blvd., NMSVH, Alamogordo, 5/16/89, C, 88001565

Bluewater Lookout Complex [National Forest Fire Lookouts in the Southwestern Region TR], Lincoln National Forest, Weed vicinity, 1/28/88, A, C, 87002486

Carrisa Lookout Complex [National Forest Fire Lookouts in the Southwestern Region TR], Lincoln National Forest, Long Canyon vicinity, 1/28/88, A, C, 87002488

Central Receiving Building [New Mexico Campus Buildings Built 1906–1937 TR], 1900 N. White Sands Blvd., NMSVH, Alamogordo, 5/16/89, C, 88001566

Circle Cross Ranch Headquarters, SW of Sacramento, Sacramento vicinity, 11/17/80, A, C, 80002563

Garcia, Juan, House [La Luz Townsite MRA], Tularosa St., La Luz, 10/23/80, C, 80002559

Hay Canyon Logging Camp [Railroad Logging Sites of the Sacramento Mountains, New Mexico MPS], Address Restricted, Mayhill vicinity, 1/02/92, D, 91001880

Hubbell Canyon Log Chute [Railroad Logging Sites of the Sacramento Mountains, New Mexico MPS], Address Restricted, Cloudcroft vicinity, 12/31/91, A, C, 91001882

Infirmary Building [New Mexico Campus Buildings Built 1906–1937 TR], 1900 N. White Sands Blvd., NMSVH, Alamogordo, 5/16/89, C, 88001567

La Luz Historic District [La Luz Townsite MRA], Off NM 83, La Luz, 10/23/80, A, C, 80002560

La Luz Pottery Factory, 2 mi. (3.2 km) E of La Luz, La Luz vicinity, 5/29/79, A, C, 79001544

Mayhill Administrative Site, US 82, 1.5 mi. N of Mayhill, Mayhill vicinity, 6/01/89, A, C, 89000476

Mexican Canyon Trestle, NW of Cloudcroft off NM 83, Cloudcroft vicinity, 5/07/79, A, C, 79001543

Queen Anne House [La Luz Townsite MRA], Kearny St., La Luz, 10/23/80, C, 80002561

Sutherland, D. H., House [La Luz Townsite MRA], Main St., La Luz, 10/23/80, B, C, 80002562

Tularosa Original Townsite District, U.S. 54/70, Tularosa, 2/02/79, C, 79001545

Weed Lookout Tower [National Forest Fire Lookouts in the Southwestern Region TR], Lincoln National Forest, Sacramento vicinity, 1/28/88, A, C, 87002487

White Sands National Monument Historic District, US 70/82, Alamogordo vicinity, 6/23/88, A, C, NPS, 88000751

Wills Canyon Spur Trestle [Railroad Logging Sites of the Sacramento Mountains, New Mexico MPS], Address Restricted, Cloudcroft vicinity, 12/31/91, A, C, 91001881

Wofford Lookout Complex [National Forest Fire Lookouts in the Southwestern Region TR], Lincoln National Forest, Cloudcroft vicinity, 1/28/88, A, C, 87002484

Quay County

Blue Swallow Motel [Route 66 Through New Mexico MPS], 815 E. Tucumcari Blvd., Tucumcari, 11/22/93, A, C, g, 93001210

Nara Visa School, US 54, Nara Visa, 10/31/83, A, C, 83004151

Richardson Store, Off I-40, Montoya, 11/16/78, A, 78001819

Rio Arriba County

Abiquiu Mesa Grid Gardens, Address Restricted, Abiquiu vicinity, 12/07/82, C, D, 82001051

Adams Canyon Site (LA 55824) [Navajo—Refugee Pueblo TR], Address Restricted, Tierrra Amarilla vicinity, 1/21/87, C, D, 86003631

Rio Arriba County—Continued

Adolfo Canyon Site (LA 5665) [Navajo—Refugee Pueblo TR], Address Restricted, Tierra Amarilla vicinity, 1/21/87, C, D, 86003605

Archeological Site No. AR-03-10-02-357 [Gallina Culture Developments in North Central New Mexico MPS], Address Restricted, Llaves vicinity, 5/14/89, D, 89000345

Becker, George, House, Bunk House and Barn [La Tierra Amarilla MRA], E. of La Puente Rd. and S. of Hatchery Rd., Los Ojos vicinity, 4/04/85, C, 85000777

Blanton Log House [La Tierra Amarilla MRA], E. of La Puente Rd. and S. of Hatchery Rd., Los Ojos vicinity, 4/04/85, C, 85000778

Bond, Frank, House, Bond St., Espanola, 3/06/80, B, C, 80002564

Boulder Fortress (LA 55828) [Navajo—Refugee Pueblo TR], Address Restricted, Tierra Amarilla vicinity, 1/21/87, C, D, 86003630

Burns Lake Bungalow [La Tierra Amarilla MRA], 1/2 mile S. of E. end of Hatchery Rd., Los Ojos vicinity, 4/04/85, C, 85000780

Cabresto Mesa Tower Complex (LA 2138) [Navajo—Refugee Pueblo TR], Address Restricted, Tierra Amarilla vicinity, 1/21/87, C, D, 86003611

Cagle's Site (LA 55826) [Navajo—Refugee Pueblo TR], Address Restricted, Tierra Amarilla vicinity, 1/21/87, C, D, 86003629

Canyon View Ruin (LA 55827) [Navajo—Refugee Pueblo TR], Address Restricted, Tierra Amarilla vicinity, 1/21/87, C, D, 86003628

Casa Mesa Diablo (LA 11100) [Navajo—Refugee Pueblo TR], Address Restricted, Tierra Amarilla vicinity, 1/21/87, C, D, 86003641

Casados House [La Tierra Amarilla MRA], Off junction of U.S. 84 and NM Rd. 95, Los Ojos vicinity, 4/04/85, A, C, 85000825

Castles of the Chama (AR-03-10-01-216) [Gallina Culture Developments in North Central New Mexico MPS], Address Restricted, Llaves vicinity, 5/14/89, D, 89000344

Citadel, The (LA 55828) [Navajo—Refugee Pueblo TR], Address Restricted, Tierra Amarilla vicinity, 1/21/87, C, D, 86003627

Compressor Station Ruin (LA 5658) [Navajo—Refugee Pueblo TR], Address Restricted, Tierra Amarilla vicinity, 1/21/87, C, D, 86003592

Corral Canyon Pueblo Site [Cultural Developments on the Pajarito Plateau MPS], Address Restricted, Espanola vicinity, 11/07/90, D, 90001581

Corral Mesa Cavate Pueblo Site [Cultural Developments on the Pajarito Plateau MPS], Address Restricted, Espanola vicinity, 11/07/90, D, 90001584

Crevice Ruin (LA 13218) [Navajo—Refugee Pueblo TR], Address Restricted, Tierra Amarilla vicinity, 1/21/87, C, D, 86003639

Crow Canyon Archeological District, Address Restricted, Farmington vicinity, 7/15/74, A, C, D, 74001200

Crow Canyon Site (LA 20219) [Navajo—Refugee Pueblo TR], Address Restricted, Tierra Amarilla vicinity, 1/21/87, C, D, 86003638

Cumbres and Toltec Scenic Railroad, Between Antonito and Chama, NM, Chama, vicinity, 2/16/73, A, C, 73000462

Delgadito Pueblito (LA 5649) [Navajo—Refugee Pueblo TR], Address Restricted, Tierra Amarilla vicinity, 1/21/87, C, D, 86003590

El Barranco Community Ditch [La Tierra Amarilla MRA], Exdending from the Chama River at Chama Division to Upper Brazos Ditch, Los Brazos, 9/29/86, A, 86002296

El Porvenir Community Ditch [La Tierra Amarilla MRA], Extending from 4.5 mi. E of Encenada to 0.5 mi. N of Encenada, Encenada vicinity, 9/29/86, A, 86002300

Embudo Historic District, U.S. 64, Embudo, 3/12/79, A, C, 79001547

Encenada Community Ditch [La Tierra Amarilla MRA], Extending from 4.5 mi. E of Encenada to 0.3 mi. W of US 85 0.5 mi. NE of State Fish Hatchery, Encenada vicinity, 9/29/86, A, 86002303

Foothold Ruin (LA 9073) [Navajo—Refugee Pueblo TR], Address Restricted, Tierra Amarilla vicinity, 1/21/87, C, D, 86003602

Foster Hotel, Fourth and Terrace, Chama, 2/13/86, A, 86000225

Frances Canyon Ruin [Navajo—Refugee Pueblo TR (AD)], Address Restricted, Blanco vicinity, 9/04/70, D, 70000404

Frances Canyon Ruin (LA 2135) (Boundary Increase) [Navajo—Refugee Pueblo TR], Address Restricted, Tierra Amarilla vicinity, 1/21/87, C, D, 87000244

Garcia Canyon Pueblito (LA 36608) [Navajo—Refugee Pueblo TR], Address Restricted, Tierra Amarilla vicinity, 1/21/87, C, D, 86003636

Gomez Canyon Ruin (LA 55831) [Navajo—Refugee Pueblo TR], Address Restricted, Tierra Amarilla vicinity, 1/21/87, C, D, 86003626

Gomez Point Site (LA 58832) [Navajo—Refugee Pueblo TR], Address Restricted, Tierra Amarilla vicinity, 1/21/87, C, D, 86003625

Gould Pass Ruin (LA 5659) [Navajo—Refugee Pueblo TR], Address Restricted, Tierra Amarilla vicinity, 1/21/87, C, D, 86003594

Hill Road Ruin (LA 55833) [Navajo—Refugee Pueblo TR], Address Restricted, Tierra Amarilla vicinity, 1/21/87, C, D, 86003624

Hooded Fireplace Ruin (LA 5662) [Navajo—Refugee Pueblo TR], Address Restricted, Tierra Amarilla vicinity, 1/21/87, C, D, 86003607

Hupobi-ouinge, Address Restricted, Ojo Caliente vicinity, 1/18/85, D, 85000111

Jaramillo, Ramon, House and Barn [La Tierra Amarilla MRA], Encenada Rd., Encenada, 9/29/86, C, 86002309

Jicarilla Apache Historic District, Main St., NM 17, Apache, Keliiaa, and Sand Hill Drs., Dulce, 3/01/84, A, 84002956

Kin Naa daa (Maize House) (LA 1872) [Navajo—Refugee Pueblo TR], Address Restricted, Tierra Amarilla vicinity, 1/21/87, C, D, 86003612

Ku-ouinge [Late Prehistoric Cultural Developments Along the Rio Chama and Tributaries MPS], Address Restricted, Espanola vicinity, 8/05/93, D, 93000674

La Puente Community Ditch [La Tierra Amarilla MRA], Extending from Parkview discharge pt. to 0.7 mi. SW of La Puente on the Chama River, La Puente vicinity, 9/29/86, A, 86002294

La Puente Historic District [La Tierra Amarilla MRA], Roughly bounded by Main Rd. in La Puente from drop-off of 2nd to 1st plateau E. to Church on West., Los Ojos vicinity, 4/04/85, C, 85000826

Largo School Ruin (LA 5657) [Navajo—Refugee Pueblo TR], Address Restricted, Tierra Amarilla vicinity, 1/21/87, C, D, 86003621

Leaf Water Pueblo(LA 300), Address Restricted, Hernandez vicinity, 12/01/83, D, 83004155

Los Brazos Historic District [La Tierra Amarilla MRA], Roughly bounded by US 84, North Rd., fence line and drop-off to Rio Brazos, Los Ojos vicinity, 4/04/85, C, 85000827

Los Luceros Hacienda, Off NM 389, Los Luceros vicinity, 10/20/83, A, C, D, a, 83004157

Los Ojos (Parkview) Fish Hatchery [La Tierra Amarilla MRA], E. end of Hatchery Rd., Los Ojos vicinity, 4/04/85, C, 85000779

Los Ojos (Parkview) Historic District [La Tierra Amarilla MRA], Roughly bounded by US 84, jct. of Old Hwy w/US 84, drop-off from 1st plateau to Chama R. Valley and E.-W. Hatchery Rd., Los Ojos vicinity, 4/04/85, A, C, 85000828

Manzanares, Tony, House [La Tierra Amarilla MRA], E. of Los Ojos Rd. and N. of La Puente Church, Los Ojos vicinity, 4/04/85, C, 85000829

Martinez, Gilbert, Barn [La Tierra Amarilla MRA], E. of La Puente Rd and S. of Hatchery Rd., Los Ojos vicinity, 4/04/85, A, C, 85000781

Martinez, Teodoro, House [La Tierra Amarilla MRA], E. of La Puente Rd and N. of Hatchery Rd., Los Ojos vicinity, 4/04/85, C, 85000782

Nogales Cliff House (AR-03-10-02-124) [Gallina Culture Developments in North Central New Mexico MPS], Address Restricted, Llaves vicinity, 5/14/89, C, D, 89000346

Old Fort (LA 1869) [Navajo—Refugee Pueblo TR], Address Restricted, Tierra Amarilla vicinity, 1/21/87, C, D, 86003614

Ortega, Victor, Cabin [National Forest Fire Lookouts in the Southwestern Region TR], Carson National Forest, Cebolla vicinity, 1/28/88, A, C, 87002456

Our Lady of Lourdes Grotto [La Tierra Amarilla MRA], Old Highway, Los Ojos, 3/27/87, A, C, a, 86002318

Overlook Site (LA 10732) [Navajo—Refugee Pueblo TR], Address Restricted, Tierra Amarilla vicinity, 1/21/87, C, D, 86003601

Parkview Community Ditch [La Tierra Amarilla MRA], Extending from 4.5 mi. E of Encenada to 1 mi. SW of State Fish Hatchery, Los Ojos vicinity, 9/29/86, A, 86002305

Plaza Blanca Community Ditch [La Tierra Amarilla MRA], Extending from 2 mi. WSW of State Fish Hatchery to 1 mi. SSW of Plaza Blanca, Plaza Blanca vicinity, 9/29/86, A, 86002298

Rio Arriba County—Continued

Plaza Blanca Historic District [La Tierra Amarilla MRA], Roughly Plaza Blanca and Old Puente Ford Rds. adjacent to Plaza Blanca Ditch, Plaza Blanca, 9/29/86, A, C, a, 86002322

Pointed Butte Ruin (LA 10733) [Navajo—Refugee Pueblo TR], Address Restricted, Tierra Amarilla vicinity, 1/21/87, C, D, 86003600

Ponsipa'Akeri [Late Prehistoric Cultural Developments Along the Rio Chama and Tributaries MPS], Address Restricted, Ojo Caliente vicinity, 8/05/93, D, 93000673

Pork Chop Pass Site (LA 5661) [Navajo—Refugee Pueblo TR], Address Restricted, Tierra Amarilla vicinity, 1/21/87, C, D, 86003597

Posi-ouinge [Late Prehistoric Cultural Developments Along the Rio Chama and Tributaries MPS], Address Restricted, Ojo Caliente vicinity, 8/05/93, D, 93000675

Pueblito Canyon Ruin (LA 1684) [Navajo—Refugee Pueblo TR], Address Restricted, Tierra Amarilla vicinity, 1/21/87, C, D, 86003615

Pueblito East Ruin (LA 55834) [Navajo—Refugee Pueblo TR], Address Restricted, Tierra Amarilla vicinity, 1/21/87, C, D, 86003623

Puye Ruins, Address Restricted, Espanola vicinity, 10/15/66, D, NHL, 66000481

Rattlesnake Ridge Site [Gallina Culture Developments in North Central New Mexico MPS], Address Restricted, Llaves vicinity, 10/27/92, D, 92001405

Ridge Top House (LA 6287) [Navajo—Refugee Pueblo TR], Address Restricted, Tierra Amarilla vicinity, 1/21/87, C, D, 86003603

Rincon Largo Ruin (LA 2436 and LA 2435) [Navajo—Refugee Pueblo TR], Address Restricted, Tierra Amarilla vicinity, 1/21/87, C, D, 86003589

Rincon Rockshelter (LA 55835) [Navajo—Refugee Pueblo TR], Address Restricted, Tierra Amarilla vicinity, 1/21/87, C, D, 86003622

Romine Canyon Ruin (LA 55836) [Navajo—Refugee Pueblo TR], Address Restricted, Tierra Amarilla vicinity, 1/21/87, C, D, 86003620

Romine Ranch Site (LA 55837) [Navajo—Refugee Pueblo TR], Address Restricted, Tierra Amarilla vicinity, 1/21/87, C, D, 86003619

San Antonio de Padua del Quemado Chapel, off NM 76, Cordova, 11/02/78, A, C, a, 78001821

San Gabriel de Yungue-Ouinge, Address Restricted, Espanola vicinity, 10/15/66, A, D, NHL, 66000482

San Joaquin Church [La Tierra Amarilla MRA], NM 162, Encenada, 9/29/86, C, a, 86002310

San Juan Pueblo, N of Sante Fe, Sante Fe vicinity, 7/30/74, A, C, D, a, 74001201

Sanchez, Samuel, Barns [La Tierra Amarilla MRA], Off US 64, Los Brazos vicinity, 9/29/86, C, 86002317

Sanchez, Samuel, House [La Tierra Amarilla MRA], Off US 64, Los Brazos vicinity, 9/29/86, C, 86002315

Sanchez-March House [La Tierra Amarilla MRA], W of US 84 and N of NM 95, Los Ojos vicinity, 4/04/85, C, 85000830

Santa Clara Pueblo, S of Espanola off NM 30, Espanola vicinity, 11/05/74, A, C, D, 74001199

Santa Rosa de Lima de Abiquiu, Address Restricted, Abiquiu vicinity, 4/14/78, A, C, D, 78001820

Shaft House (LA 5660) [Navajo—Refugee Pueblo TR], Address Restricted, Tierra Amarilla vicinity, 1/21/87, C, D, 86003595

Split Rock Ruin (LA 5664) [Navajo—Refugee Pueblo TR], Address Restricted, Tierra Amarilla vicinity, 1/21/87, C, D, 86003606

Tapicito Ruin (LA 2298) [Navajo—Refugee Pueblo TR], Address Restricted, Tierra Amarilla vicinity, 1/21/87, C, D, 86003610

Three Corn Ruin (LA 1871) [Navajo—Refugee Pueblo TR], Address Restricted, Tierra Amarilla vicinity, 1/21/87, C, D, 86003613

Tierra Amarilla Community Ditch [La Tierra Amarilla MRA], Extending from 2 mi. ESE of Tierra Amarilla to 0.2 mi. N of La Corridera Rd., Tierra Amarilla vicinity, 9/29/86, A, 86002307

Tierra Amarilla Historic District [La Tierra Amarilla MRA], Roughly along La Puente Rd. on both sides of US 84 and along Old Highway and Creek Rd., Tierra Amarilla, 9/29/86, A, C, 86002327

Tower of the Standing God (LA 55839) [Navajo—Refugee Pueblo TR], Address Restricted, Tierra Amarilla vicinity, 1/21/87, C, D, 86003618

Truby's Tower (LA 2434) [Navajo—Refugee Pueblo TR], Address Restricted, Tierra Amarilla vicinity, 1/21/87, C, D, 86003608

Trujillo, Manuelita, House [La Tierra Amarilla MRA], Off US 84 S. of Los Brazos River, Los Ojos vicinity, 4/04/85, C, 85000831

Trujillo, Sr., Fernando, House [La Tierra Amarilla MRA], W. of US 84 and N. of NM 95, Los Ojos vicinity, 4/04/85, C, 85000832

Tsama Pueblo, Address Restricted, Abiquiu vicinity, 11/17/83, D, 83004158

Tsiping, Address Restricted, Canones vicinity, 9/04/70, D, 70000405

Unreachable Rockshelter (LA 55841) [Navajo—Refugee Pueblo TR], Address Restricted, Tierra Amarilla vicinity, 1/21/87, C, D, 86003616

Valdez, Miguel, Barn [La Tierra Amarilla MRA], San Joaquin Church Loop Rd., Encenada, 9/29/86, C, 86002314

Vicenti Site, Address Restricted, Dulce vicinity, 5/14/79, D, 79001546

Wall, The (LA 55840) [Navajo—Refugee Pueblo TR], Address Restricted, Tierra Amarilla vicinity, 1/21/87, C, D, 86003617

Roosevelt County

Administration Building [New Mexico Campus Buildings Built 1906–1937 TR], S side of University Pl. and campus green., ENMU, Portales, 9/22/88, C, 88001558

Anderson Basin, Address Restricted, Clovis vicinity, 10/15/66, D, NHL, 66000483

Bank of Portales, 123 Main, Portales, 12/27/84, A, C, 84000635

US Post Office—Portales Main [US Post Offices in New Mexico MPS], 116 W. First St., Portales, 2/23/90, A, C, D, 90000140

San Juan County

Abrams, H. D., House [Aztec New Mexico Historic MRA], 403 N. Church St., Aztec, 2/21/85, C, 85000322

American Hotel [Aztec New Mexico Historic MRA], 300 S. Main, Aztec, 2/21/85, A, C, 85000323

Archeological Site OCA-CGP-56, Address Restricted, Fruitland vicinity, 2/23/78, D, 78001822

Austin-McDonald House [Aztec New Mexico Historic MRA], 501 Rio Grande, Aztec, 2/21/85, C, 85000324

Aztec Main Street Historic District [Aztec New Mexico Historic MRA], Bounded by Main E., Chuska S., alley between Park and Main W., and Chaco N., Aztec, 2/21/85, A, C, 85000321

Aztec Motor Company Building [Aztec New Mexico Historic MRA], 301 S. Main, Aztec, 2/21/85, A, C, 85000325

Aztec Ruins National Monument, 1 mi. N of Aztec, Aztec vicinity, 10/15/66, A, C, D, NPS, 66000484

Ball, D. C., House [Aztec New Mexico Historic MRA], 300 San Juan, Aztec, 2/21/85, C, 85000326

Building at 202 Park Avenue [Aztec New Mexico Historic MRA], 202 Park Ave., Aztec, 2/21/85, C, 85000328

Building at 500 White Avenue [Aztec New Mexico Historic MRA], 500 White Ave., Aztec, 2/21/85, C, 85000327

Christmas Tree Ruin (LA 11097) [Navajo—Refugee Pueblo TR], Address Restricted, Farmington vicinity, 1/21/87, C, D, 86003646

Church Avenue-Lovers Lane Historic District [Aztec New Mexico Historic MRA], Bounded by Rio Grande E., Zia S., Park W. and NM hwy 550, Aztec, 2/21/85, A, C, 85000329

Cottonwood Divide Site (LA 55829) [Navajo—Refugee Pueblo TR], Address Restricted, Farmington vicinity, 1/21/87, C, D, 86003644

Daws-Keys House [Aztec New Mexico Historic MRA], 421 N. Church, Aztec, 2/21/85, C, 85000330

Denver and Rio Grande Western Railway Depot [Aztec New Mexico Historic MRA], 314 Rio Grande, Aztec, 2/21/85, A, C, 85000331

East Side Rincon Site, Address Restricted, Farmington vicinity, 12/15/85, D, 85003154

Engleman-Thomas Building [Aztec New Mexico Historic MRA], 200 S. Main, Aztec, 2/21/85, A, C, 85000332

Gallegos Wash Archeological District, Address Restricted, Farmington vicinity, 11/20/75, D, 75001165

Hadlock's Crow Canyon No. 1 (LA 55830) [Navajo—Refugee Pueblo TR], Address Restricted, Farmington vicinity, 1/21/87, D, 86003642

San Juan County—Continued

Halfway House Archeological Site [Anasazi Sites Within the Chacoan Interaction Sphere TR], Address Restricted, Bloomfield vicinity, 10/10/80, D, 80002565

Jaquez Site Ruin, Address Restricted, Farmington vicinity, 12/10/84, D, 84001281

Lower Animas Ditch [Aztec New Mexico Historic MRA], Lower Animas Ditch from Church Ave. to Lovers Lane Historic District, Aztec, 3/19/87, A, 87001116

McCoy, Harvey, House [Aztec New Mexico Historic MRA], 725 Pioneer, Aztec, 2/21/85, C, 85000333

McCoy-Maddox House [Aztec New Mexico Historic MRA], NW corner of Maddox and NE Aztec Blvd., Aztec, 2/21/85, A, C, 85000334

McGee House [Aztec New Mexico Historic MRA], 501 Sabena St., Aztec, 2/21/85, C, 85000335

Morris' No. 41 Archeological District [Anasazi Sites Within the Chacoan Interaction Sphere TR (AD)], Address Restricted, La Plata vicinity, 5/17/79, A, C, D, 79001548

Prieta Mesa Site (LA 11251) [Navajo—Refugee Pueblo TR], Address Restricted, Farmington vicinity, 1/21/87, C, D, 86003647

Salmon Ruin, Address Restricted, Farmington vicinity, 9/04/70, D, 70000406

Simon Canyon (LA 5047) [Navajo—Refugee Pueblo TR], Address Restricted, Farmington vicinity, 1/21/87, C, D, 86003645

Site No. OCA-CGP-54-1, Address Restricted, Fruitland vicinity, 4/19/78, D, 78001823

Site OCA-CGP-605, Address Restricted, Fruitland vicinity, 2/17/78, D, 78003261

Star Rock Refuge (LA 55838) [Navajo—Refugee Pueblo TR], Address Restricted, Farmington vicinity, 1/21/87, C, D, 86003643

Twin Angels Archeological Site [Anasazi Sites Within the Chacoan Interaction Sphere TR], Address Restricted, Bloomfield vicinity, 10/10/80, D, 80002566

San Miguel County

AT & SF Roundhouse [Las Vegas New Mexico MRA], NE of Grand Ave., Las Vegas, 9/26/85, A, C, 85002621

Acequia Madre [Las Vegas New Mexico MRA], Roughly from Gallinas River to intersection of S. Pacific and US 85, Las Vegas, 3/19/87, A, 87001118

Angel, Arturo, House [Las Vegas New Mexico MRA], 926 S. Pacific, Las Vegas, 9/26/85, C, 85002604

Arthur, Charles and Lewis, E. N. House [Las Vegas New Mexico MRA], Douglas Ave., Las Vegas, 9/26/85, C, 85002605

Baca-Korte House [Las Vegas New Mexico MRA], 615 S. Pacific, Las Vegas, 9/26/85, C, 85002658

Bean-Newlee House [Las Vegas New Mexico MRA], 1045 5th St., Las Vegas, 9/26/85, C, 85002625

Bell Ranch Headquarters, N and E of the Conchas Reservoir, Bell Ranch vicinity, 10/06/70, A, C, 70000407

Bridge Street Historic District [Las Vegas New Mexico MRA (AD)], 100 block of Bridge St., Las Vegas, 7/26/78, A, C, 78001824

Building at 1202 9th Street [Las Vegas New Mexico MRA], 1202 9th St., Las Vegas, 9/26/85, C, 85002632

Building at 1214 Bridge [Las Vegas New Mexico MRA], 1214 Bridge, Las Vegas, 9/26/85, A, C, 85002660

Building at 1406 Romero [Las Vegas New Mexico MRA], 1406 Romero, Las Vegas, 9/26/85, C, 85002656

Building at 2005 Montezuma [Las Vegas New Mexico MRA], 2005 Montezuma, Las Vegas, 9/26/85, C, 85002655

Clevenger, Lowery, House [Las Vegas New Mexico MRA], 1013 2nd, Las Vegas, 9/26/85, C, 85002594

Cook, James, House [Las Vegas New Mexico MRA], 1017 11th, Las Vegas, 9/26/85, C, 85002647

Distrito de las Escuelas [Las Vegas New Mexico MRA (AD)], S. Pacific and S. Gonzales Sts., Las Vegas, 3/18/80, C, 80002567

Douglas Avenue School [Las Vegas New Mexico MRA (AD)], 900 Douglas Ave., Las Vegas, 8/05/83, A, C, 83001625

Douglas-Sixth Street Historic District [Las Vegas New Mexico MRA (AD)], Roughly bounded by Grand, Lincoln, and 7th Sts., and University Ave., Las Vegas, 7/21/83, C, 83001626

Eldorado Hotel [Las Vegas New Mexico MRA], 514 Grand, Las Vegas, 9/26/85, C, 85002626

Elks Lodge Building [Las Vegas New Mexico MRA (AD)], 819 Douglas Ave., Las Vegas, 2/28/85, A, C, 85000377

First Baptist Church [Las Vegas New Mexico MRA], 700 University, Las Vegas, 9/26/85, A, C, a, 85002612

Gatignole, Eugenio, House [Las Vegas New Mexico MRA], 1114 S. Gonzales, Las Vegas, 9/26/85, C, 85002606

Glorieta Baldy Lookout Tower [National Forest Fire Lookouts in the Southwestern Region TR], Santa Fe National Forest, La Cueva vicinity, 1/27/88, A, C, g, 87002492

Glorieta Pass Battlefield, 10 mi. SE of Santa Fe on U.S. 84–85, Santa Fe vicinity, 10/15/66, A, NHL, 66000486

Herrera, Esperansa, House [Las Vegas New Mexico MRA], 2231 Church, Las Vegas, 9/26/85, C, 85002613

House at 1007 11th Street [Las Vegas New Mexico MRA], 1007 11th St., Las Vegas, 9/26/85, C, 85002648

House at 1025 Railroad [Las Vegas New Mexico MRA], 1025 Railroad, Las Vegas, 9/26/85, C, 85002631

House at 1114 10th [Las Vegas New Mexico MRA], 1114 10th, Las Vegas, 9/26/85, C, 85002649

House at 1116 Columbia [Las Vegas New Mexico MRA], 1116 Columbia, Las Vegas, 9/26/85, C, 85002641

House at 119 Railroad [Las Vegas New Mexico MRA], 119 Railroad, Las Vegas, 9/26/85, C, 85002624

House at 12 Grand [Las Vegas New Mexico MRA], 12 Grand, Las Vegas, 9/26/85, C, 85002622

House at 1221 San Francisco [Las Vegas New Mexico MRA], 1221 San Francisco, Las Vegas, 9/26/85, C, 85002644

House at 1513 8th [Las Vegas New Mexico MRA], 1513 8th, Las Vegas, 9/26/85, C, 85002634

House at 16 Grand [Las Vegas New Mexico MRA], 16 Grand, Las Vegas, 9/26/85, C, 85002623

House at 1616 8th [Las Vegas New Mexico MRA], 1616 8th, Las Vegas, 9/26/85, C, 85002645

House at 1717 8th [Las Vegas New Mexico MRA], 1717 8th, Las Vegas, 9/26/85, C, 85002646

House at 2203 New Mexico [Las Vegas New Mexico MRA], 2203 New Mexico, Las Vegas, 9/26/85, C, 85002654

House at 2501 Taos Alley [Las Vegas New Mexico MRA], 2501 Taos Alley, Las Vegas, 9/26/85, C, 85002652

House at 309 Railroad [Las Vegas New Mexico MRA], 309 Railroad, Las Vegas, 9/26/85, C, 85002628

House at 312 Tecolote [Las Vegas New Mexico MRA], 312 Tecolote, Las Vegas, 9/26/85, C, 85002609

House at 508 University [Las Vegas New Mexico MRA], 508 University, Las Vegas, 9/26/85, C, 85002611

House at 514 University [Las Vegas New Mexico MRA], 514 University, Las Vegas, 9/26/85, C, 85002610

House at 521 S. Pacific [Las Vegas New Mexico MRA], 521 S. Pacific, Las Vegas, 9/26/85, C, 85002659

House at 613 Mora [Las Vegas New Mexico MRA], 613 Mora, Las Vegas, 9/26/85, C, 85002650

House at 618 Mora [Las Vegas New Mexico MRA], 618 Mora, Las Vegas, 9/26/85, C, 85002651

House at 733 Railroad [Las Vegas New Mexico MRA], 733 Railroad, Las Vegas, 9/26/85, C, 85002629

House at 800 Pecos [Las Vegas New Mexico MRA], 800 Pecos, Las Vegas, 9/26/85, C, 85002633

House at 810 Douglas [Las Vegas New Mexico MRA], 810 Douglas, Las Vegas, 9/26/85, C, 85002603

House at 812 Douglas [Las Vegas New Mexico MRA], 812 Douglas, Las Vegas, 9/26/85, C, 85002602

House at 814 Douglas [Las Vegas New Mexico MRA], 814 Douglas, Las Vegas, 9/26/85, C, 85002601

House at 818 Douglas [Las Vegas New Mexico MRA], 818 Douglas, Las Vegas, 9/26/85, C, 85002600

San Miguel County—Continued

House at 821 12th [Las Vegas New Mexico MRA], 821 12th, Las Vegas, 9/26/85, C, 85002643

House at 822 Douglas [Las Vegas New Mexico MRA], 822 Douglas, Las Vegas, 9/26/85, C, 85002599

House at 913 2nd [Las Vegas New Mexico MRA], 913 2nd, Las Vegas, 9/26/85, C, 85002597

House at 915 2nd [Las Vegas New Mexico MRA], 915 2nd, Las Vegas, 9/26/85, C, 85002596

House at 919 2nd [Las Vegas New Mexico MRA], 919 2nd, Las Vegas, 9/26/85, C, 85002595

House at 919 Railroad [Las Vegas New Mexico MRA], 919 Railroad, Las Vegas, 9/26/85, C, 85002630

House at 921 Chavez [Las Vegas New Mexico MRA], 921 Chavez, Las Vegas, 9/26/85, C, 85002653

House at 921 S. Pacific [Las Vegas New Mexico MRA], 921 S. Pacific, Las Vegas, 9/26/85, C, 85002608

House at 931 Prince [Las Vegas New Mexico MRA], 931 Prince, Las Vegas, 9/26/85, C, 85002620

House at 933 12th [Las Vegas New Mexico MRA], 933 12th, Las Vegas, 9/26/85, C, 85002642

Ilfeld, Adele, Auditorium [Las Vegas New Mexico MRA (AD)], New Mexico Highlands University campus, Las Vegas, 1/08/80, C, 80002568

Ilfeld, Charles, Memorial Chapel [Las Vegas New Mexico MRA], Colonias & Romero, Las Vegas, 9/26/85, C, a, 85002657

Johnsen House [Las Vegas New Mexico MRA], 1523 8th, Las Vegas, 9/26/85, C, 85002635

Johnsen Mortuary [Las Vegas New Mexico MRA], 801 Douglas, Las Vegas, 9/26/85, C, 85002607

Las Vegas Iron Works [Las Vegas New Mexico MRA], Off NM 65/104, Las Vegas, 9/26/85, C, 85002636

Las Vegas Plaza [Las Vegas New Mexico MRA (AD)], Bounded by Valencia and Moreno Sts. and rear property line of building on Gonzales St. and Hot Springs Blvd., Las Vegas, 12/16/74, A, C, 74001202

Las Vegas Railroad and Power Company Building [Las Vegas New Mexico MRA], 12th and San Francisco, Las Vegas, 9/26/85, C, 85002640

Library Park Historic District [Las Vegas New Mexico MRA (AD)], Liberty Park and environs, Las Vegas, 3/12/79, C, 79001549

Lincoln Park Historic District [Las Vegas New Mexico MRA (AD)], 7th, 8th, Lincoln and Jackson Sts, Las Vegas, 8/06/79, B, C, 79001550

Lincoln Park Historic District (Boundary Increase) [Las Vegas New Mexico MRA], Roughly bounded by Douglas and Grand Aves. and Gallinas and Twelfth Sts., Las Vegas, 3/19/87, C, 87001120

Montezuma Hotel Complex, 6 mi. NW of Las Vegas in Gallinas Canyon, Las Vegas vicinity, 5/03/74, A, C, 74001203

Nolan House [Las Vegas New Mexico MRA], 110 10th St., Las Vegas, 9/26/85, C, 85002619

North New Town Historic District [Las Vegas New Mexico MRA (AD)], Roughly bounded by National, Friedman, 3rd and 8th Sts., Las Vegas, 8/18/83, C, g, 83001627

Old Las Vegas Post Office [Las Vegas New Mexico MRA], 901 Douglas, Las Vegas, 9/26/85, C, 85002598

Old Town Residential Historic District [Las Vegas New Mexico MRA (AD)], Roughly bounded by Perey St. to Mills Ave. and from New Mexico to Gonzales St., Las Vegas, 10/28/83, C, 83004161

Our Lady of Sorrows Church, W. National Ave., Las Vegas, 9/08/76, A, C, a, 76001197

Pecos National Monument, S of Pecos on NM 63, Pecos vicinity, 10/15/66, A, C, D, a, f, NHL, NPS, 66000485

Pecos National Monument, NM 63 SW of jct. with NM 50, Pecos, 7/02/91, A, B, C, D, NPS, 91000822

Pendaries Grist Mill, 1 mi. (1.6 km) E of Rociada off NM 105, Rociada vicinity, 2/02/79, A, C, 79001552

Pimter-O'Neil Rooming House [Las Vegas New Mexico MRA], 313 Railroad, Las Vegas, 9/26/85, C, 85002627

Presbyterian Mission Church, 1413 Chavez St., Las Vegas, 11/17/78, A, C, a, 78001825

Railroad Avenue Historic District [Las Vegas New Mexico MRA (AD)], U.S. 85, Las Vegas, 8/06/79, C, 79001551

Rogers Administration Building [New Mexico Campus Buildings Built 1906–1937 TR], National Ave., NMHU, Las Vegas, 9/22/88, C, 88001559

Salazar, Vidal and Elisa, House [Las Vegas New Mexico MRA], 824 Railroad, Las Vegas, 9/26/85, C, 85002637

San Antonio de Padua Church, NM 63, Pecos, 9/13/78, A, C, a, 78001826

San Geronimo Historic District, Off NM 283, San Geronimo, 11/15/83, A, C, a, 83004163

San Miguel del Vado Historic District, SE of San Jose on NM 3, off U.S. 84, San Jose vicinity, 7/17/72, A, 72000809

Schmitt-Laemmle House [Las Vegas New Mexico MRA], 1106 Columbia, Las Vegas, 9/26/85, C, 85002639

Serna-Blanchard House [Las Vegas New Mexico MRA], 2203 N. Gonzales, Las Vegas, 9/26/85, C, 85002614

Shawn-Guerin House [Las Vegas New Mexico MRA], 140 Delgado, Las Vegas, 9/26/85, C, 85002615

St. Anthony's Hospital Annex [Las Vegas New Mexico MRA], 700 Friedman, Las Vegas, 9/26/85, C, 85002592

St. Paul's Memorial Episcopal Church and Guild Hall, 714–716 National Ave., Las Vegas, 11/07/76, A, C, a, 76001198

Sundt, M. M., House [Las Vegas New Mexico MRA], 1607 8th, Las Vegas, 9/26/85, C, 85002638

Taichert Building [Las Vegas New Mexico MRA], 1201 National, Las Vegas, 9/26/85, A, C, 85002616

Taichert Warehouse [Las Vegas New Mexico MRA], 623 12th, Las Vegas, 9/26/85, C, 85002618

Truder Park [Las Vegas New Mexico MRA], Roughly bounded by 2nd, Washington & Grand, Las Vegas, 9/26/85, C, 85002661

Trujillo-Gonzales House [Las Vegas New Mexico MRA], 935 New Mexico, Las Vegas, 9/26/85, C, 85002617

Valencia Ranch Historic Archaeological District, Address Restricted, Pecos vicinity, 2/09/84, A, C, D, 84002975

Ward, C. W. G., House [Las Vegas New Mexico MRA], 1301 8th, Las Vegas, 9/26/85, C, 85002593

Sandoval County

Abenicio Salazar Historic District, U.S. 85, Bernalillo, 6/06/80, C, 80002569

Amoxiumqua Site (FS-530, LA481) [Jemez Springs Pueblo Sites TR], Address Restricted, Jemez Springs vicinity, 5/21/84, D, 84002979

Archeological Site FS-18, LA-5920 [Jemez Springs Pueblo Sites TR], Address Restricted, Jemez Springs vicinity, 5/21/84, D, 84002986

Archeological Site FS-199, LA-135 [Jemez Springs Pueblo Sites TR], Address Restricted, Jemez Springs vicinity, 5/21/84, D, 84002989

Archeological Site FS-3 [Jemez Springs Pueblo Sites TR], Address Restricted, Jemez Springs vicinity, 5/21/84, D, 84002982

Archeological Site FS-535, LA-385 [Jemez Springs Pueblo Sites TR], Address Restricted, Jemez Springs vicinity, 5/21/84, D, 84002991

Archeological Site FS-554, LA-386 [Jemez Springs Pueblo Sites TR], Address Restricted, Jemez Springs vicinity, 5/21/84, D, 84002993

Archeological Site FS-574 [Jemez Springs Pueblo Sites TR], Address Restricted, Jemez Springs vicinity, 5/21/84, D, 84002997

Archeological Site FS-575 [Jemez Springs Pueblo Sites TR], Address Restricted, Jemez Springs vicinity, 5/21/84, D, 84003001

Archeological Site FS-580, LA-137 [Jemez Springs Pueblo Sites TR], Address Restricted, Jemez Springs vicinity, 5/21/84, D, 84003002

Archeological Site FS-647, LA-128 [Jemez Springs Pueblo Sites TR], Address Restricted, Jemez Springs vicinity, 5/21/84, D, 84003005

Archeological Site FS-688 [Jemez Springs Pueblo Sites TR], Address Restricted, Jemez Springs vicinity, 5/21/84, D, 84003007

Archeological Site FS-689, LA-403 [Jemez Springs Pueblo Sites TR], Address Restricted, Jemez Springs vicinity, 5/21/84, D, 84003008

Archeological Site FS-8 [Jemez Springs Pueblo Sites TR], Address Restricted, Jemez Springs vicinity, 5/21/84, D, 84002984

Archeological Site No. AR-03-10-03-620 [Jemez Cultural Developments in North-Central New Mexico MPS], Address Restricted, Jemez Springs vicinity, 4/19/90, D, 90000590

Sandoval County—Continued

Astialakwa Archeological District (FS-360, LA-1825) [Jemez Springs Pueblo Sites TR], Address Restricted, Jemez Springs vicinity, 5/21/84, A, B, D, 84003010

Bandelier National Monument, 12 mi. S of Los Alamos on NM 4, Los Alamos vicinity, 10/15/66, D, NPS, 66000042

Big Bead Mesa, Address Restricted, Casa Salazar vicinity, 10/15/66, D, NHL, 66000958

Boletsakwa Site (FS-2, LA-136) [Jemez Springs Pueblo Sites TR], Address Restricted, Jemez Springs vicinity, 5/21/84, A, D, 84003011

Borrego Mesa Agricultural Site [Jemez Cultural Developments in North-Central New Mexico MPS], Address Restricted, Jemez Springs vicinity, 4/19/90, D, 90000591

Cochiti Pueblo, 27 mi. SW of Santa Fe on the Rio Grande, Santa Fe vicinity, 11/20/74, A, C, D, a, 74001205

Espinaso Ridge Pueblo, Address Restricted, Budagher's vicinity, 1/27/84, D, 84003012

Forset Service Archeological Site No. FS-7 [Jemez Springs Pueblo Sites TR], Address Restricted, Jemez Springs vicinity, 5/21/84, D, 84003050

Guacamayo Site (FS0572, LA-189) [Jemez Springs Pueblo Sites TR], Address Restricted, Jemez Springs vicinity, 5/21/84, D, 84003016

Guadalupe Ruin, Address Restricted, Guadalupe vicinity, 3/24/80, A, C, D, 80002571

Hanakwa Site (FS-578) [Jemez Springs Pueblo Sites TR], Address Restricted, Jemez Springs vicinity, 5/21/84, D, 84003019

Holiday Mesa Logging Camp [Railroad Logging Era Resources of the Canon de San Diego Land Grant in North—Central New Mexico MPS], Address Restricted, Jemez Springs vicinity, 9/11/92, A, D, 92001181

Hot Springs Pueblo (FS-505, Bj-73) [Jemez Springs Pueblo Sites TR], Address Restricted, Jemez Springs vicinity, 5/21/84, D, 84003022

Jemez Cave [Jemez Cultural Developments in North-Central New Mexico MPS], Address Restricted, Jemez Springs vicinity, 4/19/90, D, 90000593

Jemez Pueblo, 28 mi. N of Bernalillo on NM 4, Bernalillo vicinity, 5/02/77, A, C, a, 77000926

Jemez State Monument, NM 4, Jemez Springs, 3/14/73, A, C, D, a, 73001147

Kiashita Site [Jemez Springs Pueblo Sites TR], Address Restricted, Jemez Springs vicinity, 5/21/84, D, 84003023

Kiatsukwa Site (FS-31 and 504, LA-132 and 133) [Jemez Springs Pueblo Sites TR], Address Restricted, Jemez Springs vicinity, 5/21/84, D, 84003026

Kuaua Ruin, Address Restricted, Bernalillo vicinity, 1/01/76, A, C, D, a, e, 76001199

Kwastiyukwa Site (FS-11, LA-482) [Jemez Springs Pueblo Sites TR], Address Restricted, Jemez Springs vicinity, 5/21/84, D, 84003029

Nanishagi Site (FS-320, LA-541) [Jemez Springs Pueblo Sites TR], Address Restricted, Jemez Springs vicinity, 5/21/84, D, 84003033

Our Lady of Sorrows Church, U.S. 85, Bernalillo, 4/29/77, A, C, a, 77000927

Patokwa Site (FS-5, LA-96) [Jemez Springs Pueblo Sites TR], Address Restricted, Jemez Springs vicinity, 5/21/84, A, D, 84003037

Pejunkwa Site (FS-571, LA-130) [Jemez Springs Pueblo Sites TR], Address Restricted, Jemez Springs vicinity, 5/21/84, D, 84003039

Pueblo Tuerto, Address Restricted, Budagher's vicinity, 1/19/84, D, 84003042

Pueblo of Santo Domingo (Kiua), 35 mi. NE of Albuquerque, off I-25, Albuquerque vicinity, 12/12/73, A, C, D, a, 73001145

San Jose de las Huertas, Address Restricted, Placitas vicinity, 7/05/90, A, D, 90001029

San Juan Mesa Ruin, Address Restricted, Jemez Spring vicinity, 7/09/70, D, 70000408

San Ysidro Church, Church Rd., Corrales, 7/30/80, C, a, 80002570

Sandia Cave, Address Restricted, Bernalillo vicinity, 10/15/66, A, D, NHL, 66000487

Tamaya, N of Bernalillo, Bernalillo vicinity, 11/01/74, A, C, D, a, 74001204

Tonque Pueblo, Address Restricted, Tejon Grant vicinity, 1/12/84, A, D, 84003045

Tostaskwinu Site (FS-579, LA-479) [Jemez Springs Pueblo Sites TR], Address Restricted, Jemez Springs vicinity, 5/21/84, D, 84003047

Tovakwa Site [Jemez Springs Pueblo Sites TR], Address Restricted, Jemez Springs vicinity, 5/21/84, D, 84003049

Unshagi Site (FS-337, LA-123) [Jemez Springs Pueblo Sites TR], Address Restricted, Jemez Springs vicinity, 5/21/84, D, 84003051

Virgin Canyon Logging Camp No. 1 [Railroad Logging Era Resources of the Canon de San Diego Land Grant in North—Central New Mexico MPS], Address Restricted, Jemez Springs vicinity, 9/11/92, A, D, 92001180

Virgin Mesa Logging Camp No. 1 [Railroad Logging Era Resources of the Canon de San Diego Land Grant in North—Central New Mexico MPS], Address Restricted, Jemez Springs vicinity, 9/11/92, A, D, 92001182

Virgin Mesa Logging Camp No. 2 [Railroad Logging Era Resources of the Canon de San Diego Land Grant in North—Central New Mexico MPS], Address Restricted, Jemez Springs vicinity, 9/11/92, A, D, 92001183

Virgin Mesa Logging Camp No. 3 [Railroad Logging Era Resources of the Canon de San Diego Land Grant in North—Central New Mexico MPS], Address Restricted, Jemez Springs vicinity, 9/11/92, A, D, 92001184

Virgin Mesa Rock Art Site [Jemez Cultural Developments in North-Central New Mexico MPS], Address Restricted, Jemez Springs vicinity, 4/19/90, D, a, 90000592

Wabakwa Site (FS-400, LA-478) [Jemez Springs Pueblo Sites TR], Address Restricted, Jemez Springs vicinity, 5/21/84, D, 84003052

Wahajhamka (FS-573) [Jemez Springs Pueblo Sites TR], Address Restricted, Jemez Springs vicinity, 5/21/84, D, 84003053

Zia Pueblo, 18 mi. W of Bernalillo on NM 44, Bernalillo vicinity, 4/03/73, D, 73001146

Santa Fe County

Acequia System of El Rancho de las Golondrinas, 12 mi. SE of Santa Fe, Santa Fe vicinity, 2/01/80, A, C, 80002572

Alarid, Ricardo, House, 534 Alarid St., Santa Fe, 8/30/84, B, C, 84003054

Allison Dormitory, 433 Paseo de Peralta, Santa Fe, 11/29/84, A, C, a, 84000431

Apache Canyon Railroad Bridge, 3 mi. (4.8 km) NE of Lamy over Galisteo Creek, Lamy vicinity, 4/27/79, A, C, 79001553

Archbishop Lamy's Chapel, Bishop's Lodge Rd., Santa Fe, 8/19/88, B, a, 88000897

Barrio de Analco Historic District, Roughly bounded by E. De Vargas and College Sts., Santa Fe, 11/24/68, C, NHL, 68000032

Bergere, Alfred M., House, 135 Grant Ave., Santa Fe, 10/01/75, A, C, 75001166

Bouquet, Jean, Historic/Archeological District, Address Restricted, Pojoaque vicinity, 1/05/83, C, D, 83001628

Camino del Monte Sol Historic District, Roughly bounded by Acequia Madre, Camino del Monte Sol, El Caminito, and Garcia St., Santa Fe, 7/11/88, A, B, C, g, 88000440

Connor Hall [New Mexico Campus Buildings Built 1906–1937 TR], 1060 Cerrillos Rd., NMSD, Santa Fe, 9/22/88, C, 88001561

Crespin, Gregorio, House, 132 E. De Vargas St., Santa Fe, 5/29/75, A, C, 75001167

Davey, Randall, House, Upper Canyon Rd., Santa Fe, 7/09/70, C, 70000409

Digneo-Valdes House, 1231 Paseo de Peralta, Santa Fe, 11/21/78, C, 78001827

Don Gaspar Historic District, Roughly bounded by Old Santa Fe Trail, Paseo de Peralta, Don Cubero and Houghton, Santa Fe, 7/21/83, C, g, 83001629

El Santuario de Chimayo, 1 mi. NW of Santa Cruz Reservoir Dam, Chimayo vicinity, 4/15/70, C, a, NHL, 70000412

Federal Building, Cathedral Pl. at Palace St., Santa Fe, 8/15/74, C, 74001207

Fort Marcy Officer's Residence, 116 Lincoln Ave., Santa Fe, 6/20/75, B, C, 75001168

Fort Marcy Ruins, Off NM 475, Santa Fe, 4/14/75, A, 75001169

Hayt—Wientge House, 620 Paseo de la Cuma, Santa Fe, 5/06/77, C, 77000929

Hospital [New Mexico Campus Buildings Built 1906–1937 TR], 1060 Cerrillos Rd., NMSD, Santa Fe, 9/22/88, C, 88001562

La Bajada Mesa Agricultural Site, Address Restricted, La Bajada vicinity, 12/15/83, D, 83004178

La Iglesia de Santa Cruz and Site of the Plaza of Santa Cruz de la Canada, N of SR 76, Santa Cruz, 8/17/73, A, a, 73001148

Laboratory of Anthropology, 708 Camino Lejo, Santa Fe, 7/12/83, A, C, 83001630

Madrid Historic District, 25 mi. SW of Santa Fe on NM 14, Madrid, 11/09/77, A, C, 77000928

Santa Fe County—Continued

National Park Service Southwest Regional Office, Old Santa Fe Trail, Santa Fe, 10/06/70, A, C, g, NHL, 70000067

Navawi, Address Restricted, White Rock vicinity, 12/08/82, D, 82001052

Otowi Historic District, 25 mi. N of Santa Fe, on NM 4 in Rio Grande Valley, Santa Fe vicinity, 12/04/75, A, C, g, 75001170

Palace of the Governors, The Plaza, Santa Fe, 10/15/66, A, C, e, NHL, 66000489

Pflueger General Merchandise Store and Annex Saloon, NM 41, Lamy, 6/23/87, A, C, 87000519

Plaza del Cerro, SW of jct. of Rtes. 76 and 4, Chimayo vicinity, 7/17/72, A, C, a, 72000810

Pueblo of Nambe, About 16 mi. off NM 4, Santa Fe vicinity, 1/21/74, A, C, a, 74001208

Pueblo of Tesuque, About 8 mi. N of Santa Fe on W bank of Tesuque River, Santa Fe vicinity, 7/16/73, A, C, a, 73001149

Reredos of Our Lady of Light, Christo Rey Church, Canyon Rd. and Cristo Rey St., Santa Fe, 9/04/70, A, C, a, 70000411

Roybal, Ignacio, House, CR 84 W of NM 4 and US 84/285, Jacona, 2/13/86, A, C, 86000227

San Ildefonso Pueblo, SW of Espanola off NM 4, Espanola vicinity, 6/20/74, A, C, 74001206

San Lazaro, Address Restricted, Santa Fe vicinity, 10/15/66, D, a, NHL, 66000490

San Marcos Pueblo, Address Restricted, Capitan vicinity, 3/26/82, A, D, 82003326

Santa Fe Historic District, Roughly bounded by Camino Cabra, Camino de las Animas, W. Manhattan Ave., S. St. Francis Dr., and Griffin St., Santa Fe, 7/23/73, A, C, 73001150

Santa Fe Plaza, Santa Fe Plaza, Santa Fe, 10/15/66, A, NHL, 66000491

School Building Number 2 [New Mexico Campus Buildings Built 1906–1937 TR], 1060 Cerrillos Rd., NMSD, Santa Fe, 9/22/88, C, 88001560

Scottish Rite Cathedral, 463 Paseo de Peralta, Santa Fe, 3/13/87, A, C, 87000424

Second Ward School, 312 Sandoval St., Santa Fe, 3/30/78, A, C, 78001828

Seton Village, 6 mi. S of Santa Fe off U.S. 84, Santa Fe vicinity, 10/15/66, B, g, NHL, 66000492

Shonnard, Eugenie, House, Address Restricted, Santa Fe, 9/05/75, B, C, g, 75001171

Spiegelberg House, 237 E. Palace St., Santa Fe, 5/25/73, C, 73001151

Superintendent's Residence [New Mexico Campus Buildings Built 1906–1937 TR], 1060 Cerrillos Rd., NMSD, Santa Fe, 9/22/88, C, 88001563

Tully, Pinckney R., House, 136 Grant Ave., Santa Fe, 11/05/74, B, C, 74001209

U.S. Courthouse, Federal Pl., Santa Fe, 5/25/73, A, C, 73001152

Vierra, Carlos, House, 1002 Old Pecos Trail, Santa Fe, 8/03/79, B, C, 79001554

Vigil, Donaciano, House, 518 Alto St., Santa Fe, 6/28/72, B, 72000811

Wheelwright Museum of the American Indian, 704 Camino Lejo, Santa Fe, 12/18/90, A, B, C, 90001917

Sierra County

Archeological Site No. LA1119 [Prehistoric Adaptations along the Rio Grande Drainage, Sierra County, New Mexico TR], Address Restricted, Truth or Consequences vicinity, 12/16/89, D, 88000489

Archeological Site No. LA49016 [Prehistoric Adaptations along the Rio Grande Drainage, Sierra County, New Mexico TR], Address Restricted, Truth or Consequences vicinity, 12/16/89, D, 88000484

Archeological Site No. LA49030 [Prehistoric Adaptations along the Rio Grande Drainage, Sierra County, New Mexico TR], Address Restricted, Truth or Consequences vicinity, 12/16/89, D, 88000486

Archeological Site No. LA517 [Prehistoric Adaptations along the Rio Grande Drainage, Sierra County, New Mexico TR], Address Restricted, Truth or Consequences vicinity, 12/16/89, D, 88000473

Archeological Site No. LA50548 [Prehistoric Adaptations along the Rio Grande Drainage, Sierra County, New Mexico TR], Address Restricted, Truth or Consequences vicinity, 12/16/89, D, 88000488

Chambers Canyon Site (LA49028) [Prehistoric Adaptations along the Rio Grande Drainage, Sierra County, New Mexico TR], Address Restricted, Truth or Consequences vicinity, 12/16/89, D, 88000485

Elephant Butte Dam, NW of Elephant Butte off NM 51, Elephant Butte vicinity, 4/09/79, A, 79001556

Hillsboro High School, Jct. of Elenora St. and First Ave., SE corner, Hillsboro, 4/15/93, A, C, 93000254

Hillsboro Peak Lookout Tower and Cabin [National Forest Fire Lookouts in the Southwestern Region TR], Gila National Forest, Hillsboro vicinity, 1/28/88, A, C, 87002475

Horse Island Site (LA48996) [Prehistoric Adaptations along the Rio Grande Drainage, Sierra County, New Mexico TR], Address Restricted, Truth or Consequences vicinity, 5/16/88, D, 88000478

Kettle Top Butte Site (LA48995) [Prehistoric Adaptations along the Rio Grande Drainage, Sierra County, New Mexico TR], Address Restricted, Truth or Consequences vicinity, 5/16/88, D, 88000477

Longbottom Canyon Site (LA49033) [Prehistoric Adaptations along the Rio Grande Drainage, Sierra County, New Mexico TR], Address Restricted, Truth or Consequences vicinity, 12/16/89, D, 88000487

Monticello Point Archeological District [Prehistoric Adaptations along the Rio Grande Drainage, Sierra County, New Mexico TR], Address Restricted, Truth or Consequences vicinity, 5/16/88, D, 88000476

Palomas Narrows North (LA38755) [Prehistoric Adaptations along the Rio Grande Drainage, Sierra County, New Mexico TR], Address Restricted, Truth or Consequences vicinity, 12/16/89, D, 88000475

Palomas Narrows South (LA49007) [Prehistoric Adaptations along the Rio Grande Drainage, Sierra County, New Mexico TR], Address Restricted, Truth or Consequences vicinity, 12/16/89, D, 88000479

Percha Diversion Dam, 2 mi. (3.2 km) NE of Arrey, Arrey vicinity, 4/06/79, A, C, 79001555

US Post Office—Truth or Consequences Main [US Post Offices in New Mexico MPS], 400 Main St., Truth or Consequences, 2/23/90, A, C, D, 90000141

Socorro County

Aragon House [Magdalena MRA], 2nd and Oak Sts., Magdalena, 8/02/82, C, 82003327

Archeological Site No. LA 1069 [Pueblo IV Sites of the Chupadera Arroyo MPS], Address Restricted, Bingham vicinity, 4/15/93, D, 93000243

Archeological Site No. LA 1070 [Pueblo IV Sites of the Chupadera Arroyo MPS], Address Restricted, Bingham vicinity, 4/15/93, D, 93000244

Archeological Site No. LA 1071 [Pueblo IV Sites of the Chupadera Arroyo MPS], Address Restricted, Bingham vicinity, 4/15/93, D, 93000245

Archeological Site No. LA 1072 [Pueblo IV Sites of the Chupadera Arroyo MPS], Address Restricted, Bingham vicinity, 4/15/93, D, 93000246

Archeological Site No. LA 1073 [Pueblo IV Sites of the Chupadera Arroyo MPS], Address Restricted, Bingham vicinity, 4/15/93, D, 93000247

Archeological Site No. LA 1074 [Pueblo IV Sites of the Chupadera Arroyo MPS], Address Restricted, Bingham vicinity, 4/15/93, D, 93000248

Archeological Site No. LA 1075 [Pueblo IV Sites of the Chupadera Arroyo MPS], Address Restricted, Bingham vicinity, 4/15/93, D, 93000249

Archeological Site No. LA 1076 [Pueblo IV Sites of the Chupadera Arroyo MPS], Address Restricted, Bingham vicinity, 4/15/93, D, 93000250

Archeological Site No. LA 1181 [Pueblo IV Sites of the Chupadera Arroyo MPS], Address Restricted, Bingham vicinity, 4/15/93, D, 93000251

Archeological Site No. LA 1201 [Pueblo IV Sites of the Chupadera Arroyo MPS], Address Restricted, Bingham vicinity, 4/15/93, D, 93000252

Atchison, Topeka and Santa Fe Railway Depot, Off U.S. 60, Magdalena, 12/29/78, A, C, 78001829

Baca, A. B., House [Domestic Architecture in Socorro MPS], 201 School of Mines Rd., Socorro, 2/20/91, C, 91000036

Bank of Magdalena [Magdalena MRA], 1st and Main Sts., Magdalena, 8/02/82, C, 82003328

Brown Hall [New Mexico Campus Buildings Built 1906–1937 TR], New Mexico Institute of Mining and Technology, Socorro, 5/16/89, C, 88001550

Bursum House, 326 Church St., Socorro, 6/18/75, B, C, 75001172

Clemens Ranchhouse, S of Magdalena, Magdalena vicinity, 4/18/79, A, C, 79001557

Socorro County—Continued

Cooney, Captain Michael, House [Domestic Architecture in Socorro MPS], 309 McCutcheon Ave., Socorro, 2/20/91, B, C, 91000029

Cortesy, Anthony, House [Domestic Architecture in Socorro MPS], 327 McCutcheon Ave., Socorro, 2/20/91, C, 91000033

Eaton, Nestor P., House [Domestic Architecture in Socorro MPS], 313 McCutcheon Ave., Socorro, 2/20/91, C, 91000034

Fitch Hall [New Mexico Campus Buildings Built 1906–1937 TR], New Mexico Institute of Mining and Technology, Socorro, 5/16/89, C, 88001551

Fitch, James Gurden, House [Domestic Architecture in Socorro MPS], 311 McCutcheon Ave., Socorro, 2/20/91, B, C, 91000035

Fort Craig, 37 mi. S of Socorro, Socorro vicinity, 10/15/70, A, 70000414

Gallinas Springs Ruin, Address Restricted, Magdalena vicinity, 9/04/70, D, 70000413

Garcia Opera House, Terry Ave. and California St., Socorro, 8/13/74, A, C, 74001210

Garcia, Juan Nepomuceno, House [Domestic Architecture in Socorro MPS], 108 Bernard St., Socorro, 2/20/91, C, 91000027

Gutierrez House [Magdalena MRA], 3rd and Popular Sts., Magdalena, 8/02/82, C, 82003329

Hall Hotel [Magdalena MRA], 2nd and Spruce Sts., Magdalena, 8/02/82, C, 82003330

Hilton House [Magdalena MRA], US 60, Magdalena, 8/02/82, C, 82003331

Hilton, August Holver, House [Domestic Architecture in Socorro MPS], 601 Park St., Socorro, 2/20/91, C, 91000031

House at 303 Eaton Avenue [Domestic Architecture in Socorro MPS], 303 Eaton Ave., Socorro, 2/20/91, C, 91000032

House at 405 Park Street [Domestic Architecture in Socorro MPS], 405 Park St., Socorro, 2/20/91, C, 91000030

Ilfeld Warehouse [Magdalena MRA], Main St., Magdalena, 8/02/82, A, C, 82003332

Illinois Brewery, Neal Ave. and 6th St., Socorro, 9/02/75, A, C, 75001173

Lewellen House, 2nd and Chestnut Sts., Magdalena, 8/02/82, C, 82003333

MacDonald Merchandise Building, U.S. 90, Magdalena, 9/25/80, C, 80002573

MacTavish House [Magdalena MRA], Elm St., Magdalena, 8/02/82, C, 82003334

Magdaline House [Magdalena MRA], 3rd and Chestnut Sts., Magdalena, 8/02/82, C, 82003335

Main Street Commercial Building [Magdalena MRA], Main St., Magdalena, 8/02/82, C, 82003336

Sagrada Familia de Lemitar Church, Los Dulces Nombres, Off I-25, Lemitar, 2/24/83, A, 83001631

Salinas National Monument, 1 mi. E of Gran Quivira on NM 10, Gran Quivira vicinity, 10/15/66, A, C, D, a, NPS, 66000494

Salome Store [Magdalena MRA], 1st St., Magdalena, 8/02/82, A, 82003337

Salome Warehouse [Magdalena MRA], 1st St., Magdalena, 8/02/82, A, 82003338

San Felipe Pueblo Ruin, Address Restricted, Socorro vicinity, 4/25/83, A, D, 83001632

Teypama Piro Site, Address Restricted, Socorro vicinity, 10/21/83, D, 83004179

Trinity Site, 25 mi. S of U.S. 380 on White Sands Missile Range, Bingham vicinity, 10/15/66, A, g, NHL, 66000493

Val Verde Hotel, 203 Manzanares St., Socorro, 9/13/77, A, C, 77000930

Vigil, Rufina, House [Domestic Architecture in Socorro MPS], 407 Park St., Socorro, 2/20/91, C, 91000028

Taos County

Bent, Gov. Charles, House, Bent St., Taos, 11/16/78, B, C, 78001831

Blumenschein, Ernest L., House, Ledoux St., Taos, 10/15/66, B, NHL, 66000495

Carson School, NM 96, Carson, 2/13/86, C, 86000233

Carson, Kit, House, Kit Carson Ave., Taos, 10/15/66, B, NHL, 66000948

Chapel of Santa Cruz, S side of Plaza off U.S. 285, Ojo Caliente, 4/14/75, A, C, a, 75001174

Fechin, Nicholai, House, NM 3, Taos, 12/31/79, B, C, 79001558

Gaspard, Leon, House, Raton Rd., Taos, 2/23/79, C, 79001559

Harwood Foundation, LeDoux St., Taos, 12/22/76, A, C, 76001200

Hennings, E. Martin, House and Studio Historic District, SE corner of Dolan St. and Kit Carson Rd., Taos, 7/05/90, A, B, 90001028

Howiri-ouinge, Address Restricted, Ojo Caliente vicinity, 4/07/83, A, C, D, 83001633

La Loma Plaza Historic District, NM 240, Taos, 7/08/82, C, 82003339

La Morada de Nuestra Senora de Guadalupe, E of Taos off U.S. 64, Taos vicinity, 6/29/76, A, C, a, 76001201

Las Trampas Historic District, On NM 76, Las Trampas, 5/28/67, C, NHL, 67000007

Laureano Cordova Mill, Off NM 75, Vadito, 11/05/74, A, C, 74001212

Luhan, Mabel Dodge, House, Luhan Lane, Taos, 11/15/78, A, B, C, g, NHL, 78001832

Mallette, Orin, Cabin [Red River MRA], W of Red River, Red River vicinity, 2/23/84, A, B, C, 84003055

Mallette, Sylvester M., Cabin [Red River MRA], River St. and Copper King, Red River vicinity, 2/23/84, A, B, C, 84003056

Martinez, Severino, House, 2 mi. from Taos Plaza, on the Lower Ranchitos Rd., Taos, 4/23/73, A, B, C, 73001153

Melson-Oldham Cabin [Red River MRA], SE of Red River, Red River vicinity, 2/23/84, A, C, 84003057

Ojo Caliente Mineral Springs, NM 414, Ojo Caliente, 11/17/85, A, 85003496

Picuris Pueblo, S of Taos, Taos vicinity, 8/13/74, A, C, a, 74001211

Pierce-Fuller House [Red River MRA], High St., Red River vicinity, 2/23/84, A, C, 84003058

Ranchos de Taos Plaza, Off U.S. 64, Ranchos de Taos, 10/02/78, A, C, a, 78001830

Red River Schoolhouse [Red River MRA], High St., Red River vicinity, 2/23/84, A, C, 84003059

San Francisco de Assisi Mission Church, The Plaza, Ranchos de Taos, 4/15/70, C, a, NHL, 70000416

San Jose de Gracia Church, N side of the Plaza, Las Trampas, 4/15/70, C, a, NHL, 70000415

San Ysidro Oratorio, NM 240, Los Cordovas, 1/05/84, A, C, a, 84003060

Taos Downtown Historic District, NM 3 and NM 240, Taos, 7/08/82, A, C, 82003340

Taos Inn, Pueblo del Norte, Taos, 2/05/82, A, C, g, 82003341

Taos Pueblo, 3 mi. N of Taos, Taos vicinity, 10/15/66, A, NHL, 66000496

Tres Piedras Administrative Site, Old, W of US 285, N of Tres Piedras, Tres Piedras vicinity, 8/05/93, C, 92000341

Tres Piedras Railroad Water Tower, Off U.S. 285, Tres Piedras, 2/02/79, A, C, 79001560

Turley Mill and Distillery Site, 11 mi. (17.6 km) N of Taos, Taos vicinity, 11/16/78, A, B, D, 78001833

Young, Brigham J., House [Red River MRA], Main St., Red River vicinity, 2/23/84, A, B, C, 84003063

Torrance County

Abo, 3 mi. W of Abo on U.S. 60, Abo vicinity, 10/15/66, A, D, a, NHL, NPS, 66000497

Evans, Greene, Garage [Route 66 Through New Mexico MPS], Jct. of Broadway and Rt. 66, NW corner, Moriarty, 11/22/93, A, g, 93001211

Moriarty Eclipse Windmill, 2 (3.2 km) W of Moriarty off NM 222, Moriarty vicinity, 6/04/79, A, C, 79001561

Mountainair Municipal Auditorium, SW corner of Roosevelt Ave. and Beal St., Mountainair, 4/30/87, A, C, 87000651

Quarai, 1 mi. S of Punta de Agua, Punta de Agua vicinity, 10/15/66, D, a, NHL, NPS, 66000498

Rancho Bonito, S of Mountainair on Gran Quivera Rd., Mountainair vicinity, 11/29/78, C, e, g, 78001834

Shaffer Hotel, Broadway St., Mountainair, 11/15/78, C, 78003077

Union County

Folsom Hotel, SW Jct. of Grand Ave. and Wall St., Folsom, 5/14/87, A, C, 87000726

Rabbit Ears, NW of Clayton, Clayton vicinity, 10/15/66, A, NHL, 66000499

Union County Courthouse [County Courthouses of New Mexico TR], Court St., Clayton, 12/07/87, C, 87000891

Valencia County

Acoma, 13 mi. S of Casa Blanca on NM 23, Casa Blanca vicinity, 10/15/66, A, C, D, a, NHL, 66000500

Atchison, Topeka, and Santa Fe Railroad Depot, U.S. 85, Los Lunas, 8/01/79, A, C, b, 79001562

Baca, Miguel E., House, NM 47, Adelino, 12/11/78, A, C, 78001835

Belen Hotel, 200 Becker Ave., Belen, 11/12/80, C, 80002574

Chaves, Felipe, House, 325 Lala St., Belen, 7/04/80, B, C, 80002575

Dittert Site, Address Restricted, Granta vicinity, 8/22/77, D, 77000931

El Morro National Monument, 2 mi. W of El Morro Via NM 53, El Morro vicinity, 10/15/66, A, NPS, 66000043

Harvey, Belen, House, 104 N. 1st St., Belen, 10/28/83, A, C, 83004180

Hawikuh, 12 mi. SW of Zuni, Zuni Indian Reservation, Zuni vicinity, 10/15/66, A, B, NHL, 66000502

Laguna Pueblo, 45 mi. W of Albuquerque off U.S. 66, Albuquerque vicinity, 6/19/73, A, C, D, a, 73001154

Los Ojuelos (The Springs), Address Restricted, Tome vicinity, 12/10/87, B, D, 87002080

Luna, Tranquilino, House, SW of Los Lunas at jct. of U.S. 85 and NM 6, Los Lunas vicinity, 4/16/75, B, C, 75001175

San Estevan del Rey Mission Church, On NM 23, Acoma, 4/15/70, C, a, NHL, 70000417

San Jose de la Laguna Mission and Convento, Address unknown at this time, Laguna Pueblo, 1/29/73, A, C, a, 73001155

San Mateo Archeological Site [Anasazi Sites Within the Chacoan Interaction Sphere TR (AD)], Address Restricted, San Mateo vicinity, 5/17/79, D, 79001563

Tome Jail, Tome Plaza, Tome, 10/05/77, A, C, 77000932

Village of Encinal Day School, NW of Encinal, Encinal, 8/08/80, A, C, 80002576

Wittwer, Dr. William Frederick, House, NM 6, W of US 85, Los Lunas, 2/27/87, B, C, 87000131

Zuni-Cibola Complex, Address Restricted, Zuni vicinity, 12/02/74, D, NHL, 74002267

The Wheelwright Museum of the American Indian was built near Santa Fe in 1937 to house recordings of Navajo chants, sandpainting reproductions, ceremonial objects, and the anthropological notes of the museum's founder, Mary Cabot Wheelwright, who dedicated her work to the preservation of Navajo oral and cultural traditions. (Sonny Lee, 1989)

NEW YORK

Albany County

Abrams Building, 55-57 S. Pearl St., Albany, 2/14/80, C, 80002577

Albany Academy, Academy Park, Albany, 2/18/71, B, C, 71000515

Albany City Hall, Eagle St. at Maiden Lane, Albany, 9/04/72, C, 72000812

Albany Glassworks Site, Address Restricted., Guilderland vicinity, 7/22/80, D, 80002583

Albany Institute of History and Art, 135 Washington Ave., Albany, 7/12/76, C, 76001202

Albany Rural Cemetery, Cemetery Ave., Menands, 10/25/79, C, d, 79001566

Albany Union Station, E side of Broadway between Columbia and Steuben Sts., Albany, 2/18/71, A, C, 71000516

Alcove Historic District, SR 11 and Alcove Rd., Alcove, 7/24/80, A, C, 80002582

Altamont Historic District [Guilderland MRA], Main St. between Thacher Dr. and the RR station, Guilderland, 11/10/82, C, 82001054

Apple Tavern [Guilderland MRA], 4450 Altamont Rd., Guilderland, 11/10/82, C, 82001055

Arbor Hill Historic District—Ten Broeck Triangle, Irregular pattern along Ten Broeck St. from Clinton Ave. to Livingston Ave., Albany, 1/25/79, C, 79001564

Arbor Hill Historic District—Ten Broeck Triangle (Boundary Increase), Roughly Ten Broeck Pl., 1st, 2nd, and Swan Sts., Albany, 9/29/84, C, 84003865

Arnold, Benjamin Walworth, House and Carriage House, 465 State St. and 307 Washington Ave., Albany, 7/26/82, C, 82003342

Aumic House [Guilderland MRA], Leesome Ln., Guilderland, 11/10/82, C, 82001056

Bacon—Stickney House [Colonie Town MRA], 441 Loudon Rd., Colonie, 10/03/85, C, 85002709

Bethlehem House, E of Bethlehem off NY 144, Bethlehem vicinity, 4/11/73, C, 73001158

Broadway—Livingston Avenue Historic District, Broadway and Livingston Ave., Albany, 1/07/88, A, C, 87002300

Bryan's Store [New York State Route 9, Town of Colonie MRA], 435 Loudon Rd., Loudonville, 10/04/79, C, b, 79003246

Buildings at 744, 746, 748, 750 Broadway, 744–750 Broadway, Albany, 12/17/87, C, 87002180

Byrne, Senator William T., House [Colonie Town MRA], 463 Loudon Rd., Colonie, 10/03/85, B, C, g, 85002703

Cathedral of All Saints, S. Swan St., Albany, 7/25/74, C, a, 74001213

Cathedral of the Immaculate Conception, 125 Eagle St., Albany, 6/08/76, C, a, 76001203

Center Square/Hudson-Park Historic District, Roughly bounded by Park Ave., State, Lark and S. Swan Sts., Albany, 3/18/80, C, 80002578

Chapel House [Guilderland MRA], Western Ave., Guilderland, 11/10/82, C, 82001057

Cherry Hill, S. Pearl St. between 1st and McCarthy Aves., Albany, 2/18/71, B, C, 71000517

Church of the Holy Innocents, 275 N. Pearl St., Albany, 1/31/78, C, a, 78001836

Clinton Avenue Historic District, Along Clinton Ave. from Quail to N. Pearl Sts., Albany, 9/01/88, A, C, a, 88001445

Coeymans School, SW corner of Westerlo St. and Civill Ave., Coeymans, 12/29/70, B, C, 70000418

Coeymans, Ariaanje, House, Stone House Rd., Coeymans, 10/18/72, A, C, 72000819

Coppola House [Guilderland MRA], Leesome Ln., Guilderland, 11/10/82, C, 82001058

Cramer, Frederick, House [Colonie Town MRA], 410 Albany-Shaker Rd., Colonie, 10/03/85, C, 85002704

Crouse, Frederick, House [Guilderland MRA], 3960 Altamont-Voorheesville Rd., Guilderland, 11/10/82, C, 82001059

Crouse, Jacob, Inn [Guilderland MRA], 3933 Altamont Rd., Guilderland, 11/10/82, A, C, 82001060

Crouse, John and Henry, Farm Complex [Guilderland MRA], 3970 Altamont-Voorheesville Rd., Guilderland, 11/10/82, C, 82001061

D. D. T. Moore Farmhouse [New York State Route 9, Town of Colonie MRA], 352 Loudon Rd., Loudonville, 10/04/79, C, 79003244

Delaware and Hudson Railroad Passenger Station, Main St. and the Delaware and Hudson RR, Altamont, 8/12/71, A, C, 71000524

Delaware and Hudson Railroad Company Building, The Plaza on State St., Albany, 3/16/72, A, C, 72000813

Downtown Albany Historic District, Broadway, State, Pine, Lodge and Columbia Sts., Albany, 1/31/80, A, C, 80002579

Downtown Cohoes Historic District, Roughly bounded by Oneida, Van Rensselaer, Columbia, Main, and Olmstead Sts., Cohoes, 9/13/84, A, C, 84002060

Dunsbach, Martin, House [Colonie Town MRA], 140 Dunsbach Ferry Rd., Colonie, 10/03/85, C, 85002705

First Reformed Church, 56 Orange St., Albany, 1/21/74, A, C, a, 74001214

First Trust Company Building, 35 State St., Albany, 1/18/73, A, C, 73001156

Fort Orange Archeological Site, Jct. of I-787 and US 9 and 20, Albany, 11/04/93, D, NHL, 93001620

Freeman House [Guilderland MRA], 136 Main St., Guilderland, 11/10/82, C, 82001062

Fuller's Tavern [Guilderland MRA], 6861 Western Tpk., Guilderland, 11/10/82, C, 82001063

Fuller, Royal K., House [Colonie Town MRA], 294 Loudon Rd., Colonie, 10/03/85, C, 85002706

Gardner House [Guilderland MRA], 5661 Gardner Rd., Guilderland, 11/10/82, C, 82001064

Gifford Grange Hall [Guilderland MRA], Western Tpk., Guilderland, 11/10/82, C, 82001065

Gillespie House [Guilderland MRA], 2554 Western Tpk, Guilderland, 11/10/82, C, 82001066

Godfrey Farmhouse [New York State Route 9, Town of Colonie MRA], 1313 Loudon Rd., Cohoes vicinity, 10/04/79, C, 79003240

Gorham House [New York State Route 9, Town of Colonie MRA], 347 Loudon Rd., Loudonville, 10/04/79, C, 79003239

Guilderland Cemetery Vault [Guilderland MRA], In Guilderland Cemetery, NY 158, Guilderland, 11/10/82, C, c, d, 82001067

Hall, James, Office, Lincoln Park, Albany, 12/08/76, B, NHL, 76001204

Hamilton Union Church Rectory [Guilderland MRA], 2267 Western Tpk., Guilderland, 11/10/82, C, 82001068

Hamilton Union Presbyterian Church [Guilderland MRA], 2291 Western Tpk., Guilderland, 11/10/82, C, a, 82001069

Harmony Mill Historic District, Between Mohawk River and RR tracks, Cohoes, 1/12/78, A, C, 78003151

Harmony Mill No. 3, 100 N. Mohawk St., Cohoes, 2/18/71, A, C, 71000525

Haswell, Isaac M., House [Colonie Town MRA], 67 Haswell Rd., Colonie, 10/03/85, C, 85002707

Hayes House, 104 Fairview Ave., Altamont, 1/17/73, A, C, 73001157

Hedge Lawn [Colonie Town MRA], 592 Broadway, Colonie, 10/03/85, C, 85002710

Helderberg Reformed Dutch Church [Guilderland MRA], 140 Main St., Guilderland, 11/10/82, C, a, 82001070

Henry—Remsen House [Colonie Town MRA], 34 Spring St., Colonie, 10/03/85, C, 85002711

Hills, Ebenezer, Jr., Farmhouse [Colonie Town MRA], 1010 Troy-Schenectady Rd., Colonie, 10/03/85, A, C, 85002712

Hilton, Adam, House [Guilderland MRA], 6073 Leesome Ln., Guilderland, 11/10/82, C, 82001071

Houck Farmhouse [Guilderland MRA], 6156 Ostrander Rd., Guilderland, 11/10/82, C, 82001072

Hughson Mansion [New York State Route 9, Town of Colonie MRA], 374 Loudon Rd., Loudonville, 10/04/79, C, 79003245

Humphrey, Friend, House [Colonie Town MRA], 372 Albany-Shaker Rd., Colonie, 10/03/85, B, C, 85002713

Kemp, John Wolf, House [Colonie Town MRA], 216 Wolf Rd., Colonie, 10/03/85, A, C, 85002714

Knower House [Guilderland MRA], 3921 Altamont Rd., Guilderland, 11/10/82, C, 82001073

Lafayette Park Historic, Roughly bounded by State, Swan, Elk, Spruce, Chapel and Eagle Sts., Albany, 11/15/78, A, C, 78001837

Lansing, John V. A., Farmhouse and Billsen Cemetery and Archeological Site [Colonie Town MRA], Address Restricted, Colonie vicinity, 10/03/85, A, C, D, 85002715

Albany County—Continued

Lawton, George H., House [Colonie Town MRA], 27 Maxwell Rd., Colonie, 10/03/85, C, 85002741

Lock 18 of Enlarged Erie Canal, W of 252 N. Mohawk St., E of Reservoir St. near Manor Ave., Cohoes, 2/18/71, A, C, 71000526

Loudon Road Historic District [New York State Route 9, Town of Colonie MRA], Loudon Rd. from Crumite Rd. to Menands Rds., Loudonville, 10/04/79, C, 79003247

Mansion Historic District, Roughly bounded by Park Ave., Pearl, Eagle, and Hamilton Sts., Albany, 9/30/82, A, C, 82003343

McNiven Farm Complex [Guilderland MRA], 4178 Altamont Rd., Guilderland, 11/10/82, C, 82001074

Menand Park Historic District [Colonie Town MRA], Roughly bounded by Menand Rd., Broadway, and Tillinghast Ave., Colonie, 10/03/85, C, 85002708

Menand, Louis, House [Colonie Town MRA], 40 Cemetery Ave., Colonie, 10/03/85, B, C, 85002742

Menands Manor [Colonie Town MRA], 272 Broadway, Colonie, 10/03/85, C, 85002743

Music Hall, NW corner of Remsen and Oneida Sts., Cohoes, 2/18/71, C, 71000527

Mynderse-Frederick House [Guilderland MRA], 152 Main St., Guilderland, 11/10/82, A, C, 82001075

New York Executive Mansion, 138 Eagle St., Albany, 2/18/71, A, C, 71000518

New York State Capitol, Capitol Park, Albany, 2/18/71, A, C, NHL, 71000519

New York State Court of Appeals Building, Eagle St. between Pine and Columbia Sts., Albany, 2/18/71, A, C, 71000520

New York State Department of Education Building, Washington Ave. between Hawk and Swan Sts., Albany, 3/18/71, A, C, 71000521

Newtonville Post Office, 534 Loudonville Rd. (NY 9), Newtonville, 3/14/73, B, C, a, 73001162

Nut Grove, McCarty Ave., Albany, 7/30/74, B, C, 74001215

Old Post Office, NE corner of Broadway and State St., Albany, 1/20/72, C, 72000814

Olmstead Street Historic District, Olmstead St. between Ontario and Cayuga Sts., Cohoes, 6/19/73, A, C, 73001159

Onesquethaw Valley Historic District, About 10 mi. SW of Albany off NY 43, Albany vicinity, 1/17/74, A, C, D, 74001216

Palace Theatre [Movie Palaces of the Tri-Cities TR], 19 Clinton Ave., Albany, 10/04/79, A, C, g, 79003235

Pangburn, Stephen, House [Guilderland MRA], 2357 Old State, Guilderland, 11/10/82, C, 82001076

Parker, Charles, House [Guilderland MRA], 2273 Old State, Guilderland, 11/10/82, C, 82001077

Pastures Historic District, Bounded on N by Madison Ave., on E by Green St., on S by South Ferry St., on W by S. Pearl St., Albany, 3/16/72, A, C, 72000815

Prospect Hill Cemetery Building [Guilderland MRA], Western Tpk., Guilderland, 11/10/82, C, 82001078

Pruyn, Casparus F., House [Colonie Town MRA], 207 Old Niskayuna Rd., Colonie, 10/03/85, B, C, 85002744

Quackenbush House, 683 Broadway, Albany, 6/19/72, A, C, 72000816

Quackenbush Pumping Station, Albany Water Works, Quackenbush Sq., Albany, 6/30/83, A, C, 83001634

Reformed Dutch Church of Rensselaer in Watervliet [Colonie Town MRA], 210 Old Loudon Rd., Colonie, 10/03/85, C, a, 85002745

Renshaw, Alfred H., House [Colonie Town MRA], 33 Fiddlers Ln., Colonie, 10/03/85, C, 85002746

Rensselaer and Saratoga Railroad: Green Island Shops, James and Tibbits Sts. and the Delaware and Hudson RR tracks, Green Island, 5/24/73, A, C, 73001161

Rensselaerville Historic District, Old Albany, Pond Hill, Methodist Hill Rds. and Main St., Rensselaerville, 9/15/83, A, C, 83001635

Rose Hill [Guilderland MRA], 2259 Western Tpk., Guilderland, 11/10/82, C, 82001079

Sage, Henry M., Estate, 1 Sage Rd., Menands, 7/04/80, C, 80004398

Schoolcraft, John, House [Guilderland MRA], 2299 Western Tpk., Guilderland, 11/10/82, C, 82001081

Schoolhouse #6 [Guilderland MRA], 206 Main St., Guilderland, 11/10/82, C, 82001082

Schuyler Flatts, Address Restricted, Menands vicinity, 1/21/74, D, NHL, 74001217

Schuyler, Philip, Mansion, Clinton and Schuyler Sts., Albany, 12/24/67, C, NHL, 67000008

Sharp Brothers House [Guilderland MRA], 4382 Western Tpk., Guilderland, 11/10/82, C, 82001083

Sharp Farmhouse [Guilderland MRA], 4379 Western Tpk., Guilderland, 11/10/82, C, 82001084

Silliman Memorial Presbyterian Church, Mohawk and Seneca Sts., Cohoes, 8/01/79, C, a, 79001565

Simmons Stone House [Colonie Town MRA], 554 Boght Rd., Colonie, 10/03/85, C, 85002747

South End-Groesbeckville Historic District, Roughly bounded by Elizabeth, 2nd, and Morton Aves., Pearl and Franklin Sts., Albany, 9/13/84, A, C, 84002062

Springwood Manor [New York State Route 9, Town of Colonie MRA], 498 Loudon Rd., Loudonville, 10/04/79, C, 79003243

St. Mark's Episcopal Church, 69-75 Hudson Ave., Green Island, 11/07/78, C, a, 78001839

St. Mark's Lutheran Church [Guilderland MRA], Main St., Guilderland, 11/10/82, C, a, 82001080

St. Mary's Church, 10 Lodge St., Albany, 7/14/77, C, a, 77000933

St. Peter's Church, 107 State St., Albany, 3/16/72, C, a, NHL, 72000817

Strong, Jedediah, House [Colonie Town MRA], 379 Vly Rd., Colonie, 10/03/85, C, 85002748

Ten Broeck Mansion, 9 Ten Broeck Pl., Albany, 8/12/71, B, C, 71000522

Treemont Manor [Colonie Town MRA], 71 Old Niskayuna Rd., Colonie, 10/03/85, C, 85002749

Trimble, George, House [Colonie Town MRA], 158 Spring Street Rd., Colonie, 10/03/85, C, 85002750

US Post Office—Delmar [US Post Offices in New York State, 1858-1943, TR], 357 Delaware Ave., Delmar, 11/17/88, A, C, 88002480

United Traction Company Building, 598 Broadway, Albany, 5/24/76, A, C, 76001205

Van Denbergh—Simmons House [Colonie Town MRA], 537 Boght Rd., Colonie, 10/03/85, B, C, 85002751

Van Patten Barn Complex [Guilderland MRA], 4773 Western Tpk., Guilderland, 11/10/82, C, 82001086

Van Schaick House, Van Schaick Ave. and the Delaware & Hudson RR track, Cohoes, 3/18/71, A, C, 71000528

Vanderpool Farm Complex [Guilderland MRA], 3647 Settles Hill Rd., Guilderland, 11/10/82, C, 82001085

Veeder Farmhouse #1 [Guilderland MRA], 3770 Western Tpk., Guilderland, 11/10/82, C, 82001087

Veeder Farmhouse #2 [Guilderland MRA], 3858 Western Tpk, Guilderland, 11/10/82, C, 82001088

Verdoy School [Colonie Town MRA], 957 Troy-Schenectady Rd., Colonie, 10/03/85, A, C, 85002752

Washington Park Historic District, Washington Park and surrounding properties, Albany, 6/19/72, A, C, 72000818

Watervliet Arsenal, S. Broadway, Watervliet, 11/13/66, A, NHL, 66000503

Watervliet Shaker Historic District, Watervliet Shaker Rd., Colonie, 2/20/73, A, C, a, 73001160

Watervliet Shaker Historic District (Boundary Increase), Stump Pond, NE of Colonie, Colonie, 9/20/73, A, 73002247

Watervliet Side Cut Locks, 23rd St. at the Hudson River, Watervliet, 8/12/71, A, C, 71000529

Wheeler Home [New York State Route 9, Town of Colonie MRA], 485 Loudon Rd., Loudonville, 10/04/79, C, 79003241

Whipple Cast and Wrought Iron Bowstring Truss Bridge, 1000 Delaware Ave., Albany, 3/18/71, A, B, C, b, 71000523

Whitney Mansion [New York State Route 9, Town of Colonie MRA], 489 Loudon Rd., Loudonville, 10/04/79, C, 79003242

Young Men's Christian Association Building, 60-64 N. Pearl St., Albany, 11/02/78, A, C, 78001838

Allegany County

Alfred Village Historic District, Sections of N. & S. Main, Church, Ford, Glenn, Park, Sayles, Terrace & W. University Sts., Alfred, 9/11/85, A, C, 85002323

Alumni Hall, Alfred University, Alfred, 9/12/85, A, C, 85002389

Allegany County—Continued

Angelica Park Circle Historic District, Main and White Sts. and Allegany County Fairgrounds, Angelica, 1/31/78, A, C, 78001840

Belvidere, 3 mi. N of Belmont on SR 408, Belmont vicinity, 3/16/72, B, C, 72000822

Christ Episcopal Church, Gibson Hill Rd., SW of Rtes. 19 and 408, Belvidere vicinity, 5/17/74, A, C, a, 74001218

Fireman's Hall, 7 W. University St., Alfred, 3/18/80, C, 80004275

Old Allegany County Courthouse, Park Circle, Angelica, 8/21/72, A, C, 72000821

Smith, Albert, House [Stone Houses of Bergen County TR], 289 Wycoff Ave., Waldwick, 1/10/83, C, 83004698

South Street Historic District, 17, 19–89 South St., Cuba, 5/26/88, C, a, g, 88000585

Steinheim, Alfred, Museum, Alfred University Campus, Alfred, 6/04/73, A, C, 73001163

Terra Cotta Building, Main St., Alfred, 3/16/72, A, C, 72000820

US Post Office—Wellsville [US Post Offices in New York State, 1858-1943, TR], 40 E. Pearl St., Wellsville, 5/11/89, A, C, 88002445

Wellman House, Main St., Friendship, 6/20/74, C, 74001219

Wellsville Erie Depot, Depot St., Wellsville, 8/27/87, A, C, 87001426

Bronx County

48th Police Precinct Station, 1925 Bathgate Ave., New York, 5/06/83, C, 83001639

52nd Police Precinct Station House and Stable, 3016 Webster Ave., New York, 10/29/82, C, 82001091

Bartow-Pell Mansion and Carriage House, Pelham Bay Park, Shore Rd., New York, 12/30/74, C, NHL, 74001220

Bronx Borough Courthouse, E. 161st St., 3rd and Brook Aves., New York, 2/25/82, A, C, 82003344

Bronx Central Annex-U.S. Post Office, 558 Grand Concourse, New York, 5/06/80, C, g, 80002584

Bronx County Courthouse, 851 Grand Concourse, New York, 9/08/83, A, C, g, 83001636

Christ Church Complex, 5030 Riverdale Ave., New York, 9/08/83, C, a, 83001637

Colgate, Robert, House, 5225 Sycamore Ave., New York, 9/08/83, C, 83001638

Dodge, William E., House, 690 W. 247th St., New York, 8/28/77, C, 77000934

Edgehill Church of Spuyten Duyvil, 2550 Independence Ave., New York, 10/29/82, C, a, 82001089

Eighth Regiment Armory, 29 W. Kingsbridge Rd., New York, 12/21/82, C, 82001090

Fonthill Castle and the Administration Building of the College of Mount St. Vincent, W. 261st St. and Riverdale Ave., New York, 7/11/80, A, C, 80002585

Fort Schuyler, Throgs Neck at East River and Long Island Sound, New York, 6/29/76, A, C, 76001206

Grand Concourse Historic District, 730–1000, 1100–1520, 1560, and 851–1675 Grand Concourse, New York, 8/24/87, C, 87001388

Hall of Fame Complex, Bronx Community College campus, New York, 9/07/79, A, C, 79001567

High Pumping Station, Jerome Ave., New York, 11/10/83, A, C, 83003882

House at 175 Belden Street, 175 Belden St., New York, 6/03/82, C, 82003345

Longwood Historic District, Roughly bounded by Beck St., Longwood, Leggett, and Prospect Aves., New York, 9/26/83, C, 83001640

Lorillard Snuff Mill, Off U.S. 1, New York, 12/22/77, A, NHL, 77000935

Morris High School Historic District, Roughly bounded by Boston Rd., Jackson and Forrest Aves., and E. 166th and Home Sts., New York, 9/15/83, C, 83001641

Mott Avenue Control House [Interborough Rapid Transit Subway Control Houses TR], 149th St. and Grand Concourse, New York, 5/06/80, A, C, 80002590

Mott Haven Historic District, An irregular pattern along Alexander Ave. and E. 140th St., New York, 3/25/80, C, 80002586

New York Botanical Gardens, Southern and Bedford Park Blvds., New York, 5/28/67, A, NHL, 67000009

New York, Westchester and Boston Railroad Administration Building, 481 Morris Park Ave., New York, 4/23/80, A, C, 80002587

Park Plaza Apartments, 1005 Jerome Ave., New York, 6/03/82, C, 82003346

Poe Cottage, 2640 Grand Concourse, New York, 8/19/80, B, C, b, 80002588

Public School 11, 1257 Ogden Ave., New York, 9/08/83, C, 83001642

Public School 15, 4010 Dyre Ave., New York, 12/10/81, C, 81000401

Public School 17, 190 Fordham St., New York, 9/27/84, C, 84002065

Rainey Memorial Gates, New York Zoological Park, New York, 3/16/72, C, g, 72000823

Riverdale Presbyterian Church Complex, 4761-4765 Henry Hudson Parkway, New York, 10/14/82, C, a, 82001092

Spaulding, Henry F., Coachman's House, 4970 Independence Ave., New York, 11/04/82, C, b, 82001093

St. Ann's Church Complex, 295 St. Ann's Ave., New York, 4/16/80, B, C, a, d, 80002589

St. James' Episcopal Church and Parish House, 2500 Jerome Ave., New York, 9/30/82, C, 82003347

St. Peter's Church, Chapel and Cemetery Complex, 2500 Westchester Ave., New York, 9/26/83, C, a, d, e, 83001643

Sunnyslope, 812 Faile St., New York, 9/15/83, C, a, 83001644

US Post Office—Morrisania [US Post Offices in New York State, 1858-1943, TR], 442 E. 167th St., New York, 11/17/88, A, C, 88002458

United Workers Cooperatives, 2700–2870 Bronx Park E, New York, 9/11/86, A, C, 86002518

Valentine-Varian House, 3266 Bainbridge Ave., New York, 3/21/78, B, C, b, 78001841

Van Cortlandt, Frederick, House, Van Cortlandt Park at 242nd St., New York, 12/24/67, C, NHL, 67000010

Washington Bridge, Between Amsterdam and Undercliff Aves., New York, 9/22/83, C, 83001645

Wave Hill, 675 W. 252nd St., New York, 9/09/83, C, 83001646

Broome County

Binghamton City Hall, Collier St. between Court and Academy Sts., Binghamton, 3/18/71, A, C, 71000530

Broome County Courthouse, Court St., Binghamton, 5/22/73, A, C, 73001164

Christ Church, Corner of Washington and Henry Sts., Binghamton, 12/02/74, A, C, a, 74001221

Court Street Historic District, Roughly bounded by the Chenango River, Carroll, Henry, and Hawley Sts., Binghamton, 9/07/84, C, 84002066

Dunk, Alfred, House, 4 Pine St., Binghamton, 3/21/85, C, 85000593

Highland Park Carousel [Broome County Carousels MPS], Highland Park, Cooper Rd., Endwell vicinity, 1/25/92, A, C, 91001963

Hotchkiss, Jedediah, House, 10 Chestnut St., Windsor, 6/03/82, B, C, 82003348

Johnson, C. Fred, Park Carousel [Broome County Carousels MPS], C. Fred Johnson Park, Johnson City, 1/25/92, A, C, 91001968

Johnson, George F., Recreation Park Carousel [Broome County Carousels MPS], George F. Johnson Recreation Park, Binghamton, 1/25/92, A, C, 91001967

Johnson, George W., Park Carousel [Broome County Carousels MPS], George W. Johnson Park, Endicott, 1/25/92, A, C, 91001964

Phelps Mansion, 191 Court St., Binghamton, 6/04/73, C, 73001165

Railroad Terminal Historic District, Intersection of Chenango St. and Erie-Lackawanna RR tracks, Binghamton, 3/20/86, A, C, 86000488

Roberson Mansion, 30 Front St., Binghamton, 3/25/80, C, D, 80002591

Rose, Robert H., House, 3 Riverside Dr., Binghamton, 8/26/80, C, 80002592

Ross Park Carousel [Broome County Carousels MPS], Ross Park, Binghamton, 1/25/92, A, C, 91001966

South Washington Street Parabolic Bridge, S. Washington St., Binghamton, 1/30/78, A, C, 78001842

State Street—Henry Street Historic District, Roughly bounded by Lewis St., Prospect Ave., Henry St., and Water and Washington Sts., Binghamton, 6/25/86, C, 86001384

State Theater, 148 Front St., Deposit, 7/21/88, C, 88001020

US Post Office—Endicott [US Post Offices in New York State, 1858-1943, TR], 200 Washington Ave., Endicott, 11/17/88, A, C, 88002498

Broome County—Continued

US Post Office—Johnson City [US Post Offices in New York State, 1858-1943, TR], 307 Main St., Johnson City, 5/11/89, A, C, 88002336

West Endicott Park Carousel [Broome County Carousels MPS], West Endicott Park, Endicott vicinity, 1/25/92, A, C, 91001965

Whitmore, John T., House, 111 Murray St., Binghamton, 8/14/86, C, 86001653

Windsor Village Historic District, College Ave., Academy, Chapel, Church, Dewey, Elm and Main Sts., Windsor, 7/30/80, A, C, 80002593

Cattaraugus County

Ellicottville Historic District, Roughly bounded by Elizabeth, Monroe, Martha and Adams Sts., Ellicottville, 8/22/91, A, C, 91001028

Ellicottville Town Hall, Village Sq., NW corner of Washington and Jefferson Sts., Ellicottville, 4/03/73, A, a, 73001166

Gladden Windmill, Pigeon Valley Rd., Napoli, 7/16/73, A, C, 73001167

Gowanda Village Historic District, 37, 39, 41–45, 47–49, and 53 W. Main St., Gowanda, 9/22/86, A, C, 86002691

Olean Public Library, 116 S. Union St., Olean, 7/11/85, A, C, 85001498

Park Square Historic District, Park Square roughly bounded by N. Main, Pine, Chestnut, S. Main, Elm, and Church Sts., Franklinville, 9/22/86, C, 86002719

Portville Free Library, 2 N. Main St., Portville, 11/07/91, A, C, 91001671

US Post Office—Little Valley [US Post Offices in New York State, 1858-1943, TR], 115 Main St., Little Valley, 5/11/89, A, C, 88002344

US Post Office—Olean [US Post Offices in New York State, 1858-1943, TR], 102 S. Union St., Olean, 5/11/89, A, C, 88002388

Cayuga County

Aurora Steam Grist Mill, Main St., Aurora, 7/30/76, A, C, 76001207

Aurora Village-Wells College Historic District, NY 90, Aurora, 11/19/80, A, C, 80002595

Case Memorial-Seymour Library, 176 Genesee St., Auburn, 5/06/80, C, 80002594

Cayuga County Courthouse and Clerk's Office, 152–154 Genesee St., Auburn, 6/21/91, A, C, 91000721

Harriet Tubman Home for the Aged, 180–182 South St., Auburn, 5/30/74, B, NHL, 74001222

Lakeside Park, NY 38A at Owasco Lake, Owasco, 10/30/89, A, C, 89001790

Sand Beach Church, S of Auburn on NY 38, Auburn vicinity, 6/10/75, B, a, d, 75001176

Seward, William H., House, 33 South St., Auburn, 10/15/66, B, NHL, 66000504

South Street Area Historic District, Roughly, South St. and adjacent properties from Metcalf Dr. to Lincoln St., Auburn, 3/09/91, C, 91000109

US Post Office, Former, and Federal Courthouse, 151–157 Genesee St., Auburn, 6/11/91, A, C, 91000722

Willard Memorial Chapel—Welch Memorial Building, 17–19 Nelson St., Auburn, 6/08/89, C, a, 89000461

Willard, Dr. Sylvester, Mansion, 203 W. Genesee St., Auburn, 11/13/89, A, B, C, 89001948

Wood, Jethro, House, NY 34B, Poplar Ridge, 10/15/66, B, NHL, 66000505

Chautauqua County

Atwater-Stone House [Westfield Village MRA], 29 Water St., Westfield, 12/16/83, C, 83003887

Barcelona Lighthouse and Keeper's Cottage, East Lake Rd., Westfield, 4/13/72, A, 72000825

Bliss, L., House [Westfield Village MRA], 90 W. Main St., Westfield, 9/26/83, C, 83001647

Bly, Smith, House, 4 N. Maple St., Ashville, 10/01/74, C, 74001223

Busti Mill, Lawson Rd., Busti, 7/23/76, A, 76001208

Campbell-Taylor, Harriet, House [Westfield Village MRA], 145 S. Portage St., Westfield, 9/26/83, C, 83001648

Chautauqua Institution Historic District, Bounded by Chautauqua Lake, North and Lowell Aves., and NY 17-J, Chautauqua, 6/19/73, A, C, a, NHL, 73001168

Dunkirk Light [U.S. Coast Guard Lighthouses and Light Stations on the Great Lakes TR], Dunkirk Harbor, Dunkirk, 7/19/84, A, C, 84002067

East Main Street Historic District [Westfield Village MRA], E. Main St., Westfield, 12/16/83, C, 83003893

Euclid Avenue School, 28 Euclid Ave., Jamestown, 3/21/85, A, C, 85000628

Fay-Usborne Mill [Westfield Village MRA], 48 Pearl St., Westfield, 9/26/83, C, 83001649

Fenton, Gov. Reuben, Mansion, 68 S. Main St., Jamestown, 10/18/72, B, C, 72000824

Fredonia Commons Historic District, Main, Temple, Church, Day, and Center Sts., Fredonia, 10/19/78, A, C, a, 78001843

French Portage Road Historic District [Westfield Village MRA], E. Main and Portage Sts., Westfield, 12/16/83, C, 83003895

Hall, Frank A., House [Westfield Village MRA], 34 Washington St., Westfield, 9/26/83, C, 83001650

Lake Shore & Michigan Southern Freight Depot [Westfield Village MRA], English St., Westfield, 9/26/83, C, 83001651

Lake Shore & Michigan Southern Railroad Station [Westfield Village MRA], English St., Westfield, 12/16/83, C, 83003897

Lord, Dr. John, House, Forest Rd. Extension, Busti, 3/02/91, C, 91000104

Mack, Gerald, House [Westfield Village MRA], 79 N. Portage St., Westfield, 9/26/83, C, 83001652

McMahan Homestead [Westfield Village MRA], 232 W. Main Rd., Westfield, 9/26/83, A, B, C, 83001653

Miller, Lewis, Cottage, Chautauqua Institution, NY 17J, Chautauqua, 10/15/66, A, B, NHL, 66000506

Nixon Homestead [Westfield Village MRA], 119 W. Main St., Westfield, 9/26/83, B, C, 83001654

Pennsylvania Railroad Station, Water St., Mayville, 8/06/93, A, C, 93000680

Point Gratiot Lighthouse Complex, Sycamore Rd., Dunkirk, 12/18/79, A, C, 79001568

Rorig Bridge [Westfield Village MRA], Water St. at Chautauqua Creek, Westfield, 9/26/83, C, 83001655

School No. 7, Jct. of E. Lake Shore Dr. and N. Serval St., Dunkirk, 3/05/92, A, C, 92000068

Thompson, Henry Dwight, House [Westfield Village MRA], 29 Wood St., Westfield, 9/26/83, C, 83001656

US Post Office—Dunkirk [US Post Offices in New York State, 1858-1943, TR], 410 Central Ave., Dunkirk, 11/17/88, A, C, 88002488

US Post Office—Fredonia [US Post Offices in New York State, 1858-1943, TR], 21 Day St., Fredonia, 11/17/88, A, C, 88002515

Ward House [Westfield Village MRA], 118 W. Main St., Westfield, 9/26/83, C, 83001657

Welch Factory Building No. 1 [Westfield Village MRA], 101 N. Portage St., Westfield, 9/26/83, A, C, 83001658

Wright, Reuben Gridley, Farm Complex [Westfield Village MRA], 233 E. Main St., Westfield, 9/26/83, C, 83001659

Wright, Rueben, House [Westfield Village MRA], 309 E. Main St., Westfield, 9/26/83, C, 83001660

York-Skinner House [Westfield Village MRA], 31 Union St., Westfield, 9/26/83, B, C, 83001661

Chemung County

Chemung Canal Bank Building, 415 E. Water St., Elmira, 6/23/78, A, C, 78001844

Chemung County Courthouse Complex, 210-228 Lake St., between Market and E. Church Sts., Elmira, 8/12/71, A, C, 71000531

Elmira Civic Historic District, E. Church, Lake, E. Market, Baldwin, Carroll, and State Sts., Elmira, 7/30/80, A, C, 80002596

Elmira College Old Campus, Roughly bounded by College and W. Washington Aves., N. Main St. and Park Pl., Elmira, 8/23/84, A, C, 84002068

Elmira Heights Village Hall, 268 E. 14th St., Elmira Heights, 5/06/82, A, C, 82003349

Fire Station No. 4, 301 Maxwell Pl., Elmira, 3/24/88, A, C, 88000242

Hanover Square Historic District, Jct. of E. and W. Franklin and N. and S. Main Sts., Horseheads, 10/29/82, C, 82001094

Horseheads 1855 Extension Historic District, Grand Central Ave., Fletcher, Sayre, W. Mill and Center Sts., Horseheads, 7/30/80, C, 80002597

Howell, F. M., and Company, 79-105 Pennsylvania Ave., 50 Pennsylvania Ave., Elmira, 8/27/84, A, 84002069

Near Westside Historic District, Roughly bounded by Chemung River, College Ave., 2nd and Hoffman Sts., Elmira, 12/22/83, C, 83003906

Chemung County—Continued

Newtown Battlefield, 6 mi. SE of Elmira on NY 17, Elmira, 11/28/72, A, NHL, 72000826

Park Church, 208 W. Gray St., Elmira, 5/25/77, A, B, C, a, 77000936

Quarry Farm, Crane Rd., Elmira, 3/13/75, B, 75001177

St. Patrick's Parochial Residence—Convent and School, 515–517 Park Pl., Elmira, 11/05/92, C, a, 92001561

Teal Park [Zim TR], Steuben, Pine, and W. Main Sts., Horseheads, 10/07/83, B, C, 83003907

Zimmerman House [Zim TR], 601 Plne St., Horseheads, 10/07/83, B, C, 83003912

Chenango County

Bainbridge Historic District, E. Main, Juliand, N. Main, Pearl, S. Main, and W. Main Sts., Park Pl. and Railroad Ave., Bainbridge, 11/09/82, A, C, 82001095

Bates Round Barn [Central Plan Dairy Barns of New York TR], NY 12, Greene vicinity, 9/29/84, C, 84002071

Burr, Theodore, House, Fort Hill Sq., Oxford, 9/11/81, B, C, 81000402

Chenango County Courthouse District, Irregular pattern between Hayes and Mechanic Sts. and Maple Ave. and City Hall, Norwich, 6/10/75, A, C, 75001178

Clinton-Rosekrans Law Building, 62 Genessee St, Greene, 7/27/79, A, C, 79001569

Columbus Community Church, NY 80, Columbus, 3/20/86, C, a, 86000487

Earlville Historic District, Fayette, N., S., E., and W. Main Sts., Earlville, 10/29/82, C, 82001096

Earlville Opera House, 12-20 E. Main St., Earlville, 1/22/73, A, C, 73001169

Greene Historic District, Chenango, Genesee, and Jackson Sts., Greene, 9/09/82, A, C, 82003350

Main Street Historic District, 169-191 and 158-180 Main St., Afton, 6/30/83, C, 83001662

Moss, Horace O., House, 45 S. Main St., New Berlin, 5/17/74, C, 74001224

New Berlin Historic District, Roughly along Main, West and Genesee Sts., New Berlin, 8/12/82, A, C, 82005025

Newton Homestead, Ridge Rd., South Otselic, 6/03/82, C, 82003351

North Broad Street Historic District, Broad St., Norwich, 11/21/78, C, 78001845

Oxford Village Historic District, Roughly Washington Ave., State St., Chenango River, Merchant & Green Sts., Washington Park, Albany & Pleasant Sts., Oxford, 9/17/85, A, C, 85002481

Sherburne High School, 16 Chapel St., Sherburne, 11/03/88, A, C, 88002185

Sherburne Historic District, N. and S. Main, E. and W. State, Classic, Summit and Church Sts. and Park Ave., Sherburne, 10/29/82, C, 82001097

South Otselic Historic District, Gladding, N. and S. Main Sts., Clarence Church and Plank Rds.,

and Potter Ave., South Otselic, 9/08/83, A, C, 83001663

US Post Office—Norwich [US Post Offices in New York State, 1858-1943, TR], 20–22 E. Main St., Norwich, 5/11/89, A, C, 88002380

US Post Office—Oxford [US Post Offices in New York State, 1858-1943, TR], S. Washington Ave., Oxford, 5/11/89, A, C, 88002392

Young Round Barn [Central Plan Dairy Barns of New York TR], NY 12, Greene vicinity, 9/29/84, C, 84002072

Clinton County

Adirondack Forest Preserve, NE New York State, Adirondack State Forest Preserve, 10/15/66, A, NHL, 66000891

Bailey, William, House [Plattsburgh City MRA], 176 Cornelia St., Plattsburgh, 11/12/82, C, 82001098

Brinkerhoff Street Historic District [Plattsburgh City MRA], Brinkerhoff St. between Oak and N. Catherine Sts., Plattsburgh, 11/12/82, C, 82001099

Carpenter, John B., House [Plattsburgh City MRA], 42 Prospect Ave., Plattsburgh, 11/12/82, C, 82001100

Church of St. Dismas, the Good Thief, Clinton Correctional Facility, Cook St., Dannemora, 11/21/91, A, C, a, 91001673

City Hall, City Hall Pl., Plattsburgh, 12/12/73, C, 73001170

Clinton County Courthouse Complex [Plattsburgh City MRA], 135 Margaret St., Plattsburgh, 11/12/82, C, 82001101

Court Street Historic District [Plattsburgh City MRA], Court St. between Oak and Beekman Sts., Plattsburgh, 2/24/83, C, 83001664

D & H Railroad Complex [Plattsburgh City MRA], Bridge St., Plattsburgh, 11/12/82, C, 82001102

D'Youville Academy [Plattsburgh City MRA], 100 Cornelia St., Plattsburgh, 11/12/82, C, 82001103

Double-Span Metal Pratt Truss Bridge [Keeseville Village MRA], AuSable St., Keeseville, 5/20/83, C, 83001665

First Presbyterian Church [Plattsburgh City MRA], 34 Brinkerhoff St., Plattsburgh, 11/12/82, C, a, 82001104

Fort Brown Site, Address Restricted, Plattsburgh vicinity, 12/15/78, A, D, 78001846

Fort Montgomery, Address Restricted, Rouses Point vicinity, 8/22/77, A, C, D, 77000937

Hartwell, W. W., House & Dependencies [Plattsburgh City MRA], 77 Brinkerhoff St., Plattsburgh, 11/12/82, A, C, 82001105

Hawkins Hall [Plattsburgh City MRA], Beekman St., Plattsburgh, 11/12/82, C, 82001106

House at 56 Cornelia Street [Plattsburgh City MRA], 56 Cornelia St., Plattsburgh, 11/12/82, C, 82001107

Keeseville Historic District [Keeseville Village MRA], Roughly bounded by Vine, Chesterfield, Clinton, Hill, Pleasant, Front, and Beech Sts., Keeseville, 5/20/83, A, C, 83001666

Kent-Delord House, 17 Cumberland Ave., Plattsburgh, 2/18/71, C, 71000532

Marshall, Paul, House [Plattsburgh City MRA], 24-26 Cornelia St., Plattsburgh, 11/12/82, C, 82001108

Old Stone Barracks, Rhode Island Ave., Plattsburgh Air Force Base, Plattsburgh, 2/18/71, A, C, 71000533

Platt, Charles C., Homestead [Plattsburgh City MRA], 96-98 Boynton Ave., Plattsburgh, 11/12/82, C, 82001109

Plattsburgh Bay, Cumberland Bay, E of Plattsburgh, Plattsburgh vicinity, 10/15/66, A, D, NHL, 66000507

Point, The, Historic District [Plattsburgh City MRA], Roughly bounded by Jay, Hamilton, Peru, and Bridge Sts., Plattsburgh, 11/12/82, A, C, 82001110

Ritchie, Z., House [Plattsburgh City MRA], 26 S. Catherine St., Plattsburgh, 11/12/82, C, 82001111

St. John the Baptist R. C. Church and Rectory [Plattsburgh City MRA], 20 Broad St., Plattsburgh, 11/12/82, C, 82001112

United States Oval Historic District [Plattsburgh City MRA], Plattsburgh Air Force Base, Plattsburgh, 8/30/89, A, C, 85003766

Valcour Bay, 7 mi. S of Plattsburgh on the W shore of Lake Champlain, Plattsburgh vicinity, 10/15/66, A, B, NHL, 66000508

Valcour Island Lighthouse, Valcour Island, Lake Champlain, Peru, 8/26/93, A, C, 93000873

Vilas, S. F., Home for Aged & Infirmed Ladies [Plattsburgh City MRA], Beekman and Cornelia Sts., Plattsburgh, 11/12/82, C, 82001113

Wilcox, W. G., House [Plattsburgh City MRA], 45-51 Lorraine St., Plattsburgh, 2/24/83, C, 83001667

Winslow-Turner Carriage House [Plattsburgh City MRA], 210 Cornelia St., Plattsburgh, 11/12/82, C, 82001114

Columbia County

Bouwerie [Clermont MRA], Buckwheat Bridge Rd., Clermont, 10/07/83, A, C, 83003918

Brodhead, Thomas, House [Clermont MRA], US 9, Clermont, 10/07/83, C, 83003919

Bronson, Dr. Oliver, House and Stables, S of Hudson off U.S. 9, Hudson vicinity, 2/20/73, C, 73001173

Church of St. John the Evangelist, Chittenden Rd., Stockport, 4/13/72, C, a, 72000827

Clarkson Chapel [Clermont MRA], NY 9G, Clermont, 10/07/83, A, C, a, 83003920

Clermont, Clermont State Park, Germantown, 2/18/71, B, C, NHL, 71000535

Clermont Academy [Clermont MRA], US 9, Clermont, 10/07/83, A, B, C, 83003931

Clermont Estates Historic District, S of Germantown, Germantown vicinity, 5/07/79, B, C, 79001572

Coons House [Clermont MRA], NY 9G, Clermont, 10/07/83, C, 83003932

Columbia County—Continued

Double-Span Whipple Bowstring Truss Bridge, Van Wyck Lane, Claverack, 4/17/80, A, C, 80002598

Evans, Cornelius H., House, 414–416 Warren St., Hudson, 11/01/74, C, 74001226

First Presbyterian Church, Church St., Valatie, 9/07/79, C, a, 79001574

Front Street-Parade Hill-Lower Warren Street Historic District, Front and Warren Sts., Hudson, 3/05/70, C, 70000420

German Reformed Sanctity Church Parsonage, Maple Ave., Germantown, 1/30/76, C, a, 76001209

Gilbert, Elisha, House, US 20, New Lebanon, 9/07/84, A, C, 84002098

Hickory Hill [Clermont MRA], Buckwheat Bridge Rd., Clermont, 10/07/83, C, 83003934

House at New Forge, 128 New Forge Rd., New Forge, 12/14/87, C, 87002143

Hudson Historic District [Hudson MRA], Roughly bounded by Warren and State Sts., Eighth and Seventh Sts., E. Allen and Allen St., and Penn Central RR, Hudson, 10/21/85, A, C, 85003363

Hudson/Athens Lighthouse [Hudson River Lighthouses TR], S of Middle Ground Flats in Hudson River, Hudson vicinity, 5/29/79, A, C, 79003796

Kinderhook Village District, Both sides of U.S. 9, Kinderhook, 7/24/74, C, 74001227

Knollcroft, CR 9, New Concord, 8/14/85, C, 85002287

Lace House, NY 22 and Miller Rd., Canaan, 2/21/85, C, 85000336

Lebanon Springs Union Free School, NY 22 E of jct. with Cemetery Rd., New Lebanon, 11/21/91, A, C, 91001727

Livingston Memorial Church and Burial Ground, CR 10 & Wire Rd., Linlithgo, 9/12/85, B, C, a, d, 85002271

Livingston, Henry W., House, N of Bell's Pond, Livingston, 2/18/71, B, C, 71000536

Mount Lebanon Shaker Society, U.S. 20, New Lebanon, 10/15/66, A, a, NHL, 66000511

Oak Hill, N of Linlithgo on Oak Hill Rd., Linlithgo vicinity, 6/26/79, C, 79001573

Olana, Church Hill, E end of Rip Van Winkle Bridge, Church Hill, 10/15/66, B, NHL, 66000509

Old Parsonage [Clermont MRA], Buckwheat Bridge Rd., Clermont, 10/07/83, C, a, 83003935

Richmond Hill, CR 31, Livingston, 7/06/88, A, B, C, 88000917

Rossman—Prospect Avenue Historic District [Hudson MRA], Prospect and Rossman Aves., Hudson, 10/21/85, C, 85003364

Scott, R. and W., Ice Company Powerhouse and Ice House Site, River Rd., Stuyvesant vicinity, 2/21/85, A, C, 85000337

Simons General Store, Ancram Sq., Ancram, 4/23/73, A, C, 73001171

Sixteen Mile District [Rhinebeck Town MRA (AD)], W of Clermont along Hudson River, Clermont vicinity, 3/07/79, A, B, C, D, 79001571

Spencertown Academy, NY 203, E of jct. with CR 7, Spencertown, 4/03/73, C, 73001174

Spengler Bridge, Spengler Rd. over Kinderhook Creek, Chatham vicinity, 2/23/73, C, 73001172

St. Luke's Church [Clermont MRA], US 9, Clermont, 10/07/83, C, a, 83003936

Steepletop, NE of Austerlitz on E. Hill Rd., Austerlitz vicinity, 11/11/71, B, NHL, 71000534

Stone Jug, S of Germantown at NY 9G and Jug Rd., Germantown vicinity, 4/20/78, B, C, D, 78001847

Stuyvesant Falls Mill District, New St. and SR 22, Stuyvesant Falls, 9/15/76, A, D, 76001210

US Post Office [US Post Offices in New York State, 1858-1943, TR], 402 Union St., Hudson, 11/17/88, A, C, 88002508

Union Station, NY 66 at intersection with NY 295, Chatham, 5/01/74, A, C, 74001225

Van Alen, Johannis L., Farm, School House Rd., Stuyvesant, 4/26/73, C, 73001175

Van Alen, Luycas, House, E of Kinderhook on NY 9H off U.S. 9, Kinderhook vicinity, 12/24/67, A, C, NHL, 67000011

Van Buren, Martin, National Historic Site, E of Kinderhook on NY 9H, Kinderhook vicinity, 10/15/66, B, NHL, NPS, 66000510

Van Hoesen, Jan, House, NY 66, Claverack, 8/01/79, B, C, 79001570

Van Rensselaer, Henry (Hendrick) I., House, Jct. of Yates Rd. and NY 9H/23, Greenport, 9/16/93, B, C, 93000947

Van Rensselaer, Jacob Rutsen, House and Mill Complex, NY 23, Claverack, 9/09/82, A, C, 82003352

Wild's Mill Complex, U.S. 9 and NY 203, Valatie, 6/14/82, A, C, 82003353

Wild, Nathan, House, 3007 Main St., Valatie, 5/30/91, A, B, C, 91000612

Wiswall, Oliver, House, W of Hudson, Hudson vicinity, 9/04/80, C, 80002599

Cortland County

Cincinnatus Historic District, Main St. and Taylor Ave., Cincinnatus, 9/07/84, C, 84002208

Cortland County Courthouse, Courthouse Park, Cortland, 10/09/74, C, 74001228

Cortland County Poor Farm, NE of Cortland off NY 13, Cortland vicinity, 10/29/82, A, C, 82001115

Cortland Fire Headquarters, 21 Court St., Cortland, 7/12/74, C, 74001229

Hatheway Homestead, NY 41, Solon, 1/20/78, C, 78001848

Little York Pavilion, S of Preble off NY 281, Preble vicinity, 7/27/79, A, C, 79001575

Main Street Historic District, Roughly on Main St. between South and Washington Sts., McGraw, 9/25/86, C, 86002773

Old Homer Village Historic District, N.and S. Main St., Central Park, Clinton, James, Cayuga, and Albany Sts., Homer, 10/02/73, B, C, 73001176

Peck Memorial Library, 28 E. Main St., Marathon, 5/19/92, C, 92000557

Presbyterian Church of McGraw, 3 W. Main St., McGraw, 9/11/86, C, a, 86002517

Tompkins Street Historic District, Tompkins and intersecting streets from Main St. to Cortland Rural Cemetery, Cortland, 3/18/75, A, C, 75001179

Tompkins Street/Main Street Historic District (Boundary Increase), Main St. from Tompkins St. to Clinton Ave., Cortland, 11/17/82, A, C, 82001116

US Post Office—Cortland [US Post Offices in New York State, 1858-1943, TR], 88 Main St., Cortland, 11/17/88, A, C, 88002475

US Post Office—Homer [US Post Offices in New York State, 1858-1943, TR], 2 S. Main St., Homer, 5/11/89, A, C, 88002502

Unitarian Universalist Church [Cobblestone Architecture of New York State MPS], 3 Church St., Courtland, 7/01/93, C, a, 93000592

Water, Wall, and Pine Streets Lenticular Truss Bridges, Wall, Water and Pine Sts., Homer, 10/05/77, A, C, 77000938

Delaware County

Andes Historic District, Delaware Ave., Main and High Sts., and Tremperskill Rd., Andes, 6/28/84, C, 84002215

Burroughs, John, Home, 2 mi. from Roxbury on Roxbury Rd., Roxbury vicinity, 10/15/66, B, NHL, 66000512

Churchill Park Historic District, NY 10 and NY 23 and W. Main St., Stamford, 11/17/80, C, 80004609

Delaware County Courthouse Square District, Roughly bounded by 2nd, Church, Main, and Court Sts., Delhi, 7/16/73, A, C, 73001177

Franklin Village Historic District, Wakeman and Institute Aves., Main, Center, Maple, Water, 2nd, 3rd, and West Sts., Franklin, 9/07/84, A, C, d, 84002220

Frisbee, Judge Gideon, House, NE of Delhi on NY 10, Delhi vicinity, 12/12/76, B, C, 76001211

Gardiner Place Historic District, Gardiner Place, Walton, 5/24/84, C, 84002222

Hanford Mill, On CR 12, East Meredith, 3/26/73, A, C, 73001178

Kelly Round Barn [Central Plan Dairy Barns of New York TR], NY 30, Halcottsville vicinity, 9/29/84, C, 84003857

MacDonald Farm, Elk Creek and Monroe Rds., Meredith, 4/03/73, B, C, 73001179

Main Street Historic District, Main St., Roxbury, 2/29/88, C, b, g, 88000111

McArthur-Martin Hexadecagon Barn [Central Plan Dairy Barns of New York TR], McArthur Hill Rd., Bloomville vicinity, 9/29/84, A, C, 84002237

Murray Hill, Murray Hill Rd., Delhi, 6/03/82, B, C, 82003354

New Stone Hall, Center St., Franklin, 5/06/80, A, C, 80002600

Pakatakan Artists Colony Historic District, NY 28 at jct. with Dry Brook Rd., Arkville, 2/21/89, A, C, 89000046

Delaware County—Continued

US Post Office—Delhi [US Post Offices in New York State, 1858-1943, TR], 10 Court St., Delhi, 11/17/88, A, C, 88002477

US Post Office—Walton [US Post Offices in New York State, 1858-1943, TR], 34–36 Gardner Pl., Walton, 5/11/89, A, C, 88002439

Dutchess County

Academy Street Historic District [Poughkeepsie MRA], Academy St. between Livingston and Montgomery Sts., Poughkeepsie, 11/26/82, A, C, 82001117

Adriance Memorial Library [Poughkeepsie MRA], 93 Market St., Poughkeepsie, 11/26/82, C, 82001118

Akin Free Library, 97 Quaker Hill Rd., Pawling, 11/21/91, A, C, 91001726

Amrita Club [Poughkeepsie MRA], 170 Church St., Poughkeepsie, 11/26/82, C, 82001119

Astor Home for Children [Rhinebeck Town MRA], 36 Mill St., Rhinebeck, 7/09/87, A, C, a, 87001098

Bain Commercial Building [Wappingers Falls MRA], 59-61 W. Main St., Wappingers Falls, 9/29/84, C, 84002369

Balding Avenue Historic District [Poughkeepsie MRA], Balding Ave. between Mansion and Marshall Sts., Poughkeepsie, 11/26/82, C, 82001120

Bannerman's Island Arsenal [Hudson Highlands MRA], Pollepel Island, off NY 9-D, Fishkill, 11/23/82, A, B, C, 82001121

Bard Infant School and St. James Chapel, East Market St., Hyde Park, 8/19/93, C, 93000848

Barrett House [Poughkeepsie MRA], 55 Noxon St., Poughkeepsie, 11/26/82, C, 82001122

Barringer Farmhouse [Rhinebeck Town MRA], US 9, Rhinebeck, 7/09/87, C, 87001076

Beekman Meeting House and Friends' Cemetery [Dutchess County Quaker Meeting Houses TR], Emans Rd., LeGrangeville, 4/27/89, A, C, a, 89000303

Benner House [Rhinebeck Town MRA], 77 Mill St., Rhinebeck, 7/09/87, C, 87001067

Bergh-Stoutenburgh House, U.S. 9, Hyde Park, 9/27/72, C, 72000829

Bloomvale Historic District, Jct. of NY 82, Co. Rd. 13 and E. Branch Wappingers Cr., Pleasant Valley and Washington Townships, Salt Point vicinity, 12/30/91, A, C, 91001874

Bogardus—DeWindt House, 16 Tompkins Ave., Beacon, 4/19/93, C, 93000280

Booth, O. H., Hose Company [Poughkeepsie MRA], 532 Main St., Poughkeepsie, 11/26/82, C, 82001123

Boughton/Haight House [Poughkeepsie MRA], 73-75 S. Hamilton St., Poughkeepsie, 11/26/82, C, 82001124

Brett, Madam Catharyna, Homestead, 50 Van Nydeck Ave., Beacon, 12/12/76, A, C, 76001212

Brower, Abraham, House [New Hamburg MRA], 2 Water St., New Hamburg, 2/27/87, C, 87000116

Brower, Adolph, House [New Hamburg MRA], 1 Water St., New Hamburg, 2/27/87, A, C, 87000114

Bykenhulle, 21 Bykenhulle Rd., Hopewell Junction vicinity, 12/30/91, C, 91001872

Carman, Cornelius, House [Chelsea MRA], River Rd. S., Chelsea, 12/30/87, B, C, 87001372

Cedarcliff Gatehouse [Poughkeepsie MRA], 66 Ferris Lane, Poughkeepsie, 11/26/82, C, 82001125

Chelsea Grammar School [Chelsea MRA], Liberty St., Chelsea, 8/25/87, C, 87001371

Church Street Row [Poughkeepsie MRA], Church St. from Academy to Hamilton St., Poughkeepsie, 11/26/82, C, 82001126

Church of the Holy Comforter, 13 Davies St., Poughkeepsie, 4/13/72, C, a, 72000831

Clark House [Poughkeepsie MRA], 85 Cedar Ave., Poughkeepsie, 11/26/82, C, 82001127

Clark, Ezra, House, Mill Rd., Millerton vicinity, 2/21/85, C, 85000338

Clinton Corners Friends Church [Dutchess County Quaker Meeting Houses TR], Salt Point Tnpk./Main St., Clinton Corners, 4/27/89, A, C, a, 89000305

Clinton House [Poughkeepsie MRA], 547 Main St., Poughkeepsie, 11/26/82, C, 82001128

Coleman Station Historic District, Coleman Station, Indian Lake, Regan and Sheffield Hill Rds., Millerton vicinity, 9/30/93, A, C, 93000945

Collingwood Opera House and Office Building, 31–37 Market St., Poughkeepsie, 10/20/77, A, C, 77000939

Collyer, Capt. Moses W., House [Chelsea MRA], River Rd. S, Chelsea, 8/25/87, B, C, 87001370

Cox Farmhouse [Rhinebeck Town MRA], Old Post Rd. N, Rhinebeck, 7/09/87, C, 87001078

Creek Meeting House and Friends' Cemetery [Dutchess County Quaker Meeting Houses TR], Salt Point Tnpk./Main St., Clinton Corners, 4/27/89, A, C, a, 89000299

Crum Elbow Meeting House and Cemetery [Dutchess County Quaker Meeting Houses TR], Quaker Ln., East Park vicinity, 4/27/89, A, C, a, 89000302

De Peyster, Watts, Fireman's Hall, 86 Broadway at Pine St., Tivoli, 11/16/89, A, B, C, 89002005

Delamater, Henry, House [Rhinebeck Town MRA (AD)], 44 Montgomery St., Rhinebeck, 5/07/73, C, 73001185

Dixon House [Poughkeepsie MRA], 49 N. Clinton St., Poughkeepsie, 11/26/82, C, 82001129

Duchess Company Superintendent's House [Wappingers Falls MRA], 120 Market St., Wappingers Falls, 9/29/84, A, C, 84002371

Dutchess County Court House [Poughkeepsie MRA], 10 Market St., Poughkeepsie, 11/26/82, A, C, 82001130

Dutchess Manor [Hudson Highlands MRA], 400 Breakneck Rd., Fishkill, 11/23/82, C, 82001131

Dwight-Hooker Avenue Historic District [Poughkeepsie MRA], Dwight St. from Hamilton to Hooker, and 79-85 Hooker Ave., Poughkeepsie, 11/26/82, A, C, 82001132

Eastman Terrace [Poughkeepsie MRA], 1-10 Eastman Terr., Poughkeepsie, 11/26/82, C, 82001133

Elmendorph Inn, 43–45 N. Broadway, Red Hook, 9/20/78, A, C, 78001850

Ethol House [Poughkeepsie MRA], 171 Hooker Ave., Poughkeepsie, 11/26/82, C, 82001134

Eustatia, 12 Monell Pl., Beacon, 2/26/79, C, 79001576

Evangelical Lutheran Church of St. Peter [Rhinebeck Town MRA (AD)], 2.25 mi. N of Rhinebeck on U.S. 9, Rhinebeck vicinity, 4/24/75, C, a, 75001182

Evergreen Lands [Rhinebeck Town MRA], Delano Dr., Rhinebeck, 7/09/87, C, 87001096

Farmer's and Manufacturer's Bank [Poughkeepsie MRA], 43 Market St., Poughkeepsie, 11/26/82, C, 82001135

First Presbyterian Church [Poughkeepsie MRA], 25 S. Hamilton St., Poughkeepsie, 11/26/82, C, a, 82001136

First Presbyterian Church Rectory [Poughkeepsie MRA], 98 Cannon St., Poughkeepsie, 11/26/82, C, a, 82001137

Fishkill Supply Depot Site, Address Restricted, Fishkill vicinity, 1/21/74, A, D, 74001230

Fishkill Village District, Roughly along NY 52 from Cary St. to Hopewell St., Fishkill, 3/20/73, C, 73001181

Fredenburg House [Rhinebeck Town MRA], Old Post Rd., Rhinebeck, 7/09/87, C, 87001068

Free Church Parsonage [Rhinebeck Town MRA], Jct. of William and Grinnell Sts., Rhinecliff, 7/09/87, C, a, 87001090

Freer House [Poughkeepsie MRA], 70 Wilbur Blvd., Poughkeepsie, 11/26/82, A, C, 82001138

Garfield Place Historic District, Both sides of Garfield Pl., Poughkeepsie, 11/29/72, C, 72000832

Glebe House [Poughkeepsie MRA], 635 Main St., Poughkeepsie, 11/26/82, C, 82001139

Grasmere [Rhinebeck Town MRA], Mill Rd., Rhinebeck, 7/09/87, A, C, 87001093

Gregory House [Poughkeepsie MRA], 140 S. Cherry St., Poughkeepsie, 11/26/82, C, 82001140

Grey Hook [Poughkeepsie MRA], 5 Ferris Lane, Poughkeepsie, 11/26/82, C, 82001141

Grove, The [Rhinebeck Town MRA], Jct. of Miller Rd. and NY 308, Rhinebeck, 7/09/87, A, C, 87001094

Halfway Diner, 39 N. Broadway, Red Hook, 1/07/88, A, C, b, 87002297

Harlow Row [Poughkeepsie MRA], 100-106 Market St., Poughkeepsie, 11/26/82, C, 82001142

Hasbrouck House [Poughkeepsie MRA], 75-77 Market St., Poughkeepsie, 11/26/82, C, 82001143

Heermance Farmhouse, N of Red Hook on W. Kerley Corner Rd., Red Hook vicinity, 5/06/80, C, 80002604

Heermance House and Law Office [Rhinebeck Town MRA], Jct. of Rhinecliff and Long Dock Rds., Rhinecliff vicinity, 7/09/87, C, 87001091

Hendricks, John, House and Dutch Barn, Old Post Rd., Staatsburg, 9/07/84, C, 84002373

Dutchess County—Continued

Hershkind House [Poughkeepsie MRA], 30 Hooker Ave., Poughkeepsie, 11/26/82, C, 82001144

Hiddenhurst, Sheffield Hill Rd. NW of jct. with Sharon Station Rd., Millerton, 2/21/91, C, 91000102

Hillside Methodist Church [Rhinebeck Town MRA], US 9, Rhinebeck, 7/09/87, C, a, 87001084

Home of Franklin D. Roosevelt National Historic Site, 2 mi. S of Hyde Park on U.S. 9, Hyde Park, 10/15/66, A, B, c, NPS, 66000056

Horton, Joseph, House, NY 376, New Hackensack Rd., New Hackensack, 11/02/88, A, C, 88000916

Howard Mansion and Carriage House, Howard Blvd., Hyde Park, 8/19/93, C, 93000862

Howland Library, 477 Main St., Beacon, 5/07/73, C, 73001180

Hudson River Heritage Historic District, E. side Hudson R. between Germantown and Staatsburg, Staatsburg, 12/14/90, A, B, C, NHL, 90002219

Hudson River State Hospital, Main Building, US 9, Poughkeepsie, 6/29/89, C, NHL, 89001166

Hyde Park Elementary School, Post Rd. N of jct. with Fuller Ln., Hyde Park, 9/02/93, A, C, 93000860

Hyde Park Firehouse, Post Rd. S of jct. with Market St., Hyde Park, 9/02/93, C, 93000859

Hyde Park Railroad Station, River Rd., Hyde Park, 9/11/81, C, 81000403

Italian Center, 225-227 Mill St., Poughkeepsie, 4/19/72, A, C, 72000833

Kane, John, House, 126 E. Main St., Pawling, 10/20/80, A, C, 80002603

Kip—Beekman—Heermance Site (A027-16-0223) [Rhinebeck Town MRA], Address Restricted, Rhinecliff vicinity, 4/19/89, A, D, 89000260

Lady Washington Hose Company [Poughkeepsie MRA], 20 Academy St., Poughkeepsie, 11/26/82, C, 82001145

Langdon Estate Gatehouse, US 9, N of jct. with Market St., Hyde Park, 9/02/93, C, b, 93000865

Locust Grove, 370 South St., Poughkeepsie, 10/15/66, B, NHL, 66000515

Lower Main Street Historic District, 142–192 & 131–221 Main Sts., Beacon, 1/07/88, C, 87002198

Luckey, Platt & Company Department Store [Poughkeepsie MRA], 332-346 Main Mall, Poughkeepsie, 11/26/82, C, 82001146

Lynfeld, South Rd., Washington, 3/19/87, C, 87000474

Mader House [Poughkeepsie MRA], 101 Corlies Ave., Poughkeepsie, 11/26/82, C, 82001147

Main Building, Vassar College, Vassar College campus, Poughkeepsie, 9/19/73, A, C, NHL, 73001183

Main Mall Row [Poughkeepsie MRA], 315 Main Mall to 11 Garden St., Poughkeepsie, 11/26/82, A, C, 82001148

Main Street Historic District [New Hamburg MRA], Main St. roughly bounded by Stone and Bridge Sts., New Hamburg, 2/27/87, A, C, 87000122

Main Street—Albertson Street—Park Place Historic District, Roughly, Main St. between Park Pl. and US 9, Park between Main and Albertson St. and Albertson adjacent to Park, Hyde Park, 9/02/93, C, 93000856

Maizefield, 75 W. Market St., Red Hook, 11/26/73, C, 73001184

Mansakenning [Rhinebeck Town MRA], Ackert Hook Rd., Rhinebeck, 7/09/87, C, 87001095

Maples, The [Rhinebeck Town MRA], 108 Montgomery St., Rhinebeck, 7/09/87, C, 87001092

Market Street Row [Poughkeepsie MRA], 88-94 Market St., Poughkeepsie, 11/26/82, C, 82001149

Marquardt Farm [Rhinebeck Town MRA], Wurtemburg Rd., Wurtemburg vicinity, 7/09/87, C, 87001075

Melius-Bentley House, N of Pine Plains on Mt. Ross Rd., Pine Plains vicinity, 8/11/82, C, 82005024

Mill Street-North Clover Street Historic District, Mill, Mansion, Vassar, and N. Clover Sts., Davies and Lafayette Pl., Poughkeepsie, 2/07/72, A, C, a, 72000834

Mill Street-North Clover Street Historic District (Boundary Increase), 101–115 Main and 25, 27, 29, and 32 N. Bridge Sts., Poughkeepsie, 5/21/87, C, 87000812

Montgomery Place, Address Restricted, Tivoli vicinity, 5/02/75, A, C, NHL, 75001184

Moore House [Poughkeepsie MRA], 37 Adriance Ave., Poughkeepsie, 11/26/82, C, 82001150

Moore, J. W., House [Rhinebeck Town MRA], Mill Rd., Rhinebeck, 7/09/87, C, 87001085

Morton Memorial Library [Rhinebeck Town MRA], Kelly St., Rhinecliff, 7/09/87, C, 87001089

Mount Beacon Incline Railway and Power House [Hudson Highlands MRA], Howland Ave. and Wolcott St., Beacon/Fishkill, 11/23/82, C, 82001151

Mount Gulian, N of Beacon off I-84, Beacon vicinity, 11/19/82, A, B, C, D, b, e, 82001152

Mulhern House [Wappingers Falls MRA], 14-16 Market St., Wappingers Falls, 9/29/84, A, C, 84002376

Mulrien House [Poughkeepsie MRA], 64 Montgomery St., Poughkeepsie, 11/26/82, C, 82001153

New York State Armory [Poughkeepsie MRA], 61-65 Market St., Poughkeepsie, 11/26/82, C, 82001154

Newcomb—Brown Estate, Brown Rd. at US 44, Pleasant Valley, 10/07/88, A, C, 88001704

Niagara Engine House [Poughkeepsie MRA], 8 N. Hamilton St., Poughkeepsie, 11/26/82, C, 82001155

Nine Partners Meeting House and Cemetery [Dutchess County Quaker Meeting Houses TR], NY 343, Millbrook vicinity, 4/27/89, A, C, a, 89000300

O'Brien General Store and Post Office [Rhinebeck Town MRA], Jct. of Schatzell Ave. and Charles St., Rhinecliff, 7/09/87, C, 87001088

Oblong Friends Meetinghouse, Meetinghouse Rd. on Quaker Hill, Pawling, 1/12/73, A, C, a, 73001182

Oswego Meeting House and Friends' Cemetery [Dutchess County Quaker Meeting Houses TR], Oswego Rd. at jct. with Smith Rd., Moore's Mill vicinity, 4/27/89, A, C, a, 89000301

Pelton Mill [Poughkeepsie MRA], 110 Mill St., Poughkeepsie, 11/26/82, A, 82001156

Phillips House [Poughkeepsie MRA], 18 Barclay St., Poughkeepsie, 11/26/82, C, 82001157

Pier, Jan, House [Rhinebeck Town MRA], NY 308, Rhinebeck, 7/09/87, C, 87001073

Pilgrim's Progress Road Bridge [Rhinebeck Town MRA], Miller Rd. S of NY 308, Rhinebeck, 7/09/87, A, C, 87001102

Pines, The, Maple St., Pine Plains, 9/26/83, C, 83001668

Post-Williams House [Poughkeepsie MRA], 44 S. Clinton St., Poughkeepsie, 11/26/82, C, 82001158

Poughkeepsie Almshouse and City Infirmary, 20 Maple St., Poughkeepsie, 12/04/78, A, C, 78001849

Poughkeepsie City Hall, 228 Main St., Poughkeepsie, 1/20/72, A, C, 72000835

Poughkeepsie Meeting House (Montgomery Street) [Dutchess County Quaker Meeting Houses TR], 112 Montgomery St., Poughkeepsie, 4/27/89, A, C, a, 89000304

Poughkeepsie Meeting House (Hooker Avenue) [Dutchess County Quaker Meeting Houses TR], 249 Hooker Ave., Poughkeepsie, 4/27/89, A, C, a, 89000306

Poughkeepsie Railroad Bridge, Spans Hudson River, Poughkeepsie, 2/23/79, A, C, 79001577

Poughkeepsie Railroad Station, Main St., Poughkeepsie, 11/21/76, A, C, 76001214

Poughkeepsie Trust Company [Poughkeepsie MRA], 236 Main St., Poughkeepsie, 11/26/82, C, 82001159

Poughkeepsie Underwear Factory [Poughkeepsie MRA], 6-1 N. Cherry St., Poughkeepsie, 11/26/82, A, 82001160

Progue House [Rhinebeck Town MRA], Primrose Hill Rd., Rhinebeck, 7/09/87, A, C, 87001072

Pultz Farmhouse [Rhinebeck Town MRA], Wurtemburg Rd., Wurtemburg vicinity, 7/09/87, A, C, 87001074

Reformed Dutch Church of Fishkill Landing, 44–50 Ferry St., Beacon, 8/31/88, A, C, a, d, 88001438

Reformed Dutch Church, Parsonage and Lecture Hall, US 9 N of jct. with Market St., Hyde Park, 9/02/93, C, a, d, 93000861

Reynolds House [Poughkeepsie MRA], 107 S. Hamilton St., Poughkeepsie, 11/26/82, C, 82001161

Rhinebeck Village Historic District [Rhinebeck Town MRA (AD)], U.S. 19 and NY 308, Rhinebeck, 8/08/79, A, C, 79001578

Rhinecliff Hotel [Rhinebeck Town MRA], Schatzell Ave., Rhinecliff, 7/09/87, A, C, 87001087

Riverside Methodist Church and Parsonage [Rhinebeck Town MRA], Charles and Orchard Sts., Rhinecliff, 7/09/87, C, a, 87001086

Rock Ledge [Rhinebeck Town MRA], Roughly Ackert Hook Rd., Haggerty Hill Rd., and Troy Dr., Rhinebeck vicinity, 11/28/89, C, 89002010

Dutchess County—Continued

Rogers, Archibald, Estate, Jct. of Mansion and Garden Sts., Hyde Park, 9/02/93, C, a, 93000864

Rokeby, S of Barrytown between Hudson River and River Rd., Barrytown, 3/26/75, C, 75001181

Rombout House [Poughkeepsie MRA], New Hackensack Rd., Poughkeepsie, 11/26/82, C, 82001162

Roosevelt Point Cottage and Boathouse, River Point Rd. at the Hudson R., Hyde Park, 9/02/93, C, 93000851

Roosevelt, Eleanor, National Historic Site, Violet Ave., Hyde Park, 3/20/80, A, B, NPS, 80000357

Roosevelt, Isaac, House, Riverview Cir., E side, Hyde Park, 9/02/93, C, 93000857

Rymph, George, House, US 9 S of jct. with S. Cross Rd., Hyde Park, 8/19/93, C, 93000863

Sague House [Poughkeepsie MRA], 167 Hooker Ave., Poughkeepsie, 11/26/82, C, 82001164

Saint Mark's Episcopal Church [Chelsea MRA], Liberty St., Chelsea, 8/25/87, C, a, 87001369

Salisbury Turnpike Bridge [Rhinebeck Town MRA], Old Turnpike Rd., Rhinebeck, 7/09/87, A, C, 87001100

Sands, Robert, Estate [Rhinebeck Town MRA (AD)], 1.5 mi. E of Rhinebeck at NY 308 and NY 9, Rhinebeck vicinity, 2/24/75, C, 75001183

Second Baptist Church, 36 Vassar St., Poughkeepsie, 1/20/72, A, C, a, 72000836

Shay's Warehouse and Stable [New Hamburg MRA], Rear of 32 Point St., New Hamburg, 2/27/87, C, 87000123

Shay, William, Double House [New Hamburg MRA], 18 Point St., New Hamburg, 2/27/87, C, 87000121

Sipperly Lown Farmhouse [Rhinebeck Town MRA], US 9, Rhinebeck, 7/09/87, A, C, 87001101

Slate Quarry Road Dutch Barn [Rhinebeck Town MRA], Slate Quarry Rd., Rhinebeck, 7/09/87, A, C, 87001077

Smith Metropolitan AME Zion Church, Jct. of Smith and Cottage Sts., Poughkeepsie, 11/21/91, A, C, a, 91001724

South Hamilton Street Row [Poughkeepsie MRA], 81-87 S. Hamilton St., Poughkeepsie, 11/26/82, C, 82001165

St. Paul's Episcopal Church [Poughkeepsie MRA], 161 Mansion Ave., Poughkeepsie, 11/26/82, C, a, 82001163

St. Paul's Lutheran Church, Parsonage and Cemetery [Rhinebeck Town MRA], Wurtemburg Rd., Wurtemburg vicinity, 7/09/87, A, C, a, 87001083

Steenburg Tavern [Rhinebeck Town MRA], US 9, Rhinebeck, 7/09/87, C, 87001070

Stone Street Historic District [New Hamburg MRA], Stone St. from Division St. to Bridge St., New Hamburg, 2/27/87, C, 87000120

Stonecrest [Rhinebeck Town MRA], Old Post Rd., Rhinebeck, 7/09/87, C, 87001097

Stony Kill Farm, W of Fishkill on NY 9D, Fishkill vicinity, 3/20/80, B, C, 80002601

Stoutenburgh, William, House, U.S. 9G, East Park, Hyde Park, 9/27/72, C, 72000830

Strawberry Hill [Rhinebeck Town MRA], Ackert Hook Rd., Rhinebeck, 7/09/87, C, 87001071

Sylvan Lake Rock Shelter, Address Restricted, Sylvan Lake vicinity, 7/12/74, D, 74001231

Tabor-Wing House, NY 22 and Cemetery Rd., Dover Plains, 6/03/82, C, 82003355

Thompson House [Poughkeepsie MRA], 100 S. Randolph Ave., Poughkeepsie, 11/26/82, C, 82001166

Tioronda Bridge, South Ave., Beacon, 10/08/76, A, C, 76001213

Traver House [Rhinebeck Town MRA], Wynkoop Ln., Rhinebeck, 7/09/87, C, 87001069

Traver, J. E., Farm [Rhinebeck Town MRA], Violet Hill Rd., Rhinebeck, 7/09/87, C, 87001082

Traver, John H., Farm [Rhinebeck Town MRA], Wurtemburg Rd., Wurtemburg, 7/09/87, C, 87001081

Travis House [Poughkeepsie MRA], 131 Cannon St., Poughkeepsie, 11/26/82, A, C, 82001167

Trinity Methodist Episcopal Church and Rectory [Poughkeepsie MRA], 1-3 Hooker Ave., Poughkeepsie, 11/26/82, C, a, 82001168

US Post Office—Beacon [US Post Offices in New York State, 1858-1943, TR], 369 Main St., Beacon, 11/17/88, A, C, 88002456

US Post Office—Hyde Park [US Post Offices in New York State, 1858-1943, TR], E. Market St. and US 9, Hyde Park, 5/11/89, A, B, C, 88002511

US Post Office—Poughkeepsie [US Post Offices in New York State, 1858-1943, TR], Mansion St., Poughkeepsie, 5/15/89, A, C, 88002413

US Post Office—Rhinebeck [US Post Offices in New York State, 1858-1943, TR], 14 Mill St., Rhinebeck, 5/11/89, A, C, 88002419

US Post Office—Wappingers Falls [US Post Offices in New York State, 1858-1943, TR], 2 South Ave., Wappingers Falls, 5/11/89, A, C, 88002440

Union Free School [New Hamburg MRA], Academy St., New Hamburg, 2/27/87, C, 87000117

Union Street Historic District, About 8 blocks in downtown Poughkeepsie centered around Union St., Poughkeepsie, 12/09/71, A, C, 71000537

Upper-Mill Street Historic District [Poughkeepsie MRA], Roughly Mill St. from Center Plaza to Catherine St., Poughkeepsie, 11/26/82, A, C, 82001169

Van Vredenburg Farm [Rhinebeck Town MRA], Cedar Heights Rd., Rhinebeck, 7/09/87, C, 87001079

Van Wyck-Wharton House, S of Fishkill on U.S. 9, Fishkill vicinity, 4/13/72, A, C, 72000828

Vanderbilt Lane Historic District, Jct. of Vanderbilt Ln. and US 9, Hyde Park, 9/02/93, C, 93000855

Vanderbilt Mansion National Historic Site, N edge of Hyde Park, U.S. 9, Hyde Park, 10/15/66, A, C, NPS, 66000059

Vassar College Observatory, Raymond Ave., Poughkeepsie, 7/17/91, A, B, NHL, 91002051

Vassar Home for Aged Men, 1 Vassar St., Poughkeepsie, 4/13/72, A, C, 72000837

Vassar Institute, 12 Vassar St., Poughkeepsie, 1/20/72, A, C, 72001540

Vassar, Matthew, Estate, Academy and Livingston Sts., Poughkeepsie, 8/11/69, C, NHL, 69000141

Vassar-Warner Row [Poughkeepsie MRA], S. Hamilton from Montgomery to 40 Hamilton St., Poughkeepsie, 11/26/82, C, 82001170

Wales House, 23 W. Market St., Hyde Park, 8/19/93, C, 93000858

Wappingers Falls Historic District [Wappingers Falls MRA], Roughly bounded by South Ave., Elm, Main, Park, Walker, Market, and McKinley Sts., Wappingers Falls, 9/29/84, A, C, 84002380

Wheeler Hill Historic District, Wheeler Hill Rd., Wappinger, 6/14/91, A, C, 91000678

Williams Farm [Rhinebeck Town MRA], Enterprise Rd., Rhinebeck, 7/09/87, C, 87001080

Windswept Farm, Sunset Trail, Clinton, 9/07/89, A, C, 89001390

Winegar, Hendrik, House, SE of Amenia on SR 2 off NY 343, Amenia vicinity, 4/15/75, C, 75001180

Young Men's Christian Association [Poughkeepsie MRA], 58 Market St., Poughkeepsie, 11/26/82, C, 82001171

Zion Memorial Chapel [New Hamburg MRA], 37 Point St., New Hamburg, 2/27/87, C, 87000119

Erie County

33–61 Emerson Place Row [Masten Neighborhood Rows TR], 33–61 Emerson Pl., Buffalo, 3/19/86, C, 86000691

Albright-Knox Art Gallery, 1285 Elmwood Ave., in Delaware Park, Buffalo, 5/27/71, C, 71000538

Allentown Historic District, Off NY 384, Buffalo, 4/21/80, A, C, 80002605

Berkeley Apartments, 24 Johnson Park, Buffalo, 10/15/87, C, 87001852

Blessed Trinity Roman Catholic Church Buildings, 317 LeRoy Ave., Buffalo, 8/03/79, A, C, a, 79001579

Buffalo Gas Light Company Works, 249 W. Genesee St., Buffalo, 9/01/76, A, C, 76001215

Buffalo Main LIght [U.S. Coast Guard Lighthouses and Light Stations on the Great Lakes TR], Buffalo River, Buffalo, 7/19/84, A, C, 84002383

Buffalo North Breakwater South End Light [U.S. Coast Guard Lighthouses and Light Stations on the Great Lakes TR], Buffalo Harbor, Buffalo, 8/04/83, A, C, 83001669

Buffalo State Asylum for the Insane, 400 Forest Ave., Buffalo, 6/24/86, C, NHL, 86003557

Buffalo State Hospital, 400 Forest Ave., Buffalo, 1/12/73, C, 73001186

Buffalo and Erie County Historical Society, 25 Nottingham Ct., Buffalo, 4/23/80, A, C, NHL, 80002606

Buffalo, Rochester & Pittsburgh Railroad Station, 227 W. Main St., Springville, 11/07/91, C, 91001669

Cazenovia Park-South Park System [Olmsted Parks and Parkways TR], South Park, NW along McKinley Pkwy. to Cazenovia Park, NW along McKinley Pkwy. to Heacock Park, Buffalo, 3/30/82, C, 82005028

Erie County—Continued

Chapel of Our Lady Help of Christians, 4125 Union Rd., Cheektowaga, 12/14/78, A, C, a, 78001851

County and City Hall, 95 Franklin St., Buffalo, 5/24/76, A, C, 76001216

Delaware Avenue Historic District, W side of Delaware Ave. between North and Bryant Sts., Buffalo, 1/17/74, A, C, a, 74001232

Delaware Park-Front Park System [Olmsted Parks and Parkways TR], Front Park, Porter Ave. to Symphony Cir., N along Richmond Ave., Bidwell Pkwy., Gates Cir. and Delaware Park, Buffalo, 3/30/82, C, 82005029

Dorsheimer, William, House, 434 Delaware Ave., Buffalo, 11/21/80, C, 80002607

Durham Memorial A.M.E. Zion Church, 174 E. Eagle St., Buffalo, 9/15/83, A, a, 83001670

Eaton Site, Address Restricted, West Seneca, 4/03/79, D, 79001581

Eberhardt Mansion, 2746 Delaware Ave., Kenmore, 9/08/83, C, 83001671

Eshelman, J., and Company Store, 6000 Goodrich Rd., Clarence Center, 5/06/82, C, 82003356

Fillmore, Millard, House, 24 Shearer Ave., East Aurora, 5/30/74, B, b, NHL, 74001235

Forest Lawn Cemetery, 1411 Delaware Ave., Buffalo, 5/10/90, C, 90000688

Fosdick-Masten Park High School, Masten Ave. and E. North St., Buffalo, 6/30/83, C, 83001672

Gamel Hexadecagon Barn [Central Plan Dairy Barns of New York TR], Shirley Rd., North Collins vicinity, 9/29/84, C, 84002386

Hull, Warren, House, 5976 Genesee St., Lancaster, 5/11/92, A, C, 92000456

Johnson-Jolls Complex, S-4287 S. Buffalo St., Orchard Park, 5/06/80, C, 80002611

King, Martin Luther, Jr., Park [Olmsted Parks and Parkways TR], Roughly bounded by Northampton St., E. Parade Ave., Best St. and Kensington Expressway, Buffalo, 3/30/82, C, 82005027

Kleinhans Music Hall, Symphony Circle, Buffalo, 6/29/89, C, NHL, 89001235

Kleis Site, Address Restricted, Hamburg vicinity, 4/20/79, D, 79001580

Lafayette High School, 370 Lafayette Ave., Buffalo, 12/03/80, C, 80002608

Laurel and Michigan Avenues Row [Masten Neighborhood Rows TR], 1335–1345 Michigan Ave., Buffalo, 3/19/86, C, 86000688

Macedonia Baptist Church, 511 Michigan Ave., Buffalo, 2/12/74, A, a, 74001233

Martin, D. D., House Complex [Olmsted Parks and Parkways TR (AD)], 123 Jewett Pkwy., Buffalo, 12/30/75, C, 75001185

Martin, Darwin D., House, 125 Jewett Pkwy., Buffalo, 2/24/86, C, NHL, 86000160

NASH (harbor tug), 1776 Niagara St., Buffalo, 12/04/91, A, C, g, NHL, 91002059

New York Central Terminal, 495 Paderewski Dr., Buffalo, 9/07/84, A, C, 84002389

Parkside East Historic District [Olmsted Parks and Parkways TR], Roughly bounded by Parkside Ave., Amherst St., Colvin Ave., NY Central RR

tracks, Main St., and Humboldt Ave., Buffalo, 10/17/86, A, C, 86002817

Parkside West Historic District [Olmsted Parks and Parkways TR], Roughly bounded by Amherst St., Nottingham Terr., Middlesex Rd., and Delaware Ave., Buffalo, 12/10/86, C, g, 86003372

Pierce Arrow Factory Complex, Elmwood and Great Arrow Aves., Buffalo, 10/01/74, A, C, 74001234

Prudential Building, Church and Pearl Sts., Buffalo, 3/20/73, A, C, NHL, 73001187

Riverside Park [Olmsted Parks and Parkways TR], Roughly bounded by Vulcan, Tonawanda, Crowley, and Niagara St., Buffalo, 3/30/82, C, 82005026

Roosevelt, Theodore, Inaugural National Historic Site, 641 Delaware Ave., Buffalo, 11/02/66, B, NPS, 66000516

Roycroft Campus, Main and W. Grove Sts., East Aurora, 11/08/74, A, B, C, a, g, NHL, 74001236

Scheidemantel, George and Gladys, House, 363 Oakwood Ave., East Aurora, 8/05/93, B, C, 93000778

Shea's Buffalo Theater, 646 Main St., Buffalo, 5/06/75, A, C, 75001186

South Buffalo North Side Light [U.S. Coast Guard Lighthouses and Light Stations on the Great Lakes TR], Buffalo Harbor, Buffalo, 8/04/83, A, 83001673

St. Andrew's Evangelical Lutheran Church Complex, Sherman and Peckham Sts., Buffalo, 9/08/83, A, C, a, 83001674

St. Paul's Cathedral, 139 Pearl St., Buffalo, 12/23/87, C, a, NHL, 87002600

St. Paul's Episcopal Cathedral, 125 Pearl St., Buffalo, 3/01/73, C, a, 73002298

Thomas Indian School, NY 438 on Cattaraugus Reservation, Irving, 1/25/73, A, C, 73001188

U.S. Post Office, 121 Ellicott St., Buffalo, 3/16/72, C, 72000839

US Post Office—Akron [US Post Offices in New York State, 1858-1943, TR], 118 Main St., Akron, 11/17/88, A, C, 88002449

US Post Office—Angola [US Post Offices in New York State, 1858-1943, TR], 80 N. Main St., Angola, 11/17/88, A, C, 88002452

US Post Office—Depew [US Post Offices in New York State, 1858-1943, TR], Warsaw St., Depew, 11/17/88, A, C, 88002481

US Post Office—Lancaster [US Post Offices in New York State, 1858-1943, TR], 5064 Broadway, Lancaster, 5/11/89, A, C, 88002340

US Post Office—Springville [US Post Offices in New York State, 1858-1943, TR], 75 Franklin St., Springville, 5/11/89, A, C, 88002433

US Post Office—Tonawanda [US Post Offices in New York State, 1858-1943, TR], 96 Seymour St., Tonawanda, 5/11/89, A, C, 88002437

USS THE SULLIVANS (destroyer), 1 Naval Cove Pk., Buffalo, 1/14/86, A, g, NHL, 86000085

West Village Historic District, Roughly bounded by S. Elmwood Ave., Chippewa, Georgia, Prospect, Carolina and Tracy Sts., Buffalo, 5/06/80, C, 80002610

Williamsville Water Mill Complex, 56 and 60 Spring St., Williamsville, 9/22/83, A, C, 83001675

Woodlawn Avenue Row [Masten Neighborhood Rows TR], 75–81 Woodlawn Ave., Buffalo, 3/19/86, C, 86000690

Young Men's Christian Association Central Building, 45 W. Mohawk St., Buffalo, 9/08/83, A, C, 83001676

Essex County

Adirondack Iron and Steel Company, Address Restricted, Tahawus vicinity, 10/05/77, A, D, 77000940

Adsit Log House, Point Rd. N of Ligonier Pt., Willsboro, 8/18/92, A, C, 92001053

Aiken, Abraham, House, NY 22/Lakeshore Rd., Willsboro, 6/08/89, C, 89000465

Amherst Avenue Historic District [Ticonderoga MRA], 322–340 Amherst Ave., Ticonderoga, 6/16/89, C, 89000473

Barngalow [Saranac Lake MPS], 108 1/2 Park Ave., Saranac Lake, 11/06/92, A, C, 92001427

Black Watch Library [Ticonderoga MRA], 161 Montcalm St., Ticonderoga, 11/15/88, C, 88002199

Bogie Cottage [Saranac Lake MPS], 59 Franklin St., Saranac Lake, 11/06/92, A, C, 92001464

Brown, John, Farm, John Brown Rd., Lake Placid, 6/19/72, A, B, c, 72000840

Burleigh, H. G., House [Ticonderoga MRA], 307 Champlain Ave., Ticonderoga, 11/15/88, C, 88002192

Camp Dudley Road Historic District, Roughly bounded by NY 22, Stacy Br., Lake Champlain and the Westport village line, Westport, 10/21/93, A, C, 93001136

Camp Santanoni [Great Camps of the Adirondacks TR], N of NY 28N, Newcomb vicinity, 4/03/87, C, 86002955

Central School [Ticonderoga MRA], 324 Champlain Ave., Ticonderoga, 11/15/88, A, C, 88002202

Church of the Nazarene, W of Essex on NY 22, Essex vicinity, 6/19/73, C, a, 73001189

Clark House [Ticonderoga MRA], 331 Montcalm St., Ticonderoga, 11/15/88, C, 88002204

Clark, Peyton, Cottage [Saranac Lake MPS], 9 Rockledge Rd., Saranac Lake, 11/06/92, A, C, 92001435

Community Building [Ticonderoga MRA], Montcalm and Champlain Sts., Ticonderoga, 11/15/88, C, 88002198

Coulter Cottage [Saranac Lake MPS], 34 Shepard Ave., Saranac Lake, 11/06/92, A, C, 92001438

Delano, Clayton H., House [Ticonderoga MRA], 25 Father Jogues Pl., Ticonderoga, 11/15/88, B, C, 88002195

Denny Cottage [Saranac Lake MPS], 76 Bloomingdale Ave., Saranac Lake, 11/06/92, A, C, 92001452

Edgewater Farm, 470 Point Rd., Willsboro Point vicinity, 2/17/88, A, C, b, 88000035

Essex County—Continued

Essex County Home and Farm, SW of Whallonsburg on NY 22, Whallonsburg vicinity, 9/23/82, A, C, 82003357

Essex Village Historic District, Town of Essex and surroundings on W bank of Lake Champlain, Essex and vicinity, 5/28/75, A, C, 75001187

Fallon Cottage Annex [Saranac Lake MPS], 31 Franklin St., Saranac Lake, 11/06/92, A, C, 92001463

Ferris House [Ticonderoga MRA], 16 Carillon Rd., Ticonderoga, 11/15/88, C, 88002203

First Congregational and Presbyterian Society Church of Westport, Main St./CR 10, Westport, 12/19/88, C, a, b, 88002750

Fort Crown Point, Crown Point Reservation, SW of Lake Champlain Bridge and NY 8, Crown Point vicinity, 11/24/68, A, C, D, NHL, 68000033

Fort St. Frederic, Jct. of NY 8 and 9N, Crown Point, 10/15/66, D, NHL, 66000517

Fort Ticonderoga, 2.5 mi. S of Ticonderoga on NY 22, Ticonderoga vicinity, 10/15/66, A, D, NHL, 66000519

Fried, Samson, Estate, NY 74, Severance, 2/26/87, C, 87000225

Gilligan and Stevens Block [Ticonderoga MRA], 115 Montclam St., Ticonderoga, 11/15/88, C, 88002193

Hancock House [Ticonderoga MRA], Montcalm and Wicker Sts., Ticonderoga, 11/15/88, C, 88002197

Hand-Hale Historic District, River and Maple Sts., Elizabethtown, 3/05/79, B, C, 79001582

Highland Park Historic District [Saranac Lake MPS], Roughly, Park Ave. from Military Rd. to 170 Park Ave., Saranac Lake, 11/06/92, A, C, 92001474

Ironville Historic District, Area surrounding Ironville including Furnace St. and Penfield Pond, Ironville, 12/27/74, A, B, C, 74001237

Kennedy Cottage [Saranac Lake MPS], 26 Shepard St., Saranac Lake, 11/06/92, A, C, 92001437

Lake George Avenue Historic District [Ticonderoga MRA], 301–331 Lake George Ave., Ticonderoga, 6/16/89, C, 89000472

Lane Cottage [Saranac Lake MPS], 4 Rockledge Rd., Saranac Lake, 11/06/92, A, C, 92001434

Larom—Welles Cottage [Saranac Lake MPS], 110 Park Ave., Saranac Lake, 11/06/92, A, C, 92001478

Leetch, Dr. Henry, House [Saranac Lake MPS], 3 Johnson Rd., Saranac Lake, 11/06/92, A, C, 92001471

Lent Cottage [Saranac Lake MPS], 18 Franklin Ave., Saranac Lake, 11/06/92, A, C, 92001462

Liberty Monument [Ticonderoga MRA], NY 9N at Montcalm St., Ticonderoga, 11/16/89, C, 89002014

Marquay Cottage [Saranac Lake MPS], 6 Slater St., Saranac Lake, 11/06/92, A, C, 92001439

Marvin Cottage [Saranac Lake MPS], 15 Franklin St., Saranac Lake, 11/06/92, A, C, 92001461

Moore, Silas B., Gristmill [Ticonderoga MRA], 218 Montcalm St., Ticonderoga, 11/15/88, C, 88002190

Morgan Cottage [Saranac Lake MPS], 100 Park Ave., Saranac Lake, 11/06/92, A, C, 92001426

NYS Armory [Ticonderoga MRA], 315 Champlain Ave., Ticonderoga, 11/15/88, C, 88002200

Octagonal Schoolhouse, On Rte. 22 in Bouquet, Essex vicinity, 1/17/73, A, C, 73001190

PAD Factory, The [Ticonderoga MRA], 109 Lake George Ave., Ticonderoga, 11/15/88, A, C, 88002205

Partridge Cottage [Saranac Lake MPS], 15 South St., Saranac Lake, 11/06/92, A, C, 92001440

Pittenger Cottage [Saranac Lake MPS], 14 Forest Hill Ave., Saranac Lake, 11/06/92, A, C, 92001460

Rembrandt Hall [Keeseville Village MRA], Clinton St., Keeseville, 5/20/83, C, 83001677

Sheldon—Owens Farm, Lake Shore Rd. SE of jct. with Middle and West Rds., Willsboro vicinity, 4/01/93, A, C, 93000171

State Theater [Ticonderoga MRA], 18 Montcalm St., Ticonderota, 4/30/92, A, C, 92000454

Stevenson Cottage [Saranac Lake MPS], Stevenson Ln., Saranac Lake, 11/06/92, A, C, 92001441

Ticonderoga High School [Ticonderoga MRA], Calkins Pl., Ticonderoga, 11/15/88, C, 88002201

Ticonderoga National Bank [Ticonderoga MRA], 101 Montcalm St., Ticonderoga, 11/15/88, C, 88002194

Ticonderoga Pulp and Paper Company Office [Ticonderoga MRA], Montcalm St., Ticonderoga, 11/15/88, A, C, 88002191

Tomlinson House [Keeseville Village MRA], Kent St., Keeseville, 5/20/83, C, 83001678

US Post Office—Lake Placid [US Post Offices in New York State, 1858-1943, TR], 201 Main St., Lake Placid, 11/17/88, A, C, 88002339

US Post Office-Ticonderoga [US Post Offices in New York State, 1858-1943, TR], 123 Champlain Ave., Ticonderoga, 5/11/89, A, C, 88002436

Van Ornam & Murdock Block, Main St., Port Henry, 11/14/82, A, C, 82001172

Watson, Elkanah, House, 3 mi. E of U.S. 9, Port Kent, 10/15/66, B, NHL, 66000518

Will Rogers Memorial Hospital, NY 86, Saranac Lake, 9/08/83, A, C, 83001679

Willsboro Congregational Church, NY 22, Willsboro, 5/31/84, C, a, 84002391

Witherbee Memorial Hall, Broad St. E of jct. with Office Rd., Mineville, 4/22/91, A, C, 91000421

Franklin County

Allen, Dr. A. H., Cottage [Saranac Lake MPS], 22 Catherine St., Saranac Lake, 11/06/92, A, C, 92001454

Ames Cottage [Saranac Lake MPS], 43 Church St., Saranac Lake, 11/06/92, A, C, 92001458

Baird Cottage [Saranac Lake MPS], Glenwood Rd., Saranac Lake, 11/06/92, A, C, 92001466

Berkeley Square Historic District, 30–84 Main St., 2–29 Broadway, Saranac Lake, 2/11/88, A, B, C, 88000114

Camp Intermission [Saranac Lake MPS], Northwest Bay Rd., Saranac Lake, 11/06/92, A, C, 92001421

Camp Topridge [Great Camps of the Adirondacks TR], S of Keese Mills Rd., Upper St. Regis Lake, Keese Hill vicinity, 11/07/86, C, 86002952

Camp Wild Air [Great Camps of the Adirondacks TR], Upper St. Regis Lake, Upper St. Regis, 11/07/86, C, 86002930

Church Street Historic District [Saranac Lake MPS], Roughly, Church St. from Main St. to St. Bernard St., Saranac Lake, 11/06/92, A, C, a, 92001472

Colbath Cottage [Saranac Lake MPS], 30 River St., Saranac Lake, 11/06/92, A, C, 92001433

Cottage Row Historic District [Saranac Lake MPS], Roughly, Park Ave. N side from Rosemont Ave. to Catherine St., Saranac Lake, 11/06/92, A, C, 92001473

Distin Cottage [Saranac Lake MPS], 11 Kiwassa Rd., Saranac Lake, 11/06/92, A, C, 92001416

Drury Cottage [Saranac Lake MPS], 29 Bloomingdale Ave., Saranac Lake, 11/06/92, A, C, 92001450

Duane Methodist Episcopal Church, NY 26 E of jct. with Kenny Rd., Duane, 8/09/91, C, a, 91001027

Eagle Island Camp [Great Camps of the Adirondacks TR], Eagle Island, Upper Saranac Lake, Saranac Inn vicinity, 4/03/87, C, 86002941

Ellenberger Cottage [Saranac Lake MPS], 183 Broadway, Saranac Lake, 11/06/92, A, C, 92001453

Feisthamel—Edelberg Cottage [Saranac Lake MPS], 11 Neil St., Saranac Lake, 11/06/92, A, C, 92001420

Feustmann Cottage [Saranac Lake MPS], 28 Catherine St., Saranac Lake, 11/06/92, A, C, 92001455

First Congregational Church, 2 Clay St., Malone, 6/06/91, A, C, a, 91000627

Freer Cottage [Saranac Lake MPS], 40 Kiwassa St., Saranac Lake, 11/06/92, A, C, 92001417

Gray, E. L., House [Saranac Lake MPS], 15 Helen St., Saranac Lake, 11/06/92, A, C, 92001469

Hathaway Cottage [Saranac Lake MPS], 6 Charles St., Saranac Lake, 11/06/92, A, C, 92001457

Hill Cottage [Saranac Lake MPS], 36 Franklin Ave., Saranac Lake, 11/06/92, A, C, 92001475

Hillside Lodge [Saranac Lake MPS], Harrietstown Rd., Saranac Lake, 11/06/92, A, C, 92001467

Homestead, The [Saranac Lake MPS], 3 Maple Hill, Saranac Lake, 11/06/92, A, C, 92001418

Hooey Cottage [Saranac Lake MPS], 24 Park Pl., Saranac Lake, 11/06/92, A, C, 92001429

Hopkins Cottage [Saranac Lake MPS], 5 Birch St., Saranac Lake, 11/06/92, A, C, 92001448

Horton Gristmill, Mill St., Malone, 4/21/75, A, C, 75001188

Jennings Cottage [Saranac Lake MPS], 16 Marshall St., Saranac Lake, 11/06/92, A, C, 92001419

Johnson Cottage [Saranac Lake MPS], 6 1/2 St. Bernard St., Saranac Lake, 11/06/92, A, C, 92001436

Joseph, Beth, Synagogue, Lake and Mill Sts., Tupper Lake, 9/01/88, C, a, 88001441

Franklin County—Continued

Larom Cottage [Saranac Lake MPS], 112 Park Ave., Saranac Lake, 11/06/92, A, C, 92001428

Leis Block [Saranac Lake MPS], 3–5 Bloomingdale Ave., Saranac Lake, 11/06/92, A, C, 92001449

Leis Cottage [Saranac Lake MPS], 26 Algonquin Ave., Saranac Lake, 11/06/92, A, C, 92001444

Lincoln, Anselm, House, 49 Duane St., Malone, 4/21/75, A, C, 75001189

Little Red [Saranac Lake MPS], Algonquin Ave., Saranac Lake, 11/06/92, A, C, b, 92001446

Magill Cottage [Saranac Lake MPS], 37 Riverside Dr., Saranac Lake, 11/06/92, A, C, 92001430

Malone Freight Depot, 99 Railroad St., Malone, 12/12/76, A, C, 76001217

McBean Cottage [Saranac Lake MPS], 89 Park Ave., Saranac Lake, 11/06/92, A, C, 92001425

Moss Ledge [Great Camps of the Adirondacks TR], Off NY 30, Upper Saranac Lake, Saranac Inn vicinity, 11/07/86, C, 86002942

Musselman Cottage [Saranac Lake MPS], 25 Riverside Dr., Saranac Lake, 11/06/92, A, C, 92001431

Noyes Cottage [Saranac Lake MPS], 16 Helen St., Saranac Lake, 11/06/92, A, C, 92001468

Paddock Building, 34 W. Main St., Malone, 11/07/76, A, C, 76001218

Pomeroy Cottage [Saranac Lake MPS], 26 Baker St., Saranac Lake, 11/06/92, A, C, 92001447

Prospect Point Camp [Great Camps of the Adirondacks TR], E of NY 30, Saranac Inn vicinity, 11/07/86, C, a, 86002947

Radwell Cottage [Saranac Lake MPS], 2 Charles St., Saranac Lake, 11/06/92, A, C, 92001456

Ryan Cottage [Saranac Lake MPS], 62 Algonquin Ave., Saranac Lake, 11/06/92, A, C, 92001445

Sarbanes Cottage [Saranac Lake MPS], 72 Bloomingdale Ave., Saranac Lake, 11/06/92, A, C, 92001451

Savage, Orin, Cottage [Saranac Lake MPS], 33 Olive St., Saranac Lake, 11/06/92, A, C, 92001422

Schrader—Griswold Cottage [Saranac Lake MPS], 49 Riverside Dr., Saranac Lake, 11/06/92, A, C, 92001432

Seeley Cottage [Saranac Lake MPS], 27 Olive St., Saranac Lake, 11/06/92, A, C, 92001423

Sloan Cottage [Saranac Lake MPS], 21 View St., Saranac Lake, 11/06/92, A, C, 92001442

Smith Cottage [Saranac Lake MPS], 12 Jenkins St., Saranac Lake, 11/06/92, A, C, 92001470

Smith's, Paul, Electric Light and Power and Railroad Company Complex, 2 Main St., Saranac Lake, 11/02/87, A, C, 87001898

Stonaker Cottage [Saranac Lake MPS], Glenwood Rd., Saranac Lake, 11/06/92, A, C, 92001465

Stuckman Cottage [Saranac Lake MPS], 6 Clinton Ave., Saranac Lake, 11/06/92, A, C, 92001459

US Post Office—Malone [US Post Offices in New York State, 1858-1943, TR], E. Main and Washington Sts., Malone, 5/11/89, A, C, 88002350

Walker Cottage [Saranac Lake MPS], 67 Park Ave., Saranac Lake, 11/06/92, A, C, 92001424

Wilson Cottage [Saranac Lake MPS], 8 Williams St., Saranac Lake, 11/06/92, A, C, 92001443

Witherspoon Cottage [Saranac Lake MPS], 3 Kiwassa Rd., Saranac Lake, 11/06/92, A, C, 92001415

Fulton County

Dolge Company Factory Complex, S. Main St., Dolgeville, 9/17/74, A, B, C, 74001238

Downtown Gloversville Historic District, Roughly bounded by Spring, Prospect, E. Fulton, N. and S. Main and Elm Sts., Gloversville, 9/12/85, A, C, 85002367

Fulton County Courthouse, N. William St., Johnstown, 7/24/72, A, C, 72000841

Fulton County Jail, Perry and Montgomery Sts., Johnstown, 10/19/81, A, C, 81000404

Garoga Site, Address Restricted, Ephratah vicinity, 7/22/80, D, 80002613

Gloversville Free Library, 58 E. Fulton St., Gloversville, 5/24/76, A, C, 76001219

Johnson Hall, Hall St., Johnstown, 10/15/66, B, C, D, NHL, 66000520

Kingsboro Historic District, Area surrounding Kingsboro Ave. Park to N side of cemetery and S to include both sides of Gregory St., Gloversville, 2/24/75, A, C, a, 75001190

Klock Site, Address Restricted, Ephratah vicinity, 7/22/80, D, 80002614

Pagerie, Smith, Site, Address Restricted, Ephratah vicinity, 4/22/80, D, 80002615

Teviotdale, Wire Rd., Linlithgo vicinity, 10/10/79, B, C, 79003794

US Post Office—Johnstown [US Post Offices in New York State, 1858-1943, TR], 14 N. William St., Johnstown, 5/11/89, A, C, 88002337

Genesee County

Alexander Classical School, Buffalo St., Alexander, 10/25/73, A, C, 73001191

Batavia Club, Main and Bank Sts., Batavia, 6/19/73, A, C, 73001192

Genesee County Courthouse, Main and Ellicott Sts., Batavia, 6/18/73, C, 73001193

Genesee County Courthouse Historic District, Bounded by Porter and Jefferson Aves., and Main, Court, and Ellicott Sts., Batavia, 12/10/82, C, f, 82001173

Gifford-Walker Farm, 7083 N. Bergen Rd., North Bergen, 1/10/80, C, 80004276

Holland Land Office, W. Main St., Batavia, 10/15/66, A, NHL, 66000521

Keeney House, 13 W. Main St, LeRoy, 9/11/79, B, C, 79001583

Lake Street Historic District, 10 and 12 S. Lake St. & 11–27 N. Lake St., Village of Bergen, 9/05/85, C, 85001953

Morganville Pottery Factory Site, Address Restricted, Morganville vicinity, 2/15/74, A, D, 74001240

Mount Pleasant, 2032 Indian Falls Rd., Corfu, 8/09/84, C, 84002393

Richmond Memorial Library, 19 Ross St., Batavia, 7/24/74, A, C, 74001239

Stafford Village Four Corners Historic District, Jct. U.S. 5 and U.S. 237, Stafford, 10/08/76, A, C, a, 76001220

US Post Office—Le Roy [US Post Offices in New York State, 1858-1943, TR], 2 Main St., Le Roy, 5/11/89, A, C, 88002342

Greene County

All Souls Church, Rt. 23-C N of Tannersville, Tannersville vicinity, 11/24/93, A, C, a, 93001223

Athens Lower Village Historic District [Village of Athens MRA], Roughly bounded by Hudson River, NY 385, Vernon and Market Sts., Athens, 11/28/80, A, C, a, 80002616

Botsford, Henry T., House, NY 81 W of jct. with NY 32, Greenville, 11/12/93, C, 93001224

Brick Row Historic District [Village of Athens MRA], Off NY 385, Athens, 11/28/80, A, C, 80002617

Bronck Farm 13-Sided Barn [Central Plan Dairy Barns of New York TR], Old Kings Rd., Coxsackie vicinity, 9/29/84, A, C, 84002395

Bronck, Pieter, House, 2 mi. W of Coxsackie on W side of U.S. 9W, Coxsackie vicinity, 12/24/67, C, NHL, 67000012

Centre Presbyterian Church, Main and Church Sts, Windham, 9/07/79, C, a, 79001586

Cole, Thomas, House, 218 Spring St., Catskill, 10/15/66, B, NHL, 66000522

ELEANOR (Sailing Sloop), Off Lower Main St. in Catskill Creek, Catskill, 12/27/82, C, 82001174

East Side Historic District, Roughly bounded by Catskill Creek, Hudson River, River, Harrison, Day, and Gardner Sts., Catskill, 8/09/82, A, C, 82004779

Elka Park Historic District, SE of Hunter town center, Hunter vicinity, 5/22/93, A, C, 93000399

Flint Mine Hill Archeological District, Address Restricted, Coxsackie vicinity, 11/29/78, D, 78001852

Forestville Commonwealth, Address Restricted, Earlton vicinity, 11/20/74, D, 74001242

Greenville Presbyterian Church Complex, North St., NY 32, Greenville, 3/28/85, A, C, a, 85000657

Houghtaling, Peter, Farm and Lime Kiln, Lime Kiln Rd., West Coxsackie, 3/20/86, A, C, 86000491

Lexington House, NY 42, Lexington, 9/04/86, A, C, 86002175

Morss Homestead/Federal City Homestead, NY 23, Red Falls, 9/30/83, A, B, C, 83001680

Newkirk Homestead, NW of Leeds on Sandy Plains Rd., Leeds vicinity, 7/22/79, A, C, 79001584

Pratt Rock Park, NY 23 NW of jct. with NY 23A, Prattsville, 12/10/92, A, B, C, 92001645

Pratt, Zadock, House, Main St., Prattsville, 8/14/86, B, C, 86001654

Greene County—Continued

Prevost Manor House, W of Greenville off NY 81, Greenville vicinity, 11/15/72, B, C, a, 72000842

Reed Street Historic District, Reed, Ely, Mansion, and River Sts., Coxsackie, 5/06/80, A, C, 80002621

Salisbury Manor, NW of Leeds on NY 145, Leeds vicinity, 6/19/79, A, C, 79001585

Stranahan-DelVecchio House [Village of Athens MRA], N. Washington St., Athens, 11/28/80, C, 80002618

Susquehannah Turnpike, Beginning at Catskill, follows the Mohican Trail (NY 145) and CR 20 and 22 NW to the Schoharie County line, Catskill, 1/02/74, A, 74001241

US Post Office—Catskill [US Post Offices in New York State, 1858-1943, TR], 270 Main St., Catskill, 11/17/88, A, C, 88002471

Van Bergen House, Jct. of NY 9W and Schiller Park Rd., New Baltimore, 4/25/91, B, C, 91000444

Van Loon, Albertus, House [Village of Athens MRA], N. Washington St., Athens, 11/28/80, A, C, 80002619

West Athens Hill Site, Address Restricted, Athens vicinity, 3/20/73, D, 73001194

Zion Lutheran Church [Village of Athens MRA], N. Washington St., Athens, 11/28/80, C, a, 80002620

Hamilton County

Blue Mountain House Annex, NY 30, Blue Mountain, 12/07/77, A, C, 77000941

Camp Pine Knot [Great Camps of the Adirondacks TR], Long Point, Raquette Lake, Raquette Lake vicinity, 11/07/86, C, 86002934

Camp Uncas [Great Camps of the Adirondacks TR], Mohegan Lake, Raquette Lake vicinity, 4/03/87, C, 86002937

Church of the Transfiguration, N of Blue Mountain Lake on NY 30, Blue Mountain Lake vicinity, 7/26/77, C, a, 77000942

Echo Camp [Great Camps of the Adirondacks TR], Long Point, Raquette Lake, Raquette Lake vicinity, 11/07/86, C, 86002939

Hamilton County Courthouse Complex, Jct. of NY 8 and S. Shore Rd., Lake Pleasant, 9/24/92, A, C, 92001280

Sagamore, Off NY 28 at W end of Sagamore Lake, Racquette Lake vicinity, 1/11/76, C, 76001221

Sagamore Lodge (Boundary Increase) [Great Camps of the Adirondacks TR], Sagamore Rd., Raquette Lake, 11/07/86, C, 86002940

Wells Baptist Church, Main St., Wells, 9/01/88, C, a, 88001440

Whelan Camp, Mick Rd., Long Lake, 12/21/89, A, C, 89002089

Herkimer County

Cold Brook Feed Mill, NY 8, Cold Brook, 10/09/74, A, 74001243

Fort Herkimer Church, NY 5S, East Herkimer vicinity, 7/24/72, A, C, a, 72000843

Herkimer County Courthouse, 320 N. Main St., Herkimer, 1/14/72, A, 72000844

Herkimer County Historical Society, 400 N. Main St., Herkimer, 4/13/72, C, 72000845

Herkimer County Jail, 327 N. Main St., Herkimer, 1/14/72, C, 72000846

Herkimer County Trust Company Building, Corner of Ann and Albany Sts., Little Falls, 3/05/70, A, C, 70000421

Herkimer House, Near NY 5 S., Danube, 2/12/71, B, C, 71000539

Indian Castle Church, NY 5S, Indian Castle vicinity, 2/18/71, A, C, a, 71000540

Jordanville Public Library, Main St., Jordanville, 5/24/84, C, 84002397

Mohawk Upper Castle Historic District, Address Restricted, Danube vicinity, 11/04/93, B, D, NHL, 93001621

Newport Stone Arch Bridge, Bridge St. across W. Canada Cr., Newport, 2/10/92, C, 91002035

Reformed Church, The, 405 N. Main St., Herkimer, 3/16/72, C, a, 72000847

Remington Stables, 1 Remington Ave., Ilion, 10/29/76, A, C, 76001222

Richardson, Thomas, House, 317 W. Main St., Ilion, 9/07/84, C, 84002400

Salisbury Center Covered Bridge, Fairview Rd. over Spruce Creek, Salisbury Center, 6/19/72, A, C, 72000848

Trinity Episcopal Church—Fairfield, NY 29 (Salisbury St.), Fairfield, 6/10/93, A, C, a, 93000499

US Post Office—Dolgeville [US Post Offices in New York State, 1858-1943, TR], 41 S. Main St., Dolgeville, 11/17/88, A, C, 88002486

US Post Office—Frankfort [US Post Offices in New York State, 1858-1943, TR], E. Main St., Frankfort, 5/11/89, A, C, 88002512

US Post Office—Herkimer [US Post Offices in New York State, 1858-1943, TR], 135 Park Ave., Herkimer, 5/11/89, A, C, 88002501

US Post Office—Ilion [US Post Offices in New York State, 1858-1943, TR], 48 First St., Ilion, 5/11/89, A, C, 88002513

US Post Office—Little Falls [US Post Offices in New York State, 1858-1943, TR], 25 W. Main St., Little Falls, 5/11/89, A, C, 88002343

Zoller-Frasier Round Barn [Central Plan Dairy Barns of New York TR], Fords Bush Rd., Newville vicinity, 9/29/84, C, 84002401

Jefferson County

Anthony, Levi, Building [Cape Vincent Town and Village MRA], Broadway, Cape Vincent, 9/27/85, A, C, 85002451

Archer, William, House [Stone Houses of Brownville TR], 112 Washington St., Brownville, 11/19/80, A, C, 80002623

Aubertine Building [Cape Vincent Town and Village MRA], Broadway, Cape Vincent, 9/27/85, A, C, 85002452

Bedford Creek Bridge [Hounsfield MRA], Campbell's Point Rd. over Bedford Creek, Hounsfield, 10/18/89, A, C, 89001617

Benton, Dr. Abner, House, Main St., Oxbow, 8/23/84, A, C, 84002405

Boldt, George C., Yacht House, NW of Alexandria Bay on Wellesley Island, Alexandria Bay vicinity, 4/26/78, A, C, 78001853

Borland, John, House [Cape Vincent Town and Village MRA], Market St., Cape Vincent, 9/27/85, A, C, 85002453

Broadway Historic District [Cape Vincent Town and Village MRA], St. Lawrence River, W. edge of Village of Cape Vincent, on Broadway & Tibbetts Point, Cape Vincent, 9/27/85, A, B, C, 85002455

Brown, Gen. Jacob, Mansion [Stone Houses of Brownville TR], Brown Blvd., Brownville, 11/19/80, B, C, 80002624

Brownville Hotel [Stone Houses of Brownville TR], Brown Blvd. and W. Main St., Brownville, 11/19/80, C, 80002625

Buckley, James, House [Cape Vincent Town and Village MRA], Joseph St., Cape Vincent, 9/27/85, C, 85002454

Burnham, E. K., House [Cape Vincent Town and Village MRA], 565 Broadway, Cape Vincent, 9/27/85, B, C, 85002456

Camp, Elisha, House, 310 General Smith Dr., Sackets Harbor, 4/23/73, C, 73001196

Cedar Grove Cemetery [Lyme MRA], Washington St., Chaumont, 9/06/90, A, C, d, 90001324

Chaumont Grange Hall and Dairymen's League Building [Lyme MRA], Main St., Chaumont, 9/06/90, C, 90001337

Chaumont Historic District [Lyme MRA], Along Main St., roughly between Washington and Church Sts., Chaumont, 9/06/90, C, 90001336

Chaumont House [Lyme MRA], Main St., Chaumont, 9/06/90, A, B, C, 90001341

Chaumont Railroad Station [Lyme MRA], Main St., Chaumont, 9/06/90, C, 90001332

Chevalier, Xavier, House [Cape Vincent Town and Village MRA], Gosier Rd., Cape Vincent, 9/27/85, A, C, 85002457

Clayton Historic District, 203–215 & 200–326 James St., 500–544 & 507–537 Riverside Dr., Clayton, 9/12/85, C, 85002368

Cocaigne, Nicholas, House [Cape Vincent Town and Village MRA], Favret Rd., Cape Vincent, 9/27/85, C, 85002458

Conklin Farm [Hounsfield MRA], Evans Rd., Hounsfield, 10/18/89, A, C, 89001624

Cornwall Brothers' Store, 2 Howell Pl., Alexandria Bay, 5/02/75, A, 75001191

Densmore Methodist Church of the Thousand Islands, Rt. 100 at Densmore Bay, Alexandria, 5/19/88, C, a, 88000591

Dezengremel, Remy, House [Cape Vincent Town and Village MRA], Rosiere Rd., Cape Vincent, 9/27/85, B, C, 85002459

District School No. 19 [Hounsfield MRA], Co. Rd. 69, Hounsfield, 10/18/89, A, C, 89001618

District School No. 20 [Hounsfield MRA], NY 3, S of Co. Rd. 75, Hounsfield, 10/18/89, A, C, 89001619

Jefferson County—Continued

District School No. 3 [Lyme MRA], Jct. NY 3 and County Rd. 57, Putnam Corners, Chaumont vicinity, 9/06/90, A, C, 90001326

Docteur, Joseph, House [Cape Vincent Town and Village MRA], Rosiere Rd., Cape Vincent, 9/27/85, C, 85002460

Duvillard Mill [Cape Vincent Town and Village MRA], Broadway, Cape Vincent, 9/27/85, A, C, 85002461

Dyer, Reuter, House [Cape Vincent Town and Village MRA], Rosiere Rd., Cape Vincent, 9/27/85, A, C, 85002462

East Hounsfield Christian Church [Hounsfield MRA], NY 3, Hounsfield, 10/18/89, C, a, 89001621

Evans—Gaige—Dillenback House [Lyme MRA], Evans Rd., Chaumont, 9/06/90, B, C, 90001340

Flower, Roswell P., Memorial Library, 229 Washington St., Watertown, 1/10/80, A, C, 80002628

Fort Haldimand Site, Address Restricted, Cape Vincent vicinity, 12/15/78, A, C, D, 78001854

Galband du Fort, Jean Philippe, House [Cape Vincent Town and Village MRA], James St., Cape Vincent, 9/27/85, C, 85002463

Galloo Island Light [U.S. Coast Guard Lighthouses and Light Stations on the Great Lakes TR], Galloo Island, Sackets Harbor vicinity, 8/04/83, A, C, 83001682

George Brothers Building [Lyme MRA], Mill St., Chaumont, 9/06/90, C, 90001334

George House [Lyme MRA], Washington St., Chaumont, 9/06/90, C, 90001338

Getman Farmhouse [Lyme MRA], S. Shore Rd., Chaumont vicinity, 9/06/90, C, 90001322

Glen Building [Cape Vincent Town and Village MRA], Broadway, Cape Vincent, 9/27/85, A, C, 85002465

Guthrie, Dr. Samuel, House [Hounsfield MRA], Co. Rd. 75/Military Rd., Hounsfield, 10/18/89, A, B, C, 89001616

Ingleside, W of Alexandria Bay on Cherry Island, Alexandria Bay vicinity, 4/16/80, C, 80002622

Irwin Brothers Store, NY 180, Stone Mills, 9/15/83, A, C, 83001681

Jefferson County Courthouse Complex, SE corner of Arsenal and Sherman Sts., Watertown, 6/07/74, C, 74001248

Johnson House [Cape Vincent Town and Village MRA], Tibbetts Point Rd., Cape Vincent, 9/27/85, A, C, 85002466

Johnston, Capt. Simon, House, 507 Riverside Dr., Clayton, 6/17/82, C, 82003358

Lance Farm [Lyme MRA], S. Shore Rd., Chaumont vicinity, 9/06/90, A, C, 90001323

LeRay Hotel, Main and Noble Sts., Evans Mills, 10/29/82, C, 82001175

LeRay Mansion, NE of Black River on Camp Drum Military Reservation, Black River vicinity, 7/11/74, B, C, 74001245

LeRay, Vincent, House [Cape Vincent Town and Village MRA], Broadway (NY 12E), Cape Vincent, 11/15/73, A, C, 73001195

Lewis House [Cape Vincent Town and Village MRA], Market St., Cape Vincent, 9/27/85, C, 85002467

Longue Vue Island, St. Lawrence River, Alexandria Bay, 11/04/82, C, 82001176

Madison Barracks, Military Rd., Sackets Harbor, 11/21/74, A, C, 74001246

Paddock Arcade, Washington St. between Arsenal and Store Sts., Watertown, 6/15/76, A, C, 76001224

Paddock Mansion, 228 Washington St., Watertown, 12/11/79, B, C, 79001587

Peugnet, Captain Louis, House [Cape Vincent Town and Village MRA], Tibbetts Point Rd., Cape Vincent, 9/27/85, C, 85002469

Pierrepont Manor Complex, N of Mannsville on Ellisburg St., Mannsville vicinity, 9/15/77, A, C, a, 77000943

Point Salubrious Historic District [Lyme MRA], Point Salubrious Rd., Chaumont vicinity, 9/06/90, C, 90001339

Public Square Historic District, Roughly Court, Arsenal, Washington, Franklin and State Sts., Watertown, 9/07/84, A, C, 84002409

Ressequie Farm [Hounsfield MRA], Parker Rd., Hounsfield, 10/18/89, A, C, 89001622

Reynolds, George, House [Cape Vincent Town and Village MRA], River Rd., Cape Vincent, 9/27/85, C, 85002470

Rock Island Light Station, N of Fishers Landing on Rock Island, Fishers Landing vicinity, 11/14/78, A, 78001855

Row, The [Lyme MRA], Main St. at Shaver Creek, Three Mile Bay, Chaumont vicinity, 9/06/90, C, 90001329

Roxy Hotel [Cape Vincent Town and Village MRA], 310 Broadway, Cape Vincent, 9/27/85, A, 85002472

Sacket, Cornelius, House [Cape Vincent Town and Village MRA], 571 Broadway, Cape Vincent, 9/27/85, C, 85002473

Sacket, General, House [Cape Vincent Town and Village MRA], 4407 James St., Cape Vincent, 9/27/85, B, C, 85002464

Sackets Harbor Battlefield, Coastline and area from Sackets Harbor SW to and including Horse Island, Sackets Harbor, 12/31/74, A, C, D, 74001247

Sackets Harbor Village Historic District, Main, Washington, Pike, Edmund, Hill, Hamilton, Broad, and Ambrose Sts., Sackets Harbor, 9/15/83, A, C, 83001683

Shore Farm [Hounsfield MRA], Military Rd., E of Mill Creek, Hounsfield, 10/18/89, A, C, 89001623

Simmons, Stephen, House [Hounsfield MRA], Camps Mills Rd., W of Old Slat Points Rd., Hounsfield, 10/18/89, C, 89001615

St. John's Episcopal Church [Cape Vincent Town and Village MRA], Market St., Cape Vincent, 9/27/85, C, a, d, 85002476

St. Vincent of Paul Catholic Church [Cape Vincent Town and Village MRA], Kanady St., Cape Vincent, 9/27/85, C, a, d, 85002477

Star Grange No. 9 [Hounsfield MRA], Sulphur Springs Rd. between Jericho and Spencer Rds., Hounsfield, 10/18/89, C, 89001626

Starkey, Otis, House [Cape Vincent Town and Village MRA], Point St., Cape Vincent, 9/27/85, C, 85002478

State Street Historic District, 249-401 State St., 246-274 State St. and 106-108 Mechanic St., Carthage, 9/22/83, C, 83001684

Stevenson—Frink Farm [Hounsfield MRA], Salt Point Rd., Hounsfield, 10/18/89, A, C, 89001625

Stone Mills Union Church, NY 180 near jct. with Carter St., Stone Mills, 12/12/76, C, a, 76001223

Stone Shop, Old [Lyme MRA], Main St., Three Mile Bay, Chaumont vicinity, 9/06/90, C, 90001328

Sulphur Springs Cemetery [Hounsfield MRA], Co. Rd. 62, SW of Spencer Rd., Hounsfield, 10/18/89, A, C, d, 89001620

Taft House [Lyme MRA], Main St., Three Mile Bay, Chaumont vicinity, 9/06/90, C, 90001297

Talcott Falls Site, Address Restricted, Adams vicinity, 6/05/74, B, D, 74001244

Taylor Boathouse [Lyme MRA], Bay View Dr., Three Mile Bay, Chaumont vicinity, 9/06/90, A, C, 90001330

Thousand Island Park Historic District, S tip of Wellesley Island, Orleans, 11/14/82, C, 82001177

Three Mile Bay Historic District [Lyme MRA], Jct. of Church and Depot Sts., Three Mile Bay, Chaumont vicinity, 9/06/90, C, a, 90001327

Tibbetts Point Light [U.S. Coast Guard Lighthouses and Light Stations on the Great Lakes TR], Tibbetts Point, Cape Vincent, 7/19/84, A, C, 84002412

US Post Office—Carthage [US Post Offices in New York State, 1858-1943, TR], 521 State St., Carthage, 11/17/88, A, C, 88002470

Union Hall [Lyme MRA], S. Shore Rd., Chaumont vicinity, 9/06/90, A, C, 90001333

Union Hotel, Main and Ray Sts., Sackets Harbor, 6/19/72, C, 72000849

Union Meeting House [Cape Vincent Town and Village MRA], Millens Bay Rd., Cape Vincent, 9/27/85, A, C, a, 85002479

United Methodist Church [Lyme MRA], S. Shore Rd., Chaumont vicinity, 9/06/90, C, a, 90001325

Vautrin, Claude, House [Cape Vincent Town and Village MRA], Mason Rd., Cape Vincent, 9/27/85, A, C, 85002480

Vogt House [Stone Houses of Brownville TR], 110 Main St., Brownville, 11/19/80, C, 80002626

Walrath, Arthur, House [Stone Houses of Brownville TR], 114 Corner Pike, Brownville, 11/19/80, A, C, 80002627

Watertown Masonic Temple, 240 Washington St., Watertown, 1/23/80, A, C, 80002629

Wheeler, Menzo, House [Lyme MRA], Main and Depot Sts., Chaumont vicinity, 9/06/90, C, 90001335

Wilcox Farmhouse [Lyme MRA], Carrying Place Rd., Three Mile Bay vicinity, 9/06/90, C, 90001331

Jefferson County—Continued

Wilson, Warren, House [Cape Vincent Town and Village MRA], Favret Rd., Cape Vincent, 9/27/85, C, 85002482

Kings County

68th Police Precinct Station House and Stable, 4302 4th Ave., New York, 6/03/82, C, 82003359

83rd Precinct Police Station and Stable, 179 Wilson Ave., New York, 4/14/82, C, 82003360

Albemarle-Kenmore Terraces Historic District, Albemarle Terrace, Kenmore Terrace , and E. 21st St., New York, 6/30/83, A, C, 83001685

Astral Apartments, 184 Franklin St., New York, 10/29/82, C, 82001178

Atlantic Avenue Control House [Interborough Rapid Transit Subway Control Houses TR], Flatbush and Atlantic Aves., New York, 5/06/80, A, C, 80002643

Atlantic Avenue Tunnel, Below Atlantic Ave. between Boerum Pl. and Columbia St., New York City, 9/07/89, A, C, D, 89001388

Boathouse on the Lullwater of the Lake in Prospect Park, Prospect Park, New York, 1/07/72, C, 72000850

Boerum Hill Historic District, Roughly bounded by Pacific, Wyckoff, Bergen, Nevins, Bond and Hoyt Sts., New York, 9/26/83, C, 83001686

Boy's High School, 832 Marcy Ave., New York, 2/25/82, C, 82003361

Brooklyn Borough Hall, 209 Joralemon St., New York, 1/10/80, A, C, 80002630

Brooklyn Bridge, Across the East River from Brooklyn to Manhattan, New York, 10/15/66, C, NHL, 66000523

Brooklyn Heights Historic District, Borough of Brooklyn, bounded by Atlantic Ave., Court and Fulton Sts. and the East River, New York, 10/15/66, C, NHL, 66000524

Brooklyn Historical Society, 128 Pierrepont St., Brooklyn, 7/17/91, C, NHL, 91002054

Brooklyn Museum, Eastern Parkway and Washington Ave., New York, 8/22/77, C, 77000944

Buildings at 375-379 Flatbush Avenue and 185-187 Sterling Place, 375-379 Flatbush Ave. and 185-187 Sterling Pl., New York, 9/07/84, C, 84002440

Carroll Gardens Historic District, Carroll and President Sts. between Smith and Hoyt Sts., New York, 9/26/83, A, C, 83001687

Casemate Fort, Whiting Quadrangle, Fort Hamilton, off NY 27, New York, 8/07/74, A, C, 74001249

Clinton Hill Historic District, Roughly bounded by Willoughby and Grand Aves., Fulton St. and Vanderbilt Ave., New York, 6/19/85, C, 85001335

Clinton Hill South Historic District, Roughly Lefferts and Brevoort Pl. between Washington Ave. and Bedford Pl., New York, 7/17/86, C, 86001675

Cobble Hill Historic District, Roughly bounded by Atlantic Ave., Court, Degraw and Hicks Sts., New York, 6/11/76, C, 76001225

Coney Island Fire Station Pumping Station, 2301 Neptune Ave., New York, 12/08/81, C, g, 81000405

Cronyn, William B., House, 271 9th St., New York, 6/03/82, C, 82005030

Cyclone Roller Coaster, 834 Surf Ave. at W. 10th St., Brooklyn, 6/25/91, A, 91000907

Ditmas Park Historic District, Bounded by Marlborough Rd., Dorchester, Ocean, and Newkirk Aves., New York, 9/30/83, C, 83001688

Eastern Parkway, Eastern Pkwy from Grand Army Plaza to Ralph Ave., New York, 9/26/83, C, 83001689

Emmanuel Baptist Church, 279 LaFayette Ave., New York, 12/16/77, C, a, 77000945

Erasmus Hall Academy, Between Flatbush, Bedford, Church, and Snyder Aves., New York, 11/11/75, A, C, 75001192

Federal Building and Post Office, 271 Cadman Plaza, E., New York, 10/09/74, A, C, 74001250

Feuchtwanger Stable, 159 Carlton Ave., New York, 3/20/86, C, 86000485

Flatbush Dutch Reformed Church Complex, 890 Flatbush Ave. and 2101-2103 Kenmore Terr., New York, 9/08/83, C, a, 83001690

Flatbush Town Hall, 35 Snyder Ave., New York, 7/24/72, A, C, 72000851

Flatlands Dutch Reformed Church, Kings Hwy. and E. 40th St., New York, 8/30/79, A, C, D, a, d, 79001588

Floyd Bennett Field Historic District, Flatbush Ave., New York, 4/11/80, A, B, NPS, 80000363

Fort Greene Historic District, Roughly bounded by Ft. Greene Pl., Fulton St., Vanderbilt and Myrtle Aves., New York, 9/26/83, C, a, 83001691

Fort Greene Historic District (Boundary Increase), Roughly bounded by Ashland Pl., DeKalb Ave., Hanson Pl., and Oxford St., Adelphi, Vanderbilt and Myrtle Aves., New York, 9/07/84, C, 84002451

Friends Meetinghouse and School, 110 Schermerhorn St., New York, 11/04/82, C, a, 82001179

Fulton Ferry District, Roughly bounded by the East River and Washington, Water, Front, and Doughty Sts., New York, 6/28/74, A, C, 74001251

Gage and Tollner Restaurant, 372 Fulton St., New York, 6/03/82, C, 82003362

Grecian Shelter, Prospect Park near Parkside Ave., New York, 1/20/72, C, 72000852

Greenpoint Historic District, Roughly bounded by Kent, Calyer, Noble, and Franklin Sts., Clifford Pl. and Manhattan Ave., New York, 9/26/83, C, 83001692

Hanson Place Seventh Day Adventist Church, 88 Hanson Pl., New York, 4/23/80, C, a, 80002631

Holy Trinity Church (Protestant Episcopal), 157 Montague St., New York, 12/23/87, C, a, NHL, 87002590

Houses on Hunterfly Road District, 1698, 1700, 1702, 1704, 1706, 1708 Bergen St., New York, 12/05/72, C, 72000853

Kings County Savings Bank, 135 Broadway, New York, 4/16/80, C, 80002632

Knickerbocker Field Club, 114 E. 18th St., New York, 10/29/82, C, 82001180

Lefferts Manor Historic District, Roughly bounded by Lincoln Rd., Fenimore St., Rogers Ave. and Flatbush Ave., Brooklyn, 5/18/92, A, C, 83004872

Lefferts-Laidlaw House, 136 Clinton St., New York, 9/12/85, C, 85002279

Lincoln Club, 65 Putnam Ave., New York, 1/27/83, C, 83001693

Litchfield Villa, Prospect Park W. and 5th St., New York, 9/14/77, B, C, 77000946

Manhattan Bridge, Spans East River between Front and Canal St., New York, 8/30/83, C, 83001694

McGolrick, Monsignor, Park and Shelter Pavilion, Bounded by Nassau and Driggs Aves., Russell and Monitor Sts., New York, 5/06/80, C, 80002633

New England Congregational Church and Rectory, 177-179 S. 9th St., New York, 9/15/83, C, a, 83001695

New Lots Reformed Church and Cemetery, 630 New Lots Ave., New York, 5/19/83, C, 83001696

New Utrecht Reformed Church and Buildings, 18th Ave. and 83rd St., New York, 4/09/80, C, a, 80002634

Ocean Parkway, From Church Ave. to Seabreeze Ave., New York, 9/08/83, A, 83001697

Old Brooklyn Fire Headquarters, 365–367 Jay St., New York, 1/20/72, C, 72000854

Old Gravesend Cemetery, Gravesend Neck Rd. and MacDonald Ave., New York, 9/17/80, A, d, 80002635

Parachute Jump, Coney Island, New York, 9/02/80, A, C, b, g, 80002645

Park Slope Historic District, Roughly bounded by Prospect Park West, Berkeley Pl., 15th St., 6th, 7th and Flatbush Aves., New York, 11/21/80, C, 80002636

Plymouth Church of the Pilgrims, 75 Hicks St., New York, 10/15/66, B, a, NHL, 66000525

Prospect Heights Historic District, Roughly bounded by Pacific and Bergen Sts., Flatbush and Vanderbilt Aves., and Park Pl., New York, 9/15/83, C, 83001698

Prospect Park, Bounded by Parkside, Ocean and Flatbush Aves., Prospect Park W. and Prospect SW., New York, 9/17/80, C, f, 80002637

Prospect Park South Historic District, Roughly bounded by BMT RR Tracks, Beverly Rd., and Coney Island and Church Aves., New York, 7/21/83, A, C, 83001699

Public Bath No. 7, 227–231 Fourth Ave., New York, 9/12/85, A, C, 85002275

Public School 108, 200 Lindwood St., New York, 12/10/82, C, 82003363

Public School 111 and Public School 9 Annex, 249 Sterling Place and 251 Sterling Place, New York, 12/14/81, A, C, 81000407

Public School 39, 417 6th Ave., New York, 4/17/80, A, C, 80002646

Public School 65K, 158 Richmond St., New York, 12/10/81, C, 81000408

Public School 7, 131-143 York St., New York, 11/03/83, A, C, 83003986

Public School 71K, 119 Heyward St., New York, 11/04/82, C, 82001181

Kings County—Continued

Quarters A, U.S. Naval Facility, New York, 5/30/74, B, C, NHL, 74001252

Rankin, John, House, 440 Clinton St., New York, 11/16/78, C, 78001856

Robinson, John Roosevelt "Jackie", House, 5224 Tilden St., New York, 5/11/76, B, g, NHL, 76001226

Rockwood Chocolate Factory Historic District, 54-88 Washington, 13-53 Waverly, and 255-275 Park Aves., New York, 10/06/83, C, 83003991

Russian Orthodox Cathedral of the Transfiguration of Our Lord, 228 N. 12th St., New York, 4/16/80, A, C, a, 80002638

South Bushwick Reformed Protestant Dutch Church Complex, 855-857 Bushwick Ave., New York, 11/04/82, C, a, 82001182

South Congregational Church, President and Court Sts., New York, 11/04/82, C, a, 82001183

St. Bartholomew's Protestant Episcopal Church and Rectory, 1227 Pacific St., New York, 4/23/80, C, 80002639

St. George's Protestant Episcopal Church, 800 Marcy Ave., New York, 9/08/83, C, a, 83001700

St. Luke's Protestant Episcopal Church, 520 Clinton Ave., New York, 9/16/82, C, a, 82003364

St. Mary's Episcopal Church, 230 Classon Ave., New York, 7/21/83, C, a, 83001701

St. Paul's Protestant Episcopal Church, 199 Carroll St., New York, 12/21/89, C, a, 89002086

State Street Houses, 291-299, 290-324 State St., New York, 1/17/80, C, 80002640

Stoothoff-Baxter-Kouwenhaven House, 1640 E. 48th St., New York, 11/14/82, A, C, b, 82001184

Stuyvesant Heights Historic District, Roughly bounded by Macon, Tompkins, Decatur, Lewis, Chauncey, and Stuyvesant, New York, 12/04/75, C, 75001193

Sunset Park Historic District, Roughly bounded by Fourth Ave., Thirty-eighth St., Seventh Ave. and Sixty-fourth St., Brooklyn, 9/15/88, C, 88001464

Twentythird Regiment Armory, 1322 Bedford Ave., New York, 5/06/80, A, C, 80002641

U.S. Army Military Ocean Terminal, 58th-65th St. and 2nd Ave., New York, 9/23/83, A, C, g, 83001702

US Post Office—Flatbush Station [US Post Offices in New York State, 1858-1943, TR], 2273 Church Ave., New York, 11/17/88, A, C, 88002460

US Post Office—Kensington [US Post Offices in New York State, 1858-1943, TR], 421 McDonald Ave., New York, 11/17/88, A, C, 88002461

US Post Office—Metropolitan Station [US Post Offices in New York State, 1858-1943, TR], 47 Debevoise St., New York, 11/17/88, A, C, 88002462

US Post Office—Parkville Station [US Post Offices in New York State, 1858-1943, TR], 6618 20th Ave., New York, 11/17/88, A, C, 88002463

Weir Greenhouse, 750-751–5th Ave., New York, 5/10/84, C, 84002487

Williamsburgh Savings Bank, 175 Broadway, New York, 4/09/80, C, 80002642

Willoughby-Suydam Historic District [Ridgewood MRA], Suydam St., Willoughby, St. Nicholas, and Wyckoff Aves., New York, 9/30/83, C, 83001782

Wyckoff, Pieter, House, 5902 Canarsie Lane, New York, 12/24/67, C, NHL, 67000013

Wyckoff-Bennett Homestead, 1669 E. 22nd St., New York, 12/24/74, C, NHL, 74001253

Lewis County

Collins, Jonathan C., House and Cemetery, West Rd., Constableville, 11/09/88, B, C, d, 88002137

Constable Hall, Off NY 26, Constableville, 3/07/73, C, 73001197

Constableville Village Historic District, Roughly bounded by Sugar River, Main, N. Main, W. Main, Church, High, West and James Sts., Constableville, 9/15/83, C, 83001703

Gould Mansion Complex, Main St., Lyons Falls, 4/19/78, B, C, 78001857

Hough, Franklin B., House, Collins St., Lowville, 10/15/66, B, NHL, 66000526

House at 58 Eighteenth Avenue [Sea Cliff Summer Resort TR], 58 Eighteenth Ave., Sea Cliff, 2/18/88, A, C, 88000002

Methodist Episcopal Church of West Martinsburg, W. Martinsburg Rd., West Martinsburg, 9/15/83, C, a, 83001704

Wilson, Edmund, House, S of Port Leyden off NY 12 on Talcottville Rd., Port Leyden vicinity, 11/26/73, A, B, C, 73001198

Livingston County

Alverson—Copeland House [Lima MRA], 1612 Rochester St., Lima, 8/31/89, C, 89001133

Avon Inn, 55 E. Main St., Avon, 4/16/91, C, 91000423

Barber-Mulligan Farm, NE of Avon at 5403 Barber Rd., Avon vicinity, 5/19/80, A, C, 80002647

Barnard Cobblestone House [Lima MRA], 7192 W. Main St., Lima, 8/31/89, C, 89001122

Black and White Farm Barn, 7420 Dansville—Mt. Morris Rd., NY 36, Sonyea vicinity, 2/08/88, A, C, 88000031

Bristol House [Lima MRA], 1950 Lake Ave., Lima, 8/31/89, C, 89001135

Cargill House [Lima MRA], 1839 Rochester St., Lima, 8/31/89, C, 89001126

Clark Farm Complex [Lima MRA], 7646 E. Main Rd., Lima, 8/31/89, A, C, 89001125

Claud No. 1 Archeological Site, Address Restricted, Groveland vicinity, 8/19/75, D, 75001195

Dansville Library, 200 Main St., Dansville, 9/14/77, C, 77000947

Dayton House [Lima MRA], 7180 W. Main St., Lima, 8/31/89, C, 89001131

DePuy, William, House [Lima MRA], 1825 Genesee St., Lima, 8/31/89, C, 89001127

Draper House [Lima MRA], 1764 Rochester St., Lima, 8/31/89, C, 89001140

Edgerley, S of Oakland at 9303 Creek Rd., Oakland vicinity, 7/16/80, C, 80002649

Ganoung Cobblestone Farmhouse [Lima MRA], 2798 Popular Hill Rd., Lima, 8/31/89, A, C, 89001120

Genesee Wesleyan Seminary and Genesee College Hall, College St., Lima, 7/19/76, A, C, a, 76001227

Godfrey House and Barn Complex [Lima MRA], 1325 Rochester Rd., Lima, 8/31/89, A, C, 89001134

Harden House [Lima MRA], 7343 E. Main St., Lima, 8/31/89, C, 89001142

Harmon, William, House [Lima MRA], 1847 Genesee St., Lima, 8/31/89, C, 89001130

Hillcrest, 7242 W. Main St., Lima, 5/06/80, C, 80002648

Homestead, The, NY 39 and U.S. 20A, Geneseo, 8/30/74, A, B, C, b, 74001254

Kemp, R. P., No. 1 Site, Address Restricted, West Sparta vicinity, 8/22/77, D, 77000950

Leech—Lloyd Farmhouse and Barn Complex [Lima MRA], 1589 and 1601 York St., Lima, 8/31/89, A, C, 89001117

Leech—Parker Farmhouse [Lima MRA], 1537 York St., Lima, 8/31/89, A, C, 89001116

Lima Village Historic District, 1881–1885 & 1818–1870 Rochester St., Lima Presbyterian Church, 7304–7312 & 7303–7315 E. Main St., Lima, 11/20/87, C, 87002042

Livonia Baptist Church, 9 High St., Livonia, 3/25/77, C, a, 77000949

Main Street Historic District, Main St. from the courthouse at Court and North Sts., Geneseo, 7/09/77, C, NHL, 77000948

Main Street Historic District (Boundary Increase), Roughly bounded by NY 39, Temple Hills Cemetery, South St. and Main, Geneseo, 3/21/85, C, NHL, 85000642

Markham Cobblestone Farmhouse and Barn Complex [Lima MRA], 6857 Heath—Markham Rd., Lima, 8/31/89, A, C, 89001119

Martin Farm Complex [Lima MRA], 1301 Bragg St., Lima, 8/31/89, A, C, 89001136

Mills, Gen. William A., House, 14 Main St., Mount Morris, 12/19/78, A, C, 78001858

Morgan Cobblestone Farmhouse [Lima MRA], 6870 W. Main Rd., Lima, 8/31/89, C, 89001118

Moses, Ogilvie, Farmhouse [Lima MRA], 2150 Clay St., Lima, 8/31/89, A, C, 89001123

Moses, Zebulon, Farm Complex [Lima MRA], 2770 Clay Rd., Lima, 8/31/89, A, C, 89001132

North Bloomfield School, 7840 Martin Rd., North Bloomfield, 5/28/81, A, C, a, 81000409

Peck, J. Franklin, House [Lima MRA], 7347 E. Main St., Lima, 8/31/89, C, 89001128

Peck, Thomas, Farmhouse [Lima MRA], 7955 E. Main Rd., Lima, 8/31/89, A, C, 89001137

Pioneer Farm, S of Dansville on NY 36, Dansville vicinity, 12/18/70, C, 70000422

School No. 6 [Lima MRA], 6679 Jenks Rd., Lima, 8/31/89, A, C, 89001121

Spencer House [Lima MRA], 7372 E. Main St., Lima, 8/31/89, C, 89001124

Livingston County—Continued

St. John's Episcopal Church, Jct. of State and Stanley Sts., Mount Morris, 7/19/91, C, a, 91000892

St. Rose Roman Catholic Church Complex, Lake Ave., Lima, 8/25/88, A, C, a, b, 88001345

Stanley House [Lima MRA], 7364 E. Main St., Lima, 8/31/89, C, 89001129

US Post Office—Dansville [US Post Offices in New York State, 1858-1943, TR], 100 Main St., Dansville, 11/17/88, A, C, 88002476

Vary, William L., House [Lima MRA], 7378 E. Main St., Lima, 8/31/89, C, 89001141

Wadsworth Fort Site, Address Restricted, Geneseo vicinity, 6/11/75, D, 75001194

Warner, Asahel, House [Lima MRA], 7136 W. Main St., Lima, 8/31/89, A, C, 89001139

Warner, Matthew, House [Lima MRA], 7449 E. Main St., Lima, 8/31/89, C, 89001138

Westerly, Chandler Rd., Piffard, 12/19/74, A, C, 74001255

Madison County

Abell Farmhouse and Barn [Cazenovia Town MRA], Ballina Rd., Cazenovia vicinity, 11/02/87, A, C, 87001860

Albany Street Historic District, Irregular pattern along Albany St., Cazenovia, 10/10/78, A, C, 78001859

Annas Farmhouse [Cazenovia Town MRA], 4812 Ridge Rd., Cazenovia vicinity, 2/18/88, A, C, 87001861

Beckwith Farmhouse [Cazenovia Town MRA], 4652 Syracuse Rd., Cazenovia vicinity, 11/02/87, C, 87001862

Brick House [Cazenovia Town MRA], 3318 Rippleton Rd., Cazenovia vicinity, 2/18/88, A, C, 87001863

Canal Town Museum [Canastota Village MRA], 122 Canal St., Canastota, 5/23/86, C, 86001292

Canastota Methodist Church [Canastota Village MRA], Main and New Boston Sts., Canastota, 5/23/86, C, a, 86001293

Canastota Public Library [Canastota Village MRA], 102 W. Center St., Canastota, 5/23/86, C, 86001294

Cazenovia Village Historic District [Cazenovia Town MRA], Roughly bounded by Union, Lincklean and Chenango Sts., and Rippleton Rd. and Foreman St., Cazenovia, 6/19/86, A, C, 86001352

Cedar Cove [Cazenovia MRA], W side of E. Lake Rd., Cazenovia vicinity, 7/15/91, A, C, 91000867

Chappell Farmhouse [Cazenovia Town MRA], Ridge Rd., Cazenovia vicinity, 11/02/87, A, C, 87001864

Chittenango Landing Dry Dock Complex, Lakeport Rd. at Old Erie Canal, Sullivan, 4/30/92, A, C, 92000458

Cobblestone House [Cazenovia Town MRA], Syracuse Rd., Cazenovia vicinity, 11/02/87, C, 87001865

Comstock, Zephnia, Farmhouse [Cazenovia Town MRA], 2363 Nelson St., Cazenovia, 11/02/87, A, C, 87001866

Cottage Lawn, 435 Main St., Oneida, 11/06/80, A, C, 80002650

Crandall Farm Complex [Cazenovia Town MRA], 2430 Ballina Rd., Cazenovia vicinity, 11/02/87, A, C, 87001867

Evergreen Acres [Cazenovia Town MRA], Syracuse Rd., Cazenovia vicinity, 11/02/87, A, C, 87001868

First National Bank of Morrisville, Main St., Morrisville, 9/12/85, A, C, 85002365

Hamilton Village Historic District, Roughly Kendrick Ave., Broad, Payne, Hamilton, Madison, Pleasant and Lewbanon Sts., Hamilton, 9/13/84, C, 84002494

Hillcrest [Cazenovia MRA], Ridge Rd. S of Hoffman, Cazenovia, 7/15/91, A, C, 91000869

House at 107 Stroud Street [Canastota Village MRA], 107 Stroud St., Canastota, 5/23/86, C, 86001302

House at 115 South Main Street [Canastota Village MRA], 115 S. Main St., Canastota, 5/23/86, C, 86001289

House at 205 North Main Street [Canastota Village MRA], 205 N. Main St., Canastota, 5/23/86, C, 86001296

House at 233 James Street [Canastota Village MRA], 233 James St., Canastota, 5/23/86, C, 86001295

House at 313 North Main Street [Canastota Village MRA], 313 N. Main St., Canastota, 5/23/86, C, 86001298

House at 326 North Peterboro Street [Canastota Village MRA], 326 N. Peterboro St., Canastota, 5/23/86, C, 86001299

House at 328 North Peterboro Street [Canastota Village MRA], 328 N. Peterboro St., Canastota, 5/23/86, C, 86001301

Lehigh Valley Railroad Depot [Cazenovia MRA], William St., Cazenovia, 7/15/91, A, C, 91000874

Lorenzo, Ledyard St. (U.S. 20), Cazenovia, 2/18/71, C, 71000541

Main-Broad-Grove Streets Historic District, Roughly bounded by Main, Broad, E. Grove, W. Grove, Wilbur, Elizabeth, E. Walnut, W. Walnut, and Stone Sts., Oneida, 9/15/83, C, 83001705

Maples, The [Cazenovia Town MRA], 2420 Nelson Rd., Cazenovia vicinity, 11/02/87, A, C, 87001876

Meadows Farm Complex [Cazenovia Town MRA], Rippleton Rd., Cazenovia vicinity, 11/02/87, A, C, 87001869

Middle Farmhouse [Cazenovia Town MRA], 4875 W. Lake Rd., Cazenovia vicinity, 11/02/87, C, 87001870

Nelson Welsh Congregational Church, Jct. of Welsh Church and Old State Rds., Nelson vicinity, 8/06/93, A, C, a, d, 93000681

Niles Farmhouse [Cazenovia Town MRA], Rippleton Rd., Cazenovia vicinity, 11/02/87, A, C, 87001871

Notleymere [Cazenovia MRA], 4641 E. Lake Rd., Cazenovia vicinity, 7/15/91, A, C, 91000868

Old Biology Hall, Colgate University, Hamilton, 9/20/73, C, 73001199

Old Madison County Courthouse, E. Main St., Morrisville, 6/15/78, A, C, 78001860

Old Trees [Cazenovia MRA], W side of Rippleton Rd., Cazenovia vicinity, 7/15/91, A, C, 91000865

Oneida Community Mansion House, Sherrill Rd., Oneida, 10/15/66, A, B, a, NHL, 66000527

Ormonde [Cazenovia MRA], Between E. Lake Rd. and Ormonde Dr., Cazenovia vicinity, 7/15/91, A, C, 91000866

Parker Farmhouse [Cazenovia Town MRA], 3981 East Rd., Cazenovia vicinity, 11/02/87, A, C, 87001872

Peterboro Land Office, Peterboro Rd., Peterboro, 9/07/84, A, C, 84002498

Peterboro Street Elementary School [Canastota Village MRA], 220 N. Peterboro St., Canastota, 5/23/86, C, 86001304

Roberts, Judge Nathan S., House [Canastota Village MRA], W. Seneca Ave., Canastota, 5/23/86, C, 86001305

Rolling Ridge Farm [Cazenovia Town MRA], 3937 Number Nine Rd., Cazenovia vicinity, 11/02/87, A, C, 87001873

Shattuck House [Cazenovia MRA], W. Lake Rd., Cazenovia vicinity, 7/15/91, A, C, 91000873

Smith, Adon, House, 3 Broad St., Hamilton, 5/02/74, C, 74001256

South Peterboro Street Commercial Historic District [Canastota Village MRA], Roughly bounded by NY 76, Diamond St., Penn Central RR tracks, and Commerce Ave., Canastota, 5/23/86, C, 86001287

South Peterboro Street Residential Historic District [Canastota Village MRA], S. Peterboro St. between Terrace and Rasbach Sts., Canastota, 5/23/86, C, 86001288

Sweetland Farmhouse [Cazenovia Town MRA], Number Nine Rd., Cazenovia vicinity, 11/02/87, C, 87001874

Tall Pines [Cazenovia Town MRA], Ridge Rd., Cazenovia vicinity, 11/02/87, C, 87001875

The Hickories [Cazenovia MRA], 47 Forman St., Cazenovia, 7/15/91, A, C, 91000870

US Post Office—Canastota [US Post Offices in New York State, 1858-1943, TR], 118 S. Peterboro St., Canton, 11/17/88, A, C, 88002467

US Post Office—Hamilton [US Post Offices in New York State, 1858-1943, TR], 32 Broad St., Hamilton, 5/11/89, A, C, 88002522

US Post Office—Oneida [US Post Offices in New York State, 1858-1943, TR], 133 Farrier Ave., Oneida, 5/11/89, A, C, 88002390

United Church of Canastota [Canastota Village MRA], 144 W. Center St., Canastota, 5/23/86, C, a, 86001306

Upenough [Cazenovia MRA], Rippleton St., Cazenovia vicinity, 7/15/91, A, C, 91000871

Wheeler House Complex, NY 8, Leonardsville, 9/22/83, C, 83001706

York Lodge [Cazenovia MRA], 4448 E. Lake Rd., Cazenovia vicinity, 7/15/91, A, C, 91000872

Monroe County

Adams-Ryan House, 425 Washington St., Adams Basin, 9/05/85, A, C, 85001957

Andrews Street Bridge [Inner Loop MRA; Stone Arch Bridge TR], Andrews St. at Genesee River, Rochester, 10/11/84, A, C, 84000182

Anthony, Susan B., House, 17 Madison St., Rochester, 10/15/66, B, NHL, 66000528

Aquinas Institute, 1127 Dewey Ave., Rochester, 6/08/89, A, C, a, 89000464

Bevier Memorial Building, Washington St., Rochester, 10/25/73, A, C, 73001201

Blackwell, Antoinette Louisa Brown, Childhood Home, 1099 Pinnacle Rd., Henrietta, 11/16/89, B, C, 89002003

Brick Presbyterian Church Complex [Inner Loop MRA], 121 N. Fitzhugh St., Rochester, 3/12/92, A, C, a, 92000152

Bridge Square Historic District [Inner Loop MRA], Roughly bounded by Inner Loop, Centre Park, Washington and W. Main Sts., Rochester, 10/11/84, A, C, 84000273

Brown's Race Historic District, Brown's Race St. from Platt St. to Conrail railroad tracks, Rochester, 3/02/89, A, C, D, 89000067

Brown, Adam, Block [Inner Loop MRA], 480 E. Main St., Rochester, 10/04/85, C, 85002857

Building at 551–555 North Goodman Street, 551–555 N. Goodman St., Rochester, 3/20/86, C, 86000448

Campbell-Whittlesey House, 123 S. Fitzhugh St., Rochester, 2/18/71, C, 71000542

Chamber of Commerce [Inner Loop MRA], 55 Saint Paul St., Rochester, 10/04/85, C, 85002859

Child, Jonathan, House & Brewster-Burke House Historic District, 37 S. Washington St. and 130 Spring St., Rochester, 2/18/71, B, C, 71000543

Chili Mills Conservation Area, 1 mi. SW of West Chili off Stuart Rd. along Black Creek, West Chili vicinity, 3/12/75, C, D, 75001198

City Hall Historic District, S. Fitzhugh St. between Broad and W. Main Sts., Rochester, 9/17/74, C, a, 74001258

Cohen, H. C., Company Building—Andrews Building [Inner Loop MRA], 216 Andrews St., Rochester, 10/04/85, A, C, 85002853

Court Exchange Building—National Casket Company [Inner Loop MRA], 142 Exchange St., Rochester, 10/04/85, C, 85002850

Court Street Bridge [Inner Loop MRA; Stone Arch Bridge TR], Court St. at Genesee River, Rochester, 10/11/84, A, C, 84000276

Cox Building [Inner Loop MRA; Department Store TR], 36-48 St. Paul St., Rochester, 10/11/84, A, C, 84000279

Daisy Flour Mill, Inc., 1880 Blossom Rd., Rochester, 6/26/72, A, C, 72000855

DeLand, Henry, House, 99 S. Main St., Fairport, 4/17/80, C, 80004610

Dewey, Chester, School No. 14 [Inner Loop MRA], 200 University Ave., Rochester, 10/04/85, C, 85002847

East Avenue Historic District, Irregular pattern along East Ave. from Probert St. to Alexander St., Rochester, 4/17/79, A, C, 79001589

East High School, 410 Alexander St., Rochester, 6/30/83, C, 83001707

Eastman Dental Dispensary, 800 E. Main St., Rochester, 4/28/83, B, C, 83001708

Eastman, George, House, 900 East Ave., Rochester, 11/13/66, B, NHL, 66000529

Edwards Building [Inner Loop MRA; Department Store TR], 26-34 St. Paul St., Rochester, 10/11/84, A, C, 84000287

Ely, Hervey, House, 138 Troup St., Rochester, 8/12/71, C, 71000544

English Evangelical Church of the Reformation and Parish House [Inner Loop MRA], 111 N. Chestnut St., Rochester, 3/12/92, C, a, 92000150

Erie Canal: Second Genesee Aqueduct, Broad St., Rochester, 9/29/76, A, C, 76001228

Federal Building, N. Fitzhugh and Church Sts., Rochester, 4/13/72, C, 72000856

First National Bank of Rochester—Old Monroe County Savings Bank Building [Inner Loop MRA], 35 State St., Rochester, 10/04/85, C, 85002861

First Presbyterian Church, 101 S. Plymouth Ave., Rochester, 10/25/73, C, a, 73001202

First Universalist Church, SE corner of S. Clinton Ave. and Court St., Rochester, 5/27/71, C, a, 71000545

Gannett Building [Inner Loop MRA], 55 Exchange St., Rochester, 10/04/85, A, C, 85002862

Genesee Lighthouse, 70 Lighthouse St., Rochester, 8/13/74, A, 74001259

German United Evangelical Church Complex [Inner Loop MRA], 60–90 Bittner St., Rochester, 3/12/92, C, a, 92000151

Granite Building [Inner Loop MRA; Department Store TR], 124 E. Main St., Rochester, 10/11/84, A, C, 84000290

Grove Place Historic District [Inner Loop MRA], Gibbs, Selden, Grove and Windsor Sts., Rochester, 10/11/84, A, C, 84000299

Hinchey, Franklin, House, 634 Hinchey Rd., Gates, 11/10/83, C, 83004045

Honeoye Falls Village Historic District, Roughly, jct. of Main, Monroe and Ontario Sts. and adjacent areas, Honeoye Falls, 11/24/93, C, 93001225

House at 235–237 Reynolds Street, 235–237 Reynolds St., Rochester, 9/12/85, C, 85002272

Immaculate Conception Roman Catholic Church Complex, 445 Frederick Douglass St. and 187 and 205 Edinburgh St., Rochester, 3/31/92, C, a, 92000381

Jewish Young Men's and Women's Association [Inner Loop MRA], 400 Andrews St., Rochester, 10/04/85, C, 85002848

Kirstein Building [Inner Loop MRA], 242 Andrews St., Rochester, 10/04/85, A, C, 85002844

Lehigh Valley Railroad Station [Inner Loop MRA], 99 Court St., Rochester, 10/04/85, A, C, 85002858

Leopold Street Shule, 30 Leopold St., Rochester, 6/07/74, A, C, a, 74001260

Little Theatre [Inner Loop MRA], 240 East Ave., Rochester, 10/04/85, A, C, 85002860

Lower Mill, N. Main St., Honeoye Falls, 5/17/73, A, C, 73001200

Madison Square—West Main Street Historic District, Roughly bounded by Silver, Canal, W. Main and Madison Sts., Rochester, 11/03/88, A, C, 88002382

Main Street Bridge [Inner Loop MRA; Stone Arch Bridge TR], Main St. at Genesee River, Rochester, 10/11/84, A, C, 84000303

Michaels—Stern Building [Inner Loop MRA], 87 N. Clinton Ave., Rochester, 10/04/85, A, C, 85002854

Morgan—Manning House, 151 Main St., Brockport, 4/25/91, B, C, 91000443

Mt. Hope-Highland Historic District, Bounded roughly by the Clarissa St. Bridge, Genesee River, Grove and Mt. Hope Aves., plus, Rochester, 1/21/74, B, C, 74001261

Mud House, 1000 Whalen Rd., Penfield, 10/11/78, C, 78001862

National Company Building [Inner Loop MRA; Department Store TR], 159 E. Main St., Rochester, 10/11/84, A, C, 84000291

Naval Armory—Convention Hall [Inner Loop MRA], 75 Woodbury Blvd., Rochester, 10/04/85, A, 85002852

Nazareth House, 94 Averill Ave., Rochester, 4/12/84, A, C, a, 84002734

O'Kane Market and O'Kane Building, 104–106 Bartlett St. & 239–255 Reynolds St., Rochester, 9/12/85, C, 85002288

Old Stone Warehouse, 1 Mt. Hope Ave., Rochester, 10/15/73, A, C, 73001203

Our Lady of Victory Roman Catholic Church [Inner Loop MRA], 210 Pleasant St., Rochester, 3/12/92, C, 92000153

Our Mother of Sorrows Roman Catholic Church Complex, 1785 Latta Rd., Greece, 11/30/89, A, C, a, d, 89002001

Phoenix Building, S. Main and State Sts., Pittsford, 8/07/74, A, C, 74001257

Pittsford Village Historic District, Roughly bounded by the Canal, Jefferson Ave., Sutherland, and South Sts., Pittsford, 9/07/84, C, 84002736

Powers Building, W. Main and State Sts., Rochester, 4/03/73, A, C, 73001204

Reynolds Arcade [Inner Loop MRA], 16 E. Main St., Rochester, 10/04/85, C, 85002855

Rich, Samuel, House, 2204 Five Mile Line Rd., Penfield vicinity, 12/30/87, A, B, C, 87002199

Richardson's Tavern, 1474 Marsh Rd., Perinton, 5/06/80, A, C, 80002652

Riga Academy, 3 Riga-Mumford Rd., Riga, 11/21/80, A, C, 80002653

Rochester City School #24, Meigs St., Rochester, 9/15/83, C, 83001709

Rochester Fire Department Headquarters and Shops [Inner Loop MRA], 185 North St., Rochester, 10/21/85, C, g, 85003361

Rochester Savings Bank, 40 Franklin St., Rochester, 3/16/72, A, C, 72000857

Rochester Street Historic District, Both sides of Rochester St., Scottsville, 10/25/73, C, 73001205

Monroe County—Continued

Rundel Memorial Library [Inner Loop MRA], 115 South Ave., Rochester, 10/04/85, C, 85002845

Shingleside, 476 Beach Ave., Rochester, 9/13/84, C, 84002737

Sibley Triangle Building [Inner Loop MRA], 20–30 East Ave., Rochester, 10/04/85, C, 85002849

Sibley, Hiram, Homestead, 29 Sibley Rd., Sibleyville, 9/12/85, B, C, b, 85002291

Spring House, 3001 Monroe Ave., Pittsford vicinity, 11/20/75, A, C, 75001199

St. John's Episcopal Church, 11 Episcopal Ave., Honeoye Falls, 7/07/88, C, a, 88001014

St. Joseph Roman Catholic Church and Rectory, 108 Franklin St., Rochester, 5/29/75, A, C, a, 75001197

St. Luke's Episcopal Church, 17 Main St., Brockport, 4/26/90, C, a, 90000686

St. Mary's Roman Catholic Church and Rectory [Inner Loop MRA], 15 St. Mary's Pl., Rochester, 3/12/92, C, a, 92000154

St. Paul-North Water Streets Historic District [Inner Loop MRA], St. Paul, N. Water, and Andrews Sts., Rochester, 10/11/84, A, C, 84000398

State Street Historic District [Inner Loop MRA], 109-173 State St., Rochester, 10/11/84, A, C, 84000402

Stone-Tolan House, 2370 E. Ave., Brighton, 7/21/83, A, C, e, 83001710

Third Ward Historic District, Roughly bounded by Adams and Peach Sts., I-490, and both sides of Troup and Fitzhugh Sts., Rochester, 7/12/74, A, B, C, 74001262

Totiakton Site, Address Restricted, Honeoye Falls vicinity, 9/21/78, D, 78001861

US Post Office—East Rochester [US Post Offices in New York State, 1858-1943, TR], 206 W. Commercial St., East Rochester, 11/17/88, A, C, 88002495

US Post Office—Honeoye Falls [US Post Offices in New York State, 1858-1943, TR], W. Main St. and Episcopal Ave., Honeoye Falls, 5/11/89, A, C, 88002505

University Club [Inner Loop MRA], 26 Broadway, Rochester, 10/04/85, C, 85002851

Vanderbeck House, 1295 Lake Ave., Rochester, 4/09/84, C, 84002739

Warner, H. H., Building [Inner Loop MRA], 72–82 St. Paul St., Rochester, 10/04/85, A, C, 85002846

Washington Street Rowhouses [Inner Loop MRA], 30–32 N. Washington St., Rochester, 10/04/85, C, 85002856

Webster Baptist Church, 59 South Ave., Webster, 11/07/91, C, a, 91001672

Wilbur House, 187 S. Main St., Fairport, 5/06/80, C, 80002651

Wilder Building [Inner Loop MRA], 1 E. Main St., Rochester, 10/04/85, A, C, 85002863

Youngs, Thomas, House, 50 Mitchell Rd., Pittsford, 6/24/93, C, b, 93000546

Montgomery County

Bates—Englehardt Mansion, 19 Washington St., St. Johnsville, 12/07/89, C, 89002091

Butler, Walter, Homestead, NE of Fonda on Old Trail Rd., Fonda vicinity, 6/23/76, B, 76001229

Caughnawaga Indian Village Site, Address Restricted, Fonda vicinity, 8/28/73, D, 73001207

Ehle House Site, Address Restricted, Nelliston, 6/14/82, A, D, 82004780

Ehle, Peter, House [Nelliston MRA], E. Main St., Nelliston, 9/27/80, B, C, 80002655

Erie Canal, 6 mi. W of Amsterdam on NY 5S, Fort Hunter vicinity, 10/15/66, A, C, D, NHL, 66000530

Fort Johnson, Jct. of NY 5 and 67, Fort Johnson, 11/28/72, B, C, NHL, 72000858

Fort Klock, 2 mi. E of St. Johnsville on NY 5, St. Johnsville, 11/28/72, A, NHL, 72000859

Fort Plain Conservation Area, Address Restricted, Fort Plain vicinity, 11/15/79, A, C, D, d, 79001591

Greene Mansion, 92 Market St., Amsterdam, 12/31/79, B, C, 79001590

Guy Park, W. Main St., Amsterdam, 2/06/73, B, C, 73001206

Jones, Samuel and Johanna, Farm, NY 67 W of jct. with NY 296, Amsterdam vicinity, 5/27/93, A, C, 93000460

Lasher-Davis House [Nelliston MRA], U.S. 5, Nelliston, 9/27/80, C, 80002656

Nellis Tavern, SR 5, St. Johnsville, 5/10/90, A, B, C, 90000685

Nellis, Jacob, Farmhouse [Nelliston MRA], Nellis St., Nelliston, 9/27/80, B, C, 80002657

Nelliston Historic District [Nelliston MRA], Prospect, River, Railroad and Berthoud Sts., Nelliston, 9/27/80, C, 80002658

Palatine Bridge Freight House, E of Palatine Bridge on NY 5, Palatine Bridge vicinity, 3/07/73, A, C, 73001208

Palatine Church, Mohawk Tpke., Palatine, 1/25/73, A, C, a, 73001209

Reformed Dutch Church of Stone Arabia, E of Nelliston on NY 10, Nelliston vicinity, 9/14/77, A, C, a, d, 77000951

Rice's Woods, Address Restricted, Canajoharie vicinity, 7/18/80, D, d, 80002654

Sweet, Samuel, Canal Store, 65 Bridge St., Amsterdam, 9/19/89, A, C, 89001389

Temple of Israel, 8 Mohawk Pl., Amsterdam, 8/27/92, C, a, 92001043

US Post Office—Amsterdam [US Post Offices in New York State, 1858-1943, TR], 12–16 Church St., Amsterdam, 11/17/88, A, C, 88002451

US Post Office—Canajoharie [US Post Offices in New York State, 1858-1943, TR], 50 W. Main St., Canajoharie, 11/17/88, A, C, 88002464

US Post Office—Fort Plain [US Post Offices in New York State, 1858-1943, TR], 41 River St., Fort Plain, 5/11/89, A, C, 88002510

US Post Office—St. Johnsville [US Post Offices in New York State, 1858-1943, TR], Main St., St. Johnsville, 5/11/89, A, C, 88002434

Van Alstyne House, Moyer St., Canajoharie, 9/08/83, A, C, 83001711

Vrooman Avenue School, Vrooman Ave., Amsterdam, 6/30/83, A, C, 83001712

Wagner, Webster, House, E. Grand St., Palatine Bridge, 3/07/73, B, C, 73001210

Walrath-Van Horne House [Nelliston MRA], W. Main St., Nelliston, 9/27/80, A, C, 80002659

Waterman-Gramps House [Nelliston MRA], School St., Nelliston, 9/27/80, C, 80002660

Nassau County

Adam-Derby House, 166 Lexington Ave., Oyster Bay, 5/17/79, C, 79001597

Aldred, John E., Estate, Lattingtown Rd., Lattingtown, 8/03/79, C, a, 79001594

Beekman, James William, House, West Shore Rd., Oyster Bay, 12/12/73, C, D, 73001212

Cedarmere—Clayton Estates, Bryant Ave. and Northern Blvd., Roslyn Harbor, 9/29/86, B, C, 86002634

Central Hall [Sea Cliff Summer Resort TR], 93 Central Ave., Sea Cliff, 2/18/88, A, C, 88000019

Crowell House [Sea Cliff Summer Resort TR], 375 Littleworth La., Sea Cliff, 2/18/88, A, C, 88000020

Denton, George W., House, West Shore Rd., Flower Hill, 8/29/85, C, 85001937

Dodge, Lillian Sefton, Estate, Frost Mill Rd., Mill Neck, 7/22/79, C, 79001595

Dodge, Thomas, Homestead, 58 Harbor Rd., Port Washington, 6/26/86, C, 86001387

East Williston Village Historic District, Roughly bounded by E. Williston Ave., Roslyn Rd., Atlanta Ave. and Village Green, East Williston, 7/18/85, A, C, 85001603

Eastman Cottage [Roslyn Village MRA], 130 Mott Ave., Roslyn, 10/02/86, C, 86002635

Elmwood, E side of Cove Rd., Oyster Bay, 4/03/75, C, 75001200

First Presbyterian Church of Oyster Bay, E. Main St., Oyster Bay, 12/12/76, C, a, 76001232

Fort Massapeag Archeological Site, Address Restricted, Oyster Bay, 4/19/93, D, NHL, 93000610

Grace Church Complex, Merrick and Dover Rds., Massapequa, 6/30/83, A, C, a, d, 83001713

Grace and Thomaston Buildings, 11 Middle Neck Rd. and 8 Bond St., Great Neck Plaza, 12/14/78, C, 78001865

Granada Towers, 310 Riverside Blvd., Long Beach, 5/31/84, A, C, 84002750

Heitz Place Courthouse, Heitz Pl., Hicksville, 7/30/74, A, C, 74001263

Hicks Lumber Company Store [Roslyn Village MRA], 1345 Old Northern Blvd., Roslyn, 10/02/86, C, 86002636

House at 103 Roslyn Avenue [Sea Cliff Summer Resort TR], 103 Roslyn Ave., Sea Cliff, 2/18/88, A, C, 88000018

House at 112 Sea Cliff Avenue [Sea Cliff Summer Resort TR], 112 Sea Cliff Ave., Sea Cliff, 2/18/88, A, C, a, 88000015

House at 115 Central Avenue [Sea Cliff Summer Resort TR], 115 Central Ave., Sea Cliff, 2/18/88, A, C, 88000014

House at 137 Prospect Avenue [Sea Cliff Summer Resort TR], 137 Prospect Ave., Sea Cliff, 2/18/88, A, C, 88000016

Nassau County—Continued

House at 173 Sixteenth Avenue [Sea Cliff Summer Resort TR], 173 Sixteenth Ave., Sea Cliff, 2/18/88, A, C, 88000013

House at 176 Prospect Avenue [Sea Cliff Summer Resort TR], 176 Prospect Ave., Sea Cliff, 2/18/88, A, C, 88000012

House at 18 Seventeenth Avenue [Sea Cliff Summer Resort TR], 18 Seventeenth Ave., Sea Cliff, 2/18/88, A, C, 88000011

House at 19 Locust Place [Sea Cliff Summer Resort TR], 19 Locust Pl., Sea Cliff, 2/18/88, A, C, 88000010

House at 195 Prospect Avenue [Sea Cliff Summer Resort TR], 195 Prospect Ave., Sea Cliff, 2/18/88, A, C, 88000009

House at 199 Prospect Avenue [Sea Cliff Summer Resort TR], 199 Prospect Ave., Sea Cliff, 2/18/88, A, C, 88000008

House at 207 Carpenter Avenue [Sea Cliff Summer Resort TR], 207 Carpenter Ave., Sea Cliff, 2/18/88, A, C, 88000007

House at 240 Sea Cliff Avenue [Sea Cliff Summer Resort TR], 240 Sea Cliff Ave., Sea Cliff, 2/18/88, A, C, a, 88000006

House at 285 Sea Cliff Avenue [Sea Cliff Summer Resort TR], 285 Sea Cliff Ave., Sea Cliff, 2/18/88, A, C, 88000005

House at 332 Franklin Avenue [Sea Cliff Summer Resort TR], 332 Franklin Ave., Sea Cliff, 2/18/88, A, C, 88000038

House at 362 Sea Cliff Avenue [Sea Cliff Summer Resort TR], 362 Sea Cliff Ave., Sea Cliff, 2/18/88, A, C, 88000037

House at 378 Glen Avenue [Sea Cliff Summer Resort TR], 378 Glen Ave., Sea Cliff, 2/18/88, A, C, 88000033

House at 52 Eighteenth Avenue [Sea Cliff Summer Resort TR], 52 Eighteenth Ave., Sea Cliff, 3/18/88, A, C, 88000032

House at 65 Twentieth Avenue [Sea Cliff Summer Resort TR], 65 Twentieth Av., Sea Cliff, 2/18/88, A, C, 88000001

House at 9 Locust Place [Sea Cliff Summer Resort TR], 9 Locust Pl., Sea Cliff, 2/18/88, A, C, 88000030

Justice Court Building, Jct. of Town Path Ext. and Glen Cove Hwy., Glen Cove, 4/26/90, A, C, 90000691

Long Island Rail Road Station at Farmingdale, Along LIRR tracks between Farmingdale and Forest Aves., Farmingdale, 11/13/91, A, C, 91001677

Mackay Estate Dairyman's Cottage, 40 Elm Dr., East Hills, 3/14/91, C, 91000238

Mackay Estate Gate Lodge, Jct. of Harbor Hill and Roslyn Rds., East Hills, 3/14/91, C, 91000240

Mackay Estate Water Tower, Redwood Dr. between Lincoln Dr. and Lufbery Dr., East Hills, 3/14/91, C, 91000239

Main Street Historic District, Main St. from N. Hempstead Tpke. to E. Broadway, including Tower St. and portions of Glen Ave. and Paper Mill Rd., Roslyn, 1/21/74, C, 74001266

Main Street School, Main and S. Washington St., Port Washington, 2/10/83, C, 83001714

Matinecock Friends Meetinghouse, Piping Rock and Duck Pond Rds., Locust Valley, 7/19/76, A, C, a, d, 76001231

Monfort Cemetery, E of Main St. and Port Washington Blvd., Port Washington, 1/07/88, A, C, d, 87002301

Moore, Benjamin, Estate, N of Muttontown on NY 25A, Muttontown vicinity, 5/14/79, C, 79001596

Old Nassau County Courthouse, 1550 Franklin Ave., Garden City, 2/17/78, A, C, 78001863

Old Westbury Gardens, 71 Old Westbury Rd., Westbury vicinity, 11/08/76, C, 76001234

Onderdonk, Horatio Gates, House, 1471 Northern Blvd., Manhasset, 4/16/80, C, 80002661

Pagan-Fletcher House, 127 Hendrickson Ave., Valley Stream, 9/08/83, A, 83001715

Planting Fields Arboretum, W of Oyster Bay on Planting Fields Rd., Oyster Bay vicinity, 1/25/79, A, C, 79001598

Raynham Hall, 20 W. Main St., Oyster Bay, 6/05/74, B, C, 74001264

Rectory of St. George's Episcopal Church, 217 Peninsula Blvd., Hempstead, 5/03/88, C, a, 88000510

Rescue Hook & Ladder Company No. 1 Firehouse [Roslyn Village MRA], Jct. of School St. and Skillman St., Roslyn, 5/06/91, C, 91000480

Rock Hall, 199 Broadway, Lawrence, 11/21/76, A, C, 76001230

Roosevelt, James Alfred, Estate, 360 Cove Neck Rd., Cove Neck, 5/17/79, B, C, 79001592

Roslyn Cemetery, Northern Blvd. W of jct. with Glen Cove Rd., Roslyn vicinity, 10/28/91, A, d, 91001534

Roslyn Grist Mill [Roslyn Village MRA], 1347 Old Northern Blvd., Roslyn, 10/02/86, A, C, 86002638

Roslyn House, Jct. of Lincoln Ave. and Roslyn Rd., Roslyn Heights, 6/07/90, C, 90000880

Roslyn National Bank and Trust Company Building [Roslyn Village MRA], 1432 Old Northern Blvd., Roslyn, 10/02/86, C, 86002639

Roslyn Savings Bank Building [Roslyn Village MRA], 1400 Old Northern Blvd., Roslyn, 10/02/86, C, 86002640

Roslyn Village Historic District [Roslyn Village MRA], Roughly bounded by Old Northern Blvd., Vernon and E. Broadway Sts., Main, Glen Ave., and Tower St., Roslyn, 4/15/87, A, C, 86002650

Saddle Rock Grist Mill [Long Island Wind and Tide Mills TR], Grist Mill Lane and Little Neck Bay, North Hempstead, 12/27/78, A, C, 78001866

Sagamore Hill National Historic Site, End of Cove Neck Rd., Oyster Bay, 10/15/66, A, B, C, e, NPS, 66000096

Sands Family Cemetery, Off Sands Point Rd. just S of jct. with Middle Neck Rd., Sands Point, 3/12/92, A, C, d, 92000092

Sands—Willets Homestead, 336 Port Washington Blvd., Port Washington, 9/19/85, A, C, 85002425

Sea Cliff Railroad Station [Sea Cliff Summer Resort TR], Sea Cliff Ave., Glen Cove, 2/18/88, A, C, 88000021

Seawanhaka Corinthian Yacht Club, Centre Island Rd., Oyster Bay, 1/08/74, C, 74001265

Shell House, The, 26 Westland Dr., East Island vicinity, 6/02/88, A, C, 88000600

Sousa, John Philip, House, 14 Hicks Lane, Sands Point, Port Washington, 10/15/66, B, NHL, 66000532

St. George's Church, 319 Front St., Hempstead, 3/07/73, C, a, 73001211

St. Lukes Protestant Episcopal Church [Sea Cliff Summer Resort TR], 253 Glen St., Sea Cliff, 2/18/88, A, C, a, 88000017

Stewart, A. T., Era Buildings, 4th, 5th, and 6th Sts., Cathedral and Cherry Valley Aves., Garden City, 11/14/78, B, C, 78001864

Swan, Edward H., House, Cove Neck Rd., Oyster Bay, 5/24/76, C, 76001233

Titus, Willet, House [Roslyn Village MRA], 1441 Old Northern Blvd., Roslyn, 10/02/86, C, 86002652

Toll Gate House, Northern Blvd., Greenvale, 8/16/77, C, 77000952

Trinity Church Complex [Roslyn Village MRA], Northern Blvd., Roslyn, 10/02/86, C, a, 86002653

US Post Office—Freeport [US Post Offices in New York State, 1858-1943, TR], 132 Merrick Rd., Freeport, 5/11/89, A, C, 88002517

US Post Office—Garden City [US Post Offices in New York State, 1858-1943, TR], 600 Franklin St., Garden City, 5/11/89, A, C, 88002521

US Post Office—Glen Cove [US Post Offices in New York State, 1858-1943, TR], 2 Glen Cove St., Glen Cove, 5/11/89, A, C, 88002525

US Post Office—Great Neck [US Post Offices in New York State, 1858-1943, TR], 1 Welwyn Rd., Great Neck Plaza, 5/11/89, A, C, 88002526

US Post Office—Hempstead [US Post Offices in New York State, 1858-1943, TR], 200 Fulton Ave., Hempstead, 11/17/88, A, C, 88002499

US Post Office—Long Beach [US Post Offices in New York State, 1858-1943, TR], 101 E. Park Ave., Long Beach, 5/11/89, A, C, 88002347

US Post Office—Mineola [US Post Offices in New York State, 1858-1943, TR], Main and First Sts., Mineola, 5/11/89, A, C, 88002354

US Post Office—Oyster Bay [US Post Offices in New York State, 1858-1943, TR], Shore Ave., Oyster Bay, 5/11/89, A, C, 88002393

US Post Office—Rockville Centre [US Post Offices in New York State, 1858-1943, TR], 250 Merrick Rd., Rockville Centre, 5/11/89, A, C, 88002425

Valley Road Historic District, S of Manhasset on Community Dr., Manhasset vicinity, 4/08/77, A, D, a, d, 77000953

Wantagh Railroad Complex, 1700 Wantagh Ave., Wantagh, 6/30/83, A, C, b, 83001716

Warner, Samuel Adams, House [Roslyn Village MRA], 1 Railroad Ave., Roslyn, 10/02/86, C, 86002654

Woolworth Estate, 77 Crescent Beach Rd., Glen Cove, 5/17/79, B, C, 79001593

New York County

75 Murray Street Building, 75 Murray St., New York, 4/03/73, C, 73001213

AMBROSE (lightship), Pier 16, East River, Manhattan, New York, 9/07/84, A, C, NHL, 84002758

Admiral's House, Governors Island, New York, 7/24/72, A, C, 72000860

African Burying Ground, Vicinity of Broadway and Reade St., New York, 4/19/93, A, D, NHL, 93001597

Alwyn Court Apartments, 180 W. 58th St., New York, 12/26/79, C, 79001599

American Fine Arts Society, 215 W. 57th St., New York, 5/06/80, A, C, 80002662

American Museum of Natural History, Central Park West and 77th St., New York, 6/24/76, A, C, 76001235

American Radiator Building, 40–52 W. 40th St., New York, 5/07/80, C, 80002663

American Stock Exchange, 86 Trinity Pl., New York, 6/02/78, A, NHL, 78001867

Andrews United Methodist Church, 95 Richmond St., Brooklyn, 1/22/92, C, a, 91001977

Ansonia Hotel, 2101–2119 Broadway, New York, 1/10/80, B, 80002665

Apartment at 1261 Madison Avenue, 1261 Madison Ave., New York, 10/29/82, C, 82001185

Apollo Theater, 253 W. 125th St., New York, 11/17/83, A, C, 83004059

Appellate Division Courthouse of New York State, 27 Madison Ave., New York, 7/26/82, A, C, 82003366

Apthorp Apartments, 2201–2219 Broadway, New York, 1/30/78, C, 78001868

Arthur, Chester A., House, 123 Lexington Ave., New York, 10/15/66, B, NHL, 66000534

Association Residence Nursing Home, 891 Amsterdam Ave., New York, 2/20/75, A, C, 75001201

Association of the Bar of the City of New York, 42 W. 44th St., New York, 1/03/80, A, C, 80002666

Audubon Terrace Historic District, Bounded by Broadway, Riverside Dr., W. 155th and W. 156th Sts., New York, 5/30/80, A, B, C, 80002667

Bailey House, 10 St. Nicholas Pl., New York, 4/23/80, C, 80002668

Baker, George F., Jr. and Sr., Houses, 67, 69, and 75 E. 93rd St., New York, 6/03/82, C, a, 82003367

Barbizon Hotel for Women, 140 E. 63rd St., New York, 10/29/82, C, 82001186

Battery Park Control House [Interborough Rapid Transit Subway Control Houses TR], State St. and Battery Pl., New York, 5/06/80, A, C, 80002669

Bayard-Condict Building, 65–69 Bleecker St., New York, 12/08/76, C, NHL, 76001236

Beacon Theater and Hotel, 2124 Broadway, New York, 11/04/82, A, C, 82001187

Bell Telephone Laboratories, 463 West St., New York, 5/15/75, A, NHL, 75001202

Belnord Apartments, 225 W. 86th St., New York, 4/23/80, C, 80002670

Bialystoker Synagogue, 7–13 Willett St., New York, 4/26/72, A, C, a, 72000861

Blackwell House, Welfare Island, New York, 2/25/72, C, 72000862

Block House, The, Governors Island, New York, 7/24/72, C, 72000863

Bouwerie Lane Theater, 330 Bowery St., New York, 4/23/80, C, 80002671

Bowery Savings Bank, 130 Bowery St., New York, 4/23/80, C, 80002672

Bowling Green Fence and Park, Broadway and Beaver Sts., New York, 4/09/80, A, 80002673

Brown, James, House, 326 Spring St., New York, 8/11/83, C, 83001717

Building at 361 Broadway, 361 Broadway, New York, 9/15/83, C, 83001718

Building at 376–380 Lafayette Street, 376–380 Lafayette Street, New York, 12/28/79, C, 79001600

Building at 45 East 66th Street, 45 E. 66th St., New York, 5/06/80, C, 80002674

Building at 85 Leonard Street, 85 Leonard St., New York, 4/23/80, C, 80002675

Candler Building, 220 42nd St. and 221 41st St., New York, 7/08/82, C, 82003368

Carnegie Hall, 7th Ave., 56th to 57th Sts., New York, 10/15/66, A, NHL, 66000535

Carnegie, Andrew, Mansion, 2 E. 91st St., New York, 11/13/66, B, NHL, 66000536

Cary Building, 105-107 Chambers St., New York, 9/15/83, C, 83001719

Casa Italina, 1151-1161 Amsterdam Ave., New York, 10/29/82, C, 82001188

Castle Clinton National Monument, South Ferry, New York, 10/15/66, A, C, NPS, 66000537

Castle Williams, Governors Island, New York, 7/31/72, A, C, 72000864

Central Park, Bounded by Central Park S., 5th Ave., Central Park W., 110th St., New York, 10/15/66, C, NHL, 66000538

Central Park West Historic District, Central Park West between 61st and 97th Sts., New York, 11/09/82, C, g, 82001189

Central Savings Bank, 2100-2108 Broadway, New York, 9/08/83, C, 83001720

Central Synagogue, 646–652 Lexington Ave., New York, 10/09/70, A, C, a, NHL, 70000423

Century Association Building, 5-7 W. 43rd St., New York, 7/15/82, C, 82003369

Chamber of Commerce Building, 65 Liberty St., New York, 2/06/73, A, C, NHL, 73001214

Chanin Building, 122 E. 42nd St., New York, 4/23/80, C, 80002676

Chapel of the Good Shepherd, Welfare Island, New York, 3/16/72, C, a, 72000865

Chapel of the Intercession Complex and Trinity Cemetery, 550 W. 155th St., New York, 7/24/80, A, C, a, d, 80002677

Charles Street House at No. 131, 131 Charles St., New York, 11/03/72, C, 72000866

Charlton-King-Vandam Historic District, Roughly bounded by Varick, Vandam, MacDougal and King Sts., New York, 7/20/73, C, 73001215

Chelsea Historic District, Roughly bounded by 19th and 22nd Sts., 9th and 10th Aves., New York, 12/06/77, C, 77000954

Chelsea Historic District (Boundary Increase), Roughly W. 22 to W. 23 Sts. and 8th to 10th Aves., New York, 12/16/82, A, C, 82001190

Christodora House, 147 Ave. B, New York, 3/20/86, A, 86000486

Chrysler Building, 405 Lexington Ave., New York, 12/08/76, B, C, f, g, NHL, 76001237

Church Missions House, 281 Park Ave., S., New York, 6/03/82, A, C, a, 82003370

Church of Notre Dame and Rectory, 405 W. 114th St. and 40 Morningside Dr., New York, 5/06/80, C, a, 80002678

Church of St. Ignatius Loyola Complex, Park Ave., 83rd and 84th Sts., New York, 7/24/80, A, C, a, 80002679

Church of St. Mary the Virgin Complex, 145 W. 46th St., New York, 4/16/90, A, C, a, 90000606

Church of St. Paul the Apostle, 415 W. 59th St., New York, 12/05/91, C, a, 91001723

Church of the Ascension (Protestant Episcopal), 36–38 Fifth Ave., New York, 12/23/87, C, a, NHL, 87002593

Church of the Holy Apostles, 300 9th Ave., New York, 4/26/72, A, C, a, 72000867

Church of the Holy Communion and Buildings, 656-662 6th Ave., New York, 4/17/80, A, B, C, 80002680

Church of the Immaculate Conception and Clergy Houses, 406-414 E. 14th St., New York, 3/28/80, A, C, a, 80002681

Church of the Incarnation and Parish House, 205-209 Madison Ave., New York, 7/08/82, B, C, a, 82003371

Church of the Transfiguration and Rectory, 1 E. 29th St., New York, 6/04/73, A, C, a, 73001216

Church of the Transfiguration, 25 Mott St., New York, 4/16/80, C, a, 80002682

City Hall, Broadway and Chambers St., New York, 10/15/66, A, NHL, 66000539

City Hospital, Welfare Island, New York, 3/16/72, C, 72000868

City Pier A, S end of Battery Pl. at Hudson River, New York, 6/27/75, A, C, 75001203

City and Suburban Homes Company's First Avenue Estate Historic District, 1168–1200 First Ave., 401–429 E. Sixty-fourth, and 402–430 E. Sixty-fifth Sts., New York, 8/01/86, A, C, 86002622

Civic Club, 243 E. 34th St., New York, 9/16/82, A, C, 82003372

Claremont Stables, 173-177 W. 89th St., New York, 4/16/80, A, C, 80002683

College of the City of New York, Bounded by Amsterdam Ave., St. Nicholas Terr., W. 138th, and W. 140th Sts., New York, 9/07/84, C, 84002763

Congregation B'nai Jeshurun Synagogue and Community House, 257 W. 88th St. and 270 W. 89th St., New York, 6/02/89, A, C, a, 89000474

Control House on 72nd Street [Interborough Rapid Transit Subway Control Houses TR], W. 72nd St. and Broadway, New York, 5/06/80, A, C, 80002684

Cook, Will Marion, House, 221 W. 138th St., New York, 5/11/76, B, NHL, 76001238

Cooper Union, Cooper Square, 7th St., and 4th Ave., New York, 10/15/66, A, NHL, 66000540

Croton Aqueduct Gate House, 135th St. and Convent Ave., New York, 9/22/83, C, 83001721

New York County—Continued

Dahlgren, Lucy Drexel, House, 15 E. 96th St., New York, 7/20/89, C, 89000946

Daily News Building, 220 E. 42nd St., New York, 11/14/82, A, C, NHL, 82001191

Dakota Apartments, 1 W. 72nd St., New York, 4/26/72, C, NHL, 72000869

DeLamar Mansion, 233 Madison Ave., New York, 8/25/83, C, 83001722

Devinne Press Building, 393–399 Lafayette St., New York, 9/14/77, A, C, 77000955

Dorilton, 171 W. 71st St., New York, 9/08/83, C, 83001723

Douglas, Adelaide L. T., House, 57 Park Ave., New York, 7/15/82, C, 82003373

Duke Residence, 1009 Fifth Ave., New York, 12/07/89, C, 89002090

Duke, James B., Mansion, 1 E. 78th St., New York, 11/10/77, A, C, 77000956

Dunbar Apartments, Bounded by 7th and 8th Aves. and W. 149th and 150th Sts., New York, 3/29/79, A, C, 79001601

Dyckman, William, House, 4881 Broadway, New York, 12/24/67, C, NHL, 67000014

East 73rd Street Historic District, 161–179 and 166–182 E. 73rd St., New York, 7/22/82, C, 82003374

East 78th Street Houses, 157, 159, 161, and 163-165 E. 78th St., New York, 3/25/80, C, 80002685

East 80th Street Houses, 116-130 E. 80th St., New York, 3/26/80, C, 80002686

Eldridge Street Synagogue, 12-16 Eldridge St., New York, 3/28/80, A, C, a, 80002687

Ellington, Edward Kennedy "Duke", House, 935 St. Nicholas Ave., Apt. 4A, New York, 5/11/76, B, g, NHL, 76001239

Empire State Building, 350 Fifth Ave., New York, 11/17/82, C, NHL, 82001192

Equitable Building, 120 Broadway, New York, 6/02/78, A, NHL, 78001869

Federal Hall National Memorial, Wall and Nassau Sts., New York, 10/15/66, A, C, NPS, 66000095

Federal Office Building, 641 Washington St., New York, 8/30/74, C, 74001267

Federal Reserve Bank of New York, 33 Liberty St., New York, 5/06/80, C, 80002688

Film Center Building, 630–9th St., New York, 9/07/84, C, 84002768

Firehouse, Engine Company 31, 87 Lafayette St., New York, 1/20/72, A, C, 72000870

Firehouse, Engine Company 33, 44 Great Jones St., New York, 3/16/72, C, 72000871

First Houses, E. 3rd St. and Ave. A, New York, 12/18/79, A, C, g, 79001602

First National City Bank, 55 Wall St., New York, 8/18/72, C, 72000872

First Police Precinct Station House, South St. and Old Slip, New York, 10/29/82, C, 82001193

First Shearith Israel Graveyard, 55-57 St. James Pl., New York, 4/17/80, A, d, 80002689

Fish, Hamilton, House, 21 Stuyvesant St., New York, 7/31/72, B, NHL, 72001456

Flatiron Building, 5th Ave. and Broadway St, New York, 11/20/79, C, NHL, 79001603

Former Emigrant Industrial Savings Bank, 51 Chambers St., New York, 2/25/82, C, 82003375

Former New York Life Insurance Company Building, 346 Broadway, New York, 6/28/82, C, 82003376

Former Police Headquarters Building, 240 Centre St., New York, 3/28/80, C, 80002690

Fort Jay, Governor's Island, New York, 3/27/74, A, 74001268

Fort Tryon Park and the Cloisters, Broadway and Dyckman St., New York, 12/19/78, A, C, g, 78001870

Fort Washington Site, Address Restricted, New York vicinity, 12/06/78, A, D, 78001871

Founder's Hall, The Rockefeller University, 66th St. and York Ave., New York, 9/13/74, A, B, NHL, 74001269

Fourteenth Ward Industrial School, 256-258 Mott St., New York, 1/27/83, A, C, 83001724

Fraunces Tavern Block, Bounded by Pearl, Water, Broad Sts. and Coenties Slip, New York, 4/28/77, C, 77000957

General Grant National Memorial, Riverside Dr. and W. 122nd St., New York, 10/15/66, B, C, c, f, NPS, 66000055

Gilsey Hotel, 1200 Broadway, New York, 12/14/78, C, 78001872

Gouverneur Hospital, 621 Water St., New York, 10/29/82, C, 82001194

Governor's House, Governors Island, New York, 4/26/73, A, C, 73001217

Governor's Island, Governor's Island, New York, 2/04/85, A, C, NHL, 85002435

Grace Church and Dependencies, Broadway, 10th St., and 4th Ave., New York, 6/28/74, C, a, NHL, 74001270

Gracie, Archibald, Mansion, East End Ave. at 88th St., New York, 5/12/75, C, 75001205

Gramercy Park Historic District, Roughly bounded by 3rd and Park Aves., S., E. 18th and 22nd Sts., New York, 1/23/80, A, a, 80002691

Grand Central Terminal, 71–105 E. 42nd St., New York, 1/17/75, A, C, NHL, 75001206

Grand Central Terminal (Boundary Increase: Park Avenue Viaduct), 71-105 E. 42nd St., Park Ave. between E. 40th and E. 42nd Sts., New York, 8/11/83, A, C, 83001726

Grand Hotel, 1232-1238 Broadway, New York, 9/15/83, C, 83001725

Greenwich Village Historic District, Roughly bounded by W. 13th St., St. Luke's Pl., University Pl., and Washington St., New York, 6/19/79, A, C, 79001604

Hamilton Grange National Memorial, 287 Convent Ave., New York, 10/15/66, B, C, b, NHL, NPS, 66000097

Hamilton Heights Historic District, Roughly bounded by St. Nicholas and Amsterdam Aves, W. 145 and W. 140th Sts., New York, 9/30/83, C, 83001727

Harlem Courthouse, 170 E. 121st St., New York, 4/16/80, A, C, 80002692

Harlem Fire Watchtower, Garvey Park at E. 122nd St., New York, 6/21/76, A, C, 76001240

Harlem River Houses, 151st to 153rd St., Macombs Pl. and Harlem River Dr., New York, 12/18/79, A, C, g, 79001605

Harvard Club of New York City, 27 W. 44th St., New York, 3/28/80, C, 80002693

Hatch, Barbara Rutherford, House, 153 E. 63rd St., New York, 6/09/83, B, C, 83001728

Haughwout, E. V., Building, 488-492 Broadway, New York, 8/28/73, A, C, 73001218

Henderson Place Historic District, Henderson Pl., New York, 6/20/74, C, 74001271

Henry Street Settlement and Neighborhood Playhouse, 263–267 Henry St. and 466 Grand St., New York, 9/13/74, B, NHL, 74001272

Henson, Matthew, Residence, 246 W. 150th St., Apt. 3F, New York, 5/15/75, B, C, NHL, 75001207

High Bridge Aqueduct and Water Tower, Harlem River at W. 170th St. and High Bridge Park, New York, 12/04/72, C, 72001560

Holland Tunnel, Connecting Lower Manhattan and Jersey City, running under the Hudson R., New York, 11/04/93, A, C, NHL, 93001619

Holy Trinity Church, St. Christopher House and Parsonage, 312-316 and 332 E. 88th St., New York, 5/30/80, C, a, 80002694

Hopper, Isaac T., House, 110 Second Ave., New York, 5/22/86, A, C, 86001155

Hotel Chelsea, 222 W. 23rd St., New York, 12/27/77, B, C, 77000958

Hotel Gerard, 123 W. 44th St., New York, 2/10/83, C, 83001729

House at 17 West 16th Street, 17 W. 16th St., New York, 5/26/83, A, B, C, 83001730

House at 203 East 29 Street, 203 E. 29th St., New York, 7/08/82, C, 82003377

House at 203 Prince Street, 203 Prince St., New York, 5/26/83, C, 83001731

House at 37 East 4th Street, 37 E. 4th St., New York, 1/03/80, C, 80002695

House at 51 Market St., 51 Market St., New York, 7/29/77, C, 77000959

Houses at 120 and 122 East 92nd Street, 120-122 East 92nd St., New York, 10/29/82, C, 82001195

Houses at 146–156 East 89th Street, 146–156 E. 89th St., New York, 6/03/82, C, 82003378

Houses at 208-218 East 78th Street, 208-218 E. 78th St., New York, 6/30/83, C, 83001732

Houses at 26, 28 and 30 Jones Street, 26, 28 and 30 Jones St., New York, 6/03/82, C, 82003379

Houses at 311 and 313 East 58th Street, 311-313 E. 58th St., New York, 11/14/82, C, 82001197

Houses at 326, 328 and 330 East 18th Street, 326–330 E. 18th St., New York, 9/30/82, C, 82003380

Houses at 437-459 West 24th Street, 437-459 W. 24th St., New York, 10/29/82, C, 82001196

Houses at 647, 651-53 Fifth Avenue and 4 East 52nd Street, 647, 651-53 5th Ave. and 4 E. 52nd St., New York, 9/08/83, A, C, 83001733

Houses at 83 and 85 Sullivan Street, 83–85 Sullivan St., New York, 11/17/80, C, 80002696

Hughes, Langston, House, 20 E. 127th St., New York, 10/29/82, B, 82001198

IRT Broadway Line Viaduct, W. 122nd St. to W. 135th St., Broadway, New York, 9/15/83, A, C, 83001749

New York County—Continued

International Mercantile Marine Company Building, 1 Broadway, New York, 3/02/91, C, 91000108

J. P. Morgan & Co. Building, 23 Wall St., New York, 6/19/72, A, C, 72000874

JOHN A. LYNCH (ferryboat), Pier 15, East River, Manhattan, New York, 9/07/84, A, 84002775

Jeffrey's Hook Lighthouse [Hudson River Lighthouses TR], Fort Washington Park, New York, 5/29/79, A, C, 79003130

John Street Building No. 170–176, 170-176 John St., New York, 5/13/71, A, C, 71000546

John Street Methodist Church, 44 John St., New York, 6/04/73, C, a, 73001219

Johnson, James Weldon, House, 187 W. 135th St., New York, 5/11/76, B, g, NHL, 76001241

Judson Memorial Church, Campanile, and Judson Hall, Washington Sq. at Thompson St., New York, 10/16/74, C, a, 74001274

Jumel Terrace Historic District, W. 160th and 162nd Sts. between St. Nicholas and Edgecombe Aves., New York, 4/03/73, C, 73001220

Knickerbocker Hotel, 142 W. 42nd St., New York, 4/11/80, C, 80002697

Knox Building, 452 5th Ave., New York, 6/03/82, B, C, 82003381

Kreischer House, 4500 Arthur Kill Rd., New York, 10/29/82, C, 82001199

LETTIE G. HOWARD (schooner), South Street Seaport Museum, New York, 9/07/84, A, C, NHL, 84002779

LaGrange Terrace, 428–434 Lafayette St., New York, 12/12/76, C, 76001242

Lamb's Club, 128 W. 44th St., New York, 6/03/82, A, C, a, 82003382

Lanier, James F. D., Residence, 123 E. 35th, New York, 6/03/82, C, 82003383

LeRoy, Daniel, House, 20 St. Mark's Pl., New York, 10/29/82, C, 82001200

Lescaze House, 211 E. 48th St., New York, 5/19/80, C, g, 80002698

Level Club, 253 W. 73rd St., New York, 4/09/84, C, 84002784

Lever House, 390 Park Ave., New York, 10/02/83, C, g, 83004078

Liberty Tower, 55 Liberty St., New York, 9/15/83, C, 83001734

Lighthouse, Welfare Island, New York, 3/16/72, A, C, 72000876

Lincoln Building, 1 Union Sq. W., New York, 9/08/83, C, 83001735

Loew, William Goadby, House, 56 E. 93rd St., New York, 7/15/82, B, C, 82003384

Low Memorial Library, Columbia University, W. Sixteenth St. between Broadway and Amsterdam Ave., New York, 12/23/87, C, NHL, 87002599

MACHIGONNE (ferry), Pier 25, New York, 12/03/92, A, C, 92001610

MacDougal-Sullivan Gardens Historic District, 74-76 MacDougal St., 170-188 Sullivan St., New York, 6/30/83, A, C, 83001736

Macy, R. H., and Company Store, 151 W. 34th St., New York, 6/02/78, A, NHL, 78001873

Madison Avenue Facade of the Squadron A Armory, Madison Ave. between 94th and 95th Sts., New York, 3/24/72, A, C, 72000877

Manhattan Avenue—West 120th—123rd Streets Historic District, 242–262 W. 120th St., 341–362 W. 121st St., 341–362 W. 122nd St., 344–373 123rd St., 481–553 Manhattan Ave. W side, New York, 1/17/92, C, 91001920

Marble Collegiate Reformed Church, 275 5th Ave., New York, 4/09/80, C, a, 80002699

Mariner's Temple, 12 Oliver St., New York, 4/16/80, C, a, 80002700

McGraw-Hill Building, 326 W. 42nd St., New York, 3/28/80, C, g, NHL, 80002701

McKay, Claude, Residence, 180 W. 135th St., New York, 12/08/76, B, g, NHL, 76002143

Mecca Temple, 131 N. 55th St., New York, 9/07/84, C, 84002788

Merchants Refrigerating Company Warehouse, 501 W. 16th St., New York, 5/31/85, C, 85001171

Metropolitan Life Insurance Company, 1 Madison Ave., New York, 6/02/78, A, NHL, 78001874

Metropolitan Museum of Art, Fifth Ave. at Eighty-second St., New York, 6/24/86, A, C, g, NHL, 86003556

Metropolitan Savings Bank, 9 E. 7th St., New York, 12/12/76, C, a, 76001243

Mills, Florence, House, 220 W. 135th St., New York, 12/08/76, B, NHL, 76001244

Minton's Playhouse, 206–210 W. One Hundred Eighteenth St., New York, 9/18/85, A, g, 85002423

Mooney, Edward, House, 18 Bowery, New York, 12/12/76, C, 76001245

Moore, William H., House, 4 E. 54th St., New York, 3/16/72, C, 72000878

Morgan, Pierpont, Library, 33 E. 36th St., New York, 11/13/66, A, B, C, NHL, 66000544

Morris, Lewis G., House, 100 E. 85th St., New York, 2/12/77, C, 77000960

Morris-Jumel Mansion, 160th St. and Edgecombe Ave., New York, 10/15/66, A, C, NHL, 66000545

Mount Morris Bank, E. 125th St. and Park Ave., New York, 12/07/89, C, 89002087

Mount Morris Park Historic District, Bounded roughly by Lenox Ave., Mount Morris Park West, and W. 124th and W. 119th Sts., New York, 2/06/73, C, a, 73001221

Municipal Asphalt Plant, Between 90th and 91st Sts., New York, 5/23/80, C, g, 80002702

Municipal Building, Chambers at Centre St., New York, 10/18/72, A, C, 72000879

Municipal Ferry Pier, 11 South St., New York, 12/12/76, A, C, 76001246

National City Bank, 55 Wall St., New York, 6/02/78, A, C, NHL, 78001875

New Amsterdam Theater, 214 W. 42nd St., New York, 1/10/80, C, 80002664

New York Amsterdam News Building, 2293 7th Ave., New York, 5/11/76, A, NHL, 76001247

New York Cancer Hospital, 2 W. 106th St., New York, 4/29/77, A, C, 77000961

New York City Marble Cemetery, 52-74 E. 2nd St., New York, 9/17/80, A, d, 80002703

New York Cotton Exchange, 1 Hanover Sq., New York, 1/07/72, A, C, NHL, 72001586

New York County Lawyers Association Building, 14 Vesey St., New York, 10/29/82, C, 82001201

New York Life Building, 51 Madison Ave., New York, 6/02/78, A, NHL, 78001876

New York Marble Cemetery, Between East 2nd and 3rd Sts., 2nd Ave. and Bowery, New York, 9/17/80, A, C, d, 80004475

New York Presbyterian Church, 151 W. 128th St., New York, 6/03/82, C, a, 82003385

New York Public Library, 5th Ave. and 42nd St., New York, 10/15/66, A, C, 66000546

New York Public Library, 222 E. 79th St., New York, 7/15/82, C, 82003386

New York Public Library and Bryant Park, Avenue of the Americas, 5th Ave., 40th and 42nd Sts., New York, 10/15/66, A, C, NHL, 66000547

New York Public Library, 115th Street Branch, 203 W. 115th St., New York, 5/06/80, C, 80002704

New York Public Library, Hamilton Grange Branch, 503 and 505 W. 145th St., New York, 7/23/81, A, C, 81000410

New York School of Applied Design, 160 Lexington Ave., New York, 12/16/82, A, C, 82001202

New York Shakespeare Festival Public Theater, 425 Lafayette St., New York, 12/02/70, C, 70000424

New York Stock Exchange, 11 Wall St., New York, 6/02/78, A, NHL, 78001877

New York Studio School of Drawing, Painting and Sculpture, 8–14 W. 8th St., New York, 4/27/92, A, B, NHL, 92001877

New York Yacht Club, 37 W. 44th St., New York, 10/29/82, A, C, NHL, 82001203

No. 8 Thomas Street Building, 8 Thomas St., New York, 4/30/80, A, C, 80002705

Norwood, Andrew S., House, 241 W. 14th St., New York, 7/09/79, B, C, 79001606

Octagon, The, Welfare Island, New York, 3/16/72, A, C, 72000880

Odd Fellows Hall, 165-171 Grand St., New York, 9/22/83, C, 83001737

Old Colony Club, 120 Madison Ave., New York, 4/23/80, A, C, 80002706

Old Grolier Club, 29 E. 32nd St., New York, 4/23/80, A, C, 80002707

Old Merchant's House, 29 E. 4th St., New York, 10/15/66, C, NHL, 66000548

Old New York Evening Post Building, 20 Vessy St., New York, 8/16/77, A, B, C, 77000963

Old St. Patrick's Cathedral Complex, Mott and Prince Sts., New York, 8/29/77, A, C, a, 77000964

Osborne Apartments, 205 W. 57th St., New York, 4/22/93, C, 93000333

Ottendorfer Public Library and Stuyvesant Polyclinic Hospital, 135 and 137 2nd Ave., New York, 7/22/79, A, B, C, 79001607

Park Avenue Houses, 680, 684, 686 and 690 Park Ave., New York, 1/03/80, C, 80002708

Park East Synagogue, Congregation Zichron Ephraim, 163 E. 67th St., New York, 8/18/83, C, a, 83001738

Players, The, 16 Gramercy Park, New York, 10/15/66, A, B, NHL, 66000549

New York County—Continued

Plaza Hotel, Fifth Ave. and Fifty-ninth St., New York, 11/29/78, A, C, NHL, 78001878

Pomander Walk District, 261-267 W. 94th St., 260-274 W. 95th St. and Pomander Walk, New York, 9/08/83, A, C, 83001739

Public Baths, Asser Levy Pl. and E. 23rd St., New York, 4/23/80, A, C, 80002709

Public School 157, 327 St. Nicholas Ave., New York, 12/10/82, C, 82003387

Public School 35, 931 1st Ave., New York, 10/27/80, C, 80002710

Public School 9, 466 W. End Ave., New York, 8/03/87, C, 87001258

Puck Building, 295-309 Lafayette St., New York, 7/21/83, A, C, 83001740

Pupin Physics Laboratories, Columbia University, Broadway and 120th St., New York, 10/15/66, A, B, g, NHL, 66000550

Queensboro Bridge, 59th St., New York, 12/20/78, C, 78001879

R & S Building, 492 First Ave., New York, 9/22/86, C, 86002683

Racquet and Tennis Club Building, 370 Park Ave., New York, 7/13/83, C, 83001741

Radio City Music Hall, 1260 Avenue of the Americas, New York, 5/08/78, A, C, g, 78001880

Red House, 350 W. 85th St., New York, 9/08/83, C, 83001742

Residences at 5-15 West 54th Street, 5-15 W. 54th St., New York, 1/04/90, C, 89002260

Rice, Isaac L., Mansion, 346 W. 89th St., New York, 6/25/80, B, C, a, 80002711

Riverside Drive-West 80th-81st Streets Historic District, Riverside Dr., W. 80th and W. 81st Sts., New York, 5/10/84, C, 84002790

Riverside Park and Drive, From 72nd St. to 129th St., New York, 9/02/83, C, g, 83001743

Riverside-West 105th Street Historic District, Roughly bounded by W. End Ave., Riverside Dr., W. 104th and W. 106th Sts., New York, 8/19/80, C, 80002712

Robbins & Appleton Building, 1-5 Bond St., New York, 10/29/82, C, 82001204

Robeson, Paul, Home, 555 Edgecombe Ave., New York, 12/08/76, B, g, NHL, 76001248

Rockefeller Center, Bounded by Fifth Ave., W. Forty-eighth St., Seventh Ave., & W. Fifty-first St., New York, 12/23/87, A, C, NHL, 87002591

Rogers, John S., House, 53 E. 79th St., New York, 6/30/83, C, 83001744

Roosevelt, Sara Delano, Memorial House, 47 and 49 E. 65th St., New York, 3/28/80, B, 80002713

Rowhouses at 322-344 East 69th Street, 322-344 E. 69th St., New York, 9/07/84, C, 84002793

Saint Mark's Historic District (Boundary Increase), E. 9th, 10th & N Sts. & S. side of Stuyvesant St., New York, 9/05/85, C, 85001956

Salmagundi Club, 47 5th Ave., New York, 7/25/74, A, B, C, 74001275

Sanger, Margaret, Clinic, 17 W. 16th St., New York, 9/14/93, A, B, NHL, 93001599

Schermerhorn Row Block, Block bounded by Front, Fulton, and South Sts., and Burling Slip, New York, 2/18/71, A, C, 71000547

Schinasi House, 351 Riverside Dr., New York, 4/23/80, C, 80002714

Schomburg Center for Research in Black Culture, 103 W. 135th St., New York, 9/21/78, A, 78001881

Scott, Gen. Winfield, House, 24 W. 12th St., New York, 11/07/73, B, NHL, 73001222

Scribner Building, 153–157 5th Ave., New York, 5/06/80, C, 80002715

Sea and Land Church, 61 Henry St., New York, 4/09/80, A, C, a, 80002716

Seventh Regiment Armory, 643 Park Ave., New York, 4/14/75, A, C, NHL, 75001208

Sidewalk Clock at 1501 3rd Avenue, Manhattan [Sidewalk Clocks of New York City TR], 1501 3rd Ave., New York, 4/18/85, A, C, 85000926

Sidewalk Clock at 200 5th Avenue, Manhattan [Sidewalk Clocks of New York City TR], 200 5th Ave., New York, 4/18/85, A, C, 85000927

Sidewalk Clock at 519 3rd Avenue, Manhattan [Sidewalk Clocks of New York City TR], 519 3rd Ave., New York, 4/18/85, A, C, 85000928

Sidewalk Clock at 522 5th Avenue, Manhattan [Sidewalk Clocks of New York City TR], 522 5th Ave., New York, 4/18/85, A, C, b, 85000929

Sidewalk Clock at 783 5th Avenue, Manhattan [Sidewalk Clocks of New York City TR], 783 5th Ave., New York, 4/18/85, A, C, 85000930

Sinclair, Harry F., House, 2 E. 79th St., New York, 6/02/78, B, NHL, 78001882

Smallpox Hospital, Welfare Island, New York, 3/16/72, A, C, 72000881

Smith, Abigail Adams, Museum, 421 E. 61st St., New York, 1/12/73, C, 73001223

Smith, Alfred E., House, 25 Oliver St., New York, 11/28/72, B, NHL, 72000882

Smith, Fleming, Warehouse, 451-453 Washington St., New York, 5/26/83, C, 83001745

Sniffen Court Historic District, E. 36th St., between Lexington and 3rd Aves., New York, 11/28/73, C, 73001224

Society for the Lying-In Hospital, 305 2nd Ave., New York, 9/01/83, A, C, 83001746

Sofia Warehouse, 43 W. 61st St., New York, 9/27/84, C, 84002801

Soho Historic District, Roughly bounded by W. Broadway, Houston, Crosby, and Canal Sts., New York, 6/29/78, A, C, NHL, 78001883

South Street Seaport, Bounded by Burling (John St.) and Peck Slips, and Water and South Sts., New York, 10/18/72, A, C, 72000883

South Street Seaport Historic District, Roughly bounded by East River, Brooklyn Bridge, Fletcher Allry, Pearl, and South Sts., New York, 12/12/78, A, C, D, 78001884

St. Andrew's Episcopal Church, 2067 5th Ave., New York, 3/18/80, C, a, b, 80002717

St. Augustine's Chapel, 290 Henry St., New York, 5/06/80, C, a, 80002718

St. Bartholomew's Church and Community House, 109 E. 50th St., New York, 4/16/80, C, a, 80002719

St. Cecilia's Church and Convent, 112-120 E. 160th St., New York, 2/02/84, C, a, 84002796

St. George's Episcopal Church, 3rd Ave. and E. 16th St., New York, 12/08/76, B, a, NHL, 76001249

St. James Church, 32 James St., New York, 7/24/72, C, a, 72000884

St. Jean Baptiste Church and Rectory, 1067-1071 Lexington Ave., New York, 4/23/80, C, a, 80002720

St. Mark's Historic District, Roughly bounded by 2nd and 3rd Aves. and E. 9th and 11th Sts., New York, 11/13/74, A, C, 74001276

St. Nicholas Historic District, W. 138th and W. 139th Sts. (both sides) between 7th and 8th Aves., New York, 10/29/75, C, 75001209

St. Patrick's Cathedral, Bounded by 5th and Madison Aves., E. 50th and E. 51st Sts., New York, 12/08/76, A, C, a, NHL, 76001250

St. Paul's Chapel, Broadway between Fulton and Vesey Sts., New York, 10/15/66, C, a, NHL, 66000551

St. Peter's Roman Catholic Church, 22 Barclay St., New York, 4/23/80, C, a, 80002721

St. Thomas Church and Parish House, 1–3 W. 53rd St., New York, 4/09/80, C, a, 80002722

St. Vincent Ferrer Church and Priory, 869 and 871 Lexington Ave., New York, 6/14/84, C, a, 84002800

St.-Marks-In-The-Bowery, E. 10th St. and 2nd Ave., New York, 6/19/72, A, B, C, a, c, 72000885

Stables at 167, 169 and 171 West 89th Street, 167-171 W. 89th St., New York, 8/25/83, C, 83001747

Statue of Liberty National Monument, Ellis Island and Liberty Island, Liberty Island, New York Harbor, New York, 10/15/66, A, C, f, NPS, 66000058

Stewart, A. T., Company Store, 280 Broadway, New York, 6/02/78, B, C, NHL, 78001885

Strecker Memorial Laboratory, Welfare Island, New York, 3/16/72, A, C, 72000886

Studio Apartments, 44 W. 77th St., New York, 5/19/83, C, 83001748

Stuyvesant Square Historic District, Roughly bounded by Nathan D. Perleman Pl., 3rd Ave., E. 18th and E. 15th Sts., New York, 11/21/80, C, 80002723

Surrogate's Court, 31 Chambers St., New York, 1/29/72, C, NHL, 72000888

Sutton Place Historic District, 1–21 Sutton Pl. & 4–16 Sutton Sq., New York, 9/12/85, C, 85002294

Tenement Building at 97 Orchard Street, 97 Orchard St., New York, 5/19/92, A, C, 92000556

Theodore Roosevelt Birthplace National Historic Site, 28 E. 20th St., New York, 10/15/66, B, c, e, NPS, 66000054

Third Judicial District Courthouse, 425 Avenue of the Americas, New York, 11/09/72, C, NHL, 72000875

Tiffany and Company Building, 401 5th Ave., New York, 6/02/78, A, C, NHL, 78001886

Tilden, Samuel J., House, 14–15 Gramercy Park South, New York, 5/11/76, B, C, NHL, 76001251

Town Hall, 113–123 W. 43rd St., New York, 4/23/80, A, C, 80002724

New York County—Continued

Triangle Shirtwaist Factory, 23–29 Washington Pl., New York, 7/17/91, A, NHL, 91002050

Trinity Chapel Complex, 15 W. 25th St., New York, 12/16/82, C, a, 82001205

Trinity Church and Graveyard, Broadway and Wall St., New York, 12/08/76, A, C, a, d, NHL, 76001252

Tudor City Historic District, Roughly bounded by Fourty-third St., First Ave., Fourty-first St., and Second Ave., New York, 9/11/86, C, 86002516

Turtle Bay Gardens Historic District, 226-246 E. 49th St. and 227-245 E. 48th St., New York, 7/21/83, A, C, 83001750

Tweed Courthouse, 52 Chambers St., New York, 9/25/74, B, C, NHL, 74001277

U.S. Customhouse, Bowling Green, New York, 1/31/72, C, NHL, 72000889

U.S. General Post Office, 8th Ave. between 31st and 33rd Sts., New York, 1/29/73, C, 73002257

US Courthouse, 40 Foley Sq., New York, 9/02/87, A, C, 87001596

US Post Office—Canal Street Station [US Post Offices in New York State, 1858-1943, TR], 350 Canal St., New York, 5/11/89, A, C, 88002358

US Post Office—Church Street Station [US Post Offices in New York State, 1858-1943, TR], 90 Church St., New York, 5/11/89, A, C, 88002359

US Post Office—Cooper Station [US Post Offices in New York State, 1858-1943, TR], 96 Fourth St., New York, 5/11/89, A, C, 88002360

US Post Office—Inwood Station [US Post Offices in New York State, 1858-1943, TR], 90 Vermilyea Ave., New York, 5/11/89, A, C, 88002361

US Post Office—Knickerbocker Station [US Post Offices in New York State, 1858-1943, TR], 130 E. Broadway, New York, 5/11/89, A, C, 88002362

US Post Office—Lenox Hill Station [US Post Offices in New York State, 1858-1943, TR], 221 E. 70th St., New York, 5/11/89, A, C, 88002363

US Post Office—Madison Square Station [US Post Offices in New York State, 1858-1943, TR], 149–153 E. 23rd St., New York, 5/11/89, A, C, 88002364

US Post Office—Old Chelsea Station [US Post Offices in New York State, 1858-1943, TR], 217 W. 18th St., New York, 5/11/89, A, C, 88002365

USS EDSON (DD-946), Intrepid Sq., foot of 46th St., New York, 6/21/90, C, g, NHL, 90000333

USS INTREPID (aircraft carrier), Intrepid Sq., New York, 1/14/86, A, g, NHL, 86000082

Union Theological Seminary, W. 120th St. and Broadway, New York, 4/23/80, A, C, a, 80002725

United Charities Building Complex, 105 E. 22nd St, . 289 Park Ave. S. and 111-113 E. 22nd St., New York, 3/28/85, B, C, NHL, 85000661

University Club, 1 W. 54th St., New York, 4/16/80, C, 80002726

University Settlement House, 184 Eldridge St., New York, 9/11/86, A, 86002515

Upper East Side Historic District, Roughly bounded by 3rd and 5th Aves., 59th and 79th Sts., New York, 9/07/84, C, 84002803

Van Rensselar, Stephen, House, 149 Mulberry St., New York, 6/16/83, C, 83001751

Vanderbilt, Mrs. Graham Fair, House, 60 E. 93rd St., New York, 10/29/82, C, 82001206

Verdi, Giuseppe, Monument, Verdi Square Park, New York, 10/04/90, A, C, 90002223

Villard Houses, 29 1/2 50th St., 24–26 E. 51st St., and 451, 453, 455, and 457 Madison Ave., New York, 9/02/75, B, C, a, 75001210

WAVERTREE, Pier 17, foot of Fulton St., New York, 6/13/78, A, C, 78001887

Waldo, Gertrude Rhinelander, Mansion, 867 Madison Ave., New York, 5/06/80, C, 80002727

Warburg, Felix M., Mansion, 1109 5th Ave., New York, 10/29/82, C, 82001207

Watson, James, House, 7 State St., New York, 7/24/72, C, a, 72000891

Webster Hotel, 40 W. 45th St., New York, 9/07/84, C, 84002806

West 67th Street Artists' Colony Historic District, 1–39 and 40–50 W. 67th St., New York, 7/11/85, A, C, 85001522

West 73rd-74th Street Historic District, 73rd, 74th Sts. and Columbus Ave., New York, 9/08/83, C, 83001752

West 76th Street Historic District, W. 76th St., New York, 7/24/80, C, 80002728

West End Collegiate Church and Collegiate School, W. End Ave. and W. 77th St., New York, 5/06/80, C, a, 80002729

Westchester House, 541–551 Broome St., New York, 3/20/86, A, C, 86000450

Woolworth Building, 233 Broadway, New York, 11/13/66, A, C, NHL, 66000554

Yiddish Art Theatre, 189 Second Ave., New York, 9/19/85, A, C, 85002427

Niagara County

Adams Power Plant Transformer House, Buffalo Ave. near Portage Rd., Niagara Falls, 6/11/75, A, C, NHL, 75001212

Deveaux School Historic District, 2900 Lewiston Rd., Niagara Falls, 6/05/74, A, a, NHL, 74001281

Fort Niagara Light [U.S. Coast Guard Lighthouses and Light Stations on the Great Lakes TR], Niagara River, Youngstown, 7/19/84, A, C, 84002809

Frontier House, 460 Center St., Lewiston, 7/08/74, A, C, 74001278

Herschell, Allan, Carousel Factory, 180 Thompson St., North Tonawanda, 4/18/85, A, C, 85000856

Holley-Rankine House, 525 Riverside Dr., Niagara Falls, 10/04/79, B, C, 79003793

Lewiston Mound, Address Restricted, Lewiston vicinity, 1/21/74, D, 74001279

Lewiston Portage Landing Site, Address Restricted, Lewiston vicinity, 7/18/74, A, D, 74001280

Lockport Industrial District, Bounded roughly by Erie Canal, Gooding, Clinton, and Water Sts., Lockport, 11/11/75, A, C, 75001211

Lowertown Historic District, Roughly bounded by Erie Canal and New York Central RR, Lockport, 6/04/73, A, C, 73001225

Moore, Benjamin C., Mill, Pine St. on the Erie Canal, Lockport, 6/19/73, A, C, 73001226

Niagara Falls Public Library, 1022 Main St., Niagara Falls, 6/05/74, A, C, 74001282

Niagara Reservation, Niagara Reservation, Niagara Falls, 10/15/66, A, NHL, 66000555

Old Fort Niagara, N of Youngstown on NY 18, Youngstown vicinity, 10/15/66, A, D, NHL, 66000556

Riviera Theatre, 27 Webster St., North Tonawanda, 3/20/80, A, C, 80002731

St. John's Episcopal Church, 117 Main St., Youngstown, 5/10/90, C, a, 90000687

Thirty Mile Point Light [U.S. Coast Guard Lighthouses and Light Stations on the Great Lakes TR], Niagara River, Somerset, 7/19/84, A, C, 84003922

U.S. Customhouse, 2245 Whirlpool St., Niagara Falls, 7/16/73, A, C, 73001227

US Post Office—Lockport [US Post Offices in New York State, 1858-1943, TR], 1 East Ave., Lockport, 5/11/89, A, C, 88002345

US Post Office—Middleport [US Post Offices in New York State, 1858-1943, TR], 42 Main St., Middleport, 5/11/89, A, C, 88002353

US Post Office—Niagara Falls Main [US Post Offices in New York State, 1858-1943, TR], Main and Walnut Sts., Niagara Falls, 5/11/89, A, C, 88002379

US Post Office—North Tonawanda [US Post Offices in New York State, 1858-1943, TR], 141 Goundry St., North Tonawanda, 5/11/89, A, C, 88002357

Union Station, 95 Union Ave., Lockport, 12/02/77, A, C, 77000966

Van Horn Mansion, 2165 Lockport—Olcott Rd., Newfane vicinity, 9/09/91, A, C, 91001149

Whitney Mansion, 335 Buffalo Ave., Niagara Falls, 1/17/74, B, C, 74001283

Williams, Johann, Farm, 10831 Cayuga Dr., Niagara Falls, 1/10/80, A, C, a, 80002730

Oneida County

Arsenal House, 514 W. Dominick St., Rome, 7/18/74, A, C, 74001284

Ava Town Hall, NY 26 S of jct. with Ava Rd., Ava, 5/18/92, C, 92000453

Boonville Historic District, Schuyler, Post, W. Main and Summit Sts., Boonville, 11/16/79, A, C, 79001608

Byington Mill (Frisbie & Stansfield Knitting Company), 421–423 Broad St., Utica, 5/27/93, A, C, 93000458

Clinton Village Historic District, North, South, East, West Park Rows, Marvin, Williams, Chestnut, Fountain, College and Utica Sts., Clinton, 6/14/82, A, C, 82003389

Oneida County—Continued

Conkling, Roscoe, House, 3 Rutger St., Utica, 5/15/75, B, NHL, 75001214

Doyle Hardware Building, 330–334 Main St., Utica, 6/10/93, A, C, 93000498

Erwin Library and Pratt House, 104 and 106 Schuyler St., Boonville, 8/14/73, A, B, C, 73001228

First Baptist Church of Deerfield, Herkimer Rd., Utica, 7/11/85, C, a, d, 85001497

First Congregational Free Church, 177 N. Main St., Oriskany Falls, 1/25/79, A, C, a, 79001609

First Presbyterian Church, 1605 Genesee St., Utica, 11/03/88, C, a, 88002172

Five Lock Combine and Locks 37 and 38, Black River Canal, NY 46, Boonville, 3/20/73, A, C, 73001229

Floyd, Gen. William, House, W side of Main St., Westernville, 7/17/71, B, NHL, 71000549

Fort Stanwix National Monument, Bounded by Dominick, Spring, Liberty, and James Sts., Rome, 10/15/66, A, e, NHL, NPS, 66000057

Fountain Elms, 318 Genesee St., Utica, 11/03/72, B, C, 72001599

Gansevoort-Bellamy Historic District, Roughly bounded by Liberty, Stuben, and Huntington Sts. to Bissel, Rome, 11/12/75, C, a, g, 75001213

Hamilton College Chapel, Hamilton College campus, Clinton, 11/03/72, A, C, a, 72000892

Holland Patent Stone Churches Historic District, Roughly bounded by Main St., Park Ave., Park Pl. and Willow Cr., Holland Patent, 11/21/91, A, C, a, 91001670

Hurd & Fitzgerald Building, 400 Main St., Utica, 6/25/93, A, C, 93000500

Jervis Public Library, 613 N. Washington St., Rome, 11/04/82, B, C, 82001208

Lower Genesee Street Historic District, Roughly bounded by Genesee, Liberty, Seneca, and Whitesboro Sts. (both sides), Utica, 10/29/82, A, C, 82001209

Mappa Hall, Mappa Ave., Barneveld, 5/12/82, B, C, 82003388

Middle Mill Historic District, NY 5A, New York Mills, 5/28/76, A, C, a, 76001254

New Century Club, 253 Genesee St., Utica, 9/12/85, A, C, 85002289

New York Central Railroad Adirondack Division Historic District, NYCRR Right-of-Way, Remson vicinity, 12/23/93, A, C, 93001451

Norton, Rev. Asahel, Homestead, Norton Rd., Kirkland vicinity, 7/11/85, A, B, 85001546

Oriskany Battlefield, 5 mi. E of Rome on NY 69, Rome vicinity, 10/15/66, A, f, NHL, 66000558

Root, Elihu, House, 101 College Hill Rd., Clinton, 11/28/72, B, NHL, 72000893

Rutger-Steuben Park Historic District, Roughly bounded by Taylor and Howard Aves. including both sides of Rutger Ave. and Steuben Park, Utica, 9/19/73, C, 73001230

St. Joseph's Church, 704–708 Columbia St., Utica, 8/22/77, A, C, a, 77000967

Stanley Theater, 259 Genesee St., Utica, 8/13/76, A, C, g, 76001255

Tower Homestead and Masonic Temple, 210 Tower St. and Sanger St., Waterville, 10/05/77, B, C, 77000968

US Post Office—Boonville [US Post Offices in New York State, 1858-1943, TR], 101 Main St., Boonville, 11/17/88, A, C, 88002457

Union Station, Main St. between John and 1st Sts., Utica, 4/28/75, A, C, 75001215

Utica Daily Press Building, 310–312 Main St., Utica, 6/10/93, A, C, 93000501

Utica Public Library, 303 Genesee St., Utica, 10/29/82, A, C, 82001210

Utica State Hospital, 1213 Court St., Utica, 10/26/71, A, C, NHL, 71000548

Vernon Center Green Historic District, Roughly bounded by Park St., Vernon, 9/19/85, C, a, 85002431

Waterville Triangle Historic District, Stafford Ave., Main and White Sts., Waterville, 4/04/78, A, C, 78001888

Weaver, Gen. John G., House, 711 Herkimer Rd., Utica, 12/07/89, C, 89002093

Welsh Calvinistic Methodist Church, Prospect St., Remsen, 1/13/88, A, C, a, 87002275

Whitestown Town Hall, 8 Park Ave., Whitesboro, 11/26/73, B, C, 73001231

Onondaga County

Alvord House, N of Syracuse on Berwick Rd., Syracuse vicinity, 8/27/76, A, D, 76001257

Amos Block, 210–216 W. Water St., Syracuse, 11/16/78, A, C, 78001890

Armory Square Historic District, S. Clinton, S. Franklin, Walton, W. Fayette, and W. Jefferson Sts., Syracuse, 9/07/84, A, C, 84002816

Bradley, Dan, House, 59 South St., Marcellus, 12/12/78, C, 78001889

Brown, Alexander, House, 726 W. Onondaga St., Syracuse, 11/03/88, B, C, 88002376

Camillus Union Free School, Jct. of First and LeRoy Sts., Camillus, 5/28/91, A, C, 91000628

Central New York Telephone and Telegraph Building, 311 Montgomery St., Syracuse, 4/03/73, A, C, 73001234

Central Technical High School, Central Ave. and Main St., Syracuse, 4/09/81, A, C, 81000662

Community Place, S of Skaneateles at 725 Sheldon Rd., Skaneateles vicinity, 4/20/79, A, C, a, 79001611

Crouse College, Syracuse University, Syracuse University campus, Syracuse, 7/30/74, A, C, 74001285

Delphi Baptist Church, Oran-Delphi Rd., Delphi Falls, 8/24/79, A, C, a, d, 79001610

Delphi Village School, East Rd., Delphi Falls, 5/22/86, A, C, 86001152

Elbridge Hydraulic Industry Archeological District, Address Restricted, Elbridge vicinity, 6/15/82, A, D, 82003391

Genesee Street Hill-Limestone Plaza Historic District, Roughly both sides of Genesee St., from Chapel St. to Limestone Plaza, Fayetteville, 7/29/82, C, 82003392

Gere Bank Building, 121 E. Water St., Syracuse, 3/16/72, C, 72000894

Gillett, William J., House, 515 W. Onondaga St., Syracuse, 5/06/82, C, 82003393

Gleason, Lucius, House, 314 Second St., Liverpool, 5/10/90, B, C, 90000693

Grace Episcopal Church, 819 Madison St., Syracuse, 3/20/73, C, a, 73001235

Gridley, John, House, 205 E. Seneca Tnpk., Syracuse, 8/16/77, A, C, 77000969

Hall of Languages, Syracuse University, Syracuse University campus, Syracuse, 9/20/73, A, C, 73001236

Hanover Square Historic District, 101–203 E. Water, 120–200 E. Genesee, 113 Salina, 109–114 S. Warren Sts., Syracuse, 6/22/76, A, C, 76001258

Hawley-Green Street Historic District, Green St. and Hawley Ave., Syracuse, 5/02/79, C, 79001613

Hutchinson, Gen. Orrin, House, 4311 W. Seneca Tpke., Onondaga, 4/13/73, C, 73001233

Ives, Dr. John, House, 6575 E. Seneca Turnpike, Jamesville, 8/29/85, C, 85001938

Jordan Village Historic District, Roughly bounded by N. Main, S. Main, Elbridge, Clinton, Hamilton, Lawrence, and Mechanic Sts., Jordan, 9/15/83, C, 83001753

Kelsey-Davey Farm, NE of Skaneateles on Old Seneca Tpke., Skaneateles vicinity, 4/16/80, A, C, 80004277

King, Polaski, House, 2270 Valley Dr., Syracuse, 4/20/79, B, C, 79001614

Loew's State Theater, 362–374 S. Salina St., Syracuse, 5/02/77, A, C, 77000970

Manlius Village Historic District, Pleasant, Franklin, North, Clinton, and E. Seneca Sts., Manlius, 11/06/73, A, C, 73001232

Montgomery Street-Columbus Circle Historic District, E. Jefferson, E. Onondaga, Montgomery and E. Fayette Sts., Syracuse, 2/19/80, C, 80004278

Mycenae Schoolhouse, NY 5, Manlius, 8/11/83, C, 83001754

Nine Mile Creek Aqueduct, NE of Camillus on Thompson Rd., Camillus vicinity, 5/17/76, A, C, 76001256

North Salina Street Historic District, 517–519 to 947–951 & 522–524 to 850–854 N. Salina St., 1121 N. Townsend St. & 504–518 Prospect Ave., Syracuse, 9/19/85, C, a, 85002441

Onondaga County Savings Bank Building, 101 S. Salina St., Syracuse, 2/24/71, C, 71000550

Onondaga County War Memorial, 200 Madison St., Syracuse, 12/19/88, C, f, g, 88002754

Oswego-Oneida Streets Historic District, Oswego, East and West Sts., and Sunset Terr., Baldwinsville, 7/29/82, C, 82003390

Pi Chapter House of Psi Upsilon Fraternity, 101 College Pl., Syracuse, 5/16/85, A, C, 85001124

Robinson Site (AO67-02-0001), Address Restricted, Cicero, Brewerton vicinity, 3/28/85, D, 85000660

Skaneateles Historic District, Jordan, Fennell, E. and W. Genesee Sts., Skaneateles, 5/10/84, C, 84002818

Onondaga County—Continued

Smith, Reuel E., House, 28 W. Lake St., Skaneateles, 7/27/79, C, 79001612

Snell, Levi, House, 416 Brooklea Dr., Fayetteville, 8/20/87, C, 87001365

South Salina Street Historic District, 111 W. Kennedy St. and 1555–1829 and 1606–1830 S. Salina St., Syracuse, 3/27/86, A, C, a, 86000671

St. Paul's Cathedral and Parish House, 310 Montgomery St., Syracuse, 12/01/78, A, C, a, 78001891

Stickley, Gustav, House, 438 Columbus Ave., Syracuse, 8/23/84, C, 84002820

Syracuse City Hall, 233 E. Washington St., Syracuse, 8/27/76, A, C, 76001259

Syracuse Savings Bank, 102 N. Salina St., Syracuse, 2/18/71, A, C, 71000551

Syracuse University-Comstock Tract Buildings, Syracuse University campus, Syracuse, 7/22/80, C, 80004279

Third National Bank, 107 James St., Syracuse, 9/22/72, A, C, 72000896

Walnut Park Historic District, Walnut Pl. and Walnut Ave., Syracuse, 9/15/83, C, 83001755

Weighlock Building, SE corner of Erie Blvd. E. and Montgomery St., Syracuse, 2/18/71, A, C, 71000552

Whig Hill and Dependencies, E. of Plainville at jct. of W. Genesee and Gates Rds., Plainville vicinity, 5/12/75, B, C, 75001217

White Memorial Building, 106 E. Washington St., Syracuse, 2/06/73, A, C, 73001237

White, Hamilton, House, 307 S. Townsend St., Syracuse, 7/20/73, B, C, 73001238

Wilcox Octagon House, 5420 W. Genesee St., Camillus, 7/28/83, C, 83001756

Ontario County

Adelaide Avenue School [Canandaigua MRA], 108-116 Adelaide Ave., Canandaigua, 4/26/84, A, C, 84002822

Ashcroft, 112 Jay St., Geneva, 11/20/75, C, 75001218

Barron, Thomas, House, 1160 Canandaigua Rd., Seneca, 10/06/88, C, 88001854

Belhurst Castle, Lochland Rd., Geneva, 1/29/87, C, 86003728

Benham House [Canandaigua MRA], 280-282 S. Main St., Canandaigua, 4/26/84, C, 84002823

Boughton Hill, Address Restricted, Victor vicinity, 10/15/66, D, NHL, 66000559

Brigham Hall [Canandaigua MRA], 229 Bristol St., Canandaigua, 9/29/84, A, C, 84002827

Building at 426 South Main Street [Canandaigua MRA], 426 S. Main St., Canandaigua, 4/26/84, C, 84002850

Canandaigua Historic District [Canandaigua MRA], Roughly Main St. from Chapel to Saltonstall Sts.; Howell, Gibson, Gorham, Bristol, Bemis and Center Sts., Canandaigua, 4/26/84, C, 84002856

Chapin, Thaddeus, House [Canandaigua MRA], 128 Thad Chapin St., Canandaigua, 4/26/84, C, 84002861

Clifton Springs Sanitarium, 11 and 9 E. Main St, Clifton Springs, 4/06/79, B, C, 79001615

Clifton Springs Sanitarium Historic District, E. Main St. between Crane and Prospect, Clifton Springs, 5/24/90, A, C, 90000818

Cobblestone Manor [Canandaigua MRA], 495 N. Main St., Canandaigua, 4/26/84, C, 84002862

Cobblestone Railroad Pumphouse [Cobblestone Architecture of New York State MPS], Main St., Victor, 5/22/92, A, C, 92000551

East Bloomfield Historic District, Roughly Main, South, Park Sts. and NY 5, East Bloomfield, 11/13/89, A, C, 89001947

Felt Cobblestone General Store [Cobblestone Architecture of New York State MPS], 6452 Victor—Manchester Rd., Victor, 5/22/92, C, 92000553

First Baptist Church of Phelps [Cobblestone Architecture of New York State MPS], 40 Church St., Phelps, 5/22/92, C, a, 92000554

Geneva Hall and Trinity Hall, Hobart & William Smith College, S. Main St., Geneva, 7/16/73, A, C, 73001241

Granger Cottage [Canandaigua MRA], 60 Granger St., Canandaigua, 4/26/84, C, b, 84002865

Granger, Francis, House [Canandaigua MRA], 426 N. Main St., Canandaigua, 4/26/84, C, 84002867

Harmon Cobblestone Farmhouse and Cobblestone Smokehouse [Cobblestone Architecture of New York State MPS], 983 Smith Rd., Phelps, 5/22/92, C, 92000552

Marshall House [Canandaigua MRA], 274 Bristol St., Canandaigua, 4/26/84, C, 84002869

Nester House, 1001 Lochland Rd., Geneva vicinity, 4/09/84, C, 84002873

North Main Street Historic District, Between RR tracks and Buffalo-Chapel St., Canandaigua, 7/20/73, C, 73001239

Osborne House, 146 Maple Ave., Victor, 7/11/80, C, 80002732

Parrott Hall, W. North St. between Castle St. and Preemption Rd., Geneva, 8/12/71, A, C, 71000553

Rippey Cobblestone Farmhouse [Cobblestone Architecture of New York State MPS], 1227 Leet Rd., Seneca, 10/06/92, C, 92001051

Saltonstall Street School [Canandaigua MRA], 47 Saltonstall St., Canandaigua, 4/26/84, A, C, 84002877

Seneca Presbyterian Church, E of Stanley off NY 245 on Number Nine Rd., Stanley vicinity, 5/25/73, A, C, a, 73001242

Sonnenberg Gardens, 151 Charlotte St., Canandaigua, 9/28/73, C, 73001240

South Main Street Historic District, Irregular pattern along S. Main St., Geneva, 12/31/74, A, B, C, 74001286

St. Bridget's Roman Catholic Church Complex, 15 Church St., between Church and Michigan Sts., Bloomfield, 8/28/92, A, C, a, d, 92001052

St. John's Episcopal Church, Church St., Phelps, 11/07/78, A, C, a, 78001892

US Post Office—Canandaigua [US Post Offices in New York State, 1858-1943, TR], 28 N. Main St., Canandaigua, 11/17/88, A, C, 88002465

US Post Office—Geneva [US Post Offices in New York State, 1858-1943, TR], 67 Castle St., Geneva, 5/11/89, A, C, 88002523

Warner, Oliver, Farmstead, NY 88, Clifton Springs vicinity, 11/17/88, A, C, 88002189

Orange County

1841 Goshen Courthouse, 101 Main St., Goshen, 3/04/75, A, C, 75001219

Arden, NY 17, Harriman, 11/13/66, B, NHL, 66000561

Barr, Amelia, House [Hudson Highlands MRA], Mountain Rd., Cornwall-on-Hudson, 11/23/82, B, C, 82001211

Blake, John, House, 924 Homestead Ave., Maybrook, 12/20/84, A, B, C, D, 84000521

Bridge Street Historic District [Montgomery Village MRA], Bridge St., Montgomery, 11/21/80, C, 80002736

Bull Stone House, Hamptonburgh Rd., Campbell Hall, 7/18/74, A, C, 74001287

Bull, William, III, House, Bart Bull Rd., Montgomery vicinity, 9/25/86, C, 86002772

Bull-Jackson House, NY 416, NW of Campbell Hall, Campbell Hall vicinity, 5/17/74, A, C, 74001288

Camp Olmsted [Hudson Highlands MRA], 114 Bayview Ave., Cornwall-on-Hudson, 11/23/82, A, C, a, 82001212

Church Park Historic District, Park Pl., Main and Webster Sts., Goshen, 11/17/80, A, C, 80002735

Church of the Holy Innocents and Rectory [Hudson Highlands MRA], 112 Main St., Highland Falls, 11/23/82, C, a, 82001213

Cornwall Friends Meeting House, 275 Quaker Ave., Cornwall, 12/08/88, A, C, a, d, 88002751

Cragston Dependencies [Hudson Highlands MRA], NY 218, Highlands, 11/23/82, B, C, 82001214

Crawford, David, House, 189 Montgomery St., Newburgh, 9/27/72, B, C, 72000899

Deer Hill [Hudson Highlands MRA], 58 Deerhill Rd., Cornwall, 11/23/82, C, 82001215

Delaware and Hudson Canal, Delaware and Hudson Canal, Cuddebackville vicinity, 11/24/68, A, C, NHL, 68000051

District School No. 9, NY 17A, Goshen vicinity, 9/15/88, A, C, 88001451

Dutch Reformed Church, NE corner of Grand and 3rd Sts., Newburgh, 12/18/70, C, a, 70000425

Dutchess Quarry Cave Site, Address Restricted, Goshen vicinity, 1/18/74, D, 74001289

East End Historic District, Roughly bounded by Robinson Ave., LeRoy Pl., Water St., Bay View Terr., Monument & Renwick Sts., Newburgh, 9/12/85, A, C, 85002426

Edmonston House, NY 94, Vails Gate, 3/02/79, A, C, D, 79001616

Erie Railroad Station, Jersey Ave. and Fowler St., Port Jervis, 4/11/80, A, C, 80002739

Orange County—Continued

First Presbyterian Church of Highland Falls [Hudson Highlands MRA], 140 Main St., Highland Falls, 11/23/82, C, a, 82001216

Fort Decker, 127 W. Main St., Port Jervis, 6/13/74, A, C, 74001291

Fort Montgomery Site, Address Restricted, Fort Montgomery vicinity, 11/28/72, A, D, NHL, 72000897

Gardner, Silas, House, 1141 Union Ave., Gardnertown, 3/28/80, B, C, 80002734

Gatehouse on Deerhill Road [Hudson Highlands MRA], Deerhill Rd., Cornwall, 11/23/82, C, 82001217

Haskell House, W of New Windsor off NY 32, New Windsor vicinity, 6/04/73, C, 73001244

Highland Falls Railroad Depot [Hudson Highlands MRA], Dock Rd., Highland Falls, 11/23/82, C, 82001218

Highland Falls Village Hall [Hudson Highlands MRA], Main St., Highland Falls, 11/23/82, C, 82001219

Hill, Nathaniel, Brick House, E of Montgomery on NY 17 K, Montgomery vicinity, 1/05/78, B, C, 78001893

Historic Track, Main St., Goshen, 10/15/66, A, NHL, 66000560

Horton, Webb, House, 115 South St., Middletown, 4/26/90, C, 90000690

House at 116 Main Street [Hudson Highlands MRA], 116 Main St., Highland Falls, 11/23/82, C, 82001221

House at 37 Center Street [Hudson Highlands MRA], 37 Center St., Highland Falls, 11/23/82, C, 82001220

Knox Headquarters, Quassaick Ave. and Forge Hill Rd., Vails Gate, 11/09/72, B, NHL, 72000901

LeDoux/Healey House [Hudson Highlands MRA], 60 Deerhill Rd., Cornwall, 11/23/82, C, 82001222

Maple Lawn, 24 Downing St., Balmville, 6/28/84, C, 84002879

Mill House, Mill House Rd., Newburgh, 1/29/73, B, C, 73001245

Miller, Johannes, House [Montgomery Village MRA], 272 Union St., Montgomery, 11/21/80, B, C, 80002737

Montgomery Worsted Mills [Montgomery Village MRA], Factory St., Montgomery, 11/21/80, A, C, 80002738

Montgomery-Grand-Liberty Streets Historic District, Montgomery, Grand, and Liberty Sts., Newburgh, 7/16/73, C, a, 73001246

New Windsor Cantonment, Temple Hill Rd., New Windsor, 7/31/72, A, D, 72000898

New York State Armory, Broadway and Johnson St., Newburgh, 6/18/81, C, 81000411

Oliver Avenue Bridge, Oliver Ave., Middletown, 7/19/84, A, C, 84002882

Palisades Interstate Park, W bank of the Hudson River, Fort Lee and vicinity, 10/15/66, A, NHL, 66000890

Parry House [Hudson Highlands MRA], Michel Rd., Highland Falls, 11/23/82, C, 82001223

Patchett House [Montgomery Village MRA], 232 Ward St., Montgomery, 11/21/80, C, 80004394

Pine Terrace [Hudson Highlands MRA], Main St., Highland Falls, 11/23/82, C, 82001224

Primitive Baptist Church of Brookfield, NY 6, Slate Hill, 11/13/76, A, C, a, 76001260

River View House [Hudson Highlands MRA], 146 Bayview Ave., Cornwall, 11/23/82, C, 82001225

Smith Clove Meetinghouse, Quaker Rd., Highland Mills, 1/11/74, A, C, 74001290

Southfield Furnace Ruin, S of Monroe off NY 17, Monroe vicinity, 11/02/73, A, 73001243

Squirrels, The [Hudson Highlands MRA], 225 Main St., Highland Falls, 11/23/82, B, C, 82001226

St. Mark's Episcopal Church [Hudson Highlands MRA], Canterbury Rd. and NY 9-W, Fort Montgomery, 11/23/82, C, a, 82001227

Stonihurst [Hudson Highlands MRA], NY 218, Highland Falls, 11/23/82, A, C, 82001228

Storm King Highway [Hudson Highlands MRA], NY 218, Highlands, 11/23/82, C, 82001229

Tuxedo Park, Tuxedo Lake and environs, Tuxedo Park, 3/13/80, A, C, 80002740

U.S. Military Academy, NY 218, West Point, 10/15/66, A, D, NHL, 66000562

US Bullion Depository, West Point, New York, Address Restricted, West Point vicinity, 2/18/88, A, g, 88000027

US Post Office—Goshen [US Post Offices in New York State, 1858-1943, TR], Grand St., Goshen, 5/11/89, A, C, 88002527

US Post Office—Newburgh [US Post Offices in New York State, 1858-1943, TR], 215–217 Liberty St., Newburgh, 5/11/89, A, C, 88002367

US Post Office—Pearl River [US Post Offices in New York State, 1858-1943, TR], Franklin and Main Sts., Pearl River, 11/17/88, A, C, 88002399

US Post Office—Port Jervis [US Post Offices in New York State, 1858-1943, TR], 20 Sussex St., Port Jervis, 5/11/89, A, C, 88002408

Union Street-Academy Hill Historic District [Montgomery Village MRA], Roughly bounded by Ward St., Wallkill Ave., Sears and Hanover Sts., Montgomery, 11/21/80, C, 80004395

Warwick Village Historic District, Roughly bounded by NY 17A, High, and South Sts., Oakland, Maple, and Colonial Aves., Warwick, 9/07/84, A, C, 84002886

Washington's Headquarters, Liberty and Washington Sts., Newburgh, 10/15/66, A, B, C, NHL, 66000887

Webb Lane House [Hudson Highlands MRA], Webb Lane, Highland Falls, 11/23/82, C, 82001230

Yelverton Inn and Store, 112-116 Main St., Chester, 3/28/80, A, C, 80002733

Orleans County

Barlow, William V. N., House, 223 S. Clinton St., Albion, 9/08/83, C, 83001757

Cobblestone Historic District, Ridge Rd. (NY 104), Gaines Township, Childs, 4/19/93, C, NHL, 93001603

Mt. Albion Cemetery, NY 31, Albion, 9/27/76, C, 76001261

Orleans County Courthouse Historic District, Courthouse Sq. and environs, Albion, 8/31/79, A, C, a, 79001617

US Post Office—Albion [US Post Offices in New York State, 1858-1943, TR], Main St., Albion, 11/17/88, A, C, 88002450

US Post Office—Medina [US Post Offices in New York State, 1858-1943, TR], 128 W. Center St., Medina, 5/11/89, A, C, 88002351

Oswego County

Ames, Leonard, Farmhouse [Mexico MPS], 5707 Main St., Mexico, 11/14/91, C, 91001630

Arthur Tavern [Mexico MPS], Jct. of Clarke Rd. and NY 16, Arthur, 11/14/91, A, C, 91001632

Barlow, Smith H., House [Sandy Creek MRA], Harwood Dr., Lacona, 11/15/88, C, 88002214

Chandler, Peter, House [Mexico MPS], 5897 Main St., Mexico, 11/14/91, C, 91001626

Davis, Phineas, Farmstead [Mexico MPS], 5422 North Rd., Mexico, 6/20/91, A, C, 91000524

First Baptist Church [Sandy Creek MRA], Harwood Dr., Sandy Creek, 11/15/88, C, a, 88002218

First National Bank of Lacona [Sandy Creek MRA], Harwood Dr. and Salina St., Lacona, 11/15/88, C, 88002219

Fort Brewerton, State and Lansing Sts., Brewerton, 3/07/73, A, D, 73001247

Fort Ontario, E. 7th St. and Lake Ontario, Oswego, 12/18/70, A, C, 70000426

Fowler—Loomis House [Mexico MPS], 6022 Main St., Mexico, 11/14/91, C, 91001628

Franklin Square Historic District, Roughly bounded by 3rd, 6th, Van Buren, and Bridge Sts., Oswego, 8/04/82, C, 82003394

Holyoke Cottage [Sandy Creek MRA], Seber Shore Rd., Sandy Creek vicinity, 11/15/88, C, 88002216

Lacona Clock Tower [Sandy Creek MRA], Harwood Dr., Lacona, 11/15/88, C, 88002220

Market House, Water St., Oswego, 6/20/74, A, C, 74001292

Methodist Church [Sandy Creek MRA], Harwood Dr., Sandy Creek, 11/15/88, C, a, 88002213

Mexico Academy and Central School [Mexico MPS], 5805 Main St., Mexico, 11/14/91, C, 91001633

Mexico Octagon Barn [Mexico MPS], 5276 Ames St., Mexico, 6/20/91, A, C, 91000527

Mexico Railroad Depot [Mexico MPS], 5530 Scenic Ave., Mexico, 6/20/91, A, C, 91000523

Mexico Village Historic District [Mexico MPS], Main, Jefferson, Church and Spring Sts., Mexico, 6/20/91, A, C, 91000528

Oswego Armory, 265 W. First St., Oswego, 5/19/88, C, 88000610

Oswego City Hall, W. Oneida St., Oswego, 2/20/73, A, C, 73001248

Oswego City Library, 120 E. 2nd St., Oswego, 9/22/71, A, C, 71000554

Oswego County—Continued

Oswego Theater, 138 W. Second St., Oswego, 9/19/88, C, g, 88001590

Pitt, Newton M., House [Sandy Creek MRA], 8114 Harwood Dr., Sandy Creek, 11/15/88, C, 88002209

Pontiac Hotel, W. 1st St., Oswego, 7/21/83, C, 83001758

Pulaski Village Historic District, Jefferson, Broad, Bridge, Hubbel and Lake Sts., Pulaski, 9/08/83, C, 83004525

Red Mill Farm [Mexico MPS], 7177 Red Mill Rd., Colosse vicinity, 11/14/91, A, C, 91001629

Richardson-Bates House, 135 E. 3rd St., Oswego, 9/05/75, B, C, 75001220

Riverside Cemetery, E. River Rd. S of jct. with NY 57, Oswego vicinity, 8/19/93, C, d, 93000854

Sadler, Samuel, House [Sandy Creek MRA], N. Main St., Sandy Creek, 11/15/88, C, 88002212

Salisbury, Charles, M., House [Sandy Creek MRA], 9089 Church St., Lacona, 11/15/88, C, 88002217

Sandy Creek Historic District [Sandy Creek MRA], Jct. of Lake Rd. and US 11, Sandy Creek, 11/15/88, C, 88002208

Schroeppel House, Morgan Rd., Schroeppel, 9/09/82, C, 82003395

Selkirk Lighthouse, W of Pulaski on Lake Rd., Pulaski vicinity, 3/30/79, A, C, 79001618

Sheldon Hall, Washington Blvd., Oswego, 5/13/80, B, C, 80002741

Shoecraft, Matthew, House [Sandy Creek MRA], Ridge Rd. at Smartville Rd., Lacona, 11/15/88, C, 88002210

Skinner, Timothy, House [Mexico MPS], 5355 Scenic Ave., Mexico, 6/20/91, C, 91000526

Slack Farmstead [Mexico MPS], 5174 Row Rd., Mexico vicinity, 11/14/91, A, C, 91001627

Sloan, George B., Estate, 107 W. Van Buren St., Oswego, 8/11/88, C, 88001237

Smart, Fred, House [Sandy Creek MRA], Salina St., Lacona, 11/15/88, C, 88002215

St. John's Episcopal Church, 670 Main St., Phoenix, 5/27/93, C, a, 93000442

Stillman Farmstead [Mexico MPS], NY 104 between Co. Rt. 58 and US 11, Mexico vicinity, 6/20/91, A, C, 91000525

Sweet Memorial Building, 821 Main St., Phoenix, 4/26/90, C, 90000695

Thayer Farmstead [Mexico MPS], 5933 Church St., Mexico vicinity, 11/14/91, A, C, 91001631

Trinity Church, NY 49, Constantia, 10/29/82, A, C, a, 82001231

Tuttle, Newman, House [Sandy Creek MRA], Harwood Dr. at Ridge Rd., Lacona, 11/15/88, C, 88002211

U.S. Customhouse, W. Oneida St. between 1st and 2nd Sts., Oswego, 11/21/76, A, C, 76001262

US Post Office—Fulton [US Post Offices in New York State, 1858-1943, TR], 214 S. First St., Fulton, 5/11/89, A, C, 88002519

Van Buren, David, House, Van Buren Dr., W end at the Oswego River, Fulton vicinity, 6/09/88, C, 88000726

Van Buren, John, Tavern, NY 57 and Van Buren Dr., Fulton vicinity, 11/03/88, A, C, b, 88002377

Van Buren, Volkert, House, NY 57 and Distin Rd., Fulton vicinity, 10/07/88, C, 88001707

Walton and Willett Stone Store, 1 Seneca St., Oswego, 5/24/76, A, 76001263

Otsego County

Baker Octagon Barn [Central Plan Dairy Barns of New York TR], NY 28, Richfield Springs vicinity, 9/29/84, C, 84002887

Bresee Hall, Hardwick Dr., Oneonta, 4/12/84, A, C, 84002892

Cherry Valley Village Historic District, Roughly bounded by Alden St. and Montgomery St., Maple Ave. and Elm St., and Main St., Cherry Valley, 4/28/88, C, a, d, 88000472

Cooperstown Historic District, NY 28, NY 80 and Main St., Cooperstown, 11/18/80, A, B, C, 80002742

Fairchild Mansion, 318 Main St., Oneonta, 2/12/74, B, C, 74001294

Ford Block, 188-202 Main St., Oneonta, 9/07/84, A, C, 84002893

Fortin Site, Address Restricted, Oneonta vicinity, 11/28/80, D, 80002743

Gilbertsville Historic District, Roughly bounded by Marion Ave., Cliff and Green Sts., Grover and Sylvan Sts., Gilbertsville, 5/17/74, A, C, 74001293

Gilbertsville Historic District (Boundary Increase), Roughly bounded by incorporated village boundary, Gilbertsville, 11/04/82, A, C, 82001232

Hyde Hall, S of Springfield Center in Glimmerglass State Park, Springfield Center vicinity, 10/07/71, C, NHL, 71000555

Lunn-Musser Octagon Barn [Central Plan Dairy Barns of New York TR], S of Garrattsville, Garrattsville vicinity, 9/29/84, C, 84002897

Major's Inn and Gilbert Block, Both sides of Commercial St. near NY 51, Gilbertsville, 4/11/73, A, C, 73001249

Mann, Andrew, Inn, 33 Riverside Rd., Unadilla, 1/10/80, A, C, 80002747

Middlefield District No. 1 School, CR 35, Cooperstown vicinity, 8/13/87, A, C, 87001363

Middlefield Hamlet Historic District, CR 35, Rezen, Whiteman, and Long Patent Rds., Middlefield, 7/11/85, A, C, 85001523

Municipal Building, 238-242 Main St., Oneonta, 10/29/82, A, C, 82001233

North, Benjamin D., House, NY 166, The Plank Rd., Middlefield, 7/11/85, C, 85001499

Old Post Office, Main St., Oneonta, 11/17/78, C, 78001895

Otsdawa Creek Site, Address Restricted, Otego vicinity, 7/22/80, D, 80002746

Otsego County Courthouse, 193 Main St., Cooperstown, 6/20/72, A, C, 72000902

Russ-Johnsen Site, Address Restricted, Unadilla vicinity, 7/22/80, D, 80002748

South Worcester Historic District, Jct. of Co. Rt. 40 and Co. Rt. 39 and W along 40, South Worcester, 11/05/92, C, 92001563

Stonehouse Farm, E of Oneonta on NY 7, Oneonta, 11/19/80, A, C, 80002744

Sunnyside, 72 E. Main St., Richfield Springs, 3/10/88, C, 88000211

Swart—Wilcox House, Jct. of Wilcox Ave. and Henry St., Oneonta, 5/24/90, A, C, 90000817

Tianderah, Off NY 51, Gilbertsville, 11/02/78, C, 78001894

US Post Office—Cooperstown [US Post Offices in New York State, 1858-1943, TR], 28-40 Main St., Cooperstown, 11/17/88, A, C, 88002473

US Post Office—Richfield Springs [US Post Offices in New York State, 1858-1943, TR], 12 E. Main St., Richfield Springs, 5/11/89, A, C, 88002422

Unadilla Village Historic District [Unadilla Village MPS], Roughly, Main St. from Hopkins St. to Butternut Rd. and Bridge St. fom Main to Watson St., Unadilla, 9/04/92, A, C, 92001079

Unadilla Waterworks [Unadilla Village MPS], Jct. of Kilkenny Rd. and Clifton St. and jct. of Martin Brook Rd. and Rod & Gun Club Rd., Unadilla, 9/04/92, A, C, 92001080

Walnut Street Historic District, Ford Ave., Walnut, Dietz, Elm and Maple Sts., Oneonta, 7/30/80, A, C, 80002745

Worcester Historic District, Both sides of Main St. (NY 7) between Decatur and Cook Sts., Worcester, 6/10/75, A, C, 75001221

Wright, Roswell, House, 25 Main St., Unadilla, 9/01/88, A, C, 88001271

Putnam County

Birches, The [Hudson Highlands MRA], Cat Rock Rd., Philipstown, 11/23/82, C, 82001259

Boscobel, N of Garrison on NY 9D, Garrison vicinity, 11/07/77, C, b, 77000971

Brewster, Walter, House, Oak St., Brewster, 10/04/78, B, C, 78001896

Castle Rock, NY 9D, Garrison, 12/12/77, C, 77000972

Champlin, H. D., & Son Horseshoeing and Wagonmaking [Hudson Highlands MRA], 286 Main St., Nelsonville, 11/23/82, C, 82001234

Cold Spring Cemetery Gatehouse [Hudson Highlands MRA], Peekskill Rd., Nelsonville, 11/23/82, C, 82001236

Cold Spring Historic District [Hudson Highlands MRA], Roughly Main, Fair, Chestnut Sts., and Paulding Ave., Cold Spring, 11/23/82, A, C, 82001235

DeRham Farm, N of Garrison on Indian Brook Rd., Garrison vicinity, 3/28/80, A, C, 80002750

Dykman, J. Y., Flour and Feed Store [Hudson Highlands MRA], 289 Main St., Nelsonville, 11/23/82, C, 82001237

Dykman, J. Y., Store [Hudson Highlands MRA], 255 Main St., Nelsonville, 11/23/82, C, 82001238

Eagle's Rest [Hudson Highlands MRA], NY 9-D, Philipstown, 11/23/82, C, 82001239

Putnam County—Continued

Fair Lawn [Hudson Highlands MRA], NY 9-D, Cold Spring, 11/23/82, B, C, 82001240

First Baptist Church of Cold Spring [Hudson Highlands MRA], Main St., Nelsonville, 11/23/82, C, a, 82001241

First National Bank of Brewster, Main St., Brewster, 1/07/88, C, 87002277

Fish and Fur Club [Hudson Highlands MRA], 258 Main St., Nelsonville, 11/23/82, C, 82001242

Garrison Grist Mill Historic District, Jct. of NY 9D and Upper Station Rd., Garrison Four Corners vicinity, 12/23/93, C, 93001434

Garrison Landing Historic District [Hudson Highlands MRA], Bounded by Hudson River and NY Central RR Tracks, Garrison, 11/23/82, A, C, 82001243

Garrison Union Free School [Hudson Highlands MRA], NY 9-D, Garrison, 11/23/82, C, 82001244

Gilead Cemetery, Mechanic St., Carmel, 12/01/88, A, C, d, 88002684

Glenfields [Hudson Highlands MRA], Old Manitou Rd., Philipstown, 11/23/82, B, C, 82001245

House at 249 Main Street [Hudson Highlands MRA], 249 Main St., Nelsonville, 7/31/89, C, 82005382

House at 3 Crown Street [Hudson Highlands MRA], 3 Crown St., Nelsonville, 11/23/82, C, 82001246

Hurst-Pierrepont Estate [Hudson Highlands MRA], NY 9-D, Garrison, 11/23/82, B, C, 82001247

Hustis House [Hudson Highlands MRA], 328 Main St., Nelsonville, 11/23/82, C, 82001248

Indian Brook Road Historic District, Jct. of Indian Brook Rd. and US 9, Garrison, 8/19/93, A, C, 93000853

Mandeville House [Hudson Highlands MRA], Lower Station Hill Rd., Philipstown, 11/23/82, A, C, 82001251

Montrest [Hudson Highlands MRA], Late Gate Rd., Philipstown, 11/23/82, C, 82001252

Moore House [Hudson Highlands MRA], Nelson Ln., Garrison, 11/23/82, C, 82001249

Normandy Grange [Hudson Highlands MRA], NY 9-D, Philipstown, 11/23/82, C, 82001250

Old Albany Post Road, US 9, Philipstown vicinity, 7/08/82, A, 82003396

Old Southeast Church, N of Brewster on NY 22 off Putnam Lake Rd., Brewster vicinity, 7/24/72, C, a, 72000903

Old Southeast Town Hall, Main St., Brewster, 7/24/79, A, C, 79001619

Oulagisket [Hudson Highlands MRA], NY 9-D, Philipstown, 11/23/82, B, C, 82001253

Plumbush [Hudson Highlands MRA], NY 9D between Peekskill and Moffet Rds., Philipstown, 1/30/92, B, C, 82005386

Putnam County Courthouse, At jct. of NY 52 and NY 301, Carmel, 8/11/76, A, C, 76001264

Reed Memorial Library, 2 Brewster Ave., Carmel, 3/28/80, A, C, 80002749

Rock Lawn and Carriage House [Hudson Highlands MRA], NY 9-D, Garrison, 11/23/82, C, 82001254

Thompson, Walter, House and Carriage House [Hudson Highlands MRA], Philipsebrook Rd., Philipstown, 11/23/82, B, C, 82001255

Tompkins Corners United Methodist Church, Peekskill Hollow Rd., Putnam Valley vicinity, 3/31/83, A, C, a, 83001759

Walker House [Hudson Highlands MRA], Cat Rock Rd., Garrison, 11/23/82, C, 82001256

West Point Foundry, Foundry Cove between NY 90 and NY Central RR tracks, Cold Spring, 4/11/73, A, 73001250

Wilson House [Hudson Highlands MRA], Lower Station Rd., Garrison, 11/23/82, C, 82001257

Woodlawn [Hudson Highlands MRA], NY 9-D, Garrison, 11/23/82, C, 82001258

Queens County

68th Avenue-64th Place Historic District [Ridgewood MRA], Roughly 64th Pl. from Catalpa Ave. to 68th Ave. from 64th St. to 65th St., New York, 9/30/83, C, 83001763

75th Avenue-61st Street Historic District [Ridgewood MRA], Roughly bounded by St. Felix Ave., 60th Lane, 60th and 62nd Sts., New York, 9/30/83, C, 83001764

Allen-Beville House, 29 Center Dr., New York, 9/22/83, C, 83001760

Armstrong, Louis, House, 3456 107th St., New York, 5/11/76, B, g, NHL, 76001265

Bowne, John, House, 37-01 Bowne St., New York, 9/13/77, A, B, C, a, 77000974

Bunche, Ralph, House, 115–125 Grosvenor Rd., New York, 5/11/76, B, g, NHL, 76001266

Central Avenue Historic District [Ridgewood MRA], Roughly bounded by Myrtle and 70th Ave., and 65th and 66th Sts., New York, 9/30/83, C, 83001761

Central Ridgewood Historic District [Ridgewood MRA], Roughly bounded by Fresh Pond Rd., Putnam, 68th, Forest, Catalpa, Onderdonk, and 71st Aves., New York, 9/30/83, C, 83001762

Cooper Avenue Row Historic District [Ridgewood MRA], 6434-6446 Cooper Ave., New York, 9/30/83, C, 83001765

Cornelia-Putnam Historic District [Ridgewood MRA], Roughly bounded by Jefferson St., Putnam, Wyckoff, and Myrtle Aves., New York, 9/30/83, C, 83001766

Cornell Farmhouse, 73-50 Little Neck Pkwy, New York, 7/24/79, C, 79001620

Cypress Avenue East Historic District [Ridgewood MRA], Roughly bounded by Linden and Cornelia Sts., Seneca and St. Nicholas Aves., New York, 9/30/83, C, 83001767

Cypress Avenue West Historic District [Ridgewood MRA], Roughly bounded by St. Nicholas and Seneca Aves., Linden and Stockholm Sts., New York, 9/30/83, C, 83001768

First Reformed Church, 153 Jamaica Ave., New York, 4/16/80, C, a, 80002753

Flushing High School, 35-01 Union St., Queens, 2/10/92, C, 91002036

Flushing Town Hall, 137–35 Northern Blvd., New York, 3/16/72, A, C, 72000904

Forest-Norman Historic District [Ridgewood MRA], Forest Ave. from Summerfield to Stephen St. and Norman St. to Myrtle Ave., New York, 9/30/83, C, 83001769

Fort Tilden Historic District, Rockaway Beach Blvd., New York, 4/20/84, A, NPS, 84002917

Fort Totten Officers' Club, Totten and Murray Aves., New York, 3/17/86, A, C, 86000446

Fresh Pond-Traffic Historic District [Ridgewood MRA], Roughly bounded by Fresh Pond Rd., Traffic Ave., Woodbine and Linden Sts., New York, 9/30/83, C, 83001770

Grace Episcopal Church Complex, 15515 Jamaica Ave., New York, 9/08/83, C, a, 83001771

Grove-Linden-St. John's Historic District [Ridgewood MRA], Fairview Ave., St. John's Rd., Linden and Grove Sts., New York, 9/30/83, C, 83001772

Hunters Point Historic District, Along 45th Ave., between 21st and 23rd Sts., New York, 9/19/73, C, 73001251

Jacob Riis Park Historic District, Rockaway Beach Blvd., New York vicinity, 6/17/81, A, C, NPS, 81000081

Jamaica Chamber of Commerce Building, 8931 161st St., New York, 9/08/83, A, C, 83001773

Jamaica Savings Bank, 161-02 Jamaica Ave., New York, 5/19/83, C, 83001774

King Manor, 150th St. and Jamaica Ave., New York, 12/02/74, B, NHL, 74001295

Kingsland Homestead, 37th St. and Parsons Blvd., New York, 5/31/72, C, b, 72000905

Kurtz, J., and Sons Store Building, 162-24 Jamaica Ave., New York, 9/08/83, C, 83001775

La Casina, 90-33 160th St., New York, 3/01/90, C, 89002259

Lent Homestead and Cemetery, 78-03 19th Rd., New York, 2/02/84, A, C, D, d, 84002918

Long Island City Courthouse Complex, 25-10 Court Sq., New York, 9/26/83, A, C, 83001776

Madison-Putnam-60th Place Historic District [Ridgewood MRA], Roughly bounded by Woodbine St., 60th Pl., 67th and Forest Aves., New York, 9/30/83, C, 83001777

Marine Air Terminal, La Guardia Airport, New York, 7/09/82, A, C, g, 82003397

Office of the Register, 161–04 Jamaica Ave., New York, 1/03/80, C, 80002754

Old Quaker Meetinghouse, S side of Northern Blvd., New York, 12/24/67, A, C, a, NHL, 67000015

Paramount Studios Complex, 35th Ave., 35th, 36th, and 37th Sts., New York, 11/14/78, A, g, 78001897

Poppenhusen Institute, 114–04 14th Rd., New York, 8/18/77, A, B, C, 77000973

RKO Keith's Theater, 129-143 Northern Blvd., New York, 10/29/82, A, C, 82001260

Reformed Church of Newtown Complex, 8515 Broadway, New York, 4/23/80, C, b, 80002751

Sage, Russell, Sage Memorial Church, 1324 Beach Twelfth St., New York, 9/22/86, C, a, 86002678

Queens County—Continued

Seneca Avenue East Historic District [Ridgewood MRA], Roughly Seneca Ave. E. between Hancock and Summerfield Sts., New York, 9/30/83, C, 83001778

Seneca-Onderdonk-Woodward Historic District [Ridgewood MRA], Roughly bounded by Woodward, Seneca, Catalpa Aves., and Woodbine St., New York, 9/30/83, C, 83001779

Sidewalk Clock at 161-11 Jamaica Avenue, New York, NY [Sidewalk Clocks of New York City TR], 161-11 Jamaica Ave., New York, 4/18/85, A, C, 85000931

St. Monica's Church, 9420 160th St., New York, 4/09/80, C, a, 80002752

Steinway House, 18-22 41st St., New York, 9/08/83, A, C, 83001780

Stockholm-DeKalb-Hart Historic District [Ridgewood MRA], Roughly DeKalb and Woodward Aves., Stockholm and Hart Sts., New York, 9/30/83, C, 83004618

Summerfield Street Row Historic District [Ridgewood MRA], 5912-5948 Summerfield St., New York, 9/30/83, C, 83001781

Sunnyside Gardens Historic District, Roughly bounded by Queens Blvd., 43rd and 52nd Sts. Barnett and Skillman Aves., New York, 9/07/84, C, 84002919

US Post Office—Far Rockaway [US Post Offices in New York State, 1858-1943, TR], 18-36 Mott Ave., New York, 11/17/88, A, C, 88002500

US Post Office—Flushing Main [US Post Offices in New York State, 1858-1943, TR], 41-65 Main St., New York, 11/17/88, A, C, 88002507

US Post Office—Forest Hills Station [US Post Offices in New York State, 1858-1943, TR], 106-28 Queens Blvd., New York, 11/17/88, A, C, 88002503

US Post Office—Jackson Heights Station [US Post Offices in New York State, 1858-1943, TR], 78-02 37th Ave., New York, 11/17/88, A, C, 88002504

US Post Office—Jamaica Main [US Post Offices in New York State, 1858-1943, TR], 88-40 164th St., New York, 11/17/88, A, C, 88002335

US Post Office—Long Island City [US Post Offices in New York State, 1858-1943, TR], 46-02 21st St., New York, 5/11/89, A, C, 88002348

Van Wyck, Cornelius, House, 126 West Dr., New York, 10/06/83, A, C, 83004149

Vander Ende—Onderdonk House Site, 1820 Flushing Ave., New York, 1/31/77, A, D, 77000975

Woodbine-Palmetto-Gates Historic District [Ridgewood MRA], Roughly bounded by Forest and Fairview Aves., Woodbine and Linden Sts., New York, 9/30/83, C, 83001783

Rensselaer County

Aiken House, NE corner of Riverside and Aiken Aves., Rensselaer, 12/31/74, B, C, 74001296

Albany Avenue Historic District, Albany Ave., Nassau vicinity, 11/21/78, C, D, 78001902

Bennington Battlefield, NY 67, on VT state line, Walloomsac vicinity, 10/15/66, A, NHL, 66000564

Beverwyck Manor, Washington Ave., Rensselaer, 8/03/79, B, C, a, 79001621

Burden Iron Works Site, Address Restricted, Troy vicinity, 11/10/77, A, C, D, 77000977

Burden Ironworks Office Building, Polk St., Troy, 3/16/72, A, C, 72000907

Bussey, Esek, Firehouse, 302 10th St., Troy, 7/16/73, A, C, 73001252

Cannon Building, 1 Broadway, Troy, 3/05/70, A, C, 70000427

Central Troy Historic District, Roughly bounded by Grand St., Fifth Ave. and Third, Adams, and First and River Sts., Troy, 8/13/86, A, C, 86001527

Chatham Street Row, Chatham St., Nassau, 12/01/78, C, D, 78001900

Church Street Historic District, Church St., Nassau, 11/21/78, C, D, a, 78001901

Church of the Holy Cross, 136 8th St., Troy, 6/04/73, A, C, a, 73001253

Defreest Homestead, S of Troy at U.S. 4 and Jordan Rd., Troy vicinity, 8/02/77, A, C, D, 77000978

Estabrook Octagon House, 8 River St., Hoosick Falls, 2/08/80, C, 80002755

Fifth Avenue—Fulton Street Historic District, Bounded by Grand, William, and Union Sts., and Broadway, Troy, 3/05/70, A, C, a, 70000428

Fort Crailo, S of Columbia St. on Riverside Ave., Rensselaer, 10/15/66, A, C, NHL, 66000563

Garfield School, NY 2 and Moonlawn Rd., Eagle Mills, 6/09/88, A, C, 88000717

Glenwood, Eddy's Lane, Troy, 5/25/73, A, C, 73001254

Grand Street Historic District, Grand St. between 5th and 6th Aves., Troy, 2/27/73, C, 73001255

Hart-Cluett Mansion, 59 2nd St., Troy, 4/11/73, A, C, 73001256

Hoosick Falls Historic District, Central Ave. and Main St., Hoosick Falls, 12/03/80, A, C, 80004280

Ilium Building, NE corner of Fulton and 4th Sts., Troy, 12/18/70, A, C, 70000429

Knickerbocker Mansion, Knickerbocker Rd., Schaghticoke, 12/11/72, C, 72000906

Lansingburgh Academy, 4th and 114th Sts., Troy, 10/14/76, A, C, 76001267

Mathews, David, House, VT 67, Hoosick, vicinity, 9/10/79, C, 79000274

McCarthy Building, 255-257 River St., Troy, 3/05/70, A, C, 70000430

Mechanicville Hydroelectric Plant, At NY 32 on Hudson River, Mechanicville vicinity, 11/13/89, A, C, 89001942

Melville, Herman, House, 2 144th St., Troy, 8/21/92, B, C, 92001081

Muitzes Kill Historic District, An irregular pattern on both sides of Schodack Landing Rd., Schodack, 7/24/74, C, a, 74001297

National State Bank Building, 297 River St., Troy, 12/29/70, A, C, 70000431

Northern River Street Historic District, 403–429 and 420–430 River St., Troy, 5/19/88, A, C, 88000630

Oakwood Cemetery, 101st St., Troy, 10/04/84, B, C, c, d, 84000021

Old Troy Hospital, 8th St., Troy, 10/25/73, A, C, 73001257

Patroon Agent's House and Office, 15 Forbes Ave., Rensselaer, 8/03/79, A, C, 79001622

Poesten Kill Gorge Historic District, Address Restricted, Troy vicinity, 3/08/78, A, D, 78001903

Powers Home, 819 3rd Ave., Troy, 4/16/74, B, C, 74001298

Proctor's Theater [Movie Palaces of the Tri-Cities TR], 82 4th St., Troy, 10/04/79, A, C, 79001623

River Street Historic District, Both sides of River St. from Congress St. to jct. with 1st St., Troy, 6/03/76, A, C, 76001268

Schodack Landing Historic District, NY 9J, Schodack Landing, 9/15/77, A, C, D, a, 77000976

Second Street Historic District, Both sides of 2nd St., Troy, 8/07/74, A, C, 74001299

Smith, Henry Tunis, Farm, S of Nassau on NY 203, Nassau vicinity, 9/18/75, A, C, 75001222

St. Paul's Episcopal Church Complex, 58 3rd St., Troy, 9/07/79, A, C, a, 79001624

Staats, Joachim, House and Gerrit Staats Ruin, N of Castleton-on-Hudson, Castleton-on-Hudson vicinity, 12/15/78, A, C, D, d, 78001898

Tibbits House, S of Hoosick at jct. of NY 22 and NY 7, Hoosick vicinity, 5/22/78, A, C, 78001899

Troy Gas Light Company, NW corner of Jefferson St. and 5th Ave., Troy, 2/18/71, A, C, 71000556

Troy Public Library, 100 2nd St., Troy, 1/17/73, A, C, 73001258

Troy Savings Bank and Music Hall, 32 Second St., Troy, 4/11/89, C, NHL, 89001066

US Post Office—Hoosick Falls [US Post Offices in New York State, 1858-1943, TR], 35 Main St., Hoosick Falls, 11/17/88, A, C, 88002506

US Post Office—Troy [US Post Offices in New York State, 1858-1943, TR], 400 Broadway, Troy, 5/11/89, A, C, 88002438

W. & L. E. Gurley Building, 514 Fulton St., Troy, 3/05/70, A, NHL, 70000432

Washington Park Historic District, Washington Park and adjacent properties on 2nd, 3rd, and Washington Sts. and Washington Pl., Troy, 5/25/73, C, a, 73001259

Willard, Emma, School, Pawling and Elmgrove Aves., Troy, 8/30/79, A, C, 79001625

Richmond County

Austen, Elizabeth Alice, House, 2 Hylan Blvd., New York, 7/28/70, B, C, g, NHL, 70000925

Battery Weed, Fort Wadsworth Reservation, New York, 1/20/72, C, 72000908

Billou-Stillwell-Perine House, 1476 Richmond Rd., New York, 1/01/76, C, 76001269

Brighton Heights Reformed Church, 320 St. Mark, New York, 6/03/82, C, a, 82003399

Conference House, Hylan Blvd., New York, 10/15/66, A, NHL, 66000566

Richmond County—Continued

Edgewater Village Hall and Tappen Park, Bounded by Wright, Water, Bay and Canal Sts., New York, 5/19/80, C, 80002756

Elliott, Dr. Samuel MacKenzie, House, 69 Delafield Pl., New York, 3/28/80, A, C, 80002757

FIREFIGHTER, St. George Ferry Terminal, Staten Island, New York, 6/30/89, A, C, NHL, 89001447

Fort Tompkins Quadrangle, Building 137, Fort Wadsworth, New York, 7/30/74, A, C, 74001300

Gardiner-Tyler House, 27 Tyler St., New York, 11/23/84, C, 84000294

Garibaldi Memorial, 420 Tompkins Ave., New York, 4/17/80, A, C, 80002758

Hamilton Park Community Houses, 105 Franklin Ave., 66 Harvard Ave., and 32 Park Pl., New York, 9/26/83, C, 83003437

House at 5910 Amboy Road, 5910 Amboy Rd., New York, 12/16/82, C, 82001263

Houseman, Peter, House, 308 St.John Ave., New York, 10/29/82, C, 82001261

Houses at 364 and 390 Van Duzer Street, 364 and 390 Van Duzer St., New York, 11/14/82, C, 82001262

Kreuzer-Pelton House, 1262 Richmond Ter., New York, 1/29/73, C, 73001261

LaTourette House, Richmond Hill, New York, 3/05/82, C, 82003400

McFarlane-Bredt House, 30 Hylan Blvd., New York, 9/08/83, C, 83001784

Miller Army Air Field Historic District, New Dorp Lane, New York, 4/11/80, A, NPS, 80000362

Moore-McMillen House, 3531 Richmond Rd., New York, 4/23/80, C, 80002760

Neville House, 806 Richmond Terrace, New York, 7/28/77, C, 77000979

New Brighton Village Hall, 66 Lafayette Ave., New York, 12/15/78, C, 78001904

New Dorp Light, Altamont Ave., Staten Island, New York, 8/28/73, C, 73001260

Office Building and U.S. Light-House Depot Complex, 1 Bay St., New York, 9/15/83, A, C, 83001785

Poillon-Seguine-Britton House, 360 Great Kills Rd., New York, 2/02/84, C, 84002942

Sailors' Snug Harbor National Register District, Richmond Ter., New York, 3/16/72, C, NHL, 72000909

Sandy Ground Historic Archeological District, Address Restricted, New York vicinity, 9/23/82, A, C, D, 82003398

Scott-Edwards House, 752 Delafiel Ave., New York, 2/11/83, C, 83001786

Seguine House, 440 Seguine Ave., New York, 5/06/80, C, 80002761

St. Alban's Episcopal Church, 76 St. Alban's Place, New York, 10/29/82, C, a, b, 82001264

St. Paul's Memorial Church and Rectory, 225 St. Paul, New York, 11/21/80, C, a, 80002762

Staten Island Borough Hall and Richmond County Courthouse, Richmond Terr., New York, 10/06/83, C, 83004150

Voorlezer's House, Arthur Kill Rd., opposite Center St., New York, 10/15/66, A, NHL, 66000565

Ward's Point Conservation Area, Address Restricted, New York vicinity, 9/29/82, D, 82003402

Ward, Caleb T., Mansion, 141 Nixon Ave., New York, 7/26/82, B, C, 82003401

Wards Point Archeological Site, Address Restricted, Tottenville, 4/19/93, D, NHL, 93000609

Woodrow Methodist Church, 1109 Woodrow Rd., New York, 10/29/82, A, C, a, 82001265

Rockland County

Bear Mountain Bridge and Toll House [Hudson Highlands MRA], NY 6/202, Stony Point, 11/23/82, A, C, 82001266

Big House [Palisades MPS], US 9W near jct. with Closter Rd., Palisades, 7/12/90, C, 90001008

Blauvelt House, Zukor Rd., New City, 3/28/85, C, 85000659

Brick Church Complex, Brick Church Rd. and NY 306, West New Hempstead, 9/07/84, A, C, a, d, 84002947

Cliffside [Palisades MPS], Lawrence Ln. S of River Rd., Palisades, 7/12/90, A, B, C, 90001012

Closter Road—Oak Tree Road Historic District [Palisades MPS], Roughly, N side of Closter Rd. and S side of Oak Tree Rd. approx. 1/2 mi. W of US 9W, Palisades, 7/12/90, A, C, d, 90001014

Concklin, Abner, House, Closter Rd., Palisades, 8/06/87, C, 87001358

De Wint House, Livingston Ave. and Oak Tree Rd., Tappan, 10/15/66, B, NHL, 66000568

DeBaun, John A., Mill, NY 59, N side, opposite Highview Ave., Tallman, 9/02/93, C, 93000852

English Church and Schoolhouse, 484 New Hempstead Rd., New City, 11/23/77, C, a, 77000980

Fraser-Hoyer House, Treason Hill off U.S. 9W, West Haverstraw, 4/22/76, C, 76001270

Haddock's Hall, 300 Ferdon Ave., Piermont, 6/20/91, A, C, 91000103

Haring—Eberle House [Palisades MPS], US 9W N of Oak Tree Rd., Palisades, 7/12/90, A, C, 90001010

Homestead, 143 Hudson Ave., Haverstraw, 11/10/83, A, 83004154

Hopson—Swan Estate, US 9W E of Sparkill, Tallman Mountain State Park, Sparkill vicinity, 11/23/92, C, 92001562

Kings Daughters Public Library, Jct. of Main and Allison Sts., Haverstraw, 8/09/91, A, C, 91000950

Little House [Palisades MPS], US 9W N of Oak Tree Rd., Palisades, 7/12/90, A, C, 90001009

M/V COMMANDER, Haverstraw Marina, West Haverstraw vicinity, 9/27/84, A, C, 84002951

Neiderhurst [Palisades MPS], Ludlow Ln. S of River Rd., Palisades, 7/12/90, A, C, 90001011

Rockland County Courthouse and Dutch Gardens, Jct. of S. Main St. and New Hempstead Rd., New City, 1/03/91, A, C, 90002104

Ross-Hand Mansion, 122 S. Franklin St., South Nyack, 9/08/83, C, 83001787

Salyer, Edward, House, 241 S. Middletown Rd., Pearl River, 9/04/86, A, C, 86002178

Seven Oaks Estate [Palisades MPS], End of Ludlow Ln., Palisades, 7/12/90, A, C, 90001013

Sloat House, 19 Orange Tpke., Sloatsburg, 11/05/74, B, C, c, 74001301

Sparkill Creek Drawbridge, Bridge St. over Sparkill Creek, Piermont, 3/28/85, A, C, 85000658

Stony Point Battlefield, N of Stony Point on U.S. 2 and 202, Stony Point vicinity, 10/15/66, A, NHL, 66000567

Stony Point Lighthouse [Hudson River Lighthouses TR], Stony Point Battlefield, Stony Point, 5/29/79, A, C, 79001626

Tappan Historic District, Roughly bounded by Main St./Kings Hwy., Andre Ave. and New York Central RR, Tappan, 4/26/90, A, C, 90000689

Tappan Zee Playhouse, 20 S. Broadway, Nyack, 7/21/83, A, C, 83001788

Terneur-Hutton House, 160 Sickelton Rd., West Nyack, 4/23/73, C, 73001263

Torne Brook Farm, Torne Brook Rd., Ramapo, 5/19/88, B, C, b, 88000611

US Post Office—Haverstraw [US Post Offices in New York State, 1858-1943, TR], 86 Main St., Haverstraw, 11/17/88, A, C, 88002497

US Post Office—Nyack [US Post Offices in New York State, 1858-1943, TR], 48 S. Broadway, Nyack, 5/11/89, A, C, 88002387

US Post Office—Spring Valley [US Post Offices in New York State, 1858-1943, TR], 7 N. Madison Ave., Spring Valley, 5/11/89, A, C, 88002432

US Post Office—Suffern [US Post Offices in New York State, 1858-1943, TR], 15 Chestnut St., Suffern, 5/11/89, A, C, 88002435

Upper Nyack Firehouse, 330 N. Broadway, Upper Nyack, 9/23/82, C, 82004781

Washington Spring Road—Woods Road Historic District [Palisades MPS], Roughly, area along Washington Spring Rd. from Highland Ave. to Hudson R. and N approx. 1/2 mi. along Woods Rd., Palisades, 7/12/90, A, C, 90001015

Saratoga County

Broadway Historic District, Broadway, Washington and Rock Sts., Saratoga Springs, 9/12/79, C, 79001627

Broadway Historic District (Boundary Increase), Phila, Caroline, and Byron Sts., Maple and Woodlawn Aves., Saratoga Springs, 4/15/83, C, 83001789

Brookside, Charlton St., Ballston Spa, 5/21/75, A, 75001223

Canfield Casino and Congress Park, Roughly bounded by Spring and Circular Sts., Park Pl., and Broadway, Saratoga Springs, 2/27/87, A, NHL, 87000904

Casino-Congress Park-Circular Street Historic District, Bounded by Broadway, Spring, and Circular Sts., Saratoga Springs, 6/19/72, A, C, a, NHL, 72000910

Champlain Canal, Extends N from Troy to Whitehall, Troy vicinity, 9/01/76, A, C, 76001274

Charlton Historic District, Main St. (SR 51), Charlton, 1/01/76, C, 76001271

Saratoga County—Continued

Drinkhall, The, 297 Broadway, Saratoga Springs, 11/20/74, C, 74001302

East Side Historic District, Roughly bounded by George, Henry, East, and North Sts., Saratoga Springs, 10/29/82, C, 82001267

Ellsworth, Col. Elmer E., Monument and Grave, Hudson View Cemetery, Mechanicville, 11/13/76, B, f, 76001273

Franklin Square Historic District, In an irregular pattern from Beekman St. along both sides of Grand Ave., Franklin, and Clinton Sts. to Van Dam, Saratoga Springs, 10/09/73, A, C, 73001264

Gansevoort Mansion, Off NY 32, Gansevoort, 6/23/76, A, B, 76001272

Grant Cottage, CR 101 N of Rte. 9, Mount McGregor, 2/18/71, B, C, 71000557

Hadley Parabolic Bridge, CR 1, Hadley, 3/25/77, A, C, 77000981

Northside Historic District, Both sides of Saratoga Ave. (NY 32) from Maple Ave. to Roosevelt Bridge, Waterford, 12/04/75, A, C, 75001226

Ormsby—Laughlin Textile Companies Mill, 31 Mohawk Ave., Waterford, 3/20/86, A, C, 86000470

Peebles (Peobles) Island, At jct. of Mohawk and Hudson rivers, Waterford, 10/02/73, A, D, 73001265

Pure Oil Gas Station, 65 Spring St., Saratoga Springs, 10/18/78, A, C, b, g, 78001905

Round Lake Historic District, U.S. 9, Round Lake and vicinity, 4/24/75, A, C, D, a, 75001225

Ruhle Road Stone Arch Bridge, Ruhle Rd., Malta, 9/29/88, C, 88001699

Saratoga National Historical Park, 30 mi. N of Albany via U.S. 4 and NY 32, Albany vicinity, 10/15/66, A, f, NPS, 66000569

Saratoga Spa State Park District, US 9 & NY 50, Saratoga Springs, 9/12/85, A, C, NHL, 85002357

Todd, Hiram Charles, House, 4 Franklin Sq., Saratoga Springs, 5/31/72, C, 72000911

US Post Office—Ballston Spa [US Post Offices in New York State, 1858-1943, TR], 1 Front St., Ballston Spa, 11/17/88, A, C, 88002468

US Post Office—Saratoga Springs [US Post Offices in New York State, 1858-1943, TR], 475 Broadway, Saratoga Springs, 5/11/89, A, C, 88002427

Union Avenue Historic District, Union Ave., Saratoga Springs, 4/04/78, A, C, 78001906

Union Mill Complex, NY 50, Milton Ave., Ballston Spa, 6/17/82, A, C, 82003404

Verbeck House, 20 Church Ave., Ballston Spa, 4/07/83, C, 83001790

Vischer Ferry Historic District, SW of Clifton Park at jcts. of River View, Vischer Ferry, and Crescent Rds., Clifton Park vicinity, 10/15/75, A, C, 75001224

Waterford Village Historic District, Roughly bounded by the Hudson River, Erie Canal, and State St., Waterford, 7/14/77, A, C, 77000982

Schenectady County

Abrahams Farmhouse [Duanesburg MRA], Hardin Rd., Duanesburg, 10/11/84, C, 84003092

Avery Farmhouse [Duanesburg MRA; Boss Jones TR], NY 30, Duanesburg, 10/11/84, C, 84003106

Barney, H. S., Building, 217-229 State St., Schenectady, 7/19/84, A, C, 84002965

Becker Farmhouse [Duanesburg MRA], Creek Rd., Duanesburg, 10/11/84, C, 84003114

Braman, Joseph, House [Duanesburg MRA], Braman's Corners, Duanesburg, 4/24/87, C, 87000917

Central Fire Station, Erie Blvd., Schenectady, 4/11/85, C, 85000729

Chadwick Farmhouse [Duanesburg MRA], Schoharie Tpk., Duanesburg, 10/11/84, C, 84003175

Chapman Farmhouse [Duanesburg MRA], Miller's Corners Rd., Duanesburg, 10/11/84, C, 84003176

Christ Episcopal Church [Duanesburg MRA], NY 20, Duanesburg, 4/24/87, C, a, 87000911

Christman Bird and Wildlife Sanctuary, Schoharie Tpke., Delanson vicinity, 8/25/70, A, B, g, 70000433

Delanson Historic District [Duanesburg MRA], Main St., Delanson, 10/11/84, C, NHL, 84003181

Dellemont-Wemple Farm, W of Schenectady on Wemple Rd., Schenectady vicinity, 10/25/73, A, C, 73001266

Duane Mansion [Duanesburg MRA], NY 20, Duanesburg, 4/24/87, C, 87000910

Duanesburg-Florida Baptist Church [Duanesburg MRA], NY 30, Duanesburg, 10/11/84, C, a, 84003185

Eatons Corners Historic District [Duanesburg MRA], Eatons Corners Rd., Duanesburg, 10/11/84, C, 84003196

Ferguson Farm Complex [Duanesburg MRA], NY 20, Duanesburg, 4/24/87, C, 87000913

Foster Building, 508 State St., Schenectady, 6/03/91, C, 91000664

Franklin School, Ave. B and Mason St., Schenectady, 6/30/83, A, C, 83001791

Gaige Homestead [Duanesburg MRA], Weaver Rd., Duanesburg, 10/11/84, C, 84003202

General Electric Realty Plot, Roughly bounded by Oxford Pl., Union Ave., Nott St., Lenox and Lowell Rds., Schenectady, 11/18/80, A, B, C, 80002763

General Electric Research Laboratory, General Electric main plant, Schenectady, 5/15/75, A, NHL, 75001227

Gilbert Farmhouse [Duanesburg MRA], Thousand Acre Rd., Duanesburg, 10/11/84, C, 84003207

Green, Joseph, Farmhouse [Duanesburg MRA], NY 159, Duanesburg, 10/11/84, C, 84003209

Halladay Farmhouse [Duanesburg MRA], US 20, Duanesburg, 10/11/84, C, 84003213

Hawes Homestead [Duanesburg MRA], Herrick Rd., Duanesburg, 10/11/84, C, 84003217

Hotel Van Curler, 78 Washington Ave., Schenectady, 9/12/85, C, 85002277

Howard Homestead [Duanesburg MRA], McGuire School Rd., Duanesburg, 10/11/84, C, 84003220

Jenkins House [Duanesburg MRA], 57 Main St., Delanson, 10/11/84, C, 84003071

Jenkins Octagon House [Duanesburg MRA; Boss Jones TR], NY 395, Duanesburg, 10/11/84, C, 84003227

Jones, A.D. (Boss), House [Duanesburg MRA; Boss Jones TR], McGuire School Rd., Duanesburg, 10/11/84, C, 84003231

Ladd Farmhouse [Duanesburg MRA; Boss Jones TR], Dare Rd., Duanesburg, 10/11/84, C, 84003238

Langmuir, Irving, House, 1176 Stratford Rd., Schenectady, 1/07/76, B, NHL, 76001275

Lasher, George, House [Duanesburg MRA], Levey Rd., Duanesburg, 10/11/84, C, 84003242

Liddle, Alexander, Farmhouse [Duanesburg MRA; Boss Jones TR], Gamsey Rd., Duanesburg, 10/11/84, C, 84003256

Liddle, Robert, Farmhouse [Duanesburg MRA; Boss Jones TR], Little Dale Farm Rd., Duanesburg, 10/11/84, C, 84003265

Liddle, Thomas, Farm Complex [Duanesburg MRA], Eaton Corners Rd., Duanesburg, 10/11/84, C, 84003247

Mabee House, S of Rotterdam Junction on NY 5S, Rotterdam Junction vicinity, 5/22/78, A, C, 78001907

Macomber Stone House [Duanesburg MRA], Barton Hill Rd., Duanesburg, 10/11/84, C, 84003266

Mariaville Historic District [Duanesburg MRA], NY 159, Duanesburg, 10/11/84, C, 84003267

Niskayuna Reformed Church, 3041 Troy-Schenectady Rd., Niskayuna, 4/18/79, C, a, 79001628

North Mansion and Tenant House [Duanesburg MRA], North Mansion Rd., Duanesburg, 4/24/87, C, 87000909

Nott Memorial Hall, Union College campus, Schenectady, 5/05/72, A, C, NHL, 72000912

Proctor, F. F., Theatre and Arcade [Movie Palaces of the Tri-Cities TR], 432 State St., Schenectady, 10/04/79, A, C, 79003237

Quaker Street Historic District [Duanesburg MRA], Schoharie Tpk., Gallupville and Darby Hill Rds., Duanesburg, 10/11/84, C, 84003270

Reformed Presbyterian Church Parsonage [Duanesburg MRA], Duanesburg Churches Rd., Duanesburg, 10/11/84, C, a, 84003271

Schenectady City Hall and Post Office, Jay St., Schenectady, 10/11/78, A, C, g, 78001908

Seeley Farmhouse, 2 Freeman's Bridge Rd., Schenectady vicinity, 5/23/78, B, C, 78001909

Sheldon Farmhouse [Duanesburg MRA], NY 7, Duanesburg, 10/11/84, C, 84003273

Shute Octagon House [Duanesburg MRA; Boss Jones TR], McGuire School Rd., Duanesburg, 10/11/84, C, 84003276

Stockade Historic District, Roughly bounded by Mohawk River, RR tracks, and Union St., Schenectady, 4/03/73, A, C, D, 73001267

Stockade Historic District (Boundary Increase), 16, 18, and 20 S. Church St., Schenectady, 9/07/84, C, 84002963

US Post Office—Schenectady [US Post Offices in New York State, 1858-1943, TR], Jay and Liberty Sts., Schenectedy, 5/11/89, A, C, 88002429

US Post Office—Scotia Station [US Post Offices in New York State, 1858-1943, TR], 224 Mohawk Ave., Scotia, 5/11/89, A, C, 88002430

Schenectady County—Continued

Union Street Historic District, Union St. from Hudson River to Phoenix Ave., Schenectady, 11/17/82, A, C, 82001268

Wing, Joseph, Farm Complex [Duanesburg MRA], NY 30, Duanesburg, 10/11/84, C, 84003279

Wing, William R., Farm Complex [Duanesburg MRA], US 20, Duanesburg, 10/11/84, C, 84003281

Schoharie County

American Hotel, Main St., Sharon Springs, 9/09/75, A, C, 75001228

Becker Stone House, E of Schoharie on Murphy Rd., Schoharie vicinity, 11/20/79, B, C, 79001630

Becker-Westfall House, E of Schoharie on NY 443, Schoharie vicinity, 11/20/79, A, C, 79001631

Bramanville Mill, E of Cobleskill on Caverns Rd., Cobleskill vicinity, 8/27/76, A, 76001276

Breakabeen Historic District, Roughly bounded by River St., New Rt. 30, and Main St. to Bush Rd., Breakabeen, 12/31/74, A, C, a, 74001304

Bute-Warner-Truax Farm, Truax Rd., Charlotteville vicinity, 7/25/85, A, C, d, 85001611

Cobleskill Historic District, Irregular pattern along Washington Ave., Main, Grand, and Elm Sts., Cobleskill, 9/18/78, A, C, 78001910

Gallupville House, Main St., Gallupville, 9/07/79, C, 79001629

Lansing Manor House, 2 mi. S of North Blenheim on NY 30, Blenheim vicinity, 5/25/73, B, C, 73001268

North Blenheim Historic District, Both sides of NY 30, beside Schoharie Creek, Blenheim, 12/31/74, A, C, 74001303

Old Blenheim Bridge, NY 30 over Schoharie Creek, North Blenheim, 10/15/66, A, C, NHL, 66000570

Old Lutheran Parsonage, Adjacent to Spring St. in Lutheran Cemetery, Schoharie, 6/19/72, A, C, a, 72000913

Parker 13-Sided Barn [Central Plan Dairy Barns of New York TR], NY 10, Jefferson vicinity, 9/29/84, C, 84002967

Schoharie Valley Railroad Complex, Depot Lane, Schoharie, 4/26/72, A, 72000914

Shafer Site, Address Restricted, Fulton, 11/28/80, D, 80002764

Sternbergh House, Oak Hill Rd., Schoharie vicinity, 3/21/85, C, 85000629

US Post Office—Middleburgh [US Post Offices in New York State, 1858-1943, TR], 162 Main St., Middleburgh, 5/11/89, A, C, 88002352

Westheimer Site, Address Restricted, Schoharie, 7/22/80, D, 80002765

Westinghouse, George, Jr., Birthplace and Boyhood Home, Westinghouse Rd., Central Bridge, 3/20/86, B, c, 86000489

Schuyler County

Lamoka, Address Restricted, Tyrone vicinity, 10/15/66, D, NHL, 66000571

Lattin-Crandall Octagon Barn [Central Plan Dairy Barns of New York TR], E of Catherine, Catherine vicinity, 9/29/84, C, 84002970

Montour Falls Historic District, Main and Genesee Sts., Montour Falls, 8/31/78, A, C, D, a, 78001911

Schuyler County Courthouse Complex, Franklin St., Watkins Glen, 6/05/74, A, C, 74001305

US Post Office—Watkins Glen [US Post Offices in New York State, 1858-1943, TR], 600 N. Franklin St., Watkins Glen, 5/11/89, A, C, 88002443

Seneca County

Bloomer, Amelia, House [Women's Rights Historic Sites TR], 53 E. Bayard St., Seneca Falls, 8/29/80, A, B, NPS, 80000359

Christ Evangelical and Reformed Church, Main St., Fayette, 12/08/89, C, a, 89002092

Covert Historic District, NY 96, Covert, 11/21/80, C, 80002766

Fall Street-Trinity Lane Historic District, Address Restricted, Seneca Falls vicinity, 2/11/74, A, D, a, 74001306

Fourth Ward School, 8 Washington St., Seneca Falls, 3/19/86, C, 86000474

Hunt House [Women's Rights Historic Sites TR], 401 E. Main St., Waterloo, 8/29/80, A, B, NPS, 80000358

Lodi Methodist Church, S. Main and Grove Sts., Lodi, 5/06/82, C, a, 82003405

M'Clintock House [Women's Rights Historic Sites TR], 14 E. Williams, Waterloo, 8/29/80, A, B, NPS, 80000360

Rose Hill, W of Fayette on NY 96A, Fayette vicinity, 2/06/73, B, C, NHL, 73001269

Seneca County Courthouse Complex at Ovid, NY 414, Ovid, 12/12/76, C, 76001277

Seneca Falls Village Historic District, Roughly, properties along State and Cayuga Sts. from Butler and Auburn to Canal St., including Van Cleef Lake, Seneca Falls, 4/05/91, A, C, 91000342

Stanton, Elizabeth Cady, House, 32 Washington St., Seneca Falls, 10/15/66, B, NHL, NPS, 66000572

US Post Office—Seneca Falls [US Post Offices in New York State, 1858-1943, TR], 34–42 State St., Seneca Falls, 5/11/89, A, C, 88002431

US Post Office—Waterloo [US Post Offices in New York State, 1858-1943, TR], 2 E. Main St., Waterloo, 5/11/89, A, C, 88002442

Wesleyan Methodist Church [Women's Rights Historic Sites TR], 126 Fall St., Seneca Falls, 8/29/80, A, NPS, 80000361

Willard Asylum for the Chronic Insane, Willard State Psychiatric Center, Willard, 3/07/75, A, C, 75001229

Women's Rights National Historical Park, P.O. Box 70, Seneca Falls, 12/28/80, A, f, NPS, 80004397

St. Lawrence County

Acker and Evans Law Office, 315 State St., Ogdensburg, 9/15/83, A, C, 83001792

Chase Mills Inn, Mein and Townline Rds., Chase Mills, 11/29/78, A, 78003122

Cox, Gardner, House, Main St., Hannawa Falls, 3/20/86, B, C, 86000484

Dr. Buck-Stevens House, W. Main St., Brasher Falls, 5/17/82, C, 82004745

Fine, Judge John, House, 422 State St., Ogdenburg, 1/09/86, B, C, 86000012

Ford, Jacob, House [Morristown Village MRA], Northumberland St., Morristown, 9/02/82, A, C, 82004684

French Family Farm, SW of Potsdam on US 11, Potsdam vicinity, 11/04/82, C, 82001269

Harrison Grist Mill, NY 345, Morley, 9/16/82, A, C, 82004683

Herring-Cole Hall, St. Lawrence University, St. Lawrence University campus, Canton, 5/01/74, C, 74002203

Land Office [Morristown Village MRA], Main St., Morristown, 9/02/82, A, C, 82004685

Library Park Historic District, 303-323 Washington St., 100-112 Carolina St., and Liberty Park, Ogdensburg, 11/04/82, C, 82001270

Lisbon Town Hall, Church and Main Sts., Lisbon, 9/04/80, A, C, 80004336

Market Street Historic District, Market and Raymond Sts., Potsdam, 11/16/79, A, C, 79003171

Miller, Paschal, House [Morristown Village MRA], Main and Gouverneur Sts., Morristown, 9/02/82, A, B, C, 82004686

Morristown Schoolhouse [Morristown Village MRA], Columbia St., Morristown, 9/02/82, A, C, 82004687

New York State Armory, 100 Lafayette St., Ogdensburg, 12/12/76, A, C, 76002174

Oswegatchie Pumping Station, Mechanic St. N of Lafayette St., Ogdensburg, 6/11/90, A, C, 90000816

Pierrepont Town Buildings, Main St., Pierrepont Center, 11/04/82, C, a, 82001271

Raymondville Parabolic Bridge, Grant Rd. over Raquette River, Raymondville, 9/07/84, C, 84002961

Richardson Hall, St. Lawrence University, St. Lawrence University campus, Canton, 5/01/74, A, C, a, 74002204

Robinson Bay Archeological District, Address Restricted, Massena vicinity, 9/13/77, D, 77001524

St. Lawrence University-Old Campus Historic District, Park St., Canton, 9/15/83, A, C, 83001793

Stocking, Samuel, House [Morristown Village MRA], 83 Gouveneur St., Morristown, 9/02/82, A, C, 82004688

Stone Windmill [Morristown Village MRA], Morris St., Morristown, 9/02/82, A, C, 82004689

Trinity Episcopal Chapel, Rt. 65, S of Morley, Morley, 2/19/90, C, a, d, 90000003

U.S. Customshouse, 127 N. Water St., Ogdensburg, 10/09/74, A, C, 74002205

U.S. Post Office, 431 State St., Ogdensburg, 8/16/77, A, C, D, 77001525

St. Lawrence County—Continued

US Post Office—Canton [US Post Offices in New York State, 1858-1943, TR], Park St., Canton, 11/17/88, A, C, 88002469

US Post Office—Gouverneur [US Post Offices in New York State, 1858-1943, TR], 35 Grove St., Gouverneur, 5/11/89, A, C, 88002516

US Post Office—Potsdam [US Post Offices in New York State, 1858-1943, TR], 21 Elm St., Potsdam, 5/11/89, A, C, 88002410

United Methodist Church [Morristown Village MRA], Gouveneur St., Morristown, 9/02/82, C, a, 82004690

Village Park Historic District, Both sides of Main and Park Sts., and Park Pl., Canton, 5/06/75, A, B, C, a, 75002087

Village Park Historic District (Boundary Increase), 7-100 Main St. N, and 70, 76, 80, 90, Main St. S, Canton, 9/29/83, A, C, 83001794

Waddington Historic District, Jct. of NY 37 and La Grasse St., Waddington, 5/18/92, A, C, 92000457

West Stockholm Historic District, W. Stockholm and Livingston Rds., West Stockholm, 11/20/79, A, C, D, 79003172

Wright's Stone Store [Morristown Village MRA], Main St., Morristown, 9/02/82, A, C, 82004691

Steuben County

Addison Village Hall, Tuscarora and South Sts., Addison, 4/23/80, C, 80002771

Campbell-Rumsey House [Bath Village MRA], 225 E. Steuben St., Bath, 9/30/83, B, C, 83001795

Church of the Redeemer, Jct. of Park and Wall Sts., Addison, 11/12/92, C, a, 92001577

Cobblestone House [Bath Village MRA], 120 W. Washington St., Bath, 9/30/83, C, 83001796

Davenport Library [Bath Village MRA], W. Morris St., Bath, 9/30/83, A, B, 83001797

Delaware, Lackawanna & Western Railroad Station, Jct. of Steuben St. and Victory Hwy., Painted Post, 11/21/91, A, C, 91001674

Erie Freighthouse Historic District [Bath Village MRA], Jct. of Cohocton St. and Railroad Ave., Bath, 3/18/91, A, C, 91000235

Gansevoort/East Steuben Streets Historic District [Bath Village MRA], E. Steuben and Gansevoort Sts., Bath, 9/30/83, B, C, 83001798

Haverling Farm House [Bath Village MRA], 313 Haverling St., Bath, 9/30/83, C, 83001799

Hornell Armory, 100 Seneca St., Hornell, 5/06/80, C, 80002772

Hornell Public Library, 64 Genesee St., Hornell, 2/24/75, C, 75001230

Jenning's Tavern, 59 W. Pulteney St., Corning, 9/20/73, A, 73001270

Larrowe House, S. Main St./US 415, Cohocton, 12/07/89, C, 89002088

Liberty Street Historic District [Bath Village MRA], Roughly Liberty St. from E. Morris St. to Haverling St., Bath, 9/30/83, A, C, 83001800

Market Street Historic District, Market St. from Chestnut St. to Wall St., Corning, 3/01/74, A, C, 74001307

McMaster House [Bath Village MRA], 207 E. Washington St., Bath, 9/30/83, B, C, 83001801

Pleasant Valley Wine Company, SR 88, Rheims, 11/18/80, A, C, 80002773

Potter-Van Camp House [Bath Village MRA], 4 W. Washington St., Bath, 9/30/83, C, 83001802

Robie, Reuben, House [Bath Village MRA], 16 W. Washington St., Bath, 9/30/83, C, 83001803

Sedgwick House [Bath Village MRA], 101 Haverling St., Bath, 9/30/83, C, 83001804

Shepherd, William, House [Bath Village MRA], 110 W. Washington St., Bath, 9/30/83, C, 83001805

US Post Office—Bath [US Post Offices in New York State, 1858-1943, TR], 101 Liberty St., Bath, 11/17/88, A, C, 88002454

US Post Office—Corning [US Post Offices in New York State, 1858-1943, TR], 129 Walnut St., Corning, 11/17/88, A, C, 88002474

US Post Office—Painted Post [US Post Offices in New York State, 1858-1943, TR], 135 N. Hamilton St., Painted Post, 5/11/89, A, C, 88002395

Ward, M. J., Feed Mill Complex [Bath Village MRA], 1-9 Cameron St., Bath, 3/18/91, A, C, 91000236

Suffolk County

Balcastle [Southampton Village MRA], NW corner of Herrick and Little Plains Rds., Southampton, 10/02/86, C, 86002722

Bald Hill Schoolhouse, Horseblock Rd., Farmingville, 7/21/88, A, C, a, 88001018

Bay Crest Historic District [Huntington Town MRA], Beech Ave., Valley Rd., Woodside & Valley Drs., Huntington Bay, 9/26/85, A, C, 85002486

Baylis, M., House [Huntington Town MRA], 530 Sweet Hollow Rd., Melville, 9/26/85, C, 85002487

Beach Road Historic District [Southampton Village MRA], Between Shinnecock and Halsely Neck Rds. on Beach Rd. at Barrier Beach, Southampton, 10/02/86, C, 86002723

Beachbend [Stony Brook Harbor Estates MPS], Smith Ln., Nissequogue, 8/09/93, A, C, 93000698

Beaux Arts Park Historic District [Huntington Town MRA], Locust Ln., Upper & Lower Drs., Huntington Bay, 9/26/85, A, C, 85002489

Beebe Windmill [Long Island Wind and Tide Mills TR], SE corner of Ocean Rd. and Hildreth Ave., Bridgehampton, 12/27/78, A, C, b, 78001918

Benjamin, James, Homestead, 1182 Flanders Rd., Flanders, 8/13/86, A, C, 86001510

Bethel AME Church and Manse [Huntington Town MRA], 291 Park Ave., Huntington, 9/26/85, A, C, a, 85002490

Blydenburgh Park Historic District, Blydenburgh County Park, Smithtown, 8/11/83, A, C, 83001807

Bowers, Dr. Wesley, House [Southampton Village MRA], Beach Rd., Southampton, 10/02/86, C, 86002699

Bowes House [Huntington Town MRA], 15 Harbor Hill Dr., Huntington Bay, 9/26/85, A, C, 85002492

Box Hill Estate, NW of St. James on Moriches Rd., St. James vicinity, 12/04/73, B, C, 73001276

Bragg, Caleb, Estate, Star Island Rd., Montauk, 11/02/87, C, 87001895

Breese, James L., House, 155 Hill St., Southampton, 4/18/80, C, 80002778

Briar Patch Road Historic District [Village of East Hampton MRA], End of Briar Patch Rd. along Georgica Pond, East Hampton, 7/21/88, C, 88001029

Brown, George McKesson, Estate—Coindre Hall [Huntington Town MRA], Brown's Rd., Huntington Station, 9/26/85, A, C, 85002493

Brush Farmstead [Huntington Town MRA], 344 Greenlawn Rd., Huntington, 9/26/85, A, C, 85002500

Buell's Lane Historic District [Village of East Hampton MRA], 47–114 Buell's La., East Hampton, 7/21/88, C, a, b, 88001027

Buffett, Eliphas, House [Huntington Town MRA], 159 W. Rogues Path, Centerport, 9/26/85, B, C, d, 85002495

Buffett, Joseph, House [Huntington Town MRA], 169 W. Rogues Path, Cold Spring Harbor, 9/26/85, A, C, 85002497

Bumpstead, John, House [Huntington Town MRA], 473 Woodbury Rd., Cold Spring Harbor, 9/26/85, C, 85002499

Burr, Carll S., Mansion [Huntington Town MRA], 304 Burr Rd., Commack, 9/26/85, B, C, 85002502

Burr, Carll, Jr., House [Huntington Town MRA], 293 Burr Rd., Commack, 9/26/85, C, 85002503

By-the-Harbor [Stony Brook Harbor Estates MPS], Moriches Rd., Nissequogue, 8/09/93, A, C, 93000699

CULLODEN, H.M.S., Shipwreck Site, Address Restricted, Montauk vicinity, 3/05/79, A, D, 79003795

Carll House [Huntington Town MRA], 79 Wall St., Huntington, 9/26/85, C, 85002504

Carll House [Huntington Town MRA], 380 Deer Park Rd., Dix Hills, 9/26/85, A, C, 85002505

Carll, Ezra, Homestead [Huntington Town MRA], 49 Melville Rd., Huntington Station, 9/26/85, C, 85002506

Carll, Marion, Farm, 475 Commack Rd., Commack, 6/26/79, A, C, 79001632

Caroline Church and Cemetery, Jct. of Dyke and Bates Rds., Brookhaven, 9/09/91, C, a, d, 91001148

Chase, William Merritt, Homestead, Canoe Pl. Rd., Southampton, 6/16/83, B, C, 83001808

Chichester's Inn [Huntington Town MRA], 97 Chichester Rd., West Hills, 9/26/85, A, C, 85002508

Cold Spring Harbor Library [Huntington Town MRA], 1 Shore Rd., Cold Spring Harbor, 9/26/85, A, C, 85002509

Commack Methodist Church and Cemetery [Huntington Town MRA], 486 Townline Rd., Huntington, 9/26/85, A, C, a, d, 85002511

Suffolk County—Continued

Congregational Church of Patchogue, 95 E. Main St., Patchogue, 4/01/93, C, a, 93000279

Conklin, David, House [Huntington Town MRA], 2 High St., Cold Spring Harbor, 9/26/85, A, B, C, 85002513

Conklin, Nathaniel, House, 280 Deer Park Ave., Babylon, 12/08/88, C, 88002683

Cox, Richard, House, Mill Rd., Mattituck, 8/21/86, C, 86001721

Crowther House, 97 Beach Lane, Westhampton Beach, 3/21/85, C, 85000630

Cutting, Bayard, Estate, N of Great River on NY 27, Great River vicinity, 10/02/73, C, 73001271

Delamater-Bevin Mansion [Huntington Town MRA], Bevin Ln., Asharoken, 9/26/85, A, C, 85002514

Donnell, Harry E., House [Huntington Town MRA], 71 Locust Ln., Eatons Neck, 9/26/85, C, 85002516

Dowden Tannery [Huntington Town MRA], 210 W. Rogues Path, Cold Spring Harbor, 9/26/85, A, C, 85002519

East Farm [Stony Brook Harbor Estates MPS], Harbor Rd., N side, at Shep Jones Ln., Head of the Harbor, 8/09/93, A, C, 93000700

East Hampton Village District [Village of East Hampton MRA], Bounded by Main St. and James and Woods Lanes, East Hampton, 5/02/74, C, 74001309

East Hampton Village Historic District (Boundary Increase) [Village of East Hampton MRA], Northeastward along Main St. to Newton La. and Southwestward along Ocean and Lee Aves. and Pond La. to Hedges La., East Hampton, 7/21/88, A, C, 88001032

East Shore Road Historic District [Huntington Town MRA], East Shore Rd., Halesite, 9/26/85, A, C, 85002521

Eatons Neck Light, Eatons Neck Point at Huntington Bay and Long Island Sound off NY 25A, Huntington, 4/03/73, A, 73001273

Egypt Lane Historic District [Village of East Hampton MRA], 111, 117, and 129 Egypt La., East Hampton, 7/21/88, C, b, 88001031

Everit, John, House [Huntington Town MRA], 130 Old Country Rd., West Hills, 9/26/85, A, C, 85002522

Felix, N. J., House [Huntington Town MRA], 235 Asharoken Ave., Asharoken, 9/26/85, C, 85002523

Field, Marshall, III, Estate, Lloyd Harbor Rd., Lloyd Harbor, 4/30/79, A, C, 79001633

Fire Island Light Station, Robert Moses Causeway, Bay Shore vicinity, 9/11/81, A, C, NPS, 81000082

First Presbyterian Church, 175 E. Main St., Smithtown, 12/23/77, C, a, 77000983

Floyd, William, House, 20 Washington Ave., Mastic Beach, 4/21/71, A, B, C, NPS, 71000066

Fort Corchaug Site, Address Restricted, Cutchogue vicinity, 1/18/74, D, 74001308

Fort Golgotha and the Old Burial Hill Cemetery, Main St. and Nassau Rd., Huntington, 3/02/81, C, D, 81000415

Fort Hill Estate, Fort Hill Dr., Lloyd Harbor, 6/02/88, A, C, 88000599

Fort Salonga, Address Restricted, Fort Salonga vicinity, 5/21/82, A, C, D, 82003406

Gardiners Island Windmill [Long Island Wind and Tide Mills TR], On Gardiners Island, East Hampton, 12/27/78, A, C, 78001912

Geoghegan, Charles, House [Huntington Town MRA], 9 Harbor Hill Dr., Huntington Bay, 9/26/85, A, C, 85002524

Gildersleeve, Andrew, Octagonal Building, Main Rd. and Love Lane, Mattituck, 8/19/76, C, 76001280

Gilsey Mansion [Huntington Town MRA], 36 Browns Rd., Huntington, 9/26/85, C, 85002525

Goodale, Capt. C., House [Southampton Village MRA], 300 Hampton Rd., Southampton, 10/02/86, C, 86002725

Goose Hill Road Historic District [Huntington Town MRA], Goose Hill Rd., Cold Spring Harbor, 9/26/85, A, C, 85002528

Green, John, House [Huntington Town MRA], 167 E. Shore Rd., Huntington Bay, 9/26/85, C, 85002526

Greenport Railroad Station, Third and Wiggins St., Greenport, 7/20/89, A, C, 89000947

Greenport Village Historic District, Roughly bounded by Stirling Basin, Main, Monsell, 2nd, and Front Sts., Greenport, 9/13/84, A, C, 84002973

Halliock Inn, 263 E. Main St., Smithtown, 8/07/74, C, 74001310

Hallock Homestead, 163 Sound Ave., Northville, 6/07/84, A, C, 84002992

Halsey Estate—Tallwood [Huntington Town MRA], Sweet Hollow Rd., West Hills, 9/26/85, C, 85002527

Harbor House [Stony Brook Harbor Estates MPS], Spring Hollow Rd., Nissequogue, 8/09/93, A, C, 93000701

Harbor Road Historic District [Huntington Town MRA], Harbor Rd., Cold Spring Harbor, 9/26/85, A, B, C, 85002529

Harned, John, House [Huntington Town MRA], 26 Little Neck Rd., Centerport, 9/26/85, A, C, 85002530

Harrison, Wallace K., Estate [Huntington Town MRA], 140 Round Swamp Rd., West Hills, 9/26/85, B, C, 85002531

Havens, James, Homestead, NY 114, Shelter Island, 4/10/86, A, C, 86000701

Hawkins Homestead, 165 Christian Ave., Stony Brook vicinity, 6/09/88, A, B, C, b, 88000727

Hawkins, Robert, Homestead, Yaphank Ave., Yaphank, 4/10/86, C, 86000702

Hayground Windmill [Long Island Wind and Tide Mills TR], At Windmill Lane, East Hampton, 12/27/78, A, C, 78001913

Heckscher Park [Huntington Town MRA], Bounded by Madison St., Sabbath Day Path, Main St. & Prince Ave., Huntington, 9/26/85, C, 85002532

Hewlett House [Huntington Town MRA], 559 Woodbury Rd., Cold Spring Harbor, 9/26/85, A, C, 85002533

Homan—Gerard House and Mills, Jct. Main St. and Yaphank Rd., Yaphank, 12/16/88, A, C, 88002761

Hook Windmill [Long Island Wind and Tide Mills TR; Village of East Hampton MRA], N. Main St., East Hampton, 12/27/78, A, C, 78001914

House at 200 Bay Avenue [Huntington Town MRA], 200 Bay Ave., Huntington Bay, 9/26/85, C, 85002535

House at 244 Park Avenue [Huntington Town MRA], 244 Park Ave., Huntington, 9/26/85, A, C, 85002534

Ireland—Gardiner Farm [Huntington Town MRA], 863 Lake Rd., Greenlawn, 9/26/85, A, C, 85002537

Jagger House, Old Montauk Hwy., Westhampton, 12/12/78, C, 78001920

Jarvis—Fleet House [Huntington Town MRA], 138 Cove Rd., Huntington, 9/26/85, A, C, 85002538

Jericho Historic District [Village of East Hampton MRA], Montauk Hwy., East Hampton, 7/21/88, C, 88001028

Jones Road Historic District [Village of East Hampton MRA], Along Jones Rd. from Apaquogue Rd. to Lilly Pond La., East Hampton, 7/21/88, A, C, b, 88001030

Kane, John P., Mansion [Huntington Town MRA], 37 Kanes Ln., Huntington Bay, 9/26/85, C, 85002580

Kennan, A. P. W., House [Huntington Town MRA], Sydney Rd., Huntington Bay, 11/06/85, C, 85003502

Ketchum, B., House [Huntington Town MRA], 237 Middleville Rd., Huntington, 9/26/85, C, 85002581

LITTLE JENNIE (Chesapeake Bay bugeye), Centerport Harbor, Centerport, 5/12/86, A, C, 86001081

Land of Clover [Stony Brook Harbor Estates MPS], Long Beach Rd., S side, Nissequogue, 8/09/93, A, C, 93000702

Lloyd Harbor Lighthouse, Entrance to Lloyd Harbor, Lloyd Harbor vicinity, 5/31/89, C, 89000501

Lloyd, Joseph, House, NW of Huntington on Lloyd Harbor Rd., Huntington vicinity, 11/07/76, A, C, 76001278

Longbotham, Nathaniel, House, 1541 Stony Brook Rd., Stony Brook, 11/16/89, A, C, 89002022

Losee, Isaac, House [Huntington Town MRA], 269 Park Ave., Huntington, 9/26/85, A, C, 85002582

Main Street Historic District [Huntington Town MRA], Main St., Cold Spring Harbor, 9/26/85, A, C, 85002583

Mallows, The [Stony Brook Harbor Estates MPS], Emmet Way, Head of the Harbor, 8/09/93, A, C, 93000703

Masury Estate Ballroom, Old Neck Rd. S, Center Moriches, 9/11/86, C, 86002513

Miller Place Historic District, N. Country Rd., Miller Place, 6/17/76, C, 76001281

Mills Pond District, W of St. James on NY 25A, St. James vicinity, 8/01/73, C, 73001277

Suffolk County—Continued

Montauk Association Historic District, E of Montauk off NY 27 on DeForest Rd., Montauk vicinity, 10/22/76, A, C, 76001282

Montauk Manor, Fairmont Ave., Montauk, 8/23/84, A, C, 84002995

Montauk Point Lighthouse, Montauk Point, East Hampton vicinity, 7/07/69, A, 69000142

Montauk Tennis Auditorium, Flamingon Ave. and Edjemere St., Montauk, 2/08/88, B, C, 88000052

Moran, Thomas, House, Main St., East Hampton, 10/15/66, B, NHL, 66000574

Mount, William Sydney, House, Gould Rd. and NY 25, Stony Brook, 10/15/66, B, NHL, 66000575

North Main Street Historic District [Southampton Village MRA], N. Main St. near CR 39 and Railroad Station Plaza, Southampton, 10/02/86, A, C, 86002730

North Main Street Historic District [Village of East Hampton MRA], N. Main St., East Hampton, 7/21/88, C, a, d, 88001025

O'Donohue, C. A., House [Huntington Town MRA], 158 Shore Rd., Huntington, 9/26/85, A, C, 85002584

Oakley, John, House [Huntington Town MRA], Sweet Hollow Rd., West Hills, 11/06/85, C, b, 85003501

Ockers, Jacob, House, 965 Montauk Hwy., Oakdale, 7/10/92, B, 92000838

Old First Church [Huntington Town MRA], 126 Main St., Huntington, 11/06/85, A, C, a, 85003500

Old House, The, NY 25, Cutchogue, 10/15/66, A, C, b, NHL, 66000573

Old Town Green Historic District [Huntington Town MRA], Park Ave., Huntington, 9/26/85, A, C, 85002586

Old Town Hall Historic District [Huntington Town MRA], Main St. & Nassau Rd., Huntington, 9/26/85, A, C, 85002588

Orient Historic District, NY 25, Orient, 5/21/76, C, 76001283

Pantigo Road Historic District [Village of East Hampton MRA], Along Pantigo Rd. from Egypt La. and Accabonac Rd. to Amy's La., East Hampton, 7/21/88, C, 88001026

Phyfe, James W. and Anne Smith, Estate [Stony Brook Harbor Estates MPS], 87 Stillwater Rd., Nissequogue, 8/09/93, A, C, 93000704

Pleasants House, NY 27, Amagansett, 2/02/84, C, 84002999

Potter—Williams House [Huntington Town MRA], 165 Wall St., Huntington, 9/26/85, A, C, 85002579

Prime House [Huntington Town MRA], 35 Prime Ave., Huntington, 9/26/85, B, C, 85002568

Prime—Octagon House [Huntington Town MRA], 41 Prime Ave., Huntington, 9/26/85, B, C, 85002569

Radio Central Complex, S of Rocky Point on Rocky Point-Yaphank Rd., Rocky Point vicinity, 6/27/80, A, C, 80002777

Rassapeague [Stony Brook Harbor Estates MPS], Long Beach Rd., S side, Nissequogue, 8/09/93, A, C, 93000705

Remp, Michael, House [Huntington Town MRA], 42 Godfrey Ln., Greenlawn, 9/26/85, A, C, 85002570

Rogers House [Huntington Town MRA], 136 Spring Rd., Huntington, 9/26/85, C, 85002571

Rogers, John, House [Huntington Town MRA], 627 Half Hollow Rd., Huntington, 9/26/85, A, C, 85002572

Roosevelt, John Ellis, Estate, Middle Rd., Sayville, 11/05/87, A, C, D, 87001896

Ryan, William J., Estate [Stony Brook Harbor Estates MPS], Moriches Rd., Nissequogue, 8/09/93, A, C, 93000706

Sag Harbor Village District, Roughly bounded by Sag Harbor, Rysam, Hamilton, Marsden, Main and Long Island Ave., Sag Harbor, 7/20/73, A, C, 73001274

Sagtikos Manor, Montauk Hwy. (NY 27A), West Bay Shore, 11/21/76, A, C, 76001284

Saint James District, On NY 25A, Saint James, 7/20/73, C, a, 73001275

Sammis, Silas, House [Huntington Town MRA], 302 W. Neck Rd., Huntington, 9/26/85, B, C, 85002573

Seaman Farm [Huntington Town MRA], 1378 Carlls Straight Path, Dix Hills, 9/26/85, A, C, 85002575

Shelter Island Heights Historic District, Roughly bounded by St. Johns St., Tower Hill Rd. Sunnyside Ave., Meadow Pl., Chase Cr. and Dering Harbor, Shelter Island Heights, 5/07/93, A, C, 93000335

Shelter Island Windmill [Long Island Wind and Tide Mills TR], N of Manwaring Rd., Shelter Island, 12/27/78, A, C, b, 78001917

Shore Cottage [Stony Brook Harbor Estates MPS], Harbor Rd., E side, Head of the Harbor, 8/09/93, A, C, 93000707

Shore Road Historic District [Huntington Town MRA], Shore Rd., Cold Spring Harbor, 9/26/85, A, C, 85002578

Smith Estate, N of Brookhaven at Longwood and Smith Rds., Brookhaven vicinity, 12/10/81, A, C, 81000414

Smith, Daniel, House [Huntington Town MRA], 117 W. Shore Rd., Huntington, 9/26/85, C, 85002576

Smith, Henry, Farmstead [Huntington Town MRA], 900 Park Ave., Huntington Station, 9/26/85, A, C, 85002539

Smith, Jacob, House [Huntington Town MRA], High Hold Dr., West Hills, 9/26/85, A, C, 85002540

Smith—Rourke House, 350 S. Country Rd., East Patchogue, 11/28/89, C, 89002021

Southampton Village Historic District [Southampton Village MRA], Roughly bounded by Hill and Main Sts., Old Town Rd., Atlantic Ocean, Coopers Neck and Halsey Neck Lns., Southampton, 4/25/88, A, C, 86002726

Southampton Village Historic District (Boundary Increase) [Southampton Village MRA], Roughly, along Rogers St., Lewis St. and Meet-

ing House Ln. on E side of existing district, Southampton, 4/12/93, C, 93000239

Southside Sportsmens Club District, NE of Great River, off NY 27, Great River vicinity, 7/23/73, A, C, 73001272

St. Andrew's Episcopal Church, Main St., Yaphank, 9/15/88, A, C, a, 88001442

Stony Brook Grist Mill, Harbor Rd. W of Main St., Stony Brook, 8/03/90, A, C, 90001140

Suffolk County Almshouse Barn, Yaphank Ave., Yaphank, 9/11/86, A, C, 86002512

Suydam House [Huntington Town MRA], 1 Ft. Salonga Rd., Centerport, 10/27/88, A, C, 88002135

Sweet Hollow Presbyterian Church Parsonage [Huntington Town MRA], 152 Old Country Rd., Huntington, 9/26/85, A, C, a, 85002541

Terry—Ketcham Inn, 81 Main St., Center Moriches, 6/24/93, C, 92000555

Terry-Mulford House, NY 25, Orient, 2/07/84, A, C, 84003003

Thompson House, N. Country Rd., Setauket, 1/07/88, A, C, d, 87002283

Titus—Bunce House [Huntington Town MRA], 7 Goose Hill Rd., Cold Spring Harbor, 9/26/85, A, C, 85002542

Townsend, Henry, House [Huntington Town MRA], 231 W. Neck Rd., Huntington, 9/26/85, A, C, 85002543

Tuthill, David, Farmstead, New Suffolk Lane, Cutchogue, 11/23/84, A, C, 84000295

US Post Office—Bay Shore [US Post Offices in New York State, 1858-1943, TR], 10 Bay Shore Ave., Bay Shore, 11/17/88, A, C, 88002455

US Post Office—Northport [US Post Offices in New York State, 1858-1943, TR], 244 Main St., Northport, 5/11/89, A, C, 88002356

US Post Office—Patchogue [US Post Offices in New York State, 1858-1943, TR], 170 E. Main St., Patchogue, 5/11/89, A, C, 88002397

US Post Office—Riverhead [US Post Offices in New York State, 1858-1943, TR], 23 W. Second St., Riverhead, 5/11/89, A, C, 88002424

US Post Office—Westhampton Beach [US Post Offices in New York State, 1858-1943, TR], Main St., Westhampton Beach, 5/11/89, A, C, 88002446

Union Chapel, The Grove, Shelter Island Heights, 11/23/84, A, C, a, 84000296

United Methodist Church, S. Ocean Ave. and Church St., Patchogue, 4/19/84, C, a, 84003006

Vail-Leavitt Music Hall, Peconic Ave., Riverhead, 8/25/83, C, 83001809

Van Iderstine, Charles, Mansion [Huntington Town MRA], Idle Day Dr., Huntington, 9/26/85, A, C, 85002544

Van Wyck-Lefferts Tide Mill [Long Island Wind and Tide Mills TR], 2 mi. NE of Mill and Southdown Rds., Lloyd Harbor, 12/27/78, A, C, 78001916

Vanderbilt, William K., Estate-Eagles Nest [Huntington Town MRA], Little Neck Rd., Huntington, 9/26/85, A, B, C, 85002545

Velzer, N., House and Caretaker's Cottage [Huntington Town MRA], 22 Fort Salonga Rd., Centerport, 9/26/85, A, C, 85002546

Suffolk County—Continued

Village of Branch Historic District, Along N side of Middle Country Rd., Branch, 9/11/86, A, C, 86002514

Wainscott Windmill [Long Island Wind and Tide Mills TR], On Georgica Association grounds, East Hampton, 12/27/78, A, C, b, 78001915

Water Mill, Old Mill Rd., Water Mill, 10/13/83, A, b, 83004175

Weeks, Charles M., House [Huntington Town MRA], 76 Mill Ln., Huntington, 9/26/85, C, 85002547

West Neck Road Historic District [Huntington Town MRA], West Neck Rd., Huntington, 9/26/85, A, C, 85002567

Wetherill, Kate Annette, Estate [Stony Brook Harbor Estates MPS], Harbor Hill Rd., S side, Head of the Harbor, 8/09/93, A, C, 93000708

Whitman, Joseph, House [Huntington Town MRA], 365 W. Hills Rd., West Hills, 9/26/85, B, C, 85002548

Whitman, Walt, House [Huntington Town MRA], 246 Walt Whitman Rd., West Hills, 9/26/85, A, B, C, c, 85002549

Whitman—Place House [Huntington Town MRA], 69 Chichester Rd., West Hills, 9/26/85, B, C, 85002550

Wickapogue Road Historic District [Southampton Village MRA], Wickapogue Rd. between Narrow Ln. and Cobb Rd., Southampton, 10/02/86, A, C, 86002697

Wiggins—Rolph House [Huntington Town MRA], 518 Park Ave., Huntington, 9/26/85, A, C, 85002551

Williams, Henry, House [Huntington Town MRA], 43 Mill Ln., Huntington, 9/26/85, C, 85002552

Windmill at Water Mill [Long Island Wind and Tide Mills TR], NY 27 and Halsey Lane, Southampton, 12/27/78, A, C, b, 78001919

Wood, Harry, House [Huntington Town MRA], 481 W. Main St., Huntington, 9/26/85, A, C, 85002553

Wood, John, House [Huntington Town MRA], 121 McKay Rd., Huntington Station, 9/26/85, A, C, 85002554

Wood, William Wooden, House [Huntington Town MRA], 90 Preston St., Huntington, 9/26/85, B, C, 85002555

Woodcrest [Stony Brook Harbor Estates MPS], Moriches Rd., Nissequogue, 8/09/93, A, C, 93000709

Woodhull, Charles, House [Huntington Town MRA], 70 Main St., Huntington, 9/26/85, C, 85002564

Wyandanch Club Historic District, Jericho Tnpk. SW of jct. with Meadow Rd., Smithtown, 8/03/90, A, C, 90001143

Sullivan County

Arlington Hotel, Main St., Narrowsburg, 3/31/83, A, 83001806

Bloomingburg Reformed Protestant Dutch Church, NY 17M, Bloomingburg, 1/10/80, A, C, a, 80002779

Calkins, Ellery, House [Upper Delaware Valley MPS], Co. Rd. 114, E of Delaware R. Bridge, Cochecton, 11/27/92, C, 92001595

Callicoon Methodist Church and Parsonage [Upper Delaware Valley, New York and Pennsylvania, MPS], Church St. (NY 97) S of jct. with Seminary Rd., Town of Delaware, Callicoon, 11/04/93, C, a, 93001134

Cochecton Presbyterian Church [Upper Delaware Valley MPS], Co. Rd. 114, E of Delaware R. Bridge, Cochecton, 11/27/92, C, a, 92001597

Delaware Aqueduct, Between Minisink Ford, NY and Lackawaxen, PA, Minisink Ford, 11/24/68, C, NPS, 68000055

Delaware and Hudson Canal, Delaware and Hudson Canal, Minisink, vicinity, 11/24/68, A, C, NHL, 68000051

Drake—Curtis House [Upper Delaware Valley MPS], Co. Rd. 114, E of NY 97, Cochecton, 4/19/93, B, C, 92001598

Glen Wild Methodist Church, Old Glen Wild Rd., Glen Wild, 5/10/84, C, a, 84003035

Grahamsville Historic District, NY 55, Grahamsville, 12/06/79, A, C, a, d, 79001634

Jeffersonville School, Terrace Ave., Jeffersonville, 4/28/88, A, C, 88000519

Kirk House, Kirk's Rd., Narrowsburg, 5/10/84, C, b, 84003043

Liberty Village Historic District, N. Main, Academy, and Law Sts., Liberty, 4/11/78, C, 78001921

Millanville—Skinners Falls Bridge [Highway Bridges Owned by the Commonwealth of Pennsylvania, Department of Transportation TR], LR 63027 over Delaware River at Millanville, Skinners Falls, 11/14/88, C, 88002167

Minisink Battlefield [Upper Delaware Valley, New York and Pennsylvania, MPS], York Lake Rd. (Co. Rd. 168) N of Minisink Ford, Minisink Ford vicinity, 9/16/93, A, 93000946

Old Cochecton Cemetery [Upper Delaware Valley MPS], W of NY 97, N of jct. with Co. Rd. 114, Cochecton, 11/27/92, A, d, 92001593

Page House [Upper Delaware Valley MPS], 59 C. Meyer Rd., Cochecton, 11/27/92, C, 92001601

Parsonage Road Historic District [Upper Delaware Valley MPS], Parsonage Rd., Cochecton, 11/27/92, C, 92001600

Pond Eddy Bridge [Highway Bridges Owned by the Commonwealth of Pennsylvania, Department of Transportation TR], LR 51013 over Delaware River, Pond Eddy, vicinity, 11/14/88, C, 88002170

Reilly's Store [Upper Delaware Valley MPS], Co. Rd. 114, W of jct. with NY 97, Cochecton, 11/27/92, C, 92001594

Riverside Cemetery [Upper Delaware Valley, New York and Pennsylvania, MPS], NY 97 SE of jct. with Church St., Long Eddy vicinity, 11/18/93, C, d, 93001226

Rockland Mill Complex, Palen Pl., Rockland, 8/23/84, A, C, 84003062

St. James Church and Rectory [Upper Delaware Valley, New York and Pennsylvania, MPS], NY 17B N side, E of jct. with NY 97, Town of Delaware, Callicoon, 11/04/93, C, a, 93001135

St. Joseph's Seminary [Upper Delaware Valley MPS], Seminary Rd. W side, Callocoon, 7/08/93, C, a, 93000582

Stone Arch Bridge, N of Kenoza Lake on NY 52, Kenoza Lake vicinity, 12/12/76, A, C, 76001285

Valleau Tavern [Upper Delaware Valley MPS], Jct. of Co. Rd. 114 and NY 97, Cochecton, 11/27/92, A, C, 92001599

Tioga County

Akins, Lyman P., House [Berkshire MRA], W. Creek Rd., Berkshire, 7/02/84, C, 84003067

Akins, Robert, House [Berkshire MRA], Main St., Berkshire, 7/02/84, C, 84003069

Ball, J., House [Berkshire MRA], NY 38, Berkshire, 7/02/84, A, C, 84003072

Ball, Levi, House [Berkshire MRA], NY 38, Berkshire, 7/02/84, A, C, 84003075

Ball, Stephen, House [Berkshire MRA], Main St., Berkshire, 7/02/84, C, 84003077

Belcher Family Homestead and Farm [Berkshire MRA], NY 38, Berkshire, 7/02/84, A, C, 84003082

Bement—Billings House, NY 38, N of Newark Valley, Newark Valley, 2/19/90, A, C, 90000002

Berkshire Village Historic District [Berkshire MRA], Main St. and Leonard Ave., Berkshire, 7/02/84, A, C, 84003086

Buffington, Calvin A., House [Berkshire MRA], Depot St. and Railroad Ave., Berkshire, 7/02/84, B, C, 84003089

Collins, Nathaniel Bishop, House [Berkshire MRA], NY 38, Berkshire, 7/02/84, C, 84003096

East Berkshire United Methodist Church [Berkshire MRA], E. Berkshire Rd., Berkshire, 7/02/84, C, a, 84003098

First Congregational Church [Berkshire MRA], Main St., Berkshire, 7/02/84, C, a, 84003101

Ford, Lebbeus, House [Berkshire MRA], Jewett Hill Rd., Berkshire, 7/02/84, C, 84003104

Owego Central Historic District, North Ave., Park, Main, Lake, Court, and Fronts Sts., Owego, 12/03/80, A, C, 80002780

Platt-Cady Mansion, 18 River St., Nichols, 8/13/76, C, 76001286

Royce, Deodatus, House [Berkshire MRA], NY 38, Berkshire, 7/02/84, C, 84003109

Royce, J. B., House and Farm Complex [Berkshire MRA], NY 38, Berkshire, 7/02/84, A, C, 84003111

Tioga County Courthouse, Village Park, Owego, 12/26/72, A, C, 72000915

US Post Office—Owego [US Post Offices in New York State, 1858-1943, TR], 6 Lake St., Owego, 5/11/89, A, C, 88002391

US Post Office—Waverly [US Post Offices in New York State, 1858-1943, TR], 434–348 Waverly St., Waverly, 5/11/89, A, C, 88002444

Tompkins County

Bailey Hall [New York State College of Agriculture TR], Cornell University campus, Ithaca, 9/24/84, A, C, 84003113

Boardman House, 120 E. Buffalo St., Ithaca, 5/06/71, B, C, 71000559

Caldwell Hall [New York State College of Agriculture TR], Cornell University campus, Ithaca, 9/24/84, A, C, 84003117

Camp, Hermon, House, Camp St., Trumansburg, 12/04/73, C, 73001279

Cascadilla School Boathouse, S. shore of Cayuga Lake at the mouth of Fall Cr., Stewart Park, Ithaca, 10/04/91, A, C, 91001498

Clarke, Luther, House [Dryden Village MRA], 39 W. Main St., Dryden, 6/08/84, C, 84003119

Clinton Hall, 108–114 N. Cayuga St., Ithaca, 7/07/88, C, 88001019

Clinton House, 116 N. Cayuga St., Ithaca, 8/12/71, A, C, 71000560

Comstock Hall [New York State College of Agriculture TR], Cornell University campus, Ithaca, 9/24/84, A, C, 84003122

Cornell Heights Historic District, Roughly bounded by Kline Rd., Highland Ave., Brock Ln., Triphammer Rd., Fall Creek, Stewart Ave., and Needham Pl., Ithaca, 9/14/89, A, C, 89001205

De Witt Park Historic District, A square bounded roughly by properties fronting on E. Buffalo, E. Court, N. Cayuga, and N. Tioga Sts., Ithaca, 10/26/71, A, C, 71000561

Deke House, 13 South Ave., Ithaca, 1/11/91, A, C, 90002144

Dryden Historic District [Dryden Village MRA], Roughly bounded by E. Main, James, Lake and South Sts., Dryden, 6/15/84, C, 84003921

East Hill Historic District, Roughly bounded by Cascadilla Creek, Eddy St., Six Mile Creek, and Aurora St., Ithaca, 8/14/86, C, 86001652

East Robert Hall [New York State College of Agriculture TR], Cornell University campus, Ithaca, 9/24/84, A, C, 84003178

Ellis Methodist Episcopal Church, Ellis Hollow Rd., Ellis Hollow, 5/27/93, C, a, b, 93000443

Enfield Falls Mill and Miller's House, SW of Ithaca in Robert H. Treman State Park, Ithaca vicinity, 2/25/79, A, C, 79001637

Fernow Hall [New York State College of Agriculture TR], Cornell University campus, Ithaca, 9/24/84, A, C, 84003183

Groton High School, 177 Main St., Groton, 7/24/92, A, C, 92000953

Halsey, Nicoll, House and Halseyville Archeological Sites, Address Restricted, Halseyville, 6/24/93, A, C, D, 93000504

Indian Fort Road Site, Address Restricted, Trumansburg vicinity, 9/30/83, D, 83001810

Ithaca Pottery Site, Address Restricted, Ithaca, 7/17/79, A, D, 79001635

Jennings-Marvin House [Dryden Village MRA], 9 Library St., Dryden, 6/08/84, C, 84003184

Lacy-Van Vleet House [Dryden Village MRA], 45 W. Main St., Dryden, 6/08/84, C, 84003187

Lehigh Valley Railroad Station, W. Buffalo St. and Taughannock Blvd., Ithaca, 12/31/74, A, 74001311

Llenroc, 100 Cornell Ave., Ithaca, 4/16/80, B, C, 80002781

Methodist Episcopal Church [Dryden Village MRA], 2 North St., Dryden, 6/08/84, C, a, 84003189

Morrill Hall, Cornell University, Cornell University campus, Ithaca, 10/15/66, A, NHL, 66000576

Rice Hall [New York State College of Agriculture TR], Cornell University campus, Ithaca, 9/24/84, A, C, 84003190

Roberts Hall [New York State College of Agriculture TR], Cornell University campus, Ithaca, 9/24/84, A, C, 84003191

Rockwell House [Dryden Village MRA], 52 W. Main St., Dryden, 6/08/84, C, 84003192

Second Tompkins County Courthouse, 121 E. Court St., Ithaca, 3/18/71, A, C, 71000562

Southworth House [Dryden Village MRA], 14 North St., Dryden, 6/08/84, C, 84003193

Southworth Library [Dryden Village MRA], 24 W. Main St., Dryden, 6/08/84, C, 84003195

St. James AME Zion Church, 116–118 Cleveland Ave., Ithaca, 7/22/82, A, C, a, 82003407

Stone Hall [New York State College of Agriculture TR], Cornell University campus, Ithaca, 9/24/84, A, C, 84003860

Strand Theatre, 310 E. State St., Ithaca, 2/22/79, A, C, 79001636

US Post Office—Ithaca [US Post Offices in New York State, 1858-1943, TR], 213 N. Tioga St., Ithaca, 5/11/89, A, C, 88002514

West Dryden Methodist Episcopal Church, Jct. of W. Dryden and Sheldon Rds., Dryden, 8/09/91, C, a, 91001029

White, Andrew Dickson, House, 27 East Ave., Ithaca, 12/04/73, B, C, 73001278

Wing Hall [New York State College of Agriculture TR], Cornell University campus, Ithaca, 9/24/84, A, C, 84003204

Ulster County

Aldrich, Peter, Homestead [Shawangunk Valley MRA], 168 Decker Rd., Gardiner, 9/26/83, C, 83001811

All Saints' Chapel, Main St., Rosendale, 9/11/86, C, a, 86002511

Beaverkill Valley Inn, Beaverkill Rd., Lew Beach vicinity, 9/12/85, A, 85002280

Bevier House [Shawangunk Valley MRA], Bevier Rd., Gardiner, 9/26/83, C, 83001812

Binnewater Historic District, Sawdust Ave., Breezy Hill and Binnewater Rds., Rosendale, 11/04/82, A, C, 82001272

Brykill [Shawangunk Valley MRA], Bruynswick Rd., Gardiner, 9/26/83, C, 83001813

Burroughs, John, Cabin, W of West Park, West Park vicinity, 11/24/68, B, NHL, 68000034

Burroughs, John, Riverby Study, Between NY 9W and the Hudson River, West Park, 11/24/68, B, NHL, 68000035

Byrdcliffe Historic District, W of Woodstock at Glasco Tpke. and Larks Nest Rd., Woodstock vicinity, 5/07/79, A, B, C, 79001643

Chestnut Street Historic District, Roughly bounded by W. Chestnut St., Broadway, E. Chestnut, Livingston & Stuyvesant Sts., Kingston, 9/19/85, C, 85002443

Chetolah, S of Cragsmoor on Vista Maria Rd., Cragsmoor vicinity, 10/21/80, A, B, C, 80002782

Clinton Avenue Historic District, Clinton Ave. and Fair St., Kingston, 2/05/70, A, C, 70000434

Common School No. 10, Northside of Upper Cherrytown Rd., Accord vicinity, 9/15/88, A, C, 88001439

Community Theatre, 601 Broadway, Kingston, 7/22/79, A, C, 79001639

Crowell, J. B., and Son Brick Mould Mill Complex, Lippencott Rd., Wallkill vicinity, 6/30/83, A, 83001814

Decker, Johannes, Farm, SW of Gardiner on Red Mill Rd. and Shawangunk Kill, Gardiner vicinity, 3/05/74, A, C, 74001312

Decker, William, House [Shawangunk Valley MRA], New Prospect Rd., Shawangunk, 9/26/83, C, 83001815

Dill Farm [Shawangunk Valley MRA], Off Goebel Rd., Shawangunk, 9/26/83, C, 83001816

DuBoris, Hendrikus, House, 600 Albany Post Rd., Libertyville vicinity, 7/08/82, C, 82003410

Esopus Meadows Lighthouse [Hudson River Lighthouses TR], Spans Hudson River, Esopus, 5/29/79, A, C, 79001638

Hait, Thaddeus, Farm, 75 Allhusen Rd., Modena, 12/29/88, A, C, 88003075

Hasbrouck, Jean, House, Huguenot and N. Front Sts., New Paltz, 12/24/67, C, NHL, 67000016

Hoornbeek Store Complex, Main St. between Clinton & Church Sts., Napanoch, 2/09/84, A, C, 84003229

Huguenot Street Historic District, Huguenot St., New Paltz, 10/15/66, A, C, NHL, 66000578

Hurley Historic District, Hurley St., Hurley Mountain Rd., and Schoonmaker Lane, Hurley, 10/15/66, A, C, NHL, 66000577

Jansen, Johannes, House and Dutch Barn [Shawangunk Valley MRA], Decker Rd., Shawangunk, 9/26/83, C, 83001818

Jansen, Thomas, House [Shawangunk Valley MRA], Jansen Rd., Shawangunk, 9/26/83, C, 83001817

Kingston City Hall, 408 Broadway, Kingston, 12/09/71, A, C, 71000563

Kingston Stockade District, Area bounded by both sides of Clinton Ave., Main, Green, and Front Sts., Kingston, 6/19/75, A, C, D, 75001231

Kingston-Port Ewen Suspension Bridge, U.S. 9W, Kingston and vicinity, 4/30/80, A, C, 80002783

Kingston/Rondout 2 Lighthouse [Hudson River Lighthouses TR], Hudson River and Rondout Creek, Kingston, 5/29/79, A, C, 79001640

Lafevre, John A., House and School, NY 208, S of New Paltz, New Paltz vicinity, 11/16/89, A, C, 89002023

Lake Mohonk Mountain House Complex, NW of New Paltz, between Wallkill Valley on E and

Ulster County—Continued

Roundout Valley on W, New Paltz, 7/16/73, A, B, C, NHL, 73001280

Locust Lawn Estate, NY 32, SE of Gardiner, Gardiner vicinity, 5/17/74, A, B, C, 74001313

Loerzel Beer Hall, 213 Partition St., Saugerties, 9/07/84, C, 84003234

Main Street Historic District, US 209, Stone Ridge, 6/07/88, A, C, a, 88000666

Main-Partition Streets Historic District, Roughly bounded by Main, Partition, Market and Jane Sts., Saugerties, 7/08/82, A, C, 82003411

Miller's House at Red Mills [Shawangunk Valley MRA], Red Mills Rd. and Wallkill Ave., Shawangunk, 9/26/83, C, 83001819

National Youth Administration Woodstock Resident Work Center, NY 212 N side, E of Woodstock, Woodstock vicinity, 4/30/92, A, C, 92000455

Pearl Street Schoolhouse [Shawangunk Valley MRA], Awosting and Decker Rds., Shawangunk, 9/26/83, C, 83001820

Perrine's Bridge, Off U.S. 87 over Wallkill River, Rosendale vicinity, 4/13/73, A, C, 73001281

Ponckhockie Union Chapel, 91 Abruyn St., Kingston, 4/23/80, A, C, a, 80002784

Poppletown Farmhouse, Jct. of Old Post Rd. and Swarte Kill Rd., Esopus, 11/07/91, C, 91001656

Reformed Church of Shawangunk Complex, Hoagerburgh Rd., Bruynswick vicinity, 6/03/82, A, C, a, 82003408

Reformed Dutch Church of New Hurley, N of Wallkill on NY 208, Wallkill vicinity, 11/10/82, C, a, 82001273

Rondout-West Strand Historic District, Roughly bounded by Broadway, Roundout Creek, Ravine, Hone and McEntee Sts., Kingston, 8/24/79, A, C, 79001641

Saugerties Lighthouse [Hudson River Lighthouses TR], Hudson River at Esopus Creek, Saugerties, 5/29/79, A, C, 79001642

Senate House, NW side of Clinton Ave. near jct. with N. Front St., Kingston, 8/12/71, A, 71000564

Snyder Estate Natural Cement Historic District, NY 213, 1/2 mi. W of Rosendale, Rosendale vicinity, 6/09/92, A, C, 92000695

Terwilliger House [Shawangunk Valley MRA], Hoagerburgh Rd., Shawangunk, 9/26/83, C, 83001821

Trumpbour Homestead Farm, 1789 Old Kings Hwy., Saugerties vicinity, 9/19/85, A, C, 85002422

Tuthilltown Gristmill, Albany Post Rd., Gardiner vicinity, 6/14/82, C, 82003409

US Post Office—Ellenville [US Post Offices in New York State, 1858-1943, TR], Liberty Pl., Ellenville, 11/17/88, A, C, 88002496

West Strand Historic District, West Strand and Broadway, Kingston, 6/28/74, A, C, 74001314

Wynkoop House, NY 32, Saugerties vicinity, 9/07/84, C, 84003237

Yelverton, Anthony, House, 39 Maple Ave., Highland, 9/22/83, A, C, 83001823

Warren County

18th Separate Company Armory [Glens Falls MRA], 147 Warren St., Glens Falls, 9/29/84, C, 84003269

Argent Apartments [Glens Falls MRA], 17-18 Sherman Ave., Glens Falls, 9/29/84, C, 84003240

Bemis Eye Sanitarium Complex [Glens Falls MRA], Glen St., Glens Falls, 9/29/84, A, C, 84003243

Birdsall, Stephen T., House [Glens Falls MRA], 186-192 Ridge St., Glens Falls, 9/29/84, C, 84003245

Burnham, Thomas, House [Glens Falls MRA; Potter, Ephraim B., Buildings TR], 195 Ridge St., Glens Falls, 9/29/84, C, 84003248

Chestertown Historic District, Canada Dr. (U.S. 9), Chestertown, 8/22/77, A, C, 77000984

Colvin, Addison B., House [Glens Falls MRA], 453-455 Glen St., Glens Falls, 9/29/84, C, 84003251

Cowles, W.T., House [Glens Falls MRA; Potter, Ephraim B., Buildings TR], 43-47 William St., Glens Falls, 9/29/84, C, 84003255

Cunningham House [Glens Falls MRA; Bigelow, Henry Forbes, Buildings TR], 169 Warren St., Glens Falls, 9/29/84, C, 84003258

Delong, Zopher, House [Glens Falls MRA], 348 Glen St., Glens Falls, 9/29/84, C, 84003261

Dix, James L., House [Glens Falls MRA], 191 Ridge St., Glens Falls, 9/29/84, C, 84003268

Ferguson, Dr. James, Office [Glens Falls MRA], 5 Culvert St., Glens Falls, 9/29/84, C, 84003282

First Presbyterian Church [Glens Falls MRA], 402-410 Glen St., Glens Falls, 9/29/84, C, a, 84003314

Foster, Dr. Charles A., House [Glens Falls MRA], 162-164 Warren St., Glens Falls, 9/29/84, C, 84003321

Fredella Avenue Historic District [Glens Falls MRA; Fredella Concrete Block Structures TR], 15-21R Fredella Ave., Glens Falls, 9/29/84, C, 84003328

Fredella, Joseph J., House and Garage [Glens Falls MRA; Fredella Concrete Block Structures TR], 15-17 Mohican St., Glens Falls, 9/29/84, C, 84003331

Glens Falls Feeder Canal [Glens Falls MRA], Roughly between Richardson St. and the Old Champlain Canal, Glens Falls, 10/25/85, A, 85003401

Glens Falls High School [Glens Falls MRA; Potter, Ephraim B., Buildings TR], 421-433 Glen St., Glens Falls, 9/29/84, C, 84003335

Glens Falls Home for Aged Women [Glens Falls MRA], 178-186 Warren St., Glens Falls, 9/29/84, C, 84003340

Goodman, Stephen L., House [Glens Falls MRA], 65-67 Park St., Glens Falls, 9/29/84, C, 84003345

Hoopes House [Glens Falls MRA; Bigelow, Henry Forbes, Buildings TR], 153 Warren St., Glens Falls, 9/29/84, C, 84003348

House at 216 Warren Street [Glens Falls MRA], 216 Warren St., Glens Falls, 9/29/84, C, 84003351

Hyde House [Glens Falls MRA; Bigelow, Henry Forbes, Buildings TR], 161 Warren St., Glens Falls, 9/29/84, C, 84003358

Joubert and White Building [Glens Falls MRA], 79 Warren St., Glens Falls, 9/29/84, A, 84003360

Krum, Hiram, House [Glens Falls MRA], 133 Warren St., Glens Falls, 9/29/84, C, 84003363

Little, Russell M., House [Glens Falls MRA], 17 Center St., Glens Falls, 9/29/84, B, C, 84003367

MaGee, Merrill, House, 2 Hudson St., Warrensburg, 4/11/85, C, 85000728

McEchron, William, House [Glens Falls MRA], 65 Ridge St., Glens Falls, 9/29/84, B, C, 84003371

North Creek Railroad Station Complex, Railroad Pl., North Creek, 8/27/76, A, C, 76001287

Old Warren County Courthouse Complex, Canada and Amherst Sts., Lake George, 6/19/73, C, 73001282

Ordway, Jones, House [Glens Falls MRA], 142 Warren St., Glens Falls, 9/29/84, B, C, 84003376

Owl's Nest, NY 9L, Lake George, 11/11/71, B, NHL, 71000565

Parks, George H., House [Glens Falls MRA], 444 Glen St., Glens Falls, 9/29/84, C, 84003378

Parry, John E., House [Glens Falls MRA; Potter, Ephraim B., Buildings TR], 146 Warren St., Glens Falls, 9/29/84, C, 84003382

Peabody, Royal C., Estate, Lake Shore Dr., Lake George, 6/21/84, A, C, 84003386

Peyser and Morrison Shirt Company Building [Glens Falls MRA; Potter, Ephraim B., Buildings TR], 211-217 Warren St., Glens Falls, 9/29/84, C, 84003388

Potter, Ephraim B., House [Glens Falls MRA; Potter, Ephraim B., Buildings TR], 15 Sherman Ave., Glens Falls, 9/29/84, C, 84003391

Rosekrans, Enoch, House [Glens Falls MRA], 62 Warren St., Glens Falls, 9/29/84, B, C, a, 84003396

Rugge, A. S., House [Glens Falls MRA], 428 Glen St., Glens Falls, 9/29/84, C, 84003394

Sagamore Hotel Complex, Green Island and Federal Hill, Bolton Landing vicinity, 7/21/83, C, 83001824

Sherman House, 380 Glen St., Glens Falls, 11/07/77, B, C, a, 77000985

Silver Bay Association Complex, NY 9N, Silver Bay, 3/20/80, A, C, a, 80002785

Smith Flats [Glens Falls MRA], 53-61 Bay St., Glens Falls, 9/29/84, C, 84003404

Society of Friends Hall [Glens Falls MRA], 172-174 Ridge St., Glens Falls, 9/29/84, C, a, 84003407

St. Mary's Academy [Glens Falls MRA], 10-12 Church St., Glens Falls, 9/29/84, C, a, 84003400

Stilwell, Thomas, House [Glens Falls MRA], 134 Maple St., Glens Falls, 9/29/84, C, 84003414

Three Squares Historic District [Glens Falls MRA], Roughly South, Glen, Maple, and Ridge Sts., Glens Falls, 9/29/84, A, C, 84003420

US Post Office—Lake George [US Post Offices in New York State, 1858-1943, TR], Canada and James St., Lake George, 5/11/89, A, C, 88002338

Wait, F. W., House [Glens Falls MRA], 173-175 Ridge St., Glens Falls, 9/29/84, C, 84003422

Warren County—Continued

Warrensburg Mills Historic District, Roughly bounded by the Osborne and Woolen Mill bridges, Schroon River and the railroad right of way, Warrensburg, 9/18/75, A, C, 75001232

Wiawaka Bateaux Site, Address Restricted, Lake George vicinity, 6/14/92, A, C, D, 92000624

Wilmarth, Martin L. C., House [Glens Falls MRA; Potter, Ephraim B., Buildings TR], 528 Glen St., Glens Falls, 9/29/84, C, 84003423

Wing, Helen, House [Glens Falls MRA; Potter, Ephraim B., Buildings TR], 126 Warren St., Glens Falls, 9/29/84, C, 84003425

Washington County

Buskirk Covered Bridge [Covered Bridges of Washington County TR], Spans Hoosic River N of NY 67, Buskirk vicinity, 3/08/78, A, C, 78003457

Cambridge Historic District, Irregular pattern along Main and S. Union Sts., Cambridge, 11/15/78, A, C, 78001922

Coffin Site, Address Restricted, Greenwich vicinity, 7/22/80, D, 80002786

DeRidder Homestead, E of Schuylerville off NY 29, Schuylerville vicinity, 3/22/74, A, 74001315

Eagleville Covered Bridge [Covered Bridges of Washington County TR], Spans Batten Kill off NY 313, Eagleville, 3/08/78, A, C, 78003458

Haynes, Lemuel, House, Rte. 149, South Granville, 5/15/75, B, NHL, 75001235

Hudson Falls Historic District, Roughly bounded by Oak, Mechanic, River, Maple and Main Sts., Hudson Falls, 9/15/83, C, 83001825

Main Street Historic District, Both sides of Williams St. and both sides of Main St. Bridge to below Saunders St. Bridge, Whitehall, 4/24/75, A, C, 75001236

Miller, William, Chapel and Ascension Rock, W of Fair Haven on SR 11, Fair Haven vicinity, 7/17/75, A, C, a, 75001233

Old Fort House, 29 Lower Broadway, Fort Edward, 9/15/83, A, C, 83001826

Potter, Judge Joseph, House, Mountain Ter., Whitehall, 5/02/74, B, C, 74001316

Rexleigh Covered Bridge [Covered Bridges of Washington County TR], Off NY 22, Jackson, 3/08/78, A, C, 78003459

Rogers Island, Address Restricted, Fort Edward vicinity, 7/24/73, A, D, 73001283

Salem Historic District, Both sides of Broadway and Main Sts. from RR tracks on N and W to include White Creek on S and E, Salem, 5/28/75, A, C, 75001234

Shushan Covered Bridge [Covered Bridges of Washington County TR], Spans Batten Kill off NY 22, Shushan, 3/08/78, A, C, 78003460

US Post Office—Granville [US Post Offices in New York State, 1858-1943, TR], 41 Main St., Granville, 5/11/89, A, C, 88002520

US Post Office—Hudson Falls [US Post Offices in New York State, 1858-1943, TR], 114 Main St., Hudson Falls, 5/11/89, A, C, 88002509

US Post Office—Whitehall [US Post Offices in New York State, 1858-1943, TR], 88 Broadway, Whitehall, 5/11/89, A, C, 88002447

White Creek Historic District, SR 68, Byars and Niles Rds., White Creek, 4/26/79, C, 79001644

Wayne County

Brick Church Corners, Jct. of Brick Church and Ontario Center Rds., Ontario, 6/05/74, A, B, a, 74001317

Broad Street-Water Street Historic District, Broad and Water Sts., Lyons, 8/14/73, A, C, 73001284

Bullis, Charles, House, 1727 Canandaigua Rd., Macedon vicinity, 3/20/86, C, 86000483

Customs House, Sentell St., Sodus Point, 5/06/80, A, C, 80002787

East Main Street Commercial Historic District, Between Clinton and William-Cuyler Sts., Palmyra, 11/21/74, A, C, 74001318

Hotchkiss, H. G., Essential Oil Company Plant, 93–95 Water St., Lyons, 11/02/87, A, 87001897

LOTUS (schooner), Trestle Landing Marina, Co. Rt. 14 at Sentell Rd., Sodus Point, 5/10/90, C, 90000694

Market Street Historic District, Both sides of Market St. between Canal and Main Sts., Palmyra, 12/08/72, A, C, 72000916

Pultneyville Historic District, Sections of Lake Rd. and Jay St., Pultneyville, 9/11/85, C, 85002325

Smith—Ely Mansion, 39 W. Genesee St., Clyde, 2/10/92, C, 92000032

Sodus Point Lighthouse, Off NY 14 at Lake Ontario, Sodus Point, 10/08/76, A, 76001288

US Post Office—Clyde [US Post Offices in New York State, 1858-1943, TR], 26 S. Park St., Clyde, 11/17/88, A, C, 88002472

US Post Office—Lyons [US Post Offices in New York State, 1858-1943, TR], 1–5 Pearl St., Lyons, 5/11/89, A, C, 88002349

US Post Office—Newark [US Post Offices in New York State, 1858-1943, TR], Maple Ct. and S. Main St., Newark, 5/11/89, A, C, 88002366

Westchester County

Amawalk Friends Meeting House, Quaker Church Rd., Amawalk, 11/16/89, A, C, a, d, 89002004

Armour-Stiner House, 45 W. Clinton Ave., Irvington, 12/18/75, C, NHL, 75001238

Austin, Richard, House, 196 Croton Ave., Ossining, 9/20/88, A, C, 88001527

Bear Mountain Bridge Rd. [Hudson Highlands MRA], NY 6/202, between Bear Mt. Bridge, Cortlandt, 11/23/82, A, C, 82001274

Bedford Road Historic District, Bedford Rd., Armonk, 11/21/85, A, C, a, d, 85002903

Bedford Village Historic District, Roughly bounded by Court, Seminary, Poundridge and Greenwich Rds., Bedford, 10/02/73, C, 73001285

Beecher—McFadden Estate, E. Main St., Peekskill, 11/02/87, C, 87001894

Bell Place-Locust Avenue Historic District, Roughly bounded by Cromwell Pl., Locust Hill Ave., Baldwin Pl. & N. Broadway, Yonkers, 8/29/85, C, 85001936

Bolton Priory, 7 Priory Lane, Pelham Manor, 6/28/74, C, 74001320

Boston Post Road Historic District, Roughly bounded by Boston Post Rd. and Milton Harbor, Rye, 10/29/82, A, B, C, NHL, 82001275

Brandreth Pill Factory, Water St., Ossining, 1/10/80, B, C, 80002792

Bridge L-158, W of Goldens Bridge at Croton River, Goldens Bridge vicinity, 11/29/78, A, C, b, 78001923

Bronx River Parkway Reservation, Bronx River Pkwy. from jct. with Sprain Brook Rd. to and including Kensico Dam Plaza, Bronxville vicinity, 1/11/91, A, C, 90002143

Bush-Lyon Homestead, John Lyon Park, King St., Port Chester, 4/22/82, A, C, 82003412

Capitol Theater, 147-151 Westchester Ave., Port Chester, 6/07/84, C, 84003426

Chappaqua Railroad Depot and Depot Plaza [Greeley, Horace TR], 200 South Greeley Ave., Chappaqua, 4/19/79, A, C, 79003210

Christ Episcopal Church, Broadway and Elizabeth Sts., Tarrytown, 4/23/87, B, C, a, 87000658

Church of Saint Mary the Virgin and Greeley Grove [Greeley, Horace TR], 191 South Greeley Ave., Chappaqua, 4/19/79, B, C, a, 79003213

Copcutt, John, Mansion, 239 Nepperhan Ave., Yonkers, 9/12/85, A, B, C, a, 85002283

Crane, Gerard, House, Old Croton Falls Rd., Somers, 9/05/85, B, C, 85001954

Cropsey, Jasper F., House and Studio, 49 Washington Ave., Hastings-on-Hudson, 5/17/73, B, C, 73001287

Croton Aqueduct, Old, Runs N from Yonkers to New Croton Dam, Yonkers and vicinity, 12/02/74, A, C, NHL, 74001324

Croton North Railroad Station, Senasqua Rd., Croton-on-Hudson, 8/27/87, A, C, 87001458

Davenport House, 157 Davenport Rd., New Rochelle, 4/30/80, C, 80002791

Delavan Terrace Historic District, Roughly bounded by Delaware Terr. and Palisade and Park Aves., Yonkers, 9/15/83, C, 83001827

Downtown Ossining Historic District, Roughly along US 9, Main St., and Croton Ave., Ossining, 8/09/89, A, C, a, 88001827

Draper, John W., House, 407 Broadway, Hastings-on-Hudson, 5/15/75, B, NHL, 75001237

Drum Hill High School, Ringgold St., Peekskill, 12/31/79, A, 79003797

Dutch Reformed Church, N edge of Tarrytown on U.S. 9, North Tarrytown, 10/15/66, A, C, a, NHL, 66000581

East Irvington School, Taxter Rd., East Irvington, 10/06/83, A, 83004216

Edgewood House, 908 Edgewood Ave., Pelham Manor, 6/26/86, A, C, 86001388

Elmsford Reformed Church and Cemetery, 30 S. Central Ave., Elmsford, 9/15/83, A, C, a, d, 83001828

Estherwood and Carriage House, Clinton Ave., Dobbs Ferry, 11/20/79, C, 79001646

Westchester County—Continued

First Baptist Church and Rectory, 56 S. Broadway, Tarrytown, 7/21/83, C, a, 83001829

First Baptist Church of Ossining, S. Highland Ave. and Main St., Ossining, 1/12/73, A, C, a, 73001288

First Presbyterian Church and Pintard, Lewis, House, Pintard Ave., New Rochelle, 9/07/79, A, C, a, 79001648

Foster Memorial A.M.E. Zion Church, 90 Wildey St., Tarrytown, 6/03/82, A, a, 82003414

Friedlander, Leo, Studio, 825 W. Hartsdale Rd., White Plains, 7/29/82, B, 82003416

Grainger, Percy, Home and Studio, 7 Cromwell Pl., White Plains, 4/08/93, B, C, g, 93000234

Greeley House [Greeley, Horace TR], 100 King St., Chappaqua, 4/19/79, B, 79003212

Halcyon Place Historic District, Halcyon Pl., Yonkers, 1/11/91, A, C, 90002145

Hammond House, S of Hawthorne on Grasslands Rd., Hawthorne vicinity, 5/06/80, B, 80002790

Hart, Eleazer, House, 243 Bronxville Rd., Yonkers, 7/29/82, A, C, 82003417

Hartford, John A., House, SW of Valhalla on NY 100, Valhalla vicinity, 12/22/77, B, g, NHL, 77000987

Hastings Prototype House, 546 Farragut Pkwy., Hastings-on-Hudson, 12/19/91, C, 91001873

Haviland's, Widow, Tavern, Purchase St., Rye, 4/16/74, C, 74001322

Hyatt, Caleb, House, 937 White Plains Post Rd., Scarsdale, 1/22/73, C, 73001291

Hyatt-Livingston House, 152 Broadway, Dobbs Ferry, 10/05/72, B, C, 72000917

Irving, Washington, High School, 18 N. Broadway, Tarrytown, 4/26/84, C, 84003437

Irvington Town Hall, 85 Main St., Irvington, 11/01/84, C, 84000205

Jay, John, Homestead, Jay St., Katonah, 7/24/72, B, NHL, 72000918

Jones, John, Homestead, Oregon Rd. and Durrin Ave., Van Cortlandtville, 5/25/89, C, 89000462

Jug Tavern, Revolutionary Rd. and Rockledge Ave., Ossining, 6/07/76, A, 76001293

Katonah Village Historic District, Parkway, Valleyedge, Edgemont and Bedford Rds., Katonah, 9/15/83, C, 83001830

Knapp, Timothy, House and Milton Cemetery, 265 Rye Beach Ave. and Milton Rd., Rye, 6/14/82, A, B, C, d, 82003413

Lawrence Park Historic District, Roughly bounded by Side Hill, Prescott, Kensington, Garden and Chestnut Ave., Maidens Ln, Valley and Pondfield Rds., Bronxville, 1/23/80, B, C, g, 80002788

Leland Castle, 29 Castle Pl., New Rochelle, 8/27/76, C, 76001291

Life Savers Building, N. Main St., Port Chester, 7/11/85, A, C, 85001496

Lispenard—Rodman—Davenport House, 180 Davenport Ave., New Rochelle, 9/22/86, B, C, 86002637

Lyndhurst, 635 S. Broadway, Tarrytown, 11/13/66, B, C, NHL, 66000582

Mamaroneck Methodist Church, 514 Boston Post Rd., Mamaroneck, 10/02/92, C, a, 92001304

Mapleton, 52 N. Broadway, White Plains, 9/28/76, C, 76001295

Masterton-Dusenberry House, 90 White Plains Rd., Bronxville, 4/16/80, B, C, 80002789

Merestead, Byram Lake Rd., Mount Kisco vicinity, 9/27/84, C, 84003431

Miller House, Virginia Rd., North White Plains, 9/29/76, B, C, 76001292

Mt. Zion Methodist Church, Primrose St. S of Reis Park, Somers, 5/10/90, A, C, a, d, 90000692

Music Hall, 11 Main St., Tarrytown, 2/12/80, A, 80002795

North Grove Street Historic District, 1, 2, 8, 15, and 19 Grove St., Tarrytown, 3/13/79, C, 79001650

North Salem Town Hall, Titicus Rd., Salem Center, 9/04/80, A, C, 80002794

Nuits, Hudson Rd. and Clifton Pl., Ardsley-on-Hudson, 4/13/77, C, 77000986

Odell House, 425 Ridge Rd., Greenburgh, 3/28/73, B, C, 73001286

Old Chappaqua Historic District, Quaker Rd., Chappaqua, 7/15/74, A, C, a, 74001319

Old Croton Dam, Site of, N of Ossining on NY 129, Ossining vicinity, 6/19/73, C, 73001289

Old St. Peter's Church, Oregon Rd. and Locust Ave., Van Cortlandtville, 3/07/73, C, a, 73001292

Paine, Thomas, Cottage, 20 Sicard Ave., New Rochelle, 11/28/72, B, b, NHL, 72000920

Patriot's Park, US 9, Tarrytown, 6/14/82, A, C, f, 82003415

Pelhamdale, 45 Iden Ave., Pelham Manor, 11/04/82, B, C, 82001276

Philipsburg Manor, 381 Bellwood Ave., Upper Mills, 10/15/66, A, NHL, 66000584

Philipse Manor Hall, Warburton Ave. and Dock St., Yonkers, 10/15/66, C, NHL, 66000585

Philipse Manor Railroad Station, Jct. of Riverside Dr. and Millard, North Tarrytown, 3/14/91, A, C, 91000237

Pioneer Building, 14 Lawton St., New Rochelle, 12/29/83, A, C, 83004217

Playland Amusement Park, Playland Pkwy. and Forest Ave., Rye, 7/04/80, A, NHL, 80004529

Pound Ridge Historic District, Roughly Pound Ridge, Old Stone Hill, and Salem Rds., Trinity Pass and Westchester Ave., Pound Ridge, 12/30/85, A, B, C, 85003196

Public Bath House No. 2 [Yonkers Public Bath House TR], 27 Vineyard Ave., Yonkers, 10/21/85, A, C, a, 85003365

Public Bath House No. 3 [Yonkers Public Bath House TR], 48 Yonkers Ave., Yonkers, 10/21/85, A, C, 85003366

Public Bath House No. 4 [Yonkers Public Bath House TR], 138 Linden St., Yonkers, 10/21/85, A, C, 85003367

Purdy, Jacob, House, 60 Park Ave., White Plains, 8/31/79, B, 79001651

Purdy, Joseph, Homestead, Jct. of NY 22 and 116, Purdys, 1/25/73, B, 73001290

Putnam and Mellor Engine and Hose Company Firehouse, 46 S. Main St., Port Chester, 9/15/83, C, 83001831

Rehoboth [Greeley, Horace TR], 33 Aldrige Rd., Chappaqua, 4/19/79, B, C, 79003214

Reid Hall, Manhattanville College, Manhattanville College, Purchase St., Purchase, 3/22/74, B, C, 74001321

Rockefeller, John D., Estate, Pocantico Hills, Mt. Pleasant, 5/11/76, B, NHL, 76001290

Sarles' Tavern, NY 100, Millwood, 12/31/79, C, 79001647

Scarborough Historic District, US 9, Ossining, 9/07/84, A, C, a, 84003433

Sherwood House, 340 Tuckahoe Rd., Yonkers, 5/10/84, A, 84003434

Smith Tavern, 440 Bedford Rd., Armonk, 9/15/83, A, 83001833

Smith, Alexander, Carpet Mills Historic District, Roughly bounded by Saw Mill River Rd., Orchard St., Lake and Ashburton Aves., Yonkers, 8/11/83, A, C, 83001832

Somers Town House, Jct. of U.S. 202 and NY 100, Somers vicinity, 8/07/74, B, C, 74001323

St. John's Protestant Episcopal Church, One Hudson St., Yonkers, 7/29/82, A, C, a, 82003418

St. Mark's Cemetery, E. Main St., corner of St. Mark's Pl., Mount Kisco, 6/23/88, C, a, d, 88000918

St. Mark's Episcopal Church, Jct. of N. Bedford Rd. and E. Main St., Mt. Kisco, 11/21/91, C, a, 91001725

St. Paul's Church National Historic Site, Eastchester, Mount Vernon, 10/15/66, A, B, C, a, f, NPS, 66000580

St. Paul's Episcopal Church and Rectory, St. Paul's Pl., Ossining, 12/06/78, C, a, 78001925

Stevens, John, House, 29 W. 4th St., Mount Vernon, 4/26/72, B, C, 72000919

Sunnyside, Sunnyside Lane, Tarrytown vicinity, 10/15/66, B, NHL, 66000583

Tarrytown Lighthouse [Hudson River Lighthouses TR], Spans Hudson River, North Tarrytown, 5/29/79, A, C, 79001649

The Woodpile, Jct. of Croton Lake and Wood Rds., Mt. Kisco vicinity, 2/10/92, C, 92000030

Thompson, W. B., Mansion, 1061 N. Broadway, Yonkers, 10/29/82, C, 82001277

Trevor, John Bond, House, 511 Warburton Ave., Yonkers, 6/19/72, C, 72000921

US Post Office—Bronxville [US Post Offices in New York State, 1858-1943, TR], Pondfield Rd., Bronxville, 11/17/88, A, C, 88002459

US Post Office—Dobbs Ferry [US Post Offices in New York State, 1858-1943, TR], Main St., Dobbs Ferry, 11/17/88, A, C, 88002484

US Post Office—Harrison [US Post Offices in New York State, 1858-1943, TR], 258 Halstead Ave., Harrison, 5/11/89, A, C, 88002524

US Post Office—Larchmont [US Post Offices in New York State, 1858-1943, TR], 1 Chatsworth Ave., Larchmont, 5/11/89, A, C, 88002341

US Post Office—Mount Vernon [US Post Offices in New York State, 1858-1943, TR], 15 S. First St., Mount Vernon, 5/11/89, A, C, 88002355

US Post Office—New Rochelle [US Post Offices in New York State, 1858-1943, TR], 255 North Ave., New Rochelle, 5/11/89, A, C, 88002368

Westchester County—Continued

US Post Office—Peekskill [US Post Offices in New York State, 1858-1943, TR], 738 South St., Peekskill, 5/11/89, A, C, 88002401

US Post Office—Port Chester [US Post Offices in New York State, 1858-1943, TR], 245 Westchester Ave., Port Chester, 5/11/89, A, C, 88002406

US Post Office—Rye [US Post Offices in New York State, 1858-1943, TR], 41 Purdy Ave., Rye, 5/11/89, A, C, 88002426

US Post Office—Scarsdale [US Post Offices in New York State, 1858-1943, TR], Chase Rd., Scarsdale, 5/11/89, A, C, 88002428

US Post Office—Yonkers [US Post Offices in New York State, 1858-1943, TR], 79–81 Main St., Yonkers, 5/11/89, A, C, 88002448

Union Hall, NY 116 and Keeler Ln., North Salem, 8/28/86, C, 86001978

United Methodist Church and Parsonage, 300 E. Main and 31 Smith Ave., Mount Kisco, 11/04/82, C, a, 82001278

Untermyer Park, Warburton Ave. and N. Broadway S. of jct. with Odell Ave., Yonkers, 5/31/74, C, 74002263

Van Cortlandt Manor, U.S. 9, N of jct. with U.S. 9A, Croton-on-Hudson, 10/15/66, A, C, NHL, 66000579

Van Cortlandt Upper Manor House, Oregon Rd., Peekskill vicinity, 4/02/81, B, 81000417

Van Cortlandtville School, 297 Locust Ave., Van Cortlandtville, 4/07/89, A, C, 89000285

Villa Lewaro, N. Broadway, Irvington, 5/11/76, B, NHL, 76001289

Villa Loretto, Crompond Rd., Peekskill, 4/27/89, A, C, a, 88000148

Ward, William E., House, Comly Ave., Rye, 11/07/76, C, 76001294

Washington School, 83 Croton Ave., Ossining, 2/12/87, C, 87000080

Wayside Cottage, 1039 Post Rd., Scarsdale, 5/01/81, B, 81000418

White Plains Armory, 35 S. Broadway, White Plains, 4/16/80, A, C, 80002796

Williams—DuBois House, Grace Ln. and Pinesbridge Rd., New Castle, 5/25/89, C, 89000463

Yonkers Water Works, Roughly bounded by Saw Mill River and Grassy Sprain Rds., and Gilmare Dr., Yonkers, 7/21/82, A, C, 82003419

Yorktown Heights Railroad Station, Commerce St., Yorktown Heights, 3/19/81, A, C, 81000419

Wyoming County

Arcade and Attica Railroad, Railroad right of way from Arcade to N. Java, North Java, 11/17/80, A, C, 80002797

Gates, Seth M., House, 15 Perry Ave., Warsaw, 2/21/92, A, C, 92000031

Middlebury Academy, 22 S. Academy St., Wyoming, 1/17/73, A, 73001293

Monument Circle Historic District, Roughly, E. Court St. from N. Main St. to Park St. and adjacent parts of Main and Park, Warsaw, 5/11/92, A, C, a, 92000447

Silver Lake Institute Historic District, Roughly bounded by Wesley, Embury, Thompson, Haven, Lakeside & Lakeview Aves., Silver Lake, 9/19/85, A, C, a, 85002442

Trinity Church, W. Buffalo St., Warsaw, 3/18/80, C, a, 80002798

US Post Office—Attica [US Post Offices in New York State, 1858-1943, TR], 76 Main St., Attica, 11/17/88, A, C, 88002453

US Post Office—Warsaw [US Post Offices in New York State, 1858-1943, TR], 35 S. Main St., Warsaw, 5/11/89, A, C, 88002441

Warsaw Academy, 73 S. Main St., Warsaw, 1/03/80, A, C, 80002799

Wyoming Village Historic District, NY 19, Wyoming, 12/27/74, A, C, 74001326

Yates County

Angus Cobblestone Farmhouse and Barn Complex [Cobblestone Architecture of New York

State MPS], 612 NY 14, Benton, 5/11/92, C, 92000439

Barden Cobblestone Farmhouse [Cobblestone Architecture of New York State MPS], 2492 Ferguson Corners Rd., Benton, 5/11/92, C, 92000435

Bates Cobblestone Farmhouse [Cobblestone Architecture of New York State MPS], 5521 NY 364, Middlesex, 5/11/92, C, 92000436

Earl, Jephtha, Cobblestone Farmhouse [Cobblestone Architecture of New York State MPS], Old State Rd. N of jct. with Johnson Rd., Benton, 5/11/92, C, 92000438

Ingersoll, Robert, Birthplace, Main St., Dresden, 2/11/88, B, C, b, c, 88000110

Nichols, William, Cobblestone Farmhouse [Cobblestone Architecture of New York State MPS], Alexander Rd. W of jct. with Thistle St. Rd., Benton, 5/11/92, C, 92000437

Penn Yan Historic District, Roughly bounded by Water, Seneca, Elm, Wagener, Court, Clinton, North and Main Sts., Penn Yan, 3/14/85, C, 85000591

Spence, Dr. Henry, Cobblestone Farmhouse and Barn Complex [Cobblestone Architecture of New York State MPS], Lakemont—Himrod Rd. N of jct. with Shannon Corners Rd., Starkey, 5/11/92, C, 92000441

Supplee, Daniel, Cobblestone Farmhouse [Cobblestone Architecture of New York State MPS], 4420 Dundee—Himrod Rd., Starkey, 5/11/92, C, 92000442

US Post Office—Penn Yan [US Post Offices in New York State, 1858-1943, TR], 159 Main St., Penn Yan, 5/11/89, A, C, 88002403

Yates County Courthouse Park District, Main, Court and Liberty Sts., Penn Yan, 6/19/79, C, a, 79001652

Young—Leach Cobblestone Farmhouse and Barn Complex [Cobblestone Architecture of New York State MPS], 2601 NY 14, Torrey, 5/11/92, C, 92000440

NORTH CAROLINA

Alamance County

Alamance Battleground State Historic Site, SW of Burlington on Rte. 1, off NC 62, near jct. with Rte. 1129, Alamance vicinity, 2/26/70, A, f, 70000435

Alamance County Courthouse, [North Carolina County Courthouses TR], Elm and Main Sts., Graham, 5/10/79, A, C, 79001655

Alamance Hotel [Burlington MRA], Maple Ave. and S. Main St., Burlington, 5/31/84, A, C, 84001906

Allen House, SW of Burlington on Rte. 1, off SC 62, Burlington vicinity, 2/26/70, C, b, 70000436

Altamahaw Mill Office, SR 1002 and SR 1567, Altamahaw, 11/20/84, A, C, 84000301

Atlantic Bank and Trust Company Building [Burlington MRA], 358 S. Main St., Burlington, 5/31/84, A, C, 84001909

Bellemont Mill Village Historic District, E and W side of NC 49, S of jct. with Great Alamance Creek, Bellemont, 7/01/87, A, C, 87001099

Braxton, Hiram, House [Log Buildings in Alamance County MPS], 3440 Newlin Rd., Snow Camp vicinity, 11/22/93, C, 93001193

Cedarock Park Historic District, SR 2409, Graham vicinity, 12/04/86, A, C, 86003455

Cook, William, House [Log Buildings in Alamance County MPS], NC 2131 W side at jct. with NC 2132, Mebane vicinity, 11/22/93, C, 93001194

Cooper School, S side of SR 2143, E of jct. with SR 2142, Mebane vicinity, 12/15/86, A, C, 86003451

Cross Roads Presbyterian Church and Cemetery and Stainback Store, N of Mebane at SR 1910 and SR 1912, Mebane vicinity, 5/22/84, A, C, a, d, 84001912

Downtown Burlington Historic District, Roughly bounded by Morehead, S. Main, Davis, S. Worth, E. Webb and Spring Sts., Burlington, 9/06/90, A, C, 90001320

Efird Building [Burlington MRA], 133 E. Davis St., Burlington, 5/31/84, A, C, 84001914

Elon College Historic District, S side of Haggard Ave. between William and O'Kelly, Elon College, 3/22/88, A, C, 88000166

First Baptist Church [Burlington MRA], 400 S. Broad St., Burlington, 5/31/84, C, a, 84001917

First Christian Church of Burlington [Burlington MRA], 415 S. Church St., Burlington, 5/31/84, A, C, a, 84001919

Fogleman, Polly, House [Log Buildings in Alamance County MPS], 4331 Brick Church Rd., Burlington, 11/22/93, C, 93001197

Friends Spring Meeting House, Jct. of SR 1005 and SR 2338, Snow Camp vicinity, 3/19/87, A, C, a, d, 87000456

Glencoe Mill Village Historic District, Off NC 62 at Haw River, Glencoe, 2/16/79, A, B, C, 79001654

Graham Historic District, E. and W. Harden, E. and W. Elm, N. and S. Main and W. Pine Sts., Graham, 4/07/83, C, 83001834

Griffis-Patton House, NW of Melbane on SR 1927, Mebane vicinity, 3/17/83, C, 83001835

Guy, Thomas, House [Log Buildings in Alamance County MPS], NC 2135 N side, 0.3 mi. W of jct. with NC 2142, Mebane vicinity, 11/22/93, C, 93001195

Hawfields Presbyterian Church, SW of Mebane on NC 119, Mebane vicinity, 12/15/78, A, B, C, a, 78001926

Henderson Scott Farm Historic District, Jct. of NC 119 and SR 2135, Mebane vicinity, 9/16/87, B, C, 87000411

Holt, Charles T., House, 228 Holt St., Haw River, 6/01/82, A, B, C, 82003421

Holt, L. Banks, House, S of Alamance on NC 62, Alamance vicinity, 4/18/77, B, C, 77000988

Holt-Frost House [Burlington MRA], 130 Union Ave., Burlington, 5/31/84, A, C, 84001920

Horner Houses [Burlington MRA], 304 and 308 N. Fisher St., Burlington, 5/31/84, A, C, 84001921

Kernodle—Pickett House, Jct. of NC 1136 and NC 1131, Bellemont vicinity, 3/23/87, B, C, 87000454

Kerr—Patton House, NC 2133, Thompson, 12/05/85, A, C, D, 85003083

Lakeside Mills Historic District [Burlington MRA], 404-418 Lakeside Ave., Kent Ave., and 428-437 Hatch St., Burlington, 5/31/84, A, 84001922

McBane, Camilus, House [Log Buildings in Alamance County MPS], Off NC 2345 N side, 0.3 mi. W of jct. with NC 2340, 0.2 mi. down unnamed rd., Snow Camp vicinity, 11/22/93, C, 93001196

McCray School, NW side of NC 62, S of jct. with SR 1757, Burlington vicinity, 12/04/86, A, C, 86003438

Menagerie Carousel, Burlington City Park, S. Main St., Burlington, 8/30/82, A, B, C, b, 82003420

Moore-Holt-White House [Burlington MRA], 520 Maple ave., Burlington, 5/31/84, A, B, C, 84001924

Scott, Kerr, Farm, N and S side of SR 2123, Haw River vicinity, 10/31/87, B, C, g, 87001850

Snow Camp Mutual Telephone Exchange Building, SR 1004, .2 mi. S of SR 1005, Snow Camp, 6/09/89, A, 89000497

Southern Railway Passenger Station, Main and Webb Sts., Burlington, 5/23/80, A, C, b, 80002800

Spoon, A. L., House [Log Buildings in Alamance County MPS], NC 1107 N side, 0.7 mi. SW of jct. with NC 1005, Snow Camp vicinity, 11/22/93, C, 93001192

St. Athanasius Episcopal Church and Parish House and the Church of the Holy Comforter, 300 E. Webb Ave. and 320 E. Davis St., Burlington, 5/29/79, C, a, 79001653

Stagg House [Burlington MRA], 317 N. Park Ave., Burlington, 5/31/84, A, C, 84001926

Sunny Side, NC 1136, 3 mi. E of jct. with NC 62, Burlington vicinity, 3/23/87, B, C, 87000457

Thompson, James Monroe, House [Log Buildings in Alamance County MPS], NC 2158 E side, 0.1 mi. S of jct. with NC 2150, Saxapahaw vicinity, 11/22/93, C, 93001198

US Post Office, 430 S. Spring St., Burlington, 9/23/88, A, C, 88001594

West Davis Street-Fountain Place Historic District, Roughly Bounded by Front, W. Webb, S. Fisher, E. Willowbrook, W. Davis Sts., and Fountain Pl., Burlington, 11/05/84, A, C, g, 84000359

White Furniture Company, E. Center and N. 5th Sts., Mebane vicinity, 7/29/82, A, B, C, 82003422

Windsor Cotton Mills Office [Burlington MRA], Market and Gilmer Sts., Burlington, 5/31/84, A, C, 84001930

Woodlawn School, N side NC 1921 0.15 mi. W of jct. with NC 1920, Mebane vicinity, 11/29/91, A, C, 91001745

Alexander County

Lucas Mansion, Church St., Hiddenite, 12/02/82, B, C, 82001279

Alleghany County

Alleghany County Courthouse [North Carolina County Courthouses TR], Main and Whitehead Sts., Sparta, 5/10/79, A, C, g, 79001657

Brinegar Cabin, At mi. 238.5, Blue Ridge Pkwy., Whitehead vicinity, 1/20/72, C, NPS, 72000922

Crouse, Elbert, Farmstead, S of Whitehead on Blue Ridge Parkway, Whitehead vicinity, 7/29/82, A, C, d, 82003423

Doughton, Robert L., House, NC 18, Laurel Springs, 8/13/79, B, C, g, 79001656

Gambill, J. C., Site, Address Restricted, New Haven vicinity, 4/03/78, D, 78001927

Hash, Bays, Site, Address Restricted, Amelia vicinity, 4/19/78, D, 78003078

Jarvis House, N end NC 1439, N of jct. with NC 18, Sparta vicinity, 10/16/91, C, 91001506

Vogler, William T., Cottage, NC 1478 E side, approx. 1.3 mi. NE of US 21, Roaring Gap, 9/30/91, A, B, C, 91001492

Weaver, William, House, SW of Piney Creek on SR 1302, Piney Creek vicinity, 11/07/76, A, 76001297

Anson County

Boggan-Hammond House and Alexander Little Wing, 210 Wade St., Wadesboro, 9/14/72, B, C, b, 72000923

Anson County—Continued

Horne, Billy, Farm, NC 1246, .5 mi. W of jct. NC 1240, Polkton vicinity, 6/09/89, A, B, C, 89000496

US Post Office, 105–111 Martin St., Wadesboro, 7/06/87, A, C, 87001161

Ashe County

Alexander, Shubal V., Archeological District, Address Restricted, Crumpler vicinity, 9/01/78, D, 78001928

Ashe County Courthouse [North Carolina County Courthouses TR], Main St., Jefferson, 5/10/79, A, C, 79001658

Baptist Chapel Church and Cemetery, E of Helton on SR 1527, Helton vicinity, 11/13/76, A, a, 76001302

Bower-Cox House, SW of Scottville on SR 1595, Scottville vicinity, 11/07/76, B, 76001303

Brinegar District, Address Restricted, Crumpler vicinity, 3/21/78, D, 78001929

Cox, Samuel, House, SW of Scottville off U.S. 221 on SR 1636, Scottville vicinity, 11/07/76, A, C, 76001304

Glendale Springs Inn, NC 16 and SR 1632, Glendale Springs, 10/10/79, A, C, 79003326

Grassy Creek Historic District, SR 1535 and SR 1573, Grassy Creek, 12/12/76, A, C, 76001300

Pierce, John M., House, N of Crumpler on SR 1559, Crumpler vicinity, 11/07/76, A, C, 76001298

Poe Fish Weir, Address Restricted, Jefferson vicinity, 5/22/78, D, 78001930

Thompson's Bromine and Arsenic Springs, W of Crumpler on SR 1542, Crumpler vicinity, 10/22/76, A, D, 76001299

Tucker, John W., House, SR 1353, Tuckerdale vicinity, 7/29/85, B, C, c, 85001685

Waddell, William, House, W of Grassy Creek off NC 16 on SR 1532, Grassy Creek vicinity, 11/07/76, C, 76001301

Avery County

Avery County Courthouse [North Carolina County Courthouses TR], Montezuma St. and Courthouse Dr., Newland, 5/10/79, A, C, 79001660

Linville Historic District, U.S. 221, Linville, 3/07/79, A, C, g, 79001659

Beaufort County

Bank of Washington, West End Branch, 216 W. Main St., Washington, 2/18/71, A, C, 71000566

Bath Historic District, Bounded by Bath Creek, NC 92, and King St., Bath, 2/26/70, A, C, a, 70000437

Beaufort County Courthouse, Corner of W. 2nd and Market Sts., Washington, 3/31/71, A, C, 71000567

Belfont Plantation House, N of Latham on SR 1411, Latham vicinity, 12/12/76, B, C, 76001305

Belhaven City Hall, Main St., Belhaven, 1/27/81, A, C, 81000420

Bonner House, Front St., Bath, 2/26/70, C, 70000438

Palmer-Marsh House, Main St., S of NC 92, Bath, 2/26/70, C, NHL, 70000439

Pantego Academy, Academy St., Pantego, 10/25/84, A, C, 84000114

Rosedale, NW of Washington off SR 1407, Washington vicinity, 4/29/82, A, B, C, b, 82003424

St. Thomas Episcopal Church, Craven St., Bath, 11/20/70, A, C, a, 70000440

Washington Historic District, Roughly bounded by Jacks Creek, Pamlico River, Hackney, 3rd, Market, 5th, Harvey, and 2nd Sts., Washington, 2/09/79, A, C, a, 79001661

Bertie County

Bertie County Courthouse [North Carolina County Courthouses TR], King and Dundee Sts., Windsor, 5/10/79, A, C, 79001662

Elmwood, W of Windsor on SR 1101, Windsor vicinity, 6/08/82, A, B, C, 82003431

Freeman Hotel, York and Granville Sts., Windsor, 9/09/82, C, 82003432

Garrett-White House, Address Restricted, Colerain vicinity, 6/28/82, C, b, 82003425

Hermitage, The, N of Merry Hill, Merry Hill vicinity, 6/08/82, C, 82003427

Hope Plantation, 4 mi. NW of Windsor, off NC 308, Windsor vicinity, 4/17/70, B, C, 70000441

Jordan House, S of Windsor on SR 1522, Windsor vicinity, 8/26/71, C, 71000569

King House, NW of Windsor off NC 308, Windsor vicinity, 8/26/71, C, b, 71000570

King-Freeman-Speight House, W of Republican on NC 308, Republican vicinity, 12/02/82, A, B, C, 82001280

Liberty Hall, Off SR 1108, Windsor vicinity, 6/08/82, B, C, 82003433

Oaklana, NE of Roxobel off SR 1249, Roxobel vicinity, 4/15/82, A, C, 82003429

Pineview, Off SR 1249, Roxobel, 6/28/82, A, B, C, 82003430

Rhodes Site (31BR90), Address Restricted, Hamilton vicinity, 8/28/86, D, 86001955

Rosefield, 212 W. Gray St., Windsor, 8/26/82, C, d, 82003434

Scotch Hall, E of Merry Hill on SR 1511, Merry Hill vicinity, 4/29/82, A, B, C, 82003428

St. Frances Methodist Church, Off NC 308, Lewiston, 4/29/82, C, a, b, 82003426

Windsor Historic District, Roughly bounded by York, Water, Sutton, and Elmo Sts., Windsor, 7/29/91, A, C, 86003146

Woodbourne, W of Roxobel on SR 1139, Roxobel vicinity, 8/26/71, C, 71000568

Bladen County

Brown Marsh Presbyterian Church, N of Clarkton on SR 1700 off SR 1762, Clarkton vicinity, 9/02/75, A, a, 75001239

Clark, John Hector, House, SE corner jct. of S. Grove and E. Green Sts., Clarkton, 5/20/87, B, C, b, 87000039

Clarkton Depot, Elm and Hester Sts., Clarkton, 12/23/86, A, C, b, 86003463

Desserette, SW side of SR 1320 near jct. with SR 1318, White Oak vicinity, 10/07/87, A, C, 87001786

Harmony Hall, W of White Oak on SR 1351, White Oak vicinity, 3/24/72, B, C, 72000925

Mt. Horeb Presbyterian Church and Cemetery, SW corner of NC 87 and SR 1712 Jct., Elizabethtown vicinity, 5/13/87, A, C, a, d, 87000695

Oakland Plantation, Off SR 1730, Carvers vicinity, 4/25/72, C, 72000924

Purdie House and Purdie Methodist Church, 2.8 mi. E of Tar Heel, Tar Heel vicinity, 4/13/77, C, 77000989

Trinity Methodist Church, Broad and Lower Sts., Elizabethtown, 9/14/89, A, C, a, d, 89001419

Walnut Grove, E of Tar Heel on NC 87, Tar Heel vicinity, 5/29/75, A, C, 75001241

Brunswick County

Bald Head Island Lighthouse, S of Southport on Smith Island at Bald Head, Southport vicinity, 4/28/75, A, C, 75001242

Brunswick County Courthouse [North Carolina County Courthouses TR], Davis and Moore Sts., Southport, 5/10/79, A, C, 79001663

Brunswick Town Historic District, N of Southport off SR 133, Southport vicinity, 9/06/78, A, D, 78001932

Cape Fear Lighthouse Complex, S of Kure Beach, Kure Beach vicinity, 8/29/78, A, 78001931

Fort Johnston, Moore St., Southport, 6/07/74, A, 74001327

Orton Plantation, On Cape Fear River at jct. of NC 1530 and 1529, Smithville Township, 4/11/73, A, B, C, 73001294

Southport Historic District, Roughly bounded by Cape Fear River, Rhett, Bay, Short and Brown Sts., Southport, 11/25/80, A, C, 80002801

St. Philip's Church Ruins, S of Orton off NC 1533, Orton vicinity, 2/26/70, A, C, a, 70000442

Buncombe County

Alexander Inn, Address Restricted, Swannanoa vicinity, 5/31/84, A, C, 84001932

Alexander, Mrs. Minnie, Cottage, 218 Patton Ave., Asheville, 12/21/89, C, 89002135

All Souls Episcopal Church and Parish House [Biltmore Village MRA], 2 Angle St., Asheville, 11/15/79, B, C, a, 79001664

Buncombe County—Continued

Arcade Building, Battery Park, Battle Sq., Asheville, 5/19/76, A, C, g, 76001306

Asheville City Hall, City County Plaza, Asheville, 11/07/76, C, g, 76001307

Asheville Transfer and Storage Company Building [Asheville Historic and Architectural MRA], 192-194 Coxe Ave., Asheville, 4/26/79, C, 79001665

B & B Motor Company Building [Asheville Historic and Architectural MRA], 84-94 Coxe Ave., Asheville, 4/26/79, A, C, 79001666

Barker, Clarence, Memorial Hospital [Biltmore Village MRA], 2–6 Reed St., Asheville, 11/15/79, B, C, 79001667

Battery Park Hotel, Battle Sq., Asheville, 7/14/77, A, C, 77000990

Bent Creek Campus of the Appalachian Forest Experiment Station, Brevard Rd. S of jct. with I-26, Asheville vicinity, 4/29/93, A, C, 93000373

Biltmore Estate, Address Unknown, Asheville, 10/15/66, A, C, NHL, 66000586

Biltmore Estate Office [Biltmore Village MRA], 10 Biltmore Plaza, Asheville, 11/15/79, B, C, 79001668

Biltmore Industries, Inc., Grovewood Rd., Asheville, 2/01/80, A, 80002802

Biltmore Shoe Store [Biltmore Village MRA], 8 Lodge St., Asheville, 11/15/79, C, 79001669

Biltmore Village Commercial Buildings [Biltmore Village MRA], Brook St. and Biltmore Plaza, Asheville, 11/15/79, A, C, 79001670

Biltmore Village Cottage District [Biltmore Village MRA], Swan St., All Souls Cresent and Boston Way, Asheville, 11/15/79, B, C, 79001671

Biltmore Village Cottages [Biltmore Village MRA], 18 Angle St. and 75 Hendersonville Rd., Asheville, 11/15/79, B, C, 79001672

Biltmore-Oteen Bank Building [Biltmore Village MRA], 12 Lodge St., Asheville, 11/15/79, C, 79001673

Black Mountain College Historic District, SR 2468, Black Mountain vicinity, 10/05/82, A, B, C, 82001281

Blue Ridge Assembly Historic District, S of Black Mountain on SR 2720, Black Mountain vicinity, 9/17/79, A, B, C, a, 79003327

Breese, William E., Sr., House, 674 Biltmore Ave., Asheville, 4/28/80, A, B, C, 80002803

Bryan, William Jennings, House, 107 Evelyn Pl., Asheville, 6/23/83, B, C, 83001836

Building at 130–132 Biltmore Avenue [Asheville Historic and Architectural MRA], 130–132 Biltmore Ave., Asheville, 4/26/79, C, 79003323

Building at 134–136 1/2 Biltmore Avenue [Asheville Historic and Architectural MRA], 134–136 1/2 Biltmore Ave., Asheville, 4/26/79, C, 79003324

Building at 140 Biltmore Avenue [Asheville Historic and Architectural MRA], 140 Biltmore Ave., Asheville, 4/26/79, C, 79003325

Buncombe County Courthouse [North Carolina County Courthouses TR], College and Davidson Sts., Asheville, 5/10/79, A, C, 79001674

Camp Academy, NC 63, Leicester vicinity, 9/19/85, A, B, C, a, 85002421

Carter-Swain House, E side SR 2162, N of jct. with SR 2163, Democrat vicinity, 7/02/87, C, 87001114

Chestnut Hill Historic District, Roughly bounded by Hillside, Washington, Broad, Hollywood, Orchards Sts. and Merrimon Ave., Asheville, 3/17/83, C, 83001837

Church of St. Lawrence, 97 Haywood St., Asheville, 3/24/78, A, C, a, g, 78001933

Church of the Redeemer, 1202 Riverside Dr., Asheville vicinity, 9/19/85, A, C, a, 85002419

Claxton School, 241 Merrimon Ave., Asheville, 6/04/92, A, C, 92000671

Conabeer Chrysler Building [Asheville Historic and Architectural MRA], 162-164 Coxe Ave., Asheville, 4/26/79, A, C, 79001675

Demens-Rumbough-Crawley House, 31 Park Ave., Asheville, 6/01/82, C, 82003435

Downtown Asheville Historic District [Asheville Historic and Architectural MRA], Roughly bounded by 1240 Valley St., Hilliard Ave., and Broad Ave., Asheville, 4/26/79, A, B, C, 79001676

Downtown Asheville Historic District (Boundary Increase) [Asheville Historic and Architectural MRA], 60 and 64 Biltmore Ave., Asheville, 5/25/89, A, C, 89000468

Downtown Asheville Historic District (Boundary Increase II) [Asheville Historic and Architectural MRA], Church St. and Ravenscroft Dr., Asheville, 8/23/90, A, C, 90001342

E. D. Latta Nurses' Residence [Asheville Historic and Architectural MRA], 159 Woodfin St., Asheville, 4/26/79, C, 79001677

Eliada Home, 2 Compton Dr., Asheville, 4/22/93, A, B, C, a, 93000314

Ellington, Douglas, House, 583 Chunns Cove Rd., Asheville, 10/16/86, C, 86002881

First Baptist Church, Oak and Woodfin Sts., Asheville, 7/13/76, C, a, 76001308

George A. Mears House [Asheville Historic and Architectural MRA], 137 Biltmore Ave., Asheville, 4/26/79, C, 79001678

Grove Park Historic District, Roughly bounded by Evelyn Pl., Macon Ave., Howland Rd., Woodland Rd., Canterbury Ln., Charlotte St., and Murdock Ave., Asheville, 4/13/89, A, C, 89000247

Grove Park Historic District (Boundary Increase), Roughly, Kimberly Ave. from Maywood St. to N of Evelyn Pl., including Grove Park Inn Country Club, Asheville, 12/18/90, A, C, 90001918

Grove Park Inn, Macon Ave., Asheville, 4/03/73, C, 73001295

Guastavino, Rafael, Sr., Estate, NC 9, 0.8 mi. S of jct. with SR 2713, Black Mountain vicinity, 7/13/89, A, B, C, 89000849

Gunston Hall, 324 Vanderbilt Rd., Biltmore Forest, 10/24/91, A, C, g, 91001505

Intheoaks, 510 Vance Ave., Black Mountain, 4/10/91, B, C, 91000361

Lanning, John A., House, W of Fairview on SR 3128, Fairview vicinity, 9/23/82, A, C, 82003437

Manor and Cottages, 265 Charlotte St., Asheville, 1/26/78, A, C, 78001934

McGeahy Building [Biltmore Village MRA], 7 1/2 Biltmore Plaza, Asheville, 11/15/79, C, 79001679

Montford Area Historic District, Irregular pattern along Montford Ave., Asheville, 11/25/77, A, C, 77000991

Oteen Veterans Administration Hospital Historic District, N side of US 70, Asheville, 11/20/85, A, C, 85003529

Ottari Sanitarium, 491 Kimberly Ave., Asheville, 10/16/86, B, C, 86002876

Overlook, 710 Town Mountain Rd., Asheville, 10/22/80, A, B, C, 80002804

Ravenscroft School, 29 Ravenscroft Dr., Asheville, 12/12/78, A, C, 78001935

Reed, Samuel Harrison, House [Biltmore Village MRA], 119 Dodge St., Asheville, 11/15/79, C, 79001680

Reynolds House, 100 Reynolds Hts., Asheville, 9/13/84, B, C, 84001934

Reynolds, Dr. Carl V., House, 86 Edgemont Rd., Asheville, 8/19/82, A, C, 82003436

Richbourg Motors Building [Asheville Historic and Architectural MRA], 50 Coxe Ave., Asheville, 4/26/79, A, C, 79001681

Richmond Hill House, 45 Richmond Hill Rd., Asheville, 8/16/77, B, C, 77000992

S And W Cafeteria, Patton Ave., Asheville, 3/28/77, A, C, 77000993

Sawyer Motor Company Building [Asheville Historic and Architectural MRA], 100 Coxe Ave., Asheville, 4/26/79, A, C, 79001682

Schoenberger Hall [Asheville Historic and Architectural MRA], 60 Ravenscroft Dr., Asheville, 4/26/79, C, 79001683

Sherrill's Inn, 2.5 mi. S of Fairview off U.S. 74, Fairview vicinity, 4/16/75, A, C, 75001244

Smith-McDowell House, 283 Victoria Rd., Asheville, 8/01/75, C, 75001243

Southern Railway Passenger Depot [Biltmore Village MRA], 1 Biltmore Plaza, Asheville, 11/15/79, C, 79001684

St. Matthias Episcopal Church, Valley St., Asheville, 5/10/79, A, C, a, 79001685

Wolfe, Thomas, House, 48 Spruce St., Asheville, 11/11/71, B, NHL, 71000572

Young Men's Institute Building, Market and Eagle Sts., Asheville, 7/14/77, A, B, C, 77000994

Zealandia, 40 Vance Gap Rd., Asheville, 3/14/77, B, C, 77000995

Burke County

Avery Avenue Historic District [Morganton MRA], Roughly along parts of Avery, Lenoir, Morehead, Walker, Evans, & Short Sts., Morganton, 11/09/87, A, C, 87001915

Avery Avenue School [Morganton MRA], 200 Avery Ave., Morganton, 11/09/87, A, C, 87001925

Avery, Alphonse Calhoun, House, 408 N. Green St., Morganton, 7/12/84, B, C, 84001947

Burke County—Continued

Bellevue, On SR 1419, N of Morganton off NC 18, Morganton vicinity, 12/04/73, C, 73001296

Broughton Hospital Historic District [Morganton MRA], Roughly bounded by Broughton Hospital campus, NC 18, Bickett St., & Enola Rd., Morganton, 11/09/87, A, B, C, g, 87001918

Burke County Courthouse [Morganton MRA (AD)], Courthouse Sq., Morganton, 4/17/70, A, 70000443

Creekside, W of Morganton at jct. of U.S. 70 and 70A, Morganton vicinity, 2/01/72, C, 72000926

Dale's, USB Market [Morganton MRA], Jct. of Enola Rd. & Dale St., Morganton, 11/09/87, C, 87001924

Forney, Jacob, Jr., House, NW of Morganton on SR 1440, Morganton vicinity, 10/14/76, B, C, 76001309

Gaither House, 102 N. Anderson St., Morganton, 4/23/76, B, C, b, 76001310

Gaston Chapel, 100 Bouchelle St., Morganton, 10/11/84, A, C, a, 84000077

Gilboa Methodist Church, U.S. 64, Salem vicinity, 10/11/84, A, C, a, 84000075

Hunting Creek Railroad Bridge [Morganton MRA], Hunting Creek N of US 64 & 70 between jct. of Stonebridge Rd. & E. Union St., Morganton, 11/09/87, A, C, 87001923

Jonesboro Historic District [Morganton MRA], Roughly bounded by W. Concord, Bay, Jones, Lytle, & S. Anderson Sts., Morganton, 11/09/87, A, 87001916

Lackey, John Alexander, House [Morganton MRA], 102 Camelot Dr., Morganton, 11/09/87, C, 87001921

Magnolia Place, S of Morganton on U.S. 64, Morganton vicinity, 6/04/73, A, C, 73001297

Morganton Downtown Historic District [Morganton MRA], E. Union, S. Green, N. & S. Sterling, King & Queen Sts., Morganton, 11/09/87, A, C, g, 87001930

Mountain View, 604 W. Union St., Morganton, 10/11/84, B, C, 84000076

North Carolina School for the Deaf: Main Building [Morganton MRA (AD)], U.S. 64 and Fleming Dr., Morganton, 12/12/76, A, C, 76001311

North Carolina School for the Deaf Historic District [Morganton MRA], Jct. US 70 and US 64, Morganton, 4/20/89, A, B, C, 89000325

North Green Street—Bouchelle Street Historic District [Morganton MRA], N. Green, Bouchelle, & Patterson Sts., Morganton, 11/09/87, A, C, 87001926

Quaker Meadows, W of Morganton off NC 181, Morganton vicinity, 10/03/73, A, C, 73001298

Quaker Meadows Cemetery [Morganton MRA], Off NC 126, Morganton, 11/09/87, A, C, d, 87001922

Riddle, Dr. Joseph Bennett, House, 411 W. Union St., Morganton, 12/20/84, B, C, 84000524

South King Street Historic District [Morganton MRA], S. King St., Morganton, 11/09/87, A, C, g, 87001920

Swan Ponds, About 4 mi. W of Morganton off NC 126, Morganton vicinity, 4/24/73, A, C, 73001299

Tate House, 100 S. King St., Morganton, 5/25/73, A, C, 73001300

Tate, Franklin Pierce, House [Morganton MRA (AD)], 410 W. Union St., Morganton, 5/21/86, C, 86001171

Valdese Elementary School, 400 Main St., Valdese, 10/25/84, A, C, 84000115

Waldensian Presbyterian Church, 104 E. Main St., Valdese, 10/25/84, A, C, a, 84000116

West Union Street Historic District [Morganton MRA], Roughly parts of W. Union St., Montrose St., & Riverside Dr., Morganton, 11/09/87, A, C, g, 87001931

Western North Carolina Insane Asylum [Morganton MRA (AD)], Off NC 18, Morganton, 10/05/77, A, C, 77000996

White Street—Valdese Avenue Historic District [Morganton MRA], White St. & Valdese Ave., Morganton, 11/09/87, A, C, b, 87001927

Cabarrus County

Barber-Scotia College, 145 Cabarrus Ave. West, Concord, 2/28/85, A, B, C, a, 85000378

Bost Mill Historic District, N and S sides of NC 200 off US 601, Georgeville vicinity, 1/13/86, A, B, C, e, 86000076

Cabarrus County Courthouse, Union St., S., Concord, 6/05/74, A, C, 74001328

Favoni—Harris, Dr. Charles and William Shakespeare House, SR 1445, Poplar Tent vicinity, 3/05/86, B, C, 86000413

First Congregational Church, Corner of Wade and C Sts., Mount Pleasant, 1/09/86, A, C, 86000030

Green, John Bunyan, Farm, SR 1114 .5 mi. E of SR 1178, Midland vicinity, 6/02/88, A, C, 88000651

Lentz Hotel, College St., Mount Pleasant, 6/14/82, C, b, 82003438

McCurdy Log House, S of Concord off U.S. 601, Concord vicinity, 1/21/74, A, C, 74001329

Mill Hill, W of Kannapolis on SR 1616, Concord vicinity, 9/10/74, A, C, 74001330

Morrison, Robert Harvey, Farm and Pioneer Mills Gold Mine, 730 Morrison Rd., Midland vicinity, 12/31/90, C, D, 90001952

Mount Pleasant Collegiate Institute Historic District, Jct. of NC 49 and NC 73, Mount Pleasant, 11/15/79, A, C, 79001686

Mount Pleasant Historic District, Roughly W. and E. Franklin between N. Halifax and C and N and N. and S. Main Sts. between Boston and Broad Sts., Mount Pleasant, 5/12/86, A, C, 86001050

North Union Street Historic District, Roughly bounded by Peachtree Ave. NW, Church St. N, Cobran Ave. SW, and Georgia St. NW and Spring St. N, Concord, 4/15/86, A, B, C, 86000789

Odell-Locke-Randolph Cotton Mill, Buffalo, Church, Peachtree, and Locust Sts., Concord, 3/28/83, A, B, C, 83001838

Pressley, Rev. John E., House, N side of SR 1613 0.3 mi. E of SR 1612, Bethpage vicinity, 1/06/86, B, C, a, 86000029

Reed Gold Mine, 11 mi. SE of Concord, Concord vicinity, 10/15/66, A, NHL, 66000587

Rocky River Presbyterian Church, Jct. of NC 1139 and NC 1158, Rocky River vicinity, 3/06/86, B, C, a, d, 86000419

South Union Street Historic District, Roughly bounded by Corban Ave. SW, S. Union St., Blume Ave. SE, and Spring St. SW, Concord, 4/10/86, A, B, C, 86000736

Spears House, 1615 Morrison Rd., Concord vicinity, 8/07/89, C, 89001046

Stonewall Jackson Training School Historic District, SR 1157, Concord, 3/15/84, A, B, C, 84001966

Caldwell County

Caldwell County Courthouse [North Carolina County Courthouses TR], Main St., Lenoir, 5/10/79, A, C, 79001687

Clover Hill, E of Patterson off NC 268 on SR 1514, Patterson vicinity, 5/25/73, C, 73001301

Fort Defiance, N of Lenoir on NC 268, Lenoir, 9/15/70, A, C, 70000444

Hagler, William, House, N of Grandin on SR 1510, Grandin vicinity, 12/28/82, A, C, 82001282

Lenoir High School, 100 Willow St., Lenoir, 8/02/90, A, B, C, 90001146

Camden County

Abbott, William Riley, House, SE of South Mills on SR 1224, South Mills vicinity, 8/11/78, A, C, 78001936

Camden County Courthouse, NC 343, Camden, 2/01/72, C, 72000928

Camden County Jail, NC 343, Camden, 5/03/84, A, C, 84001950

Dismal Swamp Canal [Dismal Swamp Canal and Associated Development, Southeast Virginia and Northeast North Carolina MPS], Runs between Chesapeake, VA and South Mills, NC, South Mills, 6/06/88, A, C, g, 88000528

Grandy, Caleb, House, Off SR 1145, Belcross vicinity, 4/29/82, B, C, 82003439

Lamb-Ferebee House, NW of Camden on NC 343, Camden vicinity, 9/22/80, A, C, D, 80002805

Milford, On SR 1205, 0.5 mi. S of jct. with NC 343, Camden vicinity, 3/16/72, C, 72000929

Carteret County

Beaufort Historic District, Roughly bounded by Beaufort Channel, Pine and Fulford Sts., and Taylors Creek, Beaufort, 5/06/74, A, C, 74001331

Carteret County—Continued

Cape Lookout Coast Guard Station, Cape Lookout, Beaufort vicinity, 2/01/89, A, g, NPS, 88003436

Cape Lookout Light Station, On Core Banks, Core Banks, 10/18/72, A, NPS, 72000097

Carteret County Home, NC 101, Beaufort, 12/20/84, A, C, 84000528

Fort Macon, Bogue Point, on Fort Macon Rd., 4 mi. E of Atlantic Beach, Atlantic Beach vicinity, 2/26/70, A, C, 70000445

Gibbs House, 903 Front St., Beaufort, 3/14/73, A, C, 73001302

Henry, Jacob, House, 229 Front St., Beaufort, 5/07/73, A, B, C, 73001303

Old Burying Ground, Bounded by Ann, Craven, and Broad Sts., Beaufort, 4/08/74, A, C, d, 74001332

Portsmouth Village, N end of Portsmouth Island, Portsmouth, 11/29/78, A, NPS, 78000267

Caswell County

Brown-Graves House and Brown's Store, SW of Yanceyville on NC 150, Locust Hill vicinity, 7/15/74, B, C, 74001334

Caswell County Courthouse, Courthouse Sq., Yanceyville, 6/04/73, C, 73001309

Garland-Buford House, N of Leasburg on SR 1561, Leasburg vicinity, 1/24/74, C, 74001333

Graves House, U.S. 158 at NC 86, Yanceyville vicinity, 11/20/74, B, C, 74001335

Griers Presbyterian Church and Cemetery, SR 1710, Frogsboro vicinity, 12/30/85, C, a, 85003187

Longwood, SW of Milton on NC 62, Milton vicinity, 9/15/76, B, C, 76001312

Melrose/Williamson House, Off NC 62, Yanceyville Township vicinity, 2/28/85, A, C, 85000379

Milton Historic District, Runs along Main St. from Atlantic and Danville RR to County Line Creek, Milton, 10/25/73, A, C, 73001306

Milton State Bank, Main (Broad) St., Milton, 4/13/73, A, C, 73001307

Moore House, E of Locust Hill off U.S. 158, Locust Hill vicinity, 8/28/73, C, 73001304

Poteat House, N of Yanceyville on NC 62, Yanceyville vicinity, 10/24/79, B, C, 79001688

Rose Hill, On U.S. 158 at jct. with NC 150, Locust Hill, 10/25/73, B, C, 73001305

Saint Agnes Church, 27 Franklin St., Franklin, 6/04/87, B, C, a, 87000822

Union Tavern, Main St., Milton, 5/15/75, A, B, C, NHL, 75001245

Warren House and Warren's Store, On NC 86, Prospect Hill, 6/19/73, A, C, 73001308

Woodside, NC 57, Milton vicinity, 3/06/86, C, 86000420

Yancey, Bartlett, House, Address Restricted, Yanceyville vicinity, 12/04/73, B, C, 73001310

Yanceyville Historic District, W. Main St., Courthouse Sq., and North Ave. to Church St., Yanceyville, 10/15/73, A, C, 73001311

Catawba County

Anthony, Abraham, Farm [Catawba County MPS], W side of SR 1008, 0.5 mi. S of jct. with SR 2021, Blackburn vicinity, 5/10/90, A, C, 90000738

Balls Creek Campground [Catawba County MPS], W side of SR 1003, 0.1 mi. S of SR 1943, Bandy's Crossroads vicinity, 4/27/90, A, C, a, 90000662

Bandy Farms Historic District [Catawba County MPS], E side of SR 1003, 0.5-0.85 mi. S of SR 1813 jct., Bandy's Crossroads vicinity, 4/27/90, C, 90000663

Bolick Historic District [Catawba County MPS], First Ave. S. between US 64/70 and 12th St., Conover, 7/05/90, A, B, C, 90001032

Bost—Burris House [Catawba County MPS], Jct. of SR 1149 and SR 1154, Newton vicinity, 7/05/90, A, C, 90001033

Bunker Hill Covered Bridge, 2 mi. E of Claremont on U.S. 70, Claremont vicinity, 2/26/70, A, C, 70000446

Catawba County Courthouse [North Carolina County Courthouses TR], S. Main, W.A, S. College, and W. 1st Sts., Newton, 5/10/79, A, C, 79001690

Catawba Historic District, Roughly bounded by Second Ave. NE, Third and Second Sts. SE, Second Ave. SW and NC 10, and Second St. SW, Catawba, 4/28/86, A, C, 86000893

Claremont High School Historic District [Hickory MRA], Roughly bounded by Fifth and Third Aves., Third St., Second Ave. and N. Center St., Hickory, 10/23/86, C, g, 86003357

Elliott-Carnegie Library [Hickory MRA], 415—1st Ave. NW, Hickory, 3/15/85, A, C, 85000584

First Presbyterian Church [Hickory MRA], 2nd St. and 3rd Ave. NW, Hickory, 3/15/85, C, a, 85000585

Foil—Cline House [Catawba County MPS], 406 S. Main Ave., Newton, 7/05/90, B, C, 90001034

Geitner, Clement, House [Hickory MRA], 436 Main Ave. NW, Hickory, 3/15/85, C, 85000703

Grace Reformed Church [Catawba County MPS], 201–211 S. Main Ave., Newton, 7/05/90, C, a, 90001035

Grace Union Church and Cemetery [Catawba County MPS], Jct. of SR 1008 and SR 2030, Blackburn vicinity, 5/10/90, C, a, d, 90000739

Highland School, 1017 10th Ave. NE., Hickory, 6/01/90, A, C, 90000824

Houck's Chapel [Hickory MRA], 9th Ave. and 17th St. NW, Hickory, 3/15/85, A, C, a, d, 85000587

Huffman, George, Farm [Catawba County MPS], SR 1479, SE of jct. with Tate Blvd., Conover vicinity, 6/21/90, A, C, 90000861

Keever—Cansler Farm [Catawba County MPS], E side of SR 2024, 0.05 mi. N of jct. with SR 2026, Blackburn vicinity, 5/10/90, A, C, 90000740

Kenworth Historic District [Hickory MRA], Roughly bounded by 2nd Ave., 5th St. and 3rd Ave. Dr. SE, Hickory, 5/09/85, A, C, 85001054

Lentz, John A., House [Hickory MRA], 321 9th St. NW, Hickory, 3/15/85, C, 85000588

Long, McCorkle and Murray Houses [Catawba County MPS], 1310–1326 N. Main Ave., Newton, 9/05/90, C, 90001371

Memorial Reformed Church [Catawba County MPS], 201 E. Main St., Maiden, 6/21/90, A, C, a, 90000865

Miller—Cansler House [Catawba County MPS], N side of SR 2007, 0.5 mi. E of jct. with SR 1005, Maiden vicinity, 5/10/90, C, 90000741

Moore, Alexander, Farm [Catawba County MPS], SR 2646 0.5 mi. NW of SR 1004 jct., Catawba vicinity, 4/27/90, A, C, 90000664

Moretz, John Alfred, House [Hickory MRA], 1437—6th St. Circle NW, Hickory, 3/15/85, C, 85000589

Munday House, Address Restricted, Denver vicinity, 8/22/75, C, 75001246

Murray's Mill Historic District, SE of Catawba, Catawba vicinity, 12/31/79, A, C, 79001689

Neill—Turner—Lester House [Catawba County MPS], N side of SR 1836, 0.25 mi. NE of jct. with SR 1837, Sherrills Ford vicinity, 5/10/90, B, C, 90000742

North Main Avenue Historic District, Roughly bounded by W. Ninth St., N. Main Ave., W. Fourth and W. Sixth Sts., N. Deal Ave., and W. Eighth St., Newton, 5/22/86, B, C, 86001147

Oakwood Historic District [Hickory MRA], Roughly bounded by Oakwood Cemetery and Fourth Ave. NW, Fourth St. NW, Second Ave. NW, and Sixth St. NW, Hickory, 3/25/86, C, 86000687

Perkins House, N of Catawba off I-40, Newton vicinity, 10/01/74, B, C, 74001336

Piedmont Wagon Company [Hickory MRA], Main Ave. NW, Hickory, 3/15/85, A, B, C, 85000592

Powell-Trollinger Lime Kilns, S of Catawba, Catawba vicinity, 11/08/74, A, 74001337

Propst House, Shuford Memorial Garden, Hickory, 4/24/73, C, b, 73001312

Propst, David F., House [Catawba County MPS], Jct. of SR 1810 and SR 1878, Maiden vicinity, 6/21/90, C, 90000864

Reinhardt, Franklin D., and Harren-Hood Farms [Catawba County MPS], SR 2013 NW of jct. with SR 2012, Maiden vicinity, 6/21/90, A, C, 90000863

Reinhardt, William Pinckney, House [Catawba County MPS], Jct. of SR 2012 and SR 2013, Maiden vicinity, 7/19/90, C, 90001111

Rock Barn Farm [Catawba County MPS], W side of SR 1709, .4 mi. N of jct. with SR 1715, Claremont vicinity, 7/05/90, A, C, 90001036

Rudisill-Wilson House, SW of Newton off NC 10, Newton vicinity, 8/14/73, C, 73001315

Self—Trott—Bickett House [Catawba County MPS], 331 S. College Ave., Newton, 7/05/90, C, 90001037

Sharpe—Gentry Farm [Catawba County MPS], Jct. of NC 10 and SR 1137, Propst Crossroads vicinity, 6/21/90, A, C, 90000859

Sherrill, Miles Alexander, House [Catawba County MPS], W side of SR 1849, 0.1 mi. S of SR 1848 jct., Sherrills Ford vicinity, 4/27/90, C, 90000665

Catawba County—Continued

Shuford House, 542 2nd St. NE., Hickory, 4/24/73, B, C, 73001313

Shuford—Hoover House [Catawba County MPS], E side of SR 1008, 0.05 mi. S of jct. with SR 10, Blackburn vicinity, 5/10/90, A, C, 90000743

St. Paul's Church and Cemetery, Jct. of SR 1149 and SR 1164, Newton vicinity, 12/09/71, A, C, a, 71000573

St. Paul's Reformed Church [Catawba County MPS], Jct. of SR 1151 and SR 1005, Startown, 6/21/90, C, a, 90000860

Terrell Historic District, NC 150 and SR 1848, Terrell, 7/15/86, A, C, 86001685

Warlick—Huffman Farm [Catawba County MPS], SR 1116 NW of jct. with NC 10, Propst Crossroads vicinity, 6/21/90, A, C, 90000862

Weidner Rock House, S of Hickory on SR 1142, Hickory vicinity, 12/04/73, C, b, 73001314

Wesley's Chapel Arbor and Cemetery [Catawba County MPS], W side of SR 2033, 0.4 mi. S of jct. with SR 10, Blackburn vicinity, 5/10/90, A, C, a, d, 90000744

Wilfong—Wilson Farm [Catawba County MPS], SR 1145, SW of jct. with SR 1146, Startown vicinity, 6/21/90, A, C, 90000858

Yoder's Mills Historic District, Address Restricted, Hickory vicinity, 1/11/80, A, C, D, 80002806

Chatham County

Alston—DeGraffenried Plantation (Boundary Increase), US 64 N side, 0.4 mi. W of jct. with NC 1564, Pittsboro vicinity, 10/21/93, A, C, D, 93001132

Alston-DeGraffenried House, W of Pittsboro off U.S. 64, Pittsboro vicinity, 11/18/74, C, 74001339

Aspen Hall, W of Pittsboro on US 64, Pittsboro vicinity, 7/29/82, A, C, 82003441

Baldwin's Mill, SR 1520, Pittsboro vicinity, 1/02/86, C, 86000007

Bowen-Jordan Farm [Chatham County MRA], SR 1100, Siler City vicinity, 7/05/85, A, B, C, 85001451

Chatham County Courthouse [North Carolina County Courthouses TR], NC 15–501 and Highway 64, Pittsboro, 5/10/79, A, C, 79001691

Clegg, Luther, House [Pittsboro MRA], S of Pittsboro on SR 1012, Pittsboro, 10/05/82, A, B, C, 82001283

DeGraffenreidt-Johnson House [Chatham County MRA], SR 1346, Silk Hope vicinity, 7/05/85, A, B, C, 85001452

Ebenezer Methodist Church [Chatham County MRA], SR 1008, Bells vicinity, 7/05/85, A, C, a, b, 85001450

Freeman, Lewis, House [Pittsboro MRA], 205 W. Salisbury St., Pittsboro, 10/05/82, A, B, C, 82001284

Goldston Commercial Historic District, Roughly S. Bellevue and S. Main Sts. between W. Goldbar & Colonial Sts., Goldston, 11/25/87, A, C, 87002014

Goodwin Farm Complex [Chatham County MRA], SR 1900, Bells vicinity, 7/05/85, A, C, 85001453

Gregson-Hadley House [Chatham County MRA], 322 E. Raleigh St., Siler City, 7/05/85, A, B, C, 85001454

Hadley House and Grist Mill, NW of Pittsboro on SR 2165, Pittsboro vicinity, 11/25/80, A, B, C, D, 80002807

Hall-London House [Pittsboro MRA], 206 Hillsboro St., Pittsboro, 10/05/82, A, B, C, 82001285

Haughton-McIver House [Chatham County MRA], SR 1007, Gulf, 7/05/85, A, B, C, 85001455

Hotel Hadley [Chatham County MRA], 103 N. Chatham St., Siler City, 7/05/85, A, B, C, 85001456

Jordan, Marion Jasper, Farm [Chatham County MRA], R. Jordan Rd./SR 2145, Gulf vicinity, 2/25/88, A, C, 88000169

Kelvin [Pittsboro MRA], 503 W. Salisbury St., Pittsboro, 10/05/82, A, B, C, 82001286

Lockville Dam, Canal and Powerhouse, W of Moncure at Deep River and U.S. 1, Moncure vicinity, 11/20/84, A, C, 84000305

London Cottage [Pittsboro MRA], N of Pittsboro on SR 1516, Pittsboro, 10/05/82, A, B, C, 82001287

Mason, John A., House, SW of Durham off NC 751, Farrington vicinity, 10/23/74, C, 74001338

McClenahan House [Pittsboro MRA], Address Restricted, Pittsboro, 10/05/82, A, C, 82001288

Moore-Manning House [Pittsboro MRA], 400 Hillsboro St., Pittsboro, 10/05/82, A, B, C, 82001289

Mount Vernon Springs Historic District [Chatham County MRA], SR 1134 & SR 1135, Bonlee vicinity, 12/03/87, A, C, 87002045

New Hope Rural Historical Archeological District, Address Restricted, Wilsonville vicinity, 2/25/85, D, 85000382

Newkirk State (Site 3lCH366), Addresss Restricted, Moncure vicinity, 11/14/83, D, 83003813

O'Kelly's Chapel [Chatham County MRA], NC 751, Farrington vicinity, 7/05/85, A, B, C, a, 85001457

Paschal-Womble House, 421 Main St., Goldston, 4/26/84, C, 84001957

Pittsboro Masonic Lodge, East and Masonic Sts., Pittsboro, 1/31/78, A, C, 78001938

Pittsboro Presbyterian Church, N. East St., Pittsboro, 1/30/78, C, a, 78001939

Reid House [Pittsboro MRA], 200 W. Salisbury St., Pittsboro, 10/05/82, C, 82001290

Rives, William Alston, House [Chatham County MRA], End of SR 2183 off SR 2187, Goldston vicinity, 7/05/85, A, B, C, 85001459

St. Lawrence, Patrick, House [Pittsboro MRA], Address Restricted, Pittsboro, 10/05/82, A, B, C, b, 82001291

Stone, Joseph B., House, SR 1008, Farrington vicinity, 6/01/82, C, 82003440

Teague, William, House [Chatham County MRA], SR 1004, Siler City vicinity, 7/05/85, A, B, C, 85001458

Terry, A. P., House [Pittsboro MRA], 601 Womack St., Pittsboro, 10/05/82, A, B, C, 82001292

Thomas, James A., Farm [Chatham County MRA], SR 1941, Pittsboro vicinity, 7/05/85, A, C, 85001460

Ward, Dr. E. H., Farm [Chatham County MRA], SR 1700, Bynum vicinity, 7/05/85, A, B, C, 85001461

Whitehead-Fogleman Farm [Chatham County MRA], SR 1352 & SR 1351 jct., Crutchfield Crossroads vicinity, 7/05/85, A, C, 85001462

Cherokee County

Campbell, John C., Folk School Historic District, Off US 64, Brasstown vicinity, 8/22/83, A, B, C, 83001839

Cherokee County Courthouse [North Carolina County Courthouses TR], Peachtree and Central Sts., Murphy, 5/10/79, A, C, 79001692

Cobb, John Franklin, House, U.S. 19-129, Bell View vicinity, 10/11/84, B, C, 84000074

Cooper, Robert Lafayette, House, 109 Campbell St., Murphey, 9/05/90, C, 90001372

Cover, Franklin Pierce, House, SR 1388, Andrews, 11/12/82, A, B, C, 82001293

Harshaw Chapel and Cemetery, Church and Central Sts., Murphy, 4/05/84, C, a, d, 84001979

Walker's Inn, S of Andrews on SR 1505 off SR 1393 and NC 19, Andrews vicinity, 8/19/75, A, 75001247

Chowan County

Albania, U.S. 17 W of jct. with NC 32, Edenton, 5/13/76, A, C, 76001313

Athol, SE of Edenton on SR 1114, Edenton vicinity, 5/22/80, A, B, C, 80002808

Barker House, S Terminus of Broad St., Edenton, 3/24/72, A, C, b, 72000931

Chowan County Courthouse, E. King St., Edenton, 4/15/70, C, NHL, 70000447

Cullins-Baker House, NC 32, Smalls Crossroads vicinity, 4/29/82, A, C, d, 82003442

Cupola House, 408 S. Broad St., Edenton, 4/15/70, C, NHL, 70000889

Edenton Historic District, Roughly bounded by E. & W. Freemason, S. Oakum, E. & W. Water, and Mosely Sts., Edenton, 7/16/73, A, C, D, 73001316

Edenton Peanut Factory, E. Church St., Edenton, 9/20/79, A, C, 79003328

Greenfield Plantation, E of Edenton on SR 1109, Somer vicinity, 5/06/76, C, 76001316

Hayes Plantation, E. Water St. Extension, Edenton vicinity, 2/26/74, C, NHL, 74001341

Iredell, James, House, 107 E. Church St., Edenton, 2/26/70, A, C, 70000449

Mulberry Hill, SE of Edenton on SR 1114, Edenton vicinity, 5/13/76, C, 76001314

Pembroke Hall, W. King St., Edenton, 11/07/76, C, 76001315

Sandy Point, Off NC 32 East of NC 1114, Edenton vicinity, 4/25/85, A, C, 85000875

Chowan County—Continued

Shelton Plantation House, Off NC 32, Edenton vicinity, 10/29/74, C, 74001342

Speight House and Cotton Gin, E. Church St., Edenton, 9/22/80, B, C, 80002809

St. Paul's Episcopal Church and Churchyard, W. Church and Broad Sts., Edenton, 5/29/75, A, C, a, d, 75001248

Strawberry Hill, Church St., Edenton, 5/22/80, B, C, 80002810

Wessington House, 120 W. King St., Edenton, 3/20/73, C, 73001317

Clay County

Clay County Courthouse, Main St., Hayesville, 10/29/75, A, C, 75001250

Moore, John Covington, House, SR 1307, Tusquitee vicinity, 7/21/83, A, B, C, 83001840

Spikebuck Town Mound and Village Site, Address Restricted, Hayesville vicinity, 8/17/82, D, 82003443

Cleveland County

Banker's House, 319 N. Lafayette St., Shelby, 5/06/75, C, 75001251

Beam, Joshua, House, NE of Shelby, Shelby vicinity, 6/04/80, B, C, 80002813

Central Shelby Historic District, Roughly Washington St. from Gidney to Sumter; Graham and Warren St to Morgan; and Marion St. from Washington St to Thompson, Shelby, 6/23/83, A, C, 83001841

Cleveland County Courthouse [North Carolina County Courthouses TR], Main, Washington, Warren, and Lafayette Sts., Shelby, 5/10/79, A, C, 79001693

Hamrick, E. B., Hall, Gardner-Webb College campus, Boiling Springs, 7/12/82, A, 82003444

Irvin-Hamrick Log House, NW of Boiling Springs on SR 1153, Boiling Springs vicinity, 5/28/80, A, C, 80002811

Lattimore, John, House, NW of Polkville on SR 1372, Polkville vicinity, 8/26/82, B, C, d, 82003445

Masonic Temple Building, 203 S. Washington St., Shelby, 7/15/82, B, C, 82003446

McBrayer, Dr. Victor, House, 507 N. Morgan St., Shelby, 5/31/79, C, 79001694

Suttle, Joseph, House, SW of Shelby, Shelby vicinity, 7/17/80, B, C, a, 80002814

Webbley, 403 S. Washington St., Shelby, 9/29/80, B, C, g, 80002812

Columbus County

Columbus County Courthouse [North Carolina County Courthouses TR], Bounded by Madison and Jefferson Sts. circle, Whiteville, 5/10/79, A, C, 79001695

Lake Waccamaw Depot, Flemington Ave., Lake Waccamaw, 7/21/83, C, b, 83001842

Powell House, Main and Orange Sts., Fair Bluff, 1/31/78, A, 78001940

Craven County

Attmore-Oliver House, 513 Broad St., New Bern, 1/20/72, C, 72000932

Baxter Clock, 323 Pollock St., New Bern, 7/02/73, C, 73001319

Bellair, W of New Bern off SR 1401, New Bern vicinity, 8/25/72, C, 72000933

Blades House, 602 Middle St., New Bern, 1/14/72, B, C, 72000934

Bryan House and Office, 603-605 Pollock St., New Bern, 3/24/72, C, 72000935

Cedar Grove Cemetery, Bounded by Queen, George, Cypress, Howard, and Metcalf Sts., New Bern, 12/05/72, C, d, 72000936

Centenary Methodist Church, 209 New St., New Bern, 9/11/72, C, a, 72000937

Central Elementary School, 311–313 New St. and 517 Hancock St., New Bern, 1/20/72, A, C, 72000938

Christ Episcopal Church and Parish House, 320 Pollock St., New Bern, 4/13/73, A, C, a, 73001320

Clear Springs Plantation, N of Jasper, Jasper vicinity, 3/14/73, C, 73001318

Coor-Bishop House, 501 E. Front St., New Bern, 11/09/72, B, C, b, 72000939

Coor-Gaston House, 421 Craven St., New Bern, 2/01/72, B, C, a, 72000940

First Baptist Church, Middle St. and Church Alley, New Bern, 3/24/72, A, C, a, 72000941

First Church of Christ, Scientist, 406 and 408 Middle St., New Bern, 10/02/73, A, C, a, 73001321

First Presbyterian Church and Churchyard, New St. between Middle and Hancock Sts., New Bern, 2/01/72, A, C, a, 72000942

Ghent Historic District, Roughly bounded by Trent Blvd., First St., Park Ave., and Seventh St., New Bern, 3/17/88, A, C, g, 88000226

Gull Harbor, 514 E. Front St., New Bern, 8/14/73, C, 73001322

Harvey Mansion, 219 Tryon Palace Dr., New Bern, 11/12/71, B, C, 71000574

Hawks House, 306 Hancock St., New Bern, 3/16/72, C, 72000943

Hollister, William, House, 613 Broad St., New Bern, 6/30/72, B, C, 72000944

Jerkins, Thomas, House, 305 Johnson St., New Bern, 10/18/72, C, 72000945

Jerkins—Duffy House, 301 Johnston St., New Bern, 3/17/88, C, 88000232

Jones-Jarvis House, 528 E. Front St., New Bern, 4/11/73, C, 73001323

Mace, Ulysses S., House, 518 Broad St., New Bern, 6/04/73, C, 73001324

Masonic Temple and Theater, 516 Hancock St., New Bern, 3/16/72, A, C, 72000946

New Bern Historic District, Roughly bounded by Neuse and Trent Rivers and Queen St., New Bern, 6/19/73, A, C, 73001325

New Bern Municipal Building, Pollock and Craven Sts., New Bern, 6/04/73, C, 73001326

Rhem-Waldrop House, 701 Broad St., New Bern, 10/18/72, C, 72000947

Riverside Historic District, Roughly bounded by N. Craven St., North Ave., E St., and Guion St., New Bern, 2/09/88, A, C, a, 87002579

Sloan, Dr. Earl S., House, 3701 Country Club Rd., Trent Woods, 8/14/86, A, C, 86001627

Slover-Bradham House, 201 Johnson St., New Bern, 4/11/73, B, C, 73001327

Smallwood, Eli, House, 524 E. Front St., New Bern, 12/05/72, C, 72000948

Smith, Benjamin, House, 210 Hancock St., New Bern, 4/13/72, A, C, 72000949

Smith-Whitford House, 506 Craven St., New Bern, 4/13/72, C, 72000950

St. Paul's Roman Catholic Church, 510 Middle St., New Bern, 3/24/72, A, C, a, 72000951

Stanly, Edward R., House, 502 Pollock St., New Bern, 3/24/72, C, 72000952

Stanly, John Wright, House, 307 George St., New Bern, 2/26/70, B, C, b, 70000450

Stevenson House, 609–611 Pollock St., New Bern, 8/26/71, C, 71000575

Taylor, Isaac, House, 228 Craven St., New Bern, 12/27/72, C, 72000953

Tisdale-Jones House, 520 New St., New Bern, 4/25/72, C, 72000954

York-Gordon House, 213 Hancock St., New Bern, 6/18/73, C, 73001328

Cumberland County

Atlantic Coast Line Railroad Station [Fayetteville MRA], 472 Hay St., Fayetteville, 7/07/82, C, 82001294

Barge's Tavern [Fayetteville MRA], 519 Ramsey St., Fayetteville, 7/07/83, C, b, 83001843

Belden-Horne House, 519 Ramsey St., Fayetteville, 3/16/72, C, b, 72000955

Big Rockfish Presbyterian Church, SR 2268, Hope Mills vicinity, 7/21/83, C, a, d, 83001844

Camp Ground Methodist Church [Fayetteville MRA], Camp Ground Rd., Fayetteville, 7/07/83, A, C, a, b, 83001845

Cape Fear Baptist Church, SR 2233, Grays Creek vicinity, 10/13/83, A, C, a, d, 83003816

Cape Fear and Yadkin Valley Railway Passenger Depot [Fayetteville MRA], 148 Maxwell St., Fayetteville, 7/07/83, A, C, 83001846

Carolina Theater [Fayetteville MRA], 443 Hay St., Fayetteville, 7/07/83, C, 83001847

Confederate Breastworks, Address Restricted, Fayetteville vicinity, 10/07/81, A, D, NHL, 81000421

Cool Spring Place, 119 N. Cool Spring St., Fayetteville, 10/10/72, B, C, 72000956

Cool Springs, Off SR 1607 at Cumberland, Carvers Creek vicinity, 9/19/85, A, B, C, D, 85002417

Cumberland County—Continued

Cumberland County Courthouse [North Carolina County Courthouses TR], Franklin, Gillespie, and Russell Sts., Fayetteville, 5/10/79, A, C, 79001696

Davis, John, House [Fayetteville MRA], 910 Arsenal Ave., Fayetteville, 7/07/83, C, 83001848

Devane-MacQueen House, NC 87, Grays Creek vicinity, 7/21/83, A, C, 83001849

Ellerslie, W of Linden on SR 1607 at jct. with SR 1606, Linden vicinity, 8/07/74, B, C, 74001344

Evans Metropolitan AME Zion Church [Fayetteville MRA], 301 N. Cool Spring St., Fayetteville, 7/07/83, C, a, 83001850

Falcon Tabernacle, West St., Falcon, 10/11/83, A, C, a, b, 83003814

Fayetteville Ice and Manufacturing Company:Plant and Engineer's House [Fayetteville MRA], 436 Rowan St. and 438 Rowan St., Fayetteville, 7/07/83, A, 83001851

Fayetteville Mutual Insurance Company Building [Fayetteville MRA], 320 Hay St., Fayetteville, 7/07/83, C, 83001852

Fayetteville Women's Club and Oval Ballroom, 224 Dick St., Fayetteville, 2/06/73, A, B, C, b, 73001330

First Baptist Church [Fayetteville MRA], 200 Old St., Fayetteville, 7/07/83, A, B, C, a, 83001853

First Presbyterian Church, Ann and Bow Sts., Fayetteville, 4/30/76, C, a, 76001317

Gully Mill [Fayetteville MRA], S.R. 1839, Fayetteville vicinity, 7/07/83, A, 83001854

Hangars 4 and 5, Pope Air Force Base [Pope Air Force Base Early Expansion MPS], Bldg. 708, Pope AFB, Fayetteville, 1/16/91, A, C, 90002153

Hay Street Methodist Church [Fayetteville MRA], Hay St. at Ray and Old Sts., Fayetteville, 7/07/83, A, C, a, 83001855

Haymount District [Fayetteville MRA], Roughly Hillside Ave, from Bragg Blvd. to Pushing St., Fayetteville, 8/07/83, A, C, 83001856

Holt-Harrison House [Fayetteville MRA], 806 Hay St., Fayetteville, 7/07/83, C, 83001857

Hope Mills Historic District, Roughly bounded by Seaboard Coastline RR tracks, Lakeview Rd., Little Creek and Cross St., Hope Mills, 7/09/85, A, B, C, D, 85001515

Kyle House, 234 Green St., Fayetteville, 6/19/72, C, 72000957

Liberty Row, N Side of the first block of Person St., bounded by Market Sq. and Liberty Point, Fayetteville, 8/14/73, A, C, 73001331

M & O Chevrolet Company [Fayetteville MRA], 412 W. Russell St., Fayetteville, 7/07/83, C, 83001858

Mansard Roof House, 214 Mason St., Fayetteville, 3/20/73, C, 73001332

Market House, Market Sq., Fayetteville, 9/15/70, C, NHL, 70000451

Market House Square District [Fayetteville MRA], Hay, Person, Green, and Gillespie Sts., Fayetteville, 7/07/83, C, 83001860

Maxwell House, Off NC 24, Stedman vicinity, 2/28/85, C, 85000380

McArthur-Council House, SR 2244, Grays Creek vicinity, 7/21/83, A, C, 83001861

McCall House [Fayetteville MRA], 822 Arsenal Ave., Fayetteville, 7/07/83, A, C, b, 83001862

McDiarmid, William, House [Fayetteville MRA], 330 Dick St., Fayetteville, 7/07/83, C, 83001863

McLean, Henry, House [Fayetteville MRA], 1006 Hay St., Fayetteville, 7/07/83, C, 83001864

Nimocks House, 225 Dick St., Fayetteville, 1/20/72, C, 72000958

North Carolina Arsenal Site, Address Restricted, Fayetteville vicinity, 2/23/83, A, C, D, 83001865

Oak Grove, S of Erwin near jct. of NC 82 and SR 1875, Erwin vicinity, 2/06/73, A, C, 73001329

Oates, John A., House [Fayetteville MRA], 406 St. James Sq., Fayetteville, 7/07/83, B, C, 83001866

Old Bluff Presbyterian Church, N of Wade on SR 1709, Wade vicinity, 8/07/74, A, C, a, 74001345

Orange Street School, 500 blk. of Orange St., jct. of Orange and Chance Sts., Fayetteville, 9/22/87, A, C, g, 87001597

Patterson, John E., House [Fayetteville MRA], 445 Moore St., Fayetteville, 7/07/83, C, 83001867

Phoenix Masonic Lodge No. 8 [Fayetteville MRA], 221 Mason St., Fayetteville, 7/07/83, A, C, 83001868

Poe, Edgar Allan, House [Fayetteville MRA], 206 Bradford Ave., Fayetteville, 7/07/83, C, 83001869

Pope Air Force Base Historic District [Pope Air Force Base Early Expansion MPS], Bldgs. 300, 302, 306, and Old Family Housing Units, Fayetteville, 1/25/91, A, C, 90002152

Prince Charles Hotel [Fayetteville MRA], 430 Hay St., Fayetteville, 7/07/83, C, 83001870

Sedberry-Holmes House, 232 Person St., Fayetteville, 9/02/75, C, 75001252

St. John's Episcopal Church, Green St., Fayetteville, 9/06/74, A, C, a, 74001343

St. Joseph's Episcopal Church, Ramsey and Moore Sts., Fayetteville, 6/01/82, A, C, a, 82003447

Strange, Robert, Country House [Fayetteville MRA], 309 Kirkland Dr., Fayetteville, 7/07/83, B, C, 83001871

Taylor-Utley House [Fayetteville MRA], 916 Hay St., Fayetteville, 7/07/83, A, C, 83001872

U.S. Post Office [Fayetteville MRA], 301 Hay St., Fayetteville, 7/07/83, C, 83001873

Waddill's Store [Fayetteville MRA], 220 Hay St., Fayetteville, 7/07/83, C, 83001874

Westlawn, 1505 Fort Bragg Rd., Fayetteville, 9/22/80, B, C, 80002815

Williams, Robert, House, SR 1728, Eastover vicinity, 7/21/83, A, C, 83001875

Currituck County

Baum Site, Address Restricted, Poplar Branch vicinity, 12/08/80, D, 80002818

Culong, S of Shawboro on SR 1147, Shawboro vicinity, 2/01/80, A, B, C, 80002819

Currituck Beach Lighthouse, Northern NC Outer Banks, Corolla, 10/15/73, A, C, 73001333

Currituck County Courthouse and Jail [North Carolina County Courthouses TR], SR 1242, Currituck, 5/10/79, A, C, D, 79001697

Currituck Shooting Club, S of Corolla, Corolla vicinity, 5/28/80, A, B, C, 80002816

Shaw House, NC 34 and SR 1203, Shawboro, 4/17/80, C, 80002820

Twin Houses, On NC 168 at jct. of SR 1203 and 1147, Shawboro, 4/13/72, C, 72000959

Whalehead Club, Currituck Banks, Corolla, 4/16/80, A, C, 80002817

Dare County

Bodie Island Lifesaving/Coast Guard Station, S of Nags Head on NC 12, Nags Head vicinity, 2/09/79, A, b, g, NPS, 79000251

Caffeys Inlet Lifesaving Station, N of Duck on SR 1200, Duck vicinity, 1/30/78, A, C, 78001942

Cape Hatteras Light Station, SE of Buxton off NC 12 in Cape Hatteras National Seashore, Buxton vicinity, 3/29/78, A, C, NPS, 78000266

Chicamacomico Life Saving Station, NC 12 and SR 1247, Rodanthe, 12/12/76, A, C, b, 76000164

Creef, George Washington, House, 304 Budleigh St., Manteo, 8/12/82, B, C, 82004798

First Colony Inn, 6720 S. Virginia Dare Trail, Nags Head, 1/21/93, A, C, b, 92001835

Fort Raleigh National Historic Site, 4 mi. N of Manteo on U.S. 158, Manteo vicinity, 10/15/66, A, D, e, NPS, 66000102

Hatteras Weather Bureau Station, Off NC 12, Hatteras, 2/17/78, A, g, NPS, 78000268

Kitty Hawk Life-Saving Station, U.S. 158, Kitty Hawk, 10/11/84, A, C, b, 84000073

Meekins, Thedore S., House, 319 Sir Walter Raleigh St., Manteo, 12/17/82, B, C, 82001295

Nags Head Beach Cottages Historic District, U.S. 158, Nags Head, 8/19/77, A, C, b, g, 77000997

Oregon Inlet Station, 12 mi. N of Rodanthe on Pea Island, Rodanthe vicinity, 12/23/75, A, g, 75001253

Salvo Post Office, NC 12 W side, 0.1 mi. S of jct. with Park Rd., Salvo, 9/23/93, A, C, b, 93000997

USS HURON, Address Restricted, Nags Head vicinity, 11/15/91, A, C, D, 91001625

USS MONITOR, Address Restricted, Cape Hatteras vicinity, 10/11/74, A, C, D, NHL, 74002299

Wright Brothers National Memorial, U.S. 158, Kill Devil Hills, 10/15/66, B, e, f, NPS, 66000071

Davidson County

Abbott's Creek Primitive Baptist Church Cemetery [Anglo-German Cemeteries TR; Davidson County MRA], SR 1743, Thomasville vicinity, 7/10/84, C, a, d, 84001982

Adderton—Badgett House [Davidson County MRA], SR 2529, Denton vicinity, 7/10/84, C, 84001988

Beallmont [Davidson County MRA], SR 1133, Linwood vicinity, 7/10/84, C, 84001991

Davidson County—Continued

Beck's Reformed Church Cemetery [Anglo-German Cemeteries TR; Davidson County MRA], SR 2250, Silver Hill vicinity, 7/10/84, C, a, d, 84001992

Bethany Reformed and Lutheran Church Cemetery [Anglo-German Cemeteries TR; Davidson County MRA], SR 1716, Midway vicinity, 7/10/84, C, a, d, 84001994

Beulah Church of Christ Cemetery [Anglo-German Cemeteries TR; Davidson County MRA], SR 1457, Welcome vicinity, 7/10/84, C, a, d, 84001995

Brummell's Inn, N of Thomasville, Thomasville vicinity, 11/25/80, A, C, 80002822

Church Street School, Jasper St., W of Church St., Thomasville, 3/01/90, A, C, 90000355

Emanuel United Church of Christ Cemetery [Anglo-German Cemeteries TR; Davidson County MRA], SR 2060, Thomasville vicinity, 7/10/84, C, a, d, 84001997

Everhart, Hamilton, Farm [Davidson County MRA], US 52, Midway vicinity, 7/10/84, C, 84002000

Everhart, Riley, Farm and General Store [Davidson County MRA], SR 1468, Arnold vicinity, 7/10/84, B, C, 84002001

Fair Grove Methodist Church Cemetery [Anglo-German Cemeteries TR; Davidson County MRA], NC 109, SR 2072 and 2070, South Thomasville, 7/10/84, C, a, d, 84002004

Good Hope Methodist Church Cemetery [Anglo-German Cemeteries TR; Davidson County MRA], Jct. of NC 150 and SR 1445, Welcome vicinity, 7/10/84, C, a, d, 84002007

Grimes School, Hege Dr., Lexington, 12/28/88, A, C, 88002832

Grimes-Crotts Mill [Davidson County MRA], SR 1445, Reedy Creek vicinity, 7/10/84, A, 84002008

Haden Place [Davidson County MRA], SR 1156, Tyro vicinity, 7/10/84, C, d, 84002009

Hampton House [Davidson County MRA], SR 483, Arcadia vicinity, 7/10/84, C, 84002025

Holt, Dr. William Rainey, House, 408 S. Main St., Lexington, 6/23/83, A, B, C, 83001876

Jersey Baptist Church Cemetery [Anglo-German Cemeteries TR; Davidson County MRA], SR 1272, Linwood, 7/10/84, C, a, d, 84002027

Jersey Settlement Meeting House [Davidson County MRA], SR 1272, Linwood vicinity, 7/10/84, A, C, a, 84002032

Junior Order United American Mechanics National Orphans Home [Davidson County MRA], NC 8, Lexington vicinity, 7/10/84, A, C, 84002034

Koonts, Capt. John, Jr., Farm [Davidson County MRA], SR 1186, Tyro vicinity, 7/10/84, C, 84002131

Lambeth, Shadrach, House [Davidson County MRA], SR 2062, Thomasville vicinity, 7/10/84, C, 84002135

Moore, Eli, House [Davidson County MRA], SR 1741, High Point vicinity, 7/10/84, C, 84002137

Mount Ebal Methodist Protestant Church [Davidson County MRA], End of SR 2518, Denton, 7/10/84, A, C, a, 84002143

Old Davidson County Courthouse, Main and Center Sts., Lexington, 6/24/71, C, 71000576

Pilgrim Reformed Church Cemetery [Anglo-German Cemeteries TR; Davidson County MRA], SR 1843, Lexington vicinity, 7/10/84, C, a, d, 84002145

Reid Farm, W of Jackson Hill on SR 2537, Jackson Hill vicinity, 1/25/79, A, C, 79001700

Shoaf, Henry, Farm [Davidson County MRA], NC 64, Lexington vicinity, 7/13/84, C, 84002148

Smith Clinic, 17 Randolph St., Thomasville, 11/29/91, C, 91001746

Sowers, Philip, House, SR 1162, Churchland vicinity, 11/25/80, C, D, 80002821

Spring Hill Methodist Protestant Church Cemetery [Anglo-German Cemeteries TR; Davidson County MRA], SR 1755, High Point vicinity, 7/10/84, C, a, d, 84002151

Spurgeon House, W of High Point, High Point vicinity, 4/20/83, C, 83001877

St. Luke's Lutheran Church Cemetery [Anglo-German Cemeteries TR; Davidson County MRA], SR 1183, Tyro vicinity, 7/10/84, C, a, d, 84002147

Thomasville Railroad Passenger Depot, W. Main St., Thomasville, 7/09/81, A, C, b, 81000423

Tyro Tavern [Davidson County MRA], NC 150, Tyro, 8/16/84, B, C, 84002154

Waggoner Graveyard [Anglo-German Cemeteries TR; Davidson County MRA], SR 1814, Welcome vicinity, 7/10/84, C, d, 84002158

Wall, George W., House [Davidson County MRA], NC 109 and SR 1723, Wallburg, 7/10/84, C, 84002161

Welborn, John Henry, House [Davidson County MRA], 511 S. Main St., Lexington, 7/10/84, C, 84002163

Yadkin College Historic District [Davidson County MRA], N and S sides of SR 1194 W of SR 1436, Yadkin College, 2/25/88, A, C, a, d, 88000165

Davie County

Center Arbor, Jct. of US 64 and NC 1150, NW corner, Center, 9/03/91, A, C, a, 91001168

Clement, Jesse, House, Maple Ave., Mocksville, 4/17/80, B, C, 80002823

Cooleemee, Terminus of SR 1812, Mocksville, 3/20/73, A, C, NHL, 73001334

Davie County Courthouse [North Carolina County Courthouses TR], Courthouse Sq., Mocksville, 5/10/79, A, C, 79001702

Davie County Jail, 20 S. Main St., Mocksville, 4/24/73, A, C, 73001335

Downtown Mocksville Historic District, Roughly Main St. from Water to Gaither Sts., including Town Square, Mocksville, 6/01/90, A, C, 90000821

Fulton United Methodist Church, S of Advance off NC 801, Advance vicinity, 11/15/79, C, a, 79001701

Helper, Hinton Rowan, House, U.S. 64 off I-40, Mocksville, 11/07/73, B, NHL, 73001336

McGuire—Setzer House, NC 1139 0.2 mi. S of Mocksville town limits, Mocksville vicinity, 9/04/92, C, 92001152

North Main Street Historic District, Roughly Main St. from Church St. to Mocksville city limits, Mocksville, 6/01/90, A, C, 90000822

Salisbury Street Historic District, Roughly Salisbury St. from Kelly St. to Lexington Rd., Mocksville, 6/01/90, A, C, 90000819

Duplin County

Dickson, Roger, Farm, E side of SR 1917, Magnolia vicinity, 2/08/88, C, 88000053

Hill, Buckner, House, SE of Faison on SR 1354, Faison vicinity, 12/06/75, C, 75001255

Kenansville Historic District, Downtown area centered around Main St. and Limestone Rd. as far N as Hill St., Kenansville, 3/13/75, C, 75001256

Waterloo, 2 mi. S of Albertson on NC 111, Albertson vicinity, 1/08/75, C, 75001254

Durham County

Bassett House [Faculty Avenue Houses TR], 1017 W. Trinity Ave., Durham, 11/29/79, A, B, C, b, 79003330

Bennett Place State Historic Site, Jct. of SR 1313 and 1314, Durham, 2/26/70, A, C, e, 70000452

Blacknall, Richard D., House [Durham MRA], 300 Alexander Ave., Durham, 3/01/90, C, b, 90000350

Bull Durham Tobacco Factory, 201 W. Pettigrew St., Durham, 9/10/74, A, NHL, 74001346

Bullington Warehouse, 500 N. Duke St., Durham, 8/30/82, A, C, 82003448

Cleveland Street District [Durham MRA], Roughly Cleveland St. between Seminary & Gray Aves. & Mallard St., Durham, 9/20/85, A, B, C, 85002438

Cranford-Wannamaker House [Faculty Avenue Houses TR], 1019 W. Trinity Ave., Durham, 11/29/79, A, B, C, b, 79003331

Crowell House [Faculty Avenue Houses TR], 504 Watts St., Durham, 11/29/79, A, B, C, b, 79003332

Dillard-Gamble Houses, 1311 and 1307 N. Mangum St., Durham, 1/19/79, B, C, 79003333

Downtown Durham Historic District, Roughly bounded by Peabody, Morgan, Seminary, Cleveland, Parrish, and Queen Sts., Durham, 11/01/77, A, C, 77000998

Duke Homestead and Tobacco Factory, 0.5 mi. N of Durham on Guess Rd., E of SR 1025, Durham vicinity, 11/13/66, A, B, NHL, 66000590

Duke Memorial United Methodist Church [Durham MRA], 504 W. Chapel Hill St., Durham, 8/11/85, A, B, C, a, 85001781

Durham Cotton Mills Village Historic District [Durham MRA], Roughly bounded by Byrd

Durham County—Continued

and Middle Sts., E. Frontage Rd. and Resevoir St., Durham, 8/09/85, A, B, C, 85001793

Durham Hosiery Mill, Angier Ave., Durham, 11/14/78, A, B, C, 78001944

Durham Hosiery Mills No. 2—Service Printing Company Building [Durham MRA], 504 E. Pettigrew St., Durham, 11/27/85, A, B, 85003055

Emmanuel AME Church [Durham MRA], 710 Kent St., Durham, 8/09/85, A, B, C, a, 85001775

Ephphatha Church [Durham MRA], 220 W. Geer St., Durham, 8/09/85, A, B, C, a, 85001778

Erwin Cotton Mills Company Mill No. 1 Headquarters Building, W. Main and 9th Sts., Durham, 11/20/84, A, C, 84002724

Fairntosh Plantation, Near jct. of SR 1004 and 1632, Durham vicinity, 4/03/73, A, B, C, 73001337

Golden Belt Historic District [Durham MRA], Roughly bounded by N & W RR, Taylor, Holman Sts., Morning Glory Ave. and Main St., Durham, 8/09/85, A, B, C, 85001791

Greystone, 618 Morhead Ave., Durham, 6/01/82, B, C, 82003449

Hardscrabble, N side of SR 1002, 1.2 mi. W of jct. with SR 1003, Bahama vicinity, 1/20/72, C, 72000960

Hill, John Sprunt, House, 900 S. Duke St., Durham, 1/30/78, B, C, 78001945

Holloway Street District [Durham MRA], Roughly bounded by Holloway, Railroad & Liberty Sts., Peachtree Pl. & Dillard St., Durham, 9/20/85, A, B, C, 85002437

Horton Grove Complex, N of Durham on SR 1626, Durham vicinity, 3/17/78, A, B, C, D, 78001946

Leigh Farm, E of Chapel Hill off NC 54, Chapel Hill vicinity, 9/05/75, A, C, 75001257

Little Creek Site (31 DH 351), Address Restricted, Chapel Hill vicinity, 1/11/85, D, 85000118

Mangum, Bartlett, House [Durham MRA], 2701 Chapel Hill Rd., Durham, 5/25/89, A, C, 89000446

Meadowmont, Off NC 54, Chapel Hill vicinity, 7/11/85, A, B, C, 85001554

Morehead Hill Historic District [Durham MRA], Roughly bounded by Jackson St., East-West Expressway, S. Duke St., Lakewood Ave., Shephard St. and Arnette Ave., Durham, 8/09/85, A, B, C, 85001792

North Carolina Central University [Durham MRA], Bounded by Lawson St., Alston Ave., Nelson, and Fayette Sts., Durham, 3/28/86, A, B, C, g, 86000676

North Carolina Mutual Life Insurance Company Building, 114–116 W. Parrish St., Durham, 5/15/75, A, NHL, 75001258

North Durham-Duke Park District, Roughly bounded by Glendale Ave., W. Knox St., Roxboro Rd., Trinity Ave., Magnum & Broadway Sts., Durham, 6/20/85, A, C, a, 85001338

O'Brien, William Thomas, House [Durham MRA], 820 Wilkerson Ave., Durham, 8/09/85, B, C, 85001777

Pearl Mill Village Historic District [Durham MRA], 900 Blk. of Washington and Orient Sts. between Trinity and Dacien Aves., Durham, 8/09/85, A, B, C, 85001782

Pegram House [Faculty Avenue Houses TR], 1019 Minerva Ave., Durham, 11/29/79, A, B, C, b, 79003334

Powe House [Durham MRA], 1503 W. Pettigrew St., Durham, 8/09/85, A, B, C, 85001780

Scarborough House [Durham MRA], 1406 Fayetteville St., Durham, 8/09/85, A, B, C, 85001779

Smith Warehouse [Durham MRA], 100 N. Buchanan Blvd., Durham, 9/16/85, A, B, C, 85002429

St. Joseph's African Methodist Episcopal Church, Fayetteville St. and Durham Expwy., Durham, 8/11/76, A, C, a, 76001319

Stagville, Near jct. of SR 1004 and 1632, Durham vicinity, 5/25/73, C, 73001338

Umstead, Adolphus W., House, NC 1607, 0.5 mi. N of NC 1611, Bahama vicinity, 9/14/89, A, C, 89001418

Venable Tobacco Company Warehouse [Durham MRA], 302–304 E. Pettigrew St., Durham, 8/09/85, A, C, 85001847

Watts Hospital, Broad St. and Club Blvd., Durham, 4/02/80, A, C, 80002824

Watts and Yuille Warehouses, 905 W. Main St., Durham, 4/05/84, A, C, 84002259

West Durham Historic District [Durham MRA], Roughly bounded by Knox, Ninth, W. Main Sts., and Rutherford St. and Carolina Ave., Durham, 3/26/86, B, C, 86000680

West Point on the Eno [Durham MRA], Roxboro Rd., Durham, 8/09/85, A, B, C, D, e, g, 85001776

Edgecombe County

Barracks, The, 1100 Albemarle St., Tarboro, 2/18/71, C, 71000578

Bracebridge Hall, Macklesfield vicinity, Tarboro vicinity, 2/18/71, B, C, 71000579

Calvary Episcopal Church and Churchyard, 411 E. Church St., Tarboro, 2/18/71, C, a, 71000580

Cedar Lane, N of Tarboro off NC 44, Leggett vicinity, 4/15/82, C, 82003451

Coats House, 1503 St. Andrews St., Tarboro, 4/03/73, C, 73001339

Coolmore Plantation, Rte. 3 (W of Tarboro on U.S. 64), Tarboro vicinity, 2/18/71, C, NHL, 71000581

Cotton Press, Town Common, Tarboro, 2/18/71, A, C, 71000582

Eastern Star Baptist Church [Tarboro MRA], Church and Wagner Sts., Tarboro, 4/02/80, C, b, 80002827

Edgecombe Agricultural Works [Tarboro MRA], Roughly bounded by Main, Howard, Albemarle, and Walnut Sts., Tarboro, 4/02/80, A, C, 80002828

Grove, The, 130 Bridgers St., Tarboro, 2/18/71, B, C, 71000583

Howell Homeplace, SR 1517, Tarboro vicinity, 12/20/84, A, C, 84000532

Lone Pine, SR 1207, S of US 64, Tarboro vicinity, 11/06/87, A, C, 87001901

Mount Prospect, Jct. of SR 1409 and SR 1428, Leggett vicinity, 11/20/74, B, C, 74001347

Nobles, Dr. A. B., House and McKendree Church, NW of Mercer on SR 1224, Mercer vicinity, 6/19/80, B, C, a, 80002825

Oakland Plantation [Tarboro MRA], Edmondson St., Tarboro, 4/02/80, C, 80002829

Old Town Plantation, Off NC 97, Battleboro vicinity, 12/01/83, C, b, 72000961

Piney Prospect, 5.7 mi. S of Tarboro off SR 1601, Tarboro vicinity, 2/18/71, C, 71000584

Railroad Depot Complex [Tarboro MRA], Off N. Main St., Tarboro, 4/02/80, A, b, 80002830

Redmond-Shackelford House, 300 Main St., Tarboro, 12/12/76, B, C, 76001320

Rocky Mount Central City Historic District, Roughly bounded by Robinson and Atlantic Aves., Holly and Franklin Sts., Rocky Mount, 6/19/80, A, C, 80002826

St. John's Episcopal Church, E. Main St., Battleboro, 2/18/71, C, a, 71000577

St. Paul Baptist Church [Tarboro MRA], Edmondson St., Tarboro, 4/02/80, C, b, 80002831

Tarboro Historic District [Tarboro MRA], Roughly bounded by Albemarle Ave., Walnut, Panola, and Water Sts., and River Rd., Tarboro, 4/02/80, A, C, 80002832

Tarboro Town Common, Bounded by Wilson St., Albemarle Ave., Park Ave. and St. Patrick St., Tarboro, 9/30/70, C, 70000453

Trinity Historic District [Durham MRA], Roughly bounded by Green, Duke, Morgan and W. Main Sts. and Markham Ave., and Clarendon St., Durham, 3/26/86, A, B, C, 86000672

Vinedale, SW of NC 42/43 and SR 1122, Pinetops vicinity, 7/15/82, A, B, C, 82003450

Walston-Bulluck House, 1018 St. Andrews St., Tarboro, 2/18/71, C, b, 71000585

Wilkinson-Dozier House, SE of Tarboro off SR 1524, Conetoe vicinity, 10/23/74, C, 74001348

Worsley—Burnette House, SR 1526 N of jct. with SR 1540, Conetoe vicinity, 5/24/90, C, 90000791

Forsyth County

Arista Cotton Mill Complex, 200 Brookstown Ave., Winston-Salem, 8/18/77, A, 77000999

Atkins, S. G., House [Slater Industrial Academy Houses TR], 346 Atkins St., Winston-Salem, 7/22/79, A, B, 79001704

Bethabara Historic District, N of Winston-Salem on NC 67, Winston-Salem vicinity, 11/15/78, A, C, D, a, 78001948

Bethabara Moravian Church, 2147 Bethabara Rd., Winston-Salem, 9/28/71, A, C, a, 71000586

Bethania Historic District, N of Winston-Salem on NC 65, SR 1611, 1628, and 1688, Winston-Salem vicinity, 5/03/76, A, C, a, 76001321

Bethania Historic District (Boundary Increase), Roughly, area outside present district W and N along Muddy Cr., S to Reynolda Rd. and E

Forsyth County—Continued

along Walker Rd., Bethania, 3/25/91, A, D, 91000346

Blair, William Allen, House, 210 S. Cherry St., Winston-Salem, 4/25/85, A, B, C, 85000876

Bland, Joseph Franklin, House, 1809 Virginia Rd., Winston-Salem, 8/21/84, C, g, 84002265

Brickenstein—Leinbach House, 426 Old Salem Rd., Winston-Salem, 9/03/91, C, b, 91001169

Conrad—Starbuck House, 118 S. Cherry St., Winston-Salem, 6/04/90, C, 90000792

Crews, Thomas A., House, 4997 Main St., Walkertown, 4/26/93, B, C, 93000316

First Baptist Church [Kernersville MPS], 126 N. Main St., Kernersville, 2/25/88, C, a, 88000130

Gilmer Building, 416–424 W. 4th St., Winston-Salem, 7/29/82, A, C, 82003452

Graylyn, Reynolda Rd., Winston-Salem, 8/03/78, B, C, g, 78001949

Hill, J. S., House [Slater Industrial Academy Houses TR], 914 Stadium Dr., Winston-Salem, 7/22/79, B, 79001705

Hylehurst, 224 S. Cherry St., Winston-Salem, 7/21/83, B, C, 83001878

Jones, Dr. Beverly, House, SR 1611, Bethania vicinity, 1/20/78, C, 78001947

Kapp, John Henry, Farm, N side NC 65, 0.1 mi. E of jct. with NC 67 (4647 Bethania—Tobaccoville Rd.), Bethania vicinity, 8/31/92, A, C, 92001087

Kernersville Depot [Kernersville MPS], 121 Railroad St., Kernersville, 2/25/88, A, C, 88000133

Korner's Folly, Main St., Kernersville, 3/20/73, C, 73001340

Lowe, Cicero Francis, House, 204 Cascade Ave., Winston-Salem, 12/20/84, B, C, 84000535

Ludlow, Col. Jacob Lott, House, 434 Summit St., Winston-Salem, 3/17/83, B, C, 83001879

McKaughan, Isaac Harrison, House [Kernersville MPS], 506 Salisbury St., Kernersville, 2/11/88, C, 88000127

Nissen Building, 310 W. Fourth St., Winston-Salem, 3/17/83, A, C, 83001880

North Cherry Street Historic District [Kernersville MPS], 100 blk. N. Cherry St., Kernersville, 2/25/88, A, C, 88000118

O'Hanlon Building, 103 W. 4th St., Winston-Salem, 7/12/84, B, C, 84002269

Old Salem Historic District, Salem College campus and area near Salem Sq., Winston-Salem, 11/13/66, A, C, a, NHL, 66000591

Paisley J. W., House [Slater Industrial Academy Houses TR], 934 Stadium Dr., Winston-Salem, 7/22/79, B, 79001706

Poindexter, H. D., Houses, 124 and 130 West End Blvd., Winston-Salem, 7/31/78, A, C, b, 78001950

Reynolda Historic District, Reynolda Rd., Winston-Salem, 11/28/80, A, B, C, 80002833

Reynolds, Richard J., High School and Richard J. Reynolds Memorial Auditorium, 301 Hawthorne Rd., Winston-Salem, 1/11/91, A, C, 90002139

Richmond Courthouse Site, Address Restricted, Donnaha, 1/05/84, D, 84002273

Roberts—Justice House [Kernersville MPS], 133 N. Main St., Kernersville, 2/25/88, C, 88000129

Rogers, James Mitchell, House, 102 S. Cherry St., Winston-Salem, 7/15/82, C, 82003453

Rural Hall Depot, Depot St. (SR 1646), Rural Hall, 7/21/83, A, C, b, 83001881

Salem Tavern, 800 S. Main St., Winston-Salem, 10/15/66, A, NHL, 66000592

Salem Town Hall, 301 S. Liberty St., Winston-Salem, 3/17/83, C, 83001882

Schaub, John Jacob, House, NE of Vienna off SR 1455, Vienna vicinity, 10/07/82, A, C, 82001296

Shamrock Mills, 3rd and Marshall Sts., Winston-Salem, 5/23/78, A, C, 78001951

Shell Service Station, Sprague and Peachtree Sts., NW, Winston-Salem, 5/13/76, A, g, 76001322

Single Brothers Industrial Complex Site, Address Restricted, Winston-Salem vicinity, 12/13/79, D, 79001707

Single Brothers' House, S. Main and Academy Sts., Winston-Salem, 4/15/70, C, NHL, 70000454

Smith, W. F., and Sons Leaf House and Brown Brothers Company Building, 4th St. between Patterson and Linden, Winston-Salem, 2/23/78, C, 78001952

Sosnik-Morris-Early Commercial Block, 500 W. 4th St., Winston-Salem, 4/05/84, A, C, 84002293

South Main Street Historic District [Kernersville MPS], 100–600 blks. of S. Main St., Kernersville, 2/25/88, A, C, a, b, d, 88000137

South Trade Street Houses, 434, 440, and 448 S. Trade St., Winston-Salem, 12/11/78, A, B, C, 78001953

Spruce Street YMCA, 315 N. Spruce St., Winston-Salem, 7/12/84, A, C, 84002296

St. Philip's Moravian Church, E side, S. Church St. near Race St., Old Salem, Winston-Salem, 9/03/91, A, C, a, 91001170

Stauber, Samuel B., Farm, SR 1611, Bethania, 1/12/88, A, C, 87002232

Stuart Motor Company [Kernersville MPS], 109–111 E. Mountain St., Kernersville, 2/25/88, A, C, 88000139

Washington Park Historc District, Roughly bounded by Leonard St., Acadia Ave., Sunnyside Ave., Vintage Ave., Broad St., Bond St. and Washington Park, Winston-Salem, 1/13/92, A, C, 91001960

Washovia Bank and Trust Company Building, 8 W. 3rd St., Winston-Salem, 5/31/84, A, C, 84002306

West End Historic District, Roughly bounded by W. End Blvd., Sixth, Broad, and Fourth Sts., I-40, Sunset Dr., and Peters Creek, Winston-Salem, 12/04/86, A, C, 86003442

Winston-Salem Southbound Railway Freight Warehouse and Office, 300 S. Liberty St., Winston-Salem, 11/29/91, A, 91001747

Zevely House, 734 Oak St., Winston-Salem, 4/24/73, C, b, 73001341

Franklin County

Baker Farm, SW of Bunn on SR 1720, Bunn vicinity, 10/05/82, A, C, 82001297

Cascine, S of Louisburg on SR 1702, Louisburg vicinity, 4/26/73, A, C, 73001342

Cascine (Boundary Increase), N side of NC 1702, Louisburg vicinity, 12/04/85, A, B, C, 85003114

Clifton House and Mill Site, SR 1103, Royal vicinity, 4/17/80, A, C, 80002835

Cooke House, SW of Louisburg near jct. of SR 1114 and SR 1109, Louisburg vicinity, 10/14/75, B, 75001265

Davis, Archibald H., Plantation, SE of Louisburg off NC 581, Justice vicinity, 7/24/75, A, C, 75001266

Dean Farm, 6 mi. E of Louisburg on NC 56, Louisburg vicinity, 5/02/75, A, C, 75001267

Franklinton Depot, 201 E. Mason St., Franklinton, 12/27/90, A, C, b, 90001941

Fuller House, 307 N. Main St., Louisburg, 11/17/78, B, C, 78001954

Green Hill House, S of Louisburg near jct. of SR 1760 and 1761, Louisburg vicinity, 6/10/75, B, C, 75001268

Harris, Dr. J. H., House, 312 E. Mason St., Franklinton, 8/01/75, C, 75001260

Jeffreys, William A., House, SE of Youngsville on SR 1101, Youngsville vicinity, 6/23/76, B, C, 76001323

Jones—Wright House, NC 1003 W side, 0.2 mi. S of jct. with NC 1252, Rocky Ford vicinity, 3/12/92, C, 92000149

Kearney, Shemuel, House, 1 mi. S of Franklinton on U.S. 1, Franklinton vicinity, 6/05/75, C, 75001261

Laurel Mill and Col. Jordan Jones House, SW of Gupton at jct. of SR 1432 and 1436, Gupton vicinity, 5/30/75, B, C, 75001262

Locust Grove, N of Louisburg on U.S. 401, Ingleside, 11/20/75, A, C, 75001269

Louisburg Historic District, Roughly bounded by Allen Lane, Main and Cedar Sts., Franklin, Elm, and King St., Louisburg, 2/18/87, A, C, 87000041

Main Building, Louisburg College, Louisburg College campus, Louisburg, 12/08/78, A, C, 78001955

Massenburg Plantation, Address Restricted, Louisburg vicinity, 7/30/75, A, C, 75001270

Monreath, S of Ingleside on NC 39, Ingleside vicinity, 8/06/75, C, 75001264

Perry, Dr. Samuel, House, E of Gupton on SR 1436, Gupton vicinity, 6/05/75, C, 75001263

Person Place, 603 N. Main St., Louisburg, 6/19/72, C, 72000962

Person-McGhee Farm, US 1, Franklinton, 6/26/79, A, C, 79003343

Portridge, SR 1224, 0.3 mi. N of jct. with NC 56, Louisburg vicinity, 3/01/90, C, b, 90000351

Savage, Dr. J. A., House, 124 College St., Franklinton, 9/22/80, A, B, 80002834

Speed Farm, W side NC 1436 between NC 1432 and NC 1434, Gupton vicinity, 12/27/91, A, 91001907

Taylor, Archibald, House, Address Restricted, Wood vicinity, 5/12/75, C, 75001273

Taylor, Patty Person, House, Address Restricted, Louisburg vicinity, 2/13/75, A, C, 75001271

Vine Hill, Address Restricted, Centerville vicinity, 5/28/75, C, 75001259

Franklin County—Continued

Williamson House, 401 Cedar St., Louisburg, 6/20/75, B, C, 75001272

Gaston County

Belmont Abbey Cathedral, On SR 2093, Belmont, 4/11/73, C, a, 73001343

Belmont Abbey Historic District, 100 Belmont—Mt. Holly Rd. (NC 2093, E side), Belmont, 7/14/93, A, B, C, a, 93000584

Carpenter, Andrew, House, SR 1820, Lucia vicinity, 3/17/83, C, 83001883

Dallas Historic District, Bounded by Holland, Main, Gaston and Trade Sts., Dallas, 7/26/73, A, C, 73001344

First National Bank Building, 168–170 W. Main Ave., Gastonia, 2/20/86, A, B, C, 86000302

Gaston County Courthouse [North Carolina County Courthouses TR], N. York and S. South Sts., Gastonia, 5/10/79, A, C, 79001708

Gastonia High School, S. York St., Gastonia, 3/17/83, A, C, 83001884

Hoyle House, NC 275 S side, 1400 ft. SW of S. Fork of Catawba R., Dallas vicinity, 10/21/93, A, C, 93001140

Jenkins, David, House, 1017 Church St., Gastonia, 2/17/78, B, 78001956

St. Joseph's Catholic Church, Off NC 273, Mountain Island, 6/07/79, A, C, a, 79001709

Third National Bank Building, 195 W. Main Ave., Gastonia, 2/20/86, A, C, 86000316

Wilson, William J., House, S of Gastonia off SR 1109, Gastonia vicinity, 10/14/76, B, C, 76001324

Gates County

Buckland, NC 37 at SR 1220, Buckland, 3/05/86, A, B, C, 86000407

Elmwood Plantation, E of Gatesville near jct. of SR 1400 and NC 37, Gatesville vicinity, 2/01/72, C, 72000963

Freeman House, N of Gates on US 13, Gates vicinity, 9/23/82, C, c, 82003454

Gates County Courthouse, Court St., Gatesville, 10/22/76, C, 76001325

Roberts-Carter House, Off NC 37, Gatesville vicinity, 3/01/84, A, C, D, 84002310

Graham County

George, Charles Noden, House, Off US 129, Topton vicinity, 4/05/84, A, C, 84002314

Snowbird Mountain Lodge, 275 Santeetlah Rd., Robbinsville vicinity, 9/02/93, A, C, 93000885

Granville County

Abrams Plains, NW of Stovall, Stovall vicinity, 11/29/79, A, B, C, 79001711

Adoniram Masonic Lodge [Granville County MPS], Jct. of NC 1410 and NC 1300, Cornwall vicinity, 8/31/88, A, C, b, 88001253

Allen—Mangum House [Granville County MPS], NC 1700, Grissom vicinity, 4/28/88, A, C, 88000410

Amis, Rufus, House and Mill [Granville County MPS], Address Restricted, Virgilina vicinity, 4/28/88, A, C, 88000416

Blackwell, James, House [Granville County MPS], NC 1411, Cornwall vicinity, 4/28/88, A, C, 88000407

Bobbitt—Rogers House and Tobacco Manufactory District [Granville County MPS], Address Restricted, Wilton vicinity, 8/31/88, A, C, b, 88001262

Brassfield Baptist Church [Granville County MPS], NC 96 and NC 1700, Wilton vicinity, 8/31/88, C, a, d, 88001267

Brookland [Granville County MPS], NC 1443, Grassy Creek vicinity, 4/28/88, A, C, 88000412

Central Orphanage [Granville County MPS], Antioch Dr. and Raleigh Rd., Oxford, 8/31/88, A, B, C, 88001257

Edgewood [Granville County MPS], NC 1437, Grassy Creek vicinity, 4/28/88, A, C, 88000421

Ellixson, William, House [Granville County MPS], Address Restricted, Wilbourns vicinity, 4/28/88, A, C, 88000404

Elmwood [Granville County MPS], Address Restricted, Lewis vicinity, 4/28/88, A, C, 88000406

First National Bank Building [Granville County MPS], 302 Main St., Creedmoor, 8/31/88, A, C, 88001254

Freeman, James W., House [Granville County MPS], NC 1623, Wilton vicinity, 4/28/88, A, C, 88000411

Granville County Courthouse [North Carolina County Courthouses TR], Main and Williamsboro Sts., Oxford, 5/10/79, A, C, 79001710

Harris—Currin House [Granville County MPS], Address Restricted, Wilton vicinity, 8/31/88, A, C, 88001258

Hart, Maurice, House [Granville County MPS], NC 1430, Stovall vicinity, 4/28/88, A, C, 88000420

Hill Airy, S of Stovall, Stovall vicinity, 10/29/74, C, 74001349

Hunt, Joseph P., Farm [Granville County MPS], NC 1514, Dexter vicinity, 8/31/88, A, C, 88001265

Lawrence, John P., Plantation [Granville County MPS], NC 1700, Grissom vicinity, 8/31/88, A, C, 88001264

Littlejohn, Joseph B., House [Granville County MPS], 219 Devin St., Oxford, 8/31/88, A, C, 88001268

Locust Lawn [Granville County MPS], Address Restricted, Oxford vicinity, 4/28/88, A, C, d, 88000422

Mount Energy Historic District [Granville County MPS], NC 1636 and NC 56, Mount Energy, 8/31/88, A, C, 88001266

Oak Lawn [Granville County MPS], Address Restricted, Huntsboro vicinity, 4/28/88, A, C, 88000408

Oliver—Morton Farm [Granville County MPS], NC 1417, Oak Hill vicinity, 8/31/88, A, C, 88001269

Oxford Historic District [Granville County MPS], Roughly bounded by College, New College and Gilliam and Raliegh, Front, Broad and Goshen and Hayes Sts., Oxford, 4/28/88, A, C, a, b, d, 88000403

Paschall—Daniel House [Granville County MPS], Address Restricted, Oxford vicinity, 6/04/92, A, C, 88001263

Peace, John, Jr., House [Granville County MPS], NC 1627, Wilton vicinity, 4/28/88, A, C, d, 88000405

Puckett Family Farm [Granville County MPS], NC 1333, Satterwhite vicinity, 4/28/88, A, C, 88000423

Red Hill, NC 1501, Bullock vicinity, 8/14/86, C, D, 86001632

Rose Hill [Granville County MPS], NC 1442, Grassy Creek vicinity, 4/28/88, A, C, 88000415

Royster, John Henry, Farm [Granville County MPS], Address Restricted, Bullock vicinity, 8/31/88, A, C, 88001260

Royster, Marcus, Plantation [Granville County MPS], NC 96, Wilbourns vicinity, 4/28/88, A, C, 88000409

Salem Methodist Church [Granville County MPS], NC 1522, Huntsboro vicinity, 8/31/88, C, a, d, 88001259

Sherman, Elijah, Farm [Granville County MPS], US 158, Berea vicinity, 8/31/88, A, C, d, 88001256

Smith, William G., House [Granville County MPS], NC 1527, Bullock vicinity, 4/28/88, A, C, 88000417

Stovall, John W., Farm [Granville County MPS], NC 1507, Stovall vicinity, 8/31/88, A, C, 88001270

Sycamore Valley [Granville County MPS], NC 1400, Grassy Creek vicinity, 4/28/88, A, C, 88000419

Taylor, Col. Richard P., House [Granville County MPS], NC 1524, Huntsboro vicinity, 4/28/88, A, C, 88000414

Thorndale [Granville County MPS], 213 W. Thorndale Dr., Oxford, 4/28/88, A, C, 88000413

Tunstall, Eldon B., Farm [Granville County MPS], NC 1500, Bullock vicinity, 8/31/88, A, C, 88001255

Wimbish, Lewis, Plantation [Granville County MPS], NC 1443, Grassy Creek vicinity, 4/28/88, A, C, 88000418

Winston, Obediah, Farm [Granville County MPS], NC 1638, Creedmoor vicinity, 8/31/88, A, C, 88001261

Greene County

Carr, Titus W., House, SR 1244, Walstonburg vicinity, 11/25/87, A, C, 87002013

Greene County—Continued

Greene County Courthouse [North Carolina County Courthouses TR], Greene and 2nd Sts., Snow Hill, 5/10/79, A, C, 79001712

Speight—Bynum House, NC 1231 W side, 0.4 mi. N of jct. with NC 1232, Walstonsburg vicinity, 3/12/92, C, 92000148

St. Barnabas Episcopal Church, SE 4th St. and St. Barnabas Rd., Snow Hill, 10/10/79, C, a, 79003337

Guilford County

Agricultural and Technical College of North Carolina Historic District, E. side of Dudley St. between Bluford St. and Headen Dr., Greensboro, 10/20/88, A, C, 88002046

Beeson, Col. Isaac, House, S of Colfax, Colfax vicinity, 10/16/80, C, 80002836

Benbow, Charles, House, S of Oak Ridge on NC 150, Oak Ridge, 8/19/82, A, B, C, 82004842

Benbow, Jesse, House II, NC 150, Oak Ridge vicinity, 9/08/83, B, C, 83001885

Bennett College Historic District [Greensboro MPS], Roughly bounded by E. Washington, Bennett and Gorrell Sts., Greensboro, 4/03/92, A, C, a, 92000179

Blandwood, 447 W. Washington St., Greensboro, 4/17/70, B, C, NHL, 70000455

Bumpas-Troy House, 114 S. Mendenhall St., Greensboro, 12/06/77, B, 77001000

Caldwell, David, Log College Site, Address Restricted, Greensboro vicinity, 1/13/82, A, B, D, 82003456

Central Fire Station, 318 N. Greene St., Greensboro, 4/28/80, C, 80002837

College Hill Historic District [Greensboro MPS], Roughly bounded by W. Market St., S. Cedar St., Oakland Ave. and McIver St., Greensboro, 11/04/93, A, C, 93001191

Dixon-Leftwich-Murphy House, 507 Church St., Greensboro, 9/23/82, A, B, C, 82003457

Downtown Greensboro Historic District, Elm, S. Davie, S. Green, and E. and W. Washington Sts., Greensboro, 6/17/82, A, C, 82003458

East White Oak School, Former [Greensboro MPS], 1801 Tenth St., Greensboro, 4/21/92, A, 92000360

Endsley-Morgan House, Off U.S. 421, Colfax vicinity, 10/25/84, C, 84000117

Fields, William, House, 447 Arlington St., Greensboro, 12/05/85, A, B, C, 85003084

Fisher Park Historic District [Greensboro MPS], Roughly bounded by Fisher and Bessemer Aves. and Wharton and Church Sts., Greensboro, 1/22/92, A, C, a, 91002006

Forney, Edward J., House [Greensboro MPS], 1402 Spring Garden St., Greensboro, 4/21/92, A, B, C, 92000359

Foust, Julius I., Building, 1000 W. Spring Garden St., Greensboro, 9/11/80, A, B, C, 80002838

Galloway, John Marion, House, 1007 N. Elm St., Greensboro, 7/21/83, B, C, 83001886

Gardner House, E of Jamestown on SR 1383, Jamestown vicinity, 10/15/74, C, 74001350

Green Hill Cemetery Gatekeeper's House, 700 Battleground Ave., Greensboro, 5/29/79, C, 79001713

Greensboro Historical Museum, 130 Summit Ave., Greensboro, 4/25/85, A, C, a, d, 85000877

Guilford College, 5800 W. Friendly Ave., Greensboro vicinity, 6/21/90, A, C, a, 90000855

Guilford County Courthouse [North Carolina County Courthouses TR], Market St., Greensboro, 5/10/79, A, C, 79001714

Guilford County Office and Court Building, 258 S. Main St., High Point, 12/20/88, A, C, 88002843

Guilford Courthouse National Military Park, 5 mi. NW of Greensboro near U.S. 220, Greensboro vicinity, 10/15/66, A, B, c, f, NPS, 66000069

Guilford Mill, SE of Oak Ridge on NC 68, Oak Ridge vicinity, 8/02/82, C, 82003462

Haley, John, House, 1805 E. Lexington Ave., High Point, 8/26/71, C, 71000587

Hardee Apartments, 1102 N. Main St., High Point, 3/14/91, C, 91000260

Hillsdale Brick Store, NC 150 and SR 2347, Hillsdale, 6/14/82, A, C, 82003459

Hillside, 301 Fisher Park Circle, Greensboro, 2/01/80, B, C, 80002839

Holly Gate, NC 61, Whitsett vicinity, 9/22/80, B, C, 80002840

Hoskins House Historic District, Intersection of New Garden Rd. and US 220, Greensboro, 3/15/88, A, C, b, 88000175

Ireland, Charles H., House, 602 W. Friendly Ave., Greensboro, 5/29/79, B, C, 79001715

Jamestown High School, Former, 200 W. Main St., Jamestown, 12/06/91, A, C, 91001779

Jamestown Historic District, Both sides of U.S. 29A, Jamestown, 1/22/73, A, C, a, 73001345

Jefferson Standard Building, Elm and Market Sts., Greensboro, 5/28/76, B, C, 76001326

Kilby Hotel, 627 E. Washington St., High Point, 4/22/82, A, B, C, 82003460

Kimrey—Haworth House, 5307 W. Friendly Ave., Greensboro, 3/14/91, C, 91000265

Kirkman, O. Arthur, House and Outbuildings, 501 W. High St., High Point, 1/28/88, B, C, 87002567

Kirkman, O. Arthur, House and Outbuildings (Boundary Increase), 106 Oak St., High Point, 6/09/89, A, C, 89000495

Latham-Baker House, 412 Fisher Park Circle, Greensboro, 11/12/82, A, B, C, 82001298

Low House, S of Gibsonville, Whitsett vicinity, 3/08/78, C, 78001957

Lyndon Street Townhouses [Greensboro MPS], 195–201 Lyndon St., Greensboro, 4/03/92, C, 92000178

Martin, Harden Thomas, House, 204 N. Mendenhall St., Greensboro, 12/19/85, B, C, 85003217

McCulloch's Gold Mill, Address Restricted, Jamestown vicinity, 4/24/79, A, C, 79001717

McIver, Charles D., School, Former [Greensboro MPS], 617 W. Lee St., Greensboro, 4/03/92, A, C, 92000177

Mendenhall, Richard, Plantation Buildings, U.S. 29, Jamestown, 11/03/72, C, 72000964

Oak Ridge Military Academy Historic District, NC 150 and NC 68, Oak Ridge, 3/17/83, A, C, g, 83001887

Oakdale Cotton Mill Village, SR 1352 and SR 1144, Jamestown, 3/15/76, A, 76001327

Oakwood Historic District, 100–300 blocks Oakwood St., High Point, 2/07/91, A, C, 90002197

Palmer Memorial Institute Historic District, Along US 70 W of jct. with NC 3056, Sedalia, 10/24/88, A, B, a, f, g, 88002029

Penn, William, High School, Washington Dr., High Point, 11/16/78, A, 78001959

Ragsdale Farm, 404 E. Main St., Jamestown, 9/03/91, A, B, C, 91001171

Revolution Cotton Mills, Roughly bounded by Southern RR, N. Buffalo Creek, Yanceyville and 9th Sts., Greensboro, 3/01/84, A, B, C, 84002324

Richardson, L., Memorial Hospital, Former [Greensboro MPS], 603 S. Benbow Rd., Greensboro, 4/03/92, A, C, 92000180

Scott, Thomas, House, SR 1001, Greensboro vicinity, 7/12/84, B, C, 84002328

Shaw-Cude House, Off SR 2010, Colfax vicinity, 6/01/82, A, C, 82003455

Sherrod Park, 200–300 blocks Woodrow Ave., High Point, 3/14/91, A, C, 91000278

Sherwood, Michael, House, 426 W. Friendly Ave., Greensboro, 1/31/78, B, C, 78001958

Siceloff, J. C., House, 1104 N. Main St., High Point, 3/14/91, C, 91000264

Smith, Francis Marion, House, 204 Railroad Ave., Gibsonville, 7/12/84, A, C, 84002330

South Greensboro Historic District [Greensboro MPS], Roughly bounded by Gorrell, Martin, E. Bragg, Sevier, Omaha, Broad, Caldwell, Andrew, Vance, McCulloch, and King Dr., Greensboro, 12/20/91, A, C, 91001812

Sternberger, Sigmund, House [Greensboro MPS], 712 Summit Ave., Greensboro, 4/16/93, C, 93000302

Summit Avenue Historic District [Greensboro MPS], Roughly bounded by Chestnut, E. Bessemer, Cypress, Dewey, Park, and Percy Sts., Greensboro, 8/05/93, A, C, 93000768

Tomlinson Chair Manufacturing Company Complex, 305 W. High St., High Point, 3/17/83, C, 83001888

Union Cemetery [Greensboro MPS], 900 block S. Elm St., Greensboro, 10/21/93, A, C, d, 93001142

Wafco Mills, 801 McGee St., Greensboro, 5/30/79, A, C, 79001716

Wagoner, Simeon, House, 5838 NC 61 (Friedens Church Rd.), Gibsonville vicinity, 9/03/91, C, 91001172

Weir, Dr. David P., House, 223 N. Edgeworth St., Greensboro, 7/12/84, B, C, 84002332

West Market Street Methodist Episcopal Church, South, 302 W. Market St., Greensboro, 12/19/85, A, B, C, a, 85003198

White Oak New Town Historic District [Greensboro MPS], 2400–2418 N. Church, 2312–2509 Spruce, 2310–2503 Hubbard and 2401–2503 Cypress Sts., Greensboro, 4/03/92, A, C, 92000176

Halifax County

Bell—Sherrod House, 207 SE Railroad St., Enfield, 10/20/88, A, C, 88002027

Bellamy's Mill, SW of Enfield, Enfield vicinity, 11/05/74, A, 74001351

Branch, Samuel Warren, House, NC 481, Enfield vicinity, 6/14/82, C, 82003464

Cellar, The, 404 Whitfield St., Enfield, 9/20/79, C, 79003336

Davie, William R., House, Norman St., Halifax, 6/19/73, B, C, 73001348

Eagle Tavern, Main St., Halifax, 4/24/73, C, b, 73001349

Edmunds-Heptinstall House, NW of Aurelian Springs on NC 1001, Aurelian Springs vicinity, 3/12/79, C, 79001718

Garner Farm, Jct. of NC 125 and I-95, Days Crossroads vicinity, 6/07/90, A, C, 90000826

Grace Episcopal Church, 404 Washington Ave., Weldon, 10/01/91, A, C, a, 91001493

Gray-Brownlow-Wilcox House, S of Brinkleyville on NC 58, Brinkleyville vicinity, 8/03/82, A, B, C, d, 82003463

Halifax County Courthouse [North Carolina County Courthouses TR], Main St., Halifax, 5/10/79, A, C, 79001719

Halifax County Home and Tubercular Hospital, NC 903, Halifax vicinity, 12/10/85, A, C, 85003338

Halifax Historic District, Roughly bounded by St. David St., Owens House Drainage Ditch, Roanoke River, and Magazine Spring Gut, Halifax, 1/21/70, A, C, 70000456

Hermitage, The, 1 mi. W of Tillery off NC 481, Tillery vicinity, 5/29/75, C, 75001274

Hoffman—Bowers—Josey—Riddick House, 1103 Church St., Scotland Neck, 12/29/88, A, C, 88003080

Magnolia, N of Scotland Neck on U.S. 258, Scotland Neck vicinity, 4/17/80, C, 80002842

Matthews Place, SE of Hollister, Hollister vicinity, 11/11/74, C, 74001352

Myrtle Lawn, SR 1003, Enfield vicinity, 6/20/85, A, C, 85001341

Oakland, At Airlie, NE corner of NC 4 and SR 1310, Airlie, 7/02/73, C, 73001346

Roanoke Canal, Roanoke Rapids Lake SE to Weldon, Roanoke Rapids and vicinity, 10/08/76, A, C, 76001328

Roanoke Rapids Junior-Senior High School, 800 Hamilton St., Roanoke Rapids, 12/29/88, A, C, 88003081

Sally-Billy House, St. Andrews St. extended, Halifax, 2/08/73, C, 73001350

Shell Castle, W of Enfield on NC 481, Enfield vicinity, 4/11/73, C, 73001347

Strawberry Hill, E of Enfield on SR 1100, Enfield vicinity, 1/15/80, C, 80002841

Tillery—Fries House, SE side of NC 481, 0.3 mi. N of jct. with NC 1117, Tillery vicinity, 7/08/92, C, 92000830

Trinity Church, N of Scotland Neck on U.S. 258, Scotland Neck vicinity, 11/25/80, A, B, C, 80002843

White Rock Plantation, N of Hollister on NC 1315, Hollister vicinity, 2/14/79, B, C, 79001720

Woodstock, N of Scotland Neck on U.S. 258, Scotland Neck, 11/25/80, C, 80002844

Harnett County

Campbell, James Archibald, House, U.S. 421, Buies Creek, 11/17/77, A, 77001001

Howard, Kenneth L., House, 400 S. Layton Ave., Dunn, 8/19/82, A, B, C, 82003465

Ivy Burne, NC 217, E side 0.4 mi. S of jct. with NC 2027, Linden vicinity, 9/05/91, A, B, C, 91001377

Lebanon, 4.5 mi. SW of Dunn on NC 82, Dunn vicinity, 1/29/73, A, C, 73001351

Lee, Gen. William C., House, 209 W. Divine St., Dunn, 11/25/83, B, C, 83003968

McKay, John A., House and Manufacturing Company, 100 E. Divine St., Dunn, 4/10/86, B, C, g, 86000739

Summer Villa and the McKay-Salmon House, SR 1291, Lillington vicinity, 4/25/85, C, D, 85000902

Summerville Presbyterian Church and Cemetery, Off SR 1291, Lillington vicinity, 4/25/85, C, a, d, 85000903

Thorbiskope, Off SR 2049 at SR 2050, Bunn Level vicinity, 1/23/86, A, B, C, 86000132

Haywood County

Boone-Withers House, 305 Church St., Waynesville, 7/21/83, A, C, 83001889

Citizens Bank and Trust Company Building, Former, 161 N. Main St., Waynesville, 3/14/91, A, 91000261

Gwyn, James M., House, NC 276, Cruso vicinity, 7/12/84, A, B, C, 84002335

Haywood County Courthouse [North Carolina County Courthouses TR], Main and Depot Sts., Waynesville, 5/10/79, A, C, g, 79001721

Lambeth Inn, Lambeth Dr., Lake Junaluska, 7/29/82, C, 82003466

Masonic Hall, 114 Church St., Waynesville, 6/09/88, A, C, 88000729

Mount Zion United Methodist Church, SR 1503, Crabtree vicinity, 2/05/86, A, C, a, 86000156

Patton Farm, SW of Canton, Phillipsville vicinity, 11/10/80, A, C, 80002845

Shelton House, 307 Shelton St., Waynesville, 1/31/79, C, 79001722

US Post Office Building, Former, 106 S. Main St., Waynesville, 3/14/91, A, C, 91000262

Way, Dr. J. Howell, House, 301 S. Main St., Waynesville, 9/11/80, B, C, 80002846

Henderson County

Aloah Hotel [Hendersonville MPS], 201 3rd Ave. West, Hendersonville, 2/24/89, A, C, 89000036

Brookland, N of Flat Rock on SR 1863, Flat Rock vicinity, 8/19/82, A, B, C, 82003467

Carl Sandburg Home National Historic Site, W of Flat Rock, Flat Rock vicinity, 10/17/68, B, g, NHL, NPS, 68000013

Cedars, The [Hendersonville MPS], 219 7th Ave. West, Hendersonville, 2/24/89, A, C, 89000033

Chewning House [Hendersonville MPS], 755 N. Main St., Hendersonville, 2/24/89, A, C, 89000034

Clarke—Hobbs—Davidson House [Hendersonville MPS], 229 5th Ave. West, Hendersonville, 2/24/89, C, 89000031

Flat Rock Historic District, W of East Flat Rock, Flat Rock, 10/15/73, A, C, 73001352

Henderson County Courthouse [North Carolina County Courthouses TR], 1st and Main Sts., Hendersonville, 5/10/79, A, C, 79001723

King—Waldrop House [Hendersonville MPS], 103 S. Washington St., Hendersonville, 6/28/89, A, C, 89000030

Main Street Historic District [Hendersonville MPS], Main St. between Sixth Ave. East and First Ave. East, Hendersonville, 3/30/89, A, C, 89000028

Meadows, The, N of Fletcher on SR 1547, Fletcher vicinity, 1/11/80, C, 80002847

Mills River Chapel, SR 1328, 0.7 mi. N of jct. with NC 280, Mills River vicinity, 12/02/88, C, a, d, 88002660

Moss—Johnson Farm, 3346 Haywood Rd., Hendersonville vicinity, 2/10/87, A, C, 87000021

Rugby Grange, Address Restricted, Fletcher vicinity, 5/05/87, A, C, 86003748

Seventh Avenue Depot District [Hendersonville MPS], Seventh Ave. between Grove and Ash, Hendersonville, 3/30/89, A, C, 89000029

Smith—Williams—Durham Boarding House [Hendersonville MPS], 247 5th Ave. West, Hendersonville, 2/24/89, A, C, 89000032

Waverly, The [Hendersonville MPS], 783 N. Main St., Hendersonville, 2/24/89, A, C, 89000035

Hertford County

Ahoskie Downtown Historic District, Roughly bounded by W. North St., Seaboard Coastline RR, W. Main St., S. and N. Mitchell Sts., Ahoskie, 4/25/85, A, C, 85000906

Brown, C. S., School Auditorium, Off NC 45, Winton, 7/29/85, A, B, C, 85001657

Cedars, The, SE of Murfreesboro off SR 1167, Murfreesboro vicinity, 9/22/83, A, C, 83001890

Columns, The, Jones Dr., Murfreesboro, 2/18/71, A, C, 71000590

Cowper—Thompson House, 405 North St., Murfreesboro, 1/09/92, C, 91001908

Deane House, Off SR 1446, Cofield vicinity, 4/15/82, A, C, 82003468

Freeman House, 200 E. Broad St., Murfreesboro, 2/18/71, A, C, 71000591

Gray Gables, Main St., Winton, 6/01/82, C, 82003470

Hare Plantation House, 1.6 mi. W of jct. of SR 1317 and U.S. 258, Como vicinity, 2/18/71, C, 71000588

Hertford County—Continued

King-Casper-Ward-Bazemore House, W of Ahoskie on NC 11, Ahoskie vicinity, 11/26/82, C, b, 82001299

Melrose, 100 E. Broad St., Murfreesboro, 3/31/71, C, 71000592

Mitchell, William, House, 3 mi. E of Ahoskie on NC 350, Ahoskie vicinity, 12/04/72, C, 72000965

Mulberry Grove, SW of Ashoskie, Ashoskie vicinity, 11/25/80, A, B, C, D, 80002848

Murfreesboro Historic District, Roughly bounded by Broad, 4th, Vance, and Winder Sts., Murfreesboro, 8/26/71, A, C, 71000593

Myrick House, 402 Broad St., Murfreesboro, 3/31/71, C, 71000594

Myrick-Yeates-Vaughan House, 327 W. Main St., Murfreesboro, 3/17/83, C, 83001891

Newsome, James, House, NC 11 at jct. NC 42, Ahoskie vicinity, 12/28/84, A, C, b, 84000803

Rea, William, Store, E. Williams St., Murfreesboro, 9/15/70, A, 70000457

Riddick House, 1 mi. S of jct. of SR 1319 and 1322, Como vicinity, 2/18/71, C, 71000589

Roberts-Vaughan House, 130 E. Main St., Murfreesboro, 2/18/71, C, 71000595

Vernon Place, N of Como off US 258, Como vicinity, 4/29/82, B, C, 82003469

Wheeler, John, House, 403 E. Broad St., Murfreesboro, 3/31/71, C, 71000596

Hoke County

Hoke County Courthouse [North Carolina County Courthouses TR], Main and Edenborough Sts., Raeford, 5/10/79, A, C, 79001725

Long Street Church, W of Fayetteville on SR 1300, Fayetteville vicinity, 1/21/74, C, a, 74001353

Mill Prong, Address Restricted, Edinburgh vicinity, 12/13/79, A, C, 79001724

Puppy Creek Plantation, NW of Rockfish on SR 1409, Rockfish vicinity, 12/12/76, C, 76001329

Hyde County

Credle, George V., House and Cemetery, US 264, Rose Bay vicinity, 7/29/85, A, B, C, d, 85001670

Fairfield Historic District, SR 1308, 1309, 1305 and NC 94, Fairfield, 7/05/85, A, B, C, D, 85001448

Hyde County Courthouse [North Carolina County Courthouses TR], Bounded by SR 1129, 1132, and 1128, Swansboro, 5/10/79, A, C, 79001726

Inkwell, E of Lake Landing on U.S. 264, Lake Landing vicinity, 9/01/78, C, 78001960

Lake Landing Historic District, Roughly bounded by Mattamuskeet Refuge Boundary, Middletown, Nebraska, SR 1110, and US 264, Lake Landing vicinity, 3/10/86, A, C, 86000786

Lake Mattamuskeet Pump Station, E of Swanquarter, Swanquarter vicinity, 5/28/80, A, C, 80002849

Ocracoke Historic District, SW tip of Ocracoke Island, around Silver Lake, Ocracoke, 9/28/90, A, C, g, NPS, 90001465

Ocracoke Light Station, SR 1326, Ocracoke, 11/25/77, A, C, NPS, 77000110

Swindell, Albin B., House and Store, US 264, Swindell Fork, 8/14/86, A, B, C, b, 86001641

Wynne's Folly, W of Engelhard on U.S. 264, Engelhard vicinity, 12/06/77, C, 77001002

Iredell County

Academy Hill Historic District [Iredell County MRA], Western Ave., Bell, Mulberry, Wise and Armfield Sts., Statesville, 11/24/80, B, C, 80002867

Bethesda Presbyterian Church, Session House and Cemetery [Iredell County MRA], SR 2359, Houstonville vicinity, 12/08/80, A, C, a, d, 80002855

Brawley, Espy Watts, House [Iredell County MRA], 601 William St., Mooresville, 11/24/80, B, C, 80002859

Campbell, Perciphull, House [Iredell County MRA], SR 1832, Union Grove vicinity, 12/08/80, C, 80002881

Center Street A.M.E. Zion Church [Iredell County MRA], S. Center St., Statesville, 11/24/80, A, C, a, 80002868

Centre Presbyterian Church, Session House and Cemeteries [Iredell County MRA], SR 1245, Mount Mourne vicinity, 11/24/80, C, a, d, 80002863

Coddle Creek Associate Reformed Presbyterian Church, Session House and Cemetery [Iredell County MRA], SR 1146, Mount Mourne vicinity, 11/24/80, A, C, a, d, 80002864

Cornelius House [Iredell County MRA], SR 1378 and SR 1302, Mooresville vicinity, 11/24/80, C, 80002860

Daltonia [Iredell County MRA], SR 2115, Houstonville vicinity, 12/08/80, B, C, 80002856

Damascus Baptist Church Arbor [Iredell County MRA], Off SR 1158 and SR 1582, Harmony vicinity, 11/24/80, A, C, a, 80002850

Davidson House [Iredell County MRA], SR 1337, Troutman vicinity, 11/24/80, C, 80002880

East Broad Street-Davie Avenue Historic District [Iredell County MRA], Davie Ave., Broad and Elm Sts., Statesville, 11/24/80, C, 80002869

Ebenezer Academy, Bethany Presbyterian Church and Cemetery [Iredell County MRA], U.S. 21, Houstonville vicinity, 12/08/80, A, B, C, a, d, 80002857

Eccles, Henry, House [Iredell County MRA], SR 2145 and SR 2180, Statesville, 11/24/80, C, 80002870

Falls-Hobbs House [Iredell County MRA], SR 1303, Statesville vicinity, 6/24/82, C, 82003471

Farmville Plantation [Iredell County MRA (AD)], SE of Elmwood off U.S. 70 on SR 2362, Elmwood vicinity, 6/19/73, C, 73001353

Feimster House [Iredell County MRA], SR 1516, Statesville vicinity, 6/24/82, C, 82003472

Fort Dobbs [Iredell County MRA (AD)], Fort Dobbs Rd., Statesville vicinity, 9/15/70, A, 70000458

Gaither House [Iredell County MRA], NC 901, Harmony vicinity, 11/24/80, C, 80002851

Hargrave House [Iredell County MRA], NC 152 and NC 150, Statesville vicinity, 6/24/82, C, 82003473

Holland-Summers House [Iredell County MRA], Off SR 1904, Harmony vicinity, 11/24/80, C, 80002852

Houston, George, House [Iredell County MRA], NC 115, Mount Mourne vicinity, 11/24/80, A, C, 80002865

Iredell County Courthouse [North Carolina County Courthouses TR], S. Center St. between W. Prospect St. and Court Pl., Statesville, 5/10/79, A, C, 79003434

Johnson-Neel House [Iredell County MRA (AD)], 4 mi. W of Mooresville off NC 150, Mooresville vicinity, 6/20/75, C, 75001275

Key Memorial Chapel [Iredell County MRA], 150 E. Sharpe St., Statesville, 11/24/80, A, C, a, 80002871

King-Flowers-Keaton House [Iredell County MRA], NC 115 and SR 1905, Statesville, 11/24/80, C, 80002872

Main Building, Mitchell College [Iredell County MRA (AD)], Broad St., Statesville, 1/25/73, A, C, 73001354

McClelland-Davis House [Iredell County MRA], SR 1551, Statesville, 11/24/80, A, C, 80002873

McElwee Houses [Iredell County MRA], 122, 126, 134 and 140 Water St., Statesville, 11/24/80, B, C, 80002874

Mitchell College Historic District [Iredell County MRA], NC 90 and U.S. 70, Statesville, 11/24/80, A, B, C, a, d, 80002875

Mooresville Historic District [Iredell County MRA], NC 115 and NC 152, Mooresville, 11/24/80, A, C, 80002861

Morrison-Campbell House [Iredell County MRA], Off SR 2125, Harmony vicinity, 11/24/80, C, 80002853

Morrison-Mott House [Iredell County MRA], 332 N. Center St., Statesville, 11/24/80, B, C, 80002876

Mount Mourne [Iredell County MRA (AD)], Off NC 115, Mount Mourne, 10/29/74, B, C, 74001354

Sharpe, Col. Silas Alexander, House [Iredell County MRA], 402 S. Center St., Statesville, 11/24/80, B, C, 80002877

Snow Creek Methodist Church and Burying Ground [Iredell County MRA], Off SR 1904, Harmony vicinity, 11/24/80, A, C, a, d, 80002854

South Broad Street Row [Iredell County MRA], 251-311 S. Broad St., Mooresville, 11/24/80, C, 80002862

Statesville Commercial Historic District [Iredell County MRA], Roughly bounded by Front, Meeting, Broad and Tradd Sts., Statesville, 11/24/80, A, C, 80002878

Turner, Henry, House and Caldwell-Turner Mill Site [Iredell County MRA], SR 2145, Statesville, 11/24/80, B, C, D, 80002879

Iredell County—Continued

U.S. Post Office and County Courthouse, 227 S. Center St., Statesville, 1/24/74, C, 74001355

Waddle-Click Farm [Iredell County MRA], SR 2309, Statesville vicinity, 6/24/82, C, 82003474

Welch-Nicholson House and Mill Site [Iredell County MRA], Statesville vicinity, Houstonville vicinity, 12/08/80, A, C, 80002858

Wood Lawn [Iredell County MRA], SR 1138, Mount Mourne vicinity, 11/24/80, C, 80002866

Jackson County

Backus, E. M., Lodge, Cold Mountain Gap Rd., Lake Toxaway vicinity, 6/09/88, A, C, 88000689

Balsam Mountain Inn, SR 1700 and SR 1701, Balsam, 7/15/82, A, C, 82003475

Church of the Good Shepherd, NC 107 at SR 1118, Cashiers, 2/20/86, A, C, a, 86000317

Fairfield Inn, U.S. 64, Cashiers vicinity, 6/14/82, C, 82003476

Hall, Lucius Coleman, House, Off NC 116, 0.1 mi. E of jct. with SR 1367, Webster vicinity, 3/09/90, A, C, 90000365

Hedden, Elisha Calor, House, Main St. and Old Webster-Sylva Rd., Webster, 12/21/89, A, C, 89002133

High Hampton Inn Historic District, NC 107 E side, 1.5 mi. S of US 64, Cashiers vicinity, 9/26/91, A, C, 91001468

Jackson County Courthouse [North Carolina County Courthouses TR], Main St., Sylva, 5/10/79, A, C, 79001727

Joyner Building, Western Carolina University Campus, Cullowhee, 12/08/78, A, 78001961

Moore, Walter E., House, Main St., Webster, 2/23/90, B, C, 90000322

Mount Beulah Hotel, US 23 and 44, Dillsboro, 3/01/84, A, C, 84002337

Webster Baptist Church, NC 116 and SR 1340, Webster, 12/21/89, C, a, 89002137

Webster Methodist Church, NC 116/Main St., Webster, 12/21/89, C, a, 89002130

Webster Rock School, Main St., Webster, 1/04/90, A, C, 89002262

Johnston County

Atkinson-Smith House, 10 mi. E of Smithfield off SR 1007, Smithfield vicinity, 6/05/75, B, C, 75001276

Benson Historic District, Roughly bounded by E. Hill, N. Lee, E. Parish and Farmers Dr. on Main and Church Sts., Benson, 5/09/85, A, B, C, 85001053

Bentonville Battleground State Historic Site, S of Princeton, off U.S. 70! and SR 1008, Princeton vicinity, 2/26/70, A, 70000460

Boyette Slave House, NW of Kenly on SR 2110, Kenly vicinity, 9/20/79, A, C, 79003329

Downtown Smithfield Historic District, S. Third and Market Sts., Smithfield, 10/14/93, A, C, 93001120

Edgerton, Noah Edward, House [Selma, North Carolina MRA], 301 W. Railroad St., Selma, 6/24/82, B, C, 82003477

Ellington-Ellis Farm, SR 1004, Clayton vicinity, 7/21/83, A, B, C, d, 83001892

Hannah's Creek Primitive Baptist Church, NC 301 SW of jct. with NC 1171, Benson vicinity, 1/25/91, A, C, a, 90002181

Harper House, Near jct. of SR 1008 and 1188, Harper, 2/26/70, A, C, 70000459

Hastings-McKinnie House, 201 S. Pierce St., Princeton, 9/08/83, A, B, C, 83001893

Hood Brothers Building, 100–104 S. Third St., Smithfield, 8/14/86, C, 86001623

Hood—Strickland House, 415 S. 4th St., Smithfield, 8/23/90, C, 90001310

Johnston County Courthouse [North Carolina County Courthouses TR], Martin and 2nd Sts, Smithfield, 5/10/79, A, C, 79001728

Nowell-Mayerburg-Oliver House [Selma, North Carolina MRA], 312 W. Anderson St., Selma, 6/24/82, C, 82003478

Sanders-Hairr House, S of Clayton on SR 1525, Clayton vicinity, 5/06/71, C, 71000597

Smith, William E., House [Selma, North Carolina MRA], 309 W. Railroad St., Selma, 6/24/82, B, C, 82003480

Stallings-Carpenter House, SR 1713, Clayton vicinity, 3/28/83, B, C, 83001894

Stevens, Everitt P., House [Selma, North Carolina MRA], SR 1003, Selma, 6/24/82, A, C, 82003481

US Post Office, Former, 405 E. Market St., Smithfield, 4/22/93, A, 93000315

Union Station [Selma, North Carolina MRA], E. Railroad St., Selma, 6/24/82, A, C, 82003482

Jones County

Bryan—Bell Farm, NC 58, 1 mi. E of SR 1119, Pollocksville vicinity, 12/21/89, A, C, d, 89002155

Eagle Nest, SE of Pink Hill off NC 41, Pink Hill vicinity, 11/13/74, C, 74001356

Foscue Plantation House, Off U.S. 17 near jct. with SR 1002, Pollocksville vicinity, 11/19/71, C, 71000598

Grace Episcopal Church, Lake View Dr. and Weber St., Trenton, 1/20/72, A, C, a, 72000966

Lavender, Bryan, House, Off US 17 South of Trent River Bridge, Pollocksville, 4/25/85, C, 85000904

Sanderson House, SW of Pollocksville on SR 1115, Pollocksville vicinity, 12/16/71, C, 71000599

Trenton Historic District, Roughly bounded by Trent, Lower and Pollock Sts., and Brock Mill Pond, Trenton, 7/03/74, A, C, a, 74001357

Lee County

Downtown Sanford Historic District, Roughly bounded by Gordon St., Horner Blvd., Cole and Chatham Sts., Sanford, 9/28/85, A, C, 85002561

Endor Iron Furnace, SE of Cumnock, Cumnock vicinity, 8/13/74, A, C, 74001358

Farrar, Obediah, House [Lee County MPS], 9910 Barringer Rd., Haywood vicinity, 8/18/93, A, C, 93000728

Lee County Courthouse [North Carolina County Courthouses TR], Horner Blvd., between Courtland and McIntosh Sts., Sanford, 5/10/79, A, C, 79001729

McIver, John D., Farm [Lee County MPS], 2007 Windmill Dr., Sanford, 8/18/93, C, 93000729

Railroad House, Carthage St. at Hawkins Ave., Sanford, 1/29/73, A, C, b, 73001355

Temple Theatre, 120 Carthage St., Sanford, 9/08/83, A, C, 83001895

Lenoir County

Atlantic and North Carolina Railroad Freight Depot [Kinston MPS], E. Blount St. between N. Queen and N. McLewean Sts., Kinston, 11/08/89, A, C, 89001768

Baptist Parsonage [Kinston MPS], 211 S. McLewean St., Kinston, 11/08/89, C, 89001767

Blalock, Robert L., House [Kinston MPS], 300 S. McLewean St., Kinston, 11/08/89, C, 89001772

Candy, B. W., House [Kinston MPS], 600 N. Queen St., Kinston, 11/08/89, B, C, 89001771

Cedar Dell, SE of Falling Creek on SR 1338, Falling Creek vicinity, 8/26/71, C, 71000600

Herring House, NW of LaGrange off SR 1503, LaGrange vicinity, 10/25/73, C, 73001356

Hill—Grainger Historic District [Kinston MPS], Roughly bounded by Summit Ave., N. East St., E. & W. Vernon Ave., and N. Heritage St., Kinston, 11/08/89, A, C, 89001764

Hotel Kinston [Kinston MPS], 503 N. Queen St., Kinston, 11/08/89, A, C, 89001770

Jackson, Jesse, House, SE of Kinston on NC 11, Kinston vicinity, 6/24/71, C, 71000602

Kinston Baptist—White Rock Presbyterian Church [Kinston MPS], 516 Thompson St., Kinston, 11/08/89, A, C, a, b, 89001773

Kinston Fire Station—City Hall [Kinston MPS], 118 S. Queen St., Kinston, 11/08/89, A, C, 89001769

LaGrange Presbyterian Church, 201 S. Caswell St., LaGrange, 8/14/86, C, a, 86001646

Lenoir County Courthouse [North Carolina County Courthouses TR], Queen and Kings Sts., Kinston, 5/10/79, A, C, 79001730

Mitchelltown Historic District [Kinston MPS], Roughly bounded by W. Vernon Ave., N. Heritage St., W. Blount St., College St., Atlantic Ave., and Rhem St., Kinston, 11/08/89, A, C, 89001766

Peebles House, 109 E. King St., Kinston, 8/26/71, A, C, 71000603

Queen—Gordon Streets Historic District [Kinston MPS], Roughly N. Queen and Gordon Sts., Kinston, 11/08/89, A, C, 89001765

Sumrell and McCoy Building [Kinston MPS], 400 N. Queen St., Kinston, 12/21/89, A, C, 89002134

Lenoir County—Continued

Trianon Historic District [Kinston MPS], Roughly E. Gordon St. from N. Tiffany to N. Orion Sts. and Water St. from N. Vance to N. Orion Sts., Kinston, 11/08/89, A, B, C, 89001763

Tull—Worth—Holland Farm, NC 1579 N side, .5 mi. E of jct. with NC 1578, Kinston vicinity, 9/22/92, A, C, 92001260

Wood, Dempsey, House, SW of Falling Creek on SR 1324, Kinston vicinity, 8/26/71, C, 71000601

Lincoln County

Caldwell—Cobb—Love House, 218 E. Congress St., Lincolnton, 2/06/86, B, C, 86000159

Graham, William A., Jr., Farm, S of Denver on SR 1360, Kidville vicinity, 5/06/77, B, C, 77001004

Ingleside, S of jct. of NC 73 and SR 1383, Iron Station vicinity, 4/13/72, B, C, 72000967

Lincoln County Courthouse [North Carolina County Courthouses TR], Courthouse Sq., Lincolnton, 5/10/79, A, C, 79001731

Loretz House, NW of Lincolnton off SR 1204, Lincolnton vicinity, 3/16/72, C, 72000969

Magnolia Grove, Jct. of SR 1309 and 1313, Iron Station vicinity, 3/16/72, C, 72000968

Mount Welcome, Jct. of NC 1511 and NC 1412, Mariposa vicinity, 9/13/91, B, C, 91001413

Pleasant Retreat Academy, 129 E. Pine St., Lincolnton, 5/29/75, A, C, 75001277

Rock Springs Camp Meeting Ground, SR 1373 off NC 16, Lincolnton vicinity, 9/22/72, A, a, 72000970

Seagle, Andrew, Farm, N of Reepsville off SR 1205, Reepsville vicinity, 2/24/75, A, 75001278

Shadow Lawn, 301 W. Main St., Lincolnton, 3/24/72, C, 72000971

St. Luke's Church and Cemetery, 303–321 N. Cedar St., 322 E. McBee St., Lincolnton, 1/14/92, C, a, d, 91001914

Tucker's Grove Camp Meeting Ground, N of Machpelah off SR 1360, Machpelah vicinity, 10/18/72, A, a, 72000972

Vesuvius Furnace, On SR 1382, N of NC 73, Catawba Springs vicinity, 8/13/74, A, B, C, 74001359

Woodside, W of jct. of U.S. 182 and 27, Lincolnton vicinity, 3/07/73, B, C, c, 73001357

Macon County

Brabson, Dr. Alexander C., House, SR 1118, 0.6 mile S. of jct. with SR 1115, Otto vicinity, 8/23/90, A, C, 90001312

Bryson, Albert Swain, House, Pine Lane, Franklin, 12/20/84, C, 84000541

Cowee Mound and Village Site, Address Restricted, Wests Mill vicinity, 1/18/73, D, 73002238

Edwards Hotel, Jct. of Main and Fourth Sts., SE corner, Highlands, 11/20/92, A, C, 92001614

Franklin Presbyterian Church, 45 Church St., Franklin, 2/05/87, C, a, 86003718

Franklin Terrace Hotel, 67 Harrison Ave., Franklin, 7/29/82, A, C, 82003483

Highlands Inn, Jct. of Main and Fourth Sts., Highlands, 12/18/90, A, 90001916

Nequasee, Address Restricted, Franklin, 11/26/80, A, 80004598

Pendergrass Building, 6 W. Main St., Franklin, 9/26/91, A, C, 91001469

Siler, Jesse R., House, 115 W. Main St., Franklin, 4/29/82, C, 82003484

Madison County

California Creek Missionary Baptist Church, US 23, Mars Hill vicinity, 7/12/84, A, C, a, 84002342

Dorland Memorial Presbyterian Church, Bridge St. at Meadow Ln., Hot Springs, 7/24/86, A, B, C, a, 86001907

Madison County Courthouse [North Carolina County Courthouses TR], Main St., Marshall, 5/10/79, A, C, 79001732

Ottinger, Henry, House, 391 Boys Home Rd., Hot Springs vicinity, 3/06/86, A, C, D, a, 86000410

Sunnybank, NC 209 and Walnut St., Hot Springs, 5/23/80, B, C, 80002883

White, James H., House, 5 Hill St., Marshall, 12/21/89, B, 89002136

White, Jeff, House, NE of Marshall on NC 213, Marshall vicinity, 6/05/75, C, 75001279

Martin County

Biggs, Asa, House and Site, 100 E. Church St., Williamston, 10/10/79, B, C, D, 79003335

Burras House, On U.S. 64, Jamesville, 3/30/78, A, C, 78001962

Darden Hotel, Main St., Hamilton, 12/30/75, A, C, 75001280

Fort Branch Site, SE of Hamilton on SR 1416, Hamilton vicinity, 6/18/73, A, 73001358

Hamilton Historic District, NC 125, Hamilton, 6/03/80, A, C, a, d, 80002884

Hickory Hill, NC 903, Hamilton vicinity, 12/20/84, A, C, 84000546

Jamesville Primitive Baptist Church and Cemetery, E side of NC 171, Jamesville, 12/20/84, A, B, C, a, 84000556

Jones, Jesse Fuller, House, Off SR 1409, Spring Green vicinity, 4/29/82, A, B, C, 82003485

Little, W. J., House, 109 N. Main St., Robersonville, 9/19/85, A, B, C, 85002420

Martin County Courthouse [North Carolina County Courthouses TR], Main St., Williamston, 5/10/79, A, C, 79001733

Sherrod Farm, W side of NC 125/903, Hamilton vicinity, 12/20/84, A, C, 84000552

McDowell County

Artz, Welsford Parker, House, 205 Maple St., Old Fort, 8/23/90, A, C, 90001311

Carson House, W of Marion on U.S. 70, Marion, 9/15/70, A, B, C, 70000843

Depot Historic District [Downtown Marion MPS], SE end Depot St., bounded on S by Southern RR tracks, and 111 Railroad St. S of tracks, Marion, 3/28/91, A, C, 91000293

First Presbyterian Church [Downtown Marion MPS], 12 W. Fort St., Marion, 3/28/91, C, a, 91000291

Main Street Historic District [Downtown Marion MPS], Roughly bounded by US 70 and Garden, State and Logan Sts., Marion, 3/28/91, A, C, 91000292

McDowell County Courthouse [North Carolina County Courthouses TR], Main and E. Court Sts., Marion, 5/10/79, A, C, 79003131

St. John's Episcopal Church [Downtown Marion MPS], 315 S. Main St., Marion, 3/28/91, C, a, 91000290

St. Matthew's Lutheran Church [Downtown Marion MPS], 307 W. Court St., Marion, 3/28/91, C, a, 91000289

Mecklenburg County

Addison Apartments, 831 E. Morehead St., Charlotte, 8/23/90, C, 90001314

Alexander, Hezekiah, House, 3420 Shamrock Dr., Charlotte, 4/17/70, B, C, 70000461

Beaver Dam Plantation House, SE of Davidson on NC 73, Davidson vicinity, 3/19/79, A, B, 79001735

Biddle Memorial Hall, Johnson C. Smith University, Beatties Ford Rd. and W. Trade St., Charlotte, 10/14/75, A, C, 75001281

Carey, Philip, Building, 301 E. 7th St., Charlotte, 3/01/84, A, C, 84002408

Carr, John Price, House, 200-206 N. McDowell St., Charlotte, 10/22/80, B, C, 80002885

Cedar Grove, 3 mi. W of Huntersville off U.S. 21, Huntersville vicinity, 2/01/72, C, 72000976

Charlotte Supply Company Building, 500 S. Mint St., Charlotte, 3/01/84, A, C, 84002348

Commercial Building at 500 North Tryon Street, 500 N. Tryon St., Charlotte, 11/20/92, A, C, 92001615

Craven, Dr. Walter Pharr, House [Rural Mecklenburg County MPS], 7648 Mt. Holly—Huntersville Rd., Charlotte vicinity, 1/31/91, A, C, 90002187

Davidson, Benjamin W., House, W of Huntersville on SR 2138, Huntersville vicinity, 4/26/76, C, 76001331

Dilworth Historic District, Roughly bounded by Myrtle, Morehead, Berkeley, Dilworth Rd. W, Charlotte, Park, Tremont, Cleveland and Rensalaer, Charlotte, 4/09/87, A, B, C, g, 87000610

Dinkins House, NW side of SR 1126, 1.2 mi. from SR 1136 (Nation's Ford Rd.), Pinville, 12/04/73, C, 73001360

Duke, James Buchanan, House, 400 Hermitage Rd., Charlotte, 1/20/78, B, C, 78001963

Elizabeth Historic District, Roughly bounded by Central Ave., Seaboard Coast Line Railroad, E.

Mecklenburg County—Continued

5th St., Kenmore Ave., Park Dr., and E. Independence, Charlotte, 1/03/89, A, C, 88003003

Eumenean Hall, Davidson College, Davidson College campus, Davidson, 4/13/72, A, C, 72000974

Ewart, John F., Farm [Rural Mecklenburg County MPS], 12920 Huntersville—Concord Rd., Huntersville vicinity, 2/04/91, A, C, 91000023

Fire Station No. 2, 1212 South Blvd., Charlotte, 10/22/80, A, C, 80002886

First Presbyterian Church, 200 W. Trade St., Charlotte, 11/12/82, C, a, 82001300

Hayes—Byrum Store and House [Rural Mecklenburg County MPS], NC 160 S of jct. with Shopton Rd., Charlotte vicinity, 1/31/91, C, 90002186

Highland Park Manufacturing Company Mill No. 3, 2901 N. Davidson St., Charlotte, 10/20/88, A, C, 88001855

Hodges, Eugene Wilson, Farm [Rural Mecklenburg County MPS], 2900 Rocky River Church Rd., Charlotte vicinity, 2/21/91, A, C, 91000077

Holly Bend, W of Huntersville on SR 2720, Huntersville vicinity, 3/24/72, C, 72000977

Hoskins Mill, 201 S. Hoskins Rd., Charlotte, 10/05/88, A, C, 88001702

Hotel Charlotte, 327 W. Trade St., Charlotte, 7/02/79, A, C, 79003344

Independence Building, 100–102 W. Trade St., Charlotte, 9/18/78, A, C, 78001964

Jonas, Charles R., Federal Building, 401 W. Trade St., Charlotte, 6/07/78, C, g, 78001965

Latta Arcade, 320 S. Tryon St., Charlotte, 10/29/75, B, C, 75001282

Latta House, 6 mi. S of Huntersville on SR 2125, Huntersville vicinity, 3/16/72, C, 72000978

Liddell-McNinch House, 511 N. Church St., Charlotte, 12/12/76, B, C, 76001330

Mayes House, 435 E. Morehead St., Charlotte, 8/05/93, C, 93000735

McAuley Farm [Rural Mecklenburg County MPS], 10724 Alexanderana Rd., Charlotte vicinity, 2/04/91, A, C, 91000024

McElroy, Samuel J., House [Rural Mecklenburg County MPS], 10915 Beatties Ford Rd., Huntersville vicinity, 2/21/91, C, 91000078

McKinney, John Washington, House [Rural Mecklenburg County MPS], 7332 Providence Rd. W., Charlotte vicinity, 2/21/91, C, 91000079

Mecklenburg County Courthouse [North Carolina County Courthouses TR], E. Trade, Alexander, and E. 4th Sts., Charlotte, 5/10/79, A, C, 79001734

Mecklenburg Investment Company Building, 233 S. Brevard St., Charlotte, 8/19/82, A, B, C, 82003486

Merchants and Farmers National Bank Building, 123 E. Trade St., Charlotte, 3/01/84, A, C, 84002344

Morris, Green, Farm [Rural Mecklenburg County MPS], W side of NC 3628 approx. 1 mi. S of jct. with Providence Rd. W., Charlotte vicinity, 2/21/91, A, C, 91000080

Morrocroft, 2525 Richardson Dr., Charlotte, 11/28/83, B, C, 83003970

Myers Park Historic District, Roughly bounded by NC 16, E and W Queens Rd., and Lillington Ave., Charlotte, 8/10/87, A, C, g, 87000655

Nebel Knitting Mill, Former, 101 W. Worthington Ave., Charlotte, 9/05/91, A, C, 91001376

North Charlotte Historic District, Roughly bounded by the Southern Railroad, Herrin St., Spencer St., and Charles Ave., Charlotte, 3/16/90, A, C, 90000367

Overcarsh House, 326 W. 8th St., Charlotte, 7/21/83, C, 83001896

Philanthropic Hall, Davidson College, Davidson College campus, Davidson, 4/13/72, A, C, 72000975

Providence Presbyterian Church and Cemetery, 10140 Providence Rd., Matthews, 6/01/82, A, B, C, a, d, 82003487

Ramah Presbyterian Church and Cemetery [Rural Mecklenburg County MPS], NC 2439 .3 mi. N of jct. with NC 2426, Huntersville vicinity, 2/21/91, A, C, a, d, 91000081

Rosedale, 3427 N. Tryon St., Charlotte, 9/11/72, C, 72000973

Seaboard Air Line Railroad Passenger Station, 1000 N. Tryon St., Charlotte, 10/24/80, A, C, 80002887

St. Mark's Episcopal Church, SR 2004, Huntersville vicinity, 3/01/84, C, a, 84002410

St. Mark's Episcopal Church (Boundary Increase) [Mecklenburg County MPS], S side NC 2004 E of jct. with NC 2074, Huntersville vicinity, 2/21/91, C, 91000076

Steele Creek Presbyterian Church and Cemetery [Rural Mecklenburg County MPS], 7407 Steele Creek Rd., Charlotte vicinity, 2/21/91, A, C, a, d, 91000082

VanLandingham Estate, 2010 The Plaza, Charlotte, 10/13/83, B, C, 83003971

Victoria, 1600 The Plaza, Charlotte, 4/11/73, C, b, 73001359

White Oak Plantation, E of Charlotte on SR 2826, Charlotte vicinity, 2/07/78, C, 78001966

Mitchell County

Mitchell County Courthouse [North Carolina County Courthouses TR], Main St., Bakersville, 5/10/79, A, C, 79001736

Peterson, John N., Farm, E side of SR 1321 just N of jct. with SR 1322, Poplar, 12/06/90, A, B, C, 90001859

Willis, Henry, House, SR 1164, Penland vicinity, 7/14/88, C, 88001051

Montgomery County

Montgomery County Courthouse [North Carolina County Courthouses TR], E. Main St. between S. Main and S. Pearl Sts., Troy, 5/10/79, A, C, 79001737

Site 31Mg22, Address Restricted, Badin vicinity, 8/05/85, D, 85001750

Town Creek Indian Mound, Address Restricted, Mount Gilead vicinity, 10/15/66, D, e, NHL, 66000594

Moore County

Aberdeen Historic District, Roughly bounded by Maple Ave., Bethesda Ave., Campbell St., Main St., Pine St., South St., and Poplar St., Aberdeen, 6/28/89, A, B, C, 89000663

Alston House, SE of Glendon on SR 1624, Glendon vicinity, 2/26/70, B, C, 70000462

Bethesda Presbyterian Church, NC 5, Aberdeen, 7/22/79, A, C, a, d, 79003345

Black-Cole House, NW of Eastwood, Eastwood vicinity, 9/18/78, C, 78001967

Blue, Daniel, House, SR 1836, Carthage vicinity, 7/21/83, C, 83001897

Blue, John, House, 200 Blue St., Aberdeen, 7/29/82, B, C, 82003488

Blue, Malcolm, Farm, Bethesda Rd. and Ernest L. Ives Dr., Aberdeen vicinity, 6/01/82, C, 82003489

Boyd, James, House, Ridge Rd. and Connecticut Ave., Southern Pines, 5/12/77, B, 77001005

Bruce-Dowd-Kennedy House, Monroe and Rockingham Sts., Carthage, 9/29/80, C, 80002888

Bryant, James, House, On SR 1210, Harris Crossroads vicinity, 4/15/82, C, 82003490

Cameron Historic District, Carthage St. from US 1 to Seaboard RR Tracks, Cameron, 3/17/83, A, C, 83001898

Carthage Historic District, Roughly, McReynolds St. between Barrett St. and Glendons Rd. and parts of Barrett, Ray, Pinecrest and Brooklyn Sts., Carthage, 3/19/92, A, C, 92000182

Gordon Payne Site (31MR15), Address Restricted, High Falls vicinity, 9/24/86, D, 86001954

Lloyd-Howe House, SW of Pinehurst, Pinehurst vicinity, 9/08/83, A, B, C, 83001899

McLeod Family Rural Complex, .4 miles west of US 1, Pine Bluff vicinity, 12/20/84, A, C, D, 84000561

Moore County Courthouse [North Carolina County Courthouses TR], Ray, Dowd, Monroe, and Sanders Sts. circle, Carthage, 5/10/79, A, C, 79001738

Pinehurst Historic District, Roughly bounded by Norfolk & Southern RR tracks, McLean Rd. and NC 5, Pinehurst, 8/14/73, A, C, 73001361

Pinehurst Race Track, Jct. of Morgantown Rd. and NC 5, SE corner, Pinehurst vicinity, 11/27/92, A, B, C, 92001628

Shaw House, 780 SW. Broad St., Southern Pines vicinity, 6/17/93, A, C, 93000542

Southern Pines Historic District, Bounded by Saylor St., New Jersey Ave., Illinois Ave. and Massachusetts Ave. Ext., Southern Pines, 12/27/91, A, C, 91001875

Nash County

Arrington, Gen. Joseph, House, SE of Hilliardston on SR 1500, Hilliardston vicinity, 7/15/74, C, 74001361

Nash County—Continued

Bellamy-Philips House, SR 1522, Battleboro vicinity, 7/12/82, A, C, 82003491

Bellemonte, 3400 N. Wesleyan Blvd., Rocky Mount, 12/21/89, A, C, b, 89002132

Benvenue, 330 Southern Blvd., Rocky Mount vicinity, 4/29/82, B, C, 82003493

Bissette—Cooley House, N. First & E. Washington Sts., Nashville, 9/19/85, B, C, g, 85002414

Black Jack, N of Red Oak, Red Oak vicinity, 7/31/74, C, 74001362

Brantley, Dr. Hassell, House, 301 Branch St., Spring Hope, 8/14/86, B, C, 86001647

Dortch House, SR 1527 off NC 43, Dortches, 12/26/72, C, 72000979

Hart, Dr. Franklin, Farm, NC 48, Drake vicinity, 7/21/88, A, C, 88001050

Machaven, 306, S. Grace St., Rocky Mount, 11/25/80, C, 80002890

Meadows, The, NW of Battleboro on SR 1510, Battleboro vicinity, 5/16/74, C, 74001360

Nash County Courthouse [North Carolina County Courthouses TR], Washington St. between Drake and N. Court Sts., Nashville, 5/10/79, A, C, 79001739

Nashville Historic District, Roughly 100–400 W. Washington and 100–300 E. Washington Sts., Nashville, 7/22/87, A, C, 87001185

Rocky Mount Electric Power Plant, 217 Andrews St., Rocky Mount, 7/15/82, A, B, C, 82003494

Rocky Mount Mills, NC 43 and NC 48, Rocky Mount, 2/01/80, A, C, 80002891

Rose Hill, N of Nashville off NC 58, Nashville vicinity, 4/28/82, A, C, 82003492

Spring Hope Historic District, Roughly bounded by Franklin, Louisburg, Second and Community Sts., Spring Hope, 9/15/88, A, C, 88001591

Stonewall, Falls Rd. extension, Rocky Mount vicinity, 6/02/70, C, 70000463

Taylor's Mill, SR 1120 W of SR 1124, Middlesex vicinity, 5/28/80, A, D, 80002889

New Hanover County

Audubon Trolley Station, Jct. of Park Ave. and Audubon Blvd., Wilmington, 8/05/93, A, 93000736

Bradley—Latimer Summer House, S side SR 1411 E of jct. with US 76, Wrightsville Beach, 7/20/87, A, C, 87001181

Cape Fear Civil War Shipwreck Discontiguous District, Address Restricted, Wilmington Beach vicinity, 12/23/85, A, C, D, 85003195

Carolina Place Historic District, Bounded by Market St., Wallace Park, Gibson Ave., Wrightsville Ave. and S. Eighteenth St., Wilmington, 8/31/92, A, C, 92001086

City Hall/Thalian Hall, 100 N. 3rd. St., Wilmington, 4/03/70, A, C, 70000464

Federal Building and Courthouse, N. Water between Market and Princess St., Wilmington, 5/02/74, C, 74001363

Fort Fisher, 18 mi. S of Wilmington on U.S. 421, Wilmington vicinity, 10/15/66, A, NHL, 66000595

Market Street Mansion District, 1704, 1705, 1710, 1713 Market St., Wilmington, 4/21/75, A, C, 75001284

Masonboro Sound Historic District, E side Magnolia Dr. and 7301–7601, 7424 and 7506 Masonboro Sound Rd., Wilmington vicinity, 10/22/92, A, C, D, b, 92001334

Mount Lebanon Chapel and Cemetery, SR 1411, Wrightsville Beach, 10/16/86, C, a, d, 86002879

U.S.S. PETERHOFF, Address Restricted, Fort Fisher vicinity, 8/06/75, D, 75001283

USS NORTH CAROLINA, Cape Fear River, Wilmington, 7/23/81, A, C, g, 81000424

USS NORTH CAROLINA (BB-55) National Historic Landmark, W bank of the Cape Fear River, Wilmington, 11/10/82, A, g, NHL, 82004893

Walker, James, Nursing School Quarters, 1020 Rankin St., Wilmington, 7/20/89, A, 89000944

Wilmington Historic and Archeological District, Roughly bounded by Wright, S. 7th, and Harnett Sts., and N/S line 100 yds. W of North East Cape Fear River, Wilmington, 5/06/74, A, C, D, 74001364

Northampton County

Duke-Lawrence House, E of Rich Square off NC 305/561, Rich Square vicinity, 10/22/80, C, 80002892

Garysburg United Methodist Church and Cemetery, SR 1207, Garysburg, 6/20/85, A, C, a, 85001350

Mowfield, 2 mi. W of Jackson on U.S. 158, Jackson vicinity, 2/13/75, A, C, 75001285

Northampton County Courthouse Square, Jefferson St. between Atherton and Brown Sts., Jackson, 4/11/77, A, C, 77001006

Parker, Francis, House, W of Murfreesboro on US 158, Murfreesboro vicinity, 10/21/83, C, 83001900

Princeton Site, Address Restricted, Murfreesboro vicinity, 11/25/80, D, 80004281

Verona, W of Jackson, Jackson vicinity, 5/29/75, B, C, 75001286

Onslow County

Alum Spring [Onslow County MPS], SR 1211 1.6 mi. S of SR 1001, Catherine Lake, 1/31/90, A, 89002349

Avirett—Stephens Plantation [Onslow County MPS], US 258/24 .25 mi. N of NC 1227, Richlands vicinity, 4/18/91, A, C, 91000465

Bank of Onslow and Jacksonville Masonic Temple [Onslow County MPS], 214–216 Old Bridge St., Jacksonville, 11/13/89, A, C, 89001850

Catherine Lake Historic District [Onslow County MPS], Jct. SR 1001 and 1211, Catherine Lake, 11/13/89, A, C, 89001853

Futral Family Farm [Onslow County MPS], SR 1210, 1 mi. SE of jct. with SR 1209, Fountain vicinity, 11/13/89, A, C, 89001851

Mattocks, William Edward, House, 109 Front St., Swansboro, 3/22/89, C, 89000166

Mill Avenue Historic District [Onslow County MPS], Roughly bounded by Bluff, College, Court, W. Railroad, Wantland, Mill, and First, Jacksonville, 3/16/90, A, B, C, g, 90000439

Palo Alto Plantation, SR 1434, Palopato, 10/10/79, A, C, 79003338

Pelletier House and Wantland Spring [Onslow County MPS], Old Bridge St. at New River, Jacksonville, 11/13/89, A, C, 89001852

Richlands Historic District [Onslow County MPS], Roughly bounded by Foy, Trenton, Hargett, Wilmington, Franck, and Church Sts., Richlands, 3/16/90, A, C, 90000441

Southwest Historic District [Onslow County MPS], NC 53 and SR 1217, Waltons Store vicinity, 11/13/89, A, C, a, d, 89001854

Swansboro Historic District [Onslow County MPS], Roughly bounded by Walnut, Main, and Elm Sts., NC 24, White Oak River, and Church, Water, and Broad Sts., Swansboro, 3/16/90, A, C, 90000440

Venters Farm Historic District, US 258 and NC 1229, Richlands vicinity, 5/07/87, A, C, g, 86003504

Orange County

Alberta Mill Complex, NE corner Weaver and N. Greensboro Sts., Carrboro, 1/19/76, A, 76001332

Ayr Mount, St. Mary's Rd., Hillsborough, 8/26/71, C, 71000606

Bingham School, NC 54 and SR 1007, Oaks, 1/18/78, A, C, 78001969

Burwell School, N. Churton St., Hillsborough, 9/15/70, A, C, 70000465

Carrboro Commercial Historic District, 100 Blk. of E. Main St. between Greensboro Rd. & Roberson St., Carrboro, 6/20/85, A, C, 85001339

Chapel Hill Historic District, Battle Park, E. Franklin and E. Rosemary Sts. residences, and central campus of University of North Carolina, Chapel Hill, 12/16/71, A, C, 71000604

Chapel Hill Town Hall, Rosemary and Columbia Sts., Chapel Hill, 3/20/90, A, C, 90000364

Chapel of the Cross, 304 E. Franklin St., Chapel Hill, 2/01/72, C, a, 72000980

Commandant's House, Barracks Rd., Hillsborough, 11/09/72, A, C, 72000981

Eagle Lodge, 142 W. King St., Hillsborough, 4/16/71, A, C, 71000607

Faucett Mill and House, Faucette Mill Rd. on the E side of Eno River, Hillsborough vicinity, 8/04/88, A, C, 88001175

Gimghoul Neighborhood Historic District, Roughly bounded by Gimghoul Rd., Ridge Ln., and Gladon Dr., Chapel Hill, 8/05/93, A, C, 93000807

Orange County—Continued

Hazel-Nash House, 116 W. Queen St., Hillsborough, 3/31/71, B, C, 71000608

Heartsease, 113 E. Queen St., Hillsborough, 4/11/73, B, C, 73001362

Hillsborough Historic District, Roughly bounded by N. Nash and W. Corbin Sts., Highland Loop Rd., and Eno River, Hillsborough, 10/15/73, A, C, D, 73001363

Lloyd, Thomas F., Historic District, Roughly bounded by E. Carr St., Maple Ave., and S. Greensboro St., Carrboro, 8/14/86, A, B, b, 86001625

Moorefields, N of jct. of SR 1134 and 1135, Hillsborough vicinity, 4/25/72, B, C, 72000982

Nash Law Office, 143 W. Margaret Lane, Hillsborough, 9/28/71, A, B, C, 71000609

Nash-Hooper House, 118 W. Tryon St., Hillsborough, 11/11/71, B, NHL, 71000610

Old East, University of North Carolina, University of North Carolina campus, Chapel Hill, 10/15/66, A, NHL, 66000596

Old Orange County Courthouse, 106 E. King St., Hillsborough, 6/24/71, A, C, 71000611

Paisley-Rice Log House, N of Mebane, Mebane vicinity, 1/31/79, A, B, C, 79001740

Playmakers Theatre, Cameron Ave., University of North Carolina campus, Chapel Hill, 6/24/71, A, C, g, NHL, 71000605

Rigsbee's Rock House, Jct. of Lawrence Rd. and US 70W Bypass, Hillsborough vicinity, 10/20/88, A, C, 88002026

Rocky Ridge Farm Historic District, Roughly bounded by Rocky Ridge Rd., Country Club Rd., Laurel Hill Rd., Laurel Hill Cir., and Buttons Dr., Chapel Hill, 8/08/89, A, C, 89001039

Ruffin-Roulhac House, Churton and Orange Sts., Hillsborough, 8/05/71, B, C, 71000612

Sans Souci, E. Corbin St., Hillsborough, 8/26/71, C, 71000613

St. Mary's Chapel, NE of Hillsborough, Hillsborough vicinity, 7/12/78, A, C, a, 78001968

St. Matthew's Episcopal Church and Churchyard, St. Mary's Rd., Hillsborough, 6/24/71, A, C, a, 71000614

Pamlico County

China Grove, 3 mi. SW of Oriental on SR 1302, Oriental vicinity, 2/06/73, C, 73001364

Pasquotank County

Elizabeth City Historic District, Irreg. pattern along Main St., Elizabeth City, 10/18/77, A, C, 77001007

Morgan House, S of South Mills off U.S. 17, South Mills, 2/01/72, C, 72000984

Newland Road Site, U.S. 17, Morgan's Corner vicinity, 4/14/83, C, D, 83001901

Old Brick House, 182 Brick House Lane, Elizabeth City, 3/16/72, C, 72000983

Pender County

Bannerman House, NE of Burgaw off NC 53 on SR 1520, Burgaw vicinity, 5/31/74, C, b, 74001365

Belvidere Plantation House, Off SR 1565, Hampstead vicinity, 6/14/82, C, 82003495

Burgaw Depot, 102 E. Fremont, Burgaw, 7/24/86, A, C, 86001910

Moore's Creek National Military Park (Boundary Increase), NW of Wilmington on NC 210, Wilmington vicinity, 2/13/87, A, NPS, 86003649

Moores Creek National Battlefield, 25 mi. NW of Wilmington on NC 210, Wilmington vicinity, 10/15/66, A, NPS, 66000070

Pender County Courthouse [North Carolina County Courthouses TR], Wright, Wilmington, Walker, and Fremont Sts., Burgaw, 5/10/79, A, C, g, 79001741

Poplar Grove, US 17, Scotts Hill, 7/16/79, B, C, 79003346

Sloop Point, NE of Vista off SR 1561, Vista vicinity, 1/20/72, B, C, 72000985

US Naval Ordnance Testing Facility Assembly Building [US Naval Ordnance Test Facilities, Topsail Island MPS], Jct. Of Channel Blvd. and Flake Ave., Topsail Beach, 9/14/93, A, g, 93000909

US Naval Ordnance Testing Facility Control Tower [US Naval Ordnance Test Facilities, Topsail Island MPS], SW corner of S. Anderson Blvd. and Flake Ave., Topsail Beach, 9/14/93, A, g, 93000910

US Naval Ordnance Testing Facility Observation Tower No. 2 [US Naval Ordnance Test Facilities, Topsail Island MPS], 1000 blk. S. Anderson Blvd., Topsail Beach, 9/14/93, A, g, 93000911

Perquimans County

Belvidere, NC 37, W of Perquimans River, Belvidere, 8/02/77, C, 77001008

Cove Grove, E of Hertford near SR 1301 and 1302, Hertford vicinity, 8/07/74, C, 74001366

Land's End, SE of Hertford near jct. of SR 1300 and 1324, Hertford vicinity, 9/20/73, C, 73001365

Myers-White House, NE of Bethel on SR 1347, Bethel vicinity, 1/20/72, C, 72000986

Newbold-White House, SE of Hertford off SR 1336, Hertford vicinity, 6/24/71, B, C, 71000615

Nixon, Samuel, House, NW of Hertford on SR 1121, Hertford vicinity, 10/15/73, B, C, 73001366

Perquimans County Courthouse [North Carolina County Courthouses TR], Market St., Hertford, 5/10/79, A, C, 79001743

Stockton, S of Woodville, Woodville vicinity, 6/07/74, C, 74001368

Sutton-Newby House, E of Hertford, Hertford vicinity, 9/10/74, B, C, 74001367

White, Isaac, House, NE of Bethel on SR 1339, Bethel vicinity, 3/23/79, A, C, 79001742

Person County

Burleigh, NW of Concord on NC 57, Concord vicinity, 5/01/80, B, C, 80002893

Henry-Vernon House, SW of Bushy Fork on NC 49, Bushy Fork vicinity, 2/03/83, A, C, 83001902

Holloway—Jones—Day House, US 501 and SR 1322, Roxboro vicinity, 6/09/88, C, 88000698

Holloway-Walker Dollarhite House, SR 1514, Bethel Hill vicinity, 6/01/82, A, B, C, d, 82003496

Person County Courthouse [North Carolina County Courthouses TR], Main St. between Aggitt and Court Sts., Roxboro, 5/10/79, A, C, g, 79001744

Roxboro Commercial Historic District, Roughly bounded by Courthouse Sq., Court, Abbit, Reams, Depot, N. and S. Main Sts., Roxboro, 3/01/84, A, C, 84002415

Roxboro Male Academy and Methodist Parsonage, 315 N. Main St., Roxboro, 7/29/82, A, B, C, 82003497

Waverly Plantation, S of U.S. 58, Cunningham vicinity, 10/09/74, B, C, 74001369

Pitt County

College View Historic District, Roughly bounded by Holly, Eastern, E. First and E. Fifth Sts., Greenville, 3/19/92, A, C, 92000181

Farmville Historic District, Roughly bounded by Turnage, Pine, Jones, and Waverly Sts., Farmville, 10/21/93, A, C, 93001121

Ficklen, E. B., House, 508 W. 5th St., Greenville, 12/20/84, B, C, 84000564

Fleming, James L., House, 302 S. Greene St., Greenville, 7/21/83, C, 83001903

Greenwreath, W of Greenville, Greenville vicinity, 4/29/82, A, B, C, 82003498

Grimesland Plantation, E of Grimesland on SR 1569, Grimesland vicinity, 3/31/71, B, C, 71000616

Humber, Robert Lee, House, 117 W. 5th St., Greenville, 7/09/81, B, C, g, 81000425

Jones-Lee House, 805 E. Evans St., Greenville, 11/25/80, C, 80002894

Lang, Robert J., Jr., House, SR 1231, 0.1 mile S. of jct. with SR 1200, Fountain vicinity, 8/23/90, C, 90001313

Long, Willian H., House, 200 E. 4th St., Greenville, 4/15/82, C, 82003499

May-Lewis, Benjamin, House, US 264-A, Farmville vicinity, 6/20/85, A, C, 85001337

Pitt County Courthouse [North Carolina County Courthouses TR], N. 3rd St. between Washington and S. Evan St., Greenville, 5/10/79, A, C, 79001745

St. John's Episcopal Church, SE corner of SR 1917 and SR 1753, St. John's, 12/02/86, C, a, 86003268

US Post Office, 215 S. Evans St., Greenville, 2/06/86, A, C, 86000784

Polk County

Blackberry Hill, E of Tryon on SR 1516, Tryon vicinity, 11/21/74, C, b, 74001372

Blockhouse Site, E of U.S. 176, Tryon vicinity, 10/15/70, A, 70000466

Church of the Transfiguration, Henderson and Charles Sts., Saluda, 11/12/82, C, a, 82001301

Green River Plantation, E of Columbus off SR 1005, Columbus vicinity, 3/28/74, B, C, 74001370

Hughes, J. G., House, N. Peak St., Columbus, 5/05/89, C, 89000347

Jones, Rev. Joshua D., House, NC 1526 S side, 0.4 mi. from NC 108, Mill Spring, 9/26/91, A, 91001476

Mills-Screven Plantation, NE of Tryon on SR 1509, Tryon, 2/17/83, C, 83001904

Pine Crest Inn, Pine Crest Lane, Tryon, 4/15/82, A, B, C, 82003500

Polk County Courthouse, Courthouse St., Columbus, 11/08/74, A, C, 74001371

Seven Hearths, N of Tryon at jct. of U.S. 176 and Harmon Field Rd., Tryon vicinity, 3/26/76, C, b, e, 76001333

Randolph County

Central School, 414 Watkins St., Asheboro, 11/12/93, A, C, 93001342

Coleridge Historic District, NC 22, Coleridge, 11/13/76, A, 76001334

Deep River-Columbia Manufacturing Company, Main St., Ramseur, 11/15/78, A, 78001970

Franklinville Historic District, Roughly bounded by Deep River, Sunrise Ave., Clark St., and Greensboro Rd., Franklinville, 12/20/84, A, C, D, 84000587

Hammond, Moses, House, 118 Trindale Rd., Archdale, 6/12/89, B, C, 89000466

Harper House, SW of Archdale, Archdale, 7/22/79, B, C, 79003347

Kindley, Wilson, Farm and Kindley Mine, NC 1408, E side, 1 mi. N of US 64, Asheboro vicinity, 6/11/92, A, C, 91001412

Marley House, N side of US 64 .1 mi. W of jct. with SR 2475, Staley vicinity, 12/18/90, A, C, 90001919

Mount Shepherd Pottery Site, Address Restricted, Asheboro vicinity, 2/01/80, D, 80002895

Pisgah Community Covered Bridge, SE of Pisgah on SR 1109 off SR 1112, Pisgah vicinity, 1/20/72, C, 72000988

Randolph County Courthouse [North Carolina County Courthouses TR], Worth St., Asheboro, 5/10/79, A, C, 79001746

Skeen's Mill Covered Bridge, 1.7 mi. W of Flint Hill on SR 1406 off SR 1408, Flint Hill vicinity, 1/20/72, C, 72000987

Thayer Farm Site (31RD10), Address Restricted, Asheboro vicinity, 8/28/86, D, 86001953

Richmond County

Bank of Pee Dee Building [Rockingham MRA], 201 E. Washington St., Rockingham, 9/22/83, A, C, 83001905

Covington Plantation House, SW of Rockingham, Rockingham vicinity, 5/28/80, C, 80002897

Dockery, Alfred, House, E side SR 1005, 0.1 mile S of jct. with SR 1143, Rockingham vicinity, 11/20/86, A, B, C, D, 86003350

Ellerbe Springs Hotel, N of Ellerbe, Ellerbe vicinity, 6/04/80, A, C, 80002896

Hannah Pickett Mill No. 1 [Rockingham MRA], 300 King Edward St., Rockingham, 9/22/83, A, C, 83001906

Little, John Phillips, House, Off NC 73, Little's Mills vicinity, 12/20/84, A, C, 84000590

Main Street Commercial Historic District, 2–105 Main St., Hamlet, 3/19/92, A, B, C, 92000169

Manufacturers Building, 220 E. Washington St., Rockingham, 5/29/79, A, B, 79003348

Richmond County Courthouse [North Carolina County Courthouses TR], Franklin St. between Hancock and Lee Sts., Rockingham, 5/10/79, A, C, 79001747

Roberdel Mill No. 1 Company Store [Rockingham MRA], 1106 Roberdel Rd., Rockingham, 9/22/83, A, C, 83001907

Rockingham Historic District [Rockingham MRA], Roughly bounded by LeGrand and Brookwood Aves., Leak and Ann Sts., Rockingham, 11/21/83, A, B, C, 83003981

Seaboard Coast Line Passenger Depot, Main St., Hamlet, 11/19/71, C, 71000617

U. S. Post Office and Federal Building [Rockingham MRA], 125 S. Hancock St., Rockingham, 9/22/83, C, 83001908

Watson, H. C., House [Rockingham MRA], 526 Caroline St., Rockingham, 9/22/83, C, 83001909

Robeson County

Ashpole Presbyterian Church, NW of Rowland of SR 1138, Rowland vicinity, 10/19/82, A, C, a, d, 82001302

Caldwell, Luther Henry, House, 209 Caldwell St., Lumberton, 9/18/78, B, C, 78001971

Carolina Theatre, 319 N. Chestnut St., Lumberton, 7/09/81, A, C, 81000426

Humphrey—Williams Plantation (Boundary Increase), NC 211 between SR 1001 and SR 1769, Lumberton vicinity, 11/16/88, A, C, 88002608

Humphrey-Williams House, W of Lumberton on NC 211, Lumberton vicinity, 7/24/73, C, 73001367

Lumberton Commercial Historic District, Roughly Sixth St., Elm St., Fifth St., Chestnut St., Second St., Walnut St., Seaboard Coast Railroad tracks, & Water St., Lumberton, 12/21/89, A, C, 89002131

MacDonald, Flora, College, College St. and 2nd Ave., Red Springs, 4/03/76, A, 76001336

Old Main, Pembroke State University, W of jct. of NC 711 and SR 1340, Pembroke, 5/13/76, A, 76001335

Philadelphus Presbyterian Church, SR 1318 SW of jct. with NC 72, Philadelphus, 10/03/75, C, a, 75001287

Planters Building, 312 N. Chestnut St., Lumberton, 11/03/87, A, C, 87001913

US Post Office—Lumberton, 606 N. Elm St., Lumberton, 3/06/85, C, 85000483

Williams-Powell House, SR 2256, Orrum vicinity, 4/09/84, C, 84002453

Rockingham County

Academy Street Historic District, Academy St., Madison, 7/15/82, A, B, C, 82003502

Boone Road Historic District, Roughly 400 and 500 blks.of Boone Rd., 400 blk. of Chestnut and 500 blk. Glovenia Sts., and 200 blk. of Highland Dr., Eden, 8/31/87, A, C, 87001455

Boxwoods, The, Penn Lane, Madison, 5/28/80, A, B, C, 80002898

Bullard-Ray House, 650 Washington St., Eden, 6/11/82, A, B, C, 82003501

Cascade Plantation, NE of Eden off NC 770, Eden vicinity, 10/14/75, C, 75001288

Central Leaksville Historic District, Roughly bounded by Lindsay, Monroe, Jay, Washington, & Kemp Sts., Eden, 12/09/86, A, C, d, 86003376

Chinqua—Penn Plantation, NC 1998 N side, 0.2 mi. W of jct. with NC 1987, Reidsville vicinity, 4/08/93, A, C, 93000235

Cross Rock Rapid Sluice [Dan River Navigation System in North Carolina TR], Address Restricted, Madison vicinity, 3/19/84, A, C, D, 84002459

Dead Timber Ford Sluices [Dan River Navigation System in North Carolina TR], Address Restricted, Wentworth vicinity, 6/29/84, D, 84002455

Dempsey-Reynolds-Taylor House, 610 Henry St., Eden, 9/08/83, A, B, C, 83001910

Eagle Falls Sluice [Dan River Navigation System in North Carolina TR], Address Restricted, Wentworth vicinity, 3/19/84, A, C, D, 84002462

Fewell-Reynolds House, Address Restricted, Madison vicinity, 7/16/79, C, 79003349

First Baptist Church [Reidsville MRA], 401 S. Scales St., Reidsville, 12/11/86, A, C, a, 86003386

First Baptist Church, 538 Greenwood St., Eden, 3/22/89, C, a, 89000178

Gravel Shoals Sluice [Dan River Navigation System in North Carolina TR], Address Restricted, Madison vicinity, 3/19/84, A, C, D, 84002458

High Rock Farm, SE of Reidsville on SR 2619, Williamsburg vicinity, 4/26/74, C, 74001373

Jacob's Creek Landing [Dan River Navigation System in North Carolina TR], Address Restricted, Madison vicinity, 3/19/84, A, C, D, 84002522

Jennings—Baker House [Reidsville MRA], 608 Vance St., Reidsville, 3/12/87, A, B, C, 86003387

Rockingham County—Continued

King, Dr. Franklin, House—Idlewild, 700 blk. of Bridge St., Eden, 9/19/85, A, B, C, 85002415

Leaksville Commercial Historic District, 622–656 Washington & 634 Monroe Sts., Eden, 10/23/87, A, C, g, 87001422

Leaksville—Spray Institute, 609 College St., Eden, 3/09/89, A, C, 89000179

Lower Sauratown Plantation, Address Restricted, Eden vicinity, 10/11/84, B, C, D, 84000071

Mayo River Sluice [Dan River Navigation System in North Carolina TR], Address Restricted, Madison vicinity, 3/19/84, A, C, D, 84002466

Mt. Sinai Baptist Church, 512 Henry St., Eden, 6/25/87, A, C, a, 87000914

North Washington Avenue Workers' House [Reidsville MRA], E side of 300 blk. of N. Washington Ave., Reidsville, 12/11/86, A, C, 86003388

Penn House, 324 Maple Ave., Reidsville, 11/25/83, A, B, C, 83003992

Reid, Gov. David S., House, 219 SE Market St., Reidsville, 4/26/74, B, 74001374

Reidsville Historic District [Reidsville MRA], Roughly bounded by W. Morehead, Southern Railway tracks, Lawson Ave., Main, Piedmontg, Vance and Lindsey Sts., Reidsville, 3/12/87, A, B, C, g, 86003391

Richardson Houses Historic District [Reidsville MRA], NW side of Richardson Dr. between Coach Rd. and Woodland Dr., Reidsville, 12/11/86, A, B, C, 86003390

Roberson's Fish Trap Shoal Sluice [Dan River Navigation System in North Carolina TR], Address Restricted, Madison vicinity, 3/19/84, A, C, D, 84002468

Rockingham County Courthouse [North Carolina County Courthouses TR], Highway 65, Wentworth, 5/10/79, A, C, 79001748

Scales, Alfred Moore, Law Office, 307 Carter St., Madison, 4/29/82, A, 82003503

Site 31RK1, Address Restricted, Eden vicinity, 5/24/84, D, 84002474

Slink Shoal Sluice and Wing Dams [Dan River Navigation System in North Carolina TR], Address Restricted, Madison vicinity, 3/19/84, A, C, D, 84002475

Spray Industrial Historic District, Roughly bounded by Warehouse, Rhode Island, River Dr., Washburn Rd., the Smith River, E. Early Ave., and Church, Eden, 12/09/86, A, B, C, 86003371

Tanyard Shoal Sluice [Dan River Navigation System in North Carolina TR], Address Restricted, Eden vicinity, 3/19/84, A, C, D, 84002478

Three Ledges Shoal Sluice [Dan River Navigation System in North Carolina TR], Address Restricted, Eden vicinity, 3/19/84, A, C, D, 84002481

Troublesome Creek Ironworks, Address Restricted, Monroeton vicinity, 9/29/72, D, 72000989

Wentworth Methodist Episcopal Church and Cemetery, NC 65 W of SR 2124, Wentworth vicinity, 3/13/86, B, C, a, 86000391

Wide Mouth Shoal Sluice [Dan River Navigation System in North Carolina TR], Address Restricted, Eden vicinity, 3/19/84, A, C, D, 84002484

Wright Tavern, NC 65, Wentworth, 9/15/70, C, 70000467

Rowan County

Back Creek Presbyterian Church and Cemeterey, SR 1763, Mt. Villa vicinity, 12/29/83, A, C, a, d, 83003998

Bernhardt House, 305 E. Innes St., Salisbury, 6/11/92, C, 92000701

Bernhardt, George Matthias, House, S of Rockwell on SR 2361, Rockwell vicinity, 11/26/82, A, C, 82001303

Bost, Henry Connor, House, E of Woodleaf off US 601, South River vicinity, 11/12/82, B, C, 82001304

Braun, Michael, House, NW of Granite Quarry on SR 2308 off U.S. 52, Granite Quarry vicinity, 9/28/71, C, 71000618

Brooklyn-South Square Historic District, Roughly bounded by Fisher, Shaver, Walls and Lee Sts., Salisbury, 7/05/85, A, B, C, 85001449

Chambers, Maxwell, House, 116 S. Jackson St., Salisbury, 1/20/72, C, a, b, 72000992

China Grove Roller Mill, 308 N. Main St., China Grove, 12/29/83, A, B, C, 83003995

Community Building, 200 N. Main St., Salisbury, 3/05/70, A, C, 70000468

Corriher Grange Hall, NW of Five Points on SR 1555, Five Points vicinity, 9/23/82, A, C, 82003507

Grace Evangelical and Reformed Church, S of Rockwell on SR 1221, Rockwell vicinity, 1/20/72, C, a, 72000990

Grimes Mill, 600 N. Church St., Salisbury, 2/06/84, A, C, 84002492

Hall Family House, NE of Bear Poplar on NC 801, Bear Poplar vicinity, 10/05/82, A, C, 82001305

Henderson, Archibald, Law Office, Church and Fisher Sts., Salisbury, 1/20/72, A, C, 72000993

Kerr Mill, W of Mill Bridge on Sloan Rd., S of NC 1768, Mill Bridge vicinity, 5/11/76, A, C, 76001337

Kerr, Gen. William, House, NW of Enochville on SR 1353, Enochville vicinity, 9/23/82, B, C, 82003505

Kesler Manufacturing Co.-Cannon Mills Co. Plant No. 7 Historic District, Park Ave. and Boundary St., Salisbury, 6/20/85, A, C, 85001346

Knox Farm Historic District, Knox and Amity Hill Rds., Cleveland vicinity, 4/01/83, A, C, 83001914

Knox—Johnstone House, 100 Beaumont Farm Rd., Cleveland, 8/05/93, C, 93000737

Livingstone College Historic District, W. Monroe St., Salisbury, 5/27/82, A, B, C, 82003509

Long, Alexander, House, N of Spencer on Sowers Ferry Rd., Spencer vicinity, 2/01/72, C, 72000995

Lyerly Building for Boys, Crescent Rd./Rt. 3, Gold Hill Township, 1/05/89, A, C, a, 88003006

McNeely-Strachan House, 226 S. Jackson St., Salisbury, 2/01/72, A, C, 72000994

Mingus, Joseph H., Farm, S side SR 1947, NE of jct. with SR 1702, Woodleaf, 10/28/87, A, C, 87001551

Mount Vernon, SR 1003 and SR 1986, Woodleaf vicinity, 5/27/80, B, C, D, 80002899

Mount Zion Baptist Church, 413 N. Church St., Salisbury, 12/30/85, A, a, 85003188

North Long Street-Park Avenue Historic District, North Long St. and Park Ave., Salisbury, 6/20/85, A, B, C, 85001347

North Main Street Historic District, Roughly bounded by N. Main, 17th, Lee and Lafayette Sts., Salisbury, 7/29/85, A, B, C, 85001674

Owen-Harrison House, Entrance off north side of SR 1768, Mill Bridge vicinity, 7/21/83, A, B, C, 83001911

Phifer, John, Farm, Jct. of Phifer Rd. and SR 1978, Cleveland vicinity, 12/28/90, A, C, 90001991

Rankin-Sherrill House, NC 801, Mt. Ulla, 9/23/82, A, B, C, 82003508

Salisbury Historic District, Roughly bounded by Jackson, Innis, Caldwell, Marsh, Church, E. Bank, Lee, and Liberty Sts., Salisbury, 11/12/75, A, C, b, c, g, 75001289

Salisbury Historic District (Boundary Increase I), 117 S. Lee St., Salisbury, 1/06/88, C, 88000141

Salisbury Historic District (Boundary Increase II), Roughly bounded by Ellis St., Monroe St., Church St., Bank St., S. Main St., and McCubbins St., Salisbury, 7/06/89, A, C, 89000760

Salisbury Railroad Corridor Historic District, Roughly East Council, Liberty, Kerr, Cemetery, Franklin, Lee, and Depot Sts., Salisbury, 5/13/87, A, C, 86003460

Salisbury Southern Railroad Passenger Depot, E side of Depot St. between Kerr and Council Sts., Salisbury, 7/30/75, A, C, 75001290

Shaver Rental Houses District, 303, 309 & 315 W. Council & 120 N. Jackson, Salisbury, 1/12/88, C, b, 87002233

Shuping's Mill Complex, S of Faith on NC 152, Faith vicinity, 9/23/82, A, B, C, 82003506

Southern Railway Spencer Shops, Salisbury Ave. between 3rd and 8th Sts., Spencer, 3/17/78, A, 78001972

Spencer Historic District, Roughly bounded by N to S Salisbury Ave., 8th St., Whitehead Ave., and Jefferson St., Spencer, 12/20/84, A, B, C, 84000619

St. Andrew's Episcopal Church and Cemetery, NE of Woodleaf on SR 1950, Woodleaf vicinity, 8/19/82, A, C, a, d, 82003510

Stigerwalt, John, House, E of Kannapolis off SR 1221 (Old Beatty Ford Rd.), Bostian Heights vicinity, 12/20/84, A, C, 84000595

Third Creek Presbyterian Church and Cemetery, SR 1973, Cleveland vicinity, 7/21/83, B, C, a, d, 83001912

Rowan County—Continued

Thyatira Presbyterian Church, Cemetery, and Manse, Off NC 150, Mill Bridge, 2/17/84, A, B, C, 84002488

Wiley, Calvin H., School, 200 blk. of Ridge Ave., Salisbury, 10/20/88, A, C, 88002028

Wood Grove, E of Bear Poplar on SR 1743, Bear Poplar vicinity, 9/23/82, B, C, 82003504

Zion Lutheran Church, SW of Rockwell on SR 1006 off SR 1221, Rockwell vicinity, 1/20/72, A, C, a, 72000991

Rutherford County

Carrier Houses, 415 and 423 N. Main St., Rutherfordton, 6/19/92, C, b, 92000681

Forest City Baptist Church, 301 W. Main St., Forest City, 9/14/89, C, a, 89001417

Fox Haven Plantation, SW of Rutherfordton off SR 1157, Rutherfordton vicinity, 9/14/72, C, 72000996

Ledbetter, James Dexter, House, Off US 74, Forest City vicinity, 6/14/82, B, C, 82003511

Logan, George W., House, SR 1555 at US 64, Rutherfordton vicinity, 2/20/86, B, C, 86000312

Melton-Fortune Farmstead, SR 1006 S of NC 226, Golden Valley vicinity, 7/11/85, A, C, D, d, 85001553

Rutherford County Courthouse [North Carolina County Courthouses TR], Main St. between 2nd and 3rd Sts., Rutherfordton, 5/10/79, A, C, 79001749

Rutherfordton—Spindale Central High School, Jct. of Charlotte Rd. (US 74 Bus.) and US 74, NW corner, Rutherfordton, 2/03/93, A, C, 92001843

St. Luke's Chapel, Jct. of Hospital Dr. and Old Twitty Ford Rd., Rutherfordton, 9/26/91, A, B, a, b, 91001470

Trinity Lutheran Church, 702 N. Main St., Rutherfordton, 3/24/72, A, C, a, 72000997

Sampson County

Beatty—Corbett House [Sampson County MRA], SR 701 at SR 1200, Ivanhoe vicinity, 3/17/86, A, B, C, 86000549

Bethune—Powell Buildings [Sampson County MRA], 118–120 E. Main St., Clinton, 3/17/86, A, C, 86000580

Bizzell, Asher W., House [Sampson County MRA], US 13 and SR 1845, Rosin, 5/21/86, A, C, b, 86001125

Black River Presbyterian and Ivanhoe Baptist Churches [Sampson County MRA], SR 1102 E of SR 1100, Ivanhoe, 3/17/86, C, a, d, 86000550

Boykin, Gen. Thomas, House [Sampson County MRA], SR 1214 SW of SR 1222, Clinton vicinity, 3/17/86, A, B, C, 86000551

Butler, Marion, Birthplace [Sampson County MRA], NC 242 at SR 1414, Salemburg vicinity, 3/17/86, B, C, c, 86000552

Caison, Dan E., Sr., House [Sampson County MRA], Broad St., Roseboro, 5/21/86, C, 86001124

Cherrydale [Sampson County MRA], SR 1919 at SR 1952, Turkey vicinity, 3/17/86, A, C, 86000554

Clear Run [Sampson County MRA], NC 411 at Black River, Clear Run, 3/17/86, A, B, C, b, 86000548

Clinton Depot [Sampson County MRA], W. Elizabeth St., Clinton, 3/17/86, A, C, 86000555

College Street Historic District [Sampson County MRA], 600–802 College St., Clinton, 3/17/86, A, B, C, 86000553

Dell School Campus [Sampson County MRA], US 421 and SR 1003, Delway, 5/21/86, A, C, 86001126

Delta Farm [Sampson County MRA], SR 1100 N of SR 1105, Ivanhoe vicinity, 3/17/86, A, B, C, 86000556

Graves-Stewart House, 600 College St., Clinton, 9/08/83, A, B, C, b, 83001913

Herring, Robert, House [Sampson County MRA], 216 Sampson St., Clinton, 3/17/86, B, C, 86000557

Herring, Troy, House [Sampson County MRA], Broad St. S of NC 24, Roseboro, 3/17/86, C, 86000558

Highsmith, Lewis, Farm [Sampson County MRA], US 421 S of NC 41, Harrells vicinity, 3/17/86, A, C, 86000559

Hollingsworth—Hines Farm [Sampson County MRA], SR 1926 S of SR 1004, Turkey vicinity, 3/17/86, A, C, b, 86000547

Howard—Royal House [Sampson County MRA], 202 N. Main St., Salemburg, 3/17/86, C, 86000561

Howell—Butler House [Sampson County MRA], Broad and McLamb Sts., Roseboro, 3/17/86, A, C, 86000560

Johnson, Samuel, House and Cemetery [Sampson County MRA], SR 1157 S of SR 1004, Ingold vicinity, 3/17/86, C, c, 86000562

Kerr, James, House [Sampson County MRA], SR 1005 S of SR 1007, Kerr vicinity, 3/17/86, A, B, C, 86000563

Killett, Marcheston, Farm [Sampson County MRA], SR 1222 N of US 701, Clinton vicinity, 3/17/86, A, C, 86000564

Kornegay, Marshall, House and Cemetery [Sampson County MRA], SR 1725 and SR 1720, Suttontown, 3/17/86, C, 86000565

Lamb, James H., House [Sampson County MRA], SR 1135 N of NC 411, Garland vicinity, 3/17/86, A, B, C, 86000566

Lee, Lovett, House [Sampson County MRA], SR 1725 and SR 1730, Giddensville vicinity, 3/17/86, C, 86000567

Matthews, Dr. James O., Office [Sampson County MRA], SR 1960 S of SR 1004, Taylors Bridge vicinity, 3/17/86, A, C, 86000568

Matthis, Fleet, Farm [Sampson County MRA], US 421 S of SR 1146, Taylors Bridge vicinity, 3/17/86, A, B, C, 86000569

McPhail, Jonas, House and McPhail, Annie, Store [Sampson County MRA], US 13 E of SR 1845, Rosin, 3/17/86, A, C, 86000571

Murphy—Lamb House and Cemetery [Sampson County MRA], SR 1135 S of US 701, Garland vicinity, 3/17/86, A, C, c, 86000570

Oak Plain Presbyterian Church [Sampson County MRA], SR 1943 S of SR 1945, Waycross vicinity, 5/21/86, A, C, a, 86001127

Oates, Livingston, Farm [Sampson County MRA], SR 1748 W of NC 403, Clinton vicinity, 3/17/86, A, C, 86000572

Owen Family House and Cemetery [Sampson County MRA], SR 1212 N of SR 1214, McDaniels vicinity, 3/17/86, A, C, d, 86000573

Patrick—Carr—Herring House, 226 McKoy St., Clinton, 1/14/93, C, 92001791

Pigford House [Sampson County MRA], SR 1751 S of US 701, Clinton vicinity, 3/17/86, C, 86000574

Pope House [Sampson County MRA], SR 1146 N of SR 1145, Clinton vicinity, 3/17/86, C, 86000575

Pugh, Francis, House [Sampson County MRA], SR 1751 at NC 403, Clinton vicinity, 3/17/86, A, C, 86000577

Pugh—Boykin House [Sampson County MRA], 306 Elizabeth St., Clinton, 3/17/86, C, 86000576

Royal—Crumpler—Parker House [Sampson County MRA], 512 Sunset Ave., Clinton, 3/17/86, A, C, 86000578

Seavey, Dr. John B., House and Cemetery [Sampson County MRA], SR 1100 S of SR 1007, Harrells vicinity, 5/21/86, C, d, 86001128

Sloan, Dr. David Dickson, Farm [Sampson County MRA], US 701 N of the South River, Garland vicinity, 3/17/86, B, C, 86000579

Thirteen Oaks [Sampson County MPS], Jct. of US 13 and SR 1647, Newton Grove vicinity, 6/07/90, A, C, 90000879

West Main—North Chesnutt Streets Historic District [Sampson County MRA], Roughly N. Chesnutt, Fayetteville, and Williams Sts. between W. Main and Margaret Sts., Clinton, 3/17/86, A, C, 86000546

Williams, Isaac, House, NC 55, Newton Grove vicinity, 3/01/84, A, C, 84002523

Williams, Isaac, House (Boundary Increase), NC 55 at jct. with NC 50, Newton Grove vicinity, 6/12/89, A, d, 89000467

Wilson, John E., House [Sampson County MRA], SR 1631 at SR 1630, Dunn vicinity, 3/17/86, A, C, b, 86000545

Scotland County

Blue, John, House, W of Laurinburg on SR 1108, Laurinburg vicinity, 12/08/78, B, C, 78003192

Blue, Mag, House, W of Laurinburg on SR 1118, Laurinburg, 9/23/82, B, C, 82003512

Scotland County—Continued

Gill, Thomas J., House, 203 Cronly St., Laurinburg, 7/15/82, B, C, 82003513

Laurel Hill Presbyterian Church, SR 1321 and SR 1323, Laurinburg vicinity, 8/18/83, A, B, C, a, b, 83001915

McRae-McQueen House, SW of Johns on US 501, Johns vicinity, 11/25/80, B, C, 80004469

Monroe, Robert Nancy, House, SR 1328, Silver Hill vicinity, 3/17/83, C, 83001916

Richmond Temperance and Literary Society Hall, 1 mi. SW of Wagram on SR 1405, Wagram vicinity, 4/11/73, A, C, 73001368

Shaw Family Farms, SR 1405, Wagram vicinity, 10/13/83, A, C, 83003999

Stewart-Hawley-Malloy House, SE of Laurinburg at jct. of SR 1610 and 1609, Laurinburg vicinity, 8/01/75, B, C, 75001291

Villa Nova, SR 1438, Laurinburg, 8/26/82, A, B, C, 82003514

Stanly County

Badin Historic District [Badin MRA], Roughly bounded by NC 740, Pine St., and Country Club property line, Badin, 10/12/83, A, C, 83004000

Hardaway Site (31ST4), Address Restricted, Badin vicinity, 3/01/84, D, NHL, 84002529

Narrows Dam and Power Plant Complex [Badin MRA], Yadkin River and SR 1704, Badin, 10/12/83, A, C, 83004001

Randle House, S side of NC 1802 at jct. with NC 1743, Norwood vicinity, 9/08/92, C, 92001172

West Badin Historic District [Badin MRA], Roughly bounded by Sims, Lincoln, Marion, and Lee Sts., Badin, 10/12/83, A, 83004002

Stokes County

Danbury Historic District, Main St. between Danbury Cemetery Rd. and NC 89, Danbury, 7/15/86, A, C, a, d, 86001686

Hanging Rock State Park Bathhouse, End of NC 2015 S of jct. with NC 1001, Hanging Rock State Park, Danbury vicinity, 10/24/91, A, C, 91001507

Jessup's Mill, SR 4132, Collinstown vicinity, 7/15/82, A, B, C, 82003515

Moore, Matthew, House, W of Danbury, Danbury vicinity, 10/29/74, B, C, 74001375

Moratock Iron Furnace, E of Danbury off NC 89, Danbury vicinity, 7/30/74, A, 74001376

Pine Hall, SR 1901 and NC 772, Pine Hall, 7/16/79, A, C, d, 79003350

Rock House, N of King on SR 1186, King vicinity, 10/01/75, B, C, 75001292

St. Philip's Episcopal Church, NC 65 and 8 and SR 1957, Germantown, 7/15/82, C, a, 82003516

Stokes County Courthouse [North Carolina County Courthouses TR], Main St. between

North St. and Courthouse Rd., Danbury, 5/10/79, A, C, 79001750

Surry County

Carter, W. F., House, 418 S. Main St., Mount Airy, 8/18/83, B, C, 83001917

Carter, William, House, SR 1626, 0.35 mi. W of jct. with SR 1625, Mount Airy vicinity, 3/15/90, C, 90000349

Cundiff, C. C., House, SR 2230, Siloam vicinity, 7/21/83, B, C, d, 83001918

Franklin, Bernard, House, NW of Dobson on SR 1331, Dobson vicinity, 4/24/73, B, C, 73001369

Haystack Farm, S of Oak Grove on SR 1480, Oak Grove vicinity, 12/02/82, B, C, 82001306

Hennis, Edgar Harvey, House, 1056 N. Main St., Mount Airy, 2/20/86, B, C, 86000318

Moore, William Alfred, House, 202 Moore Ave., Mount Airy, 3/05/86, C, 86000406

Mount Airy Historic District, Main, Brown, Market, Franklin, W. Pine, Rockford, Worth, Cherry, and Gilmer Sts., Moore, and Hines Aves., Mount Airy, 10/03/85, A, C, 85002931

North Carolina Granite Corporation Quarry Complex, E of Mount Airy on NC 103, Mount Airy vicinity, 8/06/80, A, B, 80002900

Rockford Historic District, SR 2221, Rockford, 8/27/76, A, C, a, e, 76001338

Surry County Courthouse [North Carolina County Courthouses TR], N. Main St. between School and Kapp Sts., Dobson, 5/10/79, A, C, 79001751

Trinity Episcopal Church, 472 N. Main St., Mount Airy, 1/09/86, C, a, 86000031

Swain County

Frye-Randolph House and Fryemont Inn, Fryemont Rd., Bryson City, 2/18/83, A, C, 83001919

Governor's Island, Address Restricted, Bryson City vicinity, 6/04/73, D, 73002239

Hall Cabin, 15 mi. NE of Fontana in Great Smoky Mountains National Park, Fontana vicinity, 1/30/76, C, NPS, 76000162

Hyatt, Abel, House, E. side NC 1168, 0.2 mi. N of jct with NC 1191, Bryson City vicinity, 3/22/91, C, 91000340

Nununyi Mound and Village Site, Address Restricted, Cherokee vicinity, 1/22/80, D, 80002901

Oconaluftee Archeological District, Address Restricted, Cherokee vicinity, 2/19/82, D, NPS, 82001715

Oconaluftee Baptist Church, 6 mi. N of Cherokee on U.S. 441 in Great Smoky Mountains National Park, Cherokee vicinity, 1/01/76, A, a, NPS, 76000163

Swain County Courthouse [North Carolina County Courthouses TR], Main and Fry Sts., Bryson City, 5/10/79, A, C, 79001752

Transylvania County

Biltmore Forest School, NW of Brevard off U.S. 276 in Pisgah National Forest, Brevard vicinity, 11/19/74, A, e, g, 74001377

Breese, William, Jr., House, 401 E. Main St., Brevard, 6/23/83, B, C, 83001920

Brevard College Stone Fence and Gate [Transylvania County MPS], Jct. of N. Broad St. and French Broad Ave., NW corner, Brevard, 12/21/93, C, 93001436

Deaver, William, House, N of Pisgah Forest on NC 280, Pisgah Forest vicinity, 8/13/79, C, 79001755

Godfrey—Barnette House [Transylvania County MPS], 411 S. Broad St., Brevard, 12/30/93, C, 93001437

Hillmont, W side of Lake Toxaway 3 mi. N of US 64, Lake Toxaway, 10/16/86, A, C, 86002871

Morgan's Mill, SW of Brevard on SR 1331, Brevard vicinity, 8/16/79, A, C, 79001753

Silvermont, E. Main St., Brevard, 7/09/81, B, C, 81000427

Transylvania County Courthouse [North Carolina County Courthouses TR], N. Broad and E. Main St., Brevard, 5/10/79, A, C, 79001754

Tyrrell County

Scuppernong River Bridge, US 64 Bus. across the Scuppernong R., Columbia, 3/05/92, A, C, 92000078

Tyrrell County Courthouse [North Carolina County Courthouses TR], Main and Broad Sts., Columbia, 5/10/79, A, C, 79001756

Union County

Lee, Malcolm K., House, Address Restricted, Monroe, 1/05/88, B, C, 87002200

Monroe City Hall, 102 W. Jefferson St., Monroe, 7/27/71, C, 71000619

Monroe Downtown Historic District, Roughly bounded by Jefferson, Church, Windsor & Stewart Sts., Monroe, 1/06/88, A, C, 87002202

Monroe Residential Historic District, Roughly bounded by Hough, Franklin, Jefferson, McCarten, Windsor, Sanford, Washington. Braden, Church & Hudson Sts., Monroe, 1/06/88, A, C, a, b, d, g, 87002204

Pleasant Grove Camp Meeting Ground, NE of Waxhaw on SR 1327, Waxhaw vicinity, 4/03/73, A, C, a, 73001370

Sikes, John C., House, 1301 E. Franklin St., Monroe, 4/15/82, B, C, 82003518

US Post Office—Monroe, 407 N. Main St., Monroe, 3/06/85, C, 85000482

Union County Courthouse, Courthouse Sq., Monroe, 6/24/71, C, 71000620

Waxhaw Historic District, Portions of Main, Broad, Church, Broom, Providence, Old Providence, Brevard and McKibben Sts., Waxhaw, 12/06/91, A, C, 91001773

Union County—Continued

Waxhaw—Weddington Roads Historic District, Jct. of NC 75, NC 34 & W. Franklin St., Monroe vicinity, 1/05/88, B, C, g, 87002201

Vance County

Ashburn Hall, W of Kittrell on SR 1101, Kittrell vicinity, 8/16/77, C, 77001009

Ashland, N of Henderson on Satterwhite Point Rd., Henderson vicinity, 3/14/73, B, C, 73001371

Belvidere, NC 1329, NE end, Williamsboro vicinity, 11/12/92, C, 92001603

Burnside Plantation House, On SR 1335, Williamsboro vicinity, 4/16/71, C, 71000621

Capehart, Thomas, House, W of Kittrell on SR 1105, Kittrell vicinity, 5/06/77, C, 77001010

Crudup, Josiah, House, S of Kittrell on US 1, Kittrell vicinity, 9/25/79, C, 79003342

Henderson Central Business Historic District, Garnett St. from Church to Young Sts., Henderson, 8/24/87, A, B, C, 87001249

Henderson Fire Station and Municipal Building, Garnett and Young Sts., Henderson, 8/10/78, C, 78001973

LaGrange, S of Townsville off SR 1308, Harris Crossroads vicinity, 4/27/82, A, C, 82003519

Mistletoe Villa, Young Ave., Henderson, 8/10/78, C, 78001974

Pleasant Hill/Hawkins House, W of Middleburg on SR 1371, Middleburg vicinity, 3/19/79, B, C, 79001758

Pool Rock Plantation, NE of Williamsboro on SR 1380, Williamsboro vicinity, 11/29/78, C, 78001977

St. James Episcopal Church and Rectory, Jct. of SR 1551 and SR 1555, Kittrell, 12/14/78, C, a, 78001976

St. John's Episcopal Church, SR 1329, Williamsboro, 4/16/71, C, 71000622

Stone, Daniel, Plank House, Address Restricted, Henderson vicinity, 7/12/84, C, b, 84002531

Vance County Courthouse [North Carolina County Courthouses TR], Young St., Henderson, 5/10/79, A, C, 79001757

Zollicoffer's Law Office, 215 N. Garnett St., Henderson, 6/13/78, B, C, 78001975

Wake County

Agriculture Building, E. Edenton St., Raleigh, 6/16/76, C, 76001341

Andrews-Duncan House, 407 N. Blount St., Raleigh, 1/20/72, B, C, 72000998

Apex City Hall, N. Salem St., Apex, 12/05/85, A, C, 85003077

Apex Union Depot, SE corner N. Salem St. and Center St., Apex, 12/01/88, A, C, 88002697

Beaver Dam, SR 2049 at SR 2233, Knightdale, 1/06/87, C, 86003529

Boylan Heights [Early Twentieth Century Raleigh Neighborhoods TR], Roughly bounded by Norfolk & Southern RR, Mountford, Martin and Florence Sts. and Dorothea Dr., Raleigh, 7/29/85, A, B, C, 85001671

Briggs Hardware Building, 220 Fayetteville St., Raleigh, 10/25/73, B, C, 73001372

Bunn, Bennett, Plantation, NC 97, Zebulon vicinity, 2/04/86, A, C, 86000157

Cameron Park [Early Twentieth Century Raleigh Neighborhoods TR], Roughly bounded by Clark Ave., W. Peace and Saint Mary's Sts., College Pl., Hillsborough St. and Oberlin Rd., Raleigh, 7/29/85, A, B, C, 85001673

Capehart House, N. Blount St., Raleigh, 1/17/75, C, b, 75001293

Capital Club Building, 16 W. Martin St., Raleigh, 12/05/85, A, B, C, 85003076

Capitol Area Historic District, State Capitol building and environs, Raleigh, 4/15/78, A, C, a, 78001978

Christ Church, 120 E. Edenton St., Raleigh, 7/28/70, C, a, NHL, 70000469

Christ Episcopal Church, 120 E. Edenton St., Raleigh, 12/23/87, C, a, NHL, 87002597

Daniels, Josephus, House, 1520 Caswell St., Raleigh, 12/08/76, B, NHL, 76001342

Dix Hill, Roughly bounded by Dorothea Dr., Lake Wheeler Rd. and the Norfolk Southern RR tracks, Raleigh, 11/07/90, A, C, 90001638

Dodd-Hinsdale House, 330 Hillsborough St., Raleigh, 11/12/71, C, 71000623

Downtown Garner Historic District, Roughly Garner Rd. and Main St. from New Rand Rd. to Broughton St., Garner, 12/21/89, A, d, 89002157

DuBois, W. E. B., School [Wake County MPS], 536 Franklin St., Wake Forest, 10/05/93, A, 93000998

East Raleigh—South Park Historic District, Roughly bounded by Bragg, East, E. Lenoir, Alston, Camden, Hargett, Swain, Davis, and S. Blount Sts., Raleigh, 10/11/90, A, C, 90001527

Edenwood [Wake County MPS], 7620 Old Stage Rd., Garner vicinity, 7/02/93, C, 93000544

Elmwood, 16 N. Boylan Ave., Raleigh, 10/29/75, B, C, 75001294

Estey Hall, E. South St. on Shaw University campus, Raleigh, 5/25/73, A, C, 73001373

Fadum House, 3056 Granville Dr., Raleigh, 6/10/93, C, g, 93000440

Falls of the Neuse Manufacturing Company, Neuse River at SR 2000, Falls, 9/19/83, A, C, 83001921

Federal Building, 300 Fayetteville St., Raleigh, 5/06/71, C, 71000624

Forestville Baptist Church, U.S. 1-A, Forestville, 10/25/84, C, a, 84000118

Fuquay Mineral Spring, NE corner of Main and W. Spring Sts., Fuquay-Varina, 12/04/86, A, 86003457

Glenwood [Early Twentieth Century Raleigh Neighborhoods TR], Roughly bounded by Wade Ave., Norfolk and Southern Railway, Belmont St. and Glenwood Ave., Raleigh, 7/29/85, A, B, C, 85001672

Green—Hartsfield House, SR 2303 at jct. with SR 2304, Rolesville vicinity, 12/21/89, C, 89002158

Grosvenor Gardens Apartments, 1101 Hillsborough St., Raleigh, 11/12/92, A, C, 92001602

Hawkins-Hartness House, 310 N. Blount St., Raleigh, 2/01/72, C, 72000999

Haywood Hall, 211 New Bern Ave., Raleigh, 7/28/70, B, C, 70000470

Haywood, Richard B., House, 127 E. Edenton St., Raleigh, 7/28/70, B, C, 70000471

Heck-Andrews House, 309 N. Blount St., Raleigh, 1/20/72, C, 72001000

Heck-Lee, Heck-Wynne, and Heck-Pool Houses, 503 and 511 E. Jones St. and 218 N. East St., Raleigh, 4/13/73, C, 73001374

Henderson, Isabelle Bowen, House and Gardens, 2134 Oberlin Rd., Raleigh, 8/07/89, C, 89001049

J. S. Dorton Arena, North Carolina State Fairgrounds, W. Hillsborough St., Raleigh, 4/11/73, C, g, 73001375

Johnson, J. Beale, House, 6321 Johnson Pond Rd., Fuquay-Varina vicinity, 9/05/91, C, 91001375

Jones, Alpheus, House, NE of Raleigh on U.S. 401, Raleigh vicinity, 7/07/75, A, 75001295

Jones, Crabtree, House, N of Raleigh off Old Wake Forest Rd., Raleigh vicinity, 6/04/73, C, 73001376

Jones, Nancy, House, NC 54, Cary vicinity, 3/01/84, A, C, 84002540

Jones—Johnson—Ballentine Historic District, SR 1301–522 Sunset Rd., Fuquay-Varina vicinity, 1/26/90, A, C, 89002352

Knight, Henry H. and Bettie S., Farm, US 64, Knightdale vicinity, 1/12/88, A, B, 87002234

Lane, Joel, House, 728 W. Hargett St., Raleigh, 7/28/70, B, b, 70000472

Lane-Bennett House, 7408 Ebenezer Church Rd., Raleigh vicinity, 6/30/83, B, C, b, 77001011

Lea Laboratory, Southeastern Baptist Theological Seminary campus, Wake Forest, 5/29/75, A, C, 75001298

Lewis-Smith House, N. Blount St., Raleigh, 12/11/72, B, C, b, 72001001

Lumsden-Boone Building, 226 Fayetteville St. Mall, Raleigh, 9/08/83, A, C, 83001923

Mangum, James, House, SW of Durham off NC 751, Creedmore vicinity, 11/18/74, B, C, 74001379

Marshall—Harris—Richardson House, 116 N. Person St., Raleigh, 3/05/86, C, b, 86000403

Masonic Temple Building, 133 Fayetteville St. Mall, Raleigh, 9/17/79, C, 79003341

Masonic Temple Building, 427 S. Blount St., Raleigh, 5/03/84, A, B, 84002533

Merrimon House, 526 N. Wilmington St., Raleigh, 9/05/75, B, C, 75001296

Midway Plantation, E of Raleigh on U.S. 64, Raleigh vicinity, 9/15/70, B, 70000473

Montford Hall, 308 Boylan Ave., Raleigh, 3/08/78, C, 78001979

Moore Square Historic District, Roughly bounded by Person, Morgan, Wilmington, and Davie Sts., Raleigh, 8/03/83, A, C, a, 83001924

Mordecai House, Mimosa St., Raleigh, 7/01/70, C, a, b, c, 70000474

Norburn Terrace, 216 Lafayette St., Raleigh, 2/01/80, B, C, 80002902

Wake County—Continued

North Carolina Executive Mansion, 210 N. Blount St., Raleigh, 2/26/70, B, C, 70000475

North Carolina School for the Blind and Deaf Dormitory, 216 W. Jones St., Raleigh, 8/11/76, A, C, 76001343

North Carolina State Capitol, Capitol Sq., Raleigh, 2/26/70, A, C, NHL, 70000476

North Carolina State Fair Commercial & Education Buildings, NW corner Jct. of Blue Ridge Rd. and Hillsborough St., Raleigh, 6/05/87, A, C, 87000855

Oak View, Jct. of Poole Rd. and Raleigh Beltline, Raleigh, 4/03/91, A, B, C, 91000359

Oakwood Historic District, Roughly bounded by N. Boundary, Person, Jones, and Linden Sts., and Oakwood Cemetery, Raleigh, 6/25/74, A, C, 74001380

Oakwood Historic District (Boundary Increase), E side of Linden Ave. & N side of 700 blk. E. Lane St., Raleigh, 10/21/87, A, C, 87001787

Oakwood Historic District (Boundary Increase II), Portions of N. & S. Bloodworth Sts., N. & S. East Sts., N. Person St., E. Morgan St., New Bern Ave. & E. Edenton St., Raleigh, 1/06/88, A, C, 87002235

Oakwood Historic District (Boundary Increase III), Roughly bounded by E. Franklin St., Wautauga St., Boundary St., and N. Bloodworth St., Raleigh, 1/09/89, A, C, 88003044

Oaky Grove [Wake County MPS], Jct. of NC 2506 and NC 2507, SE corner, Shotwell vicinity, 9/30/93, A, C, 93001021

Page-Walker Hotel, 119 Ambassador St., Cary, 5/29/79, B, C, 79003339

Peace College Main Building, Peace St. and N end of Wilmington St., Raleigh, 6/19/73, C, 73001377

Pilot Mill, 1121 Haynes St., Raleigh, 6/05/89, A, C, 89000441

Polk, Leonidas L., House, 612 N. Blount St., Raleigh, 4/13/77, B, 77001012

Powell House, SW of Wake Forest off U.S. 1, Wake Forest vicinity, 10/15/74, C, 74001381

Professional Building, 123-127 W. Hargett and McDowell Sts., Raleigh, 9/08/83, A, B, C, 83001925

Pullen Park Carousel, Pullen Park, Western Blvd., Raleigh, 9/08/76, C, b, 76001344

Purefoy—Dunn Plantation, E side US 1, .3 mi. N of US 1A, Wake Forest vicinity, 3/24/88, B, C, 88000238

Raleigh Banking and Trust Company Building, 5 W. Hargett St., Raleigh, 6/17/93, A, C, 93000543

Raleigh Water Tower, 115 W. Morgan St., Raleigh, 12/16/71, C, 71000625

Raleigh, Sir Walter, Hotel, 400–412 Fayetteville St., Raleigh, 8/11/78, A, C, 78001980

Rogers—Whitaker—Haywood House, SR 2044 & US 401, Wake Crossroads vicinity, 9/19/85, A, B, C, 85002418

Rogers-Bagley-Daniels-Pegues House, 125 E. South St., Raleigh, 3/21/79, B, C, 79001759

Royall Cotton Mill Commissary, Jct. of Brick and Brewer Sts., Wake Forest, 10/16/91, A, C, 91001504

Seaboard Coast Line Railroad Company Office Building, Wilmington St., Raleigh, 5/06/71, C, b, 71000626

Spring Hill, 705 Barbour Dr., Raleigh, 12/29/83, A, B, 83004003

St. Augustine's College Campus, Oakwood Ave., Raleigh, 3/28/80, A, 80002903

St. Mary's Chapel, 900 Hillsborough St., Raleigh, 11/20/70, C, a, 70000477

St. Mary's College, St. Marys and Hillsborough Sts., Raleigh, 12/19/78, A, C, a, 78001981

St. Paul A.M.E. Church, 402 W. Edenton St., Raleigh, 11/05/87, A, B, C, a, 80004607

State Bank of North Carolina, 11 New Bern Ave., Raleigh, 7/01/70, A, a, b, 70000478

Tucker Carriage House, 100 block of St. Mary, Raleigh, 2/13/75, B, C, 75001297

Varina Commercial Historic District, Broad and Fayetteville Sts. between Stewart St. and Ransdell Rd., Fuquay-Varina, 1/31/90, A, 89002351

Wakefields, SE of Creedmoor off U.S. 15A, Wake Forest vicinity, 10/16/74, B, C, 74001378

Wakelon School, Arendell St., Zebulon, 5/13/76, C, 76001345

Walnut Hill Cotton Gin, NC 2509, Knightdale vicinity, 8/14/86, A, B, C, D, 86001631

White-Holman House, New Bern Ave., Raleigh, 4/16/71, B, C, 71000627

Wyatt, Leonidas R., House, 107 S Bloodworth St., Raleigh, 7/05/90, C, b, 90001030

Yates Mill, Lake Wheeler Rd., Raleigh, 2/26/70, A, C, 70000479

Warren County

Browne, Mary Ann, House, NC 1530, Vaughan vicinity, 7/24/86, C, 86001912

Buck Spring Plantation, N of Vaughan on SR 1348, Vaughan vicinity, 10/15/70, B, D, 70000480

Buxton Place, NC 58 W side, 0.2 mi. N of jct. with NC 1628, Inez vicinity, 4/22/93, A, C, 93000323

Chapel of the Good Shepherd, E of Ridgeway, Ridgeway vicinity, 9/16/77, A, C, a, 77001013

Cherry Hill, SE of Warrenton on NC 58, Inez vicinity, 11/05/74, C, 74001384

Coleman-White House, Halifax and Hall Sts., Warrenton, 10/25/73, C, 73001380

Dalkeith, SW of Arcola off NC 43, Arcola vicinity, 12/16/74, B, C, 74001382

Duke, Green, House, SE of Manson off SR 1100, Manson vicinity, 8/07/74, C, 74001383

Elgin, SE of Warrenton on SR 1509, Warrenton vicinity, 2/06/73, C, 73001381

Hawkins, William J., House, W of Norlina on SR 1103, Ridgeway vicinity, 5/22/78, B, C, 78001982

Hebron Methodist Church, SR 1306, Oakville vicinity, 4/19/84, A, C, a, 84002547

Lake O'Woods, S of Inez of SR 1512, Inez vicinity, 1/19/79, A, C, b, 79001760

Little Manor, Address Restricted, Littleton vicinity, 4/24/73, C, 73001378

Person's Ordinary, SR 1001, Littleton, 4/24/73, B, C, 73001379

Reedy Rill, S of Warrenton off SR 1600, Warrenton vicinity, 12/03/74, C, 74001385

Shady Oaks, SE of Warrenton on SR 1600, Warrenton vicinity, 3/15/76, C, 76001346

Sledge-Hayley House, Frankin and Hayley Sts., Warrenton, 4/17/80, B, C, 80002904

Thornton, Mansfield, House, SE of Warrenton, Warrenton vicinity, 12/02/77, B, 77001014

Tusculum, SE of Warrenton off SR 1635, Arcola vicinity, 10/23/74, C, 74001386

Warrenton Historic District, U.S. 401, Warrenton, 8/11/76, A, C, a, 76001347

Watson, John, House, Petway Burwell Rd., 1/4 mi. W of NC 401, Warrenton vicinity, 12/28/90, C, 90001954

Washington County

Belgrade and St. David's Church, E of Creswell St., Creswell vicinity, 1/26/78, B, C, 78001983

Latham House, 311 E. Main St., Plymouth, 12/12/76, A, B, C, 76001348

Perry-Spruill House, 326 Washington St., Plymouth, 4/25/85, C, 85000905

Plymouth Historic District [Plymouth MPS], Roughly bounded by Monroe St., the Roanoke R., Latham La., Third St., Washington St. and the Norfolk Southern RR tracks, Plymouth, 1/16/91, A, C, 90002140

Rehoboth Methodist Church, E of Skinnersville on U.S. 64, Skinnersville vicinity, 5/13/76, A, C, 76001349

Somerset Place State Historic Site, In Pettigrew State Park, Creswell vicinity, 2/26/70, A, C, 70000481

Washington County Courthouse [North Carolina County Courthouses TR], Main and Adams Sts., Plymouth, 5/10/79, A, C, 79001761

Watauga County

Daniel Boone Hotel, E. King St., Boone, 12/27/82, C, 82001307

East Tennessee & Western North Carolina Railroad Locomotive No. 12, Tweetsie RR theme park, jct. of Tweetsie RR Rd. and US 321, Blowing Rock vicinity, 3/12/92, A, 92000147

Farthing, Ben, Farm, NC 1121 (Rominger Rd.) W side, just N of Watauga R., Sugar Grove vicinity, 1/04/93, A, 92001736

Gragg House, On U.S. 221, Blowing Rock vicinity, 10/25/73, C, 73001382

Green Park Inn, U.S. 321, Blowing Rock, 6/03/82, A, C, 82004637

Jones House, 124 E. King St., Boone, 3/25/87, C, 87000483

Mast Farm, E of Valle Crucis off SR 1112, Valle Crucis vicinity, 1/20/72, A, C, 72001002

Watauga County—Continued

Mast General Store, S of Valle Crucis on SR 1112, Valle Crucis vicinity, 4/03/73, A, 73001383

Randall Memorial Building, Former, Greenway Ct., Blowing Rock, 3/14/91, A, C, 91000263

Valle Crucis Episcopal Mission, NC 194 N side, 1 mi. SW of jct. with NC 1112, Valle Crucis vicinity, 9/09/93, A, a, 93000938

Westglow, W of Blowing Rock on U.S. 221, Blowing Rock vicinity, 8/13/79, B, C, 79001762

Wayne County

Aycock, Charles B., Birthplace, 6 mi. from jct. of SR 1542 and U.S. 117, Fremont, 2/26/70, B, C, b, c, 70000482

Eureka United Methodist Church, Church St., Eureka, 8/26/82, A, C, a, 82003520

First Presbyterian Church, 111 W. Ash St., Goldsboro, 5/29/79, A, C, a, 79003340

Giddens, L. D., and Son Jewelry Store, 135 S. Center St., Goldsboro, 3/19/79, A, C, 79001763

Goldsboro Union Station, 101 North Carolina St., Goldsboro, 4/13/77, A, C, 77001015

Lee, Harry Fitzhugh, House, 310 W. Walnut St., Goldsboro, 3/01/84, C, 84002542

Odd Fellows Lodge, 111–115 N. John St., Goldsboro, 8/03/78, A, C, 78001984

Perry—Cherry House, 308 W. Main St., Mount Olive, 3/13/86, C, 86000392

Southerland—Burnette House, 201 N. Chesnut St., Mount Olive, 2/08/88, C, 88000057

Vernon, Address Restricted, Mt. Olive vicinity, 10/09/74, C, 74001387

Weil, Solomon and Henry, Houses, 204 and 200 W. Chestnut St., Goldsboro, 12/22/76, B, C, b, 76001350

Wilkes County

Brown-Cowles House and Cowles Law Office [Wilkesboro MRA], 200 and 106 E. Main St., Wilkesboro, 8/24/82, B, C, 82003522

Claymont Hill, W side of SR 2303 along Ronda-Clingman Rd., Ronda vicinity, 9/12/85, A, C, 85002369

Cleveland, Robert, Log House, E of Purlear near jct. of SR 1300 and 1317, Purlear vicinity, 2/01/72, C, 72001003

Elkin Creek Mill, SR 2045, West Elkin vicinity, 4/29/82, A, B, C, 82003521

Federal Building [Wilkesboro MRA], 201 W. Main St., Wilkesboro, 9/24/82, C, 82003523

Ferguson, J. T., Store [Wilkesboro MRA], 11 E. Main St., Wilkesboro, 8/24/82, C, 82003524

Finley, Thomas B., Law Office [Wilkesboro MRA], Broad and North Sts., Wilkesboro, 8/24/82, A, B, C, 82003525

Hemphill, J. L., House [Wilkesboro MRA], 203 N. Brook St., Wilkesboro, 8/24/82, C, 82003526

Holbrook Farm, W of Traphill on SR 1743, Traphill vicinity, 11/29/78, C, 78001985

Johnson-Hubbard House [Wilkesboro MRA], 113 E. Main St., Wilkesboro, 8/24/82, C, 82003527

Old Wilkes County Jail, N. Bridge St., Wilkesboro, 2/18/71, A, C, 71000628

St. Paul's Episcopal Church and Cemetery [Wilkesboro MRA], Cowles St. between Woodland Blvd. and West St., Wilkesboro, 10/19/82, A, C, a, d, 82001308

Traphill Historic District, SR 1002 and SR 1749, Traphill, 5/22/80, A, C, a, 80002905

Wilkes County Courthouse [North Carolina County Courthouses TR], E. Main St. between Bridge and Broad Sts., Wilkesboro, 5/10/79, A, C, 79001764

Wilkesboro Presbyterian Church [Wilkesboro MRA], 205 E. Main St., Wilkesboro, 8/24/82, A, C, 82003528

Wilkesboro-Smithey Hotel [Wilkesboro MRA], Broad and E. Main Sts., Wilkesboro, 8/24/82, A, B, C, 82003529

Wilson County

Applewhite, W. H., House [Wilson MRA], Off NC 58, Stantonsburg vicinity, 2/13/86, A, C, 86000696

Aycock, Manalcus, House [Wilson MRA], Center St., Black Creek, 2/13/86, C, 86000765

Barnes, Gen. Joshua, House [Wilson MRA], W side of SR 1326 at SR 1327, Wilson vicinity, 2/13/86, B, C, 86000764

Black Creek Rural Historic District [Wilson MRA], Along NC 1628, Black Creek, 10/14/86, A, B, C, 86001659

Branch Banking, 124 W. Nash St., Wilson, 8/11/78, A, C, 78001986

Broad—Kenan Streets Historic District, Roughly bounded by Pine, Broad, Hines and Cone, Wilson, 10/27/88, A, C, 88002084

Bullock—Dew House [Wilson MRA], NC 581, Sims vicinity, 2/13/86, C, 86000759

Cherry Hotel, 333 E. Nash St., Wilson, 8/26/82, A, C, 82003531

Davis-Whitehead-Harriss House, 600 W. Nash St., Wilson, 6/14/82, C, 82003532

East Wilson Historic District, Roughly bounded by E. Gold and Academy Sts., Ward Blvd., Woodard Street Ave. and Elvie St., and Railroad and Pender Sts., Wilson, 4/11/88, A, B, C, a, g, 88000371

Edmondson—Woodward House [Wilson MRA], NC 58 and SR 1542, Stantonsburg vicinity, 2/13/86, B, C, 86000767

Elm City Municipal Historic District [Wilson MRA], Roughly bounded by North, Pender and Branch, Wilson, and Anderson Sts., Elm City, 2/13/86, A, B, C, a, 86000770

Langley, W. H., House [Wilson MRA], N side of SR 1003, Elm City vicinity, 2/13/86, A, C, 86000763

Lucama Municipal Historic District [Wilson MRA], Roughly bounded by US 301 and Rail-

road St., Main St., Black Creek Rd., and Goldsboro St., Lucama, 2/13/86, A, C, a, 86000772

Lucas, Dr. H. D., House [Wilson MRA], Center St., Black Creek, 2/13/86, C, 86000771

Old Wilson Historic District, Roughly bounded by Nash, N. Cone, Gold and Railroad Sts. and Maplewood Cemetery, Wilson, 12/20/84, A, C, 84000736

Pender, Joseph John, House [Wilson MRA], SR 1418 and SR 1002, Wilson vicinity, 2/13/86, B, C, 86000766

Rountree, Moses, House, 107 N. Rountree St., Wilson, 4/26/82, B, C, b, 82003533

Scarborough, Maj. James, House, NC 222, Saratoga vicinity, 6/14/82, B, C, 82003530

Upper Town Creek Rural Historic District [Wilson MRA], Roughly bounded by NC 1003, NC 1411, NC 1414, and Town Creek, Wilson vicinity, 8/29/86, A, B, C, 86001656

Ward—Applewhite—Thompson House [Wilson MRA], S side of SR 1539, Stantonsburg, 2/13/86, A, C, 86000695

Webb—Barron—Wells House [Wilson MRA], E side SR 1512, Elm City vicinity, 2/13/86, A, C, 86000769

West Nash Street Historic District, West Nash St., Wilson, 12/20/84, A, C, 84001033

Williams, Olzie Whitehead, House, SR 1332, Wilson vicinity, 12/19/83, C, b, 83004004

Wilson Central Business-Tobacco Warehouse Historic District, Roughly bounded by Pender, Green, Pine, S. Jackson, and Hines Sts., Wilson, 12/20/84, A, B, C, 84003876

Wilson County Courthouse [North Carolina County Courthouses TR], Nash at Goldsboro St., Wilson, 5/10/79, A, C, 79001765

Woodard Family Rural Historic District [Wilson MRA], Along US 264, Wilson vicinity, 8/29/86, A, B, C, 86001657

Yadkin County

Donnaha Site, Address Restricted, East Bend vicinity, 12/06/78, D, 78001987

Glenwood, E of Enon on SR 1549, Enon vicinity, 8/13/79, A, B, C, 79001766

Richmond Hill Law School, N of Richmond Hill on SR 1530, Richmond Hill vicinity, 10/15/70, A, B, 70000483

Second Yadkin County Jail, 241 E. Hemlock St., Yadkinville, 7/21/88, A, C, 88001113

White House, Shallowford Rd., Huntsville, 6/01/82, C, 82003534

Yancey County

Citizens Bank Building, Town Sq., Burnsville, 3/29/90, A, C, 90000545

McElroy, John Wesley, House, 11 Academy St., Burnsville, 11/29/90, C, 90001802

Nu-Wray Inn, Off US 19E, Burnsville, 4/15/82, A, C, 82003535

Yancey County Courthouse [North Carolina County Courthouses TR], W. Main at Town Square, Burnsville, 5/10/79, A, C, 79001767

NORTH DAKOTA

Adams County

Adams County Courthouse [North Dakota County Courthouses TR], 600 Adams Ave., Hettinger, 11/14/85, A, C, 85002977

US Post Office—Hettinger [US Post Offices in North Dakota, 1900–1940 MPS], Lake St. and Adams Ave., Hettinger, 11/01/89, A, C, 89001751

Barnes County

All Saints' Episcopal Church [Episcopal Churches of North Dakota MPS], 516 N. Central Ave., Valley City, 12/03/92, A, C, a, 92001605

Barnes County Courthouse [North Dakota County Courthouses TR], 491 Second Ave. NW, Valley City, 11/14/85, A, C, 85002978

Rudolf Hotel, Central Ave. and 2nd St., Valley City, 2/10/83, A, C, 83001926

US Post Office—Valley City [US Post Offices in North Dakota, 1900–1940 MPS], 149 NE. Third St., Valley City, 11/01/89, A, C, 89001758

Valley City Carnegie Library, 413 Central Ave., Valley City, 10/18/79, A, C, 79003724

Benson County

Benson County Courthouse [North Dakota County Courthouses TR (AD)], B Ave., Minnewaukan, 11/02/78, A, C, 78001988

Fort Totten, S of Fort Totten off ND 57, Fort Totten vicinity, 12/09/71, A, 71000629

Pierson Farm, 3.5 mi. S of York off US 2, York vicinity, 8/29/85, C, 85001939

St. Boniface Cemetery, Wrought-Iron Cross Site [German-Russian Wrought-Iron Cross Sites in Central North Dakota MPS], Address Restricted, Selz vicinity, 10/23/89, A, C, a, d, 89001686

Viking Lutheran Church, SE of Maddock, Maddock vicinity, 11/14/79, A, C, a, 79001768

Billings County

Billings County Courthouse [North Dakota County Courthouses TR (AD)], 4th St. and 4th Ave., Medora, 12/16/77, A, C, 77001016

Chateau de Mores, SW of Medora on W bank of Little Missouri River, Medora vicinity, 4/16/75, B, 75001299

De Mores Packing Plant Ruins, NW of Medora boundary, Medora vicinity, 2/18/75, B, 75001300

Initial Rock, SE of Medora in Custer National Forest, Medora vicinity, 11/07/76, A, 76002271

Myers School Timbered Lodge (32BI401), Address Restricted, Medora vicinity, 8/06/80, C, D, 80002906

St. Mary's Catholic Church, 4th St. and 3rd Ave., Medora, 12/02/77, C, a, 77001017

Von Hoffman House, Broadway and 5th St., Medora, 11/21/77, A, C, 77001018

Bottineau County

Crogen, Ole, Farm District, 4 mi. NW of Bottineau, Carbury & Bottineau vicinity, 10/16/87, A, 87001779

State Bank of Antler, Antler Sq., Antler, 6/30/88, A, B, C, 88000986

Bowman County

Fort Dilts, Address Unknown, Rhame vicinity, 11/10/80, A, 80002907

Burke County

Burke County Courthouse [North Dakota County Courthouses TR], Main St., Bowbells, 11/14/85, A, C, 85002979

Burleigh County

Bismarck Civic Auditorium, 201 N. 6th St., Bismarck, 6/07/76, A, C, 76001351

Bismarck Tribune Building, 22 N. 4th St., Bismarck, 10/22/82, A, C, 82001309

Burleigh County Courthouse [North Dakota County Courthouses TR], E. Thayer Ave., Bismarck, 11/14/85, A, C, 85002980

Camp Hancock Site, 101 Main Ave., Bismarck, 2/23/72, A, b, 72001004

Cathedral Area Historic District, Roughly bounded by Hannifan and N 1st Sts., Aves. C and A West, Bismarck, 5/08/80, C, 80002908

Double Ditch Earth Lodge Village Site (32BL8), Address Restricted, Bismarck vicinity, 1/29/79, D, 79001769

Former North Dakota Executive Mansion, 320 Ave. B, E., Bismarck, 4/16/75, A, 75001301

Menoken Indian Village Site, Address Restricted, Menoken vicinity, 10/15/66, D, NHL, 66000599

Northern Pacific Railway Depot, 410 E. Main Ave., Bismarck, 9/19/77, A, C, 77001022

Patterson Hotel, 422 E. Main Ave., Bismarck, 12/08/76, B, C, 76001352

Patterson, E. G., Building, 412-414 Main St., Bismarck, 10/22/82, A, B, C, 82001310

Soo Hotel, 112-114 5th St., N., Bismarck, 5/09/83, C, 83001927

Towne-Williams House, 722 7th St., N., Bismarck, 4/14/75, B, C, g, 75001302

U.S. Post Office and Courthouse, 304 E. Broadway, Bismarck, 6/23/76, C, 76001353

Van Horn Hotel, 114 N. 3rd St., Bismarck, 5/10/84, A, 84002759

Ward Earth Lodge Village Site (32BL3), Eastern edge of Pioneer Park, Bismarck vicinity, 11/21/78, D, 78001990

Webb Brothers Block, 317 E. Main Ave., Bismarck, 10/13/83, A, C, 83004060

Yegen House and Pioneer Grocery, 808–810 E. Main Ave., Bismarck, 10/05/77, B, C, b, 77001023

Cass County

Burlington Northern Depot, Woodard Ave., Amenia, 8/29/77, A, C, b, 77001024

Cass County Court House, Jail, and Sheriff's House [North Dakota County Courthouses TR (AD)], S. 9th St. between S. 2nd and 3rd Aves., Fargo, 12/22/83, A, C, 83004062

Casselton Commercial Historic District, Roughly bounded by Front and 1st St. between 6th and 8th Ave., Casselton, 10/28/82, A, C, 82001311

Cole Hotel, 401-407 Northern Pacific Ave., Fargo, 5/09/83, A, B, 83001928

DeLendrecie's Department Store, 620–624 Main St., Fargo, 10/22/79, A, C, 79003725

Dibley House, 331 8th Ave., S, Fargo, 11/25/80, C, 80004282

Downtown Fargo District, Roughly Roberts St., from S. 1st Ave. to 5th Ave. N., and Main Ave., Fargo, 10/13/83, A, C, 83004064

Fargo City Detention Hospital [North Side Fargo MRA], 57 Eleventh Ave. N, Fargo, 4/07/87, C, 86003741

Fargo South Residential District, Roughly bounded by 5th and 17th Aves. S., 7th and 9th Sts. S., Fargo, 9/19/83, C, 83001929

Fargo Theatre Building, 314 Broadway, Fargo, 10/21/82, A, C, 82001312

Grand Lodge of North Dakota, Ancient Order of United Workmen, 112-114 N. Roberts St., Fargo, 8/24/79, A, C, 79001770

Great Northern Freight Warehouse, 420 N. Seventh St., Fargo, 11/21/90, A, C, 90001749

Holes, James, House [North Side Fargo MRA], 1230 Fifth St. N, Fargo, 4/07/87, A, C, 86003740

Knerr Block, Floyd Block, McHench Building and Webster and Cole Building, 13, 15, 17-19, and 21-23 8th St., S., Fargo, 5/12/83, C, 83001930

Lewis House, 1002 3rd Ave., S., Fargo, 10/18/79, B, C, 79003726

Masonic Block, 11 S. 8th St., Fargo, 8/03/79, A, C, 79001771

Cass County—Continued

North Dakota State University District, Roughly bounded by N. University Dr., Twelfth Ave. N, Service Dr., and Campus Ave., Fargo, 10/06/86, A, C, 86003261

North Side Fargo Builder's Residential Historic District [North Side Fargo MRA], Roughly bounded by Benjamin Franklin School area and Golf Course, First St., Twelfth Ave. N, and Fourth St., Fargo, 4/07/87, A, C, g, 86003737

North Side Fargo High Style Residential Historic District [North Side Fargo MRA], Roughly bounded by Twelfth Ave. N, Fourth St., Eleventh Ave. N, and Seventh St., Fargo, 4/07/87, A, C, g, 86003739

Northern Pacific Railway Depot, 701 Main Ave., Fargo, 2/13/75, A, C, 75001304

Powers Hotel, 400 Broadway, Fargo, 5/12/83, C, 83001931

Research Plot 2, Near jct. of Centennial Ave. and 18th St. N., North Dakota State University campus, Fargo, 10/08/91, A, 91001474

Research Plot 30, Near jct. of Centennial Ave. and 18th St. N., North Dakota State University campus, Fargo, 10/08/91, A, B, 91001475

Smith, Chesebro, House [North Side Fargo MRA], 1337 Broadway, Fargo, 4/07/87, C, 86003744

St. Stephen's Episcopal Church [Episcopal Churches of North Dakota MPS], Jct. of 3rd Ave. and 5th St., SE corner, Casselton, 12/03/92, A, C, a, 92001609

Watts Free Library [Philanthropically Established Libraries in North Dakota MPS], 101 3rd St. N., Leonard, 5/31/90, A, C, 89002304

Cavalier County

US Post Office—Langdon [US Post Offices in North Dakota, 1900–1940 MPS], 323 Eighth Ave., Langdon, 11/01/89, A, C, 89001752

Dickey County

Dickey County Courthouse [Buechner and Orth Courthouses in North Dakota TR; North Dakota County Courthouses TR (AD)], Off U.S. 281, Ellendale, 11/25/80, A, C, 80004283

Ellendale Opera House Block, 105–111 Main St., Ellendale, 4/22/92, A, C, 92000354

Klein and Sutmar Block [Oakes MPS], 419 Main Ave., Oakes, 10/16/87, C, 87001792

Noonan, Walter T., House [Oakes MPS], 215 S. Seventh St., Oakes, 10/16/87, C, 87001791

Oakes National Bank Block [Oakes MPS], 501 Main Ave., Oakes, 10/16/87, C, 87001790

US Post Office—Oakes [US Post Offices in North Dakota, 1900–1940 MPS], 611 Main Ave., Oakes, 11/01/89, A, C, 89001753

Divide County

Divide County Courthouse [Buechner and Orth Courthouses in North Dakota TR; North Dakota County Courthouses TR (AD)], In Crosby, Crosby, 11/25/80, A, C, 80002910

Nielsen, Niels, Fourteen-Side Barn Farm [North Dakota Round Barns TR], ND 38, Noonan vicinity, 10/07/86, C, 86002743

Dunn County

Dunn County Courthouse [North Dakota County Courthouses TR], Owens St., Manning, 3/26/86, A, 86000620

Hutmacher Farm, NW of Manning, Manning vicinity, 12/17/79, A, C, g, 79001772

Saints Peter and Paul Church, N/A, New Hradec, 2/03/86, A, a, 86000161

Eddy County

Eddy County Courthouse [North Dakota County Courthouses TR], 524 Central Ave., New Rockford, 11/14/85, A, C, 85002981

Marriage, Sylvanus, Octagonal Barn [North Dakota Round Barns TR], ND 38, New Rockford vicinity, 10/07/86, C, 86002748

Myhre, Jens, Round Barn [North Dakota Round Barns TR], ND 30, New Rockford vicinity, 10/01/86, C, 86002749

US Post Office—New Rockford [US Post Offices in North Dakota, 1900–1940 MPS], 821 N. First Ave., New Rockford, 11/01/89, A, C, 89001750

Emmons County

Emmons County Courthouse [North Dakota County Courthouses TR], Fifth St., Linton, 11/14/85, A, C, 85002982

Goldade, Johannes, House, SE of Linton off ND 13, Linton vicinity, 1/27/83, A, C, 83001932

Holy Trinity Cemetery, Wrought-Iron Cross Site A [German-Russian Wrought-Iron Cross Sites in Central North Dakota MPS], Address Restricted, Strasburg vicinity, 10/23/89, A, C, a, d, 89001692

Holy Trinity Cemetery, Wrought-Iron Cross Site B [German-Russian Wrought-Iron Cross Sites in Central North Dakota MPS], Address Restricted, Strasburg vicinity, 10/23/89, A, C, a, d, 89001693

Holy Trinity Cemetery, Wrought-Iron Cross Site C [German-Russian Wrought-Iron Cross Sites in Central North Dakota MPS], Address Restricted, Strasburg vicinity, 10/23/89, A, C, a, d, 89001694

Holy Trinity Cemetery, Wrought-Iron Cross Site D [German-Russian Wrought-Iron Cross Sites in Central North Dakota MPS], Address Re-

stricted, Strasburg vicinity, 10/23/89, A, C, a, d, 89001695

Old St. Mary's Cemetery, Wrought-Iron Cross Site [German-Russian Wrought-Iron Cross Sites in Central North Dakota MPS], Address Restricted, Hague vicinity, 10/23/89, A, C, a, d, 89001679

Sacred Heart Cemetery, Wrought-Iron Cross Site [German-Russian Wrought-Iron Cross Sites in Central North Dakota MPS], Address Restricted, Linton vicinity, 10/23/89, A, C, a, d, 89001691

Saints Peter and Paul Catholic Church Complex, First Ave., Strasburg, 9/25/86, C, a, 86002786

St. Aloysius Cemetery, Wrought-Iron Cross Site A [German-Russian Wrought-Iron Cross Sites in Central North Dakota MPS], Address Restricted, Hague vicinity, 10/23/89, A, C, a, d, 89001696

St. Aloysius Cemetery, Wrought-Iron Cross Site B [German-Russian Wrought-Iron Cross Sites in Central North Dakota MPS], Address Restricted, Hague vicinity, 10/23/89, A, C, a, d, 89001697

St. Mary's Cemetery, Wrought-Iron Cross Site A [German-Russian Wrought-Iron Cross Sites in Central North Dakota MPS], Address Restricted, Hague vicinity, 10/23/89, A, C, a, d, 89001676

St. Mary's Cemetery, Wrought-Iron Cross Site B [German-Russian Wrought-Iron Cross Sites in Central North Dakota MPS], Address Restricted, Hague vicinity, 10/23/89, A, C, a, d, 89001677

St. Mary's Cemetery, Wrought-Iron Cross Site C [German-Russian Wrought-Iron Cross Sites in Central North Dakota MPS], Address Restricted, Hague vicinity, 10/23/89, A, C, a, d, 89001678

St. Mary's Church Non-Contiguous Historic District, Off ND 11, Hague, 10/13/83, A, C, a, d, 83004066

Tirsbol Cemetery, Wrought-Iron Cross Site [German-Russian Wrought-Iron Cross Sites in Central North Dakota MPS], Address Restricted, Strasburg vicinity, 10/23/89, A, C, a, d, 89001698

Welk, Ludwig and Christina, Homestead, 2.5 NW of Strasburg, Strasburg vicinity, 10/28/93, A, C, 93001102

Foster County

Foster County Courthouse [Buechner and Orth Courthouses in North Dakota TR; North Dakota County Courthouses TR (AD)], In Carrington, Carrington, 11/25/80, A, C, 80002911

Hall, Ralph, Farm District, N of Carrington on W side of Burlington Northern RR tracks, Carrington vicinity, 10/01/87, C, 87001781

Lincoln Building, Off U.S. 281, Carrington, 4/30/80, A, C, 80002912

McHenry Railroad Loop, E side of ND 20, McHenry vicinity, 10/02/86, A, 86002751

Foster County—Continued

Putnam, Thomas Nichols, House, 533 Main St., Carrington, 11/24/92, C, 92001604

US Post Office—Carrington [US Post Offices in North Dakota, 1900–1940 MPS], 87 N. Ninth Ave., Carrington, 11/01/89, A, C, 89001754

Golden Valley County

Golden Valley County Courthouse [North Dakota County Courthouses TR], First Ave. SE, Beach, 11/14/85, A, C, 85002983

Sentinel Butte Public School, Byron St., Sentinel Butte, 10/21/82, A, C, 82001313

Grand Forks County

Avalon Theater, 210 Towner Ave., Larimore, 2/04/91, A, C, 90002191

BPOE Lodge: Golden Block [Downtown Grand Forks MRA], 12 N. 4th St., Grand Forks, 10/26/82, C, 82001314

Blome, R. S., Granitoid Pavement in Grand Forks, Roughly, Lewis Blvd. S of Conklin Ave. and area around jcts. of Walnut St. and 3rd Ave. and Minnesota Ave. and 5th St., Grand Forks, 11/05/91, A, C, 91001583

Building at 201 S. 3rd St. [Downtown Grand Forks MRA], 201 S. 3rd St., Grand Forks, 10/26/82, C, 82001315

Building at 205 DeMers Ave. [Downtown Grand Forks MRA], 205 DeMers Ave., Grand Forks, 10/26/82, C, 82001316

Building at 312 Kittson Ave. [Downtown Grand Forks MRA], 312 Kittson Ave., Grand Forks, 10/26/82, C, 82001317

Building at 317 S. 3rd St. [Downtown Grand Forks MRA], 317 S. 3rd St., Grand Forks, 10/26/82, A, 82001318

Campbell, Thomas D., House, 2405 Belmont Rd., Grand Forks, 9/29/87, C, e, 87002010

Clifford Annex [Downtown Grand Forks MRA], 407-411 DeMers Ave., Grand Forks, 10/26/82, C, 82001319

Clifford, George B., House, 406 Reeves Dr., Grand Forks, 9/30/86, B, C, 86002655

Dakota Block [Downtown Grand Forks MRA], 21 S. 4th St., Grand Forks, 10/26/82, C, 82001320

DeRemer, Joseph Bell, House, 625 Belmont Rd., Grand Forks, 6/09/83, C, 83001933

Dinnie Block [Downtown Grand Forks MRA], 109 N. 3rd Ave., Grand Forks, 10/26/82, C, 82001321

Edgar Building [Downtown Grand Forks MRA], 314 Kittson Ave., Grand Forks, 4/15/83, C, 83001934

Electric Construction Co. Building [Downtown Grand Forks MRA], 16 S. 4th St., Grand Forks, 10/26/82, C, 82001322

Finks and Gokey Block [Downtown Grand Forks MRA], 414-420 DeMers Ave., Grand Forks, 4/20/83, A, C, 83001935

First National Bank [Downtown Grand Forks MRA], 322 DeMers Ave., Grand Forks, 10/26/82, C, 82001323

Flatiron Building [Downtown Grand Forks MRA], 323 Kittson Ave., Grand Forks, 10/26/82, A, 82001324

Funseth, Carlott, Round Barn [North Dakota Round Barns TR], ND 38, Kempton vicinity, 10/07/86, C, 86002752

Grand Forks City Hall [Downtown Grand Forks MRA], 404 N. 2nd Ave., Grand Forks, 10/26/82, C, 82001325

Grand Forks County Courthouse [Buechner and Orth Courthouses in North Dakota TR; North Dakota County Courthouses TR (AD)], S. 5th St, Grand Forks, 11/25/80, A, C, 80002913

Grand Forks Herald [Downtown Grand Forks MRA], 120-124 N. 4th St., Grand Forks, 11/30/82, C, 82001326

Grand Forks Mercantile Co. [Downtown Grand Forks MRA], 124 N. 3rd St., Grand Forks, 10/26/82, A, 82001327

Grand Forks Woolen Mills [Downtown Grand Forks MRA], 301 N. 3rd St., Grand Forks, 10/26/83, A, C, 83001936

Great Northern Freight Warehouse and Depot, 899 Second Ave. N., Grand Forks, 1/29/90, A, C, 89002031

Hook and Ladder No. 1 and Hose Co. No. 2 [Downtown Grand Forks MRA], 215 S. 4th St., Grand Forks, 10/26/82, A, 82001328

Iddings Block [Downtown Grand Forks MRA], 9 N. 3rd St., Grand Forks, 10/26/82, A, C, 82001329

Larimore City Hall, Block 64, bounded by Towner, 3rd, Terry and Main, Larimore, 5/31/90, A, C, 90000600

Linwell, Martin V., House, 316 S. Raymond St., Northwood, 2/28/80, C, 80002914

Lyons Garage [Downtown Grand Forks MRA], 214-218 N. 4th St., Grand Forks, 10/26/82, A, C, 82001330

Masonic Temple [Downtown Grand Forks MRA], 413-421 Bruce Ave., Grand Forks, 10/26/82, C, 82001331

New Hampshire Apartments [Downtown Grand Forks MRA], 105 N. 3rd St., Grand Forks, 10/26/82, C, 82001332

North Dakota Mill and Elevator, 1823 Mill Rd., Grand Forks, 5/11/92, A, 92000433

Northern Pacific Depot and Freight House [Downtown Grand Forks MRA], 202 N. 3rd St., Grand Forks, 10/26/82, A, C, 82001333

Odd Fellows Block [Downtown Grand Forks MRA], 23-25 S. 4th St., Grand Forks, 10/26/82, A, C, 82001334

Oxford House, University of North Dakota campus, Grand Forks, 5/02/73, A, C, 73001384

Red River Valley Brick Co. [Downtown Grand Forks MRA], 215 S. 3rd St., Grand Forks, 10/26/82, A, C, 82001335

Roller Office Supply [Downtown Grand Forks MRA], 7 N. 3rd St., Grand Forks, 10/26/82, C, 82001336

Speed Printing [Downtown Grand Forks MRA], 220 S. 3rd St., Grand Forks, 10/26/82, C, 82001337

St. John's Block Commercial Exchange [Downtown Grand Forks MRA], 2 N. 3rd St., Grand Forks, 10/26/82, C, 82001338

St. Michael's Church, 520 N. Sixth St., Grand Forks, 6/30/88, C, a, 88000983

Stratford Building [Downtown Grand Forks MRA], 311 DeMers Ave., Grand Forks, 10/26/82, C, 82001339

Telephone Co. Building [Downtown Grand Forks MRA], 24 N. 4th St., Grand Forks, 10/26/82, C, 82001340

U.S. Post Office and Courthouse, 102 N. 4th St., Grand Forks, 6/03/76, C, 76001354

United Lutheran Church, 324 Chestnut St., Grand Forks, 12/30/91, C, a, 91001906

Viets Hotel [Downtown Grand Forks MRA], 309-311 3rd St., S., Grand Forks, 10/26/82, A, C, 82001341

Washington School, 422 N. Sixth St., Grand Forks, 2/24/92, C, 92000035

Wheeler, Dr. Henry, House, 420 Franklin St., Grand Forks, 1/16/86, B, C, 86000166

Wright Block [Downtown Grand Forks MRA], 408-412 DeMers Ave., Grand Forks, 10/26/82, C, 82001342

Grant County

Carson Roller Mill, S side of Carson, Carson, 4/30/80, A, 80002915

Hope Lutheran Church, W of ND 49 S of Lake Tschida, Elgin vicinity, 1/16/92, A, C, a, 91001924

Medicine Rock State Historic Site, Address Restricted, Heil vicinity, 9/25/86, A, a, 86002757

Griggs County

Griggs County Courthouse [North Dakota County Courthouses TR (AD)], Rollin Ave., Cooperstown, 7/21/77, A, C, 77001025

Northern Lights Masonic Lodge, Ninth St., Cooperstown, 10/16/87, C, 87001775

Hettinger County

Hettinger County Courthouse [North Dakota County Courthouses TR], 336 Pacific St., Mott, 11/14/85, A, C, 85002984

Hill, Dr. S. W., Drug Store, Off ND 21, Regent, 11/10/80, B, C, 80002916

Riverside, 418 Main St., New England, 5/12/83, A, 83001937

Kidder County

Kidder County Courthouse [North Dakota County Courthouses TR], Broadway Ave., Steele, 11/14/85, A, 85002985

La Moure County

La Moure County Courthouse [Buechner and Orth Courthouses in North Dakota TR; North Dakota County Courthouses TR (AD)], In La Moure, La Moure, 11/25/80, A, C, 80004284

Rodman Octagonal Barn [North Dakota Round Barns TR], ND 30, Edgeley vicinity, 10/07/86, C, 86002753

Logan County

Abell, Robert, Round Barn [North Dakota Round Barns TR], ND 38, Burnstad vicinity, 10/07/86, C, g, 86002754

Logan County Courthouse [North Dakota County Courthouses TR], 301 Broadway, Napoleon, 11/14/85, A, C, 85002986

McHenry County

Granville State Bank, Main and 2nd Sts., Granville, 9/13/77, A, C, 77001509

Hotel Berry, 100 W. Central Ave., Velva, 10/20/82, A, C, 82001343

Liberty Baptist Church [Ukrainian Immigrant Dwellings and Churches in North Dakota from Early Settlement Until the Depression MPS], Fifth & Christina Sts., Kief, 10/16/87, A, a, b, 87001789

McHenry County Courthouse [Buechner and Orth Courthouses in North Dakota TR; North Dakota County Courthouses TR (AD)], In Towner, Towner, 11/25/80, A, C, 80002917

Old Saint John Nepomocene Cemetery, Wrought-Iron Cross Site [German-Russian Wrought-Iron Cross Sites in Central North Dakota MPS], Address Restricted, Orrin vicinity, 10/23/89, A, C, a, d, 89001683

Old Saints Peter and Paul Cemetery, Wrought-Iron Cross Site [German-Russian Wrought-Iron Cross Sites in Central North Dakota MPS], Address Restricted, Karlsruhe vicinity, 10/23/89, A, C, a, d, 89001682

McIntosh County

McIntosh County Courthouse [Buechner and Orth Courthouses in North Dakota TR; North Dakota County Courthouses TR (AD)], In Ashley, Ashley, 11/25/80, A, C, 80002918

St. Andrews Evangelical German Lutheran Church, W of SR 3 near S. Branch, Beaver Cr., Zeeland vicinity, 7/12/90, A, C, a, 90001027

St. John's Cemetery, Wrought-Iron Cross Site A [German-Russian Wrought-Iron Cross Sites in Central North Dakota MPS], Address Restricted, Zeeland vicinity, 10/23/89, A, C, a, d, 89001687

St. John's Cemetery, Wrought-Iron Cross Site B [German-Russian Wrought-Iron Cross Sites in Central North Dakota MPS], Address Restricted, Zeeland vicinity, 10/23/89, A, C, a, d, 89001688

St. John's Cemetery, Wrought-Iron Cross Site C [German-Russian Wrought-Iron Cross Sites in Central North Dakota MPS], Address Restricted, Zeeland vicinity, 10/23/89, A, C, a, d, 89001689

St. John's Cemetery, Wrought-Iron Cross Site D [German-Russian Wrought-Iron Cross Sites in Central North Dakota MPS], Address Restricted, Zeeland vicinity, 10/23/89, A, C, a, d, 89001690

McKenzie County

Grassy Butte Post Office, Off U.S. 85, Grassy Butte, 11/26/80, A, C, 80002919

McLean County

Former McLean County Courthouse [North Dakota County Courthouses TR], Main St., Washburn, 11/14/85, A, C, 85002987

Holy Trinity Ukrainian Greek Orthodox Church, Bismarck Ave. and 6th St., Wilton, 10/22/82, A, C, a, 82001344

McLean County Courthouse [North Dakota County Courthouses TR], Fifth Ave., Washburn, 11/14/85, A, C, 85002998

Semevolos Farm [Ukrainian Immigrant Dwellings and Churches in North Dakota from Early Settlement Until the Depression MPS], SE of Butte, Butte vicinity, 10/16/87, C, 87001788

Soo Line Depot, 1st St. and McLean Ave., Wilton, 3/29/78, A, C, 78003079

Zion Lutheran Cemetery, Wrought-Iron Cross Site [German-Russian Wrought-Iron Cross Sites in Central North Dakota MPS], Address Restricted, Mercer vicinity, 10/23/89, A, C, a, d, 89001684

Mercer County

Big Hidatsa Village Site, N bank of Knife River, 1 mi. N of Stanton, Stanton vicinity, 10/15/66, A, D, NHL, NPS, 66000600

Fort Clark Archeological District, Address Restricted, Stanton vicinity, 10/19/86, A, D, 86002800

High Butte Effigy and Village Site (32ME13), Address Restricted, Riverdale vicinity, 5/22/78, D, 78001991

Knife River Indian Villages National Historic Site Archeological District, Address Restricted, Stanton vicinity, 10/26/74, A, B, D, NPS, 74002220

Krause, Fred, House, 321 W. Main St., Hazen, 4/14/92, C, 92000344

Morton County

Dunlap, Stuart, House, 201 7th Ave., Mandan, 6/08/92, B, C, 92000587

Huff State Historic Site (32MO11), SE of Huff, Huff vicinity, 7/23/80, D, 80002920

Lewis and Clark Hotel, 404 W. Main St., Mandan, 5/09/83, B, C, 83001938

Mandan Commercial Historic District, Roughly bounded by Main and 1st Sts. between 1st Ave., NE and 4th Ave., NW, Mandan, 2/21/85, A, C, 85000341

Welsh House, 208 5th Ave., NW, Mandan, 4/22/80, C, 80002921

Mountrail County

Evans Site, Address Restricted, New Town vicinity, 2/08/80, D, 80002922

Mountrail County Courthouse [North Dakota County Courthouses TR (AD); Buechner and Orth Courthouses in North Dakota TR (AD)], N. Main St., Stanley, 12/22/78, A, C, 78001992

Nelson County

Tofthagen Library Museum [Philanthropically Established Libraries in North Dakota MPS], 116 W. B Ave., Lakota, 9/26/91, A, B, C, 91001467

Oliver County

Cross Ranch Archeological District, Address Restricted, Hensler vicinity, 11/04/85, D, 85003484

Pembina County

Drayton United Methodist Church, ND 44, Drayton, 12/10/79, C, a, 79001773

Gingras House and Trading Post, NE of Walhalla off ND 32, Walhalla vicinity, 5/21/75, A, C, e, 75001305

O'Connor House, Off US 81, St. Thomas, 7/03/80, C, 80004544

Pembina County Courthouse [Buechner and Orth Courthouses in North Dakota TR; North Dakota County Courthouses TR (AD)], Off ND 5, Cavalier, 11/25/80, A, C, 80002923

US Customs House and Post Office—Pembina [US Post Offices in North Dakota, 1900–1940 MPS], 125 S. Cavalier St., Pembina, 11/01/89, A, C, 89001755

Pierce County

Great Northern Passenger Depot, 201 W. Dewey St., Rugby, 9/26/91, A, C, 91001466

Pierce County—Continued

Old Mt. Carmel Cemetery, Wrought-Iron Cross Site [German-Russian Wrought-Iron Cross Sites in Central North Dakota MPS], Address Restricted, Balta vicinity, 10/23/89, A, C, a, d, 89001685

Pierce County Courthouse [Buechner and Orth Courthouses in North Dakota TR; North Dakota County Courthouses TR (AD)], In Rugby, Rugby, 11/25/80, A, C, 80002924

St. Anselm's Cemetery, Wrought-Iron Cross Site [German-Russian Wrought-Iron Cross Sites in Central North Dakota MPS], Address Restricted, Berwick vicinity, 10/23/89, A, C, a, d, 89001681

St. Mathias Cemetery, Wrought-Iron Cross Site [German-Russian Wrought-Iron Cross Sites in Central North Dakota MPS], Address Restricted, Orrin vicinity, 10/23/89, A, C, a, d, 89001680

St. Paul's Episcopal Church [Episcopal Churches of North Dakota MPS], 404 DeSmet St., Rugby, 12/03/92, C, a, 92001608

US Post Office—Rugby [US Post Offices in North Dakota, 1900–1940 MPS], 205 SE. Second St., Rugby, 11/01/89, A, C, 89001748

Ramsey County

Bangs—Wineman Block, 402–408 Fourth St., Devils Lake, 11/14/85, A, B, C, 85002797

Devils Lake Commercial District, Roughly bounded by 2nd Ave., 5th St., 5th Ave., 3rd St., and Railroad Ave., Devils Lake, 10/24/89, A, C, 89001675

Locke Block, 405 Fifth St., Devils Lake, 7/24/86, C, 86001915

Newport Apartments, 601 Seventh St., Devils Lake, 7/11/88, A, C, 88000985

Ramsey County Sheriff's House, 420 6th St., Devils Lake, 1/31/78, A, C, 78003452

St. Mary's Academy, E. 7th St., Devils Lake, 2/24/83, A, C, 83001939

US Post Office and Courthouse, 502 4th St., Devils Lake, 6/22/78, A, C, 78001993

Ransom County

Biesterfeldt Site (32RM1), Address Restricted, Lisbon vicinity, 2/08/80, D, 80002925

Bradford Hotel, 18 Fourth Ave. W., Lisbon, 10/01/87, A, 87001766

Lisbon Opera House, 413 Main Ave., Lisbon, 10/18/79, A, C, 79003727

Ransom County Courthouse [North Dakota County Courthouses TR], Fifth Ave. W, Lisbon, 11/25/85, A, C, g, 85002988

US Post Office—Lisbon [US Post Offices in North Dakota, 1900–1940 MPS], 17 W. Fourth Ave., Lisbon, 11/01/89, A, C, 89001749

Walker, T. J., Historic District, At Sheyenne River, Fort Ransom, 12/05/79, B, C, 79001774

Renville County

Mckinney Cemetery, N of Tolley, Tolley vicinity, 12/28/78, A, B, b, d, 78001994

Renville County Courthouse [North Dakota County Courthouses TR], Main St., Mohall, 11/25/85, A, C, g, 85002989

Richland County

Adams—Fairview Bonanza Farm [Bonanza Farming in North Dakota MPS], 17170 82 R St. SE, Wahepton vicinity, 11/20/90, A, C, 90001838

Bagg Bonanza Farm District, Off ND 13 on Section Rd., Mooreton vicinity, 11/14/85, A, b, 85002832

Leach Public Library [Philanthropically Established Libraries in North Dakota MPS], 417 Second Ave. N., Wahpeton, 1/26/90, A, C, 89002303

Nelson's Grocery, Main and 3rd Sts., Christine, 10/05/77, A, C, 77001027

Post Office, Main and 3rd Sts., Christine, 10/05/77, B, C, b, 77001028

Red River Valley University, N. 6th St., Wahpeton, 4/26/84, A, 84002770

Richland County Courthouse [Buechner and Orth Courthouses in North Dakota TR; North Dakota County Courthouses TR (AD)], Off ND 13, Wahpeton, 11/25/80, A, C, 80002926

South Wild Rice Church, SE of Galchutt at US 81 and CR 8, Galchutt vicinity, 10/22/82, A, a, d, 82001345

St. Alban's Episcopal Church [Episcopal Churches of North Dakota MPS], Jct. of Hammond and Eastern Aves., SW corner, Lidgerwood, 12/03/92, C, a, 92001607

US Post Office—Wahpeton [US Post Offices in North Dakota, 1900–1940 MPS], 620 Dakota Ave., Wahpeton, 11/01/89, A, C, 89001759

Wahpeton Hospital, 720-722 Dakota Ave., Wahpeton, 9/29/83, A, C, 83001940

Sargent County

Sargent County Courthouse [Buechner and Orth Courthouses in North Dakota TR; North Dakota County Courthouses TR (AD)], Off ND 32, Forman, 11/25/80, A, C, 80002927

Sheridan County

Sheridan County Courthouse [North Dakota County Courthouses TR], 215 E. Second St., McClusky, 11/25/85, A, C, g, 85002990

Winter House, NE Sheridan County, Goodrich vicinity, 11/29/79, A, C, 79001775

Sioux County

Former Sioux County Courthouse [North Dakota County Courthouses TR], Belden St., Fort Yates, 11/14/85, A, 85002993

Slope County

H-T Ranch, 10 mi. W of Amidon, Amidon vicinity, 7/05/85, A, C, 85001491

Mystic Theatre, Main St., Marmarth, 9/13/77, A, C, 77001029

Original Slope County Courthouse [North Dakota County Courthouses TR], Second St., Amidon, 11/14/85, A, b, 85002994

Stark County

Gerhardt Octagonal Pig House [North Dakota Round Barns TR], ND 38, Gladstone vicinity, 10/07/86, C, 86002758

Stark County Courthouse [North Dakota County Courthouses TR], Third St. N, Dickinson, 11/25/85, A, C, g, 85002991

US Post Office—Dickinson [US Post Offices in North Dakota, 1900–1940 MPS], 15 E. First St., Dickinson, 11/01/89, A, C, 89001757

Steele County

Baldwin's Arcade, Steele Ave. and 3rd St., Hope, 2/18/75, A, C, 75001306

Steele County Courthouse [North Dakota County Courthouses TR], Washington Ave., Finley, 11/14/85, A, C, 85002995

Stutsman County

Baker, Cecil, Round Barn [North Dakota Round Barns TR], ND 38, Kensal vicinity, 10/07/86, C, 86002759

Dickey, Alfred E., Free Library, 105 3rd St., SE, Jamestown, 7/03/80, A, C, 80004545

Elizabeth Apartments, 402 Second Ave. NW, Jamestown, 4/21/86, A, C, 86000871

Grace Episcopal Church [Episcopal Churches of North Dakota MPS], Jct. of 2nd Ave. NE. and 4th St. NE., NW corner, Jamestown, 12/03/92, A, C, a, 92001606

Jamestown Historic District [Jamestown MPS], Roughly bounded by First St., Fourth Ave., SE, Fifth St., and Second Ave., Jamestown, 9/08/89, A, C, a, 88000987

Seiler Building, 110 First St. E, Jamestown, 1/16/86, B, C, 86000080

St. James Catholic Church, 622 1st Ave., S., Jamestown, 10/22/82, C, a, 82001346

Stutsman County Courthouse and Sheriff's Residence/Jail [North Dakota County Court-

Stutsman County—Continued

houses TR (AD)], 504 3rd Ave., SE, Jamestown, 9/08/76, A, C, 76001356

Voorhees Chapel, Jamestown College campus, Jamestown, 7/22/77, A, C, a, 77001030

Towner County

Towner County Courthouse [North Dakota County Courthouses TR], Second St. S, Cando, 11/14/85, A, C, 85002996

Traill County

Delchar Theater, 20 W. Main St., Mayville, 11/14/85, A, 85002831

Eielson, Carl Ben, House, 405 8th St., Hatton, 4/11/77, B, C, 77001031

Ellingson Farm District, 1 mi. N and 2.5 mi. W of Hillsboro, Hillsboro vicinity, 9/12/85, A, C, 85002343

First National Bank, 22 W. Main St., Mayville, 11/20/85, C, 85002906

First State Bank of Buxton, 423 Broadway St., Buxton, 2/14/78, A, B, C, 78001995

Goose River Bank, 45 Main St. E, Mayville, 11/14/85, B, C, 85002793

Grandins' Mayville Farm District, 2 Brunsdale W, Mayville, 11/19/85, A, B, 85002905

Great Northern Railway Depot, Front St., Mayville, 10/05/77, A, C, 77001033

Grinager Mercantile Building, 37 Main St. E, Mayville, 11/20/85, C, 85003354

Lucken Farm, N of Portland, Portland vicinity, 5/14/86, B, C, 86001049

Lura Building, 29 W. Main St., Mayville, 11/14/85, A, B, C, 85002794

Mayville Historic District, Roughly bounded by Third St. NE, Fifth Ave. NE, Main St. E, and Third Ave. NE and Second Ave. NE, Mayville, 11/19/85, A, C, 85002904

Mayville Public Library, Center Ave., N., Mayville, 4/11/77, A, C, 77001034

Ness, Andres O., House, Oak Ave. and 6th St., Hatton, 7/15/77, A, C, 77001032

Robinson, Col. William H., House, 127 4th Ave., NE, Mayville, 4/11/77, B, C, 77001035

Sarles, O. C., House, 2nd Ave. and 3rd St., NE, Hillsboro, 3/12/85, B, C, 85000562

Stomner House, 32 3rd St., NE, Mayville, 10/11/79, B, C, 79003728

Traill County Courthouse [Buechner and Orth Courthouses in North Dakota TR; North Dakota County Courthouses TR (AD)], Off U.S. 81, Hillsboro, 11/25/80, A, C, 80002928

Union Block, 21–25 Main St. W, Mayville, 11/20/85, C, 85003353

Walsh County

Elmwood, P.O. Box 654, Grafton, 2/21/85, C, 85000339

Minto School, Jct. of Major Ave. and Third St., Minto, 1/30/92, A, C, 91002002

St. Stanislaus Church Historic District, Off I-29, Warsaw, 8/03/79, A, C, a, 79001776

US Post Office—Grafton [US Post Offices in North Dakota, 1900–1940 MPS], 506 S. Griggs Ave., Grafton, 11/01/89, A, C, 89001756

Walsh County Courthouse [North Dakota County Courthouses TR], 638 Cooper Ave., Grafton, 11/25/85, C, g, 85002992

Ward County

Carr, Andrew, Sr., House, 510 4th Ave., NW, Minot, 4/26/84, B, C, 84002771

Eastwood Park Bridge, Central Ave. and 6th St., SE, Minot, 4/21/75, A, C, 75001307

Eastwood Park Historic District [Minot MRA], Bounded by Old Souris Oxbow, Minot, 10/16/86, C, 86002824

Glick, Levi, Round Barn [North Dakota Round Barns TR], ND 38, Surrey vicinity, 3/25/87, C, 86002760

Minot Carnegie Library, 105 2nd Ave., SE, Minot, 11/10/80, C, 80002929

Minot Commercial Historic District [Minot MRA], Roughly bounded by Soo Line RR tracks, Burdick Expressway, and Broadway, Minot, 10/16/80, A, C, 86002823

Minot Industrial Historic District [Minot MRA], Roughly bounded by Souris River, Fifth St. NE, First Ave. SE, First St. NE, Soo Line RR tracks, and Broadway, Minot, 10/16/86, A, 86002818

Soo Line Passenger Depot, 11 N. Main St., Minot, 1/20/78, A, C, 78001996

Tufveson House, 426 4th Ave., NW, Minot, 4/12/84, C, 84002773

U.S. Post Office, 100 1st St., SW, Minot, 10/14/80, A, 80002930

Union National Bank and Annex, 2 N. Main and 7-11 E. Central Ave., Minot, 1/27/83, A, C, 83001941

Ward County Courthouse [North Dakota County Courthouses TR], 315 Third St. SE, Minot, 11/14/85, A, C, 85002997

Westland Oil Filling Station [Minot MRA], 510 E. Central Ave., Minot, 2/27/87, A, C, 86002816

Wells County

Beiseker Mansion, 2nd St. and Roberts Ave., Fessenden, 4/13/77, B, C, 77001036

Hurd Round House, 7 mi. SE of Hurdsfield, Hurdsfield vicinity, 4/11/77, B, C, 77001038

Wells County Courthouse [North Dakota County Courthouses TR (AD)], Railway St., N., Fessenden, 9/15/77, A, C, 77001037

Wells County Fairgrounds, Jct. of US 52 and ND 15, Fessenden, 2/28/91, A, C, b, 91000073

Williams County

Fort Buford State Historic Site, SW of Williston at confluence of Yellowstone and Missouri Rivers, Williston vicinity, 4/01/75, A, 75001308

Fort Union Trading Post National Historic Site, W of Buford, Buford vicinity, 10/15/66, A, D, NHL, NPS, 66000103

James Memorial Library, 621 1st Ave., W., Williston, 11/14/79, A, C, 79001777

Old Armory, 320 1st Ave., E., Williston, 4/11/85, C, 85000787

Old US Post Office, 322 Main Ave., Williston, 10/22/79, A, C, 79003729

Ray Opera House, 111 Main St., Ray, 11/02/78, A, C, 78001997

OHIO

Adams County

Adams County Paleo-Indian District, Address Restricted, Sandy Springs vicinity, 10/18/74, D, 74001389

Buckeye Station, E of Manchester off U.S. 52, Manchester vicinity, 5/01/74, C, 74001388

Cockerill House, 115 E. Main St., West Union, 11/21/78, B, 78001998

Dayton Power And Light Company Mound, Address Restricted, Wrightsville vicinity, 7/30/74, D, 74001391

Harshaville Covered Bridge, SR 1, Harshaville, 3/16/76, A, C, 76001357

Kirker Covered Bridge, SW of West Union off SR 136, West Union vicinity, 10/29/75, C, 75001309

Kirker, Gov. Thomas, Homestead, SW of West Union on SR 136, West Union vicinity, 11/03/75, B, 75001310

Lewis, Dr. A. C., House, 103 South St., Winchester, 10/31/80, B, C, 80002931

Serpent Mound, 5 mi. NW of Locust Grove on OH 73, Locust Grove vicinity, 10/15/66, D, NHL, 66000602

The Ridge, 503 E. 8th St., Manchester, 10/08/92, B, C, 92001352

Treber Inn, 5 mi. NE of West Union on OH 41, West Union vicinity, 5/17/76, A, B, 76001358

Wamsley Village Site, Address Restricted, Stout vicinity, 7/30/74, D, 74001390

West Union Presbyterian Church, 108 S. 2nd St., West Union, 11/18/76, B, a, 76001359

Wickerham Inn, NE of Peebles on OH 41, Peebles vicinity, 5/07/79, C, 79001778

Wilson, John T., Homestead, NE of Seaman on OH 32, Seaman vicinity, 4/11/77, B, 77001039

Woods, Tet, Building, 307 Main St., West Union, 3/25/82, C, 82003536

Allen County

Adgate Block [Lima MRA], 300-306 S. Main St., Lima, 10/07/82, C, 82001347

Allen County Courthouse, Courthouse Sq., Lima, 7/24/74, C, 74001392

Armory-Latisona Building [Lima MRA], 440 S. Main St., Lima, 10/07/82, C, 82001348

Barr Hotel, 201–209 E. High and 200–218 N. Union Sts., Lima, 5/15/86, A, 86001053

Breese, Griffith, Farm, S of Lima at 2775 Fort Amanda Rd., Lima vicinity, 1/11/83, C, 83001942

Cahill, Beck and R. C., Buildings [Lima MRA], 200-206 S. Main St., Lima, 10/07/82, C, 82001349

Dorsey Building [Lima MRA], 208 S. Main St., Lima, 10/07/82, C, 82001350

Elks Lodge [Lima MRA], 138 W. North St., Lima, 10/07/82, C, 82001865

First National Bank and Trust Building [Lima MRA], 43-53 Public Sq., Lima, 10/07/82, C, 82001351

Hotel Argonne [Lima MRA], 201 N. Elizabeth St., Lima, 10/07/82, C, 82001352

Klaus Block [Lima MRA], 401-405 N. Main St., Lima, 10/07/82, C, 82001864

Lima Cleaning and Pressing Company [Lima MRA], 436-438 S. Main St., Lima, 10/07/82, C, 82001353

Lima Memorial Hall, W. Elm and S. Elizabeth Sts., Lima, 5/07/79, A, C, 79001779

Linneman Building [Lima MRA], 210-212 S. Main St., Lima, 10/07/82, C, 82001867

Macdonell House, 632 W. Market St., Lima, 9/20/78, B, C, 78001999

Marks-Family House, 233 N. Franklin St., Delphos, 4/01/82, C, 82003537

Martin Block and Kibby Block [Lima MRA], 140-146 S. Main St., Lima, 10/07/82, C, 82001868

Metropolitan Block, 300 N. Main St, Lima, 11/29/79, A, C, 79001780

Miami And Erie Canal, Deep Cut, 2 mi. S of Spencerville on OH 66, Spencerville vicinity, 10/15/66, A, NHL, 66000603

Neal Clothing [Lima MRA], 74 Public Sq., Lima, 10/07/82, C, 82001870

Neely-Sieber House, 620 W. Spring St., Lima, 12/12/76, C, 76001360

Ohio Theatre [Lima MRA], 122 W. North St., Lima, 10/07/82, C, 82001866

Renz Block [Lima MRA], 320 N. Main St., Lima, 10/07/82, C, 82001354

Round Barn [Round Barns in the Black Swamp of Northwest Ohio TR], Address Restricted, Lima vicinity, 4/17/80, A, C, 80002934

St. John Catholic Church, 110 N. Franklin St., Delphos, 1/03/80, C, a, 80002933

U.S. Post Office [Lima MRA], 326 W. High St., Lima, 10/07/82, C, 82001356

Union Block [Lima MRA], 28-38 Public Sq., Lima, 10/07/82, C, 82001355

Ashland County

Anderson Schoolhouse, SW of Ashland on U.S. 42, Ashland vicinity, 3/25/77, A, C, 77001040

Ashland County Courthouse, W. 2nd St., Ashland, 12/21/79, C, 79003786

Black, Philip J., House, 303 N. Water St., Loudonville, 5/29/80, C, 80002935

Center Street Historic District, Center St. from Vernon to 414 Center St., Ashland, 6/18/76, C, 76001362

Center Street Historic District (Boundary Increase), Center St. between Town Cr. and Walnut St. and between Samaritan and Morgan Aves., Ashland, 5/06/93, C, 93000397

Crittenden Farm, NW of Savannah on US 224 and US 250, Savannah vicinity, 4/22/82, A, C, 82003540

Crumrine, John, Farm, 792 Co. Rd. 40, Nova vicinity, 12/07/90, A, C, 90001778

Crumrine, Michael, Farm, 871 Co. Rd. 40, Nova vicinity, 12/07/90, A, C, 90001779

Garst, John, House, NE of Loudonville on OH 95, Loudonville, 4/29/82, C, 82003539

Hayesville Opera House, 1 E. Main St., Hayesville, 5/06/76, A, C, 76001364

Lakefork School, SE of Jeromesville, Jeromesville vicinity, 3/05/82, A, C, 82003538

Sprott's Hill Mounds Site, Address Restricted, Ashland vicinity, 1/31/76, D, 76001363

Vermilion Institute, Main and College Sts., Hayesville, 3/29/78, A, C, 78002000

Ashtabula County

Ashtabula County Courthouse Group, NW corner of Jefferson and Chestnut Sts., Jefferson, 6/30/75, A, B, C, 75001316

Ashtabula Harbor Light [U.S. Coast Guard Lighthouses and Light Stations on the Great Lakes TR], Ashtabula Harbor, Ashtabula, 8/04/83, A, C, 83001943

Ashtabula Harbour Commercial District, Both sides of W. 5th St. from 1200 block to Ashtabula River, Ashtabula, 9/05/75, A, C, 75001311

Austin, Eliphalet, House, 1879 OH 45, Austinburg, 2/24/75, B, C, 75001313

Boice Fort And Village Site, Address Restricted, Wayne vicinity, 7/24/74, D, 74001398

Cahill, Michael, House, 1106 Walnut Blvd., Ashtabula, 10/05/88, C, 88001711

Congregational Church Of Austinburg, OH 307, Austinburg, 12/22/78, A, C, a, 78002001

Conneaut Harbor West Breakwater Light [Light Stations of Ohio MPS], W breakwater pierhead, harbor entrance, Conneaut, 4/10/92, A, C, 92000243

Conneaut Light Station Keeper's Dwelling [Light Stations of Ohio MPS], 1059 Harbor St., Conneaut, 8/21/92, A, C, 92001078

Conneaut Works, Address Restricted, Conneaut vicinity, 7/30/74, D, 74001393

Cummins, David, Octagon House, 301 Liberty St., Conneaut, 9/09/74, C, 74001394

Giddings, Joshua Reed, Law Office, 112 N. Chestnut St., Jefferson, 5/30/74, B, NHL, 74001396

Harmon, Francis E., House, 1641 E. Prospect Rd., Ashtabula, 2/24/75, C, 75001312

Harpersfield Covered Bridge, SR 154 over the Grand River, Harpersfield, 11/03/75, C, 75001315

Harwood Block, 246, 250, 256 Main St., Coneaut, 3/21/78, A, C, 78002002

Henderson, John, House, 5248 Stanhope-Kelloggsville Rd., West Andover, 11/07/76, C, 76001368

Hotel Ashtabula, 4726 Main Ave., Ashtabula, 6/20/85, A, C, 85001342

Ashtabula County—Continued

House, Col. Erastus, House, OH 46 and Richmond-Footville Rd., Rays Corner, 7/30/74, B, C, 74001397

Hubbard, Col. William, House, Corner of Lake Ave. and Walnut Blvd., Ashtabula, 3/20/73, B, 73001385

Jefferson Town Hall, 27 E. Jefferson St., Jefferson, 6/18/81, A, 81000428

Kilpi Hall, 1025 Buffalo St., Conneaut, 12/12/76, A, C, 76001365

Lake Shore & Michigan Southern Railroad Station, 147 E. Jefferson St., Jefferson, 10/14/82, A, C, 82001357

Lake Shore And Michigan Southern Passenger Depot, 342 Depot St., Conneaut, 3/27/75, A, C, 75001314

New Lyme Institute, 929 Brownville Rd., South New Lyme vicinity, 1/01/76, A, 76001367

New Lyme Town Hall, N of South New Lyme at 6000 NC 46, South New Lyme vicinity, 8/06/75, C, 75001317

Peck, L. W., House, 2646 Eagleville Rd., Eagleville vicinity, 1/01/76, C, 76001366

Shandy Hall, 6333 S. Ridge Rd., Geneva vicinity, 6/28/74, B, C, 74001395

West Fifth Street Bridge, SR 531 over Ashtabula River, Ashtabula, 8/23/85, C, 85001801

Windsor Corners District, U.S. 322 and OH 534, Windsor, 9/05/75, A, C, a, 75001318

Windsor Mills Christ Church Episcopal, Wisell Rd. and U.S. 322, Windsor Mills, 5/29/75, A, C, a, 75001319

Windsor Mills Fort And Village Site, Address Restricted, Windsor vicinity, 10/21/75, D, 75001321

Wiswell Road Covered Bridge, Wiswell Rd. over Phelps Creek, Windsor Mills vicinity, 4/11/73, C, 73001386

Athens County

Athens B & O Train Depot, Depot St., Athens, 1/11/83, A, 83001944

Athens Downtown Historic District, N. Court St. between Carpenter and Union Sts. and Congress and College Sts., Athens, 9/30/82, A, C, 82003541

Athens Governmental Buildings, E. State, E. Washington, Court, and W. Union Sts, Athens, 11/29/79, A, C, 79001782

Athens State Hospital, OH 682 and Richland Ave., Athens, 3/11/80, A, C, 80002936

Athens State Hospital Cow Barn, SW of Athens off U.S. 33, Athens vicinity, 4/25/78, A, C, 78002003

Beasley Building, 93 W. Union St., Athens, 10/07/82, A, C, 82001358

Blackwood Covered Bridge, S of Athens on SR 46, Athens vicinity, 6/23/78, A, C, 78002004

Clester, Joseph, House, SE of Chauncey on SR 111, Chauncey, 11/26/80, C, 80002940

Dew House, Public Sq., Nelsonville, 10/02/78, A, 78002006

Federalton, 51 State St., Stewart, 8/13/76, B, C, 76001369

Herrold, Thomas Jefferson, House and Store, 234 W. Washington St., Athens, 11/21/80, B, 80002937

Hocking Valley Railway Historic District, Roughly between Bridge #494 in Logan and Bridge #629 in Nelsonville, Nelsonville, 5/05/88, A, C, 88000451

Kidwell Covered Bridge, 1 mi. N of Truetown, Truetown vicinity, 4/11/77, A, C, 77001042

Manasseh Cutler Hall, Ohio University, Ohio University campus, Athens, 10/15/66, A, NHL, 66000604

Mount Zion Baptist Church, Congress and Carpenter Sts., Athens, 10/03/80, A, a, 80002938

Ohio University Campus Green Historic District, Ohio University campus, Athens, 6/11/79, B, C, 79001783

Palos Covered Bridge, 1 mi. N of Gloucester off OH 13, Glouster vicinity, 11/11/77, A, C, 77001041

Savage-Stewart House, SE of Canaanville on U.S. 50, Canaanville vicinity, 2/08/80, A, C, 80002939

Sheltering Arms Hospital, Clark St., Athens, 6/25/82, A, g, 82003542

Stuart's Opera House, Public Sq. and Washington St., Nelsonville, 12/29/78, A, 78002007

Sunday Creek Coal Company Mine No. 6, E of East Millfield, East Millfield vicinity, 5/23/78, A, 78002005

Weethee Historic District, N of Millfield, Millfield vicinity, 1/07/80, A, B, 80002941

White's-Vale Mill, OH 682, Athens vicinity, 7/29/82, A, C, b, 82003543

Wolf Plains, Address Restricted, Athens vicinity, 5/31/74, D, 74001399

Auglaize County

Auglaize County Courthouse, Courthouse Sq., Wapakoneta, 5/07/73, C, 73001387

Boesel, Adolph, House, 110 S. Franklin St, New Bremen, 11/29/79, C, 79001784

Boesel, Julius, House, N of New Bremen on Quellhorst Rd., New Bremen vicinity, 3/30/78, C, 78002008

Egypt Catholic Church [Cross-Tipped Churches of Ohio TR], Minster-Egypt Rd. and OH 364, Egypt, 7/26/79, A, C, a, 79002819

Egypt Catholic Church and Rectory, jct. of Minster-Egypt Rd. and OH 364, Egypt, 7/26/79, A, C, a, 79003455

Egypt Rectory [Cross-Tipped Churches of Ohio TR], Minster-Egypt Pike, Jackson Township, 7/26/79, C, a, 79002860

First Presbyterian Church of Wapakoneta, 106 W. Main St., Wapakoneta, 8/23/85, B, C, a, 85001797

Fledderjohann, H. E., House, Doctor's Office and Summer Kitchen, 107 E. German St., New Knoxville, 12/10/93, B, 93001388

Fort Amanda Site, 9 mi. NW of Wapakoneta on OH 198, Wapakoneta vicinity, 11/10/70, A, f, 70000484

Glynnwood Catholic Church [Cross-Tipped Churches of Ohio TR], NE of St. Mary's on Glynnwood Rd., Glynnwood vicinity, 7/26/79, A, C, a, 79002826

Glynnwood Catholic Church [Cross-Tipped Churches of Ohio TR], 6 mi. NE of St. Marys on Glynnwood Rd., GLynnwood, 7/26/79, C, a, 79003454

Holy Rosary Catholic Church [Cross-Tipped Churches of Ohio TR], E. Spring and S. Pine Sts., St. Marys, 7/26/79, A, C, a, 79002818

Holy Rosary Catholic Church [Cross-Tipped Churches of Ohio TR], jct. E Spring and S Pine Sts., St. Marys, 7/26/79, C, a, 79003456

Luelleman, William, House, 122 N. Main St., New Bremen, 5/21/75, C, 75001322

Minster Elementary School [Cross-Tipped Churches of Ohio TR], Lincoln St., Minster, 7/26/79, C, a, 79002850

Minster Elementary School, Lincoln St., Minster, 7/26/79, C, a, 79003452

Nichols, John H., House, 103 S. Blackhoof St., Wapakoneta, 7/14/88, C, 88001064

Rinehart, Hugh T., House, E of Uniopolis on OH 67, Uniopolis vicinity, 11/27/78, B, C, 78002009

Round Barn [Round Barns in the Black Swamp of Northwest Ohio TR], Address Information Restricted., New Hampshire vicinity, 4/17/80, A, C, 80002942

St. Augustine Catholic Church [Cross-Tipped Churches of Ohio TR], N Hanover St., Minster, 7/26/79, C, a, 79003457

St. Augustine's Catholic Church [Cross-Tipped Churches of Ohio TR], N. Hanover St., Minster, 7/26/79, C, a, 79002815

St. John Catholic Church and Parish Hall [Cross-Tipped Churches of Ohio TR], SW Corner of Schlemel and Van Buren Sts., Fryburg, 7/26/79, C, a, 79003451

St. John Parish Hall [Cross-Tipped Churches of Ohio TR], Van Buren St., Fryburg, 7/26/79, C, a, 79002845

St. John's Catholic Church [Cross-Tipped Churches of Ohio TR], Schemel and Van Buren Sts., Fryburg, 7/26/79, C, a, 79002814

St. Joseph Catholic Church [Cross-Tipped Churches of Ohio TR], 309 S. Perry St., Wapakoneta, 7/26/79, C, a, 79002839

St. Joseph Catholic Church and School [Cross-Tipped Churches of Ohio TR], 309 S Perry St., Wapakoneta, 7/26/79, A, C, a, 79003453

St. Joseph Parochial School [Cross-Tipped Churches of Ohio TR], Pearl and Blackhoof Sts., Wapakoneta, 7/26/79, A, C, a, 79002849

Wapakoneta Commercial Historic District, Roughly bounded by Auglaize, Park, Main, and Blackhoof Sts., Wapakoneta, 1/05/89, A, C, 88003131

Williams, Dr. Issac Elmer, House And Office, 407–411 N. Main St., St. Marys, 5/08/79, A, C, 79001785

Belmont County

B & O Railroad Viaduct, 31st St., Bellaire, 6/22/76, A, C, 76001370

Belmont County—Continued

Barnesville Baltimore and Ohio Railroad Depot, 300 E. Church St., Barnesville, 8/08/85, A, C, 85001694

Barnesville Historic District, Roughly bounded by Arch, Main, Gardner, Chestnut, Bond and Cherry Sts., Barnesville, 7/19/84, A, C, 84002899

Barnesville Petroglyph, Address Restricted, Barnesville vicinity, 7/15/74, D, 74001400

Belmont Historic District, Roughly bounded by Barrister, John, Jefferson, Sycamore, and Bridge Sts., Belmont, 3/13/87, A, C, 87000422

Brokaw Site, Address Restricted, St. Clairsville vicinity, 6/17/76, D, 76001371

Finney-Darrah House, Scenary Hill, Martin's Ferry, 3/15/82, B, 82003546

Frasier, Thomas T. and Wesley B. Houses, 898 and 920 National Rd., Brookside, 11/17/82, C, 82001359

Great Western Schoolhouse, W of St. Clairsville on U.S. 40, St. Clairsville vicinity, 5/07/79, A, C, 79001787

Imperial Glass Company, 29th and Belmont Sts., Bellaire, 9/08/83, A, C, 83001945

Kirkwood, Joseph, House, 329 Bennett St., Bridgeport, 2/13/86, B, C, 86000239

Morristown Historic District, Church, Main, W. Cross, E. Cross, and Middle Cross Sts., Morristown, 3/06/80, A, C, 80002943

Opatrny Village Site, Address Restricted, St. Clairsville vicinity, 5/21/75, D, 75001323

Schooley, Dr. Lindley, House and Office, Main St., Belmont, 4/01/82, B, C, 82003545

Tower Site, Address Restricted, Barnesville vicinity, 6/11/82, D, 82003544

Brown County

Aberdeen Mound, Address Restricted, Aberdeen vicinity, 7/15/74, D, 74001401

Bailey-Thompson House, 112 N. Water St., Georgetown, 11/07/76, C, 76001373

Buckner, Dr. Philip, House And Barn, 610 S. Main St., Georgetown, 3/30/78, B, C, 78002010

Burgett House And Barn, W of Ripley on White Rd., Ripley vicinity, 11/14/78, A, C, 78002013

DONALD B, 3106 Old A&P Rd. E, Georgetown, 12/20/89, A, C, NHL, 89002458

Eagle Creek Covered Bridge, 3 mi. S of Decatur on OH 763, Decatur vicinity, 12/06/75, C, 75001324

Eagle Township Works I Mound, Address Restricted, Fincastle vicinity, 9/10/71, D, 71000630

Farmers Branch, State Bank of Ohio, 14 Front St., Ripley, 4/21/83, C, 83001946

Georgetown Historic District, Roughly bounded by Water Alley, Pleasant, Short, and State Sts., Georgetown, 5/23/78, A, C, 78002011

Georgetown Public School, 307 W. Grant Ave., Georgetown, 1/25/91, A, C, 90002215

Grant, Ulysses S., Boyhood Home, 219 E. Grant Ave., Georgetown, 10/08/76, B, NHL, 76001374

Martin, Henry, Farm, 2 mi. N of Ripley on U.S. 68, Ripley vicinity, 8/15/75, A, 75001326

Mount Orab Station, N. High and Front Sts., Mount Orab, 10/14/75, A, 75001325

Murphy, Daniel, Log House, Anderson State Rd., St. Martin, 6/17/82, C, 82003548

Parker, John P., House, 300 Front St., Ripley, 1/07/80, B, 80002944

Pisgah Christian Church, NW of Ripley on Pisgah Rd., Wilmington, 11/21/80, C, a, 80002945

Rankin, John, House, E of Ripley, Liberty Hill, Ripley vicinity, 11/10/70, B, 70000485

Red Oak Presbyterian Church, Cemetery Rd., Ripley, 6/17/82, B, C, 82003547

Ripley Historic District, Roughly bounded by Main, Front, 2nd, 3rd and 4th Sts., Ripley, 3/07/85, A, B, C, a, 85000552

Stonehurst, 2 mi. N of Ripley off U.S. 68, Ripley vicinity, 10/10/75, A, C, 75001327

Sutton House, 0.3 mi. E of Decatur on OH 125, Decatur vicinity, 3/25/77, C, 77001043

Thompson Farm, W of Georgetown off OH 221, Georgetown vicinity, 1/01/76, C, 76001375

Thompson-Bullock House, W of Georgetown on OH 221, Georgetown vicinity, 2/23/78, C, 78002012

Thumann Log House, 1 mi. S of St. Martin at jct. of OH 251 and U.S. 50, St. Martin vicinity, 3/27/75, C, 75001328

Ursuline Center, NE of Fayetteville off OH 251, Fayetteville vicinity, 6/29/76, C, a, 76001372

Butler County

Alexander, Dr. William S., House, 22 N. College Ave., Oxford, 3/18/87, A, B, C, 86003498

Anderson-Shaffer House, 404 Ross Ave., Hamilton, 1/18/74, B, C, 74001402

Augspurger Grist Mill [Augspurger Amish-/Mennonite Settlement TR], Wayne-Madison Rd., Woodsdale, 11/01/84, A, 84000211

Augspurger Paper Company Rowhouse #2 [Augspurger Amish/Mennonite Settlement TR], Kennedy Rd., Woodsdale, 11/01/84, A, 84000215

Augspurger Paper Company Rowhouse #1 [Augspurger Amish/Mennonite Settlement TR], Wayne-Madison Rd., Woodsdale, 11/01/84, A, 84000216

Augspurger Schoolhouse [Augspurger Amish-/Mennonite Settlement TR], Wayne-Madison Rd., Woodsdale, 11/01/84, A, 84000212

Augspurger, Frederick, Farm [Augspurger Amish/Mennonite Settlement TR], 1856 Wayne-Madison Rd., Trenton vicinity, 8/03/84, A, C, 84002900

Augspurger, John, Farm No. 2 [Augspurger Amish/Mennonite Settlement TR], 3046 Pierson Rd., Trenton vicinity, 11/01/84, A, C, 84000208

Augspurger, John, Farm No. 1 [Augspurger Amish/Mennonite Settlement TR], 2731 Woodsdale Rd., Trenton vicinity, 8/03/84, A, C, 84002901

Augspurger, Samuel, Farm [Augspurger Amish/Mennonite Settlement TR], 2070 Woodsdale Rd., Trenton vicinity, 11/01/84, A, C, d, 84000209

Augspurger, Samuel, House [Augspurger Amish/Mennonite Settlement TR], Wayne-Madison and Kennedy Rds., Woodsdale, 11/01/84, A, B, 84000213

Austin-Magie Farm and Mill District, Section 14, Oxford Township., Oxford vicinity, 12/21/82, A, C, 82001360

Beckett-Manrod House, 2019 Stillwell-Beckett Rd., Hamilton vicinity, 11/11/77, B, C, 77001044

Benninghofen House, 327 N. 2nd St., Hamilton, 5/17/73, B, C, 73001388

Butler County Courthouse, 2nd and High Sts., Hamilton, 6/22/81, A, C, 81000429

Cochran Farm, 2900 OH 129, Millville vicinity, 7/16/73, C, 73001390

Dayton-Campbell Historic District, Primarily Dayton, High and Campbell Ave. between 6th and 11th Sts., Hamilton, 6/30/83, A, C, 83001947

Demoret Mound, Address Restricted, Ross vicinity, 10/21/75, D, 75001337

Deuscher, Henry P., House, 2385 Woodsdale Rd., Trenton vicinity, 2/09/84, B, C, 84002902

Dewitt, Zachariah Price, Cabin, E of Oxford on U.S. 73, Oxford vicinity, 4/13/73, C, 73001392

Edgeton, 575 Harrison Ave., Hamilton, 4/03/75, C, 75001331

Ehresman, Christian, Farm [Augspurger Amish/Mennonite Settlement TR], 900 Woodsdale Rd., Trenton vicinity, 8/03/84, A, C, 84002903

Elliott and Stoddard Halls, Miami University, Miami University campus, Oxford, 4/03/73, C, 73001391

Fairfield Township Works I, Address Restricted, Hamilton vicinity, 11/05/71, D, 71000631

Fitz Randolph-Rogers House, 5467 Liberty-Fairfield Rd., Hamilton vicinity, 2/08/78, A, C, 78002014

Fortified Hill Works, Address Restricted, Hamilton vicinity, 7/12/74, D, 74001403

Garver Barn, Address Restricted, Hamilton, 8/11/80, C, 80002947

German Village Historic District, Roughly bounded by Vine, Dayton, Riverfront Plaza and Martin Luther King, Jr. Blvd., Hamilton, 2/07/91, B, C, 90002216

Great Mound, Address Restricted, Middletown vicinity, 10/07/71, D, 71000633

Hamilton Catholic High School, 533 Dayton St., Hamilton, 7/24/86, A, C, a, 86001917

Harding-Jones Paper Company District, Both sides of S. Main St. at jct. with railroad tracks, Excello, 5/29/75, A, B, C, 75001330

Herron Gymnasium, Miami University campus, Oxford, 11/29/79, A, C, 79001788

Hidley, James P., Cottage, 1820 Oxford-Reily Rd., Reily, 8/18/80, C, 80002951

Hogan—Borger Mound Archeological District, Address Restricted, Ross vicinity, 10/21/75, D, 75001338

Howe Tavern, US 27, College Corner, 1/30/76, A, C, 76001376

Butler County—Continued

Hueston, Matthew, House, 1320 Four Mile Creek Rd., Hamilton vicinity, 9/16/77, B, C, 77001045

Hughes School, 5994 Princeton Rd., Hamilton vicinity, 1/02/76, B, C, 76001377

Hunting Lodge Farm, NE of Oxford at 5349 Bonham Rd., Oxford vicinity, 10/20/82, B, C, 82001361

Iutzi, Christian, Farm [Augspurger Amish-/Mennonite Settlement TR], 2180 Woodsdale Rd., Trenton vicinity, 8/03/84, A, C, 84002904

Kennel, John Sr., Farm [Augspurger Amish-/Mennonite Settlement TR], 5506 Kennel Rd., Trenton vicinity, 8/03/84, A, C, 84002906

Kennel, John, Jr., Farm [Augspurger Amish-/Mennonite Settlement TR], 2251 Wayne-Madison Rd., Trenton vicinity, 8/03/84, A, C, 84002907

Kumler, Elias, House, 120 S. Main St., Oxford, 1/03/80, C, 80002948

Lane's Mill Historic Buildings, S of Oxford at 3884 Wallace Rd., Oxford vicinity, 10/03/80, A, 80002950

Lane-Hooven House, 319 N. 3rd St., Hamilton, 10/25/73, C, 73001389

Langstroth Cottage, 303 Patterson Ave., Oxford, 6/22/76, B, NHL, 76001378

Maltby, Henry, House, 216 E. Church St, Oxford, 11/29/79, A, B, C, 79001789

Mann Mound, Address Restricted, Jacksonburg vicinity, 10/07/71, D, 71000632

McGuffey, William H., House, 401 E. Spring St., Oxford, 10/15/66, B, NHL, 66000605

Miami-Erie Canal Site Historic District, 5171–5251 Rialto Rd., West Chester vicinity, 12/18/78, A, C, 78002016

Mill Office and Post Office [Augspurger Amish/Mennonite Settlement TR], Woodsdale Rd., Woodsdale, 11/01/84, A, 84000214

Morgan—Hueston House, Ross Rd. between Mack Rd. and Woodridge Blvd., Fairfield, 10/01/90, C, 90001495

Oxford Female Institute, High St. and College Ave., Oxford, 4/26/76, A, 76001379

Oxford Railroad Depot and Junction House, S. Elm and W. Spring St., Oxford, 2/08/80, A, C, 80002949

Pugh's Mill Covered Bridge, 1 mi. N of Oxford off SR 732, Oxford vicinity, 6/05/75, C, 75001336

Rentschler House, 643 Dayton St., Hamilton, 4/21/83, B, C, g, 83001948

Roberts Mound, NW of Auburn, Auburn vicinity, 3/27/75, D, 75001329

Rose, D. S., Mound, Address Restricted, Huntsville vicinity, 5/28/75, D, 75001333

Ross Trails Adena Circle, Address Restricted, Ross vicinity, 10/10/75, D, 75001339

Rossville Historic District, Roughly bounded by B, E, Main and Amberly Dr., Hamilton, 10/06/75, A, C, 75001332

Schrock, Peter, Jr., Farm [Augspurger Amish-/Mennonite Settlement TR], Edgewood Dr., Trenton vicinity, 11/01/84, A, C, 84000210

Shaw Farm, 3357 Cincinnati-Brookville Rd., Ross vicinity, 7/24/74, C, 74001405

South Main Street District, S. Main St., Middletown, 3/21/78, B, C, 78002015

St. Stephen Church and Rectory, 224 Dayton St., Hamilton, 7/29/82, A, a, 82003549

Symmes Mission Chapel, 5139 Pleasant Ave., Fairfield, 6/12/80, C, a, 80002946

Thomas Select School, 3637 Millville-Shandon Rd., Shandon, 4/11/77, A, C, a, 77001046

Tytus, John B., House, 300 S. Main St., Middletown, 5/27/75, B, C, NHL, 75001335

Union Township Works II, Address Restricted, Pisgah vicinity, 10/07/71, D, 71000635

Unzicker-Cook House, 2975 Oxford-Middletown Rd., Oxford vicinity, 7/24/74, A, C, 74001404

Vaughan, John, House, 3756 Hamilton-New London Rd., Shandon vicinity, 5/29/75, C, 75001340

Williamson Mound Archeological District, Address Restricted, Maud vicinity, 5/29/75, D, 75001334

Carroll County

Carroll County Courthouse, Courthouse Sq., Carrollton, 10/22/74, C, 74001406

Herrington, John, House and Herrington Bethel Church, 4070 Arbor Rd. NE, Mechanicstown, 1/19/83, A, C, a, d, 83001949

Hull, Patrick, House, 8187 Blade Rd., Oneida, 12/15/82, A, 82001362

McCook, Daniel, House, Public Sq., Carrollton, 11/10/70, B, f, 70000486

Petersburg Mill, 4.3 mi. S of Carrollton on OH 332, Carrollton vicinity, 11/20/70, A, 70000487

St. Mary's Of Morges, 8012 Bachelor Rd., NW., Waynesburg vicinity, 4/11/77, A, C, a, 77001047

Van Horn Building, Public Sq., jct. of W. Main and N. Lisbon Sts., Carrollton, 9/03/87, C, 87001375

Champaign County

Baker, Maj. John C., House [Mechanicsburg MRA], 202 W. Main St., Mechanicsburg, 8/29/85, B, C, 85001875

Barr House [Mechanicsburg MRA], Locust & Sandusky Sts., Mechanicsburg, 8/29/85, B, C, 85001876

Burnham, Henry, House [Mechanicsburg MRA], N. Main St. & Rt. 559, Mechanicsburg, 8/29/85, A, C, 85001877

Church Of Our Savior [Mechanicsburg MRA], S. Main St., Mechanicsburg, 8/29/85, C, a, 85001878

Clark, Dr., House [Mechanicsburg MRA], 21 N. Main St., Mechanicsburg, 8/29/85, A, C, 85001879

Culbertson, William, House [Mechanicsburg MRA], 103 Race St., Mechanicsburg, 8/29/85, B, C, 85001880

Demand-Gest House [Mechanicsburg MRA], 37 N. Main St., Mechanicsburg, 8/29/85, A, C, 85001881

Hamer's General Store [Mechanicsburg MRA], 88 S. Main St., Mechanicsburg, 8/29/85, C, 85001882

Hunter, Norvall, Farm [Mechanicsburg MRA], S. Main St., Mechanicsburg, 8/29/85, A, B, C, 85001883

Kimball House [Mechanicsburg MRA], 115 N. Main St., Mechanicsburg, 8/29/85, A, C, 85001884

Lowler's Tavern [Mechanicsburg MRA], N. Main St., Mechanicsburg, 8/29/85, C, 85001885

Magruder Building [Mechanicsburg MRA], 16 S. Main St., Mechanicsburg, 8/29/85, C, 85001886

Masonic Temple [Mechanicsburg MRA], N. Main St., Mechanicsburg, 8/29/85, A, C, 85001887

Mechanicsburg Baptist Church [Mechanicsburg MRA], Walnut & Sandusky Sts., Mechanicsburg, 8/29/85, C, a, 85001888

Mechanicsburg Commercial Historic District [Mechanicsburg MRA], 1–11 S. Main St., Mechanicsburg, 8/29/85, A, C, 85001895

Monitor House, 375 W. Main St., Saint Paris, 5/02/74, C, 74001408

Mosgrove, Dr. Adam, House, 127 Miami St., Urbana, 7/15/82, B, C, 82003550

Ninchelser, Dr., House [Mechanicsburg MRA], 28 N. Main St., Mechanicsburg, 8/29/85, B, C, 85001889

Nutwood Place, 1428 Nutwood Place, Urbana, 12/12/76, C, 76002265

Potter, Carl, Mound, Address Restricted, Mechanicsburg vicinity, 8/13/74, D, 74001407

Scioto Street Historic District, Scioto St. from Locust to E. Lawn Ave., Urbana, 2/09/84, C, 84002908

Second Baptist Church [Mechanicsburg MRA], Sandusky St., Mechanicsburg, 8/29/85, A, C, a, 85001891

St. Michael Catholic Church [Mechanicsburg MRA], 40 Walnut St., Mechanicsburg, 8/29/85, C, a, 85001892

United Methodist Church [Mechanicsburg MRA], N. Main & Race Sts., Mechanicsburg, 8/29/85, C, a, 85001893

Urbana College Historic Buildings, College Way, Urbana, 10/03/80, A, 80002952

Urbana Monument Square Historic District, Roughly bounded by Market, Walnut, Church, and Locust Sts., Urbana, 3/01/84, A, C, 84002909

Village Hobby Shop [Mechanicsburg MRA], N. Main St., Mechanicsburg, 8/29/85, A, C, 85001894

Ward, John Q. A., House, 335 College St., Urbana, 7/30/74, B, C, 74001409

Clark County

Arcade Hotel, Fountain Ave. and High St., Springfield, 10/16/74, A, C, 74001410

Bookwalter, Francis, House, 611 S. Fountain Ave., Springfield, 1/03/80, B, C, 80002954

Brewer Log House, 2665 Old Springfield Rd., Springfield vicinity, 8/13/74, C, 74001411

Clark County—Continued

Crabill, David, House, 5 mi. E of Springfield off OH 4, Springfield vicinity, 10/10/75, B, C, 75001341

East High Street District, Roughly bounded by E. High, S. Sycamore, and Walnut Sts., Springfield, 10/09/74, C, 74001412

Enon Mound, Address Restricted, Enon vicinity, 2/23/72, D, 72001005

Green Plain Monthly Meetinghouse, Clifton Rd., South Charleston vicinity, 4/01/82, C, a, d, 82003551

Hertzler, Daniel, House, W of Springfield off OH 4, Springfield vicinity, 2/07/78, A, B, C, 78002018

Kenton-Hunt Farm, N of Springfield at 4690 Urbana Rd., Springfield vicinity, 2/08/80, B, C, 80002955

Lagonda Club Building, NW corner of High and Spring Sts., Springfield, 5/28/75, A, C, 75001342

Main Street Buildings, 6–14 E. Main St., Springfield, 3/02/79, C, 79001790

Marquart-Mercer Farm, SW of Springfield, Springfield vicinity, 7/26/79, A, C, 79001791

Municipal Building, S. Fountain Ave. between High and Washington Sts., Springfield, 5/25/73, A, C, 73001394

Myers Hall, Wittenberg Ave. and Ward St., Springfield, 6/30/75, B, C, 75001343

Newlove Works, Address Restricted, Springfield vicinity, 6/04/73, D, 73001395

Odd Fellows' Home for Orphans, Indigent and Aged, 404 E. McCreight Ave., Springfield, 4/16/80, A, C, 80002956

Pennsylvania House, 1311 W. Main St., Springfield, 4/11/73, A, C, 73001396

Pickaway Settlements Battlesite, N of Enon, Enon vicinity, 5/08/80, A, 80002953

Reeser, C. A., House, 1425 Innisfallen Ave., Springfield, 6/20/80, B, 80002957

Shawnee Hotel, Main and Limestone Sts., Springfield, 12/05/85, C, 85003044

South Charleston Historic District, OH 70, South Charleston, 7/17/78, C, 78002017

South Fountain Avenue Historic District, Roughly Fountain Ave. and Limestone St. from Perrin to Monroe Sts., Springfield, 12/29/83, A, C, 83004114

St. Joseph Roman Catholic Church, 802 Kenton St., Springfield, 3/15/82, C, a, 82003552

St. Raphael Church, 225 E. High St., Springfield, 6/22/76, C, a, 76001381

Third Presbyterian Church, 714 N. Limestone St., Springfield, 1/03/80, C, a, 80002958

Warder Public Library, E. High and Spring Sts., Springfield, 2/17/78, B, C, 78002019

Westcott House, 1340 E. High St., Springfield, 7/24/74, C, 74001413

Clermont County

Bethel Methodist Church, 1 mi. N of Bantam on Elk Lick Rd., Bantam vicinity, 8/11/78, B, C, a, 78002020

Bullskin Creek Site, Address Restricted, Felicity vicinity, 3/30/78, D, 78002022

Clarke Farm Site, Address Restricted, Point Pleasant vicinity, 11/19/74, D, 74001420

Devanney Site, Address Restricted, Goshen vicinity, 3/30/78, D, 78002023

East Fork Site, Address Restricted, Batavia vicinity, 3/30/78, D, 78002021

Edgington Mound, Address Restricted, Neville vicinity, 7/15/74, D, 74001415

Elk Lick Road Mound, Address Restricted, Bantam vicinity, 2/20/75, D, 75001344

Ferris Site, Address Restricted, Neville vicinity, 10/29/74, D, 74001416

Gaskins-Malany House, 726 Bradbury Rd., Withamsville vicinity, 10/29/75, A, C, 75001345

Gatch Site, Address Restricted, Milford vicinity, 10/15/74, D, 74001414

McKever, Lewis, Farmhouse, 4475 McKeever Rd., Williamsburg vicinity, 4/01/82, A, C, 82003555

New Richmond Water Works and Electric Station, 701 Washington St., New Richmond, 12/23/93, A, 93001389

Pfarr Log House, SE of Milford on Shayler Run Rd., Milford vicinity, 9/16/77, C, b, 77001048

Promont, 906 Goshen Pk., Milford, 11/21/80, B, C, 80002959

Roas-Ilhardt Farm and Winery, N of New Richmond at 3233 Cole Rd., New Richmond vicinity, 9/16/82, A, C, 82003553

Ross-Gowdy House, 125 George St., New Richmond, 6/01/82, B, 82003554

Salt House, SW of Bethel on OH 222, Bethel vicinity, 6/22/76, B, C, 76001382

Schafer House, E of Neville off U.S. 52, Neville vicinity, 5/13/74, C, 74001417

Snead Mound, Address Restricted, Neville vicinity, 7/30/74, D, c, 74001418

Stonelick Covered Bridge, E of Perintown, Perintown vicinity, 9/10/74, C, 74001419

Winter, William, Stone House, N of Mt. Olive on OH 133, Mt. Olive vicinity, 3/25/77, B, C, 77001049

Clinton County

College Hall, Wilmington College, E of College St. between Douglas St. and Fife Ave. on Wilmington, Wilmington, 4/23/73, A, C, 73001399

Cowan Creek Circular Enclosure, SW of Wilmington, Wilmington vicinity, 7/15/74, D, 74001422

Doan House, 822 Fife Ave, Wilmington, 6/20/79, B, C, 79001792

Haines, Frank, House, 149 W. Elm St., Sabina, 4/01/82, B, C, 82003556

Harvey, Eli, House, 1133 Lebanon Rd., Clarksville vicinity, 2/14/78, A, B, 78002024

Hillside Haven Mound, Address Restricted, Oakland vicinity, 11/21/78, D, 78002026

Hurley Mound, Address Restricted, Lumberton vicinity, 5/05/78, D, 78002025

Keiter Mound, Address Restricted, Wilmington vicinity, 10/21/75, D, 75001346

Lynchburg Covered Bridge, East Fork of Little Miami River, Lynchburg, 3/16/76, C, 76001456

Main Building, Sugartree St., Wilmington, 11/21/80, C, 80002960

Martinsville Road Covered Bridge, W of Martinsville, Martinsville vicinity, 9/10/74, C, 74001421

Pansy Methodist Church and School Historic District, S of Clarksville on OH 730, Clarksville vicinity, 3/20/73, C, a, 73001398

Rombach Place, 149 E. Locust St, Wilmington, 6/20/79, B, 79001793

South South Street Historic District, 151–515 S. South St., Wilmington, 5/06/93, A, C, 93000396

Wilmington Commercial Historic District, Roughly bounded by Columbus, Walnut, Sugartree, and Mulberry Sts., Wilmington, 10/14/82, A, C, 82001363

Columbiana County

Beginning Point of the U.S. Public Land Survey, On the OH/PA Border, E of East Liverpool, East Liverpool, 10/15/66, A, C, f, NHL, 66000606

Carnegie Public Library, 219 E. 4th St., East Liverpool, 3/11/80, C, 80002963

Cawood, Richard L., Residence, 2600 St. Clair Ave., East Liverpool, 1/21/88, B, C, 87002502

Cherry Valley Coke Ovens, Jct. of Cherry Valley and Butcher Rds., Leetonia, 5/06/93, A, 93000404

Church Hill Road Covered Bridge, 3 mi. E of Lisbon off SR 867, Lisbon vicinity, 6/11/75, C, b, 75001347

City Hall [East Liverpool Central Business District MRA], Sixth St., East Liverpool, 11/14/85, A, C, 85003511

Columbiana County Infirmary, W of Lisbon on County Home Rd, Lisbon vicinity, 6/20/79, A, C, 79001795

Diamond Historic District [East Liverpool Central Business District MRA], Market and E. Sixth Sts., East Liverpool, 11/14/85, A, C, 85003508

East Fifth Street Historic District [East Liverpool Central Business District MRA], Along E. Fifth St. between Market St. and Broadway, East Liverpool, 11/14/85, A, C, 85003510

East Liverpool Post Office, 5th and Broadway Sts., East Liverpool, 11/21/76, C, 76001384

East Liverpool Pottery, SE corner of 2nd and Market Sts., East Liverpool, 10/07/71, A, 71000636

Eckis, Nicholas, House, High St., East Fairfield, 1/03/80, C, 80002962

Elks Club [East Liverpool Central Business District MRA], 139 W. Fifth St., East Liverpool, 11/14/85, A, C, 85003512

Episcopal Church of the Ascension and Manse, 1101 and 1109 Eleventh St., Wellsville, 5/15/86, C, a, 86001061

Gaston's Mill-Lock No. 36, Sandy And Beaver Canal District, About 1 mi. S of Clarkson in Beaver Creek State Forest, Clarkson vicinity, 5/23/74, A, C, 74001423

Godwin—Knowles House [East Liverpool Central Business District MRA], 422 Broadway, East Liverpool, 11/14/85, A, 85003515

Columbiana County—Continued

Hanoverton Canal Town District, U.S. 30, Hanoverton, 8/03/77, C, 77001050

Hostetter Inn, NW of Lisbon, 32901 OH 172, Lisbon vicinity, 9/27/80, A, C, 80002965

Ikirt House, 200 6th St., East Liverpool, 5/29/80, B, C, 80002964

Jones-Bowman House, 540 Pittsburgh St., Columbiana, 12/12/76, C, 76001383

Laughlin, Homer, House [East Liverpool Central Business District MRA], 414 Broadway, East Liverpool, 11/14/85, A, B, C, 85003513

Lisbon Historic District, U.S. 30 and OH 45, Lisbon, 8/24/79, A, C, 79001794

Morgan, John H., Surrender Site, 3.1 mi. W of West Point on OH 518, West Point vicinity, 4/23/73, A, B, 73001401

Odd Fellows Temple [East Liverpool Central Business District MRA], 120 W. Sixth St., East Liverpool, 11/14/85, A, C, 85003514

Patterson, Mary A., Memorial [East Liverpool Central Business District MRA], E. Fourth St., East Liverpool, 11/14/85, A, C, 85003516

Potters National Bank [East Liverpool Central Business District MRA], Broadway and Fourth St., East Liverpool, 11/14/85, A, C, 85003518

Potters Savings and Loan [East Liverpool Central Business District MRA], Washington and Broadway, East Liverpool, 11/14/85, A, C, 85003517

Schmick, Charles Nelson, House, 110 Walnut St., Leetonia, 3/21/91, B, C, 91000250

South Lincoln Avenue Historic District, S. Lincoln Ave., roughly between Pershing and Summit Sts., Salem, 8/26/93, C, 93000876

Street, John, House, 631 N. Ellsworth Ave., Salem, 10/10/73, C, 73001400

Thompson, Cassius Clark, House, 305 Walnut St., East Liverpool, 9/28/71, B, C, 71000637

Travelers Hotel [East Liverpool Central Business District MRA], 115 E. Fourth St., East Liverpool, 7/15/86, A, 86001718

YMCA [East Liverpool Central Business District MRA], Washington and Fourth St., East Liverpool, 11/14/85, A, C, 85003509

Coshocton County

Adams-Gray House, SE of Trinway on Tobacco Hill Rd, Trinway vicinity, 12/05/79, B, C, 79001797

Chalfant Church, S of Warsaw off OH 60, Warsaw vicinity, 3/15/82, A, C, a, d, 82004416

Coshocton County Courthouse, Courthouse Sq., Coshocton, 5/22/73, C, 73001402

Ferguson, Andrew, House, E of West Lafayette on OH 751, West Lafayette vicinity, 11/30/78, B, C, 78002028

Helmick Covered Bridge, E of Blissfield on Twnshp. Rd. 25, Blissfield, 6/18/75, C, 75001348

Johnson, Thomas, House, OH 541, Plainfield, 5/14/82, C, 82004415

Johnson-Humrickhouse House, 302 S. 3rd St., Coshocton, 10/09/74, C, 74001424

Lamberson-Markley Houses, 713 Main St., Canal Lewisville, 10/18/84, C, 84000125

Lee, Samuel, House, 306 4th St, Coshocton, 12/06/79, A, C, 79001796

Meek, J.F., Buildings, 546 Chestnut St. and 213-215 N. Sixth St., Coshocton, 1/02/85, B, C, 85000033

Miller, Daniels, House, W of West Lafayette at 52357 SR 16, West Lafayette vicinity, 1/03/80, C, 80002967

Milligan, Cuthbert, House, N of Coshocton, Coshocton vicinity, 11/25/80, C, 80002966

Nichols, Eli, Farm, Address Restricted, Howard vicinity, 11/29/82, C, 82001364

Old Union School, 310 Sycamore St., Coshocton, 10/18/84, A, C, 84000127

Rodrick Bridge, 8.5 mi. (13.6 km) SE of Coshocton, Coshocton vicinity, 11/29/78, A, C, 78002027

Roscoe Village, Whitewoman and High Sts., Coshocton, 4/03/73, A, C, 73001403

Walhounding Canal Lock No. 9, OH 715, Warsaw, 2/24/86, A, C, 86000307

Crawford County

Beer, Judge Thomas, House, 306 W. Southern Ave., Bucyrus, 3/24/80, B, C, 80002968

Big Four Depot, SE corner of Church and Washington Sts., Galion, 7/07/75, A, C, 75001350

Blair, Herbert S., House, 212 S. Lane St., Bucyrus, 3/24/80, C, 80002969

Brownella Cottage and Grace Episcopal Church and Rectory, S. Union and Walnut Sts., Galion, 9/27/80, B, C, a, 80002975

Bucyrus Commercial Historic District, Sandusky Ave. and Mansfield St., Bucyrus, 2/28/85, A, C, 85000401

Bucyrus Mausoleum, Southern Ave., Bucyrus, 9/27/80, C, 80002970

Central Hotel, Hackedorn and Zimmerman Buildings, SW corner of Harding Way E. and Market Sts., Galion, 11/13/76, C, 76001386

Chesney, Dr. John, House, 225 E. Mansfield St., Bucyrus, 3/24/80, C, 80002971

Crawford, Col. William, Capture Site [Leesville Village MRA], .5 mi. E of OH 598 and CR 229, Leesville, 4/03/79, B, 79002812

Crestline City Hall, 121 W. Bucyrus St., Crestline, 5/08/74, C, 74001427

Harris, Stephen R., House, 548 East St., Bucyrus, 7/24/80, C, 80002972

Heckler Farmhouse, N of Crestline off OH 61 on Oldfield Rd., Crestline vicinity, 5/03/76, C, 76001385

Hoffman House, 211 Thoman St., Crestline, 11/29/78, C, 78002030

Hosford House, 6288 Hosford Rd., Galion vicinity, 4/30/76, B, C, 76001387

Howard, Adam, House, 230 S. Boston St., Galion, 3/30/78, B, C, 78002032

J & M Trading Post [Leesville Village MRA], 6867 Leesville Rd., Leesville, 4/03/79, B, 79002811

J & M Trading Post—Annex [Leesville Village MRA], Leesville Rd., Leesville, 4/03/79, A, 79002809

Leesville Town Hall [Leesville Village MRA], OH 598 and CR 229, Leesville, 4/03/79, B, 79002810

Mcgraw House, 116 S. Walnut St., Bucyrus, 7/18/75, C, 75001349

Methodist Episcopal Church, Thoman and Union Sts., Crestline, 10/27/78, A, C, a, 78002031

Monnett Memorial M. E. Chapel, 999 OH 98, Bucyrus, 12/29/86, C, a, 86003494

Picking, D., And Company, 119 S. Walnut St., Bucyrus, 7/11/74, A, 74001425

Scroggs House, 202 S. Walnut St., Bucyrus, 10/09/74, C, 74001426

Smith Road Bridge, NW of Bucyrus, Bucyrus vicinity, 10/07/80, A, C, 80002973

Toledo and Ohio Central Depot, 700 E. Rensselaer St., Bucyrus, 10/03/80, A, C, 80002974

Cuyahoga County

Adams, John And Maria, House, 7315 Columbia Rd., Olmsted Falls, 10/10/75, A, C, 75001368

Adelbert Hall, Case Western Reserve University, Case Western Reserve University campus, Cleveland, 10/30/73, A, C, 73001405

Alcazar Hotel, Surrey and Derbyshire Rds., Cleveland Heights, 4/17/79, A, C, 79001805

Aldrich, Aaron, House, 30663 Lake Rd., Bay Village, 12/04/78, B, C, 78002033

Allen Memorial Medical Library, 11000 Euclid Ave., Cleveland, 11/30/82, C, 82001365

Annis, John M., House, 9271 State Rd., North Royalton, 3/19/92, C, 92000174

Archwood Avenue Historic District [Brooklyn Centre MRA], Archwood Ave. roughly bounded by W. Thirty-first Pl. and W. Thirty-seventh St., Cleveland, 3/19/87, C, 87000428

Bay View Hospital, 23200 Lake Rd., Bay Village, 8/27/74, A, C, 74001428

Beehive School, 4345 Lee Rd., Cleveland, 4/05/84, A, 84002910

Bell, Dr. James, House, 1822 E. Eighty-ninth St., Cleveland, 10/16/86, C, 86002878

Benedict, Sarah, House [Upper Prospect MRA], 3751 Prospect Ave., Cleveland, 11/01/84, C, 84000220

Berea District 7 School, 323 E. Bagley Rd., Berea, 4/03/75, C, 75001355

Berea Union Depot, 30 Depot St., Berea, 11/21/80, A, C, 80002976

Bingham Company Warehouse, 1278 W. 9th St., Cleveland, 11/02/73, A, C, 73001406

Blossom, Elizabeth B., Subdivision Historic District, Jct. of Richmond and Cedar Rds., Beachwood, 9/22/87, A, B, C, g, 87001543

Bohemian National Hall, 4939 Broadway St., Cleveland, 5/28/75, A, C, 75001359

Bolton, Chester and Frances, House, Address Restricted, Lyndhurst vicinity, 3/29/84, B, C, 84002911

Bomante House [Brooklyn Centre MRA], 3000 Mapledale Ave., Cleveland, 3/19/87, C, 87000441

Cuyahoga County—Continued

Brecksville Town Hall, Public Sq., Brecksville, 7/02/73, C, 73001404

Brecksville Trailside Museum, Chippewa Cr. Dr. SE of jct. with OH 82, Brecksville, 8/14/92, A, C, 92000988

Brecksville-Northfield High Level Bridge, Carries OH 82 over the Cuyahoga River, Brecksville, 1/16/86, C, 86000078

Broadway Avenue Historic District, Broadway and Hamlet Aves. and E. Fifty-fifth St., Cleveland, 10/19/88, A, C, 88001860

Brooklyn Bank Building, 3764 W. 25th St., Cleveland, 7/19/84, C, 84002912

Brown, John Hartness, House, 2380 Overlook Rd., Cleveland Heights, 11/07/76, B, C, 76001389

Buehl House, 118 E. Bridge St., Berea, 4/30/76, A, C, 76001388

Burdick, Harold B., House, 2424 Stratford Rd., Cleveland Heights, 9/17/74, C, g, 74001434

Burt, William, House, 9525 Brecksville Rd., Brecksville, 3/22/79, A, C, NPS, 79000286

Caxton Building, 812 Huron Rd., SE., Cleveland, 10/30/73, A, C, 73001407

Central YMCA [Upper Prospect MRA], 2200 Prospect Ave., Cleveland, 11/01/84, C, 84000221

Cermak Building, 3503 E. 93rd St., Cleveland, 10/18/84, A, B, 84000128

Chagrin Falls Township Hall, 83 N. Main St., Chagrin Falls, 10/01/74, C, 74001432

Chagrin Falls Triangle Park Commercial District, Main, Franklin, and Washington Sts., Chagrin Falls, 12/29/78, A, C, 78002036

Chagrin Falls West Side District, Bounded by W. Washington, Church, Maple, and Franklin Sts., Chagrin Falls, 10/09/74, A, C, 74001433

Clague House, 1371 Clague Rd., Westlake, 1/11/76, A, C, 76001408

Clark, Jared, House, 6241 Wallings Rd., Broadview Heights, 8/01/75, C, 75001357

Cleveland And Pittsburgh Railroad Bridge, Tinker's Creek, Bedford, 7/24/75, A, C, 75001351

Cleveland Arcade, 401 Euclid Ave., Cleveland, 3/20/73, C, NHL, 73001408

Cleveland Discount Building, 815 Superior Ave. NE., Cleveland, 10/02/91, B, C, 91001416

Cleveland Grays Armory, 1234 Bolivar Rd., Cleveland, 3/28/73, C, 73001409

Cleveland Harbor Station, U.S. Coast Guard, New West Pier, Cleveland, 1/01/76, C, g, 76001390

Cleveland Home For Aged Colored People [Black History TR], 4807 Cedar Ave., Cleveland, 12/17/82, A, 82001366

Cleveland Mall, Roughly T-shaped mall area between E. 9th and W. 3rd Sts., Cleveland, 6/10/75, C, 75001360

Cleveland Municipal Stadium, Erieview Dr., Cleveland, 11/13/87, A, C, 87002287

Cleveland Packard Building [Upper Prospect MRA], 5100-5206 Prospect Ave., Cleveland, 11/01/84, A, C, 84000222

Cleveland Public Square, Superior Ave. and Ontario St., Cleveland, 12/18/75, C, f, 75001361

Cleveland Trust Company, 900 Euclid Ave. at E. 9th St., Cleveland, 11/26/73, C, 73001410

Cleveland Warehouse District, Roughly bounded by Front and Superior Aves., Railroad, Summit, 3rd, and 10th Sts., Cleveland, 9/30/82, A, C, 82003558

Cleveland West Pierhead Light [U.S. Coast Guard Lighthouses and Light Stations on the Great Lakes TR], Cleveland Harbor on Lake Erie, Cleveland, 8/04/83, A, C, 83001950

Cleveland Worsted Mills Company, 5846-6116 Broadway, Cleveland, 8/08/85, A, C, 85001695

Clifton Park Lakefront District, Roughly bounded by Clifton Blvd., Rocky River, Lake Erie, and Webb Rd., Lakewood, 11/20/74, B, C, 74001459

Colonial and Euclid Arcades, 508 and 600 Euclid Ave., Cleveland, 5/08/87, C, 87000660

Commodore Apartment Building, 15610 Van Aken Blvd., Shaker Heights, 4/21/83, C, 83001951

Cook Building [Upper Prospect MRA], 4600-4800 Prospect Ave., Cleveland, 11/01/84, A, C, 84000224

Cooley Farms, N of Warrensville Heights off OH 175, Warrensville Heights vicinity, 8/08/79, A, C, 79001823

Coonrad, Jonas, House, SE of Brecksville at 10340 Riverview Rd., Brecksville vicinity, 7/24/79, A, C, NPS, 79000287

Cozad, Justus L., House, 1508 Mayfield Rd., Cleveland, 1/18/74, C, 74001435

Crawford-Tilden Apartments, 1831-1843 Crawford Rd. and 1878-1888 E. 84th St., Cleveland, 3/21/78, C, 78002038

Dall, Andrew, Jr. and James, Houses, 2225 and 2229 E. 46th St., Cleveland, 7/19/84, B, 84002913

Day, Erastus, House, 16807 Hilliard Rd., Lakewood, 5/08/79, B, 79001812

Detroit Avenue Bridge, Detroit Ave. at Rocky River, Rocky River—Lakewood, 2/23/73, A, C, 73001428

Detroit—Warren Building, 14801-14813 Detroit Ave., Lakewood, 5/15/86, C, 86001055

Detroit-Superior High Level Bridge, Over Cuyahoga River Valley, between Detroit Ave. and Superior Ave., Cleveland, 1/18/74, A, C, 74001437

Division Avenue Pumping Station, Division Ave., at the foot of W. 45th St., Cleveland, 1/18/74, C, 74001438

Dixon Hall Apartments [Upper Prospect MRA], 3814 Prospect Ave., Cleveland, 11/01/84, C, 84000225

Doan School, 1350 E. 105th St., Cleveland, 8/23/84, C, 84002915

Drake, Alonzo, House, 24262 Broadway, Oakwood, 11/28/78, C, 78002047

Dunham Tavern, 6709 Euclid Ave., Cleveland, 7/25/74, A, C, 74001439

Dunham, Hezekiah, House, 729 Broadway, Bedford, 6/18/75, B, C, 75001352

East 89th Street Historic District, E. Eighty-ninth St. roughly between Chester and Hough Aves., Cleveland, 5/26/88, C, 88000678

East Cleveland District 9 School, 14391 Superior Rd, Cleveland Heights, 7/26/79, A, C, 79001806

East Fourth Street Historic District, Roughly on E. Fourth St. between Euclid and Prospect Aves., Cleveland, 7/09/87, C, 87001179

Ensworth, Jeremiah, House [Upper Prospect MRA], 3214 Prospect Ave., Cleveland, 11/01/84, C, 84000226

Erie Railroad Cleveland Powerhouse, 1246 River Rd., Cleveland, 7/19/84, A, 84003614

Euclid Avenue Presbyterian Church, 11205 Euclid Ave., Cleveland, 3/12/80, C, a, 80002977

Fairhill Road Village Historic District, 12309-12511 Fairhill Rd., Cleveland, 5/10/90, A, C, 90000758

Fairmount Boulevard District, 2485-3121 Fairmount Blvd., Cleveland Heights, 12/12/76, A, C, 76001391

Federal Reserve Bank Of Cleveland, E. 6th St. and Superior Ave., Cleveland, 10/08/76, C, 76001392

First Church of Christ in Euclid, 16200 Euclid Ave., East Cleveland, 11/28/78, A, C, a, 78002044

First Universalist Church of Olmsted, 5050 Porter Rd., North Olmsted, 11/25/80, A, C, a, b, 80002983

Ford Motor Company Cleveland Plant, 11610 Euclid Ave., Cleveland, 3/17/76, A, C, 76001393

Forest City Bank Building, 1400 W. Twenty-fifth St., Cleveland, 8/31/92, C, 86003827

Forest City Brewery, 6920-6922 Union Ave., Cleveland, 5/03/76, A, C, 76001394

Forest Hill Historic District, Roughly bounded by Glynn Rd., Northdale Blvd. and Cleviden Rd., Mt. Vernon Blvd. and Wyatt Rd., and Lee Blvd., Cleveland, 8/14/86, C, 86001662

Fort Hill, E of North Olmsted off OH 252, North Olmsted vicinity, 7/25/74, D, 74001460

Franklin Boulevard Historic District, Franklin Blvd. from W. 52nd to W. 38th Sts., Cleveland, 5/31/89, C, 89000430

Franklin Boulevard—West Clinton Avenue Historic District, 5207-7625 Franklin Blvd., 5802-7325 W. Clinton Ave., Cleveland, 12/06/93, C, 93001334

Frazee, Stephen, House, 7733 Canal Rd., Valley View, 5/04/76, A, C, NPS, 76000211

Froelich, John, House, 7095 Broadview Rd., Seven Hills, 7/30/74, C, 74001461

Gabel, Daniel, House, 1102 E. Ridgewood Dr., Seven Hills, 5/23/78, A, C, 78002049

Gaensslen, Phillip, House [Upper Prospect MRA], 3056 Prospect Ave., Cleveland, 11/01/84, B, C, 84000227

Garfield Memorial, 12316 Euclid Ave. in Lakeview Cemetery, Cleveland, 4/11/73, C, c, f, 73001411

Gates Mills Methodist Episcopal Church, Old Mill Rd. off U.S. 322, Gates Mills, 7/18/75, A, C, a, b, 75001367

Gates, Holsey, House, 762 Broadway, Bedford, 6/30/75, B, C, 75001354

Gifford, Dr. William, House [Upper Prospect MRA], 3047 Prospect Ave., Cleveland, 11/01/84, C, 84000228

Gleason, Edmund, Farm (Boundary Increase) [Agricultural Resources of the Cuyahoga Valley MPS], 7243 Canal Rd., Valley View vicinity, 3/12/93, A, C, NPS, 93000075

Cuyahoga County—Continued

Gleason, Edmund, House, 7243 Canal Rd., Valley View, 12/18/78, C, NPS, 78000377

Glidden, Francis K., House, 1901 Ford Dr., Cleveland, 2/08/88, C, 88000054

Goldsmith, Jacob, House, 2200 E. 40th St., Cleveland, 3/08/78, A, C, 78002039

Gordon Square Building, 6500-6616 Detroit Ave. and 1396-1490 W. 65th St., Cleveland, 4/30/85, C, 85000944

Grand Pacific Hotel, 8112 Columbia Rd., Olmsted Falls, 10/10/75, A, C, 75001369

Gwinn Estate, 12407 Lake Shore Blvd., Bratenahl, 10/01/74, A, B, C, 74001430

Hackenberg, Harvey, House, 1568 Grace Ave., Lakewood, 7/07/83, C, 83001952

Halle Building, 1228 Euclid Ave., Cleveland, 9/08/83, A, C, g, 83001953

Hangar, The, 24400 Cedar Rd., Beachwood, 1/09/86, C, 86000032

Hanna, Howard M., Jr., House, 11505 Lake Shore Blvd., Bratenahl, 7/24/74, B, C, 74001431

Hay-McKinney and Bingham-Hanna House, 10825 E. Blvd., Cleveland, 6/18/76, A, C, 76001395

Heights Rockfeller Building, 3091 Mayfield Rd., Cleveland Heights, 5/15/86, C, 86001058

Henry, Robert W., House, 6607 Pearl Rd., Parma Heights, 12/08/78, B, C, 78002048

Hessler Court Wooden Pavement, 11330 East Blvd. between Bellflower and Hessler Rds., Cleveland, 3/03/75, C, 75001362

Hilliard Apartment Building, 2804–2906 Sackett Ave., Cleveland, 3/17/87, C, 86003502

Holy Rosary Church, 12021 Mayfield Rd., Cleveland, 6/16/76, A, C, a, 76001397

Honam, John, House, 14710 Lake Ave., Lakewood, 4/13/77, A, C, b, 77001054

House of Wills [Black History TR], 2491 E. 55th St., Cleveland, 12/17/82, C, 82001367

Hoyt Block, 608 W. St. Clair St., Cleveland, 1/18/74, B, C, 74001440

Hruby Conservatory of Music, 5417 Broadway St., Cleveland, 11/29/79, A, C, 79001807

Huntington, John, Pumping Tower, 28600 Lake Rd., Bay Village, 2/29/79, B, C, 79001798

Independence Presbyterian Church, U.S. 21, Independence, 4/13/77, C, a, 77001053

Ireland, Joseph, House [Upper Prospect MRA], 2074 E. 36th St., Cleveland, 11/01/84, C, 84000229

Irishtown Bend Archeological District, Address Restricted, Cleveland vicinity, 5/25/90, A, C, D, 90000757

Jaite Mill Historic District, SE of Brecksville at Riverview and Vaughan Rds., Brecksville vicinity, 5/21/79, A, NPS, 79000288

Jennings Apartments, 2711 W. 14th St., Cleveland, 3/29/84, C, 84003618

Karamu House [Black History TR], 2355 E. 89th St., Cleveland, 12/17/82, A, g, 82001368

Kennedy Apartments and Commercial Block, 6425 Detroit Ave., Cleveland, 7/06/89, C, 85003764

Keyt, Gideon, House, Chagrin River and Deerfield Rds., Gates Mills, 6/01/82, C, 82003560

Kindra, W. H., Apartments [Brooklyn Centre MRA], 3802–2812 Mapledale Ave., Cleveland, 3/19/87, C, 87000434

Knapp, William, House, 7101 Canal Rd., Valley View, 3/19/79, A, C, NPS, 79000289

Knowlton, Dr. William A., House, 8937 Highland Dr., Brecksville, 12/04/78, A, C, 78002035

Krause Building—Otto Moser's Cafe, 2042–2044 E. Fourth St., Cleveland, 11/14/85, A, 85002834

Kuenzer, Joseph II, House, 2345 Rockside Rd., Independence vicinity, 8/13/74, C, 74001458

Kulas, E. J., Estate Historic District, W. Hill Dr., Gates Mills, 3/23/88, C, 88000206

Lay, Samuel, House, 7622 Columbia Rd., Olmstead Falls, 6/20/79, B, C, 79001814

League Park, Lexington and 66th Sts, Cleveland, 8/08/79, A, 79001808

Lindner Building, 1331 Euclid Ave., Cleveland, 9/13/78, A, C, 78002040

Lock No. 37 and Spillway [Ohio and Erie Canal TR], Fitzwater Rd., Valley View, 12/11/79, A, C, NPS, 79000290

Lock No. 38 and Spillway [Ohio and Erie Canal TR], Hillside Rd., Valley View, 12/11/79, A, C, NPS, 79000291

Lock No. 39 and Spillway [Ohio and Erie Canal TR], Canal Rd., Valley View, 12/11/79, A, C, NPS, 79000292

Lock Tender's House and Inn [Ohio and Erie Canal TR], 7104 Canal Rd., Valley View, 12/11/79, A, C, NPS, 79000293

Lorain-Carnegie Bridge, Spans Cuyahoga River between Lorain and Carnegie Aves., Cleveland, 10/08/76, A, C, g, 76001398

Lyceum Village Square And German Wallace College, Seminary St., Berea, 10/29/75, A, C, 75001356

Magnolia—Wade Park Historic District, Roughly bounded by Asbury Ave., E. 118th St., Wade Park Ave., Mistletoe Dr., Magnolia Dr., and E. 105th St., Cleveland, 10/25/90, A, C, 90001566

Malio House [Brooklyn Centre MRA], 3781 W. Twenty-fifth St., Cleveland, 3/19/87, C, 87000439

March, George, House, 126 E. Washington St., Chagrin Falls, 4/20/78, A, B, 78002037

Mather, Flora Stone, College District, Bellflower Rd. at Ford Dr., Cleveland, 2/15/74, A, C, 74001442

May Company, 158 Euclid Ave. at Public Sq., Cleveland, 1/18/74, A, C, 74001443

McKinley Terrace, 1406–1426 W. 81st St., Cleveland, 7/09/85, C, 85001527

Medical Centre Building, 1001 Huron Rd., Cleveland, 12/20/84, A, C, 84000621

Merwin, George, House, 3028 Prospect Ave., Cleveland, 6/04/73, C, b, 73001412

Miles Park Historic District, Miles Park Ave. around Miles Park, Cleveland, 5/17/74, A, C, a, 74001444

Miller Block, 3202-3214 Lorain Ave., Cleveland, 7/19/84, C, 84003624

Montana Apartments [Upper Prospect MRA], 2061 E. 36th St., Cleveland, 11/01/84, C, 84000230

Morgan, Garrett, House [Black History TR], 5202 Harlem Ave., Cleveland, 12/17/82, B, 82001369

Murray Hill School, 2026 Murray Hill Rd. and 2043 Random Rd., Cleveland, 4/28/88, A, C, 88000436

Neff Apartments [Upper Prospect MRA], 3606 Prospect Ave., Cleveland, 11/01/84, C, 84000231

Nela Park, Entrance at 1901 Noble Rd., East Cleveland, 5/29/75, A, C, 75001365

Newton Avenue Historic District, 9700–10003 Newton Ave., Cleveland, 8/31/88, C, 88001298

Nicholson, James, House, 13335 Detroit Ave, Lakewood, 8/24/79, B, C, 79001813

North Olmsted Town Hall, 5186 Dover Center Rd., North Olmsted, 11/25/80, A, g, 80002984

North Presbyterian Church, 4001 Superior Ave., Cleveland, 10/29/74, A, C, a, 74001445

North Union Shaker Site, Address Restricted, Cleveland vicinity, 8/13/74, D, 74001446

Northrop, Julia Carter, House, 7872 Columbia Rd., Olmsted Falls, 10/14/75, B, C, 75001370

Notre Dame Academy, 1325 Ansel Rd., Cleveland, 5/26/88, C, a, 88000637

Notre Dame College of Ohio, 4545 College Rd., South Euclid, 12/08/83, C, 83004267

Ohio Bell Henderson-Endicott Exchange Building [Upper Prospect MRA], 5400-5420 Prospect Ave., Cleveland, 11/01/84, A, C, 84000232

Ohio City Preservation District, Bounded by W. 26th, Clinton, W. 38th, and Carroll Sts., Cleveland, 10/09/74, A, C, 74001447

Ohio City Preservation District (Boundary Increase), Roughly Franklin Blvd. NW., W. 38th St., Bridge Ave. NW., & W. 44th St., & Stone, W. 25th, Bridge Ave. NW., & W. 28th, Cleveland, 5/25/89, C, 89000435

Ohio and Erie Canal, OH 631, Valley View Village, 11/13/66, A, NHL, NPS, 66000607

Old Center School, 784 S.O.M. Center Rd., Mayfield Village, 4/03/73, C, 73001426

Old District 10 Schoolhouse, Corner of Sheldon and Fry Rds., Middleburg Heights, 10/15/73, A, C, 73001427

Old Euclid District 4 Schoolhouse, Richmond Rd., Lyndhurst, 4/16/80, A, 80002982

Old Federal Building and Post Office, 201 Superior Ave., NE, Cleveland, 5/03/74, C, 74001448

Old Stone Church, 91 Public Sq., Cleveland, 2/23/73, C, a, 73001414

Olney, Charles, House and Gallery, 2241–2255 W. Fourteenth St., Cleveland, 6/06/88, A, B, C, 88000633

Overlook Road Carriage House District, 1–5 Herrick Mews, Cleveland Heights, 5/06/74, B, C, 74001449

Packard-Doubler House, 7634 Riverview Rd., Independence, 3/09/79, A, C, NPS, 79000294

Panek Block, 3154 E. Fourty-ninth St., Cleveland, 12/18/86, C, 86003503

Peerless Motor Company Plant No. 1, 9400 Quincy Ave., Cleveland, 5/29/75, A, C, 75001364

Cuyahoga County—Continued

Perry-Payne Building, 740 Superior Ave., Cleveland, 7/16/73, C, 73001415

Pickands, Jay M., House, 9619 Lake Shore Blvd, Bratenahl, 8/24/79, C, 79001799

Pilgrim Congregational Church, 2592 W. 14th St., Cleveland, 3/17/76, A, C, a, 76001399

Playhouse Square Group, 2067 E. 14th St.; 1422, 1501, 1515, 1621 Euclid Ave., Cleveland, 10/05/78, A, C, 78002041

Plaza Apartments [Upper Prospect MRA], 3206 Prospect ave., Cleveland, 11/01/84, C, 84000233

Pomeroy, Alanson, House, Pearl Rd. at Westwood Dr., Strongsville, 6/20/75, B, C, 75001371

Prospect Avenue Row House Group, 3645, 3649, 3651, 3657 Prospect Ave., Cleveland, 3/27/74, C, 74001450

Quad Hill, 7500 Euclid Ave., Cleveland, 5/26/88, C, 88000642

Rich, Charles B., House, 9367 Brecksville Rd., Brecksville, 2/22/79, A, C, NPS, 79000295

Riverside Cemetery Building [Brooklyn Centre MRA], 3607 W. Twenty-fifth St., Cleveland, 3/19/87, C, 87000445

Riverside Cemetery Chapel [Brooklyn Centre MRA], 3607 Pearl Rd., Cleveland, 3/19/87, C, a, 87000446

Rockefeller Building, 614 Superior Ave., Cleveland, 6/04/73, C, 73001416

Rockefeller Park Bridges, Rockefeller Park, Cleveland, 9/27/77, C, 77001051

Rocket Engine Test Facility, Lewis Research Center, Cleveland, 10/03/85, A, C, g, NHL, 85002800

Root and McBride-Bradley Building, 1220-1230 W. 6th St., Cleveland, 7/18/80, A, C, 80002978

Schweinfurth, Charles, House, 1915 E. 75th St., Cleveland, 5/22/73, B, C, 73001417

Shaker Square, Shaker and Moreland Blvds., Cleveland, 7/01/76, A, C, g, 76001400

Shaker Square Historic District (Boundary Increase), Shaker and Moreland Blvds., Cleveland, 12/09/83, A, C, 83004367

Shaker Village Historic District, Roughly bounded by Fairmount and Lomond Blvds., Green, Warrensville Center, Becket, and Coventry Rds., Shaker Heights, 5/31/84, A, B, C, 84003650

Shaker Village Historic District, Roughly bounded by Fairmount and Lomand Blvds., Green, Warrensville Center, Becket and Coventry Rd., Shaker Heights, 5/31/84, A, C, D, 84003882

Shiloh Baptist Church [Black History TR], 5500 Scovill Ave., Cleveland, 12/17/82, C, a, 82001371

Snow, Russ and Holland, Houses, 12911 and 13114 Snowville Rd., Brecksville, 9/28/82, A, C, NPS, 82001873

Society for Savings Building, Public Sq., Cleveland, 11/07/76, C, 76001401

South Park Site, Address Restricted, Independence vicinity, 6/22/76, D, NPS, 76000212

Southworth House [Upper Prospect MRA], 3334 Prospect Ave., Cleveland, 11/01/84, B, C, 84000234

St. Elizabeth's Magyar Roman Catholic Church, 9016 Buckeye Rd., Cleveland, 1/30/76, A, C, a, 76001402

St. Ignatius High School, 1911 W. 30th St. at Carroll Ave., Cleveland, 1/21/74, A, C, a, 74001451

St. John's AME Church [Black History TR], 2261 E. 40th St., Cleveland, 12/17/82, C, a, 82001370

St. John's Episcopal Church, 2600 Church St., Cleveland, 2/23/73, A, a, 73001418

St. Joseph's Church and Friary, 2543 E. 23rd St. at Woodland, Cleveland, 6/17/76, A, C, a, 76001403

St. Michael the Archangel Catholic Church, 3114 Scranton Rd., Cleveland, 1/18/74, A, C, a, 74001452

St. Paul's Episcopal Church, 4120 Euclid Ave., Cleveland, 11/25/80, C, a, 80002979

St. Paul's Episcopal Church of East Cleveland, 15837 Euclid Ave., East Cleveland, 10/18/84, C, a, 84000130

St. Stanislaus Church, Forman and E. 65th Sts., Cleveland, 6/22/76, A, C, a, 76001404

St. Stephen Church, 1930 W. 54th St., Cleveland, 11/25/77, C, a, 77001052

St. Theodosius Russian Orthodox Cathedral, 733 Starkweather Ave., Cleveland, 1/18/74, A, C, a, 74001453

Stager-Beckwith House, 3813 Euclid Ave., Cleveland, 4/20/78, A, C, 78002042

Station Road Bridge, E of Brecksville at Cuyahoga River, Brecksville vicinity, 3/07/79, C, NPS, 79000312

Stearns, Lyman, Farm, 6975 Ridge Rd., Parma, 10/01/81, A, 81000431

Stockbridge Apartment Building, 3328 Euclid Ave., Cleveland, 8/08/85, B, C, 85001693

Stone, Valerius C., House, 21706 Lunn Rd., Strongsville, 12/22/78, C, 78002050

Stoneman, Joseph, House, 18 E. Orange St., Chagrin Falls, 5/29/75, B, C, 75001358

Strong, John Stoughton, House, 18910 Westwood St., Strongsville, 11/24/80, B, 80002985

Superior Avenue Viaduct, Superior Ave., Cleveland, 6/09/78, A, C, 78002043

Tavern Club [Upper Prospect MRA], 3522 Prospect Ave., Cleveland, 11/01/84, C, 84000235

Taylor Mansion—Lakehurst, 193 Bratenahl Rd., Bratenahl, 7/10/86, B, C, a, 86001573

Telling, William E., House, 4645 Mayfield Rd., South Euclid, 10/16/74, C, 74001463

Templar-Farrell Motor Sales Building [Upper Prospect MRA], 3134 Prospect Ave., Cleveland, 11/01/84, A, C, 84000237

Temple on the Heights, 3130 Mayfield Rd., Cleveland Heights, 3/29/84, A, C, a, 84003653

Temple, The, University Circle at Silver Park, Cleveland, 8/30/74, A, C, a, 74001455

Terra Vista Archeological District, Address Restricted, Independence vicinity, 5/23/78, D, NPS, 78000378

Third Church of Christ Scientist [Brooklyn Centre MRA], 3648 W. Twenty-fifth St., Cleveland, 3/19/87, C, a, 87000444

Thorp, W. A., House, 6183–6185 Mayfield Rd., Mayfield Heights, 12/04/78, C, 78002046

Tiedemann, Hannes, House, 4308 Franklin Blvd., Cleveland, 3/15/82, A, C, 82004417

Tinkers Creek Aqueduct [Ohio and Erie Canal TR], Tinkers Creek, Valley View, 12/11/79, A, C, NPS, 79000296

Townes, Clayton, House [Brooklyn Centre MRA], 3800 W. Thirty-third St., Cleveland, 3/19/87, B, C, 87000435

Tremaine-Gallagher Residence, 3001 Fairmount Blvd., Cleveland Heights, 10/30/73, A, C, 73001419

Trinity Cathedral, Euclid Ave. at E. 22nd St., Cleveland, 6/04/73, C, 73001420

Trinity Cathedral Church Home [Upper Prospect MRA], 2227 Prospect Ave., Cleveland, 11/01/84, C, a, 84000239

USS COD (submarine), N. Marginal Dr., Cleveland, 1/14/86, A, g, NHL, 86000088

Ulyatt, Abraham, House, 6579 Canal Rd., Valley View, 2/27/79, C, NPS, 79000297

Union Club, 1211 Euclid Ave., Cleveland, 2/15/74, C, 74001456

Union Steel Screw Office Building, 1675-7 E. 40th St., Cleveland, 1/13/89, A, 88003193

Union Terminal Group, Public Sq., Cleveland, 3/17/76, A, C, g, 76001405

United Motor Service Building [Upper Prospect MRA], 4019 Prospect Ave., Cleveland, 11/01/84, C, 84000240

Universal Terminal Company Dock and Warehouse, 5451 N. Marginal Rd., Cleveland, 9/08/83, A, 83001954

University Hall, Cleveland State University, 2605 Euclid Ave., Cleveland, 2/06/73, C, 73001421

Upson-Walton Company Building, 1310 Old River Rd. (W. 11th St.), Cleveland, 1/21/74, A, C, 74001457

Valley Railway Historic District, Cuyahoga Valley between Rockside Rd. at Cuyahoga National Recreation Area and Howard St. at Little Cuyahoga Valley, Independence to Akron, 5/17/85, A, 85001123

Variety Store Building and Theatre, 11801-11825 Lorain Ave., Cleveland, 4/01/82, A, C, 82003559

Vaughn Site (33CU65), Address Restricted, Brecksville vicinity, 11/12/87, D, NPS, 87001902

Vaughn, Richard, Farm [Agricultural Resources of the Cuyahoga Valley MPS], 9570 Riverview Rd., Brecksville vicinity, 3/12/93, A, C, NPS, 93000081

Venice Building, 8401–8417 Euclid Ave., Cleveland, 10/01/90, C, 90001496

Wade Memorial Chapel, 12316 Euclid Ave., inside Lakeview Cemetery, Cleveland, 6/18/73, C, a, 73001422

Wade Park District, Roughly bounded by E. 105 St., East Blvd., Chester and Euclid Aves., Cleveland, 10/02/82, C, 82001372

Walker and Weeks Office Building [Upper Prospect MRA], 2341 Carnegie Ave., Cleveland, 11/01/84, C, 84000259

Warren, Moses, House, 3535 Ingleside Rd., Shaker Heights, 10/22/74, B, C, 74001462

Warszawa Neighborhood District, E. 65th St. and Forman Ave., Cleveland, 11/28/80, A, C, a, 80002980

Cuyahoga County—Continued

Watterson School, 1422 W. 74th St., Cleveland, 10/08/92, C, 92001354

Weizer Building, 8935 Buckeye Rd., Cleveland, 2/08/88, A, C, 88000055

West Side Market, W. 24th St. and Lorain Ave., Cleveland, 12/18/73, A, C, 73001423

Western Reserve Building, 1468 W. 9th St., Cleveland, 10/30/73, A, C, 73001424

Westlake Hotel, 19000 Lake Rd., Rocky River, 10/20/83, A, 83004278

Wheatley, Phillis, Association, 4450 Cedar Ave., Cleveland, 8/24/79, A, C, 79001809

Wheeler, John, House, 445 S. Rocky River Dr., Berea, 12/01/78, B, C, 78002034

White, Henry P., House, NW corner of Euclid Ave. and E. 90th St., Cleveland, 7/16/73, C, 73001425

Whitney, George W., House, 330 S. Rocky River Dr., Berea, 10/22/74, A, B, C, 74001429

Wilson Feed Mill [Ohio and Erie Canal TR], 7604 Canal Rd., Valley View, 12/17/79, A, C, NPS, 79000298

Wilson's Mills Settlement District, Chagrin River Rd., Gates Mills, 5/29/80, A, a, 80002981

Woodland Avenue and West Side Railroad Powerhouse, 1180 Cathan Ave., NW, Cleveland, 6/04/79, A, C, 79001810

Woodland Cemetery, 6901 Woodland Ave., Cleveland, 6/04/86, A, C, d, 86001253

Zero Gravity Research Facility (B-2), Lewis Research Center, Cleveland, 10/03/85, A, C, g, NHL, 85002801

Zion Lutheran Church [Upper Prospect MRA], 2062 E. 30th St., Cleveland, 11/01/84, A, C, a, 84000261

Zion Lutheran School [Upper Prospect MRA], 2074 E. 30th St., Cleveland, 11/01/84, C, 84000264

Darke County

Bear's Mill, 5 mi. W of Greenville off U.S. 36 on Bear Mill Rd., Greenville vicinity, 6/10/75, A, C, 75001372

Beir, Anna, House, 214 E. 4th St., Greenville, 4/11/77, B, C, 77001055

Brown Township Building, Main and Weller Sts., Ansonia, 8/30/83, A, C, g, 83001955

Carnegie Library and Henry St. Clair Memorial Hall, 520 Sycamore St. and W. 4th St., Greenville, 11/26/80, B, C, 80002986

Coppess, Benjamin Franklin House, 209 Washington St., Greenville, 3/10/78, C, 78002052

Darke County Courthouse, Sheriff's House, And Jail, 4th and Broadway, Greenville, 12/12/76, C, 76001409

English, William, House, 11291 OH 47, Versailles vicinity, 6/02/82, C, d, 82003562

Fort Jefferson Site, OH 121, Fort Jefferson, 11/10/70, A, 70000488

Garst House, 205 N. Broadway, Greenville, 11/16/77, A, C, 77001056

Greenville Mausoleum, West St., Greenville Cemetery, Greenville, 10/21/76, C, d, 76001410

Greenville South Broadway Commercial District, Roughly S. Broadway from Main to Washington and Martin Sts., Greenville, 3/01/84, A, C, 84003657

Holy Family Catholic Church [Cross-Tipped Churches of Ohio TR], OH 185, Frenchtown, 7/26/79, A, C, a, 79002817

Lambert-Parent House, 631 E. Elm St., Union City, 5/23/80, B, C, 80002987

Lansdowne House, 338 E. 3rd St., Greenville, 4/20/79, B, 79001824

Leftwich House, 203 S. Washington St., Greenville, 10/21/75, C, 75001373

Robeson, Dr. Donovan, House, 330 W. 4th St., Greenville, 12/12/76, C, 76001411

St. Louis Catholic Church and Rectory [Cross-Tipped Churches of Ohio TR], E of U.S. 127, North Star vicinity, 7/26/79, C, a, 79002835

St. Nicholas Catholic Church and Rectory [Cross-Tipped Churches of Ohio TR], OH 705 and Washington St., Osgood, 7/26/79, A, C, a, 79002841

St. Peter Evangelical Lutheran Church, S of Versailles on St. Peter Rd., Versailles vicinity, 6/04/80, A, C, a, 80002988

Studebaker-Scott House And Beehive School, S of Greenville on OH 49, Greenville vicinity, 6/15/78, B, C, 78002053

Versailles Town Hall and Wayne Township House, 4 W. Main St., Versailles, 2/18/81, A, C, 81000432

Walker, Cristopher C., House and Farm, SW of New Madison, N of OH 121, New Madison vicinity, 4/07/82, A, C, 82003561

Waring House, 304 W. 3rd St., Greenville, 9/16/77, C, 77001057

Defiance County

Brooke Site, Address Restricted, Defiance vicinity, 1/01/76, D, 76001412

Defiance Public Library, 320 Fort St., Defiance, 10/31/85, A, C, 85003446

Eagles Building, 575 Broadway, Lorain, 4/24/86, A, C, 86000850

East Side Fire Station, Douglas and Hopkins Sts., Defiance, 12/12/76, A, 76001413

Fort Defiance Park, Fort St., Defiance, 6/23/80, A, 80002989

Holgate Avenue Historic District, 328–716 Holgate Ave., Defiance, 10/11/90, B, C, 90001497

Latty, Judge Alexander, House, 718 Perry St., Defiance, 1/25/91, B, C, 90002214

Riverside Chapel, S. Clinton St. in Riverside Cemetery, Defiance, 4/11/77, C, a, 77001058

St. Paul's Episcopal Church, High St., Hicksville, 6/07/76, C, a, 76001414

Delaware County

Austin Hall [Ohio Wesleyan University TR], OWU, W. Central Ave. & Elizabeth St., Delaware, 3/18/85, A, C, 85000631

Bieber, George, House and Farm [Historic Mill-Related Resources of Liberty and Delaware Townships MPS], 2010 Stratford Rd., Delaware vicinity, 10/03/91, A, B, C, 91001426

Building at 101 North Franklin Street [Eastlake Houses of Ashley TR], 101 N. Franklin St., Ashley, 11/25/80, C, 80002990

Building at 223 West High Street [Eastlake Houses of Ashley TR], 223 W. High St., Ashley, 11/25/80, C, 80002991

Building at 500 East High Street [Eastlake Houses of Ashley TR], 500 E. High St., Ashley, 11/25/80, C, 80002992

Building at 505 East High Street [Eastlake Houses of Ashley TR], 505 E. High St., Ashley, 11/25/80, C, 80002993

Center Inn, SE of Sunbury on OH 37, Sunbury vicinity, 1/11/83, C, 83001956

Chambers Road Covered Bridge, 1.5 mi. NE of Olive Green, Olive Green vicinity, 11/21/74, C, 74001465

Cook, John, Farm, E of Harlem at Miller Paul Rd. and Gorsuch Rd., Harlem vicinity, 4/11/77, A, 77001059

Cooper, Samuel, Farmhouse, 695 Lawrence Rd., Radnor vicinity, 5/06/93, C, 93000395

Curtiss, Marcus, Inn, E of Galena at 3860 Sunbury Rd., Galena vicinity, 12/12/76, A, C, 76001415

Delaware County Courthouse, N. Sandusky St. and Central Ave., Delaware, 5/22/73, C, 73001429

Delaware County Jail and Sheriff's Residence, 20 W. Central Ave., Delaware, 7/12/90, A, C, 90001083

Delaware Public Library, 101 N. Sandusky St., Delaware, 1/11/83, A, C, 83001957

Detwiller, John, Tavern and Farmstead, 2877 N. OH 257, Radnor, 4/16/93, A, C, 93000294

Edwards Gymnasium/Pfieffer Natatorium [Ohio Wesleyan University TR], OWU Main Campus, S. Sandusky St., Delaware, 3/18/85, A, B, C, 85000632

Elliott Hall, Sturges Library, And Merrick Hall, Ohio Wesleyan University campus, Delaware, 4/23/73, A, C, b, 73001430

Felkner—Anderson House, 9716 Fontanelle Rd., Ostrander vicinity, 2/11/88, C, 88000074

Greenwood Farms, S of Delaware off U.S. 42, Delaware vicinity, 4/17/79, B, C, 79001825

High House, 2360 Panhandle Rd., Delaware vicinity, 2/13/86, C, 86000238

Highbank Park Works, Address Restricted, Worthington vicinity, 2/15/74, D, 74001466

Highbanks Metropolitan Park Mounds I and II, Address Restricted, Powell vicinity, 3/19/75, D, 75001375

Keeler, Diadatus, House, SE of Galena at 4567 Red Bank Rd., Galena vicinity, 2/29/79, C, 79001826

Lewis, Samuel, Farmhouse, 5979 Radnor Rd., Radnor vicinity, 4/16/93, C, 93000295

Limestone Vale, 3490 Olentangy River Rd., Delaware vicinity, 10/02/78, C, 78002055

Meeker, Forrest, House and Farm [Historic Mill-Related Resources of Liberty and Delaware

Delaware County—Continued

Townships MPS], 2690 Stratford Rd., Delaware vicinity, 10/03/91, A, B, C, 91001427

Mill Worker House No. 1 [Historic Mill-Related Resources of Liberty and Delaware Townships MPS], 2665 Stratford Rd., Delaware vicinity, 10/03/91, A, C, 91001431

Mill Worker House No. 3 [Historic Mill-Related Resources of Liberty and Delaware Townships MPS], 2505 Stratford Rd., Delaware vicinity, 10/03/91, A, C, 91001433

Mill Worker House No. 4 [Historic Mill-Related Resources of Liberty and Delaware Townships MPS], 2441 Stratford Rd., Delaware vicinity, 10/03/91, A, C, 91001434

Mill Worker House No. 5 [Historic Mill-Related Resources of Liberty and Delaware Townships MPS], 2441 Stratford Rd., Delaware vicinity, 10/03/91, A, C, 91001435

Neff, Edward E., House, 123 N. Franklin St., Delaware, 1/28/88, C, 87002546

O'Shaughnessy Dam and Bridge, Co. Rd. 126 between OH 257 and 745, Shawnee Hills vicinity, 7/05/90, A, C, 90000482

Ohio Wesleyan University Student Observatory [Ohio Wesleyan University TR], OWU, W. William St., Delaware, 3/18/85, A, C, 85000633

Perry, Norman Dewey, House [Historic Mill-Related Resources of Liberty and Delaware Townships MPS], 2367 Stratford Rd., Delaware vicinity, 10/03/91, A, B, C, 91001429

Richey, James, Farmhouse, 1395 South OH 257, Delaware vicinity, 9/02/93, C, 93000891

Sanborn Hall [Ohio Wesleyan University TR], OWU, W. Campus, Delaware, 3/18/85, A, C, 85000634

Sandusky Street Historic District, 44 S. to 92 N. Sandusky, 46 E. to 31 W. Winter, and 9 E. to 17 W. William, Delaware, 12/17/82, A, C, 82001373

Selby Field [Ohio Wesleyan University TR], OWU, Henry St., Delaware, 3/18/85, A, C, 85000635

Sharp, Samuel, House, 7436 Horseshoe Rd., Ashley vicinity, 7/29/82, C, 82003563

Sharp, Stephen, House, 8025 Africa Rd, Westerville vicinity, 9/30/82, C, 82003564

Slocum Hall [Ohio Wesleyan University TR], OWU Main Campus, Sandusky St., Delaware, 3/18/85, A, C, 85000636

Spruce Run Earthworks, Address Restricted, Galena vicinity, 7/16/73, D, 73001431

St. Mary's Church and Rectory, 82 E. William St., Delaware, 5/23/80, C, a, 80002994

Stratford Methodist Episcopal Church [Historic Mill-Related Resources of Liberty and Delaware Townships MPS], Jct. of US 23 and OH 315, Delaware vicinity, 10/03/91, A, a, 91001436

Stuyvesant Hall [Ohio Wesleyan University TR], OWU, W. William St., Delaware, 3/18/85, A, C, 85000637

Sunbury Tavern, NW corner OH 37 and Galena Rd., Sunbury, 2/24/75, C, 75001376

Sunbury Township Hall, Town Sq., Sunbury, 2/20/75, C, 75001377

Ufferman Site, Address Restricted, Delaware vicinity, 7/24/74, D, 74001464

University Hall-Gray's Chapel [Ohio Wesleyan University TR], OWU Main Campus, Sandusky St., Delaware, 3/18/85, A, C, 85000638

Van Deman, Henry, House, 6 Darlington Rd., Delaware, 5/31/84, B, C, 84003662

Warren Tavern Complex, U.S. 36, Delaware vicinity, 8/03/83, C, 83001958

Erie County

Abbott-Page House, 2.5 mi. NE of Milan on Mason Rd., Milan vicinity, 5/27/75, B, C, 75001383

Adams Street Double House, 106–108 E. Adams St., Sandusky, 10/10/75, C, 75001384

Andrews, Ebenezer, House, 200 S. Main St., Milan, 7/25/74, B, C, 74001467

BOECKLING, G.A., (side-paddlewheel steamboat), Jackson Street Dock, Sandusky, 3/03/83, A, 83001959

Barker School [Sandusky MRA], 1925 Barker St., Sandusky, 10/20/82, C, 82001374

Barney, Freeland T., House [Sandusky MRA], 215-213 Fulton St., Sandusky, 10/20/82, C, 82001375

Bates-Cockrem House [Sandusky MRA], 325 Lawrence St., Sandusky, 10/20/82, A, 82001376

Bavarian Brewery [Sandusky MRA], 1816-1820 W. Jefferson St., Sandusky, 10/20/82, A, 82001377

Beatty, Louis, House, South Shore Dr., Kelleys Island, 10/25/84, B, C, 84000106

Beecher, Lucas, House, 215 W. Washington Row, Sandusky, 5/07/79, B, C, 79001827

Bing's Hotel [Sandusky MRA], 302 E. Water St., Sandusky, 10/20/82, A, C, 82001378

Boalt, John, House [Sandusky MRA], 631 Wayne St., Sandusky, 10/20/82, C, 82001379

Boeckling Building [Sandusky MRA], 103-105 W. Shoreline Dr., Sandusky, 10/20/82, B, C, 82001380

Boeckling, G. A., House [Sandusky MRA], 614 Columbus Ave., Sandusky, 1/20/83, A, B, C, 83001960

Boy with the Boot Fountain [Sandusky MRA], W. Washington St. Park, Sandusky, 10/20/82, C, 82001381

Butler, Cyrus, House, Edison Hwy., Birmingham, 3/17/76, B, C, 76001416

Cable Park Historic District, 1103–1234 Wayne St., Sandusky, 1/21/88, A, C, 87002506

Cable, Frank, House [Sandusky MRA], 809 W. Washington St., Sandusky, 10/20/82, C, 82001382

Cable, Laurence House [Sandusky MRA], 910 W. Monroe St., Sandusky, 10/20/82, B, C, 82001383

Campbell School [Sandusky MRA], 1215 Campbell St., Sandusky, 10/20/82, A, C, 82001384

Carnegie Library, Adams and Columbus Ave., Sandusky, 11/12/75, A, C, 75001385

Cedar Point Light [U.S. Coast Guard Lighthouses and Light Stations on the Great Lakes TR], Cedar Point, Sandusky, 7/19/84, A, C, 84003667

Christ Episcopal Church, Park and Ohio Sts., Huron, 3/04/75, A, C, a, 75001379

Coliseum [Sandusky MRA], Midway at Cedar Point, Sandusky, 10/20/82, A, C, 82001385

Columbus Avenue Historic District [Sandusky MRA], 102-162 Columbus Ave., Sandusky, 1/20/83, A, C, 83001961

Commercial Banking & Trust Co. [Sandusky MRA], 115 E. Washington Row, Sandusky, 10/20/82, C, a, 82001386

Converse-Mertz Apartments [Sandusky MRA], 301-303 E. Washington St., Sandusky, 10/20/82, C, 82001388

Cooke, Eleutheros, House [Sandusky MRA], 1415 Columbus Ave., Sandusky, 10/20/82, C, 82001389

Cooke, Eleutheros, House [Sandusky MRA], 410 Columbus Ave., Sandusky, 10/20/82, C, 82001390

Cooke-Robertson House [Sandusky MRA], 412 Columbus Ave., Sandusky, 10/20/82, C, 82001387

Curtis, William D., House [Sandusky MRA], 1411 Hayes Ave., Sandusky, 10/20/82, A, 82001391

Dentzel, William H., 1921 Carousel [Sandusky MRA], Frontiertown, Cedar Point Amusement Park, Sandusky, 11/08/90, A, b, 90000627

Dentzel, William H., 1924 Carousel [Sandusky MRA], Kiddieland, Cedar Point Amusement Park, Sandusky, 11/08/90, C, b, 90000625

Doerzbach, George J., House, 1208–1210 Central Ave., Sandusky, 4/23/87, C, 87000639

Edison, Thomas Alva, Birthplace, Edison Dr., Milan, 10/15/66, B, c, NHL, 66000608

Emmanuel Church [Sandusky MRA], 334 Columbus Ave., Sandusky, 10/20/82, A, a, 82001392

Engels And Krudwig Wine Company Buildings, 220 E. Water St., Sandusky, 7/30/76, A, C, 76001417

Engels, Herman, House [Sandusky MRA], 117 Hancock St., Sandusky, 10/20/82, B, 82001393

Engine House No. 1 [Sandusky MRA], 901 W. Market St., Sandusky, 10/20/82, A, C, 82001394

Engine House No. 3, Meigs St. and Sycamore Line, Sandusky, 4/01/75, A, C, 75001386

Erie County Infirmary, S of Sandusky on Columbus Rd., Sandusky vicinity, 9/05/75, A, C, 75001387

Erie County Jail [Sandusky MRA], 204 W. Adams St., Sandusky, 10/20/82, C, 82001395

Erie County Office Building, 1202 Sycamore Line, Sandusky, 11/20/74, A, C, 74001470

Erie County Oil Products Co. [Sandusky MRA], 649 Tiffin Ave., Sandusky, 10/20/82, A, 82001396

Exchange Hotel, 202–204 E. Water St., Sandusky, 10/29/85, B, C, 75001388

FRANCIS, JOSEPH, IRON SURF BOAT, 480 Main St, Vermilion, 9/13/79, A, 79001829

Facer's Store [Sandusky MRA], 279 E. Market St., Sandusky, 10/20/82, B, C, 82001397

First Church of Christ Scientist [Sandusky MRA], 128 E. Adams St., Sandusky, 10/20/82, C, 82001398

First Congregational Church [Sandusky MRA], 431 Columbus Ave., Sandusky, 10/20/82, C, 82001399

Erie County—Continued

Florence Corners School, OH 113 at Division St., Florence, 3/19/75, A, C, 75001378

Follett-Moss-Moss Residences, 404, 414, 428 Wayne St., Sandusky, 12/31/74, B, C, 74001471

Fox's Brewery-Diamond Wine Co. [Sandusky MRA], 334 Harrison St., Sandusky, 10/20/82, A, 82001400

Godfrey-Johnson House [Sandusky MRA], 417 Columbus Ave., Sandusky, 10/20/82, C, 82001401

Grace Episcopal Church [Sandusky MRA], 315 Wayne St., Sandusky, 10/20/82, A, a, 82001402

Graefe, Henry, House [Sandusky MRA], 1429 Columbus Ave., Sandusky, 10/20/82, C, 82001403

Great American Racing Derby [Sandusky MRA], Midway, Cedar Point Amusement Park, Sandusky, 11/08/90, C, b, 90000626

Harper, Rice, House [Sandusky MRA], 403 E. Washington St., Sandusky, 10/20/82, A, B, 82001404

Hemminger Saloon [Sandusky MRA], 333 W. Market St., Sandusky, 10/20/82, C, 82001405

Hinde & Dauch Paper Co. [Sandusky MRA], 409 W. Water St., Sandusky, 10/20/82, A, 82001406

Hinde & Dauch Paper Co. [Sandusky MRA], 401 W. Shoreline Dr., Sandusky, 10/20/82, A, 82001407

Hinde & Dauch Paper Co. [Sandusky MRA], 407 Decatur St., Sandusky, 10/20/82, A, 82001408

Hinde, James J., House [Sandusky MRA], 317 Fulton St., Sandusky, 10/20/82, B, C, 82001409

Holy Angels Church [Sandusky MRA], W. Jefferson St. at Tiffin Ave. and Clinton St., Sandusky, 10/20/82, C, a, 82001410

Hotel Breakers, Cedar Point, Sandusky, 4/22/82, A, C, NHL, 82003565

Hubbard, Lester, House [Sandusky MRA], 134 E. Adams St., Sandusky, 10/20/82, C, 82001411

Hubbard, S. B., House [Sandusky MRA], 1205 Columbus Ave., Sandusky, 10/20/82, C, 82001412

Inscription Rock, Kelleys Island, Kelleys Island vicinity, 6/18/73, C, D, 73001432

Jackson Jr. High School [Sandusky MRA], 414 W. Madison St., Sandusky, 10/20/82, A, 82001413

Jenkins-Perry House, 37 W. Front St., Milan, 10/29/74, C, 74001468

Kelleys Island Historic District (Boundary Increase), Address Restricted, Kelleys Island, 12/15/88, A, C, D, 88002734

Kelleys Island South Shore District, Water St., S side of Kelleys Island, Kelleys Island, 3/27/75, A, C, 75001380

Kerber's Marine Grocery [Sandusky MRA], 1006 Tiffin Ave., Sandusky, 10/20/82, A, 82001414

Kuebeler, August, House [Sandusky MRA], 1319 Tiffin Ave., Sandusky, 10/20/82, C, 82001416

Kuebeler-Stang Block [Sandusky MRA], 634 Hancock St., Sandusky, 10/20/82, A, C, 82001415

Lake Shore And Michigan Southern Railroad Depot, N. Depot at Carr St., Sandusky, 7/17/75, A, C, 75001389

Lane, Ebenezer, House [Sandusky MRA], 318 Huron Ave., Sandusky, 10/20/82, C, 82001417

Lea Block [Sandusky MRA], 174-186 E. Market St., Sandusky, 10/20/82, C, 82001418

Lockwood, J. C., House, 30 Edison Dr., Milan, 12/04/74, B, C, 74001469

Lotz, Henry, Stone [Sandusky MRA], 1119 W. Washington St., Sandusky, 10/20/82, A, 82001419

Mad River Block, 1002-1018 W. Adams St., Sandusky, 10/16/74, A, C, 74001472

Mallory, Ogden, House [Sandusky MRA], 410 Warren St., Sandusky, 10/20/82, C, 82001420

March, George, House [Sandusky MRA], 532 Wayne St., Sandusky, 10/20/82, C, 82001421

Marshall, James E., House [Sandusky MRA], 514 Wayne St., Sandusky, 10/20/82, A, B, C, 82001422

McKenster-Groff House [Sandusky MRA], 334 E. Washington St., Sandusky, 10/20/82, C, 82001423

Melville-Milne, William Gordon, House, 319 Lawrence St., Sandusky, 3/28/79, A, C, 79001828

Mertz, John, House, 610 W. Washington St., Sandusky, 8/21/92, C, 92001077

Milan Historic District, Main and Church Sts., both sides of Front St., and Edison Dr., Milan, 3/13/75, A, C, 75001381

Mitchell Historic District, 115–137 and 118–136 Center St., Milan, 3/13/75, C, 75001382

Monroe School [Sandusky MRA], 328 E. Monroe St., Sandusky, 10/20/82, C, 82001424

Moss-Foster House [Sandusky MRA], 621 Wayne St., Sandusky, 10/20/82, B, 82001425

Muller, Daniel C., Carousel [Sandusky MRA], Midway at Cedar Point, Sandusky, 10/20/82, A, C, 82001426

Murschel House [Sandusky MRA], 1221 N. Depot St., Sandusky, 10/20/82, A, 82001427

No. 5 Fire Station [Sandusky MRA], W. Madison and Tiffin Ave., Sandusky, 10/20/82, A, C, 82001428

Oakland Cemetery Chapel and Superintendent's House and Office, 2917 Milan Rd., Sandusky, 5/06/83, C, a, 83001962

Ohio Soldiers' And Sailors' Home, NE of Sandusky between U.S. 250 and S. Columbus Ave., Sandusky vicinity, 9/13/76, A, C, 76001418

Old First Church [Sandusky MRA], 265 Jackson St., Sandusky, 10/20/82, C, 82001430

Osborne School [Sandusky MRA], 922 W. Osborne St., Sandusky, 10/20/82, C, 82001431

Red Popcorn Wagon [Sandusky MRA], 102 W. Washington Row, Sandusky, 10/20/82, A, 82001432

Root, Joseph, House [Sandusky MRA], 231 E. Adams St., Sandusky, 10/20/82, C, 82001433

Ross Hardware [Sandusky MRA], 708 Hancock St., Sandusky, 10/20/82, C, 82001434

Schine State Theatre [Sandusky MRA], 101-109 Columbus Ave., Sandusky, 10/20/82, C, 82001435

Simpson, Walter, House [Sandusky MRA], 521 Hancock St., Sandusky, 10/20/82, C, 82001436

Simpson, William A., House [Sandusky MRA], 230 E. Washington St., Sandusky, 10/20/82, C, 82001437

Sloane, Rush R., House, 403 E. Adams St., Sandusky, 2/24/75, B, C, 75001390

Spacecraft Propulsion Research Facility, Lewis Research Center, Plum Brook Station, Sandusky, 10/03/85, A, C, g, NHL, 85002802

St. Mary's Catholic Church, 429 Central Ave., Sandusky, 10/10/75, A, C, a, 75001391

St. Mary's Girls Grade School [Sandusky MRA], 514 Decatur St., Sandusky, 10/20/82, A, 82001438

St. Mary's Rectory [Sandusky MRA], 429 Central Ave., Sandusky, 10/20/82, A, 82001439

St. Mary's School [Sandusky MRA], 410 W. Jefferson St., Sandusky, 10/20/82, A, 82001440

St.Stephens' AME Church [Sandusky MRA], 312 Neil St., Sandusky, 10/20/82, A, C, 82001441

Stang, John, House [Sandusky MRA], 629 Columbus Ave., Sandusky, 10/20/82, C, 82001442

Starr-Truscott House, OH 133, Birmingham, 4/20/78, A, C, 78002056

Stoffel, Henry, Blacksmith Shop [Sandusky MRA], 321 E. Market St. (Rear), Sandusky, 10/20/82, A, C, 82001443

Stoll, Adam J., House [Sandusky MRA], 531 Wayne St., Sandusky, 10/20/82, B, C, 82001444

Stone's Block [Sandusky MRA], 202 Columbus Ave., Sandusky, 10/20/82, C, 82001445

Sts. Peter & Paul Church and Rectory [Sandusky MRA], Columbus Ave. at E. Jefferson St., Sandusky, 1/20/83, A, C, a, 83001963

Sycamore School, 3rd and Sycamore Sts., Sandusky, 11/19/74, C, 74001473

Taylor-Frohman House [Sandusky MRA], 1315 Columbus Ave., Sandusky, 10/20/82, C, 82001446

Third National Bank [Sandusky MRA], 220 W. Market St., Sandusky, 10/20/82, C, 82001447

Townsend, William T., House [Sandusky MRA], 515 W. Washington St., Sandusky, 10/20/82, C, 82001448

U.S. Coast Guard Building [Sandusky MRA], Cedar Point, Off Perimeter Rd., Sandusky, 10/20/82, A, 82001449

U.S. Post Office [Sandusky MRA], W. Washington & Jackson Sts., Sandusky, 10/20/82, C, 82001450

Vermilion Town Hall, 736 Main St., Vermilion, 11/20/74, C, 74001474

Von Schulenburg, Ernst, House [Sandusky MRA], 922 W. Adams St., Sandusky, 10/20/82, B, C, 82001451

Wadsworth, James, House [Sandusky MRA], 519 Huron Ave., Sandusky, 10/20/82, C, 82001452

Wagner Palace [Sandusky MRA], 804-806 Hayes Ave., Sandusky, 10/20/82, C, 82001453

Water Street Commercial Buildings, 101–165 E. Water St. and 101–231 W. Water St., Sandusky, 3/18/75, A, C, 75001392

West Market School [Sandusky MRA], 211 Fulton St., Sandusky, 10/20/82, A, 82001454

White, Samuel M., House, 304 E. Adams St., Sandusky, 6/16/76, C, 76001419

White, Samuel M., house, 304 E. Adams Street, Sandusky, 6/16/76, C, 76002163

Wichman's Grocery [Sandusky MRA], 1118 W. Washington St., Sandusky, 10/20/82, A, 82001455

Erie County—Continued

Willdred Flats, 1116 Columbus Ave., Sandusky, 3/11/93, C, 93000152

Zion Lutheran Church [Sandusky MRA], 501-503 Columbus Ave., Sandusky, 10/20/82, A, C, a, 82001456

Fairfield County

Allen, Lyman, House And Barn, NW of Amanda on OH 188, Amanda vicinity, 11/18/76, C, 76001420

Artz, John, Farmhouse, 5125 Duffy Rd., Lancaster vicinity, 4/23/87, C, 87000644

Barr House, 350 W. Main St., Amanda, 11/26/80, C, 80002995

Bright, John, Covered Bridge, 2.5 mi. SW of Baltimore over Poplar Creek, Baltimore vicinity, 5/28/75, A, C, 75001393

Bush, Samuel, House, 1934 Cold Spring Dr., Lancaster, 10/01/74, C, 74001478

Chestnut Ridge Farm, 3375 Cincinnati-Zanesville Rd., SW., Lancaster vicinity, 7/24/72, C, 72001006

Concord Hall, 1445 Cincinnati-Zanesville Rd., SW. (U.S. 22), Lancaster vicinity, 10/25/72, C, 72001007

Coon Hunters Mound, Address Restricted, Carroll vicinity, 5/02/74, D, 74001475

Crawfis Institute, Crawfis and Old Sugar Grove Rds, Sugar Grove vicinity, 11/29/79, A, C, 79001833

Dilger Store, 7640 Main St., West Rushville, 8/08/85, A, C, 85001691

Dovel, J. H., Farm, 660 N. Hill Rd., Pickerington vicinity, 3/15/82, C, 82003566

Dovel—Bowers House, 380 W. Columbus St., Pickerington, 9/02/93, C, 93000890

Ety Enclosure, Address Restricted, Carroll vicinity, 7/12/74, D, 74001476

Ety Habitation Site, Address Restricted, Carroll vicinity, 7/12/74, D, 74001477

Fortner Mounds I, II, Address Restricted, Pinkerington vicinity, 7/12/74, D, 74001481

Hizey Covered Bridge, E of Pickerington on SR 235, Pickerington vicinity, 10/08/76, A, C, 76001423

Ijams, Joseph, House, Broad and Main Sts., West Rushville, 6/16/83, C, 83001965

John Bright No. 1 Iron Bridge, 2 mi. (3.2 km) NE of Carroll on Havensport Rd., Carroll vicinity, 9/20/78, A, C, 78002060

Lancaster Historic District, Roughly bounded by 5th Ave., Penn Central RR tracks, OH 33 and Tennant St., Lancaster, 8/11/83, C, 83003438

Lancaster Methodist Episcopal Camp Ground Historic District, Roughly bounded by Hocking River, W. Fair Ave., and Ety Rd., Lancaster, 9/10/87, A, C, a, 87001560

Lancaster West Main Street Historic District, W. Main St. from Columbus to Broad St., Lancaster, 2/29/79, A, C, 79001830

Lockville Canal Locks, Off Pickerington-Lockville Rd., Lockville, 9/10/74, A, 74001480

Medill, William, House, 319 N. High St., Lancaster, 3/30/78, B, b, 78002061

Miller Farm, S of Baltimore on Pleasantville Rd., Baltimore vicinity, 5/22/78, A, d, 78002058

Musser, Henry, House, SE of Baltimore at 7079 Millersport Rd., Baltimore vicinity, 5/05/78, C, 78002059

Old Maid's Orchard Mound, Address Restricted, Lithopolis vicinity, 7/15/74, D, 74001479

Pickerington Carnegie Library, 15 W. Columbus St., Pickerington, 9/02/93, A, 93000892

Pickerington Depot, 50 N. Center St., Fairfield, 7/26/90, A, 90001119

Pugh-Kittle House, 2140 Bickel Church Rd., Baltimore vicinity, 6/16/83, C, 83001964

Reber, Valentine, House, W of Lancaster at 8325 Lancaster-Circleville Rd. (OH 188), Lancaster vicinity, 7/30/75, C, 75001395

Rock Mill, Rock Mill Rd. on S bank of the Hocking R., Lancaster vicinity, 6/01/90, A, C, D, 90000850

Rock Mill Covered Bridge, SR 41, Rock Mill, 4/26/76, C, 76001424

Royalton House, Amanda Northern Rd., Royalton, 7/30/75, C, 75001396

Rushville Historic District, Bremen Ave., Main and Market Sts., Rushville, 11/24/80, C, 80002996

Schaer, Theodore B., Mound, Address Restricted, Canal Winchester vicinity, 6/20/75, D, 75001394

Sherman, John, Birthplace, 137 E. Main St., Lancaster, 10/15/66, B, c, NHL, 66000609

Square 13 Historic District, Roughly area along Broad and High Sts. between Mulberry and Chestnut Sts., Lancaster, 7/24/72, C, 72001008

St. Peter's Evangelical Lutheran Church, Broad and Mullberry Sts., Lancaster, 4/16/79, C, a, 79001831

Tallmadge-Mithoff House, 720 Lincoln Ave., Lancaster, 5/06/76, B, C, 76001422

Tarlton Cross Mound, Address Restricted, Tarlton vicinity, 11/10/70, D, 70000489

Willow Lane Farm, SW of Lancaster on U.S. 22, Lancaster vicinity, 10/26/72, C, 72001009

Winegardner Village, Address Restricted, Rushville vicinity, 7/30/74, D, 74001482

Fayette County

Burnett, William, House, 1613 US 62 SW, Washington Court House, 3/22/89, C, 89000176

Fayette County Courthouse, Main and Columbus Sts., Washington Courthouse, 7/02/73, C, 73001433

Jackson Mound, Address Restricted, Pancoastburg vicinity, 10/21/75, D, 75001397

Kelley, Barney, House, 321 E. East St., Washington Courthouse, 4/17/79, B, C, 79001834

Light, Jacob, House, 234 W. Circle Ave., Washington Court House, 1/13/89, C, 88003191

Mark Road Bridge, Mark Rd. over Sugar Cr., Staunton vicinity, 7/26/90, C, 90001118

McCafferty, William, Farmhouse, 7099 OH 207 NE, Mt. Sterling vicinity, 4/23/87, C, 87000633

Rawlings—Brownell House, 318 Rawlings St., Washington Court House, 3/10/88, B, C, 88000207

Robinson—Pavey House, 421 W. Court St., Washington Court House, 4/23/87, C, 87000638

Sharp, Morris, House, 517 Columbus St., Washington Court House, 1/21/74, C, 74001483

Smith, Edward, Jr., Farm, 2085 US 62, Washington Court House vicinity, 12/09/87, C, 87002110

Washington Court House Commercial Historic District, Roughly bounded by N. North, East, Hinde & Market Sts., Washington Court House, 9/12/85, A, C, 85002351

Woodlawn Farm, 3789 OH 41 NW, Washington Courthouse vicinity, 2/13/86, A, C, 86000237

Franklin County

Adams, Demas, House [Worthington MRA], 721 High St., Worthington, 4/17/80, B, C, 80003005

Agler-La Follette House, 2621 Sunbury Rd., Columbus vicinity, 12/14/78, C, 78002062

Alkire House, 259 N. State St., Westerville, 3/30/78, C, 78002068

American Insurance Union Citadel, 50 W. Broad St., Columbus, 3/21/75, C, 75001398

Arendt—Seymour House [Canal Winchester MPS], 53 W. Columbus St., Canal Winchester, 8/15/89, C, 89001024

Artz House [Washington Township MRA], 56 N. High St., Dublin, 4/11/79, C, 79002901

Barnhardt—Bolenbaugh House [Canal Winchester MPS], 113 E. Waterloo St., Canal Winchester, 8/15/89, C, 89001027

Beery, Dr. L. W., House [Canal Winchester MPS], 68 Washington St., Canal Winchester, 8/15/89, C, 89001033

Bergstresser Covered Bridge, W of OH 674 over Walnut Creek, Canal Winchester vicinity, 5/03/74, A, C, 74001484

Berry Brothers Bolt Works, 350 E. First Ave., Columbus, 2/19/88, A, C, D, 88000051

Boles, E., Cottage [Washington Township MRA], 5350 Hayden Run Rd., Dublin vicinity, 4/11/79, C, 79002886

Bowman, Thomas, Barn #2 [Washington Township MRA], 6665 Shier-Rings Rd., Amlin vicinity, 4/11/79, A, 79002763

Brand, Asher, Residence [Washington Township MRA], 5381 Brand Rd., Dublin vicinity, 4/11/79, C, 79002740

Brelsford-Seese House [Washington Township MRA], 129 Riverview St., Dublin, 4/11/79, A, C, 79002888

Broad Street Apartments [East Broad Street MRA], 880–886 E. Broad St., Columbus, 12/16/86, A, C, 86003404

Broad Street Christian Church [East Broad Street MRA], 1051 E. Broad St., Columbus, 12/16/86, A, C, a, 86003448

Broad Street United Methodist Church, 501 E. Broad St., Columbus, 11/26/80, C, a, 80002997

Franklin County—Continued

Bruns—Wynkoop House [Canal Winchester MPS], 129 Washington St., Canal Winchester, 8/15/89, C, 89001023

Butler, J.G., House [Washington Township MRA], 35 S. High St., Dublin, 4/11/79, C, 79002759

Buttles, Aurora, House [Worthington MRA], 12 E. Strafford Ave., Worthington, 4/17/80, C, 80003007

Buttles—Johnson House [Worthington MRA (AD)], 956 High St., Worthington, 4/03/73, B, C, 73001443

Camp Chase Site, 2900 Sullivant Ave., Columbus, 4/11/73, A, d, NPS, 73001434

Campbell Mound, McKinley Ave., Columbus, 11/10/70, D, 70000490

Canal Winchester Methodist Church, S. Columbus and High St., Canal Winchester, 3/15/82, C, a, 82003567

Cannon, Tom, Mound, Address Restricted, Georgesville vicinity, 5/02/74, D, 74001498

Capital University Historic District, E. Main St. at College Ave., Columbus, 12/17/82, C, 82001457

Carty, J.—R. J. Tussing House [Canal Winchester MPS], 48 Elm St., Canal Winchester, 8/15/89, B, C, 89001025

Central Assurance Company [East Broad Street MRA], 741 E. Broad St., Columbus, 12/19/86, C, g, 86003421

Central Building of the Columbus Young Men's Christian Association, 40 W. Long St., Columbus, 5/06/93, A, C, 93000402

Central College Presbyterian Church [Central College MRA], 6891 Sunbury Rd., Westerville vicinity, 11/24/80, A, C, a, 80004068

Central High School, 75 S. Washington Blvd., Columbus, 3/07/85, A, C, 85000484

Central Ohio Lunatic Asylum, 1960 W. Broad St., Columbus, 4/24/86, A, C, 86000851

Chaney, O. P., Grain Elevator, W. Oak and N. High Sts., Canal Winchester, 1/28/88, A, C, 87002551

Chapman-Hutchinson House [Washington Township MRA], 37 S. Riverview St., Dublin, 4/11/79, B, C, 79002688

Coe Mound, Address Restricted, Columbus vicinity, 7/18/74, D, 74001486

Coffman, Fletcher, House [Washington Township MRA], 6659 Coffman Rd., Dublin vicinity, 4/11/79, A, C, 79002751

Columbia Building, 161-167 N. High St., Columbus, 8/12/83, C, 83001967

Columbus Country Club Mound, Address Restricted, Columbus vicinity, 2/15/74, D, 74001487

Columbus Gallery of Fine Arts, 480 E. Broad St., Columbus, 3/19/92, A, C, 92000173

Columbus Near East Side District, Roughly bounded by Parsons Ave., Broad and Main Sts., and the railroad tracks, Columbus, 5/19/78, A, B, C, 78002063

Columbus Near East Side Historic District-Parsons Avenue (Boundary Increase), 43-125 Parsons Ave. including 684 Oak St. and 690 Franklin Ave., Columbus, 12/09/83, A, C, 83004287

Columbus Savings and Trust Building, 8 E. Long St., Columbus, 9/15/77, C, 77001060

Columbus Street Historic District, 8–129 E. Columbus St. and 57 S. High St., Canal Winchester, 5/05/88, C, a, 88000559

Columbus Transfer Company Warehouse, 55 Nationwide Blvd., Columbus, 2/24/83, C, 83001966

Columbus, Hocking Valley and Toledo Railway Depot, 100 N. High St., Canal Winchester, 1/28/88, A, C, 87002550

Datz, Walter, House [Washington Township MRA], 5040 Tuttle Rd., Dublin vicinity, 4/11/79, A, C, 79002889

David's Reformed Church [Canal Winchester MPS], 80 W. Columbus St., Canal Winchester, 8/15/89, C, a, 89001017

Davis, Alexander, Cabin [Washington Township MRA], 5436 Dublin Rd. (rear house), Dublin, 4/11/79, B, 79002892

Davis, Alexander, House [Washington Township MRA], 5436 Dublin Rd. (front house), Dublin, 4/11/79, B, C, 79002746

Davis, Anson, House [Washington Township MRA], 4900 Hayden Run Rd., Dublin vicinity, 7/07/75, A, C, 75001402

Davis, Anson, Springhouse [Washington Township MRA], 4900 Hayden Run Rd., Dublin vicinity, 4/11/79, C, 79002907

Davis, James, Barn [Washington Township MRA], 5707 Dublin Rd., Dublin, 4/11/79, A, C, 79002789

Davis, James, Farm [Washington Township MRA], 5707 Dublin Rd., Dublin, 4/11/79, C, 79002772

Davis, Samuel Henry, House [Washington Township MRA], 5083 Rings Rd., Dublin, 4/11/79, B, C, 79002692

Davis, Samuel, House, 4264 Dublin Rd., Columbus vicinity, 2/15/74, C, 74001488

Decker, Elias, Farmhouse [Canal Winchester MPS], 6170 Lithopolis Rd., Canal Winchester, 8/15/89, A, C, 89001034

Deitz, Samuel, Farmhouse [Canal Winchester MPS], 280 Ashbrook Rd., Canal Winchester, 8/15/89, A, C, 89001021

Drake, Elam, House, 2738 Ole Country Lane, Columbus, 4/06/78, C, 78002064

Dublin Cemetery Vaults [Washington Township MRA], Rt. 161, 1/4 mi. W of intersection of 161 and Dublin River Rd., Dublin, 4/11/79, C, d, 79002790

Dublin Christian Church [Washington Township MRA], 81 W. Bridge St. (Rt. 161), Dublin, 4/11/79, A, C, a, 79002742

Dublin Christian Church [Washington Township MRA], 53 N. High St., Dublin, 4/11/79, A, C, a, 79002896

Dublin High Street Historic District [Washington Township MRA], 6-126 High St. (both sides of street), Dublin, 4/11/79, A, C, 79003645

Dublin Veterinary Clinic [Washington Township MRA], 32 W. Bridge St., Dublin, 4/11/79, B, C, 79002884

Dun, John, Homestead [Washington Township MRA], 8055 Dublin-Bellpoint Rd. (at intersection of Ashford Rd.), Dublin vicinity, 4/11/79, A, C, 79002691

East Broad Street Commercial Building [East Broad Street MRA], 747, 749, 751 E. Broad St., Columbus, 12/16/86, A, C, 86003424

East Broad Street Historic District [East Broad Street MRA], Along E. Broad St. between Monypenny and Ohio Aves., Columbus, 3/17/87, A, C, 86003393

East Broad Street Presbyterian Church [East Broad Street MRA], 760 E. Broad St., Columbus, 3/17/87, A, C, a, 86003397

East Town Street Historic District, Roughly bounded by Grant and Franklin Aves., Lester Dr., and E. Rich St., Columbus, 7/30/76, B, C, 76001425

Epley, Henry J., House [Canal Winchester MPS], 55 Franklin St., Canal Winchester, 8/15/89, C, 89001020

Evans, Richard W., House [Worthington MRA], 92 E. Granville Rd., Worthington, 4/17/80, C, 80003020

Everal, John W., Farm Buildings, 7610 Cleveland Ave., Westerville vicinity, 9/18/75, B, C, 75001404

Fairfield Building [Central College MRA], Sunbury Rd., Westerville vicinity, 11/25/80, A, C, 80004245

Felton School, Leonard Ave. at N. Monroe St., Columbus, 5/31/84, C, 84003677

Fifth Avenue and North High Historic District [Short North MPS], N. High St. roughly between 4th Ave. and Clark Pl., Columbus, 4/19/90, A, C, 90000584

Foor—Alspach House [Canal Winchester MPS], 92 E. Waterloo St., Canal Winchester, 8/15/89, C, 89001035

Fort Hayes, Cleveland Ave. and I-71, Columbus, 1/26/70, A, C, 70000491

Franklin Park Conservatory, 1547 E. Broad St., Columbus, 1/18/74, A, C, b, 74001489

Franklinton Post Office, 72 S. Gift St., Columbus, 3/20/73, A, 73001435

Frantz House [Washington Township MRA], 6152 Frantz Rd., Dublin, 4/11/79, C, 79002741

Galbreath, John, Mound, Address Restricted, Galloway vicinity, 7/15/74, D, 74001497

Gantz Homestead, 2233 Gantz Rd., Grove City, 6/20/79, B, C, 79001842

Gardner House [Worthington MRA], 80 W. Granville Rd., Worthington, 4/17/80, B, C, 80003009

Garfield—Broad Apartments [East Broad Street MRA], 775 E. Broad St., Columbus, 12/16/86, A, C, 86003427

Gayman, Christian, House [Canal Winchester MPS], 110 E. Waterloo St., Canal Winchester, 8/15/89, B, C, 89001037

German Village, Roughly bounded by Livingston Ave., Pear Alley, Nursery Lane, Blackberry Alley, and Lathrop St., Columbus, 12/30/74, C, 74001490

German Village (Boundary Increase), Briggs between E. Beck and Sycamore, S. Ninth between E. Blenkner and Sycamore., Columbus, 11/28/80, C, 80002998

Franklin County—Continued

Gilbert House [Worthington MRA], 72 E. Granville Rd., Worthington, 4/17/80, C, 80003016

Gilbert—Wilcox House [Worthington MRA], 196 E. Granville Rd., Worthington, 4/17/80, A, C, 80003021

Great Southern Hotel and Theatre, S. High and E. Main Sts., Columbus, 12/02/82, C, 82001458

Griffith, James, House [Canal Winchester MPS], 172 Waterloo St., Canal Winchester, 8/15/89, C, 89001019

Griswold Memorial Young Women's Christian Association, 65 S. Fourth St., Columbus, 7/22/93, A, C, 93000671

Groveport Log Houses, Wirt Rd., Groveport, 5/06/76, A, C, b, 76001428

Groveport Town Hall Historic Group, 628, 632 Main and Main and Front Sts., Groveport, 7/31/78, A, C, 78002067

Haffey, Parley, Farm Complex [Canal Winchester MPS], 525 Gender Rd., Canal Winchester, 8/15/89, C, 89001022

Hamilton Park Historic District, Broad and Long Sts., Franklin, 7/28/83, A, C, 83001968

Hamilton, Gilbert H., House, 290 Cliffside Dr., Columbus, 12/16/92, C, 89000175

Hamilton, J. L., Residence [Washington Township MRA], 6273 Cosgray Rd., Amlin vicinity, 4/11/79, A, C, 79002887

Hanby, Benjamin, House, 160 W. Main St., Westerville, 11/10/70, B, b, 70000493

Hanna House, 1021 E. Broad St., Columbus, 4/19/79, B, C, 79001835

Harrison, Gen. William Henry, Headquarters, 570 W. Broad St., Columbus, 12/15/72, B, 72001010

Hart, Gideon, House, 7328 Hempstead Rd., Westerville, 8/14/73, C, 73001442

Hart, Lucy, House [Worthington MRA], 64 W. Granville Rd., Worthington, 4/17/80, C, 80003008

Hartley Mound, Address Restricted, Columbus vicinity, 7/15/74, D, 74001491

Hartman Stock Farm Historic District, S of Columbus on U.S. 23, Columbus vicinity, 10/09/74, B, 74001492

Helpman—Chaney House [Canal Winchester MPS], 132 W. Columbus St., Canal Winchester, 8/15/89, C, 89001032

Herr, Christian S., House, N of Lockbourne at 1451 Rathmell Rd., Lockbourne vicinity, 3/05/82, C, 82003571

Heyne—Zimmerman House [East Broad Street MRA], 973 E. Broad St., Columbus, 3/17/87, A, C, 86003450

Higgins, H. A., Building, 129 E. Naghten St, Columbus, 8/27/79, C, 79001836

Hilliard Methodist Episcopal Church, 4066 Main St., Hilliard, 8/04/88, C, a, 88000634

Holder-Wright Works, Address Restricted, Dublin vicinity, 2/15/74, D, 74001496

Holy Cross Church, Rectory and School, 212 S. 5th St., Columbus, 4/26/79, A, C, a, 79001837

Home for the Aged Deaf [Central College MRA], 6971 Sunbury Rd., Westerville vicinity, 11/25/80, A, C, 80004522

Hotel Central [Worthington MRA], New England and High Sts., Worthington, 4/17/80, A, C, 80003012

House at 753 East Broad Street [East Broad Street MRA], 753 E. Broad St., Columbus, 12/17/86, A, C, 86003425

Huntington, Franz, House, 81 N. Drexel Ave., Bexley, 5/29/80, C, 80002999

Indian Run Cemetery Stone Walls [Washington Township MRA], North High St., Dublin, 4/11/79, C, d, 79002863

Indianola Junior High School, 420 E. 19th Ave., Columbus, 6/30/80, A, C, 80003000

Iuka Ravine Historic District, Roughly bounded by E. Lane and E. Northwood., N. Fourth, Twentieth and E. Nineteenth, and Indianola Aves., Columbus, 5/08/86, C, 86001023

Jackson Fort, Address Restricted, Columbus vicinity, 12/16/74, D, 74001493

Jacobs, Felix A., House, 1421 Hamlet St., Columbus, 12/19/86, B, C, 86003434

Jaeger Machine Company Office Building, 550 W. Spring St., Columbus, 6/16/83, A, C, g, 83001969

Jeffers, H. P., Mound, Address Restricted, Worthington vicinity, 5/02/74, D, 74001499

Jefferson Avenue Historic District, Roughly bounded by I-71, E. Broad, 11th, and Long Sts., Columbus, 12/02/82, A, B, C, 82001459

Jeffrey, Malcolm, House, 358 N. Parkview, Bexley, 5/06/83, A, B, 83001970

Johnson—Campbell House [East Broad Street MRA], 1203 E. Broad St., Columbus, 12/17/86, A, C, 86003414

Jones, W. H., Mansion, 731 E. Broad St., Columbus, 10/02/78, C, 78002065

Joseph—Cherrington House [East Broad Street MRA], 785 E. Broad St., Columbus, 12/17/86, A, C, 86003429

Karrer Barn [Washington Township MRA], 6199 Dublin Rd., Dublin, 4/11/79, C, 79002788

Karrer, Henry, House [Washington Township MRA], 19 S. Riverview, Dublin, 4/11/79, A, C, 79002744

Kauffman, Linus B., House [East Broad Street MRA], 906 E. Broad St., Columbus, 12/17/86, A, C, 86003410

Kaufman, Frank J., House [East Broad Street MRA], 1231 E. Broad St., Columbus, 12/17/86, A, C, 86003420

Kilbourn Commercial Building [Worthington MRA], 679-681 High St., Worthington, 4/17/80, B, C, 80003010

King, William, House [Canal Winchester MPS], 80 E. Waterloo St., Canal Winchester, 8/15/89, C, 89001031

Krumm House, 975-979 S. High St., Columbus, 9/30/82, B, C, 82003568

Landes, Samuel, House, 590 Hibbs Rd., Lockbourne vicinity, 5/08/87, C, 87000688

Lehman, Abraham, Farmhouse [Canal Winchester MPS], 40 Lehman Dr., Canal Winchester, 8/15/89, A, C, 89001016

Leppert, C., Barn [Washington Township MRA], 5280 Pinney Rd., Dublin, 4/11/79, A, C, 79002784

Leppert, C., Cabin [Washington Township MRA], 5280 Pinney Rd., Dublin, 4/11/79, C, b, 79002785

Leppert, C., Farm [Washington Township MRA], 5280 Pinney Rd., Dublin, 4/11/79, A, C, 79002783

Levy, Soloman, House [East Broad Street MRA], 929 E. Broad St., Columbus, 12/17/86, A, C, 86003437

Lincoln Theatre, 77 E. Long St., Columbus, 10/08/92, A, 92001355

Long and Third Commercial Building, 104-114 E. Long St., Columbus, 7/01/82, C, 82003569

Longenecker, Doctor, Office Building, 633–5 High St., Worthington, 3/09/90, C, 90000379

Lovejoy, Carrie, House [East Broad Street MRA], 807 E. Broad St., Columbus, 12/17/86, A, C, 86003435

Marshall, David, House [Washington Township MRA], 7455 Cosgray Rd., Dublin vicinity, 4/11/79, C, 79002686

Mattoon—Woodrow House [Worthington MRA], 72 E. North St., Worthington, 4/17/80, B, C, b, 80003011

McCracken-Sells House, 3983 Dublin Rd., Columbus vicinity, 11/29/84, C, 84000440

McDannald Homestead, NE of Columbus at 5847 Sunbury Rd., Columbus vicinity, 2/17/78, C, 78002066

McDowell, Austin, House [Washington Township MRA], 6189 Dublin Rd., Dublin, 4/11/79, A, C, 79002906

McKitrick, Dr., House [Washington Township MRA], 16 N. High St., Dublin, 4/11/79, B, C, 79002687

McKitrick, Dr., Office [Washington Township MRA], 22 N. High St., Dublin, 4/11/79, B, C, 79002882

Merryman, Dr. James, House, 5232 Norwich St., Hilliard, 5/26/88, C, 88000638

Methodist Church Parsonage [Canal Winchester MPS], 59 W. Columbus St., Canal Winchester, 8/15/89, C, a, 89001030

Miller, Frederick A., House-Broad Gables, 2065 Barton Pl. & 140 Park Dr., Columbus, 8/08/85, A, C, 85001689

Miller, J.F., House, 1600 Roxbury Rd., Marble Cliff, 5/31/84, C, 84003682

Mitchell, Charles, House [Washington Township MRA], 6992 Dublin-Bellpoint, Washington Township, 4/11/79, B, C, 79002890

Morris, C. E., House [East Broad Street MRA], 875 E. Broad St., Columbus, 12/17/86, A, C, 86003398

Myer House [Washington Township MRA], 5827 Rings Rd., Sandy Corners vicinity, 4/11/79, C, 79002689

Near Northside Historic District, Off OH 315, Columbus, 6/04/80, C, 80003001

New England Lodge [Worthington MRA], 634 N. High St., Worthington, 3/20/73, B, 73001444

New Indianola Historic District, Roughly bounded by Chittenden and Grant Aves., Fifth

Franklin County—Continued

St., Seventh Ave., and Fourth St., Columbus, 4/30/85, A, C, 85000947

Niles Car & Manufacturing Company Electric Railway Interurban Combine No. 21, 990 Proprietor's Rd., Worthington, 6/19/87, A, C, b, 87000762

Noble, Jonathan, House, 5030 Westerville Rd. (SR 3), Columbus vicinity, 12/03/75, B, C, 75001400

Noble, Lewis, House [Worthington MRA], 48 W. South St., Worthington, 4/17/80, C, 80003006

North High School, 100 Arcadia Ave., Columbus, 7/02/87, C, 87000984

North High Street Historic District [Canal Winchester MPS], Roughly N. High St. and E. and W. Mound St., Canal Winchester, 8/15/89, A, C, 89001038

North Market Historic District, Roughly bounded by W. Goodale, Park, High, Front and Vine Sts., Columbus, 12/30/82, A, C, 82001460

Odd Fellows Hall, 4065 Main St., Hilliard, 5/26/88, C, 88000636

Ohio Asylum for the Blind, 240 Parsons Ave., Columbus, 7/26/73, A, C, 73001436

Ohio Farm Bureau Federation Offices, 620 and 630 E. Broad St., Columbus, 3/13/87, A, C, 87000466

Ohio Institution for the Education of the Deaf and Dumb, 408 E. Town St., Columbus, 10/25/84, A, C, 84000107

Ohio National Bank, 167 S. High St., Columbus, 11/26/80, C, 80003002

Ohio Stadium, 404 W. 17th Ave., Columbus, 3/22/74, A, C, 74001494

Ohio State Arsenal, 139 W. Main St., Columbus, 7/18/74, A, C, 74001495

Ohio State Office Building, 65 S. Front St., Columbus, 12/18/90, A, C, 90001908

Ohio Statehouse, SE corner of High and Broad Sts., Columbus, 7/31/72, A, C, NHL, 72001011

Ohio Theatre, 39 E. State St., Columbus, 4/11/73, A, C, g, NHL, 73001437

Old Beechwold Historic District, Roughly bounded by W. Jeffrey Pl., N. High, River Park Dr., and Olentangy Blvd., Columbus, 9/22/87, A, C, g, 87001146

Old Governor's Mansion, 1234 E. Broad St., Columbus, 6/05/72, A, C, 72001012

Old Ohio Union, 154 W. 12th Ave., Columbus, 4/20/79, A, C, 79001838

Old Peace Lutheran Church, 78–82 N. High St., Gahanna, 4/23/87, C, a, 87000640

Old Port Columbus Airport Control Tower, 420 E. 5th Ave, Columbus, 7/26/79, A, 79001839

Orton Memorial Laboratory, 1445 Summit St., Columbus, 11/25/83, B, C, f, g, 83004292

Osborn, Charles S., House, 5785 Cooper Rd., Westerville vicinity, 3/28/77, B, 77001061

Otterbein Mausoleum, W. Walnut St, Westerville, 11/29/79, C, d, 79001845

Park, Jonathan, House [Worthington MRA], 91 E. Granville Rd., Worthington, 4/17/80, C, 80003013

Peoples Bank Company Building [Canal Winchester MPS], 10 N. High St., Canal Winchester, 8/15/89, C, 89001026

Pierce, Elijah, Properties, 534 E. Long St. and 142-44 N. Everett Alley, Columbus, 8/03/83, B, g, 83001971

Pinney Road Log Cabin [Washington Township MRA], Pinney Rd., Dublin, 4/11/79, C, 79002786

Pinney, Dr. Eli, House [Washington Township MRA], 109 S. Riverview St., Dublin, 4/11/79, B, C, 79002761

Plaza Hotel, 736-740 E. Long St., Columbus, 12/20/84, C, 84001041

Prentiss, Frederick, House [East Broad Street MRA], 706 E. Broad St., Columbus, 12/17/86, A, C, 86003396

Prentiss—Tulford House [East Broad Street MRA], 1074 E. Broad St., Columbus, 12/17/86, A, C, 86003413

Presbyterian Parsonage [Central College MRA], 6972 Sunbury Rd., Westerville vicinity, 11/25/80, A, C, a, b, 80004246

Principal's Cottage [Worthington MRA], 38 Short St., Worthington, 4/17/80, A, C, b, 80003014

Pythian Temple and James Pythian Theater, 861-867 Mt. Vernon Ave., Columbus, 11/25/83, A, C, 83004295

Rager, John, Farmhouse [Canal Winchester MPS], 8020 Groveport Rd., Canal Winchester, 10/01/90, C, 90001498

Rankin Building, 22 W. Gay St., Columbus, 3/10/82, C, 82003570

Rickenbacker, Capt. Edward V., House, 1334 E. Livingston Ave., Columbus, 5/11/76, B, NHL, 76001426

Riley, F., House [Washington Township MRA], 182 S. High St., Dublin, 4/11/79, C, 79002738

Rings, Louis, Barn #1 [Washington Township MRA], 6665 Shiers-Rings Rd., Dublin vicinity, 4/11/79, A, 79002769

Rings, Louis, Barn #2 [Washington Township MRA], 6665 Shiers-Rings Rd., Amlin vicinity, 4/11/79, A, 79002767

Rings, Louis, Residence [Washington Township MRA], 665 Shiers-Rings Rd., Dublin vicinity, 4/11/79, A, C, 79002765

Ripley House [Worthington MRA], 623 High St., Worthington, 4/17/80, C, 80003015

Russell, Mark, House, 5751 N. High St., Riverlea, 12/12/76, C, 76001429

Saint Paul's Episcopal Church [East Broad Street MRA], 787 E. Broad St., Columbus, 12/17/86, A, C, a, 86003430

Sandy House [Washington Township MRA], 63 S. Riverview St., Dublin, 4/11/79, B, 79002894

Schlee Brewery Historic District, 526, 543, 560, and rear 526 S. Front St. and NE corner of Beck St. and Wall Alley, Columbus, 3/28/88, A, B, C, 88000208

Schlee-Kemmler Building, 328 S. High St., Columbus, 12/02/82, C, 82001461

Schueller, Erwin W., House [East Broad Street MRA], 904 E. Broad St., Columbus, 12/17/86, A, C, 86003406

Scofield—Sanor House [East Broad Street MRA], 1031 E. Broad St., Columbus, 12/17/86, A, C, 86003447

Second Presbyterian Church, 132 S. Third St., Columbus, 1/11/83, C, a, 83001972

Sells, Benjamin, Barn #1 [Washington Township MRA], 4586 Hayden Run Rd., Dublin vicinity, 4/11/79, B, 79003133

Sells, Benjamin, Barn #2 [Washington Township MRA], 4586 Hayden Run Rd., Dublin vicinity, 4/11/79, B, 79003134

Sells, Benjamin, House [Washington Township MRA], 4586 Hayden Run Rd., Dublin vicinity, 7/30/75, B, C, 75001403

Sells, Benjamin, Wash House [Washington Township MRA], 4586 Hayden Run Rd., Dublin vicinity, 4/11/79, C, 79002893

Sells, David, Barn [Washington Township MRA], 4586 Hayden Run Rd., Dublin vicinity, 4/11/79, B, 79003135

Sells, Eliud, House [Washington Township MRA], 83 S. Riverview St., Dublin, 4/11/79, B, C, 79002891

Sells, William Henry, House [Washington Township MRA], 6028 Dublin Rd., Dublin, 4/11/79, B, e, 79002895

Seneca Hotel, 361 E. Broad St., Columbus, 12/29/83, C, 83004300

Sessions Village, Both sides of Sessions Dr., Columbus, 2/20/75, C, g, 75001401

Sharon Township Town Hall [Worthington MRA], Granville Rd. and Hartford St., Worthington, 4/17/80, A, C, 80003017

Sharp—Page House [East Broad Street MRA], 935 E. Broad St., Columbus, 12/17/86, A, C, 86003440

Shedd—Dunn House [East Broad Street MRA], 965 E. Broad St., Columbus, 12/17/86, A, C, 86003445

Shepard Street School, 106 Short St., Gahanna, 11/29/79, A, 79001841

Shier, Carl H., Barn [Washington Township MRA], 7026 Shier-Rings Rd., Amlin vicinity, 4/11/79, A, 79002873

Shier, Carl H., Chicken House [Washington Township MRA], 7026 Shier-Rings Rd., Amlin vicinity, 4/11/79, A, 79002868

Shier, Carl H., House [Washington Township MRA], 7026 Shier-Rings Rd., Amlin vicinity, 4/11/79, A, C, 79002865

Short North Historic District [Short North MPS], N. High St. roughly between Poplar St. and Cedar Ave., Columbus, 4/19/90, A, C, 90000583

Skeele, Capt. J. S., House [Worthington MRA], 700 Hartford St., Worthington, 4/17/80, C, b, 80003018

Smith, Benjamin, House, 181 E. Broad St., Columbus, 6/04/73, C, 73001438

Snow, John, House [Worthington MRA (AD)], 41 W. New England Ave., Worthington, 7/26/73, B, C, 73001445

South High Street Commercial Grouping, Bounded by Pearl, Mound, Main, and High Sts., Columbus, 12/29/83, A, C, 83004301

Squire's Glen Farm, 6770 Sunbury Rd., Central College vicinity, 8/13/74, C, 74001485

Franklin County—Continued

St. John's Episcopal Church [Worthington MRA], 700 High St., Worthington, 4/17/80, A, C, a, 80003019

St. John's Lutheran Church [Washington Township MRA], 6135 Rings Rd., Sandy Corners, 4/11/79, A, a, 79002877

Sullivant, Lucas, Building, 714 W. Gay St., Columbus, 3/20/73, B, b, 73001439

Third Avenue and North High Historic District [Short North MPS], N. High St. in the vicinity of 2nd and 3rd, Columbus, 4/19/90, A, C, 90000585

Thompson, -Builder House [Washington Township MRA], 5051 Brand Rd., Dublin P.O., 4/11/79, B, C, 79002749

Thrush, Morgan, Farm Complex [Canal Winchester MPS], 375 Gender Rd., Canal Winchester, 8/15/89, C, 89001036

Thurber, James, House, 77 Jefferson Ave., Columbus, 11/08/79, B, C, 79001840

Times Building—Lodge Hall [Canal Winchester MPS], 19 E. Waterloo St., Canal Winchester, 8/15/89, A, C, 89001028

Toledo and Ohio Central Railroad Station, 379 W. Broad St., Columbus, 6/18/73, A, C, 73001440

Towers Hall, Otterbein College, Main and Grove Sts., Otterbein College campus, Westerville, 3/04/71, A, C, 71000638

Trinity Episcopal Church, 125 E. Broad St., Columbus, 11/13/76, A, C, a, 76001427

Trinity German Evangelical Lutheran Church, 404 S. Third St., Columbus, 10/10/85, A, C, a, 85003132

U.S. Post Office and Courthouse, 121 E. State St., Columbus, 4/11/73, C, 73001441

University, Hayes and Orton Halls, The Oval, Ohio State university, Columbus, 7/16/70, A, C, 70000492

Upper Arlington Historic District, Roughly bounded by Lane Ave., Andover Rd., Fifth Ave., Cambridge Blvd. & Riverside Dr., Upper Arlington, 9/30/85, A, C, g, 85002694

Valley Dale Ballroom, 1590 Sunbury Rd., Columbus, 12/17/82, A, g, 82001462

Washburn, Rev. Ebenezer, House [Central College MRA], 7121 Sunbury Rd., Westerville vicinity, 11/25/80, B, C, 80003004

Washington Township School [Washington Township MRA], 4915 Brand Rd., Dublin vicinity, 4/11/79, A, C, 79002762

Washington Township Voting Hall [Washington Township MRA], Rings Rd., 4th bldg. E of RR tracks, Amlin, 4/11/79, A, 79002880

Welsbach Building, 116-118 E. Chestnut St., Columbus, 11/27/84, C, 84000444

Welsh Presbyterian Church, 315 E. Long St., Columbus, 11/24/80, C, a, 80003003

Wesley Chapel, SE of Hilliard at 3299 Dublin Rd., Hilliard vicinity, 2/27/79, C, a, 79001843

West Mound Street Historic District, 10–54 West Mound St., 23 Elm St., Canal Winchester, 2/11/88, C, a, 88000072

Westerville High School-Vine Street School, 44 N. Vine St., Westerville, 5/29/75, A, C, 75001405

Whitmer, Frieda, House [Washington Township MRA], 5530 Houchard Rd., Amlin vicinity, 4/11/79, A, C, 79002690

Wilcox, Jacob, Farm [Washington Township MRA], 7495 Rings Rd., Amlin, 4/11/79, B, C, 79002899

Wilcox, James, House [Washington Township MRA], 7590 Rings Rd., Amlin, 4/11/79, B, C, 79002898

Winterringer Building and House, 5344 Center St., Hilliard, 6/09/88, C, 88000720

Worthington Historical Society Museum [Worthington MRA], 50 W. New England Ave., Worthington, 4/17/80, C, b, 80003022

Worthington Manufacturing Company Boardinghouse [Worthington MRA (AD)], 25 Fox Lane, Worthington, 6/19/73, A, 73001446

Worthington Public Square [Worthington MRA], Village Green, Worthington, 4/17/80, C, 80003024

Worthington United Presbyterian Church [Worthington MRA], High St. and W. Granville Rd., Worthington, 4/17/80, C, a, 80003023

Wright, Horace, House [Worthington MRA], 137 E. Granville Rd., Worthington, 4/17/80, B, C, 80003025

Wright, J.E. Farm [Washington Township MRA], 167 S. High St., Dublin, 4/11/79, C, 79002905

Wright, Potter, House [Worthington MRA], 174 E. New England Ave., Worthington, 4/17/80, B, b, 80003026

Wyandotte Building, 21 W. Broad St., Columbus, 2/23/72, C, 72001013

York Lodge No. 563, 1276 N. High St., Columbus, 7/19/84, C, 84003691

Zellers—Langel House [Canal Winchester MPS], 163 W. Waterloo St., Canal Winchester, 8/15/89, C, 89001029

Fulton County

Clement, George S., House, 137 Clinton St., Wauseon, 4/21/83, B, C, 83001973

Fulton County Courthouse, S. Fulton and Chestnut Sts., Wauseon, 5/07/73, C, 73001447

Jones—Read—Touvelle House, 435 E. Park St., Wauseon, 5/08/87, C, 87000632

Lake Shore and Michigan Southern (LS&MS) Railroad Depot—Wauseon, Depot St. S side, between Fulton and Brunell Sts., Wauseon, 3/11/93, A, C, 93000151

Old US Post Office, 169 E. Church St., Marion, 11/28/90, A, C, 90001777

Winameg Mounds, Address Restricted, Delta vicinity, 12/31/74, D, 74001500

Gallia County

Davis Mill, NE of Patriot on Cora Mill Rd., Patriot vicinity, 11/28/80, A, 80003028

Evans House, Coal Valley Rd., Vinton vicinity, 7/19/84, C, 84003692

Ewington Academy, Ewington Rd., Ewington, 9/30/82, A, 82003572

Gallipolis Public Square and Garden Lots Historic District, Court and State Sts., 1st and 2nd Aves., Gallipolis, 1/08/80, A, C, 80003027

Gatewood, 76 State St., Gallipolis, 10/16/86, B, C, c, g, 86002877

Ohio Hospital For Epileptics Stone Water Towers, Mill Creek Rd., Gallipolis, 9/13/78, C, 78002069

Our House, 434 1st Ave., Gallipolis, 11/10/70, A, C, 70000494

Wood Old Homestead, 1253 Jackson Pike, Rio Grande, 12/14/87, A, C, 87002144

Geauga County

Batavia House, 14979 S. State St., Middlefield, 7/16/87, A, 87001213

Burton Village Historic District, Surrounding Public Sq., Burton, 11/20/74, A, B, C, 74001501

Chardon Courthouse Square District, Public Green, roughly bounded by Main and Center Sts., Chardon, 10/18/74, A, C, 74001502

Chester Township District School No. 2, 7798 Mayfield Rd., Chesterland, 11/04/82, A, 82001463

Claridon Congregational Church, U.S. 322, Claridon, 8/13/74, C, a, 74001503

Domestic Arts Hall And Flower Hall, N. Cheshire St, Burton, 8/24/79, A, C, 79001846

Fox—Pope Farm, 17767 Rapids Rd., Welshfield vicinity, 8/12/92, A, B, C, b, 92000971

Free Will Baptist Church Of Auburn, 11742 E. Washington St., Auburn Corners, 5/28/76, A, C, a, 76001430

Goodwin, Dr. Erastus, House, 14485 Main St., Burton, 8/01/75, C, 75001406

Hathaway, Lot, House, 12236 Old State Rd., East Claridon, 10/16/74, C, 74001504

Lost Lane Farm, Address Restricted, Chagrin Falls vicinity, 8/30/84, B, C, 84003693

Tambling, Lucius T., House, 14025 Chillicothe Rd., Novelty, 3/15/84, C, b, 84003695

White, Walter C., Estate, E of Mayfield Heights at U.S. 322 and County Line Rd., Mayfield Heights vicinity, 10/08/76, B, C, 76001431

Greene County

Antioch Hall, North And South Halls, Hyde Rd., Antioch College campus, Yellow Springs, 6/30/75, B, C, 75001411

Ballard Road Covered Bridge, NW of Jamestown on Ballard Rd. over Caesars Creek, Jamestown vicinity, 5/29/75, C, 75001408

Bank Of Xenia, NE corner of Detroit and E. 2nd Sts., Xenia, 5/07/73, C, 73001450

Barrett, George, Concrete House, 4 E. Main St., Spring Valley, 4/10/86, B, C, 86000699

Bath Township Consolidated School, 221 N. Central Ave., Fairborn, 9/22/83, C, 83001974

Greene County—Continued

Berryhill-Morris House, S of Bellbrook at 3113 Ferry Rd., Bellbrook vicinity, 11/12/75, C, 75001407

Cedarville Opera House, 78 N. Main St., Cedarville, 2/09/84, A, C, 84003697

Conner, Alexander, House, 99 E. Second St., Xenia, 7/28/87, C, 87000460

Dean Family Farm, 5 mi. NW of Jamestown off U.S. 35 on Ballard Rd., Jamestown vicinity, 5/29/75, A, C, 75001409

East Second Street District, 235 and 209-213-215 E. 2nd St., Xenia, 3/20/73, B, C, 73001451

East Second Street District(Boundary Increase), 184-271 E. 2nd St, Xenia, 9/10/79, C, 79001847

Grinnell Mill Historic District, 3536 Bryan Park Rd., Yellow Springs vicinity, 11/29/82, A, C, 82001464

Harper Mausoleum and Harper, George W., Memorial Entrance, North Cemetery, OH 72, Cedarville, 2/11/88, C, d, 88000115

Hollencamp House, 339 E. 2nd St., Xenia, 7/18/80, B, C, 80003029

Huffman Field, Wright-Patterson Air Force Base, 1 mi. SW of Fairborn, Fairborn vicinity, 5/06/71, A, B, C, NHL, 71000640

Main Street Historic District, Roughly E. and W. Main St. from Elm to Water Sts., Spring Valley, 5/19/89, A, B, C, 89000431

Mercer Log House, 41 N. 1st St., Fairborn, 10/16/81, C, 81000433

Millen-Schmidt House, 184 N. King St., Xenia, 11/07/76, C, 76001432

Old Chillicothe Site, Address Restricted, Xenia vicinity, 4/21/75, D, 75001410

Old Hotel, The, 100–101 1/2 W. Main St., Spring Valley, 8/25/88, A, C, 88001296

Orators Mound, Address Restricted, Yellow Springs vicinity, 7/15/74, D, 74001507

Patterson, Samuel N., House, 364 N. King St., Xenia, 6/03/76, C, 76001433

Pollock Works, Address Restricted, Cedarville vicinity, 2/23/72, D, 72001014

Reid, Whitelaw, House, SW of Cedarville at 2587 Conley Rd., Cedarville vicinity, 5/07/73, B, C, c, 73001448

South School, 909 S. High St., Yellow Springs, 10/04/89, A, C, 89001459

Waterstreet Historic District, Roughly bounded by Shawnee Creek, S. Detroit, S. Church and W. 2nd Sts., Xenia, 8/11/80, A, C, 80003030

Whitehall Farm, N of Yellow Springs off U.S. 68, Yellow Springs vicinity, 7/31/80, B, C, 80003031

Whiteman, Benjamin, House, E of Clifton, Clifton vicinity, 4/03/73, C, 73001449

Williamson Mound State Memorial, Off OH 42, Cedarville vicinity, 12/13/71, D, 71000639

Wright Brothers Memorial Mound Group, Address Restricted, Fairborn vicinity, 2/12/74, D, 74001505

Wright-Patterson Air Force Base Mound, Address Restricted, Fairborn vicinity, 2/23/72, D, 72001015

Yellow Springs Historic District, Roughly bounded by RR tracks, Yellow Springs-Fairfield Rd., High and Herman Sts., Yellow Springs, 4/01/82, A, C, 82003573

Young, Col. Charles, House, Columbus Pike between Clifton and Stevenson Rds., Wilberforce, 3/30/74, B, NHL, 74001506

Guernsey County

Barnett-Criss House, SW of Cambridge off U.S. 22, Cambridge, 12/08/78, C, 78002070

Berwick Hotel, 600–615 Wheeling Ave., Cambridge, 3/29/83, A, 83001975

Bethel Methodist Episcopal Church, W of Pleasant City on OH 146, Pleasant City vicinity, 11/24/78, A, C, a, 78002072

Booth Homestead, N of Guernsey at 8433 Wheeling Twnshp. Rd, Guernsey vicinity, 9/06/79, C, 79001851

Broom Building, 701 Wheeling Ave., Cambridge, 2/17/83, C, 83001976

Broom-Braden Stone House, N of Cambridge at 66715 Reed Rd., Cambridge vicinity, 7/18/80, B, C, 80003032

Claysville School, N of Claysville on SR 15, Claysville vicinity, 2/22/79, A, C, 79001850

Finley, Ebenezer, House, E of Buffalo on OH 313, Buffalo vicinity, 2/28/86, B, 86000417

Guernsey County Courthouse, Courthouse Sq., Cambridge, 7/16/73, C, 73001452

Harper, Samuel, Stone House, N of New Concord on SR 416, New Concord vicinity, 1/03/80, C, 80003033

Kennedy Stone House, SE of North Salem off OH 271, North Salem vicinity, 10/03/75, C, 75001412

McCracken-McFarland House, 216 N. 8th St., Cambridge, 2/16/79, B, C, b, 79001848

McCracken-Scott House, 819 Steubenville Ave., Cambridge, 12/20/78, B, C, 78002071

McCreary-Burnworth House, 220 Highland Ave., Cambridge, 3/12/82, C, 82003574

National Road, Center Township Rd. 650, Cambridge vicinity, 8/23/85, A, C, 85001842

Old Washington Historic District, Both sides of Main St., Old Washington, 5/29/75, C, 75001413

S Bridge, National Road, 4 mi. E of Old Washington on U.S. 40, Old Washington vicinity, 10/15/66, A, C, NHL, 66000610

Sarchet, Peter B., House, N of Cambridge on SR 365, Cambridge vicinity, 2/22/79, B, C, 79001849

Sarchet-Burgess House, 145 W. Eighth St., Cambridge, 5/21/87, C, 87000808

Wheeling Avenue Historic District, Roughly bounded by Steubenville, Tenth, Wheeling, and Fourth Aves., Cambridge, 5/11/87, A, C, 87000919

Hamilton County

Aklemeyer Commercial Buildings, 19-23 W. Court St., Cincinnati, 12/09/80, A, C, 80003034

Alms and Doepke Dry Goods Company [Samuel Hannaford and Sons TR in Hamilton County], 222 E. Central Pkwy., Cincinnati, 3/03/80, C, 80003035

Anderson Ferry, Off U.S. 50, Cincinnati, 6/10/82, A, b, 82003575

Apostolic Bethlehem Temple Church, 1205 Elm St., Cincinnati, 4/11/73, A, C, a, 73001453

B & O Freight Terminal, 700 Pete Rose Way, Cincinnati, 12/29/86, A, C, 86003521

Baker, John S., House, 1887 Madison Rd., Cincinnati, 6/06/79, C, 79001852

Balch House [Samuel Hannaford and Sons TR in Hamilton County], 267 Greendale Ave., Cincinnati, 3/03/80, C, 80003036

Baldwin, Joseph W., House [Wyoming MRA], 217 Springfield Pike, Wyoming, 8/25/86, B, C, 86001628

Bates Building [Columbia-Tusculum MRA], 3819 Eastern Ave., Cincinnati, 8/24/79, C, 79002700

Bauer Apartments, 2015-2017 Madison Rd., Cincinnati, 12/02/82, C, 82001465

Becker House, 179 W. Crescentville Rd., Springdale vicinity, 7/18/74, C, 74001522

Beech Avenue Houses, 1120 and 1128 Beech Ave., Cincinnati, 2/16/79, B, C, 79001853

Benham Mound, Address Restricted, Cincinnati vicinity, 7/30/74, D, 74001508

Bennett, George, House, 10281 Harrison Pike, Harrison vicinity, 5/29/75, C, 75001426

Bepler, August, House, 805 Tusculum Ave., Cincinnati, 4/13/77, B, C, 77001062

Bernheim House, 195 Greenhills Rd., Cincinnati, 3/29/83, C, 83001977

Betts-Longworth Historic District, Roughly bounded by Ezzard Dr., Central Ave., and Mound and Old Court Sts., Cincinnati, 11/29/83, C, D, 83004304

Blair House, 7844 Remington Rd (at West St.), Montgomery, 11/30/82, C, 82001466

Bramble, Ayres L., House, 4416 Homer Ave., Cincinnati, 4/01/82, B, C, 82003576

Brittany Apartment Building [Samuel Hannaford and Sons TR in Hamilton County], 100-104 W. 9th St., Cincinnati, 3/03/80, C, 80003037

Broadwell, Cyrus, House, NE of Newton at 3882 Mount Carmel Rd., Newtown vicinity, 5/29/75, C, 75001433

Bromwell, Jacob, House [Wyoming MRA], 69 Mt. Pleasant Ave., Wyoming, 8/25/86, B, C, 86001629

Burchenal Mound, Address Restricted, Woodland vicinity, 5/29/75, D, 75001437

Burckhardt, A. E., House [Samuel Hannaford and Sons TR in Hamilton County], 400 Forest Ave., Cincinnati, 3/03/80, C, 80003038

Burdsal, Samuel, House, 1342 Broadway St., Cincinnati, 6/10/82, B, C, 82003577

Burroughs, C. H., House [Samuel Hannaford and Sons TR in Hamilton County], 1010 Chapel St., Cincinnati, 3/03/80, C, 80003039

Butler, Wesley, Archeological District, Address Restricted, Elizabethtown vicinity, 7/24/76, D, 76001446

Calvary Episcopal Church Sunday School [Samuel Hannaford and Sons TR in Hamilton

Hamilton County—Continued

County], 3770 Clifton Ave., Cincinnati, 3/03/80, C, a, 80003040

Campbell, Hugh, House, 332 Weathervane Rd., Harrison vicinity, 11/07/76, C, 76001448

Capt. Stone House [Samuel Hannaford and Sons TR in Hamilton County], 405 Oak St., Cincinnati, 3/03/80, C, 80003041

Carew Tower, W. 5th St. and Fountain Sq., Cincinnati, 8/05/82, C, 82003578

Cincinnati City Hall [Samuel Hannaford and Sons TR in Hamilton County], 801 Plum St., Cincinnati, 12/11/72, C, 72001017

Cincinnati Enquirer Building, 617 Vine St., Cincinnati, 11/13/85, A, C, 85002787

Cincinnati Gymnasium and Athletic Club, 111 Shillito Pl., Cincinnati, 2/17/83, C, 83001978

Cincinnati Music Hall [Samuel Hannaford and Sons TR in Hamilton County], 1243 Elm St., Cincinnati, 1/26/70, A, C, NHL, 70000496

Cincinnati Observatory Building [Samuel Hannaford and Sons TR in Hamilton County], Observatory Pl., Cincinnati, 3/03/80, C, 80003043

Cincinnati Street Gas Lamps, 1109 Street lamps at various locations throughout Cincinnati, Cincinnati, 12/22/78, A, C, 78002073

Cincinnati Tennis Club, Dexter and Wold Aves., Cincinnati, 3/29/83, A, g, 83001979

Cincinnati Union Terminal, 1301 Western Ave., Cincinnati, 10/31/72, A, C, g, NHL, 72001018

Cincinnati Work House and Hospital [Samuel Hannaford and Sons TR in Hamilton County], 3208 Colerain Ave., Cincinnati, 3/03/80, C, 80003044

Cincinnati Zoo Historic Structures, 3400 Vine St., Cincinnati, 2/27/87, A, NHL, 87000905

Clauder's Pharmacy [Columbia-Tusculum MRA], 4026 Eastern Ave., Cincinnati, 8/24/79, C, 79002696

Clifton Avenue Historic District, Irregular pattern along Clifton Ave., Cincinnati, 12/08/78, A, C, a, 78002074

Clough Creek and Sand Ridge Archeological District, Address Restricted, Cincinnati vicinity, 10/01/74, D, 74001509

Clovernook, 7000 Hamilton Ave., Cincinnati, 6/18/73, B, 73001454

Coca-Cola Bottling Corporation, 1507 Dana Ave., Cincinnati, 7/02/87, C, g, 87000985

Colerain Works Archeological District, Address Restricted, Dunlap vicinity, 6/18/76, D, 76001445

College Hill Town Hall [Samuel Hannaford and Sons TR in Hamilton County], Belmont Ave. and Larch St., Cincinnati, 3/17/78, A, C, 78002075

Columbia Baptist Cemetery [Columbia-Tusculum MRA], Northside of Wilmer Rd., Cincinnati, 8/24/79, A, d, 79002709

Conrad Mound Archeological Site, Address Restricted, Cleves vicinity, 6/20/75, D, 75001420

Cote Bonneville, 4850 Colerain Ave., Cincinnati, 11/29/84, B, C, a, 84000448

Court Street Firehouse, 311 W. Court St., Cincinnati, 7/18/74, C, 74001510

Courtland Flats, 117-121 E. Court St., Cincinnati, 12/20/84, C, 84001046

Covenant First Presbyterian Church, 8th and Elm Sts., Cincinnati, 1/29/73, A, C, a, 73001455

Covington and Cincinnati Suspension Bridge, Spans Ohio River between Covington, KY and Cincinnati, OH, Cincinnati, 5/15/75, C, NHL, 75000786

Cox, George B., House [Samuel Hannaford and Sons TR in Hamilton County], Brookline and Jefferson Aves., Cincinnati, 11/06/73, B, C, 73001456

Cox, Jacob D., House, 241–243 Gilman Ave., Cincinnati, 4/14/75, B, C, 75001416

Cummins School [Samuel Hannaford and Sons TR in Hamilton County], 824 Wiliam H. Taft Rd., Cincinnati, 1/09/86, C, 86000014

Cuvier Press Club [Samuel Hannaford and Sons TR in Hamilton County], 22 Garfield Pl., Cincinnati, 10/26/72, A, C, 72001019

Davidson, Tyler, Fountain, 5th St., Cincinnati, 10/11/79, C, b, 79001854

Dayton Street Historic District, Roughly bounded by Bank, Linn, and Poplar Sts. and Winchell Ave., Cincinnati, 1/25/73, C, 73001457

Decker, Stephen, Rowhouse [Columbia-Tusculum MRA], 531-541 Tusculum Ave., Cincinnati, 8/24/79, C, 79002693

Derby, H. W., Building [Samuel Hannaford and Sons TR in Hamilton County], 300 W. 4th St., Cincinnati, 3/03/80, C, 80003045

Detmer, A. M., House [Samuel Hannaford and Sons TR in Hamilton County], 1520 Chapel St., Cincinnati, 3/03/80, C, 80003046

Doctors' Building, 19 Garfield Pl., Cincinnati, 12/04/86, A, C, 86003317

Domhoff Buildings, 4201-4203 Hamilton Ave. and 1604-1614 Chase Ave., Cincinnati, 3/11/80, C, 80003047

Dravo Gravel Site, Address Restricted, Cleves vicinity, 12/22/78, D, 78002083

Dunlap Archeological District, Address Restricted, Dunlap vicinity, 10/21/75, D, 75001421

East Fourth Street Historic District, 123, 127, and 135–137 E. Fourth St., Cincinnati, 2/22/88, C, 88000078

East Walnut Hills Firehouse, Madison Rd. and Hackberry St., Cincinnati, 2/17/83, C, 83001980

Eckert Building, 2600 Woodburn Ave., Cincinnati, 9/29/83, C, 83001981

Eden Park Stand Pipe [Samuel Hannaford and Sons TR in Hamilton County], Eden Park Dr., Cincinnati, 3/03/80, C, 80003048

Eden Park Station No. 7 [Samuel Hannaford and Sons TR in Hamilton County], 1430 Martin Dr., Cincinnati, 3/03/80, C, 80003049

Edgecliff [Samuel Hannaford and Sons TR in Hamilton County], 2220 Victory Pkwy., Cincinnati, 3/03/80, C, 80003050

Edgecliff Area Historic Group, 2220 Victory Parkway, Cincinnati, 11/11/77, B, C, 77001063

Edwards, William, Farmhouse, 3851 Edwards Rd., Newtown, 10/04/89, C, 89001455

Eighteen Mile House, 2 mi. SE of Harrison at Harrison Pike and Patriot Dr., Harrison vicinity, 10/10/75, A, C, 75001427

Eighteenth District School [Samuel Hannaford and Sons TR in Hamilton County], 1326 Hopple St., Cincinnati, 3/03/80, C, 80003051

Elliott House, 9352 Given Rd., Remington, 10/29/76, A, C, 76001451

Elsinore Arch [Samuel Hannaford and Sons TR in Hamilton County], 1700 Gilbert Ave., Cincinnati, 3/03/80, C, 80003052

Episcopal Church of the Resurrection [Samuel Hannaford and Sons TR in Hamilton County (AD)], 7346–48 Kirkwood La., Cincinnati, 4/13/77, C, a, 77001064

Fay, Charles, House [Wyoming MRA], 325 Reily Rd., Wyoming, 8/25/86, C, 86001630

Fenwick Club Annex, 426 E. 5th St., Cincinnati, 3/07/73, A, C, a, 73001458

Ferris, Eliphalet, House, 3915 Plainville Rd., Mariemont, 5/29/75, C, 75001431

Ferris, Joseph, House, 5729 Dragon Way, Cincinnati, 6/30/75, C, 75001417

Field, Walter, House [Samuel Hannaford and Sons TR in Hamilton County], 3725 Reading Rd., Cincinnati, 3/03/80, C, 80003053

Findlay Market Building, Esplanade at Elder St., between Elm and Race Sts., Cincinnati, 6/05/72, A, C, 72001020

First Congregational-Unitarian Church, 2901 Reading Rd., Cincinnati, 5/28/76, C, a, 76001434

First German Methodist Episcopal Church [Samuel Hannaford and Sons TR in Hamilton County], 1310 Race St., Cincinnati, 3/03/80, C, a, 80003054

First Universalist Church [Samuel Hannaford and Sons TR in Hamilton County], 2600 Essex Pl., Cincinnati, 3/03/80, C, a, 80003055

Ford Motor Company Cincinnati Plant, 660 Lincoln Ave., Cincinnati, 5/25/89, A, C, 89000460

Friedlander, Abraham J., House, 8 W. 9th St., Cincinnati, 5/07/79, B, C, 79001855

Fulton-Presbyterian Cemetery [Columbia-Tusculum MRA], Carrel St., Cincinnati, 8/24/79, A, B, 79002706

Gerrard, Stephen A., Mansion, 748 Betula Ave., Cincinnati, 11/05/87, C, 87001940

Gilbert Row, 2152-2166 Gilbert Ave., Cincinnati, 5/13/82, C, 82003579

Gilbert-Sinton Historic District, Roughly bounded by Morris, Gilbert and Sinton Aves., Cincinnati, 10/06/83, A, C, 83004306

Glendale Historic District, OH 747, Glendale, 7/20/76, A, C, NHL, 76001447

Glendale Police Station, 305 E. Sharon Ave., Glendale, 3/27/75, A, 75001425

Goldsmith, Moses, Building, 356 Bryant, Cincinnati, 6/10/82, C, 82003580

Goodall Building, 324 W. 9th St., Cincinnati, 2/09/84, C, 84003710

Goshorn, Sir Alfred T., House, 3540 Clifton Ave., Cincinnati, 4/03/73, C, 73001459

Grace Church, 3626 Reading Rd., Cincinnati, 9/16/82, C, a, 82003581

Hamilton County—Continued

Greenhills Historic District, Roughly Damon Rd., Enfield St., Farragut Rd., Flanders Ln., Winton Rd., Andover Rd., Burley Cir., and Cromwell Rd., Greenhills, 1/12/89, A, 88003066

Gwynne Building, 6th and Main Sts, Cincinnati, 8/03/79, C, 79001856

Haddon Hall, 3418 Reading Rd., Cincinnati, 7/22/82, A, C, 82003582

Hahn Field Archeological District, Address Restricted, Newtown vicinity, 10/29/74, D, 74001519

Hamilton County Memorial Building, Elm and Grant Sts., Cincinnati, 12/04/78, A, C, 78002076

Hannaford, Samuel, House [Samuel Hannaford and Sons TR in Hamilton County], 768 Derby Ave., Cincinnati, 3/03/80, B, C, 80003056

Harrison, William Henry, Tomb State Memorial, Mount Nebo on OH 128, North Bend, 11/10/70, B, c, d, g, 70000499

Harrison-Landers House, 3881 Newtown Rd., Newtown vicinity, 5/29/75, C, 75001434

Hemann, Joseph A., House, 49 W. McMillan St., Cincinnati, 4/16/80, B, C, 80003057

Hess, Elmer, House [Wyoming MRA], 333 Springfield Pike, Wyoming, 8/25/86, B, C, 86001633

Hewson-Gutting House, 515 Lafayette Ave., Cincinnati, 12/21/79, C, 79001857

Hill, Jediah, Covered Bridge, 7 mi. N of Cincinnati off U.S. 127 on Covered Bridge Rd., Cincinnati vicinity, 3/28/73, A, C, 73001460

Hoadley, George, Jr., House, 2337 Grandin Rd., Cincinnati, 3/09/90, C, 90000380

Hoffner Historic District, Bounded by Bluerock, Moline Court, Langland, and Hamilton Aves., Cincinnati, 10/03/78, C, 78002077

Holy Cross Monastery and Chapel, 1055 St. Paul Pl., Cincinnati, 9/13/78, A, C, a, 78002078

Hoodin Building [Columbia-Tusculum MRA], 3719-3725 Eastern Ave., Cincinnati, 8/24/79, C, 79002708

Hooper Building [Samuel Hannaford and Sons TR in Hamilton County], 139-151 W. 4th St., Cincinnati, 3/03/80, C, 80003058

Houston House [Columbia-Tusculum MRA], 3708 Mead Ave., Cincinnati, 8/24/79, C, 79002704

Hulbert House and McAlpin Bridal Cottage, 333 and 341 Lafayette Ave., Cincinnati, 4/29/82, C, 82003583

Hummel, George, House [Samuel Hannaford and Sons TR in Hamilton County], 3423 Whitfield Ave., Cincinnati, 3/03/80, C, 80003059

Ida Street Viaduct, Ida St. between Monastery and Paradrome Sts., Cincinnati, 11/28/80, A, C, g, 80003060

Immaculate Conception Church, School, and Rectory, Pavilion and Guido Sts., Cincinnati, 12/29/78, A, C, a, 78002079

Ingalls Building, 6 E. 4th St., Cincinnati, 3/07/75, C, 75001418

Jefferson Schoolhouse, Indian Hill and Drake Rds., Indian Hill, 3/17/76, A, C, 76001450

John, Jehu, House, E of Harrison on Stone Dr., Harrison vicinity, 10/31/75, B, C, 75001428

Kellogg House [Columbia-Tusculum MRA], 3807 Eastern Ave., Cincinnati, 8/24/79, C, 79002702

Kestler Building [Columbia-Tusculum MRA], 4024 Eastern Ave., Cincinnati, 8/24/79, C, 79002695

Kirby, Josiah, House [Wyoming MRA], 65 Oliver Rd., Wyoming, 8/25/86, B, C, 86001634

Krippendorf-Dittman Company [Samuel Hannaford and Sons TR in Hamilton County], 628 Sycamore St., Cincinnati, 3/03/80, C, 80003061

Krumberg, Theodore, Building, 1201 Main St., Cincinnati, 12/17/82, C, 82001467

Landt Building [Columbia-Tusculum MRA], 3815-3817 Eastern Ave., Cincinnati, 8/24/79, C, 79002703

Langdon House, 3626 Eastern Ave., Cincinnati, 4/16/69, C, 69000143

Laurel Homes Historic District, Roughly bounded by Liberty and John Sts., Ezzard Charles Dr., and Linn St., Cincinnati, 5/19/87, A, C, 87000690

Lillybanks, 2386 Grandin Rd., Cincinnati, 7/07/83, C, 83001982

Lloyd, John Uri, House, 3901 Clifton Ave., Cincinnati, 3/07/73, B, C, 73001461

Lombardy Apartment Building [Samuel Hannaford and Sons TR in Hamilton County], 318-326 W. 4th St., Cincinnati, 3/03/80, C, 80003062

Looker, Othniel, House, 10580 Marvin Rd., Harrison, 6/05/75, B, C, b, 75001429

Lower Price Hill Historic District, Roughly bounded by W. 8th, State, Burns, and English St., Cincinnati, 11/15/88, C, 88002536

LuNeack House [Columbia-Tusculum MRA], 3718 Mead Ave., Cincinnati, 8/24/79, C, 79002705

Luethstrom—Hurin House [Wyoming MRA], 30 Reily Rd., Wyoming, 8/25/86, B, C, 86001635

Lunkenheimer, Frederick, House, 2133 Luray, Cincinnati, 8/08/85, B, C, 85001690

Lytle Park Historic District, Roughly bounded by 3rd, 5th, Sycamore, Commercial Sq., and Butler Sts., Cincinnati, 3/26/76, A, C, 76001435

MAJESTIC, Ohio River below Central Bridge, Cincinnati, 12/20/89, A, g, NHL, 89002456

Madam Fredin's Eden Park School and Neighboring Row House, 938–946 Morris St. and 922–932 Morris St., Cincinnati, 11/29/79, B, C, 79001858

Madison and Woodburn Historic District, Woodburn Ave. and Madison Rd., Cincinnati, 6/30/83, A, C, 83001983

Madison-Stewart Historic District, Jct. of Madison and Stewart Sts., Cincinnati, 5/29/75, C, 75001419

Main and Third Street Cluster, 300-302, 304-306 Main St., and 208-210 E. 3rd St., Cincinnati, 7/15/83, A, C, 83001984

Mardot Antique Shop [Columbia-Tusculum MRA], 3964 Eastern Ave., Cincinnati, 8/24/79, C, 79002698

Mariemont Embankment And Village Site, Address Restricted, Mariemont vicinity, 10/16/74, D, 74001517

Mariemont Historic District, U.S. 50, Mariemont, 7/24/79, C, 79001862

Martin House, 6500 Beechmont Ave., Cincinnati, 3/21/79, C, a, 79001859

Mathew Mound, Address Restricted, Evendale vicinity, 5/29/75, D, 75001424

Mayer, S. C., House [Samuel Hannaford and Sons TR in Hamilton County], 1614 Main St., Cincinnati, 3/03/80, C, 80003063

McKinley School [Columbia-Tusculum MRA], 3905 Eastern Ave., Cincinnati, 8/24/79, C, 79002697

Mecklenburg's Garden, 302 E. University Ave., Cincinnati, 11/07/76, A, 76001436

Melbourne Flats, 39 W. McMillan St., Cincinnati, 10/18/84, C, 84000132

Miller, Charles A., House [Samuel Hannaford and Sons TR in Hamilton County], 1817 Chase St., Cincinnati, 3/03/80, C, 80003064

Miller-Leuser Log House, Clough Pike and Newton Rd., Cincinnati vicinity, 8/30/74, C, 74001511

Mills' Row, 2201–2209 Park Ave., Cincinnati, 4/29/77, C, 77001065

Mitchell, Richard H., House [Samuel Hannaford and Sons TR in Hamilton County], 3 Burton Woods Lane, Cincinnati, 3/03/80, C, 80003065

Montgomery Saltbox Houses, 7789 and 7795 Cooper Rd., Montgomery, 7/28/87, A, C, 87001254

Moore, Charles H., House [Wyoming MRA], 749 Stout Ave., Wyoming, 8/25/86, B, C, 86001636

Moormann, Bernard H., House, 1514 E. McMillan St., Cincinnati, 3/20/73, C, 73001462

Morrison House [Samuel Hannaford and Sons TR in Hamilton County], 750 Ludlow Ave., Cincinnati, 4/03/73, C, 73001463

Mount Adams Public School, 1125 St. Gregory St., Cincinnati, 11/24/80, A, C, 80003066

Mount Auburn Historic District, Both sides of Auburn Ave. from Ringgold St. to Howard Taft Rd., Cincinnati, 3/28/73, A, B, C, 73001464

Mt. Healthy Public School, Compton & Harrison Aves., Mt. Healthy, 5/02/85, C, 85000946

Mt. Nebo Archeological District, Address Restricted, North Bend vicinity, 3/03/75, D, 75001435

Ninth Street Historic District, 9th St. between Vine and Plum Sts., Cincinnati, 11/25/80, B, C, 80003067

Northside United Methodist Church [Samuel Hannaford and Sons TR in Hamilton County], 1674 Chase, Cincinnati, 3/03/80, C, a, 80003068

Norwell Residence [Columbia-Tusculum MRA], 506 Tusculum Ave., Cincinnati, 8/24/79, C, 79002707

Norwood Mound, Address Restricted, Norwood vicinity, 5/02/74, D, 74001520

Norwood Municipal Building, 4645 Montgomery Rd., Norwood, 3/11/80, C, 80003093

Observatory Historic District, Observatory Pl. and Ave., Cincinnati, 9/20/78, A, C, 78002080

Odd Fellows' Cemetery Mound, Address Restricted, Newtown vicinity, 6/18/73, D, 73001474

Hamilton County—Continued

Ohio National Guard Armory [Samuel Hannaford and Sons TR in Hamilton County], 1437-1439 Western Ave., Cincinnati, 3/03/80, C, 80003069

Old College Hill Post Office, 1624 Pasadena Ave., Cincinnati, 6/16/76, C, 76001437

Old Gothic Barns, 6058 Colerain Ave., Cincinnati, 7/20/76, C, 76001438

Old St. Mary's Church, School and Rectory, 123 E. 13th St., Cincinnati, 3/13/76, A, C, a, 76001439

Our Lady of Mercy High School [Samuel Hannaford and Sons TR in Hamilton County], 1409 Western Ave., Cincinnati, 3/03/80, C, a, 80003070

Over-the-Rhine Historic District, Roughly bounded by Dorsey, Sycamore, Liberty, Reading, Central Pkwy, McMicken Ave., and Vine Sts., Cincinnati, 5/17/83, A, C, 83001985

Pabodie, Professor William, House [Wyoming MRA], 731 Brooks Ave., Wyoming, 8/25/86, C, 86001638

Palace Hotel [Samuel Hannaford and Sons TR in Hamilton County], 6th and Vine Sts., Cincinnati, 3/03/80, C, 80003071

Palace Theatre, 12 E. 6th St., Cincinnati, 3/24/80, A, 80004067

Park Flats, 2378-2384 Park Ave., Cincinnati, 9/08/83, C, 83001986

Peeble's Corner Historic District, Roughly E. McMillan St. and Gilbert Ave., Cincinnati, 11/14/85, A, C, 85002835

Pendleton, George Hunt, House, 559 E. Liberty St., Cincinnati, 10/15/66, B, NHL, 66000611

Perin Village Site, Address Restricted, Newtown and vicinity vicinity, 3/25/77, D, 77001067

Peters-Kupferschmid House, 2167 Grandin Rd., Cincinnati, 10/18/84, B, 84000134

Pfleger Family Houses, 216 and 218 Erkenbrecker Ave., Cincinnati, 3/11/80, C, 80003072

Phoenix Building/Cincinnati Club, 30 Garfield Pl. and 812 Race St., Cincinnati, 1/11/85, A, C, 85000068

Phoenix Club [Samuel Hannaford and Sons TR in Hamilton County], 9th and Race Sts., Cincinnati, 3/03/80, C, 80003073

Pilgrim Presbyterian Church, 1222 Ida St., Cincinnati, 7/18/80, A, C, a, 80003074

Pine Meer, 5336 Cleves-Warsaw Pk., Cincinnati vicinity, 11/30/82, C, 82001468

Pitman, Benn, House, 1852 Columbia Pkwy., Cincinnati, 7/07/69, B, C, 69000144

Plum Street Temple, 8th and Plum Sts., Cincinnati, 12/27/72, A, C, a, NHL, 72001021

Police Station No. 2 [Patrol Stations in Cincinnati, Ohio TR], 314 Broadway, Cincinnati, 5/18/81, A, C, 81000655

Police Station No. 3 [Patrol Stations in Cincinnati, Ohio TR], 3201 Warsaw Ave., Cincinnati, 5/18/81, A, C, 81000435

Police Station No. 5 [Samuel Hannaford and Sons TR in Hamilton County], 1024-1026 York St., Cincinnati, 3/03/80, A, C, 80003075

Police Station No. 6 [Patrol Stations in Cincinnati, Ohio TR], Delta Ave. and Columbia Pkwy., Cincinnati, 5/18/81, A, C, 81000436

Police Station No. 7 [Patrol Stations in Cincinnati, Ohio TR], 355 McMillan St., Cincinnati, 5/18/81, A, C, 81000437

Pollock, John C., House [Wyoming MRA], 88 Reily Rd., Wyoming, 8/25/86, C, 86001639

Powell, Henry, House [Samuel Hannaford and Sons TR in Hamilton County], 2209 Auburn Ave., Cincinnati, 3/03/80, C, 80003076

Probasco Fountain [Samuel Hannaford and Sons TR in Hamilton County], Clifton Ave., Cincinnati, 3/03/80, C, 80003077

Probasco, Henry, House, 430 W. Cliff Lane, Cincinnati, 11/09/72, C, 72001022

Procter and Collier-Beau Brummell Building, 440 E. McMillan St., Cincinnati, 10/18/84, A, C, 84002714

Prospect Hill Historic District, Roughly bounded by Liberty Hill, Highland, Pueblo, Channing, and Sycamore Sts., Cincinnati, 9/04/80, C, 80003078

Ransley Apartment Building [Samuel Hannaford and Sons TR in Hamilton County], 2390 Kemper Lane, Cincinnati, 3/03/80, C, 80003079

Ratterman, Bernard, House, 1349 Broadway, Cincinnati, 9/30/82, C, 82003584

Rattermann, Heinrich A., House, 510 York St., Cincinnati, 5/23/80, B, C, 80003080

Rawson House, 3767 Clifton Ave., Cincinnati, 7/24/73, A, B, C, 73001465

Reily, Robert, House [Wyoming MRA], 629 Liddle Ln., Wyoming, 8/25/86, B, C, 86001640

Rennert Mound Archeological District, Address Restricted, Elizabethtown vicinity, 3/04/75, D, 75001422

Resor, William, House, 254 Greendale Ave., Cincinnati, 3/07/73, C, b, 73001466

Retszch, W. C., House [Wyoming MRA], 129 Springfield Pike, Wyoming, 8/25/86, B, C, 86001642

Riddle—Friend House [Wyoming MRA], 507 Springfield Pike, Wyoming, 8/25/86, B, C, 86001643

Robb, L. B., Drugstore [Columbia-Tusculum MRA], 4030 Eastern Ave., Cincinnati, 8/24/79, C, 79002694

Rookwood Pottery, Celestial and Rookwood Pl., Cincinnati, 12/05/72, C, 72001023

Ropes, Nathaniel, Building, 917 Main St., Cincinnati, 9/30/82, C, 82003585

Roudebush Farm, 8643 Kilby Rd., Harrison vicinity, 6/17/76, C, 76001449

Russell, Charles B., House [Samuel Hannaford and Sons TR in Hamilton County], 3416 Brookline Ave., Cincinnati, 3/03/80, C, 80003081

SHOWBOAT MAJESTIC, Broadway St., Cincinnati, 1/03/80, A, 80003085

Sacred Heart Academy [Samuel Hannaford and Sons TR in Hamilton County], 525 Lafayette St., Cincinnati, 4/11/73, C, 73001467

Salem Methodist Church Complex, 6137 Salem Rd., Cincinnati vicinity, 4/29/82, B, C, a, d, 82003586

Sawyer, Louis, House [Wyoming MRA], 315 Reily Rd., Wyoming, 8/25/86, C, 86001645

Saxony Apartment Building [Samuel Hannaford and Sons TR in Hamilton County], 105-111 W. 9th St., Cincinnati, 3/03/80, C, 80003083

Scarlet Oaks, 440 Lafayette Ave., Cincinnati, 3/07/73, C, a, 73001468

Scott, George, House [Samuel Hannaford and Sons TR in Hamilton County], 565 Purcell Ave., Cincinnati, 3/03/80, C, 80003084

Shawnee Lookout Archeological District, Address Restricted, Cleves vicinity, 12/02/74, D, 74001516

Shield's, Edwin M., House, 220 Riverside Ave., Loveland, 4/01/82, A, C, 82003592

Short Woods Park Mound, Address Restricted, Sayler Park vicinity, 10/01/74, D, 74001521

Smith-Jessup House, 1038 W. North Bend Rd., Cincinnati, 8/23/84, C, 84003717

Spencer Town Hall [Columbia-Tusculum MRA], 3833 Eastern Ave., Cincinnati, 8/24/79, C, 79002701

Spring Grove Cemetery, 4521 Spring Grove Ave., Cincinnati, 5/13/76, C, d, 76001440

Spring Grove Cemetery Chapel [Samuel Hannaford and Sons TR in Hamilton County], 4521 Spring Grove Ave., Cincinnati, 3/03/80, C, a, 80003086

St. Francis De Sales Church Historic District, Woodburn Ave. and Madison Rd., Cincinnati, 3/01/74, A, C, a, 74001512

St. Francis Hospital, 1860 Queen City Ave., Cincinnati, 4/19/84, A, C, 84003714

St. Francis Xavier Church, 607 Sycamore St., Cincinnati, 7/18/80, A, C, a, 80003087

St. George Parish and Newman Center [Samuel Hannaford and Sons TR in Hamilton County], 42 Calhoun St., Cincinnati, 3/03/80, C, a, 80003088

St. Patrick's Catholic Church, 1662 Blue Rock, Cincinnati, 12/04/78, A, C, a, 78002081

St. Paul Church Historic District, Spring, 12th and Pendleton Sts., Cincinnati, 1/18/74, A, C, a, 74001513

St. Peter's Lick Run Historic District, 2145–2153 Queen City Ave., Cincinnati, 10/04/89, A, a, 89001453

St. Peter-In-Chains Cathedral, 325 W. 8th St., Cincinnati, 1/18/73, A, C, a, 73001469

St. Rosa Church, 2501 Eastern Ave., Cincinnati, 4/01/82, A, C, a, 82003587

State Line Archeological District, Address Restricted, Elizabethtown vicinity, 7/24/75, D, 75001423

Stearns, Edward R., House [Wyoming MRA], 333 Oliver Rd., Wyoming, 8/25/86, B, C, 86001648

Stearns, William, House [Wyoming MRA], 320 Reily Rd., Wyoming, 8/25/86, B, C, 86001649

Stites House [Columbia-Tusculum MRA], 315 Stites Ave., Cincinnati, 8/24/79, C, 79002699

Story Mound, Address Restricted, Sayler Park vicinity, 6/11/75, D, 75001436

Stowe, Harriet Beecher, House, 2950 Gilbert Ave., Cincinnati, 11/10/70, B, 70000497

Sycamore-13th Street Grouping, 12th, 13th, and Sycamore Sts., Cincinnati, 6/01/82, C, 82003588

Hamilton County—Continued

Taft Museum, 316 Pike St., Cincinnati, 1/29/73, C, NHL, 73001470

Tangeman, John, House [Wyoming MRA], 550 Larchmont, Wyoming, 8/25/86, B, C, 86001650

Thomson, Peter G., House, 5870 Belmont Ave., Cincinnati, 11/29/79, B, C, 79001860

Times-Star Building, 800 Broadway, Cincinnati, 11/25/83, A, C, 83004309

Tonkens, Gerald B. and Beverley, House, 6980 Knoll Rd., Cincinnati, 10/03/91, C, g, 91001414

Turpin Site, Address Restricted, Cincinnati vicinity, 12/27/74, D, 74001514

Twelve Mile House, 11006 Reading Rd., Sharonville, 9/01/76, A, C, 76001452

Twentieth Century Theatre, 3023–3025 Madison Rd., Cincinnati, 8/26/93, C, 93000879

Twin Oaks, 629 Liddle Lane, Wyoming, 5/29/75, B, C, 75001438

Underwriters Salvage Corps, 110-112 E. 8th St., Cincinnati, 7/15/82, A, 82003589

United Brethren in Christ, S of Cincinnati off I-275, Cincinnati vicinity, 6/13/78, A, C, a, d, 78002082

United Methodist Church, 5125 Drake Rd., NE of Mariemont, Mariemont vicinity, 12/04/75, A, B, C, a, d, 75001432

Universalist Church Historic District, Montgomery Rd. from 9433 N to Remington Ave., Montgomery, 12/02/70, A, C, a, 70000498

Village Historic District [Wyoming MRA], Roughly bounded by Wentworth Ave., B & O RR tracks, E. Mill Ave., and Springfield Pike, Wyoming, 8/25/86, A, B, C, 86001626

Village of Addyston Historic District, Roughly, along Main, Sekitan, Church, First and Second Sts. and Three Rivers Pkwy., Addyston, 9/13/91, A, C, 91001388

Waldschmidt-Camp Dennison District, 7509 and 7567 Glendale-Milford Rd., Cincinnati, 3/07/73, A, C, 73001471

Wallace, Charlton, House, 2563 Hackberry St., Cincinnati, 1/30/76, A, C, a, 76001441

Walnut Hills United Presbyterian Church [Samuel Hannaford and Sons TR in Hamilton County], 2601 Gilbert Ave., Cincinnati, 3/03/80, C, a, 80003089

Warder, John Aston, House, E of North Bend off Shady Lane, North Bend vicinity, 5/19/78, B, C, 78002084

Washington Heights School, 8100 Given Rd., Indian Hill, 7/30/75, C, 75001430

West Fourth Street Historic District, Bounded by Central Ave., W. 5th, Plum, and McFarland Sts., Cincinnati, 8/13/76, A, C, 76001443

West Fourth Street Historic District (Amendment), W. 5th and Perry Sts. between Central Ave. and Plum St., 4thSt. between Central Ave. and Race St., Cincinnati, 8/13/79, A, C, 79001861

Westwood Town Center Historic District, Epworth and Harrison Aves., Cincinnati, 12/02/74, C, 74001515

Westwood United Methodist Church [Samuel Hannaford and Sons TR in Hamilton County],

Epworth and Edwiler Sts., Cincinnati, 3/03/80, C, a, 80003090

Whallon, James, House, 11000 Winton Rd., Greenhills, 5/17/73, B, C, 73001473

Whitewater Shaker Settlement, 11813, 11347, 11081 Oxford Rd., New Haven vicinity, 1/21/74, A, C, 74001518

Wilder-Swaim House, 7650 Cooper Rd., Montgomery, 5/20/81, C, 81000438

William Howard Taft National Historic Site, 2038 Auburn Ave., Cincinnati, 10/15/66, B, C, c, NPS, 66000612

Williams, W. L., House, 280 Anderson Ferry Rd., Cincinnati vicinity, 3/25/77, C, 77001066

Wilson-Gibson House, 425 Oak St., Cincinnati, 3/17/76, C, 76001444

Winton Place Methodist Episcopal Church [Samuel Hannaford and Sons TR in Hamilton County], 700 E. Epworth Ave., Cincinnati, 3/03/80, C, a, 80003091

Withrow High School, 1488 Madison Rd., Cincinnati, 1/19/83, A, C, 83001987

Wolfe, Mary A., House [Samuel Hannaford and Sons TR in Hamilton County], 965 Burton Ave., Cincinnati, 3/03/80, C, 80003092

Woodruff, Charles, House [Wyoming MRA], 411 Springfield Pike, Wyoming, 8/25/86, B, C, a, 86001651

Worth, Gorham A., House, 2316 Auburncrest Ave., Cincinnati, 4/11/73, C, 73001472

Wright, Daniel Thew, House, 3716 River Rd., Cincinnati, 9/28/82, A, C, 82003590

Wyoming Presbyterian Church [Samuel Hannaford and Sons TR in Hamilton County], Wyoming and Burns Aves., Wyoming, 3/03/80, C, a, 80003094

Yost Tavern, 7872 Cooper Rd., Montgomery, 5/06/93, A, 93000406

Young Women's Christian Association of Cincinnati, 9th and Walnut Sts., Cincinnati, 9/16/82, A, C, 82003591

Hancock County

Dana, Marcus, House, 707 N. County Line St., Fostoria, 3/24/80, B, C, 80003095

Findlay Downtown Historic District, Roughly along Main, W. Sandusky and W. Main Cross Sts., Findlay, 2/28/85, A, C, 85000402

First Hancock County Courthouse, 819 Park St., Findlay, 3/13/76, C, b, 76001454

Fostoria Mausoleum, 702 Van Buren St., Fostoria, 8/25/78, C, d, 78002085

Hancock County Courthouse, Courthouse Sq., Findlay, 5/07/73, C, 73001475

Hull, Jasper G., House, 422 W. Sandusky St., Findlay, 5/07/73, B, C, 73001476

Jones, Elijah Pelton, House, 313 East Sandusky St., Findlay, 3/14/85, B, C, 85000563

Linaweaver, Dr. Albert, House, 1224 S. Main St., Findlay, 9/29/83, B, C, 83001988

Paulding County Carnegie Library, 205 S. Main St., Paulding, 4/21/83, A, C, 83002021

Powell, Andrew, Homestead, 9821 CR 313, Findlay vicinity, 12/19/86, A, B, C, 86003449

Hardin County

Hardin County Courthouse, Courthouse Sq., Kenton, 3/21/79, A, C, 79001863

Kenton Courthouse Square Historic District, Roughly Main, Detroit, Market, Columbus and Franklin Sts., Kenton, 8/23/84, A, C, 84003722

Kenton Public Library, 121 N. Detroit St., Kenton, 12/29/83, A, B, C, 83004311

North Main-North Detroit Street Historic District, Roughly Main St. bounded by Marie, Cherry, Carroll and Detroit Sts., Kenton, 4/18/85, A, C, a, 85000867

Zimmerman Kame, Address Restricted, Roundhead vicinity, 7/30/74, D, 74001523

Harrison County

Franklin College Building No. 5, Main St., New Athens, 5/08/87, A, C, 87000687

Harrison County Courthouse, Courthouse Sq., Cadiz, 7/18/74, C, 74001524

Harrison National Bank, 101 E. Market St., Cadiz, 12/23/93, A, C, 93001438

Reaves, John, House, Public Sq., Freeport, 7/15/77, C, 77001068

Henry County

First Presbyterian Church, 303 W. Washington, Napoleon, 3/09/90, C, a, 90000381

Henry County Courthouse, N. Perry and E. Washington Sts., Napoleon, 2/28/73, A, C, 73001477

Henry County Sheriff's Residence and Jail, 123 E. Washington St., Napoleon, 6/24/81, A, C, 81000439

St. Augustine's Catholic Church, 221 E. Clinton St. at corner of Monroe, Napoleon, 9/02/82, C, a, 82003593

Highland County

Barretts Mills, CR 1A and Rocky Fork Creek, Rainsboro vicinity, 12/26/72, A, 72001024

Barretts Mills (Boundary Increase), On Factory Branch Creek, Rainsboro vicinity, 7/24/79, A, 79003168

Bell Mansion [Bell, C.S., TR], 225 Oak St., Hillsboro, 11/25/80, B, 80003099

Bell's First Home [Bell, C.S., TR], 222 Beech St., Hillsboro, 11/25/80, B, 80003096

Bell's Opera House [Bell, C.S., TR], 109-119 S. High St., Hillsboro, 11/25/80, B, 80003097

Bell, C.S., Foundry and Showroom [Bell, C.S., TR], 154-158 W. Main St., Hillsboro, 11/25/80, B, 80003098

Highland County—Continued

East Main Street Historic District, E. Main and E. Walnut Sts., Hillsboro, 6/01/82, A, C, a, 82003594

Eubanks-Tytus House, SE of Hillsboro on OH 41, Hillsboro vicinity, 2/27/79, C, 79001865

Fort Hill State Park, SE of Hillsboro on OH 41, Sinking Springs vicinity, 11/10/70, D, 70000500

Highland County Courthouse, Main and High Sts., Hillsboro, 8/24/78, A, C, 78002087

Hillsboro Historic Business District, Roughly bounded by Beech, Walnut, East and West Sts., Hillsboro, 4/19/84, A, C, 84003727

Hirons-Brown House, SW of Buford on Guernsey Rd., Buford vicinity, 12/12/76, A, C, 76001455

Lilley, Robert D., House, 7915 OH 124, Hillsboro, 6/17/82, C, 82003595

Morrow-Overman-Fairley House, 404 N. High St., Hillsboro, 5/31/84, B, C, 84003729

Mother Thompson House, 133 Willow St., Hillsboro, 6/01/82, B, C, 82003596

Rocky Fork Park Group, Address Restricted, Marshall vicinity, 6/18/73, D, 73001478

Rocky Fork Park Site, Address Restricted, Rainsboro vicinity, 6/18/73, D, 73001479

Saint Mary's Episcopal Church and Parish House, 232 N. High St., Hillsboro, 9/08/88, C, a, 88001421

Scott, William, House, 338 W. Main St., Hillsboro, 11/05/87, C, 87001981

Smith, Samuel, House And Tannery, 103 Jefferson St., Greenfield, 7/05/78, B, C, 78002086

Travellers' Rest Inn, Jefferson St. and McArthur Way, Greenfield, 5/15/79, A, C, b, 79001864

Trop Farm, 6250 Mad River Rd., Hillsboro vicinity, 4/01/82, A, C, 82003597

Workman Works, Address Restricted, Salem Township vicinity, 10/26/71, D, 71000641

Hocking County

Davis Works, Address Restricted, Laurelville vicinity, 7/15/74, D, 74001525

Deffenbaugh, George, Mound, Address Restricted, Laurelville vicinity, 7/15/74, D, 74001526

Greek Revival Commercial Building [Fredericktown MRA], 67–69 N. Main St., Fredericktown, 11/06/79, C, 79003866

Haydenville Historic Town, Haydenville, Haydenville, 3/20/73, A, C, 73001480

James, Charles Worth, House, 75 Hill St., Logan, 9/11/80, B, 80003100

Karshner Mound, Address Restricted, Laurelville vicinity, 7/15/74, D, 74001527

Ladies Comfort Station, S. Mulberry St., Logan, 3/09/90, A, C, 90000382

Logan City Hall, 101 E. Main St., Logan, 2/11/80, C, 80003101

McCarthy-Blosser-Dillon Building, 4 W. Main St., Logan, 11/29/84, A, C, 84000449

Ross, Edith, Mound, Address Restricted, Laurelville vicinity, 6/18/73, D, 73001481

Woodruff, William H., House, 35330 Linton Rd., Logan vicinity, 7/29/82, B, C, 82003598

Holmes County

Adams, G., House [Millersburg MRA], 103 N. Clay St., Millersburg, 7/17/84, B, C, 84003730

Armstrong, Joseph, Farm, SE of Fredericksburg, Fredericksburg vicinity, 11/27/78, A, C, 78002088

Boyd School, NW of Berlin on Fryburg-Fredericksburg-Boyd Rd., Berlin vicinity, 10/03/80, C, 80003103

Brightman House, Wooster Rd. and Walnut St., Millersburg, 10/29/74, C, 74001528

Cary, G.W., House [Millersburg MRA], 200 N. Washington St., Millersburg, 7/17/84, C, 84003734

Cary, Hiram W., House [Millersburg MRA], 101 N. Clay St., Millersburg, 7/17/84, B, C, 84003736

Croco House, OH 83, Holmesville vicinity, 6/20/85, C, 85001343

DeYarmon, Joseph L. House, SW Corner of Co. 129 and Twp. 273, Lakeville vicinity, 5/04/82, C, 82003599

Disciple-Christian Church [Millersburg MRA], 100 N. Clay St., Millersburg, 7/17/84, C, a, 84003738

Holmes County Courthouse And Jail, Courthouse Sq., Millersburg, 7/25/74, C, 74001529

Koch, John E., Jr., House [Millersburg MRA], 107 N. Washington St., Millersburg, 7/17/84, B, 84003740

Millersburg Historic District [Millersburg MRA], Jackson, Clay, and Washington Sts., Millersburg, 7/17/84, A, C, 84003743

Pomerene House, U.S. 62, Berlin, 10/20/80, B, C, 80003102

Shull-Lugenbuhl Farm, N of Winesburgh, Winesburgh vicinity, 4/26/79, A, C, 79001866

United Methodist Church [Millersburg MRA], N. Washington St., Millersburg, 7/17/84, C, a, 84003744

Wise, Peter, House, S of Berlin on OH 557, Berlin vicinity, 4/16/80, C, 80003104

Huron County

Benedict, Dr. David De Forest, House, 80 Seminary St., Norwalk, 1/23/75, B, C, 75001439

Brown, Seth, House, 29 Brown St., Monroeville, 5/03/74, C, 74001531

Dunton House, 130 Benedict Ave., Norwalk, 12/16/82, C, 82001469

Gregory House, 1 E. Main St., New London, 2/24/84, A, C, 84003746

Hosford, John, House, 64 Sandusky St., Monroeville, 5/03/74, C, 74001532

Hunts Corners, Jct. of Sandhill Rd. and OH 547, Monroeville vicinity, 9/02/93, A, 93000896

Huron County Courthouse And Jail, E. Main St. and Benedict Ave., Norwalk, 7/12/74, C, 74001534

Macksville Tavern, Peru Hollow Rd., Peru, 5/03/76, A, C, 76001457

Mead-Zimmerman House, E of Greenwich on OH 13, Greenwich vicinity, 3/30/78, C, 78002089

Phoenix Mills, E of Steuben on Mill Rd., Steuben vicinity, 5/28/75, A, C, 75001440

West Main Street District, In an irregular pattern, both sides of W. Main St. for 6 blocks from W edge of business district, Norwalk, 2/27/74, C, a, 74001535

Wright, John, Mansion, OH 113, W of OH 4, Bellevue vicinity, 2/27/74, C, 74001530

Zion Episcopal Church, Ridge St. at Monroe St., Monroeville, 5/03/74, C, a, 74001533

Jackson County

Buckeye Furnace, 10 mi. E of Jackson, Jackson vicinity, 11/10/70, A, e, 70000503

Buckeye Furnace Covered Bridge, 3 mi. SE of Wellston on SR 165, Wellston vicinity, 2/24/75, C, 75001442

Byer Covered Bridge, SR 31, Byer, 10/21/75, C, 75001441

Clutts House, 16 E. Broadway St., Wellston, 11/26/80, B, C, 80003105

Gibson House, 187 Main St., Jackson, 12/05/85, A, B, C, 85003045

Johnson Road Covered Bridge, Johnson Rd., Petersburg vicinity, 8/23/84, C, 84003749

Keystone Furnace, Address Restricted, Pattonsville vicinity, 3/18/82, D, 82003600

Leo Petroglyph, W of Leo, Coalton vicinity, 11/10/70, D, 70000501

Miner's Supply Store, Main and 2nd Sts., Coalton, 11/01/77, A, B, C, 77001069

Morgan Mansion, Broadway and Pennsylvania Aves., Wellston, 2/16/79, B, C, 79001867

Oak Hill Welsh Congregational Church, 412 E. Main St., Oak Hill, 5/23/78, A, C, a, 78002090

Jefferson County

Bantam Ridge School, Bantam Ridge Rd., Wintersville vicinity, 10/01/81, A, b, 81000442

Carnegie Library of Steubenville, 407 S. Fourth St., Steubenville, 9/16/92, C, 92001160

Central High School [Mingo Junction MRA], 110 Steuben Ave., Mingo Junction, 3/17/87, C, 87000471

Central Public School [Mingo Junction MRA], 109 Saint Clair Ave., Mingo Junction, 3/17/87, C, 87000472

Commercial Street Historic District [Mingo Junction MRA], Roughly Commercial St. between McLister and Highland Aves., May, and RR tracks, Mingo Junction, 3/17/87, A, C, 87000468

Federal Land Office, U.S. 22 and OH 7, Steubenville, 4/03/73, A, C, b, 73001482

Friends Meetinghouse, Near OH 150, Mount Pleasant, 11/10/70, A, C, a, 70000504

Hamilton-Ickes House, N of Adena on OH 10, Adena vicinity, 11/26/80, B, C, 80003106

Jefferson County—Continued

Hodgen's Cemetery Mound, Address Restricted, Tiltonsville vicinity, 9/25/75, D, d, 75001443

Independent School District No. 2 Building, 64520 OH 213, Steubenville vicinity, 7/10/86, A, C, 86001569

Lundy, Benjamin, House, Union and 3rd Sts., Mt. Pleasant, 5/30/74, B, NHL, 74001537

Market Street Section, Retaining Wall and Water Trough, Old Market St. between Market St. off ramp and Lawson Ave., Steubenville, 10/08/92, A, C, 92001353

North End Neighborhood Historic District, Roughly, N. Fourth St. from Dock St. to Franklin Ave. and E side of jct. of Franklin and N. Fifth St., Steubenville, 10/01/91, A, C, 91001486

North Hill Historic District [Mingo Junction MRA], Bounded by Logan, George, Western, and Alley W of Logan Ave., Mingo Junction, 3/17/87, C, 87000469

Ohio Valley Clay Company, Washington and Water Sts., Steubenville, 8/10/79, A, 79001868

Speedway Mound, Address Restricted, Warrenton vicinity, 9/05/75, D, 75001444

Steubenville Commercial Historic District, Roughly bounded by Washington, Court and Third, Market, and Eight and Commercial Sts., Steubenville, 8/21/86, A, C, 86001877

Steubenville YMCA Building, 214 N. 4th St., Steubenville, 6/01/82, A, C, 82003601

Stringer Stone House, 224 Warren St., Rayland, 7/10/74, C, 74001538

Union Cemetery—Beatty Park, 1720 W. Market St. and Lincoln Ave., Steubenville, 2/27/87, A, C, d, 86003507

Village of Mount Pleasant Historic District, Roughly bounded by 3rd, North, High, and South Sts., Mount Pleasant, 6/28/74, A, C, a, 74001536

Knox County

Beers, Samuel, House [Fredericktown MRA], W. Sandusky St., Fredericktown, 11/06/79, C, 79003855

Bell House [Fredericktown MRA], 53–57 N. Main St., Fredericktown, 11/06/79, C, 79003856

Brick Commercial Block [Fredericktown MRA], Main and College Sts., Fredericktown, 11/06/79, C, 79003857

Burch, William, House [Fredericktown MRA], Edgehill Dr. and Mount Vernon Ave., Fredericktown, 11/06/79, C, 79003858

Cassell, Henry, House [Fredericktown MRA], 23 High St., Fredericktown, 11/06/79, C, 79003859

Christ Church At The Quarry, E of Gambier at jct. of SR 235 and 233, Gambier vicinity, 9/25/75, A, C, a, 75001446

Cummings, Wilson S., House [Fredericktown MRA], Sandusky and Taylor Sts., Fredericktown, 11/06/79, C, 79003860

Davis and Dague Grocery Store, Old [Fredericktown MRA], Main and College Sts., Fredericktown, 11/06/79, C, 79003869

Delashment, Elias, House [Fredericktown MRA], Second St. and Edgehill Dr., Fredericktown, 11/06/79, C, 79003861

Early Greek Revival Cottage [Fredericktown MRA], Secon and Chestnut Sts., Fredericktown, 11/06/79, C, 79003862

Early Greek Revival House [Fredericktown MRA], Main and Second Sts., Fredericktown, 11/06/79, C, 79003863

East Gambier Street District, 100–519 E. Gambier St., Mount Vernon, 11/18/76, C, 76001459

East High Street Historic District, Roughly bounded by E. Chestnut St., S. Catherine St., E. Vine St., and S. Gay St., Mount Vernon, 3/18/87, C, 86003490

Fredericktown Presbyterian Church [Fredericktown MRA], Main St. and Public Sq., Fredericktown, 11/06/79, C, a, 79003864

Gothic Revival House [Fredericktown MRA], High and N. Main Sts., Fredericktown, 11/06/79, C, 79003865

Greek Revival Farmhouse, Old [Fredericktown MRA], W. Sandusky St., Fredericktown, 11/06/79, C, 79003870

Hosack House [Fredericktown MRA], W. College St., Fredericktown, 11/06/79, C, 79003867

Kenyon College, OH 229 and OH 308, Gambier, 12/06/75, C, 75001447

King, Dr., House [Fredericktown MRA], Main and Second Sts., Fredericktown, 11/06/79, C, 79003868

Knox County Courthouse, High St., Mount Vernon, 6/04/73, C, 73001484

Knox County Infirmary, 7516 Johnstown Rd., Mount Vernon vicinity, 7/10/86, C, a, 86001567

Kokosing House, 221 Kokosing Dr., Gambier, 2/19/85, B, C, 85000450

McFarland, James, House, 7864 Newark Rd., Mount Vernon vicinity, 3/09/90, C, 90000384

McLaughlin Mound, Address Restricted, Mount Vernon vicinity, 12/11/72, D, 72001025

Methodist Church, Old [Fredericktown MRA], Sandusky St. and Public Sq., Fredericktown, 11/06/79, A, C, a, 79003871

Mill Road Bowstring Bridge, Mill Rd, Bladensburg, 12/05/79, C, 79001869

Mount Liberty Tavern, U.S. 36, Mount Liberty, 5/03/74, C, 74001539

North Main—North Gay Streets Historic District, Roughly bounded by Curtis St., N. Gay St., Public Sq., and N. Main St., Mount Vernon, 3/09/90, A, B, C, 90000383

Raleigh Mound, Address Restricted, Fredericktown vicinity, 10/14/75, D, 75001445

Reed, James, House [Fredericktown MRA], E. College St., Fredericktown, 11/06/79, C, 79003873

Round Hill, E. Pleasant and N. McKenzie Sts., Mount Vernon, 12/12/76, B, C, 76001460

Second Hosack House [Fredericktown MRA], College and Chestnut Sts., Fredericktown, 11/06/79, C, 79003874

Sprague—Deaver House [Fredericktown MRA], Sandusky and Pleasant Sts., Fredericktown, 11/06/79, C, 79003875

Stackhouse Mound and Works, Address Restricted, Fredericktown vicinity, 6/18/73, D, 73001483

Telephone Building, Old [Fredericktown MRA], College and Chestnut Sts., Fredericktown, 11/06/79, C, 79003872

Thompson, Enoch, House, SW of Mount Vernon on OH 661, Mount Vernon vicinity, 11/25/80, C, 80003107

Tuttle House [Fredericktown MRA (AD)], 33 E. College St., Fredericktown, 7/12/76, B, C, 76001458

Woodward Opera House, Main and Vine Sts., Mount Vernon, 10/10/75, A, 75001448

Wright, Lyman, Building [Fredericktowb MRA], Main and Second Sts., Fredericktown, 11/06/79, C, 79003876

Lake County

Administration Building, Lake Erie College, 391 W. Washington St., Painesville, 3/20/73, A, C, 73001486

Brick Vernacular House No. 1 [Madison MRA], 98 Lake St., Madison, 10/20/80, C, 80003108

Brick Vernacular House No. 2 [Madison MRA], 120 N. Lake St., Madison, 10/20/80, C, 80003109

Casement House, 436 Casement Ave., Painesville, 7/30/75, A, 75001454

Cheese-vat Factory [Madison MRA], 16 Eagle St., Madison, 10/20/80, C, 80003110

Childs, Alpha Charles, House [Madison MRA], 319 W. Main St., Madison, 10/20/80, A, C, 80003111

Childs, Robertus W., House [Madison MRA], 307 W. Main St., Madison, 10/20/80, C, 80003112

Connecticut Land Company Office, 7071 E. Main St., Unionville, 8/14/73, A, C, 73001491

Corning-White House, 8353 Mentor Ave., Mentor, 11/07/72, C, 72001027

Coulby, Harry, Mansion, 28730 Ridge Rd, Wickliffe, 8/24/79, C, 79001875

Damon, George, House [Madison MRA], 841 W. Main St., Madison, 10/20/80, C, 80003113

Dayton, James, House [Madison MRA], 939 W. Main St., Madison, 10/20/80, B, C, 80003114

Dayton, James, House, II [Madison MRA], 417 W. Main St., Madison, 10/20/80, B, C, 80003115

DeHeck, Albert, House [Madison MRA], 431 W. Main St., Madison, 10/20/80, C, 80003116

Fairport Harbor West Breakwater Light [Light Stations of Ohio MPS], W breakwater pierhead, harbor entrance, Fairport Harbor, 4/10/92, A, C, 92000242

Fairport Marine Museum, 129 2nd St., Fairport Harbor, 11/05/71, A, C, 71000642

Fuller, Frances Ensign, House [Madison MRA], 790 W. Main St., Madison, 10/20/80, B, C, 80003117

Garfield Library, 7300 Center St., Mentor, 2/23/79, C, 79001872

Gilbert, Jane, House [Madison MRA], 189-195 W. Main St., Madison, 10/20/80, B, b, 80003118

Lake County—Continued

Gill, H., House [Madison MRA], 232 River St., Madison, 10/20/80, C, 80003119

Grantham, Norma, Site (33-La-139), Address Restricted, Fairport Harbor vicinity, 5/31/84, D, 84003757

Gray-Coulton House, 8607-8617 Mentor Ave., Mentor, 12/03/75, C, 75001452

Green, Lucius, House, 4160 Main St., Perry, 7/12/76, C, 76001462

Hanna, Leonard C., Jr., Estate, Little Mountain Rd., Kirtland Hills, 3/12/79, A, C, b, e, g, 79001870

Hendry, Francis, House [Madison MRA], 239-243 W. Main St., Madison, 10/20/80, B, C, 80003120

Indian Point Fort, E of Painesville, Painesville vicinity, 7/30/74, D, 74001543

Ingersoll, Cyrus J., House [Madison MRA], 249 W. Main St., Madison, 10/20/80, A, C, 80003121

James A. Garfield National Historic Site, 8095 Mentor Ave., Mentor, 10/15/66, B, NHL, NPS, 66000613

Jones, John J., House [Madison MRA], 298 Lake St., Madison, 10/20/80, C, 80003122

Kellogg, John, House and Barn [Madison MRA], 30 E. Main St., Madison, 10/20/80, B, C, 80003123

Kimball, Addison, House [Madison MRA (AD)], 390 W. Main St., Madison, 3/27/75, B, C, 75001449

Kimball, Lemuel II, House [Madison MRA (AD)], 467 W. Main St., Madison, 10/15/74, B, C, 74001540

Kimball, Solomon, House [Madison MRA], 391 W. Main St., Madison, 10/20/80, B, 80003124

Kirtland Temple, 9020 Chillicothe Rd., Kirtland, 6/04/69, A, C, a, NHL, 69000145

Ladd's Tavern, 5466 S. Ridge Rd., Madison vicinity, 5/22/78, A, 78002091

Lake Shore and Michigan Southern RR Depot and Freight House, 8445 Station St., Mentor, 1/31/78, C, 78002092

Lutz's Tavern, 792 Mentor Ave., Painesville, 4/23/73, C, 73001487

Lyman, William, House [Madison MRA], 734 W. Main St., Madison, 10/20/80, C, 80003125

Madison Fort, Address Restricted, Madison vicinity, 7/30/74, D, 74001541

Madison Seminary And Home, N of Madison at 6769 Middle Ridge Rd., Madison vicinity, 2/22/79, A, C, 79001871

Mason, James, House, 8125 Mentor Ave., Mentor, 9/18/75, C, 75001453

Mathews House, 309 W. Washington St., Painesville, 4/23/73, C, b, 73001488

Mentor Avenue District, Wood St. and Mentor Ave. from Liberty to Washington St., Painesville, 8/03/78, B, C, a, 78002093

Metcalf, Rev. Harlan, House [Madison MRA], 275 W. Main St., Madison, 10/20/80, C, 80003126

Moore, Edward W. and Louise C., Estate, 7960 Garfield Rd., Mentor, 3/10/88, A, B, C, 88000209

Morley, Lewis, House, 231 N. State St., Painesville, 3/30/78, C, 78002094

Norfolk and Western Freight Station [Madison MRA], Lake St., Madison, 10/20/80, A, 80003127

Old South Church, 9802 Chillicothe Rd., Kirtland, 9/20/73, C, a, 73001485

Oliver, John G., House, 7645 Little Mountain Rd., Mentor, 10/01/81, C, 81000444

Paige, David R., House [Madison MRA (AD)], 21-29 W. Main St., Madison, 12/23/75, B, C, 75001450

Painesville City Hall, 7 Richmond St., Painesville, 7/24/72, A, C, 72001028

Pease, George, House [Madison MRA], 553 W. Main St., Madison, 10/20/80, C, 80003128

Sawyer-Wayside House, 9470 Mentor Ave., Mentor vicinity, 10/29/74, C, 74001542

Seeley, Uri, House, 969 Riverside Dr., Painesville, 8/14/73, C, 73001489

Selby, Orland, House [Madison MRA], 564 E. Main St., Madison, 10/20/80, C, 80003129

Sessions House, 157 Mentor Ave., Painesville, 8/14/73, C, 73001490

Smart Building, 4143-4145 Erie St., Willoughby, 9/29/83, A, 83001989

Smead House, 187 Mentor Ave., Painesville, 11/21/74, C, 74001544

Smead, David, House [Madison MRA], 269 E. Main St., Madison, 10/20/80, B, C, 80003130

South Leroy Meetinghouse, NE of Painesville at OH 86 and Brakeman Rd., Painesville vicinity, 5/08/79, A, a, 79001873

St. James Episcopal Church, 141 N. State St., Painesville, 7/07/75, C, a, 75001455

Talcott, Joseph, House [Madison MRA], 354 River St., Madison, 10/20/80, B, C, 80003131

Tappan, Judge Abraham, House, 7855 S. Ridge Rd., Unionville, 5/08/79, B, C, 79001874

Town Center District [Madison MRA], Main St. between River and Lake Sts., Madison, 10/20/80, A, C, 80004247

Unionville District School, 3480 West St., Unionville, 12/29/78, A, C, 78002095

Unionville Tavern, On OH 84, Unionville, 7/26/73, A, C, 73001492

Ware, Edwin L., House [Madison MRA], 293 W. Main St., Madison, 10/20/80, C, 80003132

Whitney, Newel K., Store, 8881 Chillicothe Rd., Kirtland, 8/30/84, A, B, 84003759

Wilson, George D., House [Madison MRA], 367 River St., Madison, 10/20/80, C, 80003133

Winans, Dr. J. C., House [Madison MRA (AD)], 143 River St., Madison, 4/26/76, C, 76001461

Lawrence County

Erlich, F. W., House, 1908 S. 6th St., Ironton, 10/03/80, C, 80003134

Fifth and Lawrence Streets Residential District, 5th and Lawrence Sts., Ironton, 8/02/78, B, C, a, 78002098

Johnston, William C., House And General Store, Washington and Davidson Sts., Burlington, 9/07/76, A, 76001463

Macedonia Church, N of Burlington, Burlington vicinity, 2/07/78, A, C, a, b, 78002096

Maplewood, W of Chesapeake on Maplewood La., Chesapeake vicinity, 4/13/77, A, C, 77001070

Norfolk And Western Railroad Depot, 1st St. and Park Ave., Ironton, 9/13/78, A, C, 78002099

Old Lawrence County Jail, Court St., Burlington, 12/22/78, A, C, 78002097

Rankin Historic District, Roughly bounded by Vernon, 7th, Monroe and 4th Sts, Ironton, 7/26/79, B, C, a, 79001876

Scottown Covered Bridge, E of Scottown on SR 67, Scottown vicinity, 11/12/75, C, 75001456

Vesuvius Furnace, Co. Hwy. 29 at Storms Creek in Vesuvius Recreation Area of Wayne National Forest, Ironton vicinity, 6/14/90, A, C, 89001714

Licking County

Alligator Effigy Mound, Address Restricted, Granville vicinity, 11/05/71, D, 71000643

Avery-Hunter House, 221 E. Broadway, Granville, 12/27/79, C, 79001877

Bancroft, A. A., House [Granville MRA], N. Pearl St. and Washington Dr., Granville, 11/28/80, C, 80003135

Belle Hall Covered Bridge, E of Croton on Dutch Cross Rd., Croton vicinity, 10/22/76, A, C, 76001464

Bethel Baptist Church [Pataskala MRA], Vine and Cedar Sts., Pataskala, 9/22/83, C, a, 83001990

Bryn Mawr, 3758 Lancaster Rd., SW, Granville vicinity, 3/29/83, C, 83001991

Buxton Inn, 313 E. Broadway, Granville, 12/26/72, A, C, 72001029

Carpenter, Wallace W., House [Granville MRA], 323 Summit Dr., Granville, 11/28/80, C, 80003136

Casterton House [Pataskala MRA], 105 Broadway, Pataskala, 9/22/83, C, b, 83001992

Cedar Hill Cemetery Buildings, Cedar St., Newark, 4/13/77, C, d, 77001071

Courthouse Center, 35–37 S. Park Pl. and jct. of S. Park and S. 2nd St., Newark, 11/29/79, A, C, 79001879

Dixon Mound, Address Restricted, Homer vicinity, 6/04/73, D, 73001494

Dustin Cabin [Granville MRA], 597 N. Pearl St., Granville, 11/28/80, C, 80003137

Elliot House [Pataskala MRA], 301 S. Main St., Pataskala, 11/14/83, C, 83004315

Etna Township Mounds I And II, Address Restricted, Reynoldsburg vicinity, 9/05/75, D, 75001457

Evans—Holton—Owens House, 162 W. Locust St., Newark, 10/16/86, C, 86002874

Flint Ridge State Memorial, 2 mi. N of Brownsville, Brownsville vicinity, 11/10/70, D, 70000505

Fuller House, 203 N. Main St., Utica, 3/22/91, C, 91000304

Granville Historic District [Granville MRA], OH 37, Granville, 11/28/80, C, 80003138

Home Building Association Bank, 6 W. Main St., Newark, 7/02/73, C, 73001495

Licking County—Continued

Hudson Avenue Historic District, Hudson Ave. between Stevens St. and OH 37, Newark, 3/18/87, B, C, 86003506

Hull Place, 686 W. Main St., Newark, 12/21/79, C, 79001880

Kauber, Warren F., Funeral Home [Pataskala MRA], 289 S. Main St., Pataskala, 9/22/83, B, C, 83001993

Licking County Courthouse, Courthouse Sq., Newark, 3/20/73, C, 73001496

Lynnwood Farm, S of Johnstown at 4986 Caswell Rd., Johnstown vicinity, 6/22/79, C, 79001878

McCune's Villa, 537 Jones Rd., Granville vicinity, 4/22/82, C, 82003602

McDaniel Mound, Address Restricted, Utica vicinity, 5/02/74, D, 74001545

McNamar-McLure-Miller Residence, 124 W. Main St., Newark, 6/17/82, C, 82003603

Mead House [Pataskala MRA], 245 S. Main St., Pataskala, 9/22/83, B, C, 83001994

Melick Mound, Address Restricted, Utica vicinity, 3/27/74, D, 74001546

Monroe Township Hall-Opera House, 1 S. Main St., Johnstown, 7/06/81, A, C, 81000446

Newark Earthworks, Roughly bounded by Union, 30th, James, and Waldo Sts., and OH 16, Newark, 10/15/66, D, NHL, 66000614

Oakwood, 64-70 Penney Ave., Newark, 5/29/80, C, 80003141

Ohio Canal Groundbreaking Site, OH 79, Heath, 5/24/73, A, 73001493

Pataskala Banking Company [Pataskala MRA], 354 S. Main St., Pataskala, 9/22/83, C, 83001996

Pataskala Elementary School [Pataskala MRA], 396 S. High St., Pataskala, 9/22/83, C, 83001995

Pataskala Jail [Pataskala MRA], Main St., Pataskala, 9/22/83, C, 83001997

Pataskala Presbyterian Church [Pataskala MRA], Atkinson and Main Sts., Pataskala, 11/14/83, C, a, 83004323

Pataskala Town Hall [Pataskala MRA], 430 Main St., Pataskala, 9/22/83, C, 83001998

Pataskala United Methodist Church [Pataskala MRA], 458 S. Main St., Pataskala, 9/22/83, C, a, 83001999

Pennsylvania Railway Station, 25 E. Walnut St., Newark, 11/29/79, A, C, 79001881

Pitzer, Anthony, Jr., House, 6019 White Chapel Rd., Newark vicinity, 8/25/88, C, 88001297

Rhoads, Peter F., House, 74 Granville St., Newark, 11/28/80, C, 80003142

Rogers House [Granville MRA], 304 N. Pearl St., Granville, 11/28/80, C, 80003139

Rose, Capt. Levi, House [Granville MRA], 631 N. Pearl St., Granville, 11/28/80, C, 80003140

Shaub, Martin, Mill Site/House, 8259 Duncan Plains Rd., Alexandria vicinity, 1/23/85, C, 85000119

Sherwood-Davidson And Buckingham Houses, W. Main and 6th Sts., Newark, 11/10/77, C, b, 77001072

Shield's Block, 23–29 S. Park Pl., Newark, 11/29/78, A, C, 78002101

St. Luke's Episcopal Church, 111 E. Broadway St., Granville, 4/26/76, C, a, 76001465

Stanbery, Edwin, Office, 1 mi. (1.6 km) E of Granville, Granville vicinity, 11/30/78, C, b, 78002100

Upham-Wright House, 342 Granville St., Newark, 6/22/79, C, 79001882

Upland Farm, N of Newark off OH 657, Newark vicinity, 12/01/78, C, 78002102

West Side Planing Mill (rear), 197 Maholm St., Newark, 1/21/83, C, 83002000

Williams, Elias, House, 565 Granville St., Newark, 4/16/79, C, 79001883

Logan County

Dunns Pond Mound, Address Restricted, Huntsville vicinity, 7/30/74, D, NHL, 74001548

First Concrete Street In U.S., E. Court Ave., Bellefontaine, 2/25/74, B, C, 74001547

Lake Ridge Island Mounds, Address Restricted, Russells Point vicinity, 10/16/74, D, 74001549

Lawrence, William, House, 325 N. Main St., Bellefontaine, 8/24/79, B, 79001884

Logan County Courthouse, Public Sq., Bellefontaine, 6/04/73, C, 73001497

Marmon, Martin, House, CR 153, Zanesfield vicinity, 2/20/86, A, B, C, 86000322

McColly Covered Bridge, 2 mi. SE of Bloom Center, Bloom Center vicinity, 5/28/75, C, 75001458

Piatt, Abram S., House and Piatt, Donn S., House, TR and SR 245 (Mac-a-Cheek); Ch 1 and SR 287 (Mac-o-Chee), West Liberty, 5/03/82, B, C, 82003604

Lorain County

103rd Ohio Volunteer Infantry Association Barracks, 5501 E. Lake Rd., Sheffield Lake, 7/14/78, A, 78002115

Allen, Darlon, House [Wellington-Huntington Road MRA], S of Wellington on OH 58, Huntington Township, Wellington vicinity, 6/15/79, A, C, 79003877

Amherst Town Hall, 206 S. Main St., Amherst, 5/29/75, A, C, 75001459

Antlers Hotel, SW Erie and Washington Aves., Lorain, 11/30/82, C, 82001470

Avery, Carlos, House, 18797 SR 58, Wellington vicinity, 5/31/84, C, 84003762

Baker, O. T., House [Wellington-Huntington Road MRA], S of Wellington on OH 58, Huntington Township, Wellington vicinity, 6/15/79, C, 79003878

Baptist Parsonage, Old [Wellington-Huntington Road MRA], S of Wellington on OH 58, Huntington Township, Wellington vicinity, 6/15/79, C, 79003890

Bradford, Henry, Farm, N of Rochester on OH 511, Rochester vicinity, 9/30/82, B, C, 82003608

Breckenridge, Justin, House, 37174 S. East Main St., Grafton vicinity, 11/29/78, C, 78002107

Broadway Building, SE corner of W. Erie Ave. and Broadway, Lorain, 11/14/85, A, C, 85002833

Brownhelm Historic District, Along N. Ridge Rd., Vermilion, 6/28/79, B, C, a, 79003748

Bryant, George, House [Elyria MRA], 333 3rd. St., Elyria, 8/13/79, C, 79002727

Burrell Fort, Address Restricted, Sheffield Village vicinity, 4/04/78, D, 78002111

Burrell Orchard Site, Address Restricted, Sheffield Lake vicinity, 9/15/77, D, 77001073

Burrell, Jabez and Robbins, House and Cheese Factory, N of Lorain off OH 301, Sheffield Township vicinity, 1/01/76, A, B, C, 76001471

Burrell-King House, 317 E. College St., Oberlin, 3/07/79, B, C, 79001886

Cahoon, Samuel C., House, 38369 Center Ridge Rd., North Ridgeville, 9/20/78, C, 78002113

Cahoon, Wilbur, House, 2940 Stoney Ridge Rd., Avon, 4/06/78, B, 78002104

Carlin, Patrick, House [Elyria MRA], 1182 W. River Rd., N., Elyria, 8/13/79, C, 79002710

Central School, 474 Church St., Amherst, 11/19/87, C, 87001985

Century Block [Elyria MRA], NE corner of Broad St. and Washington Ave. and N side of Broad St., Elyria, 8/13/79, C, 79002718

Chapman, John A., House [Wellington-Huntington Road MRA], S of Wellington on OH 58, Huntington Township, Wellington vicinity, 6/15/79, A, C, 79003879

Christ Episcopal Church, 156 S. Main St., Oberlin, 11/30/78, A, C, a, 78002114

Clark, Ansel, House [Wellington-Huntington Township MRA], S of Wellington on OH 58, Huntington Township, Wellington vicinity, 6/15/79, C, 79003880

Clark, Whitney, House [Wellington-Huntington Road MRA], S of Wellington on OH 58, Huntington Township, Wellington vicinity, 6/15/79, C, 79003881

Columbia Baptist Church, 25514 Royalton Rd., Columbia Center, 7/12/76, C, a, 76001466

Columbia Town Hall, 25496 Royalton Rd., Columbia Center, 3/17/76, A, C, 76001468

Commercial Building [Elyria MRA], NE corner 2nd St. and Middle Ave., Elyria, 8/13/79, C, 79002724

Congregational Church of Christ, W. Lorain and N. Main Sts., Oberlin, 8/13/74, A, C, a, 74001554

Dean Road Bridge, W of South Amherst at Dean Rd. and Vermilion River, South Amherst vicinity, 11/28/78, C, 78002119

Duane Block, 387–401 Broadway, Lorain, 7/16/87, A, C, 87001248

Eiden Prehistoric District, Address Restricted, Lorain vicinity, 11/21/78, D, 78002112

Ely Block [Elyria MRA], N side of Broad St. between Washington and East Ave., Elyria, 8/13/79, C, 79002717

Elyria Elks Club [Elyria MRA], 246 2nd St., Elyria, 8/13/79, C, 79002726

Elyria High School—Washington Building [Elyria MRA], SW corner of 6th St. and Middle Ave., Elyria, 8/13/79, C, 79002735

Evans, Wilson Bruce, House, 33 E. Vine St., Oberlin, 4/16/80, B, 80003143

First Church Of Christ, Scientist, 309 East Ave., Elyria, 7/18/75, C, a, 75001460

Lorain County—Continued

First National Bank Building [Elyria MRA], Broad St., Elyria, 8/13/79, C, 79002719

First United Methodist Church [Elyria MRA], 312 3rd St., Elyria, 8/13/79, C, a, 79002730

Garfield, Halsey, House, 4789 Detroit Rd., Sheffield, 5/22/78, C, 78002116

Garfield, Milton, House, 4921 Detroit Rd., Sheffield, 9/21/78, B, C, 78002117

Garford, Arthur L., House, 509 Washington Ave., Elyria, 12/30/74, B, C, 74001551

Gregg House [Wellington-Huntington Road MRA], S of Wellington on OH 58, Huntington Township, Wellington vicinity, 6/15/79, C, b, 79003882

Gunn House [Huntington-Wellington Road MRA], S of Wellington on OH 58, Wellington Township, Wellington vicinity, 6/15/79, C, 79003883

Huntington Grange [Wellington-Huntington Road MRA], S of Wellington at jct. of OH 58 and 162, Huntington Township, Wellington vicinity, 6/15/79, C, a, 79003884

Huntington Inn, Old [Wellington-Huntington Road MRA], S of Wellington at jct. of OH 58 and 162, Huntington Township, Wellington vicinity, 6/15/79, A, C, 79003891

Huntington Public School [Wellington-Huntington Road MRA], S of Wellington at jct. of OH 58 and 162, Huntington Township, Wellington vicinity, 6/15/79, C, 79003885

Huntington Township Hall [Wellington-Huntington Road MRA], S of Wellington on OH 58, Huntington Township, Wellington vicinity, 6/15/79, C, a, 79003886

Hurst, William E., House, 33065 Detroit Ave., Avon, 9/11/74, C, 74001550

Immaculate Conception Church, 708 Erie St., Grafton, 3/16/76, A, C, a, 76001469

Jewett, Frank, House, 73 S. Professor St., Oberlin, 7/24/79, B, 79001887

Johnson Steel Street Railway Company General Offices Building, 1807 E. 28th St., Lorain, 7/16/92, A, C, 92000887

Johnson, E. J., House [Elyria MRA], Middle Ave. and 9th St., Elyria, 8/13/79, A, 79002737

Langston, John Mercer, House, 207 E. College St., Oberlin, 5/15/75, B, NHL, 75001464

Laundon, Thomas W., House, 307 West Ave., Elyria, 10/21/75, B, C, 75001462

Lersch, John, House [Elyria MRA], 121 Harrison St., Elyria, 8/13/79, C, 79002711

Lorain County Courthouse, 308 2nd St., Elyria, 6/18/75, C, 75001463

Lorain Fire Station No. 1, 605 W. Fourth St., Lorain, 8/20/87, A, C, 87001374

Lorain Lighthouse, Lorain Harbor, Lorain, 12/29/78, A, C, 78002108

Lorain YMCA Building, Jct. of E. 28th St. and Pearl Ave., Lorain, 7/16/92, A, 92000886

Methodist Parsonage, Old [Wellington-Huntington Road MRA], S of Wellington on OH 58, Huntington Township, Wellington vicinity, 6/15/79, C, 79003892

Mill Hollow House, The, SE of Vermilion on N. Ridge Rd., Vermilion vicinity, 6/29/76, C, 76001472

Miller, Peter, House, 33740 Lake Rd., Avon Lake, 8/25/78, B, 78002106

Monteith Hall, 218 East Ave., Elyria, 10/09/74, B, C, 74001552

Moore, Leonard M., House, 309 5th St., Lorain, 12/30/93, B, 93001439

Morris—Franks Site, Address Restricted, Vermilion vicinity, 9/05/75, D, 75001465

Mosher House [Wellington-Huntington Road MRA], S of Wellington on OH 58, Wellington Township, Wellington vicinity, 6/15/79, C, 79003887

New York Central Freight House, 412 E. River St., Elyria, 6/01/82, A, 82003605

Nichols, Walter, House [Elyria MRA], SE corner of 4th St. and West Ave., Elyria, 8/13/79, C, 79002733

Nimocks House [Wellington-Huntington Road MRA], S of Wellington on OH 58, Huntington Township, Wellington vicinity, 6/15/79, C, 79003888

Nooney, William , House [Wellington-Huntigton Road MRA], S of Wellington on OH 58, Huntington Township, Wellington vicinity, 6/15/79, C, a, 79003889

North Ridgeville City Hall, U.S. 20, North Ridgeville, 12/30/74, C, 74001553

Oberlin College, Tappan Sq., Oberlin, 10/15/66, A, f, NHL, 66000615

Oberlin Lake Shore And Michigan Southern Station, Depot Park, Oberlin, 3/02/79, A, C, 79001888

Old Amherst Freight Depot, Franklin St., Amherst, 11/21/78, C, 78002103

Old City Hall [Elyria MRA], Court St. facing Elyria Square, Elyria, 8/13/79, A, 79002725

Old District Nine Schoolhouse [Elyria MRA], Chestnut St., Elyria, 8/13/79, A, 79002715

Old Elyria Water Tower [Elyria MRA], S side of W. 15th St., 100 ft. W. of Black River Bridge, Elyria, 8/13/79, A, 79002739

Old Railroad Station [Elyria MRA], 49 East Ave., Elyria, 8/13/79, C, 79002714

Old St. John's Church [Elyria MRA], 600 W. Broad St., Elyria, 8/13/79, C, a, 79002721

Old St. Patrick's Church, 512 N. Main St., Wellington, 3/21/79, C, a, 79001890

Palace Theatre Building, Broadway and 6th St., Lorain, 3/30/78, C, 78002109

Reamer Barn, Address Restricted, Oberlin vicinity, 3/21/79, C, 79001889

Redington Block [Elyria MRA], E side of Middle Ave. between Broad and 2nd Sts. 2nd bldg from Ind. St., Elyria, 8/13/79, C, 79002723

Reefy, Frederick, House [Elyria MRA], 3rd St. between West Ave. and Court St., Elyria, 8/13/79, C, 79002729

Root, William H., House, 3535 E. Erie Ave., Lorain, 9/20/78, B, C, 78002110

Sage House [Wellington-Huntington Road MRA], S of Wellington on OH 58, Huntington Township, Wellington vicinity, 6/15/79, C, a, 79003893

Seher, William, House, 329 W. 9th St., Lorain, 6/17/76, C, 76001470

Sheffield Village Hall, Detroit Rd., Sheffield, 10/05/78, A, C, d, 78002118

Shepherd, John J., House [Elyria MRA], NW corner of East Ave. and 8th St., Elyria, 8/13/79, A, 79002736

Soldiers and Sailors Monument [Elyria MRA], Elyria Square (Downtown), Elyria, 8/13/79, C, f, 79002722

South Ridge Schoolhouse, OH 113 and Bechtel Rd., Amherst Township, 8/08/85, A, C, 85001692

Sprague House [Wellington-Huntington Road MRA], S of Wellington at jct. of OH 58 and Jones Rd., Wellington Township, Wellington vicinity, 6/15/79, C, 79003894

St. Andrew's Episcopal Church [Elyria MRA], 300 3rd St., Elyria, 8/13/79, C, a, 79002731

St. Ladislaus Roman Catholic Church, 2908 Wood Ave., Lorain, 4/01/82, C, a, 82003607

St. Mary's Catholic School [Elyria MRA], 320 Middle Ave., Elyria, 8/13/79, C, a, 79002734

St. Mary's Roman Catholic Church [Elyria MRA], 320 Middle Ave., Elyria, 8/13/79, C, a, 79002732

Starr, Horace C., House and Carriage Barns, 276 Washington Ave., Elyria, 4/03/79, A, C, a, 79001885

U.S. Post Office [Elyria MRA], NE corner of Broad and East Sts., Elyria, 8/13/79, C, 79002720

U.S. Post Office, Ninth St. and Broadway Ave., Lorain, 12/09/82, C, 82001471

Union Church, 511 Church St., Kipton, 3/15/82, C, a, 82003606

United Church of Huntington [Wellington-Huntington Road MRA], S of Wellington on OH 58, Huntington Township, Wellington vicinity, 6/15/79, C, a, 79003895

Wadsworth, Benjamin, House [Wellington-Huntington Road MRA], S of Wellington on OH 58, Huntington Township, Wellington vicinity, 6/15/79, C, 79003896

Washington Avenue Historic District [Elyria MRA], Roughly Ohio, Columbus, Harrison, and Saint Clair Sts. between Washington Ave. and Glenwood St., Elyria, 8/20/87, B, C, 87001376

Washington Terrace Apartments [Elyria MRA], Washington Ave., Elyria, 8/13/79, C, 79002713

Webber, A. R., House [Elyria MRA], 251 Washington Ave., Elyria, 8/13/79, B, 79002712

Wellington Center Historic District, Main St. and Herrick Ave., Wellington, 11/21/74, A, C, 74001556

Wellington Historic District, Irregular pattern along Main St. from Kelley St. to W and L E RR, Wellington, 5/30/79, A, C, 79001891

West House [Wellington-Huntington Road MRA], S of Wellington on OH 58, Huntington Township, Wellington vicinity, 6/15/79, C, 79003897

Westervelt Hall, 39 S. Main St., Oberlin, 5/03/74, A, C, 74001555

Wilber, J. B., House [Wellington-Huntington Road MRA], S of Wellington on OH 58, Huntington Township, Wellington vicinity, 6/15/79, A, C, 79003898

Williams, Henry Harrison, House, 37392 Detroit Rd., Avon, 7/12/78, A, C, 78002105

Lorain County—Continued

Wooster Block [Elyria MRA], N side of Broad St. between Lodi St. and Washington Ave., Elyria, 8/13/79, C, 79002716

Lucas County

Ashland Avenue Baptist Church, Ashland and Woodruff Sts., Toledo, 11/26/80, C, a, 80003144

Berdan Building, 601 Washington St., Toledo, 5/29/75, C, 75001468

Birckhead Place Historic District, Birckhead Pl., Toledo, 10/13/83, C, 83004316

Brand, R., and Company, 120–124 St. Clair St., Toledo, 5/27/75, C, 75001469

Bronson Place, Roughly bounded by Cherry St., Central and Franklin Aves., Toledo, 11/29/84, C, 84000459

Burt's Theater, 719–723 Jefferson St., Toledo, 11/01/77, A, C, 77001074

Bush Street Historic District, Bush and Erie Sts., Toledo, 6/01/82, A, B, C, 82003609

Central YMCA, 1110 Jefferson Ave., Toledo, 4/15/82, C, 82003610

Columbian House, River and Farnsworth Rds., Waterville, 12/17/69, B, C, 69000146

East Side Commercial Block, 107–117 Main St., Toledo, 5/03/76, A, 76001473

Eckenrode And Breisach Houses, 202 and 204 E. Dudley St., Maumee, 4/06/78, C, 78002120

Fallen Timbers Battlefield, 2 mi. W of Maumee on U.S. 24, Maumee vicinity, 10/15/66, A, f, NHL, 66000616

First Church of Christ, Scientist, 2704 Monroe St., Toledo, 11/29/78, A, C, a, 78002125

First Presbyterian Church Of Maumee Chapel, 200 E. Broadway, Maumee, 8/13/73, C, a, 73001498

Forsythe—Puhl House, 106 E. Harrison Ave., Maumee, 5/18/89, B, C, 89000429

Fort Industry Square, Bounded by Summit, Monroe, and Water Sts. and Jefferson Ave., Toledo, 7/23/73, A, C, 73001501

Fort Miamis Site, Address Restricted, Maumee vicinity, 6/18/75, D, 75001466

Gendron, Peter, House, 1413 Walnut St., Toledo, 3/03/83, A, B, 83002001

Gillett-Shoemaker-Welsh House, 133 N. 4th St., Waterville vicinity, 7/18/75, C, 75001474

Governor's Inn, 301 River Rd., Maumee, 10/18/74, C, 74001557

Griswold, Peck, House, 228 E. Broadway, Maumee, 5/22/78, C, 78002121

Hanson House, 405 E. Broadway, Maumee, 5/22/78, C, 78002122

Haskins, Liberty Whitcomb, House, N of Waterville at 625 Canal Rd., Waterville vicinity, 7/01/75, C, 75001475

House Of Four Pillars, 322 E. Broadway, Maumee, 7/16/73, B, C, 73001499

Hull, Isaac, Store, 114 E. Harrison St., Maumee, 3/30/78, B, 78002123

Hull-Wolcott House, 1031 River Rd., Maumee, 1/26/70, B, C, 70000506

Huron—Superior Streets Warehouse—Produce Historic District, Roughly bounded by Erie, Monroe, Superior and Market Sts., Toledo, 3/24/93, A, C, 93000153

Interurban Bridge, 1 mi. S of Waterville over Maumee River, Waterville vicinity, 6/19/72, A, C, 72001036

Inverness Club, 4601 Dorr St., Toledo, 5/10/93, A, C, 93000398

Isham, John, Farmstead, 8460 S. River Rd., Waterville, 9/16/92, A, C, 92001159

Isham, John, House, 8460 S. River Rd., Waterville vicinity, 8/09/82, C, 82005388

Libbey, Edward D., House, 2008 Scottwood Ave., Toledo, 5/04/83, B, NHL, 83004379

Lucas County Courthouse and Jail, Courthouse Sq. and 810–814 Jackson, Toledo, 5/11/73, C, 73002295

Ludwig, Isaac R., Historical Mill, Mill Rd. in Providence Park, Providence, 6/28/74, A, 74001558

Maumee Sidecut, N of Maumee River, SW of Ewing Island, Maumee, 4/11/73, A, C, 73001500

Maumee Uptown Historic District, Conant, Wayne, and Dudley Sts., Maumee, 3/01/84, A, C, 84003766

Monroe Street Commercial Buildings, 513–623 Monroe St., Toledo, 12/12/76, C, 76001474

Morehouse-Downes House, 4 S. River Rd., Waterville, 5/29/75, C, 75001476

Neukom, Albert, House, 301 Broadway, Toledo, 3/04/71, C, 71000644

Old Central Post Office, 13th St. between Madison and Jefferson Aves., Toledo, 2/23/72, C, 72001030

Old West End District, Roughly bounded by Delaware, Collingwood, and Glenwood Aves. and Grove Pl., Toledo, 3/14/73, B, C, 73001503

Old West End Historic District (Boundary Increase/Decrease), Roughly bounded by Glenwood, Glover, Ashland, Collingwood, and Central Aves., Toledo, 3/30/84, A, C, 84003771

Pray-Starkweather House, 144 N. River Rd., Waterville vicinity, 5/29/75, C, 75001477

Providence Historic District, Court and Main Sts., Ludwig and Providence-Neopolis Rds., Providence, 8/13/75, B, 75001467

Pythian Castle, 801 Jefferson Ave., Toledo, 2/23/72, A, C, 72001032

Reed, Henry, Jr., House, 511–513 White St., Maumee, 4/20/78, B, C, 78002124

Riverview Apartments, 1829-1837 Summit St., Toledo, 4/21/83, C, 83002002

Saint Peter and Saint Paul Historic District—Oliver's Second addition, 600 and 700 blks. of S. Saint Clair St., Toledo, 3/13/87, A, C, a, 87000465

Secor Hotel, 413–423 Jefferson Ave., Toledo, 4/30/76, A, C, 76001475

Secor, Joseph K., House, 311 Bush St., Toledo, 6/11/79, A, B, 79003108

Spitzer Building, 514-526 Madison Ave., Toledo, 4/21/83, C, 83002004

St. Ann Roman Catholic Church Complex, 1105 W. Bancroft and 1120 Horace Sts., Toledo, 5/05/83, C, a, 83002003

St. Clair Street Historic District, Both sides of St. Clair St. from Perry St. to S side of Lafayette St., Toledo, 5/29/75, C, 75001471

St. Patrick's Catholic Church, 13th St. and Avondale Ave., Toledo, 2/23/72, A, C, a, 72001033

Standart-Simmons Hardware Company, 36 S. Erie St., Toledo, 5/29/75, C, 75001472

Successful Sales Company, 27 Broadway, Toledo, 5/06/71, A, C, 71000645

Toledo Club, 14th St. and Madison Ave., Toledo, 12/01/78, A, C, 78002127

Toledo Harbor Light [U.S. Coast Guard Lighthouses and Light Stations on the Great Lakes TR], Toledo Harbor, Toledo, 8/04/83, A, C, 83002005

Toledo Olde Towne Historic District, Roughly bounded by Central Ave., Cherry St., Franklin Ave., Bancroft St., and Collingwood Ave., Toledo, 9/21/89, A, C, 89001454

Toledo Yacht Club, Bay View Park, Toledo, 12/12/76, A, C, 76001476

Trinity Episcopal Church, 316 Adams St., Toledo, 12/29/83, C, a, 83004317

Valentine Theater Building, 405–419 Saint Clair and 402–412 Adams, Toledo, 5/19/87, C, 87000686

Vistula Historic District, Roughly bounded by Champlain, Summit, Walnut and Magnolia Sts., Toledo, 12/06/78, A, C, a, 78002128

Waterville Commercial District, 3rd St., Waterville, 12/12/76, A, C, 76001477

West Sister Island Light [U.S. Coast Guard Lighthouses and Light Stations on the Great Lakes TR], West Sister Island, Toledo vicinity, 8/04/83, A, C, 83002006

Westmoreland Historic District, Roughly bounded by Parkside Blvd., Bancroft St., Upton Ave., and Oakwood Ave. and Allenby Rd., Toledo, 2/03/86, A, C, g, 86000208

Wright, Dr. John A., House, 1822 Cherry St., Toledo, 10/05/78, B, C, 78002129

Madison County

Cary Village Site, Address Restricted, Plain City vicinity, 5/13/75, D, 75001479

London Commercial Business Historic District, Roughly bounded by Adams, Superior and Clair Sts., Madison Ave., and Huron St., London, 12/17/85, C, 85003212

Madison County Courthouse, Public Sq., London, 3/14/73, C, 73001504

Mount Sterling Historic District, Both sides of London St., Mount Sterling, 10/01/74, C, 74001559

Red Brick Tavern, 1700 Cumberland Rd., Lafayette, 9/05/75, C, 75001478

Skunk Hill Mounds, Address Restricted, West Jefferson vicinity, 7/30/74, D, 74001560

Swetland House, 147 E. High St., London, 1/11/83, B, C, 83002007

Wilson, Valentine, House, About 1 mi. N of Somerford off I 70, Somerford vicinity, 5/22/73, C, 73001505

Mahoning County

Alliance Clay Product Company, 1500 S. Mahoning Ave., Alliance vicinity, 12/08/78, A, 78002130

Anderson, Judge William Shaw, House, 7171 Mahoning Ave., Austintown vicinity, 3/17/76, B, C, 76001479

Arlington Avenue District, 304-373 Arlington Ave., Youngstown, 8/13/74, A, C, 74001565

Austintown Log House, W of Youngstown on Raccoon Rd., Youngstown vicinity, 7/30/74, A, C, 74001566

Baltimore & Ohio Railroad Terminal, 530 Mahoning Ave., Youngstown, 7/10/86, A, C, 86001565

Butler Institute Of American Art, 524 Wick Ave., Youngstown, 10/29/74, C, 74001567

Central Tower Building [Seven Early Office Buildings at Central Square TR], 1 Federal Plaza West, Youngstown, 2/08/80, A, C, 80003146

City Hall Annex [Downtown Youngstown MRA], 9 W. Front St., Youngstown, 7/23/86, A, C, 86001918

Crandall Park—Fifth Avenue Historic District, Roughly bounded by Tod Ln., Ohio Ave., Redondo Rd., Catallina, and Guadalupe Ave., & Fifth Ave. from Gypsy to Fairgreen, Youngstown, 3/22/90, A, C, 90000474

Damascus Grade School, 14923 Morris St., Damascus, 9/21/89, C, 89001456

Erie Terminal Building—Commerce Plaza Building [Downtown Youngstown MRA], 112 W. Commerce St., Youngstown, 7/23/86, A, C, 86001914

Federal Building [Seven Early Office Buildings at Central Square TR], 18 N. Phelps St., Youngstown, 2/08/80, A, C, 80003147

First National Bank Building [Seven Early Office Buildings at Central Square TR], 6 Federal Plaza West, Youngstown, 2/08/80, A, C, 80003148

Helen Chapel [Downtown Youngstown MRA], NW corner of E. Wood and Champion Sts., Youngstown, 7/23/86, A, C, a, 86001923

Hopewell Furnace Site, Address Restricted, Struthers vicinity, 11/10/75, D, 75001481

Idora Park, SE of the jct. of McFarland and Parkview Aves., Youngstown, 9/13/93, A, C, 93000895

Jay's Lunch [Downtown Youngstown MRA], 258 Federal Plaza W, Youngstown, 7/23/86, A, C, 86001925

Jones Hall, Youngstown State University, 410 Wick Ave., Youngstown, 10/18/84, A, C, 84000151

Kirtland, Jared P., House, 113 W. McKinley Way, Poland, 5/13/76, B, C, 76001481

Kress Building [Downtown Youngstown MRA], 111-121 Federal Plaza W, Youngstown, 7/23/86, A, C, 86001926

Lake Hamilton Dam, 1.5 miles NE of Poland off SR 616, Struthers vicinity, 5/07/84, A, C, 84003774

Lanterman Mill, Canfield Rd. (U.S. 62) in Mill Creek Park, Youngstown, 7/10/74, A, C, 74001568

Liberty Theatre, 142 Federal Plaza W., Youngstown, 2/09/84, C, 84003776

Lowellville Railroad Station, Penn Central RR., Lowellville, 7/30/76, A, 76001480

Mahoning County Courthouse, 120 Market St., Youngstown, 8/13/74, C, 74001569

Mahoning National Bank Building [Seven Early Office Buildings at Central Square TR], 23 Federal Plaza West, Youngstown, 2/08/80, A, C, 80003149

Maple-Dell, 14737 Garfield Rd., Salem vicinity, 12/20/90, B, 90001821

McCrory Building [Downtown Youngstown MRA], 9-13 Federal Plaza W and 17-19 Central Sq., Youngstown, 7/23/86, A, C, 86001928

McGuffey, William H., Boyhood Home Site, McGuffey Rd., near OH 616, Coitsville Township, 10/15/66, B, NHL, 66000617

McKelvey—Higbee Co. Buildings [Downtown Youngstown MRA], 210-226 Federal Plaza W and 18-26 N. Hazel St., Youngstown, 7/23/86, A, C, 86001930

McMillan, Reuben, Free Library, 305 Wick Ave., Youngstown, 3/27/86, C, 86000526

Mill Creek Park Suspension Bridge, Mill Creek Park, Youngstown, 10/29/76, C, 76001482

Neff, Conrad, House, 3967 Canfield-Boardman Rd., Canfield vicinity, 10/09/74, A, C, 74001561

Newton, Judge Eben, House, 105 N. Broad St., Canfield, 7/18/74, B, C, 74001562

Ohio One—Ohio Edison [Downtown Youngstown MRA], 25 E. Boardman and 102-112 S. Champion, Youngstown, 7/23/86, A, C, 86001931

Old Mahoning County Courthouse, 7 Court St., Canfield, 10/07/74, C, 74001563

Our Lady of Mount Carmel Church, Off OH 289, Youngstown, 5/10/79, A, C, a, 79001893

Peggy Ann Building [Downtown Youngstown MRA], 101 Federal Plaza W and 2-10 S. Phelps, Youngstown, 7/23/86, A, C, 86001937

Poland Center School, US 224 and Struthers Rd., Poland, 5/31/84, A, C, 84003779

Rayen School, 222 Wick Ave., Youngstown, 10/22/74, A, C, 74001570

Realty Building [Seven Early Office Buildings at Central Square TR], 47 Federal Plaza, Youngstown, 2/08/80, A, C, 80003150

Renner, George J., Jr., House, 277 Park Ave., Youngstown, 10/08/76, C, 76001483

Republic Iron and Steel Office Building [Downtown Youngstown MRA], 415 S. Market St., Youngstown, 7/23/86, A, C, 86001940

Ruggles, Charles, House, 17 Court St., Canfield, 8/01/75, C, 75001480

Sebring, Frank, House, 385 W. Ohio Ave., Sebring, 9/21/89, B, C, 88000545

South Main Street District, Both sides of S. Main St., Poland, 10/01/74, A, B, C, 74001564

South Main Street District (Boundary Increase), 101 and 111 S. Main St., Poland, 10/18/84, A, C, 84000136

Southern Park Stable, 126 Washington Blvd., Boardman, 7/10/86, A, 86001564

St. James Episcopal Church, 375 Boardman-Poland Rd., Boardman, 6/20/79, A, C, a, b, 79001892

Stambaugh Building [Seven Early Office Buildings at Central Square TR], 44 Federal Plaza, Youngstown, 2/08/80, A, C, 80003151

Stambaugh, Henry H., Memorial Auditorium, 1000 5th Ave., Youngstown, 2/09/84, A, C, 84003781

State Theater [Downtown Youngstown MRA], 213 Federal Plaza W, Youngstown, 7/23/86, A, C, 86001942

Strouss—Hirschberg Company [Downtown Youngstown MRA], 14-28 Federal Plaza W, Youngstown, 7/23/86, A, C, 86001944

Tod Homestead Cemetery Gate, Belmont Ave., Youngstown, 10/22/76, C, 76001484

Vaughn, Daniel, Homestead, 694 Pine Dr., Lake Milton, 7/18/80, A, C, 80003145

Warner Theater, 260 W. Federal Plaza, Youngstown, 5/31/80, B, C, g, 80003152

Wells Building [Downtown Youngstown MRA], 201-205 Federal Plaza W, Youngstown, 7/23/86, A, C, 86001946

Welsh Congregational Church [Downtown Youngstown MRA], 220 N. Elm St., Youngstown, 7/23/86, A, C, a, 86001947

White Bridge, .07 miles E of SR 616 crossing Yellow Creek, Poland Village, 12/11/83, A, C, 83004319

Wick Avenue Historic District, Bounded by Wick, Bryson, Expwy., Spring, and Wick Oval, Youngstown, 11/20/74, B, C, 74001571

Wick Avenue Historic District (Boundary Decrease), Get this later, Youngstown, 11/20/74, 74002347

Wick Building [Seven Early Office Buildings at Central Square TR], 34 Federal Plaza West, Youngstown, 2/08/80, A, C, 80003153

Wick Park Historic District, Roughly bounded by 5th and Elm Aves., Elm St. and Broadway, Youngstown, 4/05/90, A, C, 90000601

YWCA Building [Downtown Youngstown MRA], 25 W. Rayen Ave., Youngstown, 7/23/86, A, C, 86001949

Youngstown Sheet and Tube Company Housing, Jackson and Chambers St., Campbell, 6/01/82, C, 82003611

Marion County

Bretz Farm, 197 Morrall-Kirkpatrick Rd., Morrall vicinity, 1/08/80, A, C, 80003155

Caledonia Bowstring Bridge, N of Caledonia, Caledonia vicinity, 5/23/78, A, C, 78002131

Harding Tomb, Marion Cemetery, Marion, 6/16/76, B, C, c, f, g, 76001485

Harding, Warren G., House, 380 Mount Vernon Ave., Marion, 10/15/66, B, NHL, 66000618

Hotel Harding, 267 W. Center St., Marion, 3/11/80, C, 80003154

Marion County—Continued

Marion County Courthouse, Courthouse Sq., Marion, 7/25/74, C, 74001572

Palace Theater, 272 W. Center St., Marion, 3/26/76, A, C, g, 76001486

Wyatt's Tavern-Fort Morrow Site, Address Restricted, Waldo vicinity, 12/22/78, D, 78002132

Medina County

Black River Viaduct, Baltimore And Ohio Railroad, 1 mi. W of Lodi off OH 421, Lodi vicinity, 5/06/76, A, C, 76001488

Blake, H. G., House, 314 E. Washington St., Medina, 9/30/82, B, C, 82003612

Blakslee, Burritt, House, 3756 Fenn Rd., Medina vicinity, 12/04/74, C, 74001573

Burr, George, House, 740 Wooster Rd., Lodi vicinity, 5/03/76, A, C, 76001489

Chandler, Matthew, House, S of Sharon Center at 6908 Ridge Rd., Sharon Center vicinity, 3/30/78, A, C, 78002134

Cook, Zimri, House, 6994 Spieth Rd., Lester, 6/22/76, C, 76001487

Frank, Charles, House And Store, W of Valley City at jct. of OH 303 and SR 23, Valley City vicinity, 9/05/75, B, C, 75001485

Gayer, Jacob, House, N of Medina at 4508 Marks Rd., Medina vicinity, 6/22/79, A, C, 79001894

Hulburt, Halsey, Homestead, 5484 Seville Rd., Seville vicinity, 12/01/88, B, C, 88002747

King-Phillips-Deibel House, 506 N. Broadway St., Medina, 12/16/82, C, b, 82001472

Medina County Courthouse, Liberty St. and Broadway, Public Sq., Medina, 7/16/70, A, C, 70000507

Medina Public Square Historic District, Public Sq. and surrounding properties, Medina, 6/11/75, A, C, 75001483

Munson, Judge Albert, House, 231 E. Washington St., Medina, 11/26/80, B, 80003156

Paleo Crossing Site, Address Restricted, Sharon Center vicinity, 7/30/92, D, 92000972

Parmelee House, 1328 W. River Rd, Valley City, 11/29/79, B, C, 79001895

Root, A. I. And E. R., Homestead, 662 W. Liberty St., Medina, 6/10/75, B, C, 75001484

Seymour, William H., House, 3306 S. Weymouth Rd., Weymouth, 6/04/79, A, C, 79001896

Sharon Center Public Square Historic District, OH 94 and OH 162, Sharon Center, 10/03/80, A, C, 80003157

St. Mark's Episcopal Church, 146 College St., Wadsworth, 2/06/73, C, a, 73001506

St. Martin's Catholic Church, SW of Valley City on Station Rd. (CR 23), Valley City vicinity, 11/12/75, C, a, 75001486

St. Paul's Episcopal Church, 317 E. Liberty St., Medina, 6/01/82, C, a, 82003613

Universalist Church Of Westfield Center, LeRoy and Greenwich Rds., Westfield Center, 11/29/78, A, C, a, 78002135

York United Methodist Church, Norwalk Rd., Mallet Creek, 2/17/78, A, C, a, 78002133

Meigs County

Buffington Island, 20 mi. SE of Pomeroy on OH 124, Pomeroy vicinity, 11/10/70, A, 70000508

Downing, John, Jr., House, 220–232 N. Second Ave., Middleport, 5/06/93, B, C, 93000403

Grant, William H., House, 453 Grant St., Middleport, 3/30/78, A, C, a, 78002136

Meigs County Fairgrounds, Grandstand and Racetrack, OH 124, Rock Springs, 11/29/82, A, C, 82001473

Middleport Public Library, 178 S. Third St., Middleport, 1/06/86, A, C, 86000033

Mound Cemetery Mound, N of Chester in Mound Cemetery, Chester vicinity, 5/02/74, D, d, 74001575

Old Meigs County Courthouse And Chester Academy, OH 248, Chester, 6/30/75, A, C, 75001488

Pomeroy Historic District, 2nd and Main Sts., Pomeroy, 11/14/78, A, C, 78003551

Pomeroy Historic District (Boundary Increase), Second St., Pomeroy, 11/22/80, A, C, a, 80004248

Reeves Mound, Address Restricted, Alfred vicinity, 7/15/74, D, 74001574

Mercer County

Cassella Catholic Church and Rectory [Cross-Tipped Churches of Ohio TR], RT. 119, Cassella, 7/26/79, A, C, a, 79002822

Celina Main Street Commercial Historic District, Roughly bounded by Walnut, W. Livingston, Ash and Warren Sts., Celina, 11/30/82, C, 82001474

Chickasaw School and Rectory [Cross-Tipped Churches of Ohio TR], Maple St., Chickasaw, 7/26/79, A, C, a, 79002848

Coldwater Catholic Church Complex [Cross-Tipped Churches of Ohio TR], E. Main and 2nd Sts., Coldwater, 7/26/79, A, C, a, 79002832

Fort Recovery Site, OH 49, Fort Recovery, 11/10/70, A, 70000509

Gast, Matthias, House and General Store, OH 119, Maria Stein, 12/29/78, A, B, C, 78002139

Godfrey, Sen. Thomas J., House, 602 W. Market St., Celina, 11/26/80, B, C, 80003159

Grand Lake St. Marys Lighthouse, Grand Lake St. Marys-Northwood Addition, Celinda vicinity, 6/02/82, C, 82003614

Gruenwald Convent [Cross-Tipped Churches of Ohio TR], .5 mi. S of Cassella, Cassella vicinity, 7/26/79, A, B, a, 79002813

Immaculate Conception Catholic Church Complex [Cross-Tipped Churches of Ohio TR], Anthony and Walnut Sts., Celina, 7/26/79, C, a, 79002833

Maria Stein Catholic Church and Rectory [Cross-Tipped Churches of Ohio TR], St. John's Rd. and OH 119, Maria Stein, 7/26/79, C, a, 79002828

Maria Stein Convent [Cross-Tipped Churches of Ohio TR (AD)], St. John's and Rolfes Rd., Maria Stein vicinity, 5/06/76, A, a, 76001490

Mendon Town Hall, S. Main St., Mendon, 12/29/78, A, C, 78002140

Otis Hospital, 441 E. Market St., Celina, 11/25/80, A, C, 80003160

Philothea Catholic Church and Priest House [Cross-Tipped Churches of Ohio TR], Philothea Rd. between St. Henry and Coldwater, Philothea, 7/26/79, C, a, 79002823

Riley, Calvin E., House, 130 E. Market St., Celina, 11/30/78, A, C, 78002137

St. Aloysius Catholic Church [Cross-Tipped Churches of Ohio TR], OH 274 and OH 127, Carthagena, 7/26/79, C, a, 79002824

St. Anthony Catholic Church, Padua [Cross-Tipped Churches of Ohio TR], Rt. 49 and St. Anthony Rd., St. Anthony, 7/26/79, C, a, 79002821

St. Bernard Catholic Church and Rectory [Cross-Tipped Churches of Ohio TR], Main St., Burketsville, 7/26/79, C, a, 79002842

St. Charles Seminary and Chapel [Cross-Tipped Churches of Ohio TR], .5 mi. S of Carthagena, off OH 127, Carthagena vicinity, 7/26/79, C, a, 79002840

St. Francis Catholic Church and Rectory [Cross-Tipped Churches of Ohio TR], Cranberry and Ft. Recovery-Minster Rd., Cranberry Prairie, 7/26/79, A, C, a, 79002837

St. Henry Catholic Church [Cross-Tipped Churches of Ohio TR], Main St., St. Henry, 7/26/79, A, C, a, 79002829

St. Joseph Catholic Church and Rectory [Cross-Tipped Churches of Ohio TR], Sawmill and St. Joe Rds., St. Joe, 7/26/79, A, C, a, 79002820

St. Paul's Catholic Church and Rectory [Cross-Tipped Churches of Ohio TR], R.R. 1, Ft. Recovery, Sharpsburg, 7/26/79, A, C, a, 79002827

St. Peter Catholic Church and Rectory [Cross-Tipped Churches of Ohio TR], St. Peter and Philothea Rds., St. Peter, 7/26/79, C, a, 79002831

St. Rose Catholic Church Complex [Cross-Tipped Churches of Ohio TR], Main St., St. Rose, 7/26/79, C, a, 79002838

St. Sebastian Catholic Church and Rectory [Cross-Tipped Churches of Ohio TR], Sebastian Rd. and OH 716-A, St. Sebastian, 7/26/79, C, a, 79002830

St. Wendelin Catholic Church, School, and Rectory [Cross-Tipped Churches of Ohio TR], Ft. Recovery-Minster Rd. and Township Line, Wendelin, 7/26/79, C, a, 79002885

Wallischeck Homestead, N of Fort Recovery, Fort Recovery vicinity, 11/27/78, A, C, 78002138

Miami County

African Jackson Cemetery, N of Piqua on Zimmerlin Rd., Piqua, 12/16/82, A, d, 82001475

Miami County—Continued

Arrowston, 1220 Park Ave., Piqua, 2/08/80, C, 80003162

Baumgardner, William, House and Farm Buildings, 8390 National Rd., New Carlisle vicinity, 2/17/78, A, C, 78002141

Casstown Lutheran Stone Church, 11 S. Main St., Casstown, 5/31/84, A, C, a, 84003783

Covington Historic Government Building, Spring and Pearl Sts., Covington, 6/22/81, A, 81000447

Culbertson, Robert, House, 304 E. Franklin St., Troy, 10/10/75, C, 75001489

Dunlap, William K., House, 16 E. Franklin St., Troy, 12/12/76, B, C, 76001492

Dye, John Minor, Stone House, 9 S. Children's Home Rd., Troy vicinity, 7/07/83, A, C, 83002008

Eldean Covered Bridge, N of Troy across Miami River on CR 33, Troy vicinity, 2/20/75, C, 75001492

First Presbyterian Church, Franklin and Walnut Sts., Troy, 12/12/76, A, C, a, 76001493

Fort Piqua Hotel, 114 W. Main St., Piqua, 2/15/74, A, C, 74001576

Hayner, Mary Jane, House, 301 W. Main St., Troy, 1/30/76, C, 76001494

Hobart Circle Historic District [Hobart Welded Steel Houses TR], 2–9 Hobart Cir. and 11 and 23 Hobart Dr., Troy, 5/25/89, A, C, g, 89000419

Hobart, E. A., House [Hobart Welded Steel Houses TR], 172 S. Ridge, Troy, 5/25/89, A, C, g, 89000420

Hobart, William, Vacation House [Hobart Welded Steel Houses TR], 905 Polecat Rd., Troy vicinity, 5/25/89, A, C, g, 89000421

House at 1022 West Main Street [Hobart Welded Steel Houses TR], 1022 W. Main St., Troy, 5/25/89, A, C, g, 89000424

House at 121 South Ridge [Hobart Welded Steel Houses TR], 121 S. Ridge, Troy, 5/25/89, A, C, g, 89000425

House at 129 South Ridge [Hobart Welded Steel Houses TR], 129 S. Ridge, Troy, 5/25/89, A, C, g, 89000423

House at 145 South Ridge [Hobart Welded Steel Houses TR], 145 S. Ridge, Troy, 5/25/89, A, C, g, 89000426

House at 203 Penn Road [Hobart Welded Steel Houses TR], 203 Penn Rd., Troy, 5/25/89, A, C, g, 89000422

Iddings, Benjamin, Log House, 6.5 mi. W of Troy, Troy vicinity, 11/21/76, B, 76001497

Lockington Locks Historical Area, Miami Canal between Lockington and Washington Twshp., Lockington and vicinity, 12/17/69, A, C, 69000147

Miami County Courthouse and Power Station, Bounded by Main, Short, Plum, and Water Sts., Troy, 5/30/75, C, 75001490

Old Tippecanoe Main Street Historic District, 5-439 W. Main St. and 3-225 E. Main St., Tipp City, 7/07/83, A, C, 83002009

Overfield Tavern, 201 E. Water St., Troy, 1/30/76, A, B, 76001495

Piqua Historical Area State Memorial, OH 66, 1 mi. N of Piqua, Piqua vicinity, 4/07/71, B, C, D, 71000646

Piqua-Caldwell Historic District, N. Main, Wayne, Downing, Caldwell Sts; W. Ash to Camp Sts., Piqua, 1/11/85, A, C, 85000069

Plainview Farm, 535-545 Weddle Rd., Casstown vicinity, 4/18/85, B, 85000857

Rial, York, House, McFarland St., Piqua, 8/12/86, B, C, 86002620

Saunders, Elizabeth Sheets, Farm, 4525 McCandless Rd., Casstown vicinity, 11/21/76, A, C, 76001491

Sheets, Andrew, House, 6880 LaFevre Rd., Elizabeth Township, 2/01/88, C, 87002522

Staley Farm, N of Brandt at 7095 Staley Rd., Brandt vicinity, 3/24/80, A, C, 80003161

Troy Public Square, Property surrounding jct. of Main and Market Sts., Troy, 6/30/75, A, C, 75001491

Twin Arch Stone Culvert, N of Troy at SR 25A, Troy vicinity, 7/17/78, A, C, 78002142

Weddle, Callahill and Priscilla, House, 5710 LeFevre Rd., Troy vicinity, 6/18/87, C, 87000986

Wheeling and Lake Erie RR Minerva Station, 301 Valley St., Minerva, 9/10/92, A, 92001246

Williams, Judge Henry, House, 16 S. Cherry St., Troy, 1/01/76, B, C, 76001496

Monroe County

Foreaker Bridge, 3 mi. E of Graysville on SR 40, Graysville vicinity, 6/05/75, C, 75001493

Hollister-Parry House, 217 Eastern Ave., Woodsfield, 4/16/80, C, 80003166

Kindleberger, Frederick, Stone House and Barn, NW of Clarington on SR 25, Clarington vicinity, 2/08/80, A, C, 80003163

Knowlton Covered Bridge, N of Rinards Mills on SR 387-A, Rinards Mills vicinity, 3/11/80, A, 80003165

Monroe Bank, 117 Main St., Woodsfield, 3/11/80, A, C, 80003167

Monroe County Courthouse, Main St., Woodsfield, 7/21/80, A, C, 80003168

Mooney, William C., House, 122 N. Paul St., Woodsfield, 3/15/82, B, C, 82003615

Ring, Walter, House and Mill Site, Address Restricted, Graysville vicinity, 11/28/80, A, C, D, 80003164

Salem Church, 48452 OH 255, Sardis vicinity, 8/18/92, C, a, 92000989

Montgomery County

Arnold Homestead, N of Dayton on OH 201, Dayton vicinity, 11/07/77, A, B, a, 77001077

Ausenbaugh-McElhenry House, 7373 Taylorsville Rd., Dayton, 7/18/75, C, 75001503

Biltmore Hotel, 210 N. Main St., Dayton, 2/03/82, C, 82003616

Bossler, Marcus, House, 136 S. Dutoit St., Dayton, 9/27/80, C, 80003170

Bradford, Robert, House, S of Centerville on Social Row Rd., Centerville vicinity, 3/21/79, A, C, 79001897

Brooks, James, House, 41 E. 1st St., Dayton, 5/29/75, B, C, 75001495

Brown, Samuel N., House, 1633 Wayne Ave., Dayton, 4/11/77, B, C, 77001075

Carlisle Fort, Address Restricted, Germantown vicinity, 2/15/74, D, 74001584

Centerville Historic District, Irregular pattern at Franklin and Main Sts., Centerville, 12/17/74, B, C, 74001577

Central Avenue Historic District, 201-338 Central Ave., Dayton, 12/16/82, C, 82001476

Classic Theater, 815 W. 5th St., Dayton, 2/10/75, A, C, g, 75001496

Commercial Building, 44 S. Ludlow St., Dayton, 12/02/82, B, C, 82001477

Conover Building, 4 S. Main St., Dayton, 10/14/75, C, 75001497

Dayton Arcade, From Ludlow to Main St. between 3rd and 4th Sts., Dayton, 6/18/75, A, C, 75001498

Dayton Art Institute, Forest and Riverview Aves., Dayton, 11/19/74, C, g, 74001579

Dayton Daily News Building, 4th and Ludlow Sts., Dayton, 11/30/78, B, C, 78002144

Dayton Fire Department Station No. 16, 31 S. Jersey St., Dayton, 5/23/80, C, 80003171

Dayton Fire Station No. 14, 1422 N. Main St., Dayton, 9/27/80, A, C, 80003172

Dayton Motor Car Company Historic District, 15, 101, 123-5 Bainbridge; 9-111 and 122-124 McDonough, Dayton, 5/31/84, A, C, 84003785

Dayton Stove and Cornice Works, 24-28 N. Patterson Blvd., Dayton, 11/26/80, A, C, 80003173

Dayton Terra-Cotta Historic District, S. Ludlow and W. 5th Sts., Dayton, 5/31/84, B, C, 84003789

Dayton View Historic District, Roughly bounded by Broadway, Harvard Blvd., Superior and Salem Aves., Dayton, 7/19/84, A, C, 84003787

Dayton Woman's Club, 225 N. Ludlow St., Dayton, 2/24/75, B, C, 75001494

Dayton Young Men's Christian Association Building, 117 W. Monument Ave., Dayton, 8/25/88, A, C, 88001299

Deeds' Barn, 35 Moraine Circle South, Kettering, 12/04/79, C, b, 79001904

Deerwood Farm, N of Dayton at 7200 Peters Pike, Dayton vicinity, 11/12/75, B, C, 75001507

Dunbar Historic District, N. Summit St., Dayton, 6/30/80, A, B, C, 80003174

Dunbar, Paul Lawrence, House, 219 N. Summit St., Dayton, 10/15/66, B, NHL, 66000619

Duncarrick, Webster and Keowee Sts., Dayton, 6/30/83, B, C, 83002010

Eagles Building, 320 S. Main St., Dayton, 11/04/82, C, 82001478

East Second Street District, 3-27 E. 2nd St., Dayton, 3/07/79, A, C, 79001898

Emmanuel's Evangelical Lutheran Church [Pennsylvania German Churches of Ohio MPS], 30 W. Warren St., Germantown, 9/06/90, A, C, a, 90001292

Montgomery County—Continued

Fire Blocks Historic District, Roughly bounded by Jefferson, Fourth, St. Clair and Second Sts., Dayton, 10/15/92, A, B, C, 92001374

First Lutheran Church, 138 W. 1st St., Dayton, 3/29/83, C, a, 83002011

Flory, Joseph, House, NW of Clayton on Diamond Mill Rd., Clayton vicinity, 3/29/78, B, C, 78002143

Gilbert, Philip E., Houses, 1012 Huffman Ave. and 18-30 Belpre Pl., Dayton, 8/03/79, C, b, 79001899

Gottschall, Oscar M., House, 20 Livingston Ave., Dayton, 4/11/77, C, 77001076

Gummer House, 1428 Huffman Ave., Dayton, 2/17/78, C, 78002145

Gunckel's Town Plan Historic District, Roughly bounded by Mulberry and Walnut Sts., and Warren and Market Sts., Germantown, 5/13/76, A, B, C, 76001502

Hanitch-Huffman House, 139 W. Monument Ave., Dayton, 3/29/82, B, C, b, 82003617

Hawthorn Hill, Harman and Park Aves., Oakwood, 10/18/74, B, C, NHL, 74001585

Holy Cross Lithuanian Roman Catholic Church [European Ethnic Communities, Dayton MPS], 1924 Leo St., Dayton, 11/05/91, A, C, a, f, g, 91001582

Huffman Historic District, Roughly bounded by E. 3rd., Hamilton, Van Lear and Beckel Sts., Dayton, 8/24/82, B, C, 82003618

Incinerator Site, Address Restricted, Dayton vicinity, 4/01/75, D, NHL, 75001500

Independent Order of Oddfellows, Dayton Lodge No. 273, 8 LaBelle St., Dayton, 10/25/84, A, C, 84000109

Jacob's Church [Pennsylvania German Churches of Ohio MPS], 213 E. Central Ave., Miamisburg, 9/06/90, A, C, a, 90001290

Joyce, Jacob O., House, 6 Josie St., Dayton, 11/25/83, B, C, 83004321

Kellog, Ethol, House, W of Centerville off SR 755 on Yankee St., Centerville vicinity, 6/18/76, B, 76001498

Kelly Family Home, 657 S. Main St., Dayton, 6/30/75, B, C, 75001501

Kemp, Lewis, House, 4800 Burkhardt Ave., Dayton, 1/23/75, B, C, 75001502

Kettering, Charles F., House, 3965 Southern Blvd., Kettering, 12/22/77, B, NHL, 77001080

Koehne—Poast Farm, W of Germantown off OH 725, Germantown vicinity, 4/11/77, B, C, 77001079

Kossuth Colony Historic District, Baltimore St., Mack and Notre Dame Aves., Dayton, 12/21/79, B, C, 79001900

Krug House, 3473 Sweet Potato Ridge Rd., Union vicinity, 8/12/92, C, 92000973

Kuhns, Benjamin F., Building, 43 S. Main St., Dayton, 4/24/78, C, 78002146

Lafee Building, 22 E. 3rd St., Dayton, 11/25/80, C, 80003175

Lichliter Mound And Village Site, Address Restricted, Dayton vicinity, 6/04/73, D, 73001510

Lindsey Building, 25 S. Main St., Dayton, 3/14/85, A, C, 85000564

Long—Mueller House, 986 Laurelwood Rd., Kettering, 4/23/87, C, 87000637

Long—Romspert House, 1947 Far Hills Ave., Oakwood, 12/21/87, A, 87001522

Market Square, Both sides of Main St. including jcts. at Central and Linden Aves., Miamisburg, 11/10/75, C, 75001510

Martindale, Samuel, House, NE of Englewood off U.S. 40, Englewood vicinity, 5/22/78, B, C, 78002148

McPherson Town Historic District, Roughly bounded by Main St., Great Miami River, and I-75, Dayton, 9/29/88, C, 88001712

Memorial Hall, 125 E. First St., Dayton, 7/14/88, A, C, 88001062

Miami-Erie Canal Lock No. 70, Fishburg and Endicott Rds., Huber Heights, 12/20/82, A, C, 82001479

Miamisburg Mound, SE of Miamisburg on OH 725, Miamisburg vicinity, 11/10/70, D, 70000511

Miller, Daniel, House, 3525 Dandridge Ave., Dayton, 5/29/75, C, 75001504

Montgomery County Courthouse, NW corner 3rd and Main Sts., Dayton, 1/26/70, B, C, 70000510

Mumma, Jacob H. W., House, 2239 Kipling Dr., Dayton, 5/29/80, B, C, 80003176

Mutual Home & Savings Association Building, 120 W. 2nd St., Dayton, 12/16/82, C, 82001480

Newcom House, 53 Sherman St., Dayton, 7/21/80, C, 80003177

Normandy Farms, 450 W. Alex-Bell Rd., Centerville vicinity, 11/25/83, B, C, a, 83004322

Ohmer, Nicholas, House, 1350 Creighton St., Dayton, 10/16/74, B, C, 74001580

Old Post Office And Federal Building, SE corner of W. 3rd and Wilkinson Sts., Dayton, 3/10/75, A, C, 75001505

Oregon Historic District, Between Patterson Blvd. and Wayne Ave. N to Gates St. and S to U.S. 35, Dayton, 3/27/75, B, C, 75001506

Pease Homestead, 2123 Alexander-Bellbrook Rd., Centerville, 8/11/80, B, C, 80003169

Pollack, Isaac, House, 319 W. 3rd St., Dayton, 12/16/74, B, C, b, 74001581

Pretzinger, Rudolph, House, 908 S. Main St, Dayton, 8/24/79, C, 79001901

Reynolds, John R., House, 24 Klee St., Dayton, 11/21/76, B, C, 76001499

Rohr, David, Mansion And Carriage House, Astoria Rd. and OH 725, Germantown, 5/22/78, B, C, 78002149

Rubicon Farm, 1815 Brown St., Dayton, 9/29/76, B, C, 76001500

Sachs and Pruden Ale Company Building, 127 Wyandot St., Dayton, 8/12/91, A, C, 91000973

Sacred Heart Church, 217 W. Fourth St., Dayton, 10/22/87, C, a, 87001885

Saint Anne's Hill Historic District, Roughly bounded by Fourth, McClure, Josie, and High and Dutoit Sts., Dayton, 6/05/86, A, C, 86001214

Salem Bear Creek Church, Salem Evangelical Lutheran Church [Pennsylvania German Churches of Ohio MPS], Roughly bounded by Union Rd., Dayton Germantown Pike, and Bear Creek, Germantown, 9/06/90, A, C, a, d, 90001291

Schantz Park Historic District, Roughly bounded by Far Hills, Irving, Mahart and Schenck Aves., Oakwood, 10/16/92, A, B, C, 92001492

Schantz, Adam Sr., House, 314-316 Schantz Ave., Dayton, 3/07/80, B, C, 80003178

Schriber, Hyman, Building, 306–308 Washington St., Dayton, 5/26/88, C, 88000667

Schuter Carpenter Shop and House, 3224 W. Alexandersville-Bellbrook Rd., West Carrollton, 9/27/80, B, C, 80003179

Shawen Acres, 3304 N. Main St., Dayton, 10/09/91, A, C, 91001487

Shuey's Mill, Main St., Germantown, 9/05/75, A, C, 75001508

Sig's General Store, 1400 Valley St., Dayton, 8/12/91, A, C, 91000974

Smith, Edwin, House, 131 W. 3rd St., Dayton, 8/13/74, C, 74001582

South Park Historic District, Roughly bounded by Park, Morton, Hickory, and Wayne Ave., Dayton, 8/23/84, A, C, 84003794

South Park Historic District (Boundary Increase), Roughy bounded by Wayne, Wyoming, Nathan, Oak, Alberta and Blaine, Dayton, 6/16/88, A, B, C, 88000857

Southern Ohio Lunatic Asylum, 2335 Wayne Ave., Dayton, 11/15/79, A, C, 79001902

Spitler, Samuel, House, 14 Market St., Brookville, 9/28/73, C, b, 73001507

St. Adalbert Polish Catholic Church [European Ethnic Communities, Dayton MPS], 1511 Valley St., Dayton, 11/07/91, A, C, a, 91001581

St. Mary Roman Catholic Church, 543 Xenia Ave., Dayton, 4/21/83, C, a, 83002012

St. Mary's Hall, University Of Dayton, 300 College Park, Dayton, 5/25/73, C, 73001508

Steele's Hill-Grafton Hill Historic District, Roughly bounded by Grand, Plymouth, Forest, and Salem, Dayton, 6/05/86, A, C, 86001237

Stengel, John S., House, 325 W. 2nd St., Dayton, 4/21/83, A, C, g, 83002013

Stump, John, House And Mill, SW of Germantown at jct. of Signal and Oxford Rds., Germantown vicinity, 7/07/75, B, C, 75001509

Taylorsville Canal Inn, 4240 Taylorsville Rd., Dayton vicinity, 11/16/77, A, C, 77001078

Trailsend, 3500 Governors Trail, Kettering, 5/22/79, B, C, 79001905

Traxler Mansion, 42 Yale Ave., Dayton, 4/24/79, C, 79001903

Trotwood Railroad Station and Depot, 2 W. Main St., Trotwood, 1/26/81, A, b, 81000448

United Brethren Publishing House, 40–46 S. Main St. (7–21 E. Fourth St.), Dayton, 12/10/93, A, C, 93001391

Victory Theater Building, 138 N. Main St., Dayton, 6/22/72, B, 72001037

Walters, Dr. Jefferson A., House, 35 E. 1st St., Dayton, 11/20/74, B, C, 74001583

Watkins House, 9950 Lebanon Pike, Centerville vicinity, 12/24/74, C, 74001578

West Third Street Historic District, Roughly W. Third St. between Broadway and Shannon St., Dayton, 1/25/89, B, C, 88003194

Montgomery County—Continued

Westbrock Funeral Home, 1712 Wayne Ave., Dayton, 3/10/88, A, 88000205

Wolf Creek Mound, Address Restricted, Trotwood vicinity, 6/04/73, D, 73001511

Women's Christian Association, 800 W. 5th St., Dayton, 5/13/76, A, 76001501

Woodland Cemetery Gateway, Chapel And Office, 118 Woodland Ave., Dayton, 11/30/78, C, d, 78002147

Wright Cycle Company—Wright and Wright Printing Offices, 22 S. Williams St., Dayton, 2/13/86, A, B, C, NHL, 86000236

Wright Flyer III, Carillon Park, 2001 S Patterson Blvd., Dayton, 6/21/90, A, B, C, e, NHL, 90001747

Morgan County

Big Bottom Massacre Site, 1 mi. SE of Stockport on OH 266, Stockport vicinity, 11/10/70, A, f, 70000512

McConnelsville Historic District, OH 376 and OH 77, McConnelsville, 6/14/79, A, C, 79001906

Rock Hollow School, S of Ringgold on SR 67, Ringgold vicinity, 1/11/83, C, 83002014

Morrow County

Brown, Samuel, P., House, S of Fulton on Worthington-New Haven Rd., Fulton vicinity, 3/15/82, C, 82003619

Chester Town Hall [Chesterville MRA], Sandusky and South Sts., Chesterville, 8/21/79, A, C, 79002752

Chesterville Methodist Church [Chesterville MRA], Sandusky and East Sts., Chesterville, 8/21/79, A, C, a, 79002754

Floral Hall, Morrow County Fairgrounds, Mount Gilead, 12/12/76, A, 76001503

Jarvis House [Chesterville MRA], Portland St., Chesterville, 8/21/79, C, 79002756

Levering Hall, 12 S. Main St., Mount Gilead, 5/29/80, A, B, C, 80003180

Miles, Enos, House [Chesterville MRA], Portland St., Chesterville, 8/21/79, B, C, 79002758

Morrow County Courthouse And Jail, Courthouse Sq., Mount Gilead, 7/25/74, C, 74001586

Old Bartlett and Goble Store [Chesterville MRA], Sandusky and Portland Sts., Chesterville, 8/21/79, C, 79002748

Old Union School [Chesterville MRA], Off of OH 314, Chesterville, 8/21/79, C, 79002743

Sears, A. B., House [Chesterville MRA], Sandusky St., Chesterville, 8/21/79, C, 79002745

Trimble, James S., House, 187 Iberia St., Mount Gilead, 11/30/82, C, 82001481

U.S. Post Office [Chesterville MRA], Sandusky and South Sts., Chesterville, 8/21/79, C, 79002750

Wood Commercial Building [Chesterville MRA], Sandusky and Portland Sts., Chesterville, 8/21/79, C, b, 79002747

Muskingum County

"S" Bridge II, U.S. 40 W of New Concord, New Concord vicinity, 4/23/73, A, C, 73001513

Adams, George W., House, S of Trinway on Bottom Rd, Trinway vicinity, 11/29/79, B, C, 79001912

Adena Court Apartments, 41 S. 4th St., Zanesville, 9/27/80, C, 80003190

Alameda Apartments, 7th St., Zanesville, 6/17/82, C, 82003623

Arlington Hotel, 722 Main St., Zanesville, 12/16/82, C, 82001482

Baughman Memorial Park, W of Frazeysburg on OH 586, Frazeysburg vicinity, 8/27/79, C, f, 79001909

Belt Line and New York Central Freight House [Zanesville Historic Railroad Depots TR], 3rd and Market Sts., Zanesville, 3/24/83, A, C, 83002015

Black-Elliott Block, 525 Main St., Zanesville, 5/08/79, C, 79001914

Blocksom-Rolls House, 960 Eastman St., Zanesville, 2/21/79, C, 79001915

Brendel, Charles, House, 427 Wayne Ave., Zanesville, 11/25/80, C, 80003191

Brighton-Drydon Historic District, Dryden Rd., Brighton Blvd., Lexington and Stanberry Aves., Zanesville, 6/01/82, A, C, 82003624

Buckingham-Petty House, Mound Rd., Duncan Falls, 8/11/80, C, 80003182

Christman, Nicholas, House, 532 Wayne Ave., Zanesville, 5/22/78, C, 78002159

Clossman Hardware Store, 621-623 Main St., Zanesville, 11/25/80, B, C, 80003192

Crescent Hill, 44 W. Fifth St., Dresden, 1/09/86, B, 86000034

Denison, William, House, 7115 Adamsville Rd. (OH 93), Adamsville vicinity, 4/29/82, A, C, 82003620

Dresden Suspension Bridge, OH 208 and OH 666, Dresden, 12/01/78, A, C, 78002153

Emery, Abram, House, 413 Pershing Rd., Zanesville, 12/06/78, A, C, 78002160

Factory Site [Robinson-Ransbottom Pottery TR], Moxahala Creek, Ironspot, 3/11/80, A, 80003183

Fairmont Avenue Historic District, Fairmont Ave., Zanesville, 11/30/82, C, 82001483

Five Mile House, S of Zanesville off U.S. 22, Zanesville vicinity, 4/11/77, A, C, 77001081

Galigher, James, House, S of Zanesville on S. River Rd., Zanesville vicinity, 2/22/79, B, C, 79001916

Gorsuch, Ernest J., House, 1869 Norwood Blvd., Zanesville, 3/11/80, B, C, 80003193

Grant School, Off U.S. 22, Zanesville, 11/25/80, A, C, 80003194

Hardesty, Ralph, Stone House, Main St., Norwich, 3/11/80, C, 80003184

Harper, William Rainey, Log House, E. Main St., New Concord, 4/06/78, B, C, b, c, 78002154

Harper-Cosgrave Block, N. 3rd St., Zanesville, 1/03/80, A, C, 80003195

Harris, William B., House, 1320 Newman Dr., Zanesville, 5/22/78, A, C, 78002161

Headley Inn., Smith House And Farm, 5255 West Pike, Zanesville vicinity, 4/26/78, A, C, 78002162

Hunter, James, Stone House, E of Adamsville on Mercer Rd., Adamsville vicinity, 1/03/80, C, 80003181

Johnston-Crossland House, N. 7th St., Zanesville, 3/15/82, C, 82003625

Kearns, George and Edward, Houses, 306 and 320 Luck Ave., Zanesville, 2/02/79, B, C, 79001917

Lafayette Lodge No. 79, 333 Market St., Zanesville, 9/13/78, A, C, 78002163

Lash, William D., House, 2261 Dresden Rd., Zanesville, 2/17/78, B, C, 78002164

Lilienthal Building, 44 S. 6th St., Zanesville, 7/21/80, B, 80003196

Lind Arcade, 48 N. 5th St., Zanesville, 6/01/82, C, 82003626

Locust Site (33MU160), Address Resticted, Nashport vicinity, 8/01/85, D, 85001696

Masonic Temple Building, 36–42 N. Fourth St., Zanesville, 5/25/90, A, C, 90000756

McClelland, Harry S., House, 908 Laurel Ave., Zanesville, 9/27/80, B, C, 80003197

McCully Log House, N of New Concord on Wharton Lane, New Concord vicinity, 3/15/82, C, 82003622

McIntire Terrace Historic District, Roughly bounded by Peter Alley, McIntire, Moorehead, Findley, Blue, and Adair Aves., Zanesville, 9/06/79, B, C, 79001918

Mound House, 400 Mound Rd., Duncan Falls, 6/06/79, B, C, 79001908

Mount Zion Presbyterian Church, E of Chandlersville off OH 146, Chandlersville vicinity, 12/19/78, A, C, a, 78002152

Muskingum College Campus Historic District, U.S. 22, New Concord, 6/11/79, A, C, a, 79001910

Muskingum County Courthouse And Jail, 4th and Main Sts., Zanesville, 7/16/73, C, 73001515

Muskingum River Lock No. 10 And Canal, N bank of Muskingum River, N of RR bridge S to lock terminals, Zanesville, 12/19/78, A, C, 78002165

Nashport Mound, Address Restricted, Nashport vicinity, 5/24/73, D, 73001512

Ohio Power Company, 604 Main St., Zanesville, 11/25/80, C, 80003198

Paul Hall, Muskingum College, Layton Dr., Muskingum College campus, New Concord, 4/23/73, A, C, 73001514

Peairs Homestead, E of Zanesville on OH 146, Zanesville vicinity, 2/27/79, A, C, 79001919

Philo II Archeological District, Address Restricted, Philo vicinity, 11/29/78, D, 78002156

Pittsburg, Cincinnati, and St. Louis Depot [Zanesville Historic Railroad Depots TR], Market St., Zanesville, 3/24/83, A, C, 83002016

Prospect Place, S of Trinway on OH 77, Trinway vicinity, 5/10/79, B, C, 79001913

Muskingum County—Continued

Putnam Historic District, Bounded by Penn Central RR. tracks, Van Buren St., and the Muskingum River, Zanesville, 6/30/75, A, C, 75001511

Ransbottom, C. W., House [Robinson-Ransbottom Pottery TR], 291 Washington St., Roseville, 3/11/80, B, 80003185

Ransbottom, Edward, House [Robinson-Ransbottom Pottery TR], 99 Main St., Roseville, 3/11/80, B, 80003186

Ransbottom, Frank M., House [Robinson-Ransbottom Pottery TR], 289 Washington St., Roseville, 3/11/80, B, 80003187

Ransbottom, Mort, House [Robinson-Ransbottom Pottery TR], 152 N. Main St., Roseville, 3/11/80, B, 80003188

Rider, Adam, House, Rt 2, 9350 Athens Rd., Roseville vicinity, 11/29/79, A, C, 79001911

Roseville High School, Stokeley and Perry Sts., Roseville, 3/30/78, A, C, 78002157

Salt Creek Covered Bridge, 3 mi. NW of Norwich, Norwich vicinity, 9/10/74, C, 74001587

Seborn, Frederick Augustus, House, 1115–1119 Maysville Pike, Zanesville, 4/04/78, B, C, 78002166

Smith, William R., House, 920 Marietta St., Zanesville, 6/01/82, C, 82003627

St. James Episcopal Church, 155 N. 6th St., Zanesville, 10/02/78, A, C, a, 78002167

St. John's Evangelical Lutheran Church, S of Stovertown on OH 555, Stovertown vicinity, 1/03/80, C, a, 80003189

St. John's Lutheran Church, Market and N. 7th Sts., Zanesville, 12/02/82, C, a, 82001484

St. Nicholas's Catholic Church, 925 Main St., Zanesville, 9/25/75, C, a, 75001512

St. Thomas Aquinas Church, 130 N. 5th St., Zanesville, 3/11/80, A, C, 80003199

Stormont, David, House, 103 W. Main St., New Concord, 4/21/83, C, 83002017

Tannehill, Capt. James Boggs, House, 367 Taylor St, Zanesville, 8/27/79, B, C, 79001921

Tanner, William C., House, NW of Zanesville, Zanesville vicinity, 9/17/79, B, C, 79001922

Tavener-Sears Tavern, Main St., Mount Sterling, 4/29/82, A, 82003621

US Post Office and Federal Building—Zanesville, 65 S. Fifth St., Zanesville, 2/11/88, C, 88000071

West Union School, S of Norwich on SR 200, Norwich vicinity, 3/30/78, A, C, 78002155

West View, 444 Sunkel Blvd., Zanesville, 3/05/82, C, 82003628

Wiles, Perry, Grocery Company, 32–36 N. 3rd St., Zanesville, 11/25/80, A, C, 80003200

Y Bridge, At foot of Main St., over the Licking and Muskingum rivers, Zanesville, 11/02/73, A, C, 73001516

Zanesville YMCA, 34 S. Fifth St., Zanesville, 10/29/85, A, C, 83002018

Zanesville YWCA, 49 N. 6th St., Zanesville, 7/17/78, A, C, 78002168

Noble County

Caldwell, Samuel, House, East and Locust Sts., Caldwell, 3/11/80, A, B, 80003201

Danford, Samuel, Farm, Church and Cemetery, N of Summerfield on SR 5-A, Summerfield vicinity, 3/27/80, A, C, a, d, 80003204

Huffman Covered Bridge, 1.5 mi. S of Middleburg off SR 564, Middleburg vicinity, 3/04/75, C, 75001513

SHENANDOAH Crash Sites, Near I-77 and Co. Rt. 37 and OH 78 W of Caldwell, Caldwell vicinity, 7/25/89, A, B, 89000942

St. Henry Roman Catholic Church and Rectory, 36573 County Rd. 47, Harriettsville, 12/02/82, A, C, a, 82001485

St. Mary's Church of the Immaculate Conception, Off OH 564, Fulda, 7/21/80, A, C, a, 80003202

Williams, Abner, Log House, NE of Lashley, Lashley vicinity, 6/20/79, B, C, 79001923

Young-Shaw House, E of Sarahsville on OH 146, Sarahsville vicinity, 2/08/80, B, 80003203

Ottawa County

Carroll Township Hall, Toussaint E. Rd. and Behlman Rd., Oak Harbor vicinity, 3/09/90, A, C, 90000385

Catawba Island Wine Company, 3845 Wine Celler Rd., Port Clinton vicinity, 5/05/83, A, g, 83002019

Clemons, Alexander, House, 133 Clemons St., Marblehead, 9/17/87, B, C, 87001628

Cooke, Jay, House, Put-in-Bay, Lake Erie, Gibraltar Island, 11/13/66, B, NHL, 66000620

East Point Manor, S. Shore Dr., Middle Bass Island, 6/15/90, C, 87000804

Foster—Gram House, Langrum Rd., South Bass Island, Put-In-Bay vicinity, 3/19/92, A, C, 92000175

Genoa Town Hall, Main and 6th Sts., Genoa, 6/07/76, C, 76001504

Gill—Luchsinger—Bahnsen House and Barn, 426 E. 4th St., Port Clinton, 7/16/92, C, 92000888

Golden Eagle Wine Cellars, Fox and Lonz Rds., Middle Bass Island, 4/24/86, A, C, 86000868

Green Island Light [Light Stations of Ohio MPS], Green Island in Lake Erie, Put-in-Bay vicinity, 12/18/90, A, C, 90001909

Inselruhe, NE of Put-in-Bay at jct. of Bayview Ave. and Chapman Rd. on South Bass Island, Put-in-Bay vicinity, 12/12/76, C, 76001506

Johnson Island Civil War Prison and Fort Site, E shore area of Johnson Island, Danbury, 3/27/75, A, D, d, f, NHL, 75001514

Lakeside Historic District, Roughly bounded by Lake Erie, RR tracks, Poplar and Oak Aves., Lakeside, 3/29/83, A, C, a, 83002020

Main Street Historic District, Roughly bounded by Eighth, Washington, Fifth and West Sts., Genoa, 9/22/92, A, C, 92001261

Marblehead Lighthouse, OH 163, Marblehead, 12/17/69, A, 69000148

Middle Bass Club Historic District, Grape and Grove Aves., MIddle Bass Island, 8/23/85, A, C, 85001843

Mo-John, Betsy, Cabin, About 4 mi. E of Port Clinton off OH 53, Port Clinton vicinity, 5/06/76, C, b, 76001505

Old School Privy, 310 Main St., Genoa, 7/31/75, A, 75001515

Ottawa County Courthouse, W. 4th and Madison Sts., Port Clinton, 5/03/74, C, 74001588

Perry's Victory and International Peace Memorial, South Bass Island, Put-in-Bay, 10/15/66, A, C, f, NPS, 66000118

South Bass Island Light [Light Stations of Ohio MPS], Langram Rd., on SW point of South Bass Island, South Bass Island, 4/05/90, A, C, 90000473

War Of 1812 Battle Site, East Bay Shore Rd., 1 mi. W of jct. with T-142, Mineyahta-on-the-Bay, 2/23/72, A, f, 72001038

Wolcott, Benajah, House, 9999 E. Bay Shore Rd., Lakeside—Marblehead vicinity, 3/14/91, A, C, 91000251

Paulding County

Antwerp Norfolk and Western Depot, W. Water St., Antwerp, 9/23/80, A, C, b, 80003205

Paulding County Courthouse, Courthouse Sq., Paulding, 5/03/74, C, 74001589

Round Barn [Round Barns in the Black Swamp of Northwest Ohio TR], Address Information Restricted., Paulding vicinity, 4/17/80, A, C, 80003206

Perry County

Bowman Mill Covered Bridge, S of New Reading on Sr 86, New Reading vicinity, 2/08/78, A, C, 78002169

Glenford Bank, Main and Broad Sts., Glenford, 3/09/90, C, 90000389

Glenford Fort, Address Restrocted, Glenford vicinity, 10/26/71, D, 71000649

Mitchell, Randolph, House, Rush Creek Rd., New Reading, 12/08/78, B, C, 78002170

Parks Covered Bridge, N of Somerset on CR 33, Chalfunts vicinity, 9/10/74, A, C, 74001590

Perry County Courthouse and Jail, Main and Brown Sts., New Lexington, 10/08/81, A, C, 81000449

Saint Joseph's Catholic Church, 5757 OH 383, Somerset vicinity, 8/07/86, C, a, 86002267

Shawnee Historic District, Both sides of Main St., 2nd St. to Walnut St., Shawnee, 3/17/76, A, C, 76001507

Sheridan House, S. Columbus St., Somerset, 11/28/80, B, C, 80003208

Somerset Historic District, Main St. from High St. to properties facing Market Sq; Columbus St. from jct. with Sheridan and Gay Sts., Somerset, 9/05/75, B, C, 75001516

Perry County—Continued

West School, Off OH 93, Crooksville, 4/10/80, A, 80003207

Whitmer, Solaman, House, N of Thornville at 13917 Zion Twnshp. Rd., NW, Thornville vicinity, 9/05/79, C, 79001924

Pickaway County

Anderson, William Marshall, House, 131 W. Union St, Circleville, 11/29/79, C, 79001925

Arledge Mounds I and II, Address Restricted, Circleville vicinity, 7/30/74, D, 74001591

Ashville Depot, Madison and Cromley Sts., Ashville, 2/25/80, A, C, b, 80003209

Bazore Mill, S of Williamsport on OH 138 at Deer Creek, Williamsport vicinity, 12/19/78, A, 78002172

Bellevue, N of Kingston on OH 159, Kingston vicinity, 3/17/76, B, C, 76001508

Circleville Historic District, Main and Court Sts., Circleville, 5/16/78, C, 78002171

Clemmons, W.C., Mound, Address Restricted, Fox vicinity, 5/02/74, D, 74001594

Fridley-Oman Farm, W of Marcy in Slate Run Metropolitan Park, Marcy vicinity, 12/06/75, A, C, 75001517

Gill—Morris Farm, 10104 OH 56, Circleville vicinity, 8/14/86, C, 86001658

Horn Mound, Address Restricted, Tarlton vicinity, 8/07/74, D, 74001595

Horsey-Barthelmas Farm, W of Circleville on OH 104, Circleville vicinity, 7/24/80, C, 80003210

Lawndale Farm Complex, 26476 Gay Dreisbach Rd., Circleville vicinity, 4/19/84, A, C, 84003795

Luthor List Mound, Address Restricted, Circleville vicinity, 10/16/74, D, 74001592

McCrea, Matthew, House, 428 E. Main St., Circleville, 9/29/88, C, 88001714

Memorial Hall, 165 E. Main St., Circleville, 11/21/80, C, 80003211

Morris House, 149 W. Union St, Circleville, 8/03/79, C, 79001926

Mount Oval, Off U.S. 23, Circleville vicinity, 7/25/74, C, 74001593

Perrill-Goodman Farm House, Rt. 1, Box 106, Groveport vicinity, 3/14/85, C, 85000565

Peters, Stevenson, House, 9860 SR 188, Circleville vicinity, 2/09/84, C, 84003797

Redlands, 1960 N. Court St., Circleville vicinity, 5/14/82, C, 82003630

Renick Farm, N of South Bloomfield on US 23., South Bloomfield vicinity, 3/05/82, C, 82003631

Saint Philip's Episcopal Church, 129 W. Mound St., Circleville, 5/15/86, C, a, 86001064

Scioto Township District No. 2 Schoolhouse, 8143 Snyder Rd., Orient vicinity, 5/06/87, C, 87000634

Shack, The, NW of Williamsport, Williamsport vicinity, 5/23/74, B, 74001596

Tick Ridge Mound District, Address Restricted, Williamsport vicinity, 6/11/75, D, 75001518

Walling, Ansel T., House, 146 W. Union St., Circleville, 12/14/87, B, C, 87002145

Watt-Groce-Fickhardt House, 360 E. Main St., Circleville, 8/23/85, B, C, 85001804

Pike County

Eager Inn, N of Morgantown off OH 772, Morgantown vicinity, 11/08/74, C, 74001597

Friendly Grove, OH 220, E of Piketon, Piketon, 1/26/70, B, C, 70000513

Jones-Cutler House, Bridge St., Jasper, 4/26/76, C, 76001509

Piketon Historic District, Bounded by West and 3rd Sts., U.S. 23, and the Scioto River, Piketon, 2/28/74, A, C, 74001598

Piketon Mounds, Address Restricted, Piketon vicinity, 5/02/74, D, 74001599

Scioto Township Works I, Address Restricted, Wakefield vicinity, 10/09/74, D, 74001600

Vanmeter Stone House and Outbuildings, S of Piketon at jct. of U.S. 23 and OH 124, Piketon vicinity, 3/31/75, C, b, 75001519

Waverly Canal Historic District, Walnut, North, Emmitt (US 23), Second, Third and Fourth Sts between Lock and East, Waverly, 12/20/78, A, C, 78002182

Portage County

Atwater Congregational Church, 1237 OH 183, Atwater, 2/23/73, C, a, 73001517

Aurora Center Historic District, Roughly both sides of OH 306 from and including Pioneer Trail to Rte. 82, also Maple Lane, Aurora, 6/20/74, A, C, 74001601

Aurora Train Station, 13 New Hudson Rd., Aurora, 5/22/86, A, C, 86001131

Beebe, Horace Y., House, 6538 Cleveland Rd., Ravenna vicinity, 6/16/83, B, C, 83002022

Cleveland Worsted Mills Redfern Mill, S. Chestnut St., Ravenna, 12/29/88, A, C, 88003065

Cottage Hill Farm, 5555 Newton Falls Rd., Ravenna Township, Ravenna vicinity, 5/06/93, B, C, 93000401

Crafts William H., House, 4619 W. Prospect St., Mantua, 4/29/82, B, C, 82003634

Crystal Lake Stock Farm, 4655 Hayes Rd., Ravena vicinity, 4/10/86, A, C, 86000698

Davey, John, House, 338 Woodard St., Kent, 5/29/75, B, C, 75001524

Diver, John, House and Storebuilding, 9465 Akron-Canfield Rd., Deerfield, 9/16/82, A, C, 82003632

East Main Street Historic District, E. Main St. between Clinton and Linden Sts., Ravenna, 10/10/85, B, C, 85003123

Ellenwood House, NW of Garretsville on OH 82, Garrettsville vicinity, 6/20/75, C, 75001523

Etna House [Ravenna Commercial Center MRA], 219 1/2 W. Main St., Ravenna, 7/25/85, A, C, 85001641

Ferrey, Aaron, House, 5058 Sunny Brook Rd., Kent vicinity, 8/13/74, C, 74001605

Franklin Township Hall, 218 Gougler Ave., Kent, 10/10/75, A, 75001525

Freedom Congregational Church, Public Green on OH 88, Freedom, 7/07/75, C, a, 75001521

Griffin, A. B., —O. H. Griffin House, 409 S. Walnut St., Ravenna, 3/07/85, B, C, 85000485

Griffin, Alexander B., House, 417 S. Walnut St., Ravenna, 7/02/87, B, C, 87000987

Hine, Horace L., House, 4624 W. Prospect St., Mantua, 12/12/76, A, C, 76001513

Hopkins, Benjamin F., Stone Building, Standing Rock Cemetery, Kent, 11/25/82, D, d, 82003633

Howard, C. R., House, 411 E. Garfield St., Aurora, 8/13/74, C, 74001602

Johnson, John, Farm, 6203 Pioneer Trail, Hiram vicinity, 12/12/76, B, C, a, 76001512

Kent Industrial District, Roughly bounded by Main, River, and S. Franklin Sts. and S property line of Portage Co., Kent, 12/30/74, A, C, 74001603

Kent Jail, 124 W. Day St., Kent, 8/10/78, A, C, 78002173

Kent, Charles House, 125 N. Pearl St., Kent, 2/23/78, C, b, 78002174

Kent, Zeno, House, 2.5 mi. SW of Aurora on Aurora-Hudson Rd., Aurora vicinity, 4/23/73, C, 73001518

Mantua Center District, Roughly bounded by OH 82 and Mantua Center Rd., Mantua Center, 10/09/74, C, a, 74001607

Mantua Station Brick Commercial District, Main and Prospect Sts., Mantua, 12/24/74, A, C, 74001606

Masonic Temple, 409 W. Main St., Kent, 7/18/74, B, C, 74001604

Nelson, Luman, House, 8219 OH 44, Ravenna vicinity, 12/22/93, C, 93001393

Ohio State Normal College At Kent, Hilltop Dr. on Kent State University campus, Kent, 5/30/75, A, C, 75001526

Palmyra Center Hotel, OH 225 and SR 18, Palmyra, 4/30/76, A, C, 76001514

Phoenix Block [Ravenna Commercial Center MRA], NE corner of Main and Chestnut Sts., Ravenna, 3/18/85, C, 85000624

Reed, C. A., House, 299 W. Riddle St., Ravenna, 10/10/85, B, C, 85003116

Riddle Block, Public Sq., Chestnut, and Main Sts., Ravenna, 3/17/76, A, C, 76001515

Riddle Block #11 [Ravenna Commercial Center MRA], 133-137 E. Main St., Ravenna, 3/18/85, B, C, 85000626

Riddle Block #5 [Ravenna Commercial Center MRA], 141-145 E. Main St., Ravenna, 7/25/85, A, B, 85001642

Riddle Block #9 [Ravenna Commercial Center MRA], 113-115 W. Main St., Ravenna, 3/18/85, B, C, 85000625

Wadsworth, Frederick, House, 4889 OH 14, Edinburg vicinity, 5/29/75, B, C, 75001520

West Main Street District, 409-625 W. Main St., Kent, 6/17/77, A, C, 77001082

Young, Thomas F., House, Wakefield and Garfield Sts., Hiram, 10/22/76, A, C, 76001511

Preble County

Acton House, 115 W. Main St., Eaton, 9/05/85, B, C, 85001944

Brubaker Covered Bridge, W of Gratis on Aukerman Creek Rd., Gratis vicinity, 6/11/75, A, C, 75001527

Christman Covered Bridge, 1.5 mi. NW of Eaton on SR 12, Eaton vicinity, 10/22/76, A, C, 76001516

Christman, Daniel, Homestead, W of Eaton on US 35, Eaton vicinity, 11/04/82, A, 82001486

Fort St. Clair Site, 1 mi. W of Eaton, Eaton vicinity, 11/10/70, A, 70000514

Geeting Covered Bridge, 2 mi. W of Lewisburg on Price Rd., Lewisburg vicinity, 8/19/75, A, C, 75001528

Harshman Covered Bridge, 4 mi. N of Fairhaven on Concord-Fairhaven Rd. spanning Four Mile Creek, Fairhaven vicinity, 9/29/76, A, C, 76001517

Hueston Woods Park Mound, Address Restricted, College Corner vicinity, 11/05/71, D, 71000650

Lange Hotel, 1 W. Dayton St., West Alexandria, 1/25/91, A, 90002213

Roberts Covered Bridge, 3 mi. S of Eaton over Seven Mile Creek, Eaton vicinity, 9/03/71, C, 71000651

St. Clair Street Bridge, over Seven Mile Creek, Eaton, 9/21/78, A, C, 78002175

Unger, George B., House, 29 E. Dayton St., West Alexandria, 11/15/78, A, C, 78002176

Warnke Covered Bridge, NE of Lewisburg on Swamp Creek Rd., Lewisburg vicinity, 10/08/76, A, C, 76001518

Putnam County

Edwards, John, House, 305 W. Main St., Leipsic, 11/27/78, C, 78002177

Gilboa Main Street Historic District, Main St., Gilboa, 2/27/79, A, 79001927

Huber, Dr. H., Block, Main St. and Taft Ave., Ottawa, 6/04/80, C, 80003213

Leipsic City Hall, Belmore St., Leipsic, 6/20/79, A, C, 79001928

Ottawa Waterworks Building, 1035 E. 3rd St., Ottawa, 9/13/76, A, C, 76001519

Putnam County Courthouse, Courthouse Sq., Ottawa, 5/03/74, C, 74001608

Round Barn [Round Barns in the Black Swamp of Northwest Ohio TR], Address Information Restricted., Columbus Grove vicinity, 4/17/80, A, C, 80003212

St. John The Baptist Roman Catholic Church, OH 694 and Main St., Glandorf, 6/17/77, A, C, a, 77001083

Richland County

All Souls Unitarian-Universalist Church, 125 Church St., Bellville, 1/01/76, A, C, a, 76001520

Barr, Jacob H., House [Park Avenue West MRA], 646 Park Ave., W., Mansfield, 7/08/83, C, 83002023

Bellville Bandstand, North Bellville Municipal Park, Bellville, 11/26/73, C, 73001519

Bellville Village Hall, Park Pl. and Church St., Bellville, 3/17/76, A, 76001521

Bissman Block, 193 N. Main St., Mansfield, 10/16/86, A, C, 86002882

Bissman, B.F., House [Park Avenue West MRA], 458 Park Ave., W., Mansfield, 7/08/83, C, 83002024

Bissman, Peter, House [Park Avenue West MRA], 462 Park Ave., W., Mansfield, 7/08/83, C, 83002025

Building at 240 Park Avenue West [Park Avenue West MRA], 240 Park Ave., W., Mansfield, 7/08/83, C, 83002026

Building at 252-254 Park Avenue West [Park Avenue West MRA], 252-254 Park Ave., W., Mansfield, 2/02/84, C, 84003802

Building at 309 Park Avenue West [Park Avenue West MRA], 309 Park Ave., W., Mansfield, 2/02/84, C, 84003801

Building at 415 Park Avenue West [Park Avenue West MRA], 415 Park Ave., W., Mansfield, 2/02/84, C, 84003799

Bushnell, Martin, House, 34 Sturges Ave., Mansfield, 4/26/74, B, C, 74001609

Central United Methotist Church [Park Avenue West MRA], 378 Park Ave., W., Mansfield, 7/08/83, C, a, 83002027

City Mills Building, 160 N. Main St., Mansfield, 12/18/86, A, C, 86003500

Colonial, The [Park Avenue West MRA], 283 Park Ave., W., Mansfield, 7/08/83, C, 83002028

Cook, J.M., House [Park Avenue West MRA], 429 Park Ave., W., Mansfield, 7/08/83, C, 83002029

Douglas, S.M., House [Park Avenue West MRA], 437 Park Ave., W., Mansfield, 7/08/83, C, 83002030

Dow House [Park Avenue West MRA], 564 Park Ave., W., Mansfield, 7/08/83, C, 83002031

Ferrell, Silas, House, 25 E. Main St., Shiloh, 12/14/87, C, 87002146

First Congregational Church And Lexington School, 47 Delaware St. and 51 W. Church St., Lexington, 2/23/79, A, C, a, 79001929

First English Lutheran Church [Park Avenue West MRA], 53 Park Ave., W., Mansfield, 7/08/83, C, a, 83002032

Fraser House [Park Avenue West MRA], 681 Park Ave., W., Mansfield, 7/08/83, C, 83002033

Gilbert, F.A., House [Park Avenue West MRA], 343 Park Ave., W., Mansfield, 2/02/84, C, 84003800

Gurney-Kochheiser House, 174 Main St., Bellville, 4/30/76, C, 76001522

Hancock and Dow Building, 21 E. Fourth St., Mansfield, 2/26/87, C, 86002864

Kern, Rufus A., House [Park Avenue West MRA], 608 Park Ave., W., Mansfield, 7/08/83, C, 83002034

Kingwood Center, 900 Park Ave., W., Mansfield, 11/07/76, C, g, 76001523

Krause, John, House [Park Avenue West MRA], 428 Park Ave., W., Mansfield, 7/08/83, C, 83002035

Lewis, Samuel, House, 291 N. Stewart Rd., Mansfield vicinity, 6/01/82, C, 82003636

Malabar Farm, SE of Lucas on Pleasant Valley Rd., Lucas vicinity, 4/11/73, A, B, g, 73001520

Mansfield Savings Bank, 4 W. Fourth St., Mansfield, 10/16/86, C, 86002872

Mansfield Woman's Club [Park Avenue West MRA], 145 Park Ave., W., Mansfield, 7/08/83, C, 83002037

Mansfield, Judge, House [Park Avenue West MRA], 228 Park Ave., W., Mansfield, 7/08/83, C, 83002036

Marvin Memorial Library, 34 N. Gamble St., Shelby, 8/13/87, A, C, 86003493

May Realty Building, 22–32 S. Park St., Mansfield, 10/16/86, C, 86002865

Mechanics Building and Loan Company [Park Avenue West MRA], 2 S. Main St., Mansfield, 7/08/83, C, 83002038

Most Pure Heart Of Mary Church, West St. and Raymond Ave., Shelby, 11/30/78, C, a, 78002179

Oak Hill Cottage, 310 Springmill St., Mansfield, 6/11/69, A, C, 69000149

Ohio State Reformatory, Olivesburg Rd., Mansfield, 4/14/83, A, C, 83002039

Ohio Theatre [Park Avenue West MRA], 136 Park Ave., W., Mansfield, 5/31/83, C, 83002040

Old Carriage Barn [Park Avenue West MRA], 337 Park Ave., W., Mansfield, 7/08/83, C, 83002041

Pacific Curios Antiques [Park Avenue West MRA], 365 Park Ave., W., Mansfield, 7/08/83, C, 83002042

Park Avenue Baptist Church [Park Avenue West MRA], 296 Park Ave., W., Mansfield, 7/08/83, C, a, 83002043

Richland Trust Building [Park Avenue West MRA], 3 Park Ave., W., Mansfield, 7/08/83, C, 83002044

Ritter, William, House, 181 S. Main St., Mansfield, 12/29/78, C, 78002178

Rummell Mill, NE of Butler on SR 349., Butler vicinity, 4/07/82, A, C, 82003635

Sacred Heart of Jesus Churches, OH 61, Bethlehem, 1/06/86, A, C, a, 86000035

Sandiford, Robert, House [Park Avenue West MRA], 544 Park Ave., W., Mansfield, 7/08/83, C, 83002045

Shambaugh, George, House, Frontz Rd., Perrysville vicinity, 4/01/82, C, 82003637

Shelby Center Historic District, E. and W. Main Sts., Shelby, 5/13/82, A, C, 82003638

Sherman, John, Memorial Gateway [Park Avenue West MRA], 699 Park Ave., W., Mansfield, 7/08/83, C, 83002046

Soldiers and Sailors Memorial Building and Madison Theater, 36 Park Ave., W., Mansfield, 5/27/80, A, C, g, 80003214

St. Peters Church, 54 S. Mulberry St, Mansfield, 11/29/79, C, a, 79001930

Stewart Towers [Park Avenue West MRA], 13 Park Ave., W., Mansfield, 7/08/83, C, 83002048

Richland County—Continued

Sturges, Susan, House [Park Avenue West MRA], 317 Park Ave., W., Mansfield, 7/08/83, C, 83002049

Tappan House [Park Avenue West MRA], 308 Park Ave., W., Mansfield, 7/08/83, C, 83002050

Upson House [Park Avenue West MRA], 234 Park Ave., W., Mansfield, 7/08/83, C, 83002051

Ward, W. S., House [Park Avenue West MRA], 350 Park Ave., W., Mansfield, 7/08/83, C, 83002052

Ross County

Adena, W. Allen Ave. extended, Chillicothe vicinity, 11/10/70, B, C, 70000515

Adena Mound, Address Restricted, Chillicothe vicinity, 6/05/75, D, 75001529

Anderson, Levi, House, W of Chillicothe on Anderson Station Rd., Chillicothe vicinity, 12/12/76, A, C, 76001524

Baum, Howard, Site (33RO270), Address Restricted, Bainbridge vicinity, 8/14/86, D, 86001663

Brown, Austin, Mound, Address Restricted, Chillicothe vicinity, 2/15/74, D, 74001613

Buchwalter House-Applethorpe Farm, 292 Whissler Rd., Hallsville vicinity, 5/26/83, C, 83002053

Campbell, T. C., Mound, Address Restricted, Bainbridge vicinity, 7/15/74, D, 74001610

Canal Warehouse, Main and Mulberry Sts., Chillicothe, 4/24/73, A, 73001522

Cedar-Bank Works, Address Restricted, Chillicothe vicinity, 2/15/74, D, 74001614

Chillicothe Business District, Roughly bounded by Water, 4th, Walnut and Hickory Sts., Chillicothe, 6/11/79, A, C, 79001931

Chillicothe Water And Power Company Pumping Station, Enderlin Circle, Chillicothe, 11/15/79, C, 79001932

Chillicothe's Old Residential District, Roughly bounded by 4th, S. Mulberry, S. Walnut and 7th Sts., Chillicothe, 11/28/73, A, C, 73001523

Frankfort Works Mound, Address Restricted, Frankfort vicinity, 5/17/73, D, 73001530

Grandview Cemetery, 240 S. Walnut St., Chillicothe, 12/19/78, A, C, d, 78002180

Great Seal Park Archeological District, Address Restricted, Chillicothe vicinity, 12/02/74, D, 74001615

Harris, Dr. John, Dental School, Main St., Bainbridge, 7/23/73, A, 73001521

Higby House, S of Chillicothe on Three Locks Rd, Chillicothe vicinity, 11/29/79, C, 79001933

High Banks Works, Address Restricted, Chillicothe vicinity, 7/16/73, D, 73001524

Highbank Farm, SE of Chillicothe on OH 35, Chillicothe vicinity, 10/20/80, B, C, 80003215

Hopeton Earthworks, Address Restricted, Hopetown vicinity, 10/15/66, D, NHL, 66000623

Hopewell Mound Group, Address Restricted, Chillicothe vicinity, 2/12/74, D, 74001616

Kinzer Mound, Address Restricted, South Salem vicinity, 1/17/74, D, 74001617

Macomb, Mary Worthington, House, 490 S. Paint St., Chillicothe, 4/26/76, A, C, 76001525

Metzger, Charles, Mound, Address Restricted, Chillicothe vicinity, 6/18/73, D, 73001526

Mound City Group National Monument, N of Chillicothe, Chillicothe vicinity, 10/15/66, A, D, NPS, 66000119

Mountain House, Highland Ave., Chillicothe, 12/29/78, B, C, 78002181

Oak Hill, Dun Rd., Chillicothe, 4/03/73, C, 73001527

Renick House, Paint Hill, 17 Mead Dr., Chillicothe, 5/09/73, B, C, 73001528

Seip Earthworks and Dill Mounds District, Address Restricted, Bainbridge vicinity, 8/13/74, D, 74001611

Seip House, 345 Allen Ave., Chillicothe, 5/12/81, C, 81000450

South Salem Academy, Church St., South Salem, 2/23/79, A, C, 79001937

South Salem Covered Bridge, W of South Salem on Lower Twin Rd. across Buckskin Creek, South Salem vicinity, 3/04/75, C, 75001530

Spruce Hill Works, Address Restricted, Bourneville vicinity, 2/23/72, D, 72001039

Stitt, David, Mound, Address Restricted, Chillicothe vicinity, 11/09/72, D, 72001040

Story Mound State Memorial, East of junction of Cherokee and Delano Streets, Chillicothe, 3/07/73, D, 73001529

Tanglewood, 177 Belleview Ave., Chillicothe, 6/20/79, C, 79001934

Vanmeter Church Street House, 178 Church St., Chillicothe, 2/21/79, A, C, 79001935

Wesley Chapel, Off U.S. 23, Hopetown, 2/02/79, A, C, a, 79001936

Sandusky County

Bartlett, Joseph and Rachel, House, 212 Park Ave., Fremont, 3/21/90, C, 90000388

Buckland, Ralph P., House, 300 S. Park Ave., Fremont, 12/17/74, C, a, 74001620

Cronenwett, Georg, House, 606 W. Main St., Woodville, 12/01/78, B, C, a, 78002184

Fabing, Frederick, House, 201 S. Park Ave., Fremont, 5/26/83, B, C, 83002054

Hayes, Rutherford B., House, Hayes and Buckland Aves., Fremont, 10/15/66, B, d, NHL, 66000624

Layman, Christopher C., Law Office, 212 W. First St., Woodville, 5/15/86, B, C, 86001062

Mcpherson, Maj. Gen. James B., House, 300 E. McPherson Hwy., Clyde, 10/18/74, B, 74001619

Mull Covered Bridge, E of Burgoon between OH 12 and 53, Burgoon vicinity, 10/15/74, C, 74001618

Overmyer-Waggoner-Roush Farm, 654 S. Main St., Lindsey vicinity, 9/08/83, A, C, 83002055

Soldiers Memorial Parkway and McKinley Memorial Parkway, Soldiers Memorial Pkwy. and McKinley Memorial Pkwy., Fremont, 1/25/91, A, C, f, 90002212

St. Paul's Episcopal Church, 200 N. Park Ave., Fremont, 6/09/77, C, a, 77001085

Scioto County

All Saints Episcopal Church, 4th and Court Sts., Portsmouth, 3/25/82, C, a, 82003639

Bennett Schoolhouse Road Covered Bridge, SE of Minford, Minford vicinity, 10/11/78, A, C, 78002185

Bigelow United Methodist Church [Boneyfiddle MRA], 415 Washington St., Portsmouth, 12/08/87, C, a, 87002073

Boneyfiddle Commercial Disrict, Roughly bounded by Front, Washington, 3rd and Scioto Sts., Portsmouth, 6/06/79, A, C, 79001938

Cunningham—Maier House [Boneyfiddle MRA], 506 Sixth, Portsmouth, 12/08/87, C, 87002074

Dole-Darrell House [Boneyfiddle MRA], 322 Market St., Portsmouth, 12/08/87, C, 87002075

Elden House [Boneyfiddle MRA], 634 Fourth St., Portsmouth, 12/08/87, C, 87002076

Evangelical Church of Christ [Boneyfiddle MRA], 701 Fifth St., Portsmouth, 12/08/87, C, a, 87002077

Feurt Mounds And Village Site, Address Restricted, Portsmouth vicinity, 6/18/73, D, 73001531

Feurt Mounds and Village Site (Boundary Increase), Address Restricted, Portsmouth vicinity, 1/09/75, D, 75002080

First Presbyterian Church, 221 Court St., Portsmouth, 11/28/73, A, C, a, 73001532

Gharky, George H., House [Boneyfiddle MRA], 638 Fourth St., Portsmouth, 12/08/87, C, 87002078

Greenlawn Cemetery Chapel, Offnere St., Portsmouth, 1/03/80, C, 80003216

Horseshoe Mound, Within Mound Park, Portsmouth, 5/02/74, D, 74001621

Hurth Hotel, 222 Chillicothe St., Portsmouth, 7/28/83, C, 83002056

Kinney, Aaron, House, Waller St., Portsmouth, 7/02/73, B, 73001533

Kinney, Eli, House [Boneyfiddle MRA], 317 Court St., Portsmouth, 3/10/88, B, C, 87002079

Labold House and Gardens [Boneyfiddle MRA], 633 Fourth St., Portsmouth, 12/08/87, C, 87002085

Marsh, Joseph, House [Boneyfiddle MRA], 701 Market St., Portsmouth, 12/08/87, C, 87002087

Meyer House [Boneyfiddle MRA], 309 Washington St., Portsmouth, 3/10/88, C, 87002088

Moore, Philip, Stone House, S of West Portsmouth on OH 239, West Portsmouth vicinity, 10/21/75, A, 75001531

Newman, William, House [Boneyfiddle MRA], 716 Second St., Portsmouth, 12/08/87, B, C, 87002089

Odd Fellows Hall [Boneyfiddle MRA], 500–506 Court St., Portsmouth, 12/08/87, C, 87002090

Otway Covered Bridge, N of OH 348, Otway, 5/03/74, C, 74002280

Scioto County—Continued

Peck, Judge William V., House, 601 Market St, Portsmouth, 11/15/79, B, C, 79001939

Portsmouth Fire Department No. 1 [Boneyfiddle MRA], 642 Seventh St., Portsmouth, 12/08/87, C, 87002091

Portsmouth Foundry and Machine Works [Boneyfiddle MRA], 401 Third St., Portsmouth, 12/08/87, C, 87002095

Purdum—Tracy House [Boneyfiddle MRA], 626 Fourth St., Portsmouth, 12/08/87, C, 87002097

Reed, Joseph G., Company [Boneyfiddle MRA], 700 Second St., Portsmouth, 12/08/87, C, 87002099

Scioto County Courthouse [Boneyfiddle MRA], Bounded by Seventh, Court, Sixth, & Washington Sts., Portsmouth, 12/08/87, C, 87002101

Second Street Historic District, 2nd St., Portsmouth, 11/30/83, A, C, 83004336

Sixth Street Historic District [Boneyfiddle MRA], 533, 534, 537, 538, 541, 542, 543, 547, & 548 Sixth St., W of Court St., Portsmouth, 3/10/88, C, 87002103

St. Mary's Roman Catholic Church, 5th and Markets Sts, Portsmouth, 8/24/79, C, a, 79001940

Steindam House [Boneyfiddle MRA], 725 Court St., Portsmouth, 12/08/87, C, 87002104

Streich Apartments [Boneyfiddle MRA], 716–722 Washington St., Portsmouth, 12/08/87, C, 87002105

Tremper Mound And Works, Address Restricted, West Portsmouth vicinity, 12/08/72, D, 72001041

Tripp—Bauer Building, 51–53 N. Jackson St., South Webster, 6/09/88, C, 88000719

Seneca County

Aigler Alumni Building [Heidelberg College MRA], 315 E. Market St., Tiffin, 2/12/79, C, 79002779

Bagby—Hossler House, 530 Sycamore St., Tiffin, 7/10/86, B, C, 86001562

Beatty Glass Company [Tiffin Industrial Buildings TR], 4th Ave. and Vine St., Tiffin, 1/07/80, A, C, 80003217

Black Student Union Center [Heidelberg College MRA], 120 Hedges St., Tiffin, 2/12/79, C, 79002780

Bowman's Distillery [Tiffin Industrial Buildings TR], 215 Riversdale Dr., Tiffin, 1/07/80, A, C, 80003218

College Hall [Heidelberg College MRA], 310 E. Market St., Tiffin, 2/12/79, C, 79002778

Cory, Ambrose, House, 957 N. Union St., Fostoria, 6/20/79, C, 79001942

Downtown Tiffin Historic District, Roughly bounded by Riverside Dr., Jefferson, S. Washington, E. Market, Madison, and Court Sts., Tiffin, 5/02/78, A, C, a, 78002186

Fine Arts Building [Heidelberg College MRA], 338 E. Perry St., Tiffin, 2/12/79, C, 79002770

Fort Ball-Railroad Historic Disrict, Roughly bounded by Sandusky River, Perry, Sandusky and Washington Sts., Tiffin, 6/20/79, A, C, a, 79001944

Founders Hall, Heidelberg College [Heidelberg College MRA (AD)], Perry St. (OH 18), Tiffin, 3/20/73, C, 73001534

France Hall [Heidelberg College MRA], 119 Greenfield St., Tiffin, 2/12/79, C, 79002776

Gerhart-Rust Residence [Heidelberg College MRA], 285 E. Perry St., Tiffin, 2/12/79, C, 79002766

Great Hall [Heidelberg College MRA], 44 Greenfield St., Tiffin, 2/12/79, C, 79002777

Hanson Machinery Company [Tiffin Industrial Buildings TR], 235 Miami St., Tiffin, 1/07/80, A, C, g, 80003219

Hedges-Hunter-Keller-Bacon Gristmill [Tiffin Industrial Buildings TR], 255 Riverside Dr., Tiffin, 1/07/80, A, C, 80003220

Henny Barn, W 1/2, SW 1/4, section 1, N side of Country Road 34 east of Northwestern RR tracks, Flat Rock vicinity, 11/06/79, C, 79003646

Heter Farm, NW of Bellevue, Bellevue vicinity, 3/29/79, A, C, 79001941

Hunter, William, House [Tiffin Industrial Buildings TR], 260 Riverside Dr., Tiffin, 1/07/80, B, C, 80003221

Laird Hall [Heidelberg College MRA], 70 Greenfield St., Tiffin, 2/12/79, C, 79002775

Miami Street Grade School, 155 Miami St., Tiffin, 3/21/79, C, 79001945

Michaels Farm, S of Kansas on OH 635, Kansas vicinity, 11/29/79, A, C, 79001943

Mueller Brewery [Tiffin Industrial Buildings TR], 146-164 Riverside Dr., Tiffin, 1/07/80, A, C, 80003222

Mueller, Christ, House [Tiffin Industrial Buildings TR], 140-142 Riverside Dr., Tiffin, 1/07/80, B, C, 80003223

National Orphans' Home, Junior Order United American Mechanics, 600 N. River Rd., Tiffin, 10/01/90, A, C, 90001499

North Sandusky Street Historic District, N. Sandusky St., Tiffin, 5/27/80, B, C, 80003224

Northeast Tiffin Historic District, Clinton, Ohio, and Hunter Sts., Tiffin, 5/28/80, C, g, 80003225

Octagon, The [Heidelberg College MRA], 297 E. Perry St., Tiffin, 2/12/79, C, 79002764

Ohio Lantern Company [Tiffin Industrial Buildings TR], 60-72 Hudson St., Tiffin, 1/07/80, A, C, 80003226

Omar Chapel, 408 OH 4, Attica vicinity, 11/05/87, A, C, a, 87001982

Pfleiderer Center for Religion and the Humanities [Heidelberg College MRA], 28 Greenfield St., Tiffin, 2/12/79, C, 79002773

Pleasant Ridge United Methodist Church and Cemetery, Jct. of OH 101 and Co. Rd. 38, Tiffin vicinity, 9/10/93, C, a, 93000880

President's House [Heidelberg College MRA], 67 Greenfield St., Tiffin, 2/12/79, C, 79002768

Social Science House [Heidelberg College MRA], 266 E. Market St., Tiffin, 2/12/79, C, 79002782

Springdale, 318 Sycamore St., Tiffin, 8/26/93, B, C, 93000878

St. Boniface Roman Catholic Church, School, Rectory, and Convent of the Sister of the Precious Blood, N. Perry St., New Riegel, 11/17/82, A, C, a, d, 82001487

Tiffin Agricultural Works [Tiffin Industrial Buildings TR], 40 Harrison St., Tiffin, 1/07/80, A, C, 80003227

Tiffin Art Metal Company [Tiffin Industrial Buildings TR], 450 Wall St., Tiffin, 1/07/80, A, C, 80003228

Tiffin Waterworks [Tiffin Industrial Buildings TR], 170 Ella St., Tiffin, 1/07/80, A, C, 80003229

Umsted Farm, N of Tiffin on SR 38, Tiffin vicinity, 4/27/79, A, C, 79001946

Wagner Brothers Bottling Works [Tiffin Industrial Buildings TR], 250–258 Benner St., Tiffin, 1/07/80, A, C, 80003230

Webster Manufacturing [Tiffin Industrial Buildings TR], 325 Hall St., Tiffin, 1/07/80, A, C, 80003231

Williard Hall [Heidelberg College MRA], 116 Greenfield St., Tiffin, 2/12/79, C, 79002771

Shelby County

Anna Town Hall, Main St., Anna, 9/20/78, A, C, 78002187

Botkins Elementary School [Cross-Tipped Churches of Ohio TR], Main St., Botkins, 7/26/79, C, a, 79002851

Emanuel Lutheran Church of Montra, Montra Rd., Montra, 5/13/82, A, a, 82003640

Fulton Farm, 804 S. Brooklyn Ave., Sidney, 5/08/79, A, C, 79001947

Immaculate Conception Rectory at Botkins [Cross-Tipped Churches of Ohio TR], 116 N. Mill St., Botkins, 7/26/79, A, C, a, 79002876

Lockington Covered Bridge, 1 mi. E of Lockington on SR 132, Lockington vicinity, 6/10/75, C, 75001532

People's Federal Savings and Loan Association, 101 E. Court St., Sidney, 6/05/72, C, NHL, 72001042

Port Jefferson School, Wall and Spring Sts., Port Jefferson, 6/02/82, A, 82003641

Sacred Heart of Jesus Rectory [Cross-Tipped Churches of Ohio TR], OH 119 and OH 29, McCartyville, 7/26/79, C, a, 79002874

Shelby House, 403 W. State St., Botkins, 12/08/78, A, C, 78002188

Sidney Courthouse Square Historic District, Roughly bounded by North and South Sts., West and Miami Aves., Sidney, 9/27/80, C, 80003232

Sidney Walnut Avenue Historic District, Walnut Ave. from Poplar to Michigan Sts., and 228, 228 1/2, and 238 W. North St., Sidney, 12/29/83, A, C, 83004338

Sidney Waterworks And Electric Light Building, 121 N. Brooklyn Ave., Sidney, 12/29/78, A, C, 78002190

St. Michael Catholic Church Complex [Cross-Tipped Churches of Ohio TR], U.S. 705 east of U.S. 66, Fort Loramie, 7/26/79, A, C, 79002825

Shelby County—Continued

St. Patrick Catholic Church and Rectory [Cross-Tipped Churches of Ohio TR], Hoying and Wright-Puthoff Rds., St. Patrick, 7/26/79, C, a, 79002836

St. Remy Catholic Church [Cross-Tipped Churches of Ohio TR], Main St. and Russia-Versailles Rd., Russia, 7/26/79, C, a, 79002834

Whitby Mansion, 429 N. Ohio Ave., Sidney, 12/12/76, C, 76001526

Wilson-Lenox House, W of Sidney at 9804 Houston Rd., Sidney vicinity, 3/27/80, C, 80003233

Stark County

Bair, Jacob H., House, N of Canton at 7225 N. Market Ave., Canton vicinity, 12/29/78, A, C, 78002194

Barber-Whitticar House, 519 Cleveland Ave, SW., Canton, 7/15/82, C, 82003642

Bender's Restaurant—Belmont Buffet [Architecture of Guy Tilden in Canton, 1885–1905, TR], 137 Court Ave. SW, Canton, 7/21/87, C, 87001193

Bordner House, 4522 7th St., SW., Canton, 2/17/78, C, 78002191

Brewster Railroad YMCA/Wandle House, 45 S. Wabash Ave., Brewster, 3/07/85, A, 85000486

Canal Fulton Historic District, Ohio-Erie Canal, Market, Canal, Cherry and High Sts., Canal Fulton, 12/02/82, A, C, 82001488

Canton Public Library [Architecture of Guy Tilden in Canton, 1885–1905, TR], 236 3rd St., SW., Canton, 7/15/82, C, 82003643

City National Bank Building, 205 Market Ave., S, Canton, 7/15/82, A, C, 82003644

Dewalt Building, 122 Market Ave., N, Canton, 7/15/82, C, 82003645

Eagles' Temple, 601 S. Market St., Canton, 7/15/82, A, 82003646

Earley-Hartzell House, 840 N. Park Ave., Alliance, 12/21/87, B, C, 87002147

Fife, Harry E., House [Architecture of Guy Tilden in Canton, 1885–1905, TR], 606 McKinley Ave. SW, Canton, 7/21/87, C, 87001196

First Methodist Episcopal Church, 120 Cleveland Ave., SW, Canton, 4/16/79, C, a, 79001948

First Methodist Episcopal Church of Alliance, Ohio, 470 E. Broadway St., Alliance, 5/02/85, C, a, 85000945

First Methodist Episcopal Church, 301 Lincoln Way E., Massillon, 8/22/85, C, a, 85001803

First National Bank Building, 11 Lincoln Way W, Massillon, 5/08/87, C, 87000689

First Reformed and First Lutheran Churches, 901 and 909 E. Tuscarawas St., Canton, 9/28/82, A, a, 82003647

Five Oaks, 210 4th St., NE., Massillon, 4/11/73, C, 73001535

Fourth Street Historic District, Roughly bounded by 3rd, 5th and Cherry St. and Federal Ave., Massillon, 3/25/82, C, 82003654

Frances Apartment Building, 534 Cleveland Ave., SW, Canton, 6/06/88, C, 88000668

Glamorgan, 1025 S. Union Ave., Alliance, 10/05/72, B, C, 72001043

Haines House, 186 W. Market St., Alliance, 7/30/74, A, C, 74001623

Hartville Hotel, 101 N. Prospect St., Hartville, 1/03/80, A, 80003235

Harvard Company—Weber Dental Manufacturing Company [Architecture of Guy Tilden in Canton, 1885–1905, TR], 2206 Thirteenth St. NE, Canton, 7/21/87, A, C, 87001194

Hoover Farm, S of North Canton on Easton St, North Canton vicinity, 8/03/79, A, C, 79001955

Hotel Courtland [Architecture of Guy Tilden in Canton, 1885–1905, TR], 209 W. Tuscarawas Ave., Canton, 7/21/87, C, 87001195

Ideal Department Store Building, 55–59 Lincoln Way E., Massillon, 9/10/92, A, C, 92001245

Lake Township School, E of Uniontown at 1101 Lake Center St., Uniontown vicinity, 6/22/76, A, C, 76001528

Landmark Tavern, 501 E. Tuscarawas St., Canton, 3/12/82, A, 82003648

Loew-Define Grocery Store and Home, 202 S. Market St, Navarre, 11/29/79, A, C, 79001954

Massillon Cemetery Building, 1827 Erie St. S., Massillon, 3/12/82, C, d, 82003655

Maudru House, Address Restricted, Alliance vicinity, 11/25/80, C, 80003234

McKinley, William, Tomb, 7th St., NW., Canton, 11/10/70, B, c, f, NHL, 70000516

Mellett-Canton Daily News Building, 401 W. Tuscarawas St., Canton, 4/21/83, A, 83002058

Mount Union College District, Hartshorn St., Miller and Aultman Aves., Alliance, 10/05/72, A, C, 72001044

New Baltimore Inn, 14722 Ravenna Ave., New Baltimore, 12/18/75, A, C, 75001535

Old McKinley High School, 800 N. Market St., Canton, 6/30/82, A, C, 82003649

Onesto Hotel, 2nd and Cleveland, NW, Canton, 7/15/82, A, C, 82003650

Palace Theater, 605 Market Ave., N., Canton, 4/26/79, A, C, 79001949

Putman, Walter S., House, 303 Lawnford Ave., Wilmot, 9/10/92, B, C, 92001247

Renkert, Harry S., House, 1414 Market Ave., N., Canton, 6/18/81, B, C, 81000451

Ridgewood Historic District, Roughly bounded by Market and Gibbs Ave. and 21st and 24th Sts., Canton, 12/19/82, C, 82001489

Saxton House, 331 S. Market St., Canton, 4/26/79, B, 79001950

Schuffenecker, August Building, 134 6th St. SW, Canton, 9/02/82, A, C, 82003651

Serquet, Emanuel and Frederick, Farm, N of Wilmot at 14091 Stoneford, Wilmont vicinity, 12/02/82, C, 82001490

Seven Ranges Terminus, W of Magnolia at jct. of Stark, Tuscarawas, and Carroll counties, Magnolia vicinity, 12/12/76, B, 76001527

Spring Hill, Wales Rd., NE., Massillon, 4/14/72, B, 72001045

St. John's Catholic Church, 6th St. and McKinley Ave., NW., Canton, 5/27/75, C, a, 75001533

St. Louis Church, 300 N. Chapel St., Louisville, 2/22/79, C, a, 79001951

St. Mary's Catholic Church, 206 Cherry Rd., NE, Massillon, 4/16/79, C, a, 79001952

St. Peter Church, 720 Cleveland Ave., NW., Canton, 3/22/90, C, a, 90000472

St. Timothy's Protestant Episcopal Church, 226 SE. 3rd St., Massillon, 2/22/79, C, a, 79001953

Stark County Courthouse and Annex, Market and Tuscarawas Sts., Canton, 4/03/75, A, C, 75001534

Stewart, Harry Bartlett, Property, 13340 Congress Lake Rd., Hartville vicinity, 4/29/82, C, 82003653

Third Street Bridge, 3rd St., SE., Canton, 5/05/78, C, b, 78002192

Timken, Henry H., Estate Barn, 13th St., NW and I-77, Canton, 12/29/78, C, 78002193

Trinity Lutheran Church [Architecture of Guy Tilden in Canton, 1885–1905, TR], 415 W. Tuscarawas St., Canton, 8/23/85, A, C, a, 85001802

Vicary House, 3730 Market Ave. N., Canton, 3/15/82, C, 82003652

Werner Inn, 131 E. Nassau St., East Canton, 9/17/87, A, C, 87001635

Wilmot United Brethren Church, Massillon St. (OH 62), Wilmot, 6/22/76, C, 76001529

Summit County

Akron Jewish Center, 220 S. Balch St., Akron, 7/24/86, A, C, 86001919

Akron Post Office and Federal Building, 168 E. Market St., Akron, 5/26/83, A, C, 83002059

Akron Public Library, 69 E. Market St., Akron, 1/19/83, A, C, 83002060

Akron Rural Cemetery Buildings, 150 Glendale Ave., Akron, 9/27/80, C, 80003236

Akron Y.M.C.A. Building, 80 W. Center St., Akron, 10/31/80, C, 80003237

Alling, Francis D., House, 323 East Ave., Tallmadge, 11/30/87, C, 87002093

Anna-Dean Farm, OH 619, Barberton, 7/14/77, B, C, 77001086

Barber, O. C., Barn No. 1, 115 3rd St., Barberton, 2/28/73, B, C, 73001538

Barber, O. C., Colt Barn, Austin Dr., Barberton, 10/09/74, B, 74001626

Barber, O. C., Creamery, 365 Portsmouth Ave., Barberton, 5/22/73, B, C, 73001539

Barber, O. C., Machine Barn, Austin Dr., Barberton, 10/09/74, B, 74001627

Barber, O. C., Piggery, 248 Robinson Ave., Barberton, 5/22/73, B, C, 73001540

Barder, Byron R., House, 1041 W. Market St., Akron, 9/17/87, C, 87001598

Barker Village Site, Address Restricted, Akron vicinity, 4/19/78, D, NPS, 78000379

Barker, William, Residence [Bath Township MRA], 805 Wye Rd., Ghent, 6/11/79, C, 79002797

Bath Township Hall [Bath Township MRA], 1241 N. Cleveland-Massilon Rd., Bath Center, 6/11/79, A, C, 79002805

Summit County—Continued

Bath Township School [Bath Township MRA], 4655 Akron-Medina Rd., Ghent vicinity, 6/11/79, A, C, 79002801

Boston Mills Historic District, Roughly, Riverview, Boston Mills and Stanford Rds. and Main St., Boston Mills, 11/09/92, A, C, NPS, 92001490

Brown, Jim, House, S of Peninsula at 3491 Akron Peninsula Rd., Peninsula vicinity, 3/02/79, B, C, NPS, 79000299

Brown, Jim, Tavern [Ohio and Erie Canal TR], Boston Mills Rd., Boston, 12/11/79, A, C, NPS, 79000300

Brown, John, Farmhouse, 1842 Hines Hill Rd., Hudson vicinity, 9/22/77, B, 77001088

Brown—Bender Farm (Boundary Increase) [Agricultural Resources of the Cuyahoga Valley MPS], 3491 Akron—Peninsula Rd., Cuyahoga Falls vicinity, 3/12/93, A, NPS, 93000076

Carkhuff, Stacy G., House, 1225 W. Market St., Akron, 8/30/84, B, C, 84003804

Cascade Locks Historic District, Roughly bounded by North, Howard, Innerbelt Rt. 59 and the canal from Locks 10 to 16, including discontiguous parts N, Akron, 12/10/92, A, C, 92001627

Chuckery Race, S of and in Cuyahoga Falls, Cuyahoga Falls, 12/15/72, A, C, 72001047

Corbusier, John William Creswell, House [Hudson MPS], 226 College St., Hudson, 10/05/89, C, 89001451

Cranz, Edward, Farm [Agricultural Resources of the Cuyahoga Valley MPS], 2780 Oak Hill Dr., Peninsula vicinity, 3/12/93, A, C, NPS, 93000077

Cranz, William and Eugene, Farm [Agricultural Resources of the Cuyahoga Valley MPS], 2401 Ira Rd., Peninsula vicinity, 3/12/93, A, B, C, NPS, 93000078

Duffy, Michael, Farm [Agricultural Resources of the Cuyahoga Valley MPS], 4965 Quick Rd., Peninsula vicinity, 3/12/93, A, C, NPS, 93000079

Eagles Temple, 131-137 E. Market St., Akron, 6/01/82, A, C, 82003656

East Market Street Church of Christ, 864 E. Market St., Akron, 2/07/89, C, a, 88003440

Everett Historic District, 4731–4642 Riverview Rd. and 2151–2279 Everett Rd., Cuyahoga Valley National Recreation Area, Peninsula vicinity, 1/14/93, A, C, D, NPS, 93001467

Everett Knoll Complex, Address Restricted, Everett vicinity, 5/25/77, D, NPS, 77000157

First Congregational Church of Cuyahoga Falls, 130 Broad Blvd., Cuyahoga Falls, 11/03/75, C, a, 75001538

Fort Island Works, Address Restricted, Akron vicinity, 12/02/70, D, NPS, 70000087

Furnace Run Aqueduct [Ohio and Erie Canal TR], Furnace Run, Everett vicinity, 12/11/79, A, C, NPS, 79000301

Gayer, Jacob M., House, 406 Sumner St., Akron, 10/18/84, C, 84003442

Goodyear Airdock, S side of the Akron Airport, Akron, 4/11/73, A, C, g, 73002259

Grace Reformed Church, 172 W. Bowery St., Akron, 7/19/84, C, a, 84003806

Hale, Elijah, Residence [Bath Township MRA], 3243 Ira Rd., Bath, 6/11/79, C, 79002795

Hale, Jonathan, Homestead, 2686 Oak Hill Rd., Bath, 4/23/73, C, NPS, 73000258

Harshey, John, Residence [Bath Township MRA], 4270 Bath Rd., Bath Center vicinity, 6/11/79, C, 79002804

Heller, Edward, Residence [Bath Township MRA], 3891 Granger Rd., Ghent, 6/11/79, C, 79002798

Hershey, J., Residence [Bath Township MRA], 286 Cleveland-Massilon Rd., Ghent vicinity, 6/11/79, C, 79002802

Hopkins, Roswell, Residence [Bath Township MRA], 299 Hametown Rd., Ghent vicinity, 6/11/79, C, 79002799

Hower Mansion, 60 Fir Hill, Akron, 4/11/73, C, 73001536

Hudson Historic District, Roughly bounded by College, Streetsboro, S. Main, and Baldwin Sts., Hudson, 11/28/73, A, C, 73001542

Hudson Historic District (Boundary Increase) [Hudson MPS], Roughly bounded by Hudson St., Old Orchard Dr., Aurora St., Oviatt St., Streetsboro St., and College St. to Aurora, Hudson, 10/05/89, A, B, C, 89001452

Hunt—Wilke Farm [Agricultural Resources of the Cuyahoga Valley MPS], 2049 Bolanz Rd., Cuyahoga Falls vicinity, 3/12/93, A, C, NPS, 93000080

Izant, Grace Goulder, House [Hudson MPS], 250 College St., Hudson, 10/04/89, B, C, g, 89001450

Jackson, Andrew, House, 277 E. Mill St., Akron, 2/13/75, B, C, 75001537

Johnson, Dustin, Residence [Bath Township MRA], 1946 Cleveland-Massilon Rd., Bath, 6/11/79, C, 79002806

Kent, J., Residence [Bath Township MRA], 1727 Medina Line Rd., Bath vicinity, 6/11/79, C, 79002792

Kirby, James, Mill, W of West Richfield off OH 303, West Richfield vicinity, 12/14/78, A, C, 78002197

Kittinger, David, Residence [Bath Township MRA], 1904 Cleveland-Massilon Rd., Bath, 6/11/79, C, 79002808

Ligget, J., Residence [Bath Township MRA], 481 Cleveland-Massilon Rd., Ghent vicinity, 6/11/79, C, 79002803

Lock No. 26 [Ohio and Erie Canal TR], 3.3 mi. N of Ira Rd., Ira, 12/11/79, A, C, NPS, 79000302

Lock No. 27 [Ohio and Erie Canal TR], Approx. 400 ft. E of intersection of Riverview and Everett Rds., Everett, 12/11/79, A, C, NPS, 79000303

Lock No. 28 [Ohio and Erie Canal TR], Deep Lock Q Quarry Metro Park, Peninsula, 12/11/79, A, C, NPS, 79000304

Lock No. 29 and Aqueduct [Ohio and Erie Canal TR], off SR 303, Peninsula, 12/11/79, A, C, NPS, 79000305

Lock No. 30 and Feeder Dam [Ohio and Erie Canal TR], Off SR 303, Peninsula, 12/11/79, A, C, NPS, 79000306

Lock No. 31 [Ohio and Erie Canal TR], 200 ft. E of Cuyahoga River and approx. 0.5 mi. S of Ohio Turnpike, Peninsula, 12/11/79, A, C, NPS, 79000307

Lock No. 32 [Ohio and Erie Canal TR], 800 ft. N of Boston Mills, Boston, 12/11/79, A, C, NPS, 79000308

Lock No. 33 [Ohio and Erie Canal TR], 1 mi. S of Highland Rd., Boston vicinity, 12/11/79, A, C, NPS, 79000309

Lock No. 34 [Ohio and Erie Canal TR], Highland Rd., Sagamore Hills, 12/17/79, A, C, NPS, 79000310

Lock No. 35 [Ohio and Erie Canal TR], Off SR 82, Sagamore Hills, 12/11/79, A, C, NPS, 79000311

Loew's Theatre, 182 S. Main St., Akron, 7/16/73, A, C, 73001537

McKisson, Robert, House, 7878 N. Gannett Rd., Sagamore Hills, 12/04/74, A, C, 74001632

Merriman, Wells E., House, 641 W. Market St., Akron, 9/29/83, B, C, 83002061

Miller, Harvey, Residence [Bath Township MRA], 188 Hametown Rd., Ghent vicinity, 6/11/79, C, 79002800

Miller, Lewis, House, 142 King Dr., Akron, 1/30/76, B, C, 76001531

O'Neil's Department Store, 226–250 S. Main St., Akron, 11/28/90, A, 90001776

Ohio and Erie Canal Deep Lock, S of Peninsula on Riverview Rd., Peninsula vicinity, 9/09/74, A, C, NPS, 74000345

Old Akron Post Office, 70 E. Market St., Akron, 6/19/72, C, 72001046

Palmer House, 9370 Olde Eight Rd., Northfield Center, 8/13/74, C, b, 74001628

Peninsula Village Historic District, Both sides of OH 303, Peninsula, 8/23/74, A, C, NPS, 74000346

Perkins, Col. Simon, Mansion, 550 Copley Rd., Akron, 8/13/74, C, 74001624

Portage Hotel, 10 N. Main St., Akron, 10/17/88, A, C, 80004611

Porter, Orin, House [Hudson MPS], 240 College St., Hudson, 10/05/89, B, C, 89001449

Quaker Oats Cereal Factory, 120 E. Mill St., Akron, 12/08/78, A, 78002195

Randall, Dr. Rufus, Residence [Bath Township MRA], 3675 Ira Rd., Bath, 6/11/79, C, 79002796

Ranney, Luther B., Farm, 6484 Old Rt. 8, Boston Heights vicinity, 12/01/88, C, 88002749

Richard, John, Residence [Bath Township MRA], 1924 Cleveland-Massilon Rd., Bath, 6/11/79, C, 79002807

Robinson, Byron W., House, 715 E. Buchtel Ave., Akron, 9/20/91, C, 91001415

Seiberling, Charles Willard, House, 1075 W. Market St., Akron, 5/06/93, B, C, 93000405

Shaw, Samuel, Residence [Bath Township MRA], 1588 Hametown Rd., Bath, 6/11/79, C, 79002794

Shaw, Sylvester, Residence [Bath Township MRA], 1786 Medina Line Rd., Bath vicinity, 6/11/79, C, 79002793

Smith, Dr. Robert, House, 855 Ardmore Ave., Akron, 10/31/85, B, 85003411

St. Bernard's Church, 240 S. Broadway St., Akron, 3/09/89, C, a, 89000174

Summit County—Continued

St. Paul's Sunday School and Parish House, E. Market and Forge Sts., Akron, 11/07/76, A, C, a, 76001532

Stan Hywet Hall-Frank A. Seiberling House, 714 N. Portage Path, Akron, 1/17/75, A, B, C, NHL, 75002058

Stanford, George, Farm, 6093 Stanford Rd., Peninsula vicinity, 2/17/82, A, C, NPS, 82001874

Stewart—Hanson Farm, 2832 Call Rd., Stow, 10/15/92, A, C, 92001376

Stumpy Basin [Ohio and Erie Canal TR], 200 ft. E of Cuyahoga River and approx. 0.5 mi. S of Ohio Turnpike, Peninsula vicinity, 12/11/79, A, NPS, 79000313

Summit County Courthouse and Annex, 209 S. High St., Akron, 10/15/74, C, 74001625

Tallmadge Town Square Historic District, Public Sq., Tallmadge, 5/06/71, A, C, a, 71000652

Thornton-Guise Kitchen And House, 147 S. Main St., Munroe Falls, 5/06/76, A, C, 76001534

Thorp, Manville, Residence [Bath Township MRA], 1907 Medina Lane Rd., Bath vicinity, 6/11/79, C, 79002791

Tilden, Daniel, House, 2325 Stine Rd., Peninsula, 6/20/85, C, NPS, 85001340

Tuscarawas Avenue—Alexander Square Commercial Historic District, Bounded by Park Ave., Tuscarawas Ave., 4th and 5th Sts., Barberton, 5/17/90, A, C, 90000755

Twinsburg Congregational Church, Twinsburg Public Sq., Twinsburg, 5/03/74, C, a, 74001634

Twinsburg Institute, 8996 Darrow Rd., Twinsburg, 1/01/76, A, C, 76001535

Wallace Farm, 8230 Brandywine Rd., Northfield Center vicinity, 6/27/85, A, NPS, 85001387

Ward House, 1410 Hines Hill Rd., Hudson vicinity, 3/17/87, C, b, 87000629

Welton, Allen, House, SW of Peninsula at 2485 Major Rd., Peninsula vicinity, 5/07/79, A, C, NPS, 79000314

Werner Company Building, 109 N. Union, Akron, 12/12/76, A, C, 76001533

Western Reserve Academy, Roughly bounded by Aurora St. and both sides of Oviatt, High, , Hudson, 6/30/75, A, C, 75001539

Westmont Building, 22 Rhodes Ave., Akron, 5/31/84, C, 84003807

Wolcott House, 56 E. Twinsburg Rd., Northfield vicinity, 5/05/88, C, 88000468

Young Woman's Christian Association, 146 S. High St., Akron, 11/04/82, C, 82001491

Trumbull County

Allen, Dr. Peter, House, W. Williamsfield State Rd., N of intersection of OH 87, Kinsman vicinity, 9/03/71, C, 71000653

Barnhisel, Henry II, House, 1011 N. State St., Girard, 12/19/82, A, B, 82001492

Brookfield Center Historic District, Roughly W side of OH 7 from Sharon-Warren Rd. to N.

Wood St. and Brookfield Village Green, Brookfield, 10/10/85, C, a, 85002922

Brown, Charles, Gothic Cottage, OH 45 S., North Bloomfield, 5/28/75, A, C, 75001545

Brown-Wing House, Park West Rd., North Bloomfield, 6/20/75, A, C, 75001546

Brownwood, OH 45, North Bloomfield, 9/03/71, C, 71000655

Congregational-Presbyterian Church, Near OH 5 and 7, Kinsman, 9/03/71, C, a, 71000654

Darrow, Clarence, Octagon House, OH 5 and 7, Kinsman, 9/10/71, B, 71001025

Edwards, John Stark, House, 309 South St., SE., Warren, 7/17/78, B, C, b, 78002199

Fowler Center Historic District, Roughly area around Fowler Twp. Village Green at OH 305 and OH 193, Fowler, 10/10/85, C, 85002921

Garlick, Richard, House, 1025 Ravine Dr., Youngstown vicinity, 10/10/90, A, C, 90001500

Greene Township Center, E of North Bloomfield on OH 87, North Bloomfield vicinity, 3/08/78, C, a, 78002198

Gustavus Center Historic District, Town of Gustavus situated at jct. of OH 193 and OH 87, Gustavus and vicinity, 8/06/75, A, C, 75001542

Harshman, Charles, House, 3932 Painesville-Warren State Rd., NW, Southington Township, 7/07/83, C, 83002062

Mahoning Avenue Historic District, 241–391 Mahoning Ave., NW., Warren, 10/26/71, A, C, 71000656

Mahoning Avenue Historic District (Boundary Increase), Mahoning Ave. between Perkins Dr. and High St., Warren, 5/22/78, B, C, 78003115

Mason, John Wesley, Gothic Cottage, NW of Braceville on OH 534, Braceville vicinity, 11/12/75, A, C, 75001541

McCorkle, Almon G., House, 1180 Saltsprings Rd., Lordstown, 3/10/82, B, C, 82003659

McKinley Memorial, 40 N. Main St., Niles, 10/31/75, A, B, C, f, 75001544

McLain-Gillmer House, 720 Mahoning Ave., NW., Warren, 6/15/78, B, C, 78002200

Mesopotamia Village District, OH 534 and 87, Mesopotamia, 12/24/74, C, 74001635

Newton Falls Covered Bridge, Off OH 534, Newton Falls, 10/16/74, C, 74001636

Packard, James Ward, House, 319 Oak Knoll Ave. NE, Warren, 10/31/85, B, C, 85003577

Raymond, Liberty G., Tavern and Barn, OH 87 and Dennison-Ashtabula Rd., Kenilworth, 6/20/75, A, C, 75001543

Seely, Dr. John W., House, 2245 Niles-Cortland Rd., Howland Corners vicinity, 4/14/72, B, C, 72001048

Trumbull County Courthouse, 160 High St., NW., Warren, 12/31/74, C, 74001637

Upton, Harriet Taylor, House, 380 Mahoning Ave. NW., Warren, 10/05/92, B, NHL, 92001884

Ward-Thomas House, 503 Brown St., Niles, 2/09/84, B, C, 84003809

Warren Commercial Historic District, Roughly bounded by Mahoning, Monroe, Franklin and Pine Sts., Warren, 6/16/83, A, C, 83002063

Warren Public Library, 120 High St., NW., Warren, 3/20/73, A, C, 73001543

Wells—Clark—Strouss House, 50 Warner Rd. at Logan Rd., Youngstown vicinity, 9/10/93, B, C, a, 93000877

Woodrow, William, House, 138 Champion St., E, Champion vicinity, 7/15/82, B, C, 82003658

Tuscarawas County

Bernhard, Frederick, House, 211 E. Front St., Dover, 12/09/88, B, C, 88002748

Deis, John, House, 203 W. Sixth St., Dover, 6/30/88, C, 88000980

Fort Laurens Site, Near OH 212, 0.5 mi. S of Bolivar, Bolivar vicinity, 11/10/70, A, 70000518

Garver Brothers Store, 134 N. Wooster Ave., Strasburg, 11/26/80, A, 80003238

Gnadenhutten Massacre Site, S of Gnadenhutten on county rte., Gnadenhutten vicinity, 11/10/70, A, a, 70000519

Johnson Site II, Address Restricted, Strasburg vicinity, 2/09/84, D, 84003808

Lebold John, House, Smokehouse and Springhouse, Rt. 1, Bolivar vicinity, 7/15/82, A, C, 82003660

Pennsylvania Railroad Depot And Baggage Room, Center St., Dennison, 9/08/76, A, 76001536

Pershing, Christian, Barn, Off OH 39 W of Dover, Dover vicinity, 3/19/92, C, 92000172

Port Washington Town Hall, Main St., Port Washington, 2/22/79, A, C, 79001971

Reeves, Jeremiah, House and Carriage House, 325 E. Iron Ave., Dover, 7/15/82, B, C, 82003661

Rinderknecht, Christian H., House, 602 N. Wooster Ave., Dover, 7/31/91, C, 91000972

Schoenbrunn Site, U.S. 250, New Philadelphia, 11/10/70, A, a, 70000520

Tuscarawas County Courthouse, Courthouse Sq., New Philadelphia, 7/16/73, C, 73001544

Zoar Historic District, Bounded by 5th, Foltz, and 1st Sts. and by rear property lines of properties, Zoar, 6/23/69, A, C, a, 69000150

Zoar Historic District (Boundary Increase), Town of Zoar along OH 212, Zoar and vicinity, 8/11/75, A, C, D, a, 75002124

Union County

Ellis Mounds, Address Restricted, Marysville vicinity, 7/30/74, D, 74001638

Elmwood Place, SW of Irwin on OH 161, Irwin vicinity, 11/29/79, C, 79001972

Fort, The, 26953 N. Lewisburg Rd., North Lewisburg, 7/08/82, A, C, 82003662

Gilcrist House, 3.5 mi. SE of Marysville off SR 33, Marysville vicinity, 8/13/76, C, 76001537

Marysville Historic District, Roughly bounded by Maple, Plum, 4th, and 7th Sts., Marysville, 2/01/78, C, 78002201

Reed Covered Bridge, 3.5 mi. S of Marysville off SR 38, Marysville vicinity, 3/04/75, C, 75001547

Van Wert County

Bredeick-Lang House, 508 W. 2nd St, Delphos, 4/07/82, C, 82003663

Brumback Library, 215 W. Main St., Van Wert, 1/29/79, A, C, 79001973

Marsh, George H., Homestead and the Marsh Foundation School, Ridge Rd., Van Wert, 11/28/80, B, C, 80003239

Round Barn [Round Barns in the Black Swamp of Northwest Ohio TR], Off SR 224, Van Wert vicinity, 4/17/80, A, C, 80003240

Van Wert Bandstand, Van Wert County Fairgrounds, OH 127, Van Wert, 10/14/82, A, C, b, 82001493

Van Wert County Courthouse, 121 E. Main St., Van Wert, 7/30/74, C, 74001639

Willshire School, Green St., Willshire, 11/25/80, A, C, 80003241

Vinton County

Eakin Mill Covered Bridge, Mound Hill Rd., Arbaugh, 3/16/76, A, C, 76001539

Hope Furnace, 5 mi. NE of Zaleski on OH 278, Zaleski vicinity, 5/25/73, A, 73001546

Markham Mound, Address Restricted, Zaleski vicinity, 5/03/74, D, 74001640

Mt. Olive Road Covered Bridge, 1 mi. NE of Allensville on Mt. Olive Rd., Allensville vicinity, 10/08/76, A, C, 76001538

Ponn Humpback Covered Bridge, 4 mi. SW of Wilkesville over Raccoon Creek, Wilkesville vicinity, 4/11/73, C, 73001545

Ranger Station Mound, Address Restricted, Zaleski vicinity, 7/15/74, D, 74001641

Ratcliffe Mound, Address Restricted, Londonderry vicinity, 8/28/75, D, 75001548

Trinity Episcopal Church, Sugar and High Sts., McArthur, 3/16/76, C, a, 76001540

Zaleski Methodist Church Mound, Address Restricted, Zaleski vicinity, 7/15/74, D, 74001642

Warren County

Armco Park Mound I, Address Restricted, Otterbein vicinity, 5/29/75, D, 75001550

Armco Park Mound II, Address Restricted, Otterbein vicinity, 5/29/75, D, 75001551

Bone Mound II, Address Restricted, Oregonia vicinity, 7/15/74, D, 74001643

Bone Stone Graves, Address Restricted, Oregonia vicinity, 7/15/74, D, 74001644

Butler, Charles, House, 13 E. Jackson St., Franklin, 4/29/82, C, 82003664

Coffeen, Goldsmith, House [Lebanon MRA], 419 Cincinnati Ave., Lebanon, 10/10/84, C, 84000165

Corwin House [Lebanon MRA], 1255 OH 48, Lebanon, 10/10/84, C, 84000166

Corwin-Bolin House [Lebanon MRA], 1443 OH 48, Lebanon, 10/10/84, C, 84000167

Crane, Jonathan, Farm, S of Franklin on OH 741, Franklin vicinity, 2/17/78, B, C, 78002202

Crossed Keys Tavern, E of Lebanon on OH 350, Lebanon vicinity, 10/21/76, C, 76001542

Deardoff, Daniel L., House, 4374 Union Rd., Franklin vicinity, 5/31/84, A, C, 84003810

East End Historic District [Lebanon MRA], Roughly bounded by South, Mound, Pleasant, and Cherry Sts., Lebanon, 10/10/84, A, C, a, 84000419

Ferney, John, House [Lebanon MRA], 475 Glosser Rd., Lebanon, 10/10/84, C, 84000423

Floraville Historic District [Lebanon MRA], Roughly bounded by Cincinnati and Orchard Aves., East and Keever Sts., Lebanon, 10/10/84, A, C, 84002102

Fort Ancient, OH 350, Lebanon vicinity, 10/15/66, D, NHL, 66000625

Glendower, U.S. 42 (Cincinnati Ave.), Lebanon, 11/10/70, C, 70000521

Golden Lamb, 27–31 S. Broadway, Lebanon, 1/12/78, A, C, 78002204

Harvey, Elizabeth, Free Negro School, North St., Harveysburg, 11/17/77, B, 77001089

Hatton Farm, E of Harveysburg on OH 73, Harveysburg vicinity, 3/29/78, C, 78002203

Hill-Kinder Mound, Address Restricted, Franklin vicinity, 11/05/71, D, 71000657

Kern Effigy (33WA372), Address Restricted, Oregonia vicinity, 7/21/86, A, D, 86001922

Landen Mounds I and II, Address Restricted, Foster vicinity, 5/27/75, D, 75001549

Lebanon Academy [Lebanon MRA], 190 New St., Lebanon, 10/10/84, A, 84000427

Lebanon Cemetery Entrance Arch [Lebanon MRA], Hunter St., Lebanon, 10/18/84, A, C, d, 84000157

Lebanon Cemetery Superintendent's House [Lebanon MRA], 416 W. Silver St., Lebanon, 10/18/84, C, 84000159

Lebanon Commercial District [Lebanon MRA], Roughly Broadway, Mechanic, Silver, Mulberry, and Main Sts., Lebanon, 10/10/84, A, C, 84000429

Mackinaw Historic District, Off OH 123, Franklin, 7/21/80, B, C, 80003242

Maplewood Sanitorium [Lebanon MRA], Maple and Deerfield Sts., Lebanon, 10/10/84, A, 84000432

McKay, Moses, House, E of Waynesville, on New Burlington Rd., Waynesville vicinity, 2/17/78, A, C, 78002207

Moar Mound And Village, Address Restricted, Morrow vicinity, 1/01/76, D, 76001543

Mohrman-Jack-Evans House [Lebanon MRA], 342 Columbus Ave., Lebanon, 10/10/84, C, a, 84000433

North Broadway Historic District [Lebanon MRA], Roughly Broadway, Warren, Pleasant, New and Mechanic Sts., Lebanon, 10/10/84, A, C, 84000435

Old Log Post Office, 5th and River Sts., Franklin, 3/17/76, C, b, 76001541

Peters Cartridge Company, 1915 Grandin Rd., Kings Mills, 10/10/85, A, C, 85003115

Robinson, Edmund, House, N of Lebanon at 3208 OH 48, Lebanon vicinity, 4/16/79, C, 79001974

Satterthwaite, John, House, 498 N. Third St., Waynesville, 3/30/88, A, B, C, 88000239

Smith-Davis House [Lebanon MRA], 206 W. Silver St., Lebanon, 2/06/85, C, 85000245

Stanton Farm, N of Springboro on Lytle-Five Points Rd., Springboro vicinity, 5/29/80, B, C, 80003243

Stokes, Benjamin A., House, 5587 OH 60, Lebanon vicinity, 7/18/83, A, C, 83002064

Stubbs Earthworks, Address Restricted, Morrow vicinity, 4/04/78, D, 78002205

Taylor Mound And Village Site, Address Restricted, Oregonia vicinity, 3/31/78, D, 78002206

Trevey Mound (33WA193), Address Restricted, Morrow vicinity, 6/20/86, D, 86001345

Waynesville Greek Revival Houses, 5303 and 5323 Wilkerson Lane, Waynesville, 8/08/79, C, 79001976

West Baptist Church [Lebanon MRA], 500 W. Mulberry St., Lebanon, 10/18/84, A, C, a, 84000161

Wright, Dr. Aaron, House, 155 W. Central Ave., Springboro, 8/03/79, B, C, 79001975

Washington County

Ames, Charles Rice, House, 2212 Miller Ave., Belpre, 2/14/78, C, 78002208

Barker, Col. Joseph, House, N of Marietta on Masonic Park Rd., Marietta vicinity, 6/23/78, B, C, 78002210

Barker, Judge Joseph, Jr., House, SW of Newport on OH 7, Newport vicinity, 7/26/79, B, C, 79001979

Becker Lumber and Manufacturing Company, 121 Pike St., Marietta, 6/18/87, C, 87000988

Cisler Terrace, 7th and Ephraim Cutler Sts., Marietta, 1/19/83, B, C, 83002065

Curtis, Walter, House, S of Little Hocking, Little Hocking vicinity, 10/03/80, B, C, 80003244

Deming, Col. Simeon, House, NE of Watertown on Willis Rd., Watertown vicinity, 3/24/80, B, C, 80003245

Erwin Hall, Marietta College, 5th St. on Marietta College campus, Marietta, 4/23/73, C, 73001547

First Unitarian Church Of Marietta, 232 3rd St., Marietta, 10/03/73, B, C, a, 73001548

Harmar Historic District, Roughly bounded by the Ohio and Muskingum Rivers and the rear property line of Lancaster, George, and Franklin Sts., Marietta, 12/19/74, A, B, C, 74001645

Harmar Historic District (Boundary Increase), Roughly bounded by Lancaster, Harmar, Putnam and Franklin Sts. and the Ohio R., Fort Harmar Dr. and the Muskingum R., Marietta, 9/16/93, A, C, 93000987

Harra Covered Bridge, 2 mi. NW of Watertown on SR 172, Watertown vicinity, 10/08/76, A, C, 76001547

Hildreth Covered Bridge, 5 mi. (8 km) E of Marietta off OH 26, Marietta vicinity, 2/08/78, A, C, 78002211

Washington County—Continued

Hune Covered Bridge, 2.5 mi. N of Dart on SR 34, Dart vicinity, 10/08/76, A, C, 76001545

Hune, William, Farm, OH 26 N of Dart, Reno, 3/28/91, A, C, b, 91000303

Kaiser, John, House, 300 Bellevue St., Marietta, 12/10/93, C, 93001392

MISSISSIPPI III, 237 Front St., Marietta, 9/21/83, A, 83002066

Marietta Historic District, Roughly bounded by the Muskingum and Ohio Rivers and Warren, 3rd, 5th, and 6th Sts., Marietta, 12/19/74, A, B, C, D, a, 74001646

Mason House, OH 393, Coal Run, 11/29/79, C, 79001978

Mound Cemetery Mound, 5th and Scammel Sts., Marietta, 2/23/73, D, d, 73001549

Ohio Company Land Office, Washington and 2nd Sts., Campus Martius Museum, Marietta, 11/10/70, B, b, 70000523

Putnam, Rufus, House, Campus Martius Museum, corner of 2nd and Washington Sts., Marietta, 11/10/70, B, C, 70000524

Rinard Covered Bridge, NE of Marietta on SR 406, Marietta vicinity, 10/08/76, A, C, 76001546

Root Covered Bridge, 0.5 mi. N of Decaturville on SR 6, Decaturville vicinity, 3/27/75, C, 75001552

Sawyer-Curtis House, Off U.S. 50, Little Hocking, 10/18/84, B, C, 84002696

Shinn Covered Bridge, NE of Bartlett off OH 555, Bartlett vicinity, 10/08/76, A, C, 76001544

Spencer's Landing, 4 E. Fifth St., Belpre, 8/18/92, C, 92001035

Sprague, Jonathan, House, W of Lowell Off OH 60, Lowell vicinity, 1/11/83, A, C, 83002067

St. Mary's School, Old, 132 S. Fourth St., Marietta, 10/03/89, C, a, 89001457

Stone, Capt. Jonathan, House, 612 Blennerhassett Ave., Belpre, 2/07/78, B, C, b, 78002209

W.P. SNYDER, JR. (steamboat), On Muskingum River at Sacra Via, Marietta, 11/10/70, A, C, NHL, 70000522

Waernicke-Hille House And Store, SR 36, Archer's Fork, 11/29/79, B, C, 79001977

Watertown Historic District, E of OH 339 and N of OH 676, Watertown, 4/10/86, C, 86000728

Wilcox-Milis House, 301 5th St., Marietta, 4/13/73, C, 73001550

Wayne County

Akey, James, Farm, Address Restricted, Mount Eaton vicinity, 12/22/78, A, C, 78002212

Barnet-Hoover Log House, NW of Orrville, Orrville vicinity, 8/13/74, C, 74001648

Beall, Gen. Reasin, House, 46 E. Bowman St., Wooster, 6/07/76, B, 76001548

College of Wooster, OH 3, Wooster, 2/25/80, A, C, 80003246

Deerlick Farm, 7482 Britton Rd., West Salem vicinity, 6/20/86, A, C, 86001365

Gasche, Charles, House, 340 Bever St., Wooster, 1/13/89, C, 88003192

Gertenslager Carriage and Wagon Company, 572 E. Liberty, Wooster, 2/13/86, A, C, 86000240

Kister Mill, Jct. of Twnshp. Rds. 34 and 228, Millbrook, 7/10/74, A, 74001647

McSweeney, John, House, 531 N. Market St., Wooster, 7/30/74, B, 74001649

Old Wayne County Jail, W. North St., Wooster, 4/29/82, A, C, 82003665

Overholt House, 1473 Beall Ave., Wooster, 12/06/83, C, b, 83004345

Walnut Street School, 237 S. Walnut St., Wooster, 3/01/84, A, C, 84003811

Wayne County Courthouse District, Liberty and Market Sts., Wooster, 7/26/73, A, C, 73001551

Wooster Public Square Historic District (Boundary Increase), Market and Liberty Sts., Wooster, 11/30/78, A, C, 78002213

Zimmerman, Ezekiel B., Octagon House, NW of Marshallville on OH 57, Marshallville vicinity, 5/28/75, A, C, 75001553

Williams County

Bryan Downtown Historic District, Roughly bounded by Walnut, Beech, Maple, and Bryan Sts., Bryan, 12/29/83, A, C, 83004347

Fountain City Historic District, Roughly bounded by Butler, Lynn, W. Wilson, Center, Portland and Beech Sts., Bryan, 10/01/90, C, 90001501

Kunkle Log House, 1 mi. E of jct. CR 17 and 0, Kunkle vicinity, 8/05/76, A, C, 76001549

Nettle Lake Mound Group, Address Restricted, Nettle Lake vicinity, 3/27/74, D, 74001650

Stryker Depot, N. Depot St., Stryker, 8/07/89, A, C, 89001014

Williams County Courthouse, Main and High Sts., Bryan, 5/07/73, C, 73001552

Wood County

Boom Town Historic District, Roughly bounded by W. Wooster, S. Church, N. Grove, N. Maple, and Buttonwood, Bowling Green, 5/08/87, C, 87000693

Dodge Site, Address Restricted, Bowling Green vicinity, 3/29/78, D, 78002214

Eagle Point Colony Historic District, Colony Rd., Riverside, Eagle Point, Park, and Forest Drs., Rossford, 9/22/83, C, 83002068

East River Road Historic District II, 577 E. Front St. to 28589 E. River Rd., Perrysburg and vicinity, 11/21/76, C, g, 76001550

East River Road Historic District I, 29455–30465 E. River Rd. (N side only), Rossford vicinity, 11/21/76, C, 76001551

Empire House, 5535 U.S. 20, Stony Ridge, 11/28/78, A, 78002216

Floral Hall, City Park on Conneaut Ave., Bowling Green, 7/27/82, A, C, 82003666

Fort Meigs, 1.3 mi. SW of Perrysburg, Perrysburg vicinity, 8/04/69, A, e, NHL, 69000151

Graham, William, House, 7056 Jerry City Rd., Wayne, 3/01/84, C, 84003812

Heeter-Russo House, 24570 2nd St., Grand Rapids, 5/29/75, C, 75001554

Hood-Simmons House, 202 W. 5th St., Perrysburg, 12/30/74, C, 74001652

Indian Hills Site, Address Restricted, Rossford vicinity, 9/20/79, D, 79001983

Kerr, Benjamin F., House, 17605 Beaver St., Grand Rapids, 12/21/79, C, 79001982

MacNichol Site, Address Restricted, Perrysburg vicinity, 11/24/78, D, 78002215

Main Street Historic District, Main and Wooster Sts., Bowling Green, 11/28/80, B, C, 80003247

North Baltimore Town Hall, 207 North Main St., North Baltimore, 10/29/81, C, 81000453

Old Wood County Jail, 240 W. Indiana Ave., Perrysburg, 12/17/69, A, C, 69000152

Perrysburg Historic District, Front St. (between E. Boundary St. & W. Boundary Ln.) 2nd St. (between Pine & Hickory Sts.) & 3rd St. (at Louisiana Av.), Perrysburg, 4/14/75, A, C, 75001557

Perrysburg Historic District (Boundary Increase), Roughly Maumee R. frontage from Pine to E. Boundary and S side of E. Second St. from Locust to Hickory, Perrysburg, 6/21/90, A, C, 90000948

Perrysburg Water Maintenance Building, 130 W. Indiana Ave., Perrysburg, 5/10/90, C, 90000754

Schaller Memorial Building, 130 W. Indiana St., Perrysburg, 5/10/90, C, 90000753

Simmons, Edwin H., House, 10302 Fremont Pike, Perrysburg, 2/07/91, C, 90002211

Spafford House, 27338 W. River Rd., Perrysburg vicinity, 7/15/74, C, 74001653

Thurston Building, Front St., Grand Rapids, 5/29/75, B, C, 75001555

Town Hall, Front St., Grand Rapids, 5/27/75, C, 75001556

U.S. Post Office, 305 N. Main St., Bowling Green, 3/28/79, C, 79001980

Wood County Courthouse And Jail, 200 E. Court St., Bowling Green, 6/25/74, C, 74001651

Wood County Home and Infirmary, N of Bowling Green at 13660 County Home Rd., Bowling Green vicinity, 4/16/79, A, C, 79001981

Yeager, John J., House, 343 W. Indiana Ave., Perrysburg, 3/19/85, B, C, 85000619

Wyandot County

Armstrong Farm, 13706 OH 199, Upper Sandusky vicinity, 1/17/86, A, B, C, 86000070

Crawford, Col., Burn Site Monument, NE of Crawford, Crawford, 4/15/82, B, f, 82003667

Indian Mill, 3.5 mi. NE of Upper Sandusky on Crane Twnshp. Rd., Upper Sandusky vicinity, 11/10/70, A, 70000525

Parker Covered Bridge, 5 mi. NE of Upper Sandusky on SR 40A, Upper Sandusky vicinity, 3/31/75, C, 75001558

South Sandusky Avenue Historic District, S. Sandusky Ave., Upper Sandusky, 10/22/80, C, 80003248

Swartz Covered Bridge, NW of Wyandot on SR 130A, Wyandot vicinity, 10/08/76, C, 76001553

Wyandot County—Continued

Walker, William, Jr., House, 132–134 S. 4th St., Upper Sandusky, 3/11/80, A, B, a, 80003249

West End Elementary School, 200 West St., Carey, 11/05/87, C, 87001989

Wyandot County Courthouse and Jail, Courthouse Sq., Upper Sandusky, 7/02/73, C, 73001553

Wyandot Mission Church, N of Upper Sandusky off Church St., Upper Sandusky vicinity, 1/20/76, A, a, 76001552

This 1940s WPA stone bridge contributes to the Vesuvius Furnace property in Lawrence County, Ohio. (Mary A. Wilson, 1988)

OKLAHOMA

Adair County

Adair County Courthouse [County Courthouses of Oklahoma TR], Division St., Stilwell, 8/23/84, A, C, 84002927

Buffington Hotel, Main St., Westville, 2/23/84, A, 84002929

Golda's Mill, 12 mi. NW of Stilwell, Stilwell vicinity, 11/09/72, A, 72001049

Opera Block, Main St., Westville, 2/23/84, A, 84002934

Alfalfa County

Alfalfa County Courthouse [County Courthouses of Oklahoma TR], Grand Ave., Cherokee, 8/23/84, A, C, 84002937

Aline IOOF Lodge No. 263 [IOOF Buildings in Alfalfa County TR], Off Main and Broadway, Aline, 3/08/84, A, 84002941

Carmen IOOF Home [IOOF Buildings in Alfalfa County TR], N of Carmen, Carmen vicinity, 3/08/84, A, a, 84002944

Carmen IOOF Lodge No. 84 [IOOF Buildings in Alfalfa County TR], Main and 4th St., Carmen, 3/08/84, A, 84002948

Cherokee Armory [WPA Public Bldgs., Recreational Facilities and Water Quality Improvements in Northwestern Oklahoma, 1935–1943 TR], Second and Kansas Sts., Cherokee, 9/08/88, A, C, 88001371

Cherokee IOOF Lodge No. 219 [IOOF Buildings in Alfalfa County TR], Grand Ave. and 2nd St., Cherokee, 3/08/84, A, 84002953

Farmers' Exchange Elevator [Clay Tile Grain Elevators in Northwestern Oklahoma TR], OK 45, Goltry, 10/07/83, A, C, 83004152

Farmers' Federation Elevator [Clay Tile Grain Elevators in Northwestern Oklahoma TR], Ohio Ave. and 4th St., Cherokee, 10/07/83, A, C, 83004153

Ingersoll Tile Elevator [Clay Tile Grain Elevators in Northwestern Oklahoma TR], Off US 64, Ingersoll, 10/07/83, A, C, 83004156

Sod House   , About 4 mi. N of Cleo Springs, Cleo Springs vicinity, 9/29/70, A, C, 70000526

Atoka County

Atoka Armory [WPA Public Bldgs., Recreational Facilities and Cemetery Improvements in Southeastern Oklahoma, 1935–1943 TR], Ohio and C Sts., Atoka, 9/08/88, A, C, 88001372

Atoka Community Building [WPA Public Bldgs., Recreational Facilities and Cemetery Improvements in Southeastern Oklahoma, 1935–1943 TR], First and Delaware Sts., Atoka, 9/08/88, A, C, 88001373

Billy, Isaac, Homestead and Family Cemetery, NE of Daisy, Daisy vicinity, 4/17/80, B, C, d, 80003256

Boggy Depot Site, 14 mi. SW of Atoka, Atoka vicinity, 4/19/72, A, C, 72001050

First Methodist Church Building, 105 W. 1st St., Atoka, 6/30/80, A, C, a, 80003250

First Oil Well in Oklahoma, 4 mi. NE of Wapanucka, Wapanucka vicinity, 4/13/72, A, 72001053

Indian Citizen Building, 115 N. Ohio Ave., Atoka, 10/04/79, A, 79001984

LeFlore, Capt. Charles, House, 0.5 mi. N of Limestone Gap on U.S. 69, Limestone Gap vicinity, 6/13/72, B, 72001052

Masonic Temple, 301 Court St., Atoka, 9/08/80, A, C, 80003251

McAlister, Bo, Site, Address Restricted, Wapanucka vicinity, 4/21/78, D, 78002217

Middle Boggy Battlefield Site and Confederate Cemetery, 1 mi. N of Atoka, Atoka vicinity, 4/19/72, A, d, 72001051

Old Atoka County Courthouse, Pennsylvania and Court Sts., Atoka, 12/06/79, A, C, 79001985

Old Atoka State Bank, Court and Ohio Sts., Atoka, 8/29/80, A, C, 80003252

Pioneer Club, 1st and Mississippi Sts., Atoka, 6/27/80, A, 80003253

Ralls, Joe, House, 303 S. Pennsylvania St., Atoka, 6/27/80, A, C, 80003254

Standley, Capt. James S., House, 207 N. Ohio Ave., Atoka, 12/11/79, B, C, 79001986

Waddell's Station Site, About 3 mi. SW of Wesley, Wesley vicinity, 4/13/72, A, 72001054

Zweigel Hardware Store Building, 405 and 407 Court St., Atoka, 9/08/80, A, C, 80003255

Beaver County

Beaver County Courthouse [County Courthouses of Oklahoma TR], Off US 270, Beaver City, 8/23/84, A, 84002964

Floris Grain Elevator [Woodframe Grain Elevators of Oklahoma Panhandle TR], Off US 64, Floris, 10/07/83, A, 83004159

Knowles Grain Elevator [Woodframe Grain Elevators of Oklahoma Panhandle TR], U.S. 64, Knowles, 5/13/83, A, C, 83002069

Lane Cabin, Main St. and Ave. C, Beaver City, 6/05/74, A, 74001654

Lonker Archeological Site, Address Restricted, Gate vicinity, 11/27/78, D, 78002218

Presbyterian Church, 3rd St. and Ave. E, Beaver City, 5/16/74, A, a, 74001655

Rose, Billy, Archeological Site, Address Restricted, Mocane vicinity, 9/01/78, D, 78002219

Sharps Creek Crossing Site, Address Restricted, Turpin vicinity, 4/04/75, D, 75001559

Turpin Grain Elevator [Woodframe Grain Elevators of Oklahoma Panhandle TR], Off U.S. 64, Turpin, 5/13/83, A, C, 83002071

Beckham County

Beckham County Courthouse [County Courthouses of Oklahoma TR], Courthouse Sq., Sayre, 8/23/84, A, C, 84002968

Edwards Archeological Site, Address Restricted, Carter vicinity, 9/19/73, D, 73001554

First National Bank, 101 S. Main St., Erick, 12/11/79, A, 79001987

Hedlund Motor Company Building, 206 S. Main, Elk City, 9/22/83, A, C, 83002072

Storm House, 721 W. Broadway, Elk City, 10/06/83, C, 83004162

Whited Grist Mill, 306 E. 7th St., Elk City, 1/01/76, A, e, g, 76001554

Blaine County

Blaine County Courthouse [County Courthouses of Oklahoma TR], N. Weigle St., Watonga, 8/23/84, A, C, 84002972

Cantonment, N of Canton, Canton vicinity, 4/28/70, A, a, 70000527

Chisholm, Jesse, Grave Site, NE of Geary near N. Canadian River, Geary vicinity, 12/16/71, B, c, 71000658

Cronkhite Ranch House, N of Watonga off OK 51A, Watonga vicinity, 9/22/83, A, C, 83002073

Ferguson, Thompson Benton, House, 521 N. Weigel St., Watonga, 5/17/73, B, e, 73001555

Gillespie Building, 102 E. Main St., Geary, 11/13/89, A, 89001963

Okeene Flour Mill, Off OK 51, Okeene, 11/07/76, A, 76001555

Old Plant Office Building, U.S. Gypsum Co., OK 51A, Southard, 5/13/83, A, 83002074

Old Salt Works, SE of Southard, Southard vicinity, 7/28/83, A, 83002075

Public Water Trough, Jct. Main, Canadian, and Northeast Blvd., Geary, 11/15/89, A, 89001965

Shinn Family Barn, SE of Okeene, Okeene vicinity, 3/10/83, A, C, 83002076

Wagner, J. H., House, 521 N. Prouty Ave., Watonga, 3/10/83, A, C, 83002077

Bryan County

Armstrong Academy Site, 3 mi. NE of Bokchito, Bokchito vicinity, 4/13/72, A, 72001056

Bloomfield Academy Site, S of Achille off OK 78, Achille vicinity, 11/15/72, A, 72001055

Bryan County Courthouse [County Courthouses of Oklahoma TR], 4th Ave. and Evergreen St., Durant, 8/23/84, A, C, 84002974

Caddo Community Building [WPA Public Bldgs., Recreational Facilities and Cemetery Improvements in Southeastern Oklahoma, 1935–1943

Bryan County—Continued

TR], E. Buffalo St., Caddo, 9/08/88, A, C, 88001376

Carriage Point, 4 mi. W of Durant, Durant vicinity, 6/29/72, A, 72001058

Colbert's Ferry Site, 3 mi. SE of Colbert, Colbert vicinity, 6/29/72, A, 72001057

Fort McCulloch, 2 mi. SW of Kenefic, Kenefic vicinity, 6/21/71, A, 71000659

Fort Washita, SW of Nida on OK 199, Nida vicinity, 10/15/66, A, NHL, 66000626

Lee, Robert E., School [WPA Public Bldgs., Recreational Facilities and Cemetery Improvements in Southeastern Oklahoma, 1935–1943 TR], Ninth and Louisiana Sts., Durant, 9/08/88, A, C, 88001374

Nail's Station, 2 mi. SW of Kenefick, Keneflick vicinity, 6/29/72, A, 72001059

Oklahoma Presbyterian College, 601 N. 16th St., Durant, 12/12/76, A, 76001556

Roberta School Campus [WPA Public Bldgs., Recreational Facilities and Cemetery Improvements in Southeastern Oklahoma, 1935–1943 TR], Off OK E70, Durant vicinity, 9/08/88, A, C, 88001377

Williams, Robert Lee, Public Library [WPA Public Bldgs., Recreational Facilities and Cemetery Improvements in Southeastern Oklahoma, 1935–1943 TR], Fourth and Beech Sts., Durant, 9/08/88, A, C, 88001375

Wilson, J. L., Building, 202 W. Evergreen St., Durant, 4/20/82, A, C, 82003668

Caddo County

Amphlett Brothers Drug and Jewelry Store, Evans and Coblake Aves., Apache, 5/11/82, A, 82003669

Anadarko Downtown Historic District, Roughly bounded by the Chicago, Rock Island, and Pacific Railroad, E. 2nd and W. 3rd Sts., Anadarko, 12/10/90, A, C, 82005385

Apache State Bank, Evans and Coblake, Apache, 7/17/72, A, 72001060

Fort Cobb Site, 1 mi. E of Fort Cobb, Fort Cobb vicinity, 3/01/73, A, 73001556

Rock Mary, 4 mi. W of Hinton, Hinton vicinity, 6/22/70, A, 70000528

Canadian County

Canadian County Jail, 300 S. Evans, El Reno, 11/14/85, A, 85002790

Carnegie Library, 215 E. Wade St., El Reno, 8/29/80, A, 80003257

Czech Hall, S of Yukon, Yukon vicinity, 11/25/80, A, 80003258

Darlington Agency Site, About 6 mi. NW of El Reno, El Reno vicinity, 8/14/73, A, 73001557

El Reno Hotel, 300 S. Choctaw St., El Reno, 3/21/79, A, 79001988

Fort Reno, 3 mi. W and 2 mi. N of El Reno, El Reno vicinity, 6/22/70, A, 70000529

Goff, William I. and Magdalen M., House, 506 S. Evans, El Reno, 9/08/88, C, 88001317

Mennoville Mennonite Church, N of El Reno on U.S. 81, El Reno vicinity, 10/04/79, A, a, 79001989

Mulvey Mercantile, 425 W. Main, Yukon, 9/20/82, A, 82003670

Red Cross Canteen, Rock Island Depot, El Reno, 9/05/75, A, b, 75001560

Richardson Building, NE of Main and Division, Union City, 10/06/83, A, 83004164

Rock Island Depot, 400 W. Wade St., El Reno, 3/07/83, A, 83002078

Southern Hotel, 319 S. Grand St., El Reno, 8/02/78, A, 78002220

West Point Christian Church, SW of Yukon, Yukon vicinity, 9/02/83, C, a, 83002079

Yukon Public Library, 512 Elm St., Yukon, 2/02/84, A, 84002977

Carter County

Ardmore Historic Commercial District, Main St. and Hinkle Ave., Ardmore, 3/14/83, A, C, 83002080

Black Theater of Ardmore, 536 E. Main St., Ardmore, 6/22/84, A, 84002978

Brady Cabin, 38 mi. NW of Ardmore, Ardmore vicinity, 12/05/77, C, 77001090

Carter County Courthouse [County Courthouses of Oklahoma TR], 1st and B Sts., SW, Ardmore, 3/22/85, A, 85000678

Douglass High School Auditorium, 800 M St., NE, Ardmore, 7/11/84, A, 84002981

Dunbar School, 13 6th St., SE, Ardmore, 6/22/84, A, 84002985

Galt—Franklin Home [Historic Homes of Ardmore Petroleum Executives TR], 400 Country Club Rd., Ardmore, 5/22/86, B, C, 86001132

Healdton Oil Field Bunk House, N of Wilson, Wilson vicinity, 9/26/85, A, C, 85002518

Johnson Home [Historic Homes of Ardmore Petroleum Executives TR], 400 Country Club Rd., Ardmore, 5/22/86, B, C, 86001133

Oklahoma, New Mexico and Pacific Railroad Depot, N. Washington and NE. 3rd, Ardmore, 7/22/82, B, 82003671

Sayre-Mann House, 323 F, SW, Ardmore, 5/11/82, B, C, b, 82003672

Zaneis School Teacher's Dormitory, Off US 70, Healdton vicinity, 8/15/85, A, C, 85001800

Cherokee County

Cherokee Female Seminary, Northeastern State College campus, Tahlequah, 4/05/73, A, 73001558

Cherokee National Capitol, Restricted Address, Tahlequah, 10/15/66, A, NHL, 66000627

Cherokee National Jail, Choctaw St. and Water Ave., Tahlequah, 6/28/74, A, 74001656

Cherokee Supreme Court Building, Keetoowah St. and Water Ave., Tahlequah, 6/28/74, A, 74001657

First Cherokee Female Seminary Site, SE of Tahlequah, Tahlequah vicinity, 4/30/74, A, 74001658

French-Parks House, 209 W. Keetoowah St., Tahlequah, 3/18/85, C, 85000618

Indian University of Tahlequah, 320 Academy, Tahlequah, 7/06/76, A, a, 76001557

Loeser, Dr. Irwin D., Log Cabin, 121 E. Smith St., Tahlequah, 11/17/78, B, 78002221

Murrell Home, 4 mi. S of Tahlequah, Park Hill, 6/22/70, A, C, NHL, 70000530

Thompson, Joseph M., House, 300 S. College Ave., Tahlequah, 3/11/93, A, C, 93000155

Choctaw County

Chief's House, 1.5 mi. NE of Swink, Swink vicinity, 6/21/71, A, 71000660

Doaksville Site, Address Restricted, Fort Towson vicinity, 5/29/75, A, D, 75001561

Everidge Cabin and Cemetery, Off RR, Hugo vicinity, 3/31/82, A, C, d, 82003674

Fort Towson, 1 mi. NE of Fort Towson, Fort Towson vicinity, 9/29/70, A, 70000531

Hugo Armory [WPA Public Bldgs., Recreational Facilities and Cemetery Improvements in Southeastern Oklahoma, 1935–1943 TR], Jefferson and Third Sts., Hugo, 9/08/88, A, C, 88001378

Hugo Frisco Railroad Depot, N. A and Jackson Sts., Hugo, 6/06/80, A, 80003259

Hugo Historic District, U.S. 70 and U.S. 271, Hugo, 11/12/80, A, 80003260

Hugo Public Library [WPA Public Bldgs., Recreational Facilities and Cemetery Improvements in Southeastern Oklahoma, 1935–1943 TR], E. Jefferson St., Hugo, 9/08/88, A, C, 88001379

Speer School [WPA Public Bldgs., Recreational Facilities and Cemetery Improvements in Southeastern Oklahoma, 1935–1943 TR], Off US 271 E on a county road, Hugo vicinity, 9/08/88, A, C, 88001380

Spencer Academy, 10 mi. N of Fort Towson, Fort Towson vicinity, 5/21/75, A, a, 75001562

Spencerville School Campus [WPA Public Bldgs., Recreational Facilities and Cemetery Improvements in Southeastern Oklahoma, 1935–1943 TR], S of Spencerville, Spencerville vicinity, 9/08/88, A, C, 88001381

Wilson, Willie W., House, Cincinatti and Main Sts., Fort Towson, 4/20/82, B, C, 82003673

Cimarron County

Bat Cave Archeological Site, Address Restricted, Kenton vicinity, 9/01/78, D, 78002223

Camp Nichols, 3 mi. NE of Wheeless on Ranch Rd., Wheeless vicinity, 10/15/66, A, NHL, 66000628

Cimarron County—Continued

Cedar Breaks Archeological District, Address Restricted, Felt vicinity, 10/10/78, D, 78002222

Cimarron County Courthouse [County Courthouses of Oklahoma TR], Cimarron Ave., Boise City, 8/23/84, A, C, 84002988

Red Ghost Cave Archeological District, Address Restricted, Kenton vicinity, 11/15/78, D, 78002224

Three Entrance Cave Archeological District, Address Restricted, Kenton vicinity, 11/29/78, D, 78002225

Cleveland County

Beta Theta Pi Fraternity House, The University of Oklahoma, 800 S. Chautauqua Ave., Norman, 6/02/82, C, 82003675

Casa Blanca, 103 W. Boyd, Norman, 2/21/90, C, 90000123

DeBarr Historic District, Roughly bounded by Boyd St., DeBarr Ave., Duffy St. and the A T & S F RR tracks, Norman, 12/27/91, A, C, 91001904

Gimeno, Patricio, House, 800 Elm St., Norman, 12/30/91, C, a, 91001902

Jacobson, Oscar B., House, 609 S. Chatauqua Ave., Norman, 12/23/86, B, C, 86003466

Mardock Mission, SE of Stella off OK 9, Stella vicinity, 3/14/83, A, 83002081

Moore Public School Building, NW First and Broadway, Moore, 11/08/84, A, 84000379

Moore-Lindsay House, 508 N. Peters, Norman, 11/14/85, C, 85002788

Norman Historic District, 105 W. Main and 100–232 E. Main St., Norman, 10/10/78, A, C, 78002226

President's House, University of Oklahoma, 401 W. Boyd St., Norman, 7/06/76, A, 76001558

Santa Fe Depot, Jct.of Abner Norman Dr. and Comanche St., Norman, 1/25/91, A, C, 90002203

Sooner Theater Building, 101 E. Main St., Norman, 8/31/78, A, C, g, 78002227

Coal County

Coalgate School Gymnasium—Auditorium [WPA Public Bldgs., Recreational Facilities and Cemetery Improvements in Southeastern Oklahoma, 1935–1943 TR], Fox and Frey Sts., Coalgate, 9/08/88, A, C, 88001382

Smallwood, Benjamin Franklin, House, W of Lehigh, Lehigh vicinity, 3/10/82, B, 82003676

Comanche County

Arrastra Site, Wichita Mountains Wildlife Refuge, Cache vicinity, 5/11/81, D, 81000455

Beal, Mattie, House, 5th St. and Summit Ave., Lawton, 8/19/75, A, C, 75001564

Blockhouse on Signal Mountain, Off Mackenzie Hill Rd., Fort Sill, 11/29/78, A, e, 78002228

Boulder Cabin, NW of Cache, Cache vicinity, 5/11/81, A, C, 81000456

Buffalo Lodge, NW of Cache, Cache vicinity, 5/11/81, A, C, 81000457

Building 309, Fort Sill Indian School, E edge of Lawton, off U.S. 62, Lawton vicinity, 10/15/73, A, C, 73001559

Camp Comanche Site, Address Restricted, Fort Sill vicinity, 5/12/77, A, 77001091

Carnegie Library, B Ave. and 5th St., Lawton, 8/19/76, A, 76001560

Chiefs Knoll, Macomb and Burrill Rds., Fort Sill, 5/16/78, A, d, 78002229

Ferguson House, NW of Cache, Cache vicinity, 5/11/81, A, C, 81000458

First Christian Church, 701 D Ave., Lawton, 3/12/85, C, a, 85000566

First Presbyterian Church of Lawton, 8th St. and D Ave., Lawton, 12/14/79, A, C, a, 79001990

First State Bank of Indiahoma, Main St., Indiahoma, 11/06/80, A, 80003261

Fort Sill, US 62, Fort Sill, 10/15/66, A, NHL, 66000629

General Officers Quarters, 1310 Shanklin Circle, Fort Sill, 4/14/75, A, C, 75001563

Gore Pit District, Address Restricted, Lawton vicinity, 11/21/80, D, 80004520

Indian Cemeteries, Fort Sill Military Reservation, Fort Sill, 8/10/77, A, d, 77001510

Ingram House, NE of Cache, Cache vicinity, 5/11/81, A, C, 81000459

Mahoney-Clark House, 513-515 W. Gore Ave., Lawton, 12/08/82, A, 82001494

Medicine Bluffs, Medicine Bluff Creek, Fort Sill, 12/31/74, A, 74001659

Medicine Park Hotel and Annex, E. Lake Dr., Medicine Park, 9/25/79, A, 79001991

Meers Mining Camp, 20 mi. (32 km) NW of Lawton, Lawton, 1/20/78, A, 78002230

Methodist Episcopal Church, South, 702 D Ave., Lawton, 3/12/85, C, a, 85000567

Old Tower Two, NW of Lawton at jct. of Signal Mountain and Tower Two Rds., Lawton vicinity, 12/31/74, A, 74001660

Parker, Quanah, Star House, Eagle Park, Cache vicinity, 9/29/70, B, C, b, 70000532

Penateka, 3.5 mi. W of Elgin on U.S. 277, Elgin vicinity, 11/07/76, A, 76001559

Post, Henry, Air Field, N of Lawton on Fort Sill, Lawton vicinity, 1/30/78, A, 78002231

Cotton County

Cotton County Courthouse [County Courthouses of Oklahoma TR], 301 N. Broadway, Walters, 8/23/84, A, C, 84002990

First United Methodist Church, 202 E. Oklahoma, Walters, 9/15/83, C, a, 83002082

Craig County

Craig County Courthouse [County Courthouses of Oklahoma TR], 214 W. Canadian Ave., Vinita, 8/23/84, A, C, 84002994

Creek County

Bristow Presbyterian Church, 6th and Elm Sts., Bristow, 10/03/79, C, a, 79001992

Creek County Courthouse [County Courthouses of Oklahoma TR], 222 E. Dewey Ave., Sapulpa, 3/22/85, A, 85000679

Drumright Gasoline Plant No. 2, N of Drumright, Drumright vicinity, 7/27/82, A, 82003677

Drumright, Aaron, House, 403 S. Creek Ave., Drumright, 8/17/82, B, 82003678

First United Methodist Church of Drumright, 115 N. Pennsylvania Ave., Drumright, 3/31/82, A, C, a, 82003679

Fulkerson, J. W., House, 508 E Broadway, Drumright, 3/23/82, B, 82003680

Jackson, Barnett, No. 11 Oil Well, S of Drumright, Drumright vicinity, 7/27/82, A, 82003681

Markham School and Teacherage, SW of Oilton, Oilton vicinity, 4/21/82, A, 82003683

McClung House, 708 S. Main St., Sapulpa, 6/27/80, B, C, 80003262

Meacham Building, 102 E. Main St., Oilton, 4/21/82, A, 82003682

Santa Fe Depot, Broadway and Harley Sts., Drumright, 4/02/81, A, 81000460

Tidal School, S of Drumright off OK 16, Drumright vicinity, 4/02/81, A, 81000461

Washington School, 214 W. Federal St., Drumright, 1/28/81, A, 81000462

Wheeler No. 1 Oil Well, Off OK 99, Drumright vicinity, 3/14/83, A, a, 83002083

Custer County

Broadway Hotel [Custer City Commercial Buildings TR], Off OK 33, Custer, 3/06/85, A, 85000489

Crawford House, 600 N. 13th St., Clinton, 3/08/84, A, C, a, 84002998

First National Bank of Custer City [Custer City Commercial Buildings TR], Off OK 33, Custer, 10/31/85, A, 85003426

Hodge Site, Address Restricted, Hammon vicinity, 12/15/78, D, 78002232

Little Deer Site, Address Restricted, Weatherford vicinity, 11/27/78, D, 78002233

Owl Blacksmith Shop, 208 W. Rainey, Weatherford, 7/27/83, A, 83002084

Pyeatt's, J. J., General Store [Custer City Commercial Buildings TR], Off OK 33, Custer, 3/06/85, A, 85000488

Science Building, State St., Weatherford, 2/23/84, A, 84003004

Delaware County

Bassett Grove Ceremonial Grounds, Address Restricted, Grove vicinity, 7/20/83, A, a, d, g, 83002085

Corey House/Hotel, N. Main at 2nd St., Grove, 12/17/82, A, 82001495

Hildebrand Mill, 10 mi. W of Siloam Springs, Siloam Springs vicinity, 10/18/72, A, 72001062

Polson Cemetery, NE of Jay, Jay vicinity, 11/21/77, A, B, d, 77001092

Saline Courthouse, 1 mi. SE of Rose off OK 33, Rose vicinity, 1/01/76, A, 76001561

Splitlog Church, About 9 mi. NE of Grove, Grove vicinity, 10/26/72, B, a, 72001061

Dewey County

Dewey County Courthouse [County Courthouses of Oklahoma TR], Broadway and Ruble St., Taloga, 3/22/85, A, 85000680

Seiling Milling Company, 4th and Orange St., Seiling, 12/08/83, A, 83004167

Ellis County

Bank of Gage [Banking Facilities in Ellis County TR], 18 Main St., Gage, 10/07/83, A, 83004169

Carr, George, Ranch House [Ranching Properties in Northwestern Oklahoma TR], NW of Camargo, Camargo vicinity, 4/10/85, A, 85000788

Davison Silo, 20 mi. (32 km) SE of Arnett, Arnett, 11/14/78, A, C, 78002234

Eggleston Springs, Address Restricted, Arnett vicinity, 11/27/78, D, 78002235

Ellis County Courthouse [County Courthouses of Oklahoma TR], Town Sq., Arnett, 3/22/85, A, 85000681

First State Bank [Banking Facilities in Ellis County TR], 239 S. Main St., Shattuck, 10/07/83, A, 83004170

Grand Town Site, 14 mi. S of Arnett, Arnett vicinity, 6/05/72, A, 72001063

Shattuck National Bank Building [Banking Facilities in Ellis County TR], 100 S. Main St., Shattuck, 10/07/83, A, 83004171

Stock Exchange Bank [Banking Facilities in Ellis County TR], Main St., Fargo, 10/07/83, A, 83004173

Garfield County

Bank of Hunter, Cherokee and Main Sts., Hunter, 6/22/84, A, C, 84003014

Broadway Tower, 114 E. Broadway St., Enid, 11/14/85, A, C, 85002789

Champlin, H. H., House, 612 S. Tyler, Enid, 1/21/93, C, 92001833

Eason, T. T., Mansion, 1305 W. Broadway, Enid, 3/24/87, B, C, 87000417

Enid Armory [WPA Public Bldgs., Recreational Facilities and Water Quality Improvements in Northwestern Oklahoma, 1935–1943 TR], Sixth and Elm Sts., Enid, 9/08/88, A, C, 88001370

Garfield County Courthouse [County Courthouses of Oklahoma TR], W. Broadway, Enid, 8/23/84, A, C, 84003018

Hoy, R. E., No. 1 Oil Well, Off US 64, Covington vicinity, 9/26/86, A, 86002357

Jackson School, 415 E. Illinois, Enid, 7/19/89, C, 89000848

Kaufman, H. L., House, 1708 W. Maine, Enid, 12/12/85, C, 85003339

Kimmell Barn, NE of Covington, Covington vicinity, 1/30/84, C, 84003021

McCristy—Knox Mansion, 1323 W. Broadway, Enid, 3/24/87, C, 87000418

Rock Island Depot, 200 Owen K. Garriott Blvd., Enid, 7/18/79, A, 79003639

Garvin County

Erin Springs Mansion, S of Washita River, Erin Springs, 6/22/70, B, 70000534

Eskridge Hotel, 114 E. Robert S. Kerr St., Wynnewood, 10/03/79, A, C, 79001994

Fort Arbuckle Site, About 0.5 mi. N of Hoover on SR, Hoover, 6/13/72, A, 72001064

Garvin County Courthouse [County Courthouses of Oklahoma TR], Courthouse Sq. and Grant Ave., Pauls Valley, 11/08/85, A, 85002758

Hargis-Mitchell-Cochran House, 204 E. Robert S. Kerr, Wynnewood, 6/02/82, A, C, 82003684

Initial Point, About 7.5 mi. W of Davis on Garvin, Davis vicinity, 10/06/70, A, 70000533

Moore-Settle House, 508 E. Cherokee St., Wynnewood, 3/25/83, C, 83002086

Pauls Valley Historic District, Roughly bounded by RR tracks, Grant Ave., Joy and, Pauls Valley, 2/01/79, A, C, 79001993

Santa Fe Depot of Lindsay [Territorial Era Santa Fe Depots in South Central Oklahoma TR], 120 N. Main, Lindsay, 4/25/86, A, C, 86000863

Grady County

Jewett Site, Address Restricted, Bradley vicinity, 2/14/79, D, 79001995

Rock Island Depot, Chickasha Ave., Chickasha, 3/29/85, A, C, 85000699

Grant County

Dayton School [WPA Public Bldgs., Recreational Facilities and Water Quality Improvements in Northwestern Oklahoma, 1935–1943 TR], SE of Lamont, Lamont vicinity, 9/08/88, A, C, 88001369

Deer Creek General Merchandise Store, S. Main St., Deer Creek, 3/08/84, A, 84003024

Grant County Courthouse [County Courthouses of Oklahoma TR], W. Guthrie St., Medford, 8/23/84, A, C, 84003027

Medford Bathhouse and Swimming Pool [WPA Public Bldgs., Recreational Facilities and Water Quality Improvements in Northwestern Oklahoma, 1935–1943 TR], Guthrie and Fifth Sts., Medford, 9/08/88, A, 88001368

Greer County

Greer County Courthouse [County Courthouses of Oklahoma TR], Courthouse Sq., Mangum, 3/22/85, A, 85000682

Harmon County

Harmon County Courthouse [County Courthouses of Oklahoma TR], W. Hollis St., Hollis, 8/23/84, A, C, 84003031

Harper County

Beagley-Stinson Archeological Site, Address Restricted, Laverne vicinity, 11/16/78, D, 78003394

Buffalo City Park Pavilion [WPA Public Bldgs., Recreational Facilities and Water Quality Improvements in Northwestern Oklahoma, 1935–1943 TR], US 64, Buffalo, 9/08/88, A, C, 88001367

Clover Hotel [Laverne's Early Commercial Development MRA], Main St. and Oklahoma Ave., Laverne, 3/08/84, A, C, 84003034

Farmers' Co-op Elevator [Clay Tile Grain Elevators in Northwestern Oklahoma TR], Off US 64, Buffalo, 10/07/83, A, C, 83004176

Feuquay Elevator [Clay Tile Grain Elevators in Northwestern Oklahoma TR], Off US 64, Buffalo, 10/07/83, A, C, 83004177

Fox Hotel, Broadway and NE 1st St., Laverne, 1/30/78, A, 78002236

Harper County Courthouse [County Courthouses of Oklahoma TR], Elm, Maple, 1st, and 2nd Sts. SE, Buffalo, 8/23/84, A, C, 84003041

I.O.O.F. Building of Buffalo, 110 W. Turner St., Buffalo, 7/14/83, A, C, 83002087

Laverne's North Main Street District [Laverne's Early Commercial Development MRA], Main St. and Broadway, Laverne, 3/08/84, A, C, 84003044

M.K. and T. Depot in Laverne [Laverne's Early Commercial Development MRA], Main St., Laverne, 3/08/84, A, C, 84003046

Monhollow Artificial Stone House, Off US 183, Buffalo, 7/14/83, C, 83002088

Old Settler's Irrigation Ditch, Intersects US 283 N of Rosston, Rosston vicinity, 7/27/83, A, 83002070

Page Soddy, SE of Buffalo, Buffalo vicinity, 3/24/83, A, C, 83002089

Harper County—Continued

Sharp Lumberyard [Laverne's Early Commercial Development MRA], 124 N. Broadway, Laverne, 3/08/84, A, C, 84003048

Haskell County

Cotton Storage House, Off OK 2, Kinta, 1/10/80, A, 80003263

Haskell County Courthouse [County Courthouses of Oklahoma TR], 202 E. Main St., Stigler, 8/23/84, A, C, 84003061

Kinta High School [WPA Public Bldgs., Recreational Facilities and Cemetery Improvements in Southeastern Oklahoma, 1935–1943 TR], OK 2, Kinta, 9/26/88, A, C, 88001383

McCurtain, Edmund, House, NE of Kinta, Kinta vicinity, 6/27/80, B, 80003265

McCurtain, Green, House, NE of Kinta, Kinta vicinity, 6/21/71, B, 71000661

Mule Creek Site, Address Restricted, Stigler vicinity, 9/13/78, D, 78002237

Otter Creek Archeological Site, Address Restricted, Keota vicinity, 12/31/74, D, 74001661

Scott Store, OK 2, Kinta, 1/11/80, B, 80003264

Stigler School Gymnasium—Auditorium [WPA Public Bldgs., Recreational Facilities and Cemetery Improvements in Southeastern Oklahoma, 1935–1943 TR], Fourth and E Sts., Stigler, 9/08/88, A, C, 88001384

Tamaha Jail and Ferry Landing, NE of Stigler, Stigler vicinity, 11/14/80, A, 80003266

Hughes County

Dustin Agricultural Building [WPA Public Bldgs., Recreational Facilities and Cemetery Improvements in Southeastern Oklahoma, 1935–1943 TR], Rutherford and Fourth Sts., Dustin, 9/08/88, A, C, 88001385

Holdenville Armory [WPA Public Bldgs., Recreational Facilities and Cemetery Improvements in Southeastern Oklahoma, 1935–1943 TR], US 270 and N. Butts St., Holdenville, 9/08/88, A, C, 88001386

Holdenville City Hall, 102 Creek St., Holdenville, 9/11/81, A, 81000463

Levering Mission, NE of Wetumka, Wetumka vicinity, 5/16/74, A, a, 74001662

Moss School Gymnasium [WPA Public Bldgs., Recreational Facilities and Cemetery Improvements in Southeastern Oklahoma, 1935–1943 TR], Off the intersection of US 270 and US 75, Holdenville vicinity, 9/08/88, A, C, 88001388

Spaulding School Gymnasium—Auditorium [WPA Public Bldgs., Recreational Facilities and Cemetery Improvements in Southeastern Oklahoma, 1935–1943 TR], Section Line Hwy. and Second St., Spaulding, 9/08/88, A, C, 88001389

Stuart Hotel, Off US 270, Stuart, 10/07/82, A, 82001496

Turner, John E., House, 401 E. 10th St., Holdenville, 1/27/83, B, C, 83002090

Wetumka Armory [WPA Public Bldgs., Recreational Facilities and Cemetery Improvements in Southeastern Oklahoma, 1935–1943 TR], St. Louis and Wetumka Sts., Wetumka, 9/08/88, A, C, 88001390

Wetumka Cemetery Pavilion and Fence [WPA Public Bldgs., Recreational Facilities and Cemetery Improvements in Southeastern Oklahoma, 1935–1943 TR], E of Wetumka, Wetumka vicinity, 9/08/88, A, C, d, 88001391

Jackson County

Fullerton Dam, 7 mi. NW of Olustee, Olustee vicinity, 11/07/76, A, C, 76001562

Jackson County Courthouse [County Courthouses of Oklahoma TR], Main St. and Broadway, Altus, 8/23/84, A, C, 84003064

Jefferson County

Jefferson County Courthouse [County Courthouses of Oklahoma TR], N. Main St., Waurika, 8/23/84, A, C, 84003065

San Bernardo, Address Restricted, Ringling vicinity, 3/10/82, D, 82003685

Johnston County

Chickasaw National Capitols, Capitol Ave. between 8th and 9th Sts., Tishomingo, 11/05/71, A, C, 71000663

Murray, Gov. William H., House, Off OK 78, Tishomingo, 8/02/84, B, 84003066

Poe, Bessie, Hall, Murray State College campus, Tishomingo, 9/11/81, A, 81000464

Tishomingo City Hall, W. Main St., Tishomingo, 5/21/75, A, 75001565

Wapanucka Academy Site, Address Restricted, Bromide vicinity, 6/13/72, D, a, 72001065

White House of the Chickasaws, NW of Emet, Emet vicinity, 8/05/71, A, B, C, 71000662

Kay County

Big V Ranch House [Ranching Properties in Northwestern Oklahoma TR], Off OK 156, Ponca City vicinity, 8/23/84, A, 84003068

Blackwell Armory [WPA Public Bldgs., Recreational Facilities and Water Quality Improvements in Northwestern Oklahoma, 1935–1943 TR], Sixth and Doolin Sts., Blackwell, 9/08/88, A, C, 88001366

Blaine Stadium and Fieldhouse [WPA Public Bldgs., Recreational Facilities and Water Quality Improvements in Northwestern Oklahoma,

1935–1943 TR], Fifth and Brookfield Sts., Ponca City, 9/08/88, A, C, 88001364

Bryson Archeological Site, Address Restricted, Newkirk vicinity, 9/20/79, D, 79001997

Deer Creek Site, Address Restricted, Newkirk vicinity, 10/15/66, D, NHL, 66000630

Donahoe, Daniel J., House, 302 S. 7th St., Ponca City, 3/10/82, B, C, 82003686

Electric Park Pavilion, 300 S. Main, Blackwell, 9/29/76, A, C, 76001563

Jenkins, Gov. William W., Homestead Site, Address Restricted, Newkirk vicinity, 10/14/76, D, 76001564

Kaw City Depot, W of Kaw City on Washungah Dr., Kaw City vicinity, 10/03/79, A, C, b, 79001996

Kaw Indian Agency, N of the Arkansas River, Washunga, 4/11/73, A, 73001562

Kay County Courthouse [County Courthouses of Oklahoma TR], Courthouse Sq., Newkirk, 8/23/84, A, C, 84003070

Mahoney House and Garage, 302 N. Main Ave., Tonkawa, 7/03/84, C, 84003074

Marland, E. W., Mansion, Monument Rd., Ponca City, 4/11/73, B, NHL, 73001561

Marland-Paris House, 1000 E. Grand, Ponca City, 9/28/76, B, C, 76001565

Newkirk Central Business District, Main and 7th Sts., Newkirk, 2/23/84, A, C, 84003079

Newkirk Water Purification Plant [WPA Public Bldgs., Recreational Facilities and Water Quality Improvements in Northwestern Oklahoma, 1935–1943 TR], Tenth and Elm Sts., Newkirk, 9/08/88, A, C, 88001365

Nez Perce Reservation, Address Restricted, Tonkawa vicinity, 2/15/74, D, 74001663

One-hundred-and-one Ranch, 12 mi. SW of Ponca City on OK 156, Ponca City vicinity, 4/11/73, A, B, NHL, 73001560

Pioneer Woman Statue, Monument Cir., Ponca City, 8/31/78, A, C, f, g, 78002238

Poncan Theatre, 104 E. Grand Ave., Ponca City, 11/13/84, C, 84000455

Soldani Mansion, 819 E. Central St., Ponca City, 6/24/82, B, C, 82003687

Tonkawa Armory [WPA Public Bldgs., Recreational Facilities and Water Quality Improvements in Northwestern Oklahoma, 1935–1943 TR], Third and North Sts., Tonkawa, 9/08/88, A, C, 88001363

Kingfisher County

Farmers and Merchants National Bank, 197 S. Main St., Hennessey, 2/23/84, A, 84003085

Kingfisher College Site, 1 mi. E of Kingfisher, Kingfisher vicinity, 10/22/76, A, a, 76001566

Kingfisher Post Office, Main and Robberts Sts., Kingfisher, 1/20/78, A, 78002239

Seay Mansion, 11th St. and Zellers Ave., Kingfisher, 3/24/71, B, C, 71000664

Kiowa County

Camp Radziminski, Address Restricted, Mountain Park vicinity, 4/13/72, D, 72001067

Devil's Canyon, Address Restricted, Lugert vicinity, 6/20/72, D, 72001066

Hobart City Hall, Main and 3rd Sts., Hobart, 5/22/78, A, 78002240

Hobart Public Library, 200 S. Main St., Hobart, 10/31/80, A, 80003267

Kiowa County Courthouse [County Courthouses of Oklahoma TR], Courthouse Sq., Hobart, 8/23/84, A, C, 84003094

Latimer County

Ash Creek School [WPA Public Bldgs., Recreational Facilities and Cemetery Improvements in Southeastern Oklahoma, 1935–1943 TR], Off Ash Creek Rd., Wilburton vicinity, 9/08/88, A, C, 88001392

Bowers School [WPA Public Bldgs., Recreational Facilities and Cemetery Improvements in Southeastern Oklahoma, 1935–1943 TR], Off US 270 on county road, Wilburton vicinity, 9/08/88, A, C, 88001393

Cambria School [WPA Public Bldgs., Recreational Facilities and Cemetery Improvements in Southeastern Oklahoma, 1935–1943 TR], NE of Hartshorne, Hartshorne vicinity, 9/08/88, A, C, a, 88001394

Colony Park Pavilion [WPA Public Bldgs., Recreational Facilities and Cemetery Improvements in Southeastern Oklahoma, 1935–1943 TR], Veterans Colony, Wilburton vicinity, 9/08/88, A, C, 88001395

Cupco Church, S of Yanush off OK 2, Yanush vicinity, 11/06/80, A, a, 80003273

Degnan School [WPA Public Bldgs., Recreational Facilities and Cemetery Improvements in Southeastern Oklahoma, 1935–1943 TR], NW of Wilburton off OK 2, Wilburton vicinity, 9/08/88, A, C, a, 88001396

Edwards Store, 8 mi. NE of Red Oak, Red Oak vicinity, 4/13/72, A, 72001069

Great Western Coal and Coke Company Building [Latimer County Coal Mining TR], 701 E. Main St., Wilburton, 11/06/80, A, 80003268

Great Western Coal and Coke Company Mine No. 3 [Latimer County Coal Mining TR], Off U.S. 270, Wilburton, 11/06/80, A, 80003269

Holloway's Station, About 5 mi. NE of Red Oak, Red Oak vicinity, 4/13/72, A, 72001070

Lake Wister Locality, Address Restricted, Wister vicinity, 8/19/75, D, 75001566

McLaughlin Site, Address Restricted, Red Oak vicinity, 6/28/72, D, 72001071

Mitchell Hall [Latimer County Coal Mining TR], Eastern Oklahoma State College campus, Wilburton, 11/06/80, A, 80003270

Panola High School and Gymnasium [WPA Public Bldgs., Recreational Facilities and Cemetery Improvements in Southeastern Oklahoma, 1935–1943 TR], Off US 270, on the southside of the railroad tracks, Panola, 9/08/88, A, C, 88001397

Pusley's Station, 2 mi. SW of Higgins, Higgins vicinity, 4/13/72, A, 72001068

Riddle's Station Site, About 3 mi. E of Wilburton, Wilburton vicinity, 6/13/72, A, d, 72001072

Rosenstein Building, 111 E. Main St., Wilburton, 6/27/80, A, C, 80003271

Sacred Heart Catholic Church and Rectory [Latimer County Coal Mining TR], 102 Center Point Rd., Wilburton, 11/06/80, A, C, a, 80003272

Le Flore County

Arkoma School [WPA Public Bldgs., Recreational Facilities and Cemetery Improvements in Southeastern Oklahoma, 1935–1943 TR], Arkoma and Blocker Sts., Arkoma, 9/08/88, A, C, 88001398

Choctaw Agency, 1 mi. E of Skullyville on SR, Spiro vicinity, 5/05/72, A, 72001074

Conser, Peter, House, 3.5 mi. W of Hodgens, Hodgens vicinity, 6/21/71, A, B, 71000665

Dog Creek School [WPA Public Bldgs., Recreational Facilities and Cemetery Improvements in Southeastern Oklahoma, 1935–1943 TR], SW of Shady Point, Shady Point vicinity, 9/08/88, A, C, 88001399

Jenson Tunnel, NE of Cameron off OK 112, Cameron vicinity, 5/13/76, A, 76001567

LeFlore County Courthouse [County Courthouses of Oklahoma TR], Courthouse Sq., Poteau, 8/23/84, A, 84003099

Old Military Road, 7 mi. NE of Talihina in Ouachita National Forest, Talihina vicinity, 10/22/76, A, 76002155

Overstreet House, NE of Cowlington off U.S. 59, Cowlington vicinity, 11/25/80, B, C, 80004285

Poteau Community Building [WPA Public Bldgs., Recreational Facilities and Cemetery Improvements in Southeastern Oklahoma, 1935–1943 TR], Hill and Hopkins Sts., Poteau, 9/08/88, A, C, a, 88001403

Poteau School Gymnasium—Auditorium [WPA Public Bldgs., Recreational Facilities and Cemetery Improvements in Southeastern Oklahoma, 1935–1943 TR], Walter and Parker Sts., Poteau, 9/08/88, A, C, 88001404

Reynolds, James E., House, E of Cameron off OK 112, Cameron vicinity, 4/13/77, B, C, 77001093

Shady Point School [WPA Public Bldgs., Recreational Facilities and Cemetery Improvements in Southeastern Oklahoma, 1935–1943 TR], NE edge of the community, Shady Point, 9/08/88, A, C, 88001405

Skullyville County Jail, W of Panama, Panama vicinity, 11/06/80, A, 80004286

Spiro Mound Group, Address Restricted, Redland vicinity, 9/30/69, D, 69000153

Summerfield School [WPA Public Bldgs., Recreational Facilities and Cemetery Improvements in Southeastern Oklahoma, 1935–1943 TR], Off US 271, Summerfield, 9/08/88, A, C, 88001406

Terry House, Terry Hill, Poteau, 6/27/80, C, 80004287

Trahern's Station, 9 mi. W of Shadypoint, Shadypoint, 4/25/72, A, d, 72001073

Tucker School [WPA Public Bldgs., Recreational Facilities and Cemetery Improvements in Southeastern Oklahoma, 1935–1943 TR], Off US 59, Spiro vicinity, 9/08/88, A, C, 88001407

Twyman Park [WPA Public Bldgs., Recreational Facilities and Cemetery Improvements in Southeastern Oklahoma, 1935–1943 TR], West St., Poteau vicinity, 9/08/88, A, C, 88001402

Williams School [WPA Public Bldgs., Recreational Facilities and Cemetery Improvements in Southeastern Oklahoma, 1935–1943 TR], NW of Cameron, Cameron vicinity, 9/08/88, A, C, 88001408

Lincoln County

Bank of Agra, 400 Grant Ave., Agra, 2/21/90, A, C, 90000122

Bon Ton House, 404 N. Fourth St., Stroud, 9/26/86, C, 86002350

Boston Store [Territorial Commercial Buildings of Chandler TR], 917 Manvel Ave., Chandler, 4/05/84, A, 84003107

Carpenter, Joseph, House, 204 W. Sixth St., Stroud, 9/26/86, C, 86002346

Chandler Armory, Jct. of Mickey Clarkson Ave. and First St., Chandler, 3/14/91, A, C, 91000276

Chandler Bookstore [Territorial Commercial Buildings of Chandler TR], 713 Manvel Ave., Chandler, 4/05/84, A, C, 84003110

Clapp-Cunningham Building [Territorial Commercial Buildings of Chandler TR], 1021 Manvel Ave., Chandler, 4/05/84, A, C, 84003112

Conklin House [Territorial Homes of Chandler TR], 206 W. 8th St., Chandler, 9/28/84, A, C, 84003116

First Presbyterian Church of Chandler [Territorial Era Carpenter Gothic Churches TR], 8th and Blaine Sts., Chandler, 9/28/84, A, C, a, 84003118

Graham Hotel, Main St. and 2nd Ave., Stroud, 5/22/79, A, 79001998

Hadley House, 622 N. 4th Ave., Stroud, 11/13/84, C, 84000457

Hadley, Walter, House, 424 W. Seventh St., Stroud, 9/26/86, C, 86002308

Hughes, George, House, 308 W. Fifth St., Stroud, 9/26/86, C, 86002370

Johnson House [Territorial Homes of Chandler TR], 503 Marvel Ave., Chandler, 9/28/84, A, C, 84003121

Keokuk, Moses, House, 6 mi. S of Stroud, Stroud vicinity, 6/19/73, A, 73001563

Mascho Building and Public Privy [Territorial Commercial Buildings of Chandler TR], 717-719 Manvel Ave., Chandler, 4/05/84, A, C, 84003127

Oleson-Crane Building [Territorial Commercial Buildings of Chandler TR], 721 Manvel Ave., Chandler, 4/05/84, A, C, 84003129

Lincoln County—Continued

Southwestern Bell Telephone Building, 301 W. Seventh St., Stroud, 5/14/86, C, 86001093

St. Cloud Hotel [Territorial Commercial Buildings of Chandler TR], 1216 Manvel Ave., Chandler, 4/05/84, A, C, 84003131

Stroud Trading Company Building, Main St. and 2nd Ave., Stroud, 12/27/79, A, C, 79001999

Stroud, James W., House, 110 E. 2nd St., Stroud, 3/08/84, B, C, 84003134

Tilghman, Marshal William M., Homestead, 2 mi. NW of Chandler off U.S. 66, Chandler vicinity, 1/11/76, B, 76001568

Wolcott Building [Territorial Commercial Buildings of Chandler TR], 725 Manvel Ave., Chandler, 4/05/84, A, C, 84003136

ZCBJ Lodge No. 46, S. Barta Ave., Prague, 3/08/84, A, 84003138

Logan County

Carnegie Library, Oklahoma Ave. and Ash St., Guthrie, 6/21/71, A, 71000666

Co-Operative Publishing Company Building, Harrison Ave. and 2nd St., Guthrie, 3/07/73, A, 73001564

Guthrie Historic District, Roughly bounded by 14th St., College Ave., Pine St., and Lincoln Ave., Guthrie, 6/13/74, A, C, 74001664

Logan County Courthouse [County Courthouses of Oklahoma TR], 301 E. Harrison St., Guthrie, 10/26/84, C, 84003141

Methodist Church of Marshall [Territorial Era Carpenter Gothic Churches TR], Off OK 74, Marshall, 9/28/84, A, C, a, b, 84003143

Mulhall United Methodist Church, Bryant and Craig Sts., Mulhall, 6/22/84, A, C, a, 84003145

Oklahoma State Bank Building, Baty and Main Sts., Mulhall, 6/22/84, A, C, 84003146

Scottish Rite Temple, 900 E. Oklahoma, Guthrie, 4/09/87, A, C, 87000503

St. Joseph Convent and Academy, Off OK 33, Guthrie, 12/19/79, A, C, a, 79002000

Love County

Love County Courthouse [County Courthouses of Oklahoma TR], 100 S. 4th St., Marietta, 8/23/84, A, C, 84003148

Washington, Bill, Ranchhouse, About 4 mi. SW of Marietta, Marietta vicinity, 7/27/71, B, C, 71000667

Major County

Major County Courthouse [County Courthouses of Oklahoma TR], Courthouse Sq., Fairview, 8/23/84, A, C, 84003153

Marshall County

Haley's Point Site, Address Restricted, Lebanon, 5/24/91, D, 91000613

Marshall County Courthouse [County Courthouses of Oklahoma TR], Courthouse Sq., Madill, 8/23/84, A, C, 84003154

Worth Hotel, 203 E. Main St., Madill, 4/12/85, A, C, 85000846

Mayes County

Cabin Creek Battlefield, 3 mi. N of Pensacola, Pensacola vicinity, 7/27/71, A, 71000669

Farmers and Merchants Bank, 201 W. Main St., Chouteau, 7/14/83, A, C, 83002091

Lewis Ross/Cherokee Orphan Asylum Springhouse, Off OK 20, Salina, 8/18/83, A, B, C, 83002092

Territorial Commercial District, Main St., Chouteau, 9/22/83, A, C, 83002093

Union Mission Site, About 5 mi. NE of Mazie, Mazie vicinity, 9/10/71, A, a, 71000668

McClain County

McClain County Courthouse [County Courthouses of Oklahoma TR], Courthouse Sq., Purcell, 8/23/84, A, C, 84003347

McCurtain County

Barnes-Steverson House, 3 Adams St., SE, Idabel, 11/17/78, B, C, 78003083

Davis, Grobin, Mound Group, Address Restricted, Wright City vicinity, 11/23/84, D, 84002637

Frisco Station, Texas Ave., Idabel, 5/21/79, A, 79003137

Gardner, Jefferson, House, 3 mi. W of Eagletown off U.S. 70, Eagletown vicinity, 4/04/75, B, D, 75002068

Garvin Rock Church, Love and Williams Sts., Garvin, 6/16/80, C, a, 80003275

Harkey Site, Address Restricted, Idabel vicinity, 12/19/78, D, 78003084

Harris House, 6 mi. (9.6 km.) S of Haworth, Haworth vicinity, 9/01/78, B, 78003082

Idabel Armory [WPA Public Bldgs., Recreational Facilities and Cemetery Improvements in Southeastern Oklahoma, 1935–1943 TR], Washngton and SE Avenue F Sts., Idabel, 9/08/88, A, C, 88001409

Pine Creek Mound Group, Address Restricted, Bethel vicinity, 1/21/74, D, 74002194

Spaulding-Olive House, 601 Adams, SE, Idabel, 9/28/79, B, C, 79003138

Tiner School, E of Broken Bow, Broken Bow vicinity, 11/21/80, A, 80003274

Valliant School Gymnasium—Auditorium [WPA Public Bldgs., Recreational Facilities and Cemetery Improvements in Southeastern Okla-

homa, 1935–1943 TR], Wilbor and Lucas Sts., Valliant, 9/08/88, A, C, 88001410

Waterhole Cemetery, S of Garvin, Garvin vicinity, 12/11/79, A, B, c, d, 79002001

Wheelock Academy, E of Millerton on U.S. 70, Millerton vicinity, 10/15/66, A, a, NHL, 66000949

Wheelock Church, 2 mi. NE of Millerton, Millerton vicinity, 11/09/72, B, a, c, d, 72001464

McIntosh County

Checotah Business District, Gentry Ave. between W. 1st and W. Main Sts. and Broadway Ave. between Lafayette and Spaulding Aves., Checotah, 9/13/82, A, C, 82003688

Checotah MKT Depot, Paul Carr Dr., Checotah, 9/05/91, C, b, 91001371

Cooper, C. L., Building, 5B and Harrison, Eufaula, 3/22/85, A, B, 85000684

Eufaula Business District, Main St. between Pine and Grand Sts., Eufaula, 4/14/88, A, a, 88000400

First Soil Conservation District Dedication Site, N of Eufaula, Eufaula vicinity, 9/20/82, A, g, 82003689

Honey Springs Battlefield, N of Rentiesville, Rentiesville vicinity, 9/29/70, A, 70000848

Johnson Lake Shelters, Address Restricted, Warner vicinity, 12/15/78, D, 78003086

McIntosh County Courthouse [County Courthouses of Oklahoma TR], 110 N. 1st St., Eufaula, 3/22/85, A, 85000683

Methodist Episcopal Church, South, 419 W. Gentry St., Checotah, 11/13/84, C, a, 84000462

Rock Front, Broadway, Vernon, 6/22/84, A, 84003152

Slippery Moss Shelter, Address Restricted, Texanna vicinity, 12/15/78, D, 78003085

Murray County

Lowrance Springs Site, Address Restricted, Sulphur vicinity, 3/10/75, D, 75001567

Murray County Courthouse [County Courthouses of Oklahoma TR], Wyandotte Ave., Sulphur, 8/23/84, A, C, 84003352

Muskogee County

Administration Building—Post Hospital [Fort Gibson Post-Civil War Military Buildings TR], 803 Garrison Ave., Fort Gibson, 11/14/85, A, 85002828

Central Baptist Church [Black Protestant Churches of Muskogee TR], 515 N. 4th St., Muskogee, 9/25/84, A, a, 84003157

Cherokee National Cemetery, 1.5 mi. (2.4 km) E of Fort Gibson, Fort Gibson vicinity, 3/19/79, B, c, d, 79002002

Muskogee County—Continued

Commandant's Quarters [Fort Gibson Post-Civil War Military Buildings TR], 905 Coppinger Ave., Fort Gibson, 11/14/85, A, 85002830

Coss, V. R., House [Territorial Homes of Muskogee TR], 1315 W. Okmulgee St., Muskogee, 5/02/84, A, C, 84003159

Dragoon Commandant's Quarters, 409 Creek St., Fort Gibson, 3/13/80, A, C, 80003276

DuBois, W.E.B., School [Educational Resources of All-Black Towns in Oklahoma TR], Off US 69, Summit, 9/28/84, A, 84003161

Escoe Building, 228-230 N. 2nd St., Muskogee, 7/14/83, A, C, 83002094

First Baptist Church [Black Protestant Churches of Muskogee TR], 6th and Denison Sts., Muskogee, 9/25/84, A, a, 84003164

Fite, F. B., House and Servant's Quarters, 443 N. 16th St., Muskogee, 10/06/83, B, C, 83004198

Foreman, Grant, House, 1419 W. Okmulgee St., Muskogee, 9/19/73, B, g, 73001565

Fort Davis, 2.5 mi. NE of Muskogee, Muskogee vicinity, 11/23/71, A, 71000670

Fort Gibson, Lee and Ash Sts., Fort Gibson, 10/15/66, A, NHL, 66000631

Manhattan Building [Pre-Depression Muskogee Skyscrapers TR], 325 W. Broadway, Muskogee, 8/11/83, A, C, 83002095

Manual Training High School for Negroes, 704 Altamont St., Muskogee, 6/22/84, A, 84003168

Murphy, George A., House [Territorial Homes of Muskogee TR], 1321 W. Okmulgee St., Muskogee, 5/02/84, A, B, C, 84003170

Muskogee County Courthouse [County Courthouses of Oklahoma TR], 216 State St., Muskogee, 8/23/84, A, C, 84003173

Nancy Taylor No. 1 Oil Well Site, Haskell Lake Rd., W of US 64, Haskell vicinity, 11/15/89, A, B, 89001962

Nash-Swindler House, Maple and Jackson Sts., Fort Gibson, 7/13/79, B, C, 79003640

Officer's Quarters [Fort Gibson Post-Civil War Military Buildings TR], 907 Coppinger Ave., Fort Gibson, 11/14/85, A, 85002826

Oktaha School, Off U.S. 69, Oktaha, 8/24/78, A, 78002242

Patterson, A. W., House [Territorial Homes of Muskogee TR], 1320 W. Okmulgee St., Muskogee, 5/02/84, A, B, C, 84003322

Post Adjutant's Office [Fort Gibson Post-Civil War Military Buildings TR], 905 Garrison Ave., Fort Gibson, 11/14/85, A, 85002827

Post Blacksmith Shop [Fort Gibson Post-Civil War Military Buildings TR], 905 Garrison Ave., Fort Gibson, 11/14/85, A, 85002829

Pre-Statehood Commercial District, Main, Broadway, Okmulgee, and 2nd Sts., Muskogee, 10/06/83, A, 83004210

Railroad Exchange Building [Pre-Depression Muskogee Skyscrapers TR], 2nd and Court Sts., Muskogee, 8/11/83, A, C, 83002096

Robb, Andrew W., House, 1321 Boston, Muskogee, 5/11/82, B, C, 82003690

Seawell-Ross-Isom House, Beauregard and Elm Sts., Fort Gibson, 1/30/78, C, 78002241

Severs Hotel, 200 N. State St., Muskogee, 9/12/82, C, 82003691

Sheltered Shelter District, Address Restricted, Warner vicinity, 12/15/78, D, 78002243

Surety Building [Pre-Depression Muskogee Skyscrapers TR], 117 N. Third, Muskogee, 9/04/86, A, C, 86002156

Taft City Hall [Historic Government Buildings in Oklahoma's All-Black Towns TR], Elm and Seminole Sts., Taft, 9/28/84, A, 84003330

Trumbo, A. C., House [Territorial Homes of Muskogee TR], 1321 W. Broadway St., Muskogee, 5/02/84, A, B, C, 84003334

Union Agency, Agency Hill in Honor Heights Park, Muskogee, 10/06/70, A, 70000535

Ward Chapel AME Church [Black Protestant Churches of Muskogee TR], 319 N. 9th St., Muskogee, 9/25/84, A, a, 84003338

Welch, J. C., House [Territorial Homes of Muskogee TR], 1403 W. Okmulgee St., Muskogee, 5/02/84, A, C, 84003343

Noble County

First National Bank and Trust Company Building, 300 W. 6th St., Perry, 5/16/79, C, 79002003

Morison Baptist Church [Territorial Era Carpenter Gothic Churches TR], 202 3rd St., Morrison, 9/28/84, A, C, a, 84003357

Morrison Suspension Bridge, E of Morrison off U.S. 64, Morrison vicinity, 5/23/80, C, 80003277

Noble County Courthouse [County Courthouses of Oklahoma TR], Courthouse Sq., Perry, 8/23/84, A, C, 84003361

Perry Armory [WPA Public Bldgs., Recreational Facilities and Water Quality Improvements in Northwestern Oklahoma, 1935–1943 TR], Delaware and Fourteenth Sts., Perry, 9/08/88, A, C, 88001362

Rein School [WPA Public Bldgs., Recreational Facilities and Water Quality Improvements in Northwestern Oklahoma, 1935–1943 TR], Off US 177, Ponca City vicinity, 9/08/88, A, C, 88001361

Renfrow Building [Renfrow, T.F., Historic Properties TR], 127 W. Main St., Billings, 9/28/84, B, C, 84003365

Renfrow House [Renfrow, T.F., Historic Properties TR], Graves St. and Broadway, Billings, 9/28/84, B, C, 84003373

Wollenson-Nacewonder Building, 611 Delaware St., Perry, 5/16/79, A, C, 79002004

Nowata County

Nowata County Courthouse [County Courthouses of Oklahoma TR], 229 N. Maple St., Nowata, 8/23/84, A, C, 84003375

Okfuskee County

Boley Historic District, Roughly bounded by Seward Ave., Walnut and Cedar Sts. and the southern city limits, Boley, 5/15/75, A, a, NHL, 75001568

Guthrie, Woody, House, 301 S. 1st St., Okemah, 12/04/75, B, 75001569

Okfuskee County Courthouse [County Courthouses of Oklahoma TR], 3rd and W. Atlanta, Okemah, 8/23/84, A, C, 84003377

Weleetka Town Hall and Jail, Jct. of OK 75 and Seminole, Weleetka, 3/25/93, A, 93000156

Oklahoma County

"Ringing the Wild Horse" Site, NW of Jones, Jones vicinity, 1/25/71, B, 71001081

American Legion Hut, Jct. of Fifth and Little Sts., SW corner, Edmond, 12/02/93, A, C, 93001336

Arcadia Round Barn, U.S. 66, Arcadia, 12/23/77, B, C, 77001094

Avery Building [Red Brick Warehouses of Oklahoma City TR], 15 E. California Ave., Oklahoma City, 8/12/83, A, C, 83002097

Booher Site (OK48), Address Restricted, Luther vicinity, 2/14/79, D, 79003641

Bourne Dairy, 5801 Eastern St., Oklahoma City, 10/03/79, A, 79003642

Braniff Building, 324 N. Robinson St., Oklahoma City, 2/28/80, B, C, 80003281

Buttram, Frank and Merle, House and Grounds, 7316 Nichols Rd., Nichols Hills, 9/11/90, C, 90001367

Cain's Coffee Building, 1 12th St., NW, Oklahoma City, 2/04/82, A, 82004854

Calvary Baptist Church, 2nd and Walnut Sts., Oklahoma City, 12/19/78, A, B, C, a, g, 78002244

Capitol-Lincoln Terrace Historic District, Irregular pattern roughly bounded by 13th, 23rd, Lincoln Blvd., and Kelley Ave., Oklahoma City, 9/30/76, A, B, C, g, 76001569

Case, J. I., Plow Works Building [Red Brick Warehouses of Oklahoma City TR], 2 E. California Ave., Oklahoma City, 8/12/83, A, C, 83002098

Central High School, 700 block of N. Robinson, Oklahoma City, 11/07/76, A, C, 76001570

Citizens State Bank, 102 S. Broadway, Edmond, 3/13/80, A, C, 80003279

Colcord Building, Robinson and Sheridan, Oklahoma City, 11/07/76, C, 76001571

Cotton-Exchange Building, 218 N. Harvey St., Oklahoma City, 3/18/80, A, C, 80003282

Edgemere Park Historic District, Roughly bounded by Robinson and Walker and NW 30 and NW 36, Oklahoma City, 11/12/80, B, C, g, 80003283

Edmond Armory, 431 S. Blvd., Edmond, 3/14/91, A, C, 91000275

Elks Lodge Building, 401 N. Harvey St., Oklahoma City, 3/10/80, B, C, 80003284

Engels' Dry Goods Store, 114 S. Main St., Luther, 3/03/80, A, B, 80003280

Oklahoma County—Continued

Fairchild Winery, 1600 81st St., NE, Oklahoma City, 3/13/75, B, 75001570

Farmers Public Market, 311 S. Klein St., Oklahoma City, 12/02/82, A, C, 82001497

First Christian Church, 1104 N. Robinson Ave., Oklahoma City, 3/08/84, C, a, 84003383

Goodholm House, 3101 W. Gen. Pershing Blvd., Oklahoma City, 3/30/83, C, 83002099

Gower Cemetery, Covel Rd. between Douglas and Post Rds., Edmond, 12/27/91, A, d, 91001895

Hales, W. T., House, 1521 N. Hudson Ave., Oklahoma City, 3/29/78, B, C, a, 78002245

Harbour-Longmire Building, 420 W. Main St., Oklahoma City, 3/03/80, B, C, 80003285

Harn House, NE 17th St. and Stiles, Oklahoma City, 4/13/73, B, 73001566

Heierding Building, 35 Harrison Ave., Oklahoma City, 3/10/82, B, g, 82003692

Heritage Hills Historic and Architectural District, Roughly bounded by Robinson and Walker Aves., 14th, 15th, and 21st Sts. and Classen Blvd., Oklahoma City, 6/04/79, A, B, C, g, 79002006

India Temple Shrine Building, 621 N. Robinson Ave., Oklahoma City, 3/26/80, A, C, 80003286

Kaiser's Ice Cream Parlour, 1039 N. Walker Ave., Oklahoma City, 11/28/78, A, B, 78002246

Kingman-More Building [Red Brick Warehouses of Oklahoma City TR], 100 E. California Ave., Oklahoma City, 8/12/83, A, C, 83002100

Luster, Melvin F., House, 300 3rd St., NE, Oklahoma City, 6/07/83, B, 83002101

Magnolia Petroleum Building, 722 N. Broadway St., Oklahoma City, 10/04/79, A, C, 79002007

Maney Historic District, 725 NW. 11th St., 1200 and 1224 N. Shartel Ave., Oklahoma City, 7/18/79, B, C, b, 79002008

Mesta Park, Roughly bounded by NW 16th and 23rd Sts. and Western and Walker Aves., Oklahoma City, 7/26/83, C, 83002102

Mid-Continent Life Building, 1400 Classen Dr., Oklahoma City, 3/12/79, B, C, 79002009

Mideke Supply Building [Red Brick Warehouses of Oklahoma City TR], 100 E. Main St., Oklahoma City, 8/12/83, A, C, 83002103

Miller-Jackson Building [Red Brick Warehouses of Oklahoma City TR], 121 E. California Ave., Oklahoma City, 8/12/83, A, C, 83002104

Montgomery Ward Building, 500 W. Main St., Oklahoma City, 3/13/80, A, C, 80003287

Nagle Site, Address Restricted, Spencer vicinity, 2/14/79, D, 79002011

Oklahoma City Discovery Well, SE 57th St. and ITIO Blvd., Oklahoma City, 12/09/77, A, g, 77001095

Oklahoma City University, 2501 N. Blackwelder Ave., Oklahoma City, 12/19/78, A, a, 78002247

Oklahoma County Courthouse [County Courthouses of Oklahoma MPS], 321 Park Ave., Oklahoma City, 3/05/92, C, 92000126

Oklahoma County Home for Girls, 6300 N. Western Ave., Oklahoma City, 3/21/78, A, 78002248

Oklahoma Gas and Electric Company Building, 321 N. Harvey Ave., Oklahoma City, 4/09/80, A, C, g, 80003288

Oklahoma Hardware Building [Red Brick Warehouses of Oklahoma City TR], 27 E. California Ave., Oklahoma City, 8/12/83, A, C, 83002105

Oklahoma Historical Society Building, 2100 Lincoln Blvd., Oklahoma City, 2/21/90, A, C, 90000124

Oklahoma Publishing Company Building, 500 N. Broadway, Oklahoma City, 9/18/78, B, C, 78002249

Oklahoma State Capitol, 22nd St. and Lincoln Blvd., Oklahoma City, 10/08/76, A, 76001572

Old North Tower, Central State College, 400 E. Hurd St., Central State College campus, Edmond, 6/21/71, A, 71000671

Overholser House, 405 15th St., NW, Oklahoma City, 6/22/70, B, C, 70000536

Pilgrim Congregational Church, 1433 Classen Dr., Oklahoma City, 2/23/84, C, a, 84003389

Pioneer Building, 401 N. Broadway St., Oklahoma City, 3/03/80, A, C, 80003289

Plaza Court, 1100 Classen Dr., Oklahoma City, 9/08/80, B, C, 80003290

Point 8 Site, Address Restricted, Oklahoma City vicinity, 9/06/78, D, 78002250

Post Office, Courthouse, and Federal Office Building, Robinson at 3rd St., Oklahoma City, 8/30/74, C, g, 74001665

Putnam Heights Historic Preservation District, Georgia and McKinley Blvds., 35th, 37th, and 38th Sts., Oklahoma City, 6/02/82, A, B, C, g, 82003693

Quillin Site, Address Restricted, Midwest City vicinity, 2/14/79, D, 79002005

Rock Island Plow Building [Red Brick Warehouses of Oklahoma City TR], 29 E. Reno Ave., Oklahoma City, 8/12/83, A, C, 83002106

Sherman Machine and Iron Works Building [Red Brick Warehouses of Oklahoma City TR], 26 E. Main St., Oklahoma City, 8/12/83, A, C, 83002107

Sinopoulo, John, House, 4000 N. Kelley, Oklahoma City, 11/28/78, B, C, 78002251

Skirvin Hotel, 1 Park Ave., Oklahoma City, 10/10/79, B, C, 79002010

Snyder's Super Service Station, 1325 N. Broadway Ave., Oklahoma City, 3/26/80, C, g, 80003291

Spanish Village Historic District, 2909-3024 Paseo, Oklahoma City, 2/24/83, A, C, g, 83002108

Spencer No. 2 Site, Address Restricted, Oklahoma City vicinity, 11/27/78, D, 78002252

St. Joseph's Cathedral, 225 4th St., NW, Oklahoma City, 1/30/78, A, C, a, 78002253

St. Paul's Cathedral, 127 7th St., NW, Oklahoma City, 4/11/77, A, C, a, 77001096

Stanford Furniture Co. Building [Red Brick Warehouses of Oklahoma City TR], 1 E. Sheridan Ave., Oklahoma City, 8/12/83, A, C, 83002109

Stockyards City Historic District, An irregular pattern along Agnew and Exchange Aves., Oklahoma City, 8/24/79, A, 79003643

Tradesman's National Bank Building, 101 N. Broadway St., Oklahoma City, 11/05/80, C, 80003292

Tuton's Drugstore, 1st and Main Sts., Arcadia, 3/03/80, B, C, 80003278

Union Depot, 300 7th St., NW, Oklahoma City, 5/16/78, A, C, g, 78002254

Walcourt Building, 1401 Walnut Ave., NE, Oklahoma City, 3/19/82, C, 82003694

Weather Service Building, 1923 Classen Blvd., Oklahoma City, 7/12/78, A, B, 78002255

Wells Fargo and Company Livery Stable, 115 E. Reno Ave., Oklahoma City, 7/09/82, A, 82003695

Okmulgee County

Creek National Capitol, 6th St. and Grand Ave., Okmulgee, 10/15/66, A, NHL, 66000632

Eastside Baptist Church [Black Baptist Churches in Okmulgee TR], 219 N. Osage Ave., Okmulgee, 11/23/84, A, a, 84000306

First Baptist Central Church [Black Baptist Churches in Okmulgee TR], 521 N. Central Ave., Okmulgee, 11/23/84, A, a, 84000307

Henry, Hugh, House, N. 3rd St., Henryetta, 8/18/83, B, C, 83002110

Isparhecher House and Grave, About 4 mi. W of Beggs off OK 16, Beggs vicinity, 7/12/76, B, c, 76001573

Nuyaka Mission, 9 mi. W of Okmulgee, Okmulgee vicinity, 4/13/72, A, a, 72001075

Okmulgee Black Hospital, 320 N. Wood Dr., Okmulgee, 6/22/84, A, 84003387

Okmulgee County Courthouse [County Courthouses of Oklahoma TR], 300 W. 7th St., Okmulgee, 8/23/84, A, C, 84003390

Okmulgee Downtown Historic District, Roughly bounded by 4th St., Frisco Ave., 8th St. and Okmulgee Ave., Okmulgee, 12/17/92, A, C, 92001693

Okmulgee Public Library, 218 S. Okmulgee Ave., Okmulgee, 7/28/83, A, C, 83002111

Severs Block, 101 E. 6th St., Okmulgee, 3/22/91, A, 91000311

St. Anthony's Catholic Church, 515 S. Morton St., Okmulgee, 7/14/83, C, 83002112

Wilson School, NW of Henryetta, Henryetta vicinity, 1/28/81, A, 81000465

Osage County

Bank of Bigheart [Richardsonian Romanesque Banks of Osage County TR], 308 W. Main St., Barnsdall, 11/23/84, A, C, 84000311

Bank of Burbank [Richardsonian Romanesque Banks of Osage County TR], McCorkle and 1st Sts., Burbank, 11/23/84, A, C, 84000314

Bank of Hominy [Richardsonian Romanesque Banks of Osage County TR], 102 W. Main St., Hominy, 11/23/84, A, C, 84000316

Blacksmith's House, 210 W. Main St., Pawhuska, 5/07/79, A, 79002014

Chief Ne-Kah-Wah-She-Tun-Kah Grave and Statue, Off OK 18, Fairfax, 5/22/79, A, B, c, f, g, 79002012

Osage County—Continued

City Hall, Main and Grandview Ave., Pawhuska, 1/01/76, A, 76001574

Drummond, Fred, House, 305 N. Price Ave., Hominy, 4/16/81, B, C, 81000466

First National Bank and Masonic Lodge, 301 N. Main St., Fairfax, 6/22/84, A, C, 84003393

Hominy Osage Round House, Round House Sq. in Indian Village, Hominy, 5/16/79, A, C, 79002013

Hominy School, 200 blk., S. Pettit St., Hominy, 8/12/88, A, 88001183

Immaculate Conception Church, 1314 Lynn Ave., Pawhuska, 5/21/79, A, C, a, 79002015

Osage Agency, Agency Hill, Pawhuska, 5/17/74, A, b, 74001666

Osage Bank of Fairfax [Richardsonian Romanesque Banks of Osage County TR], 250 N. Main St., Fairfax, 11/23/84, A, C, 84000315

Osage County Courthouse [County Courthouses of Oklahoma TR], 6th and Grandview Sts., Pawhuska, 8/23/84, A, C, 84003395

Pawhuska Downtown Historic District, Roughly bounded by Grand View Ave., E. Eighth St., Leahy Ave., and E. Fifth St., Pawhuska, 11/26/86, A, C, 86002355

Ottawa County

Coleman Theatre, 1st and Main Sts., Miami, 5/19/83, A, C, 83002114

Coleman, George L., Sr., House, 1001 Rockdale St., Miami, 5/09/83, B, C, 83002113

Commerce Building/Hancock Building, 103 E. Central, Miami, 5/09/83, A, 83002115

McNaughton, John Patrick, Barn, OK 137, 1.5 mi. N of OK 10, Quapaw vicinity, 12/27/91, C, 91001903

Modoc Mission Church and Cemetery, SE of Miami, Miami vicinity, 2/15/80, A, a, b, d, 80003293

Peoria Indian School [Confederated Peoria Indian TR], E of Miami, Miami vicinity, 3/21/83, A, 83002116

Peoria Tribal Cemetery [Confederated Peoria Indian TR], E of Miami, Miami vicinity, 3/21/83, A, B, 83002117

Pawnee County

Arkansas Valley National Bank, 547 6th St., Pawnee, 11/17/78, A, C, 78002256

Blackburn Methodist Church [Territorial Era Carpenter Gothic Churches TR], D St. and 4th Ave., Blackburn, 9/28/84, A, C, a, 84003398

Blue Hawk Peak Ranch, W of Pawnee on U.S. 64, Pawnee vicinity, 10/10/75, B, 75001571

Corliss Steam Engine, Pawnee County Fairgrounds, Pawnee, 5/07/79, A, 79002016

Mullendore Mansion, 910 N. Phillips St., Cleveland, 6/22/84, B, C, 84003402

Pawnee County Courthouse [County Courthouses of Oklahoma TR], Courthouse Sq., Pawnee, 8/23/84, A, C, 84003406

Pawnee Indian Agency, E edge of Pawnee, Pawnee, 4/11/73, A, 73001567

Ralston Opera House, 501–503 Main St., Ralston, 7/28/87, A, 87001257

Payne County

Berry, James E., House, 502 S. Duck St., Stillwater, 11/21/80, B, C, g, 80003294

Citizens Bank Building, 107 E. 9th St., Stillwater, 2/24/81, A, C, 81000467

Cottonwood Community Center, NW of Stillwater, Stillwater vicinity, 3/13/80, A, C, b, 80004291

Frick, William, House, 1016 S. West St., Stillwater, 9/08/80, C, 80004292

Hoke Building [Commercial Buildings in Stillwater TR], 121 W. 7th Ave., Stillwater, 9/12/83, A, 83002118

Hopkins Sandstone House and Farmstead, NE of Ripley, Ripley vicinity, 5/07/79, D, 79002017

Irvings Castle, 2.5 mi. (4 km) S of Ingalls, Ingalls vicinity, 2/17/78, A, 78002257

Magruder Plots, Oklahoma State University, Stillwater, 8/29/79, A, b, 79002018

Murphy House, 419 S. Monroe, Stillwater, 9/18/86, C, 86002173

Old Central, Oklahoma State University, Oklahoma State University campus, Stillwater, 7/27/71, A, 71000672

Payne County Courthouse [County Courthouses of Oklahoma TR], 606 S. Husband St., Stillwater, 8/23/84, A, C, 84003410

Pleasant Valley School, 1901 S. Sangre Rd., Stillwater, 1/25/91, A, 90002182

Selph Building [Commercial Buildings in Stillwater TR], 119 W. 7th Ave., Stillwater, 9/12/83, A, 83002119

Stillwater Santa Fe Depot, 400 E. 10th St., Stillwater, 3/03/80, A, 80004293

Thorpe, Jim, House, 704 E. Boston St., Yale, 3/24/71, B, 71000673

Walker Building [Commercial Buildings in Stillwater TR], 117 W. 7th Ave., Stillwater, 9/12/83, A, 83002120

Pittsburg County

Blackburn's Station Site, 9 mi. SE of Pittsburg, Pittsburg vicinity, 3/07/73, A, 73001568

Busby Office Building, 113 E. Carl Albert Pkwy., McAlester, 12/06/79, A, C, 79002021

Busby Theatre, Washington Ave. and 2nd St., McAlester, 12/06/79, A, C, a, 79002022

Canadian Jail and Livery Stable, Off OK 113, Canadian, 11/06/80, A, 80003295

Choate Cabin, 2nd and Walnut Sts., Indianola, 10/03/79, B, C, b, 79002019

Cole Chapel School [WPA Public Bldgs., Recreational Facilities and Cemetery Improvements in Southeastern Oklahoma, 1935–1943 TR], N of Hartshorne, Hartshorne vicinity, 9/08/88, A, C, a, 88001411

First Presbyterian Church, 101 E. Washington Ave., McAlester, 12/11/79, A, C, a, 79003139

Hokey's Drugstore, Main and Washington Sts, Krebs, 12/06/79, A, 79002020

Lee, Jeff, Park Bath House and Pool [WPA Public Bldgs., Recreational Facilities and Cemetery Improvements in Southeastern Oklahoma, 1935–1943 TR], Third and Fillmore Sts., McAlester, 9/08/88, A, C, 88001413

Mass Grave of the Mexican Miners, Mount Calvary Cemetery, McAlester, 11/14/80, A, d, 80003297

McAlester Armory [WPA Public Bldgs., Recreational Facilities and Cemetery Improvements in Southeastern Oklahoma, 1935–1943 TR], Third and Polk Sts., McAlester, 9/08/88, A, C, 88001412

McAlester DX, 5th St. and Carl Albert Pkwy., McAlester, 8/29/80, A, C, g, 80004288

McAlester House, 14 E. Smith Ave., McAlester, 8/29/80, B, C, 80004289

McAlester Scottish Rite Temple, 2nd St. and Adams Ave., McAlester, 11/22/80, A, C, 80004521

Mine Rescue Station Building, 507-509 E. 3rd St., McAlester, 3/13/80, A, 80004290

New State School [WPA Public Bldgs., Recreational Facilities and Cemetery Improvements in Southeastern Oklahoma, 1935–1943 TR], S of Hartshorne near North Fork Elm Creek, Hartshorne vicinity, 9/08/88, A, C, 88001414

Perryville, SW of McAlester on U.S. 69, McAlester vicinity, 5/05/72, A, 72001076

Pittsburg County Courthouse [County Courthouses of Oklahoma TR], Washington Ave., McAlester, 8/23/84, A, C, 84003415

Pittsburg School and Gymnasium [WPA Public Bldgs., Recreational Facilities and Cemetery Improvements in Southeastern Oklahoma, 1935–1943 TR], Off OK 63, Pittsburg, 9/08/88, A, C, 88001415

Southern Ice and Cold Storage Company, 338 E. Choctaw Ave., Pittsburg, 10/11/79, A, 79002023

St. Joseph's Catholic Church, Off OK 31, Krebs, 11/12/80, A, C, a, 80003296

Tipton Ridge School [WPA Public Bldgs., Recreational Facilities and Cemetery Improvements in Southeastern Oklahoma, 1935–1943 TR], N of Blocker, Blocker vicinity, 9/08/88, A, C, 88001417

Pontotoc County

Ada Public Library, 400 S. Rennie, Ada, 11/13/89, C, 89001950

Bebee Field Round House, OK 13, Ada vicinity, 8/05/85, A, 85001699

East Central State Normal School, East Central University campus, Ada, 12/23/86, A, 86003470

Mijo Camp Industrial District, N. side of Pontotoc Cty. Rd. # 148, Ada vicinity, 9/26/85, C, 85002560

Pontotoc County—Continued

Pontotoc County Courthouse [County Court-houses of Oklahoma TR], 12th and Broadway, Ada, 8/24/84, A, C, 84003418

Pottawatomie County

Beard Cabin [Shawnee Historic Homes TR], Woodland Park, Shawnee, 4/08/83, A, C, 83002121

Billington Building, 23 E. Ninth, Shawnee, 9/26/85, A, C, 85002512

Douglas, H. T., Mansion and Garage, 100 E. Federal, Shawnee, 9/26/85, C, 85002517

Governors Mansion [Shawnee Historic Homes TR], 618 N. Park St., Shawnee, 1/21/83, A, 83002122

Kerfoot House [Shawnee Historic Homes TR], 740 N. Beard St., Shawnee, 1/21/83, C, 83002123

Nuckolls House [Shawnee Historic Homes TR], 200 E. Federal St., Shawnee, 1/21/83, B, 83002124

Pottawatomie County Courthouse [County Court-houses of Oklahoma TR], 300 N. Broadway, Shawnee, 8/24/84, A, C, 84003424

Rose—Fast Site (34PT28), Address Restricted, Harjo vicinity, 12/24/86, D, 86003479

Sacred Heart Mission Site, Off OK 39, Asher vicinity, 9/15/83, A, a, d, g, 83002125

Santa Fe Depot, Main St. and Minnesota Ave., Shawnee, 6/05/74, A, C, 74001667

Shawnee Friends Mission, 2 mi. S of Shawnee, Shawnee vicinity, 3/07/73, A, a, 73001569

St. Gregory's Abbey and College, 1900 W. Mac-Arthur Dr., Shawnee, 8/15/75, A, C, a, 75001572

Walker House [Shawnee Historic Homes TR], 1801 N. Broadway, Shawnee, 4/08/83, C, 83002126

Pushmataha County

Albion State Bank, Off U.S. 271, Albion, 12/11/79, A, C, 79002024

Antlers Frisco Depot and Antlers Spring, Main St., Antlers, 6/27/80, A, 80003298

Clayton High School—Auditorium [WPA Public Bldgs., Recreational Facilities and Cemetery Improvements in Southeastern Oklahoma, 1935–1943 TR], W. Pine St., Clayton, 9/08/88, A, C, 88001418

Fewell School [WPA Public Bldgs., Recreational Facilities and Cemetery Improvements in Southeastern Oklahoma, 1935–1943 TR], Off OK 144, Nashoba vicinity, 9/08/88, A, C, 88001419

Kosyk, Mato, House, E of Albion off U.S. 271, Albion vicinity, 12/11/79, B, 79002025

Snow School [WPA Public Bldgs., Recreational Facilities and Cemetery Improvements in Southeastern Oklahoma, 1935–1943 TR], US 271, Snow, 9/08/88, A, C, 88001420

Tuskahoma, 2 mi. N of Tuskahoma, Tuskahoma vicinity, 7/28/70, A, 70000537

Roger Mills County

Allee Site, Address Restricted, Hammon vicinity, 11/08/78, D, 78002260

Antelope Hills, N of Durham, Durham vicinity, 12/14/78, A, 78002259

Dorroh-Trent House, 11th and Conley Sts., Hammon, 10/03/79, B, 79002026

Goodwin-Baker Archeological Site, Address Restricted, Berlin vicinity, 7/07/78, D, 78002258

Lamb-Miller Site, Address Restricted, Hammon vicinity, 10/02/78, D, 78002261

Washita Battlefield, NW of Cheyenne on U.S. 283, Cheyenne vicinity, 10/15/66, A, NHL, 66000633

Rogers County

Belvedere, The, 109 N. Chickasaw Ave., Claremore, 3/24/82, B, C, 82003696

Eastern University Preparatory School, College Hill, Claremore, 2/19/82, A, 82003697

Hanes Home, Off OK 88, Sageeyah vicinity, 7/12/82, A, C, 82003700

Hogue House, 1001 S. Olive St., Chelsea, 12/17/82, C, 82001498

Mendenhall's Bath House, 601 E. 7th St., Claremore, 3/23/83, A, 83002127

Meyer, Maurice, Barracks, College Hill, Claremore, 3/01/82, A, 82003698

Oologah Bank, 105 S. Maple St., Oologah, 5/10/82, A, 82003699

Oologah Pump, Maple & Cooweescoowee Sts., Oologah, 12/17/82, A, 82001499

Rogers, Will, Birthplace, About 4 mi. NE of Oologah, Oologah vicinity, 9/29/70, B, C, b, c, 70000538

Seminole County

Brown, Alice, House, Chestnut St., Sasakwa, 3/31/82, B, 82003701

Brown, Jackson, House, 1200 S. Muskogee Pl., Wewoka, 6/27/80, A, C, 80003299

Brown, Silas L., House, 107 S. Seminole, Wewoka, 8/05/85, B, 85001697

Grisso, W. E., Mansion, 612 Hwy. 9E, Seminole, 1/27/75, C, g, 75001573

Home Stake Oil and Gas Company Building, 315 E. Broadway, Seminole, 5/14/86, A, 86001094

Hotel Aldridge, Third and Wenoka Sts., Wenoka, 5/14/86, A, C, 86001083

Johnson, J. Coody, Building, 124 N. Wewoka St., Wewoka, 8/05/85, B, 85001744

Mekasukey Academy, SW of Seminole, Seminole vicinity, 3/28/74, A, 74001668

Rosenwald Hall [Educational Resources of All-Black Towns in Oklahoma TR], College St., Lima, 9/28/84, A, 84003427

Roulston-Rogers Site, Address Restricted, Sasakwa vicinity, 11/27/78, D, 78002262

Seminole County Courthouse [County Court-houses of Oklahoma TR], S. Wewoka St., Wewoka, 8/24/84, A, C, 84003429

Seminole Whipping Tree, Wewoka Ave., Wewoka, 5/22/81, A, 81000468

Sinclair Loading Rack, US 270, Seminole vicinity, 8/05/85, A, 85001698

Wewoka Switch and Side Tracks, OK 56, Wewoka, 9/26/85, A, 85002475

Sequoyah County

Baker "A" Archeological Site (34SQ269), Address Restricted, Short vicinity, 3/02/90, D, 90000125

Citizen's State Bank, Seminole and Main Sts., Marble City, 9/08/80, A, C, 80003300

Dwight Mission, 3 mi. SW of Marble City, Marble City vicinity, 3/20/73, A, a, 73001570

Ellison No. 2 Site (34SQ85), Address Restricted, Short vicinity, 8/11/88, D, 88001234

Faulkner, Judge Franklin, House, E. Cherokee St., Sallisaw, 3/13/80, B, C, b, 80003301

Fears Site (34SQ76), Address Restricted, Nicut vicinity, 8/11/88, D, 88001235

Hines Round Barn, 401 S. Adams St., Sallisaw, 3/08/84, C, 84003432

Kirby—Steely Archeological Site, Address Restricted, Short vicinity, 4/03/91, D, 91000356

Lee's Creek Ceremonial Center Site (Boundary Increase), Address Restricted, Short vicinity, 7/03/79, D, 79003741

Lee's Creek Ceremonial Site, Address Restricted, Short vicinity, 1/31/76, D, 76001575

Sequoyah's Cabin, OK 101, in Sequoyah's Cabin State Park, Akins vicinity, 10/15/66, B, NHL, 66000634

Starr Pasture Archeological Site (34SQ224), Address Restricted, Short vicinity, 3/02/90, D, 90000126

Tall Cane Archeological Site (34SQ294), Address Restricted, Short vicinity, 3/02/90, D, 90000127

Stephens County

Chrislip, H. C., House, 709 N. 14th St., Duncan, 8/06/93, C, 93000677

Johnson Hotel and Boarding House, 314 W. Mulberry, Duncan, 5/14/86, A, 86001098

Montgomery-Liman House, 301 N. 5th St., Marlow, 9/22/83, C, 83002128

Texas County

Adams Woodframe Grain Elevator [Woodframe Grain Elevators of Oklahoma Panhandle TR], N of OK 3, Adams, 5/13/83, A, C, 83002129

Baker Woodframe Elevator [Woodframe Grain Elevators of Oklahoma Panhandle TR], SR 2847, Baker, 5/13/83, A, C, 83002130

Texas County—Continued

Baker Woodframe Grain Elevator [Woodframe Grain Elevators of Oklahoma Panhandle TR], Off U.S. 64, Baker, 5/13/83, A, C, 83002131

CCC Ranch Headquarters, W of Texhoma, Texhoma vicinity, 12/01/83, A, 83004218

Easterwood Archeological Site, Address Restricted, Guymon vicinity, 11/16/78, D, 78002264

Eva Woodframe Grain Elevator [Woodframe Grain Elevators of Oklahoma Panhandle TR], OK 95, Eva, 5/13/83, A, C, 83002132

Hooker Woodframe Grain Elevator [Woodframe Grain Elevators of Oklahoma Panhandle TR], Off Texas Ave., Hooker, 5/13/83, A, C, 83002133

Hough Woodframe Elevator [Woodframe Grain Elevators of Oklahoma Panhandle TR], OK 95, Hough, 5/13/83, A, C, 83002134

Johnson-Cline Archeological Site, Address Restricted, Texhoma vicinity, 11/16/78, D, 78002267

Mouser Grain Elevator [Woodframe Grain Elevators of Oklahoma Panhandle TR], Off SR 136, Mouser, 10/07/83, A, 83004220

Mouser Woodframe Grain Elevator/Collingwood Elevator [Woodframe Grain Elevators of Oklahoma Panhandle TR], Off SR 136, Mouser, 5/13/83, C, a, 83002135

Nash II-Clawson Archeological Site, Address Restricted, Guymon vicinity, 10/02/78, D, 78002265

Old Hardesty, Address Restricted, Hardesty vicinity, 6/20/74, D, 74001669

Optima Grain Elevator [Woodframe Grain Elevators of Oklahoma Panhandle TR], U.S. 54, Optima, 5/13/83, A, C, 83002136

Penick House, 218 N. East St., Texhoma, 9/28/84, C, 84003436

Shores Archeological Site, Address Restricted, Eva vicinity, 11/27/78, D, 78002263

Stamper Site, Address Restricted, Optima vicinity, 10/15/66, D, NHL, 66000635

Texas County Courthouse [County Courthouses of Oklahoma TR], 319 N. Main St., Guymon, 8/24/84, A, C, 84003439

Tracey Woodframe Grain Elevator [Woodframe Grain Elevators of Oklahoma Panhandle TR], N of U.S. 64, Muncey, 5/13/83, A, C, 83002137

Two Sisters Archeological Site, Address Restricted, Guymon vicinity, 10/02/78, D, 78002266

Tillman County

Hubbard, William and Mabel Donahoo, House, 323 E. 5th St., Grandfield, 3/21/91, C, 91000310

Humphreys Drugstore Building, 106 E. 2nd St., Grandfield, 6/18/92, A, C, 92000797

Laney, J. D., House, SW of Frederick, Frederick vicinity, 2/03/84, C, 84003441

Ramona Theatre, 114 S. 9th St., Frederick, 11/08/84, C, 84000377

Tillman County Bank of Grandfield, 123 W. 2nd St., Grandfield, 6/18/92, A, C, 92000796

Tillman County Courthouse [County Courthouses of Oklahoma TR], Gladstone and Main Sts., Frederick, 8/24/84, A, C, 84003455

Tulsa County

Boston Avenue Methodist Church, Boston Ave. and 13th St., Tulsa, 8/31/78, C, a, g, 78002270

Brady Heights Historic District, Roughly bounded by Marshall and Easton Sts., Denver and Cheyenne Aves., Tulsa, 6/27/80, C, 80003302

Clinton-Hardy House, 1322 S. Guthrie, Tulsa, 1/23/79, C, 79002027

Convention Hall, 105 W. Brady St., Tulsa, 8/29/79, A, 79002028

Cosden Building, 409 S. Boston, Tulsa, 2/01/79, B, C, 79002029

Creek Council Tree Site, 18th and Cheyenne Sts., Tulsa, 9/29/76, A, 76001576

Fort Arbuckle Site, W of Sand Springs, Sand Springs vicinity, 12/22/78, A, 78002269

Gillette Historic District, Bounded by S. Yorktown and S. Lewis Aves, E. 15th and E. 17th Sts., Tulsa, 9/20/82, C, 82003702

Gillette-Tyrell Building, 423 S. Boulder Ave., Tulsa, 1/21/82, C, 82003703

Harwelden, 2210 S. Main St., Tulsa, 2/08/78, B, C, 78002271

Haskell State School of Agriculture, 808 E. College St., Broken Arrow, 12/19/78, A, 78002268

Holy Family Cathedral, Rectory, and School, W. 8th St. and S. Boulder Ave., Tulsa, 2/11/82, C, a, 82003704

Hooper Brothers Coffee Company Building, 731–733 E. Admiral Blvd., Tulsa, 12/19/78, C, 78002272

Maple Ridge Historic Residential District, Roughly bounded by Hazel Blvd., S. Peoria Ave., 14th St., and Railroad, Tulsa, 4/06/83, A, C, 83002138

Mayo Hotel, 115 W. 5th St., Tulsa, 6/27/80, C, 80003303

McBirney, James H., House, 1414 S. Galveston, Tulsa, 11/13/76, B, C, 76001577

McFarlin Building, 11 E. 5th St, Tulsa, 12/06/79, C, 79002030

McFarlin, Robert M., House, 1610 Carson, Tulsa, 1/25/79, C, 79002031

McLean, B. W., House and Office, 123 E. A St., Jenks, 3/22/91, C, 91000309

Mincks-Adams Hotel, 403 S. Cheyenne St., Tulsa, 11/07/78, C, 78002273

Moore Manor, 228 W. 17th Pl., Tulsa, 2/19/82, A, C, 82003705

Oklahoma Natural Gas Company Building [Zig-Zag Art Deco Style Public Utility Buildings TR], 624 S. Boston Ave., Tulsa, 4/10/84, A, C, 84003458

Petroleum Building, 420 S. Boulder St., Tulsa, 4/15/82, B, C, 82003706

Philcade Building, 511 S. Boston Ave., Tulsa, 9/18/86, C, 86002196

Phillips, Waite, Mansion, 2727 S. Rockford Rd., Tulsa, 12/01/78, C, 78002274

Philtower, 427 S. Boston Ave, Tulsa, 8/29/79, B, C, 79002032

Pierce Block, 301 E. 3rd St., Tulsa, 12/11/79, A, C, 79002033

Public Service of Oklahoma Building [Zig-Zag Art Deco Style Public Utility Buildings TR], 600 S. Main St., Tulsa, 4/10/84, A, C, 84003443

Skelly, William G., House, 2101 S. Madison, Tulsa, 11/28/78, B, C, 78002275

Southwestern Bell Main Dial Building [Zig-Zag Art Deco Style Public Utility Buildings TR], 424 Detroit Ave., Tulsa, 6/22/84, A, C, 84003445

St. John Vianney Training School for Girls, 4001 E. 101st St., Tulsa, 6/07/83, C, a, 83002139

Tracy Park Historic District, Roughly bounded by Norfolk, Peoria, 11th and 13th Sts., Tulsa, 9/20/82, A, C, 82003707

Tribune Building, 20 E. Archer St., Tulsa, 7/16/79, A, C, a, 79003644

Tulsa Municipal Building, 124 E. 4th St., Tulsa, 7/18/75, C, 75001574

Veasey, James Alexander, House, 1802 S. Cheyenne Ave., Tulsa, 7/27/89, C, 89001006

Westhope, 3704 S. Birmingham St., Tulsa, 4/10/75, C, g, 75001575

Wagoner County

Cobb Building, 203 E. Cherokee St., Wagoner, 9/13/82, A, C, 82003709

First National Bank of Wagoner, 114 E. Cherokee St., Wagoner, 3/10/83, A, 83002140

Gibson, John W., House [Territorial Homes of Wagoner, Oklahoma TR], 402 S. McQuarrie, Wagoner, 7/06/82, B, 82003710

Koweta Mission Site, 1 mi. S of Cowetah off OK 58B, Cowetah vicinity, 6/19/73, A, 73001571

Mason, A. J., Building, Lincoln St., Tullahassee, 8/05/85, A, 85001743

McAnally, William, House [Territorial Homes of Wagoner, Oklahoma TR], 702 7th St., SE, Wagoner, 7/06/82, B, 82003711

McKinney, Collin, House [Territorial Homes of Wagoner, Oklahoma TR], 1106 7th St., SE, Wagoner, 7/06/82, B, 82003708

Miller-Washington School [Educational Resources of All-Black Towns in Oklahoma TR], Market St., Red Bird, 9/28/84, A, 84003448

Newport Hotel and Restaurant, 202 S. Main, Wagoner, 12/04/85, A, 85003079

Parkinson, Amos, House [Territorial Homes of Wagoner, Oklahoma TR], 601 N. Parkinson, Wagoner, 7/06/82, B, 82003712

Parkinson, Frederick, House [Territorial Homes of Wagoner, Oklahoma TR], 407 3rd St., NE, Wagoner, 7/06/82, B, 82003713

Red Bird City Hall [Historic Government Buildings in Oklahoma's All-Black Towns TR], Boston St., Red Bird, 9/28/84, A, 84003450

Rio Grande Ranch Headquarters Historic District, OK 251A, 3 mi. E of Okay, Okay vicinity, 9/09/92, A, C, 92001191

Wagoner County—Continued

St James Episcopal Church, 303 S. Church St., Wagoner, 5/11/82, A, a, b, 82003714

Tullahassee Mission Site, Address Restricted, Tullahassee vicinity, 9/10/71, D, 71000674

Van Tuyl Homeplace, N of Porter, Porter vicinity, 2/07/78, C, 78002276

Way House [Territorial Homes of Wagoner, Oklahoma TR], 411 2nd St., NE, Wagoner, 7/06/82, B, 82003715

Washington County

Bartlesville Downtown Historic District, Roughly bounded by SE Second St., SE Cherokee Ave., SE Fourth St. and the A T & S F RR tracks, Bartlesville, 12/27/91, A, C, 91001905

Civic Center, Johnstone Ave. between 6th St. and Adams Blvd., Bartlesville, 12/29/89, A, C, 89002122

Dewey Hotel, Delaware and Don Tyler Ave., Dewey, 4/04/75, A, B, 75001578

LaQuinta, 2201 Silver Lake Rd., Bartlesville, 7/15/82, B, C, 82003716

Nellie Johnstone No. 1, Johnstone Park, Bartlesville, 4/11/72, A, 72001077

Old Washington County Courthouse, 400 Frank Phillips Blvd., Bartlesville, 1/26/81, C, 81000469

Phillips, Frank, House, 1107 Cherokee Ave., Bartlesville, 3/13/75, B, 75001576

Price Tower, 6th St. and Dewey Ave., Bartlesville, 9/13/74, C, g, 74001670

Washita County

Cedar Creek District, Address Restricted, Carnegie vicinity, 5/29/75, D, 75001577

Cordell Carnegie Public Library, 105 E. First St., Cordell, 11/13/89, A, C, 89001966

McLemore Site, Address Restricted, Colony vicinity, 10/15/66, D, NHL, 66000636

Washita County Courthouse [County Courthouses of Oklahoma TR], Courthouse Sq., Cordell, 8/24/84, A, C, 84003452

Woods County

Alva Armory [WPA Public Bldgs., Recreational Facilities and Water Quality Improvements in Northwestern Oklahoma, 1935–1943 TR], Choctaw and Third Sts., Alva, 9/08/88, A, C, 88001360

Branson Building [Territorial Buildings in Downtown Alva TR], 531 Barnes St., Alva, 1/05/84, A, C, 84000700

Building at 405-407 College Avenue [Territorial Buildings in Downtown Alva TR], 405 College Ave., Alva, 1/05/84, C, 84000702

Building at 409 College Avenue [Territorial Buildings in Downtown Alva TR], 409 College Ave., Alva, 1/05/84, A, 84000703

Building at 500 Flynn Street [Territorial Buildings in Downtown Alva TR], 500 Flynn St., Alva, 1/05/84, A, C, 84000704

Central National Bank [Territorial Buildings in Downtown Alva TR], 401 College Ave., Alva, 1/05/84, A, C, 84000705

I.O.O.F. Hall [Territorial Buildings in Downtown Alva TR], 527 Barnes St., Alva, 1/05/84, A, C, 84000706

Kavanaugh and Shea Building [Territorial Buildings in Downtown Alva TR], 403 College Ave., Alva, 1/05/84, C, 84000707

Sante Fe Depot and Reading Room, Sante Fe Tracks, Waynoka, 6/20/74, A, 74001671

Science Hall, Northwestern Oklahoma State University, Alva, 7/14/83, A, C, 83002141

Stine Building, 601 Barnes St., Alva, 4/21/82, B, 82003717

Woodward County

Fort Supply Historic District, Western State Hospital grounds, Fort Supply, 6/21/71, A, 71000675

Stein, L. L., House [Woodward MRA], 1001 10th St., Woodward, 10/07/83, B, C, 83004225

Woodward Crystal Beach Park [WPA Public Bldgs., Recreational Facilities and Water Quality Improvements in Northwestern Oklahoma, 1935–1943 TR], Jim Ben and Temple Houston Sts., Woodward, 9/08/88, A, C, 88001359

These fuel storage tanks were built in 1917 when the Drumright Gasoline Plant No. 2 opened to process natural gas from the Cushing oil field in Creek County, Oklahoma. The silver painted, riveted steel tanks continue to be used to hold present day gasoline products. (Robert C. Sweet, 1980)

OREGON

Baker County

Antlers Guard Station [USDA Forest Service Administrative Buildings in Oregon and Washington Built by the CCC MPS], SE of Whitney, Wallowa—Whitman NF, Whitney vicinity, 3/06/91, A, C, 91000166

Baker Historic District, Irregular pattern along Main St. from Madison to Estes Sts., Baker, 12/14/78, A, C, 78002277

Baker Municipal Natatorium, 2470 Grove St., Baker, 10/17/77, A, C, 77001097

Clark, Robert F. and Elizabeth, House, 1522 Washington Ave., Baker, 10/30/89, C, 89001857

Maxwell, James O., Farmstead, Rt. 2, Box 82 on N side Muddy Creek Rd., Haines vicinity, 11/06/86, B, C, 86003086

Oregon Commercial Company Building, 40–50 E. Washington St., Huntington, 6/04/92, A, C, 92000666

Rand, Ed, House, 1700 4th St., Baker, 12/09/81, B, C, 81000709

SUMPTER VALLEY GOLD DREDGE (dredge), SW of Sumpter near Cracker Creek, Sumpter, 10/26/71, A, g, 71000676

St. Elizabeth Hospital (Old), 2365 Fourth St., Baker, 2/21/89, A, C, 89000047

Sumpter Valley Railway Historic District, Roughly between Baker and Prairie City starting near the McEwen station site and W to the Dixie Pass area, Sumpter, 8/03/87, A, 87001065

Unity Ranger Station [Depression-Era Buildings TR], Wallowa-Whitman National Forest, Unity, 4/11/86, A, C, b, g, 86000823

Benton County

Benton County Courthouse, NW 4th St. between Jackson and Monroe Sts., Corvallis, 1/30/78, A, C, 78002278

Benton County State Bank Building, 155 SW Madison Ave., Corvallis, 3/07/79, B, C, 79002035

Benton Hotel, 408 SW Monroe, Corvallis, 5/20/82, A, C, 82003719

Bexell, John, House, 3009 NW. Van Buren Ave., Corvallis, 2/26/92, B, C, 92000064

Bosworth, Dr. Ralph Lyman, House, 833 NW Buchanan Ave., Corvallis, 12/09/81, B, C, b, 81000471

Bryson, J. R., House, 242 NW 7th St., Corvallis, 11/15/79, B, C, 79002036

Burnap-Rickard House, 518 SW 3rd St., Corvallis, 8/01/84, B, C, 84002931

Caton, Jesse H., House, 602 NW 4th St., Corvallis, 9/27/79, B, C, 79002037

Corvallis Hotel, 201–211 S.W. Second St., Corvallis, 9/10/87, A, C, 87001533

Episcopal Church of the Good Samaritan, 700 SW Madison Ave., Corvallis, 9/10/71, A, C, a, b, 71000677

Fairbanks, J. Leo, House, 316 NW 32nd, Corvallis, 2/14/85, B, C, 85000290

Farra, Dr. George R., House, 660 SW Madison Ave., Corvallis, 12/09/81, B, C, 81000472

Fiechter, John, House, William L. Finley National Wildlife Refuge, Corvallis vicinity, 4/11/85, A, C, D, 85000789

First Congregational Church, 8th and Madison Sts., Corvallis, 12/09/81, A, C, a, 81000473

Fort Hoskins Site, Address Restricted, Kings Valley vicinity, 5/01/74, A, D, 74001672

Gaylord, Charles, House, 600 NW. Seventh St., Corvallis, 6/21/91, A, C, b, 91000805

Hadley-Locke House, 704 NW 9th St., Corvallis, 12/21/81, B, C, 81000474

Harris Bridge [Oregon Covered Bridges TR], W of Wren, Wren vicinity, 11/29/79, A, C, g, 79002040

Hayden Bridge [Oregon Covered Bridges TR], W of Alsea, Alsea vicinity, 11/29/79, A, C, 79002034

Helm-Hout House, 844 SW 5th St., Corvallis, 6/06/85, C, 85001176

Irwin, Richard S., Barn, 26208 Finley Refuge Rd., Corvallis vicinity, 7/07/88, A, C, 88000954

Julian Hotel, 105 SW 2nd St., Corvallis, 3/22/84, A, B, C, 84002933

King, Charles, House, 22930 Harris Rd., Philomath vicinity, 6/01/90, C, 90000833

King, Isaac, House and Barn, N of Philomath off OR 223, Philomath vicinity, 10/29/75, A, C, 75001579

Kline, Lewis G., Building, 146 S.W. Second St., Corvallis, 2/27/86, C, 86000293

Kline, Lewis G., House, 308 NW 8th St., Corvallis, 12/09/81, B, C, 81000475

Lewisburg Hall and Warehouse Company Building, 6000 NE. Elliott Cir., Corvallis, 6/19/91, A, 91000804

Monroe State Bank Building, 190 S. Fifth St., Monroe, 2/26/92, A, B, C, 92000065

Pernot, Dr. Henry S., House, 242 SW 5th St., Corvallis, 4/29/82, B, C, 82003720

Philomath College, Main St., Philomath, 12/11/72, A, C, a, 72001078

Pi Beta Phi Sorority House, 3002 NW Harrison Blvd., Corvallis, 6/14/82, C, 82003721

Rickard, Peter, Farmstead, SW of Corvallis, Corvallis vicinity, 9/15/83, A, B, C, 83002142

Schuster, Charles L., House, 228 N.W. Twenty-eighth, Corvallis, 10/09/86, A, B, C, a, 86002843

Soap Creek School, 37465 Soap Creek Rd., Corvallis vicinity, 6/19/91, A, C, 91000803

Starr, Edwin and Anna, House, 26845 McFarland Rd., Monroe, 10/09/86, C, 86000840

Taylor, George, House, 504 SW 6th St., Corvallis, 12/09/81, B, C, 81000476

Taylor, Jack, House, 806 SW 5th St., Corvallis, 12/09/81, A, C, 81000470

Wilson, James O., House, 340 SW 5th St., Corvallis, 11/06/80, B, C, 80004546

Woodward, Elias, House, 442 NW 4th St., Corvallis, 8/11/83, B, C, 83002143

Clackamas County

Ainsworth, Capt. John C., House, 19131 S. Leland Rd., Oregon City vicinity, 3/26/73, B, C, 73001573

Albright, Daniel, Farm, E of Marquam, Marquam vicinity, 10/30/79, C, 79003734

Anthony, Herman, Farm, NE of Canby at 10205 S. New Era Rd., Canby vicinity, 3/26/79, A, C, 79002041

Babcock, Charles C., House, 1214 Washington St., Oregon City, 10/29/82, B, C, 82001966

Bailey, Lawrence D., House, 13908 SE. Fair Oaks Ave., Milwaukie vicinity, 2/23/90, C, 90000290

Baker, Horace, Log Cabin, S of Carver off OR 224, Carver vicinity, 12/12/76, B, C, 76001578

Barclay, Dr. Forbes, House, 719 Center St., Oregon City, 11/05/74, B, C, b, 74001676

Barlow Road, Roughly, N of Salmon and White Rivers from Rhododendron to SW of Wamic, Mt. Hood NF, Rhodendron vicinity, 4/13/92, A, 92000334

Barlow, William, House, SW of Canby, 24670 U.S. 99E, Canby vicinity, 2/15/77, B, C, 77001098

Bates, John M. and Elizabeth, House No. 3 [Wade Pipes Residences for John and Elizabeth Bates MPS], 16884 SW. Bryant Rd., Lake Oswego, 6/14/90, C, 90000831

Bates, John M. and Elizabeth, House No. 4 [Wade Pipes Residences for John and Elizabeth Bates MPS], 4101 South Shore Blvd., Lake Oswego, 6/13/90, C, g, 90000832

Bates, John M. and Elizabeth, House No. 2 [Wade Pipes Residences for John and Elizabeth Bates MPS], 16948 SW. Bryant Rd., Lake Oswego, 6/13/90, C, 90000847

Bell Station Store, 9300 S.E. Bell Ave., Portland, 9/10/87, A, 87001558

Black, Dr. Walter, House, 1125 Maple St., Lake Oswego, 2/20/91, C, 91000045

Boutwell, W. S. and Gladys, House, 920 SW Fairway Rd., Lake Oswego, 2/20/91, C, 91000052

Broetje, John F. and John H., House, 3101 S.E. Courtney Rd., Oak Grove, 9/15/87, A, B, C, 87001498

Canemah Historic District, Roughly bounded by Willamette River, 5th Ave., Marshall and Paquet Sts., Oregon City, 10/11/78, A, C, 78002279

Clackamas Lake Ranger Station Historic District [Depression-Era Buildings TR (AD)], S of Government Camp on Skyline Rd., Government Camp vicinity, 4/22/81, A, C, g, 81000477

Clark, Elizabeth, House, 812 John Adams St., Oregon City, 10/25/90, C, 90001590

Cross, Harvey, House, 809 Washington St., Oregon City, 10/30/79, B, C, b, 79002043

Clackamas County—Continued

Damascus School, 14711 SE Anderson Rd., Damascus, 12/03/80, A, C, 80003304

Dana, Marshall, House, 15725 SE. Dana Ave., Milwaukee vicinity, 3/09/92, B, C, 92000083

Dibble, Horace L., House, 616 S. Molalla Ave., Molalla, 12/19/74, A, C, 74001675

Ermatinger, Francis, House, 619 Sixth St., Oregon City, 9/17/87, B, C, b, 77001099

Ertz, Charles W., House, 1650 North Shore Rd., Lake Oswego, 3/05/92, C, 92000081

First Congregational Church of Oregon City, 6th and John Adams Sts., Oregon City, 8/26/82, C, a, 82003723

Foster, Philip, Farm, Off OR 211, Eagle Creek, 8/15/80, A, B, C, 80003305

Francis, Clarence E., House, 9717 SE. Cambridge Ln., Milwaukie, 2/19/93, B, C, 93000015

Hackett, Erwin Charles, House, 415 17th St., Oregon City, 2/14/85, B, C, 85000292

Hall—Chaney House, 10200 SE Cambridge La., Milwaukie, 9/08/88, C, 88001522

Holmes, William L., House, 534 Holmes Lane, Oregon City, 12/02/74, A, B, C, 74001678

Howard's Gristmill, 26401 S. Hwy. 213, Mulino, 12/10/81, B, 81000478

Jackson, C. S. "Sam", Log House, 14999 S. Springwater Rd., Oregon City vicinity, 12/09/81, B, C, 81000479

Jantzen, Carl C., Estate, 1850 N. Shore Rd., Lake Oswego, 2/23/90, B, 90000277

Knight, William, House, 525 S.W. Fourth Ave., Canby, 11/05/86, B, 86002961

Kraft-Brandes-Culberston Farmstead, N of Canby at 2525 N. Baker Dr., Canby vicinity, 11/01/82, A, B, C, 82001500

Ladd Estate Company Model House, 432 Country Club Rd., Lake Oswego, 10/30/89, A, C, 89001859

Lake Oswego Hunt Club Ensemble, 2725 SW Iron Mountain Blvd., Lake Oswego, 1/04/88, A, g, 87002236

Lake Oswego Odd Fellows Hall, Durham and Church Sts., Lake Oswego, 3/07/79, A, 79002042

Latourette, Charles David, House, 503 High St., Oregon City, 2/27/80, B, C, 80003306

Latourette, DeWitt Clinton, House, 914 Madison St., Oregon City, 3/05/92, B, C, 92000127

Macksburg Lutheran Church, 10210 S. Macksburg Rd., Canby, 6/14/82, A, C, a, 82003722

Mathieson—Worthington House, 885 McVey Ave., Lake Oswego, 6/01/90, C, 90000837

McCarver, Morton Matthew, House, 554 Warner-Parrot Rd., Oregon City, 1/21/74, C, 74001677

McLoughlin House National Historic Site, McLoughlin Park, between 7th and 8th Sts., Oregon City, 10/15/66, B, b, f, NPS, 66000637

Milne, James, House, 224 Center St., Oregon City, 3/12/79, C, b, 79002044

Oregon Iron Company Furnace, George Rogers Park, Lake Oswego, 2/12/74, A, 74001674

Oregon Trail, Barlow Road Segment, NW of Wemme, Wemme vicinity, 11/20/74, A, 74001679

Petzold, Richard B., Building, 714 Main St., Oregon City, 3/05/92, C, 92000084

Petzold, Richard, House, 504 Sixth St., Oregon City, 10/31/85, C, 85003452

Robbins—Melcher—Schatz Farmstead, 4875 SW. Schatz Rd., Tualatin, 2/19/93, C, 93000017

Rock Corral on the Barlow Road, W of Brightwood off U.S. 26 near Sandy River, Brightwood vicinity, 12/19/74, A, 74001673

Rock Creek Methodist Church, W of Molalla off OR 211, Molalla vicinity, 10/29/75, A, C, a, 75001580

Sherrard—Fenton House, 13100 SW Riverside Dr., Lake Oswego vicinity, 2/20/91, C, 91000051

Shindler, William, House, 3235 SE. Harrison St., Milwaukie, 1/18/90, B, 89001867

Silcox Hut, Timberline Rd., Timberline Lodge vicinity, 1/19/85, C, g, 85000144

St. John the Evangelist Roman Catholic Church, SW of Zigzag on Truman Rd., Zigzag vicinity, 12/21/79, A, C, a, b, g, 79002045

Storey, George Lincoln, House, 910 Pierce St., Oregon City, 3/10/83, B, C, 83002144

Straight, Hiram A., House, 16000 S. Depot Lane, Park Place, 2/17/78, B, C, 78002280

Timberline Lodge, 6 mi. (9.6 km) N of Government Camp in Mount Hood National Forest, Government Camp vicinity, 11/12/73, A, C, g, NHL, 73001572

Vaughan, William Hatchette, House, 14900 S. Macksburg Rd., Molalla, 5/27/93, B, C, 93000456

Vonder Ahe, Fred, House and Summer Kitchen, 625 Metzler Ave., Molalla, 3/26/76, C, b, 76001580

Walden, Nicholas O., House, 1847 SE 5th Ave., West Linn, 9/07/84, B, C, 84002935

Weinstein, Clara and Samuel B., House, 16847 SW. Greenbriar Rd., Lake Oswego, 3/05/92, C, 92000082

White—Kellogg House, 19000 S. Central Point Rd., Oregon City vicinity, 5/16/89, B, 89000415

Willamette Falls Locks, W bank of Willamette River, West Linn, 2/05/74, A, C, 74001680

Wilson, Andrew P., House, 11188 SE. 27th Ave., Milwaukie, 6/01/90, C, 90000838

Zigzag Ranger Station [Depression-Era Buildings TR], Mt. Hood National Forest, Zigzag vicinity, 4/08/86, A, C, 86000842

Clatsop County

Astor Building, 1203 Commercial St., Astoria, 9/07/84, A, C, 84002938

Astor, John Jacob, Hotel, 1401 Commercial St., Astoria, 11/16/79, A, C, 79002046

Astoria City Hall, 1618 Exchange St., Astoria, 9/07/84, A, C, 84002940

Astoria Column, Coxcomb Hill, Astoria, 5/02/74, C, g, 74001681

Astoria Elks Building, 453 Eleventh St., Astoria, 6/01/90, A, C, 90000843

Astoria Fire House No. 2, 2968 Marine Dr., Astoria, 9/07/84, A, C, 84002946

Astoria Victory Monument, Columbia St., Bond and W. Marine Dr., Astoria, 11/15/84, A, C, f, 84000466

Astoria Wharf and Warehouse Company, Water St. between 3rd & 4th Sts., Astoria, 6/14/84, A, C, 84002949

Bartlett, Robert Rensselaer, House, 1215 Fifteenth St., Astoria, 6/05/86, B, C, 86001236

Cherry, Peter L., House, 836 15th St., Astoria, 9/07/84, B, C, 84002952

Clatsop County Courthouse, 749 Commerical St., Astoria, 4/05/84, A, C, 84002954

Clatsop County Jail (Old), 732 Duane St., Astoria, 5/19/83, A, C, 83002145

Erickson—Larsen Ensemble, 3025–3027 Marine Dr., Astoria, 2/20/91, A, 91000055

Ferguson, Albert W., House, 1661 Grand Ave., Astoria, 9/07/84, C, 84002955

Fisher, Ferdinand, House, 687 Twelfth St., Astoria, 5/06/87, C, 87000668

Flavel, Capt. George, House and Carriage House, 441 8th St., Astoria, 11/28/80, B, C, 80003307

Flavel, Captain George Conrad, House, 627 Fifteenth St., Astoria, 6/05/86, C, 86001222

Flavel, George C. and Winona, House, 818 Grand Ave., Astoria, 2/19/91, B, C, b, 91000054

Foard, Martin, House, 690 Seventeenth St., Astoria, 6/05/86, C, 86001221

Fort Astoria, 15th and Exchange Sts., Astoria, 10/15/66, A, B, NHL, 66000639

Fort Clatsop National Memorial, 4.5 mi. S of Astoria, Astoria vicinity, 10/15/66, B, e, f, NPS, 66000640

Fort Stevens, Fort Stevens State Park, Hammond, 9/22/71, A, C, g, 71000678

Fullam, William and Nellie, House [Seaside MPS], 781 S. Prom, Seaside, 10/25/91, A, C, 91001570

Gilbert, Rev. William S., House, 725 Eleventh St., Astoria, 6/03/93, B, a, 93000457

Goodwin—Wilkinson Farmhouse, US 26/101 W of Cullaby Lake, Warrenton vicinity, 3/09/92, A, C, 92000128

Grace Episcopal Church Rectory, Old, 637 16th St., Astoria, 3/09/90, B, a, 90000375

Grace Episcopal Church and Rectory, 1545 Franklin Ave., Astoria, 9/07/84, C, a, 84002957

Gray, Capt. J. H. D., House, 1687 Grand Ave., Astoria, 9/07/84, B, C, 84002958

Griffin, John N., House, 1643 Grand Ave., Astoria, 10/25/84, C, 84000119

Haller—Black House [Seaside MPS], 841 South Prom, Seaside, 10/25/91, A, C, 91001568

Herschell, Allan, Two-Abreast Carousel [Oregon Historic Wooden Carousels TR], 300 Broadway, Seaside, 8/26/87, A, C, 87001382

Hlilusqahih Site (35CLT37), Address Restricted, Knappa vicinity, 4/26/84, D, 84002959

Hobson, John, House, 469 Bond St., Astoria, 2/17/78, B, C, 78002281

Holmes, Gustavus, House, 682 34th St., Astoria, 10/25/84, B, C, 84000121

ISABELLA Shipwreck Site and Remains, Address Restricted, Astoria vicinity, 9/21/89, A, C, D, 89001385

Clatsop County—Continued

Indian Point Site (35 CLT 34), Address Restricted, Svensen vicinity, 5/09/84, D, 84002960

Kinney, Marshall J., Cannery, 1 Sixth St., Astoria, 6/30/89, A, C, 89000515

Larson, Peter and Maria, House, 611 31st St., Astoria, 3/09/90, A, C, 90000374

Latourette, Charles, David, House, 683 D St., Gearhart, 3/22/84, A, B, C, 84002962

Lightship WAL-604, COLUMBIA, 1792 Maritime Dr., Astoria, 12/20/89, A, C, g, NHL, 89002463

Noonan—Norblad House, 1625 Grand Ave., Astoria, 3/31/88, B, C, 88000303

Page, Judge C. H., House, 1393 Franklin Ave., Astoria, 6/06/85, C, 85001177

Preston, Charles, House [Seaside MPS], 141 Ave. I, Seaside, 10/25/91, A, C, 91001569

Staples, Norris, House, 1031 14th St., Astoria, 10/25/84, B, C, 84000126

Stevens, Charles, House, 1388 Franklin Ave., Astoria, 6/06/85, B, C, 85001178

Svenson Blacksmith Shop, 1769 Exchange St., Astoria, 11/06/86, A, 86003015

Tillamook Rock Lighthouse, SW of Seaside, Seaside vicinity, 12/09/81, A, C, 81000480

US Post Office and Custom House [Significant US Post Offices in Oregon 1900-1941 TR], 750 Commercial St., Astoria, 3/04/85, C, 85000542

Union Fishermen's Cooperative Packing Company Alderbrook Station, 4900 Ash St., Astoria, 2/20/91, A, 91000053

Uniontown—Alameda Historic District, Marine Dr. and Alameda Ave., between Hume and Hull Aves., Astoria, 8/25/88, A, C, a, b, f, 88001311

Warren Investment Company Housing Group, 656, 674, and 690 Eleventh St., Astoria, 6/05/86, C, 86001223

Warren, Daniel Knight, House, 107 Skipanon Rd., Warrenton, 9/08/88, B, C, 88001521

West, Oswald, Coastal Retreat, 1981 Pacific Ave., Cannon Beach, 2/26/92, B, C, 92000066

Young, Andrew, House, 3720 Duane Ave., Astoria, 6/26/86, B, C, 86001391

Young, Benjamin, House and Carriage House, 3652 Duane St., Astoria, 3/07/79, B, C, 79002047

Columbia County

Cox-Williams House, 280 S. 1st St., St. Helens, 11/01/82, C, 82001501

Flippin, Thomas J., House, 620 Tichenor St., Clatskanie, 3/07/79, B, C, 79002048

Longview Bridge [Historic Bridges/Tunnels in Washington State TR], Spans Columbia river, RAINIER, 7/16/82, A, C, 82004208

Moeck, George F., House, 713 B St., W., Rainier, 4/14/78, B, 78002283

Portland and Southwestern Railroad Tunnel, Address Restricted, Scappoose vicinity, 8/17/81, A, C, g, 81000481

St. Helens Downtown Historic District, Roughly Strand, 1st, 2nd, 3rd, Cowlitz, St. Helens Sts., and Columbia Blvd., St. Helens, 10/25/84, A, C, a, 84000137

Watts, James Grant, House, 206 SE 1st St., Scappoose, 11/28/80, B, C, 80003308

Coos County

Abernethy, Edwin and Ethel, House, Box 103, Sitkum Route, Myrtle Point vicinity, 9/22/88, A, 88001532

Black, A. H. and Company, Building, 531 Spruce St., Myrtle Point, 10/25/90, C, 90001586

Breuer Building, 460 W. First Ave., Bandon, 10/02/92, A, 92001308

Cape Arago Lighthouse [Lighthouse Stations of Oregon MPS], Gregory Point, N of Cape Arago and about 2 mi. SW of Coos Bay entrance, Charleston vicinity, 5/13/93, A, C, 73002338

Cary, Leo J., House [Coquille MPS], 572 E. First St., Coquille, 10/14/92, B, C, 92001317

Chandler Hotel and Annex, 187 W. Central Ave., Coos Bay, 6/14/84, A, C, 84002966

Coke, J. S., Building, 150 Central Ave., Coos Bay, 2/20/91, A, B, 91000048

Coos Bay Carnegie Library, 515 Market St., Coos Bay, 2/27/86, A, C, 86000297

Coos Bay National Bank Building, 201 Central Ave., Coos Bay, 10/30/89, A, C, 89001868

Coquille City Hall [Coquille MPS], 99 E. Second St., Coquille, 10/14/92, A, C, 92001318

Coquille River Life Boat Station, 390 SW 1st St., Bandon, 8/03/84, A, C, 84002969

Coquille River Light, Bullard's Beach State Park, Bandon, 3/22/74, A, C, g, 74001682

Harlocker, Judge Lintner, House [Coquille MPS], 18 S. Collier St., Coquille, 10/14/92, C, 92001315

Hub Department Store Building, 125 Central Ave., Coos Bay, 10/02/92, A, B, 92001307

Marshfield Elks Temple, 195 S. 2nd St., Coos Bay, 5/19/83, A, C, 83002146

Marshfield Hotel, 275 Broadway, Coos Bay, 3/22/84, A, C, 84002971

Marshfield Sun Printing Plant, 1049 N. Front St., Coos Bay, 3/21/73, A, 73001574

Myrtle Arms Apartment Building, Sixth and Central Sts., Coos Bay, 10/31/85, C, 85003478

Nasburg—Lockhart House, 687 N. Third St., Coos Bay, 12/02/85, B, C, 85003038

Nerdrum, Hjalte, House, 955 S. Fifth St., Coos Bay, 5/27/93, A, C, 93000435

Olsson, Captain Bror W., House, 631 S. Tenth St., Coos Bay, 11/02/86, B, g, 86002905

Paulson, John E. and Christina, House, 86 N. Dean St., Coquille, 8/11/83, B, C, 83002147

Philpott Site (35 CS 1), Address Restricted, Bandon vicinity, 10/18/79, D, 79002049

Powers Hotel, 310 Second Ave., Powers, 6/05/86, A, 86001216

Reorganized Church of Latter Day Saints, 7th and Maple Sts., Myrtle Point, 10/18/79, A, C, a, 79002050

Sandy Creek Bridge [Oregon Covered Bridges TR], Sandy Creek Rd., Remote, 11/29/79, A, C, 79002051

Sherwood, A. J., House [Coquille MPS], 257 E. Main St., Coquille, 10/14/92, C, 92001314

St. James Episcopal Church [Coquille MPS], 210 E. Third St., Coquille, 10/14/92, A, C, a, 92001316

Tower, Maj. Morton, House, 486 Schetter Ave., Coos Bay, 10/31/85, B, C, 85003453

Tower-Flanagan House, 476 Newmark Ave., Coos Bay, 2/16/84, A, C, 84002976

Tribal Hall of the Confederated Tribes of Coos, Lower Umpqua and Siuslaw Indians, 338 Wallace St., Coos Bay, 3/29/89, A, g, 89000202

Crook County

Baldwin, Thomas M., House, 126 W. First St., Prineville, 9/10/87, B, C, 87001523

Crook County Bank Building, 246 N. Main St., Prineville, 6/19/91, C, 91000802

Elliott, Marion Reed, House, 305 W. First St., Prineville, 2/21/89, C, 89000049

Lamonta Compound—Prineville Supervisor's Warehouse [Depression-Era Buildings TR], Ochoco National Forest, Prineville, 4/08/86, A, C, 86000846

Old First National Bank of Prineville, and Foster and Hyde Store, 247 N. Main St., Prineville, 12/02/85, A, C, 85003035

Curry County

Cape Blanco Lighthouse [Lighthouse Stations of Oregon MPS], Westernmost part of Cape Blanco, W of Sixes, Sixes vicinity, 4/21/93, A, C, 73002339

Cape Blanco Lithic Site, Address Restricted, Port Orford vicinity, 6/04/92, D, 92000667

Central Building, 703 Chetco Ave., Brookings, 4/01/80, B, C, 80003309

Gold Beach Ranger Station [Depression-Era Buildings TR], Siskiyou National Forest, Gold Beach, 4/08/86, A, C, 86000818

HUME, MARY D., Port of Gold Beach, Gold Beach, 8/01/79, B, b, 79002052

Hughes, Patrick, House, Cape Blanco State Park, Sixes vicinity, 11/28/80, B, C, 80003310

Indian Sands, Address Restricted, Brookings vicinity, 6/04/92, D, 92000668

Rogue River Ranch, E of Agness near confluence of Mule Creek and Rogue River, Agness vicinity, 12/29/75, A, 75001581

Sixes Hotel, 93316 Sixes River Rd., Sixes, 10/22/92, A, b, 92001325

Deschutes County

Bend Amateur Atheletic Club Gymnasium [Historic Development of the Bend Company in Bend, Oregon MPS], NE of Wall and Idaho Sts., Bend, 11/25/83, A, C, 83004165

Deschutes County—Continued

Bend High School [Historic Development of The Bend Company in Bend, Oregon MPS], 529 NW. Wall St., Bend, 9/23/93, A, C, 93000916

Bend Skyliners Lodge, 11 mi. (17.6 km) W of Bend in Deschutes National Forest, Bend vicinity, 6/13/78, C, g, 78002285

Boyd, Charles, Homestead Group, N of Bend at 20410 Rivermall Ave., Bend vicinity, 8/31/82, B, b, 82003724

Deschutes County Library [Historic Development of The Bend Company in Bend, Oregon MPS], 507 NW. Wall St., Bend, 9/23/93, A, 93000914

I.O.O.F. Organization Camp, Paulina Lake, Deschutes National Forest, LaPine vicinity, 7/14/83, C, 83002148

McCann, Thomas, House, 440 NW Congress St., Bend, 4/01/80, B, C, 80003311

New Redmond Hotel, 521 S. 6th St., Redmond, 10/28/80, A, C, 80003312

New Taggart Hotel, 215 NW Greenwood Ave., Bend, 2/29/88, C, 88000087

O'Kane Building, 115 NW Oregon Ave., Bend, 11/06/86, A, C, 86002965

Old US Post Office, 745 NW Wall, Bend, 2/14/85, A, C, 85000293

Paulina Lake Guard Station [Depression-Era Buildings TR], Deschutes National Park, Bend vicinity, 4/11/86, A, C, g, 86000825

Reid School [Historic Development of the Bend Company in Bend, Oregon MPS], 460 NW Wall St., Bend, 10/16/79, A, C, 79002053

Rock O' the Range Bridge [Oregon Covered Bridges TR], N of Bend, Bend vicinity, 11/29/79, A, C, g, 79002054

Smith, N. P., Pioneer Hardware Store, 935-937 NW Wall St., Bend, 4/05/84, A, B, C, 84002980

Stover, B. A. and Ruth, House, 1 NW. Rocklyn Rd., Bend, 2/20/92, B, C, 92000061

Trinity Episcopal Church [Historic Development of The Bend Company in Bend, Oregon MPS], 469 NW. Wall St., Bend, 9/23/93, A, a, 93000915

Douglas County

Applegate, Charles, House, NE of Yoncalla on Halo Trail, Yoncalla vicinity, 3/17/75, B, C, 75001583

Brown, Henry, House, W of Elkton off OR 38, Elkton vicinity, 10/30/79, B, C, 79002057

Brown, Will Q., House and Wash House, 274 S. Main St., Riddle, 9/10/87, B, C, 87001539

Canyonville Methodist Church, 2nd and Pine Sts., Canyonville, 4/05/84, A, C, a, 84002983

China Ditch, Upper reaches of N. Myrtle Cr., Myrtle Creek vicinity, 5/22/91, A, 91000616

Curry, Nathaniel, House, 1458 Quail Lane, Roseburg, 11/25/83, A, C, 83004166

Drain, Charles D., Jr., House, 100 E. Main St., Drain, 12/12/78, B, C, 78002286

First Presbyterian Church of Roseburg, 823 SE Lane St., Roseburg, 7/28/88, C, a, 88001162

Floed, Creed, House, 544 SE Douglas St., Roseburg, 12/31/74, B, C, 74001684

Glide Ranger Station [Depression-Era Buildings TR], Umpqua National Forest, Glide, 4/08/86, A, C, g, 86000820

Howell—Kohlhagen House, 848 SE Jackson St., Roseburg, 7/28/88, B, C, 88001145

Laurelwood Historic District, Roughly bounded by the S. Umpqua R., Laurelwood Ct., and Bowden Ave., Roseburg, 10/16/90, A, C, 90001521

Methodist Episcopal Church South, 809 SE Main St., Roseburg, 6/06/85, A, C, a, g, 85001179

Mill-Pine Neighborhood Historic District, Roughly bounded by Short St., Mosher Ave., Stephens St. and Rice Ave., Roseburg, 6/20/85, A, C, 85001348

Miller's Mountain House, 1195 Roberts Mountain Rd., Roseburg vicinity, 10/25/84, A, C, 84000129

Milo Academy Bridge [Oregon Covered Bridges TR], SE of Days Creek, Days Creek vicinity, 11/29/79, A, C, g, 79002055

Moyer, C. E., Nurseries Property, 8374 Old Hwy. 99, S, Winston vicinity, 7/22/88, A, B, 88001114

Oakland Historic District, Roughly bounded by Chestnut, 1st, Cedar, and 8th Sts., Oakland, 3/30/79, A, C, a, 79002058

Parrott, Moses, House, 1772 SE Jackson St., Roseburg, 11/06/80, B, C, 80003313

Rice Brothers and Adams Building, 136 Main St., Myrtle Creek, 8/11/83, A, C, 83002149

Rice, Napoleon, House, 709 Kane St., Roseburg, 12/09/81, B, C, 81000482

Roaring Camp Bridge [Oregon Covered Bridges TR], W of Drain, Drain vicinity, 11/29/79, A, C, 79002056

Roseburg, Oregon, National Guard Armory, 1034 SE. Oak St., Roseburg, 5/27/93, A, C, 93000447

Smith, Bernard Pitzer, House, 15892 Old Hwy. 99, S, Myrtle Creek vicinity, 8/25/88, C, b, 88001313

Stephens Community Historic District, Fort McKay and Scott Henry Rds., Sutherlin vicinity, 10/25/84, A, C, a, 84000135

Susan Creek Indian Mounds Site, Address Restricted, Glide vicinity, 11/20/74, D, a, 74001683

Sutherlin Bank Building, 101 W. Central Ave., Sutherlin, 8/01/84, A, C, 84002987

Tiller Ranger Station [USDA Forest Service Administrative Buildings in Oregon and Washington Built by the CCC MPS], OR 227, Umpqua NF, Tiller, 3/06/91, A, C, 91000162

U.S. Post Office, 704 SE Cass Ave., Roseburg, 6/18/79, A, C, 79002059

US Goast Guard Station—Umpqua River, Administration and Equipment Buildings, Douglas Co. Rd. 87, Winchester Bay vicinity, 6/04/92, A, C, 92000662

Umpaqua River Light House, SW of Winchester Bay off U.S. 101, Winchester Bay vicinity, 10/21/77, A, 77001100

Weaver-Worthington Farmstead, E of Canyonville, Canyonville vicinity, 8/01/84, B, C, 84002996

Willis, Judge William R., House, 744 SE Rose St., Roseburg, 6/05/75, B, C, b, 75001582

Wimer, James, Octagonal Barn, 1191 Coos Bay Wagon Rd., Lookingglass, 12/02/85, C, 85003039

Winston, William C. and Agnes, House, Winston Section Rd., Winston, 9/10/87, A, 87001540

Gilliam County

Barker, S. B., Building, 333 S. Main St., Condon, 2/21/89, B, C, 89000053

Rice, Silas A., Log House, OR 19 at Burns Park, Condon, 10/31/91, A, C, b, 91001556

Grant County

Advent Christian Church, 261 W. Main St., John Day, 6/10/92, C, a, 92000665

Cant, James, Ranch Historic District, OR 19, Dayville vicinity, 6/21/84, A, C, NPS, 84003000

Fremont Powerhouse, Umatilla National Forest, Granite vicinity, 8/19/83, A, C, g, 83002151

John Day Compound, Supervisor's Warehouse [Depression-Era Buildings TR], Malheur National Forest, John Day, 4/11/86, A, C, g, 86000836

Kam Wah Chung Company Building, Canton St., John Day City Park, John Day, 3/20/73, A, 73001575

St. Thomas' Episcopal Church, 135 Washington St., Canyon City, 11/21/74, A, C, a, 74001685

Sumpter Valley Railway Passenger Station, Main and Bridge Sts., Prairie City, 5/05/81, A, C, 81000483

Sumpter Valley Railway, Middle Fork-John Day River, Sumpter Valley Railway's Middle Fork Spur between Bates and Susanville, Bates vicinity, 8/03/87, A, 87001066

Supervisor's House No. 1001 [Depression-Era Buildings TR], Malheur National Forest, John Day, 4/11/86, A, C, g, 86000833

Harney County

Allison Ranger Station, NE of Burns, Burns vicinity, 9/12/80, A, C, 80003314

Double-O Ranch Historic District, Double-O County Rd., Burns vicinity, 10/25/82, A, C, 82001502

French, Pete, Round Barn, N of Diamond Station, Burns vicinity, 9/10/71, A, 71000679

Frenchglen Hotel, OR 205, Frenchglen, 11/15/84, A, 84000469

P Ranch, S of Burns, Burns vicinity, 1/29/79, A, C, 79002060

Riddle Ranch, Little Blitzen R., E of Donner and Blitzen R., Frenchglen vicinity, 5/23/91, A, C, 91000614

Sod House Ranch, S of Burns, Burns vicinity, 1/29/79, A, C, 79002061

Hood River County

Cascade Locks Marine Park, On the Columbia River, Cascade Locks, 5/15/74, A, C, 74001686

Cascade Locks Work Center [Depression-Era Buildings TR], Mt. Hood National Forest, Cascade Locks, 4/11/86, A, C, g, 86000829

Cloud Cap Inn, NE flank of Mt. Hood in Mt. Hood National Forest, Mt. Hood, 10/18/74, A, C, 74001687

Cloud Cap-Tilly Jane Recreation Area Historic District [Depression-Era Buildings TR (AD)], S of Parkdale, Parkdale vicinity, 3/22/81, A, C, 81000485

Columbia Gorge Hotel, W of Hood River at 9000 Westcliffe Dr., Hood River, 9/21/79, A, B, C, 79003736

Copple, Simpson, House, 911 Montello Ave., Hood River, 3/06/87, B, C, 87000362

Davidson—Childs House, 725 Oak St., Hood River, 10/30/89, B, C, b, 89001864

DeHart, Edward J., House, 3820 Westcliff Dr., Hood River vicinity, 2/23/90, C, 90000276

Duckwall, John C., House, 811 Oak St., Hood River, 6/16/89, B, 89000512

Hartley, Orrin B., House, 1029 State St., Hood River, 10/30/89, C, 89001860

IOOF—Paris Fair Building, 315 Oak St., Hood River, 10/25/90, A, 90001598

Loomis, Robert and Mabel, House, 1100 State St., Hood River, 10/25/90, C, 90001599

Mt. Hood School House, OR 35, Mt. Hood, 4/30/87, A, C, 87000680

Murphy, Lester and Hazel, House, 1006 Sherman St., Hood River, 10/25/90, C, 90001600

Oak Grove Schoolhouse, SW of Hood River at 2121 Reed Rd., Hood River vicinity, 3/05/79, A, C, 79002062

Oregon—Washington Railroad & Navigation Company Passenger Station, Foot of First St., Hood River, 7/28/88, A, C, 88001159

Parkdale Ranger Station [Depression-Era Buildings TR], Mt. Hood National Forest, Parkdale, 4/11/86, A, C, g, 86000822

Potter, Miles B. and Eleanor, House, 4095 Belmont Dr., Hood River vicinity, 10/08/92, B, C, 92001326

Ries—Thompson House, 4993 Baseline Rd., Parkdale, 10/08/92, A, 92001327

Roe—Parker House, 416 State St., Hood River, 3/09/88, C, 88000085

Shaw—Dumble House, 318 Ninth St., Hood River, 10/30/90, B, C, 90001601

Slade, J. E., House, 1209 State St., Hood River, 2/23/89, C, 89000065

Smith, E. L., Building, 213–215 Oak St., Hood River, 6/19/91, A, C, 91000801

Thompson, Clark, House, 22 NW Cragmont, Cascade Locks, 3/02/89, C, 89000124

Valley Theater, 4945 Baseline Rd., Parkdale, 6/01/90, A, 90000842

Waucoma Hotel, 2nd St., Hood River, 12/10/81, A, C, 81000484

Jackson County

Ahlstrom, Nils, House, 248 5th St., Ashland, 2/15/80, B, C, 80003315

Anderson, Thomas N., House, 719 Second Ave., Gold Hill, 6/01/90, C, 90000845

Ashland Depot Hotel, South Wing, 624 A St., Ashland, 2/19/91, A, b, 91000047

Ashland Masonic Lodge Building, 25 N. Main St., Ashland, 6/04/92, A, 92000663

Ashland Municipal Powerhouse, Ashland Creek Canyon, Ashland, 9/10/87, A, C, 87001563

Ashland Oregon National Guard Armory, 208 Oak St., Ashland, 9/10/87, A, C, 87001564

Atkinson, W. H., House, 125 N. Main St., Ashland, 10/16/79, B, C, 79002063

BPOE Lodge No. 1168, 202 N. Central Ave., Medford, 11/28/80, A, C, 80003323

Baker, Sophenia Ish, House, 902 W. McAndrews Rd., Medford vicinity, 9/09/93, A, C, 93000924

Barclay—Klum House, 102 E. Main St., Ashland, 6/01/90, C, 90000835

Barnum Hotel, 204 N. Front St., Medford, 3/22/84, A, C, 84003009

Beach, Baldwin, House, 348 Hargadine St., Ashland, 3/28/79, B, C, 79002064

Beall, Robert Vinton, House, S of Central Point at 1253 Beall Lane, Central Point vicinity, 10/18/79, B, C, 79002069

Boslough-Claycomb House, 1 Hillcrest St., Ashland, 12/09/81, C, 81000486

Bowne, Walter, House, 1845 Old Stage Rd., Jacksonville vicinity, 2/23/90, C, 90000279

Buckhorn Mineral Springs Resort, 2200 Buckhorn Springs Rd., Ashland, 3/03/89, A, 89000064

Bursell, Victor and Bertha, House, 3075 Hanley Rd., Central Point vicinity, 4/29/82, B, C, 82003725

Butte Falls Ranger Station [Depression-Era Buildings TR], Rogue River National Forest, Butte Falls, 4/11/86, A, C, g, 86000824

Bybee, Frank E., House, 4491 Jacksonville Hwy., Jacksonville vicinity, 12/09/81, A, C, 81000492

Bybee, William, House, 883 Old Stage Rd., Medford vicinity, 2/15/77, B, C, 77001102

Campbell, Richard Posey, House, 94 Bush St., Ashland, 2/12/80, C, 80003316

Carter, E. V., House, 505 Siskiyou Blvd., Ashland, 3/07/79, B, C, 79002065

Carter, H. B., House, 91 Gresham St., Ashland, 11/02/77, C, 77001101

Carter-Fortmiller House, 514 Siskiyou Blvd., Ashland, 12/21/81, B, C, 81000487

Central Point Public School, 450 S. 4th St., Central Point, 12/03/80, A, C, 80003321

Chappell-Swedenburg House, 990 Siskiyou Blvd., Ashland, 11/30/82, B, C, 82001503

Citizen's Banking & Trust Co. Building, 232–242 E. Main St., Ashland, 2/28/85, C, 85000364

Clark, Frank Chamberlain, House, 1917 E. Main St., Medford, 10/29/82, C, 82001504

Colver, Samuel, House, 150 Main St., Phoenix, 10/25/90, B, C, 90001596

Coolidge, Orlando, House, 137 N. Main St., Ashland, 2/12/80, B, C, b, 80003317

Corning Court Ensemble, 5–16 Corning Ct., Medford, 2/19/91, A, b, 91000043

Driver, E. Raymond, House, 4140 Old Stage Rd., Central Point vicinity, 3/09/90, C, 90000372

Dunn, Patrick, Ranch, SE of Ashland on OR 66, Ashland vicinity, 3/08/78, B, 78002287

Eddings-Provost House, 364 Vista St., Ashland, 11/06/80, A, C, 80003318

Enders Building, 250–300 E. Main St., Ashland, 10/23/86, A, B, C, 86002902

Fiero, Conro, House, 4615 Hamrick Rd., Central Point, 12/09/81, A, B, C, 81000490

First Baptist Church, 241 Hargadine St., Ashland, 3/28/79, A, C, a, 79002066

First National Bank, Vaupel Store and Oregon Hotel Buildings, 15 S. Pioneer St. and 70 E. Main St., Ashland, 2/29/80, A, C, 80003319

Fluhrer Bakery Building, 29 N. Holly St., Medford, 5/16/83, A, C, 83002152

Fort Lane Military Post Site, Address Restricted, Central Point vicinity, 9/20/88, A, B, 88001121

Fredenburg, Andrew J., House, 234 S. Holly St., Medford, 6/17/82, B, C, 82003726

Furry, Frederic E., House, SE of Medford at 1720 N. Phoenix Rd., Medford vicinity, 2/29/80, A, C, 80003324

Gates, C. E. "Pop", House, 1307 Queen Anne Ave., Medford, 2/19/91, B, C, 91000042

Glenview Orchard Ensemble, 1395 Carpenter Hill Rd., Phoenix vicinity, 10/23/86, A, C, 86002925

Gold Hill High School, 806 6th Ave., Gold Hill, 2/20/91, A, C, 91000046

Grainger, G. M. and Kate, House, 35 Granite St., Ashland, 2/23/90, B, C, 90000289

Hafer, Edgar F., House, 426 W. 6th St., Medford, 9/01/83, A, B, C, g, 83002153

Hanley, Michael, Farmstead, 1053 Hanley Rd., Medford, 11/25/83, A, B, C, 83004172

Hillcrest Orchard Historic District, 3285 Hillcrest Rd., Medford, 2/16/84, A, B, C, 84003013

Hover, George A., House, 4192 Coleman Creek Rd., Medford vicinity, 9/08/80, B, C, 80003325

IOOF Building, 49–57 N. Main St., Ashland, 2/17/78, A, C, 78002288

Imnaha Guard Station [Depression-Era Buildings TR], Rogue River National Forest, Butte Falls vicinity, 4/11/86, A, C, g, 86000835

Jackson County Courthouse, S. Oakdale Ave. at Eighth St., Medford, 10/23/86, A, C, 86002921

Jacksonville Historic District, Jacksonville city limits, Jacksonville, 11/13/66, A, NHL, 66000950

Jacksonville-to-Fort Klamath Military Wagon Road, S of Butte Falls, Butte Falls vicinity, 5/16/79, A, 79002068

Kane, E. C., House, 386 B St., Ashland, 11/06/86, A, B, C, 86002964

Liberty Building, 201 W. Main St., Medford, 3/14/78, C, 78002292

Lithia Park, 59 Winburn Way, Ashland, 11/22/82, A, C, 82001505

Lodgepole Guard Station [USDA Forest Service Administrative Buildings in Oregon and Washington Built by the CCC MPS], SE of Prospect, Rogue R. NF, Butte Falls vicinity, 3/06/91, A, C, 91000164

Jackson County—Continued

Lost Creek Bridge [Oregon Covered Bridges TR], SE of Lakecreek, Lakecreek vicinity, 11/29/79, A, C, 79002070

Lucas, Robert and Ruth, House and Mary E. Rose House, 59, 77 Sixth St., Ashland, 7/21/88, C, 88001115

Mark Antony Motor Hotel, 212 E. Main St., Ashland, 3/14/78, C, 78002289

McCall, John, House, 153 Oak St., Ashland, 12/09/81, B, C, 81000488

McCredie, William, House, 2685 Old Stage Rd., Central Point vicinity, 9/17/80, B, C, 80003326

McKee Bridge [Oregon Covered Bridges TR], S of Ruch, Ruch vicinity, 11/29/79, A, C, 79002074

McManus, Patrick F., House, 117 W. 1st St., Phoenix, 3/08/78, B, C, 78002293

Medford Carnegie Library, 413 W. Main St., Medford, 7/30/81, A, C, 81000493

Merritt, John W., House and Store, 117 E. Pine St., Central Point, 3/09/92, B, C, 92000129

Nininger, Amos and Vera, House, 80 Hargadine St., Ashland, 10/29/82, A, C, 82001506

Orth, John, House, Main and 3rd Sts., Jacksonville, 4/11/72, C, 72001080

Patton, Hamilton and Edith, House, 245 Valley View Dr., Medford, 9/09/93, C, 93000923

Pedigrift, S. and Sarah J., House, 407 Scenic Ave., Ashland, 2/20/92, C, 92000063

Peerless Rooms Building, 243–249 Fourth St., Ashland, 10/08/92, A, 92001328

Peil, Emil and Alice Applegate, House, 52 Granite St., Ashland, 2/20/92, B, 92000062

Pelton, John and Charlotte, House, 228 B St., Ashland, 9/09/93, C, 93000922

Perozzi, Domingo, House, 88 Granite St., Ashland, 2/12/80, B, C, 80003320

Pickel, Dr. E. B., Rental House, 815 W. Main St., Medford, 10/29/82, C, 82001507

Pracht, Humboldt, House, 234 Vista St., Ashland, 12/23/81, C, 81000489

Prospect Hotel, 39 Mill Creek Dr., Prospect, 2/12/80, A, C, 80003327

Reames, Alfred Evan, House, 816 W. Tenth St., Medford, 2/20/91, B, 91000049

Reddy, Dr. John F. and Mary, House, 122 Oregon Terr., Medford, 9/10/87, B, C, 87001538

Rock Point Hotel, 40 N. River Rd., Gold Hill, 9/04/80, A, C, 80003322

Rogue Elk Hotel, 27390 OR 62, Trail, 2/22/80, A, C, 80003329

Roper, Fordyce, House—Southern Oregon Hospital, 35 S. Second St., Ashland, 12/02/85, A, B, C, b, 85003075

Schuler Apartment Building, 38 N. Oakdale Ave., Medford, 6/19/91, C, 91000800

Shone-Charley House, 305 N. Grape St., Medford, 10/25/84, C, 84000131

Silsby, Col. William H., House, 111 3rd St., Ashland, 2/28/85, C, 85000365

Snowy Butte Flour Mill, Off OR 62, Eagle Point, 9/01/76, A, 76001581

South Oakdale Historic District, Irregular pattern along S. Oakdale Ave. from Stewart Ave. to W. 10th St., Medford, 3/15/79, A, B, C, 79002072

Sparta Building, 12 N. Riverside St., Medford, 10/08/92, A, 92001329

Star Ranger Station [USDA Forest Service Administrative Buildings in Oregon and Washington Built by the CCC MPS], E of Applegate R., Rogue R. NF, Ruch vicinity, 3/06/91, A, C, 91000168

Sweeney, Dr. Charles T. and Mary, House, 2336 Table Rock Rd., Medford, 6/04/92, B, C, 92000664

Taverner, George, House, 912 Siskiyou Blvd., Ashland, 11/07/78, C, 78002290

Tayler—Phipps Building, 221–225 E. Main St., Medford, 2/23/90, C, 90000280

Trinity Episcopal Church, 44 N. 2nd St., Ashland, 4/05/84, A, C, a, 84003015

U.S. Post Office and Courthouse, 310 W. 6th St., Medford, 4/30/79, A, C, 79002073

Union Creek Historic District [Depression-Era Buildings TR (AD)], OR 62, Prospect vicinity, 10/29/80, A, C, g, 80003328

Van Hoevenberg, Henry, Jr., House, 9130 Ramsey Canyon Rd., Gold Hill vicinity, 12/10/81, B, C, 81000491

Wagner Creek School, 8448 Wagner Creek Rd., Talent vicinity, 10/08/92, A, 92001331

Walker, John P., House, 1521 E. Main St., Ashland, 3/14/78, A, C, 78002291

West Side Feed and Sale Stable, 29 S. Grape St., Medford, 12/21/81, A, C, 81000494

White John B., House, 86 N. River Rd., Rock Point, 11/02/78, B, C, 78002294

Wilkinson-Swem Building, 217 E. Main St., Medford, 8/26/82, B, C, 82003727

Wimer Bridge [Oregon Covered Bridges TR], E. Evans Creek Rd, Wimer, 11/29/79, A, C, g, 79002075

Women's Civic Improvement Clubhouse, 59 Winburn Way, Ashland, 6/16/89, A, 89000513

Woolen, Isaac, House, 131 N. Main St., Ashland, 10/16/79, B, C, 79002067

Jefferson County

Oregon Trunk Passenger and Freight Station, Washington St. at the foot of Sixth St., Metolius, 2/27/86, A, C, a, b, 86000285

Josephine County

Ahlf, John and Susanna, House, 762 NW 6th St., Grants Pass, 5/09/83, B, C, 83002154

Calhoun, George, House, 612 NW 5th St., Grants Pass, 12/02/81, B, C, 81000495

Cedar Guard Station No. 1019 [Depression-Era Buildings TR], Illinois Valley Rd., Siskiyou National Forest, Cave Junction, 4/08/86, A, C, 86000837

Clark-Norton House, 127 N.W. D St., Grants Pass, 2/27/86, B, C, 86000290

Clemens, Michael, House, 612 NW 3rd St., Grants Pass, 4/29/82, B, C, 82003728

Croxton, Thomas, House, 1002 NW Washington Blvd., Grants Pass, 3/29/79, B, a, 79002076

Fetzner, Joseph, House, 314 NE. Fetzner St., Grants Pass, 10/25/90, C, 90001595

Flanagan, Dr. William H., House, 720 NW 6th St., Grants Pass, 5/09/83, C, 83002155

Grant Pass City Hall and Fire Station, 4th and H Sts., Grants Pass, 9/07/84, A, C, 84003017

Grants Pass G Street Historic District, Bounded by SW. G and H Sts. and 4th and 6th Sts., Grants Pass, 10/07/93, A, C, 93001030

Grants Pass Supervisor's Warehouse [USDA Forest Service Administrative Buildings in Oregon and Washington Built by the CCC MPS], 200 NE. Greenfield Rd., Grants Pass, 3/06/91, A, C, 91000163

Grave Creek Bridge [Oregon Covered Bridges TR], N of Grants Pass, Sunny Valley vicinity, 11/29/79, A, C, 79002077

Hugo Community Baptist Church, 6501 Hugo Rd., Grants Pass vicinity, 10/25/90, A, a, b, 90001587

Kienlen-Harbeck Building, 147 SW G St., Grants Pass, 5/13/82, C, 82003729

Lundburg, George H., House, 404 N.W. A St., Grants Pass, 3/06/87, B, C, 87000365

McLean, Robert and Lucy, House, 724 NW 4th St., Grants Pass, 4/05/84, A, B, C, 84003020

Newell, Edwin, House, 591 SW G St, Grants Pass, 11/15/79, C, 79002078

Newman United Methodist Church, 128 NE B St., Grants Pass, 12/23/77, C, a, 77001103

Oregon Caves Chateau, Off SR 46, Oregon Caves National Monument, 5/28/87, C, NHL, NPS, 87001346

Oregon Caves Historic District, Caves Hwy., Oregon Caves NM, Siskiyou NF, Cave Junction vicinity, 2/25/92, A, C, NPS, 92000058

Redwoods Hotel, 310 NW 6th St, Grants Pass, 10/25/79, A, C, 79002079

Rogue River Valley Grange No. 469, 2064 Upper River Rd., Grants Pass vicinity, 3/09/92, A, 92000130

Smith, Herbert and Katherine, House, 139 SW I St., Grants Pass, 5/09/83, B, C, 83002156

Speed's Place on the Rogue, 11407 Merlin—Galice Rd., Galice vicinity, 6/21/91, A, 91000808

Store Gulch Guard Station No. 1020 [Depression-Era Buildings TR], Illinois Valley Rd., Siskiyou National Forest, Cave Junction vicinity, 4/08/86, A, C, 86000838

Voorhies, Amos E., House, 421 NW. B St., Grants Pass, 2/23/90, B, 90000282

Whisky Creek Cabin, 10 mi. W of Wolf Creek at Rogue River, Wolf Creek vicinity, 9/05/75, A, 75001584

Wolf Creek Tavern, About 22 mi. N of Grants Pass, Wolf Creek, 9/22/72, A, C, 72001081

Klamath County

Baldwin Hotel, 31 Main St., Klamath Falls, 10/02/73, B, C, 73001576

Klamath County—Continued

Benson, Judge Henry L., House, 137 High St., Klamath Falls, 12/02/81, B, C, 81000496

Bly Ranger Station, OR 140, Bly, 3/11/81, A, C, g, 81000650

Comfort Station No. 68 [Crater Lake National Park MRA], Rim Dr., near Rim Village Campground, Fort Klamath vicinity, 12/01/88, A, C, NPS, 88002624

Comfort Station No. 72 [Crater Lake National Park MRA], Rim Dr., in Rim Village Campground, Fort Klamath vicinity, 12/01/88, A, C, NPS, 88002625

Crater Lake Lodge, Crater Lake National Park, Klamath Falls vicinity, 5/05/81, A, C, NPS, 81000096

Crater Lake Superintendent's Residence, Munson Valley, Crater Lake National Park, 5/28/87, C, NHL, NPS, 87001347

Fort Klamath Site, SE of Fort Klamath, Fort Klamath vicinity, 10/07/71, A, 71000680

Klamath Falls City Hall, 226 S. 5th St., Klamath Falls, 10/30/89, A, 89001861

Klamath Falls City Library, Old, 500 Klamath Ave., Klamath Falls, 10/30/89, A, 89001863

Lake of the Woods Ranger Station—Work Center [Depression-Era Buildings TR], Winema National Forest, Klamath Falls vicinity, 4/08/86, A, C, 86000845

Lower Klamath National Wildlife Refuge, Lower Klamath Lake, E of Dorris, Worden, vicinity, 10/15/66, A, NHL, 66000238

Mills, Warren, House, 123 High St., Klamath Falls, 2/11/93, C, 93000016

Munson Valley Historic District [Crater Lake National Park MRA], Jct. of Crater Lake Hwy. and Rim Dr., Fort Klamath vicinity, 12/01/88, A, C, g, NPS, 88002622

Oregon Bank Building, 905 Main St., Klamath Falls, 9/10/87, A, C, 87001525

Point Comfort Lodge, 27505 Rocky Point Rd., Klamath Falls vicinity, 12/31/79, A, C, 79002080

Richardson—Ulrich House, 636 Conger Ave., Klamath Falls, 8/11/88, A, C, 88001244

Sinnott Memorial Building No. 67 [Crater Lake National Park MRA], Rim Dr., near Rim Village Campground, Fort Klamath vicinity, 12/01/88, A, C, f, NPS, 88002623

Valley Hospital, 405 Pine St., Klamath Falls, 9/08/88, A, 88001524

Watchman Lookout Station No. 68 [Crater Lake National Park MRA], Off Rim Dr. on The Watchman, Fort Klamath vicinity, 12/01/88, A, C, NPS, 88002626

Winthrow-Melhase Block, 4th and Main Sts., Klamath Falls, 6/14/82, C, 82003730

Lake County

Abert Lake Petroglyphs, Address Restricted, Lakeview vicinity, 11/20/74, A, D, 74002292

Bailey and Massingill Store, 4 N. E St., Lakeview, 10/25/84, A, C, 84000133

Cabin Lake Guard Station [Depression-Era Buildings TR], Deschutes National Forest, Bend vicinity, 4/11/86, A, C, g, 86000827

East Lake Abert Archeological District, Address Restricted, Valley Falls vicinity, 11/29/78, A, D, 78002295

Eskelin, Ed, Ranch Complex, HC 61, Fort Rock Valley, Silver Lake vicinity, 2/25/91, A, C, b, 91000062

Fort Rock Cave, Address Restricted, Fort Rock vicinity, 10/15/66, D, NHL, 66000641

Greaser Petroglyph Site, Address Restricted, Adel vicinity, 11/20/74, A, D, 74002293

Heryford Brothers Building, 524 Center St., Lakeview, 4/30/80, C, 80003330

Heryford, William P., House, 108 S. F St., Lakeview, 5/22/80, B, C, 80003331

Nevada-California-Oregon Railway Passenger Station, 1400 Center St., Lakeview, 8/22/83, A, C, 83002157

Picture Rock Pass Petroglyphs Site, Address Restricted, Silver Lake vicinity, 8/28/75, A, D, 75001585

Post and King Saloon, N. 2nd and E Sts., Lakeview, 3/17/77, A, C, 77001104

Stone Bridge and the Oregon Central Military Wagon Road, The Narrows S of Plush, Plush vicinity, 11/08/74, A, 74001689

Watson, John N. and Cornelia, House, 5 N. H St., Lakeview, 2/21/89, C, 89000051

Lane County

Alpha Phi Sorority House [Eugene West University Neighborhood MPS], 1050 Hilyard St., Eugene, 10/24/91, C, 91001564

Alpha Tau Omega Fraternity House (Old), 1143 Oak St., Eugene, 9/01/83, A, C, 83002158

Ax Billy Department Store, E. 10th Ave. and Willamette St., Eugene, 8/26/82, B, C, 82003731

Belknap Bridge [Oregon Covered Bridges TR], Off SR 126, Rainbow, 11/29/79, A, C, g, 79002097

Benedict, Edwin E., House, E of Florence on Cox Island, Florence vicinity, 10/18/79, A, 79002090

Beta Theta Pi Fraternity House, Old, 379–381 E. 12th Ave., Eugene, 10/30/89, A, C, 89001858

Calkins, Windsor W., House, 588 E. 11th Ave., Eugene, 12/09/81, B, C, 81000498

Campbell, Robert E., House, 890 Aspen Dr., Springfield vicinity, 11/01/79, A, C, 79002088

Chambers Bridge [Oregon Covered Bridges TR], S. River Rd., Cottage Grove, 11/29/79, A, C, g, 79002081

Chambers, Frank L. and Ida H., House, 1006 Taylor St., Eugene, 9/14/87, B, C, b, 87001537

Chi Psi Fraternity House [Eugene West University Neighborhood MPS], 1018 Hilyard St., Eugene, 3/18/93, C, 91001563

Christian—Patterson Rental Property [Eugene West University Neighborhood MPS], 244 E. 16th Ave., Eugene, 10/24/91, C, 91001567

Coburg Historic District, Roughly bounded by Van Duyn Rd., Diamond and Miller Sts., Dixon St. and Tax lots 1700 and 201, and Bottom Loop Rd., Coburg, 1/07/86, A, 86000036

Cochran—Rice Farm Complex, 993 N. Lane St., Cottage Grove, 10/17/91, A, 91001558

Coyote Creek Bridge [Oregon Covered Bridges TR], SE of Crow, Crow vicinity, 11/29/79, A, C, 79002084

Currin Bridge [Oregon Covered Bridges TR], E of Cottage Grove, Cottage Grove vicinity, 11/29/79, A, C, 79002082

Deadwood Creek Bridge [Oregon Covered Bridges TR], NE of Swisshome, Swisshome vicinity, 11/29/79, A, C, g, 79002099

Deady Hall, University of Oregon campus, Eugene, 4/11/72, A, C, NHL, 72001082

Dorena Bridge [Oregon Covered Bridges TR], NW of Dorena, Dorena vicinity, 11/29/79, A, C, g, 79002086

Dorris Apartments [Eugene West University Neighborhood MPS], 963 Ferry Ln., Eugene, 10/24/91, C, 91001565

Dorris Ranch, S. Second St. at Dorris Ave., Springfield vicinity, 6/22/88, A, B, 88000724

East Skinner Butte Historic District, Pearl and High Sts., and 2nd and 3rd Aves., Eugene, 9/23/82, A, C, 82003732

Ernest Bridge [Oregon Covered Bridges TR], NE of Marcola, Marcola vicinity, 11/29/79, A, C, g, 79002094

Eugene Blair Boulevard Historic Commercial Area, Blair Blvd. between W. 3rd and W. 5th Aves., including Van Buren St. between Blair and W. 3rd, Eugene, 9/21/93, A, B, b, g, 93000928

Eugene Hotel, 222 E. Broadway, Eugene, 10/07/82, A, C, 82001508

First Congregational Church, 492 E. 13th Ave., Eugene, 2/12/80, B, C, a, 80003333

First Presbyterian Church, 216 S. 3rd St., Cottage Grove, 12/31/74, C, a, g, 74001690

Fitch, Charles C., Farmstead, 26689 Pickens Rd., Eugene vicinity, 6/16/89, A, 89000510

Flanagan Site (35 LA 218), Address Restricted, Eugene vicinity, 7/20/77, D, 77001106

Gamma Phi Beta Sorority House [Eugene West University Neighborhood MPS], 1021 Hilyard St., Eugene, 10/24/91, C, 91001566

Goodpasture Bridge [Oregon Covered Bridges TR], W of Vida, Vida vicinity, 11/29/79, A, C, g, 79002100

Hall, Howard A., House, 1991 Garden Ave., Eugene, 7/14/88, C, 88001036

Harlow, Elmer, House, 2991 Harlow Rd., Eugene, 2/12/80, B, C, 80003334

Hayse Blacksmith Shop, 357 Van Buren St., Eugene, 11/07/80, C, 80003335

Heceta Head Lighthouse and Keepers Quarters, N of Florence on U.S. 101, Florence vicinity, 11/28/78, A, C, 78002296

Honeyman, Jessie M., Memorial State Park Historic District, U.S. 101, Florence vicinity, 11/28/84, A, C, g, 84000473

Johnson Hall, E. 13th between University and Kincaid Sts., Eugene, 6/20/85, A, C, 85001351

Kyle, William, and Sons, Building, 1297 Bay St., Florence, 12/02/81, B, C, 81000499

Lane County—Continued

Lake Creek Bridge [Oregon Covered Bridges TR], W of Greenleaf, Greenleaf vicinity, 11/29/79, A, C, 79002091

Lane County Clerk's Building, 740 W. 13th Ave., Eugene, 11/25/83, A, B, C, 83004174

Lane County Farmers' Union Cooperative Wholesalers' Association Building, 532 Olive St., Eugene, 10/17/91, A, 91001560

Lee, Dr. Norman L., House, 655 Holly St., Junction City, 11/02/77, B, C, 77001108

Lowell Bridge [Oregon Covered Bridges TR], E of Dexter, Lowell vicinity, 11/29/79, A, C, g, 79002085

Masonic Cemetery and Hope Abbey Mausoleum, 25th and University Sts., Eugene, 9/15/80, B, C, d, 80003336

Mathews, Nelson and Margret, House, 231 E. Pearl St., Coburg, 6/14/84, A, C, 84003025

McDonald Theater Building, 1004-1044 Willamette St., Eugene, 8/26/82, A, C, 82003733

McMorran and Washburne Department Store Building, 795 Willamette St., Eugene, 3/02/89, A, C, 89000125

Methodist Episcopal Church of Goshen, 85896 First St., Goshen, 10/17/91, C, a, 91001559

Mosby Creek Bridge [Oregon Covered Bridges TR], E of Cottage Grove, Cottage Grove vicinity, 11/29/79, A, C, 79002083

Musick Guard Station [USDA Forest Service Administrative Buildings in Oregon and Washington Built by the CCC MPS], NE of Bohemia Mtn., Umpqua NF, Cottage Grove vicinity, 3/06/91, A, C, 91000170

Office Bridge [Oregon Covered Bridges TR], Crosses N. Fork Middle Fork Willamette River, Westfir, 11/29/79, A, C, g, 79003768

Oregon Electric Railway Passenger Station, 27 E. 5th St., Eugene, 3/13/79, A, C, 79002087

Oregon Railway and Navigation Company Bridge, SE of Coburg, Coburg vicinity, 3/13/80, C, b, 80003332

Pacific Cooperative Poultry Producers Egg-Taking Station, 506 Olive St., Eugene, 9/08/88, A, 88001523

Palace Hotel, 488 Willamette St., Eugene, 12/23/77, A, B, C, 77001105

Parvin Bridge [Oregon Covered Bridges TR], S of Dexter off Lost Creek Rd., Dexter vicinity, 11/29/79, A, C, 79003767

Patterson—Stratton House [Eugene West University Neighborhood MPS], 1605 Pearl St., Eugene, 9/29/92, C, 92001262

Pengra Bridge [Oregon Covered Bridges TR], SE of Jasper, Jasper vicinity, 11/29/79, A, C, g, 79002092

Peters, A. V., House, 1611 Lincoln St., Eugene, 10/25/90, C, b, 90001597

Quackenbush Hardware Store, 160 E. Broadway, Eugene, 9/23/82, B, 82003734

Schaefers Building, 1001 Willamette St., Eugene, 10/30/79, C, 79003735

Shelton—McMurphey House and Grounds, 303 Willamette St., Eugene, 6/14/84, C, 84003028

Smeede Hotel, 767 Willamette St., Eugene, 1/17/74, C, 74001691

Southern Pacific Railroad Passenger Station and Freight House, 101 S. A St., Springfield, 2/24/93, A, C, 82005088

Spores, Jacob C., House, N of Eugene at 90311 Coburg Rd., Eugene vicinity, 11/02/77, B, C, f, 77001107

Springfield General Hospital, 846 F St., Springfield, 9/01/83, A, B, C, 83002159

Stewart Bridge [Oregon Covered Bridges TR], SE of Walden, Walden vicinity, 11/29/79, A, C, g, 79002102

US Post Office [Significant US Post Offices in Oregon 1900-1941 TR], 520 Willamette St., Eugene, 8/14/85, B, C, g, 85001805

Unity Bridge [Oregon Covered Bridges TR], N of Lowell, Lowell vicinity, 11/29/79, A, C, g, 79002093

University of Oregon Library and Memorial Quadrangle, Kincaid St. at E. Fifteenth Ave., Eugene, 3/09/90, A, C, 90000370

University of Oregon Museum of Art, University of Oregon, off OR 99, Eugene, 6/05/86, B, C, 86001224

Villard Hall, University of Oregon, Eugene, 4/11/72, A, C, NHL, 72001083

Washburne Historic District, Roughly bounded by G, N. Tenth, A, and N. Second Sts., Springfield, 2/10/87, A, C, g, 87000042

Wendling Bridge [Oregon Covered Bridges TR], NE of Marcola, Wendling vicinity, 11/29/79, A, C, g, 79002095

Wildcat Creek Bridge [Oregon Covered Bridges TR], W of Eugene, Walton vicinity, 11/29/79, A, C, 79002089

Williams, C. S., House, 1973 Garden Ave., Eugene, 7/14/88, C, 88001037

Wilson, Woodrow, Junior High School, 650 W. Twelfth Ave., Eugene, 10/25/90, A, C, 90001602

Women's Memorial Quadrangle Ensemble [Architecture of Ellis F. Lawrence MPS], Bounded by University St., Johnson Ln. and Pioneer Cemetery, University of Oregon campus, Eugene, 10/02/92, A, C, 92001320

Lincoln County

Cape Perpetua Shelter and Parapet, 3 mi. S of Yachats, Yachats vicinity, 3/17/89, A, C, 88002016

Chitwood Bridge [Oregon Covered Bridges TR], Off SR 20, Chitwood, 11/29/79, A, C, g, 79002103

Dorchester House, 2701 U.S. 101, Lincoln City, 2/29/80, C, 80003337

Drift Creek Bridge [Oregon Covered Bridges TR], SE of Lincoln City, Lincoln City vicinity, 11/29/79, A, C, 79002106

Fisher School Bridge [Oregon Covered Bridges TR], Five Rivers Rd., Fisher, 11/29/79, A, C, 79002105

New Cliff House, 267 N.W. Cliff St., Newport, 11/06/86, A, C, 86002962

North Fork of the Yachats Bridge [Oregon Covered Bridges TR], NE of Yachats, Yachats vicinity, 11/29/79, A, C, g, 79002108

Old Yaquina Bay Lighthouse, Yaquina Bay State Park, Newport, 5/01/74, C, 74001692

Roper, Charles and Theresa, House, 620 SW Alder St., Newport, 12/09/81, B, C, 81000500

Siletz Agency Site, Siletz-Logsden Rd., Siletz, 1/01/76, A, 76001582

St. John's Episcopal Church [Architecture of Ellis F. Lawrence MPS], 110 NE Alder St., Toledo, 10/17/90, C, a, 90001510

TRADEWINDS KINGFISHER (Cruiser), Depoe Bay Boat Basin, Depoe Bay, 10/29/91, A, C, 91001562

US Spruce Production Railroad XII, Spur 5 [Blodgett Tract MPS], E of Yachats, Yachats vicinity, 6/08/89, A, 88002032

Yaquina Head Lighthouse [Lighthouse Stations of Oregon MPS], Yaquina Head, about 4 mi. N of Yaquina R. entrance, Newport vicinity, 5/13/93, A, C, 73002340

Linn County

Albany Custom Mill, 213 Water St., Albany, 2/12/80, A, C, 80003338

Albany Downtown Commercial Historic District, Roughly bounded by Williamette River, Montgomery, Washington, 5th Sts., Albany, 12/09/82, A, C, 82001509

Angell—Brewster House, 34191 Brewster Rd., Lebanon vicinity, 10/08/92, A, C, 92001330

Baber, Granville H., House, NE of Albany off U.S. 99, Albany vicinity, 10/29/75, C, 75001588

Booth, Dr. J. C., House, 486 Park St., Lebanon, 4/01/80, B, C, 80003344

Boston Flour Mill, E of Shedd on Boston Mill Rd., Shedd vicinity, 8/21/79, A, C, 79002117

Brown, Hugh Leeper, Barn, SE of Brownsville on OR 228, Brownsville vicinity, 11/15/79, A, C, 79002112

Brown, John and Amelia, Farmhouse, SE of Brownsville on OR 228, Brownsville vicinity, 11/22/78, C, 78003408

Cascadia Cave, Address Restricted, Cascadia vicinity, 10/25/90, D, 90001589

Chamberlain, George Earle, House, 208 SE 7th St., Albany, 2/22/80, B, C, 80003339

Cooley, George C., House, 220 Blakely Ave., Brownsville, 5/09/83, B, C, b, 83002160

Crabtree Creek—Hoffman Covered Bridge [Oregon Covered Bridges TR], Hungry Hill Dr., 1.8 mi. N of Crabtree, Crabtree, 2/17/87, A, C, 87000017

Crandall, Louis A., House, 959 Main St., Lebanon, 10/25/90, C, 90001588

Crawfordsville Bridge [Oregon Covered Bridges TR], SR 228, Crawfordsville, 11/29/79, A, C, g, 79002115

Dawson, Alfred, House, 731 SW Broadalbin St., Albany, 2/12/80, C, 80003340

Fields, Hugh, House, 36176 OR 228, Brownsville vicinity, 7/19/89, B, C, 89000853

First Baptist Church of Brownsville, 515 N. Main St., Brownsville, 6/19/91, C, a, 91000807

Linn County—Continued

First Evangelical Church of Albany, 1120 SW 12 Ave., Albany, 8/01/84, A, C, a, 84003030

Flinn Block, 222 SW 1st Ave., Albany, 3/02/79, B, C, 79002109

Hackleman Historic District, Roughly bounded by Pacific Blvd., Lyons, 2nd and Madison Sts., Albany, 3/15/82, A, B, C, 82003735

Hannah Bridge [Oregon Covered Bridges TR], Burmester Creek Rd., Scio vicinity, 11/29/79, A, C, g, 79002116

Harrisburg Odd Fellows Hall, 190 Smith St., Harrisburg, 10/15/92, A, C, 92001382

Hochstedler, George, House, 237 SE 6th Ave., Albany, 10/10/80, B, C, 80004549

Howe, C. J., Building, 104 Spaulding Ave., Brownsville, 4/01/80, C, 80003343

Independence Prairie Ranger Station, Willamette National Forest, Marion Forks vicinity, 3/29/83, A, C, 83002161

Larwood Bridge [Oregon Covered Bridges TR], E of Crabtree, Crabtree vicinity, 11/29/79, A, C, g, 79003733

Methodist Episcopal Church South, 238 E. 3rd St, Albany, 11/16/79, A, C, a, b, 79002110

Monteith Historic District, Roughly bounded by 2nd, Lyon, 12th and Elm Sts., Albany, 2/29/80, A, C, a, 80003341

Monteith, Thomas and Walter, House, 518 W. 2nd Ave., Albany, 5/21/75, B, C, b, 75001586

Moyer, John M., House, 204 Main St., Brownsville, 1/21/74, B, C, 74001693

Mt. Pleasant Presbyterian Church, S of Stayton on Stayton-Jordan Rd., Stayton vicinity, 1/24/74, A, C, a, 74001694

Parker, Moses, House, 638 SE 5th St., Albany, 8/25/80, B, C, 80003342

Porter-Brasfield House, 31838 Fayetteville Dr., Shedd, 11/25/80, A, B, C, 80003345

Ralston, John, House, 632 SE Baker St., Albany, 12/09/81, C, 81000501

Rock Hill School, Rock Hill Dr., 2.2 mi. E of Sand Ridge Rd., Lebanon, 6/04/92, A, C, 92000661

Ross—Averill House, 420 Averill St., Brownsville, 2/20/91, C, 91000061

Short Bridge [Oregon Covered Bridges TR], High Deck Rd., Cascadia, 11/29/79, A, C, g, 79002113

Starr and Blakely Drug Store, 421 N. Main St., Brownsville, 10/29/82, B, C, 82001510

Thomas Creek—Gilkey Covered Bridge [Oregon Covered Bridges TR], Goar Rd., 3 mi. N of Crabtree, Crabtree vicinity, 2/19/87, A, C, 87000016

Thomas Creek—Shimanek Covered Bridge [Oregon Covered Bridges TR], Richardson Gap Rd., 2 mi. E of Scio, Scio vicinity, 2/19/87, A, C, g, 87000013

United Presbyterian Church and Rectory, 510 SW 5th Ave., Albany, 4/18/79, C, a, 79002111

Wesely, Joseph, House and Barn, 38712 OR 226, Scio, 10/23/86, C, 86002903

Wigle, Jacob and Maranda K., Farmstead, 1119 Kirk Ave., Brownsville, 3/05/92, A, C, 92000131

Malheur County

Charbonneau, Jean Baptiste, Memorial and Inskip Station RuinS, N of Danner off US 95, Danner vicinity, 3/14/73, A, B, c, 73001577

First Bank of Vale, 148 Main St. S., Vale, 3/05/92, C, 92000132

Old Stone House, 283 S. Main St., Vale, 5/19/72, A, 72001085

Oregon Trail Historic District, 5 mi. SE of Vale at Lytle Blvd., Vale vicinity, 10/29/75, A, d, 75001589

Pelota Fronton, Bassett St. (U.S. 95), Jordan Valley, 5/19/72, A, C, 72001084

Sheep Ranch Fortified House, W of Arock, Arock vicinity, 11/01/74, A, C, 74001695

Vale Hotel and Grand Opera House, 123 S. Main St., Vale, 8/01/84, A, C, 84003032

Marion County

Adolph Block, 360–372 State St., Salem, 2/01/80, C, 80003348

Adolph, Samuel, House, 2493 State St., Salem, 10/02/78, B, C, 78002297

Anderson, James Mechlin, House, Off I-5, Jefferson, 10/16/79, A, C, 79002118

Aurora Colony Historic District, Roughly bounded by Cemetery Rd., Bobs Ave., and Liberty St., Aurora, 4/16/74, A, C, a, 74001696

Beers, Oliver, House, 10602 Wheatland Rd., Gervais, 8/01/84, C, D, a, 84003036

Bents, Frederick, House, 22776 Bents Rd., NE, Aurora vicinity, 12/09/81, B, C, b, 81000502

Boise, R. P., Building, 217 State St., Salem, 12/02/81, C, 81000504

Boon Brick Store, 888 Liberty St., NE, Salem, 11/20/75, A, C, 75001590

Boon, John D., House, 1313 Mill St., S.E., Salem, 1/17/75, B, b, 75001591

Breitenbush Guard Station [Depression-Era Buildings TR], Willamette National Forest, Detroit, 4/08/86, A, C, 86000843

Brown, Sam, House, E of Gervais, Gervais vicinity, 11/05/74, B, C, 74001697

Burggraf-Burt-Webster House, 901 13th St., SE, Salem, 4/01/80, B, C, 80003349

Bush and Brey Block and Annex, 179–197 Commercial St., NE, Salem, 12/21/81, A, B, C, 81000505

Bush, Asahel, House, 600 Mission St., SE, Salem, 1/21/74, B, C, 74001700

Bush-Breyman Block, 141–147 N. Commercial St., Salem, 2/17/78, B, C, 78002298

Calvary Lutheran Church & Parsonage, 314 Jersey St., Silverton, 6/06/85, A, C, a, b, 85001182

Campbell, Hamilton, House, N of Jefferson, Jefferson vicinity, 3/13/79, B, C, 79002119

Case, William, Farm, SE of Champoeg off Arbor Grove Rd., Champoeg vicinity, 3/21/73, B, C, 73001578

Champoeg State Park Historic Archeological District, Address Restricted, St. Paul vicinity, 8/01/84, A, B, D, 84003038

Chemawa Indian School Site, 3700 Chemawa Rd., NE., Salem, 12/16/92, A, d, 92001333

Chemeketa Lodge No. 1 Odd Fellows Buildings, 185–195 High St. NE, Salem, 4/08/88, A, C, 88000275

Collins, George, House, 1340 Chemeketa St. NE., Salem, 12/01/89, C, b, 89002063

Conser, Jacob, House, 114 Main St., Jefferson, 1/21/74, B, C, 74001699

Court Street—Chemeketa Street Historic District, Roughly bounded by Chemeketa St., Mill Creek, Court, and Fourteenth St., Salem, 8/26/87, A, C, 87001373

Cross, Curtis, House, 1635 Fairmount Ave., S., Salem, 12/18/81, B, C, 81000506

Cusick, Dr. William A., House, 415 Lincoln St. S., Salem, 2/23/90, C, 90000281

Daue, Alexander, House, 1095 S. Saginaw St., Salem, 6/06/85, A, C, 85001181

Despard, Joseph, Cabin Site [Early French-Canadian Settlement MPS], Address Restricted, Newberg vicinity, 10/31/91, A, D, 91001573

Farrar Building, 351-373 State St., Salem, 8/26/82, A, C, 82003737

Fawk, Henry, House, 310 Lincoln St. S., Salem, 2/20/91, C, 91000060

First Methodist Episcopal Church of Salem, 600 State St., Salem, 5/09/83, A, C, a, 83002162

Gaiety Hill—Bush's Pasture Park Historic District, Roughly bounded by Pringle Creek, Mission St., Bush's Pasture Pk., Cross, High, and Liberty Sts., Salem, 10/10/86, A, B, C, g, 86002849

Gallon House Bridge [Oregon Covered Bridges TR], NW of Silverton, Silverton vicinity, 11/29/79, A, C, 79002124

Geer, R. C., Farmhouse, E of Salem at 12390 Sunnyview Rd., Salem vicinity, 2/12/80, A, B, C, 80003353

Gilbert, Andrew T., House, 116 Marion St., NE, Salem, 11/06/80, B, C, 80003350

Gill, J. K., Building, 356 State St., Salem, 2/01/80, A, C, 80003351

Harding, Benjamin F., House, 1043 High St., SE, Salem, 12/21/81, C, 81000507

Hudson's Bay Company Granary and Clerk's House Site [Early French-Canadian Settlement MPS], Address Restricted, Newberg vicinity, 10/31/91, A, D, 91001574

Jarman, Daniel B., House and Garden, 567 High St., SE, Salem, 12/06/79, C, 79002120

Jefferson Methodist Church, 310 and 342 N. 2nd St., Jefferson, 11/06/80, C, a, 80003346

Jones-Sherman House, 835 D St., NE, Salem, 12/21/81, B, C, 81000508

Kay, Thomas, Woolen Mill, 260 12th St., SE, Salem, 5/08/73, A, C, 73001579

Kirk, John W., and Thomas F., House, 4686 Saint Paul Hwy. NE, St. Paul vicinity, 6/17/87, A, B, 87000867

Lamport, Frederick S., House, 590 Lower Ben Lomond Dr. SE., Salem, 6/19/91, C, 91000806

Lee Mission Cemetery, D St., Salem, 12/29/78, B, a, d, 78002299

Lee, Jason, House, 1313 Mill St., SE, Salem, 4/23/73, B, a, b, 73001580

Marion County—Continued

Livesley, T. A., House, 533 Lincoln St., S., Salem, 4/26/90, B, C, 90000684

Manning, S. A., Building, 200 State St., Salem, 2/10/87, A, 87000035

Marion County Housing Committee Demonstration House, 140 Wilson St., S, Salem, 8/11/88, A, C, b, 88001243

Marion Forks Guard Station [USDA Forest Service Administrative Buildings in Oregon and Washington Built by the CCC MPS], OR 22, Willamette NF, Marion Forks, 3/06/91, A, C, 91000167

McCallister-Gash Farmhouse, SW of Silverton at 9626 Kaufman Rd., Silverton vicinity, 11/06/80, B, C, 80003354

McCully, David, House, 1365 John St., S., Salem, 2/14/78, B, C, b, 78002300

Methodist Mission Parsonage, 1313 Mill St., S.E., Salem, 12/31/74, A, a, b, 74001701

Miller Cemetery Church, 2 mi. (3.2 km) NE of Silverton on Cascade Hwy. NE, Silverton vicinity, 8/10/78, C, a, 78002304

Minto, John and Douglas, Houses, 841, 835 and 821 Saginaw St., S., Salem, 12/18/81, B, C, b, 81000509

Olallie Lake Guard Station [USDA Forest Service Administrative Buildings in Oregon and Washington Built by the CCC MPS], S of Pinhead Buttes, Mt. Hood NF, Estacada vicinity, 3/06/91, A, C, 91000169

Old First National Bank Building, 388 State St. NE, Salem, 10/09/86, C, 86002851

Old Garfield School, 528 Cottage St., NE, Salem, 12/02/81, A, C, 81000510

Old Woodburn City Hall, 550 N. 1st St., Woodburn, 3/30/79, C, 79002125

Oregon State Capitol, Capitol Mall, Salem, 6/29/88, A, C, 88001055

Oregon State Forester's Office Building, 2600 State St., Salem, 4/15/82, A, C, g, 82003738

Paris Woolen Mill, 535 E. Florence St., Stayton, 12/21/81, A, B, 81000511

Paulus, Christopher, Building, 355, 357 and 363 Court St. NE., Salem, 3/05/92, A, C, 92000133

Pleasant Grove Presbyterian Church, 1313 Mill St. SE, Salem, 2/10/87, A, C, a, b, 74001703

Port, Dr. Luke A., House, 1116 Mission St., SE, Salem, 10/02/73, C, 73001581

Port-Manning House, 4922 Halls Ferry Rd., S., Salem, 10/02/78, B, C, b, 78002301

Queen of Angels Priory, 840 S. Main St., Mount Angel, 7/08/82, A, C, a, 82003736

Reed Opera House and McCornack Block Addition, 189 and 177 Liberty St., NE, Salem, 3/08/78, A, C, 78002302

Robertson, Dr. and Mrs. Charles G., House and Garden, 460 S. Leffelle St., Salem, 5/19/83, A, C, 83002163

Scheurer, William Riley, House, 23707 1st St., NE, Butteville, 12/23/81, B, C, 81000503

Settlemier, Jesse H., House, 355 N. Settlemier Ave., Woodburn, 12/19/74, B, C, 74001704

Silver Falls State Park Concession Building Area, 20024 Silver Falls Hwy., Sublimity vicinity, 6/30/83, A, C, g, 83002164

Silverton Commercial Historic District, Roughly bounded by High, and Oak Sts., Silver Creek, Lewis, Water, and First Sts., Silverton, 7/29/87, A, C, 87000878

Smith-Ohmart House, 2655 E. Nobb Hill, SE, Salem, 11/16/79, B, C, 79002121

South First National Bank Block, 241-247 Commercial St., NE, Salem, 3/31/83, C, 83002165

St. Mary's Roman Catholic Church, Off OR 214, Mount Angel, 10/22/76, C, a, 76001583

St. Paul Historic District, Off OR 219, St. Paul, 3/15/82, A, B, C, D, a, d, 82003739

St. Paul Roman Catholic Church, Off OR 219, St. Paul, 10/16/79, A, B, C, a, 79002098

St. Pierre, Edward W., House, 2425 Eola Dr., Salem vicinity, 2/21/89, B, 89000050

Starkey-McCully Block, 223-233 Commercial St., NE, Salem, 3/12/79, A, C, 79002122

Stauffer, John, House and Barn, NE of Hubbard, Hubbard vicinity, 5/01/74, C, 74001698

Stratton, C. C., House, 1599 State St., Salem, 11/15/84, B, C, 84000475

Wade, William Lincoln, House, 1305 John St., S., Salem, 2/17/78, A, B, C, b, 78002303

Waller Hall, Willamette University, 900 State St., Salem, 11/20/75, A, 75001593

Williamette Station Site, Methodist Mission in Oregon, Address Restricted, Gervais vicinity, 8/01/84, A, B, D, 84003040

Windischar's General Blacksmith Shop, 110 Sheridan St., Mount Angel, 11/07/80, A, b, 80003347

Witzel, Robert, House, 6576 Joseph St., SE, Salem vicinity, 11/15/79, A, C, 79002123

Zorn, Casper, Farmhouse, NE of St. Paul at 8448 Champoeg Rd., NE, St. Paul vicinity, 2/12/80, A, B, C, 80003355

Morrow County

Gilliam and Bisbee Building, SE corner of Main and May Sts., Heppner, 6/01/90, A, C, 90000840

Heppner Hotel, 124 N. Main St., Heppner, 10/29/82, A, B, C, 82001511

Morrow County Courthouse, 100 Court St., Heppner, 2/28/85, C, 85000366

Oregon Trail, Wells Springs Segment, S of Boardman, Boardman vicinity, 9/13/78, A, d, 78002305

Multnomah County

Adams, Charles F., House, 2363 NW Flanders, Portland, 12/09/81, B, C, 81000513

Ainsworth, Maud and Belle, House, 2542 S.W. Hillcrest Dr., Portland, 2/27/86, B, C, 86000288

Albee, H. Russell, House, 3360 SE. Ankeny St., Portland, 10/22/92, B, C, 92001332

Albers Brothers Milling Company, 1118-1130 Front Ave., Portland, 11/15/84, A, 84000480

Ambassador Apartments, 1209 SW 6th Ave., Portland, 2/26/79, B, C, 79003738

American Apartment Building, 2093 NW. Johnson St., Portland, 5/27/93, C, 93000452

Arminius Hotel, 1022–1038 SW Morrison St., Portland, 7/14/88, A, C, 88001038

Ashley, Mark A. M., House, 2847 NW Westover Rd., Portland, 3/02/79, C, 79002126

Auditorium and Music Hall, 920, 924, 926, 928 SW 3rd Ave., Portland, 2/22/80, C, 80003357

Autzen, Thomas J., House, 2425 NE. Alameda, Portland, 3/09/92, B, C, 92000088

Ayer, W. B., House, 811 NW. Nineteenth Ave., Portland, 2/22/91, B, C, 91000144

Ayer-Shea House, 1809 NW Johnson St., Portland, 6/14/82, B, C, a, 82003741

Bader, Louis J., House and Garden, 3604 SE. Oak St., Portland, 10/30/89, C, 89001856

Bagdad Theatre [Portland Eastside MPS], 3708–26 SE Hawthorne, Portland, 3/08/89, A, C, 89000099

Ball—Ehrman House, 2040 SW. Laurel St., Portland, 2/22/91, C, 91000143

Ballou & Wright Company Building, 327 N.W. Tenth Ave., Portland, 4/30/87, A, C, 87000698

Bank of California Building, 330 SW 6th Ave., Portland, 3/14/78, A, C, 78002306

Barber Block, 532–538 SE Grand Ave., Portland, 2/15/77, C, 77001109

Barnes, Frank C., House, 3533 NE Klickitat, Portland, 9/01/83, B, C, 83002166

Bartman, Gustave, House [Portland Eastside MPS], 1817 SE 12th, Portland, 3/08/89, C, 89000098

Bates, John M. and Elizabeth, House No. 1 [Wade Pipes Residences for John and Elizabeth Bates MPS], 1837 SW. Edgewood Rd., Portland, 6/12/90, C, 90000846

Bates-Seller House, 2381 NW Flanders St., Portland, 8/29/79, B, C, 79002127

Bay E, West Ankeny Car Barns, 2706 NE Couch St., Portland, 10/10/78, A, 78002307

Becker, Christine, House, 1331 NW. 25th Ave., Portland, 2/28/91, C, 91000142

Bedell Building, 520–538 SW 6th Ave., Portland, 2/23/89, A, C, 89000066

Belle Court Apartments, 120 N.W. Trinity Pl., Portland, 11/06/86, B, C, 86002966

Benson Hotel, 309 S.W. Broadway, Portland, 11/20/86, B, C, 86003175

Benson, Simon, House, 1504 SW 11th Ave., Portland, 8/11/83, B, C, 83002167

Berg, Charles F., Building, 615 SW Broadway, Portland, 9/01/83, A, C, 83002170

Bergman, Joseph, House, 2134 NW Hoyt St., Portland, 9/01/83, B, C, 83002168

Beth Israel School, 1230 SW Main St., Portland, 8/10/78, A, B, a, 78002308

Bethel Baptist Church, 101 S. Main St., Gresham, 4/15/82, C, a, b, 82003740

Biltmore Apartments, 2014 NW Glisan St., Portland, 2/20/91, C, 91000041

Bishop's House, 219–223 SW Stark St., Portland, 10/18/74, C, a, 74001706

Blake McFall Company Building, 215 SE. Ankeny St., Portland, 3/09/90, C, 90000371

Multnomah County—Continued

Bonneville Dam Historic District, Columbia River between Bradford and Cascade Islands off I-80 in Multnomah County, Oregon to WA 14 in Skamania County, WA, Bonneville, 4/09/86, A, C, g, NHL, 86000727

Bonneville Dam Historic District (Boundary Increase), Roughly bounded by Mitchell Creek Bypass, SW District boundary, Union Pacific right-of-way, and Hatchery Service Rd., Bonneville, 3/26/87, A, C, NHL, 86003598

Bowles, Joseph R., House, 1934 SW Vista Ave., Portland, 3/08/78, C, 78002309

Bowman, F. E., Apartments, 1624–1636 Tillamook St., Portland, 6/16/89, C, 89000511

Bradley, J. S., House, 2111 SW. Vista Ave., Portland, 2/22/91, C, 91000133

Brainard, William E., House, 5332 SE Morrison St., Portland, 3/01/79, B, C, 79002128

Braly, J. C., House, 2846 NW. Fairfax Terr., Portland, 2/28/91, C, 91000132

Bretnor Apartments, 931 NW Twentieth Ave., Portland, 2/20/91, C, 91000067

Broadway Hotel, 10 NW. Broadway, Portland, 9/09/93, A, C, b, 93000927

Brown Apartments, 807 SW. Fourteenth Ave., Portland, 10/17/91, C, 91001553

Buck Apartment Building, 415 NW. Twenty-first Ave., Portland, 10/25/90, C, 90001594

Buckler-Henry House, 2324 SE Ivon St., Portland, 2/12/80, B, C, g, 80003358

Buehner, Philip, House, 5511 SE Hawthorne Blvd., Portland, 10/24/80, B, C, a, 80003359

Burke-Clark House, 2610 NW Cornell Rd., Portland, 8/26/82, B, C, 82003742

Burrell, Walter F., House, 2610 SE. Hawthorne, Portland, 10/25/90, C, 90001593

Burrell, Walter F., House (Boundary Increase), 2610 SE. Hawthorne Blvd., Portland, 7/26/91, C, 91000975

Bybee-Howell House, Off Sauvie Island Rd., Sauvie Island, 11/05/74, C, 74001716

Calumet Hotel, 620 SW Park St., Portland, 9/21/84, A, C, 84003073

Calvary Presbyterian Church, 1422 SW 11th Ave., Portland, 3/29/72, C, a, 72001086

Campbell Hotel, 530 NW Twenty-third Ave., Portland, 2/22/88, C, 88000098

Campbell Townhouses, 1705–1719 NW Irving St. and 715–719 17th Ave., Portland, 2/12/80, C, 80003360

Canterbury Castle, 2910 S.W. Canterbury Ln., Portland, 9/08/87, C, 87001509

Cardwell—Parrish House, 7543 SW. Fulton Park Blvd., Portland, 2/22/91, C, 91000130

Central Building, Public Library, 801 SW 10th Ave., Portland, 6/11/79, C, 79002129

Chamberlain, George Earle, House, 1927 NE. Tillamook St., Portland, 6/19/91, B, 91000815

Chown, Francis R., House, 2030 SW. Main St., Portland, 2/23/90, C, 90000296

Clarke—Woodward Drug Company Building, 911 NW. Hoyt, Portland, 3/02/89, A, 89000121

Clovelly Garden Apartments, 6309 NE Union Ave., Portland, 5/19/83, B, C, 83002169

Cole, David, House, 1441 N. McClellan St., Portland, 8/06/80, B, C, 80003361

Coleman—Scott House, 2110 N.E. Sixteenth Ave., Portland, 11/08/85, B, C, 85003504

Columbia River Highway Historic District, Roughly bounded by the Sandy River Bridge, Troutdale, Multnomah County on the West, the Chenoweth Creek Bridge, etc., Troutdale, 12/12/83, A, C, 83004168

Commodore Hotel, 1609 SW Morrison St., Portland, 6/27/84, C, 84003076

Concord Building, 208 SW Stark St., Portland, 10/21/77, C, 77001110

Corbett, H. L. and Gretchen Hoyt, House, 01405 SW. Corbett Hill Cir., Portland vicinity, 2/28/91, B, C, 91000129

Corkish Apartments, 2734–2740 SW 2nd Ave., Portland, 12/02/81, A, C, 81000514

Cornelius Hotel, 525 S.W. Park Ave., Portland, 2/27/86, B, C, 86000286

Cotillion Hall, 406 SW 14th Ave., Portland, 3/09/79, A, C, 79002130

Couch Family Investment Development, 1721–1735 NW Irving St. and 718 NW 18th St., Portland, 2/25/80, C, 80003362

Crumpacker, Maurice, House, 12714 SW. Iron Mountain Blvd., Portland, 10/23/92, C, 92001378

Cumberland Apartments [Architecture of Ellis F. Lawrence MPS], 1405 SW Park Ave., Portland, 10/17/90, C, 90001509

Day Building, 2068 NW Flanders St., Portland, 10/02/78, C, 78002310

Dayton Apartment Building, 2056–2058 NW Flanders St., Portland, 12/21/81, C, 81000515

Deere, John, Plow Company Building [Portland Eastside MPS], 215 SE Morrison, Portland, 3/08/89, A, C, 89000097

Dekum, The, 519 SW 3rd St., Portland, 10/10/80, B, C, 80003363

Del Rey Apartments, 2555 NE Glisan St., Portland, 2/20/91, C, 91000040

Digman—Zidell House, 2959 SW. Bennington Dr., Portland, 5/27/93, B, C, 93000453

Doernbecher, Frank Silas, House, 2323 NE Tillamook St., Portland, 3/14/78, B, C, 78002311

Dooly, Frank E., House, 2670 NW Lovejoy St., Portland, 10/24/80, B, C, 80003364

Dosch, Henry E., House, 5298 SW Dosch Rd., Portland, 10/02/78, B, C, 78002312

Dosch, Henry E., Investment Property, 425 N.W. Eighteenth Ave., Portland, 6/04/87, C, 87000886

Douglas Building [Portland Eastside MPS], 3525–41 SE Hawthorne, Portland, 3/08/89, C, 89000096

Druhot, Alice, House, 1903 SW Cable St., Portland, 2/29/88, C, 88000079

Ducey, Elizabeth, House, 2773 NW. Westover Rd., Portland, 6/01/90, C, 90000839

Dupont, Edward D., House [Portland Eastside MPS], 3326 SE Main, Portland, 3/08/89, C, 89000095

Durham—Jacobs House, 2138 S.W. Salmon St., Portland, 3/06/87, C, 87000307

East Portland Branch, Public Library of Multnomah County, 1110 S.E. Alder, Portland, 9/08/87, A, C, 87001491

East Portland Grand Avenue Historic District, Bounded by Main and Ankeny Sts., SE. 7th Ave. and SE. Martin Luther King, Jr. Blvd. (SE. Union Ave.), Portland, 3/04/91, A, 91000126

Eastman-Shaver House, 2645 NW Beuhla Vista Terrace, Portland, 7/09/85, B, C, 85001528

Edwards, J. G., House, 2645 SW. Alta Vista Pl., Portland, 2/22/91, C, 91000128

Electric Building, 621 SW Alder St., Portland, 2/23/89, A, C, 89000059

Elks Temple, 614 SW 11th Ave., Portland, 2/17/78, C, 78002313

Elm Street Apartments, 1825–1837 SW Elm St., Portland, 2/20/91, C, 91000056

Envoy Apartment Building, 2336 SW Osage, Portland, 3/03/88, C, 88000093

Equitable Building, 421 SW 6th Ave., Portland, 3/30/76, C, g, 76001584

Eugenia Apartments [Portland Eastside MPS], 1314 SE Salmon, Portland, 3/08/89, C, 89000094

Farrer, Franklin W., House [Portland Eastside MPS], 2706 SE Yamhill, Portland, 3/08/89, C, 89000093

Fenton, William D., House, 626 SE 16th Ave, Portland, 8/29/79, B, C, 79002145

First Church of Christ, Scientist, 1813 NW Everett St., Portland, 10/02/78, A, C, a, 78002314

First Congregational Church, 1126 SW Park St., Portland, 5/02/75, C, a, 75001594

First National Bank, 401 SW 5th Ave., Portland, 10/15/74, C, 74001707

First Presbyterian Church of Portland, 1200 SW Alder, Portland, 12/19/74, C, a, 74002294

First Unitarian Church of Portland, 1011 SW 12th Ave., Portland, 11/22/78, C, a, 78002315

Fisher, Thaddeus, House [Portland Eastside MPS], 913–15 SE 33rd, Portland, 3/08/89, C, 89000092

Flanders, Caroline W. and M. Louise, House, 2421 SW. Arden Rd., Portland, 3/01/91, B, C, 91000127

Frank, M. Lloyd, Estate, 0615 SW Palatine Hill Rd., Portland, 4/18/79, C, 79002133

Franklin Hotel, 1337 S.W. Washington St., Portland, 10/31/85, A, C, 85003474

Freiwald, Gustav, House, 1810 NE. Fifteenth Ave., Portland, 5/27/93, C, 93000454

Frigidaire Building [Portland Eastside MPS], 230 E. Burnside, Portland, 3/08/89, A, C, 89000091

Fruit and Flower Mission, 1609 S.W. Twelfth Ave., Portland, 6/05/86, A, C, 86001225

Frye, J. O., House, 2997 SW Fairview Blvd., Portland, 6/06/85, C, 85001183

Gangware, Roy and Leola, House, 4848 SW. Humphrey Blvd., Portland vicinity, 2/23/90, C, 90000284

Gaston, Joseph, House, 1960 S.W. Sixteenth Ave., Portland, 2/21/89, B, 89000052

Gaston—Strong House, 1130 SW. King Ave., Portland, 2/23/90, B, 90000292

Gatehouse, Portland City Reservoir No. 2, 6007 SE. Division St., Portland, 6/01/90, A, C, 90000834

Multnomah County—Continued

Gedamke, William, House, 1304 E. Powell Blvd., Gresham, 11/13/89, C, 89001970

Giesy—Failing House, 1965 SW. Montgomery Pl., Portland, 2/22/91, B, 91000137

Gilbert Building, 319 SW Taylor St., Portland, 8/21/80, C, 80003365

Gilliland, Lewis T., House, 2229 NE Brazee, Portland, 2/23/89, C, 89000063

Goodman, Joseph, House, 240 NW. Twentieth Ave., Portland, 5/27/93, C, 93000455

Gowanlock, Elizabeth B., House [Portland Eastside MPS], 808 SE 28th, Portland, 3/08/89, C, 89000089

Graf, Andreas, House, SE of Corbett, Corbett vicinity, 11/13/80, A, C, 80003356

Graham, Thomas, Building, 6031 SE. Stark St., Portland, 3/05/92, C, 92000134

Grand Stable Building and Adjacent Commercial Building, 415-421 SW 2nd Ave., Portland, 10/07/82, B, C, 82001512

Grant, Henry M., House, 3114 NW. Thurman St., Portland, 2/22/91, A, C, 91000148

Green, Bertha M. and Marie A., House, 2610 SW. Vista Ave., Portland, 10/15/92, C, 92001379

Greenwood, Frederick and Grace, House, 248 SW. Kingston Ave., Portland, 6/19/91, C, 91000814

Groat—Gates House, 35 NE Twenty-second Ave., Portland, 2/23/89, C, 89000062

Hahn, Henry, House, 2636 NW. Cornell Rd., Portland, 9/09/93, C, 93000918

Hall, Hazel, House, 104–106 NW. 22nd Pl., Portland, 6/19/91, B, 91000813

Hamilton Building, 529 SW 3rd Ave., Portland, 3/17/77, C, 77001112

Hamilton, Alexander B. and Anna Balch, House, 2723–2729 NW. Savier St., Portland, 2/11/93, C, 93000021

Hancock Street Fourplex, 1414 NE. Hancock St., Portland, 2/11/93, A, C, 93000023

Harlow Block, 720–738 NW Glisan St., Portland, 10/24/80, C, 80003366

Harlow, Fred, House, 726 E. Columbia St., Troutdale, 2/16/84, A, B, C, 84003078

Harmon-Neils House, 2642 NW Lovejoy St., Portland, 2/16/84, B, C, 84003080

Haseltine, Edward Knox, House, 1616 SW Spring St., Portland, 11/15/84, C, 84000481

Haseltine, William A., House, 3231 NE. U. S. Grant Pl., Portland, 10/17/91, C, 91001551

Hawthorne, Rachel Louise, House [Portland Eastside MPS], 1007 SE 12th, Portland, 3/08/89, C, 89000090

Heintz, Albert, Oscar, and Linda, House [Architecture of Ellis F. Lawrence MPS], 2556 SW Vista Ave., Portland, 10/17/90, C, 90001508

Hendershott, Dr. Harry M., House [Architecture of Ellis F. Lawrence MPS], 824 NW. Albemarle Terr., Portland, 6/19/91, C, 91000797

Henry, C. K., Building, 309 SW 4th Ave., Portland, 5/13/82, B, C, 82003743

Herschell—Spillman Noah's Ark Carousel [Oregon Historic Wooden Carousels TR], E end of

Sellwood Bridge, Portland, 8/26/87, A, C, b, 87001380

Heusner, George F., House, 333 NW 20th Ave., Portland, 10/19/78, C, 78002316

Hexter, Levi, House, 2326 SW Park Pl., Portland, 2/12/80, B, C, 80003367

Hickey, James, House [Architecture of Ellis F. Lawrence MPS], 6719 SE 29th Ave., Portland, 10/17/90, C, 90001514

Hochapfel, Edward C., House, 1520 SW 11th Ave., Portland, 8/11/83, A, C, 83002171

Hollywood Theatre, 4122 NE Sandy Blvd., Portland, 9/01/83, A, C, 83002172

Holman, Capt. Herbert, House, 2359 NW. Overton St., Portland, 2/22/91, C, 91000136

Holman, Rufus C., House, 2116 SW. Montgomery Dr., Portland, 2/22/91, B, C, 91000147

Holt-Saylor-Liberto House, 3625 SW Condor, Portland, 11/22/78, B, C, 78002317

Honeyman Hardware Company Building, 832 NW. Hoyt, Portland, 12/15/89, A, 89002124

Honeyman, David T. and Nan Wood, House, 1728 S.W. Prospect Dr., Portland, 5/07/87, B, C, 87000677

Honeyman, John S., House, 1318 S.W. Twelfth Ave., Portland, 10/31/85, B, C, 85003436

Hyland, Olive and Ellsworth, Apartments, 1424 and 1434 SW Morrison, and 716 SW 15th Ave., Portland, 2/01/80, B, C, 80004548

Imperial Garage, 212 SW. Fourth Ave., Portland, 5/27/93, A, C, 93000451

Imperial Hotel, 422–426 S.W. Broadway, Portland, 12/02/85, A, B, C, 85003037

Inman, Clarissa McKeyes, House, 2884 NW. Cumberland, Portland, 2/23/90, C, 90000275

International Harvester Company Warehouse [Portland Eastside MPS], 79 SE Taylor, Portland, 3/08/89, C, 89000088

Irving Street Bowman Apartments, 2004–2018 NW. Irving St., Portland, 2/23/90, C, 90000291

Irvington Tennis Club [Architecture of Ellis F. Lawrence MPS], 2131 NE Thompson St., Portland, 10/17/90, C, 90001513

Italian Gardeners and Ranchers Association Market Building [Portland Eastside MPS], 1305–37 SE Union, Portland, 3/08/89, A, 89000087

Jacobberger, Josef, House, 1502 SW. Upper Hall St., Portland, 3/09/90, C, 90000369

Jacobs-Wilson House, 6461 SE Thorburn St., Portland, 12/10/81, A, C, 81000516

Jantzen Knitting Mills Company Building, 1935 NE. Glisan St., Portland, 6/24/91, A, C, g, 91000812

Jefferson Substation, 37 SW Jefferson St., Portland, 5/31/80, A, C, 80003368

Jeppesen, Peter, House, 4107 N. Albina Ave., Portland, 9/10/87, C, 87001535

Jewish Shelter Home, 4133 SW Corbett Ave., Portland, 6/14/84, A, 84003083

Johnson, C. D., House, 2582 NW. Lovejoy St., Portland, 2/22/91, B, 91000146

Jones, Clarence H., House [Portland Eastside MPS], 1834 SE Ankeny, Portland, 3/08/89, C, 89000085

Jones, Dr. Noble Wiley, House, 2187 SW Market St. Dr., Portland, 2/11/88, B, 88000088

Kamm, Jacob, House, 1425 SW 20th Ave., Portland, 11/05/74, C, b, 74001708

Kendall, Joseph, House, 3908 SE Taggart St., Portland, 8/29/79, C, 79002134

Kenton Hotel, 8303–8319 N. Denver Ave., Portland, 10/16/90, A, C, 90001522

Kerr, Albertina, Nursery, 424 NE 22nd Ave., Portland, 8/29/79, B, C, 79002135

King's Hill Historic District, Bounded by W. Burnside St., SW Canyon Rd, SW 21st St. and Washington Park, Portland, 2/19/91, B, C, 91000039

King, Samuel W., House, 1060 S.W. King Ave., Portland, 9/08/87, C, 87001471

Kingsley, Edward D., House, 2132 SW. Montgomery Dr., Portland, 2/23/90, C, 90000283

Kistner, Dr. Frank B., House, 5400 S.W. Hewett Blvd., Portland, 4/30/87, C, 87000681

Knight, F. M., Building [Portland Eastside MPS], 3300 SE Belmont, Portland, 3/08/89, C, 89000086

Knights of Columbus Building, 804 SW. Taylor St., Portland, 6/01/90, A, C, 90000830

Krouse, Nettie, Fourplex [Portland Eastside MPS], 2106–12 SE Main, Portland, 3/08/89, C, 89000084

Kuehle, Henry, Investment Property [Portland Eastside MPS], 210–13 SE 12th, Portland, 3/08/89, C, 89000083

Ladd Carriage House, 1331 SW Broadway, Portland, 2/12/80, B, C, a, 80003369

Ladd's Addition Historic District, Bounded by S.E. Division, Hawthorne, Twelfth and Twentieth Sts., Portland, 8/31/88, A, B, C, b, 88001310

Landenberger, C. A., House, 1805 N.W. Glisan St., Portland, 2/29/88, B, C, 88000097

Lauer Apartment Building, 323–337 NW. Seventeenth Ave., Portland, 3/05/92, A, C, 92000089

Lent, George P., Investment Properties [Portland Eastside MPS], 1921–1927 SE 7th and 621–637 SE Harrison, Portland, 3/08/89, C, 89000082

Lewis, William H., Model House, 2877 NW. Westover Rd., Portland, 3/06/90, A, C, 90000274

Lindquist Apartment House, 711 NE. Randall St., Portland, 2/19/93, A, C, 93000022

Linnea Hall, 2066 NW Irving St., Portland, 12/02/81, A, C, 81000517

Lipman—Wolfe and Company Building, 521 SW Fifth Ave., Portland, 9/08/88, A, C, 88001531

Loeb, Nathan, House, 726 NW 22nd Ave., Portland, 1/20/78, C, 78002318

Long, A. G., House, 1987 SW. Sixteenth Ave., Portland, 9/09/93, C, 93000917

Looff, Charles, 20-Sweep Menagerie Carousel [Oregon Historic Wooden Carousels TR], Holladay St. at NE. Eighth Ave., Portland, 3/30/89, A, C, b, 87001379

Louise Home Hospital and Residence Hall, 722 N.E. One Hundred and Sixty-second Ave., Gresham, 9/10/87, A, 87001556

Lytle, Robert F., House, 1914 NE 22nd Ave., Portland, 5/19/83, B, C, 83002173

MacMaster, William and Annie, House, 1041 SW. Vista Ave., Portland, 10/30/89, C, 89001862

Mackenzie, W. R., House, 1131 SW King Ave., Portland, 11/28/78, C, 78002319

Multnomah County—Continued

Maegly, A. H., House, 226 SW Kingston St., Portland, 12/02/81, C, 81000518

Malarkey, Daniel J., House, 2141 SW. Hillcrest Pl., Portland, 5/27/93, B, 93000450

Mangels, William F., Four-Row Carousel [Oregon Historic Wooden Carousels TR], 4033 SW Canyon Rd., Portland, 8/26/87, A, C, b, 87001383

Mann, Anna Lewis, Old People's Home, 1021 NE. 33rd Ave., Portland, 10/15/92, A, C, 92001380

Markle-Pittock House, 1816 SW Hawthorne Terr., Portland, 2/28/85, B, C, 85000368

Marks, Morris, House, 1501 SW Harrison St., Portland, 12/30/75, C, b, 75001596

Marquam Manor, 3211 SW. 10th Ave., Portland, 5/27/93, A, C, 93000449

Marshall—Wells Company Warehouse No. 2, 1420 N.W. Lovejoy St., Portland, 2/23/89, A, C, 89000061

Medical Arts Building, 1020 S.W. Taylor, Portland, 11/06/86, A, C, 86002968

Meier and Frank Building, 621 SW 5th Ave., Portland, 7/08/82, A, C, g, 82003744

Menefee, L. B., House, 1634 SW. Myrtle St., Portland, 10/30/89, A, C, 89001866

Miller, Henry B., House, 2439 NE. 21st St., Portland, 10/30/89, B, C, 89001865

Mills, Lewis H., House, 2039 NW Irving St., Portland, 8/26/82, B, C, 82003745

Mizpah Presbytarian Church of East Portland, 2456 SE Tamarack Ave., Portland, 5/19/83, A, C, b, 83002174

Mock, John, House, 4333 N. Willamette Blvd., Portland, 2/15/80, B, C, 80003370

Mohle, Wilhelmina, House [Portland Eastside MPS], 734 SE 34th, Portland, 3/08/89, C, 89000081

Monastery of the Precious Blood, 1208 SE 76th, Portland, 2/14/85, A, C, a, 85000294

Montgomery Ward & Company, 2741 NW Vaughn, Portland, 6/06/85, A, C, 85001184

Morgan, Melinda E., House, 3115 NW. Thurman St., Portland, 10/25/90, C, 90001592

Multnomah County Courthouse, 1021 SW 4th Ave., Portland, 6/11/79, C, 79002136

Multnomah County Poor Farm, 2126 SW. Halsey St., Troutdale, 6/01/90, A, 90000844

Multnomah Falls Lodge and Footpath, NE of Bridal Veil on Old Columbia River Hwy., Bridal Veil vicinity, 4/22/81, C, 81000512

Multnomah Hotel, 319 SW Pine, Portland, 2/28/85, A, C, 85000369

Munsell, William O., House [Portland Eastside MPS], 1507 SE Alder, Portland, 3/08/89, C, 89000080

Murphy, Paul C., House [Architecture of Ellis F. Lawrence MPS], 3574 E. Burnside St., Portland, 2/28/91, B, C, 91000145

Murphy, Paul F., House, 850 NW. Powhatan Terr., Portland, 2/22/91, C, 91000138

Neighborhood House, 3030 SW 2nd Ave., Portland, 7/10/79, A, C, a, 79003737

Neuberger, Isaac, House [Architecture of Ellis F. Lawrence MPS], 630 NW Alpine Ter., Portland, 10/17/90, C, 90001512

New Heathman Hotel, 712 SW Salmon St., Portland, 2/16/84, A, C, 84003087

New Houston Hotel, 230 NW Sixth Ave., Portland, 2/20/91, A, C, 91000058

New Logus Block, 523–535 SE Grand Ave., Portland, 2/01/80, B, C, 80003371

Nicholas-Lang House, 2030 SW Vista Ave., Portland, 3/13/79, C, 79002137

Nichols, Dr. A. S., House, 1961 SW. Vista Ave., Portland, 3/05/92, C, 92000090

Nichols, Dr. Herbert S., House, 1925 SW. Vista Ave., Portland, 6/01/90, C, 90000829

Nicolai, Harry T., House [Architecture of Ellis F. Lawrence MPS], 2621 NW Westover Rd., Portland, 10/17/90, C, 90001511

Odd Fellows Building, 1019 SW 10th Ave., Portland, 10/24/80, A, C, 80003372

Olds, Wortman and King Department Store, 921 SW Morrison St., Portland, 2/20/91, A, C, 91000057

Olsen and Weygandt Building, 1421–1441 NE. Broadway, Portland, 2/11/93, C, 93000024

Olympic Cereal Mill [Portland Eastside MPS], 107 SE Washington, Portland, 3/08/89, A, C, 89000115

Oregon Cracker Company Building, 616 NW Glisan St., Portland, 8/10/79, A, C, 79002138

Oregon Portland Cement Building [Portland Eastside MPS], 111 SE Madison, Portland, 3/08/89, C, 89000114

Oriental Apartments, 3562 SE. Harrison St., Portland, 10/15/92, A, C, 92001377

Ormonde Apartment Building, 2046–2048 NW Flanders, Portland, 9/08/87, C, 87001493

Osborn Hotel, 205 SE Grand Ave., Portland, 3/27/80, C, 80003373

Otis Elevator Company Building, 230 NW Tenth Ave., Portland, 2/11/88, A, C, 88000095

Pacific Building, 520 SW. Yamhill St., Portland, 3/05/92, C, 92000091

Page and Son Apartments [Portland Eastside MPS], 723–37 E. Burnside, Portland, 3/08/89, C, 89000113

Pallay Building, 231–239 N.W. Third Ave., Portland, 11/08/85, A, 85003503

Palmer, John, House, 4314 N. Mississippi Ave., Portland, 3/08/78, C, 78002320

Paramount Theatre, 1037 SW Broadway, Portland, 4/22/76, C, g, 76001585

Parelius, Martin, Fourplex [Portland Eastside MPS], 423–29 and 433–39 SE 28th, Portland, 3/08/89, C, 89000112

Parker, C. W., Four-Row Park Carousel [Oregon Historic Wooden Carousels TR], 1492 Jantzen Beach Center, Portland, 8/26/87, C, b, 87001381

Parkview Apartments, 1760 NE. Irving St., Portland, 3/06/92, C, 92000085

Piggott, Charles, House, 2591 SW Buckingham Ter., Portland, 3/28/79, B, 79002139

Pioneer Courthouse, 520 SW Morrison St., Portland, 3/20/73, A, C, NHL, 73001582

Piper, Charles, Building [Portland Eastside MPS], 3610–24 SE Hawthorne, Portland, 3/08/89, C, 89000111

Pipes, George, House, 2526 St. Helen's Ct., Portland, 2/22/91, C, 91000131

Pipes, Martin Luther, House, 2675 S.W. Vista Ave., Portland, 3/06/87, B, C, 87000310

Pittock Block, 921 S.W. Washington St., Portland, 9/08/87, A, C, 87001507

Pittock Mansion, 3229 NW Pittock Dr., Portland, 11/21/74, B, C, 74001709

Polhemus, James S., House [Portland Eastside MPS], 135 SE 16th, Portland, 3/08/89, C, 89000110

Poole, Otho, House, 506 NW. Hermosa Blvd., Portland, 2/28/91, C, 91000150

Portland Art Museum, 1219 SW Park Ave., Portland, 12/31/74, C, g, 74001710

Portland City Hall, 1220 SW 5th Ave., Portland, 11/21/74, A, C, 74001711

Portland Cordage Company Building, 1313 NW. Marshall St., Portland, 2/11/93, A, B, 93000018

Portland Fire Station No. 17, 824 N.W. Twenty-fourth Ave., Portland, 3/12/87, A, C, 87000311

Portland Fire Station No. 23 [Portland Eastside MPS], 1917 SE 7th, Portland, 5/08/89, A, B, C, 89000108

Portland Fire Station No. 7 [Portland Eastside MPS], 1036 SE Stark, Portland, 5/08/89, A, C, 89000109

Portland General Electric Company Station "L" Group, 1841 S.E. Water St., Portland, 12/02/85, A, C, 85003090

Portland New Chinatown—Japantown Historic District, Bounded by NW. Glisan, NW. 3rd Ave., W. Burnside, and NW. 5th Ave., Portland, 11/21/89, A, C, 89001957

Portland Police Block, 209 SW Oak St., Portland, 6/06/85, A, C, 85001185

Portland Skidmore/Old Town Historic District, Roughly bounded by Harbor Dr., Everett, 3rd, and Oak Sts., Portland, 12/06/75, A, C, NHL, 75001597

Portland Thirteenth Avenue Historic District, NW Thirteenth Ave. between NW Davis and NW Johnson Sts., Portland, 6/15/87, A, C, g, 87000888

Portland Yamhill Historic District, Roughly bounded by Taylor, Morrison, both sides of 2nd Ave. and Willamette River, Portland, 7/30/76, C, 76001587

Posey, John V. G., House [Architecture of Ellis F. Lawrence MPS], 02107 SW Greenwood Rd., Portland vicinity, 10/17/90, C, 90001517

Postal Building, 510 SW 3rd Ave., Portland, 3/14/78, C, 78002321

Poulsen, Johan, House, 3040 SE McLoughlin Blvd., Portland, 3/14/77, C, 77001113

Powers, Ira F., Building, 804–810 S.W. Third Ave., Portland, 12/02/85, B, C, 85003082

Prager—Lombard House, 2032 NW. Everett St., Portland, 2/22/91, C, 91000149

Price, O. L., House, 2681 SW Buena Vista, Portland, 8/11/88, C, 88001242

Prince, Thomas, House, 2903 N.E. Alameda St., Multnomah, 10/23/86, C, 86002911

Multnomah County—Continued

Raabe, Capt. George, House [Portland Eastside MPS], 1506–08 SE Taylor, Portland, 3/08/89, B, C, 89000107

Railway Exchange Building and Huber's Restaurant, 320 SW Stark St., Portland, 3/13/79, A, C, 79002132

Raymond, Jessie M., House [Portland Eastside MPS], 2944 SE Taylor, Portland, 3/08/89, C, 89000106

Reed, Rosamond Coursen and Walter R., House, 2036 SW. Main St., Portland, 2/23/90, B, 90000288

Reed, Samuel G., House [Architecture of Ellis F. Lawrence MPS], 2615 SW Vista Ave., Portland, 10/17/90, C, 90001516

Regent Apartments, 1975 NW. Everett St., Portland, 2/20/91, C, 91000044

Reinhart, Jacques and Amelia, House, 7821 S.E. Thirtieth Ave., Portland, 12/02/85, B, C, a, 85003081

Ricen, Dr. Leo, House, 2624 NW. Overton St., Portland, 3/09/92, C, 92000086

Rockey, Dr. A. E. and Phila Jane, House, 10263 S.W. Riverside Dr., Portland vicinity, 12/02/85, B, C, 85003036

Rocky Butte Scenic Drive Historic District, Rocky Butte Rd. and parts of NE. Fremont St. and 92nd Ave., Portland, 10/17/91, A, C, 91001550

Roome—Stearns House, 2146 NE. Twelfth Ave., Portland, 3/09/92, A, C, 92000087

Rosenberg, Dr. J. J., House, 1792 SW. Montgomery Dr., Portland, 6/01/90, C, 90000828

Rosenfeld, Dr. James, House, 2125 SW Twenty-first Ave., Portland, 2/23/89, B, 89000060

Santa Barbara Apartments [Portland Eastside MPS], 2052 SE Hawthorne, Portland, 3/08/89, C, 89000105

Schnabel, Charles J. and Elsa, House, 2375 S.W. Park Pl., Portland, 9/08/87, B, C, 87001496

Scott, Leslie M., House [Portland Eastside MPS], 2936 SE Taylor, Portland, 3/08/89, B, C, 89000104

Seitz, Maurice, House [Architecture of Ellis F. Lawrence MPS], 1495 SW Clifton St., Portland, 10/17/90, C, 90001515

Selling Building, 610 SW. Alder St., Portland, 10/17/91, C, 91001554

Sensel, Henry, Building [Portland Eastside MPS], 3556–62 SE Hawthorne, Portland, 3/08/89, C, 89000103

Seven Hundred Five Davis Street Apartments, 2141 NW Davis St., Portland, 10/10/80, B, C, 80003374

Seward Hotel, 611 SW 10th Ave., Portland, 2/28/85, C, 85000370

Sheffield, John and Sarah, House, 4272 SE. Washington St., Portland, 3/01/91, C, 91000139

Sherlock Building, 309 SW 3rd Ave., Portland, 10/20/77, C, 77001111

Shogren, Fred A., May, and Ann, House, 400 NE. 62nd Ave., Portland, 7/03/89, B, 89000517

Shriners Hospital for Crippled Children, 8200 NE. Sandy Blvd., Portland, 10/30/89, A, C, 89001869

Smith, Blaine, House [Architecture of Ellis F. Lawrence MPS], 5219 SE. Belmont St., Portland, 6/19/91, C, 91000798

Smith, Mary J. G., House, 2256 NW Johnson St., Portland, 12/02/81, C, 81000519

Smith, Milton W., House, 0305 SW Curry Ave., Portland, 1/11/80, C, 80004547

Smith, Percy A., House, 01837 SW. Greenwood Rd., Portland vicinity, 2/22/91, C, 91000135

Smith, Stanley C. E., House [Architecture of Ellis F. Lawrence MPS], 01905 SW. Greenwood Rd., Portland vicinity, 6/19/91, C, 91000796

Smith, Walter V., House, 1943 SW. Montgomery Dr., Portland, 2/19/93, C, 93000020

Smithson and McKay Brothers Blocks, 943 and 927 N. Russell St., Portland, 8/10/79, C, 79002140

Sovereign Hotel, 710 SW Madison St., Portland, 12/02/81, A, C, 81000520

Spalding Building, 319 SW Washington St., Portland, 10/07/82, A, C, 82001513

Sprague-Marshall-Bowie House, 2234 NW Johnson St., Portland, 2/05/80, C, b, 80003375

Sprouse, John A., Jr., House [Architecture of Ellis F. Lawrence MPS], 2826 NW Cumberland Rd., Portland, 2/19/91, C, 91000068

St. James Lutheran Church, 1315 SW Park Ave., Portland, 5/21/75, A, C, a, 75001598

St. John's Episcopal Church, Foot of SE Spokane St., Portland, 12/27/74, A, C, a, b, 74001712

St. Patrick's Roman Catholic Church and Rectory, 1635 NW 19th Ave., Portland, 5/01/74, A, C, a, 74001713

Stettler, Frank C., House, 2606 NW. Lovejoy St., Portland, 2/23/90, B, 90000287

Stratton-Cornelius House, 2182 SW Yamhill St., Portland, 3/08/78, C, 78002322

Strong, Alice Henderson, House [Architecture of Ellis F. Lawrence MPS], 2241 SW Montgomery Dr., Portland, 10/17/90, C, 90001520

Sunken Village Archeological Site (35MU4), Address Restricted, Portland vicinity, 12/20/89, D, NHL, 89002455

Swedish Evangelical Mission Covenant Church, 1624 NW Glisan St., Portland, 10/07/82, A, C, 82001514

Swigert, Ernest G., House, 720 NW. Warrenton Terr., Portland, 2/28/91, A, g, 91000134

Tanner, Albert H., House, 2248 NW Johnson St., Portland, 3/11/83, B, C, 83002175

Taylor, Fred E., House [Architecture of Ellis F. Lawrence MPS], 2873 NW Shenandoah Ter., Portland, 10/17/90, C, 90001519

Taylor, Peter, House and Haehlen, Gotlieb, House, 2806 and 2816 SW 1st Ave., Portland, 8/01/84, B, C, 84003091

Temple Beth Israel, 1931 NW Flanders St., Portland, 7/26/79, B, C, a, 79002141

Terminal Sales Building, 1220 SW. Morrison St., Portland, 10/17/91, C, 91001555

Town Club, The, 2115 S.W. Salmon St., Portland, 3/06/87, A, C, 87000328

Trenkmann Houses, 525 NW 17th Ave., 526 NW 18th Ave., 1704, 1710, 1716, 1720, 1728, 1734 NW Hoyt St., Portland, 1/30/78, C, 78002323

Trevett-Nunn House, 2347 NW Flanders St., Portland, 2/05/80, B, C, 80003376

Trinity Lutheran Church and School, 106 NE Ivy St., Portland, 5/07/80, C, a, 80003377

Trinity Place Apartments, 117 NW. Trinity Pl., Portland, 2/23/90, C, 90000294

Troutdale Methodist Episcopal Church, 302 SE. Harlow St., Troutdale, 9/09/93, A, C, a, 93000921

Troy Laundry Building [Portland Eastside MPS], 1025 SE Pine, Portland, 3/08/89, A, C, 89000102

Turner, Frederick, Fourplex, 1430 NE. Twentysecond Ave., Portland, 3/05/92, C, 92000135

U.S. Courthouse, 620 SW Main St., Portland, 4/30/79, C, g, 79002142

U.S. Customhouse, 220 NW 8th Ave., Portland, 5/02/74, A, C, 74001714

U.S. Post Office, 511 NW Broadway, Portland, 4/18/79, C, 79002143

US National Bank Building, 321 S.W. Sixth Ave., Portland, 10/09/86, A, C, 86002842

US Post Office—St. John's Station [Significant US Post Offices in Oregon 1900-1941 TR], 8720 N. Ivanhoe St., Portland, 3/04/85, C, 85000543

Union Station, NW 6th Ave., Portland, 8/06/75, C, 75001595

University Club, 1225 SW 6th Ave, Portland, 7/26/79, A, C, 79002144

Vancouver-Portland Bridge [Historic Bridges-/Tunnels in Washington State TR], Spans Columbia River, PORTLAND, 7/16/82, A, C, 82004205

Vetter, Herman, House, 5830 SE. Taylor St., Portland, 6/04/92, C, 92000660

View Point Inn, 40301 NE Larch Mountain Rd., Corbett, 2/28/85, A, C, 85000367

Vista Avenue Viaduct, SW Vista Ave., Portland, 4/26/84, A, C, 84003093

Vista House, Columbia River Scenic Hwy., Crown Point, 11/05/74, A, C, 74001705

Waldo Block, 431–433 SW 2nd Ave., Portland, 4/29/82, A, C, 82003746

Wallace, John M., Fourplex [Portland Eastside MPS], 3645–55 SE Yamhill, Portland, 5/08/89, C, 89000101

Warren, Frank M., House, 2545 NW. Westover Rd., Portland, 6/16/89, B, 89000509

Watzek, Aubrey R., House, 1061 SW Skyline Blvd., Portland, 11/01/74, C, g, 74001715

Webb, Alfred, Investment Properties [Portland Eastside MPS], 1503–17 SE Belmont and 822 SE 15th, Portland, 3/08/89, C, 89000100

Weist Apartments, 209 NW. 23rd Ave., Portland, 2/23/90, C, 90000293

Wells Fargo Building, 309 S.W. Sixth Ave., Portland, 10/09/86, C, 86002839

Wells, William Bittle, House, 1515 SW. Clifton St., Portland, 6/16/89, B, C, 89000519

Wells—Guthrie House, 6651 SE. Scott Dr., Portland, 2/23/90, C, 90000278

West Hall, 5000 N. Willamette Blvd., Portland, 9/22/77, C, a, 77001114

West's Block, 701–707 SE Grand Ave., Portland, 10/10/80, A, C, 80003378

West, Nathaniel, Buildings, 711-727 SE Grand Ave., Portland, 4/26/84, A, C, 84003095

Multnomah County—Continued

Wheeldon Apartment Building, 910 SW. Park Ave., Portland, 10/25/90, C, 90001591

Wheeler, Cora Bryant, House, 1841 SW. Montgomery Dr., Portland, 2/23/90, C, 90000295

Wheeler, James E., House [Architecture of Ellis F. Lawrence MPS], 2417 SW 16th Ave., Portland, 10/17/90, C, 90001518

Whidden—Kerr House and Garden, 11648 SW Military La., Portland vicinity, 10/13/88, C, 88001039

White, Catherine, House, 1924 SE 14th Ave., Portland, 3/10/83, C, 83002176

White, Isam, House, 311 NW. Twentieth Ave., Portland, 10/17/91, C, 91001557

Whitney and Gray Building and Jake's Famous Crawfish Restaurant, 401-409 SW 12th Ave., Portland, 8/11/83, A, C, 83002177

Wickersham Apartments, 410 NW 18th Ave., Portland, 3/10/83, B, C, 83002178

Wilcox Building, 506 SW 6th Ave., Portland, 2/23/89, A, C, 89000058

Wilcox, Theodore B., Country Estate, 3787 SW. 52nd Pl., Portland, 2/19/93, B, C, 93000019

Williams, George H., Townhouses, 133 NW 18th Ave., Portland, 3/22/84, B, C, 84003097

Wortman, H. C., House, 1111 SW Vista Ave., Portland, 8/11/88, B, C, 88001245

Young, John Eben, House, 916 S.W. King St., Portland, 8/25/88, B, C, 88001312

Zimmerman, Jacob, House, 17111 N.E. Sandy Blvd., Gresham, 6/05/86, C, 86001226

Zimmerman, Walter S., House, 1840 SW. Hawthorne Terr., Portland, 2/28/91, C, 91000141

Zimmerman—Rudeen House, 3425 NE. Beakey St., Portland, 6/19/91, C, 91000811

Polk County

Brunk, Harrison, House, Brunk Corner and OR 22, Salem vicinity, 5/06/75, B, C, 75001599

Cooper, James S. and Jennie M., House, 487 S. Third St., Independence, 2/22/88, C, b, 88000092

Dallas Tannery, 505 SW Levens St., Dallas, 11/06/80, A, 80003379

Davidson, Dr. John E. and Mary D., House, 887 Monmouth St., Independence, 2/28/85, B, C, 85000371

Domes, Walter J., House, 8240 Pacific Hwy. W., Rickreall vicinity, 3/09/90, C, 90000373

Eldridge, Kersey C., House, 675 Monmouth St., Independence, 7/14/88, C, 88001040

Fort Yamhill Site, Address Restricted, Willamina vicinity, 7/27/71, A, 71000681

Graves-Fisher-Strong House, 391 E. Jackson St., Monmouth, 6/20/85, C, 85001336

Howell, John W., House, 212 N. Knox St., Monmouth, 9/10/87, A, C, 87001536

Independence Historic District, Roughly bounded by Butler, Main, G, and Ninth Sts., Independence, 3/01/89, A, C, 89000048

Independence National Bank, 302 S. Main St., Independence, 11/06/86, A, C, 86003182

Parker School, 8900 Parker Rd., Independence vicinity, 6/16/89, C, 89000514

Phillips, John, House, NW of Salem on Spring Valley Rd., Salem vicinity, 3/15/76, C, 76001588

Polk County Bank, 295 E. Main St., Monmouth, 11/06/86, A, C, 86003179

Riley-Cutler House, 11510 Pedee Creek Rd., Pedee vicinity, 4/03/80, B, C, b, e, 80003380

Ritner Creek Bridge [Oregon Covered Bridges TR], S of Pedee, Pedee vicinity, 11/29/79, A, C, b, 79002147

Saint Patrick's Roman Catholic Church, 330 Monmouth St., Independence, 2/05/87, A, C, a, 87000040

Sherman, Eleanor, House, 175 N. Craven St., Monmouth, 2/21/89, C, 89000054

Spring Valley Presbyterian Church, SE of McCoy, Zena, 5/15/74, C, a, 74001717

Wells, George A., Jr., House, 10635 Buena Vista Rd., Independence vicinity, 12/22/81, C, 81000521

West Salem City Hall, Old, 1320 Edgewater St. NW., Salem, 6/01/90, A, C, 90000841

Wheeler, J. A., House, 386 Monmouth St., Independence, 11/06/86, C, 86003177

Sherman County

Columbia Southern Railroad Passenger Station and Freight Warehouse, Jct. of Clark and Fulton Sts., Wasco, 2/19/91, A, 91000059

Mack Canyon Archeological Site, Address Restricted, Grass Valley vicinity, 8/22/75, D, 75001600

Tillamook County

Cape Meares Lighthouse [Lighthouse Stations of Oregon MPS], Cape Meares, 5 mi. S of Tillamook Bay entrance, Tillamook vicinity, 4/21/93, A, C, 73002341

Doyle, A. E., Cottage, 37480 2nd St., Neahkahnie Beach, Nehalem vicinity, 2/19/91, C, 91000066

Isom, Mary Frances, Cottage, 37465 Beulah Reed Rd., Neahkahnie Beach, Nehalem vicinity, 2/19/91, C, 91000065

US Coast Guard Station—Tillamook Bay, US 101, Garibaldi, 12/10/93, A, C, g, 93001337

US Naval Air Station Dirigible Hangars A and B, Off US 101 2.5 mi. SE of Tillamook, Tillamook vicinity, 3/29/89, A, C, g, 89000201

US Post Office [Significant US Post Offices in Oregon 1900-1941 TR], 210 Laurel Ave., Tillamook, 3/01/85, C, g, 85000546

Wentz, Harry F., Studio, N of Manzanita off U.S. 101, Manzanita vicinity, 4/22/76, C, 76001589

Umatilla County

Bank of Echo Building, 230 W. Main, Echo, 4/15/82, A, C, 82003747

Bowman Hotel, 17 SW Frazer Ave., Pendleton, 11/06/80, A, C, 80003381

Ellis—Hampton House, 711 S.E. Byers Ave., Pendleton, 10/23/86, B, C, 86002909

Empire Block, 21–37 SW Emigrant Ave., Pendleton, 6/01/82, A, C, 82003748

Frazier, Williams, Farmstead, 1403 Chestnut St., Milton-Freewater, 6/05/86, B, C, 86001234

Greasewood Finnish Apostolic Lutheran Church, Finn Rd. at Finland Cemetery Rd., Adams vicinity, 7/14/88, A, C, a, 88001041

Hamley and Company Leather Goods Store, 30 SE Court St., Pendleton, 6/09/82, A, B, C, 82003749

Hendricks Building (K.O.T.M.), 369 S. Main St., Pendleton, 6/01/82, A, C, 82003750

Johnson—Ellis House, 326 S.E. Second St., Pendleton, 3/14/86, B, C, g, 86000347

LaDow Block, 201–239 SE. Court Ave., Pendleton, 10/22/92, A, B, C, 92001381

Masonic Temple, 18 SW Emigrant Ave., Pendleton, 6/01/82, A, C, 82003751

Matlock-Brownfield Building, 413–425 S. Main St., Pendleton, 6/01/82, A, C, 82003752

Milarkey Building, 203 S. Main St., Pendleton, 9/23/82, A, C, 82003753

Saling, Isham, House, Off OR 204, Weston, 1/01/76, A, C, 76001590

Sommerville, Edgar, House, 104 SE 5th St., Pendleton, 10/14/80, B, C, 80003382

South Main Street Commercial Historic District, Roughly bounded by Dorion Ave., S.E. First St., Union Pacific RR, and S.W. Second St., Pendleton, 10/10/86, A, C, 86003260

Still—Perkins House, 112 SE. Sixth Ave., Milton-Freewater, 9/09/93, C, b, 93000925

US Post Office and Courthouse [Significant US Post Offices in Oregon 1900-1941 TR], 104 SW Dorian Ave., Pendleton, 3/04/85, C, 85000544

Umatilla Site (35 UM 1), Address Restricted, Umatilla vicinity, 1/30/81, D, d, 81000522

Vey, Joseph, House, 1304 S.E. Court Pl., Pendleton, 2/27/86, B, C, 86000299

Walla Walla Valley Traction Company Passenger Station and Powerhouse, 403 Robbins St., Milton-Freewater, 9/09/93, A, 93000926

Watts, M. L., House, Fourth at Jefferson St., Athena, 3/09/88, C, 88000090

Weston Commercial Historic District, E. Main St. between Water and Broad St., Weston, 10/05/82, A, C, 82001515

Union County

Administration Building, Eastern Oregon State College campus, La Grande, 2/27/80, A, C, 80003384

Anthony, John, House, 1606 Sixth St., La Grande, 9/22/88, C, 88001530

Anthony-Buckley House, 1602 6th St., La Grande, 2/28/85, C, 85000372

Ascension Episcopal Church and Rectory, Church St., Cove, 12/03/74, A, C, a, 74001718

Union County—Continued

Eaton, Abel E., House, 464 N. Main St., Union, 11/02/77, C, 77001115

Elgin City Hall and Opera House, Albany and N. 8th Sts., Elgin, 10/10/80, C, 80003383

Foley Building, 206 Chestnut St., La Grande, 12/02/85, A, B, C, 85003080

Hot Lake Resort, SE of La Grande on OR 203, La Grande vicinity, 3/15/79, A, C, 79002148

La Grande Neighborhood Club, 1108 N Ave., La Grande, 7/15/88, A, b, 88001042

Slater Building, 216-224 Fir St., La Grande, 8/11/83, B, C, 83002179

Townley, W. J., House, 782 N. 5th St., Union, 11/06/80, A, C, 80003386

U.S. Post Office and Federal Building, 1010 Adams St., La Grande, 1/25/79, C, 79002149

Wallowa County

Barnard, Dr. J. W., Building and First National Bank of Joseph, 012–014 Main Sts., Joseph, 6/19/91, A, B, C, 91000810

Billy Meadows Guard Station [USDA Forest Service Administrative Buildings in Oregon and Washington Built by the CCC MPS], NE of Red Hill summit, Wallowa—Whitman NF, Joseph vicinity, 3/06/91, A, C, 91000161

Burnaugh Building, 107 N. River St., Enterprise, 5/27/93, B, C, 93000434

College Creek Ranger Station [USDA Forest Service Administrative Buildings in Oregon and Washington Built by the CCC MPS], Imnaha R., Wallowa—Whitman National Forest, Imnaha vicinity, 3/06/91, A, C, g, 91000171

First Bank of Joseph, 2nd and Main Sts., Joseph, 2/23/78, A, C, 78002324

Hells Canyon Archeological District, Address Restricted, Imnaha, vicinity, 8/10/84, A, D, 84000984

Hunter-Morelock House, 104 Holmes St., Wallowa, 2/28/85, C, 85000373

Kirkland Lookout Ground House (Guard Station) [USDA Forest Service Administrative Buildings in Oregon and Washington Built by the CCC MPS], E of Joseph Cr., Wallowa—Whitman NF, Joseph vicinity, 3/06/91, A, C, 91000165

Lick Creek Guard Station [Depression-Era Buildings TR], Wallowa-Whitman National Forest, Enterprise, 4/08/86, A, C, 86000844

Nez Perce Traditional Site, Wallowa Lake, SR 82 S of Joseph, Joseph vicinity, 5/05/89, A, NHL, 89001082

Warnock, William P., House, 501 S. 5th St., Enterprise, 11/15/84, C, 84000486

Wasco County

Anderson, Lewis, House, Barn and Granary, 508 W. 16th St., The Dalles, 3/20/80, A, C, b, 80003387

Balch Hotel, 40 S. Main, Dufur, 9/08/87, A, 87001469

Bennett-Williams House, 608 W. Sixth St., The Dalles, 2/27/86, B, C, 86000291

Columbia Southern Hotel, 4th and E Sts., Shaniko, 10/31/79, A, C, 79002150

Dalles Carnegie Library, E. 4th and Washington Sts., The Dalles, 12/08/78, A, C, 78002325

First Wasco County Courthouse, 404 2nd St., The Dalles, 11/16/77, A, C, b, 77001116

Fivemile Rapids Site (35 WS 4), Address Restricted, The Dalles vicinity, 12/19/74, D, 74001719

Fort Dalles Surgeon's Quarters, 15th and Garrison Sts., The Dalles, 9/10/71, A, C, 71000682

French, Edward, House, 515 Liberty St., The Dalles, 10/02/92, B, 92001319

Fulton—Taylor House, 704 Case St., The Dalles, 9/09/93, B, 93000920

Glenn, Hugh, House, 100 W. Ninth St., The Dalles, 2/20/91, C, 91000064

Heimrich—Seufert House, 303 E. Tenth St., The Dalles, 6/01/90, B, C, 90000827

Humason, Orlando, House, 908 Court St., The Dalles, 6/21/91, B, C, b, 91000809

Indian Shaker Church and Gulick Homestead, Jct. U.S. 80N and U.S. 197, The Dalles, 4/04/78, A, a, b, 78003087

Moody, Malcolm A., House, 300 W. 13th St., The Dalles, 10/10/80, A, B, C, 80003388

Mosier, Jefferson, House, 704 3rd Ave., Mosier, 2/23/90, B, C, 90000286

Rock Fort Campsite, Off I-80N, The Dalles, 9/04/80, A, B, 80003389

Shaniko Historic District, US 97 and OR 218, Shaniko, 3/18/82, A, C, 82003754

Sharp, Edward F., Residential Ensemble, 400 and 404 E. Fourth St. and 504 Federal St., The Dalles, 10/25/91, B, C, 91001561

St. Peter's Roman Catholic Church, 3rd and Lincoln Sts., The Dalles, 6/20/74, C, a, 74001720

The Dalles Civic Auditorium, E. 4th and Federal Sts., The Dalles, 12/12/78, A, C, 78002326

The Dalles Commercial Historic District, Roughly bounded by Columbia River, Laughlin, Fifth, and Union Sts., The Dalles, 11/04/86, A, g, 86002953

Thompson, John L., House, 209 W. 3rd St., The Dalles, 11/06/80, A, B, C, 80003390

US Post Office [Significant US Post Offices in Oregon 1900-1941 TR], 100 W. 2nd St., The Dalles, 3/04/85, C, 85000545

Van Dellen, John and Murta, House, 400 E. Eighth St., The Dalles, 2/20/91, C, 91000063

Washington County

Beaverton Downtown Historic District, Roughly bounded by S.W. Canyon Blvd., S.W. East and S.W. Washington Sts., S.W. Second, and S.W. Watson Sts., Beaverton, 1/07/86, A, g, 86000037

Beeks, Silas Jacob N., House, NE of Forest Grove, Forest Grove vicinity, 6/14/84, B, C, D, 84003100

Blank, Stephen and Parthena M., House, 2117 A St., Forest Grove, 7/14/88, C, b, 88001035

Blanton, M. E., House, 3980 SW 170th Ave., Aloha, 3/02/89, C, 89000123

Cornelius, Benjamin, Jr., House, 2314 Nineteenth Ave., Forest Grove, 7/14/88, C, b, 88001034

Crosley, Harry A., House, 2125 A St., Forest Grove, 9/09/93, C, 93000919

Dundee Lodge, Rt. 1, Box 311, Gaston vicinity, 6/06/85, C, 85001186

Fanno, Augustus, Farmhouse, 8385 SW Hall Boulevard, Beaverton, 4/05/84, A, B, C, 84003103

Feldman, Adam and Johanna, House, 8808 SW. Rambler Ln., Portland, 2/11/93, C, 93000013

Imbrie Farm, NE of Hillsboro off U.S. 26, Hillsboro vicinity, 2/15/77, A, C, 77001117

Jenkins, Belle Ainsworth, Estate, 20950 SW Farmington Rd., Beaverton vicinity, 11/28/78, C, 78002327

Linklater, Zula, House, 230 NE 2nd Ave., Hillsboro, 8/01/84, C, 84003108

Michos, Thomas, House, 4400 SW. Scholls Ferry Rd., Portland vicinity, 10/17/91, C, 91001552

Old Scotch Church, Scotch Church Rd., Hillsboro, 11/05/74, C, a, 74001723

Oleson, Ole and Polly, Farmhouse, 5430 SW. Ames Way, Portland vicinity, 2/22/91, A, C, 91000140

Rice-Gates House, 308 SE Walnut St., Hillsboro, 9/08/80, B, C, 80003391

Robb, James D., House, 2606 Seventeenth Ave., Forest Grove, 7/14/88, C, 88001033

Schanen-Zolling House, 6750 S.W. Oleson Rd., Portland, 12/10/85, B, C, 85003340

Schulmerich, Edward, House, 614 E. Main St., Hillsboro, 2/28/91, B, C, 91000050

Shaver—Bilyeu House, 16445 SW. 92nd Ave., Tigard, 2/11/93, A, C, b, 93000014

Sholes, Albert S., House, 1599 S. Alpine St., Cornelius, 9/02/82, A, C, 82003755

Shorey, Charles, House, 905 E. Main St., Hillsboro, 6/16/89, C, 89000518

Smith, Alvin T., House, S. Elm St., Forest Grove, 11/08/74, C, 74001721

Sweek, John, House, 18815 SW Boones Ferry Rd., Tualatin, 11/08/74, C, 74001724

Tigard, John W., House, 10310 SW Canterbury Lane, Tigard, 7/20/79, A, C, b, 79003739

Tualatin Academy, Pacific University campus, Forest Grove, 2/12/74, A, C, a, 74001722

Washington County Jail, 872 N.E. Twenty-eighth Ave., Hillsboro, 7/31/86, A, C, b, e, 86002090

Watkins, J. F., House, 5419 SW. Scholls Ferry Rd., Portland, 5/27/93, C, 93000448

West Union Baptist Church, W. Union Rd., West Union, 7/10/74, C, a, 74001725

Woods and Caples General Store, 2020 Main St., Forest Grove, 12/02/85, A, C, 85003028

Wheeler County

Hoover, Thomas Benton, House, 1st St. between Adams and Washington Sts., Fossil, 4/14/78, B, 78002328

Yamhill County

Avery House [Dayton MRA], 403 Church St., Dayton, 3/16/87, C, 87000329

Baxter House [Dayton MRA], 407 Church St., Dayton, 3/16/87, C, 87000331

Berry—Sigler Investment Property [Dayton MRA], 700 Church St., Dayton, 8/03/87, A, C, 87000368

Bertram, Henry, Sr., House, 6160 SE Webfoot Rd., Dayton vicinity, 2/29/88, C, 88000080

Briedwell School, 11935 SW Bellevue Hwy., Amity vicinity, 7/28/88, C, 88001156

Brookside Cemetery [Dayton MRA], S end of Third St., Dayton, 3/16/87, B, C, d, 87000332

Bunn, John Marion, House, 285 SW 3rd St., Yamhill, 10/16/79, B, C, 79002152

Cain House [Dayton MRA], 208 Alder St., Dayton, 3/16/87, C, 87000333

Carlton State and Savings Bank, 109 W. Main St., Carlton, 2/11/88, A, B, 88000082

Carter-Goodrich House [Dayton MRA], 521 Church St., Dayton, 3/16/87, C, 87000334

Cate, Asa F., Farm Ensemble, 16900 NW. Baker Creek Rd., McMinnville vicinity, 2/23/90, C, 90000285

Chambers, Joseph and Virginia, Farmstead, 30295 N. OR 99W, Newberg vicinity, 3/05/92, A, C, 92000136

Commercial Club—Stuckey, S. C., Building [Dayton MRA], 304 Ferry St., Dayton, 3/16/87, B, C, 87000335

Cook, Amos, House, NW of Dayton on OR 233, Dayton vicinity, 12/31/74, C, 74001726

Courthouse Square [Dayton MRA], Bounded by Third, Fourth, Ferry, and Main Sts., Dayton, 3/16/87, A, b, f, 87000336

Dayton Auto and Transfer Company Building [Dayton MRA], 411 Ferry St., Dayton, 3/16/87, A, 87000337

Dayton Common School [Dayton MRA], 504 Fourth St., Dayton, 3/16/87, A, 87000338

Dayton High School [Dayton MRA], 801 Ferry St., Dayton, 3/16/87, C, 87000339

Dayton Methodist Episcopal Church [Dayton MRA], 302 Fourth St., Dayton, 3/16/87, A, a, 87000340

Dayton Opera House [Dayton MRA], 318 Ferry St., Dayton, 3/16/87, C, 87000342

Diehl—Seitters House [Dayton MRA], 527 Church St., Dayton, 3/16/87, C, 87000344

Dundee Woman's Club Hall, US 99 W, Dundee, 6/05/86, A, 86001241

Edwards, Jesse, House, 402 S. College St., Newberg, 8/25/80, A, B, C, b, 80003393

Evangelical United Brethren Church [Dayton MRA], 302 Fifth St., Dayton, 8/03/87, A, C, a, 87000346

Fenton, Frank W., House, 434 N. Evans St., McMinnville, 9/01/83, B, C, 83002180

First Baptist Church [Dayton MRA (AD)], 3rd and Main Sts., Dayton, 10/16/79, C, a, 79002151

Fischer, Carl, Meats [Dayton MRA], 400 Ferry St., Dayton, 3/16/87, C, 87000348

Fletcher, Alfred P., Farmhouse, 1007 3rd St., Lafayette, 8/25/80, B, C, 80003392

Fletcher, Francis, House, W of Dayton off OR 18, Dayton vicinity, 10/29/75, C, 75001601

Fletcher—Stretch House [Dayton MRA], 401 Oak St., Dayton, 3/16/87, C, 87000349

Foster Oil Company [Dayton MRA], 216 Ferry St., Dayton, 3/16/87, C, 87000356

Free Methodist Church [Dayton MRA], 411 Oak St., Dayton, 3/16/87, A, a, 87000357

Gabriel—Filer House [Dayton MRA], 525 Church St., Dayton, 3/16/87, B, 87000358

Gabriel—Will House [Dayton MRA], 401 Third St., Dayton, 3/16/87, C, 87000359

Hagey, Levi, House, Off U.S. 99, Dundee, 12/19/74, C, 74001727

Harrington House [Dayton MRA], 212 Mill St., Dayton, 3/16/87, C, 87000360

Harris Building [Dayton MRA], 302 Ferry St., Dayton, 3/16/87, B, 87000363

Hibbert, William, House [Dayton MRA (AD)], 426 5th St., Dayton, 11/30/78, B, C, 78002329

Hole House [Dayton MRA], 623 Ferry St., Dayton, 3/16/87, B, 87000367

Jessen—Goodrich House [Dayton MRA], 324 Sixth St., Dayton, 3/16/87, C, 87000370

Kelty, James M. and Paul R., House, 675 3rd St., Lafayette, 9/23/82, B, C, g, 82003756

Kershaw, Dr. Andrew, House, 472 E. Main St., Willamina, 3/02/89, B, C, 89000122

Krietz House [Dayton MRA], 627 Church St., Dayton, 3/16/87, C, 87000372

Laughlin, Lee, House, 100 Laurel St., Yamhill, 3/26/79, B, C, 79002153

Lewis—Shippy House [Dayton MRA], 421 Sixth St., Dayton, 3/16/87, C, 87000373

Londershausen House [Dayton MRA], 402 Main St., Dayton, 3/16/87, B, 87000383

Londershausen House [Dayton MRA], 309 Main St., Dayton, 3/16/87, C, 87000384

Mabee—Mayberry House [Dayton MRA], 309 Seventh St., Dayton, 8/03/87, C, 87000385

Mattey, Joseph, House, W of Lafayette at jct. of Mattey Lane and Rutherford Rd., Lafayette vicinity, 2/15/77, C, 77001118

McMinnville Downtown Historic District, Bounded by Fifth St., Southern Pacific RR tracks, Second, and N. Adams Sts., McMinnville, 9/14/87, A, C, 87001366

McNamar Building [Dayton MRA], 310–312 Ferry St., Dayton, 3/16/87, B, 87000386

McNish House [Dayton MRA], 1005 Ferry St., Dayton, 3/16/87, C, 87000388

Mellinger House [Dayton MRA], 414 Fifth St., Dayton, 3/16/87, C, 87000389

Mellinger—Ponnay House [Dayton MRA], 603 Palmer Ln., Dayton, 8/03/87, C, 87000390

Methodist Episcopal Parsonage [Dayton MRA], 202 Fourth St., Dayton, 8/03/87, A, a, 87000393

Minthorn, Dr. Henry J., House (Herbert Hoover House), 115 S. River St., Newberg, 10/29/75, B, C, 75001602

Monahan House [Dayton MRA], 120 Fifth St., Dayton, 3/16/87, C, 87000395

Morse House [Dayton MRA], 101 Fifth St., Dayton, 3/16/87, C, 87000396

Morse House [Dayton MRA], 409 Oak St., Dayton, 3/16/87, C, 87000398

Nichols House [Dayton MRA], 303 Main St., Dayton, 3/16/87, B, 87000400

Oregon Mutual Merchant Fire Insurance Association Office [Dayton MRA], 308 Ferry St., Dayton, 3/16/87, C, 87000402

Palmer House [Dayton MRA], 600 Ferry St., Dayton, 3/16/87, B, C, 87000403

Pioneer Hall, Linfield College, Linfield College campus, McMinnville, 2/23/78, A, C, a, 78002330

Powell, Curtis W., House [Dayton MRA], 524 Ash St., Dayton, 3/16/87, C, 87000404

Rippey House [Dayton MRA], 533 Ash St., Dayton, 3/16/87, B, C, 87000405

Sigler House [Dayton MRA], 521 Ferry St., Dayton, 3/16/87, B, C, 87000406

Smith, Andrew, House [Dayton MRA (AD)], 306 5th St., Dayton, 6/23/76, B, C, 76001591

Smith, John T., House, 414 N. College St., Newberg, 11/15/84, A, B, 84000493

Spence, Jack, House, 536 E. Fifth St., McMinnville, 2/27/86, C, 86000295

Stuart, Dr., House [Dayton MRA], 103 Ferry St., Dayton, 3/16/87, B, 87000408

Travelers Home, 147 NE Yamhill St., Sheridan, 7/08/82, B, C, 82003757

Yamhill River Lock and Dam, Across the Yamhill R. at S terminus of Locks Rd., Dayton vicinity, 6/21/91, A, 91000799

Young, Ewing, Site, Address Restricted, Newberg vicinity, 11/26/89, B, D, 89001977

PALAU

Aimeliik Municipality

Ked Ra Ngchemiangel, Address Restricted, Ameliik (Babelthuap) vicinity, 9/30/76, C, D, 76002196

Airai Municipality

Bai Ra Irrai, Airai, Airai (Babelthuap), 9/20/76, A, C, e, 76002195

Melekeiok Municipality

Meteu 'L Klechem, Melekeok, Melekeok (Babelthuap), 9/30/76, A, b, 76002197
Odalmelech, Melekeok, Melekeok (Babelthuap), 9/30/76, A, 76002198
Ongeluluul, Melekeok, Melekeok (Babelthuap), 9/30/76, A, a, 76002199

Peleliu Municipality

Peleliu Battlefield, Peleliu Island, Peleliu, 2/04/85, A, g, NHL, 85001754

These stone paths in the Airai Village, Palau, converge at the Bai Ra Irrai, or men's meetinghouse, where village elders traditionally met to discuss religion, politics, and law. (Isamu Iowai, 1975)

PENNSYLVANIA

Adams County

Abbott, John, House, E. King St., Abbottstown, 2/22/80, B, C, 80003394

Adams County Courthouse, Baltimore and W. Middle Sts., Gettysburg, 10/01/74, A, C, 74001728

Black Horse Tavern, W of Gettysburg on PA 116, Gettysburg vicinity, 3/30/78, A, C, 78002331

Bridge in Cumberland Township [Highway Bridges Owned by the Commonwealth of Pennsylvania, Department of Transportation TR], LR 01002 over Marsh Creek, Greenmount vicinity, 6/22/88, C, 88000866

Carbaugh Run Rhyolite Quarry Site (36AD30), Address Restricted, Cashtown vicinity, 1/15/86, D, 86000817

Conewago Chapel, 3 mi. NW of Hanover, Conewago Township, Hanover vicinity, 1/29/75, A, C, a, 75001604

Conewago Mass House, N of McSherrystown on SR 476, Conewago Township, McSherrystown vicinity, 10/19/78, A, C, a, 78002332

Dobbin House, 89 Steinwehr Ave., Gettysburg, 3/26/73, A, C, a, 73001584

East Berlin Historic District, Portions of King, Harrisburg and Abbottstown St., East Berlin, 9/30/85, A, C, a, 85002693

Eisenhower National Historic Site, SW edge of Gettysburg National Military Park, Gettysburg vicinity, 11/27/67, A, B, f, g, NHL, NPS, 67000017

Fairfield Inn, Main St., Fairfield, 4/02/73, A, C, 73001583

Gettysburg Armory [Pennsylvania National Guard Armories MPS], 315 W. Confederate Ave., Gettysburg, 4/18/90, A, C, 90000422

Gettysburg Battlefield Historic District, Town of Gettysburg and its environs, Gettysburg and vicinity, 3/19/75, A, C, 75000155

Gettysburg National Military Park, Gettysburg National Military Park, Gettysburg, 10/15/66, A, B, f, NPS, 66000642

Great Conewago Presbyterian Church, Church Rd., Straban Township, Hunterstown, 12/27/74, A, C, a, 74001730

Heikes Covered Bridge [Covered Bridges of Adams, Cumberland, and Perry Counties TR], N of Heidlersburg on T 5857, Tyronne-/Huntington Townships, Heidlersburg vicinity, 8/25/80, A, 80003396

Hunterstown Historic District, PA 394 and Granite Station Rd., Hunterstown, 5/15/79, A, C, a, 79002154

Jacks Mountain Covered Bridge [Covered Bridges of Adams, Cumberland, and Perry Counties TR], SW of Fairfield on LR 01053, Hamiltonban Township, Iron Springs vicinity, 8/25/80, A, 80003397

John's Burnt Mill Bridge, SW of New Oxford on T 428, New Oxford, 12/16/74, A, C, 74001731

Lower Marsh Creek Presbyterian Church, SE of Orrtanna on LR 01002, Highland Township, Orrtanna vicinity, 10/15/80, C, a, 80003399

Lutheran Theological Seminary-Old Dorm, Seminary Ridge, Lutheran Theological Seminary campus, Gettysburg, 5/03/74, A, a, 74001729

Pennsylvania Hall, Gettysburg College, Gettysburg College campus, Gettysburg, 3/16/72, A, C, a, 72001087

Pond Mill Bridge [Highway Bridges Owned by the Commonwealth of Pennsylvania, Department of Transportation TR], LR 01009 over Bermudian Creek, Bermudian vicinity, 6/22/88, C, 88000816

Sauck's Covered Bridge [Covered Bridges of Adams, Cumberland, and Perry Counties TR], SW of Gettysburg on T 326, Cumberland/Freedom Townships, Gettysburg vicinity, 8/25/80, A, 80003395

Sheads House, 331 Buford Ave., Gettysburg, 12/08/76, A, C, 76001592

Spangler—Benner Farm, 230 Benner Rd., Mt. Joy Township, Gettysburg vicinity, 10/29/92, A, 92001493

Wirts House, 798 Schrivers Corner Rd. (PA 394), Straban Township, Gettysburg, 1/22/92, C, 91002010

Zeigler, John, Farm House, 1281 Mountain Rd., Latimore Township, York Springs, 5/07/92, C, 92000395

Allegheny County

Allegheny Cemetery, Roughly bounded by N. Mathilda and Butler Sts., and Penn, Stanton, and Mossfield Aves., Pittsburgh, 12/10/80, A, C, d, 80003405

Allegheny County Courthouse and Jail, 436 Grant St., Pittsburgh, 3/07/73, C, NHL, 73001586

Allegheny High School [Pittsburgh Public Schools TR], 810 Arch St., Pittsburgh, 9/30/86, A, C, 86002643

Allegheny Observatory, 159 Riverview Ave., Pittsburgh, 6/22/79, A, C, 79002157

Allegheny Post Office, Allegheny Center, Pittsburgh, 7/27/71, C, 71000683

Allegheny West Historic District, Roughly bounded by Brighton Rd., Jabok Way, Ridge and Allegheny Aves., Pittsburgh, 11/02/78, A, C, a, g, 78002334

Allerdice, Taylor, High School [Pittsburgh Public Schools TR], 2409 Shady Ave., Pittsburgh, 9/30/86, A, C, 86002641

Alpha Terrace Historic District, 716–740 and 721–743 N. Beatty St., Pittsburg, 7/18/85, C, 85001570

Armstrong Tunnel, Between Forbes and Second Aves. at S. Tenth St., Pittsburgh, 1/07/86, A, C, 86000015

Arsenal Junior High School [Pittsburgh Public Schools TR], Butler and Fortieth Sts., Pittsburgh, 9/30/86, A, C, 86002645

Baxter High School [Pittsburgh Public Schools TR], Baxter St. and Brushton Ave., Pittsburgh, 9/30/86, A, C, 86002647

Bayard School [Pittsburgh Public Schools TR], 4830 Hatfield St., Pittsburgh, 9/30/86, A, C, 86002649

Bedford School [Pittsburgh Public Schools TR], 910–918 Bingham St., Pittsburgh, 9/30/86, A, C, 86002651

Beechwood Elementary School [Pittsburgh Public Schools TR], Rockland Ave. near Sebring Ave., Pittsburgh, 9/30/86, A, C, 86002656

Beltzhoover Elementary School [Pittsburgh Public Schools TR], Cedarhurst and Estrella Sts., Pittsburgh, 9/30/86, A, C, 86002657

Beulah Presbyterian Church, Beulah and McCready Rds., Churchill, 11/03/75, C, a, 75001606

Bindley Hardware Company Building, 401 Amberson Ave., Pittsburgh, 8/08/85, B, C, 85001748

Birmingham Public School [Pittsburgh Public Schools TR], 118–128 S. Fifteenth St., Pittsburgh, 9/30/86, A, C, a, 86002658

Boggs Avenue Elementary School [Pittsburgh Public Schools TR], Boggs and Southern Aves., Pittsburgh, 2/03/87, C, 86002659

Bowman Homestead, N of McKeesport at 3500 The Lane, North Versailles Township, McKeesport vicinity, 9/07/79, A, C, 79003140

Boyce Station, 1050 Boyce Rd., Upper St. Clair, 11/14/82, A, C, b, 82001528

Bridge in Jefferson Borough [Highway Bridges Owned by the Commonwealth of Pennsylvania, Department of Transportation TR], Cochran Mill Rd. over Lick Run, Cochrans Mill vicinity, 6/22/88, C, 88000938

Bridge in Shaler Township [Highway Bridges Owned by the Commonwealth of Pennsylvania, Department of Transportation TR], Birchfield Rd. over Pine Creek, Glenshaw vicinity, 6/22/88, C, 88000797

Buhl Building, 204 5th Ave., Pittsburgh, 1/03/80, A, C, 80003406

Burke Building, 209-211 4th Ave., Pittsburgh, 9/18/78, C, 78002335

Burtner Stone House, NW of Natrona Heights on Burtner Rd., Harrison Township, Natrona Heights vicinity, 1/13/72, C, 72001088

Butler Street Gatehouse, 4734 Butler St., Pittsburgh, 7/30/74, C, d, 74001734

Byers-Lyons House, 901 Ridge Ave., Pittsburgh, 11/19/74, C, 74001735

Byrnes & Kiefer Building, 1127-1133 Penn Ave., Pittsburg, 3/07/85, A, C, 85000457

Campbell Building, 3 Crafton Sq., Crafton, 9/19/88, C, 88001157

Carnegie Free Library, 1507 Liberty Ave., McKeesport, 10/15/80, A, C, 80003402

Carnegie Free Library Of Braddock, 419 Library St., Braddock, 6/19/73, B, C, 73001585

Carnegie Free Library of Allegheny, Allegheny Center, Pittsburgh, 11/01/74, A, C, 74001736

Allegheny County—Continued

Carnegie Institute and Library, 4400 Forbes Ave., Pittsburgh, 3/30/79, A, B, C, 79002158

Carnegie, Andrew, Free Library, 300 Beechwood Ave., Carnegie, 10/08/81, B, C, 81000523

Carson, Rachel, House, 613 Marion Ave., Springdale, 10/22/76, B, C, c, g, 76001601

Cathedral of Learning, Forbes Ave. and Bigelow Blvd., Pittsburgh, 11/03/75, A, C, g, 75001608

Colfax Elementary School [Pittsburgh Public Schools TR], Beechwood Blvd. and Phillips Ave., Pittsburgh, 9/30/86, A, C, 86002660

Connelly, Clifford B., Trade School [Pittsburgh Public Schools TR], 1501 Bedford Ave., Pittsburgh, 9/30/86, A, C, 86002661

Conroy Junior High School [Pittsburgh Public Schools TR], Page and Fulton Sts., Pittsburgh, 9/30/86, A, C, 86002662

Coraopolis Armory [Pennsylvania National Guard Armories MPS], 835 Fifth Ave., Coraopolis, 11/14/91, A, C, 91001695

Coraopolis Bridge [Allegheny County Owned River Bridges TR], Ohio River Back Channel at Ferree St. and Grand Ave., Coraopolis, 1/07/86, A, C, 86000021

Coraopolis Railroad Station, Neville Ave. and Mill St., Coraopolis, 4/20/79, A, C, 79002156

Davis Island Lock and Dam Site, Off PA 65, Avalon, 8/29/80, A, C, 80003400

Deutschtown Historic District, Roughly bounded by Cedar Ave., Knoll, East, and Pressley Sts., Pittsburgh, 11/25/83, C, a, 83004181

Dilworth Elementary School [Pittsburgh Public Schools TR], Saint Marie and Collins Sts., Pittsburgh, 9/30/86, C, 86002663

Dollar Savings Bank, 4th Ave. and Smithfield St., Pittsburgh, 7/14/76, A, C, 76001594

Duquesne Incline, 1220 Grandview Ave., Pittsburgh, 3/04/75, A, C, 75001609

East Carson Street Historic District, Roughly E. Carson St. from 9th to 24th St., Pittsburgh, 11/17/83, C, 83004183

East Liberty Market, Centre Ave. and Baum Blvd., Pittsburgh, 12/12/77, A, C, 77001121

Eberhardt and Ober Brewery, Troy Hill Rd. & Vinial St., Pittsburgh, 11/05/87, A, C, 87001984

Emmanuel Episcopal Church, North and Allegheny Aves., Pittsburgh, 5/03/74, C, a, 74001737

Evergreen Hamlet, Evergreen Hamlet Rd., Ross Township, Pittsburgh, 9/17/74, A, C, 74001738

Ewart Building, 921, 923 and 925 Liberty Ave, Pittsburgh, 8/09/79, A, C, 79002159

Experimental Mine, U.S. Bureau Of Mines, S of Bruceton off Cochran Mill Rd., Bruceton vicinity, 10/18/74, A, C, 74001732

Fifth Avenue High School [Pittsburgh Public Schools TR], 1800 Fifth Ave., Pittsburgh, 10/23/86, A, C, 86002956

Firstside Historic District, 211–249 Fort Pitt Blvd.; 1–7 Wood St., Pittsburgh, 7/28/88, A, C, 88001215

Forks of the Ohio, Point Park, Pittsburgh, 10/15/66, A, D, NHL, 66000643

Fort Pitt Elementary School [Pittsburgh Public Schools TR], 5101 Hillcrest St., Pittsburgh, 9/30/86, C, 86002666

Fortieth Street Bridge [Highway Bridges Owned by the Commonwealth of Pennsylvania, Department of Transportation TR], Fortieth St. over Allegheny River, Millvale, 6/22/88, C, 88000820

Foster School [Pittsburgh Public Schools TR], 286 Main St., Pittsburgh, 9/30/86, A, C, 86002667

Fourth Avenue Historic District, Fourth Ave. & Wood St., Pittsburgh, 9/05/85, A, C, 85001961

Frick Building and Annex, 437 Grant St., Pittsburgh, 5/22/78, C, 78002336

Frick, Henry Clay, Training School for Teachers [Pittsburgh Public Schools TR], 107 Thackeray St., Pittsburgh, 9/30/86, A, C, 86002668

Fulton Elementary School [Pittsburgh Public Schools TR], Hampton and N. Saint Clair Sts., Pittsburgh, 9/30/86, A, C, 86002669

Fulton Log House, NW of Pittsburgh on Clifton-Bridgeville Rd. off PA 65, Upper St. Clair Township, Pittsburgh vicinity, 12/06/75, C, 75001610

Gardner-Bailey House, 124 W. Swissvale Ave., Edgewood Borough, Pittsburgh, 10/01/74, C, 74001739

Gilfillan Farm, 1950 Washington Rd., Upper St. Clair Township, Bridgeville vicinity, 11/20/79, A, C, 79002155

Greenfield Elementary School [Pittsburgh Public Schools TR], N of Greenfield Ave. at E end of Alger St., Pittsburgh, 9/30/86, A, C, 86002671

Hartley-Rose Belting Company Building, 425-427 1st Ave., Pittsburgh, 8/25/83, A, C, 83002212

Heathside Cottage, 416 Catoma St., Pittsburgh, 12/30/74, C, 74001740

Henderson-Metz House, 1516 Warren St., Pittsburgh, 8/22/79, C, 79003141

Highland Building, 121 S. Highland Mall, Pittsburgh, 9/06/91, A, C, 91001123

Highland Towers Apartments, 340 S. Highland Ave., Pittsburgh, 9/28/76, C, 76001595

Hoene-Werle House, 1313-1315 Allegheny Ave., Pittsburgh, 11/15/84, C, 84000533

Homestead High-Level Bridge [Allegheny County Owned River Bridges TR], Monongahela River at West St., Pittsburgh, 1/07/86, A, C, 86000016

Homestead Historic District, Eighth Ave. area roughly bounded by Mesta, Sixth, Andrew, 11th and Walnuts Sts. and Doyle and Seventh Aves., Pittsburgh, 5/10/90, A, C, 90000696

Homestead Pennsylvania Railroad Station, Amity St., Homestead, 12/26/85, A, C, 85003157

House at 200 West North Avenue, 200 W. North Ave., Pittsburgh, 2/27/86, C, 86000305

Houses at 2501-2531 Charles Street, 2501-2531 Charles St., Pittsburgh, 3/15/84, C, 84003084

Houses at 838-862 Brightridge Street, 838-862 Brightridge St., Pittsburgh, 3/01/84, C, 84003081

Hunt Armory [Pennsylvania National Guard Armories MPS], 324 Emerson St., Pittsburgh, 11/14/91, A, C, 91001697

Hutchinson Farm, Round Hill Rd. at PA 51, Elizabeth, 2/19/86, A, C, 86000321

Jerome Street Bridge [Highway Bridges Owned by the Commonwealth of Pennsylvania, De-

partment of Transportation TR], Fifth Ave. over Youghiogheny River, Glassport, 6/22/88, C, 88000818

Kennywood Park, 4800 Kennywood Blvd., West Mifflin, 2/27/87, A, NHL, 87000824

Knoxville Junior High School [Pittsburgh Public Schools TR], Charles and Grimes Aves., Pittsburgh, 2/03/87, C, 86002673

Langley High School [Pittsburgh Public Schools TR], Sheraden Blvd. and Chartiers Ave., Pittsburgh, 9/30/86, A, C, 86002674

Larimer School [Pittsburgh Public Schools TR], Larimer Ave. at Winslow St., Pittsburgh, 9/30/86, C, 86002675

Latimer School [Pittsburgh Public Schools TR], Tripoli and James Sts., Pittsburgh, 9/30/86, C, 86002676

Lawrence Public School [Pittsburgh Public Schools TR], 3701 Charlotte St., Pittsburgh, 9/30/86, A, C, 86002679

Lemington Elementary School [Pittsburgh Public Schools TR], 7060 Lemington Ave., Pittsburgh, 9/30/86, A, C, g, 86002681

Letsche Elementary School [Pittsburgh Public Schools TR], 1530 Cliff St., Pittsburgh, 9/30/86, A, C, g, 86002682

Liberty Bridge [Highway Bridges Owned by the Commonwealth of Pennsylvania, Department of Transportation TR], Over the Monongahela River, Pittsburgh, 6/22/88, A, C, 88000867

Liberty School No. 4, Friendship Building [Pittsburgh Public Schools TR], 5501 Friendship Ave., Pittsburgh, 9/30/86, C, 86002684

Lightner, Isaac, House, 2407 Mt. Royal Blvd., Shaler township, Glenshaw, 4/20/78, C, 78002333

Lincoln Elementary School [Pittsburgh Public Schools TR], Lincoln and Frankstown Aves., Pittsburgh, 9/30/86, C, 86002685

Linden Avenue School [Pittsburgh Public Schools TR], 739 S. Linden Ave., Pittsburgh, 9/30/86, A, C, 86002686

Linden Grove, Grove Rd. at Library Rd. & Willow Ave., Castle Shannon, 11/05/87, A, C, 87001970

Lobb's Cemetery and Yohogania County Courthouse Site [Whiskey Rebellion Resources in Southwestern Pennsylvania MPS], Calamity Hollow Rd. at Lobb's Run, Jefferson Borough, West Elizabeth vicinity, 11/12/92, A, d, 92001501

Longfellow School, Monroe St. and McClure Ave., Pittsburgh, 6/28/84, A, C, 84003088

Madison Elementary School [Pittsburgh Public Schools TR], Milwaukee and Orion Sts., Pittsburgh, 9/30/86, A, C, 86002687

Main Building, U.S. Bureau of Mines, 4800 Forbes Ave., Pittsburgh, 5/24/74, C, 74001741

Manchester Historic District, Irregular pattern contained with Faulsey, Chateau, Franklin, and Bidwell Sts., Pittsburgh, 9/18/75, C, 75001611

McCleary Elementary School [Pittsburgh Public Schools TR], Holmes St. and McCandless Ave., Pittsburgh, 9/30/86, C, 86002690

McKees Rocks Bridge [Highway Bridges Owned by the Commonwealth of Pennsylvania, Department of Transportation TR], LR 76, Spur 2,

Allegheny County—Continued

over Ohio River at Bellevue, Bellevue, 11/14/88, C, 88002168

McKeesport National Bank, 5th and Sinclair Sts., McKeesport, 8/29/80, A, C, 80003403

Mexican War Streets Historic District, , Irregular pattern between Brighton and Arch Sts. and between O'Hern and West Park, Pittsburgh, 5/28/75, A, C, 75001612

Mifflin Elementary School [Pittsburgh Public Schools TR], Mifflin Rd. at Lincoln Pl., Pittsburgh, 9/30/86, A, C, 86002692

Miller, James, House, E of Bethel on Manse Dr., Bethel vicinity, 1/17/75, C, 75001605

Monongahela Incline, Grandview Ave. at Wyoming Ave., Pittsburgh, 6/25/74, A, 74001742

Moreland-Hoffstot House, 5057 5th Ave., Pittsburgh, 2/23/78, C, 78002337

Morrow, John, Elementary School [Pittsburgh Public Schools TR], 1611 Davis Ave., Pittsburgh, 9/30/86, C, 86002693

Morse, Samuel F. B., School [Pittsburgh Public Schools TR], 2418 Sarah St., Pittsburgh, 9/30/86, A, C, 86002694

Neville House, S of Heidelberg on PA 50, Heidelberg vicinity, 2/05/74, B, NHL, 74001733

Ninth Street Bridge [Allegheny County Owned River Bridges TR], Allegheny River at Ninth St., Pittsburgh, 1/07/86, A, C, 86000019

Oakland Public School [Pittsburgh Public Schools TR], Dawson St. near Edith Pl., Pittsburgh, 2/03/87, C, 86002696

Oakmont Country Club Historic District, Hulton Rd., Oakmont vicinity, 8/17/84, A, C, NHL, 84003090

Old Allegheny Rows Historic District, Roughly bounded by Sedgwick, California, Marquis, Mero, Brighton, and Moorison Sts., Pittsburgh, 11/01/84, C, 84000349

Old Heidelberg Apartments, Braddock Ave. at Waverly St., Pittsburgh, 5/04/76, C, 76001596

Oliver, David P., High School [Pittsburgh Public Schools TR], Brighton Rd. and Island Ave., Pittsburgh, 2/03/87, A, C, 86002698

Osterling, Frederick J., Office and Studio, 228 Isabella St., Pittsburgh, 9/05/85, C, 85001964

Park Place School [Pittsburgh Public Schools TR], S. Braddock and Brashear Aves., Pittsburgh, 9/30/86, C, 86002701

Penn-Liberty Historic District, Roughly bounded by French & Tenth Sts., Liberty & Penn Aves., & Ninth St., Pittsburgh, 11/18/87, A, C, 87001995

Pennsalt Historic District, Roughly bounded by Federal, Penn & Pond Sts., Philadelphia and Blue Ridge Aves., Natrona, 7/18/85, A, C, 85001571

Pennsylvania Railroad Bridge, 11th St., Pittsburgh, 8/13/79, A, C, 79002160

Pennsylvania Railroad Station, 1101 Liberty Ave., Pittsburgh, 4/22/76, A, C, 76001597

Pennsylvania Railroad Station-Wilkinsburg, Hay St. at Ross Ave., Wilkinsburg, 7/18/85, A, C, 85001568

Perry High School [Pittsburgh Public Schools TR], Perrysville Ave. and Semicir St., Pittsburgh, 9/30/86, A, C, 86002702

Phipps Conservatory, Schenley Park, Pittsburgh, 11/13/76, A, C, 76001598

Pittsburgh & Lake Erie Railroad Station, Smithfield St. at Carson St., Pittsburgh, 1/11/74, A, C, 74001743

Pittsburgh Athletic Association Building, 4215 5th Ave., Pittsburgh, 12/15/78, C, 78002338

Pittsburgh Central Downtown Historic District, Roughly bounded by Liberty Ave., Grant St., Forbes Ave., and Wood St., Pittsburgh, 12/17/85, A, C, a, g, 85003216

Pittsburgh and Lake Erie Railroad Complex, Smithfield and Carson Sts., Pittsburgh, 12/31/79, A, C, 79002161

Prospect Junior High and Elementary School [Pittsburgh Public Schools TR], Prospect Ave. near Southern Ave., Pittsburgh, 9/30/86, C, 86002705

Reed Hall, W of Emsworth on Huntington Rd., Kilbuck Township, Emsworth vicinity, 11/28/80, A, 80003401

Rodef Shalom Temple, 4905 5th Ave., Pittsburgh, 11/15/79, A, C, a, 79002162

Rotunda of the Pennsylvania Railroad Station, 1100 Liberty Ave. at Grant St., Pittsburgh, 4/11/73, A, C, 73001587

Sauer Buildings Historic District, 607–717 Center Ave., Aspinwall, 9/11/85, C, g, 85002296

Schenley Farms Historic District, Roughly bounded by Andover Terr., Centre, Bellefield, and Parkman Aves., Ditbridge, Thackeray, Forbes and Mawhinney, Pittsburgh, 7/22/83, A, C, 83002213

Schenley High School [Pittsburgh Public Schools TR], Bigelow Blvd. and Centre Ave., Pittsburgh, 9/30/86, A, C, 86002706

Schenley Park, Schenley Dr. and Panther Hollow Rd., Pittsburgh, 11/13/85, A, C, 85003506

Schiller Elementary School [Pittsburgh Public Schools TR], 1018 Peralta St., Pittsburgh, 9/30/86, A, C, g, 86002707

Sellers House, 400 Shady Ave., Pittsburgh, 9/07/79, C, a, 79003142

Seventh Street Bridge [Allegheny County Owned River Bridges TR], Allegheny River at Seventh St., Pittsburgh, 1/07/86, A, C, 86000018

Shadyside Presbyterian Church, Amberson Ave. and Westminster Pl., Pittsburgh, 4/03/75, A, C, a, 75001613

Shields, David, House, Shields Lane, Edgeworth, 10/29/75, C, 75001607

Singer, John F., House, 1318 Singer Pl., Wilkinsburg Township, Pittsburgh, 11/13/74, C, 74001744

Sixteenth Street Bridge, Spans Allegheny River, Pittsburgh, 8/13/79, A, C, 79002163

Sixth Street Bridge [Allegheny County Owned River Bridges TR], Allegheny River at Sixth St., Pittsburgh, 1/07/86, A, C, 86000017

Smithfield Street Bridge, Smithfield St. at the Monongahela River, Pittsburgh, 3/21/74, C, NHL, 74001745

Snyder, William Penn, House, 852 Ridge Ave., Pittsburgh, 5/03/76, C, 76001599

Soldiers and Sailors Memorial Hall, 5th Ave. at Bigelow Blvd., Pittsburgh, 12/30/74, A, C, f, 74001746

South Side High School [Pittsburgh Public Schools TR], 900 E. Carson St., Pittsburgh, 9/30/86, A, C, 86002709

South Side Market Building, 12th and Bingham Sts., Pittsburgh, 10/14/76, C, 76001600

South Tenth Street Bridge [Allegheny County Owned River Bridges TR], Monongahela River at S. Tenth St., Pittsburgh, 1/07/86, A, C, 86000020

Springfield Public School [Pittsburgh Public Schools TR], Smallman and Thirty-first Sts., Pittsburgh, 9/30/86, C, 86002711

St. Boniface Roman Catholic Church, East St., Pittsburgh, 11/17/81, C, a, 81000525

St. John the Baptist Ukranian Catholic Church, 109 S. Carson St., Pittsburgh, 10/29/74, A, C, a, 74001747

St. Nicholas Croatian Church, 24 Maryland Ave., Millvale, 5/06/80, B, C, a, g, 80003404

St. Stanislaus Kostka Roman Catholic Church, 21st and Smallman Sts., Pittsburgh, 9/14/72, A, C, a, 72001089

Stanley Theater and Clark Building, 207 Seventh St. and 701–717 Liberty Ave., Pittsburgh, 2/27/86, A, C, 86000303

Sterrett Sub-District School [Pittsburgh Public Schools TR], 339 Lang Ave., Pittsburgh, 9/30/86, A, C, 86002713

Thornburg Historic District, Off PA 60, Thornburg, 12/08/82, A, C, 82001529

Tuberculosis Hospital of Pittsburgh, 2851 Bedford Ave., Pittsburgh, 2/25/93, A, 93000073

Union Trust Building, 435 Grant St., Pittsburgh, 1/21/74, C, 74001748

Van Kirk Farm, Round Hill Rd. at Scenery Dr., Elizabeth, 2/19/86, A, C, 86000320

Walker-Ewing Log House, NE of Oakdale on Noblestown Rd., Collier Township, Oakdale vicinity, 1/30/76, C, 76001593

Washington Vocational School [Pittsburgh Public Schools TR], 169 Fortieth St., Pittsburgh, 9/30/86, A, g, 86002715

Way, Nicholas, House, 108 Beaver Rd., Pittsburgh, 9/13/78, C, 78002339

West End-North Side Bridge, Western Ave. and Carson St., Pittsburgh, 8/24/79, C, g, 79003143

Westinghouse Air Brake Company General Office Building, Marguerite and Bluff Sts., Wilmerding, 3/06/87, A, B, C, 87000376

Westinghouse High School [Pittsburgh Public Schools TR], 1101 N. Murtland St., Pittsburgh, 9/30/86, C, 86002716

Westinghouse, George, Memorial Bridge, U.S. 30 at Turtle Creek, North Versailles Township, East Pittsburgh, 3/28/77, A, C, g, 77001120

Wightman School [Pittsburgh Public Schools TR], 5604 Solway St., Pittsburgh, 9/30/86, C, 86002717

William Penn Hotel, Mellon Sq. between 6th and Oliver Sts., Pittsburg, 3/07/85, A, C, 85000458

Allegheny County—Continued

Woods, John, House [Whiskey Rebellion Resources in Southwestern Pennsylvania MPS], 4604 Monongahela St., Pittsburgh, 4/29/93, B, C, 93000353

Woolslair Elementary School [Pittsburgh Public Schools TR], Fortieth St. and Liberty Ave., Pittsburgh, 9/30/86, A, C, 86002718

Armstrong County

Armstrong County Courthouse and Jail, E. Market St., Kittanning, 11/01/81, A, 81000526

Bradys Bend Iron Company Furnaces, PA 68, Bradys Bend, 8/11/80, A, D, 80003407

Bridge between Madison and Mahoning Townships [Highway Bridges Owned by the Commonwealth of Pennsylvania, Department of Transportation TR], LR 03178 over Mahoning Creek, Deanville vicinity, 6/22/88, C, 88000798

Colwell Cut Viaduct [Highway Bridges Owned by the Commonwealth of Pennsylvania, Department of Transportation TR], LR 66 over Pittsburgh & Shawmut RR, Seminole vicinity, 6/22/88, C, 88000796

Drake Log Cabin, Williams Alley, Apollo, 3/03/83, A, C, 83002214

Ford City Armory [Pennsylvania National Guard Armories MPS], 301 Tenth St., Ford City, 12/22/89, A, C, 89002074

Marshall, Thomas, House, State St., Dayton, 4/22/76, C, 76001602

St. Patrick's Roman Catholic Church, W of Cowansville off PA 268, Sugarcreek Township, Cowansville vicinity, 3/21/78, A, a, 78002340

St. Stephen's Church, PA 68, Bradys Bend, 6/30/80, A, C, a, 80003408

Beaver County

Beginning Point of the U.S. Public Land Survey, On the OH/PA Border, E of East Liverpool, Glasgow, 10/15/66, A, C, f, NHL, 66000606

Bridge in South Beaver Township [Highway Bridges Owned by the Commonwealth of Pennsylvania, Department of Transportation TR], Walts Mill Rd. over Little Beaver, Cannelton vicinity, 6/22/88, C, 88000868

Carnegie Free Library, Beaver Falls, 1301 7th Ave., Beaver Falls, 9/05/85, A, C, 85001967

Clow, James Beach, House, Chapel Dr. at Ann St., Ellwood City, 5/17/89, C, 89000349

Dunlap, William B., Mansion, 1298 Market St., Bridgewater, 8/29/80, B, C, 80003409

Economy Historic District, Old Economy Village roughly bounded by PA 65, 12th, Merchant, and 16th Sts., Ambridge, 5/21/85, A, C, a, 85001142

Fort McIntosh Site, Address Restricted, Beaver vicinity, 4/24/75, A, D, 75001614

Greersburg Academy, Market St., Darlington, 2/24/75, B, C, 75001616

Jones, B. F., Memorial Library, 663 Franklin Ave., Aliquippa, 12/15/78, B, C, 78002341

Legionville, Address Restricted, Harmony vicinity, 3/27/75, B, D, 75001617

Littell, David, House, PA 18, Hookstown vicinity, 10/31/86, C, 86002886

Merrick Art Gallery, 5th Ave. and 11th St., New Brighton, 8/05/83, A, B, C, 83002215

Merrill Lock No. 6, E of Midland on PA 68, Ohioview Township, Midland vicinity, 9/04/80, A, C, 80003410

Old Economy, NE of Pittsburgh on PA 65, Ambridge vicinity, 10/15/66, A, B, a, NHL, 66000644

Pittsburgh and Lake Erie Passenger Station, Aliquippa, 111 Station St., Aliquippa, 4/26/90, A, C, 90000700

Quay, Matthew S., House, 205 College Ave., Beaver, 5/15/75, B, NHL, 75001615

Racoon Creek RDA [Emergency Conservation Work (ECW) Architecture in Pennsylvania State Parks: 1933-1942, TR], 20 mi. S of Rochester on PA 18, Rochester vicinity, 5/18/87, A, C, g, 87000745

Vicary, Capt. William, House, 1251 4th St., Freedom, 11/08/74, B, C, 74001749

Bedford County

Barclay House, 230 Juliana St., Bedford, 9/18/78, C, 78002342

Bedford County Alms House, Cumberland Rd., .4 mi. S of Bedford, Bedford vicinity, 11/03/88, A, C, 88002378

Bedford Historic District, Roughly bounded by East, West, and Watson Sts., and the Raystown Branch of Juniata River, Bedford, 12/22/83, A, C, 83004187

Bedford Springs Hotel Historic District, US 220, Bedford Township, Bedford, 12/20/84, A, B, C, NHL, 84001413

Bonnet's Tavern, 4 mi. W of Bedford at jct. of U.S. 30 and PA 31, Napier Twonship, Bedford vicinity, 8/01/79, A, C, 79002164

Bridge in Snake Spring Township [Highway Bridges Owned by the Commonwealth of Pennsylvania, Department of Transportation TR], TR 30 over Raystown branch of Juniata River, Bedford, 6/22/88, C, 88000793

Chalybeate Springs Hotel, Chalybeate Rd., Bedford Borough vicinity, 7/18/85, A, 85001560

Defibaugh Tavern [Whiskey Rebellion Resources in Southwestern Pennsylvania MPS], US 30 N side, E of Bedford, Snake Spring Valley Township, Bedford vicinity, 11/12/92, A, C, 92001498

Diehls Covered Bridge [Bedford County Covered Bridges TR], S of Schellsburg on LR 09057, Harrison Township, New Buena Vista vicinity, 4/10/80, A, C, 80003420

Espy House, 123 Pitt St., Bedford, 11/19/74, B, NHL, 74001750

Feltons Mill Covered Bridge [Bedford County Covered Bridges TR], LR 05021, East Providence Township, Bedford vicinity, 4/10/80, A, C, 80003413

Fischtner Covered Bridge [Bedford County Covered Bridges TR], N of Stringtown off LR 05007, Londonderry Township, Stringtown vicinity, 4/10/80, A, C, 80003422

Halls Mill Covered Bridge [Bedford County Covered Bridges TR], N of Everett on T 528, Hopewell Township, Hopewell vicinity, 4/10/80, A, C, 80003418

Heirline Covered Bridge [Bedford County Covered Bridges TR], W of Bedford on LR 05097, Harrison/Napier Townships, Manns Choice vicinity, 4/10/80, A, C, 80003419

Hewitt Covered Bridge [Bedford County Covered Bridges TR], T 305, Southhampton Township, Hewitt vicinity, 4/10/80, A, C, 80003417

Jacksons Mill Covered Bridge [Bedford County Covered Bridges TR], T 412, East Providence Township, Bedford vicinity, 4/10/80, A, C, 80003414

Juniata Woolen Mill and Newry Manor, W of Everett on Lutzville Rd., Snake Spring Township, Everett vicinity, 3/31/83, A, 83002216

Knisley, Dr., Covered Bridge [Bedford County Covered Bridges TR], SE of Alum Bank on LR 05098, West St. Clair Township, Alum Bank vicinity, 4/10/80, A, C, 80003411

New Enterprise Public School, Off PA 869, South Woodbury Township, New Enterprise, 10/08/81, A, 81000528

New Paris Covered Bridge [Bedford County Covered Bridges TR], 1 mi. N of New Paris, Napier Township, New Paris vicinity, 4/10/80, A, C, 80003423

Osterburg Covered Bridge [Bedford County Covered Bridges TR], W of Osterburg on T 757, East St. Clair Township, Osterburg vicinity, 4/10/80, A, C, 80003421

Russell House, 203 S. Juliana St., Bedford, 6/19/79, C, 79002165

Ryot Covered Bridge [Bedford County Covered Bridges TR], S of Alum Bank on T 559, West St. Clair Township, Fishertown vicinity, 4/10/80, A, C, 80003416

Site 36BD90, Address Restricted, Bedford vicinity, 6/04/84, D, 84003102

Snooks Covered Bridge [Bedford County Covered Bridges TR], E of Alum Bank on T 578, East St. Clair Township, Alum Bank vicinity, 4/10/80, A, C, 80003412

Berks County

Allegheny Aqueduct, PA 724 and Allegheny Creek, Gibraltar vicinity, 2/23/84, A, C, 84003105

Askew Bridge, N. 6th St. near Woodward St., Reading, 3/01/73, A, C, 73001590

Astor Theater, 730–742 Penn St., Reading, 1/05/78, A, C, 78002346

Berks County—Continued

Bahr Mill Complex [Gristmills in Berks County MPS], Ironstone Dr., Colebrookdale Township, Gabelsville, 11/08/90, A, C, 90001611

Barto Bridge [Highway Bridges Owned by the Commonwealth of Pennsylvania, Department of Transportation TR], LR 284 over trib. to Perkiomen Creek, Barto vicinity, 6/22/88, C, 88000790

Bellman's Union Church, SW of Centerport off Rte. 726, Centerport vicinity, 12/04/73, C, a, 73001589

Berk, Daniel, Log House, S of Albany on Maiden Creek, Albany Township, Albany vicinity, 12/16/77, C, 77001122

Bethel A.M.E. Church, 119 N. 10th St, Reading, 9/07/79, A, a, 79002167

Bishop, John, House, Perkiomen Ave., Reading vicinity, 6/27/85, A, C, 85001390

Boone, Daniel, Homestead Site and Bertolet Cabin, 2 mi. N of Birdsboro, Albany Township, Birdsboro vicinity, 3/24/72, B, c, NHL, 72001090

Boonecroft, Oley Line Rd., Douglassville, 7/26/82, A, C, 82003758

Borneman Mill [Gristmills in Berks County MPS], Off PA 100 SW of Clayton, Washington Township, Bally vicinity, 11/08/90, A, C, 90001612

Bridge in Albany Township [Highway Bridges Owned by the Commonwealth of Pennsylvania, Department of Transportation TR], LR 06173 over Maiden Creek, Steinsville vicinity, 6/22/88, C, 88000769

Brobst Mill [Gristmills in Berks County MPS], Off T 814 on Pine Cr., Albany Township, Lenhartsville vicinity, 11/08/90, A, C, 90001613

Christman, Philip, House, 1 mi. SE of Bally at the Berks, Bally vicinity, 3/07/73, A, C, 73001588

City Hall, 8th & Washington Sts., Reading, 4/13/82, A, C, 82003760

Cotton and Maple Streets School, Cotton and Maple Sts., Reading, 7/17/86, A, C, 86001676

Dale Furnace and Forge Historic District [Iron and Steel Resources in Pennsylvania MPS], Forgedale Rd. NW of Bally, Washington Township, Bally vicinity, 9/06/91, A, C, D, 91001134

Dauberville Bridge [Highway Bridges Owned by the Commonwealth of Pennsylvania, Department of Transportation TR], Belleman's Church Rd. over Schuylkill River, Dauberville, 6/22/88, C, 88000788

Davies House, Berkley Rd., East Berkley, 11/14/82, A, C, 82001530

Deisher, H. K., Knitting Mill, 56 Noble St., Kutztown, 9/05/85, A, C, 85001963

Dreibelbis Mill [Gristmills in Berks County MPS], Jct. of Dreibelbis Mill and Bellevue Rds., Perry Township, Shoemakersville vicinity, 11/08/90, A, C, D, 90001614

Dreibelbis Station Bridge [Berks County Covered Bridges TR], S of Lenhartsville on T 745, Greenwich Township, Kutztown vicinity, 2/23/81, A, C, 81000530

Dreibelbis, Joel, Farm, PA 143, Virginville, 10/30/89, A, C, 89001820

Fisher, Henry, House, About 1.25 mi. N of Yellow House on PA 662, Oley Township, Yellow House vicinity, 6/04/73, C, 73001591

Foos, Charles S., Elementary School, Douglass and Weiser Sts., Reading, 11/10/83, A, C, 83004191

French Creek State Park Six Penny Day Use District [Emergency Conservation Work (ECW) Architecture in Pennsylvania State Parks: 1933-1942, TR], 7 mi. NE of Morgantown on PA 345, Morgantown vicinity, 2/11/87, A, C, g, 87000054

French Creek State Park: Organized Group Camp 4 District [Emergency Conservation Work (ECW) Architecture in Pennsylvania State Parks: 1933-1942, TR], 7 mi. NE of Morgantown on PA 345, Reading vicinity, 2/12/87, A, C, g, 87000104

Gehman, John, Farm [Farms in Berks County MPS], Township Rd. N of Harlem, Hereford Township, Seisholtzville, 5/07/92, A, C, 92000398

Geiger Mill [Gristmills in Berks County MPS], Jct. of Mill Rd. and PA 82, Robeson Township, Geigertown, 11/08/90, A, C, D, 90001738

Grand View Dairy Farm [Farms in Berks County MPS], Preston Rd. S of Wernersville, South Heidelberg Township, Wernersville vicinity, 7/29/92, A, C, 92000933

Greisemer's Mill Bridge [Berks County Covered Bridges TR], NW of Boyerstown on T 579, Oley Township, Oley vicinity, 2/23/81, C, 81000532

Griesemer—Brown Mill Complex [Gristmills in Berks County MPS], Brown's Mill Rd. at Monocacy Cr., Amity Township, Birdsboro vicinity, 11/08/90, A, C, 90001616

Grimshaw Silk Mill, 1200 N. 1100 St., Reading, 1/31/85, A, C, 85000176

Gruber Wagon Works, W of Reading off PA 183 in Tulpehocken Creek Park, Reading vicinity, 6/02/72, A, b, NHL, 72001092

Guldin Mill [Gristmills in Berks County MPS], Off PA 73 SE of jct. with US 222, Maiden Creek Township, Blandon, 11/08/90, A, C, D, 90001617

Hain Mill [Gristmills in Berks County MPS], Jct. of Hain Mill Rd. and T 495, Lower Heidelberg Township, Wernersville vicinity, 11/08/90, A, C, 90001618

Hamburg Armory [Pennsylvania National Guard Armories MPS], N. Fifth St., S of I-78, Hamburg, 5/09/91, A, C, 91000511

Hamburg Public Library, 35 N. Third St., Hamburg, 11/03/88, C, 88002369

Hampden Firehouse, 1101 Greenwich St., Reading, 4/13/82, A, C, 82003761

Hartman Cider Press, Keim Rd., 1.1 mi. W of Lobachsville, Lobachsville vicinity, 1/07/88, A, b, 87002205

Hendel Brothers, Sons and Company Hat Factory, 517–539 S. 5th St., Reading, 11/20/79, A, 79002168

Hopewell Furnace National Historic Site, R.D. #1, Box 345, 5 Miles S. of Birdsboro, Elverson vicinity, 10/15/66, A, C, f, NPS, 66000645

Hottenstein Mansion, 2 mi. E of Kutztown on U.S. 222, Maxatawny Township, Kutztown vicinity, 6/22/72, C, 72001091

Hunter's Mill Complex, Forgedale Rd., Herreford Twnshp., 12/22/88, A, B, C, 88003045

Ironstone Bridge [Highway Bridges Owned by the Commonwealth of Pennsylvania, Department of Transportation TR], Farmington Ave. over Ironstone Creek, Morysville vicinity, 6/22/88, C, 88000789

Joanna Furnace Complex, N of Morgantown on PA 10, Robeson Township, Morgantown vicinity, 4/23/80, C, 80003426

Johnson, Nicholas, Mill [Gristmills in Berks County MPS], Mill Crest Rd., Colebrookdale Township, New Berlinville, 11/08/90, A, C, D, 90001619

Kauffman Mill [Gristmills in Berks County MPS], Jct. of Mill and Mill Hill Rds., Upper Bern Township, Shartlesville, 11/08/90, A, C, D, 90001620

Keim Homestead, W of Lobachsville, Pike Township, Lobachsville vicinity, 5/01/74, C, 74001752

Kemp's Hotel, E of Kutztown on US 222, Maxatawny Township, Kutztown vicinity, 12/19/78, A, 78002344

Keystone Hook and Ladder Company, Second and Penn Sts., Reading, 10/31/85, C, 85003447

Kissling Farm [Farms in Berks County MPS], Brownsville Rd. E of Robesonia, Heidelberg Township, Robesonia vicinity, 7/29/92, A, C, 92000934

Knabb—Bieber Mill [Gristmills in Berks County MPS], Bieber Mill Rd. at Monocacy Cr., Oley Township, Stony Creek Mills vicinity, 11/08/90, A, C, D, 90001621

Knorr—Bare Farm [Farms in Berks County MPS], 4995 Penn Ave., Lower Heidelberg Township, Sinking Spring, 7/29/92, A, C, 92000935

Kutz Mill [Gristmills in Berks County MPS], Kutz Mill Rd. at Sacony Cr., Greenwich Township, Kutztown vicinity, 11/08/90, A, C, 90001622

Kutz's Mill Bridge [Berks County Covered Bridges TR], NW of Kutztown on T 798, Greenwich Township, Kutztown vicinity, 2/23/81, C, 81000531

Kutztown 1892 Public School Building, White Oak and Normal Ave., Kutztown, 6/27/80, C, 80003425

Leesport Lock House, Wall St., Leesport, 6/09/77, A, 77001123

Leiby, Jacob, Farm [Farms in Berks County MPS], PA 143, Perry Township, Virginville, 7/29/92, A, C, 92000936

Lenhart Farm, Jct. of U.S. 22 and PA 143, Lenhartsville, 9/18/78, C, 78002345

Lerch Tavern, 182-184 W. Penn Ave, Wernersville, 9/12/79, A, C, 79002171

Levan Farm, PA 562, Exeter Township, St. Lawrence, 12/19/78, A, 78002348

Liberty Fire Company No. 5, 501 S. 5th St., Reading, 1/18/85, A, C, 85000112

Lincoln, Mordecai, House, Lincoln Rd., Lorane, 11/03/88, A, C, 88002370

Lindbergh Viaduct [Highway Bridges Owned by the Commonwealth of Pennsylvania, Depart-

Berks County—Continued

ment of Transportation TR], US 422/Mineral Spring Rd. over Mineral Spring Creek, Reading, 6/22/88, C, 88000792

Log House, Hiester House, and Market Annex, 30 S. 4th St., Reading, 11/20/79, A, C, 79002169

Long—Hawerter Mill [Gristmills in Berks County MPS], Longsdale Rd. at Little Lehigh Cr., Longswamp Township, Topton vicinity, 11/08/90, A, C, 90001623

Mary Ann Furnace Historic District [Iron and Steel Resources in Pennsylvania MPS], Centennial Rd. SE of Longswamp, Longswamp Township, Longswamp vicinity, 9/06/91, A, C, 91001141

Meinig Glove Factory-Meinig, E. Richard, Co., 621–641 McKnight St., Reading, 8/30/85, B, C, 85001896

Merkel Mill [Gristmills in Berks County MPS], Dreibelbis Station Rd. at Maiden Cr., Greenwich Township, Lenhartsville vicinity, 11/08/90, A, C, 90001625

Merkel Mill Complex [Gristmills in Berks County MPS], Jct. of PA 662 and PA 143, Richmond Township, Virginville vicinity, 11/08/90, A, C, 90001626

Metropolitan Edison Building, 412 Washington St., Reading, 10/28/83, A, C, 83004192

Mill Tract Farm, NE of Stonersville on Mill Rd., Exeter Township, Stonersville vicinity, 9/22/77, A, C, 77001124

Mill at Lobachsville [Gristmills in Berks County MPS], Mill Rd. at Pine Cr., Pike Township, Lobachsville, 11/08/90, A, C, 90001624

Moselem Farms Mill [Gristmills in Berks County MPS], Jct. of PA 662 and Forge Rd., Richmond Township, Moselem, 11/08/90, A, C, 90001627

Old Dry Road, 3 mi. (4.8 km) NW of Wernersville on Highland Rd., Lower Heidelberg Township, Wernersville vicinity, 1/23/78, A, C, 78002349

Old Swede's House, Old Philadelphia Pike, Douglassville, 1/21/74, A, C, 74001751

Oley Township Historic District, PA 73, Oley Township, 3/11/83, A, C, 83002218

Pagoda, Mount Penn, at jct. of Duryea Dr. and Skyline Blvd., Reading, 11/07/72, C, 72001093

Pleasantville Bridge [Berks County Covered Bridges TR], S of Mantawny on T 916, Oley Township, Oley vicinity, 2/23/81, C, 81000533

Reading Hardware Company Butt Works, 537 Willow St., Reading, 11/20/79, A, C, 79002170

Reading Knitting Mills, 350 Elm St., Reading, 4/13/82, A, 82003762

Reiff Farm, SW of Oley on T 454, Oley Township, Oley vicinity, 2/25/82, A, C, 82003759

Ridgewood Farm [Farms in Berks County MPS], Jct. of PA 724 and I-176, Cumru Township, Seyfert, 5/07/92, A, C, 92000399

Rieser Mill [Gristmills in Berks County MPS], Jct. of Grange and Cross Keys Rds., Bern Township, Leesport vicinity, 11/08/90, A, C, 90001628

Rieser—Shoemaker Farm [Farms in Berks County MPS], Cross Keys Rd., Bern Township, Leesport, 7/29/92, A, C, 92000939

Robesonia Furnace Historic District [Iron and Steel Resources in Pennsylvania MPS], Furnace, S. Church and Freeman Sts. and Mountain and E. Meadow Aves., Robesonia, 9/06/91, A, C, D, 91001128

S Bridge [Highway Bridges Owned by the Commonwealth of Pennsylvania, Department of Transportation TR], LR 06024 over Tulpehocken Creek, Sheridan vicinity, 6/22/88, C, 88000794

Sally Ann Furnace Complex, SW of Topton, Rockland Township, Topton vicinity, 8/17/76, A, C, 76001604

Schaumboch's Tavern, NW of Hamburg on Hawk Mountain Rd., Albany Township, Hamburg vicinity, 11/20/79, C, 79002166

Schlegel, Christian, Farm [Farms in Berks County MPS], Fleetwood—Lyons Rd., Richmond Township, Fleetwood, 7/29/92, A, C, 92000938

Seyfert Mill [Gristmills in Berks County MPS], Jct. of Old US 22 and Campsite Rd., Upper Tulpehocken Township, Strausstown vicinity, 11/08/90, A, C, 90001629

Siegfried's Dale Farm, Siegfried's Rd., Maxatawny Township, Maxatawny vicinity, 5/10/84, A, C, 84003115

Snyder Mill [Gristmills in Berks County MPS], Oley Line Rd. at Monocacy Cr., Exeter Township, Limekiln vicinity, 11/08/90, A, C, 90001630

Spannuth Mill [Gristmills in Berks County MPS], Jct. of Frystown and Crosskill Creek Rds., Bethel Township, Frystown vicinity, 11/08/90, A, C, 90001631

Spicker, Peter, House, 150 Main St., Stouchsburg, 4/22/83, A, C, 83002217

St. Gabriel's Episcopal Church, U.S. 422, Douglassville, 3/08/78, C, a, 78002343

St. Michael's Protestant Episcopal Church, Parish House and Rectory, Mill and Church Sts., Birdsboro, 12/20/82, C, a, 82001531

Stein Mill [Gristmills in Berks County MPS], PA 737 at Mill Cr., Greenwich Township, Kutztown vicinity, 11/08/90, A, C, 90001632

Stirling, 1120 Centre Ave., Reading, 4/17/80, C, 80003427

Stouchsburg Historic District, 12 to 153 Main St., and Water St., Stouchsburg, 1/08/85, A, C, 85000071

Stupp—Oxenrider Farm [Farms in Berks County MPS], Dundore Rd. NW of Robesonia, North Heidelberg Township, Robesonia vicinity, 7/29/92, A, C, 92000932

Thompson Mill [Gristmills in Berks County MPS], Golf Course Rd. at Seidel Cr., Robeson Township, Gibraltar vicinity, 11/08/90, A, C, 90001633

Trinity Lutheran Church, 6th and Washington Sts., Reading, 6/07/76, A, C, a, d, 76001603

Tulpehocken Creek Historic District, Tulpehocken and Mill Creeks from Berks-Lebanon line to Blue March Dam between Millardsville and Bernville, Womelsdorf vicinity, 3/28/85, A, C, a, 85000672

Wanner, Peter, Mansion, 1401 Walnut St., Reading, 11/05/87, B, C, 87001950

Weidner Mill [Gristmills in Berks County MPS], Blacksmith Rd. at Manatawny Cr., Amity Township, Earlville vicinity, 11/08/90, A, C, 90001634

Weiser, Conrad, House, 2 mi. E of Womelsdorf, Womelsdorf vicinity, 10/15/66, B, NHL, 66000646

Wertz Mill [Gristmills in Berks County MPS], 60 Werner St., Wernersville, 11/08/90, A, C, 90001635

Wertz's Covered Bridge [Berks County Covered Bridges TR (AD)], NW of Reading on T 921, Bern/Spring Townships, Reading vicinity, 11/17/78, A, C, 78002347

White Horse Tavern, 509 Old Philadelphia Pike, Douglassville, 4/21/75, C, 75001618

Wilhelm Mansion and Carriage House, 730 Centre Ave., Reading, 3/01/82, C, 82003763

Womelsdorf Historic District, Roughly bounded by Water, 4th, Franklin and Jefferson Sts., Womelsdorf, 3/10/82, A, B, C, 82003764

Yoder Mill [Gristmills in Berks County MPS], Yoder Rd. at Oysterville Cr., Pike Township, Pikeville, 11/08/90, A, C, D, 90001636

Blair County

Allegheny Furnace [Iron and Steel Resources in Pennsylvania MPS], 3400 Crescent Rd., Altoona, 9/06/91, A, 91001131

Allegheny Portage Railroad National Historic Site, U.S. 22, Johnstown vicinity, 10/15/66, A, C, f, NHL, NPS, 66000648

Altoona Armory [Pennsylvania National Guard Armories MPS], 327 Frankstown Rd., Logan Township, Altoona vicinity, 5/09/91, A, C, 91000507

Baker Mansion, 3500 Baker Blvd., Altoona, 6/05/75, C, 75001619

Blair County Courthouse, 423 Allegheny St., Hollidaysburg, 6/17/76, C, 76001606

Central Trust Company Buildings, 1210-1218 11th Ave., Altoona, 11/01/84, A, C, 84000271

Downtown Altoona Historic District, Roughly bounded by 11th Ave., 11th St., 15th Ave. and 13th St., also 700–1000 Lexington and 900–1000 Howard Aves., Altoona, 7/24/92, A, C, 92000946

Dudley, Charles B., House, 802 Lexington Ave., Altoona, 5/11/76, B, NHL, 76001605

Etna Furnace [Iron and Steel Resources in Pennsylvania MPS], N of Williamsburg, Catharine Township, Williamsburg vicinity, 4/11/73, A, 73001593

Etna Furnace (Boundary Decrease) [Iron and Steel Resources in Pennsylvania MPS], Roughly, area W of Etna Furnace buildings, N and S of Roaring Run, Mt. Etna vicinity, 9/06/91, A, 91001369

Etna Furnace (Boundary Increase) [Iron and Steel Resources in Pennsylvania MPS], Roughly, area S and E of Frankstown Br. Juniata R. bend at Mt. Etna, Catherine Township, Mt. Etna, 9/06/91, A, C, D, 91001145

Fort Roberdeau, W of Culp off U.S. 220, Tyronne Township, Culp vicinity, 5/29/74, A, 74001753

Blair County—Continued

Highland Hall, 517 Walnut St., Hollidaysburg, 9/13/78, A, C, a, 78002351

Hollidaysburg Historic District, Roughly bounded by Spruce, Bella, Blair, and Juniata Sts., Hollidaysburg, 12/26/85, A, C, 85003158

Horseshoe Curve, 5 mi. W of Altoona on PA 193, Altoona vicinity, 11/13/66, A, C, NHL, 66000647

Leap-the-Dips, 700 Park Ave., Altoona, 3/15/91, A, C, 91000229

Mishler Theatre, 1208 12th Ave., Altoona, 4/11/73, A, C, 73001592

Penn Alto Hotel, 12th St. and 13th Ave., Altoona, 5/05/89, A, C, 89000350

Royer, Daniel, House, 5 mi. SW of Williamsburg on PA 866, Woodbury Township, Williamsburg vicinity, 11/03/75, A, C, 75001620

St. John's Evangelical Lutheran Church, NE of Culp, Tyronne Township, Culp vicinity, 9/18/78, C, a, 78002350

Tyrone Armory [Pennsylvania National Guard Armories MPS], 956 S. Logan Ave., Tyrone, 12/22/89, A, C, 89002083

Tyrone Borough Historic District, Roughly bounded by W. 14th St., Logan Ave., Bald Eagle Ave., the Little Juniata R., W. 8th St. and Jefferson Ave., Tyrone, 1/21/93, A, C, 92001823

Bradford County

Bliss, Phillip Paul, House, Main St., Rome, 4/24/86, B, 86000865

Bradford County Courthouse, 301 Main St., Towanda, 1/06/87, A, C, 86003573

Bridge in Athens Township [Highway Bridges Owned by the Commonwealth of Pennsylvania, Department of Transportation TR], LR 08081 over Susquehanna River, Athens vicinity, 6/22/88, C, 88000821

Knapp's Covered Bridge [Covered Bridges of Bradford, Sullivan and Lycoming Counties TR], E of Burlington on T 554, Burlington Township, Burlington vicinity, 7/24/80, A, 80003428

Methodist Episcopal Church of Burlington, US 6 at Township Rd. 357, West Burlington, 1/04/90, C, a, 89002280

Towanda Historic District, Roughly bounded by Elizabeth, Fourth and Kingsbury Sts. and the Susquehanna R., Towanda, 5/07/92, A, B, C, 92000394

Van Dyne Civic Building, Main and Elmira Sts., Troy, 1/21/74, C, 74001754

Bucks County

Andalusia, 1.4 mi. N of Philadelphia on PA 32, Philadelphia vicinity, 11/13/66, B, NHL, 66000649

Belmont, 3779 Bristol Rd., Bensalem, 5/03/88, C, 88000460

Bridge Valley Bridge, Spans Neshaminy Creek N of Hartsville, Warwick Township, Hartsville vicinity, 5/10/84, C, 84003120

Bridge in Buckingham Township [Highway Bridges Owned by the Commonwealth of Pennsylvania, Department of Transportation TR], Forest Grove Rd. over Mill Creek, Wycombe vicinity, 6/22/88, C, 88000786

Bridge in Solebury Township [Highway Bridges Owned by the Commonwealth of Pennsylvania, Department of Transportation TR], Carversville Rd. over Paunacussing Creek, Carversville vicinity, 6/22/88, C, 88000783

Bridge in Tinicum Township [Highway Bridges Owned by the Commonwealth of Pennsylvania, Department of Transportation TR], LR 920 over Pennsylvania Canal, Point Pleasant, 6/22/88, C, 88000814

Bridge in Yardley Borough [Highway Bridges Owned by the Commonwealth of Pennsylvania, Department of Transportation TR], Reading Ave. over VanHorn Creek, Scammells Corner vicinity, 6/22/88, C, 88000770

Bristol Historic District, Roughly bounded by Pond, Cedar, E. Lincoln Sts., the Delaware River, and E. Mill St., Bristol, 4/30/87, A, C, 87000665

Bristol Industrial Historic District, Roughly bounded by Pennsylvania Canal, Jefferson Ave., Canal St., Pennsylvania RR, & Beaver St., Bristol, 11/16/87, A, C, 87002016

Burroughs, John, Homestead, Wrightstown-Taylorsville Rd., Upper Makefield Township, Taylorsville vicinity, 3/05/84, A, C, 84003163

Byecroft Farm Complex, Off US 202, Buckingham Township, Buckingham vicinity, 9/09/83, A, C, 83002219

Cabin Run Covered Bridge [Covered Bridges of the Delaware River Watershed TR], S of Tinicum on LR 09099, Plumstead Township, Point Pleasant vicinity, 12/01/80, A, C, 80003443

Campbell's Bridge [Highway Bridges Owned by the Commonwealth of Pennsylvania, Department of Transportation TR], Allentown Rd. over Unami Creek, Milford Square vicinity, 6/22/88, C, 88000733

Carversville Historic District, Off PA 32, Carversville, 12/13/78, A, C, 78003418

Center Bridge Historic District, Bounded by Ely and Laurel Rds. on River Rd., Solebury Township, Center Bridge, 3/26/85, A, B, C, 85000673

Chapman, John, House, S of New Hope off PA 232 on Eagle Rd., Upper Makefield Township, New Hope vicinity, 1/24/74, B, 74001757

Cintra [New Hope MRA], 181 W. Bridge St., New Hope, 3/06/85, B, C, 85000460

Craft, Gershom, House, 105 Barnsley Ave., Morrisville, 10/16/86, C, 86002892

Delaware Division of the Pennsylvania Canal [Covered Bridges of the Delaware River Watershed TR (AD)], Parallels W bank of the Delaware River from Easton to Bristol, Easton, 10/29/74, A, C, NHL, 74001756

Dorrance Mansion, 300 Radcliffe St., Bristol, 10/16/86, B, C, 86002891

Doylestown Historic District, Roughly bounded by Union, Cottage and E. Ashland Sts, Hillside Ave. and S. and N. West Sts., Doylestown, 5/10/85, A, C, 85001012

Dungan, Pugh, House, 33 W. Court St., Doylestown, 3/20/80, B, C, 80003430

Durham Mill and Furnace, Durham Rd., Durham, 11/21/76, A, 76001608

Dyerstown Historic District, Along Old Easton Rd. near jct. of Stony Ln., Plumstead Township, 1/15/87, C, 86003574

Eagle Tavern, S of New Hope, Upper Makefield Township, New Hope vicinity, 4/20/78, A, C, 78002353

Edgemont, N of Langhorne on Bridgetown Rd., Langhorne vicinity, 12/16/77, C, 77001126

Ely, Joshua, House [New Hope MRA], Rittenhouse Circle, New Hope, 3/06/85, C, 85000463

Erwinna Covered Bridge [Covered Bridges of the Delaware River Watershed TR], N of Erwinna on LR 09098, Tinicum Township, Erwinna, 12/01/80, A, C, 80003434

Fallsington Historic District, S of U.S. 1, E of New Tyburn Rd., Fallsington, 6/19/72, A, C, a, 72001099

Fonthill, E. Court St. at intersection of PA 313, Doylestown, 6/01/72, B, C, 72001094

Fonthill, Mercer Museum and Moravian Pottery and Tile Works, Court St. and Swamp Rd. and Pine and Ashland Sts., Doylestown, 2/04/85, B, C, NHL, 85002366

Fordhook Farm, 105 New Britain Rd., Doylestown, 4/30/87, A, C, 87000674

Forest Grove Historic District, Forest Grove and Lower Mountain Rds., Buckingham Township, Buckingham vicinity, 4/20/82, A, C, 82003765

Fountain House, State and Main Sts., Doylestown, 3/16/72, A, C, 72001095

Frankenfield Covered Bridge [Covered Bridges of the Delaware River Watershed TR], N of Tinicum on T 421, Tinicum Township, Point Pleasant vicinity, 12/01/80, A, C, 80003444

Fretz Farm, Almshouse Rd. and PA 611, Doylestown Township, Doylestown vicinity, 3/07/85, A, C, 85000459

Gardenville—North Branch Rural Historic District, Roughly bounded by Durham Rd., Pt. Pleasant Pike, Valley Park Rd. and N. Branch Neshaminy Cr., Plumstead Township, Gardenville, 11/07/91, A, C, 91000954

Gilbert, Thomas and Lydia, Farm, 5042 Anderson Rd., Holicong, 5/05/89, C, 89000351

Green Hills Farm, SW of Dublin on Dublin Rd., Hilltown Township, Dublin vicinity, 2/27/74, B, g, NHL, 74001755

Grundy Mill Complex, W corner of Jefferson Ave. and Canal St., Bristol, 1/09/86, A, B, C, 86000013

Half-Moon Inn, 101 and 105 Court St., Newtown, 12/06/77, A, 77001128

Hammerstein, Oscar, II, Farm, 70 East Rd., Doylestown, 11/17/88, B, g, 88002374

Hampton Hill, 1269 Second Street Pike, Northampton Township, Richboro, 4/02/73, A, C, 73001594

Bucks County—Continued

Harewood and Beechwood, E of Langhorne off PA 213, Middletown Township, Langhorne vicinity, 2/01/80, C, 80003436

Harriman Historic District, Roughly bounded by Trenton Ave., Cleveland and McKinley Sts., Farragut Ave., and West Circle, Bristol, 4/30/87, A, C, 87000673

Hayhurst Farm, NE of Wrightstown on Eagle Rd., Upper Makefield Township, Wrightstown vicinity, 2/12/74, B, C, 74001759

Holicong Village Historic District, U.S. 202 and Holicong Rd., Buckingham Township, Holicong, 3/20/80, A, C, D, 80003435

Honey Hollow Watershed, 2.5 mi. S of the Delaware River on PA 263, New Hope vicinity, 8/04/69, A, g, NHL, 69000155

Hough, John and Phineas, House, 20 Moyer Rd., Lower Makefield Township, Yardley, 12/24/92, C, 92001721

Hulmeville Historic District, 2–4 Beaver St., 946–1101 Bellevue Ave., 1–111 Green, 4 Hulme, 3–342 Main Sts., 1–131 Trenton Ave., & 2–9 Water St., Hulmeville, 7/17/86, A, C, 86001677

James, Morgan, Homestead, NW of New Britain on Ferry Rd., New Britain Township, New Britain vicinity, 12/27/77, C, 77001127

James-Lorah House, 132 N. Main St., Doylestown, 10/17/72, C, 72001096

Jefferson Avenue School, Jefferson Ave. & Pond St., Bristol, 7/18/85, A, C, 85001569

Jefferson Land Association Historic District, Bounded by Spring St., Jefferson Ave., Garden & Mansion Sts., & Beaver Dam Rd., Bristol, 11/05/87, C, 87001994

Keith House—Washington's Headquarters, E of Pineville on Pineville Rd., Upper Makefield Township, Pineville vicinity, 11/14/78, B, C, 78002356

Kitchen, William, House [New Hope MRA], 332 S. Sugan Rd., New Hope, 3/06/85, C, 85000464

Knecht's Mill Covered Bridge [Covered Bridges of the Delaware River Watershed TR], NE of Springtown on T 424, Springfield Township, Springtown vicinity, 12/01/80, A, C, 80003432

Lacey, Gen. John, Homestead, Forest Grove Rd., Buckingham Township, Wycombe, 12/02/80, B, C, 80003448

Langhorne Historic District, Summit & Marshall Aves., Pine St., Richardson Ave., & Green St., Langhorne, 11/20/87, A, C, 87001993

Langhorne Library, 160 W. Maple Ave., Langhorne, 1/09/86, C, 86000038

Leedom, David, Farm, SW of Newtown off Richboro Rd., Newtown Township, Newtown vicinity, 1/01/76, B, C, 76001609

Liberty Hall, 1237 W. Broad St., Quakertown, 1/26/78, A, C, 78002358

Little Jerusalem AME Church, 1200 Bridwater Rd., Cornwells Heights, 12/03/80, A, a, 80003429

Loux Covered Bridge [Covered Bridges of the Delaware River Watershed TR], SE of Pipersville on LR 09060, Plumstead Township, Pipersville vicinity, 12/01/80, A, C, 80003442

Lumberville Historic District, Fleecy Dale, Carversville, River, and Green Hill Rds., Lumberville, 8/09/84, A, 84003165

Makefield Meeting, NE of Newtown at Mt. Eyre Rd. and Dolington Rd., Upper Makefield Township, Newtown vicinity, 1/18/74, A, C, a, 74001758

Mechanicsville Village Historic District, Jct. Mechanicsville Rd. and Rt. 413, Mechanicsville, 1/04/89, A, C, 88003049

Mercer Museum, Pine and Ashland Sts., Doylestown, 3/16/72, B, C, 72001097

Moland House, 1641 Old York Rd., Hartsville, 5/19/89, A, 89000352

Mood's Covered Bridge [Covered Bridges of the Delaware River Watershed TR], E of Perkasie on LR 09118, East Rockhill Township, Perkasie, 12/01/80, A, C, 80003440

Moravian Pottery and Tile Works, Court St. and PA 313, Doylestown, 6/01/72, A, B, C, 72001098

New Hope Village District [New Hope MRA], Old Mill Rd., Stockton Ave., Ferry, Bridge, Mechanic, Randolph, Main, Coryell, and Waterloo Sts., New Hope, 3/06/85, A, C, 85000462

Newtown Creek Bridge [Highway Bridges Owned by the Commonwealth of Pennsylvania, Department of Transportation TR], Richoro Rd. over Newtown Creek, Newtown vicinity, 6/22/88, C, 88000787

Newtown Friends Meetinghouse and Cemetery, Court St., Newtown, 7/21/77, A, B, C, a, d, 77001129

Newtown Historic District, PA 413 and PA 332, Newtown, 12/17/79, A, B, C, 79002174

Newtown Historic District (Boundary Increase), E side of Sycamore St. from Frost Ln. to Saint Andrew's Catholic Church, Newtown, 2/25/86, A, C, a, 86000315

Newtown Historic District (Boundary Increase: North and South Extensions), Parts of Congress, Chancellor and Liberty Sts. N of Washington Ave. and Chancellor St. S of Penn St. to S. State St., Newtown, 10/28/86, A, C, 86002867

Newtown Presbyterian Church, Sycamore St., Newtown vicinity, 7/16/87, C, a, 87001212

Palmer, Amos, House, Township Line Rd., Langhorne, 11/18/88, C, 88002661

Paxson, Isaiah, Farm, Address Restricted, Stockton vicinity, 8/23/84, A, C, 84003167

Pemberton, Phineas, House, Holly Dr., Bristol Township, Levittown, 9/28/71, B, C, 71000684

Penn's Park General Store Complex, 2310-2324 Second St. Pike, Wrightson Township, Penn's Park, 1/08/85, A, C, 85000072

Penns Park Historic District, Intersection of Second St. Pike and Penns Park Rd., Wrightstown, 3/13/86, A, C, a, 86000349

Pennsbury Manor, On the Delaware River S of Bordentown Rd., Morrisville vicinity, 10/28/69, B, D, 69000154

Phillips Mill Historic District, River Rd. between Limeport and Chapel Rd., Solebury Township, Solebury, 6/30/83, A, B, C, g, 83002220

Pine Valley Covered Bridge [Covered Bridges of the Delaware River Watershed TR], N of New

Britain on T 340, New Britain Township, New Britain vicinity, 12/01/80, A, C, 80003437

Point Pleasant Historic District, River Rd. and Point Pleasant Pike, Point Pleasant, 10/05/89, A, C, 89001652

Red Hill Church and School, Durham Rd., Ottsville, 5/22/78, A, C, a, 78002355

Richardson, Joseph, House, Bellevue and Maple Aves., Langhorne, 12/26/85, A, B, C, 85003159

Ridge Valley Rural Historic District, Roughly, all of Sheep Hole Rd. and parts of Headquarters, Geigel Hill, Red Hill, Tabor and Bunker Hill Rds., Tinicum Twp, Ottsville, 7/24/92, A, C, 92000944

Riegel, Benjamin, House, 29 Delaware Rd., Riegelsville, 1/06/87, B, C, 86003569

Riverside Farm, River and Headquarters Rds., Erwinna, 4/21/88, A, C, 88000461

Roberts, Enoch, House, 1226 W. Broad St., Quakertown, 4/24/86, C, 86000856

Shaw Historic District, Bounded by S. Main, Ashland, Bridge, and S. Clinton Sts., Doylestown, 12/17/79, A, C, 79002172

Sheard's Mill Covered Bridge [Covered Bridges of the Delaware River Watershed TR], E of Quakertown on LR 09129, Haycock/East Rockhill Townships, Richardtown vicinity, 12/01/80, A, C, 80003445

Slate Hill Cemetery, Jct. of Yardley—Morrisville Rd. and Mahlon Dr., Lower Makefield Township, Morrisville vicinity, 4/28/92, A, d, 92000397

Smith Family Farmstead, S of New Hope on River Rd., Upper Makefield Township, New Hope vicinity, 1/30/78, B, C, d, 78002354

Smith, William, House, Mud and Penns Park Rd., Wrightstown, 4/13/77, C, 77001131

Sotcher Farmhouse, 335 Trenton Rd., Fairless Hills, 12/27/77, B, C, 77001125

South Perkasie Covered Bridge [Covered Bridges of the Delaware River Watershed TR], S of Perkasie in Lenape Park, South Perkasie/Perkasie Townships, Perkasie, 12/01/80, A, C, b, 80003441

Southampton Baptist Church and Cemetery, 2nd St. Pike and Maple Ave., Southampton, 9/18/78, A, C, a, d, 78002359

Spinner House, Spinnerstown and Sleepy Hollow Rds., Spinnerstown, 6/22/79, C, 79002175

Spring Valley Historic District, Mill Rd. and US 202, Buckingham vicinity, 1/07/88, A, C, 88000140

Springdale Historic District [New Hope MRA], Mechanic St., Old York, S. Sugan, and Stoney Hill Rds., New Hope, 3/06/85, A, B, C, 85000461

St. Elizabeth's Convent, 1663 Bristol Pike, Cornwells Heights, 3/21/78, A, C, a, 78002352

Stover Mill, PA 32, Erwinna, 10/18/79, A, C, 79002174

Stover, Isaac, House, River Rd. S of Geigel Hill Rd., Erwinna, 4/26/90, C, 90000702

Stover-Myers Mill, N of Pipersville on Dark Hollow Rd., Pipersville vicinity, 9/13/78, A, 78002357

Summers, Lewis, Farm, 60 Headquarters Rd., Tinicum Township, Ottsville, 8/27/91, C, 91001124

Bucks County—Continued

Summerseat, Clymer St. and Morris Ave., Morrisville, 7/17/71, B, NHL, 71000685

Tabor Home for Needy and Destitute Children, 601 New Britain Rd., Doylestown, 7/16/87, A, C, a, 87001207

Taylor, Benjamin, Homestead, NE of Newtown off SR 532, Lower Makefield Township, Newtown vicinity, 12/06/75, C, 75001622

Taylor, Peter, Farmstead, 229 Wrights Rd., Newtown, 5/05/89, C, 89000353

Teller Cigar Factory, 340 N. Main St., Sellersville, 1/06/87, A, 86003567

Thompson, John, House, 1925 Second Street Pike, Northampton Township, Richboro vicinity, 7/16/73, B, C, 73001595

Tomlinson-Huddleston House, 109 W. Maple Ave., Langhorne, 11/10/83, C, 83004200

Trenton City/Calhoun Street Bridge, Spans Delaware River between Morrisville, PA and Trenton, NJ, Morrisville, 11/20/75, A, 75001621

Trevose Manor, 5408 Old Trevose Rd., Cornwells Heights, 5/24/76, B, C, 76001607

Twin Trees Farm, 905 2nd St. Pike, Richboro, 6/05/75, B, C, 75001623

Twining Farm, Buck Rd., Newtown Township, Newtown vicinity, 7/01/82, B, C, 82003766

Twining Ford Covered Bridge [Covered Bridges of the Delaware River Watershed TR], W of Newtown in Tyler State Park, Northampton-/Newtown Townships, Newtown vicinity, 12/01/80, A, C, 80003439

Tyler, George F., Mansion, W side of Swamp Rd./PA 313, Newtown, 7/16/87, C, 87001210

Upper Aquetong Valley Historic District, Meeting House and Aquetong Rds., between US 202 and Sugan Rd., Solebury, 7/30/87, A, C, 87001216

Van Sant Covered Bridge [Covered Bridges of the Delaware River Watershed TR], S of New Hope on T 392, Solebury Township, New Hope vicinity, 12/01/80, A, C, 80003438

Vansant Farmhouse, N of Rushland on Ceder Lane, Rushland vicinity, 8/02/77, C, 77001130

Village of Edgewood Historic District, Yardley, Langhorne, Edgewood and Stony Hill Rds., Lower Makefield Township, Edgewood, 11/28/80, A, C, 80003433

Washington Crossing State Park, Between Yardley and New Hope, on the Delaware River, Yardley vicinity, 10/15/66, A, B, NHL, 66000650

White Hall of Bristol College, 701-721 Shadyside Ave., Croyden, 1/12/84, A, C, 84003177

Wrightstown Friends Meeting Complex, PA 413, Wrightstown, 10/29/75, A, C, a, 75001624

Wycombe Village Historic District, Roughly bounded by Township Line, Mill Creek and Forest Grove Rds., Cherry Lane, Washington and Park Aves., Buckingham and Wrightstown Townships, 1/31/85, A, C, 85000177

Butler County

Butler Armory [Pennsylvania National Guard Armories MPS], 216 N. Washington St., Butler, 7/12/91, A, C, 91000903

Butler County Courthouse, S. Main and Diamond Sts., Butler, 9/15/77, A, C, 77001132

Elm Court, Between Polk and Elm Sts., Butler, 12/06/79, B, C, 79002176

Harmony Historic District, PA 68, Harmony, 3/21/73, A, B, a, NHL, 73002139

Lowrie, Sen. Walter, House, W. Diamond and S. Jackson Sts., Butler, 5/01/79, B, C, 79002177

Passavant House, 243 S. Main St., Zelienople, 4/11/77, C, 77001133

Roebling, John, House, Rebecca and Main Sts., Saxonburg, 11/13/76, B, C, b, 76001610

Cambria County

Berwind—White Mine 40 Historic District, Roughly bounded by the boney pile, Eureka No. 40 mine site, Scalp Level Borough line and Berwind—White Farmstead, Scalp Level, 4/28/92, A, 92000392

Bridge in Cassandra Borough [Highway Bridges Owned by the Commonwealth of Pennsylvania, Department of Transportation TR], PA 53 over Bens Creek, Oil City vicinity, 6/22/88, A, C, 88000782

Bridge in Johnstown City [Highway Bridges Owned by the Commonwealth of Pennsylvania, Department of Transportation TR], LR 525 spur over Stoney Creek, Johnstown, 6/22/88, A, C, 88000805

Cambria City Historic District, Roughly bounded by Broad St., Tenth Ave. and the Conemaugh R., Johnstown, 11/14/91, A, C, 91001706

Cambria County Courthouse, Center St., Ebensburg, 6/30/80, A, C, 80003449

Cambria County Jail, N. Center and Sample Sts., Ebensburg, 6/30/80, A, C, 80003450

Cambria Iron Company, Along Conemaugh River in the Johnstown vicinity, Johnstown vicinity, 6/22/89, A, B, C, NHL, 89001101

Cambria Public Library Building, 304 Washington St., Johnstown, 6/19/72, C, 72001100

Downtown Johnstown Historic District, Bounded by Washington, Clinton, Bedford, Vine, Market, Locust and Walnut Sts., Johnstown, 8/07/92, A, C, 92000941

Eliza Furnace [Iron and Steel Resources in Pennsylvania MPS], Lower Main St., Buffington and Blacklick Townships, Vintonville, 9/06/91, A, C, 91001138

Grand Army of the Republic Hall, 132 Park Pl., Johnstown, 4/17/80, A, 80003451

Johnstown Flood National Memorial, Jct. of U.S. 219 and PA 869, Johnstown vicinity, 10/15/66, A, f, NPS, 66000656

Johnstown Inclined Railway, Johns St. and Edgehill Dr., Johnstown, 6/18/73, A, C, 73001597

Lilly Bridge [Highway Bridges Owned by the Commonwealth of Pennsylvania, Department of Transportation TR], PA 53 over Burgoon Run, Lilly, 6/22/88, A, C, 88000785

Nathan's Department Store, 426-432 Main St, Johnstown, 8/10/79, A, C, 79002178

Noon, Philip, House, 114 E. High St., Ebensburg, 8/23/84, A, C, 84003179

South Fork Fishing and Hunting Club Historic District, Roughly bounded by Fourtieth, Main, and Lake Sts., St. Michael, 7/31/86, A, C, 86002091

Carbon County

Carbon County Jail, 128 Broadway St., Jim Thorpe, 11/08/74, A, C, 74001764

Carbon County Section of the Lehigh Canal, Along Lehigh River, Weissport and Vicinity, 8/10/79, A, 79002179

Central Railroad of New Jersey Station, Susquehanna St., Jim Thorpe, 1/01/76, A, C, 76001615

Little Gap Covered Bridge [Covered Bridges of the Delaware River Watershed TR], S of Little Gap on T 376, Towamensing Township, Little Gap, 12/01/80, A, C, 80004294

Mauch Chunk and Summit Hill Switchback Railroad, Between Ludlow St. in Summit Hill and F.A.P. 209 in Jim Thorpe, Jim Thorpe, 6/03/76, A, C, 76001616

Old Mauch Chunk Historic District, Broadway, Susquehanna, Race, and High Sts., Jim Thorpe, 11/10/77, A, C, 77001134

Packer, Asa, Mansion, Packer Rd., Jim Thorpe, 12/30/74, B, C, NHL, 74001765

Packer, Harry, Mansion, Packer Rd., Jim Thorpe, 11/20/74, C, 74001766

St. Mark's Episcopal Church, Race and Susquehanna Sts., Jim Thorpe, 7/26/77, C, a, NHL, 77001135

Centre County

Aaronsburg Historic District, PA 45, Aaronsburg, 9/02/80, B, C, 80003452

Ag Hill Complex, Penn State University campus, State College, 1/22/79, A, C, 79002191

Allison, William, House, 1 mi. W of Spring Mills on PA 45, Spring Mills vicinity, 4/18/77, C, 77001146

Ayres, Bucher, Farm, SW of Pine Grove Mills on Whitehall Rd., Pennsylvania Furnace, Pine Grove Mills vicinity, 12/01/80, B, C, 80003453

Bechdel II, Christian, House, S of Blanchard on Liberty Rd., Liberty Township, Blanchard vicinity, 3/01/82, B, C, 82003775

Bellefonte Academy, 225 E. Bishop St., Bellefonte, 11/07/76, B, C, 76001617

Bellefonte Armory [Pennsylvania National Guard Armories MPS], E. Bishop St., Bellefonte, 12/22/89, A, C, 89002068

Bellefonte Historic District, Roughly bounded by Stony Batter, Ardell Alley, Thomas, Armor, Penn, Ridge and Logan Sts., Bellefonte, 8/12/77, B, C, 77001136

Black Moshannon State Park Maintenance District [Emergency Conservation Work (ECW) Architecture in Pennsylvania State Parks: 1933-1942, TR], 9 mi. E of Philipsburg on PA 504, Philipsburg vicinity, 2/12/87, A, C, 87000097

Centre County—Continued

Black Moshannon State Park Day Use District [Emergency Conservation Work (ECW) Architecture in Pennsylvania State Parks: 1933-1942, TR], 9 mi. E of Philipsburg on PA 504, Philipsburg vicinity, 2/12/87, A, C, 87000101

Black Moshannon State Park Family Cabin District [Emergency Conservation Work (ECW) Architecture in Pennsylvania State Parks: 1933-1942, TR], 9 mi. E of Philipsburg on PA 504, Philipsburg vicinity, 2/12/87, A, C, 87000102

Boal Mansion, U.S. 322 and PA 45, Boalsburg, 12/04/78, B, C, 78002361

Boalsburg Historic District, U.S. 322, Boalsburg, 12/12/77, A, B, C, 77001139

Brockerhoff Hotel, High and Allegheny Sts., Bellefonte, 4/11/77, B, C, 77001137

Brockerhoff Mill, SW of Bellefonte on PA 550, Benner Township, Bellefonte vicinity, 5/01/79, B, C, 79002180

Camelot, 520 S. Fraser St., State College, 4/26/79, C, 79002192

Centre County Courthouse, High St., Bellefonte, 11/07/76, B, C, 76001618

Centre Furnace Mansion House, 1001 E. College Ave., State College, 12/27/79, A, 79002193

Centre Mills, SW of Rebersburg off PA 445, Rebersburg vicinity, 12/12/76, A, C, 76001621

Curtin Village, Off U.S. 220, Boggs Township, Curtin, 3/11/71, B, C, 71000687

Dale, Felix, Stone House, Rt. 871, Lemont, 4/20/82, B, C, 82003777

Egg Hill Church, SW of Spring Mills on Egg Hill Rd., Potter Township, Spring Mills vicinity, 6/04/79, A, C, a, 79002189

Elder, Abraham, Stone House, PA 550, Stormstown, 4/13/77, B, C, 77001148

Farmers' High School, College Ave. and Atherton St., State College, 9/11/81, A, C, g, 81000538

Fisher Farm Site, Address Restricted, Wingate vicinity, 3/03/82, D, 82003781

Fisher, Maj. Jared B., House, NE of Spring Mills on PA 45, Spring Mills vicinity, 9/14/77, B, C, 77001147

Gamble Mill, Dunlap and Lamb Sts., Bellefonte, 8/01/75, A, C, 75001627

Gray, John, House, E of Port Matilda off PA 550, S of U.S. 220, Halfmoon Township, Port Matilda vicinity, 4/03/75, C, 75001628

Gregg, Andrew, Homestead, 2 mi. E of Centre Hall off PA 192, Centre Hall vicinity, 7/28/77, B, C, 77001141

Harmony Forge Mansion, S of Milesburg on PA 144 , Boggs Township, Milesburg vicinity, 10/16/79, A, B, C, 79002183

Hill House, Tennis St., Boalsburg, 3/28/77, C, 77001140

Houserville Site (36CE65), Address Restricted, State College vicinity, 3/06/86, D, 86000401

Iddings-Baldridge House, Railroad St., Milesburg, 7/29/77, C, 77001145

Lemont Historic District, Off PA 26, Lemont, 6/06/79, A, C, 79002182

Linden Hall Historic District, Rock Hill Rd. between Linden Hall and Brush Valley Rds., Linden Hall, 9/05/90, C, 90001409

Logan Furnace Mansion, 3 mi. S of Bellefonte on PA 144, Benner Township, Bellefonte vicinity, 4/11/77, C, 77001138

McAllister-Beaver House, 817 E. Bishop St., Bellefonte, 2/24/82, B, C, 82003774

Miles-Humes House, 203 N. Allegheny St., Bellefonte, 10/21/76, C, b, 76001619

Millheim Historic District, PA 45 and PA 445, Millheim, 3/25/86, A, C, 86000787

Neff Round Barn, S of Centre Hall off PA 45, Potter Township, Centre Hall vicinity, 5/02/79, A, C, 79002181

Neff, Maj. John, Homestead, SW of Centre Hall, Centre Hall vicinity, 4/11/77, C, 77001142

Oak Hall Historic District, SR 871, College Township, Oak Hall, 10/25/79, B, C, 79002185

Penn's Cave and Hotel, 5 mi. (8 km) E of Centre Hall off PA 192, Gregg Township, Centre Hall vicinity, 4/14/78, A, C, 78002363

Philips, Hardman, House, Presquisle and 4th Sts., Philipsburg, 9/18/78, B, 78002364

Pickle, Simon, Stone House, Jct. of PA 192 and PA 445, Madisonburg, 4/18/77, A, C, 77001144

Potter-Allison Farm, SE of Centre Hall on PA 144, Potter Township, Centre Hall vicinity, 12/06/77, A, B, C, 77001143

Rebersburg Historic District, PA 192, Rebersburg, 12/07/79, A, C, 79002188

Rhone, Leonard, House, Off PA 45, Centre vicinity, 10/31/85, B, 85003448

Rowland Theater, Front St., Philipsburg, 10/18/79, A, C, 79002186

South Ward School, Bishop St., Bellefonte, 2/23/78, A, C, 78002360

Thomas, William, House, 266 N. Thomas St., Bellefonte, 11/13/76, B, C, 76001620

Thompson, Gen. John, House, E. Branch Rd., State College, 3/29/78, C, 78002366

Tudek Site, Address Restricted, State College vicinity, 2/12/82, D, 82003778

Union Church and Burial Ground, E. Presquisle St., Philipsburg, 5/23/78, B, C, a, d, 78002365

Unionville Historic District, U.S. 220 and PA 504, Unionville, 5/30/79, A, C, 79002194

Waggoner, Daniel, Log House and Barn, SW of Spring Mills, Potter Township, Spring Mills vicinity, 4/18/79, B, C, 79002190

Wilson, George, Homestead, SW of Centennial on PA 550, Centennial vicinity, 2/24/82, B, C, a, 82003776

Woodward Inn, PA 45, Woodward, 12/18/78, A, B, C, 78002367

Chester County

Ashbridge, David, Log House [West Whiteland Township MRA], 1181 King Rd., West Chester, 11/06/84, C, 84003878

Autun [West Whiteland Township MRA], 371 E. Boot Rd., West Whiteland, 9/06/84, C, 84003232

Bailey, John, Farm [East Fallowfield Township MRA], Springdell Rd., East Fallowfield Township, Coatesville vicinity, 5/20/85, A, C, 85001143

Baily Farm [West Branch Brandywine Creek MRA], Strasburg and Broad Run Rds., W. Bradford Twp., 9/16/85, C, 85002347

Barnard, William J., Residence, 920 E. Street Rd., Thornbury, 7/21/82, C, 82003779

Barns-Brinton House, E of Hamorton on U.S. 1, Pennsbury Township, Hamorton vicinity, 5/27/71, C, 71000692

Bartram's Covered Bridge [Covered Bridges of Chester County TR], W of Newtown on LR 15098, Willistown/Newtown Townships, Media vicinity, 12/10/80, A, C, 80003462

Bell, John, Farm [West Whiteland Township MRA], 463 N. Ship Rd., West Whiteland, 9/06/84, C, 84003235

Birchrunville General Store, Hollow and Flowing Springs Rds., Birchrunville, 3/21/78, A, C, 78002368

Birchrunville Historic District, Jct. of Flowing Springs Rd. and Schoolhouse Ln., West Vincent Township, Birchrunville, 4/28/92, A, C, 92000401

Birmingham Friends Meetinghouse and School, 1245 Birmingham Rd., Birmingham, 7/27/71, A, a, 71000688

Black Rock Bridge [Highway Bridges Owned by the Commonwealth of Pennsylvania, Department of Transportation TR], TR 113 over Schuylkill River, Mont Clare vicinity, 6/22/88, C, 88000735

Boyer, Riter, House [West Whiteland Township MRA], 350 W. Boot Rd., West Whiteland, 11/10/83, B, C, 83004207

Bradford Friends Meetinghouse, E side of Northbrook Rd., Marshallton, 7/27/71, C, a, 71000694

Brandywine Building and Loan Assoc. Rowhouses [East Fallowfield Township MRA], Hephzibah Hill Rd., East Fallowfield Township, Coatesville vicinity, 5/20/85, C, 85001144

Bridge Mill Farm, Marshall Rd., East Brandywine Township, Downingtown vicinity, 3/09/83, A, 83002221

Bridge in East Fallowfield Township [Highway Bridges Owned by the Commonwealth of Pennsylvania, Department of Transportation TR], Strasburg Rd. over Mill Race, Mortonville, 6/22/88, C, 88000878

Bridge in New Garden Township [Highway Bridges Owned by the Commonwealth of Pennsylvania, Department of Transportation TR], Landenberg Rd. over White Clay Creek, Landenberg, 6/22/88, C, 88000804

Bridge in Tredyffrin Township [Highway Bridges Owned by the Commonwealth of Pennsylvania, Department of Transportation TR], Gulph Rd. over Trout Run, Port Kennedy vicinity, 6/22/88, C, 88000778

Bridge in West Fallowfield Township [Highway Bridges Owned by the Commonwealth of Pennsylvania, Department of Transportation TR], Ross Fording Rd. over Octoraro Creek, Steelville vicinity, 6/22/88, C, 88000849

Chester County—Continued

Brinton's Mill, N of Chadds Ford on U.S. 100, Birmingham Township, Chadds Ford vicinity, 5/27/71, A, C, 71000689

Brinton, Edward, House, NW of Chadds Ford on PA 100, Chadds Ford vicinity, 6/19/73, A, C, 73001599

Brinton, George, House, PA 100, 1 mi. N of jct. with US 1, Birmingham Township, Chadds Ford, 10/25/90, C, D, 90001608

Brower's Bridge [Highway Bridges Owned by the Commonwealth of Pennsylvania, Department of Transportation TR], Mansion Rd. over French Creek, Warwick vicinity, 6/22/88, C, 88000754

Buckwalter Building, 11-13 S. High St., West Chester, 2/22/84, C, 84003180

Bull, Thomas, House, E of Elverson on Bulltown Rd., East Nantmeal Township, Elverson vicinity, 8/03/79, A, C, 79002198

Butler House, 228 W. Miner St., West Chester, 7/23/80, B, C, 80003470

Caln Meeting House, 901 Caln Meeting House Rd., Caln Township, Coatesville, 5/03/84, C, a, 84003182

Carter-Worth House and Farm, 450 Lucky Hill Rd., East Bradford Township, Marshallton vicinity, 9/15/77, A, C, 77001151

Cedarcroft, N of Kennett Sq., Kennett Square vicinity, 11/11/71, B, NHL, 71000693

Charlestown Village Historic District, SW of Phoenixville on Charlestown Rd., Charlestown Township, Phoenixville vicinity, 5/16/78, A, 78002374

Chester County Courthouse, 10 N. High St., West Chester, 6/05/72, C, 72001109

Church Farm School Historic District [West Whiteland Township MRA], US 30, West Whiteland, 10/26/84, A, C, 84002733

Clinger-Moses Mill Complex, S of Chester Springs on Pine Creek Lane, Chester Springs vicinity, 7/17/80, A, C, 80003454

Coates, Moses, Jr., Farm, 1416 State Rd., Schuykill Township, Phoenixville vicinity, 5/03/84, A, 84003186

Coatesville Historic District, Roughly bounded by Chesnut St., Sixth Ave., Oak St., Fifth Ave., Harmony St., and First Ave., Coatesville, 5/14/87, A, C, 87000667

Colebrook Manor [West Whiteland Township MRA], 637 W. Lincoln Hwy., Exton, 9/06/84, A, C, 84003239

Collins Mansion, 633 Goshen Rd., West Chester, 11/09/72, C, 72001110

Como Farm [West Branch Brandywine Creek MRA], Broad Run Rd., W. Bradford Twp., 9/16/85, B, 85002348

Cope's Bridge, Address Restricted, Marshallton vicinity, 3/07/85, A, C, 85000465

County Bridge No. 101 [Highway Bridges Owned by the Commonwealth of Pennsylvania, Department of Transportation TR], Wagontown Rd. over Brandywine Creek, Rock Run vicinity, 6/22/88, C, 88000780

County Bridge No. 124 [Highway Bridges Owned by the Commonwealth of Pennsylvania, Department of Transportation TR], Edge Hill Rd. over Beaver Creek, Downingtown vicinity, 6/22/88, C, 88000760

County Bridge No. 148 [Highway Bridges Owned by the Commonwealth of Pennsylvania, Department of Transportation TR], PA 926 over Chester County, Westtown, 6/22/88, C, 88000879

County Bridge No. 171 [Highway Bridges Owned by the Commonwealth of Pennsylvania, Department of Transportation TR], Cedar Hollow Rd. over Valley Creek, Malvern vicinity, 6/22/88, C, 88000762

Coventry Hall, Off PA 23, South Coventry Township, Coventryville, 12/16/74, A, C, 74001767

Coventryville Historic District, S of Pottstown on PA 23, Pottstown vicinity, 1/31/78, A, C, 78002378

Cox, Hewson, House [West Whiteland Township MRA], Church Farm Rd., West Whiteland, 8/02/84, C, 84003188

Cramond, 95 Crestline Rd., Strafford, 6/30/83, C, 83002222

Cressbrook Farm, S of Valley Forge, off U.S. 76, Valley Forge vicinity, 10/26/72, A, 72001106

Davis, Daniel, House and Barn, Birmingham and Street Rd., Birmingham Township, Birmingham vicinity, 4/11/73, C, 73001598

DeHaven, Harry, House [Strasburg Road TR; East Fallowfield Township MRA], Strasburg Rd., Coatesville vicinity, 9/18/85, A, C, 85002386

Deery Family Homestead, W of Phoenixville, West Vincent Township, Phoenixville vicinity, 12/23/77, A, C, 77001153

Derbydown Homestead [West Branch Brandywine Creek MRA], At jct. of CR 15077 and 15080, Northbrook, 4/02/73, B, a, 73001609

Dilworthtown Historic District, Jct. of CR 15199 and 15087, Dilworthtown, 1/18/73, A, C, 73001601

Doe Run Village Historic District [West Branch Brandywine Creek MRA], Highland Dairy, DuPont & Chapel Rds. & Rts. 82 & 841, W. Marlborough Twp., 9/16/85, A, 85002349

Dougherty, Edward, House [East Fallowfield Township MRA], Mt. Carmel Rd., East Fallowfield Township, Coatesville vicinity, 5/20/85, A, C, 85001145

Dougherty, Philip, House [Strasburg Road TR; East Fallowfield Township MRA], Strasburg Rd., Coatesville vicinity, 9/18/85, A, 85002390

Dougherty, Philip, Tavern [Strasburg Road TR; East Fallowfield Township MRA], Strasburg Rd., Coatesville vicinity, 9/18/85, A, B, 85002391

Downing, Hunt, House [West Whiteland Township MRA], 600 W. Lincoln Hwy., Exton vicinity, 10/11/90, C, 84003960

Downing, Hunt, House (Boundary Decrease) [West Whiteland Township MRA], 600 W. Lincoln Hwy., Exton vicinity, 9/07/90, C, 90001343

Downingtown Log House, 15 E. Lancaster Ave., Downingtown, 5/24/79, A, C, 79002195

Drovers Inn [Strasburg Road TR; East Fallowfield Township MRA], Strasburg Rd., Coatesville vicinity, 9/18/85, A, 85002388

East Bradford Boarding School for Boys, 1 mi. E of Lenape at West Chester and Sconnelltown Rds., East Bradford Township, Lenape vicinity, 3/07/73, C, 73001605

East Lancaster Avenue Historic District, An irregular pattern along E. Lancaster Ave., Downingtown, 12/11/79, A, C, 79002196

East, Nicholas, House, W of Valley Forge on Kimberton Rd., Valley Forge vicinity, 4/02/73, C, 73001614

Elverson Historic District, Main, Chestnut and Hall Sts. and Park Ave., Elverson, 4/29/93, A, C, 93000354

Embreeville Historic District [Embreeville Historic District], Rt. 162, Newlin Twp., 9/16/85, A, 85002350

Ercildoun Historic District [East Fallowfield Township MRA], PA 82 and SRs T368, 15236, T371, and 182, East Fallowfield Township, Coatesville vicinity, 5/20/85, A, C, 85001157

Esherick, Wharton, Studio, 1520 Horseshoe Trail, Malvern, 4/26/73, B, C, g, NHL, 73001615

Everhart, William, Buildings, 28 W. Market St., West Chester, 7/17/79, A, 79002206

Everhart, William, House [West Whiteland Township MRA], S. Ship and Boot Rds., West Whiteland, 8/02/84, C, 84003249

Exton Hotel [West Whiteland Township MRA], 423 E. Lincoln Hwy., Exton, 11/01/83, A, C, 83004201

Fagley House, W of Phoenixville on Art School Rd., West Pikeland Township, Phoenixville vicinity, 5/03/76, C, 76001628

Farmers and Mechanics Trust Company Building, Market and High Sts., West Chester, 1/06/83, C, 83002223

Federal Barn, Off PA 252, Valley Forge vicinity, 2/08/80, A, C, 80003469

Ferguson, William, Farm, E of Glen Moore on Marshall Rd., Glen Moore vicinity, 4/10/80, A, B, C, a, 80003460

Ferron, John, House [West Branch Brandywine Creek MRA], Saint Malachi Rd., Londonderry Township, 11/26/85, C, 85003049

First Presbyterian Church of West Chester, 130 W. Miner St., West Chester, 11/27/72, C, a, 72001111

Fox Chase Inn [West Whiteland Township MRA], 613 Swedesford Rd., West Whiteland, 9/06/84, C, 84003253

French Creek Farm, Kimberton Rd., Kimberton, 11/03/88, C, 88002372

Gay Street School, Gay and Morgan Sts., Phoenixville, 11/01/83, A, 83004202

General Washington Inn, Uwchlan and E. Lancaster Aves., Downingtown, 8/22/79, A, 79002197

Gibson's Covered Bridge [Covered Bridges of Chester County TR], SE of Downingtown on T 391, East/West Bradford Townships, Downingtown vicinity, 12/10/80, A, C, 80003456

Gladden, Joseph, House [East Fallowfield Township MRA], West Chester Rd., East Fallowfield

Chester County—Continued

Township, Coatesville vicinity, 5/20/85, C, 85001146

Glen Hope Covered Bridge [Covered Bridges of Chester County TR], W of Lewisville on T 344, Elk Township, West Grove vicinity, 12/10/80, A, C, 80003472

Glen Rose Historic District [East Fallowfield Township MRA], SRs 15178 and T371, Coatesville vicinity, 9/18/85, A, 85002384

Good News Buildings, N of Chester Springs on Art School Rd., West Pikeland Township, Chester Springs vicinity, 5/27/71, A, C, 71000691

Goodwin Acres, 600 Reservoir Rd., West Chester vicinity, 6/27/80, C, 80003471

Great Valley Mill, 72 N. Valley Rd., Tredyffrin Township, Paoli vicinity, 9/01/83, A, C, 83002224

Green Valley Historic District [West Branch Brandywine Creek MRA], Green Valley Rd., Newlin & E. Marlborough Twps., 9/16/85, A, 85002352

Greenwood School [West Whiteland Township MRA], 700 King Rd., West Whiteland, 11/10/83, C, 83004208

Grove Historic District [West Whiteland Township MRA], S. Whitford Rd., West Whiteland Township, Downington vicinity, 8/02/84, A, C, a, d, 84003264

Hall's Bridge [Covered Bridges of Chester County TR (AD)], About 3 mi. N of Chester Springs at Sheeder Rd. and Birch Run, East/West Vincent Townships, Chester Springs vicinity, 4/23/73, A, C, 73001600

Hamorton Historic District, Jct. of US 1 and SR 52, Kennett Square vicinity, 4/26/90, A, C, 90000704

Hance House and Barn [West Branch Brandywine Creek MRA], Rt. 842, E. Bradford Twp., 9/16/85, B, C, 85002354

Hanna, John, Farm [East Fallowfield Township MRA], Fairview Rd., East Fallowfield Township, Coatesville vicinity, 5/20/85, C, 85001147

Hannum, Col. John, House, NE of Marshallton at 898 Frank Rd., East Bradford Township, Marshallton vicinity, 12/10/80, A, B, 80003463

Hare's Hill Road Bridge, W of Phoenixville on Hare's Hill Rd., East Pikeland Township, Phoenixville vicinity, 3/28/78, C, 78002375

Harlan House, PA 162 and Star Gazer Rd., Embreeville vicinity, 5/09/85, A, C, 85001004

Harlan Log House, Fairville Rd., Kennett Square vicinity, 7/16/87, A, C, 87001211

Hartman, George, House, W of Phoenixville on Church Rd., East Pikeland Township, Phoenixville vicinity, 3/26/76, C, 76001629

Harvard, David, House, S of Valley Forge off U.S. 76, Valley Forge vicinity, 10/26/72, A, 72001107

Harvey, Peter, House and Barn, E of Kennett Sq. on Hillendale Rd., Mendenhall, Kennett Square vicinity, 4/20/78, C, 78002371

Harvey, William, House, NW of Chadds Ford on Brinton's Bridge Rd. off U.S. 1, Pennsbury Township, Chadds Ford vicinity, 5/27/71, A, C, 71000690

Hatfield-Hibernia Historic District, N of Wagontown, Wagontown vicinity, 6/20/84, A, C, 84003205

Hayes Homestead [West Branch Brandywine Creek MRA], Rt. 162 & Harvey's Bridge Rd., Newlin Twp., 9/16/85, C, 85002355

Hayes Mill House [West Branch Brandywine Creek MRA], Star Gazer Rd., Newlin Twp., 9/16/85, A, C, 85002358

Hayes, Jacob, House [West Branch Brandywine Creek MRA], Rt. 162, Newlin Twp., 9/16/85, B, C, 85002356

Hibernia House, N of Wagontown off PA 340, Wagontown vicinity, 11/20/75, C, 75001632

High Bridge, Spans west branch of the Brandywine, Coatesville, 3/26/76, A, C, 76001623

Hockley Mill Farm, Warwick Furnace Rd., SE of Knauertown (Warwick Township), Glen Moore, 12/18/90, A, C, 90001921

Hoffman, George, House [West Whiteland Township MRA], 1311 Grove Rd., West Whiteland, 8/02/84, C, 84003272

Hoopes, Cyrus, House and Barn [West Branch Brandywine Creek MRA], Springdell Rd., W. Marlborough Township, 11/26/85, C, 85003050

Hopewell Historic District, Roughly, Hopewell Rd. from Lower Hopewell Rd. to Roneys Corner Rd. and area S, and Lower Hopewell Rd. N past Calvery Rd., Hopewell, 2/28/91, A, C, 91000226

House at Springdell [West Branch Brandywine Creek MRA], Rt. 841, W. Marlborough Twp., 9/16/85, C, 85002360

House at Upper Laurel Iron Works [West Branch Brandywine Creek MRA], McCorkel's Rock Rd., Newlin Twp., 9/16/85, A, 85002371

Hunt, Roger, Mill, Race St., Downingtown, 1/04/80, A, 80003457

Huston, Abram, House and Carriage House, 53 S. 1st Ave., Coatesville, 9/15/77, C, 77001149

Indian Deep Farm [West Branch Brandywine Creek MRA], Glenhall & Groundhog College Rds., Newlin Twp., 9/16/85, A, C, 85002372

Isabella Furnace [Iron and Steel Resources in Pennsylvania MPS], Bollinger Dr. just N of Creek Rd., Nantmeal Township, Brandywine Manor vicinity, 9/06/91, A, 91001135

Jacobs, Benjamin, House [West Whiteland Township MRA], 325 N. Ship Rd., West Whiteland, 8/02/84, C, 84003274

Kennedy Bridge [Covered Bridges of Chester County TR (AD)], N of Kimberton off PA 23 on Seven Stars Rd. over French Creek, East Vincent Township, Kimberton vicinity, 1/21/74, C, 74001770

Kennedy, Francis W., House [West Whiteland Township MRA], 4717 Highland Ave., West Whiteland, 8/02/84, C, 84003277

Kennett Square Historic District, Roughly bounded by Sickles, Willow, Mulberry, Broad, South, Union, Cedar, Lafayette, State, and Washington, Kennett Square, 8/18/89, A, C, 89001052

Kimberton Historic District (Boundary Increase), Hare's Hill, Prizer, and Kimberton Rds., Kimberton, 7/30/87, A, B, C, 87001252

Kimberton Village Historic District, Both sides of Hares Hill Rd. between Kimberton and Cold Stream, East Pikeland Township, Kimberton, 5/06/76, A, C, 76001626

Kinbawn [West Whiteland Township MRA], 405 Highland Ave., West Whiteland, 9/06/84, C, 84003280

Kirkland Station [West Whiteland Township MRA], 1370 Kirkland Ave., West Whiteland, 11/10/83, A, C, 83004209

Knauer, John, House and Mill, PA 23, Knauertown, 5/30/85, A, C, 85001173

Lafayette's Quarters, SE of Valley Forge on Wilson Rd., Valley Forge vicinity, 6/20/74, A, B, NPS, 74001774

Lahr Farm, E of Elverson on PA 23, Elverson vicinity, 9/07/79, C, 79002199

Lapp Log House, S of Chester Springs at Conestoga and Yellow Springs Rds., East Whiteland Township, Chester Springs vicinity, 1/23/80, C, 80003455

Larkin Covered Bridge [Covered Bridges of Chester County TR], N of Downingtown in Marsh Creek State Park, Upper Uwchlan Township, Downingtown vicinity, 12/10/80, A, C, b, 80003458

Lenape Bridge [Highway Bridges Owned by the Commonwealth of Pennsylvania, Department of Transportation TR], PA 52 over parking lot, Lenape vicinity, 6/22/88, C, 88000781

Lewis, Evan, House [West Whiteland Township MRA], 117 N. Ship Rd., Exton, 8/02/84, C, 84003286

Lightfoot Mill, W of Valley Forge off PA 401, Valley Forge vicinity, 4/13/73, A, C, 73001616

Lionville Historic District, Roughly along PA 100 and S. Village Ave., Lionville, 12/01/80, A, 80003459

Lochiel Farm [West Whiteland Township MRA], 111A N. Ship Rd., West Whiteland, 9/06/84, C, 84003289

Longwood Gardens District, On U.S. 1, East Marlborough Township, Hamorton vicinity, 10/18/72, A, C, a, 72001105

Lukens Main Office Building, 50 S. 1st Ave., Coatesville, 5/24/76, C, 76001624

Lunn's Tavern, PA 896, Strickersville, 10/25/79, A, C, 79002204

Marshall's Bridge [Highway Bridges Owned by the Commonwealth of Pennsylvania, Department of Transportation TR], Marshall Rd. over Culbertson Run, Little Washington vicinity, 6/22/88, C, 88000880

Marshall, Humphry, House, Strasburg Rd. (PA 62) at jct. of Northbrook Rd., Marshallton, 5/27/71, B, C, 71000695

Marshall, Humphry, House, 1407 S. Strasburg Rd./PA 162, Marshallton, 12/23/87, B, C, NHL, 87002596

Marshallton Historic District, Strasburg Rd., Marshallton, 1/08/86, A, C, 86000056

Marshallton Inn, W. Strasburg Rd., Marshallton, 7/29/77, A, C, 77001152

Martin-Little House, S of Phoenixville off PA 113 on Church Rd., Charlestown Township, Phoenixville vicinity, 7/02/73, C, 73001611

Chester County—Continued

Meredith, Daniel, House [West Whiteland Township MRA], 1358 Glen Echo Rd., West Whiteland, 8/02/84, C, 84003291

Meredith, Simon, House, 0.5 mi. W of Pughtown on Pughtown Rd., Pughtown vicinity, 12/16/74, C, 74001772

Meredith, Stephen, House, PA 100 halfway between Bucktown and Pughtown, South Coventry Township, Bucktown vicinity, 4/29/93, C, 93000355

Michener, Nathan, House, W of Bucktown on Ridge Rd., South Coventry Township, Bucktown vicinity, 4/03/76, A, B, C, 76001622

Middle Pickering Rural Historic District, Pikeland, Yellow Springs, Merlin, Church and Pickering Rds., Phoenixville, E. Pikeland and W. Pikeland Townships, Phoenixville vicinity, 9/06/91, A, C, 91001125

Moore Hall, E of Phoenixville on Valley Forge Rd., Schuylkill Township, Phoenixville vicinity, 11/19/74, A, C, 74001771

Mortonville Bridge [Strasburg Road TR; East Fallowfield Township MRA], Straburg Rd., Coatesville vicinity, 9/18/85, A, 85002392

Mortonville Hotel [Strasburg Road TR; East Fallowfield Township MRA], Strasburg Rd., Coatesville vicinity, 9/18/85, A, 85002393

Mountain Meadow Farm [West Branch Brandywine Creek MRA], Harvey's Bridge Rd., Newlin Twp., 9/16/85, C, 85002373

National Bank of Coatesville Building, 235 E. Lincoln Highway, Coatesville, 9/14/77, C, 77001150

New Century Clubhouse, High and Lacey Sts., West Chester, 2/24/83, A, C, 83002225

Newlin Miller's House [West Whiteland Township MRA], 1240 Samuel Rd., West Whiteland, 9/06/84, A, C, 84003293

Northbrook Historic District [West Branch Brandywine Creek MRA], Northbrook, Indian Hannah & Bragg Hill Rds., Newlin, Pocopson & W. Bradford Twps., 9/16/85, A, B, 85002374

Oakdale, Hillendale Rd., Pennsbury Township, Chadds Ford, 1/13/72, A, C, 72001103

Oaklands [West Whiteland Township MRA], 349 W. Lincoln Hwy., West Whiteland, 9/06/84, C, 84003295

Okehocking Historic District, Roughly bounded by West Chester Pike, Plumsock Rd., Goshen Rd. and Garrett Mill Rd., Willistown Township, Media vicinity, 8/02/93, A, C, 93000719

Old Kennett Meetinghouse, S of West Chester on U.S. 1, E of jct. of PA 52, West Chester vicinity, 7/15/74, A, C, a, 74001776

Orthodox Meetinghouse, SW of West Chester on Birmingham Rd., West Chester vicinity, 4/26/72, A, a, 72001112

Paradise Valley Historic District, Roughly, Valley Creek Rd. from US 322 to Ravine Rd., East Bradford Township, Marshallton vicinity, 12/24/92, A, C, 92001724

Parker's Ford, Old Schuylkill Rd., East Vincent/East Coventry Townships, Parkerford, 3/17/83, A, 83002226

Parkersville Friends Meetinghouse, S of Parkersville off PA 926, Pennsbury Township, Parkersville vicinity, 3/20/73, A, C, a, 73001610

Parkesburg National Bank, Gay and Main Sts., Parkesburg, 8/29/80, C, 80003467

Passmore, Mansel, House [East Fallowfield Township MRA], Glen Rose Rd., East Fallowfield Township, Coatesville vicinity, 5/20/85, C, 85001148

Pawling, Isaac, House [Strasburg Road TR; East Fallowfield Township MRA], Strasburg Rd., Coatesville vicinity, 9/18/85, A, C, 85002394

Pennock, Martha, House [East Fallowfield Township MRA], PA 82, East Fallowfield Township, Coatesville vicinity, 5/20/85, A, C, 85001149

Pennsbury Inn, On U.S. 1 at jct. with Hickory Hill Rd., Pennsbury Township, Chadds Ford vicinity, 3/16/72, A, 72001104

Pennypacker, Benjamin, House [West Whiteland Township MRA], 800 E. Swedesford Rd., West Whiteland, 8/02/84, C, 84003298

Pennypacker, Matthias, Farm, S of Phoenixville on White Horse Rd., Phoenixville vicinity, 12/27/77, A, C, 77001154

Peters, William, House, Hillendale Rd., Pennsbury Township, Mendenhall, 5/27/71, C, b, 71000696

Phillips, Joseph and Esther, Plantation, Bailey's Crossroads, S of Glen Run Rd., Atglen vicinity, 9/05/90, C, 90001414

Phoenixville Historic District, Roughly bounded by Penn St., RR tracks, Fourth Ave., and Wheatland St., Phoenixville, 3/17/87, A, C, 87000378

Pickwick [West Whiteland Township MRA], N side of Swedesford Rd., West Whiteland, 7/28/88, C, 88001163

Pierce, Lukens, House, NW of Ercildoun on Wilmington Rd., East Fallowfield Township, Ercildoun vicinity, 3/14/73, B, C, 73001604

Pleasant Hill Plantation, Little Conestoga Rd., Glen Moore, 2/24/83, A, C, 83002227

Powell Farm [East Fallowfield Township MRA], Dupont Rd., East Fallowfield Township, Coatesville vicinity, 5/20/85, C, 85001150

Powell, John, House [East Fallowfield Township MRA], Hephzibah Hill Rd., East Fallowfield Township, Coatesville vicinity, 5/20/85, C, 85001151

Price, Joseph, House [West Whiteland Township MRA], 401 Clover Mill Rd., West Whiteland, 9/06/84, C, 84003299

Primitive Hall, 2 mi. NW of Chatham on PA 841, West Marlborough Township, Chatham vicinity, 3/19/75, C, 75001629

Prizer's Mill Complex, W of Phoenixville on Seven Stars Rd., Phoenixville vicinity, 9/06/78, A, 78002376

Pusey, Joshua, House [East Fallowfield Township MRA], Saw Mill Rd., East Fallowfield Township, Coatesville vicinity, 5/20/85, C, 85001152

Rapps Bridge [Covered Bridges of Chester County TR (AD)], W of Mont Clare off PA 724 on Mowere Rd., East Pikeland Township, Mont Clare vicinity, 6/18/73, C, 73001608

Reading Furnace Historic District, Mansion Rd., Warwick vicinity, 7/30/87, C, 87000797

Rice—Pennebecker Farm, Clover Mill Rd., Chester Springs, 8/21/86, A, C, 86001765

River Bend Farm, N of Spring City on Sanatoga Rd., Spring City vicinity, 8/29/80, A, C, 80003468

Rogers, Philip, House, Ridge Rd., Warwick Township, 5/25/73, C, 73001617

Rooke, Robert, House, N of Downingtown on Horseshoe Trail at Fellowship Rd., West Vincent Township, Downingtown vicinity, 9/19/73, C, 73001602

Ross, Moses, House [West Branch Brandywine Creek MRA], Londonderry Twp., Doe Run Valley, 9/16/85, C, 85002375

Rothrock, Joseph, House, Address Restricted, West Chester vicinity, 9/06/84, B, 84003211

Roughwood, 107 Old Lancaster Rd., Devon, 11/23/84, A, C, 84000318

Rudolph and Arthur Covered Bridge [Covered Bridges of Chester County TR], N of Lewisville on T 307, New London/Elk Townships, West Grove vicinity, 12/10/80, A, C, 80003473

Rush, Benjamin, House [West Whiteland Township MRA], Boot Rd., Kirkland, 8/02/84, C, 84003300

Sandy Hill Tavern, SE of Honey Brook on PA 340, West Caln Township, Honey Brook vicinity, 12/10/80, A, C, 80003461

Schuylkill Navigation Canal, Oakes Reach Section, N and E bank of Schuylkill River from PA 113 to Lock 61, Phoenixville vicinity, 5/06/88, A, 88000462

Scott, David, House [East Fallowfield Township MRA], Mt. Carmel Rd., East Fallowfield Township, Coatesville vicinity, 5/20/85, C, 85001153

Scott, Thomas, House [East Fallowfield Township MRA], Park Ave., East Fallowfield Township, Coatesville vicinity, 5/20/85, C, 85001154

Sharples Homestead, 22 Dean St., West Chester, 9/19/85, B, C, 85002412

Sharples Separator Works, N. Franklin and Evans Sts., West Chester, 6/28/84, A, 84003214

Ship Inn [West Whiteland Township MRA], 100 N. Ship Rd., Exton, 8/02/84, A, C, 84003301

Sleepy Hollow Hall [West Whiteland Township MRA], 109 E. Lincoln Hwy., West Whiteland, 8/02/84, A, C, 84003302

Solitude Farm [West Whiteland Township MRA], Church Farm Rd., West Whiteland, 8/02/84, C, 84003303

South Brook Farm, Jct. of Street Rd. and Bird Rd., East Marlborough Township, London Grove, 11/14/91, C, 91001710

Speakman No. 1 [Covered Bridges of Chester County TR], S of Coatesville on LR 15068, East Fallowfield Township, Modena vicinity, 12/10/80, A, C, 80003464

Speakman No. 2, Mary Ann Pyle Bridge [Covered Bridges of Chester County TR], S of Coatesville on T 371, East Fallowfield Township, Modena vicinity, 12/10/80, A, C, 80003465

Chester County—Continued

Spring Mill Complex, SW of Devault at jct. of Moores Rd. and PA 401, East Whiteland Township, Devault vicinity, 12/14/78, A, C, 78002370

Springdale Farm, NW of Mendenhall on Hillendale Rd., Mendenhall vicinity, 3/07/73, C, 73001607

Springton Manor Farm, S of Glenmoore at Springton and Creek Rds., Wallace Township, Glenmoore vicinity, 8/07/79, A, C, 79002200

Spruce Grove School [West Branch Brandywine Creek MRA], Brandywine Creek Rd., Newlin Twp., 9/16/85, A, 85002378

St. Milachi Church [West Branch Brandywine Creek MRA], St. Milachi Rd., Londonderry Twp., 9/16/85, A, a, d, 85002376

St. Paul's Church [West Whiteland Township MRA], 901 E. Lincoln Hwy., Exton, 9/06/84, C, a, 84003304

St. Peter's Church in the Great Valley, S of Phoenixville off PA 423, Phoenixville vicinity, 11/21/77, C, a, 77001155

Steen, Robert, House [East Fallowfield Township MRA], Fairview Rd., East Fallowfield Township, Coatesville vicinity, 5/20/85, A, 85001155

Stevens, Linton, Covered Bridge [Covered Bridges of Chester County TR], SW of New London on T 344, Nottingham/New London Townships, New London vicinity, 12/10/80, A, C, 80003466

Stirling, Maj. Gen. Lord, Quarters, S of Valley Forge on Yellow Springs Rd., Valley Forge vicinity, 2/15/74, B, C, NPS, 74000283

Stonorov, Oskar G., House, SW of Phoenixville on Pickering Rd., Phoenixville vicinity, 12/06/75, B, C, g, 75001631

Strafford Railroad Station, Old Eagle School Rd., Strafford, 7/26/84, A, C, 84003226

Strickland-Roberts Homestead, 3 mi. (4.8 km) S of Kimberton on St. Matthews Rd., West Vincent Township, Kimberton vicinity, 1/30/78, A, C, 78002372

Strode's Mill, Jct. of PA 100, West Chester, 5/27/71, A, C, 71000697

Strode's Mill Historic District, Jct. PA 52/100 and Birmingham Rd., West Chester vicinity, 5/05/89, A, C, 89000354

Sugartown Historic District, Sugartown, Boot, Spring, Dutton Mill, and Providence Rds., Willistown Township, Malvern vicinity, 9/07/84, A, C, 84003230

Taylor House, E of Marshallton on W. Strasburg Rd., East Bradford Township, Marshallton vicinity, 8/01/79, C, 79002202

Taylor—Cope Historic District, 890–1100 blk. of Strasburg Rd./PA 162, Marshallton vicinity, 7/16/87, A, C, 87001250

Temple-Webster-Stoner House, E of Romansville off PA 162, Romansville vicinity, 3/07/73, C, 72133612

Terracina, 76 S. 1st Ave., Coatesville, 12/13/78, A, C, 78002369

Thomas Marble Quarry Houses [West Whiteland Township MRA], Quarry Lane, West Whiteland, 8/02/84, A, C, 84003306

Thomas Mill and Miller's House [West Whiteland Township MRA], 130 W. Lincoln Hwy., West Whiteland, 9/06/84, C, 84003310

Thomas, Charles, House [West Whiteland Township MRA], 225 N. Whitford Rd., West Whiteland, 9/06/84, C, 84003305

Thompson Farm, 632 Chambers Rock Rd., London Britain Township, New London vicinity, 7/14/83, C, 83002228

Townsend House, SW of Pughtown off PA 100, Pughtown vicinity, 12/16/74, C, 74001773

Trimbleville Historic District [West Branch Brandywine Creek MRA], Northbrook, Broad Run, and Camp Linden Rds., Pocopson & West Bradford Twps., 9/16/85, A, B, C, 85002377

Unionville Village Historic District, PA 162 and PA 82, Unionville, 6/06/79, A, C, 79002205

Uwchlan Meetinghouse, N. Village Ave. (Rte. 113), Lionville, 9/20/73, A, a, 73001606

Valley Forge National Historical Park, Valley Forge State Park, Norristown vicinity, 10/15/66, A, B, NHL, NPS, 66000657

Vaughan, Rev. Joshua, House [Strasburg Road TR; East Fallowfield Township MRA], Strasburg Rd., Coatesville vicinity, 9/18/85, A, B, a, 85002395

Vincent Forge Mansion, Cook's Glen Rd. R.D., Spring City, 5/09/85, B, C, 85001003

Von Steuben, Gen. Frederick, Headquarters, PA 23, Valley Forge State Park, 11/28/72, B, NHL, NPS, 72001108

Walker, Joseph, House, 274 Anthony Wayne Dr., Tredyffrin Township, 1/06/87, A, C, 86003566

Walton, Asa, House [Strasburg Road TR; East Fallowfield Township MRA], Strasburg and Old Wilmington Rds., Coatesville, 9/18/85, A, C, 85002396

Warner Theater, 120 N. High St., West Chester, 11/20/79, A, C, g, 79002207

Warrenpoint, W of Knauertown off PA 23, Warwick Township, Knauertown vicinity, 11/11/75, A, B, C, 75001630

Warwick Furnace/Farms, S of Knauertown off PA 23 on Warwick Furnace Rd., East Nantmeal Township, Knauertown vicinity, 9/13/76, A, C, 76001627

Warwick Mills, E of Elverton off PA 23 on James Mills Rd., Warwick Township, Elverson vicinity, 12/30/74, A, C, 74001769

Waynesborough, 2049 Waynesborough Rd., Paoli, 3/07/73, B, NHL, 73001603

Wee Grimmet [West Whiteland Township MRA], 624 W. Lincoln Hwy., West Whiteland, 8/02/84, A, C, 84003312

Wentz, John, House [East Fallowfield Township MRA], PA 82, East Fallowfield Township, Coatesville vicinity, 5/20/85, C, 85001156

West Chester Boarding School for Boys, 200 E. Biddle St., West Chester, 1/04/90, A, C, 89002257

West Chester Downtown Historic District, Roughly bounded by Biddle, Matlick, Barnard and New Sts., West Chester, 7/02/85, A, C, 85001447

West Chester State College Quadrangle Historic District, Bounded by S. High and S. Church Sts., College and Rosedale Aves., West Chester, 10/08/81, A, C, g, 81000539

West Whiteland Inn [West Whiteland Township MRA], 609 W. Lincoln Hwy., Exton, 8/02/84, C, 84003313

Wetherby-Hampton-Snyder-Wilson-Erdman Log House, 251 Irish Rd., Tredyffrin, 4/02/73, C, 73001613

Wheelen House, NE of Downingtown on Fellowship Rd., Upper Uwchlan Township, Downingtown vicinity, 6/20/74, C, 74001768

White Horse Farm, 54 S. Whitehorse Rd., Phoenixville vicinity, 7/29/87, B, C, 87001206

White Horse Tavern, NW of Malvern at 480 Swedesford Rd., Malvern vicinity, 12/29/78, A, C, 78002373

White Horse Tavern [Strasburg Road TR; East Fallowfield Township MRA], Strasburg Rd., Coatesville, 9/18/85, A, B, C, 85002397

White, Hannah, Log House [West Whiteland Township MRA], 545 W. Boot Rd., West Whiteland, 8/02/84, C, 84003315

Whitford Garne [West Whiteland Township MRA], 201 W. Boot Rd., West Whiteland, 9/06/84, C, 84003317

Whitford Hall [West Whiteland Township MRA], 145 W. Lincoln Hwy., West Whiteland, 9/06/84, C, 84003319

Whitford Station House [West Whiteland Township MRA], 405 S. Whitford Rd., West Whiteland, 8/02/84, C, 84003324

Wickersham, Gideon, Farmstead, 750 Northbrook Rd., Kennett Square vicinity, 1/30/88, C, 87001992

Wilkinson House [West Branch Brandywine Creek MRA], Rt. 482, Pocopson Twp., 9/16/85, C, 85002379

Williams Deluxe Cabins [West Whiteland Township MRA], Lincoln Hwy., West Whiteland, 7/28/88, A, 88001165

Williams, John, Farm, S of Phoenixville on Union Hill Rd., Phoenixville vicinity, 12/15/78, A, C, 78002377

Wilson, Robert, House [Strasburg Road TR; East Fallowfield Township MRA], Strasburg Rd., Coatesville, 9/18/85, A, C, D, 85002398

Winings, Jacob, House and Clover Mill, SW of Phoenixville on James Mill Rd., Phoenixville vicinity, 8/17/79, C, 79002203

Wisner, Jacob, House, NW of Malvern on Yellow Springs Rd, Malvern vicinity, 8/06/79, C, 79002201

Woodland Station [West Whiteland Township MRA], 408 King Rd., West Whiteland, 9/06/84, A, C, 84003326

Woodledge [West Whiteland Township MRA], 525 W. Lincoln Hwy., West Whiteland, 7/28/88, C, 88001161

Worker's House at Lower Laurel Iron Works [West Branch Brandywine Creek MRA], Creek Rd., Newlin Twp., 9/16/85, A, 85002381

Chester County—Continued

Young, Joseph, House [West Branch Brandywine Creek MRA], Creek Rd., Newlin Twp., 9/16/85, C, 85002383

Young, Robert, House [Strasburg Road TR; East Fallowfield Township MRA], Strasburg Rd., Coatesville vicinity, 9/18/85, A, C, 85002399

Zook House [West Whiteland Township MRA (AD)], Off U.S. 30, Exton, 1/01/76, C, 76001625

Zook House (Boundary Increase) [West Whiteland Township MRA], 300 Exton Sq., Exton, 8/02/84, C, 84003333

Clarion County

Buchanan Furnace [Iron and Steel Resources in Pennsylvania MPS], Off PA 378 at Clarion R., Licking Township, Callensburg vicinity, 9/06/91, A, 91001129

Clarion County Courthouse and Jail, Main St., Clarion, 5/22/79, A, C, 79002208

Clearfield County

Bridge in Greenwood Township [Highway Bridges Owned by the Commonwealth of Pennsylvania, Department of Transportation TR], LR 17026 over W branch of Susquehanna River, Bells Landing vicinity, 6/22/88, C, 88000846

Bridge in Westover Borough [Highway Bridges Owned by the Commonwealth of Pennsylvania, Department of Transportation TR], LR 17003/TR 185 over Chest Creek, Westover, 6/22/88, C, 88000736

Clearfield Armory [Pennsylvania National Guard Armories MPS], Coal Hill Rd., Clearfield, 12/22/89, A, C, 89002072

Clearfield County Courthouse, 2nd and Market Sts., Clearfield, 4/27/79, A, C, 79002210

Commercial Hotel, Long and Brady Aves., Dubois, 11/13/85, A, 85003507

Dimeling Hotel, 2nd and Market Sts., Clearfield, 4/10/80, C, 80003474

Elliott, S. B., State Park Day Use District [Emergency Conservation Work (ECW) Architecture in Pennsylvania State Parks: 1933-1942, TR], 9 mi. N of Clearfield on PA 153, Clearfield vicinity, 2/11/87, A, C, g, 87000023

Elliott, S. B., State Park Family Cabin District [Emergency Conservation Work (ECW) Architecture in Pennsylvania State Parks: 1933-1942, TR], 9 mi. N of Clearfield on PA 153, Clearfield vicinity, 2/11/87, A, C, g, 87000024

Hogback Bridge [Highway Bridges Owned by the Commonwealth of Pennsylvania, Department of Transportation TR], LR 869 over W branch of Susquehanna River, Curwensville vicinity, 6/22/88, C, 88000848

Irvin-Patchin House, Main St., Burnside, 6/19/79, B, C, 79002209

McGees Mills Covered Bridge, W of Mahaffey, Mahaffey vicinity, 4/17/80, A, 80003475

Murray, Thomas, House, 120 S. 2nd St, Clearfield, 10/25/79, C, 79002211

Old Town Historic District, Irregular pattern along Front St., Clearfield, 5/15/79, C, 79002212

Parker Dam State Park Family Cabin District [Emergency Conservation Work (ECW) Architecture in Pennsylvania State Parks: 1933-1942, TR], 5 mi. S of Penfield off PA 153, Penfield vicinity, 2/11/87, A, C, 87000043

Parker Dam State Park—Octagonal Lodge [Emergency Conservation Work (ECW) Architecture in Pennsylvania State Parks: 1933-1942, TR], 5 mi. S of Penfield off PA 153, Penfield vicinity, 5/11/87, A, C, 87000044

Parker Dam State Park—Parker Dam District [Emergency Conservation Work (ECW) Architecture in Pennsylvania State Parks: 1933-1942, TR], 5 mi. S of Penfield off PA 153, Penfield vicinity, 2/11/87, A, C, g, 87000049

St. Severin's Old Log Church, W of Cooper Settlement off PA 53, Cooper Settlement vicinity, 6/05/75, A, C, a, 75001633

Clinton County

Farrandsville Iron Furnace [Iron and Steel Resources in Pennsylvania MPS], Jct. of Graham and Old Carrier Rds., Colebrook Township, Farrandsville, 9/06/91, A, C, 91001137

Harvey, Nathan, House, 425-427 S. Water St., Mill Hall, 1/03/85, B, 85000034

Heisey House, 362 E. Water St., Lock Haven, 3/16/72, C, 72001113

Logan Mills Covered Bridge, SW of Loganton over Fishing Creek, Loganton vicinity, 8/06/79, A, C, 79002213

Logan Mills Gristmill, Off PA 880, Logan Mills, 8/11/80, A, 80003476

Memorial Park Site, Address Restricted, Lock Haven, 4/14/82, D, 82003783

Packer, Isaac A., Farm, Farrandsville Rd. along W. Branch of the Susquehanna R., Woodward Township, Lock Haven vicinity, 2/21/91, C, 91000092

Ravensburg State Park [Emergency Conservation Work (ECW) Architecture in Pennsylvania State Parks: 1933-1942, TR], 8 mi. SE of Jersey Shore on PA 880, Loganton vicinity, 5/18/87, A, C, 87000741

Rich-McCormick Woolen Factory, Little Plum Run Rd., Woolrich vicinity, 9/05/85, A, 85001959

Water Street District, Roughly bounded by the Susquehanna River, St. Mary's Alley, Locust Ave., and 6th St., Lock Haven, 7/10/73, A, C, 73001618

Columbia County

Berwick Armory [Pennsylvania National Guard Armories MPS], 201 Pine St., Berwick, 11/14/91, A, C, 91001692

Bloomsburg Historic District, Roughly bounded by Penn, 5th, West, Willow, Millville and Light Sts., Bloomsburg, 9/08/83, A, C, 83002229

Bridge in Fishing Creek Township [Highway Bridges Owned by the Commonwealth of Pennsylvania, Department of Transportation TR], LR 19078 over Little Pine Creek, Bendertown vicinity, 6/22/88, C, 88000738

Catawissa Friends Meetinghouse, South and 3rd Sts., Catawissa, 6/09/78, A, C, a, 78002379

Creasyville Covered Bridge [Covered Bridges of Columbia and Montour Counties TR], SR 683, Millville vicinity, 11/29/79, A, C, 79003198

Davis Covered Bridge [Covered Bridges of Columbia and Montour Counties TR], SR 371, Catawissa vicinity, 11/29/79, A, C, 79003191

Eckman, Sam, Covered Bridge No. 92 [Covered Bridges of Columbia and Montour Counties TR], SR 548, Millville vicinity, 11/29/79, A, C, 79003183

Fowlersville Covered Bridge [Covered Bridges of Columbia and Montour Counties TR], SR 19039, Fowlersville vicinity, 11/29/79, A, C, 79003182

Furnace Covered Bridge No. 11 [Covered Bridges of Columbia and Montour Counties TR], SR 373, Esther vicinity, 11/29/79, A, C, 79003190

Hollingshead Covered Bridge No. 40 [Covered Bridges of Columbia and Montour Counties TR], SR 405, Catawissa vicinity, 11/29/79, A, C, 79003187

Jackson Mansion and Carriage House, 344 Market St., Berwick, 9/05/85, C, 85001965

Johnson Covered Bridge No. 28 [Covered Bridges of Columbia and Montour Counties TR], SR 320, Catawissa vicinity, 11/29/79, A, C, 79003185

Josiah Hess Covered Bridge No. 122 [Covered Bridges of Columbia and Montour Counties TR], SR 563, Forks vicinity, 11/29/79, A, C, 79003181

Jud Christie Covered Bridge No. 95 [Covered Bridges of Columbia and Montour Counties TR], SR 685, Millville vicinity, 11/29/79, A, C, 79003184

Kramer Covered Bridge No. 113 [Covered Bridges of Columbia and Montour Counties TR], SR 572, Rohrsburg vicinity, 11/29/79, A, C, 79003194

Parr's Mill Covered Bridge No. 10 [Covered Bridges of Columbia and Montour Counties TR], SR 371, Parr's Mill, 11/29/79, A, C, 79003189

Patterson Covered Bridge No. 112 [Covered Bridges of Columbia and Montour Counties TR], SR 575, Orangeville vicinity, 11/29/79, A, C, 79003193

Riegel Covered Bridge No. 6 [Covered Bridges of Columbia and Montour Counties TR], SR 312, Catawissa vicinity, 11/29/79, A, C, 79003196

Rohrbach Covered Bridge No. 24 [Covered Bridges of Columbia and Montour Counties TR], SR 369, Catawissa vicinity, 11/29/79, A, C, 79003197

Columbia County—Continued

Rupert Covered Bridge No. 56 [Covered Bridges of Columbia and Montour Counties TR], ST 449, Rupert, 11/29/79, A, C, 79003186

Shoemaker Covered Bridge [Covered Bridges of Columbia and Montour Counties TR], SR 19053, Iola vicinity, 11/29/79, A, C, 79003192

Snyder Covered Bridge No. 17 [Covered Bridges of Columbia and Montour Counties TR], SR 361, Slabtown vicinity, 11/29/79, A, C, 79003188

Stillwater Covered Bridge No. 134 [Covered Bridges of Columbia and Montour Counties TR], SR 629, Stillwater, 11/29/79, A, C, 79003177

Twin Bridges-East Paden Covered Bridge No. 120 [Covered Bridges of Columbia and Montour Counties TR], Off PA 478, Forks vicinity, 11/29/79, A, C, 79003180

Twin Bridges-West Paden Covered Bridge No. 121 [Covered Bridges of Columbia and Montour Counties TR], Off PA 487, Forks vicinity, 11/29/79, A, C, 79003179

Wagner Covered Bridge No. 19 [Covered Bridges of Columbia and Montour Counties TR], SR 468, Newlin vicinity, 11/29/79, A, C, 79003178

Wanich Covered Bridge No. 69 [Covered Bridges of Columbia and Montour Counties TR], Off PA 42, Fernville vicinity, 11/29/79, A, C, 79003195

Y Covered Bridge No. 156 [Covered Bridges of Columbia and Montour Counties TR], SR 757, Central vicinity, 11/29/79, A, C, 79003176

Crawford County

Baldwin-Reynolds House, Terrace St., Meadville, 12/30/74, B, C, 74001777

Bently Hall, Allegheny College campus, Meadville, 5/06/77, A, C, 77001156

Bridge in East Fallowfield Township [Highway Bridges Owned by the Commonwealth of Pennsylvania, Department of Transportation TR], LR 20012 over Unger Run, Atlantic vicinity, 6/22/88, C, 88000825

Bridge in Oil Creek Township [Highway Bridges Owned by the Commonwealth of Pennsylvania, Department of Transportation TR], LR 20132 over Oil Creek, Titusville vicinity, 6/22/88, C, 88000833

Bridge in Rockdale Township [Highway Bridges Owned by the Commonwealth of Pennsylvania, Department of Transportation TR], LR 20076 over French Creek, Millers Station vicinity, 6/22/88, C, 88000829

Bridge in West Mead Township [Highway Bridges Owned by the Commonwealth of Pennsylvania, Department of Transportation TR], LR 20027 over French Creek, Center Road Corners vicinity, 6/22/88, C, 88000827

Brown, John, Tannery Site, Address Restricted, New Richmond vicinity, 12/14/78, B, D, 78002383

Cambridge Springs Bridge [Highway Bridges Owned by the Commonwealth of Pennsylvania, Department of Transportation TR], LR 84 spur B over French Creek, Cambridge Springs, 6/22/88, C, 88000824

Independent Congregational Church, 346 Chestnut St., Meadville, 3/08/78, A, C, a, 78002381

Kelly, Amos, House, 325 S. Main St., Cambridge Springs, 7/23/80, B, C, 80003477

Meadville Downtown Historic District, Roughly bounded by Chancery Lane, Mulberry, Walnut and Chestnut Sts., Meadville, 10/02/84, A, C, 84000023

Mosier, Dr. J. R., Office, Terrace St., Meadville, 6/13/76, A, b, 77001157

Riverside Hotel, 1 Fountain St., Cambridge Springs, 12/13/78, A, C, g, 78002380

Roueche House, 762 Park Ave., Meadville, 3/04/82, C, 82003784

Ruter Hall, N. Main St. on Allegheny College campus, Meadville, 9/18/78, A, C, 78002382

Saeger, Edward, House, 375 Main St., Saegertown, 8/22/80, B, C, 80003479

Shippen, Judge Henry, House, 403 Chestnut St., Meadville, 6/06/84, B, C, 84003339

Titusville City Hall, 107 N. Franklin St., Titusville, 3/31/75, A, C, 75001635

Titusville Historic District, Roughly bounded by Petroleum, Spruce, Franklin, Perry, Monroe, Main and Spring Sts., Titusville, 1/31/85, A, 85000178

White, Dr. James, House, Jct. of U.S. 322 and PA 285, Hartstown, 7/24/80, C, 80003478

Cumberland County

Black, William, Homestead, Drexel Hill Park Rd., New Cumberland, 7/20/77, A, C, 77001159

Blythe, Benjamin, Homestead, 217 Means Hollow Rd., Shippensburg vicinity, 9/15/77, B, C, 77001160

Boiling Springs Historic District, Roughly bounded by High and First Sts., Boiling Springs Lake, and Yellow Britches Creek, Boiling Springs, 12/03/84, A, C, 84000566

Carlisle Armory [Pennsylvania National Guard Armories MPS], 504 Cavalry Rd., Carlisle, 12/22/89, A, C, 89002071

Carlisle Historic District, Roughly bounded by Penn, East, Walnut and College Sts., Carlisle, 6/15/79, A, C, g, 79002214

Carlisle Indian School, E edge of Carlisle on U.S. 11, Carlisle, 10/15/66, A, B, NHL, 66000658

Cumberland Valley Railroad Station and Station Master's House, 2 W. Strawberry Alley and 4 W. Strawberry Alley, Mechanicsburg, 11/17/78, A, 78002384

Cumberland Valley State Normal School Historic District, Roughly bounded by N. Prince St., Stewart, Old Main, Gilbert and Henderson Drs., Shippensburg, 1/11/85, A, C, 85000076

Eberly, Johannes, House, NE of Mechanicsburg on U.S. 11, Mechanicsburg vicinity, 4/02/73, C, 73001619

Etters Bridge, Green Lane Dr. and Yellow Breeches Creek, Lower Allen Township, 2/27/86, A, C, 86000308

Gilbert Bridge, Bishop Rd./Gilbert Rd. over Yellow Breeches Creek, Grantham vicinity, 5/05/89, A, C, 89000355

Given, James, Tavern, 1189 Walnut Bottom Rd., S. Middleton Township, Carlisle, 7/24/92, A, C, 92000943

Hessian Powder Magazine, Guardhouse and Garrison Lanes, Carlisle, 5/17/74, A, C, 74001778

Irving Female College, Filbert, Main, and Simpson Sts., Mechanicsburg, 5/06/83, A, 83002231

Market Street Bridge [Highway Bridges Owned by the Commonwealth of Pennsylvania, Department of Transportation TR], Market St./LR 34 over Susquehanna River, Harrisburg, 6/22/88, C, 88000759

McCullough, John, House, SE of Newville on PA 233, Newville vicinity, 12/20/78, C, 78002385

Mechanicsburg Commercial Historic District, Main St. from Arch to High St., Mechanicsburg, 4/21/83, A, C, 83002232

Old West, Dickinson College, Dickinson College campus, Carlisle, 10/15/66, C, NHL, 66000659

Orris, Adam, House, 318 W. Main St., Mechanicsburg, 12/30/87, B, C, 87002206

Peace Church, NW corner of Trindle and St. John's Rds., Camp Hill, 3/24/72, A, C, a, 72001114

Pine Grove Furnace, S of Dickinson on PA 233, Dickinson vicinity, 4/13/77, A, C, 77001158

Ramp Covered Bridge [Covered Bridges of Adams, Cumberland, and Perry Counties TR], E of Newburg on T 374, Hopewell Township, Newburg vicinity, 8/25/80, A, 80003480

Shippen House, 52 W. King St., Shippensburg, 11/25/75, A, B, C, 75001636

Shippensburg Historic District, Roughly bounded by Lutz Ave., Kenneth, Spring, and Fort Sts., Shippensburg, 6/07/84, A, C, 84003346

Simpson Street School, Simpson & High Sts., Mechanicsburg, 2/24/83, A, C, 83002233

Sterrett-Hassinger House, Three Squares Hollow Rd., Newville vicinity, 9/15/83, C, 83002234

Trimble, George, House, 50 Pleasant Grove Rd., Silver Spring Township, Mechanicsburg, 7/24/92, C, 92000945

Union Hotel, 240 Old Gettysburg Rd., Shepherdstown, 5/05/89, A, C, 89000362

Widow Piper's Tavern, SW corner of King and Queen Sts., Shippensburg, 1/17/74, C, 74001779

Williams, John, House, 0.5 mi. S of Williams Grove, Williams Grove vicinity, 7/28/77, B, C, 77001161

Wormley, John, House, 126 N. Front St., Wormleysburg, 11/21/76, B, C, 76001630

Dauphin County

Ayres, John, House, NW of Dauphin on PA 325, Dauphin vicinity, 9/07/79, A, C, 79002215

B'Nai Jacob Synagogue, Nissley & Water Sts., Middletown, 9/19/85, A, C, a, 85002413

Bridge in Lykens Township No. 2 [Highway Bridges Owned by the Commonwealth of Pennsylvania, Department of Transportation

Dauphin County—Continued

TR], LR 22033 over trib. to Pine Creek, Fearnot vicinity, 6/22/88, C, 88000768

Bridge in Lykens Township No. 1 [Highway Bridges Owned by the Commonwealth of Pennsylvania, Department of Transportation TR], LR 22001 over Pine Creek, Edman vicinity, 6/22/88, C, 88000773

Bridge in Reed Township [Highway Bridges Owned by the Commonwealth of Pennsylvania, Department of Transportation TR], LR 1/TR-147 over Powell's Creek, Inglenook vicinity, 6/22/88, A, C, 88000823

Broad Street Market, Verbeke St. between 3rd and 6th Sts., Harrisburg, 12/27/74, A, C, 74001780

Cameron, Simon, House and Bank, 28 and 30 E. Main St., Middletown, 11/21/76, B, C, 76001634

Cameron, Simon, School, 1839 Green St., Harrisburg, 4/24/86, A, C, 86000855

Camp Curtin Fire Station, 2504 N. 6th St., Harrisburg, 8/11/81, C, 81000541

Clemson Island Prehistoric District, Address Restricted, Halifax vicinity, 9/17/81, D, 81000540

Colonial Theatre, 3rd and Market Sts., Harrisburg, 11/09/82, A, C, 82001532

Dauphin County Bridge No. 27, Deibler's Dam Rd. (Mahantango Creek Rd.) across Mahantango Cr. (Mifflin and Lower Mahanoy Townships), Pillow vicinity, 8/02/93, C, 93000720

Dauphin County Courthouse, Jct. of Front and Market Sts., Harrisburg, 8/02/93, A, C, 93000723

Donaldson, William, House, 2005 N. Third St., Harrisburg, 4/26/90, C, 90000699

Fort Hunter Historic District, U.S. 22, Fort Hunter, 8/17/79, A, C, D, b, 79002216

GAR Building, 626–628 N. Second St., Lykens, 11/05/86, A, 86003453

German Evangelical Zion Lutheran Church, Capital and Herr Sts., Harrisburg, 11/12/75, C, a, 75001637

Greenawalt Building, 118-120 Market St., Harrisburg, 2/24/83, A, C, 83002235

Griffith, William R., House, 215 N. Front St., Harrisburg, 10/21/76, C, a, 76001631

Harris, John, Mansion, 219 S. Front St., Harrisburg, 9/20/73, B, C, NHL, 73001620

Harrisburg 19th Street Armory [Pennsylvania National Guard Armories MPS], 1313 S. 19th St., Harrisburg, 11/14/91, A, C, 91001696

Harrisburg Cemetery, 13th and Liberty Sts., Harrisburg, 3/07/85, C, d, 85000866

Harrisburg Central Railroad Station and Trainshed, Aberdeen St., Harrisburg, 6/11/75, A, C, NHL, 75001638

Harrisburg Historic District, Bounded roughly by Forster, 3rd, Hanna Sts. and the Susquehanna River, Harrisburg, 1/19/76, A, C, 76001632

Harrisburg Military Post [Pennsylvania National Guard Armories MPS], Jct. of 14th and Calder Sts., Harrisburg, 11/29/91, A, C, 91001755

Harrisburg Technical High School, 423 Walnut St., Harrisburg, 12/07/82, A, C, 82001533

Henderson, Dr. William, House, 31 E. Main St., Hummelstown, 5/14/79, C, 79002218

Henniger Farm Covered Bridge, NE of Elizabethville, Elizabethville vicinity, 12/18/78, A, 78002386

Hershey Community Center Building, 2 Chocolate Ave., Hershey, 10/15/80, A, B, C, g, 80003483

Hershey, Milton S., Mansion, Mansion Rd., Hershey, 2/07/78, B, C, NHL, 78002388

Highspire High School, 221 Penn St., Highspire, 4/26/90, A, C, 90000703

Keystone Building, 18-22 S. 3rd St, Harrisburg, 9/07/79, C, 79002217

Keystone Hotel, 40 E. Main St., Hummelstown, 5/09/85, A, C, 85001002

Kunkel Building, 301 Market St., Harrisburg, 11/09/82, C, 82001534

Matlack, Enoch, House, 250 E. Main St., Hummelstown, 6/22/79, C, 79002219

McAllister, Archibald, House, 5300 N. Front St., Harrisburg, 6/07/76, B, C, 76001633

Midtown Harrisburg Historic District, Roughly bounded by Susquehanna River, Forster, Verbeke, and 3rd Sts., Harrisburg, 4/21/83, A, C, 83002237

Mount Pleasant Historic District, Sylvan Terr. to 19th St., Market to Brookwood Sts., Harrisburg, 1/11/85, A, C, 85000079

Mount Pleasant Historic District (Boundary Increase), 1100–1321 Market St., 1142 Derry St., Harrisburg, 5/09/90, A, C, 90000710

Old Downtown Harrisburg Commercial Historic District, Dewberry, Chestnut, Blackberry, and S. 3rd Sts., Harrisburg, 7/14/83, A, C, 83002238

Old Downtown Harrisburg Commercial Historic District (Boundary Increase), Roughly Market St. from 3rd to 4th and 3rd St. from Walnut to Chestnut Sts., Harrisburg, 3/22/84, A, C, 84003198

Old Uptown Harrisburg Historic District, Roughly bounded by McClay, N. Third, Reily, N. Second, and Calder, Harrisburg, 1/04/90, C, 89002297

Pennsylvania State Lunatic Hospital, Cameron St., Harrisburg, 1/08/86, A, C, 86000057

Raymond, Charles and Joseph, Houses, 38 and 37 N. Union St, Middletown, 8/01/79, C, 79002221

Rockville Bridge, 0.5 mi. S of Marysville over Susquehanna River, Marysville, 8/15/75, A, C, 75001640

Romberger-Stover House, Market St., Berrysburg, 8/29/80, C, 80003481

Salem United Church of Christ, 231 Chestnut St., Harrisburg, 4/23/75, C, a, 75001639

Seel, William, Building, 319 Market St., Harrisburg, 12/03/80, A, C, 80003482

Senate Hotel, 122 Market St., Harrisburg, 12/16/82, C, 82001535

Sheffield Apartments, 2003 N. Third St., Harrisburg, 4/26/90, C, 90000698

Shoop Site (36DA20), Address Restricted, Jackson vicinity, 2/13/86, D, 86000241

Smith, Henry, Farm, 950 Swatara Creek Rd., Middletown, 12/22/88, C, 88003050

Soldiers and Sailors Memorial Bridge [Highway Bridges Owned by the Commonwealth of Pennsylvania, Department of Transportation TR], LR 140/State St. over LR 130 Spur and Paxton Creek, Harrisburg, 6/22/88, C, 88000761

St. Peter's Kierch, 31 W. High St., Middletown, 6/18/73, C, a, 73001621

State Capitol Building, 3rd and State Sts., Harrisburg, 9/14/77, A, C, 77001162

Swatara Ferry House, 400 Swatara St., Middletown, 9/27/76, C, 76001635

Todd, John, House, S. Meadow Ln., Hummelstown vicinity, 11/03/88, C, 88002371

Walnut Street Bridge, Walnut St. over Susquehanna River, Harrisburg, 6/05/72, A, C, 72001115

Zion Lutheran Church and Graveyard, Rosanna St., Hummelstown, 3/29/79, A, C, a, d, 79002220

Delaware County

1724 Chester Courthouse, Market St. below 5th St., Chester, 5/27/71, C, 71000702

Allgates, Coopertown Rd., Haverford, 5/15/79, A, B, C, 79002222

Brandywine Battlefield, Brandywine Battlefield Park, Chadds Ford, 10/15/66, A, NHL, 66000660

Bridge in Radnor Township No. 2 [Highway Bridges Owned by the Commonwealth of Pennsylvania, Department of Transportation TR], Bryn Mawr Ave. over Meadow Brook Creek, Villanova vicinity, 6/22/88, C, 88000784

Bridge in Radnor Township No. 1 [Highway Bridges Owned by the Commonwealth of Pennsylvania, Department of Transportation TR], Goshen Rd. over Darby Creek, Broomall vicinity, 6/22/88, C, 88000791

Camp-Woods, 745 Newtown Rd., Villanova, 9/01/83, C, 83002239

Chad House, PA 100, Chadds Ford, 3/11/71, D, 71000698

Chadds Ford Historic District, Jct. of U.S. 1 and PA 100, Chadds Ford, 11/23/71, A, C, 71000699

Chamberlain-Pennell House, W of Media off U.S. 1 at Valley Brook Rd., Media vicinity, 12/27/77, C, 77001165

Chanticleer, Address Restricted, St. Davids vicinity, 7/24/84, B, C, 84003350

Chester Creek Historic District, N, E, and S of Glen Mills along the W branch of Chester Creek, Thornbury, 3/24/72, A, B, C, D, 72001120

Cheyney, John, Log Tenant House and Farm, Station Rd., Cheyney, 11/21/78, A, C, 78002390

Chichester Friends Meetinghouse, 611 Meetinghouse Rd., Boothwyn, 3/14/73, A, a, 73001622

Collen Brook Farm, Off Mansion and Marvine Rds., Upper Darby Twnshp., 12/22/88, B, C, 88003048

Concord Friends Meetinghouse, Old Concord Rd., Concordville, 6/17/77, A, C, a, 77001164

Concordville Historic District, Concord Rd. and Baltimore Pike, Concordville, 4/03/73, A, C, a, 73001624

Crozer, George K., Mansion, 6th St., Upland, 8/14/73, C, 73001625

Delaware County—Continued

Crozer, John P., II, Mansion, 900, 922, 924 and 926 Main St., Upland, 7/23/80, C, 80003486

Darby Meeting, 1017 Main St., Darby, 9/13/78, C, a, 78002392

Delaware County National Bank, 1 W. Third St., Chester, 11/05/87, A, C, 87001947

Federal School, Haverford-Darby Rd., Haverford, 11/05/71, A, C, 71000704

Forge Hill, Off U.S. 1, Wawa, 3/07/73, C, 73001627

Gilpin Homestead, Harvey Rd., Chadds Ford, 5/27/71, B, C, 71000700

Glenays, 926 Coopertown Rd., Bryn Mawr, 12/27/77, A, C, 77001163

Grange, The, Grove Pl., Haverford, 1/11/76, C, 76001636

Handwrought, Concord and Station Rd., Concordville, 1/18/78, C, 78002391

High Hill Farm, 180 Thornton Rd., Concordville vicinity, 8/21/86, C, 86001784

Ivy Mills Historic District, Corner of Ivy Mills and Pole Cat Rds., Concord Township, 8/21/72, A, C, 72001117

Lansdowne Park Historic District, W. Greenwood, Owen, W. Baltimore, Windermere, & W. Stratford Aves., Lansdowne, 11/05/87, C, 87001986

Lansdowne Theatre, 29 N. Lansdowne Ave., Lansdowne, 1/06/87, C, 86003575

Lazaretto, The, Wanamaker Ave. and 2nd St., Essington, 3/16/72, A, C, 72001119

Leiper, Thomas, Estate, Avondale Rd., Wallingford, 12/29/70, C, 70000547

Lower Swedish Cabin, Creek Rd., Clifton Heights, 6/09/80, A, C, 80003484

Massey, Thomas, House, Lawrence and Springhouse Rds., Broomall, 11/16/70, A, C, 70000904

Media Armory [Pennsylvania National Guard Armories MPS], 12 E. State St., Media, 12/22/89, A, C, 89002077

Melrose, Hill Dr., Cheyney, 9/04/86, A, B, 86001780

Merion Golf Club, East and West Courses, Ardmore Ave., Ardmore, 12/21/89, A, B, C, NHL, 89002085

Morton Homestead, 100 Lincoln Ave., Prospect Park, 12/02/70, C, 70000546

Newlin Mill Complex, S. Cheyney Rd., Glen Mills, 3/09/83, A, C, 83002240

Newlin, Nicholas, House, Concord Rd., Concordville, 4/26/72, A, B, C, 72001118

Nitre Hall, Karakung Dr., Haverford, 12/18/70, A, C, 70000545

North Wayne Historic District, Roughly bounded by Eagle Rd., Woodland Ct., Radnor St., Poplar & N. Wayne Ave., Wayne, 7/25/85, C, 85001619

Ogden House, 530 Cedar Lane, Swarthmore, 11/20/79, C, 79002223

Old Main, 21st St. and Upland Ave., Upland, 6/18/73, A, C, g, 73001626

Old Main and Chemistry Building, 14th St. between Melrose Ave. and Walnut St., Chester, 5/22/78, A, C, 78002389

Old Rose Tree Tavern, N of Media at jct. of Rose Tree and Providence Rds., Media vicinity, 6/21/71, A, C, 71000705

Painter, William, Farm, 2 mi. NE of Chadds Ford on U.S. 1, Chadds Ford vicinity, 7/27/71, C, 71000701

Penn, William, Landing Site, Penn and Front Sts., Chester, 3/11/71, A, B, a, f, 71000703

Pont Reading, 2713 Haverford Rd., Ardmore, 10/26/72, A, B, C, 72001116

Printzhof, The, Taylor Ave. and 2nd St., Essington, 10/15/66, A, D, NHL, 66000661

Pusey, Caleb, House, 15 Race St., Upland, 3/11/71, C, 71000706

Pusey-Crozier Mill Historic District, Race St., Upland, 9/27/76, A, C, b, 76001638

Radnor Friends Meetinghouse, Sproul and Conestoga Rds., Ithan, 8/31/78, C, a, 78002393

Ridley Creek State Park, NW of Media between PA 3 and PA 352, Media vicinity, 10/08/76, A, C, D, d, 76001637

Risley, Dr. Samuel D., House, 430 N. Monroe St., Media, 4/26/90, C, 90000697

Saturday Club, 117 W. Wayne Ave., Wayne, 3/14/78, A, 78002395

Second Street Bridge [Highway Bridges Owned by the Commonwealth of Pennsylvania, Department of Transportation TR], PA 291/Second St. over Chester Creek, Chester, 6/22/88, C, 88000752

Seventeen-hundred-and-four House, Oakland Rd., near jct. of U.S. 202 and CR 15199, Dilworthtown vicinity, 12/24/67, C, NHL, 67000018

South Wayne Historic District, Roughly bounded by Lancaster Ave., Conestoga Rd. and Iven Ave., Radnor Township, Wayne, 4/18/91, A, C, 91000477

Square Tavern, Newtown Street Rd. and Goshen Rd., Newtown Square, 9/07/84, A, C, 84003353

St. David's Church and Graveyard, 7 mi. (11 km) N of Media, Media vicinity, 9/20/78, A, C, a, d, 78002394

Thompson Cottage, SE of Westchester on Thornton Rd., Westchester vicinity, 4/13/77, A, C, 77001166

Thunderbird Lodge, 45 Rose Valley Rd., Rose Valley, 8/18/89, B, C, 89001053

Twaddell's Mill and House, Rock Hill Rd. S of Chadds Ford, Chadds Ford vicinity, 3/07/73, C, 73001623

Twentieth Century Club of Lansdowne, 84 S. Lansdown Ave., Lansdowne, 7/23/80, A, C, 80003485

Wayne Hotel, 139 E. Lancaster Ave., Wayne, 11/05/87, C, 87001966

West, Benjamin, Birthplace, Swarthmore College campus, Swarthmore, 10/15/66, B, e, NHL, 66000662

Westlawn, 123 N. Providence Rd., Wallingford, 11/18/88, C, 88002188

Wolley Stille, Harvey Rd., Wallingford, 6/27/80, A, C, 80003487

Elk County

Bonifels, W of Ridgway off Laurel Mill Rd., Ridgway vicinity, 12/14/78, B, C, 78002396

Ridgway Armory [Pennsylvania National Guard Armories MPS], 72 N. Broad St., Ridgway, 12/22/89, A, C, 89002078

Weidenboerner, John E., House, 20 N. Michael St., St. Mary's, 7/24/92, C, 92000931

Erie County

Carman Covered Bridge [Covered Bridges of Erie County TR], SE of West Springfield on T 338, Springfield/Conneaut Townships, West Springfield vicinity, 9/17/80, A, C, 80003493

Cashier's House, 413 State St., Erie, 1/13/72, A, C, 72001121

Cashiers House and Coach House (Boundary Increase), 413 State St., 11 E. 4th St., Erie, 3/09/83, A, C, 83002241

Corry Armory [Pennsylvania National Guard Armories MPS], 205 E. Washington St., Corry, 5/09/91, A, C, 91000509

Dickson Tavern, 201 French St., Erie, 1/18/90, A, 89002256

Eagle Hotel, 32 High St., Waterford, 10/28/77, C, 77001167

Erie Armory [Pennsylvania National Guard Armories MPS], 6th and Parade Sts., Erie, 12/22/89, A, C, 89002073

Erie Federal Courthouse and Post Office, Jct. of 6th and State Sts., Erie, 1/22/93, A, C, 92000468

Erie Land Lighthouse, Dunn Blvd., Lighthouse Park, Erie, 3/30/78, A, C, 78002397

Federal Row, 146-162 E. 5th St.; 424-430 Holland St., Erie, 5/17/84, A, C, 84003355

Gudgeonville Covered Bridge [Covered Bridges of Erie County TR], Se of Girard on T 460, Girard Township, Girard vicinity, 9/17/80, A, C, 80003491

Hamot, Pierre S. V., House, 302 French St., Erie, 11/14/91, C, 91001707

Harrington Covered Bridge [Covered Bridges of Erie County TR], T 338, Conneaut Township, Albion vicinity, 9/17/80, A, C, 80003488

Hill, John, House, 230 W. 6th St., Erie, 12/17/79, C, 79002224

Koehler, Jackson, Eagle Brewery, 2131 State St., Erie, 4/13/82, A, g, 82003785

Main Library, 3 S. Perry St., Erie, 4/26/79, C, 79002225

Modern Tool Company, NE jct. of State and Fourth Sts., Erie, 3/06/87, A, 87000382

Nicholson House and Inn, 4838 W. Ridge Rd., Millcreek Township, Erie, 2/26/85, A, B, 85000606

North East Historic District, Roughly bounded by Division, N. Lake, Eagle, N. Pearl, and Gibson Sts., North East, 3/09/90, A, C, 90000414

Old Customshouse, 409 State St., Erie, 1/13/72, A, C, 72001122

Presque Isle Light [U.S. Coast Guard Lighthouses and Light Stations on the Great Lakes TR], Presque Isle Pennisula on Lake Erie, Erie, 8/04/83, A, C, 83002242

Qhandlery Corner, 1 and 3 E. Fourth St., and 401–403, and 405 State St., Erie, 2/05/87, A, 87000030

Erie County—Continued

Reed, Charles Manning, Mansion, 524 Peach St., Erie, 4/19/82, B, C, 82003786

SS NIAGARA (freighter), Erie Sand and Gravel Co., foot of Sassafrass St., Erie, 8/03/87, A, C, 87001255

Short's Hotel, 90 S. Pearl St., North East, 8/25/83, B, 83002243

Sommerheim Park Archeological District, Address Restricted, Mill Creek Township vicinity, 3/06/86, D, 86000397

Sturgeon House, 102 S. Garwood St., Fairview, 12/10/80, A, 80003490

Thayer—Thompson House, 605 W. Eighth St., Erie, 10/31/85, C, 85003443

U.S.S. NIAGARA, State St. at Lake Erie, Erie, 4/11/73, A, 73001628

Union City Historic District, Roughly bounded by Third, High, Main, and South Sts., Union City, 3/09/90, A, C, 90000417

Warner Theater, 811 State St., Erie, 4/13/82, C, 82003787

Waterford Bourough Historic District, Roughly bounded by N. Park Row, High, W. First, and Walnut Sts., Waterford, 3/09/90, A, C, 90000419

Waterford Covered Bridge [Covered Bridges of Erie County TR], E of Waterford on T 459, Waterford Township, Waterford vicinity, 9/17/80, A, C, 80003492

Watson-Curtze Mansion, 356 W. 6th St., Erie, 7/16/83, C, 83002244

West 21st Street Historic District, 125–262 W. 21st St. and 2014–2125 Sassafras St., Erie, 3/09/90, B, C, 90000418

West Park Place, Bounded by N. Park Row, Peach, 5th, and State Sts., Erie, 9/04/80, A, C, 80003489

West Sixth Street Historic District, W. 6th St. from Poplar to Peach St., Erie, 11/01/84, A, C, a, 84000353

Fayette County

Alliance Furnace [Iron and Steel Resources in Pennsylvania MPS], Off T 568 at Jacob's Cr., Perry Township, Perryopolis vicinity, 9/06/91, A, D, 91001130

Bowman's Castle, Front St., Brownsville, 3/03/75, C, 75001641

Brier Hill, On U.S. 40, Brier Hill, 7/02/73, A, C, 73001629

Brown—Moore Blacksmith Shop, 0.1 mi. W of PA 4020, Luzerne Township, Merrittstown, 5/07/92, A, D, 92000393

Brownsville Bridge [Highway Bridges Owned by the Commonwealth of Pennsylvania, Department of Transportation TR], LR 268 over Monongahela River, Brownsville, 6/22/88, C, 88000834

Brownsville Commercial Historic District, 105–128 Brownsville Ave. and 1–145 Market, 101–200 High, 2–6 Water, 100 Charles, 1 Seneca and 108 Bank Sts., Brownsville, 8/02/93, A, C, 93000716

Brownsville Northside Historic District, Roughly bounded by Front St., Broadway, Shaffner Rd. and Baltimore St., Brownsville, 8/02/93, A, C, 93000717

Carnegie Free Library, S. Pittsburgh St., Connellsville, 10/08/81, A, 81000542

Cochran, Philip G., Memorial United Methodist Church, Howell and Griscom Sts., Dawson, 6/04/84, C, a, 84003364

Colley, Peter, Tavern and Barn, On U.S. 40, Brier Hill, 7/24/73, A, C, 73001630

Conn, John P., House, 84 Ben Lomond St., Uniontown, 7/28/88, C, 88001164

Connellsville Armory [Pennsylvania National Guard Armories MPS], 108 W. Washington St., Connellsville, 11/14/91, A, C, 91001694

Cook, Col. Edward, House, E of Belle Vernon, Belle Vernon vicinity, 3/29/78, B, C, 78003090

Deffenbaugh Site (36FA57), Address Restricted, Nicholson Township vicinity, 5/14/84, D, 84003368

Dunlap's Creek Bridge, Spans Dunlap, Brownsville, 7/31/78, A, C, 78002398

Fallingwater, W of PA 381, Mill Run vicinity, 7/23/74, A, C, g, NHL, 74001781

Fort Necessity National Battlefield, 11 mi. E of Uniontown on U.S. 40, Uniontown vicinity, 10/15/66, A, B, d, f, NPS, 66000664

Francis Farm Petroglyphs Site (36FA35), Address Restricted, Jefferson Township vicinity, 5/10/84, D, 84003370

Gaddis, Thomas, Homestead, S of Uniontown off U.S. 119, Uniontown vicinity, 4/26/74, A, B, C, 74001782

Gallatin, Albert, House [Whiskey Rebellion Resources in Southwestern Pennsylvania MPS (AD)], 3 mi. N of Point Marion on PA 166, Point Marion vicinity, 10/15/66, B, NHL, NPS, 66000663

Laughlin, Hugh, House, TR 422, Brownsville vicinity, 4/30/87, C, 87000659

Layton Bridge [Highway Bridges Owned by the Commonwealth of Pennsylvania, Department of Transportation TR], LR 26191 over Youghiogheny River, Layton vicinity, 6/22/88, C, 88000840

Linden Hall at Saint James Park, RR 26051 NW of Dawson, Dawson vicinity, 10/11/89, C, 89001787

Locus 7 Site, Address Restricted, Fayette City vicinity, 3/20/80, D, 80003495

Marion Bridge [Highway Bridges Owned by the Commonwealth of Pennsylvania, Department of Transportation TR], LR 451 over Mon River, Point Marion vicinity, 6/22/88, C, 88000841

Meason, Isaac, House, U.S. 119 North, Mount Braddock vicinity, 1/25/71, B, C, NHL, 71000707

Mount Vernon Furnace [Iron and Steel Resources in Pennsylvania MPS], Entsey Rd. E of PA 982, Bullskin Township, Scottdale vicinity, 9/06/91, A, B, C, 91001127

Nutt, Adam Clarke, Mansion, 26 Nutt Ave., Uniontown, 10/25/90, C, 90001607

Penn-Craft Historic District, Roughly bounded by PA 4020, Twp. Rd. 326, and Twp. Rd. 549, Penn-Craft, 5/18/89, A, g, 89000356

Rabb, Andrew, House [Whiskey Rebellion Resources in Southwestern Pennsylvania MPS], Off PA 166 N of Masontown, German Township, Masontown vicinity, 11/12/92, B, C, 92001497

Rush House, U.S. 40 and PA 381, Farmington, 3/08/78, A, 78002399

Searight's Fulling Mill, Cemetery Rd., Perryopolis, 6/19/73, A, C, 73001631

Searights Tollhouse, National Road, W of Uniontown off U.S. 40, Uniontown vicinity, 10/15/66, A, NHL, 66000665

Springer Farm, PA 51, North Union Township, North Union, 7/23/82, A, C, 82003788

St. Peter's Church, Church St., Brownsville, 10/15/80, C, a, 80003494

US Post Office—Connellsville, 115 N. Arch St., Connellsville, 6/24/93, A, C, 92001495

Uniontown Downtown Historic District, Roughly Main St., between Court St. and Mill St., Uniontown, 5/19/89, A, C, 89000357

Wharton Furnace [Iron and Steel Resources in Pennsylvania MPS], Wharton Furnace—Hull Rd. S of US 40, Wharton Township, Hopwood vicinity, 9/06/91, A, C, 91001143

Forest County

Cook Forest State Park Indian Cabin District [Emergency Conservation Work (ECW) Architecture in Pennsylvania State Parks: 1933-1942, TR], Off PA 36 at Cooksburg, Cooksburg, 2/12/87, A, C, 87000019

Cook Forest State Park River Cabin District [Emergency Conservation Work (ECW) Architecture in Pennsylvania State Parks: 1933-1942, TR], Off PA 36 at Cooksburg, Cooksburg, 2/12/87, A, C, 87000053

Cook, Anthony Wayne, Mansion, River Dr., Cooksburg, 6/19/79, B, C, 79002226

West Hickory Bridge [Highway Bridges Owned by the Commonwealth of Pennsylvania, Department of Transportation TR], LR 598 over Allegheny River, West Hickory vicinity, 6/22/88, C, 88000835

Franklin County

Angle Farm, SE of Mercersburg, Mercersburg vicinity, 11/20/79, A, C, 79002231

Borough Hall of the Borough of Waynesboro, 57 E. Main St., Waynesboro, 12/02/80, A, C, 80003496

Bridge between Guilford and Hamilton Townships [Highway Bridges Owned by the Commonwealth of Pennsylvania, Department of Transportation TR], LR 28033 over Conococheque Creek, Social Island vicinity, 6/22/88, C, 88000776

Franklin County—Continued

Bridge in Metal Township [Highway Bridges Owned by the Commonwealth of Pennsylvania, Department of Transportation TR], LR 45 Spur E over W branch of Conococheaque Creek, Willow Hill vicinity, 6/22/88, C, 88000763

Brotherton Farm, SW of Chambersburg on Falling Spring Rd., Chambersburg vicinity, 3/30/79, A, C, 79002227

Brown, John, House, 225 E. King St., Chambersburg, 3/05/70, B, 70000548

Carrick Furnace [Iron and Steel Resources in Pennsylvania MPS], PA 75 N of Metal, Metal Township, Metal vicinity, 9/06/91, A, C, 91001133

Chambersburg Historic District, US 11 and US 30, Chambersburg, 8/26/82, A, C, 82003789

Chambersburg and Bedford Turnpike Road Company Toll House, W of St. Thomas on U.S. 30, St. Thomas vicinity, 1/03/78, A, C, 78002404

Church Hill Farm, NE of Mercersburg at 8941 Kings Lane, Mercersburg, 12/02/80, A, C, 80003498

Culbertson-Harbison Farm, S of Nyesville on Nyesville Rd., Nyesville vicinity, 6/27/80, A, C, 80003499

Donaldson, Widow, Place, 177 Bear Valley Rd., Fort Loudon vicinity, 11/05/87, C, 87001983

Findlay Farm, 6801 Findlay Rd., Lamasters vicinity, 4/21/83, C, 83002245

Finley, James, House, Building No. 505, Letterkenny Army Depot, Chambersburg vicinity, 11/19/74, B, C, 74001783

Franklin County Courthouse, 1 N. Main St., on Memorial Sq., Chambersburg, 1/18/74, C, 74001784

Franklin County Jail, NW corner of King and 2nd Sts., Chambersburg, 1/21/70, C, 70000549

Franklin Furnace Historic District [Iron and Steel Resources in Pennsylvania MPS], Roughly bounded by Circle Dr. and Cinder St., St. Thomas Township, Edenville vicinity, 9/06/91, A, C, 91001136

Gass House, E of Chambersburg off U.S. 30, Chambersburg vicinity, 4/11/77, C, 77001168

Greencastle Historic District, Roughly bounded by Washington, PA 2002, Jefferson, Mifflin, Chambers, Grant and Allison, and Baltimore N to Spring Grove, Greencastle, 12/24/92, A, C, 92001722

Hamilton, Alexander, House, 45 E. Main St., Waynesboro, 6/27/80, C, 80003501

Hays Bridge Historic District, E of Mercersburg on SR 331 and SR 328, Mercersburg vicinity, 7/31/78, A, C, 78002402

Horse Valley Bridge [Highway Bridges Owned by the Commonwealth of Pennsylvania, Department of Transportation TR], LR 28093 over Conodoguinet Creek, Upper Strasburg vicinity, 6/22/88, C, 88000775

Lane House, 14 N. Main St., Mercersburg, 1/13/72, B, C, 72001123

Mansfield, SE of Mercersburg, Mercersburg vicinity, 4/26/79, A, C, 79002232

Martin's Mill Covered Bridge, SW of Greencastle over Conococheague Creek, Greencastle vicinity, 2/15/74, A, 74001786

Masonic Temple, 74 S. 2nd St., Chambersburg, 6/18/76, C, 76001640

McClay's Twin Bridge (East) [Highway Bridges Owned by the Commonwealth of Pennsylvania, Department of Transportation TR], LR 28010 over trib. to Conodoguinet Creek, Middle Spring vicinity, 6/22/88, C, 88000777

McClay's Twin Bridge (West) [Highway Bridges Owned by the Commonwealth of Pennsylvania, Department of Transportation TR], LR 28010 over Conodoguinet Creek, Middle Spring vicinity, 6/22/88, C, 88000779

McCoy-Shoemaker Farm, SW of Upton on PA 995, Upton vicinity, 6/27/80, A, C, 80003500

Memorial Fountain and Statue, Memorial Sq., Chambersburg, 5/19/78, A, C, 78002400

Mercersburg Academy, PA 16, Mercersburg, 6/21/84, A, C, 84003374

Mercersburg Historic District, Main and Seminary Sts., Mercersburg, 12/13/78, A, C, 78002403

Mercersburg Historic District (Boundary Increase), S. Main St., between Linden Ave. and PA 75, Mercersburg, 5/17/89, C, 89000358

Millmont Farm, E of Mercersburg at jct. of PA 16 and PA 416, Mercersburg vicinity, 4/27/79, A, B, C, D, 79002233

Mitchell-Shook House, Leitersburg St., Greencastle, 9/17/80, C, 80003497

Monterey Historic District, Off PA 16, Blue Ridge Summit, 4/22/76, A, C, 76001639

Old Brown's Mill School, Off U.S. 11, Antrim Township, Kauffman vicinity, 3/07/73, A, C, 73001632

Royer-Nicodemus House and Farm, 1010 E. Main St., Waynesboro, 8/28/76, A, C, 76001641

Small House, About 4 mi. N of Fort Loudon on PA 75, Fort Loudon vicinity, 12/31/74, B, C, 74001785

Spring Grove Farm and Distillery, NW of Greencastle on Williamsport Pike, Greencastle vicinity, 8/10/79, A, C, 79002229

Springdale Mills, SE of Waynesboro off PA 16 on Amsterdam Rd., Waynesboro vicinity, 9/18/75, A, 75001642

Stover-Winger Farm, Leitersburg Rd., Greencastle vicinity, 8/24/79, A, B, 79002230

Townhouse Row, 57–85 N. Main St., Chambersburg, 12/18/78, A, C, 78002401

Waynesboro Armory [Pennsylvania National Guard Armories MPS], N. Grant St., Waynesboro, 12/22/89, A, C, 89002080

Welty's Mill Bridge, S of Waynesboro on PA 997, Waynesboro vicinity, 1/06/83, C, 83002246

White House Inn, 10111 Lincoln Way W, St. Thomas Township, 2/27/86, A, C, 86000304

Woodland, SW of St. Thomas on PA 416, St. Thomas vicinity, 9/20/73, A, C, 73001633

Work, Col. John, House, SE of Mercersburg, Mercersburg vicinity, 11/20/79, C, 79002234

Yeakle's Mill Bridge [Highway Bridges Owned by the Commonwealth of Pennsylvania, Depart-

ment of Transportation TR], LR 28042 over Little Cove Creek, Yeakle Mill, 11/14/88, C, 88002169

Zion Reformed Church, S. Main and W. Liberty Sts., Chambersburg, 12/17/79, A, C, a, 79002228

Fulton County

Burnt Cabins Gristmill Property, Allen's Valley Rd., Burnt Cabins, 11/28/80, A, C, 80003502

Cowans Gap State Park Family Cabin District [Emergency Conservation Work (ECW) Architecture in Pennsylvania State Parks: 1933-1942, TR], 18 mi. N of PA 75 and Chambersburg on Richmond Rd., Chambersburg vicinity, 2/11/87, A, C, g, 87000051

Fulton House, 112–116 Lincoln Way East, McConnellsburg, 7/20/77, A, C, 77001169

McConnell House, 114 Lincoln Way, McConnellsburg, 11/21/76, C, 76001642

McConnellsburg Historic District, Roughly, Lincoln Way from First St. to Fifth Ave. and Second St. from Spruce St. to Maple St., McConnellsburg, 8/09/93, A, C, 93000727

Greene County

Bridge in Franklin Township [Highway Bridges Owned by the Commonwealth of Pennsylvania, Department of Transportation TR], LR 268 over Ten Mile Creek, Morrisville vicinity, 6/22/88, C, 88000766

Carmichaels Covered Bridge [Covered Bridges of Washington and Greene Counties TR], E of Carmichael crossing Muddy Creek, Cumberland Township, Carmichael vicinity, 6/22/79, A, 79003815

Corbley, John, Farm, N of Garards Fort, Garards Fort vicinity, 5/03/84, B, C, 84003380

Crawford, William, House [Whiskey Rebellion Resources in Southwestern Pennsylvania MPS], Off jct. of Brown's Ferry Rd. and Stevenson's Ln., Cumberland Township, Carmichaels vicinity, 11/12/92, B, C, b, 92001496

Fisher Site (36GR21), Address Restricted, West Findley vicinity, 11/15/82, D, 82001536

Foley, Richard T., Site (36GR52), Address Restricted, Holbrook vicinity, 5/10/84, D, c, 84003385

Greene Academy, 314 N. Market St., Carmichaels, 12/12/76, A, 76001643

Greene Hills Farm, 3.5 mi. E of Waynesburg on PA 21, Waynesburg vicinity, 4/23/73, C, 73001634

Grimes Covered Bridge [Covered Bridges of Washington and Greene Counties TR], Off PA 221 crossing Ruff Creek, Washington Township, Waynesburg vicinity, 6/22/79, A, 79003820

Hanna Hall, College St., Waynesburg, 4/18/79, A, 79002235

Heasley, Charles Grant, House, 75 Sherman Ave., Bonar Addition, Franklin Township, Waynesburg, 2/21/91, C, 91000091

Greene County—Continued

Hughes House, Hatfield St., Jefferson Township, Jefferson, 12/27/72, B, C, 72001124

King Covered Bridge [Covered Bridges of Washington and Greene Counties TR], S of Kuhntown crossing Hoover Run, Wayne Township, Kuhntown vicinity, 6/22/79, A, 79003816

Lippincott Covered Bridge [Covered Bridges of Washington and Greene Counties TR], Off PA 221 crossing Ruff Creek, Washington Township, Waynesburg vicinity, 6/22/79, A, g, 79003823

Miller Hall, 51 W. College St., Waynesburg, 4/14/78, A, C, 78002405

Red, Neils, Covered Bridge [Covered Bridges of Washington and Greene Counties TR], E of Garards Fort crossing Whiteley Creek, Greene Township, Garads Fort vicinity, 6/22/79, A, 79003817

Rice's Landing Historic District, Roughly bounded by the Monongahela R., Water, Second, Bayard, Carmichael, High, Main and Ferry including Pumpkin Run Pk., Rice's Landing, 12/24/92, A, C, D, 92001723

Scott Covered Bridge [Covered Bridges of Washington and Greene Counties TR], Off PA 21 crossing Ten Mile Creek, Gray Township, Rogersville vicinity, 6/22/79, A, 79003819

Shriver Covered Bridge [Covered Bridges of Washington and Greene Counties TR], S of Rogersville crossing Harqus Creek, Gray Township, Rogersville vicinity, 6/22/79, A, 79003821

Sugar Grove Petroglyph Site (36GR5), Address Restricted, Monongahela Township vicinity, 3/20/86, D, 86000476

Waynesburg Historic District, Roughly bounded by 2nd Alley, Cherry Ave., East and Bowlby Sts., Waynesburg, 3/01/84, A, C, 84003392

White Covered Bridge [Covered Bridges of Washington and Greene Counties TR], W of Garards Fort crossing Whiteley Creek, Greene Township, Garards Fort vicinity, 6/22/79, A, 79003822

Woods, Nettie, Covered Bridge [Covered Bridges of Washington and Greene Counties TR], N of Oak Forest crossing Pursley Creek, Center Township, Oak Forest vicinity, 6/22/79, A, 79003818

Huntingdon County

Andrews, H. O., Feed Mill [Industrial Resources of Huntingdon County, 1780–1939 MPS], W. Main St., Union, 3/20/90, A, 90000399

Baker Bridge [Industrial Resources of Huntingdon County, 1780–1939 MPS], Twnshp. Rt. 370 over Great Trough Creek, 1 mi. E of Newburg, Newburg vicinity, 3/20/90, C, 90000411

Barree Forge and Furnace [Industrial Resources of Huntingdon County, 1780–1939 MPS], 2 mi. N of Alexandria along the Juniata River, Alexandria vicinity, 3/20/90, A, D, 90000405

Birmingham Bridge [Industrial Resources of Huntingdon County, 1780–1939 MPS], Over the Juniata River, N of Birmingham off PA 350, Birmingham vicinity, 3/20/90, C, 90000400

Brumbaugh Homestead, NE of Marklesburg off PA 26, Marklesburg vicinity, 3/28/79, A, C, 79002236

Colerain Forges Mansion [Industrial Resources of Huntingdon County, 1780–1939 MPS], PA 45, 0.75 mi. S of Franklinville, Franklinville vicinity, 3/20/90, A, C, 90000406

Corbin Bridge [Industrial Resources of Huntingdon County, 1780–1939 MPS], Twnshp. Rd. 428 over the Raystown Branch, 0.5 W of confluence with the Juniata River, Huntingdon vicinity, 3/20/90, C, 90000402

East Broad Top Railroad, 1 mi. W of Orbisonia on U.S. 522, Rockhill Furnace, 10/15/66, A, NHL, 66000666

Frehn Bridge [Industrial Resources of Huntingdon County, 1780–1939 MPS], Twnshp. Rt. 313, 2 mi. W of PA 475, Springfield, 3/20/90, C, 90000391

Greenwood Furnace [Industrial Resources of Huntingdon County, 1780–1939 MPS], PA 305 in Greenwood Furnace State Park, McAlevys Fort vicinity, 11/13/89, A, D, 89001819

Greenwood Lake Dam [Emergency Conservation Work (ECW) Architecture in Pennsylvania State Parks: 1933-1942, TR], 5 mi. N of Belleville off PA 305, Belleville vicinity, 5/11/87, A, C, 87000050

Harbison—Walker Refractories Company [Industrial Resources of Huntingdon County, 1780–1939 MPS], W. Shirley St., Mount Union, 3/20/90, A, 90000392

Hudson Grist Mill [Industrial Resources of Huntingdon County, 1780–1939 MPS], PA 829, Saltillo, 3/20/90, A, 90000390

Huntingdon Armory [Pennsylvania National Guard Armories MPS], Standing Stone Ave., Huntingdon, 12/22/89, A, C, 89002075

Huntingdon Borough Historic District, Roughly bounded by Moore, Second, Allegheny, and Ninth Sts., Huntingdon, 4/24/86, A, C, 86000852

Huntingdon Furnace [Industrial Resources of Huntingdon County, 1780–1939 MPS], Twnshp. Rd. 31106, 2 mi. NW of jct. with PA 45, Franklinville vicinity, 3/20/90, A, C, 90000407

Juniata Iron Works [Industrial Resources of Huntingdon County, 1780–1939 MPS], Off PA 885, 1.5 mil E of Alexandria, Alexandria vicinity, 3/20/90, A, C, 90000404

Leas, Benjamin B., House, US 522, Shirleysburg, 2/23/84, A, C, 84003401

Lloyd and Henry Warehouse [Industrial Resources of Huntingdon County, 1780–1939 MPS], S. 8th St., Huntingdon, 3/20/90, C, b, 90000397

Minersville Coke Ovens [Industrial Resources of Huntingdon County, 1780–1939 MPS], PA 913, 1 mi. E of Coalmont, Coalmont vicinity, 3/20/90, A, D, 90000401

Monroe Furnace [Industrial Resources of Huntingdon County, 1780–1939 MPS], Jct. PA 26 and Legislative Rt. 31076, 6 mi. NW of McAlevys Fort, McAlevys Fort vicinity, 11/13/89, A, D, 89001818

Mount Union Refractories Company [Industrial Resources of Huntingdon County, 1780–1939 MPS], Pennsylvania Ave. at Juniata River, Mount Union, 3/20/90, A, 90000398

Paradise Furnace [Industrial Resources of Huntingdon County, 1780–1939 MPS], 5 mi. SE of Entriken in Trough Creek State Park, Entriken vicinity, 3/20/90, A, 90000403

Pennsylvania Canal Guard Lock and Feeder Dam, Raystown Branch [Industrial Resources of Huntingdon County, 1780–1939 MPS], 2.5 mi. E of Huntingdon, S of US 22 on the Juniata River, Springfield, 3/20/90, A, C, D, 90000394

Pennsylvania Furnace Mansion [Industrial Resources of Huntingdon County, 1780–1939 MPS], Off PA 45, S of Centre County line, Pennsylvania Furnace, 3/20/90, A, C, 90000409

Pennsylvania Railroad Bridge over Shavers Creek [Industrial Resources of Huntingdon County, 1780–1939 MPS], Over Shavers Creek near confluence with Juniata River, Petersburg, 3/20/90, A, C, 90000395

Pennsylvania Railroad District [Industrial Resources of Huntingdon County, 1780–1939 MPS], Conrail mile markers 213.73 to 218.88, Spruce Creek, 3/20/90, A, C, 90000393

Pennsylvania Railroad Old Bridge over Standing Stone Creek [Industrial Resources of Huntingdon County, 1780–1939 MPS], S of Penn St. over Standing Stone Creek, Huntingdon, 3/20/90, A, C, 90000410

Pulpit Rocks, Old Huntingdon—Hollidaysburg Tpk., Huntingdon vicinity, 11/04/93, A, B, NHL, 93001614

Robertsdale Historic District [Industrial Resources of Huntingdon County MPS], Roughly bounded by USGS 1840 contour line, S. Main, Wood, Lincoln, Cliff and Cherry Sts., Wood Township, Robertsdale, 5/07/92, A, C, D, g, 92000391

Runk Bridge [Industrial Resources of Huntingdon County, 1780–1939 MPS], Over Aughwick Creek, 1 mi. S of Shirleysburg off US 522, Shirleysburg vicinity, 3/20/90, C, 90000408

Shade Gap Feed and Flour Mill [Industrial Resources of Huntingdon County, 1780–1939 MPS], US 522, 1 mi. N of Shade Gap, Shade Gap vicinity, 3/20/90, A, C, 90000396

Smalley, Lewis, Homestead, E of Allenport on PA 103, Allenport vicinity, 11/14/78, B, C, 78003088

Spruce Creek Rod and Gun Club, PA 45 W of Graysville, Franklin Township, Franklinville vicinity, 2/28/91, A, C, 91000228

St. Mary's Covered Bridge, 4.5 mi S of Orbisonia on U.S. 522, Orbisonia vicinity, 3/20/80, A, C, 80003503

Warrior Ridge Dam and Hydroelectric Plant [Industrial Resources of Huntingdon County MPS], 2 mi. S of Petersburg, along Conrail main line, Petersburg vicinity, 4/26/90, A, C, 90000701

Whipple Dam State Park Day Use District [Emergency Conservation Work (ECW) Architecture in Pennsylvania State Parks: 1933-1942, TR], 10 mi. S of State College, E of PA 26, Huntingdon, 2/12/87, A, C, g, 87000109

Huntingdon County—Continued

Woodvale Historic District [Industrial Resources of Huntingdon County MPS], Roughly bounded by Ash, High, North, Fulton and Broad Sts., Wood, Wells and Broad Top Townships, Woodvale, 7/24/92, A, C, 92000942

Indiana County

Blairsville Armory [Pennsylvania National Guard Armories MPS], 119 N. Walnut St., Blairsville, 12/22/89, A, C, 89002069

Breezedale, Indiana University of Pennsylvania campus, Indiana, 3/29/79, B, C, 79002238

Bridge in West Wheatfield Township [Highway Bridges Owned by the Commonwealth of Pennsylvania, Department of Transportation TR], LR 32008 over Richards Run, Robinson vicinity, 6/22/88, C, 88000774

Buffalo, Rochester & Pittsburgh Railway Indiana Passenger Station, 1125 Philadelphia St., Indiana, 5/10/93, A, C, 93000365

Clark, Silas M., House, 6th St. and Wayne Ave., Indiana, 6/15/78, A, C, 78002406

Diehl, George, Homestead, E of US 422 on Diehl Rd., Indiana vicinity, 4/30/87, C, 87000672

Downtown Indiana Historic District, Roughly bounded by Water, 7th and 6th Sts. and Wayne Ave., Indiana, 4/29/93, A, C, 93000366

Graff's Market, 27 N. 6th St., Indiana, 12/04/80, A, C, 80003504

Harmon's Covered Bridge [Covered Bridges of Indiana County TR], NE of Willet, Willet vicinity, 8/03/79, A, C, 79002242

Indiana Armory [Pennsylvania National Guard Armories MPS], 621 Wayne Ave., Indiana, 11/14/91, A, C, 91001698

Indiana Borough 1912 Municipal Building, 39 7th St., Indiana, 9/07/83, C, 83002247

Kintersburg Covered Bridge [Covered Bridges of Indiana County TR], S of Kintersburg, Kintersburg, 8/03/79, A, C, 79002241

McCormick, John B., House, W of Georgeville off PA 210, Georgeville vicinity, 5/03/74, B, C, 74001787

Mitchell, James, House, 57 S. 6th St., Indiana, 12/04/78, A, C, 78002407

Old Indiana County Courthouse, 601 Philadelphia St., Indiana, 10/29/74, A, C, 74001788

Old Indiana County Jail and Sheriff's Office, 6th St. and Nixon Ave., Indiana, 9/27/79, A, 79002240

Saltsburg Historic District, Roughly, W of Plum and Walnut Alleys to Kiskiminetas R., Saltsburg, 5/07/92, A, C, D, 92000386

St. Peter's Episcopal Church and Rectory, 36–38 W. Campbell St., Blairsville, 5/09/88, C, a, 88000463

Sutton, John, Hall, Indiana University of Pennsylvania campus, Indiana, 9/17/75, A, C, 75001643

Thomas Covered Bridge [Covered Bridges of Indiana County TR], N of Fulton Run, Creekside vicinity, 8/03/79, A, C, 79002237

Trusal Covered Bridge [Covered Bridges of Indiana County TR], W of Willet, Willet vicinity, 8/03/79, A, C, 79002243

Jefferson County

Brookville Historic District, Roughly bounded by RR tracks, Franklin Ave., Church and Main Sts., Brookville, 6/07/84, A, C, 84003409

Brookville Presbyterian Church and Manse, White and Main Sts., Brookville, 11/26/82, C, a, 82001538

Clear Creek State Park Day Use District [Emergency Conservation Work (ECW) Architecture in Pennsylvania State Parks: 1933-1942, TR], 4 mi. N of Sigel on PA 949, Sigel vicinity, 2/11/87, A, C, 87000018

Clear Creek State Park Family Cabin District [Emergency Conservation Work (ECW) Architecture in Pennsylvania State Parks: 1933-1942, TR], 4 mi. N of Sigel on PA 949, Sigel vicinity, 2/12/87, A, C, 87000106

Gray-Taylor House, 9 Walnut St., Brookville, 8/03/79, B, C, 79002244

Hall, Joseph E., House, 419 W. Main, Brookville, 12/13/78, C, 78002408

Jefferson Theater, 230 N. Findley St., Punxsutawney, 5/09/85, A, C, 85001001

Kurtz, T. M., House, 312 W. Mahoning St., Punxsutawney, 7/28/88, B, C, 88001158

Taylor, Phillip, House, Euclid Ave., Brookville, 7/22/82, B, C, 82003790

Juniata County

Academia Pomeroy Covered Bridge [Covered Bridges of Juniata and Synder Counties TR], NW of Spruce Hill, Spruce Hill vicinity, 8/10/79, A, 79002249

Book Site (36 Jul), Address Restricted, Beale vicinity, 1/03/86, D, 86000067

Dimmsville Covered Bridge [Covered Bridges of Juniata and Synder Counties TR], W of Dimmsville, Dimmsville vicinity, 8/10/79, A, 79002245

East Oriental Covered Bridge [Covered Bridges of Juniata and Synder Counties TR], NE of Oriental, Susquehanna/Perry Townships, Oriental vicinity, 8/10/79, A, 79002246

Lehman's, Port Royal Covered Bridge [Covered Bridges of Juniata and Synder Counties TR], SW of Port Royal, Port Royal, 8/10/79, A, 79002248

North Oriental Covered Bridge [Covered Bridges of Juniata and Synder Counties TR], NE of Oriental, Susquehanna/Perry Townships, Oriental vicinity, 8/10/79, A, 79002247

Tuscarora Academy, 8 mi. S of Mifflintown at jct. of SR 34005 and 34028, Mifflintown vicinity, 6/30/72, A, C, a, 72001125

Lackawanna County

Ad-Lin Building, 600 Linden St., Scranton, 11/05/87, C, 87001969

Albright Memorial Building, N. Washington Ave. and Vine St., Scranton, 5/22/78, A, C, 78002411

Carbondale City Hall and Courthouse, One N. Main St., Carbondale, 1/06/83, A, C, 83002248

Central Railroad of New Jersey Freight Station, 602 W. Lackawanna Ave, Scranton, 8/01/79, A, C, 79002250

Dalton House, E. Main St., Dalton, 5/22/78, A, C, 78002410

Delaware, Lackawanna and Western Railroad Station, Lackawanna and Jefferson Aves., Scranton, 12/06/77, A, C, 77001170

Delaware, Lackawanna and Western Railroad Yard—Dickson Manufacturing Co. Site, Roughly bounded by Cliff St., Lackawanna Ave., Mattes Ave., River St. & the Lackawanna R., Scranton, 11/21/90, A, NPS, 90001739

Dickson Works, 225 Vine St., Scranton, 5/14/79, A, C, 79002251

Dime Bank Building, Wyoming Ave. and Spruce St., Scranton, 7/14/78, A, C, 78002412

Finch Building, 424 Wyoming Ave., Scranton, 6/14/76, A, C, 76001644

First Church of Christ, Scientist, 520 Vine St., Scranton, 5/09/88, C, a, 88000467

Florence Apartments, 643 Adams Ave., Scranton, 1/05/84, C, 84003412

Grand Army of the Republic Building, 303 Linden St., Scranton, 5/17/84, A, C, 84003416

Harrison Avenue Bridge [Highway Bridges Owned by the Commonwealth of Pennsylvania, Department of Transportation TR], LR 5 over LR 35009 Par—Roaring Brook and RR, Scranton, 6/22/88, C, 88000767

Lackawanna Avenue Commerical Historic District, Roughly bounded by Adams, Franklin, Bogart Pl., and Spruce Sts., Scranton, 11/10/83, A, C, 83004215

Lackawanna Iron and Coal Company Furnace [Iron and Steel Resources in Pennsylvania MPS], 159 Cedar Ave., Scranton, 9/06/91, A, C, 91001126

Municipal Building and Central Fire Station, 340, N. Washington Ave. and 518 Mulberry St., Scranton, 9/11/81, A, C, 81000544

Powderly, Terence V., House, 614 N. Main St., Scranton, 10/15/66, B, NHL, 66000667

Scranton Armory [Pennsylvania National Guard Armories MPS], 900 Adams Ave., Scranton, 12/22/89, A, C, 89002081

Silkman House, 2006 N. Main Ave., Scranton, 12/18/78, C, 78002413

St. Peter's Cathedral Complex, 315 Wyoming Ave., Scranton, 7/19/76, A, C, a, 76001645

Tripp Family Homestead, 1101 N. Main Ave., Scranton, 6/19/72, B, C, 72001126

Lancaster County

Abbeville, 1140 Columbia Ave., Lancaster, 12/14/78, C, 78002414

Lancaster County—Continued

American/Consolidated Tobacco Companies [Tobacco Buildings in Lancaster City MPS], 820–830 N. Prince St., Lancaster, 9/21/90, A, C, 90001398

Andrews Bridge Historic District, Jct. of Rt. 896 and Sproul and Creek Rds., Colerain Twnshp, 12/22/88, A, C, 88003046

Ashley and Bailey Silk Mill, E. Walnut and Pine Sts., Marietta, 6/27/80, A, C, 80003533

B.F. Good & Company Leaf Tobacco Warehouse, 49-53 W. James St., Lancaster, 1/03/85, A, C, 85000035

Bachman and Forry Tobacco Warehouse, 125 Bank Alley, Columbia, 3/29/79, A, C, 79002252

Bangor Episcopal Church, NW corner of Main and Water Sts., Blue Ball vicinity, 4/30/87, C, a, 87000664

Basch & Fisher Tobacco Warehouse [Tobacco Buildings in Lancaster City MPS], 348 New Holland Ave., Lancaster, 9/21/90, A, C, 90001399

Baumgardner's Mill Covered Bridge [Covered Bridges of Lancaster County TR], SW of Willow Street on T 425, Pequea/Mantic Townships, Willow Street vicinity, 12/11/80, A, C, 80003541

Big and Little Indian Rock Petroglyphs, Address Restricted, Safe Harbor vicinity, 4/03/78, D, 78002421

Bird-in-Hand Hotel, 2695 Old Philadelphia Pike (PA 340), East Lampeter Township, Bird-in-Hand, 7/24/92, A, C, 92000950

Bitzer's Mill Covered Bridge [Covered Bridges of Lancaster County TR], SE of Ephrata on LR 36122, West Earl Township, Ephrata vicinity, 12/11/80, A, C, 80003516

Bowman, Jacob, Tobacco Warehouse [Tobacco Buildings in Lancaster City MPS], 226–230 E. Grant St., Lancaster, 9/21/90, A, C, 90001400

Bowmansville Roller Mill, Jct. of PA 625 and Von Nieda St., Bowmansville, 1/19/90, A, C, 89001821

Bridge in West Earl Township [Highway Bridges Owned by the Commonwealth of Pennsylvania, Department of Transportation TR], LR 36032 over Conestoga Creek, Brownstown, 6/22/88, C, 88000875

Brimmer, John, Tobacco Warehouse [Tobacco Buildings in Lancaster City MPS], 226 N. Prince St., Lancaster, 9/21/90, A, C, 90001390

Buchanan, James, House, 1120 Marietta Ave., Lancaster, 10/15/66, B, NHL, 66000669

Bucher Thal Historic District, Weaver Rd., Denver, 12/31/87, C, 87002207

Bucher, Joseph, House, 104 E. Front St, Marietta, 9/07/79, C, 79002260

Buck Hill Farm Covered Bridge [Covered Bridges of Lancaster County TR], S of Lititz E of PA 501, Warwick Township, Lititz vicinity, 12/10/80, A, C, 80003528

Butcher's Mill Covered Bridge [Covered Bridges of Lancaster County TR], S of Denver on T 955, East Cocalico Township, Denver vicinity, 12/11/80, A, C, 80003514

Cameron Estate, 2 mi. W of Mount Joy on Donegal Springs Rd., Mount Joy vicinity, 11/03/75, B, 75001646

Central Hotel, 102 N. Market St., Mount Joy, 6/04/73, A, C, 73001637

Central Market, William Henry Pl., Lancaster, 7/12/72, A, 72001127

Colemanville Covered Bridge [Covered Bridges of Lancaster County TR], NE of Pequea on T 408, Conestoga/Mantic Townships, Pequea vicinity, 12/11/80, A, C, 80003534

Columbia Historic District, Roughly bounded by Susquehanna River, Union, Cedar, 4th, and 5th Sts., Chestnut to 9th St., Columbia, 5/06/83, A, C, 83002249

Combination Baggage and Mail Car No. 5403 [Pennsylvania Railroad Rolling Stock TR], E of Strasburg, Strasburg vicinity, 12/17/79, A, 79002261

Conestoga Town, Address Restricted, Letort vicinity, 6/18/73, D, 73001636

Congregational Store, 120-122 E. Main St., Lititz, 1/06/83, A, C, 83002250

Connell Mansion, 249 W. Main St., Ephrata, 1/19/79, C, 79002254

Consolidation Freight Locomotive No. 1187 [Pennsylvania Railroad Rolling Stock TR], E of Strasburg, Strasburg vicinity, 12/17/79, A, 79002262

Consolidation Freight Locomotive No. 2846 [Pennsylvania Railroad Rolling Stock TR], E of Strasburg, Strasburg vicinity, 12/17/79, A, 79002263

Consolidation Freight Locomotive No. 7688 [Pennsylvania Railroad Rolling Stock TR], E of Strasburg, Strasburg vicinity, 12/17/79, A, 79002264

Cumberland Valley Car [Pennsylvania Railroad Rolling Stock TR], E of Strasburg, Strasburg vicinity, 12/17/79, A, 79002265

DDI Electric Locomotive No. 36 [Pennsylvania Railroad Rolling Stock TR], E of Strasburg, Strasburg vicinity, 12/17/79, A, 79002266

Davies, Edward, House, S side of PA 23, W of Water St., Caernarvon Township, Churchtown, 9/06/91, A, 91001122

Dohner, Michael, Farmhouse, E of Lancaster, Lancaster vicinity, 6/27/80, C, 80003523

Donegal Mills Plantation, SW on Mount Joy on Trout Run Rd., Mount Joy vicinity, 1/20/78, A, C, 78002418

Donegal Presbyterian Church Complex, Donegal Springs Rd., East Donegal Township, 7/02/85, A, a, d, f, 85001482

Douglass, John, House, Sproul Rd., S of PA 896, Kirkwood vicinity, 9/05/90, C, 90001411

Duncan Island (36LA60, 61), Address Restricted, Holtwood vicinity, 5/10/84, D, 84003428

Eby Shoe Corporation, 136 N. State St., Ephrata, 8/18/89, A, C, 89001050

Eisenlohr—Bayuk Tobacco Historic District [Tobacco Buildings in Lancaster City MPS], N. Water St., at W. Liberty St., Lancaster, 9/21/90, A, C, 90001397

Electric Locomotive No. 4859, PA 741, Strasburg vicinity, 8/19/82, A, C, g, 82003797

Ellicott, Andrew, House, 123 N. Prince St., Lancaster, 1/13/72, B, C, 72001128

Ephrata Cloister, Jct. of US 322 and 222, Ephrata, 12/24/67, A, C, a, NHL, 67000026

Erb's Covered Bridge [Covered Bridges of Lancaster County TR], N of Rothsville T 634, Ephrata/Warwick Townships, Rothsville vicinity, 12/10/80, A, C, 80003536

Farmer's Southern Market, 106 S. Queen St., Lancaster, 11/10/86, A, C, 86003090

Flat Car No. 473567 [Pennsylvania Railroad Rolling Stock TR], E of Strasburg, Strasburg vicinity, 12/17/79, A, 79002267

Follmer, Clogg and Company Umbrella Factory, 254–260 W. King St., Lancaster, 8/21/86, A, 86001775

Forry's Mill Covered Bridge [Covered Bridges of Lancaster County TR], NE of Columbia on T 362, Rapho/West Hempfield Townships, Columbia vicinity, 12/11/80, A, C, 80003512

Freight Locomotive No. 5741 [Pennsylvania Railroad Rolling Stock TR], E of Strasburg, Strasburg vicinity, 12/17/79, A, 79002268

Frey, Jacob L., Tobacco Warehouse [Tobacco Buildings in Lancaster City MPS], 210 W. Grant St., Lancaster, 9/21/90, A, C, 90001396

Frey—Haverstick Site (36LA6), Address Restricted, Washington Boro vicinity, 1/15/86, D, 86000819

Friedman, Henry B., Tobacco Warehouse [Tobacco Buildings in Lancaster City MPS], 309–311 Harrisburg Ave., rear, Lancaster, 9/21/90, A, C, 90001392

Fulton Opera House, 12–14 N. Prince St., Lancaster, 8/11/69, A, NHL, 69000156

Fulton, Robert, Birthplace, 8 mi. S of Quarryville on U.S. 222, Quarryville vicinity, 10/15/66, B, c, e, NHL, 66000670

Germania Turnverein Building, 33–35 N. Market St., Lancaster, 4/10/80, A, C, 80003524

Good, John B., House, PA 625, Bowmansville, 2/08/80, A, C, 80003507

Grove Mansion, 133 River Rd., Maytown, 4/21/83, C, 83002251

Hager Building, 25 W. King St., Lancaster, 10/16/79, A, C, 79002255

Hamilton Apartments, 247-249 N. Duke St. and 104-118 E. Walnut St., Lancaster, 6/28/84, A, C, 84003430

Hammer Creek Bridge [Highway Bridges Owned by the Commonwealth of Pennsylvania, Department of Transportation TR], LR 36011 over Hammer Creek, Brunnerville vicinity, 6/22/88, C, 88000872

Hand, Gen. Edward, House, 881 Rock Ford Rd., Lancaster, 11/21/76, B, C, 76001646

Harrisburg Avenue Tobacco Historic District [Tobacco Buildings in Lancaster City MPS], Harrisburg Ave. at N. Mulberry St., Lancaster, 9/21/90, A, C, 90001393

Herr's Mill Covered Bridge [Covered Bridges of Lancaster County TR], SW of Soundersburg on T 696, Paradise/East Lampeter Townships, Soundersbury vicinity, 12/10/80, A, C, 80003537

Herr, Hans, House, 1851 Hans Herr Dr., Lancaster vicinity, 5/03/71, A, a, 71000708

Lancaster County—Continued

Hess, A. B., Cigar Factory, and Warehouses [Tobacco Buildings in Lancaster MPS (AD)], 231 N. Shippen St., Lancaster, 8/24/82, A, C, 82003792

Hibshman Farm, Springville Rd., Ephrata, 6/27/80, A, 80003517

Kagerise Store and House, 84–86 W. Main St., Adamstown, 11/03/88, C, 88002174

Kaufman's Distillery Covered Bridge [Covered Bridges of Lancaster County TR], SW of Manheim on T 889, Rapho/Penn Townships, Manheim vicinity, 12/11/80, A, C, 80003529

Keller's Covered Bridge [Covered Bridges of Lancaster County TR], SW of Ephrata on T 656, Ephrata Township, Ephrata vicinity, 12/10/80, A, C, 80003518

Keller, Jacob, Farm, 900 Rettew Mill Rd., Ephrata vicinity, 7/17/86, C, 86001679

Kirk Johnson Building, 16-18 W. King St., Lancaster, 7/07/83, C, 83002252

Kirks Mills Historic District, W of Nottingham off PA 272, Nottingham vicinity, 7/17/78, A, C, 78002420

Krauskap, Henry, House, and Store, 301-303 1/2 W. King St., Lancaster, 10/07/82, A, C, 82001539

Kreider Shoe Manufacturing Company, 155 S. Poplar St., Elizabethtown, 6/27/80, A, C, 80003515

Lancaster Armory [Pennsylvania National Guard Armories MPS], 438 N. Queen St., Lancaster, 11/14/91, A, C, 91001699

Lancaster County Courthouse, 43 E. King St., Lancaster, 11/07/78, A, C, 78002415

Lancaster County House of Employment, 900 E. King St., Lancaster, 4/17/80, A, C, 80003525

Lancaster Crematorium, Greenwood Cemetery, 719 Highland Ave., Lancaster, 4/14/83, A, C, d, 83002253

Lancaster Historic District, Roughly bounded by Howard Ave., Queen, Church, Duke, Chestnut and Plum Sts., Lancaster, 11/15/79, A, C, a, 79002256

Lancaster Historic District (Boundary Increase), Bounded by E. Vine, S. Christian, Washington, S. Duke, and Church Sts., Lancaster, 11/10/83, C, 83004219

Lancaster Historic District (Boundary Increase II), E. King St., Lancaster, 6/21/84, A, C, 84003435

Lancaster Trust Company, 37-41 N. Market St., Lancaster, 11/03/83, A, C, 83004221

Lancaster Watch Company, 901 Columbia Ave., Lancaster, 8/24/82, A, C, 82003793

Landis Mill Covered Bridge [Covered Bridges of Lancaster County TR], NW of Lancaster on T 560, East Hempfield/Manheim Townships, Lancaster vicinity, 12/10/80, A, C, 80003526

Leaman Place Covered Bridge [Covered Bridges of Lancaster County TR], S of Intercourse on T 684, Paradise/Leacock Townships, Intercourse vicinity, 12/11/80, A, C, 80003519

Lime Valley Covered Bridge [Covered Bridges of Lancaster County TR], N of Refton on T 498,

West Lampeter/Strasburg Townships, Refton vicinity, 12/10/80, A, C, 80003535

Linden House, 606 E. Market St., Marietta, 1/06/83, A, C, 83002254

Lititz Moravian Historic District, Roughly bounded by E. Main, Willow and Locust, Marion and Orange, and S. Cedar and S. and N. Broad Sts., Lititz, 5/09/86, A, C, a, 86001030

Locust Grove, S of Bainbridge off PA 441, Bainbridge vicinity, 8/03/77, B, C, D, 77001171

Manor Street Elementary School, Tenth and Manor Sts., Columbia, 4/02/87, A, C, 87000572

Marietta Historic District, Roughly bounded by Market, Front, Biddle, and Waterford Sts., Marietta, 7/18/78, A, C, 78002417

Marietta Historic District (Boundary Increase), Bounded by Waterford Ave., Clay, Prospect, and Front Sts., Marietta, 8/17/84, A, C, 84003446

Martin, B. B., Tobacco Warehouse [Tobacco Buildings in Lancaster City MPS], 422–428 N. Water St., Lancaster, 9/21/90, A, C, 90001394

Mascot Roller Mills, Newport and Stumptown Rds., Mascot, 9/29/83, A, C, 83002255

McGovern, Edward, Tobacco Warehouse [Tobacco Buildings in Lancaster City MPS], 302–304 N. Plum St., Lancaster, 9/21/90, A, C, 90001395

Mentzer Building, 3 W. Main St., Ephrata, 3/07/85, A, C, 85000466

Mercer's Mill Covered Bridge [Covered Bridges of Lancaster County TR], NE of Christiana, Christiana vicinity, 12/11/80, A, C, 80003509

Mikado Freight Locomotive No. 520 [Pennsylvania Railroad Rolling Stock TR], E of Strasburg, Strasburg vicinity, 12/17/79, A, 79002269

Miller, David H., Tobacco Warehouse [Tobacco Buildings in Lancaster City MPS], 512 N. Market St., Lancaster, 9/21/90, A, C, 90001407

Milleysack, J. B. Cigar Factory [Tobacco Buildings in Lancaster City MPS], 820 Columbia Ave., rear, Lancaster, 9/21/90, A, C, 90001401

Mount Hope Estate [Iron and Steel Resources in Pennsylvania MPS], NW of Manheim on PA 72, Manheim vicinity, 12/01/80, A, C, 80003530

Mount Hope Estate (Boundary Increase) [Iron and Steel Resources in Pennsylvania MPS], Roughly, along Shearer's Cr. E of Mansion House Rd. and N of PA Tpk., Penn and Rapho Townships, Mount Hope, 9/06/91, A, C, D, 91001146

Mountain Springs Hotel, 320 E. Main St., Ephrata, 3/02/82, A, C, 82003791

Murry Site, Address Restricted, Washington vicinity, 12/10/80, D, 80003540

N. Shippen—Tobacco Avenue Historic District [Tobacco Buildings in Lancaster City MPS], Roughly bounded by N. Shippen St., Tobacco Ave., and E. Fulton St., Lancaster, 9/21/90, A, C, 90001402

Neff's Mill Covered Bridge [Covered Bridges of Lancaster County TR], W of Strasburg on T 559, West Lampeter/Strasburg Townships, Strasburg vicinity, 12/11/80, A, C, 80003538

New Era Building, 39-41 N. Queen St., Lancaster, 7/14/83, A, C, 83002256

Nissly—Stauffer Tobacco Warehouses, 322–24 N. Arch St. and 317–19 N. Mulberry St., Lancaster, 8/07/89, A, C, 89001051

North Charlotte Street Historic District, Roughly N. Charlotte St. from Harrisburg Pike to W. James St., Lancaster, 8/31/89, C, 89001206

North Prince Street Historic District, Roughly N. Prince St. and W. Lemon St., Lancaster, 8/18/89, A, C, 89001054

Northeast Lancaster Township Historic District, Roughly bounded by Marietta, Race, and Wheatland Aves., and Wilson Dr., Lancaster vicinity, 3/20/86, C, a, 86000464

Old City Hall, Penn Sq., Lancaster, 6/30/72, A, C, 72001129

Old Columbia—Wrightsville Bridge [Highway Bridges Owned by the Commonwealth of Pennsylvania, Department of Transportation TR], LR 128 over Susquehanna River and RR, Columbia, 6/22/88, A, C, 88000764

Old Main, Goethean Hall, and Diagnothian Hall, Franklin and Marshall College campus, Lancaster, 7/30/75, A, C, 75001645

Oregon Mill Complex, 1415 Oregon Rd., Oregon, 6/27/85, A, C, 85001389

Park Site 36La96, Address Restricted, Lancaster vicinity, 4/04/85, D, d, 85000698

Passenger Coach No. 3556 [Pennsylvania Railroad Rolling Stock TR], E of Strasburg, Strasburg vicinity, 12/17/79, A, 79002270

Passenger Day Coach No. 8177 [Pennsylvania Railroad Rolling Stock TR], E of Strasburg, Strasburg vicinity, 12/17/79, A, 79002271

Passenger Locomotive No. 1223 [Pennsylvania Railroad Rolling Stock TR], E of Strasburg, Strasburg vicinity, 12/17/79, A, 79002272

Passenger Locomotive No. 1737 [Pennsylvania Railroad Rolling Stock TR], E of Strasburg, Strasburg vicinity, 12/17/79, A, 79002273

Passenger Locomotive No. 460 [Pennsylvania Railroad Rolling Stock TR], E of Strasburg, Strasburg vicinity, 12/17/79, A, 79002274

Passenger Locomotive No. 7002 [Pennsylvania Railroad Rolling Stock TR], E of Strasburg, Strasburg vicinity, 12/17/79, A, 79002275

Passenger and Baggage Car No. 4639 [Pennsylvania Railroad Rolling Stock TR], E of Strasburg, Strasburg vicinity, 12/17/79, A, 79002276

Pine Grove Covered Bridge [Covered Bridges of Lancaster County TR], SE of Kirkwood on LR 36018, Little Britain/East Nottingham Townships, Kirkwood vicinity, 12/11/80, A, C, 80003521

Pinetown Covered Bridge [Covered Bridges of Lancaster County TR], E of Lancaster on T 620, Upper Leacock/Manheim Townships, Lancaster vicinity, 12/11/80, A, C, 80003527

Pool Forge Covered Bridge [Covered Bridges of Lancaster County TR], NW of Churchtown on T 773, Caernarvon Township, Churchtown vicinity, 12/11/80, A, C, 80003510

Poole Forge [Iron and Steel Resources of Pennsylvania MPS], 1936, 1938, 1940 and 1942 Main St., Caernarvon Township, Narvon, 4/29/93, A, C, 93000351

Lancaster County—Continued

Red Run Covered Bridge [Covered Bridges of Lancaster County TR], NW of Terre Hill W of T 816, Brecknock Township, Terre Hill vicinity, 12/11/80, A, C, 80003539

Reilly Brothers and Raub Building, 44-46 N. Queen St. and 45 N. Market St., Lancaster, 11/03/83, A, C, 83004222

Reinholds Station Trinity Chapel, 114 E. Main St., Reinholds, 9/05/90, C, a, 90001412

Risser's Mill Covered Bridge [Covered Bridges of Lancaster County TR], SW of Manheim on LR 36069, Rapho/Mount Joy Townships, Manheim vicinity, 12/10/80, A, C, 80004612

Roberts Farm Site (36LA1), Address Restricted, Conestoga vicinity, 4/03/86, D, 86000830

Schnader, R. K. & Sons, Tobacco Warehouse [Tobacco Buildings in Lancaster City MPS], 437–439 W. Grant St., Lancaster, 9/21/90, A, C, 90001404

Schnader, Walter, Tobacco Warehouse [Tobacco Buildings in Lancaster City MPS], 417–419 W. Grant St., Lancaster, 9/21/90, A, C, 90001391

Seigrist's Mill Covered Bridge [Covered Bridges of Lancaster County TR], NE of Columbia on T 360, Rapho/West Hempfield Townships, Columbia vicinity, 12/10/80, A, C, 80003513

Shearer's Covered Bridge [Covered Bridges of Lancaster County TR], High School Memorial Park, Manheim, 12/10/80, A, C, 80003532

Shenk's Mill Covered Bridge [Covered Bridges of Lancaster County TR], S of Manheim on T 372, East Hempfield/Rapho Townships, Manheim vicinity, 12/10/80, A, C, 80003531

Shenks Ferry Site (36LA2), Address Restricted, Pequea vicinity, 3/03/82, D, 82004655

Sherman, L. G., Tobacco Warehouse [Tobacco Buildings in Lancaster City MPS], 602 E. Marion St., Lancaster, 9/21/90, A, C, 90001405

Shultz-Funk Site (36LA7 and 36LA9), Address Restricted, Washington Boro vicinity, 3/03/82, D, 82003796

Slater Cigar Company [Tobacco Buildings in Lancaster City MPS], 625 and 626–628 Columbia Ave., Lancaster, 9/21/90, A, C, 90001403

Soldiers and Sailors Monument, Penn Sq., Lancaster, 4/02/73, A, C, f, 73001635

Sprenger Brewery, 125–131 E. King St., Lancaster, 11/27/79, A, C, 79002257

Spring Grove Forge Mansion, Spring Grove Rd., East Earl, 7/11/84, B, C, 84003447

Stauffer, Christian, House, Millcross Rd., Lancaster, 10/16/86, A, C, 86002889

Steel Hopper Car No. 33164 [Pennsylvania Railroad Rolling Stock TR], E of Strasburg, Strasburg vicinity, 12/17/79, A, 79002277

Steel Passenger Coach No. 1650 [Pennsylvania Railroad Rolling Stock TR], E of Strasburg, Strasburg vicinity, 12/17/79, A, 79002278

Steel Passenger Coach No. 1651 [Pennsylvania Railroad Rolling Stock TR], E of Strasburg, Strasburg vicinity, 12/17/79, A, 79002279

Steinman Hardware Store, 26–28 W. King St., Lancaster, 10/18/79, C, 79002258

Stevens High School, W. Chestnut and Charlotte Sts., Lancaster, 6/30/83, A, C, 83002257

Stiegel-Coleman House, PA 501 and U.S. 322, Brickerville, 11/13/66, A, B, NHL, 66000668

Stoever, John Casper, Log House, 200 W. Main St., New Holland, 1/06/87, C, 86003561

Strasburg Historic District, E. and W. Main, W. Miller, S. Decatur Sts., Strasburg, 3/03/83, A, C, 83002258

Strickler Site, Address Restricted, Washington vicinity, 6/18/73, D, 73001638

Sturgis, Julius, Pretzel House, 219-221 E. Main St., Lititz, 12/16/74, A, C, 74001789

Sutter, Johann Agust, House, 17-19 E. Main St., Lititz, 4/20/82, B, 82003795

Switcher No. 1670 [Pennsylvania Railroad Rolling Stock TR], E of Strasburg, Strasburg vicinity, 12/17/79, A, 79002280

Switcher No. 94 [Pennsylvania Railroad Rolling Stock TR], E of Strasburg, Strasburg vicinity, 12/17/79, A, 79002281

Teller Brothers—Reed Tobacco Historic District [Tobacco Buildings in Lancaster City MPS], N. Prince St., 200 block, E side, Lancaster, 9/21/90, A, C, 90001406

Totten House, 1049 E. King St., Lancaster vicinity, 2/03/89, C, 89000003

U.S. Post Office, 50 W. Chestnut St., Lancaster, 7/23/81, C, 81000545

Wagner's, Charlie, Cafe, 30 E. Grant St., Lancaster, 12/29/83, A, C, 83004223

Walter, Henry, House, Greenville Rd., Blainsport vicinity, 7/26/84, B, C, 84003449

Weaver's Mill Covered Bridge [Covered Bridges of Lancaster County TR], SW of Churchtown on T 773, Caernarvon Township, Churchtown vicinity, 12/11/80, A, C, 80003511

Weaver, Henry, Farmstead, S of Terre Hill off U.S. 322, Terre Hill vicinity, 12/15/78, A, C, 78002422

Werner, William, House, 66 E. Main St., Lititz, 5/10/84, A, C, 84003451

West Lawn, 407 W. Chestnut St., Lancaster, 5/03/84, B, C, 84003453

White Chimneys, 1 mi. NW of Gap on U.S. 30, Gap vicinity, 4/01/75, C, 75001644

White Rock Forge Covered Bridge [Covered Bridges of Lancaster County TR], S of Kirkwood on T 337, Little Britain/Colerain Townships, Kirkwood vicinity, 12/10/80, A, C, 80003522

Windsor Forge Mansion, Windsor Rd. S of Bootjack Rd., Churchtown vicinity, 1/04/90, A, B, C, 89002283

Witmer's Tavern, 2014 Old Philadelphia Pike, Lancaster vicinity, 12/01/78, A, 78002416

Wooden Baggage Express No. 6 [Pennsylvania Railroad Rolling Stock TR], E of Strasburg, Strasburg vicinity, 12/17/79, A, 79002282

Wooden Express Baggage No. 6076 [Pennsylvania Railroad Rolling Stock TR], E of Strasburg, Strasburg vicinity, 12/17/79, A, 79002283

Wooden Hopper Gondola No. 1818 [Pennsylvania Railroad Rolling Stock TR], E of Strasburg, Strasburg vicinity, 12/17/79, A, 79002284

Wright's Ferry Mansion, 38 S. 2nd St., Columbia, 11/20/79, B, C, 79002253

Yeates, Jasper, House, 24 26 S. Queen St., Lancaster, 9/23/82, B, C, 82003794

Zook's Mill Covered Bridge [Covered Bridges of Lancaster County TR], W of Brownstown on T 797, Warwick/West Earl Townships, Brownstown vicinity, 12/11/80, A, C, 80003508

Lawrence County

Banks Covered Bridge [Lawrence County Covered Bridges TR], SE of New Wilmington on T 476, Wilmington Township, New Wilmington vicinity, 6/27/80, A, C, 80003543

Lawrence County Courthouse, Court St., New Castle, 12/15/78, A, C, 78002419

McClelland Homestead, McClelland Rd., Bessemer vicinity, 5/17/89, C, 89000359

McConnell's Mill Covered Bridge [Lawrence County Covered Bridges TR], N of Portersville on T 415, Slippery Rock Township, Princeton vicinity, 6/27/80, A, C, 80003544

New Castle Armory [Pennsylvania National Guard Armories MPS], 820 Frank Ave., Shenango Township, New Castle vicinity, 5/09/91, A, C, 91000516

Old Homestead, NW of Enon Valley off PA 351, Enon Valley vicinity, 8/22/80, C, 80003542

Thompson, S. R., House, Market St., New Wilmington, 3/07/85, B, C, 85000467

Lebanon County

Annville Historic District, Roughly bounded by Quittapahilla Creek, Lebanon, Saylor and Marshall Sts., Annville, 4/30/79, A, C, 79002285

Biever House, 49 S. White Oak St., Annville, 2/14/78, C, 78002423

Bindnagles Evangelical Lutheran Church, N of Palmyra at jct. of SR 38003 and SR T330, Palmyra vicinity, 7/07/75, A, C, a, d, 75001651

Bomberger's Distillery, 7 mi. SW of Newmanstown off PA 501, Newmanstown vicinity, 6/26/75, A, C, NHL, 75001649

Brendle Farms, Jct. of PA 501 and 897, Schaefferstown, 7/24/72, A, C, 72001130

Chestnut Street Log House, 1110 Chestnut St., Lebanon, 11/20/78, A, C, 78002424

Cornwall & Lebanon Railroad Station, 161 N. 8th St., Lebanon, 12/04/74, A, C, 74001790

Cornwall Iron Furnace, Rexmont Rd. and Boyd St., Cornwall, 11/13/66, A, NHL, 66000671

Erpff, Philip, House, S. Market St., Schaefferstown, 11/20/79, C, 79002287

Funck, Josiah, Mansion, 450 Cumberland St., Lebanon, 1/31/80, C, 80003545

Gloninger Estate, 2511 W. Oak St., Lebanon, 12/10/80, B, C, 80003546

House of Miller at Millbach, SW of Newmanstown off Rte. 1, Newmanstown vicinity, 4/23/73, A, C, 73001640

Lebanon County—Continued

Immel, John, House, E of Myerstown on Flanagan Rd., Myerstown vicinity, 4/17/80, C, 80003548

Landis Shoe Company Building, N. Chestnut and E. Broad Sts., Palmyra, 8/29/80, A, 80003550

Meier, Isaac, Homestead, 5200 S. College St., Myerstown, 4/02/73, B, 73001639

Reading Railroad Station, N. 8th St., Lebanon, 7/17/75, A, C, 75001647

Rex House, N. Market St., Schaefferstown, 8/11/80, C, 80003551

St. Lukes Episcopal Church, 6th and Chestnut Sts., Lebanon, 9/04/74, A, C, a, 74001791

Stauffer, Dr. B., House, 192 W. Main St., Campbelltown, 6/22/79, B, C, 79002286

Tabor Reformed Church, 10th and Walnut Sts., Lebanon, 6/27/80, C, a, 80003547

Tulpehocken Manor Plantation, 2 mi. W of Myerstown on U.S. 422, Myerstown vicinity, 5/12/75, A, C, 75001648

Union Canal Tunnel, W of Lebanon off PA 72, Lebanon vicinity, 10/01/74, A, C, 74001792

Waterville Bridge [Highway Bridges Owned by the Commonwealth of Pennsylvania, Department of Transportation TR], Appalachian Trail over Swatara Creek, Swatara Gap, 11/14/88, C, b, 88002171

Zeller, Heinrich, House, W of Newmanstown off SR 419, Newmanstown vicinity, 5/12/75, C, 75001650

Lehigh County

Americus Hotel, 541 Hamilton St., Allentown, 8/23/84, B, C, 84003454

Bethlehem Armory [Pennsylvania National Guard Armories MPS], 301 Prospect St., Bethlehem, 11/14/91, A, C, 91001693

Biery's Port Historic District, Roughly bounded by Pineapple, Front, Race, and Mulberry Sts., Catasauqua, 8/09/84, A, 84003457

Bogert Covered Bridge [Covered Bridges of the Delaware River Watershed TR], S of Allentown on LR 39016, Little Lehigh Park, Allentown, 12/01/80, A, C, 80003552

Bridge in Heidelberg Township [Highway Bridges Owned by the Commonwealth of Pennsylvania, Department of Transportation TR], LR 39110 over branch of Jordan Creek, Germansville, 6/22/88, A, C, 88000765

Bridge in Lynn Township [Highway Bridges Owned by the Commonwealth of Pennsylvania, Department of Transportation TR], LR 39112 over Ontelaunee Creek, Steinsville vicinity, 6/22/88, C, 88000822

Burnside Plantation, Schoenersville Rd., 2 mi. SE of jct. with Easton Ave., Bethlehem, 5/02/90, A, C, 90000705

Catasauqua Residential Historic District, Roughly bounded by Howertown Rd., Railroad Ave., Oak and Bridge Sts., Catasauqua, 5/10/84, A, C, a, 84003465

Centennial Bridge [Highway Bridges Owned by the Commonwealth of Pennsylvania, Department of Transportation TR], Station Ave. over Saucon Creek, Center Valley, 6/22/88, C, 88000772

Cold Spring Bridge [Highway Bridges Owned by the Commonwealth of Pennsylvania, Department of Transportation TR], Second St. over Spring Creek, North Hampton vicinity, 6/22/88, C, 88000874

Coopersburg Historic District, Main St. and PA 309, Coopersburg, 4/26/82, A, B, C, a, 82003798

Coplay Cement Company Kilns, N. 2nd St., Coplay, 9/02/80, B, C, 80003556

Dent Hardware Company Factory Complex, 1101 Third St., Whitehall, 8/21/86, A, C, 86001772

Dillingersville Union School and Church, E of Zionsville on Zionsville Rd., Zionsville vicinity, 10/25/79, A, C, a, 79002290

Dime Savings and Trust Company, 12 N. 7th St., Allentown, 1/03/85, A, B, C, 85000036

Dorneyville Crossroad Settlement, S of Allentown at jct. of U.S. 222 and PA 29, Allentown vicinity, 12/07/77, A, C, 77001172

Fireman's Drinking Fountain, Main St., Slatington, 11/09/81, C, 81000551

Fountain Hill Historic District, Roughly bounded by Brighton, Wyandotte, W. Fourth and Seminole Sts., and Delaware Ave., Bethlehem, 4/21/88, A, B, C, 88000450

Frantz's Bridge [Highway Bridges Owned by the Commonwealth of Pennsylvania, Department of Transportation TR], LR 39060 over Jordan Creek, Weidasville vicinity, 6/22/88, C, 88000771

Gauff-Roth House, 427–443 Auburn St., Allentown, 9/05/85, C, 85001966

Geiger Covered Bridge [Covered Bridges of the Delaware River Watershed TR], SE of Schencksville on T 681, North Whiteland Township, Orefield vicinity, 12/01/80, A, C, 80003558

Haines Mill, Walnut St. and Main Blvd., Allentown, 9/11/81, A, 81000548

Helfrich's Springs Grist Mill, W of Fullerton on Mickley Rd., Fullerton vicinity, 10/14/77, A, C, 77001174

High German Evangelical Reformed Church, 620 Hamilton St., Allentown, 7/28/83, A, C, a, 83002259

Hotel Sterling, 343-345 Hamilton St., Allentown, 5/03/84, C, 84003469

Kemmerer House, 3 Iroquois St., Emmaus, 9/14/77, C, 77001173

Lehigh Canal, Walnutport to Allentown Section, Allentown and vicinity, 8/15/80, A, 80003553

Lehigh County Prison, 4th and Linden Sts., Allentown, 9/11/81, A, C, 81000549

Linden Grove Pavilion, Linden and S. Main Sts, Coopersburg, 11/30/79, B, C, 79002289

Lock Ridge Furnace Complex, Franklin and Church Sts., Alburtis, 9/11/81, A, 81000547

Manasses Guth Covered Bridge [Covered Bridges of the Delaware River Watershed TR], W of Greenawalds on T 602, South Whiteland Township, Orefield vicinity, 12/01/80, A, C, 80003559

Meyers, Albertus L., Bridge [Highway Bridges Owned by the Commonwealth of Pennsylvania, Department of Transportation TR], Eighth St. over Little Lehigh and Railroad Sts., Allentown, 6/22/88, C, 88000870

Mount Airy Historic District, Roughly Prospect Ave. between Fifteenth and Eighth Aves., Bethlehem, 5/09/88, B, C, 88000453

Neuweiler Brewery, 401 N. Front St., Allentown, 6/27/80, A, C, 80003554

Old Lehigh County Courthouse, 5th and Hamilton Sts., Allentown, 9/11/81, A, C, 81000550

Rex Covered Bridge [Covered Bridges of the Delaware River Watershed TR], S of Schencksville on T 593, North Whiteland Township, Orefield vicinity, 12/01/80, A, C, 80003560

Schlicher Covered Bridge [Covered Bridges of the Delaware River Watershed TR], LR 39058, North Whitehall Township, Allentown vicinity, 12/01/80, A, C, 80003555

Schlicher, George F., Hotel, 105–107 S. Main St., Alburtis, 5/07/92, A, C, 92000396

Shelter House, S. 4th St., Emmaus, 2/17/78, A, C, 78002426

Taylor, George, House, Front St., Catasauqua, 7/17/71, B, NHL, 71000709

Trout Hall, 414 Walnut St., Allentown, 11/14/78, C, 78002425

Troxell-Steckel House, 4229 Reliance St., Egypt, 6/27/80, B, C, 80003557

Weaver, Valentine, House, 146 S. Church St., Macungie, 6/28/84, B, C, 84003482

Wehr Covered Bridge [Covered Bridges of the Delaware River Watershed TR], W of Greenawald on T 597, South Whitehall Township, Orefield vicinity, 12/01/80, A, C, 80003561

Zollinger-Harned Company Building, 605–613 Hamilton Mall and 14016 N. 6th St., Allentown, 12/17/79, A, C, 79002288

Luzerne County

Ashley Planes, Off PA 309, Ashley and vicinity, 1/25/80, A, C, 80003562

Bittenbender Covered Bridge [Covered Bridges of the Delaware River Watershed TR], S of Huntington Mills off LR 40076, Huntington Township, Huntington Mills vicinity, 12/01/80, A, C, 80003563

Bridge in City of Wilkes-Barre [Highway Bridges Owned by the Commonwealth of Pennsylvania, Department of Transportation TR], LR 5 over Mill Creek, Wilkes-Barre, 6/22/88, C, 88000828

Catlin Hall, Wilkes College, 92 S. River St., Wilkes-Barre, 3/16/72, C, 72001132

Central Railroad of New Jersey Station, 31–35 S. Baltimore St., Wilkes-Barre 5/12/75, A, C, 75001652

Comerford Theater, 71 Public Sq., Wilkes-Barre, 12/03/80, C, g, 80003564

Denison House, 35 Denison St., Forty Fort, 12/02/70, C, 70000550

Luzerne County—Continued

Eckley Historic District, Both sides of Main St. through town of Eckley, Eckley, 10/26/71, A, C, 71000710

Evans, Benjamin, House, Off PA 93, Nescopeck vicinity, 8/25/83, B, C, 83002260

Forty Fort Meetinghouse, River St. and Wyoming Ave., Forty Fort, 11/03/88, A, C, a, 88002373

Guthrie, George W., School, 643 N. Washington St., Wilkes-Barre, 6/27/80, A, C, 80003565

Kingston Armory [Pennsylvania National Guard Armories MPS], 280 Market St., Wilkes-Barre, 12/21/89, A, C, 89002084

Luzerne County Courthouse, N. River St., Wilkes-Barre, 9/04/80, C, 80003566

Luzerne Presbyterial Institute, Institute St., Wyoming, 9/07/79, A, C, a, 79002293

Market Street Bridge [Highway Bridges Owned by the Commonwealth of Pennsylvania, Department of Transportation TR], Market St./LR 11 over Susquehanna River, Wilkes-Barre, 6/22/88, C, 88000873

McClintock Hall, 44 S. River St., Wilkes-Barre, 3/16/72, C, 72001133

Pardee, Israel Platt, Mansion, 235 N. Laurel St. and 28 Aspen St., Hazleton, 1/12/84, B, C, 84003487

River Street Historic District, Franklin, River, W. River, W. Jackson, W. Union, W. Market, W. Northampton, W. South and W. Ross Sts. & Barnum Pl., Wilkes-Barre, 9/10/85, A, C, a, 85002328

Stegmaier Brewery, Roughly bounded by Coal, Welles, Market, Lincoln and Baltimore Sts., Wilkes-Barre, 5/30/79, A, C, 79002292

Swetland Homestead, 855 Wyoming Ave., Wyoming, 12/13/78, B, C, 78002427

Weiss Hall, 98 S. River St., Wilkes-Barre, 11/27/72, C, 72001134

Wyoming Seminary, Sprague Ave., Kingston, 8/06/79, B, C, 79002291

Lycoming County

Archeological Site 36 LY 37, Address Restricted, Williamsport vicinity, 4/14/82, D, 82003799

Bridge in Brown Township [Highway Bridges Owned by the Commonwealth of Pennsylvania, Department of Transportation TR], LR 41022 over Pine Creek, Hillborn, 6/22/88, C, 88000844

Bridge in Lewis Township [Highway Bridges Owned by the Commonwealth of Pennsylvania, Department of Transportation TR], LR 41051 over Lycoming Creek, Bodines vicinity, 6/22/88, C, 88000845

Bridge in Plunkett's Creek Township [Highway Bridges Owned by the Commonwealth of Pennsylvania, Department of Transportation TR], LR 41053 over Plunkett's Creek, Proctor, 6/22/88, C, 88000830

Bridge in Porter Township [Highway Bridges Owned by the Commonwealth of Pennsylvania, Department of Transportation TR], LR 41017 over Pine Creek, Jersey Shore vicinity, 6/22/88, C, 88000842

Buttonwood Covered Bridge [Covered Bridges of Bradford, Sullivan and Lycoming Counties TR], SW of Liberty on T 816, Jackson Township, Liberty vicinity, 7/24/80, A, 80003569

Cogan House Covered Bridge [Covered Bridges of Bradford, Sullivan and Lycoming Counties TR], Se of White Pine on T 784, Cogan House township, Cogan House vicinity, 7/24/80, A, 80003567

English Center Suspension Bridge, Over Pine Creek, English Center, 12/14/78, A, C, 78002428

Hart Building, 26-30 W. 3rd St., Williamsport, 9/07/84, C, 84003490

Herdic, Peter, House, 407 4th St., Williamsport, 11/21/78, C, 78002429

Jersey Shore Historic District, Irregular shape roughly bounded by Lawshe Run, W. Branch Susquehanna River, S borough bundaries, and Tomb Ave., Jersey Shore, 3/31/75, C, 75001653

Lairdsville Covered Bridge [Covered Bridges of Bradford, Sullivan and Lycoming Counties TR], W of Lairdsville on T 664, Moreland Township, Hughesville vicinity, 7/24/80, A, 80003568

Millionaire's Row Historic District, Roughly bounded by Nichols Pl., Elmira and W. 3rd Sts., and 7th Ave., Williamsport, 1/24/85, A, C, 85000120

Muncy Historic District, Roughly bounded by Ridell Lane, Sherman, Washington and Mechanic Sts., Muncy, 7/03/80, A, C, 80003570

Reading-Halls Station Bridge, NW of Muncy off U.S. 220, Muncy vicinity, 1/17/80, A, C, 80003571

St. James Episcopal Church, 215 S. Main St., Muncy, 11/20/79, A, C, a, 79002294

U.S. Post Office, W. 4th St. between Government Pl. and West St., Williamsport, 3/16/72, C, 72001135

Williamsport Armory [Pennsylvania National Guard Armories MPS], 1300 Penn St., Williamsport, 11/14/91, A, C, 91001704

Williamsport City Hall, Pine St., Williamsport, 11/07/76, C, 76001648

McKean County

Anoatok, 230 Clay St., Kane, 1/07/86, B, C, 86000039

Barrett, Rufus, Stone House, 11 Boylston St., Bradford, 11/14/82, A, B, C, 82001540

Bradford Armory [Pennsylvania National Guard Armories MPS], 28 Barbour St., Bradford, 5/09/91, A, C, 91000508

Bradford Old City Hall, Kennedy and Boylston Sts., Bradford, 5/17/76, C, 76002156

Crook Farm, NE of Bradford on Seaward Ave. Extended, Bradford vicinity, 3/26/76, A, C, 76002157

Kane Armory [Pennsylvania National Guard Armories MPS], Jct. of Chestnut and Fraley Sts., Kane, 5/09/91, A, C, 91000512

Kane, Thomas L., Memorial Chapel, 30 Chestnut St., Kane, 3/29/78, B, C, a, 78003089

Kinzua Viaduct, 4.2 mi. NE of Mt. Jewett, Mount Jewett, 8/29/77, A, C, 77001511

New Thomson House, 2 Greeves St., Kane, 5/03/84, A, 84003493

Mercer County

Big Bend Historical Area, 6 mi. NW of Mercer on Shenango River, Mercer vicinity, 4/21/75, A, 75001654

Bridge in French Creek Township [Highway Bridges Owned by the Commonwealth of Pennsylvania, Department of Transportation TR], LR 43074 over French Creek, Carlton vicinity, 6/22/88, C, 88000862

Buhl, Frank H., Mansion, 422 E. State St., Sharon, 12/02/77, C, 77001175

Gibson House, 210 Liberty St., Jamestown, 12/01/78, C, 78002430

Johnston's Tavern, 6 mi. S of Mercer on U.S. 19, Mercer vicinity, 3/24/72, A, C, 72001136

Kidd's Mills Covered Bridge Historic District, 5 mi. S of Greenville off PA 58, Greenville vicinity, 12/02/74, A, 74001793

New Hamburg Historical Area, 7 mi. S of Greenville off PA 58, Greenville vicinity, 12/02/74, A, 74001794

Quaker Bridge [Highway Bridges Owned by the Commonwealth of Pennsylvania, Department of Transportation TR], LR 43135 over Little Shenango River, Greenville vicinity, 6/22/88, C, 88000863

Mifflin County

Lewistown Armory [Pennsylvania National Guard Armories MPS], 1101 Walnut St., Derry Township, Lewistown vicinity, 5/09/91, A, C, 91000513

McCoy House, 17 N. Main St., Lewistown, 3/14/73, B, 73001641

Mifflin County Courthouse, 1 W. Market St., Lewistown, 5/28/76, C, 76001649

Montgomery Ward Building, 3-7 W. Market St., Lewistown, 9/07/84, A, C, 84003497

Old Hoopes School, NE of Lewistown, Lewistown vicinity, 12/20/78, A, C, 78002431

Wollner Building, 16 W. Market St., Lewistown, 8/23/84, A, C, 84003499

Monroe County

Academy Hill Historic District, Roughly bounded by Sarah, 8th, Fulmer and 5th Sts., Stroudsburg, 1/04/90, C, 89002258

Christ Hamilton United Lutheran Church and Cemetery, Bossardsville Rd., Hamilton Square, 6/11/80, A, C, a, d, 80003573

Monroe County—Continued

Cold Spring Farm Springhouse, NE of Monroe, Monroe vicinity, 8/24/79, A, C, NPS, 79000246

East Stroudsburg Armory [Pennsylvania National Guard Armories MPS], 271 Washington St., East Stroudsburg, 5/09/91, A, C, 91000510

East Stroudsburg Railroad Station, Crystal St., East Stroudsburg, 6/27/80, A, C, 80003572

Fenner-Snyder Mill, U.S. 29, N of Sciota, Sciota vicinity, 5/13/76, A, 76001650

Henryville House, Jct. of PA 191 and 715, Henryville, 1/06/87, A, C, 86003572

Kitson Woolen Mill, 411 Main St., Stroudsburg, 1/12/84, A, 84003501

Michael, John, Farm, E of Stroudsburg, Stroudsburg vicinity, 7/08/80, A, C, NPS, 80000355

Quiet Valley Farm, SW of Stroudsburg off U.S. 209, Stroudsburg vicinity, 4/23/73, A, C, 73001642

Ross Common Manor, S of Saylorsburg on PA 115, Saylorsburg vicinity, 11/22/78, B, C, 78002432

Schoonover Mountain House, S of Bushkill, Bushkill vicinity, 8/21/79, A, C, NPS, 79000245

Shoemaker, Capt. Jacob, House, Off LR 45012, Bushkill vicinity, 7/17/79, C, NPS, 79000247

Stroud Mansion, Main and 9th Sts., Stroudsburg, 8/01/79, A, 79002297

Swiftwater Inn, PA 611, Swiftwater, 6/04/76, A, C, 76001651

Turn, John, Farm, NE of Stroudsburg, Stroudsburg vicinity, 7/23/79, A, C, NPS, 79000249

Zion Lutheran Church, Off River Rd., East Stroudsburg vicinity, 11/09/72, A, C, a, NPS, 72000094

Montgomery County

Abington Township High School, 1801 Susquehanna Rd., Abington, 8/02/85, A, C, 85001676

Antes, Henry, House, NE of Pottstown on Colonial Rd., Pottstown vicinity, 5/12/75, A, B, C, a, NHL, 75001657

Augustus Lutheran Church, 7th Ave. E and Main St., Trappe, 12/24/67, C, a, NHL, 67000019

Barley Sheaf Inn, N of Norristown at 420 W. Germantown Pk., Norristown vicinity, 12/10/80, A, 80003580

Bauern Freund Print Shop, PA 63, Marlborough, 7/26/82, B, C, 82003801

Bergy Bridge Historic District, NW of Harleysville off PA 63, Harleysville vicinity, 10/10/73, A, C, 73001644

Bridge in Franconia Township [Highway Bridges Owned by the Commonwealth of Pennsylvania, Department of Transportation TR], Allentown Rd. over Skippack Creek, Elvoy vicinity, 6/22/88, C, 88000856

Bridge in Hatfield Township [Highway Bridges Owned by the Commonwealth of Pennsylvania, Department of Transportation TR], Orvilla Rd. over W branch of Neshaminy Creek, Unionville vicinity, 6/22/88, C, 88000861

Bridge in Upper Frederick Township [Highway Bridges Owned by the Commonwealth of

Pennsylvania, Department of Transportation TR], Fagleysville Rd. over Swamp Creek, Fagleysville vicinity, 6/22/88, C, 88000864

Bridge in Upper Fredrick Township [Highway Bridges Owned by the Commonwealth of Pennsylvania, Department of Transportation TR], Gerloff Rd. over Swamp Creek, Zieglersville vicinity, 6/22/88, C, 88000838

Bridge in Upper Merion Township [Highway Bridges Owned by the Commonwealth of Pennsylvania, Department of Transportation TR], S. Gulph Rd. over Gulph Creek, Gulph Mills, 6/22/88, C, 88000832

Bryn Athyn—Lower Moreland Bridge [Highway Bridges Owned by the Commonwealth of Pennsylvania, Department of Transportation TR], Byberry Rd. over branch of Pennypack Creek, Lower Moreland vicinity, 6/22/88, C, 88000831

Bryn Mawr, 500 Harriton Rd., Bryn Mawr, 7/02/73, A, B, a, 73001643

Bryn Mawr College Historic District, Morris Ave., Yarrow St. and New Gulph Rd., Bryn Mawr, 5/04/79, A, C, g, 79002299

Bryn Mawr Hotel, Morris and Montgomery Aves., Bryn Mawr, 4/27/79, C, 79002300

Camptown Historic District, Roughly bounded by Penrose Ave., Graham Ln., Dennis St., and Cheltenham Ave., LaMott, 10/31/85, A, 85003434

Carson College for Orphan Girls, Between W. Mill and Wissahickon Rds., Springfield Township, Flourtown, 3/15/91, A, B, C, 91000227

Central Norristown Historic District, Roughly bounded by Stoney Creek, Walnut, Lafayette, and Fornace Sts., Norristown, 11/23/84, A, C, 84000321

Cold Point Historic District, I-276, Butler Pike, Militia Hill and Narcissa Rds., Norristown vicinity, 9/09/83, A, C, 83002261

Cole, Warren Z., House, Skippack Pike and Evansburg Rd., Skippack, 3/07/73, A, C, 73001653

Continental Stove Works, First St. above Main, Royersford, 1/09/86, A, 86000040

Corson, Alan W., Homestead, 5130 Butler Pike, Plymouth Meeting, 6/19/73, B, C, 73001649

County Bridge No. 54 [Highway Bridges Owned by the Commonwealth of Pennsylvania, Department of Transportation TR], Morris Rd. over branch of Wissahickon Creek, Prospectville vicinity, 6/22/88, C, 88000837

Dawesfield, 565 Lewis Ln., Whitpain Township, Ambler, 3/29/91, A, C, 91000318

Elkins Railroad Station, Philadelphia and Reading Railroad, Jct. of Spring and Park Aves., Cheltenham Township, Elkins Park, 10/25/90, A, C, 90001609

Englehardt, John, Homestead, W of Schwenksville off PA 73 on Keyser Rd., Schwenksville vicinity, 6/04/73, A, C, 73001650

Evansburg Historic District, On U.S. 422, bounded by Cross Key Rd., Grange Ave., Mill Rd., and Ridge Pike, Evansburg, 6/19/72, A, C, a, 72001139

Farmar Mill, N of Flourtown at jct. of U.S. 309 and PA 73, Fort Washington, 5/19/72, A, B, 72001140

General Wayne Inn, 625 Montgomery Ave., Merion, 1/01/76, A, 76001655

Gladwyne Historic District, PA 23, Gladwyne, 12/10/80, A, C, 80003577

Glencairn, 1001 Papermill Rd., Bryn Athyn, 8/31/78, C, g, 78002434

Graeme Park, Keith Valley Rd., Horsham vicinity, 10/15/66, C, NHL, 66000672

Grey Towers, Easton Rd. and Limekiln Pike, Glenside, 2/14/80, C, NHL, 80003578

Grubb Mansion, 1304 High St., Pottstown, 5/01/91, C, 91000505

Grubb, Conrad, Homestead, NW of Schwenksville off PA 73 on Perkiomenville Rd., Schwenksville vicinity, 6/19/73, A, C, 73001651

Gwynedd Hall, 1244 Meetinghouse Rd., Ambler vicinity, 9/24/85, C, 85002474

Harriton, 1401–1415 Old Guelph Rd., Villanova, 10/31/85, C, 85003472

High Street Historic District, 631–1329 High St., Pottstown, 1/28/92, C, 91001756

Highlands, The, W of Fort Washington at Skippack Pike and Sheaff Lane, Fort Washington vicinity, 12/12/76, B, C, 76001653

Hope Lodge, 553 Bethlehem Pike, Fort Washington, 4/26/72, A, C, 72001141

Horsham Friends Meeting, Jct. of Meeting House and Easton Rds., Horsham, 6/21/91, A, C, a, 91000723

Horsham—Montgomery Bridge [Highway Bridges Owned by the Commonwealth of Pennsylvania, Department of Transportation TR], Lower State Rd. over Little Neshaminy Creek, Fort Washington vicinity, 6/22/88, C, 88000836

Hovenden House, Barn and Abolition Hall, 1 E. Germantown Pike, Plymouth Meeting, 2/18/71, A, B, 71000713

Idlewild Farm Complex, 617 Williamson Rd., Bryn Mawr, 1/20/84, A, C, 84003505

Jenkins Homestead, 137 Jenkins Ave., Lansdale, 9/15/77, C, 77001176

Jenkins' Town Lyceum Building, Old York and Vista Rds., Jenkintown, 10/16/79, A, 79002303

Kenderdine Mill Complex, Jct. of Keith Valley and Davis Grove Rds., Horsham, 1/22/92, A, C, 91002011

Kennedy Mansion, 1050 Valley Forge Rd., Port Kennedy, 6/21/83, C, NPS, 83002262

Keswick Theatre, 291 Keswick Ave., Glenside, 6/30/83, A, C, 83002263

King of Prussia Inn, Jct. of U.S. 202 and PA 363, King of Prussia, 12/23/75, C, 75001656

Klein Meetinghouse, Maple Ave., Harleysville, 4/13/73, A, C, a, 73001645

Knapp Farm, S of Montgomeryville off PA 309, Montgomeryville vicinity, 10/22/76, A, C, 76001656

Knurr Log House, Meng Rd., Delphi, 11/05/74, A, C, 74001795

Kolb, Dielman, Homestead, S of Lederach on Kinsey Rd., Lederach vicinity, 8/17/73, C, 73001647

Kuster Mill, On Skippack Creek at Mill Rd. and Water St. Rd., Collegeville vicinity, 3/24/71, A, B, 71000711

Montgomery County—Continued

Lady Washington Inn, 2550 Huntington Pike, Huntingdon Valley, 11/26/82, A, 82001541

Landis Homestead, SW of Tylersport off PA 563 on Morwood Rd., Tylersport vicinity, 10/10/73, A, C, 73001654

Lee Tire and Rubber Company, 1100 Hector St., Conshohocken, 8/23/84, A, B, 84003512

Loller Academy, 424 S. York Rd., Hatboro, 8/24/78, A, B, 78002435

Long Meadow Farm, NW of Schwenksville on PA 73, Schwenksville vicinity, 6/19/73, A, C, 73001652

Merion Cricket Club, Montgomery Ave. and Grays Ln., Haverford, 2/27/87, A, g, NHL, 87000759

Mill Creek Historic District, E of Bryn Mawr, Bryn Mawr vicinity, 12/10/80, A, C, D, 80003575

Mill Grove, Pawling Rd., Audubon, 3/16/72, B, NHL, 72001138

Miller's House at Spring Mill, North Ln. and Hector St., Conshohocken, 1/04/90, C, 89002281

Morgan, Edward, Log House, Off PA 363 on Weikel Rd., Kulpsville vicinity, 5/17/73, A, C, 73001646

Morris, Anthony, House, N of Norristown on Stump Hall Rd., Norristown vicinity, 12/03/80, B, C, 80003581

Mount Joy, North Lane and Hector St., Conshohocken, 3/11/71, B, C, 71000712

Old Norriton Presbyterian Church, NW of Norristown on U.S. 422, Norristown vicinity, 4/03/79, A, C, a, 79002304

Old Pottstown Historic District, Roughly bounded by South, Race, Bailey, Adams, Lincoln, Beech, & Manatawny Sts., Pottstown, 9/05/85, A, C, a, 85001955

Old Pottstown Historic District (Boundary Increase), High St. between Hanover and Franklin Sts., Pottstown, 11/14/91, C, 91001715

Pennypacker Mansion, 5 Haldeman Rd., Schwenksville vicinity, 11/07/76, A, B, 76001657

Perikomen Bridge Hotel, Main St. and Rt. 29, Collegeville, 1/03/85, A, C, 85000037

Perkiomen Bridge [Highway Bridges Owned by the Commonwealth of Pennsylvania, Department of Transportation TR], Ridge Pike over Perkiomen Creek, Collegeville vicinity, 6/22/88, C, 88000826

Plymouth Friends Meetinghouse, Corner of Germantown and Butler Pikes, Plymouth Meeting, 2/18/71, A, a, 71000714

Plymouth Meeting Historic District, Plymouth Meeting and Whitemarsh Twshps., Plymouth Meeting, 2/18/71, A, C, 71000715

Poplar Lane, 1000 Boxwood Ct., King of Prussia, 5/22/78, C, 78002436

Pottsgrove Mansion, W of Pottstown on Benjamin Franklin Hwy. (High St.), Pottstown vicinity, 1/18/74, C, 74001796

Pottstown Roller Mill, South and Hanover Sts., Pottstown, 10/10/74, A, C, 74001797

Quaker Manor House, 1165 Pinetown Rd., Fort Washington, 11/21/76, B, C, 76001654

Reading Railroad Pottstown Station, High St. between Hanover and York Sts., Pottstown, 1/12/84, A, 84003514

Red Hill Historic District, 148, 152, and 200–600 Main St., 98–226 and 21–231 W. Sixth St., and 532–550 Adams St., Red Hill, 10/31/85, A, C, 85003428

Rieth, Andreas, Homestead, SE of Pennsburg on Geryville Pike, Pennsburg vicinity, 9/19/73, C, 73001648

Rowland House, 300 Ashbourne Rd, Cheltenham, 10/25/79, A, B, C, 79002301

Sinnott, Joseph, Mansion, Montgomery and Lendover Aves., Rosemont, 8/29/80, B, C, 80003582

Skippack Bridge, E of Evansburg on PA 422, Evansburg vicinity, 12/02/70, C, 70000551

Springfield Mill, On Northwestern Ave. between Germantown Ave. and Bethlehem Pike, Erdenheim, 5/13/76, A, 76001652

St. Paul's Episcopal Church, Old York and Ashbourne Rds., Elkins Park, 4/22/82, B, C, a, 82003800

Stewart, Gen. Thomas J., Memorial Armory [Pennsylvania National Guard Armories MPS], 340 Harding Blvd., Norristown, 7/12/91, A, C, 91000904

Stotesbury Club House, 7830 Eastern Ave., Wyndmoor, 3/07/85, B, C, 85000468

Strawbridge and Clothier Store, Old York Rd. N of Rydal Rd., Jenkintown, 12/22/88, A, C, 88003047

Sunrise Mill, 3 mi. W of Schwenksville on Neiffer Rd., Schwenksville vicinity, 4/11/77, A, B, 77001177

Sutch Road Bridge in Marlborough Township [Highway Bridges Owned by the Commonwealth of Pennsylvania, Department of Transportation TR], Sutch Rd. over Unami Creek, Milford vicinity, 6/22/88, C, 88000859

Swamp Creek Road Bridge [Highway Bridges Owned by the Commonwealth of Pennsylvania, Department of Transportation TR], Swamp Creek Rd. over Unami Creek, Sumneytown vicinity, 6/22/88, C, 88000860

Thomas, M. Carey, Library, Bryn Mawr College, Bounded by Morris, Yarrow, Wyndon and New Gulph Rds., Bryn Mawr College campus, Bryn Mawr, 7/17/91, A, B, NHL, 91002052

Union Library Company, 243 S. York Rd., Hatboro, 11/20/80, A, C, 80003579

Union School, 516–518 Bethlehem Pike, Fort Washington, 8/11/80, A, 80003576

Wall House, Wall Park Dr., Elkins Park vicinity, 6/28/79, A, B, a, 79002302

Washington Hose and Steam Fire Engine Company, No. 1, 15 W. Hector St., Conshohocken, 11/20/75, C, 75001655

Washington's Headquarters, Valley Creek Rd. near jct. of PA 252 and 23, Valley Forge State Park, 2/11/73, B, NHL, NPS, 73001655

Welsh, John, House, 8765 Stenton Ave., Wyndmoor, 9/05/90, B, C, 90001415

Wentz, Peter, Homestead, Schultz Rd., Worcester, 5/08/73, A, C, 73001656

West Laurel Hill Cemetery, 227 Belmont Ave., Lower Merion Township, Bala Cynwyd, 8/14/92, C, d, 92000991

West Norristown Historic District, Roughly bounded by Stoney Creek, Selma and Elm Sts., West Norristown, 11/23/84, A, C, 84000323

Whitehall Apartments, 410 W. Lancaster Ave., Haverford, 12/28/83, A, C, 83004238

Wyncote Historic District, Roughly bounded by Glenview Ave., SEPTA RR, Webster Ave., and Church Rd., Philadelphia vicinity, 10/16/86, A, C, 86002884

Yeakle and Miller Houses, 500 and 502 Bethlehem Pike and 9 Hillcrest Ave., Springfield Township, Erdenheim, 1/22/92, C, 91002009

Montour County

Beaver, Thomas, Free Library and Danville YMCA, E. Market and Ferry Sts., Danville, 1/15/87, B, C, 86003578

Danville West Market Street Historic District, Bounded by Courthouse Alley E., Front St S., Haney's Alley W. and Mahoning St. N., Danville, 5/29/85, C, 85001174

Keefer Covered Bridge No. 7 [Covered Bridges of Columbia and Montour Counties TR], SR 346, Washingtonville vicinity, 11/29/79, A, C, 79003174

Montgomery, Gen. William, House, 1 and 3 Bloom St., Danville, 8/09/79, B, 79002305

Mooresburg School, PA 642/45, Mooresburg, 12/30/87, A, 87002208

Northampton County

Bridge in Bangor Borough [Highway Bridges Owned by the Commonwealth of Pennsylvania, Department of Transportation TR], Pennsylvania St. over Martins Creek, Bangor, 6/22/88, C, 88000876

Bridge in Williams Township [Highway Bridges Owned by the Commonwealth of Pennsylvania, Department of Transportation TR], LR 48007 over Frey's Run, Stouts vicinity, 6/22/88, C, 88000855

Central Bethlehem Historic District, Bounded by Main, Nevada, and E. Broad Sts., and the river, Bethlehem, 5/05/72, A, B, C, 72001131

Central Bethlehem Historic District (Boundary Increase), Roughly bounded by Walnut St., Linden St., Lehigh River, and New St., Bethlehem, 11/07/88, A, C, a, d, 88000452

Chain Bridge, SW of Glendon on Hugh Moore Pkwy. across the Lehigh River, Easton vicinity, 2/12/74, A, C, 74001798

Coffeetown Grist Mill, 7 mi. S of Easton at Coffeetown and Kressman Rds., Easton vicinity, 11/16/77, A, C, 77001179

College Hill Residential Historic District, Roughly bounded by McCartney St., Pierce St., Pardee St., the Forks Township line and the Delaware R., Easton, 5/01/91, A, B, C, 91000506

Northampton County—Continued

County Bridge No. 36 [Highway Bridges Owned by the Commonwealth of Pennsylvania, Department of Transportation TR], TR 611 over Jacoby Creek, Portland, 6/22/88, C, 88000877

Easton Cemetery, 401 N. Seventh St., Easton, 10/25/90, C, d, 90001610

Easton Historic District, Roughly bounded by Riverside and Bushkill Drs., Ferry and 7th Sts., Easton, 5/06/83, A, C, 83002264

Easton House, 167-169 Northampton St., Easton, 12/03/80, A, B, C, 80003583

Ehrhart's Mill Historic District, Old Mill Rd., Hellertown vicinity, 4/30/87, A, C, 87000666

Elmwood Park Historic District, Roughly bounded by Goepp Circle, Woodruff St., Park Pl., andCarson St., Bethlehem, 4/21/88, C, 88000449

Gemeinhaus-Lewis David De Schweinitz Residence, W. Church St., Bethlehem, 5/15/75, A, B, C, a, c, NHL, 75001658

Gristmiller's House, 459 Old York Rd., Bethlehem, 6/18/73, A, C, 73001657

Heller, William Jacob, House, 501 Mixsell St., Easton, 4/20/82, B, C, 82003803

Jacobsburg Historic District, 3 mi. NE of Nazareth off PA 115, Nazareth vicinity, 10/17/77, A, C, D, 77001181

Kreiderville Covered Bridge [Covered Bridges of the Delaware River Watershed TR], N of Northampton on LR 48061, Kreiderville, 12/01/80, A, C, 80003587

Lehigh Canal, Lehigh Gap to S Walnutport boundary, Walnutport, 10/02/78, A, C, 78002439

Lehigh Canal: Eastern Section Glendon and Abbott Street Industrial Sites, Lehigh River from Hopeville to confluence of Lehigh and Delaware Rivers, Easton, 10/02/78, A, C, D, 78002437

Lehigh Canal; Allentown to Hopeville Section, Along Lehigh River, Bethlehem and vicinity, 12/17/79, A, C, 79002307

Lehigh Valley Railroad Headquarters Building, 425 Brighton St., Bethlehem, 5/24/84, A, C, 84003517

Lehigh Valley Silk Mills, Jct. of Seneca and Clewell Sts., Fountain Hill, 4/29/93, A, C, 93000356

Mixsell, Jacob, House, 101 S. 4th St., Easton, 2/14/80, C, 80003584

Moravian Sun Inn, 564 Main St., Bethlehem, 10/02/73, A, C, 73001658

Nazareth Hall Tract, Zizendorf Sq., Nazareth, 11/28/80, A, a, 80003588

Nazareth Historic District, Centered on Center and Main Sts., Nazareth, 8/11/88, A, C, a, 88001203

Nicholas, Jacob, House, 458 Ferry St., Easton, 11/21/76, C, D, 76001658

Old Waterworks, Within Historic Subdistrict A near Monocacy Creek, Bethlehem, 6/19/72, A, C, NHL, 72001142

Packer Memorial Chapel, Packer Avenue, Lehigh University, Bethlehem, 11/20/79, C, a, 79003234

Parsons-Taylor House, 4th and Ferry Sts., Easton, 8/22/80, B, C, 80003585

Pembroke Village Historic District, Roughly bounded by Radclyffe St., Carlisle St., Stefko Blvd., Arcadia St. and Minsi Trail, Bethlehem, 5/09/88, A, 88000464

Real Estate Building, 2–8 N. Main St., Bangor, 2/20/86, A, C, 86000319

Seipsville Hotel, 2912 Old Nazareth Rd., Easton, 5/06/77, A, C, 77001178

Simon, Herman, House, 41 N. 3rd St., Easton, 6/27/80, B, C, 80003586

State Theatre, 454 Northampton St., Easton, 3/04/82, A, C, 82003804

Steckel, Daniel, House, 207 W. Northampton St., Bath, 3/08/82, B, C, 82003802

Tannery, The, Within Bethlehem Historic Subdistrict A near Monocacy Creek, Bethlehem, 6/19/72, A, C, 72001143

Whitefield House and Gray Cottage, 214 E. Center St., Nazareth, 5/01/80, A, C, a, 80003589

Northumberland County

Allenwood River Bridge [Highway Bridges Owned by the Commonwealth of Pennsylvania, Department of Transportation TR], LR 460 over W branch of Susquehanna River, Allenwood, 6/22/88, C, 88000865

Beck House, 62 N. Front St., Sunbury, 1/11/76, C, 76001659

Brown, Gottlieb, Covered Bridge [Covered Bridges of Northumberland County TR], E of Potts Grove on T 594, East Chillisquauque-/Liberty Townships, Potts Grove vicinity, 8/08/79, A, 79002311

Cameron, Col. James, House, PA 405/River Rd., SE of Milton, Milton vicinity, 5/05/89, C, 89000360

Himmel's Church Covered Bridge [Covered Bridges of Northumberland County TR], NE of Rebuck on T 442, Washington Township, Rebuck vicinity, 8/08/79, A, 79002312

Hopper-Snyder Homestead, NE of Watsontown off SR 49061, Watsontown vicinity, 7/03/79, C, 79002315

Hower-Slote House, W of Turbotville, Turbotville vicinity, 8/22/79, C, D, 79002314

Keefer Station Covered Bridge [Covered Bridges of Northumberland County TR], E of Sunbury on T 698, Upper Augusta Township, Sunbury vicinity, 8/08/79, A, 79002313

Kirk, William, House, W of Turbotville, Turbotville vicinity, 12/02/80, C, 80003590

Knoebel, Lawrence L., Covered Bridge [Covered Bridges of Northumberland County TR], Knoebel's Grove, Ralpho Township, Knoebel's Grove, 8/08/79, A, b, 79002309

Kreigbaum Covered Bridge [Covered Bridges of Northumberland County TR], E of Elysburg on T 459, Ralpho/Cleveland Townships, Elysburg vicinity, 8/08/79, A, 79002316

Milton Armory [Pennsylvania National Guard Armories MPS], 133 Ridge Ave., Milton, 7/12/91, A, C, 91000905

Milton Freight Station, 90 Broadway, Milton, 4/13/77, A, C, 77001180

Milton Historic District, Roughly bounded by Eight and Upper Market Sts., Spruce Ave. and Stanton, High and Apple Sts., and the Susquehanna River, Milton, 7/24/86, A, C, 86001933

Northumberland County Courthouse, 207 Market St., Sunbury, 12/30/74, A, C, 74001800

Northumberland Historic District, Roughly bounded by Fourth and A Sts., North Shore RR and Wheatley Ave., Northumberland, 11/18/88, B, C, 88002313

Pennsylvania Canal and Limestone Run Aqueduct, Bounded by Broadway, Filbert St., Limestone Run and Bound Ave., Milton, 12/19/78, A, 78002438

Priestley, Dr. Joseph, House, 100 King St., Northumberland, 9/11/81, B, C, 81000554

Priestley, Joseph, House, Priestley Ave., Northumberland, 10/15/66, B, NHL, 66000673

Richards Covered Bridge [Covered Bridges of Northumberland County TR], E of Elysburg on T 804, Ralpho/Cleveland Townships, Elysburg vicinity, 8/08/79, A, 79002308

Rishel Covered Bridge [Covered Bridges of Northumberland County TR], E of Montandon on T 573, East/West Chillisquaque Townships, Montandon vicinity, 8/08/79, A, 79002310

Sodom Schoolhouse, E of Montandon on PA 45, Montandon vicinity, 2/12/74, A, C, 74001799

Sunbury Armory [Pennsylvania National Guard Armories MPS], Catawissa Ave., Sunbury, 12/22/89, A, C, 89002082

Sunbury Historic District, Roughly bounded by Arch, Chestnut, Front, and 5th Sts., Sunbury, 11/03/83, A, C, a, 83004240

Victoria Theatre, 46 W. Independence St., Shamokin, 11/21/85, A, C, 85002907

Warrior Run Presbyterian Church, N of McEwensville on PA 147, McEwensville vicinity, 4/02/73, C, a, 73001659

Watsontown River Bridge [Highway Bridges Owned by the Commonwealth of Pennsylvania, Department of Transportation TR], LR 240 spur over W branch of Susquehanna River, Watsontown, 6/22/88, C, 88000801

Zion Stone Church, Tulpehocken Rd., Augustaville, 11/01/84, A, C, a, d, 84000267

Perry County

Adairs Covered Bridge [Covered Bridges of Adams, Cumberland, and Perry Counties TR], E of Andersonburg on LR 50009, Southwest Madison Township, Kistler vicinity, 8/25/80, A, 80003594

Bistline Covered Bridge [Covered Bridges of Adams, Cumberland, and Perry Counties TR], S of Andersonburg on LR 50008, Southwest Madison Township, Blain vicinity, 8/25/80, A, 80003591

Book's Covered Bridge [Covered Bridges of Adams, Cumberland, and Perry Counties TR], SW

Perry County—Continued

of Blain on LR 50004, Jackson Township, Blain vicinity, 8/25/80, A, 80003592

Bridge in Newport Borough [Highway Bridges Owned by the Commonwealth of Pennsylvania, Department of Transportation TR], LR 31 over Little Buffalo Creek, Newport, 6/22/88, C, 88000854

Dellville Covered Bridge [Covered Bridges of Adams, Cumberland, and Perry Counties TR], T 456, Wheatfield Township, Dellville, 8/25/80, A, 80003593

Dunbar-Creigh House, Water St., Landisburg, 6/27/80, A, C, 80003595

Fleisher Covered Bridge [Covered Bridges of Adams, Cumberland, and Perry Counties TR], NW of Newport on T 477, Oliver Township, Newport vicinity, 8/25/80, A, 80003601

Kochendefer Covered Bridge [Covered Bridges of Adams, Cumberland, and Perry Counties TR], SE of Saville on T 332, Saville Township, Saville vicinity, 8/25/80, A, 80003602

Little Buffalo Historic District, SW of Newport off PA 34, Newport vicinity, 4/03/78, A, C, d, 78002440

Mt. Pleasant Covered Bridge [Covered Bridges of Adams, Cumberland, and Perry Counties TR], E of New Germantown on T 304, Jackson Township, New Germantown vicinity, 8/25/80, A, 80003599

New Germantown Covered Bridge [Covered Bridges of Adams, Cumberland, and Perry Counties TR], S of New Germantown on T 302, Jackson Township, New Germantown, 8/25/80, A, 80003600

O'Donel House and Farm, W of New Germantown on PA 274, Blain, 7/17/86, C, 86001687

Perry County Courthouse, Center Sq., New Bloomfield, 2/24/75, A, C, 75001659

Red Covered Bridge [Covered Bridges of Adams, Cumberland, and Perry Counties TR], E of Millerstown on LR 50023, Liverpool Township, Liverpool vicinity, 8/25/80, A, 80003597

Rice Covered Bridge [Covered Bridges of Adams, Cumberland, and Perry Counties TR], S of Landisburg on LR 50023, Tyrone Township, Landisburg vicinity, 8/25/80, A, 80003596

Saville Covered Bridge [Covered Bridges of Adams, Cumberland, and Perry Counties TR], LR 50037, Saville Township, Saville, 8/25/80, A, 80003603

Waggoner Covered Bridge [Covered Bridges of Adams, Cumberland, and Perry Counties TR], W of Loysville on T 579, Tyrone/Northwest Madison Townships, Loysville vicinity, 8/25/80, A, 80003598

Philadelphia County

1616 Building, 1616 Walnut St., Philadelphia, 10/17/83, C, 83004247

1900 Rittenhouse Square Apartments, 1900 S. Rittenhouse Sq., Philadelphia, 7/26/82, C, 82003805

26th District Police and Patrol Station, 2136-2142 E. Dauphin St., Philadelphia, 7/12/84, A, C, 84003550

32nd St. and Lancaster Ave. Philadelphia Armory [Pennsylvania National Guard Armories MPS], Jct. of 32nd St. and Lancaster Ave., Philadelphia, 11/14/91, A, C, 91001703

Academy of Music, Broad and Locust Sts., Philadelphia, 10/15/66, A, C, NHL, 66000674

Adams Avenue Bridge in Philadelphia [Highway Bridges Owned by the Commonwealth of Pennsylvania, Department of Transportation TR], Adams Ave. over Tacony Creek, Philadelphia, 6/22/88, C, 88000851

Adamson, William, School [Philadelphia Public Schools TR], 2637-2647 N. 4th St., Philadelphia, 11/18/88, C, a, 88002224

Adelphi School, 1223-1225 Spring St., Philadelphia, 9/18/78, A, C, a, 78002441

Alcorn, James, School [Philadelphia Public Schools TR], 1500 S. 32nd St., Philadelphia, 11/18/88, C, 88002225

Alden Park Manor, School House Lane and Wissahickon Ave., Philadelphia, 8/15/80, C, 80003606

Allen, Ethan, School [Philadelphia Public Schools TR], 3001 Robbins Ave., Philadelphia, 11/18/88, C, 88002227

American Baptist Publication Society, 1420-1422 Chestnut St., Philadelphia, 6/27/80, B, C, 80003607

American Philosophical Society Hall, Independence Sq., Philadelphia, 10/15/66, A, a, NHL, NPS, 66000675

Anglecot, The, Evergreen and Prospect Sts., Philadelphia, 4/19/82, C, 82003806

Arch Street Meetinghouse, 302-338 Arch St., Philadelphia, 5/27/71, C, a, 71000716

Arch Street Opera House, 1003-1005 Arch St., Philadelphia, 6/13/78, A, C, 78002442

Arch Street Presbyterian Church, 1726-1732 Arch St., Philadelphia, 5/27/71, C, a, 71000717

Athenaeum of Philadelphia, 219 S. 6th St., Philadelphia, 2/01/72, A, C, NHL, 72001144

Audenried, Charles Y., Junior High School [Philadelphia Public Schools TR], 1601 S. 33rd St., Philadelphia, 11/18/88, C, 88002239

Axe, William W., School [Philadelphia Public Schools TR], 1709-1733 Kinsey St., Philadelphia, 11/18/88, C, 88002240

BARNEGAT (lightship), Pier Thirty South, Philadelphia, 11/29/79, A, b, 79002317

Bache, Alexander Dallas, School [Philadelphia Public Schools TR], 801 N. Twenty-second St., Philadelphia, 12/04/86, A, C, 86003262

Bair, Oliver, H., Funeral Home, 1818-1820 Chestnut St., Philadelphia, 11/14/82, A, C, 82001542

Baird, Matthew, Mansion, 814 N. Broad St., Philadelphia, 12/29/83, B, C, 83004241

Baptist Institute for Christian Workers, 1425-1429 Snyder Ave., Philadelphia, 4/21/83, A, C, 83002265

Bartlett School [Philadelphia Public Schools TR], 1100 Catharine St., Philadelphia, 12/04/86, C, 86003315

Barton, Clara, School [Philadelphia Public Schools TR], 300 E. Wyoming Ave., Philadelphia, 11/18/88, C, 88002242

Bartram, John, High School [Philadelphia Public Schools TR], Sixty-seventh and Elmwood Sts., Philadelphia, 12/04/86, A, C, g, 86003263

Bartram, John, House, 54th St. and Eastwick Ave., Philadelphia, 10/15/66, B, NHL, 66000676

Beeber, Dimner, Junior High School [Philadelphia Public Schools TR], 5901 Malvern Ave., Philadelphia, 11/18/88, A, C, 88002244

Beggarstown School, 6669 Germantown Ave., Philadelphia, 11/23/71, A, 71000718

Belgravia Hotel, 1811 Chestnut St., Philadelphia, 11/14/82, C, 82001543

Bell, John C., House, 229 S. 22nd St., Philadelphia, 4/13/82, A, B, C, 82003807

Bellevue Stratford Hotel, 200 S. Broad St., Philadelphia, 3/24/77, A, C, 77001182

Belmont Avenue Bridge in Philadelphia [Highway Bridges Owned by the Commonwealth of Pennsylvania, Department of Transportation TR], Belmont Ave. over Ramp B, Philadelphia, 6/22/88, C, 88000843

Belmont School [Philadelphia Public Schools TR], 4030-4060 Brown St., Philadelphia, 11/18/88, C, 88002245

Benjamin Franklin Hotel, 822-840 Chestnut St., Philadelphia, 3/02/82, A, C, 82003808

Bergdoll Mansion, 2201-2205 Green St., Philadelphia, 11/07/76, C, 76001660

Bergdoll, Louis, House, 929 N. 29th St., Philadelphia, 1/03/85, B, C, 85000038

Billmeyer, Daniel, House, 6504 Germantown Ave., Philadelphia, 12/13/71, A, C, 71000719

Billmeyer, Michael, House, 6505-6507 Germantown Ave., Philadelphia, 1/13/72, C, 72001145

Birney, Gen. David B., School [Philadelphia Public Schools TR], 900 W. Lindley St., Philadelphia, 11/18/88, C, 88002246

Bishop Mackay-Smith House, 251 S. 22nd St., Philadelphia, 1/25/80, B, C, a, 80003608

Blankenburg, Reudolph, School [Philadelphia Public Schools TR], 4600 Girard Ave., Philadelphia, 11/18/88, C, 88002248

Board of Education Building, 21st St. and Benjamin Franklin Pkwy., Philadelphia, 8/25/83, A, C, 83002266

Boat House Row, 1-15 E. River Dr., Philadelphia, 2/27/87, A, g, NHL, 87000821

Bok, Edward, Vocational School [Philadelphia Public Schools TR], 1909 S. Ninth St., Philadelphia, 12/04/86, A, C, g, 86003264

Boone, Daniel, School [Philadelphia Public Schools TR], Hancock and Wildey Sts., Philadelphia, 12/04/86, C, 86003265

Bregy, F. Amadee, School [Philadelphia Public Schools TR], 1700 Bigler St., Philadelphia, 11/18/88, C, 88002249

Breslyn Apartments, 4624-4642 Walnut St., 201-213 S. 47th St., Philadelphia, 11/14/82, A, C, 82001544

Brewerytown Historic District, Roughly bounded by 30th St., Girard Ave., 32nd St. and Glenwood Ave., Philadelphia, 3/01/91, A, C, 91000096

Philadelphia County—Continued

Bridesburg School [Philadelphia Public Schools TR], 2624 Haworth St., Philadelphia, 4/10/89, A, C, 88002285

Broad Street Historic District, Roughly bounded by Juniper, Cherry, 15th, and Pine Sts., Philadelphia, 4/06/84, A, C, 84003529

Brooks, George L., School [Philadelphia Public Schools TR], 5629–5643 Haverford Ave., Philadelphia, 12/04/86, C, 86003266

Brown, Joseph H., School [Philadelphia Public Schools TR], 8118–8120 Frankford Ave., Philadelphia, 11/18/88, C, 88002250

Burk Brothers and Company, 913–916 N. Third St., Philadelphia, 11/14/85, A, 85003493

Carnell, Laura H., School [Philadelphia Public Schools TR], 6101 Summerdale Ave., Philadelphia, 11/18/88, C, 88002251

Carpenters' Hall, 310 Chestnut St., Philadelphia, 4/15/70, C, NHL, NPS, 70000552

Cassidy, Lewis C., School [Philadelphia Public Schools TR], 6523–6543 Lansdowne Ave., Philadelphia, 11/18/88, C, 88002252

Catharine, Joseph W., School [Philadelphia Public Schools TR], 6600 Chester Ave., Philadelphia, 11/18/88, C, 88002253

Cathedral of Saints Peter and Paul, 18th St. and the Pkwy., Philadelphia, 6/24/71, C, a, 71000720

Centennial National Bank, 3200 Market St., Philadelphia, 3/11/71, C, 71000721

Center City West Commercial Historic District, Roughly bounded by Chestnut, Fifteenth, Walnut, Sansom & Twenty-first Sts., Philadelphia, 1/07/88, A, C, g, 87002203

Central High School [Philadelphia Public Schools TR], Olney and Ogontz Aves., Philadelphia, 12/04/86, A, C, g, 86003267

Chamounix, West Fairmount Park on Chamounix Dr., Philadelphia, 4/26/72, C, 72001146

Chandler, George, School [Philadelphia Public Schools TR], 1050 E. Montgomery St., Philadelphia, 11/18/88, C, 88002255

Chateau Crillon Apartment House, 222 S. 19th St., Philadelphia, 4/25/78, C, 78002443

Chestnut Hill Historic District, Roughly bounded by Fairmount Park and Montgomery Co. Line, Philadelphia, 6/20/85, A, C, 85001334

Childs, George W., School [Philadelphia Public Schools TR], 1501 S. 17th St., Philadelphia, 11/18/88, C, 88002257

Christ Church, 22–26 N. 2nd St., Philadelphia, 4/15/70, C, a, NHL, NPS, 70000553

Christ Church Burial Ground, 5th and Arch Sts., Philadelphia, 6/24/71, B, C, d, NPS, 71000062

Church of St. James the Less, Hunting Park Ave. and Clearfield St., Philadelphia, 11/20/74, C, a, NHL, 74001801

Church of the Holy Trinity, 19th and Walnut Sts. facing Rittenhouse Sq., Philadelphia, 2/06/73, C, a, 73001660

City Line Avenue Bridge [Highway Bridges Owned by the Commonwealth of Pennsylvania, Department of Transportation TR], City

Ave. over E branch of Indian Creek, Philadelphia, 6/22/88, C, 88000802

City Park Brewery, Roughly bounded by Pennsylvania Ave., 28th, 30th, and Poplar Sts., Philadelphia, 7/18/80, A, C, 80003609

Clarkson-Watson House, 5275–5277 Germantown Ave., Philadelphia, 4/02/73, A, C, 73001661

Cliffs, The, East Fairmount Park near 33rd St., Philadelphia, 3/16/72, C, 72001147

Clinton Street Historic District, Bounded by 9th, 11th, Pine, and Cypress Sts., Philadelphia, 4/26/72, C, 72001148

Cliveden, 6401 Germantown Ave., Philadelphia, 10/15/66, A, C, NHL, 66000677

College Hall, University Of Pennsylvania, Bounded by Walnut, Spruce, 34th, and 36th Sts., Philadelphia, 2/14/78, A, C, 78002444

Colonial Germantown Historic District, Germantown Ave. between Windrim Ave. and Upsal St., Philadelphia, 10/15/66, A, C, a, NHL, 66000678

Colonial Germantown Historic District (Boundary Increase), 6500–7600 blks. of Germantown Ave. from Ft. Washington branch of PA RR to Sharpnack St., Philadelphia, 7/30/87, A, C, g, 87001239

Comly, Watson, School [Philadelphia Public Schools TR], 13250 Trevose Rd., Philadelphia, 11/18/88, C, 88002324

Commandant's Quarters, U.S. Naval Base, Philadelphia, 6/03/76, A, C, 76001661

Compton and Bloomfield, 9414 Meadowbrook Ave., Philadelphia, 12/22/78, A, C, 78002445

Conwell, Russell H., School [Philadelphia Public Schools TR], 1829–1951 E. Clearfield St., Philadelphia, 11/18/88, A, C, 88002258

Conyngham-Hacker House, 5214 Germantown Ave., Philadelphia, 1/13/72, C, 72001149

Cooke, Jay, Junior High School [Philadelphia Public Schools TR], 4735 Old York Rd., Philadelphia, 11/18/88, A, C, 88002259

Cope, Edward Drinker, House, 2102 Pine St., Philadelphia, 5/15/75, B, NHL, 75001660

Creighton, Thomas, School [Philadelphia Public Schools TR], 5401 Tabor Rd., Philadelphia, 11/18/88, C, 88002260

Crossan, Kennedy, School [Philadelphia Public Schools TR], 7341 Palmetto St., Philadelphia, 11/18/88, C, 88002261

Darrah, Lydia, School [Philadelphia Public Schools TR], 708–732 N. Seventeenth St., Philadelphia, 12/04/86, C, 86003269

Delmar Apartments, 319 W. Chelton Ave., Philadelphia, 11/14/82, A, C, 82001545

Deshler-Morris House, 5442 Germantown Ave., Philadelphia, 1/13/72, B, C, NPS, 72000095

Disston, Hamilton, School [Philadelphia Public Schools TR], 6801 Cottage St., Philadelphia, 11/18/88, C, 88002262

Disston, Mary, School [Philadelphia Public Schools TR], 4521 Longshore Ave., Philadelphia, 11/18/88, C, a, 88002319

Dobbins, Murrell, Vocational School [Philadelphia Public Schools TR], 2100 Lehigh Ave., Philadelphia, 11/18/88, C, 88002263

Dobson Mills, 4001–4041 Ridge Ave.; 33502–3530 Scott's La., Philadelphia, 7/28/88, A, C, 88001214

Dobson, James, School [Philadelphia Public Schools TR], 4665 Umbria St., Philadelphia, 11/18/88, C, 88002264

Drake Hotel, 1512–1514 Spruce St., Philadelphia, 9/18/78, A, C, 78002446

Drexel Development Historic District, Roughly bounded by Pine, Delancy, 39th and 40th Sts., Philadelphia, 11/14/82, C, 82001546

Drexel and Company Building, 135–143 S. 15th St., Philadelphia, 2/08/80, A, C, 80003610

Drexel, Francis M., School [Philadelphia Public Schools TR], 1800 S. Sixteenth St., Philadelphia, 12/04/86, C, 86003272

Drinker's Court, 236-238 Delancey St., Philadelphia, 5/27/71, C, 71000723

Dropsie University Complex, Broad and York Sts., Philadelphia, 1/17/75, A, B, C, a, 75001661

Druim Moir Historic District, Bounded by Fairmount Park, Cherokee St., Hartwell Lane and Valley Green Rd., Philadelphia, 12/11/79, C, 79002318

Dunbar, Paul Lawrence, School [Philadelphia Public Schools TR], Twelfth above Columbia Ave., Philadelphia, 12/04/86, C, 86003274

Dunlap, Thomas, School [Philadelphia Public Schools TR], 5031 Race St., Philadelphia, 12/04/86, C, 86003277

Durham, Thomas, School [Philadelphia Public Schools TR], 1600 Lombard St., Philadelphia, 11/18/88, C, 88002265

Eakins, Thomas, House, 1729 Mount Vernon Pl., Philadelphia, 10/15/66, B, NHL, 66000679

East Center City Commercial Historic District, Roughly bounded by 6th, Juniper, Market and Locust Sts., Philadelphia, 7/05/84, A, C, 84003531

Eastern State Penitentiary, 21st St. and Fairmount Ave., Philadelphia, 10/15/66, A, NHL, 66000680

Edmunds, Henry R., School [Philadelphia Public Schools TR], 1101–1197 Haworth St., Philadelphia, 11/18/88, C, 88002266

Elfreth's Alley Historic District, Between 2nd and Front Sts., Philadelphia, 10/15/66, C, NHL, 66000681

Elk's Lodge BPOE No. 2, 306-320 N. Broad St., Philadelphia, 8/23/84, A, C, 84003535

Elverson, James, Jr., School [Philadelphia Public Schools TR], 1300 Susquehanna Ave., Philadelphia, 11/18/88, C, 88002231

Emlen, Eleanor Cope, School of Practice [Philadelphia Public Schools TR], 6501 Chew St., Philadelphia, 11/18/88, A, 88002267

Equitable Trust Building, 1405 Locust St., Philadelphia, 7/03/86, C, 86001405

Estey Hall, 1701 Walnut St., Philadelphia, 10/28/83, A, C, 83004244

Eyre, Wilson, House, 1003 Spruce St., Philadelphia, 4/13/77, C, 77001183

Fairmount Park, Both banks of Schuylkill River and Wissahickon Creek, from Spring Garden St. to Northwestern Ave., Philadelphia, 2/07/72, A, C, f, 72001151

Philadelphia County—Continued

Fairmount Water Works, E banks of Schuylkill River, Philadelphia, 5/11/76, A, C, NHL, 76001662

Farragut, David, School [Philadelphia Public Schools TR], Hancock and Cumberland, Philadelphia, 12/04/86, C, 86003280

Fayette School [Philadelphia Public Schools TR], Old Bustleton and Welsh Rds., Philadelphia, 12/04/86, C, 86003295

Federal Street School [Philadelphia Public Schools TR], 1130–1148 Federal St., Philadelphia, 12/01/86, C, 86003294

Fell, D. Newlin, School [Philadelphia Public Schools TR], 900 Oregon Ave., Philadelphia, 11/18/88, C, 88002268

Feltonville School No. 2 [Philadelphia Public Schools TR], 4901 Rising Sun Ave., Philadelphia, 11/18/88, C, 88002269

Ferguson, Joseph C., School [Philadelphia Public Schools TR], 2000–2046 7th St., Philadelphia, 11/18/88, C, 88002270

Fidelity Mutual Life Insurance Company Building, Fairmount and Pennsylvania Aves., Philadelphia, 7/02/73, A, C, g, 73001662

Fidelity-Philadelphia Trust Company Building, 123–151 S. Broad St., Philadelphia, 11/27/78, C, 78002447

Finletter, Thomas K., School [Philadelphia Public Schools TR], 6101 N. Front St., Philadelphia, 11/18/88, C, 88002271

First Bank of the United States, 116 S. Third St., Philadelphia, 5/04/87, A, C, NHL, NPS, 87001292

First Unitarian Church, 2121 Chestnut St., Philadelphia, 5/27/71, C, a, 71000724

Fisher's Lane, E. Logan St., Philadelphia, 2/20/80, A, C, 80003611

Fitler School [Philadelphia Public Schools TR], SE Seymour and Knox Sts., Philadelphia, 12/04/86, C, 86003281

Fitzsimons, Thomas, Junior High School [Philadelphia Public Schools TR], 2601 W. Cumberland St., Philadelphia, 11/18/88, A, C, 88002272

Fleischer, Helen, Vocational School [Philadelphia Public Schools TR], Thirteenth and Brandywine Sts., Philadelphia, 12/04/86, A, C, 86003282

Fleisher, Samuel S., Art Memorial, 711-721 Catharine St., Philadelphia, 11/14/82, A, B, C, 82001547

Forrest, Edwin, House, 1326 N. Broad St., Philadelphia, 1/13/72, A, B, C, 72001152

Forrest, Edwin, School [Philadelphia Public Schools TR], 4300 Bleigh St., Philadelphia, 11/18/88, C, 88002273

Fort Mifflin, Marina and Penrose Ferry Rds., Philadelphia, 8/29/70, A, C, NHL, 70000554

Fort Mifflin Hospital, Marina and Penrose Ferry Rds., Philadelphia, 9/29/69, A, C, 69000157

Founder's Hall, Girard College, Corinthian and Girard Aves., Philadelphia, 8/04/69, B, f, NHL, 69000158

Frank, Henry S., Memorial Synagogue, York and Tabor Rds., Philadelphia, 7/12/83, C, a, 83002267

Frankford Arsenal, Tacony and Bridge Sts., Philadelphia, 3/16/72, A, C, 72001153

Frankford Avenue Bridge [Highway Bridges Owned by the Commonwealth of Pennsylvania, Department of Transportation TR], Frankford Ave. over Pennypack Creek, Philadelphia, 6/22/88, C, 88000803

Frankford Avenue Bridge [Highway Bridges Owned by the Commonwealth of Pennsylvania, Department of Transportation TR], Frankford Ave. over Poquessing Creek, Philadelphia, 6/22/88, A, C, 88000850

Franklin Hose Company No. 28, 730-732 S. Broad St., Philadelphia, 12/03/80, A, C, 80003604

Franklin Institute, 15 S. 7th St., Philadelphia, 8/01/79, A, B, C, 79002319

Franklin Institute Science Museum, 20th St. and the Benjamin Franklin Pkwy., Philadelphia, 1/03/85, A, C, 85000039

Franklin Square [Four Public Squares of Philadelphia TR], Race and 6th Sts., Philadelphia, 9/14/81, A, C, 81000556

Franklin, Benjamin, School [Philadelphia Public Schools TR], 5737–5741 Rising Sun Ave., Philadelphia, 11/18/88, C, 88002274

Free Quaker Meetinghouse, SW corner of 5th and Arch Sts., Philadelphia, 9/22/71, A, C, b, NPS, 71000063

Fulton, Robert, School [Philadelphia Public Schools TR], 60–68 E. Haines St., Philadelphia, 12/04/86, C, 86003284

Furness Library, 34th St. below Walnut on University of Pennsylvania campus, Philadelphia, 5/19/72, C, NHL, 72001154

Furness, Horace, Junior High School [Philadelphia Public Schools TR], 1900 S. Third St., Philadelphia, 12/01/86, C, 86003286

Garden Court Historic District, Roughly bounded by Larchwood Ave., 46th, 50th, and Pine Sts., Philadelphia, 7/05/84, C, 84003539

Garden Court Historic District (Boundary Increase), 4526–4534 and 4537–4539 Osage Ave., Philadelphia, 2/25/86, C, 86000314

General Electric Switchgear Plant, Seventh and Willow Sts., Philadelphia, 10/31/85, A, C, 85003470

George, Henry, Birthplace, 413 S. Tenth St., Philadelphia, 4/01/83, A, B, c, f, 83002268

German Society of Pennsylvania, 611 Spring Garden St., Philadelphia, 7/24/92, A, C, 92000947

Germantown Cricket Club, 5140 Morris St., Philadelphia, 2/27/87, A, NHL, 87000758

Germantown Grammar School [Philadelphia Public Schools TR], McCallum and Haines Sts., Philadelphia, 12/01/86, C, 86003287

Gilbert Building, 1315–1329 Cherry St., Philadelphia, 7/17/86, C, 86001688

Gillespie, Elizabeth Duane, Junior High School [Philadelphia Public Schools TR], 3901–3961 N. 18th St., Philadelphia, 4/10/89, C, 88002275

Girard Avenue Historic District, 1415–2028 Girard Ave. and 1700 blk. of Thompson St., Philadelphia, 10/31/85, C, 85003427

Girard College Complex, Bounded by Poplar St., Girard, W. College, S. College, and Ridge Aves., Philadelphia, 10/29/74, A, C, 74001802

Girard Group, Delaware Ave. and Arch St., Philadelphia, 5/06/83, A, C, 83002269

Glen Foerd at Torresdale, 5001 Grant Ave., Philadelphia, 11/20/79, A, C, a, 79002320

Globe Ticket Company Building, 112 N. 12th St., Philadelphia, 11/01/84, A, C, 84000268

Gloria Dei (Old Swedes') Church National Historic Site, Swanson St., between Christian and Water Sts., Philadelphia, 10/15/66, A, C, a, f, NPS, 66000682

Goodman Brothers and Hinlein Company, 1238 Callowhill St., Philadelphia, 3/07/85, C, 85000469

Graham and Laird, Schober and Mitchell Factories, 19th St. between Hamilton and Buttonwood Sts., Philadelphia, 7/07/78, A, C, 78002448

Gratz, Simon, High School [Philadelphia Public Schools TR], 3901–3961 N. 18th St., Philadelphia, 4/10/89, C, 88002276

Graver's Lane Station, Gravers Lane and Reading Railroad Line, Philadelphia, 11/07/77, A, C, 77001184

Grays Road Recreation Center, 2501 Christian St., Philadelphia, 4/21/88, A, C, 88000448

Green Tree Tavern, 260–262 E. Girard Ave., Philadelphia, 6/27/80, A, C, 80003612

Grumblethorpe, 5267 Germantown Ave., Philadelphia, 3/16/72, C, 72001155

Grumblethorpe Tenant House, 5269 Germantown Ave., Philadelphia, 6/19/72, C, 72001156

Haddington Historic District, 6000 blks. of Market, Ludlow and Chestnut, Philadelphia, 9/29/88, A, a, 88001832

Haines, Hanson, House, 4801 Springfield Ave., Philadelphia, 1/29/85, C, 85000179

Hamilton Family Estate, 4039–4041 Baltimore Ave. and 4000–4018 Pine St., Philadelphia, 6/22/79, C, 79002321

Hanna, William B., School [Philadelphia Public Schools TR], 5720–5738 Media St., Philadelphia, 12/04/86, C, 86003288

Harding, Warren G., Junior High School [Philadelphia Public Schools TR], 2000 Wakeling St., Philadelphia, 11/18/88, A, C, 88002277

Harper, Frances Ellen Watkins, House, 1006 Bainbridge St., Philadelphia, 12/08/76, B, NHL, 76001663

Harrington Machine Shop, 1640-1666 Callowhill St., Philadelphia, 5/06/83, A, 83002270

Harrison, William H., School [Philadelphia Public Schools TR], 1012–1020 W. Thompson St., Philadelphia, 11/18/88, C, 88002278

Hatfield House, Fairmount Park, 33rd St. near Girard Ave., Philadelphia, 3/16/72, C, b, 72001157

Hawthorne, Nathaniel, School [Philadelphia Public Schools TR], 712 S. Twelfth St., Philadelphia, 12/04/86, C, 86003289

Head House Square, Both sides of the 400 block of S. 2nd St., Philadelphia, 6/19/72, A, C, 72001158

Philadelphia County—Continued

Henry, Charles Wolcott, School [Philadelphia Public Schools TR], 601–645 W. Carpenter Ln., Philadelphia, 11/18/88, C, 88002279

Heywood Chair Factory, 1010-1014 Race St., Philadelphia, 8/23/84, A, C, 84003541

Hill-Physick House, 321 S. 4th St., Philadelphia, 5/27/71, B, C, NHL, 71000726

Hockley Row, 237-241 S. 21st St., 2049 Locust St., Philadelphia, 4/21/83, C, 83002272

Hogue, Robert M., House, 100 Pelham Rd., Philadelphia, 1/16/86, C, 86000165

Holman, A. J., and Company, 1222-26 Arch St., Philadelphia, 5/17/84, A, C, 84003544

Holme Avenue Bridge [Highway Bridges Owned by the Commonwealth of Pennsylvania, Department of Transportation TR], Holme Ave. over Wooden Bridge Run, Philadelphia, 6/22/88, C, 88000806

Holmes Junior High School [Philadelphia Public Schools TR], 5429–5455 Chestnut St., Philadelphia, 11/18/88, A, 88002281

Hopkinson, Francis, School [Philadelphia Public Schools TR], 1301–1331 E. Luzerne Ave., Philadelphia, 11/18/88, C, 88002282

Horn, George L., School [Philadelphia Public Schools TR], Frankford and Castor Aves., Philadelphia, 12/04/86, C, 86003292

Houses at 2000-2018 Delancey Street, 2000-2018 Delancey St., Philadelphia, 4/22/82, C, 82003809

Houston, Henry H., School [Philadelphia Public Schools TR], 135 W. Allen's Ln., Philadelphia, 4/10/89, C, 88002283

Howe, Julia Ward, School [Philadelphia Public Schools TR], 1301–1331 Grange St., Philadelphia, 11/18/88, C, 88002284

Howell House, 5218 Germantown Ave., Philadelphia, 1/13/72, C, 72001159

Independence National Historical Park, Bounded by Walnut, 6th, Chestnut, and 2nd Sts., Philadelphia, 10/15/66, A, C, a, d, e, f, g, NPS, 66000683

Institute for Colored Youth [Philadelphia Public Schools TR], Tenth and Bainbridge Sts., Philadelphia, 12/04/86, A, C, 86003324

Institute of the Pennsylvania Hospital, 111 N. 49th St., Philadelphia, 10/15/66, A, NHL, 66000684

Insurance Company of North America Building, 1600 Arch St., Philadelphia, 6/02/78, A, B, NHL, 78002449

Integrity Title Insurance, Trust and Safe Deposit Company, 4th and Green Sts., Philadelphia, 11/14/82, A, C, 82001548

Irish, Nathaniel, House, 704 S. Front St., Philadelphia, 3/16/72, C, 72001160

Ivy Lodge, 29 E. Penn St., Philadelphia, 2/01/72, C, a, 72001161

Jayne Estate Building, 2–16 Vine St., Philadelphia, 4/30/87, A, C, 87000648

Jayne, Horace, House, 320 S. 19th St., Philadelphia, 7/22/82, C, 82003810

Jefferson, Thomas, School [Philadelphia Public Schools TR], 1101–1125 N. 4th St., Philadelphia, 11/18/88, C, 88002280

Jenks, John Story, School [Philadelphia Public Schools TR], 8301–8317 Germantown Ave., Philadelphia, 11/18/88, C, 88002286

Johnson, John, House, 6306 Germantown Ave., Philadelphia, 1/13/72, C, 72001162

Jones, John Paul, Junior High School [Philadelphia Public Schools TR], 2922 Memphis St., Philadelphia, 11/18/88, A, C, 88002287

Kensington Branch of the Philadelphia YWCA, 174 W. Allegheny Ave., Philadelphia, 3/09/90, A, C, 90000415

Kensington High School for Girls [Philadelphia Public Schools TR], 2075 E. Cumberland St., Philadelphia, 11/18/88, A, C, 88002288

Key, Francis Scott, School [Philadelphia Public Schools TR], 2226–2250 S. Eighth St., Philadelphia, 12/01/86, C, 86003296

Kinsey, John L., School [Philadelphia Public Schools TR], Sixty-fifth Ave. and Limekiln Pike, Philadelphia, 12/04/86, C, 86003297

Kirkbride, Eliza Butler, School [Philadelphia Public Schools TR], 626 Dickinson St., Philadelphia, 11/18/88, C, 88002290

Knowlton, 8001 Verree Rd., Philadelphia, 10/01/74, C, 74001803

La Blanche Apartments, 5100 Walnut St., Philadelphia, 3/07/85, A, C, 85000470

Land Title Building, 1400 Chestnut St., Philadelphia, 12/15/78, C, 78002450

Landreth, David, School [Philadelphia Public Schools TR], 1201 S. Twenty-third St., Philadelphia, 12/04/86, C, 86003299

Laurel Hill Cemetery, 3822 Ridge Ave., Philadelphia, 10/28/77, C, d, 77001185

Lawndale School [Philadelphia Public Schools TR], 600 Hellerman St., Philadelphia, 11/18/88, C, a, 88002254

Lea, Henry C., School of Practice [Philadelphia Public Schools TR], 242 S. 47th St., Philadelphia, 11/18/88, A, C, 88002291

Leidy, Dr. Joseph, House, 1319 Locust St., Philadelphia, 12/04/80, A, C, 80003613

Levering, William, School [Philadelphia Public Schools TR], 5938 Ridge Ave., Philadelphia, 11/18/88, C, 88002292

Lits Department Store, Market between 7th and 8th Sts., Philadelphia, 5/15/79, A, C, 79002322

Logan Demonstration School [Philadelphia Public Schools TR], 5000 N. 17th St., Philadelphia, 11/18/88, A, C, 88002293

Logan Square [Four Public Squares of Philadelphia TR], 18th and Race Sts., Philadelphia, 9/14/81, A, C, 81000555

Longfellow, Henry, School [Philadelphia Public Schools TR], 5004–5098 Tacony St., Philadelphia, 11/18/88, C, 88002294

Lowell, James Russell, School [Philadelphia Public Schools TR], 5801–5851 N. 5th St., Philadelphia, 11/18/88, C, 88002295

Ludlow, James R., School [Philadelphia Public Schools TR], 1323–1345 N. 6th St., Philadelphia, 11/18/88, C, 88002296

Malvern Hall, 6655 McCallum St., Philadelphia, 8/25/83, C, 83002273

Manayunk Main Street Historic District, Roughly bounded by Reading RR, Flat Rock Dam, Schuylkill River, and Lot 4025 Main St., Philadelphia, 3/18/83, A, C, 83002274

Mann, William, School [Philadelphia Public Schools TR], 1835–1869 N. 54th St., Philadelphia, 11/18/88, C, 88002297

Marine Barracks, Bldg. 100, Naval Base, Broad St., Philadelphia, 7/13/76, A, 76001664

Marine Corps Supply Activity, 1100 S. Broad St., Philadelphia, 8/06/75, A, 75001662

Marshall, John, School [Philadelphia Public Schools TR], 1501–1527 Sellers St., Philadelphia, 11/18/88, C, 88002298

Martin Orthopedic School [Philadelphia Public Schools TR], 800 N. Twenty-second St., Philadelphia, 12/04/86, A, C, 86003300

Martin, James, School [Philadelphia Public Schools TR], 3340 Richmond St., Philadelphia, 11/18/88, C, 88002299

Mask and Wig Club of the University of Pennsylvania, 310 S. Quince St., Philadelphia, 11/20/79, A, C, 79002323

Masonic Temple, 1 N. Broad St., Philadelphia, 5/27/71, C, NHL, 71000727

Maxwell, Ebenezer, House, 200 W. Tulpehocken St., Philadelphia, 2/24/71, C, a, 71000728

Mayfair House, 401 W. Johnson St., Philadelphia, 4/07/82, C, 82003811

McCallum Manor, 6653 McCallum Ave., Philadelphia, 5/09/85, C, 85001000

McClure, Alexander K., School [Philadelphia Public Schools TR], 4139 N. 6th St., Philadelphia, 11/18/88, C, 88002300

McDaniel, Delaplaine, School [Philadelphia Public Schools TR], 2100 Moore St., Philadelphia, 12/04/86, C, 86003303

McIlvain, Francis, House, 1924 Arch St., Philadelphia, 11/20/79, C, 79002324

Meade, George, School [Philadelphia Public Schools TR], 1801 Oxford St., Philadelphia, 12/04/86, C, 86003305

Mechanicsville School [Philadelphia Public Schools TR], Mechanicsville Rd., Philadelphia, 12/01/86, C, 86003306

Meehan, Thomas, School [Philadelphia Public Schools TR], 5347–5353 Pulaski St., Philadelphia, 11/18/88, C, a, 88002312

Memorial Hall, West Fairmount Park, Philadelphia, 12/08/76, C, NHL, 76001665

Mennonite Meetinghouse, 6119 Germantown Ave., Philadelphia, 7/23/73, A, a, 73001663

Meredith, William M., School [Philadelphia Public Schools TR], Fifth and Fitzwater Sts., Philadelphia, 12/04/86, C, 86003307

Metropolitan Opera House, 858 N. Broad St., Philadelphia, 2/01/72, A, a, 72001163

Middishade Clothing Factory, 1600 Callowhill St., Philadelphia, 1/06/87, A, C, 86003579

Mifflin School [Philadelphia Public Schools TR], 808–818 N. Third St., Philadelphia, 12/04/86, A, C, 86003308

Philadelphia County—Continued

Mifflin, Thomas, School [Philadelphia Public Schools TR], 3500 Midvale Ave., Philadelphia, 11/18/88, C, 88002301

Mikveh Israel Cemetery, NW corner of Spruce and Darien Sts., Philadelphia, 6/24/71, A, B, a, d, NPS, 71000061

Mitchell, S. Weir, School [Philadelphia Public Schools TR], Fifty-sixth and Kingsessing St., Philadelphia, 12/04/86, C, 86003309

Monastery, The, Fairmount Park, Kitchen's Lane at Wissahickon Creek, Philadelphia, 3/16/72, C, 72001164

Monte Vista, 917-931 N. 63rd St., 6154-6160 Oxford St., 6151-6157 Nasseau St., Philadelphia, 3/03/83, A, C, 83002275

Moore, Capt. Thomas, House, 702 S. Front St., Philadelphia, 3/16/72, C, 72001165

Moore, Clarence B., House, 1321 Locust St., Philadelphia, 5/08/73, C, 73001664

Morrison, Andrew J., School [Philadelphia Public Schools TR], 300 Duncannon St., Philadelphia, 11/18/88, C, 88002302

Most Precious Blood Roman Catholic Church, Rectory and Parochial School, 2800-2818 Diamond St., Philadelphia, 1/22/92, C, a, 91002008

Mother Bethel A.M.E. Church, 419 6th St., Philadelphia, 3/16/72, A, B, C, a, NHL, 72001166

Mount Pleasant, Fairmount Park, Philadelphia, 10/15/66, C, NHL, 66000685

Mt. Airy Station, E. Gowen Ave., Philadelphia, 9/22/77, C, 77001186

Muhlenberg School [Philadelphia Public Schools TR], 1640 Master St., Philadelphia, 11/18/88, C, a, 88002247

Muhr, Simon, Work Training School [Philadelphia Public Schools TR], Twelfth and Allegheny, Philadelphia, 12/01/86, A, C, 86003310

Musical Fund Hall, 808 Locust St., Philadelphia, 3/11/71, A, NHL, 71000730

National Bank of North Philadelphia, 3701 N. Broad St., Philadelphia, 5/20/85, C, 85001131

Nebinger, George W., School [Philadelphia Public Schools TR], 601-627 Carpenter St., Philadelphia, 11/18/88, C, 88002303

Neill-Mauran House, 315-317 S. 22nd St., Philadelphia, 6/30/80, C, 80003614

New Century Guild, 1307 Locust St., Philadelphia, 11/04/93, A, NHL, 93001611

New Market, S. 2nd St., between Pine and Lombard Sts., Philadelphia, 11/13/66, A, NHL, 66000686

New York Mutual Life Insurance Company Building, 1001-1005 Chestnut St., Philadelphia, 6/06/80, C, 80003615

Nichols, Jeremiah, School [Philadelphia Public Schools TR], 1235 S. 16th St., Philadelphia, 11/18/88, C, 88002241

North Broad Street Mansion District, Roughly bounded by Broad, Jefferson, Willington, and Oxford Sts., Philadelphia, 3/29/85, C, 85000674

Northeast Manual Training School [Philadelphia Public Schools TR], 701 Lehigh St., Philadelphia, 12/04/86, A, C, 86003279

Northern Liberties Historic District, Roughly bounded by Brown, Boone and Galloway, Green and Wallace, and Fifth and Sixth Sts., Philadelphia, 10/31/85, A, C, 85003471

Northern National Bank, 2300 Germantown Ave., Philadelphia, 6/27/85, A, C, 85001388

Northern Saving Fund and Safe Deposit Company, 600 Spring Garden St., Philadelphia, 9/28/77, C, 77001187

Oakley, Violet, Studio, 627 St. George's Rd., Philadelphia, 9/13/77, B, 77001188

Ogontz Hall, 7175-7165 Ogontz Ave., Philadelphia, 11/14/91, C, 91001708

Old City Historic District, Old city area including parts of Washington Square East Development Area and Franklin Square East Development Area, Philadelphia, 5/05/72, A, C, NPS, 72000093

Old Federal Reserve Bank, 925 Chestnut St., Philadelphia, 6/28/79, A, C, 79002325

Old Germantown Academy And Headmasters' Houses, Schoolhouse Lane and Greene St., Philadelphia, 1/13/72, A, C, 72001168

Olney Elementary School [Philadelphia Public Schools TR], Tabor Rd. and Water St., Philadelphia, 12/04/86, C, 86003311

Olney High School [Philadelphia Public Schools TR], Duncannon and Front Sts., Philadelphia, 12/04/86, C, 86003312

Overbrook Farms, Roughly bounded by City Line Ave., 58th St., Woodbine Ave. and 64th St., Philadelphia, 3/21/85, A, C, 85000690

Overbrook High School [Philadelphia Public Schools TR], Fifty-ninth and Lancaster Ave., Philadelphia, 12/04/86, C, 86003313

Overbrook School [Philadelphia Public Schools TR], 6201-6231 Lebanon Ave., Philadelphia, 11/18/88, C, 88002304

Packard Motor Corporation Building, 317-321 N. Broad St., Philadelphia, 2/08/80, C, 80003616

Parkside Historic District, Bounded by Penn-Central RR track, 38th St., Girard, Parksid nd Belmont Aves., Philadelphia, 11/17/83, C, 83004248

Paterson, John M., School [Philadelphia Public Schools TR], 7001 Buist Ave., Philadelphia, 11/18/88, C, 88002305

Peale, Charles Willson, House, 2100 Clarkson Ave., Philadelphia, 10/15/66, B, NHL, 66000687

Peirce, William S., School [Philadelphia Public Schools TR], 2400 Christian St., Philadelphia, 11/18/88, C, 88002307

Penn Treaty Junior High School [Philadelphia Public Schools TR], 600 E. Thompson St., Philadelphia, 11/18/88, A, C, 88002311

Penn, William, High School for Girls [Philadelphia Public Schools TR], 1501 Wallace St., Philadelphia, 12/01/86, A, 86003316

Pennell, Joseph, School [Philadelphia Public Schools TR], 1800-1856 Nedro St., Philadelphia, 11/18/88, C, 88002309

Pennsylvania Academy of the Fine Arts, SW corner of Broad and Cherry Sts., Philadelphia, 5/27/71, C, NHL, 71000731

Pennsylvania Hospital, 8th and Spruce Sts., Philadelphia, 10/15/66, A, NHL, 66000688

Pennsylvania Institute for the Deaf and Dumb, 7500 Germantown Ave., Philadelphia, 5/09/85, A, C, 85000999

Pennypacker, Samuel W., School [Philadelphia Public Schools TR], 1800-1850 E. Washington Ln., Philadelphia, 11/18/88, C, 88002314

Philadelphia City Hall, Penn Sq., Broad and Market Sts., Philadelphia, 12/08/76, A, C, NHL, 76001666

Philadelphia College of Art, NW corner of Broad and Pine Sts., Philadelphia, 5/27/71, A, C, 71000733

Philadelphia College of Art (Boundary Increase), Broad and Pine Sts., Philadelphia, 12/15/78, A, C, 78002451

Philadelphia Contributorship, 212 S. 4th St., Philadelphia, 5/27/71, A, C, NHL, 71000732

Philadelphia High School for Girls [Philadelphia Public Schools TR], Seventeenth and Spring Garden Sts., Philadelphia, 12/04/86, A, C, 86003302

Philadelphia Racquet Club, 213-225 S. 16th St., Philadelphia, 8/01/79, A, C, 79002326

Philadelphia Savings Fund Society Building, 12 S. 19th St., Philadelphia, 12/08/76, C, g, NHL, 76001667

Philadelphia School of Design for Women, 1346 N. Broad St., Philadelphia, 11/04/93, A, NHL, 93001608

Philadelphia Stock Exchange, 1409 1411 Walnut St., Philadelphia, 8/31/82, A, C, 82003812

Philadelphia Wholesales Drug Company Building, 513-525 N. Tenth St., Philadelphia, 9/05/90, A, C, 90001410

Physicians and Dentists Building, 1831-1833 Chestnut St., Philadelphia, 11/05/87, A, C, 87001968

Pinehurst Apartments, 4511-4523 Pine and 324-334 S. Fourty-fifth Sts., Philadelphia, 1/06/87, C, 86003571

Pitcairn Building, 1027 Arch St., Philadelphia, 1/07/88, A, C, 87002209

Plays and Players, 1714 Delancey St., Philadelphia, 3/14/73, A, C, 73001665

Poe, Edgar Allan, House, 530-532 N. Seventh St., Philadelphia, 10/15/66, A, B, NHL, NPS, 66000689

Poe, Edgar Allen, School [Philadelphia Public Schools TR], 2136 Ritner St., Philadelphia, 12/04/86, C, 86003318

Portico Row, 900-930 Spruce St., Philadelphia, 12/16/77, C, 77001189

Poth and Schmidt Development Houses, 3306-3316 Arch St., Philadelphia, 4/21/83, A, C, 83002276

Poth, Frederick A., Houses, , 15, 3301-3311 Powelton Ave., Philadelphia, 4/19/79, A, C, 79002327

Powelton Historic District, Roughly bounded by Brandywine St., 32nd to 39th Sts. and Lancaster Ave., Philadelphia, 5/09/85, A, C, 85000998

Powelton, The, 3500-3520 Powelton Ave., 214-218 35th St., and 215-221 36th St., Philadelphia, 12/13/78, A, C, 78002452

Philadelphia County—Continued

Powers, Thomas, School [Philadelphia Public Schools TR], Frankford Ave. and Somerset St., Philadelphia, 12/04/86, C, 86003319

Princeton Club, 1221–1223 Locust St., Philadelphia, 12/04/80, A, C, 80003617

Protestant Episcopal Church of the Saviour, Ludlow St. and 3723-3725 Chestnut St, Philadelphia, 8/01/79, A, C, a, 79002328

Race Street Friends Meetinghouse, 1515 Cherry St., Philadelphia, 11/04/93, A, B, a, NHL, 93001610

Rafsnyder-Welsh House, 1923 Spruce St., Philadelphia, 2/14/80, C, 80003618

Ralston, Robert, School [Philadelphia Public Schools TR], 221 Bainbridge St., Philadelphia, 12/04/86, C, 86003321

Ramcat Historic District, Roughly bounded by Market, Twenty-third, and Bainbridge Sts., and RR yards, Philadelphia, 1/08/86, A, C, 86000055

Ramsey, J. Sylvester, School [Philadelphia Public Schools TR], Pine and Quince Sts., Philadelphia, 12/01/86, C, 86003322

Randolph House, East Fairmount Park, Philadelphia, 3/24/72, C, 72001169

Read, Thomas Buchanan, School [Philadelphia Public Schools TR], Seventy-eighth and Buist Ave., Philadelphia, 12/04/86, C, 86003325

Reading Company Grain Elevator, 411 N. 20th St., Philadelphia, 3/10/82, A, C, 82003813

Reading Terminal and Trainshed, 1115–1141 Market St., Philadelphia, 6/30/72, A, C, NHL, 72001170

Regent-Rennoc Court, 5100 blk. Regent St. & 1311–1327 S. 52nd St., Philadelphia, 9/12/85, C, 85002292

Reynolds, Gen. John F., School [Philadelphia Public Schools TR], 2300 Jefferson St., Philadelphia, 11/18/88, C, 88002315

Reynolds-Morris House, 225 S. 8th St., Philadelphia, 12/24/67, C, NHL, 67000020

Richmond School [Philadelphia Public Schools TR], 2942 Belgrade St., Philadelphia, 11/18/88, C, 88002316

Ridge Avenue Bridge in Philadelphia [Highway Bridges Owned by the Commonwealth of Pennsylvania, Department of Transportation TR], Ridge Ave. over Wissahickon Creek, Philadelphia, 6/22/88, C, 88000852

Ridge Avenue Farmers' Market, 1810 Ridge Ave., Philadelphia, 3/05/84, A, C, 84003547

Ringgold Place, 1900 block Waverly St., Philadelphia, 8/29/78, C, 78002453

Rittenhouse Historic District, Roughly bounded by Waverly, 15th, Sanson, Ludlow, 23rd and 25th Sts., Philadelphia, 8/25/83, A, C, 83002277

Rittenhouse Square [Four Public Squares of Philadelphia TR], Rittenhouse Sq. and 18th St., Philadelphia, 9/14/81, A, C, 81000557

RittenhouseTown Historic District, 206–210 Lincoln Dr., Philadelphia, 4/27/92, A, B, c, NHL, 92001878

Roberts-Quay House, 1035–1037 Spruce St., Philadelphia, 11/13/76, B, C, 76001668

Roosevelt, Theodore, Junior High School [Philadelphia Public Schools TR], 430 E. Washington Ln., Philadelphia, 11/18/88, A, C, 88002317

Rowen, William, School [Philadelphia Public Schools TR], 6801 N. 19th St., Philadelphia, 11/18/88, C, 88002318

Royal Theater, 1524–1534 South St., Philadelphia, 2/08/80, A, C, 80003619

Ruan, John, House, 4278–4280 Griscom St., Philadelphia, 10/31/85, C, 85003410

Ryerss Mansion, Central and Cottman Aves., Philadelphia, 11/21/76, B, C, 76001669

Sansom Row, 3402–3436 Sansom St., Philadelphia, 12/27/77, C, 77001190

Schaeffer, Charles, School [Philadelphia Public Schools TR], Germantown Ave. and Abbottsford Rd., Philadelphia, 12/04/86, C, a, 86003327

Scherer, Frank C., Wagon Works, 801 N. Twenty-seventh St., Philadelphia, 12/26/85, A, B, 85003160

Second Bank of the United States, 420 Chestnut St., Philadelphia, 5/04/87, A, C, NHL, NPS, 87001293

Seymour, Edward B., House, 260 W. Johnson St., Philadelphia, 11/05/87, C, 87001945

Sharpless, William C., House, 5446 Wayne Ave., Philadelphia, 12/29/83, A, C, 83004249

Sharswood, George, School [Philadelphia Public Schools TR], 200 Wolf St., Philadelphia, 11/18/88, C, 88002320

Shaw, Anna Howard, Junior High School [Philadelphia Public Schools TR], 5401 Warrington St., Philadelphia, 11/18/88, A, C, 88002321

Shedwick, John, Development Houses, 3433-3439 Lancaster Ave., Philadelphia, 3/10/82, C, 82003814

Sheridan, Philip H., School [Philadelphia Public Schools TR], 800–818 E. Ontario St., Philadelphia, 11/18/88, C, 88002322

Shoemaker, William, Junior High School [Philadelphia Public Schools TR], 1464–1488 N. Fifty-third St., Philadelphia, 12/04/86, C, 86003328

Smedley, Franklin, School [Philadelphia Public Schools TR], 5199 Mulberry St., Philadelphia, 11/18/88, C, 88002323

Smith, Walter George, School [Philadelphia Public Schools TR], 1300 S. Fourteenth St., Philadelphia, 12/04/86, C, 86003329

Snellenburg's Clothing Factory, 642 N. Broad St., Philadelphia, 9/02/86, A, C, 86001842

Society Hill Historic District, Bounded on the N by Walnut St., on the S by Lombard St., on the E by pier line of Delaware River, and on the W by 8th, Philadelphia, 6/23/71, C, a, g, NPS, 71000065

Solomon House, 130–132 S. 17th St., Philadelphia, 8/24/78, C, 78002454

South Front Street Historic District, 700–712 S. Front St., W side Bainbridge St. to Kenilworth St., Philadelphia, 4/25/72, C, 72001171

South, George W., Memorial Protestant Episcopal Church of the Advocate, 18th and Diamond Sts., Philadelphia, 2/08/80, A, C, a, 80003620

Southwark District, Bounded by Delaware, Washington Aves., 5th, Lombard, Front, and Catherine Sts., Philadelphia, 5/19/72, C, 72001172

Southwark School [Philadelphia Public Schools TR], Eighth and Miflin Sts., Philadelphia, 12/01/86, C, 86003330

Special Troops Armory [Pennsylvania National Guard Armories MPS], 5350 Ogontz Ave., Philadelphia, 11/14/91, A, C, 91001702

Spring Garden District, Roughly bounded by Fairmount Ave., 15th, 24th, Mt. Vernon and Spring Garden Sts., Philadelphia, 12/21/78, C, 78002455

Spring Garden District (Boundary Increase), Roughly bounded by Fairmount, Mt. Vernon, 15th and 19th Sts., Philadelphia, 9/12/83, A, C, 83002279

Spring Garden School No. 1 [Philadelphia Public Schools TR], Twelfth and Ogden Sts., Philadelphia, 12/04/86, C, 86003332

Spring Garden School No. 2 [Philadelphia Public Schools TR], Melon St. S of Twelfth St., Philadelphia, 12/04/86, C, 86003333

St. Anthony de Padua Parish School, 2317–2333 Carpenter St., Philadelphia, 5/07/92, A, C, a, 92000400

St. Augustine's Catholic Church, 4th and New Sts., Philadelphia, 6/15/76, A, C, a, 76001670

St. Clement's Protestant Episcopal Church, SW corner of 20th and Cherry Sts., Philadelphia, 11/20/70, A, C, a, 70000555

St. George's Methodist Church, 324 New St., Philadelphia, 5/27/71, A, C, a, NPS, 71000064

St. James Hotel, 1226–1232 Walnut St., Philadelphia, 11/13/76, C, 76001671

St. John's Church, 220–230 Brown St., Philadelphia, 2/24/83, C, a, 83002278

St. Mark's Episcopal Church, 1607–27 Locust St., Philadelphia, 4/19/82, C, a, NHL, 82003815

St. Peter's Episcopal Church of Germantown, 6000 Wayne Ave., Philadelphia, 9/05/85, C, a, 85001960

St. Stephen's Episcopal Church, 19 S. 10th St., Philadelphia, 6/04/79, C, a, 79002329

Stanton, Edwin M., School [Philadelphia Public Schools TR], 1616–1644 Christian St., Philadelphia, 11/18/88, C, 88002326

Stenton, 18th and Courtland Sts., Philadelphia, 10/15/66, B, C, NHL, 66000690

Stevens, Thaddeus, School of Observation [Philadelphia Public Schools TR], 1301 Spring St., Philadelphia, 12/04/86, A, 86003335

Stewart, John, Houses, 1020–1028 Spruce St., Philadelphia, 11/20/79, C, 79002330

Stokely, William J., School [Philadelphia Public Schools TR], 1844–1860 N. Thirty-second St., Philadelphia, 12/04/86, C, a, 86003336

Strickland, William, Row, 215–227 S. 9th St., Philadelphia, 9/14/77, B, C, 77001192

Suburban Station Building, 1617 John F. Kennedy Blvd., Philadelphia, 9/05/85, A, C, 85001962

Sullivan, James J., School [Philadelphia Public Schools TR], 5300 Ditman St., Philadelphia, 11/18/88, C, 88002327

Sully, Thomas, Residence, 530 Spruce St., Philadelphia, 10/15/66, B, NHL, 66000691

Sulzberger, Mayer, Junior High School [Philadelphia Public Schools TR], 701–741 N. 48th St., Philadelphia, 11/18/88, A, C, 88002328

Philadelphia County—Continued

Sun Oil Building, 1608-1610 Walnut St., Philadelphia, 8/25/83, A, C, 83002280

Tacony Music Hall, 4815–19 Longshore Ave., Philadelphia, 3/09/90, A, 90000413

Tanner, Henry O., House, 2908 W. Diamond St., Philadelphia, 5/11/76, B, NHL, 76001672

Taylor, Bayard, School [Philadelphia Public Schools TR], 3614–3630 N. Randolph St., Philadelphia, 11/18/88, C, 88002329

Thaddeus Kosciuszko National Memorial, 301 Pine St., Philadelphia, 12/18/70, B, C, NPS, 70000068

Thirtieth Street Station, W. River Dr., Market, 30th, and Arch Sts., Philadelphia, 6/07/78, C, g, 78002456

Thirty-third Street Bridge in Philadelphia [Highway Bridges Owned by the Commonwealth of Pennsylvania, Department of Transportation TR], Thirty-third St. over Master St., Philadelphia, 6/22/88, C, 88000847

Thomas Mill Covered Bridge [Covered Bridges of the Delaware River Watershed TR], Thomas Mill Rd., Philadelphia, 12/01/80, A, C, 80003621

Thomas, George C., Junior High School [Philadelphia Public Schools TR], 2746 S. 9th St., Philadelphia, 11/18/88, C, 88002330

Tilden, William J., Junior High School [Philadelphia Public Schools TR], Sixty-sixth St. and Elmwood Ave., Philadelphia, 12/01/86, C, 86003337

Touraine, The, 1520 Spruce St., Philadelphia, 4/07/82, C, 82003816

Tulpehocken Station Historic District, Roughly bounded by McCallum St., W. Walnut Ln., Penn Central RR tracks, and W. Tulpehocken, Philadelphia, 11/26/85, A, C, 85003564

U.S. Naval Home, Gray's Ferry Ave. at 24th St., Philadelphia, 8/21/72, A, C, NHL, 72001173

U.S.S. OLYMPIA, Pier 40, at foot of Chestnut St., Philadelphia, 10/15/66, A, NHL, 66000692

US Court House and Post Office Building, Jct. of Ninth and Markets Sts., Philadelphia, 10/19/90, C, 90001540

USS BECUNA (SS-319), Penn's Landing, Delaware Ave. & Spruce St., Philadelphia, 8/29/78, A, B, C, g, NHL, 78002458

Union League of Philadelphia, 140 S. Broad St., Philadelphia, 6/22/79, A, C, 79002331

Union Methodist Episcopal Church, 2019 W. Diamond St., Philadelphia, 10/15/80, B, C, a, 80003622

University of Pennsylvania Campus Historic District, Roughly bounded by Hamilton Walk, South, 32nd, Walnut, 36th, Spruce, and 39th Sts., Philadelphia, 12/28/78, A, C, 78002457

Upsala, 6430 Germantown Ave., Philadelphia, 1/13/72, C, 72001174

Uptown Theater and Office Building, 2240-2248 N. Broad St., Philadelphia, 7/22/82, A, C, 82003817

Vare, Abigail, School [Philadelphia Public Schools TR], Morris St. and Moyamensing Ave., Philadelphia, 12/04/86, C, 86003339

Vare, Edwin H., Junior High School [Philadelphia Public Schools TR], 2102 S. 24th St., Philadelphia, 11/18/88, A, C, 88002331

Vaux, Roberts, Junior High School [Philadelphia Public Schools TR], 230–2344 W. Master St., Philadelphia, 11/18/88, C, 88002332

WCAU Studios, 1618-22 Chestnut St., Philadelphia, 1/27/83, A, C, 83002281

WFIL Studio, 4548 Market St., Philadelphia, 7/28/86, A, g, 86002092

Wagner Free Institute of Science, 17th St. and Montgomery Ave., Philadelphia, 5/17/89, A, B, C, NHL, 89000361

Wagner, Gen. Louis, Junior High School [Philadelphia Public Schools TR], Seventeenth and Chelton Sts., Philadelphia, 12/04/86, C, 86003340

Walnut Street Theatre, 9th and Walnut Sts., Philadelphia, 10/15/66, A, NHL, 66000693

Walnut-Chancellor Historic District, 21st., Walnut and Chancellor Sts., Philadelphia, 12/01/80, C, 80003605

Walton, Rudolph, School [Philadelphia Public Schools TR], 2601–2631 N. Twenty-eighth St., Philadelphia, 12/04/86, C, 86003341

Wanamaker, John, Store, Juniper and Market Sts., Philadelphia, 6/02/78, A, B, NHL, 78002459

Warwick, The, 1701 Locust St., Philadelphia, 8/10/78, A, C, 78002460

Washington Avenue Historic District, Roughly bounded by Carpenter, Washington, 10th, and Broad Sts., Philadelphia, 9/07/84, A, C, 84003561

Washington Square [Four Public Squares of Philadelphia TR], Locust and 6th Sts., Philadelphia, 9/14/81, A, C, 81000558

Washington Square West Historic District, Roughly bounded by 8th, Locust, Broad, and Lombard Sts., Philadelphia, 9/20/84, C, 84003563

Washington, George, School [Philadelphia Public Schools TR], Fifth and Federal Sts., Philadelphia, 12/04/86, C, 86003343

Watson, Sally, House, 5128 Wayne Ave., Philadelphia, 3/10/82, C, 82003818

Wayne, Anthony, School [Philadelphia Public Schools TR], 2700 Morris St., Philadelphia, 12/01/86, C, 86003344

Wesley AME Zion Church, 1500 Lombard St., Philadelphia, 12/01/78, A, C, a, g, 78002461

Wesley Building, 1701-1709 Arch St., Philadelphia, 5/10/84, A, C, a, 84003581

West Diamond Street Townhouse Historic District, 3008–3146, 3011–3215 Diamond St., Philadelphia, 2/21/91, C, 91000097

West Philadelphia High School [Philadelphia Public Schools TR], 4700 Walnut St., Philadelphia, 12/04/86, A, C, 86003345

Whittier, John Greenleaf, School [Philadelphia Public Schools TR], 2600 Clearfield St., Philadelphia, 11/18/88, C, 88002334

Widow Maloby's Tavern, 700 S. Front St., Philadelphia, 3/16/72, C, 72001175

Willard, Francis E., School [Philadelphia Public Schools TR], Emerald and Orleans Sts., Philadelphia, 12/04/86, C, 86003346

Wills Hospital, 1601 Spring Garden St., Philadelphia, 7/12/84, A, C, 84003582

Wilmot, David, School [Philadelphia Public Schools TR], 1734 Meadow St., Phildelphia, 11/18/88, A, 88002289

Wilson, Woodrow, Junior High School [Philadelphia Public Schools TR], Cottman Ave. and Loretta St., Philadelphia, 12/04/86, C, 86003347

Wissahickon, Schuyler & Queen Sts., Philadelphia, 11/25/83, A, C, 83004257

Wissahickon Inn, 500 W. Willow Grove Ave., Philadelphia, 12/06/79, C, 79002333

Wissahickon Memorial Bridge [Highway Bridges Owned by the Commonwealth of Pennsylvania, Department of Transportation TR], Henry Ave. over Wissahickon Dr., Philadelphia, 6/22/88, C, 88000807

Wister, Mary Channing, School [Philadelphia Public Schools TR], 843–855 N. 8th St., Philadelphia, 11/18/88, C, 88002333

Witherspoon Building, 1319–1323 Walnut St., Philadelphia, 9/18/78, A, C, a, 78002462

Wolf, George, School [Philadelphia Public Schools TR], 8100 Lyons Ave., Philadelphia, 11/18/88, C, 88002243

Woodford, East Fairmount Park, Philadelphia, 12/24/67, C, NHL, 67000021

Woodland Terrace, 501–519, 500–520 Woodland Ter., Philadelphia, 3/16/72, C, 72001176

Woodlands, The, 40th St. and Woodland Ave., Philadelphia, 12/24/67, C, NHL, 67000022

Wright, Richardson L., School [Philadelphia Public Schools TR], 1101 Venango St., Philadelphia, 12/04/86, C, 86003348

Wyck House, 6026 Germantown Ave., Philadelphia, 10/26/71, C, NHL, 71000736

YMCA of Germantown, 5722 Greene St., Philadelphia, 11/14/91, A, C, 91001709

Young Men's Christian Association, 115 N. 15th St., Philadelphia, 12/02/80, A, C, 80003624

Young, Smyth, Field Company Building, 1216–1220 Arch St., Philadelphia, 12/24/92, C, 92001720

Pike County

Brodhead Farm, NE of Bushkill on U.S. 209, Bushkill vicinity, 7/23/79, A, C, NPS, 79000242

Callahan House, U.S. 29, Milford, 7/23/79, A, C, NPS, 79000244

D & H Canal Co. Office [Upper Delaware Valley, New York and Pennsylvania, MPS], Scenic Dr., NW side, Lackawaxen Township, Lackawaxen, 8/09/93, A, C, 93000715

Delaware Aqueduct, Between Minisink Ford, NY and Lackawaxen, PA, Lackawaxen, 11/24/68, C, NPS, 68000055

Dingman's Ferry Dutch Reformed Church, U.S. 209, Dingman's Ferry, 7/23/79, A, C, a, NPS, 79000241

Forester's Hall, Broad and Hartford Sts., Milford, 7/14/83, A, C, 83002282

Gordon, Jervis, Grist Mill Historic District, Water, Mill, and Seventh Sts., Milford, 12/26/85, A, C, 85003163

Pike County—Continued

Grey, Zane, House, Roebling Rd., Lackawaxen vicinity, 5/06/83, B, NPS, 83002283

Hotel Fauchere and Annex, 401 and 403 Broad St., Milford, 8/29/80, A, C, 80003626

Lord House, PA 739, Lords Valley, 6/30/80, A, 80003625

Mill Rift Hall [Upper Delaware Valley, New York and Pennsylvania, MPS], Bluestone Blvd., Westfall Township, Mill Rift, 8/09/93, A, 93000714

Minisink Archeological Site, Address Restricted, Bushkill vicinity, 4/19/93, D, NHL, NPS, 93000608

Nearpass House [Upper Delaware Valley, New York and Pennsylvania, MPS], Cemetery Rd., Westfall Township, Mill Rift, 8/19/93, A, C, 93000849

Nyce Farm, NW of Bushkill on U.S. 209, Bushkill vicinity, 7/23/79, A, C, NPS, 79000240

Peters House, U.S. 209, Bushkill, 8/24/79, A, C, NPS, 79000239

Pike County Courthouse, Broad and High Sts., Milford, 7/23/79, A, C, 79002340

Pinchot, Gifford, House, W edge of Milford, Milford, 10/15/66, B, NHL, 66000694

Pond Eddy Bridge [Highway Bridges Owned by the Commonwealth of Pennsylvania, Department of Transportation TR], LR 51013 over Delaware River, Pond Eddy vicinity, 11/14/88, C, 88002170

Promised Land State Park Whittaker Lodge District [Emergency Conservation Work (ECW) Architecture in Pennsylvania State Parks: 1933-1942, TR], 10 mi. N of Canadensis on PA 390, Canadensis vicinity, 2/11/87, A, C, 87000047

Promised Land State Park—Bear Wallow Cabins [Emergency Conservation Work (ECW) Architecture in Pennsylvania State Parks: 1933-1942, TR], 10 mi. N of Canadensis on PA 390, Canadensis vicinity, 2/11/87, A, C, g, 87000048

Shanna House, U.S. 209, Dingman Township, 1/08/85, A, NPS, 85000075

Turn Store and the Tinsmith's Shop, U.S. 209, Bushkill, 9/18/78, A, NPS, 78000260

Zimmerman, Marie, Farm, SW of Milford on U.S. 209, Milford vicinity, 11/01/79, C, NPS, 79000243

Potter County

Austin Dam, PA 872, Austin, 1/15/87, A, 86003570

Cherry Springs Picnic Pavilion [Emergency Conservation Work (ECW) Architecture in Pennsylvania State Parks: 1933-1942, TR], 8 mi. N of Carter Camp off PA 44, West Branch Township, 5/11/87, A, C, g, 87000052

Coudersport Historic District, Roughly bounded by Seventh, East, Water and Main Sts., Coudersport, 5/09/85, A, C, 85000997

Coudersport and Port Allegany Railroad Station, 201 S. West St., Coudersport, 11/21/76, A, C, 76001673

Potter County Courthouse, E. 2nd St., Coudersport, 2/24/75, A, C, 75001664

Schuylkill County

Anthracite Bank Building, 133 W. Broad St., Tamaqua, 9/13/78, A, C, 78002469

Cloud Home, 351 S. 2nd St., Pottsville, 5/22/78, C, 78002465

Mt. Pleasant Historic District, TR 881 & SR 901, Mt. Pleasant, 1/07/88, A, C, 87002211

New Ringgold Gristmill, SR 53062, New Ringgold, 12/18/78, A, C, 78002464

Nutting Hall, 205 S. Tulpehocken St., Pine Grove, 7/23/80, B, C, 80003627

O'Hara, John, House, 606 Mahantongo St., Pottsville, 5/22/78, B, 78002466

Ormrod, George, House, 218 W. Broad St., Tamaqua, 6/14/77, C, 77001193

Pine Grove Historic District, S. Tulpehocken & Mill Sts., & Swatara Creek, Pine Grove, 12/31/87, A, C, 87002210

Pottsville Armory [Pennsylvania National Guard Armories MPS], 502 N. Centre St., Pottsville, 11/14/91, A, C, 91001701

Pottsville Downtown Historic District, Roughly bounded by Laurel Blvd., Railroad, Morris and 4th Sts., Pottsville, 3/01/82, A, C, 82003819

Reading Railroad Passenger Station—Tamaqua, Off W. Broad St., Tamaqua, 12/26/85, A, C, 85003164

Schuylkill County Bridge No. 114, E of Rock off PA 895, Rock vicinity, 1/03/78, A, 78002467

Schuylkill County Bridge No. 113, W of Rock off PA 895, Rock vicinity, 1/03/78, A, 78002468

Swatara Furnace [Iron and Steel Resources in Pennsylvania MPS], Old Forge Rd. E of Lebanon Reservoir, Pine Grove Township, Suedberg vicinity, 9/06/91, A, C, 91001140

Yuengling, D. G., and Son Brewing Complex, 5th and Mahantongo Sts., Pottsville, 2/01/85, A, g, 85000180

Yuengling, Frank D., Mansion, 1440 Mahantongo St., Pottsville, 4/18/79, C, 79002342

Snyder County

Aline Covered Bridge [Covered Bridges of Juniata and Synder Counties TR], NW of Meiserville, Chapman/Perry Townships, Meiserville, 8/10/79, A, 79002344

Bridge between Monroe and Penn Townships [Highway Bridges Owned by the Commonwealth of Pennsylvania, Department of Transportation TR], LR 54013 over Penn's Creek, Selinsgrove vicinity, 6/22/88, C, 88000811

Dreese's Covered Bridge [Covered Bridges of Juniata and Synder Counties TR], Spans Middle Creek, Beaver Township, Beavertown vicinity, 8/10/79, A, 79002343

Gross Bridge [Covered Bridges of Juniata and Synder Counties TR (AD)], 3 mi. W of Beaver-town on SR 574, Spring Township, Beavertown vicinity, 8/29/77, A, C, 77001194

Selinsgrove Hall and Seibert Hall, Pine St., Selinsgrove, 10/25/79, A, a, 79002345

Snyder, Gov. Simon, Mansion, 119–121 N. Market St., Selinsgrove, 8/25/78, B, C, 78002470

Somerset County

Barronvale Bridge [Covered Bridges of Somerset County TR], W of Somerset off LR 55118, Middlecreek Township, Somerset vicinity, 12/11/80, A, C, 80003633

Beechdale Bridge [Covered Bridges of Somerset County TR], SW of Berlin off US 219, Brothersvalley Township, Berlin vicinity, 12/10/80, A, C, 80003628

Bollman, W., and Company Bridge, 1.5 mi. (2.4 km) N of Myersdale on U.S. 219, Meyersdale vicinity, 11/08/78, A, 78002471

Bridge in Jenner Township [Highway Bridges Owned by the Commonwealth of Pennsylvania, Department of Transportation TR], LR 55125 over Roaring Run, Pilltown, 6/22/88, C, 88000853

Glessner Bridge [Covered Bridges of Somerset County TR], NW of Shanksville off LR, 55068, Stonycreek Township, Shanksville vicinity, 12/10/80, A, C, 80003631

King's Bridge [Covered Bridges of Somerset County TR], W of Somerset off PA 653, Middlecreek Township, Somerset vicinity, 12/11/80, A, C, 80003632

Kooser State Park Family Cabin District [Emergency Conservation Work (ECW) Architecture in Pennsylvania State Parks: 1933-1942, TR], 10 mi. N of PA Turnpike Exit 10 on PA 31, Jefferson vicinity, 2/12/87, A, C, g, 87000111

Laurel Hill RDA [Emergency Conservation Work (ECW) Architecture in Pennsylvania State Parks: 1933-1942, TR], 4 mi. W of New Centerville and PA 281, Somerset, 5/18/87, A, C, g, 87000738

Lower Humbert Bridge [Covered Bridges of Somerset County TR], N of Ursina off LR 55030, Lower Turkeyfoot Township, Ursina vicinity, 12/10/80, A, C, 80003638

Miller's Store, Jct. of PA 3029 and PA 3033, Middlecreek Township, Trent, 7/24/92, A, C, 92000948

New Baltimore Bridge [Covered Bridges of Somerset County TR], Off LR 55051, Allegheny Township, New Baltimore, 12/10/80, A, C, 80003630

Packsaddle Bridge [Covered Bridges of Somerset County TR], SW of Glen Savage off LR 55005, Fairhope Township, Glen Savage vicinity, 12/10/80, A, C, 80003629

Petersburg Tollhouse, Off U.S. 40, Addison, 3/20/79, A, C, 79002346

Shaffer's Bridge [Covered Bridges of Somerset County TR], W of Tire Hill on T 634, Conemaugh Township, Tire Hill vicinity, 12/10/80, A, C, 80003637

Somerset County—Continued

Somerset County Courthouse, E. Union St. and N. Center Ave., Somerset, 6/27/80, C, 80003634

Trostletown Bridge [Covered Bridges of Somerset County TR], SE of Stoystown off US 30, Quemahonig Township, Stoystown vicinity, 12/11/80, A, C, 80003636

Walter's Mill Bridge [Covered Bridges of Somerset County TR], N of Somerset off PA 985, Somerset Township, Somerset vicinity, 12/10/80, A, C, b, 80003635

Windber Historic District, Roughly bounded by the borough line, Cambria Ave., 28th St. and the Big Paint Cr., Windber, 11/14/91, A, C, 91001705

Sullivan County

Forksville Covered Bridge [Covered Bridges of Bradford, Sullivan and Lycoming Counties TR], LR 56007 spur, Forks Township, Forksville, 7/24/80, A, 80003639

Hillsgrove Covered Bridge [Covered Bridges of Bradford, Sullivan and Lycoming Counties TR (AD)], 3 mi. E of Hillsgrove off PA 87 over Loyalsock Creek, Hillsgrove vicinity, 7/02/73, A, 73001666

Ricketts, Clemuel, Mansion, Off PA 487, Lopez vicinity, 6/09/83, A, C, 83002284

Sonestown Covered Bridge [Covered Bridges of Bradford, Sullivan and Lycoming Counties TR], S of Sonestown on T 310, Davidson Township, Sonestown, 7/24/80, A, 80003640

Sullivan County Courthouse, Main and Muncy Sts., Laporte, 12/15/78, C, 78002472

Worlds End State Park Family Cabin District [Emergency Conservation Work (ECW) Architecture in Pennsylvania State Parks: 1933-1942, TR], 2 mi. SE of Forksville on PA 154, Forksville vicinity, 5/18/87, A, C, g, 87000742

Susquehanna County

Bridge in Gibson Borough [Highway Bridges Owned by the Commonwealth of Pennsylvania, Department of Transportation TR], LR 57045 over Tunkhannock Creek, South Gibson vicinity, 6/22/88, C, 88000839

Erie Railroad Station, S bank of Susquehanna River, Susquehanna, 6/19/72, A, C, 72001177

Mulford, Sylvanus, House, 65 Church St., Montrose, 5/22/78, C, 78002473

Silver Lake Bank, 75 Church St., Montrose, 3/07/75, A, C, 75001666

Starrucca Viaduct, SR 57058 over Starrucca Creek, Lanesboro, 10/29/75, C, 75001665

Tioga County

Colton Point State Park [Emergency Conservation Work (ECW) Architecture in Pennsylvania

State Parks: 1933-1942, TR], 5 mi. S of US 6 at Ansonia, Ansonia vicinity, 2/12/87, A, C, g, 87000112

Ford, James, House, Cowanesque St., Lawrenceville, 12/06/75, B, C, 75001667

Mansfield Armory [Pennsylvania National Guard Armories MPS], Smythe Park, Mansfield, 5/09/91, A, C, 91000515

Robinson House, 120 Main St., Wellsboro, 8/03/77, A, C, 77001196

Robinson, Jesse, House, 141 Main St., Wellsboro, 2/21/91, C, 91000089

Ryon, Judge John, House, Main St., Lawrenceville, 12/16/77, C, 77001195

Wellsboro Armory [Pennsylvania National Guard Armories MPS], 2 Central Ave., Wellsboro, 5/09/91, A, C, 91000521

Union County

Buffalo Presbyterian Church, W of Lewisburg on PA 192, Lewisburg vicinity, 1/30/76, C, a, 76001675

Chamberlin Iron Front Building, 434 Market St., Lewisburg, 5/14/79, A, C, 79002347

Factory Bridge [Union County Covered Bridges TR], 1 mi. W of White Deer on T 629, White Deer Township, White Deer vicinity, 2/08/80, A, 80003645

Griffey, Benjamin, House, W of Allenwood on PA 44, Allenwood vicinity, 9/13/78, C, 78002474

Halfway Lake Dam [Emergency Conservation Work (ECW) Architecture in Pennsylvania State Parks: 1933-1942, TR], 16 mi. W of Lewisburg on PA 191, Lewisburg vicinity, 5/11/87, A, C, 87000046

Hassenplug Bridge [Union County Covered Bridges TR], N. 4th St., Mifflinburg, 2/08/80, A, 80003641

Hayes Bridge [Union County Covered Bridges TR], W of Mifflinburg on T 376, West Buffalo Township, Mifflinburg vicinity, 2/08/80, A, 80003642

Heiss, William A., House and Buggy Shop, 523 Green St., Mifflinburg, 8/06/79, A, 79002348

Lewisburg Armory [Pennsylvania National Guard Armories MPS], US 15 S of jct. with PA 45, East Buffalo Township, Lewisburg vicinity, 11/14/91, A, C, 91001700

Mifflinburg Historic District, PA 45, Mifflinburg, 4/10/80, A, C, 80003643

Millmont Red Bridge [Union County Covered Bridges TR], SW of Millmont on LR 59005, Hartley Township, Millmont vicinity, 2/08/80, A, 80003644

New Berlin Presbyterian Church, Vine and High Sts., New Berlin, 10/26/72, C, a, 72001178

Old Union County Courthouse, Market and Vine Sts., New Berlin, 11/09/72, A, 72001179

Packwood House-American Hotel, 10 Market St., Lewisburg, 9/20/78, A, C, 78002475

Reading Railroad Freight Station, Jct. of S. Fifth and St. Louis Sts., Lewisburg, 1/22/92, A, C, 91002012

Slifer House, N of Lewisburg off U.S. 15 on SR 59024, Lewisburg vicinity, 6/18/75, B, C, 75001668

Venango County

Allegheny Baptist Church, PA 27 and Main St., Pleasantville, 12/15/78, A, C, a, 78002478

Bridge in Cherrytree Township [Highway Bridges Owned by the Commonwealth of Pennsylvania, Department of Transportation TR], LR 60052 over Oil Creek, Titusville vicinity, 6/22/88, C, 88000809

Bridge in Clinton Township [Highway Bridges Owned by the Commonwealth of Pennsylvania, Department of Transportation TR], LR 60010 over Scrubgrass Creek, Kennerdell vicinity, 6/22/88, C, 88000808

Dale, Samuel F., House, 1409 Elk St., Franklin, 12/04/75, B, C, 75001670

Drake Oil Well, 3 mi. SE of Titusville on PA 36, in Drake Well Memorial Park, Titusville vicinity, 11/13/66, A, e, NHL, 66000695

Franklin Historic District, Roughly bounded by Miller Ave., Otter, 8th, Buffalo, and 16th Sts., Franklin, 1/26/84, A, C, 84003583

Indian God Rock Petroglyphs Site (36VE26), Address Restricted, Rockland Township vicinity, 5/14/84, C, D, 84003585

National Transit Building, 206 Seneca St., Oil City, 9/13/78, A, C, 78002477

Oil City Armory [Pennsylvania National Guard Armories MPS], Jct. of E. 2nd St. and State St., Oil City, 5/09/91, A, C, 91000517

Pithole City, Site of, 10 mi. SE of Titusville, Titusville vicinity, 3/20/73, A, 73001667

Pithole Stone Arch [Highway Bridges Owned by the Commonwealth of Pennsylvania, Department of Transportation TR], LR 60046 over Pithole Creek, Oleopolis vicinity, 6/22/88, C, 88000869

Rockland Furnace [Iron and Steel Resources in Pennsylvania MPS], On Shull Run N of the Allegheny R., NW of Emlenton, Emlenton vicinity, 9/06/91, A, C, 91001139

U.S. Post Office, 270 Seneca St., Oil City, 9/15/77, C, 77001197

Witherup Bridge [Highway Bridges Owned by the Commonwealth of Pennsylvania, Department of Transportation TR], LR 60007 over Scrubgrass Creek, Kennerdell vicinity, 6/22/88, C, 88000800

Warren County

Hazeltine, A. J., House, 710 Pennsylvania Ave., W., Warren, 11/21/76, B, C, 76001677

Irvine United Presbyterian Church, Off U.S. 6, Irvine, 8/27/76, C, a, 76001676

Irvine, Guy C., House, 1.5 mi. S of Russell on U.S. 62, Russell vicinity, 9/13/78, C, 78002479

Jefferson, John P., House, 119 Market St., Warren, 5/09/85, C, 85000996

Warren County—Continued

Struthers Library Building, 3rd Ave. and Liberty St., Warren, 10/10/75, A, C, 75001671

Warren Armory [Pennsylvania National Guard Armories MPS], 330 Hickory St., Warren, 5/09/91, A, C, 91000519

Warren County Courthouse, Market St. and 4th Ave., Warren, 4/18/77, C, 77001198

Wetmore House, 210 4th Ave., Warren, 4/28/75, C, 75001672

Washington County

"S" Bridge, 6 mi. W of Washington on U.S. 40, Washington vicinity, 4/04/75, A, C, 75001676

Acheson, Edward G., House, 908 Main St., Monongahela, 5/11/76, B, NHL, 76001679

Administration Building, Washington and Jefferson College, Washington and Jefferson College campus, Canonsburg, 8/16/77, C, 77001199

Bailey Covered Bridge [Covered Bridges of Washington and Greene Counties TR], Spans Ten Mile Creek, Prosperity vicinity, 6/22/79, A, 79002355

Bradford, David, House, 175 S. Main St., Washington, 7/16/73, B, C, NHL, 73001668

Brownlee, Samuel, House, N of Eighty-Four on PA 519, Eighty-Four vicinity, 11/07/76, C, 76001678

Brownlee, Scott, Covered Bridge [Covered Bridges of Washington and Greene Counties TR], Off PA 231, West Finley vicinity, 6/22/79, A, 79002360

Canonsburg Armory [Pennsylvania National Guard Armories MPS], W. College St. and N. Central Ave., Canonsburg, 12/22/89, A, C, 89002070

Charleroi—Monessen Bridge [Highway Bridges Owned by the Commonwealth of Pennsylvania, Department of Transportation TR], LR 247 over Monongahela River, Charleroi, 6/22/88, C, 88000812

Crawford Covered Bridge [Covered Bridges of Washington and Greene Counties TR], Spanning Robinson Fork Creek, West Finley vicinity, 6/22/79, A, 79002361

Danley Covered Bridge [Covered Bridges of Washington and Greene Counties TR], Spanning Robinson Fork Creek, West Finley vicinity, 6/22/79, A, 79002362

Davis, Horn, Overholtzer Bridge [Covered Bridges of Washington and Greene Counties TR], SE of Fairfield, North Fredericktown vicinity, 6/22/79, A, 79002354

Day Covered Bridge [Covered Bridges of Washington and Greene Counties TR], Spans Short Creek, Prosperity vicinity, 6/22/79, A, 79002356

Derrow, Margaret, House, W. Main St., Claysville, 11/05/74, C, 74001808

Devil's Den, McClurg Covered Bridge [Covered Bridges of Washington and Greene Counties TR], N of Paris crossing King's Creek, Hanover Township, Paris vicinity, 6/22/79, A, 79003828

Dorsey, Joseph, House, 113 Cherry Ave., West Brownsville, 11/19/74, C, 74001814

Dusmal House, E of Gastonville off Gilmore Rd., Gastonville vicinity, 2/24/75, C, 75001675

East Washington Historic District, Roughly North, East, and Wade Aves., Wheeling, Beau, and Chestnut Sts., East Washington, 11/15/84, C, 84000547

Ebenezer Covered Bridge [Covered Bridges of Washington and Greene Counties TR], W of Ginger Hill crossing South Fork of Maple Creek, Nottingham Township, Ginger Hill vicinity, 6/22/79, A, b, 79003829

Erskine Covered Bridge [Covered Bridges of Washington and Greene Counties TR], Spans Middle Wheeling Creek, West Alexander vicinity, 6/22/79, A, 79002359

Harrison House, Old Rte. 40, Centerville, 12/30/74, C, 74001807

Hawthorne School, Hawthorne and Bluff Sts., Canonsburg, 5/08/86, C, 86001028

Henry Covered Bridge [Covered Bridges of Washington and Greene Counties TR], Spans Mingo Creek, Monongahela vicinity, 6/22/79, A, 79002353

Hill's Tavern, U.S. 40, Scenery Hill, 11/19/74, A, C, 74001811

Huffman Distillery and Chopping Mill [Whiskey Rebellion Resources in Southwestern Pennsylvania MPS], LR 62155, 2 mi. N of jct. with PA 917, Somerset Township, Cokeburg vicinity, 11/12/92, A, C, 92001499

Hughes Covered Bridge [Covered Bridges of Washington and Greene Counties TR], Spans Ten Mile Creek, Prosperity vicinity, 6/22/79, A, 79002357

Jackson's Mill Covered Bridge [Covered Bridges of Washington and Greene Counties TR], NW of Burgettstown crossing Kings Creek, Hanover Township, Burgettstown vicinity, 6/22/79, A, 79003830

Kinder's Mill, LR 62194 at Piper Rd., Deemston, 10/16/86, C, 86002888

Krepps Covered Bridge [Covered Bridges of Washington and Greene Counties TR], SE of Cherry Valley, Midway vicinity, 6/22/79, A, 79002352

Leatherman Covered Bridge [Covered Bridges of Washington and Greene Counties TR], N of Cokeburg, Cokeburg vicinity, 6/22/79, A, 79002351

Lemoyne, Dr. Julius, House, 49 E. Maiden St., Washington, 10/25/73, B, C, 73001669

Longwell, David, House, 711 W. Main St., Monongahela City, 8/02/93, C, 93000718

Lyle Covered Bridge [Covered Bridges of Washington and Greene Counties TR], N of Raccoon crossing Raccoon Creek, Hanover Township, Raccoon vicinity, 6/22/79, A, 79003831

Malden Inn, W of Blainsburg on U.S. 40, Blainsburg vicinity, 1/24/74, C, 74001805

Manchester, Isaac, House, 2 mi. S of Avella on PA 231, Avella vicinity, 6/21/75, A, C, 75001673

Marianna Historic District, Roughly bounded by Ten Mile Creek, Beeson Ave. Hill, 6th, and 7th Sts., Marianna, 11/15/84, A, 84000560

Martin's Mill Covered Bridge [Covered Bridges of Washington and Greene Counties TR], W of Marianna crossing Ten Mile Creek, West Bethlehem Township, Marianna, 6/22/79, A, 79003825

Mauer, Dr. Joseph House, 97 W. Wheeling St., Washington, 12/30/93, C, 93001470

Mays, Blaney Covered Bridge [Covered Bridges of Washington and Greene Counties TR], Spans Middle Wheeling Creek, Claysville vicinity, 6/22/79, A, 79002350

Meadowcroft Rockshelter, W of Avella, Avella vicinity, 11/21/78, D, 78002480

Miller, Longdon L., Covered Bridge [Covered Bridges of Washington and Greene Counties TR], NW of West Finley, West Finley vicinity, 6/22/79, C, 79002363

Mingo Creek Presbyterian Church and Churchyard [Whiskey Rebellion Resources in Southwestern Pennsylvania MPS], Jct. of PA 88 and Mingo Church Rd., Union Township, Courtney vicinity, 11/12/92, A, B, a, d, 92001500

Montgomery House, W. Main St., Claysville, 10/25/74, C, 74001809

Old Main, California State College, California State College campus, California, 5/02/74, C, 74001806

Pennsylvania Railroad Passenger Station, Water and Wood Sts, California, 6/19/79, A, C, 79002349

Pine Bank Covered Bridge [Covered Bridges of Washington and Greene Counties TR], SW of Studa crossing Rouine, Cross Creek Township, Studa vicinity, 6/22/79, A, b, 79003824

Plant's Covered Bridge [Covered Bridges of Washington and Greene Counties TR], Spanning Templeton Fork Creek, West Finley vicinity, 6/22/79, A, 79002364

Ralston Freeman Covered Bridge [Covered Bridges of Washington and Greene Counties TR], N of Paris crossing Aunt Clara'a Fork of King's Creek, Hanover Township, Paris vicinity, 6/22/79, A, 79003827

Regester Log House, N of Fredericktown off PA 88, Fredericktown vicinity, 10/16/74, C, 74001810

Roberts House, 225 N. Central Ave., Canonsburg, 4/10/75, C, 75001674

Sackville House, 309 E. Wheeling St., Washington, 11/21/76, C, 76001680

Sawhill Covered Bridge [Covered Bridges of Washington and Greene Counties TR], PA 221, Taylorstown vicinity, 6/22/79, A, 79002358

Sprowl's Covered Bridge [Covered Bridges of Washington and Greene Counties TR], Off PA 231, West Finley vicinity, 6/22/79, A, 79002365

Taylorstown Historic District, Main St., Taylorstown, 9/05/85, A, C, 85001958

Trinity Hall, 1 mi. S of Washington on PA 18, Washington vicinity, 9/27/76, C, 76001681

US Post Office—Charleroi, 638 Fallowfield Ave., Charleroi, 1/04/90, A, C, 89002287

Ulery Mill, SE of Marianna, Marianna vicinity, 4/20/78, A, 78002481

Washington County—Continued

Washington Armory [Pennsylvania National Guard Armories MPS], 76 W. Maiden St., Washington, 5/09/91, A, C, 91000520

Washington County Courthouse, S. Main St., Washington, 7/30/74, C, 74001812

Washington County Jail, Cherry St., Washington, 7/30/74, C, 74001813

Webster Donora Bridge [Highway Bridges Owned by the Commonwealth of Pennsylvania, Department of Transportation TR], A 143 over Monongahela River, Donora, 6/22/88, C, 88000813

West Alexander Historic District, Roughly bounded by Main, N. Liberty and Mechanic Sts., West Alexander Borough, 3/07/85, A, C, 85000471

West Middletown Historic District, Main St., West Middletown Borough, 8/08/85, A, C, 85001740

Wilson's Mill Covered Bridge [Covered Bridges of Washington and Greene Counties TR], SE of Avella crossing Cross Creek, Cross Creek Township, Avella vicinity, 6/22/79, A, 79003826

Wright, Cerl, Covered Bridge [Covered Bridges of Washington and Greene Counties TR], NW of Bentleyville crossing North Fork of Pigeon Creek, Somerset Township, Bentleyville vicinity, 6/22/79, A, 79003832

Wyit Sprowls Covered Bridge [Covered Bridges of Washington and Greene Counties TR], Spanning Robinson Fork Creek, West Finley vicinity, 6/22/79, A, 79002366

Wayne County

Bridge in Dreher Township [Highway Bridges Owned by the Commonwealth of Pennsylvania, Department of Transportation TR], LR 171 over Haags Mill Creek, Haags Mill, 6/22/88, C, 88000871

Damascus Historic District [Upper Delaware Valley, New York and Pennsylvania, MPS], Roughly, PA 371 from Galilee Rd. to the Delaware R. and adjacent part of Rt. 63027 S of PA 371, Damascus, 8/14/92, A, C, 92001000

Delaware and Hudson Canal, Delaware and Hudson Canal, Honesdale, vicinity, 11/24/68, A, C, NHL, 68000051

Dorflinger, Eugene, Estate, U.S. 6 and Charles St., White Mills, 9/18/78, A, C, 78002483

Hill's Sawmill, S of Equinunk off PA 191, Equinunk vicinity, 11/08/74, A, 74001816

Lacawac, E of Ledgedale, Ledgedale vicinity, 8/09/79, A, C, 79002367

Milanville Historic District [Upper Delaware Valley, New York and Pennsylvania, MPS], Roughly, Rt. 63027 from jct. with Rt. 63029 E to Skinner's Falls Bridge via bridge approach rd., Damascus Township, Milanville, 4/29/93, A, C, 93000352

Millanville—Skinners Falls Bridge [Highway Bridges Owned by the Commonwealth of Pennsylvania, Department of Transportation TR], LR 63027 over Delaware River at Millanville, Millanville, 11/14/88, C, 88002167

Octagon Stone Schoolhouse, 1 mi. SW of South Canaan, South Canaan vicinity, 5/06/77, A, C, 77001200

Wilmot House, Wayne St., Bethany, 2/15/74, B, 74001815

Wilmot Mansion, Wayne and Sugar Sts., Bethany, 1/26/78, B, C, 78003172

Westmoreland County

Bells Mills Covered Bridge, W of Yukon, Yukon vicinity, 6/27/80, A, C, 80003648

Brush Creek Salems Church, SE of Westmoreland City on Brush Creek Rd., Westmoreland City vicinity, 5/11/87, C, a, 87000675

Brush Hill, 651 Brush Hill Rd., Irwin, 10/14/75, B, C, 75001677

Bushy Run Battlefield, 2 mi. E of Harrison City on PA 993, Harrison City vicinity, 10/15/66, A, NHL, 66000696

Byerly House, 115 Menk Rd., New Kensington, 7/18/85, C, 85001567

Fisher, Adam, Homestead, Brinkerton Rd. near jct. with Mt. Pleasant Rd., Mt. Pleasant Township, United, 2/28/91, C, 91000230

Fort Ligonier Site, S. Market St., Ligonier, 1/21/75, A, e, 75001678

Fullerton Inn, 11029 Old Trail Rd., Irwin vicinity, 6/30/83, A, 83002285

Greensburg Railroad Station, Harrison Ave., Greensburg, 11/07/77, A, C, 77001202

Household No. 1 Site (36WM61), Address Restricted, Rostraver Township vicinity, 3/20/86, D, 86000465

Kingston House, U.S. 30, Youngstown vicinity, 6/30/83, A, C, 83002286

Latrobe Armory [Pennsylvania National Guard Armories MPS], 1017 Ridge Ave., Latrobe, 12/22/89, A, C, 89002076

Laurel Hill Furnace, SE of New Florence on Baldwin Run, New Florence vicinity, 4/28/75, A, 75001679

Ligonier Armory [Pennsylvania National Guard Armories MPS], 358 W. Main St., Ligonier, 5/09/91, A, C, 91000514

Linn Run State Park Family Cabin District [Emergency Conservation Work (ECW) Architecture in Pennsylvania State Parks: 1933-1942, TR], 2 mi. SE of Rector on Linn Run Rd., Rector vicinity, 2/12/87, A, C, g, 87000107

Mount Pleasant Armory [Pennsylvania National Guard Armories MPS], Eagle and Spring Sts., Mount Pleasant, 12/22/89, A, C, 89002079

Old Hannastown, Site of, 4 mi. NE of Greensburg, Greensburg vicinity, 1/26/72, A, 72001180

Patterson, Samuel, House, RD 1—Box 155 on PA 981, New Alexandria, 3/07/85, C, 85000472

Pennsylvania Railroad Station—Latrobe, Depot St., Latrobe, 7/17/86, A, C, 86001689

Plumer House, Vine and S. Water St., West Newton, 12/06/79, B, 79002368

Ross Furnace [Iron and Steel Resources in Pennsylvania MPS], SW of Tubmill Reservoir off PA 711, Fairfield Township, West Fairfield vicinity, 9/06/91, A, C, 91001142

Salem Crossroads Historic District, Pittsburgh and Greenburg Sts., Delmont, 9/18/78, A, 78002484

Scottdale Armory [Pennsylvania National Guard Armories MPS], 501 N. Broadway St., Scottdale, 5/09/91, A, C, 91000518

Sewickley Manor, SR 64136, United vicinity, 4/19/82, A, C, 82003820

Squirrel Hill Site, Address Restricted, New Florence vicinity, 3/26/80, D, 80003647

St. Gertrude Roman Catholic Church, 311 Franklin Ave., Vandergrift, 9/23/83, A, C, a, 83002287

St. Vincent Archabbey Gristmill, SW of Latrobe off U.S. 30, Latrobe vicinity, 1/18/78, A, C, a, 78002486

West Overton Historic District, Frick Ave., East Huntingdon Township, 7/18/85, A, B, C, c, 85001572

Western Division of the PA Canal, Along the Conemaugh River, Robinson vicinity, 11/14/82, A, C, 82001537

Western Division-Pennsylvania Canal, N of Torrance, Torrance vicinity, 9/17/74, A, C, 74001817

Westmoreland County Courthouse, N. Main St., Greensburg, 3/30/78, A, C, 78002485

Wyoming County

Bridge in Nicholson Township [Highway Bridges Owned by the Commonwealth of Pennsylvania, Department of Transportation TR], LR 65021 over Tunkhannock Creeek, Starkville vicinity, 6/22/88, C, 88000810

Old White Mill, Off Welles St., Meshoppen, 9/11/75, A, C, 75001680

Tunkhannock Viaduct, 0.5 mi. E of Nicholson at Tunkhannock Creek, Nicholson vicinity, 4/11/77, A, C, 77001203

York County

Ashley and Bailey Company Silk Mill, 1237 W. Princess St., West York Borough, 2/21/91, A, C, 91000090

Billmeyer House, E. Market St., York, 11/10/70, C, 70000557

Bobb, Barnett, House, Rear of 157 West Market St., York, 10/29/75, C, 75001682

Bridge in Washington Township [Highway Bridges Owned by the Commonwealth of Pennsylvania, Department of Transportation TR], LR 66150 over Bermudian Creek, Kralltown vicinity, 6/22/88, C, 88000817

Brodbeck, S. B., Housing, Main St., Brodbecks, 9/06/90, B, C, 90001413

Burgholtshouse, S of East Prospect on PA 124, East Prospect vicinity, 6/22/79, C, 79002369

Codorus Forge and Furnace Historic District [Iron and Steel Resources in Pennsylvania MPS], Jct.

York County—Continued

of River Farm and Furnace Rds., Hellam Township, Saginaw vicinity, 9/06/91, A, C, D, 91001132

Cookes House, 438–440 Cordorus St., York, 10/05/72, A, C, b, 72001182

Coulsontown Cottages Historic District, Ridge Rd. and Main, Delta, 1/31/85, A, C, 85000175

Delta Historic District, Main St., Delta, 9/15/83, A, C, 83002288

Diamond Silk Mill, Jct. of Ridge Ave. and Hay St., East York, 7/24/92, A, C, 92000949

Dritt Mansion, 3.5 mi. S of Wrightsville on PA 624, Wrightsville vicinity, 8/16/77, A, C, 77001206

Emig Mansion, 3342 N. George St., Emigsville, 9/07/84, A, C, 84003586

Farmers Market, 380 W. Market St., York, 11/25/77, A, C, 77001207

Forry House, 149 N. Newberry St., York, 12/27/77, C, 77001208

Gates, Gen. Horatio, House, and Golden Plough Tavern, 157–159 W. Market St., York, 12/06/71, A, C, 71000737

Goldsboro Historic District, Roughly bounded by North, 3rd, Fraser, and Railroad Sts., Goldsboro, 6/14/84, A, C, 84003589

Guinston United Presbyterian Church, E of Laurel off PA 74, Laurel vicinity, 1/11/76, C, a, 76001682

Hammersly-Strominger House, NE of Lewisberry on PA 177, Lewisberry vicinity, 12/20/78, A, C, 78002487

Hanover Junction Railroad Station, PA 616, Hanover Junction, 12/29/83, A, 83004258

Indian Steps Cabin, Indian Steps Rd., Airville, 3/09/90, A, 90000416

Kise Mill Bridge [Highway Bridges Owned by the Commonwealth of Pennsylvania, Department of Transportation TR], LR 66003 over Bennett Run, Woodside vicinity, 6/22/88, C, 88000799

Kise Mill Bridge Historic District, Address Information Restricted., York Haven, 10/15/80, A, C, D, 80003650

Laurel-Rex Fire Company House, S. Duke St., York, 10/08/76, C, 76001683

Leibhart, Oscar, Site (36YO9), Address Restricted, Long Level vicinity, 5/24/84, D, 84003597

Melchinger, Englehart, House, 5 N. Main St., Dover, 8/12/92, C, a, 92000990

Nace (Neas), George, House, 113–115 W. Chestnut St., Hanover, 4/26/72, C, 72001181

Nook, The, 1101 Farquhar Dr., York Spring Garden vicinity, 3/01/82, C, 82003821

Northwest York Historic District, Roughly bounded by Carlisle, Texas, Pennsylvaia, Newberry, Park, and Linden Ave., York, 9/12/83, A, C, 83002289

Payne's Folly, Watters Rd., Fawn Township, 3/06/86, C, 86000422

Pettit's Ford, 4400 Colonial Rd., Dover, 5/03/83, B, C, 83002290

Railroad Borough Historic District, Shaub Rd. N., E., and S. Main St., Railroad, 3/22/84, A, C, 84003601

Schultz, Martin, House, 155 Emig St., Hallam, 3/11/93, C, 93000057

Shrewsbury Historic District, Roughly bounded by Highland, Sunset Drs., Park Ave., Church, and Pine Sts., Shrewsbury, 3/22/84, A, C, 84003605

Spring Grove Borough Historic District, Roughly bounded by College Ave., Jackson, Water, East, and Church Sts., Spring Grove, 5/25/84, A, C, 84003608

Stevens School, 606 W. Philadelphia St., York, 12/29/83, A, C, 83004263

Stoner, Samuel, Homestead, S of York off PA 182, York vicinity, 1/30/76, B, C, 76001684

Strickler Family Farmhouse, 1205 Williams Rd., Springettsbury Township, York, 2/21/91, A, C, 91000093

Swigart's Mill, N of Hanover on Berlin Rd., Hanover vicinity, 7/23/80, A, 80003649

US Post Office—Hanover, 141 Broadway, Hanover, 12/24/92, A, C, 92001719

Wallace-Cross Mill, S of Felton, Felton vicinity, 12/22/77, A, 77001204

Warrington Meetinghouse, PA 74, Wellsville, 2/20/75, C, a, 75001681

Wellsville Historic District, PA 74, Wellsville, 12/06/77, A, 77001205

Willis House, 135 Willis Run Rd., York, 4/20/79, A, 79002370

Wrightsville Historic District, Roughly bounded by the Susquehanna River, Vine, 4th, and Willow Sts., Wrightsville, 9/12/83, A, C, 83002291

York Armory [Pennsylvania National Guard Armories MPS], 369 N. George St., York, 4/18/90, A, C, 90000421

York Central Market, Philadelphia and Beaver Sts., York, 6/09/78, A, C, 78002488

York Dispatch Newspaper Offices, 15 and 17 E. Philadelphia St., York, 3/08/78, A, C, 78002489

York Historic District, Roughly bounded by RR tracks, Hartley St., Lilac Lane, and Cordorus Creek, York, 8/29/79, A, C, 79002371

York Iron Company Mine, N of Green Valley Rd., Spring Grove vicinity, 3/15/85, A, D, 85000580

York Meetinghouse, 134 West Philadelphia St., York, 5/06/75, A, C, a, 75001683

In the early decades of the 19th century, grain production became the dominant agricultural commodity in Berks County, Pennsylvania. During this period, more productive merchant mills like the Rieser Mill (ca. 1825) replaced smaller Colonial custom mills. (Louise Emery, 1990)

PUERTO RICO

Aguadilla Municipality

Antiguo Casino Camuyano, Estella and Munoz Rivera Sts., Camuy, 1/26/84, C, 84003123

Cardona Residence, Betances St. No. 55, Aguadilla, 1/02/85, C, 85000040

Casa de Piedra, 14 Progresso St., Aguadilla, 4/03/86, C, 86000704

Church Nuestra Senora del Carmen of Hatillo [Historic Churches of Puerto Rico TR], Luis M. Lacomba St., Hatillo, 12/10/84, A, C, a, 84000443

Church San Carlos Borromeo of Aguadilla [Historic Churches of Puerto Rico TR], Diego St., Town Plaza, Aguadilla, 9/18/84, A, a, 84003124

Church San Juan Bautista of Maricao [Historic Churches of Puerto Rico TR], Baldorioty St., Town Plaza, Maricao, 9/18/84, A, C, a, 84003125

District Courthouse, Progreso, Aguadilla, 1/02/85, C, 85000041

El Parterre—Ojo De Agua, Bounded by Munoz Rivera, Gonzalo Firpo, De Diego, and Mango Sts., Aguadilla, 1/13/86, A, C, 86000781

Faro di Punta Borinquen [Lighthouse System of Puerto Rico TR], Off IR 107, Aguadilla vicinity, 10/22/81, A, C, 81000559

Fuerte de la Conception, Stahl St., Aquadilla, 4/03/86, A, 86000703

Hacienda La Sabana, PR 119, Camuy vicinity, 2/14/85, C, 85000295

Hermitage of San Antonio de Padua de la Tuna, Address Restricted, Isabela vicinity, 12/02/83, C, D, a, 83004193

Old Urban Cemetery, Cuesta Vieja, Aguadilla, 1/02/85, A, C, d, 85000042

Puente Blanco, NE of Quebradillas off PR 485, Quebradillas, 2/23/84, C, 84003126

Residence Lopez, Progreso St. No. 67, Aguadilla, 1/02/85, C, 85000043

Silva—Benejan House, 15 Munoz Rivera St., Aguadilla, 5/20/87, C, 87000725

Aibonito Municipality

Villa Julita, 401 San Jose Ave., Aibonito, 12/19/86, C, 86003491

Arecibo Municipality

Calle Gonzalo Marin No. 61, Calle Gonzalo Marin No. 61, Arecibo, 6/09/88, C, 88000645

Casa Alcaldia de Arecibo, Jose de Diego Ave., Arecibo, 9/29/86, A, C, 86002762

Casa Cordova, 14 Gonzalo Marin St., Arecibo, 11/17/86, C, 86003185

Casa Ulanga, 7 Gonzalo Marin St., Arecibo, 7/26/82, B, C, 82003822

Casa de la Diosa Mita, 251 Fernandez Juncos St., Arecibo, 9/09/88, C, 88000966

Church Inmaculada Conception of Vega Alta [Historic Churches of Puerto Rico TR], Town Plaza, Vega Alta, 9/18/84, A, a, 84003128

Church Nuestra Senora de la Candelaria y San Matias of Manati [Historic Churches of Puerto Rico TR], Patriota Pozo St., Town Plaza, Manati, 9/18/84, A, C, a, 84003130

Church San Miguel Arcangel of Utuado [Historic Churches of Puerto Rico TR], Dr. Barbosa St., Utuado, 12/10/84, A, C, a, 84000447

Church San Sebastian Martir of San Sebastian [Historic Churches of Puerto Rico TR], Severo Arana St., Town Plaza, San Sebastian, 9/18/84, A, C, a, 84003132

Church Santa Maria del Rosario of Vega Baja [Historic Churches of Puerto Rico TR], Town Plaza, Vega Baja, 9/18/84, A, C, a, 84003133

Corregimiento Plaza Theater, Llaguerry and Toribio Pagan Sts., Arecibo, 1/06/86, A, 86000041

Edificio Oliver, 64 Jose de Diego Ave., Arecibo, 10/01/86, C, 86002764

Faro de Arecibo [Lighthouse System of Puerto Rico TR (AD)], NE of Arecibo off Route 66, Arecibo vicinity, 11/23/77, A, C, 77001546

Faro di Punta Higuero [Lighthouse System of Puerto Rico TR], NW of Rincon off IR 413, Rincon vicinity, 10/22/81, A, C, 81000560

Gonzalo Marin 101, 101 Gonzalo Marin St., Arecibo, 11/19/86, A, C, 86003183

Mercado de las Carnes, Alley connecting Mayor and Leon Sts., Ponce, 11/17/86, A, C, 86003199

Palacio del Marques de las Claras, Calle Gonzalo Marin #58, Arecibo, 7/12/88, A, B, C, 88000964

Paseo Victor Rojas, Calle Gònzalo Marin at Avenida De Diego, Arecibo, 11/19/86, C, 86003188

Pauteon Otero-Martinez, Old Bega Baja Cemetery, PR 670, Vega Baja, 7/30/84, C, 84003135

Bayamon Municipality

Farmacia Serra, Degetau No. 11, Bayamon, 5/04/89, B, C, g, 88000685

Cabo Rojo Municipality

Faro de los Morrillos de Cabo Rojo [Lighthouse System of Puerto Rico TR], SE of Pole Ojea on Cabo Rojo, Pole Ojea vicinity, 10/22/81, A, C, 81000685

Caguas Municipality

Aguayo Aldea Vocational High School [Early Twentieth Century Schools in Puerto Rico TR], Jct. of San Juan and Principal Sts., Caguas, 8/04/87, C, g, 87001311

Alcaldia de Caguas, Calle Munoz Rivera Num. 42, Caguas, 3/22/89, A, C, 88001307

Benitez, Gautier, High School, Calle Gautier Benitez and Calle Cristobal Colon, Caguas, 6/15/88, A, C, g, 88000657

Logia Union y Amparo No. 44, Calle Acosta No. 39, Caguas, 6/15/88, C, 88000661

Coamo Municipality

Casa Blanca, 17 Jose I. Quinton St., Coamo, 4/28/92, C, 92000379

Hermitage Church of Nuestra Senora de Valvanera of Coamo, Quinton and Carrion Mafuro Sts., Coamo, 3/31/86, A, a, 86000700

Pomar, Pico, Residence, Corner of Mario Braschi and Jose Quinton St., Coamo, 7/12/88, C, 88000961

Comerio Municipality

Cueva La Mora, Address Restricted, Comerio vicinity, 3/10/83, D, 83002292

Culebra Municipality

Faro Isla de Culebritas [Lighthouse System of Puerto Rico TR], SE part of Isla Culebrita, Culebra vicinity, 10/22/81, A, C, 81000686

Dorado Municipality

Casa del Rey, Calle Mendez Vigo 292, Dorado, 5/19/89, A, B, C, 89000408

Hacienda de Carlos Vassallo, SR 693, Dorado vicinity, 3/22/89, A, C, 88001848

Martinez, Jacinto Lopez, Grammar School [Early Twentieth Century Schools in Puerto Rico TR], Calle Norte and Calle San Quintin, Dorado, 10/11/88, A, C, 88001846

Ramirez, Dona Antonia, Residencia, SR 693, Dorado vicinity, 10/11/88, C, 88001847

Residencia Don Andres Hernandez, Calle Norte 196, Dorado, 5/22/89, C, 89000428

Fajardo Municipality

US Custom House [United States Custom Houses in Puerto Rico MPS], Calle Union, Fajardo, 2/10/88, A, C, 88000077

Guanica Municipality

Faro de Guanica [Lighthouse System of Puerto Rico TR (AD)], S of Guanica, Guanica vicinity, 3/28/77, C, 77001549

Guayama Municipality

Casa Cautino, Vicente Pales Ares St., Guayama, 6/11/84, C, 84003137

Casa Natal de Luis Munoz Rivera, Munez Rivera and Manuel Torres Sts., Barranquitas, 9/04/84, B, C, 84003139

Church Nuestra Senora de la Asuncion of Cayey [Historic Churches of Puerto Rico TR], Munoz Rivera St., Cayey, 12/10/84, A, C, a, 84000454

Church San Jose of Aibonito [Historic Churches of Puerto Rico TR], Emeterio Betances St., Aibonito, 12/10/84, A, C, a, 84000451

Eleuterio Derkes Grammar School [Early Twentieth Century Schools in Puerto Rico TR], Jose Maria Angueli St., Guayama, 8/04/87, C, 87001312

Faro de Punta de la Tuna [Lighthouse System of Puerto Rico TR], SE of Punta Maunabo, Guayama vicinity, 10/22/81, A, C, 81000688

Faro de Punta de las Figuras [Lighthouse System of Puerto Rico TR], SE of Arroyo, Guayama, 10/22/81, A, C, 81000687

Iglesia Parroquial de San Antonio de Padua de Guayama, 5 Ashford St., Guayama, 7/30/76, A, C, a, 76002248

Ingenio Azucarero Vives, Avenida Central, Barrio Machete, Guayama, 9/01/76, C, D, 76002249

Guaynabo Municipality

Iglesia Parroquial de San Pedro Martir de Guaynabo, Plaza de Recreo, Guaynabo, 9/08/76, C, a, 76002250

Hormigueros Municipality

Santuario de la Monserate de Hormigueros and Casa de Peregrinos, Calle Peregrinos No. 1 on Insular Rte. 344, Hormigueros, 4/17/75, C, a, 75002134

Humacao Municipality

Algodones 2 (12VPr2-204), Address Restricted, Barrio Puerto Diablo, Vieques, 8/21/91, D, 91001037

Algodones 3 (12VPr2-205), Address Restricted, Barrio Puerto Diablo, Vieques, 8/21/91, D, 91001038

Algodones 6 (12VPr2-229), Address Restricted, Barrio Puerto Diablo, Vieques, 8/21/91, D, 91001032

Camp Garcia (Campo Asilo) 3 (12VPr2-164), Address Restricted, Barrio Puerto Ferro, Vieques, 8/21/91, C, D, 91001041

Casa Roig, Antonio Lopez 66, Humacao, 11/17/77, C, 77001550

Church Dulce Nombre de Jesus of Humacao [Historic Churches of Puerto Rico TR], Town Plaza, Humacao, 9/18/84, A, C, a, 84003140

Church Nuestra Senora del Rosario of Naguabo [Historic Churches of Puerto Rico TR], Town Plaza, Naguabo, 12/10/84, A, C, a, 84000456

Church San Jose of Gurabo [Historic Churches of Puerto Rico TR], Santiago and Eugenio Sanches Lopez Sts., Gurabo, 9/18/84, A, a, 84003142

Church Santiago Apostol of Fajardo [Historic Churches of Puerto Rico TR], Town Plaza, Fajardo, 9/18/84, A, C, a, 84003144

Le Pistolet (12VPr2-168), Address Restricted, Barrio Punta Arenas, Vieques, 8/22/91, A, D, 91001040

Llave 13 (12VPr2-175), Address Restricted, Barrio Llave, Vieques, 8/21/91, A, C, D, 91001036

Loma Jalova 3 (12VPr2-219), Address Restricted, Barrio Puerto Diablo, Vieques, 8/21/91, D, 91001034

Monte Largo 2 (12VPr2-172), Address Restricted, Barrio Puerto Diablo, Vieques, 8/21/91, D, 91001042

Nuestra Senora de las Mercedes de San Miguel de Hato Grande, Colon St., San Lorenzo, 12/08/83, A, C, 83004194

Playa Grande 9 (12VPr2-212), Address Restricted, Barrio Llave, Vieques, 8/21/91, D, 91001035

Ventana 4 (12VPr2-171), Address Restricted, Barrio Punta Arenas, Vieques, 8/21/91, D, 91001039

Villa Del Mar, PR 3, Naguabo, 6/23/83, C, 83002293

Yanuel 8 (12VPr2-173), Address Restricted, Barrio Puerto Diablo, Vieques, 8/21/91, D, 91001043

Yanuel 9 (12VPr2-220), Address Restricted, Barrio Puerto Diablo, Vieques, 8/21/91, D, 91001033

Isabela Municipality

Faro de Vieques [Lighthouse System of Puerto Rico TR (AD)], Off PR 38, Isabel II, 11/17/77, C, 77001551

Fuerte de Vieques, Calle del Fuerte, Isabel II, 11/18/77, C, 77001552

Loiza Municipality

Cueva de Los Indios, Address Restricted, Loiza vicinity, 6/24/82, D, 82003823

Parroquia del Espiritu Santo y San Patricio, Plaza de Loiza, Loiza Aldea, 9/08/76, A, C, a, 76002251

Manati Municipality

Brunet—Calaf Residence, Quinones corner of Patriota Pozo St., Manati, 9/01/88, C, 88001306

Hacienda Azucarera la Esperanza, NW of Manati on PR 616, Manati vicinity, 8/11/76, A, B, C, 76002190

La Colectiva Tabacalera, 18 Quinones St., Manati, 9/01/88, A, g, 88001305

Plaza del Mercado de Manati, Quinones, Padial and Baldrioty Sts., Manati, 8/19/88, A, C, g, 88001303

Mayaguez Municipality

Asilo De Pobres, Post St., Mayaguez, 12/02/85, A, C, 85003087

Casa Consistorial De Mayaguez, Peral St., Mayaguez, 12/02/85, A, C, 85003046

Casa Franceschi Antongiorgi, 25 de Julio St., Yauco, 1/16/85, C, 85000113

Casa de los Ponce de Leon, Dr. Santiago Veve Num. 13, San German, 3/09/83, A, B, 83002295

Casona Cesari, 25th of July and Matienzo Cintron Sts., Yauco, 1/16/85, C, 85000114

Cementerio Municipal de Mayaguez [Cemeteries in Puerto Rico, 1804–1920 MPS], Southern end of Post St., Mayaguez, 8/25/88, C, d, 88001247

Chalet Amill, No. 33 Mattei Lluberas St., Yauco, 1/16/85, C, 85000115

Church San German Auxerre of San German [Historic Churches of Puerto Rico TR], De la Cruz St., San German, 12/10/84, A, C, a, 84000461

Church of San Isidro Labrador and Santa Maria de la Cabeza of Sabana Grande [Historic Churches of Puerto Rico TR], Angel G. Martinez St., Sabana Grande, 12/10/84, A, C, a, 84000460

Edificio Jose de Diego, University of Puerto Rico campus, Mayaguez, 11/18/77, A, C, 77001553

Esmoris, Duran, Residencia, Mendez Vigo B204 L204, Mayaguez, 9/07/88, C, 88000655

Faro de la Isla de la Mona [Lighthouse System of Puerto Rico TR], E side of Island, Mona Island, 10/22/81, A, C, 81000689

Filardi House, 25 de Julio St. and corner of Baldrioty St., Yauco, 1/16/85, C, 85000116

Fuentes, Ramirez, Residencia, Calle Mendez Vigo #117, Mayaguez, 7/12/88, C, 88000965

Gomez Residencia, Mendez Vigo No. 60, Mayaguez, 6/15/88, C, 88000656

Hacienda Buena Union, Address Restricted, San German vicinity, 8/23/83, D, 83002296

Hacienda Santa Rita, PR 116, Guanica vicinity, 1/05/84, A, C, a, 84003147

Isla de Mona, Address Restricted, Mayaguez vicinity, 12/17/93, A, B, D, 93001398

La Case Solariega de Jose De Diego, 52 Liceo St., Mayaguez, 4/03/86, B, C, 86000624

Logia Adelphia, 64 E. Sol St., Mayaguez, 2/19/86, A, C, 86000323

Plaza Publica, McKinley St., Mayaguez, 12/03/85, A, 85003085

Mayaguez Municipality—Continued

Residencia Heygler, Calle Liceo #51, Mayaguez, 7/12/88, C, 88000962

Residencia Ramirez De Arellano en Guanajibo, PR 102, Mayaguez, 2/05/87, C, 86003192

Rivera, Nazario, Residencia, Post St. No. 105, Mayaguez, 9/13/88, C, 88000686

Teatro Yaguez, McKinley and Basora Sts., Mayaguez, 12/02/85, A, C, 85003086

US Custom House [United States Custom Houses in Puerto Rico MPS], Ava. Gonzalez Clemente, esq. McKinley, Mayaguez, 2/10/88, A, C, 88000076

US Post Office and Courthouse, McKinley and Pilar DeFillo Sts., Mayaquez, 5/21/86, C, 86001169

Moca Municipality

Hacienda Iruena Manor House, Km. 115.7 PR Rd. No. 2, Aceituna, 8/14/87, A, C, 87000735

Ponce Municipality

Albergue Caritativo Tricoche [19th Century Civil Architecture in Ponce TR], Tricoche St., Ponce, 5/14/87, C, 87000769

Antiguo Cuartel Militar Espanol de Ponce [19th Century Civil Architecture in Ponce TR], Calle Castillo Final, Ponce, 5/14/87, C, 87000772

Antiguo Hospital Militar Espanol de Ponce [19th Century Civil Architecture in Ponce TR], Leon, Atocha and Bondad Sts., Ponce, 5/14/87, C, 87000770

Armstrong-Toro House, Calle Union No. 9, Ponce, 10/29/87, C, 87001821

Banco Credito y Ahorro Ponceno, Marina and Amor Sts., Ponce, 6/25/87, C, 87001002

Banco de Ponce, Amor and Comercio Sts., Ponce, 6/25/87, C, 87001003

Casa Alcaldia de Ponce—City Hall [19th Century Civil Architecture in Ponce TR (AD)], South, Las Delicias Square, Ponce, 11/19/86, A, C, 86003197

Casino de Ponce, Calle Marina & Calle Luna, Ponce, 10/28/87, A, C, 87001818

Castillo de Serralles, Cerro El Vigia, Ponce, 11/03/80, A, C, 80004494

Cathedral Nuestra Senora de Guadalupe of Ponce [Historic Churches of Puerto Rico TR; 19th Century Civil Architecture in Ponce TR (AD)], Town Plaza, Ponce, 12/10/84, A, C, a, 84000467

Cementerio Antiguo de Ponce, Torres no. 1 and Frontispicio St., Ponce, 1/05/84, C, d, 84003149

Cementerio Catolico San Vicente de Paul [Cemeteries in Puerto Rico, 1804–1920 MPS], Off PR 10, Ponce, 8/25/88, C, d, 88001249

Centro Ceremonial Indigena, Address Restricted, Ponce vicinity, 4/14/78, D, d, 78003381

Church San Blas de Illescas of Coamo [Historic Churches of Puerto Rico TR], Mario Braschi St., Coamo, 12/10/84, A, C, a, 84000463

Church San Juan Bautista y San Ramon Nonato of Juana Diaz [Historic Churches of Puerto Rico TR], Town Plaza, Juana Diaz, 12/10/84, A, C, a, 84000465

Faro de la Isla de Caja de Muertos [Lighthouse System of Puerto Rico TR], SE of Ponce on Isla Caja de Muertos, Ponce vicinity, 10/22/81, A, C, 81000690

Faro del Puerto de Ponce [Lighthouse System of Puerto Rico TR], S of Ponce on Cayo Cardona, Ponce vicinity, 10/22/81, A, C, 81000691

Font-Ubides House, Calle Castillo No. 34, Ponce, 10/29/87, C, 87001825

Godreau, Miguel C., Casa, 146 Calle Reina, Ponce, 4/30/86, C, 86000894

Iglesia de la Santisma Trinidad, Marina St. at jct. of Mayor and Abolicion Sts., Ponce, 9/29/86, C, a, 86002766

Missionary Society of the Methodist Episcopal Church, Calle Villa No. 135, Ponce, 10/29/87, A, C, a, 87001822

Nebot, Zaldo de, Residencia, Calle Marina No. 27, Ponce, 6/09/88, C, 88000643

Oppenheimer House, Calle Salud No. 47, Ponce, 10/29/87, C, 87001824

Parque de Bombas de Ponce, Plaza las Delicias, Ponce, 7/12/84, A, C, 84003150

Ponce High School [Early Twentieth Century Schools in Puerto Rico TR], Christina St., Ponce, 8/04/87, C, 87001310

Rosaly—Batiz House, 125 Villa St., Ponce, 9/29/86, C, 86002768

Salazar—Candal House, Calle Isabel No. 53, Ponce, 6/09/88, C, 88000663

Subira House, Calle Raina No. 107, Ponce, 10/28/87, C, 87001826

Toro, Fernando Luis, Casa, Calle Obispado No. 3, La Alhambra, Ponce, 3/05/86, C, 86000421

US Custom House [United States Custom Houses in Puerto Rico MPS], Calle Bonaire at Calle Aduana Playa de Ponce, 2/10/88, A, C, 88000073

Villaronga House, 106 Reina St., Ponce, 8/24/84, C, 84003151

Quebradillas Municipality

Teatro Liberty, Calle Rafols #157, Quebradillas, 5/04/89, A, C, g, 88000963

Sabana Grande Municipality

Lassise-Schettini House, Calle Angel Ramirez, final, Sabana Grande, 10/21/87, C, 87001823

San German Municipality

Alcantarilla Pluvial sobre la Quebrada Manzanares, Calle Ferrocarril and Calle Esperanza, San German, 4/12/90, A, C, 90000552

Convento de Porta Coeli, Plaza Porta Coeli, San German, 9/08/76, C, a, 76002252

Jaime Acosta y Fores Residence, Calle Dr. Santiago Veve, 70, San German, 5/24/90, C, 90000767

San Juan Municipality

Administration Building, Address Restricted, Santurce, 10/26/83, A, C, a, 83004195

Antiguo Casino de Puerto Rico, Avenida Ponce de Leon 1, San Juan, 9/22/77, A, C, 77001554

Biblioteca Carnegie, Ponce de Leon Ave., Puerta de Tierra, 10/20/83, A, C, 83004196

Caparra, Address Restricted, Guaynabo vicinity, 2/28/84, A, D, 84003155

Carcel de Puerta de Tierra, Avenida Ponce de Leon, Parada 8, Puerta de Tierra, San Juan, 8/11/76, A, C, 76002253

Casa Natal Dr. Jose Celso Barbosa, 13 Barbosa St., Bayamon, 8/24/84, B, C, c, 84003156

Casa de Espana, Ponce de Leon Ave., San Juan, 7/05/83, A, C, 83002294

Central High School [Early Twentieth Century Schools in Puerto Rico TR], Ponce de Leon Ave., Santurce, 8/04/87, C, 87001309

Church Nuestra Senora de la Concepcion y San Fernando of Toa Alta [Historic Churches of Puerto Rico TR], Ponce de Leon St., Town Plaza, Toa Alta, 9/18/84, A, C, a, 84003158

Church Santa Cruz of Bayamon [Historic Churches of Puerto Rico TR], Plaza de Hostos, Bayamon, 9/18/84, A, C, a, 84003162

Church of San Fernando of Carolina [Historic Churches of Puerto Rico TR], Munoz Rivera St., Town Plaza, Carolina, 9/18/84, A, C, a, 84003160

Church of San Mateo de Cangrejos of Santurce, Corner of San Jorge St. and Eduardo Conde Ave., Santurce, 1/02/85, C, a, 85000044

Church, School, Convent and Parish House of San Agustin, 265 Ponce de Leon Ave., San Juan vicinity, 12/30/85, C, a, 85003194

Colegio de las Madres del Sagrado Corazon, Ponce de Leon Ave., San Juan, 11/21/85, C, 85002908

Edificio Alcaldia, Calle Ignacio Arzuaga, Esq. De Diego, Carolina, 12/28/83, A, C, 83004197

El Capitolio de Puerto Rico, Avenida Ponce de Leon and Avenida Munoz Rivera, San Juan, 11/18/77, A, C, g, 77001555

El Falansterio de Puerta de Tierra, Bounded by RR Right-of-Way, Fernandez Juncos Ave., Matias Ledesma and San Juan Bautista Sts., San Juan, 5/03/84, A, C, g, 84003166

Escuela Brambaugh [Early Twentieth Century Schools in Puerto Rico TR], San Juan Bautista St. and Ponce de Leon Ave., San Juan, 5/05/89, A, C, 89000324

Escuela Graduado Jose Celso Barbosa [Early Twentieth Century Schools in Puerto Rico TR], Ponce de Leon Ave., San Juan, 5/19/89, A, C, 89000406

San Juan Municipality—Continued

Faro de Morro [Lighthouse System of Puerto Rico TR], Summit of San Felipe del Moro Castle, San Juan, 10/22/81, A, C, 81000693

Faro de las Cabezas de San Juan [Lighthouse System of Puerto Rico TR], NE of Soroco, Soroco vicinity, 10/22/81, A, C, 81000692

Fortin de San Geronimo de Boqueron, Puerta de Tierra, San Juan, 10/11/83, A, C, 83004199

Hotel Normandie, Ponce de Leon Ave. and San Geronimo St., San Juan, 8/29/80, C, g, 80004295

House at 659 Concordia Street, 659 Concordia St., Miramar, 10/18/91, C, 91001501

House at 659 La Paz Street, 659 La Paz St., Miramar, 1/30/92, C, 91002007

House at 663 La Paz Street, 663 La Paz St., Miramar, 10/18/91, C, 91001500

House at 665 McKinley Street, 665 McKinley St., Miramar, 10/19/91, C, 91001502

La Fortaleza, Calle Fortaleza, San Juan Island between San Juan Bay and Calle Recinto Oeste, San Juan, 10/15/66, A, NHL, 66000951

Miami Building, 868 Ashford Ave., Santurce, 8/23/84, C, g, 84003169

Nuestra Senora de Lourdes Chapel, Ponce de Leon and Miramar Aves., Santurce, 9/27/84, A, C, 84003171

Polvorin de Miraflores, Antiqua Base Naval de Miramar, Santurce, 3/09/84, A, C, a, 84003172

Puerto Rico National Cemetery, PR 168, Bayamon, 9/26/83, A, d, g, 83002298

Rafael M. Labra High School [Early Twentieth Century Schools in Puerto Rico TR], Jct. of Ponce de Leon and Roberto H. Todd Aves., Santurce, 8/04/87, C, 87001308

Residencia Aboy—Lompre, Avenida Ponce de Leon 900, Santurce, 3/22/89, C, 88001304

San Juan National Historic Site, San Juan National Historic Site, San Juan, 10/15/66, A, C, NPS, 66000930

School of Tropical Medicine, Ponce de Leon Ave., Puerta de Tierra, 9/29/83, A, C, 83002297

Superintendent of Lighthouses' Dwelling [Lighthouse System of Puerto Rico TR], La Puntilla, San Juan, 10/22/81, C, 81000694

US Custom House [United States Custom Houses in Puerto Rico MPS], Calle Puntilla, 1, San Juan, 2/10/88, A, C, 88000075

US Post Office and Courthouse, Block bounded by Calle San Justo, Calle Tanca, Calle Commercio, and Calle Recinto Sur, Old San Juan, 3/28/88, C, g, 87000694

University of Puerto Rico Tower and Quadrangle, Ponce de Leon Ave., Rio Piedras, 5/17/84, A, C, g, 84003174

Zona Historica de San Juan, NW triangle of the islet of San Juan, San Juan, 10/10/72, A, C, a, d, 72001553

San Lorenzo Municipality

Residencia Machin-Ramos, Calle Eugenio Sanchez Lopez, San Lorenzo, 5/05/89, C, 88001180

Toa Baja Municipality

Iglesia Parroquial de San Pedro Apostol de Toa Baja, Las Flores St. No. 47, Toa Baja, 4/17/75, A, C, a, 75002135

Santa Elena Hacienda, N of Hwys. 2 and 165 jct., Toa Baja, 9/24/92, A, C, 83004662

Utuado Municipality

Caguana Ceremonial Ball Courts Site, PR 11, Km. 12.3, Utuado, 12/17/92, C, D, NHL, 92001671

Vieques Municipality

Casa Delerme—Anduze No. 2, 355 Antonio Mellado St., Isabel Segunda, 11/22/93, C, 93001205

Central Playa Grande, Address Restricted, Barrio Llave, Vieques, 9/10/92, D, 92001236

Hacienda Casa del Frances, NW of Esperanza, Esperanza vicinity, 11/18/77, C, 77001548

Laguna Jalova Archeological District, Address Restricted, Barrio Puerto Diablo, Vieques, 9/10/92, D, 92001237

Paramayon 2, Address Restricted, Barrio Llave, Vieques, 9/10/92, D, 92001241

Playa Vieja, Address Restricted, Barrio Punta Arenas, Vieques, 9/10/92, D, 92001235

Punta Jalova, Address Restricted, Barrio Puerto Diablo, Vieques, 9/10/92, D, 92001239

Resolucion Historic District, Address Restricted, Barrio Punta Arenas, Vieques, 9/10/92, D, 92001242

Ventana Archeological District, Address Restricted, Barrio Llave, Vieques, 9/10/92, D, 92001238

Yauco Municipality

Casa Agostini, Calle San Rafael, Yauco, 6/09/88, B, C, 88000682

Logia Masonica Hijos de la Luz, Avenida Jose C. Barbosa, Yauco, 6/09/88, C, 88000684

Residencia Gonzalez Vivaldi, 26 Mattei Lluberas St., Yauco, 2/05/87, C, 86003201

Teatro Ideal, Calle Comerio, Yauco, 6/09/88, A, C, 88000683

The Fernando Luis Toro residence (ca. 1927) is part of the first upper class, early 20th-century suburb developed in Ponce, Puerto Rico. (Agamemnon Gus Pantel, 1985)

RHODE ISLAND

Bristol County

Barrington Civic Center, County Rd., Barrington, 12/12/76, A, C, d, 76000198

Belton Court, Middle Hwy., Barrington, 6/30/76, B, C, a, 76000037

Blithewold, Ferry Rd., Bristol, 6/27/80, A, C, 80000074

Bristol County Courthouse, High St., Bristol, 4/28/70, A, C, 70000011

Bristol County Jail, 48 Court St., Bristol, 4/24/73, C, 73000048

Bristol Customshouse and Post Office, 420–448 Hope St., Bristol, 5/31/72, C, 72000015

Bristol Ferry Lighthouse [Lighthouses of Rhode Island TR], Ferry Rd., Bristol, 2/25/88, A, C, 87001696

Bristol Waterfront Historic District, Bristol Harbor to E side of Wood St. as far N as Washington St. and S to Walker Cove, Bristol, 3/18/75, A, C, 75000053

Church, Benjamin, House, 1014 Hope St., Bristol, 9/22/71, C, 71000011

Hog Island Shoal Lighthouse [Lighthouses of Rhode Island TR], S of Hog Island, E passage, Narrangansett Bay, Portsmouth, 3/30/88, A, C, 88000282

Longfield, 1200 Hope St., Bristol, 7/17/72, C, 72000016

Mount Hope Bridge, RI 114 over Narragansett Bay, Bristol, 1/31/76, A, C, g, 76000038

Mount Hope Farm, Metacom Ave., Bristol, 5/02/77, A, B, C, D, 77000023

Nayatt Point Lighthouse [Lighthouses of Rhode Island TR], Nayatt Point, Barrington, 2/25/88, A, C, 87001694

Poppasquash Farms Historic District, Off RI 114, Bristol, 6/27/80, A, C, 80000075

Reynolds, Joseph, House, 956 Hope St., Bristol, 5/31/72, A, C, NHL, 72000017

St. Matthew's Episcopal Church, 5 Chapel Rd., Barrington, 8/22/91, A, C, a, 91001024

Warren United Methodist Church and Parsonage, 27 Church St., Warren, 8/12/71, A, C, a, 71000012

Warren Waterfront Historic District, Bounded roughly by the Warren River, Belcher Cove, and the old town line (includes Main St. to Campbell St.), Warren, 2/28/74, A, C, a, 74000035

Whalley, William, Homestead, 33 Burchard Ave., Little Compton, 8/03/88, A, C, 88001127

Kent County

Allen, Stephen, House, Sharp St., West Greenwich, 9/20/78, A, C, 78000060

Apponaug Historic District [Warwick MRA], 3376, 3384, 3387, 3391, 3397–3399, and 3404 Post Rd., Warwick, 2/23/84, C, 84001833

Arkwright Bridge, Crosses Pawtuxet River at Hill St., West Warwick vicinity, 12/12/78, C, 78000061

Armory of the Kentish Guards, Armory and Peirce Sts., East Greenwich, 4/28/70, A, C, 70000012

Arnold, John Waterman, House, 11 Roger Williams Ave., Warwick, 9/10/71, C, 71000013

Bowen, Isaac, House, NE of Coventry on Maple Valley Rd., Coventry vicinity, 6/27/80, C, 80000076

Briggs, Joseph, House—Coventry Town Farm, Town Farm Rd., Coventry, 6/18/87, A, C, 87000997

Budlong Farm [Warwick MRA], 595 Buttonwoods Ave., Warwick, 8/18/83, C, 83000165

Buttonwoods Beach Historic District [Warwick MRA], Roughly bounded by Brush Neck Cove, Greenwich Bay, Cooper and Promenade Aves., Warwick, 2/23/84, A, C, 84001834

Carbuncle Hill Archaeological District, RI-1072-1079, Address Restricted, Coventry, 9/28/85, D, 85002692

Clapp, Silas, House, E. Greenwich Ave., West Warwick, 5/07/73, C, 73000049

Conimicut Lighthouse [Lighthouses of Rhode Island TR], E of Conimicut Pt. in the Providence River, Warwick, 3/30/88, A, C, 88000269

Cowesett Pound, Cowesett Rd., Warwick, 9/04/87, A, 87000994

Crompton Free Library, Main St., West Warwick, 11/20/78, A, C, 78000062

East Greenwich Historic District, Roughly bounded by Kenyon Ave., Division, Peirce, & London Sts., Greenwich Cove and Dark Entry Brook, East Greenwich, 6/13/74, A, C, 74000036

Elizabeth Spring [Warwick MRA], Off Forge Rd., Warwick, 8/18/83, B, 83000166

Forge Farm, 40 Forge Rd., Warwick, 1/11/74, A, B, C, c, 74000037

Forge Road Historic District [Warwick MRA], Forge Rd. from Ives Rd. to the Potowomut River, Warwick, 2/23/84, C, 84001861

Fry's Hamlet Historic District, 2068, 2153, 2196, and 2233 S. County Trail, East Greenwich, 12/20/85, A, C, 85003161

Gardiner, Capt. Oliver, House [Warwick MRA], 4451 Post Rd., Warwick, 8/18/83, C, 83000167

Gaspee Point, Off Namquid Dr., Warwick, 6/08/72, A, 72000018

Gorton, Caleb, House [Warwick MRA], 987 Greenwich Ave., Warwick, 8/18/83, C, 83000168

Greene, Caleb, House, 15 Centerville Rd., Warwick, 11/28/78, B, C, a, c, 78000063

Greene, Gen. Nathanael, Homestead, 20 Taft St., Coventry, 10/07/71, B, NHL, 71000014

Greene, Moses, House [Warwick MRA], 11 Economy Ave., Warwick, 8/18/83, C, 83000169

Greene, Peter, House [Warwick MRA], 1124 W. Shore Rd., Warwick, 8/18/83, C, 83000170

Greene, Richard Wickes, House [Warwick MRA], 27 Homestead Ave., Warwick, 8/18/83, C, 83000171

Greene-Bowen House, 698 Buttonwoods Ave., Warwick, 5/02/74, A, C, 74000038

Greene-Durfee House [Warwick MRA], 1272 W. Shore Rd., Warwick, 8/18/83, C, 83000172

Greenwich Cove Site, Address Restricted, Warwick vicinity, 1/04/80, D, 80000077

Hopelands [Warwick MRA], Wampanoag Rd., Warwick, 8/18/83, C, 83000173

Indian Oaks [Warwick MRA], 836 Warwick Neck Ave., Warwick, 8/18/83, C, a, 83000174

Interlaken Mill Bridge, Spans Pawtuxet River at Arkwright, Coventry, 12/22/78, C, 78000064

Kent County Courthouse, 127 Main St., East Greenwich, 4/28/70, A, C, 70000013

Knight Estate [Warwick MRA], 486 East Ave., Warwick, 2/23/84, C, 84001864

Lambert Farm Site, RI-269, Address Restricted, Warwick, 11/03/83, D, 83003798

Lippitt Mill, 825 Main St., West Warwick, 1/11/74, A, C, 74000053

Meadows Archeological District, Address Restricted, Warwick vicinity, 11/03/83, D, 83003800

Moosup River Site (RI-1153), Address Restricted, Coventry vicinity, 12/10/87, D, 87002083

Paine House, Station St., Coventry, 5/01/74, A, C, 74000039

Pawtuxet Village Historic District, Bounded roughly by Bayside, S. Atlantic, and Ocean Aves., Pawtuxet and Providence rivers, and Post Rd., Warwick, 4/24/73, A, C, 73000050

Pontiac Mills, Knight St., Warwick, 6/05/72, A, C, 72000019

Rhode Island State Airport Terminal [Warwick MRA], 572 Occupasstuxet Rd., Warwick, 8/18/83, A, C, 83000175

Rhodes, Christopher, House, 25 Post Rd., Warwick, 3/31/71, B, C, 71000015

Rice City Historic District, W of Coventry Center at RI 14 and RI 117, Coventry vicinity, 6/09/80, A, C, a, b, d, e, 80000078

South Main Street Historic District, Cady, S. Main, and Wood Sts., Coventry, 7/10/87, A, C, 87001064

St. Mary's Church and Cemetery, Church St., Crompton, 11/21/78, A, C, a, d, 78000065

Tillinghast Mill Site, Address Restricted, East Greenwich vicinity, 3/10/88, A, D, 88000164

Tillinghast Road Historic District, Tillinghast Rd., East Greenwich, 3/09/88, A, B, C, b, 88000167

Trafalgar Site, RI-639, Address Restricted, Warwick, 11/03/83, D, 83003801

Valley Queen Mill, 700 Providence St., West Warwick, 1/19/84, A, C, 84001880

Varnum, Gen. James Mitchell, House, 57 Peirce St., East Greenwich, 8/12/71, B, C, 71000016

Warwick Civic Center Historic District, Post Rd., Warwick, 6/27/80, A, C, 80000079

Kent County—Continued

Warwick Lighthouse [Lighthouses of Rhode Island TR], 1350 Warwick Neck Ave., Warwick, 3/30/88, A, C, b, 88000268

Waterman Tavern, Maple Valley Rd., Coventry, 7/24/74, A, 74000040

Waterman, John R., House [Warwick MRA], 100 Old Homestead Rd., Warwick, 8/18/83, B, C, 83000176

Waterman, William, House, RI 102, Coventry, 11/14/80, A, C, 80000080

West Greenwich Baptist Church and Cemetery, Plain Meeting House and Liberty Hill Rds., West Greenwich Center, 11/28/78, A, C, a, d, 78000066

West Winds, 300 Wakefield St., West Warwick, 5/20/93, B, C, 93000425

Whitmarsh, Col. Micah, House, 294 Main St., East Greenwich, 2/18/71, C, 71000017

Wickes, Oliver A., House [Warwick MRA], 794 Major Potter Rd., Warwick, 8/18/83, C, 83000177

Wilson—Winslow House, 2414 Harkney Hill Rd., Coventry, 11/04/93, C, 93001182

Windmill Cottage, 144 Division St., East Greenwich, 5/22/73, A, C, 73000051

Newport County

Army and Navy YMCA, 50 Washington Sq., Newport, 12/29/88, B, C, 88003073

Artillery Park, North Rd. and Narragansett Ave., Jamestown, 3/07/73, A, d, 73000054

Bailey Farm, 373 Wyatt Rd., Middletown, 6/04/84, A, C, 84001887

Baldwin, Charles H., House, Bellevue Ave., opposite Perry St., Newport, 5/06/71, C, 71000018

Barker, Benjamin, House, 1229 Main Rd., Tiverton, 10/31/80, C, 80000081

Battle of Rhode Island Site, Lehigh Hill and both sides of RI 21 between Medley and Dexter Sts., Portsmouth, 5/30/74, A, NHL, 74002054

Beavertail Light [Lighthouses of Rhode Island TR (AD)], Beavertail Rd., Jamestown vicinity, 12/12/77, A, C, 77000024

Bell, Isaac, House, 70 Perry St., Newport, 1/13/72, C, 72000022

Bellevue Avenue Historic District, Roughly bounded Atlantic Ocean, Easton Bay, Coggeshall Ave., Spring St., and Memorial Blvd., Newport, 12/08/72, A, C, g, NHL, 72000023

Bellevue Avenue/Casino Historic District, 170-230 Bellvue Avenue, Newport, 12/08/72, A, C, 72000024

Bird's Nest, The, 526 Broadway at One Mile Corner, Newport, 6/07/82, A, C, 82000130

Breakers, The, Ochre Point Ave., Newport, 9/10/71, B, C, 71000019

Brick Market, Thames St. & Washington Sq., Newport, 10/15/66, C, NHL, 66000019

Carr, Thomas, Farmstead Site (Keeler Site RI-707), Address Restricted, Jamestown vicinity, 11/01/84, D, 84000356

Castle Hill Lighthouse [Lighthouses of Rhode Island TR], Off Ocean Ave. on Castle Hill at W end of Newport Neck, Newport, 3/30/88, A, C, 88000277

Chateau-Sur-Mer, Bellevue Ave., Newport, 11/08/68, C, 68000002

Clarke Street Meeting House, Clarke St., Newport, 1/25/71, B, a, 71000020

Commandant's Residence, Quarters Number One, Fort Adams, Harrison Ave., Fort Adams, Newport, 5/08/74, A, C, 74000043

Common Burying Ground and Island Cemetery, Farwell and Warner Sts., Newport, 5/01/74, B, C, d, 74000044

Conanicut Battery, W of Beaver Tail Rd., Jamestown, 7/02/73, A, 73000055

Conanicut Island Lighthouse [Lighthouses of Rhode Island TR], 64 N. Bay View Ave., Jamestown, 2/25/88, A, C, 87001698

Cook-Bateman Farm, Fogland and Puncatest Neck Rds., Tiverton, 10/11/79, A, C, 79003775

Cotton, Dr. Charles, House, 5 Cotton's Court, Newport, 1/13/72, C, 72000026

Covell, William King, III, House, 72 Washington St., Newport, 5/31/72, C, 72000027

Dutch Island Lighthouse [Lighthouses of Rhode Island TR], S end of Dutch Island, Jamestown, 2/25/88, A, C, 87001701

Elms, The, Bellevue Ave., Newport, 9/10/71, A, C, 71000021

Fort Adams, W of Newport at Fort Adams Rd. and Harrison Ave., Newport vicinity, 7/28/70, A, C, NHL, 70000014

Fort Barton Site, Lawton and Highland Aves., Tiverton, 3/07/73, A, 73000056

Fort Dumpling Site, Address Restricted, Jamestown, 3/16/72, A, 72000021

Friends Meetinghouse, North Rd. and Weeden Lane, Jamestown, 3/07/73, A, C, a, 73000276

Gale, Levi H., House, 89 Touro St., Newport, 5/06/71, A, C, a, b, 71000022

Gardiner Pond Shell Midden, Address Restricted, Middletown vicinity, 4/12/85, D, 85000718

Greenvale Farm, 582 Wapping Rd., Portsmouth vicinity, 1/04/80, A, C, 80000082

Griswold, John, House, 76 Bellevue Ave., Newport, 11/05/71, C, 71000023

Hazard Farmstead (Joyner Site RI-706), Address Restricted, Jamestown vicinity, 11/01/84, D, 84000365

Hicks, Joseph, House, 494 Main Rd., Tiverton, 9/10/79, C, 79000053

Hunter House, 54 Washington St., Newport, 11/24/68, C, NHL, 68000003

Ida Lewis Rock Lighthouse [Lighthouses of Rhode Island TR], On Lime Rock in Newport Harbor off Wellington Ave., Newport, 2/25/88, A, B, C, 87001700

Jamestown Archeological District, Address Restricted, Jamestown vicinity, 12/10/89, D, 83004869

Jamestown Windmill, North Rd., N of Weeden Lane, Jamestown, 3/14/73, A, C, 73000057

Joseph, Lyman C., House, 438 Walcott Ave., Middletown, 5/02/75, C, 75000054

Kay Street—Catherine Street—Old Beach Road Historic District, Newport, Newport, 5/22/73, A, C, 73000052

King, Edward, House, Aquidneck Park, Spring St., Newport, 10/15/70, C, NHL, 70000024

Kingscote, Bellevue Ave. and Bowery St., Newport, 5/17/73, C, 73000058

Lawton—Almy—Hall Farm, 559 Union St., Portsmouth, 10/11/78, A, C, 78000068

Little Compton Common Historic District, Little Compton, Little Compton, 5/03/74, C, a, 74000041

Lucas—Johnston House, 40 Division St., Newport, 5/06/71, B, C, 71000024

Luce Hall, US Naval War College and Torpedo School, Coasters Harbor Island, Newport, 9/22/72, A, 72001439

Malbone, Malbone Rd., Newport, 10/22/76, A, C, 76000039

Malbone, Francis, House, 392 Thames St., Newport, 4/28/75, A, C, 75000055

Marble House, Bellevue Ave., Newport, 9/10/71, A, C, 71000025

Mawdsley, Capt. John, House, 228 Spring St., Newport, 7/02/83, A, C, 83000180

Miantonomi Memorial Park, Between Hillside and Girard Aves., Newport, 6/23/69, A, C, f, 69000003

Newport Artillery Company Armory, 23 Clarke St., Newport, 6/30/72, A, C, 72000029

Newport Casino, 194 Bellevue Ave., Newport, 12/02/70, A, C, NHL, 70000083

Newport Harbor Lighthouse [Lighthouses of Rhode Island TR], N. end of Goat Island, Newport Harbor, Newport, 3/30/88, A, C, 88000276

Newport Historic District, Bounded roughly by Van Zandt Ave., Farewell, Sherman, High, Thomas, Golden Hill, Thames, Marsh, and Washington Sts., Newport, 11/24/68, A, C, a, NHL, 68000001

Newport Steam Factory, 449 Thames St., Newport, 1/20/72, A, C, 72000030

Oak Glen, 745 Union St., Portsmouth, 3/29/78, B, C, 78003444

Ocean Drive Historic District, Ocean Dr., Newport, 5/11/76, A, C, NHL, 76000048

Ochre Point-Cliffs Historic District, Roughly bounded by Bellevue Ave. and Coastland as far N as Memorial Blvd. and S to Sheep Point Cove, Newport, 3/18/75, A, C, 75000211

Old Colony House, Washington Sq., Newport, 10/15/66, A, C, NHL, 66000014

Paradise School, Paradise and Prospect Aves., Middletown, 5/05/78, A, C, 78000069

Perry Mill, 337 Thames St., Newport, 1/13/72, A, C, 72000020

Pine Hill Archeological Site, RI-655, Address Restricted, Portsmouth, 11/03/83, D, 83003803

Portsmouth Friends Meetinghouse Parsonage and Cemetery, 11 Middle Rd. and 2232 E. Main Rd., Portsmouth, 3/07/73, A, C, a, b, 73000053

President's House, Naval War College, Naval Education and Training Center on Coasters Harbor Island, Newport, 9/18/89, A, 89001219

Prudence Island Lighthouse [Lighthouses of Rhode Island TR], E end of Sandy Pt. on Pru-

Newport County—Continued

dence Island, Portsmouth, 3/30/88, A, C, b, 88000270

Redwood Library, 50 Bellevue Ave., Newport, 10/15/66, C, NHL, 66000015

Rogers, Joseph, House, 37 Touro St., Newport, 2/23/72, C, 72000031

Rose Island Lighthouse [Lighthouses of Rhode Island TR], SW pt. of Rose Island, Newport, 4/10/87, A, 87000033

Rosecliff, Bellevue Ave., Newport, 2/06/73, C, 73000059

Sakonnet Light Station [Lighthouses of Rhode Island TR (AD)], S of Little Compton on Little Cormorant Rock, Little Compton vicinity, 2/10/83, A, C, 83000179

Seamen's Church Institute of Newport, 18 Market Square, Newport, 8/04/83, C, a, 83000178

Sherman, William Watts, House, 2 Shepard Ave., Newport, 12/30/70, C, NHL, 70000015

Shiloh Church, 25 School St., Newport, 8/12/71, A, a, 71000026

Stiles, Ezra, House, 14 Clarke St., Newport, 3/16/72, B, C, a, b, 72000116

Taylor—Chase—Smythe House, Chase Ln., Naval Education and Training Center, Newport, 8/30/89, A, 89001220

Tillinghast, Charles, House, 243–245 Thames St., Newport, 1/20/72, A, C, 72001576

Tillinghast, John, House, 142 Mill St., Newport, 4/11/73, A, C, 73000060

Tiverton Four Corners Historic District, Roughly bounded by Main, West and East Rds., Tiverton, 6/20/74, A, C, 74000042

Touro Synagogue National Historic Site, 85 Touro St., Newport, 10/15/66, A, C, a, NPS, 66000927

Trinity Church, Spring and Church Sts., Newport, 11/24/68, C, a, d, NHL, 68000004

US Naval War College, Coaster's Harbor Island, Newport, 10/15/66, A, NHL, 66000876

Union Church, Union St. and E. Main Rd., Portsmouth, 6/13/74, A, C, a, 74000045

United Congregational Church, Spring and Pelham Sts., Newport, 11/19/71, A, C, a, 71000027

Vernon House, 46 Clarke St., Newport, 11/24/68, C, NHL, 68000005

Wanton—Lyman—Hazard House, 17 Broadway, Newport, 10/15/66, C, NHL, 66000016

White Horse Tavern, 26 Marlborough St., Newport, 2/23/72, A, C, 72000032

Whitehall, Berkeley Ave., Middletown, 4/28/70, B, C, a, 70000016

Whitehorne, Samuel, House, 414 Thames St., Newport, 5/06/71, A, C, 71000028

Windmill Hill Historic District, Eldred Ave. and N. Main Rd., Jamestown vicinity, 10/02/78, A, C, a, d, 78000067

Witherbee School [Middletown MPS], Green End Ave., Middletown, 11/27/89, A, C, 89002036

Wreck Sites of H.M.S. Cerberus and H.M.S. Lark, Waters of Narragansett Bay adjacent to Aquidneck Island, South Portsmouth vicinity, 4/26/73, A, 73000061

Providence County

1761 Milestone [Woonsocket MRA], 640 S. Main St., Woonsocket, 11/24/82, A, 82000131

Adams, John E., House [Pawtucket MRA], 11 Allen Ave., Pawtucket, 11/18/83, C, b, 83003804

Albion Historic District, Roughly bounded by Berkshire Dr., Willow Lane, Ledge Way, Kennedy Blvd., School and Main Sts., Lincoln, 7/19/84, A, C, g, 84001899

Aldrich, Nelson W., House, 110 Benevolent St., Providence, 12/08/76, B, NHL, 76000040

All Saints Memorial Church [Elmwood MRA], 674 Westminster St., Providence, 1/07/80, C, a, 80000083

Allen Street Historic District [Woonsocket MPS], Allen St., Woonsocket, 9/13/90, A, C, 90001349

Allen, Candace, House, 12 Benevolent St., Providence, 4/11/73, C, 73000062

Allendale Mill, 494 Woonasquatucket Ave., North Providence, 5/07/73, A, C, 73000063

Allenville Mill, 5 Esmond St., Esmond, 1/20/72, A, 72000033

American Street School, 22 America St., Providence, 6/18/87, A, C, 87000996

Andrew Dickhaut Cottages Historic District, 114–141 Bath St., 6–18 Duke Street., and 377 Orms St., Providence, 2/23/84, A, C, 84001904

Andrews—Luther Farm, Elmdale Rd., Scituate, 6/19/85, A, C, 85001352

Angell, Daniel, House, 15 Dean Ave., Johnston, 4/21/75, A, C, 75000056

Arcade, The, 130 Westminster St. and 65 Weybosset St., Providence, 5/06/71, A, C, NHL, 71000029

Arnold Mills Historic District, E of Cumberland Hill at Sneech Pond, Attleboro, and Abbott Run Valley Rds., Cumberland, 12/28/78, A, C, 78000070

Arnold, Dexter, Farmstead, Chopmist Hill Rd., Scituate, 11/25/77, A, C, 77001586

Arnold, Eleazer, House, Great Rd. (RI 123) near jct. with RI 126, Lincoln, 11/24/68, C, NHL, 68000006

Arnold, Israel, House, Great Rd., Lincoln, 12/18/70, C, 70000017

Arnold, John, House [Woonsocket MRA], 99 Providence St., Woonsocket, 11/24/82, A, C, 82000132

Arnold, Peleg, Tavern, Woonsocket Hill Rd., Union Village, 7/30/74, B, 74000046

Arnold—Palmer House, 33 Chestnut St., Providence, 1/20/72, C, a, 72000034

Art's Auto, 5–7 Lonsdale Ave., Pawtucket, 12/15/78, A, C, 78000071

Ashton Historic District, Roughly Mendon, Scott, and Old Angell Rds., Store Hill Rd., Front and Middle Sts., Cumberland, 11/01/84, A, C, a, d, 84000367

Aylesworth Apartments, 188–194 Broad St., Providence, 11/12/82, C, 82000133

Bailey, William L., House, Eaton St., Providence College Campus, Providence, 3/07/73, C, 73000064

Ballou House [Lincoln MRA], Albion Rd., Lincoln, 8/30/84, C, 84001908

Ballou—Weatherhead House, Tower Hill Rd. (Pole 68), Cumberland Hill vicinity, 6/25/93, C, 93000503

Battey—Barden House, Plainfield Pike, Scituate, 8/29/80, C, 80000084

Bell Street Chapel, 5 Bell St., Providence, 3/14/73, C, a, 73000065

Beneficent Congregational Church, 300 Weybosset St., Providence, 1/13/72, A, C, a, 72000035

Berkeley Mill Village, Bounded roughly by Martin St., Mendon Rd., railroad, and cemetery, Cumberland (Berkeley), 2/23/72, A, C, 72000036

Bicknell—Armington Lightning Splitter House [East Providence MRA], 3591 Pawtucket Ave., East Providence, 11/28/80, C, 80000085

Blackstone Canal, From Steeple and Promenade Sts. to the Ashton Dam, Lincoln, 5/06/71, A, C, 71000030

Blackstone Canal (Boundary Increase), From the Ashton Dam N to Massachusetts state line, Providence, 11/01/91, A, C, D, 91001536

Boston and Providence Railroad Bridge [East Providence MRA], Spans Ten Mile River, East Providence, 11/28/80, C, 80000086

Brackett, Charles, House, 45 Prospect St., Providence, 4/03/70, C, 70000018

Bradley, George M., House, Eaton St., Providence College Campus, Providence, 1/13/72, C, a, 72000037

Breezy Hill Site (RI-957), Address Restricted, Foster, 9/28/85, D, 85002700

Brick Schoolhouse, 24 Meeting St., Providence, 12/05/72, A, C, 72000038

Bridge Mill Power Plant [Pawtucket MRA], 25 Roosevelt Ave., Pawtucket, 11/18/83, C, 83003805

Bridgham Farm [East Providence MRA], 120, 148, 150 & 160 Pleasant St., East Providence, 11/28/80, A, C, a, 80000087

Bridgham—Arch—Wilson Streets Historic District, Roughly bounded by Lester and Bridgham Sts., Elmwood Ave., Warren and Dexter Sts., Providence, 9/01/88, A, C, 88001433

Broadway—Amory Historic District, Providence, Providence, 5/01/74, C, 74000047

Brown Avenue Historic District, Brown Ave., Johnston, 4/24/73, A, C, d, 73000066

Brown, John, House, 52 Power St., Providence, 11/24/68, C, NHL, 68000007

Brown, Morris, House, 317 Rochambeau Ave., Providence, 8/22/91, C, 91001025

Brown, Moses, School, 250 Lloyd Ave., Providence, 7/24/80, A, C, a, 80000088

Burlingame—Noon House, 3261 Mendon Rd., Cumberland, 2/15/74, C, 74000048

Burnham, G.A., House [Pawtucket MRA], 17 Nickerson St., Pawtucket, 11/18/83, C, 83003806

Burrows Block, 735–745 Westminster St., Providence, 9/05/90, C, 90001347

Butler Hospital, 333 Grotto Ave., Providence, 10/08/76, A, C, 76000041

Calvary Baptist Church [Elmwood MRA], 747 Broad St., Providence, 1/07/80, C, a, 80000089

Providence County—Continued

Cappelli, A. F., Block, 263–265 Atwells Ave., Providence, 3/03/80, A, C, 80000090

Carpenter, Lakeside, and Springvale Cemeteries [East Providence MRA], Newman and Pawtucket Aves., East Providence, 11/28/80, A, d, 80000091

Carr, Dr. George W., House, 29 Waterman St., Providence, 3/07/73, C, 73000067

Cathedral of Saints Peter and Paul, Cathedral Sq., Providence, 2/10/75, A, C, a, 75000057

Cato Hill Historic District [Woonsocket MRA (AD)], RI 44, Woonsocket, 8/10/76, A, C, 76002255

Cato Hill Historic District (Boundary Increase) [Woonsocket MRA], Roughly bounded by Arnold, Blackstone, Cherry, and Railroad Sts., Woonsocket, 11/24/82, A, 82000134

Central Falls Congregational Church [Central Falls MRA (AD)], 376 High St., Central Falls, 7/12/76, A, C, a, 76000042

Central Falls Mill Historic District [Central Falls MRA], Between Roosevelt Avenue and Blackstone River, Central Falls, 7/02/76, A, C, 76000007

Central Street School [Central Falls MRA], 379 Central St., Central Falls, 4/06/79, A, C, 79000004

Chemical Building, Fields Point Sewage Treatment Plant [Public Works and Utilities—Sewage Treatment Facilities in Providence, 1895–1935 TR], Ernest St. at Fields Point, Providence, 1/13/89, A, 88003106

Chepachet Village Historic District, Both Sides of US 44 (roughly from intersection of US 44 and RI 102 N to intersection of RI 100 and 102) and radiating, Glocester, 3/31/71, A, 71000031

Cherry Valley Archeological Site, RI-279, Address Restricted, Glocester vicinity, 11/01/84, D, 84000358

Childs—Brown House [Pawtucket MRA], 172 Pine St., Pawtucket, 11/18/83, A, C, 83003807

Christ Episcopal Church, 909 Eddy St., Providence, 6/30/76, A, C, a, 76000043

Church Hill Industrial District, Roughly bounded by S. Union, Pine, Baley, Commerce, Main, and Hill Sts., Pawtucket, 8/12/82, A, C, 82000135

Clayville Historic District [Foster MPS], Roughly bounded by Cole Ave., Plainfield Pike, Field Hill Rd., and Victory Hwy., Foster, 12/29/88, A, C, a, d, 88003079

Clemence—Irons House, 38 George Waterman Rd., Johnston, 7/02/73, A, B, C, 73000068

Cole, John, Farm, E of Manville on Reservoir Rd., Cumberland, 8/16/77, A, C, 77000025

College Hill Historic District, Roughly bounded by the Providence and Seekouk Rivers, Olney, Hope, and Governor Sts., Carrington and Whittier, Providence, 11/10/70, A, C, a, NHL, 70000019

Collyer Monument [Pawtucket MRA], Mineral Spring Park, Pawtucket, 11/18/83, A, C, f, 83003808

Conant Thread—Coats & Clark Mill Complex District [Pawtucket MRA], Roughly bounded by Lonsdale Ave., Pine, Conant, Carpenter, and Rand Sts., Pawtucket, 11/18/83, A, C, 83003809

Conant, Samuel B., House [Central Falls MRA], 104 Clay St., Central Falls, 4/06/79, C, 79000005

Congdon Street Baptist Church, 17 Congdon St., Providence, 6/21/71, A, C, a, 71000032

Cooke, Amos, House, Chopmist Hill Rd., Scituate, 10/30/79, C, 79000054

Corliss, John, House, 201 S. Main St., Providence, 5/01/74, C, 74000049

Corliss—Carrington House, 66 Williams St., Providence, 12/30/70, C, NHL, 70000020

Cornell—Randall—Bailey Roadhouse, 2737 Hartford Ave., Johnston, 5/10/84, A, C, 84001943

Covell Street School, 231 Amherst St., Providence, 9/30/76, A, C, 76000044

Crandall, Lorenzo, House, 221 High St., Pawtucket, 12/10/84, A, C, 78000072

Crescent Park Carousel [East Providence MRA (AD)], Bullock's Point Ave., East Providence, 4/21/76, A, C, NHL, 76000045

Customhouse Historic District, Bounded by Westminster, Exchange, Dyer, Pine, and Peck Sts., Providence, 2/20/75, A, C, 75000058

Daggett, Nathaniel, House [East Providence MRA], 74 Roger Williams Ave., East Providence, 11/28/80, C, e, 80000092

Darling, Henry, House [Woonsocket MRA], 786 Harris Ave., Woonsocket, 11/26/82, C, 82000136

Davol Rubber Company, Point and Eddy Sts., Providence, 6/27/80, C, 80000093

Deming, Richard Henry, House [Elmwood MRA], 66 Burnett St., Providence, 1/07/80, C, 80000094

Dennis, James, House [East Providence MRA], 3120 Pawtucket Ave., East Providence, 11/28/80, C, 80000095

Dexter, Edward, House, 72 Waterman St., Providence, 6/21/71, C, b, 71000033

Dexter, Jeremiah, House, 957 N. Main St., Providence, 10/08/76, C, 76000046

District 6 Schoolhouse [East Providence MRA], 347 Willett Ave, East Providence, 11/28/80, A, C, 80000096

Division Street Bridge [Pawtucket MRA], Division St. at Seekonk River, Pawtucket, 11/18/83, A, C, 83003810

Dorrance, Capt. George, House, Jencks Rd., Foster, 3/16/72, C, 72000039

Double L Site, RI-958, Address Restricted, Scituate, 9/12/85, D, 85002362

Dowler, Charles, House, 581 Smith St., Providence, 2/23/84, B, C, 84001955

Downtown Providence Historic District, Roughly bounded by Washington, Westminister, Empire and Weybosset Sts., Providence, 2/10/84, A, C, 84001967

Doyle Avenue Historic District, Doyle Ave. from N. Main St. to Hope St., Providence, 2/22/90, A, B, C, 90000104

Dyerville Mill, 610 Manton Ave, Providence, 6/18/79, A, C, 79000055

Eddy Homestead, 2543 Hartford Ave., Johnston, 8/13/86, C, 86001511

Edgewood Yacht Club, 3 Shaw Ave., Cranston, 2/23/89, C, 89000072

Elizabeth Building, 100 N. Main St., Providence, 11/05/71, C, 71000034

Elliot—Harris—Miner House [Lincoln MRA], 1406 Old Louisquisset Pike, Lincoln, 8/30/84, C, 84001984

Elmwood Historic District [Elmwood MRA], Bounded by Whitemarsh, Moore, Daboll, Mawney, and Ontario Sts. and Congress, Lexington, Atlantic, and Adelaide Aves., Providence, 1/07/80, B, C, 80004603

Ernest Street Sewage Pumping Station [Public Works and Utilities—Sewage Treatment Facilities in Providence, 1895–1935 TR], Ernest and Ellis Sts., Providence, 1/13/89, A, C, 88003103

Fales, David G., House [Central Falls MRA], 476 High St., Central Falls, 4/06/79, B, C, 79000006

Farnum, Edwin H., House, US 44 at jct. with Collins St., Johnston, 5/17/74, A, C, 74000359

Federal Building, Kennedy Plaza, Providence, 4/13/72, C, 72000040

Fenner, Thomas, House, 43 Stony Acre Dr., Cranston, 3/02/90, A, C, 90000143

Fifth Ward Wardroom [Pawtucket MRA], 47 Mulberry St., Pawtucket, 11/18/83, A, C, 83003817

Fire Station No. 4 [Pawtucket MRA], 474 Broadway, Pawtucket, 11/18/83, A, C, 83003819

First Baptist Meetinghouse, N. Main St., between Thomas and Waterman Sts., Providence, 10/15/66, C, a, NHL, 66000017

First Universalist Church, 250 Washington St., Providence, 8/16/77, A, C, a, 77000026

First Ward Wardroom [Pawtucket MRA], 171 Fountain St., Pawtucket, 11/18/83, A, C, 83003820

Fleur-de-Lis Studios, 7 Thomas St., Providence, 10/05/92, C, NHL, 92001886

Forestdale Mill Village Historic District, E and W along Main St. and N on Maple Ave., North Smithfield, 6/05/72, A, C, 72000041

Foster Center Historic District, Foster, Foster, 5/11/74, A, C, a, 74000050

Foster—Payne House [Pawtucket MRA], 25 Belmont St., Pawtucket, 11/18/83, C, 83003823

Fuller Houses [Pawtucket MRA], 339–341 and 343–345 Broadway, Pawtucket, 11/18/83, C, 83003825

Furnace Carolina Site, Address Restricted, Cumberland, 5/10/93, A, D, 93000341

Furnace Hill Brook Historic and Archeological District, Address Restricted, Cranston vicinity, 8/06/80, A, C, D, d, 80000097

Gaulin, Alphonse, Jr., House [Woonsocket MRA], 311 Elm St., Woonsocket, 11/24/82, C, 82000137

Georgiaville Historic District, Roughly bounded by Stillwater Rd., Cross St., Whipple Ave., and Farnum Pike, Smithfield vicinity, 10/03/85, A, C, 85002734

Gilbane's Service Center Building [Pawtucket MRA], 175–191 Pawtucket Avenue, Pawtucket, 11/18/83, A, C, 83003827

Glenark Mills [Woonsocket MRA], 64 East St., Woonsocket, 5/15/89, A, B, C, 89000409

Glocester Town Pound, Pound Rd. and Chopmist Hill Rd., Glocester, 9/22/70, A, C, 70000021

Providence County—Continued

Gloria Dei Evangelical Lutheran Church, 15 Hayes St., Providence, 2/23/84, C, a, 84002006

Grace Church, 175 Mathewson St., Providence, 6/19/72, C, a, 72000042

Great Road Historic District, Great Rd., Lincoln vicinity, 7/22/74, A, C, 74000051

Greene, Benjamin F., House [Central Falls MRA], 85 Cross St., Central Falls, 4/06/79, C, 79000007

Grove Street Elementary School [Woonsocket MRA], 312 Grove St., Woonsocket, 11/24/82, A, C, 82000138

Haile, Joseph, House, 106 George St., Providence, 5/19/72, C, 72000007

Hanora Mills [Woonsocket MRA], 1 Main St., Woonsocket, 11/24/82, A, C, 82000139

Harmony Chapel and Cemetery, Putnam Pike, Harmony, 6/25/80, A, C, a, d, 80000098

Harris Warehouse, 61 Railroad St., Woonsocket, 7/01/76, A, C, 76000047

Harrisville Historic District, Roughly bounded by Wood and Sherman Rds., East Ave, Main, Chapel, School, and River Sts., Burrillville, 3/21/84, A, B, C, 84002010

Hay and Owen Buildings, 101 and 117–135 Dyer St., Providence, 11/12/82, A, C, 82001859

Hearthside, Great Rd., Lincoln, 4/24/73, C, 73000069

Holy Trinity Church Complex [Central Falls MRA (AD)], 134 Fuller Ave., Central Falls, 1/03/78, A, C, a, 78000073

Honan's Block and 112–114 Main Street [Woonsocket MRA], 110–114 Main St., Woonsocket, 8/03/89, A, C, 89000941

Hope Block and Cheapside, 22–26 and 40 N. Main St., Providence, 5/21/75, C, 75000059

Hope—Power—Cooke Streets Historic District, Roughly bounded by Angell, Governor, Williams, and Brook Sts., Providence, 1/12/73, C, g, 73000070

Hopkins, Esek, House, 97 Admiral St., Providence, 5/22/73, B, 73000071

Hopkins, Gov. Stephen, House, 15 Hopkins St., Providence, 4/03/70, B, b, NHL, 70000022

Hoppin, Thomas F., House, 383 Benefit St., Providence, 2/06/73, C, 73000072

Hughes, Thomas H., House, 423 Central Ave., Johnston, 6/15/79, B, C, 79000056

Island Place Historic District [Woonsocket MPS], Island Place and S. Main St. at Market Sq., Woonsocket, 9/13/90, A, C, 90001348

Ives, Thomas P., House, 66 Power St., Providence, 12/30/70, C, NHL, 70000023

Jenckes House [Lincoln MRA], 1730 Old Louisquisset Pike, Lincoln, 10/10/84, C, 84000088

Jenckes House [Lincoln MRA], 81 Jenckes Hill Rd., Lincoln, 8/30/84, C, 84002019

Jenckes Mansion [Woonsocket MRA], 837–839 Social St., Woonsocket, 11/24/82, C, 82000140

Jenks Park & Cogswell Tower [Central Falls MRA (AD)], Adjoining 580 Broad St., Central Falls, 4/06/79, C, 79000057

Jillson, Luke, House, 2510 Mendon Rd., Cumberland, 8/12/82, C, 82000141

Jones Warehouses [Elmwood MRA], 49–63 Central St., Providence, 1/07/80, C, 80000099

Joy Homestead, 156 Scituate Ave., Cranston, 2/18/71, A, C, 71000035

Knightsville Meetinghouse, 67 Phenix Ave., Cranston, 3/08/78, A, C, a, 78000074

Kotzow, Louis, House [Pawtucket MRA], 641 East Ave., Pawtucket, 11/18/83, A, C, 83003829

L'Eglise du Precieux Sang, 94 Carrington Ave. and 61 Park Ave., Woonsocket, 7/26/82, A, C, a, 82000142

Leroy Theatre, 66 Broad St., Pawtucket, 8/04/83, A, C, 83000181

Lime Kilns [Lincoln MRA], Off Louisquisset Pike, Sherman and Dexter Rock Rds., Lincoln, 8/30/84, A, 84002015

Limerock Village Historic District, In irregular pattern along Smith, Wilbur, and Great Rds., and Old Louisquisset Pike, Lincoln, 5/23/74, A, C, 74000052

Linton Block [Woonsocket MRA], 3–5 Monument Sq., Woonsocket, 11/24/82, A, C, 82000143

Lippitt Hill Historic District, Hope Rd., Burlingame Rd., and Lippett Ave., Cranston, 3/02/89, A, C, d, 89000142

Lippitt, Gov. Henry, House, 199 Hope St., Providence, 11/27/72, C, NHL, 72000043

Little Neck Cemetery [East Providence MRA], Off Read St., East Providence, 11/28/80, A, C, d, 80000100

Loew's State Theatre, 220 Weybosset St., Providence, 8/19/77, A, C, 77000027

Logee House [Woonsocket MRA], 225 Logee St., Woonsocket, 11/24/82, A, C, 82000001

Lonsdale Historic District, Lonsdale Ave., Blackstone Ct., Front, Main, Cook, Broad, Mill, Cross and Blackstone Sts., Lonsdale, 5/25/84, A, C, 84002022

Lynch, Matthew, House, 120 Robinson St., Providence, 3/08/78, B, 78000001

Main Street Bridge [Pawtucket MRA], Main St. at Pawtucket Falls, Pawtucket, 11/18/83, A, C, 83003832

Main Street Historic District [Woonsocket MRA], Roughly, Main St. E of Market Sq. to Depot Sq., Woonsocket, 4/18/91, A, C, 91000461

Manton—Hunt—Farnum Farm, Putnam Pike, Glocester, 10/03/85, A, C, 85002735

Market House, Market Sq., Providence, 4/13/72, A, C, 72000001

Mason, Israel B., House, 571 Broad St., Providence, 8/16/77, C, 77000001

McGonagle Site, RI-1227, Address Restricted, Scituate, 9/12/85, A, D, d, 85002400

Merchants Bank Building, 32 Westminster St., Providence, 11/21/77, A, C, 77000002

Millrace Site, RI-1039, Address Restricted, Scituate, 9/12/85, D, 85002361

Mitchell—Arnold House [Pawtucket MRA], 41 Waldo St., Pawtucket, 11/18/83, C, 83003833

Modern Diner, 364 East Ave., Pawtucket, 10/19/78, A, C, b, g, 78000002

Montgomery, Nathaniel, House, 178 High St., Pawtucket, 1/19/84, A, C, 84002030

Moosup Valley Historic District [Foster MPS], Roughly bounded by Harrington, Johnson,

Moosup Valley and Barb Hill, and Cucumber Hill Rds., Foster, 5/11/88, A, B, D, a, b, d, 88000521

Moshassuck Square, Roughly bounded by Charles, Randall, N. Main, and Smith Sts., Providence, 9/08/70, A, C, 70000001

Moswansicut Pond Site, RI-960, Address Restricted, Scituate, 9/12/85, D, 85002363

Mount Vernon Tavern, Plainfield Pike (RI 14), Foster vicinity, 5/08/74, A, C, 74000001

Mowry, William, House, Farnum Pike, North Smithfield, 2/10/83, C, 83000001

Mt. Hygeia, Mt. Hygeia Rd., Foster, 8/12/77, B, C, 77000008

New England Butt Company [Elmwood MRA], 304 Pearl St., Providence, 1/07/80, C, 80000001

Newman Cemetery [East Providence MRA], Newman and Pawtucket Aves., East Providence, 11/28/80, A, C, d, 80000002

Newman Congregational Church [East Providence MRA], 100 Newman Ave., East Providence, 11/28/80, A, C, a, 80000003

Nightingale—Brown House, 357 Benefit St., Providence, 6/29/89, A, B, C, NHL, 89001242

Nopkins Mill Historic District, Old Danielson Pike, US 6, Maple Rock and Rams Trail Rds., Foster, 5/10/84, C, 84002013

North Burial Ground, Between Branch Ave. and N. Main St., Providence, 9/13/77, A, C, d, 77000100

North End Historic District [Woonsocket MRA], Roughly bounded by Verry, Highland, Winter, and Summer Sts., Woonsocket, 11/24/82, A, C, a, g, 82000002

Oak Lawn Village Historic District, Wilbur Ave. from Natick Rd. to Oaklawn Ave., includes Searle, Exchange, and Wheelock Sts., Cranston, 11/25/77, A, C, a, 77000004

Oakland Avenue Historic District, Roughly bounded by Pembroke Ave., Eaton, Malbone, and Dickens Sts., Providence, 11/01/84, A, C, 84000378

Oakland Historic District, Victory Hwy., Burrillville, 9/09/87, A, B, C, 87001359

Ochee Spring Quarry, Address Restricted, Johnston vicinity, 5/05/78, A, D, 78000003

Oddfellow's Hall [East Providence MRA], 63–67 Warren Ave., East Providence, 11/28/80, A, C, 80000004

Old Ashton Historic District [Lincoln MRA], Lower River Rd. and Blackstone Canal Towpath, Lincoln, 8/30/84, C, 84002037

Old Congregational Church, Off US 6 on Greenville Rd. (RI 116), North Scituate, 1/11/74, A, C, a, 74000002

Old Slater Mill, Roosevelt Ave., Pawtucket, 11/13/66, A, B, NHL, 66000001

Olney Street—Alumni Avenue Historic District, Roughly bounded by Olney St., Arlington, Alumni Ave., and Hope St., Providence, 5/11/89, C, 89000333

Olney, Capt. Stephen, House, 138 Smithfield Rd., North Providence, 5/01/74, C, 74000003

Our Lady of Lourdes Church Complex [Providence MPS], 901–903 Atwells Ave., Providence, 3/15/90, A, C, a, 90000343

Providence County—Continued

Parkis—Comstock Historic District [Elmwood MRA], Broad St., Parkis and Comstock Aves., Providence, 1/07/80, C, 80000005

Parkis—Comstock Historic District (Boundary Increase) [Elmwood MRA], 568, 570–572 Broad St. and 39–41, 54–56, and 60–62 Harvard Ave., Providence, 5/05/88, C, 88000512

Patterson Brothers Commercial Building and House, 157, 159 and 161 Broad St., Valley Falls, 6/10/93, A, C, 93000502

Pawtucket Armory [Pawtucket MRA], 172 Exchange St., Pawtucket, 11/18/83, A, C, 83003836

Pawtucket City Hall [Pawtucket MRA], 137 Roosevelt Ave., Pawtucket, 11/18/83, A, C, 83003838

Pawtucket Congregational Church, 40 and 56 Walcott St., Pawtucket, 9/18/78, C, a, 78000004

Pawtucket Elks Lodge Building [Pawtucket MRA], 27 Exchange, Pawtucket, 11/18/83, A, C, 83003840

Pawtucket Post Office, 56 High St., Pawtucket, 4/30/76, A, C, 76000226

Pawtucket Times Building [Pawtucket MRA], 23 Exchange St., Pawtucket, 11/18/83, A, C, 83003842

Pawtucket West High School [Pawtucket MRA], 485 East Ave., Pawtucket, 11/18/83, A, C, g, 83003845

Payne, Charles, House [Pawtucket MRA], 25 Brown St., Pawtucket, 11/18/83, C, 83003847

Pearce, Nathaniel, House, 305 Brook St., Providence, 5/19/72, C, b, 72000002

Pekin Street Historic District, Roughly bounded by Pekin and Candace Sts., Douglas and Chalkstone Aves., Providence, 11/01/84, C, 84000381

Pine Street Historic District, Irregular pattern along Pine St. from Myrtle to Seekill Sts., Providence, 9/13/78, A, C, 78000005

Pitcher—Goff House, 56 Walcott St., Pawtucket, 6/24/76, A, C, 76000001

Plain Farm House, 108 Webster Ave, Providence, 6/27/80, C, 80000006

Pomham Rocks Light Station [Lighthouses of Rhode Island TR (AD)], Riverside Rd., East Providence, 7/09/79, A, C, 79000001

Pothier House [Woonsocket MRA], 172 Pond St., Woonsocket, 11/24/82, B, 82000003

Potter—Collyer House [Pawtucket MRA], 67 Cedar St., Pawtucket, 11/18/83, C, 83003849

Potter—Remington House, 571 Natick Rd., Cranston vicinity, 12/28/78, C, 78000006

Power Street-Cooke Street Historic District, Roughly bounded by Angell, Governor, Power and Hope Sts., Providence, 7/30/74, C, 74002345

Providence City Hall, Dorrance and Washington Sts., Providence, 1/23/75, C, 75000001

Providence Jewelry Manufacturing Historic District, Bounded by Ship St., Ashcroft and Elbow and Hospital Sts., Point and South Sts., Imperial and Claverick Sts. and US 195, Providence, 12/05/85, A, B, C, 85003088

Providence Lying-In Hospital, 50 Maude St., Providence, 8/13/86, A, C, 86001512

Providence Telephone Company, 112 Union St., Providence, 8/04/83, A, C, 83000002

Providence—Biltmore Hotel, 11 Dorrance St., Providence, 5/27/77, A, C, 77000005

Pullen Corner School [Lincoln MRA], Angell and Whipple, Lincoln, 8/30/84, C, 84002039

Quality Hill Historic District [Pawtucket MRA], Roughly bounded by I-95, Cottage, Lyon, Bend, and Potter Sts., Pawtucket, 4/13/84, A, C, a, 84002041

Reservoir Avenue Sewage Pumping Station [Public Works and Utilities—Sewage Treatment Facilities in Providence, 1895–1935 TR], Reservoir and Pontiac Aves., Providence, 1/13/89, A, 88003108

Return Sludge Pumping Station, Fields Point Sewage Treatment Plant [Public Works and Utilities—Sewage Treatment Facilities in Providence, 1895–1935 TR], Ernest St., Providence, 1/13/89, A, 88003105

Rhode Island Hospital Trust Building, 15 Westminster St., Providence, 10/22/76, A, C, 76000002

Rhode Island Medical Society Building, 106 Francis St., Providence, 6/04/84, C, 84002043

Rhode Island Statehouse, 90 Smith St., Providence, 4/28/70, A, C, 70000002

Rhodes Street Historic District, Rhodes, Janes and Alphonso Sts., Providence, 11/12/82, C, 82000004

Rhodes-on-the Pawtuxet Ballroom and Gazebo, Rhodes Pl., Cranston, 12/12/78, A, C, 78000007

Riverside Cemetery [Pawtucket MRA], 724 Pleasant St., Pawtucket, 11/18/83, A, C, d, 83003853

Roger Williams National Memorial, Bounded by N. Main, Canal, Smith, and Haymarket Sts., Providence, 10/15/66, A, B, a, f, NPS, 66000942

Roger Williams Park Historic District, Roger Williams Park, Providence, 10/15/66, A, C, 66000002

Rumford Chemical Works and Mill House Historic District [East Providence MRA], N. Broadway, Newman and Greenwood Aves., East Providence, 11/28/80, A, C, 80000007

Rumford Historic District [East Providence MRA], Pleasant St., Greenwood and Pawtucket Aves, East Providence, 11/28/80, C, a, 80000008

Russell, Joseph and William, House, 118 N. Main St., Providence, 8/12/71, C, 71000001

Saint Thomas Episcopal Church and Rectory, Putnam Pike, Smithfield, 7/02/87, A, C, a, 87000993

Sassafras Site, RI-55, Address Restricted, Albion vicinity, 11/01/84, D, 84000360

Sayles, Deborah Cook, Public Library, 13 Summer St., Pawtucket, 12/06/75, A, C, 75000002

Saylesville Historic District [Lincoln MRA], Roughly bounded by Memorial Ave., Scotts Road, Industrial Circle, Smithfield Ave., and Woodland Court, Lincoln, 8/30/84, A, C, 84002049

Saylesville Meetinghouse, Smithfield Ave., Lincoln, 11/28/78, A, C, a, 78000008

Scholze—Sayles House [Pawtucket MRA], 625 East Ave., Pawtucket, 11/18/83, A, C, 83003859

Shakespeare Hall, 128 Dorrance St., Providence, 6/18/79, A, C, 79000002

Sheldon House, 458 Scituate Ave., Cranston, 1/05/89, C, 88001123

Shepard Company Building, 259 Westminster Mall, 72–92 Washington St., Providence, 8/11/76, A, C, 76000003

Sixth District Courthouse, 150 Benefit St., Providence, 4/28/70, A, C, 70000092

Slater Park, Armistice Blvd., Pawtucket, 6/30/76, A, C, 76000004

Slatersville Historic District, Main, Green, Church, and School Sts. and Ridge Rd., Slatersville, 4/24/73, A, C, 73000002

Sludge Press House, Fields Point Sewage Treatment Plant [Public Works and Utilities—Sewage Treatment Facilities in Providence, 1895–1935 TR], Ernest St. at Fields Point, Providence, 1/13/89, A, 88003104

Smith Hill Historic District, 57–65 Brownell St., 73–114 Holden St., 23–80 Jewett St., 189–240 Smith St. and 10–18 W. Park St., Providence, 11/04/93, A, C, 93001183

Smith Street Primary School, 396 Smith St., Providence, 2/23/84, C, 84002050

Smith, Joseph, House, 109 Smithfield Rd., North Providence, 11/28/78, C, 78000009

Smith—Appleby House, Stillwater Rd., SE of jct. with Capron Rd., Smithfield vicinity, 5/01/74, C, 74000005

Smithfield Friends Meeting House, Parsonage & Cemetery [Woonsocket MRA], 126 Smithfield Rd., Woonsocket, 11/24/82, A, C, a, d, 82000008

Smithfield Road Historic District, Smithfield Rd., North Smithfield, 2/18/87, A, C, 87000036

Smithville Seminary, Institute Lane, Scituate, 3/29/78, A, C, a, 78003446

Smithville—North Scituate, Danielson Pike and W Greenville Road, Scituate, 8/29/79, A, C, a, 79000003

Sons of Jacob Synagogue, 24 Douglas Ave., Providence, 8/24/89, A, C, a, 89001152

South Central Falls Historic District [Central Falls MRA], Roughly bounded by Central Falls—Pawtucket boundary, Rand, Summit, Dexter and Broad Sts., Central Falls, 1/31/91, A, C, 91000025

South Main Street Historic District [Woonsocket MRA], Roughly bounded by Mason, Coe, Andrews St., and Bernice Ave., Woonsocket, 11/24/82, A, C, 82000009

South Street Historic District [Pawtucket MRA], Roughly South Street between Meadow and Fruit Sts., Pawtucket, 11/18/83, A, C, 83003864

Spaulding, Joseph, House, 30 Fruit St., Pawtucket, 10/22/76, C, 76000005

Sprague, David, House, 263 Public St., Providence, 5/23/78, C, 78000010

Sprague, Gov. William, Mansion, 1351 Cranston St., Cranston, 2/18/71, A, C, 71000002

Squantum Association [East Providence MRA], 947 Veterans Memorial Parkway, East Providence, 11/28/80, A, C, 80000010

St. Andrews Episcopal Chapel [Woonsocket MRA], 576 Fairmont St., Woonsocket, 11/24/82, C, a, 82000005

Providence County—Continued

St. Ann's Church Complex [Woonsocket MRA], Cumberland and Elm Sts. and Gaulin Ave., Woonsocket, 11/24/82, A, C, a, g, 82000006

St. Charles Borromeo Church Complex [Woonsocket MRA], N. Main, Daniels and Earle Sts., Woonsocket, 2/24/83, A, C, a, 83000003

St. John the Baptist Church [Pawtucket MRA], 68 Slater, Pawtucket, 11/18/83, C, a, 83003855

St. Joseph's Church Complex, 1303–1317 Mendon Rd., Cumberland, 8/12/82, A, C, a, 82000007

St. Joseph's Roman Catholic Church, 86 Hope St., Providence, 7/15/74, C, a, 74000004

St. Mary's Church of the Immaculate Conception Complex [Pawtucket MRA], 103 Pine St., Pawtucket, 11/18/83, A, C, a, 83003856

St. Mary's Episcopal Church [East Providence MRA], 83 Warren Ave., East Providence, 11/28/80, C, a, 80000009

St. Matthew's Church [Central Falls MRA], Dexter & W. Hunt Sts., Central Falls, 4/06/79, C, a, 79000008

St. Michael's Roman Catholic Church, Convent, Rectory, and School, 251 Oxford St., Providence, 3/25/77, A, C, a, 77000006

St. Paul's Church [Pawtucket MRA], 50 Dark Pl., Pawtucket, 11/18/83, A, C, a, 83003857

St. Stephen's Church, 114 George St., Providence, 2/06/73, C, a, 73000001

Stadium Building, 329 Main St., Woonsocket, 6/30/76, A, C, 76000006

State Arsenal, 176 Benefit St, Providence, 4/28/70, A, C, b, 70000003

Stimson Avenue Historic District, Both sides of Stimson Ave. and Diman Pl. between Angell St. on S, Hope St. on W, and a stone wall on N., Providence, 4/24/73, C, 73000008

Swan Point Cemetery, 585 Blackstone Blvd., Providence, 10/05/77, A, C, d, 77000007

Swan Point Cemetery and Trolley Shelter (Boundary Increase), Opposite 585 Blackstone Blvd., Providence, 11/28/78, C, 78003445

Temple Beth-El, 688 Broad St., Providence, 12/29/88, A, C, a, 88003074

Three Dog Site, RI-151, Address Restricted, North Smithfield, 11/01/84, D, 84000362

Todd Farm, 670 Farnum Pike, North Smithfield, 2/10/83, C, 83000004

Tower, Lewis, House, 2199 Mendon Rd., Cumberland, 8/30/82, C, 82000010

Trinity Church, 50 Main St., Pawtucket, 1/13/72, A, C, a, 72000003

Trinity Square Historic District [Elmwood MRA], Broad St. and Elmwood Ave., Providence, 1/07/80, C, a, d, 80000011

Trinity Square Repertory Theatre, 201 Washington St., Providence, 6/05/72, A, C, 72000004

U.S. Customshouse, 24 Weybosset St., Providence, 4/13/72, C, 72000005

U.S. Post Office, 295 Main St., Woonsocket, 5/30/79, C, 79003774

Union Station, Exchange Ter., Providence, 2/20/75, A, 75000003

Union Trust Company Building, 62 Dorrance St., Providence, 3/01/73, C, 73000004

Union Village Historic District, W of Woonsocket on RI 146A, Woonsocket vicinity, 7/28/78, C, 78000011

University Hall, Brown University, Brown University Campus, Providence, 10/15/66, A, C, NHL, 66000003

Valley Falls Mill [Central Falls MRA], 1363 Broad St., Central Falls, 4/26/78, A, C, 78000012

Valley Falls Mill, Office and Bath House [Central Falls MRA (AD)], 1359 and 1361–63 Broad St., Central Falls, 4/26/78, A, C, 78000013

Veterans Memorial Auditorium—Masonic Temple, Jct. of Brownell and Park Sts., Providence, 11/16/93, C, 93001181

Walker, Phillip, House, 432 W. Massasoit Ave., East Providence, 6/24/72, C, 72000006

Wanskuck Historic District, Roughly bounded by Branch Ave., Louisquisset Pike, and town boundary, Providence, 12/01/83, A, C, a, 83003867

Washington Park Sewage Pumping Station [Public Works and Utilities—Sewage Treatment Facilities in Providence, 1895–1935 TR], Shipyard St., Providence, 1/13/89, A, 88003107

Waterman—Winsor Farm, 79 Austin Ave., Smithfield, 6/27/80, A, C, 80000012

Wesleyan Avenue Historic District, Roughly Wesleyan Ave. between Taylor and Broad Sts., Providence, 11/23/82, C, 82000011

Westcote, 101 Mountain Laurel Dr., Cranston, 8/03/88, C, 88001126

Westcott, Nathan, House, 150 Scituate Ave., Cranston, 1/05/89, C, 88001124

Whipple—Cullen House and Barn [Lincoln MPS], Old River Rd. S of jct. with George Washington Hwy., Lincoln, 11/14/91, C, 91001647

Whipple—Jenckes House, 2500 Diamond Hill Rd., Cumberland, 11/05/92, C, 92001541

Whitcomb Farm [East Providence MRA], 36 Willett Ave., East Providence, 11/28/80, C, 80000013

White, Josephine, Block [Elmwood MRA], 737–739 Cranston St., Providence, 1/07/80, C, 80000014

Wilbur, Frank, House [Woonsocket MRA], 1273 Park Ave., Woonsocket, 11/24/82, C, 82000012

Winsor, Stephen, House, 93 Austin Ave., Smithfield vicinity, 10/06/75, C, 75000004

Winsor—Swan—Whitman Farm, 416 Eaton St., Providence, 5/01/74, C, 74000006

Witherby, Constance, Park, 210 Pitman St., Providence, 11/25/75, C, g, 75000005

Wood, Arad, House, 407 Pontiac Ave., Cranston, 8/03/88, C, 88001125

Woods—Gerry House, 62 Prospect St., Providence, 2/12/71, C, 71000003

Woonasquatucket River Site (RI-163), Address Restricted, Smithville vicinity, 11/01/84, D, 84000364

Woonsocket City Hall, 169 Main St., Woonsocket, 5/01/74, A, C, 74000007

Woonsocket Civil War Monument [Woonsocket MRA], Monument Sq., Woonsocket, 11/24/82, A, C, f, 82000013

Woonsocket Company Mill Complex, 100–115 Front St., Woonsocket, 5/07/73, C, 73000005

Woonsocket District Courthouse [Woonsocket MRA], 24 Front St., Woonsocket, 11/24/82, A, C, 82000014

Woonsocket Rubber Company Mill, 60–82 S. Main St., Woonsocket, 5/01/89, A, B, C, 89000334

Washington County

Allen—Madison House, Post Rd., North Kingstown, 3/28/80, C, 80000015

Austin Farm Road Agricultural Area, 6 mi. W of Exeter of I-95, Exeter vicinity, 8/16/77, A, C, a, d, 77000009

Babcock House, Main St., Charlestown, 1/01/76, A, C, 76000008

Babcock—Smith House, 124 Granite St., Westerly, 7/24/72, A, C, 72000008

Baptist Church in Exeter, N of Arcadia on RI 165, Exeter, 11/21/78, A, C, a, 78000014

Block Island North Light [Lighthouses of Rhode Island TR (AD)], Sandy Point (off N end of Corn Neck Rd.), New Shoreham, 5/23/74, A, C, 74000008

Block Island South East Light, South East Light Rd. at Lighthouse Cove, New Shoreham, 8/06/90, A, C, 90001131

Bouchard Archeological Site, RI-1025, Address Restricted, Usquepaug vicinity, 11/01/84, D, 84000370

Bull, Jireh, Blockhouse Historic Site, Address Restricted, South Kingstown vicinity, 11/03/83, A, D, 83003869

Camp Endicott, Between Seventh and Tenth Sts., North Kingstown, 10/19/78, A, C, g, 78000015

Carolina Village Historic District, Charleston, Carolina, 5/02/74, A, C, 74000009

Casey, Silas, Farm, Boston Neck Rd., North Kingstown, 8/14/73, A, C, 73000006

Central Street Historic Distriict [Narragansett Pier MRA], Both sides of Central Street from Fifth Ave. to Boon St., Narragansett, 8/18/82, A, C, a, 82000015

Champlin, Peleg, House, Rodman Pond Lane, New Shoreham, 6/01/82, C, 82000016

Cocumscossoc Archeological Site, Address Restricted, Wickford, 4/12/93, D, NHL, 93000605

Crowfield Historic District [North Kingstown MRA], Boston Neck Rd., North Kingstown, 7/19/85, A, B, C, 85001646

Davisville Historic District [North Kingstown MRA], Davisville Rd., North Kingstown, 7/19/85, A, C, d, 85001645

Devil's Foot Cemetery Archeological Site, RI-694, Address Restricted, North Kingston vicinity, 11/15/84, D, 84000562

Dewey Cottage, 668 Matunuck Beach Rd., South Kingstown, 5/07/92, A, C, 92000467

District Schoolhouse No. 2, Old Post Rd., Charlestown, 1/04/80, A, C, b, e, 80000016

Douglas, George, House, S of Allenton at Tower Hill and Gilbert Stuart Rds., North Kingstown, 10/10/75, C, 75000006

Washington County—Continued

Druidsdream, 144 Gibson Ave., Narragansett, 7/20/89, B, C, 89000940

Earlscourt Historic District [Narragansett Pier MRA], Roughly bounded by Westmoreland, Noble, Woodward Sts., and Gibson Ave.(both sides), Narragansett, 8/18/82, C, 82000017

Eldred, Henry, Farm, 368 Old North Rd., South Kingstown, 11/18/91, A, C, 91001646

Fayerweather, George, Blacksmith Shop, Address Restricted, Kingstown vicinity, 11/29/84, A, D, 84000470

Fernwood Archeological Site, RI-702, Address Restricted, South Kingston, 9/12/85, D, d, 85002364

Fisherville Historic and Archeological District, Address Restricted, Exeter vicinity, 12/05/80, A, D, d, 80000017

Flying Horse Carousel, Bay St., Westerly, 1/11/80, A, C, NHL, 80000019

Former Immaculate Conception Church, 119 High St., Westerly, 4/24/73, A, C, a, 73000007

Fort Ninigret, Fort Neck Rd., Charlestown, 4/28/70, A, f, 70000004

Foster Cove Archeological Site, Address Restricted, Charlestown vicinity, 5/06/80, D, 80000018

Gardencourt [Narragansett Pier MRA], 10 Gibson Ave., Narragansett, 8/18/82, C, 82000018

Gardner, Ezekial, House [North Kingstown MRA], 297 Pendar Rd., North Kingstown, 7/19/85, A, C, 85001654

Gladstone Springhouse and Bottling Plant, 145a Boon St., Narrangansett, 5/10/84, A, C, 84002051

Great Salt Pond Archeological District [Indian Use of Block Island, 500 BC—AD 1676 MPS], Address Restricted, New Shoreham vicinity, 2/15/90, D, 90000107

Greene Inn, 175 Ocean Rd., Narragansett, 6/24/76, A, C, 76000009

Hallville Historic and Archeological District, Address Restricted, Exeter vicinity, 12/05/80, A, D, 80000020

Hamilton Mill Village Historic District, Boston Neck and Martha Rds., Salisbury and Web Aves., North Kingstown, 11/03/83, A, C, 83003874

Hillsdale Historic and Archeological District, Address Restricted, Wyoming vicinity, 11/24/80, A, D, 80000021

Historic Village of the Narragansetts in Charlestown, Address Restricted, Charlestown vicinity, 5/07/73, A, D, a, d, 73000008

Hopkinton City Historic District, Hopkinton, Hopkinton, 5/01/74, A, C, 74000010

Hoxsie, John, House, E of RI 112, Richmond vicinity, 5/05/78, A, C, 78000016

Indian Burial Ground, Narrow Lane, Charlestown vicinity, 4/28/70, A, 70000005

Jeffrey, Joseph, House, S of Carolina on Town House Rd., Charlestown vicinity, 3/08/78, A, C, 78000017

Kenyon's Department Store, 344 Main St., South Kingstown, 11/05/92, A, C, 92001540

Kingston Hill Farm, 549 Old North Rd., South Kingstown, 5/07/93, A, C, 93000343

Kingston Railroad Station, Kingston Rd., South Kingstown, 4/26/78, A, C, 78000018

Kingston Village Historic District, South Kingston, Kingston, 5/01/74, A, C, 74000011

Lafayette Village, Ten Rod Road, North Kingstown, 11/14/78, A, C, a, 78000019

Lambda Chi Site, RI-704, Address Restricted, Kingstown vicinity, 11/01/84, A, D, 84000372

Lawton's Mill, Ten Rod Rd., Exeter, 6/27/80, A, 80000022

Lillibridge, Simon, Farm, Summit Rd., Exeter, 11/28/78, A, C, d, 78000020

Main Street Historic District, 113–132 Main St., 8, 7–13 School St., 3–14 Maple St., Westerly, 1/09/78, A, C, a, 78000021

Marchant, Henry, Farm, S. County Trail, Kingstown vicinity, 8/16/79, A, B, C, 79000009

Miller, William Davis, House, 130 Main St., Wakefield, South Kingstown, 3/21/85, A, C, 85000627

Ministerial Rd. Site, RI-781, Address Restricted, South Kingstown vicinity, 11/15/84, D, 84000565

Mumford, Silas Site (Tappan Site RI-705), Address Restricted, South Kingstown vicinity, 11/01/84, A, D, 84000382

Narragansett Baptist Church, S. Ferry Rd., Narragansett vicinity, 11/25/77, C, a, 77000010

Narragansett Pier Life Saving Station, 40 Ocean Rd., Narragansett, 6/30/76, C, 76000010

Northrup, Stephen, House [North Kingstown MRA], 99 Featherbed Lane, North Kingstown, 7/19/85, C, 85001653

Nursery Site, RI-273, Address Restricted, Westerly vicinity, 11/01/84, D, 84000386

Ocean Road Historic District [Narragansett Pier MRA], Ocean and Wildfield Farm Rds., and Newton and Hazard Aves., Narragansett, 8/18/82, A, C, 82000019

Old Harbor Historic District, Roughly bounded by Atlantic Ocean and Main St. (includes Spring and High Sts. and Main St.), New Shoreham, 5/08/74, A, C, 74000012

Old Narragansett Cemetery [North Kingstown MRA], Shermantown Rd., North Kingstown, 7/19/85, A, C, a, d, 85001655

Old Narragansett Church, 60 Church Lane, Wickford, North Kingstown, 7/02/73, A, C, a, b, 73000009

Palmer—Northrup House, 7919 Post Rd., North Kingstown, 4/11/73, A, C, 73000010

Parris Brook Historic and Archeological District, Address Restricted, Exeter vicinity, 12/05/80, A, D, 80000023

Peace Dale Historic District, Roughly bounded by Kensey Rd., Oakwoods Dr., Kingstown Rd., School, Church and Railroad Sts., South Kingstown, 10/30/87, A, B, C, 87000493

Perry, Commodore Oliver, Farm, 184 Post Rd., South Kingstown, 8/26/82, A, C, 82000020

Perry—Carpenter Grist Mill, 364 Moonstone Beach Rd., South Kingstown, 2/22/90, A, 90000106

Pierce, Joseph, Farm [North Kingstown MRA], 933 Gilbert Stuart Rd., North Kingstown, 7/19/85, C, 85001652

Plum Beach Lighthouse [Lighthouses of Rhode Island TR], Off Plum Beach, W Passage, Narragansett Bay, North Kingston, 3/30/88, A, C, 88000281

Point Judith Lighthouse [Lighthouses of Rhode Island TR], 1470 Ocean Rd., Narragansett, 3/30/88, A, C, 88000279

Poplar Point Lighthouse [Lighthouses of Rhode Island TR], 1 Poplar Ave., North Kingston, 2/25/88, A, C, 87001703

Potter Pond Archeological District [Indian Use of the Salt Pond Region between ca. 4000 B.P. and ca. 1750 A.D. MPS], Address Restricted, South Kingstown vicinity, 12/08/87, D, 87002102

Queen's Fort, Stony Lane, Exeter vicinity, 11/26/80, D, 80000024

Rathbun House [North Kingstown MRA], 343 Beacon Dr., North Kingstown, 7/19/85, C, 85001651

Rodman, Gen. Isaac Peace, House, 1789 Kingstown Rd., South Kingstown, 4/23/90, B, C, 90000596

Sanford, Esbon, House [North Kingstown MRA], 88 Featherbed Lane, North Kingstown, 7/19/85, B, C, 85001649

Saunderstown Historic District [North Kingstown MRA], Roughly bounded by Stillman, Waterway, Willet, Boston Neck & Ferry Rds., North Kingstown, 7/19/85, A, C, 85001647

Scrabbletown Historic and Archeological District, Address Restricgted, North Kingstown vicinity, 4/11/85, A, D, d, 85000790

Shadow Farm, Kingstown Rd., South Kingston, 2/07/86, C, 86000785

Shady Lea Historic District [North Kingstown MRA], Shady Lea and Tower Hill Rds., North Kingstown, 7/19/85, A, B, 85001644

Shannock Historic District, Main St., N. Shannock and W. Shannock Rds., Charlestown, 8/04/83, A, C, 83000005

Sheffield House, Beach Rd., Charlestown, 1/01/76, C, 76000011

Six Principle Baptist Church, 85 Old Baptist Rd., North Kingstown, 11/21/78, C, a, d, 78000022

Slocum, Joseph, House [North Kingstown MRA], Slocum Rd., North Kingstown, 7/19/85, C, 85001648

Smith's Castle [North Kingstown MRA], N of Wickford on the Post Rd., North Kingstown, 2/23/72, A, C, D, d, 72000010

Sodom Mill Historic and Archeological District, Address Restricted, Exeter vicinity, 11/24/80, A, D, 80000025

Spink Farm [North Kingstown MRA], 1325 Shermantown Rd., North Kingstown, 7/19/85, A, C, d, 85001650

St. Paul's Church, 76 Main St., North Kingstown, 6/30/72, C, a, 72000009

Stanton, Joseph, House, US 1, Charlestown, 1/11/80, B, C, 80000026

Stuart, Gilbert, Birthplace, Gilbert Stuart Rd., Saunderstown, 10/15/66, B, c, NHL, 66000004

Washington County—Continued

Theatre-By-the-Sea, Card Ponds Rd., South Kingstown, 7/10/80, A, g, 80004597

Tomaquag Rock Shelters, Address Restricted, Hopkinton vicinity, 8/12/77, D, 77000011

Towers Historic District [Narragansett Pier MRA], Bounded by the Atlantic Ocean, Exchange Pl., Mathewson and Taylor Sts., Narragansett, 8/18/82, A, C, 82000021

Towers, The, Ocean Rd., Narragansett, 11/25/69, A, C, 69000001

US Post Office, High and Broad Sts., Westerly, 8/12/71, C, 71000004

US Weather Bureau Station, Beach Ave., New Shoreham, 8/04/83, A, C, 83000006

Usquepaug Road Historic District, Usquepaug Rd., South Kingstown, 10/30/87, A, C, 87001298

Washington County Court House, 3481 Kingstown Rd., South Kingstown, 11/05/92, A, C, 92001542

Watch Hill Historic District [Lighthouses of Rhode Island TR (AD)], Roughly bounded by Breen, Watch Hill & E. Hill Rds., Block Island Sound, Little Narragansett Bay, & Pawtucket River, Westerly, 9/05/85, A, C, 85001948

Westerly Downtown Historic District, Railroad Ave., High, Canal, Broad, Union, and Main Sts., Westerly, 7/19/84, A, C, 84002055

Wickford Historic District, Roughly bounded by Tower Hill and Post Rds. as far N as Mill Cove and S to Lindley Ave, North Kingstown, 12/31/74, A, C, a, 74000013

Wilcox Park Historic District, Roughly bounded by Broad, Granite, High Sts. and Grove Ave. and running along Elm St., Westerly, 5/07/73, C, 73000011

Wyoming Village Historic District, Roughly bounded by RI 138, RI 3, Old Nooseneck Hill Rd., Bridge and Prospect Sts., Hopkinton, 5/02/74, A, C, 74000014

YWCA Site, Address Restricted, North Kingstown vicinity, 11/20/80, D, 80000027

The farmhouses, outbuildings, stone fences, and agricultural systems of the Tillinghast Road Historic District convey two-and-a-half centuries of settlement and land use patterns near East Greenwich, Rhode Island. (Virginia A. Fitch, 1987)

SOUTH CAROLINA

Abbeville County

Abbeville County Courthouse [Courthouses in South Carolina Designed by William Augustus Edwards TR], Court Sq., Abbeville, 10/30/81, A, C, 81000706

Abbeville Historic District, Roughly bounded by Seaboard Coastline RR, SR 72, Rickey, Haight, Hemphill and Haigler Sts., Abbeville, 9/14/72, A, C, a, 72001183

Abbeville Historic District (Boundary Decrease), Roughly E of Magazine St., S of Whitehall St., NW along Long Branch St., W of Lemon St., N along Washington St., Abbeville, 9/14/72, A, C, 72001579

Abbeville Historic District (Boundary Increase), Roughly W along N. Main St. from Haigler to Livingston Sts., N along Greenville St., and NE on Marshall Ct., Abbeville, 5/07/84, A, C, 84002014

Abbeville Opera House, Court Sq., Abbeville, 7/01/70, A, 70000558

Burt, Armistead, House, 306 N. Main St., Abbeville, 4/03/70, A, B, C, NHL, 70000559

Calhoun, Patrick, Family Cemetery, 9.5 mi. SW of Abbeville on SC 823, Abbeville vicinity, 8/28/75, A, d, 75001684

Cedar Springs Historic District, SR 33, SR 112 and SR 47, Abbeville vicinity, 3/25/82, A, C, a, 82003824

Erskine College-Due West Historic District, Main, Church, College, Bonner, Hayne, Washington, Cleveland, Depot, & Abbeville Sts., Due West, 3/19/82, A, C, a, 82003825

Harbison College President's Home, N of Abbeville on SC 20, Abbeville vicinity, 1/13/83, A, 83002181

Trinity Episcopal Church and Cemetery, Church St., Abbeville, 5/06/71, A, C, a, 71000738

Young Place, SC 185, Due West, 10/09/74, A, C, 74001818

Aiken County

Aiken Mile Track [Aiken Winter Colony TR], Banks Mill Rd., Aiken, 5/09/85, A, g, 85000991

Aiken Training Track [Aiken Winter Colony TR], Two Notch Rd., Aiken, 5/09/85, A, g, 85000992

Aiken Winter Colony Historic District I [Aiken Winter Colony TR], Off U.S. 1/78, Aiken, 11/27/84, A, C, g, 84000484

Aiken Winter Colony Historic District II [Aiken Winter Colony TR], Roughly bounded by RR track, Colleton and 3rd Aves., Laurens, South Boundary, and Marion Sts., Aiken, 11/27/84, A, C, b, 84000498

Aiken Winter Colony Historic District III [Aiken Winter Colony TR], Roughly bounded by Edge-field Ave., Highland Park Dr., Fauburg, and Greenville St., Aiken, 11/27/84, A, C, 84000508

Carroll, Chancellor James P., House, 112 Gregg Ave., Aiken, 11/23/77, A, C, 77001209

Cedars, The, US 278, 0.3 mi E of SC 125, Beech Island vicinity, 6/17/93, C, 93000539

Chinaberry, 441 York St., SE, Aiken, 4/29/82, A, B, C, 82003826

Coker Spring, Coker Spring Rd., Aiken, 1/18/78, A, D, 78002490

Court Tennis Building [Aiken Winter Colony TR], Newberry and Park Sts., Aiken, 11/27/84, A, 84000513

Dawson-Vanderhorst House, NE of Aiken at jct. of Wire and New Bridge Rds., Aiken vicinity, 6/29/76, C, 76001685

Fort Moore-Savano Town Site, Address Restricted, Beech Island vicinity, 8/14/73, A, D, 73001670

Georgia Avenue-Butler Avenue Historic District, Georgia, Butler Aves. and Martintown Rd., North Augusta, 4/05/84, C, 84002017

Graniteville Historic District, SC 19 and Gregg St., Graniteville, 6/02/78, A, B, C, NHL, 78002491

Hammond, Charles, House, 908 Martintown Road W., North Augusta, 10/02/73, A, C, 73001672

Joye Cottage, 463 Whiskey Rd. and 129 1st Ave., Aiken, 9/29/80, A, B, C, 80003651

Legare-Morgan House, 241 Lauren St., SW, Aiken, 9/22/77, A, B, 77001210

Lookaway Hall, 103 W. Forest Ave., North Augusta, 8/13/92, A, B, C, 92000962

Phelps House, Barnwell Ave., Aiken, 6/10/74, A, C, 74001819

Pickens House, 101 Gregg Ave., Aiken, 5/19/83, B, b, 83002182

Redcliffe, 1.5 mi. NE of Beech Island on SC 125, Beech Island vicinity, 5/08/73, A, B, C, 73001671

Rosemary Hall, 804 Carolina Ave., North Augusta, 4/28/75, A, B, C, 75001685

Silver Bluff, Address Restricted, Jackson vicinity, 11/01/77, A, D, 77001211

St. Mary Help of Christians Church, York St. and Park Ave., Aiken, 3/25/82, A, C, a, 82003827

St. Thaddeus Episcopal Church [Aiken Winter Colony TR], Pendleton and Richland Sts., Aiken, 11/27/84, A, a, 84000518

Wall, B. C., House, 1008 West Ave., North Augusta, 11/27/92, C, 92001632

Whitehall [Aiken Winter Colony TR], 902 Magnolia St., Aiken, 11/27/84, C, 84000527

Willcox's, Colleton Ave., Aiken, 3/19/82, A, B, 82003828

Allendale County

Allendale Chert Quarries Archeological District, Address Restricted, Martin vicinity, 9/28/85, D, 85002699

Antioch Christian Church, SW of Allendale on SC 3, Allendale vicinity, 12/12/77, A, C, a, 77001212

Erwin House, SW of Allendale off U.S. 301, Allendale vicinity, 5/07/76, A, C, 76001687

Fennell Hill, Address Restricted, Peeples vicinity, 11/19/74, D, 74001820

Gravel Hill Plantation, SW of Allendale off U.S. 301, Allendale vicinity, 5/28/76, A, C, 76001688

Lawton Mounds, Address Restricted, Johnson's Landing vicinity, 6/19/72, D, 72001185

Red Bluff Flint Quarries, Address Restricted, Allendale vicinity, 6/22/72, D, 72001184

Roselawn, 3 mi. SW of Allendale on SC 47, Allendale vicinity, 5/28/76, A, C, 76001689

Smyrna Baptist Church, S of Allendale on SC 22, Allendale vicinity, 5/28/76, A, C, a, 76001691

Young, Virginia Durant, House, US 278, Fairfax, 8/08/83, B, 83002183

Anderson County

Anderson Downtown Historic District, Main St. between Tribble and Market Sts., Anderson, 2/23/79, A, C, 79002372

Anderson Downtown Historic District (Boundary Increase), 402 N. Main St., Anderson, 11/05/87, A, C, 87001996

Anderson Historic District, Bounded by Hampton, Main, Franklin, McDuffie, Benson, and Fant Sts., Anderson, 12/13/71, A, C, 71000739

Ashtabula, 1.25 mi. NE of Pendleton off SC 88, Pendleton vicinity, 3/23/72, B, C, b, 72001186

Belton Depot, Public Sq, Belton, 8/13/79, A, C, 79002373

Belton Standpipe, McGee St., Belton, 11/05/87, A, C, 87001948

Caldwell-Johnson-Morris Cottage, 220 E. Morris St., Anderson, 10/07/71, B, C, 71000740

Chamberlain-Kay House, 205 River St., Belton, 11/25/80, C, b, 80003652

McFall House, SR 247, Anderson vicinity, 6/28/82, B, C, 82003829

Orr, Dr. Samuel Marshall, House, 809 W. Market St., Anderson, 4/13/73, B, 73001673

Pelzer Presbyterian Church, 13 Lebby St., Pelzer, 12/13/93, C, a, 93001407

Pendleton Historic District, Bounded on W by Hopewell and Treaty Oak, N by Old Stone Church, E by Montpelier, and S by town limits, Pendleton, 8/25/70, A, B, C, D, 70000560

Prevost, Nick, House, 105 N. Prevost St., Anderson, 7/10/84, C, 84002020

Ramer, Ralph John, House, 402 Boulevard, Anderson, 2/10/92, C, 92000023

Woodburn, End of Woodburn Rd., W of Pendleton, Pendleton vicinity, 5/06/71, B, C, 71000741

Bamberg County

Bamberg Historic District, E. Railroad Ave., 2nd, Midway, Elm, Cannon, N. Carlisle, and Church Sts., Bamberg, 5/19/83, C, 83002184

Bamberg, Gen. Francis Marion, House, N. Railroad Ave. and N. Carlisle St., Bamberg, 6/29/76, B, C, 76001692

Cal Smoak Site, Address Restricted, Bamberg vicinity, 1/06/86, D, 86000042

Copeland House, SC Secondary Rd. 389, .3 mi. S of jct. with SC 64, Ehrhardt vicinity, 10/18/91, C, 91001494

Rivers Bridge State Park, 6 mi. SW of Ehrhardt, Ehrhardt vicinity, 2/23/72, A, 72001187

Voorhees College Historic District, Voorhees College Campus, Denmark vicinity, 1/21/82, B, C, b, 82003830

Woodlands, 3 mi. S of Bamberg on SC 78, Bamberg vicinity, 11/11/71, B, NHL, 71000742

Barnwell County

Banksia Hall, 108 Reynolds Rd., Barnwell, 5/31/74, A, C, 74001821

Bethlehem Baptist Church, Wall and Gilmore Sts., Barnwell, 7/10/79, A, C, a, 79002374

Church of the Holy Apostles, Episcopal, 1706 Hagood Ave., Barnwell, 4/13/72, C, a, 72001188

Church of the Holy Apostles Rectory, 1700 Hagood Ave., Barnwell, 4/13/72, A, B, C, a, 72001189

Old Presbyterian Church, 1905 Academy St., Barnwell, 4/13/72, A, C, a, b, 72001190

Beaufort County

Alston, Emanuel, House [Historic Resources of St. Helena Island c. 1740-c. 1935 MPS], Sec. Rd. 161, .25 mi. N of jct. with US 21, Frogmore vicinity, 10/06/88, C, 88001723

Anchorage, The, 1103 Bay St., Beaufort, 11/23/71, B, C, 71000743

Bailey, Dr. York, House [Historic Resources of St. Helena Island c. 1740-c. 1935 MPS], US Hwy. 21, approx. .2 mi. E of jct. with Lands End Rd., Frogmore, 10/06/88, B, C, 88001726

Barnwell, William, House, 800 Prince St., Beaufort, 3/24/71, C, b, 71000744

Barnwell-Gough House, 705 Washington St., Beaufort, 11/15/72, B, C, 72001191

Beaufort Historic District, Bounded by the Beaufort River, Bladen, Hamar, and Boundary Sts., Beaufort, 12/17/69, A, C, NHL, 69000159

Charles Forte, Address Restricted, Beaufort vicinity, 8/07/74, D, 74001822

Chester Field, Address Restricted, Laurel Bay vicinity, 10/15/70, D, 70000565

Church of the Cross, Calhoun St., Bluffton, 5/29/75, C, a, 75001686

Coffin Point Plantation, 3 mi. E of Frogmore at NE end of Seaside Rd. on St. Helena Island, Frogmore vicinity, 8/28/75, A, C, 75001687

Coffin Point Plantation Caretaker's House [Historic Resources of St. Helena Island c. 1740-c. 1935 MPS], Adjacent to Coffin Point Plantation, off Seaside Rd., Frogmore vicinity, 5/28/89, A, C, 88001730

Corner Packing Shed, The [Historic Resources of St. Helena Island c. 1740-c. 1935 MPS], US Hwy. 21, W of jct. with Land's End Rd., Frogmore, 10/06/88, A, C, 88001733

Corner Store and Office, The [Historic Resources of St. Helena Island c. 1740-c. 1935 MPS], US Hwy. 21, W of jct. with Lands End Rd., Frogmore, 10/06/88, C, 88001737

Cuthbert, John A., House, 1203 Bay St., Beaufort, 6/13/72, B, C, a, 72001192

Daufuskie Island Historic District, SW of Hilton Head, Hilton Head vicinity, 6/02/82, A, C, d, 82003831

Eddings Point Community Praise House [Historic Resources of St. Helena Island c. 1740-c. 1935 MPS], On SC Sec. Rd. 183, .1 mi. N of jct. with SC Sec. Rd. 74, Frogmore vicinity, 5/19/89, A, C, a, 88001739

Fish Haul Archaeological Site (38BU805), Address Restricted, Hilton Head Island vicinity, 6/30/88, D, 88000976

Fort Frederick, Address Restricted, Port Royal vicinity, 12/31/74, D, 74001826

Fort Fremont Hospital [Historic Resources of St. Helena Island c. 1740-c. 1935 MPS], .3 mi. from Land's End Rd., Frogmore vicinity, 5/26/89, A, C, 88001819

Fort Lyttelton Site, Address Restricted, Beaufort vicinity, 9/13/79, D, 79003322

Fripp, Edgar, Mausoleum, St. Helena Island Parish Church [Historic Resources of St. Helena Island c. 1740-c. 1935 MPS], SC Sec. Rd. 45 near jct. with SC Sec. Rd. 37, Frogmore vicinity, 10/06/88, C, d, 88001743

Fripp, Isaac, House Ruins [Historic Resources of St. Helena Island c. 1740-c. 1935 MPS], On an unpaved rd. 1.1 mi. W of jct. with SC Rd. 45, Frogmore vicinity, 10/06/88, C, D, 88001750

Frogmore Plantation Complex [Historic Resources of St. Helena Island c. 1740-c. 1935 MPS], Off SC Sec. Rd. 77 near jct. with SC Sec. Rd. 35, Frogmore vicinity, 5/26/89, B, C, 88001754

Green's Shell Enclosure, Address Restricted, Hilton Head Island vicinity, 8/07/74, D, 74001825

Green, The [Historic Resources of St. Helena Island c. 1740-c. 1935 MPS], SE corner intersection of US Hwy. 21 and Lands End Rd., Frogmore, 10/06/88, A, 88001759

Hasell Point Site, Address Restricted, Port Royal vicinity, 8/14/73, D, 73001675

Hunting Island State Park Lighthouse, 17 mi. SSW of Beaufort on U.S. 21, Beaufort vicinity, 6/05/70, A, C, b, 70000561

Indian Hill Site, Address Restricted, St. Helena Island vicinity, 3/22/74, D, 74001827

Jenkins, Mary, Community Praise House [Historic Resources of St. Helena Island c. 1740-c. 1935

MPS], On SC Sec. Rd. 74, 2.1 mi. N of its jct. with US Hwy. 21, Frogmore vicinity, 5/19/89, A, C, a, 88001770

Lands End Road Tabby Ruins [Historic Resources of St. Helena Island c. 1740-c. 1935 MPS], Address Restricted, Frogmore vicinity, 10/06/88, D, 88001771

Little Barnwell Island, N of Port Royal, Port Royal vicinity, 8/14/73, D, 73001676

Marshlands, 501 Pinckney St., Beaufort, 11/07/73, C, NHL, 73001674

Oaks, The [Historic Resources of St. Helena Island c. 1740-c. 1935 MPS], On unpaved rd. .3 mi. W of SC Sec. Rd. 165, Frogmore vicinity, 10/06/88, A, B, 88001773

Old Brass, E of Yemassee on River Rd., Yemassee vicinity, 6/03/76, C, g, 76001693

Orange Grove Plantation [Historic Resources of St. Helena Island c. 1740-c. 1935 MPS], Overlooking Wallace Creek, .25 mi. from SC 113, Frogmore vicinity, 5/26/89, A, C, 88001774

Parris Island Drydock and Commanding Generals House, Mexico and Tripoli Sts., Parris Island, 11/21/78, A, B, C, 78002492

Penn Center Historic District, S of Frogmore on SC 37, Frogmore vicinity, 9/09/74, A, NHL, 74001824

Pine Island Plantation Complex [Historic Resources of St. Helena Island c. 1740-c. 1935 MPS], Pine Island, Frogmore vicinity, 5/26/89, A, C, 88001775

Rear Lighthouse of Hilton Head Range Light Station, Arthur Hill Golf Course, Palmetto Dunes Resort off US 278, Hilton Head Island, 12/12/85, A, C, 85003349

Riverside Plantation Tabby Ruins [Historic Resources of St. Helena Island c. 1740-c. 1935 MPS], On unpaved rd. .4 mi. W of SC Sec. Rd. 45 at Lands End, Frogmore vicinity, 10/06/88, C, D, 88001776

Rose Hill Plantation House, Off U.S. 278, Bluffton vicinity, 5/19/83, C, 83002185

Sea Pines, Address Restricted, Hilton Head Island vicinity, 10/15/70, D, 70000563

Seaside Plantation, 10 mi. E of Beaufort on SC 21, Beaufort vicinity, 7/16/79, A, C, 79002375

Sheldon Church Ruins, NW of Gardens Corner on U.S. 21, Gardens Corner vicinity, 10/22/70, A, C, a, g, 70000562

Simmons, Robert, House [Historic Resources of St. Helena Island c. 1740-c. 1935 MPS], On unpaved rd. .5 mi. S of US Hwy. 21, Frogmore vicinity, 10/06/88, C, 88001779

Skull Creek, Address Restricted, Hilton Head vicinity, 11/10/70, D, 70000564

Smalls, Robert, House, 511 Prince St., Beaufort, 5/30/74, B, NHL, 74001823

St. Helena Parish Chapel of Ease Ruins [Historic Resources of St. Helena Island c. 1740-c. 1935 MPS], SC Sec. Rd. 45, near jct. with SC Sec. Rd. 37, Frogmore vicinity, 10/06/88, A, C, a, d, 88001777

St. Helenaville Archaeological Site (38BU931) [Historic Resources of St. Helena Island c. 1740-c. 1935 MPS], Address Restricted, Frogmore vicinity, 10/06/88, D, 88001778

Beaufort County—Continued

St. Luke's Church, SC 170, Pritchardville vicinity, 11/10/87, C, a, 87001951

Tabby Manse, 1211 Bay St., Beaufort, 5/14/71, B, C, 71000745

Tombee Plantation, S of Frogmore on St. Helena's Island, Frogmore vicinity, 9/18/75, A, C, 75001688

Verdier, John Mark, House, 801 Bay St., Beaufort, 8/19/71, C, 71000746

Berkeley County

Biggin Church Ruins, 2 mi. NE of Moncks Corner on SC 402, Moncks Corner vicinity, 12/13/77, A, a, d, 77001215

Cainhoy Historic District, SE of Huger, Huger vicinity, 3/11/82, A, C, 82003832

Calais Milestones, On CR 98 and 44, Cainhoy vicinity, 3/14/73, A, 73001677

Keller Site, Address Restricted, St. Stephen vicinity, 2/01/80, D, 80003654

Lawson's Pond Plantation, 5 mi. N of Cross off SC 6, Cross vicinity, 12/13/77, A, C, 77001213

Lewisfield Plantation, About 2.5 mi. S of Moncks Corner on U.S. 52, Moncks Corner vicinity, 5/09/73, A, C, 73001678

Loch Dhu, N of Cross off SC 6, Cross vicinity, 9/22/77, A, C, 77001214

Medway, E of Mount Holly off U.S. 52, Mount Holly vicinity, 7/16/70, A, B, C, D, 70000569

Middleburg Plantation, 2 mi. SW of Huger on the E branch of the Cooper River, Huger vicinity, 4/15/70, C, NHL, 70000568

Mulberry Plantation, Off U.S. 52 on Cooper River, Moncks Corner, 10/15/66, C, NHL, 66000697

Otranto Plantation, 18 Basilica Ave., Hanahan vicinity, 2/17/78, A, B, C, 78003191

Otranto Plantation Indigo Vats, SC Sec. Rd. 503, E of Goose Creek, Goose Creek vicinity, 12/21/89, A, C, b, 89002150

Pineville Historic District, Rd. S-8-204 S of jct. with SC 45, Pineville, 2/10/92, A, C, a, 92000024

Pinopolis Historic District North [Pinopolis MRA], Lake View St. South to Lake Moultrie, Pinopolis, 8/19/82, A, C, 82003834

Pinopolis Historic District South [Pinopolis MRA], CR 5, Pinopolis, 8/19/82, A, C, 82003835

Pompion Hill Chapel, 0.5 mi. SW of jct. of SC 41 and 402, Huger, 4/15/70, C, a, NHL, 70000567

Quinby Plantation House—Halidon Hill Plantation, 3 mi. W of Huger, Huger vicinity, 10/10/85, A, C, b, g, 85003122

Richmond Plantation, SE of Cordesville, Cordesville vicinity, 11/24/80, A, C, D, d, 80003653

Robertson, William, House [Pinopolis MRA], CR 5, Pinopolis, 8/19/82, C, 82003836

Santee Canal, NE of Moncks Corner, Moncks Corner vicinity, 5/05/82, A, C, 82003833

St. James' Church, Goose Creek, S of Goose Creek, Goose Creek vicinity, 4/15/70, C, a, NHL, 70000566

St. Stephen's Episcopal Church, On SC 45, St. Stephens, 4/15/70, C, a, NHL, 70000570

Strawberry Chapel and Childsbury Town Site, SE of Moncks Corner on CR 44, N of the Tee of the Cooper River, Moncks Corner vicinity, 4/26/72, D, a, 72001194

Taveau Church, S of Cordesville on SR 44, Cordesville vicinity, 2/14/78, A, C, a, 78002493

White Church, 2 mi. N of Cainhoy on CR 98, Cainhoy vicinity, 3/23/72, A, C, a, d, 72001193

Calhoun County

Baker, William, House, E of Gaston off U.S. 21, Gaston vicinity, 3/08/78, A, C, 78002494

Banks, Col. J. A., House, 104 Dantzler St., St. Matthews, 11/24/80, B, C, 80003655

Buyck's Bluff Archeological Site, Address Restricted, St. Matthews vicinity, 5/04/79, D, 79002376

Calhoun County Courthouse [Courthouses in South Carolina Designed by William Augustus Edwards TR], S. Railroad Ave., St. Matthews, 10/30/81, A, C, 81000561

Calhoun County Library, Railroad Ave., St. Matthews, 5/29/75, C, 75001690

Cherokee Path, Sterling Land Grant, 5 mi. SE of St. Matthews on SC 6, St. Matthews vicinity, 5/13/76, A, 76001696

Dantzler, Col. Olin M., House, 412 E. Bridge St., St. Matthews, 3/30/73, B, C, 73001680

Fort Motte Battle Site, Address Restricted, Fort Motte vicinity, 11/09/72, A, D, 72001195

Houser, David, House, W of St. Matthews on U.S. 176, St. Matthews vicinity, 11/25/80, A, C, 80003656

Midway Plantation, S of Fort Motte off U.S. 601, Fort Motte vicinity, 5/28/76, A, B, C, 76001694

Oakland Plantation, S of Fort Motte off SC 26 on SR 1, Fort Motte vicinity, 5/30/75, B, C, 75001689

Prehistoric Indian Village, Address Restricted, St. Matthews vicinity, 7/30/74, D, 74001828

Puritan Farm, W of St. Matthews, St. Matthews vicinity, 7/25/74, B, C, 74001829

Ulmer-Summers House, Old Orangeburg Rd. (SC 31), Cameron, 10/25/73, A, C, 73001679

Zante Plantation, SE of Fort Motte off SC 601, Fort Motte vicinity, 6/29/76, B, C, 76001695

Charleston County

Aiken, Gov. William, House, 48 Elizabeth St., Charleston, 11/21/77, B, C, D, 77001216

Aiken, William, House and Associated Railroad Structures, 456 King St., Charleston, 10/15/66, A, NHL, 66000698

Ashley Hall Plantation, Address Restricted, Charleston vicinity, 6/05/75, B, C, D, 75001691

Ashley River Road, SC 61 between Church Creek and SC 165, Summerville vicinity, 11/21/83, A, 83003831

Auld Mound, Address Restricted, Mount Pleasant vicinity, 10/15/70, D, 70000583

Bailey's Store [Edisto Island MRA], On Store Creek at jct. of SC 174 and Point of Pines Rd., Edisto Island, 11/28/86, A, C, b, 86003204

Barnwell House, S of Charleston, Charleston vicinity, 11/25/80, B, C, 80003657

Bass Pond Site, Address Restricted, Kiawah Island vicinity, 4/24/79, D, 79002379

Battery Cheves [Civil War Defenses of Charleston TR], James Island, Fort Johnson Estates, 8/11/82, A, C, 82003841

Battery Gadsden, 2017 Ion Ave., Sullivan's Island, 6/25/74, A, C, 74001842

Battery LeRoy [Civil War Defenses of Charleston TR], Riverland Dr., James Island, 8/11/82, A, C, 82004786

Battery No. 1 [Civil War Defenses of Charleston TR], Riverland Dr., James Island, 8/11/82, A, C, 82004787

Battery No. 5 [Civil War Defenses of Charleston TR], Stonefield Subdivision, James Island, 8/11/82, A, C, 82004788

Battery Thomson, 2013 Ion Ave., Sullivan's Island, 6/25/74, A, C, 74001843

Battery Tynes [Civil War Defenses of Charleston TR], Stono River, James Island, 8/11/82, A, C, 82004789

Battery Wilkes [Civil War Defenses of Charleston TR], St Andrew's Parish, Longbranch Estates vicinity, 10/21/82, A, 82001516

Bennett, Gov. Thomas, House, 69 Barre St., Charleston, 1/31/78, B, C, 78002496

Bethel Methodist Church, 57 Pitt St., Charleston, 11/20/74, C, a, 74002260

Blacklock, William, House, 18 Bull St., Charleston, 11/07/73, C, NHL, 73001681

Blake Tenements, 2–4 Courthouse Sq., Charleston, 8/25/70, C, 70000572

Bleak Hall Plantation Outbuildings, 4 mi. SE of Edisto Island off SC 174, Edisto Island vicinity, 3/07/73, A, B, C, 73001698

Branford-Horry House, 59 Meeting St., Charleston, 10/15/70, C, 70000573

Brewton, Miles, House, 27 King St., Charleston, 10/15/66, C, NHL, 66000699

Brewton, Robert, House, 71 Church St., Charleston, 10/15/66, C, NHL, 66000700

Brick House Ruin, S of Edisto Island, Edisto Island vicinity, 4/15/70, C, NHL, 70000580

Brooklands Plantation [Edisto Island MRA], Off Laurel Hill Rd. on Scanawah Island, Edisto Island vicinity, 5/05/87, A, C, 86003198

Buzzard's Island Site, Address Restricted, Mount Pleasant vicinity, 10/15/70, D, 70000584

Cape Romain Lighthouses, SE of McClellanville on Lighthouse Island, McClellanville vicinity, 11/12/81, A, C, 81000563

Cassina Point [Edisto Island MRA], Cassina Point Rd., Edisto Island, 11/28/86, A, C, 86003210

Castle Pinckney, Shute's Folly Island, Charleston vicinity, 7/16/70, A, C, D, 70000574

Central Baptist Church, 26 Radcliffe St., Charleston, 8/16/77, A, C, a, 77001217

Charleston Historic District, An area roughly bounded by Broad, Bay, S. Battery and Ashley and an area along Church bounded by Cum-

Charleston County—Continued

berland and Chalmers, Charleston, 10/15/66, C, NHL, 66000964

Charleston Historic District (Boundary Increase), An area roughly bounded by Calhoun, Archdale, Cumberland, E.Battery, Broad and Gadsden and an area along Anson St., Charleston, 1/30/70, A, C, D, a, 70000923

Charleston Historic District, Incorporates most of area S of Bee, Morris, and Mary Sts. to Waterfront, Charleston, 7/16/78, A, C, a, 78002497

Charleston Historic District (Boundary Increase), King and Calhoun Sts., Charleston, 8/02/84, C, 84002028

Charleston Old and Historic District (Boundary Increase), 25 and 25 1/2 Warren and 114 St. Phillip Sts., Charleston, 8/13/85, C, 85001833

Charleston Old and Historic District (Boundary Increase), 280 E. Bay St., Charleston, 3/27/86, C, 86000588

Charleston's French Quarter District, Bounded by Lodge Alley and Cumberland, E. Bay, and State Sts., Charleston, 9/19/73, A, C, 73001682

Christ Church, 4.6 mi. NE of Mount Pleasant on U.S. 17, Mount Pleasant vicinity, 11/27/72, A, B, C, a, 72001201

Cigar Factory, Block bounded by East Bay, Columbus, Blake and Drake Sts., Charleston, 11/25/80, A, C, 80003658

Circular Congregational Church and Parish House, 150 Meeting St., Charleston, 11/07/73, C, NHL, 73001683

Citizens and Southern National Bank of South Carolina, 50 Broad St., Charleston, 5/06/71, A, C, 71000747

College of Charleston, Glebe, George, St. Philip, and Green Sts., Charleston, 11/11/71, C, NHL, 71000748

Crawford's Plantation House [Edisto Island MRA], 8202 Oyster Factory Rd., Edisto Island, 6/08/93, C, 93000475

Dock Street Theatre, 135 Church St., Charleston, 6/19/73, A, C, 73001684

Drayton Hall, 12 mi. W of Charleston on SC 61, Charleston vicinity, 10/15/66, C, NHL, 66000701

Edisto Island Baptist Church [Edisto Island MRA (AD)], N of Edisto Island, on SC 174, Edisto Island, 4/01/82, A, a, 82003839

Edisto Island Presbyterian Church, 1.9 mi. N of Edisto Island on SC 174, Edisto Island vicinity, 6/24/71, C, a, 71000754

Exchange and Provost, E. Bay and Broad Sts., Charleston, 12/17/69, A, C, NHL, 69000160

Fairfield Plantation, N of McClellanville, McClellanville vicinity, 7/25/74, B, C, 74001838

Farmers' and Exchange Bank, 14 E. Bay St., Charleston, 11/07/73, C, NHL, 73001685

Farmfield Plantation House, Farmfield Rd., Charleston, 10/29/82, C, 82001517

Fenwick Hall, S of Charleston on John's Island, US 17, Charleston vicinity, 2/23/72, A, C, 72001196

Fig Island Site, Address Restricted, Rockville vicinity, 10/15/70, D, 70000585

Fireproof Building, 100 Meeting St., Charleston, 7/29/69, C, NHL, 69000161

Fort Johnson/Powder Magazine, About 3 mi. SE of Charleston on James Island, Charleston vicinity, 9/14/72, A, D, 72001197

Fort Palmetto [Civil War Defenses of Charleston TR], Christ Church Parish, Hamlin Sound vicinity, 8/11/82, A, C, 82003842

Fort Pemberton Site, Address Restricted, Charleston vicinity, 11/21/78, A, C, D, 78002498

Fort Pringle [Civil War Defenses of Charleston TR], Riverland Dr., James Island, 8/11/82, A, C, 82004790

Fort Sumter National Monument, Charleston Harbor, Charleston, 10/15/66, A, C, f, NPS, 66000101

Fort Trenholm [Civil War Defenses of Charleston TR], John's Island Airport, John's Island, 8/11/82, A, C, 82004791

Frogmore [Edisto Island MRA], S of Pine Landing Rd. near intersection of SC 174 and Laurel Hill Rd., Edisto Island, 5/05/87, A, C, 86003203

Gibbes, William, House, 64 S. Battery, Charleston, 4/15/70, C, NHL, 70000575

Grimball, Paul, House Ruins [Edisto Island MRA], Address Restricted, Edisto Island vicinity, 11/28/86, D, 86003190

Grove Plantation, SW of Adams Run off SC 174, Adams Run vicinity, 8/25/78, A, C, 78002495

H. L. HUNLEY (submarine), E of Charleston, Charleston vicinity, 12/29/78, A, 78003412

Hampton Plantation, 8 mi. N of McClellanville, McClellanville vicinity, 4/15/70, C, NHL, 70000582

Hanckel Mound, Address Restricted, Rockville vicinity, 10/15/70, D, 70000586

Harrietta Plantation, 5 mi. E of McClellanville off U.S. 17, McClellanville vicinity, 9/18/75, A, B, C, 75001695

Heyward, Dubose, House, 76 Church St., Charleston, 11/11/71, B, NHL, 71000749

Heyward-Washington House, 87 Church St., Charleston, 4/15/70, B, C, NHL, 70000576

Hibernian Hall, 105 Meeting St., Charleston, 11/07/73, A, NHL, 73001686

Horse Island, Address Restricted, Rockville vicinity, 11/10/70, D, 70000587

Huguenot Church, 136 Church St., Charleston, 11/07/73, C, a, NHL, 73001687

Hutchinson House [Edisto Island MRA], N side of Point of Pines Rd., Edisto Island, 5/05/87, A, C, 86003218

John's Island Presbyterian Church, 10 mi. W of Charleston on SR 20, Charleston vicinity, 11/03/75, A, C, a, 75001692

Kahal Kadosh Beth Elohim Synagogue, 90 Hasell St., Charleston, 4/04/78, A, C, a, NHL, 78002499

Laurel Hill, Off U.S. 17, McClellanville vicinity, 9/12/85, B, C, b, 85002359

Lighthouse Point Shell Ring (38CH12) [Late Archaic—Early Woodland Period Shell Rings of South Carolina MPS], Address Restricted, Charleston vicinity, 10/14/90, D, 90001505

Long Point Plantation (38CH321), Address Restricted, Mt. Pleasant vicinity, 3/20/86, D, 86000468

Lowndes Grove, 260 St. Margaret St., Charleston, 8/30/78, B, C, 78002500

Lucas, Jonathan, House, 286 Calhoun St., Charleston, 2/23/78, A, B, C, 78002501

Magnolia Cemetery, N of Charleston off U.S. 52, Charleston vicinity, 3/24/78, A, C, d, 78002502

Magnolia Plantation and Gardens, 10 mi. NW of Charleston on SC 61, Charleston vicinity, 12/11/72, B, C, 72001198

Manigault, Joseph, House, 350 Meeting St., Charleston, 11/07/73, C, NHL, 73001688

Market Hall and Sheds, 188 Meeting St., Charleston, 6/04/73, A, C, NHL, 73001689

Marshlands Plantation House, N side of Fort Sumter Dr., James Island, 3/30/73, C, b, 73001700

McClellanville Historic District, Pinckney, Lofton, Charlotte, Church, Water, Oak, Venning, Legare, Morrison, and Scotia Sts., McClellanville, 3/23/82, A, C, 82003845

McCrady's Tavern and Long Room, 153 E. Bay St., Charleston, 9/14/72, A, C, 72001199

McLeod Plantation, 325 Country Club Dr., Charleston, 8/13/74, A, C, 74001831

Middleton's Plantation, 3.5 mi. N of Edisto Island off SC 174, Edisto Island vicinity, 5/06/71, C, 71000755

Mills, Clark, Studio, 51 Broad St., Charleston, 10/15/66, B, NHL, 66000703

Morris Island Lighthouse, 6 mi. SE of Charleston, Charleston vicinity, 6/28/82, A, C, 82003837

Mount Pleasant Historic District, Bounded by Charleston Harbor, Shem Creek, Royal Ave., and McConts Dr., Mount Pleasant, 3/30/73, A, C, 73001701

Moving Star Hall, River Rd., John's Islands, 6/17/82, A, a, 82003843

Nicholson, James, House, 172 Rutledge Ave., Charleston, 8/30/74, A, B, C, 74001832

Oak Island [Edisto Island MRA], 1 mi. off Oak Island Rd. on Westbank Creek, Edisto Island, 11/28/86, A, C, 86003202

Oakland Plantation House, 7 mi. N of Charleston Harbor on U.S. 17, Mount Pleasant vicinity, 7/13/77, C, 77001218

Old Bethel United Methodist Church, 222 Calhoun St., Charleston, 4/21/75, A, C, a, b, 75001693

Old Courthouse, 331 King St., Mount Pleasant, 5/06/71, C, 71000760

Old House Plantation [Edisto Island MRA (AD)], NE of Edisto Island via SC 174, Edisto Island vicinity, 5/14/71, C, 71000756

Old House Plantation and Commissary (Boundary Increase) [Edisto Island MRA], .5 mi. E of jct. of SC 174 and Oak Island Rd., then right on dirt rd., Edisto Island vicinity, 5/05/87, A, 87000656

Old Marine Hospital, 20 Franklin St., Charleston, 11/07/73, C, NHL, 73001690

Old Slave Mart, 6 Chalmers St., Charleston, 5/02/75, A, C, 75001694

Peter's Point Plantation, SW of Edisto Island off SC 174 on CR 764, Edisto Island vicinity, 6/19/73, C, 73001699

Charleston County—Continued

Point of Pines Plantation Slave Cabin [Edisto Island MRA], Point of Pines Rd., Edisto Island, 11/28/86, A, C, 86003213

Powder Magazine, 79 Cumberland St., Charleston, 1/05/72, A, C, 72001200

Powder Magazine, 79 Cumberland St., Charleston, 9/27/89, A, NHL, 89002100

Presbyterian Manse, NW of Edisto Island off SC 174, Edisto Island vicinity, 5/14/71, A, C, a, 71000757

Presqui'ile, 2 Amherst St., Charleston, 12/08/78, C, 78002503

Pritchard, Paul, Shipyard, Address Restricted, Mount Pleasant vicinity, 9/17/74, A, D, 74001839

Prospect Hill [Edisto Island MRA], Off Laurel Hill Rd., Edisto Island, 11/28/86, A, C, 86003196

Rhett, Robert Barnwell, House, 6 Thomas St., Charleston, 11/07/73, B, NHL, 73001691

Robb, William, House, 12 Bee St., Charleston, 9/08/83, B, C, g, 83002186

Rockville Historic District, Town of Rockville on N bank of Bohicket Creek, Rockville and vicinity, 6/13/72, A, C, 72001202

Roper, Robert William, House, 9 E. Battery St., Charleston, 11/07/73, C, NHL, 73001692

Rose, Thomas, House, 57–59 Church St., Charleston, 10/15/70, C, 70000892

Russell, Nathaniel, House, 51 Meeting St., Charleston, 8/19/71, A, C, NHL, 71000750

Rutledge, Edward, House, 117 Broad St., Charleston, 11/11/71, B, NHL, 71000751

Rutledge, Gov. John, House, 116 Broad St., Charleston, 11/07/71, B, NHL, 71000752

SAVANNAH (nuclear ship), W of Mt. Pleasant on E side of Charleston Harbor, Mount Pleasant vicinity, 11/14/82, A, C, g, NHL, 82001518

Seabrook, John, Plantation Bridge, NW of Rockville off SC 700, Rockville vicinity, 10/09/74, A, C, 74001841

Seabrook, William, House, N of Edisto Island off SC 174, Edisto Island vicinity, 5/06/71, B, C, 71000758

Seaside Plantation House, Off SC 174, Edisto Island vicinity, 1/21/82, C, 82003840

Secessionville Historic District, N of Folly Beach, Folly Beach vicinity, 10/01/79, A, B, C, 79002378

Sewee Mound, Address Restricted, Awendaw vicinity, 10/15/70, D, 70000571

Simmons-Edwards House, 12–14 Legare St., Charleston, 1/25/71, C, NHL, 71000753

Site of Old Charles Towne, Albemarle Point, Charleston vicinity, 12/17/69, A, D, 69000162

Slave Street, Smokehouse, and Allee, Boone Hall Plantation, N of Mt. Pleasant off US 17, Mount Pleasant vicinity, 7/14/83, A, C, 83002187

Snee Farm, 6 mi. W of Mt. Pleasant off U.S. 17, Mount Pleasant vicinity, 4/13/73, B, C, NHL, 73001702

South Carolina National Bank of Charleston, 16 Broad St., Charleston, 6/04/73, A, C, 73001693

South Carolina State Arsenal, 2 Tobacco St. (Marion Sq.), Charleston, 7/16/70, A, C, 70000577

Spanish Mount Point, Address Restricted, Edisto Island vicinity, 8/30/74, D, 74001836

St. Andrews Episcopal Church, 5 mi. NW of Charleston on SC 61, Charleston vicinity, 10/15/73, A, C, a, 73001694

St. James Episcopal Church, Santee, 17 mi. S of Georgetown on the Santee River, Georgetown vicinity, 4/15/70, A, C, a, NHL, 70000581

St. Mary's Roman Catholic Church, 93 Hasell St., Charleston, 11/07/76, A, C, a, 76001697

St. Michael's Episcopal Church, 80 Meeting St., Charleston, 10/15/66, C, a, NHL, 66000704

St. Philip's Episcopal Church, 146 Church St., Charleston, 11/07/73, C, a, NHL, 73001695

Stiles-Hinson House, 940 Paul Revere Dr., Charleston, 10/09/74, B, C, 74001833

Stono River Slave Rebellion Site, Off U.S. 17 on W bank of Wallace River, Rantowles vicinity, 5/30/74, A, NHL, 74001840

Stuart, Col. John, House, 104–106 Tradd St., Charleston, 10/22/70, C, NHL, 70000578

Summit Plantation House, Off CR 390, Adams Run vicinity, 7/28/83, A, C, 83002188

Sunnyside [Edisto Island MRA], Off N side of Peter's Point Rd., Edisto Island, 11/28/86, A, C, 86003216

Sword Gate Houses, 32 Legare St. and 111 Tradd St., Charleston, 12/18/70, C, 70000579

Tennent, Josiah Smith, House, 729 E. Bay St, Charleston, 11/27/79, A, B, C, 79002377

Townsend's, Hephzibah Jenkins, Tabby Oven Ruins [Edisto Island MRA], Address Restricted, Edisto Island, 5/05/87, A, B, D, 86003200

Trinity Episcopal Church, About 1.2 mi. N of Edisto Island on SC 174, Edisto Island vicinity, 5/14/71, C, a, 71000759

U.S. Coast Guard Historic District, Ion Ave. between Station 18 and Station 18 1/2, Sullivans Island, 6/19/73, A, 73001703

U.S. Customhouse, 200 E. Bay St., Charleston, 10/09/74, A, C, 74001834

U.S. Post Office and Courthouse, 83 Broad St., Charleston, 8/13/74, C, 74001835

USCGC INGHAM, 40 Patriots Point Rd., Mount Pleasant, 4/27/92, A, C, NHL, 92001879

USS CLAMAGORE (SS-343), Patriot's Point, Mt. Pleasant, 6/29/89, A, C, g, NHL, 89001229

USS LAFFEY, W of Mt. Pleasant on E side of Charleston Harbor, Mount Pleasant vicinity, 4/12/83, A, C, g, NHL, 83002189

USS YORKTOWN (CV-10), W of Mt. Pleasant on E side of Charleston Harbor, Mount Pleasant vicinity, 11/10/82, A, g, NHL, 82001519

Unitarian Church, 6 Archdale St., Charleston, 11/07/73, C, a, NHL, 73001696

Unnamed Battery [Civil War Defenses of Charleston TR], St. Andrew, Shaftsbury Townhouses vicinity, 8/11/82, A, C, 82003846

Unnamed Battery No. 1 [Civil War Defenses of Charleston TR], James Island, Clark's Point vicinity, 8/11/82, A, C, 82003838

Vander Horst, Arnoldus, House, 25 mi. SW of Charleston on Kiawah Island, Charleston vicinity, 10/25/73, B, C, 73001697

Vesey, Denmark, House, 56 Bull St., Charleston, 5/11/76, B, NHL, 76001698

Wedge, The, NE of McClellanville, McClellanville vicinity, 11/25/80, C, 80003660

Wescott Road [Edisto Island MRA], W of SC 174, Edisto Island, 11/28/86, A, 86003195

Willtown Bluff, SW of Adams Run at end of CR 55 on banks of S. Edisto River, Adams Run vicinity, 1/08/74, A, D, 74001830

Windsor Plantation, E of SC 174 near Little Edisto, Edisto Island, 7/23/74, A, C, 74001837

Cherokee County

Archeological Site 38CK1 [Pacolet Soapstone Quarries TR], Address Restricted, Gaffney vicinity, 12/10/80, D, 80003661

Archeological Site 38CK44 [Pacolet Soapstone Quarries TR], Address Restricted, Gaffney vicinity, 12/10/80, D, 80003662

Archeological Site 38CK45 [Pacolet Soapstone Quarries TR], Address Restricted, Gaffney vicinity, 12/10/80, D, 80003663

Coopersville Ironworks Site (38CK2) and Susan Furnace Site (38CK67) [Early Ironworks of Northwestern South Carolina TR (AD)], Address Restricted, Gaffney vicinity, 11/13/76, A, D, 76001699

Cowpens Furnace Site (38CK73) [Early Ironworks of Northwestern South Carolina TR], Address Restricted, Gaffney vicinity, 5/08/87, D, 87000704

Cowpens National Battlefield, 2 mi. E of Chesnee at jct. of SC 11 and 110, Chesnee vicinity, 10/15/66, A, NPS, 66000072

Davis, Winnie, Hall, 1115 College Dr., Gaffney, 4/29/77, A, C, 77001219

Ellen Furnace Site (38CK68) [Early Ironworks of Northwestern South Carolina TR], Address Restricted, Gaffney vicinity, 5/08/87, D, 87000705

Gaffney Commercial Historic District [Gaffney MRA], Roughly N. Limestone St. between Cherokee Ave. and E. Meadow St., Gaffney, 3/27/86, A, C, 86000602

Gaffney Residential Historic District [Gaffney MRA], Roughly bounded by Floyd Baker Blvd., Johnson and Thompson Sts., Rutledge and Fairview Aves., and Limestone St., Gaffney, 3/27/86, C, 86000601

Hicks, Zeno, House, US 221 and Mill Gap Rd., Chesnee vicinity, 2/09/89, A, C, b, 89000002

Irene Mill Finishing Plant [Gaffney MRA], W side of Buford St. between Liberty and Logan Sts., Gaffney, 3/27/86, A, 86000591

Jefferies House [Gaffney MRA], 306 S. Grannard St., Gaffney, 3/27/86, C, 86000594

King's Creek Furnace Site (38CK71) [Early Ironworks of Northwestern South Carolina TR], Address Restricted, Kings Creek vicinity, 5/08/87, D, 87000707

Limestone Springs Historic District [Gaffney MRA], O'Neal St. extension and Limestone College campus, Gaffney, 3/27/86, A, a, 86000597

Nesbitt's Limestone Quarry (38CK69) [Early Ironworks of Northwestern South Carolina TR], Ad-

Cherokee County—Continued

dress Restricted, Gaffney vicinity, 5/08/87, D, 87000710

Robbs House [Gaffney MRA], 310 W. Burford St., Gaffney, 3/27/86, C, 86000593

Sarratt House [Gaffney MRA], 217 Marion St., Gaffney, 3/27/86, C, 86000599

Settlemyer House [Gaffney MRA], 915 N. Limehouse St., Gaffney, 3/27/86, C, 86000598

Thicketty Mountain Ore Pits (38CK74) [Early Ironworks of Northwestern South Carolina TR], Address Restricted, Shady Grove Church vicinity, 5/08/87, D, 87000711

Victor Cotton Oil Company Complex [Gaffney MRA], W side of Frederick St. between Hill and Johnson Sts., Gaffney, 3/27/86, A, 86000596

West End Elementary School [Gaffney MRA], Floyd Baker Blvd. and Broad St., Gaffney, 3/27/86, A, C, 86000600

Chester County

Catholic Presbyterian Church, 14 mi. S of Chester on SC 97 and CR 355, Chester vicinity, 5/06/71, C, a, 71000762

Chester City Hall and Opera House, Corner of West End and Columbia Sts., Chester, 3/30/73, A, C, 73001704

Chester Historic District, Commercial area centered around jct. of U.S. 321 and SC 72, Chester, 6/13/72, A, C, 72001203

Chester Historic District (Boundary Increase), Roughly bounded by Hemphill Ave., Brawley, Saluda, and FooteSts. and along Reedy St., Chester, 3/15/88, A, C, 87000684

Colvin—Fant—Durham Farm Complex, SC 22 E side, approx. 1 mi. W of jct. with SC 16, Chester vicinity, 7/30/92, A, C, 92000961

Elliott House, N of Richburg off SC 901 on CR 136, Richburg vicinity, 5/06/71, C, 71000764

Fishdam Ford, SW of Chester off SC 72, Chester vicinity, 8/14/73, D, 73001705

Great Falls Depot, Republic St., Great Falls, 11/25/80, A, 80003664

Kumler Hall, Lancaster and Cemetery Sts., Chester, 1/27/83, A, 83002190

Landsford Canal, Off US 21, Rowell, 12/03/69, A, C, D, 69000163

Landsford Plantation House, CR 595 1/2 mi. E of US 21, Landsford Township, 2/04/87, C, 86003520

Lewis Inn, NE of Chester off SC 72, Chester vicinity, 5/06/71, A, B, C, 71000763

McCollum Fish Weir, Address Restricted, Lockhart vicinity, 8/28/74, D, 74001845

McCollum Mound, Address Restricted, Chester vicinity, 3/23/72, D, 72001204

People's Free Library of South Carolina, Church St., Lowrys, 10/29/82, A, 82001520

Republic Theater, 806 Dearborn St., Great Falls, 11/26/80, A, C, 80003665

Chesterfield County

Cheraw Historic District, Bounded by Front, Kershaw, 3rd, McIver, Cedar, Greene, Christian, and Church Sts., Cheraw, 11/20/74, A, B, C, D, a, 74001844

East Main Street Historic District [Chesterfield MRA], Hursey Dr., E. Main and Craig Sts., Chesterfield, 5/04/82, A, C, 82003847

Kirkley, Evy, Site, Address Restricted, McBee vicinity, 8/03/79, D, 79002380

Lucas, Dr. Thomas E., House [Chesterfield MRA], 716 W. Main St., Chesterfield, 5/04/82, B, C, 82003848

St. David's Episcopal Church and Cemetery, Church St., Cheraw, 9/22/71, A, B, C, a, d, 71000761

West Main Street Historic District [Chesterfield MRA], W. Main, Church and Academy Sts., Chesterfield, 5/04/82, C, 82003849

Clarendon County

Davis House, S of Manning on SR 63, Manning vicinity, 1/13/83, C, 83002191

Manning Library, 211 N. Brooks St., Manning, 7/10/79, A, C, 79002381

Santee Indian Mound and Fort Watson, Addres Restricted, Summerton vicinity, 7/29/69, D, 69000164

Colleton County

Colleton County Courthouse, Corner of Hampton and Jeffries Sts., Walterboro, 5/14/71, A, C, 71000765

Hickory Valley Historic District, Roughly bounded by Ireland Creek, Jeffries Blvd., Wichman, Verdier and Ivanhoe Sts., Walterboro, 11/21/80, A, C, 80003666

Old Colleton County Jail, Jeffries Blvd., Walterboro, 5/14/71, C, 71000766

Pon Pon Chapel, NW of Jacksonboro on Parker's Ferry Rd., Jacksonboro vicinity, 1/05/72, A, a, 72001205

Walterboro Historic District, Roughly bounded by Jeffries Blvd., Sanders, Black, Church, Valley and Lemacks Sts., Walterboro, 11/10/80, C, 80003667

Walterboro Historic District (Boundary Increase), 807 Hampton St., Walterboro, 6/03/93, A, C, 93000433

Walterboro Library Society Building, 801 Wichman St., Walterboro, 10/14/71, A, C, b, 71000767

Williams, Tom, House, 0.25 mi. W of Williams on SC 362, Williams vicinity, 4/26/73, C, 73001706

Darlington County

Arcade Hotel, 204 N. Fifth St., Hartsville, 12/19/86, A, C, 86003467

Cannon, W. E., House and Store [Hartsville MPS], 612 W. Home Ave., Hartsville, 5/03/91, A, C, 91000470

Cashua Street—Spring Street Historic District [City of Darlington MRA], Cashua St. between Columbian St. and Warley St., and Spring St. between Cashua St. and N. Ervin St., Darlington, 2/10/88, C, b, 88000064

Coker Experimental Farms, W of Hartsville on SC 151, Hartsville vicinity, 10/15/66, A, B, NHL, 66000706

Coker, J. L., Company Building, 5th St. and Carolina Ave., Hartsville, 2/09/83, A, C, 83002192

Coker, James L., III, House [Hartsville MPS], 620 W. Home Ave., Hartsville, 5/03/91, B, C, 91000471

Dargan, Julius A., House [City of Darlington MRA], 488 Pearl St., Darlington, 2/10/88, C, 88000036

Darlington Industrial Historic District [City of Darlington MRA], Roughly bounded by Sixth St., Ave. B, Dargan St., and Siskron St., Darlington, 2/10/88, A, 88000062

Davidson Hall, Coker College, College Ave., Hartsville, 11/10/83, A, B, C, 83003835

Deas, Edmund H., House [City of Darlington MRA], 229 Ave. E, Darlington, 2/10/88, B, C, 88000045

Dunlap, C. K., House [Hartsville MPS], 1346 W. Carolina Ave., Hartsville, 5/03/91, B, C, 91000472

East Home Avenue Historic District [Hartsville MPS], Roughly, E. Home Ave. from N. Fifth St. to just E of First Ave., Hartsville, 5/03/91, A, B, C, a, c, d, 91000475

First Baptist Church [City of Darlington MRA], 246 S. Main St., Darlington, 10/17/91, C, a, d, 88000061

Gilbert, J. B., House [Hartsville MPS], 200 Fairfield Terr., Hartsville, 5/03/91, B, C, 91000473

Goodson, Arthur, House [Springville MRA], W of CR 133, Springville, 10/10/85, A, C, 85003137

Hart, John L., House, Home Ave., Hartsville, 11/10/83, B, b, 83003843

Hart, John L., House [Springville MRA], E of CR 133, Springville, 10/10/85, A, C, 85003138

Hart, Thomas E., House, and Kalmia Gardens [Hartsville MPS], 624 W. Carolina Ave., Hartsville, 5/03/91, A, B, C, 91000474

Hartsville Passenger Station, 114 S. 4th St., Hartsville, 6/29/76, A, 76001700

Hudson, Nelson, House [City of Darlington MRA], 521 Pearl St., Darlington, 2/10/88, C, 88000039

Japonica Hall, S. Main St., Society Hill, 12/21/89, C, 89002153

Kelley, Jacob, House, W of Hartsville on SC S-16-12, Hartsville vicinity, 5/06/71, A, C, 71000768

Lawton Park and Pavilion [Hartsville MPS], Prestwood Dr. at jct. with Lanier Dr., Hartsville, 5/03/91, A, C, 91000476

Lide, Evan J., House [Springville MRA], W of CR 228 NW of SC 34, Springville, 10/10/85, A, C, 85003139

Lide, John W., House [Springville MRA], W of CR 133, Springville, 10/10/85, A, C, 85003140

Darlington County—Continued

Manne Building [City of Darlington MRA], 129 Pearl St., Darlington, 2/10/88, A, C, 88000044

McCall, Clarence, House [City of Darlington MRA], 870 Cashua St., Darlington, 2/10/88, C, 88000058

McCullough, Charles S., House [City of Darlington MRA], 480 Pearl St., Darlington, 2/10/88, C, 88000060

Memorial Hall, 2nd St. between Home Ave. and Carolina Ave., Hartsville, 2/09/89, A, C, 89000001

South Carolina Western Railway Station [City of Darlington MRA], 129 Russell St., Darlington, 2/10/88, A, C, 88000040

St. John's Historic District, Park, St. John's Sanders and Orange Sts., Darlington, 9/04/80, A, C, 80003668

Welsh Neck-Long Bluff-Society Hill Historic District, SW of Bennettsville along U.S. 15, Bennettsville vicinity, 12/16/74, A, C, D, 74001846

West Broad Street Historic District [City of Darlington MRA], W. Broad St. between Dargan St. and Player Sts., Darlington, 2/10/88, C, 88000063

White Plains [Springville MRA], N of CR 177 and NE of CR 389, Springville, 10/10/85, B, C, 85003141

Wilds Hall [Springville MRA], W of CR 228 off SC 34, Springville, 10/10/85, A, C, 85003142

Wilds—Edwards House [City of Darlington MRA], 120 Edwards Ave., Darlington, 2/10/88, C, 88000034

Williamson, Mrs. B. F., House [City of Darlington MRA], 141 Oak St., Darlington, 2/10/88, C, 88000059

Dillon County

Allen, Joel, House, NW of Latta, Latta vicinity, 8/13/74, A, C, 74001848

Catfish Creek Baptist Church, 5 mi. NW of Latta at jct. of CR 1741 and 1763, Latta vicinity, 1/17/75, A, C, a, 75001697

Dillon County Courthouse [Courthouses in South Carolina Designed by William Augustus Edwards TR], 1303 W. Main St., Dillon, 10/30/81, A, C, 81000564

Dillon, James W., House, 1302 W. Main St., Dillon, 5/06/71, B, C, 71000769

Early Cotton Press, Near jct. of SC 917 and 38, Latta vicinity, 11/15/72, A, C, b, 72001206

Hamer Hall, N of Hamer on U.S. 301, Hamer vicinity, 5/30/75, B, C, 75001696

Latta Historic District No. 1 [Latta MRA], Church, Marion, Bethea, Rice, Dew, Mauldin, and Main Sts., Latta, 5/17/84, C, 84002038

Latta Historic District No. 2 [Latta MRA], Richardson St., Bamberg to Oak Sts., Latta, 5/17/84, C, 84002040

McMillan House [Latta MRA], 206 Maion St., Latta, 5/17/84, C, 84002042

Meekins Barn [Flue-Cured Tobacco Production Properties TR], Off SC 9, Floydale vicinity, 8/03/84, C, 84003815

Selkirk Farm, E of Bingham on Old Cashua Ferry Rd., Bingham vicinity, 7/24/74, A, B, C, 74001847

Smith Barn [Flue-Cured Tobacco Production Properties TR], E of Floydale, Floydale vicinity, 12/04/84, A, C, g, 84000568

St. Paul's Methodist Church, Off SC 9, Little Rock, 7/26/77, A, C, a, 77001220

Dorchester County

Appleby's Methodist Church, SW of St. George at jct. of SR 19 and SR 71, St. George vicinity, 2/14/78, C, a, 78002505

Carroll Place, Jct. of Quaker and Wire Rds., St. George vicinity, 7/25/74, B, C, 74001849

Cypress Methodist Camp Ground, E of Ridgeville on SC 182, Ridgeville vicinity, 4/26/78, B, C, a, 78002504

Indian Fields Methodist Campground, About 4 mi. NE of St. George on SC 73, St. George vicinity, 3/30/73, A, C, a, 73001707

Middleton Place, SE of Summerville on SC 61, Summerville vicinity, 5/06/71, B, C, NHL, 71000770

Newington Plantation, Address Restricted, Stallsville vicinity, 9/17/74, D, 74001850

Old Dorchester, 6 mi. S of Summerville on SC 642, Summerville vicinity, 12/03/69, D, 69000165

Summerville Historic District, Roughly bounded by S. Railroad Ave., Magnolia, Main Sts. and town boundary, Summerville, 5/19/76, A, C, 76001701

Edgefield County

Big Stevens Creek Baptist Church, About 8 mi. NW of North Augusta on SC 230, North Augusta vicinity, 5/06/71, A, C, a, 71000774

Blocker House, About 6 mi. NW of Edgefield on U.S. 25, Edgefield vicinity, 5/14/71, C, 71000771

Cedar Grove, 5 mi. NW of Edgefield on U.S. 25, Edgefield vicinity, 10/14/71, C, 71000772

Darby Plantation, SE of Edgefield off U.S. 25, Edgefield vicinity, 8/13/74, B, 74001851

Edgefield Historic District, Both sides of U.S. 25 through town of Edgefield, Edgefield, 3/23/72, A, C, 72001207

Horn Creek Baptist Church, S of Edgefield, Edgefield vicinity, 5/06/71, A, C, a, 71000773

Johnston Historic District, Calhoun, Edisto, Lee, Mims, Jackson, Church and Addison Sts., Edgefield, 8/25/83, A, C, 83002193

Pottersville, Address Restricted, Edgefield vicinity, 1/17/75, D, 75001698

Simkins, Paris, House, 202 Gary St., Edgefield, 4/05/84, B, 84002044

Fairfield County

Albion [Fairfield County MRA], W of Winnsboro off SC 34, Winnsboro vicinity, 12/06/84, C, 84000592

Balwearie [Fairfield County MRA], W of Winnsboro on SC 34, Winnsboro vicinity, 12/06/84, C, 84000593

Beard, James, House [Fairfield County MRA], W of Ridgeway, Ridgeway vicinity, 12/06/84, C, 84000585

Blair Mound, Address Restricted, Winnsboro vicinity, 8/23/74, D, 74001853

Blink Bonnie, About 10 mi. NE of Ridgeway, Ridgeway vicinity, 4/13/72, C, 72001209

Brice, Dr. Walter, House and Office [Fairfield County MRA], NW of Winnsboro, Winnsboro vicinity, 12/06/84, B, C, 84000594

Camp Welfare [Fairfield County MRA], Off U.S. 21, Ridgeway vicinity, 12/06/84, A, a, 84000586

Century House, SC 34, Ridgeway, 8/19/71, A, C, 71000777

Concord Presbyterian Church [Fairfield County MRA], U.S. 321, Winnsboro vicinity, 12/06/84, C, a, d, 84000598

Davis Plantation, S of Monticello on SC 215, Monticello vicinity, 5/06/71, A, B, C, 71000776

Ebenezer Associate Reformed Presbyterian Church, 4.3 mi. N of Jenkinsville on SC 213, Jenkinsville vicinity, 8/19/71, A, C, a, 71000775

Fonti Flora Plantation, 5.4 mi. NE of Monticello on SC 99, Monticello vicinity, 4/24/79, B, C, 79002382

Furman Institution Academic Building [Fairfield County MRA], SW of Winnsboro, Winnsboro vicinity, 12/06/84, A, 84000600

Furman Institution Faculty Residence [Fairfield County MRA], SW of Winnsboro, Winnsboro vicinity, 12/06/84, A, 84000601

Glenn, Dr. John, House [Fairfield County MRA], SC 215, Jenkinsville vicinity, 12/06/84, C, 84000572

High Point [Fairfield County MRA], SC 215, Jenkinsville vicinity, 12/06/84, C, 84000576

Hunstanton [Fairfield County MRA], U.S. 321, Winnsboro vicinity, 12/06/84, C, 84000604

Hunter House [Fairfield County MRA], NE of Ridgeway, Ridgeway vicinity, 12/06/84, C, 84000588

Ketchin Building, 231 S. Congress St., Winnsboro, 12/18/70, C, 70000588

Kincaid-Anderson House, NE of Jenkinsville of SC 213, Jenkinsville, 7/30/74, B, C, a, 74001852

Lemmon, Bob, House [Fairfield County MRA], Off SC 213, Winnsboro vicinity, 12/06/84, C, 84000607

Liberty Universalist Church and Feasterville Academy Historic District [Fairfield County MRA], SC 215, Winnsboro vicinity, 12/06/84, A, a, 84000612

Little River Baptist Church, 3.8 mi. N of Jenkinsville on SC 213, Jenkinsville vicinity, 4/13/72, A, C, a, 72001208

Mayfair [Fairfield County MRA], Off SC 215, Jenkinsville, 2/06/85, C, 85000246

McMeekin Rock Shelter, Address Restricted, Winnsboro vicinity, 8/23/74, D, 74001854

Monticello Methodist Church [Fairfield County MRA], Off SC 215, Monticello, 12/06/84, C, a, d, 84000578

Fairfield County—Continued

Monticello Store and Post Office [Fairfield County MRA], Off SC 215, Monticello, 12/06/84, A, C, 84000584

Mount Hope [Fairfield County MRA], SC 34, Ridgeway vicinity, 12/06/84, B, C, 84000589

Mount Olivet Presbyterian Church, Off SC 200, Winnsboro vicinity, 8/13/86, C, a, 86001523

New Hope A.R.P. Church and Session House [Fairfield County MRA], NW of Winnsboro, Winnsboro vicinity, 12/06/84, C, a, 84000652

Old Stone House [Fairfield County MRA], Off SC 34, Winnsboro vicinity, 12/06/84, C, 84000614

Ridgeway Historic District [Ridgeway MRA], US 21 and SC 34, Ridgeway, 11/25/80, A, C, 80004466

Rockton and Rion Railroad Historic District [Fairfield County MRA], S of Winnsboro from SC 34 W to SC 213, Winnsboro vicinity, 12/06/84, A, 84000617

Ruff's Chapel [Ridgeway MRA], U.S. 21 and SC 34, Ridgeway, 11/25/80, A, B, C, a, 80004400

Rural Point, Old Camden Rd., Winnsboro, 2/23/72, B, C, 72001210

Shivar Springs Bottling Company Cisterns [Fairfield County MRA], W of Winnsboro, Winnsboro vicinity, 12/06/84, A, 84000622

St. Stephen's Episcopal Church, NE of Ridgeway on CR 106, Ridgeway vicinity, 5/06/71, A, C, a, 71000778

The Oaks [Fairfield County MRA], SC 213, Winnsboro vicinity, 12/06/84, C, 84000624

Tocaland [Fairfield County MRA], Off SC 34, Winnsboro vicinity, 12/06/84, C, 84000627

Valencia, NW of Ridgeway on CR 106, Ridgeway vicinity, 5/06/71, B, C, a, 71000779

Vaughn's Stage Coach Stop [Fairfield County MRA], SC 34, Ridgeway vicinity, 12/06/84, C, 84000591

White Oak Historic District [Fairfield County MRA], Off U.S. 321, Winnsboro vicinity, 12/06/84, A, 84000631

Wilson, Monroe, House [Ridgeway MRA], Railroad Ave. and SR S20-20, Ridgeway, 11/25/80, C, 80004467

Winnsboro Historic District, Roughly bounded by Gooding, Buchanan, Garden, and Fairfield Sts., Winnsboro, 10/14/71, A, C, 71000780

Florence County

Bonnie Shade, 1439 Cherokee Rd., Florence, 11/14/78, B, C, 78002506

Browntown, SC 341, Johnsonville vicinity, 6/28/82, C, 82003850

Christ Episcopal Church, NE of Florence on SC 327, Florence vicinity, 11/14/78, A, C, a, 78002507

Poynor Junior High School, 301 S. Dargan St., Florence, 5/19/83, C, 83002194

Rankin-Harwell House, 6 mi. NE of Florence off SC 305, Florence vicinity, 10/09/74, B, C, 74001855

Red Doe, E of Florence on SC 327, Florence vicinity, 10/29/82, C, 82001521

Slave Houses, Gregg Plantation, Francis Marion College campus, Mars Bluff, 7/22/74, A, C, 74001856

Smith-Cannon House, 106 W. Market St., Timmonsville, 7/28/83, B, C, 83002195

Snow's Island, Address Restricted, Johnsonville vicinity, 3/14/73, A, B, D, NHL, 73001708

Stockade, The, Address Restricted, Florence vicinity, 11/28/80, A, D, NHL, 80003669

U.S. Post Office, Irby and W. Evan Sts., Florence, 12/21/77, A, C, 77001221

Young Farm, W of Florence on US 76, Florence vicinity, 11/10/83, B, 83003854

Georgetown County

All Saints' Episcopal Church, Waccamaw, SC 255 .2 mi. N of jct. with SC 46, Pawleys Island vicinity, 3/13/91, A, C, a, d, 91000232

Annandale Plantation, About 14 mi. S of Georgetown between SC 30 and SC 18, Georgetown vicinity, 10/25/73, A, B, C, 73001709

Arcadia Plantation, 5 mi. (8 km) E of Georgetown off U.S. 17, Georgetown vicinity, 1/03/78, A, C, 78002509

Atalaya, Off US 17, Murrells Inlet vicinity, 9/07/84, B, C, g, NHL, 84002045

Battery White, S of Georgetown on Belle Isle Rd., Georgetown vicinity, 11/16/77, A, D, 77001222

Belle Isle Rice Mill Chimney [Georgetown County Rice Culture c. 1750–1910 MPS], Cat Island, Georgetown vicinity, 10/03/88, A, C, 88000525

Beneventum Plantation House [Georgetown County Rice Culture c. 1750–1910 MPS], Off CR 431, Georgetown vicinity, 10/03/88, A, B, C, 88000526

Brookgreen Gardens, 18 mi. (28.8 km) NE of Georgetown on U.S. 17, Georgetown vicinity, 4/15/78, A, B, C, g, 78002510

Cedar Grove Plantation Chapel [Georgetown County Rice Culture MPS], SC 255 .2 mi. N of jct. with SC 46, Pawleys Island vicinity, 3/13/91, A, C, a, b, 91000231

Chicora Wood Plantation, 12 mi. NE of Georgetown on CR 52, Georgetown vicinity, 4/11/73, A, B, C, 73001710

China Grove, SC 512, Georgetown vicinity, 3/25/82, C, 82003851

Fairfield Rice Mill Chimney [Georgetown County Rice Culture c. 1750–1910 MPS], Off US 17, Georgetown vicinity, 10/03/88, A, C, 88000527

Georgetown Historic District, Along N side of Sampit River, Georgetown, 10/14/71, A, C, 71000781

Georgetown Lighthouse, On North Island, about 12 mi. SE of Georgetown, Georgetown vicinity, 12/30/74, A, 74001857

Hopsewee, 12 mi. S of Georgetown on U.S. 17, Georgetown vicinity, 1/25/71, B, C, b, NHL, 71000782

Keithfield Plantation [Georgetown County Rice Culture c. 1750–1910 MPS], Off CR 52, Georgetown vicinity, 10/03/88, A, C, 88000529

Mansfield Plantation, 5 mi. N of Georgetown off U.S. 701, Georgetown vicinity, 12/06/77, A, B, C, 77001223

Milldam Rice Mill and Rice Barn [Georgetown County Rice Culture c. 1750–1910 MPS], Off CR 30, Georgetown vicinity, 10/03/88, A, C, 88000530

Minim Island Shell Midden (38GE46), Address Restricted, Georgetown vicinity, 8/18/82, D, 82003852

Murrells Inlet Historic District, Off U.S. 17, Murrells Inlet, 11/25/80, A, B, C, 80003670

Nightingale Hall Rice Mill Chimney [Georgetown County Rice Culture c. 1750–1910 MPS], Off CR 52, Georgetown vicinity, 10/03/88, A, C, 88000531

Old Market Building, Front and Screven Sts., Georgetown, 12/03/69, A, 69000166

Pawleys Island Historic District, W side of Pawleys Island, Pawleys Island, 11/15/72, A, B, 72001211

Pee Dee River Rice Planters Historic District [Georgetown County Rice Culture c. 1750–1910 MPS], Along the Pee Dee and Waccamaw Rivers, Georgetown vicinity, 10/03/88, A, B, C, 88000532

Prince Frederick's Chapel Ruins, SE of Plantersville on Rte. 52, Plantersville vicinity, 8/28/74, A, C, a, 74001858

Prince George Winyah Church (Episcopal) and Cemetery, Corner of Broad and Highmarket Sts., Georgetown, 5/06/71, A, C, a, 71000783

Rainey, Joseph H., House, 909 Prince St., Georgetown, 4/20/84, B, NHL, 84003877

Richmond Hill Plantation Archeological Sites [Georgetown County Rice Culture c. 1750–1910 MPS], Address Restricted, Murrell's Inlet vicinity, 10/06/88, A, C, d, 88000537

Rural Hall Plantation House [Georgetown County Rice Culture c. 1750–1910 MPS], Off CR 179, Georgetown vicinity, 10/03/88, A, C, 88000533

Summer Chapel Rectory, Prince Frederick's Episcopal Church [Georgetown County Rice Culture c. 1750–1910 MPS], CR 52, Plantersville, 10/03/88, A, C, a, 88000536

Summer Chapel, Prince Frederick's Episcopal Church [Georgetown County Rice Culture c. 1750–1910 MPS], CR 52, Plantersville, 10/03/88, A, C, a, 88000535

Weehaw Rice Mill Chimney [Georgetown County Rice Culture c. 1750–1910 MPS], Off CR 325, Georgetown vicinity, 10/03/88, A, C, 88000534

Wicklow Hall Plantation, S of Georgetown on SC 30, Georgetown vicinity, 8/29/78, A, C, 78002511

Winyah Indigo School, 1200 Highmarket St., Georgetown, 11/03/88, A, C, 88002386

Greenville County

American Cigar Factory [Greenville MRA], E. Ct. St., Greenville, 7/01/82, A, C, 82003853

Barnwell, Arthur, House, S of Greer on SR 14, Greer vicinity, 3/19/82, A, C, 82003867

Greenville County—Continued

Bates, William, House, E of Greenville on SC 14, Greenville vicinity, 12/04/78, B, 78002512

Beattie, Fountain Fox, House, N. Church St., Greenville, 10/09/74, C, 74001859

Broad Margin, 9 W. Avondale Dr., Greenville, 12/08/78, C, g, 78002513

Chamber of Commerce Building [Greenville MRA], 130 S. Main St., Greenville, 7/01/82, A, C, 82003854

Cherrydale, 1500 Poinsett Hwy., Greenville, 6/17/76, B, C, 76001702

Christ Church (Episcopal) and Churchyard, 10 N. Church St., Greenville, 5/06/71, A, C, D, a, 71000784

Cureton-Huff House, SW of Simpsonville off SC 176, Simpsonville vicinity, 1/13/83, C, 83002196

Davenport Apartments [Greenville MRA], 400–402 E. Washington St., Greenville, 7/01/82, C, 82003855

Donaldson, T. Q., House, 412 Crescent Ave., Greenville, 9/04/80, B, C, 80003671

Downtown Baptist Church, 101 W. McBee Ave., Greenville, 8/16/77, A, C, a, 77001225

Earle Town House, 107 James St., Greenville, 8/05/69, A, C, 69000167

Earle, Col. Elias, Historic District [Greenville MRA], Earle, James, N. Main, and Rutherford Sts., Greenville, 7/01/82, A, C, 82003856

Fairview Presbyterian Church, W of Fountain Inn off SC 418, Fountain Inn vicinity, 8/16/77, A, C, a, 77001224

First National Bank, 102 S. Main St., Greenville, 12/21/89, C, 89002152

Gilreath's Mill, 4 mi. NW of Greer on SC 101, Greer vicinity, 5/28/76, A, 76001703

Goodwin, John H., House, SC 11 at U.S. 25, Travelers Rest vicinity, 9/08/83, C, 83002197

Greenville Gas and Electric Light Company [Greenville MRA], 211 E. Broad St., Greenville, 7/01/82, A, 82003857

Greer Depot, 311 Trade St., Greer, 3/06/87, A, C, 87000409

Hampton-Pinckney Historic District, Hampton Ave. and Pinckney St. between Butler Ave. and Lloyd St., Greenville, 12/12/77, A, C, a, g, 77001226

Hampton-Pinckney Historic District Extension [Greenville MRA], Hampton, Lloyd, Hudson Sts., Butler and Asbury Aves., Greenville, 7/01/82, A, C, 82003858

Imperial Hotel [Greenville MRA], 201 W. Washington St., Greenville, 9/12/85, C, 85002167

Isaqueena [Greenville MRA], 106 DuPont Dr., Greenville, 7/01/82, B, C, 82003859

Kilgore, Josiah, House, N. Church and Academy Sts., Greenville, 4/28/75, C, b, 75001699

Lanneau-Norwood House [Greenville MRA], 417 Belmont Ave., Greenville, 7/01/82, C, 82003860

McBee Methodist Church, Main St., Conestee, 3/23/72, C, a, 72001212

Mills Mill [Greenville MRA], Mills and Guess Sts., Greenville, 7/01/82, A, 82003861

Old Textile Hall, 322 W. Washington St., Greenville, 11/25/80, A, C, 80003672

Pelham Mills Site (38GR165), Address Restricted, Pelham vicinity, 11/19/87, A, D, 87001954

Pettigru Street Historic District [Greenville MRA], Pettigru, Whitsett, Williams, Manly, E. Washington, Broadus, Toy, and Boyce Sts., Greenville, 7/01/82, C, 82003862

Poinsett Bridge, About 4 mi. N of Tigerville on CR 42, Tigerville vicinity, 10/22/70, A, C, 70000590

Poinsett Hotel [Greenville MRA], 120 S. Main St., Greenville, 7/01/82, C, 82003863

Reedy River Falls Historic Park and Greenway, Both banks of Reedy River from the falls to Church St., Greenville, 4/23/73, A, C, 73001711

Reedy River Falls Historic Park and Greenway (Boundary Increase), Roughly bounded by S. Main and Church Sts., and Camperdown Way, Greenville, 11/17/78, A, 78003205

Reedy River Industrial District, Along Reedy River between River St. and Camperdown Way, Greenville, 2/14/79, A, 79002383

Salmon, George, House, SC 414, 1.8 mi. W of US 25, Travelers Rest vicinity, 1/21/88, B, C, b, 87002520

Simpsonville Baptist Church, 106 Church St., Simpsonville, 10/13/92, C, a, 92001309

Tullyton, 606 Hickory Tavern Rd., Fountain Inn vicinity, 7/31/90, C, 89002151

Wesley, John, Methodist Episcopal Church, 101 E. Court St., Greenville, 1/20/78, A, C, a, 78002514

West End Commercial Historic District, Roughly, jct. of Pendleton, River, Augusta and S. Main Sts. and E along Main to Camperdown Way, Greenville, 1/07/93, A, C, 92001751

Whitehall, 310 W. Earle St., Greenville, 8/05/69, B, C, 69000168

Williams-Earle House [Greenville MRA], 319 Grove Rd., Greenville, 7/01/82, C, 82003864

Woodside Cotton Mill Village Historic District, Woodside Ave. and E. Main St., Woodside, 4/30/87, A, 87000678

Working Benevolent Temple and Professional Building [Greenville MRA], Broad and Fall Sts., Greenville, 7/01/82, A, C, 82003865

Wyche, C. Granville, House, 2900 Augusta Rd., Greenville, 9/02/93, C, 93000904

Greenwood County

Barratt House, SC 67 & Bryan Dorn Rd., Greenwood vicinity, 9/12/85, B, C, 85002382

Brooks, J. Wesley, House, 2 mi. S of Greenwood on U.S. 25, Greenwood vicinity, 3/30/73, C, 73001712

Lander College Old Main Building, Stanley Ave. and Lander St., Greenwood, 8/02/84, A, C, a, 84002046

Moore-Kinard House, US 178 and S-24-44, Ninety Six vicinity, 8/04/83, C, 83002198

Mt. Pisgah A.M.E. Church, Hackett Ave. and James St., Greenwood, 8/16/79, A, C, a, 79002384

Ninety Six National Historic Site, 2 mi. S of Ninety Six between SC 248 and 27, Ninety Six vicinity, 12/03/69, A, D, e, NHL, NPS, 69000169

Old Cokesbury and Masonic Female College and Conference School, N of Greenwood at jct. of SR 246 and 254, Cokesbury vicinity, 8/25/70, A, C, a, 70000589

Old Greenwood High School, 857 S. Main St., Greenwood, 10/10/85, A, C, 85003120

Self, James C., House, 595 N. Mathis St., Greenwood vicinity, 11/20/87, B, C, 87002064

Stony Point, N of Greenwood at jct. of SC 246 and SR 39, Greenwood vicinity, 6/20/75, B, C, 75001700

Sunnyside, 105 Dargan Ave., Greenwood, 11/14/78, B, C, 78002515

Trapp and Chandler Pottery Site (38GN169), Address Restricted, Kirksey vicinity, 1/06/86, A, D, 86000043

Vance-Maxwell House, 158 E. Cambridge ST., Greenwood, 3/05/82, B, C, 82003866

Hampton County

Cohasset, US 601, Crocketville vicinity, 7/24/86, A, B, C, 86001935

Hampton Colored School, W. Holly St. E. of jct. with Hoover St., Hampton, 2/28/91, A, C, 91000233

Hampton County Courthouse, U.S. 278, Hampton, 12/12/78, A, 78002517

Oak Grove, SW of Brunson, Brunson vicinity, 7/12/76, C, 76001704

Peeples, Hattie J., House, 109 Carolina Ave. W., Varnville, 10/13/92, C, 92001299

Horry County

Ambrose, H. W., House [Conway MRA], 1503 Elm St., Conway, 8/05/86, C, 86002219

Beaty—Little House [Conway MRA], 507 Main St., Conway, 8/05/86, C, 86002220

Beaty—Spivey House [Conway MRA], 428 Kingston St., Conway, 8/05/86, B, C, 86002223

Buck's Upper Mill Farm, N of Bucksville, Bucksville vicinity, 3/25/82, B, 82003868

Burroughs School, 801 Main St., Conway, 8/02/84, A, 84002047

Burroughs, Arthur M., House [Conway MRA], 500 Lakeside Dr., Conway, 8/05/86, B, C, 86002224

Conway Methodist Church, 1898 and 1910 Sanctuaries [Conway MRA], Fifth Ave., Conway, 8/05/86, C, a, 86002225

Hebron Church, 10 mi. S of Conway off U.S. 701, Bucksville vicinity, 5/16/77, A, C, a, 77001227

Holliday, J. W., Jr., House [Conway MRA], 701 Laurel St., Conway, 8/05/86, C, 86002227

Kingston Presbyterian Church Cemetery [Conway MRA], 800 Third Ave., Conway, 8/05/86, C, d, 86002229

Old Horry County Courthouse, Main St., Conway, 4/07/71, A, C, 71000785

Horry County—Continued

Quattlebaum, C. P., House [Conway MRA], 219 Kingston St., Conway, 8/05/86, C, 86002233

Quattlebaum, C. P., Office [Conway MRA], 903 Third Ave., Conway, 8/05/86, C, b, 86002235

Quattlebaum, Paul, House [Conway MRA], 225 Kingston St., Conway, 8/05/86, C, 86002231

Waccamaw River Warehouse Historic District [Conway MRA], Roughly Main St. between the Waccamaw River and Laurel St., Conway, 8/05/86, A, C, 86002269

Winborne, W. H., House [Conway MRA], 1300 Sixth Ave., Conway, 8/05/86, C, 86002268

Jasper County

Church of the Holy Trinity, SC 13 and SC 29, Ridgeland vicinity, 3/25/82, C, a, 82003869

Gillisonville Baptist Church, U.S. 278, Gillisonville, 5/14/71, A, C, a, 71000786

Jasper County Courthouse [Courthouses in South Carolina Designed by William Augustus Edwards TR], Russell St., Ridgeland, 10/30/81, A, C, 81000566

Robertville Baptist Church, Jct. of U.S. 321 and CR 26, Robertville, 2/23/72, C, a, b, 72001213

Kershaw County

Adamson Mounds Site, Address Restricted, Camden vicinity, 7/16/70, D, 70000591

Bethesda Presbyterian Church, 502 Dekalb St., Camden, 2/04/85, C, a, NHL, 85003258

Boykin Mill Complex, 8 mi. S of Camden at jct. of SC 261 and Co. Rd. 2, Camden vicinity, 9/10/92, A, C, 92001230

Camden Battlefield, 5 mi. N of Camden on U.S. 521 and 601, Camden vicinity, 10/15/66, A, NHL, 66000707

Cantey, Zachariah, House, CR 92, Camden vicinity, 5/19/83, B, C, 83002199

Carter Hill, 10 mi. S of Camden, E of SC 521, Camden vicinity, 9/24/92, C, 92001231

City of Camden Historic District, Bounded on S by city limits, on E and W by Southern RR. right-of-way, and on N by Dicey Creek Rd., Camden, 5/06/71, A, C, 71000787

Cool Springs, 726 Kershaw Hwy., Camden vicinity, 9/28/89, C, 89001596

English, Thomas, House, SC 92, 0.6 mi. W of jct. with SC 93, Camden, 7/22/93, C, b, 82003871

Historic Camden Revolutionary War Restoration, Southern area of the city, DeKalb Township, Camden, 7/29/69, A, D, 69000170

Kendall Mill Historic District, Roughly bounded by RR tracks, Kendall Lake, Lakeshore Dr., McRae Rd., and Haile St., Camden, 3/19/82, 82003870

Liberty Hill Historic District, SC 97, Liberty Hill, 11/14/78, C, 78002519

McCoy, Benjamin, House, S of Cassatt on SR 15, Cassatt vicinity, 8/07/80, C, 80003674

McDowell Site, Address Restricted, Camden vicinity, 7/16/70, A, D, 70000592

Midfield Plantation, NE of Boykin on SR 23, Boykin vicinity, 4/20/78, A, C, 78002518

Mulberry Plantation, S of Camden on U.S. 521, Camden vicinity, 11/25/80, B, C, 80003673

Russell—Heath House, SC 522, W of jct. with Co. Rd. 2088, Stoneboro vicinity, 2/14/90, C, 90000006

Lancaster County

Allison, Robert Barnwell, House [Lancaster County MPS], 404 Chesterfield Ave., Lancaster, 1/04/90, C, 89002148

Battle of Hanging Rock Historic Site, About 3.5 mi. S of Heath Springs off U.S. 521, Heath Springs vicinity, 12/31/74, A, 74001860

Buford's Massacre Site [Lancaster County MPS], SC 522, 0.25 mi. S of SC 9, Tradesville vicinity, 2/15/90, A, 90000091

Cauthen, Dr. William Columbus, House, SR 75, Kershaw vicinity, 6/28/82, B, C, 82003872

Clinton AME Zion Church [Lancaster County MPS], Johnson and Church Sts., Kershaw, 2/16/90, A, C, a, 90000092

Craig House [Lancaster County MPS], SC 185/Craig Dr., Lancaster vicinity, 2/16/90, C, 90000093

Cureton House [Lancaster County MPS], Co. Rd. 29, S of Co. Rd. 39, City Unavailable, 9/04/90, C, 90000094

East Richland Street—East Church Street Historic District [Lancaster County MPS], Roughly bounded by E. Church St., Ingram St., E. Richland St., and Hart St., Kershaw, 1/04/90, C, 89002142

Heath Springs Depot [Lancaster County MPS], E. Railroad Ave., Heath Springs, 1/04/90, C, 89002147

Huey, Thomas Walker, House [Lancaster County MPS], Jct. of SC 200 and SC 285, Lancaster vicinity, 1/04/90, C, 89002146

Ivy, Adam, House [Lancaster County MPS], SC 55, 1.5 mi. SW of jct. with Co. Rd. 2109, Van Wyck vicinity, 9/04/90, C, 89002144

Kershaw Depot [Lancaster County MPS], Cleveland St., Kershaw, 2/16/90, C, 90000096

Kilburnie, 204 N. White St., Lancaster, 4/24/79, B, C, 79002385

Lancaster Cotton Oil Company [Lancaster County MPS], S. Main St. at Lancaster & Chester Railroad tracks, Lancaster, 2/06/90, A, C, 89002145

Lancaster County Courthouse, 104 N. Main St., Lancaster, 2/24/71, A, C, NHL, 71000788

Lancaster County Jail, 208 W. Gay St., Lancaster, 8/09/71, A, C, NHL, 71000789

Lancaster Downtown Historic District, S. Main, Gay, and Catawba Sts., Lancaster, 8/09/84, A, C, 84002048

Lancaster Presbyterian Church, W. Gay St., Lancaster, 12/16/77, A, 77001228

Massey—Doby—Nisbet House [Lancaster County MPS], SC 55, SW of Co. Rd. 2109, Van Wyck vicinity, 2/16/90, C, 90000095

Matson Street Historic District [Lancaster County MPS], Matson St. from Hilton to Pine Sts., Kershaw, 9/04/90, C, 89002143

Mount Carmel A.M.E. Zion Campground, S of Lancaster, Lancaster vicinity, 5/10/79, A, C, a, 79002386

North Carolina-South Carolina Cornerstone, Off US 521, Lancaster vicinity, 12/20/84, A, 84001115

Sapp, William Harrison, House [Lancaster County MPS], SC 522 and SC 51, Tradesville vicinity, 1/04/90, C, 89002141

Springs, Leroy, House, Catawba and Gay Sts., Lancaster, 3/20/86, B, C, 86000467

Stewart—Sapp House [Lancaster County MPS], SC 522 and SC 28, Tradesville vicinity, 2/16/90, C, 90000097

Unity Baptist Church [Lancaster County MPS], Sumter and Hart Sts., Kershaw, 2/16/90, A, C, a, 90000098

Wade—Beckham House, SC 200, Lancaster vicinity, 6/17/88, C, b, 88000669

Waxhaw Presbyterian Church Cemetery, 8 mi. N of Lancaster off U.S. 521, Lancaster vicinity, 9/11/75, A, B, C, a, c, d, 75001701

Laurens County

Albright—Dukes House [City of Laurens MRA], 127 Academy St., Laurens, 11/19/86, C, 86003149

Clinton Commercial Historic District, Main, Broad, Pitts, Musgrove and Gary Sts., Clinton, 11/15/84, A, C, 84000577

Darlington, Lyde Irby, House [City of Laurens MRA], 110 Irby Ave., Laurens, 11/19/86, C, 86003150

Dial, Allen, House, SR 729, Laurens vicinity, 1/21/82, C, 82003874

Duckett, Charles H., House [City of Laurens MRA], 105 Downs St., Laurens, 11/19/86, B, C, g, 86003151

Duncan's Creek Presbyterian Church, 5 mi. NE of Clinton, off SC 72, Clinton vicinity, 11/15/73, A, C, a, d, 73001714

Dunklin, James, House, 544 W. Main St., Laurens, 10/01/74, C, 74001861

Irby, Dr. William Claudius, House [City of Laurens MRA], 132 Irby Ave., Laurens, 11/19/86, C, 86003152

Irby-Henderson-Todd House, 112 Todd Ave., Laurens, 9/08/83, B, C, 83002200

Laurens County Courthouse, Laurens Courthouse Sq., Laurens, 6/19/72, A, C, 72001214

Laurens Historic District, U.S. 221 and U.S. 76, Laurens, 10/10/80, A, C, 80003675

Laurens Historic District (Boundary Increase) [City of Laurens MRA], Both sides of W. Main

Laurens County—Continued

St. from 742 to 964 W. Main St., Laurens, 11/19/86, A, C, 86003164

Lindley's Fort Site, Address Restricted, Madens vicinity, 11/07/78, D, 78002521

Nickels-Milam House, S of Laurens off U.S. 221, Laurens vicinity, 5/28/76, B, C, a, g, 76001705

Octagon House, 619 E. Main St., Laurens, 3/20/73, C, 73001715

Owings, John Calvin, House, 787 W. Main St., Laurens, 2/23/78, C, 78002520

Simpson, William Dunlap, House, 726 W. Main St., Laurens, 7/24/74, B, C, 74001862

Sitgreaves House [City of Laurens MRA], 428 W. Farley Ave., Laurens, 11/19/86, C, 86003158

South Harper Historic District [City of Laurens MRA], Both sides of S. Harper St. from 320 to 1037, Laurens, 11/19/86, A, C, g, 86003161

Sullivan House, 10 mi. W of Laurens on U.S. 76, Laurens vicinity, 5/22/73, C, 73001716

Thornwell-Presbyterian College Historic District, Presbyterian College Campus, Clinton, 3/05/82, A, B, C, a, 82003873

Williams—Ball—Copeland House [City of Laurens MRA], 544 Ball Dr., Laurens, 11/19/86, B, C, a, 86003159

Wilson—Clary House [City of Laurens MRA], 120 Irby Ave., Laurens, 12/11/86, C, 86003471

Lee County

Bishopville Commercial Historic District [Bishopville MRA], N. Main St. between W. Church and Cedar Ln. and along Cedar Ln., Bishopville, 1/09/86, A, C, 86000052

Carnes, James, House [Bishopville MRA], 200 S. Main St., Bishopville, 1/09/86, B, C, 86000051

Fraser, Thomas, House [Bishopville MRA], US 15, Bishopville, 1/09/86, B, C, 86000050

Lee County Courthouse [Courthouses in South Carolina Designed by William Augustus Edwards TR], 123 Main St., Bishopville, 10/30/81, A, C, 81000568

Manor, The [Bishopville MRA], 529 N. Main St., Bishopville, 1/09/86, B, C, 86000049

Rembert Church, 1 mi. E of Woodrow on SC 37, Woodrow vicinity, 2/25/75, A, C, a, 75001702

Rogers, William, House [Bishopville MRA], 531 W. Church St., Bishopville, 1/09/86, B, C, 86000047

South Main Historic District [Bishopville MRA], S. Main between E. Harris and W. Ridge Sts., Bishopville, 1/09/86, B, C, 86000048

Spencer House [Bishopville MRA], 817 N. Main St., Bishopville, 1/09/86, B, C, 86000046

Tall Oaks [Bishopville MRA], SC 341, Bishopville, 1/09/86, B, C, 86000045

Tanglewood Plantation, SE of Lynchburg on SC 341, Lynchburg vicinity, 9/22/77, A, 77001229

Lexington County

"Congarees" Site, Address Restricted, Cayce vicinity, 12/31/74, A, D, 74002261

Ballentine-Shealy House [Lexington County MRA], SR 1323, Lexington vicinity, 11/22/83, C, 83003858

Bank of Western Carolina [Lexington County MRA], 126 Main St., Lexington vicinity, 11/22/83, A, C, 83003860

Barr, D. D. D., House [Lexington County MRA], Off SC 245, Batesburg vicinity, 11/22/83, C, 83003866

Batesburg Commercial Historic District [Batesburg-Leesville MRA], Granite, Oak, Pine, Church Sts., Rutland and N. Railroad Aves., Batesburg, 7/06/82, A, 82003875

Berly, W. Q. M., House [Lexington County MRA], 122 Berly St., Lexington vicinity, 11/22/83, C, 83003870

Berly, William, House, 121 Berly St., Lexington, 11/23/77, B, C, 77001230

Boozer, Lemuel, House, 320 W. Main St., Lexington, 8/16/77, B, C, 77001231

Bouknight, Simon, House [Batesburg-Leesville MRA], Saluda Ave., Batesburg, 7/06/82, C, 82003876

Cartledge House [Batesburg-Leesville MRA], 305 Saluda Ave., Batesburg, 7/06/82, C, 82003879

Cayce, William J., House, 517 Holland Ave., Cayce, 4/16/75, A, B, 75001703

Church Street Historic District [Batesburg-Leesville MRA], Church St., Leesville, 7/06/82, A, C, a, b, 82003884

Corley, C. E., House [Lexington County MRA], 808 S. Lake Dr., Lexington vicinity, 11/22/83, C, 83003872

Dreher, Jacob Wingard, House [Lexington County MRA], Off SC 6, Irmo vicinity, 11/22/83, C, 83003875

Edwards, Broadus, House [Batesburg-Leesville MRA], 12 Peachtree St., Batesburg, 7/06/82, B, C, 82003877

Fox House, 232 Fox St., Lexington, 7/01/70, A, C, e, 70000893

George's Grist and Flour Mill [Lexington County MRA], Gibson's Pond Rd., Lexington vicinity, 11/22/83, A, 83003877

Gervais Street Bridge [Columbia MRA], Spans Congaree River, West Columbia, 11/25/80, A, C, g, 80003676

Griffith, David Jefferson, House [Lexington County MRA], Address Restricted, Gilbert vicinity, 11/22/83, C, 83003879

Gunter—Summers House [Lexington County MRA], 841 Center St., Lexington, 11/10/87, C, 87001988

Hampton Hendrix Office [Batesburg-Leesville MRA], Leesville Ave., Leesville, 7/06/82, B, C, 82003885

Harman, James, Building [Lexington County MRA], Gantt St., Lexington vicinity, 11/22/83, C, 83003903

Hartley House [Batesburg-Leesville MRA], 305 E. Columbia Ave., Batesburg, 7/09/82, A, 82003878

Hazelius, Ernest L., House, Fox St., Lexington, 5/11/73, B, C, a, 73001717

Hendrix, Henry Franklin, House [Batesburg-Leesville MRA], Hendrix Heights Plantation, Leesville, 7/06/82, B, C, 82003886

Hendrix, John Solomon, House [Lexington County MRA], Old Cherokee Rd., Lexington vicinity, 11/22/83, C, 83003904

Herbert, Rev. Walter I., House [Batesburg-Leesville MRA], 506 Trotter St., Leesville, 7/06/82, C, 82003887

Hite, John Jacob, Farm [Lexington County MRA], Address Restricted, Lexington vicinity, 11/22/83, C, 83003908

Holman, J. B., House [Batesburg-Leesville MRA], N. Peachtree St., Leesville, 7/06/82, B, C, 82003888

Home National Bank [Lexington County MRA], Main St. and North Lake Dr., Lexington vicinity, 11/22/83, A, C, 83003909

Jones, A. C., House [Batesburg-Leesville MRA], 104 Fair Ave., Batesburg, 7/06/82, C, 82003880

Leesville College Historic District [Batesburg-Leesville MRA], Railroad Ave., College, Peachtree, King, and Lee Sts., Leesville, 7/06/82, A, C, 82003889

Lybrand, Henry, Farm [Lexington County MRA], Address Restricted, Lexington vicinity, 11/22/83, C, 83003911

Manning Archeological Site, Address Restricted, Cayce vicinity, 12/14/78, D, 78002522

Meetze, Maj. Henry A., House, S of Lexington at 723 S. Lake Dr., Lexington vicinity, 7/13/79, A, B, C, 79002387

Mitchell, Crowell, House [Batesburg-Leesville MRA], Church St., Leesville, 7/06/82, C, 82003890

Mitchell, McKendree, House [Batesburg-Leesville MRA], 310 Saluda Ave., Batesburg, 7/06/82, C, 82003881

Mitchell-Shealy House [Batesburg-Leesville MRA], 419 W. Church St., Leesville, 7/06/82, C, 82003891

Mount Hebron Temperance Hall, 3041 Leaphart Rd., West Columbia, 11/24/80, A, 80003677

Music Hall Evangelical Lutheran Church [Lexington County MRA], Address Restricted, Gilbert vicinity, 11/22/83, A, a, 83003913

New Brookland Historic District, Roughly bounded by Alexander Rd., Augusta, State, Spring, and Meeting Sts., West Columbia, 10/10/78, A, C, 78002524

Old Batesburg Grade School [Batesburg-Leesville MRA], 306 E. Columbia Ave, Batesburg, 5/27/83, A, C, 83002201

Old Batesburg-Leesville High School [Batesburg-Leesville MRA], Summerland Ave., Lexington, 7/06/82, A, 82003893

Rauch, Charlton, House [Lexington County MRA], Main and Cedar Sts., Lexington vicinity, 11/22/83, C, 83003914

Lexington County—Continued

Rawl, David, House [Lexington County MRA], 201 W. Main St., Lexington vicinity, 11/22/83, C, 83003915

Rawl, John Jacob, House [Batesburg-Leesville MRA], Line St., Batesburg, 7/06/82, C, 82003882

Rawl-Couch House [Batesburg-Leesville MRA], 22 Short St., Batesburg, 7/06/82, A, C, 82003883

SAM Site, Address Restricted, Cayce vicinity, 12/06/78, D, 78002523

Saluda Factory Historic District, Along Saluda River SE of jct. of I 126 and I 26, West Columbia, 5/25/73, A, 73001718

Simmons-Harth House [Lexington County MRA], 102 Gantt St., Lexington vicinity, 11/22/83, C, 83003916

Southern Railway Depot [Batesburg-Leesville MRA], SE corner of Perry and Wilson Sts., Batesburg, 5/27/83, A, b, 83002202

Stewart, James, House [Lexington County MRA], Address Restricted, Lexington vicinity, 11/22/83, C, 83003917

Still Hopes [Lexington County MRA], Off 7th St., Cayce, 11/22/83, C, 83003921

Taylor Site, Address Restricted, Cayce vicinity, 11/21/74, D, 74001864

Timmerman Law Office [Lexington County MRA], 207 E. Main St., Lexington vicinity, 11/22/83, B, C, 83003922

Wessinger, Vastine, House [Lexington County MRA], Address Restricted, Lexington vicinity, 11/22/83, C, 83003923

Yarborough, Rev. Frank, House [Batesburg-Leesville MRA], 810 Bernard St., Leesville, 7/06/82, C, 82003892

Marion County

Buchan, A. H., Company Building [Flue-Cured Tobacco Production Properties TR], Laurel St., Mullins, 8/03/84, A, 84003817

Dew Barn [Flue-Cured Tobacco Production Properties TR], NW of Zion, Zion, 8/03/84, A, 84003818

Imperial Tobacco Company Building [Flue-Cured Tobacco Production Properties TR], 416 N. Mullins St., Mullins, 8/03/84, A, 84003820

Liberty Warehouse [Flue-Cured Tobacco Production Properties TR], Park St., Mullins, 8/03/84, A, 84003821

Marion Historic District, Roughly bounded by E. and W. Dozier, N. Montgomery, W. Baptist, and N. Wilcox Sts., Marion, 10/04/73, A, B, C, 73001720

Marion Historic District (Boundary Increase), Roughly bounded by Railroad and N. Wilcox Aves., N. Main and W. Dozier Sts., also Wheeler, Lee and Arch Sts., Marion, 4/20/79, A, C, 79003320

Neal and Dixon's Warehouse [Flue-Cured Tobacco Production Properties TR], S. Main St., Mullins, 8/03/84, A, C, 84003822

Old Brick Warehouse [Flue-Cured Tobacco Production Properties TR], Main and Wine Sts., Mullins, 8/03/84, A, C, 84003828

Old Ebenezer Church, 5 mi. S of Latta on SC 38, Latta vicinity, 3/30/73, C, a, 73001719

Rasor and Clardy Company Building, 202 S. Main St., Mullins, 10/29/82, C, 82001522

Marlboro County

Appin, U.S. 15, Bennettsville vicinity, 6/28/82, B, 82003894

Bennettsville Historic District, Irregular pattern along Main St. from Everett to Lindsey and from Parsonage to Murchison, Bennettsville, 4/20/78, C, 78002525

Bennettsville Historic District (Boundary Increase), Clyde St. between Main and Market Sts., Bennettsville, 6/03/93, C, 93000438

Clio Historic District, SC 9 and SC 381, Clio, 7/16/79, A, C, 79002388

Jennings-Brown House, 121 S. Marlboro St., Bennettsville, 2/23/72, A, C, b, 72001215

Magnolia, 508 E. Main St., Bennettsville, 3/14/73, B, C, 73001721

McLaurin House, E of Clio on SR 40, Clio vicinity, 3/24/78, B, C, 78002526

Pegues Place, N of Wallace, off U.S. 1, Wallace vicinity, 1/25/71, A, B, C, 71000790

Robertson-Easterling-McLaurin House, W of Bennettsville off SC 912, Bennettsville, 4/05/84, C, 84002090

McCormick County

Calhoun Mill, NE of Mount Carmel, Mount Carmel vicinity, 11/24/80, A, C, 80003679

Dorn Gold Mine [McCormick MRA], Address Restricted, McCormick vicinity, 12/12/85, D, 85003341

Dorn's Flour and Grist Mill, SC 28, McCormick, 7/12/76, A, C, 76002158

Dorn, Joseph Jennings, House [McCormick MRA], Gold and Oak Sts., McCormick, 12/12/85, B, C, 85003342

Eden Hall, 6 mi. NE of McCormick off U.S. 221 and SR 24, McCormick vicinity, 9/23/80, B, C, 80003678

Farmer's Bank [McCormick MRA], Main St., McCormick, 12/12/85, A, C, 85003343

Gibert, John Albert, M.D., House, SC secondary rd. 7, 0.2 mi. S of jct. with SC secondary rd. 110, McCormick vicinity, 5/27/93, C, 93000441

Guillebeau House, Hickory Knob State Park, Willington, 3/07/73, B, C, 73002136

Henderson, Otway, House [McCormick MRA], Augusta St., McCormick, 12/12/85, C, 85003344

Hotel Keturah [McCormick MRA], Main St., McCormick, 12/12/85, C, 85003345

Long Cane Massacre Site, W of Troy off SC 10, Troy vicinity, 1/27/83, A, f, 83002203

McCormick County Courthouse [McCormick MRA], Hwy. 28, McCormick, 12/12/85, A, C, 85003346

McCormick Train Station [McCormick MRA], Main St., McCormick, 12/12/85, A, C, 85003347

Mount Carmel Historic District, SC 823 and SC 81, Mount Carmel, 6/22/82, A, C, 82003895

Price's Mill, E of Parksville on SC 138 at Steven's Creek, Parksville, 11/22/72, A, C, 72001465

Sturkey, M. L. B., House [McCormick MRA], Main and Washington Sts., McCormick, 12/12/85, B, C, 85003348

Sylvania, S of Bradley off SC 10, Bradley vicinity, 11/28/77, A, C, 77001533

Newberry County

Boundary Street-Newberry Cotton Mills Historic District [Newberry MRA], Roughly bounded by Drayton, Boundary, Charles, Terrant and Crosson Sts., Newberry, 11/26/80, A, C, 80004465

Burton House [Newberry MRA], Address Restricted, Newberry, 11/26/80, C, b, 80003681

Caldwell Street Historic District [Newberry MRA], Caldwell St., Newberry, 11/26/80, C, 80004464

Coateswood, 1700 Boundary St., Newberry, 4/28/75, B, C, 75001704

College Street Historic District [Newberry MRA], College St., Newberry, 11/26/80, C, 80004461

Cousins House [Newberry MRA], Nance St. Extension, Newberry, 11/26/80, C, 80004473

Folk—Holloway House, Jct. of Holloway (Columbia Hwy. or Co. Rt. 107) and Folk Sts., Pomaria, 7/30/92, C, 92000963

Harrington Street Historic District [Newberry MRA], Harrington St., Newberry, 11/26/80, C, 80004462

Hatton House, Holloway St. between Folk St. and US 176, Pomaria, 10/01/90, C, 90001504

Higgins, Francis B., House [Newberry MRA], 1520 Boundary St., Newberry, 11/26/80, C, 80003682

Main Street Historic District [Newberry MRA], Roughly bounded by Harper, Summer, Douglas, Johnstone, Holman, and McMorris Sts., Newberry, 11/26/80, C, 80004463

Moon-Dominick House, NE of Chappells, Chappells vicinity, 3/22/82, A, C, 82003896

Mower, George, House [Newberry MRA], 1526 Boundary St., Newberry, 11/26/80, B, C, 80003683

Newberry College Historic District, 2100 College St., Newberry, 6/23/76, A, C, a, 76001706

Newberry Historic District, Bounded roughly by Friend, College, McKibben, and Harrington Sts., Newberry, 12/31/74, A, C, 74001870

Newberry Historic District (Boundary Increase) [Newberry MRA], Roughly bounded by Friend, McKibben, Harrington, Lindsay and Coates Sts., Newberry, 11/26/80, C, 80003680

Newberry Opera House, Boyce and Nance Sts., Newberry, 12/03/69, A, C, 69000171

Oakhurst, 2723 Main St., Newberry, 4/24/79, B, C, 79002389

Newberry County—Continued

Old Courthouse, 1207 Caldwell St., Newberry, 8/19/71, C, 71000791

Pomaria, SE of Pomaria on US 176, Pomaria vicinity, 4/24/79, A, C, 79003321

Reighley, Ike, House [Newberry MRA], 2304 Main St., Newberry, 11/26/80, C, 80003684

St. John's Lutheran Church, SE of Pomaria, Pomaria vicinity, 12/08/78, A, C, a, 78002527

Stewart House [Newberry MRA], 1001 Wilson St., Newberry, 11/26/80, C, 80003685

Summer Brothers Stores [Newberry MRA], 900 Main St., Newberry, 11/26/80, C, 80003686

Timberhouse [Newberry MRA], 1427 Ebenezer Rd., Newberry, 11/26/80, C, 80003687

Vincent Street Historic District [Newberry MRA], Vincent and Crosson Sts., Newberry, 11/26/80, C, 80003688

Wells Japanese Garden [Newberry MRA], Lindsay St., Newberry, 11/26/80, C, 80003689

Wells, Osborne, House [Newberry MRA], 1101 Fair St., Newberry, 11/26/80, C, 80003690

West Boundary Street Historic District [Newberry MRA], Boundary and Jessica Sts., Newberry, 11/26/80, B, C, g, 80003691

Oconee County

Alexander-Hill House, About 10 mi. N of Seneca off SC 183, Seneca vicinity, 7/24/72, B, b, 72001216

Ellicott Rock, N of Walhalla off SC 107, Walhalla vicinity, 7/24/73, A, 73001722

Long Creek Academy, CR 14, Long Creek vicinity, 11/20/87, A, a, 87002059

Newry Historic District, Broadway, River Ridge Rd., South, Branch, and Palmetto Aves., Newry, 3/19/82, A, C, 82003897

Oconee County Cage [Oconee County Penal System TR], Church St., Walhalla, 11/14/82, A, 82001523

Oconee Station and Richards House, 11 mi. N of Walhalla via SC 11 and CR 95, Walhalla vicinity, 2/24/71, C, 71000792

Seneca Historic District, Roughly bounded by S. First, S. Third, Townsville, and Poplar Sts., Seneca, 12/31/74, C, 74001871

Seneca Historic District (Boundary Increase), 300 S. Fairplay St., Seneca, 4/23/87, C, 87000643

Southern Railway Passenger Station, 129 Main St., Westminster, 11/07/76, A, 76001707

St. John's Lutheran Church, 301 W. Main St., Walhalla, 11/24/80, A, C, 80003692

Stumphouse Tunnel Complex, 5 mi. N of Walhalla via SC 28 and Rte. 226, Walhalla vicinity, 4/07/71, A, C, 71000793

Walhalla Graded School, 101 E. N. Broad St., Walhalla, 2/13/92, A, C, 92000059

Orangeburg County

Amelia Street Historic District [Orangeburg MRA], Amelia St. between Treadwell St. & Summers Ave., Orangeburg, 9/20/85, A, C, 85002322

Briggman, F. H. W., House [Orangeburg MRA], 156 Amelia St., Orangeburg, 9/20/85, A, C, 85002337

Bruce, Donald, House, SE of Orangeburg on U.S. 301, Orangeburg vicinity, 12/01/78, B, C, b, 78002528

Cattle Creek Campground, Off SC 210, Rowesville vicinity, 5/19/83, A, a, d, 83002204

Claflin College Historic District [Orangeburg MRA], On a portion of Claflin College campus, Orangeburg, 9/20/85, A, C, 85002324

Dixie Library Building [Orangeburg MRA], Bull St., Orangeburg, 9/20/85, C, b, 85002336

Dukes Gymnasium [Orangeburg MRA], South Carolina State College campus, Orangeburg, 9/20/85, A, C, 85002321

East Russell Street Area Historic District [Orangeburg MRA], Along sections of E. Russell St. between Watson & Clarendon Sts. and along portion of Oakland Pl. Dickson & Whitman Sts., Orangeburg, 9/20/85, A, C, 85002335

Ellis Avenue Historic District [Orangeburg MRA], Along portion of Ellis Ave. between Summers Ave. & Wilson St., Orangeburg, 9/20/85, C, 85002327

Enterprise Cotton Mills Building [Orangeburg MRA], U.S. 21, Orangeburg, 9/20/85, A, C, 85002340

Eutaw Springs Battleground Park, 2 mi. E of Eutawville on SC 6 and 45, Eutawville, 6/05/70, A, 70000593

Fordham, Maj. John Hammond, House [Orangeburg MRA], 415 Boulevard, Orangeburg, 9/20/85, B, C, 85002341

Gilmore House, S of intersection of State St. and Eutaw Rd., Holly Hill, 9/19/88, C, 88001470

Hodge Hall [Orangeburg MRA], South Carolina State College campus, Orangeburg, 9/20/85, A, B, C, 85002320

Hotel Eutaw [Orangeburg MRA], Russell & Centre Sts., Orangeburg, 9/20/85, A, C, 85002318

Lowman Hall, South Carolina State College [Orangeburg MRA], South Carolina State College campus, Orangeburg, 9/20/85, A, C, 85002346

Mack, Alan, Site (38OR67), Address Restricted, Orangeburg vicinity, 1/06/86, D, 86000044

Mt. Pisgah Baptist Church [Orangeburg MRA], 310 Green, Orangeburg, 9/20/85, B, C, a, 85002342

Numertia Plantation, E of Eutawville, Eutawville vicinity, 3/19/82, A, C, 82003898

Orangeburg County Fair Main Exhibit Building [Orangeburg MRA], U.S. 21, Orangeburg, 9/20/85, A, 85002344

Orangeburg County Jail, 44 Saint John St., Orangeburg, 10/02/73, C, 73001724

Orangeburg Downtown Historic District [Orangeburg MRA], Russell, Broughton, Middleton, Church, Meeting, St. John, Hampton, and Amelia Sts. around public square, Orangeburg, 9/20/85, A, C, a, 85002317

Rocks Plantation, 7 mi. E of Eutawville off SC 6, Eutawville vicinity, 7/13/76, B, C, b, 76001709

Southern Railway Passenger Depot, 110 N. Main St., Branchville, 4/23/73, A, C, 73001723

St. Julien Plantation, SC 6, Eutawville vicinity, 11/28/80, B, C, 80003693

Tingley Memorial Hall, Claflin College [Orangeburg MRA], College Ave., Orangeburg, 8/04/83, A, C, 83002205

Treadwell Street Historic District [Orangeburg MRA], Along portions of Treadwell & Amelia Sts., Orangeburg, 9/20/85, A, C, 85002315

White House United Methodist Church, N of Orangeburg on U.S. 301, Orangeburg vicinity, 5/13/74, A, C, a, 74001872

Whitman Street Area Historic District [Orangeburg MRA], Along sections of Whitman, Elliot, and E. Russell Sts., Orangeburg, 9/20/85, C, 85002326

Williams Chapel A.M.E. Church [Orangeburg MRA], 1908 Glover St., Orangeburg, 9/20/85, A, C, a, 85002345

Pickens County

Civilian Conservation Corps Quarry No. 1 and Truck Trail [South Carolina State Parks MPS], Off Section Rd. 25/Hickory Hollow Rd., .7 mi. S of SC 11, Pickens vicinity, 6/16/89, A, 89000479

Civilian Conservation Corps Quarry No. 2 [South Carolina State Parks MPS], .2 mi. N of Section Rd. 69/Sliding Rock Rd. near Oolenoy River, Pickens vicinity, 6/16/89, A, 89000480

Clemson College Sheep Barn [Clemson University MPS], S. Palmetto Blvd., Clemson University campus, Clemson, 1/04/90, A, C, 89002140

Clemson University Historic District I [Clemson University MPS], Northern portion of campus along US 76, Clemson, 1/04/90, A, C, 89002138

Clemson University Historic District II [Clemson University MPS], Center of campus, Clemson, 1/04/90, A, C, 89002139

Fort Hill, Clemson University campus, Clemson, 10/15/66, B, NHL, 66000708

Hagood Mill, 3.5 mi. NW of Pickens on U.S. 178, Pickens vicinity, 12/11/72, A, C, 72001217

Hanover House, Clemson University campus, Clemson, 6/05/70, C, b, 70000594

Old Pickens Jail, Johnson and Pendleton Sts., Pickens, 4/11/79, A, 79002390

Old Stone Church and Cemetery, 1.5 mi. N of Pendleton off U.S. 76, Pendleton vicinity, 11/05/71, B, C, a, 71000794

Roper House Complex [South Carolina State Parks MPS], SC Section Rd. 25, .1 mi. SE of SC 11, Pickens vicinity, 6/16/89, A, C, 89000482

Sheriff Mill Complex, SR 40, Easley vicinity, 11/20/87, A, C, 87002058

Table Rock Civilian Conservation Corps Camp Site [South Carolina State Parks MPS], Table Rock State Park Rd. Ext. at SC 11, Pickens vicinity, 6/16/89, A, C, 89000481

Table Rock State Park Historic District [South Carolina State Parks MPS], SC 11, 4.5 mi. E of SC Primary Rd. 45, Pickens vicinity, 6/15/89, A, C, 89000478

Richland County

Allen University, 1530 Harden St., Columbia, 4/14/75, A, g, 75001705

Alston House [Columbia MRA], 1811 Gervais St., Columbia, 3/02/79, A, C, 79003359

Arcade Building [Columbia MRA], 1332 Main St., Columbia, 11/17/82, C, 82001525

Arsenal Hill, 1800 Lincoln St., Columbia, 11/23/71, A, e, 71000795

BROWN'S FERRY VESSEL, Address Restricted, Columbia vicinity, 5/18/79, D, 79002391

Babcock Building, South Carolina State Hospital, Bull St., Columbia, 10/30/81, A, C, 81000570

Barber House [Lower Richland County MRA], Off CR 37, Hopkins vicinity, 3/27/86, A, C, 86000531

Benedict College Historic District, Roughly bounded by Laurel, Oak, Taylor and Harden Sts. on Benedict College campus, Columbia, 4/20/87, A, C, 87000809

Bethel A.M.E. Church [Columbia MRA], 1528 Sumter St., Columbia, 5/24/82, C, a, 82003899

Brevard, Keziah Goodwyn Hopkins, House [Lower Richland County MRA], Address Restricted, Columbia vicinity, 3/27/86, C, 86000535

Building at 1210–1214 Main Street [Columbia MRA], 1210–1214 Main St., Columbia, 3/02/79, A, C, 79003361

Building at 1644 Main Street [Columbia MRA], 1644 Main St., Columbia, 3/02/79, A, C, g, 79003377

Building at 1722–1724 Main Street [Columbia MRA], 1722–1724 Main St., Columbia, 11/25/80, C, 80003694

Building at 303 Saluda Avenue [Columbia MRA], 303 Saluda Ave., Columbia, 5/24/82, C, 82003900

Byrd, J. A., Mercantile Store [Lower Richland County MRA], Main St., Eastover, 3/27/86, A, C, 86000542

Caldwell-Hampton-Boylston House, 829 Richland St., Columbia, 5/06/71, B, C, 71000796

Canal Dime Savings Bank [Columbia MRA], 1530 Main St., Columbia, 11/25/80, C, 80004468

Chapelle Administration Building, 1530 Harden St., Columbia, 12/08/76, B, C, NHL, 76001710

Chappell House, Address Restricted, Cedar Creek vicinity, 3/27/86, C, 86000589

Chesnut Cottage, 1718 Hampton St., Columbia, 5/06/71, B, C, 71000797

Claussen's Bakery [Columbia MRA], 2001–2003 Green St., Columbia, 3/09/87, A, C, 87000401

Columbia Canal, E bank of the Broad and Congaree Rivers from the Diversion dam to the Southern RR Bridge, Columbia, 1/15/79, A, C, D, 79002392

Columbia City Hall, Main and Laurel Sts., Columbia, 6/19/73, A, C, 73001725

Columbia Historic District I, Roughly bounded by Elmwood, Assembly, Laurel, and Wayne Sts., Columbia, 5/06/71, A, C, 71000798

Columbia Historic District II, Roughly bounded by Taylor, Richland, Pickens, and Barnwell Sts., Columbia, 5/06/71, B, C, 71000799

Columbia Historic District II (Boundary Increase), Blanding, Laurel, Richland, Calhoun, Marion, Bull, Pickens, Henderson, and Barnwell Sts., Columbia, 6/28/82, A, C, 82003901

Columbia Mills Building [Columbia MRA], On the Congaree River, Columbia, 5/24/82, A, 82003902

Confederate Printing Plant, 501 Gervais St., Columbia, 3/28/79, A, C, 79002393

Consolidated Building [Columbia MRA], 1326–1330 Main St., Columbia, 3/02/79, C, 79003373

Debruhl-Marshall House, 1401 Laurel St., Columbia, 3/23/72, C, 72001218

Dovillers-Manning-Magoffin House [Columbia MRA], 4203 St. Clair Dr., Columbia, 3/02/79, B, C, b, 79003358

Eau Claire Town Hall and Survey Publishing Company Building [Columbia MRA], 3904 Monticello Rd., Columbia, 3/02/79, B, C, a, 79003371

Ebenezer Lutheran Chapel [Columbia MRA], 1301 Richland St., Columbia, 3/02/79, A, C, a, 79003365

Elmwood Park Historic District, Roughly bounded by Elmwood Ave., Main St. and the SAL RR tracks, Columbia, 5/03/91, A, C, 91000529

Ensor-Keenan House [Columbia MRA], 801 Wildwood Ave., Columbia, 3/02/79, B, C, 79003360

Fair-Rutherford and Rutherford Houses, 1326 and 1330 Gregg St., Columbia, 4/05/84, A, 84002093

Farmers and Merchants Bank Building [Lower Richland County MRA], Main St., Eastover vicinity, 3/27/86, A, C, 86000541

First Baptist Church, 1306 Hampton St., Columbia, 1/25/71, A, C, a, NHL, 71000800

First National Bank [Columbia MRA], 1208 Washington St., Columbia, 11/25/80, A, C, 80003695

First Presbyterian Church, 1324 Marion St., Columbia, 1/25/71, C, a, 71000801

Good Hope Baptist Church [Lower Richland County MRA], SC 378 near Sandhill Rd., Eastover vicinity, 3/27/86, A, C, a, 86000537

Goodwill Plantation [Lower Richland County MRA], Off US 378, Eastover vicinity, 3/27/86, A, C, 86000528

Granby Mill Village Historic District [Textile Mills designed by W.B. Smith Whaley MPS], Roughly bounded by Catawba, Gist, Heyward, and Church Sts., Columbia, 9/20/93, A, C, 93000905

Greyhound Bus Depot [Columbia MRA], 1200 Blanding St., Columbia, 12/28/89, C, g, 82005383

Grovewood [Lower Richland County MRA], SC 769, Congaree, 3/27/86, C, 86000530

Hale-Elmore-Seibels House, 1601 Richland St., Columbia, 5/06/71, C, 71000804

Hall, Ainsley, House, 1616 Blanding St., Columbia, 7/16/70, A, C, a, NHL, 70000595

Hampton-Preston House, 1615 Blanding St., Columbia, 7/29/69, A, B, C, 69000172

Heslep House [Columbia MRA], 203 Saluda Ave., Columbia, 3/02/79, C, 79003378

Hoffman, George P., House, N of CR 54, Blythewood, 3/27/86, A, 86000586

Hopkins Graded School [Lower Richland County MRA], Jct. of CR 37 and CR 1412, Hopkins, 3/27/86, A, C, 86000540

Hopkins Presbyterian Church [Lower Richland County MRA], Near jct. of CR 66 and CR 86, Hopkins, 3/27/86, A, C, a, 86000538

Horry-Guignard House, 1527 Senate St., Columbia, 5/06/71, B, C, 71000802

House of Peace Synagogue [Columbia MRA], Hampton and Park Sts., Columbia, 8/28/79, A, C, a, 79003354

Kaminer, John J., House [Lower Richland County MRA], Near jct. of SC 48 and SC 769, Gadsden, 3/27/86, C, 86000532

Kensington Plantation House, E of Eastover off Rte. 764, Eastover vicinity, 1/25/71, B, C, 71000806

Kirkland, B. B., Seed and Distributing Company [Columbia MRA], 912 Lady St., Columbia, 3/02/79, A, C, 79003370

Koon, John Jacob Calhoun, Farmstead, CR 27 off US 76/176, Ballentine vicinity, 3/27/86, A, C, b, 86000590

Kress Building [Columbia MRA], 1508 Main St., Columbia, 3/02/79, C, g, 79003376

Lace House, 803 Richland St., Columbia, 12/17/69, A, C, 69000173

Laurelwood [Lower Richland County MRA], Address Restricted, Columbia vicinity, 3/27/86, C, 86000529

Lever Building [Columbia MRA], 1613 Main St., Columbia, 3/02/79, C, 79003372

Logan School [Columbia MRA], 815 Elmwood Ave., Columbia, 3/02/79, C, 79003367

Lorick, Preston C., House, 1727 Hampton St., Columbia, 2/23/72, B, C, 72001219

Lutheran Theological Seminary Building: Beam Dormitory [Columbia MRA], 4201 Main St., Columbia, 8/28/79, A, C, a, 79003353

Lyles-Gudmundson House [Columbia MRA], Address Restricted, Columbia, 3/02/79, C, 79003364

Magnolia [Lower Richland County MRA], Address Restricted, Gadsden vicinity, 3/27/86, A, C, 86000536

Mann-Simons Cottage, 1403 Richland St., Columbia, 4/23/73, A, B, 73001726

McCord House [Columbia MRA], 1431 Pendleton St., Columbia, 3/02/79, B, C, 79003357

Millwood, E of Columbia on Garner's Ferry Rd., Columbia vicinity, 3/18/71, A, B, C, 71000803

Moore-Mann House [Columbia MRA], 1611 Hampton St., Columbia, 3/02/79, C, 79003363

National Loan and Exchange Bank Building [Columbia MRA], 1338 Main St., Columbia, 3/02/79, C, 79003374

Nipper Creek(38RD18), Address Restricted, Columbia vicinity, 12/24/86, D, 86003474

Oakwood [Lower Richland County MRA], SC 48, Gadsden vicinity, 3/27/86, A, C, 86000544

Old Campus District, University of South Carolina, Bounded by Pendleton, Sumter, Pickens, and Green Sts., Columbia, 6/05/70, A, C, 70000596

Palmetto Building [Columbia MRA], 1400 Main St., Columbia, 11/25/80, C, 80003696

Richland County—Continued

Palmetto Compress and Warehouse Company Building [Columbia MRA], 617 Devine St., Columbia, 10/17/85, A, C, 85003237

Richland Cotton Mill, 211-221 Main St., Columbia, 11/10/83, A, C, 83003933

Richland Presbyterian Church [Lower Richland County MRA], CR 1313, Gadsden vicinity, 3/27/86, A, C, a, 86000533

Saint Thomas' Protestant Episcopal Church [Lower Richland County MRA], Near jct. of US 601 and SC 263, Eastover vicinity, 3/27/86, A, C, a, 86000539

Scott, Claudius, Cottage [Lower Richland County MRA], CR 1182, Eastover vicinity, 3/27/86, C, 86000534

South Carolina Governor's Mansion, 800 Richland St., Columbia, 6/05/70, A, C, 70000597

South Carolina State Hospital, Mills Building, 2100 Bull St., Columbia, 6/05/70, A, C, NHL, 70000890

South Carolina Statehouse, Main St., Columbia, 6/05/70, A, C, NHL, 70000598

St. Peter's Roman Catholic Church [Columbia MRA], 1529 Assembly St., Columbia, 9/28/89, C, a, 89001610

Supreme Court of South Carolina Building, NW corner of Gervais and Sumter Sts., Columbia, 10/18/72, A, C, 72001220

Sylvan Building, 1500 Main St., Columbia, 3/23/72, C, 72001221

Taylor House [Columbia MRA], 1505 Senate St., Columbia, 7/06/82, B, C, 82003903

Town Theatre, 1012 Sumter St., Columbia, 10/09/74, A, C, 74001873

Trinity Episcopal Church, 1100 Sumter St., Columbia, 2/24/71, A, C, a, 71000805

US Courthouse [Columbia MRA], 1100 Laurel St., Columbia, 3/02/79, C, g, 79003375

Union Station, 401 S. Main St., Columbia, 6/19/73, A, C, 73001728

Wallace-McGee House [Columbia MRA], 415 Harden St., Columbia, 3/02/79, C, g, 79003379

Wardlaw Junior High School [Columbia MRA], 1003 Elmwood Ave., Columbia, 9/13/84, A, C, 84002096

Washington Street United Methodist Church, 1401 Washington St., Columbia, 12/18/70, A, C, a, 70000599

Waverly Historic District, Roughly bounded by Hampton St., Heidt St., Gervais St., and Harden St., Columbia, 12/21/89, A, C, 89002154

West Gervais Street Historic District [Columbia MRA], Roughly bounded by Gadsen, Senate, Park, and Lady Sts., Columbia, 4/27/83, A, C, 83002206

Whaley, W. B. Smith, House [Columbia MRA], 1527 Gervais St., Columbia, 3/02/79, B, C, 79003362

Wilson, Thomas Woodrow, Boyhood Home, 1705 Hampton St., Columbia, 2/23/72, B, C, 72001222

Woodrow Memorial Presbyterian Church [Columbia MRA], 2221 Washington St., Columbia, 3/02/79, B, C, a, 79003366

Zimmerman House [Columbia MRA], 1332 Pickens St., Columbia, 3/02/79, A, C, 79003355

Zimmerman School [Columbia MRA], 1336 Pickens St., Columbia, 3/02/79, A, C, 79003356

Zion Protestant Episcopal Church [Lower Richland County MRA], SC 263, Eastover, 3/27/86, A, C, a, 86000543

Saluda County

Bonham House, SE of Saluda off U.S. 178, Saluda vicinity, 12/30/74, B, C, 74001875

Butler Family Cemetery, NE of Saluda off SC 194, Saluda, 12/31/74, B, d, 74001874

Marsh-Johnson House, Intersection of S-41-21 and S-41-37, Saluda, 6/17/82, C, 82003904

Saluda Old Town Site, Address Restricted, Saluda vicinity, 6/28/72, D, 72001223

Saluda Theatre, 107 Law Range, Salude, 12/13/93, A, C, 93001406

Webb—Coleman House, 2 mi. S of Chappells, .3 mi. E of SC 39, at jct. of three dirt rds., Chappells vicinity, 4/24/92, C, 92000365

Whitehall, Etheredge Rd., Saluda, 8/21/80, B, C, 80003697

Spartanburg County

Anderson's Mill, W of Spartanburg off SC 296, Spartanburg vicinity, 11/14/78, A, 78002529

Archeological Site 38SP11 [Pacolet Soapstone Quarries TR], Address Restricted, Pacolet vicinity, 12/10/80, D, 80003698

Archeological Site 38SP12 [Pacolet Soapstone Quarries TR], Address Restricted, Pacolet vicinity, 12/10/80, D, 80003699

Archeological Site 38SP13 [Pacolet Soapstone Quarries TR], Address Restricted, Pacolet vicinity, 12/10/80, D, 80003700

Archeological Site 38SP17 [Pacolet Soapstone Quarries TR], Address Restricted, Pacolet vicinity, 12/10/80, D, 80003701

Archeological Site 38SP18 [Pacolet Soapstone Quarries TR], Address Restricted, Pacolet vicinity, 12/10/80, D, 80003702

Archeological Site 38SP19 [Pacolet Soapstone Quarries TR], Address Restricted, Pacolet vicinity, 12/10/80, D, 80003703

Archeological Site 38SP20 [Pacolet Soapstone Quarries TR], Address Restricted, Pacolet vicinity, 12/10/80, D, 80003704

Archeological Site 38SP21 [Pacolet Soapstone Quarries TR], Address Restricted, Pacolet vicinity, 12/10/80, D, 80003705

Archeological Site 38SP23 [Pacolet Soapstone Quarries TR], Address Restricted, Pacolet vicinity, 12/10/80, D, 80003706

Archeological Site 38SP52 [Pacolet Soapstone Quarries TR], Address Restricted, Pacolet vicinity, 12/10/80, D, 80003707

Archeological Site 38SP53 [Pacolet Soapstone Quarries TR], Address Restricted, Pacolet vicinity, 12/10/80, D, 80003708

Archeological Site 38SP54 [Pacolet Soapstone Quarries TR], Address Restricted, Pacolet vicinity, 12/10/80, D, 80003709

Archeological Site 38SP57 [Pacolet Soapstone Quarries TR], Address Restricted, Pacolet vicinity, 12/10/80, D, 80003710

Bon Haven, 728 N. Church St., Spartanburg, 6/29/76, A, B, C, 76001711

Camp Hill, S of Glenn Springs on SC 215, Glenn Springs vicinity, 7/06/70, B, C, 70000600

Cleveland Law Range, 171 Magnolia St., Spartanburg, 4/13/73, A, C, 73001730

Converse College Historic District, 580 E. Main St., Spartanburg, 11/12/75, A, C, 75001706

Duncan, Bishop William Wallace, House, 249 N. Church St., Spartanburg, 7/12/76, B, C, 76001712

Evins-Bivings House, 563 N. Church St., Spartanburg, 7/16/70, B, C, 70000601

Foster's Tavern, 191 Cedar Spring Rd., Spartanburg, 12/18/70, A, C, 70000602

Franklin Hotel, 185 E. Main St., Spartanburg, 7/28/83, C, 83002207

Glenn Springs Historic District, SC 150 and Rich Hill Rd., Glenn Springs, 11/04/82, A, C, 82001526

Golightly-Dean House, SC 56, Spartanburg vicinity, 9/29/88, C, 88001845

Hampton Heights Historic District, Roughly bounded by Spring, Henry, Hydrick, Peronneau Sts., Hampton Dr., and Hampton Ave., (both sides), Spartanburg, 1/27/83, C, 83002208

Ingleside, 1 mi. N of Campobello on U.S. 176, Campobello vicinity, 10/15/73, B, C, 73001729

McMakin's Tavern, NW of Lyman off SC 358, Lyman vicinity, 10/09/74, A, C, 74001876

Montgomery, Walter Scott, House, 314 S. Pine St., Spartanburg, 11/01/84, B, C, 84000345

Morgan, Daniel, Monument, Main and Church Sts., Spartanburg, 9/22/80, C, b, f, 80003711

Mountain Shoals Plantation, Jct. of U.S. 221 and SC 92, Enoree, 4/24/79, A, C, 79002394

Nicholls-Crook House, 15 mi. SW of Spartanburg off U.S. 221, Spartanburg vicinity, 3/20/73, C, 73001731

Price's Post Office, SE of Moore at jct. of CR 86, 199, 200, Moore vicinity, 10/28/69, A, B, C, 69000174

Seay, Jammie, House, Darby Rd. off Crescent Ave., Spartanburg, 10/07/71, C, 71000807

Smith's Tavern, E of SC 49, Roebuck vicinity, 7/23/74, A, C, 74001878

Spartanburg Historic District, W. Main, Magnolia, Wall, Ezell, and Spring Sts., Spartanburg, 5/19/83, A, C, 83002209

Walker Hall, SE of Spartanburg on SC 56, Spartanburg vicinity, 12/06/77, A, C, 77001232

Walnut Grove Plantation, 8 mi. SE of Spartanburg, about 1 mi. E of jct. of U.S. 921 and I-26, Spartanburg vicinity, 7/01/70, A, C, 70000603

Williams Place, SW of Glenn Springs on SR 113, Glenn Springs vicinity, 11/10/82, A, C, 82001527

Spartanburg County—Continued

Wofford College Historic District, Wofford College campus, Spartanburg, 12/27/74, A, C, 74001879

Sumter County

Borough House Plantation, Rt. 261, 0.8 mi. N of intersection of Rt. 261 and SC 76/3 78, Stateburg, 3/23/72, A, B, C, NHL, 72001224

Brogdon, J. Clinton, House, 3755 Boots Branch Rd., Sumter vicinity, 7/01/93, C, 93000585

Ellerbe's Mill, About 3 mi. S of Rembert off U.S. 521 on Rafting Creek, Rembert vicinity, 11/20/74, A, C, 74001880

Heriot—Moise House, Jct. Brewington Rd. and US 401, Sumter vicinity, 12/21/89, C, 89002149

Holy Cross Episcopal Church, SC 261, Stateburg, 11/07/73, C, a, NHL, 73001732

Mayesville Historic District, Irregular pattern along Lafayette St., Mayesville, 7/16/79, A, C, 79002395

Milford Plantation, W of Pinewood on SC 261, Pinewood, 11/19/71, A, C, NHL, 71000808

Myrtle Moor, Address Restricted, Sumter vicinity, 1/13/83, C, 83002210

Orange Grove, Jct. of SC 43 (Black River Rd.) and SC 441, Dalzell vicinity, 8/19/93, C, 93000845

Rip Raps Plantation, E of Sumter on SC 378, Sumter vicinity, 12/12/78, A, B, C, 78002532

Salem Black River Presbyterian Church, E of Sumter on SC 521, Sumter vicinity, 11/14/78, A, C, a, 78003091

Singleton's Graveyard, 6 mi. S of Wedgefield off SC 261, Wedgefield vicinity, 5/13/76, B, C, d, 76001713

St. Mark's Church, W of Pinewood on SR 51, Pinewood vicinity, 1/20/78, A, C, a, d, 78002530

Stateburg Historic District, Roughly bounded by US 76, SR 261 and 441, Sumter vicinity, 2/24/71, A, B, C, a, 71000809

Sumter Historic District, Commercial area centered around Main and Liberty Sts., Sumter, 4/21/75, A, C, 75001707

Sumter Town Hall—Opera House, N. Main St., Sumter, 5/24/73, A, C, 73001733

White, Elizabeth, House, 421 N. Main St., Sumter, 3/21/78, B, C, 78002531

Union County

Battle of Blackstock's Historic Site, W of Union off SC 49, Union vicinity, 12/16/74, A, 74001885

Buffalo Mill Historic District [Textile Mills in SC Designed by W.B. Smith Whaley MPS], Village of Buffalo and immediate surroundings, Buffalo, 10/10/90, A, C, 90001506

Cedar Bluff, SC 49, Union vicinity, 7/20/74, A, B, C, 74001886

Central Graded School, 309 Academy St., Union, 3/30/78, A, C, 78002534

Corinth Baptist Church [Union MPS], N. Herndon St., Union, 7/20/89, A, C, a, 89000939

Cross Keys House, SW of Union on SC 49, Union vicinity, 6/24/71, A, B, C, 71000811

Culp House, 300 N. Mountain St., Union, 4/09/75, C, 75001709

Dawkins, Judge Thomas, House, Dawkins Court, N of E. Main St., Union, 4/23/73, B, C, 73001735

East Main Street—Douglass Heights Historic District [Union MPS], Roughly bounded by Perrin Ave., S. Church St., and E. Main St., and 100–121 Douglass Heights, Union, 7/17/89, C, 89000796

Episcopal Church of the Nativity, Church and Pinckney Sts., Union, 8/30/74, B, C, a, 74001881

Fair Forest Hotel, 221 E. Main St., Union, 11/01/84, A, C, 84000346

Herndon Terrace, N. Pinckney St. and Catherine St., Union, 8/25/70, C, 70000604

Hillside, NW of Carlisle on SC 215, Carlisle vicinity, 2/17/78, C, 78002533

Jeter, Gov. Thomas B., House, 203 Thompson Blvd., Union, 12/02/74, B, C, 74001882

Means House, 2 mi. SW of Jonesville on SC 12, Jonesville vicinity, 4/13/73, A, C, 73001734

Meng House, 117 Academy St., Union, 7/12/76, C, 76001714

Merridun, 100 Merridun Pl., Union, 6/20/74, B, C, 74001883

Musgrove's Mill Historic Battle Site, 2.5 mi. S of Cross Anchor on SC 56, Cross Anchor vicinity, 3/04/75, A, 75001708

Padgett's Creek Baptist Church, E of Cross Keys on SC 18, Cross Keys vicinity, 5/06/71, C, a, 71000810

Pinckneyville, 13 mi. NE of Union on SC 13, Union vicinity, 12/03/69, D, 69000175

Rose Hill, 9 mi. SSW of Union on CR 16, Union vicinity, 6/05/70, A, B, C, 70000605

South Street—South Church Street Historic District, Roughly South St. between Church & Boyce Sts., Union, 5/19/83, A, C, a, c, 83002211

South Street—South Church Street Historic District (Boundary Increase) [Union MPS], Roughly S. Church St. from South St. to Henrietta St., Union, 7/17/89, C, 89000798

Union County Jail, Main St., Union, 8/30/74, A, C, 74001884

Union Downtown Historic District [Union MPS], Roughly bounded by E. Academy, N. Church, Main, and N. Herndon Sts., Sharpe Ave., and N. Gadberry St., Union, 7/17/89, A, C, 89000795

Union High School—Main Street Grammar School [Union MPS], E. Main and N. Church Sts., Union, 7/20/89, A, C, 89000797

Williamsburg County

Black Mingo Baptist Church, SE of Nesmith, Nesmith vicinity, 8/21/80, A, C, a, 80003713

Clarkson Farm Complex, US 52, 1.5 mi. S of jct. with US 521, Greeleyville vicinity, 10/06/88, A, C, b, 88001706

Gamble House, W of Nesmith off SC 502, Nesmith vicinity, 12/08/78, C, 78002535

Kingstree Historic District [Kingstree MRA], Main, Hampton and Academy Sts., Kingstree, 6/28/82, A, C, 82003906

Scott House [Kingstree MRA], 506 Live Oak St., Kingstree, 6/28/82, A, C, 82004797

Thorntree, SC 527, in Fluitt-Nelson Memorial Park, Kingstree, 10/28/70, A, C, b, 70000606

Wilson, John Calvin, House, Off SC 512, Indiantown vicinity, 6/28/82, A, C, 82003905

York County

Afro—American Insurance Company Building [Rock Hill MPS], 558 S. Dave Lyle Blvd., Rock Hill, 6/10/92, A, C, 92000651

Allison Plantation, Off SC 40 and SC 60, York vicinity, 9/29/80, B, C, 80003716

Anderson House, 227 Oakland Ave., Rock Hill, 5/13/82, A, B, C, 82003908

Banks—Mack House [Fort Mill MPS], 329 Confederate St., Fort Mill, 6/11/92, C, 92000643

Bethel Presbyterian Church, SC 557, Clover vicinity, 12/10/80, A, C, a, 80003714

Bethesda Presbyterian Church, 3.5 mi. NE of McConnells on SC 322, McConnells vicinity, 8/16/77, A, C, a, 77001233

Brattonsville Historic District, E of McConnellsville on CR 165 off SC 13, McConnellsville vicinity, 8/19/71, A, C, 71000812

Charlotte Avenue—Aiken Avenue Historic District [Rock Hill MPS], Roughly, Aiken Ave. from College Ave. to Charlotte Ave. and Charlotte from Aiken to Union Ave., Rock Hill, 6/10/92, A, C, 92000659

Ebenezer Academy, 2132 Ebenezer Rd., Rock Hill, 8/16/77, A, 77001234

First Presbyterian Church [Rock Hill MPS], 234 E. Main St., Rock Hill, 6/10/92, A, C, a, 92000653

Fort Mill Downtown Historic District [Fort Mill MPS], Main St. from Confederate Park E to 233 Main, Fort Mill, 6/11/92, A, C, 92000646

Hart House, 220 E. Liberty St., York, 12/02/77, B, C, 77001236

Hermon Presbyterian Church [Rock Hill MPS], 446 Dave Lyle Blvd., Rock Hill, 6/10/92, A, C, a, 92000652

Highland Park Manufacturing Plant and Cotton Oil Complex [Rock Hill MPS], 869 Standard St., 732 and 737 E. White St., Rock Hill, 6/10/92, A, C, 92000655

Hightower Hall, York County Rd 165, McConnells vicinity, 6/28/82, A, C, 82003907

Jackson's Furnace Site (38YK217) [Early Ironworks of Northwestern South Carolina TR], Address Restricted, Smyrna vicinity, 5/08/87, D, 87000706

Kings Mountain National Military Park, NW of Bethany on SC 161, Bethany vicinity, 10/15/66, A, c, d, NPS, 66000079

Mack—Belk House [Fort Mill MPS], 119 Banks St., Fort Mill, 6/11/92, C, 92000647

York County—Continued

Marion Street Area Historic District [Rock Hill MPS], Roughly, Marion St. from Hampton St. to Center St. and Center from State St. to Marion, Rock Hill, 6/10/92, C, 92000654

McCorkle-Fewell-Long House, 639 College Ave., Rock Hill, 8/21/80, B, C, 80003715

Mills House [Fort Mill MPS], 122 Confederate St., Fort Mill, 6/11/92, C, 92000645

Mount Prospect Baptist Church [Rock Hill MPS], 339 W. Black St., Rock Hill, 6/10/92, A, C, a, 92000656

National Guard Armory [Fort Mill MPS], Jct. of Elliott and Unity Sts., Fort Mill, 6/11/92, A, C, 92000648

Reid Street—North Confederate Avenue Area Historic District [Rock Hill MPS], Roughly, Reid St. and N. Confederate Ave. between E. Main St. and E. White St., Rock Hill, 6/10/92, C, 92000657

Rock Hill Cotton Factory [Rock Hill MPS], 215 Chatham St., Rock Hill, 6/10/92, A, C, 92000658

Rock Hill Downtown Historic District [Rock Hill MPS], Roughly, S. Oakland Ave. from S of Peoples Pl. to E. Main St., Rock Hill, 6/24/91, A, C, a, 91000828

Springfield Plantation House, US 21, Fort Mill vicinity, 9/12/85, A, C, 85002387

Stokes-Mayfield House, 353 Oakland Ave., Rock Hill, 5/17/84, C, 84002100

Thornwell—Elliott House [Fort Mill MPS], 118 Confederate St., Fort Mill, 6/11/92, C, 92000644

Tillman Hall, Oakland Ave., Winthrop College campus, Rock Hill, 12/02/77, A, C, 77001235

US Post Office and Courthouse, 102 Main St., Rock Hill, 1/21/88, A, C, 87002523

Unity Presbyterian Church Complex [Fort Mill MPS], 303 Tom Hall St., Fort Mill, 6/11/92, A, C, a, d, 92000649

White House, 258 E. White St., Rock Hill, 12/03/69, A, C, 69000176

White, John M., House, White & Skipper Sts., Fort Mill, 9/12/85, C, 85002385

White, William Elliott, House, N. White St., Fort Mill vicinity, 3/22/87, A, B, C, g, 87000381

Wilson House, 3 S. Congress St., York, 11/20/74, A, C, 74001887

Wilson House [Fort Mill MPS], 107 Clebourne St., Fort Mill, 6/11/92, C, b, 92000650

Winthrop College Historic District, Along Oakland Ave. between Cherry Rd. and Stewart Ave. on the Winthrop College campus, Rock Hill, 4/23/87, A, C, g, 86003469

Withers Building, Oakland Ave., Rock Hill, 8/20/81, A, C, 81000571

Witherspoon-Hunter House, 15 W. Liberty St., York, 2/07/78, B, C, 78002536

York County Courthouse [Courthouses in South Carolina Designed by William Augustus Edwards TR], Corner of W. Liberty and S. Congress Sts., York, 10/30/81, A, C, 81000700

York Historic District, SC 5 and U.S. 321, York, 10/18/79, A, C, 79002396

Home to the founder of the City of North Augusta, South Carolina, Lookaway Hall (ca. 1898), with its imposing portico and Beaux Arts details, is more than a local landmark: it is an official symbol of the city. (Ellen Pruitt, 1990)

SOUTH DAKOTA

Aurora County

Aurora County Courthouse [County Courthouses of South Dakota MPS], Main St. between Fourth and Fifth Sts., Plankinton, 2/10/93, A, C, 92001855

Beadle County

Archeological Site No. 39BE3 [Prehistoric Rock Art of South Dakota MPS], Address Restricted, Wolsey vicinity, 8/06/93, D, 93000802

Campbell Park Historic District of Huron, Roughly bounded by 5th, 7th, 9th, Wisconsin, California, Kansas, and Dakota Sts., Huron, 11/05/74, A, B, C, a, 74001888

Dairy Building, Off Third St. near the South Dakota State Fair Grounds, Huron, 1/25/90, A, 90001642

Drake, Hattie O. and Henry, Octagon House, 605 Third St., SW., Huron, 1/30/92, C, 91002045

Grace Episcopal Church, Fourth St. and Kansas Ave., SE., Huron, 7/19/89, C, a, 89000828

Milford Hutterite Colony [Historic Hutterite Colonies TR], NE of Lake Byron, Carpenter vicinity, 6/30/82, A, C, a, 82003909

Old Riverside Hutterite Colony [Historic Hutterite Colonies TR], Off James River, Huron vicinity, 6/30/82, A, C, a, 82003910

Pyle House, 376 Idaho Ave., SE, Huron, 12/30/74, B, C, 74002288

Site 39BE14 [James River Basin Woodland Sites TR], Address Restricted, Huron vicinity, 1/30/84, D, 84003199

Site 39BE15 [James River Basin Woodland Sites TR], Address Restricted, Huron vicinity, 1/30/84, D, 84003201

Site 39BE23 [James River Basin Woodland Sites TR], Address Restricted, Huron vicinity, 1/30/84, D, 84003206

Site 39BE46 [James River Basin Woodland Sites TR], Address Restricted, Huron vicinity, 1/30/84, D, 84003208

Site 39BE48 [James River Basin Woodland Sites TR], Address Restricted, Huron vicinity, 1/30/84, D, 84003210

Site 39BE57 [James River Basin Woodland Sites TR], Address Restricted, Yale vicinity, 1/30/84, D, 84003212

Site 39BE64 [James River Basin Woodland Sites TR], Address Restricted, Yale vicinity, 1/30/84, D, 84003215

South Dakota Dept. of Transportation Bridge No. 03-020-008 [Historic Bridges in South Dakota MPS], Local rd. over unnamed cr., Wessington vicinity, 12/09/93, A, C, 93001260

South Dakota Dept. of Transportation Bridge No. 03-327-230 [Historic Bridges in South Dakota MPS], Local rd. over Pearl Cr., Cavour vicinity, 12/09/93, C, 93001261

South Dakota Dept. of Transportation Bridge No. 03-338-100 [Historic Bridges in South Dakota MPS], Local rd. over Shue Cr., Cavour vicinity, 12/09/93, A, C, 93001269

Bon Homme County

Bon Homme County Courthouse, Walnut and Washington Sts., Tyndall, 12/13/84, A, C, 84000581

Bon Homme Hutterite Colony [Historic Hutterite Colonies TR], Om Missouri River, Tabor vicinity, 6/30/82, A, C, a, d, 82003913

Campbell, Gen. Charles T., House, 611 4th St., Scotland, 6/17/82, B, C, 82003911

Carnegie Public Library of Tyndall, State and Main Sts., Tyndall, 12/13/84, A, 84000582

Cihak Farmstead [German-Russian Folk Architecture TR], Address Restricted, Scotland vicinity, 11/28/84, A, C, 84001263

Frydrych, John, Farmstead [Czech Folk Architecture in Southeastern South Dakota MRA], N side of SD 50, Tyndall vicinity, 7/06/87, A, C, 87001053

Greenfield, Dr. John C., House, 307 W. First St., Avon, 10/19/89, C, 89001717

Hakl, John, Chalkrock House [Czech Folk Architecture in Southeastern South Dakota MRA], SW of Tabor off SD 50, Tabor vicinity, 6/07/87, A, C, 87001050

Herman, Joseph, Chalkrock House [Czech Folk Architecture in Southeastern South Dakota MRA], W side of SD 25, Tabor vicinity, 7/06/87, A, C, 87001045

Herman, Joseph, Log Stable [Czech Folk Architecture in Southeastern South Dakota MRA], W side of SD 25, Tabor vicinity, 7/06/87, A, C, 87001047

Herman, Joseph, Rubblestone Barn [Czech Folk Architecture in Southeastern South Dakota MRA], W side of SD 25, Tabor vicinity, 7/06/87, A, C, 87001046

Honner, Martin, Chalkrock House [Czech Folk Architecture in Southeastern South Dakota MRA], NW of Tabor off SD 50, Tabor vicinity, 7/06/87, A, C, 87001052

Koobs House, 431 4th St., Scotland, 8/01/84, C, 84003218

Main Hall, University of South Dakota campus, Springfield, 2/03/81, A, C, 81000572

Merkwan, John and Kate, Log and Rubblestone House [Czech Folk Architecture in Southeastern South Dakota MRA], E side of SD 25, Tabor vicinity, 7/06/87, A, C, 87001041

Merkwan, John and Kate, Rubblestone House-Barn [Czech Folk Architecture in Southeastern South Dakota MRA], E side of SD 25, Tabor vicinity, 7/06/87, A, C, 87001040

Merkwan, John, Jr., Rubblestone House [Czech Folk Architecture in Southeastern South Dakota MRA], W side of SD 25, Tabor vicinity, 7/06/87, A, C, 87001044

Methodist Episcopal Church, 811 6th St., Scotland, 9/12/79, A, C, a, 79002397

Noll, Joseph, Chalkrock Barn [Czech Folk Architecture in Southeastern South Dakota MRA], S of Tabor off SD 50, Tabor vicinity, 7/06/87, A, C, 87001049

Old St. Wenceslaus Catholic Parish House, 227 Yankton St., Tabor, 2/08/88, A, 88000023

Sedlacek, Jacob, Chalkrock House [Czech Folk Architecture in Southeastern South Dakota MRA], SW of Tabor off SD 50, Tabor vicinity, 7/06/87, A, C, 87001051

South Dakota Dept. of Transportation Bridge No. 05-028-200 [Historic Bridges in South Dakota MPS], Local rd. over Choteau Cr., Perkins vicinity, 12/09/93, A, C, 93001270

South Dakota Dept. of Transportation Bridge No. 05-032-170 [Historic Bridges in South Dakota MPS], Local rd. over Choteau Cr., Avon vicinity, 12/09/93, A, C, 93001271

South Dakota Dept. of Transportation Bridge No. 05-138-080 [Historic Bridges in South Dakota MPS], Local rd. over Emanuel Cr., Tyndall vicinity, 12/09/93, C, 93001272

South Dakota Dept. of Transportation Bridge No. 05-255-130 [Historic Bridges in South Dakota MPS], Local rd. over Beaver Cr., Tabor vicinity, 12/09/93, C, 93001273

St. Andrew's Episcopal Church, 4th and Poplar Sts., Scotland, 6/17/82, A, C, a, 82003912

St. Wenceslaus Catholic Church and Parish House, Yankton and Lidice Sts., Tabor, 12/13/84, C, a, 84000579

Tabor School, Off SD 50, Tabor, 9/02/83, A, b, 83003001

Teibel-Sykora Rubblestone Barn [Czech Folk Architecture in Southeastern South Dakota MRA], W side of SD 25, Tabor vicinity, 7/06/87, A, C, 87001048

Travnicek, John, Chalkrock House [Czech Folk Architecture in Southeastern South Dakota MRA], W side of jct. of SD 50 and SD 25, Tabor vicinity, 7/06/87, A, C, 87001043

Walker, Albion, Chalkrock House [Czech Folk Architecture in Southeastern South Dakota MRA], S of SD 52, Tabor vicinity, 7/06/87, A, C, 87001042

ZCBJ Hall, Nebraska and Washington Sts., Tyndall, 1/31/85, A, 85000181

Brookings County

Beals, William H. and Elizabeth, House, 1302 Sixth St., Brookings, 6/09/92, C, 92000685

Brookings City Hall, 4th St., Brookings, 6/17/82, A, C, 82003914

Brookings County—Continued

Brookings Commercial Historic District, Roughly along Main Ave.between the C&NW Railraod and the alley N. Fifth St., Brookings, 4/19/88, A, C, g, 88000029

Brookings County Courthouse, 4th St. and 6th Ave., Brookings, 12/12/76, A, C, 76001715

Caldwell, W. A., House, 804 Sixth Ave., Brookings, 11/03/86, B, C, 86002990

Carnegie Public Library, 524 4th St., Brookings, 5/07/80, A, C, 80003717

Chicago and Northwestern Railroad Depot, Main St., Brookings, 10/08/76, A, C, 76001716

Coolidge Sylvan Theatre, Medary Ave., Brookings, 2/26/87, A, 87000224

Coughlin Campanile, Medary Ave., Brookings, 2/26/87, C, 87000223

Experimental Rammed Earth Wall, Medary Ave. behind Dean of Agricultural and Biological Sciences House, South Dakota State University campus, Brookings, 6/28/91, C, 91000850

Experimental Rammed Earth Machine Shed, South Dakota State University campus, NW corner, Brookings, 8/26/93, C, 93000869

Fishback House, 501 8th St., Brookings, 10/08/76, B, C, 76001717

Fishback House (Boundary Increase), 501 Eighth St., Brookings, 3/09/87, B, C, 87000387

Henry-Martinson House, 405 Kasan Ave., Volga, 12/20/77, A, C, g, 77001237

Micheel, Herman F., Gothic Arched-Roof Barn, 5 Mi. N and 3 mi. W of White, White vicinity, 1/25/91, C, 90002207

Nick's Hamburger Shop, 427 Main Ave., Brookings, 11/06/86, A, C, 86003008

Sexauer, George P., House, 929 Fourth St., Brookings, 1/26/90, B, C, 89002333

Sterling Methodist Church, US 77, 5 mi. E of Bruce, Bruce vicinity, 10/19/89, A, C, a, 89001723

Stock Judging Pavilion, 11th St. and Medary Ave., Brookings, 10/19/78, A, C, 78002538

Trygstad Law and Commerce Building, 401 Main Ave., Brookings, 2/23/84, A, 84003244

Walters, Solomon, House, Railway St., Bruce, 4/26/78, C, 78002539

Wenona Hall and Wecota Hall, Medary Ave., Brookings, 5/07/80, C, 80003718

Woodbine Cottage, 929 Harvey Dunn St., Brookings, 1/26/90, C, 89002332

Woodbine Cottage Experimental Rammed Earth Wall, W of jct. of 10th St. and Medary Ave., South Dakota State University campus, Brookings, 6/28/91, C, 91000849

Brown County

Aberdeen Commercial Historic District, 1–523 S. Main St., Aberdeen, 5/23/88, C, 88000586

Aberdeen Highlands Historic District, Both sides of N. Main from 12th to 15th Ave., NE, Aberdeen, 6/05/75, A, C, g, 75001710

Aberdeen Historic District, Both sides of 3rd—6th Aves. and Jay, Kline and Arch Sts., Aberdeen, 6/05/75, C, a, g, 75001711

Augustana Swedish Lutheran Church, 4.5 mi. S of Claremont, Claremont vicinity, 12/20/88, A, C, a, 88002842

Aurland United Norwegian Lutheran Church, SE of Frederick, Frederick vicinity, 4/16/82, C, a, 82003916

Bickelhaupt, William G., House, 1003 S. Jay, Aberdeen, 10/19/89, C, 89001727

Brown County Courthouse, 1st Ave., Aberdeen, 6/03/76, C, 76001718

Brown Hall, Main St., Barnard, 2/07/90, A, b, 89002336

Brown's Post [19th Century South Dakota Trading Posts MPS], Address Restricted, Sisseton vicinity, 5/27/88, A, D, 88000583

Campbell, Colin, Post [19th Century South Dakota Trading Posts MPS], Address Restricted, Frederick vicinity, 5/27/88, A, D, 88000584

Chicago, Milwaukee, St. Paul and Pacific Railroad Depot, Main St. and Railroad Ave., Aberdeen, 9/20/77, A, C, 77001238

Dakota Farmer Building, 1216 S. Main St., Aberdeen, 8/01/84, A, C, 84003221

Easton's Castle, 1210 2nd Ave., NW, Aberdeen, 3/01/73, C, 73001736

Finnish Apostolic Lutheran Church, Address Restricted, Frederick vicinity, 5/31/84, A, C, a, 84003223

First United Methodist Church, S. Lincoln St. and SE 5th Ave., Aberdeen, 5/28/76, C, a, 76001719

Geranen, Paul and Fredriika, Farm [Architecture of Finnish Settlement TR], E of Frederick, Frederick vicinity, 11/13/85, A, B, C, 85003498

Great Northern Railway Passenger and Freight Depot, 1 Court St., Aberdeen, 1/27/83, A, C, 83003002

Martilla-Pettingel and Gorder General Merchandise Store [Architecture of Finnish Settlement TR], 515–516 Main St., Frederick, 11/13/85, A, 85003490

Masonic Temple, 503 S. Main St., Aberdeen, 5/29/80, A, C, 80003719

McKenzie—Cassels House, 508 N. Third St., Groton, 2/13/86, C, 86000242

Minneapolis and St. Louis Railroad Depot, 1100 S. Main St., Aberdeen, 9/28/76, A, C, 76001720

Pfutzenreuter, George, House, 411 Third St., Hecla, 6/21/90, B, 90000955

Robar Trading Post [19th Century South Dakota Trading Posts MPS], Address Restricted, Wilmot vicinity, 5/27/88, A, D, 88000582

Savo Hall-Finnish National Society Hall [Architecture of Finnish Settlement TR], NE of Savo, Savo Township, 11/13/85, A, C, 85003494

Simmons House, 1408 S. Main St., Aberdeen, 8/01/84, C, 84003224

Trinity Episcopal Church, 3rd Ave. E. and 3rd St. N., Groton, 1/27/83, A, C, a, 83003003

Ward, Alonzo, Hotel, 104 S. Main St., Aberdeen, 6/17/82, A, C, 82003915

Werth, Gustav and Mary, House, 1502 N. Dakota St., Aberdeen, 6/28/91, C, 91000846

Western Union Building, 21–23 S. Main St., Aberdeen, 12/12/76, A, 76001721

Wylie Park Pavilion, N of Aberdeen off U.S. 281, Aberdeen vicinity, 1/26/78, A, C, 78002540

Brule County

Holy Trinity Church, Off I-90, Kimball vicinity, 11/15/83, A, C, a, b, 83004205

Buffalo County

Crow Creek Site, Address Restricted, Chamberlain vicinity, 10/15/66, D, NHL, 66000710

Fort Thompson Archeological District [Big Bend Area MRA], Address Restricted, Fort Thompson vicinity, 8/14/86, A, D, 86002738

Fort Thompson Mounds, Adress Restricted, Fort Thompson vicinity, 10/15/66, D, NHL, 66000711

Butte County

Belle Fourche Commercial Historic District, 500–620 State St. and 608–622 5th Ave., Belle Fourche, 4/27/82, A, C, 82003917

Belle Fourche Dam, E of Belle Fourche off U.S. 212, Belle Fourche vicinity, 11/23/77, A, C, 77001239

Belle Fourche Experiment Farm, NW of Newell off SD 79, Newell vicinity, 12/22/76, A, 76001722

Belle Fourche River Bridge [Rural Butte and Meade Counties MRA], NE of Belle Fourche off US 212, Belle Fourche vicinity, 4/30/86, C, 86000923

Bolles, Charles, House, 919 State St., Belle Fourche, 7/01/82, C, 82003918

Butte—Lawrence County Fairgrounds [Rural Butte and Meade Counties MRA], SW of Nisland, Nisland vicinity, 4/30/86, A, C, 86000934

Fruitdale Bridge [Rural Butte and Meade Counties MRA], 1/2 mi. S of Fruitdale, Fruitdale vicinity, 4/30/86, C, 86000925

Fruitdale School [Rural Butte and Meade Counties MRA], High St., Fruitdale, 4/30/86, A, C, b, 86000926

Fruitdale Store [Rural Butte and Meade Counties MRA], Water and Main Sts., Fruitdale, 4/30/86, A, C, 86000927

Gartner, Carl Friedrick, Homestead [Rural Butte and Meade Counties MRA], W of SD 79, Newell vicinity, 4/30/86, A, C, b, 86000930

Gay, Thomas Haskins, House, 704 Harding, Belle Fourche, 7/19/82, C, 82003919

Harris, Fred S., House, 826 State St., Belle Fourche, 7/13/88, C, 88000575

Hay Creek Bridge [Historic Bridges in South Dakota MPS], Eighth Ave. over Hay Cr., Belle Fourche, 12/09/93, A, C, 93001274

Hoover Store [Rural Butte and Meade Counties MRA], SD 79, Hoover, 4/30/86, A, C, 86000931

Butte County—Continued

Hoover, Alexander, House [Rural Butte and Meade Counties MRA], SD 59, Hoover, 4/30/86, A, C, 86000929

Johnson, William, House [Rural Butte and Meade Counties MRA], High St., Fruitdale, 4/30/86, C, 86000928

Kenaston, William G., House, 301 Dartmouth, Newell, 2/23/84, C, 84003246

Langdon School [Rural Butte and Meade Counties MRA], Snoma Rd., Nisland vicinity, 4/30/86, A, C, 86000935

Minnesela Bridge [Historic Bridges in South Dakota MPS], Local rd. over Redwater Cr., Belle Fourche vicinity, 12/09/93, C, 93001277

Newell High School [Rural Butte and Meade Counties MRA], Dartmouth St., Newell, 5/01/86, A, C, 86000947

Nisland Bridge [Rural Butte and Meade Counties MRA], S of Nisland on Section Rd., Nisland vicinity, 4/30/86, C, 86000936

Olson Bridge [Rural Butte and Meade Counties MRA], NE of Belle Fourche, Belle Fourche vicinity, 4/30/86, C, 86000924

Scotney, John Aaron, House, 830 9th St., Belle Fourche, 1/03/78, C, 78002541

Small, Charles and Eleanor, House, 825 Fifth Ave., Belle Fourche, 11/01/91, C, 91001617

Snoma Finnish Cemetery [Architecture of Finnish Settlement TR], 3.5 mi. SE of Fruitdale, Fruitdale vicinity, 11/13/85, A, d, 85003492

Soper—Behymer Ranch [Rural Butte and Meade Counties MRA], SD 34, Belle Fourche vicinity, 6/06/86, A, C, 86001262

South Dakota Dept. of Transportation Bridge No. 10-109-360 [Historic Bridges in South Dakota MPS], Local rd. over the Diversion Dam Inlet Canal, Belle Fourche Irrigation District, Belle Fourche vicinity, 12/09/93, A, C, 93001275

South Dakota Dept. of Transportation Bridge No. 10-112-355 [Historic Bridges in South Dakota MPS], Diversion Dam rd. over Crow Cr., Belle Fourche vicinity, 12/09/93, A, C, 93001276

Stonelake Bridge [Rural Butte and Meade Counties MRA], Winkler Rd., Newell vicinity, 4/30/86, C, b, 86000932

Tri State Bakery, 705 State St., Belle Fourche, 8/05/93, A, C, 93000781

Vale Cut Off Belle Fourche River Bridge [Rural Butte and Meade Counties MRA], 7 mi. SW of Newell, Belle Fourche, 4/30/86, C, 86000937

Vale School, Off SD 79, Vale, 8/01/84, A, 84003250

Viken, Nicholas Augustus, Homestead [Rural Butte and Meade Counties MRA], N of Hope Cemetery Rd., Newell vicinity, 4/30/86, B, C, 86000933

Wide Awake Grocery Building, 520 State St., Belle Fourche, 3/30/78, A, C, 78002542

Charles Mix County

Charles Mix County Courthouse [County Courthouses of South Dakota MPS], Main St. between Fourth and Fifth Sts., Lake Andes, 2/10/93, A, C, 92001856

Church of Christ in LaRoche Township, SD 50, Academy, 7/01/82, A, C, a, 82003920

Farmers State Bank of Platte, 404 N. Main St., Platte, 1/27/83, A, C, 83003004

Geddes Historic District, Off SD 50, Geddes, 5/08/73, A, C, 73001737

Holy Fellowship Episcopal Church, SE of Greenwood, Greenwood vicinity, 6/05/75, A, C, a, 75001712

Rising Hail Colony, 5 mi. NW of Greenwood along Seven Mile Creek, Greenwood vicinity, 4/28/75, A, C, g, 75001713

South Dakota Dept. of Transportation Bridge No. 12-503-230 [Historic Bridges in South Dakota MPS], Local rd. over Choteau Cr., Wagner vicinity, 12/09/93, C, 93001278

Clark County

Elrod, Gov. S. H., House, 301 N. Commercial St., Clark, 7/27/79, B, C, 79002399

Garden City Opera House, First and Railroad Sts., Garden City, 12/20/88, A, 88002839

Southeast Merton School No. 19, N of Willow Lake, Willow Lake vicinity, 1/26/90, A, 89002338

Telemarken Lutheran Church, NW of Wallace, Wallace vicinity, 10/19/89, A, C, a, 89001720

Clay County

Anderson Homestead, E of Hub City, Hub City vicinity, 3/30/78, A, C, 78002543

Austin-Whittemore House, 15 Austin Ave., Vermillion, 10/18/72, C, 72001225

Clay County Courthouse, 211 W. Main St., Vermillion, 8/18/83, A, C, 83003005

First Baptist Church of Vermillion, 101 E. Main St., Vermillion, 3/05/82, A, C, a, 82003921

First National Bank Building of Vermillion, 1 E. Main St., Vermillion, 2/13/86, B, 86000244

Forest Avenue Historic District, Forest Ave. and Lewis Sts., Vermillion, 10/18/79, B, C, 79002400

Inman House, 415 E. Main St., Vermillion, 5/24/76, B, C, 76001723

Junker, Jens N. and Anna, Farmstead, Norway Twnshp, Section 6, Meckling vicinity, 12/20/88, A, C, 88002841

Old Main, Clark St., University of South Dakota campus, Vermillion, 3/24/73, A, 73001738

Rice Farm, W of Vermillion, Vermillion vicinity, 1/20/78, A, C, 78002544

Spirit Mound, N of Vermillion, Vermillion vicinity, 11/19/74, A, 74001889

Vermillion Historic District, Bounded by N. Yale, E. Clark, Willow and E. Main Sts., Vermillion, 2/24/75, C, 75001714

Vermillion-Andrew Carnegie Library, 12 Church St., Vermillion, 8/18/83, A, C, 83003006

Willey, E. H., House, 104 Court St., Vermillion, 6/17/82, B, C, 82003922

Codington County

Adams, E. C., House [North End Neighborhood MPS], 604 N. Maple, Watertown, 1/03/89, C, 88003032

Appleby Atlas Elevator, 6 mi. S of jct. of US 212 and I 29, Watertown vicinity, 6/21/90, A, 90000957

Carnegie Free Public Library, 27 1st Ave., SE, Watertown, 6/18/76, A, C, 76001724

Cartford, Benjamin H., House [North End Neighborhood MPS], 803 N. Maple, Watertown, 1/03/89, C, 88003025

Codington County Courthouse, 1st Ave., SE, Watertown, 7/24/78, C, g, 78002545

Davis, Amy A., House [North End Neighborhood MPS], 20 Fourth Ave. NW, Watertown, 1/03/89, C, 88003030

DeGraff, Curt E., House [North End Neighborhood MPS], 603 N. Park, Watertown, 1/03/89, C, 88003033

Emminger, Corson, Round Barn, S of Watertown on U.S. 81, Watertown vicinity, 3/30/78, C, 78002546

Evangelical United Brethren Church [North End Neighborhood MPS], 409 N. Maple, Watertown, 1/03/89, C, a, 88003026

Ferris, James W., House [North End Neighborhood MPS], 619 N. Park, Watertown, 1/03/89, C, 88003034

Florence Methodist Church, Jct. of 5th St. and Dolly Ave., Florence, 6/28/91, C, a, 91000848

Freeburg, Dr. H. M., House [North End Neighborhood MPS], 501 N. Park, Watertown, 1/03/89, C, 88003035

Gilruth, A. C., House [North End Neighborhood MPS], 218 Second Ave. NE, Watertown, 1/03/89, C, 88003031

Hanson, Nels M., Farmstead, 4 mi. N of Henry, Henry vicinity, 7/13/89, A, C, 89000831

Hanten, John B., House, 518 E. Kemp Ave., Watertown, 1/26/90, C, 89002337

Henningson, Dr. Harry, House [North End Neighborhood MPS], 802 First St. NW, Watertown, 1/03/89, C, 88003036

Holy Rosary Church, Minnesota Ave., Kranzburg, 6/06/86, A, C, a, 86001227

Johnson, A. Einar, House [North End Neighborhood MPS], 803 First St. NW, Watertown, 1/03/89, C, 88003029

Kemp Avenue Bridge [Historic Bridges in South Dakota MPS], Kemp Ave. over the Sioux R., Watertown, 12/09/93, A, C, 93001264

Kranzburg School District No. 5, Hasting St., Kranzburg, 6/28/91, A, 91000847

Larson Bridge [Historic Bridges in South Dakota MPS], Local rd. over Willow Cr., Watertown vicinity, 12/09/93, C, 93001266

Mathiesen House, 914 N. Maple, Watertown, 2/01/82, C, 82003923

Mauseth, Peter, House [North End Neighborhood MPS], 703 N. Maple, Watertown, 1/03/89, C, 88003028

Mellette House, 421 5th Ave., NW, Watertown, 8/13/76, B, C, 76001725

Codington County—Continued

Minneapolis and St. Louis Railroad Depot, 168 N. Broadway, Watertown, 10/31/85, A, C, 85003477

Mount Hope Cemetery Mausoleum, Mt. Hope Cemetery off US 81, Watertown, 8/13/86, C, d, 86001500

Olive Place, N of Watertown off U.S. 81, Watertown vicinity, 5/23/78, B, C, b, 78002547

Reeve's Resort, 6 mi. S of Florence, Florence vicinity, 10/19/89, A, 89001726

Ries, Nicholas T., Farmstead, Off Codington County Hwy. 3, Kranzburg vicinity, 2/11/88, A, C, g, 88000047

Sheafe, Gen. Mark W., House, 57 Fourth Ave. NW, Watertown, 2/26/87, B, 87000222

South Dakota Dept. of Transportation Bridge No. 15-210-136 [Historic Bridges in South Dakota MPS], Local rd. over unnamed cr., Watertown vicinity, 12/09/93, C, 93001265

Watertown Commercial Historic District, Roughly bounded by First Ave. N., Third St. E., Second Ave. S., and First St. W., Jefferson, 7/13/89, C, 89000834

Watertown Light and Power Company Plant, 524 W. Kemp St., Watertown, 7/13/89, A, 89000830

Watertown Post Office, 26 S. Broadway, Watertown, 12/12/76, C, 76001726

Willson, Walter, House [North End Neighborhood MPS], 702 Second St. NE, Watertown, 1/03/89, C, 88003027

Corson County

Antelope Creek Stage Station [South Dakota Portion of the Bismarck to Deadwood Trail MPS], Address Restricted, Morristown vicinity, 6/18/92, A, D, 92000692

Archeological Site No. 39CO39 [Prehistoric Rock Art of South Dakota MPS], Address Restricted, Mahto vicinity, 8/06/93, D, a, 93000765

Fort Manuel, Address Restricted, McIntosh vicinity, 12/02/77, B, D, 77001240

Grand River Stage Station [South Dakota Portion of the Bismarck to Deadwood Trail MPS], Address Restricted, Morristown vicinity, 6/18/92, A, D, 92000693

Harding Schoolhouse, 5.5 mi. NW of Trail City, Trail City vicinity, 7/13/89, A, 89000832

South Dakota Dept. of Transportation Bridge No. 16-570-054 [Historic Bridges in South Dakota MPS], Local rd. over Oak Cr., McLaughlin vicinity, 12/09/93, A, C, 93001279

Custer County

Archeological Site No. 39CU890 [Prehistoric Rock Art of South Dakota MPS], Address Restricted, Hermosa vicinity, 8/06/93, D, 93000803

Archeological Site No. 39CU70 [Prehistoric Rock Art of South Dakota MPS], Address Restricted, Custer vicinity, 10/20/93, D, 93001039

Ayres, Lonnie and Francis, Ranch, 2 mi. SE of Fourmile Jct. on US 16, Custer vicinity, 1/25/91, A, 90002209

Badger Hole, 1 mi. E of Legion Lake on U.S. 16A, Custer vicinity, 3/07/73, B, 73001740

Bauer, Maria, Homestead Ranch, 3 mi. SE of Jewel Cave NM, Custer vicinity, 6/09/92, A, 92000683

Beaver Creek Bridge, Wind Cave National Park, Hot Springs vicinity, 8/08/84, C, NPS, 84003254

Beaver Creek Rockshelter, Address Restricted, Pringle vicinity, 10/25/93, D, NPS, 93001130

Buffalo Gap Cheyenne River Bridge, CR 656, Buffalo Gap vicinity, 2/08/88, A, 88000024

CCC Camp Custer Officers' Cabin, 8 mi. NW of Custer on Custer Co. Rd. 292, Custer vicinity, 6/09/92, C, 92000684

Cold Springs Schoolhouse, SE of Custer off SR 336 in Black Hills National Forest, Custer vicinity, 3/07/73, A, 73001741

Custer County Courthouse, 411 Mt. Rushmore Rd., Custer, 11/27/72, A, 72001226

Custer State Game Lodge, E of Custer on US 16A, Custer vicinity, 3/30/83, A, C, 83003007

Custer State Park Museum, W of Hermosa on US 16A, Hermosa vicinity, 3/30/83, A, C, 83003008

First National Bank Building, 6th St. and Mt. Rushmore Rd., Custer, 3/05/82, C, 82003924

Fourmile School No. 21, 1/4 mi. S of Fourmile Jct. on US 16, Custer vicinity, 1/25/91, A, 90002208

Lampert, Charles and Ollie, Ranch [Ranches of Southwestern Custer Co. MPS], S of Elk Mtns., N of Dewey, Custer vicinity, 7/05/90, A, 90000951

Mann, Irene and Walter, Ranch [Ranches of Southwestern Custer Co. MPS], Schenk Canyon area, just off Co. Rt. 270, Custer vicinity, 7/05/90, A, 90000953

Norbeck, Peter, Summer House, W of Custer at Custer State Park, Custer vicinity, 9/13/77, B, C, 77001241

Red Shirt Bridge [Historic Bridges in South Dakota MPS], SD 40 over the Cheyenne R., Red Shirt vicinity, 12/09/93, A, 93001281

Roetzel, Ferdinand and Elizabeth, Ranch, 1 mi. NW of jct. of Saginaw and Roetzel Rds., Custer vicinity, 1/25/91, A, 90002210

Site No. 39 Cu 510 [Rock Art in the Southern Black Hills TR], Address Restricted, City Restricted, 5/20/82, D, 82004752

Site No. 39 Cu 511 [Rock Art in the Southern Black Hills TR], Address Restricted, City Restricted, 5/20/82, D, 82004754

Site No. 39 Cu 512 [Rock Art in the Southern Black Hills TR], Address Restricted, City Restricted, 5/20/82, D, 82004753

Site No. 39 Cu 513 [Rock Art in the Southern Black Hills TR], Address Restricted, City Restricted, 5/20/82, D, 82004755

Site No. 39 Cu 514 [Rock Art in the Southern Black Hills TR], Address Restricted, City Restricted, 5/20/82, D, 82004756

Site No. 39 Cu 515 [Rock Art in the Southern Black Hills TR], Address Restricted, City Restricted, 5/20/82, D, 82004757

Site No. 39 Cu 516 [Rock Art in the Southern Black Hills TR], Address Restricted, City Restricted, 5/20/82, D, 82004758

Site No. 39 Cu 91 [Rock Art in the Southern Black Hills TR], Address Restricted, City Restricted, 5/20/82, D, 82004759

South Dakota Dept. of Transportation Bridge No. 17-289-107 [Historic Bridges in South Dakota MPS], SD 87 over French Cr., Custer State Park, Custer vicinity, 12/09/93, A, 93001280

Stearns, William, Ranch [Ranches of Southwestern Custer Co. MPS], E of Elk Mtn., off Co. Hwy. 769, Custer vicinity, 7/05/90, A, 90000952

Towner, Francis Averill (T. A.) and Janet Leach, House, 218 Crook St., Custer, 6/21/90, C, 90000959

Tubbs, Newton Seymour, House, 35 Centennial Dr., Custer, 12/09/93, C, 93001341

Ward, Elbert and Harriet, Ranch [Ranches of Southwestern Custer Co. MPS], E of Elk Mtn., S of US 16, Custer vicinity, 7/05/90, A, 90000950

Way Park Museum, 4th St. and Rushmore Rd., Custer, 3/07/73, A, b, 73001739

Wind Cave National Park Historic District, E of Custer off US 385, Custer, 7/11/84, A, C, NPS, 84003259

Young, Edna and Ernest, Ranch [Ranches of Southwestern Custer Co. MPS], Approximately 3 mi. S of Dewey, S of Beaver Cr., Custer vicinity, 7/05/90, A, 90000949

Davison County

Anderson, John F., House, 323 N. Duff, Mitchell, 7/01/82, C, 82003925

Beckwith, Louis, House, 1311 S. Duff Dr., Mitchell, 7/01/82, B, C, b, 82003926

Chambers, C. E., House, 322 W. 11th St., Mitchell, 1/26/90, C, 89002334

Dakota Wesleyan University, Bounded by E. and W. University Aves. and McCabe St., Mitchell, 12/22/76, C, 76001727

Holy Family Church, School, and Rectory, Kimball and Davison Sts., E. 2nd and E. 3rd Aves., Mitchell, 12/12/76, C, a, 76001729

Mitchell Historic Commercial District, 210 S.—604 N. Main, 119–201 W. 3rd St., 117–219 E. 4th St., and 112–220 W. 5th St., Mitchell, 6/27/75, A, C, 75001716

Mitchell Site, Address Restricted, Mitchell vicinity, 10/15/66, D, NHL, 66000712

Site 39DV24 [James River Basin Woodland Sites TR], Address Restricted, Mitchell vicinity, 1/31/84, D, 84003260

Site 39DV9 [James River Basin Woodland Sites TR], Address Restricted, Riverside vicinity, 1/31/84, D, 84003275

South Dakota Dept. of Transportation Bridge No. 18-040-137 [Historic Bridges in South Dakota MPS], Local rd. over Enemy Cr., Mitchell vicinity, 12/09/93, C, 93001282

Davison County—Continued

South Dakota Dept. of Transportation Bridge No. 18-060-202 [Historic Bridges in South Dakota MPS], Local rd. over Twelve Mile Cr., Mitchell vicinity, 12/09/93, C, 93001283

South Dakota Dept. of Transportation Bridge No. 18-100-052 [Historic Bridges in South Dakota MPS], Local rd. over Firesteel Cr., Loomis vicinity, 12/09/93, C, 93001284

South Dakota Dept. of Transportation Bridge No. 18-142-150 [Historic Bridges in South Dakota MPS], Local rd. over Enemy Cr., Mitchell vicinity, 12/09/93, C, 93001285

Welch, L. J., House, 608 E. 4th Ave., Mitchell, 10/19/89, C, 89001722

Day County

Barber, Charles A., Farmstead, 1/4 mi. W of Lily, Lily vicinity, 2/08/88, A, 88000048

Havens, William, House, 915 E. 1st St., Webster, 1/31/85, B, C, 85000182

Waldorf Hotel, Main St., Andover, 9/13/79, A, 79002401

Zoar Norwegian Lutheran Church, 7 mi. E, 5 mi. N of Grenville, Grenville vicinity, 10/25/90, A, a, 90001644

Deuel County

Deuel County Courthouse and Jail, SD 22, Clear Lake, 6/16/76, C, 76001730

First National Bank, Off SD 22, Gary, 12/02/77, C, 77001242

Odd Fellows Building, Main St., Gary, 6/03/76, C, 76001731

Old Cochrane Road Bridge [Historic Bridges in South Dakota MPS], Abandoned local rd. over the inlet to Lake Cochrane, Brandt vicinity, 12/09/93, C, 93001268

South Dakota Dept. of Transportation Bridge No. 20-153-210 [Historic Bridges in South Dakota MPS], Local rd. over Cobb Cr., Brandt vicinity, 12/09/93, A, C, 93001286

South Dakota School for the Blind, Coteau and Third Sts., Gary, 5/26/88, A, 88000570

Dewey County

Molstad Village, Address Restricted, Mobridge vicinity, 10/15/66, D, NHL, 66000713

Douglas County

Armour Historic District, Main St. between 3rd and 7th Sts., Armour, 1/30/78, A, C, 78002548

Douglas County Courthouse and Auditor's Office, U.S. 281, Armour, 3/21/78, C, 78002549

Lenehan, Thomas, House, Main St., Delmont, 2/08/88, C, 88000003

Slettebak Grocercies, Hardware and Opera House, Address Restricted, Armour vicinity, 2/23/84, A, C, 84003278

Stevens Opera Block, Main St., Delmont, 12/20/88, A, 88002838

Edmunds County

Bank of Bowdle, 3026 Main St., Bowdle, 1/31/85, A, 85000183

Beebe, Marcus P., Library, Main St. and 2nd Ave., Ipswich, 11/16/77, B, C, g, 77001243

Beebe, Marcus, House, 4th St. and 5th Ave., Ipswich, 12/12/76, C, 76001733

Eisenbeis, John, House [German-Russian Folk Architecture TR], Address Restricted, Bowdle vicinity, 8/13/84, A, C, 84003283

Ipswich Baptist Church, Main St. and 3rd Ave., Ipswich, 1/30/78, C, a, 78002550

Ipswich State Bank, 1st Ave. and Main St., Ipswich, 5/22/78, C, 78002551

Parmley Land Office, Main St., Ipswich, 3/26/79, B, 79002402

Parmley, J. W., House, 4th St. and 4th Ave., Ipswich, 6/04/80, B, C, 80003720

Roscoe Community Hall, 202 Mitchell St., Roscoe, 8/01/84, A, 84003284

Strouckel, John, House [German-Russian Folk Architecture TR], Address Restricted, Loyalton vicinity, 11/28/84, A, C, 84001268

Fall River County

Allen Bank Building and Cascade Springs Bath House-Sanitarium, Address Restricted, Hot Springs vicinity, 2/23/84, A, C, 84003285

Archeological Site No. 39FA806 [Prehistoric Rock Art of South Dakota MPS], Address Restricted, Hot Springs vicinity, 8/06/93, D, 93000790

Archeological Site No. 39FA1049 [Prehistoric Rock Art of South Dakota MPS], Address Restricted, Hot Springs vicinity, 8/06/93, D, 93000791

Archeological Site No. 39FA1201 [Prehistoric Rock Art of South Dakota MPS], Address Restricted, Edgemont vicinity, 8/06/93, D, 93000792

Archeological Site No. 39FA678 [Prehistoric Rock Art of South Dakota MPS], Address Restricted, Edgemont vicinity, 8/06/93, D, 93000801

Archeological Site No. 39FA86 [Prehistoric Rock Art of South Dakota MPS], Address Restricted, Edgemont vicinity, 8/06/93, D, 93000804

Archeological Site No. 39FA89 [Prehistoric Rock Art of South Dakota MPS], Address Restricted, Edgemont vicinity, 8/06/93, D, 93000806

Archeological Site No. 39FA88 [Prehistoric Rock Art of South Dakota MPS], Address Restricted, Edgemont vicinity, 10/20/93, D, 93001040

Archeological Site No. 39FA90 [Prehistoric Rock Art of South Dakota MPS], Address Restricted, Hot Springs vicinity, 10/20/93, D, 93001041

Archeological Site No. 39FA99 [Prehistoric Rock Art of South Dakota MPS], Address Restricted, Edgemont vicinity, 10/20/93, D, 93001042

Archeological Site No. 39FA243 [Prehistoric Rock Art of South Dakota MPS], Address Restricted, Edgemont vicinity, 10/20/93, D, 93001043

Archeological Site No. 39FA244 [Prehistoric Rock Art of South Dakota MPS], Address Restricted, Edgemont vicinity, 10/20/93, D, 93001044

Archeological Site No. 39FA316 [Prehistoric Rock Art of South Dakota MPS], Address Restricted, Edgemont vicinity, 10/20/93, D, 93001045

Archeological Site No. 39FA321 [Prehistoric Rock Art of South Dakota MPS], Address Restricted, Edgemont vicinity, 10/20/93, D, 93001046

Archeological Site No. 39FA395 [Prehistoric Rock Art of South Dakota MPS], Address Restricted, Edgemont vicinity, 10/20/93, D, 93001047

Archeological Site No. 39FA446 [Prehistoric Rock Art of South Dakota MPS], Address Restricted, Edgemont vicinity, 10/20/93, D, 93001048

Archeological Site No. 39FA447 [Prehistoric Rock Art of South Dakota MPS], Address Restricted, Edgemont vicinity, 10/20/93, D, 93001049

Archeological Site No. 39FA448 [Prehistoric Rock Art of South Dakota MPS], Address Restricted, Edgemont vicinity, 10/20/93, D, 93001050

Archeological Site No. 39FA542 [Prehistoric Rock Art of South Dakota MPS], Address Restricted, Edgemont vicinity, 10/25/93, D, 93001051

Archeological Site No. 39FA679 [Prehistoric Rock Art of South Dakota MPS], Address Restricted, Edgemont vicinity, 10/20/93, D, 93001052

Archeological Site No. 39FA680 [Prehistoric Rock Art of South Dakota MPS], Address Restricted, Edgemont vicinity, 10/20/93, D, 93001053

Archeological Site No. 39FA682 [Prehistoric Rock Art of South Dakota MPS], Address Restricted, Edgemont vicinity, 10/20/93, D, 93001054

Archeological Site No. 39FA683 [Prehistoric Rock Art of South Dakota MPS], Address Restricted, Edgemont vicinity, 10/20/93, D, 93001055

Archeological Site No. 39FA686 [Prehistoric Rock Art of South Dakota MPS], Address Restricted, Edgemont vicinity, 10/20/93, D, 93001056

Archeological Site No. 39FA688 [Prehistoric Rock Art of South Dakota MPS], Address Restricted, Edgemont vicinity, 10/20/93, D, 93001057

Archeological Site No. 39FA690 [Prehistoric Rock Art of South Dakota MPS], Address Restricted, Edgemont vicinity, 10/20/93, D, 93001058

Archeological Site No. 39FA691 [Prehistoric Rock Art of South Dakota MPS], Address Restricted, Edgemont vicinity, 10/20/93, D, 93001059

Archeological Site No. 39FA767 [Prehistoric Rock Art of South Dakota MPS], Address Restricted, Edgemont vicinity, 10/20/93, D, 93001060

Archeological Site No. 39FA788 [Prehistoric Rock Art of South Dakota MPS], Address Restricted, Edgemont vicinity, 10/20/93, D, 93001061

Archeological Site No. 39FA819 [Prehistoric Rock Art of South Dakota MPS], Address Restricted, Edgemont vicinity, 10/20/93, D, 93001062

Fall River County—Continued

Archeological Site No. 39FA1010 [Prehistoric Rock Art of South Dakota MPS], Address Restricted, Hot Springs vicinity, 10/20/93, D, 93001063

Archeological Site No. 39FA1013 [Prehistoric Rock Art of South Dakota MPS], Address Restricted, Hot Springs vicinity, 10/20/93, D, 93001064

Archeological Site No. 39FA1046 [Prehistoric Rock Art of South Dakota MPS], Address Restricted, Edgemont vicinity, 10/20/93, D, 93001065

Archeological Site No. 39FA1093 [Prehistoric Rock Art of South Dakota MPS], Address Restricted, Hot Springs vicinity, 10/20/93, D, 93001066

Archeological Site No. 39FA1152 [Prehistoric Rock Art of South Dakota MPS], Address Restricted, Hot Springs vicinity, 10/20/93, D, 93001067

Archeological Site No. 39FA1154 [Prehistoric Rock Art of South Dakota MPS], Address Restricted, Hot Springs vicinity, 10/20/93, D, 93001068

Archeological Site No. 39FA1155 [Prehistoric Rock Art of South Dakota MPS], Address Restricted, Hot Springs vicinity, 10/20/93, D, 93001069

Archeological Site No. 39FA1190 [Prehistoric Rock Art of South Dakota MPS], Address Restricted, Edgemont vicinity, 10/20/93, D, 93001070

Archeological Site No. 39FA1204 [Prehistoric Rock Art of South Dakota MPS], Address Restricted, Hot Springs vicinity, 10/20/93, D, 93001071

Chilson Bridge [Historic Bridges in South Dakota MPS], Local rd. over Burlington Northern RR tracks, Edgemont vicinity, 12/09/93, C, 93001287

Flint Hill Aboriginal Quartzite Quarry, Address Restricted, Edgemont vicinity, 7/14/78, D, 78002552

Hot Springs High School, 146 N. 16th St., Hot Springs, 5/07/80, C, 80003721

Hot Springs Historic District, Roughly both sides of River St. from Summit Rd. S to Baltimore St., including part of Minnekahta Ave., Hot Springs, 6/25/74, A, C, 74001890

Jensen, Governor Leslie, House, 309 S. Fifth St., Hot Spring, 9/25/87, B, C, 87001731

Site No. 39 FA 277 [Rock Art in the Southern Black Hills TR], Address Restricted, City Restricted, 5/20/82, C, D, 82004761

Site No. 39 FA 389 [Rock Art in the Southern Black Hills TR], Address Restricted, City Restricted, 5/20/82, C, D, 82004762

Site No. 39 FA 554 [Rock Art in the Southern Black Hills TR], Address Restricted, City Restricted, 5/20/82, C, D, 82004764

Site No. 39 FA 58 [Rock Art in the Southern Black Hills TR], Address Restricted, City Restricted, 5/20/82, D, 82004765

Site No. 39 FA 676 [Rock Art in the Southern Black Hills TR], Address Restricted, City Restricted, 5/20/82, C, D, 82004766

Site No. 39 FA 677 [Rock Art in the Southern Black Hills TR], Address Restricted, City Restricted, 5/20/82, D, 82004767

Site No. 39 FA 681 [Rock Art in the Southern Black Hills TR], Address Restricted, City Restricted, 5/20/82, C, D, 82004769

Site No. 39 FA 684 [Rock Art in the Southern Black Hills TR], Address Restricted, City Restricted, 5/20/82, C, D, 82004768

Site No. 39 FA 685 [Rock Art in the Southern Black Hills TR], Address Restricted, City Restricted, 5/20/82, C, D, 82004906

Site No. 39 FA 687 [Rock Art in the Southern Black Hills TR], Address Restricted, City Restricted, 5/20/82, C, D, 82004770

Site No. 39 FA 7 [Rock Art in the Southern Black Hills TR], Address Restricted, City Restricted, 5/20/82, C, D, 82004771

Site No. 39 FA 75 [Rock Art in the Southern Black Hills TR], Address Restricted, City Restricted, 5/20/82, C, D, 82004760

Site No. 39 FA 79 [Rock Art in the Southern Black Hills TR], Address Restricted, City Restricted, 5/20/82, C, D, 82004772

Site No. 39 FA 91 [Rock Art in the Southern Black Hills TR], Address Restricted, City Restricted, 5/20/82, D, 82004773

Site No. 39 FA 94 [Rock Art in the Southern Black Hills TR], Address Restricted, City Restricted, 5/20/82, C, D, 82004774

Wesch, Phillip, House, 2229 Minnekahta, Hot Springs, 2/23/84, A, 84003287

Faulk County

Byrne, Gov. Frank M., House, 1017 St. John St., Faulkton, 1/30/92, B, 91002044

Faulk County Courthouse [County Courthouses of South Dakota MPS], Jct. of Ninth Ave. and Court St., Faulkton, 2/10/93, A, C, 92001857

Pickler, Maj. John A., Homestead, S edge of Faulkton city limits, Faulkton, 4/11/73, B, 73001742

South Dakota Dept. of Transportation Bridge No. 25-380-142 [Historic Bridges in South Dakota MPS], Local rd. over the S. fork of Snake Cr., Zell vicinity, 12/09/93, C, b, 93001262

South Dakota Dept. of Transportation Bridge No. 25-218-141 [Historic Bridges in South Dakota MPS], 10th Ave. over the S. Fork of Snake Cr., Faulkton, 12/09/93, A, C, 93001288

Turner, Frank and Clara, House, 1006 Main, Faulkton, 2/13/86, A, C, 86000245

Grant County

Brown Earth Presbyterian Church, NE of Stockholm, Stockholm vicinity, 8/29/84, A, C, a, 84003288

First Congregational Church of Milbank, E. 3rd Ave., Milbank, 4/19/78, A, C, a, 78002553

First National Bank of Milbank, 225 S. Main St., Milbank, 4/19/78, C, 78002554

First State Bank Building, Main Street, Revillo, 2/26/87, A, C, 87000221

Grant County Courthouse [County Courthouses of South Dakota MPS], Jct. of Park Ave. and Main St., Milbank, 2/10/93, A, C, 92001858

Hollands Grist Mill, U.S. 12, Milbank, 2/24/81, A, C, b, 81000573

Lebanon Lutheran Church, 8 mi. SW of Summit, Summit vicinity, 9/15/77, A, 77001244

Milbank Carnegie Library, S. 3rd Ave., Milbank, 11/21/78, C, 78002555

Swedish Lutheran Church of Strandburg, Main St., Strandburg, 2/17/78, C, a, 78002556

Gregory County

Dallas Carnegie Library, Off US 18, Dallas, 5/28/76, A, C, 76001734

Fort Randall, 3 mi. SW of Pickstown, Pickstown vicinity, 4/22/76, A, 76001735

Pocahontas Schoolhouse, 4.5 mi. NE of Dixon, Dixon vicinity, 4/26/73, A, b, 73001743

South Dakota Dept. of Transportation Bridge No. 27-000-201 [Historic Bridges in South Dakota MPS], Local rd. over unnamed cr., Dallas vicinity, 12/09/93, C, 93001289

South Dakota Dept. of Transportation Bridge No. 27-060-298 [Historic Bridges in South Dakota MPS], Local rd. over unnamed cr., Gregory vicinity, 12/09/93, A, C, 93001290

Haakon County

Bank of Midland Building, Main St., Midland, 8/13/86, A, C, 86001481

Hamlin County

Hendrickson, Hendrick and Waldur, Farm [Architecture of Finnish Settlement TR], Hwy. 28, Lake Norden vicinity, 11/13/85, A, C, 85003485

Kant Hotel, N of SD 28, Bryant vicinity, 10/31/85, A, 85003449

Lohr, Charles and Mary, House, 1705 State Ave., Estelline, 7/19/82, B, C, 82003927

Old St. Mary's Catholic Parish House, 5th Ave. and Underwood St., Bryant, 12/27/88, C, a, 88002840

South Dakota Dept. of Transportation Bridge No. 29-221-060 [Historic Bridges in South Dakota MPS], Local rd. over the Big Sioux R., Castlewood vicinity, 12/09/93, C, 93001291

South Dakota Dept. of Transportation Bridge No. 29-279-010 [Historic Bridges in South Dakota MPS], Local rd. over Stray Horse Cr., Castlewood vicinity, 12/09/93, C, 93001292

Tuohino, Jacob and Amelia, Farm [Architecture of Finnish Settlement TR], S of Hwy. 28, Lake Norden vicinity, 11/13/85, A, C, 85003495

Hand County

Archeological Site 39HD22 [Petroforms of South Dakota TR], Address Restricted, Danforth vicinity, 2/23/84, D, 84003296

Miller Ree Creek Bridge, W edge of Miller, Miller, 8/25/88, C, 88001314

South Dakota Dept. of Transportation Bridge No. 30-257-400 [Historic Bridges in South Dakota MPS], Local rd. over Sand Cr., Miller vicinity, 12/09/93, A, 93001293

St. Mary's Church, School and Convent, U.S. 212, Zell vicinity, 7/19/82, A, C, a, 82003928

Hanson County

Bloom Site, Address Restricted, Bloom vicinity, 10/15/66, D, NHL, 66000714

Fort James (39HS48), Address Restricted, Rosedale Colony vicinity, 3/15/84, D, 84003290

Old Rockport Hutterite Colony [Historic Hutterite Colonies TR], Off James River, Alexandria vicinity, 6/30/82, A, C, a, 82003929

Reese, Sheldon, Site (39HS23), Address Restricted, Mitchell vicinity, 3/15/84, D, 84003292

Site 39HS3 [James River Basin Woodland Sites TR], Address Restricted, Mitchell vicinity, 1/31/84, D, 84003294

South Dakota Dept. of Transportation Bridge No. 31-115-110 [Historic Bridges in South Dakota MPS], Local rd. over Pierre Cr., Fulton vicinity, 12/09/93, C, 93001294

Harding County

Archeological Site No. 39HN208 [Prehistoric Rock Art of South Dakota MPS], Address Restricted, Ludlow vicinity, 8/06/93, D, 93000794

Archeological Site No. 39HN17 [Prehistoric Rock Art of South Dakota MPS], Address Restricted, Ludlow vicinity, 8/06/93, D, 93000805

Ashcroft, Thomas, Ranch [Harding and Perkins Counties MRA], Floodplain of South Fork of Grand River, ENE of Buffalo, Buffalo vicinity, 4/10/87, A, C, 87000547

Blake Ranch House [Harding and Perkins Counties MRA], 1 mi. W of Camp Crook Rd., Gustave vicinity, 4/10/87, C, 87000534

Emmanuel Lutheran Church and Cemetery [Harding and Perkins Counties MRA], CR 858, Ralph vicinity, 4/10/87, A, C, a, 87000531

Giannonatti Ranch [Harding and Perkins Counties MRA], S side of an E-W Section Rd., Ludlow vicinity, 4/10/87, A, C, 87000546

Golden Valley Norwegian Lutheran Church [Harding and Perkins Counties MRA], N-S Section Rd. E of SD 79, Ralph vicinity, 4/10/87, C, a, 87000548

Johnson, Axel, Ranch [Harding and Perkins Counties MRA], E of SD 79 on Sorum Rd., Reva vicinity, 5/19/87, A, C, 87000541

Lightning Spring (39HN204), Address Restricted, Ludlow vicinity, 8/02/82, D, 82003930

Little Missouri Bank Building [Harding and Perkins Counties MRA], Main St., Camp Crook, 4/10/87, A, 87000536

Livingston, John and Daisy May, Ranch [Harding and Perkins Counties MRA], E of SD 79 on S side of Sorum Rd., Sorum vicinity, 4/10/87, A, C, 87000542

Peace Valley Evangelical Church and Cemetery [Harding and Perkins Counties MRA], E side of SD 79, Ralph vicinity, 4/10/87, A, C, a, 87000550

Shevling, L. W., Ranch [Harding and Perkins Counties MRA], E of Harding in the West Short Pine Hills area, Harding, 4/10/87, A, C, 87000537

Stokes, Oliver O., House [Harding and Perkins Counties MRA], W side of N-S Section Rd., Harding, 4/10/87, A, C, 87000532

Vessey School [Harding and Perkins Counties MRA], CR 859, Haley vicinity, 4/10/87, A, C, 87000553

Hughes County

Archeological Site 39HU189 [Petroforms of South Dakota TR], Address Restricted, Macs Corner vicinity, 2/23/84, D, 84003307

Archeological Site 39HU201 [Petroforms of South Dakota TR], Address Restricted, Pierre vicinity, 2/23/84, D, 84003308

Archeological Site 39HU66 [Petroforms of South Dakota TR], Address Restricted, Canning vicinity, 2/23/84, D, 84003297

Arzberger Site, Address Restricted, Pierre vicinity, 10/15/66, D, NHL, 66000715

Brandhuber Ice Company Barn, 419 S. Fort St., Pierre, 10/22/80, A, C, 80003722

Brink-Wagner House, 110 E. 4th St., Pierre, 4/26/78, C, 78002557

Cedar Islands Archeological District [Big Bend Area MRA], Address Restricted, Pierre vicinity, 8/14/86, A, C, D, 86002739

Central Block, 321–325 S. Pierre St., Pierre, 1/19/89, A, 88003201

Crawford-Pettyjohn House, 129 S. Washington St., Pierre, 9/22/77, B, C, 77001245

Farr House, 106 E. Wynoka St., Pierre, 12/04/80, B, C, 80003723

Fort George Creek Archeological District [Big Bend Area MRA], Address Restricted, Pierre vicinity, 8/14/86, A, D, 86002741

Graham, Mentor, House, U.S. 14, Blunt, 12/13/76, B, 76001736

Horner—Hyde House, 100 W. Capitol Ave., Pierre, 12/20/88, B, 88002836

Hughes County Courthouse [County Courthouses of South Dakota MPS], Capitol Ave. between Grand and Euclid Aves., Pierre, 2/10/93, A, C, 92001859

Hyde Buildings, 101 1/2, 105, 108 1/2, and 109 S. Pierre St. and 105 1/2 Capitol Ave., Pierre, 2/01/83, A, C, 83003009

Karcher Block, 366 S. Pierre St., Pierre, 8/17/93, A, 93000783

Karcher-Sahr House, 222 E. Prospect St., Pierre, 9/22/77, C, 77001246

McClure Site (39HU7) [Big Bend Area MRA], Address Restricted, Pierre vicinity, 8/14/86, D, 86002732

McDonald, Henry M., House, 1906 E. Erskine, Pierre, 10/19/89, C, 89001718

McMillen, George, House, 111 E. Broadway, Pierre, 8/18/83, A, C, 83003010

Meade, Judge C. D., House, 106 W. Prospect St., Pierre, 10/07/77, C, 77001247

Medicine Creek Archeological District [Big Bend Area MRA], Address Restricted, Lower Brule vicinity, 8/14/86, A, D, 86002740

Oahe Chapel, NW of Pierre, Pierre vicinity, 6/06/80, A, a, b, 80003725

Old Fort Sully Site (39HU52) [Big Bend Area MRA], Address Restricted, Pierre vicinity, 8/14/86, D, 86002731

Scurr, Kenneth R., House, 121 S. Washington Ave., Pierre, 8/05/93, B, 93000780

Soldiers & Sailors World War Memorial, Capitol Ave., Pierre, 1/27/83, A, C, 83003011

South Dakota State Capitol and Governor's House, Bounded by Broadway, Washington, and Capitol Aves., Pierre, 9/01/76, A, C, g, 76001737

St. Charles Hotel, 207 E. Capitol Ave., Pierre, 5/07/80, A, B, C, 80003724

Stephens-Lucas House, 123 N. Nicollette, Pierre, 5/26/77, C, 77001248

Hutchinson County

Deckert, Ludwig, House [German-Russian Folk Architecture TR], Address Restricted, Freeman vicinity, 8/13/84, A, C, 84003309

Grosz, Martin and Wilhelminn, House-Barn [German-Russian Folk Architecture TR], Address Restricted, Olivet vicinity, 8/13/84, A, C, 84003311

Hofer, Enoch, House-Barn [German-Russian Folk Architecture TR], Address Restricted, Freeman vicinity, 11/28/84, A, C, 84001278

Hofer, Michael, House [German-Russian Folk Architecture TR], Address Restricted, Freeman vicinity, 8/13/84, A, 84003316

Holzworth-Lang House [German-Russian Folk Architecture TR], Address Restricted, Freeman vicinity, 11/28/84, A, C, 84001284

Milltown Hutterite Colony [Historic Hutterite Colonies TR], On James River, Milltown vicinity, 6/30/82, A, a, 82004658

New Elmspring Colony [Historic Hutterite Colonies TR], On James River, Ethan vicinity, 6/30/82, A, a, 82004656

Old Elmspring Hutterite Colony [Historic Hutterite Colonies TR], Off James River, Parkston vicinity, 6/30/82, A, C, a, 82004659

Old Maxwell Hutterite Colony [Historic Hutterite Colonies TR], SE of Olivet, Scotland vicinity, 6/30/82, A, C, a, 82004660

Hutchinson County—Continued

Schatz, Jacob, House [German-Russian Folk Architecture TR], Address Restricted, Freeman vicinity, 8/13/84, A, C, 84003318

Schmitt, Gottlieb, House, 150 W. Poplar, Menno, 11/06/86, B, 86003011

Site 39HT14 [James River Basin Woodland Sites TR], Address Restricted, Olivet vicinity, 1/31/84, D, 84003320

Site 39HT27 [James River Basin Woodland Sites TR], Address Restricted, Clayton vicinity, 2/01/84, D, 84003323

Site 39HT29 [James River Basin Woodland Sites TR], Address Restricted, Clayton vicinity, 2/01/84, D, 84003325

Sites 39HT30 and 39HT202 [James River Basin Woodland Sites TR], Address Restricted, Clayton vicinity, 2/01/84, D, 84003327

Stern, Gottlieb, House [German-Russian Folk Architecture TR], Address Restricted, Freeman vicinity, 11/28/84, A, C, 84001287

Ulmer, J. W., House, 611 5th St., Menno, 6/17/82, B, C, 82004657

Vetter, George, House [German-Russian Folk Architecture TR], Address Restricted, Tripp vicinity, 8/13/84, A, C, 84003329

Wollman, Joseph, House [German-Russian Folk Architecture TR], Address Restricted, Freeman vicinity, 11/28/84, A, C, 84001292

Ziegler, Wihelm, House-Barn [German-Russian Folk Architecture TR], Address Restricted, Kaylor vicinity, 8/13/84, A, C, 84003332

Hyde County

Archeological Site No. 39HE331 [Prehistoric Rock Art of South Dakota MPS], Address Restricted, Holabird vicinity, 8/06/93, D, 93000793

Hyde County Courthouse, 412 Commercial St., SE, Highmore, 3/30/78, A, C, 78002558

Old Hyde County Courthouse, 110 Commercial St., SE, Highmore, 4/19/78, A, C, 78002559

Jackson County

Chicago, Milwaukee, and St. Paul Railroad Depot, South end of Kadoka adjacent to Chicago, Milwaukee, St. Paul, and Pacific RR, Kadoka, 8/13/86, A, 86001478

Jones, Tom, Ranch, 5 1/2 mi. S of Midland, Midland vicinity, 10/25/90, A, B, 90001653

Lip's Camp, Address Restricted, Wanblee vicinity, 6/11/75, D, 75002104

Prairie Homestead, N of Interior on U.S. 16A, Interior vicinity, 1/11/74, A, b, 74001891

Jerauld County

Archeological Site 39JE10 [Petroforms of South Dakota TR], Address Restricted, Wessington Springs vicinity, 2/23/84, D, 84003336

Archeological Site 39JE11 [Petroforms of South Dakota TR], Address Restricted, Gann Valley vicinity, 2/23/84, D, 84003337

Jerauld County Courthouse [County Courthouses of South Dakota MPS], Jct. of South Dakota Ave. and Burrett St., Wessington Springs, 2/10/93, A, C, 92001860

Shakespeare Garden and Shay House, Off SD 34, Wessington Springs, 11/14/79, C, g, 79003681

Vessey, Robert S., House, 118 College Ave., Wessington Springs, 4/26/78, B, C, 78002560

Wessington Springs Opera House, 111 Dakota Ave. N., Wessington Springs, 7/21/76, A, C, b, 76001738

Jones County

Capa Bridge [Historic Bridges in South Dakota MPS], Local rd. over the Bad R., Murdo vicinity, 12/09/93, A, C, 93001295

Immanuel Lutheran Church, 14 mi. N of I-90, Murdo vicinity, 2/08/88, A, C, a, 88000022

Van Metre Bridge [Historic Bridges in South Dakota MPS], Local rd. over the Bad R., Murdo vicinity, 12/09/93, C, 93001296

Kingsbury County

Chicago Northwestern Depot, SD 25, De Smet, 12/12/76, C, 76001739

Esmond Bridge [Historic Bridges in South Dakota MPS], Local rd. over Redstone Cr., De Smet vicinity, 12/09/93, C, 93001298

Ingalls House, 210 3rd St. W., De Smet, 4/21/75, A, 75001717

Kingsbury County Courthouse, SD 25, De Smet, 9/22/77, A, C, 77001249

Oldham Methodist Church, Main St. and Epton Ave., Oldham, 9/25/87, C, a, 87001728

Peterson-Loriks House, In Oldham, Oldham, 6/19/80, B, C, 80003726

Railroad Camp Shanty, 1st and Olivet Sts., De Smet, 3/20/73, A, b, 73001744

South Dakota Dept. of Transportation Bridge No. 39-006-070 [Historic Bridges in South Dakota MPS], Local rd. over Pearl Cr., Iroquois vicinity, 12/09/93, C, 93001297

South Dakota Dept. of Transportation Bridge No. 39-176-100 [Historic Bridges in South Dakota MPS], Local rd. over unnamed cr., De Smet vicinity, 12/09/93, C, 93001299

Lake County

Chapel Emmanuel Railroad Car, W of Madison on U.S. 81 in Prairie Village, Madison vicinity, 9/08/76, A, b, 76001740

Chicago, Milwaukee, St. Paul, and Pacific Railroad Depot, 315 S. Egan, Madison, 10/19/89, A, C, 89001719

Daly, Matthew W., House, 102 N. E. Ninth St., Madison, 7/13/88, C, 88000571

Lake County Courthouse [County Courthouses of South Dakota MPS], Center St. between Harth and Lee Aves., Madison, 2/10/93, A, C, 92001861

Luce, Herman, Cabin, Lake Herman State Park, Madison, 1/30/78, A, C, 78002561

Mackay, William A., House, 304 NE 4th St., Madison, 6/03/76, C, 76001741

Madison Historic District, Bounded roughly by Egan Ave. (both sides), Washington, 4th and 7th Sts., Madison, 5/11/76, A, C, e, 76001742

Madison Masonic Temple, 229 N. Egan Ave., Madison, 1/26/90, C, 89002335

St. Ann's Catholic Church of Badus, NE of Ramona, Ramona vicinity, 8/07/79, A, C, 79002403

Lawrence County

Ainsworth, Oliver N., House, 340 Kansas, Spearfish, 10/25/90, C, 90001646

Buskala, Henry Ranch [Architecture of Finnish Settlement TR], FDR 206, Dumont vicinity, 11/13/85, A, C, 85003488

Cook, Fayette, House, 840 Eighth Ave., Spearfish, 7/13/88, C, 88000573

Corbin, James A., House, 345 Main St., Spearfish, 10/25/90, C, 90001651

Court, Henry, House, 329 Main St., Spearfish, 10/25/90, C, 90001652

Deadwood Historic District, Bounded by the city limits, Deadwood, 10/15/66, A, C, NHL, 66000716

Dickey, Eleazer C. and Gwinnie, House, 735 Eighth St., Spearfish, 7/13/89, C, 89000824

Dickey, Walter, House, 815 State St., Spearfish, 5/16/88, B, C, 88000568

Driskill, William D., House, 335 Canyon St., Spearfish, 7/13/89, C, 89000822

Episcopal Church of All Angels, 129 W. Michigan, Spearfish, 4/22/76, C, a, 76001743

Evans, Robert H., House, 258 Evans Ln., Spearfish, 11/01/91, C, 91001621

Frawley Historic Ranch, 6 mi. E of Spearfish on U.S. 14, Spearfish vicinity, 12/31/74, A, C, D, NHL, 74001893

Halloran-Matthews-Brady House, 214 E. Jackson St., Spearfish, 12/12/76, B, C, 76001744

Hewes, Arthur, House, 811 St. Joe, Spearfish, 10/25/90, C, 90001650

Hill, John, Ranch—Keltomaki [Architecture of Finnish Settlement TR], NE of Brownsville, Brownsville vicinity, 11/13/85, A, C, 85003489

Homestake Workers House, 830 State St., Spearfish, 11/01/91, C, b, 91001620

Keets, Henry, House, 344 E. Illinois, Spearfish, 7/13/88, C, 88000572

Knight, Webb S., House, 514 Seventh St., Spearfish, 7/13/89, C, 89000823

Kroll Meat Market and Slaughterhouse, Spearfish City Park, Spearfish, 5/20/88, A, 88000576

Lead Historic District, Roughly bounded by city limits, Lead, 12/31/74, A, C, 74001892

Lawrence County—Continued

Lown, William Ernest, House, 745 5th St., Spearfish, 5/28/76, B, C, 76001745

Mail Building, The, 731 Main St., Spearfish, 5/16/88, A, 88000574

Old Finnish Lutheran Church [Architecture of Finnish Settlement TR], Sinking Gardens, E. Main St., Lead, 11/13/85, A, a, b, 85003487

Quillian, Thomas, House, W. Center St., St. Onge, 11/01/91, C, 91001618

Redwater Bridge, Old [Historic Bridges in South Dakota MPS], Local rd. over the Redwater R., Spearfish vicinity, 12/09/93, A, C, 93001300

Riley, Almira, House, 938 Ames, Spearfish, 7/13/89, C, 89000825

Selbie Building, 1101 Meade, Whitewood, 11/06/86, A, 86003013

Spearfish City Hall, 722 Main St., Spearfish, 10/25/90, A, 90001649

Spearfish Filling Station, 706 Main St., Spearfish, 5/16/88, A, 88000567

Spearfish Fisheries Center, S of Spearfish off US 14, Spearfish vicinity, 5/19/78, A, g, 78003438

Spearfish Historic Commercial District, 544, 545, 603–645 Main St., 114–136 W. Illinois St., and 701–703 5th St., Spearfish, 6/05/75, C, g, 75001718

St. Onge Schoolhouse, Off SD 24, St. Onge, 5/07/80, A, C, b, 80003727

Sunderland, James, House, 711 Canyon, Spearfish, 10/25/90, C, 90001648

Uhlig, Otto L., House, 230 Jackson, Spearfish, 7/13/89, C, 89000827

Walters, Benjamin F., House, 740 Seventh St., Spearfish, 7/13/89, C, 89000826

Whitney, Mary, House, 704 Eighth St., Spearfish, 10/25/90, C, 90001647

Wolzmuth, John, House, 814 Eighth Ave., Spearfish, 7/13/88, C, 88000562

Woodmen Hall, Jct. of Center and Second Sts., St. Onge, 11/14/91, A, 91001619

Lincoln County

Blood Run Site, Address Restricted, Shindlar, vicinity, 8/29/70, D, NHL, 70000246

Harney Hospital, 305 S. Main St., Lennox, 8/01/84, A, 84003341

Isakson, John, House, 504 E. 3rd St., Canton, 8/01/84, B, C, 84003342

Kruger Dam, NE of Canton, Canton vicinity, 5/01/79, A, 79002404

Old Main, Augustana Academy, Lawler and Second Sts., Canton, 12/02/85, A, C, 85003093

Penmarch Place, Penmarch P., RD 1, Box 142, Sioux Falls, 2/26/87, C, 87000220

Lyman County

Burnt Prairie Site (39LM207) [Big Bend Area MRA], Address Restricted, Lower Brule vicinity, 8/14/86, D, 86002735

Fort Lookout IV, Address Restricted, Oacoma vicinity, 12/31/90, A, D, 90001940

Jiggs Thompson Site (39LM208) [Big Bend Area MRA], Address Restricted, Lower Brule vicinity, 8/14/86, D, 86002734

Langdeau Site, Address Restricted, Lower Brule vicinity, 10/15/66, D, NHL, 66000717

Lower Brule Agency House, 1st St. and Lichtenstien Ave., Oacoma, 11/21/80, A, C, 80003728

Vernon, Edgar, House, Off U.S. 16, Presho, 3/30/78, C, 78002562

Marshall County

First Presbyterian Church of Langford, Jct. of Main and Findley Sts., Langford, 11/01/91, C, a, 91001616

Fort Sisseton, SE of Britton, Britton vicinity, 5/10/73, A, D, 73001745

Palestine Evangelical Lutheran Church, NE of Veblen, Veblen vicinity, 3/05/82, A, C, a, 82003931

McCook County

Archeological Site No. 39MK12 [Prehistoric Rock Art of South Dakota MPS], Address Restricted, Bridgewater vicinity, 8/06/93, D, 93000796

McCook County Courthouse [County Courthouses of South Dakota MPS], Essex Ave. between Nebraska and Main, Salem, 2/10/93, A, C, 92001862

South Dakota Dept. of Transportation Bridge No. 44-028-220 [Historic Bridges in South Dakota MPS], Local rd. over Wolf Cr., Bridgewater vicinity, 12/09/93, C, 93001301

South Dakota Dept. of Transportation Bridge No. 44-212-090 [Historic Bridges in South Dakota MPS], Local rd. over the E. fork of the Vermillion R., Montrose vicinity, 12/09/93, C, 93001302

St. Mary's Catholic Church, Vermont and Idaho Sts., Salem, 6/19/85, C, a, 85001354

McPherson County

Archeological Site No. 39MP3 [Prehistoric Rock Art of South Dakota MPS], Address Restricted, Long Lake vicinity, 8/06/93, D, 93000795

Eureka Lutheran College, 301 Fourth St., Eureka, 10/25/90, A, 90001643

Hoffman, Amos, House, SD 10, Leola, 8/13/86, B, 86001476

McPherson County Courthouse, SD 10, Leola, 11/03/86, A, C, 86003020

Wittmayer, Peter, House-Barn [German-Russian Folk Architecture TR], Address Restricted, Eureka vicinity, 8/13/84, A, C, 84003344

Meade County

Archeological Site No. 39MD20 [Prehistoric Rock Art of South Dakota MPS], Address Restricted, Tilford vicinity, 8/06/93, D, 93000798

Baker, Joseph, House [Rural Butte and Meade Counties MRA], CR 19A, Hereford vicinity, 4/30/86, B, C, 86000942

Bartlett, L. L., House [Rural Butte and Meade Counties MRA], CR 26, Stoneville vicinity, 4/30/86, C, 86000946

Bear Butte, NE of Sturgis, Sturgis vicinity, 6/19/73, A, NHL, 73001746

Bethel Lutheran Church [Rural Butte and Meade Counties MRA], Main and Fifth Sts., Faith, 4/30/86, A, C, a, 86000941

Black Hawk Elementaty School [Rural Butte and Meade Counties MRA], Main and Elm Sts., Black Hawk, 4/30/86, C, 86000939

Erskine School, Sherman St., Sturgis, 8/16/84, A, C, 84003354

Evans, John and Coralin, Ranch [Rural Butte and Meade Counties MRA], CR 4, Piedmont vicinity, 4/30/86, B, C, 86000943

Fort Meade District, E of Sturgis on SD 34, Sturgis vicinity, 5/22/73, A, C, 73001747

Frozenman Stage Station [South Dakota Portion of the Bismarck to Deadwood Trail MPS], Address Restricted, Bison vicinity, 6/18/92, A, D, 92000691

H O Ranch Log House, 3 mi. W of Marcus, Marcus vicinity, 6/21/90, A, 90000954

Johnson, Ole and Carris, Ranch [Rural Butte and Meade Counties MRA], CR 7, Black Hawk vicinity, 4/30/86, B, C, 86000938

Olsen, Elias B., Ranch [Rural Butte and Meade Counties MRA], CR 6, Elm Springs vicinity, 4/30/86, B, C, 86000940

Raskob, Jacob and Elizabeth, Ranch [Rural Butte and Meade Counties MRA], SD 34, Sturgis vicinity, 4/30/86, B, C, 86000945

South Dakota Dept. of Transportation Bridge No. 47-151-389 [Historic Bridges in South Dakota MPS], Local rd. over Bear Butte Cr., Sturgis vicinity, 12/09/93, C, 93001263

South Dakota Dept. of Transportation Bridge No. 47-215-363 [Historic Bridges in South Dakota MPS], SD 34 over the Belle Fourche R., Sturgis vicinity, 12/09/93, C, 93001303

Stevens Ranch [Rural Butte and Meade Counties MRA], CR 4, Piedmont vicinity, 4/30/86, A, C, 86000944

Stomprude Trail Ruts [South Dakota Portion of the Bismarck to Deadwood Trail MPS], Address Restricted, Bison vicinity, 6/18/92, A, D, 92000690

Sturgis Commercial Block, 1000–1028 Main St., Sturgis, 6/20/75, A, C, 75001719

Tallent, Annie, House, 1603 Main St., Sturgis, 5/28/76, B, C, 76001746

Wenke, John G., House, 1340 Junction Ave., Sturgis, 5/28/76, B, C, 76001747

Mellette County

South Dakota Dept. of Transportation Bridge No. 48-244-204 [Historic Bridges in South Dakota

Mellette County—Continued

MPS], Local rd. over the Little White R., White River vicinity, 12/09/93, C, 93001305

Stamford Bridge [Historic Bridges in South Dakota MPS], Local rd. over the White R., Cedar Butte vicinity, 12/09/93, A, C, 93001304

Miner County

South Dakota Dept. of Transportation Bridge No. 49-095-190 [Historic Bridges in South Dakota MPS], Local rd. over Rock Cr., Howard vicinity, 12/09/93, C, 93001306

Wheeler Hotel, 101 N. Main St., Howard, 6/19/85, A, 85001353

Minnehaha County

All Saints Historic District, Roughly Main to 2nd Ave. from 14th to 23rd Sts., and 18th to 21st Sts. to 5th Ave., Sioux Falls, 2/23/84, A, C, 84003349

All Saints School Main Building, 101 W. 17th St., Sioux Falls, 3/14/73, A, a, 73001748

Augustana College Historic Buildings, 29th and S. Summit Sts., Sioux Falls, 3/25/77, A, C, a, 77001250

Berdahl-Rolvaag House, 1009 W. 33rd St., Sioux Falls, 1/23/79, A, B, b, 79002405

Bowen, Marion E., House, 840 W. 9th St., Sioux Falls, 5/28/76, C, b, 76001748

Campbell, Gina Smith, Bathhouse, City Park, Beach Ave. extension, Dell Rapids, 2/13/86, A, 86000246

Carnegie Free Public Library, 235 W. 10th St., Sioux Falls, 3/14/73, A, C, 73001750

Carnegie Public Library, 513 N. Orleans, Dell Rapids, 2/13/86, A, 86000247

Carpenter Hotel, 221 S. Phillips Ave., Sioux Falls, 8/13/86, A, 86001499

Central Fire Station, 100 S. Minnesota Ave., Sioux Falls, 5/27/80, A, C, 80003730

Coughran, Edward, House, 1203 S. 1st Ave., Sioux Falls, 5/28/76, C, 76001749

Daniels, E. J. and Alice, House, 3901 S. Hawthorne, Sioux Falls, 10/19/89, C, b, 89001724

Dell Rapids Historic District, 335–536 E. 4th St., Dell Rapids, 2/23/78, A, C, 78002563

Dell Rapids Water Tower, 10th and Orleans, Dell Rapids, 2/23/84, C, 84003356

Eighth Street Bridge [Historic Bridges in South Dakota MPS], S. Eighth St. over the Big Sioux R., Sioux Falls, 12/09/93, C, 93001308

Federal Building and U.S. Courthouse, 400 S. Phillips Ave., Sioux Falls, 5/02/74, A, C, 74001894

First Congregational Church, 303 S. Dakota Ave., Sioux Falls, 8/18/83, A, C, a, 83003012

Glidden, Josephine Martin, Memorial Chapel, 2121 E. Twelfth St., Sioux Falls, 9/25/87, C, a, 87001732

Grand Lodge and Library of the Ancient Free and Accepted Masons, 415 S. Main Ave., Sioux Falls, 5/28/76, A, C, 76001750

Huseboe, Andrew O., House, 223 S. Prairie Ave., Sioux Falls, 7/13/88, C, 88000569

Illinois Central Passenger Depot, Big Sioux River at 8th St., Sioux Falls, 8/18/83, A, C, 83003013

Kuehn, Andrew, Warehouse, 401 N. Phillips Ave., Sioux Falls, 2/25/82, B, C, 82003933

McKennan Park Historic District, McKennan Park, 2nd and 4th Aves. from 21st to 26th Sts., and 21st St. from Phillips to 7th Aves., Sioux Falls, 6/06/84, A, C, 84003359

Miller, L. D., Funeral Home, 507 S. Main Ave., Sioux Falls, 8/18/83, A, C, 83003014

Mundt, John, Building, 103 N. Main Ave., Hartford, 2/17/81, B, C, 81000575

Old Courthouse and Warehouse Historic District, Roughly bounded by Big Sioux River, 4th and 6th Sts., and Dakota Ave., Sioux Falls, 8/18/83, A, C, g, 83003015

Old Minnehaha County Courthouse, Main Ave. at 6th St., Sioux Falls, 5/10/73, C, 73001749

Orpheum Theatre, 315 N. Phillips Ave., Sioux Falls, 6/23/83, A, C, 83003016

Pettigrew, R. F., and Tate, S. L., Building, 121–123 S. Main Ave., Sioux Falls, 11/06/86, A, C, 86002991

Phillips Block, 333–335 N. Main Ave., Sioux Falls, 1/18/78, A, C, 78002564

Presentation Children's Home, 701 S. Western Ave., Sioux Falls, 2/10/93, A, 92001852

Queen Bee Mill, N. Weber Ave., Falls Park, Sioux Falls, 8/01/84, A, C, 84003362

Renner Lutheran Sanctuary, Off U.S. 77, Renner, 5/07/80, A, C, a, b, 80003729

Rock Island Depot, 210 E. 10th St., Sioux Falls, 2/15/74, A, 74001895

Security Bank Building, 101 S. Main Ave., Sioux Falls, 2/23/84, A, B, C, 84003366

Shriver-Johnson Building, 230 S. Phillips Ave., Sioux Falls, 6/17/82, A, C, 82003934

Sioux Falls Historic District, Bounded by W. 4th and 10th Sts., Spring, Prairie, and Summit Aves., Sioux Falls, 6/05/74, A, B, C, a, 74001896

Sioux Falls Light and Power Hydro Electric Plant, N. Weber Ave. on E bank of Big Sioux R., Sioux Falls, 2/03/93, A, 92001854

Sioux Falls National Bank Building, 100 N. Phillips Ave., Sioux Falls, 3/26/79, A, C, 79002406

South Dakota Dept. of Transportation Bridge No. 50-200-035 [Historic Bridges in South Dakota MPS], Co. rd. over the Big Sioux R., Dell Rapids vicinity, 12/09/93, C, 93001267

South Dakota School for the Deaf, 1800 E. 10th St., Sioux Falls, 6/14/81, A, C, 81000576

South Dakota State Penitentiary Historic Buildings, 1600 North Dr., Sioux Falls, 4/20/78, A, C, 78002565

South Side Fire Station No. 3, 1324 S. Minnesota Ave., Sioux Falls, 2/23/84, A, 84003369

Split Rock Park Bridge [Historic Bridges in South Dakota MPS], Split Rock Park Rd. over Devils Cr. Gulch, Garretson vicinity, 12/09/93, A, 93001309

Summit Avenue Viaduct [Historic Bridges in South Dakota MPS], Summit Ave. over the Chicago and North Western RR tracks, Sioux Falls, 12/09/93, A, 93001307

Thomas, Charles A., House, 620 S. Dakota Ave., Sioux Falls, 10/31/85, C, 85003450

Washington High School, 315 S. Main, Sioux Falls, 2/13/86, A, C, 86000248

Moody County

Few, George, House, 208 1st Ave. E., Flandreau, 8/18/83, A, B, C, 83003017

Flandreau Masonic Temple, 300 E. Second Ave., Flandreau, 10/19/89, A, 89001725

Moody County Courthouse [County Courthouses of South Dakota MPS], Pipestone Ave. between Crescent and Wind Sts., Flandreau, 2/10/93, A, C, 92001863

St. Vincent's Hotel, 100 North Wind, Flandreau, 1/27/83, C, 83003018

Pennington County

Archeological Site No. 39PN376 [Prehistoric Rock Art of South Dakota MPS], Address Restricted, Custer vicinity, 10/25/93, D, 93001072

Byron, Lewis, House, Cemetery Rd., Keystone, 6/17/82, C, 82003935

Church of the Immaculate Conception, 918 5th St., Rapid City, 6/05/75, A, C, a, 75001721

Dinosaur Park, Skyline Dr. SW of Lincoln School, Rapid City, 6/21/90, A, C, 90000956

Emmanuel Episcopal Church, 717 Quincy St., Rapid City, 5/29/75, A, C, a, 75001722

First Congregational Church, 715 Kansas City St., Rapid City, 2/23/84, A, C, a, 84003372

Gambrill Storage Building, 822 Main St., Rapid City, 2/23/84, A, C, 84003379

Harney Peak Hotel, U.S. 16, Hill City, 4/11/77, A, C, 77001252

Harney Peak Lookout Tower, Dam, Pumphouse and Stairway, NE of Custer, Custer vicinity, 3/10/83, A, C, c, 83003019

Harney Peak Tin Mining Company Buildings, U.S. 16, Hill City, 7/21/77, A, b, 77001251

Holmes, Zack, House, 818 St. James St., Rapid City, 6/17/82, B, C, 82003937

Johnson Siding, House and Sawmill, Rimrock Hwy., Rapid City vicinity, 6/17/82, A, B, C, b, 82003938

Keystone School, 3rd St., Keystone, 2/22/81, A, C, 81000577

Keystone Trading Company Store, SD 40, Keystone, 6/17/82, A, C, 82003936

Milwaukee Road Freight House, 306 Seventh St., Rapid City, 1/19/89, A, 88003200

Mount Rushmore National Memorial, 3 mi. W of Keystone off U.S. 16A, Keystone vicinity, 10/15/66, A, C, f, g, NPS, 66000718

Mystic Townsite Historic District, Address Restricted, Mystic vicinity, 8/01/86, A, 86002093

Pennington County—Continued

Pennington County Courthouse, 301 St. Joseph St., Rapid City, 5/28/76, A, C, 76001751

Quinn, Michael, House, 728 Sixth St., Rapid City, 8/05/76, C, 93000782

Rapid City Carnegie Library, 604 Kansas City St., Rapid City, 2/17/81, A, C, 81000578

Rapid City Fruit Company, 320 7th St., Rapid City, 12/09/93, A, 93001340

Rapid City Garage, 827-829 Main St., Rapid City, 8/01/84, A, 84003381

Rapid City Historic Commercial District, Bounded by both sides of Main, St. Joseph, 7th, and 6th Sts., Rapid City, 10/01/74, A, C, 74001897

Rapid City Historical Museum, 515 West Blvd., Rapid City, 12/20/88, C, 88002837

Rapid City West Boulevard Historic District, Bordered by Kansas City, Fairview, 11th, 7th, and 8th Sts., Rapid City, 12/31/74, B, C, 74001898

Site No. 39 PN 108 [Rock Art in the Southern Black Hills TR], Address Restricted, City Restricted, 5/20/82, C, D, 82004775

Site No. 39 PN 438 [Rock Art in the Southern Black Hills TR], Address Restricted, City Restricted, 5/20/82, C, D, 82004776

Site No. 39 PN 439 [Rock Art in the Southern Black Hills TR], Address Restricted, City Restricted, 5/20/82, C, D, 82004777

Site No. 39 PN 57 [Rock Art in the Southern Black Hills TR], Address Restricted, City Restricted, 5/20/82, C, D, 82004778

Von Woehrmann Building, U.S. 16, Hill City, 4/13/77, B, C, 77001253

Perkins County

Beckon, Donald, Ranch [Harding and Perkins Counties MRA], 6 mi. SE of Zeona, Zeona vicinity, 4/10/87, A, C, 87000551

Bethany United Methodist Church [Harding and Perkins Counties MRA], 9.5 mi. W of Lodgepole, Lodgepole vicinity, 4/10/87, C, a, 87000559

Carr No. 60 School [Harding and Perkins Counties MRA], 12 mi. SE of Lodgepole, Lodgepole vicinity, 4/10/87, C, 87000560

Carr, Anna, Homestead, Off SD 20, Bison, 1/20/78, B, C, 78002566

Duck Creek Lutheran Church and Cemetery [Harding and Perkins Counties MRA], 7 mi. SW of Lodgepole along Duck Creek, Lodgepole vicinity, 4/10/87, A, C, a, 87000561

Foster Ranch House [Harding and Perkins Counties MRA], 4 mi. E of SD 79, Chance vicinity, 4/10/87, C, 87000557

Golden Rule Department Store, 201–203 Main St., Lemmon, 12/12/76, A, C, 76001752

Harriman, L. F., House, 111 2nd Ave., W, Lemmon, 12/12/76, C, 76001753

Immanuel Lutheran Church [Harding and Perkins Counties MRA], 15 mi. N of Mud Butte and

US 212 on gravel CR, Zeona vicinity, 4/10/87, A, C, a, 87000555

Lemmon Petrified Park, Off U.S. 12, Lemmon, 11/21/77, A, B, g, 77001254

Lemmon, G. E., House, 507 3rd Ave., W, Lemmon, 12/12/76, B, 76001754

Rockford No. 40 School [Harding and Perkins Counties MRA], 15 mi. NE of Bison, Bison vicinity, 4/10/87, A, 87000549

Sorum Cooperative Store [Harding and Perkins Counties MRA], Main St., Sorum, 4/10/87, A, C, 87000556

Sorum Hotel [Harding and Perkins Counties MRA], Main St., Sorum, 4/10/87, A, C, a, 87000552

Spring Creek School [Harding and Perkins Counties MRA], 1 mi. E of Zeona, Zeona vicinity, 4/10/87, A, C, 87000554

Veal, Thomas J., Ranch [Harding and Perkins Counties MRA], 7 mi. SE of jct. of SD 20 and SD 73, Chance vicinity, 4/10/87, A, C, 87000558

Potter County

Archeological Site No. 39PO205 [Prehistoric Rock Art of South Dakota MPS], Address Restricted, Gettysburg vicinity, 8/06/93, D, 93000799

Archeological Site No. 39PO63 [Prehistoric Rock Art of South Dakota MPS], Address Restricted, Gettysburg vicinity, 8/06/93, D, 93000800

Holland, George, House, 314 N. Exene St., Gettysburg, 10/19/89, C, 89001721

North Canton School—District No. 12, Off SD 47, Seneca, 5/08/86, A, 86001025

St. Bernard's Catholic Church, SD 20, Hoven, 5/07/80, A, C, a, 80003731

Roberts County

New Effington Hospital, Oddin Ave., New Effington, 7/13/89, A, 89000829

Roberts County Courthouse, SD 10, Sisseton, 12/12/76, A, C, 76001755

Sanborn County

Mathews, G. A., House, 423 Eighth St., Brookings, 11/26/86, B, C, 86002989

Site 39SB15 [James River Basin Woodland Sites TR], Address Restricted, Mitchell vicinity, 2/01/84, D, 84003384

Site 39SB18 [James River Basin Woodland Sites TR], Address Restricted, Forestburg vicinity, 2/01/84, D, 84003397

Site 39SB31 [James River Basin Woodland Sites TR], Address Restricted, Forestburg vicinity, 2/01/84, D, 84003399

South Dakota Dept. of Transportation Bridge No. 56-090-096 [Historic Bridges in South Dakota

MPS], Local rd. over Sand Cr., Forestburg vicinity, 12/09/93, A, C, 93001310

South Dakota Dept. of Transportation Bridge No. 56-117-123 [Historic Bridges in South Dakota MPS], Local rd. over the James R., Forestburg vicinity, 12/09/93, C, 93001311

South Dakota Dept. of Transportation Bridge No. 56-174-090 [Historic Bridges in South Dakota MPS], Local rd. over Redstone Cr., Artesian vicinity, 12/09/93, A, C, 93001312

Shannon County

Wounded Knee Battlefield, 11 mi. W of Batesland, Pine Ridge Indian Reservation, Batesland vicinity, 10/15/66, A, NHL, 66000719

Spink County

Ashton Methodist Church, NE corner of 2nd Ave. and 2nd St., Ashton, 6/17/82, A, C, a, 82003939

Chicago and Northwestern Depot, U.S. 212, Redfield, 11/21/80, A, C, 80003732

First Congregational Church, Oak and 2nd Sts., Turton, 9/14/79, A, C, a, 79002407

Hall Bridge [Historic Bridges in South Dakota MPS], Local rd. over Snake Cr., Ashton vicinity, 12/09/93, C, 93001317

Harlow Farmstead, SW of Turton, Frankfort vicinity, 2/26/82, B, C, g, 82003940

Markham Farmstead, Jct. of Co. Rts. 4 and 7, Conde vicinity, 9/13/90, A, 90000958

Old Spink Colony [Historic Hutterite Colonies TR], On James River, Frankfort vicinity, 6/30/82, A, C, a, 82003941

Redfield Carnegie Library, 5 E. 5th Ave., Redfield, 2/17/78, C, 78002568

Redfield Light Plant and Fire Station, 614 1st St., E, Redfield, 3/21/78, C, 78002569

Site 39SP12 [James River Basin Woodland Sites TR], Address Restricted, Ashton vicinity, 2/01/84, D, 84003403

Site 39SP19 [James River Basin Woodland Sites TR], Address Restricted, Spink Colony vicinity, 2/01/84, D, 84003405

Site 39SP2 [James River Basin Woodland Sites TR], Address Restricted, Frankfort vicinity, 2/01/84, D, 84003408

Site 39SP37 [James River Basin Woodland Sites TR], Address Restricted, Crandon vicinity, 2/01/84, D, 84003411

Site 39SP46 [James River Basin Woodland Sites TR], Address Restricted, Crandon vicinity, 2/01/84, D, 84003413

South Dakota Dept. of Transportation Bridge No. 58-010-376 [Historic Bridges in South Dakota MPS], Local rd. over Wolf Cr., Tulare vicinity, 12/09/93, 93001313

South Dakota Dept. of Transportation Bridge No. 58-021-400 [Historic Bridges in South Dakota MPS], Local rd. over Turtle Cr., Tulare vicinity, 12/09/93, A, C, 93001314

Spink County—Continued

South Dakota Dept. of Transportation Bridge No. 58-025-370 [Historic Bridges in South Dakota MPS], Local rd. over Turtle Cr., Tulare vicinity, 12/09/93, A, C, 93001315

South Dakota Dept. of Transportation Bridge No. 58-062-270 [Historic Bridges in South Dakota MPS], Local rd. over Turtle Cr., Redfield vicinity, 12/09/93, C, 93001316

South Dakota Dept. of Transportation Bridge No. 58-120-231 [Historic Bridges in South Dakota MPS], Local rd. over the James R., Redfield vicinity, 12/09/93, A, C, 93001318

South Dakota Dept. of Transportation Bridge No. 58-140-224 [Historic Bridges in South Dakota MPS], Local rd. over the James R., Redfield vicinity, 12/09/93, C, 93001319

South Dakota Dept. of Transportation Bridge No. 58-218-360 [Historic Bridges in South Dakota MPS], Local rd. over the James R., Frankfort vicinity, 12/09/93, A, C, 93001320

Stanley County

Antelope Creek Site (39ST55) [Big Bend Area MRA], Address Restricted, Fort Pierre vicinity, 8/14/86, D, 86002737

Bloody Hand Site (39ST230) [Big Bend Area MRA], Address Restricted, Fort Pierre vicinity, 8/14/86, D, 86002736

Carr, Jefferson Davis, House, 236 W. 2nd Ave., Fort Pierre, 3/05/82, B, C, 82003942

Fort Pierre Chouteau Site, N of Fort Pierre, Fort Pierre vicinity, 4/03/76, A, B, D, NHL, 76001756

Ft. Pierre II (39ST217) [19th Century South Dakota Trading Posts MPS], Address Restricted, Ft. Pierre vicinity, 8/15/88, A, D, 88000732

La Verendrye Site, Off U.S. 83, Fort Pierre, 8/07/74, A, B, NHL, 74001899

Lower Antelope Creek Site, Address Restricted, Fort Pierre vicinity, 9/15/82, D, 82003943

Old Fort Pierre School, 2nd Ave. and 2nd St., Fort Pierre, 11/25/77, A, 77001255

Stockgrowers Bank Building, Deadwood and Main Sts., Fort Pierre, 11/11/77, A, C, 77001256

Sumner, Gaylord, House, 2nd and Wandel Sts., Fort Pierre, 12/21/77, B, C, 77001257

United Church of Christ, Congregational, 2nd and Main St., Fort Pierre, 12/21/77, A, C, a, 77001258

Sully County

Goosen, Jacob D., Barn, Roughly 0.6 mi. E of Onida, Onida vicinity, 2/03/93, C, 92001853

Snyder, L. E., House, Jct. of Cedar and Sixth Sts., Onida, 8/05/93, C, 93000784

Todd County

Rosebud Agency, Main St. and Legion Ave., Rosebud, 5/07/80, A, 80003733

Rosebud Hotel, 7 Circle Dr., Rosebud, 5/07/80, A, 80003734

Spotted Tail Gravesite, N of Rosebud, Rosebud vicinity, 5/07/80, B, c, 80003735

St. Francis Mission, Rosebud Indian Reservation, St. Francis, 6/20/75, A, C, a, d, 75001723

Tripp County

Barnum, E. G., House, 205 Van Buren, Winner, 1/27/83, A, C, 83003020

Lewis Bridge [Highway Bridges in Nebraska MPS], Co. Rd. over the Keya Paha R., 13.6 mi. NE of Springview, Wewela, vicinity, 6/29/92, C, 92000774

South Dakota Dept. of Transportation Bridge No. 62-220-512 [Historic Bridges in South Dakota MPS], Local rd. over the Keya Paha R., Wewela vicinity, 12/09/93, C, 93001321

Turner County

Archeological Site 39TU5 [Petroforms of South Dakota TR], Address Restricted, Freeman vicinity, 2/23/84, D, 84003417

Brough-Martinson House, Off SD 19, Hurley, 3/30/78, A, C, 78002570

Farrar House, Off SD 19, Hurley, 3/21/78, C, 78002571

Graves, Dr. Harry S., House, Center Ave. and Monroe St., Hurley, 3/21/78, B, C, 78002572

Newhall, Chandler Gray and Mary Abbie, House and Homestead Shack, 5 mi. W and 4 1/4 mi. S of Parker, Parker vicinity, 6/09/92, A, C, 92000682

Thielman-Stoddard House, 132 1st St., Parker, 8/03/79, B, C, 79003691

Thomson, James S., House, 1121 Washington St., Centerville, 8/18/83, C, 83003021

Weins, Jacob, House-Barn [German-Russian Folk Architecture TR], Address Restricted, Marion vicinity, 8/13/84, A, C, 84003419

Union County

Baker House, Off SD 48, Alcester vicinity, 8/07/79, A, C, 79002409

Bulow, Governor William J., House, 207 W. Hemlock St., Beresford, 5/08/86, B, g, 86001024

Chicago and Northwestern Railroad Depot, 1 Depot Sq., Beresford, 1/31/85, A, 85000262

Larson, John August, Home, 407 W. Hemlock, Beresford, 10/31/85, C, 85003451

Murtha, Charles, House and Brick Yard, W. Main St., Elk Point, 2/01/82, A, C, b, 82003945

Reedy, J. W., House, 304 N. 2nd, Beresford, 12/13/84, B, 84000605

South Dakota Dept. of Transportation Bridge No. 64-061-199 [Historic Bridges in South Dakota MPS], Local rd. over Brule Cr., Elk Point vicinity, 12/09/93, A, C, 93001322

St. Peter's Catholic Church, 400 Main St., Jerrerson, 7/19/89, A, C, a, 89000833

Walworth County

Brown Palace Hotel, 301 Main St., Mobridge, 1/27/83, A, 83003022

Brown, A. H., Public Library, N. Main St., Mobridge, 12/22/78, A, B, C, g, 78002573

Brown—Evans House, 405 First Ave., W., Mobridge, 6/21/90, C, 90000960

Gravel Pit Site (39WW203), Address Restricted, Mobridge vicinity, 4/03/86, D, 86000834

Mobridge Auditorium, 212 Main St., Mobridge, 5/23/86, C, g, 86001189

Mobridge Masonic Temple, 6th and Main Sts., Mobridge, 3/25/77, C, 77001259

Moser, Wilhelm, House-Barn [German-Russian Folk Architecture TR], Address Restricted, Java vicinity, 11/28/84, A, C, 84001299

Ochszbner, Jacob, Sr., House [German-Russian Folk Architecture TR], Address Restricted, Java vicinity, 8/13/84, A, C, 84003421

Selby Opera House, 3409 Main St., Selby, 9/25/87, A, 87001730

Yankton County

Banton, Dr. B. M., House, 517 Locust St., Yankton, 10/08/87, B, C, 87001729

Bishop Marty Rectory, 1101 W. 5th St., Yankton, 12/27/74, B, C, a, 74001900

Brockmueller Barn [Northern and Central Townships of Yankton MRA], S of SD 46, Volin, 4/16/80, A, C, 80003757

Bruce-Donaldson House, 313 Pine St., Yankton, 3/05/82, A, C, 82003946

Chicago, Milwaukee and St. Paul Depot, 8th and Douglas Sts., Yankton, 3/05/82, A, C, 82003947

DeJong House [Northern and Central Townships of Yankton MRA], In Utica, Utica, 4/16/80, C, 80003750

Doyle, Harold A. (H. A.), House, 712 W. Third St., Yankton, 10/25/90, C, 90001645

ES Volin Farmstead [Northern and Central Townships of Yankton MRA], SE of Volin, Volin, 4/16/80, A, 80003758

Ellerman, Arthur C., House, 708 W. 5th St., Yankton, 3/05/82, C, 82003948

Excelsior Flour Mill, 2nd and Capital, Yankton, 11/07/76, A, 76001757

Fantle, William J., House, 1201 Douglas, Yankton, 10/10/89, C, 89001588

Gordon House [Northern and Central Townships of Yankton MRA], N of SD 46, Irene, 4/16/80, C, 80003736

Gorsett Farmstead [Northern and Central Townships of Yankton MRA], N of Volin, Volin, 4/16/80, C, 80003759

Gunderson, Endre B., Farmstead [Northern and Central Townships of Yankton MRA], N of Yankton, Yankton, 4/16/80, C, 80003769

Yankton County—Continued

Gurney, Charles, Hotel, 3rd and Capital Sts., Yankton, 8/03/79, A, C, 79002410

Gustad, Bernt, House [Northern and Central Townships of Yankton MRA], NW of Volin, Volin, 4/16/80, C, 80003760

Henjna Farmstead [Northern and Central Townships of Yankton MRA], N of SD 50, Yankton, 4/16/80, C, 80003770

Hoxeng Farmstead [Northern and Central Townships of Yankton MRA], NW of Volin, Volin, 4/16/80, C, 80003761

Human Services Center [Northern and Central Townships of Yankton MRA], Off US 81, Yankton, 4/16/80, A, C, 80003771

Ingebrigtsen-Hinseth Farmstead [Northern and Central Townships of Yankton MRA], W of Irene, Irene vicinity, 4/16/80, A, C, 80003737

Jencks Farmstead [Northern and Central Townships of Yankton MRA], N of Yankton, off US 81, Yankton, 4/16/80, C, 80003772

Kietzman Farmstead [Northern and Central Townships of Yankton MRA], NE of Utica, Yankton, 4/16/80, C, 80003773

Kremer House [Northern and Central Townships of Yankton MRA], In Lesterville, Lesterville, 4/16/80, C, 80003738

Larson-Simonson House [Northern and Central Townships of Yankton MRA], In Mission Hill, Mission Hill, 4/16/80, C, 80003742

Lasele, Mathias, House [Northern and Central Townships of Yankton MRA], E of Lesterville, Lesterville, 4/16/80, A, C, 80003739

Machacek Homestead [Northern and Central Townships of Yankton MRA], SW of Utica, Utica, 4/16/80, C, 80003751

Marindahl Post Office [Northern and Central Townships of Yankton MRA], NW of Volin, Volin, 4/16/80, A, 80003762

Marindahl Township Hall [Northern and Central Townships of Yankton MRA], SW of Irene, Volin, 4/16/80, A, 80003763

Martin's Evangelical Church [Northern and Central Townships of Yankton MRA], E of Lesterville, Utica, 4/16/80, C, a, 80003752

McGregor, Walker, Farmstead [Northern and Central Townships of Yankton MRA], NW of Volin, Yankton, 4/16/80, C, 80003774

Meridian Bridge [Highway Bridges in Nebraska MPS], US 81 over the Missouri R., just S of Yankton, SD, Yankton, vicinity, 6/17/93, C, 93000537

Merk, Nels, Farmstead [Northern and Central Townships of Yankton MRA], SE of Center Point, Yankton, 4/16/80, C, g, 80003775

Merkwan, Mathias, Rubblestone Barn [Czech Folk Architecture in Southeastern South Dakota MRA], E of Tabor, Tabor vicinity, 7/06/87, A, C, 87001055

Mueller Homestead [Northern and Central Townships of Yankton MRA], E of Lesterville, Utica, 4/16/80, C, 80003753

Ohlman-Shannon House, 205 Green St., Yankton, 5/28/76, B, C, 76001758

Old Catholic Church [Northern and Central Townships of Yankton MRA], N of SD 50, Yankton, 4/16/80, A, C, a, 80003776

Olson, Lewis, Log House [Northern and Central Townships of Yankton MRA], W of Mission Hill, Mission Hill, 4/16/80, C, 80003743

Pechan, Frantisek, Log House [Czech Folk Architecture in Southeastern South Dakota MRA], N of SD 50 and SD 52, Tabor vicinity, 7/06/87, A, C, 87001054

Pennington, Governor John L., House, 410 E. Third St., Yankton, 2/08/88, B, 88000025

Peterson, Mathias, Homestead [Northern and Central Townships of Yankton MRA], SW of Volin, Mission Hill, 4/16/80, C, 80003744

Ripple House [Northern and Central Townships of Yankton MRA], S of Lesterville, Lesterville, 4/16/80, C, 80003740

Schaffer Farmstead [Northern and Central Townships of Yankton MRA], N of Yankton, off US 81, Yankton, 4/16/80, A, C, 80003777

Schnauber, Fred, House, 717 Walnut St., Yankton, 1/31/85, C, 85000185

Simonson Farmstead [Northern and Central Townships of Yankton MRA], SW of Volin, Mission Hill, 4/16/80, C, e, 80003745

Sloan, John, Homestead [Northern and Central Townships of Yankton MRA], SW of Irene, Volin, 4/16/80, C, 80003764

Smith, Jessie, Farmstead [Northern and Central Townships of Yankton MRA], SW of Volin, Volin, 4/16/80, C, 80003765

St. Agnes Church [Northern and Central Townships of Yankton MRA], E of Lesterville, Utica, 4/16/80, C, a, 80003754

Stribral Homestead and Farmstead [Northern and Central Townships of Yankton MRA], S of Lesterville, Tabor vicinity, 4/16/80, A, C, 80003749

Svatos, Frank, Rubblestone Barn [Czech Folk Architecture in Southeastern South Dakota MRA], SE of Tabor off SD 50, Tabor vicinity, 7/06/87, A, C, 87001056

Trierweiler, Dr. John, House, 301 Spruce St., Yankton, 5/07/80, C, 80003778

United Church of Christ [Northern and Central Townships of Yankton MRA], In Mission Hill, Mission Hill, 4/16/80, C, a, 80003746

Utica Depot [Northern and Central Townships of Yankton MRA], In Utica, Utica, 4/16/80, A, 80003755

Utica Fire and City Hall [Northern and Central Townships of Yankton MRA], In Utica, Utica, 4/16/80, A, C, 80004591

Utica Public School [Northern and Central Townships of Yankton MRA], In Utica, Utica, 4/16/80, A, C, 80003756

Van Osdel House [Northern and Central Townships of Yankton MRA], In Mission Hill, Mission Hill, 4/16/80, B, C, 80003747

Vangen Church [Northern and Central Townships of Yankton MRA], NE Mission Hill, Mission Hill, 4/16/80, C, a, 80003748

Volin School [Northern and Central Townships of Yankton MRA], In Volin, Volin, 4/16/80, C, 80003766

Volin Town Hall [Northern and Central Townships of Yankton MRA], In Volin, Volin, 4/16/80, A, C, 80003767

Volin, Louis, House [Northern and Central Townships of Yankton MRA], NW of Volin, Volin, 4/16/80, A, B, 80003768

Walloch Farmstead [Northern and Central Townships of Yankton MRA], S of Lesterville, Lesterville, 4/16/80, C, g, 80003741

Walshtown School [Northern and Central Townships of Yankton MRA], S of SD 46, Yankton, 4/16/80, A, 80003779

Western Portland Cement Plant, W of Yankton, Yankton vicinity, 9/19/79, A, 79002411

Yankton Carnegie Library, 4th and Capitol Sts., Yankton, 8/07/79, A, B, C, 79002412

Yankton College Conservatory, Yankton College campus, Yankton, 2/24/75, A, C, 75001724

Yankton College Historic District, 12th and Douglas Sts., Yankton, 3/22/82, A, C, 82003949

Yankton County Courthouse, 3rd St. and Broadway, Yankton, 9/03/76, A, C, 76001759

Yankton Historic Commercial District, Roughly bounded by 2nd, 4th, Pine and Broadway Sts., Yankton, 6/23/82, A, C, 82003950

Yankton Historic District, Bounded by Marne Creek and 4th St., and includes both sides of Cedar, Yankton, 2/13/75, B, C, 75001725

Zion Lutheran Church [Northern and Central Townships of Yankton MRA], NW of Volin, Volin, 4/16/80, A, C, a, d, 80004527

Ziebach County

Ziebach County Courthouse [County Courthouses of South Dakota MPS], Main St. between Second and Third Sts., Dupree, 2/10/93, A, C, 92001864

TENNESSEE

Anderson County

Arnwine Cabin, TN 61, Norris, 3/16/76, C, b, 76001760

Bear Creek Road Checking Station [Oak Ridge MPS], Jct. of S. Illinois Ave. and Bear Creek Rd., Oak Ridge, 5/06/92, A, g, 92000411

Bethel Valley Road Checking Station [Oak Ridge MPS], Jct. of Bethel Valley and Scarboro Rds., Oak Ridge, 5/06/92, A, g, 92000410

Brannon, Luther, House [Oak Ridge MPS], 151 Oak Ridge Tpk., Oak Ridge, 9/05/91, A, B, g, 91001108

Edwards-Fowler House, 3.5 mi. S of Lake City on Dutch Valley Rd., Lake City vicinity, 5/29/75, C, 75001726

Freels Cabin [Oak Ridge MPS], Freels Bend Rd., Oak Ridge, 5/06/92, A, C, g, 92000407

Jones, J. B., House [Oak Ridge MPS], Old Edgemoor Rd. between Bethel Valley Rd. and Melton Hill Lake, Oak Ridge, 9/05/91, A, 91001107

Norris District, Town of Norris on U.S. 441, Norris, 7/10/75, A, B, g, 75001727

Oak Ridge Historic District [Oak Ridge MPS], Roughly bounded by East Dr., W. Outer Dr., Louisiana and Tennessee Aves., Oak Ridge, 9/05/91, A, C, g, 91001109

Oliver Springs Banking Company, 110 E. Tri County Blvd., Oliver Springs, 4/14/92, A, C, 92000357

Woodland—Scarboro Historic District [Oak Ridge MPS], Roughly bounded by Rutgers Ave., Lafayette Dr., Benedict, Wilburforce and Illinois Aves., Oak Ridge, 9/05/91, A, C, g, 91001106

Bedford County

Bedford County Jail, N. Spring and Jackson Sts., Shelbyville, 4/01/75, A, C, 75001728

Bell Buckle Historic District, Irregular pattern bounded roughly by Webb Rd., Abernathy, Maple, Cumberland, and Church Sts., Bell Buckle, 1/20/76, A, B, C, 76001762

Bivvins House, Off U.S. 41, Shelbyville, 12/06/79, A, C, 79002413

Clark, Henry A., House, Fairfield Rd., Wartrace vicinity, 8/30/85, C, 85001899

Cooper, Gov. Prentice, House, 413 E. Lane St., Shelbyville, 6/05/75, B, C, 75001729

Eakin, Spencer, Farm, 201 Nashville Dirt Rd., Shelbyville vicinity, 6/24/93, A, C, 93000564

East Shelbyville Historic District, Bounded roughly by N. Brittian, Louisville & Nashville railroad tracks, Lane, Evans, Sandusky and Madison Sts., Shelbyville, 4/23/90, C, 90000594

Evans, Winston, House, 306 E. Franklin St., Shelbyville, 11/27/89, C, 89002026

Farrar Homeplace, 170 Ike Farrar Rd., Shelbyville vicinity, 11/07/90, C, 90001657

First Presbyterian Church, 600 N. Brittain St., Shelbyville, 7/17/80, C, a, 80003780

Frierson-Coble House, 404 N. Jefferson St., Shelbyville, 4/12/82, B, C, 82003951

Gilliland, James, House, 803 Lipscomb St., Shelbyville, 5/12/75, B, 75001730

Grassland Farm, 8 mi. SW of Shelbyville on Snell Rd., Shelbyville vicinity, 3/04/75, B, C, 75001731

Heidt Tavern—Singleton House, 115 Dr. Jackson Rd., Wartrace vicinity, 6/24/91, A, C, 91000823

Landis, Absalom Lowe, House, Thompson's Creek Rd., Normandy vicinity, 6/25/87, C, 87001034

Martin House, 7 mi. NE of Wartrace off TN 64, Wartrace vicinity, 4/14/72, B, C, d, 72001227

Normandy Historic District, Roughly bounded by Maple and Poplar Sts., Tullahoma Rd., College St., and Old Manchester Rd., Normandy, 11/07/85, A, C, 85002786

Palmetto Farm, TN 64, Palmetto vicinity, 3/28/85, B, C, 85000675

Shelbyville Courthouse Square Historic District, Public Square (Main, Spring, Depot, and Holland Sts.), Shelbyville, 10/27/82, C, 82001725

Shelbyville Hydroelectric Station [Pre-TVA Hydroelectric Development in Tennessee, 1901-1933 MPS], TN 231 at Duck River, Shelbyville, 2/09/90, A, 89002354

Shelbyville Railroad Station, Depot St., Shelbyville, 3/24/88, A, C, 88000265

Sims, John Green, House, Normandy Rd., Wartrace vicinity, 11/05/87, C, 87001937

Valley Home, Potts Rd., W of Wartrace, Wartrace vicinity, 11/13/89, C, 89001956

Walking Horse Hotel, Spring St., Wartrace, 7/19/84, A, C, 84003262

Wartrace Historic District, Roughly Spring St. from Coffey to Main Sts., Vine St. from Broad to McKinley Sts. and Knob Cr. Rd. from Main to McKinley, Wartrace, 7/31/91, A, C, 91000914

Benton County

Mount Zion Church, 5.5 mi. SE of Big Sandy, Big Sandy vicinity, 10/02/73, A, C, a, 73001752

Thompson, William, House, S of Camden, off TN 69, Camden vicinity, 5/06/76, C, 76001763

US Post Office, 81 N. Forest St., Camden, 9/23/88, C, 88001577

Bledsoe County

Bridgman, John, House, 106 E. Spring St., Pikeville, 6/24/93, B, C, 93000567

Lincoln School, Old TN 28 near Rockford Rd., Pikeville, 7/15/93, A, C, 93000648

Blount County

Alcoa South Plant Office [Blount County MPS], Hall Rd., Alcoa, 8/18/89, A, g, 89001070

Alcoa West Plant Office [Blount County MPS], Lodge St., Alcoa, 7/25/89, A, 89000863

Alexander, John, House [Blount County MPS], 714 Hillside Ave., Maryville, 7/25/89, B, 89000864

Alumni Gym [Blount County MPS], Maryville College campus, Maryville, 7/25/89, A, 89000865

Anderson Hall, Maryville College campus, Maryville, 2/20/75, A, C, 75001732

Bartlett, Peter, House [Blount County MPS], 315 High St., Maryville, 7/25/89, C, 89000866

Bethlehem Methodist Church [Blount County MPS], Bethlehem Rd., 0.5 mi. S of Ellejoy Rd., Wildwood vicinity, 7/25/89, C, a, 89000867

Brick Mill Site [Blount County MPS], Brick Mill Rd., Maryville vicinity, 7/25/89, A, 89000868

Brickey, Peter, House [Blount County MPS], Wears Valley Rd., 0.1 mi. W of Bonner Hollow Rd., Townsend vicinity, 7/25/89, C, 89000869

Cades Cove Historic District, 10 mi. SW of Townsend in Great Smoky Mountains National Park, Townsend, 7/13/77, A, C, D, NPS, 77000111

Calderwood Dam [Blount County MPS], Tennessee River at end of Calderwood Rd., Calderwood vicinity, 8/21/89, A, C, 89001069

Calderwood Dam (Boundary Increase) [Pre-TVA Hydroelectric Development in Tennessee, 1901-1933, MPS], Tennessee R. at end of Calderwood Rd., Calderwood vicinity, 7/03/90, A, C, 90001016

Clark, Langston, Barn [Blount County MPS], Sixmile Rd., 0.4 mi. E of Knob Creek Rd., Maryville vicinity, 7/25/89, C, 89000870

Clover Hill Mill [Blount County MPS], Jct. of Mill Rd. and Clover Hill Rd., Maryville vicinity, 7/25/89, A, 89000871

Cloyd's Creek Presbyterian Church [Blount County MPS], Jct. of Buzzard's Roost Rd. and Kirk Rd., Friendsville vicinity, 7/25/89, C, a, 89000873

Cochrane, Mary, Barn [Blount County MPS], Binfield Rd., 0.2 mi. N of Clover Hill Rd., Maryville vicinity, 7/25/89, C, 89000872

Craig, John J., Quarry Historic District [Blount County MPS], Marmor Rd., 0.5 mi. S of Miser Station Rd., Friendsville vicinity, 7/25/89, A, 89000874

Crawford, Gideon, House [Blount County MPS], Maryville College campus, Maryville, 7/25/89, B, C, 89000875

Davis, James R., House [Blount County MPS], Jct. of River Rd. and Davis Ford Rd., Walland vicinity, 7/25/89, C, 89000876

Federal Building [Blount County MPS], 201 E. Broadway, Maryville, 8/31/89, A, C, 89001217

Fisher, A. J., House [Blount County MPS], Old Walland Hwy., Walland, 7/25/89, A, 89000877

Blount County—Continued

Frazier, Samuel, House [Blount County MPS], Jct. of Marble Hill Rd. and Big Springs Rd., Friendsville vicinity, 7/25/89, C, 89000878

Friends Church [Blount County MPS], 314 W. Broadway, Maryville, 7/25/89, A, a, 89000879

George, Samuel, House, NE of Louisville on Topside Rd., Louisville vicinity, 1/27/82, C, 82003952

Gillespie, James, House [Blount County MPS], Lowes Ferry Rd., 1 mi. N of Louisville, Louisville vicinity, 7/25/89, C, 89000880

Hackney, John, House [Blount County MPS], Front and Main Sts., Friendsville, 7/25/89, B, C, 89000881

Hackney, John, Mill Site [Blount County MPS], Main St. near Front St., Friendsville, 7/25/89, A, 89000882

Hamil, Alexander, Hosue [Blount County MPS], Morganton Rd., 0.5 mi. E of Clover Hill Rd., Maryville vicinity, 7/25/89, C, 89000883

Happy Valley School [Blount County MPS], Happy Valley Rd., Maryville vicinity, 7/25/89, A, 89000884

Harper Memorial Library [Blount County MPS], 300 E. Church St., Maryville, 7/25/89, C, 89000885

Henderson, William, House [Blount County MPS], Louisville Rd., 0.75 mi. S of Lowes Ferry Rd., Louisville vicinity, 7/25/89, C, 89000886

Henry House, SE of Binfield on Henry Lane, Binfield vicinity, 11/01/74, C, 74001901

Hitch, John, House [Blount County MPS], Lee Lambert Rd., 0.5 mi. S of Old Walland Hwy., Maryville vicinity, 4/16/93, C, 89000924

Hood, Pete, House [Blount County MPS], 827 W. Broadway, Maryville, 7/25/89, C, 89000888

Indiana Avenue Historic District [Blount County MPS], Roughly bounded by Goddard St., Court St., Indiana Ave., and Cates St., Maryville, 8/21/89, C, 89001071

Jones, David, House, 720 Tuckaleechee Pike, Maryville, 8/26/82, C, a, 82004840

Jones, David, House [Blount County MPS], 404 High St., Maryville, 7/25/89, B, C, 89000889

Kerr, Macklin, House [Blount County MPS], Big Gully Rd., 0.3 mi. N of Kyker Rd., Maryville vicinity, 7/25/89, C, 89000891

Kizer, Hezekiah, House [Blount County MPS], 0.5 mi. S of jct. of Marble Hill Rd. and Dunlap Hollow Rd., Maryville vicinity, 7/25/89, C, 89000892

Louisville Historic District, Between railroad tracks and Tennessee River, Louisville, 12/23/74, A, B, C, 74001902

Martin, James, House [Blount County MPS], Martin Rd., 1 mi. E of E. Millers Cove Rd., Walland vicinity, 7/25/89, C, 89000893

Martin, John, Mill [Blount County MPS], Mill Rd., 0.3 mi. S of W. Millers Cove Rd., Walland vicinity, 7/25/89, A, 89000894

Martin, Warner, House [Blount County MPS], Central Point Rd. at Old Nails Creek, Rockford vicinity, 7/25/89, C, 89000895

Maryville College Historic District, Washington St., Maryville, 9/09/82, A, C, 82003953

McCampbell, James, Barn [Blount County MPS], Old Cades Cove Rd., 0.1 mi. S of Dry Valley Rd., Townsend vicinity, 7/25/89, C, 89000896

McCampbell, Minnis, Barn [Blount County MPS], Old Cades Cove Rd., 0.1 mi. S of Dry Valley Rd., Townsend vicinity, 7/25/89, C, 89000897

McConnell, John, House [Blount County MPS], McConnell Rd., 0.5 mi. W of Maple Lane Rd., Maryville vicinity, 7/25/89, C, 89000898

McCullock, Thomas, House [Blount County MPS], Jct. of Martin Mill Pike and TN 33, Rockford vicinity, 7/25/89, C, 89000899

McNutt—Howard House [Blount County MPS], 825 W. Broadway Ave., Maryville, 7/25/89, C, 89000900

McNutt—McReynolds House [Blount County MPS], 803 W. Broadway Ave., Maryville, 7/25/89, C, 89000901

Miser Station Store [Blount County MPS], Jct. of Union Grove Rd. and Chestnut Hill Rd., Friendsville vicinity, 7/25/89, A, 89000902

Morningside [Blount County MPS], Maryville College campus, Maryville, 7/25/89, C, 89000904

Patton, Samuel A., Building [Blount County MPS], 114 E. Broadway Ave., Maryville, 7/25/89, C, 89000905

Peery Mill Site [Blount County MPS], Old Walland Hwy., 0.1 mi. N of Cold Springs Rd., Walland vicinity, 7/25/89, A, 89000887

People's Bank of Friendsville [Blount County MPS], College St., Friendsville, 7/25/89, A, 89000906

Pistol Creek Dam and Mill Race [Blount County MPS], Pistol Creek between Church Ave. and Ellis St., Maryville, 7/25/89, A, 89000907

Porter, Stephen, House [Blount County MPS], Martin Mill Pike, 0.2 mi. W of Glover Rd., Rockford vicinity, 7/25/89, C, 89000908

Rorex, John M., House [Blount County MPS], Jct. of Brick Mill Rd. and Old Niles Ferry Rd., Maryville vicinity, 7/25/89, C, 89000909

Russell—Lackey—Prater House [Blount County MPS], Prater Rd. off Old Lowes Ferry Rd. at Poland Creek, Louisville vicinity, 11/20/89, C, 89001961

Sam Houston Schoolhouse, NE of Maryville on TN 8, Maryville vicinity, 6/13/72, B, 72001228

Shaddon Mill Site [Blount County MPS], Ninemile Creek at jct. of Big Elm and Trigonia Rds., Maryville vicinity, 8/21/89, A, 89001094

Shea, John F., House [Blount County MPS], Old Walland Hwy., Townsend, 7/25/89, C, b, 89000910

Southern Railroad Bridge [Blount County MPS], Southern Railroad right-of-way over Little River, Rockford vicinity, 7/25/89, C, 89000911

Southern Railroad Freight Depot [Blount County MPS], Southern Railroad right-of-way between Sevierville Rd. and Washington Ave., Maryville, 7/25/89, A, 89000912

Stevenson, Dr. William P., House [Blount County MPS], Maryville College campus, Maryville, 7/25/89, A, 89000913

Thompson-Brown House, 1005 Tuckleechee Pike, Maryville, 11/02/78, C, 78002574

Trundle, Carl, Barn [Blount County MPS], Jct. Wildwood Rd. and US 411, Wildwood vicinity, 7/25/89, C, 89000890

Vineyard, Tobler, House [Blount County MPS], Hollybrook Rd., 1 mi. N of Martin Mill Pike, Rockford vicinity, 7/25/89, C, 89000914

Walland Bridge [Blount County MPS], Old Walland Rd. over Little River, Walland, 7/25/89, C, 89000915

Walland Power Plant [Blount County MPS], Old Walland Hwy., 0.75 mi. N of Walland, Walland vicinity, 7/25/89, A, 89000916

Warren, Marcus, House [Blount County MPS], Miser Station Rd., 0.2 mi. S of Middle Settlement Rd., Louisville vicinity, 7/25/89, C, 89000917

White's Mill [Blount County MPS], Old White's Mill Rd., Maryville vicinity, 7/25/89, A, 89000918

Willard—Clark House [Blount County MPS], 1125 Broadway, Maryville, 7/25/89, C, 89000919

Yearout, Isaac, House [Blount County MPS], Big Springs Rd., 0.3 mi. N of Morganton Rd., Alcoa vicinity, 7/25/89, C, 89000920

Bradley County

Broad Street United Methodist Church, 263 Broad St., NW, Cleveland, 4/05/84, C, a, 84003263

Centenary Avenue Historic District, Roughly bounded by 8th, Harle, 13th and Ocoee Sts., Cleveland, 4/01/93, C, 93000172

Charleston Cumberland Presbyterian Church, Railroad St., Charleston, 7/12/84, C, a, 84003444

Conrad, Hair, Cabin, W of Cleveland on Blythewood Rd., Cleveland vicinity, 9/13/76, B, C, 76001765

Craigmiles Hall, 170 Ocoee St., NE, Cleveland, 11/25/80, B, C, 80003781

Craigmiles, P. M., House, 833 Ocoee St., NW, Cleveland, 11/20/75, C, 75001733

Fillauer Brothers Building, Broad and First Sts., Cleveland, 6/28/89, B, C, 89000507

First Presbyterian Church, 433 Ocoee St. NW, Cleveland, 3/13/86, C, a, 86000396

Henegar House, Market St., Charleston, 7/06/76, B, C, 76001764

Hughes, W. J., Business House, 3202 Ocoee St., Cleveland, 6/10/75, B, C, 75001735

Rattlesnake Springs, NE of Cleveland off Dry Valley Rd., Cleveland vicinity, 9/05/75, A, 75001734

Red Clay Council Ground, 13 mi. S of Cleveland on Blue Springs Rd., Cleveland vicinity, 9/14/72, A, 72001229

St. Luke's Episcopal Church, Ocoee and Central Sts., NW, Cleveland, 4/12/82, C, a, 82003954

Tipton-Fillauer House, 63 Broad St., NW, Cleveland, 12/08/80, C, 80003782

U.S. Post Office, 155 Board St., NW, Cleveland, 6/30/83, C, 83003023

Campbell County

Kincaid-Howard House, TN 63, Fincastle, 3/16/76, C, 76001766

LaFollette House, Indiana Ave., LaFollette, 5/29/75, B, C, 75001736

Smith—Little—Mars House, W of Speedwell on TN 63, Speedwell vicinity, 11/07/76, C, 76001767

U.S. Post Office and Mine Rescue Station, Main and 2nd Sts., Jellico, 2/10/84, A, C, 84003467

Cannon County

Baptist Female College—Adams House, 210 S. College St., Woodbury, 6/25/87, A, B, C, 87001035

Cannon County Courthouse, Court Sq., Woodbury, 4/14/92, C, 92000347

Houston, William Cannon, House, 107 Houston Ln., Woodbury, 6/16/89, B, C, 89000503

Readyville Mill, On U.S. 70S, Readyville, 7/02/73, B, C, 73001753

Carroll County

First Cumberland Presbyterian Church—McKenzie, 305 N. Stonewall St., McKenzie, 6/17/93, C, a, 93000476

Hillsman House, Old Hinkledale-McKenzie Rd., Trezevant vicinity, 3/25/82, B, C, 82003955

Carter County

Carriger-Cowan House, E of Saim, Siam vicinity, 6/06/79, C, 79002415

Carter, John and Landon, House, E. Broad St., Elizabethton, 4/14/72, B, C, 72001230

Elizabethton Historic District, Bounded roughly by 2nd, 4th, East, and Sycamore Sts., Elizabethton, 3/14/73, B, C, f, 73001754

Hunt, Henson, House, Brookdale Rd., Johnson City, 12/26/79, C, 79002414

Sabine Hill, Off TN 67, Elizabethton, 4/11/73, B, C, 73001755

Sycamore Shoals, 2 mi. W of Elizabethton on the Watauga River, Elizabethton vicinity, 10/15/66, A, f, NHL, 66000721

U.S. Post Office, 201-203 N. Sycamore St., Elizabethton, 8/09/83, C, 83003024

Wilder, John T., House, 202 Main St., Roan Mountain, 3/13/86, B, C, 86000400

Cheatham County

Cheatham County Courthouse, Court Sq., Ashland City, 12/12/76, A, C, 76001769

Indian Town Bluff, Address Restricted, Ashland City vicinity, 8/30/74, D, 74001904

Kingston Springs Hotel and Buildings, Kingston Springs Rd., Kingston Springs, 10/31/79, B, 79002417

Mound Bottom, Address Restricted, Kingston Springs vicinity, 9/03/71, D, 71000813

Patterson Forge (40CH87) [Iron Industry on the Western Highland Rim 1790s—1920s MPS (AD)], Address Restricted, Kingston Springs vicinity, 4/16/71, B, C, 71000814

Patterson Forge (40CH87) (Boundary Increase) [Iron Industry on the Western Highland Rim 1790s—1920s MPS], Address Restricted, Lillamay vicinity, 7/27/88, B, C, D, d, 88001106

Sycamore Mills Site, Address Restricted, Ashland City vicinity, 7/09/79, B, D, 79002416

Turnbull Forge (40CH97) [Iron Industry on the Western Highland Rim 1790s—1920s MPS], Address Restricted, Kingston Springs vicinity, 7/20/88, D, 88001108

Chester County

Chester County Courthouse, Court Sq., Henderson, 3/26/79, A, C, 79002418

Hamlett-Smith House, Jacks Creek-Mifflin Rd., Jacks Creek vicinity, 12/01/83, B, C, 83004227

Claiborne County

Big Spring Union Church, Off TN 32, Springdale, 5/29/75, A, C, a, 75001739

Cumberland Gap Historic District, Roughly bounded by Colwyn, Cumberland, Pennlyn, and the L & N Railroad tracks, Cumberland Gap, 2/23/90, A, C, 90000321

Cumberland Gap Historic District, E of Middlesboro, Harrogate, vicinity, 5/28/80, A, NPS, 80000366

Cumberland Gap National Historical Park, E of Middlesboro along Kentucky-Virginia state line, Cumberland Gap, vicinity, 10/15/66, A, C, e, g, NPS, 66000353

Graham—Kivette House (Boundary Decrease), Jct. of Old Knoxville Rd. and Main St., Tazewell, 10/31/91, B, C, 91001578

Graham-Kivette House, Main St. and Old Knoxville Rd., Tazewell, 5/29/75, B, C, 75001740

Grant-Lee Hall, Lincoln Memorial University campus, Harrogate, 12/08/78, A, 78002575

Kesterson-Watkins House, Cedar Fork Rd., Tazewell vicinity, 4/26/82, C, 82003958

Kincaid House, NE of Speedwell on Russell Lane, Speedwell vicinity, 3/22/82, C, 82003957

Kincaid-Ausmus House, NE of Speedwell off TN 63, Speedwell vicinity, 6/18/75, B, C, 75001737

McClain-Ellison House, W of Speedwell on Rte. 2 off TN 63, Speedwell vicinity, 6/10/75, B, C, 75001738

Wier, James, House, , Eppes St., Tazewell, 4/18/79, C, 79002419

Clay County

Clay County Courthouse, TN 52, Celina, 9/22/77, A, B, C, 77001261

Cocke County

Beechwood Hall, N of Newport on Rankin Rd., Newport vicinity, 5/29/75, B, C, 75001741

Elm Hill, 206 W. Riverview St., Newport, 5/29/75, B, C, 75001742

Greenlawn, NW of Newport on Old Rankin Rd., Newport vicinity, 5/29/75, B, C, 75001743

O'Dell House, NE of Newport on Greeneville Hwy., Newport vicinity, 4/01/75, C, 75001744

Swaggerty Blockhouse, E of Parrottsville on U.S. 411, Parrottsville vicinity, 6/18/73, A, D, 73001756

Vinson House, 4.5 mi. S of Newport off Hartford Rd., Newport vicinity, 5/29/75, C, 75001745

Yett-Ellison House, Main St. (Greeneville Hwy.), Parrottsville, 4/16/75, C, 75001746

Coffee County

Coffee County Courthouse, Public Sq., Manchester, 2/12/74, A, C, 74001905

Farrar Distillery, Noah Fork Rd., Noah vicinity, 9/27/84, A, 84003472

Hickerson, L. D., House [Tullahoma MPS], 215 N. Washington St., ullahoma, 8/18/93, B, C, 89001395

Manchester Cumberland Presbyterian Church, Jct. of Church and W. High Sts., Manchester, 6/29/92, C, a, 92000781

North Atlantic Street Historic District, 200–500 blks. of N. Atlantic St., Tullahoma, 7/14/88, C, b, 88001052

North Washington Street Historic District [Tullahoma MPS], 603–611 N. Washington St., Tullahoma, 8/18/93, A, C, 89001396

Old Stone Fort, W of Manchester, Manchester, 2/20/73, D, 73001757

Crockett County

Bank of Alamo, 103 S. Bells St., Alamo, 6/26/86, C, 86001397

Cumberland County

Cumberland County Courthouses, Main St., Crossville, 6/17/80, A, 80003783

Cumberland Homesteads Historic District, Roughly follows County Seat and Valley Rds., Grassy Cove Rd., Deep Draw and Pigeon Ridge Rds., Crossville vicinity, 9/30/88, A, C, 88001593

Cumberland County—Continued

Cumberland Mountain School, W side, Old US 127 N, 2 mi. N of Crossville, Crossville vicinity, 8/05/93, A, a, 93000779

Pioneer Hall, Main St., Pleasant Hill, 11/21/78, B, C, a, 78002576

Davidson County

Archeological Site No. 40DV35, Address Restricted, Nashville vicinity, 12/16/92, D, 92001655

Belair, 2250 Lebanon Rd., Nashville, 5/06/71, C, 71000815

Belle Meade, Harding Rd. at Leake Ave., Nashville vicinity, 12/30/69, A, C, 69000177

Belle Meade Apartments, 715 Belle Meade Blvd., Nashville, 4/19/84, C, 84003474

Belle Vue, Old Harding Rd., off U.S. 70S, Bellevue, 10/25/73, A, C, 73001758

Belmont, Belmont Blvd., Nashville, 5/06/71, A, C, 71000816

Belmont-Hillsboro Historic District, Roughly bounded by Primrose and 20th Aves., Magnolia and Belmont Blvds., Nashville, 5/01/80, C, 80003784

Bennie-Dillon Building, 702 Church St., Nashville, 8/16/84, C, 84003483

Berger Building, 164 N. 8th Ave., Nashville, 11/08/84, C, 84000376

Brick Church Mound and Village Site, Address Restricted, Nashville vicinity, 5/07/73, D, 73001759

Broadway Historic District, Broadway between 2nd and 5th Aves., Nashville, 7/18/80, A, C, 80003785

Buchanan, James, House, 2910 Elm Hill Pike, Nashville, 3/29/84, B, C, 84003486

Buena Vista Historic District, I-265 and U.S. 41, Nashville, 4/24/80, A, C, a, 80003786

Bush-Herbert Building, 174 3rd. Ave., N., Nashville, 3/25/82, B, C, 82003959

Cane Ridge Cumberland Presbyterian Church, SE of Antioch on Old Hickory Blvd., Antioch vicinity, 12/12/76, A, C, a, 76001770

Capers C.M.E. Church [McKissack and McKissack Buildings TR], 319 15th Ave., N., Nashville, 1/02/85, A, C, a, 85000045

Carnegie Library [McKissack and McKissack Buildings TR], 17th Ave. N., Fisk University campus, Nashville, 1/02/85, A, C, 85003769

Cartwright-Moss House, Old Dickerson Pike, Goodlettsville, 8/01/79, B, C, 79002420

Chadwell, Robert, House, 712 Neeleys Bend Rd., Madison, 11/13/89, C, 89001972

Cheatham Building, 301–309 Church St., Nashville, 2/21/80, A, C, 80003787

Christ Church, 900 Broadway, Nashville, 11/14/78, C, a, 78002577

Church of the Assumption, 1227 7th Ave., N., Nashville, 8/22/77, A, C, a, 77001262

Cleveland Hall, 4041 Old Hickory Blvd., Old Hickory, 4/16/71, B, C, 71000821

Clover Bottom Mansion, 2930 Lebanon Rd., Donelson, 4/03/75, C, 75001747

Cole House, 2001 Lebanon Rd., Nashville, 12/27/74, B, C, 74001907

Cole, Anna Russell, Auditorium, Tennessee Preparatory School campus, Nashville, 4/17/80, B, 80003788

Cummins Station, Demonbreun and 10th Ave., S., Nashville, 11/17/83, A, C, 83004233

Davidson County Courthouse, Public Sq., Nashville, 3/23/87, C, 87000670

Demonbreun's Cave, 1700 Omohumdro Dr., Nashville, 2/07/80, A, 80003789

Devon Farm, S of Nashville on TN 100, Nashville vicinity, 8/28/74, B, C, 74001908

Doctor's Building, 706 Church St., Nashville, 7/25/85, A, C, 85001607

Dozier Farm, 8451 River Rd. Pike, Nashville vicinity, 11/01/90, A, 90001580

DuPont Fire Hall [Old Hickory MRA], 1010 Hadley Ave., Old Hickory, 5/24/85, C, 85001558

East Nashville Historic District, Roughly bounded by Gallatin Pike, Edgewood Pl., N 16th and Russell Sts., Nashville, 4/15/82, C, a, 82003960

Edgefield Historic District, Roughly bounded by Woodland, S. 10th and S. 5th Sts., and Shelby Ave., Nashville, 7/13/77, A, C, a, 77001263

Eighth Avenue South Reservoir [Omohundro Waterworks System TR (AD)], 8th Ave., S., Nashville, 3/30/78, C, 78002578

Ellis Service Station Garage, 2000 Old Murfreesboro Rd., Nashville, 4/15/91, A, C, 91000436

Elm Street Methodist Church [Nineteenth Century Churches of South Nashville TR], 616 5th Ave., S., Nashville, 5/15/84, C, a, 84003496

Evergreen Place, 1023 Joyce Lane, Nashville, 4/15/82, C, 82003961

Ewing, Alexander, House, 5101 Buena Vista Pk., Nashville, 11/25/80, C, 80003790

Fall School, 1116 S. 8th Ave., Nashville, 12/19/79, A, C, 79002421

Federal Office Building, Broadway, Nashville, 12/26/72, A, C, 72001232

Federal Reserve Bank of Atlanta [Marr and Holman Buildings in Downtown Nashville TR], 226 N. 3rd Ave., Nashville, 10/10/84, A, C, 84000089

Fifth Avenue Historic District, Roughly bounded by Church and Union Sts., 4th, 5th, and 6th Aves., Nashville, 12/05/83, A, C, 83004234

First Presbyterian Church, 154 5th Ave., N., Nashville, 7/08/70, A, C, a, NHL, 70000608

Fisk University Historic District, Roughly bounded by 16th and 18th Aves., Hermosa, Herman and Jefferson Sts., Nashville, 2/09/78, A, C, b, 78002579

Fort Negley, Ridley Blvd. and Chestnut St., Nashville, 4/21/75, C, 75001748

Frost Building, 161 8th Ave., N., Nashville, 11/25/80, A, C, a, 80003791

Geddes, James, Engine Company No. 6, 629 2nd Ave., S., Nashville, 1/09/78, C, 78002580

Geist, John, and Sons, Blacksmith Shop and House, 309, 311, and 313 Jefferson St., Nashville, 4/29/80, A, 80003792

Germantown Historic District, Off I-40 and U.S. 41, Nashville, 8/01/79, A, C, a, 79002422

Gilbert Mansion, 1906 West End Ave., Nashville, 3/28/79, C, 79002423

Gladstone Apartments, 3803 West End Ave., Nashville, 6/16/83, C, 83003025

Glen Oak, 2012 25th Ave., S., Nashville, 11/17/83, B, C, 83004235

Goodwill Manor, 3500 Centennial Blvd., Tennessee State University, Nashville, 3/25/82, A, B, 82003962

Grassmere, Nolensville Rd., Nashville, 7/19/84, C, 84003503

Gray, Benajah, Log House, 446 Battle Rd., Antioch vicinity, 7/11/85, A, C, 85001512

Gymnasium, Vanderbilt University, West End and 23rd Aves., Nashville, 2/23/72, A, C, 72001233

Hatch Show Print Company Building, 116-118 4th Ave., Nashville, 6/16/83, A, 83003026

Hays-Kiser House, 834 Reeves Rd., Antioch, 9/10/74, C, 74001906

Hermitage Hotel, 231 6th Ave., N., Nashville, 7/24/75, A, C, 75001749

Hermitage, The, 12 mi. E of Nashville on U.S. 70N, Nashville vicinity, 10/15/66, B, NHL, 66000722

Hillsboro—West End Historic District, Roughly bounded by West End, 31st, Blakemore and 21st Aves. and I-440, Nashville, 12/23/93, C, 93001435

Holly Street Fire Hall, 1600 Holly St., Nashville, 8/26/82, C, 82003963

Holy Trinity Church, 615 6th Ave., S., Nashville, 4/14/72, A, C, a, 72001234

Hows-Madden House, U.S. 70, Nashville vicinity, 11/23/84, B, C, 84000324

Hubbard House [McKissack and McKissack Buildings TR (AD)], 1109 1st Ave., S., Nashville, 8/14/73, B, 73001760

Hume-Fogg High School, 700 Broad St., Nashville, 10/16/74, A, C, 74001909

Jubilee Hall, Fisk University, 17th Ave., N., Nashville, 12/09/71, A, C, NHL, 71000817

Lakewood Commercial District [Old Hickory MRA], Roughly bounded by 22nd St. and Old Hickory Blvd., Lakewood, 5/24/85, C, 85001556

Lebanon Road Stone Arch Bridge [Omohundro Waterworks System TR], Over Brown's Creek at Lebanon Rd., Nashville, 5/13/87, C, 87000379

Lindsley Avenue Church of Christ [Nineteenth Century Churches of South Nashville TR], 3 Lindsley Ave., Nashville, 5/15/84, A, C, a, 84003507

Litterer Laboratory, 631 2nd Ave., S., Nashville, 1/09/78, B, C, 78002581

Little Sisters of the Poor Home for the Aged, 1400 18th Ave., S., Nashville, 7/25/85, A, C, a, 85001608

Longleat, 5819 Hillsboro Rd., Nashville, 2/16/84, B, C, 84003509

Longview, 811 Caldwell Lane, Nashville, 1/12/83, C, 83003027

McCrory-Mayfield House, 1280 Hickory Blvd., Brentwood, 12/27/82, A, B, C, 82001726

Mechanical Engineering Hall, Vanderbilt University, Grand Ave. and 21st Ave., S., Nashville, 12/13/78, A, C, 78002582

Miles House, 631 Woodland St., Nashville, 1/08/79, A, a, 79002424

Davidson County—Continued

Morris Memorial Building [McKissack and McKissack Buildings TR], 330 Charlotte Ave., Nashville, 1/02/85, A, C, 85000046

Nashville Arcade, Between 4th and 5th Aves., Nashville, 5/22/73, A, C, 73001761

Nashville Children's Museum, 724 2nd Ave., S., Nashville, 5/06/71, A, C, 71000818

Nashville City Cemetery, 1001 S. 4th Ave., Nashville, 10/18/72, B, C, d, 72001235

Nashville Union Station and Trainshed, Broadway and 10th Ave., Nashville, 12/30/69, A, C, NHL, 69000178

Newsom's Mill, W of Nashville at Big Harpeth River, Nashville vicinity, 9/13/76, A, 76001771

Noel Hotel [Marr and Holman Buildings in Downtown Nashville TR], 200-204 N. 4th Ave., Nashville, 10/10/84, C, 84000090

Old Hickory Historic District [Old Hickory MRA], Bordered by Hadley Ave., Jones St., Eight St., Riverside Dr. and 15th Ave., Old Hickory, 5/24/85, A, C, 85001555

Old Hickory Methodist Church [Old Hickory MRA], 1216 Hadley Ave., Old Hickory, 5/24/85, C, a, 85001557

Old Natchez Trace, From AL/TN border to US 100 in Davidson Co., Nashville, 5/30/75, A, 75002125

Omohundro Water Filtration Complex District [Omohundro Waterworks System TR], NE of Omohundro Dr., Nashville, 5/13/87, C, 87000380

Overbrook, 4218 Harding Rd., Nashville, 3/29/84, C, a, 84003511

Overton Lane, Kirkman Lane, Oak Hill, 7/17/80, A, 80003795

Parthenon, The, Centennial Park, Nashville, 2/23/72, C, g, 72001236

Peabody College for Teachers, 21st Ave. S. and Edgehill Ave., Nashville, 10/15/66, A, NHL, 66000723

Primitive Baptist Church [Nineteenth Century Churches of South Nashville TR], 627-629 3rd Ave., S., Nashville, 5/15/84, C, a, 84003513

Printers Alley Historic District, Roughly bounded by 3rd and 4th Aves., Bank Alley, and both sides of Church St., Nashville, 8/26/82, A, C, 82003964

Rich-Schwartz Building [Marr and Holman Buildings in Downtown Nashville TR], 202-204 N. 6th Ave., Nashville, 10/10/84, C, 84000091

Richland Hall, 4822 Charlotte Ave., Nashville, 9/01/83, A, C, 83003028

Richland-West End Historic District, Roughly bounded by RR tracks, Murphy Rd., Park Circle, Wilson and Richland Aves., Nashville, 4/16/79, C, 79002425

Riverwood, 1833 Welcome Lane, Nashville, 7/20/77, B, C, 77001264

Robertson, James, Hotel [Marr and Holman Buildings in Downtown Nashville TR], 118 N. 7th Ave., Nashville, 10/10/84, C, 84000092

Robincroft, 746 Benton Ave., Nashville, 7/10/78, B, C, 78002583

Rutledge Hill Historic District, Roughly bounded by Middleton, 2nd, Lea and Hermitage Aves., Nashville, 7/08/80, C, 80003793

Ryman Auditorium, 116 Opry Pl., Nashville, 5/06/71, A, 71000819

Savage House, 167 8th Ave., N., Nashville, 1/11/83, B, C, 83003029

Scarritt College Historic District, 19th Ave., S., Nashville, 8/26/82, A, C, a, 82003965

Second Avenue Commercial District, 2nd Ave. between Brandon St. and Broadway, Nashville, 2/23/72, A, C, 72001237

Shaw, Abner T., House, 4866 Brick Church Pike, Goodlettsville vicinity, 3/28/85, C, 85000671

Shelby Street Bridge, Over Cumberland River at Shelby St., Nashville, 11/20/86, A, C, 86003237

Smith Farmhouse, TN 100, Pasquo, 11/17/83, A, C, 83004239

Smith Farmhouse (Boundary Increase), 8600 TN 100, N and W of original boundaries, Pasquo vicinity, 6/24/91, B, 91000816

Southern Methodist Publishing House, 810 Broadway, Nashville, 9/13/84, A, C, a, 84003519

St. Ann's Episcopal Church, 419 Woodland St., Nashville, 11/18/83, C, a, 83004237

St. Cecilia Academy, 8th Ave. and Clay St., Nashville, 12/12/76, A, C, a, 76001772

St. Mary's Catholic Church, 330 5th Ave., N., Nashville, 7/08/70, A, C, a, 70000609

St. Patrick's Catholic Church and Rectory [Nineteenth Century Churches of South Nashville TR], 1219 2nd Ave., S., Nashville, 5/15/84, A, C, a, 84003516

Stump, Frederick, House, 4949 Buena Vista Pike, Nashville, 4/02/73, B, C, 73001762

Sudekum Building, 535 Church St., Nashville, 12/19/79, A, C, b, 79002426

Sunnyside, 3000 Granny White Pike, Nashville, 10/01/74, A, C, 74001910

Tennessee State Capitol, Capitol Hill, Nashville, 7/08/70, A, C, NHL, 70000894

Third Baptist Church, 906 and 908 Monroe St., Nashville, 10/31/79, A, C, a, 79002427

Travellers' Rest, Franklin Rd., Nashville, 12/30/69, B, C, 69000179

Treppard-Baldwin House, 3338 Whites Creek Pike, Nashville, 10/28/83, C, 83004242

Tulip Grove, Lebanon Rd., Hermitage, 2/26/70, B, C, 70000607

Two Rivers, 3130 McGavock Pike, Nashville, 2/23/72, C, 72001238

US Post Office [Marr and Holman Buildings in Downtown Nashville TR (AD)], 901 Broadway, Nashville, 11/15/84, A, C, 84000580

US Post Office—Old Hickory [Old Hickory MRA], 1010 Donelson Ave., Old Hickory, 8/06/85, C, 85002401

Utopia Hotel, 206 4th Ave., N., Nashville, 3/26/79, A, C, 79002428

Warner Park Historic Park, Roughly bounded by Little Harpeth River, Belle Meade Blvd., TN 100, and Chickering Rd., Nashville, 1/20/84, A, C, g, 84003528

Waverly Place Historic District, Roughly bounded by Beech, Douglas and Bradford Aves., 10th

Ave. S. and Acklen Ave., Nashville, 3/28/85, A, C, 85000676

Weakley—Truett—Clark House, 415 Rosebank Ave., Nashville, 4/13/89, C, 89000297

West Meade, Old Harding Pike, Nashville, 3/04/75, A, B, C, 75001750

Whites Creek Historic District, Whites Creek Pike and Old Hickory Blvd., Whites Creek, 8/16/84, A, C, 84003530

Woodland in Waverly Historic District, Roughly bounded by I 65, 8th, Bradford and Wedgewood Aves., Nashville, 3/25/82, C, 82003966

Woodlawn, 127 Woodmont Blvd., Nashville, 11/21/78, A, B, C, 78002584

Young Women's Christian Association Building, 211 7th Ave., N., Nashville, 12/16/82, A, C, 82001727

De Kalb County

Evans Block, 101 and 103 N. 4th St., Smithville, 8/30/84, C, 84003533

Liberty Historic District, Roughly along Main and N. Main Sts., Liberty, 6/25/87, A, C, 87001058

Decatur County

Brooks, Dr. Beauregard Martin, House, TN 114 (Clifton Ferry Rd.) E of jct. with TN 69, Bath Springs, 9/03/92, B, C, 92001074

Brownsport I Furnace (40DR85) [Iron Industry on the Western Highland Rim 1790s—1920s MPS], Address Restricted, Gumdale vicinity, 7/28/88, D, 88001144

Brownsport II Furnace [Iron Industry on the Western Highland Rim 1790s—1920s MPS (AD)], Address Restricted, Decaturville vicinity, 8/26/77, A, D, 77001265

Brownsport II Furnace (40DR86) (Boundary Increase) [Iron Industry on the Western Highland Rim 1790s—1920s MPS], Address Restricted, Decaturville vicinity, 7/20/88, C, D, 88001105

Decatur Furnace (40DR84) [Iron Industry on the Western Highland Rim 1790s—1920s MPS], Address Restricted, Bath Springs vicinity, 7/28/88, D, 88001142

Rains, John P., Hotel, 106–108 Tennessee Ave., S., Parsons, 11/21/78, A, 78002585

Dickson County

Bellview Furnace (40DS23) [Iron Industry on the Western Highland Rim 1790s—1920s MPS], Address Restricted, Charlotte vicinity, 4/09/88, D, a, 88000245

Charlotte Courthouse Square Historic District, Public Square and environs, Charlotte, 11/25/77, A, C, 77001266

Cumberland Furnace Historic District (40DS22) [Iron Industry on the Western Highland Rim

Dickson County—Continued

1790s—1920s MPS], Address Restricted, Cumberland Furnace vicinity, 9/28/88, A, C, D, a, d, 88001109

Drouillard House, Off TN 48, Cumberland Furnace, 12/27/77, B, C, 77001267

Farmers and Merchants Bank Building, 201 Main St., White Bluff, 11/08/93, A, 93001161

First National Bank of Dickson, 106 N. Main St., Dickson, 3/13/86, A, C, 86000398

Halbrook Hotel, 100 Clement Pl., Dickson, 6/14/90, A, 90000915

Jones Creek Forge (40DS30) [Iron Industry on the Western Highland Rim 1790s—1920s MPS], Address Restricted, Harpeth Valley vicinity, 7/19/88, D, 88001103

Laurel Furnace (40DS4) [Iron Industry on the Western Highland Rim 1790s—1920s MPS], Address Restricted, Burns vicinity, 4/09/88, D, 88000244

Napier, Richard C., House [Iron Industry on the Western Highland Rim 1790s—1920s MPS], Old Hwy. 48, Charlotte vicinity, 7/26/88, B, 88001110

Ruskin Colony Grounds, NW of Dickson on Yellow Creek Rd., Dickson vicinity, 10/29/74, A, D, 74001911

Shule, Peter Paul, Barn, Denny Rd., Sylvia vicinity, 5/13/82, C, 82003967

St. James Episcopal Church, Off TN 48, Cumberland Furnace, 8/22/77, C, a, 77001268

Upper Forge (40DS32) [Iron Industry on the Western Highland Rim 1790s—1920s MPS], Address Restricted, Cumberland Furnace vicinity, 9/28/88, D, 88001097

Valley Forge (40DS28) [Iron Industry on the Western Highland Rim 1790s—1920s MPS], Address Restricted, Charlotte vicinity, 7/20/88, C, D, 88001102

White Bluff Forge (40DS27) [Iron Industry on the Western Highland Rim 1790s—1920s MPS], Address Restricted, White Bluff vicinity, 9/28/88, D, 88001104

Dyer County

Bank of Dyersburg, 100 N. Main St., Dyersburg, 6/16/83, A, C, 83003030

Dyersburg Courthouse Square Historic District, Roughly bounded by Church, Main, Cedar and Court Sts., Dyersburg, 2/28/91, A, C, 91000222

Gordon—Oak Streets Historic District [Dyersburg MPS], 107–302 Gordon and 114–305 Oak Sts., and W side 711–731 Sampson Ave., Dyersburg, 5/08/92, C, 92000428

King, Edward Moody, House, 512 Finley St., Dyersburg, 10/25/90, C, 90001658

Latta House, 917 Troy Ave., Dyersburg, 11/14/78, B, C, 78002586

Newbern Illinois Central Depot, Jct. of Main and Jefferson Sts., Newbern, 3/25/93, A, C, 93000213

Troy Avenue Historic District [Dyersburg MPS], 827–1445 Troy Ave., W side, Dyersburg, 5/08/92, C, 92000429

Fayette County

Crawford General Store, Macon Rd., Williston, 7/08/75, A, C, 75001752

Crawford's Experiment Farm, Jct. of Hotel St. and Old Somerville—Williston Rd., Williston, 3/14/91, A, C, b, 91000247

Immanuel Church, 2nd and Chestnut Sts., La Grange, 4/14/72, A, C, a, 72001239

La Grange Historic District, Bounded by La Grange town boundaries and including both sides of TN 57 E to jct. with TN 18, La Grange and vicinity, 4/04/75, A, C, 75001751

Lucerne, 20 mi. S of Brownsville on TN 76, Brownsville vicinity, 12/23/77, C, 77001269

Mebane—Nuckolls House, Macon-Collierville Rd., Macon vicinity, 11/20/85, A, B, C, d, 85002910

Miller House, Raleigh-La Grange Rd., Elba vicinity, 12/08/78, C, 78002587

Somerville Historic District, Court Square, and irregular pattern along N. Main St., Somerville, 4/15/82, C, 82003968

Fentress County

Allardt Historic District [Fentress County MPS], Jct. of TN 52 and Base Line Rd., Allardt, 10/29/91, C, 91001593

Allardt Presbyterian Church [Fentress County MPS], TN 52, Allardt, 7/03/91, A, C, a, 91000818

Davidson School [Fentress County MPS], TN 85, Davidson, 1/07/93, A, C, 92001739

Forbus Historic District [Fentress County MPS], TN 28 E of Davidson, Forbus, 7/03/91, A, C, 91000821

Gernt Office [Fentress County MPS], TN 52, Allardt, 7/03/91, A, B, 91000819

Gernt, Bruno, House, Base Line Rd., Allardt, 3/06/87, B, 87000391

Old Fentress County Jail, N. Smith St. and TN 52, Jamestown, 5/24/84, C, 84003536

Sergeant York Historic Area, Off Alvin York Hwy., Pall Mall, 4/11/73, B, a, c, g, 73001763

York, Alvin C., Agricultural Institute Historic District [Fentress County MPS], US 127 S of jct. with TN 154, Jamestown, 9/20/91, A, 91001378

York, Alvin Cullom, Farm, U.S. 127, Pall Mall vicinity, 5/11/76, B, g, NHL, 76001773

Youngs Historic District [Fentress County MPS], Jct. of Indiana and Portland Aves., Allardt, 10/16/91, A, C, 91000820

Franklin County

Bank of Winchester Building, 1st Ave., Winchester, 5/23/78, A, C, 78002589

Cowan Depot, Front St., Cowan, 11/24/78, C, 78002588

Cumberland Mountain Tunnel, SE of Cowan, Cowan vicinity, 8/22/77, A, C, 77001270

Estill-Fite House, 114 Sharp Springs Rd., Winchester, 3/23/79, B, C, 79002429

Falls Mill, 1 mi. off U.S. 64, Huntland vicinity, 2/23/72, A, 72001240

Falls Mills Historic District, Old Salem-Lexie and Falls Mill Rds., Huntland vicinity, 7/09/87, A, C, 87001158

Franklin County Jail, Decherd Blvd., Winchester, 3/26/79, A, 79002430

Gray, Isaac, House, SW of Winchester off U.S. 64, Winchester vicinity, 11/21/76, B, C, 76001776

Hundred Oaks, Oak St. at U.S. 64, Winchester, 12/20/90, A, C, a, 75001753

Knies Blacksmith Shop, 118 N. Jefferson St., Winchester, 4/11/73, A, 73001765

Mann, R. N., House, N of Old Salem off U.S. 64, Old Salem vicinity, 9/22/77, C, 77001271

Simmons, Peter, House, 11 mi. SW of Winchester on U.S. 64, Winchester vicinity, 8/16/77, B, C, 77001272

Trinity Episcopal Church, 213 1st Ave., NW, Winchester, 11/25/80, C, a, 80003796

Valentine Square, 111 N. Cedar St., Winchester, 11/08/84, C, 84000375

Zaugg Bank Barn, SE of Belvidere off U.S. 64, Belvidere vicinity, 12/18/73, A, 73001764

Gibson County

Browning House, E of Milan on Milan Army Ammunition Plant, Milan vicinity, 6/28/74, B, C, g, 74001912

Dodson House, 119 N. 17th Ave., Humboldt, 3/25/82, C, 82003969

Gibson County Courthouse, Court Sq., Trenton, 11/07/76, C, 76001777

Peabody High School, S. College St., Trenton, 11/23/84, A, C, 84000326

Senter-Rooks House, 2227 Main St., Humboldt, 7/09/80, B, C, 80003797

Taylor, Col. Robert Z., House, 1008 S. College St., Trenton, 4/12/82, B, C, 82003970

Trenton Historic District, High, College, and Church Sts., Trenton, 4/15/82, C, 82003971

US Post Office, 382 S. Main St., Milan, 7/09/87, C, 87001169

US Post Office, 200 S. College St., Trenton, 9/23/88, C, 88001576

Union Central School, Union Central Rd., Milan vicinity, 7/05/85, A, 85001490

Giles County

Bass—Morrell House, TN 293/Bryson Rd., Ardmore, 11/10/88, B, C, 88002615

Bethany Presbyterian Church Complex, Elkton Rd., Bryson vicinity, 11/13/89, A, C, a, 89001968

Brown-Daly-Horne House, 307 W. Madison St., Pulaski, 12/06/79, B, C, 79002431

Church of the Messiah, W. Madison and N. 3rd Sts., Pulaski, 7/28/83, C, a, 83003031

Clifton Place, Campbellsville Rd., Wales, 4/11/73, C, 73001767

Giles County—Continued

First Presbyterian Church of Pulaski, 202 S. Second St., Pulaski, 7/28/83, C, a, 83003032

Hewitt, Austin, Home, 322 E. Washington St., Pulaski, 12/13/84, B, C, 84000611

Lynnville Historic District, Roughly bounded by Mill St., Main and School Rd. and Long St., Louisville & Nashville RR, and Water and Buggs Sts., Lynnville, 4/01/88, A, C, 88000225

Milky Way Farm, US 31, Pulaski vicinity, 9/27/84, A, B, C, 84003537

Olivet United Methodist Church, Parsonage and School, Columbia Pike, Riversburg vicinity, 7/19/84, C, a, 84003538

Pisgah United Methodist Church and Cemetery, Pisgah Rd., Pisgah vicinity, 11/23/84, C, a, d, 84000330

Pulaski Courthouse Square Historic District, First, Jefferson, Madison, and Second Sts., Pulaski, 8/11/83, A, C, 83003033

Sam Davis Avenue Historic District, Sam Davis Ave. and E. Madison St., Pulaski, 3/02/89, C, 89000148

South Pulaski Historic District, Roughly bounded by W. College, First, Cemetery, and S. Third Sts., Pulaski, 7/10/86, C, 86001556

Tillery, George W., House, US 31N, Pulaski vicinity, 7/05/85, C, 85001486

White, Elisha, House, W of Waco on Yokley Rd., Waco vicinity, 3/04/83, A, C, 83003034

White, Newton, House, Old Pigeon Roost Rd., Pulaski, 10/22/87, C, 87001884

Whitfield, Copeland, House, Bee Line Hwy., Pulaski vicinity, 7/07/88, C, 88001021

Wilkerson Place, Miller Hollow Rd., Wales vicinity, 10/23/86, C, 86002899

Wilson-Young House, SW of Dellrose off I-65, Dellrose vicinity, 4/13/73, C, 73001766

Grainger County

Cocke, William, House, NE of Rutledge, Rutledge vicinity, 7/03/80, C, 80003799

Lea Springs, 11 mi. SW of Rutledge off U.S. 11, W on Lea Lake Rd., Rutledge vicinity, 5/29/75, B, 75001754

Poplar Hill, NE of Blaine, Blaine vicinity, 7/08/80, C, 80003798

Shields' Station, U.S. 11W, Blaine, 4/24/73, A, C, 73001769

Tate Springs Springhouse, E of Bean Station on U.S. 11W, Bean Station vicinity, 4/13/73, A, C, 73001768

Greene County

Andrew Johnson National Historic Site, Depot and College Sts., Greeneville, 10/15/66, A, B, c, d, NPS, 66000073

Brown-Neas House, Old Johnson City Rd., Afton vicinity, 11/08/84, C, 84000374

Chuckey Depot, SR 2391, Chuckey, 12/19/79, C, 79002432

Doak, Samuel, House, 2.5 mi. E of Greeneville on U.S. 11, Greeneville vicinity, 2/18/75, B, C, a, 75001755

Greeneville Historic District, Roughly bounded by Irish, Nelson, E. Church, College and McKee Sts., Greeneville, 5/03/74, A, B, C, 74001913

Lowry, James, House, Asheville Hwy., Greeneville vicinity, 3/25/82, C, 82003972

Mauris-Earnest Fort House, S of Chuckey on Nolichucky River, Chuckey vicinity, 1/30/78, A, C, 78002591

New Bethel Cumberland Presbyterian Church, NW of Greeneville on TN 70, Greeneville vicinity, 10/05/78, C, a, 78002592

Rankin, David, House, Snapp's Ferry Rd., Greeneville vicinity, 8/26/83, B, C, 83003035

Ripley Stone House, E of Afton off U.S. 11, Afton vicinity, 9/18/78, C, 78002590

Tusculum College Historic District, U.S. 11 and TN 107, Tusculum, 11/25/80, A, C, 80003800

Wayside, E of Greeneville off US 411, Greeneville vicinity, 3/22/84, B, C, 84003543

Grundy County

Beersheba Springs Historic District [Grundy County MRA (AD)], TN 56, Beersheba Springs, 3/20/80, A, a, 80003801

Coalmont Bank Building [Grundy County MPS], Jct. of TN 56 and Heidenburg St., Coalmont, 3/14/91, A, C, 91000246

DuBose Memorial Church Training School [Grundy County MRA (AD)], Fairmont and College Sts., Monteagle, 11/25/80, A, C, a, 80003802

Firescald Creek Stone Arch Bridge [Grundy County MRA], Northcutts Cove Rd. over Firescald Creek, Altamont vicinity, 4/01/87, C, 87000522

Grundy Lakes Historic District [Grundy County MRA], Grundy Lakes State Pk. E of TN 56, Tracy City vicinity, 4/01/87, A, g, 87000538

Hampton, E. L., House [Grundy County MRA], Depot and Oak St., Tracy City, 4/01/87, B, 87000528

Hickory Creek Stone Arch Bridge [Grundy County MRA], Sherwood Rd. over Hickory Creek, Marvin Chapel vicinity, 4/01/87, C, 87000526

Marugg Company [Grundy County MRA], 35 Depot St., Tracy City, 4/01/87, A, 87000527

Monteagle Sunday School Assembly Historic District [Grundy County MRA (AD)], Off U.S. 64, U.S. 41, and TN 56, Monteagle, 3/25/82, A, C, a, 82003974

Northcutt, H. B., House [Grundy County MRA (AD)], TN 56, Altamont, 3/23/82, C, 82003973

Northcutts Cove Chapel [Grundy County MRA (AD)], SE of Altamont, Altamont vicinity, 4/18/79, A, a, 79002433

Patton, John E., House [Grundy County MRA], Roddy Creek Rd., Coalmont vicinity, 4/01/87, B, C, 87000540

Scott Creek Stone Arch Bridge [Grundy County MRA], Over Scott Creek at Flat Branch Rd., Coalmont vicinity, 4/01/87, C, 87000539

Shook, Col. A. M., House [Grundy County MRA], Jct. of Depot and Montgomery Sts., Tracy City, 4/01/87, B, C, 87000529

Stagecoach Inn [Grundy County MRA], Colony Rd., Gruetli, 4/02/87, A, 87000524

Stagecoach Road [Grundy County MRA], Savage Gulf State Natural Area NW of TN 108, Beersheba Springs vicinity, 4/01/87, A, 87000521

Stoker—Stampfli Farm [Grundy County MRA], Colony Cemetery Rd., Gruetli, 4/02/87, A, 87000525

Tracy City Coke Ovens [Grundy County MRA], W of Hobbs Hill Rd., Tracy City, 4/01/87, A, 87000533

White, Frank, House [Grundy County MRA], Tenth St., Tracy City, 4/01/87, C, 87000530

Wonder Cave Historic District [Grundy County MRA], Wonder Cave Rd., Monteagle vicinity, 4/01/87, A, C, 87000520

Woodlee, L. V., House [Grundy County MRA], Cumberland St., Altamont, 4/02/87, B, 87000523

Wrenn's Nest [Grundy County MRA (AD)], Eagle Cliff Rd., Monteagle, 3/13/86, C, 86000399

Hamblen County

Barton Springs, 3 mi. (4.8 km) E of Morristown, Morristown vicinity, 5/22/78, A, C, 78002594

Bethesda Presbyterian Church, About 2 mi. SW of Russellville of U.S. 11E, Russellville vicinity, 4/11/73, A, C, a, 73001771

Hamblen County Courthouse, 511 W. 2nd North St., Morristown, 4/13/73, A, C, 73001770

Morristown College Historic District, 417 N. James St., Morristown, 9/15/83, C, 83003036

Rose School, Jackson and W. 2nd North Sts., Morristown, 10/18/76, A, C, 76001778

Rural Mount, 8 mi. SE of Morristown off TN 160, Morristown vicinity, 7/30/75, B, C, 75001757

St. Paul Presbyterian Church, W of Lowland, Lowland vicinity, 8/10/79, C, a, 79002434

U. S. Post Office, 134 N. Henry St., Morristown, 4/25/83, A, C, 83003037

Watkins—Witt House, 6622 W. Andrew Johnson Hwy., Talbott vicinity, 1/31/91, C, 90001752

Hamilton County

Audubon Acres Site (40 HA 84), Address Restricted, Chattanooga vicinity, 10/07/82, D, 82001728

Bonny Oaks, 5114 Bonny Oaks Dr., Chattanooga, 8/11/80, A, C, 80003803

Brabson House, 407 E. 5th St., Chattanooga, 4/11/73, A, C, 73001772

Brainerd Junior High [Hunt, Reuben H., Buildings in Hamilton County TR], 4201 Cherryton Dr., Chattanooga, 9/15/80, C, g, 80003804

Hamilton County—Continued

Brainerd Mission Cemetery, Off U.S. 11 and U.S. 64, Chattanooga, 12/06/79, A, d, 79002435

Brown House, The, About 10 mi. NE of Ooltewah on Georgetown Pike, Ooltewah vicinity, 4/11/73, A, B, C, 73001781

Brown's Ferry Tavern, Brown's Ferry Rd., Chattanooga, 3/24/71, A, B, 71000822

Chattanooga Bank Building [Hunt, Reuben H., Buildings in Hamilton County TR], 8th St., Chattanooga, 9/15/80, C, 80003805

Chattanooga Car Barns, 301 Market St., Chattanooga, 7/09/79, A, 79002436

Chattanooga Electric Railway [Hunt, Reuben H., Buildings in Hamilton County TR], 211-241 Market St., Chattanooga, 2/29/80, A, 80003806

Chattanooga, Harrison, Georgetown & Charleston Railroad Tunnel, Below N. Crest Rd., Chattanooga, 8/24/78, A, 78002595

Chickamauga and Chattanooga National Military Park, S of Chattanooga on U.S. 27, Chattanooga, 10/15/66, A, f, g, NPS, 66000274

Civil War Fortification, Bonny Oaks Dr., Chattanooga vicinity, 1/31/76, A, 76001779

Connor Toll House, 4212 Anderson Pike, Signal Mountain vicinity, 8/22/77, A, C, 77001273

Crane Building, 1317 Chestnut St., Chattanooga, 11/10/83, A, C, 83004246

Cravens—Coleman House, 1 Cravens Ter., Chattanooga, 10/25/90, C, 90001655

Cummings, Judge Will, House, W. of Chattanooga at 4025 Cummings Rd., Chattanooga, 7/03/80, B, 80003807

Douglas, Hiram, House, About 5 mi. N of Ooltewah on Snow Hill Rd., Ooltewah vicinity, 4/24/73, B, 73001782

East Side Junior High School, 2200 E. Main St., Chattanooga, 3/06/87, A, 87000392

East Tennessee Iron Manufacturing Company Blast Furnace, Address Restricted, Chattanooga vicinity, 5/08/80, A, D, 80003808

Faxon-Thomas Mansion, 10 Bluff View Ave., Chattanooga, 11/25/80, B, C, 80003809

Ferger Place Historic District, Evening Side Dr. and Morning Side Dr., Chattanooga, 5/01/80, A, C, g, 80003810

First Baptist Church Education Building [Hunt, Reuben H., Buildings in Hamilton County TR], 317 Oak St., Chattanooga, 2/29/80, C, 80003811

Fort Wood Historic District, Roughly bounded by Palmetto, McCallie, Central and 5th Sts., Chattanooga, 4/18/79, B, C, 79002437

Fountain Square, 600–622 Georgia Ave. and 317 Oak St., Chattanooga, 3/28/79, C, 79002438

Gaskill House, 427 E. 5th St., Chattanooga, 12/06/79, B, C, 79002439

Glenwood Historic District, Roughly bounded by Parkwood Dr., Glenwood Dr., Oak St., and Derby St., Chattanooga, 7/25/89, C, 89000861

Hamilton County Courthouse [Hunt, Reuben H., Buildings in Hamilton County TR (AD)], W. 6th St. and Georgia Ave., Chattanooga, 11/21/78, C, 78002596

Hampton Place Archeological Site (40HA146) [Moccasin Bend MRA], Address Restricted, Chattanooga vicinity, 5/22/84, D, 84003548

Hardy, Richard, Junior High School [Hunt, Reuben H., Buildings in Hamilton County TR], 2115 Dodson Ave., Chattanooga, 9/15/80, C, 80003812

Highland Park Methodist Episcopal church [Hunt, Reuben H., Buildings in Hamilton County TR], Bailey Ave., Chattanooga, 2/29/80, C, a, 80003813

Hutcheson House, 360 S. Crest Rd., Chattanooga, 11/21/78, B, C, 78002597

Isbester, Caleb, House, 551 Oak St., Chattanooga, 3/25/82, B, C, 82003975

James Building [Hunt, Reuben H., Buildings in Hamilton County TR], 735 Broad St., Chattanooga, 2/29/80, C, 80003814

James County Courthouse, Mulberry St., Ooltewah, 11/07/76, A, 76001782

Kelley House, 1903 McCallie Ave., Chattanooga, 5/14/80, C, 80003815

King, M. L., Boulevard Historic District, Roughly M. L. King Blvd. between Browns and University Sts., Chattanooga, 3/20/84, A, C, 84003551

Lookout Mountain Caverns and Cavern Castle, Scenic Hwy., Chattanooga, 11/26/85, A, 85002969

Lookout Mountain Incline Railway, Off U.S. 11, Chattanooga, 4/26/73, A, C, 73001774

Maclellan Building [Hunt, Reuben H., Buildings in Hamilton County TR], 721 Broad St., Chattanooga, 4/04/85, A, C, 85000708

Mallards Dozen Archeological Site (40HA147) [Moccasin Bend MRA], Address Restricted, Chattanooga vicinity, 5/22/84, D, 84003552

Market Square-Patten Parkway, Roughly bounded by E. 8th, and E. 9th Sts., Georgia and Lindsay Aves., Chattanooga, 5/01/80, A, C, 80003816

Market Street Warehouse Historic District, 1118-1148 Market St., Chattanooga, 4/05/84, A, C, g, 84003554

Market and Main Streets Historic District, Roughly bounded by Cowart, King, Market and Main Sts., Chattanooga, 7/24/92, A, C, 92000927

Matthews, Pleasant L., House, SW of Georgetown on Ooltewah-Georgetown Rd., Georgetown vicinity, 12/12/76, B, C, 76001781

McConnell, Chancellor T. M., House, 517 E. Fifth St., Chattanooga, 4/17/92, C, 92000314

Medical Arts Building [Hunt, Reuben H., Buildings in Hamilton County TR], McCallie Ave., Chattanooga, 9/15/80, C, 80003817

Mikado Locomotive No. 4501, 2202 N. Chamberlain Ave., Chattanooga, 3/28/79, A, 79002440

Miller Brothers Department Store, 629 Market St., Chattanooga, 9/17/87, A, B, g, 87001115

Moccasin Bend Archeological District, Address Restricted, Chattanooga vicinity, 9/08/86, A, C, D, NHL, 86003510

Model Electric Home, 1516 Sunset Rd., Chattanooga, 7/15/93, A, 93000645

Municipal Building [Hunt, Reuben H., Buildings in Hamilton County TR], E. 11th St., Chattanooga, 2/29/80, C, 80003818

Newton Chevrolet Building, 329 Market St., Chattanooga, 4/02/73, A, C, 73001775

Northside United Presbyterian [Hunt, Reuben H., Buildings in Hamilton County TR], 923 Mississippi Ave., Chattanooga, 9/15/80, C, a, 80003820

Ochs Building, Georgia Ave., Chattanooga, 11/17/78, B, C, 78002598

Old Library Building [Hunt, Reuben H., Buildings in Hamilton County TR (AD)], 200 E. 8th St., Chattanooga, 3/14/73, C, 73001776

Old Post Office, E. 11th and Lindsay Sts., Chattanooga, 4/13/73, C, 73001777

Park Hotel [Hunt, Reuben H., Buildings in Hamilton County TR], 117 E. 7th St., Chattanooga, 8/18/80, C, 80003821

Read House, Broad and 9th Sts., Chattanooga, 12/23/76, A, C, 76001780

Ross's Landing, 101 Market St., Chattanooga, 6/27/74, A, 74001914

Saints Peter and Paul Catholic Church and Buildings, 214 E. 8th St., Chattanooga, 12/11/79, C, a, 79002441

Schwartz, Robert, and Company Building, 736-738 Cherry St., Chattanooga, 7/19/84, C, 84003555

Second Presbyterian Church [Hunt, Reuben H., Buildings in Hamilton County TR], 700 Pine St., Chattanooga, 2/29/80, C, a, 80003822

Shavin, Seamour and Gerte, House, 334 N. Crest Rd., Chattanooga, 3/23/93, C, g, 93000149

Shiloh Baptist Church, 506 E. 8th St., Chattanooga, 1/19/79, A, C, a, 79002442

Soldiers and Sailors Memorial Auditorium [Hunt, Reuben H., Buildings in Hamilton County TR], McCallie Ave., Chattanooga, 9/15/80, C, 80003823

Southern Railway Freight Depot, 1140 Newby St., Chattanooga, 6/16/83, A, C, e, 83003038

St. Elmo Historic District, Alabama, St. Elmo, and Tennessee Aves., Chattanooga, 4/15/82, A, C, 82003976

St. Paul's Episcopal Church, 7th and Pine Sts., Chattanooga, 9/01/78, A, C, a, 78002599

Stringer Ridge Historic District [Moccasin Bend MRA], Address Restricted, Chattanooga vicinity, 5/22/84, A, D, 84003557

Tennessee Valley Railroad Museum Rolling Stock, 2022 N. Chamberlain Ave., Chattanooga, 8/06/80, A, g, 80003824

Terminal Station, 1434 Market St., Chattanooga, 2/20/73, A, C, 73001778

Thomas, Benjamin F., House, 938 McCallie Ave., Chattanooga, 12/03/80, B, C, 80003825

Tivoli Theater [Hunt, Reuben H., Buildings in Hamilton County TR (AD)], 709 Broad St., Chattanooga, 4/11/73, C, 73001779

Topside, N of Signal Mountain off TN 8 on Wilson Ave., Signal Mountain vicinity, 4/11/73, B, C, 73001783

Trigg—Smartt Building, 701–707 Broad St., Chattanooga, 6/26/86, B, C, 86001383

Trinity Methodist Episcopal Church [Hunt, Reuben H., Buildings in Hamilton County TR], McCallie Ave., Chattanooga, 2/29/80, C, a, 80003826

Hamilton County—Continued

Turnbull Cone and Machine Company, 1400 Fort and W. Fourteenth Sts., Chattanooga, 7/15/92, A, B, g, 92000848

U.S. Post Office [Hunt, Reuben H., Buildings in Hamilton County TR], Georgia Ave., Chattanooga, 2/29/80, C, g, 80003827

Vulcan Archeological Site (40HA140) [Moccasin Bend MRA], Address Restricted, Chattanooga vicinity, 5/22/84, D, 84003558

Walnut Street Bridge, Walnut St., over the Tennessee River, Chattanooga, 2/23/90, A, C, 90000300

Wiley United Methodist Church, 504 Lookout St., Chattanooga, 8/01/79, C, a, 79002443

Willard, Frances, House [Hunt, Reuben H., Buildings in Hamilton County TR], 615 Lindsay St., Chattanooga, 2/29/80, A, 80003828

Williams Island, Address Restricted, Chattanooga vicinity, 4/11/73, D, 73001780

Woodland Mound Archeological District [Moccasin Bend MRA], Address Retricted, Chattanooga vicinity, 5/22/84, D, 84003562

Wyatt Hall [Hunt, Reuben H., Buildings in Hamilton County TR], 865 E. Third St., Chattanooga, 10/23/86, C, 86002897

Hancock County

Old Jail, Jail St., Sneedville, 4/11/73, A, C, 73001784

Vardy School Community Historic District, Blackwater Rd., Sneadville vicinity, 11/08/84, A, C, a, 84000373

Hardeman County

Bills-McNeal Historic District, Irregular pattern along Lafayette, McNeal, Bills, Union, Lauderdale and Washington Sts., Bolivar, 2/12/80, C, a, 80003829

Bolivar Court Square Historic District, TN 125 and U.S. 64, Bolivar, 1/10/80, A, C, 80003830

North Main Street Historic District, N. Main, Sycamore, Jefferson, Washing and Water Sts., Bolivar, 3/20/80, C, 80003831

Western State Hospital Historic District, US 64, Bolivar, 6/25/87, A, B, C, 87001057

Hardin County

Cherry Mansion, 101 Main St., Savannah, 8/16/77, B, C, 77001274

Graham, James, House, Jct. of TN 69 and Airport Rd., Savannah vicinity, 10/29/91, B, C, 91001594

Savannah Historic District, Irregular pattern along Main, Deford, Guinn, Church, College, Williams and Cook Sts., Savannah, 4/02/80, B, C, 80003832

Savannah Historic District (Boundary Increase), 410 and 506 Main St., Savannah, 11/08/93, C, 93001153

Shiloh Indian Mounds Site, E of Hurley in Shiloh National Military Park, Hurley vicinity, 4/27/79, D, NHL, NPS, 79000279

Shiloh National Military Park, Off TN 22, Shiloh, 10/15/66, A, C, d, NPS, 66000074

Tanyard Branch Furnace (40HR121) [Iron Industry on the Western Highland Rim 1790s—1920s MPS], Address Restricted, Bath Springs vicinity, 4/09/88, D, 88000250

White, Meady, House, Main St. (TN 69), Saltillo, 7/01/93, B, C, 93000586

Hawkins County

Amis House, E of Rogersville on Burem Pike, Rogersville vicinity, 6/19/73, B, C, 73001786

Boatyard Historic District, SW of Kingsport on Holston and S. Fork of Holston River, Kingsport, 12/12/73, A, B, 73001785

Bulls Gap Historic District, S. Main, Church, McGregor, Price and Mill Sts., Bulls Gap, 7/30/87, A, 87001232

Fudge Farm, NE of Surgoinsville on U.S. 11W, Surgoinsville vicinity, 12/12/76, B, C, 76001783

Long Meadow, N of Surgoinsville off U.S. 11W (Rte. 1), Surgoinsville vicinity, 1/11/74, C, 74001915

New Providence Presbyterian Church, Academy, and Cemetery, NE of Surgoinsville off U.S. 11, Surgoinsville vicinity, 12/01/78, A, C, a, d, 78002600

Pressmen's Home Historic District, TN 94, Pressmen's Home, 11/20/85, A, B, C, a, g, 85002970

Price Public Elementary School, Hasson and Spring Sts., Rogersville, 11/10/88, A, 88002538

Rogersville Historic District, Bounded by N. Boyd, Kyle, Clinch, and N. Bend Sts., McKinney Ave., and S. Rogen Rd., Rogersville, 2/23/73, A, C, 73001787

Stony Point, NE of Surgoinsville on U.S. 11W, Surgoinsville vicinity, 4/26/73, B, C, 73001788

Haywood County

Cedar Grove, W of Brownsville, Brownsville vicinity, 4/29/80, C, 80003833

College Hill Historic District, TN 19 and U.S. 70/79, Brownsville, 9/11/80, B, C, g, 80003834

Dancyville United Methodist Church and Cemetery, Dancyville Methodist Church St., Dancyville, 3/13/91, C, a, d, 91000224

Hutchison, Joshua K., House, 124 N. Church Ave., Brownsville, 7/07/88, C, 88001022

Stanton Masonic Lodge and School, W. Main St., Stanton, 10/22/87, C, 87001878

Temple Adas Israel, Washington and College Sts., Brownsville, 1/19/79, A, C, a, 79002445

Zion Church, College and Washington Sts., Brownsville, 11/21/78, A, C, a, 78002601

Henderson County

Edwards, Thompsie, House, 113 Main St., Lexington, 6/30/83, B, C, 83003039

Henry County

Bruce, H. L., House [Paris MRA], 202 S. Poplar St., Paris, 9/07/88, C, a, 88001431

Grove, E. W. Henry County High School, Grove Blvd., Paris, 11/25/80, A, C, 80003835

Hagler, John L., House, NW of Springville on Poplar Grove Rd., Springville vicinity, 3/13/80, A, C, 80003836

Jernigan, E. K., House [Paris MRA], 207 Dunlap St., Paris, 9/07/88, C, 88001429

Jernigan, Thomas P., House [Paris MRA], 918 Dunlap St., Paris, 9/07/88, C, 88001430

Lee, Robert E., School [Paris MRA], 402 Lee St., Paris, 9/07/88, A, 88001426

Mt. Zion Church and Cemetery, NE of Elkhorn on Tennessee River, Elkhorn vicinity, 12/23/74, A, a, d, 74001916

North Poplar Historic District [Paris MRA], Along sections of N. Poplar St. and E. Church St., Paris, 9/07/88, A, C, 88001428

Obion Mounds, Address Restricted, Paris vicinity, 5/07/73, D, 73001790

Paris Commercial Historic District [Paris MRA], Along sections of E. and W. Wood, W. Washington, N. and S. Poplar, N. and S. Market, Fentress and W. Blythe Sts., Paris, 9/07/88, A, C, 88001424

Porter House, 407 S. Dunlap St., Paris, 4/11/73, B, C, 73001789

Sweeney, Judge John C., House [Paris MRA], 1212 Chickasaw Rd., Paris, 9/07/88, C, 88001427

West Paris Historic District [Paris MRA], Along sections of W. Washington, N. College and Hudson Sts., Paris, 9/07/88, C, 88001432

White, Charles M., House [Paris MRA], 403 Whitehall Circle, Paris, 9/07/88, C, 88001425

Hickman County

Bon Aqua Springs Historic District, Old Hwy. 46, SE of Bon Aqua, Bon Aqua, 2/23/90, A, 90000303

Fairview School, 113 E. Hackberry St., Centerville, 12/08/83, A, C, 83004252

Lee and Gould Furnace (40HI125) [Iron Industry on the Western Highland Rim 1790s—1920s MPS], Address Restricted, Bucksnort vicinity, 4/09/88, C, D, 88000248

New Aetna Furnace Historic District (40HI149) [Iron Industry on the Western Highland Rim 1790s—1920s MPS], Address Restricted, Aetna vicinity, 6/13/88, A, D, 88000246

Oakland Furnace and Forge (40HI146) [Iron Industry on the Western Highland Rim 1790s—1920s MPS], Address Restricted, Texas Hollow vicinity, 4/09/88, D, 88000261

Hickman County—Continued

Old Aetna Furnace (40HI148) [Iron Industry on the Western Highland Rim 1790s—1920s MPS], Address Restricted, Aetna vicinity, 4/09/88, D, 88000247

Primm Springs Historic District, Irregular Pattern along the Puppy Branch of Dog Creek between House & Baker Rds. & Mineral Springs, Primm Springs, 7/05/85, B, C, 85001480

Shelby Bend Archeological District, Address Restricted, Greenfield Bend vicinity, 2/01/90, D, NPS, 89001760

Standard Furnace (40HI145) [Iron Industry on the Western Highland Rim 1790s—1920s MPS], Address Restricted, Nunnelly vicinity, 4/09/88, D, 88000243

Walker, James Buchanan, House, West End and S. Barnwell Aves., Centerville, 3/02/89, B, C, 89000146

Houston County

Harris, V. R., House, Main St., Erin, 8/18/83, B, C, 83003040

Humphreys County

Fairchance Furnace (40HS168) [Iron Industry on the Western Highland Rim 1790s—1920s MPS], Address Restricted, Halls Creek vicinity, 7/28/88, D, 88001143

Link Farm Site, Address Restricted, Hurricane Mills vicinity, 4/11/73, D, 73001791

McAdoo, Hugh M., House, 113 N. Church St., Waverley, 10/29/91, C, 91001595

Nolan, James N., House, Hwy. 13 N, Waverly, 3/13/86, B, C, 86000395

Sycamore Landing, Sycamore Landing Rd., Sycamore Landing, 1/04/80, B, 80003837

Jackson County

Fort Blount-Williamsburg Site, On Cumberland River S of Gainesboro, Gainesboro vicinity, 7/17/74, A, B, 74001918

Gainesboro Historic District, Roughly bounded by Cox, Minor, Montpelier and Mark Twain Sts., Gainesboro, 10/25/90, A, 90001570

Jefferson County

Branner-Hicks House, E of Jefferson City on Chucky Rd., Jefferson City vicinity, 7/09/74, B, C, 74001919

Cox's Mill, N of Jefferson City on Fielden's Store Rd., Jefferson City vicinity, 1/27/83, A, C, 83003041

Dandridge Historic District, Town center around Main, Meeting, and Gay Sts., Dandridge, 1/22/73, A, C, 73001792

Fairfax, SE of White Pine off U.S. 25E, White Pine vicinity, 4/13/73, B, C, 73001795

Fairvue, Andrew Johnson Hwy., Jefferson City vicinity, 4/12/82, C, 82003978

Franklin, Lawson D., House, SE of white Pine off U.S. 25E, White Pine vicinity, 4/13/73, B, 73001796

Glenmore, Off U.S. 11E, Jefferson City, 4/13/73, B, C, 73001794

Hill-Hance House, E of Chestnut Hill off US 411, Chestnut Hill vicinity, 8/26/82, C, 82003977

Newman, Samuel Isaac, House, Bible Rd., Jefferson City, 7/17/80, C, 80003838

Swann, Judge James Preston, House, Cherokee Dr., Dandridge, 7/16/73, C, 73001793

Johnson County

Butler House, 309 N. Church St., Mountain City, 4/11/73, B, C, 73001798

Morrison Farm and Store, TN 91, Laurel Bloomery, 4/11/73, B, 73001797

Rhea House, U.S. 421, Shouns, 4/11/73, A, 73001799

Knox County

Bleak House, 3148 Kingston Pike, Knoxville, 11/08/84, B, C, 84000369

Blount, William, Mansion, 200 W. Hill Ave., Knoxville, 10/15/66, B, C, NHL, 66000726

Boyd—Harvey House, Harvey Rd., Knoxville vicinity, 11/07/85, C, 85002774

Buffat, Alfred, Homestead, 1 mi N of Knoxville on Love Creek Rd., Knoxville vicinity, 4/01/75, B, 75001761

Burwell Building Tennessee Theater, 600 S. Gay St., Knoxville, 4/01/82, A, C, 82003979

Camp House, 1306 Broadway, NE, Knoxville, 4/24/73, C, 73001800

Chesterfield, N of Mascot off Old Rutledge Pike, Mascot vicinity, 11/16/77, C, 77001276

Concord Village Historic District, Roughly bounded by Lakeridge & Third Drs., Spring St., & the Masonic Hall & Cemetery, Concord, 10/22/87, A, C, 87001888

Cowan, McClung and Company Building, 500-504 Gay St., Knoxville, 7/12/84, A, C, 84003566

Craighead-Jackson House, 1000 State St., Knoxville, 3/20/73, C, 73001801

Dulin, H. L., House, 3100 Kingston Pike, Knoxville, 10/15/74, C, 74002265

Ebenezer Mill, Ebenezer Rd., Knoxville vicinity, 6/25/87, A, C, 87001037

Fire Station No. 5, 419 Arthur St., NW, Knoxville, 11/02/78, A, C, 78002602

Forest Hills Boulevard Historic District, 500–709 Forest Hills Blvd., Knoxville, 4/14/92, C, 92000350

Fort Sanders Historic District, Roughly bounded by White and Grand Aves., 11th and 19th Sts., Knoxville, 9/16/80, A, B, C, 80003839

Fourth and Gill Historic District, Roughly bounded by I-40, Broadway, Central and 5th Ave., Knoxville, 4/29/85, A, C, 85000948

Gay Street Commercial Historic District, Roughly along Gay St. from Summit Hill Dr. to Church Ave., Knoxville, 11/04/86, A, C, g, 86002912

General Building, 625 Market St., Knoxville, 3/08/88, B, C, 88000174

Gibbs, Nicholas, House, Emory Rd., Knoxville, 9/09/88, A, B, C, D, 88001447

Holston National Bank, 531 S. Gay St., Knoxville, 10/02/79, C, 79002446

Jackson Avenue Warehouse District, Jackson Ave., Knoxville, 4/11/73, A, C, 73001802

Jackson Avenue Warehouse District Extension, 120–124 Jackson Ave., Knoxville, 3/10/75, A, C, 75002148

Johnson, Andrew, Hotel, 912 S. Gay St., Knoxville, 7/09/80, A, C, 80003840

Knollwood, 6411 Kingston Pike, Knoxville, 5/12/75, A, C, 75001762

Knox County Courthouse, Main Ave. and Gay St., Knoxville, 4/24/73, A, C, 73001803

Knoxville Business College, 209 W. Church St., Knoxville, 1/27/83, C, 83003042

Knoxville College Historic District, 901 College St., NW, Knoxville, 5/01/80, A, a, 80003841

Knoxville Iron Foundry Complex-Nail Factory and Warehouse, 715 Western Ave., NW, Knoxville, 3/25/82, A, 82003980

Knoxville Post Office, 501 Main St., Knoxville, 5/31/84, C, 84003567

Knoxville YMCA Building, 605 Clinch Ave., Knoxville, 11/17/83, A, C, 83004256

Lamar House Hotel, 803 Gay St., SW., Knoxville, 12/04/75, A, B, C, 75001763

Louisville and Nashville Freight Depot, 700 Western Ave., NW, Knoxville, 3/25/82, A, 82003981

Louisville and Nashville Passenger Station, 700 Western Ave., NW, Knoxville, 3/25/82, A, C, 82003982

Mabry, Joseph Alexander, Jr., House, 1711 Dandridge Ave., Knoxville, 11/13/89, A, B, C, 89001974

Mall Building, 1–5 Market St., Knoxville, 8/26/82, B, C, 82003983

Marble Springs, S of Knoxville on Neubert Springs Rd., Knoxville vicinity, 5/06/71, B, C, 71000823

Market Square Commercial Historic District, Market Sq. Mall, Knoxville, 12/20/84, A, C, 84001138

McCammon, Samuel, House, 1715 Riverside Dr., Knoxville, 3/01/84, C, D, 84003571

Mechanics' Bank and Trust Company Building, 612 S. Gay St., Knoxville, 1/27/83, C, 83003043

Mechanicsville Historic District, Off TN 62, Knoxville, 7/18/80, B, C, 80003842

Medical Arts Building, 603 Main St., Knoxville, 5/24/84, C, 84003573

Middlebrook, 4001 Middlebrook Pike, Knoxville, 6/18/74, C, 74001920

New Salem United Methodist Church, 2417 Tipton Station Rd., Knoxville vicinity, 8/11/83, C, a, d, 83003044

Knox County—Continued

Old Knoxville City Hall, Summit Hill Dr., Knoxville, 5/31/72, A, C, g, 72001241

Old North Knoxville Historic District, Roughly bounded by E. Woodland, Bluff, Armstrong, E. Baxter and Central Aves., Knoxville, 5/14/92, A, C, 92000506

Old Post Office Building, Clinch and Market Sts., Knoxville, 3/20/73, C, 73001804

Ossoli Circle Clubhouse, 2511 W. Cumberland Ave., Knoxville, 3/21/85, A, C, 85000620

Park City Historic District, Roughly bounded by Washington Ave., Cherry St., Woodbine Ave., Beaman St., Magnolia Ave. and Winona St., Knoxville, 10/25/90, A, C, 90001578

Park City Junior High School, 523 Bertrand St., Knoxville, 6/30/83, C, 83003045

Park, James, House, 422 W. Cumberland Ave., Knoxville, 10/18/72, C, 72001242

Ramsey House, SE of Knoxville on Thorngrove Pike, Knoxville vicinity, 12/23/69, B, C, 69000180

Riverdale Mill, Wayland Rd. and Thorngrove Pike, Knoxville vicinity, 3/13/87, A, 87000464

Russell, Avery, House, 11409 Kingston Pike, Farragut, 6/05/75, A, B, 75001759

Southern Terminal and Warehouse Historic District, Roughly bounded by Depot Ave., N. Central Ave. and Sullivan St. and S. Central Ave., Vine Ave., and N. and S. Gay St., Knoxville, 11/18/85, A, C, 85002909

St. John's Lutheran Church, 544 Broadway, NW, Knoxville, 4/04/85, C, a, 85000700

Statesview, About 10 mi. SW of Knoxville off U.S. 70, Knoxville vicinity, 4/24/73, B, C, 73001805

Talahi Improvements, Off U.S. 129, Knoxville, 12/26/79, B, C, 79002447

Trinity Methodist Episcopal Church, 416 Lovenia Ave., Knoxville, 8/26/82, C, a, 82003984

U. T. Agriculture Farm Mound, Address Restricted, Knoxville vicinity, 3/30/78, D, 78002603

Westwood, 3425 Kingston Pike, Knoxville, 11/08/84, B, C, 84000366

Williams, Col. John, House, 2325 Dandridge Ave., Knoxville, 12/03/80, A, B, C, 80003843

Lake County

Caldwell—Hopson House, 431 Wynn St., Tiptonville, 3/11/93, C, 93000150

Lauderdale County

Fort Pillow, TN 87, Fort Pillow, 4/11/73, A, NHL, 73001806

Palmer, W. E., House, Off U.S. 51, Henning, 12/14/78, B, C, g, 78002604

US Post Office, 17 E. Jackson Ave., Ripley, 9/23/88, C, 88001582

Wardlaw-Steele House, 128 Wardlaw Pl., Ripley, 1/08/80, B, 80003844

Lawrence County

Davenport, T. D., Forge (40LR7) [Iron Industry on the Western Highland Rim 1790s—1920s MPS], Address Restricted, Lawrenceburg vicinity, 7/19/88, D, 88001101

Garner Mill, Garner Lane, Lawrenceburg, 7/12/84, A, C, 84003575

Lawrence County Jail, Waterloo St., Lawrenceburg, 3/16/76, C, 76001784

Lawrenceburg Commercial Historic District, Roughly bounded by N. Military St., Public Sq., E. Gaines St. and E. Pulaski St., Lawrenceburg, 4/14/92, A, 92000346

Lawrenceburg No. 1 Hydroelectric Station [Pre-TVA Hydroelectric Development in Tennessee, 1901-1933 MPS], Glen Spring Rd. at Horseshoe Bend of Little Shoal Creek, Lawrenceburg vicinity, 4/20/90, A, C, 90000308

Lawrenceburg No. 2 Hydroelectric Station [Pre-TVA Hydroelectric Development in Tennessee, 1901-1933, MPS], Mi. 51.7 on Shoal Cr. near old US 43, Lawrenceburg vicinity, 7/05/90, A, C, 90001005

Mount Zion Methodist Episcopal Church South, Mount Zion Rd., Fall River vicinity, 3/10/88, C, a, d, 88000201

Sacred Heart of Jesus Church [German Catholic Churches and Cemeteries of Lawrence County TR], Berger St., Lawrenceburg, 10/10/84, C, a, 84000093

Sacred Heart of Jesus Church [German Catholic Churches and Cemeteries of Lawrence County TR], Church St., Loretto, 10/10/84, C, a, 84000094

St. Joseph Church [German Catholic Churches and Cemeteries of Lawrence County TR], Spring St., St. Joseph, 10/10/84, A, C, a, d, 84000113

St. Mary's Cemetery [German Catholic Churches and Cemeteries of Lawrence County TR], Rascal Town Rd., Rascal Town vicinity, 10/10/84, A, d, 84000095

Lewis County

Blackburn, Ambrose, Farmstead, Gordonsburg Rd., Gordonsburg vicinity, 3/28/85, A, C, 85000670

Hohenwald Railroad Depot, TN 99, Hohenwald, 5/14/87, A, b, 87000730

Napier Furnaces Historic District (40LS14) [Iron Industry on the Western Highland Rim 1790s—1920s MPS], Address Restricted, Napier vicinity, 5/04/88, A, C, D, NPS, 88000459

Steele's Iron Works (40LS15) [Iron Industry on the Western Highland Rim 1790s—1920s MPS], Address Restricted, Napier vicinity, 5/04/88, D, NPS, 88000458

Tait, Netherland, House, Napier Rd., Napier vicinity, 8/09/84, B, C, 84003577

Lincoln County

Borden Powdered Milk Plant, S. Main St., Fayetteville, 7/14/88, A, 88001060

Childress House, 9 mi. W of Fayetteville on U.S. 64, Fayetteville vicinity, 2/25/82, C, 82003985

Conger, Isaac, House, NE of Fayetteville off Hamestring Rd., Fayetteville vicinity, 7/16/73, B, C, a, 73001807

Douglas, Hugh Bright, House, 301 Elk Ave., N., Fayetteville, 3/25/82, C, 82003986

Harms Mill Hydroelectric Station [Pre-TVA Hydroelectric Development in Tennessee, 1901-1933, MPS], SR 15 at Elk R., Fayetteville vicinity, 7/05/90, A, C, 90001007

Harris-Holden House, E of Howell on Daves Hollow Rd., Howell vicinity, 3/19/75, C, 75001766

Kelso Bowstring Arch Truss Bridge, N of Kelso on Stephens Creek Rd., Kelso vicinity, 1/04/83, A, C, 83003046

Lincoln County Poor House Farm, Yukon Rd., Coldwater vicinity, 7/11/85, A, 85001511

McDonald-Bolner House, 400 S. Elk, Fayetteville, 5/31/84, C, 84003579

Mimosa School, Mimosa Rd., Mimosa, 7/28/83, A, C, 83003047

Mulbery-Washington-Lincoln Historic District, Roughly Bright, Elk, Green, Main, Lincoln, Mulberry and Washington Sts., Fayetteville, 5/31/84, C, 84003580

Petersburg Historic District, Roughly bounded by Church, Railroad, Gaunt Sts., and TN 50, Petersburg, 11/07/85, A, C, 85002753

South Elk Street Historic District, Roughly bounded by E. Campbell St., Franklin St., Louisville and Nashville Railroad tracks, and S. Elk St., Fayetteville, 7/12/89, C, 89000127

Loudon County

Blair's Ferry Storehouse, 800 Main St., Loudon, 7/14/77, A, C, 77001277

Bowman House, E of Loudon on Little River Rd., Loudon vicinity, 7/08/70, B, 70000610

Bussell Island Site, Address Restricted, Lenoir City vicinity, 3/29/78, D, 78002606

Cannon-Calloway House, W of Loudon off U.S. 11, Loudon vicinity, 7/08/70, C, 70000611

Cumberland Presbyterian Church of Loudon, College St., Loudon, 4/15/82, C, a, 82003988

Griffitts, William H., House, Jackson Ferry—Greenback Rd., Greenback vicinity, 3/02/89, A, C, 89000141

Lenoir City Company, Depot St., Lenoir City, 3/19/82, A, C, 82003987

Lenoir Cotton Mill, Depot St., Lenoir City, 6/18/75, A, C, 75001767

Lenoir, Albert, House, W of Loudon on River Rd. (TN 72), Loudon, 4/11/73, B, C, 73001808

Loudon County—Continued

Loudon County Courthouse, Grove and Mulberry Sts., Loudon, 5/28/75, A, C, 75001768

Mason Place, 600 Commerce St., Loudon, 11/27/89, B, C, 89002029

McCollum Farm, SW of Greenback on Morganton Rd., Greenback vicinity, 4/15/78, A, C, 78002605

National Campground, SR 1, Greenback, 1/07/72, A, a, 72001243

Robinson Mill, TN 72, Loudon vicinity, 4/05/84, A, C, 84003592

Wilson, Orme, and Company Storehouse, Hackberry St., Loudon, 2/12/80, A, C, 80003845

Macon County

Cloyd Hotel [Early Twentieth Century Resort Buildings of Red Boiling Springs TR], Market St., Red Boiling Springs, 9/11/86, A, C, 86002855

Counts Hotel [Early Twentieth Century Resort Buildings of Red Boiling Springs TR], Market St., Red Boiling Springs, 9/11/86, A, C, 86002856

Donoho Hotel Historic District [Early Twentieth Century Resort Buildings of Red Boiling Springs TR], Market St., Red Boiling Springs, 9/11/86, A, C, 86002857

Galen Elementary School [Education Related Properties of Macon County MPS], Jct. of Galen and Tucker Rds., Galen, 2/22/93, C, 93000030

Keystone School [Education Related Properties of Macon County MPS], TN 52 W of Lafayette, just E of Gap of the Ridge, Lafayette vicinity, 2/22/93, C, 93000031

Long Creek School [Education Related Properties of Macon County MPS], Long Creek Rd. NW of Lafayette, Lafayette vicinity, 2/22/93, C, b, 93000032

Madison County

Bemis Historic District, Roughly bounded by D St., the Illinois Central Gulf RR tracks, Sixth St. and rural property lines to the W and S, Bemis, 12/16/91, A, C, g, 91001777

Deberry-Hurt House, SW of Jackson, Jackson vicinity, 7/08/80, C, 80003846

Denmark Mound Group, Address Restricted, Denmark vicinity, 12/07/92, D, 92001656

Denmark Presbyterian Church, Jackson-Denmark Rd., Denmark, 6/16/83, A, C, a, 83003048

East Main Street Historic District, Irregular pattern along E. Main St., Jackson, 7/03/80, C, 80003847

Farrar, Capt. H. P., House, 161 West Orleans St., Jackson, 4/15/82, B, C, 82003989

Greyhound Bus Station [Transportation-Related Properties of Jackson MPS], 407 E. Main St., Jackson, 2/11/93, A, C, 92001871

Illinois Central Railroad Division Office [Transportation-Related Properties of Jackson MPS],

245 W. Sycamore St., Jackson, 2/11/93, A, 92001869

Jackson Free Library, College and Church Sts., Jackson, 6/26/75, C, 75001769

Lane College Historic District, Lane Ave., Jackson, 7/02/87, A, C, a, 87001117

Lane College Historic District (Boundary Increase), Area including President's Home and Lane Ave. to present district boundary, Jackson, 11/08/91, A, B, 91001591

Murphy Hotel [Transportation-Related Properties of Jackson MPS], 545 S. Royal St., Jackson, 2/11/93, A, C, 92001872

Nashville, Chattanooga & St. Louis Passenger Depot—Jackson [Transportation-Related Properties of Jackson MPS], 590 S. Royal St., Jackson, 2/11/93, A, C, 92001870

Northwood Avenue Historic District, 1–38 Northwood Ave., Jackson, 11/07/90, C, g, 90001659

Pinson Mounds, Address Restricted, Pinson vicinity, 10/15/66, D, NHL, 66000727

Ross-Sewell House, 909 Highland Ave., Jackson, 1/27/83, B, 83003049

Southern Engine and Boiler Works [Transportation-Related Properties of Jackson MPS], 342 N. Royal St., Jackson, 2/11/93, A, 92001868

St. Luke Episcopal Church, 309 E. Baltimore St., Jackson, 5/24/84, C, a, 84003600

Walsh, William Kirby, House, 204 E. Deaderick St., Jackson, 12/10/93, B, C, 93001374

Marion County

Christ Episcopal Church and Parish House, Corner of 3rd and Holly Sts., South Pittsburg, 8/22/77, C, a, 77001278

Cumberland Avenue Bridge [Cement Construction in Richard City MPS], Cumberland Ave. over Poplar Springs Branch Cr., South Pittsburg, 10/28/91, A, C, 91001584

First National Bank of South Pittsburg, 204 W. Third St., South Pittsburg, 6/24/91, A, C, 91000826

Hardy, Richard, Memorial School, 1620 Hamilton Ave., South Pittsburg, 9/30/82, B, C, 82003990

Ketner's Mill and Bridge, E of Victoria on Ketner Mill Rd. and at Sequatchie River, Victoria vicinity, 11/23/77, A, C, 77001279

McKendree Methodist Episcopal Church, Betsy Pack Dr., Jasper, 11/21/78, C, a, 78002607

Primitive Baptist Church of Sweeten's Cove, Sweeden Cove Rd., South Pittsburg vicinity, 6/30/83, C, a, 83003050

Putnam—Cumberland Historic District of Richard City [Cement Construction in Richard City MPS], 1805–1810 Cumberland and 1805–1812 Putnam Aves., South Pittsburg, 7/25/91, A, C, 91000898

South Pittsburg Historic District, Roughly bounded by Elm and Walnut Aves. and 2nd and 7th Sts., South Pittsburg, 10/25/90, A, C, 90001573

Townsite Historic District of Richard City [Cement Construction in Richard City MPS], 402–

512 Dixie, 102–106 Lee Hunt and 2207 Cumberland Aves., South Pittsburg, 7/25/91, A, C, 91000897

Marshall County

Adams, Joe Chase, House, 327 E. Church St., Lewisburg, 12/02/93, C, 93001354

Baird-Welch House, Water St., Cornersville, 3/21/85, C, 85000621

Bear Creek Cumberland Presbyterian Church, Bear Creek Rd., Mooresville vicinity, 3/28/85, C, a, d, 85000667

Belfast Railroad Depot, US 431, Belfast, 8/09/84, A, C, b, 84003606

Berlin Historic District, US 431, Berlin, 8/30/84, A, C, 84003609

Chapel Hill Cumberland Presbyterian Church, Main St., Chapel Hill, 8/30/85, C, a, 85001897

Cornersville Methodist Episcopal Church South, 100 S. Mulberry St., Cornersville, 4/15/82, C, a, 82003991

Ewing Farm, Franklin Road, Lewisburg vicinity, 4/05/84, A, C, 84003612

Fitzpatrick House, TN 50 A, Mooresville, 8/26/82, C, 82003992

Forrest, Nathan Bedford, Boyhood Home, W of Chapel Hill, Chapel Hill vicinity, 7/13/77, B, C, 77001280

Harris, Robert C., House, W of S. Berlin on TN 50, South Berlin vicinity, 1/27/83, C, 83003051

Lillard's Mill Hydroelectric Station [Pre-TVA Hydroelectric Development in Tennessee, 1901-1933 MPS], McLean Rd. and Duck River, Milltown, 4/20/90, A, 89002370

Swaim House, Main St., Chapel Hill, 7/12/84, C, 84003613

Tate, J. C., General Merchandise Store, Old Belfast Rd., Belfast, 7/12/78, A, C, 78002608

Valley Farm, Cornersville Rd., Cornersville vicinity, 4/05/84, C, 84003616

Verona Methodist Episcopal Church, South, Verona-Berlin Rd., Verona, 11/07/85, C, a, 85002755

Maury County

Amis, Jonathan, House, Covey Hollow Rd., McCains, 4/26/84, C, 84003620

Ashwood Rural Historic District, Spans US 43 between Columbia and Mount Pleasant, Columbia vicinity, 2/10/89, A, B, C, D, a, d, 88003247

Athenaeum, The, 808 Athenaeum St., Columbia, 4/24/73, A, C, 73001809

Beechlawn Advance and Retreat, S of Columbia on U.S. 31, Columbia vicinity, 5/14/71, A, C, 71000824

Blythewood, Trotwood and Hatcher Lane, Columbia, 4/11/73, C, 73001810

Booker, Merritt H., House, Scott Hollow Rd., Culleoka vicinity, 7/18/85, B, C, 85001561

Breckenridge Hatter's Shop, N. Main St., Mt. Pleasant, 12/13/84, B, C, 84000613

Maury County—Continued

Cheairs, Martin, House, U.S. 31, Spring Hill, 12/12/76, C, 76001787

Church House, 312 W. 7th St., Columbia, 10/19/78, C, 78002609

Clifton Place, SW of Columbia on Mt. Pleasant Hwy., Columbia vicinity, 7/08/70, A, B, C, 70000613

Columbia Arsenal, W. 7th St., Columbia, 9/19/77, C, 77001281

Columbia Central High School, W. 8th St., Columbia, 4/21/80, A, C, 80003848

Columbia Commercial Historic District, Roughly bounded by 7th, 8th, Woodland, and High St., Columbia, 8/16/84, A, C, 84003625

Columbia Hydroelectric Station [Pre-TVA Hydroelectric Development in Tennessee, 1901-1933 MPS], Riverside Park, Riverside Dr. and Duck River, Columbia, 2/09/90, A, 89002364

Columbia West End Historic District, Roughly along W. Seventh St. between Frierson St. and the Seaboard System RR, Columbia, 3/13/86, C, 86000394

Culleoka Methodist Episcopal Church, South, Quality St., Culleoka, 5/22/86, A, a, 86001134

Derryberry House, New Lasea Rd. E of jct. with I-65, Spring Hill vicinity, 11/07/90, A, C, 90001656

Elm Springs, Mooresville Pike, Columbia vicinity, 3/13/86, C, 86000402

Ewell Farm, Depot Lane, Spring Hill, 5/24/76, A, C, 76001788

Fairmont, Mooresville Pike, Columbia vicinity, 9/01/83, C, 83003052

First United Methodist Church of Columbia, 222 W. 7th St., Columbia, 8/30/84, A, C, a, 84003628

Frierson, Lucius, House, W. 7th St., Columbia, 9/01/78, B, C, a, 78002610

Gordon, John, House, NW of Williamsport off TN 50, Williamsport vicinity, 4/18/74, A, B, NPS, 74000333

Grace Episcopal Church, U.S. 31, Spring Hill, 5/17/76, C, a, 76001789

Hamilton Place, Mt. Pleasant Pike, W of Columbia off U.S. 43, Columbia vicinity, 7/16/73, B, C, 73001812

Kennedy, James, House, Rogers Ford Rd., Columbia vicinity, 11/06/87, C, 87001780

Maguire, Patrick, House, 105 N. Campbell Blvd., Columbia, 12/15/83, B, C, 83004270

Mayes, Dr. Samuel, House, Jct. of Zion Ln. and Canaan Rd., Columbia vicinity, 10/25/93, C, 93000345

Mayes-Hutton House, 306 W. 6th St., Columbia, 7/08/70, C, 70000614

Mercer Hall, 902 Mercer Ct., Columbia, 12/16/82, B, C, 82001730

North Main Street Historic District [Mount Pleasant MPS], Roughly N. Main St. from Shofner St. to Third St., Mount Pleasant, 8/08/89, A, C, 89000263

Pillow Place, Campbellsville Pike, Columbia vicinity, 12/08/83, C, 83004271

Pillow—Bethel House, SW of Columbia off U.S. 43, Columbia vicinity, 12/12/76, C, 76001785

Pine Hill, Old Zion Lane, Ashwood vicinity, 12/15/83, C, 83004272

Pleasant Historic District [Mount Pleasant MPS], Roughly bounded by Haylong Ave., Pleasant, Bond, Wheeler, Adams, and Cherry St., Washington Ave., and College St., Mount Pleasant, 8/08/89, A, C, 89000264

Pleasant Mount Cumberland Presbyterian Church, SE of Columbia off TN 50, Columbia vicinity, 8/16/77, C, a, 77001282

Polk Sisters' House, 305 W. 7th St., Columbia, 5/21/75, C, 75001770

Polk, James K., House, W. 7th and S. High Sts., Columbia, 10/15/66, B, c, NHL, 66000728

Rally Hill, 319 W. 8th St., Columbia, 8/16/84, B, C, 84003638

Rattle and Snap, Andrew Jackson Hwy. (TN 43), Columbia vicinity, 11/11/71, C, NHL, 71000825

Ritter-Morton House, McLemore Ave., Spring Hill, 12/12/76, C, 76001790

Rockdale Furnace Historic District (40MU487) [Iron Industry on the Western Highland Rim 1790s—1920s MPS], Address Restricted, Rockdale vicinity, 7/21/88, A, D, 88001100

Skipwith Hall, W of Columbia on TN 50, Columbia vicinity, 11/23/77, C, 77001283

Spring Hill Presbyterian Church, S. Main St., Spring Hill, 7/19/84, C, a, 84003640

St. John's Episcopal Church, W of Columbia on U.S. 43, Columbia vicinity, 7/08/70, A, C, a, d, 70000615

St. Peter's Episcopal Church, 311 W. 7th St., Columbia, 6/27/79, C, a, 79002448

State Bank of Tennessee, 201 W. 7th St., Columbia, 11/02/78, A, C, 78002611

Thompson, Absalom, House, S of Spring Hill on Denning Rd, Spring Hill vicinity, 9/11/79, A, 79002449

Union Station, Depot St., Columbia, 10/23/86, C, 86002908

Vine Hill, Sawdust Rd., Cross Bridges vicinity, 7/15/83, A, C, 83003053

Walnut Grove, 510 N. Main St., Mt. Pleasant, 3/08/84, C, 84003641

Watkins, William, House, Canaan Rd., Mt. Pleasant vicinity, 10/23/86, C, 86002901

Webster, George, House, Sawdust Rd., Williamsport vicinity, 4/05/84, A, C, 84003646

West Sixth Street and Mayes Place Historic District, W. 6th St. and Mayes Pl., Columbia, 2/25/78, C, 78002612

White Hall, Duplex Rd., Spring Hill, 4/05/84, A, B, C, 84003661

Zion Presbyterian Church, 6.3 mi. W of Columbia off TN 99, Columbia vicinity, 6/13/72, C, a, 72001245

McMinn County

Cate, Elijah, House, W. of Niota on SR 1, Niota vicinity, 3/25/82, C, 82003993

Cleage, Samuel, House, N of Athens on Lee Hwy., Athens vicinity, 5/12/75, C, 75002069

Etowah Depot, U.S. 411, Etowah, 10/17/77, A, C, 77001513

Keith, Alexander H., House, 110 Keith Ln., Athens, 6/26/86, B, C, 86001381

Lowry, William, House, 405 E. Madison Ave., Athens, 7/19/84, C, 84003596

McClatchey-Gettys Farm, S of Riceville on SR 1, Riceville vicinity, 12/28/82, A, C, 82001731

Niota Depot, Main St., Niota, 4/01/75, A, 75002105

Old College, College St., Athens, 12/29/83, A, C, 83004259

Trew General Merchandise Store, W of Delano at TN 163 and Bowater Rd., Delano vicinity, 12/22/76, A, C, 76002159

McNairy County

Bethel Springs Presbyterian Church, 3rd Ave., Bethel Springs, 8/18/83, C, a, 83003054

Meigs County

Big Sewee Creek Bridge [Meigs County, Tennessee MRA], TN 58 and Center Point Rd., Decatur, 7/06/82, A, 82003995

Black, John M., Cabin [Meigs County, Tennessee MRA], Big Sewee Creek Rd., Ten Mile, 7/06/82, C, 82004016

Blythe Ferry [Meigs County, Tennessee MRA], N of Birchwood on TN 60 at Tennessee River, Birchwood vicinity, 1/05/83, A, g, 83003055

Buchanan House [Meigs County, Tennessee MRA], Vernon St., Decatur, 7/06/82, C, 82003996

Cowan, James, House [Meigs County, Tennessee MRA], Old Bunker Hill Rd., Big Spring, 7/06/82, B, C, 82003994

Culvahouse House [Meigs County, Tennessee MRA], River Rd., Ten Mile, 7/06/82, C, 82004017

Decatur Methodist Church [Meigs County, Tennessee MRA], Vernon St., Decatur, 7/06/82, A, C, a, 82003997

Eaves, S. S., House [Meigs County, Tennessee MRA], Eaves Ferry Rd., Decatur, 7/06/82, B, C, 82003998

Ewing House [Meigs County, Tennessee MRA], River Rd., Ten Mile, 7/06/82, C, 82004018

Feezell Barn [Meigs County, Tennessee MRA], TN 58, Ten Mile, 7/06/82, C, 82004019

Gettys, James R., House [Meigs County, Tennessee MRA], N. No Pone Valley Rd., Ten Mile, 7/06/82, B, C, 82004020

Gettys, James R., Mill [Meigs County, Tennessee MRA], N. No Pone Valley Rd., Ten Mile, 7/06/82, A, 82004021

Godsey, Jim, House [Meigs County, Tennessee MRA], TN 30, Decatur, 7/06/82, C, 82003999

Griffith, James Turk, House [Meigs County, Tennessee MRA], TN 58, Ten Mile, 7/06/82, B, C, 82004022

Grubb, Jacob L., Store [Meigs County, Tennessee MRA], TN 58, Decatur, 7/06/82, A, 82004000

Meigs County—Continued

Hastings-Locke Ferry [Meigs County, Tennessee MRA], W of Decatur on TN 30 at Tennessee River, Decatur vicinity, 1/05/83, A, 83003056

Holloway, Dr. D. W., House [Meigs County, Tennessee MRA], River Rd., Ten Mile, 7/06/82, B, C, 82004023

Hooper, Scott, Garage [Meigs County, Tennessee MRA], SR 1, Georgetown, 7/06/82, A, C, 82004010

Hutsell Truss Bridge [Meigs County, Tennessee MRA], Old Ten Mile Rd., Ten Mile, 7/06/82, A, 82004024

Hutsell, Sam, House [Meigs County, Tennessee MRA], Old Ten Mile Rd., Ten Mile, 7/06/82, C, 82004025

Johnson, R. H., Stable [Meigs County, Tennessee MRA], TN 58, Ten Mile, 7/06/82, A, C, 82004026

Kings Mill Bridge [Meigs County, Tennessee MRA], Big Sewee Rd., Decatur, 7/06/82, A, 82004001

MacPherson House [Meigs County, Tennessee MRA], Off Hurricane Valley Rd., Ten Mile, 7/06/82, C, 82004027

McKenzie Windmill [Meigs County, Tennessee MRA], TN 58, Georgetown, 7/06/82, C, 82004011

Meigs County Bank [Meigs County, Tennessee MRA], Court Sq., Decatur, 7/06/82, A, 82004003

Meigs County Courthouse [Meigs County, Tennessee MRA (AD)], Court Sq., Decatur, 8/03/78, C, 78002613

Meigs County High School Gymnasium [Meigs County, Tennessee MRA], Brown St., Decatur, 7/06/82, A, C, 82004005

Mount Zion Church [Meigs County, Tennessee MRA], Mt. Zion Hollow, Decatur, 7/06/82, C, a, 82004006

Oak Grove Methodist Church [Meigs County, Tennessee MRA], Pinhook Ferroy Rd., Ten Mile vicinity, 7/06/82, C, a, 82004028

Patterson, Alexander, House [Meigs County, Tennessee MRA], Wood Lane, Ten Mile, 7/06/82, B, C, 82004029

Rice-Marler House [Meigs County, Tennessee MRA], Goodfield Valley Rd., Decatur, 7/06/82, B, C, 82004007

Rymer, Bradford, Barn [Meigs County, Tennessee MRA], SR 1, Georgetown, 7/06/82, A, C, 82004012

Sharp, Elisha, House [Meigs County, Tennessee MRA], Old Ten Mile Rd., Ten Mile, 7/06/82, A, B, C, 82004030

Shiflett, G. W., Barn [Meigs County, Tennessee MRA], SR 1, Georgetown, 7/06/82, C, 82004013

Shiflett, H. C., Barn [Meigs County, Tennessee MRA], SR 1, Georgetown, 7/06/82, C, 82004014

Smith, Robert H., Law Office [Meigs County, Tennessee MRA], TN 58, Decatur, 7/06/82, A, C, b, 82004008

Stewart, John, House [Meigs County, Tennessee MRA], TN 58, Decatur, 7/06/82, A, C, 82004009

Surprise Truss Bridge [Meigs County, Tennessee MRA], Sewee Creek Rd., Ten Mile, 7/06/82, A, 82004031

Wood, Andy, Log House and Willie Wood Blacksmith Shop [Meigs County, Tennessee MRA], SR 1, Georgetown, 7/06/82, A, 82004015

Monroe County

Chota and Tanasi Cherokee Village Sites, Address Restricted, Vonore vicinity, 8/30/73, D, 73001813

Chota and Tanasi Cherokee Village Sites (Boundary Increase), Address Restricted, Vonore vicinity, 10/25/78, D, 78003410

Citico Site, Address Restricted, Vonore vicinity, 11/02/78, D, 78002614

Fort Loudoun, U.S. 411, Vonore vicinity, 10/15/66, A, NHL, 66000729

Fowler, William J., Mill and House, Sweetwater Rd., Eve Mills, 1/27/83, A, B, C, 83003057

Icehouse Bottom Site, Address Restricted, Vonore vicinity, 10/19/78, A, D, g, 78002615

Johnson, Elisha, Mansion, Ballplay Rd., Tellico Plains, 12/24/74, B, C, 74001923

Mialoquo Site, Address Restricted, Vonore vicinity, 10/19/78, B, D, 78002616

Scott Mansion, Scott Mansion Rd., about 1 1/4 mi. E of TN 68, Tellico Plains, 1/21/93, A, B, C, 92001816

Stickley House, W of jct. of U.S. 411 and TN 68, Madisonville, 9/10/74, A, C, 74001922

Tellico Blockhouse Site, 2 mi. E of Vonore off TN 72, Vonore vicinity, 8/11/75, A, D, 75001771

Tomotley Site, Address Restricted, Vonore vicinity, 10/19/78, D, 78002617

Toqua Site, Address Restricted, Vonore vicinity, 11/16/78, D, 78002618

Montgomery County

Allen House, N of Clarksville on Allen-Griffey Rd., Clarksville vicinity, 10/03/78, A, B, C, 78002619

Catholic Church and Rectory [Nineteenth Century Churches in Clarksville TR], 716 Franklin St., Clarksville, 8/02/82, C, a, 82004032

Clarksville Architectural District, Public Sq., Legion, 3rd, Franklin, and Commerce Sts., Clarksville, 5/13/76, A, C, 76001791

Clarksville Federal Building, Commerce and S. 2nd Sts., Clarksville, 6/13/72, C, 72001246

Clarksville Foundry and Machine Works [Iron Industry on the Western Highland Rim 1790s—1920s MPS], 96 Commerce St., Clarksville, 11/25/87, A, C, 87002007

Clarksville High School, Greenwood Ave., Clarksville, 12/08/83, A, C, 83004281

Clarksville Industrial District, Bounded by Washington St., Crossland Ave., the ICG RR., and the Cumberland River, Clarksville, 4/30/76, A, C, 76002295

Clarksville Methodist Church [Nineteenth Century Churches in Clarksville TR], 334 Main St., Clarksville, 4/06/82, A, C, a, 82004033

Cloverlands, N of St. Bethlehem on Clarksville-Trenton Rd., St. Bethlehem vicinity, 1/08/79, C, 79002451

Dog Hill Architectural District, Munford Ave., 1st, Union, Madison and 2nd Sts., Clarksville, 5/09/80, C, 80003849

Drane—Foust House, 319 Home Ave., Clarksville, 7/07/88, C, 88001023

Emerald Hill, N. 2nd St., Clarksville, 7/14/71, B, 71000826

First Presbyterian Church [Nineteenth Century Churches in Clarksville TR (AD)], 213 Main St., Clarksville, 4/30/76, C, a, 76001793

Fort Defiance CSA/Fort Bruce USA, Address Restricted, New Providence vicinity, 2/04/82, D, 82004036

Gracey—Woodward Furnace (40MT378) [Iron Industry on the Western Highland Rim 1790s—1920s MPS], Address Restricted, Clarksville vicinity, 11/25/87, D, 87002003

Home Infirmary, Riverside Dr. and Current St., Clarksville, 8/24/78, B, 78002620

Lafayette Furnace (40MT372) [Iron Industry on the Western Highland Rim 1790s—1920s MPS], Address Restricted, Southside vicinity, 11/25/87, C, D, d, 87002000

Louisa Furnace (40MT379) [Iron Industry on the Western Highland Rim 1790s—1920s MPS], Address Restricted, Slayden vicinity, 1/12/88, D, 87002004

Madison Street Methodist Church [Nineteenth Century Churches in Clarksville TR (AD)], 319 Madison St., Clarksville, 5/13/76, C, a, 76001794

Minglewood Farm, 1650 Hopkinsville Hwy., Clarksville, 10/15/87, B, C, 87001856

Oak Top, 107 Madison Ter., Clarksville, 7/08/80, C, 80003850

Old Post House, N of Clarksville on U.S. 41 A, Clarksville vicinity, 3/08/78, A, C, 78002621

Poplar Spring Furnace (40MT376) [Iron Industry on the Western Highland Rim 1790s—1920s MPS], Address Restricted, Needmore vicinity, 1/12/88, A, D, 87002002

Poston Block, Main and Telegraph Sts., Clarksville, 6/13/72, A, C, 72001247

Rexinger, Samuel, House, 703 E. College St., Clarksville, 4/13/77, B, C, 77001284

Ringgold Mill Complex, NW of Clarksville on Mill Rd., Clarksville vicinity, 7/08/80, A, 80003851

Riverview, W of Clarksville on Cumberland Heights Rd., Clarksville vicinity, 3/26/79, B, C, g, 79002450

Sailor's Rest Furnace (40MT375) [Iron Industry on the Western Highland Rim 1790s—1920s MPS], Address Restricted, Shiloh vicinity, 11/25/87, D, 87002001

Sevier Station, Walker St., S of B St., Clarksville, 5/06/71, A, 71000827

Smith, Christopher H., House, Spring and McClure Sts., Clarksville, 3/08/88, B, C, 88000173

Smith-Hoffman House, Beech and A Sts., Clarksville, 8/22/77, A, C, 77001285

Montgomery County—Continued

St. Peter African Methodist Church [Nineteenth Century Churches in Clarksville TR], 518 Franklin St., Clarksville, 4/06/82, C, a, 82004034

Tennessee Furnace (40MT383) [Iron Industry on the Western Highland Rim 1790s—1920s MPS], Address Restricted, McAllisters Crossroad vicinity, 11/25/87, D, 87002006

Trinity Church and Rectory [Nineteenth Century Churches in Clarksville TR], 317 Franklin St., Clarksville, 4/06/82, C, a, 82004035

Washington Furnace and Forge (40MT382) [Iron Industry on the Western Highland Rim 1790s—1920s MPS], Address Restricted, Excell vicinity, 1/12/88, D, 87002005

White Chapel, Rossview Rd., Rossview, 6/26/86, A, B, a, 86001395

Whitehall, NW of Clarksville off TN 12 on Mill Rd., Clarksville vicinity, 1/31/78, B, C, 78002622

Wilson, Sanford, House, Old Ashland City Hwy., Fredonia, 9/13/78, A, C, 78002623

Yellow Creek Furnace and Forge (40MT371) [Iron Industry on the Western Highland Rim 1790s—1920s MPS], Address Restricted, Needmore vicinity, 1/12/88, C, D, d, 87001999

Moore County

Green—Evans House, Old TN 55 N of Lynchburg, Lynchburg vicinity, 12/17/92, C, 92001713

Jack Daniel Distillery, TN 55, Lynchburg, 9/14/72, A, 72001248

Ledfords Mill, Ledford Mill Rd., Tullahoma vicinity, 1/10/85, A, C, 85000077

Moore County Courthouse and Jail, Court Sq., Lynchburg, 9/26/79, C, 79002452

Morgan County

Brooks, R. M., General Store and Residence, Jct. of TN 52 and Brewstertown Rd., Rugby vicinity, 4/14/92, A, 92000364

Rugby Colony, TN 52, Rugby vicinity, 4/26/72, B, C, a, 72001249

Obion County

Confederate Monument, Summer and Edwards Sts., Union City, 7/28/77, A, 77001286

Deering Building, 106 1st St., Union City, 11/25/83, A, 83004283

Dickey's Octagonal Barbershop, SW corner High and N. Church Sts., Rives, 4/29/75, A, C, 75001772

Morris, W. W., House, 305 W. State Line Rd., South Fulton, 1/27/83, B, C, 83003058

Parks Covered Bridge, N of Trimble off U.S. 51, Trimble vicinity, 11/27/78, C, 78002624

US Post Office, 114 W. Washington, Union City, 5/31/84, C, 84003671

Overton County

Overton County Courthouse, Court Sq., Livingston, 11/13/80, A, C, 80003852

Roberts, Gov. Albert H., Law Office, 114 E. Main St., Livingston, 2/20/75, B, C, 75001773

Standing Stone Rustic Park Historic District [State Parks in Tennessee Built by the CCC and the WPA, 1934-1942, TR], Standing Stone State Park, Livingston vicinity, 7/08/86, A, C, g, 86002794

Perry County

Cedar Grove Furnace [Iron Industry on the Western Highland Rim 1790s—1920s MPS (AD)], Address Restricted, Linden vicinity, 6/19/73, A, C, 73001814

Cedar Grove Furnace (40PY77)(Boundary Increase) [Iron Industry on the Western Highland Rim 1790s—1920s MPS], Address Restricted, Pope vicinity, 9/28/88, C, D, 88001107

Dickson, James, House, Lower Lick Creek Rd., Linden vicinity, 3/28/85, C, 85000668

Hufstedler Gravehouse, Hurricane Creek Rd., Linden vicinity, 6/25/87, C, d, 87001038

Pickett County

Hull, Cordell, Birthplace, About 2 mi. W of Byrdstown, Byrdstown vicinity, 5/05/72, B, C, c, 72001250

Pickett State Rustic Park Historic District [State Parks in Tennessee Built by the CCC and the WPA, 1934-1942, TR], Pickett State Park and Forest, Jamestown vicinity, 7/08/86, A, C, g, 86002795

Polk County

Burra Burra Mine Historic District, TN 68 and Burra St., Ducktown, 3/17/83, A, C, 83003059

Buzzard's Roost Historic District [Tennessee Copper Basin MPS], 301-400 College, 420-430 Ell and 129-186 Main Sts., 400-415 School House Rd. and 211 and 215 TN 68, Ducktown, 5/15/92, A, C, 92000451

Center & Abernathy Store Building [Tennessee Copper Basin MPS], 23-33 Ocoee St., Copperhill, 9/02/92, A, C, 92001071

Central Headframe [Tennessee Copper Basin MPS], TN 68 S of jct. with US 64/74, Ducktown vicinity, 9/02/92, A, C, g, 92001073

Copeland House, Cookson Creek Rd., Parksville vicinity, 4/05/84, C, 84003674

Copperhill Historic District [Tennessee Copper Basin MPS], Roughly bounded by Hill, Prospect, Main and Riverview Sts., Copperhill, 5/15/92, A, C, 92000449

Ducktown Historic District [Tennessee Copper Basin MPS], Roughly bounded by TN 68 and

alley 2 blocks NW of Main St., Ducktown, 5/15/92, A, 92000450

Isabella Managers' Row [Tennessee Copper Basin MPS], Ducktown—Isabella Rd. N of US 64, Isabella, 5/15/92, A, C, 92000448

Kimsey Junior College [Tennessee Copper Basin MPS], 244 TN 68, Ducktown, 9/02/92, A, C, 92001072

Newtown Historic District [Tennessee Copper Basin MPS], 510-521 First, 538-730 Second and 580-730 Third Sts., Copperhill vicinity, 5/15/92, A, C, 92000452

Ocoee Hydroelectric Plant No. 2, U.S. 64, Ocoee, 10/31/79, A, C, 79002453

Ocoee No. 1 Hydroelectric Station [Pre-TVA Hydroelectric Development in Tennessee, 1901-1933, MPS], Jct. of US 64 and Ocoee R., Parksville vicinity, 7/05/90, A, C, 90001003

Polk County Courthouse, Bounded by US 411 and Ward, Commerce and Main Sts., Benton, 6/24/93, C, 93000562

Reliance Historic District, Roughly bounded by New Reliance and Power House Rds., TN 30, and the Hiwassee River, Reliance, 3/13/86, B, C, 86000350

Ward, Nancy, Tomb, S of Benton on U.S. 411, Benton vicinity, 4/11/73, B, D, c, 73001815

Wiggins, William, House, Jct. of Main and Ward Sts., NE corner, Benton, 12/02/93, C, 93001355

Putnam County

Algood Methodist Church, 158 Wall St, Algood, 11/15/79, A, C, a, 79002454

Arcade, The, 7-13 S. Jefferson Ave., Cookeville, 4/17/79, A, C, 79002455

Burgess Falls Hydroelectric Station [Pre-TVA Hydroelectric Development in Tennessee, 1901-1933, MPS], SR 135 over Falling Water R., Cookeville vicinity, 7/05/90, A, 90001006

Cookeville Railroad Depot, Broad and Cedar Sts., Cookeville, 11/07/85, A, C, 85002773

Harding Studio, 43 W. Broad St., Cookeville, 4/21/92, B, 92000355

Henderson Hall, Tennessee Technological University, Dixie Ave., Cookeville, 11/07/85, A, C, 85002754

Rhea County

Hiwassee Garrison Site, Address Restricted, Dayton vicinity, 11/14/78, A, D, 78002625

Rhea County Courthouse, Market St. between 2nd and 3rd Aves., Dayton, 11/07/72, A, a, g, NHL, 72001251

Roane County

Colonial Hall, Spring and Main Sts., Oliver Springs, 9/11/75, B, 75001774

Roane County—Continued

Cornstalk Heights Historic District, Roughly bounded by Georgia Ave., Sewanee St., Morgan Ave. and Trenton St., Harriman, 1/11/91, A, C, 90002142

Harriman City Hall, Roane and Walden Sts., Harriman, 4/16/71, A, C, 71000828

Jones, George, Memorial Baptist Church [Oak Ridge MPS], Blair Rd., Oak Ridge, 5/06/92, A, C, a, g, 92000408

Morgan, Col. Gideon, House, 149 Kentucky St., Kingston, 1/27/83, B, C, 83003060

New Bethel Baptist Church [Oak Ridge MPS], Bethel Valley Rd., Oak Ridge, 5/06/92, A, C, a, f, g, 92000409

Oak Ridge Turnpike Checking Station [Oak Ridge MPS], Oak Ridge Tpk., Oak Ridge, 5/06/92, A, g, 92000412

Roane County Courthouse, Kentucky Ave., Kingston, 7/14/71, C, 71000829

Roane Street Commercial Historic District, Roughly Roane St. between Morgan Ave. NW. and Crescent Ave. NW., Harriman, 6/29/89, A, C, 89000506

Southwest Point, 1 mi. SW of Kingston, Kingston, 7/31/72, A, 72001252

X-10 Reactor, Oak Ridge National Laboratory, Oak Ridge National Laboratory, Oak Ridge, 10/15/66, A, g, NHL, 66000720

Robertson County

Beeches, The, SC 49, Springfield vicinity, 3/25/82, A, B, 82004037

Cornsilk, N of Cross Plains on Highland Rd., Cross Plains vicinity, 1/11/74, B, C, g, 74002266

Glen Raven, SW of Cedar Hill on Washington Rd., Cedar Hill vicinity, 10/02/73, A, C, 73001816

Highland Chapel Union Church, Highland Ave., Ridgetop, 10/29/91, C, a, 91001592

Mansfield Cheatham House, 7th Ave., W., Springfield, 1/30/78, B, C, 78002626

O'Bryan, George, House, O'Bryan and Highland Aves., Ridgetop, 2/23/89, B, C, 89000073

Pitt, Arthur, House and Distillery, NE of Springfield off TN 49, Springfield vicinity, 12/18/73, A, 73001820

Randolph, William, House, On TN 25, Cross Plains, 10/30/73, A, 73001818

Robertson County Courthouse, Public Sq., Springfield, 5/22/78, A, C, 78002627

Rock Jolly, NE of Cross Plains off TN 52, Cross Plains vicinity, 10/30/73, C, 73001819

Springfield Town Square Historic District, U.S. 41 and TN 49, Springfield, 8/01/79, C, 79002456

St. Michael's Catholic Church, 3.5 mi. W of TN 49, Cedar Hill, 7/05/73, A, a, 73001817

Sudley Place, N of Youngfield on State Line Rd., Youngville vicinity, 1/11/74, B, C, 74001925

Thomas Drugs, 7802 TN 25 E, Cross Plains, 11/04/93, A, C, 93001189

Wessyngton, S of Cedar Hill, Cedar Hill vicinity, 5/06/71, A, B, C, 71000830

Woodard Hall, NE of Springfield on Owens Chapel Rd., Springfield vicinity, 10/10/75, A, C, 75001775

Rutherford County

Arnold—Harrell House, 1710 E. Main St., Murfreesboro, 3/27/92, C, 92000145

Boxwood, Old Salem Pike, Murfreesboro vicinity, 10/25/84, C, 84000139

Bradley Academy, 415 S. Academy St., Murfreesboro, 6/14/90, A, 90000914

Brown's Mill, SE of Lascassas on Brown's Mill Rd., Lascassas vicinity, 12/29/78, A, 78002628

Childress-Ray House, 225 N. Academy St., Murfreesboro, 12/27/79, B, C, 79002458

Collier-Crichlow House, 511 E. Main St., Murfreesboro, 7/16/73, B, C, 73001822

Collier-Lane-Crichlow House, 500 N. Spring St., Murfreesboro, 8/23/78, B, C, 78002629

Crichlow Grammar School and Cox., E. C., Memorial Gym, 400 N. Maple St. and 105 Olive St., Murfreesboro, 12/17/92, A, C, 92001685

Davis, Sam, House, NE of Smyrna off TN 102, Smyrna vicinity, 12/23/69, A, B, C, D, b, 69000181

Dement House, Cainsville Pike, Lascassas vicinity, 6/26/86, B, C, 86001379

East Main Street Historic District, Roughly E. Main, E. Lytle, College, University and E. Vine Sts., Murfreesboro, 7/11/85, B, C, 85001516

Elmwood, NW of Murfreesboro, off U.S. 70S/41, Murfreesboro vicinity, 10/15/73, A, C, 73001823

First Presbyterian Church, 210 N. Spring St., Murfreesboro, 6/24/93, C, a, 93000561

Fortress Rosecrans Site, W of Murfreesboro at Stones River, Murfreesboro vicinity, 6/07/74, A, C, 74001926

Jarman Farm, Cainsville Pike, Lascassas vicinity, 7/06/87, C, 87001368

Jenkins, Hiram, House, 1556 Gresham Ln., Murfreesboro, 6/16/89, C, 89000504

Jordan, William B., Farm, 2665 Taylor Ln., Eagleville vicinity, 7/13/92, C, 92000825

Landsberger—Gerhardt House, 435 N. Spring St., Murfreesboro, 12/13/93, C, 93001397

Macon, Uncle Dave, House, W of Readyville on U.S. 70S, Readyville vicinity, 11/15/73, A, C, 73001827

Marymont, SW of Murfreesboro, off TN 99 on Rucker Lane, Murfreesboro vicinity, 10/30/73, C, 73001824

McCord, William Harrison, House, US 41A, Eagleville, 12/20/84, B, C, 84001121

Middle Tennessee State Teachers College Training School, 923 E. Lytle St., Murfreesboro, 1/04/93, A, C, 92001731

Morgan House, SW of Christiana, Christiana vicinity, 12/27/79, C, 79002457

Murray Farm, 9409 Bradyville Rd., Readyville vicinity, 7/31/91, A, C, 91000980

North Maney Avenue Historic District, Roughly bounded by N. Maney and N. Highland Aves.,

E. College St. and N. Academy Ave., Murfreesboro, 4/04/85, C, 85000709

Oaklands, N. Maney Ave., Murfreesboro, 2/26/70, B, C, 70000616

Palmer, Gen. Joseph B., House, 434 E. Main St., Murfreesboro, 9/20/73, B, C, 73001825

Ready, Charles, House, On U.S. 70S, Readyville, 7/02/73, A, C, 73001828

Ridley's Landing, N of Smyrna on Jones Mill Rd., at Stoves River, Smyrna vicinity, 7/16/73, A, C, 73001829

Rucker, Benjamine, House, 3978 Betty Ford Rd., Compton vicinity, 2/28/91, C, 91000223

Rutherford County Courthouse, Public Square, Murfreesboro, 7/16/73, A, C, 73001826

Rutherford Health Department, 303 N. Church St., Murfreesboro, 7/24/92, A, C, 92000960

Scales, Absalom, House, N of Eagleville off TN 16, on Rocky Glade Rd., Eagleville vicinity, 10/30/73, C, 73001821

Smith, Robert Andrew, Farm, 2568 Armstrong Valley Rd., Murfreesboro vicinity, 1/04/93, A, C, 92001712

Stones River National Battlefield, 3 mi. NW of Murfreesboro on U.S. 41, Murfreesboro vicinity, 10/15/66, A, d, f, NPS, 66000075

Walter Hill Hydroelectric Station [Pre-TVA Hydroelectric Development in Tennessee MPS], US 231 at Stones R., Murfreesboro, 11/07/90, A, C, 90001660

Scott County

Barton Chapel, US 27, Robbins, 7/12/84, C, a, 84003679

Bryant, Louis E., House, 2 mi. E of Oneida on Bear Creek Rd., Oneida vicinity, 5/29/75, A, 75001776

First National Bank of Huntsville, #4 Courthouse Square, Huntsville, 7/11/85, A, 85001510

Huntsville High School, 220 E. Main St., Huntsville, 7/02/87, C, 87001119

Old Scott County Jail, Courthouse Sq., Huntsville, 4/18/74, A, C, 74001927

Sequatchie County

Dunlap Coke Ovens, Hickory St. and Cordell Rd., Dunlap, 7/05/85, A, 85001489

Sequatchie County Courthouse, Cherry St., Dunlap, 1/20/80, A, 80003853

Sevier County

Andes, Riley H., House, Douglas Dam Rd., Sevierville, 7/08/80, C, 80003854

Brabson's Ferry Plantation, NW of Sevierville off Sevierville Pike in Boyd's Creek area, Sevierville vicinity, 6/25/75, A, C, 75001780

Sevier County—Continued

Buckingham House, W of Sevierville on Sevierville Pike, Sevierville vicinity, 3/18/71, B, C, 71000831

Cole, Alex, Cabin, 5 mi. S of Gatlinburg off U.S. 441 in Great Smoky Mountains National Park, Gatlinburg vicinity, 1/02/76, C, NPS, 76000165

Harrisburg Covered Bridge, S of Harrisburg off U.S. 411 over East Fork of Little Pigeon River, Harrisburg vicinity, 6/10/75, A, C, 75001777

King-Walker Place, W of Gatlinburg off TN 73, Great Smoky Mountains National Park, Gatlinburg vicinity, 3/16/76, A, C, NPS, 76000169

Little Greenbrier School-Church, About 9 mi. W of Gatlinburg off TN 73 in Great Smoky Mountains National Park, Gatlinburg vicinity, 1/11/76, A, a, g, NPS, 76000168

McCarter, Tyson, Place, 10 mi. E of Gatlinburg on TN 73, Great Smoky Mountains National Park, Gatlinburg vicinity, 3/16/76, A, C, NPS, 76000204

Messer Barn, SE of Gatlinburg near Greenbrier Cove in Great Smoky Mountains National Park, Gatlinburg vicinity, 1/01/76, C, NPS, 76000166

Mountain View Hotel, 400 Parkway, Gatlinburg, 9/13/84, A, C, 84003681

Ogle, Bud, Farm, 3 mi. SE of Gatlinburg, Gatlinburg vicinity, 11/23/77, A, C, NPS, 77000158

Ownby, John, Cabin, 3 mi. S of Gatlinburg off TN 73 in Great Smoky Mountains National Park, Gatlinburg vicinity, 1/01/76, C, NPS, 76000167

Perry's Camp, 101 Flat Branch Rd., Gatlinburg vicinity, 10/30/92, A, C, 92000369

Pigeon Forge Mill, Off U.S. 441, Pigeon Forge, 6/10/75, A, 75001778

Roaring Fork Historic District, 5 mi. SE of Gatlinburg off TN 73, Great Smoky Mountains National Park, Gatlinburg vicinity, 3/16/76, A, C, NPS, 76000170

Rose Glen, 4 mi. E of Sevierville on Newport Hwy., Sevierville vicinity, 7/18/75, A, C, 75001781

Sevier County Courthouse, Court Ave., Sevierville, 3/24/71, C, 71000832

Sevierville Commercial Historic District, Sections of Bruce St., Court Ave., and Commerce St., Sevierville, 10/23/86, A, C, 86002910

Sevierville Masonic Lodge, 119 Main St., Sevierville, 2/07/80, A, 80003855

Trotter-McMahan House, S of Sevierville on Middle Creek Rd., Sevierville vicinity, 10/10/75, A, C, 75001783

Walker Mill Hydroelectric Station [Pre-TVA Hydroelectric Development in Tennessee, 1901-1933, MPS], W Prong, Little Pigeon R. just off US 441, Sevierville vicinity, 11/20/90, A, C, 90001751

Waters House, 217 Cedar St., Sevierville, 6/18/75, A, C, 75001784

Wheatlands, NW of Sevierville on Old Knoxville Hwy., Sevierville vicinity, 7/07/75, C, 75001785

Shelby County

Adams Avenue Historic District, Adams and Washington Aves., Memphis, 11/25/80, A, C, a, 80004481

Allen, Walter Granville, House, 8504 Macon Rd., Cordova, 2/23/90, B, C, 90000320

Anderson—Coward House, 919 Coward Pl., Memphis, 3/13/86, B, C, 86000404

Annesdale, 1325 Lamar Ave., Memphis, 11/25/80, C, 80003856

Annesdale Park Historic District, Roughly bounded by Peabody and Goodbar Aves., Cleveland St. and Rosenstein Pl., Memphis, 12/22/78, A, C, 78002630

Annesdale-Snowden Historic District, Roughly bounded by I-255, Lamar Ave. and Heistan Pl, Memphis, 10/25/79, C, 79002460

Arlington Historic District, Brown, Campbell, Chester, Quintard, Greenlee, and Walker Sts., Arlington, 5/17/82, A, C, 82004038

Ashlar Hall, 1397 Central Ave., Memphis, 1/13/83, C, 83003061

Austin, John Alexander, House, 290 S. Front St., Memphis, 7/12/84, B, C, 84003684

Bank of Commerce and Trust Company Building, 45 S. 2nd St., Memphis, 5/07/80, C, 80003857

Beale Street Historic District, Beale St. from 2nd to 4th Sts., Memphis, 10/15/66, A, g, NHL, 66000731

Bowles, Robert S., Houses, 544-548 Vance Ave., Memphis, 12/16/79, C, 79002461

Boyce-Gregg House, 317 S. Highland St., Memphis, 12/19/79, C, 79002462

Bradford-Maydwell House, 648 Poplar Ave., Memphis, 12/26/79, C, 79002463

Brister, John Willard, Library, Memphis State University campus, Memphis, 7/11/80, A, C, 80003858

Brooks, Wilks, House, 2000 Old Oak Dr., Memphis, 5/16/80, C, b, 80003859

Calvary Episcopal Church and Parish House, 102 N. 2nd St., Memphis, 4/27/82, C, a, 82004039

Campbell, Joseph A., House [Collierville MPS], 215 South St., Collierville, 3/29/91, C, 91000314

Capleville Methodist Church, 5053 Shelby Dr., Capleville, 4/03/79, C, a, 79002459

Capt. Harris House, 2106 Young St., Memphis, 12/19/79, C, 79002464

Carrier, Robert M., House, 642 S. Willett St., Memphis, 5/27/80, C, 80003860

Central Gardens Historic District, Roughly bounded by Rembert St., York, Cleveland and Eastmoreland Aves., Memphis, 9/09/82, A, C, 82004040

Central High School [Public Schools of Memphis 1902-1915 TR], 306 S. Bellevue Blvd., Memphis, 9/17/82, A, C, 82004041

Chucalissa Indian Village, Mitchell Rd., Memphis, 5/07/73, D, 73001830

Clancy, Cornelius Lawrence, House, 911 Kerr Ave., Memphis, 11/25/83, B, C, 83004294

Collierville Historic District [Collierville MPS], Roughly N. and S. Rowlett, Poplar, and Walnut Sts., Collierville, 3/12/90, A, C, b, g, 90000305

Collins Chapel CME Church and Site, 678 Washington Ave., Memphis, 3/29/91, A, a, g, 91000307

Columbian Mutual Tower, 60 N. Main St., Memphis, 7/24/78, A, C, 78002631

Cooper—Young Historic District, Roughly bounded by L & N Railroad tracks, E. Parkway S., Southern Ave., and S. McLean Blvd., Memphis, 6/22/89, C, 89000508

Cotton Row Historic District, S. Front St. between Monroe and Gayoso Aves., Memphis, 8/01/79, A, g, 79002467

Court Square Historic District, Roughly bounded by Riverside Dr., N. 2nd St., Madison and Jefferson Aves., Memphis, 4/15/82, A, C, 82004042

Crisscross Lodge, 10056 Poplar Ave., Collierville vicinity, 4/06/89, C, 88002627

Crump, E. H., House, 1962 Peabody Ave., Memphis, 12/26/79, B, g, 79002465

Darnell, Rowland J., House, 1433 Union Ave., Memphis, 3/26/79, B, C, 79002466

Davies Manor, 9336 Davies Plantation Rd., Memphis, 3/19/75, B, C, 75001787

Dermon Building, 46 N. 3rd St., Memphis, 3/15/84, B, C, 84003688

Dudney, Jack, House [Collierville MPS], 90 W. Poplar Ave., Collierville, 3/29/91, C, 91000315

Elam Homestead, 1428 Fox St., Memphis, 9/18/80, C, 80003861

Ellis, William C., and Sons Ironworks and Machine Shop, 231-245 S. Front St., Memphis, 8/25/83, A, C, 83003062

Elmwood Cemetery Office and Entrance Bridge, 824 S. Dudley St., Memphis, 5/22/78, C, 78002632

Evergreen Historic District, Roughly bounded by N. Parkway, Kenilworth St., Watkins St., and Court Ave., Memphis, 1/11/85, A, C, 85000080

Fairview Junior High School, 750 E. Parkway S., Memphis, 10/25/90, C, 90001571

First Baptist Church, 379 Beale Ave., Memphis, 2/11/71, A, a, 71000833

First Congregational Church and Parish House, 234 S. Watkins St., Memphis, 7/21/80, C, 80003862

First Methodist Church, 204 N. 2nd St., Memphis, 3/19/76, C, 76001804

Fleming, John M., Home Place, 1545 S. Byhalia Rd., Collierville vicinity, 12/06/90, A, C, D, 90001763

Fowlkes-Boyle House, 208 Adams Ave., Memphis, 8/07/74, C, 74001928

Gartly-Ramsay Hospital, 696 Jackson Ave., Memphis, 7/12/84, A, C, 84003700

Gaston Park Historic District [Memphis Park and Parkway System MPS], 1046 S. Third St., Memphis, 7/03/89, A, C, 89000521

Gayoso-Peabody Historic District, Roughly bounded by Call Pl., S. 3rd and S. Front Sts., Monroe and Gayoso Aves., Memphis, 5/07/80, A, C, 80003863

Germantown Baptist Church, 2216 Germantown Rd., Germantown, 4/01/75, C, a, 75001786

Germantown Redoubt, Honey Tree Dr. S of jct. with Poplar Pike, Germantown, 6/06/91, D, 91000623

Goodwinslow, 4066 James Rd, Raleigh, 12/06/79, A, C, 79002482

Goodwyn Street Historic District, Goodwyn St. from Central to Southern Aves., Memphis, 3/09/90, A, C, 90000302

Shelby County—Continued

Graceland, 3764 Elvis Presley Blvd., Memphis, 11/07/91, B, g, 91001585

Greenlaw Addition Historic District, Roughly bounded by Bethel, Thomas, 7th, Auction, and 2nd Sts., Memphis, 8/16/84, A, C, 84003704

Greenlevel, 853 Collierville-Arlington Rd. S, Collierville vicinity, 3/06/87, A, B, C, 87000397

Greenstone Apartments, 1116-1118 Poplar Ave. and 200 Waldran Blvd., Memphis, 5/14/80, C, 80003864

Greenwood, 1560 Central Ave., Memphis, 7/09/79, C, 79002468

Guthrie Elementary School [Public Schools of Memphis 1902-1915 TR], 951 Chelsea Ave., Memphis, 9/17/82, A, C, 82004043

Hayley, Patrick, House, 604 Vance Ave., Memphis, 10/10/79, C, 79002469

Hein Park Historic District, Bounded by Charles Pl., Jackson Ave., Trezevant St., and N. Parkway Dr., Memphis, 11/16/88, A, C, g, 88002613

Hill, A. B., Elementary School [Public Schools of Memphis 1902-1915 TR], 1372 Latham St., Memphis, 9/17/82, A, C, 82004044

Hotel Claridge, 109 N. Main St., Memphis, 4/29/82, C, 82004045

Houston, J. W., House [Collierville MPS], 259 S. Center St., Collierville, 3/29/91, C, 91000313

Hunt-Phelan House, 533 Beale Ave., Memphis, 2/11/71, A, C, 71000834

Lauderdale Walker Elementary School [Public Schools of Memphis 1902-1915 TR], 995 S. Lauderdale St., Memphis, 9/17/82, A, C, 82004046

Lee and Fontaine Houses of the James Lee Memorial, 680–690 Adams Ave., Memphis, 2/11/71, A, C, 71000835

Lee, James, House, 239 Adams Ave., Memphis, 10/02/78, B, C, 78002633

Lenox School, 519 S. Edgewood Ave., Memphis, 7/30/81, C, 81000579

Libertyland Grand Carousel, Libertyland Theme Park, Memphis, 7/03/80, C, 80003865

Linden Station and Reichman-Crosby Warehouse, 245, 281, 291 Wagner Pl., Memphis, 9/08/78, A, 78002634

Love, George Collins, House, 619 N. 7th St., Memphis, 4/02/79, B, C, 79002472

Lowenstein House, 756 Jefferson Ave., Memphis, 3/23/79, A, B, C, 79002473

Lowenstein, Abraham, House, 217 N. Waldran Blvd., Memphis, 1/05/84, A, B, C, 84003705

Lowenstein, B., & Brothers Building, 27 S. Main St., Memphis, 6/16/83, A, C, 83003063

Madison-Monroe Historic District, Madison and Monroe Aves., Main and 2nd Sts., Memphis, 5/19/83, A, C, 83003064

Magevney House, 198 Adams Ave., Memphis, 11/06/73, B, C, 73001831

Mason Temple, Church of God in Christ, 958 Mason St., Memphis, 4/10/92, A, B, a, g, 92000286

Maury Elementary School [Public Schools of Memphis 1902-1915 TR], 272 N. Bellevue Blvd., Memphis, 9/17/82, A, C, 82004047

Maxwelton, 3105 Southern Ave., Memphis, 3/10/80, B, C, 80003866

McFerrin, John B., House [Collierville MPS], 156 W. Poplar Ave., Collierville, 3/29/91, C, 91000316

Medical Arts Building and Garage, 248 Madison Ave. and 11 N. 4th St., Memphis, 8/16/84, A, C, 84003707

Memphis Merchants Exchange, 2nd St. and Madison Ave., Memphis, 5/08/79, A, C, 79002474

Memphis Parkway System [Memphis Park and Parkway System MPS], S. Parkway W., S. Parkway E., E Parkway S., E. Parkway N., N. Parkway, Memphis, 7/03/89, A, C, 89000520

Memphis Pink Palace Museum, 3050 Central Ave., Memphis, 7/09/80, B, C, 80003870

Memphis Street Railway Company Office and Streetcar Complex, 821 Beale St., Memphis, 9/09/82, A, C, 82004048

Memphis Trust Building, 12 S. Main St., Memphis, 11/25/80, A, C, 80003867

Moore, William R., Dry Goods Building, 183 Monroe Ave., Memphis, 8/26/82, A, C, 82004049

Mosby-Bennett House, 626 Poplar Pike, Memphis, 5/27/80, C, 80003868

Nelson—Kirby House, 6792 Poplar Pike, Germantown, 10/23/86, B, C, c, 86002913

Newburger, Joseph, House, 168 E. Parkway, South, Memphis, 4/29/82, B, C, 82004050

Orpheum Theatre, 197 S. Main St., Memphis, 8/15/77, A, C, 77001289

Overton Park Historic District, Roughly bounded by Poplar Ave., E. Parkway N., N. Parkway E., and Kenilworth St., Memphis, 10/25/79, A, C, 79002475

Paisley Hall, 1822 Overton Park Ave., Memphis, 2/12/80, C, 80003869

Patton-Bejach House, 1085 Poplar St, Memphis, 7/27/79, C, 79002476

Peabody Elementary School [Public Schools of Memphis 1902-1915 TR], 2086 Young Ave., Memphis, 9/17/82, A, C, 82004051

Peabody Hotel, 149 Union Ave., Memphis, 9/14/77, A, C, 77001290

Pinch—North Main Commercial District (Boundary Increase), 122 Jackson Ave., Memphis, 10/25/90, A, 90001637

Pinch-North Main Commercial District, Roughly bounded by N. Front and N. 2nd Sts., Commerce and Auction Aves., Memphis, 10/18/79, A, C, 79002477

Pope, Leroy, Elementary School [Public Schools of Memphis TR], 190 Chelsea Ave., Memphis, 9/25/92, A, C, 82005387

Porter, Dr. D. T., Building, 10 N. Main St., Memphis, 4/18/77, A, C, 77001291

Porter—Leath Home, 850 N. Manassas St., Memphis, 5/08/79, A, C, 79002471

Rayner, Eli, House, 1020 Rayner St., Memphis, 5/09/77, B, C, 77001292

Richards, Newton Copeland, House, 975 Peabody Ave., Memphis, 7/12/84, A, C, 84003709

Rozelle Elementary School [Public Schools of Memphis 1902-1915 TR], 993 Roland St., Memphis, 9/17/82, A, C, 82004052

Saunders, Clarence, Estate, 5922 Quince, Memphis, 11/13/89, B, C, 89001969

Scimitar Building, 179 Madison Ave., Memphis, 6/30/83, A, C, 83003065

Sculptures of Dionicio Rodriguez at Memorial Park Cemetery, 5668 Poplar Ave., Memphis, 1/31/91, C, d, g, 90001867

Second Congregational Church, 764 Walker Ave., Memphis, 8/26/82, A, C, a, 82004053

Second Presbyterian Church, 280 Hernando St., Memphis, 9/04/79, A, C, a, 79002478

Shrine Building, 66 Monroe Ave., Memphis, 3/29/79, A, C, 79002479

South Bluffs Warehouse Historic District, Roughly S. Front St., Wagner Pl., and Tennesee St. from Beale St. to Calhoun Ave., Memphis, 6/04/87, A, C, 87000453

South Main Street Historic District, Roughly S. Main St. between Webster and Linden, and Mulberry between Calhoun and Vance Aves., Memphis, 9/02/82, A, B, C, g, 82004054

South Parkway-Heiskell Farm Historic District, S. Parkway E. and E. Parkway S., Memphis, 2/11/83, A, C, 83003066

Southwestern at Memphis Historic District, 2000 N. Parkway, Memphis, 7/20/78, C, a, g, 78002635

St. Mary's Cathedral, Chapel, and Diocesan House, 700, 714, and 692 Poplar Ave., Memphis, 1/19/79, A, C, a, 79002480

St. Mary's Catholic Church, 155 Market St., Memphis, 8/07/74, A, C, a, 74001929

Steele Hall, LeMoyne-Owen College campus, Memphis, 3/23/79, A, a, 79002481

Sterick Building, 8 N. 3rd St., Memphis, 10/02/78, B, C, 78002636

Stonewall Place Historic District, Stonewall St. between Poplar Ave. and North Pkwy., Memphis, 3/25/82, A, C, 82004055

Stratton, Leslie M., YMCA, 245 Madison Ave., Memphis, 6/30/83, A, C, 83003067

Tennessee Brewery, 477 Tennessee St., Memphis, 11/25/80, A, C, 80004482

Tennessee Club-Overall Goodbar Building, 128–130 Court Ave., Memphis, 4/22/82, A, C, 82004056

Tennessee Trust Building, 81 Madison Ave., Memphis, 12/09/82, A, C, 82001732

Thomas, John W., House [Collierville MPS], 245 W. Poplar Ave., Collierville, 3/29/91, C, 91000312

Toof Building, 195 Madison Ave., Memphis, 8/26/82, A, C, 82004057

Toof, John S., House, 246 Adams Ave., Memphis, 3/25/82, B, C, 82004058

Tri-State Bank, 386 Beale St., Memphis, 2/11/71, B, 71000836

U.S. Marine Hospital Executive Building and Laundry-Kitchen, 360 and 374 W. California Ave., Memphis, 7/02/80, A, 80003872

U.S. Post Office-Front Street Station, 1 N. Front St., Memphis, 6/30/80, C, g, 80003873

Union Avenue Methodist Episcopal Church, South, 2117 Union Ave., Memphis, 3/06/87, C, a, 87000399

Shelby County—Continued

Victorian Village District, Adams and Jefferson Sts., Memphis, 12/11/72, C, 72001253

Zion Cemetery, S. Pky. E. at Pillow St., Memphis, 2/23/90, A, d, 90000301

Smith County

Bradley, James, House, SE of Dixon Springs off TN 25, Dixon Springs vicinity, 9/18/78, B, C, 78002637

Carthage United Methodist Church, 609 S. Main St., Carthage, 7/05/85, C, a, 85001487

Cullum Mansion, 609 Cullum St., Carthage, 1/04/83, B, C, 83003068

Davis-Hull House, 1004 N. Main St., Carthage, 1/04/83, B, C, 83003069

Dixon Springs District, 1.75 mi. NE of Cumberland River, Dixon Springs, 2/10/75, C, 75001788

Dixona, NW of Dixon Springs on TN 25, Dixon Springs vicinity, 7/05/73, B, C, 73001832

Rome Ferry, US 70 at Cumberland River, Rome, 12/24/86, A, g, 86003477

Smith County Courthouse, Court Sq., Carthage, 4/17/79, C, 79002483

Stewart County

Bear Spring Furnace (40SW207) [Iron Industry on the Western Highland Rim 1790s—1920s MPS], Address Restricted, Dover vicinity, 4/09/88, A, C, D, 88000259

Bellwood Furnace (40SW210) [Iron Industry on the Western Highland Rim 1790s—1920s MPS], Address Restricted, Bumpus Mills vicinity, 4/21/88, D, 88000382

Brunsoni Furnace (40SW219) [Iron Industry on the Western Highland Rim 1790s—1920s MPS], Address Restricted, Cumberland City vicinity, 4/11/88, D, 88000255

Clark Furnace (40SW212) [Iron Industry on the Western Highland Rim 1790s—1920s MPS], Address Restricted, Standing Rock vicinity, 4/11/88, D, 88000249

Cross Creek Furnace (40SW217) [Iron Industry on the Western Highland Rim 1790s—1920s MPS], Address Restricted, Indian Mound vicinity, 4/11/88, D, 88000256

Dover Flint Quarries, Address Restricted, Dover vicinity, 5/07/73, D, 73001833

Eclipse Furnace (40SW213) [Iron Industry on the Western Highland Rim 1790s—1920s MPS], Address Restricted, McKinnon vicinity, 4/11/88, D, 88000260

Fort Donelson National Military Park, 1 mi. W of Dover on U.S. 79, Dover vicinity, 10/15/66, A, d, f, NPS, 66000076

Fort Henry Site, NW of Dover off U.S. 79 on Fort Henry Rd., Dover vicinity, 10/10/75, D, 75001789

Great Western Furnace, NW of Dover on TN 49, Dover vicinity, 10/06/75, A, 75001790

Hollister, Henry, House [Iron Industry on the Western Highland Rim 1790s—1920s MPS], Chapel Ridge Rd., Cumberland City vicinity, 4/09/88, B, C, D, d, 88000262

LaGrange Furnace (40SW214) [Iron Industry on the Western Highland Rim 1790s—1920s MPS], Address Restricted, McKinnon vicinity, 4/21/88, D, 88000383

Rough and Ready Furnace (40SW215) [Iron Industry on the Western Highland Rim 1790s—1920s MPS], Address Restricted, Cumberland City vicinity, 4/09/88, D, 88000251

Saline Furnace (40SW218) [Iron Industry on the Western Highland Rim 1790s—1920s MPS], Address Restricted, Bumpus Mills vicinity, 4/09/88, D, 88000258

Stacker, Samuel, House [Iron Industry on the Western Highland Rim 1790s—1920s MPS], Long Branch Rd., Dover vicinity, 4/11/88, B, C, 88000257

Sullivan County

Alison, Finlay, House, W of Piney Flats off U.S. 11, Piney Flats vicinity, 4/11/73, C, 73001851

Alison, Jesse, House, SW of Bluff City off U.S. 11E, Bluff City vicinity, 4/02/73, C, 73001839

Blountville Historic District, Center of Blountville along both sides of TN 126, Blountville, 2/23/73, C, 73001835

Bristol Municipal Stadium, 1112 Edgemont Ave., Bristol, 6/25/87, A, C, 87001039

Bristol Virginia—Tennessee Slogan Sign, E. State St., Bristol, 9/08/88, A, b, 88001568

Church Circle District, Center of Kingsport, along Sullivan St., Kingsport, 4/11/73, A, C, a, g, 73001841

Clinchfield Railroad Station, 101 E. Main St., Kingsport, 4/24/73, A, C, 73001842

DeVault-Masengill House, Andrew Johnson Hwy. US 11E, Piney Flats, 3/28/85, C, 85000669

Erwin Farm, W of Blountville off TN 75, Blountville vicinity, 4/11/73, C, 73001836

Fain Plantation, E of Bloomingdale off U.S. 11W, Arcadia vicinity, 4/11/73, B, C, 73001834

First National Bank of Bristol, 500 State St., Bristol, 7/25/85, A, C, 85001606

Grass Dale, 774 Bloomingdale Pike, Kingsport, 10/25/84, C, 84000140

Johnson, J. Fred, House, 1322 Watauga Ave., Kingsport, 4/11/73, B, 73001843

Long Island of the Holston, S fork of the Holston River, Kingsport vicinity, 10/15/66, A, NHL, 66000733

Looney, Moses, Fort House, 5436 Old Island Rd., Kingsport vicinity, 1/18/78, B, 78002638

Mount Ida, 1010–1012 Sevier Terrace Dr., Kingsport, 4/02/73, A, C, b, 73001844

Netherland Inn and Complex, 2144 Netherland Inn Rd., Kingsport, 12/23/69, A, B, 69000182

Old Deery Inn, Main St., Blountville, 5/07/73, B, C, b, 73001838

Old Kingsport Presbyterian Church, Stone Dr. (Hwy. 11W) and Afton, Kingsport, 10/02/73, B, C, a, b, 73001845

Paramount Theatre and Office Building, 516 State St., Bristol, 4/04/85, C, 85000701

Parlett House, 728 Georgia Ave., Bristol, 8/18/83, B, C, g, 83003070

Pearson Brick House, E of Kingsport on Shipley Ferry Rd., Kingsport vicinity, 4/11/73, C, 73001846

Pemberton Mansion and Oak, 9 mi. NE of Bristol on TN 34, Bristol vicinity, 3/14/73, A, 73001840

Preston Farm, 4812 Orebank Rd., Kingsport, 9/03/71, A, 71000837

Rock Ledge, 117 Stuffle Pl., Kingsport vicinity, 5/24/78, B, C, 78002639

Rocky Mount, SW of Piney Flats off U.S. 11E, Piney Flats vicinity, 2/26/70, B, 70000617

Roller-Pettyjohn Mill, W of Blountville on Creek Rd., Blountville vicinity, 12/07/77, A, C, 77001293

Roseland, S of Kingsport on Shipp St., Kingsport vicinity, 4/02/73, B, a, 73001847

Spring Place, NW of Kingsport on W. Carter's Valley Rd., off US 23, Kingsport vicinity, 4/11/73, B, a, 73001848

Steel-Seneker Houses, 4 mi. W of Bristol on TN 126, Bristol vicinity, 8/22/77, B, C, b, 77001294

Stone-Penn House, 1306 Watauga St., Kingsport, 11/15/84, A, C, 84000669

US Post Office—Shelby Street Station, 620 Shelby St., Bristol, 11/07/85, C, 85002772

Wills-Dickey Stone House, NW of Kingsport off U.S. 23 on W. Carter's Valley Rd., Kingsport vicinity, 3/30/73, C, 73001849

Yancey's Tavern, E of Kingsport on TN 126, Kingsport vicinity, 4/11/73, A, 73001850

Sumner County

Ashcrest Farm, 410 Gallatin Rd., Hendersonville, 4/14/92, A, C, 92000349

Bledsoe's Station, Address Restricted, Castalian Springs vicinity, 7/30/92, A, B, D, 92000970

Bowen-Campbell House, E of Goodlettsville on Jackson Rd., Goodlettsville vicinity, 7/25/77, B, C, 77001295

Bridal House, Red River Rd., Cottontown, 2/04/82, A, C, 82004059

Brown-Chenault House, Chenault Lane, Castalian Springs vicinity, 7/25/85, B, C, 85001614

Castalian Springs, Gallatin-Hartsville Pike, TN 25, Castalian Springs, 7/14/71, A, C, D, NHL, 71000838

Cragfont, E of Gallatin off TN 25, Gallatin vicinity, 2/26/70, A, B, C, 70000618

Donelson, Daniel Smith, House, 178 Berrywood Dr., Hendersonville, 1/04/83, B, C, 83003071

Fairvue, 4 mi. S of Gallatin on U.S. 31E, Gallatin vicinity, 6/10/75, A, B, NHL, 75002162

Ferrell, Mary Felice, House, 2144 Nashville Pike, Gallatin, 4/14/92, C, 92000348

Fite, Leonard B., House, 1154 W. Main St., Hendersonville vicinity, 3/25/82, B, C, b, 82004061

Sumner County—Continued

Gallatin Commercial Historic District, Roughly bounded by Town Creek, N. Water Ave. and Boyer and College Sts., E. Main St., and S. Water Ave. and Trimble St., Gallatin, 10/23/85, A, C, 85003369

Gallatin Presbyterian Church, 167 W. Main St., Gallatin, 3/25/82, C, a, 82004060

Greenfield, 683 Rock Springs Rd., Castalian Springs vicinity, 11/07/90, A, B, C, d, 90001579

Hazel Path, 175 E. Main St., Hendersonville, 4/05/84, A, C, 84003713

Jameson, James B., House, TN 25, Gallatin vicinity, 11/25/85, C, 85002968

King Homestead, W of Cottontown off TN 25, Cottontown vicinity, 1/30/78, B, C, 78002640

Locust Grove, N of Castalian Springs, Castalian Springs vicinity, 1/08/79, C, 79002484

Oakland, 1995 Hartsville Pike, Gallatin vicinity, 10/02/92, B, C, 92000841

Oakley, 2243 Nashville Pike, Gallatin vicinity, 7/25/85, B, C, 85001615

Parker—Bryson Historic District, Greenfield Lane, Castilian Springs vicinity, 6/25/87, A, 87001036

Rock Castle, SE of Hendersonville on Indian Lake Rd., Hendersonville vicinity, 7/08/70, B, C, 70000619

Rosemont, 810 S. Water St., Gallatin, 4/26/78, B, C, 78002641

Shackle Island Historic District, N of Hendersonville at Shackle Island Rd. and Long Hollow Pike, Hendersonville vicinity, 1/30/78, B, C, 78002643

Trousdale Place, 183 W. Main St., Gallatin, 6/05/75, B, 75001793

Walnut Grove, W of Gallatin on Red River Rd., Gallatin vicinity, 12/29/78, C, 78002642

Westmoreland Tunnel, Off TN 52, Westmoreland, 1/20/78, C, 78002644

Williamson and Adams Carriage Factory, 326 E. Main St., Gallatin, 5/12/87, A, C, 87000488

Tipton County

Hotel Lindo, 116 W. Liberty St., Covington, 12/27/82, A, C, 82001733

Mt. Carmel Presbyterian Church, Mt. Carmel Rd., Covington vicinity, 7/12/84, C, a, 84003716

Rhodes House, SE of Brighton on Clopton-Gainsville Rd., Brighton vicinity, 4/30/80, A, 80003875

Ruffin Theater, 113 W. Pleasant Ave., Covington, 3/26/92, B, C, 92000248

South Main Street Historic District, Roughly bounded by S. Main St., Sherrod Ave., S. Maple St. and Sanford and Lauderdale Aves., Covington, 5/29/92, A, C, 92000427

St. Matthew's Episcopal Church, Munford St., Covington, 8/16/77, A, C, a, 77001297

Trinity Church, Main St., Mason, 3/15/84, C, a, 84003719

Trousdale County

DeBow, James R., House, TN 25, Hartsville vicinity, 11/03/88, C, 88002381

Hartsville Depot, Broadway, Hartsville, 7/03/80, C, 80003876

Hartsville Historic District, Roughly bounded by Church, Front, River, Greentop and Court Sts., Hartsville, 6/24/93, A, C, 93000568

Turney—Hutchins House, TN 25, Hartsville, 7/01/92, C, 92000780

Unicoi County

Clarksville Iron Furnace, SW of Erwin off TN 107 in Cherokee National Forest, Erwin vicinity, 6/04/73, A, 73001852

Clinchfield Depot, Jct. of Nolichucky Ave. and Union St., Erwin, 6/22/93, A, C, 93000530

Union County

Ousley, Baite, House, 15 mi. SW of Tazewell, N of Morris Lake on Big Valley Rd., Tazewell vicinity, 3/04/75, C, 75001794

Van Buren County

Big Bone Cave, Address Restricted, Bone Cave vicinity, 4/11/73, A, D, 73001853

Crain Hill School and Church, Crain Hill Rd., Crain Hill, 3/21/85, A, a, 85000622

Warren County

Black House, 301 W. Main St., McMinnville, 11/17/83, C, 83004310

Cardwell Mountain, Address Restricted, Union vicinity, 12/14/78, D, 78002646

Falconhurst, N of McMinnville on Faulkner Springs Rd., McMinnville vicinity, 8/26/82, B, C, g, 82004062

Faulkner, Clay, House, Jct. of Faulkner Springs and Flood Rds., Faulkner Springs, 3/05/92, B, C, 92000137

Great Falls Cotton Mill, W of Rock Island off US 70S, Rock Island vicinity, 8/26/82, A, 82004063

Magness, William H. and Edgar, Community House and Library, 118 W. Main St., McMinnville, 11/04/93, A, B, C, 93001177

McMinnville Hydroelectric Station [Pre-TVA Hydroelectric Development in Tennessee, 1901–1933 MPS], State Route 55 Bypass at Barren Fork River, McMinnville, 2/26/90, A, C, 90000307

My Grandfather's House, US 70S, McMinnville vicinity, 4/04/85, C, b, 85000702

Myers Mound, Address Restricted, McMinnville vicinity, 12/14/78, D, 78002645

Northcutt Plantation, 7 mi. SW of McMinnville off TN 108 on Wheeler Lane, McMinnville vicinity, 5/12/75, C, 75001795

Oakham, US 70 Bypass, McMinnville vicinity, 8/11/83, B, C, 83003072

Philadelphia Church of Christ, Vervilla Rd., Vervilla, 11/17/88, A, a, 88002537

Stone—Pennebaker House, 229 Towles Ave., McMinnville, 11/17/88, C, 88002648

US Post Office—Main, Morford St. and Court Sq., McMinnville, 12/03/85, C, 85003089

Walling, Joseph Daniel, House, River Cliff and Old Viola Rds., McMinnville, 8/06/80, C, 80003877

Washington County

Aquone, 110 Barberry Rd., Johnson City, 11/04/93, B, C, 93001199

Bashor Mill, NE of Johnson City, Johnson City vicinity, 7/08/80, A, 80003878

Broylesville Historic District, Roughly bounded by TN 34, Taylor Mill and Gravel Hill Rds. along Little Limestone Creek, Washington vicinity, 3/28/85, A, B, C, 85000677

Cooper, Isaac, House, Glendale Rd., Limestone vicinity, 9/07/84, C, 84003723

DeVault Tavern, W of Jonesboro on Leesburg Rd., Jonesboro vicinity, 6/04/73, A, C, 73001855

DeVault, Valentine, House, 5 mi. N of Johnson City off DeVault Lane, Johnson City vicinity, 7/29/77, C, 77001298

Dungan's Mill and Stone House, NE of Johnson City on Watauga Rd., Johnson City vicinity, 7/02/73, A, 73001854

Embree House, SW of Telford on Walker's Mill Rd., Telford vicinity, 2/14/78, A, B, C, 78002647

Gillespie, Col. George, House, Off U.S. 411, Limestone, 8/22/77, A, B, C, 77001299

Hammer, Isaac, House, N of Johnson City off U.S. 11, Johnson City vicinity, 3/19/76, C, 76001805

Hoss, Henry, House, Blountville Rd., Jonesboro, 12/16/82, C, 82001734

Jonesboro Historic District, Roughly bounded by Depot and College Sts., 3rd Ave., and jct. of Main St. and Franklin Ave., Jonesboro, 12/23/69, A, 69000183

Kitzmiller, Martin, House, US 23, Boon's Creek, Gray, 7/25/85, C, 85001609

Knob Creek Historic District, Gray Station, Knob Creek, and Fair Ridge Rds., Johnson City, 7/10/86, A, C, d, 86001543

Montrose Court Apartments, Montrose Ct., Johnson City, 4/21/80, C, 80003879

Plum Grove Archaeological Site, Address Restricted, Jonesboro vicinity, 9/05/85, D, 85002353

Range, Peter, Stone House, 307 Twin Falls Dr., Johnson City, 12/15/83, B, C, 83004312

Robin's Roost, S. Roane St., Johnson City, 1/20/76, B, C, 76001806

Salem Presbyterian Church, 147 Washington College Rd., Washington College, 9/22/92, A, C, a, 92001255

Washington County—Continued

Sulphur Springs Methodist Campground, N of Jonesboro off TN 81 in Sulphur Springs Community, Jonesboro vicinity, 5/12/75, C, a, e, 75001796

Taylor, Christopher, House, Main St., Jonesboro, 12/09/71, A, 71000839

Telford, Thomas, House, Old Jonesboro Water Plant Rd., Limestone vicinity, 2/10/82, C, 82004064

Tipton-Haynes House, SE of Johnson City on U.S. 19W, Johnson City vicinity, 2/26/70, A, B, C, 70000620

Wayne County

Collinwood Railroad Station, Old RR Bed, Collinwood, 3/24/88, A, C, 88000264

First Presbyterian Church of Clifton, Main St., Clifton, 3/08/88, C, a, 88000172

Forty-eight Forge (40WY63) [Iron Industry on the Western Highland Rim 1790s—1920s MPS], Address Restricted, Waynesboro vicinity, 4/11/88, D, 88000254

Marion Furnace (40WY61) [Iron Industry on the Western Highland Rim 1790s—1920s MPS], Address Restricted, Eagle Creek vicinity, 4/09/88, D, 88000252

Water Street Historic District, Water St. (TN 128) between Polk and Cedar Sts., Clifton, 7/08/92, C, 92000829

Waynesboro Cumberland Presbyterian Church, High St., Waynesboro, 10/22/87, C, a, 87001877

Weakley County

Bandy, Dr. Robert W., House, College St., Gleason, 8/09/84, B, C, 84003726

Caldwell, William Parker, House, Off TN 22, Gardner, 3/09/79, B, C, 79002485

Cary Lawn, 321 Linden St., Dresden, 6/18/92, C, 92000779

Ivandale, 115 N. McCombs St., Martin, 3/25/82, B, C, 82004067

Lawler, W. T., House, 229 University St., Martin, 3/25/82, C, 82004068

Marshalldale, 115 Ryan Ave., Martin, 3/25/82, B, C, 82004069

Oakland, SR 22 and TN 89, Dresden, 4/22/82, B, C, 82004065

Sims, Capt. William, House, Rte. 2, Liberty Rd., Greenfield vicinity, 3/25/82, C, 82004066

White County

Cherry Creek Mound, Address Restricted, Key vicinity, 12/15/78, D, 78002648

Great Falls Hydroelectric Station [Pre-TVA Hydroelectric Development in Tennessee, 1901-1933,

MPS], Caney Fork R. Mi. 91.1 off US 70, Rock Island vicinity, 7/05/90, A, C, 90001004

Indian Cave Petroglyphs, Address Restricted, Onward vicinity, 12/14/78, D, 78002649

Oldham Theater, W. Liberty Sq., Sparta, 11/04/93, A, C, 93001188

Sparta Electric Building [Pre-TVA Hydroelectric Power Development in Tennessee MPS], S. Main St., Sparta, 3/25/93, A, 93000238

Sparta Hydroelectric Station [Pre-TVA Hydroelectric Development in Tennessee, 1901–1933 MPS], TN 111 at Calfkiller River, Sparta vicinity, 4/20/90, A, C, 90000306

Sparta Nashville, Chattanooga and St. Louis Railroad Depot, Jct.of Depot and Clark Sts., Sparta, 12/07/92, A, C, 92001658

Sparta Residential Historic District, Roughly bounded by N. Main, College, Everett and Church Sts., Sparta, 10/28/91, C, 91001586

Sparta Rock House, 3 mi. E of Sparta on U.S. 70, Sparta vicinity, 8/14/73, A, C, 73001856

Williamson County

Allison, William, House [Williamson County MRA], US Alt. 31, 2 mi. S of College Grove, College Grove vicinity, 4/13/88, B, C, 88000288

Anderson Site, Address Restricted, Franklin, 6/14/90, D, 90000913

Bank of College Grove, The [Williamson County MRA], US Alt. 31, College Grove, 4/13/88, A, 88000289

Bank of Nolensville [Williamson County MRA], US Alt. 41, Nolensville, 4/13/88, A, 88000287

Beasley—Parham House [Williamson County MRA], Lick Creek Rd. 1 mi. N of Natchez Trace, Greenbrier vicinity, 4/13/88, C, 88000286

Bostick Female Academy, Hwy. 41 A, College Grove vicinity, 4/15/82, A, C, 82004070

Boyd Mill Ruins [Williamson County MRA], E bank of the West Harpeth River, 1/10 mi. S of Boxley Valley Rd. and Boyd Mill Pike, Franklin vicinity, 4/13/88, A, 88000285

Boyd, William, House [Williamson County MRA], Boyd Mill Pike 1/10 mi. N of Boxley Valley Rd., Franklin vicinity, 4/13/88, B, C, 88000284

Buford, Spencer, House [Williamson County MRA], US 31 1/2 mi. S of Critz Ln., Thompsons Station vicinity, 4/13/88, C, 88000346

Campbell, William S., House, TN 96, Franklin, 10/29/75, B, C, 75001798

Carnton, Confederate Cemetery Lane, Franklin, 1/18/73, A, C, d, 73001857

Carothers, John Henry, House [Williamson County MRA], Liberty Pike, Franklin vicinity, 11/27/89, A, C, 89002028

Cedarmont, Off TN 96, Franklin vicinity, 7/12/84, A, C, 84003747

College Grove Methodist Church [Williamson County MRA], US Alt. 31, College Grove, 4/13/88, C, a, 88000345

Collins, James E., House [Williamson County MRA], Hillsboro Rd./US 431 1/2 mi. S of Spen-

cer Creek Rd., Franklin vicinity, 4/13/88, C, 88000344

Cox House, 150 Franklin Rd., Franklin, 2/28/80, B, C, 80003881

Crafton, John, House [Williamson County MRA], N. Chapel Rd. 2 mi. E of Arno Rd., Franklin vicinity, 4/13/88, C, 88000347

Critz, Jacob, House [Williamson County MRA], Evergreen Rd. 1 1/2 mi. E of Pope Chapel Rd., Thompsons Station vicinity, 4/13/88, C, 88000343

Critz, Thomas L., House [Williamson County MRA], Critz Ln. 1 mi. E of Columbia Pike/US 31, Thompsons Station vicinity, 4/13/88, C, 88000342

Crockett, Andrew, House [Williamson County MRA], 8230 Wikle Ln., Brentwood, 4/13/88, B, C, 88000302

Crockett, Samuel, House [Williamson County MRA], Crockett Rd. and Wilson Pike, Brentwood vicinity, 4/14/88, A, C, 88000296

Douglass—Reams House [Williamson County MRA], Henpeck Ln. 1/4 mi. W of Lewisburg Pike, Franklin vicinity, 4/13/88, C, 88000293

Elliston, Joseph, House [Williamson County MRA], Hillsboro Rd./US 431 1 mi. N of Sneed Rd., Brentwood, 4/13/88, C, 88000291

Fewkes Group Archeological Site, Address Restricted, Brentwood vicinity, 4/21/80, A, C, D, 80003880

Forest Hills School [Williamson County MRA], Carters Creek Pike 2/10 mi. S of Bear Creek Rd., Franklin vicinity, 4/13/88, A, 88000290

Fort Granger, Off Liberty Pike, Franklin, 1/08/73, A, D, 73001858

Franklin Battlefield, S of Franklin on U.S. 31, Franklin vicinity, 10/15/66, A, NHL, 66000734

Franklin Historic District [Williamson County MRA (AD)], Centered around Main St. (TN 96) and 3rd Ave. (U.S. 31), Franklin, 10/05/72, A, B, C, a, 72001254

Franklin Historic District (Boundary Increase) [Williamson County MRA], Third Ave. S between S. Margin St. and the RR, Franklin, 4/13/88, C, 88000378

Frost, John, House [Williamson County MRA], Old Smyrna Rd. 1 1/2 mi. E of Wilson Pike, Brentwood, 4/13/88, A, 88000308

Giddens, James, House [Williamson County MRA], Farm Ln. at N boundary of Thompsons Station, Thompsons Station, 4/13/88, C, 88000301

Glass, Samuel F., House [Williamson County MRA], TN 96 at Boyd Mill Pike, Franklin, 4/13/88, C, 88000309

Glen Echo, N of Franklin off U.S. 31 on Spencer Creek Rd., Franklin vicinity, 11/07/76, B, C, 76001808

Glenn, Abram, House [Williamson County MRA], McCanless Rd. 1 1/2 mi. E of US Alt. 41, Triune vicinity, 4/13/88, C, 88000310

Gray, Henry P., House [Williamson County MRA], Old Hillsboro Rd. at Boyd Mill Rd., Franklin vicinity, 4/13/88, C, 88000313

Williamson County—Continued

Green, Sherwood, House [Williamson County MRA], Rocky Fork Rd. 1/2 mi. E of Nolensville, Nolensville vicinity, 4/13/88, C, d, 88000311

Hadley, Denny P., House [Williamson County MRA], Off US 31/Franklin Rd. S of Brentwood, Brentwood, 4/14/88, C, 88000283

Hardeman, Franklin, House [Williamson County MRA], Lewisburg Pike 1 mi. S of Goose Creek Bypass, Franklin vicinity, 4/13/88, B, C, 88000280

Harpeth Furnace (40WM83) [Iron Industry on the Western Highland Rim 1790s—1920s MPS], Address Restricted, Fernvale vicinity, 4/11/88, D, 88000253

Harrison House, S of Franklin on Columbia Pike, Franklin vicinity, 6/18/75, A, C, 75001799

Herbert, John, House [Williamson County MRA], Clovercroft Rd. 3/4 mi. E of Wilson Pike, Franklin vicinity, 4/13/88, C, 88000278

Hincheyville Historic District, W. Main, Fair, 6th, 7th, 8th, 9th, and 10th Sts., Franklin, 4/15/82, C, 82004071

Hiram Masonic Lodge No. 7, S. 2nd Ave., Franklin, 11/07/73, A, NHL, 73001859

Holt, Thomas, House [Williamson County MRA], Crockett Rd. 1 mi. E of Wilson Pike, Brentwood vicinity, 4/14/88, C, 88000274

Homestead Manor, N of Thompson Station on U.S. 31, Thompson Station vicinity, 4/29/77, A, C, 77001300

Huff Store [Williamson County MRA], Carters Creek Pike, Burwood, 4/13/88, A, 88000321

Hunter, John, House [Williamson County MRA], Old TN 96 at Carl Rd., Franklin vicinity, 4/13/88, C, 88000319

Hyde, Hartwell B., House [Williamson County MRA], TN 96, 1 mi. E of US Alt. 41, Triune vicinity, 4/13/88, C, 88000318

Johnson, James P., House [Williamson County MRA], US 31 3/10 mi. S of W. Harpeth Rd., Thompsons Station vicinity, 4/13/88, B, C, 88000316

Johnson, William W., House [Williamson County MRA], Farm Ln. 1/2 mi. S of Clovercroft Rd. 1/2 mi. E of Pleasant Hill Rd., Franklin vicinity, 4/13/88, C, 88000314

Johnston, James, House, S of Brentwood on U.S. 31, Brentwood vicinity, 3/26/76, A, C, 76001807

Jordan, Newton, House [Williamson County MRA], New Rd. 1 mi. E of US Alt. 41, Triune vicinity, 4/13/88, C, 88000298

Jordan—Williams House [Williamson County MRA], Rocky Fork Rd. 2 mi. E of Nolensville, Nolensville vicinity, 4/13/88, C, 88000341

King, William, House [Williamson County MRA], TN 96, 1 1/2 mi. W of US Alt. 41, Franklin vicinity, 4/13/88, C, 88000297

Kinnard, Claiborne, House [Williamson County MRA], Carters Creek Pike 1/2 mi. N of Bear Creek Rd., Franklin vicinity, 4/13/88, C, 88000355

Knight—Moran House [Williamson County MRA], Off Old Natchez Trace 1/10 mi. S of

Moran Rd., Franklin vicinity, 4/13/88, C, 88000295

Knights of Pythias Pavilion [Williamson County MRA], TN 96, Franklin, 4/14/88, C, 88000292

Lamb—Stephens House [Williamson County MRA], Burke Hollow Rd. 1 1/2 mi. E of Wilson Pike, Franklin vicinity, 4/13/88, C, 88000299

Leaton, William, House [Williamson County MRA], Hillsboro Rd./US 431 at Manely Ln., Franklin vicinity, 4/13/88, C, 88000357

Lee, Samuel B., House [Williamson County MRA], Duplex Rd. 1/2 mi. W of Lewisburg Pike, Duplex, 4/13/88, C, 88000300

Lewisburg Avenue Historic District [Williamson County MRA], Roughly bounded by S. Margin St., Lewisburg Ave., and Adams St., Franklin, 4/13/88, C, 88000312

Liberty Hill School [Williamson County MRA], Crow Cut Rd., Liberty Hill, 4/13/88, A, 88000315

Liberty School [Williamson County MRA], Liberty Church Rd. 1/4 mi. N of Concord Rd., Brentwood vicinity, 6/22/88, C, 88000317

Lotz House, 1111 Columbia Ave., Franklin, 12/12/76, C, 76001809

Maney—Sidway House [Williamson County MRA], Myles Manor Ct. W of Franklin Rd./US 31, Franklin, 4/13/88, C, 88000333

Maplewood Farm (Boundary Increase) [Williamson County MPS], 3085 Duplex—Spring Hill Rd., Spring Hill vicinity, 1/12/93, A, C, 92001758

Martin, William, House [Williamson County MRA], 5215 Seward Rd., Brentwood, 4/13/88, C, 88000334

Mayberry, H. G. W., House [Williamson County MRA], Bear Creek Rd. 1/2 mi. W of Carters Creek Pike, Franklin vicinity, 4/13/88, C, 88000363

Mayberry, Henry H., House [Williamson County MRA], US 31 just across the Harpeth River N of Franklin, Franklin, 4/13/88, C, 88000335

McEwen, Christopher, House [Williamson County MRA], Franklin Rd. 2/10 mi. S of Berrys Chapel Rd., Franklin vicinity, 4/13/88, C, 88000320

McEwen, David, House [Williamson County MRA], Off the E side of Franklin Rd./US 31 2/10 mi. N of Spencer Creek Rd., Franklin vicinity, 4/13/88, B, 88000360

McGavock—Gaines House [Williamson County MRA], Caruthers Rd. 1 mi. E of Lewisburg Pike, Franklin vicinity, 4/13/88, C, 88000329

McMahan, Daniel, House [Williamson County MRA], Spencer Creek Rd. 1/2 mi. W of Franklin Rd., Franklin vicinity, 4/13/88, B, C, 88000331

Meeting-of-the-Waters, NW of Franklin on Del Rio Pike, Franklin vicinity, 8/26/82, B, C, 82004072

Montpier, NW of Franklin off Old Hillsboro Pike, Franklin vicinity, 8/26/82, C, 82004073

Mooreland, Off U.S. 31, Brentwood, 7/24/75, C, 75001797

Morton, George W., House [Williamson County MRA], US Alt. 41 1/2 mi. N of Sunset Rd., Nolensville vicinity, 4/13/88, C, 88000337

Morton, Samuel S., House [Williamson County MRA], Carters Creek Pike 3/10 mi. N of Bear

Creek Rd., Franklin vicinity, 4/13/88, C, 88000365

Motheral, John, House [Williamson County MRA], Moran Rd. at Big Harpeth River, Franklin vicinity, 4/13/88, C, 88000339

Mountview, 913 Franklin Rd., Brentwood, 11/20/86, C, 86003293

Neely, John, House [Williamson County MRA], Sedberry Rd. 2 mi. S of W. Harpeth Rd., Thompsons Station vicinity, 4/13/88, C, 88000366

Oak Hall, 1704 Wilson Pike, Brentwood vicinity, 3/13/86, C, 86000393

Oden, Dr. Hezekiah, House [Williamson County MRA], Lewisburg Pike 1/2 mi. S of Henpeck Ln., Franklin vicinity, 4/13/88, C, 88000322

Ogilvie, William, House [Williamson County MRA], W side of US Alt. 31, 1 mi. S of College Grove, College Grove vicinity, 4/14/88, A, B, C, 88000323

Old Town [Williamson County MRA], Old Natchez Trace 1 1/2 mi. S of Moran Rd., Franklin vicinity, 4/14/88, C, 88000324

Old Town Archeological Site (40WM2) [Mississippian Cultural Resources of the Central Basin (AD 900—AD 1450) MPS], Address Restricted, Franklin vicinity, 9/16/89, D, 89000159

Old Town Bridge [Williamson County MRA], Over Brown's Creek just W of Old Natchez Trace Rd., Franklin vicinity, 4/13/88, A, 88000325

Owen Chapel Church of Christ, 1101 Franklin Rd., Brentwood, 10/23/86, C, a, 86002914

Owen, Dr. Urban, House [Williamson County MRA], US Alt. 31, College Grove, 4/13/88, C, 88000326

Owen—Cox House [Williamson County MRA], Moores Ln. 1 mi. E of I-65, Brentwood vicinity, 4/13/88, B, 88000327

Owen—Primm House [Williamson County MRA], Moores Ln. at Wilson Pike, Brentwood vicinity, 4/13/88, C, 88000328

Parks Place, Cox Rd., College Grove vicinity, 9/27/84, C, 84003753

Perkins, Nicholas Tate, House [Williamson County MRA], Del Rio Pike 2/10 mi. W of Cotton Rd., Franklin vicinity, 4/13/88, C, 88000330

Pointer, Henry, House [Williamson County MRA], US 31 S of Thompsons Station, Thompsons Station vicinity, 4/13/88, C, 88000332

Pollard, George, House [Williamson County MRA], Wilson Pike 1 2/10 mi. S of Peytonsville Rd., Franklin vicinity, 4/13/88, C, 88000336

Pope, John, House [Williamson County MRA], Pope Chapel Rd., Burwood vicinity, 4/13/88, C, 88000338

Puryear, Mordecai, House [Williamson County MRA], Lewisburg Pike, 2/10 mi. N of Henpeck Ln., Franklin vicinity, 4/13/88, C, 88000340

Rainey House, 244 1st Ave., Franklin, 7/08/70, A, C, 70000621

Ravenswood, Wilson Pike, Brentwood vicinity, 7/07/83, B, C, 83003073

Rizer, Y. M., House [Williamson County MRA], Del Rio Pike 3/4 mi. W of Hillsboro Rd., Franklin vicinity, 4/13/88, C, 88000348

Williamson County—Continued

Russwurm, John S., House [Williamson County MRA], Spann Town Rd. 1/2 mi. E of US Alt. 41, Triune vicinity, 4/13/88, C, 88000349

Scales, James, House [Williamson County MRA], US Alt. 31, Kirkland, 4/13/88, C, 88000350

Scales, Joseph, House [Williamson County MRA], Off Cox Rd. 1 mi. W of US Alt. 41, Triune vicinity, 4/13/88, C, 88000351

Seward, John, House [Williamson County MRA], Liberty Pike 3/4 mi. W of Wilson Pike, Franklin vicinity, 4/13/88, C, 88000352

Shute, Thomas, House [Williamson County MRA], US 31/Franklin Rd. at Spencer Creek Rd., Franklin vicinity, 4/13/88, C, 88000367

Smithson, Nathaniel, House [Williamson County MRA], Peytonsville—Bethesda Rd., Peytonsville, 4/13/88, C, 88000353

Sneed, Constantine, House [Williamson County MRA], 9135 Old Smyrna Rd., Brentwood, 4/13/88, C, 88000354

St. Paul's Episcopal Church, 510 Main St., Franklin, 2/23/72, A, C, a, 72001255

Steele, William, House [Williamson County MRA], Bethesda—Arno Rd. 1/2 mi. E of Bethesda, Franklin, 4/13/88, C, 88000356

Thompson Station Bank [Williamson County MRA], Thompson Station Rd., Thompsons Station, 4/13/88, A, 88000358

Thompson Store [Williamson County MRA], Duplex Rd. and Lewisburg Pike, Duplex, 4/13/88, A, 88000359

Toon, Beverly, House [Williamson County MRA], Arno Rd. 1/2 mi. W of Peytonsville Rd., Franklin vicinity, 4/14/88, C, 88000361

Trinity United Methodist Curch [Williamson County MRA], Wilson Pike 1 1/2 mi. S of Clovercroft Rd., Franklin vicinity, 4/13/88, C, a, 88000362

Truett, Alpheus, House [Williamson County MRA], US 31/Franklin Rd.3/10 mi. N of the Franklin Sq., Franklin, 4/13/88, A, C, 88000364

Vaughn, Andrew C., House [Williamson County MRA], 501 Murfreesboro Rd., Franklin, 4/13/88, C, 88000368

Webb, James, House [Williamson County MRA], US Alt. 31 at Taliaferro Rd., Triune vicinity, 4/13/88, C, 88000369

Wilhoite, James, House [Williamson County MRA], US Alt. 31, Allisona, 4/13/88, C, 88000370

Wilson, Joseph, House [Williamson County MRA], Clovercroft Rd. 2/10 mi. W of Wilson Pike, Franklin vicinity, 4/13/88, C, 88000372

Winstead Hill, 2 mi. S of Franklin on U.S. 31, Franklin vicinity, 11/29/74, A, 74001930

Winstead House, S. Margin St., Franklin, 4/18/79, C, 79002486

Winstead, John M., Houses [Williamson County MRA], Concord Rd. 1 mi. E of Edmondson Pike, Brentwood vicinity, 4/13/88, C, 88000373

Wyatt Hall, U.S. 31, Franklin, 7/02/80, B, C, 80003882

Wilson County

Buchanan, I. W. P., House, 428 W. Main St., Lebanon, 1/08/79, B, C, 79002487

Camp Bell, Coles Ferry Pike, Lebanon vicinity, 4/15/82, B, 82004074

Campbell, Dr. John Owen, House, W of Lebanon on U.S. 70, Lebanon vicinity, 12/08/80, C, 80003884

Cloyd, John, House, NW of Mount Juliet on U.S. 70, Mount Juliet vicinity, 10/01/74, A, C, 74001931

Fite-Fessenden House, 326 West Main St., Lebanon, 7/05/85, A, C, 85001488

Memorial Hall, Cumberland University, Cumberland University campus, Lebanon, 4/29/77, C, 77001301

Mitchell House, W. Main St., on grounds of Castle Heights Military Academy, Lebanon, 12/06/79, C, 79003435

Pickett Chapel Methodist Church, E. Market St., Lebanon, 4/18/77, A, C, a, 77001302

Rest Hill Cemetery, TN 141 E of jct. with TN 24 Bypass, Lebanon, 3/25/93, A, d, 93000212

Sellars Indian Mound, Address Restricted, Lebanon vicinity, 12/11/72, D, 72001256

Smith, Warner Price Mumford, House, 10277 Lebanon Rd., Mount Juliet vicinity, 7/22/93, C, 93000647

Graceland, listed in the National Register under Criterion B and Criterion Consideration G, is exceptionally significant as the home of legendary singer Elvis Presley, who bought the house in 1957 at the start of a career that revolutionized the American music industry, and who died there in 1977. (Jennifer Tucker, 1990)

TEXAS

Anderson County

Anderson Camp Ground, W of Brushy Creek on SR 837, Brushy Creek vicinity, 12/27/82, A, C, a, 82001735

Anderson County Courthouse, 1 Public Sq., Palestine, 9/28/92, C, 92001256

Broyles, William and Caroline, House, 1305 S. Sycamore St., Palestine, 11/10/88, C, 88002614

Howard House, 1011 N. Perry St., Palestine, 3/14/93, C, 93000072

Link House, 925 N. Link St., Palestine, 5/29/80, C, 80004073

Pace McDonald Site, Address Restricted, Palestine vicinity, 8/12/82, A, D, 82004488

Palestine Carnegie Library, 502 N. Queen St., Palestine, 10/17/88, C, 88001944

Palestine High School, 400 Micheaux Ave., Palestine, 9/24/86, A, C, 86002295

Sacred Heart Catholic Church and School, 503 N. Queen St., Palestine, 12/06/79, C, 79002909

Saunders, A. C., Site, Address Restricted, Frankston vicinity, 7/15/82, D, 82004487

Andrews County

Andrews Lake Sites, Address Restricted, Andrews vicinity, 11/22/78, D, 78002886

Angelina County

Abercrombie—Cavanaugh House [Angelina County MRA], 304 Paul, Lufkin, 12/22/88, C, 88002794

Angelina River Bridge [Angelina County MRA], US 59 over Angelina River, Lufkin, 12/22/88, A, C, 88002801

Banks—Ogg House [Angelina County MRA], 602 Groesbeck St., East, Lufkin, 12/22/88, C, 88002771

Behannon—Kenley House [Angelina County MRA], 317 Shephard, Lufkin, 12/22/88, C, 88002798

Binion—Casper House [Angelina County MRA], 404 Mantooth, Lufkin, 7/19/89, C, 88002785

Bowers—Felts House [Angelina County MRA], 1213 Lotus Ln., Lufkin, 12/22/88, C, 88002780

Boynton—Kent House [Angelina County MRA], 107 Kerr St., West, Lufkin, 12/22/88, C, 88002779

Brookshire, Houston—Yeates House [Angelina County MRA], 304 Howe St., East, Lufkin, 12/22/88, C, 88002776

Byus—Kirkland House [Angelina County MRA], 411 Mantooth, Lufkin, 12/22/88, C, 88002786

Clark—Whitton House [Angelina County MRA], 1865 Old Mill Rd., Lufkin, 12/22/88, C, 88002792

Corstone Sales Company [Angelina County MRA], 109–111 Shepherd St., East, Lufkin, 12/22/88, C, 88002797

Dunham Hill [Angelina County MRA], US 69, Huntington, 12/22/88, C, 88002803

Everitt—Cox House [Angelina County MRA], 418 Moore, Lufkin, 12/22/88, C, 88002789

Fenley Commercial Building [Angelina County MRA], 112 Lufkin Ave., East, Lufkin, 12/22/88, C, 88002781

Gibbs—Flournoy House [Angelina County MRA], TX 844, Manning vicinity, 12/22/88, C, 88002804

Henderson, S. W.—Bridges House [Angelina County MRA], 202 Henderson, Lufkin, 12/22/88, C, 88002775

Humason—Pinkerton House [Angelina County MRA], 602 Grove, Lufkin, 12/22/88, C, 88002773

Keltys Worker Housing [Angelina County MRA], 109 Maas, Lufkin, 12/22/88, C, 88002784

Kennedy, A. C.—Runnells House [Angelina County MRA], 603 Groesbeck St., East, Lufkin, 12/22/88, C, 88002772

Kennedy, R. A.—J. M. Lowrey House [Angelina County MRA], 519 Groesbeck St., East, Lufkin, 12/22/88, C, 88002770

Kurth, J. H., House [Angelina County MRA], 1860 Old Mill Rd., Lufkin, 12/22/88, C, 88002791

Kurth—Glover House [Angelina County MRA], 1847 Old Mill Rd., Lufkin, 12/22/88, C, 88002790

Lawrence, G. E., House [Angelina County MRA], 2005 Chestnut St., South, Lufkin, 12/22/88, C, 88002766

Lufkin Land—Long Bell—Buck House [Angelina County MRA], 1218 Lufkin St., Lufkin, 12/22/88, C, 88002783

Marsh—Smith House [Angelina County MRA], 503 Raguet St., North, Lufkin, 12/22/88, C, 88002796

McClendon—Abney Hardware Company [Angelina County MRA], 119 Lufkin Ave., East, Lufkin, 12/22/88, C, 88002782

McGilbert House [Angelina County MRA], 1902 Old Mill Rd., Lufkin, 12/22/88, C, 88002793

Newsom—Moss House [Angelina County MRA], 420 Mantooth, Lufkin, 12/22/88, C, 88002787

Old Federal Building—Federal Courthouse [Angelina County MRA], 104 Third St., North, Lufkin, 12/22/88, C, 88002799

Parker—Bradshaw House [Angelina County MRA], 213 Raguet St., North, Lufkin, 12/22/88, C, 88002795

Percy, Dr. Edward—Abney House [Angelina County MRA], 466 Jefferson, Lufkin, 12/22/88, C, 88002778

Perry, A. F. and Myrtle—Pitmann House [Angelina County MRA], 402 Bynum St., South, Lufkin, 12/22/88, C, 88002765

Perry, C. W. Archie—Hallmark House [Angelina County MRA], 302 S. Bynum, Lufkin, 12/22/88, C, 88002764

Pines Theatre [Angelina County MRA], 113 First St., South, Lufkin, 12/22/88, C, a, 88002767

Rastus—Read House [Angelina County MRA], 1509 First St., South, Lufkin, 12/22/88, C, 88002768

Russell—Arnold House [Angelina County MRA], 121 Menefee St., West, Lufkin, 12/22/88, C, 88002788

Standley House [Angelina County MRA], 1607 Tulane, Lufkin, 12/22/88, C, 88002800

Temple, Henry G., House [Angelina County MRA], 501 Hines Rd., Diboll, 12/22/88, C, 88002802

Texas Highway Department Complex [Angelina County MRA], 110 Forest Park, Lufkin, 12/22/88, C, 88002769

Trout, Walter C.—White House [Angelina County MRA], 444 Jefferson, Lufkin, 12/22/88, C, 88002777

Walker, Howard, House [Angelina County MRA], 503 Harmony Hill Rd., Lufkin, 12/22/88, C, 88002774

Aransas County

Aransas Pass Light Station, N of Port Aransas on Harbor Island, Port Aransas vicinity, 8/03/77, A, C, g, 77001423

Fulton, George W., Mansion, Fulton Beach Rd., Fulton, 4/24/75, B, C, 75001945

Kent-Crane Shell Midden, Address Restricted, Fulton vicinity, 6/21/84, D, 84001565

Mathis, T. H., House, 612 Church St., Rockport, 6/21/71, B, C, 71000918

Archer County

Archer County Courthouse and Jail, Public Sq. and Sycamore and Pecan Sts., Archer City, 12/23/77, C, 77001424

Armstrong County

J A Ranch, Palo Duro Canyon, Palo Duro vicinity, 10/15/66, B, NHL, 66000807

Palo Duro Pen (41AM5) [New Mexican Pastor Sites in Texas Panhandle TR], Address Restricted, Claude vicinity, 7/12/84, D, NHL, 84001568

Palo Duro Shelter (41AM6) [New Mexican Pastor Sites in Texas Panhandle TR], Address Restricted, Claude vicinity, 7/12/84, A, D, 84001569

Austin County

Allens Creek Ossuary Site, Address Restricted, Wallis vicinity, 3/21/75, A, D, 75001946

Austin County Jail, 36 S. Bell St., Bellville, 11/12/80, C, 80004074

Church of the Guardian Angel [Churches with Decorative Interior Painting TR], 5614 Demel St., Wallis, 6/21/83, A, C, a, 83003074

Old Masonic Hall, 15 N. Masonic St., Bellville, 8/14/86, A, 86001611

Roesler House, W of Nelsonville on TX 159, Nelsonville vicinity, 5/10/84, A, C, 84001570

Wesley Brethren Church [Churches with Decorative Interior Painting TR (AD)], S of Wesley, Wesley vicinity, 1/18/79, A, C, a, 79002910

Bandera County

Bandera County Courthouse and Jail, Public Sq., 12th and Maple Sts., Bandera, 10/31/79, C, 79002911

Jureczki House, 607 Cypress St., Bandera, 1/11/80, B, C, 80004075

Bastrop County

Allen-Bell House [Bastrop Historic and Architectural MRA (AD)], 1408 Church St., Bastrop, 1/25/71, C, 71000919

Baron, August, House [Bastrop Historic and Architectural MRA], 1707 Pecan, Bastrop, 12/22/78, B, 78003277

Bastain-Haralson, Ed, House [Bastrop Historic and Architectural MRA], 1006 Chestnut, Bastrop, 12/22/78, C, 78003350

Bastrop Commercial District [Bastrop Historic and Architectural MRA], Roughly bounded by Church, Water, Spring, and Walnut Sts., Bastrop, 12/22/78, A, C, 78003262

Bastrop County Courthouse and Jail Complex [Bastrop Historic and Architectural MRA (AD)], Bounded by Pine, Walnut, Pecan, and Water Sts., Bastrop, 11/20/75, C, 75001947

Batts, Judge R., House [Bastrop Historic and Architectural MRA], 609 Pecan, Bastrop, 12/22/78, B, C, 78003336

Brannon, S. L., House [Bastrop Historic and Architectural MRA], 1301 Main, Bastrop, 12/22/78, B, C, 78003264

Brieger, R. J., House [Bastrop Historic and Architectural MRA], 1508 Hill, Bastrop, 12/22/78, C, 78003278

Brooks, Jennie, House [Bastrop Historic and Architectural MRA], 1009 Walnut, Bastrop, 12/22/78, A, 78003317

Brooks-Wilbarger House [Bastrop Historic and Architectural MRA], 1403 Main St., Bastrop, 12/22/78, B, C, 78003269

Buchanan, J. C., House [Bastrop Historic and Architectural MRA], 1010 Pecan, Bastrop, 12/22/78, C, 78003326

Casino Hall [Bastrop Historic and Architectural MRA], NE corner of Farm and Fayette, Bastrop, 12/22/78, A, C, 78003291

Colorado River Bridge at Bastrop [Bastrop MPS], SR 150 over the Colorado R., Bastrop, 7/19/90, A, C, 90001031

Combs, H. B., House [Bastrop Historic and Architectural MRA], 1208 Church, Bastrop, 12/22/78, C, 78003294

Cornelsum, John, House [Bastrop Historic and Architectural MRA], 702 Main, Bastrop, 12/22/78, A, C, 78003301

Crocheron-McDowall House [Bastrop Historic and Architectural MRA (AD)], 1502 Wilson St., Bastrop, 4/20/78, C, 78003357

Crysup, J. T., House [Bastrop Historic and Architectural MRA], 1607 Main, Bastrop, 12/22/78, B, 78003274

Davis, George W., House [Bastrop Historic and Architectural MRA], 1010 Chestnut, Bastrop, 12/22/78, C, 78003343

Dawson House [Bastrop Historic and Architectural MRA], 1002 Chestnut, Bastrop, 12/22/78, C, 78003351

Duval, Mary, House [Bastrop Historic and Architectural MRA], 1502 Pecan, Bastrop, 12/22/78, C, 78003268

Elzner House [Bastrop Historic and Architectural MRA], 800 Main, Bastrop, 12/22/78, B, C, 78003302

Elzner, August, House [Bastrop Historic and Architectural MRA], 1701 Main, Bastrop, 12/22/78, C, 78003273

Elzner, Prince, House [Bastrop Historic and Architectural MRA], 1303 Pecan, Bastrop, 12/22/78, C, 78003283

Erhard House [Bastrop Historic and Architectural MRA], 907 Cedar, Bastrop, 12/22/78, A, 78003280

Erhard, A. A., House [Bastrop Historic and Architectural MRA], 1106 Pecan, Bastrop, 12/22/78, C, 78003329

Erhard, Adolph A., House [Bastrop Historic and Architectural MRA], 1205 Pecan, Bastrop, 12/22/78, B, C, 78003284

Erhard, E. C., House [Bastrop Historic and Architectural MRA], 1507 Pecan, Bastrop, 12/22/78, C, 78003279

Farm House [Bastrop Historic and Architectural MRA], End of Pecan, Bastrop, 12/22/78, C, 78003334

Fowler House [Bastrop Historic and Architectural MRA], 1404 Wilson, Bastrop, 12/22/78, C, 78003321

Fowler-Jenkins House [Bastrop Historic and Architectural MRA], 1302 Pecan, Bastrop, 12/22/78, B, C, 78003263

Fry, P. A., House [Bastrop Historic and Architectural MRA], 1403 Government, Bastrop, 12/22/78, C, b, 78003337

Green, Rufus A., House [Bastrop Historic and Architectural MRA], 1501 Church, Bastrop, 12/22/78, C, 78003280

Griesenbeck House [Bastrop Historic and Architectural MRA], 805 Pecan, Bastrop, 12/22/78, C, 78003349

Griesenbeck, Alf, House [Bastrop Historic and Architectural MRA], 1302 Hill, Bastrop, 12/22/78, C, 78003282

Griesenbeck, Erna, House [Bastrop Historic and Architectural MRA], 908 Pine, Bastrop, 12/22/78, C, 78003338

Griesenbeck, R. J., House [Bastrop Historic and Architectural MRA], 1005 Chestnut, Bastrop, 12/22/78, C, 78003308

Grimes, Dr. C. A., House [Bastrop Historic and Architectural MRA], 1201 Farm, Bastrop, 12/22/78, B, 78003355

Hall-Sayers-Perkins House [Bastrop Historic and Architectural MRA], 1307 Church, Bastrop, 12/22/78, B, C, 78003293

Harlson, Eugene, House [Bastrop Historic and Architectural MRA], 803 Jefferson, Bastrop, 12/22/78, C, 78003344

Hasler, Emelia, House [Bastrop Historic and Architectural MRA], 1004 Pine, Bastrop, 12/22/78, C, 78003307

Hasler, T. A., House [Bastrop Historic and Architectural MRA], 1109 Pecan, Bastrop, 12/22/78, C, 78003330

Hill, Abraham Wiley, House, 5 mi. SW of Hills Prairie, Hills Prairie vicinity, 3/11/71, C, 71000920

House at 1002 Pine [Bastrop Historic and Architectural MRA], 1002 Pine, Bastrop, 12/22/78, C, 78003304

House at 1002 Walnut [Bastrop Historic and Architectural MRA], 1002 Walnut, Bastrop, 12/22/78, C, 78003303

House at 1105 Hill [Bastrop Historic and Architectural MRA], 1105 Hill, Bastrop, 12/22/78, C, 78003312

House at 1108 Hill [Bastrop Historic and Architectural MRA], 1108 Hill, Bastrop, 12/22/78, A, C, 78003306

House at 1301 Hill [Bastrop Historic and Architectural MRA], 1301 Hill, Bastrop, 12/22/78, C, 78003286

House at 1308 Fayette [Bastrop Historic and Architectural MRA], 1308 Fayette, Bastrop, 12/22/78, C, 78003285

House at 1316 Farm [Bastrop Historic and Architectural MRA], 1316 Farm, Bastrop, 12/22/78, C, 78003290

House at 311 Pecan [Bastrop Historic and Architectural MRA], 311 Pecan, Bastrop, 12/22/78, C, 78003327

House at 604 Elm [Bastrop Historic and Architectural MRA], 604 Elm, Bastrop, 12/22/78, C, 78003310

House at 806 Jefferson [Bastrop Historic and Architectural MRA], 806 Jefferson, Bastrop, 12/22/78, C, 78003342

Houses at 703 and 704 Austin [Bastrop Historic and Architectural MRA], 703 and 704 Austin, Bastrop, 12/22/78, C, 78003316

Hubbard-Trigg House [Bastrop Historic and Architectural MRA], 1508 Pecan, Bastrop, 12/22/78, A, C, 78003266

Iron Bridge [Bastrop Historic and Architectural MRA], Over Piney Creek, Bastrop, 12/22/78, A, 78003292

Bastrop County—Continued

Jenkins House [Bastrop Historic and Architectural MRA], 1710 Main, Bastrop, 12/22/78, C, 78003299

Jenkins House [Bastrop Historic and Architectural MRA], 801 Pecan, Bastrop, 12/22/78, C, 78003345

Jones, George Washington, House [Bastrop Historic and Architectural MRA], Fayette and Mill, Bastrop, 12/22/78, B, D, 78003335

Jones, Oliver P., House [Bastrop Historic and Architectural MRA], 1009 Pecan, Bastrop, 12/22/78, C, 78003331

Jung Storage Building [Bastrop Historic and Architectural MRA], 108 Government, Bastrop, 12/22/78, A, 78003323

Jung, Alf, House [Bastrop Historic and Architectural MRA], 508 Pecan, Bastrop, 12/22/78, A, C, 78003322

Jung, Joe, House [Bastrop Historic and Architectural MRA], 909 Pecan, Bastrop, 12/22/78, B, C, 78003333

Kerr Community Center [Bastrop Historic and Architectural MRA], 1308 Walnut, Bastrop, 12/22/78, A, 78003339

Kerr, Beverly and Lula, House [Bastrop Historic and Architectural MRA], 1305 Pine, Bastrop, 12/22/78, A, C, 78003356

Kleinert House [Bastrop Historic and Architectural MRA], 1801 Hill, Bastrop, 12/22/78, C, 78003288

Kohler-McPhaul House [Bastrop Historic and Architectural MRA], 1901 Pecan, Bastrop, 12/22/78, B, C, 78003275

Luckett, H. P., House [Bastrop Historic and Architectural MRA], 1402 Church, Bastrop, 12/22/78, B, C, 78003296

MKT Depot [Bastrop Historic and Architectural MRA], NW Chestnut and Fayette, Bastrop, 12/22/78, A, C, 78003354

Manlove, Bartholomew, House [Bastrop Historic and Architectural MRA], 502 Elm, Bastrop, 12/22/78, B, C, 78003311

Maynard, Powell C., House [Bastrop Historic and Architectural MRA], 1408 Pecan, Bastrop, 12/22/78, B, C, 78003267

Maynard, W. E., House [Bastrop Historic and Architectural MRA], 1310 Hill, Bastrop, 12/22/78, C, 78003281

McNeil, Harriet and Charlie, House [Bastrop Historic and Architectural MRA], 1805 Pecan, Bastrop, 12/22/78, A, 78003276

McNeil, Marcellus, House [Bastrop Historic and Architectural MRA], 1809 Wilson, Bastrop, 12/22/78, B, C, 78003298

Miley, Willis, House [Bastrop Historic and Architectural MRA], 1320 Farm, Bastrop, 12/22/78, C, 78003289

Old Bastrop Co. Pavilion [Bastrop Historic and Architectural MRA], 1800 block of Hawthorne, Bastrop, 12/22/78, A, b, 78003287

Olive, L. W., House [Bastrop Historic and Architectural MRA], 1507 Main, Bastrop, 12/22/78, C, 78003270

Orgain, Elbert S., House [Bastrop Historic and Architectural MRA], 1704 Main, Bastrop, 12/22/78, C, 78003300

Orgain, Sarah Jane, House [Bastrop Historic and Architectural MRA], 602 Cedar, Bastrop, 12/22/78, B, C, 78003309

Page, Paul D., House [Bastrop Historic and Architectural MRA], 1792 Pecan, Bastrop, 12/22/78, B, C, 78003272

Pearcy, J. H., House [Bastrop Historic and Architectural MRA], 1602 Pecan, Bastrop, 12/22/78, C, 78003271

Phieffer House [Bastrop Historic and Architectural MRA], 1802 Main, Bastrop, 12/22/78, B, 78003314

Pledger, J. W., House [Bastrop Historic and Architectural MRA], 1704 Wilson, Bastrop, 12/22/78, C, 78003318

Ploeger-Kerr-White House [Bastrop Historic and Architectural MRA], 806 Marion, Bastrop, 12/22/78, B, 78003346

Rabensburg House [Bastrop Historic and Architectural MRA], 707 Pecan, Bastrop, 12/22/78, C, 78003348

Reding, Mrs. William R., House [Bastrop Historic and Architectural MRA], 901 Pecan, Bastrop, 12/22/78, C, 78003340

Sayers, Gov. Joseph, House [Bastrop Historic and Architectural MRA], 1703 Wilson, Bastrop, 12/22/78, B, C, 78003297

Schaeffer, W. F., House [Bastrop Historic and Architectural MRA], 608 Pecan, Bastrop, 12/22/78, C, 78003324

Smithville Commercial Historic District, 2nd, 3rd, and Main Sts., Smithville, 6/17/82, A, C, 82004489

Starcke, Richard, House [Bastrop Historic and Architectural MRA], 703 Main, Bastrop, 12/22/78, C, 78003315

Starcke, Richard, House [Bastrop Historic and Architectural MRA], 710 Water, Bastrop, 12/22/78, C, 78003328

Taylor, Campbell and Greenlief Fisk, House [Bastrop Historic and Architectural MRA], 1005 Hill, Bastrop, 12/22/78, B, C, 78003353

Waugh House [Bastrop Historic and Architectural MRA], 1801 Main, Bastrop, 12/22/78, C, 78003313

White House [Bastrop Historic and Architectural MRA], 1307 Main, Bastrop, 12/22/78, C, 78003265

Wilke House [Bastrop Historic and Architectural MRA], 807 Pecan, Bastrop, 12/22/78, C, 78003341

Wilkes, Minnie, House [Bastrop Historic and Architectural MRA], 1101 Hill, Bastrop, 12/22/78, C, 78003352

Bee County

Medio Creek Bridge, CR 241, Normanna vicinity, 10/13/88, C, 88002000

Praeger Building, 110 W. Corpus Christi St., Beeville, 9/09/82, C, 82004490

Bell County

Anderson House and Store [Salado MRA], Main St., Salado, 4/05/83, A, C, 83003076

Armstrong-Adams House [Salado MRA], Main St. and Thomas Arnold Rd., Salado, 4/05/83, C, 83003077

Austin, F. K. and Mary, House [Belton MPS], 702 N. Penelope St., Belton, 12/26/90, C, 90001891

Baggett, Ele, House [Belton MPS], 1019 N. Main St., Belton, 12/26/90, C, 90001882

Baggett, Silas and Ellen, House [Belton MPS], 1018 N. Main St., Belton, 12/26/90, C, 90001881

Baines, George Washington, House [Salado MRA], Royal St., Salado, 4/05/83, B, C, 83003078

Barbee-Berry Mercantile Building [Salado MRA], Main and Royal St., Salado, 8/22/84, A, C, 84001571

Barclay-Bryan House, 804 S. 25th St., Temple, 5/10/84, C, 84001572

Bartlett Commercial Historic District, E. Clark St., Bartlett, 9/30/80, C, 80004076

Barton House [Salado MRA], Main St., Salado, 4/05/83, C, 83003079

Baylor Female College Historic District [Belton MPS], Bounded by King, College and W. Ninth Sts., Belton, 12/26/90, A, C, 90001869

Beamer, William, House [Belton MPS], 1202 S. Beal St., Belton, 12/26/90, C, 90001875

Bell County Courthouse, Public Sq., Belton, 12/12/76, A, C, 76002004

Belton Academy [Belton MPS], 404 E. Ninth St., Belton, 12/26/90, A, C, 90001937

Belton Commercial Historic District [Belton MPS], Roughly bounded by Nolan Valley Rd., Penelope St. and Nolan Cr.., Belton, 12/26/90, A, C, 90001868

Belton Farmers' Gin Coop [Belton MPS], 219 S. East Ave., Building 4, Belton, 12/26/90, A, C, 90001870

Belton Standpipe [Belton MPS], NW of jct. of TX 317 & I-35, Belton, 12/26/90, A, C, 90001900

Belton Yarn Mill [Belton MPS], 805 E. Fourth St., Belton, 12/26/90, C, 90001899

Birdwell, T. Hamp and Beulah, House [Belton MPS], 503 N. Wall, Belton, 12/26/90, C, 90001896

Burford, R. F. and Lena, House [Belton MPS], 920 N. Penelope St., Belton, 12/26/90, C, 90001893

Carnegie Public Library, 201 N. Main St., Belton, 3/04/85, A, C, 85000473

Cornelison House [Belton MPS], 1102 N. Pearl St., Belton, 12/26/90, C, 90001886

Davis House [Salado MRA], Main St., Salado, 4/05/83, C, 83003080

Elliott, Joel, House [Belton MPS], 716 N. College St., Belton, 12/26/90, C, 90001876

Farr, Dr. R. S., House [Belton MPS], 801 E. Central Ave., Belton, 12/26/90, C, 90001935

Ferguson House, 518 N. 7th St., Temple, 12/08/78, B, 78002888

Ferguson, James A., House [Belton MPS], 1123 N. Beal St., Belton, 12/26/90, C, 90001874

Bell County—Continued

Ferguson, James E. and Miriam, House [Belton MPS], 604 N. Penelope St., Belton, 12/26/90, C, 90001889

First Christian Church Parsonage [Belton MPS], 608 N. Penelope St., Belton, 12/26/90, C, 90001890

Fowler House [Salado MRA], Main St., Salado, 4/05/83, B, C, 83003081

Frazier, Dr. Jacob Moore, House [Belton MPS], 618 N. Wall, Belton, 12/26/90, C, 90001897

Gray Rental Houses [Belton MPS], 702–708 N. Pearl St., Belton, 12/26/90, C, 90001934

Halley, Capt. Robert, House [Salado MRA], Main St., Salado, 4/05/83, B, C, 83003082

Hammersmith, John P., House [Belton MPS], 520 S. Main St., Belton, 12/26/90, C, 90001883

Harris, Capt. Andrew Jackson, House [Belton MPS], 1001 W. Tenth St., Belton, 12/26/90, C, 90001871

House at 402 N. East St. [Belton MPS], 402 N. East St., Belton, 12/26/90, C, 90001878

House at 730 N. Beal St. [Belton MPS], 730 N. Beal St., Belton, 12/26/90, C, 90001936

Hudson, Dr. Taylor, House [Belton MPS], 324 N. Main St., Belton, 12/26/90, C, 90001879

James House [Belton MPS], 805 N. Beal St., Belton, 12/26/90, C, 90001873

Kinchion, L. B., House [Belton MPS], 702 S. Pearl St., Belton, 12/26/90, C, 90001887

Kyle Hotel, 111 Main St., Temple, 8/05/93, A, 93000772

Lee, Walter J., House [Belton MPS], 804 N. College St., Belton, 12/26/90, C, 90001877

McWhirter, George and Martha, House [Belton MPS], 400 N. Pearl St., Belton, 12/26/90, B, C, a, 90001884

Means, V. R., House [Belton MPS], 609 E. 14th St., Belton, 12/26/90, C, 90001938

Miller, J. Z., House [Belton MPS], 804 N. Penelope St., Belton, 12/26/90, C, 90001892

Miller-Curtis House, 1004 N. Main St., Belton, 4/07/83, C, 83003083

Missouri, Kansas & Texas Railroad Bridge at the Leon River [Belton MPS], Across the Leon R. at Taylor's Valley Rd., Belton, 12/26/90, A, 90001898

Morey House [Belton MPS], 328 N. Main St., Belton, 12/26/90, C, 90001880

Mount Zion United Methodist Church [Belton MPS], 218 Alexander St., Belton, 12/26/90, A, C, a, 90001872

Naismith, Robert, House [Belton MPS], 440 N. Penelope St., Belton, 12/26/90, C, 90001888

Norton—Orgain House [Salado MRA], Main St., Salado, 3/25/92, C, 92000185

Old St. Luke's Episcopal Church, 401 N. Wall St., Belton, 1/17/74, A, C, a, g, 74002056

Potts, Arthur, House [Belton MPS], 445 N. Wall, Belton, 12/26/90, C, 90001895

Robertson, Col. Elijah Sterling Clack, Plantation [Salado MRA], I-35, Salado, 4/05/83, B, C, 83003084

Rose, Maj. A. J., House, Wm. Rose Way and Royal St., Salado, 5/22/78, C, 78002887

Salado College Archeological Site [Salado MRA], Address Restricted, Salado vicinity, 3/01/85, A, D, 85000403

Salado United Methodist Chruch [Salado MRA], Thomas Arnold Rd. and Church St., Salado, 8/22/84, C, a, 84001573

Stagecoach Inn [Salado MRA], Main and Front Sts., Salado, 4/05/83, A, C, 83003085

Tenney, Levi, House [Salado MRA], Pace Park Dr., Salado, 4/05/83, B, C, 83003086

Twelve Oaks [Salado MRA], Center Cirlce, Salado, 4/05/83, A, C, 83003088

Tyler House [Salado MRA], Main St., Salado, 4/05/83, B, C, 83003087

Venable, W. J., House [Belton MPS], 426 N. Wall, Belton, 12/26/90, C, 90001894

Vickrey House [Salado MRA], Main St., Salado, 4/05/83, C, 83003089

Ware, H. A. and Helena, House [Belton MPS], 401 N. Pearl St., Belton, 12/26/90, C, 90001885

White-Aiken House [Salado MRA], I-35, Salado, 4/05/83, B, C, 83003090

Bexar County

Alamo Methodist Church, 1150 S. Alamo St., San Antonio, 6/11/79, C, a, 79003446

Alamo National Bank Building, 316 E. Commerce St., San Antonio, 1/05/84, A, C, 84001574

Alamo Plaza Historic District, Roughly bounded by S. Broadway, Commerce, Bonham and Travis Sts., San Antonio, 7/13/77, A, C, a, 77001425

Alamo Portland and Roman Cement Works, Brackenridge Park, San Antonio, 12/12/76, A, 76002005

Alamo, The, Alamo Plaza, San Antonio, 10/15/66, A, a, NHL, 66000808

Aue Stagecoach Inn, Boerne Stage Rd. and I-10, Leon Springs vicinity, 8/01/79, A, 79002912

Aztec Theater, 104 N. St. Mary's St., San Antonio, 10/22/92, C, 92001403

Barnes—Laird House, 103 W. Ashby Pl., San Antonio, 7/28/88, C, 88001146

Barr Building, 213-219 Broadway, San Antonio, 4/11/85, B, C, 85000766

Base Administration Building, Randolph AFB, Randolph AFB, 8/27/87, C, 87001434

Bexar County Courthouse, Main Plaza, San Antonio, 8/29/77, A, C, 77001426

Bonham, James Butler, Elementary School, 925 S. St. Mary's St., San Antonio, 11/17/78, A, C, 78002890

Bushnell, 240 Bushnell, San Antonio, 8/26/82, C, 82004491

Central Trust Company Building, 603 Navarro St., San Antonio, 8/11/82, C, 82004492

Church of Nuestra Senora de la Candelaria y Guadalupe, 115 Main Ave., San Antonio, 2/25/75, A, C, a, 75001949

City of San Antonio Municipal Auditorium, 100 Auditorium Circle, San Antonio, 9/14/81, A, C, a, 81000624

Clegg, L. B., House, 123 W. Park Ave., San Antonio, 12/07/79, C, 79002913

Elmendorf, Emil, House, 509 Burleson St., San Antonio, 5/19/80, B, C, 80004077

Espada Aqueduct, Espada Rd., E of U.S. 281S, San Antonio, 10/15/66, A, C, NHL, NPS, 66000809

Fairmount Hotel, The, 401 S. Alamo, San Antonio, 6/30/88, A, C, b, 88000753

First National Bank of San Antonio, 213 W. Commerce St., San Antonio, 3/16/72, B, C, 72001348

Fort Sam Houston, N edge of San Antonio, San Antonio, 5/15/75, A, NHL, 75001950

Fourth Ward School, 141 Lavaca St., San Antonio, 11/17/78, A, C, 78002891

Franklin, Thomas H., House, 105 E. French Pl., San Antonio, 5/22/86, C, 86001135

Garcia-Garza House, 214 W. Salinas St., San Antonio, 7/07/83, C, 83003091

Guenther, Carl Hilmar, House, 205 E. Guenther St., San Antonio, 10/11/90, C, 90001539

Halff, A. H., House, 601 Howard St., San Antonio, 9/04/86, C, 86002180

Hangar 9, Brooks Air Force Base Inner Circle Rd., San Antonio, 5/21/70, A, g, NHL, 70000895

Havana, The, 1015 Navarro St., San Antonio, 4/10/86, C, 86000725

International & Great Northern Railroad Passenger Station, Medina and Houston Sts., San Antonio, 9/09/75, A, C, 75001951

King William Historic District, Roughly bounded by Durango, Alamo, Guenther Sts. and the San Antonio River, San Antonio, 1/20/72, C, 72001349

La Villita Historic District, Bounded by Durango, Navarro, Alamo Sts. and San Antonio River, San Antonio, 1/20/72, C, e, 72001350

Live Oak Park Site, Address Restricted, Live Oak vicinity, 12/15/78, D, 78002889

Main and Military Plazas Historic District, Roughly bounded by San Antonio River, E. Nueva, Laredo, and Houston Sts., San Antonio, 6/11/79, A, C, D, a, 79002914

Majestic Theatre, 230 E. Houston St., San Antonio, 10/01/75, B, C, g, NHL, 75001952

Maverick—Altgelt Ranch and Fenstermaker-Fromme Farm, Address Restricted, San Antonio vicinity, 4/12/79, A, C, D, 79002915

Meerscheidt, Otto, House, 322 Adams St., San Antonio, 7/04/80, C, 80004488

Menger Soap Works, 400 block of N. Laredo St., San Antonio, 12/12/73, A, C, 73001958

Meyer Pottery Archeological Complex (41BX128), Address Restricted, Atascosa vicinity, 3/09/90, D, 90000299

Mission Concepcion, 807 Mission Rd., San Antonio, 4/15/70, A, C, a, NHL, NPS, 70000740

Mission Parkway, Along San Antonio River, San Antonio, 10/06/75, A, C, D, NPS, 75001953

Mission San Francisco de la Espada, Espada Rd., San Antonio, 2/23/72, A, C, D, a, NPS, 72001351

Mission San Francisco de la Espada (Boundary Increase), Espada Rd., San Antonio, 1/28/74, A, a, NPS, 74002324

Mission San Juan Capistrano, Mission Rd., San Antonio, 2/23/72, A, C, D, a, NPS, 72001352

Bexar County—Continued

Morrison, William J., Jr., House, 710 N. Olive St., San Antonio, 7/12/90, C, 90001078

Navarro, Jose Antonio, Elementary School, 623 S. Pecos St., San Antonio, 11/29/78, A, C, 78002892

Navarro, Jose Antonio, House Complex, 228–232 S. Loredo St., San Antonio, 3/24/72, B, C, c, 72001353

Old Lone Star Brewery, 110–116 Jones Ave., San Antonio, 10/26/72, A, C, 72001354

Old Lone Star Brewery (Boundary Increase), 110–116 Jones Ave., San Antonio, 9/25/79, A, C, 79003544

Partee, Hiram, House, 605 Belknap Pl., San Antonio, 9/20/84, C, 84001576

Pershing House, Staff Post Rd., Fort Sam Houston, San Antonio, 7/30/74, B, 74002058

Plehwe Complex, W of Leon Springs on Boerne Stage Rd., Leon Springs vicinity, 12/15/83, C, 83003755

Post Chapel, Fort Sam Houston, Bldg. 2200, Wilson St., San Antonio, 5/17/74, A, a, 74002057

Prospect Hill Missionary Baptist Church, 1601 Buena Vista, San Antonio, 9/18/86, C, a, 86002185

Quadrangle, The, Grayson St., Fort Sam Houston, San Antonio, 7/30/74, A, 74002059

Saint Anthony Hotel, 300 Travis St., San Antonio, 9/19/86, A, 86002186

Salado Battlefield and Archeological Site, Address Restricted, San Antonio vicinity, 11/21/78, A, D, 78002893

San Antonio Casino Club Building, 102 W. Crockett St., San Antonio, 1/08/80, A, C, 80004078

San Antonio Loan and Trust Building, 235 E. Commerce St., San Antonio, 7/12/76, A, C, 76002006

San Antonio Missions National Historical Park, Mission and Espada Rds. and San Jose Dr., San Antonio, 11/10/78, A, C, a, NPS, 78003147

San Antonio Water Works Pump Station No. 2, Brackenridge Park, San Antonio, 8/21/81, A, B, 81000625

San Jose Mission National Historic Site, 6519 San Jose Dr., San Antonio, 10/15/66, A, C, a, NPS, 66000810

San Pedro Springs Park, San Pedro Ave., San Antonio, 11/01/79, A, C, 79002916

Schroeder-Yturri House, 1040 E. Commerce St., San Antonio, 4/14/75, C, 75001954

Smith—Young Tower, 310 S. St. Mary's St., San Antonio, 11/13/91, C, 91001682

Source of the River District, Address Restricted, San Antonio vicinity, 7/31/78, A, C, D, NHL, 78002894

South Alamo Street-South Mary's Street Historic District, Bounded by the San Antonio River, S. Alamo, S. St. Mary's, and Temple Sts., San Antonio, 10/04/84, A, C, 84000026

Southern Pacific Depot Historic District, Roughly bounded by Crockett, Chestnut, Galveston, and Cherry Sts., San Antonio, 2/01/79, A, C, a, 79002917

Southern Pacific Railroad Passenger Station, 1174 E. Commerce St., San Antonio, 5/29/75, A, C, 75001955

Spanish Governor's Palace, 105 Military Plaza, San Antonio, 4/15/70, A, C, NHL, 70000741

Staacke Brothers Building, 309 E. Commerce St., San Antonio, 9/02/80, A, C, 80004079

Stevens Building, 315 E. Commerce St., San Antonio, 5/10/84, B, C, 84001614

Thiele House and Thiele Cottage, 411 and 415 Sixth St., San Antonio, 3/03/83, C, 83003092

Thomas Jefferson High School, 723 Donaldson Ave., San Antonio, 9/22/83, A, C, 83003093

U.S. San Antonio Arsenal, Roughly bounded by S. Flores and E. Arsenal Sts., and the San Antonio River, San Antonio, 12/30/69, A, 69000200

Ursuline Academy, 300 Augusta St., San Antonio, 11/25/69, A, C, a, 69000201

Vogel Belt Complex, 111–121 Military Plaza, San Antonio, 4/10/75, A, C, 75001956

Walker Ranch, Address Restricted, San Antonio vicinity, 2/24/75, A, D, 75001957

Wright, L. T., House, 342 Wilkins Ave., San Antonio, 4/01/83, C, 83003094

Ximenes Chapel, 113 Ruiz St., San Antonio, 9/08/80, B, C, a, 80004080

Blanco County

Blanco Historic District, Roughly bounded by Fifth St., Live Oak St., Town Cr. and rear property lines W of Main St., Blanco, 7/16/91, A, C, 91000890

Conn, Adrian Edwards, House, Jct. of U.S. 281 and SW boundary of courthouse square, Blanco, 11/19/71, C, 71000921

Lyndon B. Johnson National Historical Park, Lyndon B. Johnson National Historical Park, Johnson City, 12/02/69, B, c, e, f, NPS, 69000202

Round Mountain Stage-Coach Inn and Stable, SR 962 off U.S. 281, Round Mountain, 3/31/78, A, C, 78002896

Bosque County

Bekken, J. H., House [Norwegian Settlement of Bosque County TR], NW of Clifton, Clifton vicinity, 7/22/83, A, C, 83003095

Bosque County Courthouse, Public Sq., Meridian, 4/13/77, A, C, 77001427

Bosque County Jail, 203 E. Morgan, Meridian, 1/29/79, A, C, 79002918

Brandhagen Houses [Norwegian Settlement of Bosque County TR], W of Clifton on FM 182, Clifton vicinity, 7/22/83, A, C, 83003096

Bridges-Johnson House, Off TX 6, SW of Meridian, Meridian vicinity, 10/25/79, C, 79003447

Brogdon Farm [Norwegian Settlement of Bosque County TR], W of Clifton, Clifton vicinity, 7/22/83, A, C, 83003097

Bronstad House [Norwegian Settlement of Bosque County TR], SW of Clifton, Clifton vicinity, 7/22/83, A, C, 83003098

Colwick, John and Mary, Farm [Norwegian Settlement of Bosque County TR], SW of Clifton, Clifton vicinity, 7/22/83, A, C, 83003099

Dahl, Peder, Farm [Norwegian Settlement of Bosque County TR], SW of Clifton on FM 219, Clifton vicinity, 7/22/83, A, C, 83003100

Ellingson Farm [Norwegian Settlement of Bosque County TR], W of Clifton, Clifton vicinity, 7/22/83, A, C, 83003101

Erickson, Even and Petrine, Farm [Norwegian Settlement of Bosque County TR], NW of Clifton, Clifton vicinity, 7/22/83, A, C, 83003102

Finstad, Ole and Elizabeth, Homesite [Norwegian Settlement of Bosque County TR], SW of Clifton on FM 219, Clifton vicinity, 7/22/83, A, C, 83003103

First National Bank Building, Main and Morgan Sts., Meridian, 11/07/79, A, B, C, 79002919

Godager, Adolf and Christine, Homesite [Norwegian Settlement of Bosque County TR], NW of Clifton, Clifton vicinity, 7/22/83, A, C, 83003104

Grimland, Gunsten and Lofise, House [Norwegian Settlement of Bosque County TR], SW of Clifton on FM 219, Clifton vicinity, 7/22/83, A, C, 83003105

Grimland, Keddel and Liv, Farm [Norwegian Settlement of Bosque County TR], SW of Clifton on FM 219, Clifton vicinity, 7/22/83, A, C, 83003106

Hoff-Ulland Farm [Norwegian Settlement of Bosque County TR], SW of Clifton, Clifton vicinity, 7/22/83, A, C, 83003107

Hog Creek Archeological District, Address Restricted, Mosheim vicinity, 7/20/77, D, 77001428

Jenson, James Jens and Martha, House [Norwegian Settlement of Bosque County TR], NW of Clifton on FM 2136, Clifton vicinity, 7/22/83, A, C, 83003108

Knudson, Christen and Johanne, Farm [Norwegian Settlement of Bosque County TR], SW of Clifton on FM 219, Clifton vicinity, 7/22/83, A, C, 83003109

Lahlum, A. H., House [Norwegian Settlement of Bosque County TR], SW of Clifton, Clifton vicinity, 7/22/83, A, C, b, 83003110

Larson, Martin, House [Norwegian Settlement of Bosque County TR], SW of Clifton, Clifton vicinity, 7/22/83, A, C, 83003111

Linberg, Eric and Martha, Farm [Norwegian Settlement of Bosque County TR], W of Clifton, Clifton vicinity, 7/22/83, A, C, 83003112

Norway Mill [Norwegian Settlement of Bosque County TR], SW of Clifton on FM 182, Clifton vicinity, 7/22/83, A, C, 83003113

Olson, Joseph and Anna, Farm [Norwegian Settlement of Bosque County TR], SW of Clifton on FM 182, Clifton vicinity, 7/22/83, A, C, 83003114

Olson-Hanson Farm [Norwegian Settlement of Bosque County TR], SW of Clifton on FM 219, Clifton vicinity, 7/22/83, A, C, 83003115

Olson-Nelson Farm [Norwegian Settlement of Bosque County TR], W of Clifton, Clifton vicinity, 7/22/83, A, C, 83003116

Bosque County—Continued

Pederson, John, Farm [Norwegian Settlement of Bosque County TR], SW of Clifton on FM 219, Clifton vicinity, 7/22/83, A, C, 83003117

Pierson, Ole and Ann, Farm [Norwegian Settlement of Bosque County TR], W of Clifton, Clifton vicinity, 7/22/83, A, C, 83003118

Questad, Carl and Sedsel, Farm [Norwegian Settlement of Bosque County TR], W of Clifton, Clifton vicinity, 7/22/83, A, B, C, 83003119

Reeder-Omenson Farm [Norwegian Settlement of Bosque County TR], SW of Clifton on FM 182, Clifton vicinity, 7/22/83, A, C, 83003120

Reierson, Hans and Berthe, House [Norwegian Settlement of Bosque County TR], SW of Clifton, Clifton vicinity, 7/22/83, A, C, 83003121

Ringness, Jens and Kari, Farm [Norwegian Settlement of Bosque County TR], Sw of Clifton on FM 219, Clifton vicinity, 7/22/83, A, C, 83003122

Rogstad, Tom and Martha, Farm [Norwegian Settlement of Bosque County TR], W of Clifton, Clifton vicinity, 7/22/83, A, C, 83003123

Schultz, Tobias and Wilhelmine, Farm [Norwegian Settlement of Bosque County TR], SW of Clifton, Clifton vicinity, 7/22/83, A, C, 83003124

Shefstad, Gunarus and Ingerborg, House [Norwegian Settlement of Bosque County TR], N of Clifton, Clifton vicinity, 7/22/83, A, C, 83003125

Upper Settlement Rural Historic District [Norwegian Settlement of Bosque County TR], E of Granfills Gap off TX 22, Granfills Gap vicinity, 7/22/83, A, C, 83003126

Wilson Homesite [Norwegian Settlement of Bosque County TR], W of Clifton, Clifton vicinity, 7/22/83, A, C, 83003127

Bowie County

Bowie County Courthouse and Jail, Public Sq., Boston, 11/16/77, A, C, 77001429

Draughn-Moore House, 420 Pine St., Texarkana, 6/29/76, C, 76002007

Hotel McCartney, State Line Ave., Texarkana, 9/06/79, A, C, 79002920

Offenhauser Insurance Building, State Line Ave. and 3rd St., Texarkana, 2/25/71, A, 71000922

Rialto Building, 317 State Line Ave., Texarkana, 6/17/82, A, C, 82004493

Roseborough Lake Site, Address Restricted, Texarkana vicinity, 7/06/76, D, 76002008

Saenger Theater, 219 Main St., Texarkana, 7/12/78, A, C, 78002897

Texarkana Phase Archeological District, Address Restricted, Texarkana vicinity, 8/14/73, D, 73001959

Texarkana Union Station, State Line and Front St., Texarkana, 11/19/78, A, C, 78000611

Tilson Mounds—Summerhill Lake Place (41BW14), Address Restricted, Texarkana vicinity, 1/16/87, A, D, 86003637

Whitaker House, 517 Whitaker St., Texarkana, 11/07/79, C, 79002921

Brazoria County

Brazoria Bridge, 0.9 mi. E of TX 36 on TX 332, Brazoria, 6/14/91, A, C, 91000783

Durazno Plantation, S of Jones Creek off TX 36, Jones Creek vicinity, 9/02/80, B, C, D, d, 80004081

East Columbia Historic District [East Columbia MPS], S. Main St., East Columbia, 10/28/91, A, C, 91001602

McCroskey, John, Cabin, 2 mi. NE of Cedar Lake on Stringfellow Ranch, Cedar Lake, 8/28/75, B, C, 75001958

Old Brazoria County Courthouse, Public Sq., Angleton, 3/12/79, A, C, 79002922

Underwood, Ammon, House, Main St., East Columbia, 6/24/76, A, B, C, b, 76002011

Varner-Hogg Plantation, 2 mi. NE of West Columbia off SR 2852, West Columbia vicinity, 4/09/80, A, B, 80004082

Brazos County

Allen Academy Memorial Hall [Bryan MRA], 1100 blk. of Ursuline, Bryan, 9/25/87, A, 87001603

Allen Block [Bryan MRA], 400–422 N. Main, Bryan, 9/25/87, C, 87001604

Allen, R. O., House-Allen Academy [Bryan MRA], 1120 Ursuline, Bryan, 9/25/87, C, 87001605

Armstrong House-Allen Academy [Bryan MRA], 1200 Ursuline, Bryan, 9/25/87, C, 87001606

Astin, R. Q., House [Bryan MRA], 508 W. Twenty-sixth, Bryan, 9/25/87, C, 87001607

Blazek, E. J., House [Bryan MRA], 409 W. Thirtieth, Bryan, 9/25/87, C, 87001608

Bryan Carnegie Library, 111 S. Main St., Bryan, 10/27/76, A, C, 76002009

Bryan Compress and Warehouse [Bryan MRA], 911 N. Bryan, Bryan, 9/25/87, A, 87001609

Bryan Ice House [Bryan MRA], 107 E. Martin Luther King, Bryan, 9/25/87, C, 87001610

CSPS Lodge—Griesser Bakery [Bryan MRA], 304 N. Logan, Bryan, 9/25/87, A, 87001611

Cavitt House, 713 E. 30th St., Bryan, 10/27/76, C, 76002010

Chance, James O., House [Bryan MRA], 102 S. Parker, Bryan, 9/25/87, C, 87001612

East Side Historic District [Bryan MRA], Roughly bounded by Houston, Twenty-ninth, Haswell, and E. Thirtieth Sts., Bryan, 9/25/87, C, 87001613

Edge, Eugene, House [Bryan MRA], 609 S. Ennis, Bryan, 9/25/87, B, C, 87001614

English—Dansby House [Bryan MRA], 204 W. Twenty-eighth, Bryan, 9/25/87, C, 87001615

English—Poindexter House [Bryan MRA], 206 W. Twenty-eighth, Bryan, 9/25/87, C, 87001616

First Baptist Church [Bryan MRA], 201 S. Washington, Bryan, 9/25/87, C, a, 87001617

First National Bank and Trust Building [Bryan MRA], 120 N. Main, Bryan, 9/25/87, C, 87001618

First State Bank and Trust Building [Bryan MRA], 100 W. Twenty-fifth, Bryan, 9/25/87, C, 87001619

Higgs, Walter J., House [Bryan MRA], 609 N. Tabor, Bryan, 9/25/87, C, 87001620

House at 109 N. Sterling [Bryan MRA], 109 N. Sterling, Bryan, 9/25/87, C, 87001623

House at 1401 Baker [Bryan MRA], 1401 Baker, Bryan, 9/25/87, C, 87001621

House at 407 N. Parker [Bryan MRA], 407 N. Parker, Bryan, 9/25/87, C, 87001624

House at 600 N. Washington [Bryan MRA], 600 N. Washington, Bryan, 9/25/87, C, 87001626

House at 603 E. Thirty-first [Bryan MRA], 603 E. Thirty-first, Bryan, 9/25/87, C, 87001627

House at 604 E. Twenty-seventh [Bryan MRA], 604 E. Twenty-seventh, Bryan, 9/25/87, C, 87001629

Humpty Dumpty Store [Bryan MRA], 218 N. Bryan, Bryan, 9/25/87, A, 87001631

Jenkins, Edward J., House [Bryan MRA], 607 E. Twenty-seventh, Bryan, 9/25/87, C, 87001633

Jones, J. M., House [Bryan MRA], 812 S. Ennis, Bryan, 9/25/87, B, C, 87001634

Kemp, E. A., House [Bryan MRA], 606 W. Seventeenth, Bryan, 9/25/87, B, C, 87001636

McDougal—Jones House [Bryan MRA], 600 E. Twenty-seventh, Bryan, 9/25/87, C, 87001637

Moore House [Bryan MRA], 500 E. Twenty-fifth, Bryan, 9/25/87, C, 87001638

Noto House [Bryan MRA], 900 N. Parker, Bryan, 9/25/87, C, 87001639

Oliver, Dr. William Holt, House [Bryan MRA], 602 W. Twenty-sixth, Bryan, 9/25/87, B, 87001640

Parker Lumber Company Complex [Bryan MRA], 419 N. Main, Bryan, 9/25/87, A, C, 87001641

Parker, Milton, House [Bryan MRA], 200 S. Congress, Bryan, 9/25/87, C, 87001642

Saint Andrew's Episcopal Church [Bryan MRA], 217 W. Twenty-sixth, Bryan, 9/25/87, C, a, 87001646

Saint Anthony's Catholic Church [Bryan MRA], 306 S. Parker, Bryan, 9/25/87, A, a, 87001647

Sausley House [Bryan MRA], 700 N. Washington, Bryan, 9/25/87, C, 87001643

Sinclair Station, (Old) [Bryan MRA], 507 S. Texas, Bryan, 9/25/87, C, 87001644

Smith—Barron House [Bryan MRA], 100 S. Congress, Bryan, 6/20/88, B, C, 87001645

Stone, Roy C., House [Bryan MRA], 715 E. Thirty-first, Bryan, 9/25/87, C, 87001649

Temple Freda, 205 Parker St., Bryan, 9/22/83, A, C, a, 83003128

Zimmerman, Minnie Zulch, House [Bryan MRA], 308 N. Washington, Bryan, 9/25/87, C, 87001650

Brewster County

Brewster County Courthouse and Jail, Courthouse Sq., Alpine, 7/17/78, A, C, 78002899

Burro Mesa Archeological District, Address Restricted, Panther Junction vicinity, 9/11/85, A, D, NPS, 85002309

Brewster County—Continued

Castolon Historic District, Along Rio Grande at jct. of Park Rtes. 5, 9, and 35, Big Bend National Park, 9/06/74, A, NPS, 74000276

Daniels Farm House, W of Rio Grande Village in Big Bend National Park, Rio Grande Village vicinity, 10/20/89, A, NPS, 89001627

Hot Springs, W of Rio Grande Village, Big Bend National Park, 9/17/74, A, g, NPS, 74000278

Luna Jacal, At base of Pena Mountain in Big Bend National Park, Big Bend National Park, 11/08/74, A, B, C, NPS, 74000282

Mariscal Mine, River Rd., Big Bend National Park, 9/13/74, A, NPS, 74000279

Rancho Estelle, On the Rio Grande River, Big Bend National Park, 9/03/74, A, C, NPS, 74000280

Wilson, Homer, Ranch, 8 mi. S of Santa Elena Junction on Park Rte. 5, Big Bend National Park, Santa Elena Junction vicinity, 4/14/75, A, g, NPS, 75000153

Briscoe County

Lake Theo Folsom Site Complex, Address Restricted, Quitaque vicinity, 4/28/75, D, 75001960

Mayfield Dugout, 7 mi. NW of Silverton, Silverton vicinity, 6/18/73, C, 73001960

Brown County

Brown County Jail, 401 W. Broadway, Brownwood, 9/22/83, C, 83003129

Santa Fe Railroad Station, Washington Ave. between E. Depot and E. Adams Sts., Brownwood, 1/02/76, A, C, 76002012

St. John's Episcopal Church, 700 Main Ave, Brownwood, 9/04/79, A, C, a, 79002923

Walker, J. A., House and Rogers, R. B., House, 701 and 707 Center Ave., Brownwood, 7/19/82, C, 82004494

Burleson County

Reeves—Womack House, 405 W. Fox St., Caldwell, 2/04/93, C, 93000002

Burnet County

Krause Spring Site, Address Restricted, Spicewood vicinity, 11/15/78, D, 78002901

Page, Louis, Archeological Site, Address Restricted, Marble Falls vicinity, 3/30/78, D, 78002900

Roper Hotel, TX 281 and 3rd St., Marble Falls, 1/08/80, A, C, 80004083

Caldwell County

Caldwell County Courthouse Historic District, Courthouse Sq. and environs, Lockhart, 1/03/78, A, C, 78002902

Emmanuel Episcopal Church, SE corner of N. Church and Walnut Sts., Lockhart, 6/05/74, A, C, a, 74002065

Withers, M. A., House, W of Lockhart on Borchert Loop Rd., Lockhart vicinity, 8/27/76, B, C, 76002013

Calhoun County

Matagorda Island Lighthouse, Matagorda Island, Port O'Connor vicinity, 9/18/84, A, C, 84001624

Cameron County

Brazos Santiago Depot (41CF4), Address Restricted, Port Isabel vicinity, 7/14/71, A, D, 71000923

Brooks, Samuel Wallace, House, 623 E. St. Charles St., Brownsville, 11/22/88, C, b, 88002530

Browne-Wagner House, 245 E. St. Charles St., Brownsville, 8/29/77, C, 77001430

Cameron County Courthouse, 1150 E. Madison St., Brownsville, 9/27/80, A, C, 80004084

Celaya, Augustine, House, 504 E. Saint Francis St., Brownsville, 4/11/86, C, 86000726

Celaya—Creager House, 441 E. Washington St., Brownsville, 5/05/88, B, C, 88000523

Fernandez, Miguel, Hide Yard, 1101–1121 E. Adams St., Brownsville, 10/01/90, A, C, 90001485

Fort Brown, S edge of Brownsville off International Blvd., Brownsville, 10/15/66, A, NHL, 66000811

Garcia Pasture Site, Address Restricted, Port Isabel vicinity, 2/23/72, D, 72001355

Immaculate Conception Church, 1218 E. Jefferson St., Brownsville, 3/26/80, A, C, a, 80004085

La Madrilena, 1002 E. Madison, Brownsville, 11/17/88, C, 88002384

La Nueva Libertad, 1301 E. Madison St., Brownsville, 6/14/84, A, C, 84001628

Manautou House, 5 E. Elizabeth St., Brownsville, 7/14/83, C, 83003130

Old Brulay Plantation, E of Brownsville off TX 4, Brownsville vicinity, 10/10/75, A, C, D, 75001961

Palmito Ranch Battlefield, Between TX 4 (Boca Chica Hwy.) and the Rio Grande, approximately 12 mi. E of Brownsville, Brownsville vicinity, 6/23/93, A, D, 93000266

Palo Alto Battlefield, 6.3 mi. N of Brownsville at jct. of FR 1847 and 511, Brownsville vicinity, 10/15/66, A, NHL, NPS, 66000812

Point Isabel Lighthouse, Off TX 100, Port Isabel, 4/30/76, A, 76002014

Resaca de la Palma Battlefield, N edge of Brownsville on Parades Line Rd., Brownsville, 10/15/66, A, f, NHL, 66000813

Southern Pacific Railroad Passenger Depot, 601 E. Madison St., Brownsville, 11/17/78, A, C, 78002903

Stillman, Charles, House, 1305 E. Washington St., Brownsville, 11/19/79, B, C, 79003448

The Gem, 400 E. 13th St., Brownsville, 6/28/91, A, B, C, 91000852

Carson County

Carson County Square House Museum, 5th and Elsie Sts., Panhandle, 3/07/73, B, C, 73001961

Cass County

Cass County Courthouse, Public Sq., Linden, 5/25/79, A, C, 79002924

Mathews-Powell House, Miller St., Queen City, 9/22/77, B, C, 77001431

Chambers County

Archeological Site 41 CH 110, Address Restricted, Cove vicinity, 7/14/71, D, 71000924

Chambersea, Washington and Cummings Sts, Anahuac, 11/19/79, B, C, D, 79002925

Fort Anahuac, TX 564, Anahuac, 7/01/81, A, D, 81000626

Old Wallisville Town Site, Address Restricted, Wallisville vicinity, 3/30/82, D, b, 82004495

Orcoquisac Archeological District, Address Restricted, Wallisville vicinity, 7/14/71, A, D, 71000925

Cherokee County

Aber and Haberle Houses, 823 and 833 S. Bolton St., Jacksonville, 8/21/84, A, C, 84001630

Davis, George C., Site, Address Restricted, Alto vicinity, 10/15/70, A, D, 70000742

Davis, George C., Site (Boundary Increase), Address Restricted, Alto vicinity, 11/15/79, D, 79003449

Newton, William Walter, House, 401 N. Bolton St., Jacksonville, 7/15/82, C, 82004496

Clay County

Clay County Courthouse and Jail, 100 N. Bridge St., Henrietta, 10/03/78, A, C, 78002904

Coke County

Fort Chadbourne, Address Restricted, Bronte vicinity, 4/02/73, A, D, 73001962

Collin County

Aston Building, 113 S. Main St., Farmersville, 6/30/83, C, 83003131

Beverly—Harris House [McKinney MPS], 604 Parker, McKinney, 10/08/87, C, 87001661

Bingham, John H., House [McKinney MPS], 800 S. Chestnut, McKinney, 6/27/88, C, 87001662

Board—Everett House [McKinney MPS], 507 N. Bradley, McKinney, 10/08/87, C, 87001663

Brown, John R., House [McKinney MPS], 509 N. Church, McKinney, 10/08/87, C, 87001666

Burrus—Finch House [McKinney MPS], 405 N. Waddill, McKinney, 6/27/88, B, C, 87001671

Clardy, U. P., House [McKinney MPS], 315 Oak, McKinney, 10/08/87, C, 87001679

Cline—Bass House [McKinney MPS], 804 Tucker, McKinney, 6/27/88, B, 87001681

Coggins, J. R., House [McKinney MPS], 805 Howell, McKinney, 10/08/87, C, 87001682

Collin County Mill and Elevator Company [McKinney MPS], 407 E. Louisiana, McKinney, 10/08/87, A, C, 87001685

Crouch—Perkins House [McKinney MPS], 205 N. Church, McKinney, 10/08/87, C, 87001691

Davis, H. L., House [McKinney MPS], 705 N. College, McKinney, 10/08/87, C, 87001695

Davis—Hill House [McKinney MPS], 710 N. Church, McKinney, 10/08/87, C, 87001697

Dowell, J. S., House [McKinney MPS], 608 Parker, McKinney, 10/08/87, C, 87001699

Dulaney, Joe E., House [McKinney MPS], 311 S. Chestnut, McKinney, 10/08/87, C, 87001704

Dulaney, Joseph Field, House [McKinney MPS], 315 S. Chestnut, McKinney, 10/08/87, C, 87001702

Faires, F. C., House [McKinney MPS], 505 S. Chestnut, McKinney, 10/08/87, C, 87001705

Faires—Bell House [McKinney MPS], S side Chestnut Sq., McKinney, 10/08/87, C, 87001706

Ferguson, John H., House [McKinney MPS], 607 N. Church, McKinney, 10/08/87, C, 87001707

Foote—Crouch House [McKinney MPS], 401 N. Benge, McKinney, 6/27/88, C, 87001708

Fox, S. H., House [McKinney MPS], 808 Tucker, McKinney, 10/08/87, C, 87001709

Goodner, Jim B., House [McKinney MPS], 302 S. Tennessee, McKinney, 10/08/87, C, 87001688

Gouch—Hughston House [McKinney MPS], 1206 W. Louisiana, McKinney, 6/27/88, C, 87001710

Heard—Craig House [McKinney MPS], 205 W. Hunt, McKinney, 10/08/87, B, C, 87001711

Hill, Ben, House [McKinney MPS], 509 Tucker, McKinney, 10/08/87, C, 87001712

Hill, John B., House [McKinney MPS], 605 N. College, McKinney, 10/08/87, C, 87001713

Hill, Moran, House [McKinney MPS], 203 N. Waddill, McKinney, 10/08/87, C, 87001714

Hill, W. R., House [McKinney MPS], 601 N. College, McKinney, 10/08/87, C, 87001715

Hill—Webb Grain Elevator [McKinney MPS], 400 E. Louisiana, McKinney, 10/08/87, A, 87001716

House at 1303 W. Louisiana [McKinney MPS], 1303 W. Louisiana, McKinney, 10/08/87, C, 87001717

House at 201 N. Graves [McKinney MPS], 201 N. Graves, McKinney, 10/08/87, C, 87001718

House at 301 E. Lamar [McKinney MPS], 301 E. Lamar, McKinney, 10/08/87, C, 87001719

House at 610 Tucker [McKinney MPS], 610 Tucker, McKinney, 10/08/87, C, 87001720

House at 704 Parker [McKinney MPS], 704 Parker, McKinney, 10/08/87, C, 87001721

Houses at 406 and 408 Heard [McKinney MPS], 406 & 408 Heard, McKinney, 10/08/87, C, 87001722

Johnson, John, House [McKinney MPS], 302 Anthony, McKinney, 10/08/87, C, 87001723

King, Mrs. J. C., House [McKinney MPS], 405 W. Louisiana, McKinney, 10/13/88, C, 87001737

Kirkpatrick, E. W., House and Barn [McKinney MPS], 903 Parker, McKinney, 10/08/87, B, C, 87001738

McKinney Commercial Historic District, Roughly bounded by Herndon, Wood, Cloyd, Davis, Louisiana, MacDonald, and Virginia Sts., McKinney, 1/10/83, C, 83003132

McKinney Cotton Compress Plant [McKinney MPS], 300 blk. Throckmorton, McKinney, 6/27/88, A, 87001739

McKinney Cotton Mill Historic District [McKinney MPS], Roughly bounded by Elm, RR tracks, Burrus, Fowler, & Amscott, McKinney, 10/08/87, A, C, 87001740

McKinney Hospital, Old [McKinney MPS], 700–800 S. College, McKinney, 10/08/87, A, C, 87001743

McKinney Residential Historic District [McKinney MPS], Roughly bounded by W. Lamar, N. Benge, W. Louisiana, & N. Oak, McKinney, 10/08/87, C, 87001744

Neathery, Sam, House [McKinney MPS], 215 N. Waddill, McKinney, 6/27/88, C, 87001745

Nenney, J. P., House [McKinney MPS], 601 N. Church, McKinney, 6/27/88, C, 87001746

Newsome, R. F., House [McKinney MPS], 609 Tucker, McKinney, 10/08/87, C, 87001747

Newsome—King House [McKinney MPS], 401 W. Louisiana, McKinney, 10/08/87, C, 87001748

Rhea, John C., House [McKinney MPS], 801 N. College, McKinney, 6/27/88, C, 87001749

Scott, A. M., House [McKinney MPS], 1109 W. Louisiana, McKinney, 10/08/87, C, 87001750

Scott, L. A., House [McKinney MPS], 513 W. Louisiana, McKinney, 6/27/88, B, C, 87001751

Sister Grove Creek Site, Address Restricted, Farmersville vicinity, 8/22/77, D, 77001432

Smith, W. D., House [McKinney MPS], 703 N. College, McKinney, 10/08/87, C, 87001752

Taylor, J. H., House [McKinney MPS], 211 N. Waddill, McKinney, 10/08/87, C, 87001753

Thompson House [McKinney MPS], 1207 W. Louisiana, McKinney, 10/08/87, C, 87001754

Waddill, R. L., House [McKinney MPS], 302 W. Lamar, McKinney, 10/08/87, C, 87001755

Wiley, Thomas W., House [McKinney MPS], 105 S. Church, McKinney, 10/08/87, C, 87001756

Wilson, A. G., House [McKinney MPS], 417 N. Waddill, McKinney, 10/08/87, C, 87001757

Wilson, Ammie, House, 1900 W. 15th St., Plano, 12/28/78, B, C, g, 78002906

Colorado County

Colorado County Courthouse, Bounded by Milam, Spring, Travis and Walnut Sts., Columbus, 7/12/76, C, 76002015

Colorado County Courthouse Historic District, Roughly bounded by Preston, Walnut, Milam, Front, Washington, and Live Oak Sts., Columbus, 6/23/78, A, C, 78002907

Stafford Bank and Opera House, Milan and Spring Sts., Columbus, 5/08/73, A, C, 73002276

Stafford, John, House, S of Columbus on U.S. 71, Columbus vicinity, 5/03/76, A, C, 76002016

Comal County

Breustedt, Andreas, House, 1370 Church Hill Dr., New Braunfels, 7/22/82, C, b, 82004497

Comal County Courthouse, N. Sequin Ave., New Braunfels, 12/12/76, A, C, 76002017

Comal Hotel and Klein-Kuse House, 295 E. San Antonio and 165 Market St., New Braunfels, 6/26/86, A, C, 86001373

First Protestant Church, 296 S. Sequin St., New Braunfels, 7/14/71, A, C, a, 71000926

Gruene Historic District, Both sides of Sequin, New Braunfels, and Austin Sts., Gruene, 4/21/75, A, C, 75001962

Guadalupe Hotel, 471 Main Plaza, New Braunfels, 3/13/75, A, C, 75001963

Hotel Faust, 240 S. Sequin St., New Braunfels, 5/02/85, A, C, 85000922

Klein, Stephen, House, 131 S. Seguin St., New Braunfels, 8/25/70, C, 70000743

Lindheimer House, 489 Comal Ave., New Braunfels, 8/25/70, B, C, 70000744

Concho County

Bishop Site, Address Restricted, Salt Gap vicinity, 6/17/77, D, 77001434

Concho County Courthouse, Public Sq., Paint Rock, 11/07/77, A, C, 77001433

Paint Rock Indian Pictograph Site, Address Restricted, Paint Rock vicinity, 6/21/71, A, D, 71000927

Cooke County

Cloud-Stark House, 327 S. Dixon St., Gainesville, 6/01/82, C, 82004498

Cooke County—Continued

Cooke County Courthouse, Public Square, bounded by California, Dixon, Main and Commerce Sts., Gainesville, 3/22/91, A, C, 91000336

Davis, William and Anna, House, 505 S. Denton St., Gainesville, 5/10/84, B, C, 84001633

Santa Fe Passenger Depot, 505 E. Broadway, Gainesville, 10/06/83, A, C, 83003757

St. Peter's Roman Catholic Church [Churches with Decorative Interior Painting TR], Ash St., Lindsay, 5/25/79, A, C, a, 79002927

Thomason-Scott House, Off TX 51 and SR 922, Era, 9/30/80, B, C, 80004086

Coryell County

Copperas Cove Stagestop and Post Office, 1.6 mi. SW of Copperas Cove off U.S. 190, Copperas Cove vicinity, 9/26/79, A, C, 79002928

Coryell County Courthouse, Public Sq., Gatesville, 8/18/77, A, C, 77001435

Mother Neff State Park and F. A. S. 21-B(1) Historic District, Jct. of TX 236 and the Leon R., Moody vicinity, 10/02/92, A, C, 92001303

Crane County

Insley, Merritt, House and Outbuildings, 602 Seneca St., Leavenworth, 10/02/86, B, C, 86002801

Crockett County

Camp Melvin Site, Address Restricted, Iraan vicinity, 11/15/78, A, D, 78002909

Crockett County Courthouse, 907 Ave. D, Ozona, 12/27/74, C, 74002066

Fort Lancaster, 10 mi. E of Sheffield on U.S. 290, Sheffield vicinity, 3/11/71, A, 71000928

Harris Ranch Petroglyph Site 41 CX 110, Address Restricted, Iraan vicinity, 5/05/78, D, 78002908

Live Oak Creek Archeological District, Address Restricted, Sheffield vicinity, 4/02/76, D, 76002018

Turkey Roost Petroglyph Site, Address Restricted, Ozona vicinity, 10/19/78, D, 78002910

Culberson County

Clark Hotel, 112 Broadway St., Van Horn, 7/19/79, A, 79002929

First Presbyterian Church, Fannin and 3rd Sts., Van Horn, 12/01/78, A, C, a, 78002912

Granado Cave, Address Restricted, Toyah vicinity, 3/25/77, D, 77001436

Guadalupe Ranch, NE of Salt Flat in Guadalupe Mountains National Park, Salt Flat vicinity, 11/21/78, C, NPS, 78000259

Lobo Valley Petroglyph Site, Address Restricted, Lobo vicinity, 10/25/88, C, D, 88002012

McKittrick Canyon Archeological District, Guadalupe Mountains National Park, Address Restricted, Salt Flat vicinity, 9/26/91, A, D, NPS, 91001381

Pinery Station, Off U.S. 62/180, Gaudalupe Mountain National Park, 10/09/74, A, NPS, 74000281

Pratt, Wallace, Lodge, At jct. of N and S branch of McKittrick Canyon, Gaudalupe Mountain National Park, 3/26/75, B, C, NPS, 75000154

Dallam County

Dallam County Courthouse, Jct. of Fifth and Denrock Sts., Dalhart, 10/15/92, A, C, 92001375

Dallas County

Angle, D. M., House [Cedar Hill Texas MRA], 800 Beltline, Cedar Hill, 3/27/85, C, 85000710

Belo, Alfred Horatio, House, 2115 Ross Ave., Dallas, 10/29/75, A, C, 75001965

Bryant, William, Jr., House [Cedar Hill Texas MRA], S. Broad and Cooper, Cedar Hill, 3/27/85, B, C, 85000711

Busch Building, 1501–1509 Main St., Dallas, 7/04/80, A, C, 80004489

Cedar Springs Place, 2531 Lucas Dr., Dallas, 12/30/91, A, C, 91001901

Clements Hall [Georgian Revival Buildings of Southern Methodist University TR], 3200 Dyer St., Dallas, 9/27/80, A, C, 80004087

Continental Gin Company, 3301-3333 Elm St., 212 and 232 Trunk Ave., Dallas, 2/14/83, C, 83003134

Dallas County Courthouse, Houston and Commerce Sts., Dallas, 12/12/76, C, 76002019

Dallas Hall [Georgian Revival Buildings of Southern Methodist University TR (AD)], Southern Methodist University campus, Dallas, 11/17/78, A, C, 78002913

Dallas Scottish Rite Temple, Harwood and Young Sts., Dallas, 3/26/80, A, C, 80004088

Dallas Union Terminal, 400 S. Houston St., Dallas, 5/29/75, A, C, 75001966

DeGolyer Estate, 8525 Garland Rd., Dallas, 12/28/78, A, B, C, 78002914

Dealey Plaza Historic District, Roughly bounded by Pacific Ave., Market St., Jackson St. and right of way of Dallas Right of Way Management Company, Dallas, 4/19/93, A, B, C, f, g, NHL, 93001607

Florence, Fred, Hall [Georgian Revival Buildings of Southern Methodist University TR], 3330 University Blvd., Dallas, 9/27/80, A, C, 80004089

Gilbert, Samuel and Julia, House, 2540 Farmers Branch Ln., Farmers Branch, 11/10/88, C, D, 88002063

Grace Methodist Episcopal Church, 4105 Junius St., Dallas, 11/04/82, A, C, a, 82001736

Hawkes, Z. T. (Tip), House [Cedar Hill Texas MRA], 132 N. Potter St., Cedar Hill, 3/27/85, C, 85000712

Hilton Hotel, 1933 Main St., Dallas, 12/05/85, A, C, 85003092

Hotel Adolphus, 1315 Commerce St., Dallas, 7/14/83, A, C, 83003133

Houston Street Viaduct, Houston St. roughly between Arlington St. and Lancaster Ave., Dallas, 8/09/84, A, C, 84001641

Hyer Hall [Georgian Revival Buildings of Southern Methodist University TR], 6424 Hill Lane, Dallas, 9/27/80, A, C, 80004090

Interstate Forwarding Company Warehouse, 3200 Main St., Dallas, 2/14/92, A, C, 92000021

Magnolia Building, 108 S. Akard St., Dallas, 1/30/78, A, C, 78002915

Majestic Theatre, 1925 Elm St., Dallas, 11/14/77, A, B, C, 77001437

McFarlin Memorial Auditorium [Georgian Revival Buildings of Southern Methodist University TR], 6405 Hillcrest Rd., Dallas, 9/27/80, A, C, 80004091

McIntosh, Roger D., House, 1518 Abrams Rd., Dallas, 4/07/83, A, 83003135

Miller, John Hickman, House, 3506 Cedar Springs, Dallas, 5/23/80, C, 80004092

Mitchell, John E., Company Plant, 3800 Commerce St., Dallas, 3/04/91, A, 91000118

Munger Place Historic District, Roughly bounded by Henderson, Junius, Prairie, and Reiger Sts., Dallas, 9/13/78, C, 78002916

Number 4 Hook and Ladder Company, Cedar Springs Rd. and Reagan St., Dallas, 5/04/81, C, 81000627

Oak Lawn Methodist Episcopal Church, South, 3014 Oak Lawn Ave., Dallas, 3/16/88, C, a, 88000176

Ownby, Jordan C., Stadium [Georgian Revival Buildings of Southern Methodist University TR], 5900 Ownby Dr., Dallas, 9/27/80, A, C, 80004093

Patterson, Stanley, Hall [Georgian Revival Buildings of Southern Methodist University TR], 3128 Dyer St., Dallas, 9/27/80, A, C, 80004094

Perkins Hall of Administration [Georgian Revival Buildings of Southern Methodist University TR], 6425 Hillcrest Rd., Dallas, 9/27/80, A, C, 80004095

Randlett House, 401 S. Centre St., Lancaster, 8/11/78, C, 78002920

Rawlins, Capt. R. A., House, 2219 Dowling St., Lancaster, 11/15/78, A, C, 78002921

Roberts, Dr. Rufus A., House [Cedar Hill Texas MRA], 210 S. Broad St., Cedar Hill, 3/27/85, A, C, 85000713

Sanger Brothers Complex, Block 32, bounded by Elm, Lamar, Main and Austin Sts., Dallas, 4/08/75, A, C, 75001967

Snider Hall [Georgian Revival Buildings of Southern Methodist University TR], 3305 Dyer St., Dallas, 9/27/80, A, C, 80004096

South Boulevard-Park Row Historic District, South Blvd. and Park Row from Central, Dallas, 2/05/79, C, 79002930

Dallas County—Continued

Spake, Jacob and Eliza, House, 2600 State St., Dallas, 11/21/85, B, C, 85002912

Strain, W. A., House, 400 E. Pecan St., Lancaster, 11/29/78, A, C, 78002922

Straus House [Cedar Hill Texas MRA], 400 Cedar, Cedar Hill, 7/12/85, B, C, 85001495

Swiss Avenue Historic District, Swiss Ave. between Fitzhugh and LaVista, Dallas, 3/28/74, C, 74002068

Texas Centennial Exposition Buildings (1936–1937), Bounded by Texas and Pacific RR, Pennsylvania, Second, and Parry Aves., Dallas, 9/24/86, A, g, NHL, 86003488

Viola Courts Apartments, 4845 Swiss Ave., Dallas, 1/19/84, C, 84001643

Virginia Hall [Georgian Revival Buildings of Southern Methodist University TR], 3325 Dyer St., Dallas, 9/27/80, A, C, 80004097

Waples-Platter Buildings, 2200–2211 N. Lamar St., Dallas, 3/24/78, A, C, 78002917

Westend Historic District, Bounded by Lamar, Griffin, Wood, Market, and Commerce Sts., Dallas, 11/14/78, A, C, g, 78002918

Wilson Block, 2902, 2906, 2910 and 2922 Swiss Ave., Dallas, 12/15/78, B, C, 78002919

Wilson Building, 1621-1623 Main St., Dallas, 7/24/79, B, C, 79002931

Winnetka Heights Historic District, Roughly bounded by Davis and 12th Sts., and Rosemont and Willomet Aves., Dallas, 11/03/83, A, C, 83003758

Dawson County

Lamesa Farm Workers Community Historic Ditrict, Jct. of US 87 and US 180, Los Ybanez, 8/09/93, A, C, 93000771

De Witt County

Bates—Sheppard House [Cuero MRA], 312 E. Broadway, Cuero, 10/31/88, B, 88001948

Bell, John Y., House [Cuero MRA], 304 E. Prairie, Cuero, 10/31/88, C, 88001982

Bennett, M. D., House [Cuero MRA], 208 N. Hunt, Cuero, 10/31/88, C, 88001963

Billow—Thompson House [Cuero MRA], 402 E. Broadway, Cuero, 10/31/88, C, 88001949

Breeden—Runge Wholesale Grocery Company Building [Cuero MRA], 108 N. Frederick William, Cuero, 10/31/88, A, C, 88001957

Buchel, Floyd, House [Cuero MRA], 407 E. Broadway, Cuero, 10/31/88, C, 88001950

Burns, Arthur, House [Cuero MRA], 130 E. Sarah, Cuero, 10/31/88, C, 88001987

Burns, John W., House [Cuero MRA], 311 E. Broadway, Cuero, 10/31/88, C, 88001947

Callaway—Gillette House [Cuero MRA], 306 E. Sarah, Cuero, 10/31/88, C, 88001989

Chaddock, J. B., House [Cuero MRA], 202 S. Valley, Cuero, 10/31/88, C, b, 88001995

City Water Works [Cuero MRA], 208 S. Esplanade, Cuero, 10/31/88, C, 88001956

Clement—Nagel House [Cuero MRA], 701 E. Morgan, Cuero, 10/31/88, B, C, b, e, 88001974

Colston—Gohmert House [Cuero MRA], 309 E. Prairie, Cuero, 10/31/88, C, 88001983

Cook, Charles, House [Cuero MRA], 103 E. Sarah, Cuero, 10/31/88, C, 88001986

Crain, W. H., House [Cuero MRA], 508 E. Courthouse, Cuero, 10/31/88, C, 88001953

Cuero Commercial Historic District [Cuero MRA], Roughly bounded by Gonzales, Main, Terrell and Courthouse, Cuero, 11/17/88, A, C, 88001996

Cuero Gin [Cuero MRA], 501 W. Main, Cuero, 10/31/88, A, 88001970

Cuero High School [Cuero MRA], 405 E. Sarah, Cuero, 10/31/88, A, C, 88001990

Cuero Hydroelectric Plant, 2 mi. N of Cuero on Guadalupe Plant, Cuero vicinity, 9/19/77, A, 77001514

Cuero I Archeological District, Address Restricted, Cuero vicinity, 10/09/74, A, D, 74002271

Daule, E. A., House [Cuero MRA], 201 W. Newman, Cuero, 10/31/88, B, C, 88001981

De Witt County Courthouse, Bounded by N. Gonzales, E. Live Oak, N. Clinton, and E. Courthouse Sts., Cuero, 5/06/71, C, 71000929

East Main Street Residential Historic District [Cuero MRA], 400 to 800 blks. of E. Main St., Cuero, 10/31/88, C, 88001998

Eckhardt Stores, Eckhardt and Main St., Yorktown, 6/29/76, A, C, 76002020

Eichholz, William and L. F., House [Cuero MRA], 308 E. Courthouse, Cuero, 10/31/88, B, C, 88001954

English-German School [Cuero MRA], 201 E. Newman, Cuero, 10/31/88, A, 88001978

Farris, J. B., House [Cuero MRA], 502 N. Gonzales, Cuero, 10/31/88, C, 88001960

First Methodist Church [Cuero MRA], 301 E. Courthouse, Cuero, 10/31/88, C, a, 88001952

Friar, Alfred, House [Cuero MRA], 703 N. Gonzales, Cuero, 10/31/88, C, 88001961

Frobese, William, Sr., House [Cuero MRA], 305 E. Newman, Cuero, 10/31/88, B, C, a, b, e, 88001980

Grace Episcopal Church [Cuero MRA], 401 N. Esplanade, Cuero, 10/31/88, C, a, 88001955

House at 1002 Stockdale [Cuero MRA], 1002 Stockdale, Cuero, 10/31/88, C, b, 88001993

House at 404 Stockdale [Cuero MRA], 404 Stockdale, Cuero, 10/31/88, C, 88001992

House at 609 East Live Oak [Cuero MRA], 609 E. Live Oak, Cuero, 10/31/88, C, 88001968

Keller—Grunder House [Cuero MRA], 409 E. Morgan, Cuero, 10/31/88, C, b, e, 88001973

Leinhardt, Albert and Kate, House [Cuero MRA], 818 E. Morgan, Cuero, 10/31/88, C, b, 88001976

Leonardt, Emil, House [Cuero MRA], 804 E. Morgan, Cuero, 11/04/88, C, 88001975

Leske Bar [Cuero MRA], 432 W. Main, Cuero, 10/31/88, C, 88001969

Ley, Valentine, House [Cuero MRA], 206 E. Newman, Cuero, 10/31/88, C, b, 88001979

Lynch—Probst House [Cuero MRA], 502 E. Broadway, Cuero, 10/31/88, C, 88001951

Macedonia Baptist Church [Cuero MRA], 512 S. Indianola, Cuero, 10/31/88, A, C, a, b, 88001967

Marie, Frank, House [Cuero MRA], 402 E. French, Cuero, 10/31/88, C, 88001959

May—Hickey House, FM 682 1.7 mi. S of jct. with TX 111, Yoakum vicinity, 10/27/88, C, b, 88002129

Meissner—Pleasants House [Cuero MRA], 108 N. Hunt, Cuero, 10/31/88, C, 88001962

Mugge, Edward, House [Cuero MRA], 218 N. Terrell, Cuero, 10/31/88, C, 88001994

Old Beer and Ice Warehouse [Cuero MRA], 104 SW Railroad, Cuero, 10/31/88, C, 88001985

Ott, Charles J. and Alvina, House [Cuero MRA], 306 N. Hunt, Cuero, 10/31/88, C, 88001965

Ott, S. I., House [Cuero MRA], 302 N. Hunt, Cuero, 10/31/88, C, 88001964

Prigden, O. F. and Mary, House [Cuero MRA], 401 E. French, Cuero, 10/31/88, C, 88001958

Reuss, J. M., House [Cuero MRA], 315 Stockdale, Cuero, 10/31/88, A, B, b, 88001991

St. Michael's Catholic Church [Cuero MRA], 202 N. McLeod, Cuero, 10/31/88, C, a, 88001971

Stevens, Elisha, House [Cuero MRA], 408 E. Prairie, Cuero, 10/31/88, C, 88001984

Terrell—Reuss Streets Historic District [Cuero MRA], 300 to 900 blks. of Terrell, 500 to 900 blks. of Indianola, and 200 blk. of W. Reuss to 400 blk. of E. Reuss, Cuero, 10/31/88, B, C, b, 88001997

Thomson, W. F., House [Cuero MRA], 608 N. McLeod, Cuero, 10/31/88, C, 88001972

Wittenbert, Dane, House [Cuero MRA], 402 S. Hunt, Cuero, 10/31/88, C, 88001966

Wittmer, Charles, House [Cuero MRA], 110 E. Newman, Cuero, 10/31/88, C, b, 88001977

Wofford—Finney House [Cuero MRA], 202 E. Prairie St., Cuero, 8/14/92, C, 92000984

Deaf Smith County

Black, E. B., House, 508 W. 3rd St., Hereford, 7/17/78, A, C, 78002923

Denton County

Cranston Site [19th Century Pottery Kilns of Denton Co. TR], Address Restricted, Denton vicinity, 8/21/82, A, D, 82004499

Denton County Courthouse, Public Sq., Denton, 12/20/77, A, C, 77001438

Lambert, J. C., Site [19th Century Pottery Kilns of Denton Co. TR], Address Restricted, Denton vicinity, 8/21/82, D, 82004500

Old Alton Bridge, Copper Canyon Rd., Copper Canyon vicinity, 7/08/88, C, 88000979

Old Continental State Bank, 312 Oak St., Roanoke, 7/22/86, A, C, 86001939

Denton County—Continued

Roark-Griffith Site [19th Century Pottery Kilns of Denton Co. TR], Address Restricted, Denton vicinity, 8/21/82, A, D, 82004501

Serren, A. H., Site [19th Century Pottery Kilns of Denton Co. TR], Address Restricted, Denton vicinity, 8/21/82, A, D, 82004502

Wilson-Donaldson Site [19th Century Pottery Kilns of Denton Co. TR], Address Restricted, Denton vicinity, 8/21/82, A, D, 82004503

Dickens County

Dickens County Courthouse and Jail, Public Sq., Dickens, 9/04/80, A, 80004098

Dimmit County

Dimmit County Courthouse, Public Square, Carrizo Springs, 8/14/84, C, 84001652

Richardson, Asher and Mary Isabelle, House, US 83, Asherton, 11/22/88, C, 88002539

Valenzuela Ranch Headquarters, Valenzuela Creek, Catarina vicinity, 7/18/85, A, B, C, 85001562

Donley County

Donley County Courthouse and Jail, Public Sq., Clarendon, 2/17/78, A, C, 78002924

Martin—Lowe House, 507 W. Fifth, Clarendon, 11/21/85, C, 85002911

Eastland County

Cisco Historic District, Roughly bounded by Conrad Hilton Ave., W. 3rd St., Ave. K, W. 8th and 9th Sts., Cisco, 11/20/84, A, C, 84000334

Mobley Hotel, 4th St. and Conrad Hilton Ave., Cisco, 5/13/81, A, 81000628

Ector County

White-Pool House, 112 E. Murphy St., Odessa, 1/08/80, A, C, 80004099

Edwards County

Edwards County Courthouse and Jail, Public Sq., Rocksprings, 11/07/79, A, C, 79002932

El Paso County

1800's Mexican Consulate, 612 E. San Antonio St., El Paso, 5/23/75, A, C, 75001969

Abdou Building [Commercial Structures of El Paso by Henry C. Trost TR], 115 N. Mesa St., El Paso, 9/24/80, C, 80004100

Bassett, O. T., Tower [Commercial Structures of El Paso by Henry C. Trost TR], 301 Texas Ave., El Paso, 9/24/80, B, C, 80004101

Caples, Richard, Building [Commercial Structures of El Paso by Henry C. Trost TR], 300 E. San Antonio Ave., El Paso, 9/24/80, C, 80004102

Castner Range Archeological District, Address Restricted, El Paso vicinity, 4/22/76, D, 76002021

Chamizal National Memorial, Paisano Dr., El Paso, 2/04/74, A, f, NPS, 74002069

Doyle, Sgt., Site, Address Restricted, El Paso vicinity, 4/11/77, A, C, D, 77001439

El Paso High School, 1600 N. Virginia St., El Paso, 11/17/80, A, C, 80004103

El Paso Union Passenger Station, SW corner of Coldwell at San Francisco St., El Paso, 4/03/75, A, C, 75001970

First Mortage Company Building, 109 N. Oregon St., El Paso, 6/13/78, A, C, 78002925

Franklin Canal, Roughly, S of the Texas and Pacific—Southern Pacific RR tracks from western El Paso to Fabens, El Paso vicinity, 6/19/92, A, 92000696

Fusselman Canyon Rock Art District, Address Restricted, El Paso vicinity, 6/03/76, A, D, 76002022

Hills, W. S., Commercial Structure [Commercial Structures of El Paso by Henry C. Trost TR], 215–219 San Antonio Ave., El Paso, 9/24/80, C, 80004104

Hot Well Archeological Site, Address Restricted, El Paso vicinity, 4/30/76, A, C, D, 76002023

Hotel Cortez [Commercial Structures of El Paso by Henry C. Trost TR], 300 N. Mesa St., El Paso, 9/24/80, C, 80004105

Hotel Paso del Norte [Commercial Structures of El Paso by Henry C. Trost TR (AD)], 115 El Paso St., El Paso, 1/05/79, A, C, 79002933

Hueco Tanks, Address Restricted, El Paso vicinity, 7/14/71, A, D, 71000930

Magoffin Homestead, 1120 Magoffin Ave., El Paso, 3/31/71, B, C, 71000931

Manhattan Heights Historic District, Roughly bounded by Grant, Louisiana and Richmond Aves., El Paso, 9/27/80, C, a, 80004107

Martin Building, 215 N. Stanton St., El Paso, 8/08/84, C, 84001655

Mission Socorro Archeological Site, Address Restricted, Socorro, 1/22/93, A, D, d, 92001741

Newberry, J. J., Company [Commercial Structures of El Paso by Henry C. Trost TR], 201–205 N. Stanton St., El Paso, 9/24/80, C, 80004108

Northgate Site, Address Restricted, El Paso vicinity, 3/16/72, A, C, 72001356

Old Bnai Zion Synagogue, 906 N. El Paso St., El Paso, 8/16/84, A, C, a, 84001658

Old Fort Bliss, 1800 block of Doniphan St., El Paso, 2/23/72, A, 72001357

Old San Francisco Historic District, Missouri St. between No. 325 and 527, El Paso, 5/21/85, C, 85001132

Palace Theatre [Commercial Structures of El Paso by Henry C. Trost TR], 209 S. El Paso St., El Paso, 9/24/80, C, 80004109

Plaza Hotel [Commercial Structures of El Paso by Henry C. Trost TR], Oregon and Mills Sts., El Paso, 9/24/80, C, 80004110

Plaza Theatre, 125 Pioneer Plaza, El Paso, 6/04/87, A, C, 87000902

Popular Department Store [Commercial Structures of El Paso by Henry C. Trost TR], 102 N. Mesa St., El Paso, 9/24/80, B, C, b, 80004111

Presidio Chapel of San Elizario, S side of plaza, San Elizario, 9/14/72, A, C, D, a, b, 72001358

Quarters Number 1, 228 Sheridan Rd., Fort Bliss, 4/09/87, A, C, 87000484

Roberts-Banner Building [Commercial Structures of El Paso by Henry C. Trost TR], 215 N. Mesa St., El Paso, 9/24/80, C, 80004112

Silver Dollar Cafe, 1021 S. Mesa, El Paso, 8/14/86, A, C, 86002618

Singer Sewing Company [Commercial Structures of El Paso by Henry C. Trost TR], 211 Texas Ave., El Paso, 9/24/80, C, 80004113

Socorro Mission, Moon Rd. and TX 258, Socorro, 3/16/72, C, D, a, 72001359

State National Bank [Commercial Structures of El Paso by Henry C. Trost TR], 114 E. San Antonio Ave., El Paso, 9/24/80, C, 80004114

Sunset Heights Historic District, Roughly bounded by Heisig Ave., River Ave., N. El Paso St., and I-10, El Paso, 12/08/88, A, B, C, 88002672

Toltec Club, 602 Magoffin Ave., El Paso, 3/12/79, C, 79002934

Trost, Henry C., House, 1013 W. Yandell Dr., El Paso, 7/12/76, C, 76002024

U.S. Post Office, 219 Mills Ave., El Paso, 7/19/84, C, 84001662

White House Department Store and Hotel McCoy [Commercial Structures of El Paso by Henry C. Trost TR], 109 Pioneer Plaza, El Paso, 9/24/80, C, 80004115

Women's Club, 1400 N. Mesa St., El Paso, 7/22/79, A, C, 79002935

Ysleta Mission, U.S. 80 near jct. with Zaragosa Rd., Ysleta, 7/31/72, C, D, a, 72001360

Ellis County

Adamson, F. R., House [Waxahachie MRA], 309 University, Waxahachie, 9/24/86, C, 86002485

Alderdice, J. M., House [Waxahachie MRA], 1500 W. Main, Waxahachie, 9/24/86, C, 86002443

Alderman, G. H., House [Waxahachie MRA], 317 E. Marvin, Waxahachie, 9/24/86, C, 86002446

Allen, I. R., House [Ennis MRA], 601 N. Dallas, Ennis, 9/25/86, C, 86002387

Atwood, E. K., House [Ennis MRA], 605 N. Preston, Ennis, 9/25/86, C, 86002504

Barkley—Floyd House [Ennis MRA], 709 N. Dallas, Ennis, 9/25/86, C, 86002389

Ellis County—Continued

Barrington House [Ennis MRA], 206 W. Belknap, Ennis, 9/25/86, C, 86002365

Berry, J. S., House [Waxahachie MRA], 201 E. University, Waxahachie, 9/24/86, C, 86002386

Boren, E. T., House [Ennis MRA], 616 W. Denton, Ennis, 9/25/86, C, 86002436

Building at 441 East Main [Waxahachie MRA], 441 E. Main, Waxahachie, 9/24/86, A, 86002437

Building at 500–502 East Main [Waxahachie MRA], 500–502 E. Main, Waxahachie, 9/24/86, A, 86002440

Bullard, T. J., House [Waxahachie MRA], 221 Patrick, Waxahachie, 9/24/86, C, 86002340

Central Presbyterian Church [Waxahachie MRA], 402 N. College, Waxahachie, 9/11/87, C, a, 86002362

Chapman, Oscar H., House [Waxahachie MRA], 201 Overhill, Waxahachie, 9/24/86, C, 86002479

Cohn, Joe, House [Waxahachie MRA], 501 Sycamore, Waxahachie, 9/24/86, C, 86002492

Cole—Hipp House [Waxahachie MRA], 309 E. Marvin, Waxahachie, 9/24/86, C, 86002445

Coleman—Cole House [Waxahachie MRA], 1219 E. Marvin, Waxahachie, 9/24/86, C, 86002522

Connally, Roy, House [Waxahachie MRA], 205 E. University, Waxahachie, 9/24/86, C, 86002388

Dillon, George C., House [Waxahachie MRA], 123 E. University, Waxahachie, 9/24/86, C, 86002378

Dunkerly, G. G., House [Ennis MRA], 607 W. Baylor, Ennis, 9/25/86, C, 86002364

Eastham, D. D., House [Waxahachie MRA], 401 E. Marvin, Waxahachie, 9/24/86, C, 86002526

Ellis County Courthouse Historic District [Waxahachie MRA], Roughly bounded by both sides of Waxahachie Creek N to Union Pacific RR tracks & between both sides of Elm and Flat Sts., Waxahachie, 4/23/75, A, C, 75001971

Ennis Commercial Historic District [Ennis MRA], Roughly bounded by W. Baylor, N. Main, W. Crockett, and McKinney Sts., Ennis, 9/25/86, A, C, 86002547

Ennis Cotton Compress [Ennis MRA], 111 E. Lampasas, Ennis, 9/25/86, A, 86002449

Ennis High School [Ennis MRA], 501 N. Gaines, Ennis, 9/25/86, A, C, 86002425

Erwin, J. R., House [Waxahachie MRA], 414 W. Marvin, Waxahachie, 9/24/86, C, 86002520

Fain House [Ennis MRA], 403 N. Preston, Ennis, 9/25/86, C, 86002501

Farrar House [Ennis MRA], 601 S. Main W, Ennis, 9/25/86, C, 86002454

Ferris School [Waxahachie MPS], 411 Gibson, Waxahachie, 12/06/90, A, C, 90001858

Forrest, W. B., House [Waxahachie MRA], 500 Royal, Waxahachie, 9/24/86, C, 86002451

Graham, Dr. L. H., House [Waxahachie MRA], 909 W. Marvin, Waxahachie, 9/24/86, C, 86002497

Hines, E. M., House [Waxahachie MRA], 124 Kaufman, Waxahachie, 9/24/86, C, 86002430

House at 104 Kaufman [Waxahachie MRA], 104 Kaufman, Waxahachie, 9/24/86, C, 86002417

House at 106 East Denton [Ennis MRA], 106 E. Denton, Ennis, 9/25/86, C, 86002397

House at 106 Kaufman [Waxahachie MRA], 106 Kaufman, Waxahachie, 9/24/86, C, 86002419

House at 111 Brown [Waxahachie MRA], 111 Brown, Waxahachie, 9/24/86, C, 86002347

House at 111 Williams [Waxahachie MRA], 111 Williams, Waxahachie, 9/24/86, C, 86002476

House at 113 East Ross [Waxahachie MRA], 113 E. Ross, Waxahachie, 9/24/86, C, 86002448

House at 1301 East Marvin [Waxahachie MRA], 1301 E. Marvin, Waxahachie, 9/24/86, C, 86002521

House at 1423 Sycamore [Waxahachie MRA], 1423 Sycamore, Waxahachie, 9/24/86, C, 86002488

House at 301 Turner [Waxahachie MRA], 301 Turner, Waxahachie, 9/24/86, C, 86002487

House at 320 East Marvin [Waxahachie MRA], 320 E. Marvin, Waxahachie, 9/24/86, C, 86002527

House at 404 East Crockett [Ennis MRA], 404 E. Crockett, Ennis, 9/25/86, C, 86002379

House at 418 North College [Waxahachie MRA], 418 N. College, Waxahachie, 9/24/86, C, 86002367

House at 500 North Main, East [Ennis MRA], 500 N. Main E, Ennis, 9/25/86, C, 86002439

House at 501 North Grand [Waxahachie MRA], 501 N. Grand, Waxahachie, 9/24/86, C, 86002408

House at 508 North Dallas [Ennis MRA], 508 N. Dallas, Ennis, 9/25/86, C, 86002381

House at 509 West Brown [Ennis MRA], 509 W. Brown, Ennis, 9/25/86, C, 86002371

House at 512 North Grand [Waxahachie MRA], 512 N. Grand, Waxahachie, 9/24/86, C, 86002409

House at 523 Highland [Waxahachie MRA], 523 Highland, Waxahachie, 9/24/86, C, 86002416

House at 625 Cantrell [Waxahachie MRA], 625 Cantrell, Waxahachie, 9/24/86, C, 86002352

House at 700 South Rogers [Waxahachie MRA], 700 S. Rogers, Waxahachie, 9/24/86, C, 86002344

House at 703 South College [Waxahachie MRA], 703 S. College, Waxahachie, 9/24/86, C, 86002372

House at 708 East Brown [Ennis MRA], 708 E. Brown, Ennis, 9/25/86, C, 86002368

House at 712 East Marvin [Waxahachie MRA], 712 E. Marvin, Waxahachie, 9/24/86, C, 86002525

House at 722 West Madison [Ennis MRA], 722 W. Madison, Ennis, 9/25/86, C, 86002426

House at 802 East Ennis [Ennis MRA], 802 E. Ennis, Ennis, 9/25/86, C, 86002429

House at 803 Cantrell [Waxahachie MRA], 803 Cantrell, Waxahachie, 9/24/86, C, 86002353

House at 806 South Dallas [Ennis MRA], 806 S. Dallas, Ennis, 9/25/86, C, 86002393

House at 807 North Preston [Ennis MRA], 807 N. Preston, Ennis, 9/25/86, C, 86002529

House at 810 North Preston [Ennis MRA], 810 N. Preston, Ennis, 9/25/86, C, 86002532

House at 816 Cantrell [Waxahachie MRA], 816 Cantrell, Waxahachie, 9/24/86, C, 86002358

House at 816 West Water [Waxahachie MRA], 816 W. Water, Waxahachie, 9/24/86, A, C, 86002480

House at 901 Cantrell [Waxahachie MRA], 901 Cantrell, Waxahachie, 9/24/86, C, 86002360

Jolesch House [Ennis MRA], 504 W. Knox, Ennis, 9/25/86, C, 86002452

Joshua Chapel A.M.E. Church [Waxahachie MRA], 110 Ailen, Waxahachie, 9/24/86, A, C, a, 86002345

Kirven, J. D., House [Waxahachie MRA], 601 Sycamore, Waxahachie, 9/24/86, C, 86002489

Koger, William, House [Waxahachie MRA], 409 Kaufman, Waxahachie, 9/24/86, C, 86002435

Langsford, Samuel, House [Waxahachie MRA], 1208 E. Marvin, Waxahachie, 9/24/86, C, 86002523

Lewis, William, House [Waxahachie MRA], 1201 E. Marvin, Waxahachie, 9/24/86, C, 86002524

Matthews—Atwood House [Ennis MRA], 307 N. Sherman, Ennis, 9/25/86, C, 86002537

Matthews—Templeton House [Ennis MRA], 606 W. Denton, Ennis, 9/25/86, C, 86002410

McCanless—Williams House [Ennis MRA], 402 W. Tyler, Ennis, 9/25/86, C, 86002540

McCartney House [Waxahachie MRA], 603 W. Marvin, Waxahachie, 9/24/86, C, 86002519

Meredith—McDowal House [Ennis MRA], 701 N. Gaines, Ennis, 9/25/86, C, 86002500

Moore House [Ennis MRA], 400 W. Denton, Ennis, 9/25/86, C, 86002398

Moore, W. B., House [Waxahachie MRA], 912 E. Marvin, Waxahachie, 9/24/86, C, 86002447

Morton House [Ennis MRA], 1007 N. McKinney, Ennis, 9/25/86, C, 86002457

National Compress Company Building [Waxahachie MRA], 503 S. Flat, Waxahachie, 9/11/87, A, 86002400

Neal House [Ennis MRA], 704 N. Preston, Ennis, 9/25/86, C, 86002505

North Rogers Street Historic District [Waxahachie MRA], 500–600 blks. of N. Rogers, 500–600 blks. of N. Monroe, and 100–200 blks. of W. Marvin Sts., Waxahachie, 9/24/86, C, 86002465

Novy, Joe, House [Ennis MRA], 401 N. Clay, Ennis, 9/25/86, C, 86002376

Odom, Frank, House [Waxahachie MRA], 910 W. Marvin, Waxahachie, 9/24/86, C, 86002496

Old City Mills [Ennis MRA], 212 E. Ennis and 108 E. Brown, Ennis, 9/25/86, A, 86002431

Oldham Avenue Historic District [Waxahachie MRA], Oldham Ave. between N. Jackson and Bethel Sts., Waxahachie, 9/24/86, C, 86002461

Paillet House [Waxahachie MRA], 800 S. College, Waxahachie, 9/24/86, C, 86002339

Patrick, Marshall T., House [Waxahachie MRA], 233 Patrick, Waxahachie, 9/24/86, C, 86002341

Payne, M. S., House [Waxahachie MRA], 521 N. Grand, Waxahachie, 9/24/86, C, 86002413

Phillips, E. F., House [Waxahachie MRA], 902 W. Marvin, Waxahachie, 9/24/86, C, 86002498

Plumhoff House [Waxahachie MRA], 612 S. Rogers, Waxahachie, 9/24/86, C, 86002342

Ellis County—Continued

Ralston, Mary, House [Waxahachie MRA], 116 E. University, Waxahachie, 9/24/86, C, 86002375

Ransom House [Ennis MRA], 501 N. McKinney, Ennis, 9/25/86, C, 86002456

Raphael House [Ennis MRA], 500 W. Ennis, Ennis, 9/25/86, C, 86002428

Ray, M. B., House [Waxahachie MRA], 401 N. Monroe, Waxahachie, 9/24/86, C, 86002477

Reinmiller, W. B., House [Waxahachie MRA], 206 E. Marvin, Waxahachie, 9/24/86, C, 86002444

Rockett, Paris Q., House [Waxahachie MRA], 321 E. University, Waxahachie, 9/24/86, C, 86002343

Rosemont House [Waxahachie MRA], 701 S. Rogers, Waxahachie, 7/08/82, C, 82004504

Saint Paul's Episcopal Church [Waxahachie MRA], 308 N. Monroe, Waxahachie, 9/24/86, C, a, 86002495

Sanderson, James S., House [Ennis MRA], 201 N. Gaines, Ennis, 9/25/86, C, 86002420

Second Trinity University Campus [Waxahachie MRA], 1200 blk. of Sycamore, Waxahachie, 9/11/87, A, C, a, 86002458

Sharp House [Ennis MRA], 208 N. Gaines, Ennis, 9/25/86, C, 86002423

Sims, O. B., House [Waxahachie MRA], 1408 W. Main, Waxahachie, 9/24/86, C, 86002441

Solon, John, House [Waxahachie MRA], 617 Solon Rd., Waxahachie, 9/11/87, C, 86002453

Story, Jesse and Mary, House [Ennis MRA], 510 W. Brown, Ennis, 9/25/86, C, 86002373

Strickland-Sawyer House [Waxahachie MRA], 500 Oldham St., Waxahachie, 10/18/84, B, C, 84000168

Telfair House [Ennis MRA], 209 N. Preston, Ennis, 9/25/86, C, 86002473

Templeton, Judge M. B., House [Waxahachie MRA], 203 N. Grand, Waxahachie, 9/24/86, C, 86002402

Thompson, D. H., House [Waxahachie MRA], 312 Kaufman, Waxahachie, 9/24/86, B, 86002433

Trippet-Shive House [Waxahachie MRA], 209 N. Grand, Waxahachie, 9/24/86, C, 86002404

Vickery, Richard, House [Waxahachie MRA], 1104 E. Marvin, Waxahachie, 9/25/86, C, 86002528

Waxahachie Chautauqua Building [Waxahachie MRA], Getzendaner Park, Waxahachie, 5/03/74, A, C, 74002070

Waxahachie Lumber Company [Waxahachie MRA], 123 Kaufman, Waxahachie, 9/11/87, A, C, 86002424

Weatherford House [Ennis MRA], 501 N. Preston, Ennis, 9/25/86, C, 86002503

Weekley, John M., House [Ennis MRA], 510 W. Denton, Ennis, 9/25/86, C, 86002406

West End Historic District [Waxahachie MRA], Roughly bounded by Central, W. Water, Monroe, Madison and W. Jefferson, Waxahachie, 9/24/86, A, C, 86002474

Williams, Porter L., House [Waxahachie MRA], 200 E. University, Waxahachie, 9/24/86, C, 86002383

Williams-Erwin House [Waxahachie MRA], 412 W. Marvin St., Waxahachie, 7/07/78, A, C, 78002926

Witten, Pat, House [Waxahachie MRA], 204 Brown, Waxahachie, 9/24/86, C, 86002349

Wyatt Street Shotgun House Historic District [Waxahachie MRA], E side 300 blk. of Wyatt St., Waxahachie, 9/24/86, A, C, 86002463

Erath County

Berry House, 525 E. Washington St., Stephenville, 5/15/80, C, 80004116

Bluff Dale Suspension Bridge, Berry's Creek Rd., Bluff Dale, 12/20/77, A, C, b, 77001440

Erath County Courthouse, Public Sq., Stephenville, 8/18/77, A, C, 77001441

Thurber Historic District, S of Thurber, Thurber vicinity, 8/17/79, A, C, D, g, 79002936

Wyatt—Hickie Ranch Complex, Off US 281 NW of TX 913, Stephenville vicinity, 12/26/85, A, C, e, 85003162

Fannin County

Clendenen-Carleton House, 803 N. Main St., Bonham, 5/14/79, C, 79002937

Haden House, 603 W. Bonham St., Ladonia, 1/08/80, C, 80004118

Nunn House, 505 W. 5th St., Bonham, 5/06/80, B, C, 80004117

Rayburn, Samuel T., House, 1.5 mi. W of Bonham on U.S. 82, Bonham, 6/05/72, B, g, NHL, 72001361

Trout, Thomas and Katherine, House, 705 Poplar St., Honey Grove, 8/23/84, C, 84001664

Fayette County

Bethlehem Lutheran Church, White St., Round Top, 8/10/78, A, C, a, 78002928

Cummins Creek Bridge, 2 mi. NW of Round Top over Cummins Creek, Round Top vicinity, 4/21/75, A, 75001975

Fayette County Courthouse and Jail, Courthouse Sq. and 104 Main St., La Grange, 1/23/75, C, 75001973

Kreische, Henry L., Brewery and House, S of La Grange off U.S. 77 on Monument Hill, La Grange, 4/16/75, A, C, 75001974

Mount Eliza, 3 mi. (4.8 km) S of La Grange on U.S. 77, La Grange vicinity, 7/17/78, A, B, C, 78002927

Mulberry Creek Bridge, 2.5 mi. SW of Schulenburg on Old Praha Rd., Schulenburg vicinity, 4/21/75, A, C, 75001976

Nativity of Mary, Blessed Virgin Catholic Church [Churches with Decorative Interior Painting TR], FM 2672, High Hill, 6/21/83, A, C, a, 83003136

Neese, William, Sr., Homestead, TX 237, Warrenton, 2/18/75, C, 75001977

Pytlovany, Simon, House, 1.5 mi. S of Dubina on FR 1383, Dubina vicinity, 4/14/75, C, 75001972

Schulenburg Cotton Compress, James and Main Sts., Schulenburg, 9/13/79, A, C, 79002938

St. James Episcopal Church, Monroe and Colorado Sts., La Grange, 6/18/76, A, C, a, 76002026

St. John the Baptist Catholic Church [Churches with Decorative Interior Painting TR], FM 1383, Ammansville, 6/21/83, A, C, a, 83003137

St. Mary's Church of the Assumption [Churches with Decorative Interior Painting TR], FM 1295, Praha, 6/21/83, A, C, a, 83003138

Winedale Inn Complex, Off FM 1457, Winedale, 6/22/70, C, 70000745

Zapp Building, Fayette and Washington Sts., Fayetteville, 6/23/83, A, C, 83003139

Fisher County

Steadman, Foy, Site, Address Restricted, Noodle vicinity, 3/11/71, D, 71000932

Floyd County

Floyd County Stone Corral [New Mexican Pastor Sites in Texas Panhandle TR], Address Restricted, Floydada vicinity, 9/27/84, D, 84001666

Floydada Country Club Site, Address Restricted, Floydada vicinity, 11/07/79, D, 79002939

Quitaque Railway Tunnel, 10 mi. SW of Quitaque, Quitaque vicinity, 9/13/77, A, C, g, 77001442

Fort Bend County

Fort Bend County Courthouse, 400 Jackson St., Richmond, 3/13/80, A, C, 80004119

Franklin County

Rogers-Drummond House, SE of Mount Vernon, Mount Vernon vicinity, 9/08/80, C, 80004120

Freestone County

Trinity and Brazos Valley Railroad Depot and Office Building, 208 S. 3rd Ave., Teague, 3/21/79, A, C, 79002940

Frio County

Old Frio County Jail, E. Medina and S. Pecan Sts., Pearsall, 11/19/79, C, 79002941

Galveston County

Ashbel Smith Building, 914–916 Ave. B, Galveston, 10/28/69, A, C, 69000203

Ashton Villa, 2328 Broadway, Galveston, 10/28/69, C, 69000204

Beissner, Henry, House, 2818 Ball Ave., Galveston, 4/03/78, C, 78002929

Bishop's Palace, 1402 Ave. J (Broadway), Galveston, 8/25/70, B, C, a, 70000746

Building at 1921-1921 1/2 Avenue D [Central Business District MRA], 1921-1921 1/2 Ave. D, Galveston, 8/14/84, C, 84001671

Building at 1925-1927 Market Street [Central Business District MRA], 1925-1927 Market St., Galveston, 8/14/84, C, 84001668

City Hall [Central Business District MRA], 823 25th St., Galveston, 8/14/84, A, C, 84001676

City National Bank [Central Business District MRA], 2219 Ave. D, Galveston, 8/14/84, A, C, 84001680

Davison, Frank B., House, 109 3rd Ave., Texas City, 6/29/76, A, C, 76002033

ELISSA, Seawolf Park, Galveston, 3/21/78, A, g, NHL, 78002930

East End Historic District, Irregular pattern including both sides of Broadway and Market Sts., Galveston, 5/30/75, A, C, NHL, 75001979

Eiband's [Central Business District MRA], 2001 Central Plaza, Galveston, 8/14/84, A, 84001683

First Evangelical Lutheran Church [Central Business District MRA], 2401 Ave. G, Galveston, 8/14/84, A, 84001688

First Presbyterian Church, 1903 Church St., Galveston, 1/29/79, C, a, 79002942

Galveston Causeway, Spans Galveston Bay from Virginia Point to Galveston Island, Galveston, 12/12/76, A, C, 76002028

Galveston Orphans Home, 1315 21st St., Galveston, 3/21/79, A, C, 79002943

Galveston Seawall, Seawall Blvd., Galveston, 8/18/77, A, C, 77001443

Galvez Hotel, 2024 Seawall Blvd., Galveston, 4/04/79, A, C, 79002944

Garten Verein Pavilion, 27th St. and Avenue O (Kempner Park), Galveston, 7/20/77, A, C, 77001444

Grace Episcopal Church, 1115 36th St., Galveston, 4/03/75, C, a, 75001980

Grand Opera House, 2012–2020 Ave. E, Galveston, 1/02/74, A, C, 74002071

Hagemann, John, House, 3301 Ave. L, Galveston, 6/01/82, C, 82004505

House at 2017-2023 Avenue I [Central Business District MRA], 2017-2023 Ave. I, Galveston, 8/14/84, C, 84001698

House at 2528 Postoffice St. [Central Business District MRA], 2528 Postoffice St., Galveston, 8/14/84, A, 84001700

I.O.O.F. Lodge [Central Business District MRA], 505 20th St., Galveston, 8/14/84, A, 84001703

Jean Lafitte Hotel [Central Business District MRA], 2105 Ave. F, Galveston, 8/14/84, A, C, 84001705

Kempner, Daniel Webster, House, 2504 Ave. O, Galveston, 3/30/79, B, C, c, g, 79002945

Lasker Home for Homeless Children, 1019 16th St., Galveston, 4/14/83, A, B, C, 83003140

Marschner Building [Central Business District MRA], 1914-1916 Mechanic St., Galveston, 8/14/84, C, 84001706

McKinney-McDonald House, 926 Winnie St., Galveston, 5/04/76, C, 76002030

Menard, Michel B., House, 1605 33rd St., Galveston, 12/12/76, B, C, 76002031

Merimax Building [Central Business District MRA], 521 22nd St., Galveston, 1/24/85, A, C, 85000121

Model Laundry [Central Business District MRA], 513-523 25th St., Galveston, 8/14/84, A, C, 84001707

Moser House [Central Business District MRA], 509 19th St., Galveston, 8/14/84, C, 84001711

Mosquito Fleet Berth, Pier 19, N end of 20th St., Pier 19, Galveston, 4/21/75, A, g, 75001981

Old Galveston Customhouse, SE corner 20th and Post Office (Ave. E) Sts., Galveston, 8/25/70, A, C, 70000747

Pix Building [Central Business District MRA], 2128 Postoffice St., Galveston, 8/14/84, C, 84001713

Point Bolivar Lighthouse, TX 87, Port Bolivar, 8/18/77, A, C, 77001445

Powhatan House, 3427 Ave. O, Galveston, 10/06/75, B, C, b, 75001982

Reedy Chapel-AME Church, 2013 Broadway, Galveston, 9/14/84, C, a, 84001717

Robinson Building [Central Business District MRA], 2009-2011 Postoffice St., Galveston, 8/14/84, C, 84001720

Rosenberg Library [Central Business District MRA], 2310 Sealy St., Galveston, 8/14/84, A, C, 84001722

Scottish Rite Cathedral [Central Business District MRA], 2128 Church St., Galveston, 8/14/84, C, a, 84001724

Sealy, George, House, 2424 Broadway, Galveston, 10/28/69, C, 69000205

Shaw, M. W., Building [Central Business District MRA], 2427 Ave. D, Galveston, 8/14/84, A, C, 84001728

St. Joseph's Church, 2202 Ave. K, Galveston, 12/12/76, A, C, a, 76002032

St. Mary's Cathedral, 2011 Church Ave., Galveston, 6/04/73, A, C, a, 73001964

Star Drug Store [Central Business District MRA], 510 23rd St., Galveston, 8/14/84, A, C, 84001731

Steffens—Drewa House Complex, 2701, 2705, and 2709 Ave. O, Galveston, 12/01/88, C, 88002671

Strand Historic District, The, Roughly bounded by Ave. A, 20th St., alley between Aves. C and D, and railroad depot, Galveston, 1/26/70, A, C, NHL, 70000748

Sweeney-Royston House, 2402 Ave. L, Galveston, 9/01/78, A, C, 78002931

Texas Building [Central Business District MRA], 2200 Central Plaza, Galveston, 8/14/84, C, 84001734

Texas Heroes Monument [Central Business District MRA], 25th and Broadway, Galveston, 8/14/84, C, f, 84001737

Trinity Protestant Episcopal Church, 22nd St. and Ave. G, Galveston, 9/04/79, C, a, 79002946

Trueheart-Adriance Building, 212 22nd St., Galveston, 7/14/71, A, C, 71000933

U.S. National Bank [Central Business District MRA], 2201 Ave. D, Galveston, 8/14/84, A, C, 84001739

USS HATTERAS (41GV68), Address Restricted, Galveston vicinity, 1/28/77, A, 77001567

Williams, Samuel May, House, 361 Ave. P, Galveston, 7/14/71, B, C, 71000934

Garza County

Cooper's Canyon Site 41 GR 25, Address Restricted, Post vicinity, 11/07/78, A, D, 78002933

O.S. Ranch Petroglyphs 41 GR 57, Address Restricted, Post vicinity, 1/31/78, A, D, 78002934

Old Algerita Hotel, S corner of Main and Ave. I, Post, 4/23/75, A, 75001983

Old Post Sanitarium, 117 North Ave. N, Post, 5/21/75, A, B, 75001984

Post West Dugout, Address Restricted, Post vicinity, 5/22/78, A, D, 78002935

Post-Montgomery Site 41 GR 188, Address Restricted, Post vicinity, 11/07/78, D, 78002936

Gillespie County

Enchanted Rock Archeological District, Address Resticted, Enchanted Rock vicinity, 8/29/84, D, 84001740

Fort Martin Scott, Address Restricted, Fredericksburg vicinity, 1/20/80, A, D, 80004121

Fredericksburg Historic District, Roughly bunded by Elk, Schubert, Acorn, and Creek Sts., Fredericksburg, 10/14/70, A, C, g, 70000749

Fredericksburg Memorial Library, Courthouse Sq., Fredericksburg, 3/11/71, C, 71000935

Morris Ranch Schoolhouse, Morris Ranch Rd., Fredericksburg vicinity, 3/29/83, A, C, 83003142

St. Mary's Catholic Church [Churches with Decorative Interior Painting TR], 306 W. San Antonio, Fredericksburg, 6/21/83, A, C, a, 83003143

Goliad County

Baker, Charles H. and Catherine B., House, 401 S. Commercial St., Goliad, 7/25/85, C, 85001616

Goliad County Courthouse Historic District, Roughly bounded by E. Franklin, S. Washington, E. Fannin, and S. Chilton Sts., Goliad, 6/29/76, A, C, 76002034

Nuestra Senora del Espiritu Santo de Zuniga Site, Address Restricted, Goliad vicinity, 8/22/77, A, C, D, a, b, 77001446

Goliad County—Continued

Old Market House Museum, S. Market and Franklin Sts., Goliad, 10/18/72, A, 72001362

Peck, Capt. Barton, House, W of Goliad at Hill and Post Oak St., Goliad vicinity, 2/23/79, C, 79002947

Presidio Nuestra Senora de Loreto de la Bahia, 1 mi. S of Goliad State Park on U.S. 183, Goliad vicinity, 12/24/67, A, a, NHL, 67000024

Ruins of Mission Nuestra Senora del Rosario de los Cujanes, Address Restricted, Goliad vicinity, 9/22/72, A, C, D, a, 72001363

Stoddard, Jessie W., House, Jct. of US 183, Fannin and Hord Sts., Goliad, 1/29/92, C, 91002020

Gonzales County

Braches House, 12 mi. SE of Gonzales off U.S. 90A, Gonzales vicinity, 3/11/71, A, C, 71000936

Gonzales County Courthouse, Bounded by St. Louis, St. Paul. St. Lawrence, and St. Joseph Sts., Gonzales, 6/19/72, C, 72001364

Gonzales County Jail, Courthouse Sq. on St. Lawrence St., Gonzales, 5/21/75, A, 75001985

Kennard House, 621 St. Louis St., Gonzales, 1/25/71, C, 71000937

Leesville Schoolhouse, E of Leesville off TX 80, Leesville vicinity, 5/25/78, A, 78002937

Gray County

Schneider Hotel, 120 S. Russell, Pampa, 12/19/85, A, C, 85003215

US Post Office—Pampa Main, 120 E. Foster, Pampa, 11/17/86, A, C, 86003236

Grayson County

Birge, Capt. Noble Allan, House, 727 W. Birge, Sherman, 9/18/86, B, C, 86002187

Braun, George, House, 421 N. Austin Ave., Denison, 11/20/75, C, 75001986

Denison Commercial Historic District, Roughly Woodard, Main and Chestnut Sts., Denison, 11/10/83, A, C, 83003772

Kohl, Ernst Martin, Building, 300 E. Main St., Denison, 7/12/76, A, C, 76002035

Old Sherman Public Library, 301 S. Walnut, Sherman, 10/23/86, C, 86002927

Umphress—Taylor House, 301 Paris St., Van Alstyne, 9/12/86, C, 86001956

Gregg County

Everett Building, 214–216 Fredonia St., Longview, 11/15/79, A, C, 79002948

Northcutt House, 313 S. Fredonia St., Longview, 5/22/78, A, B, C, 78002938

Whaley House, 101 E. Whaley St., Longview, 5/23/80, A, C, 80004122

Grimes County

Anderson Historic District, Anderson and environs, Anderson, 3/15/74, A, C, a, 74002072

Foster House, E of Navasota on TX 90, Navasota vicinity, 9/08/80, A, 80004123

Navasota Commercial Historic District, Roughly bounded by La Salle, Holland, 9th, and Brule Sts., Navasota, 11/30/82, A, C, 82001737

P. A. Smith Hotel, Railroad St., Navasota, 4/16/76, A, B, C, 76002036

Piedmont Springs Archeological Site, Address Restricted, Anderson vicinity, 7/29/82, D, 82004506

Steele House, 217 Brewer St., Navasota, 6/13/78, A, C, 78002939

Guadalupe County

Erskine House No. 1, 902 N. Austin St., Seguin, 8/25/70, A, 70000750

Hall, Robert, House, 214 S. Travis St, Seguin, 10/25/79, A, C, 79002949

Johnson, Joseph F., House, 761 Johnson Ave., Seguin, 6/23/78, A, B, C, 78002940

Los Nogales, S. River and E. Live Oak Sts., Seguin, 3/24/72, C, 72001365

Park Hotel, 217 S. River St., Seguin, 5/23/80, C, 80004124

Saffold Dam, Off TX 123, Seguin, 11/15/79, A, 79002950

Sebastopol, NE corner of W. Court and N. Erkel Sts., Seguin, 8/25/70, B, C, 70000751

Seguin Commercial Historic District, Roughly bounded by Camp, Myrtle, Washington, and Crockett Sts., Seguin, 12/15/83, A, C, 83003773

Wilson Utility Pottery Kilns Archeological District, Address Restricted, Seguin vicinity, 4/16/75, A, C, D, 75001987

Hale County

Plainview Commercial Historic District, Roughly bounded by E. 4th, Austin, E. 9th, and Ash Sts. (both sides), Plainview, 12/02/82, A, C, 82004855

Plainview Site, Address Restricted, Plainview vicinity, 10/15/66, A, D, NHL, 66000814

Hall County

Hotel Turkey, Jct. of 3rd and Alexander Sts., Turkey, 10/24/91, A, C, 91001521

Hamilton County

Hamilton County Courthouse, Public Sq., Hamilton, 9/04/80, A, C, 80004125

Hardeman County

Quanah, Acme and Pacific Depot, 100 Mercer St., Quanah, 10/15/79, A, C, 79002951

Hardin County

Ada Belle Oil Well, N of Batson, Batson vicinity, 1/20/80, A, C, 80004126

Harris County

1879 Houston Waterworks, 27 Artesian St., Houston, 5/06/76, A, 76002037

1884 Houston Cotton Exchange Building, 202 Travis St., Houston, 5/06/71, A, C, 71000938

All Saints Roman Catholic Church [Houston Heights MRA], 201 E. 10th St., Houston, 6/22/83, C, a, 83004425

Allbach House [Houston Heights MRA], 2023 Arlington St., Houston, 6/22/83, C, 83004426

Anderson, John W., House [Houston Heights MRA], 711 Columbia, Houston, 1/15/88, C, 87002241

Annunciation Church, 1618 Texas Ave., Houston, 11/03/75, A, C, a, 75001988

Antioch Missionary Baptist Church, 313 Robin St., Houston, 12/22/76, A, C, a, 76002038

Apollo Mission Control Center, Lyndon B. Johnson Space Flight Center, Houston, 10/03/85, A, C, g, NHL, 85002815

Armand Bayou Archeological District, Address Restricted, Seabrook vicinity, 12/12/78, D, 78002952

Autry, James L., House, 5 Courtlandt Pl., Houston, 6/14/79, A, C, 79002953

Banta House [Houston Heights MRA], 119 E. 20th St., Houston, 6/22/83, C, 83004427

Baring, Otto H., House [Houston Heights MRA], 1030 Rutland, Houston, 1/15/88, C, 87002242

Barker House [Houston Heights MRA], 121 E. 16th St., Houston, 5/14/84, B, 84001754

Barker-Cypress Archeological Site (41HR436), Address Restricted, Houston vicinity, 4/24/84, D, 84001753

Bayou Bend, 1 Westcott St., Houston, 12/06/79, A, B, C, 79002954

Beaconsfield, 1700 Main St., Houston, 3/29/83, C, 83004428

Borgstrom House [Houston Heights MRA], 1401 Cortlandt St., Houston, 5/14/84, C, 84001755

Broadacres Historic District, 1300-1506 North Blvd. and 1305-1515 South Blvd., Houston, 4/16/80, A, C, 80004128

Burge House [Houston Heights MRA], 1801 Heights Blvd., Houston, 6/22/83, C, 83004430

Harris County—Continued

Burlingame, George L., House [Houston Heights MRA], 1238 Harvard, Houston, 1/15/88, C, 87002243

Carden, David A., House [Houston Heights MRA], 718 W. 17th Ave., Houston, 7/17/90, C, 90001048

Carroll, J. J., House, 16 Courtlandt Pl., Houston, 6/14/79, C, 79002955

Carter, W. T., Jr., House, 18 Courtlandt Pl., Houston, 6/14/79, C, 79002956

Cedar Bayou Archeological District, Address Restricted, Baytown vicinity, 3/02/79, D, 79002952

Christ Church, 1117 Texas Ave., Houston, 6/15/79, A, C, a, g, 79002957

Clanton, Moses A., House [Houston Heights MRA], 1025 Arlington, Houston, 7/17/90, C, 90001040

Clare, J. H., House [Houston Heights MRA], 939 Arlington, Houston, 1/15/88, C, 87002244

Clayton, William L., Summer House, 3376 Inwood Dr., Houston, 2/02/84, C, 84001756

Cleveland, A. S., House, 8 Courtlandt Pl., Houston, 6/14/79, C, 79002958

Cohn, Arthur B., House, 1711 Rusk Ave., Houston, 11/07/85, B, C, a, 85002771

Coombs, Charles E., House [Houston Heights MRA], 1037 Columbia, Houston, 7/17/90, C, 90001041

Coop, Dr. B. F., House [Houston Heights MRA], 1536 Heights Blvd., Houston, 5/14/84, C, 84001757

Copeland, Austin, House I [Houston Heights MRA], 921 Arlington, Houston, 1/15/88, C, 87002248

Copeland, Austin, House II [Houston Heights MRA], 925 Arlington, Houston, 1/15/88, C, 87002245

Countryman House [Houston Heights MRA], 402 E. 9th St., Houston, 6/22/83, C, 83004431

Courtlandt Place Historic District, 2–25 Courtlandt Pl., Houston, 12/03/80, C, 80004129

Cummings House [Houston Heights MRA], 1418 Heights Blvd., Houston, 6/22/83, C, 83004432

DePelchin Faith Home, 2700 Albany St., Houston, 8/09/84, A, C, f, 84001759

Dexter House [Houston Heights MRA], 224 W. 17th St., Houston, 5/14/84, A, C, 84001761

Donoghue, Thomas J., House, 17 Courtlandt Pl., Houston, 6/14/79, A, C, 79002959

Dorrance, John M., House, 9 Courtlandt Pl., Houston, 6/14/79, A, C, 79002960

Doughty, Lula J., House [Houston Heights MRA], 1233 Yale St., Houston, 7/17/90, C, 90001046

Durham, Jay L., House [Houston Heights MRA], 921 Heights Blvd., Houston, 1/15/88, C, 87002246

Eaton House [Houston Heights MRA], 510 Harvard St., Houston, 6/22/83, B, C, 83004433

Elkins House [Houston Heights MRA], 602 E. 9th St., Houston, 6/22/83, C, 83004434

Ellis, Dr. Billie V., House [Houston Heights MRA], 1515 Heights Blvd., Houston, 6/22/83, C, 83004435

Ezzell House [Houston Heights MRA], 1236 Rutland St., Houston, 5/14/84, C, 84001762

Fire Engine House No. 9, 1810–1812 Keene St., Houston, 10/17/85, A, C, 85003238

Fluegel, William F., House [Houston Heights MRA], 1327 Ashland, Houston, 1/15/88, C, 87002247

Foley, W. L., Building, 214–218 Travis St., Houston, 10/11/78, A, C, 78002942

Forum of Civics, 2503 Westheimer Rd., Houston, 10/13/88, A, 88001053

Freedmen's Town Historic District, Roughly Bounded by Genesse, West Dallas, Arthur and W. Gray Sts., Houston, 1/17/85, A, C, 85000186

Gerloff House [Houston Heights MRA], 221 E. 12th Ave., Houston, 7/17/90, C, 90001047

Gillette House [Houston Heights MRA], 301–303 E. 15th St., Houston, 5/14/84, C, 84001764

Gulf Building, 710-724 Main St., Houston, 8/30/83, A, B, C, 83004436

Harris County Boy's School Site, Address Restricted, Houston vicinity, 5/02/79, D, 79002961

Harris County Courthouse of 1910, 301 Fannin St., Houston, 5/13/81, A, C, 81000629

Hartley House [Houston Heights MRA], 315 W. 17th St., Houston, 6/22/83, C, 83004437

Hawkins House [Houston Heights MRA], 1015 Heights Blvd., Houston, 5/14/84, B, 84001765

Heights Boulevard Esplanade [Houston Heights MRA], Heights Boulevard from White Oak Bayou to 20th St., Houston, 5/14/84, C, 84001766

Heights Christian Church [Houston Heights MRA], 1703 Heights Blvd., Houston, 6/22/83, C, a, 83004438

Heights State Bank Building [Houston Heights MRA], 3620 Washington St., Houston, 6/22/83, A, C, 83004439

Hogg Building, 401 Louisiana St., Houston, 7/14/78, A, B, C, 78002943

House at 1111 Heights Boulevard [Houston Heights MRA], 1111 Heights Blvd., Houston, 5/14/84, C, 84001768

House at 112 W. 4th Street [Houston Heights MRA], 112 W. 4th St., Houston, 5/14/84, C, 84001771

House at 1210 Harvard Street [Houston Heights MRA], 1210 Harvard St., Houston, 5/14/84, C, 84001774

House at 1217 Harvard [Houston Heights MRA], 1217 Harvard, Houston, 1/15/88, C, 87002249

House at 122 East Fifth Street [Houston Heights MRA], 122 E. 5th St., Houston, 5/14/84, C, 84001776

House at 1220 Harvard [Houston Heights MRA], 1220 Harvard, Houston, 1/15/88, C, 87002250

House at 1222 Harvard Street [Houston Heights MRA], 1222 Harvard St., Houston, 7/17/90, C, 90001043

House at 1227 Rutland Street [Houston Heights MRA], 1227 Rutland St., Houston, 5/14/84, C, 84001777

House at 1230 Oxford Street [Houston Heights MRA], 1230 Oxford St., Houston, 5/14/84, C, 84001780

House at 1237 Rutland Street [Houston Heights MRA], 1237 Rutland St., Houston, 6/22/83, C, 83004456

House at 1304 Cortlandt Street [Houston Heights MRA], 1304 Cortlandt St., Houston, 5/14/84, C, 84001784

House at 1343 Allston Street [Houston Heights MRA], 1343 Allston St., Houston, 6/22/83, C, 83004443

House at 1421 Harvard St. [Houston Heights MRA], 1421 Harvard St., Houston, 6/22/83, C, 83004449

House at 1421 Heights Boulevard [Houston Heights MRA], 1421 Heights Blvd., Houston, 6/22/83, C, 83004452

House at 1421-1423 Waverly Street [Houston Heights MRA], 1421-1423 Waverly St., Houston, 6/22/83, C, 83004459

House at 1435 Heights Boulevard [Houston Heights MRA], 1435 Heights Blvd., Houston, 1/15/88, C, 87002251

House at 1437 Heights Boulevard [Houston Heights MRA], 1437 Heights Blvd., Houston, 6/22/83, C, 83004453

House at 1437 Waverly Street [Houston Heights MRA], 1437 Waverly St., Houston, 6/22/83, C, 83004458

House at 1443 Allston Street [Houston Heights MRA], 1443 Allston St., Houston, 6/22/83, C, 83004442

House at 1509 Allston Street [Houston Heights MRA], 1509 Allston St., Houston, 6/22/83, C, 83004441

House at 1515 Allston Street [Houston Heights MRA], 1515 Allston St., Houston, 6/22/83, C, 83004440

House at 1517 Cortland Street [Houston Heights MRA], 1517 Cortland St., Houston, 6/22/83, C, 83004446

House at 1537 Tulane Street [Houston Heights MRA], 1537 Tulane Street, Houston, 6/22/83, C, b, 83004457

House at 1640 Harvard Street [Houston Heights MRA], 1640 Harvard St., Houston, 6/22/83, C, 83004450

House at 201 W. 15th Street [Houston Heights MRA], 201 W. 15th St., Houston, 6/22/83, C, 83004460

House at 2035 Rutland Street [Houston Heights MRA], 2035 Rutland St., Houston, 6/22/83, C, 83004455

House at 217 E. 5th Street [Houston Heights MRA], 217 E. 5th St., Houston, 5/14/84, C, 84001786

House at 2402 Rutland Street [Houston Heights MRA], 2402 Rutland St., Houston, 6/22/83, C, 83004454

House at 402 E. 11th Street [Houston Heights MRA], 402 E. 11th Street, Houston, 6/22/83, C, 83004447

House at 444 West 24th Street [Houston Heights MRA], 444 W. 24th St., Houston, 5/14/84, C, 84001788

House at 505 W. 18th Street [Houston Heights MRA], 505 W. 18th St., Houston, 5/14/84, C, 84001791

Harris County—Continued

House at 532 Harvard Street [Houston Heights MRA], 532 Harvard St., Houston, 6/22/83, C, 83004448

House at 825 Heights Boulevard [Houston Heights MRA], 825 Heights Blvd., Houston, 6/22/83, C, 83004451

House at 844 Columbia Street [Houston Heights MRA], 844 Columbia St., Houston, 6/22/83, C, 83004445

House at 844 Courtlandt [Houston Heights MRA], 844 Courtlandt, Houston, 6/22/83, C, 83004444

House at 917 Heights Boulevard [Houston Heights MRA], 917 Heights Blvd., Houston, 5/14/84, C, 84001793

House at 943 1/2 Cortlandt Street [Houston Heights MRA], 943 1/2 Cortlandt St., Houston, 1/07/93, C, b, 84003972

Houston City Hall, 901 Bagby St., Houston, 9/18/90, A, C, 90001471

Houston Fire Station No. 7, 2304 Milam St., Houston, 4/17/86, C, 86000798

Houston Heights Fire Station [Houston Heights MRA], Yale and 12th Sts., Houston, 6/22/83, A, C, 83004461

Houston Heights Waterworks Reservoir [Houston Heights MRA], W. 20 and Nicolson Sts., Houston, 6/22/83, A, 83004462

Houston Heights Woman's Club [Houston Heights MRA], 1846 Harvard St, Houston, 6/22/83, A, 83004463

Houston Negro Hospital, 3204 Ennis St., Houston, 12/27/82, A, 82004856

Houston Negro Hospital School of Nursing Building, Holman Ave. and Ennis St., Houston, 12/27/82, A, C, 82004857

Houston Public Library [Houston Heights MRA], 1302 Heights Blvd., Houston, 5/14/84, C, 84001795

Houston Turn-Verein, 5202 Almeda Rd., Houston, 3/21/78, A, C, 78002944

Ideson, Julia, Building, 500 McKinney St., Houston, 11/23/77, A, C, 77001447

Immanuel Lutheran Church [Houston Heights MRA], 1448 Cortlandt St., Houston, 6/22/83, C, a, 83004464

Isbell House [Houston Heights MRA], 639 Heights Blvd., Houston, 6/22/83, A, C, 83004465

Jensen, James L., House [Houston Heights MRA], 721 Arlington, Houston, 7/17/90, C, 90001039

Jones House [Houston Heights MRA], 1115-1117 Allston St., Houston, 6/22/83, A, C, 83004466

Jones-Hunt House, 24 Courtlandt Pl., Houston, 6/14/79, C, 79002962

Keller House [Houston Heights MRA], 1448 Heights Blvd., Houston, 5/14/84, C, 84001797

Kellum-Noble House, 212 Dallas St., Houston, 4/03/75, A, C, 75001989

Kennedy Bakery, 813 Congress St., Houston, 7/27/79, A, 79002963

Kennedy, Marshall W., House [Houston Heights MRA], 1122 Harvard, Houston, 1/15/88, C, 87002252

Kleinhaus House [Houston Heights MRA], 803 Yale St., Houston, 6/22/83, C, 83004467

Knittel House [Houston Heights MRA], 1601 Ashland St., Houston, 6/22/83, C, 83004468

Kronenberger House [Houston Heights MRA], 612 W. 26th St., Houston, 6/22/83, C, 83004469

Lindenburg, Emil, House [Houston Heights MRA], 1445 Harvard, Houston, 1/15/88, C, 87002253

Lowry, Fayette C., House [Houston Heights MRA], 2009 Harvard, Houston, 7/19/90, C, 90001045

Lund House [Houston Heights MRA], 301 E. 5th St., Houston, 6/22/83, C, 83004470

Main Street/Market Square Historic District, Roughly bounded by Buffalo Bayou, Fannin, Texas, and Milamsts, Houston, 7/18/83, A, C, 83004471

Main Street/Market Square Historic District (Boundary Increase), 110 Milam, 112-114 Milam, 202-204 Milam, 715 Franklin, Houston, 2/23/84, A, C, 84001811

Mansfield House [Houston Heights MRA], 1802 Harvard St., Houston, 6/22/83, C, 83004472

Mansfield Street Archeological Site, Address Restricted, Houston vicinity, 5/22/78, D, 78002945

McCain, Henry Hicks, House [Houston Heights MRA], 1026 Allston, Houston, 1/15/88, C, 87002254

McCollum, D. C., House [Houston Heights MRA], 433 W. 24th St., Houston, 7/17/90, C, 90001049

McDonald House [Houston Heights MRA], 1801 Ashland St., Houston, 6/22/83, C, 83004473

Meitzen House [Houston Heights MRA], 725 Harvard St., Houston, 5/14/84, C, 84001813

Merchants and Manufacturers Building, 1 Main St., Houston, 9/17/80, A, C, 80004130

Miller House [Houston Heights MRA], 1245 Yale St., Houston, 5/14/84, C, 84001814

Miller, Ezekial and Mary Jane, House, 304 Hawthorne St., Houston, 10/06/83, C, 83003788

Milroy House [Houston Heights MRA], 1102 Heights Blvd., Houston, 6/22/83, A, C, 83004474

Milroy, John, House, 1102 Heights Blvd., Houston, 11/12/80, C, 80004131

Milroy-Muller House [Houston Heights MRA], 1602 Harvard St., Houston, 5/14/84, A, C, 84001816

Morris, Glenn W., House [Houston Heights MRA], 1611 Harvard St., Houston, 7/17/90, C, 90001044

Morton Brothers Grocery [Houston Heights MRA], 401 W. Ninth, Houston, 1/15/88, C, 87002255

Mulcahy House [Houston Heights MRA], 1046 Harvard St., Houston, 5/14/84, C, 84001819

Myer, Sterling, House, 4 Courtlandt Pl., Houston, 6/14/79, C, 79002964

Nairn, Forrest A., House [Houston Heights MRA], 1148 Heights Blvd., Houston, 11/12/91, C, 87002256

Nash, William R., House, 215 Westmoreland Ave., Houston, 8/23/90, C, 90001293

Neuhaus, C. L., House, 6 Courtlandt Pl., Houston, 6/14/79, C, 79002965

Ogle, Joseph, House [Houston Heights MRA], 530 Harvard St., Houston, 6/22/83, C, 83004475

Old Houston National Bank, 202 Main St., Houston, 7/17/75, C, g, 75001990

Old Sixth Ward Historic District, Bounded by Washington, Union, Houston, Capitol and Glenwood Cemetery, Houston, 1/23/78, A, C, 78002946

Oriental Textile Mill [Houston Heights MRA], 2201 Lawrence St., Houston, 6/22/83, A, C, 83004476

Otto House [Houston Heights MRA], 835 Rutland St., Houston, 5/14/84, C, 84001820

Palmer, Edward Albert, Memorial Chapel and Autry House, 6221 and 6265 Main St., Houston, 10/31/84, C, a, 84000388

Parker, John W., House, 2 Courtlandt Pl., Houston, 6/14/79, C, 79002966

Paul Building, 1018 Preston Ave., Houston, 4/06/79, A, C, 79002967

Paul, Allen, House, 2201 Fannin St., Houston, 9/27/80, C, 80004127

Peden, D. D., House, 2 Longfellow Ln., Houston, 7/16/91, C, 91000889

Perry-Swilley House [Houston Heights MRA], 1101 Heights Blvd., Houston, 6/22/83, C, 83004477

Pillot Building, 106 Congress St., Houston, 6/13/74, C, 74002073

Reed, Thomas B., House [Houston Heights MRA], 933 Allston St., Houston, 7/17/90, C, 90001038

Rice Hotel, Main St. and Texas Ave., Houston, 6/23/78, A, C, 78002947

Roessler, Charles, House [Houston Heights MRA], 736 Cortland, Houston, 1/15/88, C, 87002257

Rogers, Ghent W., House [Houston Heights MRA], 1150 Cortlandt, Houston, 7/17/90, C, 90001042

San Felipe Courts Historic District, 1 Allen Pkwy. Village, Houston, 2/16/88, A, C, g, 88000042

San Jacinto Battlefield, 22 mi. E of Houston on TX 134, Houston vicinity, 10/15/66, A, NHL, 66000815

Scanlan Building, 405 Main St., Houston, 5/23/80, B, C, 80004132

Schauer Filling Station [Houston Heights MRA], 1400 Oxford St., Houston, 6/22/83, A, C, 83004478

Schlesser-Burrows House [Houston Heights MRA], 1123 Harvard St., Houston, 5/14/84, C, 84001823

Sewall, Cleveland Harding, House, 3452 Inwood St., Houston, 4/14/75, C, 75001991

Sheridan Apartments, 802-804 McGowen St., Houston, 8/02/84, C, 84001825

Shoaf, John H., House [Houston Heights MRA], 2030 Arlington, Houston, 1/15/88, C, 87002258

South Texas National Bank, 215 Main St., Houston, 12/08/78, A, C, 78002948

Space Environment Simulation Laboratory, Lyndon B. Johnson Space Center, Houston, 10/03/85, A, C, g, NHL, 85002810

State National Bank Building, 412 Main St., Houston, 8/11/82, C, 82004843

Sterling, Ross, S., House, 515 Bayridge Rd., Morgan's Point, 10/29/82, B, C, 82004858

Harris County—Continued

Sterling-Berry House, 4515 Yoakum Blvd., Houston, 7/14/83, C, 83004479

Sweeney, Coombs & Fredericks Building, 301 Main St., Houston, 6/20/74, C, 74002074

Taylor, Judson L., House, 20 Courtlandt Pl., Houston, 6/14/79, B, C, 79002968

Temple Beth Israel, 3517 Austin St., Houston, 3/01/84, C, a, 84001826

Thornton, Dr. Penn B., House [Houston Heights MRA], 1541 Tulane St., Houston, 6/22/83, A, C, 83004480

Trinity Church, 3404 S. Main St., Houston, 5/26/83, C, a, 83004481

U.S. Customhouse, San Jacinto at Rusk St., Houston, 8/28/74, C, 74002075

U.S.S. TEXAS, 22 mi. E of Houston on TX 134 at San Jacinto Battleground, Houston, 12/08/76, A, C, g, NHL, 76002039

Union Station, 501 Crawford St., Houston, 11/10/77, A, C, 77001448

Upchurch House [Houston Heights MRA], 301 E. 14th St., Houston, 6/22/83, C, 83004482

Ward House [Houston Heights MRA], 323 W. 17th St., Houston, 6/22/83, C, 83004483

Webber House [Houston Heights MRA], 1011 Heights Blvd., Houston, 5/14/84, C, 84001829

Webber, Samuel H., House [Houston Heights MRA], 407 Heights Blvd., Houston, 6/22/83, C, 83004484

Wilkins House [Houston Heights MRA], 1541 Ashland St., Houston, 5/14/84, A, 84001831

Williams-Brueder House [Houston Heights MRA], 245 W. 18th St., Houston, 6/22/83, C, 83004485

Wilson House [Houston Heights MRA], 1206 Cortlandt St., Houston, 5/14/84, B, C, 84001841

Wimberly House [Houston Heights MRA], 703 Harvard St., Houston, 5/14/84, C, 84001843

Wisnoski House [Houston Heights MRA], 1651 Columbia St., Houston, 5/14/84, C, 84001844

Woodard House [Houston Heights MRA], 740 Rutlant St., Houston, 5/14/84, C, 84001847

Woodward House [Houston Heights MRA], 1605 Heights Blvd., Houston, 6/22/83, A, C, 83004486

Wray, Andrew Jackson and Margaret Cullinan, House, 3 Remington Ln., Houston, 8/19/93, C, 93000844

Wunsche Bros. Saloon and Hotel, 103 Midway St., Spring, 2/16/84, A, C, 84001849

Harrison County

Arnot House, 306 W. Houston St, Marshall, 7/27/79, A, C, 79002970

Dial-Williamson House, 3 mi.(4.8 km) W of Marshall on Old Longview Rd., Marshall vicinity, 3/02/79, C, 79002971

Edgemont, W of Marshall, Marshall vicinity, 9/22/77, B, C, 77001449

First Methodist Church, 300 E. Houston St., Marshall, 7/16/80, A, C, a, 80004133

Fry-Barry House, 314 W. Austin, Marshall, 11/21/78, A, B, C, 78002950

Ginocchio Historic District, Bounded by Grand Ave., and N. Franklin, Willow, and Lake Sts., Marshall, 12/31/74, A, B, C, 74002076

Hagerty House, 505 E. Rusk St., Marshall, 9/13/78, B, C, 78002951

Harrison County Courthouse, Public Square, Marshall, 8/16/77, A, C, 77001450

Hochwald House, 211 W. Grand Ave., Marshall, 7/14/83, A, C, 83004487

Locust Grove, Off TX 134, Jonesville, 6/20/79, C, 79002969

Marshall Arsenal, CSA, Address Restricted, Marshall vicinity, 7/01/76, A, D, 76002040

Mimosa Hall, S of Leigh off SR 134, Leigh vicinity, 11/02/78, A, C, 78002949

Old Pierce House, 303 N. Columbus St., Marshall, 4/13/73, C, 73001965

Starr House, 407 W. Travis St., Marshall, 12/11/79, A, C, 79002972

Stinson, John R., House, 313 W. Austin St., Marshall, 11/07/79, A, C, 79002973

Turner, James, House, 406 W. Washington Ave., Marshall, 11/07/79, A, B, C, b, 79002974

Weisman-Hirsch House, 313 S. Washington St., Marshall, 7/07/83, C, 83004488

Hartley County

Hartley County Courthouse and Jail, Railroad Ave., Channing, 12/31/87, A, C, 87002237

Proctor Pen I(41HT13) [New Mexican Pastor Sites in Texas Panhandle TR], Address Restricted, Amarillo vicinity, 7/12/84, D, 84001852

Tafoya, Miguel, Place(41HT17) [New Mexican Pastor Sites in Texas Panhandle TR], Address Restricted, Amarillo vicinity, 7/12/84, A, D, 84001854

XIT General Office, Railroad Ave. and 5th St., Channing, 5/06/85, A, 85000960

Hays County

Barber House [San Marcos MRA], 100 Burleson St., San Marcos, 8/26/83, B, C, 83004489

Belger-Cahill Lime Kiln [San Marcos MRA], Lime Kiln Rd., San Marcos, 8/26/83, A, 83004490

Belvin Street Historic District [San Marcos MRA], 700, 800, 900 blocks of Belvin St., and 227 Mitchell St., San Marcos, 12/01/83, A, C, 83003792

Burleson-Knispel House, 1.5 mi. N of San Marcos on Lime Kiln Rd, San Marcos vicinity, 8/03/79, A, B, C, 79002975

Caldwell House [San Marcos MRA], 619 Maury St., San Marcos, 8/26/83, C, 83004491

Cape House [San Marcos MRA], 316 W. Hopkins St., San Marcos, 8/26/83, B, C, 83004492

Cemetery Chapel, San Marcos Cemetery [San Marcos MRA], TX 12, San Marcos, 12/01/83, C, a, 83003793

Cock House, 402 E. Hopkins St., San Marcos, 4/02/73, C, 73001966

Dobie, John R., House, 282 Old Kyle Rd., Wimberley, 8/18/92, C, 92001024

Episcopalian Rectory [San Marcos MRA], 225 W. Hopkins St., San Marcos, 8/26/83, C, a, 83004493

Farmers Union Gin Company [San Marcos MRA], 120 Grove St., San Marcos, 8/26/83, A, C, 83004494

Fire Station and City Hall [San Marcos MRA], 224 N. Guadalupe St., San Marcos, 8/26/83, A, C, 83004495

First United Methodist Church, 129 W. Hutchison, San Marcos, 11/08/74, A, C, a, 74002269

Fisher Hall [San Marcos MRA], 1132 Belvin St., San Marcos, 8/26/83, A, C, 83004496

Fort Street Presbyterian Church [San Marcos MRA], 516 W. Hopkins St., San Marcos, 3/23/84, C, a, 84001860

Freeman, Harry, Site, Address Restricted, San Marcos vicinity, 11/07/78, D, 78002953

Goforth-Harris House [San Marcos MRA], 401 Comanche St., San Marcos, 8/26/83, B, C, 83004497

Green and Faris Buildings [San Marcos MRA], 136-144 E. San Antonio St., San Marcos, 8/26/83, A, C, 83004498

Hardy-Williams Building [San Marcos MRA], 127 E. Hopkins St., San Marcos, 8/26/83, A, C, 83004499

Hays County Courthouse, Public Sq., San Marcos, 5/23/80, A, C, 80004134

Hays County Courthouse Historic District [San Marcos MRA], Roughly bounded by the alleys behind N. Guadalupe, E. Hopkins, N. LBJ and E. San Antonio Sts., San Marcos, 9/10/92, C, 92001233

Hays County Jail [San Marcos MRA], 170 Fredericksburg St., San Marcos, 8/26/83, A, C, 83004500

Heard House [San Marcos MRA], 620 W. San Antonio St., San Marcos, 8/26/83, C, 83004501

Hofheinz, Augusta, House [San Marcos MRA], 1104 W. Hopkins St., San Marcos, 8/26/83, C, 83004502

Hofheinz, Walter, House [San Marcos MRA], 819 W. Hopkins St., San Marcos, 12/01/83, C, 83003794

Hutchison House [San Marcos MRA], LBJ Dr. and University St., San Marcos, 8/26/83, C, b, 83004503

Johnson House [San Marcos MRA], 1030 Belvin St., San Marcos, 8/26/83, C, 83004504

Kone-Cliett House [San Marcos MRA], 724 Burleson St., San Marcos, 12/01/83, B, C, 83003795

Kyle, Claiborne, Log House, SW of Kyle, Kyle vicinity, 5/28/81, A, B, C, D, 81000630

Main Building, Southwest Texas Normal School [San Marcos MRA], Old Main St., Southwest Texas State University campus, San Marcos, 8/26/83, A, C, 83004505

McKie-Bass Building [San Marcos MRA], 111 N. Guadalupe St., San Marcos, 12/01/83, C, 83003797

Moore Grocery Company [San Marcos MRA], 101 S. Edward Gary St., San Marcos, 8/26/83, A, 83004506

Hays County—Continued

Norman, Ruskin C., Site (41 HY 86), Address Restricted, San Marcos vicinity, 11/21/78, D, 78002954

Ragsdale-Jackman-Yarbough House [San Marcos MRA], 621 W. San Antonio St., San Marcos, 8/26/83, A, C, 83004507

Rylander-Kyle House [San Marcos MRA], 711 W. San Antonio St., San Marcos, 8/26/83, B, C, 83004508

San Marcos Milling Company [San Marcos MRA], Nicola Alley, San Marcos, 12/01/83, A, 83003799

San Marcos Telephone Company [San Marcos MRA], 138 W. San Antonio St., San Marcos, 8/26/83, A, C, 83004509

Simon Building [San Marcos MRA], 124-126 W. Hopkins St., San Marcos, 8/26/83, C, 83004510

Smith House [San Marcos MRA], 322 Scott St., San Marcos, 8/26/83, C, 83004511

Williams-Tarbutton House [San Marcos MRA], 626 Lindsey St., San Marcos, 8/26/83, B, C, 83004512

Henderson County

Faulk and Gauntt Building, 217 N. Prairieville St., Athens, 6/09/80, C, 80004135

Hidalgo County

El Sal Del Rey Archeological District, Address Restricted, Linn vicinity, 8/27/79, A, D, 79002977

La Lomita Historic District, 5 mi. S of Mission on FM 1016, Mission vicinity, 5/28/75, A, C, a, 75002165

Old Hidalgo Courthouse and Buildings, Flora and 1st Sts., Hidalgo, 2/01/80, A, C, 80004136

Old Hidalgo School, Flora and 4th Sts., Hidalgo, 10/24/79, A, C, 79002976

Rancho Toluca, FM 1015, Progreso, 7/21/83, A, B, 83004513

Hill County

Baker, J. T., Farmstead, 1.2 mi. N of Blum between TX 174 and the Nolan R., Blum vicinity, 3/17/92, C, D, 92000138

Bear Creek Shelter Site, Address Restricted, Huron vicinity, 10/19/78, D, 78002955

Buzzard Cave, Address Restricted, Lake Whitney vicinity, 7/18/74, D, 74002270

Farmers National Bank [Hillsboro MRA], 68 W. Elm St., Hillsboro, 3/30/84, A, C, 84001871

Gebhardt Bakery [Hillsboro MRA], 119 E. Franklin St., Hillsboro, 3/30/84, A, C, 84001873

Grimes Garage [Hillsboro MRA], 110 N. Waco St., Hillsboro, 3/30/84, A, C, 84001875

Grimes House [Hillsboro MRA], Country Club Rd. and Corporation St., Hillsboro, 3/30/84, A, C, 84001877

Hill County Courthouse, Courthouse Sq., Hillsboro, 6/21/71, C, 71000939

Hill County Jail, N. Waco St., Hillsboro, 5/28/81, C, 81000631

Hillsboro Cotton Mills [Hillsboro MRA], 220 N. Houston St., Hillsboro, 3/30/84, A, C, 84001878

Hillsboro Residential Historic District [Hillsboro MRA], Roughly bounded by Country Club Rd., Thompson, Corsicana, Pleasant, Franklin, and Elm Sts., Hillsboro, 7/09/84, B, C, 84001879

Kyle Shelter, Address Restricted, Lake Whitney Estates vicinity, 7/09/74, D, 74002078

McKenzie Site, Address Restricted, Hillsboro vicinity, 11/25/77, D, 77001451

Missouri-Kansas-Texas Company Railroad Station, Covington St., Hillsboro, 12/19/79, A, C, b, 79002978

Old Rock Saloon [Hillsboro MRA], 58 W. Elm St., Hillsboro, 3/30/84, A, C, 84001881

Pictograph Cave, Address Restricted, Lake Whitney vicinity, 3/13/74, D, 74002079

Sheep Cave, Address Restricted, Blum vicinity, 7/09/74, D, 74002077

Sturgis National Bank [Hillsboro MRA], S. Waco and W. Elm Sts., Hillsboro, 3/30/84, A, C, 84001889

Tarlton Building [Hillsboro MRA], 110 E. Franklin St., Hillsboro, 3/30/84, A, C, 84001892

Turner, Joe E., House, 3 mi. E of Itasca on SR 934, Itasca vicinity, 4/13/77, A, C, 77001452

U.S. Post Office [Hillsboro MRA], 118 S. Waco St., Hillsboro, 3/30/84, C, 84001894

Western Union Building [Hillsboro MRA], 107 S. Covington St., Hillsboro, 3/30/84, A, C, 84001896

Hood County

Hood County Courthouse Historic District, Courthouse Sq., bounded by Bridge, Pearl, and Houston Sts., Granbury, 6/05/74, A, C, 74002080

Wright-Henderson-Duncan House, 703 Spring St., Granbury, 12/19/78, C, 78002956

Hopkins County

Hopkins County Courthouse, Church and Jefferson Sts., Sulphur Springs, 4/11/77, C, 77001453

Houston County

Downes-Aldrich House, 206 N. 7th St., Crockett, 4/19/78, B, C, 78002957

Mary Allen Seminary for Colored Girls, Administration Building, 803 N. 4th St., Crockett, 5/12/83, A, C, 83004514

Monroe-Crook House, 707 E. Houston St., Crockett, 3/31/71, C, 71000940

Westerman Mound, Address Restricted, Kennard vicinity, 6/21/71, D, 71000941

Howard County

Potton-Hayden House, SW corner Gregg and 2nd Sts., Big Spring, 4/14/75, C, 75001992

Hudspeth County

Alamo Canyon—Wilkey Ranch Discontiguous Archeological District, Address Restricted, Fort Hancock vicinity, 10/28/88, C, D, a, 88002151

Archeological Site No. 41 HZ 1 [Indian Hot Springs MPS], Address Restricted, Sierra Blanca vicinity, 1/11/91, D, 90002015

Archeological Site No. 41 HZ 7 [Indian Hot Springs MPS], Address Restricted, Sierra Blanca vicinity, 1/11/91, D, 90002016

Archeological Site No. 41 HZ 181 [Indian Hot Springs MPS], Address Restricted, Sierra Blanca vicinity, 1/11/91, D, 90002017

Archeological Site No. 41 HZ 182 [Indian Hot Springs MPS], Address Restricted, Sierra Blanca vicinity, 1/11/91, D, 90002018

Archeological Site No. 41 HZ 183 [Indian Hot Springs MPS], Address Restricted, Sierra Blanca vicinity, 1/11/91, D, 90002019

Archeological Site No. 41 HZ 184 [Indian Hot Springs MPS], Address Restricted, Sierra Blanca vicinity, 1/11/91, D, 90002020

Archeological Site No. 41 HZ 190 [Indian Hot Springs MPS], Address Restricted, Sierra Blanca vicinity, 1/11/91, D, 90002021

Archeological Site No. 41 HZ 200 [Indian Hot Springs MPS], Address Restricted, Sierra Blanca vicinity, 1/11/91, D, 90002022

Archeological Site No. 41 HZ 220 [Indian Hot Springs MPS], Address Restricted, Sierra Blanca vicinity, 1/11/91, D, 90002023

Archeological Site No. 41 HZ 227 [Indian Hot Springs MPS], Address Restricted, Sierra Blanca vicinity, 1/11/91, A, D, 90002024

Archeological Site No. 41 HZ 228 [Indian Hot Springs MPS], Address Restricted, Sierra Blanca vicinity, 1/11/91, A, D, d, 90002025

Archeological Site No. 41 HZ 283 [Indian Hot Springs MPS], Address Restricted, Sierra Blanca vicinity, 1/11/91, D, 90002026

Archeological Site No. 41 HZ 284 [Indian Hot Springs MPS], Address Restricted, Sierra Blanca vicinity, 1/11/91, D, 90002027

Archeological Site No. 41 HZ 285 [Indian Hot Springs MPS], Address Restricted, Sierra Blanca vicinity, 1/11/91, D, 90002028

Archeological Site No. 41 HZ 286 [Indian Hot Springs MPS], Address Restricted, Sierra Blanca vicinity, 1/11/91, D, 90002029

Archeological Site No. 41 HZ 287 [Indian Hot Springs MPS], Address Restricted, Sierra Blanca vicinity, 1/11/91, D, 90002030

Hudspeth County—Continued

Archeological Site No. 41 HZ 288 [Indian Hot Springs MPS], Address Restricted, Sierra Blanca vicinity, 1/11/91, D, 90002031

Archeological Site No. 41 HZ 289 [Indian Hot Springs MPS], Address Restricted, Sierra Blanca vicinity, 1/11/91, D, 90002032

Archeological Site No. 41 HZ 290 [Indian Hot Springs MPS], Address Restricted, Sierra Blanca vicinity, 1/11/91, D, 90002033

Archeological Site No. 41 HZ 291 [Indian Hot Springs MPS], Address Restricted, Sierra Blanca vicinity, 1/11/91, D, 90002034

Archeological Site No. 41 HZ 292 [Indian Hot Springs MPS], Address Restricted, Sierra Blanca vicinity, 1/11/91, D, 90002035

Archeological Site No. 41 HZ 293 [Indian Hot Springs MPS], Address Restricted, Sierra Blanca vicinity, 1/11/91, D, 90002036

Archeological Site No. 41 HZ 294 [Indian Hot Springs MPS], Address Restricted, Sierra Blanca vicinity, 1/11/91, D, 90002037

Archeological Site No. 41 HZ 295 [Indian Hot Springs MPS], Address Restricted, Sierra Blanca vicinity, 1/11/91, D, 90002038

Archeological Site No. 41 HZ 296 [Indian Hot Springs MPS], Address Restricted, Sierra Blanca vicinity, 1/11/91, D, 90002039

Archeological Site No. 41 HZ 297 [Indian Hot Springs MPS], Address Restricted, Sierra Blanca vicinity, 1/11/91, D, 90002040

Archeological Site No. 41 HZ 298 [Indian Hot Springs MPS], Address Restricted, Sierra Blanca vicinity, 1/11/91, D, 90002041

Archeological Site No. 41 HZ 299 [Indian Hot Springs MPS], Address Restricted, Sierra Blanca vicinity, 1/11/91, D, 90002042

Archeological Site No. 41 HZ 300 [Indian Hot Springs MPS], Address Restricted, Sierra Blanca vicinity, 1/11/91, D, 90002043

Archeological Site No. 41 HZ 301 [Indian Hot Springs MPS], Address Restricted, Sierra Blanca vicinity, 1/11/91, D, 90002044

Archeological Site No. 41 HZ 302 [Indian Hot Springs MPS], Address Restricted, Sierra Blanca vicinity, 1/11/91, D, 90002045

Archeological Site No. 41 HZ 303 [Indian Hot Springs MPS], Address Restricted, Sierra Blanca vicinity, 1/11/91, D, 90002046

Archeological Site No. 41 HZ 304–305 [Indian Hot Springs MPS], Address Restricted, Sierra Blanca vicinity, 1/11/91, D, 90002047

Archeological Site No. 41 HZ 306 [Indian Hot Springs MPS], Address Restricted, Sierra Blanca vicinity, 1/11/91, D, 90002048

Archeological Site No. 41 HZ 307 [Indian Hot Springs MPS], Address Restricted, Sierra Blanca vicinity, 1/11/91, D, 90002049

Archeological Site No. 41 HZ 308 [Indian Hot Springs MPS], Address Restricted, Sierra Blanca vicinity, 1/11/91, D, 90002050

Archeological Site No. 41 HZ 309 [Indian Hot Springs MPS], Address Restricted, Sierra Blanca vicinity, 1/11/91, D, 90002051

Archeological Site No. 41 HZ 311 [Indian Hot Springs MPS], Address Restricted, Sierra Blanca vicinity, 1/11/91, D, 90002052

Archeological Site No. 41 HZ 312 [Indian Hot Springs MPS], Address Restricted, Sierra Blanca vicinity, 1/11/91, D, 90002053

Archeological Site No. 41 HZ 313 [Indian Hot Springs MPS], Address Restricted, Sierra Blanca vicinity, 1/11/91, D, 90002054

Archeological Site No. 41 HZ 339 [Indian Hot Springs MPS], Address Restricted, Sierra Blanca vicinity, 1/11/91, D, 90002055

Archeological Site No. 41 HZ 340 [Indian Hot Springs MPS], Address Restricted, Sierra Blanca vicinity, 1/11/91, D, 90002056

Archeological Site No. 41 HZ 409 [Indian Hot Springs MPS], Address Restricted, Sierra Blanca vicinity, 1/11/91, D, 90002057

Archeological Site No. 41 HZ 410 [Indian Hot Springs MPS], Address Restricted, Sierra Blanca vicinity, 1/11/91, D, 90002058

Archeological Site No. 41 HZ 411 [Indian Hot Springs MPS], Address Restricted, Sierra Blanca vicinity, 1/11/91, D, 90002059

Archeological Site No. 41 HZ 412 [Indian Hot Springs MPS], Address Restricted, Sierra Blanca vicinity, 1/11/91, D, 90002060

Archeological Site No. 41 HZ 413 [Indian Hot Springs MPS], Address Restricted, Sierra Blanca vicinity, 1/11/91, D, 90002061

Archeological Site No. 41 HZ 414 [Indian Hot Springs MPS], Address Restricted, Sierra Blanca vicinity, 1/11/91, D, 90002062

Archeological Site No. 41 HZ 415 [Indian Hot Springs MPS], Address Restricted, Sierra Blanca vicinity, 1/11/91, D, 90002063

Archeological Site No. 41 HZ 416 [Indian Hot Springs MPS], Address Restricted, Sierra Blanca vicinity, 1/11/91, D, 90002064

Archeological Site No. 41 HZ 417 [Indian Hot Springs MPS], Address Restricted, Sierra Blanca vicinity, 1/11/91, D, 90002065

Archeological Site No. 41 HZ 418 [Indian Hot Springs MPS], Address Restricted, Sierra Blanca vicinity, 1/11/91, D, 90002066

Archeological Site No. 41 HZ 419 [Indian Hot Springs MPS], Address Restricted, Sierra Blanca vicinity, 1/11/91, D, 90002067

Archeological Site No. 41 HZ 420 [Indian Hot Springs MPS], Address Restricted, Sierra Blanca vicinity, 1/11/91, D, 90002068

Archeological Site No. 41 HZ 421 [Indian Hot Springs MPS], Address Restricted, Sierra Blanca vicinity, 1/11/91, D, 90002069

Archeological Site No. 41 HZ 422 [Indian Hot Springs MPS], Address Restricted, Sierra Blanca vicinity, 1/11/91, D, 90002070

Archeological Site No. 41 HZ 423 [Indian Hot Springs MPS], Address Restricted, Sierra Blanca vicinity, 1/11/91, D, 90002071

Archeological Site No. 41 HZ 424 [Indian Hot Springs MPS], Address Restricted, Sierra Blanca vicinity, 1/11/91, D, 90002072

Archeological Site No. 41 HZ 425 [Indian Hot Springs MPS], Address Restricted, Sierra Blanca vicinity, 1/11/91, D, 90002073

Archeological Site No. 41 HZ 426 [Indian Hot Springs MPS], Address Restricted, Sierra Blanca vicinity, 1/11/91, D, 90002074

Archeological Site No. 41 HZ 427 [Indian Hot Springs MPS], Address Restricted, Sierra Blanca vicinity, 1/11/91, D, 90002075

Archeological Site No. 41 HZ 428 [Indian Hot Springs MPS], Address Restricted, Sierra Blanca vicinity, 1/11/91, D, 90002076

Archeological Site No. 41 HZ 429 [Indian Hot Springs MPS], Address Restricted, Sierra Blanca vicinity, 1/11/91, D, 90002077

Archeological Site No. 41 HZ 430 [Indian Hot Springs MPS], Address Restricted, Sierra Blanca vicinity, 1/11/91, D, 90002078

Archeological Site No. 41 HZ 431 [Indian Hot Springs MPS], Address Restricted, Sierra Blanca vicinity, 1/11/91, D, 90002079

Archeological Site No. 41 HZ 432 [Indian Hot Springs MPS], Address Restricted, Sierra Blanca vicinity, 1/11/91, D, 90002080

Archeological Site No. 41 HZ 433 [Indian Hot Springs MPS], Address Restricted, Sierra Blanca vicinity, 1/11/91, D, 90002081

Archeological Site No. 41 HZ 434 [Indian Hot Springs MPS], Address Restricted, Sierra Blanca vicinity, 1/11/91, D, 90002082

Archeological Site No. 41 HZ 435 [Indian Hot Springs MPS], Address Restricted, Sierra Blanca vicinity, 1/11/91, D, 90002083

Archeological Site No. 41 HZ 436 [Indian Hot Springs MPS], Address Restricted, Sierra Blanca vicinity, 1/11/91, D, 90002084

Archeological Site No. 41 HZ 437 [Indian Hot Springs MPS], Address Restricted, Sierra Blanca vicinity, 1/11/91, D, 90002085

Archeological Site No. 41 HZ 438 [Indian Hot Springs MPS], Address Restricted, Sierra Blanca vicinity, 1/11/91, D, 90002086

Archeological Site No. 41 HZ 439 [Indian Hot Springs MPS], Address Restricted, Sierra Blanca vicinity, 1/11/91, D, 90002087

Archeological Site No. 41 HZ 440 [Indian Hot Springs MPS], Address Restricted, Sierra Blanca vicinity, 1/11/91, D, 90002088

Archeological Site No. 41 HZ 441 [Indian Hot Springs MPS], Address Restricted, Sierra Blanca vicinity, 1/11/91, D, 90002089

Archeological Site No. 41 HZ 442 [Indian Hot Springs MPS], Address Restricted, Sierra Blanca vicinity, 1/11/91, D, 90002090

Archeological Site No. 41 HZ 443 [Indian Hot Springs MPS], Address Restricted, Sierra Blanca vicinity, 1/11/91, D, 90002091

Archeological Site No. 41 HZ 445 [Indian Hot Springs MPS], Address Restricted, Sierra Blanca vicinity, 1/11/91, C, D, 90002093

Archeological Site No. 41 HZ 448 [Indian Hot Springs MPS], Address Restricted, Sierra Blanca vicinity, 1/11/91, D, 90002094

Archeological Site No. 41 HZ 464 [Indian Hot Springs MPS], Address Restricted, Sierra Blanca vicinity, 1/11/91, D, 90002095

Archeological Site No. 41 HZ 465 [Indian Hot Springs MPS], Address Restricted, Sierra Blanca vicinity, 1/11/91, D, 90002096

Hudspeth County—Continued

Hudspeth County Courthouse, Millican St., Sierra Blanca, 5/21/75, C, 75001993

Indian Hot Springs Health Resort Historic District [Indian Hot Springs MPS], Address Restricted, Sierra Blanca vicinity, 1/11/91, A, C, D, 90002092

Johnson, Rod, Site, Address Restricted, Sierra Blance vicinity, 11/01/79, D, 79002979

Red Rock Archeological Complex, Address Restricted, Allamore vicinity, 5/02/77, D, 77001454

Tinaja de las Palmas Battle Site, Address Restricted, Sierra Blanca vicinity, 11/07/79, A, D, 79002980

Hunt County

Camp, William and Medora, House, 2620 Church St., Greenville, 11/14/88, C, 88002130

Post Office Building, Lee at King St., Greenville, 8/07/74, B, C, g, 74002081

Hutchinson County

Adobe Walls, Address Restricted, Stinnet vicinity, 5/22/78, A, D, 78002958

Antelope Creek Archeological District, Address Restricted, Fritch vicinity, 9/22/72, D, 72001366

Irion County

Irion County Courthouse, Public Sq., Sherwood, 8/29/77, C, 77001455

Jack County

Fort Richardson, S of Jacksboro on U.S. 281, Jacksboro vicinity, 10/15/66, A, NHL, 66000816

Jackson County

Texana Presbyterian Church, Apollo Dr. and Country Club Lane, Edna, 9/12/79, A, C, a, 79002982

Jasper County

Blake-Beaty-Orton House, 206 S. Main St., Jasper, 4/16/75, C, 75001994

Doom, Col. Randolph C., House, 7.5 mi. W of Jasper on FM 1747, Jasper vicinity, 12/30/75, B, C, b, 75001995

Jasper County Courthouse, Public Sq., Jasper, 9/06/84, A, 84001898

Smyth, Andrew, House, W of Jasper, Jasper vicinity, 5/25/79, C, 79002983

Turner-White-McGee House, Off U.S. 96, Roganville, 6/19/79, C, 79002984

Jeff Davis County

Fort Davis National Historic Site, Jct. of TX 17 and 118, Fort Davis, 10/15/66, A, C, NPS, 66000045

Grierson-Sproul House, Court Ave., Fort Davis, 8/11/82, C, 82004508

Jefferson County

Beaumont Commercial District, Roughly bounded by Orleans, Bowie, Neches, Crockett, Laurel, Willow, Broadway, Pearl, Main, and Gilbert Sts., Beaumont, 4/14/78, A, C, 78002959

Beaumont Y.M.C.A., 934 Calder St., Beaumont, 3/30/79, C, 79002985

Duke, Holmes, House, 694 Forrest St., Beaumont, 10/04/84, C, 84000028

French Home Trading Post, 2995 French Rd., Beaumont, 10/15/70, B, C, 70000752

Gates Memorial Library, 317 Stilwell Blvd., Port Arthur, 5/04/81, C, 81000632

Hinchee House, 1814 Park St., Beaumont, 11/21/78, C, 78002960

Idle Hours, 1608 Orange St., Beaumont, 5/22/78, C, 78002961

Jefferson County Courthouse, 1149 Pearl St., Beaumont, 6/17/82, C, 82004509

Jefferson Theater, 345 Fannin St., Beaumont, 1/30/78, A, 78002962

Lucas Gusher, Spindletop Oil Field, 3 mi. S of Beaumont on Spindletop Ave., Beaumont vicinity, 11/13/66, A, NHL, 66000818

McFaddin House Complex, 1906 McFaddin St., Beaumont, 1/25/71, C, 71000942

Mildred Buildings, 1400 block of Calder Ave., Beaumont, 12/01/78, B, C, 78002963

Pompeiian Villa, 1953 Lakeshore Dr., Port Arthur, 5/23/73, A, C, 73001967

Port Arthur Federated Women's Clubhouse, 1924 Lakeshore Dr., Port Arthur, 7/18/85, A, 85001559

Rose Hill, 100 Woodworth Blvd., Port Arthur, 10/31/79, A, C, 79002986

Sanders House, 479 Pine, Beaumont, 12/13/78, C, 78002964

US Post Office and Federal Building, 500 Austin Ave., Port Arthur, 5/12/86, C, 86001099

Jim Wells County

Hinojosa Site, Address Restricted, Alice vicinity, 3/30/78, D, 78002965

Johnson County

Cleburne Carnegie Library, 201 N. Caddo St., Cleburne, 12/12/76, C, 76002042

Ham Creek Site, Address Restricted, Rio Vista vicinity, 2/15/74, D, 74002082

Hart, Meredith, House, E of Rio Vista on SR 916, Rio Vista vicinity, 4/13/77, C, 77001456

Johnson County Courthouse, 1 Public Sq., Cleburne, 4/14/88, A, C, 88000439

Jones County

Astin, J. P., House [Stamford MRA], 111 E. Campbell, Stamford, 9/24/86, C, 86002390

Buena Vista Hotel [Stamford MRA], 123 N. Wetherbee, Stamford, 9/24/86, A, 86002369

Bunkley, Dr. E. P., House and Garage [Stamford MRA], 1034 E. Reynolds, Stamford, 9/24/86, C, 86002380

First Baptist Church [Stamford MRA], E. Oliver and N. Swenson, Stamford, 9/24/86, C, a, 86002359

Fort Phantom Hill, N of Abilene on Ranch Rd. 600, Abilene vicinity, 9/14/72, A, D, 72001367

House at 501 North Swenson [Stamford MRA], 501 N. Swenson, Stamford, 9/24/86, C, 86002374

House at 502 South Orient [Stamford MRA], 502 S. Orient, Stamford, 9/24/86, C, 86002377

House at 610 East Oliver [Stamford MRA], 610 E. Oliver, Stamford, 9/24/86, C, 86002394

House at 709 East Reynolds [Stamford MRA], 709 E. Reynolds, Stamford, 9/24/86, C, 86002384

House at 719 East Reynolds [Stamford MRA], 719 E. Reynolds, Stamford, 9/24/86, C, 86002385

House at 815 East Campbell [Stamford MRA], 815 E. Campbell, Stamford, 9/24/86, C, 86002392

Jackson, A. J., House [Stamford MRA], 305 S. Ferguson, Stamford, 9/24/86, C, 86002366

Old Bryant—Link Building [Stamford MRA], 120 S. Swenson, Stamford, 9/24/86, C, 86002361

Old Penick—Hughes Company [Stamford MRA], 100–106 E. Hamilton, Stamford, 9/24/86, A, 86002354

Old West Texas Utilities Company [Stamford MRA], 127 E. McHarg, Stamford, 9/24/86, C, 86002335

Old Wooten, H. O., Grocery [Stamford MRA], 128 E. Rotan, Stamford, 9/24/86, C, 86002363

SMS Building [Stamford MRA], 101 S. Wetherbee and 210 E. McHarg, Stamford, 9/24/86, B, C, 86002336

Saint John's Methodist Church [Stamford MRA], S. Ferguson St., Stamford, 9/24/86, C, a, 86002351

Stamford City Hall [Stamford MRA], 201 E. McHarg, Stamford, 9/24/86, C, 86002348

Swenson, A. J., House [Stamford MRA], 305 E. Oliver, Stamford, 9/24/86, B, C, 86002395

US Post Office [Stamford MRA], Town Sq., Stamford, 9/24/86, C, 86002332

Karnes County

Panna Maria Historic District, TX 123, Panna Maria and vicinity, 5/13/76, A, C, a, 76002043
Ruckman, John, House, 6 mi. N of Karnes City off TX 80, Karnes City vicinity, 6/19/79, C, 79002987

Kaufman County

Brooks, William and Blanche, House, 500 S. Center St., Forney, 7/06/93, B, C, 93000566
Cartwright, Matthew, House, 505 Griffith Ave., Terrell, 4/04/79, B, C, 79002988
First National Bank Building, 101 E. Moore, Terrell, 1/11/85, A, C, 85000073
Porter, Walter C., Farm, 2 mi. N of Terrell on FR 986, Terrell vicinity, 10/15/66, A, NHL, 66000819
Terrell Times Star Building, 108 S. Catherine St., Terrell, 5/02/85, A, B, C, 85000923
Warren-Crowell House, 705 Griffith Ave., Terrell, 5/23/80, C, 80004137

Kendall County

Brinkmann, Otto, House, 701 High St., Comfort, 12/12/77, C, 77001457
Comfort Historic District, TX 27, Comfort, 5/29/79, A, C, 79002989
Dienger, Joseph, Building, 106 W. Blanco Rd., Boerne, 1/19/84, C, 84001901
Hygieostatic Bat Roost, E of Comfort, Comfort vicinity, 3/28/83, A, B, C, 83003144
Kendall County Courthouse and Jail, Public Sq., Boerne, 2/15/80, A, C, 80004138
Kendall Inn, Off U.S. 87, Boerne, 6/29/76, A, C, 76002045
Sisterdale Valley District, SR 1376, Sisterdale, 1/08/75, A, C, 75001996
Treue Der Union Monument, High St., Comfort, 11/29/78, A, f, 78002966

Kenedy County

King Ranch, Kingsville and its environs, Kingsville and vicinity, 10/15/66, A, NHL, 66000820
Mansfield Cut Underwater Archeological District, Address Restricted, Port Isabel vicinity, 1/21/74, D, 74002083

Kerr County

Masonic Building, 211 Earl Garrett St., Kerrville, 1/12/84, B, C, 84001903
Old Camp Verde, Address Restricted, Camp Verde vicinity, 5/25/73, A, D, 73001968
Schreiner, Capt. Charles, Mansion, 216 Earl Garrett St., Kerrville, 4/14/75, C, 75001997
Tulahteka, S of Kerrville on TX 16, Kerrville vicinity, 8/11/82, C, 82004510

Kimble County

Brambletye, Off SR 2291, Junction, 7/15/82, A, C, 82004511

Kinney County

Fort Clark Historic District, Off U.S. 90, Brackettville, 12/06/79, A, C, 79002990

Kleberg County

Dunn Ranch, Novillo Line Camp, S of Corpus Christi in Padre Island National Seashore, Corpus Christi vicinity, 10/01/74, A, NPS, 74000277
King, Henrietta M., High School, Kleberg Ave. and 3rd St., Kingsville, 5/09/83, A, C, 83003145
Ragland, John B., Mercantile Company Building, 201 E. Kleberg Ave., Kingsville, 1/21/93, C, 92001820

Lamar County

Atkinson—Morris House [Paris MRA], 802 Fitzhugh, Paris, 10/26/88, C, 88001914
Bailey—Ragland House [Paris MRA], 433 W. Washington, Paris, 10/26/88, C, 88001917
Baldwin, Benjamin and Adelaide, House [Paris MRA], 714 Graham, Paris, 10/26/88, C, 88001925
Baty—Plummer House [Paris MRA], 708 Sherman, Paris, 10/26/88, C, 88001931
Brazelton, Thomas and Bettie, House [Paris MRA], 801 W. Sherman, Paris, 10/26/88, C, 88001932
Carlton—Gladden House [Paris MRA], 2120 Bonham, Paris, 10/26/88, C, 88001933
Church Street Historic District [Paris MRA], Roughly bounded by E. Austin, 3rd, SE, Washington and 1st, SW Sts., Paris, 10/26/88, C, 88001936
Daniel, J. M. and Emily, House [Paris MRA], 216 4th, SW, Paris, 10/26/88, C, 88001921
Ellis II Site, Address Restricted, Pin Hook vicinity, 3/30/78, D, 78002967
Emerson Site, Address Restricted, Pin Hook vicinity, 12/01/78, D, 78002968
First Church of Christ, Scientist [Paris MRA], 339 W. Kaufman, Paris, 10/26/88, C, a, 88001912
First Presbyterian Church [Paris MRA], 410 W. Kaufman, Paris, 10/26/88, C, a, 88001913
First United Methodist Church [Churches with Decorative Interior Painting TR], 322 Lamar St., Paris, 6/21/83, A, C, a, 83003146
Gibbons, John Chisum, House [Paris MRA], 623 6th, SE, Paris, 10/26/88, B, C, 88001923
High House [Paris MRA], 352 Washington, Paris, 10/26/88, C, 88001920
House at 705 3rd Street, SE [Paris MRA], 705 3rd St., SE, Paris, 10/26/88, C, 88001935

Jenkins, Edwin and Mary, House [Paris MRA], 549 5th, NW, Paris, 10/26/88, C, 88001927
Johnson—McCuistion House [Paris MRA], 730 Clarksville, Paris, 10/26/88, C, 88001911
Lamar County Hospital [Paris MRA], 625 W. Washington, Paris, 10/26/88, C, 88001918
Latimer, William and Etta, House [Paris MRA], 707 Sherman, Paris, 10/26/88, C, 88001930
Loma Alto Site, Address Restricted, Pin Hook vicinity, 3/29/78, D, 78002969
Mackin, A. C., Archeological Site, Address Restricted, Faulkner vicinity, 5/16/74, D, 74002085
Maxey, Samuel Bell, House, 812 E. Church St., Paris, 3/18/71, B, C, 71000943
McCormic—Bishop House [Paris MRA], 603 8th St., SE, Paris, 10/26/88, C, 88001910
Means—Justiss House [Paris MRA], 537 6th St., SE, Paris, 10/26/88, C, 88001934
Morris—Moore House [Paris MRA], 744 3rd, NW, Paris, 10/26/88, C, 88001926
Paris Commercial Historic District [Paris MRA], Roughly bounded by Price, 3rd, SE, Sherman and 4th, SW, Paris, 12/22/88, A, C, 88001937
Pine Bluff—Fitzhugh Historic District [Paris MRA], 500-900 blks of Pine Bluff and 300-600 blks of Fitzhugh, Paris, 10/26/88, C, 88001938
Preston, Thaddeus and Josepha, House [Paris MRA], 731 E. Austin, Paris, 10/26/88, C, 88001915
Ragland House [Paris MRA], 208 5th St., SW, Paris, 10/26/88, C, 88001922
Rodgers—Wade Furniture Company [Paris MRA], 401 3rd, SW, Paris, 10/26/88, A, B, 88001919
Scott—Roden Mansion, 425 S. Church St., Paris, 9/15/83, C, 83003147
St. Paul's Baptist Church [Paris MRA], 454 2nd, NE, Paris, 10/26/88, C, a, 88001928
Swindle Site, Address Restricted, Pin Hook vicinity, 3/29/78, D, 78002970
Trigg, W. S. and Mary, House [Paris MRA], 441 12th St., SE, Paris, 10/26/88, C, 88001924
Wise—Fielding House and Carriage House [Paris MRA], 418 W. Washington, Paris, 12/22/88, C, 88001916
Wright, Edgar and Annie, House [Paris MRA], 857 Lamar, Paris, 10/26/88, C, 88001929

Lampasas County

Lampasas County Courthouse, Bounded by S. Live Oak, E. 4th, S. Pecan, and E. 3rd Sts., Lampasas, 6/21/71, C, 71000944
Phillips and Trosper Buildings, 408 and 410 E. Third St., Lampasas, 4/30/87, C, 87000676

Lavaca County

Ascension of Our Lord Catholic Church [Churches with Decorative Interior Painting TR], FM 957, Moravia, 6/21/83, A, C, a, 83003148

Lavaca County—Continued

Church of the Blessed Virgin Mary, the Queen of Peace [Churches with Decorative Interior Painting TR], FM 340, Sweet Home, 6/21/83, A, C, a, 83003149

Church of the Immaculate Conception of Blessed Virgin Mary [Churches with Decorative Interior Painting TR], FM 2672, St. Mary's, 6/21/83, A, C, a, g, 83003150

Lavaca County Courthouse, Bounded by La-Grange, 2nd, 3rd, and Main Sts., Hallettsville, 3/11/71, C, 71000945

Lay-Bozka House, 205 Fairwinds, Hallettsville, 1/25/71, C, 71000946

Sts. Cyril and Methodius Church [Churches with Decorative Interior Painting TR], 100 St. Lud-milla St., Shiner, 6/21/83, A, C, a, g, 83003151

Lee County

Droemer Brickyard Site, 1 mi. SW of Giddings on Old Serbin Rd, Giddings vicinity, 11/07/79, A, C, 79002991

Lee County Courthouse, Bounded by Hempstead, Grimes, E. Richmond, and Main Sts., Giddings, 5/30/75, C, 75001998

Schubert House, 183 Hempstead St., Giddings, 8/25/70, B, C, 70000753

Leon County

Leon County Courthouse and Jails, Public Sq., Centerville, 12/12/77, C, 77001458

Liberty County

Black Cloud, Address Restricted, Liberty vicinity, 10/22/92, A, D, 92001401

Cleveland-Partlow House, 2131 Grand Ave., Liberty, 2/16/84, C, 84001907

Site 41 Lb 4, Address Restricted, Dayton vicinity, 7/14/71, D, 71000947

Limestone County

Booker T. Washington Emancipation Proclamation Park, W side of Lake Mexia, 9 mi. W of Mexia, Mexia vicinity, 5/24/76, A, f, 76002046

Johnston, Joseph E., Confederate Reunion Grounds, 4 mi. W of Mexia on SR 1633, Mexia vicinity, 4/02/76, A, C, 76002048

Texas Hall, Old Trinity University, College and Westminister Sts., Tehuacana, 7/12/78, A, C, 78002971

Vinson Site, Address Restricted, Tehuacana vicinity, 1/17/91, D, 90001530

Live Oak County

Fort Merrill, Address Restricted, Dinero vicinity, 11/22/91, A, D, 91001686

Pagan Site, 41 LK 58, Address Restricted, Calliham vicinity, 8/10/78, D, 78002972

Llano County

Badu Building, 601 Bessemer Ave., Llano, 6/06/80, A, B, 80004139

Llano County Courthouse Historic District, Roughly bounded by the Llano River, Ford St., Sandstone St., and Berry St., Llano, 2/10/89, A, C, f, g, 88002542

Llano County Courthouse and Jail, Public Sq., Oatman and Haynie Sts., Llano, 12/02/77, A, C, a, 77001459

Southern Hotel, 201 W. Main St, Llano, 10/10/79, A, 79002992

Lubbock County

Bacon, Warren and Myrta, House, 1802 Broadway, Lubbock, 7/15/82, C, a, 82004512

Canyon Lakes Archeological District, Address Restricted, Lubbock vicinity, 3/26/76, D, 76002049

Fort Worth and Denver South Plains Railway Depot, 1801 Ave. G, Lubbock, 7/26/90, A, C, 90001120

Kress Building, 1109 Broadway, Lubbock, 10/02/92, C, 92001305

Lubbock High School, 2004 19th St., Lubbock, 5/01/85, A, C, 85000924

Lubbock Lake Site, Address Restricted, Lubbock vicinity, 6/21/71, D, NHL, 71000948

Snyder, Fred and Annie, House, 2701 19th St., Lubbock, 1/28/92, C, 91002019

Texas Technological College Dairy Barn, Texas Tech University campus, Lubbock, 4/02/92, A, C, 92000336

Tubbs—Carlisle House, 602 Fulton Ave., Lubbock, 11/02/90, C, 90001719

Lynn County

Lynn County Courthouse, Public Sq., Tahoka, 7/08/82, A, C, 82004513

Madison County

Shapira Hotel, 209 N. Madison St., Madisonville, 9/08/80, A, C, 80004140

Marion County

Alley-Carlson House, 501 Walker St., Jefferson, 10/28/69, C, 69000206

Beard House, 212 N. Vale St., Jefferson, 8/25/70, C, 70000754

Epperson-McNutt House, 409 S. Alley St., Jefferson, 10/28/69, B, C, 69000207

Excelsior Hotel, Austin St., between Market and Vale Sts., Jefferson, 10/28/69, A, 69000208

Freeman Plantation House, 0.8 mi. W of Jefferson on TX 49, Jefferson vicinity, 11/25/69, C, 69000209

Jefferson Historic District, Roughly bounded by Owens, Dixon, Walnut, Camp, and Taylor Sts., Jefferson, 3/31/71, A, C, 71000949

Jefferson Playhouse, NW corner of Market and Henderson Sts., Jefferson, 10/28/69, C, a, 69000374

Magnolias, The, 209 E. Broadway, Jefferson, 3/31/71, A, C, 71000951

Old U.S. Post Office and Courts Building, 223 Austin St., Jefferson, 10/28/69, C, 69000210

Perry, Capt. William, House, NW corner of Walnut and Clarksville Sts., Jefferson, 8/25/70, A, C, 70000755

Planters Bank Building, 224 E. Austin St., Jefferson, 3/11/71, A, C, 71000952

Presbyterian Manse, NE corner of Alley and Delta Sts., Jefferson, 10/28/69, C, a, 69000211

Sedberry House, 211 N. Market St., Jefferson, 8/25/70, C, 70000756

Singleton, Capt. William E., House, 204 N. Soda St., Jefferson, 8/25/70, C, 70000757

Woods, Perry M., House, 502 Walker St., Jefferson, 3/31/71, C, 71000953

Mason County

Hasse, Heinrich and Fredericka, House, TX 29, W of Art, Art vicinity, 3/14/90, C, 90000336

Mason Historic District, Irregular pattern along both sides of U.S. 87 and TX 29, Mason, 9/17/74, A, C, 74002086

Mason Historic District (Boundary Increase), Roughly, Post Hill Rd. from College Ave. to Spruce St., Mason, 10/16/91, A, C, 91001526

Reynolds-Seaquist House, 400 Broad St., Mason, 11/20/74, C, 74002087

Matagorda County

Hotel Blessing, Ave. B, Blessing, 2/01/79, C, 79002993

Maverick County

Fort Duncan, Bounded by Monroe and Garrison Sts., . city limits on the S, and the Rio Grande on the W, Eagle Pass, 12/09/71, A, 71000954

Maverick County Courthouse, Public Sq., Eagle Pass, 2/15/80, A, C, 80004141

McCulloch County

McCulloch County Courthouse, Public Sq., Brady, 12/16/77, C, 77001515
Old McCulloch County Jail, 117 N. High St., Brady, 4/03/75, C, 75002073

McLennan County

Artesian Manufacturing and Bottling Company Building, 300 S. 5th St., Waco, 5/26/83, A, C, 83003152
Brown—Mann House, 725 W. Sixth St., McGregor, 10/22/87, C, 87001887
Cooper, Madison, House, 1801 Austin Ave., Waco, 7/08/82, A, B, C, 82004514
Earle-Napier-Kinnard House, 814 S. 4th St., Waco, 3/11/71, C, 71001017
Fort House, 503 E. 4th St., Waco, 10/15/70, C, 70000849
Hippodrome, 724 Austin Ave., Waco, 4/28/83, B, C, 83003153
Mann, John Wesley, House, 100 Mill St., Waco, 4/19/72, C, 72001466
McClennan County Courthouse, Public Sq., Waco, 12/14/78, A, C, 78003095
McCulloch House, 406 Columbus Ave., Waco, 9/14/72, C, 72001467
Praetorian Building, 601 Franklin Ave., Waco, 7/26/84, A, C, 84001911
Rotan-Dossett House, 1503 Columbus Ave., Waco, 1/29/79, A, C, 79003151
Torrey's Trading House No. 2 Site, Address Restricted, Waco vicinity, 6/05/75, A, D, 75002074
Waco Suspension Bridge, At Bridge St., over the Brazos River, Waco, 6/22/70, A, C, 70000850

McMullen County

Mustang Branch Site, Address Restricted, Calliham vicinity, 8/10/78, D, 78003096

Medina County

Castroville Historic District, Roughly bounded by Medina River, SR 471, Gime, Houston, and Constantinople, Castroville, 4/03/70, C, a, 70000758
D'Hanis Historic District, 7 mi. W of Hondo, D'Hanis, 6/24/76, A, C, a, 76002051
Devine Opera House, Transportation Blvd., Devine, 4/24/75, A, 75001999
Landmark Inn Complex, Florella and Florence Sts., Castroville, 1/07/72, C, 72001368
Medina Dam, N of Castroville on the Medina River, Castroville vicinity, 3/15/76, A, C, 76002050
Saathoff House, Quihi-Stormhill Rd., Quihi, 9/09/82, A, C, 82004515
de Montel, Charles, House, NW of Castroville, Castroville vicinity, 11/25/80, A, C, 80004142

Menard County

Fort McKavett Historic District, S bank of the San Saba River, Fort McKavett, 7/14/71, A, 71000955
Site of Presidio San Luis de las Amarillas, Address Restricted, Menard vicinity, 8/25/72, A, D, 72001369

Midland County

Brown-Dorsey House, 213 N. Weatherford, Midland, 6/17/82, A, C, 82004516
Turner, Fred and Juliette, House, 1705 W. Missouri, Midland, 8/15/88, A, B, 88001148

Milam County

Cass, Dr. Nathan and Lula, House, 502 N. Travis Ave., Cameron, 2/08/91, C, 91000037
Milam County Courthouse and Jail, Public Sq. and S. Fannin and E. 1st St., Cameron, 12/20/77, A, C, 77001460
San Xavier Mission Complex Archeological District, Address Restricted, Rockdale vicinity, 7/27/73, D, 73001969

Mills County

Mills County Jailhouse, Fisher and 5th Sts., Goldthwaite, 5/08/79, A, C, 79002994
Regency Suspension Bridge, 0.75 mi. S of Regency at Colorado River, Regency vicinity, 12/12/76, C, g, 76002052

Mitchell County

Scott-Majors House, 425 Chestnut St., Colorado City, 2/05/79, B, C, 79002995

Montague County

Spanish Fort Site, Address Restricted, Spanish Fort vicinity, 4/14/75, A, D, 75002000

Montgomery County

Arnold-Simonton House, Rankin St., Montgomery, 12/11/79, B, C, b, 79002996
Kirbee Kiln Site, Address Restricted, Montgomery vicinity, 8/28/73, D, 73001970

Morris County

Old Morris County Courthouse, 101 Linda Dr., Daingerfield, 12/11/79, A, C, 79002997

Motley County

Traweek House, 927 Lariat St., Matador, 5/02/91, B, C, 91000486

Nacogdoches County

Barret, Tol, House, S of Nacogdoches, Nacogdoches vicinity, 7/27/79, B, C, b, 79002998
Blount, Eugene H., House [Nacogdoches MPS], 1801 North St., Nacogdoches, 2/14/92, C, 92000014
Blount, Stephen William and Mary Price, House, 310 N. Mound St., Nacogdoches, 1/30/91, B, C, 90002180
Cotton Exchange Building, Old [Nacogdoches MPS], 305 E. Commerce St., Nacogdoches, 2/14/92, C, 92000008
Davidson, Maria A., Apartments [Nacogdoches MPS], 214 S. Fredonia St., Nacogdoches, 2/14/92, C, 92000009
Hayter Office Building [Nacogdoches MPS], 112 E. Main St., Nacogdoches, 2/14/92, C, 92000010
Hoya Land Office Building [Nacogdoches MPS], 120 E. Pilar St., Nacogdoches, 2/14/92, B, C, 92000015
Jones, Roland, House [Nacogdoches MPS], 141 N. Church St., Nacogdoches, 2/14/92, C, 92000007
Oil Springs Oil Field Discovery Well, 4 mi. SE of Woden, Woden vicinity, 11/23/77, A, C, 77001461
Old Nacogdoches University Building, Washington Sq., Nacogdoches, 6/21/71, A, C, 71000956
Post Office Building, Old [Nacogdoches MPS], 206 E. Main St., Nacogdoches, 2/14/92, C, 92000011
Roberts Building [Nacogdoches MPS], 216 E. Pilar St., Nacogdoches, 2/14/92, C, 92000016
Southern Pacific Railroad Depot [Nacogdoches MPS], 500 W. Main St., Nacogdoches, 2/14/92, A, C, 92000013
Sterne, Adolphus, House, 211 S. Lanana St., Nacogdoches, 11/13/76, B, D, 76002053
Sterne—Hoya Historic District [Nacogdoches MPS], 100–200 blocks of S. Lanana St., 500 block of E. Main St. (S side), 500 block of E. Pilar St., Nacogdoches, 2/14/92, C, 92000017
Virginia Avenue Historic District [Nacogdoches MPS], 500 block of Bremond (W side), 500–1800 blocks of Virginia Ave., 521 Weaver, Nacogdoches, 2/14/92, C, 92000018
Washington Square Historic District [Nacogdoches MPS], Roughly bounded by Houston, Logansport, N. Lanana, E. Hospital and N. Fredonia Sts., Nacogdoches, 2/14/92, C, 92000019
Woodmen of the World Building [Nacogdoches MPS], 412 E. Main St., Nacogdoches, 2/14/92, C, 92000012
Zion Hill Historic District [Nacogdoches MPS], Roughly bounded by Park St., Lanana Cr., Oak Grove Cemetery and N. Lanana St., Nacogdoches, 1/07/93, A, C, 92001759

Navarro County

Corsicana Oil Field Discovery Well, 400 block S. 12th St., Corsicana, 8/22/77, A, C, 77001462

Temple Beth-El, 208 S. Fifteenth St., Corsicana, 2/03/87, C, a, 86003687

Newton County

Newton County Courthouse, Off TX 190, Newton, 7/19/79, A, C, 79002999

West Log House, NE of Salem, Salem vicinity, 12/13/79, C, 79003000

Nolan County

First National Bank Building, 101 E. 3rd St., Sweetwater, 5/26/83, A, C, 83003154

Ragland, R. A., Building, 113–117 3rd St., Sweetwater, 5/14/79, A, B, 79003001

Sweetwater Commercial Historic District, Roughly between 1st and 5th, and Ash and Texas and Pacific RR tracks, Sweetwater, 6/07/84, A, C, g, 84001915

Nueces County

Britton-Evans House, 411 N. Broadway, Corpus Christi, 12/12/76, B, C, 76002054

Broadway Bluff Improvement, Roughly bounded by Upper and Lower Broadway, I-37, Mann and Mesquite Sts., Corpus Christi, 10/11/88, A, C, 88001829

Gugenheim, Simon, House, 1601 N. Chaparral St., Corpus Christi, 3/10/83, B, C, b, 83003155

King, Richard, House, 611 S. Upper Broadway, Corpus Christi, 3/17/93, C, 93000129

Lichtenstein, S. Julius, House, 1617 N. Chaparral St., Corpus Christi, 3/10/83, C, b, 83003156

Nueces County Courthouse, Mesquite and Belden Sts., Corpus Christi, 6/24/76, C, 76002055

Old St. Anthony's Catholic Church, S. Violet Rd. and TX 44, Violet, 9/07/79, C, a, b, 79003003

Oso Dune Site (41NU37), Address Restricted, Corpus Christi vicinity, 8/23/85, D, 85001799

Sidbury, Charlotte, House, 1609 N. Chaparral St., Corpus Christi, 3/10/83, B, C, b, 83003157

Tarpon Inn, 200 E. Cotter St, Port Aransas, 9/14/79, A, C, 79003002

Tucker Site (41NU46), Address Restricted, Corpus Christi vicinity, 8/29/85, D, 85001940

Ochiltree County

Buried City Site (41OC1), Address Restricted, Perryton vicinity, 9/13/84, D, 84001923

Plainview Hardware Company Building, 210 S. Main St., Perryton, 6/14/90, A, C, 90000904

Oldham County

Chavez City Ruins (41OL253) [New Mexican Pastor Sites in Texas Panhandle TR], Address Restricted, Amarillo vicinity, 7/12/84, A, D, 84001925

Chavez Suburbs East and West (41OL254) [New Mexican Pastor Sites in Texas Panhandle TR], Address Restricted, Amarillo vicinity, 7/12/84, A, D, 84001928

Green No. 5 (41OL257) [New Mexican Pastor Sites in Texas Panhandle TR], Address Restricted, Amarillo vicinity, 7/12/84, D, 84001936

Griffin Site (41OL246) [New Mexican Pastor Sites in Texas Panhandle TR], Address Restricted, Amarillo vicinity, 7/12/84, A, D, 84001938

Landergin Mesa, Address Restricted, Vega vicinity, 10/15/66, D, NHL, 66000821

Mansfield I (41OL50) [New Mexican Pastor Sites in Texas Panhandle TR], Address Restricted, Amarillo vicinity, 7/12/84, D, 84001940

Maston I (41OL256) [New Mexican Pastor Sites in Texas Panhandle TR], Address Restricted, Amarillo vicinity, 7/12/84, D, 84001942

Maston No. 13 Stone Wall (41OL249) [New Mexican Pastor Sites in Texas Panhandle TR], Address Restricted, Adrian vicinity, 9/10/84, D, 84001945

Maston No. 52 (41OL235) [New Mexican Pastor Sites in Texas Panhandle TR], Address Restricted, Amarillo vicinity, 7/12/84, A, D, 84001948

Rocky Dell, Address Restricted, Adrian vicinity, 2/23/72, D, 72001370

Stone Corrals No. 1-6 (41OL250) [New Mexican Pastor Sites in Texas Panhandle TR], Address Restricted, Amarillo vicinity, 7/12/84, A, D, 84001951

Orange County

Lutcher Memorial Church Building, 902 W. Green Ave., Orange, 9/09/82, B, C, a, 82004517

Sims House, 905 Division St., Orange, 3/26/80, A, B, C, b, 80004143

Stark, W. H., House, 611 W. Green Ave., Orange, 12/12/76, B, C, 76002056

Palo Pinto County

Baker Hotel, 200 E. Hubbard St., Mineral Wells, 6/23/82, A, C, 82004518

First Presbyterian Church, 410 NW 2nd St., Mineral Wells, 6/14/79, C, a, 79003004

Palo Pinto County Jail, Elm St. and 5th Ave, Palo Pinto, 9/26/79, C, 79003005

Weatherford-Mineral Wells and Northwestern Railroad Depot, S. Oak St., Mineral Wells, 1/05/84, A, C, 84001953

Panola County

International Boundary Marker, SE of Deadwood off SR 31 at LA State line, Deadwood vicinity, 4/13/77, A, 77001463

Methodist Church Concord, SE of Carthage off TX 59, Carthage vicinity, 9/08/80, A, C, a, 80004144

Panola County Jail, 110 N. Shelby St., Carthage, 6/29/76, C, 76002057

Parker County

Parker County Courthouse, Courthouse Sq., Weatherford, 6/21/71, C, 71000957

Weatherford Downtown Historic District [Weatherford MPS], Roughly bounded by Waco, Water, Walnut and Lee Sts., Weatherford, 11/23/90, A, C, a, 90001745

Pecos County

Canon Ranch Archeological District, Address Restricted, Sheffield vicinity, 8/11/82, D, 82004519

Canon Ranch Railroad Eclipse Windmill, W of Sheffield on Canon Ranch, Sheffield vicinity, 9/22/77, A, C, 77001465

Fort Stockton Historic District, E edge of town, Fort Stockton, 4/02/73, C, 73001971

Potter County

Alibates Flint Quarries National Monument, SW of Fritch on the Canadian River, Fritch vicinity, 10/15/66, A, D, NPS, 66000822

Amarillo College Administration Building and Gymnasium, 2201 S. Washington St. and 2221 S. Washington St., Amarillo, 1/28/92, A, C, 91002023

Atchison, Topeka and Santa Fe Railway Company Depot and Locomotive No. 5000, 307 S. Grant, Amarillo, 9/18/86, A, C, 86002189

Bivins House, 1000 Polk St., Amarillo, 12/31/74, A, B, C, 74002088

Bivins, Miles and Myda, House, 2311 W. 16th Ave., Amarillo, 10/02/92, C, 92001306

Central Presbyterian Church, 1100 Harrison St., Amarillo, 11/13/91, C, a, 91001649

Curtis, Alice Ghormley, House, 1626 S. Washington St., Amarillo, 8/14/92, C, 92000980

First Baptist Church [Churches with Decorative Interior Painting TR], 218 W. 13th St., Amarillo, 6/21/83, A, C, a, 83003158

Jons—Gilvin House, 1500 S. Buchanan St., Amarillo, 8/14/92, C, 92000983

Kouns—Jackson House, 1118 S. Harrison St., Amarillo, 8/14/92, C, 92000981

Landergin-Harrington House, 1600 Polk St., Amarillo, 12/16/77, B, C, 77001466

McBride Canyon Ruin, Address Restricted, Fritch vicinity, 7/05/85, D, NPS, 85001483

Potter County—Continued

McBride Ranch House, N of Amarillo in Lake Meredith Recreation Area, Amarillo vicinity, 4/23/75, A, NPS, 75000152

Plemons—Mrs. M. D. Oliver-Eakle Additions Historic District, Roughly bounded by 16th Ave., Taylor St., 26th Ave., Van Buren St., I-40 and Madison St., Amarillo, 4/21/92, A, C, 92000370

Polk Street Methodist Church, 1401 S. Polk St., Amarillo, 1/28/92, C, a, 91002021

Sanborn, Henry B. and Ellen M., House, 1311 S. Madison St., Amarillo, 8/14/92, B, C, b, 92000982

Shelton-Houghton House, 1700 Polk St., Amarillo, 8/29/80, C, 80004145

Wolflin Historic District, Roughly bounded by Wolflin Ave., Washington St., SW. 34th Ave., Parker St., SW. 30th Ave. and Lipscomb St., Amarillo, 5/21/92, A, C, 92000581

Presidio County

El Paisano Hotel, N. Highland and W. Texas Sts., Marfa, 8/01/78, A, C, 78002973

Fort Leaton, 4 mi. E of Presidio on FM 170, Presidio vicinity, 6/18/73, A, B, D, NHL, 73001972

Fortin de la Cienega, 15 mi. NE of Shafter on Cienega Creek, Shafter vicinity, 10/08/76, C, D, 76002059

La Junta de los Rios Archeological District, Address Restricted, Presidio vicinity, 2/14/78, D, 78002974

Presidio County Courthouse, Public Sq., Marfa, 12/20/77, A, C, 77001467

Shafter Historic Mining District, 20 mi. N of Presidio on U.S. 67, Shafter, 5/17/76, A, 76002058

Tapalcomes, Address Restricted, Redford vicinity, 3/25/77, D, 77001468

Rains County

Gilbert Site, Address Restricted, Emory vicinity, 4/13/77, D, 77001469

Koons Site, Address Restricted, Emory vicinity, 4/13/77, D, 77001470

Yandell Site, Address Restricted, Emory vicinity, 4/13/77, D, 77001471

Randall County

Lester, L. T., House, 310 8th St., Canyon, 9/13/78, B, C, 78002975

Llano Cemetery Historic District, 2900 South Hayes, Amarillo, 5/21/92, A, C, d, 92000584

St. Mary's Catholic Church [Churches with Decorative Interior Painting TR], Off U.S. 60, Umbarger, 6/21/83, A, C, a, 83003159

Reagan County

Old Reagan County Courthouse, Off TX 137, Stiles, 5/05/78, A, C, 78002976

Real County

Mission San Lorenzo de la Santa Cruz, Address Restricted, Camp Wood vicinity, 7/14/71, D, a, 71000958

Red River County

Kaufman, Sam, Site, Address Restricted, Blakeney vicinity, 8/14/73, D, 73001973

Kiomatia Mounds Archeological District, Address Restricted, Kiomatia vicinity, 1/11/74, D, 74002089

McCarty Site, Address Restricted, Pin Hook vicinity, 12/01/78, D, 78003377

Neely Site 41 RR 48, Address Restricted, Manchester vicinity, 8/20/82, D, 82004520

Red River County Courthouse, Public Sq., Clarksville, 8/31/78, A, C, 78002977

Smathers-Demorse House, E. Comanche St., Clarksville, 5/17/76, B, C, 76002060

Refugio County

Wood, John Howland, House, 1 Copano Bay St., Bayside, 10/13/83, C, 83003811

Robertson County

Allen, Robert C., House, 402 Cedar St., Hearne, 8/11/82, C, 82004521

Calvert Historic District, Roughly bounded by Main, Garritt, Pin Oak, Maple, and Barton Sts., Calvert, 4/03/78, C, d, 78002978

Hammond House, Bounded by Burnet, China, Elm, and Hanna Sts., Calvert, 10/28/70, C, 70000759

Robertson County Courthouse and Jail, Public Sq., Franklin, 12/22/77, C, 77001472

Runnels County

Ballinger Carnegie Library, 204 N. 8th St., Ballinger, 6/18/75, A, 75002002

Day, Edwin and Hattie, House, 302 N. Broadway, Ballinger, 1/03/85, C, 85000047

Thiele, J., Building, Robinson and 2nd Sts., Miles, 6/29/76, A, 76002061

Van Pelt House, 209 10th St., Ballinger, 12/03/80, C, 80004146

Rusk County

Harmony Hill Site, Address Restricted, Tatum vicinity, 5/13/76, D, 76002062

Hudnall—Pirtle Site, Address Restricted, Easton vicinity, 9/11/91, D, 91001159

Musgano Site, Address Restricted, Tatum vicinity, 6/24/76, D, 76002063

Sabine County

Oliphant House, 7 mi. E of Milam off TX 21, Milam vicinity, 8/18/77, A, C, 77001473

San Augustine County

Blount, Capt. Thomas William, House, 2.5 mi. W of San Augustine on TX 21, San Augustine vicinity, 3/07/73, B, C, 73001974

Cartwright, Matthew, House, 912 E. Main St., San Augustine, 1/25/71, C, 71000959

Cullen, Ezekiel, House, 207 S. Congress St., San Augustine, 6/21/71, B, C, e, 71000960

Garrett, William, Plantation House, 1 mi. W of San Augustine on TX 21, San Augustine vicinity, 3/25/77, C, d, 77001474

Horn-Polk House, 717 W. Columbia St., San Augustine, 11/07/76, B, C, 76002064

Mission Nuestra Senora de los Dolores de los Ais Site, Address Restricted, San Augustine vicinity, 12/16/77, D, a, 77001475

San Jacinto County

San Jacinto County Jail, Slade and Loyd St., Coldspring, 7/15/80, A, C, 80004148

San Patricio County

McGloin, James, Homestead, 1 mi. NW of San Patricio on FM 666, San Patricio vicinity, 7/14/71, A, C, e, 71000961

McGloin, James, Homestead (Boundary Increase), NW of San Patricio off TX 666, San Patricio vicinity, 11/15/79, A, C, 79003678

Schleicher County

Mittel Site, Address Restricted, Eldorado vicinity, 1/04/90, D, 89002278

Shackelford County

Fort Griffin, 15 mi. N of Albany on U.S. 283, Albany vicinity, 3/11/71, A, 71000962

Shackelford County—Continued

Fort Griffin Brazos River Bridge, NE of Fort Griffin, Fort Griffin vicinity, 10/16/79, A, 79003006

Shackelford County Courthouse Historic District, Roughly bounded by S. 1st, S. 4th, S. Jacobs, and S. Pecan Sts., Albany, 7/30/76, A, C, 76002065

Shelby County

Shelby County Courthouse, Courthouse Sq., Center, 3/31/71, C, 71001074

Shelby County Courthouse Square (Boundary Increase), Courthouse Sq., Center, 11/29/90, A, C, 90001819

Smith County

Carnegie Public Library, 125 S. College St., Tyler, 3/26/79, A, 79003007

Dewberry, Col. John, House, 1 mi. N of Teaselville on FM 346, Teaselville vicinity, 5/06/71, C, 71000963

Goodman-LeGrand House, 624 N. Broadway, Tyler, 11/07/76, B, C, 76002066

Ramey House, 605 S. Broadway, Tyler, 10/29/82, C, 82001738

Tyler Hydraulic-Fill Dam, W of Tyler off TX 31, Tyler vicinity, 8/29/77, C, 77001543

Whitaker-McClendon House, 806 W. Houston St., Tyler, 6/02/82, C, 82004522

Somervell County

Barnard's Mill, 307 SW Barnard St., Glen Rose, 9/09/82, A, C, 82004523

Somervell County Courthouse, Off TX 144, Glen Rose, 8/01/79, A, C, 79003008

Starr County

Fort Ringgold Historic District, Rio Grande City School grounds, 1/4 mi. SE of jct. of US 83 and TX 755, Rio Grande City, 3/26/93, A, C, 93000196

LaBorde House, Store and Hotel, 601 E. Main St., Rio Grande City, 5/29/80, C, 80004149

Roma Historic District, Properties along Estrella and Hidalgo Sts. between Garfield St. and Bravo Alley, Roma, 7/31/72, A, C, a, NHL, 72001371

Roma-San Pedro International Bridge, SW of Hidalgo St. and Bravo Alley, Roma-Los Saenz, 3/23/84, A, C, 84001959

de la Pena, Silverio, Drugstore and Post Office, 423 E. Main St., Rio Grande City, 9/02/80, C, 80004150

Stephens County

Fort Davis Family Fort, Address Restricted, Breckenridge vicinity, 10/28/92, A, D, 92001363

Sutton County

Old Mercantile Building, 222 Main St., Sonora, 1/30/78, C, 78002979

Sutton County Courthouse, Public Sq., Sonora, 7/15/77, C, 77001476

Tarrant County

Allen Chapel AME Church, 116 Elm St., Fort Worth, 10/18/84, C, a, 84000169

Anderson, Neil P., Building, 411 W. 7th St., Fort Worth, 3/08/78, A, C, 78002981

Austin, Stephen F., Elementary School, 319 Lipscomb St., Fort Worth, 3/10/83, A, C, 83003160

Benton, M. A., House, 1730 6th Ave., Fort Worth, 5/22/78, B, C, 78002982

Blackstone Hotel, 601 Main St., Fort Worth, 2/02/84, A, C, 84001961

Bryce Building, 909 Throckmorton St., Fort Worth, 2/23/84, B, C, 84001963

Bryce, William J., House, 4900 Bryce Ave., Fort Worth, 3/01/84, C, 84001965

Buck Oaks Farm, 6312 White Settlement Rd., Westworth, 7/06/87, A, B, C, 87000995

Burnett, Burk, Building, 500–502 Main St., Fort Worth, 11/12/80, A, C, 80004151

Eddleman-McFarland House, 1110 Penn St., Fort Worth, 10/18/79, A, C, 79003009

Elizabeth Boulevard Historic District, 1001–1616 Elizabeth Blvd., Fort Worth, 11/16/79, A, C, 79003010

Fairmount—Southside Historic District, Roughly bounded by Magnolia, Hemphill, Eighth, and Jessamine, Fort Worth, 4/05/90, A, C, 90000490

First Christian Church, 612 Throckorton St., Fort Worth, 10/06/83, A, C, a, 83003812

Flatiron Building, 1000 Houston St., Fort Worth, 3/31/71, B, C, 71000964

Fort Worth Elks Lodge 124, 512 W. 4th St., Fort Worth, 2/16/84, C, 84001969

Fort Worth Public Market, 1400 Henderson St., Fort Worth, 1/05/84, A, C, 84001981

Fort Worth Stockyards Historic District, Roughly bounded by 23rd, Houston, and 28th Sts., and railroad, Fort Worth, 6/29/76, A, C, 76002067

Grand Avenue Historic District, Roughly Grand Ave. from Northside to Park, Fort Worth, 3/01/90, A, C, 90000337

Grapevine Commercial Historic District, 404–432 S. Main St., Grapevine, 3/09/92, A, C, 92000097

Gulf, Colorado and Sante Fe Railroad Passenger Station, 1601 Jones St., Fort Worth, 10/15/70, A, C, 70000760

Hotel Texas, 815 Main St., Fort Worth, 7/03/79, A, C, 79003011

Hutcheson-Smith House, 312 N. Oak St., Arlington, 8/02/84, C, 84001993

Johnson-Elliott House, 3 Chase Ct., Fort Worth, 5/10/84, C, 84001996

Knights of Pythias Building, 315 Main St., Fort Worth, 4/28/70, A, C, 70000761

Marrow Bone Spring Archeological Site, Address Restricted, Arlington vicinity, 11/21/78, D, 78002980

Masonic Widows and Orphans Home Historic District, Roughly bounded by E. Berry St., Mitchell Blvd., Vaughn St., Wichita St. and Glen Garden Dr., Fort Worth, 1/28/92, A, C, 91002022

Paddock Viaduct, Main St., Fort Worth, 3/15/76, A, C, 76002068

Pollock-Capps House, 1120 Penn St., Fort Worth, 6/19/72, C, 72001372

Rogers-O'Daniel House, 2230 Warner Rd., Fort Worth, 7/05/85, B, 85001484

Sanguinet, Marshall R., House, 4729 Collinwood Ave., Fort Worth, 6/07/83, C, 83003162

Sinclair Building, 512 Main St., Fort Worth, 1/07/92, C, 91001913

South Side Masonic Lodge No. 1114, 1301 W. Magnolia, Fort Worth, 1/03/85, C, 85000048

St. Mary of the Assumption Church, 501 W. Magnolia Ave., Fort Worth, 5/10/84, A, C, a, 84001998

St. Patrick Cathedral Complex, 1206 Throckmorton, Fort Worth, 1/07/85, A, C, a, 85000074

Tarrant County Courthouse, Bounded by Houston, Belknap, Weatherford, and Commerce Sts., Fort Worth, 10/15/70, A, C, 70000762

Texas & Pacific Steam Locomotive No. 610, Felix and Hemphill Sts., Fort Worth, 3/25/77, A, C, 77001477

Texas and Pacific Terminal Complex, Lancaster and Throckmorton Sts., Fort Worth, 5/26/78, A, C, 78002983

US Post Office, Lancaster and Jennings Ave., Fort Worth, 4/15/85, C, 85000855

Waggoner, W. T. Building, 810 Houston St., Fort Worth, 7/10/79, A, C, 79003012

Westover Manor, 8 Westover Rd., Westover Hills, 12/15/88, A, B, C, 88002709

Wharton-Scott House, 1509 Pennsylvania Ave., Fort Worth, 4/14/75, C, 75002003

Taylor County

1915 Taylor County Courthouse [Abilene MPS], 301 Oak St., Abilene, 3/23/92, A, C, 92000225

Abilene Christian College Administration Building [Abilene MPS], Campus Court Dr., Abilene Christian University, Abilene, 3/23/92, A, C, 92000193

Abilene Commercial Historic District [Abilene MPS], Roughly bounded by Hickory, N. Third and Pine Sts. and the S side of the Missouri Pacific RR tracks, Abilene, 12/18/91, A, C, 91001811

Abilene Fire Station No. 2 [Abilene MPS], 441 Butternut, Abilene, 3/23/92, C, 92000200

Taylor County—Continued

Abilene Street Railway Company Barn [Abilene MPS], 1037 Clinton St., Abilene, 3/23/92, A, 92000205

Ackers, William and Mary, House [Abilene MPS], 802 Mulberry St., Abilene, 3/23/92, C, 92000214

Blanton, Thomas L., House [Abilene MPS], 3425 S. Seventh St., Abilene, 3/23/92, B, 92000234

Boyd—Hall House [Abilene MPS], 502 Poplar St., Abilene, 3/23/92, C, 92000229

Caldwell Hall [Abilene MPS], Intracampus Dr., Hardin—Simmons University, Abilene, 3/23/92, A, C, 92000206

Cash, W. A. V., House [Abilene MPS], 1302 Amarillo, Abilene, 3/23/92, C, 92000195

Castle, David S., House [Abilene MPS], 1742 N. Second St., Abilene, 3/23/92, B, C, 92000218

Chambers, Samuel A., House [Abilene MPS], 224 Merchant, Abilene, 3/23/92, C, 92000211

Davis, George R., House [Abilene MPS], 718 Victoria, Abilene, 3/23/92, C, 92000237

Dillingham, O. D. and Ada, House [Abilene MPS], 1625 Belmont, Abilene, 3/23/92, C, 92000199

Dodd—Harkrider House [Abilene MPS], 2026 N. Third St., Abilene, 3/23/92, B, 92000222

Evans, J. W., House [Abilene MPS], 258 Clinton St., Abilene, 3/23/92, C, 92000204

Federal Building [Abilene MPS], 341 Pine, Abilene, 7/20/92, C, 92000228

Finley, Eugene L., House [Abilene MPS], 208 Merchant, Abilene, 3/23/92, C, 92000210

First Presbyterian Church [Abilene MPS], 402 Orange St., Abilene, 3/23/92, C, 92000226

Fritz, David C. and Docia, House [Abilene MPS], 1325 N. Eighteenth St., Abilene, 3/23/92, C, 92000215

Goodloe, Albert S. and Ruth, House [Abilene MPS], 1302 Sayles Blvd., Abilene, 3/23/92, C, 92000232

Green, Roland A. D., House [Abilene MPS], 1358 Highland St., Abilene, 3/23/92, B, 92000207

Higginbotham, J. G., House [Abilene MPS], 2102 Swenson, Abilene, 3/23/92, C, 92000236

Hilton Hotel, 986 N. Fourth St., Abilene, 12/23/93, A, C, 85003658

House at 1127 Ash Street [Abilene MPS], 1127 Ash St., Abilene, 3/23/92, C, 92000196

Hughes, Ed S., Company Warehouse [Abilene MPS], 135 Oak St., Abilene, 3/23/92, A, B, C, 92000224

Jones, A. T., House [Abilene MPS], 418 Merchant, Abilene, 3/23/92, C, 92000212

Lanius, C. A., House [Abilene MPS], 1942 N. Third St., Abilene, 3/23/92, C, 92000221

Luce Hall [Abilene MPS], Campus Court Dr., N of Administration Building, Abilene Christian University, Abilene, 3/23/92, C, 92000194

Magee, J. D., House [Abilene MPS], 1910 N. Third St., Abilene, 3/23/92, C, 92000220

McDaniel, George W. and Lavina, House [Abilene MPS], 774 Butternut, Abilene, 3/23/92, C, 92000201

McDonald Hall [Abilene MPS], 2083 N. Second St., Abilene, 3/23/92, A, 92000219

McMurry College Administration Building [Abilene MPS], Off Hunt, McMurry College, Abilene, 3/23/92, A, 92000209

Minter, William A., House [Abilene MPS], 340 Beech St., Abilene, 3/23/92, B, 92000198

Motz, Charles, House [Abilene MPS], 1842 N. Fifth St., Abilene, 3/23/92, C, 92000216

Old Taylor County Courthouse and Jail, William St. between North and Elm Sts., Buffalo Gap, 6/09/78, A, 78002984

Paramount Theater, 352 Cypress St., Abilene, 12/27/82, C, 82001739

Parramore Historic District, Bounded by Orange, N. 8th, alley between Grape and Mulberry, and N. 7th Sts., Abilene, 8/29/91, C, 91001153

Parramore, D. D., House [Abilene MPS], 542 Poplar St., Abilene, 3/23/92, C, 92000230

Radford, James M., Grocery Company Warehouse [Abilene MPS], 101 Oak St., Abilene, 3/23/92, A, B, 92000223

Reading, Jhules, House [Abilene MPS], 421 Reading St., Abilene, 3/23/92, C, 92000231

Roberts, Nathan J. and Nancy, House [Abilene MPS], 1430 S. Sixth St., Abilene, 3/23/92, C, 92000235

Sacred Heart Catholic Church [Abilene MPS], 1633 S. Eighth St., Abilene, 3/23/92, C, 92000233

Sayles Boulevard Historic District [Abilene MPS], Roughly bounded by S. Fifth, Meander and S. Tenth Sts. and Highland Ave., Abilene, 3/09/92, A, C, 92000095

Sayles, Henry, House, 642 Sayles Blvd., Abilene, 6/24/76, A, B, C, 76002069

State Epileptic Colony Historic District, Roughly bounded by S. 24th, Lakeside and Plum, also area roughly bounded by SH 322, FM 1750 and Industrial Blvd., Abilene, 10/30/91, A, C, 91001539

Stith, William and Evla, House [Abilene MPS], 346 Mulberry St., Abilene, 3/23/92, C, 92000213

Swenson, William and Shirley, House, 1726 Swenson Ave., Abilene, 12/22/87, B, C, 87002148

Thomas, Oscar P., House [Abilene MPS], 210 Clinton St., Abilene, 3/23/92, C, 92000203

U.S. Weather Bureau Building, 1482 N. 1st St., Abilene, 7/08/82, A, C, 82004524

Universal Manufacturing Company Building [Abilene MPS], 150 Locust St., Abilene, 3/23/92, A, C, 92000208

West Texas Utilities Company Power Plant [Abilene MPS], 100 Block of N. Second St., Abilene, 3/23/92, A, 92000217

Williamson, E. D., House [Abilene MPS], 641 Chestnut St., Abilene, 3/23/92, C, 92000202

Wooten, Horace O., Grocery Company Warehouse [Abilene MPS], 101 Walnut, Abilene, 3/23/92, A, B, C, 92000238

Wooten, Horace O., House [Abilene MPS], 242 Beech St., Abilene, 3/23/92, B, 92000197

Zabloudil—Hendrick House [Abilene MPS], 802 Orange St., Abilene, 3/23/92, B, 92000227

Terrell County

Bullis' Camp Site, Address Restricted, Dryden vicinity, 8/02/78, A, D, 78002985

Geddis Canyon Rock Art Site, Address Restricted, Dryden vicinity, 5/22/78, A, D, 78002986

Meyers Springs Pictograph Site, Address Restricted, Dryden vicinity, 9/14/72, A, D, 72001373

Wroe Ranch Shelter No. 1, Address Restricted, Sheffield vicinity, 1/04/90, D, 89002279

Throckmorton County

Throckmorton County Courthouse and Jail, Public Sq. and Chestnut St., Throckmorton, 8/10/78, A, C, 78002987

Titus County

Hale Mound Site, Address Restricted, Winfield vicinity, 7/07/90, D, 90000983

Tom Green County

Angelo Heights Historic District [San Angelo MRA], Roughly bounded by Colorado St., the Concho River, Live Oak St., S. Bishop St., Twohig St., and S. Washington St., San Angelo, 11/25/88, C, 88002605

Aztec Cleaners and Laundry Building [San Angelo MRA], 119 S. Irving, San Angelo, 11/25/88, C, 88002577

Beck, Frederick, Farm [San Angelo MRA], 1231 Culberson, San Angelo, 11/25/88, C, 88002566

Blakeney, J. B., House [San Angelo MRA], 438 W. Twohig, San Angelo, 11/25/88, C, 88002600

Broome, C. A., House [San Angelo MRA], 123 S. David, San Angelo, 11/25/88, C, 88002567

Brown, R. Wilbur, House [San Angelo MRA], 1004 Pecos, San Angelo, 11/25/88, C, 88002585

Building at 113–119 East Concho [San Angelo MRA], 113–119 E. Concho, San Angelo, 9/13/90, C, 88002564

Clayton House [San Angelo MRA], 1101 S. David, San Angelo, 11/25/88, C, 88002570

Collyns House [San Angelo MRA], 315 W. Twohig, San Angelo, 11/25/88, C, 88002597

Develin House [San Angelo MRA], 913 S. David, San Angelo, 11/25/88, C, 88002568

Eckert House [San Angelo MRA], 503 Koberlin, San Angelo, 11/25/88, C, 88002578

Emmanuel Episcopal Church [San Angelo MRA], 3 S. Randolph, San Angelo, 11/25/88, C, a, 88002590

First Presbyterian Church [San Angelo MRA], 32 N. Irving, San Angelo, 11/25/88, C, a, 88002604

Fisher, O. C., Federal Building [San Angelo MRA], 33 E. Twohig, San Angelo, 11/25/88, C, 88002592

Fort Concho Historic District, S edge of San Angelo, San Angelo, 10/15/66, A, D, e, NHL, 66000823

Tom Green County—Continued

Greater St. Paul AME Church [San Angelo MRA], 215 W. 3rd St., San Angelo, 11/25/88, A, a, 88002548

Hagelstein Commercial Building [San Angelo MRA], 616–620 S. Chadbourne, San Angelo, 11/25/88, C, 88002560

Hall, R. A., House [San Angelo MRA], 215 W. Twohig, San Angelo, 11/25/88, C, 88002595

Henderson, S. L., House [San Angelo MRA], 1303 S. Park, San Angelo, 11/25/88, C, 88002583

Hilton Hotel, 36 E. Twohig St., San Angelo, 9/20/84, A, C, 84001999

Holcomb—Blanton Print Shop [San Angelo MRA], 24 W. Beauregard, San Angelo, 11/25/88, C, 88002554

House at 1017 South David [San Angelo MRA], 1017 S. David, San Angelo, 11/25/88, C, 88002569

House at 123 Allen [San Angelo MRA], 123 Allen, San Angelo, 11/25/88, C, 88002601

House at 1325 South David [San Angelo MRA], 1325 S. David, San Angelo, 11/25/88, C, 88002571

House at 140 Allen [San Angelo MRA], 140 Allen, San Angelo, 11/25/88, C, 88002550

House at 1621 North Chadbourne [San Angelo MRA], 1621 N. Chadbourne, San Angelo, 11/25/88, C, 88002559

House at 221 North Magdalen [San Angelo MRA], 221 N. Magdalen, San Angelo, 11/25/88, C, 88002579

House at 405 Preusser [San Angelo MRA], 405 Preusser, San Angelo, 11/25/88, C, 88002586

House at 410 Summit [San Angelo MRA], 410 Summit, San Angelo, 9/13/90, C, 88002591

House at 419 West Avenue C [San Angelo MRA], 419 West Ave. C, San Angelo, 11/25/88, C, 88002544

House at 421 West Twohig [San Angelo MRA], 421 W. Twohig, San Angelo, 11/25/88, C, 88002598

House at 427 West Twohig [San Angelo MRA], 427 W. Twohig, San Angelo, 9/13/90, C, 88002599

House at 521 West Highland Boulevard [San Angelo MRA], 521 W. Highland Blvd., San Angelo, 11/25/88, C, 88002575

House at 715 Austin [San Angelo MRA], 715 Austin, San Angelo, 11/25/88, C, 88002551

House at 731 Preusser [San Angelo MRA], 731 Preusser, San Angelo, 11/25/88, C, 88002589

Household Furniture Co. [San Angelo MRA], 11 N. Chadbourne, San Angelo, 11/25/88, C, 88002558

Iglesia Santa Maria [San Angelo MRA], 7 West Ave. N, San Angelo, 11/25/88, C, a, 88002547

Lone Wolf Crossing Bridge [San Angelo MRA], Ave. K extension, E of Oakes, San Angelo, 11/25/88, A, 88002546

Masonic Lodge 570 [San Angelo MRA], 130 S. Oakes, San Angelo, 11/25/88, C, 88002580

McClelland, J. T. and Minnie, House [San Angelo MRA], 715 W. Highland, San Angelo, 11/25/88, C, 88002576

Monogram Square [San Angelo MRA], 305 W. Concho, San Angelo, 11/25/88, C, 88002602

Montgomery Ward Building [San Angelo MRA], 10 W. Beauregard, San Angelo, 11/25/88, C, 88002553

Municipal Swimming Pool [San Angelo MRA], 18 East Ave. A, San Angelo, 11/25/88, A, C, 88002543

Murrah House [San Angelo MRA], 212 W. Twohig, San Angelo, 11/25/88, C, 88002594

Oakes Hotel Building [San Angelo MRA], 204 S. Oakes, San Angelo, 11/25/88, C, 88002581

Princess Ice Cream Co. [San Angelo MRA], 217 W. Beauregard, San Angelo, 11/25/88, C, 88002556

Rackley, J. J., Building, 118 S. Chadbourne, San Angelo, 6/30/83, A, C, 83003163

San Angelo City Hall [San Angelo MRA], City Hall Plaza, San Angelo, 11/25/88, C, 88002563

San Angelo National Bank Building, 201 S. Chadbourne St., San Angelo, 12/16/82, A, C, 82001740

San Angelo National Bank, Johnson and Taylor, and Schwartz and Raas Buildings, 20–22, 24, 26 E. Concho Ave., San Angelo, 4/07/78, A, C, 78002988

San Angelo Telephone Company Building [San Angelo MRA], 14 W. Twohig, San Angelo, 11/25/88, C, 88002593

Santa Fe Passenger Depot [San Angelo MRA], 700 S. Chadbourne, San Angelo, 11/27/89, A, C, 88002561

Santa Fe Railway Freight Depot [San Angelo MRA], 700 S. Chadbourne, San Angelo, 11/27/89, A, C, 88002562

Schneemann, William, House [San Angelo MRA], 724 Preusser St., San Angelo, 11/25/88, C, 88002588

Shepperson House [San Angelo MRA], 716 Preusser, San Angelo, 11/25/88, C, 88002587

Texas Highway Department Building, Warehouse and Motor Vehicle Division [San Angelo MRA], 100 Paint Rock Rd., San Angelo, 11/25/88, A, 88002582

Tom Green County Courthouse [San Angelo MRA], 100 W. Beauregard, San Angelo, 11/25/88, C, 88002555

Tom Green County Jail, US 67, San Angelo, 10/22/76, A, C, 76002246

Walsh, C. C., House [San Angelo MRA], 922 Pecos, San Angelo, 9/13/90, C, 88002584

Wardlaw, Dr. Herbert A., House [San Angelo MRA], 233 W. Twohig, San Angelo, 11/25/88, C, 88002596

West Texas Utilities Office [San Angelo MRA], 15 E. Beauregard, San Angelo, 11/25/88, C, 88002552

Westbrook, John C., House [San Angelo MRA], 600 West Ave. C, San Angelo, 11/25/88, C, 88002545

Willeke, John and Anton, House [San Angelo MRA], 941 E. Harris, San Angelo, 11/25/88, C, 88002573

Willeke, John, Jr., House [San Angelo MRA], 1005 E. Harris, San Angelo, 11/25/88, C, a, 88002574

Willeke, John, Sr., House [San Angelo MRA], 931 E. Harris, San Angelo, 11/25/88, C, 88002572

Woodward, Dr. M. M., House [San Angelo MRA], 44 W. 25th St., San Angelo, 11/25/88, C, 88002549

Travis County

Administration Building [East Austin MRA], 1820 E. Eighth St., Austin, 10/21/93, A, C, 86003845

Austin Public Library, 810 Guadalupe St., Austin, 5/06/93, C, 93000389

Aynesworth-Wright House, N of Austin at 11693 Research Blvd., Austin vicinity, 9/27/80, B, C, b, 80004156

Bailetti House [East Austin MRA], 1006 Waller St., Austin, 9/17/85, B, C, 85002268

Barnes, Charles W., House [East Austin MRA], 1105 E. 12th St., Austin, 9/17/85, C, 85002266

Barr, William Braxton, House, NE of Austin at 10463 Sprinkle Rd., Austin vicinity, 1/10/83, C, 83003164

Barton Springs Archeological and Historical District, Address Restricted, Austin vicinity, 11/27/85, A, B, C, D, g, 85003213

Battle Hall, South Mall, University of Texas campus, Austin, 8/25/70, C, 70000763

Batts, Judge Robert Lynn, House, 1505 Windsor Rd., Austin, 8/22/84, B, C, 84002002

Bluebonnet Tourist Camp [Hyde Park MPS], 4407 Guadalupe St., Austin, 8/16/90, C, 90001188

Boardman-Webb-Bugg House, 602 W. 9th St., Austin, 1/08/80, B, C, 80004152

Bremond Block Historic District, Roughly bounded by Guadalupe, San Antonio, 7th and 8th Sts., Austin, 4/03/70, C, 70000764

Brizendine House, 507 W. 11th St., Austin, 7/22/74, C, 74002090

Carrington-Covert House, 1511 Colorado St., Austin, 8/25/70, C, 70000765

Caswell, Daniel H. and William T., Houses, 1404 and 1502 West Ave., Austin, 4/21/75, B, C, 75002004

Central Christian Church, 1110 Guadalupe St., Austin, 7/16/92, C, a, 92000889

City Cemetery [East Austin MRA], 16th & Navasota, Austin, 9/17/85, C, d, 85002297

Clarksville Historic District, Bounded by W. Lynn, Waterson, W. 10th and MO-PAC Expwy., Austin, 12/76/76, A, C, 76002070

Commercial Building at 4113 Guadalupe Street [Hyde Park MPS], 4113 Guadalupe St., Austin, 8/16/90, C, 90001187

Community Center [East Austin MRA], 1192 Angelina St., Austin, 9/17/85, A, C, 85002267

Congress Avenue Historic District, Congress Ave. from 1st to 11th Sts., Austin, 8/11/78, A, C, 78002989

Covert, Frank M. and Annie G., House [Hyde Park MPS], 3912 Ave. G, Austin, 8/16/90, C, 90001185

Cox, Andrew M., Ranch Site, Address Restricted, Austin vicinity, 12/06/75, D, 75002009

Travis County—Continued

Dobie, J. Frank, House, 702 E. 26th St., Austin, 5/20/91, B, g, 91000575

Driskill Hotel, 117 E. 7th St., Austin, 11/25/69, C, 69000212

Evans Industrial Building, Huston-Tillotson College Campus, 1820 E. 8th, Austin, 6/17/82, A, 82004525

Fischer House, 1008 West Ave., Austin, 12/16/82, C, 82001741

French Legation, 802 San Marcos St., Austin, 11/25/69, A, C, 69000213

Gethsemane Lutheran Church, 1510 Congress Ave., Austin, 8/25/70, A, C, a, 70000766

Gilfillan House, 603 W. 8th St., Austin, 9/27/80, C, 80004153

Goodman Building, 202 W. 13th St., Austin, 4/13/73, C, 73001976

Governor's Mansion, 1010 Colorado St., Austin, 8/25/70, A, C, NHL, 70000896

Green Pastures, 811 W. Live Oak St., Austin, 9/27/80, C, 80004154

Haehnel Building [East Austin MRA], 1101 E. 11th St., Austin, 9/17/85, A, C, 85002295

Hancock, John, House, 1306 Colorado St., Austin, 4/13/73, C, 73001977

Haynes-DeLashwah House, 1209 Rosewood Ave., Austin, 3/03/83, A, C, 83004033

Hildreth—Flanagan—Heierman House [Hyde Park MPS], 3909 Ave. G, Austin, 8/16/90, C, 90001184

Hirshfeld, Henry, House and Cottage, 303 and 305 W. 9th St., Austin, 4/13/73, C, 73001978

Hofheintz-Reissig Store, 600 E. 3rd St., Austin, 6/23/83, A, C, 83003165

Horton-Porter, Goldie, House, 2402 Windsor Rd., Austin, 10/04/90, B, C, 90001535

House at 1170 San Bernard Street [East Austin MRA], 1170 San Bernard St., Austin, 9/17/85, C, 85002269

House at 1400 Canterbury Street [East Austin MRA], 1400 Canterbury St., Austin, 9/17/85, C, 85002274

Hyde Park Historic District [Hyde Park MPS], Roughly bounded by Ave. A, 45th St., Duval St., and 40th St., Austin, 8/16/90, C, 90001191

Hyde Park Presbyterian Church [Hyde Park MPS], 3915 Ave. B, Austin, 8/16/90, C, a, b, 90001175

Irvin, Robert, House [East Austin MRA], 1008 E. 9th St., Austin, 9/17/85, C, 85002270

Jernigan, A. J., House, 602 Harthan, Austin, 9/22/83, B, C, 83003166

Jobe, Phillip W., House [East Austin MRA], 1113 E. 9th St., Austin, 9/17/85, C, 85002278

Johnson, C. E., House [East Austin MRA], 1022 E. 7th St., Austin, 9/17/85, C, 85002282

Laguna Gloria, 3809 W. 35th St., Austin, 12/06/75, B, C, 75002005

Ledbetter, Charles P., House [Hyde Park MPS], 3904 Ave. C, Austin, 8/16/90, C, 90001178

Levi Rock Shelter, Address Restricted, Austin vicinity, 6/21/71, D, 71000965

Little Campus, Bounded by 18th, Oldham, 19th, and Red River Sts., Austin, 8/13/74, A, C, 74002091

Littlefield House, 24th St. and Whitis Ave., Austin, 8/25/70, A, C, 70000767

Long Hog Hollow Archeological District, Address Restricted, Austin vicinity, 5/25/84, A, D, 84002003

Maddox, John W., House [East Austin MRA], 1115 E. 3rd St., Austin, 9/17/85, C, 85002293

Mansbendel, Peter and Clotilde Shipe, House [Hyde Park MPS], 3824 Ave. F, Austin, 8/16/90, C, 90001183

Mather-Kirkland House, 402 Academy, Austin, 12/08/78, A, C, 78002990

McCauley, Robert H. and Edith Ethel, House [Hyde Park MPS], 4415 Ave. A, Austin, 8/16/90, C, 90001236

McGown, Floyd, House [East Austin MRA], 1202 Garden St., Austin, 9/17/85, C, 85002290

McKinney Homestead, SW of Austin between TX 71 and U.S. 183, Austin vicinity, 10/16/74, D, 74002093

Millett Opera House, 110 E. 9th St., Austin, 3/21/78, A, C, 78002991

Missouri, Kansas and Texas Land Co. House [Hyde Park MPS], 3908 Ave. C, Austin, 8/16/90, C, 90001179

Moonlight Towers, Austin and vicinity, Austin, 7/12/76, A, C, 76002071

Moreland, Charles B., House [East Austin MRA], 1301 E. 1st St., Austin, 9/17/85, B, C, 85002276

Neill-Cochran House, 2310 San Gabriel St., Austin, 8/25/70, C, 70000768

Newton House [East Austin MRA], 1013 E. Ninth St., Austin, 4/02/87, C, 87000578

Ney, Elisabet, Studio and Museum, 304 E. 44th St., Austin, 11/29/72, A, B, 72001374

Old Bakery, 1006 Congress Ave., Austin, 12/17/69, A, 69000214

Old Land Office Building, 108 E. 11th St., Austin, 8/25/70, A, B, C, 70000769

Oliphant—Walker House [Hyde Park MPS], 3900 Ave. C, Austin, 8/16/90, B, C, 90001177

Page—Gilbert House [Hyde Park MPS], 3913 Ave. G, Austin, 8/16/90, C, 90001186

Paggi, Michael, House, 200 Lee Barton Dr., Austin, 4/16/75, C, 75002006

Paramount Theatre, 713 Congress Ave., Austin, 6/23/76, A, C, 76002072

Parker, James F. and Susie R., House [Hyde Park MPS], 3906 Ave. D, Austin, 8/16/90, C, 90001181

Peterson, George A., House [East Austin MRA], 1012 E. 8th St., Austin, 9/17/85, C, 85002273

Polhemus, Joseph O., House [East Austin MRA], 912 E. 2nd St., Austin, 9/17/85, C, 85002299

Porter, William Sidney, House, 409 E. 5th S., Austin, 6/18/73, B, C, b, 73001979

Rainey Street Historic District [East Austin MRA], 70–97 Rainey St., Austin, 9/17/85, C, 85002302

Ramsey, F. T. and Belle, House [Hyde Park MPS], 4412 Ave. B, Austin, 8/16/90, B, C, 90001176

Rather House, 3105 Duval St., Austin, 10/24/79, C, a, 79003013

Raymond-Morley House, 510 Baylor St., Austin, 11/20/74, C, 74002092

Reuter, Louis and Mathilde, House, 806 Rosedale Terrace, Austin, 12/07/87, B, C, 87002100

Robbins, Alice H., House [Hyde Park MPS], 4311 Ave. A, Austin, 8/16/90, C, 90001235

Robinson-Macken House, 702 Rio Grande St., Austin, 9/12/85, C, b, 85002300

Rogers, Edward H., Homestead, N of Austin off TX 1325, Austin vicinity, 12/27/74, A, C, 74002094

Rogers—Bell House [East Austin MRA], 1001 E. Eighth St., East Austin, 6/24/88, C, 88000703

Sampson, George W., House, 1003 Rio Grande, Austin, 7/08/82, C, 82004526

Schneider, J. P., Store, 401 W. 2nd St., Austin, 1/29/79, A, C, 79003014

Scholz Garten, 1607 San Jacinto, Austin, 7/27/79, A, 79003015

Schulze, Walter, House and Industrial Structure [East Austin MRA], 102 Chicon St., Austin, 4/25/86, C, 86000864

Sears, Rev. Henry M. and Jennie, House [Hyde Park MPS], 209 W. 39th St., Austin, 8/16/90, C, 90001174

Shadow Lawn Historic District [Hyde Park MPS], Roughly bounded by Ave. G, 38th St., Duval St., and 39th St., Austin, 8/16/90, C, 90001192

Sheeks-Robertson House, 610 W. Lynn St., Austin, 6/24/76, B, C, 76002073

Shipe, Col. Monroe M., House, 3816 Ave. G, Austin, 3/29/83, B, C, 83003167

Shotgun at 1206 Canterbury Street [East Austin MRA], 1206 Canterbury St., Austin, 9/17/85, C, 85002285

Shotguns at 1203–1205 Bob Harrison [East Austin MRA], 1203–1205 Bob Harrison, Austin, 9/17/85, C, b, 85002284

Sixth Street Historic District, Roughly bounded by 5th, 7th, Lavaca Sts. and I-35, Austin, 12/30/75, A, C, 75002132

Smith Rock Shelter, Address Restricted, Austin vicinity, 10/01/74, D, 74002095

Smith, B. J., House, 700 W. 6th St., Austin, 4/19/78, B, C, 78002992

Smith—Marcuse—Lowry House [Hyde Park MPS], 3913 Ave. C, Austin, 8/16/90, C, 90001180

Smith-Clark and Smith-Bickler Houses, 502 and 504 W. 14th St., Austin, 4/20/79, C, 79003016

Smoot, Richmond Kelley, House, 1316 W. 6th St., Austin, 8/12/82, B, C, a, 82004527

Southgate-Lewis House [East Austin MRA], 1501 E. 12th St., Austin, 9/17/85, B, C, 85002265

Southwestern Telegraph and Telephone Building, 410 Congress Ave., Austin, 2/14/78, C, 78002993

St. David's Episcopal Church, 304 E. 7th St., Austin, 8/02/78, A, C, a, 78002994

St. Edward's University Main Building and Holy Cross Dormitory, 3001 S. Congress St., Austin, 3/07/73, A, C, a, 73001980

St. Mary's Cathedral, 201–207 10th St., Austin, 4/02/73, A, C, a, 73001981

State Cemetery of Texas [East Austin MRA], 901 Navasota St., Austin, 5/12/86, A, d, 86001085

State Lunatic Asylum, 4110 Guadalupe, Austin, 12/04/87, A, C, 87002115

Travis County—Continued

Stavely-Kunz-Johnson House, 1402 E. 1st, Austin, 8/19/80, C, 80004155

Swedish Hill Historic District [East Austin MRA], 900–1000 blks. of E. Fourteenth St. and 900 blk. of E. Fifteenth St., Austin, 5/12/86, C, 86001088

Texas Federation of Women's Clubs Headquarters, 2312 San Gabriel St., Austin, 10/24/85, A, C, 85003377

Texas State Capitol, Congress and 11th Sts., Austin, 6/22/70, C, NHL, 70000770

U.S. Post Office and Federal Building, 126 W. 6th St., Austin, 8/25/70, C, 70000771

Wahrenberger House, 208 W. 14th St., Austin, 2/23/78, A, C, 78002995

Walnut Creek Archeological District, Address Restricted, Austin vicinity, 9/24/81, D, 81000633

Wesley United Methodist Church [East Austin MRA], 1164 San Bernard St., Austin, 9/17/85, A, C, a, 85002281

Westhill, 1703 West Ave., Austin, 7/26/79, C, 79003017

Williams, W. T. and Clotilde V., House [Hyde Park MPS], 3820 Ave. F, Austin, 8/16/90, C, 90001182

Willow-Spence Streets Historic District [East Austin MRA], Portions of Willow, Spence, Canterbury, San Marcos & Waller Sts., Austin, 9/17/85, C, a, 85002264

Woodlawn, 6 Niles Rd., Austin, 8/25/70, C, 70000772

Wooldridge Park, Guadalupe St., Austin, 8/01/79, C, 79003018

Wooten, Goodall, House, 700 W. 19th St., Austin, 4/03/75, C, 75002008

Youth Council Site (41TV382), Address Restricted, Austin vicinity, 4/24/79, D, 79003450

Uvalde County

Fort Inge Archeological Site, Address Restricted, Uvalde, 9/12/85, A, D, 85002298

Garner, John Nance, House, 333 N. Park St., Uvalde, 12/08/76, B, NHL, 76002074

Grand Opera House, E. North and N. Getty Sts., Uvalde, 5/22/78, B, C, 78002996

Leona River Archeological Site, Address Restricted, Uvalde vicinity, 5/06/76, D, 76002075

Taylor Slough Archeological Site, Address Restricted, Uvalde vicinity, 5/04/76, D, 76002076

Uvalde Flint Quarry, Address Restricted, Uvalde vicinity, 6/03/76, D, 76002077

Willingham Site, Address Restricted, Uvalde vicinity, 4/26/76, D, 76002078

Val Verde County

Cassinelli Gin House, Corner of Pecan and Academy Sts., Del Rio, 9/04/86, A, C, 86002188

Lower Pecos Canyon Archeological District, Address Restricted, Comstock vicinity, 3/31/71, D, 71000966

Mile Canyon, Address Restricted, Langtry vicinity, 10/15/70, D, 70000773

Rattlesnake Canyon Site, Address Restricted, Langtry vicinity, 9/28/71, D, 71000968

San Felipe Creek Archeological District, Address Restricted, Del Rio vicinity, 10/16/74, D, 74002096

Seminole Canyon Archeological District, Address Restricted, Comstock vicinity, 1/25/71, D, 71000967

Seminole Canyon District (Boundary Increase), Address Restricted, Comstock vicinity, 12/21/85, D, 85003181

Seven Mile Ranch Archeological District, Address Restricted, Comstock vicinity, 11/16/90, D, 90001733

Val Verde County Courthouse And Jail, 400 Pecan St., Del Rio, 8/18/77, A, 77001478

West of Pecos Railroad Camps District, Address Restricted, Comstock vicinity, 4/03/73, A, D, 73001982

Victoria County

Alden, C. R., Building [Victoria MRA], 106–110 W. Juan Linn, Victoria, 12/09/86, C, 86002533

Alonso, Frank, House [Victoria MRA], 401 S. Cameron, Victoria, 12/09/86, B, C, 86002585

B'nai Isreal [Victoria MRA], 604 N. Main, Victoria, 12/09/86, A, C, a, 86002613

Barden—O'Connor House [Victoria MRA], 305 N. Moody, Victoria, 12/09/86, B, C, 86002609

Barnes, W. C., House [Victoria MRA], 106 W. Stayton, Victoria, 12/09/86, B, C, 86002568

Bendt, E. H. D., House [Victoria MRA], 407 S. DeLeon, Victoria, 12/09/86, C, 86002570

Bettin, Max, House [Victoria MRA], 602 E. Santa Rosa, Victoria, 12/09/86, B, C, 86002564

Braman House [Victoria MRA], 206 W. Stayton, Victoria, 12/09/86, C, 86002593

Buhler, Theodore, House [Victoria MRA], 202 W. Stayton, Victoria, 12/09/86, C, 86002594

Building at 205 East Constitution [Victoria MRA], 205 E. Constitution, Victoria, 12/09/86, C, 86002475

Burrough—Daniel House [Victoria MRA], 502 W. North, Victoria, 12/09/86, C, 86002604

Calhoun Bakery [Victoria MRA], 209 N. Wheeler, Victoria, 12/09/86, C, 86002534

Callender House, 404 W. Guadelupe St, Victoria, 9/26/79, C, 79003019

City of Victoria Pumping Plant—Waterworks [Victoria MRA], 105 W. Juan Linn, City of Victoria, 12/09/86, A, 86002610

Clark House [Victoria MRA], 606 S. Liberty, Victoria, 12/09/86, C, 86002507

Clark, Robert, House [Victoria MRA], 317 N. Main, Victoria, 12/09/86, B, C, 86002615

Clegg, John H., House [Victoria MRA], 507 N. Vine, Victoria, 12/09/86, C, 86002548

Crain, F. H., House [Victoria MRA], 307 N. Vine, Victoria, 12/09/86, C, 86002549

DeLeon Plaza and Bandstand [Victoria MRA], 100 blk. W. Constitution, Victoria, 3/24/87, A, C, b, 86002584

Diebel—Hyak House [Victoria MRA], 501 S. Cameron, Victoria, 12/12/86, C, 86002484

Farmers and Merchants Cotton Gin Warehouse [Victoria MRA], 402 S. East, Victoria, 12/09/86, A, C, 86002561

Fleming—Welder House [Victoria MRA], 607 N. Craig, Victoria, 12/09/86, C, 86002581

Fort St. Louis Site, Address Restricted, Inez vicinity, 3/31/71, A, D, 71000969

Fossati's [Victoria MPS], 302 S. Main, Victoria, 5/20/91, A, 91000578

Fossati, E. J., House [Victoria MRA], 607 S. DeLeon, Victoria, 12/09/86, C, 86002563

Fox, Jacob, House [Victoria MRA], 708 W. Power, Victoria, 12/09/86, B, C, 86002596

Gaylord—Levy House [Victoria MRA], 402 N. Bridge, Victoria, 12/09/86, B, C, 86002589

Gervais House [Victoria MRA], 507 W. Forrest, Victoria, 7/05/90, C, 90001052

Goldman's Cotton Gin Warehouse [Victoria MRA], 901 E. Murray, Victoria, 12/09/86, A, C, 86002606

Goldman, A., Building [Victoria MRA], 207 E. Constitution, Victoria, 12/09/86, C, 86002499

Gramann House [Victoria MRA], 302 E. Goodwin, Victoria, 12/09/86, C, 86002542

Hauschild, George H., Building [Victoria MRA], 206 N. Liberty, Victoria, 12/09/86, A, C, 86002530

Hauschild, George and Adele, House [Victoria MRA], 208 N. Liberty, Victoria, 12/09/86, B, C, 86002510

Hill—Howard House [Victoria MRA], 802 W. Power, Victoria, 12/09/86, C, 86002558

Hiller House [Victoria MRA], 501 E. Church, Victoria, 12/09/86, C, 86002459

Hiller House [Victoria MRA], 3003 N. Vine, Victoria, 12/09/86, C, 86002482

House at 1602 North Moody [Victoria MRA], 1602 N. Moody, Victoria, 12/09/86, C, 86002608

House at 1907 Southwest Ben Jordan [Victoria MRA], 1907 S.W. Ben Jordan, Victoria, 12/09/86, C, 86002590

House at 304 West Stayton [Victoria MRA], 304 W. Stayton, Victoria, 12/09/86, C, 86002591

House at 306 East Forrest [Victoria MRA], 306 E. Forrest, Victoria, 12/09/86, C, 86002557

House at 401 East Stayton [Victoria MRA], 401 E. Stayton, Victoria, 12/09/86, C, 86002572

House at 402 W. Colorado [Victoria MPS], 402 W. Colorado, Victoria, 5/20/91, C, 91000576

House at 407 East Convent [Victoria MRA], 407 E. Convent, Victoria, 12/09/86, C, 86002583

House at 4402 East Juan Linn [Victoria MRA], 4402 E. Juan Linn, Victoria, 12/09/86, A, C, b, 86002535

House at 604 East Santa Rosa [Victoria MRA], 604 E. Santa Rosa, Victoria, 12/09/86, C, 86002562

House at 702 Siegfried [Victoria MRA], 702 Siegfried, Victoria, 12/09/86, C, 86002577

House at 706 Siegfried [Victoria MRA], 706 Siegfried, Victoria, 12/09/86, C, 86002576

House at 804 Siegfried [Victoria MRA], 804 Siegfried, Victoria, 12/09/86, C, 86002574

Hull House [Victoria MRA], 1002 NE Water, Victoria, 12/09/86, B, C, 86002543

Victoria County—Continued

Jecker, E. J., House [Victoria MRA], 201 N. Wheeler, Victoria, 12/09/86, C, 86002539

Jecker, J. T., House [Victoria MRA], 104 N. Liberty, Victoria, 3/24/87, C, 86002531

Jordan—Koch House [Victoria MRA], 307 N. DeLeon, Victoria, 12/09/86, C, 86002579

Kaufman, E. C., House [Victoria MRA], 502 S. DeLeon, Victoria, 12/09/86, C, 86002567

Keef—Filley Building [Victoria MRA], 214 S. Main, Victoria, 3/24/87, A, C, 86002612

Krenek House [Victoria MRA], 607 N. Main, Victoria, 12/09/86, C, 86002611

Lander—Hopkins House [Victoria MRA], 202 W. Power at N. Bridge, Victoria, 12/09/86, C, 86002600

Lane—Tarkington House [Victoria MRA], 1207 N. Bridge, Victoria, 12/09/86, C, 86002617

Lawrence House [Victoria MRA], 1203 N. Bridge, Victoria, 12/09/86, C, 86002588

Leffland, Jules, House [Victoria MPS], 302 E. Convent, Victoria, 5/20/91, C, 91000577

Levi—Welder House [Victoria MRA], 403 N. Main, Victoria, 12/09/86, C, 86002614

Little House [Victoria MRA], 502 N. Victoria, Victoria, 12/09/86, C, 86002551

Martin—Fiek-Thumford, Vera, House [Victoria MRA], 507 N. William, Victoria, 12/09/86, C, 86002597

McCabe Building [Victoria MRA], 508 N. Wheeler, Victoria, 12/19/86, C, 86002464

McCan—Nave House [Victoria MRA], 401 N. Glass, Victoria, 12/09/86, B, C, 86002555

McDonald House [Victoria MRA], 406 E. Constitution, Victoria, 12/09/86, C, 86002460

McFaddin, James, House [Victoria MRA], 207 W. Commercial, Victoria, 3/24/87, B, C, 86002506

McNamara—O'Conner House [Victoria MRA], 502 N. Liberty, Victoria, 12/09/86, C, 86002509

Mission Creek Dam and Acequia Site, Address Restricted, Victoria vicinity, 4/09/80, C, D, 80004157

Mitchell, Guy, House [Victoria MRA], 402 W. Goodwin, Victoria, 12/09/86, C, 86002541

Moeller House [Victoria MRA], 901 S. East, Victoria, 12/09/86, C, 86002559

Mohris—Abschier House [Victoria MRA], 101 N. DeLeon, Victoria, 12/09/86, C, 86002580

Murphy, Mrs. J. V., House [Victoria MRA], 204 E. Santa Rosa, Victoria, 12/09/86, C, 86002554

Nave, Royston, Memorial [Victoria MRA], 306 W. Commercial, Victoria, 12/09/86, B, C, f, 86002502

O'Conner, Thomas M., House [Victoria MRA], 303 S. Bridge, Victoria, 12/09/86, B, C, 86002587

O'Conner—Procter Building [Victoria MRA], 202 N. Main, Victoria, 12/09/86, A, C, 86002546

Old Brownson School [Victoria MRA], 500 blk. of W. Power, Victoria, 12/09/86, A, C, 86002598

Old Federal Building and Post Office [Victoria MRA], 210 E. Constitution, Victoria, 12/09/86, A, C, 86002493

Old Municipal Assembly Hall [Victoria MRA], 800 E. Pine, Victoria, 12/09/86, A, C, 86002603

Old Nazareth Academy [Victoria MRA], 105 W. Church, Victoria, 12/09/86, C, a, 86002462

Old Victoria County Courthouse, 101 N. Bridge St., Victoria, 8/18/77, A, C, 77001479

Our Lady of Lourdes Church [Victoria MRA], 105 N. William, Victoria, 12/09/86, C, a, 86002601

Pela House [Victoria MRA], 309 E. Santa Rosa, Victoria, 12/09/86, C, 86002552

Phillips, Judge Alexander H., House, 705 N. Craig St., Victoria, 11/03/83, B, C, 83003824

Pickering House [Victoria MRA], 403 N. Glass, Victoria, 12/09/86, B, C, 86002553

Pippert House [Victoria MRA], 207 E. Third, Victoria, 12/09/86, C, 86002578

Presbyterian Iglesia Nicea [Victoria MRA], 401 S. DeLeon, Victoria, 10/28/92, C, a, b, 86002571

Proctor House [Victoria MRA], 507 N. Glass, Victoria, 12/06/86, B, C, 86002544

Proctor—Vandenberge House [Victoria MRA], 604 N. Craig, Victoria, 12/09/86, C, 86002575

Randall Building [Victoria MRA], 103–105 W. Santa Rosa, Victoria, 12/09/86, A, C, 86002560

Regan, D. H., House [Victoria MRA], 507 S. De-Leon, Victoria, 12/09/86, C, b, 86002565

Roselle—Smith House [Victoria MRA], 301 E. Commercial, Victoria, 7/05/90, C, 90001050

Saint Mary's Catholic Church [Victoria MRA], 101 W. Church, Victoria, 12/09/86, C, a, 86002450

Schroeder House [Victoria MRA], 1507 N. Vine, Victoria, 12/09/86, C, 86002545

Schummacker Company Building [Victoria MRA], 402 E. Power, Victoria, 12/09/86, C, 86002602

Sengele, Alphonse T., House [Victoria MRA], 502 E. Juan Linn, Victoria, 10/28/92, C, b, 86002538

Shrader, Henry, House [Victoria MRA], 607 S. Cameron, Victoria, 12/09/86, C, 86002483

Sigmund House [Victoria MRA], 508 E. Santa Rosa, Victoria, 12/09/86, C, 86002566

South Bridge Street Historic District [Victoria MRA], W side 700 blk. of S. Bridge and N side 700 blk. of W. Water Sts., Victoria, 9/24/86, A, C, b, 86002592

Stuart House [Victoria MRA], 506 S. Bridge, Victoria, 12/09/86, C, 86002586

Tasin House [Victoria MRA], 202 N. Wheeler, Victoria, 12/09/86, C, 86002536

Texas Company Filling Station [Victoria MRA], 102 S. Williams St., Victoria, 12/09/86, C, 86002595

Tonkawa Bank Site, Address Restricted, Victoria vicinity, 2/13/81, D, 81000634

Townsend—Wilkins House [Victoria MRA], 106 N. Navarro, Victoria, 12/09/86, B, C, 86002605

Trinity Lutheran Church [Victoria MRA], 402 E. Constitution, Victoria, 12/09/86, C, a, 86002486

Urban, Fred, House [Victoria MRA], 501 E. River, Victoria, 10/28/92, C, 86002556

Vandenberge, J. V., House [Victoria MRA], 301 N. Vine, Victoria, 12/09/86, B, C, 86002550

Victoria Colored School [Victoria MRA], 702 E. Convent, Victoria, 12/09/86, A, 86002582

Victoria Grist Windmill, Memorial Park in Victoria, Victoria, 4/30/76, C, b, 76002079

Weber—Schuchert House [Victoria MRA], 302 E. Constitution, Victoria, 12/09/86, C, 86002490

Webster Chapel United Methodist Church [Victoria MRA], 405 S. Wheeler, Victoria, 12/09/86, A, a, 86002478

Wheeler, William, House [Victoria MRA], 303 N. William St., Victoria, 12/09/86, B, C, 86002599

Willeke Site, Address Restricted, Victoria vicinity, 11/20/78, D, 78002997

Williams, B. F., House [Victoria MRA], 401 E. Murray, Victoria, 12/09/86, C, 86002607

Woodhouse House [Victoria MRA], 609 N. Wheeler, Victoria, 12/09/86, C, 86002481

Zahn, Herman and Alvina, House [Victoria MRA], 107 S. DeLeon, Victoria, 12/09/86, C, 86002573

Walker County

Houston, Sam, House, Ave. L, Sam Houston State University, Huntsville, 5/30/74, B, NHL, 74002097

Riverside Swinging Bridge, NE of Riverside, Riverside vicinity, 9/12/79, C, 79003020

Thomason, John W., House, 1207 Ave. J, Huntsville, 8/11/82, B, C, f, 82004528

Waller County

Foster Hall, Prairie View A and M University campus, Prairie View, 12/07/79, A, C, 79003021

Liendo Plantation, 2 mi. NE of Hempstead off FM 1488, Hempstead vicinity, 6/21/71, B, C, 71000970

Washington County

Applewhite, Isaac, House [Chappell Hill MRA], Church St., Chappell Hill, 2/20/85, B, C, 85000342

Bassett and Bassett Banking House, 222 E. Main St., Brenham, 4/21/83, A, C, 83003168

Becker—Hildebrandt House [Brenham MPS], 1402 S. Church, Brenham, 3/29/90, C, 90000456

Blinn College [Brenham MPS], Roughly bounded by Third, Jackson, Fifth, Green, College, and High, Brenham, 3/29/90, A, C, 90000446

Blue Bell Creameries Complex [Brenham MPS], 602 Creamery, Brenham, 3/29/90, A, 90000468

Brenham High School [Brenham MPS], 1301 S. Market, Brenham, 3/29/90, C, 90000466

Brenham High School Gymnasium [Brenham MPS], 1301 S. Market, Brenham, 3/29/90, C, 90000467

Brenham School [Brenham MPS], 600 E. Alamo, Brenham, 3/29/90, A, C, 90000454

Brenham Water Works [Brenham MPS], 1105 S. Austin, Brenham, 3/29/90, A, C, 90000465

Brockschmidt—Miller House [Brenham MPS], 806 S. Day, Brenham, 3/29/90, C, 90000451

Brown, John M., House, S of Washington on FM 912, Washington vicinity, 4/16/75, C, 75002010

Washington County—Continued

Browning, W. W., House, S of Chappell Hill near jct. of U.S. 290 and FM 1155, Chappell Hill vicinity, 1/20/72, C, 72001376

Burton Commercial Historic District [Burton MPS], Roughly bounded by Railroad, Live Oak, Brazos and Burton, including area S of Railroad between Washington and Texas Sts., Burton, 6/11/91, A, C, 91000709

Burton Farmers Gin [Burton MPS], Main St. SE of Burton St., Burton, 6/11/91, A, C, 91000712

Burton High School [Burton MPS], Jct. of Main St. and FM 390, Burton, 6/11/91, A, C, 91000711

Chappell Hill Circulating Library [Chappell Hill MRA], Cedar St., Chappell Hill, 2/20/85, C, 85000343

Chappell Hill Methodist Episcopal Church [Chappell Hill MRA], Church St., Chappell Hill, 2/20/85, C, a, 85000344

Chappell Hill Public School and Chappell Hill Female College Bell [Chappell Hill MRA], Poplar St., Chappell Hill, 2/20/85, A, C, f, 85000345

East Brenham [Brenham MPS], Roughly bounded by Crockett, Embrey, E. Academy, Ross, E. Main, Market, Sycamore, Cottonwood, Botts, McIntyre, and Alma, Brenham, 3/29/90, C, 90000445

Felder, E. King, House [Chappell Hill MRA], Haller st., Chappell Hill, 2/20/85, C, 85000346

Gantt-Jones House, 1.5 mi. NW of Burton off SR 1697, Burton vicinity, 11/16/79, C, 79003022

Giddings-Stone Mansion, 204 E. Stone St., Brenham, 6/24/76, B, C, 76002080

Giddings-Wilkin House, 805 Crocket St., Brenham, 12/12/76, C, 76002081

Hatfield Plantation, NW of Brenham off FM 912, Brenham vicinity, 1/25/71, C, 71000971

Hodde Drugstore [Burton MPS], Main St. SE of Burton St., Burton, 6/11/91, A, C, 91000713

Holle, Edmund, House [Brenham MPS], 1002 S. Day, Brenham, 3/29/90, C, 90000458

Houston, Mrs. Sam, House, FM 390, 1 block E of jct. with FM 50, Independence, 10/22/70, C, 70000775

Hoxey, Asa, House, W of Independence, Independence vicinity, 6/29/76, B, C, 76002083

Kneip—Bredthauer House [Burton MPS], SE corner of Colorado and Cedar, Burton, 6/11/91, C, 91000719

Laas, Dr. Charles, House [Burton MPS], NE corner of Live Oak and Colorado Sts., Burton, 6/11/91, C, 91000717

Lenert, Dr. Robert, House [Brenham MPS], 602 S. Market, Brenham, 3/29/90, C, 90000457

Main Building, Blinn College, 804 College Ave., Brenham, 12/06/78, A, 78002998

Main Street Historic District [Chappell Hill MRA], Main St., Chappell Hill, 5/15/85, A, C, 85001175

Matchett, Edgar, House [Brenham MPS], 502 W. Main, Brenham, 3/29/90, C, 90000462

Mt. Zion Methodist Church [Brenham MPS], 500 High, Brenham, 3/29/90, C, a, 90000450

Neumann, William, House [Burton MPS], Navasota St. W of Washington St., Burton, 6/18/91, C, 91000710

Nienstedt, Herbert, House [Burton MPS], NE corner of Brazos and Washington Sts., Burton, 6/11/91, C, 91000718

Nienstedt, William, House [Burton MPS], SE corner of Brazos and Texas Sts., Burton, 6/11/91, C, 91000715

Pampell-Day House, 409 W. Alamo St., Brenham, 10/15/70, C, 70000774

Red House, NE of Gay Hill via TX 36 and FM 390, Gay Hill vicinity, 1/25/71, B, C, 71000972

Reichardt—Low House [Brenham MPS], 609 S. Austin, Brenham, 3/29/90, C, 90000455

Rogers, William S., House [Chappell Hill MRA], Cedar St., Chappell Hill, 2/20/85, C, 85000347

Routt, J. R., House [Chappell Hill MRA], Chestnut St., Chappell Hill, 2/20/85, C, 85000348

Sanders, William Edward, House [Burton MPS], Railroad St. SE of US 290, Burton, 6/11/91, C, 91000716

Santa Fe Railway Company Freight Depot [Brenham MPS], 214 S. Austin, Brenham, 3/29/90, A, C, 90000459

Schlenker, Almot, House [Brenham MPS], 405 College, Brenham, 3/29/90, C, 90000461

Schlenker—Kolwes House [Brenham MPS], 1304 S. Market, Brenham, 3/29/90, C, 90000460

Schmidt House [Brenham MPS], 906 W. 5th St., Brenham, 12/10/90, B, C, 90001806

Schuerenberg, F. W., House [Brenham MPS], 503 W. Alamo, Brenham, 3/29/90, C, 90000469

Schuerenberg, R. A., House [Brenham MPS], 703 S. Market, Brenham, 3/29/90, C, 90000463

Seelhorst, W. E., House [Brenham MPS], 702 Seelhorst, Brenham, 3/29/90, C, 90000470

Smith, John Sterling, Jr., House [Chappell Hill MRA], Chestnut St., Chappell Hill, 2/20/85, C, 85000349

Southern Pacific Railroad Freight Depot [Brenham MPS], 306 S. Market, Brenham, 3/29/90, A, C, 90000453

St. Mary's Catholic Church [Brenham MPS], 701 Church, Brenham, 3/29/90, C, a, 90000452

Stage Coach Inn, Main and Chestnut Sts., Chappell Hill, 12/12/76, A, C, 76002082

Synagogue B'nai Abraham [Brenham MPS], 302 N. Park, Brenham, 3/29/90, C, a, 90000464

US Post Office—Federal Building—Brenham [Brenham MPS], 105 S. Market, Brenham, 3/29/90, C, 90000449

Walker, James, Log House, Co. Rd. 80, Brenham vicinity, 8/21/89, A, C, b, 89001143

Washington County Courthouse [Brenham MPS], 110 E. Main, Brenham, 3/29/90, A, C, 90000447

Waverly, FR 2447, Chappell Hill, 4/14/83, B, C, 83003169

Wehring Shoe Shop and Residence [Burton MPS], Main St. SE of Burton St., Burton, 6/11/91, A, 91000714

Wood—Hughes House [Brenham MPS], 614 S. Austin, Brenham, 3/29/90, C, 90000448

Webb County

Fort McIntosh, Laredo Junior College campus, Laredo, 6/25/75, A, C, a, 75002011

Hamilton Hotel, 815 Salinas St., Laredo, 4/14/92, C, 92000363

Los Ojuelos, 2.5 mi. S of Mirando City on SR 649, Mirando City vicinity, 12/22/76, C, D, a, 76002084

San Augustin de Laredo Historic District, Roughly bounded by Grant and Water Sts., Convent and San Bernardino Aves., Laredo, 9/19/73, C, a, 73001983

San Jose de Palafox Historic/Archeological District, Address Restricted, Laredo vicinity, 7/24/73, A, C, D, 73001984

Webb County Courthouse, 1000 Houston St., Laredo, 5/04/81, C, 81000635

Wharton County

Banker, Willie, Jr., House [Wharton MPS], 401 N. Rusk, Wharton, 3/18/93, C, 93000118

Bernstein, Moses, House [Wharton MPS], 1705 N. Richmond, Wharton, 3/18/93, C, 93000116

Bolton—Outlar House [Wharton MPS], 517 N. Richmond, Wharton, 3/18/93, C, 93000108

Colorado River Bridge [Wharton MPS], S. Richmond Rd. (Old US 59) across the Colorado R., Wharton, 3/18/93, A, 93000117

Croom, Wiley J., House [Wharton MPS], 205 E. Milam, Wharton, 3/18/93, C, 93000099

Dannon, F. F., House [Wharton MPS], 612 W. Caney, Wharton, 3/18/93, C, 93000095

Davidson, Dr. Green, House [Wharton MPS], 404 Bolton, Wharton, 3/18/93, C, b, 93000111

Davis, Ben and Mary, House [Wharton MPS], 100 S. Resident, Wharton, 3/18/93, C, 93000104

Elkins, Nettie, House [Wharton MPS], 109 E. Alabama, Wharton, 3/18/93, C, 93000114

Elliott, E. Clyde and Mary, House [Wharton MPS], 707 N. Walnut, Wharton, 3/18/93, C, 93000122

First Methodist Episcopal Church South, Old [Wharton MPS], 200 N. Fulton, Wharton, 3/18/93, C, a, 93000097

Garrett, Henry B., House [Wharton MPS], 504 N. Fulton, Wharton, 3/18/93, C, 93000098

Garrett, John A. and Sophie, House [Wharton MPS], 401 E. Alabama, Wharton, 3/18/93, C, 93000115

Gifford, George C. and Annie, House [Wharton MPS], 615 W. Caney, Wharton, 3/18/93, C, 93000096

Hamilton, Joseph Andrew, House [Wharton MPS], 325 N. Richmond, Wharton, 3/18/93, C, 93000106

Harrison, Gerard A., House [Wharton MPS], 209 E. Caney, Wharton, 3/18/93, B, C, 93000112

Harrison—Dennis House [Wharton MPS], 409 W. Burleson, Wharton, 3/18/93, B, C, 93000110

Hawes, Edwin, House [Wharton MPS], 309 N. Resident, Wharton, 3/18/93, C, 93000102

Hawes, Edwin, Jr., House [Wharton MPS], 119 S. Resident, Wharton, 3/18/93, C, 93000105

Wharton County—Continued

House at 401 North Richmond [Wharton MPS], 401 N. Richmond, Wharton, 3/18/93, C, 93000107

House at 512 North Resident [Wharton MPS], 512 N. Resident, Wharton, 3/18/93, C, 93000103

Linn Street Historic District [Wharton MPS], Roughly, the 500 blocks of Richmond Rd. and Houston St. and the 100–200 blocks of Linn St., Wharton, 3/18/93, C, 93000124

Merrill—Roten House [Wharton MPS], 520 Ave. A, Wharton, 3/18/93, C, 93000113

Moran—Moore House [Wharton MPS], 501 N. Walnut, Wharton, 3/18/93, C, 93000120

Speaker, J. H., House [Wharton MPS], 414 E. Alabama, Wharton, 3/18/93, C, 93000109

St. John's Evangelical Lutheran Church [Wharton MPS], 612 N. Pecan, Wharton, 3/18/93, C, a, 93000100

Texas and New Orleans Railroad Depot [Wharton MPS], 100 block of N. Sunset, Wharton, 3/18/93, A, C, 93000119

Texas and New Orleans Railroad Bridge [Wharton MPS], Southern Pacific RR tracks, 0.25 mi. W of Old US 59, over the Colorado R., Wharton, 3/18/93, A, 93000123

West Milam Street Mercantile Historic District [Wharton MPS], Roughly 637–668 W. Milam St., Wharton, 3/18/93, C, 93000125

Wharton County Courthouse Historic Commercial District, Roughly bounded by the alley N of Milam St., Rusk St., Elm St. and Richmond St., Wharton, 11/05/91, A, C, 91001624

Worthing, Louis F., House [Wharton MPS], 620 N. Walnut, Wharton, 3/18/93, C, 93000121

Wichita County

Hamilton, William Benjamin, House, 1106 Brook Ave., Wichita Falls, 10/28/83, C, 83003826

Hodges-Hardy-Chambers House, 1100 Travis St., Wichita Falls, 5/02/85, A, C, 85000925

Kell, Frank, House, 900 Bluff St., Wichita Falls, 11/28/78, B, C, 78003378

Morningside Historic District, Roughly bounded by 9th St., Morningside Dr., Pembroke Lane and Buchanan St., Wichita Falls, 5/16/85, A, C, 85001122

Weeks House, 2112 Kell Blvd., Wichita Falls, 12/03/80, A, C, 80004158

Wichita Falls Route Building, 503 8th St., Wichita Falls, 11/29/78, A, C, 78002999

Wilbarger County

Doan's Adobe House, E of Odell off U.S. 283, Odell vicinity, 2/08/79, A, C, 79003023

Willacy County

Old Lyford High School, High School Circle, Lyford, 11/07/85, A, 85002770

Williamson County

Amos, Martin C., House [Georgetown MRA], 1408 Olive, Georgetown, 4/29/86, C, 86000989

Arnold—Torbet House [Georgetown MRA], 908 Pine, Georgetown, 4/29/86, C, 86000990

Atkinson House [Georgetown MRA], 911 Walnut, Georgetown, 4/29/86, C, 86000992

Belford Historic District [Georgetown MRA], Roughly bounded by University Ave., Main, E. Eighteenth, and Austin, Georgetown, 4/29/86, C, 86000991

Bowlen House [Georgetown MRA], 1405 Forest, Georgetown, 1/14/86, C, 86000180

Bryson Stage Coach Stop, NW of Liberty Hill on TX 29, Liberty Hill vicinity, 12/01/78, A, C, 78003000

Burcham House [Georgetown MRA], 1310 College, Georgetown, 4/29/86, C, 86000993

Casey House [Georgetown MRA], 705 E. Third, Georgetown, 1/14/86, C, 86000184

Caswell House [Georgetown MRA], 207 E. Ninth, Georgetown, 4/29/86, C, 86000994

Chesser—Morgan House [Georgetown MRA], 1202 E. Fifteenth, Georgetown, 1/14/86, C, 86000185

Daughtrey, E. M., House [Georgetown MRA], 1316 E. University, Georgetown, 4/29/86, C, 86000984

Easley, S. A., House [Georgetown MRA], 1310 Olive, Georgetown, 4/29/86, C, 86000983

First Methodist Church [Georgetown MRA], 410 E. University, Georgetown, 6/17/86, C, a, 86001368

Fowler, D. D., House [Georgetown MRA], 1531 Ash, Georgetown, 4/29/86, C, 86000985

Grace Episcopal Church [Georgetown MRA], 1314 E. University, Georgetown, 4/29/86, C, a, b, 86000986

Harper—Chesser House [Georgetown MRA], 1309 College, Georgetown, 4/29/86, C, 86000969

Harrell, Moses, House [Georgetown MRA], 1001 Church, Georgetown, 1/14/86, B, C, 86000169

Harris, E. M., House [Georgetown MRA], 404 E. Seventh, Georgetown, 1/14/86, C, 86000168

Hawnen, A. W., House [Georgetown MRA], 1409 Olive, Georgetown, 4/29/86, C, 86000967

House at 214 W. University [Georgetown MRA], 214 W. University, Georgetown, 4/29/86, C, 86000987

House at 801 West [Georgetown MRA], 801 West, Georgetown, 1/14/86, C, 86000172

House at 907 Pine [Georgetown MRA], 907 Pine, Georgetown, 1/14/86, C, 86000171

Hyer, Dr. Robert, House [Georgetown MRA], 904 Ash, Georgetown, 1/14/86, B, C, 86000175

Imhoff House [Georgetown MRA], 208 Austin, Georgetown, 1/14/86, C, 86000176

Inn at Brushy Creek, Taylor Exit off U.S. 79, off I-35, Old Round Rock, 10/15/70, C, 70000777

Irvine, George, House [Georgetown MRA], 409 E. University, Georgetown, 4/29/86, B, C, 86000973

Johnson, J. J., Farm [Georgetown MRA], Rabbitt Hill Rd., Georgetown, 1/14/86, C, 86000178

Kenney's Fort Site (41WM465), Address Restricted, Round Rock vicinity, 4/20/87, A, D, 87000565

Lane—Riley House [Georgetown MRA], 1302 College, Georgetown, 4/29/86, C, 86000975

Leake, Will and Mary, House [Georgetown MRA], 313 E. Seventh, Georgetown, 4/29/86, C, 86000976

Leavell, John, House [Georgetown MRA], 803 College, Georgetown, 4/29/86, B, C, 86000979

Lockett, M. B. and Annie, House [Georgetown MRA], 811 E. University, Georgetown, 4/29/86, B, C, 86000981

Love, Frank and Mellie, House [Georgetown MRA], 1415 Ash, Georgetown, 4/29/86, B, C, 86000977

Makemson, W. K. and Kate, House [Georgetown MRA], 1002 Ash, Georgetown, 1/14/86, A, C, 86000190

McFadin House, N of Taylor, Taylor vicinity, 4/09/80, B, C, 80004160

McKnight—Ebb House [Georgetown MRA], 502 W. Eighteenth, Georgetown, 1/14/86, C, 86000191

McMurray House [Georgetown MRA], 611 Church, Georgetown, 1/14/86, C, 86000192

Merrell, Capt. Nelson, House, NE of Round Rock on U.S. 79, Round Rock vicinity, 10/15/70, C, 70000778

Miller—Ellyson House [Georgetown MRA], 303 E. Ninth, Georgetown, 1/14/86, C, 86000193

Old Georgetown High School [Georgetown MRA], 507 E. University, Georgetown, 1/14/86, C, 86000195

Paige—DeCrow—Weir House [Georgetown MRA], I-35 and SR 2243, Georgetown, 1/14/86, C, 86000194

Patrick, Woodson and Margaret, House [Georgetown MRA], 211 E. Fifth, Georgetown, 1/14/86, C, 86000197

Pegues House [Georgetown MRA], 904 E. University, Georgetown, 1/14/86, C, 86000196

Price, R. H. and Martha, House [Georgetown MRA], 209 E. Tenth, Georgetown, 4/29/86, C, 86000982

Railroad Produce Depot, 401 W. 6th St., Georgetown, 11/07/79, C, 79003024

Reedy, J. H., House [Georgetown MRA], 908 E. University, Georgetown, 4/29/86, C, 86000949

Round Rock Commercial Historic District, 100 and 200 blks E. Main St., Round Rock, 6/09/83, A, C, 83003170

Round Rock Post Office and William M. Owen House, Chisholm Trail and Emanuel St., Round Rock, 7/07/83, A, C, 83003171

Rouser House [Georgetown MRA], 602 Myrtle, Georgetown, 1/14/86, C, 86000198

Saint John's Methodist Church [Georgetown MRA], 301 E. University, Georgetown, 4/29/86, A, C, a, 86000950

Sansom—Schmalenbeck House [Georgetown MRA], 813 Church, Georgetown, 1/14/86, C, 86000199

Williamson County—Continued

Saxon Motor Car Store [Georgetown MRA], 316 E. Sixth St., Georgetown, 6/17/86, C, b, 86001366

Sillure, A. W., House [Georgetown MRA], 1414 Ash, Georgetown, 4/29/86, C, 86000951

Southwestern University Administration Building and Mood Hall, University Ave., Southwestern University campus, Georgetown, 4/23/75, C, 75002013

Stone, Robert and Lula, House [Georgetown MRA], 1102 Ash, Georgetown, 1/14/86, C, 86000200

Taylor National Bank, 200 Main St., Taylor, 5/23/80, A, C, 80004159

Taylor—Cooper House [Georgetown MRA], 105 E. Fifth, Georgetown, 1/14/86, B, C, 86000203

Tinnen House, 1220 Austin St., Georgetown, 8/25/70, C, 70000776

University Avenue-Elm Street Historic District, E. University and Elm Sts., Georgetown, 12/06/79, C, 79003025

Vaden, W. C. and Kate, House [Georgetown MRA], 711 E. University, Georgetown, 4/29/86, C, 86000952

Wesley Chapel A.M.E Church [Georgetown MRA], 508 W. Fourth, Georgetown, 1/14/86, C, a, 86000204

Wilcox, D. K. and Inez, House [Georgetown MRA], 1307 Olive, Georgetown, 4/29/86, C, 86000954

Wilcox—Graves House [Georgetown MRA], 1403 Olive, Georgetown, 4/29/86, C, 86000953

Williamson County Courthouse Historical District, Rock and 9th Sts., Main and 7th Sts. (includes both sides), Georgetown, 7/26/77, A, C, 77001480

Williamson County Courthouse Historic District (Boundary Increase) [Georgetown MRA], 114–124 and 113 E. Eighth St., Georgetown, 4/29/86, A, C, 86000955

Wilson County

Rancho de las Cabras, Address Restricted, Floresville vicinity, 3/20/73, D, 73001985

Whitehall, N of Sutherland Springs on SR 539, Sutherland Springs vicinity, 2/01/80, B, C, 80004161

Wilson County Courthouse and Jail, Public Sq., Floresville, 5/05/78, C, 78003001

Wise County

Administration Building, Decatur Baptist College, 1602 S. Trinity St., Decatur, 3/11/71, A, C, a, 71000973

Brown, J. T., Hotel, E. Decatur St, Chico, 10/16/79, A, C, 79003026

Waggoner Mansion, 1003 E. Main, Decatur, 5/01/74, C, 74002098

Wise County Courthouse, Public Sq., Decatur, 12/12/76, C, 76002085

Wood County

Haines, George W., Site, Address Restricted, Hainesville vicinity, 5/10/90, D, 90000764

Howle Site, Address Restricted, Quitman vicinity, 4/13/77, D, 77001482

Moody, Joseph and Martha, Farmstead, Address Restricted, Hainesville vicinity, 5/10/90, D, 90000765

Moody, Ned, Site, Address Restricted, Hainesville vicinity, 5/04/90, D, 90000724

Osborn Site, Address Restricted, Quitman vicinity, 12/15/76, D, 76002086

Sadler Site, Address Restricted, Alba vicinity, 4/13/77, D, 77001481

Young County

Fort Belknap, 1 mi. S of jct. of TX 24 and 251, Newcastle vicinity, 10/15/66, A, e, NHL, 66000824

Harrell Site, Address Restricted, South Bend vicinity, 10/15/66, D, NHL, 66000825

National Theater, 522 Oak St., Graham, 6/24/93, C, 93000565

Street, Spencer Boyd, Houses, 800 and 804 3rd St., Graham, 8/16/84, C, 84002005

Zapata County

Corralitos Ranch, 2 mi. N of San Ygnacio off U.S. 83, San Ygnacio vicinity, 8/02/77, A, C, D, 77001483

Dolores Nuevo, Address Restricted, Laredo vicinity, 11/27/73, C, D, 73001986

Dolores Viejo, Address Restricted, San Ygnacio vicinity, 8/17/73, D, 73001987

San Francisco Ranch, 1 mi. N of San Ygnacio, San Ygnacio vicinity, 3/25/77, A, C, 77001484

San Ygnacio Historic District, Town of San Ygnacio, San Ygnacio, 7/16/73, C, 73001988

Commissioned by Fort Worth oilman Richard Otto Dulaney, the Sinclair Building (ca. 1930) is an outstanding local example of a Zigzag Moderne commercial office building. (Danny Biggs, 1989)

U.S. MINOR ISLANDS

Midway Islands Territory

World War II Facilities at Midway, Sand and Eastern Islands, Midway Islands, 5/28/87, A, g, NHL, 87001302

Wake Island Territory

Wake Island, In the North Pacific, Pacific Ocean, 9/16/85, A, g, NHL, 85002726

UTAH

Beaver County

Ashworth, John, House [Beaver MRA], 1105 S. 1st West, Beaver, 11/29/83, C, 83003828

Ashworth, John, House [Beaver MRA], 115 S. 200 West, Beaver, 11/29/83, C, 83003830

Atkin, James, House [Beaver MRA], 260 W. 300 North, Beaver, 9/17/82, C, 82004075

Atkins and Smith House [Beaver MRA], 390 N. 400 West, Beaver, 4/15/83, C, 83004390

Baldwin, Caleb, House [Beaver MRA], 195 S. 400 East, Beaver, 11/30/83, C, 83003834

Barton, William, House [Beaver MRA], 295 N. 300 East, Beaver, 9/17/82, C, 82004076

Beaver City Library [Beaver MRA], 50 W. Center St., Beaver, 4/15/83, C, 83004391

Beaver County Courthouse, 90 E. Center St., Beaver, 10/06/70, C, 70000622

Beaver High School [Beaver MRA], 150 N. Main St., Beaver, 9/17/82, C, 82004077

Beaver Opera House, 55 E. Center St., Beaver, 2/11/82, C, 82004078

Beaver Relief Society Meetinghouse [Beaver MRA], 35 N. 1st East, Beaver, 11/29/83, A, a, 83003837

Bird, Edward, House [Beaver MRA], Center and 300 East, Beaver, 4/15/83, C, 83004392

Black, John, House [Beaver MRA], 595 N. 100 West, Beaver, 9/17/82, C, 82004079

Bohn, Joseph, House [Beaver MRA], 355 S. 200 West, Beaver, 9/17/82, C, 82004080

Boyter, Alexander, House [Beaver MRA], 590 N. 200 West, Beaver, 4/15/83, C, 83004393

Boyter, James, House [Beaver MRA], 90 W. 200 North, Beaver, 4/15/83, C, 83004394

Boyter, James, Shop [Beaver MRA], 50 W. 200 North, Beaver, 4/15/83, C, 83004395

Bradshaw, George Albert, House [Beaver MRA], 265 N. 200 West, Beaver, 11/29/83, C, 83003839

Burt, William, House [Beaver MRA], 515 E. Center St., Beaver, 11/30/83, C, 83003841

Cowdell, Enoch E., House [Beaver MRA], 595 N. 4th West, Beaver, 9/17/82, A, C, 82004081

Cox, Silas, House [Beaver MRA], 1st South and 4th East, Beaver, 11/29/83, C, 83003844

Crosby, Alma, House [Beaver MRA], 115 E. 1st North, Beaver, 4/15/83, C, 83004396

Dalten, Charles A., House [Beaver MRA], 270 S. 1st West, Beaver, 9/17/82, C, 82004082

Dean, James Heber, House [Beaver MRA], 390 W. 500 North, Beaver, 9/17/82, C, 82004083

Erickson House [Beaver MRA], 290 N. 300 West, Beaver, 9/17/82, C, 82004084

Farnsworth, Julia P. M., Barn [Beaver MRA], 180 W. Center St. (rear), Beaver, 9/17/82, C, 82004085

Farnsworth, Julia, House [Beaver MRA], 180 W. Center St., Beaver, 9/17/82, C, 82004086

Fennemore, Dr. George, House, 90 S. 100 West, Beaver, 2/01/80, C, 80003885

Fennemore, James, House [Beaver MRA], 195 N. 2nd East, Beaver, 4/15/83, C, 83004397

Fernley, Edward, House [Beaver MRA], 215 E. 200 North, Beaver, 11/29/83, C, 83003846

Fernley, William, House [Beaver MRA], 1045 E. 200 North, Beaver, 11/30/83, C, 83003848

Fort Cameron, E of Beaver on UT 153, Beaver vicinity, 9/09/74, A, a, 74001932

Fotheringham, Caroline, House [Beaver MRA], 290 N. 600 East, Beaver, 9/17/82, C, 82004087

Fotheringham, William, House [Beaver MRA], 190 W. 1st North, Beaver, 4/15/83, C, 83004403

Frazer, David L., House [Beaver MRA], 817 E. 200 North, Beaver, 11/30/83, B, C, 83003850

Frazer, Thomas, House, 590 N. 300 West, Beaver, 11/16/78, B, 78002650

Frisco Charcoal Kilns, W of Milford off UT 21, Milford vicinity, 3/09/82, A, 82004793

Gale, Henry C., House [Beaver MRA], 495 N. 1st East, Beaver, 11/29/83, C, 83003851

Gale, Henry C., House [Beaver MRA], 95 E. 500 North, Beaver, 4/15/83, C, 83004404

Greenwood, William, House [Beaver MRA], 190 S. 1st West, Beaver, 9/17/82, B, 82004088

Grimshaw, Duckworth, House, 95 N. 400 West, Beaver, 2/01/80, C, 80003886

Grimshaw, John, House [Beaver MRA], 290 N. 200 East, Beaver, 9/17/82, C, 82004089

Harris, Louis W., Flour Mill [Beaver MRA], 915 E. 200 North, Beaver, 9/17/82, A, 82004090

Harris, Louis W., House [Beaver MRA], 55 E. 200 North, Beaver, 4/15/83, C, 83004405

Harris, Sarah Eliza, House [Beaver MRA], 375 E. 200 North, Beaver, 4/15/83, C, 83004406

Hawkins, William and Eliza, House [Beaver MRA], 95 E. 200 North, Beaver, 11/29/83, C, 83003852

House at 110 S. 3rd West [Beaver MRA], 110 S. 3rd West, Beaver, 11/30/83, C, 83003861

House at 325 S. Main St. [Beaver MRA], 325 S. Main St., Beaver, 11/30/83, C, 83003862

Huntington, Joseph, House [Beaver MRA], 215 S. 2nd West, Beaver, 4/15/83, C, 83004407

Jackson, Samuel, House [Beaver MRA], 215 S. 2nd East, Beaver, 11/30/83, C, 83003863

Jenner-Griffiths House, 10 N. 300 East, Minersville, 5/16/85, C, 85001118

Jones, Thomas, House [Beaver MRA], 635 N. 400 West, Beaver, 9/17/82, C, 82004091

Lee, John Ruphard, House [Beaver MRA], 195 N. 1st West, Beaver, 9/17/82, C, 82004092

Limb, Lester, House [Beaver MRA], 495 N. 400 West, Beaver, 9/17/82, C, 82004093

Low Hotel [Beaver MRA], 95 N. Main St., Beaver, 11/29/83, C, 83003865

Maeser, Reinhard, House [Beaver MRA], 295 E. 200 North, Beaver, 11/29/83, C, 83003871

Mansfield, Murdock and Co. Store [Beaver MRA], W. Center and N. Main Sts., Beaver, 11/29/83, A, 83003868

McEvan, Mathew, House [Beaver MRA], 205 N. 100 West, Beaver, 4/15/83, C, 83004408

Meeting Hall [Beaver MRA], 1st North and 3rd East, Beaver, 9/17/82, C, a, 82004094

Minersville City Hall [Public Works Buildings TR], 600 W. Main St., Minersville, 4/01/85, A, 85000795

Morgan, William, House [Beaver MRA], 110 W. 600 North, Beaver, 4/15/83, C, 83004409

Morris, Andrew James, House [Beaver MRA], 110 N. 400 East, Beaver, 9/17/82, C, 82004095

Moyes, William, Jr., House [Beaver MRA], 395 N. 100 West, Beaver, 11/29/83, C, 83003873

Mud Spring [Great Basin Style Rock Art TR], Address Restricted, Garrison vicinity, 6/04/85, D, 85001231

Muir, David, House, 295 N. 300 West, Beaver, 11/25/80, A, C, 80003887

Murdock, Almira Lott, House [Beaver MRA], 85 W. 1st North, Beaver, 11/29/83, A, 83003878

Murdock, John Riggs and Wolfenden, Mary Ellen, House [Beaver MRA], 90 W. 1st North, Beaver, 11/29/83, A, 83003884

Nowers, Wilson G., House [Beaver MRA], 195 E. 1st North, Beaver, 11/29/83, C, 83003876

Odd Fellows Hall [Beaver MRA], 33-35 N. Main St., Beaver, 11/29/83, C, 83003885

Olcott, Frances A., House [Beaver MRA], 590 E. 100 North, Beaver, 11/30/83, C, 83003886

Orwin, Jessie, House [Beaver MRA], 390 W. 600 North, Beaver, 11/29/83, C, 83003888

Powell, David, House [Beaver MRA], 115 N. 400 West, Beaver, 4/15/83, C, 83004410

Puffer, Ephraim Orvel, House [Beaver MRA], 195 S. 2nd East, Beaver, 11/29/83, C, 83003889

Reeves, Sylvester H., House [Beaver MRA], 90 N. 2nd West, Beaver, 11/29/83, C, 83003890

Robinson, James E., House [Beaver MRA], 415 E. 400 North, Beaver, 9/17/82, C, 82004096

Robinson, William, House [Beaver MRA], E of Beaver on UT 153, Beaver vicinity, 11/30/83, C, 83003891

Robinson, William, House [Beaver MRA], 95 N. 300 West, Beaver, 4/15/83, C, 83004411

Ryan Ranch (42 BE 618) [Great Basin Style Rock Art TR], Address Restricted, Beaver vicinity, 6/04/85, D, 85001232

School House [Beaver MRA], 325 N. 200 West, Beaver, 11/29/83, A, C, 83003892

Shepherd, Dr. Warren, House [Beaver MRA], 50 W. 1st North, Beaver, 4/15/83, C, 83004412

Shepherd, Harriet S., House, 190 N. 200 East, Beaver, 2/08/80, C, 80003888

Skinner, Horace A., House [Beaver MRA], 185 S. Main St., Beaver, 11/29/83, C, 83003894

Smith, Ellen, House [Beaver MRA], 395 N. 300 West, Beaver, 11/29/83, C, 83003896

Smith, Seth W., House [Beaver MRA], 190 N. 600 East, Beaver, 9/17/82, C, 82004097

Smith, William P., House [Beaver MRA], 190 E. Center St., Beaver, 11/29/83, C, 83003898

Beaver County—Continued

Stephens, Mitchell M., House [Beaver MRA], 495 N. 200 East, Beaver, 11/29/83, C, 83003899

Stoney, Robert W., House [Beaver MRA], 305 W. 300 North, Beaver, 11/30/83, C, 83003900

Stoney, Robert, House [Beaver MRA], 295 N. 400 West, Beaver, 9/17/82, C, 82004098

Structure at 490 E. 200 North [Beaver MRA], 490 E. 200 North, Beaver, 9/17/82, C, 82004099

Tanner, Henry M., House [Beaver MRA], 400 North and 300 East, Beaver, 4/15/83, C, 83004413

Tanner, Jake, House [Beaver MRA], 580 S. 200 West, Beaver, 11/30/83, C, 83003901

Tanner, Sidney, House [Beaver MRA], 195 E. 200 North, Beaver, 4/15/83, C, 83004414

Tattersall, Joseph, House [Beaver MRA], 195 N. 400 West, Beaver, 9/17/82, C, 82004100

Thompson, Mary I., House [Beaver MRA], 25 N. 400 East, Beaver, 11/30/83, C, 83003902

Thompson, W. O., House [Beaver MRA], 415 N. 400 West, Beaver, 9/17/82, C, 82004101

Thompson, William, House [Beaver MRA], 160 E. Center St., Beaver, 9/17/82, C, 82004102

Thompson, William, Jr., House [Beaver MRA], 10 W. 400 North, Beaver, 9/17/82, C, 82004103

Tolton, Edward, House [Beaver MRA], 210 W. 400 North, Beaver, 9/17/82, C, 82004104

Tolton, J. F., Grocery [Beaver MRA], 25 N. Main St., Beaver, 11/29/83, C, 83003905

Tolton, Walter S., House [Beaver MRA], 195 W. 500 North, Beaver, 11/29/83, C, 83003910

Twitchell, Ancil, House [Beaver MRA], 100 S. 200 East, Beaver, 2/23/84, C, 84002146

Tyler, Daniel, House [Beaver MRA], 310 N. Main St., Beaver, 11/29/83, C, 83003943

US Post Office—Beaver Main [US Post Offices in Utah 1900–1941 MPS], 20 S. Main St., Beaver, 11/27/89, A, C, 89001992

Upper Beaver Hydroelectric Power Plant Historic District [Electric Power Plants of Utah MPS], UT 153 10 mi. E of Beaver, Beaver vicinity, 4/20/89, A, B, C, 89000282

White, Charles Dennis, House, 115 E. 400 North St., Beaver, 2/14/80, C, 80003889

White, Maggie Gillies, House [Beaver MRA], 200 North, Beaver, 2/23/84, C, 84002149

White, Samuel, House [Beaver MRA], 315 N. 100 East, Beaver, 11/29/83, C, 83003944

White, William H., House [Beaver MRA], 510 N. 100 East, Beaver, 2/23/84, C, 84002153

Wildhorse Canyon Obsidian Quarry, Address Restricted, Milford vicinity, 5/13/76, D, 76001810

Willden, Charles, House [Beaver MRA], 180 E. 300 South, Beaver, 11/30/83, C, 83003945

Willden, Elliot, House [Beaver MRA], 340 S. Main St., Beaver, 11/30/83, C, 83003946

Willden, Feargus O'Connor, House [Beaver MRA], 120 E. 1st South, Beaver, 11/29/83, C, 83003947

Willden, John, House [Beaver MRA], 495 N. 200 West, Beaver, 9/17/82, A, C, 82004105

Yardley, John, House [Beaver MRA], 210 S. 1st West, Beaver, 11/29/83, C, 83003948

Box Elder County

Bear River High School Science Building [Public Works Buildings TR], 1450 S. Main St., Garland, 4/01/85, A, g, 85000797

Box Elder County Courthouse, 1 N. Main St., Brigham City, 4/07/88, A, C, 88000399

Box Elder Flouring Mill [Brigham City MPS], 327 East 200 North, Brigham City, 1/24/90, A, B, C, a, 89000452

Box Elder High School Gymnasium [Public Works Buildings TR], 18 N. 400 East, Brigham City, 4/01/85, A, C, 85000796

Box Elder Stake Tabernacle, Main St. between 2nd and 3rd South Sts., Brigham City, 5/14/71, A, C, a, 71000840

Brigham City Carnegie Library [Carnegie Library TR], 26 E. Forest St., Brigham City, 10/25/84, A, 84000143

Brigham City Fire Station/City Hall, 6 N. Main St., Brigham City, 4/07/88, A, C, 88000389

Brigham City Mercantile and Manufacturing Association Mercantile Store [Brigham City MPS], 5 N. Main St., Brigham City, 1/24/90, A, C, a, 89000453

Central Pacific Railroad Grade Historic District, 87 mi. segment between Umbria jct. 9 mi. E. of NV border around N end of Great Salt Lake to Golden Spike NHS, Park Valley vicinity, 5/15/87, A, D, g, 87000699

Compton, Alma, House, 142 S. 100 East, Brigham City, 4/07/88, B, 88000381

Corinne Methodist Episcopal Church, Corner of Colorado and S. 600 Sts., Corinne, 5/14/71, A, a, 71000842

Cutler Hydroelectric Power Plant Historic District [Electric Power Plants of Utah MPS], Off UT 30 at Bear River, Beaver Dam vicinity, 4/20/89, A, C, 89000280

Elberta Theatre [Brigham City MPS], 53 S. Main St., Brigham City, 10/17/91, A, 91001544

Fryer Hotel, 3274 W. 11300 North, Deweyville, 4/07/88, A, C, 88000379

Garland Carnegie Library [Carnegie Library TR], 86 W. Factory St., Garland, 10/25/84, A, 84000146

Golden Spike National Historic Site, NE of Great Salt Lake, Promontory vicinity, 10/15/66, A, C, D, NPS, 66000080

Granary of the Relief Society [Brigham City MPS], 100 North 400 East, Brigham City, 1/24/90, A, a, 89000455

Hampton's Ford Stage Stop and Barn, NW of Collinston on UT 154 at Bear River, Collinston vicinity, 8/12/71, A, 71000841

Hogup Cave (42BO36), Address Restricted, Park Valley vicinity, 5/08/86, A, D, g, 86001016

Hotel Brigham [Brigham City MPS], 13 and 17 W. Forest St., Brigham City, 10/17/91, A, 91001543

Knudson Brothers Building [Brigham City MPS], 63 S. Main St., Brigham City, 7/16/92, A, 92000893

Lower Bear River Archeological Discontiguous District, Address Restricted, Brigham City vicinity, 2/13/86, D, 86000249

Oregon Short Line Depot, 800 West and Forest St., Brigham City, 7/16/92, A, C, 92000891

Planing Mill of Brigham City Mercantile and Manufacturing Association [Brigham City MPS], 547 E. Forest St., Brigham City, 1/24/90, A, a, 89000454

Plymouth School [Public Works Buildings TR], 135 S. Main, Plymouth, 4/09/86, A, C, 86000733

Southern Pacific Railroad: Ogden-Lucin Cut-Off Trestle, 30 mi. W of Ogden at N arm of Great Salt Lake, Ogden vicinity, 4/14/72, C, 72001257

Tanner, A. N., House, Grouse Creek, Grouse Creek, 2/11/82, C, 82004107

Union Block [Brigham City MPS], 57 S. Main St., Brigham City, 10/17/91, A, 91001545

Willard Historic District, Roughly bounded by 200 W., 200 N., 100 E., and 200 S. Sts., Willard, 6/25/74, A, C, 74001933

Cache County

Baker, George Washington, House, 115 N. 100 West, Mendon, 2/10/83, C, 83004416

Baker, Samuel, House, 150 W. 200 North, Mendon, 3/31/83, A, C, 83004417

Benson Elementary School [Public Works Buildings TR], 3440 N. 3000 West, Benson, 4/01/85, A, 85000798

Bradshaw, George, House and Joshua Salisbury/George Bradshaw Barn, 73 S. Ceneter St., Wellsville, 11/19/82, C, 82004846

Clarkston Tithing Granary [Tithing Offices and Granaries of the Mormon Church TR], 10212 N. 8700 West, Clarkston, 1/25/85, A, C, a, 85000250

Douglas General Mercantile, 100 Main St., Smithfield, 8/04/82, A, 82004113

Eccles, David, House, 250 W. Center St., Logan, 7/30/76, B, C, 76001811

Gardner, James, House, 173 N. Main St., Mendon, 2/11/82, C, 82004111

Hanson, Soren, House, 166 W. Main St., Hyrum, 2/11/82, B, C, 82004109

Harris, Martin, Gravesite, N of Clarkston, Clarkston vicinity, 11/28/80, B, c, 80003890

Holley—Globe Grain and Milling Company Elevator, 100 North and Center St., Hyrum, 10/24/85, C, 85003386

Home Economics/Commons Building [Public Works Buildings TR], Off US 89, Utah State University, Logan, 4/01/85, A, C, 85000800

Howell-Theurer House, 30 S. 100 East, Wellsville, 10/18/79, B, C, 79002490

Hyrum First Ward Meetinghouse, 290 S. Center St., Hyrum, 2/15/80, A, C, a, 80003891

Hyrum Stake Tithing Office [Tithing Offices and Granaries of the Mormon Church TR], 26 W. Main St., Hyrum, 1/25/85, A, a, 85000251

Lee, John E., House, 123 W. Center St., Hyde Park, 2/11/82, C, 82004108

Lewiston Community Building [Public Works Buildings TR], 29 S. Main St., Lewiston, 4/01/85, A, 85000799

Lewiston Tithing Office and Granary [Tithing Offices and Granaries of the Mormon Church

Cache County—Continued

TR], 87 E. 800 South, Lewiston, 1/25/85, A, C, a, 85000252

Logan Center Street Historic District, Roughly bounded by 200 North, 200 South, 200 East and 600 West, Logan, 4/26/79, A, C, 79002488

Logan Fish Hatchery Caretaker's Residence [Public Works Buildings TR], 1469 W. 200 North, Logan, 4/01/85, A, 85000801

Logan High School Gymnasium [Public Works Buildings TR], 162 W. 100 South, Logan, 8/07/85, A, C, 85001844

Logan LDS Sixth Ward Church, 395 S. Main St., Logan, 7/17/79, A, C, a, 79002489

Logan Municipal Slaughterhouse [Public Works Buildings TR], 265 N. 600 West, Logan, 4/01/85, A, 85000802

Logan Tabernacle, Bounded by Center, 1st North, Main, and 1st East Sts., Logan, 10/10/75, A, C, a, 75001800

Logan Temple, Between 2nd and 3rd East and 1st and 2nd North, Logan, 11/20/75, A, C, a, 75001801

Logan Temple Barn, 368 E. Two Hundred N, Logan, 12/19/85, A, C, a, 85003199

Mendon Elementary School [Public Works Buildings TR], Off UT 23, Mendon, 4/01/85, A, g, 85000803

Mitton, Samuel Crowthers, House, 242 E. Main St., Wellsville, 11/19/82, C, 82004847

Newton Reservoir, 3 mi. N of Newton, Newton vicinity, 11/30/73, A, 73001860

Old Main, Utah State University, Utah State University campus, Logan, 2/23/72, A, C, 72001258

Paradise Tithing Office [Tithing Offices and Granaries of the Mormon Church TR], 8970 S. 200 West, Paradise, 1/25/85, A, C, a, 85000253

Providence LDS Chapel and Meetinghouse, 20 S. Main St., Providence, 2/11/82, A, C, a, 82004112

Richmond Carnegie Library [Carnegie Library TR], 6 W. Main St., Richmond, 10/25/84, A, 84000147

Richmond Community Building [Public Works Buildings TR], 6 W. Main, Richmond, 4/09/86, A, C, g, 86000731

Richmond Tithing Office [Tithing Offices and Granaries of the Mormon Church TR], 31 S. State St., Richmond, 1/25/85, A, C, a, 85000256

Riggs, Zial, House, 94 S. 100 E St., Wellsville, 2/11/82, C, 82004114

Smith, William McNeil, House, 116 S. 100 East, Logan, 2/11/82, C, 82004110

Smithfield Public Library, 25 N. Main St., Smithfield, 2/17/81, A, C, 81000580

Smithfield Tithing Office [Tithing Offices and Granaries of the Mormon Church TR], 35 W. Center, Smithfield, 1/25/85, A, a, 85000258

Tony Grove Ranger Station Historic District, US 89, 23 mi. NE of Logan, Wasatch—Cache NF, Logan vicinity, 4/13/92, A, C, 92000338

Wellsville Relief Society Meeting House [Mormon Church Buildings in Utah, 1847–1936 MPS], 67 S. Center, Wellsville, 2/13/89, A, a, 88003439

Wellsville Tabernacle, 75 S. 100 East St., Wellsville, 11/26/80, C, a, 80003893

Willie, James G., House, 97 N. 100 West, Mendon, 4/13/83, A, C, 83004418

Women's Residence Hall [Public Works Buildings TR], Utah State University, Logan, 4/09/86, A, C, g, 86000735

Zollinger, Ferdinand, Jr., House, 193 N. 100 East, Providence, 7/16/92, C, 92000892

Carbon County

Desolation Canyon, Address Unknown, Green River, 11/24/68, B, NHL, 68000057

Flat Canyon Archeological District, Address Restricted, Price vicinity, 12/12/78, D, 78002654

Harmon, Oliver John, House, 211 S. 200 East, Price, 8/18/92, C, 92001058

Hellenic Orthodox Church of the Assumption, 61 S. 2nd East, Price, 4/11/73, A, a, 73001861

Helper Commercial District, Bounded by RR tracks, Janet, 1st, West, and Locust Sts, Helper, 7/24/79, A, C, 79002491

Loofbourow, James W. and Mary K., House, 187 N. One Hundred E, Price, 4/10/86, C, 86000722

Millarich, Martin, Hall, Main St., Spring Glen, 10/31/80, A, g, 80003894

Notre Dame de Lourdes Catholic Church, 200 N. Carbon Ave., Price, 1/09/78, A, 78002651

Parker and Weeter Block, 85 W. Main St., Price, 3/09/82, C, 82004115

Price Municipal Building, 200 East and Main St., Price, 2/17/78, A, 78002652

Price Tavern/Braffet Block, E. 100 South and Carbon Ave., Price, 8/11/78, A, 78002653

Star Theatre, 20 E. Main St., Price, 8/09/82, A, C, 82004116

Topolovec Farmstead, Main St., Spring Glen, 8/09/82, A, C, 82004117

US Post Office—Helper Main [US Post Offices in Utah 1900–1941 MPS], 45 S. Main, Helper, 11/27/89, A, C, D, 89001995

US Post Office—Price Main [US Post Offices in Utah 1900–1941 MPS], 95 S. Carbon Ave., Price, 11/27/89, A, C, 89001998

Daggett County

John Jarvie Historic Ranch District, Green River and Indian Crossing Bridge SW of Jarvis, Brown's Park, 1/14/86, A, 86000232

Manila Petroglyphs, Address Restricted, Manila vicinity, 10/06/75, D, 75001802

Parson, Dr. John, Cabin Complex, SW of Bridgeport, Bridgeport vicinity, 11/21/76, A, B, 76001812

Swett Ranch, NE of Dutch John, Dutch John vicinity, 7/10/79, A, C, g, 79002492

Ute Mountain Fire Tower, SW of Manila, Manila vicinity, 4/10/80, A, C, g, 80003895

Davis County

Adams, Joseph, House, 300 N. Adamswood Rd., Layton, 2/17/78, A, C, 78002655

Barnes, John George Moroni, House, 42 W. Center St., Kaysville, 2/11/82, B, C, 82004120

Barnes, John R., House, 10 S. 100 West, Kaysville, 7/23/82, B, C, 82004121

Blood, Henry, House, 95 S. 300 West, Kaysville, 4/29/80, B, C, 80003897

Bountiful Tabernacle, Main and Centre Sts., Bountiful, 1/01/76, A, C, a, 76001813

Capener, William, House, 252 N. 400 East, Centerville, 1/05/84, C, 84002172

Farmer's Union Building, State and W. Gentile Sts., Layton, 11/30/78, A, 78002656

Farmington Tithing Office [Tithing Offices and Granaries of the Mormon Church TR], 108 N. Main St., Farmington, 3/28/85, A, C, a, 85000686

Fielding Garr Ranch, Off UT 127, Antelope Island, 1/21/83, A, 83004402

Green, James, House, 206 N. 100 East, Bountiful, 2/11/82, C, 82004118

Haight, Hector C., House, 208 N. Main St., Farmington, 5/17/85, A, C, 85001141

Layton, George W., House, W. Gentile St., Layton vicinity, 7/23/82, C, 82004122

Layton, John Henry, House, 683 W. Gentile St., West Layton, 2/11/82, A, C, 82004123

Randall, Melvin Harley, House, 390 E. Porter Lane, Centerville, 6/20/80, B, C, 80003896

Richards House, 386 N. 100 East, Farmington, 12/23/77, B, 77001303

Tingey, Thomas, House, 20 N. 300 East, Centerville, 7/28/83, C, 83004401

VanFleet Hotel, 88 E. State St., Farmington, 12/19/91, A, C, 91001819

Wilcox, James D., House, 93 E. One Hundred N, Farmington, 11/26/85, C, 85003051

Duchesne County

Simmons Ranch, 8 mi. S of US 40, Fruitland vicinity, 8/18/92, A, 92000463

Toyack Future Farmers of America Chapter House, 340 N. 300 West, Roosevelt, 5/18/84, A, 84002175

Emery County

Black Dragon Canyon Pictographs, Address Restricted, Green River vicinity, 9/04/80, D, 80003905

Buckhorn Wash Rock Art Sites, Address Restricted, Castle Dale vicinity, 8/01/80, D, 80003898

Castle Dale High School Shop [Public Works Buildings TR], 300 N. Center St., Castle Dale, 4/01/85, A, g, 85000804

Castle Dale School, 100 North and 100 East, Castle Dale, 9/06/78, C, 78002657

Emery County—Continued

Christensen, Paul C., House, Off UT 10, Castle Dale, 12/02/80, B, C, 80003899

Denver and Rio Grande Lime Kiln, SE of Cleveland, Cleveland vicinity, 8/26/80, A, 80003901

Emery LDS Church, Off UT 10, Emery, 2/22/80, C, a, 80003903

Ferron Box Pictographs and Petroglyphs, Address Restricted, Ferron, 7/11/80, D, 80003904

Ferron Presbyterian Church and Cottage, Mill Rd. and 3rd West, Ferron, 9/06/78, A, C, a, 78002658

Green River Presbyterian Church, 134 W. Third Ave., Green River, 1/05/89, A, C, a, 88002998

Huntington Roller Mill and Miller's House, 400 North St., Huntington, 9/27/79, A, C, 79002495

Huntington Tithing Granary [Tithing Offices and Granaries of the Mormon Church TR], 65 W. 300 North, Huntington, 1/25/85, A, a, b, 85000261

Johansen, Peter, House, N of Castle Dale off UT 29, Castle Dale vicinity, 3/19/80, B, 80003900

Larson, Lars Peter, House, Off UT 155, Cleveland, 2/13/80, B, C, 80003902

Rochester-Muddy Creek Petroglyph Site, Address Restricted, Emery vicinity, 6/26/75, D, 75001803

Seeley, Justis Wellington II, House, Center and 100 South Sts., Castle Dale, 11/15/79, B, C, 79002493

Singleton, Samuel, House, S of Ferron on UT 10, Ferron vicinity, 11/08/79, B, C, 79002494

Temple Mountain Wash Pictographs, Address Restricted, Hanksville vicinity, 3/15/76, D, 76001814

Garfield County

Boulder Elementary School [Public Works Buildings TR], Off UT 51, Boulder, 4/01/85, A, g, 85000805

Bryce Canyon Airport, SE of Panguitch off UT 12, Panguitch vicinity, 10/19/78, A, C, g, 78002660

Bryce Canyon Lodge and Deluxe Cabins, SR 63, Bryce Canyon National Park, 5/28/87, A, C, NHL, NPS, 87001339

Coombs Village Site, UT 117, Boulder, 1/01/76, D, 76001815

Friendship Cove Pictograph, Address Restricted, Escalante vicinity, 12/21/78, D, 78002659

Hole-in-the-Rock Trail, A trail commencing at Escalante, Utah and terminating at Bluff, Utah, Escalante vicinity, 8/09/82, A, C, NPS, 82004792

Kolb Brothers "Cat Camp" Inscription [Canyonlands National Park MRA], Big Drop #2 vicinity, Moab vicinity, 10/07/88, A, NPS, 88001250

Panguitch Carnegie Library [Carnegie Library TR], 75 E. Center St., Panguitch, 10/25/84, A, 84000148

Pole Hollow Archeological Site, Address Restricted, Panguitch vicinity, 7/16/81, D, 81000581

Starr Ranch, 46 mi. S of Hanksville, Hanksville vicinity, 4/23/76, A, C, 76001816

Grand County

Courthouse Wash Pictographs, 1 mi. NW of Moab in Arches National Park on UT 163, Moab vicinity, 4/01/76, C, D, NPS, 76000207

Dewey Bridge, NE of Moab on UT 128, Moab vicinity, 7/12/84, A, C, 84002179

Elk Mountain Mission Fort Site, NW of Moab off U.S. 160, Moab vicinity, 6/15/78, A, D, a, 78002661

Julien Incription Panel [Arches National Park MRA], Dark Angel vicinity, Moab vicinity, 10/06/88, A, NPS, 88001184

Julien, Denis, Inscription, Mouth of Hell Roaring Canyon, Green River Canyon, Moab vicinity, 5/23/91, A, 91000617

Moab Cabin, E. 1st St., Moab, 2/14/80, A, B, 80003906

Moab LDS Church, Off U.S. 160, Moab, 11/28/80, C, a, 80003907

Old Spanish Trail [Arches National Park MRA], Visitor Center vicinity, Moab vicinity, 10/06/88, A, NPS, 88001181

Pinhook Battleground, E of Moab, Moab vicinity, 3/01/82, A, 82004125

Ringhoffer Inscription [Arches National Park MRA], Tower Arch, Moab vicinity, 10/06/88, A, B, f, NPS, 88001185

Robidoux Inscription, Westwater Creek in Book Cliffs, Cisco vicinity, 7/23/82, B, 82004124

Rock House—Custodian's Residence [Arches National Park MRA], Visitor Center vicinity, Moab vicinity, 10/06/88, A, g, NPS, 88001186

Star Hall, 159 E. Center St., Moab, 5/14/93, A, C, a, 93000416

Taylor, Arthur, House, U.S. 163, Moab, 2/28/80, B, 80003908

Thompson Wash Rock Art District, Address Restricted, Thompson vicinity, 8/01/80, D, 80003909

Warner, Orlando W., House, Mill Creek Rd., Moab, 9/20/77, B, 77001304

Wolfe Ranch Historical District, N of Moab in Arches National Monument, Moab vicinity, 11/20/75, A, C, NPS, 75000167

Iron County

Caretaker's Cabin, Off UT 14, Cedar City vicinity, 8/04/83, C, g, NPS, 83004385

Cedar City Railroad Depot, 220 N. Main St., Cedar City, 8/09/84, A, C, 84002184

Ensign-Smith House, 96 N. Main St., Paragonah, 5/19/83, B, C, 83004400

Evans Mound (42IN40), Address Restricted, Summit vicinity, 10/24/85, D, 85003387

Gold Spring, Address Restricted, Modena vicinity, 7/21/77, A, 77001305

Hunter, Joseph S., House, 86 E. Center St., Cedar City, 2/11/82, C, 82004126

Long Flat Site, Address Restricted, Parowan vicinity, 11/01/79, D, 79002496

Modena Elementary School [Public Works Buildings TR], Off UT 56, Modena, 4/01/85, A, g, 85000806

Old Irontown, About 22 mi. W of Ceder City, 3 mi. S of UT 56, Cedar City vicinity, 5/14/71, A, 71000843

Old Main and Science Buildings, Southern Utah State College campus, Cedar City, 8/21/84, A, 84002186

Page, Daniel R. and Sophia G., House, Richie Flat at W. edge of Harmony Mountains, Page Ranch vicinity, 5/09/85, A, C, 85000961

Parowan Gap Petroglyphs, Address Restricted, Parowan vicinity, 10/10/75, D, 75001806

Parowan Meetinghouse, Center block of Main St., between Center and 100 South St., Parowan, 5/06/76, A, C, a, 76001818

Smith, Jesse N., House, 45 W. 100 South, Parowan, 6/20/75, B, C, 75001807

US Post Office—Cedar City Main [US Post Offices in Utah 1900–1941 MPS], 10 N. Main, Cedar City, 11/27/89, A, C, 89001993

Visitor Center, Off UT 14, Cedar City vicinity, 8/04/83, C, g, NPS, 83004386

Wood, George H., House, 432 N. Main St., Cedar City, 11/14/78, C, 78002662

Juab County

Booth, Edwin Robert, House, 94 W. 300 South, Nephi, 12/06/79, B, 79002497

Booth, Oscar M., House, 395 E. 100 South, Nephi, 4/18/83, C, 83004399

Centennial-Eureka Mine [Tintic Mining District MRA], S of Eureka, Eureka vicinity, 3/14/79, C, 79003481

Diamond Cemetery [Tintic Mining District MRA], S of Mammoth, Mammoth vicinity, 3/14/79, A, d, 79003474

Eagle and Blue Bell Mine [Tintic Mining District MRA], S of Eureka, Eureka vicinity, 3/14/79, C, 79003482

Eureka City Cemetery [Tintic Mining District MRA], SW of Eureka off US 50, Eureka vicinity, 3/14/79, D, d, 79003469

Eureka Historic District [Tintic Mining District MRA], Roughly bounded by city limits, Eureka vicinity, 3/14/79, A, C, 79002514

Fish Springs Caves Archeological District, Address Restricted, Callao vicinity, 5/11/81, D, 81000582

Fitch Cemetery [Tintic Mining District MRA], SR 36, Eureka vicinity, 3/14/79, A, d, 79003471

Grand Central Mine [Tintic Mining District MRA], N of Mammoth, Mammoth vicinity, 3/14/79, C, 79003480

Juab County Jail, 45 W. Center, Nephi, 11/20/87, A, 87002060

Knight Grain Elevator [Tintic Mining District MRA], SR 36, Eureka vicinity, 3/14/79, C, 79003470

Knightsville School Foundation [Tintic Mining District MRA], E of Eureka, Eureka vicinity, 3/14/79, A, 79003485

Juab County—Continued

Mammoth Historic District [Tintic Mining District MRA], Roughly bounded by city limits, Mammoth, 3/14/79, A, 79003468

Nephi Mounds, Address Restricted, Nephi vicinity, 9/09/75, D, 75001808

Showers Mine and Headframe [Tintic Mining District MRA], SE of Mammoth, Mammoth vicinity, 3/14/79, C, 79003475

Silver City Cemetery [Tintic Mining District MRA], SW of Mammoth, Mammoth vicinity, 3/14/79, D, d, 79003473

Sunbeam Mine [Tintic Mining District MRA], S of Mammoth, Mammoth vicinity, 3/14/79, A, 79003476

Tintic Smelter Site [Tintic Mining District MRA], Off US 50, Eureka vicinity, 3/14/79, A, 79003472

US Post Office—Eureka Main [US Post Offices in Utah 1900–1941 MPS], Main and Wallace, Eureka, 11/27/89, A, C, 89001994

US Post Office—Nephi Main [US Post Offices in Utah 1900–1941 MPS], 10 N. Main, Nephi, 11/27/89, A, C, 89001996

Union Pacific Railroad Depot [Tintic Mining District MRA], SE of Mammoth, Mammoth vicinity, 3/14/79, A, b, 79003478

Whitmore, George Carter, Mansion, 106 S. Main, Nephi, 12/12/78, B, C, 78002663

Kane County

Bowman-Chamberlain House, 14 E. 100 South, Kanab, 7/08/75, B, C, 75001811

Cottonwood Canyon Cliff Dwelling, Address Restricted, Kanab vicinity, 8/18/80, D, 80003910

Davis Gulch Pictograph Panel, Address Restricted, Glen Canyon vicinity, 6/05/75, D, NPS, 75000166

Hole-In-The-Rock, SE of Escalante in Glen Canyon National Recreation Area, Escalante, 11/03/75, A, NPS, 75000165

Mt. Carmel School and Church, Off UT 89, Mt. Carmel, 11/20/87, A, a, 87002061

Valley School [Public Works Buildings TR], Off US 89, Orderville, 4/01/85, A, C, g, 85000807

Millard County

Archeological Site No. 42Md300, Address Restricted, Millard vicinity, 8/06/80, D, 80003911

Cottonwood Wash (42 MD 183) [Great Basin Style Rock Art TR], Address Restricted, Milford vicinity, 6/04/85, D, 85001233

Cove Fort, 2 mi. E of I-15 on UT 4, Cove Fort vicinity, 10/06/70, A, 70000623

Deseret (42 MD 55) [Great Basin Style Rock Art TR], Address Restricted, Deseret vicinity, 6/04/85, D, 85001234

Fort Deseret, 2 mi. S of Deseret on UT 257, Deseret vicinity, 10/09/70, A, 70000624

Gunnison Massacre Site, 6 mi. SW of Hinckley on the Sevier River, Hinckley vicinity, 4/30/76, A, 76001819

Hinckley High School Gymnasium [Public Works Buildings TR], Off US 5/50, Hinckley, 4/01/85, A, C, g, 85000809

Kanosh Tithing Office [Tithing Offices and Granaries of the Mormon Church TR], Off U.S. 91, Kanosh, 1/25/85, A, C, a, 85000263

Meadow Tithing Granary [Tithing Offices and Granaries of the Mormon Church TR], Off U.S. 91, Meadow, 1/25/85, A, a, b, 85000276

Millard Academy, Off US 6 50, Hinckley, 2/11/82, A, a, 82004127

Millard High School Gymnasium [Public Works Buildings TR], 35 N. 200 West, Fillmore, 4/01/85, A, C, g, 85000808

Mountain Home Wash [Great Basin Style Rock Art TR], Address Restricted, Milford vicinity, 6/04/85, D, 85001235

Partridge, Edward and Elizabeth, House, 10 S. 200 West, Fillmore, 5/14/93, C, 93000414

Pharo Village, S of Scipio, Scipio vicinity, 10/10/75, D, 75001813

Quarnberg, Peter, House, Off UT 63, Scipio, 7/26/82, C, 82004128

Scipio Town Hall, UT 63, Scipio, 12/22/88, A, 88002999

Site 42 MD 284 [Great Basin Style Rock Art TR], Address Restricted, Fillmore vicinity, 6/04/85, D, 85001236

Thuesen-Petersen House [Scandinavian-American Pair-houses TR], 260 W. Center St., Scipio, 2/01/83, C, b, 83004398

Topaz War Relocation Center Site, 16 mi. NW of Delta, Delta vicinity, 1/02/74, A, g, 74001934

Utah Territorial Capitol, Center St. between Main and 100 West St., Fillmore, 9/22/70, A, C, 70000625

Morgan County

Devil's Gate—Weber Hydroelectric Power Plant Historic District [Electric Power Plants of Utah MPS], I-84 E of jct. with I-89, Ogden vicinity, 4/20/89, A, B, C, 89000276

Heiner, Daniel, House, 543 N. 700 East, Morgan, 12/20/78, B, 78002664

Morgan Elementary School [Public Works Buildings TR], 75 N. One Hundred E, Morgan, 4/09/86, A, C, 86000737

Morgan High School Mechanical Arts Building [Public Works Buildings TR], 20 N. One Hundred E, Morgan, 4/09/86, A, C, 86000738

Mormon Flat Breastworks [Utah War Fortifications MPS], Address Restricted, Porterville vicinity, 10/27/88, A, 88001943

Piute County

Piute County Courthouse, Main St. at Center St., Junction, 4/16/71, C, 71000844

Rich County

Randolph Tabernacle, Off UT 16, Randolph, 4/10/86, C, a, 86000724

Salt Lake County

19th Ward Meetinghouse and Relief Society Hall, 168 W. 500 North, Salt Lake City, 5/28/76, A, C, a, 76001820

Allen, J. R., House, 1047 E. 13200 South, Draper, 8/28/80, B, C, 80003912

Anderson, John A., House [Sandy City MPS], 510 E. 8800 South, Sandy, 8/28/92, A, C, 92001066

Anselmo, Fortunato, House, 164 S. 900 East, Salt Lake City, 5/21/79, A, 79002499

Arbuckle, George, House, 747 E. 17th South, Salt Lake City, 2/12/82, C, 82004130

Armista Apartments [Salt Lake City MPS], 555 E. 100 South, Salt Lake City, 10/20/89, A, C, 89001736

Armstrong, Francis, House, 667 E. 1st South, Salt Lake City, 5/23/80, A, B, C, 80003914

Avenues Historic District, Roughly bounded by 1st and 9th Aves., State and Virginia Sts., Salt Lake City, 8/27/80, A, C, a, 80003915

B'nai Israel Temple, 249 S. 400 East, Salt Lake City, 11/16/78, A, a, 78002666

Baldwin, Charles, House, 229 S. 1200 East, Salt Lake City, 2/11/82, B, C, 82004131

Baldwin, Nathaniel, House, 2374 Evergreen Ave., Salt Lake City vicinity, 5/09/85, B, C, 85000963

Bamberger, Simon, House, 623 E. 100 South, Salt Lake City, 5/30/75, A, C, 75001814

Beattie, Jeremiah, House, 655 E. 200 South, Salt Lake City, 7/07/83, C, 83004421

Beehive House, 67 E. South Temple St., Salt Lake City, 2/26/70, B, C, a, 70000626

Beer, William F., Estate, 181 B St. and 222 4th Ave., Salt Lake City, 12/06/77, C, 77001306

Beesley, Ebenezer, House, 80 W. 200 North, Salt Lake City, 7/16/79, B, C, 79002500

Bertolini Block, 143 1/2 W. 200 South, Salt Lake City, 9/29/76, A, C, 76001822

Best-Cannon House, 1146 S. 900 East, Salt Lake City, 10/03/80, C, 80003916

Bingham Canyon Open Pit Copper Mine, 16 mi. SW of Salt Lake City on UT 48, Salt Lake City vicinity, 11/13/66, A, NHL, 66000736

Brinton, David B., House, 1981 E. 4800 South, Holladay, 5/22/78, B, C, a, 78002665

Brinton-Dahl House, 1501 Spring Lane, Salt Lake City, 2/14/80, C, 80003917

Broadway Hotel [Salt Lake City Business District MRA], 222 W. 3rd South, Salt Lake City, 8/17/82, A, C, 82004132

Brooks Arcade [Salt Lake City Business District MRA], 260 S. State St., Salt Lake City, 8/17/82, B, C, 82004133

Building at 561 W. 200 South [Salt Lake City Business District MRA], 561 W. 200 South, Salt Lake City, 12/27/82, A, 82004848

Salt Lake County—Continued

Building at 592–98 West 200 South [Salt Lake City Business District MRA], 592–98 W. 200 South, Salt Lake City, 8/17/82, A, 82004134

Building at Rear, 537 W. 200 South [Salt Lake City Business District MRA], Rear, 537 W. 200 South, Salt Lake City, 12/27/82, B, 82004849

Cahoon, John P., House, 4872 S. Poplar St., Murray, 3/03/83, B, C, 83003186

Cannon, George M., House, 720 E. Ashton Ave., Salt Lake City, 7/18/83, B, C, 83004419

Capitol Building, Capitol Hill, Salt Lake City, 10/11/78, A, C, 78002667

Capitol Hill Historic District, Roughly bounded by Beck, Main and Wall Sts., 300 N. Victory Rd. and Capitol Blvd., Salt Lake City, 8/02/82, A, C, a, 82004135

Casto, Santa Anna, House, 2731 Casto Lane, Salt Lake City, 2/03/83, C, 83004422

Cathedral of the Madeleine, 331 E. South Temple St., Salt Lake City, 3/11/71, A, C, a, 71000845

Central Warehouse [Salt Lake City Business District MRA], 520 W. 200 South, Salt Lake City, 8/17/82, A, 82004136

Chapman Branch Library, 577 S. 900 West, Salt Lake City, 1/20/80, A, C, 80003918

Chase, Isaac, Mill, Liberty Park, 6th East, Salt Lake City, 6/15/70, A, 70000627

Cheesman, Morton A., House, 2320 Walker Lane, Salt Lake City, 7/23/82, C, 82004137

City Creek Canyon Historic District, Bounded by Capitol Blvd., A St., 4th Ave. and Canyon Rd., Salt Lake City, 3/12/80, A, C, 80003919

Clayton Building [Salt Lake City Business District MRA], 214 S. State St., Salt Lake City, 8/17/82, C, 82004138

Clift Building [Salt Lake City Business District MRA], 272 S. Main St., Salt Lake City, 8/17/82, C, 82004139

Cluff Apartments [Salt Lake City MPS], 1270–1280 E. 200 South, Salt Lake City, 10/20/89, A, C, 89001739

Congregation Montefiore [Jewish Synagogue TR], 355 S. 300 East, Salt Lake City, 6/27/85, A, C, a, 85001395

Congregation Sharey Tzedek Synagogue [Jewish Synagogue TR], 833 S. 200 East, Salt Lake City, 6/27/85, A, a, 85001396

Continental Bank Building [Salt Lake City Business District MRA], 200 S. Main St., Salt Lake City, 12/27/82, B, 82004850

Converse Hall, 1840 S. 13th East, Salt Lake City, 4/20/78, A, C, a, 78002685

Copperton Historic District, Roughly bounded by SR 48, Fifth E, Hillcrest, and Second West Sts., Copperton, 8/14/86, A, C, g, 86002642

Cornell Apartments [Salt Lake City MPS], 101 S. 600 East, Salt Lake City, 10/20/89, A, C, 89001741

Corona Apartments [Salt Lake City MPS], 335 S. 200 East, Salt Lake City, 10/20/89, A, C, 89001742

Council Hall, Capitol Hill at head of State St., Salt Lake City, 5/14/71, A, NHL, 71000846

Covey, Almon A., House, 1211 E. 100 South, Salt Lake City, 10/03/80, C, 80003920

Covey, Hyrum T., House, 1229 E. 100 South, Salt Lake City, 10/03/80, C, 80003921

Cramer House [Salt Lake City Business District MRA], 241 Floral St., Salt Lake City, 8/17/82, C, 82004140

Culmer, William, House, 33 C St., Salt Lake City, 4/18/74, C, 74001935

Cummings, Byron, House [Perkins Addition Streetcar Suburb TR], 936 E. 1700 South, Salt Lake City, 10/13/83, A, B, C, 83003949

Daft Block, 128 S. Main St., Salt Lake City, 5/28/76, A, B, C, 76001823

Dansie, George Henry, Farmstead, 12494 S. 1700 West, Riverton, 9/27/79, B, C, g, 79002498

Denver and Rio Grande Railroad Station, 3rd South and Rio Grande, Salt Lake City, 9/25/75, A, C, 75001815

Devereaux House, 334 W. South Temple St., Salt Lake City, 3/11/71, A, C, 71000847

Dininny, Harper J., House [Perkins Addition Streetcar Suburb], 925 E. Logan Ave., Salt Lake City, 10/13/83, A, C, 83003950

Dinwoody, Henry, House, 411 E. 100 South, Salt Lake City, 7/24/74, B, C, 74001936

Draper Park School, 12441 S. 900 East, Draper, 5/07/80, A, C, 80003913

Draper—Steadman House, 13518 S. 1700 West, Riverton, 8/21/92, C, 92001057

Emigration Canyon, E edge of Salt Lake City on UT 65, Salt Lake City, 10/15/66, A, f, NHL, 66000737

Empress Theatre, 9104 W. 2700 South, Magna, 5/09/85, A, C, 85000962

Exchange Place Historic District, Exchange Pl, and S. Main St., Salt Lake City, 8/10/78, A, C, 78002669

Fairbanks, J. Leo, House, 1228 Bryan Ave., Salt Lake City, 4/26/84, A, C, 84002198

Farrer, Benjamin and Jane Cook, House [Sandy City MPS], 530 E. 8800 South, Sandy, 8/28/92, A, C, 92001065

Farrer, John William, House [Sandy City MPS], 39 E. Pioneer, Sandy, 8/28/92, A, C, 92001064

Felt Electric [Salt Lake City Business District MRA], 165 S. Regent St., Salt Lake City, 8/17/82, A, 82004141

Fifth Ward Meetinghouse, 740 S. 300 West, Salt Lake City, 12/08/78, A, a, 78002670

Firestation No. 8, 258 S. 1300 East, Salt Lake City, 7/28/83, A, C, 83004423

First Church of Christ Scientist, 352 E. 3rd South, Salt Lake City, 7/30/76, C, a, 76001824

First National Bank, 163 S. Main St., Salt Lake City, 5/24/76, A, C, 76001825

Fort Douglas, Fort Douglas Military Reservation, Salt Lake City, 6/15/70, A, NHL, 70000628

Fritsch, J. A., Block, 158 E. 200 South, Salt Lake City, 7/30/76, C, 76001826

Gardner Mill, 1050 W. 7800 South, West Jordan, 9/29/82, A, C, 82004153

Garside-McMullin House, 10481 S. 1300 West, South Jordan, 12/17/82, B, C, 82004852

General Engineering Company Building, 159 W. Pierpont Ave., Salt Lake City, 1/21/80, A, B, 80003922

Gibbs-Thomas House, 137 NW Temple St., Salt Lake City, 7/12/84, B, C, 84002202

Granite Hydroelectric Power Plant Historic District [Electric Power Plants of Utah MPS], UT 152, Salt Lake City vicinity, 4/20/89, A, C, 89000283

Granite Paper Mill, 6900 Big Cottonwood Canyon Rd., Salt Lake City, 4/16/71, A, e, 71000848

Grant Steam Locomotive No. 223, Liberty Park, Salt Lake City, 5/23/79, A, b, 79002501

Greenwald Furniture Company Building [Salt Lake City Business District MRA], 35 W. 300 South, Salt Lake City, 12/27/82, A, 82004851

Hall, Nels G., House, 1340 2nd Ave., Salt Lake City, 10/03/80, C, 80003923

Harris Apartments [Salt Lake City MPS], 836 S. 500 East, Salt Lake City, 9/24/91, A, C, 91001445

Hawarden, 4396 S. 3200 West, Salt Lake City, 2/14/80, C, 80003924

Hawk, William, Cabin, 458 N. 3rd West, Salt Lake City, 12/29/78, B, C, b, 78002671

Henderson Block, 375 W. 200 South, Salt Lake City, 1/30/78, A, B, C, 78002672

Herald Building, 165–169 S. Main St., Salt Lake City, 7/30/76, C, 76001827

Hills, Lewis S., House, 126 S. 200 West, Salt Lake City, 8/18/77, B, C, 77001307

Hills, Lewis S., House, 425 E. 100 South, Salt Lake City, 8/03/90, B, C, 90001141

Hintze-Anders House [Scandinavian-American Pair-houses TR], 4249 S. 2300 East, Salt Lake City, 2/01/83, C, 83004424

Holman, Abba R., Block [Sandy City MPS], 142 E. Main St. (8720 South), Sandy, 8/28/92, A, C, 92001063

Holy Trinity Greek Orthodox Church, 279 S. 200 West, Salt Lake City, 7/08/75, A, C, a, 75001816

Hotel Albert [Salt Lake City Business District MRA], 121 SW Temple St., Salt Lake City, 8/17/82, A, C, 82004142

Hotel Utah, S. Temple and Main St., Salt Lake City, 1/03/78, A, C, 78002673

Hotel Victor [Salt Lake City Business District MRA], 155 W. 200 South, Salt Lake City, 8/17/82, C, 82004143

Immanuel Baptist Church, 401 E. 200 South, Salt Lake City, 12/12/78, A, C, a, 78002668

Independent Order of Odd Fellows Hall, 41 Post Office Pl., Salt Lake City, 11/07/77, A, C, 77001308

Irving Junior High School, 1179 E. 2100 South, Salt Lake City, 12/22/78, A, C, 78002674

Ivanhoe Apartments [Salt Lake City MPS], 417 E. 300 South, Salt Lake City, 10/20/89, A, C, 89001738

Japanese Church of Christ [Salt Lake City Business District MRA], 268 W. 100 South, Salt Lake City, 8/17/82, A, a, 82004144

Jordan High School, 9351 S. State St., Sandy, 5/17/84, A, C, 84002203

Jordan School District Administration Building [Public Works Buildings TR], 9361 W. 400 East, Sandy, 4/01/85, A, 85000810

Salt Lake County—Continued

Judd, John W., House [Perkins Addition Streetcar Suburb TR], 918 E. Logan Ave., Salt Lake City, 10/13/83, A, B, C, 83003952

Judge Building, 8 E. 300 South, Salt Lake City, 12/26/79, C, 79002502

Kahn, Emanuel, House, 678 E. South Temple St., Salt Lake City, 7/21/77, B, C, 77001309

Karrick Block, 236 S. Main St., Salt Lake City, 6/16/76, C, 76001828

Kearns Building [Salt Lake City Business District MRA], 132 S. Main St., Salt Lake City, 8/17/82, B, C, 82004145

Kearns, Thomas, Mansion and Carriage House, 603 E. South Temple St., Salt Lake City, 2/26/70, B, C, 70000631

Kearns-St. Ann's Orphanage, 430 E. 2100 South, Salt Lake City, 10/03/80, A, C, a, 80003925

Keith-Brown Mansion and Carriage House, 529 E. South Temple St., Salt Lake City, 5/14/71, B, C, 71000849

Keith-O'Brien Building, 242–256 S. Main St., Salt Lake City, 8/16/77, A, C, 77001310

Kelly, Albert H., House, 418 S. 200 West, Salt Lake City, 7/20/83, C, 83004420

Kelly, John B., House, 422 S. 200 West, Salt Lake City, 7/20/83, C, 83003172

Kuhre, William D., House, 8586 S. One Hundred and Fiftieth E, Sandy, 7/06/87, B, C, 87001175

Ladies Literary Club Clubhouse, 850 E. South Temple St., Salt Lake City, 10/11/78, A, C, 78002675

Langton, James and Susan R., House, 648 E. 100 South, Salt Lake City, 11/19/82, C, 82001750

Lefler—Woodman Building, 859 E. 900 South, Salt Lake City, 12/17/92, A, C, 92001687

Liberty Park, Roughly bounded by 5th East, 7th East, 9th South and 13th South, Salt Lake City, 12/11/80, A, C, 80003926

Lincoln Arms Apartments [Salt Lake City MPS], 242 E. 100 South, Salt Lake City, 10/20/89, A, C, 89001737

Little Dell Station, W of Salt Lake City in Mountain Dell Canyon, near jct. of UT 239 and 65, Salt Lake City vicinity, 8/12/71, A, 71000850

Lollin Block, 238 S. Main St., Salt Lake City, 8/18/77, A, C, 77001311

Luce, Henry, House [Perkins Addition Streetcar Suburb TR], 921 E. 1700 South, Salt Lake City, 10/13/83, A, C, 83003953

Lyne, Walter C., House, 1135 E. South Temple St., Salt Lake City, 3/09/79, C, 79003495

Mabry-Van Pelt House [Perkins Addition Streetcar Suburb TR], 946 E. 1700 South, Salt Lake City, 10/13/83, A, C, 83003954

Magna Community Baptist Church, 2908 S. Eight Thousand Nine Hundred W, Magna, 6/05/86, A, a, b, 86001233

Malin, Millard F., House, 133 S. 400 East, Salt Lake City, 7/07/83, C, 83003173

McAllister, James G., House, 306 Douglas St., Salt Lake City, 12/17/82, C, 82001751

McCornick Building, 10 W. 100 South, Salt Lake City, 8/24/77, B, C, 77001312

McCune, Alfred W., Mansion, 200 N. Main St., Salt Lake City, 6/13/74, B, C, 74001937

McDonald, David, House, 4659 Highland Dr., Salt Lake City, 5/29/80, B, C, 80003927

McDonald, J. G., Chocolate Company Building, 155–159 W. 300 South, Salt Lake City, 3/29/78, A, B, 78002676

McIntyre Building, 68–72 S. Main St., Salt Lake City, 7/15/77, B, C, 77001313

McIntyre House, 259 7th Ave., Salt Lake City, 7/17/78, C, a, 78002677

McLachlan, William, Farmhouse, 4499 S. 3200 West, Salt Lake City, 2/14/80, A, C, 80003928

Meyer, Frederick A. E., House, 929 E. 200 South, Salt Lake City, 7/07/83, C, 83003174

Mitchell, Alexander, House [Perkins Addition Streetcar Suburb TR], 1620 S. 1000 East, Salt Lake City, 10/13/83, A, C, 83003955

Morris, Richard Vaughen, House, 314 Quince St., Salt Lake City, 4/29/80, B, C, 80003929

Mountain Dell Dam, N of Salt Lake City, Salt Lake City vicinity, 6/20/80, C, 80003930

Nelden, William A., House, 1172 E. 100 South, Salt Lake City, 10/19/78, C, 78002678

Nelson, Nels A., House [Sandy City MPS], 8840 S. 90 East, Sandy, 8/28/92, A, C, 92001062

Nelson-Beesley House, 533 11th Ave., Salt Lake City, 6/20/80, B, C, 80003931

Neuhausen, Carl M., House, 1265 E. 100 South, Salt Lake City, 10/03/80, C, 80003932

New York Hotel, 42 Post Office Pl., Salt Lake City, 3/10/80, C, 80003933

Oakwood, 2610 Evergreen St., Salt Lake City, 11/16/79, A, B, C, 79002503

Old Clock at Zion's First National Bank [Salt Lake City Business District MRA], SW corner of 1st South and Main St., Salt Lake City, 12/27/82, C, 82001752

Old Pioneer Fort Site, 400 South and 200 West, Salt Lake City, 10/15/74, A, 74001938

Oregon Shortline Railroad Company Building, 126–140 Pierpont Ave., Salt Lake City, 6/23/76, C, 76001829

Orem, Frank M., House, 274 S. 1200 East, Salt Lake City, 8/05/83, B, 83003175

Orpheum Theatre, 46 W. 2nd South, Salt Lake City, 9/30/76, A, C, 76002257

Ottinger Hall, 233 Canyon Rd., Salt Lake City, 4/16/71, A, 71000851

Park Hotel [Salt Lake City Business District MRA], 422–432 W. 300 South, Salt Lake City, 12/17/92, A, 92001690

Pearsall, Clifford R., House [Perkins Addition Streetcar Suburb TR], 950 E. Logan Ave., Salt Lake City, 10/13/83, A, C, 83003957

Peery Hotel, 270–280 S. West Temple, 102–120 W. 300 South, Salt Lake City, 2/17/78, A, 78002679

Peterson, Charles, House [Sandy City MPS], 82 E. 8880 South, Sandy, 8/28/92, A, C, 92001061

Platts, John, House, 364 Quince St., Salt Lake City, 8/25/72, C, 72001259

Pugh, Edward, House, 1299 E. 4500 South, Salt Lake City, 8/31/78, B, C, 78002680

Rowland Hall-St. Mark's School, 205 1st Ave., Salt Lake City, 7/26/79, A, B, a, 79002504

Royle, Jonathan C. and Eliza K., House, 635 E. 100 South, Salt Lake City, 1/03/83, B, C, 83003176

Rumel, Eliza Gray, House, 358 S. 500 East, Salt Lake City, 7/07/83, C, 83003177

Salt Lake City Public Library, 15 S. State St, Salt Lake City, 8/07/79, A, C, 79002505

Salt Lake City and County Building, 451 Washington Sq., Salt Lake City, 6/15/70, A, C, 70000629

Salt Lake County Library [Public Works Buildings TR], 80 E. Center St., Midvale, 7/26/82, A, g, 82004129

Salt Lake Stamp Company Building [Salt Lake City Business District MRA], 43 W. 200 South, Salt Lake City, 12/27/82, C, 82001753

Salt Lake Stock and Mining Exchange Building, 39 Exchange Pl., Salt Lake City, 7/30/76, A, C, 76001830

Salt Lake Union Pacific Railroad Station, S. Temple at 400 West, Salt Lake City, 7/09/75, A, C, 75001818

Sandy Co-Op Block [Sandy City MPS], 8750 S. Center St. (150 East), Sandy, 8/28/92, A, C, 92001060

Sandy Tithing Office [Tithing Offices and Granaries of the Mormon Church TR], 326 S. 280 East, Sandy, 1/25/85, A, a, 85000279

Smith Apartments [Salt Lake City MPS], 228 S. 300 East, Salt Lake City, 10/20/89, A, C, 89001740

Smith, Albert, House, 349 S. 200 West, Salt Lake City, 7/07/83, C, 83003178

Smith, George Albert, House, 1302 E. Yale Ave., Salt Lake City, 3/12/93, B, a, g, 93000066

Smith, Lauritz, House, 1350 E. 12400 South, Draper, 6/24/83, A, C, 83003179

Smith-Bailey Drug Company Building [Salt Lake City Business District MRA], 171 W. 200 South, Salt Lake City, 8/17/82, C, 82004146

South Temple Historic District, S. Temple St., Salt Lake City, 7/14/82, A, C, a, 82004147

St. Mark's Episcopal Cathedral, 231 E. 100 South, Salt Lake City, 9/22/70, A, C, a, 70000630

Stairs Station Hydroelectric Power Plant Historic District [Electric Power Plants of Utah MPS], UT 152, Salt Lake City vicinity, 4/20/89, A, C, 89000284

Stratford Hotel [Salt Lake City Business District MRA], 175 E. 200 South, Salt Lake City, 12/27/82, A, C, 82001754

Tampico Restaurant [Salt Lake City Business District MRA], 169 Regent St., Salt Lake City, 12/27/82, A, C, 82001755

Technical High School, 241 N. 300 West, Salt Lake City, 2/19/80, C, 80003934

Temple Square, Temple Sq., Salt Lake City, 10/15/66, A, a, NHL, 66000738

Tenth Ward Square, 400 South and 800 East, Salt Lake City, 11/11/77, A, C, a, 77001314

Tracy Loan and Trust Company Building, 151 S. Main St., Salt Lake City, 10/10/78, B, 78002681

Trinity A.M.E. Church, 239 E. 600 South, Salt Lake City, 7/30/76, A, a, 76001831

University of Utah Circle, University of Utah campus, Salt Lake City, 4/20/78, A, C, 78002682

Utah Commercial and Savings Bank Building, 22 E. 100 South, Salt Lake City, 6/18/75, C, 75001819

Salt Lake County—Continued

Utah Copper Company Mine Superintendent's House, 104 E. State Hwy, Copperton, 10/31/85, A, C, 85003422

Utah Slaughter Company Warehouse [Salt Lake City Business District MRA], 370 W. 100 South, Salt Lake City, 8/17/82, B, C, 82004148

Utah State Fair Grounds, 10th West and N. Temple Sts., Salt Lake City, 1/27/81, A, 81000583

Warehouse District [Salt Lake City Business District MRA], 200 South and Pierpont Ave. between 300 and 400 West, Salt Lake City, 8/17/82, C, 82004149

Wasatch Mountain Club Lodge, SE of Salt Lake City, Salt Lake City vicinity, 11/10/80, A, C, 80003935

Wasatch Springs Plunge, 840 N. 300 West, Salt Lake City, 5/15/80, A, C, 80003936

Weeks, Charles H., House [Perkins Addition Streetcar Suburb TR], 935 E. Logan Ave., Salt Lake City, 10/13/83, A, C, 83003959

Wheeler, Henry J., Farm, 6343 S. 900 East, Salt Lake City, 5/04/76, A, C, 76001832

Whipple, Nelson Wheeler, House, 564 W. 400 North, Salt Lake City, 9/26/79, B, C, 79002506

Whitaker, John M., House, 975 Garfield Ave., Salt Lake City, 3/30/78, B, a, 78002684

Woodruff Villa [Woodruff, Wilford, Family Historic Residences TR], 1622 S. 5th East, Salt Lake City, 7/14/82, B, a, 82004150

Woodruff, Asahel Hart, House [Woodruff, Wilford, Family Historic Residences TR], 1636 W. 5th East, Salt Lake City, 7/14/82, A, a, 82004151

Woodruff, Wilford, Farm House [Woodruff, Wilford, Family Historic Residences TR], 1604 S. 5th East, Salt Lake City, 7/14/82, B, a, 82004152

Woodruff-Riter House, 225 N. State St, Salt Lake City, 7/26/79, B, C, g, 79002507

Yardley, Thomas, House [Perkins Addition Streetcar Suburb TR], 955 E. Logan Ave., Salt Lake City, 10/13/83, A, C, 83003961

Young, Brigham, Complex, 63–67 E. South Temple St., Salt Lake City, 10/15/66, A, B, a, NHL, 66000739

Z.C.M.I. Cast Iron Front, 15 S. Main St., Salt Lake City, 9/22/70, A, C, 70000632

San Juan County

Adams, Joseph Frederick, House, Off US 163, Bluff, 10/24/85, A, C, 85003390

Alkali Ridge, Address Restricted, Monticello vicinity, 10/15/66, D, NHL, 66000740

Aneth Terrace Archeological District, Address Restricted, Aneth vicinity, 8/01/80, D, 80003937

Big Westwater Ruin, Address Restricted, Blanding vicinity, 7/16/80, D, 80003938

Butler Wash Archeological District, Address Restricted, Blanding vicinity, 7/11/81, D, 81000584

Cave Springs Cowboy Camp [Canyonlands National Park MRA], Cave Springs vicintiy, Moab vicinity, 10/07/88, A, B, NPS, 88001233

Decker, James Bean, House, UT 47, Bluff, 8/04/83, A, 83003180

Defiance House, Address Restricted, Blanding vicinity, 12/20/78, D, NPS, 78000347

Edge of Cedars Indian Ruin, W of Blanding, Blanding vicinity, 8/12/71, D, 71000853

Goulding's Trading Post, Off UT 47, Gouldings, 10/20/80, A, B, 80003941

Grand Gulch Archeological District, Address Restricted, Blanding vicinity, 6/14/82, A, D, 82004154

Indian Creek State Park, 14 mi. N of Monticello, Monticello vicinity, 3/15/76, D, 76001833

Julien Inscription [Canyonlands National Park MRA], Lower Red Lake vicinity, Moab vicinity, 10/07/88, A, NPS, 88001248

Kirk's Cabin Complex [Canyonlands National Park MRA], Upper Salt Walsh, Moab vicinity, 10/07/88, A, NPS, 88001252

Lost Canyon Cowboy Camp [Canyonlands National Park MRA], Lost Canyon vicinity, Moab vicinity, 10/07/88, A, B, NPS, 88001232

Murphy Trail and Bridge [Canyonlands National Park MRA], Murphy Point vicinty, Moab vicinity, 10/07/88, A, NPS, 88001236

Nielson, Jens, House, Off UT 47, Bluff, 2/22/82, A, B, 82004155

Oljato Trading Post, SW of Blanding, Blanding vicinity, 6/20/80, A, 80003939

Owachomo Bridge Trail, Armstrong Canyon, Blanding vicinity, 2/02/89, A, NPS, 88001166

Patterson, Nancy, Site, Address Restricted, Blanding vicinity, 11/21/80, D, 80004495

Poncho House, Address Restricted, Mexican Hat vicinity, 10/10/75, D, 75001821

Redd, Lemuel H., Jr., House, UT 47, Bluff, 5/18/83, A, B, 83003181

Salt Creek Archeological District, Address Restricted, Monticello vicinity, 3/31/75, D, NPS, 75000164

Sand Island Petroglyph Site, Address Restricted, Bluff vicinity, 7/11/81, D, 81000585

Scorup, John Albert, House, UT 47, Bluff, 4/13/83, B, C, 83003182

Westwater Canyon Archeological District, Address Restricted, Blanding vicinity, 9/04/80, D, 80003940

Sanpete County

Andersen, Claus P., House [Scandinavian-American Pair-houses TR], 2nd South St., Ephraim, 2/01/83, A, C, 83003183

Andersen, Lars S., House [Scandinavian-American Pair-houses TR], 213 N. 200 East, Ephraim, 2/01/83, A, C, 83003184

Anderson, James, House, 15 S. 200 East, Fairview, 10/03/80, C, 80003945

Anderson, Niels Ole, House, 306 S. 100 East, Ephraim, 10/05/78, B, C, 78002687

Arilsen, Ole, House, Off UT 116, Mount Pleasant, 10/03/80, C, 80003953

Barentsen, Andrew, House [Scandinavian-American Pair-houses TR], UT 30, Fountain Green, 2/01/83, A, C, 83003185

Bessey, Anthony W., House, Off U.S. 89, Manti, 10/22/80, C, 80003947

Billings-Hougaard House, Off U.S. 89, Manti, 10/14/80, C, 80003948

Casino Theatre, 78 S. Main St., Gunnison, 9/22/89, A, C, 89001416

Cox-Shoemaker-Parry House, 50 N. 100 West, Manti, 8/04/82, B, C, 82004157

Crawforth, Charles, Farmstead, SW of Spring City on Pigeon Hollow Rd., Spring City vicinity, 2/19/80, A, C, 80003956

Dorius, John, Jr., House, 46 W. 100 North, Ephraim, 5/09/85, B, C, 85000964

Ephraim Carnegie Library [Carnegie Library TR], 30 S. Main St., Ephraim, 10/25/84, A, 84000149

Ephraim United Order Cooperative Building, Main and 1st North Sts., Ephraim, 3/20/73, A, 73001862

Fairview City Hall [Public Works Buildings TR], 85 S. State, Fairview, 4/09/86, A, C, 86000745

Fairview Tithing Office/Bishop's Storehouse [Tithing Offices and Granaries of the Mormon Church TR], 60 W. 100 South, Fairview, 1/25/85, A, a, 85000281

Faux, Jabez, House And Barn, UT 132, Moroni, 11/07/76, B, C, 76001835

Fountain Green Hydroelectric Plant Historic District [Electric Power Plants of Utah MPS], NW of Fountain Green, Fountain Green vicinity, 4/20/89, A, C, 89000277

Greaves-Deakin House, 118 S. Main St., Ephraim, 10/03/80, C, 80003942

Hansen, Hans A., House, 75 W. 100 North, Ephraim, 10/22/80, C, 80003943

Hansen, Peter, House [Scandinavian-American Pair-houses TR], 247 S. 200 East, Manti, 2/01/83, A, C, 83003187

Hjort, Niels P., House, N. Main St., Fairview, 10/03/80, C, 80003946

Jensen, Frederick C., House, 2nd West and 2nd South, Mount Pleasant, 4/19/82, B, C, 82004158

Jensen, Hans C., House [Scandinavian-American Pair-houses TR], 263 E. 100 South, Ephraim, 2/01/83, A, C, 83003188

Jensen, Rasmus, House [Scandinavian-American Pair-houses TR], 97 E. 100 South, Ephraim, 2/01/83, A, C, 83003189

Johnson, Robert, House, Off U.S. 89, Manti, 10/14/80, C, 80003949

Johnson-Nielson House, 351 N. Main St., Ephraim, 7/26/82, A, C, 82004156

Jolley, Francis Marion, House, Off U.S. 89, Manti, 10/14/80, C, 80003950

Larsen, Oluf, House [Scandinavian-American Pair-houses TR], 75 S. 100 West, Ephraim, 2/01/83, A, C, 83003190

Larsen-Noyes House, 96 E. Center St., Ephraim, 12/01/78, B, C, 78002688

Lewellyn, John T., House, Main St., Wales, 10/03/80, C, 80003958

Manti Carnegie Library [Carnegie Library TR], 12 S. Main St., Manti, 10/25/84, A, 84000150

Manti City Hall, 191 N. Main, Manti, 6/27/85, A, C, 85001397

Sanpete County—Continued

Manti National Guard Armory [Public Works Buildings TR], 50 E. One Hundred N, Manti, 4/09/86, A, C, g, 86000744

Manti Presbyterian Church, U.S. 89, Manti, 3/27/80, B, C, a, 80003951

Manti Temple, N edge of Manti, on U.S. 89, Manti, 8/12/71, B, C, a, 71000854

Moroni High School Mechanical Arts Building [Public Works Buildings TR], 350 N. Center St., Moroni, 4/01/85, A, g, 85000812

Mount Pleasant Carnegie Library [Carnegie Library TR], 24 E. Main St., Mount Pleasant, 10/25/84, A, 84000152

Mount Pleasant Commercial Historic District, U.S. 89 and UT 116, Mount Pleasant, 10/26/79, A, C, g, 79002508

Mount Pleasant High School Mechanical Arts Building [Public Works Buildings TR], 150 N. State St., Mount Pleasant, 4/01/85, A, g, 85000813

Mount Pleasant National Guard Armory [Public Works Buildings TR], 10 N. State, Mount Pleasant, 4/09/86, A, C, g, 86000740

Nielsen, Jens, House [Scandinavian-American Pair-houses TR], 192 W. 200 South, Ephraim, 2/01/83, A, C, 83003191

Nielson, N. S., House, 179 W. Main St., Pleasant, 7/26/82, A, C, 82004160

Olsen, Hans Peter, House, UT 11, Fountain Green, 4/22/76, C, 76001834

Ottesen, Hans, House [Scandinavian-American Pair-houses TR], 202 S. 200 W, Manti, 8/06/87, C, 87001177

Patten, John, House, 95 W. 400 North, Manti, 8/22/77, B, C, 77001315

Peterson, Canute, House, 10 N. Main St., Ephraim, 7/17/78, B, C, 78002689

Rasmussen, Morten, House, 417 W. Main St., Mount Pleasant, 8/18/77, B, C, 77001317

Sanpete County Courthouse [Public Works Buildings TR], 160 N. Main St., Manti, 4/01/85, A, g, 85000811

Seeley, William Stuart, House, 150 S. State St., Mt. Pleasant, 7/16/92, A, B, C, 92000894

Seely, John H., House, 91 S. 5th West, Mount Pleasant, 3/09/82, B, C, 82004159

Snow Academy Building, 150 College Ave., Ephraim, 11/20/87, A, a, 87002062

Sorensen, Dykes, House [Scandinavian-American Pair-houses TR], 2nd East St., Ephriam, 10/20/82, A, C, 82001756

Sorensen, Fredrick Christian, House, E. Center St., Ephraim, 10/14/80, C, 80003944

Spring City Historic District, UT 17, Spring City, 10/22/80, A, C, a, b, 80003957

Spring City School, Off UT 117, Spring City, 11/14/78, A, C, 78002691

Staker, Alma, House, 81 E. 300 South, Mount Pleasant, 7/09/79, C, 79002509

Staker, James B., House, U.S. 89, Mount Pleasant, 10/03/80, C, 80003954

Tuttle-Folsom House, 195 W. 300 North, Manti, 7/21/77, B, C, 77001316

US Post Office—Springville Main [US Post Offices in Utah 1900–1941 MPS], 309 S. Main, Springville, 11/27/89, A, C, 89002000

Wasatch Academy, Off U.S. 89, Mount Pleasant, 10/02/78, A, a, g, 78002690

Wheelock, Cyrus, House, 200 E. 100 North, Mount Pleasant, 10/03/80, C, 80003955

Sevier County

Aspen-Cloud Rock Shelters, Address Restricted, Salina vicinity, 11/01/79, D, 79002510

Elsinore Sugar Factory, E of Elsinore, Elsinore vicinity, 6/17/80, A, 80003959

Elsinore White Rock Schoolhouse, 25 S. 100 East, Elsinore, 1/18/78, A, 78002692

Glenwood Cooperative Store, 15 W. Center St., Glenwood, 4/29/80, A, 80003960

Gooseberry Valley Archeological District, Address Restricted, Salina vicinity, 9/04/80, D, 80003968

Jenson, Jens Larson, Lime Kiln, 2 mi. N of Richfield, Richfield vicinity, 12/22/78, A, 78002693

Johnson, Martin, House [Scandinavian-American Pair-houses TR], 45 W. 400 South, Glenwood, 10/20/82, A, C, 82001757

Monroe City Hall [Public Works Buildings TR], 10 N. Main St., Monroe, 4/01/85, A, C, 85000814

Monroe Methodist Episcopal Church, 55 W. 100 West, Monroe, 5/23/80, C, a, 80003962

Monroe Presbyterian Church, 20 E. 100 North, Monroe, 3/27/80, A, C, a, 80003963

Parker, Joseph William, Farm, 2.5 mi. NE of Joseph, Joseph vicinity, 3/25/77, B, C, b, 77001318

Ramsay, Ralph, House, 57 E. 2nd North, Richfield, 7/08/75, B, C, 75001824

Redmond Hotel, 15 E. Main St., Redmond, 6/20/80, A, 80003964

Redmond Town Hall, 18 W. Main St., Redmond, 9/13/76, A, a, 76001836

Richfield Carnegie Library [Carnegie Library TR], 83 E. Center St., Richfield, 10/25/84, A, 84000153

Salina Hospital, 330 W. Main St., Salina, 6/19/80, A, C, 80003966

Salina Municipal Building and Library [Public Works Buildings TR], 90 W. Main, Salina, 4/09/86, A, C, g, 86000742

Salina Presbyterian Church, 204 S. 1st East, Salina, 3/27/80, A, C, a, 80003967

Sevier Ward Church, E of Sevier U.S. 89, Sevier vicinity, 6/24/80, C, a, 80003969

Simonsen, Soren, House [Scandinavian-American Pair-houses TR], 55 W. 200 North, Monroe, 10/20/82, A, C, 82001758

Sudden Shelter (42SV6), Address Restricted, Salina vicinity, 1/04/89, D, 88003009

US Post Office—Richfield Main [US Post Offices in Utah 1900–1941 MPS], 93 N. Main, Richfield, 11/27/89, A, C, 89001999

Wall, Joseph, Gristmill, 355 S. 250 East, Glenwood, 6/20/80, A, 80003961

Young Block, 3-17 S. Main St., Richfield, 6/24/80, A, 80003965

Summit County

Allen, Thomas L., House, 98 N. Main St., Coalville, 7/23/82, C, 82004161

Austin, William, House [Mining Boom Era Houses TR], 247 Ontario Ave., Park City, 7/11/84, C, 84002226

Barnes, Charles, House [Mining Boom Era Houses TR], 413 Ontario Ave., Park City, 7/12/84, C, 84002230

Barrett, Richard, House [Mining Boom Era Houses TR], 36 Prospect Ave., Park City, 7/11/84, C, 84002238

Barry, George J., House [Mining Boom Era Houses TR], 250 Grant Ave., Park City, 7/12/84, C, 84002239

Beggs, Ellsworth J., House [Mining Boom Era Houses TR], 703 Park Ave., Park City, 7/11/84, C, 84002240

Birch, Annie, House [Scandinavian-American Pair-houses TR], Off I-80, Hoytsville vicinity, 10/22/84, C, 84000163

Bogan Boarding House [Mining Boom Era Houses TR], 221 Main St., Park City, 10/22/84, A, C, 84000154

Boyden, John, House, 47 W. Center St., Coalville, 2/11/82, A, C, 82004162

Brown, Otis L., House [Mining Boom Era Houses TR], 713 Woodside Ave., Park City, 7/11/84, C, 84002241

Buck, John W., House [Mining Boom Era Houses TR], 1110 Woodside Ave., Park City, 7/12/84, C, 84002242

Campbell, William, House [Mining Boom Era Houses TR], 164 Norfolk St., Park City, 7/11/84, C, 84002243

Carling, Benedictus, House [Mining Boom Era Houses TR], 660 Rossie Hill Dr., Park City, 7/12/84, C, 84002244

Cassidy, James, House [Mining Boom Era Houses TR], 33 King Rd., Park City, 7/11/84, C, 84002245

Cavanaugh, James House [Mining Boom Era Houses TR], 564 Woodside Ave., Park City, 7/12/84, C, 84002246

Clark, Peter, House [Mining Boom Era Houses TR], 1135 Park Ave., Park City, 7/11/84, C, 84002247

Condon, David F. and Elizabeth, House [Mining Boom Era Houses TR], 1304 Park Ave., Park City, 7/12/84, C, 84002248

Cunningham, John F., House [Mining Boom Era Houses TR], 606 Park Ave., Park City, 7/11/84, C, 84002249

Cunningham, Thomas, House [Mining Boom Era Houses TR], 139 Main St., Park City, 7/12/84, C, 84002250

Diem, John, House [Mining Boom Era Houses TR], 401 Park Ave., Park City, 10/22/84, C, 84000155

Doyle, John, House [Mining Boom Era Houses TR], 339 Park, Park City, 2/06/86, C, 86000162

Durkin Boarding House [Mining Boom Era Houses TR], 176 Main St., Park City, 7/12/84, C, 84002253

Summit County—Continued

Durkin, Joseph, House [Mining Boom Era Houses TR], 22 Prospect Ave., Park City, 7/11/84, C, 84002262

Echo Canyon Breastworks [Utah War Fortifications MPS], Address Restricted, Echo vicinity, 10/27/88, A, 88001942

Echo Church and School, Temple Ln., Echo, 1/05/89, A, a, 88003000

Ecker Hill Ski Jump, Off I-80, Synderville vicinity, 6/04/86, A, g, 86001251

Farthelos, Peter, House [Mining Boom Era Houses TR], 1150 Park Ave., Park City, 7/12/84, C, 84002267

Frkovich, Mike, House [Mining Boom Era Houses TR], 162 Daly Ave., Park City, 7/12/84, C, 84002270

Gray, Levins D., House [Mining Boom Era Houses TR], 355 Ontario Ave., Park City, 7/12/84, C, 84002272

Hansen, Frank, House [Mining Boom Era Houses TR], 1025 Park Ave., Park City, 7/12/84, C, 84002274

Harris, Joseph D., House [Mining Boom Era Houses TR], 959 Park Ave., Park City, 7/12/84, C, 84002277

Harris, William H., House [Mining Boom Era Houses TR], 39 King Rd., Park City, 7/12/84, C, 84002279

Haumann, Harry W., House [Mining Boom Era Houses TR], 939 Empire Ave., Park City, 7/12/84, C, 84002281

Hewlett, Verner O., Ranch House [Stewart Ranch TR], Off UT 35, Woodland, 5/23/85, A, 85001133

Hinsdill, Henry M., House [Mining Boom Era Houses TR], 662 Norfolk St., Park City, 7/12/84, C, 84002283

Holman, Samuel, House [Mining Boom Era Houses TR], 307 Norfolk St., Park City, 7/12/84, C, 84002290

House at 101 Prospect Street [Mining Boom Era Houses TR], 101 Prospect St., Park City, 10/22/84, C, 84000156

House at 1101 Norfolk Avenue [Mining Boom Era Houses TR], 1101 Norfolk Ave., Park City, 7/12/84, C, 84002294

House at 343 Park Avenue [Mining Boom Era Houses TR], 343 Park Ave., Park City, 7/12/84, C, 84002297

House at 555 Deer Valley Road [Mining Boom Era Houses TR], 555 Deer Valley Rd., Park City, 7/12/84, C, 84002299

House at 577 Deer Valley Road [Mining Boom Era Houses TR], 577 Deer Valley Rd., Park City, 7/12/84, C, 84002301

House at 62 Daly Avenue [Mining Boom Era Houses TR], 62 Daly Ave., Park City, 7/12/84, C, 84002304

House at 622 Rossie Hill Drive [Mining Boom Era Houses TR], 622 Rossie Hill Dr., Park City, 7/12/84, C, 84002308

Howe Flume Historic District, NE of Oakley on Wasatch National Forest, Oakley vicinity, 12/12/78, D, 78002695

Hoyt, Samuel P., House, Off I-80, Hoytsville, 4/19/82, B, C, 82004163

IOOF Relief Home [Mining Boom Era Houses TR], 232 Woodside Ave., Park City, 7/12/84, C, 84002311

Jenkins, Joseph J., House [Mining Boom Era Houses TR], 27 Prospect Ave., Park City, 7/12/84, C, 84002315

Johnson, Carl G., House [Mining Boom Era Houses TR], 147 Grant Ave., Park City, 4/12/84, C, 84002318

Jones, Elizabeth M., House [Mining Boom Era Houses TR], 412 Marsac Ave., Park City, 7/12/84, C, 84002322

Kimball Stage Stop, US 40, W of Silver Creek jct., Park City vicinity, 4/16/71, A, 71000855

Kimball, Burt, House [Mining Boom Era Houses TR], 817 Park Ave., Park City, 7/12/84, C, 84002325

Kimball, Ernest Lynn, House [Mining Boom Era Houses TR], 911 Empire Ave., Park City, 7/12/84, C, 84002329

LDS Park City Meetinghouse, 424 Park Ave., Park City, 5/22/78, A, C, a, 78002696

Lindorff, Alfred, House [Mining Boom Era Houses TR], 40 Sampson Ave., Park City, 7/12/84, C, 84002331

Lyons, Oscar F., House, Woodenshoe Rd., Peoa, 7/14/83, A, C, 83003192

Marsac Elementary School [Public Works Buildings TR], 431 Marsac, Park City, 4/01/85, A, C, g, 85000815

Meadowcroft, Charles, House [Mining Boom Era Houses TR], 951 Woodside Ave., Park City, 7/12/84, C, 84002333

Mitchell, Byron T., House, US 189 and UT 35, Francis, 5/18/84, C, 84002336

Morgan, Jesse, House [Mining Boom Era Houses TR], 1027 Woodside Ave., Park City, 7/12/84, C, 84002338

Murdock, Jack M., House [Mining Boom Era Houses TR], 652 Rossie Hill Dr., Park City, 7/12/84, C, 84002340

Murray, George, House [Mining Boom Era Houses TR], 44 Chambers Ave., Park City, 7/12/84, C, 84002343

Myrick, William and Martha, House, N of Kamas, Kamas vicinity, 3/09/82, A, C, 82004164

Park City Community Church, 402 Park Ave., Park City, 11/25/80, A, C, a, 80003970

Park City Main Street Historic District, Main St., Park City, 3/26/79, A, C, 79002511

Park City Miner's Hospital, Off UT 97, Park City, 12/08/78, A, 78002697

Raddon, LaPage H., House [Mining Boom Era Houses TR], 817 Woodside Ave., Park City, 7/12/84, C, 84002345

Raddon, Samuel L., House [Mining Boom Era Houses TR], 325 Park Ave., Park City, 7/12/84, C, 84002349

Richardson, Jacob F., House [Mining Boom Era Houses TR], 245 Park Ave., Park City, 7/12/84, C, 84002354

Rogers, John H. and Margaretta, House [Mining Boom Era Houses TR], 455 Park Ave., Park City, 4/14/88, A, C, 88000386

Rowe, Nicholas, House [Mining Boom Era Houses TR], 150 Main St., Park City, 10/22/84, C, 84000158

Silver King Ore Loading Station, Park Ave., Park City, 10/04/78, A, 78002698

Snyder, Wilson I., House [Mining Boom Era Houses TR], 1010 Woodside Ave., Park City, 7/12/84, B, C, 84002356

St. Luke's Episcopal Church, 523 Park Ave., Park City, 11/28/80, A, C, a, 80003971

St. Mary Of The Assumption Church and School, 121 Park Ave., Park City, 1/25/79, A, a, 79002512

Streeter, Eugene, House [Mining Boom Era Houses TR], 335 Ontario Ave., Park City, 7/12/84, C, 84002357

Sullivan, James R. and Mary E., House [Mining Boom Era Houses TR], 146 Main St., Park City, 7/12/84, C, 84002360

Summit County Courthouse, Main St., Coalville, 12/15/78, A, C, 78002694

Sutton, Ephraim D. and William D., House [Mining Boom Era Houses TR], 713 Norfolk St., Park City, 7/12/84, C, 84002362

Thomas, Milton and Minerva, House [Mining Boom Era Houses TR], 445 Park Ave., Park City, 7/12/84, C, 84002363

Tretheway, William, House [Mining Boom Era Houses TR], 335 Woodside Ave., Park City, 7/12/84, C, 84002364

Urie, Matthew, House [Mining Boom Era Houses TR], 157 Park Ave., Park City, 7/12/84, C, 84002366

Walker, Samuel D., House [Mining Boom Era Houses TR], 1119 Park Ave., Park City, 7/12/84, C, 84002368

Washington School, 541 Park Ave., Park City, 12/08/78, A, C, 78002699

Watson, Irinda, House [Mining Boom Era Houses TR], 610 Park Ave., Park City, 7/12/84, C, 84002370

Welch-Sherman House [Mining Boom Era Houses TR], 59 Prospect Ave., Park City, 7/12/84, B, C, 84002372

Wells, Hannah, House [Mining Boom Era Houses TR], 1103 Woodside Ave., Park City, 7/12/84, C, 84002375

Whitehead, Charles C., House [Mining Boom Era Houses TR], 937 Park Ave., Park City, 10/22/84, C, 84000160

Wilcocks, Walter and Ann, House [Mining Boom Era Houses TR], 363 Park Ave., Park City, 7/12/84, C, 84002378

Wilkinson-Hawkinson House [Mining Boom Era Houses TR], 39 Sampson Ave., Park City, 7/12/84, C, 84002418

Williams, Nathaniel J., House [Mining Boom Era Houses TR], 945 Norfolk Ave., Park City, 7/12/84, C, 84002419

Williams, Reese, House [Mining Boom Era Houses TR], 421 Park Ave., Park City, 7/12/84, A, C, 84002420

Willis, Joseph S., House [Mining Boom Era Houses TR], 1062 Park Ave., Park City, 7/12/84, C, 84002421

Summit County—Continued

Wilson-Shields House [Mining Boom Era Houses TR], 139 Park Ave., Park City, 7/12/84, B, C, 84002422

Tooele County

Benson Mill, SW of Mills Junction on UT 138, Mills Junction vicinity, 4/14/72, C, 72001260

Bonneville Salt Flats Race Track, 3 mi. E of Wendover off U.S. 40, Wendover vicinity, 12/18/75, A, 75001826

Danger Cave, 1 mi. E of Wendover on U.S. 40, Wendover vicinity, 10/15/66, D, NHL, 66000741

GAPA Launch Site and Blockhouse, NE of Knolls, Knolls vicinity, 8/26/80, A, g, 80003972

Grantsville First Ward Meetinghouse, 297 Clark St., Grantsville, 2/11/82, A, C, a, 82004165

Iosepa Settlement Cemetery, Skull Valley, Iosepa, 8/12/71, A, 71000856

Lincoln Highway Bridge, In Dog Area on 2nd St. over Government Creek, Dugway Proving Ground, 5/21/75, A, C, 75001825

Ophir Town Hall, 43 S. Main St., Ophir, 6/09/83, A, C, 83003193

Rich, John T., House, 275 W. Clark St., Grantsville, 5/02/84, C, 84002423

Sharp, John C., House, Off UT 36, Vernon, 7/13/84, A, C, 84002424

Soldier Creek Kilns, Address Restricted, Stockton vicinity, 8/19/80, A, D, 80003973

Stockton Jail, Off UT 36, Stockton, 5/09/85, A, 85000965

Tooele Carnegie Library [Carnegie Library TR], 47 E. Vine St., Tooele, 10/29/84, A, 84000420

Tooele County Courthouse and City Hall, 71 E. Vine St., Tooele, 7/21/83, A, C, 83003194

Tooele Valley Railroad Complex, 35 N. Broadway, Tooele, 5/17/84, A, 84002426

Wendover Air Force Base, S of Wendover off U.S. 40, Wendover vicinity, 7/01/75, A, g, 75001827

Uintah County

Cockleburr Wash Petroglyphs, Address Restricted, Jensen vicinity, 9/04/80, D, 80003974

Curry, Lewis, House, 189 S. Vernal Ave., Vernal, 7/26/82, B, 82004166

Douglass, Earl, Workshop—Laboratory [Dinosaur National Monument MRA], US 40, Dinosaur National Monument, 12/19/86, A, B, NPS, 86003400

Little Brush Creek Petroglyphs, Address Restricted, Vernal vicinity, 3/15/76, D, 76001837

McConkie Ranch Petroglyphs, SE of Dry Fork, Vernal vicinity, 9/25/75, D, 75001828

Morris, Josie Bassett, Ranch Complex [Dinosaur National Monument MRA], US 40, Dinosaur National Monument, 12/19/86, A, B, NPS, 86003394

Quarry Visitor Center [Dinosaur National Monument MRA], US 40, Dinosaur National Monument, 12/19/86, A, g, NPS, 86003401

St. Paul's Episcopal Church and Lodge, 226 W. Main St., Vernal, 1/03/85, A, C, a, 85000049

Vernal Tithing Office [Tithing Offices and Granaries of the Mormon Church TR], NW Corner of 500 West and 200 South, Vernal, 1/25/85, A, a, b, 85000286

Whiterocks Village Site, Address Restricted, Whiterocks vicinity, 1/01/76, D, 76001838

Utah County

Adams, John Alma, House [Pleasant Grove Soft-Rock Buildings TR], 625 E. Two Hundred S, Pleasant Grove, 6/09/87, C, 87000825

Alexander, William D., House, 91 W. 200 South, Provo, 7/28/83, C, 83003195

Allen, Dr. Samuel H., House and Carriage House, 135 E. 200 North, Provo, 5/18/79, B, C, 79002515

Alpine City Hall [Public Works Buildings TR], 20 N. Main St., Alpine, 12/19/91, A, C, 91001820

Alpine LDS Church Meetinghouse [Mormon Church Buildings in Utah MPS], 50 N. Main, Alpine, 5/24/90, A, C, a, 90000794

American Fork Presbyterian Church, 75 N. 1st East St., American Fork, 5/23/80, A, a, 80003975

American Fork Second Ward Meetinghouse, 130 W. 100 South, American Fork, 3/10/92, C, a, 92000101

Ashton—Driggs House [Pleasant Grove Soft-Rock Buildings TR (AD)], 119 E. Battlecreek Rd., Pleasant Grove, 4/14/72, C, 72001261

Austin, Thomas, House, 427 E. 500 North, Lehi, 7/26/82, C, 82004168

Bank of American Fork, 5 E. Main St., American Fork, 3/09/93, A, C, 93000065

Beck No. 2 Mine [Tintic Mining District MRA], SE of Eureka, Eureka vicinity, 3/14/79, A, C, 79003483

Beebe, Angus, George and Martha Ansil, House, 489 W. 100 South, Provo, 10/31/80, C, 80003979

Bird, Roswell Darius, Sr., House, 115 S. Main St., Mapleton, 11/28/80, C, 80003977

Booth, John E., House, 59 W. 500 North, Provo, 2/11/82, B, C, 82004171

Brown, George M., House, 284 E. 100 North, Provo, 12/01/82, C, 82001759

Bullock, Benjamin Kimball, Farmhouse, 1705 S. State, Provo, 12/04/85, B, C, 85003042

Camp Floyd Site, 0.5 mi. S of Fairfield, Fairfield vicinity, 11/11/74, A, d, 74001939

Camp Williams Hostess House/Officers' Club [Public Works Buildings TR], Off UT 68, Camp W. G. Williams, 4/01/85, A, C, g, 85000816

Charcoal Kilns [Tintic Mining District MRA], NE of Eureka, Eureka vicinity, 3/14/79, A, 79003491

Clark-Taylor House, 306 N. 500 West, Provo, 10/07/75, A, C, 75001829

Cluff, Harvey H., House, 174 N. 100 East, Provo, 8/04/82, B, C, 82004172

Crandall Houses, 112 and 136 E. 200 North, Springville, 1/19/83, C, 83003196

Cutler, Thomas R., Mansion, 150 E. State St., Lehi, 7/12/84, B, C, 84002427

Davies, Charles E., House, 388 W. 300 North, Provo, 8/04/82, C, 82004173

Dixon, Christopher F., Jr., House, 248 N. Main St., Payson, 11/07/77, A, C, 77001319

Dixon, John, House, 218 N. Main St., Payson, 2/17/78, C, 78002701

Douglass, Samuel, House, 215 N. Main St., Payson, 8/21/92, C, 92001059

Dunn, Frederick and Della, House, 145 N. Main St., Springville, 8/03/90, C, 90001142

Eggertsen, Simon P. Sr., House, 390 S. 500 West, Provo, 9/13/77, C, 77001321

Eureka Lilly Headframe [Tintic Mining District MRA], E of Eureka, Eureka vicinity, 3/14/79, A, C, 79003487

Fairfield District School, 59 N. Church St., Fairfield, 8/06/87, A, C, 87000992

Frisby, Joseph H., House, 209 E. 400 West, Provo, 7/13/84, B, C, 84002428

Fugal Dugout House, 630 N. Four Hundred E, Pleasant Grove, 3/27/86, C, 86000611

Gardner, Ira W., House, 10 N. Main St., Salem, 7/28/77, C, 77001323

Goode, Charles T.H., House [Pleasant Grove Soft-Rock Buildings TR], 1215 E. Main, American Fork, 6/09/87, C, 87000826

Green, Samuel, House [Pleasant Grove Soft-Rock Buildings TR], 264 E. Two Hundred S., Pleasant Grove, 6/09/87, C, 87000827

Hafen, John, House, 956 S. Main St., Springville, 7/23/82, B, 82004182

Harper, Alfred William, House [Pleasant Grove Soft-Rock Buildings TR], 125 W. Four Hundred N, Lindon, 6/09/87, C, 87000828

Harrington Elementary School, 50 N. Center St., American Fork, 3/04/93, A, C, 93000064

Hines Mansion, 125 S. 4th West, Provo, 7/12/78, A, C, 78002702

Hotel Roberts, 192 S. University Ave, Provo, 7/26/79, B, 79002516

Johnson, Peter Axel, House [Scandinavian-American Pair-houses TR], 1075 N. 100 East, Pleasant Grove, 10/22/84, C, 84000164

Jones, David H., House, 143 S. Main, Spanish Fork, 10/24/85, B, C, 85003392

Kelly, T.R., House, 164 W. 200 South, Springville, 12/09/83, C, 83003972

Knight Block, 1–13 E. Center St., 20–24 N. University Ave., Provo, 12/02/77, B, C, 77001322

Knight, Jesse, House [Entreprenurial Residences of Turn-of-the-Century Provo TR], 185 E. Center St., Provo, 7/23/82, B, C, 82004174

Knight-Allen House [Entreprenurial Residences of Turn-of-the-Century Provo TR], 390 E. Center St., Provo, 7/23/82, B, C, 82004175

Knight-Mangum House [Entreprenurial Residences of Turn-of-the-Century Provo TR], 318 E. Carter St., Provo, 7/23/82, B, C, 82004176

Lakeview Tithing Office [Tithing Offices and Granaries of the Mormon Church TR], Off UT 114, Provo, 1/25/85, A, a, 85000289

Larsen, Christen, House [Scandinavian-American Pair-houses TR], 990 N. 400 E, Pleasant Grove, 7/13/87, C, 87001178

Utah County—Continued

Larsen, Neils Peter, House [Pleasant Grove Soft-Rock Buildings TR], 1146 N. One Hundred E, Pleasant Grove, 6/09/87, C, 87000829

Lehi City Hall, 51 N. Center St., Lehi, 3/01/82, C, 82004169

Lehi Fifth Ward Meetinghouse, 121 N. 100 East, approximately, Lehi, 12/30/92, C, a, 92001688

Lewis Terrace, 68-82 N. 700 East, Provo, 4/07/83, C, 83003197

Lime Kilns [Tintic Mining District MRA], NE of Eureka, Eureka vicinity, 3/14/79, A, C, 79003490

Maeser School, 150 S. 500 East, Provo, 7/26/82, A, C, 82004177

Merrihew, Harry B., Drugstore, 1st West and Main Sts., Lehi, 7/23/82, C, 82004170

Morgan, David, House, Off US 6, Goshen, 2/19/82, C, 82004167

Moyle House and Indian Tower, 606 E. 770 North, Alpine, 12/23/92, A, C, e, 92001689

Nunn Power Plant, Off U.S. 189, Provo, 12/13/79, A, 79002517

Old Goshen Site, Address Restricted, Goshen vicinity, 8/26/80, A, D, 80003976

Olmsted Station Powerhouse, 5 mi. N of Provo on U.S. 189, Provo vicinity, 6/26/72, A, 72001262

Olpin, Joseph, House [Pleasant Grove Soft-Rock Buildings TR (AD)], 510 Locust Ave., Pleasant Grove, 11/07/77, A, C, 77001320

Payson Presbyterian Church, 160 S. Main, Payson, 3/27/86, A, C, a, 86000610

Peteetneet School, 50 N. 500 East, Payson, 5/30/90, A, C, 90000795

Pleasant Grove School, 65 South 100 E., Pleasant Grove, 2/20/80, A, 80003978

Pleasant Grove Tithing Office [Tithing Offices and Granaries of the Mormon Church TR], 7 S. 300 East, Pleasant Grove, 1/25/85, A, a, 85000288

Pleasant Grove Town Hall [Pleasant Grove Soft-Rock Buildings TR (AD)], 107 S. 100 East, Pleasant Grove, 6/27/85, A, C, 85001391

Provo Canyon Guard Quarters, Off US 189, Provo, 6/12/86, A, 86001291

Provo Downtown Historic District, Center St. and University Ave., Provo, 5/01/80, A, C, 80003980

Provo Tabernacle, 50 S. University Ave., Provo, 9/09/75, A, C, a, 75001830

Provo Third Ward Chapel and Amusement Hall, 105 N. 500 West, Provo, 4/02/79, A, C, 79002518

Provo West Co-op, 450 W. Center St., Provo, 7/13/84, A, 84002429

Ray, William H., House [Entreprenurial Residences of Turn-of-the-Century Provo TR], 415 S. University, Provo, 7/23/82, C, 82004178

Recreation Center for the Utah State Hospital [Public Works Buildings TR], 1300 E. Center, Provo, 4/09/86, A, C, g, 86000746

Reynolds, John T. and Henry T., Jr., House, 101 E. 200 South, Springville, 6/27/85, A, C, 85001393

Richins, Thomas A., House [Pleasant Grove Soft-Rock Buildings TR], 405 N. Five Hundred E, Pleasant Grove, 6/09/87, C, 87000831

Roberts, William D., House, 212 N. 500 West, Provo, 7/24/84, C, 84002430

Santaquin Junior High School [Public Works Buildings TR], 75 W. 100 South, Santaquin, 4/01/85, A, 85000817

Silver Row, 621–645 W. 100 North, Provo, 8/04/82, C, 82004179

Smith, Hannah Maria Libby, House, 315 E. Center St., Provo, 2/14/80, B, C, 80003981

Smith, Warren B., House, 589 E. Main St., American Fork, 6/19/79, C, 79002513

Smoot, Reed, House, 183 E. 100 South, Provo, 10/14/75, A, B, C, a, NHL, 75001831

Spanish Fork Fire Station [Public Works Buildings TR], 365 N. Main St., Spanish Fork, 4/01/85, A, C, 85000818

Spanish Fork High School Gymnasium [Public Works Buildings TR], 300 S. Main St., Spanish Fork, 4/01/85, A, C, 85000819

Spanish Fork National Guard Armory [Public Works Buildings TR], 360 N. Main, Spanish Fork, 4/09/86, A, C, g, 86000749

Springville Carnegie Library [Carnegie Library TR], 175 S. Main St., Springville, 12/13/91, A, 91001821

Springville High School Art Gallery [Public Works Buildings TR], 126 E. Four Hundred S, Springville, 4/09/86, A, C, g, 86000750

Springville High School Mechanical Arts Building, 443 S. 200 East, Springville, 5/14/93, A, 93000415

Springville Presbyterian Church, 251 S. 200 East, Springville, 10/24/80, A, a, 80003983

Stagecoach Inn, Address unknown at this time, Fairfield, 5/14/71, A, 71000857

Startup Candy Factory, 534 S. 100 West, Provo, 10/28/83, A, 83003973

Superintendent's Residence at the Utah State Hospital [Public Works Buildings TR], 1079 E. Center, Provo, 4/09/86, A, C, 86000748

Talmage, James E. and Albert, House, 345 E. 400 North, Provo, 2/20/80, B, 80003982

Taylor, George, Jr., House, 187 N. 400 West, Provo, 8/09/83, C, 83004185

Taylor, Thomas N., House [Entreprenurial Residences of Turn-of-the-Century Provo TR], 342 N. 500 West, Provo, 7/23/82, B, C, 82004180

Timpanogos Cave Historic District, UT 80, Pleasant Grove vicinity, 10/13/82, A, C, NPS, 82001760

Tintic Standard Reduction Mill, E of Goshen off U.S. 6, Goshen vicinity, 9/13/78, A, C, 78002700

Twelves, John R., House [Entreprenurial Residences of Turn-of-the-Century Provo TR], 287 E. 100 North, Provo, 7/23/82, B, C, 82004181

Upper American Fork Hydroelectric Power Plant Historic District [Electric Power Plants of Utah MPS], UT 80, Highland vicinity, 4/20/89, A, C, 89000278

Wadley, Edward, House [Pleasant Grove Soft-Rock Buildings TR], 2445 N. Canyon Rd., Pleasant Grove, 6/09/87, C, 87000832

Water Lily Shaft [Tintic Mining District MRA], NE of Eureka, Eureka vicinity, 3/14/79, A, C, 79003489

Wentz, Peter, House, 575 N. University Ave., Provo, 4/26/78, C, 78002703

White, Jacob Hanmer, House [Pleasant Grove Soft-Rock Buildings TR], 599 E. One Hundred S, Pleasant Grove, 6/09/87, C, 87000833

Wood-Harrison House, 310 S. 300 West, Springville, 1/19/83, C, 83003198

Yankee Headframe [Tintic Mining District MRA], E of Eureka, Eureka vicinity, 3/14/79, A, C, 79003484

Young, Brigham, Academy, 5th and 6th North Sts. and University Ave. and 1st East St., Provo, 1/01/76, A, C, 76001839

Young, William Friend, House [Pleasant Grove Soft-Rock Buildings TR], 550 E. Five Hundred N, Pleasant Grove, 6/09/87, C, 87000834

Wasatch County

Austin-Wherritt House, 315 E. Center, Heber City, 1/25/79, A, C, 79002520

Blackley, George, House, 421 E. 200 North, Heber City, 6/27/85, C, 85001392

Bonner, George, Jr., House [Architecture of John Watkins TR], 90 E. Main, Midway, 6/17/86, C, 86001357

Bonner, George, Sr., House [Architecture of John Watkins TR], 103 E. Main, Midway, 6/17/86, C, 86001359

Bonner, William, House [Architecture of John Watkins TR], 110 E. Main, Midway, 6/17/86, C, 86001361

Cloud Rim Girl Scout Lodge [Public Works Buildings TR], Lake Brimhall, Brighton vicinity, 4/09/86, A, C, g, 86000751

Coleman, William, House [Architecture of John Watkins TR], 180 N. Center, Midway, 6/17/86, C, 86001362

Crook, John, House, 188 W. 3rd North, Heber City, 11/16/78, A, C, 78002705

Fisher, David, House, 125 E. 400 South, Heber City, 4/16/80, C, 80003984

Hatch, Abram, House, 81 E. Center St., Heber City, 10/10/75, C, 75001832

Heber Second Ward Meetinghouse, 1st West and Center Sts., Heber City, 12/12/78, A, C, a, 78002706

Hewlett, Lester F. and Margaret Stewart, Ranch House [Stewart Ranch TR], Off UT 35, Woodland vicinity, 5/23/85, A, 85001134

Huber, John, House and Creamery, Off Snake Creek Rd., Midway vicinity, 8/11/88, B, a, 88001182

Murdoch, John, House, 261 N. 400 West, Heber City, 2/28/80, C, 80003985

Murdock, Joseph S., House, 115 E. Three-hundred N, Heber City, 5/01/87, A, B, C, a, 87000701

Schneitter Hotel, 700 N. Homestead Dr., Midway, 12/17/92, A, C, 92001691

Snake Creek Hydroelectric Power Plant Historic District [Electric Power Plants of Utah MPS], UT 220, Heber City vicinity, 4/21/89, B, C, 89000279

Wasatch County—Continued

Stewart Ranch Foreman's House [Stewart Ranch TR], Off UT 35, Woodland vicinity, 5/23/85, A, 85001135

Stewart, Barnard J., Ranch House [Stewart Ranch TR], Off UT 35, Woodland vicinity, 5/23/85, A, 85001136

Stewart, Charles B., Ranch House [Stewart Ranch TR], Off UT 35, Woodland vicinity, 5/23/85, A, 85001137

Stewart, Samuel W., Ranch House [Stewart Ranch TR], Off UT 35, Woodland vicinity, 5/23/85, A, 85001138

Stewart-Hewlett Ranch Dairy Barn [Stewart Ranch TR], Off UT 35, Woodland vicinity, 5/23/85, A, 85001139

Wasatch Saloon, Main St., Heber City, 9/23/80, C, 80003986

Wasatch Stake Tabernacle and Heber Amusement Hall, Main St. at 100 North St. and 100 West St. corners, Heber City, 12/02/70, A, C, a, 70000633

Wasatch Wave Publishing Company Building, 55 W. Center St., Heber City, 12/27/79, A, C, 79002519

Watkins, John and Margaret, House [Architecture of John Watkins TR], 22 W. Hundred S, Midway, 6/17/86, C, 86001364

Watkins-Coleman House, 5 E. Main St., Midway, 5/14/71, C, 71000858

White, Ethelbert and Stewart, William M., Ranch House [Stewart Ranch TR], Off UT 35, Woodland vicinity, 5/23/85, A, b, 85001140

Wootton, Attewall, Jr., House, 270 E. Main St., Midway, 4/10/80, A, C, 80003987

Washington County

Angels Landing Trail—West Rim Trail [Zion National Park MRA], S of Scout Lookout across the Virgin River and Refrigerator Canyon, Springdale, 2/14/87, C, NPS, 86003707

Blake, Wallace, House, S of St. George, St. George vicinity, 11/14/78, C, 78002709

Bradshaw House—Hotel, 85 S. Main St., Hurricane, 9/26/91, A, 91001443

Butler, William F., House, 168 S. 300 West, St. George, 7/13/84, B, C, 84002433

Cable Mountain Draw Works [Zion National Park MRA (AD)], N of Springdale in Zion National Park, Springdale vicinity, 5/24/78, A, C, NPS, 78000281

Canyon Overlook Trail [Zion National Park MRA], Across hwy. from parking area at E end of Zion-Mt. Carmel Tunnel to a point directly above the Great Arch of Zion, Springdale, 2/14/87, C, NPS, 86003722

Covington, Robert D., House, 200 N. 200 East, Washington, 4/20/78, B, C, 78002711

Crawford Irrigation Canal [Zion National Park MRA], W bank of Virgin River from 1 mi. N of Virgin River Bridge to base of Virgin River For-

mation and .5 mi up Oak Creek, Springdale, 7/07/87, A, NPS, 86003732

Deseret Telegraph and Post Office, On UT 15, Rockville, 2/23/72, A, 72001263

East Entrance Checking Station [Zion National Park MRA], Island in middle of UT 9, Springdale, 2/14/87, C, NPS, 86003711

East Entrance Residence [Zion National Park MRA], E Entrance 150 ft. N of UT 9, Springdale, 2/14/87, C, NPS, 86003712

East Entrance Sign [Zion National Park MRA], East Entrance Checking Station on N and S sides of UT 9, Springdale, 7/07/87, C, NPS, 86003710

East Rim Trail [Zion National Park MRA], Between Weeping Rock Parking Area and Observation Pt., Springdale, 7/07/87, A, C, NPS, 86003723

Emerald Pools Trail [Zion National Park MRA], Foot Bridge across hwy. from Utah Parks Lodge proceeding W to the Lower Emerald Pool, Springdale, 2/14/87, C, NPS, 86003725

Enterprise Meetinghouse [Mormon Church Buildings in Utah MPS], Approximately 24 S. Center St., Enterprise, 5/14/93, A, C, a, 93000410

Forsyth, Thomas, House, Off UT 15, Toquerville, 2/11/82, A, C, 82004184

Fort Harmony Site, E of New Harmony on I-15, New Harmony vicinity, 11/16/79, A, 79003493

Fort Pearce, 12 mi. SE of Washington off I-15, Washington vicinity, 11/20/75, A, 75001834

Gateway to the Narrows Trail [Zion National Park MRA], Temple of Sinawava at the end of Zion Canyon Scenic Dr. to a pt. 1 mi. N on Virgin River, Springdale, 7/07/87, A, C, NPS, 86003726

Grotto Camping Ground North Comfort Station [Zion National Park MRA], Grotto Picnic Area near Grotto Residence E of Scenic Dr., Springdale, 2/14/87, C, NPS, 86003705

Grotto Camping Ground South Comfort Station [Zion National Park MRA], Grotto Picnic Area near Grotto Residence, E of Scenic Dr., Springdale, 2/14/87, C, NPS, 86003704

Hamblin, Jacob, House, US 91, Santa Clara, 3/11/71, B, a, 71000860

Hidden Canyon Trail [Zion National Park MRA], Hidden Canyon jct. on the E Rim Trail to the mouth of Hidden Canyon, Springdale, 2/14/87, C, NPS, 86003731

Hurricane Canal, E of Hurricane, Hurricane vicinity, 8/29/77, A, C, 77001324

Hurricane High School [Public Works Buildings TR], 34 S. One Hundred W, Hurricane, 4/09/86, A, C, 86000752

Hurricane Library—City Hall, 35 W. State St., Hurricane, 9/26/91, A, 91001444

Isom, Samuel and Elizabeth, House, 188 S. 100 West, Hurricane, 3/04/93, A, C, 93000063

Judd, Thomas, House, 269 S. 200 East, St. George, 1/31/78, B, C, 78002710

Leeds CCC Camp Historic District, 96 W. Mulberry, Leeds, 3/04/93, A, 93000062

Leeds Tithing Office [Tithing Offices and Granaries of the Mormon Church TR], SW Corner 100 West and 100 North, Leeds, 1/25/85, A, a, 85000291

Main Building of Dixie College, 86 S. Main St., St. George, 6/19/80, A, C, 80003988

Mountain Meadows Historic Site, 7 mi. S of Enterprise on UT 18, Enterprise vicinity, 8/28/75, A, d, 75001833

Museum—Grotto Residence [Zion National Park MRA], SE of Grotto Picnic Area, Springdale, 2/14/87, C, NPS, 86003721

Naegle Winery, Main and 5th Sts., Toquerville, 2/20/80, A, 80003990

Oak Creek Historic District [Zion National Park MRA], Off US 9 along bank of Oak Creek, Springdale, 7/07/87, C, g, NPS, 86003706

Oak Creek Irrigation Canal [Zion National Park MRA], W side of the N Fork of Virgin River 1/8 mi. N of Virgin River Bridge to the N side of Watchman Campground Entrance Rd., Springdale, 7/07/87, A, NPS, 86003738

Old Washington County Courthouse, 85 E. 100 North, St. George, 9/22/70, A, 70000634

Pine Creek Irrigation Canal [Zion National Park MRA], E bank of the Virgin River .25 mi. N of Virgin River Bridge to the SW end of Watchman Residential Loop, Springdale, 7/07/87, A, NPS, 86003734

Pine Creek Residential Historic District [Zion National Park MRA], W side of UT 9 500 ft. S of Virgin River Bridge, Springdale, 7/07/87, C, NPS, 86003736

Pine Valley Chapel and Tithing Office, Main and Grass Valley Sts., Pine Valley, 4/16/71, A, C, a, 71000859

Pratt, Orson, House, 76 W. Tabernacle St., St. George, 8/11/83, B, 83003199

Santa Clara Hydroelectric Power Plants Historic District [Electric Power Plants of Utah MPS], Off UT 18 on Santa Clara River, Veyo vicinity, 4/21/89, A, C, 89000281

South Campground Amphitheater [Zion National Park MRA], South Campground, Springdale, 2/14/87, C, NPS, 86003717

South Campground Comfort Station [Zion National Park MRA], South Campground at N end of campsite loop, Springdale, 2/14/87, C, NPS, 86003708

South Entrance Sign [Zion National Park MRA], South Entrance, Springdale, 2/14/87, C, NPS, 86003713

Southern Paiute Archeological District, Address Restricted, Washington vicinity, 6/11/82, D, 82004185

St. George Elementary School [Public Works Buildings TR], 120 S. 100 West, St. George, 4/01/85, A, g, 85000820

St. George Social Hall, 212 N. Main St., St. George, 4/03/91, A, 91000360

St. George Tabernacle, Jct. of Tabernacle and Main Sts., St. George, 5/14/71, A, C, a, 71000862

St. George Temple, Bounded by 200 East, 300 East, 400 South, and 500 South, St. George, 11/07/77, A, C, a, 77001325

Stanworth, Emanuel and Ursella, House, 198 S. Main St., Hurricane, 12/17/92, C, 92001692

Steele, John, House, 263 N. Toquerville Blvd., Toquerville, 4/07/88, B, C, 88000401

Washington County—Continued

Washington Cotton Factory, On U.S. 91 (Frontage Rd. West), Washington, 4/16/71, A, 71000864

Washington Relief Society Hall, 100 West and Telegraph Sts., Washington, 8/27/80, A, C, 80003991

Washington School, Main and Telegraph Sts., Washington, 11/23/80, A, C, 80003992

Wells Fargo and Company Express Building, Main St., Silver Reef, 3/11/71, A, 71000861

Woodward School, 100 West and Tabernacle Sts., St. George, 11/23/80, A, C, 80003989

Young, Brigham, Winter Home and Office, Corner of 200 North and 100 West, St. George, 2/22/71, B, C, a, 71000863

Zion Lodge Historic District, N of Springdale in Zion National Park, Springdale vicinity, 8/24/82, C, NPS, 82001718

Zion Lodge—Birch Creek Historic District (Boundary Increase) [Zion National Park MRA], W of UT 9 on the W and E sides of The Zion Canyon Scenic Drive near Birch Creek, Springdale vicinity, 7/07/87, C, NPS, 86003753

Zion Nature Center—Zion Inn [Zion National Park MRA], N of South Campground facilities, Springdale, 2/14/87, C, NPS, 86003719

Zion-Mount Carmel Highway [Zion National Park MRA], Between US 9 and US 89, Springdale, 7/07/87, A, C, NPS, 86003709

Wayne County

Bull Creek Archeological District, Address Restricted, Hanksville vicinity, 4/30/81, D, c, 81000586

Cowboy Caves, Address Restricted, Green River vicinity, 8/27/80, D, 80003993

D.C.C. & P. Inscription "B" [Canyonlands National Park MRA], Confluence vicinity, Moab vicinity, 10/07/88, A, NPS, 88001251

Fruita Schoolhouse, Capitol Reef National Park on UT 24, Fruita, 2/23/72, A, NPS, 72000098

Grover School [Public Works Buildings TR], Off UT 117, Grover, 4/09/86, A, 86000753

Hanksville Meetinghouse—School [Mormon Church Buildings in Utah MPS], Sawmill Basin Rd., Hanksville, 12/18/90, A, C, a, 90001825

Harvest Scene Pictograph, Address Restricted, Green River vicinity, 4/01/75, C, D, NPS, 75000241

Horseshoe (Barrier) Canyon Pictograph Panels, Address Restricted, Green River vicinity, 2/23/72, C, D, NPS, 72000099

Loa Tithing Office [Tithing Offices and Granaries of the Mormon Church TR], 100 West and Center St., Loa, 3/28/85, A, C, a, 85000687

Nielson, Hans Peter, Gristmill, 3 mi. SE of Bicknell, Bicknell vicinity, 6/18/75, A, 75001835

Teasdale Tithing Granary [Tithing Offices and Granaries of the Mormon Church TR], Off UT 117, Teasdale, 3/28/85, A, C, a, b, 85000688

Torrey Log Church—Schoolhouse [Mormon Church Buildings in Utah MPS], Approximately

49 E. Main St., Torrey, 5/14/93, A, C, a, b, 93000411

Wayne County High School [Public Works Buildings TR], 55 N. Center St., Bicknell, 4/01/85, A, g, 85000821

Weber County

Arvondor Apartments [Three-Story Apartment Buildings in Ogden, 1908–1928 MPS], 823 Twenty-third St., Odgen, 12/31/87, A, C, 87002156

Avelan Apartments [Three-Story Apartment Buildings in Ogden, 1908–1928 MPS], 449 Twenty-seventh St., Ogden, 12/31/87, A, C, 87002157

Avon Apartments [Three-Story Apartment Buildings in Ogden, 1908–1928 MPS], 961 Twenty-fifth St., Ogden, 12/31/87, A, C, 87002158

Barnhart Apartments [Three-Story Apartment Buildings in Ogden, 1908–1928 MPS], 336 Twenty-seventh St., Ogden, 12/31/87, A, C, 87002159

Becker, Gustav, House, 2408 Van Buren Ave., Ogden, 7/21/77, B, C, 77001327

Bertha Eccles Community Art Center, 2580 Jefferson Ave., Ogden, 5/14/71, A, C, 71000865

Bigelow—Ben Lomond Hotel, 2510 Washington Blvd., Ogden, 4/19/90, A, C, 90000637

Browning Apartments, 2703 Washington Blvd., Ogden, 12/19/85, B, C, a, 85003200

Browning, John Moses, House, 505 27th St., Ogden, 4/24/73, B, 73001863

Burch-Taylor Mill, 4287 Riverdale Rd., Ogden, 7/14/82, A, 82004186

Congregation B'rith Sholem Synagogue [Jewish Synagogue TR], 2750 Grant, Ogden, 6/27/85, A, a, 85001394

Cross, Charles W., House, 451 17th St., Ogden, 7/12/84, C, 84002434

Dalton, John L. and Elizabeth, House, 2622 Madison Ave., Ogden, 3/11/87, C, 86003659

Downing Apartments [Three-Story Apartment Buildings in Ogden, 1908–1928 MPS], 357–359 Twenty-seventh St., Ogden, 12/31/87, A, C, 87002160

Eccles Avenue Historic District, Bounded by 25th and 26th Sts., Van Buren and Jackson Aves., Ogden, 12/12/76, C, 76001840

Eccles Building, 385 24th St., Ogden, 7/14/82, B, C, 82004187

El Monte Golf Course Clubhouse [Public Works Buildings TR], 1300 Valley Dr., Ogden, 4/01/85, A, C, 85000823

Episcopal Church of the Good Shepherd, 2374 Grant Ave., Ogden, 4/03/73, A, a, 73001864

Fairview Apartments [Three-Story Apartment Buildings in Ogden, 1908–1928 MPS], 579–587 Twenty-seventh St., Ogden, 12/31/87, A, C, 87002161

Farnsworth Apartments [Three-Story Apartment Buildings in Ogden, 1908–1928 MPS], 2539 Jefferson Ave., Ogden, 12/31/87, A, C, 87002162

Farr, Valasco, House, 700 Canyon Rd., Ogden, 6/13/78, C, 78002712

Fern—Marylyn Apartments [Three-Story Apartment Buildings in Ogden, 1908–1928 MPS], 2579 Adams Ave., Ogden, 12/31/87, A, C, 87002163

Flowers Apartments [Three-Story Apartment Buildings in Ogden, 1908–1928 MPS], 2681 Madison Ave., Ogden, 12/31/87, A, C, 87002166

Fontenelle Apartments [Three-Story Apartment Buildings in Ogden, 1908–1928 MPS], 2465–2475 Monroe Ave., Ogden, 12/31/87, A, C, 87002167

Geffas Apartments [Three-Story Apartment Buildings in Ogden, 1908–1928 MPS], 2675 Grant Ave., Ogden, 12/31/87, A, C, 87002168

Goodyear, Miles, Cabin, Tabernacle Sq., Ogden, 2/24/71, A, b, 71000866

Helms Apartments [Three-Story Apartment Buildings in Ogden, 1908–1928 MPS], 2248–2250 Jefferson Ave., Ogden, 12/31/87, A, C, 87002169

Hillcrest Apartments [Three-Story Apartment Buildings in Ogden, 1908–1928 MPS], 2485 Monroe Ave., Ogden, 12/31/87, A, C, 87002170

La Frantz Apartments [Three-Story Apartment Buildings in Ogden, 1908–1928 MPS], 461 Twenty-seventh St., Ogden, 12/31/87, A, C, 87002172

Ladywood Apartments [Three-Story Apartment Buildings in Ogden, 1908–1928 MPS], 670–690 Twenty-sixth St., Odgen, 12/31/87, A, C, 87002171

Lower 25th Street Historic District, 25th St. between Wall and Grant Aves., Ogden, 1/31/78, C, 78003260

Lower 25th Street Historic District (Boundary Increase), Grant Ave., Ogden, 2/25/83, A, C, 83003200

Madison Elementary School, 2418 Madison Ave., Ogden, 2/19/82, A, 82004188

Maguire, Don, Duplex, 549-551 25th St., Ogden, 2/26/79, B, C, 79002521

McGregor Apartments [Three-Story Apartment Buildings in Ogden, 1908–1928 MPS], 802–810 Twenty-fifth St., Ogden, 12/31/87, A, C, 87002173

Mountain View Auto Court, 563 W. Twenty-fourth St., Ogden, 11/24/87, A, C, g, 87002063

New Brigham Hotel, 2402–2410 Wall Ave., Ogden, 6/14/79, A, 79002522

North Ogden Elementary School [Public Works Buildings TR], 474 E. 2650 North, North Ogden, 4/01/85, A, C, g, 85000822

Ogden High School [Ogden Art Deco Building TR], 2828 Harrison Blvd., Ogden, 6/07/83, A, C, 83003201

Ogden Union Depot, 25th St. at Wall Ave., Ogden, 4/11/71, A, g, 71000867

Ogden/Weber Municipal Building [Ogden Art Deco Building TR], 2541 Washington Blvd., Ogden, 6/07/83, A, C, g, 83003202

Patton, Augustus B., House, 1506 24th St., Ogden, 2/19/82, B, C, 82004189

Peery Apartments [Three-Story Apartment Buildings in Ogden, 1908–1928 MPS], 2461 Adams Ave., Ogden, 12/31/87, A, C, 87002174

Weber County—Continued

Peery's Egyptian Theatre, 2439 Washington Blvd., Ogden, 12/12/78, A, C, 78002714

Pioneer Hydroelectric Power Plant Historic District [Electric Power Plants of Utah MPS], 12th St. at Canyon Rd., Ogden, 4/21/89, A, C, 89000275

Rose Apartments [Three-Story Apartment Buildings in Ogden, 1908–1928 MPS], 302–308 Twenty-seventh St., Ogden, 12/31/87, A, C, 87002175

Scowcroft Warehouse, 23rd St., Ogden, 11/30/78, B, C, 78002715

Scowcroft, Heber, House, 795 24th St., Ogden, 12/13/91, B, C, 91001818

Shupe-Williams Candy Company Factory, 2605 Wall Ave., Ogden, 3/30/78, A, C, 78002716

Skeen, William D., House, Address unknown at this time, Plain City, 8/09/82, C, 82004191

Smyth, Dennis A., House, 635 25th St., Ogden, 2/11/82, B, C, 82004190

Stevens, Sidney, House, 2593 N. 400 East, North Ogden, 12/02/77, B, 77001326

U.S. Post Office and Courthouse, 298 W. 24th St., Ogden, 7/26/79, C, 79002523

Upton Apartments [Three-Story Apartment Buildings in Ogden, 1908–1928 MPS], 2300–2314 Jefferson Ave., Ogden, 12/31/87, A, C, 87002176

Utah School for the Deaf and Blind Boys' Dormitory [Public Works Buildings TR], 846 20th St., Ogden, 4/01/85, A, 85000824

Warner, Andrew J., House, 726 25th St., Ogden, 12/13/77, C, 77001328

Weber Stake Relief Society Building [Mormon Church Buildings in Utah, 1847–1936 MPS], 2148 Grant Ave., Ogden, 2/13/89, A, a, 88003438

Several architectural features, including a central passage plan, stone construction, diagonal brick chimney stacks, and casement windows make the Partridge House (ca. 1871–72) in Fillmore, Utah, a unique local residence. (Roger Roper, 1992)

VERMONT

Addison County

Addison Baptist Church, jct. of VT 22A and VT 17, Addison, 11/02/78, A, C, a, 78003202

Bristol Downtown Historic District, Main St., Bristol, 2/03/83, C, 83003203

Cedar Swamp Covered Bridge, W of West Salisbury over Otter Creek, West Salisbury vicinity, 9/10/74, A, C, 74000386

Chimney Point Tavern, VT 125, Addison, 3/31/71, A, C, 71000073

Cornwall Town Hall, VT 30, Cornwall, 5/08/86, A, C, 86001035

District School No. 1, Lake Rd., Panton, 4/17/80, A, 80000323

District Six Schoolhouse, N of Shoreham on Worcester Rd., Shoreham vicinity, 8/18/77, A, C, 77000093

East Shoreham Covered Railroad Bridge, SE of Shoreham over Lemon Fair River, Shoreham, 6/13/74, A, C, 74000198

Frost, Robert, Farm, 1 mi. N of VT 125, 3 mi. E of Ripton, Ripton vicinity, 5/23/68, B, g, NHL, 68000046

Halpin Covered Bridge, NE of Middlebury, Middlebury vicinity, 9/10/74, A, C, 74000199

Hamilton, John, Farmstead [Agricultural Resources of Vermont MPS], VT 125 W of Lemon Fair R., Bridport vicinity, 6/17/93, A, C, 93000531

Hand's Cove, SW of Shoreham, Shoreham vicinity, 5/22/80, A, C, D, 80000324

Hawley's Ferry House, NW of Ferrisburg on Kingsland Bay, Ferrisburg vicinity, 11/02/78, A, C, 78000224

Heights, The, South St./VT 30, Middlebury, 12/29/88, C, 88003082

Hoag Gristmill and Knight House Complex, NW of Starksboro on State Prison Hollow Rd., Starksboro vicinity, 4/22/80, A, C, 80000325

Larrabee's Point Complex, SW of Shoreham, Shoreham vicinity, 5/01/80, A, C, 80000423

Leicester Meeting House, US 7 and Town Hwy. 1, Leicester, 7/28/88, C, a, 88001043

Middlebury Gorge Concrete Arch Bridge [Metal Truss, Masonry, and Concrete Bridges in Vermont MPS], Vermont 125 over the Middlebury R., Middlebury, 11/14/91, A, C, 91001604

Middlebury Village Historic District, U.S. 7, Middlebury, 11/13/76, A, B, C, 76000223

Middlebury Village Historic District (Boundary Increase), U.S. 7, VT 125 and VT 30, Middlebury, 9/17/80, A, C, 80000422

Monkton Borough Baptist Church, Town Hwy. 1, Monkton, 1/05/89, C, a, 88003121

Monkton Town Hall, N of Monkton on Monkton Ridge Rd., Monkton vicinity, 1/03/78, C, 78000225

Mount Independence, On Lake Champlain opposite Fort Ticonderoga, NW of Orwell, Orwell vicinity, 9/03/71, A, D, NHL, 71000079

New Haven Junction Depot, jct. U.S. 7 and VT 17, New Haven, 10/19/78, A, C, 78000226

Old Stone Blacksmith Shop, N of Cornwall on VT 30, Cornwall vicinity, 4/21/75, A, C, 75000136

Orwell Site, Address Restricted, Orwell vicinity, 4/11/77, D, 77000094

Pulp Mill Covered Bridge, NW of Middlebury off VT 23, Middlebury vicinity, 9/10/74, A, C, 74000200

Ripton Community House, On VT 125, Ripton, 7/03/73, C, 73000180

Rokeby, N of Ferrisburg off U.S. 7, Ferrisburg vicinity, 6/20/74, B, 74000201

School House and Town Hall, US 7 and Town Hwy. 1, Leicester, 6/14/88, C, 88001045

Shard Villa, Jct. Shard Villa and Columbus Smith Rds., Salisbury, 10/30/89, A, B, C, 89001789

South Starksboro Friends Meeting House and Cemetery, Dan Sargent Rd., Starksboro, 11/07/85, C, a, b, 85002769

Stagecoach Inn, U.S. 7, Leicester, 11/15/84, C, b, 84000674

Starksboro Village Meeting House, VT 116, Starksboro Village, 11/07/85, C, a, 85002768

Stone Mill, Mill St., Middlebury, 4/11/73, A, C, 73000181

Strong, Gen. Samuel, House, 64 W. Main St., Vergennes, 4/11/73, C, 73000182

Strong, John, House, SW of Addison VT A, Addison vicinity, 5/15/80, B, C, 80000326

Strong, Samuel Paddock, House, 82 W. Main St., Vergennes, 8/15/79, C, 79000216

Union Meetinghouse, U.S. 7, Ferrisburg, 2/23/78, C, a, 78000227

University of Vermont Morgan Horse Farm, Morgan Horse Farm Rd. Off U.S. 7, Weybridge, 4/11/73, A, C, 73000183

Vergennes Historic District, U.S. 7, Vergennes, 9/03/76, A, C, 76000136

Waybury Inn, VT 125, East Middlebury vicinity, 7/14/83, C, 83003204

Wilcox-Cutts House, 2 mi. S of Orwell on VT 22A, Orwell vicinity, 12/02/74, A, C, 74000202

Willard, Emma, House, Middlebury College campus, Middlebury, 10/15/66, B, NHL, 66000798

Witherell Farm [Agricultural Resources of Vermont MPS], Town Hwy. 74 (Witherell Rd.) W of Lakeview and St. Genevieve cemeteries, Shoreham Township, Shoreham vicinity, 4/01/93, A, C, 93000241

Bennington County

Arlington Green Covered Bridge, Off VT 313, W of Arlington, Arlington vicinity, 8/28/73, A, C, 73000184

Arlington Village Historic District, Roughly Main St., School St., E. Arlington Rd., and Battenkill Dr., Arlington, 11/02/89, A, B, C, 89001936

Bennington Battle Monument, Monument Circle, Bennington, 3/31/71, C, f, 71000054

Bennington Falls Covered Bridge, NW of Bennington off VT 67A, Bennington vicinity, 8/28/73, A, C, 73000185

Bennington Post Office, 118 South St., Bennington, 12/12/76, C, 76000137

Bennington Railroad Station, Depot and River Sts., Bennington, 11/09/88, C, 88001301

Center Shaftsbury Historic District, VT 7A, Shaftsbury, 11/09/88, A, C, 88002052

Dorset Village Historic District, Roughly bounded by Main and Church Sts. and Dorset Hollow Rd., Dorset, 4/18/85, A, C, 85000868

Downtown Bennington Historic District, U.S. 7 and VT 9, Bennington, 4/01/80, A, C, 80000327

Equinox House, Main St., Manchester, 11/21/72, A, C, 72000107

Equinox House Historic District, Main and Union Sts., Manchester, 6/03/80, A, C, 80000384

First Congregational Church of Bennington, Monument Ave., Bennington, 4/24/73, C, a, 73000186

Frost, Robert, Farm, 0.25 mi. W of U.S. 7 on Buck Hill Rd., South Shaftsbury, 5/23/68, B, g, NHL, 68000047

Galusha, Gov. Jonas, Homestead, U.S. 7, Center Shaftsbury vicinity, 11/30/79, B, C, 79000217

Hard, Zera, House, River Rd., Manchester, 11/09/88, C, 88002230

Henry Covered Bridge, NW of Bennington off VT 67A, Bennington vicinity, 8/28/73, A, C, 73000187

Henry, William, House, River Rd., Bennington, 11/09/88, A, C, 88001302

Hildene, S of Manchester off U.S. 7, Manchester vicinity, 10/28/77, C, 77000095

Holden—Leonard Mill Complex, 160 Benmont Ave., Bennington, 11/14/88, A, C, e, 88002085

Kent Neighborhood Historic District, S of Dorset at Dorset West and Nichols Hill Rds., Dorset, 7/14/78, A, C, 78003203

Lawrence, Amos, House, Richville Rd., Manchester, 5/21/85, C, 85001245

Manchester Village Historic District, US 7A, Union St., and Taconic Ave., Manchester, 1/26/84, A, C, 84003438

Manley—Lefevre House, Dorset West Rd., Town Hwy. 1, Dorset, 1/26/90, A, C, 89002324

Mathews, David, House, VT 67, Bennington vicinity, 9/10/79, C, 79000274

Munro-Hawkins House, 0.5 mi. S of Shaftsbury Center on U.S. 7, Shaftsbury Center vicinity, 5/17/73, C, 73000188

North Bennington Depot, Main St. at the Vermont Ry tracks, North Bennington, 4/11/73, A, C, 73000189

North Bennington Historic District, VT 67 and VT 67A, North Bennington, 8/29/80, A, C, 80000328

Old Bennington Historic District, Roughly bounded by Rutland RR, Monument Ave. and

Bennington County—Continued

Circle, West Rd., Seminary Lane, Elm and Fairview Sts., Bennington vicinity, 10/04/84, A, C, 84000030

Park-McCullough House, SW corner of West and Park Sts., North Bennington, 10/26/72, B, C, 72000090

Ritchie Block, 465–473 Main St., Bennington, 11/06/86, C, 86003060

Silk Covered Bridge, NW of Bennington off VT 67A, Bennington vicinity, 8/28/73, A, C, 73000190

Squire, Frederick, House, 185 North St., Bennington, 7/30/92, C, 92000964

Tudor House, VT 8, Stamford, 9/10/79, A, C, 79000218

Yester House, West Rd., Manchester, 11/10/88, C, 88002051

Caledonia County

Barnet Center Historic DIstrict, Off US 5, Barnet, 7/12/84, A, C, a, 84003440

Bradley Covered Bridge, N of Lyndon on VT 122 over Miller Run, Lyndon vicinity, 6/13/77, A, C, 77000096

Burklyn Hall, Bemis Hill Rd., East Burke, 5/07/73, C, 73000191

Burrington Covered Bridge, NE of Lyndon off VT 114 over East Branch of the Passumpsic River, Lyndon vicinity, 6/13/74, A, C, 74000203

Centre Covered Bridge, NE of Lyndon off U.S. 5, over Passumpsic River, Lyndon vicinity, 6/20/74, A, C, b, 74000204

Chamberlin Mill Covered Bridge, W of VT 114 over South Wheelock Branch of Passumpsic River, Lyndon, 7/30/74, A, C, 74000205

Christian Union Society Meetinghouse, Bayley-Hazen Military Rd., South Walden, 5/23/80, A, C, a, 80000385

Cobb School [Educational Resources of Vermont MPS], Jct. of Hardwick Town Hwy. 10 (Cobb School Rd.) and Sanborn Cemetery Rd., Hardwick, 9/30/93, A, C, 93001007

Darling Inn, Depot St., Lyndonville, 11/24/80, A, C, 80000386

Downtown Hardwick Village Historic District, Main, Church, Maple and Mill Sts., Hardwick, 9/30/82, A, C, 82001698

Elkins Tavern, Bailey-Hazen Rd., Peacham, 12/18/78, A, C, 78000228

Fairbanks, Franklin, House, 30 Western Ave., St. Johnsbury, 9/27/80, B, C, 80000329

Gilkerson, William and Agnes, Farm [Agricultural Resources of Vermont MPS], Town Hwy. 5 W of jct. with US 5, Barnet, 10/29/92, A, C, 92001504

Greenbanks Hollow Covered Bridge, S of Danville over Joes Brook, Danville vicinity, 6/13/74, A, C, 74000206

Grouselands, Town Hwy. 26, Danville, 12/22/83, C, 83004224

Hardwick Street Historic District, NE of Hardwick, Hardwick vicinity, 6/22/79, A, C, 79000321

Lee Farm, SR 25, Waterford, 5/26/83, C, 83003205

Lind Houses, Pleasant St., South Ryegate, 9/27/88, C, 88001589

McIndoes Academy, Main St., McIndoe Falls, 5/06/75, A, C, 75000137

Methodist-Episcopal Church, Off VT 16, Stannard, 1/05/78, A, C, a, 78000229

Old Schoolhouse Bridge, S. Wheelock Rd. over Cold Hill Brook, Lyndon, 3/31/71, A, C, 71000055

Railroad Street Historic District, Roughly bounded N and S by Railroad St. and Canadian Pacific RR tracks, St. Johnsbury, 6/25/74, A, C, 74000354

Riverside, Lily Pond R. S of Lyndonville, Lyndonville vicinity, 6/17/93, C, 93000532

St. Johnsbury Historic District, U.S. 5 and U.S. 2, St. Johnsbury, 4/17/80, A, C, 80000424

St. Johnsbury Main Street Historic District, Area along Main St. including intersecting streets, St. Johnsbury, 5/28/75, C, 75000238

Stannard Schoolhouse, Off VT 16, Stannard, 12/12/77, A, C, 77000097

Thurston, Phineas, House, Barnet Town Hwy. 12, Barnet, 10/30/89, C, 89001788

Whitehill House, N of Ryegate on Groton-Peacham Rd., Ryegate vicinity, 5/30/75, A, C, 75000138

Whittier House, US 2, Danville, 8/23/84, C, 84003456

Chittenden County

Allen, Ethan, Homestead, Off Van Patten Pkwy., Burlington, 7/24/86, A, B, 86002265

Bates, Martin M., Farmstead [Agricultural Resources of Vermont MPS], Huntington Rd. N of Huntington, Richmond, 11/21/91, A, C, 91001676

Battery Street Historic District, Roughly bounded by Lake Champlain, Main, Maple, and St. Pauls Sts. (both sides), Burlington, 11/02/77, A, C, D, 77000098

Battery Street Historic District (Boundary Increase), Roughly bounded by Brown's Court, King, Adams, and Union Sts., Burlington, 6/28/84, C, 84003459

Bentley, Wilson Alwyn "Snowflake", House, SE of Jerico on Nashville Rd., Jerico vicinity, 7/03/80, B, C, 80004501

Burlington Bay Horse Ferry, Address Restricted, Burlington vicinity, 12/15/93, A, C, D, 93001384

Burlington Montgomery Ward Building, 52–54 Church St., Burlington, 5/30/91, A, C, 91000673

Carnegie Building of the Fletcher Free Library, College St. and S. Winooski Ave., Burlington, 8/18/76, C, 76000138

Champlain School, 809 Pine St., Burlington, 12/10/82, C, 82001761

Charlotte Center Historic District, Church Hill and Hinesburg Rds., Charlotte, 7/19/84, C, 84003460

Chittenden County Courthouse, 180 Church St., Burlington, 4/11/73, A, C, 73000192

Chittenden, Giles, Farmstead, Governor Chittenden Rd., NE of Williston village center, Williston, 10/29/93, A, C, 93001160

Chittenden, Martin, House, W of Jericho on VT 117, Jericho vicinity, 1/09/78, A, B, C, 78000230

City Hall Park Historic District, Church, College, Main and St. Paul Sts., Burlington, 6/09/83, C, 83003206

Ethan Allen Engine company No. 4, Church St., Burlington, 4/16/71, C, 71000056

First Methodist Church of Burlington, S. Winooski Ave., Burlington, 10/05/78, A, C, a, 78000231

Follett House, 63 College St., Burlington, 10/30/72, C, 72000091

Galusha House, S of Jericho, Jericho vicinity, 10/10/78, C, 78000232

Grassemount, 411 Main St., Burlington, 4/11/73, C, 73000193

Head of Church Street Historic District, Pearl and Church Sts., Burlington, 7/15/74, C, a, 74000207

Holmes Creek Covered Bridge, NW of Charlotte over Holmes Creek, Charlotte vicinity, 9/06/74, A, C, 74000326

Huntington Lower Village Church, Huntington Lower Village Church, Huntington, 8/23/84, C, a, 84003463

Jericho Center Historic District, Brown's Trace, Bolger Hill and Varney Rds., Jericho, 5/26/83, C, 83003207

Jericho Village Historic District, VT 15, Plains Rd., Mill St. and Old Pump Rd., Jericho, 11/05/92, A, C, 92001533

Johnson, Dan, Farmstead [Agricultural Resources of Vermont MPS], Jct. of US 2 and Johnson Ln., Williston, 11/04/93, A, C, 93001178

Jonesville Academy, S of Jonesville at Cochran and Waterbury Rds., Jonesville vicinity, 11/02/82, C, 82001762

Kelsey, Martin L., House, 43 Elmwood Ave, Burlington, 2/24/83, C, 83003208

Lakeside Development, Lakeside, Central, Conger, Wright, and Harrison Aves., Burlington, 4/12/82, A, C, 82001699

Main Street-College Street Historic District, Roughly bounded by College, S. Williams and Main Sts., and S. Winooski Ave., Burlington, 10/13/88, C, 88001850

McNeil Homestead, Lake Champlain off VT F5, Charlotte, 6/17/82, A, C, 82001700

Murray—Isham Farm [Agricultural Resources of Vermont MPS], 741 Oak Hill Rd. (Town Hwy. 1), Williston, 12/07/92, A, 92001668

Old Ohavi Zedex Synagogue, Archibald and Hyde Sts., Burlington, 1/31/78, A, C, a, 78000233

Old Red Mill and Mill House, VT 15, Jericho, 7/31/72, A, C, 72000113

Old Red Mill and Mill House (Boundary Increase), VT 15, Jericho, 6/03/76, A, B, C, 76002245

Old Stone House, 73 E. Allen St., Winooski, 5/08/73, A, C, 73000271

Pearl Street Historic District, Roughly 184 to 415 Pearl St., Orchard Terr., and Winooski Ave., Burlington, 11/01/84, C, 84000416

Chittenden County—Continued

Porter Screen Company, 110 E. Spring St., Winooski, 11/15/79, A, C, 79000219

Quinlan's Covered Bridge, S of East Charlotte over Lewis Creek, East Charlotte vicinity, 9/10/74, A, C, 74000208

Richmond Underwear Company Building, Millet St., Richmond, 5/07/92, C, 92000465

Robinson, Daniel Webster, House, 384 and 388 Main St., Burlington, 4/22/82, A, C, 82001701

Round Church, Bridge St. and Cochran Rd., Richmond, 6/20/74, A, C, a, 74000355

Sequin Covered Bridge, SE of East Charlotte over Lewis Creek, East Charlotte vicinity, 9/06/74, A, C, 74000209

Shelburne Farms, Off U.S. 7, Shelburne vicinity, 8/11/80, B, C, b, 80000330

Shelburne Village Historic District, Area N and S of jct. of US 7, Harbor Rd. and Falls Rd., including area S and E of La Platte R. and US 7, Shelburne, 7/27/90, C, 90001055

South Union Street Historic District, S. Union St. between Howard and Main, Burlington, 10/31/88, C, 88001946

South Willard Street Historic District, S. Willard St., Burlington, 11/03/88, C, 88002226

TICONDEROGA, Shelburne Museum, Shelburne, 10/15/66, A, NHL, 66000797

Tavern on Mutton Hill, Church Hill Rd., Charlotte, 12/10/82, C, 82001763

Tracy, Lee, House, US 7, Shelburne, 12/22/83, C, 83004226

U.S. Post Office and Customhouse, SE corner of Main and Church Sts., Burlington, 11/21/72, C, 72000114

University Green Historic District, University of Vermont campus, Burlington, 4/14/75, A, C, 75000139

Wells, Edward, House, 61 Summit St., Burlington, 10/03/79, B, C, 79000220

Wells-Jackson Carriage House Complex, 192-194 Jackson Court and 370 Maple St., Burlington, 12/10/82, A, C, 82001764

Wells-Richardson District, Main, Pine, College, and St. Paul Sts., Burlington, 3/05/79, A, C, 79000221

West Milton Bridge [Metal Truss, Masonry, and Concrete Bridges in Vermont MPS], Town Hwy. 40 over the Lamoille R., Milton, 9/08/92, A, C, 92001173

Whitcomb, M. S., Farm [Agricultural Resources of Vermont MPS], US 2, Richmond, 9/30/93, A, C, 93001010

Williston Congregational Church, Center of Williston Village on VT 2, Williston, 5/17/73, A, C, 73000194

Williston Village Historic District, U.S. 2, Williston, 12/19/79, C, 79000222

Williston Village Historic District (Boundary Increase), US 2 over Allen Brook, Williston, 9/04/92, C, 92001151

Winooski Archeological Site, Address Restricted, Winooski vicinity, 1/05/78, A, D, 78000234

Winooski Block, E. Allen and Main Sts., Winooski, 11/20/74, A, C, 74000210

Winooski Falls Mill District, N. bank of Winooski River to Center and Canal Sts., S bank to Bartlet St., Winooski, 2/09/79, A, C, 79000223

Winooski Falls Mill Historic District (Boundary Increase), 485–497 Colchester Ave., 5–21 Mill St., 8–32 Barrett St., Burlington, 9/30/93, A, C, 93001009

Winooski River Bridge [Metal Truss, Masonry, and Concrete Bridges in Vermont MPS], SR 2 over the Winooski R., Richmond, 5/30/90, A, C, 90000775

Winterbotham Estate, 163 S. Willard St., Burlington, 5/12/75, C, 75000140

Essex County

Bloomfield—Nulhegan River Route 102 Bridge [Metal Truss, Masonry, and Concrete Bridges in Vermont MPS], VT 102 over the Nulhegan R., Bloomfield, 11/14/91, A, C, 91001605

Columbia Covered Bridge, Across Connecticut River between US 3 and VT 102, Lemington, 12/12/76, A, C, 76000123

Guildhall Village Historic District, VT 102, Guildhall, 9/27/80, A, C, 80000331

Island Pond Historic District, Jct. of VT 105 and VT 114, Island Pond, 1/31/79, A, C, 79000275

Jacobs Stand, W. Park St., Canaan, 6/03/80, A, B, C, 80000332

Mount Orne Covered Bridge, SW of Lancaster off NH 135, Lunenburg, vicinity, 12/12/76, A, C, 76000124

Franklin County

Ballard Farm [Agricultural Resources of Vermont MPS], Jct. of Ballard Rd. and Town Hwy. 6, Georgia, 11/04/93, A, C, 93001241

Boright, Sheldon, House, 122 River St., Richford, 6/02/89, C, 89000433

Central Vermont Railroad Headquarters, Bounded roughly by Federal, Catherine, Allen, Lower Welden, Houghton, and Pine Sts., St. Albans, 1/21/74, A, C, 74000211

Comstock Covered Bridge, Off VT 118 over Trout River, Montgomery, 11/19/74, A, C, 74000212

Douglas & Jarvis Patent Parabolic Truss Iron Bridge, Rte. 2 over Missisquoi River, Highgate Falls vicinity, 3/21/74, A, C, 74000213

Downtown Richford Historic District, Main and River Sts., Richford, 8/22/80, A, C, 80000333

East Fairfield Covered Bridge, Off VT 108, over Black Creek, East Fairfield, 11/19/74, A, C, 74000214

Enosburg Opera House, 31 Depot St., Enosburg Falls, 9/20/78, A, C, 78000235

Evarts-McWilliams House, Georgia Shore Rd., Georgia, 10/21/82, C, 82001765

Fairfax Covered Bridge, Off VT 104 over Mill Brook, Fairfax, 11/05/74, A, C, 74000215

Fletcher Union Church, SR 1, Fletcher, 5/17/82, A, C, 82001702

Fuller Covered Bridge, Town Rd. over Black Falls Brook at Montgomery Village, Montgomery, 12/23/74, A, C, 74000216

Hathaway's Tavern, 255 N. Main St., St. Albans, 7/14/83, C, 83003209

Hectorville Covered Bridge, 1.8 mi. S of Montgomery Center over South Branch of Trout River, Montgomery Center vicinity, 11/20/74, A, C, 74000217

Hopkins Covered Bridge, Town Rd. over Trout River, Enosburg, 11/20/74, A, C, 74000218

Houghton House, 86 S. Main St., St. Albans, 9/04/72, C, 72000092

Hutchins Covered Bridge, S of Montgomery Center over South Branch of Trout River, Montgomery Center vicinity, 12/30/74, A, C, 74000219

Kendall, Dr. B. J., Company, 228 N. Main St., Enosburg, 8/02/93, A, C, 93000721

L'Ecole Saintes-Anges, 247 Lake St., St. Albans, 11/28/80, A, C, a, 80000334

Longley Covered Bridge, NW of Montgomery over Trout River, Montgomery vicinity, 12/30/74, A, C, 74000220

Missisquoi River Bridge [Metal Truss, Masonry, and Concrete Bridges in Vermont MPS], VT 105-A over the Missisquoi R., Richford, 10/11/90, A, C, 90001494

Montgomery House, VT 118, Montgomery, 8/20/92, A, C, 92000997

Richwood Estate, N of St. Albans off US 7, St. Albans vicinity, 11/03/88, C, 88002175

St. Albans Historic District, U.S. 7 and VT 36, St. Albans, 5/01/80, A, C, a, 80000335

St. Bartholomew's Episcopal Church, VT 118, Montgomery, 9/01/88, C, a, e, f, 88001467

St. John's Episcopal Churdh, Highgate Falls Village Green, Highgate Falls, 9/03/76, C, a, 76000139

Swanton Covered Railroad Bridge, S of Swanton over Missisquoi River, Swanton vicinity, 6/18/73, A, C, 73000195

Warner Home, 133 High St., St. Albans, 10/20/88, C, 88002034

West Berkshire School [Educational Resources of Vermont MPS], Jct. of Town Hwy. 26 and Town Hwy. 3, Berkshire, 11/04/93, A, C, 93001174

West Hill Covered Bridge, 3.2 mi. S of Montgomery over West Hill Brook, Montgomery vicinity, 12/31/74, A, C, 74000221

Grand Isle County

Gordon—Center House, West Shore Rd., Grand Isle, 4/17/86, A, C, 86000808

Hyde Log Cabin, U.S. 2, Grand Isle, 3/11/71, C, b, 71000057

South Hero Inn, South St. and U.S. 2, South Hero, 4/16/75, C, 75000141

Lamoille County

Cambridge Meetinghouse, Church St., Jefferson-ville, 2/06/81, A, C, 81000077

Fisher Covered Railroad Bridge, SE of Wolcott, over Lamoille River, Wolcott vicinity, 10/01/74, A, C, 74000222

Gates Farm Covered Bridge, Off VT 15, over Seymour River, Cambridge, 11/19/74, A, C, b, 74000223

Gold Brook Covered Bridge, S of Stowe, Stowe vicinity, 10/01/74, A, C, 74000224

Grist Mill Covered Bridge, E of Cambridge over Brewster River, Cambridge, 6/13/74, A, C, 74000225

Jaynes Covered Bridge, NE of Waterville, over North Branch of Lamoille River, Waterville vicinity, 10/01/74, A, C, 74000226

Jeffersonville Bridge [Metal Truss, Masonry, and Concrete Bridges in Vermont MPS], VT 108 over the Lamoille R., Cambridge, 11/14/91, A, C, 91001606

Jeffersonville Historic District, Church, Main, Maple, and School Sts., Carlton Ave., VT 108, and Brewster Ave., Cambridge, 4/10/87, A, C, g, 86002929

Johnson Railroad Depot, Railroad St., Johnson, 11/28/80, A, C, 80000336

Lamoille River Route 15-A Bridge [Metal Truss, Masonry, and Concrete Bridges in Vermont MPS], VT 15-A over the Lamoille R., Morristown, 11/14/91, A, C, 91001607

Mill Covered Bridge, Off VT 109 over North Branch of Lamoille River, Belvidere, 11/19/74, A, C, 74000227

Montgomery Covered Bridge, NE of Waterville over North Branch of Lamoille River, Waterville vicinity, 10/18/74, A, C, 74000228

Morgan Covered Bridge, Off VT 109, over North Branch of Lamoille River, Belvidere, 11/19/74, A, C, 74000229

Morrisville Historic District, Portland, Main, Railroad and Foundry Sts., Morrisville, 1/19/83, C, 83003210

Nye Block, Main and Railroad Sts., Johnson, 8/19/77, C, 77000144

Poland Covered Bridge, Off VT 15, over Lamoille River, Cambridge Junction, 10/09/74, A, C, 74000230

Power House Covered Bridge, Off VT 100, over Gihon River, Johnson, 10/09/74, A, C, 74000231

Red Covered Bridge, SW of Morristown, over Sterling Brook, Morristown vicinity, 10/16/74, A, C, 74000232

Scribner Covered Bridge, E of Johnson over Gihon River, Johnson vicinity, 10/01/74, A, C, 74000233

Stowe Village Historic District, VT 100 and VT 108, Stowe, 11/15/78, C, 78000236

Village Covered Bridge, Over North Branch of Lamoille River, Waterville, 12/16/74, A, C, 74000234

Waterman Covered Bridge, S of Johnson over Waterman Brook, Johnson vicinity, 6/13/74, A, C, 74000235

Orange County

Bayley Historic District, VT 5 and Oxbow St., Newbury, 7/28/83, C, 83003211

Bedell Covered Bridge, Crosses Connecticut River between Haverhill and Newbury, Newbury, 5/28/75, A, C, 75002171

Bradford Village Historic District, Residential area along Main, Depot, Pleasant, High, and Mill Sts., Wrights Ave., Goshen Rd., and U.S. 5, Bradford, 5/28/75, A, C, 75000142

Braley Covered Bridge, E of Randolph off VT 14, over Second Branch of White River, Randolph vicinity, 6/13/74, A, C, 74000236

Brookfield Village Historic District, Sunset Lake area, Brookfield, 3/28/74, A, C, 74000237

Chandler Music Hall and Bethany Parish House, 71 Main St., Randolph, 7/16/73, A, C, a, 73000196

Chase, Elwin, House, Off VT 25, East Topsham, 11/02/77, C, 77000099

Chelsea Village Historic District, N. and S. Main, Jail, School, Court and Church Sts., Maple and Highland Aves., Chelsea, 9/29/83, C, 83003212

Cilley Covered Bridge, SW of Tunbridge, over First Branch of White River, Tunbridge vicinity, 9/10/74, A, C, 74000238

Congregational Church of Chelsea, Chelsea Green, Chelsea, 9/03/76, C, a, 76000140

Depot Square Historic District, Both sides of Main, Pleasant and Salisbury Sts., and both sides of Central Vermont Rwy. tracks, Randolph, 5/29/75, A, C, 75000143

Flint Covered Bridge, NE of Tunbridge off VT 110, over First Branch of White River, Tunbridge vicinity, 9/10/74, A, C, 74000239

Gifford Covered Bridge, S of Randolph off VT 14 over Second Branch of White River, East Randolph vicinity, 7/30/74, A, C, 74000240

Goshen Church, N of Bradford on Goshen Rd., Bradford vicinity, 9/03/76, C, a, 76000141

Hayward and Kibby Mill, Spring Rd. at First Branch, White R., Tunbridge, 3/12/92, A, C, 92000094

Howe Covered Bridge, S of Tunbridge off VT 110, over First Branch of White River, Tunbridge vicinity, 9/10/74, A, C, 74000241

Kimball Public Library, 67 Main St., Randolph, 3/14/85, C, 85000568

Kingsbury Covered Bridge, S of East Randolph off VT 14 over Second Branch of White River, East Randolph vicinity, 7/30/74, A, C, 74000242

Larkin Covered Bridge, NE of North Tunbridge off VT 110 over First Branch of White River, North Tunbridge vicinity, 7/30/74, A, C, 74000327

Mari-Castle, 41 S. Main St., Randolph, 5/24/90, B, C, 90000796

May, Asa, House, Town Hwy. 4 (Blood Brook Rd.) SE of West Fairlee Center, West Fairlee Township, West Fairlee vicinity, 4/07/93, C, 93000240

Mill Covered Bridge, W of VT 110, over First Branch of White River, Tunbridge, 7/30/74, A, C, 74000243

Morrill, Justin Smith, Homestead, S of the Common, Strafford, 10/15/66, B, NHL, 66000795

Moxley Covered Bridge, S of Chelsea over First Branch of White River, Chelsea vicinity, 9/10/74, A, C, 74000244

Newbury Town House, Scotch Hollow Rd., Newbury, 7/28/83, C, 83003213

Newbury Village Historic District, Main, Pulaski, Cross, and Pine Sts., Chapel Rd. and Romance Lane, Newbury, 8/04/83, C, 83003214

Newton, Marvin, House, Ridge Rd., Brookfield Center, 6/11/80, C, 80000337

Oxbow Historic District, VT 5, Newbury, 7/28/83, C, 83003215

Peabody Library, VT 113, Thetford vicinity, 9/27/84, C, 84003466

Post Mills Church, VT 244 E of jct. with VT 113, Thetford, 10/29/92, C, a, 92001489

Randolph Center Historic District, West and Main Sts., Randolph, 11/21/74, A, C, 74000245

South Newbury Village Historic District, US 5 and Doe Hill Rd., South Newbury, 7/28/83, C, 83003216

Strafford Village Historic District, Roughly both sides of Morrill Hwy. and Sharon Brook Rd., Strafford, 6/20/74, C, 74000246

Stratton's Inn, E of Brookfield on East St., Brookfield vicinity, 7/29/82, C, 82001703

Thetford Center Covered Bridge, Over Ompompanoosuc River, Thetford, 9/17/74, A, C, 74000247

Thetford Hill Historic District, Roughly Rt. 113 and Academy Rd., Thetford, 10/27/88, C, 88002134

Union Village Covered Bridge, Over Ompompanoosuc River, Union Village, 9/17/74, A, C, 74000248

Waits River Schoolhouse, VT 25 N of Waits River, Waits River vicinity, 9/27/88, A, C, 88002656

Well River Graded School, Main St., Wells River, 9/03/76, C, 76000142

Wells River Village Historic District, Main, Center, Grove, Cross, and Water Sts., Newbury, 7/28/83, C, 83003217

West Newbury Village Historic District, Snake and Tucker Mtn. Rds., West Newbury, 9/15/83, C, 83003218

Whitcomb, Harlie, Farm, NE of Barre off U.S. 302, Barre vicinity, 9/11/79, A, C, 79000224

Wildwood Hall, SW of Newbury off U.S. 5, Newbury vicinity, 10/02/78, C, 78000237

Orleans County

Brownington Village Historic District, Hinman and Brownington Centers Rd., Brownington, 5/09/73, A, B, C, a, 73000197

Fox Hall, VT 56, Westmore, 9/27/84, C, 84003468

Goodrich Memorial Library, Main and Field St., Newport, 11/23/83, C, 83004228

Greensboro Depot, W side of Main St. at R.R. track jct., Greensboro Bend, 4/21/75, A, C, 75000144

Haskell Free Library and Opera House, Caswell Ave., Derby Line, 9/08/76, A, C, 76000143

Orleans County—Continued

Hayden, William, House, S of Albany on VT 14, Albany vicinity, 1/31/78, C, 78000238

Holland Congregational Church, W. Holland Rd., Holland, 12/04/86, C, a, 86003411

Orleans County Courthouse and Jail Complex, Main St., Newport, 11/23/84, C, 84000336

Orne Covered Bridge, SW of Coventry off VT 14, over Black River, Coventry vicinity, 11/20/74, A, C, 74000328

River Road Covered Bridge, S of North Troy off VT 101, over Missisquni River, North Troy vicinity, 11/19/74, A, C, 74000249

Sweeney, J. S., Store, Barn, Livery and Hall, Jct. of VT 105 and Town Hwy. 3 (Main St.), Charleston, 8/18/92, A, C, 92000993

U.S. Courthouse, Post Office and Customs House, Main St. at 2nd St., Newport, 12/12/76, C, 76000144

Rutland County

Allen, Nathan, House, VT 30, Pawlet vicinity, 10/27/88, C, 88002069

Baxter, H. H., Memorial Library, 96 Grove St., Rutland, 8/24/78, A, B, C, a, f, 78000239

Benson Village, Stage and Benson Landing Sts., Benson, 11/17/78, A, C, 78000240

Brandon Village Historic District, U.S. 7, Brandon, 12/22/76, A, C, 76000145

Brown Covered Bridge, 2.9 mi. E of North Clarendon across the Cold River, North Clarendon vicinity, 1/21/74, A, C, 74000250

Castleton Medical College Building, South St., Castleton, 3/11/71, A, C, b, 71000058

Castleton Village Historic District, Irregular pattern along Main and South Sts., Castleton, 4/26/79, C, 79000225

Clarendon Congregational Church, Middle Rd., Clarendon, 7/12/84, C, a, 84003471

Clarendon House, Off VT 133, Clarendon Springs, 5/17/76, A, C, 76000146

Clementwood, Clement Rd., Rutland, 9/27/80, A, C, 80000338

Colburn Bridge [Metal Truss, Masonry, and Concrete Bridges in Vermont MPS], US 7 over Sugar Hollow Brook, Pittsford, 10/11/90, A, C, 90001493

Cold River Bridge [Metal Truss, Masonry, and Concrete Bridges in Vermont MPS], VT 7B over the Cold R., Clarendon, 11/14/91, A, C, 91001608

Cooley Covered Bridge, 1.2 mi. S of Pittsford across Furnace Brook, Pittsford vicinity, 1/24/74, A, C, 74000251

Crowley Cheese Factory, SW of Healdville on Healdville Rd., Healdville vicinity, 10/11/79, A, 79000226

Danby Village Historic District, Main St., Mt. Tabor Ave., Depot St., and Borough Hill Rd., Danby, 2/10/83, C, 83003219

Dean Covered Bridge, S of Brandon, over Otter Creek, Brandon vicinity, 9/10/74, A, C, 74000252

Depot Covered Bridge, 0.8 mi. W of Pittsford across Otter Creek, Pittsford vicinity, 1/21/74, A, C, 74000253

East Poultney Historic District, Village Green and environs, East Poultney, 1/31/78, C, 78000241

Fair Haven Green Historic District, Park Pl., Adams and Main Sts., Fair Haven, 11/24/80, A, C, 80000339

Forestdale Iron Furnace, VT 73 and Furnace Rd., Brandon, 6/13/74, D, 74000254

Fox—Cook Farm [Rural Otter Creek Valley MRA], Off US 7 on Cook Rd., Wallingford, 11/26/86, A, C, 86003228

Gorham Covered Bridge, N of Proctor across Otter Creek off VT 3, Proctor vicinity, 2/12/74, A, C, 74000255

Hager Farm [Rural Otter Creek Valley MRA], US 7, Wallingford, 11/26/86, A, C, 86003224

Hall, Gen. Robinson, House [Rural Otter Creek Valley MRA], US 7, Wallingford, 11/26/86, A, C, 86003221

Hammond Covered Bridge, NW of Pittsford across Otter Creek, Pittsford vicinity, 1/21/74, A, C, 74000256

Hubbardton Battlefield, Jct. of Castleton-Hubbardton Rd. and Old Military Rd. to Independence, Hubbardton, 3/11/71, A, 71000059

Hulett Farm [Rural Otter Creek Valley MRA], US 7, Wallingford, 11/26/86, A, C, 86003220

Hyde's Hotel, S. of Sudbury on VT 30, Sudbury vicinity, 4/11/80, A, C, 80000340

Hydeville School, W of Castleton on VT 4A, Castleton vicinity, 11/21/78, A, C, 78000242

Kingsley Covered Bridge, SW of East Clarendon across the Mill River, East Clarendon vicinity, 2/12/74, A, C, 74000257

Longfellow School, 6 Church St., Rutland, 12/12/76, A, C, 76000147

Marble Bridge [Metal Truss, Masonry, and Concrete Bridges in Vermont MPS], Main St. over Otter Cr., Proctor, 11/14/91, A, C, 91001609

Marble Street Historic District, 87–132 Marble St. and 10 Smith Ave., West Rutland, 3/01/90, A, C, 90000338

Middletown Springs Historic District, East, North, South, and West Sts., Montvert Ave., and Schoolhouse Rd., Middletown Springs, 10/17/85, A, B, C, 85003239

Mission of the Church of Our Savior, Mission Farm Rd., Sherburne, 10/29/92, C, a, 92001479

Mountain View Stock Farm, VT 22A, N of Lake Rd., Benson, 10/30/89, A, C, 89001817

Palmer, Thomas H., House, SE of Pittsford on U.S. 7, Pittsford vicinity, 12/29/78, A, B, C, 78000243

Perkins, Arthur, House, 242 S. Main St., Rutland, 9/27/88, C, 88001579

Pittsford Green Historic District, Main St., Pittsford, 5/13/82, C, 82001704

Poultney Central School, Main St., Poultney, 3/25/77, C, 77000100

Poultney Main Street Historic District, Roughly Main St., E. Main St., Depot St., Knapp Ave., Beaman St., Grove St., Maple Ave., and College Ave., Poultney, 6/02/88, C, 88000649

Proctor-Clement House, Field Ave., Rutland, 6/17/82, B, C, 82001705

Rural Otter Creek Valley Historic District [Rural Otter Creek Valley MRA], Roughly US 7 W of Otter Creek, Wallingford, 3/31/87, A, C, 86003212

Rutland Courthouse Historic District, U.S. 7, Rutland, 9/08/76, A, C, 76000148

Rutland Downtown Historic District, Roughly bounded by Strong Ave., State, Wales, Washington, Pine and Cottage Sts., Rutland, 8/22/80, A, C, 80000387

Sanderson Covered Bridge, W of Brandon over Otter Creek, Brandon vicinity, 6/13/74, A, C, 74000258

Smith, Simeon, House, W. Haven Rd., West Haven, 3/03/83, C, 83003220

Smith, Simeon, Mansion, Smith Rd. W of jct. with VT 22A, West Haven, 11/21/91, C, 91001675

St. Peter's Church and Mount St. Joseph Convent Complex, Convent Ave., Meadow and River Sts., Rutland, 10/03/80, A, C, a, 80000388

Sudbury Congregational Church, VT 30, Sudbury, 10/28/77, C, 77000101

Sudbury School No. 3, jct. of VT 30 and VT 73, Sudbury, 11/02/78, A, C, 78000244

Tinmouth Historic District, VT 140 and SR 2, Tinmouth, 6/25/80, A, C, 80000425

Waldo, Homer, Farm [Rural Otter Creek Valley MRA], Waldo Ln., Wallingford, 11/26/86, A, C, 86003215

Wallingford Main Street Historic District, Main and School Sts., Wallingford, 11/01/84, C, a, d, 84000424

Wells Village School [Educational Resources of Vermont MPS], N side of Main St. (VT Rt. 30), Wells, 10/07/93, A, C, 93001004

West Rutland Town Hall, Main and Marble Sts., West Rutland, 7/28/83, C, 83003221

Washington County

Allenwood Farm, US 2, Plainfield, 12/22/83, A, C, 83004229

Athenwood and Thomas W. Wood Studio, 41 and 39 Northfield St., Montpelier, 6/13/74, C, 74000259

Barre City Hall and Opera House, 12 N. Main St., Barre, 1/18/73, A, C, 73000198

Barre Downtown Historic District, VT 302, Barre, 9/04/79, A, C, 79000227

Central Vermont Railway Depot, W end of Depot Sq., Northfield, 4/01/75, A, C, 75000145

Coburn Covered Bridge, NE of East Montpelier between VT 14 and U.S. 2, over Winooski River, East Montpelier vicinity, 10/09/74, A, C, 74000260

Colby Mansion, N of Waterbury on VT 100, Waterbury vicinity, 9/10/79, C, 79000228

College Hall, Vermont College campus, Ridge St., Montpelier, 4/23/75, C, 75000146

Currier Park Historic District, Properties bordering Currier Park on Park, North, East and Academy Sts. and adjacent properties on Averill and Cliff Sts, Barre City, 9/27/90, C, 90001454

Washington County—Continued

Davis, Parley, House, Address Restricted, East Montpelier, 9/18/89, A, B, C, 89000242

East Village Meetinghouse, U.S. 2 and U.S. 14, East Montpelier, 6/30/80, A, C, a, 80000341

Gale-Bancroft House, Brook Rd., Plainfield, 11/15/84, C, 84000741

Great Eddy Covered Bridge, E of VT 100 over Mad River, Waitsfield, 9/06/74, A, C, 74000261

Green Mountain Seminary, off VT 100, Waterbury Center, 1/30/78, A, C, 78000245

Italian Baptist Church, 10 N. Brook St., Barre, 4/23/75, A, C, a, 75000147

Joslin Farm, E. Warren Rd., 1.5 mi. E of jct. with Bridge St., Waitsfield, 10/27/88, A, C, 88002058

Kent's Corner Historic District, Kent's Corner, Calais, 5/08/73, A, C, 73000199

Lower Cox Brook Covered Bridge, Off VT 12, Northfield Falls, 10/15/74, A, C, 74000262

Martin Covered Bridge, NE of Plainfield, over Winooski River, Plainsfield vicinity, 10/09/74, A, C, 74000358

Mayo Building, Main & East Sts., Northfield, 7/14/83, C, 83003222

Middlesex—Winooski River Bridge [Metal Truss, Masonry, and Concrete Bridges in Vermont MPS], US 2 over the Winooski R., Middlesex, 11/14/91, A, C, 91001610

Mill Village Historic District, Roughly bounded by VT 100, I-89, and Stowe St., Waterbury, 6/12/79, A, 79000229

Montpelier Historic District, U.S. 2 and VT 12, Montpelier, 11/03/78, A, C, 78000246

Montpelier Historic District (Boundary Increase), 70–101 E. State St. and 1 West St., Montpelier, 4/17/89, C, 89000248

Nichols House, SW of East Barre off VT 110, East Barre vicinity, 1/31/78, C, 78000247

Northfield Falls Covered Bridge, N of Northfield off VT 12, over Dog River, Northfield vicinity, 8/13/74, A, C, 74000263

Old Red Mill, VT 12, South Northfield, 10/20/77, A, 77000102

Old West Church, 0.8 mi. S of Kent's Corner, Calais, 5/08/73, A, C, a, 73000200

Pine Brook Covered Bridge, NE of Waitsfiel over Pine Brook, Waitsfield vicinity, 6/13/74, A, C, 74000264

Plainfield Village Historic District, High, School, Main and Water Sts., and Brook Rd., Plainfield, 2/03/83, C, 83003223

Slaughterhouse Covered Bridge, N of Northfield off VT 12 over Dog River, Northfield, 6/13/74, A, C, 74000265

Stony Brook Covered Bridge, SW of Northfield off VT 12A, over Stony Brook, Northfield vicinity, 11/20/74, A, C, 74000266

Twing, Joshua, Gristmill, 450 N. Main St., Barre, 12/29/78, A, C, 78000248

Union Meetinghouse, Center Rd., East Montpelier, 6/30/80, A, C, a, 80000342

Upper Cox Brook Covered Bridge, N of Northfield off VT 12 over Cox Brook, Northfield vicinity, 10/01/74, A, C, 74000267

Vermont Statehouse, State St., Montpelier, 12/30/70, A, C, NHL, 70000739

Waitsfield Village Historic District, VT 100 and Bridge St., Waitsfield vicinity, 8/11/83, C, 83003224

Warren Covered Bridge, Off VT 100, over Mad River, Warren, 8/07/74, A, C, 74000269

Warren Village Historic District [Mad River Valley MPS], Along Town Hwys. 1, 4, 16 and 17, Warren, 11/20/92, A, C, 92001532

Waterbury Center Methodist Church, VT 100, Waterbury Center, 1/09/78, A, C, a, 78000251

Waterbury Village Historic District, U.S. 2, Waterbury, 8/24/78, A, B, C, 78000249

Wheelock Law Office, 135 N. Main St., Barre City, 6/18/75, C, 75000148

Woodbury Graded School [Educational Resources of Vermont MPS], Jct. of Town Hwy. 22 and VT 14, Woodbury, 9/30/93, A, C, 93001008

Windham County

Adams Gristmill Warehouse [Bellows Falls Island MRA], Bridge St., Rockingham, 1/22/90, C, 88002162

Bartonsville Covered Bridge, Across Williams River at S end of Bartonsville, Bartonsville, 7/02/73, A, C, 73000201

Bellows Falls Co-operative Creamery Complex [Bellows Falls Island MRA], Island St., Rockingham, 1/22/90, A, C, 88002164

Bellows Falls Downtown Historic District, Depot, Canal, Rockingham, Bridge, Mill and Westminster Sts., Bellows Falls, 8/16/82, A, C, 82001706

Bellows Falls Petroglyph Site (VT-WD-8) [Bellows Falls Island MRA], Address Restricted, Bellows Falls, 1/22/90, D, 88002166

Bellows Falls Times Building [Bellows Falls Island MRA], Bridge and Island Sts., Rockingham, 1/22/90, C, 88002160

Brattleboro Downtown Historic District, Main St. from Vernon to Walnut, Flat, Elliot, High, and Grove Sts., Brattleboro, 2/17/83, A, C, 83003225

Brattleboro Retreat, Linden St. and Upper Dummerston Rd., Brattleboro, 4/12/84, A, C, 84003478

Brooks House, 4 High St. and 128 Main St., Brattleboro, 2/01/80, B, C, 80000343

Canal Street Schoolhouse, Canal St., Brattleboro, 8/19/77, C, 77000103

Canal Street—Clark Street Neighborhood Historic District, Roughly bounded by Canal, S. Main, Lawrence and Clark Sts., Brattleboro, 7/08/93, C, 93000593

Christ Church, Melendy Rd. and US 5, Guilford, 5/13/82, A, C, a, 82001707

Creamery Covered Bridge, W of Brattleboro off VT 9, Brattleboro vicinity, 8/28/73, A, C, 73000202

District No. 1 Schoolhouse, Somerset Rd., Somerset, 4/20/92, C, 92000337

Dover Town Hall, School House Rd., Dover, 9/01/88, C, a, 88001466

East Putney Brook Stone Arch Bridge, Spans East Putney Brook off River Rd., East Putney, 12/12/76, A, C, 76000149

Estey Organ Company Factory, Birge St., Brattleboro, 4/17/80, A, C, 80000344

Follett Stone Arch Bridge Historic District, W of Townshend off VT 30, Townshend vicinity, 12/12/76, A, C, 76000150

Gratton Congregational Church and Chapel, Main St., Grafton, 12/10/79, A, C, a, 79000230

Green River Covered Bridge, Across the Green River, Green River, 8/28/73, A, C, 73000203

Guilford Center Meetinghouse, Guilford Center Rd., Guilford, 5/13/82, C, a, 82001708

Hall Covered Bridge, W of Bellows Falls Across Saxtons River, off VT 121, Bellows Falls vicinity, 8/28/73, A, C, 73000204

Harris, William, House, 140 Western Ave., Brattleboro, 12/18/78, A, C, 78000250

Holbrook, Deacon John, House, Corner Linden & Chapin Streets NE, Brattleboro, 3/19/82, C, 82001709

Howard Hardware Storehouse [Bellows Falls Island MRA], Bridge St., Rockingham, 1/22/90, C, 88002163

Kidder Covered Bridge, SE of Grafton, Grafton vicinity, 7/02/73, A, C, 73000205

Londonderry Town House, Middletown Rd., South Londonderry vicinity, 7/14/83, C, 83003227

Medburyville Bridge [Metal Truss, Masonry, and Concrete Bridges in Vermont MPS], Town Hwy. 31 over the Deerfield R., Wilmington, 11/08/90, A, C, 90001746

Milldean and Alexander—Davis House, Main St. near town center, Grafton, 5/24/90, C, 90000815

Miss Bellows Falls Diner, 90 Rockingham St., Bellows Falls, 2/15/83, C, 83003226

Moore and Thompson Paper Mill Complex [Bellows Falls Island MRA (AD)], Bridge St., Bellows Falls, 3/16/84, A, C, 84003475

Naulakha, Off U.S. 5, Dummerston, 4/11/79, B, C, NHL, 79000231

Newfane Village Historic District, Main, West, Church, Court, Depot, and Cross Sts., Newfane, 7/21/83, C, 83003228

Oak Hill Cemetery Chapel, Off Pleasant St., Bellows Falls, 11/14/91, C, 91001613

Old Brick Church, Off VT 35, Athens, 11/30/79, A, C, a, 79000340

Parker Hill Rural Historic District, Parker Hill and Lower Parker Hill Rds., Rockingham, 5/20/93, A, C, 93000431

Pond Road Chapel, Pond Rd., Town Hwy. #2, Vernon, 5/09/85, C, a, 85000959

Putney Village Historic District, Westminster W Rd., US 5, Christian Sq., Old US 5, and Depot Rd., Putney, 2/20/86, B, C, a, 86000324

Robertson Paper Company Complex [Bellows Falls Island MRA], Island St., Rockingham, 1/22/90, A, C, 88002165

Rockingham Meetinghouse, Off VT 103, Rockingham, 9/10/79, A, C, a, d, 79000232

Round Schoolhouse, S of Brookline, Brookline vicinity, 11/23/77, A, C, 77000104

Windham County—Continued

Sacketts Brook Stone Arch Bridge, Off U.S. 5 on Mill Rd., Putney, 12/12/76, A, C, 76000151

Saxtons River Village Historic District, Roughly bounded by Burk Hill and Belleview Rds., Oak St., Saxtons River, and Westminster West Rd., Saxtons River, 9/29/88, A, C, 88001851

Scott Covered Bridge, W of Townshend off VT 30, Townshend vicinity, 8/28/73, A, C, 73000206

Simpsonville Stone Arch Bridge, N of Townshend on VT 35, Townshend vicinity, 4/11/77, A, C, 77000105

South Londonderry Village Historic District, Church, Main, River, School, and Farnum Sts., and Melendy Hill Rd., South Londonderry, 7/24/86, C, 86001943

South Newfane Bridge [Metal Truss, Masonry, and Concrete Bridges in Vermont MPS], Town Hwy. 26 (Parish Rd.) over the Rock R., Newfane, 9/08/92, A, C, 92001174

South Windham Village Historic District, TH 1 and TH 26, Windham, 10/27/88, C, 88002061

Stratton Mountain Lookout Tower, Summit of Stratton Mountain, Green Mountain NF, Stratton, 6/17/92, A, C, 92000687

Union Station, Jct. of Bridge St. and Boston and Maine RR. tracks, Brattleboro, 6/07/74, A, C, 74000268

West Dover Village Historic District, Rt. 100, Valley View, Cross Town, Parsonage, Dorr Fitch, and Bogle Rds., Dover, 10/24/85, C, 85003381

West Dummerston Covered Bridge, Dummerston Center Rd. and VT 30, over West River, Dummerston, 5/08/73, A, C, 73000207

West Townshend Stone Arch Bridge, Spans Tannery Brook, West Townshend, 4/18/77, A, C, 77000106

West Townshend Village Historic District, Roughly Main St. from Old Rt. 30 to VT 30 and Town Rds. 7, 23, 47, 49, and 50, West Townshend, 9/11/86, C, 86001502

Westminster Village Historic District, Main and School Sts., and Grout Ave., Westminster, 7/14/88, A, C, a, b, d, 88001058

Wheelock House, CR 30, Townshend vicinity, 5/08/86, C, 86001033

Williams River Route 5 Bridge [Metal Truss, Masonry, and Concrete Bridges in Vermont MPS], US 5 over the Williams R., Rockingham, 11/14/91, A, C, 91001603

Williamsville Covered Bridge, SW of Newfane at Williamsville, Newfane vicinity, 8/14/73, A, C, 73000208

Wilmington Village Historic District, VT9 and VT 100, Wilmington, 8/11/80, A, C, 80000389

Windham Village Historic District, Town Hill Rd., Windham, 11/01/84, C, 84000428

Worrall Covered Bridge, N of Rockingham across the Williams River, Rockingham vicinity, 7/16/73, A, C, 73000209

Windsor County

Aiken Stand Complex, E of Bernard off VT 12, Barnard vicinity, 1/27/83, A, C, 83003229

Best's Covered Bridge, About 8 mi. W of Windsor off VT 44, Windsor vicinity, 7/02/73, A, C, 73000210

Bethel Village Historic District, Both sides of S. Main, Main, N. Main, and Church Sts., Bethel, 9/03/76, A, C, 76000199

Bethel Village Historic District (Boundary Increase), SR 107 across the White R. and N to Central Vermont Railway tracks, Bethel, 5/24/90, C, 90000797

Black River Academy, High St., Ludlow, 11/15/72, A, B, C, 72000108

Bowers Covered Bridge, W of Windsor, Windsor vicinity, 8/28/73, A, C, 73000211

Boyd, Theron, Homestead [Agricultural Resources of Vermont MPS], Town Hwy. 6, Hartford, 5/20/93, A, C, 93000381

Bridgewater Corners Bridge [Metal Truss, Masonry, and Concrete Bridges in Vermont MPS], VT 100A over the Ottauquechee R., Bridgewater, 10/29/92, A, C, 92001525

Bridgewater Woolen Mill, U.S.4, Bridgewater, 7/06/76, A, C, 76002240

Brook Farm [Agricultural Resources of Vermont MPS], Twenty Mile Stream Rd. NW of Cavendish, Cavendish vicinity, 7/22/93, A, C, 93000676

Cavendish Universalist Church, VT 131, Cavendish, 4/24/73, C, 73000252

Chester Village Historic District, Roughly bounded by Lovers Lane Brook, Maple St., Williams River, Middle Branch & Lovers Lane, Chester, 8/08/85, C, 85001739

Coolidge, Calvin, Homestead District, Off VT 100A, Plymouth Notch, 10/15/66, B, NHL, 66000794

Cornish—Windsor Covered Bridge, W of Cornish City, Windsor, vicinity, 11/21/76, A, C, 76000135

Daman, Rev. George, House, Wyman Ln., Woodstock, 6/22/89, C, 89000759

Damon Hall, US 5 and VT 12, Hartland, 6/02/88, C, 88000654

Eureka Schoolhouse, Carleston Rd., Goulds Mill, 3/11/71, A, b, 71000074

Fowler-Steele House, N. Main St., Windsor, 6/17/82, C, 82001710

Gate of the Hills, Jct. of North and Royalton Hill Rds., Bethel, 11/18/91, B, C, 91001648

Gay, Daniel, House, VT 107, Gaysville, 1/09/78, C, 78000252

Gilead Brook Bridge [Metal Truss, Masonry, and Concrete Bridges in Vermont MPS], VT 12 over Gilead Brook, Bethel, 10/11/90, A, C, 90001492

Glimmerstone, VT 131, Cavendish, 11/14/78, C, 78000253

Greenwood House, VT 103, Chester, 10/31/85, C, 85003442

Harrington House, River St. and VT 107, Bethel, 3/16/83, C, 83003230

Hartness House, 30 Orchard St., Springfield, 12/20/78, B, C, 78000254

Historic Crown Point Road, Off VT 131, Weathersfield, 12/02/74, A, B, 74000270

Indian Stones, VT 106, Reading, 11/20/74, A, C, b, f, 74000356

Iron Bridge at Howard Hill Road, Howard Hill Rd. and VT 131, Cavendish, 9/09/82, C, 82001711

Jeffrey House, North St., Chester, 6/13/74, C, 74000271

Juniper Hill Farm—Maxwell Evarts House, Juniper Hill Rd., Windsor, 7/14/88, C, 88001044

Kendron Brook Bridge [Metal Truss, Masonry, and Concrete Bridges in Vermont MPS], Town Hwy. 65 over Kendron Brook, Woodstock, 8/27/92, A, C, 92001037

Lincoln Covered Bridge, SW of Woodstock off U.S. 4, Woodstock vicinity, 8/28/73, A, C, 73000212

Lockwood-Boynton House, 1 School St., North Springfield, 5/04/82, C, 82001712

Locust Creek House Complex, VT 12, Bethel, 12/10/82, C, 82001766

Ludlow Graded School, High St., Ludlow, 11/29/79, A, 79000276

Marsh, George Perkins, Boyhood Home, 54 Elm St., Woodstock, 6/11/67, B, NHL, 67000023

Martin's Mill Covered Bridge, S of Hartland off U.S. 5, Hartland vicinity, 8/28/73, A, C, 73000213

McKenstry Manor, N of Bethel on VT 12, Bethel vicinity, 12/01/78, C, 78000255

Moon, Owen, Farm, S of South Woodstock off VT 106, South Woodstock vicinity, 1/27/83, C, 83003231

Morris, Gen. Lewis R., House [Agricultural Resources of Vermont MPS], 456 Old Connecticut River Rd., Springfield, 6/25/92, A, C, 92000813

NAMCO Block, 1–17 Union St., Windsor, 11/14/91, C, 91001615

Norwich Village Historic District, Main St. from S of Elm St. to Turnpike Rd. and adjacent portions of Elm, Church, Mechanic, Hazen and Cliff Sts., Norwich, 1/03/91, C, 90002116

Old Constitution House, 16 N. Main St., Windsor, 3/11/71, A, C, b, 71000075

Ottauquechee River Bridge [Metal Truss, Masonry, and Concrete Bridges in Vermont MPS], US 5 over the Ottauquechee R., Hartland, 10/11/90, A, C, 90001491

Plymouth Historic District, VT 100A, Plymouth, 12/12/70, A, B, C, c, 70000084

Quechee Gorge Bridge [Metal Truss, Masonry, and Concrete Bridges in Vermont MPS], US 4 over Quechee Gorge, Hartford, 10/11/90, A, C, 90001490

Raymond, Isaac M., Farm [Agricultural Resources of Vermont MPS], Jct. of Woodstock Town Hwys. 95 and 18, Woodstock Township, Woodstock vicinity, 4/01/93, A, C, 93000242

Robbins and Lawrence Armory and Machine Shop, S. Main St., Windsor, 11/13/66, A, NHL, 66000796

Royalton Mill Complex, N of South Royalton on Town Rd. 12, South Royalton vicinity, 2/03/83, C, 83003232

Simons' Inn, SW of Andover on VT 11, Andover vicinity, 3/02/79, A, C, 79000233

South Reading Schoolhouse, Felchville-Tyson's Corner Rd., South Reading, 2/03/83, C, 83003233

Windsor County—Continued

South Royalton Historic District, E of Royalton on VT 14, Royalton vicinity, 9/03/76, A, B, C, 76000200

South Woodstock Village Historic District, Both sides of VT 106, TH 61, and Church Hill Rd., Woodstock vicinity, 8/12/82, A, C, 82001713

Spaulding, Zachariah, Farm [Agricultural Resources of Vermont MPS], Town Hwy. 38 S of Ludlow town center, Ludlow, 11/04/93, A, C, 93001175

Springfield Downtown Historic District, Roughly bounded b Black River, Mineral, Pearl, Main, and Valley Sts., Springfield, 8/11/83, A, C, 83003234

Springfield Downtown Historic District (Boundary Increase), Roughly Brookline Apts. on Wall St., Park St., and along the Black River, Springfield, 9/11/86, A, C, 86001995

Stellafane Observatory, S of North Springfield off Breezy Hill Rd., North Springfield vicinity, 11/07/77, A, B, NHL, 77000107

Stockbridge Common Historic District, Area around Stockbridge Common, including Maplewood Cemetery, Stockbridge, 5/24/90, B, C, 90000800

Stockbridge Four Corners Bridge [Metal Truss, Masonry, and Concrete Bridges in Vermont MPS], VT 100 over the White R., Stockbridge, 11/14/91, A, C, 91001611

Stone Village Historic District, Both sides of VT 103, Chester, 5/17/74, C, 74000329

Strong, Jedediah II, House, Clubhouse and Dewey's Mills Rds., Hartford, 8/13/74, C, 74000272

Sumner, David, House, US 5, Hartland, 3/02/89, B, C, 89000027

Taftsville Covered Bridge, E of Woodstock off U.S. 4, Woodstock vicinity, 8/28/73, A, C, 73000214

Upper Falls Covered Bridge, N of Perkinsville off VT 131, Perkinsville vicinity, 8/28/73, A, C, 73000215

Weathersfield Center Historic District, Center Rd., Weathersfield Center, 6/30/80, C, a, 80000345

West Hartford Bridge [Metal Truss, Masonry, and Concrete Bridges in Vermont MPS], Town Hwy. 14 at VT 14 over the White R., Hartford, 10/29/92, A, C, 92001524

West Woodstock Bridge [Metal Truss, Masonry, and Concrete Bridges in Vermont MPS], Town Hwy. 50 over the Ottauquechee R., West Woodstock, 8/27/92, A, C, 92001038

Weston Village Historic District, Main, Park & School Sts., Lawrence Hill, Landgrove & Trout Club Rds., Mill Lane & Chester Mountain Rd., Weston, 8/29/85, C, D, a, d, 85001934

White River Junction Historic District, Railroad Row, Main, Currier, Bridge, and Gates Sts., Hartford, 8/22/80, A, C, 80000390

Wilder, John, House, Lawrence Hill Rd., Weston, 11/10/83, C, 83004231

Willard Covered Bridge, NE of Hartland off U.S.5, Hartland vicinity, 8/28/73, A, C, 73000216

Windsor House, N. Main St., N of jct. of Main and State Sts., Windsor, 12/29/71, A, C, 71000060

Windsor Village Historic District, Area centered around Main, Depot Ave., State St., and Court Sq., Windsor, 4/23/75, A, C, 75000212

Woodstock Village Historic District, Along the Ottauquechee River, Woodstock, 1/22/73, B, C, 73000274

Woodstock Warren Through Truss Bridge [Metal Truss, Masonry, and Concrete Bridges in Vermont MPS], Town Hwy. 24 across the Ottauquechee R., Woodstock vicinity, 8/18/92, A, C, 92000987

The grand Shard Villa (ca. 1872–74) in Addison County is significant not only for its elaborate Second Empire architecture and details, but also for its architect (Warren Thayer of Burlington), original owner (internationally known probate lawyer Columbus Smith), interior artwork, landscaped grounds, and its function as one of the first and continuously operated elderly care facilities in Vermont. (Max Peterson, 1987)

VIRGIN ISLANDS

St. Croix Island

Aklis Archeological Site, Address Restricted, Frederiksted vicinity, 7/01/76, D, 76001852

Bethlehem Middle Works Historic District, King's Quarter, Christiansted vicinity, 7/06/88, A, C, D, 87001932

Christiansted Historic District, Roughly bounded by Christiansted Harbor, New, Peter's Farm Hospital, and West Sts., Christiansted, 7/30/76, A, C, NPS, 76002266

Christiansted National Historic Site, Bounded by King, Queen, and Queens Cross Sts. and Christiansted Harbor, Christiansted, 10/15/66, A, C, a, NPS, 66000077

Coakley Bay Estate, E of Christiansted, Christiansted vicinity, 7/23/76, A, C, 76001841

Columbus Landing Site, E of Greig Hill on Salt River Bay, Salt River Bay, 10/15/66, A, B, NHL, 66000743

Danish West India and Guinea Company Warehouse, Church and Company Sts., Christiansted, 10/09/74, A, C, 74001940

Diamond School, W of Christiansted on Center-line Rd., Christiansted vicinity, 7/01/76, A, C, 76001842

Estate Butler's Bay, N of Frederiksted, Frederiksted vicinity, 8/25/78, A, C, 78002722

Estate Grove Place, 4 mi. (6.4 km) E of Frederiksted off Centerline Rd., Frederiksted vicinity, 7/17/78, C, 78002721

Estate Hogansborg, E of Frederiksted off Center-line Rd., Frederiksted vicinity, 2/17/78, A, C, 78002723

Estate Judith's Fancy, 4 mi. (3.2 km) NW of Christiansted, Christiansted vicinity, 7/17/78, A, C, 78002717

Estate La Reine, 20 Kings Quarter and 19 Queens Quarter, Christiansted vicinity, 11/24/80, A, C, D, 80003994

Estate Little Princess, NW of Christiansted, Christiansted vicinity, 6/09/80, B, C, D, 80003995

Estate Mount Victory, NE of Frederiksted, Frederiksted vicinity, 2/17/78, C, 78002724

Estate Prosperity, N of Frederiksted, Frederiksted vicinity, 2/17/78, C, 78002725

Estate Saint George Historic District, Prince Quarter, Frederiksted vicinity, 10/24/86, A, C, a, 86003351

Estate St. John, 3 mi. (4.8 km) NW of Christiansted, Christiansted vicinity, 6/09/78, C, 78002718

Fair Plain Archeological District, Address Restricted, Christiansted vicinity, 9/29/76, D, 76001843

Fairplain Historic and Archeological District, Address Restricted, Christiansted vicinity, 7/06/88, A, C, D, 87001903

Frederiksted Historic District, Roughly bounded by Fisher St., the cemetery, Fort Frederick, , Frederiksted, 8/09/76, A, C, 76001853

Friedensfeld Midlands Moravian Church and Manse, W of Christiansted, Christiansted vicinity, 7/01/76, A, C, a, 76001844

Friedensthal Mission, SW of Christiansted, Christiansted vicinity, 8/25/78, A, C, a, 78002719

Great Pond Archeological Site, Address Restricted, Christiansted vicinity, 7/12/76, D, 76001845

Green Kay, E of Christiansted, Christiansted vicinity, 7/19/76, C, 76001846

La Grande Princesse School, NE of Christiansted, Christiansted vicinity, 7/12/76, A, C, 76001847

Little La Grange, NE of Frederiksted, Frederiksted vicinity, 10/22/76, A, C, 76001854

Lower Granard Archeological District, Address Restricted, Christiansted vicinity, 7/01/76, D, 76001849

Prosperity Archeological Site, Address Restricted, Frederiksted vicinity, 7/12/76, D, 76001855

Richmond Prison Detention and Workhouse, W of Christiansted, Christiansted vicinity, 2/14/78, A, C, 78002720

River Archeological Site, Address Restricted, Frederiksted vicinity, 7/01/76, D, 76001856

Sion Hill, W of Christiansted, Christiansted vicinity, 7/19/76, A, C, 76001850

Slob Historic District, King's Quarter, Christiansted vicinity, 11/12/87, A, C, D, 87001929

St. Georges Archeological Site, Address Restricted, Frederiksted vicinity, 9/29/76, D, 76001857

Strawberry Hill Historic District, Queen's Quarter, Christiansted vicinity, 10/02/87, A, B, C, D, 87001934

Upper Salt River Archeological District, Address Restricted, Christiansted vicinity, 9/01/76, D, 76001851

Whim, 1.7 mi. SE of Frederiksted on Centerline Rd., Frederiksted vicinity, 7/30/76, A, C, 76001858

St. John Island

Annaberg Historic District [Virgin Islands National Park MRA], NW of Coral Bay, Leinster Bay, 7/23/81, A, NPS, 81000090

Brown Bay Plantation Historic District [Virgin Islands National Park MRA], N of Palestina, Brown Bay, 7/23/81, A, NPS, 81000089

Catherineberg-Jockumsdahl-Herman Farm [Virgin Islands National Park MRA (AD)], E of Cruz Bay, Cruz Bay vicinity, 3/30/78, A, C, D, NPS, 78000270

Cinnamon Bay Plantation [Virgin Islands National Park MRA (AD)], NE of Cruz Bay on Cinnamon Bay, Cruz Bay vicinity, 7/11/78, A, C, D, NPS, 78000269

Congo Cay Archeological District, Address Restricted, Cruz Bay vicinity, 12/01/78, D, 78003166

Dennis Bay Historic District [Virgin Islands National Park MRA], NE of Cruz Bay off North Shore Rd., Dennis Bay, 7/23/81, A, C, D, NPS, 81000095

Emmaus Moravian Church and Manse, W of Palestina, Coral Bay, 11/07/77, A, C, a, 77001531

Enighed, Cruz Bay Quarter, Cruz Bay, 7/01/76, C, 76002219

Estate Beverhoudt, 1.5 mi. E. of Cruz Bay off Center Line Rd., Cruz Bay vicinity, 8/29/78, C, 78003170

Estate Carolina Sugar Plantation, W of Coral Bay on King Hill Rd., Coral Bay vicinity, 7/19/76, A, C, 76002217

Fortsberg, SE of Coral Bay, Coral Bay vicinity, 9/01/76, A, C, D, 76002218

HMS Santa Monica, Address Restricted, Coral Bay vicinity, 2/17/78, D, 78003163

Hermitage Plantation Historic District [Virgin Islands National Park MRA], East End Rd., Hurricane Hole vicinity, 7/23/81, A, D, NPS, 81000094

Jossie Gut Historic District [Virgin Islands National Park MRA], W of Coral Bay off Center Line Rd., Reef Bay vicinity, 7/23/81, A, D, NPS, 81000086

L'Esperance Historic District [Virgin Islands National Park MRA], E of Cruz Bay off Center Line Rd., Reef Bay, 7/23/81, A, B, C, D, NPS, 81000099

Lameshur Plantation [Virgin Islands National Park MRA (AD)], E of Cruz Bay on Little Lameshur Bay, Cruz Bay vicinity, 6/23/78, A, C, D, NPS, 78000271

Liever Marches Bay Historic District [Virgin Islands National Park MRA], E of Brown Bay, Brown Bay vicinity, 7/23/81, A, D, NPS, 81000087

Lind Point Fort [Virgin Islands National Park MRA], NW of Cruz Bay, Cruz Bay, 7/23/81, A, D, NPS, 81000085

Mary Point Estate [Virgin Islands National Park MRA (AD)], NE of Cruz Bay, Cruz Bay vicinity, 5/22/78, A, C, D, NPS, 78000272

More Hill Historic District [Virgin Islands National Park MRA], Off East End Rd., East End vicinity, 7/23/81, A, C, D, NPS, 81000092

Petroglyph Site, Address Restricted, Reef Bay vicinity, 7/07/82, D, NPS, 82001716

Reef Bay Great House Historic District [Virgin Islands National Park MRA], W of Bordeaux, Reef Bay, 7/23/81, C, D, NPS, 81000091

Reef Bay Sugar Factory Historic District [Virgin Islands National Park MRA], E of Cruz Bay, Reef Bay, 7/23/81, A, C, D, NPS, 81000084

Rustenberg Plantation South Historic District [Virgin Islands National Park MRA], W of Coral Bay off Center Line Rd., Cinnamon Bay, 7/23/81, A, D, NPS, 81000093

St. John Island—Continued

Trunk Bay Sugar Factory [Virgin Islands National Park MRA], NE of Cruz Bay on North Shore Rd., Trunk Bay, 7/23/81, A, D, NPS, 81000088

St. Thomas Island

Bordeaux, W of Charlotte Amalie, Charlotte Amalie vicinity, 11/15/78, A, C, 78002726

Botany Bay Archeological District, Address Restricted, Charlotte Amalie vicinity, 7/01/76, D, 76001859

Charlotte Amalie Historic District, Roughly bounded by Nytvaer, Berg and Government Hills, Bjebre Gade and St. Thomas Harbor, Charlotte Amalie, 7/19/76, A, C, 76001860

Estate Botany Bay, W of Charlotte Amalie, Charlotte Amalie vicinity, 7/30/76, A, C, 76001861

Estate Brewers Bay, 2 mi. (3.2 km) W of Charlotte Amalie at Brewers Bay, Charlotte Amalie vicinity, 7/31/78, A, C, 78002727

Estate Hafensight, S of Charlotte Amalie, Charlotte Amalie vicinity, 2/17/78, C, 78002728

Estate Neltjeberg, NW of Charlotte Amalie, Charlotte Amalie vicinity, 2/17/78, A, C, 78002729

Estate Niesky, 1.5 mi. W of Charlotte Amalie off Harwood Hwy., Charlotte Amalie vicinity, 8/29/78, A, C, a, 78003092

Estate Perseverance, W of Charlotte Amalie, Charlotte Amalie vicinity, 2/17/78, A, C, 78002730

Fort Christian, At St. Thomas Harbor, Charlotte Amalie, 5/05/77, A, NHL, 77001329

Hamburg-America Shipping Line Administrative Offices, 48B Tolbod Gade, Charlotte Amalie, 10/10/78, A, C, 78002731

Hassel Island, S of Charlotte Amalie in St. Thomas Harbor, Charlotte Amalie vicinity, 7/19/76, A, C, 76001862

Hassel Island Historic District (Boundary Increase), S of Charlotte Amalie, Charlotte Amalie vicinity, 8/29/78, A, C, D, 78003093

Hull Bay Archeological District, Address Restricted, Charlotte Amalie vicinity, 9/01/76, D, 76001863

Krum Bay Archeological District, Address Restricted, Charlotte Amalie vicinity, 8/28/76, D, 76001864

Mafolie Great House, N of Charlotte Amalie, Charlotte Amalie vicinity, 2/17/78, C, 78002732

Magens Bay Archeological District, Address Restricted, Charlotte Amalie vicinity, 7/30/76, D, 76001865

New Herrnhut Moravian Church, E of Charlotte Amalie, Charlotte Amalie vicinity, 10/08/76, A, C, a, 76001866

Skytsborg, 39 Donningens Gade, Charlotte Amalie, 12/20/91, A, B, C, 91001844

Tutu Plantation House, 3 mi. NE of Charlotte Amalie, Charlotte Amalie vicinity, 7/12/76, C, 76001867

Venus Hill, N of Charlotte Amalie, Charlotte Amalie vicinity, 2/17/78, A, 78002733

The stone base of a cane-crushing windmill (ca. 1760) on the Estate Slob, St. Croix Island, is one of several structures associated with the estate's 250 year history as a sugar plantation. (William Chapman, 1979)

VIRGINIA

Accomack County

Accomac Historic District, Business Rte. 13, Accomac, 7/21/82, A, C, 82004529

Arbuckle Place, Seaside Rd./VA 679, Assawoman, 5/22/86, C, 86001136

Assateague Lighthouse, S of Chincoteague at S end of Assateague Island, Chincoteague vicinity, 6/04/73, A, C, 73001989

Bank Building, No. 1 Court House Ave., Accomac, 7/23/74, A, C, 74002099

Bayly, Edmund, House, VA 615, Craddockville vicinity, 6/28/82, C, 82004530

Bowman's Folly, SE of jct. of Rtes. 652 and 13, Accomac vicinity, 11/12/69, C, 69000216

Corbin Hall, E of Horntown on VA 679, Horntown vicinity, 11/09/72, C, 72001377

Debtors' Prison, VA 764, Accomac, 11/07/76, A, C, 76002087

Hopkins and Brother Store, Market St., Onancock, 11/12/69, A, C, 69000217

Kerr Place, NE corner of Crockett Ave. and Market St., Onancock, 2/26/70, C, 70000780

Mason House, N of Guilford off VA 658, Guilford vicinity, 11/21/74, C, 74002100

Onancock Historic District, Roughly bounded by Joynes Branch, Onancock Cr. and Lake, Kerr, Jackson, Market, Justice, Johnson and Holly Sts., Onancock, 10/08/92, A, C, 92001266

Pitts Neck, 6 mi. W of New Church on VA 709, New Church vicinity, 10/21/76, C, 76002088

Scarborough House Archaeological Site (44AC4), Address Restricted, Davis Wharf vicinity, 5/16/85, A, D, 85001125

Shepherd's Plain, W of Pungoteague, Pungoteague vicinity, 6/28/82, B, C, 82004531

St. George's Church, VA 178, NE of jct. with VA 180, Pungoteague, 9/15/70, A, C, a, 70000781

St. James Church, Daugherty Rd. between Back St. and Ocean Hwy., Accomac, 6/11/69, C, a, 69000215

Wessells Root Cellar, NE of jct. of Rtes. 701 and 692, Hallwood vicinity, 2/26/70, A, C, 70000779

Wharton Place, 0.7 mi. NE of jct. of VA 762 and 679, Mappsville vicinity, 11/03/72, C, 72001378

Albemarle County

Arrowhead, E side US 29, 1.5 mi. NE of jct. with VA 608, Charlottesville vicinity, 7/09/91, C, 91000885

Aspen Hall [Berkeley County Multiple Resource Area], End of Boyd Ave., Martinsburg, 12/10/80, 80004882

Bellair, Cty. Rt. 708 S side, 3.8 mi. E of jct. with VA 20, Charlottesville vicinity, 10/15/92, B, C, 92001372

Blenheim, S of Charlottesville on VA 727, Blenheim vicinity, 5/17/76, B, C, b, 76002089

Blue Ridge Farm, Jct. of VA 691 and VA 692, Greenwood vicinity, 1/25/91, C, 90002163

Carrsbrook, VA 1424, Charlottesville vicinity, 7/08/82, B, C, 82004532

Casa Maria, VA 691 S of jct. with US 250, Greenwood vicinity, 12/28/90, C, 90001999

Castle Hill, NE of Cismont near jct. of VA 231 and 640, Cismont vicinity, 2/23/72, A, B, C, 72001379

Cedars, The, US 250, W of US 64, Greenwood, 12/27/90, C, 89001909

Christ Church Glendower, On VA 713, 0.4 mi. SW of jct. with VA 712, Keene vicinity, 7/02/71, C, a, 71000974

Cliffside, N of Scottsville on VA 6, Scottsville vicinity, 9/16/82, C, 82004536

Clifton, VA 729 at Rivanna River, Shadwell vicinity, 11/02/89, B, C, 89001922

Cobham Park, S of VA 22, Cobham vicinity, 7/18/74, C, 74002101

Cocke's Mill House and Mill Site, VA 712 N of jct. with VA 719, North Garden vicinity, 12/06/90, A, C, 90001828

Cove Presbyterian Church, US 29, N of VA 699, Covesville, 11/02/89, C, a, 89001935

Crossroads Tavern, VA 692, Crossroads, 8/16/84, A, C, 84003481

D. S. Tavern, U.S. 250, Ivy vicinity, 9/29/83, A, C, 83003255

Edgehill, N of Shadwell on VA 22, Shadwell vicinity, 9/09/82, A, B, C, 82004537

Edgemont, SE of Colesville on VA 712, Covesville vicinity, 11/28/80, C, 80004162

Ednam House, US 250, Ednam vicinity, 7/08/82, C, 82004533

Emmanuel Church, US 250, Greenwood vicinity, 7/08/82, B, C, a, 82004535

Enniscorthy, VA 627 .5 mi. S of jct. with VA 712, Keene vicinity, 9/24/92, C, 92001273

Esmont, N of Esmont, Esmont vicinity, 5/06/80, C, 80004163

Estouteville, SE of Powell Corner off VA 712, Powell Corner vicinity, 1/30/78, C, 78003002

Farmington, W of jct. of U.S. 250 and U.S. 29, Charlottesville vicinity, 9/15/70, C, 70000782

Faulkner House, 2201 Old Ivy Rd., Charlottesville vicinity, 5/03/84, A, C, 84003484

Gallison Hall, 24 Farmington Dr., Charlottesville vicinity, 12/28/90, C, 90002013

Grace Church, NE of Cismont on VA 231, Cismont vicinity, 10/21/76, C, a, 76002091

Guthrie Hall, N of Esmont on VA 719, Esmont vicinity, 9/23/82, C, 82004534

High Meadows, Off VA 20, Scottsville vicinity, 5/30/86, C, 86001185

Highland, SE of Charlottesville off VA 53, Simeon vicinity, 8/14/73, B, 73001990

Midway, SE of Millington off VA 678, Millington vicinity, 2/31/79, A, C, 79003152

Miller School of Albemarle, SE of Yancey Mills off VA 635, Yancey Mills vicinity, 2/15/74, A, C, 74002102

Mirador, U.S. 250, Greenwood vicinity, 4/07/83, B, C, 83003256

Monticello, 2 mi. S of Charlottesville on VA 53, Charlottesville vicinity, 10/15/66, B, NHL, 66000826

Monticola, SR 602 N of jct. with SR 724, Howardsville, 6/22/90, C, 90000872

Morven, W of Simeon off VA 20, Simeon vicinity, 4/24/73, C, 73001991

Mount Fair, Jct. of VA 673 and VA 810, Browns Cove vicinity, 12/28/90, C, 90001997

Mountain Grove, NW of Esmont on VA 717, Esmont vicinity, 9/08/80, C, 80004164

Piedmont, Jct. of I-64 and VA 691, Greenwood vicinity, 2/01/91, C, 90002184

Pine Knot, VA 712, Glendower vicinity, 2/01/89, A, B, 88003211

Plain Dealing, E of Keene, Keene vicinity, 5/06/80, C, 80004165

Redlands, Jct. of Rtes. 708 and 627, Covesville vicinity, 11/12/69, C, 69000218

Scottsville Historic District, VA 6, Scottsville, 7/30/76, A, C, 76002093

Seven Oaks Farm and Black's Tavern, US 250, W of US 64, Greenwood vicinity, 12/26/89, A, C, 89001906

Shack Mountain, 2 mi. NNW of Charlottesville near jct. of VA 657 and 743, Charlottesville vicinity, 9/01/76, B, C, g, NHL, 76002090

Southwest Mountains Rural Historic District, Roughly bounded by I-64, VA 20, Orange Co. line and C & O RR tracks, Keswick vicinity, 2/27/92, A, B, C, 92000054

Spring Hill, VA 637 and 786, Ivy vicinity, 11/21/83, A, C, 83004232

Sunny Bank, NE of Covesville, W of jct. of VA 712 and VA 631, South Garden vicinity, 12/12/76, C, 76002092

Sunnyfields, VA 53 W side at jct. with VA 732, Simeon vicinity, 6/10/93, B, C, 93000509

The Rectory, Jct. of VA 712 and VA 713, Keene vicinity, 11/07/91, C, a, 91001579

Walker House, VA 627 S of jct. with VA 726, Warren vicinity, 12/28/90, C, 90002001

Wavertree Hall Farm, S side VA 692, 3500 ft. W of jct. with VA 637, Batesville vicinity, 7/09/91, C, 91000886

Woodlands, VA 676, Charlottesville (Independent City) vicinity, 11/02/89, B, C, 89001931

Woodstock Hall Tavern, VA 637, Ivy vicinity, 1/29/87, A, C, 86003735

Alexandria Independent City

Alexandria Canal Tide Lock, Address Restricted, Alexandria (Independent City) vicinity, 1/15/80, A, D, 80004305

Alexandria City Hall, 301 King St., Alexandria (Independent City), 3/08/84, A, C, 84003491

Alexandria Independent City— Continued

Alexandria Historic District, Bounded by, Alexandria (Independent City), 11/13/66, A, C, NHL, 66000928

Bank of Alexandria, 133 N. Fairfax St., Alexandria (Independent City), 6/04/73, A, C, 73002202

Bayne—Fowle House, 811 Prince St., Alexandria (Independent City), 11/06/86, C, 86003136

Carlyle House, 121 N. Fairfax St., Alexandria (Independent City), 11/12/69, C, 69000333

Christ Church, SE corner of Cameron and Columbus Sts., Alexandria (Independent City), 5/10/70, C, a, NHL, 70000899

Fairfax—Moore House, 207 Prince St., Alexandria (Independent City), 1/17/91, A, C, 90002113

Ford, President Gerald R., Jr., House, 514 Crown View Dr., Alexandria (Independent City), 12/17/85, B, g, NHL, 85003048

Fort Ward, 4301 W. Braddock Rd., Alexandria (Independent City), 8/26/82, A, C, D, 82004538

Franklin and Armfield Office, 1315 Duke St., Alexandria (Independent City), 6/02/78, A, NHL, 78003146

Gadsby's Tavern, 128 N. Royal St., Alexandria (Independent City), 10/15/66, A, NHL, 66000913

Jones Point Lighthouse and District of Columbia South Cornerstone, Jones Point Park, Alexandria (Independent City), 5/19/80, A, NPS, 80000352

Lee, Robert E., Boyhood Home, 607 Oronoco St., Alexandria (Independent City), 6/05/86, B, C, c, 86001228

Lee-Fendall House, 614 Oronoco St., Alexandria (Independent City), 6/22/79, B, C, D, g, 79003277

Lloyd House, 220 N. Washington St., Alexandria (Independent City), 7/12/76, B, C, 76002222

Lyceum, The, 201 S. Washington St., Alexandria (Independent City), 5/27/69, A, C, 69000334

Mount Vernon Memorial Highway, Washington St. and George Washington Memorial Pkwy., Alexandria (Independent City), 5/18/81, A, C, NPS, 81000079

Old Dominion Bank Building, 201 Prince St., Alexandria (Independent City), 3/20/80, A, C, 80004307

Protestant Episcopal Theological Seminary, 3737 Seminary Rd., Alexandria (Independent City), 11/17/80, A, C, a, 80004166

Rosemont Historic District, Roughly bounded by Commonwealth AVe., W. Walnut St., Russell Rd., Rucker Pl. and King St., Alexandria (Independent City), 9/24/92, A, C, 92001275

Southwest No. 1 Boundary Marker of the Original District of Columbia [Boundary Markers of the Original District of Columbia MPS], 1220 Wilkes St., Alexandria (Independent City), 2/01/91, A, b, 91000006

Southwest No. 2 Boundary Marker of the Original District of Columbia [Boundary Markers of the Original District of Columbia MPS], E side of Russell Rd., N of jct. with King St., Alexandria (Independent City), 2/01/91, A, b, e, 91000007

Southwest No. 3 Boundary Marker of the Original District of Columbia [Boundary Markers of the Original District of Columbia MPS], 2952 King St., Alexandria (Independent City), 2/01/91, A, 91000008

St. Paul's Episcopal Church, 228 S. Pitt St., Alexandria (Independent City), 5/09/85, A, C, a, 85000987

Stabler-Leadbeater Apothecary Shop, 105-107 S. Fairfax, Alexandria (Independent City), 11/24/82, A, C, 82001796

Town of Potomac, Roughly bounded by Commonwealth Ave., US 1, E. Bellefonte Ave. and Ashby Ave., Alexandria (Independent City), 9/10/92, A, C, 92001186

Alleghany County

Clifton Furnace, SE of Clifton Forge off U.S. 220, Clifton Forge vicinity, 8/16/77, A, 77001485

Douthat State Park Historic District, VA 629, Millboro vicinity, 9/20/86, A, C, g, 86002183

Fudge House, 620 Parklin Dr., Covington, 4/29/93, C, 93000348

Humpback Bridge, Over Dunlop Creek, SW of jct. of U.S. 60 and CR 651, Callaghan vicinity, 10/01/69, C, 69000219

Massie House, US 220, Falling Spring vicinity, 7/08/82, A, C, 82004669

Oakland Grove Presbyterian Church, VA 696, Selma vicinity, 7/08/82, A, C, a, 82004670

Persinger House, VA 788, Covington, 7/08/82, B, C, 82004668

Sweet Chalybeate Springs, S of Earlhurst on VA 311, Sweet Chalybeate vicinity, 1/21/74, A, C, 74002103

Wood Hall, VA 600, Callaghan, 7/26/82, A, C, 82004667

Amelia County

Dykeland, VA 632, Chula vicinity, 5/08/87, B, C, 87000721

Egglestetton, NW of Chula, Chula vicinity, 3/28/80, B, C, 80004167

Farmer House, 3 mi. (4.8 km) SE of Deatonville on VA 647, Deatonville vicinity, 11/17/78, C, 78003004

Haw Branch, N of Amelia off VA 667, Amelia vicinity, 4/02/73, A, C, 73001992

Sayler's Creek Battlefield, VA 617, 618, and 619, Farmville vicinity, 2/04/85, A, NHL, 85002436

St. John's Church, 3.8 mi (6 km) W of Chula on VA 609, Chula vicinity, 11/16/78, A, C, a, 78003003

Wigwam, 8 mi. NW of Chula, Chula vicinity, 11/25/69, B, C, 69000220

Amherst County

Athlone, Jct. of VA 151 and VA 674, Amherst vicinity, 8/24/92, C, 92001029

Fort Riverview (44AH91 and 44AH195), Address Restricted, Madison Heights vicinity, 11/16/89, C, D, 89001921

Geddes, SR 700, Clifford vicinity, 2/24/83, A, C, 83003257

Red Hill Farm, W of Pedlar Mills on VA 647, Pedlar Mills vicinity, 6/09/80, B, C, 80004168

Sweet Briar House, SW of jct. of U.S. 29 and VA 624, Sweet Briar, 9/15/70, B, C, 70000783

Winton, W of VA 151, Clifford, 5/02/74, B, C, d, 74002104

Appomattox County

Appomattox Court House National Historical Park, 3 mi. NE of Appomattox on VA 24, Appomattox vicinity, 10/15/66, A, B, C, b, d, e, NPS, 66000827

Pamplin Pipe Factory, Address Restricted, Pamplin, 11/25/80, A, D, 80004169

Arlington County

Arlington House, The Robert E. Lee Memorial, Arlington National Cemetery, Arlington, 10/15/66, B, C, f, NPS, 66000040

Ball-Sellers House, 5620 S. 3rd St., Arlington, 7/17/75, C, 75002014

Benjamin Banneker: SW 9 Intermediate Boundary Stone, 18th and Van Buren Sts., Arlington, 5/11/76, A, B, f, NHL, 76002094

Carlin Hall, 5711 4th St., S., Arlington, 8/12/93, A, C, 93000833

Colonial Village, Roughly bounded by Wilson Blvd., Lee Hwy., N. Veitch St. and Queens Lane, Arlington vicinity, 12/09/80, A, C, g, 80004170

Drew, Charles Richard, House, 2505 1st St., S., Arlington, 5/11/76, B, NHL, 76002095

Fort Myer Historic District, Arlington Blvd. (U.S. 50), Arlington, 11/28/72, A, NHL, 72001380

Glebe, The, 4527 17th St., N., Arlington, 2/23/72, C, 72001381

Hume School, 1805 S. Arlington Ridge Rd., Arlington, 6/18/79, A, C, 79003027

Mount Vernon Memorial Highway, Washington St. and George Washington Memorial Pkwy., Arlington, 5/18/81, A, C, NPS, 81000079

Northwest No. 1 Boundary Marker of the Original District of Columbia [Boundary Markers of the Original District of Columbia MPS], 3607 Powhatan St., Arlington, 2/01/91, A, b, 91000003

Northwest No. 2 Boundary Marker of the Original District of Columbia [Boundary Markers of the Original District of Columbia MPS], 5145 N. 38th St., Arlington, 2/01/91, A, 91000004

Pentagon Office Building Complex, Jefferson Davis Hwy./VA 110 at I-395, Arlington, 7/27/89, A, B, C, g, NHL, 89000932

Quarters 1, Fort Myer, Grant Ave., Arlington, 11/28/72, A, NHL, 72001382

Southwest No. 4 Boundary Marker of the Original District of Columbia [Boundary Markers of the Original District of Columbia MPS], King St. N

Arlington County—Continued

of jct. with Wakefield St., Alexandria, 2/01/91, A, b, 91000009

Southwest No. 5 Boundary Marker of the Original District of Columbia [Boundary Markers of the Original District of Columbia MPS], NE of jct. of King St. and Walter Reed Dr., Arlington, 2/01/91, A, b, 91000010

Southwest No. 6 Boundary Marker of the Original District of Columbia [Boundary Markers of the Original District of Columbia MPS], S. Jefferson St. S of jct. with Columbia Pike, in median strip, Bailey's Crossroads, 2/01/91, A, b, 91000011

Southwest No. 7 Boundary Marker of the Original District of Columbia [Boundary Markers of the Original District of Columbia MPS], Behind 3101 S. Manchester St., Fairfax, 2/01/91, A, 91000012

Southwest No. 8 Boundary Marker of the Original District of Columbia [Boundary Markers of the Original District of Columbia MPS], Jct. of Wilson Blvd. and John Marshall Dr., behind apt. bldg., Arlington, 2/01/91, A, b, 91000013

US Post Office—Arlington, 3118 N. Washington Blvd., Arlington, 2/07/86, A, C, g, 86000151

West Cornerstone [Boundary Markers of the Original District of Columbia MPS], W side Meridian St., S of jct. with Williamsburg Blvd., Falls Church, 2/01/91, A, b, 91000014

Augusta County

Alexander, James, House, N of Spottswood on VA 671, Spottswood vicinity, 9/16/82, A, C, 82004543

Archeological Site No. AU-154, Address Restricted, Luray vicinity, 12/13/85, D, NPS, 85003171

Augusta County Training School [Public Schools in Augusta County Virginia 1870–1940 TR], VA 693, Cedar Green, 6/19/86, A, C, g, 86001400

Augusta Military Academy, N of Staunton on U.S. 11, Fort Defiance vicinity, 2/10/83, A, B, C, 83003258

Augusta Stone Church, U.S. 11, Fort Defiance, 5/09/73, A, C, a, 73001994

Bethel Green, Rte. 701, Greenville vicinity, 8/26/82, C, 82004539

Blackrock Springs Site, Address Restricted, Luray vicinity, 12/13/85, D, NPS, 85003169

Chapel Hill, E of Mint Spring on VA 654, Mint Spring vicinity, 11/16/78, C, 78003006

Clover Mount, W of Greenvile on VA 674, Greenville vicinity, 9/16/82, B, C, 82004540

Coiner House, NW of Crimora off VA 865, Crimora vicinity, 3/30/78, C, 78003005

Craigsville School [Public Schools in Augusta County Virginia 1870–1940 TR], Railroad Ave., Craigsville, 2/27/85, A, C, 85000383

Crimora School [Public Schools in Augusta County Virginia 1870–1940 TR], VA 612, Crimora, 2/27/85, A, C, 85000384

Deerfield School [Public Schools in Augusta County Virginia 1870–1940 TR], VA 600, Deerfield, 6/19/86, A, C, g, 86001402

Estaline Schoolhouse [Public Schools in Augusta County Virginia 1870–1940 TR], VA 601, Estaline Valley, 2/27/85, A, C, 85000385

Folly, S of Staunton on U.S. 11, Staunton vicinity, 10/25/73, C, 73001995

Glebe Burying Ground, S of Swoope on VA 876, Swoope vicinity, 10/01/85, A, C, d, 85002722

Glebe Schoolhouse [Public Schools in Augusta County Virginia 1870–1940 TR], VA 876, Summerdean vicinity, 2/27/85, A, C, 85000386

Hanger Mill, Jct. of VA 801 and US 250, Churchville vicinity, 11/08/91, A, C, 91001596

Harnsberger Octagonal Barn, VA 256 and VA 865, Grottoes vicinity, 7/08/82, A, C, 82004541

Intervale, VA 720, Swoope, 2/14/85, A, C, 85000296

Middlebrook High School [Public Schools in Augusta County Virginia 1870–1940 TR], VA 670, Middlebrook, 2/27/85, A, C, 85000387

Middlebrook Historic District, Jct. VA 252 and 876, Middlebrook, 2/10/83, A, C, D, 83003259

Middlebrook School [Public Schools in Augusta County Virginia 1870–1940 TR], VA 670, Middlebrook, 2/27/85, A, C, 85000388

Miller, A. J., House, VA 639, Middlebrook vicinity, 7/08/82, B, 82004542

Miller, Hannah, House, N of Mossy Creek off VA 747, Mossy Creek vicinity, 5/24/79, B, C, 79003028

Miller, Henry, House, E of Mossy Creek on VA 42, Mossy Creek vicinity, 5/23/79, B, C, 79003029

Mish, Henry, Barn, N of Middlebrook on VA 876, Middlebrook vicinity, 2/10/83, A, C, 83003260

Moffett's Creek Schoolhouse [Public Schools in Augusta County Virginia 1870–1940 TR], VA 681, Newport vicinity, 2/27/85, A, C, 85000389

Mt. Meridian Schoolhouse [Public Schools in Augusta County Virginia 1870–1940 TR], VA 865, Mt. Meridian, 2/27/85, A, C, 85000390

Mt. Pleasant, VA 732 N of Staunton, Staunton vicinity, 10/30/89, B, C, 89001792

Mt. Sidney School [Public Schools in Augusta County Virginia 1870–1940 TR], VA 11, Mt. Sidney, 2/27/85, A, C, 85000391

Mt. Torry Furnace, SW of Waynesboro on VA 664 in the George Washington National Forest, Sherando vicinity, 2/25/74, A, 74002231

Mt. Zion Schoolhouse [Public Schools in Augusta County Virginia 1870–1940 TR], VA 747, Mt. Solon vicinity, 2/27/85, A, C, b, 85000392

New Hope High School [Public Schools in Augusta County Virginia 1870–1940 TR], VA 608, New Hope, 2/27/85, A, C, 85000393

North River High School [Public Schools in Augusta County Virginia 1870–1940 TR], VA 42, Moscow vicinity, 2/27/85, A, C, 85000394

Old Providence Stone Church, Jct. of VA 613 and VA 620, Spottswood vicinity, 12/05/72, A, C, a, 72001383

Paine Run Rockshelter, Address Restricted, Luray vicinity, 12/13/85, D, NPS, 85003170

Shuey, Lewis, House, S of Swoope on VA 713, Swoope vicinity, 2/10/83, A, C, 83003261

Sugar Loaf Farm, W of jct. of VA 695 and VA 710, Staunton vicinity, 7/09/91, A, C, 91000884

Swannanoa, S of jct. of VA 610 and U.S. 250, Waynesboro vicinity, 10/01/69, C, 69000221

Tinkling Spring Presbyterian Church, VA 608, 1 mi. S of jct. with VA 636 and VA 631, Fishersville vicinity, 4/11/73, A, C, a, 73001993

Valley Railroad Stone Bridge, S of Jolivue off VA 654, Jolivue vicinity, 11/19/74, A, C, 74002105

Verona School [Public Schools in Augusta County Virginia 1870–1940 TR], VA 11, Verona, 2/27/85, A, C, b, 85000395

Walker's Creek Schoolhouse [Public Schools in Augusta County Virginia 1870–1940 TR], VA 602, Newport vicinity, 2/27/85, A, C, 85000396

West View Schoolhouse [Public Schools in Augusta County Virginia 1870–1940 TR], VA 774 and 773, Weyers Cave vicinity, 2/27/85, A, C, 85000397

Weyers Cave School [Public Schools in Augusta County Virginia 1870–1940 TR], VA 276, Weyers Cave, 2/27/85, A, C, 85000398

Bath County

Hidden Valley, N of Bacova near jct. of Rtes. 621 and 39 in George Washington National Forest, Bacova vicinity, 2/26/70, C, 70000784

Hidden Valley Rock Shelter (44BA31), Address Restricted, Warm Springs vicinity, 7/22/86, D, 86001945

Homestead, The, US 220, Hot Springs, 5/03/84, A, C, NHL, 84003494

Old Stone House, SW of Milboro Springs on VA 664, Millboro Springs vicinity, 2/10/83, C, 83003262

Warm Springs Bathhouses, NE of Warm Springs off Rt. 220, Warm Springs vicinity, 10/08/69, A, C, 69000222

Warm Springs Mill, E side of VA 645, Warm Springs, 9/11/89, A, g, 88001448

Bedford County

Cifax Rural Historic District, Jct. of VA 644 and VA 643 and surrounding valley area, Cifax, 2/20/92, A, C, 92000052

Elk Hill, NW of Forest on VA 663, Forest vicinity, 4/02/73, C, 73001996

Fancy Farm, On VA 43, N of jct. with VA 682, Bedford vicinity, 1/07/72, C, 72001384

Hope Dawn, NW of Lynchburg off VA 761, Lynchburg vicinity, 10/09/74, B, C, 74002106

Locust Level, US 460 W of jct. with VA 695, Montvale, 12/21/90, A, B, C, 90001841

Mount Airy, Jct. of VA 630 and VA 631, Leesville vicinity, 12/19/90, B, C, 90001823

New London Academy, Near jct. of VA 297 and VA 211, Forest vicinity, 4/13/72, A, 72001385

Old Rectory, S of Perrowville on VA 663, Perrowville vicinity, 7/24/73, C, 73001998

Poplar Forest, S of jct. of Rtes. 661 and 460, Lynchburg vicinity, 11/12/69, C, NHL, 69000223

Bedford County—Continued

Rothsay, US 221 N side, 2000 ft. E of jct. with VA 811, Forest, 10/30/92, C, 92001387

Saint Stephen's Episcopal Church, VA 663, Forest vicinity, 11/07/85, A, C, a, 85002766

Three Otters, W of jct. of Rte. 838 and VA 43, Bedford vicinity, 9/15/70, C, 70000785

Woodbourne, NE of Forest off VA 609, Forest vicinity, 7/02/73, C, 73001997

Bedford Independent City

Avenel, 413 Avenel Ave., Bedford (Independent City), 1/30/92, C, 92000003

Bedford Historic District, Roughly bounded by Longwood, Bedford, and Mountain Aves., Peaks, Oak, Grove, and Washington Sts., Bedford (Independent City), 10/04/84, A, C, 84000031

Bedford Historic Meetinghouse, 153 W. Main St., Bedford (Independent City), 1/31/78, A, C, a, 78003182

Bellevue, VA 643, 1 mi. E of Goode, Goode vicinity, 12/19/90, A, B, C, 89001917

Burks—Guy—Hagen House, 520 Peaks St., Bedford (Independent City), 12/19/85, B, C, 85003201

Bland County

Mountain Glen, 1 mi. SE of Ceres, Ceres vicinity, 1/24/91, C, 90002161

Sharon Lutheran Church and Cemetery, W of Ceres on VA 42, Ceres vicinity, 2/31/79, C, a, 79003030

Botetourt County

Annandale, VA 608, 1.5 mi. E of jct. with VA 609, Gilmore Mills vicinity, 2/11/93, C, 93000039

Bessemer Archaeological Site (44 BO 26), Address Restricted, Eagle Rock vicinity, 12/15/84, D, 84000807

Breckinridge Mill, W of Fincastle on VA 600, Fincastle vicinity, 7/30/80, A, B, C, 80004172

Callie Furnace, 1.5 mi. N of Glen Wilton in the George Washington National Forest, Glen Wilton vicinity, 1/21/74, A, 74002108

Fincastle Historic District, Roughly bounded by Carper, Hancock, Catawba, and Back Sts., and Griffin Alley, Fincastle, 11/12/69, A, C, 69000224

Looney Mill Creek Site, Address Restricted, Buchanan vicinity, 8/03/78, D, 78003007

Nininger's Mill, S of Daleville, Daleville vicinity, 7/30/80, A, C, 80004171

Phoenix Bridge, NW of Eagle Rock off VA 615 over Craig Creek, Eagle Rock vicinity, 6/10/75, A, C, 75002015

Prospect Hill, Off VA 606, Fincastle vicinity, 12/28/79, C, 79003031

Roaring Run Furnace, NW of Eagle Rock on VA 621, Eagle Rock vicinity, 3/21/83, A, C, D, 83003263

Santillane, W of U.S. 220, Fincastle vicinity, 7/24/74, C, 74002107

Springwood Truss Bridge, VA 630 over James River, Springwood, 4/15/78, C, 78003009

Varney's Falls Dam, 1 mi. E of jct. of VA 608 and VA 609 on the James R., Gillmore Mills vicinity, 10/14/93, A, C, 93001127

Wheatland Manor, N side VA 639 1/4 mi. SE of jct. with VA 638, Fincastle vicinity, 2/05/92, C, 91002040

Wiloma, Off US 220, Fincastle vicinity, 11/22/85, C, 85002913

Wilson Warehouse, Lower and Washington Sts., Buchanan, 1/26/78, A, C, 78003008

Bristol Independent City

Bristol Railroad Station, State and Washington Sts., Bristol (Independent City), 11/28/80, A, C, 80004173

Bristol Virginia—Tennessee Slogan Sign, E. State St., Bristol (Independent City), 9/08/88, A, b, 88001568

Virginia Intermont College, Moore and Harmeling Sts., Bristol (Independent City), 10/04/84, A, C, 84000032

Brunswick County

Bentfield, SW of Lawrenceville off U.S. 58 and VA 656, Lawrenceville vicinity, 1/24/74, C, 74002109

Brick House, VA 659, White Plains vicinity, 7/08/82, A, B, C, 82004544

Brunswick County Courthouse Square, U.S. 58, Lawrenceville, 12/31/74, C, 74002110

Fort Christanna, Address Restricted, Lawrenceville vicinity, 7/16/80, D, 80004175

Gholson Bridge, S of Lawrenceville on VA 715 at Meherrin River, Lawrenceville vicinity, 5/05/78, C, 78003010

Hobson's Choice, E of Alberta on VA 606, Alberta vicinity, 3/18/80, B, C, 80004174

St. Paul's College, St. Paul's College campus, Lawrenceville, 6/27/79, A, 79003032

Buchanan County

Buchanan County Courthouse, Walnut and Main Sts., Grundy, 9/16/82, A, C, 82004545

Buckingham County

Bryn Arvon and Gwyn Arvon, VA 675, Arvonia, 1/03/91, A, C, 90002111

Buckingham Courthouse Historic District, Both sides of U.S. 60, Buckingham, 11/12/69, C, 69000225

Buckingham Female Collegiate Institute Historic District, VA 617, Gravel Hill, 10/04/84, A, 84000035

Francisco, Peter, House, SE of Dillwyn, 0.9 mi. S of SR 626, Dillwyn vicinity, 3/16/72, B, C, 72001386

Mount Ida, VA 610, New Canton vicinity, 4/27/87, C, 87000624

Perry Hill, VA 56, Saint Joy vicinity, 10/30/80, C, 80004176

Seven Islands Archeological and Historic District, Address Restricted, Arvonia vicinity, 7/03/91, C, D, 91000832

Stanton Family Cemetery, VA 677 E side, 0.4 mi. N of jct. with VA 676, Diana Mills vicinity, 4/29/93, A, d, 93000350

Woodside, VA 631 N side, 0.5 mi. SW of jct. with US 60, Buckingham vicinity, 11/16/93, C, 93000040

Buena Vista Independent City

Old Courthouse, 2110 Magnolia Ave., Buena Vista (Independent City), 5/25/79, A, C, 79003297

Southern Seminary Main Building, Jct. of Ivy and Park Aves., Buena Vista (Independent City), 4/13/72, A, C, 72001501

Campbell County

Avoca, N of Altavista on US 29, Altavista vicinity, 9/16/82, C, 82004546

Blenheim, 2.4 mi. SW of Spring Mills, Spring Mills vicinity, 5/31/79, C, 79003033

Campbell County Courthouse, US 501, Rustburg, 10/29/81, A, C, 81000638

Cat Rock Sluice of the Roanoke Navigation, W of Brookneal, Brookneal vicinity, 3/25/80, A, C, 80004177

Federal Hill, S of Forest on VA 623, Forest vicinity, 9/09/82, A, B, C, 82004547

Green Hill, SW of Long Island near jct. of Rtes. 633 and 728, Long Island vicinity, 11/12/69, A, C, 69000226

Mansion Truss Bridge, VA 640 over Staunton River, Mansion vicinity, 4/15/78, C, 78003011

Mount Athos, Address Restricted, Kelly vicinity, 7/24/75, A, D, 75002016

Shady Grove, E of Gladys on VA 650, Gladys vicinity, 8/26/82, C, 82004548

Caroline County

Camden, Address Restricted, Port Royal vicinity, 11/12/69, C, D, NHL, 69000228

Caroline County Courthouse, Main St. and Court House Lane, Bowling Green, 5/25/73, C, 73001999

Caroline County—Continued

Edge Hill, W of Woodford on VA 632, Woodford vicinity, 2/10/83, A, B, C, D, 83003264

Gay Mont, Off U.S. 17 near jct. with U.S. 301, Port Royal vicinity, 5/19/72, C, e, g, 72001387

Hazelwood, Address Restricted, Port Royal vicinity, 1/11/74, A, B, D, 74002111

Old Mansion, S of jct. of U.S. 301 and VA 207, Bowling Green vicinity, 11/12/69, C, 69000227

Port Royal Historic District, Roughly bounded by Rappahannock River, Roys Run, Rt. 17, and Goldenville Creek, Port Royal, 2/16/70, A, C, 70000786

Prospect Hill, SE of Fredericksburg off U.S. 17, Fredericksburg vicinity, 12/12/76, C, 76002096

Santee, Off VA 610, Corbin vicinity, 5/07/79, A, C, 79003034

Spring Grove, Address Restricted, Oak Corner vicinity, 12/12/76, C, 76002097

Carroll County

Allen, Sidna, House, N of Fancy Gap on U.S. 52, Fancy Gap vicinity, 7/15/74, B, C, 74002112

Carroll County Courthouse, 515 Main St., Hillsville, 7/08/82, A, C, 82004549

Snake Creek Farm Historic District, VA 670 S of jct. with VA 674, Hillsville vicinity, 1/11/91, C, 90002138

Charles City County

Belle Air, N of VA 5, Charles City vicinity, 7/18/74, C, 74002232

Berkeley, 8 mi. W of Charles City, Charles City vicinity, 11/11/71, B, C, NHL, 71001040

Cary, Lott, Birth Site, NW of Charles City on VA 602, Charles City vicinity, 7/30/80, A, 80004883

Charles City County Courthouse, VA 5, Charles City, 11/12/69, C, 69000335

Edgewood, W of Charles City on VA 5, Charles City vicinity, 2/10/83, A, C, 83003265

Eppes Island, Address Restricted, Hopewell vicinity, 11/12/69, A, D, 69000337

Evelynton, VA 5 E of VA 609, Charles City vicinity, 8/17/89, C, 89000486

Glebe of Westover Parish, SW of Ruthville off VA 615, Ruthville vicinity, 6/05/75, A, C, a, 75002108

Greenway, On VA 5, Charles City, 11/12/69, B, C, 69000336

Hardens, W of Lamptie Hill on VA 5, Lamptie Hill vicinity, 2/10/83, A, C, 83003266

Kittiewan, 2.5 mi. SE of New Hope, New Hope vicinity, 12/28/79, C, D, 79003316

Margots, NE of Tettington off VA 621, Tettington vicinity, 8/17/73, C, 73002203

Mount Stirling, VA 155 E side, 3200 ft. NNE of jct. with VA 614, Providence Forge vicinity, 2/04/93, C, 93000005

North Bend, VA 619, Weyanoke vicinity, 8/21/89, C, 89001107

Piney Grove, VA 615, Holdcroft vicinity, 11/26/85, A, C, 85003052

Rowe, The, 3 mi. SW of Rustic, Rustic vicinity, 3/28/80, C, 80004442

Shirley, 5 mi. N of Hopewell off VA 608, Hopewell vicinity, 10/01/69, C, NHL, 69000328

Tyler, John, House, 4 mi. E of Charles City on VA 5, Charles City vicinity, 10/15/66, B, NHL, 66000922

Upper Shirley, W of Charles City on SR 608, Charles City vicinity, 10/29/82, C, 82001884

Upper Weyanoke, S. of Charles City on VA 619, Charles City vicinity, 12/09/80, C, D, 80004441

Westover, 7 mi. W of Charles City on VA 5, Charles City vicinity, 10/15/66, B, C, NHL, 66000923

Westover Church, 5 mi. W of Charles City off VA 5, Charles City, 12/05/72, A, C, a, 72001502

Weyanoke, Address Restricted, Charles City vicinity, 3/10/80, A, C, D, 80004406

Woodburn, NW of Charles on VA 618, Charles City vicinity, 12/12/78, B, C, 78003183

Charlotte County

Charlotte County Courthouse, VA 40 and VA 47, Charlotte Court House, 5/07/80, C, 80004178

Greenfield, E of Charlotte Court House on VA 656, Charlotte Court House vicinity, 4/02/73, A, C, 73002000

Mulberry Hill, N of Randolph on VA 641, Randolph vicinity, 3/20/73, B, C, 73002001

Red Hill, SE of Brookneal on SR 677, Brookneal vicinity, 2/14/78, A, B, c, e, f, 78003012

Roanoke Plantation, W of Saxe off VA 746, Saxe vicinity, 4/11/73, A, B, 73002002

Staunton Hill, SW of jct. of Rtes. 619 and 693, Brookneal vicinity, 10/01/69, C, 69000229

Charlottesville Independent City

Albemarle County Courthouse Historic District, Courthouse Sq. and surrounding properties, Charlottesville (Independent City), 6/30/72, A, C, 72001503

Anderson Brothers Building [Charlottesville MRA], 1417-1427 University Ave., Charlottesville (Independent City), 10/21/82, C, 82001797

Armstrong Knitting Factory [Charlottesville MRA], 700 Harris St., Charlottesville (Independent City), 10/21/82, A, C, 82001798

Barringer Mansion [Charlottesville MRA], 1404 Jefferson Park Ave., Charlottesville (Independent City), 10/21/82, C, 82001799

Belmont [Charlottesville MRA], 759 Belmont Ave., Charlottesville (Independent City), 10/21/82, C, 82001800

Carter-Gilmer House [Charlottesville MRA], 802 E. Jefferson St., Charlottesville (Independent City), 10/21/82, C, 82001801

Charlottesville and Albemarle County Courthouse Historic District, Roughly bounded by Park, Water, Saxton, and Main Sts., Charlottesville (Independent City), 7/28/82, A, C, 82004904

Dabney-Thompson House [Charlottesville MRA], 1602 Gordon Ave., Charlottesville (Independent City), 1/10/84, C, 84003498

Delevan Baptist Church [Charlottesville MRA], 632 W. Main St., Charlottesville (Independent City), 10/21/82, C, a, 82001802

Enderly [Charlottesville MRA], 603 Watson Ave., Charlottesville (Independent City), 10/21/82, C, 82001803

Ficklin-Crawford Cottage [Charlottesville MRA], 1200 Carlton Ave., Charlottesville (Independent City), 10/21/82, C, 82001804

Four Acres [Charlottesville MRA], 1314 Rugby Rd., Charlottesville (Independent City), 10/21/82, C, 82001805

Gardner-Mays Cottage [Charlottesville MRA], 1022 Grove St., Charlottesville (Independent City), 10/21/82, C, 82001806

Hard Bargain [Charlottesville MRA], 1105 Park St., Charlottesville (Independent City), 1/10/84, C, 84003521

Hotel Gleason/Albemarle Hotel, Imperial Cafe [Charlottesville MRA], 617-619 W. Main St., Charlottesville (Independent City), 8/10/83, C, 83003267

House at Pireus [Charlottesville MRA], 302 Riverside Ave., Charlottesville (Independent City), 8/10/83, A, a, 83003268

King Lumber Company Warehouse [Charlottesville MRA], 608 Preston Ave., Charlottesville (Independent City), 8/10/83, A, 83003269

King-Runkle House [Charlottesville MRA], 201 14th St., NW, Charlottesville (Independent City), 8/10/83, C, 83003270

Lewis Farm [Charlottesville MRA], 1201 Jefferson St., Charlottesville (Independent City), 10/21/82, C, 82001807

Locust Grove [Charlottesville MRA], 810 Locust Ave., Charlottesville (Independent City), 10/21/82, C, 82001808

McConnell-Neve House [Charlottesville MRA], 228 14th St., NW, Charlottesville (Independent City), 8/10/83, C, 83003271

Morea, 209-211 Sprigg Lane, Charlottesville (Independent City), 5/03/84, A, C, 84003522

Mount Zion Baptist Church, 105 Ridge St., Charlottesville (Independent City), 10/15/92, A, a, 92001388

Oak Lawn, Cherry Ave. and 9th St., Charlottesville (Independent City), 5/25/73, C, 73002204

Patton Mansion [Charlottesville MRA], 1018 W. Main St., Charlottesville (Independent City), 10/21/82, C, 82001809

Paxton Place [Charlottesville MRA], 503 W. Main St., Charlottesville (Independent City), 10/21/82, C, 82001810

Peyton-Ellington Building [Charlottesville MRA], 711 W. Main St., Charlottesville (Independent City), 10/21/82, C, a, 82001811

Piereus Store [Charlottesville MRA], 1901 E. Market St., Charlottesville (Independent City), 8/10/83, A, 83003272

Charlottesville Independent City— Continued

Pitts-Inge [Charlottesville MRA], 331-333 W. Main St., Charlottesville (Independent City), 10/21/82, C, 82001812

Ridge Street Historic District [Charlottesville MRA], 200-700 Ridge St., Charlottesville (Independent City), 10/21/82, A, C, 82001813

Rose Cottage/Peyton House [Charlottesville MRA], 800 Delevan St., Charlottesville (Independent City), 8/10/83, C, 83003273

Rotunda, University of Virginia, University of Virginia, Charlottesville (Independent City), 10/15/66, A, e, NHL, 66000937

Rugby Road-University Corner Historic District, Roughly bounded by University Ave., Wayside Pl., 14th St., and US 29, Charlottesville (Independent City), 2/16/84, A, C, 84003523

Stonefield [Charlottesville MRA], 1204 Rugby Rd., Charlottesville (Independent City), 1/10/84, A, C, 84003524

Timberlake-Branham House [Charlottesville MRA], 1512 E. Market St., Charlottesville (Independent City), 1/10/84, C, 84003525

Tonsler, Benjamin, House [Charlottesville MRA], 327 6th St., Charlottesville (Independent City), 8/10/83, B, 83003274

Turner-LaRowe House [Charlottesville MRA], 1 University Court, Charlottesville (Independent City), 8/10/83, C, 83003275

University Of Virginia Historic District, Bounded by University and Jefferson Park Aves., and Hospital and McCormick Rds., Charlottesville (Independent City), 11/20/70, A, B, NHL, 70000865

Updike, Robert L., House [Charlottesville MRA], 620 Prospect Ave., Charlottesville (Independent City), 8/10/83, C, 83003276

Vowles, John, House, 1111–1113 W. Main St., Charlottesville (Independent City), 11/02/89, C, 89001928

Wertland Street Historic District [Charlottesville MRA], Wertland St. between 10th and 14th Sts., Charlottesville (Independent City), 2/14/85, A, C, 85000298

White Cross-Huntley Hall [Charlottesville MRA], 152 Stribling Ave., Charlottesville (Independent City), 10/21/82, C, 82001814

Woolen Mills Chapel [Charlottesville MRA], 1819 E. Market St., Charlottesville (Independent City), 10/21/82, C, a, 82001815

Wynhurst [Charlottesville MRA], 605 Preston Pl., Charlottesville (Independent City), 10/21/82, C, 82001816

Young Building [Charlottesville MRA], 1102 Carlton Ave., Charlottesville (Independent City), 10/21/82, C, 82001817

Chesapeake Independent City

Dismal Swamp Canal [Dismal Swamp Canal and Associated Development, Southeast Virginia and Northeast North Carolina MPS], Runs between Chesapeake, VA and South Mills, NC, Chesapeake, 6/06/88, A, C, g, 88000528

Great Bridge Battle Site, Both sides of the Albemarle and Chesapeake Canal between Oak Grove and Great Bridge, Chesapeake (Independent City), 3/28/73, A, 73002205

South Norfolk Historic District, Roughly bounded by Hull St., Poindexter, D St., 16th St., B St., Seaboard Ave., Richmond Ave., and Byrd Ave., Chesapeake (Independent City), 1/27/89, C, 88003133

Chesterfield County

Azurest South, 2900 Boisseau St., Petersburg vicinity, 12/30/93, C, 93001464

Bellona Arsenal, Off VA 673, NW of jct. with Rte. 147, Midlothian vicinity, 5/06/71, A, C, 71000975

Bellwood, Address Restricted, Richmond vicinity, 12/12/78, A, C, 78003013

Bon Air Historic District, Roughly bounded by Forest Hill Rd., N. Robert, W. Bon View Dr., and McRae Rd., Richmond vicinity, 11/15/88, A, C, 88002178

Castlewood, VA 10, Chesterfield, 11/21/76, C, 76002099

Chester Presbyterian Church, Jct. of Osborne Rd. and VA 10, Chester, 11/21/76, A, C, a, b, 76002098

Chesterfield County Courthouse and Courthouse Square, N side VA 10, 350 ft. E of jct. with VA 655, Chesterfield, 8/18/92, A, C, 92001008

Dinwiddie County Pullman Car, Hallsboro Yard, NE of jct. of VA 606 and VA 671, Midlothian vicinity, 7/03/91, A, C, 91000834

Eppington, S of jct. of VA 621 and 602, Winterpock vicinity, 11/12/69, C, 69000230

Hallsborough Tavern, W of Midlothian on U.S. 60, Midlothian vicinity, 3/17/80, A, C, 80004181

Kingsland, 1608 Willis Rd., Chimney Corner vicinity, 9/18/75, C, 75002019

Magnolia Grange, VA 10, Chesterfield, 3/17/80, A, C, 80004179

Olive Hill, 0.5 mi. W of Matoaca off VA 36, Matoaca vicinity, 4/03/75, C, 75002017

Pleasant View, 1.5 mi. E of Midlothian on VA 677, Midlothian vicinity, 6/10/75, A, C, 75002018

Swift Creek Mill, N of Colonial Heights on U.S. 1, Colonial Heights vicinity, 1/11/74, A, C, 74002113

Vawter Hall and Old President's House, Virginia State University campus, Ettrick, 5/07/80, A, C, 80004180

Clarke County

Annefield, E of jct. of Rtes. 633 and 652, Boyce vicinity, 11/12/69, C, 69000231

Berryville Historic District, Jct. of US 7 & 340, Main, Church, & Buckmarsh Sts., Berryville, 11/03/87, A, C, g, 87001881

Bethel Memorial Church, Co. Rt. 622, White Post vicinity, 2/07/91, C, a, 89001927

Blandy Experimental Farm Historic District, US 50/17 S side, 4 mi. W of the Shenandoah R., Boyce vicinity, 11/12/92, A, C, 92001580

Burwell-Morgan Mill, At jct. of Rtes. 723 and 255, Millwood, 11/12/69, A, B, 69000233

Carter Hall, NE of Millwood off VA 255, Millwood, 7/24/73, B, C, 73002003

Clarke County Courthouse (Old), 104 N. Church St., Berryville, 7/07/83, C, 83003277

Fairfield, E of jct. of Rtes. 340 and 610, Berryville vicinity, 2/26/70, B, C, 70000787

Farnley, VA 658 at VA 622, White Post vicinity, 11/02/89, C, 89001914

Greenway Court, 1 mi. S of White Post on VA 277, White Post vicinity, 10/15/66, A, NHL, 66000829

Greenway Historic District, Roughly bounded by the Shenandoah R., the Warren Co. line, VA 340 and VA 618, Boyce vicinity, 11/04/93, A, B, C, 93001133

Guilford, VA 644 S side, 0.5 mi. W of jct. with VA 658, White Post vicinity, 2/04/93, C, 93000004

Huntingdon, N of Boyce, Boyce vicinity, 5/25/79, A, C, 79003035

Long Branch, W of jct. of CR 626 and 624, Millwood vicinity, 10/01/69, C, 69000232

Lucky Hit, VA 628 S side, 4500 ft. NE of jct. with VA 658, White Post vicinity, 8/12/93, C, 93000834

Old Chapel, 3 mi. N of Millwood off U.S. 340, Millwood vicinity, 4/02/73, A, C, a, d, 73002004

River House, US 17/50, 2.5 mi. E of Millwood, Millwood vicinity, 12/23/93, C, 93001440

Saratoga, SE of jct. of Rtes. 723 and 617, Boyce vicinity, 2/26/70, B, C, NHL, 70000788

Scaleby, Co. Rd. 723 S of jct. with US 340, Boyce vicinity, 12/28/90, C, 90002000

Tuleyries, The, 1.5 mi. E of White Post off VA 628, White Post vicinity, 8/07/72, C, 72001388

White Post Historic District, VA 658 and 628, White Post, 9/29/83, B, C, 83003278

Clifton Forge Independent City

Clifton Forge Commercial Historic District, Roughly, E. Ridgeway St. from Roxbury St. to Main St. and Main from Commercial Ave. to Railroad St., Clifton Forge (Independent City), 1/28/92, A, C, 91002015

Colonial Heights Independent City

Conjurer's Field Archeological Site (44CF20), Address Restricted, Colonial Heights (Independent city), 10/25/90, D, 90001139

Ellerslie, Ellerslie Rd., Colonial Heights (Independent City), 12/04/73, A, C, 73002206

Fort Clifton Archeological Site, Address Restricted, Colonial Heights (Independent City) vicinity, 2/03/81, A, D, 81000639

Oak Hill, 151 Carroll Ave., Colonial Heights (Independent City), 7/30/74, C, 74002233

Colonial Heights Independent City—Continued

Violet Bank, Royal Oak Ave., Colonial Heights (Independent City), 7/30/74, A, C, 74002234

Covington Independent City

Covington Historic District, Roughly bounded by the Jackson R., Monroe Ave., CSX RR tracks, and Maple Ave., Covington, 2/21/91, A, C, 91000099

Craig County

Craig Healing Springs, VA 658, Craig Springs, 7/21/82, C, a, 82004551
New Castle Historic District, Main and Court Sts., New Castle, 10/25/73, A, C, 73002005
New Castle Historic District (Boundary Increase), Boyd, Broad, Court, Main, Market, Middle, Race and Walnut Sts., VA 42 and VA 311, Mitchell Dr. and Salem Ave., New Castle, 6/10/93, A, C, 93000497

Culpeper County

Culpeper Historic District, Roughly bounded by Edmonson St., Southern RR, Stevens, & West Sts., Culpeper, 10/22/87, A, C, 87001809
Elmwood, US 522 W, Culpeper vicinity, 1/16/86, C, 86000075
Farley, N of Brandy Station on VA 679, S of Hazel River, Brandy Station vicinity, 5/06/76, A, C, 76002100
Greenville, NE of Raccoon's Ford, Raccoon's Ford vicinity, 3/17/80, C, 80004184
Greenwood, 1931 Orange Rd., Culpeper, 11/22/85, C, 85002914
Hill Mansion, 501 East St., Culpeper, 3/17/80, A, C, 80004182
Hill, A. P., Boyhood Home, 102 N. Main St., Culpeper, 10/02/73, B, C, 73002006
Little Fork Church, Jct. of Rtes. 624 and 726, Rixeyville vicinity, 11/12/69, C, a, 69000234
Locust Grove, Locust Grove Farm, VA 736, Rapidan, 10/10/85, C, 85003131
Madden's Tavern, VA 610, Lignum vicinity, 8/16/84, A, 84003526
Mitchells Presbyterian Church, VA 652, Mitchells, 5/07/80, B, C, 80004183
Rapidan Historic District, Jct. of VA 614, VA 615, and VA 673, Rapidan, 5/08/87, A, C, 87000723
Salubria, E of jct. of Rtes. 3 and 663, Stevensburg vicinity, 2/16/70, A, C, 70000789
Slaughter—Hill House, 306 N. West St., Culpeper, 3/16/89, C, 89000203

Cumberland County

Ampthill, W side of VA 602, 3 mi. N of jct. with VA 45, Cartersville vicinity, 4/13/72, C, 72001389
Cartersville Bridge, VA 45 over James River, Cartersville vicinity, 9/14/72, A, C, 72001390
Cartersville Historic District, Roughly bounded by VA 45, VA 649 and VA 656, Cartersville, 6/10/93, A, C, 93000505
Clifton, N of Hamilton off VA 690, Hamilton vicinity, 6/19/73, B, C, 73002007
Grace Church, W of Cumberland on VA 632, Ca Ira vicinity, 10/30/80, A, C, a, 80004185
Morven, VA 45, 1/2 mi. S of Cartersville, Cartersville vicinity, 12/28/90, C, 90002014
Muddy Creek Mill, S of Cartersville off VA 684, Tamworth vicinity, 10/09/74, A, C, 74002114
Needham, VA 45, 1.4 mi. N of jct. with US 460, Farmville vicinity, 11/10/88, A, B, C, 88002059
Thornton, Charles Irving, Tombstone, W of Cumberland on Oak Hill Rd., Cumberland vicinity, 11/25/80, B, 80004186

Danville Independent City

Danville Historic District, Roughly bounded by Main, Green, and Paxton Sts., and Memorial Hospital, Danville (Independent City), 4/11/73, A, C, 73002207
Danville Public Library, 975 Main St., Danville (Independent City), 11/12/69, A, C, 69000338
Danville Tobacco Warehouse and Residential District, Off U.S. 58, Danville (Independent City), 7/14/82, A, C, D, 82004552
Downtown Danville Historic District, Roughly bounded by Memorial Dr. and High, Patton and Ridge Sts., Danville (Independent City), 8/12/93, A, C, 93000830
Hotel Danville, 600 Main St., Danville (Independent City), 12/06/84, A, C, 84000658
Main Street Methodist Episcopal Church South, 767 Main St., Danville (independent City), 12/06/90, C, a, 90001822
Penn-Wyatt House, 862 Main St., Danville (Independent City), 9/07/79, C, 79003317

Dickenson County

Dickenson County Courthouse, Main and McClure Sts., Clintwood, 9/16/82, C, 82004553

Dinwiddie County

Burlington, W of Petersburg off VA 600, Petersburg vicinity, 4/30/76, C, 76002102
Burnt Quarter, SW of jct. of Rtes. 627, 613, and 645, Dinwiddie vicinity, 11/25/69, A, C, 69000235
Conover Archaeological Site, Address Restricted, Carson vicinity, 3/28/85, D, 85000647

Dinwiddie County Courthouse, Jct. of U.S. 1 and VA 619, Dinwiddie, 3/21/73, A, C, 73002008
Five Forks Battlefield, 12 mi. W of Petersburg on CR 627 at Church Rd., Petersburg vicinity, 10/15/66, A, NHL, NPS, 66000830
Mansfield, W of Petersburg on VA 601, Petersburg vicinity, 5/28/76, C, 76002103
Mayfield Cottage, Central State Hospital Grounds, Petersburg vicinity, 11/12/69, A, C, 69000236
Petersburg National Battlefield, SE, S, and SW of Petersburg, Petersburg vicinity, 10/15/66, A, d, f, NPS, 66000831
Rose Bower, VA 665 S of jct. with VA 40, Stoney Creek vicinity, 2/05/91, A, C, 91000020
Sappony Church, S of Sappony Creek off VA 692, McKenny vicinity, 4/30/76, B, C, a, 76002101
Wales, W of Petersburg off VA 632, Petersburg vicinity, 12/23/74, B, C, 74002115
Williamson Site, Address Restricted, Dinwiddie vicinity, 12/03/69, D, 69000237

Emporia Independent City

Greensville County Courthouse Complex, S. Main St., Emporia (Independent City), 7/21/83, A, C, 83003279
Klugel, H. T., Architectural Sheet Metal Work Building, 135 Atlantic Ave., Emporia (Independent City), 4/02/73, C, 73002208
Old Merchants and Farmers Bank Building, S. Main St., Emporia (Independent City), 5/07/79, A, C, 79003278
Village View, 221 Briggs St., Emporia (Independent City), 9/16/82, A, C, 82004554

Essex County

Blandfield, E of jct. of Rtes. 624 and U.S. 17, Caret vicinity, 11/12/69, C, 69000238
Brooke's Bank, 1 mi. E of Loretto, 1.4 mi. N of VA 17, Loretto vicinity, 9/28/71, C, 71000976
Cherry Walk, S of Dunbrooke on VA 620, Dunbrooke vicinity, 2/10/83, C, 83003280
Elmwood, SW of jct. of Rtes. 640 and U.S. 17, Loretto vicinity, 9/15/70, C, 70000790
Glebe House of St. Anne's Parish, 2.5 mi. NE of Champlain on N bank of Farmers Hall Creek, Champlain vicinity, 3/03/75, A, C, a, 75002020
Glencairn, N of Chance off U.S. 17, Chance vicinity, 5/14/79, C, 79003036
Linden, US 17 SW side, 0.5 mi. S of Champlain, Champlain vicinity, 10/15/92, C, 92001397
Port Micou, VA 674, at Rappahannock R., Loretto vicinity, 2/06/92, A, C, 91002041
Tappahannock Historic District, Roughly bounded by Queen St., Church Lane, Rappahannock River and the grounds of St. Margaret's School, Tappahannock, 4/02/73, A, C, 73002009
Vauter's Church, 1 mi. NW of Loretto on U.S. 17, Loretto vicinity, 12/05/72, A, C, a, 72001391

Essex County—Continued

Wheatland, VA 638 between US 17 and the Rappahanock River, Loretto, 12/19/90, A, C, 89001918

Woodlawn, NE of Millers Tavern, Millers Tavern vicinity, 7/16/80, C, 80004187

Fairfax County

Belvoir Mansion Ruins and the Fairfax Grave, SE of intersection of 23rd St. and Belvoir Rd., Fort Belvoir, 6/04/73, D, 73002337

Civil War Fort Sites (Boundary Increase), S of Washington on Rosier Bluff, N of Washington off George Washington Parkway, McLean, vicinity, 9/13/78, A, NPS, 78003439

Clifton Historic District, Roughly bounded by Popes Head Creek, Water St., Dell Ave., Chestnut & Chapel Rds., Clifton, 8/15/85, A, C, 85001786

Colvin Run Mill, S of Great Falls at 10017 Colvin Run Rd., Great Falls vicinity, 8/16/77, A, C, 77001487

Cornwell Farm, SE of Great Falls, 9414 Georgetown Pike, Great Falls vicinity, 4/13/77, C, 77001488

Dranesville Tavern, 11919 Leesburg Pike, Dranesville vicinity, 11/09/72, A, C, b, 72001393

Fairfax Arms, 10712 Old Colchester Rd., Colchester, 5/21/79, A, C, 79003037

Fort Hunt, Mount Vernon Memorial Hwy., Alexandria vicinity, 3/26/80, A, NPS, 80000353

Frying Pan Meetinghouse, 2615 Centreville Rd., Floris vicinity, 2/05/91, A, C, a, 91000016

Gunston Hall, 15 mi. S of Alexandria on VA 242, Lorton vicinity, 10/15/66, B, C, NHL, 66000832

Herndon Depot, Elden St., Herndon, 6/18/79, A, 79003039

Herndon Historic District, Roughly bounded by Locust, Spring, Pearl, Monroe, Station and Vine Sts., Herndon, 1/11/91, A, C, 90002121

Hope Park Mill and Miller's House, 12124 Pope's Head Rd., Fairfax vicinity, 8/15/77, A, 77001486

Huntley, 6918 Harrison Lane, Alexandria vicinity, 11/03/72, A, C, 72001392

Langley Fork Historic District, Jct. of Georgetown Pike and Old Chain Bridge Rd., Langley, 10/19/82, A, C, a, 82001818

Moorefield, Moorefield Hill Pl., Vienna, 4/19/78, B, a, 78003014

Mount Vernon, 7 mi. S of Alexandria on George Washington Memorial Pkwy., Alexandria vicinity, 10/15/66, B, NHL, 66000833

Northwest No. 3 Boundary Marker of the Original District of Columbia [Boundary Markers of the Original District of Columbia MPS], 4013 N. Tazewell St., Arlington, 2/01/91, A, b, 91000005

Pohick Church, 9201 Richmond Hwy., Lorton, 10/16/69, A, C, a, 69000239

Pope-Leighey House, E of Accotink off U.S. 1, Accotink vicinity, 12/18/70, C, b, e, g, 70000791

Potomac Canal Historic District, E of Great Falls, Great Falls vicinity, 10/18/79, A, C, NHL, NPS, 79003038

Salona, 1214 Buchanan St., McLean, 7/24/73, A, C, 73002011

St. Mary's Church, 5605 Vogue Rd., Fairfax Station, 7/01/76, A, B, a, 76002104

Sully, N of jct. of Rtes. 28 and U.S. 50, Chantilly vicinity, 12/18/70, A, C, 70000793

Woodlawn Plantation, W of jct. of U.S. 1 and Rte. 235, Accotink vicinity, 2/26/70, A, C, 70000792

Fairfax Independent City

29 Diner, 10536 Lee Hwy., Fairfax (Independent City), 10/29/92, C, g, 92001370

City of Fairfax Historic District, Jct. of VA 236 and VA 123, Fairfax (Independent City), 8/27/87, A, C, 87001432

Fairfax County Courthouse, 4000 Chain Bridge Rd., Fairfax (Independent City), 5/03/74, A, C, 74002235

Fairfax County Courthouse and Jail (Boundary Increase), 4000 Chain Bridge Rd., Fairfax (Independent City), 10/01/81, C, 81000673

Fairfax Public School, 10209 Main St., Fairfax (Independent City), 10/21/92, A, 92001367

Ratcliffe-Logan-Allison House, 200 E. Main St., Fairfax (Independent City), 2/16/73, A, C, 73002209

Falls Church Independent City

Birch House, 312 E. Broad St., Falls Church (Independent City), 10/26/77, B, C, D, 77001534

Cherry Hill, 312 Park Ave., Falls Church (Independent City), 7/26/73, B, C, 73002210

Falls Church, 115 E. Fairfax St., Falls Church (Independent City), 2/26/70, A, C, a, 70000870

Mount Hope, 203 Oak St., Falls Church (Independent City), 10/04/84, C, 84000037

Fauquier County

Ashleigh, S of Delaplane, off U.S. 17, Delaplane vicinity, 8/14/73, C, 73002012

Brentmoor, 173 Main St., Warrenton, 1/20/78, B, C, 78003016

Germantown Archeological Sites, Address Restricted, Midland vicinity, 9/16/82, D, 82004555

Loretta, US 17 E side, 3500 ft. N of Warrenton town limits, Warrenton vicinity, 12/23/93, C, 93001442

Melrose, N of Casanova on VA 602, Casanova vicinity, 2/10/83, A, C, 83003281

Mill House, US 50, Middleburg vicinity, 1/12/84, A, C, 84003527

Monterosa, 343 Culpeper St., Warrenton, 1/25/91, B, C, 90002193

Oak Hill, 2.2 mi. S of Delaplane, Delaplane vicinity, 6/18/73, B, C, 73002013

Oakley, E of Upperville on U.S. 50, Upperville vicinity, 2/24/83, A, C, 83003282

Old Fauquier County Jail, Fauquier County Courthouse Sq., Warrenton, 1/20/78, A, C, 78003015

Upperville Historic District, Including the entire village extending approximately 1 mi. along Rt. 50, Upperville, 10/18/72, A, C, a, 72001394

Warrenton Historic District, Roughly Main, Waterloo, Alexandria, Winchester, Culpeper, High, Falmouth, Lee, and Horner Sts., Warrenton, 10/13/83, A, B, C, 83004243

Waverly, S of Middleburg on VA 626, Middleburg vicinity, 3/26/79, C, 79003040

Floyd County

Floyd Presbyterian Church, U.S. 221, Floyd, 5/17/76, A, C, a, 76002105

Fluvanna County

Bremo Plantation, W of Bremo Bluff off U.S. 15, Bremo Bluff vicinity, 11/12/69, A, C, NHL, 69000241

Bremo Slave Chapel, N of Bremo Bluff, Bremo Bluff vicinity, 3/17/80, A, C, a, b, 80004189

Fluvanna County Courthouse Historic District, Roughly bounded by VA 601, VA 15, and the Rivanna River, Palmyra, 9/22/71, C, 71000977

Glen Arvon, E of Bremo Bluff near jct. of VA 655 and VA 656, Bremo Bluff vicinity, 5/28/76, A, C, 76002106

Point of Fork Arsenal, Address Restricted, Columbia vicinity, 10/01/69, D, 69000242

Point of Fork Plantation, W of Columbia off VA 624, Columbia vicinity, 8/13/74, A, C, 74002116

Franklin County

Booker T. Washington National Monument, 15 mi. E of Rocky Mount on VA 122, Rocky Mount vicinity, 10/15/66, B, c, f, NPS, 66000834

Brooks—Brown House, VA 646, N of VA 890, Dickinson vicinity, 11/02/89, A, 89001930

Farm, The, US 220, Rocky Mount, 11/02/89, A, C, 89001910

Greer House, 206 E. Court St., Rocky Mount, 12/28/90, C, 90002011

Otter Creek Archaeological Site (44FR31), Address Restricted, Ferrum vicinity, 5/09/85, D, 85000986

Washington Iron Furnace, 108 Old Furnace Rd., Rocky Mount, 3/20/73, A, C, 73002014

Woods-Meade House, 118 Maple St., Rocky Mount, 7/08/82, C, 82004557

Franklin Independent City

Elms, The, Clay St., Franklin (Independent City), 9/09/82, B, C, 82004556

Franklin Independent City—Continued

Franklin Historic District, US 58 and US 258, Franklin (Independent City), 5/09/85, A, C, 85000988

Frederick County

Cather, Willa, Birthplace, NW of Gore on U.S. 50, Gore vicinity, 11/16/78, B, C, c, 78003017

Cedar Creek Battlefield and Belle Grove, On I-81 between Middletown and Strasburg, Middletown vicinity, 8/11/69, A, NHL, 69000243

Frederick County Poor Farm, VA 654 E side, S of jct. with VA 679, Round Hill vicinity, 8/12/93, A, C, 93000823

Hite, John, House, US 11, Bartonsville vicinity, 7/08/82, A, C, 82004558

Hopewell Friends Meetinghouse, W of Clear Brook off VA 672, Clear Brook vicinity, 3/28/80, A, C, a, 80004190

Monte Vista, 8100 US 11, Middletown vicinity, 11/16/87, A, C, 87002018

Newtown—Stephensburg Historic District, Roughly, Main St. from city limit to Farm View Dr. and adjacent areas of Mulberry and German Sts., Stephens City, 8/18/92, A, C, 92001033

Springdale Mill Complex, US 11, Bartonville vicinity, 7/08/82, A, C, 82004559

St. Thomas Chapel, Jct. of SR 1102 and 1105, Middletown, 4/11/73, A, C, a, 73002015

Willow Shade, Jct. of Frederick Co. Rd. and US 50, Winchester vicinity, 12/18/90, B, C, 90001925

Fredericksburg Independent City

Brompton, Hanover St. and Sunken Rd., Fredericksburg (Independent City), 7/24/79, A, C, 79003279

Chimneys, The, 623 Caroline St., Fredericksburg (Independent City), 4/03/75, C, 75002109

Farmers Bank of Fredericksburg, 900 Princess Anne St., Fredericksburg (Independent City), 8/11/83, A, C, 83003283

Federal Hill, S side of Hanover St. between Jackson and Prince Edward Sts., Fredericksburg (Independent City), 3/26/75, C, 75002110

Fredericksburg Gun Manufactory Site, Address Restricted, Fredericksburg (Independent City), 11/14/78, D, 78003184

Fredericksburg Historic District, Roughly bounded by Rappahannock River, Hazel Run, Prince Edward and Canal Sts., Fredericksburg (Independent City), 9/22/71, C, 71001053

Fredericksburg and Spotsylvania County Battlefields Memorial National Military Park, Fredericksburg and W and SW areas in Spotsylvania County, Fredericksburg (Independent City) vicinity, 10/15/66, A, B, C, d, f, NPS, 66000046

Kenmore, 1201 Washington Ave., Fredericksburg (Independent City), 6/04/69, C, NHL, 69000325

Monroe Law Office, 908 Charles St., Fredericksburg (Independent City), 11/13/66, B, NHL, 66000917

Presbyterian Church of Fredericksburg, SW of Princess Anne and George Sts., Fredericksburg (Independent City), 3/01/84, A, C, a, 84003534

Rising Sun Tavern, 1306 Caroline St., Fredericksburg (Independent City), 10/15/66, A, NHL, 66000919

Sentry Box, 133 Caroline St., Fredericksburg, 2/26/92, B, C, 90002135

Washington, Mary, House, 1200 Charles St., Fredericksburg (Independent City), 6/05/75, B, C, 75002111

Giles County

Giles County Courthouse, VA 100 and US 460, Pearisburg, 9/09/82, A, C, f, 82004560

Johnston, Andrew, House, 208 N. Main St., Pearisburg, 2/11/93, C, 93000041

Pearisburg Historic District, Roughly, Wenonah Ave. from Tazewell St. to Main St. and adjacent parts of N. and S. Main, Pearisburg, 1/30/92, A, C, 92000004

Gloucester County

Abingdon Church, U.S. 17, S of jct. with VA 614, White Marsh vicinity, 9/15/70, A, C, a, 70000796

Abingdon Glebe House, S of jct. of U.S. 17 and VA 615, Gloucester vicinity, 9/15/70, A, C, a, 70000794

Airville, VA 629 S of jct. with VA 626, Gloucester vicinity, 12/06/90, B, C, 90001824

Burgh Westra, E of Gloucester off VA 3, Gloucester vicinity, 10/08/76, B, C, 76002107

Fairfield Site, Address Restricted, White Marsh vicinity, 7/16/73, D, 73002019

Gloucester County Courthouse Square Historic District, Main St. and Gloucester County Courthouse Sq., Gloucester, 10/03/73, A, C, 73002016

Gloucester Point Archaeological District, Address Restricted, Gloucester vicinity, 6/10/85, A, D, 85001251

Gloucester Women's Club, On U.S. 17, Gloucester, 1/24/74, C, 74002117

Holly Knoll, Off RR 662, Capahosic vicinity, 12/21/81, B, g, NHL, 81000640

Kempsville, E of Shacklefords on VA 33, Shacklefords vicinity, 12/21/78, C, 78003018

Lands End, SE of Naxera on VA 614, Naxera vicinity, 11/06/74, A, B, C, 74002118

Little England, E of Gloucester on VA 672, Gloucester vicinity, 12/18/70, C, 70000795

Lowland Cottage, SW of Ware Neck, 0.5 mi. S of VA 623, Ware Neck vicinity, 9/22/71, C, e, 71001104

Reed, Walter, Birthplace, SW of Gloucester at jct. of VA 614 and 616, Belroi vicinity, 9/20/73, B, C, c, 73002017

Roaring Spring, 0.3 mi. E of VA 616, Gloucester vicinity, 9/22/72, C, 72001395

Rosewell, Address Restricted, Gloucester vicinity, 10/01/69, D, 69000244

Shelly Archeological District, Address Restricted, Hayes vicinity, 7/12/90, D, 89001932

Timberneck, E of Wicomico off VA 635, Wicomico vicinity, 9/10/79, A, C, 79003041

Toddsbury, E of jct. of Rtes. 662 and 14, Gloucester vicinity, 11/12/69, C, 69000245

Ware Parish Church, NE of Gloucester on VA 14, Gloucester vicinity, 3/20/73, A, C, a, 73002018

Warner Hall, VA 629, Gloucester vicinity, 11/25/80, A, B, C, D, 80004191

White Hall, VA 668, Zanoni vicinity, 8/16/84, C, 84003540

Goochland County

Bolling Hall, W of Goochland off VA 600, Goochland vicinity, 12/27/72, A, C, 72001397

Bolling Island, Stokes Station Rd., Goochland vicinity, 12/27/90, C, 89001926

Elk Hill, W of Goochland off VA 6, Goochland vicinity, 2/31/79, C, 79003042

Goochland County Court Square, On VA 6, Goochland, 9/15/70, C, 70000797

Howard's Neck Plantation, 1 mi. NW of Pemberton, Pemberton vicinity, 2/23/72, A, C, 72001398

Lock-Keeper's House, Off VA 6 at James River, Cedar Point, 11/21/74, A, 74002119

Powell's Tavern, On VA 650, Manakin vicinity, 4/02/73, A, C, 73002020

Rock Castle, SR 600, Rock Castle vicinity, 9/15/70, C, b, 70000798

Tuckahoe, SE of Manakin near jct. of Rtes. 650 and 647, Manakin vicinity, 11/22/68, B, C, NHL, 68000049

Woodlawn, SE of Oilville at jct. of VA 250 and VA 612, Oilville vicinity, 12/16/71, C, 71000978

Grayson County

Grayson County Courthouse, Main St., Independence, 1/26/78, C, 78003019

Ripshin, Near jct. of VA 603 and 732, Trout Dale vicinity, 9/22/71, B, g, NHL, 71000979

Snowville Historic District, VA 693, Snowville, 1/07/87, A, B, C, 86003650

Greene County

Gibson Memorial Chapel and Martha Bagby Battle House at Blue Ridge School, VA 627 W side, NW of jct. with VA 810, Dyke vicinity, 4/29/93, C, a, 93000349

Greene County Courthouse, S of jct. of U.S. 33 and VA 649, Stanardsville, 2/26/70, C, 70000799

Locust Grove, VA 641, Amicus vicinity, 9/25/87, B, C, 87001733

Octonia Stone, N of Stanardsville, off VA 637, Stanardsville vicinity, 9/15/70, A, 70000800

Greensville County

Batte, Alexander Watson, House, S side VA 612, 1500 ft. W of jct. with VA 651, Jarratt vicinity, 7/03/91, C, 91000831

Green, John, Archaeological Sites, Address Restricted, Emporia vicinity, 5/09/85, D, 85000985

Spring Hill, VA 730, Emporia vicinity, 12/02/85, C, 85003094

Weaver House, VA 614, Cowie Corner vicinity, 7/08/82, A, C, 82004561

Halifax County

Berry Hill, S of jct. of Rtes. 659 and 682, South Boston vicinity, 11/25/69, C, NHL, 69000246

Black Walnut, VA 600, 850 ft. S of jct. with VA 778, Clover vicinity, 10/29/91, A, C, 91001597

Buckshoal Farm, VA 737, Omega vicinity, 9/16/87, B, C, g, 87001473

Carter's Tavern, SE of Ingram, Pace's vicinity, 10/11/74, C, 74002120

Eldridge, Bowling, House, VA 622 W side, 1.5 mi. N of jct. with VA 659, Elmo vicinity, 8/12/93, C, 93000824

Fourqurean House, 2.4 mi. SW of South Boston, South Boston vicinity, 5/06/80, A, C, 80004192

Glennmary, SW of South Boston on U.S. 58, South Boston vicinity, 2/31/79, C, 79003043

Halifax County Courthouse, Jct. US 360 and US 501, Halifax, 9/16/82, A, C, 82004563

Indian Jim's Cave, Address Restricted, Brookneal vicinity, 8/26/82, D, 82004562

Mountain Road Historic District, Roughly Mountain Rd. from Mimosa Dr. to Academy St., Halifax, 10/06/83, C, a, 83004245

Old Providence Presybterian Church, VA 624, Providence, 7/07/88, C, a, 88001013

Redfield, 3 mi. SE of Oak Level on VA 683, Oak Level vicinity, 9/20/78, B, C, 78003020

Seaton, N of South Boston on U.S. 501, South Boston vicinity, 5/19/80, B, C, 80004193

Tarover, W of South Boston on VA 659, South Boston vicinity, 9/20/78, B, C, 78003021

Hampton Independent City

Buckroe Beach Carousel, 602 Settlers Landing Rd., Hampton (Independent City), 10/27/92, A, C, b, 92001396

Chesterville Plantation Site, Address Restricted, Hampton (Independent City) vicinity, 8/14/73, D, 73002211

Clark, Reuben, House, 125 S. Willard Ave., Hampton (Independent City), 8/16/84, B, C, 84003542

Eight-Foot High Speed Tunnel, Langley Research Center, Hampton (Independent City), 10/03/85, A, C, g, NHL, 85002798

Fort Monroe, Old Point Comfort, Hampton (Independent City), 10/15/66, A, B, NHL, 66000912

Fort Wool, Island between Willoughby Spit and Old Point Comfort, Hampton (Independent City), 11/25/69, A, C, 69000339

Full Scale Tunnel, Langley Research Center, Hampton (Independent City), 10/03/85, A, C, g, NHL, 85002796

Hampton Institute, NW of jct. of U.S. 60 and the Hampton Roads Bridge Tunnel, Hampton (Independent City), 11/12/69, A, NHL, 69000323

Herbert House, E end of Marina Rd. on Hampton Creek, Hampton (Independent City), 2/23/72, C, 72001504

Little England Chapel, 4100 Kecoughtan Rd., Hampton (Independent City), 7/08/82, A, C, a, 82004564

Lunar Landing Research Facility, Langley Research Center, Hampton (Independent City), 10/03/85, A, C, g, NHL, 85002808

Old Point Comfort Lighthouse, Fenwick Rd., SW of E gate of Fort Monroe, Hampton (Independent City), 3/01/73, A, C, 73002212

Rendezvous Docking Simulator, Langley Research Center, Hampton (Independent City), 10/03/85, A, C, g, NHL, 85002809

St. John's Church, NW corner of W. Queen and Court Sts., Hampton (Independent City), 2/26/70, A, C, a, d, 70000871

Trusty, William H., House, 76 W. County St., Hampton (Independent City), 6/22/79, B, C, 79003280

Variable Density Tunnel, Langley Research Center, Hampton (Independent City), 10/03/85, A, C, g, NHL, 85002795

Victoria Boulevard Historic District, Roughly bounded by Sunset Creek, Armisted and Linden Aves., and Bridge St., Hampton (Independent City), 10/04/84, A, C, 84000039

Hanover County

Ashland Historic District, Center, Racecourse, James, Howard, Clay Sts., Hanover and Railroad Aves., Ashland, 2/11/83, A, C, 83003284

Beaverdam Depot, On C & O RR tracks at jct. of VA 715 and 739, Beaverdam, 11/08/88, A, C, 88002060

Clover Lea, E of Mechanicsville off VA 629, Mechanicsville vicinity, 2/31/79, C, 79003045

Fork Church, At jct. of Rtes. 738 and 685, Ashland vicinity, 2/26/70, C, a, d, 70000801

Hanover County Courthouse, Jct. of Rte. 1006 and U.S. 301, Hanover Court House, 10/01/69, B, C, NHL, 69000247

Hanover County Courthouse Historic District, US 301, Hanover vicinity, 9/22/71, A, C, 71000980

Hanover Meeting House, Address Restricted, Mechanicsville vicinity, 9/04/91, A, B, D, a, d, 91001089

Hanover Town, Address Restricted, Mechanicsville vicinity, 9/17/74, D, 74002122

Hickory Hill, E of Ashland off VA 646, Ashland vicinity, 11/21/74, B, C, 74002121

Oakland, N of Montpelier, Montpelier vicinity, 7/30/74, B, 74002123

Patrick Henry's Birthplace Archeological Site, Address Restricted, Studley vicinity, 8/02/82, B, D, b, c, 82001819

Pine Slash, VA 643, Studley vicinity, 11/19/87, C, 87001946

Randolph-Macon College Buildings, Randolph-Macon College campus, Ashland, 6/19/79, A, C, a, 79003044

Richmond National Battlefield Park, E of Richmond, Richmond vicinity, 10/15/66, A, f, NPS, 66000836

Ruffin, Edmund, Plantation, 11 mi. NE of Richmond on U.S. 360, Richmond vicinity, 10/15/66, B, NHL, 66000837

Rural Plains, 6 mi. N of Mechanicsville off VA 606, Mechanicsville vicinity, 6/05/75, B, C, 75002021

Scotchtown, 10 mi. NW of Ashland on VA 685, Ashland vicinity, 10/15/66, B, NHL, 66000835

Slash Church, VA 656, N of jct. with VA 657, Ashland vicinity, 9/22/72, A, C, a, 72001399

Sycamore Tavern, W of U.S. 33, Montpelier, 7/24/74, B, C, 74002124

Totomoi, W of Studley on VA 643, Studley vicinity, 12/12/76, C, 76002108

Trinity Church, Jct. of VA 738 and VA 658, Beaverdam vicinity, 12/27/90, C, a, 90001923

Williamsville, Off VA 615, Studley vicinity, 11/18/85, A, C, 85002915

Harrisonburg Independent City

Harrison, Thomas, House, 30 W. Bruce St., Harrisonburg (Independent City), 7/26/73, B, C, 73002213

Hockman, Anthony, House, E. Market and Broad Sts., Harrisonburg (Independent City), 7/08/82, C, 82004565

Rockinghan County Courthouse, Courthouse Square, Harrisonburg (Independent City), 9/16/82, C, 82004566

Wilton, Joshua, House, 412 S. Main St., Harrisonburg (Independent City), 5/24/79, C, 79003281

Henrico County

Flood Marker of 1771, 0.8 mi. SE of jct. of VA 5 and VA 156, Richmond vicinity, 9/22/71, A, f, 71000981

Henrico, Address Restricted, Dutch Gap vicinity, 4/13/72, D, 72001400

James River and Kanawha Canal Historic District, Extends from Ship Locks to Bosher's Dam, Richmond vicinity, 8/26/71, A, C, 71000982

Laurel Industrial School Historic District, N & S sides of Hungary Rd. W of Old Staples Mill Rd., Laurel vicinity, 6/12/87, A, C, 87001149

Malvern Hill, SE of jct. of Rtes. 5 and 156, Richmond vicinity, 11/12/69, A, C, 69000248

Mankin Mansion, 4300 Oakleys Ln., Richmond vicinity, 10/14/93, B, C, 93001124

Meadow Farm, Mountain and Courtney Rds., Glen Allen vicinity, 8/13/74, A, C, 74002125

Henrico County—Continued

Randolph, Virginia, Cottage, 2200 Mountain Rd., Glen Allen, 12/02/74, B, f, g, NHL, 74002126

Tree Hill, VA 5, Richmond vicinity, 10/17/74, C, 74002127

Varina Plantation, Address Restricted, Varina vicinity, 4/29/77, A, B, C, D, 77001489

Walkerton, Mountain Rd., Glen Allen vicinity, 12/06/84, A, C, 84000676

Woodside, SW of Tuckahoe off VA 157, Tuckahoe vicinity, 7/24/73, C, 73002021

Henry County

Beaver Creek Plantation, VA 108, Martinsville vicinity, 5/09/85, C, 85000984

Belleview, S of VA 641, Ridgeway vicinity, 6/10/74, B, C, 74002129

Carter, John Waddey, House, 324 E. Church St., Martinsville, 11/03/88, C, 88002180

Martinsville Fish Dam, Address Restricted, Martinsville vicinity, 1/21/74, D, 74002128

Stoneleigh, VA 606, Stanleytown, 11/24/82, B, C, 82001820

Highland County

GW Jeep Site, Address Restricted, Monterey, vicinity, 12/23/93, D, 93001443

McClung Farm Historic District, Address Restricted, McDowell vicinity, 1/25/91, C, 90002195

Monterey Hotel, Main St. (U.S. 250), Monterey, 1/18/74, A, C, 74002130

Hopewell Independent City

Appomattox Manor, Cedar Lane, at confluence of James and Appomattox Rivers, Hopewell (Independent City), 10/01/69, A, NPS, 69000015

City Point Historic District, Off VA 10/156, Hopewell (Independent City), 10/15/79, A, C, 79000248

Weston Manor, Off VA 10 on S bank of Appomattox River, Hopewell (Independent City), 4/13/72, A, C, 72001505

Isle Of Wight County

Basses Choice—Days Point Archeological District, Address Restricted, Rushmere, 7/28/83, A, D, 83003285

Boykin's Tavern, W of U.S. 258, Isle of Wight, 6/19/74, A, C, 74002131

Fort Boykin Archaeological Site (44IW20), Address Restricted, Smithfield vicinity, 8/01/85, A, D, 85001675

Four Square, W. of Smithfield on VA 620, Smithfield vicinity, 7/26/79, A, C, 79003047

Jordan, Joseph, House, NE of Raynor on VA 683, Raynor vicinity, 6/22/79, A, C, 79003046

Old Isle of Wight Courthouse, NE corner of Main and Mason Sts., Smithfield, 9/15/70, C, 70000802

Scott, William, Farmstead, VA 603 E of jct. with VA 600, Windsor vicinity, 1/25/91, C, 90002194

Smithfield Historic District, Roughly bounded by Pagan River, Little Creek, and town line, Smithfield, 7/02/73, A, C, 73002022

St. Luke's Church, 4 mi. S of Smithfield on VA 10, Smithfield vicinity, 10/15/66, C, a, NHL, 66000838

Wolftrap Farm, NW of Smithfield off VA 627, Smithfield vicinity, 10/15/74, C, 74002132

James City County

Archeological Site No. 44JC308, Address Restricted, Williamsburg vicinity, 6/26/93, A, D, 93000507

Carter's Grove, SE of jct. of Rte. 667 and U.S. 60, Williamsburg vicinity, 11/12/69, C, NHL, 69000249

Chickahominy Shipyard Archeological Site, Address Restricted, Toano vicinity, 6/28/79, D, 79003048

Colonial National Historical Park, VA 359, Jamestown and vicinity, 10/15/66, A, C, D, f, NPS, 66000839

Croaker Landing Archaeological Site (44JC70), Address Restricted, Croaker vicinity, 5/14/87, D, 87000753

Governor's Land Archeological District, Address Restricted, Jamestown vicinity, 9/21/73, D, 73002025

Green Spring, Address Restricted, Williamsburg vicinity, 12/29/78, A, C, NPS, 78000261

Hickory Neck Church, N of Toano on U.S. 60, Toano vicinity, 7/02/73, C, a, 73002023

Jamestown National Historic Site, Jamestown Island, Jamestown, 10/15/66, A, D, f, NPS, 66000840

Kingsmill Plantation, 5 mi. S of Williamsburg, Williamsburg vicinity, 4/26/72, C, D, 72001401

Pinewoods, 1.4 mi. SW of jct. of VA 613 and 614, Lightfoot vicinity, 11/12/71, C, 71000983

Powhatan, N of jct. of Rtes. 615 and 5, Five Forks vicinity, 9/15/70, A, C, 70000803

Stone House Site, Address Restricted, Toano vicinity, 8/14/73, C, D, 73002024

Windsor Castle, 1812 Forge Rd., Toano vicinity, 12/14/87, C, 87002149

King And Queen County

Bewdley, S of St. Stephens Church on Mattaponi River, St. Stephens Church vicinity, 11/16/78, B, C, 78003024

Hillsborough, 2 mi. SE of Walkerton off SR 633, Walkerton vicinity, 9/22/71, A, C, 71000984

Holly Hill, NE of Aylett off U.S. 360, Aylett vicinity, 7/24/73, C, 73002026

Mattaponi Church, 0.5 mi. S of Cumnor off VA 14, Cumnor vicinity, 3/20/73, A, C, a, 73002027

Newtown Historic District, VA 721 and 625, Newtown, 10/29/82, A, C, d, 82001821

Upper Church, Stratton Major Parish, SE of Shanghai on VA 14, Shanghai vicinity, 4/02/73, A, C, a, 73002030

King George County

Belle Grove, On U.S. 301, Port Conway, 4/11/73, B, C, c, 73002029

Cleydael, Off VA 206, Weedonville vicinity, 12/18/86, A, C, 86003495

Eagle's Nest, VA 642 E of jct. of VA 218 and VA 682, Ambar vicinity, 10/29/92, C, b, 90002160

Emmanuel Church, US 301, Port Conway, 1/07/87, C, a, 86003593

Lamb's Creek Church, VA 607, Sealston vicinity, 9/22/72, A, C, a, 72001403

Marmion, NE of jct. of SR 649 and 609, Comorn vicinity, 2/26/70, A, C, 70000804

Nanzatico, S of jct. of SR 650 and 625, King George Court House vicinity, 11/12/69, C, 69000250

Office Hall, Jct. of VA 3 and US 301, King George Court House vicinity, 1/24/91, C, 90002164

Powhatan Rural Historic District, Jct. of VA 607 and VA 610, King George, 2/20/92, B, C, 92000020

St. Paul's Church, W of Owens off VA 206, Owens vicinity, 5/25/73, A, C, a, 73002028

Woodlawn Historic and Archeological District, Between VA 625 and the Rappahannock R., E of US 301, Port Conway, 1/03/91, A, C, D, 90002012

King William County

Burlington, Address Restricted, Aylett vicinity, 1/30/78, A, C, D, 78003023

Chelsea, N of jct. of Chelsea Rd. and Rte. 30, West Point vicinity, 11/12/69, A, C, 69000253

Chericoke, W of Falls on VA 666, Falls vicinity, 9/08/80, A, C, c, 80004195

Elsing Green, SW of jct. of SR 632 and 623, Tunstall vicinity, 11/12/69, B, C, NHL, 69000252

Horn Quarter, NW of Manquin on VA 614, Manquin vicinity, 6/09/80, B, C, 80004196

King William County Courthouse, Rte. 619, off VA 30, King William, 10/01/69, C, 69000251

Mangohick Church, VA 638, S of VA 30, Mangohick, 12/05/72, C, a, 72001402

Mount Columbia, Off VA 649, 2.7 mi. W of VA 605, Manquin vicinity, 1/19/89, C, 88003208

Pamunkey Indian Reservation Archaeological District, Address Restricted, Lanesville vicinity, 9/16/82, D, 82004567

Seven Springs, W of Enfield, Enfield vicinity, 5/06/80, C, 80004194

King William County—Continued

St. John's Church, N of Sweet Hall on VA 30, Sweet Hall vicinity, 4/24/73, A, C, a, 73002214

Sweet Hall, S of King William, King William vicinity, 11/07/77, C, 77001490

Windsor Shades, SW of Sweet Hall off VA 30, Sweet Hall vicinity, 5/22/78, A, C, 78003025

Wyoming, N of Studley on VA 615, Studley vicinity, 2/08/80, C, 80004197

Lancaster County

Belle Isle, SW side of W end of VA 683, Lancaster vicinity, 2/06/73, C, 73002031

Christ Church, 3 mi. S of Kilmarnock on VA 3, Irvington vicinity, 10/15/66, C, a, NHL, 66000841

Corotoman, Address Restricted, Weems vicinity, 9/15/70, D, 70000805

Fox Hill Plantation, SW of Lively off VA 201, Lively vicinity, 11/17/78, C, D, 78003026

Lancaster Court House Historic District, VA 3, Lancaster, 8/11/83, A, C, 83003286

Pop Castle, VA 659 on the Rappahannock River, White Stone vicinity, 6/16/89, A, C, b, 89000505

St. Mary's Whitechapel, NW of jct. of Rtes. 354 and 201, Lively vicinity, 11/12/69, C, a, 69000254

Verville, VA 611, Merry Point vicinity, 4/24/87, A, B, C, a, 87000609

Lee County

Cumberland Gap Historic District, E of Middlesboro, Gibson Station, vicinity, 5/28/80, A, NPS, 80000366

Cumberland Gap National Historical Park, E of Middlesboro along Kentucky-Virginia state line, Cumberland Gap, vicinity, 10/15/66, A, C, e, g, NPS, 66000353

Dickinson—Milbourn House, US 58, Jonesville, 8/12/93, A, C, 93000825

Ely Mound, Address Restricted, Rose Hill vicinity, 7/28/83, D, 83003287

Jonesville Methodist Campground, W of Jonesville at jct. of VA 652 and U.S. 58, Jonesville vicinity, 5/16/74, A, a, 74002133

Lexington Independent City

Alexander-Withrow House, Main and Washington Sts., Lexington (Independent City), 7/02/71, C, 71001055

Barracks, Virginia Military Institute, N edge of Lexington on U.S. 11, Lexington, 10/15/66, C, NHL, 66000956

Col Alto, Nelson and Spottswood Dr., Lexington (Independent City), 11/19/90, B, C, 89001925

Jackson, Stonewall, House, 8 E. Washington St., Lexington (Independent City), 4/24/73, B, 73002215

Lee Chapel, Washington and Lee University, Washington and Lee University campus, Lexington (Independent City), 10/15/66, B, a, c, NHL, 66000914

Lexington Historic District, Roughly bounded by Chesapeake and Ohio RR, Graham and Jackson Aves., and Estill and Jordan Sts., Lexington (Independent City), 7/26/72, A, C, 72001506

Lexington Presbyterian Church, Main and Nelson Sts., Lexington (Independent City), 5/24/79, C, a, 79003282

Mulberry Hill, Liberty Hall Rd., Lexington (Independent City), 9/09/82, C, 82004671

Stono, At U.S. 11 and U.S. 11A, Lexington (Independent City), 4/01/75, B, C, 75002112

Virginia Military Institute Historic District, VMI campus, Lexington (Independent City), 5/30/74, A, NHL, 74002219

Washington and Lee University Historic District, W and L University campus, Lexington (Independent City), 11/11/71, A, C, NHL, 71001047

Loudoun County

Aldie Mill Historic District, Both sides of U.S. 50 from E of Rte. 612 to W of Rte. 732, Aldie, 9/15/70, B, C, 70000806

Ball's Bluff Battlefield and National Cemetery, Ball's Bluff, Leesburg vicinity, 4/27/84, A, NHL, 84003880

Belmont, 1.8 mi. N. of Ashburn, Ashburn vicinity, 2/08/80, A, C, 80004198

Benton, VA 774, Middleburg vicinity, 6/14/84, C, 84003545

Bluemont Historic District, VA 734 and 760, Bluemont, 2/23/84, A, C, 84003546

Broad Run Bridge and Tollhouse, Jct. of Rtes. 7 and 28 with Broad Run, Sterling vicinity, 4/17/70, A, 70000808

Carlheim, N of Leesburg on U.S. 15, Leesburg vicinity, 12/28/79, B, C, 79003050

Catoctin Creek Bridge, Rte. 673, N of Waterford, Waterford vicinity, 6/25/74, A, C, b, 74002136

Douglass High School, 408 E. Market St., Leesburg, 9/24/92, A, 92001274

Exeter, E of Leesburg on Edwards Ferry Rd., Leesburg vicinity, 8/14/73, A, C, 73002032

Farmer's Delight, About 3 mi. N of Middleburg off Rte. 745, Leithtown vicinity, 6/02/73, B, C, 73002033

Fleetwood Farm, VA 621 S of jct. with VA 617, Arcola vicinity, 2/01/91, C, 90002172

Glebe of Shelburne Parish, 3.5 mi. S of Lincoln off VA 728, Lincoln vicinity, 4/01/75, A, C, a, 75002023

Goose Creek Historic District, Roughly bounded by Purcellville, VA 611, 728, 797, 622, 704, and 709, Lincoln vicinity, 11/14/82, A, C, 82001822

Goose Creek Meetinghouse Complex, S of VA 7, Lincoln, 7/24/74, A, C, a, d, 74002135

Goose Creek Stone Bridge, NW of Atoka off U.S. 50, Atoka vicinity, 10/09/74, A, C, 74002134

Harpers Ferry National Historical Park, At confluence of Shenandoah and Potomac rivers, Harpers Ferry, 10/15/66, A, B, C, D, b, e, NPS, 66000041

Hillsboro Historic District, VA 9, Hillsboro, 5/07/79, A, C, 79003049

Janelia, N side of VA 7, 6 mi. E of Leesburg, Ashburn vicinity, 3/20/87, C, 86003596

Leesburg Historic District, Area of the original town centered at jct. of U.S. 15 and VA 9, Leesburg, 2/26/70, C, 70000807

Loudoun Agricultural and Mechanical Institute, VA 650, Aldie vicinity, 7/08/82, A, 82004568

Lucketts School, 42361 Lucketts Rd., Leesburg vicinity, 10/14/93, C, 93001125

Middleburg Historic District, US 50, VA 626 and 776, Middleburg, 10/29/82, A, B, C, 82001823

Mitchell, Gen. William, House, 0.5 mi. S of Middleburg on VA 626, Middleburg vicinity, 12/08/76, B, g, NHL, 76002112

Morven Park, 1 mi. NW of Leesburg off U.S. 15, Leesburg vicinity, 2/18/75, B, C, 75002022

Much Haddam, US 50 W of jct. with VA 626, Middleburg, 12/28/90, C, 90001988

Nichols, Edward, House, 330 W. Market St., Leesburg, 12/04/87, C, 87002117

Oak Hill, 8 mi. S of Leesburg on U.S. 15, Leesburg vicinity, 10/15/66, B, NHL, 66000842

Oatlands, S of jct. of Rtes. 15 and 651, Leesburg vicinity, 11/12/69, C, NHL, 69000255

Oatlands Historic District, S of Leesburg off U.S. 15, Leesburg vicinity, 5/03/74, A, C, D, a, 74002327

Old Stone Church Archeological Site (44LD376), Address Restricted, Leesburg vicinity, 9/07/89, A, D, a, d, 89001402

Rockland, E side of US 15, N of Leesburg, Leesburg vicinity, 5/14/87, C, 87000752

Rokeby, 2.4 mi. SW of Leesburg off VA 650, Leesburg vicinity, 5/30/76, A, C, 76002109

Taylorstown Historic District, Around jct. of Rtes. 633 and 688 at Catoctin Creek, Taylorstown, 1/30/78, A, C, 78003027

Waterford Historic District, NW of Leesburg on Rte. 665, Waterford, 6/03/69, A, C, a, NHL, 69000256

Waverly, 212 S. King St., Leesburg, 2/10/83, B, C, 83003288

Welbourne, NW of jct. of VA 743 and 6111, Middleburg vicinity, 2/23/72, A, C, 72001404

Woodburn, 3 mi. SW of Leesburg off VA 704, Leesburg vicinity, 12/12/76, A, C, 76002111

Louisa County

Anderson-Foster House, N of Holly Grove, Holly Grove vicinity, 11/17/78, C, D, 78003028

Boswell's Tavern, Jct. of VA 22 and U.S. 15, Gordonsville vicinity, 11/25/69, B, C, 69000257

Grassdale, W of Trevilians off U.S. 15, Trevilians vicinity, 7/02/73, C, 73002035

Green Springs, 0.2 mi. S of VA 617 and 1.5 mi. SW of jct. with VA 640, Trevilians vicinity, 6/30/72, C, 72001406

Green Springs Historic District, NE of Zion Crossroads on U.S. 15, Zion Crossroads vicinity, 3/07/73, A, C, NHL, NPS, 73002036

Louisa County—Continued

Hawkwood, S of Gordonsville off U.S. 15, Gordonsville vicinity, 9/17/70, C, 70000809

Ionia, 0.1 mi. E of VA 640 and 0.8 mi. N of jct. with VA 613, Trevelians vicinity, 6/30/72, C, 72001405

Jerdone Castle, N of Bumpas, Bumpas vicinity, 10/04/84, B, C, 84000042

Louisa County Courthouse, Jct. of Main St. and VA 208, Louisa, 12/28/90, C, 90001998

Providence Presbyterian Church, NW of Gum Spring off U.S. 250, Gum Spring vicinity, 4/13/73, A, C, a, 73002034

Westend, S of jct. of Rtes. 22 and 638, Trevelians vicinity, 9/17/70, C, 70000810

Lunenburg County

Flat Rock, SW of Kenbridge on VA 655, Kenbridge vicinity, 5/21/79, B, C, 79003051

Lunenburg Courthouse Historic District, Jct. of SR 40 and 49 and CR 675, Lunenburg vicinity, 2/23/72, A, C, 72001509

Lynchburg Independent City

Academy of Music, 522–526 Main St., Lynchburg (Independent City), 6/11/69, A, C, 69000340

Allied Arts Building, 725 Church St., Lynchburg (Independent City), 12/19/85, C, 85003203

Aviary, 402 Grove St., Lynchburg (Independent City), 7/30/80, A, C, 80004309

Bragassa Toy Store, 323–325 Twelfth St., Lynchburg, 1/11/91, A, 90002136

Court Street Baptist Church, 6th and Court Sts., Lynchburg (Independent City), 7/08/82, A, C, a, 82004569

Daniel's Hill Historic District, Cabell, Norwood, Hancock, Stonewall from 6th to H St., Lynchburg (Independent City), 2/24/83, C, 83003289

Diamond Hill Historic District, Roughly bounded by Dunbar Dr., Main, Jackson and Arch Sts., Lynchburg (Independent City), 10/01/79, A, C, 79003283

Diamond Hill Historic District (Boundary Increase), Grace St., Lynchburg (Independent City), 4/14/83, A, C, 83003290

Federal Hill Historic District, Roughly bounded by 8th, 12th, Harrison and Polk Sts., Lynchburg (Independent City), 9/17/80, A, C, 80004310

First Baptist Church, 1100 Court St., Lynchburg (Independent City), 9/09/82, A, C, a, 82004570

Garland Hill Historic District, Bounded roughly by 5th St., Federal Ave., and Norfolk Western Ry. tracks, Lynchburg (Independent city), 9/07/72, A, C, 72001507

Glass, Carter, House, 605 Clay St., Lynchburg (Independent City), 12/08/76, B, a, NHL, 76002183

Hayes Hall, Dewitt St. and Garfield Ave., Lynchburg (Independent City), 6/19/79, A, C, 79003284

Jones Memorial Library, 434 Rivermont Ave., Lynchburg (Independent City), 10/30/80, B, C, 80004311

Kentucky Hotel, 900 Fifth St., Lynchburg (Independent City), 12/11/86, C, 86003468

Locust Grove, US 501 S side, 3000 ft. E of jct. with VA 644, Lynchburg (Independent City), 12/17/92, C, 92001704

Lower Basin Historic District, 700–1300 blks. of Jefferson St., 600–1300 blks. of Commerce St., and 1200–1300 Blks. of Main St., Lynchburg (Independent City), 4/24/87, A, C, 87000601

Lynchburg Courthouse, 9th St. between Court and Church Sts., Lynchburg (Independent City), 5/19/72, C, 72001508

Main Hall, Randolph-Macon Women's College, 2500 Rivermont Ave., Lynchburg (Independent City), 6/19/79, A, C, 79003285

Miller, Samuel, House, 1433 Nelson Dr., Lynchburg (Independent City), 11/12/92, B, 92001579

Miller-Claytor House, Treasure Island Rd. at Miller-Claytor Lane, Lynchburg (Independent City), 5/06/76, C, b, 76002223

Montview, Liberty University campus between VA 670 and US 29, Lynchburg (Independent City), 6/05/87, B, a, g, 87000854

Old City Cemetery, 4th, Monroe, 1st Sts. and Southern RR. tracks, Lynchburg (Independent City), 4/02/73, A, C, d, 73002216

Point of Honor, 112 Cabell St., Lynchburg (Independent City), 2/26/70, A, C, 70000872

Rosedale, Old Graves Mill Rd., Lynchburg (Independent City), 7/07/83, A, C, 83003291

Rosedale (Boundary Increase), Graves Mill Rd. W of jct. with VA 291, Lynchburg (Independent City) vicinity, 4/10/92, A, C, 92000240

Sandusky House, 757 Sandusky Dr., Lynchburg (Independent City), 7/26/82, A, C, 82004571

South River Friends Meetinghouse, 5810 Fort Ave., Lynchburg (Independent City), 8/28/75, A, C, a, d, 75002113

Spencer, Anne, House, 1313 Pierce St., Lynchburg (Independent City), 12/06/76, B, 76002224

St. Paul's Church, 605 Clay St., Lynchburg (Independent City), 9/09/82, C, a, 82004572

Virginia Episcopal School, 400 Virginia Episcopal School Rd., Lynchburg (Independent City), 10/28/92, A, C, a, 92001392

Western Hotel, 5th and Madison Sts., Lynchburg (Independent City), 7/22/74, C, 74002236

Wood, J. W., Building, 23-27 Ninth St., Lynchburg (Independent City), 2/17/83, A, C, 83003292

Madison County

Big Meadows Site, Address Restricted, Luray vicinity, 12/13/85, D, NPS, 85003172

Brampton, VA 671, Orange vicinity, 12/12/85, A, C, 85003350

Camp Hoover, Shenandoah National Park, Graves Mill vicinity, 6/07/88, A, B, NHL, NPS, 88001825

Cliff Kill Site, Address Restricted, Luray vicinity, 12/15/85, D, NPS, 85003153

Corbin, George T., Cabin, 1.5 mi. off Skyline Dr. at jct. of Corbin Cabin Trail and Nicholson Hollow Trail, Nethers vicinity, 1/13/89, C, NPS, 88003067

Gentle Site, Address Restricted, Luray vicinity, 12/13/85, D, NPS, 85003174

Greenway, US 15, Madison Mills vicinity, 11/16/88, C, 88002385

Hebron Lutheran Church, 1 mi. NE of Madison off U.S. 29, Madison vicinity, 7/02/71, A, C, a, 71000986

Madison County Courthouse, U.S. 29, Madison, 11/12/69, C, 69000258

Madison County Courthouse Historic District, Main St., Madison, 8/16/84, A, C, 84003549

Residence, The, Woodberry Forest School, Woodberry Forest, 6/19/79, B, C, 79003052

Robertson Mountain Site, Address Restricted, Luray vicinity, 12/13/85, D, NPS, 85003173

Manassas Independent City

Manassas Historic District, Roughly bounded by Quarry Rd., Prescott and Fairview Aves., the Southern RR, and Grant Ave., Manassas (Independent City), 6/29/88, A, C, a, 88000747

Mathews County

Billups House, E of Moon, Moon vicinity, 3/26/80, C, 80004199

Fort Cricket Hill, Address Restricted, Hudgins vicinity, 6/15/70, A, D, 70000811

Hesse, E of Cobbs Creek off VA 631, Blakes vicinity, 2/12/74, A, C, 74002137

Mathews County Courthouse Square, VA 611, Mathews, 8/18/77, A, C, 77001491

Methodist Tabernacle, SE of Mathews on VA 611 at jct. with VA 644, Mathews vicinity, 5/21/75, A, C, a, 75002024

New Point Comfort Lighthouse, Jct. of Chesapeake Bay and Mobjack Bay, New Point vicinity, 3/01/73, A, C, 73002037

Poplar Grove Mill and House, SW of jct. of Rtes. 14 and 613, Williams vicinity, 11/12/69, A, C, 69000259

Mecklenburg County

Boyd's Tavern, Washington St., Boydton, 9/29/76, A, B, C, 76002113

Elm Hill, SE of Baskerville off VA 4, Baskerville vicinity, 7/27/79, B, C, 79003053

Elm Hill Archaeological Site, Address Restricted, Castle Heights vicinity, 3/14/85, D, 85000569

Eureka, SE of Baskerville, Baskerville vicinity, 9/17/80, C, 80004200

Mecklenburg County Courthouse, SW corner of jct. of U.S. 58 and VA 92, Boydton, 7/17/75, A, C, 75002025

Mecklenburg County—Continued

Moss Tobacco Factory, Main and 7th Sts., Clarksville, 5/21/79, A, C, 79003054

Prestwould, N of Clarksville, Clarksville vicinity, 10/01/69, B, C, 69000260

Red Fox Farm, VA 688 E side, 0.7 mi. S of jct. with VA 695, Skipwith vicinity, 6/10/93, A, C, 93000508

Shadow Lawn, 27 N. Main St., Chase City, 10/19/82, C, 82001824

Middlesex County

Christ Church, Off VA 638, N of jct. with VA 33, Saluda vicinity, 11/03/72, A, C, a, 72001408

Deer Chase, SE of Saluda off VA 629, Saluda vicinity, 8/14/73, C, 73002039

Hewick, NW of Urbanna, Urbanna vicinity, 11/17/78, A, C, 78003030

Lansdowne, Virginia St. at Upton Lane, Urbanna, 11/08/74, B, C, 74002138

Lower Church, W of Hartfield on VA 33, Hartfield vicinity, 4/24/73, A, C, a, 73002038

Middlesex County Courthouse, Off VA 602, Urbanna, 11/21/76, A, C, 76002114

Middlesex County Courthouse, Jct. of U.S. 17, Saluda, 11/21/78, A, C, 78003029

Mills, James, Storehouse, S side of Rte. T-1002, Urbanna, 11/07/72, A, C, 72001409

Rosegill, E of Urbanna off VA 227, Urbanna vicinity, 11/27/73, C, 73002040

Urbanna Historic District, Roughly bounded by Virginia St., Rappahannock Ave., Watling St. and Urbanna Cr., Urbanna, 2/07/91, A, C, 90002196

Wilton, S of Wilton on VA 3, Wilton vicinity, 2/31/79, C, 79003055

Wormeley Cottage, Virginia St., Urbanna, 5/23/80, C, 80004201

Montgomery County

Alleghany Springs Springhouse [Montgomery County MPS], VA 637, Alleghany Springs, 11/13/89, A, C, 89001807

Amiss—Palmer House [Montgomery County MPS], Mountain View Dr. and Penn St. off Eakin St., Blacksburg, 11/13/89, C, 89001804

Barnett House [Montgomery County MPS], US 460/11, 0.3 mi. S of jct. with VA 631, Elliston vicinity, 11/13/89, C, 89001810

Barnett, William, House [Montgomery County MPS], Off VA 637, 0.1 mi. N of VA 638, Alleghany Springs vicinity, 11/13/89, C, b, 89001806

Big Spring Baptist Church [Montgomery County MPS], VA 631, 0.1 mi. E of US 460/11, Elliston, 11/13/89, A, C, a, d, 89001809

Bishop House [Montgomery County MPS], 0.1 mi. N of jct. of VA 693 and 613, Graysontown vicinity, 11/13/89, C, 89001812

Blacksburg Historic District [Montgomery County MPS], Roughly, area N of jct. of Main and Jackson Sts. including sections out along Lee and Progress Sts., Blacksburg, 1/31/91, A, C, D, 90002165

Blankenship Farm [Montgomery County MPS], 0.4 mi. S of jct. of VA 733 and 603, Ellett vicinity, 11/13/89, C, 89001808

Bowyer—Trollinger Farm [Montgomery County MPS], VA 600 N of jct. with VA 693, Childress vicinity, 2/01/91, C, 90002167

Bridge over North Fork of Roanoke River [Montgomery County MPS], S of jct. of VA 637 and 603 over North Fork of Roanoake River, Ironto vicinity, 1/10/91, C, b, 89001802

Callaway, Pompey, House [Montgomery County MPS], VA 754, 0.2 mi. E of US 460, Elliston vicinity, 11/13/89, C, 89001811

Cambria Freight Station, 630 Depot St., Christiansburg, 12/12/85, A, C, 85003351

Cambria Historic District [Montgomery County MPS], 500–600 blocks Depot St., 500–600 block Montgomery St., 900–1000 blocks Cambria St., and railroad depots, Christiansburg, 1/10/91, A, C, 90002002

Charlton, James, Farm [Montgomery County MPS], VA 666, 1.3 mi. SW of VA 724, Radford, 11/13/89, C, 89001816

Christiansburg Presbyterian Church, 107 W. Main St., Christiansburg, 1/30/78, C, a, 78003031

Crockett Springs Cottage [Montgomery County MPS], 1 mi. S of jct. of VA 637 and 609, Piedmont vicinity, 11/13/89, C, 89001814

Cromer House [Montgomery County MPS], Off VA 787, 0.25 mi. E of VA 693, Childress vicinity, 11/13/89, C, 89001893

Earhart House [Montgomery County MPS], VA 723, 0.3 mi. W of VA 603, Ellett vicinity, 11/13/89, C, 89001801

Earhart, George, House [Montgomery County MPS], VA 712, 0.5 mi. N of VA 723, New Ellett, 11/13/89, C, 89001886

East Main Street Historic District [Montgomery County MPS], E. Main St. from Roanoke and Pepper Sts. to the old high school and Park St. from E. Main to Lester St., Christiansburg, 1/10/91, C, D, 90002008

Edgemont Church [Montgomery County MPS], VA 666, 1 mi. E of VA 645, Christiansburg vicinity, 11/13/89, C, a, 89001902

Evans House No. 2 [Montgomery County MPS], VA 685, 0.5 mi. W of VA 657, Prices Fork vicinity, 11/13/89, C, 89001890

Fotheringay, S of jct. of Rtes. 11 and 631, Elliston vicinity, 11/12/69, C, 69000262

Gordon, Nealy, Farm [Montgomery County MPS], Off VA 637, 0.5 mi. S of jct. with VA 603, Brush Harbor vicinity, 11/13/89, C, 89001805

Grayson, John, House [Montgomery County MPS], 0.5 mi. NE of VA 613 bridge over Little River, Graysontown vicinity, 11/13/89, C, 89001896

Grayson—Gravely House [Montgomery County MPS], VA 613 at Little River Bridge, Graysontown vicinity, 11/13/89, C, 89001813

Graysontown Methodist Church [Montgomery County MPS], VA 613, Graysontown, 11/13/89, C, a, 89001889

Guerrant House [Montgomery County MPS], VA 612 at VA 615, Pilot, 11/13/89, C, 89001815

Hall, Thomas, House [Montgomery County MPS], VA 667, 0.5 mi. SE of VA 600, Childress vicinity, 11/13/89, C, 89001898

Harrison—Hancock Hardware Company Building [Montgomery County MPS], 24 E. Main St., Christiansburg, 11/13/89, A, C, 89001877

Hornbarger Store [Montgomery County MPS], VA 659, 0.1 mi. E of VA 719, Vicker, 11/13/89, C, 89001888

Howard—Bell—Feather House [Montgomery County MPS], VA 669 at Elliot Creek, Riner vicinity, 11/13/89, C, 89001887

Ingles Bottom Archeological Sites, Address Restricted, Radford vicinity, 12/05/78, B, C, D, 78003032

Keister House [Montgomery County MPS], 607 Giles Rd., Blacksburg, 11/13/89, C, 89001880

Kentland Farm Historic and Archeological District [Montgomery County MPS], At end of VA 623 along New R., Blacksburg vicinity, 7/03/91, A, B, C, D, 91000833

Kinzer, Michael, House [Montgomery County MPS], VA 655, 1 mi. E of VA 624, Blacksburg vicinity, 11/13/89, A, C, D, 89001901

Lafayette Historic District [Montgomery County MPS], Roughly, High St. from Main to Washington Sts., Main from High to Water Sts. and Church St. from Main to Washington, Lafayette, 1/10/91, A, C, 90002005

Lawrence, Frank, House [Montgomery County MPS], VA 612, 0.5 mi. E of VA 614, Basham vicinity, 11/13/89, C, 89001897

Linkous—Kipps House [Montgomery County MPS], VA 657, Merrimac, 11/13/89, C, 89001885

Madison Farm Historic and Archeological District [Montgomery County MPS], E and W sides of US 460 N of jct. with VA 633, Elliston vicinity, 1/25/91, C, D, 90002190

McDonald, Joseph, Farm [Montgomery County MPS], VA 657 NW of jct. with VA 685, at end of Spur Rd., Prices Fork vicinity, 2/01/91, C, 90002166

Miller—Southside Residential Historic District [Montgomery County MPS], Roughly bounded by Miller St., S. Main St., Airport Rd. and Preston Ave., Blacksburg, 1/11/91, C, 90002110

Montgomery Primitive Baptist Church [Montgomery County MPS], VA 624, SW of jct. with US 460/11, Merrimac vicinity, 11/13/89, C, a, 89001803

Montgomery White Sulphur Springs Cottage [Montgomery County MPS], Depot and New Sts., Christiansburg, 11/13/89, A, C, b, 89001884

Murdock, Elijah, Farm [Montgomery County MPS], Off VA 643, 1 mi. N of US 460, Yellow Sulphur vicinity, 11/13/89, C, D, 89001882

North Fork Valley Rural Historic District [Montgomery County MPS], Along the North Fork of the Roanoke R. from the Roanoke Co. line S to Lusters Gate, Blacksburg vicinity, 2/01/91, A, C, D, 90002169

Montgomery County—Continued

Old Christiansburg Industrial Institute, 570 High St., Christiansburg, 4/06/79, A, B, C, a, 79003056

Phillips—Ronald House [Montgomery County MPS], Draper Rd. at Washington St., Blacksburg, 11/13/89, C, 89001904

Phlegar Building [Montgomery County MPS], 2 S. Franklin St., Christiansburg, 11/13/89, A, C, 89001892

Piedmont Camp Meeting Grounds Historic District [Montgomery County MPS], Jct. of VA 637 and VA 602, Piedmont, 1/10/91, C, a, 90002003

Prices Fork Historic District [Montgomery County MPS], Prices Fork Rd. from VA 737 roughly to VA 654, Prices Fork, 1/10/91, C, 90002004

Rife House [Montgomery County MPS], VA 633 at US 460/11, Shawsville vicinity, 11/13/89, C, 89001900

Riner Historic District [Montgomery County MPS], Roughly, E and S of jct. of Main St. and Franklin Sts., Riner, 1/10/91, C, 90002006

Shawsville Historic District [Montgomery County MPS], Main St. E and W of jct. with VA 637, Shawsville, 1/10/91, C, 90002009

Smithfield, W of Blacksburg, Blacksburg vicinity, 11/12/69, B, C, 69000261

Solitude, Greenhouse Rd. on Virginia Polytechnic Institute campus, Blacksburg, 5/05/89, C, 89000363

South Franklin Street Historic District [Montgomery County MPS], 100–308 S. Franklin St., Christiansburg, 1/10/91, C, 90002007

Surface House [Montgomery County MPS], High St., E of Depot St., Christiansburg, 11/13/89, C, 89001883

Trinity United Methodist Church [Montgomery County MPS], VA 723, 0.1 mi. S of VA 603, Ellett, 11/13/89, C, a, 89001894

US Post Office—Christiansburg [Montgomery County MPS], NW corner of public square, Christiansburg, 2/01/91, C, 90002168

Virginian Railway Underpass [Montgomery County MPS], Jct. of Norfolk Southern Railroad tracks and VA 723, S of New Ellett, New Ellett, 11/13/89, C, 89001903

Wall, Adam, House [Montgomery County MPS], VA 657, 0.5 mi. S of VA 685, Prices Fork vicinity, 11/13/89, C, 89001891

Walnut Grove Farm [Montgomery County MPS], VA 609, 0.2 mi. SE of US 460/11, Shawsville vicinity, 1/17/91, A, C, 89001899

Walnut Spring [Montgomery County MPS], VA 655, 0.5 mi. E of jct. with VA 654, Kanodes Mill vicinity, 11/13/89, C, 89001878

Whitethorn [Montgomery County MPS], VA 685, 1 mi. W of jct. with US 460, Blacksburg vicinity, 11/13/89, C, 89001879

Yellow Sulphur Springs, N of Christiansburg on VA 643, Christiansburg vicinity, 9/20/79, C, 79003057

Nelson County

Bon Aire, E of Shipman on VA 626, Shipman vicinity, 7/30/80, B, C, 80004203

Midway Mill, On the James River at end of VA 743, Midway Mills, 4/11/73, C, 73002042

Montezuma, NE of Norwood on VA 626, Norwood vicinity, 7/30/80, B, C, 80004202

Nelson County Courthouse, Off U.S. 29, Lovingston, 5/17/73, C, 73002041

Oak Ridge Railroad Overpass, SW of Shipman on VA 653, Shipman vicinity, 4/15/78, A, C, 78003033

River Bluff, S of Wintergreen on VA 151, Wintergreen vicinity, 7/30/80, C, 80004205

Soldier's Joy, SE of Shipman on VA 626, Wingina vicinity, 11/28/80, B, C, 80004204

Woodson's Mill, VA 778 E of jct. with VA 666, Lowesville vicinity, 12/17/92, C, 92001703

New Kent County

Cedar Grove, NW of Providence Forge on VA 609, Providence Forge vicinity, 12/28/79, B, C, 79003058

Criss Cross, SW of New Kent off VA 608, New Kent vicinity, 5/11/73, C, 73002043

Emmaus Baptist Church, VA 106 W side, 0.4 mi. S of I-64, Providence Forge vicinity, 6/10/93, C, a, 93000506

Foster's Castle, NE of Tunstall off VA 608, Tunstall vicinity, 4/11/73, C, 73002044

Hampstead, 1 mi. NW of jct. of Rtes. 606 and 607, Tunstall vicinity, 12/18/70, A, C, 70000812

Marl Hill, VA 642 E of jct. with VA 609, Talleysville vicinity, 12/21/90, C, 90001832

Moysonec, Address Restricted, Toano vicinity, 6/20/75, D, 75002026

Olivet Presbyterian Church, 2.7 mi. (4.3 km) NW of Providence Forge on VA 618, Providence Forge vicinity, 1/26/78, A, C, a, 78003034

St. Peter's Church, CR 642, New Kent, 10/01/69, A, C, 69000263

Newport News Independent City

Boldrup Plantation Archeological Site, Address Restricted, Newport News (Independent City) vicinity, 9/16/82, D, d, 82004573

Denbigh Plantation Site, Address Restricted, Newport News (Independent City) vicinity, 2/16/70, A, 70000873

First Denbigh Parish Church Archeological Site, Address Restricted, Newport News (Independent City) vicinity, 9/07/82, D, a, 82004574

Fort Crafford, Fort Eustis Military Reservation on Mulberry Island Point, Newport News (Independent City), 5/17/74, A, 74002237

Hilton Village, Bounded by the James River, Post St., Chesapeake and Ohio RR tracks, and Hopkins St., Newport News (Independent City), 6/23/69, C, 69000341

Hotel Warwick, 25th St. and West Ave., Newport News (Independent City), 10/04/84, A, C, 84000044

Jones, Matthew, House, MacAuliffe Rd. and James River Rd., Fort Eustis, Newport News (Independent City), 6/11/69, C, 69000342

Lee Hall, Near jct. of U.S. 60 and VA 238, Newport News (Independent City), 12/05/72, B, C, 72001510

Newsome, J. Thomas, House, 2803 Oak Ave., Newport News (Independent City), 12/19/90, B, 90001831

North End Historic District, Roughly bounded by Sixty-eighth St., Warwick Blvd., Fiftieth St., and Huntington Ave., Newport News (Independent City), 8/28/86, A, C, 86001999

Queen Hith Plantation Complex Site [Oakland Farm Industrial Park MRA], Address Restricted, Newport News (Independent City), 2/24/83, D, 83003293

Richneck Plantation Site, Address Restricted, Newport News (Independent City) vicinity, 7/08/77, B, D, 77001535

Riverside Apartments, 4500-4600 Washington Ave., Newport News (Independent City), 7/28/83, A, C, 83003294

S.S. JOHN W. BROWN, Fort Eustis, Newport News (Independent City) vicinity, 3/01/85, A, C, g, 85000399

Skiffes Creek Sand Spit Site [Oakland Farm Industrial Park MRA], Address Restricted, Newport News (Independent City), 2/24/83, D, 83003295

Southern Terminal Redoubt [Oakland Farm Industrial Park MRA], Address Restricted, Newport News (Independent City), 2/24/83, A, D, 83003296

Warwick County Courthouses, Old Courthouse Way, Newport News (Independent City), 11/03/88, A, C, 88002186

Norfolk Independent City

Allmand-Archer House, 327 Duke St., Norfolk (Independent City), 9/22/71, C, 71001056

Attucks Theatre, 1008–1012 Church St., Norfolk (Independent City), 9/16/82, A, C, 82004575

Boush-Tazewell House, 6225 Powhaten Ave., Norfolk (Independent City), 7/18/74, B, C, b, 74002238

Christ and St. Luke's Church, 560 W. Olney Rd., Norfolk (Independent City), 6/18/79, A, C, a, 79003286

Downtown Norfolk Historic District, Granby, Main, and Plume Sts., City Hall Ave., and Bank St., Norfolk (Independent City), 3/20/87, A, C, 87000475

First Baptist Church, 418 E. Bute St., Norfolk (Independent City), 7/21/83, A, C, a, 83003297

First Calvary Baptist Church, 1036–1040 Wide St., Norfolk (Independent City), 10/15/87, A, C, a, 87001853

Fort Norfolk, 803 Front St., Norfolk (Independent City), 10/29/76, A, 76002225

Freemason Street Baptist Church, NE corner of Freemason and Bank Sts., Norfolk (Independent City), 9/22/71, B, C, a, 71001057

Norfolk Independent City—Continued

Ghent Historic District, Roughly bounded by Olney Rd., Virginia Beach Blvd., Smith's Creek, and Brambleton Ave., Norfolk (Independent City), 7/04/80, A, C, 80004455

Jamestown Exposition Site Buildings, Bounded by Bacon, Powhatan, Farragut, Gilbert, Bainbridge, and the harbor, Norfolk (Independent City), 10/20/75, A, C, b, 75002114

Kenmure, 420 W. Bute St., Norfolk (Independent City), 6/01/88, B, C, 88000601

Lafayette Grammar and High School, 3109 Tidewater Dr., Norfolk (Independent City), 2/10/83, A, C, 83003298

Monticello Arcade, In 200 block E. City Hall Ave.; between City Hall Ave. and Plume St., Norfolk (Independent City), 5/21/75, A, C, 75002115

Myers, Moses, House, SW corner of E. Freemason and N. Bank Sts., Norfolk (Independent City), 2/16/70, B, C, 70000874

Norfolk Academy, 420 Bank St., Norfolk (Independent City), 11/12/69, C, 69000343

Norfolk City Hall, 421 E. City Hall Ave., Norfolk (Independent City), 3/16/72, A, B, C, c, f, g, 72001511

Old Norfolk City Hall, 235 E. Plume St., Norfolk (Independent City), 10/29/81, A, C, 81000674

St. John's African Methodist Episcopal Church, 539–545 E. Bute St., Norfolk (Independent City), 12/04/86, A, C, a, 86003441

St. Mary's Church, 232 Chapel St., Norfolk (Independent City), 5/25/79, A, C, 79003287

St. Paul's Church, 201 St. Paul's Blvd., Norfolk (Independent City), 7/02/71, A, C, a, 71001058

Taylor-Whittle House, 225 W. Freemason St., Norfolk (Independent City), 9/22/71, C, 71001059

U.S. Customhouse, 101 E. Main St., Norfolk (Independent City), 4/17/70, A, C, 70000901

US Post Office and Courthouse, 600 Granby St., Norfolk (Independent City), 10/10/84, A, C, 84000098

Virginia Bank and Trust Building, 101 Granby St., Norfolk (Independent City), 2/23/84, A, C, 84003553

Wells Theatre, Tazewell St. and Monticello Ave., Norfolk (Independent City), 5/19/80, A, C, 80004312

West Freemason Street Area Historic District, Both sides of Bute and Freemason Sts. between Elizabeth River, and York and Duke Sts., Norfolk (Independent City), 11/07/72, A, C, 72001512

Willoughby-Baylor House, 601 Freemason St., Norfolk (Independent City), 9/22/71, C, 71001060

Northampton County

Brownsville, SW of jct. of Rtes. 608 and 600, Nassawadox vicinity, 2/26/70, C, 70000819

Cape Charles Historic District, Roughly bounded by Washington, Bay and Mason Aves. and Fig St., Cape Charles, 1/03/91, A, C, 90002122

Caserta, NW of jct. of Rtes. 630 and US 13, Eastville vicinity, 2/26/70, C, 70000816

Custis Tombs, NW of jct. of Rtes. 644 and 645, Cheapside vicinity, 4/17/70, A, B, 70000815

Eyre Hall, N of jct. of Rte. 680 and U.S. 13, Cheriton vicinity, 11/12/69, A, 69000265

Glebe of Hungar's Parish, NW of jct. of Rtes. 622 and 619, Franktown vicinity, 2/26/70, A, C, a, 70000817

Grapeland, Address Restricted, Wardtown vicinity, 5/06/80, C, 80004207

Hungars Church, E of jct. of Rtes. 619 and 622, Bridgetown, 10/15/70, A, C, a, 70000813

Kendall Grove, VA 674, Eastville vicinity, 6/21/82, A, C, 82004576

Northampton County Courthouse Historic District, E. by Rt.13 & extending from Rt. 13 .1 mi. west, & extendingfrom the intersection of Rt. 631 .1 mi north & .1 mi. south, Eastville, 4/13/72, A, C, 72001410

Oak Grove, VA 630 N side, 1 mi. W of jct. with US 13, Eastville vicinity, 2/04/93, C, 93000006

Pear Valley, S of jct. of Rtes. 689 and 628, Eastville vicinity, 11/12/69, A, 69000266

Somers House, SE of jct. of Rtes. 183 and 691, Jamesville vicinity, 2/26/70, C, 70000818

Stratton Manor, SE of Cape Charles off VA 642, Cape Charles vicinity, 11/28/80, C, 80004206

Vaucluse, S of jct. of Rtes. 619 and 657, Bridgetown vicinity, 9/15/70, A, B, C, 70000814

Westerhouse House, W of Bridgetown off VA 619, Bridgetown vicinity, 11/19/74, C, 74002139

Westover, VA 630, Eastville vicinity, 6/28/82, B, C, 82004577

Winona, NE of jct. of Rtes. 619 and 622, Bridgetown vicinity, 10/01/69, C, 69000264

Northumberland County

Ditchley, VA 607 N side, 2000 ft. E of jct. with VA 669, Kilmarnock vicinity, 9/24/92, C, 92001272

Heathsville Historic District, US 360 at jct. with VA 634 and VA 201, Heathsville, 2/26/92, A, C, 92000053

Holley Graded School, US 360, N of VA 614, Lottsburg, 12/19/90, C, 89001934

Howland Chapel School, Jct. of VA 201 and VA 642, Heathsville vicinity, 1/25/91, B, C, 90002206

Hurstville, VA 605 E side, 3500 ft. S of jct. with VA 606, Kilmarnock vicinity, 9/24/92, C, 92001264

Kirkland Grove Campground, VA 779, 1.6 mi. S of Heathsville, Heathsville vicinity, 10/15/92, A, C, a, 92001391

Reedville Historic District, VA 644 at VA 722, Reedville, 8/16/84, A, C, 84003556

Rice's Hotel, Jct. of Co. Rts. 1001 and 1002, Heathsville, 10/15/92, C, D, 92001389

Shalango, VA 666, Wicomico Church vicinity, 11/06/86, C, 86003135

Shiloh School, Jct. of VA 605 and VA 606, Kilmarnock vicinity, 1/22/92, C, 91001976

Springfield, SR 360, Heathsville, 12/23/79, C, 79003059

St. Stephen's Church, SR 360, Heathsville, 12/28/79, A, C, a, 79003060

Wheatland, VA 624, Callao vicinity, 11/15/88, C, 87000015

Nottoway County

Blackstone Historic District, Roughly bounded by Mann, Dillard, Tavern, S. High, Oak, Eighth and Freeman Sts. and the Norfolk and Western RR tracks, Blackstone, 1/25/91, A, C, 90002174

Burke's Tavern, 1.5 mi. W of Burkeville at jct. of VA 621 and VA 607, Burkeville vicinity, 7/17/75, A, C, 75002027

Little Mountain Pictograph Site, Address Restricted, Blackstone vicinity, 2/15/91, C, D, 91000021

Nottoway County Courthouse, Off U.S. 460 on VA 625, Nottoway, 8/13/73, A, C, 73002045

Oakridge, W of Blackstone off VA 626, Blackstone vicinity, 1/30/78, A, C, 78003035

Schwartz Tavern, 111 Tavern St., Blackstone, 6/28/74, C, 74002140

Orange County

Ballard—Marshall House, 158 E. Main St., Orange, 10/27/88, C, 88002138

Barboursville, S of jct. of Rtes. 777 and 678, Barboursville vicinity, 11/12/69, A, C, 69000267

Berry Hill, S of Orange on VA 647, Orange Vicinity, 5/07/80, A, C, 80004208

Bloomsbury, Off VA 20 W of jct. with VA 600, Orange vicinity, 2/27/92, C, 92000044

Exchange Hotel, S. Main St., Gordonsville, 8/14/73, A, C, 73002046

Frascati, S of Somerset on VA 231, Somerset vicinity, 6/28/82, A, B, C, 82004579

Germanna Site, Address Restricted, Culpepper vicinity, 8/24/78, A, C, D, 78003036

Gordonsville Historic District, VA 15 and vicinity, Gordonsville, 10/13/83, A, C, a, 83004250

Greenwood, 13011 Greenwood Rd., Orange vicinity, 12/17/92, C, 92001702

Hampstead Farm Archeological District, Address Restricted, Barboursville vicinity, 8/16/84, D, 84003559

Hare Forest Farm, VA 700 W of jct. with VA 615, Orange vicinity, 1/28/92, C, 91002016

Madison—Barbour Rural Historic District, Roughly bounded by US 15, the Rapidan R. and the Albemarle and Greene County lines, Barboursville vicinity, 1/17/91, A, B, C, D, 90002115

Mayhurst, SW of jct. of Rte. 647 and U.S. 15, Orange vicinity, 11/12/69, A, C, 69000268

Montpelier, 4 mi. W of Orange on VA 20, Orange vicinity, 10/15/66, B, NHL, 66000843

Orange County Courthouse, Madison Rd. and N. Main St., Orange, 12/28/79, A, C, 79003062

Orange Springs, VA 629 E of jct. with US 522, Unionville vicinity, 2/27/92, A, C, 90002134

Orange County—Continued

Rocklands, N of Gordonsville on VA 231, Gordonsville vicinity, 9/23/82, A, C, 82004578

Somerset Christian Church, VA 20, Old Somerset, 2/31/79, A, C, a, 79003061

St. Thomas Church, 119 Caroline St., Orange, 12/06/76, A, C, a, 76002115

Tetley, VA 64 E of jct. with VA 231, Somerset vicinity, 2/05/91, C, 91000018

Waddell Memorial Presbyterian Church, SE of Rapidan on VA 615, Rapidan vicinity, 8/28/75, A, B, C, a, 75002028

Willow Grove, 2 mi. (3.2 km) NW of Orange on U.S. 15, Madison Mills vicinity, 5/07/79, C, 79003063

Page County

Aventine Hall, 143 S. Court St., Luray, 2/26/70, A, 70000820

Beaver, John, House, N of Stanley on VA 615, Salem vicinity, 6/22/79, C, 79003065

Catherine Furnace, 2 mi. W of Newport in George Washington National Forest, Newport vicinity, 1/21/74, A, 74002141

Fort Egypt, NW of Hamburg, Hamburg vicinity, 6/18/79, A, C, 79003064

Fort Philip Long, Off VA 616 on Shenandoah River, Stanley vicinity, 4/11/73, A, C, 73002048

Fort Rodes, NW of Luray off VA 615, Luray vicinity, 5/22/78, A, C, 78003190

Heiston-Strickler House, NW of Luray off VA 75, Luray vicinity, 11/16/78, A, B, C, 78003037

Jeremey's Run Site, Address Restricted, Luray vicinity, 12/13/85, D, NPS, 85003175

Massanutton Heights, W of Luray on U.S. 211, Luray vicinity, 7/30/76, A, C, 76002117

Mauck's Meetinghouse, Off U.S. 211, Hamburg, 6/18/76, A, C, a, 76002116

Page County Courthouse, 116 S. Court St., Luray, 6/25/73, A, C, 73002047

Shenandoah Land and Improvement Company Office, 201 Maryland Ave., Shenandoah, 7/14/78, A, C, 78003038

Stover House, N of Luray off VA 660, Luray vicinity, 5/22/78, A, C, 78003189

Patrick County

Aurora, VA 629 S of jct. with US 58, Spencer vicinity, 2/04/91, C, 91000015

Bob White Covered Bridge, About 2.5 mi. S of Woolwine off VA 618, over Smith River, Woolwine vicinity, 5/22/73, A, C, 73002049

Cockram Mill, US 58 E of jct. with VA 632, Meadows of Dan vicinity, 12/06/90, A, 90001842

Jack's Creek Covered Bridge, About 2 mi. S of Woolwine off VA 8, over Jack, Woolwine vicinity, 5/22/73, A, C, 73002050

Patrick County Courthouse, SE corner of Main and Blue Ridge Sts., Stuart, 12/27/74, A, C, 74002142

Reynolds Homestead, N of Critz on VA 798, Critz vicinity, 9/22/71, B, C, NHL, 71000987

Petersburg Independent City

Appomattox Iron Works, 20–28 Old St., Petersburg (Independent City), 8/11/76, C, 76002226

Battersea, 793 Appomattox St., Petersburg (Independent City), 11/12/69, B, C, 69000344

Blandford Cemetery, 319 S. Crater Rd., Petersburg (Independent City), 10/15/92, C, d, 92001371

Blandford Church, 319 S. Crater Rd., Petersburg (Independent City), 5/31/72, C, a, 72001513

Centre Hill, Center Hill Lane, Petersburg (Independent City), 12/27/72, C, 72001514

Centre Hill Historic District, Henry, N. Adams, N. Jefferson, Franklin, and E. Washington Sts., Centre Hill Ct., and Centre Hill Ave., Petersburg (Independent City), 6/13/86, A, C, 86001277

City Market, Rock, W. Old and River Sts., and Cockade Alley, Petersburg (Independent City), 6/11/69, C, 69000345

Exchange Building, 15–19 W. Bank St., Petersburg (Independent City), 6/11/69, A, C, NHL, 69000322

Farmers' Bank, NW corner of Bollingbrook St. and Cockade Alley, Petersburg (Independent City), 4/13/72, A, C, e, 72001515

Folly Castle Historic District, Perry and W. Washington Sts., Petersburg (Independent City), 7/16/80, A, C, 80004313

Folly Castle Historic District (Boundary Increase), 235–618 Washington, 235–580 Hinton, 15–37 Guarantee, 18–115 Lafayette and 18–42 Perry Sts., Petersburg, 4/14/92, A, C, 92000343

Friend, Nathaniel, House, 27–29 Bollingbrook St., Petersburg (Independent City), 8/11/76, B, 76002227

McIlwaine House, Market Square at corner of Pelham and Cockade Alleys, Petersburg (Independent City), 7/16/73, C, b, 73002217

McKenney, William, House, 250 S. Sycamore St., Petersburg (Independent City), 12/06/90, C, 90001830

Petersburg City Hall, 129–141 N. Union St., Petersburg (Independent City), 11/16/78, C, 78003185

Petersburg Courthouse, Court House Sq., Petersburg (Independent City), 5/14/73, A, C, 73002218

Petersburg Courthouse Historic District, Roughly bounded by W. Bank, N. Adams, W. Washington and N. Market Sts., Petersburg (Independent City), 12/21/90, A, C, 90001572

Petersburg Old Town Historic District, U.S. 1 and VA 36, Petersburg (Independent City), 7/04/80, A, C, D, 80004314

Poplar Lawn Historic District, Roughly bounded by Surrey Lane, St. Jefferson, Mars and Harrison Sts., Petersburg (Independent City), 5/23/80, A, C, 80004315

Saint Paul's Church, 102 N. Union St., Petersburg (Independent City), 5/30/86, C, a, 86001191

Second Presbyterian Church, 419 W. Washington St., Petersburg (Independent City), 1/14/91, A, C, a, 90002114

South Market Street Historic District, S. Market St. from Washington St. to Halifax St., Petersburg (Independent City), 4/22/92, A, C, 92000345

Strawberry Hill, 231–235–237 Hinton St., Petersburg (Independent City), 12/23/74, C, 74002239

Tabb Street Prebyterian Church, 21 W. Tabb St., Petersburg (Independent City), 5/31/79, C, a, 79003288

Wallace, Thomas, House, SW corner of Brown and S. Market Sts., Petersburg (Independent City), 5/02/75, A, C, 75002116

Washington Street Methodist Church, 14–24 E. Washington St., Petersburg (Independent City), 11/24/80, A, C, a, 80004209

Pittsylvania County

Berry Hill, SW of Berry Hill, Berry Hill vicinity, 5/06/80, A, C, 80004210

Clerk's Office, Main St., Chatham, 7/08/82, A, C, 82004580

Dan's Hill, 4 mi. (6.4 km) W of Danville, Danville vicinity, 5/30/79, C, 79003067

Leesville Dam Archeological Site (44PY30), Address Restricted, Altavista vicinity, 11/02/89, D, 89001916

Little Cherrystone, N of jct. of Rtes. 703 and 832, Chatham vicinity, 11/12/69, C, 69000269

Mountain View, 2 mi. S of Chatham on VA 703, Chatham vicinity, 9/10/79, C, 79003066

Oak Hill, VA 863, Oak Ridge vicinity, 12/28/79, B, C, 79003068

Pittsylvania County Courthouse, US 29, Chatham, 10/29/81, A, C, NHL, 81000643

Windsor, Address Restricted, Cascade vicinity, 7/30/80, B, C, 80004211

Yates Tavern, S of Gretna on U.S. 29, Gretna vicinity, 12/19/74, C, 74002143

Portsmouth Independent City

Cedar Grove Cemetery, 301 Fort Ln., Portsmouth (Independent City), 10/15/92, C, d, 92001366

Craddock Historic District, Bounded by Paradise Creek, Victory Blvd., and George Washington Hwy., Portsmouth (Independent City), 6/20/74, C, 74002240

Drydock No. 1, Norfolk Naval Shipyard, Portsmouth (Independent City), 2/26/70, A, NHL, 70000862

LIGHTSHIP No. 101, PORTSMOUTH, London Slip, Elizabeth River, Portsmouth (Independent City), 5/05/89, A, C, NHL, 89001080

Park View Historic District, Roughly bounded by Elm and Parkview Aves., Fort Lane, Blair, and Harrell Sts., Portsmouth (Independent City), 10/04/84, A, C, 84000047

Portsmouth Independent City— Continued

Port Norfolk Historic District, Roughly bounded by Bayview Blvd., Chatauqua Ave., Hartford St., Douglas Ave. and Hull Creek, Portsmouth (Independent City), 9/30/83, A, C, 83003299

Portsmouth Courthouse, NE corner of Court and High Sts., Portsmouth (Independent City), 4/29/70, A, C, 70000876

Portsmouth Historic District (Boundary Increase), Green and Queen Sts., Portsmouth (Independent City), 10/06/83, A, C, a, 83004251

Portsmouth Naval Hospital, On Hospital Point at Washington and Crawford Sts., Portsmouth (Independent City), 4/13/72, A, C, 72001516

Portsmouth Olde Town Historic District, Bounded by Crawford Pkwy., London St., the Elizabeth River, and extending 0.1 mi. W of Washington St., Portsmouth (Independent City), 9/08/70, C, 70000877

Pythian Castle, 610-612 Court St., Portsmouth (Independent City), 10/30/80, A, C, 80004316

Quarters A, B, and C, Norfolk Naval Shipyard, Norfolk Naval Shipyard, Portsmouth (Independent City), 12/19/74, A, C, 74002242

Seaboard Coastline Building, 1 High St., Portsmouth (Independent city), 10/10/85, A, C, 85003129

Trinity Episcopal Church, High and Court Sts., Portsmouth (Independent City), 5/14/73, C, a, 73002219

Truxtun Historic District, Portsmouth and Deep Creek Blvds., Manly, Dahlin, Hobson, Dewey and Bagley Sts., Portsmouth (Independent City), 9/16/82, A, C, 82004581

Powhatan County

Beaumont, VA 313, Michaux vicinity, 4/02/87, C, 87000571

Belmead, NW of jct. of Rtes. 663 and 600, Powhatan vicinity, 11/12/69, A, C, a, 69000270

Belnemus, W of Powhatan off U.S. 60, Powhatan vicinity, 4/20/79, C, d, 79003069

Blenheim, 6177 Blenheim Rd., Ballsville vicinity, 12/11/86, C, 86003475

Emmanuel Episcopal Church, Emmanuel Church Rd. S of US 60, Powhatan vicinity, 12/27/90, C, a, 90001924

French's Tavern, 6100 Old Buckingham Rd., Ballsville vicinity, 4/21/89, A, 89000293

Huguenot Memorial Chapel and Monument, VA 711, Manakin vicinity, 3/23/88, A, a, b, f, 88000214

Keswick, NE of Powhatan off VA 711, Powhatan vicinity, 12/19/74, A, C, 74002144

Norwood, NE of Powhatan, Powhatan vicinity, 5/19/80, A, C, 80004212

Paxton, 3032 Genito Rd., Powhatan vicinity, 12/28/90, C, 90001987

Powhatan Courthouse Historic District, Jct. of Rtes. 13 and 300, Powhatan, 2/16/70, A, C, 70000821

St. Luke's Episcopal Church, 2245 Huguenot Trail, Fine Creek Mill vicinity, 3/29/89, C, a, 89000193

Prince Edward County

Briery Church, N of jct. of Rtes. 747 and 671, Briery vicinity, 11/29/69, A, C, a, 69000371

Debtor's Prison, On U.S. 15, Worsham, 9/22/72, A, C, 72001412

Falkland, NW of Meherrin on VA 632, Redd Shop vicinity, 6/22/79, B, C, 79003071

Farmville Historic District, Roughly bounded by Main, Venable, High, Ely, School, First Ave., Irving, Second Ave., Oak, W. Third St., and Mill, Farmville, 10/30/89, A, C, 89001822

Hampden-Sydney College Historic District, Bounded approximately by the Hampden-Sydney College campus, Hampden-Sydney, 2/26/70, A, C, a, 70000822

Longwood House, Johnson Dr., Farmville vicinity, 3/08/84, C, 84003564

Old Prince Edward County Clerk's Office, U.S. 15, Worsham, 9/10/79, A, C, 79003072

Prince George County

Brandon, W bank of the James River at the end of Rte. 611, Burrowsville vicinity, 11/12/69, A, C, NHL, 69000271

Evergreen, E. of Hopewell on VA 644, Hopewell vicinity, 7/24/79, B, C, 79003070

Flowerdew Hundred Plantation, Address Restricted, Garysville vicinity, 8/01/75, D, 75002030

Hatch Archeological Site (44PG51), Address Restricted, Hopewell vicinity, 11/06/89, D, 89001923

Martin's Brandon Church, VA 10 and VA 1201, Burrowsville vicinity, 10/31/80, A, C, a, d, 80004213

Merchant's Hope Church, W of jct. of Rte. 641 and VA 10, Hopewell vicinity, 10/08/69, C, a, 69000274

Prince William County

Bel Air, W of Rte. 640, Minnieville vicinity, 2/26/70, B, C, 70000823

Ben Lomond, NW of Manassas at 10914 Sudley Manor Dr., Manassas vicinity, 7/30/80, A, C, 80004214

Beverley Mill, Jct. of VA 600 and 55, Plains vicinity, 2/23/72, A, 72001411

Brentsville Courthouse and Jail [Civil War Properties in Prince William County MPS], 12239 and 12249 Bristow Rd., Brentsville, 8/18/89, A, C, 89001060

Brentsville Historic District [Civil War Properties of Prince William Co. MPS], Roughly Bristow Rd. from Old Church Rd. to Isaac Walton Rd., Bristow vicinity, 12/21/90, A, C, 90001829

Buckland Historic District, 7980–8205 Buckland Mill Rd. and 16206, 16208, 16210, and 16211 Lee Hwy., Buckland, 6/17/88, A, C, a, b, d, 88000681

Conner House, Conner Dr., Manassas Park vicinity, 10/06/81, A, C, 81000645

Davis—Beard House, 10726 Bristow Rd., Bristow, 11/09/89, A, C, 89001794

Effingham, 14103 Aden Rd., Aden vicinity, 11/09/89, B, C, 89001793

Freestone Point Confederate Battery [Civil War Properties in Prince William County MPS], At Potomac River off VA 610 in Leesylvania State Park, Woodbridge vicinity, 8/18/89, A, 89001059

Goodwill Historic District, Chopawamsic RDA Camp 1 [ECW Architecture at Prince William Forest Park 1933–1942 MPS], Off VA 234 W of I-95, Triangle vicinity, 6/12/89, A, C, NPS, 89000456

Greenwich Presbyterian Church and Cemetery [Civil War Properties in Prince William County MPS], 9510 Burwell Rd., Greenwich, 8/18/89, A, C, a, d, 89001065

Lawn, The, 15027 Vint Hill Rd./VA 215, Nokesville vicinity, 10/30/89, C, 89001798

Leesylvania Archeological Site (44PW7), Address Restricted, Dumfries vicinity, 9/13/84, D, 84003565

Liberia, 8700 Centreville Rd., Manassas, 3/20/80, A, C, d, 80004215

Locust Bottom, 2520 Logmill Rd., Haymarket vicinity, 2/11/91, A, C, 89001796

Louisiana Brigade Winter Camp [Civil War Properties in Prince William County MPS], Address Restricted, Manassas Park vicinity, 11/16/89, D, 89001912

Manassas National Battlefield Park, NW of Manassas off VA 215, Manassas vicinity, 10/15/66, A, D, NPS, 66000039

Mawavi Historic District, Chopawamsic RDA Camp 2 [ECW Architecture at Prince William Forest Park 1933–1942 MPS], Off VA 619 W of I-95, Triangle vicinity, 6/12/89, A, C, NPS, 89000457

Mayfield Fortification (44PW226) [Civil War Properties in Prince William County MPS], Address Restricted, Manassas vicinity, 8/08/89, A, D, 89001063

Mitchell's Ford Entrenchments [Civil War Properties in Prince William County MPS], Address Restricted, Manassas Park vicinity, 8/08/89, A, 89001064

Moor Green, 1.3 mi. N of Brentsville off 692, Brentsville vicinity, 11/17/78, C, 78003039

Mt. Atlas, 4105 Mt. Atlas Ln., Haymarket vicinity, 10/30/89, C, 89001799

Nokesville Truss Bridge, NE of Nokesville on VA 646, Nokesville vicinity, 4/15/78, C, 78003040

Occoquan Historic District, Roughly bounded by the Occoquan River, Center Lane, Washington St. and western end of Mill St., Occoquan, 10/06/83, A, C, 83004255

Old Hotel, U.S. 1, Dumfries, 11/12/69, C, 69000273

Orange and Alexandria Railroad Bridge Piers [Civil War Properties in Prince William County

Prince William County—Continued

MPS], Address Restricted, Manassas Park vicinity, 8/08/89, A, 89001061

Orenda/SP-26 Historic District, Chopawamsic RDA Camp 3 [ECW Architecture at Prince William Forest Park 1933–1942 MPS], Off VA 619 W of I-95, Triangle vicinity, 6/12/89, A, C, NPS, 89000458

Park Gate, 11508 Park Gate Dr., Nokesville, 4/03/87, B, C, 87000580

Pilgrim's Rest, 14102 Carriage Ford Rd., Nokesville vicinity, 10/30/89, C, 89001797

Pleasant Historic District, Chopawamsic RDA Camp 4 [ECW Architecture at Prince William Forest Park 1933–1942 MPS], Off VA 234 W of I-95, Triangle vicinity, 6/12/89, A, C, NPS, 89000459

Rippon Lodge, 0.8 mi. N of jct. of U.S. 1 and VA 642, Woodbridge vicinity, 7/02/71, A, C, 71000988

Rockledge, Telegraph Rd., Occoquan, 6/25/73, A, C, 73002051

Signal Hill [Civil War Properties in Prince William County MPS], Signal Hill Rd. and Blooms Rd., Manassas vicinity, 8/08/89, A, 89001062

St. Paul's Episcopal Church, Off VA 55, Haymarket, 1/20/75, A, a, 75002031

Weems-Botts House, SW corner of Duke and Cameron Sts., Dumfries, 5/12/75, B, C, 75002029

White House, 12320 Bristow Rd., Brentsville, 10/30/89, C, 89001795

Pulaski County

Back Creek Farm, NW of Dublin off VA 100, Dublin vicinity, 5/21/75, C, 75002032

Belle-Hampton, VA 627, 0.3 mi. N of VA 617, Dublin vicinity, 11/13/89, A, B, C, 89001911

Dalton Theatre Building, Washington Ave., Pulaski, 5/07/79, A, C, 79003074

Dublin Historic District, Roughly, Giles Ave. from Long to Main Sts., Church St. from Giles to Linkous Ave. and E. Main from Giles to Ziegler St., Dublin, 10/15/92, A, C, 92001369

Harvey, Nathaniel Burwell, House, Off VA 812, Dublin vicinity, 2/13/86, B, C, 86000250

Hoge, John, House, NW side of VA 617, Belspring vicinity, 8/25/88, C, 88001320

Ingles Ferry, N of jct. of Rtes. 611 and 624, Radford vicinity, 11/25/69, A, C, 69000275

Newbern Historic District, VA 611, Newbern, 6/04/79, A, C, 79003073

Pulaski County Courthouse, Main St., Pulaski, 7/08/82, A, C, 82004582

Pulaski Historic Commercial District, Roughly bounded by Third St., Madison Ave., Norfolk & Western RR tracks, and Randolph Ave., Pulaski, 3/13/86, A, C, 86000405

Pulaski Historic Residential District, Roughly bounded by Eleventh St., Prospect, Madison and Washington Aves., Second St., and Henry Ave., Pulaski, 8/11/88, C, a, 88001216

Pulaski South Historic Residential and Industrial District, Roughly bounded by Bertha St., Commerce St., Pierce Ave., 5th St. and Pulaski St., Pulaski, 10/29/91, A, C, 91001580

Snowville Christian Church, VA 693, Snowville, 4/02/87, A, C, a, 87000563

Radford Independent City

Harvey House, 706 Harvey St., Radford (Independent City), 7/30/76, C, 76002228

Rappahannock County

Ben Venue, NE of Washington on VA 729, Washington vicinity, 12/28/79, A, C, 79003075

Caledonia Farm, Jct. of VA 628 and VA 606, Flint Hall, 12/28/90, C, 90001996

Calvert Mill/Washington Mill, E of Washington on US 211, Washington vicinity, 9/02/82, A, C, 82004583

Miller, John W., House, Jct. of VA 707 and VA 604, Boston vicinity, 1/03/91, C, 90002010

Montpelier, S of Sperryville on VA 231, Sperryville vicinity, 4/11/73, A, C, 73002052

Mount Salem Baptist Meetinghouse, SE of Washington on VA 626, Washington vicinity, 5/24/79, A, C, a, 79003076

Sperryville Historic District, VA 522, 600, 1001, and 1002, Sperryville, 2/10/83, C, 83003300

Washington Historic District, Residential area N of U.S. 211/522, Washington and vicinity, 5/28/75, A, C, 75002033

Richmond County

Bladensfield, NE of Warsaw off VA 203, Warsaw vicinity, 10/31/80, A, C, 80004219

Farnham Church, VA 3, Farnham, 8/14/73, A, C, a, 73002053

Grove Mount, Jct. of VA 635 and VA 624, Warsaw vicinity, 1/03/91, C, 90001995

Indian Banks, Address Restricted, Simonson vicinity, 3/20/80, C, D, 80004218

Linden Farm, N of Farnham on VA 3, Farnham vicinity, 4/13/77, C, 77001492

Menokin, NW of jct. of Rtes. 690 and 621, Warsaw vicinity, 10/01/69, B, C, NHL, 69000276

Mount Airy, W of Warsaw on U.S. 360, Warsaw vicinity, 10/15/66, C, NHL, 66000845

Richmond County Courthouse, Jct. of U.S. 360 with VA 3, Warsaw, 12/05/72, C, 72001413

Sabine Hall, S of jct. of Rtes. 624 and 360, Tappahannock vicinity, 11/12/69, C, NHL, 69000277

Woodford, VA 610, Simons Corner vicinity, 2/24/83, C, 83003311

Richmond Independent City

2900 Block Grove Avenue Historic District, 2901, 2905, 2911, and 2915 Grove Ave., Richmond (Independent City), 2/20/73, C, 73002223

Agecroft, 4305 Sulgrave Rd., Richmond (Independent City), 12/13/78, A, C, 78003186

Almshouse, The, 210 Hospital St., Richmond (Independent City), 10/29/81, A, C, 81000647

Almshouse, The (Boundary Increase), 210 Hospital St., Richmond (Independent City), 6/13/90, A, C, 89001913

Bacon, Nathaniel, School [Public Schools of Richmond MPS], 815 N. 35th St., Richmond, 8/24/92, A, C, 92001031

Barret House, 15 S. 5th St., Richmond (Independent City), 2/23/72, B, C, 72001517

Beers, William, House, 1228 E. Broad St., Richmond (Independent City), 4/16/69, C, 69000346

Bell Tower, Capitol Sq., Richmond (Independent City), 6/11/69, A, C, 69000347

Block 0-100 East Franklin Street Historic District, Roughly bounded by 1st, Main, Foushee and Grace Sts., Richmond (Independent City), 2/27/80, C, 80004216

Blues Armory, 6th and Marshall Sts., Richmond (Independent City), 5/17/76, A, C, 76002229

Boulevard Historic District, 10–300 S. Boulevard and 10–800 N. Boulevard, Richmond (Independent City), 9/18/86, A, C, 86002887

Branch Building, 1015 E. Main St., Richmond (Independent City), 4/17/70, C, 70000878

Branch House, 2501 Monument Ave., Richmond (Independent City), 2/23/84, C, 84003569

Broad Street Commercial Historic District, Along Broad St. area roughly bounded by Belvidere, Marshall, Fourth and Grace, Richmond (Independent City), 4/09/87, A, C, 87000611

Broad Street Station, Broad and Robinson Sts., Richmond (Independent City), 2/23/72, A, C, 72001518

Byrd Theatre, 2908 W. Cary St., Richmond (Independent City), 9/24/79, A, C, 79003289

Cabell, Henry Coalter, House, 116 S. 3rd St., Richmond (Independent City), 12/27/72, C, 72001519

Cary, John B., School [Public Schools of Richmond MPS], 2100 Idlewood Ave., Richmond (Independent City), 8/24/92, A, C, 92001030

Cathedral of the Sacred Heart, Floyd Ave. and Laurel St., Richmond (Independent City), 7/08/82, A, C, a, 82004584

Centenary Church, 411 E. Grace St., Richmond (Independent City), 12/28/79, A, C, a, 79003077

Central National Bank, 3rd and Broad Sts., Richmond (Independent City), 9/20/79, A, C, 79003290

City Hall, Bounded by 10th, Broad, 11th, and Capitol Sts., Richmond (Independent City), 10/01/69, C, NHL, 69000327

Columbia, 1142 W. Grace St., Richmond (Independent City), 9/16/82, A, C, b, 82004585

Commonwealth Club Historic District, 319-415 and 400-500 W. Franklin St., Richmond (Independent City), 4/07/83, A, C, 83003301

Richmond Independent City— Continued

Confederate Memorial Chapel, 2900 Grove Ave., Richmond (Independent City), 2/23/72, A, C, a, 72001520

Crozet House, 100 E. Main St., Richmond (Independent City), 2/23/72, B, C, 72001521

Donnan-Asher Iron-Front Building, 1207–1211 E. Main St., Richmond (Independent City), 2/26/70, A, C, 70000879

Egyptian Building, SW corner of E. Marshall and College Sts., Richmond (Independent City), 4/16/69, A, C, NHL, 69000321

English Village, 3418-3450 Grove Ave., Richmond (Independent City), 9/29/83, A, C, 83003302

Fan Area Historic District, Roughly bounded by by N. Harrison, W. Main, W. Grace and N. Mulberry Sts., Richmond (Independent City), 9/12/85, C, 85002243

Fan Area Historic District (Boundary Increase), Roughly bounded by W. Main St., S. Harrison St., Richmond Metropolitan Expressway, and S. Boulevard, Richmond (Independent City)00000, 5/30/86, A, C, 86001190

First African Baptist Church, NE corner of College and E. Broad Sts., Richmond (Independent City), 4/16/69, C, a, 69000348

First Baptist Church, NW corner of 12th and E. Broad Sts., Richmond (Independent City), 4/16/69, C, a, 69000349

First National Bank Building, 825–27 East Main St., Richmond (Independent City), 4/12/82, A, C, 82004586

Fourth Baptist Church, 2800 P St., Richmond (Independent City), 9/07/79, A, C, a, 79003291

Ginter Park Historic District, Roughly bounded by North Ave., Moss Side and Hawthorne and Chamberlayne Aves., Brookland Park Blvd., and Brook Rd., Richmond (Independent City), 9/22/86, A, C, a, 86002688

Glasgow, Ellen, House, 1 W. Main St., Richmond (Independent City), 11/11/71, B, C, NHL, 71001041

Governor's Mansion, Capitol Sq., Richmond (Independent City), 6/04/69, A, B, C, NHL, 69000360

Grant, William H., House, 1008 E. Clay St., Richmond (Independent City), 4/16/69, C, 69000356

Hancock-Wirt-Caskie House, 2 N. 5th St., Richmond (Independent City), 4/17/70, B, C, 70000881

Hasker and Marcuse Factory, 2401-2413 Venable St., Richmond (Independent City), 8/11/83, A, 83003303

Haxall, Bolling, House, 211 E. Franklin St., Richmond (Independent City), 3/16/72, A, C, 72001522

Highland Park Public School, 2928 Second Ave., Richmond (Independent City), 10/22/91, A, C, 91001683

Holly Lawn, 4015 Hermitage Rd., Richmond (Independent City), 8/26/82, B, C, 82004587

Hollywood Cemetery, 412 S. Cherry St., Richmond (Independent City), 11/12/69, C, d, 69000350

Home For Confederate Women, 301 N. Sheppard St., Richmond (Independent City), 11/07/85, A, C, 85002767

Jackson Ward Historic District, Roughly bounded by 5th, Marshall, and Gilmer Sts., and the Richmond-Petersburg Tpke., Richmond (Independent City), 7/30/76, A, a, NHL, 76002187

Jefferson Hotel, 104 W. Main St., Richmond (Independent City), 6/04/69, C, 69000351

Kent-Valentine House, 12 E. Franklin St., Richmond (Independent City), 12/18/70, C, 70000882

Leigh Street Baptist Church, 517 N. 25th St., Richmond (Independent City), 3/16/72, A, C, a, 72001523

Leigh, Benjamin Watkins, House, 1000 E. Clay St., Richmond (Independent City), 4/16/69, C, 69000352

Linden Row, 100–114 E. Franklin St., Richmond (Independent City), 11/23/71, A, C, 71001061

Loews Theatre, 6th and Grace Sts., Richmond (Independent City), 11/20/79, A, C, 79003292

Main Street Station and Trainshed, 1020 E. Main St., Richmond (Independent City), 10/15/70, A, C, NHL, 70000867

Manchester Cotton and Wool Manufacturing Co., Hull St. at Mayo's Bridge, Richmond (Independent City), 7/21/83, A, C, 83003304

Marshall, John, House, 9th and Marshall Sts., Richmond (Independent City), 10/15/66, B, NHL, 66000916

Mason's Hall, 1807 E. Franklin St., Richmond (Independent City), 7/02/73, A, C, 73002220

Masonic Temple, 101-107 W. Broad St., Richmond (Independent City), 2/10/83, A, C, 83003305

Maymont, Hampton St. (Spottswood Rd.), Richmond (Independent City), 12/16/71, A, C, 71001062

Monroe Park Historic District, Roughly bounded by Belvidere, Main, Cherry, Park, Laurel, and Franklin Sts., Richmond (Independent City), 7/05/84, C, a, 84003572

Monroe, James, Tomb, Hollywood Cemetery, 412 S. Cherry St., Richmond (Independent City), 11/11/71, B, C, c, NHL, 71001044

Monument Avenue Historic District, Bounded by Grace and Birch Sts., Park Ave., and Roseneath Rd., Richmond (Independent City), 2/16/70, A, B, C, f, 70000883

Monument Avenue Historic District (Boundary Increase), Roughly, Franklin St. from Roseneath Rd. to Cleveland St., Richmond (Independent City), 1/17/91, C, 90002098

Monumental Church, 1224 E. Broad St., Richmond (Independent City), 4/16/69, C, a, f, NHL, 69000326

Moore's Auto Body and Paint Shop, 401 W Broad St., Richmond, 10/14/93, A, C, 93001123

Morson's Row, 219–223 Governor St., Richmond (Independent City), 6/11/69, C, 69000354

Old Stone House, 1914 E. Main St., Richmond (Independent City), 11/14/73, C, 73002222

Oregon Hill Historic District, Roughly bounded by W. Cary St., Belvidere St., Oregon Hill Park, S. Cherry St. and S. Linden St., Richmond (Independent City), 2/05/91, A, B, C, 91000022

Pace-King House, 205 N. 19th St., Richmond (Independent City), 7/30/76, B, C, 76002230

Planters National Bank, 12th and E. Main Sts., Richmond (Independent City), 2/10/83, A, C, 83003306

Putney Houses, 1010–1012 E. Marshall St., Richmond (Independent City), 6/11/69, A, C, 69000355

Randolph School, 300 S. Randolph St., Richmond (Independent City), 10/04/84, A, C, 84000050

Reveille, 4200 Cary Street Rd., Richmond (Independent City), 2/01/79, C, a, 79003293

Richmond Academy of Medicine, 1200 E. Clay St., Richmond (Independent City), 8/16/84, A, C, 84003574

Scott-Clarke House, 9 S. 5th St., Richmond (Independent City), 4/13/72, A, B, C, 72001524

Second Presbyterian Church, 9 N. 5th St., Richmond (Independent City), 3/29/72, B, C, a, 72001525

Shockoe Slip Historic District, Roughly along E. Carey St. between S. 14th and S. 12 Sts., Richmond (Independent City), 3/29/72, A, C, 72001526

Shockoe Slip Historic District (Boundary Increase), Roughly bounded by Seaboard RR tracks, Downtown Expressway, Main, Dock, and 12th Sts., Richmond (Independent City), 4/20/83, A, C, 83003307

Shockoe Valley and Tobacco Row Historic District, Roughly bounded by Dock, 15th, Clay, Franklin, and Peach Sts., Richmond (Independent City), 2/24/83, A, C, d, 83003308

Springfield School [Public Schools of Richmond MPS], 608 N. 26th St., Richmond, 8/24/92, A, C, 92001032

St. Alban's Hall, 300–302 E. Main St., Richmond (Independent City), 9/09/82, A, C, 82004588

St. Andrew's Church, 223, 224, and 227 S. Cherry St., Richmond (Independent City), 6/22/79, A, C, a, 79003294

St. John's Church Historic District, Bounded roughly by 22nd, Marshall, 32nd, Main, and Franklin Sts. and Williamsburg Ave., Richmond (Independent City), 9/15/70, A, B, C, a, 70000884

St. John's Church Historic District (Boundary Increase), Roughly bounded by 21st, E. Marshall, 22nd and E. Franklin Sts., Richmond (Independent City), 1/17/91, C, 90002097

St. John's Episcopal Church, E. Broad St. between 24th and 25th Sts., Richmond (Independent City), 10/15/66, B, a, NHL, 66000920

St. Luke Building, 900 St. James St., Richmond (Independent City), 9/16/82, A, C, 82004589

St. Paul's Church, 815 E. Grace St., Richmond (Independent City), 6/04/69, C, a, 69000357

St. Peter's Church, 800 E. Grace St., Richmond (Independent City), 6/23/69, C, a, 69000358

St. Sophia Home of the Little Sisters of the Poor, 16 N. Harvie St., Richmond (Independent City), 5/07/80, A, C, a, 80004217

Richmond Independent City— Continued

Stearns Iron-Front Building, 1007–1013 E. Main St., Richmond (Independent City), 2/26/70, A, C, 70000885

Stewart-Lee House, 707 E. Franklin St., Richmond (Independent City), 5/05/72, A, B, C, 72001527

Stonewall Jackson School, 1520 W. Main St., Richmond (Independent City), 5/03/84, A, C, 84003576

Taylor Farm, 4012 Walmsley Blvd., Richmond (Independent City), 1/24/91, C, 90002158

Taylor-Mayo House, 110 W. Franklin St., Richmond (Independent City), 4/02/73, C, a, 73002221

Third Street Bethel A.M.E. Church, 616 N. 3rd St., Richmond (Independent City), 6/05/75, A, a, 75002117

Thomas Jefferson High School [Public Schools of Richmond MPS], 4100 W. Grace St., Richmond (Independent City), 12/23/93, A, C, 93001441

Tredegar Iron Works, 500 Tredegar St., Richmond (Independent City), 7/02/71, A, NHL, 71001048

Trinity Methodist Church, 2000 E. Broad St., Richmond (Independent City), 4/16/87, C, a, 87000625

Two Hundred Block West Franklin Street Historic District, 200 block of W. Franklin St., Richmond (Independent City), 11/17/77, A, C, 77001536

U.S. Post Office and Customhouse, 1000 E. Main St., Richmond (Independent City), 6/04/69, A, C, 69000359

Union Seminary, 3401 Brook Rd., Richmond (Independent City), 4/14/83, A, C, a, 83003309

Valentine Museum, 1005–1015 E. Clay St., Richmond (Independent City), 6/11/69, C, NHL, 69000329

Virginia House, 4301 Sulgrave Rd., Richmond (Independent City), 6/13/90, C, 89001933

Virginia Mutual Building, 821 E. Main St., Richmond (Independent City), 11/07/77, A, C, 77001537

Virginia State Capitol, Capitol Sq., Richmond (Independent City), 10/15/66, A, C, NHL, 66000911

Virginia Union University, Lombardy St. and Brook Rd., Richmond (Independent City), 2/26/70, A, C, 70000886

Virginia Union University, 1500 N. Lombardy St., Richmond (Independent City), 7/26/82, A, C, a, 82004590

Virginia War Memorial Carillon, 1300 Blanton Ave., Richmond (Independent City), 10/04/84, A, C, f, 84000053

Virginia, The, 1 N. Fifth St., Richmond (Independent City), 2/10/83, A, C, 83003310

Walker, Maggie Lena, House, 110A E. Leigh St., Richmond (Independent City), 5/12/75, B, C, NHL, NPS, 75002100

West Franklin Street Historic District, W. Franklin St. between Laurel and Ryland Sts., Richmond (Independent City), 9/14/72, A, C, 72001528

White House of the Confederacy, Clay and 12th Sts., Richmond (Independent City), 10/15/66, A, B, NHL, 66000924

Wilton, S of Richmond, on N bank of James River, Richmond (Independent City), 4/30/76, A, B, C, b, 76002231

Winston, Joseph P., House, 101–103 E. Grace St., Richmond (Independent City), 6/11/79, A, C, 79003295

Woodward House, 3017 Williamsburg Ave., Richmond (Independent City), 6/19/74, A, C, 74002243

Young Women's Christian Association, 6 N. 5th St., Richmond (Independent City), 5/03/84, A, C, 84003578

Roanoke County

Belle Aire, U.S. 11, Salem vicinity, 4/15/75, C, 75002034

Harshbarger House, 316 John Richardson Rd. (Co. Rt. 743), Roanoke (Independent City) vicinity, 10/15/92, A, C, 92001390

Hollins College Quadrangle, Hollins College Campus, Hollins, 11/05/74, A, C, 74002145

Lone Oaks, 3402 Grandin Road Extension SW., Roanoke vicinity, 4/11/73, C, 73002054

Monterey, Tinker Creek Lane, NE, Roanoke vicinity, 7/30/74, C, 74002146

Old Roanoke County Courthouse, 301 E. Main St., Salem, 5/14/87, A, C, 87000727

Old Tombstone, N of Roanoke, Roanoke vicinity, 3/25/80, C, c, 80004222

Roanoke Independent City

Boxley Building, 416 Jefferson St. SW, Roanoke (Independent City), 3/08/84, C, 84003587

Buena Vista, Penmar Ave. and 9th St., Roanoke (Independent City), 7/30/74, B, C, 74002244

Campbell Avenue Complex, 118–128 Campbell Ave., SW., Roanoke (Independent City), 1/24/91, A, C, 90002171

Colonial National Bank, 202-208 Jefferson St., Roanoke (Independent City), 12/17/83, A, C, 83004035

Crystal Spring Steam Pumping Station, 2016 Lake St., SE, Roanoke (Independent City), 5/23/80, A, C, 80004220

Fire Station No. 1, 13 E. Church Ave., Roanoke (Independent City), 5/07/73, A, C, 73002224

First Baptist Church, 407 N. Jefferson St., NW, Roanoke (Independent City), 12/06/90, A, B, C, a, 90001840

First National Bank, 101 S. Jefferson St., Roanoke (Independent City), 6/14/82, A, C, 82004591

Harrison School, 523 Harrison Ave., NW, Roanoke (Independent City), 9/09/82, A, 82004592

Henry, Patrick, Hotel, 617 Jefferson St. S., Roanoke (Independent City), 7/03/91, C, 91000829

Huntingdon, 320 Huntingdon Blvd., Roanoke (Independent City), 11/08/91, C, 91001598

Mountain View, 714 13th St., SW, Roanoke (Independent City), 10/31/80, B, C, 80004221

Roanoke City Firehouse No. 6, 1015 Jamison Ave., SE., Roanoke (Independent City), 1/24/91, A, 90002162

Roanoke City Market Historic District, Roughly bounded by Williamson Rd., Norfolk Ave., S. Jefferson St., and Church Ave., Roanoke (Independent City), 4/20/83, A, C, g, 83003312

Roanoke Warehouse Historic District, 109-133 Norfolk Ave., SW, Roanoke (Independent City), 3/29/83, A, C, 83003313

Southwest Historic District, Roughly bounded by Salem Ave., Jefferson St., Roanoke River and 20th St., Roanoke (Independent City), 6/19/85, A, C, 85001349

St. Andrew's Roman Catholic Church, 631 N. Jefferson St., Roanoke (Independent City), 5/07/73, C, a, 73002225

St. John's Episcopal Church, Jct. of Jefferson St. and Elm Ave., SW corner, Roanoke (Independent City), 8/23/91, A, C, a, 91001083

Rockbridge County

Anderson Hollow Archaeological District, Address Restricted, Lexington vicinity, 7/21/83, D, g, 83003314

Brownsburg Historic District, Including the entire village extending .5 mi. along Rte. 252, Brownsburg, 7/02/73, A, C, 73002055

Church Hill, 6.5 mi. NE of Lexington off U.S.11 at I-64, Lexington vicinity, 2/26/79, C, 79003079

Glen Maury, W of Buena Vista, Buena Vista vicinity, 5/24/79, C, 79003078

Goshen Land Company Bridge, E of Goshen on VA 746, Goshen vicinity, 5/15/78, A, C, 78003041

Kennedy-Wade Mill, 2.3 mi. NE of Brownsburg on VA 606, Brownsburg vicinity, 7/13/79, A, C, D, 79003296

Level Loop, VA 724 1 mi. W of Brownsburg and 0.5 mi. E of McClung's Mill, Brownsburg vicinity, 8/12/93, C, 93000822

Liberty Hall Site, Address Restricted, Lexington vicinity, 8/16/77, A, C, D, 77001493

Locust Hill, VA 608, Mechanicsville vicinity, 5/12/86, C, 86001066

Mackey, William, House, VA 716, .5 mi SE of jct. with US 11, Cornwall vicinity, 10/29/93, C, 93001126

Maple Hall, Jct. of US 11 and I-81 and I-64, Lexington vicinity, 1/29/87, C, 87000006

McCormick, Cyrus, Farm and Workshop, S of Staunton on U.S. 11 and CR 606 at Walnut Grove, Steele's Tavern vicinity, 10/15/66, B, NHL, 66000846

New Providence Presbyterian Church, NE of Brownsburg, Brownsburg vicinity, 3/26/80, C, a, 80004223

Rockbridge Alum Springs Historic District, Address Restricted, California vicinity, 1/19/89, A, C, D, 88003204

Stone House, W of Lexington on Ross Rd., Lexington vicinity, 5/24/79, B, C, 79003080

Rockbridge County—Continued

Tankersley Tavern, VA 631, Lexington vicinity, 11/03/88, A, 88002179

Thorn Hill, SW of Lexington off VA 251, Lexington vicinity, 6/18/75, B, C, 75002035

Timber Ridge Presbyterian Church, SW of jct. of Rtes. 11 and 716, Lexington vicinity, 11/12/69, A, a, 69000278

Vine Forest, US 11, 2 mi. W of Natural Bridge, Natural Bridge vicinity, 8/23/91, C, 91001084

Virginia Manor, VA 130, Natural Bridge vicinity, 9/10/87, B, C, 87001549

Rockingham County

Baxter House, N of Harrisonburg on VA 42, Edom vicinity, 10/03/73, C, 73002057

Beery, John K., Farm, N of Harrisonburg off VA 42, Edom vicinity, 9/19/73, A, C, a, 73002058

Bethlehem Church, VA 798, Broadway, 6/27/85, A, a, 85001414

Big Run Quarry Site, Address Restricted, Luray vicinity, 12/13/85, D, NPS, 85003177

Bridgewater Historic District, Roughly Main St. from North River to Crawford Ave., E. College, Gravel Lane and Bank St., Bridgewater, 11/01/84, A, C, 84000477

Dayton Historic District, Roughly bounded by Main, Mason, Walnut, Summit, and Bowman Sts., Dayton, 8/16/84, A, C, 84003590

Earman, George, House, 109 Pleasant Hill Rd., Harrisonburg vicinity, 7/15/82, C, 82004594

Funk, Joseph, House, VA 613, Singers Glen, 2/24/75, B, 75002036

Harnsberger Farm, Jct. of VA 601 and VA 602, Shenandoah vicinity, 1/22/92, C, 91001974

Harnsberger, Stephen, House, Holly Ave., Grottoes, 7/08/82, C, 82004593

Harrison, Daniel, House, NE of Dayton on VA 42, Dayton, 7/24/73, A, C, 73002056

Inglewood, VA 753, Harrisonburg vicinity, 5/30/85, C, 85001172

Lincoln Homestead and Cemetery, S of jct. of VA 684 and 42, Broadway vicinity, 12/05/72, C, 72001414

Linville Creek Bridge, S of Broadway on SR 1421, Broadway vicinity, 4/15/78, A, C, 78003042

Miller-Kite House, 302 Rockingham St., Elkton, 2/01/79, A, B, C, 79003083

Paul, Peter, House, N of Dayton on VA 701, Dayton vicinity, 12/28/79, A, C, 79003082

Port Republic Historic District, VA 605 and VA 865, Port Republic, 9/08/80, A, C, D, b, 80004224

Singers Glen Historic District, Jct. of VA 613 and VA 712, Singers Glen, 1/20/78, B, C, b, d, 78003043

Sites House, NW of Broadway off VA 617, Broadway vicinity, 4/03/79, A, C, 79003081

Tunker House, S of Broadway at jct. of VA 786 and 42, Broadway, 7/02/71, A, a, 71000989

Russell County

Daugherty's Cave and Breeding Site, Address Restricted, Lebanon vicinity, 6/23/78, D, 78003044

Old Russell County Courthouse, W of Dickensonville on U.S. 58A, Dickensonville vicinity, 7/16/73, A, C, 73002059

Salem Independent City

Academy Street School, Academy St., Salem (Independent City), 10/01/81, A, C, 81000648

Evans House, 312 Broad St., Salem (Independent City), 5/19/72, C, 72001529

Main Campus Complex, Roanoke College, Roanoke College, Salem (Independent City), 3/07/73, C, a, 73002226

Salem Post Office, 103 E. Main St., Salem (Independent City), 9/24/92, C, 92001265

Salem Presbyterian Church, E. Main and Market Sts., Salem (Independent City), 10/15/74, C, a, 74002245

Salem Presbyterian Parsonage, 530 E. Main St., Salem (Independent City), 1/28/92, C, a, 91002017

Williams-Brown House and Store, 523 E. Main St., Salem (Independent City), 11/23/71, A, C, 71001050

Scott County

Carter, A. P. and Sara, House [Carter Family TR], Rt. 614, Maces Spring vicinity, 6/12/85, B, C, 85001410

Carter, A. P., Homeplace [Carter Family TR (AD)], SE of Maces Spring near jct. of VA 614 and VA 691, Maces Spring vicinity, 7/30/76, A, B, C, c, 76002118

Carter, A. P., Store [Carter Family TR], Rt. 614, Maces Spring vicinity, 6/14/85, B, C, g, 85001411

Carter, Maybelle and Ezra, House [Carter Family TR], Rt. 614, Maces Spring vicinity, 6/12/85, B, C, 85001412

Flanary Archeological Site (44SC13), Address Restricted, Dungannon vicinity, 7/07/83, D, 83003315

Killgore Fort House, SW of Nickelsville off VA 71, Nickelsville vicinity, 5/19/72, A, C, 72001415

Mt. Vernon Methodist Church [Carter Family TR], Rt. 614, Maces Spring vicinity, 6/12/85, B, C, a, 85001413

Shenandoah County

Campbell Farm, VA 675, near Lantz Mills, Edinburg vicinity, 8/15/90, A, C, 90001416

Edinburg Mill, U.S. 11, Edinburg, 9/07/79, A, C, 79003084

Fort Bowman, NE of jct. of Rtes. 660 and U.S. 11, Middletown vicinity, 11/25/69, B, C, 69000279

Hockman, Dr. Christian, House, US 11, Edinburg vicinity, 2/23/84, C, 84003593

Lantz Hall, 614 S. Main St. (US 11), Woodstock, 12/30/92, C, a, 92001711

Meems Bottom Covered Bridge, S of Mt. Jackson on VA 720 over North Fork of Shenandoah River, Mt. Jackson vicinity, 6/10/75, C, 75002037

Mount Jackson Historic District, Main, King, Gospel, Broad, Bridge, Race, Clifford, Tisinger and Wunder Sts. and Orkney Dr., Mount Jackson, 6/17/93, A, C, 93000541

New Market Battlefield Park, N of jct. of U.S. 11 and U.S. 211, New Market vicinity, 9/15/70, A, 70000824

New Market Historic District, Jct. of U.S. 11 and 211, New Market, 9/22/72, A, C, 72001416

Orkney Springs Hotel, VA 263, W of jct. with VA 610, Orkney Springs, 4/22/76, A, C, 76002119

Shenandoah County Courthouse, W. Court and S. Main Sts., Woodstock, 6/19/73, A, C, 73002060

Shenandoah County Farm, N side VA 654, 4000 ft. E of jct. with US 11, Maurertown vicinity, 10/29/93, A, C, 93001122

Snapp House, SW of Fishers Hill on VA 757, Fishers Hill vicinity, 5/07/79, A, C, 79003085

Strasburg Historic District, Roughly bounded by RR tracks, 3rd, High, and Massanutten Sts., Strasburg, 8/16/84, A, C, 84003595

Strasburg Stone and Earthenware Manufacturing Company, E. King St., Strasburg, 6/19/79, A, 79003086

Zirkle Mill, W of Quicksburg on VA 42, Quicksburg vicinity, 2/10/83, A, C, 83003316

Smyth County

Aspenvale Cemetery, Off U.S. 11, Seven Mile Ford vicinity, 12/05/80, B, d, 80004226

Chilhowie Methodist Episcopal Church, 501 Old Stage Rd., Chilhowie, 7/03/91, C, a, 91000830

Fox Farm Site, Address Restricted, McMullin vicinity, 6/23/78, D, 78003045

Henderson Building, Southwestern State Hospital, E. Main St., Marion, 12/21/90, A, C, 89001919

Lincoln Theatre, 117 E. Main St., Marion, 12/17/92, C, 92001710

Marion Male Academy, 343 College St., Marion vicinity, 11/02/89, A, C, 89001915

Old Stone Tavern, US 11, Atkins vicinity, 7/08/82, A, C, 82004595

Preston House, S of jct. of Rtes. 645 and U.S. 11, Marion vicinity, 11/25/69, A, C, 69000280

Preston House, VA 107, Saltville, 7/30/76, A, B, C, 76002120

Thomas, Abijah, House, SW of Marion on VA 657, Marion vicinity, 11/28/80, C, 80004225

South Boston Independent City

Reedy Creek Site, Address Restricted, South Boston (Independent City), 4/26/78, D, 78003187

South Boston Independent City—Continued

South Boston Historic District, Along Railroad Ave., Ferry, Factory, and Main Sts., Wilborn Ave., N. Main St., Washington and Peach Aves., and Jeffress, South Boston (Independent City), 9/26/86, A, C, 86002471

Southampton County

Beechwood, NE of Courtland on VA 643, Beales vicinity, 2/01/79, B, C, g, 79003088

Belmont, NE of Capron off VA 652, Capron vicinity, 10/03/73, A, C, 73002061

Brown's Ferry, E of Drakes Corner off VA 684, Drakes Corner vicinity, 6/18/79, B, C, c, 79003090

Elm Grove, NE of Courtland on VA 646, Courtland vicinity, 7/24/79, A, C, 79003089

Rose Hill, NE of Capron on VA 635, Capron vicinity, 12/31/79, C, D, 79003087

Sunnyside, VA 673, Newsoms vicinity, 7/08/82, A, C, 82004596

Spotsylvania County

Andrews Tavern, 2.6 mi. NE of Glenora on VA 601, Glenora vicinity, 7/30/76, A, C, 76002121

Fairview, 2020 Whitelake Dr., Fredericksburg vicinity, 12/30/93, C, 93001460

Fall Hill, NW of Fredericksburg off VA 639, Fredericksburg vicinity, 6/18/73, A, C, 73002062

Kenmore, 8300 Courthouse Rd., Spotsylvania vicinity, 6/24/93, C, 93000569

Massaponax Baptist Church, Jct. of US 1 and Co. Rt. 608, Massaponax vicinity, 1/24/91, A, B, C, a, 90002137

Prospect Hill, N of Mineral on VA 612, Mineral vicinity, 9/09/82, A, B, C, 82004597

Rapidan Dam Canal of the Rappahannock Navigation, Extending from the mouth of the Rapidan River down the Rappahannock River for 1.5 mi., Fredericksburg vicinity, 7/26/73, A, C, 73002063

Spotsylvania Court House Historic District, VA 208, Spotsylvania, 9/08/83, A, C, d, 83003317

St. Julien, S of Fredericksburg between VA 609 and VA 2, Fredericksburg vicinity, 6/05/75, B, C, 75002038

Stirling, Co. Rt. 607 at I-95, Massaponax vicinity, 5/05/89, C, 89000366

Tubal Furnace Archeological Site, Address Restricted, Chancellor vicinity, 10/19/82, A, B, D, 82001825

Stafford County

Accokeek Furnace Archeological Site (44ST53), Address Restricted, Stafford vicinity, 5/15/84, D, 84003598

Aquia Church, N of jct. of U.S. 1 and VA 610, Garrisonville vicinity, 11/12/69, C, a, NHL, 69000282

Belmont, Off U.S. 1, Falmouth, 10/15/66, B, NHL, 66000848

Carlton, 501 Melchers Dr., Falmouth, 10/03/73, C, 73002064

Clearview, Off Telegraph Rd. near VA 664 and U.S. 1, Falmouth, 2/24/75, C, 75002039

Falmouth Historic District, Jct. of U.S. 1 and U.S. 17, Falmouth, 2/26/70, A, C, a, 70000825

Ferry Farm Site, E of Fredericksburg at 712 Kings Hwy., Fredericksburg vicinity, 5/05/72, B, f, 72001417

Hartwood Presbyterian Church, Jct. VA 705 and 612, Hartwood, 11/13/89, C, a, 89001929

Hunter's Ironworks, W of Falmouth off U.S. 17, Falmouth vicinity, 1/18/74, A, C, 74002147

Potomac Creek Site, Address Restricted, Brooke vicinity, 12/03/69, D, 69000281

White Oak Church, 8 Caisson Rd., Falmouth, 1/03/91, C, a, 90002112

Staunton Independent City

Augusta County Courthouse, 1 E. Johnson St., Staunton (Independent City), 10/26/82, A, C, 82001826

Beverley Historic District, U.S. 250 and VA 254, Staunton (Independent City), 7/14/82, A, C, 82004598

Breezy Hill, 1220 N. Augusta St., Staunton (Independent City), 7/08/82, C, 82004599

Catlett House, 303 Berkeley Pl., Staunton (Independent City), 7/15/82, C, 82004600

Gospel Hill Historic District, Roughly bounded by E. Beverly, N. Market, E. Frederick and Kalorama Sts., Staunton (Independent City), 2/14/85, A, C, 85000299

Hilltop, Mary Baldwin College campus, Staunton (Independent City), 6/19/79, B, C, 79003298

Hoge, Arista, House, 215 Kalorama St., Staunton (Independent City), 7/15/82, B, C, 82004601

Kable House, 310 Prospect St., Staunton (Independent City), 6/19/79, A, 79003299

Mary Baldwin College, Main Building, Mary Baldwin College campus, Staunton (Independent City), 7/26/73, A, C, 73002227

Merrillat, J. C. M., House, 521 E. Beverley St., Staunton (Independent City), 9/16/82, B, C, 82004602

Michie, Thomas J., House, 324 E. Beverley St., Staunton (Independent City), 9/09/82, B, C, 82004603

Miller, C. W., House, 210 N. New St., Staunton (Independent City), 6/19/79, C, 79003300

National Valley Bank, 12–14 W. Beverly St., Staunton (Independent City), 6/19/79, A, C, 79003301

Newtown Historic District, Roughly bounded by Lewis St. and S. Jefferson Sts., C&O RR, Allegheny and Churchville Aves., incl. Thornrose cemetery, Staunton (Independent City), 9/08/83, A, C, d, 83003318

Oakdene, 605 E. Beverley St., Staunton (Independent City), 11/24/82, A, C, 82001827

Oaks, The, 437 E. Beverly St., Staunton (Independent City), 6/19/79, B, C, 79003302

Old Main, 235 W. Frederick St., Staunton (Independent City), 8/13/74, A, C, 74002246

Rose Terrace, 150 N. Market St., Staunton (Independent City), 6/19/79, C, 79003303

Sears House, Sears Hill Rd. in Woodrow Wilson City Park, Staunton (Independent City), 2/23/72, B, C, 72001530

Steephill, 200 Park Blvd., Staunton (Independent City), 2/23/84, C, 84003599

Stuart Addition Historic District, Roughly bounded by Augusta, Sunnyside, Market, and New Sts., Staunton (Independent City), 5/03/84, A, C, a, 84003604

Stuart House, 120 Church St., Staunton (Independent City), 5/05/72, B, C, 72001531

Trinity Episcopal Church, Beverley and Lewis Sts., Staunton (Independent City), 5/05/72, A, C, a, 72001532

Virginia School for the Deaf and Blind, E. Beverly St. and Pleasant Ter., Staunton (Independent City), 11/12/69, A, C, 69000361

Waverly Hill, 3001 N. Augusta St., Staunton (Independent City), 7/08/82, B, C, 82004604

Western State Hospital Complex, Jct. of U.S. 11 and U.S. 250, Staunton (Independent City), 11/25/69, A, C, 69000362

Wharf Area Historic District, Middlebrook Ave. between S. New and S. Lewis Sts., including S. Augusta St. to Johnson St., Staunton (Independent City), 11/09/72, A, C, 72001533

Wharf Area Historic District (Boundary Increase), Boundary extended on E to Lewis Creek, Staunton (Independent City), 7/19/82, A, C, g, 82004605

Wilson, Woodrow, Birthplace, N. Coalter St. between Beverly and Frederick Sts., Staunton (Independent City), 10/15/66, B, a, c, NHL, 66000926

Suffolk Independent City

Building at 216 Bank Street, 216 Bank St., Suffolk (Independent City), 11/07/85, B, C, 85002765

Glebe Church, W of Chesapeake City on VA 337, Driver vicinity, 5/25/73, A, C, a, 73002148

Godwin—Knight House, 140 King's Hwy., Chuckatuck, 8/24/92, C, 92001028

Phoenix Bank of Nansemond, 339 E. Washington St., Suffolk (Independent City), 1/24/91, A, 90002159

Riddick House, 510 Main St., Suffolk (Independent City), 5/02/74, A, C, 74002247

St. John's Church, E of Chuckatuck on VA 125, Chuckatuck vicinity, 4/11/73, C, a, 73002149

Suffolk Historic District, Roughly bounded by RR tracks, Hill St., Central Ave., Holladay, Washington, N. Saratoga and Pine Sts., Suffolk (Independent City), 6/22/87, A, C, 87000631

Surry County

Bacon's Castle, Off VA 10, Bacon's Castle, 10/15/66, A, C, NHL, 66000849

Chippokes Plantation, Chippokes State Park, VA 634 and 633, Jamestown vicinity, 10/01/69, A, C, D, 69000283

Enos House, Address Restricted, Surry vicinity, 12/07/77, C, 77001494

Four Mile Tree, NE of the jct. of VA 618 and VA 610, Surry vicinity, 12/18/70, C, 70000826

Glebe House of Southwark Parish, E of Spring Grove on VA 10, Spring Grove vicinity, 5/17/76, A, B, C, a, 76002123

Melville, E of Surry, Surry vicinity, 5/06/80, B, C, 80004228

Montpelier, 1.4 mi. SW of Cabin Point, Cabin Point vicinity, 3/26/80, B, C, 80004227

Old Brick Church, VA 10, Bacon's Castle vicinity, 1/02/86, A, C, a, 86000002

Pleasant Point, 1 mi. S of Scotland on VA 637, Scotland vicinity, 7/16/76, A, B, C, D, 76002122

Rich Neck Farm, E of Surry, Surry vicinity, 5/19/80, A, C, 80004229

Second Southwark Church Archeological Site (44SY65), Address Restricted, Surry vicinity, 2/23/84, D, a, 84003610

Smith's Fort, Address Restricted, Surry vicinity, 6/15/70, D, 70000827

Snow Hill, VA 40, Gwaltney Corner vicinity, 12/28/79, C, 79003091

Surry County Courthouse Complex, VA 10, Surry, 4/10/86, A, C, 86000719

Swann's Point Plantation Site, Address Restricted, Scotland vicinity, 4/01/75, B, D, 75002040

Warren House, NE of Surry off VA 31, Surry vicinity, 11/14/73, C, 73002065

Sussex County

Carpenter, Miles B., House, US 460, Waverly, 11/13/89, B, g, 89001920

Chester, N of jct. of Rtes. 625 and 35, Homeville vicinity, 12/18/70, C, 70000829

Fortsville, SE of the jct. of Rtes. 612 and 611, Grizzard vicinity, 9/15/70, B, C, 70000828

Little Town, W of Littleton on VA 622, Littleton vicinity, 11/18/76, C, 76002124

Nottoway Archeological Site (44SX6, 44SX7, 44SX98, 44SX162), Address Restricted, Stony Creek vicinity, 11/03/88, D, 88002181

Sussex County Courthouse Historic District, Jct. of VA 634 and 626, Sussex, 7/24/73, A, C, 73002066

Tazewell County

Big Crab Orchard Site, Address Restricted, Tazewell vicinity, 8/11/80, A, D, 80004230

Bull Thistle Cave Archeological Site (44TZ92), Address Restricted, Tazewell vicinity, 9/10/87, D, 87001531

Burke's Garden Central Church And Cemetery, SE of Burke's Garden on VA 623, Burke's Garden vicinity, 5/07/79, A, C, a, d, 79003092

Burke's Garden Rural Historic District, Valley encircled by Garden Mountain, Tazewell vicinity, 2/25/86, A, C, D, 86000306

Chimney Rock Farm, VA 91, Tazewell vicinity, 7/08/82, C, 82004607

Clinch Valley Roller Mills, River Street Dr., Cedar Bluff, 10/04/84, A, C, 84000056

Indian Paintings, Address Restricted, Maiden Spring vicinity, 12/03/69, C, D, 69000284

Pocahontas Historic District, Corporate boundaries of Pocahontas including cemetery, Pocahontas and vicinity, 11/03/72, A, C, 72001418

St. Clair, Alexander, House, W of Bluefield on VA 650, Bluefield vicinity, 6/28/82, C, 82004606

Thompson, George Oscar, House, U.S. 604, Tazewell vicinity, 6/28/82, C, 82004608

Williams House, 102 Suffolk Ave., Richlands, 7/07/83, A, 83003319

Wynn, James, House, 408 S. Elk St., Tazewell, 10/28/92, C, 92001368

Virginia Beach Independent City

Bayville Farm, Off VA 650, Virginia Beach (Independent City), 5/19/80, C, 80004317

Cape Henry Lighthouse, Atlantic Ave. at U.S. 60, Virginia Beach (Independent City), 10/15/66, A, NHL, 66000910

Keeling House, 3157 Adam Keeling Rd., Virginia Beach (Independent City), 6/19/73, C, 73002297

Land, Francis, House, 3133 Virginia Beach Blvd., Virginia Beach (Independent City), 5/12/75, C, 75002118

Old Donation Church, 4449 N. Witch Duck Rd., Virginia Beach (Independent City), 4/13/72, C, a, 72001534

Pembroke Manor, E of jct. of Rtes. 627, 647, and U.S. 58, Virginia Beach (Independent City), 2/26/70, C, 70000887

Pleasant Hall, 5184 Princess Anne Rd., Virginia Beach (Independent City), 1/25/73, C, 73002229

Thoroughgood House, E of Norfolk on Lynnhaven River, Virginia Beach (Independent City), 10/15/66, C, NHL, 66000921

U.S. Coast Guard Station, Atlantic Ave. and 24th St., Virginia Beach (Independent City), 7/11/79, A, C, b, 79003304

Upper Wolfsnare, E of jct. of Rtes. 635 and 632, Virginia Beach (Independent City), 3/26/75, C, 75002119

Weblin House, 5588 Moore's Pond Rd., Virginia Beach (Independent City), 11/08/74, C, 74002248

Wishart-Boush House, E of jct. of VA 649 and Absalom Rd., Virginia Beach (Independent City), 11/12/69, C, 69000363

de Witt Cottage, 1106 Atlantic Ave., Virginia Beach (Independent City), 6/16/88, A, C, 88000748

Warren County

Compton Gap Site, Address Restricted, Luray vicinity, 12/13/85, D, NPS, 85003176

Erin, NE of Front Royal on U.S. 340/522, Front Royal vicinity, 12/28/79, B, C, 79003093

Fairview Farm, VA 658, Front Royal vicinity, 6/05/86, C, 86001249

Flint Run Archeological District, Address Restricted, Front Royal vicinity, 12/22/76, D, 76002125

Front Royal Recreational Park Historic District, VA 665, 1.1 mi. N of Riverton from VA 522, Front Royal, 10/27/92, A, 91001975

Killahevlin, 1401 N Royal Ave., Front Royal, 10/14/93, B, C, 93001128

Mount Zion, NE of jct. of Rtes. 624 and 639, Milldale, 2/26/70, C, 70000830

Sonner Hall, Third St., Front Royal, 1/29/87, A, C, 87000007

Thunderbird Archeological District, Address Restricted, Limeton vicinity, 5/05/77, D, NHL, 77001495

Washington County

Abingdon Bank, 225 E. Main St., Abingdon, 11/12/69, C, 69000285

Abingdon Historic District, Both sides of Main St. between Cummings and Deadmore Sts., Abingdon, 2/26/70, A, C, 70000831

Abingdon Historic District (Boundary Increase), Roughly bounded by Russell Rd. and Jackson St., Whites Mill Rd., E. Main and E. Park and W. Main Sts., and Academy Dr., Abingdon, 9/17/86, A, C, 86002193

Crabtree-Blackwell Farm, 1 mi. S of Blackwell on SR 686, Blackwell vicinity, 4/01/75, A, C, 75002041

Emory and Henry College, VA 609, Emory vicinity, 1/30/89, A, C, a, 85003695

Mont Calm, W of VA 75, Abingdon, 7/18/74, B, C, 74002148

White's Mill, NW of Abingdon on White Mill Rd., Abingdon vicinity, 9/10/74, A, C, 74002149

Waynesboro Independent City

Coiner-Quesenbery House, 332 W. Main St., Waynesboro (Independent City), 11/07/76, C, 76002232

Fairfax Hall, Winchester Ave., Waynesboro (Independent City), 9/09/82, A, C, 82004609

Fishburne Military School, 225 S. Wayne Ave., Waynesboro (Independent City), 10/04/84, A, B, C, 84000058

Plumb House, 1012 W. Main St., Waynesboro (Independent City), 1/24/91, C, 90002178

Westmoreland County

Bell House, 821 Irving Ave., Colonial Beach, 9/21/87, A, B, C, 87000692

Westmoreland County—Continued

Blenheim, N of Wakefield Corner off VA 204, Wakefield Corner vicinity, 6/05/75, B, C, 75002042

Chantilly, Address Restricted, Montross vicinity, 12/16/71, B, D, 71000990

George Washington Birthplace National Monument, E of Fredericksburg off U.S. 301 and VA 3, Fredericksburg vicinity, 10/15/66, B, c, e, f, g, NPS, 66000850

Ingleside, S of Oak Grove on VA 638, Oak Grove vicinity, 3/15/79, A, C, 79003094

Jones, Morgan, 1677 Pottery Kiln, Address Restricted, Hague vicinity, 10/16/74, A, D, 74002150

Monroe, James, Family Home Site, Address Restricted, Oak Grove vicinity, 7/24/79, B, D, 79003095

Rochester House, Co. Rt. 613, 1 mi. NE of Lyells off VA 3, Lyells vicinity, 1/25/91, C, 90002205

Roxbury, 1.7 mi. S of Oak Grove, Oak Grove vicinity, 3/15/79, C, 79003096

Spence's Point, On Sandy Point Neck, on VA 749, Westmoreland, 11/11/71, B, g, NHL, 71000991

Spring Grove, VA 202, Mt. Holly vicinity, 10/10/85, C, 85003130

Stratford Hall, N of Lerty on VA 214, Lerty vicinity, 10/15/66, B, C, NHL, 66000851

Wirtland, S of Oak Grove on VA 638, Oak Grove vicinity, 3/15/79, C, 79003097

Yeocomico Church, SW of Tucker Hill on Rte. 66, Tucker Hill vicinity, 11/12/69, C, a, NHL, 69000331

Williamsburg Independent City

Bruton Parish Church, Duke of Gloucester St., Williamsburg (Independent City), 5/10/70, C, a, NHL, 70000861

College Landing, Address Restricted, Williamsburg (Independent City), 7/12/78, A, D, 78003188

Randolph, Peyton, House, Corner of Nicholson and N. England Sts., Williamsburg (Independent City), 4/15/70, C, NHL, 70000863

Semple, James, House, S side of Frances St. between Blair and Walker Sts., Williamsburg (Independent City), 4/15/70, C, NHL, 70000864

Williamsburg Historic District, Bounded by Francis, Waller, Nicholson, N. England, Lafayette, and Nassau Sts., Williamsburg (Independent City), 10/15/66, A, C, e, g, NHL, 66000925

Wren Building, College of William and Mary, College of William and Mary campus, Williamsburg (Independent City), 10/15/66, A, NHL, 66000929

Wythe House, W side of the Palace Green, Williamsburg (Independent City), 4/15/70, B, C, NHL, 70000866

Winchester Independent City

Abram's Delight, Parkview St. and Rouss Spring Rd., Winchester (Independent City), 4/11/73, A, C, 73002230

Glen Burnie, 801 Amherst St., Winchester (Independent City), 9/10/79, A, C, 79003305

Handley Library, NW corner of Braddock and Piccadilly Sts., Winchester (Independent City), 11/12/69, C, 69000364

Hexagon House, 530 Amherst St., Winchester (Independent City), 9/10/87, C, 87001550

Jackson, Thomas J., Headquarters, 415 N. Braddock St., Winchester (Independent City), 5/28/67, A, B, NHL, 67000027

Kurtz, Adam, House, NE corner of Braddock and Cork Sts., Winchester (Independent City), 5/17/76, B, C, 76002233

Old Stone Church, 304 E. Piccadilly St., Winchester (Independent City), 8/18/77, A, C, a, 77001538

Winchester Historic District, U.S. 522, U.S. 11 and U.S. 50/17, Winchester (Independent City), 3/04/80, A, B, C, 80004318

Wise County

"June Tolliver" House, On VA 613, Big Stone Gap, 8/28/73, B, 73002067

Christ Episcopal Church, 100 Clinton Ave., Big Stone Gap, 12/19/90, C, a, 89001905

Colonial Hotel, Jct. of Main and Spring Sts., Wise, 2/05/91, A, C, 91000019

Country Cabin, Jct. of US 23 and VA 790, Norton vicinity, 10/27/92, A, 92001395

Fox, John, Jr., House, 117 Shawnee Ave., Big Stone Gap, 6/07/74, B, 74002151

U.S. Post Office and Courthouse, U.S. 58, Big Stone Gap, 12/23/75, A, C, 75002043

Wise County Courthouse, VA 640, Wise, 3/02/81, A, C, 81000649

Wythe County

Cornett Archeological Site (44WY1), Address Restricted, Austinville vicinity, 9/29/83, D, 83003320

Crockett's Cove Presbyterian Church, VA 600 E of jct. with VA 603, Wytheville vicinity, 10/15/92, C, a, 92001373

Fort Chiswell Mansion, I-81 near jct. of U.S. 52 and VA 121, Max Meadows vicinity, 5/06/71, C, 71000992

Fort Chiswell Site, Address Restricted, Fort Chiswell vicinity, 8/29/78, A, D, 78003046

Graham, Maj. David, House, VA 619 and 626, Fosters Falls vicinity, 2/14/85, A, C, 85000300

Haller-Gibboney Rock House, Monroe and Tazewell Sts., Wytheville, 11/09/72, C, 72001419

Kimberling Lutheran Cemetery, NW of Rural Retreat, Rural Retreat vicinity, 3/26/80, A, C, a, d, 80004231

Martin Site, Address Restricted, Fosters Falls vicinity, 8/13/74, D, 74002152

McGavock Family Cemetery, E of Fort Chiswell off I-81, Fort Chiswell vicinity, 6/22/79, B, C, d, 79003098

Shot Tower, W of jct. of Rte. 608 and U.S. 52, Max Meadows vicinity, 10/01/69, A, C, 69000286

St. John's Lutheran Church and Cemetery, NW of Wytheville at jct of U.S. 21/52 and I-81, Wytheville vicinity, 1/26/78, A, C, a, d, 78003047

Zion Evangelical Lutheran Church Cemetery, NW of Speedwell, Speedwell vicinity, 2/01/79, A, C, a, d, 79003099

York County

Bruton Parish Poorhouse Archeological Site, Address Restricted, Williamsburg vicinity, 9/02/82, A, D, a, 82004610

Bryan Manor, Address Restricted, Williamsburg vicinity, 11/14/78, C, D, 78003048

Gooch, William, Tomb and York Village Archeological Site, Address Restricted, Yorktown vicinity, 1/18/74, A, C, D, d, 74002153

Grace Church, Rte. 1003 and Main St., Yorktown, 9/15/70, A, C, a, 70000832

Kiskiack, NE of jct. of VA 238 and 168, Lackay vicinity, 11/12/69, C, 69000287

Porto Bello, On Queens Creek, in Camp Peary Military Reservation, Williamsburg vicinity, 4/13/73, B, C, D, 73002068

Yorktown Wrecks, Address Restricted, Yorktown vicinity, 10/09/73, A, D, 73002069

WASHINGTON

Adams County

Burroughs, Dr. Frank R., House, 408 Main St., Ritzville, 11/20/75, B, C, 75001838

Denver and Rio Grande Western Railroad Business Car No. 101, Bruce and Lee Rds., Othello, 6/16/88, C, b, 88000740

Greene, Nelson H., House, 502 S. Adams St., Ritzville, 3/07/80, B, C, 80003996

Ritzville Carnegie Library [Carnegie Libraries of Washington TR], 302 W. Main St., Ritzville, 8/03/82, A, C, 82004192

Ritzville Historic District, Roughly bounded by Broadway, Division St., Railroad Ave., and Washington St., Ritzville, 5/02/90, A, C, 90000676

Seivers Brothers Ranchhouse and Barn, SE of Lind on Providence Rd., Lind vicinity, 6/19/79, A, C, 79002524

Strap Iron Corral, 5 mi. N of Hooper on Harder Ranch, Hooper vicinity, 8/01/75, A, 75001837

Asotin County

Clarkston Public Library [Carnegie Libraries of Washington TR], 6th and Chestnut Sts., Clarkston, 8/03/82, A, C, 82004193

Cloverland Garage, CR 01050, Cloverland, 5/02/86, A, C, 86000895

Full Gospel Church, 1st and Monroe Sts., Asotin, 1/19/72, C, a, 72001266

Indian Timothy Memorial Bridge [Historic Bridges/Tunnels in Washington State TR], Spans Alpowa Creek, Pomeroy, 7/16/82, A, C, 82004194

Nez Perce Snake River Archeological District, Address Restricted, Asotin, vicinity, 12/22/78, D, 78001086

Snake River Archeological District, Address Restricted, Asotin vicinity, 5/13/76, D, 76001868

US Post Office—Clarkston Main [Historic US Post Offices in Washington MPS], 949 6th St., Clarkston, 5/30/91, A, C, 91000642

Van Arsdol, C. C., House, 15th and Chestnut Sts., Clarkston, 5/06/75, B, 75001839

Benton County

Benton County Courthouse, Dudley Ave. and Market St., Prosser, 12/12/76, A, C, 76001869

Carey, J. W., House, Byron Rd., W of Prosser, Prosser vicinity, 12/07/89, C, 89002096

Glade Creek Site, Address Restricted, Prosser vicinity, 10/21/77, D, 77001330

Hanford B Reactor, Near jct. of WA 24 and WA 240, Hanford Site, Richland vicinity, 4/03/92, A, 92000245

Hanford Island Archeological Site, Address Restricted, Richland vicinity, 8/28/76, D, 76001870

Hanford North Archeological District, Address Restricted, Richland vicinity, 8/28/76, D, 76001871

Locke Island Archeological District, Address Restricted, Richland vicinity, 8/28/76, D, 76001872

Rattlesnake Springs Sites, Address Restricted, Richland vicinity, 5/04/76, D, 76001873

Ryegrass Archeological District, Address Restricted, Richland vicinity, 1/31/76, D, 76001874

Snively Canyon Archeological District, Address Restricted, Richland vicinity, 8/28/76, D, 76001875

Telegraph Island Petroglyphs, Address Restricted, Paterson vicinity, 3/10/75, D, 75001840

US Post Office—Prosser Main [Historic US Post Offices in Washington MPS], 1103 Meade Ave., Prosser, 8/07/91, A, C, 91000653

Wooded Island Archeological District, 7 mi. N of Richland, Richland vicinity, 7/19/76, D, 76001876

Chelan County

Black Warrior Mine, N of Stehekin in North Cascades National Park, Stehekin vicinity, 10/15/74, A, NPS, 74000914

Blewett Arrastra, S of Cashmere on U.S. 97, Cashmere vicinity, 9/17/74, A, C, 74001941

Bridge Creek Cabin—Ranger Station [North Cascades National Park Service Complex MRA], Bridge Creek Campground off Stehekin Valley Rd., Stehekin vicinity, 2/10/89, A, C, NPS, 88003458

Bridge Creek Shelter [North Cascades National Park Service Complex MRA], Bridge Creek Campground off Stehekin Valley Rd., Stehekin vicinity, 2/10/89, C, NPS, 88003445

Buckner Cabin, Lake Chelan National Recreation Area, Stehekin, 5/17/74, A, NPS, 74000912

Buckner Homestead Historic District [North Cascades National Park Service Complex MRA], Address Restricted, Stehekin, 2/10/89, A, NPS, 88003441

Burbank Homestead Waterwheel, Cottage Ave., Cashmere, 6/19/73, A, C, b, 73002277

Chatter Creek Guard Station [Depression-Era Buildings TR], Wenatchee National Forest, Leavenworth, 4/08/86, A, C, 86000812

Chelan Butte Lookout [USDA Forest Service Fire Lookouts on Wenatchee NF MPS], Summit of Chelan Butte, Chelan vicinity, 12/27/90, A, C, 90001912

Columbia River Bridge [Historic Bridges/Tunnels in Washington State TR], Spans Columbia River between Wenatchee and East Wenatchee, Wenatchee, 7/16/82, A, C, 82004198

Courtney Cabin, Lake Chelan National Recreation Area, Stehekin, 5/31/74, A, NPS, 74000910

Flick Creek Shelter [North Cascades National Park Service Complex MRA], E side of Lake Chelan S of Flick Creek, Stehekin vicinity, 2/10/89, C, NPS, 88003444

Golden West Lodge Historic District [North Cascades National Park Service Complex MRA], Stehekin Landing, Stehekin, 2/10/89, A, g, NPS, 88003442

High Bridge Ranger Station Historic District [North Cascades National Park Service Complex MRA], Stehekin Valley Rd., Stehekin, 2/10/89, A, C, g, NPS, 88003443

High Bridge Shelter [North Cascades National Park Service Complex MRA], High Bridge Campground off Stehekin Valley Rd., Stehekin vicinity, 2/10/89, C, NPS, 88003461

Horan, Michael, House, 2 Horan Rd., Wenatchee, 3/31/92, B, C, 92000281

Lake Chelan Hydroelectric Power Plant [Hydroelectric Power Plants in Washington State, 1890–1938 MPS], Lake Chelan, Chelan vicinity, 12/15/88, A, C, 88002739

Lake Wenatchee Residence No. 1200 [USDA Forest Service Administrative Buildings in Oregon and Washington Built by the CCC MPS], WA 207, N shore of Lake Wenatchee, Wenatchee NF, Leavenworth vicinity, 3/06/91, A, C, 91000158

Leavenworth Ranger Station [Depression-Era Buildings TR], Wenatchee National Forest, Leavenworth, 4/11/86, A, C, g, 86000840

Lucas Homestead, SW of Chelan, Chelan vicinity, 12/14/78, B, C, 78002734

Lucerne Guard Station [USDA Forest Service Administrative Buildings in Oregon and Washington Built by the CCC MPS], S shore of Lake Chelan, Wenatchee NF, Lucerne, 3/06/91, A, C, 91000160

Miller, George, House [North Cascades National Park Service Complex MRA], E side Lake Chelan on Stehekin Valley Rd., Stehekin, 2/10/89, A, C, NPS, 88003464

Penstock Bridge [Historic Bridges/Tunnels in Washington State TR], Spans Wenatchee River, N of Leavenworth on US 2, Leavenworth vicinity, 7/16/82, A, C, 82004196

Purple Point—Stehekin Ranger Station House [North Cascades National Park Service Complex MRA], E side of Lake Chelan, Stehekin, 2/10/89, C, NPS, 88003460

Rock Island Railroad Bridge [Historic Bridges/Tunnels in Washington State TR (AD)], SW of Rock Island over the Columbia River, Rock Island vicinity, 7/30/75, A, C, 75001842

Ruby Theater [Movie Theaters in Washington State MPS], 135 E. Woodin Ave., Chelan, 10/07/91, A, 91001495

St. Andrews Episcopal Church, 120 E. Woodin Ave., Chelan, 3/31/92, C, a, 92000283

Stehekin School, Lake Chelan National Recreation Area, Stehekin, 5/31/74, A, NPS, 74000913

Chelan County—Continued

Steliko Ranger Station [USDA Forest Service Administrative Buildings in Oregon and Washington Built by the CCC MPS], E of Entiat R., Wenatchee NF, Ardenvoir vicinity, 3/06/91, A, C, 91000159

Stevens Pass Guard Station [USDA Forest Service Administrative Buildings in Oregon and Washington Built by the CCC MPS], I-2 at Stevens Pass, Skykomish vicinity, 3/06/91, A, C, 91000156

Sugarloaf Peak Lookout [USDA Forest Service Fire Lookouts on Wenatchee NF MPS], Summit of Sugarloaf Peak, Leavenworth vicinity, 12/27/90, A, C, 90001914

Sulphide—Frisco Cabin [North Cascades National Park Service Complex MRA], Bridge Creek Trail, 9 mi. N of Stehekin Valley Rd., Stehekin vicinity, 2/10/89, A, C, NPS, 88003459

Tyee Mountain Lookout [USDA Forest Service Fire Lookouts on Wenatchee NF MPS], Summit of Tyee Mountain, Entait vicinity, 12/27/90, C, 90001913

U.S. Post Office and Annex, Mission and Yakima Sts., Wenatchee, 5/27/77, A, g, 77001331

Wells House, 1300 5th St., Wenatchee, 6/04/73, B, C, 73001865

Wenatchee Carnegie Library [Carnegie Libraries of Washington TR], 2 S. Chelan St., Wenatchee, 8/03/82, A, C, 82004199

Wenatchee Flat Site, Address Restricted, Wenatchee vicinity, 8/14/73, D, 73001866

West Monitor Bridge [Historic Bridges/Tunnels in Washington State TR], Spans Wenatchee River, Monitor vicinity, 7/16/82, A, C, 82004197

Clallam County

Aircraft Warning Service Observation Tower, 216 Spring Rd., Agnew vicinity, 4/29/93, A, b, 93000363

Beaver School [Rural Public Schools of Washington State MPS], US 101 N, W side, Beaver, 11/19/92, A, 92001591

Blue Mountain School [Rural Public Schools in Washington from Early Settlement to 1945 MPS], Blue Mountain Rd., Port Angeles vicinity, 11/05/87, A, b, d, 87001938

Clallam County Courthouse, 319 Lincoln St., Port Angeles, 9/02/87, A, C, 87001459

Dungeness River Bridge [Historic Bridges-/Tunnels in Washington State TR], Spans Dungeness River, Sequim, 7/16/82, A, C, 82004201

Dungeness School [Rural Public Schools in Washington from Early Settlement to 1945 MPS], 657 Towne Rd., Dungeness, 5/19/88, A, C, 88000627

Elwha River Bridge [Historic Bridges/Tunnels in Washington State TR], Old Hwy. 112, Elwha, 7/16/82, A, C, 82004200

Elwha River Hydroelectric Power Plant [Hydroelectric Power Plants in Washington State, 1890–

1938 MPS], N end of Lake Aldwell, Port Angeles vicinity, 12/15/88, A, C, 88002741

Emery Farmstead, Emery Rd., Port Angeles vicinity, 12/16/88, C, 88002746

Glines Canyon Hydroelectric Power Plant [Hydroelectric Power Plants in Washington State, 1890–1938 MPS], N end of Lake Mills at Elwha River, Port Angeles vicinity, 12/15/88, A, C, 88002742

Hoko River Archeological Site, Address Restricted, Pysht vicinity, 3/21/78, D, 78002735

Hoko River Rockshelter Archeological Site, Address Restricted, Sekiu vicinity, 3/27/80, D, 80003997

Humes Ranch Cabin, S of Port Angeles on Elwha River, Port Angeles vicinity, 9/14/77, A, C, NPS, 77001332

Manis Mastodon Site, Address Restricted, Sequim vicinity, 3/21/78, D, 78002736

Masonic Temple, 622 S. Lincoln St., Port Angeles, 5/11/89, A, C, 89000400

McAlmond House, N of Sequim on Dungeness Bay, Sequim vicinity, 8/09/76, B, C, 76001879

Naval Lodge Elks Building, 131 E. First St., Port Angeles, 5/02/86, A, C, 86000956

New Dungeness Light Station, Dungeness Spit, Sequim vicinity, 11/30/93, A, 93001338

Ozette Indian Village Archeological Site, Address Restricted, La Push vicinity, 1/11/74, D, NPS, 74000916

Paris, Joseph, House, 101 E. Fifth St., Port Angeles, 11/05/87, C, 87001939

Rosemary Inn, SW of Port Angeles on Barnes Point, Port Angeles vicinity, 7/17/79, A, C, NPS, 79001033

Sekiu School [Rural Public Schools in Washington State MPS], Rice St., Sekiu, 5/01/91, A, C, 91000539

Sequim Opera House, 119 N. Sequim Ave., Sequim, 5/28/91, A, 91000632

St. Andrew's Episcopal Church, 206 S. Peabody St., Port Angeles, 11/05/87, C, a, 87001942

Tatoosh Island, NW of Cape Flattery, Olympic Peninsula, 3/16/72, A, 72001267

U.S. Post Office, W. 1st and Oak Sts., Port Angeles, 9/01/83, C, 83003321

US Quarantine Station Surgeon's Residence, 101 Discovery Way, Diamond Point, Sequim, 5/11/89, A, 89000401

Wedding Rock Petroglyphs, Address Restricted, Forks vicinity, 4/03/76, A, D, NPS, 76000951

Clark County

Anderson—Beletski Prune Farm, 4119 N.W. McCann Rd., Vancouver, 5/15/86, A, 86001100

Arndt Prune Dryer, SE of Ridgefield at 2109 NW 219th St., Ridgefield vicinity, 10/04/79, A, 79002527

Basalt Cobblestone Quarries District, Ridgefield National Wildlife Refuge, Ridgefield vicinity, 12/14/81, A, C, 81000587

Cedar Creek Grist Mill, 9 mi. E of Woodland on Cedar Creek, Woodland vicinity, 3/26/75, A, 75001844

Covington House, 4208 Main St., Vancouver, 5/05/72, C, b, 72001268

Elks Building, 916 Main St., Vancouver, 7/14/83, A, C, 83003322

Evergreen Hotel, 500 Main St., Vancouver, 1/01/79, A, 79002529

Fort Vancouver National Historic Site, NE of Vancouver, Vancouver, 10/15/66, A, NPS, 66000370

Glenwood School [Rural Public Schools in Washington State MPS], Jct. of NE. 87th Ave. and NE. 134th St., SE corner, Glenwood vicinity, 6/11/92, A, 92000697

Green, Albert and Letha, House and Barn, 25716 NE Lewisville Hwy., Battle Ground vicinity, 2/19/82, A, C, 82004202

Heisen, Henry, House, 27904 NE 174th Ave., Heisson, 10/04/79, A, C, 79002526

Hidden Houses, 100 and 110 W. 13th St., Vancouver, 11/29/78, B, C, 78002737

House of Providence, 400 E. Evergreen Blvd., Vancouver, 12/01/78, A, B, C, a, 78002738

Lambert School [Rural Public Schools in Washington from Early Settlement to 1945 MPS], 21814 NW 11th, Ridgefield vicinity, 3/16/89, A, 89000216

Lancaster, Judge Columbia, House, N of Ridgefield on Lancaster Rd., Ridgefield vicinity, 2/20/75, A, B, b, 75001843

Lewisville Park, 26411 N.E. Lewisville Hwy., Battle Ground vicinity, 5/28/86, A, C, g, 86001202

Officers Row, Fort Vancouver Barracks, 611-1616 E. Evergreen Blvd., Vancouver, 11/11/74, B, C, 74001948

Parkersville Site, Address Restricted, Camas vicinity, 8/11/76, A, D, 76001880

Pittock House, N of Camas at 114 NE Leadbetter Rd., Camas vicinity, 7/03/79, C, 79003148

Pomeroy Farm, 20902 N.E. Lucia Falls Rd., Yacolt vicinity, 3/13/87, A, B, b, 87000413

Roffler, John, House, 1437 NE. Everett St., Camas, 4/29/93, B, C, 93000368

Shobert, William Henry, House, 621 Shobert Lane, Ridgefield, 10/04/79, A, C, 79002528

Slocum House, 605 Esther St., Vancouver, 1/18/73, C, 73001867

Stanger, John, House, 9213 Evergreen Hwy., Vancouver vicinity, 5/17/90, A, 90000785

U.S. National Bank Building, 601 Main St., Vancouver, 12/29/88, C, 84004010

US Post Office—Camas Main [Historic US Post Offices in Washington MPS], 440 NE. Fifth Ave., Camas, 8/07/91, A, C, 91000639

US Post Office—Vancouver Main [Historic US Post Offices in Washington MPS], 1211 Daniels, Vancouver, 5/30/91, A, C, 91000659

Vancouver Public Library [Carnegie Libraries of Washington TR], 1511 Main St., Vancouver, 8/03/82, A, C, 82004204

Vancouver Telephone Building, 112 W. Eleventh, Vancouver, 11/06/86, A, C, 86003092

Vancouver-Portland Bridge [Historic Bridges-/Tunnels in Washington State TR], Spans Columbia River, Vancouver, 7/16/82, A, C, 82004205

Venersborg School [Rural Public Schools in Washington from Early Settlement to 1945

Clark County—Continued

MPS], NE 209th St at NE 242nd Ave., Battle Ground vicinity, 3/16/89, A, 89000215

Washington School for the Blind, 2214 E. 13th St., Vancouver, 5/14/93, A, C, 93000370

Yale Bridge [Historic Bridges/Tunnels in Washington State TR], Spans Lewis River on WA 502, Yale, 7/16/82, A, C, 82004206

Columbia County

Bank of Starbuck, Main and McNeil Sts., Starbuck, 2/08/78, A, 78002739

Bishop, A. H., House [Historic Houses of Dayton TR], 622 E. Richmond, Dayton, 8/13/86, C, 86001516

Brining, John, House [Historic Houses of Dayton TR], 410 N. First, Dayton, 8/13/86, C, 86001517

Columbia County Courthouse, 341 E. Main, Dayton, 2/10/75, A, C, 75001845

Dayton Depot, 2nd and Commercial Sts., Dayton, 11/19/74, A, C, b, 74001949

Dexter House No. 1 [Historic Houses of Dayton TR], 515 S. Fourth, Dayton, 8/13/86, C, 86001519

Dexter House No. 2 [Historic Houses of Dayton TR], 507 N. Third, Dayton, 8/13/86, C, 86001520

Flintner, Frank, House [Historic Houses of Dayton TR], 214 S. Sixth, Dayton, 8/13/86, C, 86001522

Guernsey—Sturdevant Building, 225 E. Main St., Dayton, 1/12/93, A, B, 92001589

Isreal, Grover J., House [Historic Houses of Dayton TR], 305 S. Sixth, Dayton, 8/13/86, C, 86001525

Kelley, Mancel, House [Historic Houses of Dayton TR], 1301 S. Fifth, Dayton, 8/13/86, C, 86001526

Mill House [Historic Houses of Dayton TR], 504 N. First, Dayton, 8/13/86, A, C, 86001528

Nilsson, Andrew, House [Historic Houses of Dayton TR], 312 E. Patit, Dayton, 8/13/86, C, 86001530

Pietrzycki, Dr. Marcel, House [Historic Houses of Dayton TR], 415 E. Clay, Dayton, 8/13/86, B, C, 86001531

Snake River Bridge [Historic Bridges/Tunnels in Washington State TR], N of SR 12, Lyons Ferry, 7/16/82, A, C, b, e, 82004207

South Side Historic District [Historic Houses of Dayton TR], Roughly bounded by Clay, Third, Park, and First Sts., Dayton, 8/13/86, C, 86001515

Thronson, J. A., House [Historic Houses of Dayton TR], 510 S. Fourth, Dayton, 8/13/86, C, 86001532

Washington Street Historic District [Historic Houses of Dayton TR], Roughly Washington St. between Patit Creek and Third St., Dayton, 8/13/86, C, 86001514

Weinhard, Jacob, House [Historic Houses of Dayton TR], NW of Dayton, Dayton vicinity, 8/13/86, B, C, 86001524

Cowlitz County

Big Four Furniture Building [Civic, Cultural, and Commercial Resources of Longview TR], 1329 Commerce Ave., Longview, 12/05/85, C, 85003013

Columbia Theater [Civic, Cultural, and Commercial Resources of Longview TR], 1225 Vandercook Way, Longview, 12/05/85, A, C, 85003014

First Christian Church [Civic, Cultural, and Commercial Resources of Longview TR], 2000 E. Kessler Blvd., Longview, 12/05/85, A, C, a, 85003015

Klager, Hulda, Lilac Gardens, 115 S. Pekin Rd., Woodland, 7/17/75, B, 75001847

Lake Sacajawea Park [Civic, Cultural, and Commercial Resources of Longview TR], Bounded by Nichols and Kessler Blvds., Longview, 12/05/85, A, C, 85003011

Laughlin Round Barn, 8249 Barnes Dr., Castle Rock vicinity, 5/15/86, C, 86001080

Long, Robert Alexander, High School [Civic, Cultural, and Commercial Resources of Longview TR], 2903 Nichols Blvd., Longview, 12/05/85, A, C, 85003010

Longview Bridge [Historic Bridges/Tunnels in Washington State TR], Spans Columbia river, Longview, 7/16/82, A, C, 82004208

Longview Civic Center Historic District [Civic, Cultural, and Commercial Resources of Longview TR], Bounded by Maple St., Sixteenth Ave., Hemlock St., and Eighteenth Ave., Longview, 12/05/85, A, C, 85003012

Longview Community Church [Civic, Cultural, and Commercial Resources of Longview TR], 2323 Washington Way, Longview, 12/05/85, A, C, a, 85003016

Longview Community Church—Saint Helen's Addition [Civic, Cultural, and Commercial Resources of Longview TR], 416 Twentieth Ave., Longview, 12/05/85, A, C, a, 85003017

Longview Community Store [Civic, Cultural, and Commercial Resources of Longview TR], 421 Twentieth Ave., Longview, 12/05/85, A, C, 85003027

Longview Women's Clubhouse [Civic, Cultural, and Commercial Resources of Longview TR], 835 Twenty-first Ave., Longview, 12/05/85, A, C, 85003018

Mills Building [Civic, Cultural, and Commercial Resources of Longview TR], 1239 Commerce Ave., Longview, 12/05/85, C, 85003019

Pacific Telephone and Telegraph Building [Civic, Cultural, and Commercial Resources of Longview TR], 1304 Vandercook Way, Longview, 12/05/85, A, C, 85003020

Pounder Building [Civic, Cultural, and Commercial Resources of Longview TR], 1208 Commerce Ave., Longview, 12/05/85, B, C, 85003021

Schumann Building [Civic, Cultural, and Commercial Resources of Longview TR], 1233 Commerce Ave., Longview, 12/05/85, A, C, 85003022

Sevier and Weed Building [Civic, Cultural, and Commercial Resources of Longview TR], 1266

Twelfth Ave., Longview, 12/05/85, A, C, 85003023

Smith, Nat, House, 110 W. Grant St., Kelso, 3/03/75, B, C, 75001846

Stella Blacksmith Shop, 8530 Ocean Beach Hwy., Stella, 12/19/85, A, 85003204

Tennant, J. D., House, 420 Rutherglen Rd., Longview, 4/12/84, B, C, 84003461

Tyni Building [Civic, Cultural, and Commercial Resources of Longview TR], 1166 Commerce Ave., Longview, 12/05/85, A, C, 85003024

US Post Office—Kelso Main [Historic US Post Offices in Washington MPS], 304 Academy St., Kelso, 8/07/91, A, C, 91000646

US Post Office—Longview Main [Historic US Post Offices in Washington MPS], 1603 Larch St., Longview, 5/30/91, A, C, 91000647

Washington Gas and Electric Building [Civic, Cultural, and Commercial Resources of Longview TR], 1346 Fourteenth Ave., Longview, 12/05/85, A, C, 85003025

Willard Building [Civic, Cultural, and Commercial Resources of Longview TR], 1403 Twelfth Ave., Longview, 12/05/85, A, C, 85003026

Douglas County

Badger Mountain Lookout [USDA Forest Service Fire Lookouts on Wenatchee NF MPS], Near summit of Badger Mountain, East Wenatchee vicinity, 12/27/90, A, C, 90001915

Canton, William J., House, 305 W. Ash St., Waterville, 6/16/88, B, C, 88000737

Douglas County Courthouse, Off U.S. 2, Waterville, 9/05/75, A, C, 75001849

Downtown Waterville Historic District, Locust and Chelan Sts., Waterville, 5/19/88, A, C, 88000629

Gallaher House, 11.5 mi. NW of Mansfield on Dyer Rd., Mansfield vicinity, 8/01/75, C, 75001848

Lutheran St. Paul's Kirche, Lake Ave., Douglas, 4/12/82, A, C, a, 82004209

Pangborn-Herndon Memorial Site, 3 mi. NE of East Wenatchee, East Wenatchee vicinity, 3/16/72, A, g, 72001269

Smith Hospital and Douglas County Press Building, 109 N. Chelan, Waterville, 5/11/89, A, 89000402

Waterville Hotel, 102 S. Central St., Waterville, 10/18/84, A, C, 84000170

Ferry County

Ansorge Hotel, River St. and Railroad Ave., Curlew, 3/26/79, A, 79002530

Creaser Hotel, 702 S. Jefferson St., Republic, 4/12/82, B, C, 82004211

Curlew Bridge [Historic Bridges/Tunnels in Washington State TR], Spans Kettle River, Curlew, 7/16/82, A, C, 82004210

Curlew School, Off WA 4A, Curlew, 11/28/80, A, 80003998

Ferry County—Continued

St. Paul's Mission, W of Kettle Falls on Roosevelt Lake, Kettle Falls vicinity, 11/20/74, A, D, a, e, NPS, 74002259

Franklin County

Allen Rockshelter, Address Restricted, Pasco vicinity, 11/16/78, D, 78002741

Burr Cave, Address Restricted, Walker vicinity, 12/15/78, D, 78002742

Franklin County Courthouse, 1016 N. 4th St., Pasco, 2/08/78, A, C, 78002740

Lower Snake River Archaeological District, Address Restricted, Pasco vicinity, 10/29/84, D, 84000471

Marmes Rockshelter, Address Restricted, Lyons Ferry vicinity, 10/15/66, D, NHL, 66000745

Moore, James, House, Off U.S. 12, Pasco, 5/31/79, A, 79002532

Palouse Canyon Archaeological District, Address Restricted, Starbuck vicinity, 10/29/84, D, 84000464

Pasco Carnegie Library [Carnegie Libraries of Washington TR], 305 N. 4th St., Pasco, 8/03/82, A, C, 82004212

Savage Island Archeological District, Address Restricted, Richland vicinity, 8/28/76, D, 76001881

Strawberry Island Village Archeological Site, Address Restricted, Pasco vicinity, 8/21/80, D, 80003999

Tri-Cities Archaeological District, Address Restricted, Richland vicinity, 10/29/84, D, 84000468

Windust Caves Archaeological District, Address Restricted, Windust vicinity, 10/29/84, D, 84000479

Garfield County

Garfield County Courthouse, 8th and Main Sts., Pomeroy, 7/24/74, A, C, 74001951

Lewis and Clark Trail-Travois Road, 5 mi. E of Pomeroy, U.S. 12, Pomeroy vicinity, 1/11/74, A, D, 74001952

Grant County

Beverly Railroad Bridge [Historic Bridges-/Tunnels in Washington State TR], Spans Columbia River, Beverly, 7/16/82, A, C, 82004214

Grant County Courthouse, C St., NW, Ephrata, 9/05/75, A, C, 75001850

Lind Coulee Archaeological Site, Address Restricted, Warden vicinity, 1/21/74, D, 74001953

Mesa 36, Address Restricted, Soap Lake vicinity, 12/08/78, D, 78002744

Paris Archeological Site, Address Restricted, Richland vicinity, 9/20/78, D, 78002743

Stratford School [Rural Public Schools in Washington from Early Settlement to 1945 MPS], Just off WA 7, Stratford, 10/25/90, A, C, 90001606

Wilson Creek State Bank, Off WA 7, Wilson Creek, 9/25/75, A, C, 75001851

Grays Harbor County

Carnegie Library [Carnegie Libraries of Washington TR], 621 K St., Hoquiam, 8/03/82, A, C, 82004216

Cooney, Neil, Mansion, 802 E. 5th St., Cosmopolis, 7/14/83, A, C, 83003324

Finch Building, Heron and H Sts., Aberdeen, 10/13/83, C, 83004230

Grays Harbor Light Station, W of Westport, Westport vicinity, 11/02/77, A, C, 77001333

Hoquiam River Bridge [Historic Bridges/Tunnels in Washington State TR], N of SR 12, Hoquiam, 7/16/82, A, C, 82004217

Hoquiam's Castle, 515 Chenault Ave., Hoquiam, 4/11/73, A, C, 73001868

Lytle, Joseph, Home, 509 Chenault, Hoquiam, 7/12/90, C, 90001073

McTaggert, Lachlin, House, 2240 L St., Hoquiam, 8/29/85, C, 85001942

Mickelson, Ole, Cabin, Lot 46, S shore Lake Quinault, between Willaby Cr. and Falls Cr., Quinault vicinity, 5/06/93, C, 92001291

Polson, F. Arnold, House and Polson, Alex, Grounds, 1611 Riverside Ave., Hoquiam, 6/19/79, C, 79002533

SIERRA (motor ship), 1401 Sargent Blvd., Aberdeen, 3/29/78, A, 78002745

Seventh Street Theater, 313 Seventh St., Hoquiam, 8/06/87, A, C, 87001334

US Post Office—Hoquiam Main [Historic US Post Offices in Washington MPS], 620 Eighth St., Hoquiam, 5/30/91, A, C, 91000645

US Post Office—Montesano Main [Historic US Post Offices in Washington MPS], 211 Pioneer Ave. N., Montesano, 5/30/91, A, C, 91000649

Island County

Central Whidbey Island Historic District, S of Oak Harbor, roughly 6 mi. either side of Coupeville, Oak Harbor vicinity, 12/12/73, A, C, a, b, 73001869

Loers, Benjamin, House, 2046 Swantown Rd., Oak Harbor, 8/29/77, C, 77001334

Olympic Club, 230 1st St., Langley, 5/28/91, A, 91000630

Smith Island Light Station, N of Port Townsend, Port Townsend vicinity, 4/06/78, A, 78002746

Jefferson County

Bartlett, Frank, House, 314 Polk St., Port Townsend, 4/24/73, C, 73001870

Bash, Henry, House [Victorian Residences in Port Townsend TR], 718 F St., Port Townsend, 5/16/85, C, 85001099

Bishop, Senator William, House and Office [Eastern Jefferson County MRA], Chimacum-Center Rd., Chimacum, 10/10/84, B, 84000099

Chimacum Post Office [Eastern Jefferson County MRA], Chimacum-Center Rd., Chimacum, 7/14/83, C, 83003323

City Hall, Water and Madison Sts., Port Townsend, 5/14/71, A, 71000868

Coleman-Furlong House [Victorian Residences in Port Townsend TR], 1253 Umatilla Ave., Port Townsend, 5/16/85, C, 85001100

Duckabush River Bridge [Historic Bridges-/Tunnels in Washington State TR], Spans Duckabush River, Duckabush, 7/16/82, A, C, g, 82004219

Edwards, Joel, House [Victorian Residences in Port Townsend TR], 913 25th St., Port Townsend, 5/16/85, C, 85001101

Fitzgerald, Thomas, House [Victorian Residences in Port Townsend TR], 832 T St., Port Townsend, 5/16/85, C, 85001102

Fort Flagler, SE of Port Townsend on Marrowstone Island, Port Townsend vicinity, 5/03/76, A, C, 76001882

Fort Worden, Cherry and W Sts., Port Townsend, 3/15/74, A, C, NHL, 74001954

Fowler, Capt. Enoch S., House, Corner of Polk and Washington Sts., Port Townsend, 9/29/70, C, 70000635

Gagen-Sherlock House [Victorian Residences in Port Townsend TR (AD)], 1906 Cherry St., Port Townsend, 3/19/82, A, C, 82004220

Galster House [Eastern Jefferson County MRA], Water St., Lower Hadlock, 7/14/83, A, B, 83003325

Griffiths, J. W., House [Victorian Residences in Port Townsend TR], 2030 Monroe St., Port Townsend, 5/16/85, C, 85001103

Harper, F. C., House [Victorian Residences in Port Townsend TR], 502 Reed St., Port Townsend, 5/16/85, C, 85001104

House at 1723 Holcomb Street [Victorian Residences in Port Townsend TR], 1723 Holcomb St., Port Townsend, 5/16/85, C, 85001105

House at 30 Tremont Street [Victorian Residences in Port Townsend TR], 30 Tremont St., Port Townsend, 5/16/85, C, 85001106

House at 503 Fir Street [Victorian Residences in Port Townsend TR], 503 Fir St., Port Townsend, 5/16/85, C, 85001107

Irondale Historic District [Eastern Jefferson County MRA], Port Townsend Bay and Admirally Inlet, Port Townsend vicinity, 7/14/83, A, 83003326

Irondale Jail [Eastern Jefferson County MRA], Moore St., Irondale, 7/14/83, A, 83003327

James, Francis Wilcox, House, Corner of Washington and Harrison Sts., Port Townsend, 9/29/70, A, 70000636

Jefferson County Courthouse, Jefferson and Case Sts., Port Townsend, 4/24/73, C, 73001871

Jefferson County—Continued

Johnson House [Eastern Jefferson County MRA], 287 Flagler Rd., Nordland, 7/14/83, A, C, 83003328

Kuhn Spit Archeological Site, Address Restricted, Chimacum vicinity, 12/22/78, D, 78002747

Lake-Little House [Victorian Residences in Port Townsend TR], 1607 Sheridan St., Port Townsend, 5/16/85, C, 85001108

Laubach, J. N., House [Victorian Residences in Port Townsend TR], 613 F St., Port Townsend, 5/16/85, C, 85001109

Leader Building, 226 Adams St., Port Townsend, 9/29/70, A, 70000637

Manresa Hall, Sheridan St., Port Townsend, 9/29/70, C, 70000638

Methodist Epscopal Church of Port Hadlock [Eastern Jefferson County MRA], Randolph and Curtiss Sts., Hadlock, 7/14/83, A, C, a, 83003329

Morgan, O. L. and Josephine, House [Victorian Residences in Port Townsend TR], 1033 Pierce St., Port Townsend, 5/16/85, C, 85001110

Nelson House [Eastern Jefferson County MRA], Freeman Rd., Nordland vicinity, 10/10/84, C, 84000101

Oatman, Earl, House [Eastern Jefferson County MRA], Muncie St., Quilcene, 7/14/83, B, C, 83003330

Old German Consulate, 313 Walker St., Port Townsend, 2/24/71, C, 71000869

Pearson House [Victorian Residences in Port Townsend TR], 1939 27th St., Port Townsend, 5/16/85, C, 85001111

Petersen, H. S., House [Victorian Residences in Port Townsend TR], 50th and Kuhn St., Port Townsend, 5/16/85, C, 85001112

Pettygrove, Benjamin S., House [Victorian Residences in Port Townsend TR], 1000 G St., Port Townsend, 9/25/85, C, 85002662

Point Wilson Lighthouse, On a point of land between Juan de Fuca Strait and Admiralty Inlet, Port Townsend, 3/24/71, A, 71000870

Port Townsend Carnegie Library [Carnegie Libraries of Washington TR], 1220 Lawrence, Port Townsend, 8/03/82, A, C, 82004908

Port Townsend Historic District, Roughly bounded by Scott, Blaine, Walker, and Taft Sts., and the Waterfront, Port Townsend, 5/17/76, A, C, NHL, 76001883

Quilcene-Quinault Battleground Site, Address Restricted, Quilcene vicinity, 12/29/78, A, D, 78002748

Ralston, Judge, House [Victorian Residences in Port Townsend TR], 1523 Madison St., Port Townsend, 5/16/85, C, 85001113

Rothschild House, Taylor and Franklin Sts., Port Townsend, 9/29/70, B, C, 70000639

Rover, Hanna, House [Eastern Jefferson County MRA], Chimacum-Center Rd., Center, 7/14/83, C, 83003331

Saint's Rest, Tukey's Pioneer Cabin and Homestead House [Eastern Jefferson County MRA],

Chevy Chase Rd., Port Townsend vicinity, 7/14/83, A, 83003332

Saunders, James C., House [Victorian Residences in Port Townsend TR (AD)], Sims Way, Port Townsend, 10/18/77, B, C, 77001335

Schlager, Ferdinand, House [Victorian Residences in Port Townsend TR], 810 Rose St., Port Townsend, 5/16/85, C, 85001114

Seal Rock Shell Mounds (45JE15), Address Restricted, Brinnon vicinity, 6/12/85, D, 85001247

Shibles, Capt. Peter, House [Eastern Jefferson County MRA], Curtiss St., Hadlock, 7/14/83, B, C, 83003333

Sole, Tollef, House [Eastern Jefferson County MRA], 275 Flagler Rd., Nordland, 7/14/83, A, C, 83003334

St. Paul's Episcopal Church, Corner of Jefferson and Tyler Sts., Port Townsend, 9/29/70, A, C, a, b, 70000640

Starrett House, 744 Clay St., Port Townsend, 9/29/70, B, C, 70000641

Stegerwald, Andrew, House [Victorian Residences in Port Townsend TR], 1710 Fir St., Port Townsend, 5/16/85, C, 85001115

Swanson, Hans, House [Eastern Jefferson County MRA], Swansonville Rd., Port Ludlow vicinity, 7/14/83, A, B, 83003335

Trumbull, John, House [Victorian Residences in Port Townsend TR], 925 Wilson St., Port Townsend, 5/16/85, C, 85001116

Tucker, Horace, House, 706 Franklin St., Port Townsend, 1/18/73, C, 73001872

US Post Office—Port Townsend Main [Historic US Post Offices in Washington MPS], 1322 Washington, Port Townsend, 5/30/91, A, C, 91000652

Uncas School [Eastern Jefferson County MRA], E. Uncas, Discovery, 2/05/87, A, 87000025

Van Trojen House [Eastern Jefferson County MRA], Van Trojen Rd., Chimacum, 10/10/84, C, 84000100

Ward, Milo P., House [Victorian Residences in Port Townsend TR], 1707 Jackson St., Port Townsend, 5/16/85, C, 85001117

Williams, Hattie, House [Eastern Jefferson County MRA], Moore St., Irondale, 7/14/83, C, 83003336

King County

12th Avenue South Bridge [Historic Bridges-/Tunnels in Washington State TR], 12th Ave., S. over Dearborn St., Seattle, 7/16/82, A, C, 82004227

1411 Fourth Avenue Building, 1411 Fourth Ave., Seattle, 5/28/91, C, 91000633

14th Avenue South Bridge [Historic Bridges-/Tunnels in Washington State TR], Spans Duwamish River, Seattle, 7/16/82, A, C, 82004228

ADVENTURESS, Lake Union Drydock, Seattle, 4/11/89, A, C, NHL, 89001067

ARTHUR FOSS (tugboat), Moss Bay waterfront, Kirkland, 4/11/89, A, C, g, NHL, 89001078

Alaska Trade Building, 1915–1919 1st Ave., Seattle, 5/06/71, A, 71000871

Arboretum Sewer Trestle [Historic Bridges-/Tunnels in Washington State TR], Crosses 26th Ave., E. between Roanoke and E. Miller St., Seattle, 7/16/82, A, C, 82004229

Arctic Building, 306 Cherry St., Seattle, 11/28/78, A, C, 78002749

Assay Office, 613 9th Ave., Seattle, 3/16/72, A, C, 72001271

Auburn Public Library [Carnegie Libraries of Washington TR], 306 Auburn Ave., Auburn, 8/03/82, A, C, 82004221

Aurora Avenue Bridge [Historic Bridges/Tunnels in Washington State TR], Aurora Ave., N. over Lake Washington Ship Canal, Seattle, 7/16/82, A, C, 82004230

Ballard Avenue Historic District, Ballard Ave. from NW Market to NW Dock Sts., Seattle, 7/01/76, A, C, 76001885

Ballard Bridge [Historic Bridges/Tunnels in Washington State TR], Spans Lake Washington Ship Canal, Seattle, 7/16/82, A, C, 82004231

Ballard Carnegie Library [Carnegie Libraries of Washington TR (AD)], 2026 N. West Market St., Seattle, 6/15/79, A, C, 79002535

Ballard-Howe House, 22 W. Highland Dr., Seattle, 3/26/79, B, C, 79002536

Ballinger, Richard A., House, 1733 39th Ave., Seattle, 5/28/76, B, C, 76001886

Barnes Building, 2320–2322 1st Ave., Seattle, 2/24/75, C, 75001853

Bell Apartments, 2326 1st Ave., Seattle, 7/12/74, C, 74001957

Blomeen, Oscar, House, 324 B St. NE., Auburn, 6/21/91, A, C, 91000781

Boeing, William E., House, Huckleberry Ln., Highlands, 12/16/88, B, 88002743

Bowles, Jesse C., House, 2540 Shoreland Dr. S, Seattle, 11/06/86, C, 86003162

Building No. 105, Boeing Airplane Company, Purcell Ave., Seattle, 8/26/71, A, B, b, 71000872

Butterworth Building, 1921 1st Ave., Seattle, 5/14/71, C, 71000873

Camp North Bend, 45509 SE. 150th St., North Bend, 4/29/93, A, 93000372

Chase, Dr. Reuben, House [Historic Resources of Bothell MPS], 17819 113th Ave. NE, Bothell, 8/27/90, B, C, 90001246

Chelsea Family Hotel, 620 W. Olympic Pl., Seattle, 12/14/78, C, 78002750

Chinese Baptist Church, 925 S. King St., Seattle, 7/31/86, A, a, 86002094

Chittenden Locks and Lake Washington Ship Canal, Salmon Bay, Seattle, 12/14/78, A, C, 78002748

Church of the Blessed Sacrament, Priory, and School, 5040-5041 9th Ave., NE, Seattle, 1/12/84, C, a, 84003479

Clise, James W., House, 6046 Lake Sammamish Pkwy., NE, Redmond, 6/19/73, B, C, 73001874

Cobb Building, 1301-1309 4th Ave., Seattle, 8/03/84, A, C, 84003485

Coliseum Theater, 5th Ave. and Pike St., Seattle, 7/07/75, C, 75001854

King County—Continued

Colman Building, 811 1st Ave., Seattle, 3/16/72, B, C, 72001272

Colonial Hotel, 1119–1123 1st Ave., Seattle, 4/29/82, C, 82004232

Columbia City Historic District, Roughly bounded by S. Hudson and S. Alaska Sts., 35th and Rainier Aves., Seattle, 9/08/80, A, C, 80004000

Cornish School, 710 E. Roy St., Seattle, 8/29/77, A, 77001337

Cowen Park Bridge [Historic Bridges/Tunnels in Washington State TR], 15th Ave., N., Seattle, 7/16/82, A, C, g, 82004233

DUWAMISH, Lake Washington Ship Canal, Chittenden Locks, Seattle, 6/30/89, A, C, NHL, 89001448

De La Mar Apartments, 115 W. Olympic Pl., Seattle, 8/18/80, C, 80004001

Dockton Hotel, 260th St., SE and 99th Ave., SW, Dockton, 7/28/83, A, 83003337

Dr. Trueblood House [Kirkland Land Improvement Company TR], 127 7th Ave., Kirkland, 8/03/82, A, 82004222

Duwamish Number 1 Site, Address Restricted, Seattle vicinity, 10/18/77, D, 77001338

Eagles Auditorium Building, 1416 7th Ave., Seattle, 7/14/83, A, C, 83003338

Eddy, James G., House and Grounds, 1005 Evergreen Point Rd., Medina, 2/19/82, B, C, 82004226

Eddy, James G., House and Grounds (Boundary Increase), 1005 Evergreen Point Rd., Medina, 11/06/86, B, C, 86003139

Federal Office Building, 909 1st Ave., Seattle, 4/30/79, C, g, 79003155

Ferry, Pierre P., House, 1531 10th Ave., E., Seattle, 4/18/79, C, 79002537

Fire Station No. 18, 5427 Russell Ave., NW, Seattle, 6/19/73, A, C, 73001876

Fire Station No. 23, 18th Ave. and Columbia St., Seattle, 9/10/71, A, C, 71000874

Fire Station No. 25, 1400 Harvard Ave., Seattle, 4/14/72, A, C, 72001273

First Methodist Protestant Church of Seattle, 128 16th Ave. E., Seattle, 5/14/93, A, C, a, 93000364

Fort Lawton, On Magnolia Bluff, Seattle, 8/15/78, A, C, 78002752

Fremont Bridge [Historic Bridges/Tunnels in Washington State TR], Spans Lake Washington Ship Canal, Seattle, 7/16/82, A, C, 82004234

Fremont Building, 3419 Fremont Ave. N., Seattle, 11/12/92, A, C, 92001587

Galland, Caroline Kline, House, 1605 17th Ave., Seattle, 2/08/80, B, C, 80004002

Globe Building, Beebe Building and Hotel Cecil, 1001–1023 1st Ave., Seattle, 4/29/82, A, C, 82004235

Graham, J. S., Store, 119 Pine St., Seattle, 12/07/89, C, 89002094

Grand Pacific Hotel, 1115–1117 1st Ave., Seattle, 5/13/82, C, 82004236

Guiry and Schillestad Building, 2101–2111 1st Ave., Seattle, 8/28/85, A, 85001941

Harvard-Belmont District, Bellevue Pl., Broadway, Boylston and Harvard Aves., Seattle, 5/13/82, A, C, 82004237

Hill, Samuel, House, 814 E. Highland Dr., Seattle, 5/03/76, B, C, 76001887

Hoge Building, 705 2nd Ave., Seattle, 4/14/83, C, 83003339

Hollywood Farm, SE of Woodinville at 14111 NE 145th St., Woodinville vicinity, 12/15/78, A, B, C, 78002757

Holyoke Building, 1018–1022 1st Ave., Seattle, 6/03/76, A, C, 76001888

Home of the Good Shepherd, Sunnyside, N. and 50th St., Seattle, 5/23/78, A, 78002753

Hull Building, 2401–2405 1st Ave., Seattle, 1/27/83, C, 83003340

Hyde, Samuel, House, 3726 E. Madison St., Seattle, 4/12/82, C, 82004238

Immanuel Lutheran Church, 1215 Thomas St., Seattle, 2/25/82, C, a, 82004239

Interlake Public School, 4416 Wallingford Ave., N., Seattle, 7/14/83, A, C, 83003341

Iron Pergola, 1st Ave. and Yesler Way, Seattle, 8/26/71, C, 71000875

Issaquah Depot, Rainier Ave. N, Issaquah, 9/13/90, A, 90001461

King Street Station, 3rd St., S. and S. King St., Seattle, 4/13/73, A, 73001877

Kirk, Peter, Building, 620 Market St., Kirkland, 8/14/73, A, B, 73001873

Kirkland Woman's Club, 407 First St., Kirkland, 1/26/90, A, 89002321

Kraus, Joseph, House, 2812 Mt. Saint Helens Pl., Seattle, 2/25/82, C, 82004240

Lakeview School [Rural Public Schools in Washington from Early Settlement to 1945 MPS], Island Crest Way and S.E. Sixty-eighth St., Mercer Island, 6/16/88, A, 88000742

Leary, Eliza Ferry, House, 1551 10th Ave., E., Seattle, 4/14/72, B, C, 72001274

Lester Depot, US Forest Service Rd. 212, Green River Watershed, Lester, 9/10/87, A, C, 87001534

Loomis House [Kirkland Land Improvement Company TR], 304 8th Ave., W., Kirkland, 8/03/82, A, 82004223

M. V. VASHON, Pier 52, Seattle, 4/29/82, A, 82004241

Marsh, Louis S., House, 6604 Lake Washington Blvd., Kirkland, 6/30/89, B, C, 89000500

Marymoor Prehistoric Indian Site, Address Restricted, Redmond vicinity, 11/20/70, D, 70000642

Masonic Lodge Building [Kirkland Land Improvement Company TR], 700 Market St., Kirkland, 8/03/82, A, 82004224

Merrill, R. D., House, 919 Harvard Ave., E., Seattle, 8/22/77, C, 77001339

Montlake Bridge [Historic Bridges/Tunnels in Washington State TR], Spans Lake Union Ship Canal, Seattle, 7/16/82, A, C, 82004242

Moore Theatre and Hotel, 1932 2nd Ave., Seattle, 8/30/74, C, 74001958

Mount Baker Ridge Tunnel [Historic Bridges/Tunnels in Washington State TR], E of WA 90, Seattle, 7/16/82, A, C, g, 82004243

National Building, 1006–1024 Western Ave., Seattle, 4/29/82, A, 82004244

Naval Military Hangar—University Shell House, University of Washington campus, Seattle, 7/01/75, A, C, 75001856

Neely, Aaron, Sr., Mansion, E of Auburn off WA 18, Auburn vicinity, 10/15/74, A, C, 74001955

New Washington Hotel, 1902 Second Ave., Seattle, 9/28/89, A, C, 89001607

Nihon Go Gakko, 1414 S. Weller St., Seattle, 6/23/82, A, 82004245

Nippon Kan, 622 S. Washington St., Seattle, 5/22/78, A, 78002754

North Bend Ranger Station [USDA Forest Service Administrative Buildings in Oregon and Washington Built by the CCC MPS], 42404 SE. North Bend Way, North Bend, 3/06/91, A, C, 91000157

Northern Life Tower, 1212 3rd Ave., Seattle, 5/30/75, C, g, 75001857

Old Georgetown City Hall, 6202 13th Ave., S., Seattle, 4/14/83, A, C, 83003342

Old Public Safety Building, 4th Ave. and Terrace St. and 5th Ave. and Yesler Way, Seattle, 6/19/73, A, C, 73001878

Olson, Louis and Ellen, House, 1513 Griffin Ave., Enumclaw, 8/30/84, B, C, 84003492

Olympic Hotel, 1200–1220 4th Ave., Seattle, 6/15/79, A, C, 79002538

Pacific Coast Company House No. 75, N of Renton at 7210 138th St., SE, Renton vicinity, 12/21/79, A, C, 79002534

Paramount Theatre, 901 Pine St., Seattle, 10/09/74, A, C, g, 74001959

Park Department, Division of Playgrounds, 301 Terry Ave., Seattle, 3/16/72, A, C, 72001275

Parsons, William, House, 2706 Harvard Ave. E., Seattle, 6/21/91, B, 91000782

Phillips House, 711–713 E. Union St., Seattle, 4/29/93, C, 93000359

Pickering Farm, 21809 SE 56th St., Issaquah, 7/07/83, A, C, 83003343

Pike Place Public Market Historic District, Roughly bounded by 1st and Western Aves. and Virginia and Pike Sts., Seattle, 3/13/70, A, C, 70000644

Pioneer Building, Pergola, and Totem Pole, 5th Ave. and Yesler Way, Seattle, 5/05/77, A, C, NHL, 77001340

Pioneer Hall, 1642 43rd Ave., E., Seattle, 6/05/70, C, 70000645

Pioneer Square—Skid Road Historic District (Boundary Increase), 500 blk. of First Ave., S, Seattle, 6/16/88, A, C, 88000739

Pioneer Square-Skid Road District, Roughly bounded by Elliott Bay, King, 3rd, Columbia, and Cherry Sts., Seattle, 6/22/70, A, NPS, 70000086

Pioneer Square-Skid Road District (Boundary Increase), Roughly bounded by the Viaduct, King St., 6th and 5th Aves., James and Columbia Sts., Seattle, 7/07/78, A, C, NPS, 78000341

Queen Anne Club, 1530 N. Queen Anne Ave., Seattle, 1/27/83, A, 83003344

Queen Anne High School, 215 Galer St., Seattle, 11/21/85, A, C, 85002916

King County—Continued

Queen Anne Public School, 515 W. Galer St., Seattle, 7/30/75, C, 75001858

RELIEF (lightship), Central Waterfront at Moss Bay, Kirkland, 4/23/75, A, C, NHL, 75001852

Rainier Club, 810 4th Ave., Seattle, 4/22/76, A, C, 76001889

Ravenna Park Bridge [Historic Bridges/Tunnels in Washington State TR], 20th Ave., Spans Ravenna Park Ravine, Seattle, 7/16/82, A, C, 82004246

Raymond-Ogden Mansion, 702 35th Ave., Seattle, 6/15/79, C, 79002539

Redelsheimer—Ostrander House, 200 40th Ave. E., Seattle, 1/12/90, C, 89002298

Ronald, Judge James T., House, 421 30th St., Seattle, 2/20/75, B, g, 75001859

S.S. SAN MATEO, Seattle waterfront, Seattle, 4/07/71, A, C, b, g, 71000876

Sanders, Erick Gustave, Mansion, 5516 S. Two Hundred and Seventy-seventh St., Kent vicinity, 11/06/86, C, a, 86003163

Schmitz Park Bridge [Historic Bridges/Tunnels in Washington State TR], Spans Schmitz Park Ravine, Seattle, 7/16/82, A, C, g, 82004247

Sears, Joshua, Building [Kirkland Land Improvement Company TR], 701 Market St., Kirkland, 8/03/82, A, 82004225

Seattle Chinatown Historic District, Roughly bounded by Main, Jackson, I-5, Waller, and Fifth, Seattle, 11/06/86, A, C, 86003153

Seattle Electric Company Georgetown Steam Plant, Off WA 99 at King County Airport, Seattle, 8/01/78, C, NHL, 78002755

Seattle Public Library [Carnegie Libraries of Washington TR], 2306 42nd Ave., SW, Seattle, 8/03/82, A, C, 82004249

Seattle Public Library [Carnegie Libraries of Washington TR], 400 W. Garfield St., Seattle, 8/03/82, A, C, 82004250

Seattle Public Library [Carnegie Libraries of Washington TR], 5009 Roosevelt Way, NE, Seattle, 8/03/82, A, C, 82004251

Seattle Public Library [Carnegie Libraries of Washington TR], 731 N. 35th St., Seattle, 8/03/82, A, C, 82004252

Seattle Public Library [Carnegie Libraries of Washington TR], 7364 E. Green Lake Dr., N., Seattle, 8/03/82, A, C, 82004253

Seattle Public Library [Carnegie Libraries of Washington TR], 4721 Rainier Ave. South, Seattle, 8/03/82, A, C, 82004909

Seattle, Chief of the Suquamish, Statue, 5th Ave., Denny Way, and Cedar St., Seattle, 4/19/84, C, f, 84003502

Selleck Historic District, SE 252nd, Selleck vicinity, 3/16/89, A, 89000214

Showboat Theatre, University of Washington, 1705 N.E. Pacific St., Seattle, 4/25/86, A, g, 86000970

Skinner Building, 1300–1334 5th Ave., Seattle, 11/28/78, C, 78002756

Snoqualmie Depot, 109 King St., Snoqualmie, 7/24/74, A, C, 74001963

Snoqualmie Falls Cavity Generating Station, N of Snoqualmie on Snoqualmie River, Snoqualmie vicinity, 4/23/76, A, C, 76001895

Snoqualmie Falls Hydroelectric Power Plant Historic District [Hydroelectric Plants in Washington State MPS], WA 202, .5 mi. N of Snoqualmie, Snoqualmie vicinity, 10/24/92, A, C, 92001324

Snoqualmie School Campus, Silva and King Sts., Snoqualmie, 3/16/89, A, 89000209

Stevens Pass Historic District, W of Berne on U.S. 2, Berne vicinity, 10/22/76, A, C, 76001884

Stimson-Green House, 1204 Minor Ave., Seattle, 5/04/76, B, C, 76001890

Storey, Ellsworth, Cottages Historic District, 1706–1816 S. Lake Washington Blvd. and 1725–1729 S. 36th Ave., Seattle, 7/06/76, C, 76001891

Storey, Ellsworth, Residences, 260, 270 E. Dorffel Dr., Seattle, 4/14/72, C, 72001276

Stuart House and Gardens, 619 W. Comstock St., Seattle, 4/14/83, B, C, 83003345

Summit School, E. Union St. and Summit Ave., Seattle, 10/04/79, C, 79002540

Temple de Hirsch, 15th Ave. and E. Union St., Seattle, 1/05/84, A, C, a, 84003506

Thompson, Will H., House, 3119 S. Day St., Seattle, 11/29/79, C, 79002541

Times Building, 414 Olive Way, Seattle, 1/27/83, A, C, 83003346

Triangle Hotel and Bar, 551 1st Ave., S., Seattle, 5/03/76, A, C, 76001892

Trinity Parish Church, 609 Eighth Ave., Seattle, 9/26/91, A, C, a, 91001440

Tukwila School, 14475 59th Ave., S., Tukwila, 11/29/79, A, 79002544

Turner-Koepf House, 2336 15th Ave., S., Seattle, 4/22/76, A, C, b, 76001893

U.S. Courthouse, 1010 5th Ave., Seattle, 1/08/80, A, C, g, 80004003

U.S. Immigrant Station and Assay Office, 815 Airport Way, S., Seattle, 1/01/79, A, C, g, 79002542

U.S. Marine Hospital, 1131 14th Ave., S., Seattle, 12/21/79, C, g, 79002543

US Immigration Building, 84 Union St., Seattle, 9/14/87, A, 87001524

USCGC FIR, 1519 Alaskan Way, S., Seattle, 4/27/92, A, C, NHL, 92001880

Union Station, 4th, S. and S. Jackson Sts., Seattle, 8/30/74, A, C, 74001960

United Shopping Tower, 217 Pine St., Seattle, 8/18/80, C, 80004004

University Bridge [Historic Bridges/Tunnels in Washington State TR], Spans Lake Washington Ship Canal, Seattle, 7/16/82, A, C, 82004254

VIRGINIA V, 4250 21st Ave., W., Seattle, 4/24/73, A, C, NHL, 73001875

Victorian Apartments, 1234–1238 S. King St., Seattle, 12/18/90, C, b, 90001864

Volker, William, Building, 1000 Lenora St., Seattle, 10/13/83, C, 83004236

Volunteer Park, Between E. Prospect and E. Galer Sts., and Federal and E. 15th Aves., Seattle, 5/03/76, A, C, g, 76001894

WAWONA (schooner), Seattle Police Harbor Patrol Dock, foot of Densmore St., Seattle, 7/01/70, A, 70000643

Wagner Houseboat, 2770 Westlake Ave., N., Seattle, 2/19/82, A, C, g, 82004255

Wallingford Fire and Police Station, 1629 N. 45th St., Seattle, 1/27/83, A, C, 83003347

Ward House, 520 E. Denny Way, Seattle, 3/16/72, C, 72001277

Washington Street Public Boat Landing Facility, S. Washington St. W of Alaskan Way, Seattle, 6/10/74, A, C, 74001961

West Point Light Station, W of Fort Lawton, Fort Lawton vicinity, 8/16/77, A, C, 77001336

Wilke Farmhouse, 1920 2nd North St., Seattle, 11/01/74, A, C, 74001962

Winters, Frederick W., House, 2102 Bellevue Way, SE., Bellevue, 4/21/92, A, C, 92000367

Wurdemann, Harry Vanderbilt, House, 17602 Bothell Way NE., Lake Forest Park, 12/27/90, A, C, 90002154

Ye College Inn, 4000 University Way, NE, Seattle, 2/25/82, A, C, 82004256

Yellowstone Road, The, 196th St. between the Fall City Hwy. and 80th, NE, Redmond, 12/02/74, A, C, 74001956

ZODIAC (schooner), Lake Union Dry Dock, Seattle, 4/29/82, C, 82004248

Kitsap County

Fort Ward Historic District, S of Winslow, Winslow vicinity, 1/12/78, A, C, 78002759

Hospital Reservation Historic District [Puget Sound Naval Shipyard Shore Facilities TR], Roughly bounded by Mahan Ave., Hoogewerf Rd., Decatur Ave., and Dewey St., Bremerton, 7/16/90, A, 88003052

Marine Reservation Historic District [Puget Sound Naval Shipyard Shore Facilities TR], Bounded by Cole St., Dewey St., Decatur Ave., and Doyen St., Bremerton, 7/16/90, A, 88003051

Navy Yard Puget Sound, N shore of Sinclair Inlet, Bremerton, 8/27/92, A, NHL, 92001883

Nelson, Charles F., House, Corner of Nelson and Crescent Valley Rds., Olalla, 8/28/73, A, C, 73001879

Officers' Row Historic District [Puget Sound Naval Shipyard Shore Facilities TR], Roughly bounded by Mahan Ave., Decatur Ave., and Coghlan Rd., Bremerton, 7/16/90, A, 88003054

Old-Man-House Site (45KP2), Old Man House State Park, Suquamish vicinity, 1/12/90, A, D, 89002299

Point No Point Light Station, E of Hansville, Hansville vicinity, 8/10/78, A, 78002758

Port Gamble Historic District, NW end of Kitsap Peninsula near entrance to Hood Canal, Puget Sound, Port Gamble, 11/13/66, A, NHL, 66000746

Puget Sound Radio Station Historic District [Puget Sound Naval Shipyard Shore Facilities TR], Roughly bounded by Mahan Ave., Coghlan Rd., and Cottman Rd., Bremerton, 7/16/90, A, 88003053

U.S.S. MISSOURI, Puget Sound Naval Shipyard, Bremerton, 5/14/71, A, g, 71000877

Kitsap County—Continued

US Post Office—Bremerton Main [Historic US Post Offices in Washington MPS], 602 Pacific Ave., Bremerton, 8/07/91, A, C, 91000638

USS HORNET, Puget Sound Naval Shipyard, Bremerton, 12/04/91, A, g, NHL, 91002065

Kittitas County

Cabin Creek Historic District, W of Easton, Easton vicinity, 8/17/79, A, 79002545

Chicago, Milwaukee, St. Paul & Pacific Railroad—Kittitas Depot [Milwaukee Road MPS], Jct. of Railroad Ave. and Main St., Kittitas, 11/19/92, A, 92001582

Cle Elum-Roslyn Beneficial Association Hospital, 505 Power St., Cle Elum, 12/03/80, A, 80004005

Downtown Ellensburg Historic District, Roughly bounded by 3rd and 6th Aves., and Main and Ruby Sts., Ellensburg, 7/01/77, A, C, 77001341

First Railroad Addition Historic District, Roughly bounded by Tenth Ave., D St., Ninth Ave., and A St., Ellensburg, 5/08/87, C, 87000722

Kinkade, John W., Farmstead, Off U.S. 7B, Ellensburg vicinity, 2/25/82, A, C, 82004257

Liberty Historic District, Both sides of Williams Creek Wagon Rd., Liberty, 10/15/74, A, C, 74001965

Milwaukee Road Bunkhouse, 526 Marie, South Cle Elum, 3/31/89, A, b, 89000210

Nelson, Albert, Farmstead, Manastash Rd., Ellensburg vicinity, 2/25/82, A, C, 82004258

Northern Pacific Railway Passenger Depot, 606 W. Third St., Ellensburg, 9/26/91, A, 91001438

Northwestern Improvement Company Store, 1st St. and Pennsylvania Ave., Roslyn, 4/13/73, A, 73001881

Olmstead Place State Park, 4 mi. E of Ellensburg near the Kittitas Hwy., Ellensburg vicinity, 3/31/71, A, 71000878

Ramsay House, 215 E. Ninth, Ellensburg, 5/02/86, C, 86000957

Roslyn Historic District, WA 2E, Roslyn, 2/14/78, A, C, d, 78002760

Salmon la Sac Guard Station, N of Cle Elum in Wenatchee National Forest, Cle Elum vicinity, 7/15/74, A, 74001964

Shoudy House, 309 W. Fifth Ave., Ellensburg, 11/12/92, B, C, 92001585

Springfield Farm, 9 mi. N of Ellensburg, Ellensburg vicinity, 4/13/77, B, C, 77001342

Tekison Cave, Address Restricted, Wenatchee vicinity, 11/24/78, D, 78002761

Thorp Mill, Thorp Highway off U.S. 10, Thorp, 11/23/77, A, 77001343

Washington State Normal School Building, 8th Ave., Ellensburg, 12/12/76, A, C, 76001896

Klickitat County

Appleton Log Hall, 835 Appleton Rd., Appleton, 10/02/92, A, C, 92001294

First Day Advent Christian Church, Jct. of Maryhill Hwy. and Stonehenge Ave., Maryhill, 9/26/91, C, a, 91001439

Goldendale Free Public Library [Carnegie Libraries of Washington TR], 131 W. Burgen, Goldendale, 8/03/82, A, C, 82004259

Maryhill, SW of Goldendale on U.S. 197, Goldendale vicinity, 12/31/74, A, C, g, 74001966

Newell, Charles, House, 114 Sentinel St., Goldendale, 8/18/77, B, C, 77001344

Rattlesnake Creek Site, Address Restricted, Husum vicinity, 5/22/78, D, 78002762

Whitcomb Cabin, 8 mi. S of Glenwood on SR 163, Glenwood vicinity, 6/10/75, B, C, 75001860

Wishram Indian Village Site, Address Restricted, The Dalles vicinity, 3/16/72, D, 72001278

Lewis County

Birge, George E., House, 715 E St., Centralia, 12/01/86, C, 86003375

Boistfort High School [Rural Public Schools in Washington from Early Settlement to 1945 MPS], 983 Boistfort Rd., Curtis, 8/06/87, A, 87001335

Borst, Joseph, House, 302 Bryden Ave., Centralia, 12/27/77, B, C, 77001345

Burlington Northern Depot, Off U.S. 99, Chehalis, 11/06/74, A, 74001967

Centralia Union Depot, 210 Railroad St., Centralia, 5/19/88, A, 88000608

Claquato Church, Off WA 12, Claquato, 4/24/73, A, a, 73001882

Everest, Wesley, Gravesite [Centralia Armistice Day, 1919 MPS], Sticklin—Greenwood Memorial Park, 1905 Johnson Rd., Centralia, 12/17/91, A, B, c, 91001781

Holy Cross Polish National Catholic Church, Third and Queen, Pe Ell, 9/02/87, A, C, a, 87001456

Jackson, John R., House, At Mary's Corner, 11 mi. S of Chehalis on Jackson Hwy., Chehalis vicinity, 1/11/74, B, e, 74001968

La Wis Wis Guard Station No. 1165 [Depression-Era Buildings TR], Gifford Pinchot National Forest, Packwood vicinity, 4/08/86, A, C, 86000813

McFadden, O. B., House, 1639 Chehalis Ave., Chehalis, 4/01/75, B, C, 75001861

Mineral Log Lodge, E side of Mineral Lake on Hill Rd., Mineral, 3/26/75, C, 75001862

North Fork Guard Station No. 1142 [Depression-Era Buildings TR], Randle Ranger Station, Gifford Pinchot National Forest, Randle vicinity, 4/11/86, A, C, g, 86000815

Ohanapecosh Comfort Station No. O-302 [Mt. Rainier National Park MPS], Mt. Rainier National Park, Ohanapecosh vicinity, 3/13/91, A, C, NPS, 91000203

Ohanapecosh Comfort Station No. O-303 [Mt. Rainier National Park MPS], Mt. Rainier National Park, Ohanapecosh vicinity, 3/13/91, A, C, NPS, 91000204

Olsen, Ben, House, S end of D St., Vader, 11/07/76, B, C, 76001897

Olympic Club Saloon, 112 N. Tower St., Centralia, 3/10/80, A, C, 80004006

Palmer, O. K., House, 673 N.W. Pennsylvania, Chehalis, 5/15/86, B, C, 86001067

Pennsylvania Avenue—West Side Historic District [Chehalis MPS], 600 block NW. St. Helens and 440–723 Pennsylvania Aves., Chehalis, 12/03/91, B, C, 91001721

Randle Ranger Station—Work Center [Depression-Era Buildings TR], Gifford Pinchot National Forest, Randle, 4/08/86, A, C, 86000816

St. Helens Hotel [Chehalis MPS], 440 N. Market Blvd., Chehalis, 10/08/91, A, C, 91001497

The Sentinel [Centralia Armistice Day, 1919 MPS], Washington Park, bounded by Main, Pearl, Locust and Silver, Centralia, 12/17/91, A, C, f, 91001782

Three Lakes Patrol Cabin [Mt. Rainier National Park MPS], Mt. Rainier National Park, Ohanapecosh vicinity, 3/13/91, A, C, NPS, 91000189

US Post Office—Centralia Main [Historic US Post Offices in Washington MPS], 214 W. Locust, Centralia, 8/07/91, A, C, 91000640

US Post Office—Chehalis Main [Historic US Post Offices in Washington MPS], 1031 NW. Cascade, Chehalis, 5/30/91, A, C, 91000641

Wolfenbarger Site, Address Restricted, Curtis vicinity, 5/02/77, D, 77001346

Lincoln County

Fort Spokane Military Reserve, Rt. 25, Miles vicinity, 11/23/88, A, C, D, NPS, 88002621

Goose Creek Rockshelter, Address Restricted, Wilbur vicinity, 5/22/78, D, 78002763

Harrington Bank Block and Opera House, Jct. of Third and Willis Sts., NW corner, Harrington, 10/02/92, A, C, 92001288

Mary Queen of Heaven Roman Catholic Church, N. First and B St., Sprague, 4/26/90, C, a, 90000675

Mason County

Cushman No. 1 Hydroelectric Power Plant [Hydroelectric Power Plants in Washington State, 1890–1938 MPS], S end of Lake Cushman, Hoodsport vicinity, 12/15/88, A, C, 88002759

Cushman No. 2 Hydroelectric Power Plant [Hydroelectric Power Plants in Washington State, 1890–1938 MPS], Skokomish River, Hoodsport vicinity, 12/15/88, A, C, 88002757

Goldsborough Creek Bridge [Historic Bridges/Tunnels in Washington State TR], WA 3, Shelton, 7/16/82, A, C, 82004264

High Steel Bridge [Historic Bridges/Tunnels in Washington State TR], Spans Skokomish South Fork, Shelton, 7/16/82, A, C, 82004265

North Hamma Hamma River Bridge [Historic Bridges/Tunnels in Washington State TR],

Mason County—Continued

Spans North Hamma Hamma River, Eldon, 7/16/82, A, C, 82004262

Shelton Public Library and Town Hall, 5th St. and Railroad Ave., Shelton, 7/14/83, A, C, 83003348

Simpson Logging Company Locomotive No. 7 and Peninsular Railway Caboose No. 700, 3rd and Railroad Aves., Shelton, 1/12/84, A, 84003532

South Hamma Hamma River Bridge [Historic Bridges/Tunnels in Washington State TR], Spans South Hamma Hamma River, Eldon, 7/16/82, A, C, 82004263

Vance Creek Bridge [Historic Bridges/Tunnels in Washington State TR], NW of Shelton, Shelton vicinity, 7/16/82, A, C, 82004266

Okanogan County

Bonaparte Mountain Cabin, E of Tonasket in Okanogan National Forest, Tonasket vicinity, 4/20/81, A, 81000588

Chief Joseph Memorial, Near jct. of WA 10A and Cache Creek Rd., Nespelem, 5/15/74, B, c, 74001970

Early Winters Ranger Station Work Center [Depression-Era Buildings TR], Okanogan National Forest, Winthrop vicinity, 4/11/86, A, C, g, 86000841

Enloe Dam and Powerplant, 4 mi. (6.4 km) W of Oroville, Oroville vicinity, 10/18/78, C, 78002764

Fort Okanogan, Sites of, N of Bridgeport between the Columbia and Okanogan Rivers, Bridgeport vicinity, 6/04/73, A, 73001883

Grand Coulee Bridge [Historic Bridges/Tunnels in Washington State TR], Spans Columbia River, Grand Coulee, 7/16/82, A, C, g, 82004267

Lost Lake Guard Station [Depression-Era Buildings TR], Okanogan National Forest, Tonasket, 4/11/86, A, C, g, 86000814

Okanogan Project: Conconully Resevoir Dam, S of Conconully, Conconully vicinity, 9/06/74, A, C, 74001969

Parson Smith Tree, 40 mi. N of Winthrop on the Canadian border in Okanogan National Forest, Winthrop vicinity, 3/16/72, A, 72001279

Smith, Hiram F., Orchard, 2 mi. N of Oroville on Osoyoos Lake, Oroville vicinity, 11/12/75, B, 75001863

US Post Office—Okanogan Main [Historic US Post Offices in Washington MPS], 212 Second Ave. N., Okanogan, 5/30/91, A, C, 91000650

US Post Office—Omak Main [Historic US Post Offices in Washington MPS], 104 S. Main St., Omak, 5/30/91, A, C, 91000651

Waring, Guy, Cabin, 285 Castle Ave., Winthrop, 3/19/82, B, 82004268

Pacific County

Cape Disappointment Historic District, From 0.5 mi. S of Ilwaco to WA/OR boundary, Ilwaco vicinity, 8/15/75, A, D, 75001864

Chinook Point, 5 mi. SE of Fort Columbia Historical State Park on U.S. 101, Chinook vicinity, 10/15/66, A, B, NHL, 66000747

Colbert House, Quaker and Lake Sts., Ilwaco, 10/18/77, B, C, b, 77001347

Columbia River Quarantine Station, SW of Knappton on WA 401, Knappton vicinity, 2/08/80, A, b, 80004007

Klipsan Beach Life Saving Station, WA 103, Klipsan Beach, 7/05/79, A, b, 79002546

Lumber Exchange Building, Robert Bush Dr./US 101 and Willapa Ave., South Bend, 5/19/88, A, C, 88000604

Oysterville Historic District, WA 103, Oysterville, 4/21/76, A, B, C, 76001898

Pacific County Courthouse, Cowlitz and Vine Sts., South Bend, 7/20/77, A, C, 77001348

Raymond Public Library, 507 Duryea St., Raymond, 11/29/79, A, C, 79002548

Raymond Theater, 325 N. Third St., Raymond, 5/01/91, A, C, 91000540

Russell House, 902 E. Water St., South Bend, 11/25/77, C, 77001349

Schulderman, Peter, House, Thirty-seventh and K Sts., Seaview, 5/19/88, C, 88000597

Shelburne Hotel, WA 103 and K St., Seaview, 12/15/78, A, 78002765

South Bend Carnegie Public Library [Carnegie Libraries of Washington TR], W. 1st and Pacific Sts., South Bend, 8/03/82, A, C, 82004269

Tokeland Hotel, Kindred Ave. and Hotel Rd., Tokeland, 4/11/78, A, 78002766

US Post Office—Raymond Main [Historic US Post Offices in Washington MPS], 406 Duryea St., Raymond, 5/30/91, A, C, 91000654

Willapa Bay Boathouse, US Coast Guard Station, Willapa Bay, Tokeland, 3/13/86, A, 86000358

Wreckage, The, 256th Pl., Ocean Park, 9/18/79, B, C, 79002547

Pend Oreille County

Idaho and Wash. Northern RR Bridge [Historic Bridges/Tunnels in Washington State TR], Spans Pend Oreille River, off WA 31, Metaline Falls, 7/16/82, A, C, 82004270

Larson, Lewis P., House. 5th and Pend Oreille Blvd., Metaline Falls, 3/26/79, B, C, 79002549

Metaline Falls School, 302 Park, Metaline Falls, 9/08/88, A, C, 88001518

Washington Hotel, 5th and Washington St., Metaline Falls, 3/26/79, B, 79002550

Pierce County

Adjutant General's Residence, Camp Murray, Tacoma vicinity, 5/01/91, A, B, 91000537

Alderton School [Rural Public Schools in Washington from Early Settlement to 1945 MPS], 9512 Orting Hwy., E., Alderton, 7/15/87, A, 87001171

Anderson Island School [Rural Public Schools in Washington from Early Settlement to 1945 MPS], Eckenstam-Johnson Rd., Anderson Island, 7/15/87, A, b, 87001165

Arletta School [Rural Public Schools in Washington from Early Settlement to 1945 MPS], Jct. Ninety-sixth Ave. and Thirty-sixth St. NW, Gig Harbor vicinity, 9/28/87, A, C, g, 87001163

Ashford House, Off WA 5, Ashford, 8/30/84, A, C, 84003560

Bisson, William, House, Washington and Emery Sts., South Prairie, 2/19/82, B, C, 82004276

Boatman-Ainsworth Hose, 6000 12th St., SW, Tacoma, 2/19/82, B, C, 82004277

Bowes Building, 100 S. 9th St, Tacoma, 11/23/79, A, B, C, 79002553

Browns Point Lighthouse and Keeper's Cottage, 201 Tulalip NE, Tacoma vicinity, 3/29/89, A, C, 89000208

Cabin No. 97, NW of Tacoma on Salmon Beach, Tacoma vicinity, 12/13/77, A, 77001354

Camp Muir [Mt. Rainier National Park MPS], Mt. Rainier National Park, Paradise vicinity, 3/13/91, A, C, NPS, 91000176

Camp Six, Point Defiance Park, Tacoma, 3/07/73, A, C, b, 73001885

Chinook Pass Entrance Arch [Mt. Rainier National Park MPS], Mt. Rainier National Park, Chinook Pass Entrance, 3/13/91, A, C, NPS, 91000202

Christine Falls Bridge [Mt. Rainier National Park MPS], Mt. Rainier National Park, Paradise vicinity, 3/13/91, A, C, NPS, 91000196

City Waterway Bridge [Historic Bridges/Tunnels in Washington State TR], 20th Ave., Spans Ravenna Park Ravine, Tacoma, 7/16/82, A, C, 82004278

Coke Ovens, SE of Wilkeson at RR tracks, Wilkeson vicinity, 6/10/74, A, C, 74001976

Custer School [Rural Public Schools in Washington from Early Settlement to 1945 MPS], 7700 Steilacoom Blvd. SW, Tacoma, 7/15/87, A, 87001162

Davidson House, 1802 Commercial St., Steilacoom, 7/27/73, B, C, 73001884

DeVoe, Emma Smith, House, 308 E. 133rd St., Tacoma vicinity, 5/06/93, B, 93000369

Drum, Henry, House, 9 St. Helens St., Tacoma, 7/20/77, B, C, 77001351

DuPont Village Historic District, Roughly bounded by Santa Cruz, Brandywine, DuPont, and Penniman, DuPont, 9/10/87, A, 87001542

East 34th Street Bridge [Historic Bridges/Tunnels in Washington State TR], Pacific to A St., Tacoma, 7/16/82, A, C, g, 82004279

Edith Creek Chlorination House [Mt. Rainier National Park MPS], Mt. Rainier National Park, Paradise vicinity, 3/13/91, A, C, NPS, 91000201

Elbe Evangelical Lutheran Church, WA 5, Elbe, 10/08/76, A, C, a, 76001899

Engine House No. 11 [Historic Fire Stations of Tacoma, Washington TR], 3802 McKinley Ave., Tacoma, 5/02/86, A, C, 86000965

Engine House No. 13 [Historic Fire Stations of Tacoma, Washington TR], 3825 N. Twenty-fifth St., Tacoma, 5/02/86, A, C, 86000964

Engine House No. 4, 220-224 E. 26th St., Tacoma, 10/18/84, A, C, 84002425

Pierce County—Continued

Engine House No. 8 [Historic Fire Stations of Tacoma, Washington TR], 4301 S. L St., Tacoma, 5/02/86, A, C, 86000968

Engine House No. 9, 611 N. Pine St., Tacoma, 7/30/75, A, C, 75001866

FIREBOAT NO.1, Marine Park on Ruxton Way, Tacoma, 12/02/83, A, C, NHL, 83004254

Fairfax Bridge [Historic Bridges/Tunnels in Washington State TR], Spans Carbon River, S of Wilkeson, Melmont, 7/16/82, A, C, 82004273

Fire Alarm Station [Historic Fire Stations of Tacoma, Washington TR], 415 S. Tacoma Ave., Tacoma, 5/02/86, A, C, 86000980

Fire Station No. 1 [Historic Fire Stations of Tacoma, Washington TR], 425 S. Tacoma Ave., Tacoma, 5/02/86, A, C, 86000974

Fire Station No. 10 [Historic Fire Stations of Tacoma, Washington TR], 7247 S. Park Ave., Tacoma, 5/02/86, A, C, 86000966

Fire Station No. 14 [Historic Fire Stations of Tacoma, Washington TR], 4701 N. Fourty-first St., Tacoma, 5/02/86, A, C, 86000962

Fire Station No. 15 [Historic Fire Stations of Tacoma, Washington TR], 3510 E. Eleventh St., Tacoma, 5/02/86, A, C, 86000961

Fire Station No. 2 [Historic Fire Stations of Tacoma, Washington TR], 2701 S. Tacoma Ave., Tacoma, 5/02/86, A, C, 86000972

Fire Station No. 5 [Historic Fire Stations of Tacoma, Washington TR], 1453 S. Twelfth St., Tacoma, 5/02/86, A, C, 86000971

Fireboat Station [Historic Fire Stations of Tacoma, Washington TR], 302 E. Eleventh St., Tacoma, 5/02/86, A, C, 86000978

Fort Nisqually Granary and Factor's House, Point Defiance Park, Tacoma, 4/15/70, A, C, b, NHL, 70000647

Fort Nisqually Site, NW of Dupont off I-5, Dupont vicinity, 10/16/74, A, 74001971

Fort Steilacoom, NE of Steilacoom, Steilacoom vicinity, 11/25/77, A, C, 77001350

Fox Island School [Rural Public Schools in Washington from Early Settlement to 1945 MPS], Gway Dr. and Ninth St., Fox Island, 7/15/87, A, 87001167

Galbraith, John, House, 140 Oak St., E., Eatonville, 3/19/82, B, g, 82004271

Glencove Hotel, W of Gig Harbor off WA 302, Gig Harbor vicinity, 5/22/78, A, C, 78002767

Gobbler's Knob Fire Lookout [Mt. Rainier National Park MPS], Mt. Rainier National Park, Nisqually Entrance vicinity, 3/13/91, A, NPS, 91000191

Haddaway Hall, 4301 N. Stevens, Tacoma, 1/27/83, A, C, 83003349

Holy Trinity Orthodox Church, 433 Long St., Wilkeson, 9/28/89, A, C, a, 89001606

Home School, 6th and C Sts., Home, 4/12/82, A, 82004272

Huckleberry Creek Patrol Cabin [Mt. Rainier National Park MPS], Mt. Rainier National Park, Sunrise vicinity, 3/13/91, A, C, NPS, 91000178

Indian Bar Trail Shelter [Mt. Rainier National Park MPS], Mt. Rainier National Park, Paradise vicinity, 3/13/91, A, C, NPS, 91000179

Indian Henry's Patrol Cabin [Mt. Rainier National Park MPS], Mt. Rainier National Park, Longmire vicinity, 3/13/91, A, C, NPS, 91000180

Ipsut Creek Patrol Cabin [Mt. Rainier National Park MPS], Mt. Rainier National Park, Carbon River Entrance vicinity, 3/13/91, A, C, NPS, 91000181

Lake George Patrol Cabin [Mt. Rainier National Park MPS], Mt. Rainier National Park, Longmire vicinity, 3/13/91, A, C, NPS, 91000182

Longbranch School Gymnasium [Rural Public Schools in Washington from Early Settlement to 1945 MPS], Gig Harbor-Longbranch Rd., Lakebay vicinity, 9/28/87, A, C, g, 87001164

Longmire Buildings, Longmire, Mount Rainier National Park, 5/28/87, C, NHL, NPS, 87001338

Longmire Campground Comfort Station No. L-302 [Mt. Rainier National Park MPS], Mt. Rainier National Park, Longmire vicinity, 3/13/91, A, C, NPS, 91000209

Longmire Campground Comfort Station No. L-303 [Mt. Rainier National Park MPS], Mt. Rainier National Park, Longmire vicinity, 3/13/91, A, C, NPS, 91000210

Longmire Campground Comfort Station No. L-304 [Mt. Rainier National Park MPS], Mt. Rainier National Park, Longmire vicinity, 3/13/91, A, C, NPS, 91000211

Longmire Historic District [Mt. Rainier National Park MPS], Mt. Rainier National Park, Longmire, 3/13/91, A, C, NPS, 91000173

Lotz, J. H., House, 1004 2nd Ave., NW, Puyallup, 3/10/80, C, 80004401

Masonic Temple Building—Temple Theater [Movie Theaters in Washington State MPS], 47 St. Helens Ave., Tacoma, 4/29/93, A, C, 93000357

McMillin Bridge [Historic Bridges/Tunnels in Washington State TR], Spans Puyallup River on SR E5, Puyallup vicinity, 7/16/82, A, C, g, 82004275

McMillin School [Rural Public Schools in Washington from Early Settlement to 1945 MPS], WA 162, McMillin, 7/15/87, A, 87001172

Meeker, Ezra, Mansion, 321 Pioneer Ave., E., Puyallup, 8/26/71, B, C, 71000879

Midway School [Rural Public Schools in Washington from Early Settlement to 1945 MPS], 5115 Thirty-eighth Ave. NW, Gig Harbor vicinity, 7/15/87, C, 87001166

Mowich Lake Patrol Cabin [Mt. Rainier National Park MPS], Mt. Rainier National Park, Carbon River Entrance vicinity, 3/13/91, A, C, NPS, 91000183

Mt. Fremont Fire Lookout [Mt. Rainier National Park MPS], Mt. Rainier National Park, Sunrise vicinity, 3/13/91, A, C, NPS, 91000193

Murray, Frederick H., House, 402 N. Sheridan Ave., Tacoma, 8/23/85, C, 85001810

Narada Falls Bridge [Mt. Rainier National Park MPS], Mt. Rainier National Park, Paradise vicinity, 3/13/91, A, C, NPS, 91000197

Narada Falls Comfort Station [Mt. Rainier National Park MPS], Mt. Rainier National Park, Paradise vicinity, 3/13/91, A, C, NPS, 91000208

Nihon Go Gakko, 1715 S. Tacoma Ave., Tacoma, 8/30/84, A, 84003568

Nisqually Entrance Historic District [Mt. Rainier National Park MPS], Mt. Rainier National Park, Nisqually Entrance, 3/13/91, A, C, NPS, 91000172

North 21st Street Bridge [Historic Bridges/Tunnels in Washington State TR], Spans Buckley Gulch, N. Fife and Oakes, Tacoma, 7/16/82, A, C, 82004280

North 23rd Street Bridge [Historic Bridges/Tunnels in Washington State TR], Spans Buckley Gulch, N. Fife and Oakes, Tacoma, 7/16/82, A, C, 82004281

North Mowich Trail Shelter [Mt. Rainier National Park MPS], Mt. Rainier National Park, Mowich Lake Entrance vicinity, 3/13/91, A, C, NPS, 91000184

Northern Pacific Office Building, NE corner of 7th St. and Pacific Ave., Tacoma, 5/04/76, A, 76001901

Old City Hall, 7th Ave. between Commerce and Pacific Ave., Tacoma, 5/17/74, A, C, 74001973

Old City Hall Historic District, Roughly bounded by St. Helens Ave., Court C, freeway spur, 7th and 9th Sts., Tacoma, 12/23/77, A, C, 77001352

Old Main, Park Ave., S. and Garfield St., Tacoma, 1/27/84, A, C, 84003570

Orr, Nathaniel, House and Orchard, 1807 Rainier St., Steilacoom, 11/21/72, B, 72001280

Orton, Charles W., House, 7473 Riverside Rd., E., Sumner, 7/28/83, B, 83003350

Pacific Brewing and Malting Company, S. 25th St. between C St. and Jefferson Ave., Tacoma, 7/31/78, A, C, 78002768

Pacific National Bank Building, 1302 Pacific Ave., Tacoma, 3/07/80, A, C, 80004008

Pantages Theatre, 901 and 909 Broadway, Tacoma, 11/07/76, A, C, 76001902

Paradise Historic District [Mt. Rainier National Park MPS], Mt. Rainier National Park, Paradise, 3/13/91, A, C, NPS, 91000174

Paradise Inn, Paradise, Mount Rainier National Park, 5/28/87, A, C, NHL, NPS, 87001336

Purdy Bridge [Historic Bridges/Tunnels in Washington State TR], Spans Henderson Bay, Purdy, 7/16/82, A, C, g, 82004274

Pythian Temple, 924-926 1/2 Broadway, Tacoma, 8/23/85, A, C, 85001811

Red Shield Inn, Main St., Fort Lewis, 2/14/79, A, C, 79002552

Rhodes Medical Arts Building, 740 St. Helens Ave., Tacoma, 11/21/78, A, C, g, 78002769

Rhodesleigh, 10815 Greendale Dr., SW, Tacoma, 1/27/83, B, C, 83003352

Rialto Theater [Movie Theaters in Washington State MPS], 310 Ninth St., Tacoma, 8/21/92, A, 92001041

Rust, William Ross, House, 1001 N. I St., Tacoma, 8/23/85, B, C, 85001806

Ryan House, 1228 Main St., Sumner, 6/30/76, B, 76001900

Pierce County—Continued

Sequalitchew Archeological Site, Address Restricted, Dupont vicinity, 2/14/79, D, 79002551

Shriner Peak Fire Lookout [Mt. Rainier National Park MPS], Mt. Rainier National Park, Ohanapecosh vicinity, 3/13/91, A, NPS, 91000194

Silver Creek Ranger Station [USDA Forest Service Buildings in Oregon and Washington Built by the CCC MPS], WA 410 on eastern border of Mt. Rainier National Park, Mt. Baker—Snoqualmie National Forest, Crystal Mountain vicinity, 6/07/91, A, C, 91000707

Slavonian Hall, 2306 N. 30th St., Tacoma, 11/07/76, A, 76001903

South J Street Historic District, W Side of S. J St. between S. Seventh and S. Eighth Sts., Tacoma, 5/08/86, A, C, 86001020

South Puyallup River Bridge [Mt. Rainier National Park MPS], Mt. Rainier National Park, Nisqually Entrance vicinity, 3/13/91, A, C, NPS, 91000198

Sprague Building, 1501–1505 Pacific Ave., Tacoma, 11/21/85, B, C, 85002920

St. Andrews Creek Bridge [Mt. Rainier National Park MPS], Mt. Rainier National Park, Nisqually Entrance vicinity, 3/13/91, A, C, NPS, 91000199

St. Andrews Patrol Cabin [Mt. Rainier National Park MPS], Mt. Rainier National Park, Nisqually Entrance vicinity, 3/13/91, A, C, NPS, 91000188

St. Peter's Episcopal Church, Starr between 29th and 30th Sts., Tacoma, 11/05/74, A, a, 74001974

Stadium-Seminary Historic District, Roughly bounded by 1st, I, 10th Sts., and shoreline, Tacoma, 5/26/77, C, 77001353

Steilacoom Catholic Church, 1810 Nisqually St., Steilacoom, 7/30/74, A, a, b, 74001972

Steilacoom Historic District, Between Nisqually St. and Puget Sound, Steilacoom, 11/24/75, A, C, 75001865

Summerland Trail Shelter [Mt. Rainier National Park MPS], Mt. Rainier National Park, Sunrise vicinity, 3/13/91, A, C, NPS, 91000185

Sunrise Comfort Station [Mt. Rainier National Park MPS], Mt. Rainier National Park, Sunrise vicinity, 3/13/91, A, C, NPS, 91000207

Sunrise Historic District [Mt. Rainier National Park MPS], Mt. Rainier National Park, Sunrise, 3/13/91, A, C, NPS, 91000175

Sunset Park Patrol Cabin [Mt. Rainier National Park MPS], Mt. Rainier National Park, Mowich Lake Entrance vicinity, 3/13/91, A, C, NPS, 91000186

Sunset Park Trail Shelter [Mt. Rainier National Park MPS], Mt. Rainier National Park, Mowich Lake Entrance vicinity, 3/13/91, A, C, NPS, 91000187

Sunset Telephone & Telegraph Building, 1101 Fawcett Ave., Tacoma, 8/23/85, A, 85001809

Suntop Lookout [USDA Forest Service Fire Lookouts on Mt. Baker—Snoqualmie National Forest TR], White River Ranger District on Suntop Mountain, 15 mi. NE of Mt. Rainier, Enumclaw, 7/14/87, A, C, 87001192

Tacoma Narrows Bridge Ruins, WA 16 over the Tacoma Narrows, Tacoma, 8/31/92, A, 92001068

Tahoma Vista Comfort Station [Mt. Rainier National Park MPS], Mt. Rainier National Park, Nisqually Entrance vicinity, 3/13/91, A, C, NPS, 91000205

Thornewood, 8601, 8307 N. Thorne Lane, SW and 4 Thornewood Lane, SW, Tacoma, 3/18/82, B, C, 82004283

Tipsoo Lake Comfort Station [Mt. Rainier National Park MPS], Mt. Rainier National Park, Chinook Pass vicinity, 3/13/91, A, C, NPS, 91000206

Tolmie Peak Fire Lookout [Mt. Rainier National Park MPS], Mt. Rainier National Park, Mowich Lake Entrance vicinity, 3/13/91, A, NPS, 91000195

US Post Office—Tacoma Downtown Station—Federal Building [Historic US Post Offices in Washington MPS], 1102 S. A St., Tacoma, 5/30/91, A, C, 91000657

Union Depot-Warehouse Historic District, Roughly bounded by RR tracks, 15th, 23rd and Market Sts., Tacoma, 4/02/80, A, C, 80004009

Union Passenger Station, 1713 Pacific Ave., Tacoma, 3/15/74, A, C, 74001975

Walker Cut Stone Company, E of Wilkeson, Wilkeson vicinity, 6/07/78, A, 78002770

White River Bridge [Mt. Rainier National Park MPS], Mt. Rainier National Park, White River Entrance vicinity, 3/13/91, A, C, NPS, 91000200

White River Entrance [Mt. Rainier National Park MPS], Mt. Rainier National Park, White River Entrance, 3/13/91, A, C, NPS, 91000177

White River Mess Hall and Dormitory [Mt. Rainier National Park MPS], Mt. Rainier National Park, White River Entrance, 3/13/91, A, C, NPS, 91000328

White River Patrol Cabin [Mt. Rainier National Park MPS], Mt. Rainier National Park, White River Entrance vicinity, 3/13/91, A, C, NPS, 91000190

Wilkeson School, Off WA 165, Wilkeson, 10/08/76, A, C, a, 76001905

Williams, Herbert, House, 1711 Elm St., Sumner, 10/18/84, B, C, 84000172

Williams, Sidney, House, 15003 E. Elm St., Sumner, 10/18/84, B, C, 84000179

Wollochet—Point Fosdick School [Rural Public Schools in Washington from Early Settlement to 1945 MPS], 3409 E. Bay Dr., Gig Harbor vicinity, 7/15/87, A, 87001168

Woolrey-Koehler Hop Kiln, 176th St., E. (Leach Rd.), Orting, 10/13/83, A, C, 83004260

Wright Park and Seymour Conservatory, Division Ave. to 6th Ave., between S. G and I Sts., Tacoma, 10/08/76, A, C, 76001904

Y.M.C.A. Building, 714 Market St., Tacoma, 1/27/83, A, 83003353

Yakima Park Stockade Group, Sunrise (Yakima Park), Mount Rainier National Park, 5/28/87, C, g, NHL, NPS, 87001337

Yuncker, John F., House, 519 S. G St., Tacoma, 8/23/85, C, 85001807

San Juan County

Alderbrook Farmhouse, Point Lawrence Rd., Doe Bay vicinity, 11/21/85, C, 85002919

Crow Valley School [Rural Public Schools in Washington from Early Settlement to 1945 MPS], Crow Valley Rd., Eastsound vicinity, 8/27/87, A, 87001457

Doe Bay General Store and Post Office, End of County Rd., Doe Bay, Orcas Island, 5/08/86, A, 86001017

Krumdiack Homestead, N. coast, between Fishery Pt. and Pt. Hammond, Waldron Island, 4/29/93, A, C, 93000367

Little Red Schoolhouse, Corner of Hoffman Cove and Neck Point Cove Rd., Shaw Island, 6/19/73, A, 73001886

Orcas Hotel, In Orcas, Orcas, 8/24/82, A, C, 82004284

Patos Island Light Station, N of East Sound on Patos Island, East Sound vicinity, 10/21/77, A, C, 77001355

Roche Harbor, Northern San Juan Island, San Juan Island, 8/29/77, A, C, 77001356

Rosario, S of East Sound on Orcas Island, Orcas Island, 11/02/78, A, B, C, 78002772

San Juan County Courthouse, 350 N. Court St., Friday Harbor, 4/12/84, A, C, 84003603

San Juan Island National Historic Site, Between Haro Strait and San Juan Channel, Friday Harbor vicinity, 10/15/66, A, d, NHL, NPS, 66000369

San Juan Island, Lime Kiln Light Station, W of Friday Harbor on CR 1, Friday Harbor vicinity, 12/15/78, C, 78002771

Skagit County

Anacortes Public Library [Carnegie Libraries of Washington TR (AD)], 1305 8th St., Anacortes, 10/21/77, A, C, 77001357

Backus—Marblemount Ranger Station House No. 1009 [North Cascades National Park Service Complex MRA], Ranger Station Rd., 1 mi. N of WA 20, Marblemount, 2/10/89, C, NPS, 88003462

Backus—Marblemount Ranger Station House No. 1010 [North Cascades National Park Service Complex MRA], Ranger Station Rd., 1 mi. N of WA 20, Marblemount, 2/10/89, C, NPS, 88003463

Baker River Bridge [Historic Bridges/Tunnels in Washington State TR (AD)], On WA 17A, over Baker River, Concrete vicinity, 5/04/76, A, C, 76001906

Bethsaida Swedish Evangelical Lutheran Church Parsonage, 1754 Chilberg Rd., Pleasant Ridge, La Conner vicinity, 12/06/90, A, 90001863

Burlington Carnegie Library [Carnegie Libraries of Washington TR], 901 Fairhaven St., Burlington, 8/03/82, A, C, 82004286

California Fruit Store, 909 Third St., Anacortes, 11/05/87, C, b, 87001949

Causland Park, 8th St. and M Ave., Anacortes, 5/07/81, C, 81000589

Skagit County—Continued

Curtis Wharf, Jct. of O Ave. & Second St., Anacortes, 11/05/87, A, B, 87001941

Deception Pass [Historic Bridges/Tunnels in Washington State TR], Rte. 20, Anacortes, 7/16/82, A, C, g, 82004285

Gilbert's Cabin [North Cascades National Park Service Complex MRA], Cascade River Rd. W of Gilbert Creek, Stehekin vicinity, 2/10/89, A, NPS, 88003453

Great Northern Depot, R Ave. & Seventh St., Anacortes, 11/05/87, A, C, 87001935

Hidden Lake Peak Lookout [USDA Forest Service Fire Lookouts on Mt. Baker—Snoqualmie National Forest TR], Mt. Baker Ranger District, Southernmost peak of Hidden Lake Peaks near North Cascades National Park boundary, Marblemount, 7/14/87, A, C, 87001184

LA MERCED, Anacortes Waterfront off Oakes Ave., Anacortes, 4/17/90, A, C, g, 90000588

La Conner Historic District, Roughly bounded by 2nd, Morris and Commercial Sts., and Snohomish Channel, La Conner, 4/24/74, A, C, 74001977

Lincoln Theater and Commercial Block, 301–329 Kincaid St. & 710–740 First St., Mt. Vernon, 11/05/87, A, 87001987

Lower Baker River Hydroelectric Power Plant [Hydroelectric Power Plants in Washington State, 1890–1938 MPS], Baker River at S end of Shannan Lake, Concrete vicinity, 7/17/90, A, C, 88002736

Marine Supply and Hardware Complex, 202–218 Commercial Ave. & 1009 Second St., Anacortes, 11/05/87, C, 87001943

Minkler, Birdsey D., House, 201 S. Main St., Lyman, 12/01/88, B, C, 88002745

Rock Cabin [North Cascades National Park Service Complex MRA], Fisher Creek Trail S of Diablo Lake, Diablo vicinity, 2/10/89, B, C, NPS, 88003457

Semar Block, 501 Q Ave., Anacortes, 11/05/87, A, C, 87001967

Skagit City School, 3.5 mi. S of Mount Vernon on Moore Rd., Mount Vernon vicinity, 7/15/77, A, 77001358

Swamp—Meadow Cabin East [North Cascades National Park Service Complex MRA], Thunder Creek Trail S of Diablo Lake, Diablo vicinity, 2/10/89, A, C, NPS, 88003456

Swamp—Meadow Cabin West [North Cascades National Park Service Complex MRA], Thunder Creek Trail S of Diablo Lake, Diablo vicinity, 2/10/89, A, C, NPS, 88003455

US Post Office—Sedro Woolley Main [Historic US Post Offices in Washington MPS], 111 Woodworth St., Sedro Woolley, 8/07/91, A, C, 91000655

W. T. PRESTON (snagboat), Anacortes waterfront, R Ave., at foot of 7th St., Anacortes, 3/16/72, A, C, g, NHL, 72001270

Skamania County

Bonneville Dam Historic District, Columbia River between Bradford and Cascade Islands off I-80

in Multnomah County, Oregon to WA 14 in Skamania County, WA, N. Bonneville, 4/09/86, A, C, g, NHL, 86000727

North Bonneville Archeological District, Address Restricted, North Bonneville vicinity, 2/02/87, D, 87000498

Snohomish County

COASTER II, C Dock South, Port of Everett, Everett, 9/28/89, C, 89001605

Carnegie, Andrew, Library [Carnegie Libraries of Washington TR (AD)], 118 5th Ave., N., Edmonds, 4/24/73, A, 73001887

Commerce Building, 1801 Hewitt Ave., Everett, 10/01/92, C, 92001290

Community Center and War Memorial Building, 1611 Everett Ave., Everett, 2/26/79, A, C, 79002554

Darrington Ranger Station [USDA Forest Service Administrative Buildings in Oregon and Washington Built by the CCC MPS], 1405 Emmens St., Darrington, 3/06/91, A, C, 91000155

EQUATOR (schooner), 14th St. Yacht Basin, Everett, 4/14/72, A, 72001281

Everett Carnegie Library [Carnegie Libraries of Washington TR (AD)], 3001 Oakes Ave., Everett, 12/06/75, A, C, 75001868

Everett City Hall, 3002 Wetmore Ave., Everett, 5/02/90, A, C, 90000674

Everett Fire Station No. 2, 2801 Oakes Ave., Everett, 5/02/90, A, 90000673

Evergreen Mountain Lookout [USDA Forest Service Fire Lookouts on Mt. Baker—Snoqualmie National Forest TR], Skykomish Ranger District on SW ridgecrest of Evergreen Mountain, Skykomish, 7/14/87, A, C, 87001187

Floral Hall, Forest Park, Everett, 4/26/90, A, C, 90000671

Green Mountain Lookout [USDA Forest Service Fire Lookouts on Mt. Baker—Snoqualmie National Forest TR], Darrington Ranger District, Darrington, 2/22/88, A, C, 88000117

Hartley, Roland, House, 2320 Rucker Ave., Everett, 5/02/86, B, C, 86000958

Horseshoe Bend Placer Claim, N of Sultan, Sultan vicinity, 5/07/81, C, 81000590

Indian Shaker Church, W of Marysville, Tulalip Reservation, N. Meridan Ave., Marysville vicinity, 5/04/76, A, C, a, 76001910

Keeler's Korner, 16401 U.S. 99, Lynnwood, 4/29/82, A, 82004287

Marysville Opera House, 1225 3rd St., Marysville, 2/25/82, A, C, 82004288

McCabe Building, 3120 Hewitt Ave., Everett, 10/21/77, A, C, 77001359

Miners Ridge Lookout [USDA Forest Service Fire Lookouts on Mt. Baker—Snoqualmie National Forest TR], Darrington Ranger District in Glacier Peak Wilderness area 5 mi. W of Pacific Crest trail, Darrington, 7/19/87, A, C, g, 87001183

Monte Cristo Hotel, 1507 Wall St., Everett, 6/03/76, A, C, 76001907

Mukilteo Light Station, WA 525, Mukilteo, 10/21/77, C, 77001360

Pearson, D. O., House, Pearson and Market Sts., Stanwood, 5/25/73, C, 73001890

Red Men Hall, Index Ave. at 6th St., Index, 4/13/73, A, 73001889

Rucker Hill Historic District, Roughly bounded by 32nd, Tulalip Ave., Bell Ave., Snohomish Ave., Laurel, and Warren, Everett, 11/08/89, C, 89000399

Rucker House, 412 Laurel Dr., Everett, 12/04/75, A, C, 75001869

Snohomish County Courthouse, Wetmore Ave. between Wall St. and Pacific Ave., Everett, 12/06/75, A, C, 75001870

Snohomish Historic District, Roughly bounded by Ave. E, 5th St., Union Ave., Northern Pacific RR and Snohomish River, Snohomish, 10/22/74, A, C, 74001978

St. Anne's Roman Catholic Church, W of Marysville on Mission Beach Rd., Marysville vicinity, 6/18/76, A, C, a, 76001911

Suiattle Guard Station, Suiattle R. E of Buck Cr., Mt. Baker—Snoqualmie NF, Darrington vicinity, 12/18/90, A, C, 90001865

Swalwell Block and Adjoining Commercial Buildings, 2901–2909 and 2915 Hewitt Ave., Everett, 5/17/76, A, C, 76001908

Swalwell Cottage, 2712 Pine St., Everett, 11/28/78, A, C, 78002773

Three Fingers Lookout [USDA Forest Service Fire Lookouts on Mt. Baker—Snoqualmie National Forest TR], Darrington Ranger District on the southernmost peak, Darrington, 7/14/87, A, C, 87001190

Tulalip Indian Agency Office, 3901 Mission Beach Rd., Tulalip Reservation, Marysville vicinity, 5/03/76, A, 76001912

U.S. Post Office and Customshouse, 3006 Colby Ave., Everett, 6/22/76, A, C, 76001909

Verlot Ranger Station—Public Service Center [Depression-Era Buildings TR], Mt. Baker, Snoqualmie National Forest, Granite Falls, 4/08/86, A, C, 86000839

Weyerhouser Office Building, 1710 W. Marine View Dr., Everett, 5/14/86, A, C, b, 86001079

Spokane County

American Firebrick Company, WA 27, Mica, 3/09/82, A, 82004289

Amman [Apartment Buildings by Albert Held TR], W. 1516 Riverside, Spokane, 2/12/87, C, 87000086

Benewah Milk Bottle, S. 321 Cedar, Spokane, 8/13/86, C, 86001521

Binkley, J. W., House, 628 S. Maple, Spokane, 3/31/89, B, 89000211

Breslin [Apartment Buildings by Albert Held TR], S. 729 Bernard, Spokane, 2/12/87, C, 87000095

Browne's Addition Historic District, Roughly bounded by Sunset Blvd., Maple, Latah Creek, and Spokane River, Spokane, 7/30/76, C, 76001916

Spokane County—Continued

California Ranch, E of Mica on Jackson and Belmont Rds., Mica vicinity, 8/11/80, A, B, C, 80004010

Cambern Dutch Shop Windmill, S. 1102 Perry, Spokane, 3/16/89, C, 89000213

Campbell House, W. 2316 1st Ave., Spokane, 5/31/74, B, C, 74001979

Central Schoolhouse (District No. 49) [Rural Public Schools in Washington State MPS], Jct. of Ritchey and Four Mound Rds., NW corner, Nine Mile Falls vicinity, 8/27/92, A, 92001040

Cheney Interurban Depot, 505 2nd St., Cheney, 3/26/79, A, 79002555

Cheney Odd Fellows Hall, 321 First St., Cheney, 10/25/90, A, 90001639

Clark Mansion, W. 2208 2nd Ave., Spokane, 10/31/75, B, C, 75001873

Clemmer Theater, W. 901 Sprague Ave., Spokane, 12/01/88, A, 88002758

Commercial Block [Single Room Occupancy Hotels in the Central Business District of Spokane MPS], 1111–1119 First Ave. W., Spokane, 10/15/93, A, 93001103

Coolidge—Rising House, W. 1405 Ninth Ave., Spokane, 5/19/88, B, 88000598

Corbin Park Historic District, Waverly Pl. (W205–733), Park Pl. (W203–738), W. Oval and E. Oval, Spokane, 11/12/92, A, B, C, 92001584

Cowley Park, S. Division St. between 6th and 7th Aves., Spokane, 2/06/73, B, D, a, f, 73001891

Davenport Hotel, 807 W. Sprague, Spokane, 9/05/75, A, B, C, 75001874

Dybdall Gristmill, 10 mi. S of Cheney at Chapman Lake, Cheney vicinity, 1/11/76, A, B, C, 76001913

Eldridge Building, 1319–1325 W. First Ave., Spokane, 11/12/92, A, C, 92001588

Empire State Building, W. 901 Riverside St., Spokane, 8/18/77, B, C, 77001361

Felts Field Historic District, Roughly, Rutter Ave. between Fancher and Dollar Rds., Spokane, 9/24/91, A, 91001442

Finch House, W. 2340 1st Ave., S. 104 Poplar, Spokane, 7/12/76, B, C, 76001917

Finch, John A., Memorial Nurses Home, N. 852 Summit Blvd., Spokane, 5/28/91, A, 91000631

First Congregational Church of Spokane, W. 311–329 4th Ave., Spokane, 4/26/78, A, C, a, 78002775

Fort George Wright Historic District, W. 4000 Randolph Rd., Spokane vicinity, 5/17/76, A, C, 76001918

Frequency Changing Station, E. 1420 Celesta Ave., Spokane, 6/19/79, A, B, 79002556

Glover House, W. 321 8th Ave., Spokane, 8/14/73, B, C, a, 73001892

Grace Baptist Church, 1527 W. Mallon St., Spokane, 10/02/92, C, a, 92001289

Hallett House, E. 623 Lake, SE, Medical Lake, 6/17/76, B, C, 76001915

Ham-McEachern House, Pine and 5th Sts., Latah, 2/08/78, A, B, C, 78002774

Holley-Mason Building, S. 157 Howard, Spokane, 10/13/83, A, C, 83004262

Holy Names Academy Building, 1216 N. Superior St., Spokane, 5/02/86, A, a, 86000959

Hutton Building, 9 S. Washington St., Spokane, 1/27/83, B, C, 83004037

Hutton Settlement, 9907 Wellesley, Spokane vicinity, 1/01/76, A, B, C, 76001919

Italian Rock Ovens, S of Cheney, Cheney vicinity, 9/29/76, A, 76001914

Knickerbocker [Apartment Buildings by Albert Held TR], S. 501–507 Howard, Spokane, 2/12/87, C, 87000096

Lewis & Clark High School, W. 521 4th Ave., Spokane, 12/06/90, A, C, 90001860

Lowe, David, House, 306 F St., Cheney, 10/13/83, C, 83004264

Marycliff-Cliff Park Historic District, Roughly bounded by Lincoln St., 7th, 12th, and 14th Aves., Spokane, 12/21/79, A, C, g, 79002557

Mission Avenue Historic District, E. 220–824 Mission Ave., Spokane, 8/14/86, C, g, 86002644

Monroe Street Bridge [Historic Bridges/Tunnels in Washington State TR (AD)], Monroe St. between Ide Ave. and Riverfalls Blvd., Spokane, 5/13/76, A, C, 76001920

Natatorium Carousel, Spokane Falls Blvd., Spokane, 9/19/77, A, B, b, 77001362

Nine Mile Hydroelectric Power Plant Historic District [Hydroelectric Power Plants in Washington State, 1890-1938 MPS], Charles Rd. at Spokane R., Nine Mile Falls vicinity, 12/06/90, A, 90001861

Peaceful Valley Historic District, Roughly bounded by the Spokane River, Wilson Ave., Elm, and Cedar Sts., Spokane, 4/19/84, A, C, 84003617

Review Building, SE corner, Riverside Ave. and Monroe St., Spokane, 2/24/75, B, C, 75001875

Riblet, Royal, House, E of Spokane on Fruit Hill Rd., Spokane vicinity, 3/26/79, B, C, 79002558

Riverside Avenue Historic District, Riverside Ave., Spokane, 7/30/76, A, C, a, g, 76001921

San Marco [Apartment Buildings by Albert Held TR], W. 1229 Riverside, Spokane, 2/12/87, C, 87000090

Sears, Roebuck Department Store, W. 902 Main Ave., Spokane, 6/04/91, C, 91000629

Smith, Edwin A., House, N. 1414 Summit Blvd., Spokane, 8/23/85, B, C, 85001808

Spokane City Hall Building, N. 221 Wall St. and W. 711 Spokane Falls Blvd., Spokane, 2/21/85, A, C, 85000350

Spokane County Courthouse, W. 1116 Broadway, Spokane, 1/21/74, A, C, 74001980

Spokane Flour Mill, W. 621 Mallon Ave., Spokane, 2/08/78, A, C, 78002778

Spokane Public Library [Carnegie Libraries of Washington TR], 25 Altamont St., Spokane, 8/03/82, A, C, 82004290

Spokane Public Library [Carnegie Libraries of Washington TR], 525 Mission St., Spokane, 8/03/82, A, C, 82004291

Spokane Public Library [Carnegie Libraries of Washington TR], 925 W. Montgomery St., Spokane, 8/03/82, A, C, 82004292

Spokane Public Library [Carnegie Libraries of Washington TR], 10 S. Cedar, Spokane, 8/03/82, A, C, 82004910

Sunset Boulevard Bridge [Historic Bridges/Tunnels in Washington State TR], Spans Latah Creek, Spokane, 7/16/82, A, C, 82004293

Sutton Barn, 0.5 mi. SW of Cheney off U.S. 395, Cheney vicinity, 11/20/75, A, C, 75001871

Turnbull Pines Rock Shelter, Address Restricted, Cheney vicinity, 5/06/75, D, 75001872

US Post Office, Courthouse, and Custom House, W. 904 Riverside Ave., Spokane, 12/08/83, A, C, 83004269

Upper Kepple Rockshelters (45SP7), Address Restricted, Cheney vicinity, 7/26/85, D, 85001640

Washington State Normal School at Cheney Historic District, Jct. of Fifth and C Sts., Cheney, 10/01/92, A, B, C, 92001287

Washington Street Bridge [Historic Bridges/Tunnels in Washington State TR], Spans Spokane River, Spokane, 7/16/82, A, C, 82004294

West Valley High School [Rural Public Schools of Washington State MPS], N. 2805 Argonne Rd., Millwood, 11/21/91, A, C, 91001736

Whitten Block, N. 1 Post St., Spokane, 5/14/93, A, C, 93000362

Stevens County

Hudsons Bay Gristmill Site on Colville River, Address Restricted, Kettle Falls vicinity, 4/12/82, A, B, D, 82004295

Keller House, 700 N. Wynne St., Colville, 4/18/79, C, 79002559

Kettle Falls District, Address Restricted, Kettle Falls vicinity, 11/20/74, D, NPS, 74000352

Little Falls Hydroelectric Power Plant [Hydroelectric Power Plants in Washington State, 1890–1938 MPS], Spokane River, Reardon vicinity, 12/15/88, A, C, 88002737

Long Lake Hydroelectric Power Plant [Hydroelectric Power Plants in Washington State, 1890–1938 MPS], Spokane River, Ford vicinity, 12/15/88, A, C, 88002738

Long Lake Pictographs, Address Restricted, Ford vicinity, 5/24/76, D, 76001922

Loon Lake School [Rural Public Schools in Washington State MPS], 4000 Colville Rd., Loon Lake, 11/19/92, A, 92001592

McCauley, H. M., House, 285 Oak St., Colville, 4/18/79, C, 79002560

Northport School, South and 7th Sts., Northport, 10/04/79, A, 79002561

Old Indian Agency, 3rd St., Chewelah, 5/17/74, A, C, 74001981

Orient Bridge [Historic Bridges/Tunnels in Washington State TR], Richardson Rd., Spans Kettle River, Orient, 7/16/82, A, C, 82004297

Red Mountain Railroad Bridge [Historic Bridges/Tunnels in Washington State TR], Spans Little Sheep Creek, Northport, 7/16/82, A, C, 82004296

US Post Office—Colville Main [Historic US Post Offices in Washington MPS], 204 S. Oak, Colville, 8/07/91, A, C, 91000644

Stevens County—Continued

Winslow Railroad Bridge [Historic Bridges-/Tunnels in Washington State TR], S of Colville, Colville vicinity, 7/16/82, A, C, 82004298

Winslow, Colburn T., House, 458 E. 2nd St., Colville, 4/26/90, B, 90000670

Thurston County

Allen House Hotel [Downtown Olympia MRA], 114–118 N. Jefferson, Olympia, 6/17/87, C, 87000872

Bigelow, Daniel R., House, 918 Glass St, Olympia, 8/07/79, B, 79002562

Black Lake School [Rural Public Schools in Washington from Early Settlement to 1945 MPS], 6000 Black Lake Blvd. SW., Olympia vicinity, 5/10/90, A, 90000709

Capital Boulevard Crossing [Historic Bridges-/Tunnels in Washington State TR], Spans Deschutes River, Tumwater, 7/16/82, A, C, g, 82004300

Cloverfields, 1100 Carlyon Ave., SE, Olympia, 5/22/78, B, 78002779

Colvin House [Thurston County MRA], 16828 Old Hwy. 99, Tenino vicinity, 6/23/88, A, B, 88000693

Delphi School [Rural Public Schools in Washington from Early Settlement to 1945 MPS], 7601 SW. Delphi Rd., Olympia vicinity, 7/19/90, A, 90001075

Elks Building [Downtown Olympia MRA], 607–613 S. Capitol Way, Olympia, 4/21/88, A, 88000690

Funk House, 1202 E. Olympia Ave., Olympia, 5/08/87, C, 87000691

Gate School [Rural Public Schools in Washington from Early Settlement to 1945 MPS], 16925 Moon Rd. SW., Rochester vicinity, 7/19/90, A, 90001094

Hale, Calvin and Pamela, House, 902 Tullis St., NE, Olympia, 1/12/84, A, C, 84003632

Jaaska House and Warehouse [Thurston County MRA], 11300 Independence Rd., Rochester vicinity, 6/23/88, A, C, 88000702

Jeffers Studio [Downtown Olympia MRA], 500 and 502 S. Washington, Olympia, 6/17/87, A, C, 87000870

Johnson House [Thurston County MRA], 19540 Johnson Rd., Yelm vicinity, 6/23/88, C, 88000695

LOTUS (motor vessel), Fiddlehead Marina, B Dock, Olympia, 5/18/87, C, 87000715

Lackamas School [Rural Public Schools in Washington from Early Settlement to 1945 MPS], 16240, 16312 Bald Hill Rd. SE., Yelm vicinity, 5/10/90, A, 90000707

Long Lake Recreation Hall [Thurston County MRA], 3054 Carpenter Rd., SE, Lacey vicinity, 6/23/88, A, C, 88000697

Lord, C. J., Mansion, 211 W. 21st Ave., Olympia, 5/07/81, B, C, 81000591

McCleary, Henry, House, 111 W. 21st Ave., Olympia, 10/02/78, B, C, 78002780

Meyer House, 1136 E. Bay Dr., Olympia, 2/21/85, C, 85000351

Miller—Brewer House [Thurston County MRA], 17915 Guava, Rochester vicinity, 6/23/88, A, B, 88000694

Mottman Building [Downtown Olympia MRA (AD)], 101-105 N. Capitol Way, Olympia, 6/16/83, A, B, 83003354

Nisqually School [Rural Public Schools in Washington from Early Settlement to 1945 MPS], 341 Nisqually Cut-Off Rd. SE, Olympia vicinity, 8/23/90, A, 90001248

Old Capitol Building [Downtown Olympia MRA (AD)], 600 block Washington St., Olympia, 5/30/75, A, 75001877

Olympia National Bank [Downtown Olympia MRA], 422 S. Capitol Way, Olympia, 6/17/87, A, C, 87000869

Olympia Public Library [Carnegie Libraries of Washington TR; Downtown Olympia MRA (AD)], S. Franklin and E. 7th, Olympia, 8/03/82, A, C, 82004299

Patnude, Charles, House, 1239 8th Ave., Olympia, 5/22/78, C, 78002781

Reinhart—Young House, 1106 E. Olympia Ave., Olympia, 5/08/87, C, 87000712

Rice, L. N., House [Thurston County MRA], 12247 Vail Rd., SE, Yelm vicinity, 9/23/88, B, 88000700

Rochester Elementary School [Rural Public Schools in Washington from Early Settlement to 1945 MPS], 10140 US 12 SW., Rochester vicinity, 5/17/90, A, 90000784

Rudkin, Frank, House, 1005 E. Olympia Ave., Olympia, 5/08/87, B, C, 87000713

Salsich Lumber Company Superintendent's House [Thurston County MRA], 10808 Vail Rd., Yelm vicinity, 6/23/88, A, C, 88000696

Seatco Prison Site, Off WA 507, Bucoda, 5/02/75, A, 75001876

South Capitol Neighborhood Historic District, Roughly bounded by Capitol Lake, US 5 and 16th Ave., Olympia, 10/22/91, B, C, 91001516

State Training School for Girls Administration Building [Thurston County MRA], 20311 S.W. Old Hwy. 99, Rochester vicinity, 6/23/88, A, 88000697

Steele, Alden Hatch, House, 1010 S. Franklin St., Olympia, 6/18/92, B, C, 92000783

Tenino Depot, Off WA 507, Tenino, 12/27/74, A, b, 74001982

Tenino Stone Company Quarry, City Park, Tenino, 7/28/83, A, 83003355

Thurston County Courthouse [Downtown Olympia MRA (AD)], Capitol Way, Olympia, 7/23/81, A, C, 81000592

Ticknor School [Rural Public Schools in Washington from Early Settlement to 1945 MPS], 7212 Skookumchuck Rd. SE., Tenino vicinity, 5/10/90, A, 90000708

Town Square [Downtown Olympia MRA], Bounded by Seventh, Legion, Capitol Way, and S. Washington, Olympia, 6/17/87, A, C, 87000868

Tumwater Historic District, Roughly bounded by I-5, Capitol Way and Capitol Lake, Tumwater, 5/22/78, A, C, D, 78002782

Tumwater Methodist Church, 219 W. B St., Tumwater, 1/12/84, A, C, 84003636

U.S. Post Office [Downtown Olympia MRA (AD)], 801 Capitol Way, Olympia, 11/30/79, C, 79002563

Union Mills Superintendent's House [Thurston County MRA], 7716 Union Mills Rd., Olympia vicinity, 6/23/88, A, 88000699

Washington State Capitol Historic District, State Capitol and environs, Olympia, 6/22/79, A, C, g, 79002564

Weyerhaeuser South Bay Log Dump Rural Historic Landscape, 609 Whitham Rd., Olympia vicinity, 10/02/91, A, D, 91001441

Women's Club, 1002 Washington St., Olympia, 6/15/79, A, C, 79002565

Wahkiakum County

Columbia River Gillnet Boat, Altoona Cannery, Altoona, 2/14/78, A, 78002783

Deep River Pioneer Lutheran Church, N of Deep River, Deep River vicinity, 8/07/74, A, C, a, 74001983

Grays River Covered Bridge [Historic Bridges-/Tunnels in Washington State TR (AD)], WA 4, 1.5 mi. E of Grays River, Grays River vicinity, 11/23/71, A, 71000880

Pioneer Church, Alley St., Cathlamet, 4/11/73, A, C, a, 73001893

Skamokawa Historic District, WA 4, Skamokawa, 4/21/76, A, b, g, 76001923

Walla Walla County

Boyer, John F., House, 204 Newell St., Walla Walla, 8/11/80, B, 80004011

Bruce, William Perry, House, 4th and Main Sts., Waitsburg, 11/20/75, C, 75001878

Butler, Norman Francis, House, 207 E. Cherry St., Walla Walla, 11/12/92, C, 92001586

Dacres Hotel, 4th and Main Sts., Walla Walla, 11/05/74, A, 74001984

Dixie High School, Off U.S. 410, Dixie, 7/23/81, C, 81000593

Fort Walla Walla Historic District, 77 Wainwright Dr., Walla Walla, 4/16/74, A, D, 74001985

Green Park School, 1105 Isaacs Ave., Walla Walla, 11/08/90, A, C, 90001604

Johnson Bridge [Historic Bridges/Tunnels in Washington State TR], Spans Touchet River, Lowden, 7/16/82, A, C, 82004302

Kirkman House, 214 N. Colville St., Walla Walla, 12/27/74, C, 74001986

Liberty Theater [Movie Theaters in Washington State MPS], 50 E. Main St., Walla Walla, 4/29/93, A, C, 93000358

Ludwigs, George, House, 125 Newell St., Walla Walla, 4/12/82, B, C, 82004303

Walla Walla County—Continued

Memorial Building, Whitman College, 345 Boyer Ave., Walla Walla, 12/03/74, A, 74001987

Moore, Miles C., House, 720 Bryant, Walla Walla, 11/13/89, B, C, 89001949

Northern Pacific Railway Passenger Depot, 416 N. Second Ave., Walla Walla, 12/06/90, A, 90001862

Osterman House, 508 Lincoln St., Walla Walla, 10/19/83, C, 83004274

Preston Hall, 600 Main St., Waitsburg, 1/12/93, A, B, C, 92001590

Saturno-Breen Truck Garden, E of College Place on Rt. 5, College Place vicinity, 3/01/82, A, 82004301

Small-Elliott House, 314 E. Poplar St., Walla Walla, 3/01/82, B, C, b, 82004304

US Post Office—Walla Walla Main [Historic US Post Offices in Washington MPS], 128 N. Second St., Walla Walla, 5/30/91, A, C, 91000660

Waitsburg Historic District, Main St., Waitsburg, 3/31/78, A, C, g, 78002784

Walla Walla Public Library [Carnegie Libraries of Washington TR (AD)], 109 S. Palouse St., Walla Walla, 11/20/74, A, 74001988

Walla Walla Valley Traction Company Car Barn, 1102 W. Cherry, Walla Walla, 12/07/89, A, 89002097

Washington School, 501 N. Cayuse, Walla Walla, 11/21/91, A, C, 91001737

Whitman Mission National Historic Site, 6 mi. W of Walla Walla off U.S. 410, Walla Walla vicinity, 10/15/66, A, B, D, a, f, NPS, 66000749

Whatcom County

Aftermath Clubhouse, 1300 Broadway, Bellingham, 12/14/78, A, C, 78002785

Austin Pass Warming Hut, SE of Bagley Lakes, Mt. Baker—Snoqualmie NF, Glacier vicinity, 12/21/90, A, C, 90001866

B. P. O. E. Building, 1412–1414 Cornwall Ave., Bellingham, 3/26/92, A, C, 92000282

Bacon, George H., House, 2001 Eldridge Ave., Bellingham, 11/21/74, C, 74001989

Beaver Pass Shelter [North Cascades National Park Service Complex MRA], Beaver Pass, 14 mi. W of Ross Lake, Diablo vicinity, 2/10/89, C, NPS, 88003448

Bellingham National Bank Building, 101-111 E. Holly St., Bellingham, 10/13/83, A, C, 83004275

Black, Alfred L., House, 158 S. Forest St., Bellingham, 12/04/80, C, 80004012

Boundary Marker No. 1, Marine Dr. at U.S./Canada border, Point Roberts, 5/30/75, A, 75001881

Citizen's Dock, 1201 Roeder Ave., Bellingham, 5/14/81, A, 81000594

Copper Mountain Fire Lookout [North Cascades National Park Service Complex MRA], On Copper Mountain, 10 mi. E of Hannegan Campground, Newhalem vicinity, 2/10/89, A, NPS, 88003446

Deer Lick Cabin [North Cascades National Park Service Complex MRA], E of Ross Lake on Lightening Creek Trail, S of Three Fools Trail, Hozomeen vicinity, 2/10/89, C, NPS, 88003452

Desolation Peak Lookout [North Cascades National Park Service Complex MRA], On Desolation Peak E of Ross Lake, 6 mi. S of Canadian border, Hozomeen vicinity, 2/10/89, A, C, NPS, 88003451

Devil's Corner Cliff Walk [Historic Bridges-/Tunnels in Washington State TR (AD)], N of Newhalem in Ross Lake National Recreation Area, Newhalem vicinity, 6/07/74, A, NPS, 74000909

Diablo Hydroelectric Power Plant [Hydroelectric Power Plants in Washington State, 1890–1938 MPS], Off WA 20 at W end of Diablo Lake, Newhalem vicinity, 6/30/89, A, C, 89000498

Donovan, J. J., House, 1201 Garden St., Bellingham, 1/27/83, B, C, 83003356

Eldridge Avenue Historic District, Eldridge Ave. and environs, Bellingham, 7/27/79, A, C, g, 79002566

Eldridge Homesite and Mansion, 2915 Eldridge Ave., Bellingham, 1/27/83, C, 83003357

Fairhaven Historic District, Roughly bounded by 10th and 13th Sts., Columbia and Larrabee Aves., Bellingham, 8/19/77, A, C, g, 77001363

Fairhaven Library [Carnegie Libraries of Washington TR], 1105 12th St., Bellingham, 8/03/82, A, C, 82004907

Fish and Game—Hozomeen Cabin [North Cascades National Park Service Complex MRA], Hozomeen Lake—Lightening Creek trailhead on E side of Ross Lake, Hozomeen, 2/10/89, C, NPS, 88003454

Flatiron Building, 1311-1319 Bay St., Bellingham, 1/27/83, C, 83003358

Gamwell House, 1001 16th St., Bellingham, 3/16/72, B, C, 72001282

Glacier Ranger Station [Depression-Era Buildings TR (AD)], Mount Baker Hwy., Glacier, 9/17/80, A, g, 80004013

Gorge Hydroelectric Power Plants [Hydroelectric Power Plants in Washington State, 1890–1938 MPS], Off WA 20 at W end of Gorge Lake, Newhalem vicinity, 6/30/89, A, C, 89000499

Great Northern Passenger Station, S end of D St., Bellingham, 5/30/75, A, C, g, 75001879

Hovander Homestead, 5299 Neilson Rd., Ferndale, 10/16/74, B, C, 74001990

International Boundary US—Canada [North Cascades National Park Service Complex MRA], Along US—Canada border between eastern boundary of Ross Lake NRA and western boundary of North Cascades National Park, Hozomeen vicinity, 2/10/89, A, NPS, 88003450

Koma Kulshan Ranger Station [USDA Forest Service Buildings in Oregon and Washington Built by the CCC MPS], Forest Rd. 11, W of Baker Lake, Mt. Baker National Forest, Concrete vicinity, 6/10/91, A, C, 91000708

Larrabee House, 405 Fieldstone Rd., Bellingham, 5/30/75, B, C, 75001880

Leopold Hotel, 1224 Cornwall Ave., Bellingham, 2/19/82, A, 82004306

Middle Fork Nooksack River Bridge [Historic Bridges/Tunnels in Washington State TR], Mosquito Lake Rd., Acme, 7/16/82, A, C, b, 82004305

Montague and McHugh Building, 114 W. Magnolia St., Bellingham, 4/29/93, A, C, 93000371

Morse, Robert I., House, 1014 N. Garden St., Bellingham, 11/07/77, B, C, 77001364

Mount Baker Theatre, 106 N. Commercial St., Bellingham, 12/14/78, A, C, 78002786

Nooksack Falls Hydroelectric Power Plant [Hydroelectric Power Plants in Washington State, 1890–1938 MPS], Rt. 542 on Nooksack River, Glacier vicinity, 12/15/88, A, C, 88002735

Old Main, Western Washington State College, 516 High St., Bellingham, 11/07/77, A, C, 77001365

Park Butte Lookout [USDA Forest Service Fire Lookouts on Mt. Baker—Snoqualmie National Forest TR], Mt. Baker Ranger District, SW of the Easton Glacier of Mt. Baker, Sedro Wooley, 7/14/87, A, C, 87001189

Perry Creek Shelter [North Cascades National Park Service Complex MRA], On Little Beaver Trail, 5 mi. W of Ross Lake, Hozomeen vicinity, 2/10/89, C, NPS, 88003447

Pickett House, 910 Bancroft St., Bellingham, 12/13/71, B, 71000881

Roeder, Victor A., House, 2600 Sunset Dr., Bellingham, 11/07/77, B, C, 77001366

Roth, Lottie, Block, 1106 W. Holly St., Bellingham, 12/12/78, B, C, 78002787

Sourdough Mountain Lookout [North Cascades National Park Service Complex MRA], On Sourdough Mountain, 5 mi. NE of Diablo, Diablo vicinity, 2/10/89, A, C, NPS, 88003449

U.S. Post Office and Courthouse, 104 W. Magnolia St., Bellingham, 4/30/79, C, 79003157

US Post Office—Lyden Main [Historic US Post Offices in Washington MPS], 600 Front St., Lyden, 8/07/91, A, C, 91000648

Wardner, James F., House, 1103 15th St., Bellingham, 12/01/88, B, C, 88002744

Whatcom Museum of History and Art, 121 Prospect St., Bellingham, 4/03/70, C, 70000648

Wild Goose Pass Tree, Address Restricted, Glacier vicinity, 6/07/91, A, 91000706

Winchester Mountain Lookout [USDA Forest Service Fire Lookouts on Mt. Baker—Snoqualmie National Forest TR], Mt. Baker Wilderness Area overlooking the N fork of Nooksack River and W fork of Silesia Creek, Sedro Wooley, 7/14/87, A, C, 87001188

Young Women's Christian Association, 1026 N. Forest St., Bellingham, 4/21/77, A, C, 77001367

Whitman County

Barron, J. C., Flour Mill, 1st and Jackson Sts., Oakesdale, 2/08/78, A, 78002788

Canyon Grain Bin and Chutes [Grain Production Properties in Eastern Washington MPS], E of County Rd. 7030, 2 mi. NE of jct. County Rds. 7030 and 7010, Hay vicinity, 9/22/88, A, g, 88001539

Whitman County—Continued

Collins House and Granary, SE of Uniontown off U.S. 195, Uniontown vicinity, 7/30/74, B, 74001993

F Street Bridge [Historic Bridges/Tunnels in Washington State TR], Spans Palouse River, Palouse, 7/16/82, A, C, 82004308

Hanford, Edwin H., House, N of WA 217, Oakesdale vicinity, 5/15/86, B, C, 86001068

Heilsberg, Gustave, Farm [Grain Production Properties in Eastern Washington MPS], Rt. 2, Colfax vicinity, 9/22/88, A, C, 88001534

Henley Site, Address Restricted, Hay vicinity, 9/19/77, D, 77001369

Interior Grain Tramway [Grain Production Properties in Eastern Washington MPS], Snake River Canyon, 2 mi. N of Wawawai, Pullman vicinity, 9/22/88, A, 88001538

Leonard, T. A., Barn, S side of Old Moscow Hwy., Pullman vicinity, 5/02/86, C, 86000963

Manning-Rye Covered Bridge [Historic Bridges/Tunnels in Washington State TR], Spans Palouse River, Colfax, 7/16/82, A, C, 82004307

Masonic Hall, Corner of Main and Second Sts., Farmington, 2/12/87, C, 87000057

McCroskey, R. C., House, 4th and Manring Sts., Garfield, 11/21/74, B, C, 74001992

McGregor Ranch [Grain Production Properties in Eastern Washington MPS], 6 mi. S of Hooper, Hooper vicinity, 9/22/88, A, B, 88001535

Oakesdale City Hall, E. 101 Steptoe, Oakesdale, 4/29/93, A, 93000360

Palouse Main Street Historic District, Main St. between K and Mary Sts., Palouse, 5/08/86, A, C, 86001026

Perkins, James A., House, N. 623 Perkins St., Colfax, 12/11/72, A, C, 72001283

Rosalia Railroad Bridge [Historic Bridges/Tunnels in Washington State TR], WA 271, Rosalia, 7/16/82, A, C, 82004310

Steinke, Max, Barn [Grain Production Properties in Eastern Washington MPS], Rt. 1, Box 130, St. John vicinity, 9/22/88, C, 88001536

Steptoe Battlefield Site, SE of Rosalia, Rosalia vicinity, 5/06/76, A, 76001924

Stevens Hall, Campus and Administration Sts., Pullman, 3/26/79, A, 79002567

Tekoa Grain Company Elevator & Flathouse [Grain Production Properties in Eastern Washington MPS], 4 mi. W of Tekoa, Lone Pine vicinity, 9/22/88, A, 88001537

Thompson, Albert W., Hall, Administration Rd. on Washington State University campus, Pullman, 3/01/73, A, C, 73001894

US Post Office—Colfax Main [Historic US Post Offices in Washington MPS], S. 211 Main St., Colfax, 5/30/91, A, C, 91000643

United Presbyterian Church, 430 Maple St., Pullman, 12/07/89, C, a, 89002095

Yakima County

Brackett, E. William, House, 2606 Tieton Dr., Yakima, 10/25/90, B, C, 90001605

Brooker—Taylor House [Yakima TR], 203 S. Naches Ave., Yakima, 2/18/87, C, 87000061

Buckeye Ranch House, 10881 WA 410, Naches vicinity, 11/02/90, B, C, 90001735

Capitol Theatre, 19 S. 3rd St., Yakima, 4/11/73, A, C, 73001895

Carbonneau Mansion, 620 S. 48th Ave., Yakima, 12/12/76, B, C, 76001927

Card, Rupert, House [Yakima TR], 1105 W. A St., Yakima, 2/18/87, C, 87000063

Carmichael, Elizabeth Loudon, House, 108 W. Pine St., Union Gap, 5/01/91, B, C, 91000538

Carmichael—Loudon House [Yakima TR], 2 Chicago Ave., Yakima, 2/18/87, B, C, 87000065

Cornell Farmstead [Grandview MRA], Pleasant Rd. and Old Prosser Rd., Grandview vicinity, 2/17/87, A, C, 87000055

Dills, Harrison, House [Yakima TR], 4 N. Sixteenth Ave., Yakima, 2/18/87, B, C, 87000066

Donald House, 304 N. 2nd St., Yakima, 12/12/76, B, C, 76001928

Fort Simcoe State Park, SW of Yakima on WA 220, Yakima vicinity, 6/27/74, A, C, D, 74001994

Gilbert, H. M., House, 2109 W. Yakima Ave., Yakima, 8/23/85, B, C, 85001812

Gleed, James, Barn, 1960 Old Naches Hwy., Naches vicinity, 5/10/90, C, 90000672

Goodman, Daniel, House, 701 S. 3rd Ave., Yakima, 10/02/92, B, C, 92001286

Grandview Herald Building [Grandview MRA], 107 Division St., Grandview, 2/17/87, A, C, 87000056

Grandview High School [Grandview MRA], 913 W. Second St., Grandview, 2/17/87, A, C, 87000058

Grandview State Bank [Grandview MRA], 100 W. Second Ave., Grandview, 2/17/87, A, C, 87000060

Grave of the Legendary Giantess, 9 mi. (14.4 km) S of Toppenish on U.S. 97, Toppenish vicinity, 12/14/78, A, 78002789

Greene, James, House [Yakima TR], 203 N. Ninth St., Yakima, 5/06/87, C, 87000059

Howard, A. E., House [Yakima TR], 602 N. First St., Yakima, 2/18/87, B, C, 87000067

Howay—Dykstra House [Grandview MRA], 114 Birch St., Grandview, 2/17/87, C, 87000062

Irish, William N., House, 210 S. 28th Ave., Yakima, 3/31/92, B, 92000280

Kamiakin's Gardens, W of Union Gap on Lower Ahtanum Rd., Union Gap vicinity, 12/22/76, B, 76001926

Knuppenburg, James, House [Yakima TR], 111 S. Ninth St., Yakima, 2/18/87, C, 87000070

LaFramboise Farmstead, 5204 Mieras Rd., Yakima, 2/28/85, A, C, a, 85000400

Larson, A. E., Building, 6 S. 2nd St., Yakima, 9/11/84, C, 84003647

Larson—Hellieson House [Yakima TR], 208 N. Naches Ave., Yakima, 5/06/87, C, b, 87000073

Lindsey, William, House [Yakima TR], 301 N. Eighth St., Yakima, 2/18/87, C, b, 87000075

Lund Building, 5 N. Front St., Yakima, 10/13/83, C, 83004276

Mabton High School, High School Rd., Mabton, 11/21/85, A, 85002917

Mattoon Cabin, S of Sawyer on U.S. 12, Sawyer vicinity, 10/28/77, A, 77001371

McAllister, Alexander, House, 402 W. White St., Union Gap, 10/25/90, C, 90001603

Miller, John J., House [Yakima TR], 9 S. Tenth Ave., Yakima, 2/18/87, B, C, 87000078

Mineau, Francis, House [Yakima TR], 216 N. Seventh St., Yakima, 2/18/87, C, 87000079

Moore, Edward B., House [Yakima TR], 222 N. Second St., Yakima, 2/18/87, C, 87000081

Morse House [Grandview MRA], 404 E. Main St., Grandview, 2/17/87, C, 87000064

Old North Yakima Historic District, Roughly bounded by E. A St., S. First St., E. Yakima Ave., and the Northern Pacific RR tracks, Yakima, 5/02/86, A, C, 86000960

Perrin, Winfield, House [Yakima TR], 12 S. Eleventh Ave., Yakima, 2/18/87, C, 87000083

Potter, H. W., House [Yakima TR], 305 S. Fourth St., Yakima, 2/18/87, C, 87000084

Powell House [Yakima TR], 207 S. Ninth St., Yakima, 2/18/87, C, 87000085

Richey, James, House [Yakima TR], 206 N. Naches Ave., Yakima, 5/06/87, C, 87000087

Rosedell, 1811 W. Yakima Ave., Yakima, 7/12/90, B, C, 90001074

Sawyer, W. P., House And Orchard, U.S. 12, Sawyer, 11/23/77, B, C, 77001370

Sharp, James, House [Yakima TR], 111 N. Ninth St., Yakima, 2/18/87, C, 87000088

St. Joseph's Mission, E of Tampico on Tampico Rd., Tampico vicinity, 12/22/76, A, a, 76001925

Sweet, Reuben, House [Yakima TR], 6 Chicago Ave., Yakima, 2/18/87, C, 87000089

Teapot Dome Service Station, Old State HW 12, Zillah vicinity, 8/29/85, C, b, 85001943

U. S. Post Office and Courthouse, 25 S. 3rd St, Yakima, 11/27/79, C, 79002568

US Post Office—Sunnyside Main [Historic US Post Offices in Washington MPS], 713 E. Edison Ave., Sunnyside, 5/30/91, A, C, 91000656

US Post Office—Toppenish Main [Historic US Post Offices in Washington MPS], 14 Jefferson Ave., Toppenish, 8/07/91, A, C, 91000658

Union Pacific Freight Building, 104 W. Yakima Ave., Yakima, 9/08/88, A, 88001519

Watt, William, House [Yakima TR], 1511 W. Chestnut Ave., Yakima, 2/18/87, C, 87000091

West, Dr. Edmond, House [Yakima TR], 202 S. Sixteenth Ave., Yakima, 2/18/87, B, C, 87000092

Wilcox, Charles, House [Yakima TR], 220 N. Sixteenth Ave., Yakima, 2/18/87, C, 87000093

Yakima Indian Agency Building, 1 S. Elm, Toppenish, 5/19/88, A, 88000605

Yakima Valley Transportation Company, Third Ave. and Pine St., Yakima, 10/08/92, A, C, 84004012

Young Women's Christian Association Building, 15 N. Naches Ave., Yakima, 4/29/93, A, 93000361

WEST VIRGINIA

Barbour County

Barbour County Courthouse, Court Sq., Philippi, 2/22/80, A, C, 80004014

Carrolton Covered Bridge [West Virginia Covered Bridges TR], SR 36, Carrollton, 6/04/81, A, C, 81000595

Crim, J. N. B., House, WV 57, Elk City, 8/24/84, C, 84003462

Peck-Crim-Chesser House, 14 N. Walnut St., Philippi, 8/23/84, C, 84003464

Philippi B & O Railroad Station, 146 N. Main St., Philippi, 5/16/86, A, C, 86001082

Philippi Covered Bridge [West Virginia Covered Bridges TR], U.S. 250 at jct. with U.S. 119, Philippi, 9/14/72, A, C, 72001284

Philippi Historic District, Roughly bounded by Pike, High, Walnut, Wolfe, Main, Wilson Sts., and Tygart Valley River, Philippi, 8/29/90, A, C, 90001241

Whitescarver Hall, Circle Dr. on the Alderson-Broaddus College campus, Philippi, 2/05/90, A, C, 89002317

Berkeley County

Apollo Theatre, 128 E. Martin St, Martinsburg, 10/11/79, A, C, 79002569

Ar-Qua Springs, CR 37, Arden vicinity, 12/12/76, A, a, 76001929

Baltimore and Ohio and Related Industries Historic District [Berkeley County MRA], Roughly bounded by B&O RR from S side of Burke St. underpass to N side of B&O & PA RR bridge, Martinsburg, 12/10/80, A, C, 80004415

Boomtown Historic District [Berkeley County MRA], Roughly along Winchester Ave. to Arden Rd., W. King St. to Red Hill Rd., W. Stephen, W. Addition St, and Raleigh Sts., Martinsburg, 12/10/80, A, C, a, 80004414

Boydville, 601 S. Queen St., Martinsburg, 10/15/70, A, B, 70000649

Boydville Historic District [Berkeley County MRA], Roughly bounded by W. Stephen, S. Spring, and S. Queen Sts., including Boydville grounds, Martinsburg, 12/10/80, A, C, a, d, 80004413

Brown, Thomas, House, , CR 30, Inwood vicinity, 1/16/86, A, C, 86000202

Bunker Hill Historic District [Berkeley County MRA], Jct. of US 11 and Rt. 26, Bunker Hill, 12/10/80, A, C, a, 80004412

Burwell, James Nathanial, House, E of US 11, N of WV state line, Ridgeway vicinity, 5/16/91, C, 91000553

Campbellton [Berkeley County MRA], Address Unknown, Gerrardstown, 12/10/80, A, C, 80004411

Continental Clay Brick Plant [Berkeley County MRA], SE of Martinsburg on Rt. 9, Martinsburg, 12/10/80, A, 80004439

Cunningham, Samuel, House, SE of Hedgesville off WV 9, Hedgesville vicinity, 12/12/76, A, C, 76001930

Darkesville Historic District [Berkeley County MRA], US 11 at Middle Creek, Darkesville, 12/10/80, A, C, D, a, 80004410

Downs, Charles, II, House, WV Secondary Rt. 1, W of US 11, Marlowe vicinity, 5/17/91, B, C, 91000554

Downtown Martinsburg Historic District [Berkeley County MRA], Roughly bounded by W. Race, Water, Stephen, and Charles Sts., Martinsburg, 12/10/80, A, C, a, 80004416

Drinker, John, House [Berkeley County MRA], Sam Mason Rd., Bunker Hill vicinity, 12/10/80, A, B, C, D, 80004409

East Martinsburg Historic District [Berkeley County MRA], Roughly bounded by B&O RR right-of-way , N. Queen St., Moler Ave., and High St., Martinsburg, 12/10/80, A, C, a, 80004417

Edgewood [Berkeley County MRA], Address Unknown, Bunker Hill, 12/10/80, A, C, D, 80004431

Faraway Farm [Berkeley County MRA], Rt. 8, Martinsburg vicinity, 12/10/80, C, 80004432

Federal Aviation Administration Records Center, 300 W. King St., Martinsburg, 9/10/74, C, 74001995

French, Teter Myers, House [Berkeley County MRA], Jct. of Rts. 1 and 3, Hedgesville vicinity, 12/10/80, A, C, 80004434

Gerrardstown Historic District, Roughly, along WV 51 and Virginia Line Rd., Gerrardstown, 8/05/91, A, C, 91001008

Gold, Washington, House, S of Gerrardstown on CR 51/2, Gerrardstown vicinity, 1/12/84, A, C, 84003470

Green Hill Cemetery Historic District [Berkeley County MRA], 486 E. Burke St., Martinsburg, 12/10/80, A, C, d, 80004433

Harlan Spring Historic District [Berkeley County MRA], Harlan Spring, Hedgesville, 12/10/80, A, C, 80004435

Harmony Cemetery [Berkeley County MRA], Rt. 1/1, Marlow vicinity, 12/10/80, A, D, a, d, 80004436

Hays-Gerrard House, Congress St., Gerrardstown, 9/16/85, B, C, a, 85002409

Hedges, Decatur, House, WV 9, Hedgesville vicinity, 1/12/84, C, 84003473

Hedges, Samuel, House, CR 9/10, Hedgesville vicinity, 12/12/76, A, 76001931

Hedges—Lemen House, Co. Rt. 4, .7 mi. N of jct. with WV 9, Hedgesville vicinity, 5/02/91, A, C, 91000556

Hedges-Robinson-Myers House [Berkeley County MRA], Rte. 3, Hedgesville vicinity, 12/10/80, A, C, 80004418

Hedgesville Historic District [Berkeley County MRA], Roughly bounded by N. and S. Mary St., and E. and W. Main St., Hedgesville, 12/10/80, A, C, D, a, 80004419

Hughes-Cunningham House, Harlan Springs Rd., Hedgesville vicinity, 7/08/85, A, C, 85001518

Jones Mill Run Historic District [Berkeley County MRA], Address Unknown, Martinsburg vicinity, 12/10/80, A, C, D, 80004421

Kearfott-Bane House, SR 36/1, Baker Heights vicinity, 7/08/85, C, 85001520

Kunkel, Elizabeth, House, W side of US 11, 2.4 mi. N of Martinsburg, Martinsburg vicinity, 5/17/91, C, 91000557

Lick Run Plantation, Off US 11, Bedington vicinity, 1/12/84, A, C, 84003476

Maidstone Manor Farm [Berkeley County MRA], CR 1/4, Hedgesville vicinity, 12/10/80, A, B, C, 80004408

McKown, Gilbert and Samuel, House, WV 51, Gerrardstown vicinity, 1/12/84, A, C, 84003477

Mill Creek Historic District [Berkeley County MRA], Runs along Mill Creek extending both E and W of Bunker Hill, Bunker Hill vicinity, 12/10/80, A, C, D, 80004420

Morgan Chapel and Graveyard, N side of Secondary Rt. 26 W of jct. with U.S. 11, Bunker Hill vicinity, 1/12/84, A, C, a, d, 84003480

Morgan, William G., House, On Secondary Rt. 24, S of jct. with Secondary Rt. 26, Bunker Hill vicinity, 1/12/84, A, C, D, 84003489

Morgan-Gold House, SR 26, Bunker Hill vicinity, 7/08/85, A, C, 85001519

Mount Zion Baptist Church [Berkeley County MRA], Opequon Lane, Martinsburg, 12/10/80, A, C, a, 80004422

Mulliss, George W. F., House, W side of US 11, 1 mi. S of Martinsburg, Martinsburg vicinity, 5/02/91, B, C, 91000549

Myers House [Berkeley County MRA], Union Corner at end of Rt. 37/1, Martinsburg, 12/10/80, A, C, 80004423

Power Plant and Dam No. 4 [Berkeley County MRA], On Potomac River N of CR 5 at Scrabble, Sheperdstown vicinity, 12/10/80, A, C, 80004437

Power Plant and Dam No. 5 [Berkeley County MRA], On Potomac River W of Marlow, Marlow vicinity, 12/10/80, A, 80004438

Redbud Hollow [Berkeley County MRA], Address Unknown, Martinsburg vicinity, 12/10/80, A, C, 80004424

Rees, John, David, and Jacob, House, Off US 11, Bunker Hill vicinity, 1/12/84, A, C, 84003495

Ridge Road Historic District [Berkeley County MRA], S along Ridge Rd. from Nollville, Nollville vicinity, 12/10/80, A, C, D, 80004429

Rush-Miller House, On WV 45, Smoketown vicinity, 7/08/85, B, C, 85001521

Seibert, Henry J., II, House, Off W.VA 45, Martinsburg vicinity, 7/08/85, C, 85001526

Berkeley County—Continued

Snodgrass Tavern, W of Hedgesville on WV 3, Hedgesville vicinity, 4/24/73, C, 73001896

South Water Street Historic District [Berkeley County MRA], Roughly bounded by E. John, Water, and E. Burke Sts., and B&O RR, Martinsburg, 12/10/80, A, C, 80004430

Stephen, Adam, House, 309 E. John St., Martinsburg, 10/15/70, A, B, 70000650

Stuckey House, Co. Rt. 7/8, along Wilson Ridge, Jones Spring vicinity, 5/17/91, B, C, 91000555

Swan Pond, CR 5/3, Martinsburg vicinity, 7/29/77, A, C, 77001372

Swan Pond Manor Historic District [Berkeley County MRA], Swan Pond, Martinsburg, 12/10/80, A, C, D, 80004425

Tabb, Edward, House, On CR 4 S of jct. with WV 9, Hedgesville, 1/12/84, A, C, 84003500

Tuscarora Creek Historic District [Berkeley County MRA], Roughly bounded by N. Tennessee Ave., S on Old Mill Rd. to Rt. 15, Martinsburg vicinity, 12/10/80, A, C, D, a, 80004426

Union Bryarly's Mill [Berkeley County MRA], Address Unknown, Darkesville, 12/10/80, A, C, D, 80004440

Van Metre Ford Stone Bridge, E of Martinsburg across Opequon Creek on SR 36, Martinsburg vicinity, 8/22/77, A, C, 77001373

VanDoren, Jacob, House, 1 mi. SW of jct. of CR 45/3 and CR 40, Martinsburg vicinity, 1/12/84, A, C, 84003504

Watkins Ferry Toll House [Berkeley County MRA], Rt. 11, Martinsburg, 12/10/80, A, C, 80004427

White Bush [Berkeley County MRA], Rt. 11/3, Falling Waters, 12/10/80, C, D, 80004428

Wilson, Mary Park, House, SR 51/2, Gerrardstown vicinity, 7/08/85, C, 85001524

Wilson, William, House, WV 51, Gerrardstown vicinity, 1/12/84, A, C, 84003508

Boone County

Boone County Courthouse, State St., Madison, 4/09/81, C, 81000596

Braxton County

Cunningham House and Outbuildings [Bulltown MRA], E of Napier, Napier vicinity, 3/21/84, C, 84003510

Old Sutton High School, N. Hill Rd, Sutton, 8/29/79, A, C, 79002570

Sutton Downtown Historic District, Roughly bounded by Main St., River View Dr., and First St., Sutton, 7/10/87, A, C, 87001059

Union Civil War Fortification [Bulltown MRA], Address Restricted, Napier vicinity, 3/21/84, A, C, D, 84003515

Windy Run Grade School, Jct. of CR 38 and CR 19/48, Telsa vicinity, 1/12/84, A, 84003518

Brooke County

Beallmore [Pleasant Avenue MRA], 1500 Pleasant Ave., Wellsburg, 5/16/86, B, C, 86001069

Bethany Historic District, WV 67, Bethany, 4/01/82, A, B, C, a, 82004311

Brooke Cemetery [Pleasant Avenue MRA], 2200 Pleasant Ave., Wellsburg, 5/16/86, B, C, d, 86001070

Brown, Danforth, House, 555 Washington Pike (US 27), Wellsburg vicinity, 10/29/92, A, B, 92001484

Campbell, Alexander, Mansion, E of Bethany on WV 67, Bethany vicinity, 10/15/70, B, a, 70000651

Delta Tau Delta Founders House, 211 Main St., Bethany, 5/29/79, A, 79002571

Duval, Gen. I. H., Mansion [Pleasant Avenue MRA], 1222 Pleasant Ave., Wellsburg, 5/16/86, B, C, 86001071

Elmhurst [Pleasant Avenue MRA], 1606 Pleasant Ave., Wellsburg, 5/16/86, B, C, 86001072

Fleming, David and Lucy Tarr, Mansion [Pleasant Avenue MRA], 2000 Pleasant Ave., Wellsburg, 5/16/86, B, C, 86001073

Hall, Lewis, Mansion [Pleasant Avenue MRA], 1300 Pleasant Ave., Wellsburg, 5/16/86, B, C, 86001074

Inn at Fowlerstown, 1001 Washington Pike (WV 27), Wellsburg vicinity, 10/29/92, A, C, 92001483

Kirker House [Pleasant Avenue MRA], 1520 Grand Ave., Wellsburg, 9/15/86, C, 86002883

Miller's Tavern, 6th and Main Sts., Wellsburg, 12/14/78, A, C, 78002790

Old Bethany Church, Main and Church Sts., Bethany, 12/12/76, A, B, a, 76001932

Old Main, Bethany College, Bethany College campus, Bethany, 8/25/70, A, B, C, NHL, 70000652

Paull, Harry and Louisiana Beall, Mansion [Pleasant Avenue MRA], 1312 Pleasant Ave., Wellsburg, 5/16/86, B, C, 86001075

Pendleton Heights, Bethany College campus, Bethany, 6/26/75, A, B, C, 75001882

Tarr, Lucy, Mansion [Pleasant Avenue MRA], 1456 Pleasant Ave., Wellsburg, 5/16/86, B, C, 86001076

Vancroft, Brinker Rd., Wellsburg vicinity, 9/15/86, A, C, a, 86002885

Wellsburg Historic District, WV 2, Wellsburg, 4/01/82, A, C, 82004312

Wellsburg Wharf, 6th and Main Sts, Wellsburg, 11/27/79, A, C, 79002572

Cabell County

Baltimore and Ohio Railroad Depot, 1100 block of 2nd Ave., Huntington, 10/30/73, A, 73001897

Cabell County Courthouse, 5th Ave. and 8th St., Huntington, 9/02/82, A, C, 82004313

Campbell-Hicks House, 1102 Fifth Ave., Huntington, 8/19/85, B, C, a, 85001814

Carnegie Public Library, 900 5th St., Huntington, 4/03/80, A, C, 80004015

Carroll, Thomas, House, 234 Guyan St., Huntington, 6/01/73, A, C, 73001898

Clover Site, Address Restricted, Lesage, 4/27/92, D, NHL, 92001881

Douglass Junior and Senior High School, Tenth Ave. and Bruce St., Huntington, 12/05/85, A, 85003091

Harvey House, 1305 3rd Ave., Huntington, 8/21/72, B, C, 72001285

Huntington Downtown Historic District, Roughly bounded by Third Ave., Tenth St., Fifth Ave., Seventh and Eighth Sts., Huntington, 2/24/86, A, C, a, 86000309

Jenkins, Gen. Albert Gallatin, House, 8814 Ohio River Rd., Green Bottom vicinity, 5/22/78, B, C, 78002791

Masonic Temple—Watts, Ritter, Wholesale Drygoods Company Building, 1100–1108 E. Third Ave., Huntington, 8/26/93, A, 93000614

Memorial Arch, Memorial Park, Huntington, 4/16/81, C, f, 81000597

Mud River Covered Bridge [West Virginia Covered Bridges TR], Off U.S. 60 on SR 25 over Mud River, Milton, 6/10/75, A, C, 75001883

Ninth Street West Historic District, 9th St., Madison and Jefferson Aves., Huntington, 11/28/80, A, C, 80004016

Old Main, Marshall University, 16th St., Marshall University campus, Huntington, 7/16/73, A, 73001899

Ritter Park Historic District, Ritter Park, including northern boundary streets, Huntington, 11/28/90, A, C, 90001774

Thornburg House, 700 Main St., Barboursville, 4/25/91, B, C, 91000451

U.S. Post Office and Courthouse, 9th St. and 5th Ave., Huntington, 4/15/82, C, 82004314

Calhoun County

Alberts Chapel, U.S. 119/33, Sand Ridge, 4/15/82, A, C, a, 82004315

Clay County

Old Clay County Courthouse, Main St., Clay, 4/20/79, A, C, 79002573

Doddridge County

Center Point Covered Bridge, Off WV 23, Center Point vicinity, 8/29/83, C, 83003235

Charter, Lathrop Russell, House, 109 High St., West Union, 3/25/93, C, 93000219

Doddridge County Courthouse, Court Sq., West Union, 3/18/82, C, 82004316

Gamsjager—Wysong Farm, CR 66, St. Clara, 9/04/86, A, B, C, 86002181

Krenn School, Co. Rt. 66/Little Buck Run Rd., New Milton, 3/29/89, A, C, 89000181

Doddridge County—Continued

Stuart, W. Scott, House, 104 Chancery St., West Union, 3/25/93, C, 93000220

Fayette County

Altamont Hotel, 110 Fayette Ave, Fayetteville, 8/29/79, A, 79002574

Bank of Glen Jean, Main St., Glen Jean, 2/10/83, B, C, g, 83003236

Camp Washington-Carver Complex, CR 11/3, Clifftop vicinity, 6/20/80, A, C, g, 80004017

Contentment, Along U.S. 60, Ansted, 12/30/74, B, 74001996

Fayette County Courthouse, Court St. between Wiseman and Maple Aves., Fayetteville, 9/06/78, A, C, 78002793

Fayetteville Historic District, Roughly bounded by SR 16, Maple and Fayette Aves., Fayetteville, 12/20/90, A, C, g, 90001845

Gauley Bridge Railroad Station, Off WV 16/39, Gauley Bridge, 5/15/80, A, 80004018

Glen Ferris Inn, US 60 overlooking Kanawha Falls, Glen Ferris, 4/25/91, A, B, 91000449

Halfway House, Off old U.S. 60, Ansted, 12/18/78, A, C, 78002792

Hawkins, E. B., House, 120 Fayette Ave., Fayetteville, 1/18/90, B, C, 89002319

Kay Moor, Along the New R. S of US 19, Fayetteville vicinity, 11/08/90, A, C, NPS, 90001641

Main Building, West Virginia Institute of Technology campus, Montgomery, 6/25/80, A, 80004019

Page-Vawter House, Rt. Box 20, Ansted, 8/21/85, B, C, 85001813

Prince Brothers General Store—Berry Store, WV 41, Prince, 4/17/86, A, NPS, 86000810

Thurmond Historic District, WV 25 at New River, Thurmond, 1/27/84, A, C, NPS, 84003520

Tyree Stone Tavern, E of Clifftop off U.S. 19 on SR 10, Clifftop vicinity, 6/20/75, A, C, 75001884

Whipple Company Store, Jct. of Co. Rds. 15 and 21/20, Whipple, 4/26/91, A, C, 91000448

Gilmer County

Arbuckle, John E., House, 213 Court St., Glenville, 11/21/91, C, 91001729

Job's Temple, W of Glenville on WV 5, Glenville vicinity, 5/29/79, A, C, a, 79002575

Little Kanawha Valley Bank, 5 Howard St., Glenville, 8/05/91, C, b, 91001012

Grant County

Fairfax Stone Site, N of William at corner of Grant, Preston, and Tucker counties, William vicinity, 1/26/70, A, 70000653

Grant County Courthouse [South Branch Valley MRA (AD)], Virginia Ave., Petersburg, 10/26/79, A, C, 79003306

Hermitage Motor Inn [South Branch Valley MRA], Virginia Ave., Petersburg, 1/14/86, A, 86000776

Manor, The, N of Petersburg off WV 42, Petersburg vicinity, 12/18/75, A, C, 75001886

Rohrbaugh Cabin, Smokehole Rd. (WV 28/11), 3 mi. S of jct. with WV 28/55, Monongahela NF, Petersburg vicinity, 11/03/93, A, 93000490

Snyder, Noah, Farm [South Branch Valley MRA (AD)], 1.5 mi. S of Lahmansville on Rte. 5, Lahmansville vicinity, 6/10/75, A, C, 75001885

Greenbrier County

Alderson Bridge, Monroe St. across the Greenbrier R., Alderson, 12/04/91, A, C, 91001730

Alderson Historic District, Roughly, along Monroe St., Riverview Dr., Railroad Ave. and adjacent streets, Alderson, 11/12/93, A, B, C, 93001231

Arbuckle, Alexander W., I, House, 2 mi. N of Lewisburg on Arbuckle Lane, Lewisburg vicinity, 5/03/76, C, 76001933

Blue Sulphur Springs Pavilion, Co. Rt. 25, 9 mi. N of Alderson, Blue Sulphur Springs, 10/29/92, A, C, 92001481

Confederate Cemetery at Lewisburg, Maple St. and US 60, Library Park, Lewisburg, 2/02/88, A, d, 87002535

Creigh, David S., House, SW of Lewisburg off the Davis-Stuart Rd., Lewisburg vicinity, 11/12/75, B, C, 75001888

Deitz Farm, Jct. of WV 20 and WV 28, Meadow Bluff vicinity, 4/17/92, A, B, d, 92000304

Elmhurst, U.S. 60, Caldwell, 6/05/75, A, C, 75001887

Elmhurst (Boundary Increase), US 60 at the Greenbrier R., Caldwell, 12/20/90, A, C, 90001846

Greenbrier County Courthouse and Lewis Spring, Corner of Court and Randolph Sts., Lewisburg, 8/17/73, A, C, 73001900

Greenbrier, The, Off U.S. 60, White Sulphur Springs, 10/09/74, A, B, C, NHL, 74002000

Hartland, 2 mi. W of Lewisburg on Houfnaggle Rd., Lewisburg vicinity, 6/10/75, A, C, 75001889

Herns Mill Covered Bridge [West Virginia Covered Bridges TR], Secondary Rt. 40 at jct. of Secondary Rt. 60/11, Lewisburg vicinity, 6/04/81, A, C, 81000598

Hokes Mill Covered Bridge [West Virginia Covered Bridges TR], Secondary Rt. 62 at Hokes Mill crossing of Second Creek, Lewisburg vicinity, 6/04/81, A, C, 81000599

John Wesley Methodist Church, E. Foster St., Lewisburg, 6/05/74, A, C, a, 74001997

Lewisburg Historic District, Irregular pattern along U.S. 60 and U.S. 219, Lewisburg, 7/07/78, A, C, a, 78002795

Maple Street Historic District, 107–121 Maple St., Lewisburg, 4/06/88, A, C, 87002529

Miller, Alexander McVeight, House, Hemlock Ave., Alderson, 12/15/78, A, B, g, 78002794

Morlunda, NW of Lewisburg on SR 40, Lewisburg vicinity, 3/25/77, A, C, 77001374

Mountain Home, SW of White Sulphur Springs on U.S. 60, White Sulphur Springs vicinity, 11/28/80, C, 80004020

Mt. Tabor Baptist Church, Court and Foster Sts., Lewisburg, 12/12/76, A, a, 76001934

North, John A., House, 100 Church St., Lewisburg, 10/09/74, B, C, 74001998

Old Stone Church, Church and Foster Sts., Lewisburg, 2/23/72, A, a, d, 72001286

Price, Gov. Samuel, House, 224 N. Court St., Lewisburg, 6/20/75, B, C, 75001890

South Church Street Historic District, S. Church St., Lewisburg, 2/02/88, B, C, 87002528

Stuart Manor, SW of Lewisburg off U.S. 219, Lewisburg vicinity, 7/27/73, B, C, 73001901

Supreme Court Library Building, U.S. 60W and Courtney Dr., Lewisburg, 2/23/72, A, 72001287

Tuckwiller Tavern, 2 mi. NW of Lewisburg on U.S. 60, Lewisburg vicinity, 3/04/75, A, B, C, 75001891

Tuscawilla, S of Lewisburg off U.S. 219, Lewisburg vicinity, 12/19/79, A, C, 79002576

Withrow, James, House, 200 N. Jefferson St., Lewisburg, 12/31/74, B, C, 74001999

Wylie, James, House, 208 E. Main St., White Sulphur Springs, 2/05/90, A, C, 89002318

Hampshire County

Capon Springs, Address Restricted, Capon Springs, 11/12/93, A, C, 93001228

Kuykendall Polygonal Barn [Round and Polygonal Barns of West Virginia TR], River Rd., Romney vicinity, 7/09/85, A, C, 85001549

Literary Hall, Main and High Sts., Romney, 5/29/79, A, C, 79002577

Scanlon Farm, Three Churches Run Rd., Three Churches, 2/03/88, B, 87002521

Sloan-Parker House, E of Junction on U.S. 50, Junction vicinity, 6/05/75, A, C, 75001892

Sycamore Dale, W of Romney off SR 8, Romney vicinity, 12/02/80, A, C, 80004021

Wilson-Wodrow-Mytinger House, 51 W. Gravel Lane, Romney, 8/22/77, A, C, 77001375

Hancock County

Marland Heights Park and Margaret Manson Weir Memorial Pool, Jct. of Williams Dr. and Riverview Dr., Weirton, 11/15/93, A, C, 93001230

Murray, James F., House, 530 Louisiana Ave., Chester, 7/12/90, B, C, 90001066

Tarr, Peter, Furnace Site, Address Restricted, Weirton vicinity, 1/01/76, A, D, 76001935

Hardy County

Allen, Judge J. W. F., House [South Branch Valley MRA (AD)], South Fork Rd., Moorefield, 2/10/83, B, C, 83003237

Buena Vista Farms [South Branch Valley MRA], US 220, Old Fields vicinity, 7/10/85, C, 85001594

Fort Pleasant [South Branch Valley MRA (AD)], N of Moorefield, Moorefield vicinity, 7/16/73, A, C, 73001903

Hickory Hill [South Branch Valley MRA], US 220, Petersburg vicinity, 7/10/85, C, 85001596

Inskeep, P. W., House [South Branch Valley MRA], W.VA 55, Moorefield, 7/10/85, C, 85001597

Lee, Lighthorse Harry, Cabin, W of Mathias in Lost River State Park, Mathias vicinity, 7/30/74, B, C, 74002001

Maslin, Thomas, House, 131 Main St., Moorefield, 8/29/79, B, C, 79002578

Mathias, John, House, WV 259, Mathias, 11/24/78, B, C, 78002796

Meadows, The [South Branch Valley MRA], US 220, Moorefield vicinity, 1/14/86, B, C, 86000777

Mill Island [South Branch Valley MRA (AD)], S of Moorefield, Moorefield vicinity, 7/02/73, A, C, 73001904

Moorefield Historic District [South Branch Valley MRA], Portions of Main, Elm, Washington, and Winchester Sts., Moorefield, 1/15/86, A, C, 86000774

Oakland Hall [South Branch Valley MRA], US 220, Moorefield vicinity, 7/10/85, C, 85001598

Old Hardy County Courthouse, Winchester Ave. and Elm St., Moorefield, 10/09/74, A, 74002002

Old Stone Tavern, 117 Main St., Moorefield, 12/10/79, A, C, 79002579

Westfall Place [South Branch Valley MRA], US 220, Moorefield vicinity, 7/10/85, C, 85001599

Willow Wall [South Branch Valley MRA (AD)], S of Old Fields, Old Fields vicinity, 7/02/73, C, 73001906

Willows, The [South Branch Valley MRA (AD)], S of Moorefield, Moorefield vicinity, 7/02/73, A, C, 73001905

Wilson-Kuykendall Farm [South Branch Valley MRA], US 220, Moorefield vicinity, 7/10/85, C, 85001600

Harrison County

Clarksburg Downtown Historic District, Roughly bounded by Elk, Creek, 7th, and Main Sts., Clarksburg, 4/12/82, A, C, 82004794

Fletcher Covered Bridge [West Virginia Covered Bridges TR], SR 5/29 at jct. of SR 5, Maken vicinity, 6/04/81, A, C, 81000601

Glen Elk Historic District, Roughly bounded by Elk Cr. and the Baltimore & Ohio RR tracks, Clarksburg, 11/24/93, A, C, 93001232

Indian Cave Petroglyphs, Address Restricted, Good Hope vicinity, 3/16/76, D, 76001937

Johnson, Governor Joseph, House, 424 Oakdale Ave., Bridgeport, 3/19/87, B, C, 87000490

Quality Hill Historic District, East Main St., Clarksburg, 8/22/85, A, B, C, 85001815

Salem College Administration Building, 223 W. Main St., Salem, 3/30/89, A, C, 89000184

Salem Historic District, WV 23, Salem, 12/02/80, A, C, 80004022

Shinn, Levi, House, Clarksburg Rd. (U.S. 19), Shinnston, 7/16/73, B, C, 73001907

Simpson Creek Covered Bridge [West Virginia Covered Bridges TR], Secondary Rt. 24/2 at jct. of Secondary Rt. 24, Bridgeport vicinity, 6/04/81, A, C, 81000600

Smith, Watters, Farm on Duck Creek, CR 25/6, Lost Creek vicinity, 5/16/74, A, C, 74002003

Stealey-Goff-Vance House, 123 W. Main St., Clarksburg, 9/25/79, B, C, 79002580

Templemoor, WV 20, Clarksburg vicinity, 4/15/82, B, C, 82004318

Trinity Memorial Methodist Episcopal Church, 420 Ben St., Clarksburg, 4/26/84, A, C, a, 84003584

Waldomore, W. Pike and N. 4th Sts., Clarksburg, 10/04/78, B, C, 78002797

Jackson County

Armstrong House, 315 North St., Ripley, 2/12/80, B, C, 80004023

Clerc—Carson House, 121 North St., Ripley, 10/29/92, C, 92001482

Lemley—Wood—Sayer House, 301 Walnut St., Ravenswood, 10/30/85, B, C, 85003409

Rankin Octagonal Barn [Round and Polygonal Barns of West Virginia TR], CR 3, Silverton vicinity, 7/09/85, A, C, 85001551

Sarvis Fork Covered Bridge [West Virginia Covered Bridges TR], NE of New Era, Sandyville vicinity, 6/04/81, A, C, 81000602

Staats Mill Covered Bridge [West Virginia Covered Bridges TR], SR 40, Staats Mill, 5/29/79, A, C, 79002582

Jefferson County

Allstadt House and Ordinary, Jct. of U.S. 340 and CR 27, Harper's Ferry vicinity, 4/09/85, A, C, d, 85000767

Aspen Hill, N of Charles Town on WV 9, Charles Town vicinity, 3/13/80, A, C, 80004024

B & O Railroad Potomac River Crossing, At confluence of the Shenandoah and Potomac Rivers, Harper's Ferry, vicinity, 2/14/78, A, C, g, 78001484

Beall-Air, W of Halltown off U.S. 340, Halltown vicinity, 8/17/73, A, 73001914

Belvedere, 811 Belvedere Farm Dr., Charles Town vicinity, 1/12/84, A, C, 84003588

Beverley, US 340, Charles Town vicinity, 3/20/87, A, C, 87000486

Blakeley, SR 13/3, Charles Town vicinity, 4/15/82, B, 82004319

Bower, The, CR 1/1, Leetown vicinity, 4/15/82, A, B, C, 82004321

Burr, Peter, House, Warm Springs Rd., Shenandoah Junction vicinity, 4/09/82, B, C, 82004322

Cedar Lawn, 3.5 mi. W of Charles Town off VA 51 and S on CR 51/1, Charles Town, 12/04/74, A, C, 74002004

Claymont Court, SW of Charles Town off U.S. 340, Charles Town vicinity, 7/25/73, B, C, 73001908

Cold Spring, S of Shepherdstown on CR 17, Shepherdstown vicinity, 8/14/73, B, 73001917

Elmwood, S of Shepherdstown off CR 17, Shepherdstown vicinity, 8/17/73, B, 73001918

Falling Spring—Morgan's Grove, SR 480, Shepherdstown vicinity, 2/15/89, A, B, C, 88002670

Fruit Hill, Shepherd Grade, Shepherdstown vicinity, 9/26/88, C, 88001588

Gibson-Todd House, 515 S. Samuel St., Charles Town, 9/16/83, A, B, C, 83003238

Glenburnie, CR 16/Ridge Rd., Shenandoah Junction vicinity, 11/29/88, B, C, 88002668

Grubb, William, Farm, Co. Rd. 340/2, W of jct. with US 340, Charles Town vicinity, 11/21/91, A, C, a, d, 91001735

Halltown Union Colored Sunday School, Off US 340, Halltown, 1/12/84, A, C, a, 84003591

Harewood, W of Charles Town off WV 51, Charles Town vicinity, 3/14/73, C, 73001909

Harpers Ferry Historic District, Off U.S. 340, Harpers Ferry, 10/15/79, A, C, D, 79002584

Harpers Ferry National Historical Park, At confluence of Shenandoah and Potomac rivers, Harpers Ferry, 10/15/66, A, B, C, D, b, e, NPS, 66000041

Hazelfield, Off CR 48/2, Shenandoah Junction vicinity, 12/12/76, C, 76001938

Hillside, Old Cave Rd., Charles Town vicinity, 12/12/85, C, 85003521

Jacks-Manning Farm, US 340, Charles Town vicinity, 1/12/84, A, C, 84003594

Jefferson County Courthouse, N. George and E. Washington Sts., Charles Town, 7/10/73, A, 73001910

Lee-Longsworth House, 1141 Washington St., Harpers Ferry, 9/23/85, C, 85002471

Lucas, Capt. William and Lucas, Robert, House, SE of Shepherdstown on SR 31, Shepherdstown vicinity, 9/02/82, B, C, 82004323

Marshall, James, House, Shepherd Grade, Shepherdstown vicinity, 9/27/88, C, 88001596

Middleway Historic District, SR 1/8, Middleway, 3/13/80, A, C, 80004025

Morgan-Bedinger-Dandridge House, SW of Shepherdstown on WV 48, Shepherdstown vicinity, 5/13/83, A, B, g, 83003239

New Opera House, 200–204 N. George St., Charles Town, 11/24/78, A, C, 78002798

Prato Rio, WV 48, Leetown, 4/11/73, B, 73001916

Richwood Hall, About 4 mi. W of Charles Town off WV 51, Charles Town, 6/19/73, C, 73001911

Rion Hall, E of Charles Town off US 340, Charles Town vicinity, 9/20/82, B, C, 82004320

Ripon Lodge, N of Rippon, Rippon vicinity, 8/18/83, B, C, 83003240

Rockland, SR 480, Shepherdstown vicinity, 2/05/90, B, C, 89002316

Jefferson County—Continued

Rose Hill Farm, Off SR 48 SE of jct. with Warm Springs Rd., Shepherdstown vicinity, 5/18/90, C, 90000716

Rumsey Hall, German and Princess Sts., Shepherdstown, 3/30/73, A, C, 73001919

Shepherd's Mill, High St., Shepherdstown, 5/06/71, A, 71000882

Shepherdstown Historic District, Bounded roughly by Mill, Rocky, Duke, and Washington Sts., Shepherdstown, 8/17/73, A, C, 73001920

Shepherdstown Historic District (Boundary Increase), Jct. of High and German Sts. E to Ray and High Sts. and the Potomac River S to Fairmont Ave., Shepherdstown, 7/22/87, A, B, C, 87001205

St. Peter's Roman Catholic Church, Church St. and Jefferson Rock Trail, Harpers Ferry, 3/30/73, A, C, a, 73001915

Strider Farm, WV 27, Harpers Ferry vicinity, 2/01/88, A, B, C, a, 87002524

The Hermitage, Cabletown Rd. (Co. Rd. 25) N of jct. with Mt. Hammond Rd., Charles Town vicinity, 12/23/93, B, C, 93001444

Traveller's Rest, 3.3 mi. NW of Leetown on WV 48, Kearneysville, 11/15/72, B, NHL, 72001288

Van Swearingen-Shepherd House, N of Shepherdstown, Shepherdstown vicinity, 8/18/83, A, C, 83003241

Washington, Charles, House, Blakely Pl., Charles Town vicinity, 7/02/73, B, C, 73001912

White House Farm, E of Summit Point of SR 13, Summit Point vicinity, 8/29/79, A, 79002583

Woodbury, On CR 1/4, Leetown vicinity, 10/09/74, B, C, 74002005

Worthington, Robert, House, 2 mi. W of Charles Town off WV 51, Charles Town vicinity, 7/02/73, C, 73001913

Kanawha County

African Zion Baptist Church, 4104 Malden Dr., Malden, 12/27/74, A, B, a, 74002010

Bank of St. Albans Building, 80 Olde Main Plaza, St. Albans, 2/01/88, C, 87002518

Barnes-Wellford House [South Hills MRA], 66 Abney Circle, Charleston, 10/26/84, C, 84000390

Beeches, The, 805 Kanawha Ter., St. Albans, 4/20/79, B, C, 79002586

Bird Haven [South Hills MRA], 733 Myrtle Rd., Charleston, 10/26/84, B, 84000393

Bougemont Complex [South Hills MRA], Bougemont Dr., Charleston, 10/26/84, B, C, 84000395

Breezemont, 915 Breezemont Dr., Charleston, 4/15/82, B, C, 82004324

Briarwood [South Hills MRA], 1240 Staunton Rd., Charleston, 10/26/84, C, 84000396

Canty House, WV 25, Institute, 9/23/88, B, C, b, 88001587

Cedar Grove, SE of jct. of U.S. 60 and Kanawha and James River Tpke., Cedar Grove, 3/10/75, B, C, 75001893

Charleston City Hall, Court and Virginia Sts., Charleston, 6/06/88, A, C, 88000639

Chesapeake and Ohio Depot [South Hills MRA], 305 MacCorkle Ave., Charleston, 10/26/84, A, C, 84000782

Chilton House, Off U.S. 60, St. Albans, 4/29/77, C, b, 77001376

Chilton, W. E. II, House [South Hills MRA], 1266 Louden Heights Rd., Charleston, 10/26/84, C, 84000397

Cox-Morton House [South Hills MRA], 640 Holley Rd., Charleston, 10/26/84, C, 84000399

Cox-Parks House [South Hills MRA], 710 Myrtle Rd., Charleston, 10/26/84, C, 84000400

Craik-Patton House, U.S. 60 in Daniel Boone Roadside Park, Charleston, 8/12/70, B, C, b, 75001894

Crawford-Gardner House [South Hills MRA], 743 Myrtle Rd., Charleston, 10/26/84, B, C, 84000401

Dalgain [South Hills MRA], 1223 Staunton Rd., Charleston, 10/26/84, C, 84000404

Daniel Boone Hotel, 405 Capitol St., Charleston, 8/21/84, A, C, 84003602

Danner-Fletcher House [South Hills MRA], 626 Holley Rd., Charleston, 10/26/84, C, 84000405

Dutch Hollow Wine Cellars, Dutch Hollow Rd., Dunbar, 12/18/70, A, C, 70000654

East End Historic District, Roughly bounded by the Kanawha River, Bradford, Quarrier, and Greenbriar Sts., Charleston, 4/20/78, A, C, 78002800

East Hall, West Quadrangle, West Virginia State College, Institute, 9/26/88, A, b, 88001585

Ebenezer Chapel, Ohio Ave., S at Hillview Dr., Marmet, 12/16/74, A, a, 74002011

Edgewood Historic District, Roughly bounded by Edgewood Dr., Highland, Beech, Chester, and Lower Chester, Charleston, 11/09/89, A, C, 89001800

Edwards William H. & William S., House, SR 61 NE of Cabin Creek, Coalburg, 5/11/90, B, 90000713

Fort Scammon, Address Restricted, Charleston vicinity, 3/26/76, A, D, 76001939

Garnet High School, 422 Dickinson St., Charleston, 7/24/90, A, g, 90001068

Gilliland, William S., Log Cabin and Cemetery [South Hills MRA], Louden Heights and Bridge Rd., Charleston, 10/26/84, A, d, e, 84000407

Gilmore, Elizabeth Harden, House, 514 Broad St., Charleston, 9/17/88, B, C, g, 88001462

Good Shepherd Church, SR 61 SW of East Bank, Coalburg, 4/26/90, B, a, 90000712

Grosscup Road Historic District [South Hills MRA], Grosscup, Roscommon, Roller, and Bridge Rds., Charleston, 1/26/84, A, B, C, 84003607

Hansford, Felix G., House, Centre and 14th Sts., Hansford, 1/12/84, A, C, 84003611

Harriman, John, House, 2233 3rd Ave., East Bank, 12/15/78, B, C, 78002803

Holly Grove Mansion, 1710 E. Kanawha Blvd., Charleston, 8/28/74, B, 74002007

Kanawha County Courthouse, Virginia and Court Sts., Charleston, 9/06/78, A, C, 78002801

Kanawha State Forest Historic District, Co. Rd. 42/43 2.6 mi. S of Charleston, Loundendale vicinity, 3/25/93, A, C, 93000228

Kearse Theater, 161, 165, 167 Summers St., Charleston, 11/28/80, A, C, 80004026

Laidley-Summers-Quarrier House, 800 Orchard St., Charleston, 12/13/78, B, C, 78002802

Lee, Mattie V., Home 810 Donnally St., Charleston, 6/16/92, A, g, 92000303

Little Brick Church, 0.75 mi. E of Kelley's Creek on U.S. 60, Cedar Grove, 12/16/74, A, a, 74002006

Littlepage Stone Mansion, 1809 W. Washington St., Charleston, 9/02/82, A, B, C, 82004325

Loewenstein and Sons Hardware Building, 223–225 Capitol St., Charleston, 11/01/85, A, C, 85003475

MacFarland House, 1310 Kanawha Blvd., Charleston, 12/10/79, C, 79002585

Malden Historic District, Roughly bounded by RR tracks, Kanawha River, Georges Dr. and U.S. 60, Malden, 7/18/80, A, C, D, 80004028

McAndrews-Gallaher House [South Hills MRA], 601 Briarwood Rd., Charleston, 10/26/84, C, 84000409

Mohler, William E., House, 819 Pennsylvania Ave., St. Albans, 2/10/83, B, C, g, 83003242

Mother Jones' Prison, 305 Center St., Pratt, 4/27/92, A, B, NHL, 92001876

Plaza Theatre, 123 Summers St., Charleston, 10/30/85, A, C, 85003408

Pratt Historic District, Roughly bounded by Ferry St., Kanawha River, Charles and Pratt Aves. incl. cemetery, Pratt, 1/12/84, A, C, 84003615

Shrewsbury, Samuel, Sr., House, 310 Stubb Dr., Belle, 11/02/78, A, C, 78002799

Simpson Memorial Methodist Episcopal Church, 607 Shrewsbury St., Charleston, 8/05/91, A, a, 91001011

South Charleston Mound, US 60, in city park, South Charleston, 10/15/70, D, 70000655

Spring Hill Cemetery Historic District, 1554 Farnsworth Dr., Charleston, 10/18/85, A, C, d, 85003360

St. Albans Site, Address Restricted, St. Albans vicinity, 5/03/74, D, 74002012

St. John's Episcopal Church, 11105 Quarrier St., Charleston, 11/02/89, A, B, C, a, 89001782

St. Mark's Episcopal Church, 405–407 B St., St. Albans, 11/07/77, A, C, a, 77001377

Starks, Samuel, House, 413 Shrewsbury St., Charleston, 2/01/88, B, 87002526

Stoneleigh [South Hills MRA], 909 Ridgeway Rd., Charleston, 10/26/84, C, 84000411

Sunrise, 746 Myrtle Rd., Charleston, 7/24/74, B, C, 74002008

Thomas-McJunkin-Love House [South Hills MRA], 920 Newton Rd., Charleston, 10/26/84, B, C, 84000413

West Virginia Capitol Complex, Along Kanawha Blvd., E., Charleston, 12/31/74, A, C, 74002009

Wood, Col. Henry Hewitt, House, 6560 Roosevelt Ave., SE, Charleston, 11/28/80, B, C, 80004027

Young—Noyes House, 2122 Kanawha Ave., Charleston, 4/25/91, C, 91000446

Lewis County

Annamede, RD 1, Box 126, US 19, Walkersville vicinity, 3/11/87, B, C, 87000218

Bennett, Jonathan M., House, Court Ave., Weston, 6/09/78, A, C, 78002804

Jackson's Mill, E of Jackson Mill on Rte. 1, Jackson Mill vicinity, 2/23/72, A, 72001289

St. Bernard Church and Cemetery, Cty. Rds. 20/6 & 17/2, Camden vicinity, 7/12/85, B, a, d, 85001583

Walkersville Covered Bridge [West Virginia Covered Bridges TR], On CR 19/17 near U.S. 19, Walkersville vicinity, 6/04/81, A, C, 81000603

Weston Colored School, 345 Center St., Weston, 4/09/93, A, C, g, 93000224

Weston Downtown Historic District, Parts of Main, Center & Court Aves., Second & Third Sts., Weston, 9/28/85, A, C, 85002468

Weston State Hospital, River St., Weston, 4/19/78, A, C, NHL, 78002805

Lincoln County

Holley Hills Estate, S of Alum Creek on Coal River Rd., Alum Creek vicinity, 12/01/80, A, 80004029

Logan County

Hatfield Cemetery [Hatfield Cemeteries in Southwestern West Virginia TR], S of Sarah Ann on U.S. 119, Sarah Ann vicinity, 11/28/80, A, B, C, d, 80004030

Marion County

Barrackville Covered Bridge [West Virginia Covered Bridges TR], WV 21, over Buffalo Creek, Barrackville, 3/30/73, A, C, 73001921

Fleming, Thomas W., House, 300 1st St., Fairmont, 8/29/79, B, C, 79002587

Hamilton Round Barn [Round and Polygonal Barns of West Virginia TR], CR 11, Mannington vicinity, 7/09/85, A, C, 85001548

High Gate, 801 Fairmont Ave., Fairmont, 4/15/82, A, C, 82004326

High Level Bridge, Jefferson St. across the Monongahela R., Fairmont, 12/04/91, A, C, 91001734

Marion County Courthouse and Sheriff's House, Adams and Jefferson Sts., Fairmont, 5/29/79, A, C, 79003149

Masonic Temple, 320 Jefferson St., Fairmont, 4/09/93, A, C, 93000218

Prickett's Fort, Address Restricted, Fairmont vicinity, 2/13/74, A, D, 74002404

Prickett, Jacob, Jr., Log House, S of Montana off SR 72, Montana vicinity, 4/20/79, A, C, 79002588

Shaw House, 425 Morgantown Ave., Fairmont, 9/14/88, B, C, 88001461

Marshall County

Cameron City Pool—PWA Project 1196, Park St., Cameron, 7/14/93, A, C, 93000612

Ferrell-Holt House, 609 Jefferson Ave., Moundsville, 2/03/87, B, C, 86003678

Grave Creek Mound, Off SR 2, Moundsville vicinity, 10/15/66, D, NHL, 66000751

McMechen Lockmaster Houses on the Ohio River, 623–625 Grant St., McMechen, 11/12/92, A, 92001485

Mason County

Couch-Artrip House, US 35, Southside vicinity, 8/23/84, A, C, 84003623

Eastham House, US 35, Point Pleasant vicinity, 2/24/89, A, C, 88002669

Elm Grove, 2283 US 35 N, Southside, 7/16/92, C, 92000897

Lewis-Capehart-Roseberry House, 1 Roseberry Lane, Point Pleasant, 8/29/79, A, C, 79002590

McCausland, Gen. John, House, WV 35, Leon vicinity, 6/16/80, B, C, 80004031

Point Pleasant Battleground, SW corner of Main and 1st Sts., Point Pleasant, 1/26/70, A, D, 70000656

Point Pleasant Historic District, Main St. between 1st & 11th and Viand St. between 8th & 10th, Point Pleasant, 7/01/85, A, C, 85001465

Powell-Redmond House, 23 Columbia St., Clifton, 2/10/83, B, C, 83003243

Shumaker-Lewis House, Brown St., Mason, 3/26/79, B, C, 79002589

McDowell County

Algoma Coal and Coke Company Store [Coal Company Stores in McDowell County MPS], Co. Rt. 17, Algoma, 4/17/92, A, C, 92000323

Carter Coal Company Store [Coal Company Stores in McDowell County MPS], Co. Rt. 2, Coalwood, 4/17/92, A, C, 92000328

Carter Coal Company Store [Coal Company Stores in McDowell County MPS], Jct. of WV 16 and Co. Rt. 12/8, Caretta, 4/17/92, A, C, 92000329

Empire Coal Company Store [Coal Company Stores in McDowell County MPS], US 52, Landgraff, 4/17/92, A, C, 92000321

Houston Coal Company Store [Coal Company Stores in McDowell County MPS], US 52, Kimball, 4/17/92, A, C, 92000331

Jones, James Ellwood, House, N of US 52, E of Turkey Gap Branch, Switchback, 4/02/92, A, B, C, 92000306

Lincoln, John J., House, N of US 52, Elkhorn, 7/16/92, A, B, C, 92000900

McDowell County Courthouse, Wyoming St., Welch, 8/29/79, A, C, 79003256

Page Coal and Coke Company Store [Coal Company Stores in McDowell County MPS], WV 161, Pageton, 4/17/92, A, C, 92000325

Peerless Coal Company Store [Coal Company Stores in McDowell County MPS], S of US 52, Vivian, 4/17/92, A, C, 92000322

Pocahontas Fuel Company Store [Coal Company Stores in McDowell County MPS], US 52, Maybeury, 4/17/92, A, C, 92000324

Pocahontas Fuel Company Store and Office Buildings [Coal Company Stores in McDowell County MPS], Co. Rt. 8, Jenkinjones, 4/17/92, A, C, 92000326

Pocahontas Fuel Company Store [Coal Company Stores in McDowell County MPS], US 52, Switchback, 4/17/92, A, C, 92000330

U.S. Coal and Coke Company [Coal Company Stores in McDowell County MPS], Co. Rt. 13/2, Ream, 4/17/92, A, C, 92000327

Welch Commercial Historic District, Roughly bounded by Wyoming St., Elkhorn Cr. and the Tug R., Welch, 4/02/92, A, C, 92000305

World War Memorial, US 52, Kimball, 4/09/93, A, C, f, 93000227

Mercer County

Bluefield Downtown Commercial Historic District, Roughly bounded by Princeton Ave., Scott, High, and Russell Sts., Bluefield, 3/18/87, A, C, 87000630

Bramwell Historic District, Main, Rose, Bloch, Duhring, Wyatt, Church, N. and S. Rivers Sts., Bramwell, 2/10/83, A, B, C, 83003244

Easley House [South Bluefield MPS], 1500 College Ave., Bluefield, 7/29/92, A, B, C, 92000879

French, Col. William Henderson, House, S of Athens off WV 20, Athens vicinity, 3/12/76, B, C, 76001940

Hale, Dr. James W., House, 1034 Mercer St., Princeton, 3/12/76, B, C, 76001941

Hancock House, 300 Sussex St., Bluefield, 1/17/90, A, B, C, g, 89001783

Jefferson Street Historic District [South Bluefield MPS], Along Jefferson St. between Cumberland Rd. and College Ave., Bluefield, 7/29/92, A, C, 92000877

Mercer County Courthouse, Courthouse Sq., Princeton, 11/28/80, C, 80004032

Municipal Building, 514 Bland St., Bluefield, 5/29/79, A, C, 79002591

South Bluefield Historic District [South Bluefield MPS], Along Mountain View Rd., Bland Rd., Oakhurst and Parkway, Bluefield, 7/29/92, A, B, C, 92000876

Upper Oakhurst Historic District [South Bluefield MPS], Along Oakhurst Ave., Groveland Dr., Edgewood Rd. and Mountain View Rd., Bluefield, 7/29/92, A, C, 92000875

Mineral County

Burlington Historic District, WV 11 S from jct. with US 50/220, Burlington, 12/07/92, A, C, 92001660

Mineral County—Continued

Carskadon House, Rt. 1, Box 93A, Beaver Run Rd., Burlington vicinity, 3/20/87, B, C, 87000487

Fairview, Jct. of Patterson Creek Dr. and Russelldale Rds., Burlington vicinity, 12/07/92, B, C, 92001631

Fort Ashby, South St., Fort Ashby, 12/18/70, A, 70000657

Vandiver-Trout-Clause House, U.S. 50 and 220, Ridgeville, 5/29/79, A, 79002592

Mingo County

Coal House, 2nd Ave. and Court St., Williamson, 3/06/80, A, C, g, 80004297

Hatfield Cemetery [Hatfield Cemeteries in Southwestern West Virginia TR], S of New Town on SR 6, New Town vicinity, 11/28/80, A, d, 80004033

Matewan Historic District, Roughly bounded by McCoy Alley, Railroad Alley, Mate St. underpass and Warm Hollow to the head of the hollow, Matewan, 4/27/93, A, B, C, 93000303

Price, R. T., House, 2405 W. Third Ave., Williamson, 1/10/91, B, C, 90001989

Monongalia County

Brown Building, 295 High St., Morgantown, 7/08/85, A, C, 85001514

Camp Rhododendron [Coopers Rock State Forest MPS], off US 48, 8 mi. E of Morgantown, Morgantown vicinity, 5/15/91, A, C, 91000545

Coopers Rock State Forest Superintendent's House and Garage [Coopers Rock State Forest MPS], off US 48, 8 mi. E of Morgantown, Morgantown vicinity, 5/15/91, A, C, 91000546

Cox, Judge Frank, House, 206 Spruce St., Morgantown, 1/12/84, A, C, 84003626

Dents Run Covered Bridge [West Virginia Covered Bridges TR], SR 43/4 at jct. of SR 43 crossing Dents Run, Laurel Point vicinity, 6/04/81, A, C, 81000604

Easton Roller Mill, E of Morgantown on SR 119/17, Morgantown vicinity, 12/19/78, A, C, 78002806

Ford House, 310 Ford St., Morgantown, 11/15/93, C, 93001227

Hamilton Farm Petroglyphs, SE of Ringgold on U.S. 119, Ringgold vicinity, 8/07/74, 74002015

Harmony Grove Meeting House, Off I-79, Harmony Grove, 9/16/83, A, C, a, 83003245

Harner Homestead, 1818 Listravia St., Morgantown, 1/12/84, A, C, 84003629

Henry Clay Furnace, SE of Cheat Neck in Cooper's Rock State Forest, Cheat Neck vicinity, 1/26/70, A, 70000658

Kern's Fort, 305 Dewey St., Morgantown, 4/09/93, A, B, C, 93000225

Mason and Dixon Survey Terminal Point, 2.25 mi. NE of Pentress on WV 39, Pentress vicinity, 6/25/73, C, f, 73001922

Men's Hall [West Virginia University MPS], Prospect and High Sts., Morgantown, 2/05/90, A, C, 89002309

Metropolitan Theatre, 371 S. High St., Morgantown, 1/12/84, A, C, 84003631

Monongalia County Courthouse, 243 High St., Morgantown, 7/08/85, A, C, 85001525

Moore, Elizabeth, Hall [West Virginia University Neo-Classical Revival Buildings TR], University Ave., Morgantown, 12/19/85, A, C, 85003208

Oglebay Hall [West Virginia University Neo-Classical Revival Buildings TR], University Ave., Morgantown, 12/19/85, A, C, 85003207

Old Morgantown Post Office, 107 High St., Morgantown, 3/28/79, C, 79002593

Old Stone House, Chestnut St., Morgantown, 12/27/72, C, 72001290

Old Watson Homestead House, WV 73, Smithtown, 12/07/84, B, C, 84003871

Purinton House [West Virginia University Neo-Classical Revival Buildings TR], University Ave., Morgantown, 12/19/85, A, C, 85003206

Rogers House, 293 Willey St., Morgantown, 12/04/84, C, 84000683

Second Ward Negro Elementary School, Jct. of White and Posten Aves., Morgantown, 7/28/92, A, g, 92000896

Seneca Glass Company Building, 709 Beechurst Ave., Morgantown, 12/19/85, A, C, 85003214

South Park Historic District, Roughly bounded by Elgin St., Kingwood St., Cobun Ave., Prairie Ave., Jefferson St., Lincoln Ave., and Grand St., Morgantown, 7/23/90, A, C, 90001054

St. Mary's Orthodox Church, W. Park and Holland Aves., Westover, 2/03/88, A, C, a, 87002525

Stalnaker Hall [West Virginia University Neo-Classical Revival Buildings TR], Maiden Ln., Morgantown, 12/19/85, A, C, 85003205

Stewart Hall, West Virginia University campus, Morgantown, 6/25/80, A, C, 80004034

Vance Farmhouse, 1535 Mileground, West Virginia University, Morgantown vicinity, 11/21/91, A, B, 91001731

Wade, Alexander, House, 256 Prairie St., Morgantown, 10/15/66, B, NHL, 66000752

Walters House, 221 Willey St., Morgantown, 8/18/83, C, 83003246

Willey, Waitman T., House, 128 Wagner Rd., Morgantown, 4/15/82, A, C, 82004327

Women's Christian Temperance Union Community Building, 160 Fayette St., Morgantown, 10/30/85, A, C, 85003406

Woodburn Circle, University Ave., West Virginia University, Morgantown, 12/04/74, A, C, 74002014

Monroe County

Byrnside—Beirne—Johnson House, Co. Rd. 13 S of Union, Union vicinity, 12/02/93, A, B, C, 93001358

Caperton, William Gaston, Jr., House, WV 3 E of Union, Union vicinity, 11/21/91, A, C, 91001733

Cook's Mill, Rt. 2, Greenville vicinity, 2/06/89, A, B, C, 88001857

Echols, Brig. Gen. John, House, Elmwood & 2nd St. N., Union, 6/27/85, B, C, 85001415

Elmwood, N of Union off U.S. 219, Union vicinity, 5/13/76, B, C, 76001942

Estill, Wallace, Sr., House, WV 122, Union vicinity, 4/09/84, A, B, C, 84003634

Indian Creek Covered Bridge [West Virginia Covered Bridges TR], 1.5 mi. S of Salt Sulphur Springs on US 219, Salt Sulphur Springs vicinity, 4/01/75, A, C, 75001806

Laurel Creek Covered Bridge [West Virginia Covered Bridges TR], SR 23/4 at jct. of SR 219/1 crossing Laurel Creek, Lillydale vicinity, 6/04/81, A, C, 81000605

Lynnside Historic District, Jct. of WV 3 and Cove Cr. Rd., Sweet Springs vicinity, 4/26/91, B, C, a, d, 91000452

McNeer House, US 219 at Gin Run, Salt Sulphur Springs vicinity, 4/26/91, C, 91000453

Old Sweet Springs, WV 3, Sweet Springs, 1/26/70, A, 70000659

Reed's Mill, Co. Rd. 219/1, Second Creek, 4/09/93, A, C, 93000226

Rehoboth Church, 2 mi. E of Union off WV 3, Union vicinity, 12/31/74, A, C, a, 74002016

Salt Sulphur Springs Historic District, US 219, Union vicinity, 10/31/85, A, C, a, 85003412

Spring Valley Farm, NE of Union on U.S. 219, Union vicinity, 12/30/74, A, C, 74002017

Spring Valley Farm (Boundary Increase), NE of Union on US 219, Union vicinity, 7/16/92, A, C, 92000901

Union Historic District, Roughly along Main, Dunlap, Pump and Elmwood Sts. N from Royal Oak Field, including Paradise and Monument Fields, Union, 12/06/90, A, B, C, 90001844

Walnut Grove, N of Union on U.S. 219, Union vicinity, 8/22/77, A, B, 77001378

Morgan County

Berkeley Springs State Park, S. Washington and Fairfax Sts., Berkeley Springs, 5/24/76, A, 76001943

Chesapeake and Ohio Canal National Historical Park, Bordering the Potomac River from Georgetown, D.C. to Cumberland, Maryland, Shepardstown, 10/15/66, A, C, NPS, 66000036

Dawson, T. H. B., House, 300 S. Green St., Berkeley Springs, 2/10/83, B, C, 83003247

Quick, John Herbert, House, Off US 522, Berkeley Springs vicinity, 8/23/84, B, C, 84003639

Sloat-Horn-Rossell House, 415 Fairfax St., Berkeley Springs, 8/23/84, C, 84003643

Suit, Samuel Taylor, Cottage, WV 9, Berkeley Springs, 11/28/80, A, C, 80004035

Western Maryland Railroad Right-of-Way, Milepost 126 to Milepost 160, Milepost 126 to Milepost 160, Jerome, vicinity, 7/23/81, A, C, NPS, 81000078

Wright, Judge John W., Cottage, 305 S. Green St., Berkeley Springs, 4/28/86, B, C, 86000896

Nicholas County

Brock Hotel, 1400 Webster Rd., Summersville, 7/09/93, A, 93000615

Carnifex Ferry State Park, S of Kesslers Cross Lanes off WV 129, Kesslers Cross Lanes vicinity, 7/24/74, A, 74002018

Nicholas County Courthouse, 700 Main St., Summersville, 8/16/91, A, C, 91001014

Nicholas County High School, Main St., Summerville, 3/27/89, B, C, 89000185

Ohio County

Beagle Hotel [National Road MPS], National Rd. .1 mi. W of Valley Grove Rd., Valley Grove vicinity, 2/11/93, A, C, 92000863

Carter Farm, Boggs Hill Rd., Wheeling vicinity, 8/18/83, A, C, g, 83003248

Center Wheeling Market, Market St. between 22nd and 23rd Sts., Wheeling, 2/20/75, A, C, 75001896

Centre Market Square Historic District, Roughly Market St. between 20th and 23rd Sts., Wheeling, 1/12/84, A, C, 84003651

Centre Market Square Historic District (Boundary Increase), S side of Main from Alley 19 to 20th St., and Chapline, Eoff and Charles Sts. bounded by Lane 22nd, and 24th Sts., Wheeling, 2/25/87, A, C, g, 87000127

Chapline Street Row Historic District, 2301-2323 Chapline St., Wheeling, 1/12/84, A, C, 84003655

Edemar, 1330 National Rd., Wheeling, 5/28/92, B, C, g, 91001728

Elm Grove Stone Arch Bridge, U.S. 40, Wheeling, 8/21/81, A, C, 81000606

Elm Hill, WV 88 NE of Wheeling Country Club, Wheeling, 12/04/91, B, C, 91001732

Feay Inn [National Road MPS], 9 Burkham Ct., Wheeling, 2/11/93, A, C, 92000872

Franzheim, Harry C. and Jessie F., House, 404 S. Front St., Wheeling, 3/27/89, B, C, 89000183

Good, L. S., House, 95 14th St., Wheeling, 11/28/88, B, C, 88002667

Hazlett, Robert W., House, 921 N. Main St., Wheeling, 5/02/91, A, B, C, 91000552

Highland Park Historic District, Highland Park, jct. of Lincoln Dr. and National Rd., Wheeling, 4/07/93, A, C, 93000222

List, Henry K., House, 827 Main St., Wheeling, 10/04/78, B, C, 78002807

McKinley, Johnson Camden, House, 147 Bethany Pike, Wheeling, 8/18/83, A, C, 83003251

McLure, John, House, 203 S. Front St., Wheeling, 8/05/91, A, C, 91001013

Monroe Street East Historic District, 12th and Byron Sts., Wheeling, 2/12/80, A, C, a, 80004036

Mount de Chantal Visitation Academy, Washington Ave., Wheeling, 11/27/78, A, C, a, 78002808

National Road Corridor Historic District [National Road MPS], National Rd. from Bethany Pike to Park View Ln., Wheeling, 2/11/93, C, d, 92000874

National Road Mile Markers Nos. 8, 9, 10, 11, 13, 14 [National Road MPS], Along National Rd. from Mt. Echo to Triadelphia, Mt. Echo vicinity, 2/11/93, A, 92000873

North Wheeling Historic District, Roughly bounded by Main Street Ter., Market St., I-70, and N. Main St., Wheeling, 12/09/88, A, C, 88002693

Ogden, H. C., House, 12 Park Rd., Wheeling, 7/12/90, B, C, 90001067

Oglebay Mansion Museum, Oglebay Park, Wheeling, 8/29/79, A, C, 79002595

Russell, Charles W., House, 75 Twelfth St., Wheeling, 11/12/93, A, B, C, 93001229

Shepherd Hall, Monument Place and Kruger St., Wheeling, 12/18/70, B, C, 70000661

Stewart, David, Farm, Dallas Pike, CR 43, Triadelphia vicinity, 5/29/79, A, C, 79002594

Stone Tavern at Roney's Point [National Road MPS], Jct. of E. National and Roney's Point Rds., Roney's Point, 2/11/93, A, C, 92000864

Tiernan, William Miles, House, 5 Kenwood Pl., Wheeling, 3/25/93, C, 93000223

West Liberty Presbyterian Church, Main St., West Liberty, 7/03/80, C, a, 80004407

West Virginia Independence Hall, 1524 Market St., Wheeling, 1/26/70, A, C, NHL, 70000660

Wheeling Baltimore and Ohio Railroad Passenger Station, College Sq., Wheeling, 3/26/79, A, C, 79002596

Wheeling Country Club, 355 Oglebay Dr., Wheeling vicinity, 4/26/90, A, C, 90000711

Wheeling Historic District, Roughly bounded by RR tracks, Eoff, Water, and 10th Sts., Wheeling, 12/31/79, A, C, 79002597

Wheeling Island Historic District, Roughly bounded by Stone, Front, North, Ontario, Erie and Wabash Sts., Wheeling, 4/02/92, C, 92000320

Wheeling Suspension Bridge, Over Ohio River from 10th St., Wheeling, to Virginia St., Wheeling Island, Wheeling, 1/26/70, C, NHL, 70000662

Woods, Robert C., House, 923 N. Main St., Wheeling, 5/02/91, A, B, C, 91000551

Pendleton County

Bowers House [South Branch Valley MRA], Brandywine-Sugar Grove Rd., Sugar Grove, 7/10/85, C, 85001593

Cunningham-Hevener House [South Branch Valley MRA], US 220, Upper Tract, 7/10/85, C, 85001595

Franklin Historic District [South Branch Valley MRA], Roughly bounded by US 33, Main St., the Potomac River, and High St., Franklin, 1/15/86, A, C, 86000773

McCoy House, Main St., Franklin, 12/10/82, A, B, C, 82004328

McCoy Mill [South Branch Valley MRA], Johnstown Rd., Franklin vicinity, 1/14/86, A, 86000780

Old Judy Church [South Branch Valley MRA (AD)], 10 mi. S of Petersburg on U.S. 220, Petersburg vicinity, 5/13/76, A, C, a, 76001944

Old Probst Church [South Branch Valley MRA], CR 21/9, Brandywine vicinity, 1/14/86, A, C, a, 86000779

Pendleton County Poor Farm [South Branch Valley MRA], US 220, Upper Tract, 1/14/86, A, 86000775

Sites Homestead, Seneca Rocks Visitor Center, Seneca Rocks, 5/20/93, C, D, 93000382

Pleasants County

Cain House, Creel St. and Riverside Dr., St. Marys, 6/25/80, A, 80004037

Pocahontas County

Buck, Pearl, House, NE of Hillsboro on U.S. 219, Hillsboro vicinity, 6/15/70, B, a, c, 70000663

Camp Allegheny, Address Restricted, Bartow vicinity, 9/28/90, A, C, D, d, 90001446

Cass Historic District, SR 1 and SR 7, Cass, 11/28/80, A, C, 80004038

Cass Scenic Railroad, Along railroad tracks from Cass to Bald Knob, Cass, 7/12/74, A, 74002019

Droop Mountain Battlefield, About 14 mi. S of Marlinton on U.S. 219, Marlinton vicinity, 1/26/70, A, 70000664

GW Jeep Site, Address Restricted, Greenbank vicinity, 12/23/93, D, 93001443

Hunter, Frank and Anna, House, U.S. 219, Marlinton, 5/13/76, C, 76001945

Huntersville Presbyterian Church, CR 21 at WV 39, Huntersville, 10/04/78, A, a, 78002809

Locust Creek Covered Bridge [West Virginia Covered Bridges TR], SR 31, Hillsboro vicinity, 6/04/81, A, C, 81000607

Marlinton Chesapeake and Ohio Railroad Station, 8th St. and 4th Ave., Marlinton, 8/29/79, A, C, 79002598

McNeel Mill, US 219, Mill Point, 8/08/85, A, 85001783

Pocahontas Times Print Shop, 810 2nd Ave., Marlinton, 9/22/77, A, C, 77001379

Reber Radio Telescope, National Radio Astronomy Observatory, NE of Green Bank on WV 28, Green Bank vicinity, 11/09/72, A, B, b, g, NHL, 72001291

Preston County

Arthurdale Historic District, E and W of WV 92, Arthurdale, 2/01/89, A, B, 88001862

Elkins Coal and Coke Company Historic District, Off WV 7, Bretz, 7/01/83, A, C, NHL, 83003249

Gaymont, US 50 W of jct. with WV 24, Aurora vicinity, 4/14/92, A, C, 92000351

Preston County—Continued

Hagans Homestead, WV 26, 1 mi. N of jct. with I-68E (Exit 23), Brandonville, 7/14/93, B, 93000617

McGrew, James Clark, House, 109 E. Main St., Kingwood, 7/09/93, B, 93000618

Ralphsnyder Decagonal Barn [Round and Polygonal Barns of West Virginia TR], CR 52/2, Masontown vicinity, 12/02/85, A, C, b, 85003111

Reckart Mill, W of Cranesville at jct. of WV 28 and SR 47/2, Cranesville vicinity, 6/03/80, A, C, 80004039

Red Horse Tavern, 1 mi. E of Aurora on U.S. 50, Aurora vicinity, 7/02/73, A, C, 73001923

Red Horse Tavern (Boundary Increase), US 50, 1 mi E. of Aurora, Brookside, 5/04/79, A, 79003443

Putnam County

Buffalo Indian Village Site, Address Restricted, Buffalo vicinity, 1/25/71, D, 71000883

Buffalo Town Square Historic District, Jct. of WV 62 and High St., Buffalo, 8/16/91, B, C, a, 91001009

Raleigh County

Phillips—Sprague Mine, Address Restricted, Beckley vicinity, 3/25/88, A, C, g, 88000266

St. Colman's Roman Catholic Church and Cemetery, WV 26, Sandstone vicinity, 8/23/84, A, a, d, 84003658

Trump—Lilly Farmstead, WV 26/3, 2.5 mi. from WV 26, Hinton vicinity, 11/08/90, A, C, NPS, 90001640

Wildwood, 117 Laurel Ter., Beckley, 8/25/70, B, 70000665

Randolph County

Albert and Liberal Arts Halls, Davis and Elkins College campus, Elkins, 8/29/79, A, C, 79002599

Beverly Historic District, WV 92 and U.S. 219 and 250, Beverly, 1/11/80, A, C, 80004040

Blackman-Bosworth Store, Main and Court Sts., Beverly, 4/14/75, A, 75001897

Butcher Hill Historic District, E of Beverly, Beverly vicinity, 11/09/89, A, B, C, d, 89001784

Cheat Summit Fort, Address Restricted, Huttonsville vicinity, 9/28/90, A, C, D, 90001445

Davis Memorial Presbyterian Church, 450 Randolph Ave., Elkins, 4/20/84, A, C, a, 84003664

Day—Vandevander Mill, WV 32, Harmon vicinity, 7/21/87, A, C, 87001173

Elkins, Senator Stephen Benton, House, Davis and Elkins College Campus, Elkins, 9/02/82, B, C, NHL, 82004329

Graceland, Davis and Elkins College campus, Elkins, 9/17/70, B, C, 70000666

Helvetia, SR 45 and SR 46, Helvetia, 11/29/78, A, C, 78002810

Hutton, E. E., House, Jct. of U.S. 219 and 250 and, Union St., Huttonsville, 6/11/75, C, 75001898

Kump, Gov. H. Guy, House, US 33 and 250, Elkins, 8/18/83, B, C, g, 83003250

Middle Mountain Cabins, E side of Middle Mountain Rd. at Camp Five Run, Monongahela National Forest, Wymer vicinity, 9/27/90, B, C, 90001447

Perly, Fred A., House, Address Restricted, Jenningston vicinity, 9/14/88, B, C, 88001453

Pinecrest, Kerens Hill, Elkins, 12/11/79, B, C, 79002600

Randolph County Courthouse and Jail, Randolph Ave. and High St., Elkins, 11/28/80, C, 80004041

Rich Mountain Battlefield, 6 mi. W of Beverly on Rich Mountain Rd., Co. Rt. 37/8, Beverly vicinity, 7/17/92, A, B, 92000899

See—Ward House, US 219/250, Mill Creek vicinity, 8/25/88, A, B, C, 88000671

Taylor-Condrey House, 1700 Taylor Ave., Elkins, 8/18/83, B, C, 83003252

Tygarts Valley Church, US 219, Huttonsville, 4/15/86, C, a, 86000797

Ritchie County

Old Stone House, 310 W. Myles Ave., Pennsboro, 7/21/78, A, 78002811

Roane County

Robey Theatre, 318 Main St., Spencer, 3/29/89, A, 89000182

Summers County

Graham, Col. James, House, SW of Lowell on WV 3, Lowell vicinity, 3/16/76, A, C, 76001946

Gwinn, Samuel, Plantation, County Rt. 15, Lowell vicinity, 3/08/89, A, B, C, 88002956

Hinton Historic District, Roughly bounded by C & O RR, James St., 5th Ave., and Roundhouse, Hinton, 2/17/84, A, C, NPS, 84003670

Jordan's Chapel, NW of Pipestem on SR 18, Pipestem vicinity, 2/22/80, A, a, 80004042

Pence Springs Hotel Historic District, Roughly bounded by Buggy Branch, Buggy Branch Rd., WV 3 and Pence Springs Access Rd., Pence Springs, 2/27/85, A, C, 85000404

Summers County Courthouse, Ballangee St. and 1st Ave., Hinton, 3/02/81, A, C, 81000608

Taylor County

Andrews Methodist Church, E. Main St. between St. John and Luzader Sts., Grafton, 12/18/70, A, B, a, NHL, 70000667

Clelland House, Off CR 250/4, Grafton vicinity, 6/23/80, C, 80004043

Grafton Downtown Commercial Historic District, Main and Latrobe Sts. between Bridge and St.Mary's, Grafton, 4/09/84, A, C, 84003675

Grafton National Cemetery, 431 Walnut St., Grafton, 2/19/82, A, d, 82004330

Jarvis, Anna, House, U.S. 119 and 250, Webster, 5/29/79, A, B, 79002601

Tucker County

Cottrill Opera House, East Ave., Thomas, 8/29/79, A, 79002602

Tucker County Courthouse and Jail, 1st and Walnut Sts., Parsons, 8/23/84, C, 84003680

Tyler County

Durham, E. A., House, 110 Chelsea St., Sistersville, 6/19/73, A, C, 73001924

Middlebourne Historic District, Main, East, and Dodd Sts., Middlebourne, 7/09/93, A, C, 93000613

Sistersville City Hall, City Sq., Main and Diamond Sts., Sistersville, 10/05/72, A, C, 72001292

Sistersville Historic District, From Chelsea to the Ohio River between Catherine and both sides of Virginia Sts., Sistersville, 8/13/75, A, C, 75001899

Tyler County Courthouse and Jail, Main and Dodd Sts., Middlebourne, 6/23/80, A, C, 80004044

Wells Inn, 316 Charles St., Sistersville, 10/05/72, A, C, 72001293

Wells, William, House, WV 18, Tyler City, 7/21/87, A, B, C, 87001176

Wells—Schaff House, 500 S. Wells, Sistersville, 1/07/86, A, B, C, d, 86000054

Wells—Twyford House, Jct. of WV 2 and Kahle St., Sistersville vicinity, 4/29/91, C, 91000447

Upshur County

Agnes Howard Hall, West Virginia Wesleyan College campus, Buckhannon, 8/18/83, A, C, 83003253

French Creek Presbyterian Church, Rte. 2, French Creek, 12/24/74, A, C, a, 74002020

Post, William, Mansion, 8 Island Ave., Buckhannon, 7/13/93, B, C, 93000619

Southern Methodist Church Building, 81 W. Main St., Buckhannon, 7/29/92, A, C, a, 92000898

Wayne County

Miller, Joseph S., House, 748 Beech St., Kenova, 3/29/89, B, C, 89000180

Ramsdell, Z. D., House, 1108 B St., Ceredo, 8/18/83, B, 83003254

Wayne County—Continued

Wildcat Branch Petroglyphs, Address Restricted, Fort Gay vicinity, 7/22/79, D, 79002603

Webster County

Craig Run East Fork Rockshelter [Rockshelters on the Gauley Ranger District, Monongahela National Forest MPS], Address Restricted, Mills Mountain vicinity, 6/03/93, D, 93000493

Laurel Run Rockshelter [Rockshelters on the Gauley Ranger District, Monongahela National Forest MPS], Address Restricted, Coe vicinity, 6/03/93, D, 93000491

Mollohan Mill, On CR 8, Replete vicinity, 9/02/82, A, C, 82004331

Morton House, Union St., Webster Springs, 4/15/86, C, 86000795

Wetzel County

Fish Creek Covered Bridge [West Virginia Covered Bridges TR], SR 13, Hundred vicinity, 6/04/81, A, C, 81000609

New Martinsville Downtown Historic District, Main, Washington Sts., and Monroe Alley, New Martinsville, 9/23/88, A, B, C, 88000675

North Street Historic District, North St. between Florida and the railroad tracks, New Martinsville, 6/07/88, A, 88000677

Wirt County

Beauchamp-Newman House, Court St., Elizabeth, 7/24/74, A, 74002021

Buffalo Church, Jct. Co. Rts. 28 and 14, Palestine vicinity, 1/29/90, C, a, 89001781

Burning Springs Complex, Along the N bank of the Kanawha River from the confluence of Burning Springs Run, Burning Springs, 5/06/71, A, 71000884

Kanawha Hotel, 111 Court St., Elizabeth, 11/25/86, A, C, 86003232

Ruble Church, Jct. of CR 34/1 and 34/2, Burning Springs, 4/09/82, A, C, a, 82004332

Wood County

Avery Street Historic District, Roughly bounded by Nineteenth, Spring and Quincy, Eighth, and Market Sts., Parkersburg, 4/15/86, A, C, 86000849

Bethel AME Church [Downtown Parkersburg MRA], 820 Clay St., Parkersburg, 10/08/82, A, C, a, 82001767

Blennerhassett Hotel [Downtown Parkersburg MRA], 316 Market St., Parkersburg, 12/10/82, A, C, 82001768

Blennerhassett Island Historic District, On the Ohio River, 1.7 mi. S of Parkersburg, Parkersburg vicinity, 9/07/72, A, D, 72001294

Carnegie Library [Downtown Parkersburg MRA], 725 Green St., Parkersburg, 10/08/82, A, C, 82001769

Case House [Downtown Parkersburg MRA], 710 Ann St., Parkersburg, 10/08/82, C, 82001770

Citizens National Bank [Downtown Parkersburg MRA], 219 4th St., Parkersburg, 10/08/82, C, 82001772

Cook House, 1301 Murdoch Ave., Parkersburg, 6/07/78, A, C, 78002812

Cooper, Henry, House, Park Ave., Parkersburg, 2/06/86, A, 86000828

Elks Club [Downtown Parkersburg MRA], 515 Juliana St., Parkersburg, 10/08/82, C, 82001773

First Baptist Church [Downtown Parkersburg MRA], 813 Market St., Parkersburg, 12/10/82, C, a, 82001774

First Presbyterian Church/Calvary Temple Evangelical Church [Downtown Parkersburg MRA], 946 Market St., Parkersburg, 12/10/82, C, a, 82001775

Gould House/Greater Parkersburg Chamber of Commerce [Downtown Parkersburg MRA], 720 Juliana St., Parkersburg, 10/08/82, C, 82001776

Henderson Hall Historic District, CR 21/2 off WV 14, Williamstown vicinity, 4/17/86, A, B, C, D, c, 86000811

House at 10th and Avery Streets [Downtown Parkersburg MRA], 10th and Avery Sts., Parkersburg, 12/10/82, C, 82001777

Jackson Memorial Fountain, Park Ave. and 17th St., Parkersburg, 8/23/84, C, 84003686

Julia—Ann Square Historic District, Both sides of Juliana and Ann Sts. from cemetery to 9th St., Parkersburg, 5/24/77, A, C, 77001380

Logan, Henry, Memorial AME Church [Downtown Parkersburg MRA], Ann & 6th Sts., Parkersburg, 12/16/82, C, a, 82001778

Masonic Temple [Downtown Parkersburg MRA], 900 Market St., Parkersburg, 10/08/82, C, 82001779

Mather Building/Franklin & DeHaven Jewelers [Downtown Parkersburg MRA], 405 Market St., Parkersburg, 10/08/82, C, 82001780

Meldahl House, Washington Bottom Rd. off WV 892, Washington vicinity, 5/17/91, A, B, 91000550

Neale, George, Jr., House, 331 Juliana St., Parkersburg, 1/10/80, B, C, 80004045

Oakland, 1131 7th St., Parkersburg, 5/29/79, B, C, 79002604

Oeldorf Building/Wetherell's Jewelers [Downtown Parkersburg MRA], 809 Market St., Parkersburg, 12/10/82, C, 82001781

Parkersburg High School—Washington Avenue Historic District, Washington Ave. from Park Ave. to Dudley Ave., including 2101 Dudley, Parkersburg, 7/16/92, A, C, 92000895

Parkersburg Women's Club [Downtown Parkersburg MRA], 323 9th St., Parkersburg, 10/08/82, C, 82001782

Sharon Lodge No. 28 IOOF [Downtown Parkersburg MRA], 316 5th St., Parkersburg, 10/08/82, C, 82001784

Sixth Street Railroad Bridge [Downtown Parkersburg MRA], 6th Street, Parkersburg, 12/10/82, C, 82001785

Smith Building [Downtown Parkersburg MRA], 310 1/2 Market St., Parkersburg, 12/10/82, C, 82001786

Smoot Theater [Downtown Parkersburg MRA], 213 5th St., Parkersburg, 10/08/82, C, 82001787

St. Francis Xavier Church, 532 Market St., Parkersburg, 12/22/78, B, C, a, 78002813

Tavenner House, 2401 Camden Ave., Parkersburg, 11/10/82, A, 82001788

Tomlinson Mansion, 901 W. 3rd St., Williamstown, 7/24/74, B, C, 74002022

Tracewell House, WV 95 W of Gihon Rd., Parkersburg vicinity, 4/26/91, B, C, 91000450

Trinity Episcopal Church Rectory [Downtown Parkersburg MRA], 430 Juliana St., Parkersburg, 12/10/82, C, a, 82001789

Trinity Protestant Episcopal Church [Downtown Parkersburg MRA], 424 Juliana St., Parkersburg, 12/10/82, C, a, 82001790

Union Trust & Deposit Co./Union Trust National Bank [Downtown Parkersburg MRA], 700 Market St., Parkersburg, 10/08/82, C, 82001791

Van Winkle, Peter G., House [Downtown Parkersburg MRA], 600 Juliana St., Parkersburg, 10/08/82, C, 82001792

Wait, Walton, House [Downtown Parkersburg MRA], 1232 Murdoch Ave., Parkersburg, 12/10/82, C, b, 82001793

Windmill Quaker State [Downtown Parkersburg MRA], 800 Murdoch Ave., Parkersburg, 10/08/82, C, 82001795

Wood County Courthouse, Court Sq. at 3rd and Market St., Parkersburg, 8/29/79, C, 79002606

Wyoming County

Itmann Company Store and Office, WV 10/16, Itmann, 11/28/90, A, C, 90001775

Mullens Historic District, Roughly bounded by Lusk and Highland Aves., the Norfolk & Southern RR tracks and Water St., Mullens, 11/16/93, A, C, 93001233

Wyoming County Courthouse and Jail, Main St., Pineville, 11/27/79, A, C, 79002607

WISCONSIN

Adams County

Adams County Courthouse [County Courthouses of Wisconsin TR], 402 Main St., Friendship, 3/09/82, C, 82000627

Roche-a-Cri Petroglyphs, , Friendship vicinity, 5/11/81, C, D, 81000031

Ashland County

Apostle Islands Lighthouses, N and E of Bayfield on Michigan, raspberry, Outer, Sand and Devils Islands, Bayfield vicinity, 3/08/77, A, NPS, 77000145

Ashland County Courthouse [County Courthouses of Wisconsin TR], 201 W. 2nd St., Ashland, 3/09/82, C, 82000628

Ashland Middle School [Wildhagen, Henry, Schools of Ashland TR], 1000 Ellis Ave., Ashland, 7/17/80, C, 80000101

Bass Island Brownstone Company Quarry, N of La Pointe on Basswood Island, La Pointe vicinity, 3/29/78, A, NPS, 78000075

Beaser School [Wildhagen, Henry, Schools of Ashland TR], 612 Beaser Ave., Ashland, 7/17/80, C, 80000102

Ellis School [Wildhagen, Henry, Schools of Ashland TR], 310 Stuntz Ave., Ashland, 7/17/80, C, 80000103

Hadland Fishing Camp, N of La Pointe on Rocky Island, La Pointe vicinity, 8/18/77, A, b, g, NPS, 77000146

LUCERNE (Shipwreck), Address Restricted, La Pointe vicinity, 12/18/91, A, C, D, 91001775

La Pointe Indian Cemetery, S. Old Main St., La Pointe, 8/03/77, A, D, a, d, 77000028

La Pointe Light Station [U.S. Coast Guard Lighthouses and Light Stations on the Great Lakes TR], Long Island in Chequamagon Bay, Bayfield vicinity, 8/04/83, A, C, 83003366

Manitou Camp, Manitou Island, Apostle Islands National Lakeshore, 1/19/83, A, C, b, NPS, 83003367

Marina Site, Address Restricted, La Pointe vicinity, 12/22/78, A, D, d, 78000076

Marion Park Pavilion, Marion Park, Glidden vicinity, 6/04/81, A, C, 81000032

Mellen City Hall, Bennett and Main Sts., Ashland, 9/20/79, A, 79000341

Morty Site (47AS40), Address Restricted, Bayfield vicinity, 6/13/88, D, NPS, 88000145

NOQUEBAY (Schooner—Barge) Shipwreck Site [Great Lakes Shipwrecks of Wisconsin MPS], Address Restricted, La Pointe, 6/04/92, C, D, 92000593

Old Ashland Post Office, 601 West Second St., Ashland, 1/21/74, C, 74000054

P-Flat Site (47AS47), Address Restricted, Bayfield vicinity, 9/19/88, D, NPS, 88000144

R. G. STEWART (Shipwreck), Address Restricted, La Pointe vicinity, 12/27/91, D, 91001850

Security Savings Bank, 212-214 W. 2nd St., Ashland, 12/27/74, C, 74000055

Soo Line Depot, Third Ave. W, at Fourth St., Ashland, 11/03/88, A, C, 88002177

Trout Point Logging Camp, Address Restricted, Bayfield vicinity, 12/16/88, D, NPS, 88002756

Union Depot, 417 Chapple Ave., Ashland, 3/23/79, A, C, 79000058

West Second Street Historic District, W. 2nd St. from Ellis Ave. to 6th Ave., Ashland, 2/02/84, A, C, 84003619

Wheeler Hall, Northland College, 1411 Ellis Ave., Ashland, 9/13/77, A, 77000029

Wilmarth School [Wildhagen, Henry, Schools of Ashland TR], 913 3rd Ave. W., Ashland, 7/17/80, C, 80000104

Barron County

Barron County Pipestone Quarry, E of Rice Lake, Rice Lake vicinity, 12/22/78, D, 78000077

Cumberland Public Library [Public Library Facilities of Wisconsin MPS], 1305 Second Ave., Cumberland, 6/25/92, A, C, 92000804

Rice Lake Mounds (47 BN-90), , Rice Lake, 9/07/79, D, 79000059

ZCBJ Hall, 320 W. 3rd St., Haugen, 4/11/85, A, 85000768

Bayfield County

Bank of Washburn, Bayfield St. and Central Ave., Washburn, 1/17/80, C, 80000105

Bayfield County Courthouse, 117 E. 5th St., Washburn, 1/17/75, C, 75000060

Bayfield Fish Hatchery, WI 13, Salmo vicinity, 7/22/81, A, C, 81000033

Bayfield Historic District, WI J and WI 13, Bayfield, 11/25/80, A, C, 80000106

Booth Cooperage, 1 East Washington St., Bayfield, 8/13/76, A, 76000049

Boutin, Frank, Jr., House, 7 Rice St., Bayfield, 12/27/74, C, 74000056

Christ Episcopal Church, 121-125 North 3rd. St., Bayfield, 12/27/74, C, a, 74000057

Hokenson Fishing Dock, N of Bayfield at Little Sand Bay, Bayfield vicinity, 6/18/76, A, NPS, 76000050

Island Lake Camp, Island Lake Rd., Drummond vicinity, 3/12/82, A, B, 82000629

OTTAWA (Tug) Shipwreck Site [Great Lakes Shipwreck Sites of Wisconsin MPS], Address Restricted, Russell, 6/08/92, A, C, D, 92000594

Old Bayfield County Courthouse, Washington St. between 4th and 5th Sts., Bayfield, 12/27/74, C, 74000058

Pureair Sanatorium, S of Bayfield, Bayfield vicinity, 8/20/81, A, 81000034

SEVONA (Bulk Carrier) Shipwreck Site [Great Lakes Shipwrecks of Wisconsin MPS], Address Restricted, Bayfield vicinity, 4/09/93, C, D, 93000229

Sevona Cabin, N of Bayfield on Sand Island, Bayfield vicinity, 9/29/76, B, C, NPS, 76000051

Shaw Farm, Sand Island, Bayfield vicinity, 6/18/76, A, NPS, 76000052

Washburn Public Library, Washington Ave. and W. 3rd St., Washburn, 3/01/84, C, 84003621

Brown County

Astor Historic District, WI 57, Green Bay, 2/27/80, A, C, 80000107

Baird Law Office, 2640 South Webster Avenue, Green Bay, 10/15/70, A, C, b, 70000025

Brown County Courthouse, 100 S. Jefferson St., Green Bay, 1/01/76, C, 76000053

Cotton House, 2640 South Webster Ave., Green Bay, 4/28/70, C, b, 70000026

Fisk, Joel S., House, 123 N. Oakland Ave., Green Bay, 8/11/78, C, 78000420

Fort Howard Hospital, 2640 S. Webster Ave., Green Bay, 7/22/79, A, C, b, 71001075

Fort Howard Officers' Quarters, 2640 S. Webster Ave., Green Bay, 7/22/79, A, C, b, 72001548

Fort Howard Ward Building, 2640 S. Webster Ave., Green Bay, 7/22/79, A, b, 72001547

Hazelwood, 1008 S. Monroe Ave., Green Bay, 4/28/70, A, C, 70000027

Henry House, 1749 Riverside Dr., Suamico, 1/31/80, A, C, 80000108

Kellogg Public Library and Neville Public Museum, 125 S. Jefferson St., Green Bay, 6/09/81, A, C, 81000035

Lawton, C. A., Company, 233 N. Broadway, De Pere, 1/30/92, A, C, 91001985

Main Hall, Third St. and College Ave., De Pere, 10/28/88, A, C, a, 88002001

Mueller-Wright House, Washington and Mueller Sts., Wrightstown, 3/29/78, B, C, 78000078

North Broadway Street Historic District, Broadway, Ridgeway Blvd., Morris, Fulton, Franklin, Cass, Front, and Wisconsin Sts., De Pere, 9/08/83, B, C, 83003368

Oakland—Dousman Historic District, Roughly bounded by Dousman St., Oakland Ave., Shawano Ave., Antoinette and Francis Sts., Green Bay, 4/27/88, B, C, 88000455

Tank Cottage, 2640 South Webster Avenue, Green Bay, 4/28/70, A, C, b, 70000028

Wisconsin State Reformatory, SE corner of Riverside Dr. and SR 172, Allouez, 5/03/90, A, C, 90000641

Buffalo County

Alma Historic District [Alma MRA], Roughly bounded by RR tracks, 2nd, Swift, and Cedar Sts., Alma, 5/13/82, A, B, C, 82000631

Berni, Jacob, House [Alma MRA], 911 Riverview Dr., Alma, 5/13/82, C, 82000632

Burlington Hotel [Alma MRA], 809 N. Main St., Alma, 5/13/82, C, 82000633

Fugina House, 348 S. Main St., Fountain City, 5/08/79, B, C, 79000061

Laue, Frederick, House, 1111 S. Main St., Alma, 5/14/79, A, C, 79000062

Laue, Frederick, Jr., House [Alma MRA], 1109 S. Main St., Alma, 5/13/82, C, 82000634

Senn, John L., House [Alma MRA], 811 S. 2nd St., Alma, 5/13/82, C, 82000635

Sherman House, 301 S. Main St., Alma, 8/14/79, B, C, 79000063

Steiner, John, Store [Alma MRA], 1101 S. Main St., Alma, 5/13/82, C, 82000636

Tenny, Dr. J. T., House [Alma MRA], 305 N. 2nd St., Alma, 5/13/82, C, 82000637

Tester and Polin General Merchandise Store, 215 N. Main St., Alma, 5/14/79, A, B, C, 79000064

Walser, Ulrich, House [Alma MRA], 711 N. 2nd St., Alma, 5/13/82, C, 82000638

Burnett County

Altern Site, Address Restricted, Hertel vicinity, 3/31/80, D, 80000391

Burnett County Abstract Company, 214 N. Oak St., Grantsburg, 5/07/80, A, C, 80000109

Ebert Mound Group (47Bt28), , Yellow Lake vicinity, 7/09/82, D, 82000639

Fickle Site (47BT25), Address Restricted, Siren vicinity, 1/26/90, D, 89002310

Jacobson House and Mill Site, E of Gransburg on SR M, Grantsburg vicinity, 4/22/80, B, 80000110

Northwest and XY Company Trading Post Sites, Address Restricted, Webster vicinity, 2/15/74, D, 74000059

Sandrock Cliffs, Address Restricted, Grantsburg vicinity, 5/01/90, D, NPS, 90000632

Yellow River Swamp Site 47-Bt-36, Address Restricted, Webster vicinity, 2/28/85, D, 85000405

Calumet County

Aebischer Site (47CT30), Address Restricted, Chilton vicinity, 10/10/85, D, 85003136

Calumet County Courthouse [County Courthouses of Wisconsin TR], 206 Court St., Chilton, 3/09/82, C, 82000640

Haese Memorial Village Historic District, Milwaukee and Randolph Sts, Forest Junction, 3/02/82, A, B, C, 82000641

Ridge Group, Address Restricted, Chilton vicinity, 12/08/78, D, 78000079

Stockridge Indian Cemetery, N of Stockridge off WI 55, Stockbridge vicinity, 10/22/80, A, d, 80000111

Chippewa County

Cook-Rutledge House, 509 W. Grand Ave., Chippewa Falls, 8/07/74, A, C, 74000060

Cornell Pulpwood Stacker, Cornell Mill Yard Park, Cornell, 12/23/93, A, C, 93001425

Marsh Rainbow Arch Bridge, Spring St., Chippewa Falls, 6/25/82, C, 82000642

McDonell High School [Notre Dame Parish TR], 3 S. High St., Chippewa Falls, 10/06/82, C, 82001840

Moon, D. R., Memorial Library, E. Fourth Ave., Stanley, 12/02/85, A, C, 85003096

Notre Dame Church and Goldsmith Memorial Chapel [Notre Dame Parish TR], 117 Allen St., Chippewa Falls, 4/07/83, C, a, 83003369

Roe, L.I., House, 410 N. Franklin St., Stanley, 8/27/80, B, 80000112

Sheeley House, 236 W. River St., Chippewa Falls, 9/05/85, A, C, 85001949

Z. C. B. J. Hall, WI 27, 7 mi. N of Cadott, Arthur, 6/25/92, A, 92000812

Clark County

Clark County Jail, 215 E. 5th St., Neillsville, 12/08/78, A, C, 78000080

Schofield, Robert, House, 303 W. Schofield Ave., Greenwood, 9/09/82, B, C, 82000643

Columbia County

Bellmont Hotel, 120 N. Main St., Pardeeville, 11/04/93, C, 93001170

Bennett, H. H., Studio, 215 Broadway, Wisconsin Dells, 10/08/76, A, B, 76000054

Bowman House, 714 Broadway St., Wisconsin Dells, 4/03/86, C, 86000621

Chadbourn, F. A., House, 314 S. Charles St., Columbus, 12/28/90, C, 90001961

Columbus City Hall, 105 N. Dickason St., Columbus, 9/04/79, A, C, 79000065

Columbus Downtown Historic District, Roughly bounded by Mill, Water and Harrison Sts. and Dickason Blvd., Columbus, 3/05/92, A, C, 92000113

Columbus Public Library [Public Library Facilities of Wisconsin MPS], 112 S. Dickason Blvd., Columbus, 11/15/90, A, C, 90001704

Cox, Angie Williams, Library [Public Library Facilities of Wisconsin MPS], 129 N. Main St., Pardeeville, 11/15/90, A, B, 90001703

Durward's Glen, NE of Merrimac off WI 78, Merrimac vicinity, 11/07/78, A, C, 78000081

Farmers and Merchants Union Bank, 159 W. James St., Columbus, 10/18/72, C, NHL, 72000044

Fort Winnebago Site, Address Restricted, Portage vicinity, 5/17/79, D, 79000066

Fort Winnebago Surgeon's Quarters, 0.1 mi. & of corporate city limits on WI 33, Portage vicinity, 10/28/70, A, 70000029

Fox-Wisconsin Portage Site, Address Restricted, Portage vicinity, 3/14/73, A, 73000074

Gale, Zona, House, 506 W. Edgewater St., Portage, 10/24/80, B, C, 80000113

Holsten Family Farmstead, W1391 Weiner Rd., Columbia, 9/08/92, A, C, 92001189

Kilbourn Public Library, 429 Broadway, Wisconsin Dells, 12/27/74, C, 74000061

Kurth, John H., and Company Office Building, 729–733 Park Ave., Columbus, 12/02/93, A, C, 93001359

Lewis, Gov. James T., House, 711 W. James St., Columbus, 4/09/82, B, C, 82000644

Merrell, Henry, House, 505 E. Cook St., Portage, 7/08/93, C, b, 93000545

Merrimac Ferry, WI 113 at the Wisconsin River, Merrimac, 12/31/74, A, 74000330

Nashold 20-sided Barn, Trunk Z, 0.4 mi. E of WI 146, Fall River vicinity, 2/11/88, A, C, 88000091

Old Indian Agency House, NE end of old Agency House Rd. (Rte.1) near NE city limits, Portage, 2/01/72, A, B, C, 72000045

Pardeeville Presbyterian Church, 105 S. Main St., Pardeeville, 1/15/80, C, a, 80000114

Portage Canal, Between Fox and Wisconsin Rivers, Portage, 8/26/77, A, 77000030

Society Hill Historic District, Roughly bounded by W. Wisconsin, Cass and W. Emmett Sts. and MacFarlane Rd., Portage, 3/05/92, C, a, 92000112

Wawbeek-Horace A.J. Upham House, WI 13, Wisconsin Dells, 6/19/85, A, C, 85001355

Weber, Jacob, House, 825 Oak St., Wisconsin Dells, 1/20/78, B, C, 78000083

Crawford County

Astor Fur Warehouse, Water St., St. Feriole Island, Prairie du Chien, 10/15/66, A, NHL, 66000800

Brisbois, Michael, House, Water St., St. Feriole Island, Prairie du Chien, 10/15/66, A, C, NHL, 66000801

Crawford County Courthouse [County Courthouses of Wisconsin TR], 220 N. Beaumont Rd., Prairie du Chien, 3/09/82, A, C, 82000645

Dousman Hotel, Fisher St. and River Rd., Prairie du Chien, 10/15/66, A, C, NHL, 66000122

Foley Mound Group, Address Restricted, Lynxville vicinity, 7/15/74, D, 74000062

Folsom, W.H.C., House, 109 Blackhawk Ave., Prairie du Chien, 12/06/84, A, C, 84000692

Fort Crawford Military Hospital, Rice Street and South Beaumont Rd., Prairie du Chien, 10/15/66, A, NHL, 66000121

Old Rock School, S. Marquette Rd. at Parrish St., Prairie du Chien, 12/01/83, A, C, 83004265

Olson Mound Group, Address Restricted, Seneca vicinity, 2/12/74, D, 74000063

Crawford County—Continued

Pedretti III, Address Restricted, Prairie du Chien vicinity, 12/18/78, D, 78000084

Powers, Strange, House, 338 N. Main St., Prairie du Chien, 8/27/79, C, 79000067

Reed, Alfred, Mound Group (47Cr311), Address Restricted, Prairie du Chien vicinity, 9/07/82, D, 82000646

Rolette House, NE corner of N. Water and Fisher Sts., Prairie du Chien, 2/01/72, B, 72000046

Vertefeuille, Francois, House, Hwy. K, 0.35 mi. S of jct. with Limery Rd., Prairie du Chien, 3/18/93, A, C, 93000142

Villa Louis, Villa Rd. and Bolvin St., Prairie du Chien, 10/15/66, B, C, NHL, 66000123

Wall-Smethurst Mound Group, Address Restricted, Lynxville vicinity, 6/13/74, D, 74000064

Dane County

Agricultural Chemistry Building, 420 Henry Mall, University of Wisconsin campus, Madison, 6/19/85, A, C, 85001356

Agricultural Dean's House, 10 Babcock Dr., Madison, 9/20/84, A, B, C, 84003627

Agricultural Engineering Building, 460 Henry Mall, University of Wisconsin Campus, Madison, 6/27/85, A, C, 85001404

Agricultural Heating station, 1535 Observatory Dr., Univ. of WI, Madison, 3/14/85, C, 85000570

Agriculture Hall, 1450 Linden Dr., University of Wisconsin campus, Madison, 3/14/85, A, C, 85000571

American Exchange Bank, 1 N. Pinckney St., Madison, 8/18/80, A, C, 80000115

Ames, Francis Marian, Farmstead, 221 US 14, Rutland, 11/05/92, C, 92001555

Badger State Shoe Company, 123 N. Blount St., Madison, 4/11/89, A, C, 89000232

Bascom Hill Historic District, Bounded by Observatory Dr., University Ave., and N. Park, Langdon, and State Sts., Madison, 9/12/74, A, C, g, 74000065

Bashford, Robert M., House, 423 N. Pinckney St., Madison, 3/14/73, B, C, 73000075

Baskerville Apartment Building, 121-129 S. Hamilton St., Madison, 10/13/88, C, 88002006

Bellevue Apartment Building, 29 E. Wilson St., Madison, 3/13/87, C, 87000433

Belmont Hotel, 101 E. Mifflin St., Madison, 1/18/90, A, C, 89002311

Bernard-Hoover Boathouse, 622 E. Gorham St., Madison, 7/30/81, A, 81000036

Biederstaedt Grocery, 851-853 Williamson St., Madison, 3/25/82, A, 82000647

Blackhawk Country Club Mound Group (47 DA 131), Address Restricted, Madison vicinity, 8/01/79, D, 79000068

Bowen, James B., House, 302 S. Mills St., Madison, 3/01/82, A, C, 82000648

Bradley, Harold C., House, 106 N. Prospect Ave., Madison, 2/23/72, C, NHL, 72000047

Braley, Judge Arthur B., House, 422 N. Henry St., Madison, 11/28/80, B, 80000116

Bram Mound Group [Late Woodland Stage in Archeological Region 8 MPS], Address Restricted, Dunn, 3/25/93, D, 93000216

Brittingham Park Boathouse, N. Shore Dr., Madison, 6/30/82, A, C, 82000649

Brown, Charles E., Indian Mounds, Address Restricted, Madison vicinity, 1/05/84, D, 84003630

Burrows Park Effigy Mound and Campsite, Address Restricted, Madison vicinity, 12/31/74, D, 74000066

Camp Randall, Camp Randall Memorial Park, Madison, 6/07/71, A, 71000036

Cardinal Hotel, 416 E. Wilson St., Madison, 9/02/82, A, C, 82000650

City Market, 101 N. Blount St., Madison, 11/28/78, C, 78000085

Clarke, Bascom B., House, 1150 Spaight St., Madison, 11/28/80, B, 80000117

Collins, William, House, 704 E. Gorham St., Madison, 12/03/74, C, 74000067

Commons, John R., House, 1645 Norman Way, Madison, 3/14/85, B, 85000572

Crosse, Dr. Charles G., House, 133 W. Main St., Sun Prairie, 2/24/93, C, 93000029

Curtis-Kittleson House, 1102 Spaight St., Madison, 4/10/80, A, B, C, 80000118

Cutter, Judson C., House, 1030 Jenifer St., Madison, 7/12/78, C, 78000086

Dean, Nathaniel W., House, 4718 Monona Dr., Madison, 11/07/80, B, 80000119

Donald Farm, 1972 WI 92, Mount Horeb vicinity, 6/07/84, B, 84003633

Drohman Cabin, 6701 E. Broadway, Madison vicinity, 9/28/81, C, 81000037

Dunroven House, 7801 Dunroven Rd., Dane vicinity, 11/28/80, B, C, 80000120

East Dayton Street Historic District, 649–53 E. Dayton St. and 114 N. Blount St., Madison, 12/27/88, A, 88000217

East Wilson Street Historic District, 402–524 E. Wilson and 133 S. Blair Sts., Madison, 4/03/86, A, C, 86000618

Edgewood College Mound Group Archeological District [Late Woodland Stage in Archeological Region 8 MPS], Address Restricted, Madison, 6/07/91, D, 91000669

Elliott, Edward C., House, 137 N. Prospect Ave., Madison, 8/11/78, C, 78000087

Elmside Park Mounds [Late Woodland Stage in Archeological Region 8 (AD 650–1300) MPS], Address Restricted, Madison, 4/10/91, D, 91000358

Ely, Richard T., House, 205 N. Prospect Ave., Madison, 12/16/74, B, C, 74000068

Farwell's Point Mound Group, Address Restricted, Madison vicinity, 12/27/74, D, 74000069

Fess Hotel, 123 E. Doty Street, Madison, 9/21/78, A, C, 78003204

Fire Station No. 4, 1329 W. Dayton St., Madison, 3/01/84, A, 84003637

First Church of Christ Scientist, 315 Wisconsin Ave., Madison, 11/24/82, C, a, 82001841

First Lutheran Church, Pleasant View Rd. at Old Sauk Rd., Middleton, 6/16/88, A, C, a, d, 88000728

First Unitarian Society Meetinghouse, 900 University Bay Dr., Shorewood Hills, 4/11/73, C, a, g, 73000076

Forest Hill Cemetery Mound Group, Address Restricted, Madison vicinity, 12/27/74, D, d, 74000070

Fox Hall, 5183 County Hwy. M, Fitchburg vicinity, 12/01/83, C, 83004273

Gilmore, Eugene A., House, 120 Ely Pl., Madison, 3/14/73, C, 73000077

Grace Episcopal Church, 6 N. Carroll St., Madison, 1/01/76, A, C, a, 76000055

Graves, Sereno W., House [Graves Stone Buildings TR], 4006 Old Stage Rd., Rutland, 9/29/82, B, C, 82000651

Grimm Book Bindery, 454 W. Gilman St., Madison, 4/03/86, C, 86000625

Haight, Nicholas, Farmstead, 4926 Lacy Rd., Fitchburg, 10/29/93, C, 93001162

Hall, Samuel, House, 924 Hillside Rd., Albion, 12/23/93, A, C, 93001445

Halvorson Mound Group [Late Woodland Stage in Archeological Region 8 MPS], Address Restricted, Madison, 3/25/93, D, 93000215

Hauge Log Church, 1 mi. N of Daleyville on CR Z, Daleyville vicinity, 12/31/74, A, C, a, 74000071

Heiney's Meat Market, 1221 Mills St., Black Earth, 9/27/84, C, 84003642

Henry Mall Historic District, 420, 425, 440, 445, 460 and 465 Henry Mall and 1450 Linden Dr., Madison, 1/22/92, A, C, 91001986

Hiram Smith Hall and Annex, 1545 Observatory Dr., Univ. of WI, Madison, 3/14/85, A, C, 85000573

Hirsig, Louis, House, 1010 Sherman Ave., Madison, 12/02/74, C, 74000072

Hoff Department Store, 101–103 Main St., Mount Horeb, 2/14/89, A, C, 89000005

Horticulture and Agricultural Physics and Soil Science Building, 1525 Observatory Dr., Univ. of WI, Madison, 3/14/85, A, B, C, 85000574

Hunt, Samuel, House [Graves Stone Buildings TR], 632 Center Rd., Rutland, 9/30/82, C, 82000652

Hyer's Hotel, 854 Jenifer St., Madison, 9/22/83, A, C, 83003370

Ingebretson, Gaute, Loft House, 1212 Pleasant Hill Rd., Stoughton vicinity, 3/13/87, A, C, 87000437

Iverson—Johnson House, 327 E. Washington St., Stoughton, 1/21/88, B, C, 87002501

Jackman Building, 111 S. Hamilton St., Madison, 3/27/80, C, 80000121

Jacobs, Herbert A., House, 441 Toepfer Ave., Madison, 7/24/74, C, g, 74000073

Jacobs, Herbert, Second House, 7033 Old Sauk Rd., Middleton, 12/31/74, C, g, 74000074

Kayser, Adolph H., House, 802 E. Gorham St., Madison, 11/28/80, C, 80000122

Kehl Winery, E of Prairie du Sac on WI 188, Prairie du Sac vicinity, 1/02/76, A, C, 76000056

Dane County—Continued

Kohlmann, Friederich, House, W of Springfield Corners off WI 19, Springfield Corners vicinity, 12/27/74, A, C, 74000075

LaFollette, Robert M., House, 733 Lakewood Blvd., Maple Bluff, 10/15/66, B, NHL, 66000020

Lake Farms Archeological District, Address Restricted, Madison vicinity, 12/22/78, D, 78000088

Lake View Sanatorium, 1204 Northport Dr., Madison, 4/15/93, A, C, 93000258

Lamb Building, 114 State St., Madison, 8/02/84, C, 84003645

Lamp, Robert M., House, 22 N. Butler St., Madison, 1/03/78, C, 78000089

Langdon Street Historic District, Roughly bounded by Lake Mendota, Wisconsin Ave., Langdon, and N. Lake Sts., Madison, 6/26/86, A, B, C, 86001394

Lathrop Hall, 1050 University Ave., University of Wisconsin Campus, Madison, 7/11/85, A, C, 85001503

Leitch, William T., House, 752 E. Gorham St., Madison, 7/18/75, B, C, 75000061

Leonard, William Ellery, House, 2015 Adams St., Madison, 2/25/93, B, 93000071

Lewis Mound Group (47-Da-74), Address Restricted, McFarland vicinity, 12/15/84, D, 84000809

Library Park, Bounded by Vine, Main, Park and Pearl Sts., Belleville, 1/26/81, A, C, 81000038

Lie, Aslak, Cabin, 3022 County Trunk P, Mount Horeb, 4/03/86, B, C, 86000622

Lincoln School, 728 E. Gorham St., Madison, 8/28/80, C, 80000123

Lockwood Barn [Graves Stone Buildings TR], Old Stage Rd, Rutland, 9/29/82, C, 82000653

Lougee, George A., House, 620 S. Ingersoll St., Madison, 6/07/78, C, 78000090

Machinery Row, 601-627 Williamson St., Madison, 4/12/82, A, C, 82000654

Madison Masonic Temple, 301 Wisconsin Ave., Madison, 9/13/90, A, C, 90001456

Madison Waterworks, N. Hancock St., Madison, 8/18/80, A, C, 80000125

Mann, John, House, 6261 Nesbitt Rd., Fitchburg vicinity, 7/08/82, C, 82000655

Mazomanie Downtown Historic District, 1–118 Brodhead, 2–46 Hudson, 37–105 Crescent and 113 E. Exchange Sts., Mazomanie, 8/19/92, A, C, 92000406

Mazomanie Town Hall, 51 Crescent St., Mazomanie, 10/22/80, A, 80000126

McCoy Farmhouse, S of Madison at 2925 Syene Rd., Fitchburg, 5/29/80, A, B, 80000124

McFarland House, 5923 Exchange St., McFarland, 11/03/88, A, B, C, 88002228

Mendota State Hospital Mound Group, , Madison vicinity, 12/27/74, D, 74000076

Merrill Springs Mound Group II Archeological District [Late Woodland Stage in Archeological Region 8 MPS], Address Restricted, Madison, 6/07/91, D, 91000670

Miller House, 647 E. Dayton St., Madison, 11/08/79, B, b, 79000339

Mills Woods Mound [Late Woodland Stage in Archeological Region 8 MPS], Address Restricted, Madison, 6/07/91, D, 91000667

Mills, Simeon, House, 2709 Sommers Ave., Madison, 8/13/87, B, C, 87001386

Monona Mound (47DA275), Address Restricted, Monona vicinity, 12/01/89, D, 89002064

Moore Mound Group [Late Woodland Stage in Archeological Region 8 MPS], Address Restricted, Dunn, 8/05/93, D, 93000809

Mt. Horeb Opera Block, 109–117 E. Main St., Mt. Horeb, 2/23/89, A, C, 89000068

Naeset, Jens, House, 126 E. Washington, Stoughton, 3/14/85, B, C, 85000577

North Hall, University of Wisconsin, University of Wisconsin campus, Madison, 10/15/66, A, B, NHL, 66000021

Old Executive Mansion, 130 E. Gilman St., Madison, 4/11/73, A, C, 73000078

Old Spring Tavern, 3706 Nakoma Rd., Madison, 1/21/74, A, C, 74000077

Old Synagogue, E. Gorham St. at N. Butler St., Madison, 12/29/70, A, a, 70000030

Old U.S. Forest Products Laboratory, 1509 University Ave., University of Wisconsin campus, Madison, 9/12/85, A, C, 85002332

Oregon Masonic Lodge, 117–119 S. Main St., Oregon, 6/18/92, A, C, 92000803

Orton Park, 1100 Spaight St., Madison, 12/18/78, A, d, 78000091

Orton Park Historic District, Roughly bounded by Spaight St., S. Few St., Lake Monona, and S. Ingersoll St., Madison, 10/31/88, B, C, 88000221

Ott, John George, House, 754 Jenifer St., Madison, 9/23/82, B, C, 82000656

Paoli Mills, 6890 Sun Valley Pkwy., Paoli, 3/30/79, A, 79000337

Phlaum—McWilliams Mound Group [Late Woodland Stage in Archeological Region 8 MPS], Address Restricted, Madison, 6/07/91, D, 91000666

Pierce, Carrie, House, 424 N. Pinckney St., Madison, 10/18/72, C, 72000048

Plough Inn, 3402 Monroe St., Madison, 5/29/80, A, 80000127

Pond, Daniel, Farmhouse, E of Brooklyn on U.S. 14, Brooklyn vicinity, 6/30/80, A, C, 80000128

Quisling Towers Apartments, 1 E. Gilman St., Madison, 1/09/84, C, 84003648

Roe, Ole K., House, 404 S. 5th St., Stoughton, 9/07/84, B, C, 84003652

Savage House [Cooksville MRA], SR 1, Stoughton vicinity, 9/17/80, B, 80000392

Schumann, Frederick, Farmstead, 8313 WI 19, Berry, 12/10/93, C, 93001426

Sherman Avenue Historic District, Sherman Ave. roughly between Marston Ave. and N. Brearly St., Madison, 3/22/88, C, g, 88000216

Siggelkow Park Mound Group (47-Da-504), Address Restricted, McFarland vicinity, 3/14/85, D, 85000576

Simeon Mills Historic District, 102–118 King and 115–123 E. Main Sts., Madison, 6/25/87, A, C, 87001063

South School, 1009 Summit Ave., Stoughton, 9/12/85, C, 85002319

Spring Harbor Mound Group [Late Woodland Stage in Archeological Region 8 MPS], Address Restricted, Madison, 6/07/91, D, 91000668

St. Patrick's Roman Catholic Church, 404 E. Main St., Madison, 9/16/82, C, a, 82000657

St. Peter's Roman Catholic Church, W I K, Ashton, 9/23/80, A, C, a, 80000130

State Historical Society of Wisconsin, 816 State St., Madison, 2/23/72, A, C, 72000049

State Office Building, 1 W. Wilson St., Madison, 1/28/82, C, g, 82000658

Steensland, Halle, House, 315 N. Carroll St., Madison, 11/30/82, A, B, C, 82001843

Stock Pavilion, 1675 Linden Dr., University of Wisconsin Campus, Madison, 7/11/85, C, 85001504

Stoner, Joseph J., House, 321 S. Hamilton St., Madison, 1/17/80, A, B, C, 80000129

Stoughton Main Street Commercial Historic District, Main St. from the Yahara River to Forest St., Stoughton, 10/21/82, C, 82001842

Stoughton Universalist Church, 324 S. Page St., Stoughton, 9/30/82, A, C, a, 82000659

Stricker Pond I Site (47 DA 424), Address Restricted, Middleton, 7/16/79, D, 79000069

Suhr, John J., House, 121 Langdon St., Madison, 6/17/82, B, C, 82000660

Thompson's Block, 119 E. Main St., Madison, 6/07/84, C, 84003654

Thorstrand, 1-2 Thorstrand Rd., Madison, 8/11/80, B, 80000131

University Heights Historic District, Roughly bounded by Regent, Allen, Lathrop Sts., and Kendall Ave. (both sides), Madison, 12/17/82, B, C, 82001844

University of Wisconsin Armory and Gymnasium, 716 Langdon St., Madison, 11/04/93, A, NHL, 93001618

University of Wisconsin Science Hall, 550 N. Park St., Madison, 11/04/93, A, B, NHL, 93001616

Vilas Circle Bear Effigy Mound and the Curtis Mounds, Address Restricted, Madison vicinity, 12/30/74, D, 74000078

Vilas Park Mound Group [Late Woodland Stage in Archeological Region 8 (AD 650–1300) MPS], Address Restricted, Madison, 4/10/91, D, 91000357

Wakeley—Giles Commercial Building, 117–119 E. Mifflin St., Madison, 2/23/88, A, B, 88000081

Washburn Observatory and Observatory Director's Residence, 1401 and 1225 Observatory Dr., Univ. of WI, Madison, 3/14/85, A, B, C, 85000575

Waunakee Railroad Depot, South and Main Sts., Waunakee, 2/14/78, A, 78000092

West Madison Depot, Chicago, Milwaukee, and St. Paul Railway, 640 W. Washington Ave., Madison, 5/09/85, A, C, 85000990

West School, 404 Garfield St., Stoughton, 1/22/92, A, 91001992

Wiedenbeck—Dobelin Warehouse, 619 W. Mifflin St., Madison, 12/23/86, A, C, 86003473

Wisconsin Industrial School for Girls, 5212 WI M, Fitchburg, 9/13/91, A, 91001391

Dane County—Continued

Wisconsin Memorial Hospital Historic District, 816 Troy Dr., Madison, 11/03/88, A, 88002183

Wisconsin State Capitol, Capitol Sq., Madison, 10/15/70, A, C, 70000031

Dodge County

Beaumont Hotel, 45 Main St., Mayville, 1/13/88, C, 87002238

Central State Hospital Historic District, Lincoln St. between Beaver Dam and Mason Sts., Waupun, 9/13/91, A, 91001395

Dahl, Martin K., House, 314 Beaver Dam St., Waupun, 9/11/75, B, C, 75000062

Dodge County Courthouse [County Courthouses of Wisconsin TR], 220 E. State St., Juneau, 3/09/82, C, g, 82000661

Dodge County Historical Museum, 127 S. Spring St., Beaver Dam, 7/07/81, C, 81000039

Fox Lake Railroad Depot, Cordelia St. and S. College Avenue, Fox Lake, 5/22/78, A, 78000093

Greenfield, Willard, Farmstead, N-7436 WI Trunk Hwy. 26, Burnett Township, Horicon vicinity, 11/05/92, C, 92001557

Hartwig, Ferdinand C., House, 908 Country Lane, Watertown, 6/17/82, A, 82000662

Hollenstein Wagon and Carriage Factory, Bridge and German Sts., Mayville, 7/27/79, A, 79000070

Horicon Site, E of Waupun, Waupun vicinity, 1/31/79, D, 79003492

Hotel Rogers, 103 E. Maple Ave., Beaver Dam, 3/02/89, A, C, 89000120

Hustis, John, House, N. Ridge St., Hustisford, 3/10/83, B, b, 83003371

Hutchinson Memorial Library [Public Library Facilities of Wisconsin MPS], 228 N. High St., Randolph, 11/15/90, A, C, 90001705

Indian Point Site, Address Restricted, Fox Lake vicinity, 9/13/90, D, 90001459

Schoenicke Barn, NE of Watertown on Venus Rd., Watertown vicinity, 9/19/79, C, 79000071

St. Joseph's Roman Catholic Church, WI Q and Rich Rd., Shields, 7/02/80, A, C, a, 80004480

St. Mark's Episcopal Church, 130 E. Maple St., Beaver Dam, 11/28/80, C, a, b, 80000132

Swan House and Vita Spring Pavilion, 230 Park Ave., Beaver Dam, 4/09/80, B, C, 80000133

Van Brunt, Daniel C., House, 139 W. Lake St., Horicon, 9/14/81, B, C, 81000040

Waupun Public Library, 22 S. Madison St., Waupun, 9/04/79, A, C, 79000072

White Limestone School, N. Main St. between Dayton and Buchanan Sts., Mayville, 10/22/76, A, C, 76000057

Williams Free Library, 105 Park Ave., Beaver Dam, 8/07/74, C, 74000079

Wisconsin State Prison Historic District, 200 S. Madison St., Waupun, 1/22/92, A, C, 91001994

Door County

Anderson Dock Historic District [Ephraim MRA], Roughly bounded by Anderson Lane and North Water St., Ephraim, 6/11/85, A, 85001249

Baileys Harbor Range Light, Roughly Co. Rd. Q, Ridges Rd., and WI 57, Baileys Harbor, 9/21/89, A, C, 89001466

Bohjanen's Door Bluff Pictographs [Indian Rock Art Sites MPS], Address Restricted, Liberty Grove vicinity, 9/02/93, D, 93000881

Cana Island Lighthouse, NE of Baileys Harbor on E side of Cana Island, Baileys Harbor vicinity, 11/21/76, A, 76000201

Carnegie Free Library, 354 Michigan St., Sturgeon Bay, 12/29/88, A, C, 88003069

Chambers Island Lighthouse, 7 mi. NW of Fish Creek at NW tip of Chambers Island, Fish Creek vicinity, 8/19/75, A, 75000063

Church of the Atonement, Fire No. 9410, Fish Creek, 3/07/85, A, C, a, 85000487

Clearing, The, Off WI 42, Ellison Bay, 12/31/74, B, C, 74000080

Cupola House, 7836 Egg Harbor Rd., Egg Harbor, 7/16/79, B, C, 79000073

Eagle Bluff Lighthouse, 3.5 mi. N of Fish Creek on Shore Rd., in Peninsula State Park, Fish Creek vicinity, 10/15/70, A, C, 70000032

Ephraim Moravian Church [Ephraim MRA], 9970 Moravia St., Ephraim, 3/27/85, A, a, b, 85000662

Ephraim Village Hall [Ephraim MRA], 9996 S. Water St., Ephraim, 3/27/85, A, C, 85000663

Free Evangelical Lutheran Church—Bethania Scandinavian Evangelical Lutheran Congregation [Ephraim MRA], 3028 Church St., Ephraim, 3/27/85, A, a, 85000664

Gibraltar District School No. 2 [Ephraim MRA], 9988 Moravia St., Ephraim, 6/11/85, A, 85001250

Globe Hotel, 8090 Main St., Baileys Harbor, 1/28/82, B, C, 82000663

Globe Hotel, 8090 Main St., Baileys Harbor, 1/28/82, B, C, 82004661

Hillside Hotel [Ephraim MRA], 9980 S. Water St., Ephraim, 3/27/85, A, 85000665

Jischke's Meat Market, 414 Maple Dr., Sister Bay, 9/11/86, A, C, 86002306

LOUISIANA (Shipwreck) [Great Lakes Shipwrecks of Wisconsin MPS], Address Restricted, Washington vicinity, 3/19/92, C, D, 92000104

Larson, L. A., & Co. Store, 306 S. 3rd Ave., Sturgeon Bay, 6/19/85, A, C, 85001357

Louisiana Street/Seventh Avenue Historic District, Roughly bounded by Louisiana and Kentucky Sts., N. 5th, N. 7th, and N. 8th Aves., Sturgeon Bay, 9/22/83, C, 83003372

Namur Belgian-American District, Roughly bounded by CR K, Brussels Rd., WI 57, Belgian Dr., and the Green Bay, Namur vicinity, 11/06/89, A, C, a, d, NHL, 87002553

Peterson, Peter, House [Ephraim MRA], 10020 N. Water St., Ephraim, 3/27/85, A, B, a, 85000666

Pilot Island Light, Portes des Norts Passage, Gills Rock vicinity, 11/21/83, A, 83004279

Pilot Island NW Site [Great Lakes Shipwrecks of Wisconsin MPS], Address Restricted, Washington vicinity, 3/19/92, D, 92000103

Plum Island Range Rear Light [U.S. Coast Guard Lighthouses and Light Stations on the Great Lakes TR], Plum Island, Gills Rock vicinity, 7/19/84, A, C, 84003659

Porte des Morts Site, Address Restricted, Northport vicinity, 3/16/76, D, 76000058

Pottawatomie Lighthouse, NW Rock Island, Washington Island vicinity, 4/20/79, A, 79000074

Rock Island Historic District, Rock Island, off NE tip of Washington Island, Washington vicinity, 5/19/72, D, 72000050

Sherwood Point Light Station [U.S. Coast Guard Lighthouses and Light Stations on the Great Lakes TR], Sherwood Point Road on Green Bay, Sturgeon Bay vicinity, 7/19/84, A, C, 84003663

Sturgeon Bay Canal Lighthouse [U.S. Coast Guard Lighthouses and Light Stations on the Great Lakes TR], Sturgeon Bay Canal, Sturgeon Bay vicinity, 7/19/84, A, C, 84003666

Third Avenue Historic District, Roughly bounded by Kentucky St., N. 2nd, N. 3rd, and S. 3rd Aves., Sturgeon Bay, 10/06/83, A, C, 83004282

Thordarson Estate Historic District [Chester H. Thordarson Estate TR], Rock Island State Park, Washington Island vicinity, 3/21/85, C, 85000641

Water Tower [Chester H. Thordarson Estate TR], Rock Island State Park, Washington Island vicinity, 3/21/85, C, 85000640

Whitefish Dunes—Bay View Site, Address Restricted, Sevastopol vicinity, 12/28/90, D, 90001960

Douglas County

Berkshire Block [Speculative Commercial Blocks of Superior's Boom Period 1888–1892 TR], 917–927 Tower Ave., Superior, 6/27/85, A, C, 85001466

Brule-St. Croix Portage, Brule River State Park, Solon Springs vicinity, 10/15/70, A, 70000033

Davidson Windmill, SE of Superior on WI 13, Superior vicinity, 8/03/79, A, C, 79000075

Douglas County Courthouse [County Courthouses of Wisconsin TR], 1313 Belknap St., Superior, 3/09/82, C, 82000664

Empire Block [Speculative Commercial Blocks of Superior's Boom Period 1888–1892 TR], 1202–1208 Tower Ave., Superior, 6/27/85, A, C, 85001467

Lake Nebagamon Auditorium, 1st St., Lake Nebagamon, 9/14/81, A, C, g, 81000041

METEOR (Whaleback carrier), NW tip of Barkers Island, Superior, 9/09/74, A, 74000081

Maryland Block [Speculative Commercial Blocks of Superior's Boom Period 1888–1892 TR], 1221–1227 Tower Ave., Superior, 6/27/85, A, C, 85001468

Douglas County—Continued

Massachusetts Block [Speculative Commercial Blocks of Superior's Boom Period 1888–1892 TR], 1525–1531 Tower Ave., Superior, 6/27/85, A, C, 85001469

Minnesota Block-Board of Trade Bldg. [Speculative Commercial Blocks of Superior's Boom Period 1888–1892 TR], 1501–1511 Tower Ave., Superior, 6/27/85, A, C, 85001470

New Jersey Building, 1422-1432 Tower Ave. and 1705-1723 Belknap Ave., Superior, 9/22/83, A, C, 83003373

New York Block [Speculative Commercial Blocks of Superior's Boom Period 1888–1892 TR], 1402–1412 Tower Ave., Superior, 6/27/85, A, 85001472

Northern Block [Speculative Commercial Blocks of Superior's Boom Period 1888–1892 TR], 2229 East 5th St., Superior, 6/27/85, A, C, 85001471

Pattison, Martin, House, 906 E. 2nd St., Superior, 2/12/81, B, 81000042

Trade and Commerce Building, 916 Hammond Ave., Superior, 5/08/79, A, C, 79000076

Washington Block [Speculative Commercial Blocks of Superior's Boom Period 1888–1892 TR], 1517–1523 Tower Ave., Superior, 6/27/85, A, C, 85001473

Wemyss Building [Speculative Commercial Blocks of Superior's Boom Period 1888–1892 TR], 1301–1305 Tower Ave., Superior, 6/27/85, A, C, 85001474

Dunn County

Menomonie Downtown Historic District, Roughly bounded by Main and Crescent Sts., Fifth St., Wilson, and Second St. and Broadway, Menomonie, 7/14/86, A, B, C, 86001667

Tainter, Louis Smith, House, Broadway at Crescent, Menomonie, 7/18/74, B, C, 74000082

Tainter, Mabel, Memorial Building, 205 Main St., Menomonie, 7/18/74, B, C, 74000083

Eau Claire County

Barber, James, House [Eau Claire MRA], 132 Marston Ave., Eau Claire, 1/28/83, B, C, 83003374

Barnes Block, 15-21 S. Barstow St., Eau Claire, 1/22/82, C, 82000665

Barron, Martin Van Buren, House [Eau Claire MRA], 221 Washington St., Eau Claire, 1/28/83, C, 83003375

Brice, Orlando, House [Eau Claire MRA], 120 Marston Ave., Eau Claire, 1/28/83, C, 83003376

California Wine and Liquor Store, 201 Farmers St., Fairchild, 3/01/82, C, 82000666

Chicago, St. Paul, Minneapolis & Omaha Railroad Depot [Eau Claire MRA], 324 Putnam Ave., Eau Claire, 10/24/85, C, 85003383

Christ Church Cathedral and Parish House [Eau Claire MRA], 510 S. Farwell St., Eau Claire, 1/28/83, C, a, 83003377

City Hall [Eau Claire MRA], 203 S. Farwell St., Eau Claire, 1/28/83, C, 83003378

Cobblestone House, 1011 State St., Eau Claire, 11/19/74, C, 74000084

Community House, First Congregational Church, 310 Broadway, Eau Claire, 7/18/74, C, a, 74000085

Dells Mill, About 3 mi. NNW of Augusta off WI 27, Augusta vicinity, 12/24/74, A, 74000086

Drummond, David, House, 1310 State St., Eau Claire, 7/30/74, B, C, 74000087

Eau Claire High School [Eau Claire MRA], 314 Doty St., Eau Claire, 1/28/83, C, 83003379

Eau Claire Public Library [Eau Claire MRA], 217 S. Farwell St., Eau Claire, 1/28/83, C, 83003380

Eichert, Christine, House [Eau Claire MRA], 527 N. Barstow St., Eau Claire, 1/28/83, C, 83003381

Emery Street Bungalow District [Eau Claire MRA], Emery St. between Chauncey and Agnes Sts., Eau Claire, 5/20/83, C, 83003382

Johnson, John, Saloon [Eau Claire MRA], 216 Fifth Ave., Eau Claire, 1/28/83, C, 83003383

Kaiser Lumber Company Office [Eau Claire MRA], 1004 Menomonie St., Eau Claire, 1/28/83, A, C, 83003384

Kenyon, A. L., House [Eau Claire MRA], 333 Garfield Ave., Eau Claire, 1/28/83, C, 83003385

Kline's Department Store [Eau Claire MRA], 6-10 S. Barstow St., Eau Claire, 6/14/84, C, 84003669

Merrill, Levi, House [Eau Claire MRA], 120 Ferry St., Eau Claire, 6/20/85, C, 85001358

Ottawa House [Eau Claire MRA], 602 Water St., Eau Claire, 1/28/83, C, 83003386

Owen, John S., House [Eau Claire MRA], 907 Porter Ave., Eau Claire, 1/28/83, B, 83003387

Pioneer Block, 401-409 Water St., Eau Claire, 8/27/80, C, 80000134

Randall Park Historic District [Eau Claire MRA], Roughly bounded by Lake and Niagara Sts., 3rd and 5th Aves., Eau Claire, 5/20/83, C, 83003390

Randall, Adin, House [Eau Claire MRA], 526 Menomonie St., Eau Claire, 1/28/83, B, 83003389

Sacred Heart Church [Eau Claire MRA], 418 N. Dewey St., Eau Claire, 3/03/83, C, a, 83003391

Schofield Hall [Eau Claire MRA], 105 Garfield Ave., Eau Claire, 1/28/83, A, 83003393

St. Joseph's Chapel, Sacred Heart Cemetery, Omaha St., Eau Claire, 1/14/88, C, a, 87002436

St. Patrick's Church [Eau Claire MRA], 322 Fulton St, Eau Claire, 1/28/83, C, a, 83003392

Steven House, 216 Hudson Ave., Eau Claire, 3/01/82, C, 82000667

Temple of Free Masonry, 616 Graham Ave., Eau Claire, 1/14/88, C, 87002450

Third Ward Historic District [Eau Claire MRA], Roughly bounded by Chippewa River, Park Pl., Gilbert Ave., and Farwell St., Eau Claire, 5/20/83, C, 83003394

US Post Office and Courthouse, 500 S. Barstow Commons, Eau Claire, 7/25/91, A, C, 91000899

Union National Bank [Eau Claire MRA], 131 S. Barstow St., Eau Claire, 1/28/83, C, 83003395

Walter-Heins House, 605 N. Barstow St., Eau Claire, 3/19/82, C, 82000668

Wilcox, Roy, House [Eau Claire MRA], 104 Wilcox St, Eau Claire, 1/28/83, B, 83003396

Winslow, George F., House, 210 Oakwood Pl., Eau Claire, 12/08/78, C, 78000094

Florence County

Fay Outlet Site (47FL13), Address Restricted, Long Lake vicinity, 1/17/89, D, 88000647

Fern School, SW of Florence on WI 101, Florence vicinity, 3/20/81, A, 81000043

Florence County Courthouse and Jail [County Courthouses of Wisconsin TR], 501 Lake St., Florence, 12/02/85, C, 85003029

Fond Du Lac County

Aetna Station No. 5, 193 N. Main St., Fond du Lac, 12/12/76, A, C, 76000059

Ceresco Site, Bounded by North, Church, Union, and both sides of Warren Sts., Ripon, 9/05/75, A, 75000064

Chicago and Northwestern Railroad Depot, 182 Forest Ave., Fond du Lac, 8/10/90, A, C, b, 90001232

Club Harbor, Jct. of WI 151 and WI W, Pipe, 1/22/80, A, 80000135

El Dorado Apartments, 130 Forest Ave., Fond du Lac, 1/22/92, C, 91001979

End of the Trail, Madison St. (Shaler Park), Waupun, 8/29/80, A, 80000136

First Baptist Church of Fond du Lac, 90 S. Macy St., Fond du Lac, 12/29/86, C, a, 86003522

First Congregational Church, 220 Ransom St., Ripon, 9/04/79, C, a, 79000077

Galloway, Edwin H., House, 336 E. Pioneer Rd., Fond du Lac, 5/28/76, B, C, 76000060

Horner, John Scott, House, 336 Scott St., Ripon, 9/27/84, B, C, 84003672

Hotel Calumet, 170 Forest Ave., Fond du Lac, 3/20/92, C, 92000111

Hotel Retlaw, 15 E. Division St., Fond du Lac, 9/07/84, A, C, 84003673

Little White Schoolhouse, SE corner of Blackburn and Blossom Sts., Ripon, 8/14/73, A, b, NHL, 73000079

Moose Temple, 17–23 Forest Ave., Fond du Lac, 4/22/93, A, C, 93000340

Octagon House, 276 Linden St., Fond du Lac, 11/03/72, C, 72000051

Pedrick, Marcellus, House, 515 Ransom Ave., Ripon, 9/29/76, C, 76000061

Pipe Site, NE of Fond du Lac, Fond du Lac vicinity, 12/22/78, D, 78000095

Raube Road Site, Address Restricted, Springvale, 6/04/92, A, C, D, 92000589

Recording Angel, The, Forest Mound Cemetery, N. Madison St., Waupun, 7/15/74, C, f, 74000088

Saint John Evangelical Lutheran Church, 670 County Trunk Hwy. S, New Fane, 4/15/86, C, a, 86000794

Fond Du Lac County—Continued

South Main Street Historic District, Roughly, 71–213 S. Main St., Fond du Lac, 3/11/93, A, C, 93000160

St. John the Baptist Catholic Church, Off WI Q, Johnsburg, 10/29/80, A, C, a, 80000137

St. Matthias Mission, 1081 County Trunk S, New Fane vicinity, 10/13/88, A, a, 88001838

St. Peter's Episcopal Church, 217 Houston St., Ripon, 12/31/74, C, a, 74000089

Watson Street Commercial Historic District, Roughly, Watson St. from Seward to Jackson Sts. and Jackson and Scott Sts. from Watson to Blackburn Sts., Ripon, 9/27/91, A, C, 91001396

Woodruff, Jacob, House, 610 Liberty St., Ripon, 12/30/74, C, 74000090

Forest County

Chicago and North-Western Land Office [Public Library Facilities of Wisconson MPS], 4556 N. Branch St., Waubeno, 12/23/93, A, 93001446

Franklin Lake Campground, National Forest Rd. 2181, Alvin vicinity, 9/28/88, A, C, 88001573

Grant County

Agriculture and Manual Arts Building/Platteville State Normal School, Univ. of WI, Platteville, Platteville, 3/14/85, A, C, 85000578

Arthur, L. J., House, 210 N. Jefferson St., Lancaster, 9/05/85, C, 85001951

Ballantine, James, House, 720 North 4th Street, Bloomington, 6/07/76, C, 76000062

Bass Site (47Gt25), Address Restricted, Lancaster vicinity, 9/09/82, D, 82000669

Beebe House, 390 W. Adams St., Platteville, 8/07/79, B, C, 79000078

Boscobel High School, 207 Buchanan St., Boscobel, 12/30/86, A, C, 86003518

Denniston House, 117 E. Front St, Cassville, 2/20/75, A, B, 75000213

Evans, Jonathan H., House, 440 W. Adams St., Platteville, 6/01/82, A, B, 82000670

First Congregational Church, 80 Market, Platteville, 6/19/85, C, a, 85001359

Grant County Courthouse, 126 W. Main St., Lancaster, 10/19/78, A, C, 78000096

Hazel Green Town Hall, 2130 N. Main St., Hazel Green, 1/26/89, A, C, 88003231

Lancaster Municipal Building, 206 S. Madison St., Lancaster, 3/10/83, C, 83003397

Main Street Commercial Historic District, Roughly bounded by Chestnut, Furnace, Bonson, Mineral, Oak, and Pine, Platteville, 3/09/90, A, C, 90000377

Mitchell-Rountree House, Jewett and Lancaster Sts., Platteville, 2/23/72, C, 72000052

Parker, Dwight T., Public Library, 925 Lincoln Ave., Fennimore, 3/10/83, C, 83003398

Potosi Brewery, Main St., Potosi, 11/19/80, A, 80000138

Rountree Hall, 30 North Elm St., Platteville, 12/17/74, A, C, 74000091

Rountree, J. H., Mansion, 150 Rountree Ave., Platteville, 6/13/86, B, C, 86001307

St. John Mine, WI 133, Potosi, 6/04/79, A, 79000079

Stonefield, 2.5 mi. W of Cassville, on CR VV, Cassville vicinity, 5/19/70, B, C, 70000034

Green County

Bingham, Judge John A., House, 621 14th Ave., Monroe, 1/02/76, B, 76000063

Bintliff, Gen. James, House, 723 18th Ave., Monroe, 5/14/79, B, C, 79000080

Blumer, Dr. Samuel, House, 112 Sixth Ave., New Glarus, 11/05/92, A, C, 92001556

Caradine Building, 1007 16th Ave., Monroe, 5/08/79, A, C, 79000081

Chenoweth, Frank L., House, 2004 10th St., Monroe, 10/08/76, C, 76000064

Exchange Square Historic District, Roughly bounded by 10th, RR tracks, E. 2nd and W. 3rd Aves., Brodhead, 11/15/84, A, C, 84000724

First Methodist Church, 11th St. and 14th Ave., Monroe, 2/25/75, A, C, a, 75000065

Freitag's Pure Oil Service Station, 1323 9th St., Monroe, 1/15/80, A, C, 80000139

Green County Courthouse, Courthouse Sq., Monroe, 3/21/78, A, B, C, 78000097

Hulburt, C.D., House, 1205 13th Ave., Monroe, 5/08/79, C, 79000082

Jennings, Janet, House, 612 22nd Ave., Monroe, 1/02/76, B, b, 76000065

Monroe Commerical District, Roughly bounded by 15th and 18th Aves., 9th and 13th Sts., Monroe, 5/06/82, A, C, g, 82000671

Regez, Jacob, Sr., House, 2121 7th St., Monroe, 1/17/80, A, B, C, 80000140

Smith, Francis West, House, 1002 W. 2nd Ave., Brodhead, 4/17/79, C, 79000083

West, Gen. Francis H., House, 1410 17th Ave., Monroe, 1/01/75, C, 75000066

White, F. F., Block, 1514-1524 11th St., Monroe, 1/31/79, A, B, C, 79000084

Green Lake County

Beckwith House Hotel, 101 W. Huron St., Berlin, 9/13/91, A, 91001389

Beckwith, Nelson F., House, 179 E. Huron St., Berlin, 4/06/90, C, 90000575

Green Lake County Courthouse [County Courthouses of Wisconsin TR], 492 Hill St., Green Lake, 3/09/82, C, 82000672

Hamilton-Brooks Site, S of Berlin, Berlin vicinity, 12/19/78, D, 78000098

Huron Street Historic District, Roughly, Huron St. from Fox R. to 124 E. Huron, including adjacent side streets, Berlin, 8/31/92, A, C, 92001140

Wisconsin Power and Light Berlin Power Plant, 142 Water St., Berlin, 3/19/92, A, C, 92000157

Iowa County

Archeological Site No. 47Ia168 [Wisconsin Indian Rock Art Sites MPS], Address Restricted, Brigham, 8/21/92, D, 92001025

Archeological Site No. 47Ia167 [Wisconsin Indian Rock Art Sites MPS], Address Restricted, Brigham, 8/21/92, D, 92001026

Brisbane, William Henry, House, Reimann Rd., .6 mi. S of US 14, Arena, 9/13/90, C, 90001458

Carden Rockshelter [Wisconsin Indian Rock Art Sites MPS], Address Restricted, Brigham, 8/05/93, D, 93000808

Cassidy Farmhouse [Barneveld MRA], Off WI K N of US 18/151, Barneveld, 9/29/86, C, 86002297

DNR #4 Rockshelter [Wisconsin Indian Rock Art Sites MPS], Address Restricted, Brigham vicinity, 1/30/91, D, 90002156

DNR No. 5 Archeological Site [Wisconsin Indian Rock Art Sites MPS], Address Restricted, Brigham, 5/21/92, D, 92000592

Gottschall Site (47Ia80), Address Restricted, Highland vicinity, 6/30/83, D, 83003399

Grove Street Historic District [Barneveld MRA], 304–316 Grove St., Barneveld, 9/29/86, A, C, 86002313

Harris House [Barneveld MRA], 202 W. Wood St., Barneveld, 9/29/86, C, 86002299

Hole-in-the-Wall #1 Cave [Wisconsin Indian Rock Art Sites MPS], Address Restricted, Brigham vicinity, 1/30/91, D, 90002157

Hyde Chapel, 1 mi. S of CTH H on CTH T, Ridgeway, 10/13/88, C, a, d, 88002002

Ihm House [Barneveld MRA], 203 N. Garfield St., Barneveld, 9/29/86, C, 86002301

Iowa County Courthouse, NW corner of Iowa and Chapel Sts., Dodgeville, 2/01/72, C, 72000053

Kittleson House [Barneveld MRA], 104 W. Wood St., Barneveld, 9/29/86, C, 86002304

Linden High School, 344 E. Main St., Linden, 11/04/93, A, C, 93001168

Linden Methodist Church, Main and Church Sts., Linden, 10/19/78, A, C, a, 78000099

Mayland Cave, Address Restricted, Dodgeville vicinity, 12/22/78, D, 78000100

McCoy Rock Art Site [Wisconsin Indian Rock Art Sites MPS], Address Restricted, Moscow, 4/19/91, D, 91000467

Mineral Point Hill, Roughly bounded by WI 23, Copper, Dodge, and Shake Rag Sts., Mineral Point, 10/26/72, A, C, 72000054

Mineral Point Historic District, Roughly bounded by Ross, Shake Rag, 9th, and Bend Sts., Mineral Point, 7/30/71, A, C, 71000037

Old Rock School, 914 Bequette St., Dodgeville, 12/18/78, A, C, e, 78000101

Pendarvis, 114 Shake Rag St., Mineral Point, 1/25/71, A, C, 71000038

Roberts House [Barneveld MRA], 302 Front St., Barneveld, 9/01/88, C, 86002311

Iowa County—Continued

Roethlisberger House [Barneveld MRA], 205 N. Grove St., Barneveld, 9/29/86, C, 86002312

Sawle Mound Group Archeological District [Late Woodland Stage in Archeological Region 8 MPS], Address Restricted, Arena, 6/07/91, D, 91000672

Shiprock Rockshelter [Wisconsin Indian Rock Art Sites MPS], Address Restricted, Pulaski, 5/21/92, D, 92000591

Shot Tower, SE of Spring Green in Tower Hill State Park, Spring Green vicinity, 4/03/73, A, C, 73000080

Taliesin, 2 mi. S of Spring Green on WI 23, Spring Green vicinity, 4/14/73, A, C, g, NHL, 73000081

Unity Chapel, S of Spring Green off WI 23, Spring Green vicinity, 7/18/74, C, a, 74000092

Iron County

Annala Round Barn, S of Hurley, Hurley vicinity, 8/27/79, A, C, 79000085

Montreal Company Location Historic District, WI 77, Montreal, 5/23/80, A, 80000141

Old Iron County Courthouse, 303 Iron St., Hurley, 7/26/77, A, C, 77000031

Jackson County

Gullickson's Glen, Address Restricted, Black River Falls vicinity, 12/21/78, D, 78000102

Silver Mound Archeological District, Address Restricted, Alma Center vicinity, 1/17/75, D, 75000067

Union High School, N. 3rd St., Black River Falls, 1/20/78, C, 78000103

Jefferson County

Aztalan, Near Lake Mills on WI 89, Aztalan State Park, Lake Mills vicinity, 10/15/66, D, e, NHL, 66000022

Beals and Torrey Shoe Co. Building, 100 W. Milwaukee St., Watertown, 12/06/84, A, 84000699

Bean Lake Islands Archeological District, Address Restricted, Lake Mills, 8/12/82, D, 82000673

Carcajou Point (47 Je 2), Address Restricted, Busseyville vicinity, 9/18/79, D, 79000088

Carcajou Point Site (Boundary Increase), Address Restricted, Sumner, 9/05/91, D, 91001370

Chicago and Northwest Railroad Passenger Station, 725 W. Main St., Watertown, 3/28/79, A, C, 79000086

Copeland—Ryder Company, 411 Wisconsin Dr., Jefferson, 4/13/89, A, 89000233

Crab Apple Point Site, Address Restricted, Edgerton vicinity, 12/22/78, D, 78000104

Enterprise Building, 125 W. Main St., Palmyra, 6/05/75, A, C, 75000068

Fargo, Enoch J., House, 406 Mulberry St., Lake Mills, 7/08/82, B, C, 82000674

Fargo, L. D., Public Library, 120 E. Madison St., Lake Mills, 1/18/82, A, C, 82000675

First Kindergarten, 919 Charles St., Watertown, 2/23/72, A, B, b, 72000055

Fuermann, August, Jr., and Eliza, House, 500 S. Third St., Watertown, 7/27/89, C, 89001002

Haight Creek Mound Group (47-Je-38), Address Restricted, Fort Atkinson vicinity, 8/05/85, D, 85001751

Highsmith Site, NE of Fort Atkinson, Fort Atkinson vicinity, 12/01/78, D, 78000106

Hoard Mound Group (47JE33), Address Restricted, Fort Atkinson vicinity, 5/10/84, D, 84003678

Hoard's Dairyman Farm, N of Fort Atkinson, Fort Atkinson vicinity, 8/29/78, A, B, 78000105

Hoard, Arthur R., House, 323 Merchants Ave., Fort Atkinson, 11/30/82, B, C, 82001845

Jefferson Fire Station, 146 E. Milwaukee St., Jefferson, 12/06/84, A, C, 84000695

Jefferson Public Library, 305 S. Main St., Jefferson, 1/17/80, C, 80000142

Jones Dairy Farm, Jones Ave., Fort Atkinson, 12/27/78, A, B, g, 78000107

Main Street Commercial Historic District, Roughly Main St. from N. Washington St. to S. Seventh St., Watertown, 6/02/89, A, C, 89000483

Main Street Historic District, Roughly Main St. from Sherman Ave. to S. 3rd St., Fort Atkinson, 6/07/84, A, C, 84003683

May, Eli, House, 407 E. Milwaukee Ave., Fort Atkinson, 9/14/72, A, D, 72000056

McKenzie, Monroe, House, 226 Main St., Palmyra, 6/19/85, C, 85001360

Merchants Avenue Historic District, Roughly bounded by S. Third St. E and S. Milwaukee Ave. E, Foster St., Whitewater, and Merchant Aves., Fort Atkinson, 6/13/86, B, C, 86001303

Octagon House, 919 Charles St., Watertown, 11/23/71, C, 71000039

Panther Intaglio Effigy Mound, Address Restricted, Fort Atkinson vicinity, 10/15/70, D, 70000035

Pioneer Aztalan Site, SE corner at jct. of SR B and Sr Q, Aztalan, 2/25/75, A, C, b, 75000069

Pitzner Site (47 Je 676), , Jefferson vicinity, 7/06/82, D, 82000676

Puerner Block-Breunig's Brewery, 101-115 E. Racine, 110-112 N. Main St., Jefferson, 6/14/84, A, C, 84003687

Smith, Richard C., House, 332 E. Linden St., Jefferson, 4/19/79, C, g, 79000338

St. Paul's Episcopal Church, 413 S 2nd St., Watertown, 11/07/79, C, a, 79000087

St. Wenceslaus Roman Catholic Church, SE of Waterloo at jct. of Blue Point and Island Rds., Waterloo vicinity, 5/12/75, A, C, a, 75000070

Juneau County

Boorman, Benjamin, House, 211 N. Union St., Mauston, 5/04/76, B, C, 76000066

Cranberry Creek Archeological District, Address Restricted, Necedah National Wildlife Refuge vicinity, 7/19/84, D, 84003689

Gee's Slough Mound Group, Address Restricted, New Lisbon vicinity, 3/08/78, D, 78000108

Juneau County Courthouse [County Courthouses of Wisconsin TR], 220 E. State St., Mauston, 11/04/82, A, g, 82001846

Lemonweir Glyphs [Wisconsin Indian Rock Art Sites MPS], Address Restricted, Kildare, 11/04/93, D, 93001173

Weston-Babcock House, Main St., Necedah, 1/29/79, A, C, 79000089

Kenosha County

Barnes Creek Site, Address Restricted, Kenosha vicinity, 7/20/77, D, NHL, 77000032

Boys and Girls Library, 5810 8th Ave., Kenosha, 10/24/80, A, B, C, 80000144

Chesrow Site, S of Kenosha on WI 32, Kenosha vicinity, 11/30/78, D, 78000109

Civic Center Historic District, Roughly bounded by 55th St., 8th Ave., 58th St., and 10th Ave., Kenosha, 7/26/89, A, C, b, 89000069

Kemper Hall, 6501 3rd Ave., Kenosha, 6/07/76, B, C, a, 76000067

Kenosha County Courthouse and Jail [County Courthouses of Wisconsin TR], 912 56th St., Kenosha, 3/09/82, A, C, 82000677

Kenosha Light Station, 5117 Fourth Ave., Kenosha, 6/28/90, A, 90000995

Library Park Historic District, Roughly bounded by 59th St., 7th Ave., 61st St., and 8th Ave., Kenosha, 11/29/88, A, B, C, a, 88002657

Manor House, 6536 3rd Ave., Kenosha, 10/29/80, C, 80000145

McCaffary, John, House, 5732 13th Court, Kenosha, 1/31/78, A, B, 78000110

Simmons, Gilbert M., Memorial Library, 711 59th Pl., Kenosha, 12/17/74, C, f, 74000093

St. Matthew's Episcopal Church, 5900 7th Ave., Kenosha, 6/06/79, A, C, a, 79000090

Third Avenue Historic District, Along Third Ave. between 61st and 66th Sts., Kenosha, 11/01/88, A, B, C, b, 88002022

Weed, Justin, House, 3509 Washington Rd., Kenosha, 12/03/74, C, 74000094

Wehmhoff Mound (47KN15), Address Restricted, Wheatland vicinity, 11/21/85, A, D, 85002971

Kewaunee County

Dettman, Art, Fishing Shanty, Church St. at the Ahnapee R., Algoma, 12/10/93, A, 93001428

Halada, George, Farmstead, E-1113 Co. Trunk Hwy. F, Montpelier Township, Ellisville vicinity, 2/11/93, C, 93000026

Marquette Historic District, Roughly bounded by Lake Michigan and Center, Juneau and Lincoln Sts., Kewaunee, 11/04/93, C, 93001167

Kewaunee County—Continued

Pilgrim Family Farmstead, SW of Kewanee on Church Rd., Kewaunee, 5/08/79, A, B, C, 79000091

St. Lawrence Catholic Church, Jct. of WI 163 and County Hwy. J, Stangelville, 2/21/89, A, C, a, b, d, 89000056

La Crosse County

Agger Rockshelter, Address Restricted, Stevenstown vicinity, 3/25/88, D, 87002239

Anderson, Mons, House, 410 Cass St., La Crosse, 5/06/75, B, C, 75000071

Barron, E.R., Building, 426–430 Main St., LaCrosse, 6/19/85, A, C, 85001362

Bridge No. 1 [Van Loon Wildlife Area Truss Bridge TR], NW of La Crosse, La Crosse vicinity, 2/27/80, A, C, 80000146

Bridge No. 2 [Van Loon Wildlife Area Truss Bridge TR], NW of La Crosse, La Crosse vicinity, 2/27/80, A, C, 80000147

Bridge No. 3 [Van Loon Wildlife Area Truss Bridge TR], NW of La Crosse, La Crosse vicinity, 2/27/80, A, C, 80000148

Bridge No. 4 [Van Loon Wildlife Area Truss Bridge TR], NW of La Crosse, La Crosse vicinity, 2/27/80, A, C, 80000149

Bridge No. 5 [Van Loon Wildlife Area Truss Bridge TR], NW of La Crosse, La Crosse vicinity, 2/27/80, A, C, 80000150

Bridge No. 6 [Van Loon Wildlife Area Truss Bridge TR], NW of La Crosse, La Crosse vicinity, 2/27/80, A, C, 80000151

Chambers—Markle Farmstead, 6104 WI 35, La Crosse, 3/22/91, C, 91000341

Chase, Dr. H. H., and Henry G. Wohlhuter Bungalows, 221 and 223 S. 11th St., La Crosse, 6/30/83, C, 83003400

Christ Church of LaCrosse, 831 Main St., LaCrosse, 6/19/85, C, a, 85001361

Freight House, 107-109 Vine St., La Crosse, 3/02/82, A, C, 82000678

Garland, Hamlin, House, 357 W. Garland St., West Salem, 11/11/71, B, NHL, 71000040

Hixon, Gideon C., House, 429 N. 7th St., La Crosse, 12/30/74, B, C, 74000095

La Crosse County School of Agriculture and Domestic Economy, 700 Wilson Ave., Onalaska, 3/13/87, A, C, 87000438

Laverty-Martindale House, 237 S. 10th St., La Crosse, 11/23/77, C, 77000033

Main Hall/La Crosse State Normal School, 1724 State St., Univ. of WI, La Crosse, La Crosse, 3/14/85, A, C, 85000579

Midway Village Site, W of Holmen, Holmen vicinity, 12/18/78, D, 78000111

Nichols, Frank Eugene, House, 421 N. Second St., Onalaska, 2/11/93, B, 93000027

Ott, Will, House, 1532 Madison St., La Crosse, 1/15/80, B, C, 80000152

Our Lady of Sorrows Chapel, 519 Losey Blvd. S, La Crosse, 9/11/86, C, a, 86002302

Overhead Site, S of La Crosse, La Crosse vicinity, 12/18/78, D, 78000112

Palmer Brother's Octagons, 358 N. Leonard St. and WI 16, West Salem and Vicinity, 8/07/79, C, b, 79000092

Physical Education Building/La Crosse State Normal School, UW La Crosse Campus off US 16, La Crosse, 4/11/85, A, C, 85000791

Powell Place, 200-212 Main St., La Crosse, 12/22/83, B, C, 83004299

Roosevelt, W. A., Company, 230 N. Front St., La Crosse, 2/16/84, A, C, 84003690

Samuels' Cave, Address Restricted, Barre Mills vicinity, 6/11/91, A, D, 86003275

Sand Lake Archeological District, Address Restricted, Onalaska vicinity, 4/20/84, D, 84003694

Sand Lake Site (47Lc44), Address Restricted, Onalaska vicinity, 6/30/83, D, 83003401

Smith Valley School, 4130 Smith Valley Rd., La Crosse vicinity, 7/30/81, A, 81000044

Swennes Archaeological District, Address Restricted, Onalaska vicinity, 7/18/85, D, 85001573

U.S. Fish Control Laboratory, Riverside Park, La Crosse, 9/17/81, A, 81000045

Valley View Site, N of Medary, Medary vicinity, 12/15/78, D, 78000113

Vincent, James, House, 1024 Cass St., La Crosse, 10/20/88, C, 88002024

Waterworks Building, 119 King St., La Crosse, 7/27/79, C, 79000093

Wisconsin Telephone Company Building, 125 N. 4th St., La Crosse, 3/07/85, C, 85000491

Zeisler, George, Building, 201 Pearl St., La Crosse, 2/25/93, C, 93000069

Lafayette County

First Capitol, N of Belmont off U.S. 151, Belmont vicinity, 4/28/70, A, 70000036

Gratiot House, S of Shullsburg on Rennick Rd., Shullsburg vicinity, 1/08/80, A, C, 80000153

Lafayette County Courthouse, 626 Main St., Darlington, 12/22/78, A, C, 78000114

St. Augustine Church, Off CR W, New Diggings, 2/23/72, C, a, 72000057

Star Theatre, 200 S. North St., Argyle, 11/07/80, A, C, 80000154

Water Street Commercial Historic District, Roughly Water St. from Judgement to Kennedy Sts. and Gratiot St. from Water to Church Sts., Shullsburg, 6/28/90, A, C, a, 90000998

Langlade County

Antigo Depot, 522 Morse St., Antigo, 2/10/92, A, C, 92000029

Antigo Opera House, 1016 5th Ave., Antigo, 1/12/84, A, 84003699

Antigo Public Library and Deleglise Cabin, 404 Superior St., Antigo, 12/18/78, A, B, C, b, 78000115

Langlade County Courthouse, 800 Clermont St., Antigo, 7/25/77, C, 77000034

Lincoln County

Lincoln County Courthouse, 1110 E. Main St., Merrill, 4/19/78, A, C, 78000116

Merrill City Hall, 717 E. 2nd St., Merrill, 7/12/78, A, 78000117

Scott, T. B., Free Library, E. 1st St., Merrill, 1/21/74, A, B, C, 74000096

Manitowoc County

Eighth Street Historic District, Roughly bounded by Buffalo St., Eighth and Seventh Sts., Hancock St., and Tenth, Ninth and Quay Sts., Manitowoc, 3/17/88, A, C, 88000215

Frenchside Fishing Village, Twenty-first, Jackson, East, Sixteenth, Harbor, and Rogers Sts., Two Rivers, 1/06/87, A, 86003580

Loreto Shrine Chapel [Colony of St. Gregory of Nazianzen TR], Off WI A, St. Nazianz, 6/07/82, A, a, 82000679

Lutze Housebarn, 13634 S. Union Rd., Newton vicinity, 6/07/84, A, C, 84003702

Manitowoc County Courthouse, 8th and Washington Sts., Manitowoc, 4/16/81, A, C, 81000047

Rawley Point Light Station [U.S. Coast Guard Lighthouses and Light Stations on the Great Lakes TR], Point Beach State Forest, Two Rivers vicinity, 7/19/84, A, C, 84003706

Rock Mill, Off U.S. 141, Maribel, 6/21/82, C, 82000680

St. Gregory's Church [Colony of St. Gregory of Nazianzen TR], 212 Church St., St. Nazianz, 6/07/82, A, a, 82000681

USS COBIA (submarine), 809 S. Eighth St., Manitowoc, 1/14/86, A, g, NHL, 86000087

Vilas, Joseph, Jr., House, 610-616 N. 8th St., Manitowoc, 4/29/77, B, C, 77000035

Marathon County

Andrew Warren Historic District, Roughly bounded by Fulton, Grant, 4th, and 7th Sts., Wausau, 1/05/84, A, C, 84003708

Bird, C. B., House [Eschweiler TR of Marathon County], 522 McIndoe St., Wausau, 5/01/80, B, C, 80000155

Dessert, Joseph, Library [Eschweiler TR of Marathon County], 123 Main St., Mosinee, 5/01/80, B, C, 80000156

Dunbar, C. F., House [Eschweiler TR of Marathon County], 929 McIndoe St., Wausau, 5/01/80, C, 80000157

Everest, D. C., House [Eschweiler TR of Marathon County], 1206 Highland Park Blvd., Wausau, 5/01/80, B, C, 80000158

Marathon County—Continued

First Universalist Church [Eschweiler TR of Marathon County], 504 Grant St., Wausau, 5/01/80, C, a, 80000159

Fricke—Menzner House, 105 Main St., Marathon, 7/16/92, B, C, 92000856

Fromm, Walter and Mabel, House, Off WI 107, Hamburg, 6/17/82, C, 82000682

Jones, Granville D., House, 915 Grant St., Wausau, 12/07/77, B, C, 77000036

Maine Site (47MR22), Address Restricted, Brokaw vicinity, 7/19/84, D, 84003711

Marathon County Fairgrounds [Eschweiler TR of Marathon County], Stewart Ave., Wausau, 5/01/80, A, C, 80000160

Mathie, Karl, House [Eschweiler TR of Marathon County], 202 Water St., Mosinee, 5/01/80, B, C, 80000161

Miller, Henry, House, 1314 Grand Ave., Wausau, 6/14/82, B, C, b, 82000683

Schuetz, E.K., House [Eschweiler TR of Marathon County], 930 Franklin St., Wausau, 5/01/80, B, C, 80000162

Single, Benjamin, House, W of Wausau at 4708 Stettin Dr., Wausau vicinity, 11/24/80, B, C, 80000163

Stewart, Hiram C., House, 521 Grant St., Wausau, 8/30/74, C, 74000097

Wausau Club, 309 McClellan St., Wausau, 9/14/89, A, C, 89001420

Wegner, C. H., House [Eschweiler TR of Marathon County], 906 Grant St., Wausau, 5/01/80, B, C, 80000164

Wright, Ely, House, 901 6th St., Wausau, 3/01/82, C, 82000684

Yawkey, Cyrus C., House, 403 McIndoe St., Wausau, 12/31/74, B, C, 74000098

Marinette County

Amberg Town Hall, Grant St., Amberg, 3/20/81, A, C, 81000048

Bijou Theatre Building, 1722-1726 Main St., Marinette, 3/11/93, C, 93000159

Dunlap Square Building, 1821 Hall St., Marinette, 2/24/92, C, 92000026

Lauerman Brothers Department Store, 1701-1721 Dunlap Sq., Marinette, 2/24/92, A, C, b, 92000027

Lauerman, F.J., House, 383 State St., Marinette, 8/14/79, A, B, C, 79000094

Peshtigo Fire Cemetery, Oconto Ave. between Peck and Ellis Aves., Peshtigo, 10/15/70, A, f, 70000037

Marquette County

Bonnie Oaks Historic District, Grouse Dr., Briggsville vicinity, 4/03/86, B, D, 86000626

Fountain Lake Farm, Co. Hwy. F and Gillette Rd., Montello vicinity, 6/21/90, B, NHL, 90000471

Marquette County Courthouse and Marquette County Sheriff's Office and Jail [County Courthouses of Wisconsin TR], 77 W. Park St., Montello, 3/09/82, C, 82000685

Milwaukee County

Abbot Row, 1019-1043 E. Ogden Ave., Milwaukee, 3/03/83, C, 83003402

Abresch, Charles, House [West Side Area MRA], 2126 W. Juneau Ave., Milwaukee, 1/16/86, B, C, 86000095

Adler, Emanuel D., House, 1681 N. Prospect Ave., Milwaukee, 9/13/91, C, 91001397

All Saints' Episcopal Cathedral Complex, 804-828 E. Juneau Ave., Milwaukee, 12/27/74, A, C, a, 74000099

Allis, Charles, House, 1630 E. Royall Pl., Milwaukee, 1/17/75, B, C, 75000072

American System Built Homes-Burnham Street District, W. Burnham St., Milwaukee, 9/12/85, C, 85002166

Annunciation Greek Orthodox Church, 9400 W. Congress St., Wauwatosa, 12/19/74, C, a, g, 74000100

Arndt, Rufus, House [Ernest Flagg Stone Masonry Houses of Milwaukee County TR], 4524 N. Cramer St., Whitefish Bay, 9/12/85, C, 85002016

Astor on the Lake, 924 E. Juneau Ave., Milwaukee, 9/06/84, C, 84003715

Baasen House-German YMCA [Brewers' Hill MRA], 1702 N. 4th St., Milwaukee, 8/02/84, A, 84003718

Barfield-Staples House [Ernest Flagg Stone Masonry Houses of Milwaukee County TR], 5461-5463 Danbury Rd., Whitefish Bay, 9/12/85, C, 85002017

Baumbach Building, 302 N. Broadway St., Milwaukee, 3/03/83, C, 83003403

Bay View Historic District, Roughly bounded by Lake Michigan, Meredith, Superior, Nock, Wentworth, Pryor, Clair, RR tracks and Conway St., Milwaukee, 8/23/82, A, C, 82000686

Blatz Brewery Complex, 1101-1147 N. Broadway, Milwaukee, 4/15/86, A, C, 86000793

Blatz, Valentin, Brewing Company Office Building, 1120 N. Broadway, Milwaukee, 3/31/83, A, C, 83003404

Bogk, Frederick C., House, 2420 N. Terrace Ave., Milwaukee, 10/18/72, C, 72000058

Bossert, Thomas, House [Ernest Flagg Stone Masonry Houses of Milwaukee County TR], 2614 E. Menlo Blvd., Shorewood, 9/12/85, C, 85002018

Brown Deer School, 4800 W. Green Brook Dr., Brown Deer, 12/10/93, A, C, b, 93001427

Buemming, Herman W., House, 1012 E. Pleasant St., Milwaukee, 1/18/90, C, 89002315

Burnham, J. L., Block, 907-911 W. National Ave., Milwaukee, 2/11/88, A, C, 88000086

Calkins, Elias A., Doublehouse, 1612-1614 E. Kane Pl., Milwaukee, 1/18/90, C, 89002313

Calvary Presbyterian Church [West Side Area MRA], 935 W. Wisconsin Ave., Milwaukee, 3/10/86, C, a, 86000098

Carpenter, Michael, House [West Side Area MRA], 1115 Thirty-fifth St., Milwaukee, 1/16/86, C, a, 86000096

Cass—Juneau Street Historic District, Roughly bounded by E. Knapp and Marshall Sts., Juneau Ave., and Van Buren St., Milwaukee, 11/03/88, C, a, 88002389

Cass—Wells Street Historic District, 712, 718, and 724 E. Wells St. and 801, 809, 815, 819, and 823 N. Cass St., Milwaukee, 6/13/86, C, 86001325

Central Library, 814 W. Wisconsin Ave., Milwaukee, 12/30/74, C, 74000101

Chief Lippert Fire Station, 642 W. North Ave., Milwaukee, 10/28/88, C, 88002007

Christ Evangelical Lutheran Church, 2235 W. Greenfield Ave., Milwaukee, 9/25/87, C, a, 87001735

Church Street Historic District, 1448-1630 Church St. and 7758 W. Menomonee River Pkwy., Wauwatosa, 8/10/89, C, 89001099

Church, Benjamin, House, Parkway Dr., Eastabrook Park, Shorewood, 2/23/72, C, b, 72000059

Coast Guard Station, Old, 1600 N. Lincoln Memorial Dr., Milwaukee, 8/07/89, A, C, 89001047

Concordia Historic District [West Side Area MRA], Roughly bounded by West State, N. 27th, W. Killbourn Ave. and N. 35th St., Milwaukee, 7/30/85, A, B, C, g, 85001688

Congregation Beth Israel Synagogue, 2432 N. Teutonia Ave., Milwaukee, 3/05/92, A, C, a, 92000107

Cook, Thomas, House [West Side Area MRA], 853 N. Seventeenth St., Milwaukee, 1/16/86, C, 86000104

Cords, Erwin, House [Ernest Flagg Stone Masonry Houses of Milwaukee County TR], 1913 E. Olive St., Shorewood, 9/12/85, C, 85002019

Curtin, Jeremiah, House, 8685 W. Grange Ave., Greendale, 11/07/72, B, C, 72000060

Dahinden, Edward J., House [West Side Area MRA], 3316 W. Wisconsin Ave., Milwaukee, 2/25/86, C, 86000313

Damon, Lowell, House, 2107 N. Wauwatosa Ave., Wauwatosa, 2/23/72, C, 72000061

Davis, H. R., House [Ernest Flagg Stone Masonry Houses of Milwaukee County TR], 6839 Cedar St., Wauwatosa, 9/12/85, C, 85002020

Desmond—Farnham—Hustis House, 1535 N. Marshall St., Milwaukee, 1/18/90, C, 89002314

Eagles Club [West Side Area MRA], 2401 W. Wisconsin Ave., Milwaukee, 7/29/86, C, g, 86002096

East Brady Street Historic District, E. Brady St. from N. Farwell Ave. to N. Van Buren St., Milwaukee, 3/09/90, A, C, a, b, 90000363

East Side Commercial Historic District, Roughly bounded by E. Wells St., N. Jefferson St. and N. Broadway, Michigan and E. Clybourn, and N. Water Sts., Milwaukee, 9/23/86, A, C, g, 86002325

Elderwood, 6789 N. Elm Tree Rd., Glendale, 12/04/80, C, 80000165

Esbenshade, Abraham H., House [West Side Area MRA], 3119 W. Wells St., Milwaukee, 1/16/86, C, 86000106

Milwaukee County—Continued

Federal Building, 515-519 E. Wisconsin Ave., Milwaukee, 3/14/73, C, 73000082

Fiebing, J. H., House [Ernest Flagg Stone Masonry Houses of Milwaukee County TR], 7707 Stickney, Wauwatosa, 9/12/85, C, 85002021

Fiebing, Otto F., House [Ernest Flagg Stone Masonry Houses of Milwaukee County TR], 302 N. Hawley Rd., Milwaukee, 9/12/85, C, 85002022

First Church of Christ, Scientist, 1443-1451 N. Prospect Ave., Milwaukee, 3/08/89, C, a, 89000070

First Unitarian Church, 1009 E. Ogden Ave., Milwaukee, 12/30/74, C, a, 74000102

First Ward Triangle Historic District, Roughly Franklin Pl., N. Prospect and E. Juneau Aves., and E. Knapp St., Milwaukee, 3/19/87, B, C, 87000489

Forest Home Cemetery and Chapel, 2405 Forest Home Ave., Milwaukee, 11/03/80, A, B, C, d, g, 80000166

Foth, Christian, House, 1209–1211 S. Seventh St., Milwaukee, 3/22/88, C, 88000218

Fourth Street School [Brewers' Hill MRA], 333 W. Galena St., Milwaukee, 8/02/84, B, C, NHL, 84003720

Gabel, George, House [Ernest Flagg Stone Masonry Houses of Milwaukee County TR], 4600 N. Cramer St., Whitefish Bay, 9/12/85, C, 85002023

Gallun Tannery Historic District [Brewers' Hill MRA], Holton and Water Sts., Milwaukee, 8/02/84, A, C, 84003721

Garden Homes Historic District, Roughly bounded by W. Ruby and N. Teutonia Aves., N. 24th Pl., W. Atkinson Ave. and N. 27th St., Milwaukee, 5/04/90, A, 90000669

George, Warren B., House [Ernest Flagg Stone Masonry Houses of Milwaukee County TR], 7105 Grand Pkwy., Wauwatosa, 9/12/85, C, 85002024

German-English Academy, 1020 N. Broadway, Milwaukee, 4/11/77, A, C, 77000037

Germania Building, 135 W. Wells St., Milwaukee, 7/07/83, A, B, C, g, 83003405

Gesu Church [West Side Area MRA], 1145 W. Wisconsin Ave., Milwaukee, 1/16/86, C, a, 86000108

Graham Row, 1501, 1503, and 1507 N. Marshall St., Milwaukee, 7/27/79, C, 79000095

Grand Avenue Congregational Church [West Side Area MRA], 2133 W. Wisconsin Ave., Milwaukee, 1/16/86, C, a, 86000110

Grant, Paul S., House [Ernest Flagg Stone Masonry Houses of Milwaukee County TR], 984 E. Circle Dr., Whitefish Bay, 9/12/85, C, 85002025

Greene, Thomas A., Memorial Museum, 3367 N. Downer Ave., Milwaukee, 11/04/93, A, B, NHL, 93001615

Hardie, Harrison, House [Ernest Flagg Stone Masonry Houses of Milwaukee County TR], 4540 N. Cramer St., Whitefish Bay, 9/12/85, C, 85002026

Hart, Thomas B., House, 1609 Church St., Wauwatosa, 10/10/85, B, C, 85003135

Hatch, Horace W., House [Ernest Flagg Stone Masonry Houses of Milwaukee County TR], 739 E. Beaumont, Whitefish Bay, 9/12/85, C, 85002027

Henni Hall, 3257 S. Lake Dr., St. Francis, 7/24/74, A, C, a, 74000103

Highland Avenue Methodist Church [West Side Area MRA], 2024 W. Highland Ave., Milwaukee, 1/16/86, A, C, a, 86000114

Highland Boulevard Historic District [West Side Area MRA], W. Highland Blvd. roughly bounded by N. 33rd and N. 29th Sts., Milwaukee, 7/30/85, A, B, C, 85001686

Historic Third Ward District, Bounded by the Milwaukee River, C and NW RR, and E. St. Paul and N. Jackson Sts., Milwaukee, 3/08/84, A, C, 84003724

Hoelz, Alfred M., House [Ernest Flagg Stone Masonry Houses of Milwaukee County TR], 3449–3451 Frederick Ave., Milwaukee, 9/12/85, C, 85002029

Holy Trinity Roman Catholic Church, 605 S. 4th St., Milwaukee, 11/07/72, A, C, a, 72000062

Home Office, Northwestern Mutual Life Insurance Company, 605-623 N. Broadway, Milwaukee, 3/20/73, A, C, 73000083

Hopkins, Willis, House [Ernest Flagg Stone Masonry Houses of Milwaukee County TR], 325 Glenview, Wauwatosa, 9/12/85, C, 85002030

Howie, David W., House [West Side Area MRA], 3026 W. Wells St., Milwaukee, 1/16/86, C, 86000116

Immanuel Presbyterian Church, 1100 N. Astor St., Milwaukee, 12/27/74, C, a, 74000104

Iron Block, 205 E. Wisconsin Ave., Milwaukee, 12/27/74, C, 74000105

Jenkins, Halbert D., House [Ernest Flagg Stone Masonry Houses of Milwaukee County TR], 1028 E. Lexington Blvd., Whitefish Bay, 9/12/85, C, 85002031

Johnston Hall [West Side Area MRA], 1121 W. Wisconsin Ave., Milwaukee, 1/16/86, A, C, 86000118

Kalvelage, Joseph B., House, 2432 W. Kilbourn Ave., Milwaukee, 5/23/78, C, 78000118

Kane, Sanford R., House, 1841 N. Prospect Ave., Milwaukee, 9/13/91, C, 91001398

Ketter, Frederick, Warehouse [Brewers' Hill MRA], 325 W. Vine St., Milwaukee, 8/02/84, C, 84003725

Kilbourn Avenue Row House Historic District [West Side Area MRA], Roughly bounded by N. Fourteenth St., W. Kilbourn Ave., and N. Fifteenth St., Milwaukee, 2/25/86, C, 86000311

Kilbourn Masonic Temple [West Side Area MRA], 827 N. Eleventh St., Milwaukee, 1/16/86, C, 86000121

Knapp-Astor House, 930 E. Knapp St. and 1301 N. Astor St., Milwaukee, 3/27/80, C, 80000167

Kneeland—Walker House, 7406 Hillcrest Dr., Wauwatosa, 1/19/89, C, 88003212

Knickerbocker Hotel, 1028 E. Juneau Ave., Milwaukee, 6/02/88, C, 88000680

LIGHT VESSEL No. 57 (Shipwreck), Address Restricted, Milwaukee vicinity, 12/23/91, D, 91001823

Lake Park, 2900 N. Lake Dr. and 2800 E. Kenwood Blvd., Milwaukee, 4/22/93, C, D, 93000339

Lohman Funeral Home and Livery Stable, 804 W. Greenfield and 1325 S. Eighth, Milwaukee, 3/17/88, A, C, 88000220

Machek, Robert, House, 1305 N. 19th St., Milwaukee, 10/28/77, C, 77000038

Mackie Building, 225 E. Michigan St., Milwaukee, 4/03/73, A, C, 73000084

Mayer Boot and Shoe Company Building [Brewers' Hill MRA], 116 E. Walnut St., Milwaukee, 8/02/84, A, C, 84003728

McEwens, John F., House [Ernest Flagg Stone Masonry Houses of Milwaukee County TR], 829 E. Lake Forest, Whitefish Bay, 9/12/85, C, 85002032

McKinley Boulevard Historic District [West Side Area MRA], W. McKinley Blvd. between N. 34th & N. 27th Sts., Milwaukee, 7/30/85, A, C, 85001687

Meyer, Henry A., House [Ernest Flagg Stone Masonry Houses of Milwaukee County TR], 3559 N. Summit Ave., Shorewood, 9/12/85, C, 85002033

Meyer, Starke, House [Ernest Flagg Stone Masonry Houses of Milwaukee County TR], 7896 N. Club Circle, Fox Point, 9/12/85, C, 85002034

Milwaukee City Hall, 200 E. Wells St., Milwaukee, 3/14/73, C, 73000085

Milwaukee County Courthouse [County Courthouses of Wisconsin TR], 901 N. 9th St., Milwaukee, 3/09/82, A, C, 82000687

Milwaukee County Dispensary and Emergency Hospital, 2430 W. Wisconsin Ave., Milwaukee, 3/21/85, A, B, C, 85000639

Milwaukee County Historical Center, 910 N. 3rd St., Milwaukee, 3/14/73, A, C, 73000086

Milwaukee Fire Department High Pressure Pumping Station, 2011 S. 1st St., Milwaukee, 7/07/81, A, C, 81000049

Milwaukee News Building and Milwaukee Abstract Association Building, 222 E. Mason St., Milwaukee, 3/01/82, A, C, 82000688

Milwaukee Normal School—Milwaukee Girls' Trade and Technical High School [West Side Area MRA], 1820 W. Wells St., Milwaukee, 1/16/86, A, B, C, 86000123

Milwaukee—Western Fuel Company Building, 2150 N. Prospect Ave., Milwaukee, 3/05/92, C, 92000108

Milwaukee-Downer "Quad", NW corner of Hartford and Downer Aves., Milwaukee, 1/17/74, A, C, 74000106

Mitchell Building, 207 E. Michigan St., Milwaukee, 4/03/73, A, C, 73000087

Morgan, George E., House [Ernest Flagg Stone Masonry Houses of Milwaukee County TR], 4448 N. Maryland Ave., Shorewood, 9/12/85, C, 85002035

New Coeln House, 5905 S. Howell Ave., Milwaukee, 2/11/88, A, C, 88000083

North First Street Historic District [Brewers' Hill MRA], Roughly 1st and 2nd Sts. between North

Milwaukee County—Continued

and Center Sts., Milwaukee, 8/02/84, A, C, 84003731

North Point Lighthouse [U.S. Coast Guard Lighthouses and Light Stations on the Great Lakes TR], Wahl St. at Terrace, Milwaukee, 7/19/84, A, C, 84003732

North Point South Historic District, Roughly bounded by North Ave., Summit, Terrace, and Lafayette Sts., Milwaukee, 9/04/79, C, 79000322

North Point Water Tower, E. North Ave. between N. Lake Dr. and N. Terrace Ave., Milwaukee, 2/23/73, C, 73000088

North Third Street Historic District [Brewers' Hill MRA], Roughly N. 3rd St. between N. 3rd Ave. and Vine St., Milwaukee, 8/02/84, A, C, 84003733

Norton, Pearl C., House [Ernest Flagg Stone Masonry Houses of Milwaukee County TR], 2021 Church St., Wauwatosa, 9/12/85, C, 85002036

Old St. Mary's Church, 844 N. Broadway, Milwaukee, 3/07/73, A, C, a, 73000253

Old World Third Street Historic District, N. Old World Third St., W. Highland Ave., and W. State St., Milwaukee, 3/19/87, A, C, 87000494

Oliver, Joseph B., House, 1516 E. Brady St., Milwaukee, 1/18/90, C, b, 89002312

Oneida Street Station, 108 E. Wells and 816 N. Edison Sts., Milwaukee, 12/06/84, A, C, 84000701

Pabst Brewery Saloon [West Side Area MRA], 1338–1340 W. Juneau Ave., Milwaukee, 1/16/86, C, a, 86000125

Pabst Theater, 144 E. Wells St., Milwaukee, 4/11/72, A, C, NHL, 72000063

Pabst, Frederick, House, 2000 W. Wisconsin Ave., Milwaukee, 4/21/75, B, C, 75000073

Painesville Chapel, 2740 W. Ryan Rd., Franklin, 11/07/77, A, C, a, 77000039

Plankinton—Wells—Water Street Historic District, Roughly bounded by Wells, Bridge, N. Water, E. Mason, W. Wells, and N. Second Sts., Milwaukee, 6/13/86, A, C, 86001328

Prospect Avenue Apartment Buildings Historic District, N. Prospect Ave. area roughly between E. Kane Pl. and E. Windsor St., Milwaukee, 4/19/90, C, 90000640

Prospect Avenue Mansions Historic District, 1363–1551 N. Prospect Ave., Milwaukee, 4/07/90, C, 90000478

Public School No. 27 [Brewers' Hill MRA], 2215 N. 4th St., Milwaukee, 8/02/84, C, 84003735

Pythian Castle Lodge, 1925 W. National Ave., Milwaukee, 2/25/88, A, C, 88000089

Quarles, Charles, House, 2531 N. Farwell Ave., Milwaukee, 7/27/79, B, C, 79000096

Saint George Melkite Catholic Church [West Side Area MRA], 1617 W. State St., Milwaukee, 1/16/86, A, C, a, 86000128

Saint Peter's Evangelical Lutheran Church, 1204, 1213, 1214, and 1215 S. Eighth St., Milwaukee, 9/25/87, C, a, 87001736

Saint Vincent's Infant Asylum, 809 W. Greenfield Ave., Milwaukee, 9/25/87, A, C, 87001742

Saints Peter and Paul Roman Catholic Church Complex, 2474 and 2490 N. Cramer St. and 2479 and 2491 N. Murray Ave., Milwaukee, 9/13/91, C, a, 91001392

Salem Evangelical Church, 1025 & 1037 S. Eleventh St., Milwaukee, 10/01/87, C, a, 87001760

Schlitz, Joseph, Brewing Company Saloon, 2414 S. St. Clair St., Milwaukee, 4/11/77, A, C, 77000040

Schlitz, Victor, House [West Side Area MRA], 2004 W. Highland Ave., Milwaukee, 1/16/86, C, 86000145

Schuster, George, House and Carriage Shed [West Side Area MRA], 3209 W. Wells St., Milwaukee, 1/16/86, C, 86000137

Second Church of Christ Scientist [West Side Area MRA], 2722 W. Highland Blvd., Milwaukee, 1/16/86, C, a, 86000139

Shorecrest Hotel, 1962 N. Prospect Ave., Milwaukee, 9/07/84, C, 84003737

Shorewood Village Hall, 3930 N. Murray Ave., Shorewood, 9/07/84, A, 84003739

Sivyer, Fred, House [West Side Area MRA], 761 N. Twenty-fifth St., Milwaukee, 1/16/86, C, 86000141

Sixth Church of Christ, Scientist, 1036 N. Van Buren St., Milwaukee, 3/27/80, A, C, a, 80000168

Smith, Lloyd R., House, 2220 N. Terrace Ave., Milwaukee, 12/30/74, A, C, 74000107

Soldiers' Home Reef, NE of jct. of Wood Ave. and General Mitchell Blvd., Clement J. Zablocki Veterans Affairs Medical Center grounds, Milwaukee, 11/04/93, A, B, NHL, 93001617

South Branch Library, 931 W. Madison St., Milwaukee, 2/11/88, A, C, 88000084

South First and Second Street Historic District, Roughly bounded by Menomonee River, Chicago & N. Western RR, Seeboth, S. First, Oregon, & S. Second Sts., Milwaukee, 11/30/87, A, C, 87002092

South Milwaukee Passenger Station, Milwaukee Ave., South Milwaukee, 8/03/78, A, C, 78000119

Spence, William G., House, 1741 N. Farwell Ave., Milwaukee, 9/13/91, C, 91001393

Sperling, Frederick, House [Ernest Flagg Stone Masonry Houses of Milwaukee County TR], 1016 E. Lexington Blvd., Whitefish Bay, 9/12/85, C, 85002037

Spring Grove Site, Address Restricted, Milwaukee vicinity, 9/10/79, A, D, 79000097

St. James Episcopal Church, 833 W. Wisconsin Ave., Milwaukee, 6/27/79, A, C, a, 79000098

St. John's Evangelical Lutheran Church Complex, 804–816 W. Vliet St., Milwaukee, 5/18/92, C, a, 92000459

St. John's Roman Catholic Cathedral, 812 N. Jackson St., Milwaukee, 12/31/74, A, C, a, e, 74000108

St. Josaphat Basilica, 601 W. Lincoln Ave., Milwaukee, 3/07/73, A, C, a, 73000089

St. Martini Evangelical Lutheran Church, 1557 W. Orchard St., Milwaukee, 9/25/87, C, a, 87001741

St. Patrick's Roman Catholic Church, 1105 S. 7th St., Milwaukee, 12/16/74, C, a, 74000109

St. Paul's Episcopal Church, 904 E. Knapp St., Milwaukee, 12/27/74, C, a, 74000110

State Bank of Wisconsin, 210 E. Michigan St., Milwaukee, 3/08/84, A, C, 84003742

Steinmeyer, William, House [Brewers' Hill MRA], 1716-1722 N. 5th St., Milwaukee, 10/11/84, C, 84000102

Sunnyhill Home, 8000 W. Milwaukee Ave., Wauwatosa, 5/07/80, B, C, 80000169

Town of Milwaukee Town Hall, 5909 N. Milwaukee River Pkwy., Glendale, 10/09/86, A, C, b, 86002852

Trimborn Farm, 8801 W. Grange Ave., Greendale, 7/31/80, A, C, 80000170

Trinity Evangelical Lutheran Church, 1046 N. 9th St., Milwaukee, 5/08/79, A, C, a, 79000099

Tripoli Temple [West Side Area MRA], 3000 W. Wisconsin Ave., Milwaukee, 1/16/86, A, C, 86000142

Turner Hall, 1034 N. 4th St., Milwaukee, 11/07/77, A, C, 77000041

Uihlein, Herman, House, 5270 N. Lake Dr., Whitefish Bay, 12/22/83, C, 83004313

Ullius, Fred W., Jr., House [Ernest Flagg Stone Masonry Houses of Milwaukee County TR], 5775 N. Santa Monica Blvd., Whitefish Bay, 1/07/87, C, 86003658

Van Altena, William, House [Ernest Flagg Stone Masonry Houses of Milwaukee County TR], 1916 E. Glendale, Whitefish Bay, 9/12/85, C, 85002038

Van Devan, G. B., House [Ernest Flagg Stone Masonry Houses of Milwaukee County TR], 4601 N. Murray Ave., Whitefish Bay, 9/12/85, C, 85002039

Vine-Reservoir Historic District [Brewers' Hill MRA], Vine, Reservoir, Palmer, 1st, 2nd, and Brown Sts., Milwaukee, 8/02/84, C, 84003745

Walker's Point Historic District, Roughly bounded by the Freeway, Menomonee Canal, Scott, 2nd, and W. VA. Sts., Milwaukee, 12/19/78, A, C, 78000120

Walker, Harry B., House [West Side Area MRA], 3130 W. Wells St., Milwaukee, 1/16/86, C, 86000144

Ward Memorial Hall, 5000 W. National Ave., Wood, 9/06/84, A, C, 84003748

Washington Highlands Historic District, Bounded by N. 68th St., W. Lloyd St., N. 60th St., and Milwaukee Ave., Wauwatosa, 12/18/89, A, C, g, 89002121

Williams, Frank J., House [Ernest Flagg Stone Masonry Houses of Milwaukee County TR], 912 E. Lexington Blvd., Whitefish Bay, 9/12/85, C, 85002040

Woman's Club of Wisconsin, 813 E. Kilbourn Ave., Milwaukee, 10/04/82, A, C, 82001847

Monroe County

Kendalls Depot, N. Railroad St., Kendall, 8/12/81, C, 81000050

Monroe County Courthouse [County Courthouses of Wisconsin TR], 418 W. Main St., Sparta, 3/09/82, C, 82000689

Monroe County—Continued

Sparta Free Library, Court and Main Sts., Sparta, 9/03/81, C, 81000051

Sparta Masonic Temple, 200 W. Main St., Sparta, 9/25/87, C, 87001734

St. John's Episcopal Church, 400 N. Water St., Sparta, 3/18/83, C, a, 83003406

Tomah Public Library, 716 Superior Ave., Tomah, 5/28/76, C, 76000068

Water Street Commercial Historic District, Roughly bounded by K, Main, Bridge and Spring Sts. and Jefferson Ave., Sparta, 11/12/92, A, C, g, 92001554

Oconto County

Beyer Home Museum, 917 Park Ave., Oconto, 8/14/79, B, C, 79000100

Campbell, John G., House, 916 Park Ave., Oconto, 1/15/80, C, 80000171

First Church of Christ, Scientist, Chicago and Main Sts., Oconto, 11/19/74, A, C, a, 74000111

Holt and Balcom Logging Camp No.1, E of Lakewood, Lakewood vicinity, 12/22/78, A, C, 78000121

Holt-Balcom Lumber Company Office, 106 Superior Ave., Oconto, 11/13/76, A, 76000069

Jones, Huff, House, 1345 Main St, Oconto, 12/22/78, A, 78000122

Oconto County Courthouse [County Courthouses of Wisconsin TR], 300 Washington St., Oconto, 3/09/82, C, 82000690

Oconto Main Post Office, 141 Congress St., Oconto, 8/28/80, B, C, 80004479

Oconto Site, Copper Culture State Park, Oconto, 10/15/66, D, NHL, 66000023

Scofield, Gov. Edward, House, 610 Main St., Oconto, 4/11/73, B, 73000090

St. Mark's Episcopal Church, Guild Hall and Vicarage, 408 Park Ave., Oconto, 8/01/85, C, a, 85001684

St. Peter's and St. Joseph's Catholic Churches, 516 Brazeau Ave. and 705 Park Ave., Oconto, 11/10/80, A, C, a, 80000172

West Main Street Historic District, Main St. from Duncan to Erie Sts., Oconto, 5/14/79, B, C, 79000101

Oneida County

First National Bank, 8 W. Davenport St., Rhinelander, 8/14/73, C, 73000091

Little St. Germain Creek Site, Address Restricted, Newbold, 3/25/93, D, 93000217

Mecikalski General Store, Saloon, and Boardinghouse, 465 Max Rd., Jennings, 3/22/84, C, 84003751

Oneida County Courthouse, S. Oneida Ave., Rhinelander, 3/20/81, C, 81000052

Tomahawk Lake Camp Historic District, 8500 Raven Rd., Lake Tomahawk, 1/30/92, A, 91001987

Outagamie County

Black, Merritt, House [Kaukauna MRA], 104 River Rd., Kaukauna, 3/29/84, C, 84003752

Brokaw, Norman, House [Kaukauna MRA], 714 Grignon St., Kaukauna, 3/29/84, B, 84003754

College Avenue Historic District, 215 W. to 109 E., and 110 W. to 102 E. College Ave.; 106-114n. Onida St., Appleton, 12/02/82, A, C, 82001848

Courtney, J. B., Woolen Mills, 301 E. Water St., Appleton, 7/15/93, A, C, 93000650

Fargo's Furniture Store [Kaukauna MRA], 172-176 W. Wisconsin Ave., Kaukauna, 3/29/84, C, 84003755

Fox River Paper Company Historic District, 405-406, 415 S. Olde Oneida St., Appleton, 4/19/90, A, C, 90000639

Free Public Library of Kaukauna [Kaukauna MRA], 111 Main Ave., Kaukauna, 3/29/84, A, 84003756

Geenen, William and Susanna, House, 416 N. Sidney St., Kimberly, 2/25/93, C, 93000070

Greenville State Bank, 252 Municipal Dr., Greenville, 9/23/82, A, 82000691

Grignon, Charles A., House, Augustine St., Kaukauna, 10/18/72, A, B, C, 72000064

Hearthstone, 625 W. Prospect Ave., Appleton, 12/02/74, A, C, 74000112

Holy Cross Church [Kaukauna MRA], 309 Desnoyer St., Kaukauna, 3/29/84, C, a, 84003758

Hortonville Community Hall, 312 W. Main St., Hortonville, 1/23/81, A, C, 81000053

Klein Dairy Farmhouse [Kaukauna MRA], 1018 Sullivan Ave., Kaukauna, 3/29/84, A, C, 84003760

Kronser, Joseph, Hotel and Saloon, 246 Municipal Dr., Greenville, 7/28/88, A, C, 88001153

Kuehn Blacksmith Shop-Hardware Store [Kaukauna MRA], 148-152 E. 2nd St., Kaukauna, 3/29/84, C, 84003761

Lindauer and Rupert Block [Kaukauna MRA], 137-141 E. 2nd St., Kaukauna, 3/29/84, A, C, 84003763

Main Hall, Lawrence University, 400-500 E. College Ave., Appleton, 1/18/74, A, C, 74000113

Martens, Julius J., Company Building [Kaukauna MRA], 124-128 E. 3rd St., Kaukauna, 3/29/84, A, B, C, 84003764

Masonic Temple, 330 E. College Ave., Appleton, 9/12/85, A, C, 85002330

Meade, Capt. Matthew J., House [Kaukauna MRA], 309 Division St., Kaukauna, 3/29/84, B, 84003765

Nicolet Public School [Kaukauna MRA], 109 E. 8th St., Kaukauna, 3/29/84, C, 84003767

Peters, George, House, 305 N. Maple St., Black Creek, 6/18/87, C, 87000989

St. Andrews, Frank, House [Kaukauna MRA], 320 Dixon St., Kaukauna, 3/29/84, C, 84003768

St. Mary's Catholic Church [Kaukauna MRA], 119 W. 7th St., Kaukauna, 3/29/84, A, C, 84003769

Stribley, Charles W., House [Kaukauna MRA], 705 W. Wisconsin Ave., Kaukauna, 3/29/84, C, 84003770

Temple Zion and School, 320 N. Durkee St. and 309 E. Harris St., Appleton, 9/18/78, A, B, C, a, 78000123

Tompkins, James, House, 523 S. State St., Appleton, 4/03/86, C, 86000623

US Post Office, Former, 112 Main Ave., Kaukauna, 1/22/92, A, C, 91001990

Washington School, 818 W. Lorain St., Appleton, 6/07/84, C, 84003772

Whorton, John Hart, House, 315 W. Prospect Ave., Appleton, 11/19/74, B, C, 74000114

Zion Lutheran Church, 912 N. Oneida St., Appleton, 6/13/86, C, a, 86001309

Ozaukee County

Bolens, Harry W., House, 824 W. Grand Ave., Port Washington, 8/25/83, B, g, 83003407

Cedarburg Mill, 215 E. Columbia Ave., Cedarburg, 5/08/74, C, 74000115

Cedarburg Woolen Co. Worsted Mill [Mills of Grafton TR], 1350 14th Ave., Grafton, 6/30/83, A, 83003408

Clark, Jonathan, House, 13615 N. Cedarburg Rd., Mequon, 6/02/82, C, 82000692

Columbia Historic District, Roughly bounded by Cedar Cr., Highland Dr. and Bridge Rd., Cedarburg, 1/22/92, C, 91001980

Concordia Mill, 252 Green Bay Rd., Cedarburg vicinity, 4/26/74, C, 74000116

Covered Bridge, 1 Mi. N of Five Corners over Cedar Creek, Cedarburg vicinity, 3/14/73, A, C, 73000092

Dodge, Edward, House, 126 E. Grand Ave., Port Washington, 7/24/75, C, b, 75000074

Grafton Flour Mill [Mills of Grafton TR], 1300 14th Ave., Grafton, 6/30/83, A, C, 83003409

Hamilton Historic District, Hamilton and Green Bay Rds., Cedarburg, 7/01/76, A, C, D, 76000070

Hilgen and Wittenberg Woolen Mill, N70 W6340 Bridge Rd., Cedarburg, 12/22/78, A, C, 78000124

Hoffman House Hotel, 200 W. Grand Ave., Port Washington, 3/01/84, A, 84003773

Old Ozaukee County Courthouse [County Courthouses of Wisconsin TR (AD)], 109 W. Main St., Port Washington, 12/12/76, C, 76000071

Payne Hotel, 310 E. Green Bay Ave., Saukville, 3/14/91, A, B, 91000220

Reichert, John, Farmhouse, 14053 N. Wauwatosa Rd., Mequon, 7/01/82, C, 82000693

St. Mary's Roman Catholic Church, 430 N. Johnson St., Port Washington, 12/12/77, A, C, a, 77000042

Stony Hill School, NE of Waubeka on SR 1, waubeka vicinity, 10/08/76, A, B, 76000072

Washington Avenue Historic District, Roughly bounded by Elm St., Cedar Creek, Hamilton

Ozaukee County—Continued

Rd., and Washington Ave., Cedarburg, 1/17/86, A, B, C, 86000218

Wayside House, W61 N439 Washington Ave., Cedarburg, 3/17/82, C, 82000694

Pepin County

Durand Free Library, 315 W. 2nd Ave., Durand, 2/20/80, C, 80000173

Pepin County Courthouse and Jail [County Courthouses of Wisconsin TR], 307 W. Madison, Durand, 3/09/82, A, C, 82000695

Pierce County

Diamond Bluff Site-Mero Mound Group, Address Restricted, Diamond Bluff vicinity, 8/01/75, D, 75000075

Mero Archeological District (Boundary Increase), Address Restricted, Diamond Bluff, 6/04/92, D, 92000590

North Hall—River Falls State Normal School, University of Wisconsin, River Falls, 4/03/86, A, C, 86000627

Pierce County Courthouse [County Courthouses of Wisconsin TR], 411 W. Main St., Ellsworth, 3/09/82, C, 82000696

Smith, Daniel, House, 331 N. Lake St., Prescott, 3/15/84, B, 84003775

South Hall, River Falls State Normal School, 320 E. Cascade Ave., River Falls, 11/07/76, A, 76000073

Polk County

Dalles Bluff Site, Address Restricted, St. Croix Falls vicinity, 9/05/81, D, 81000054

Geiger Building—Old Polk County Courthouse, 201 Cascade St., Osceola, 12/02/85, A, 85003030

Heald, Alvah A., House, 202 Sixth Ave., Osceola, 12/02/85, B, C, 85003097

Lamar Community Center, NE of St. Croix Falls, St. Croix Falls vicinity, 3/01/82, A, 82001860

Polk County Courthouse [County Courthouses of Wisconsin TR], Main St., Balsam Lake, 3/09/82, C, 82000697

Seven Pines Lodge, SE of Lewis of WI 35, Lewis vicinity, 12/08/78, B, C, 78000125

Thompson, Thomas Henry, House, 205 N. Adams St., St. Croix Falls, 3/08/84, B, C, 84003777

Portage County

Folding Furniture Works Building, 1020 First St., Stevens Point, 7/29/93, A, C, 93000666

Fox Theater, 1116-1128 Main St., Stevens Point, 7/26/82, A, B, C, 82000698

Hatch, Seneca W. & Bertha, House [Ernest Flagg Stone Masonry Houses of Milwaukee County TR], 3821 N. Prospect Ave., Shorewood, 9/12/85, C, 85002028

Hotel Whiting, 1408 Strongs Ave., Stevens Point, 9/13/90, A, C, 90001457

Jensen, J. L., House, 1100 Brawley St., Stevens Point, 7/28/88, C, 88001151

Kuhl, Christina, House, 1416 Main St., Stevens Point, 1/09/78, C, 78000126

Mathias Mitchell Public Square—Main Street Historic District, Roughly Main St. from Strongs Ave. to Second St., Stevens Point, 8/13/86, A, C, 86001513

McMillan, David, House, 1924 Pine St., Stevens Point, 12/16/74, C, 74000117

Morgan, J. H., House, 1308 Madison Ave., Plover, 10/01/74, C, 74000118

Old Plover Methodist Church, Madison Ave., Plover, 3/27/80, C, 80000393

Pipe School, Jct. of Pipe Rd. and Co. Hwy. T, Lanark, 11/04/93, A, 93001171

Pomeroy, L. A., House, 203 Laconia St., Amherst, 11/05/92, B, C, 92001560

Severance—Pipe Farmstead, Pipe Rd., 1/8 mi. E of Co. Hwy. T, Lanark, 10/29/93, C, 93001163

Stevens Point State Normal School, 2100 Main St., Stevens Point, 12/12/76, A, 76000074

Price County

Bloom's Tavern, Store and House, 396 S. Avon Ave., Phillips, 3/07/85, A, 85000490

Deadman Slough [Paleo-Indian Tradition in Wisconsin MPS], Address Restricted, Flambeau vicinity, 8/20/93, D, 93000750

Fifield Town Hall, Pine St. and Flambeau Ave., Fifield, 2/17/78, A, 78000339

Flambeau Paper Company Office Building, 200 N. First Ave., Park Falls, 9/12/85, A, C, 85002331

Johnson, Albin, Log House, E of Ogema, Ogema vicinity, 1/20/78, A, C, 78000127

Johnson, Matt, Log House, S of Brantwood off U.S. 8, Brantwood vicinity, 12/08/78, A, C, 78000128

Prentice Co-operative Creamery Company, 700 Main St., Prentice, 9/12/85, A, 85002329

Round Lake Logging Dam, NE of Fifield, Fifield vicinity, 9/17/81, A, C, 81000055

Racine County

Badger Building, 610 Main St., Racine, 12/03/80, C, 80000174

Beardsley, Elam, Farmhouse, 5601 Northwest Hwy., Waterford vicinity, 3/01/82, C, 82000699

Collins, John, House, 6409 Nicholson Rd., Caledonia, 11/20/74, C, 74000119

Cooley, Eli R., House, 1135 S. Main St., Racine, 4/11/73, C, 73000273

First Presbyterian Church, 716 College Ave., Racine, 3/20/73, C, a, 73000093

Hall, Chauncey, Building, 338-340 Main St., Racine, 10/10/80, C, 80000175

Hall, Chauncey, House, 1235 S. Main St., Racine, 1/02/76, C, 76000075

Hansen House, 1221 N. Main St., Racine, 6/06/79, C, 79000103

Hardy, Thomas P., House, 1319 S. Main St., Racine, 12/03/74, C, 74000120

Hazelo, Franklyn, House, 34108 Oak Knoll Rd., Burlington vicinity, 12/30/74, C, 74000121

Historic Sixth Street Business District, Roughly bounded by Water St. and Fifth St., Main Seventh St., and Grand Ave., Racine, 3/24/88, A, C, a, f, 88000263

Johnson, Herbert F., House, 33 E. Four Mile Rd., Wind Point vicinity, 1/08/75, C, g, NHL, 75000076

Johnson, Peter, House, 1601 State St., Racine, 1/06/86, C, 86000053

Johnson, S.C., and Son Administration Building and Research Tower, 1525 Howe St., Racine, 12/27/74, C, NHL, 74002275

Jonas, Karel, House, 1337 N. Erie St., Racine, 3/01/82, B, f, 82000700

Kaiser's, 218 6th St., Racine, 11/25/80, C, 80000176

McClurg Building, 245 Main St., Racine, 7/13/77, A, C, 77000044

Memorial Hall, 72 7th St., Racine, 4/10/80, A, C, 80000177

Murray, George, House, 2219 Washington Ave., Racine, 6/06/79, C, a, 79000104

No. 4 Engine House, 1339 Lincoln St., Racine, 6/27/79, A, C, 79000102

Norwegian Buildings at Heg Park, NE of Waterford on Heg Park Rd., Waterford vicinity, 7/17/80, A, B, a, b, f, 80000178

Old Main Street Historic District, Roughly bounded by Second St., Lake Ave., Fifth St., and Wisconsin Ave., Racine, 8/11/87, A, B, C, 87000491

Racine College, 600 21st St., Racine, 12/12/76, A, C, a, 76000076

Racine County Courthouse, 730 Wisconsin Ave., Racine, 7/28/80, A, C, 80000179

Racine Depot, 1402 Liberty St., Racine, 10/10/80, C, 80000180

Racine Elks Club, Lodge No. 252, 601 Lake Ave., Racine, 9/07/84, C, 84003778

Racine Harbor Lighthouse and Life Saving Station, Racine Harbor North Pier, Racine, 9/09/75, A, 75000077

Racine Public Library, 701 S. Main St., Racine, 3/20/81, C, 81000056

Rickeman Grocery Building, 415 6th St., Racine, 3/01/82, C, 82000701

Shoop Building, 215 State St., Racine, 4/26/78, A, C, 78000129

Southern Wisconsin Home Historic District, 21425 Spring St., Dover, 9/27/91, A, 91001394

Southside Historic District, Roughly bounded by Lake Michigan, DeKoven Ave., Villa and Eighth Sts., Racine, 10/18/77, C, 77000147

St. Luke's Episcopal Church, Chapel, Guildhall, and Rectory, 614 S. Main St., Racine, 7/27/79, C, a, 79000105

Racine County—Continued

St. Patrick's Roman Catholic Church, 1100 Erie St., Racine, 7/05/79, C, a, 79000106

US Post Office—Racine Main, 603 Main St., Racine, 5/08/85, C, 85000989

United Laymen Bible Student Tabernacle, 924 Center St., Racine, 12/08/83, C, 83004318

Uptown Theater, 1426-1430 Washington Ave., Racine, 3/01/82, C, 82000702

Whitman-Belden House, 108 N. State St., Rochester, 1/17/80, B, C, 80000181

Windpoint Light Station [U.S. Coast Guard Lighthouses and Light Stations on the Great Lakes TR], Windridge Dr. at Lake Michigan, Racine, 7/19/84, A, C, 84003780

Young Men's Christian Association Building, 314-320 6th St., Racine, 3/01/82, C, 82000703

Richland County

A. D. German Warehouse, 316 S. Church St., Richland Center, 12/31/74, C, 74000122

Coumbe, John, Farmstead, Jct. of WI Trunk Hwy. 60 and Co. Trunk Hwy. X, Town of Richwood, Port Andrew, 6/25/92, C, 92000827

Court Street Commercial Historic District, Roughly bounded by Mill, Church, Haseltine, and Main Sts., Richland Center, 11/13/89, A, C, 89001955

Fiedler, Henry, House, Putnam and Washington Sts., Muscoda vicinity, 12/29/86, C, 86003515

Richland Center Archeological District, Address Restricted, Richland Center vicinity, 9/30/93, D, 93001006

Richland Center City Auditorium, 182 N. Central Ave., Richland Center, 8/18/80, A, 80000182

Syttende Mai Site, Address Restricted, Richland vicinity, 12/30/91, D, 91001869

Rock County

Alexander, John, Wheat Warehouse [Grout Buildings in Milton TR], 304 S. Janesville St., Milton, 9/13/78, A, B, C, 78003383

Allen, Abram, House [Grout Buildings in Milton TR], 205 E. Madison Ave., Milton, 9/13/78, C, 78003386

Armory, The, 10 S. High St., Janesville, 11/21/78, A, 78000130

Bartlett Memorial Historical Museum, 2149 St. Lawrence Ave., Beloit, 4/11/77, A, C, 77000048

Beloit Water Tower [Beloit MRA], 1005 Pleasant St., Beloit, 1/07/83, A, C, 83003410

Blodgett, Selvy, House, 417 Bluff St., Beloit, 5/23/80, A, C, 80000183

Bluff Street Historic District [Beloit MRA], Roughly both sides of Bluff St. from Shirland Ave. to Merrill St., Beloit, 1/07/83, A, C, 83003411

Brasstown Cottage [Beloit MRA], 1701 Colley Rd., Beloit, 3/04/83, C, b, 83003412

Church of St. Thomas the Apostle [Beloit MRA], 822 E. Grand Ave., Beloit, 1/07/83, C, a, 83003413

Citizens Bank [Clinton MRA], Front & Allen Sts., Clinton, 8/01/85, C, 85001661

City of Beloit Waterworks and Pump Station, 1005 Pleasant St., Beloit, 9/13/90, A, 90001460

Clark-Brown House [Cobblestone Buildings of Rock County TR], 3457 Riverside Dr., Beloit, 9/13/85, C, 85002126

Clinton Village Hall [Clinton MRA], 301 Cross St., Clinton, 8/01/85, C, 85001660

Clinton Water Tower [Water Works Structures of Rock County—19th Century TR], High St., Clinton, 3/07/85, A, 85000493

Conrad Cottages Historic District, 235–330 Milton Ave., Janesville, 3/11/93, C, 93000157

Cooksville Cheese Factory [Cooksville MRA], SR 1, Evansville vicinity, 9/17/80, A, 80000395

Cooksville Historic District, Both sides of streets bordering the Public Sq. and Rock St., Cooksville, 10/25/73, A, C, 73000254

Cooksville Mill and Mill Pond Site [Cooksville MRA], SR 1, Evansville, 9/17/80, A, D, 80000394

Cooper-Gillies House [Cooksville MRA], SR 1, Evansville vicinity, 9/17/80, C, 80000397

Court Street Methodist Church, 36 S. Main St., Janesville, 11/17/77, A, C, a, 77000045

Courthouse Hill Historic District, Roughly bounded by E. Milwaukee St., Garfield and Oakland Aves., S. Main St., and E. Court St. and Milton Ave., Janesville, 1/17/86, B, C, 86000205

Crist, J. W., House [Beloit MRA], 2601 Afton Rd., Beloit, 1/07/83, C, 83003414

Crosby Block [Clinton MRA], 102 Allen St., Clinton, 8/01/85, C, 85001658

Culton, Charles L., House, 708 Washington St., Edgertown, 8/22/77, A, C, 77000046

De Jean House [Grout Buildings in Milton TR], 27 Third St., Milton, 9/13/78, C, 78003388

DeLong, Homer B., House [Clinton MRA], 500 Milwaukee Rd., Clinton, 8/01/85, C, 85001659

Dean, Erastus, Farmstead, E of Janesville on U.S. 14, Janesville vicinity, 12/04/78, B, b, 78000131

Dougan Round Barn [Centric Barns in Rock County TR], 444 West Colley Rd., Beloit, 6/04/79, A, C, 79000108

Dow, J.B., House and Carpenter Douglas Barn [Beloit MRA; Cobblestone Buildings of Rock County TR (AD)], 910 Board St., Beloit, 1/07/83, C, 83003415

Dow, John T., House [Cooksville MRA], SR 1, Evansville vicinity, 9/17/80, B, C, 80000396

Eager Free Public Library, 39 W. Main St., Evansville, 8/16/77, C, 77000047

East Milwaukee Street Historic District, N. Parker Dr. and E. Milwaukee St., Janesville, 2/08/80, A, C, 80000184

Edgerton Public Grade Schools, 116 N. Swift St., Edgerton, 1/14/87, A, C, 86003568

Emerson Hall, Beloit College campus, Beloit, 9/20/79, A, C, 79000109

Evansville Historic District, roughly bounded by Allens Creek, Liberty, 4th and Garfield Sts., Evansville, 11/16/78, A, C, 78000132

Fairbanks Flats [Beloit MRA], 205, 215 Birch Ave. and 206, 216 Carpenter Ave., Beloit, 1/07/83, A, 83003416

First Congregational Church, 801 Bushnell St., Beloit, 1/23/75, C, a, 75000078

Footville Condensery [Footville MRA], Beloit St., Footville, 5/07/82, A, C, 82000704

Footville State Bank [Footville MRA], 158 Depot St., Footville, 5/07/82, A, C, 82000705

Fredendall Block, 33-39 S. Main St., Janesville, 3/25/82, C, 82000706

Fulton Congregational Church, Fulton St., Fulton, 6/07/76, A, C, a, 76000077

Gempeler Round Barn [Centric Barns in Rock County TR], SW of Orfordville, Orfordville vicinity, 6/04/79, A, C, 79000110

Gifford House [Grout Buildings in Milton TR], 308 Vernal, Milton, 9/13/78, C, 78003387

Gilley-tofsland Octagonal Barn [Centric Barns in Rock County TR], NW of Edgerton, Edgerton vicinity, 6/04/79, A, C, 79000111

Goodrich Blacksmith Shop [Grout Buildings in Milton TR], 28 S. Janesville St., Milton, 9/13/78, B, C, 78003382

Goodrich House and Log Cabin [Grout Buildings in Milton TR (AD)], 18 S. Janesville St., Milton, 2/01/72, A, B, C, 72000065

Goodrich-Buten House [Grout Buildings in Milton TR], 528 E. Madison St., Milton, 9/13/78, B, C, 78003385

Hanchett Block, 307 State St., Beloit, 3/20/80, A, 80000185

How-Beckman Mill, Address Restricted, Beloit vicinity, 9/07/77, A, g, NHL, 77000049

Janesville Cotton Mill, 220 N. Franklin St., Janesville, 7/16/80, A, 80000186

Janesville Public Library, 64 S. Main St., Janesville, 7/01/81, A, C, 81000057

Janesville Pumping Station [Water Works Structures of Rock County—19th Century TR], 500 Blk. River St., Janesville, 3/07/85, A, 85000494

Jones, Samuel S., Cobblestone House [Cobblestone Buildings of Rock County TR (AD)], E of Clinton on Milwaukee Rd., Clinton vicinity, 2/23/78, C, 78000133

Kinney Farmstead-Tay-e-he-Dah Site, Address Restricted, Edgerton vicinity, 2/17/78, A, C, D, 78000134

LaPrairie Grange Hall No. 79, SE of Janesville on Town Hall Rd., Janesville vicinity, 4/11/77, A, 77000050

Lappin-Hayes Block, 20 E. Milwaukee St., Janesville, 11/07/76, A, C, 76000224

Lathrop-Munn Cobblestone House [Cobblestone Buildings of Rock County TR (AD)], 524 Bluff St., Beloit, 8/22/77, C, 77000051

Leedle Mill Truss Bridge [Cooksville MRA], SR 1, Evansville, 9/17/80, A, 80000398

Look West Historic District, Roughly bounded by Mineral Point Ave., N. Franklin and Race Sts., Laurel Ave., and N. Chatham St., Janesville, 3/26/87, A, C, 87000506

Look West Historic District (Boundary Increase), Roughly bounded by Laurel Ave. and N. Madison, W. Court and N. Palm Sts., Janesville, 12/10/93, C, 93001429

Rock County—Continued

Lovejoy and Merrill-Nowlan Houses, 220 and 202 St. Lawrence Ave., Janesville, 1/21/80, A, C, 80000187

McEwan, Peter, Warehouse [Grout Buildings in Milton TR], 711 E. High St., Milton, 9/13/78, C, 78003384

Merrill Avenue Historic District, 103, 107, 111, 115 Merrill Ave., Beloit, 2/19/93, A, C, 93000028

Miller House [Cooksville MRA], SR 1, Evansville vicinity, 9/17/80, C, 80000399

Milton College Historic District, College St., Milton, 5/27/80, A, B, C, 80000188

Moran's Saloon [Beloit MRA], 312 State St., Beloit, 1/07/83, C, 83003417

Mouth of the Yahara Archeological District, Address Restricted, Fulton vicinity, 4/28/75, D, c, 75000079

Murray-George House [Cobblestone Buildings of Rock County TR], SR P, Beloit, 9/13/85, C, 85002125

Myers, Peter, Pork Packing Plant and Willard Coleman Building, 117-123 N. Main St., Janesville, 7/07/83, A, C, 83003418

Myers-Newhoff House, 121 N. Parker Dr., Janesville, 5/18/79, C, A, 79000277

Near East Side Historic District [Beloit MRA], Roughly bounded by Pleasant, Clary Sts., Wisconsin and E. Grand Aves., Beloit, 1/07/83, A, C, 83003419

Neese, Elbert, House [Beloit MRA], 1302 Bushnell St, Beloit, 1/07/83, B, C, 83003420

North Main Street Historic District, N. Main St. and N. Parker Dr., Janesville, 2/08/80, A, C, 80000189

Nye, Clark, House [Beloit MRA], 2501 Spring Creek Rd., Beloit, 1/07/83, C, 83003422

Old Fourth Ward Historic District, Roughly bounded by Washington St., Center Ave., Court St., Franklin St., and Monterey Park, Janesville, 5/30/90, A, C, 90000789

Orfordville Depot, Beliot St., Orfordville, 10/13/88, A, C, b, 88002004

Owen, William J., Store [Footville MRA], 220 Depot St., Footville, 5/07/82, A, C, b, 82000707

Pangborn, J. L., House [Clinton MRA], 300 Allen St., Clinton, 8/01/85, C, 85001664

Payne—Craig House, 2200 W. Memorial Dr., Janesville, 7/02/87, B, C, 87000990

Pearsons Hall of Science, Beloit College campus, Beloit, 6/30/80, A, C, 80000190

Porter, J. K., Farmstead [Cooksville MRA], SR 1, Evansville vicinity, 9/17/80, A, b, 80000400

Prospect Hill Historic District, Roughly bounded by Eisenhower, Prospect and Atwood Aves., Milwaukee St., Parker Dr. and Centerway, Janesville, 11/05/92, C, 92001558

Randall, Brewster, House, 1412 Ruger Ave., Janesville, 3/01/84, C, 84003782

Rasey House, 517 Prospect St., Beloit, 12/27/74, A, C, 74000123

Rau, Charles, House [Beloit MRA], 757 Euclid Ave., Beloit, 1/07/83, C, 83003423

Richardson Grout House [Cooksville MRA], SR 1, Evansville vicinity, 9/17/80, C, 80000402

Richardson, Hamilton, House, 429 Prospect Ave., Janesville, 7/17/78, B, C, 78000135

Richardson-Brinkman Cobblestone House [Cobblestone Buildings of Rock County TR (AD)], 607 W. Milwaukee Rd., Clinton, 7/28/77, C, 77000052

Rindfleisch Building [Beloit MRA], 512 E. Grand Ave., Beloit, 1/07/83, C, 83003424

Risum Round Barn [Centric Barns in Rock County TR], SW of Orfordville, Orfordville vicinity, 6/04/79, A, C, 79000112

Shopiere Congregational Church, Buss Rd., near Shopiere Rd., Shopiere vicinity, 8/13/76, A, C, a, 76000078

Slaymaker, Stephen, House [Beloit MRA], 348 Euclid Ave., Beloit, 1/07/83, C, 83003425

Smiley, Samuel, House, SE of Orfordville on WI 213, Orfordville vicinity, 10/21/82, C, 82001849

Smith, John, House [Clinton MRA], 312 Pleasant St., Clinton, 8/01/85, C, 85001663

South Main Street Historic District, Roughly S. Main St. from Milwaukee St. to Rock Co. Courthouse grounds and E. Court St. from Parker Dr. to Rock R., Janesville, 6/01/90, A, C, 90000820

St. Paul's Episcopal Church, 212 W. Grand Ave., Beloit, 4/04/78, C, a, 78000136

Stark-Clint House [Cobblestone Buildings of Rock County TR], Creek Rd., Tiffany, 9/13/85, C, 85002124

Stebbins, Harrison, House [Cooksville MRA], SR 1, Evansville vicinity, 9/17/80, B, C, 80000401

Strang, Soloman J., House [Footville MRA], 231 North Gilbert, Footville, 5/07/82, C, 82000708

Strong Building [Beloit MRA], 400-408 E. Grand Ave., Beloit, 1/07/83, C, 83003426

Tallman House, 440 N. Jackson St., Janesville, 10/15/70, B, C, 70000085

Taylor, A. E., House [Clinton MRA], 318 Durand St., Clinton, 8/01/85, C, 85001662

Turtleville Iron Bridge, N of Beloit on Lathers Rd., Beloit vicinity, 9/15/77, A, C, 77000053

West Luther Valley Lutheran Church, SW of Orfordville on W. Church Rd., Ordfordville vicinity, 5/27/80, A, B, a, 80000191

West Milwaukee Street Historic District, Roughly bounded by Wall, River, Court, and Academy Sts., Janesville, 5/17/90, A, C, 90000790

Willard, Frances, Schoolhouse, Craig Ave., Janesville, 10/05/77, B, b, 77000054

Wyman-Rye Farmstead, N of Clinton on Wyman-Rye Dr., Clinton vicinity, 11/07/77, A, C, 77000055

Yates, Florence, House [Beloit MRA], 1614 Emerson St., Beloit, 1/07/83, C, 83003427

Rusk County

Flambeau Mission Church, W of Ladysmith, Ladysmith vicinity, 8/07/79, A, C, a, 79000113

State Bank of Ladysmith, 102 W. 2nd St., Ladysmith, 1/17/80, A, C, 80000192

Sauk County

Baraboo Public Library, 230 4th Ave., Baraboo, 9/14/81, C, 81000058

Chicago and North Western Depot [Reedsburg MRA], Railroad St., Reedsburg, 12/26/84, A, C, 84000639

City Hotel [Reedsburg MRA], 125 Main St., Reedsburg, 12/26/84, C, 84000642

Clark, William, House, 320 Walnut St., Baraboo, 4/08/80, C, 80000193

Derleth, August W., House, S10431a Lueders Rd., Sauk City vicinity, 4/30/91, B, g, 91000468

Durst-Bloedau Site, N of Leland, Leland vicinity, 12/19/78, D, 78000137

Freethinkers' Hall, 309 Polk St., Sauk City, 3/31/88, A, B, C, a, 88000237

Hackett, Edward M., House [Reedsburg MRA], 612 E. Main St., Reedsburg, 12/26/84, C, 84000644

Harris, Abner L., House [Reedsburg MRA], 226 N. Pine St., Reedsburg, 12/26/84, B, C, 84000649

Honey Creek Swiss Rural Historic District, SE of Prairie du Sac, Prairie du Sac vicinity, 4/06/90, A, C, d, 89000484

Hulburt Creek Garden Beds, Address Restricted, Delton, 8/08/91, D, 91000958

Leopold, Aldo, Shack, Central Wisconsin, Columbus vicinity, 7/14/78, A, B, g, 78000082

Main Street Commercial Historic District [Reedsburg MRA], Roughly bounded by N. Park, S. Park, N. Walnut, and S. Walnut Sts. on Main, Reedsburg, 12/26/84, A, C, 84000654

Man Mound, E of Baraboo off WI 33, Baraboo vicinity, 11/30/78, D, c, 78000138

Manchester Street Bridge, Ochsner Park, Baraboo, 10/13/88, C, b, 88002005

Marshall Memorial Hall, 30 Wisconsin Dells Pkwy. S., Lake Delton, 4/01/93, C, 93000264

Our Lady of Loretto Roman Catholic Church and Cemetery, Co. Hwy. C, 1 mi. W of Denzer, Honey Creek, 3/09/90, C, a, d, 90000378

Park Street Historic District [Reedsburg MRA], On N. Park St. roughly bounded by 6th, Locust, N. Pine and Main Sts., Reedsburg, 12/26/84, C, 84000656

Peterson, Seth, Cottage, Dell Ave., Lake Delton vicinity, 11/09/81, C, g, 81000059

Raddatz Rockshelter, Address Restricted, Leland vicinity, 12/18/78, D, 78000139

Reedsburg Brewery [Reedsburg MRA], 401 N. Walnut St., Reedsburg, 12/26/84, A, C, 84000661

Reedsburg Woolen Mill Office [Reedsburg MRA], 26 Main St., Reedsburg, 12/26/84, A, 84000664

Riggert, William, House [Reedsburg MRA], 547 S. Park St., Reedsburg, 12/26/84, C, 84000666

Ringling Brothers Circus Headquarters, Bounded roughly by Water, Brian, Lynn, and East Sts., Baraboo, 8/04/69, A, NHL, 69000032

Ringling, Al, Theatre, 136 4th Ave., Baraboo, 5/17/76, B, C, 76000202

Ringling, Albrecht C., House, 623 Broadway, Baraboo, 5/17/76, B, C, 76000079

Sauk County—Continued

Salem Evangelical Church, Jct. of CR PF and Church Rd., Plain vicinity, 3/29/88, A, C, a, 86003576

Sauk City High School, 713 Madison St., Sauk City, 2/23/89, A, C, 89000071

Sauk County Courthouse [County Courthouses of Wisconsin TR], 515 Oak St., Baraboo, 3/09/82, C, 82000711

Seven Gables, 215 6th St., Baraboo, 1/20/78, C, 78000140

Stolte, William, Jr., House [Reedsburg MRA], 432 S. Walnut St., Reedsburg, 12/26/84, C, 84000667

Stolte, William, Sr., House [Reedsburg MRA], 444 S. Walnut St., Reedsburg, 12/26/84, C, 84000670

Tripp Memorial Library and Hall, 565 Water St., Prairie du Sac, 9/14/81, B, 81000060

Tuttle, A.G., Estate, N. Elizabeth St., Baraboo, 11/06/80, B, C, 80000194

Sawyer County

Hall-Raynor Stopping Place, N of Ojibwa on WI G, Ojibwa vicinity, 8/14/79, A, C, 79000115

North Wisconsin Lumber Company Office, Florida Ave., Hayward, 5/07/80, A, B, 80000403

Ojibwa Courier Press Building, E of Raddison at 110 Ojibwa Mall, Raddison vicinity, 3/01/82, A, B, 82000712

Shawano County

Lutheran Indian Mission, NE of Gresham on WI G, Gresham vicinity, 10/22/80, A, a, 80000195

Sheboygan County

American Club, High St., Kohler, 5/22/78, A, 78000141

Balzer, John, Wagon Works Complex, 818–820, 820A Pennsylvania Ave., Sheboygan, 12/23/93, A, C, 92000028

Cole Historic District, 501 and 517 Monroe St. and 504, 508, and 516-518 Water St., Sheboygan Falls, 12/01/88, A, B, b, 88002696

Downtown Historic District, Roughly bounded by Broadway, Monroe, Pine, and Buffalo Sts., and the Sheboygan River, Sheboygan Falls, 12/27/84, A, C, 84000691

Franklin Feed Mill [19th Century Grist and Flouring Mills of Sheboygan County TR], Franklin Rd., Franklin, 4/11/85, A, 85000792

Friendship House, 721 Ontario Ave., Sheboygan, 7/10/74, A, C, 74000331

Glenbeulah Mill/Grist Mill [19th Century Grist and Flouring Mills of Sheboygan County TR], Gardner St., Glenbeulah, 12/27/84, A, 84000678

Gooseville Mill/Grist Mill [19th Century Grist and Flouring Mills of Sheboygan County TR], Silver Creek-Cascade Rd., Adell, 12/27/84, A, 84000673

Hotel Laack, 52 Stafford St., Plymouth, 12/02/85, A, C, 85003095

Huson, Henry H., House and Water Tower, 405 Collins St., Plymouth, 11/28/80, B, C, 80000196

Jung Carriage Factory, 829-835 Pennsylvania Ave., Sheboygan, 7/10/74, A, C, 74000125

Jung Shoe Manufacturing Company Factory, 620 S. Eighth St., Sheboygan, 1/22/92, C, 91001993

Kletzien Mound Group (47-SB-61), Address Restricted, Sheboygan vicinity, 7/23/81, D, 81000061

Kohler, John Michael, House, 608 New York Ave., Sheboygan, 11/30/82, A, B, C, 82001850

Mission House Historic District, County Trunk M, Town Herman, 12/20/84, A, C, a, 84001221

Onion River Flouring Mill/Grist Mill [19th Century Grist and Flouring Mills of Sheboygan County TR], Hwy 57, Waldo, 12/27/84, A, 84000679

Riverbend, Lower Falls Rd., Kohler, 12/04/80, B, C, 80000197

Robinson, Charles, House, Center St., Old Wade House State Park, Greenbush, 12/20/84, B, C, 84001125

Robinson-Herrling Sawmill, Old Wade House State Park, Greenbush, 12/27/84, D, 84000685

Roth, Henry and Henriette, House, 822 Niagara Ave., Sheboygan, 4/29/93, B, 93000337

Sheboygan County Courthouse [County Courthouses of Wisconsin TR], 615 N. 6th St., Sheboygan, 3/12/82, A, C, g, 82000713

St. Patrick's Roman Catholic Church, WI 1, Adell vicinity, 9/08/83, C, a, 83003428

Taylor, David, House, 3110 Erie Ave., Sheboygan, 1/02/76, B, 76000080

Third Ward School, 1208 S. 8th St., Sheboygan, 9/03/81, A, C, 81000062

Thomas, I. C., Drug Store, 632 N. 8th St., Sheboygan, 7/10/74, A, C, 74000126

Villa Laun, 402 Lake Side Park Dr., Elkhart Lake, 1/28/82, C, 82000714

Villa Von Baumbach, 754 Elkhart Lake Dr., Elkhart Lake, 11/30/82, C, b, 82001851

Wade, Sylvanus, House, At jct. of WI 23 and Kettle Maraine Dr. in Old Wade House State Park, Greenbush, 10/26/71, A, C, 71000041

Windway, CTH Y, N of CTH O, Sheboygan, 7/28/88, C, 88001149

Wolff—Jung Company Shoe Factory, 531 S. Eighth St., Sheboygan, 1/30/92, C, 91001989

St. Croix County

Bell, Marcus Sears, Farm [New Richmond MRA], 1100 Heritage Dr., New Richmond, 5/31/88, C, b, 88000614

Bernd, William J., House [New Richmond MRA], 210 Second St., E, New Richmond, 5/31/88, C, 88000615

Bernd, William J., House [New Richmond MRA], 143 Arch Ave., N, New Richmond, 5/31/88, C, 88000616

Chicago, St. Paul, Minneapolis and Omaha Railroad Car Shop Historic District [Hudson and North Hudson MRA], Roughly bounded by Gallahad Rd., Sommer, 4th and St. Croix Sts., North Hudson, 10/04/84, A, C, 84000072

Darling, Frederick L., House [Hudson and North Hudson MRA], 617 3rd St., Hudson, 10/04/84, C, 84000060

Dwelley, William, House [Hudson and North Hudson MRA], 1002 4th St., Hudson, 10/04/84, C, 84000061

Epley, Dr. Frank W., Office [New Richmond MRA], 137 Third St., E, New Richmond, 5/31/88, B, 88000617

First English Lutheran Church [New Richmond MRA], 354 Third St., N, New Richmond, 5/31/88, A, a, 88000618

Glover, Ezra, Jr., House [New Richmond MRA], 415 Second St., E, New Richmond, 5/31/88, A, C, 88000619

Hudson Public Library [Hudson and North Hudson MRA], 304 Locust St., Hudson, 10/04/84, A, C, 84000062

Humphrey, Herman L., House [Hudson and North Hudson MRA], 803 Orange St., Hudson, 10/04/84, B, C, 84000063

Johnson, August, House [Hudson and North Hudson MRA], 427 St. Croix St., Hudson, 10/04/84, C, 84000064

Johnson, Dr. Samuel C., House [Hudson and North Hudson MRA], 405 Locust St., Hudson, 10/04/84, B, C, 84000065

Kell, William H., House [New Richmond MRA], 215 Green Ave., S, New Richmond, 5/31/88, C, 88000620

Lewis Farmhouse, Farm Dr., Boardman vicinity, 3/19/82, C, 82000709

Lewis-Williams House [Hudson and North Hudson MRA], 101 3rd St., Hudson, 1/02/85, B, C, 85000050

Merritt, Samuel T., House [Hudson and North Hudson MRA], 904 7th St., Hudson, 10/04/84, B, 84000066

Mielke, Joseph, House [New Richmond MRA], 326 Second St., W, New Richmond, 5/31/88, C, 88000621

Moffat, John S., House, 1004 3rd St., Hudson, 7/18/74, C, 74000124

New Richmond News Building [New Richmond MRA], 145 Second St., W, New Richmond, 5/31/88, A, 88000625

New Richmond Roller Mills Co. [New Richmond MRA], 201 Knowles Ave., N, New Richmond, 5/31/88, A, 88000622

New Richmond West Side Historic District [New Richmond MRA], Roughly bounded by Willow River, Minnesota Ave., W. Second St., S. Washington Ave., New Richmond, 5/31/88, A, B, C, 88000626

Opera Hall Block, 516 2nd St., Hudson, 3/07/79, A, 79000114

Phipps, William H., House, 1005 Third St., Hudson, 6/18/87, B, C, 87000991

Second Street Commercial District [Hudson and North Hudson MRA], Roughly 1st, 2nd, Walnut,

St. Croix County—Continued

and Locust Sts., Hudson, 10/04/84, A, C, 84000067

Sixth Street Historic District [Hudson and North Hudson MRA], Roughly 6th St. between Myrtle and Vine Sts., Hudson, 10/04/84, C, 84000069

Soo Line Depot [New Richmond MRA], 120 High St., New Richmond, 5/31/88, A, 88000623

Soo Line High Bridge [Washington County MRA (AD)], Address Restricted, Somerset vicinity, 8/22/77, A, C, NPS, 77000056

St Croix County Courthouse [County Courthouses of Wisconsin TR], 904 3rd St., Hudson, 3/09/82, C, 82000710

Stillwater Bridge, MN 36/WI 64 over St. Croix River, Houlton, 5/25/89, C, 89000445

Thompson, Erick J., House [New Richmond MRA], 350 Second St., W, New Richmond, 5/31/88, C, 88000624

Williams, T.E., Block [Hudson and North Hudson MRA], 321 2nd St., Hudson, 10/04/84, C, 84000070

Taylor County

Benn, J. W., Building, 202-204 S. Main St., Medford, 12/22/83, C, 83004320

Big Indian Farms, Address Restricted, Perkinstown vicinity, 7/11/88, D, 87001827

Jump River Town Hall, S of WI 73, Jump River, 3/28/74, C, 74000127

Medford Free Public Library [Public Library Facilities of Wisconsin MPS], 104 E. Perkins St., Medford, 4/01/93, A, C, 93000259

Mondeaux Dam Recreation Area, Roughly bounded by Mondeaux River and Forest Rd., Westboro vicinity, 8/21/84, A, C, 84003784

Taylor County Courthouse, 224 S. 2nd, Courthouse Sq., Medford, 5/14/80, A, C, 80000198

Trempealeau County

Arnold, Capt. Alexander A., Farm, N of Galesville off U.S. 53, Galesville vicinity, 3/21/78, B, C, 78000142

Bartlett Blacksmith Shop-Scandinavian Hotel [Galesville MRA], 218 E. Mill Rd., Galesville, 9/18/84, C, 84003786

Bohrnstedt, John, House [Galesville MRA], 830 Clark St., Galesville, 9/18/84, C, 84003788

Cance, John, F., House [Galesville MRA], 807 W. Ridge Ave., Galesville, 9/18/84, B, C, 84003790

Coman [Trempealeau MRA], 581 3rd St., Trempealeau, 11/15/84, C, 84000747

Downtown Historic District [Galesville MRA], Roughly Gale Ave., Main and Davis Sts., Galesville, 9/18/84, A, C, 84003791

Jensen, Tollef, House [Galesville MRA], 806 W. Gale Ave., Galesville, 9/18/84, C, 84003793

Main Street Historic District [Trempealeau MRA], Roughly Main St. between 1st and 3rd Sts., Trempealeau, 11/15/84, A, C, 84000763

Melchoir Hotel and Brewery Ruins [Trempealeau MRA], Address Restricted, Trempealeau vicinity, 11/15/84, A, D, 84000769

Ridge Avenue Historic District [Galesville MRA], Roughly Ridge Ave. from 4th to 6th Sts., Galesville, 9/18/84, C, 84003792

Schwert Mound Group, , Trempealeau vicinity, 11/01/74, D, 74000128

Trempealeau Platform Mounds Site, Address Restricted, Trempealeau, 12/23/91, D, c, 91001822

Vernon County

Archeological Site No. 47 VE-881, Address Restricted, Sterling vicinity, 9/30/93, D, 93001005

B. Lawrence Site I, Address Restricted, Rockton vicinity, 6/30/75, D, 75000080

Cade Archeological District, Address Restricted, Newton vicinity, 11/03/88, D, 88002176

Goose Island Archeological Site Ve-502, Address Restricted, Stoddard vicinity, 7/17/80, D, 80000199

Hanson Petroglyphs, , Viola vicinity, 12/31/74, D, 74000129

Hay Valley Archeological District, , Ontario vicinity, 12/31/74, D, 74000130

Larson Cave, Address Restricted, Westby vicinity, 1/06/88, A, D, 87002240

Markee Site, Address Restricted, Rockton vicinity, 8/22/75, D, 75000081

Norwegian Evangelic Lutheran Church and Cemetery, Coon Prairie and E. Coon Prairie Rds., Westby vicinity, 7/14/86, C, a, d, 86001719

Rockton Archeological District, , Ontario vicinity, 12/31/74, D, 74000131

Skumsrud, Nils, House, SE of jct. of SR 162 and U.S. 14/61, Coon Valley vicinity, 7/11/90, A, C, 90000571

Vernon County Courthouse, N. Dunlap Ave., Viroqua, 1/08/80, A, C, 80000200

Viola Rockshelter (47 Ve 640), Addres Restricted, Kickapoo Center vicinity, 12/10/87, D, 87002081

Vilas County

Presque Isle State Graded School, Jct. of Co. Trunk Hwy. B and School Loop St., Presque Isle, 3/25/93, A, C, 93000158

Strawberry Island Site, Address Restricted, Lac du Flambeau vicinity, 3/08/78, A, D, 78000340

Sunset Point, 1024 Everett Rd., Eagle River, 11/04/93, C, 93001169

Wallila Farm, Address Restricted, Phelps, 7/23/92, D, 92000851

Walworth County

Allyn, A. H., House, 511 E. Walworth Ave., Walworth, 9/05/85, C, 85001950

Bonnie Brae, 78 Snake Rd., Linn, 4/03/86, B, C, 86000614

Bradley Knitting Company, 902 Wisconsin St., Delavan, 3/19/92, A, C, 92000168

Buena Vista House, 2090 Church St., East Troy, 1/18/78, C, 78000143

Davidson Hall, 550 S. Shore Dr., Lake Geneva, 7/02/87, B, C, 87000443

Douglass—Stevenson House, Main and Mill Sts., Fontana, 4/03/86, B, C, 86000615

East Wing (Old Main), University of Wisconsin, Whitewater, 12/13/84, A, C, 84000609

Elderkin, Edward, House, 127 S. Lincoln St., Elkhorn, 5/03/74, C, 74000132

Grace and Pearl Historic District, Roughly bounded by Pearl, Park, Dougall, Grace and Martin Sts., Sharon, 8/05/93, C, 93000810

Halverson Log Cabin, University of Wisconsin-Whitewater Campus, Whitewater, 1/08/85, A, b, 85000070

Heart Prairie Lutheran Church, S of Whitewater on Town Line Rd., Whitewater vicinity, 12/27/74, A, C, a, 74000133

Johnson, A.P., House, 3455 S. Shore Dr., Delavan, 7/09/82, C, 82000715

Jones, Fred B., Estate, 3335 S. Shore Dr., Delavan Lake vicinity, 12/27/74, C, 74000134

Loomis, Horace, House, 2.4 mi. S of East Troy, East Troy vicinity, 12/03/74, C, 74000357

Main Street Historic District, Roughly W. Main St./US 12 from Prairie St. to Fremont St. and Church St. from Forest Ave. to W. Main St., Whitewater, 12/21/89, A, C, 89002116

Maples Mound Group [Late Woodland Stage in Archeological Region 8 MPS], Address Restricted, Whitewater, 6/07/91, D, 91000671

Metropolitan Block, 772 Main St., Lake Geneva, 4/19/90, C, 90000559

Meyerhofer Cobblestone House, E of Lake Geneva on Townline Rd., Lake Geneva vicinity, 12/08/80, C, 80000202

Mile Long Site, Address Restricted, Delavan vicinity, 6/23/77, D, 77000057

Phoenix Hall—Wisconsin Institute for the Education of the Deaf and Dumb, 309 W. Walworth St., Delavan, 3/19/87, A, 87000492

Redwood Cottage, 327 Wrigley Dr., Lake Geneva, 9/07/84, A, C, 84003796

Reynolds-Weed House, 12 N. Church St., Elkhorn, 3/31/83, C, 83003429

Riviera, The, 810 Wrigley Dr., Lake Geneva, 4/03/86, A, C, 86000616

Smith and Meadows Store Buildings, 2888–2890 Main St., East Troy, 3/12/93, C, 93000067

Smith, T. C., House, 865 Main St., Lake Geneva, 11/30/82, A, B, C, 82001852

Stowell, Israel, Temperance House, 61-65 E. Walworth Ave., Delavan, 8/11/78, A, 78000145

Strang, James Jesse, House, W of Burlington on WI 11, Burlington vicinity, 1/24/74, B, C, 74000135

Webster, Joseph P., House, 9 E. Rockwell St., Elkhorn, 2/23/72, B, 72000066

Younglands, 880 Lake Shore Dr., Lake Geneva, 9/18/79, B, C, 79000116

Washburn County

Polson, Mrs. Richard, House, N of Spooner, Spooner vicinity, 2/08/84, C, 84003798

Siegner, George V., House, 513 Dale St., Spooner, 3/01/82, B, C, 82000716

Washington County

Barton Historic District, Roughly bounded by Harrison and Jefferson Sts., Barton Ave., Salisbury Rd., Monroe St. and the Milwaukee R., West Bend, 3/05/92, A, C, a, 92000109

Christ Evangelical Church, W188 N12808 Fond du Lac Avenue, Germantown vicinity, 11/09/83, A, C, 83004324

Frisby, Leander F., House, 304 S. Main St., West Bend, 6/19/85, B, C, 85001363

Gadow's Mill, 1784 Barton Ave., West Bend, 12/24/74, A, 74000136

Holy Hill, 1525 Carmel Rd., Erin, 3/12/92, A, C, a, d, 92000139

Kissel's Addition Historic District [Kissel, Louis, & Sons of Hartford TR], Rural St. and W. Root Ave., Hartford, 11/03/88, A, 88002071

Kissel's Wheelock Addition Historic District [Kissel, Louis, & Sons of Hartford TR], Roughly bounded by Church St., Wheelock and Linden Aves., Branch St., and Teddy Ave., Hartford, 11/03/88, A, 88002072

Kissel, George A., House [Kissel, Louis, & Sons of Hartford TR], 215 E. Sumner, Hartford, 11/03/88, B, 88002075

Kissel, Louis, House [Kissel, Louis, & Sons of Hartford TR], 407 E. Sumner, Hartford, 11/03/88, B, 88002077

Kissel, William L., House [Kissel, Louis, & Sons of Hartford TR], 67 South St., Hartford, 11/03/88, B, 88002073

Lizard Mound State Park, NE of West Bend, West Bend vicinity, 10/15/70, D, 70000038

Ritger Wagonmaking and Blacksmith Shop, , 4928 WI 175, Hartford vicinity, 6/01/82, A, C, 82000717

Schunk, Jacob, Farmhouse, Donges Bay Rd., Germantown vicinity, 12/08/83, C, 83004325

St. Augustine Catholic Church and Cemetery, Co. Hwy. Y 3 mi. S of jct. of Co. Hwy. Y and SR 33, Trenton, 5/03/90, C, a, d, 90000638

St. John of God Roman Catholic Church, Convent, and School, E of Kewaskum at 1488 Highland Dr., Kewaskum vicinity, 8/09/79, A, C, a, 79000117

St. Peter's Church, 1010 Newark Dr., West Bend vicinity, 6/30/83, C, a, 83003430

Washington County Courthouse and Jail [County Courthouses of Wisconsin TR], 320 S. 5th Ave., West Bend, 3/09/82, C, 82000718

Waukesha County

Andrews, Sewall, House, 103 Main St., Mukwonago, 7/07/81, B, C, 81000063

Arcadian Bottling Works [Waukesha MRA], 900 N. Hartwell Ave., Waukesha, 10/28/83, A, 83004326

Arlington Apartments [Waukesha MRA], 309 Arlington St., Waukesha, 1/21/87, C, 86003651

Baer, Albert R., House [Menomonee Falls MRA], W166 N8990 Grand Ave., Menomonee Falls, 9/21/88, C, 88001645

Bailie, Ralph C., House [Hartland MRA], 530 North Ave., Hartland, 12/08/86, C, 86003407

Bank of Hartland [Hartland MRA], 112 E. Capitol Dr., Hartland, 4/21/88, C, 86003415

Barfoth-Blood Mound Group (47 WK 63), Address Restricted, Mukwonago vicinity, 9/02/82, D, d, 82000720

Barnes, Andrew, House [Menomonee Falls MRA], N89 W16840 Appleton Ave., Menomonee Falls, 9/21/88, C, 88001652

Beaumont Hop House, Address Restricted, Hartland vicinity, 11/23/77, A, 77000058

Big Bend Mound Group No. 2, S of Big Bend, Big Bend vicinity, 12/19/78, D, 78000146

Bishopstead, 153 W. Oakwood Dr., Delafield, 3/01/84, B, 84003803

Blair, Sen. William, House [Waukesha MRA], 434 Madison St., Waukesha, 10/28/83, B, C, 83004327

Booth, J. C., House, About 1 mi. SW of Saylesville on Saylesville Rd., Saylesville vicinity, 1/25/73, C, 73000094

Buckley, Patrick J., House, 1101 Buckley St., Waukesha, 2/28/91, C, 91000075

Burr Oak Tavern [Hartland MRA], 315–317 E. Capitol Dr., Hartland, 12/28/88, A, B, C, g, 86003403

Camp, Thomas, Farmhouse [Menomonee Falls MRA], W204 N8151 Lannon Rd., Menomonee Falls, 9/21/88, C, 88001670

Caples' Park Historic District [Waukesha MRA], Roughly bounded by E. Newhall Ave., S. Hartwell Ave., Windsor Dr. and Oxford Rd., and S. East Ave., Waukesha, 3/17/88, C, 88000219

Chandler, Walter S., House, 151 W. College Ave., Waukesha, 12/27/74, C, 74000137

Chapel of St. Mary the Virgin, 2 mi. SW of Nashotah on Nashotah House Rd., Nashotah vicinity, 2/23/72, A, C, a, 72000067

Cobb, George N., House, S of Oconomowoc at 1505 N. Golden Lake Rd., Oconomowoc vicinity, 3/02/82, C, 82000719

College Avenue Historic District [Waukesha MRA], Fountain St., S. East and College Aves., Waukesha, 10/28/83, A, C, 83004328

Cook, Alexander, House [Waukesha MRA], 600 E. North St., Waukesha, 10/28/83, B, 83004329

Cutler Mound Group, Address Restricted, Waukesha vicinity, 11/03/88, D, 88002184

Cutler, Morris, House, 401 Central Ave., Waukesha MRA, 10/28/83, B, C, 83004330

Dansk Evangelical Lutheran Kirke [Hartland MRA], 400 W. Capitol Dr., Hartland, 4/21/88, A, C, a, 86003422

Davis, Cyrus, Farmstead [Menomonee Falls MRA], W204 N7776 Lannon Rd., Menomonee Falls, 3/15/89, C, 88001674

Davis, Cyrus—Davis Brothers Farmhouse [Menomonee Falls MRA], W204 N7818 Lannon Rd., Menomonee Falls, 9/21/88, C, 88001672

Delafield Fish Hatchery, Main St., Delafield, 5/13/81, A, C, 81000064

Dewey Mound Group, Address Restricted, Big Bend vicinity, 12/19/78, D, 78000147

Dousman Inn, 15670 Blue Mound Rd., Brookfield, 1/15/79, A, C, 79000118

Downtown Historic District [Waukesha MRA], Roughly bounded by Broadway, Grand Ave., Clinton and South Sts., Waukesha, 10/28/83, A, C, 83004331

Dwinnell, George, House [Waukesha MRA], 442 W. College Ave., Waukesha, 10/28/83, C, 83004332

East Capitol Drive Historic District [Hartland MRA], 337–702 E. Capitol Dr., Hartland, 9/11/86, C, 86002319

Elliot, Dr. F. C., House [Waukesha MRA], 501 Dunbar Ave., Waukesha, 10/28/83, C, 83004333

First Baptist Church [Waukesha MRA], 247 Wisconsin Ave., Waukesha, 10/28/83, C, a, 83004334

First Congregational Church [Hartland MRA], 214 E. Capitol Dr., Hartland, 12/08/86, C, a, 86003405

First Congregational Church, 100 E. Broadway, Waukesha, 1/30/92, C, a, 91001991

First German Reformed Church, 413 Wisconsin Ave., Waukesha, 9/13/91, C, a, 91001390

First Methodist Church [Waukesha MRA], 121 Wisconsin Ave., Waukesha, 12/01/83, C, a, 83004335

Frame, Andrew, House [Waukesha MRA], 507 N. Grand Ave., Waukesha, 10/28/83, B, C, 83004337

Friederich Farmstead Historic District [Menomonee Falls MRA], N96 W15009 County Line Rd., Menomonee Falls, 9/21/88, A, C, 88001631

Genesee Town Hall, Genesee St., Genesee Depot, 6/25/81, A, 81000065

Goodwin-McBean Site (47 WK 184), Address Restricted, Big Bend vicinity, 9/17/82, D, 82000721

Grace, Perry, House [Waukesha MRA], 307 N. West Ave., Waukesha, 10/28/83, C, 83004339

Grand View Health Resort [Waukesha MRA], 500 Riverview Ave., Waukesha, 1/31/84, A, g, 84003805

Gredler-Gramins House, 20190 Davidson Rd., Brookfield vicinity, 11/24/80, C, 80000203

Hadfield Company Lime Kilns [Lime Kilns of Waukesha County TR], N of Waukesha, Waukesha vicinity, 3/12/82, A, C, 82000722

Hartland Railroad Depot [Hartland MRA], 301 Pawling Ave., Hartland, 4/21/88, A, C, b, 86003417

Haseltine Cobblestone House, N of Big Bend on Big Bend Dr., Big Bend vicinity, 1/15/80, C, 80000204

Hawks Inn, 428 Wells St., Delafield, 2/23/72, A, C, b, 72000068

Hemlock, David, J., House [Waukesha MRA], 234 Carroll St., Waukesha, 12/01/83, C, 83004340

Waukesha County—Continued

Henze, LeRoy A., House [Menomonee Falls MRA], N89 W15781 Main St., Menomonee Falls, 9/21/88, C, 88001638

Hinkley, Ahira R., House, NE of Eagle off WI 59, Eagle vicinity, 1/21/74, C, 74000138

Hoeltz, Herbert, House [Menomonee Falls MRA], N87 W15714 Kenwood Blvd., Menomonee Falls, 9/21/88, C, 88001636

Hoos, Elizabeth, House [Menomonee Falls MRA], W164 N9010 Water St., Menomonee Falls, 9/21/88, C, 88001640

Hoos—Rowell House [Menomonee Falls MRA], W164 N8953 Water St., Menomonee Falls, 9/21/88, C, 88001644

Hornburg, Harold, House [Hartland MRA], 213 Warren Ave., Hartland, 12/08/86, C, 86003431

Howitt, John, House [Waukesha MRA], 407 N. Grand Ave., Waukesha, 10/28/83, C, 83004341

Jackson House [Hartland MRA], 235 North Ave., Hartland, 12/08/86, C, 86003409

Johnston, William, Lime Kiln [Lime Kilns of Waukesha County TR], E of Genesse Depot, Saylesville vicinity, 3/12/82, A, C, 82000723

Jones, Robert O., House [Waukesha MRA], 501 W. College Ave., Waukesha, 10/28/83, C, 83004342

Koehler, Frank, House and Office [Menomonee Falls MRA], N88 W16623 Appleton Ave., Menomonee Falls, 9/21/88, B, C, 88001669

Koepsel House, Old World Wisconsin, off WI 59, Eagle vicinity, 10/25/73, C, b, e, 73000095

Laflin Avenue Historic District [Waukesha MRA], W. Laflin and Garfield Aves., Waukesha, 10/28/83, A, C, 83004343

Lain-Estburg House, 229 Wisconsin Ave., Waukesha, 12/27/74, B, C, 74000139

Mace, Garwin A., House [Menomonee Falls MRA], W166 N8941 Grand Ave., Menomonee Falls, 9/21/88, C, 88001650

Mace, Garwin, Lime Kilns [Lime Kilns of Waukesha County TR], LimeKiln Park, Menomonee Falls, 3/12/82, A, C, 82000724

Madison Street Historic District, Jct. of Madison, Randall, and Third Sts., Waukesha, 3/22/90, C, 90000489

Main Street Historic District [Menomonee Falls MRA], Main and Appleton Sts., Menomonee Falls, 9/21/88, A, C, 88001629

Mann, William G., House [Waukesha MRA], 346 Maple Ave., Waukesha, 10/28/83, A, C, 83004349

McCall Street Historic District [Waukesha MRA], McCall and James Sts., and N. East and Hartwell Aves., Waukesha, 12/01/83, B, C, 83004348

McCall Street Historic District (Boundary Increase) [Waukesha MRA], Roughly, Charles and James Sts. from College Ave. to McCall St. and Hartwell Ave. from College to Grove St., Waukesha, 3/29/93, C, 93000154

Menomonee Falls City Hall [Menomonee Falls MRA], N88 W16631 Appleton Ave., Menomonee Falls, 9/21/88, A, C, 88001667

Menomonee Golf Club [Menomonee Falls MRA], N73 W13430 Appleton Ave., Menomonee Falls, 9/21/88, C, 88001663

Miller-Davidson House, On County Line Rd., E of U.S. 41, Menomonee Falls, 4/24/73, C, 73000096

Moore, Dr. Volney L., House [Waukesha MRA], 307 E. Main St., Waukesha, 10/28/83, C, 83004350

National Guard Armory 127th Regiment Infantry Company G, 103 E. Jefferson at Main St., Oconomowoc, 12/06/84, A, 84000709

National Hotel [Waukesha MRA], 235 W. Main St., Waukesha, 10/28/83, A, 83004344

Nelson, Charles E., Sr., House, 520 N. Grand Ave., Waukesha, 4/05/90, C, 90000560

Nickell, William, A., House [Waukesha MRA], 511 Lake St., Waukesha, 10/28/83, C, 83004346

Oconomowoc City Hall, 174 E. Wisconsin Ave., Oconomowoc, 4/10/80, A, C, 80000205

Oconomowoc Depot, 115 Collins St., Oconomowoc, 1/29/80, A, C, 80000206

Okauchee House, 34880 Lake Dr., Okauchee, 8/11/78, A, C, 78000149

Old Waukesha County Courthouse, 101 W. Main St., Waukesha, 3/27/75, C, D, 75000082

Pabst, Gustave, Estate, 36100 Genesee Lake Rd., Summit, 11/27/89, C, a, 89002033

Peck, Clarence, Residence, 430 and 434 N. Lake Rd., Oconomowoc, 1/28/88, B, C, 87002569

Peck, Walter L., House, 38928 Islandale Dr., Oconomowoc, 4/10/86, C, 86000715

Peterson Site (47 WK 199), Address Restricted, Big Bend vicinity, 9/02/82, D, 82000726

Pokrandt Blacksmith Shop [Waukesha MRA], 128 E. St. Paul Ave., Waukesha, 10/28/83, A, 83004351

Pratt, Hannah, House [Waukesha MRA], 501 Barney St., Waukesha, 10/28/83, C, 83004352

Pratt, John A., House [Menomonee Falls MRA], N88 W15634 Park Blvd., Menomonee Falls, 9/21/88, C, 88001634

Putney Block, 301 W. Main St., 816 and 802 Grand Ave., Waukesha, 9/23/82, C, 82000727

Putney, Frank H., House [Waukesha MRA], 223 Wisconsin Ave., Waukesha, 10/28/83, C, 83004353

Resthaven Hotel [Waukesha MRA], 915 N. Hartwell Ave., Waukesha, 10/28/83, A, C, 83004354

Sanger, Casper M., House [Waukesha MRA], 507 E. College Ave., Waukesha, 10/28/83, A, C, a, 83004357

Schuttler, Henry and Mary, House, 371 E. Lisbon Rd., Oconomowoc, 7/16/87, C, 87001122

Sign of the Willows [Hartland MRA], 122 E. Capitol Dr., Hartland, 12/08/86, C, 86003428

Silurian Mineral Springhouse [Waukesha MRA], Post Office Circle, Waukesha, 1/31/84, A, C, 84003814

Sloan, William P., House [Waukesha MRA], 912 N. Barstow St., Waukesha, 10/28/83, C, b, 83004368

Smith, Camillia, House [Waukesha MRA], 603 N. West Ave., Waukesha, 10/28/83, C, 83004358

St. John Chrysostom Church, 1111 Genesee St., Delafield, 2/23/72, C, a, 72000069

St. John's Military Academy, Genessee St., Delafield, 10/28/77, A, B, C, g, 77000059

St. Joseph's Catholic Church Complex [Waukesha MRA], 818 N. East Ave., Waukesha, 10/28/83, A, C, a, 83004355

St. Matthias Episcopal Church [Waukesha MRA], 111 E. Main St., Waukesha, 10/28/83, C, a, 83004356

Statesan Historic District, Boys School Rd., Wales vicinity, 4/21/88, A, a, 88000454

Third Street Bridge [Menomonee Falls MRA], Roosevelt Dr., Menomonee Falls, 9/21/88, C, 88001647

Totten-Butterfield House [Waukesha MRA], 515 N. Grand Ave., Waukesha, 1/31/84, C, b, 84003816

Trapp Filling Station [Hartland MRA], 252–256 W. Capitol Dr., Hartland, 12/08/86, C, 86003419

Turck, Christian, House, Off WI 59 in Old World Wisconsin, Eagle vicinity, 10/25/73, C, b, e, 73000097

United Unitarian and Universalist Church, 216 Main St., Mukwonago, 10/01/87, A, C, a, 87001759

Van Buren, Sarah Belle, House [Hartland MRA], 128 Hill St., Hartland, 12/08/86, C, 86003426

Village Park Bandstand [Menomonee Falls MRA], Village Park on Garfield Dr., Menomonee Falls, 9/21/88, A, 88001653

Ward District No. 3 Schoolhouse, WI 67 and Betts Rd., Eagle vicinity, 7/07/81, A, C, 81000066

Warren, Stephen, House [Hartland MRA], 235 E. Capitol Dr., Hartland, 12/08/86, B, C, 86003432

Waukesha Post Office [Waukesha MRA], 235 W. Broadway Ave., Waukesha, 10/28/83, C, 83004359

Waukesha Pure Food Company [Waukesha MRA], 550 Elizabeth St., Waukesha, 10/28/83, A, C, 83004360

Welch, C. A., House [Waukesha MRA], 1616 White Rock Ave., Waukesha, 10/28/83, A, C, 83004361

West, Deacon, Octagon House, 370 High St., Pewaukee, 5/12/75, C, 75000083

Wick, Michael, Farmhouse and Barn [Menomonee Falls MRA], N72 W13449 Good Hope Rd., Menomonee Falls, 9/21/88, C, 88001665

Wisconsin Avenue Historic District [Waukesha MRA], Wisconsin, Waukesha, 10/28/83, C, 83004362

Wisconsin Industrial School for Boys [Waukesha MRA], 621 and 627 W. College Ave., Waukesha, 1/21/87, A, C, 86003652

Yanke, Louis, Saloon [Waukesha MRA], 200 Madison Ave., Waukesha, 10/28/83, C, 83004363

Zimmer, Johann, Farmhouse [Menomonee Falls MRA], W156 N9390 Pilgrim Rd., Menomonee Falls, 9/21/88, C, 88001632

Zion Evangelical Lutheran Church [Hartland MRA], 403 W. Capitol Dr., Hartland, 12/08/86, C, a, 86003423

Waupaca County

Browne Law Office, 202 E. Union St., Waupaca, 8/18/80, A, B, 80000208

Waupaca County—Continued

Commandant's Residence Home [Wisconsin Home for Veterans TR], Off WI 22, KIng, 6/19/85, A, C, 85001364

Crescent Roller Mills, 213 Oborn St., Waupaca, 12/20/78, A, 78000150

Danes Hall, 303 N. Main St., Waupaca, 1/17/80, A, 80000209

Halfway House, Potts Ave., King vicinity, 3/01/82, A, B, 82000728

Kasper, Philip H., Cheese Factory, W of Bear Creek on WI 22, Bear Creek vicinity, 8/27/76, A, B, 76000081

Old Hospital [Wisconsin Home for Veterans TR], Off WI 22, King, 6/19/85, A, C, 85001365

Rural on the Crystal Historic District, Roughly bounded by Arbor St., Rapley St., Rural Rd., and Cleghorn St., Rural, 4/12/89, A, C, 89000231

Sanders Site (47WP26 and 47WP70), Address Restricted, Fremont vicinity, 2/09/84, D, 84003819

Shearer-Cristy House, 315 E. Lake St., Waupaca, 12/22/83, C, 83004364

Veterans Cottages Historic District [Wisconsin Home for Veterans TR], Off WI 22, King, 6/19/85, A, C, 85001367

Veterans Home Chapel [Wisconsin Home for Veterans TR], Off WI 22, King, 6/19/85, A, C, a, 85001366

Wipf, J. & C., Mills, 280 N. Main St., Iola, 12/08/87, A, b, 87002108

Waushara County

Kimball, Alanson M., House, 204 Middleton St., Pine River, 10/20/88, C, 88002023

Waushara County Courthouse, Waushara County Sheriff's Residence and Jail [County Courthouses of Wisconsin TR], 209 St. Marie St., Wautoma, 3/09/82, C, 82000729

Whistler Mound Group, Address Restricted, Hancock, 9/18/93, D, 93000882

Winnebago County

Algoma Boulevard Methodist Church, 1174 Algoma Blvd., Oshkosh, 12/03/74, C, a, 74000140

Augustin, Gustav, Block, 68 Racine St., Menasha, 5/30/86, C, 86001181

Babcock, Havilah, House, 537 E. Wisconsin Ave., Neenah, 8/07/74, B, C, 74000141

Bergstrom, George O., House, 579 E. Wisconsin Ave., Neenah, 3/22/93, B, C, 93000144

Black Oak School, 5028 S. Green Bay Rd., Nekimi, 6/25/87, C, b, 87001062

Bowen, Abraham Briggs, House, 1010 Bayshore Dr., Oshkosh, 4/22/82, C, 82000731

Brainerd Site, Address Restricted, Neenah vicinity, 9/07/84, D, 84003823

Brin Building, 1 Main St., Menasha, 7/10/86, A, 86001541

Buckstaff Observatory, 2119 N. Main St., Oshkosh, 5/17/79, A, B, 79000119

Carpenter Site (47 Wn 246), Address Restricted, Eureka vicinity, 4/07/82, D, 82000725

Cole Watch Tower, W of Omro on WI 21, Omro vicinity, 6/09/78, A, g, 78000148

Daily Northwestern Building, 224 State St., Oshkosh, 5/13/82, A, C, 82000732

Doty Island (47-WN-30), Address Restricted, Menasha vicinity, 6/20/85, D, 85001368

Eureka Lock and Lock Tender's House, S of Eureka on Fox River, Eureka vicinity, 9/29/76, A, 76000082

First Presbyterian Church, 110 Church Ave., Oshkosh, 12/27/74, C, a, 74000142

Frontenac, 132-140 High St. and 9 Brown St., Oshkosh, 4/22/82, C, 82000733

Gram, Hans, House, 345 E. Wisconsin Ave., Neenah, 7/02/87, C, 87001123

Grand Loggery, Doty Park (Lincoln St.), Neenah, 3/22/74, B, b, e, 74000143

Grignon, Augustin, Hotel, SE corner of Main and Washington Sts., Butte des Morts, 4/14/75, A, C, 75000084

Guenther, Richard, House, 1200 Washington Ave., Oshkosh, 3/01/84, A, B, C, 84003824

Hooper, Jessie Jack, House, 1149 Algoma Blvd., Oshkosh, 12/18/78, B, C, 78000151

Jennings, Ellis, House, 711 E. Forest Ave., Neenah, 3/20/92, C, 92000110

Kamrath Site, Address Restricted, Winneconne vicinity, 5/06/75, D, 75000085

Koch, Carl, Block, 2 Tayco St., Menasha, 7/10/86, A, C, 86001539

Larson Brothers Airport, WI 150, Clayton, 4/05/84, A, C, 84003825

Lasley's Point Site, Address Restricted, Winneconne vicinity, 9/06/79, D, 79000120

Lutz, Robert, House, 1449 Knapp St., Oshkosh, 5/27/82, B, C, 82000734

Metzig Garden Site (47WN283), Address Restricted, Wolf vicinity, 12/29/88, D, 88003070

Morgan, John R., House, 234 Church Ave., Oshkosh, 10/14/83, B, C, 83004365

Neenah United States Post Office, 307 S. Commercial St., Neenah, 11/08/90, C, 90001743

Omro High School, Annex and Webster Manual Training School, 515 S. Webster St., Omro, 6/19/85, A, C, 85001369

Orville Beach Memorial Manual Training School, 240 Algoma Blvd., Oshkosh, 9/12/85, A, C, 85002334

Oshkosh Grand Opera House, 100 High Ave., Oshkosh, 1/21/74, A, 74000144

Oshkosh State Normal School Historic District, Buildings at 800, 842, and 912 Algoma Blvd., and 845 Elmwood Ave., Oshkosh, 12/06/84, A, C, 84000722

Overton Archeological District, Address Restricted, Oshkosh vicinity, 5/02/75, D, 75000086

Oviatt House, 842 Algoma Blvd., Oshkosh, 8/27/79, A, B, C, 79000121

Paepke, Henry, House, 251 E. Doty Ave., Neenah, 3/13/87, C, 87000462

Paine Art Center and Arboretum, 1410 Algoma Blvd., Oshkosh, 12/01/78, B, C, 78000152

Paine Lumber Company Historic District, Off Congress Ave. roughly between High, New York, and Summit Aves., and Paine Lumber Access Rd., Oshkosh, 6/26/86, A, C, 86001392

Pollock, William E., Residence, 765 Algoma Blvd., Oshkosh, 12/06/84, C, 84000728

Read School, 1120 Algoma Blvd., Oshkosh, 2/11/93, C, 93000025

Shattuck, Franklyn C., House, 547 E. Wisconsin Ave., Neenah, 12/04/78, B, C, 78000153

Smith, Charles R., House, 824 E. Forest Ave., Neenah, 7/16/79, A, B, 79000122

Smith, Henry Spencer, House, 706 E. Forest Ave., Neenah, 6/25/82, B, 82000735

Tayco Street Bridge, Tayco and Water Sts., Menasha, 5/30/86, C, 86001182

Trinity Espicopal Church, 203 Algoma Blvd., Oshkosh, 12/30/74, C, a, 74000145

US Post Office—Menasha, 84 Racine St., Menasha, 8/22/86, C, 86001518

Upper Main Street Historic District, 163-240 Main, 3 Mill, 56 Racine, and 408 Water Sts., Menasha, 12/06/84, A, C, 84000714

Vining, Gorham, P., House, 1590 Oakridge Rd., Neenah, 12/08/83, C, 83004366

Wall, Thomas R., Residence, 751 Algoma Blvd., Oshkosh, 12/06/84, C, 84000732

Washington Avenue Historic District, Roughly bounded by Merritt Ave., Linde and Lampert Sts., Washington Ave., Bowen and Evan Sts., Oshkosh, 5/22/86, C, 86001129

Washington Street Historic District, 214–216 Washington St., Menasha, 5/30/86, C, a, 86001180

Waterman, S. H., House, 1141 Algoma Blvd., Oshkosh, 2/25/93, C, 93000068

Wing, William C., House, 143 N. Park Ave., Neenah, 5/06/93, C, 93000400

Winnebago County Courthouse [County Courthouses of Wisconsin TR], 415 Jackson St., Oshkosh, 6/23/82, C, g, 82000736

Wisconsin Avenue Historic District, 106-226 W. Wisconsin Ave., 110 Church St., Neenah, 6/14/84, A, C, 84003827

Wisconsin National Life Insurance Building, 220 Washington Ave., Oshkosh, 4/29/82, C, 82000737

Wood County

Daly, Elizabeth, House, 641 Baker St., Wisconsin Rapids, 11/04/93, C, 93001172

Marshfield Central Avenue Historic District, Roughly, Central Ave. from Depot St. to Third St., Marshfield, 11/04/93, A, C, 93001166

Purdy, Willard D., Junior High and Vocational School, 110 W. Third St., Marshfield, 9/08/92, C, 92001188

Upham, Gov. William H., House, 212 W. 3rd St., Marshfield, 12/12/76, B, 76000083

Wahle—Laird House, 208 S. Cherry Ave., Marshfield, 1/30/92, A, B, C, 91001988

Wakeley's Tavern, W end of Wakeley Rd., Nekoosa, 12/27/74, A, 74000146

WYOMING

Albany County

Ames Monument, 3 mi. NW of Sherman, Sherman vicinity, 7/24/72, B, C, f, 72001296
Barn at Oxford Horse Ranch, 868 US 287, Laramie vicinity, 6/25/86, B, C, 86001398
Bath Ranch, Herrick Lane Rd., Laramie vicinity, 12/13/85, A, C, 85003211
Bath Row, 155, 157, and 159 N. Sixth St. and 611 University Ave., Laramie, 5/08/86, A, C, 86001015
Blair, Charles E., House, 170 N. 5th St., Laramie, 10/31/80, C, 80004298
Boswell, N. K., Ranch, S of Woods Landing off WY 230, Woods Landing vicinity, 7/21/77, A, B, C, 77001381
Brooklyn Lodge, WY 130, 7.5 mi. W of Centennial, Centennial vicinity, 10/24/89, A, B, 89001068
Centennial Depot, WY 130, Centennial, 11/08/82, A, C, b, 82001828
Como Bluff, On U.S. 30, along Como Ridge, Rock River—Medicine Bow vicinity, 1/18/73, A, B, 73001925
Conley, John D., House, 718 Ivinson St., Laramie, 5/15/80, B, C, 80004299
Cooper Mansion, 1411 Grand Ave., Laramie, 8/08/83, A, C, 83003359
DOE Bridge over Laramie River [Vehicular Truss and Arch Bridges in Wyoming TR], Cty. Rd. CNA-740, Bosler vicinity, 2/22/85, A, C, b, 85000411
Dale Creek Crossing (48AB145), 4 mi. W of Sherman, Ames Monument vicinity, 5/09/86, A, D, 86001027
East Side School, Off U.S. 30, Laramie, 3/17/81, A, C, g, 81000610
First National Bank of Rock River, 131 Ave. C, Rock River, 11/21/88, A, 88002532
Fort Sanders Guardhouse, Kiowa St., Laramie, 5/01/80, A, 80004300
Goodale, William, House, 214 S. Fourteenth St., Laramie, 8/05/91, C, 91000996
Ivinson Mansion and Grounds, Lots 1–8, block 178, Laramie, 2/23/72, B, C, 72001295
Jelm-Frank Smith Ranch Historic District, S of Woods Landing, Woods Landing vicinity, 8/31/78, A, B, C, 78002816
Laramie Downtown Historic District, Roughly bounded by University Ave., 6th St., Grand Ave., 3rd St., Garfield Ave., and 1st Ave., Laramie, 11/10/88, A, 88002541
Lehman-Tunnell Mansion, 618 Grand Ave., Laramie, 11/08/82, C, 82001829
Libby Lodge, NW of Centennial on WY 130, Centennial vicinity, 9/30/76, A, C, 76001947
Old Main, University of Wyoming campus, Ninth St. and Ivinson Ave., Laramie, 7/11/86, A, C, 86001536
Parker Ranch House, Address Restricted, Laramie Peak vicinity, 12/13/85, C, 85003209

Richardson's Overland Trail Ranch, 111 Hart Rd., Laramie, 3/05/92, A, 92000122
St. Matthew's Cathedral Close, 104 S. 4th St., Laramie, 4/12/84, A, C, a, 84003622
St. Paulus Kirche, 602 Garfield, Laramie, 11/25/83, A, a, 83004266
Union Pacific Athletic Club, Off U.S. 30, Laramie, 9/13/78, A, C, 78002814
Vee Bar Ranch Lodge, 2087 WY 130, Laramie, 6/30/86, A, C, 86001468
Woods Landing Dance Hall, 2731 WY 230, Woods Landing, 12/13/85, C, 85003210
Wyoming Territorial Penitentiary, Off WY 130, Laramie, 3/29/78, A, C, 78002815

Big Horn County

Bad Pass Trail, E of Warren along Big Horn River in Bighorn Canyon National Recreation Area, Warren, vicinity, 10/29/75, A, D, NPS, 75000215
Basin Republican-Rustler Printing Building, 409 W. C St., Basin, 7/19/76, A, B, 76001948
Bear Creek Ranch Medicine Wheel (48BH48), Address Restricted, Greybull vicinity, 5/04/87, A, D, 87000661
Big Horn Academy Historic District, 25 and 35 E. First South, Cowley, 3/26/92, A, 92000285
Black Mountain Archeological District (48BH900/902/1064/106 7/1126/1127/1128/1129), Address Restricted, Shell vicinity, 7/02/87, D, 86003459
Black Mountain Archeological District (Boundary Increase), Address Restricted, Shell vicinity, 4/16/90, D, 90000557
Bridger Immigrant Road-Dry Creek Crossing, 26 mi. E of Cody on U.S. 14, Cody vicinity, 1/17/75, A, 75001900
EJE Bridge over Shell Creek [Vehicular Truss and Arch Bridges in Wyoming TR], Cty. Rd. CN9-57, Shell vicinity, 2/22/85, A, C, 85000415
EJP County Line Bridge [Vehicular Truss and Arch Bridges in Wyoming TR], Rd. CN9-60, Hyattville vicinity, 2/22/85, A, C, 85000412
EJZ Bridge over Shoshone River [Vehicular Truss and Arch Bridges in Wyoming TR], Cty. Rd. CN9-111, Lovell vicinity, 2/22/85, A, C, 85000413
Hanson Site, Address Restricted, Shell vicinity, 12/15/78, A, D, g, 78002817
Lower Shell School House, U.S. 14, Greybull vicinity, 2/07/85, A, 85000247
M L Ranch, Off Alt. US 14 near E shore of Bighorn Lake, 13 mi. E of Lovell, Bighorn Canyon National Recreation Area, Lovell vicinity, 7/15/92, A, B, NPS, 92000836
Medicine Lodge Creek Site, Address Restricted, Hyattville vicinity, 7/05/73, A, D, 73001926
Medicine Wheel, Address Restricted, Kane vicinity, 4/16/69, D, NHL, 69000184
Paint Rock Canyon Archeological Landscape District, Address Restricted, Hyattville vicinity, 7/12/90, D, 80004881

Rairden Bridge [Vehicular Truss and Arch Bridges in Wyoming TR], S of Big Horn Cty. Rd. CN9-30, Manderson vicinity, 2/22/85, A, C, 85000414
US Post Office—Basin Main [Historic US Post Offices in Wyoming, 1900–1941, TR], 402 W. C St., Basin, 5/19/87, A, C, 87000779
US Post Office—Greybull Main [Historic US Post Offices in Wyoming, 1900–1941, TR], 401 Greybull Ave., Greybull, 5/22/87, A, C, D, g, 87000780

Campbell County

Basin Oil Field Tipi Rings (48CA1667), Address Restricted, Piney vicinity, 12/13/85, D, 85003165
Bishop Road Site (48CA1612), Address Restricted, Piney vicinity, 12/13/85, D, 85003202
Nine Mile Segment, Bozeman Trail (48CA264) [Bozeman Trail in Wyoming MPS], Address Restricted, Pine Tree Junction vicinity, 7/23/89, A, 89000813

Carbon County

Allen, Garrett, Prehistoric Site, Address Restricted, Elk Mountain vicinity, 8/07/74, D, 74002023
Arlington, S of I-180, Arlington, 11/25/83, A, 83004268
Baker, Jim, Cabin, Off WY 70, Savery, 11/08/82, A, B, C, b, 82001830
Bridger's Pass, SW of Rawlins, Rawlins vicinity, 4/28/70, A, 70000669
DFU Elk Mountain Bridge [Vehicular Truss and Arch Bridges in Wyoming TR], CR 120-1, Elk Mountain vicinity, 2/22/85, A, C, 85000416
DMJ Pick Bridge [Vehicular Truss and Arch Bridges in Wyoming TR], Rd. CN6-508 (Pick Bridge Rd.), Saratoga vicinity, 2/22/85, A, C, b, 85000418
DML-Butler Bridge [Vehicular Truss and Arch Bridges in Wyoming TR], Cty. Rd. CN6-203, Encampment vicinity, 2/22/85, A, C, 85000417
Divide Sheep Camp, NE of Baggs, Baggs vicinity, 2/09/84, A, 84003635
Downtown Rawlins Historic District, Roughly 2nd to 6th Sts. and Front to Buffalo Sts., Rawlins, 5/16/85, A, C, 85001119
Duck Lake Station Site, Address Restricted, Wamsutter vicinity, 12/06/78, A, D, 78002825
Elk Mountain Hotel, Bridge St. and CR 402, Elk Mountain, 10/10/86, A, 86003233
Ferris, George, Mansion, 607 W. Maple St., Rawlins, 11/01/82, A, C, 82001831
First State Bank of Baggs, 10 S. Miles St., Baggs, 9/13/84, C, 84003644

Carbon County—Continued

Fort Halleck, SW of Elk Mountain, Elk Mountain vicinity, 4/28/70, A, 70000668

Fort Steele, On North Platte River at point of Union Pacific RR. crossing, Fort Fred Steele vicinity, 4/16/69, A, 69000185

France Memorial United Presbyterian Church, 3rd and Cedar Sts., Rawlins, 5/14/84, A, C, a, 84003649

Grand Encampment Mining Region: Boston Wyoming Smelter Site, E of Encampment on Encampment River, Encampment vicinity, 7/02/73, A, 73001927

Grand Encampment Mining Region: Ferris-Haggarty Mine Site, W of Encampment, Encampment vicinity, 7/02/73, A, 73001928

Hanna Community Hall, Front St., Hanna, 11/26/83, A, a, 83004277

Hotel Wolf, 101 E. Bridge St., Saratoga, 11/21/74, A, C, 74002024

Hugus Hardware, 123 E. Bridge St., Saratoga, 4/05/84, A, 84003656

Jack Creek Guard Station, Off FDR 452, Saratoga vicinity, 5/15/86, A, C, 86001101

Medicine Bow Union Pacific Depot, 405 Lincoln Hwy., Medicine Bow, 11/01/82, A, 82001832

Midway Station Site, Address Restricted, Rawlins vicinity, 12/06/78, A, D, 78002819

Parco Historic District, Roughly bounded by Monroe Ave., N. Fourth St., Union and Lincoln Aves., and N. Ninth St., Sinclair, 5/06/87, A, C, 87000918

Pine Grove Station Site, Address Restricted, Rawlins vicinity, 11/21/78, A, D, 78002820

Platte River Crossing, 17 mi. W of Saratoga, Saratoga vicinity, 8/12/71, A, d, f, 71000885

Ryan Ranch, S of Saratoga off WY 130, Saratoga vicinity, 3/29/78, B, C, 78002823

Sage Creek Station Site, Address Restricted, Rawlins vicinity, 12/06/78, A, D, 78002821

Saratoga Masonic Hall, 1st and Main Sts., Saratoga, 3/29/78, A, a, 78002824

Stockgrowers Bank, Third St., Dixon, 6/25/86, A, 86001393

Stone Wall Ranch, Star Rt., Box 1300, Savery vicinity, 9/29/86, A, 86002329

Sun, Tom, Ranch, 6 mi. W of Independence Rock on WY 220, Independence Rock vicinity, 10/15/66, A, NHL, 66000753

Union Pacific Railroad Depot, Jct. of N. Front and Fourth Sts., Rawlins, 9/02/93, A, 93000883

Virginian Hotel, U.S. 30, Medicine Bow, 5/22/78, A, C, 78002818

Washakie Station Site, Address Restricted, Rawlins vicinity, 12/12/78, A, D, 78002822

Wyoming State Penitentiary District, 6th and Walnut Sts., Rawlins, 5/26/83, A, C, g, 83003360

Converse County

Antelope Creek Crossing (48CO171 and 48CO165) [Bozeman Trail in Wyoming MPS],

Address Restricted, City Unavailable vicinity, 7/23/89, A, 89000816

Christ Episcopal Church and Rectory, 4th and Center Sts., Douglas, 11/17/80, A, C, a, 80004046

College Inn Bar, 103 N. 2nd St., Douglas, 7/10/79, A, 79002608

Fort Fetterman, 7 mi. N of I-25 on Orpha Rd., Orpha vicinity, 4/16/69, A, 69000187

Glenrock Buffalo Jump, Address Restricted, Glenrock vicinity, 4/16/69, A, D, 69000186

Holdup Hollow Segment, Bozeman Trail (48CO165) [Bozeman Trail in Wyoming MPS], Address Restricted, City Unavailable vicinity, 7/23/89, A, 89000818

Hotel Higgins, 416 W. Birch, Glenrock, 11/25/83, A, 83004280

Ross Flat Segment, Bozeman Trail (48CO165) [Bozeman Trail in Wyoming MPS], Address Restricted, City Unavailable vicinity, 7/23/89, A, 89000811

Sage Creek Station (48CO104) [Bozeman Trail in Wyoming MPS], Address Restricted, Glenrock vicinity, 7/23/89, A, 89000812

Stinking Water Gulch Segment, Bozeman Trail (48CO165) [Bozeman Trail in Wyoming MPS], Address Restricted, City Unavailable vicinity, 7/23/89, A, 89000817

US Post Office—Douglas Main [Historic US Post Offices in Wyoming, 1900–1941, TR], 129 N. Third St., Douglas, 5/19/87, A, C, 87000781

Crook County

Arch Creek Petroglyphs (48CK41), Address Restricted, Moorcroft vicinity, 12/04/86, D, 86003458

DXN Bridge over Missouri River [Vehicular Truss and Arch Bridges in Wyoming TR], Crook Cty. Rd. 18-200, Hulett vicinity, 2/22/85, A, C, 85000419

Inyan Kara Mountain, About 15 mi. S of Sundance in Black Hills National Forest, Sundance vicinity, 4/24/73, A, D, 73001929

McKean Archeological Site (48CK7), Address Restricted, Moorcroft vicinity, 4/01/91, A, D, 91000326

Sundance School, 108 N. Fourth St., Sundance, 12/02/85, A, C, 85003099

Sundance State Bank, 301 Main St., Sundance, 3/23/84, A, C, 84003660

Vore Buffalo Jump, Address Restricted, Sundance vicinity, 4/11/73, A, D, 73001930

Wyoming Mercantile, WY 24, Aladdin, 4/16/91, A, 91000435

Fremont County

Atlantic City Mercantile, Rt. 62, Box 260, Atlantic City, 4/25/85, A, C, 85000869

BMU Bridge over Wind River [Vehicular Truss and Arch Bridges in Wyoming TR], WY 132, Ethete vicinity, 2/22/85, A, C, 85000421

Brooks Lake Lodge, Lower Brooks Lake-Shoshone National Forest, Dubois vicinity, 9/29/82, A, C, 82004333

CM Ranch and Simpson Lake Cabins, State Fish Hatchery Rd. S of Dubois off US 287, Dubois vicinity, 9/15/92, A, 92001249

Castle Gardens Petroglyph Site, Address Restricted, Moneta vicinity, 4/16/69, D, 69000189

Decker, Dean, Site (48FR916; 48SW541), Address Restricted, Honeycomb Buttes vicinity, 3/12/86, D, 86000354

Delfelder Schoolhouse, N of Riverton off U.S. 26, Riverton vicinity, 3/29/78, A, 78002826

Diamond A Ranch [Pioneer Ranches/Farms in Fremont County MPS], Off US 26/287 NE of Whiskey Mtn., Dubois vicinity, 8/19/91, A, C, 91001026

ELS Bridge over Big Wind River [Vehicular Truss and Arch Bridges in Wyoming TR], Cty. Rd. CN10-21, Dubois vicinity, 2/22/85, A, C, 85000420

ELY Wind River Diversion Dam Bridge [Vehicular Truss and Arch Bridges in Wyoming TR], Cty. Rd. CN10-24, Morton vicinity, 2/22/85, A, C, 85000422

Fort Washakie Historic District, Wind River Indian Reservation on US 287, Fort Washakie vicinity, 4/16/69, A, C, g, 69000188

Green Mountain Arrow Site (48FR96), Address Restricted, Stratton Rim vicinity, 3/12/86, C, D, 86000351

Hamilton City, NE of Atlantic City, Atlantic City vicinity, 6/04/80, A, d, 80004047

Lander Downtown Historic District, Main St. between Second and Fourth Sts., Lander, 5/05/87, A, C, 87000700

Quien Sabe Ranch [Pioneer Ranches/Farms in Fremont County MPS], Quien Sabe Ranch Rd., 18 mi. NE of Shoshoni, Shoshoni vicinity, 4/18/91, A, 91000434

Riverton Railroad Depot, 1st and Main Sts., Riverton, 5/22/78, A, C, 78002827

Shoshone-Episcopal Mission, 3 mi. SW of Fort Washakie on Moccasin Lake Rd., Fort Washakie vicinity, 4/11/73, B, C, a, 73001931

South Pass, About 10 mi. SW of South Pass City on WY 28, South Pass City vicinity, 10/15/66, A, NHL, 66000754

South Pass City, South Pass Rd., South Pass City, 2/26/70, A, NHL, 70000670

Split Rock Prehistoric Site (48FR1484), Address Restricted, Split Rock Ranch vicinity, 5/04/87, A, D, 87000662

St. Michael's Mission, In Ethete, Ethete, 6/21/71, A, B, a, 71000886

Torrey Lake Club/Ranch Historic District, Along W shores of Lake Julia, Torrey Lake and Ring Lake, Dubois, 8/12/91, A, 91000999

Torrey Lake Petroglyph District, Address Restricted, Dubois vicinity, 10/04/93, C, D, 93000983

Twin Pines Lodge and Cabin Camp, 218 W. Ramshorn, Dubois, 12/10/93, C, 93001382

US Post Office and Courthouse—Lander Main [Historic US Post Offices in Wyoming, 1900–

Fremont County—Continued

1941, TR], 177 N. Third St., Lander, 5/19/87, A, C, 87000782

Union Pass, On the Continental Divide in Teton National Forest, Unknown vicinity, 4/16/69, A, 69000367

Welty's General Store, 220 Ramshorn St., Dubois, 11/15/79, A, C, b, 79003680

Goshen County

Cheyenne-Black Hills Stage Route and Rawhide Buttes and Running Water Stage Stations, 1 mi. W to about 15 mi. SW of Lusk, Lusk vicinity, 4/16/69, A, 69000190

Fort Laramie National Historic Site, 3 mi. SW of Fort Laramie, Fort Laramie vicinity, 10/15/66, A, f, NPS, 66000755

Fort Laramie Three-Mile Hog Ranch, 5.5 mi. W of Fort Laramie along Laramie River, Fort Laramie vicinity, 4/23/75, A, 75001901

Jay Em Historic District, Main St., Jay Em, 4/12/84, A, 84003665

South Torrington Union Pacific Depot, U.S. 85, Torrington, 12/31/74, A, g, 74002025

US Post Office—Torrington Main [Historic US Post Offices in Wyoming, 1900–1941, TR], 2145 Main St., Torrington, 5/19/87, A, C, 87000783

Hot Springs County

Bates Battlefield, Bates Creek, Unknown vicinity, 11/20/74, A, 74002286

CQA Four Mile Bridge [Vehicular Truss and Arch Bridges in Wyoming TR], WY 173, Thermopolis vicinity, 2/22/85, A, C, 85000423

Callaghan Apartments, 116 E. Park St., Thermopolis, 3/29/93, A, 93000231

Downtown Thermopolis Historic District, Broadway, 5th and 6th Sts., Thermopolis, 5/10/84, A, C, 84003668

EFP Bridge over Owl Creek [Vehicular Truss and Arch Bridges in Wyoming TR], Cty. Rd. CN15-28, Thermopolis vicinity, 2/22/85, A, C, 85000424

Legend Rock Petroglyph Site, Address Restricted, Grass Creek vicinity, 7/05/73, D, 73001932

US Post Office—Thermopolis Main [Historic US Post Offices in Wyoming, 1900–1941, TR], 440 Arapahoe St., Thermopolis, 5/19/87, A, C, 87000784

Woodruff Cabin Site, 26 mi. NW of Thermopolis, Thermopolis vicinity, 2/26/70, B, 70000671

Johnson County

AJX Bridge over South Fork and Powder River [Vehicular Truss and Arch Bridges in Wyoming TR], I-25 W. Service Rd. (old hwy 87), Kaycee vicinity, 2/22/85, A, C, 85000426

Cantonment Reno, 5 mi. N of Sussex at Powder River, Sussex vicinity, 7/29/77, A, 77001382

Carnegie Public Library, 90 N. Main, Buffalo, 11/07/76, A, C, 76001949

Dull Knife Battlefield, N of Barnum, Barnum vicinity, 8/15/79, A, 79002609

EDL Peloux Bridge [Vehicular Truss and Arch Bridges in Wyoming TR], Cty. Rd. CN16-40, Buffalo vicinity, 2/22/85, A, C, 85000425

EDZ Irigary Bridge [Vehicular Truss and Arch Bridges in Wyoming TR], Cty. Rd. CN16-254, Sussex vicinity, 2/22/85, A, C, b, 85000427

Fort McKinney, About 2 mi. W of Buffalo on U.S. 16, Buffalo vicinity, 7/30/76, A, 76001950

Fort Phil Kearny and Associated Sites, On SR W off U.S. 87, Story vicinity, 10/15/66, A, NHL, 66000756

Fort Reno, E of Sussex on Powder River, Sussex vicinity, 4/28/70, A, 70000672

HF Bar Ranch Historic District, NW of Buffalo, Buffalo vicinity, 11/07/84, A, 84000392

Holland House, 312 N. Main St., Buffalo, 11/04/93, A, B, 93001185

Johnson County Courthouse, 76 N. Main, Buffalo, 11/07/76, A, C, 76001951

Lake Desmet Segment, Bozeman Trail [Bozeman Trail in Wyoming MPS], Address Restricted, City Unavailable vicinity, 7/23/89, A, 89000814

Main Street Historic District, Main St., Buffalo, 4/12/84, A, 84003676

Methodist Episcopal Church, Fort and N. Adams Sts., Buffalo, 9/13/76, A, C, a, 76001952

Powder River Station—Powder River Crossing (48JO134 and 48JO801) [Bozeman Trail in Wyoming MPS], Address Restricted, Sussex vicinity, 7/23/89, A, 89000810

St. Luke's Episcopal Church, 178 S. Main, Buffalo, 11/07/76, A, C, a, 76001953

TA Ranch Historic District, E of Wy 196 on N. Fork, Crazy Woman Cr., Buffalo vicinity, 3/26/93, A, 93000198

Trabing Station—Crazy Woman Crossing [Bozeman Trail in Wyoming MPS], Address Restricted, City Unavailable vicinity, 7/23/89, A, 89000815

US Post Office—Buffalo Main [Historic US Post Offices in Wyoming, 1900–1941, TR], 193 S. Main St., Buffalo, 5/19/87, A, C, 87000785

Union Congregational Church and Parsonage, 110 Bennett St., Buffalo, 2/07/85, A, a, 85000248

Laramie County

Atlas Theatre, 213 W. 16th St., Cheyenne, 4/03/73, A, 73001933

Baxter Ranch Headquarters Buildings, 912–122 E. 18th St. and 1810–1920 Morris Ave., Cheyenne, 6/14/79, B, C, b, 79002610

Beatty, Charles L., House, 2320 Capitol Ave., Cheyenne, 6/28/90, A, C, 90001001

Boeing/United Airlines Terminal Building, Hangar and Fountain, 200 E. 8th Ave., Cheyenne, 2/07/85, A, C, 85000249

Capitol North Historic District, Roughly bounded by E. 29th, and E. 25th St., Warren and Pioneer Aves., Cheyenne, 12/10/80, A, C, 80004048

Castle on 19th Street, 1318 E. 19th St., Cheyenne, 7/10/79, B, C, 79002611

City and County Building, 19th St. and Carey Ave., Cheyenne, 11/30/78, A, C, 78002828

Crook House, 314 E. 21st St., Cheyenne, 7/10/79, B, C, 79002612

Dereemer Ranch Historic District, E of Horse Creek, Horse Creek vicinity, 11/25/83, A, C, b, 83004290

Downtown Cheyenne Historic District, Roughly bounded by 15th and 16th Sts., Central and Pioneer Aves., Cheyenne, 12/22/78, A, C, 78003434

Downtown Cheyenne Historic District (Boundary Increase), Roughly bounded by 17th and 18th Sts., Pioneer and Carey Aves., also along Central Ave. and 17th St., Cheyenne, 12/22/80, A, C, 80004049

Downtown Cheyenne Historic District (Boundary Increase), Roughly bounded by Nineteenth St., Capital Ave., Seventeenth St., and Carey Ave., Cheyenne, 5/20/88, A, C, g, 88000522

First United Methodist Church, NE corner of 18th St. and Central Ave., Cheyenne, 2/25/75, A, C, a, 75001902

Fort David A. Russell, West side of Cheyenne, Cheyenne, 10/01/69, A, NHL, 69000191

Frewen, Moreton, House, 506 E. 23rd St., Cheyenne, 4/14/75, A, B, C, 75001904

Governor's Mansion, 300 E. 21st St., Cheyenne, 9/30/69, A, 69000192

Hynds Lodge, Curt Gowdy State Park, Cheyenne, 3/23/84, A, 84003685

Keefe Row, E. 22nd St. and Evans Ave, Cheyenne, 8/03/79, C, 79002613

Lafrentz, Ferdinand, House, 2015 Warren Ave., Cheyenne, 7/17/79, B, C, 79003679

Masonic Temple, 1820 Capitol Ave., Cheyenne, 10/25/84, A, C, 84000162

McDonald Ranch, 14 mi. SW of Chugwater on S side Laramie Cty. line, Chugwater vicinity, 5/14/87, A, C, 87000777

Nagle-Warren Mansion, 222 E. 17th St., Cheyenne, 7/12/76, B, C, 76001955

Rainsford Historic District, Roughly bounded by Morrie, Twenty-second, Warren, and Seventeenth Sts., Cheyenne, 11/06/84, A, C, 84003884

Remount Ranch, Remount Ranch Rd., 1 mi. S of US 80, Cheyenne vicinity, 9/19/90, A, B, 90001389

St. Mark's Episcopal Church, 1908 Central Ave., Cheyenne, 2/26/70, C, a, 70000673

St. Mary's Catholic Cathedral, 2107 Capitol Ave., Cheyenne, 11/20/74, C, a, 74002026

Sturgis, William, House, 821 E. 17th St., Cheyenne, 11/08/82, B, C, 82001833

Union Pacific Depot, 121 W. 15th St., Cheyenne, 1/29/73, A, C, 73001934

Union Pacific Roundhouse, Turntable and Machine Shop, 121 W. 15th St., Cheyenne, 7/24/92, A, C, 92000930

Van Tassell Carriage Barn, 1010 E. 16th St., Cheyenne, 9/13/78, B, C, b, 78002829

Laramie County—Continued

Whipple-Lacey House, 300 E. 17th St., Cheyenne, 5/15/80, B, C, 80004050

Wyoming State Capitol and Grounds, 24th St. and Capitol Ave., Cheyenne, 1/29/73, A, C, NHL, 73001935

Lincoln County

Emigrant Springs, Address Restricted, Kemmerer vicinity, 1/11/76, A, 76001956

Johnston Scout Rocks, Address Restricted, Kemmerer vicinity, 11/07/76, A, 76001957

Kemmerer Hotel, Pine and Sapphire, Kemmerer, 12/02/85, A, 85003064

Lincoln County Courthouse, Sage and Garnet Sts., Kemmerer, 11/08/84, A, C, 84000385

Names Hill, On the Green River, 5 mi. S of La-Barge and W of U.S. 189, La Barge vicinity, 4/16/69, A, 69000193

Penney, J. C., Historic District, J. C. Penney Ave. and S. Main St., Kemmerer, 6/02/78, A, b, NHL, 78002830

Penney, J. C., House, Railroad Park, Kemmerer, 6/18/76, B, b, 76001958

Rock Church, Second W and First S Sts., Auburn, 12/13/85, A, C, a, 85003222

Salt River Hydroelectric Powerplant, End of Co. Rd. 12-104, .7 mi W of US 89, Etna vicinity, 12/02/93, A, 93000889

US Post Office—Kemmerer Main [Historic US Post Offices in Wyoming, 1900–1941, TR], Sapphire Ave. and Cedar St., Kemmerer, 5/19/87, A, C, 87000786

Natrona County

Big Horn Hotel, Main St., Arminto, 12/18/78, A, C, b, 78002831

Bridger Immigrant Road—Waltman Crossing, 49 mi. W of Casper on U.S. 20, Casper vicinity, 1/17/75, A, 75001905

Casper Buffalo Trap, Address Restricted, Casper vicinity, 6/25/74, D, 74002027

Casper Fire Department Station No. 1, 302 S. David St., Casper, 11/04/93, A, C, 93001187

Chicago and Northwestern Railroad Depot, 35231 W. Dakota Ave., Powder River, 1/07/88, A, 87002296

Consolidated Royalty Building, 137–141 S. Center St., Casper, 11/04/93, A, 93001186

DUX Bessemer Bend Bridge [Vehicular Truss and Arch Bridges in Wyoming TR], Cty. Rd. CN1-58, Bessemer Bend, 2/22/85, A, C, 85000428

Fort Caspar, 14 Fort Caspar Rd., Casper, 8/12/71, A, D, e, 71000887

Fort Caspar (Boundary Increase), Area on N side of fort along Platte River, Casper, 7/19/76, C, D, 76002282

Independence Rock, 60 mi. SW of Casper on WY 220, Casper vicinity, 10/15/66, A, NHL, 66000757

Martin's Cove, W of Casper, Casper vicinity, 3/08/77, A, a, 77001383

Midwest Oil Company Hotel, 136 E. 6th St., Casper, 11/17/83, A, C, 83004302

Pathfinder Dam, 45 mi. SW of Casper, Casper vicinity, 8/12/71, A, C, 71000888

Rialto Theater, 102 E. Second St., Casper, 2/11/93, A, 93000037

South Wolcott Street Historic District, Roughly bounded by S. Center St., E. Ninth St., S. Wolcott St., E. Seventh St., S. Beech St., and E. Thirteenth St., Casper, 11/23/88, A, B, 88002609

Split Rock, Twin Peaks, NW of Muddy Gap, Muddy Gap vicinity, 12/22/76, A, 76001959

Stone Ranch Stage Station, NW of Casper on US 20/26, Casper vicinity, 11/01/82, A, 82001834

Teapot Rock, Off US 87, Midwest vicinity, 12/30/74, A, 74002028

Townsend Hotel, 115 N. Centre St., Casper, 11/25/83, C, 83004303

Niobrara County

Agate Basin Site, Address Restricted, Mule Creek vicinity, 2/15/74, D, 74002029

DSD Bridge over Cheyenne River [Vehicular Truss and Arch Bridges in Wyoming TR], Cty. Rd. CN14-46, Riverview vicinity, 2/22/85, A, C, 85000429

Lusk Water Tower, Along C & NW RR tracks across from US 20, Lusk, 8/12/91, A, b, 91000997

Site of Ferdinand Branstetter Post No. 1, American Legion, US 20, Van Tassell, 9/30/69, A, 69000194

Park County

Anderson Lodge, Greybull Ranger District, Shoshone National Forest, Meeteetse, 9/14/87, A, B, C, 87001548

Blair, Quintin, House, 5588 Greybull Hwy., Cody, 9/27/91, C, g, 91000998

Buffalo Bill Boyhood Home, 720 Sheridan Ave., Cody, 6/05/75, C, b, 75001906

Buffalo Bill Dam, 7 mi. W of Cody, Cody vicinity, 8/12/71, A, C, 71000890

Buffalo Bill Statue, 720 Sheridan Ave., Cody, 12/31/74, C, f, 74002319

Colter's Hell, W of Cody on U.S. 14, Cody vicinity, 8/14/73, A, B, 73001937

Dead Indian Campsite, Address Restricted, Cody vicinity, 5/03/74, D, 74002030

Downtown Cody Historic District, 1155 to 1313 and 1192 to 1286 Sheridan Ave., Cody, 8/15/83, A, C, 83003361

First National Bank of Meeteetse, 1033 Park Ave., Meeteetse, 9/05/90, A, 90001388

Hayden Arch Bridge [Vehicular Truss and Arch Bridges in Wyoming TR], Old US 14/16 (Cody

Yellowstone Hwy), Cody vicinity, 2/22/85, A, C, 85000430

Heart Mountain Relocation Center, Off US Alt. 14, Ralston vicinity, 12/19/85, A, g, 85003167

Horner Site, Address Restricted, Cody vicinity, 10/15/66, D, NHL, 66000758

Irma Hotel, 1192 Sheridan Ave., Cody, 4/03/73, A, C, 73001936

Lake Fish Hatchery Historic District [Yellowstone National Park MRA], Yellowstone National Park, Canyon Village, 6/25/85, A, C, NPS, 85001416

Lamar Buffalo Ranch [Yellowstone National Park MRA], E of Mammoth Hot Springs on Northeast Entrance Rd., Mammoth Hot Springs vicinity, 12/07/82, A, NPS, 82001835

Mummy Cave, Address Restricted, Cody vicinity, 2/18/81, D, 81000611

Norris Museum/Norris Comfort Station [Yellowstone National Park MRA], Grand Loop Rd., Yellowstone National Park, 7/21/83, A, C, NHL, NPS, 83003362

Norris, Madison, and Fishing Bridge Museums, Norris Geyser Basin, Madison Junction, and Fishing Bridge, Yellowstone National Park, 5/28/87, C, NHL, NPS, 87001445

Obsidian Cliff Kiosk [Yellowstone National Park MRA], Yellowstone National Park, Mammoth vicinity, 7/09/82, A, C, NPS, 82001719

Pahaska Tepee, 2 mi. E of E entrance to Yellowstone National Park on U.S. 14, Cody vicinity, 3/20/73, A, C, 73001938

Pioneer School, Co. Rd. 1-AG N of Badger Basin, Clark vicinity, 10/05/93, A, 93001011

Roosevelt Lodge Historic District [Yellowstone National Park MRA], Grand Loop Rd., Yellowstone National Park, 4/04/83, A, C, NPS, 83003363

Stock Center, 836 Sheridan Ave., Cody, 1/01/76, A, C, f, g, 76001960

T E Ranch Headquarters, 30 mi. SW of Cody on South Fork Rd., Cody vicinity, 4/03/73, A, B, C, 73001939

US Post Office—Powell Main [Historic US Post Offices in Wyoming, 1900–1941, TR], 270 N. Bent St., Powell, 5/22/87, A, C, D, g, 87000787

US Post Office—Yellowstone Main [Historic US Post Offices in Wyoming, 1900–1941, TR], Mammoth, off Grand Loop Rd., Yellowstone, 5/19/87, C, 87000789

Wapiti Ranger Station, Shoshone National Forest, Wapiti vicinity, 10/15/66, A, NHL, 66000759

Platte County

Diamond Ranch, NW of Chugwater, Chugwater vicinity, 9/28/84, A, C, 84003696

EWZ Bridge over East Channel of Laramie River [Vehicular Truss and Arch Bridges in Wyoming TR], Cty. Rd. CN8-204, Wheatland vicinity, 2/22/85, A, C, 85000431

Guernsey Lake Park, 1 mi. (1.6 km) NW of Guernsey, Guernsey vicinity, 8/26/80, A, C, g, 80004051

Platte County—Continued

Oregon Trail Ruts, S side of the North Platte River, 0.5 mi. S of Guernsey, Guernsey vicinity, 10/15/66, A, NHL, 66000761

Patten Creek Site (48PL68) [Aboriginal Lithic Source Areas in Wyoming MPS], Address Restricted, Hartville vicinity, 9/11/89, D, 89001204

Register Cliff, SE of Guernsey on N. Platte River, Guernsey vicinity, 4/03/70, A, 70000674

Swan Land and Cattle Company Headquarters, E side of Chugwater, Chugwater, 10/15/66, A, NHL, 66000760

Sheridan County

Big Goose Creek Buffalo Jump, Address Restricted, Sheridan vicinity, 2/12/74, A, D, 74002031

Big Red Ranch Complex, Off U.S. 14/16, Ucross, 10/11/84, A, e, 84000437

CKW Bridge over Powder River [Vehicular Truss and Arch Bridges in Wyoming TR], US 14/16, Arvada vicinity, 2/22/85, A, C, 85000432

Clearmont Jail, Water St., Clearmont, 5/14/84, A, 84003698

Connor Battlefield, City park on the Tongue River, Ranchester, 8/12/71, A, 71000891

EAU Arvada Bridge [Vehicular Truss and Arch Bridges in Wyoming TR], Cty. Rd. CN3-38, Arvada vicinity, 2/22/85, A, C, 85000433

EBF Bridge over Powder River [Vehicular Truss and Arch Bridges in Wyoming TR], Cty. Rd. CN3-269, Leiter vicinity, 2/22/85, A, C, 85000434

ECR Kooi Bridge [Vehicular Truss and Arch Bridges in Wyoming TR], Cty. Rd. CN3-93, Monarch vicinity, 2/22/85, A, C, 85000436

ECS Bridge over Big Goose Creek [Vehicular Truss and Arch Bridges in Wyoming TR], Cty. Rd. CN3-93, Sheridan vicinity, 2/22/85, A, C, 85000435

Fort MacKenzie, N of Sheridan on WY 337, Sheridan vicinity, 6/18/81, A, C, g, 81000612

Johnson Street Historic District, Johnson, 1st, and 2nd Sts., Big Horn, 4/09/84, A, C, 84003701

Odd Fellows Hall, Jackson St., Big Horn, 12/09/80, A, 80004052

Quarter Circle A Ranch, 2 mi. SW of Big Horn, Big Horn vicinity, 8/10/76, A, 76001961

Sheridan County Courthouse, Burkett and Main St., Sheridan, 11/15/82, A, C, 82001836

Sheridan Inn, Broadway and 5th St., Sheridan, 10/15/66, A, B, NHL, 66000762

Sheridan Main Street Historic District, Main St. from Burkitt to Mandel Sts., Sheridan, 11/09/82, A, C, 82001837

Trail End, 400 Claredon Ave., Sheridan, 2/26/70, B, C, 70000675

Wissler, Susan, House, 406 Main St., Dayton, 3/08/84, B, 84003703

Sublette County

Circle Ranch, 4 mi. SW of Big Piney off WY 350, Big Piney vicinity, 5/14/87, A, B, C, 87000778

DDZ Bridge over New Fork River [Vehicular Truss and Arch Bridges in Wyoming TR], Cty. Rd. 136, Boulder vicinity, 2/22/85, A, C, 85000437

Daniel School, US 189, Daniel, 9/05/90, A, 90001387

ENP Bridge over Green River [Vehicular Truss and Arch Bridges in Wyoming TR], Cty. Rd. CN23-145, Daniel vicinity, 2/22/85, A, C, 85000438

Father DeSmet's Prairie Mass Site, Off US 187, Daniel vicinity, 4/28/70, A, B, a, 70000676

Fort Bonneville, Off US 189, Pinedale vicinity, 4/28/70, A, 70000677

Jensen Ranch, Martin Jensen County Rd., Boulder vicinity, 5/05/88, A, 88000552

Log Cabin Motel, 49 E. Magnolia St., Pinedale, 3/25/93, A, C, 93000230

New Fork, 3 mi. S of Boulder on US 187, Boulder vicinity, 7/16/87, A, C, 87000773

Redick Lodge, N of Pinedale, Pinedale vicinity, 3/18/83, A, C, 83003364

Steele Homestead, WY 191, Boulder vicinity, 4/25/85, A, C, 85000870

Upper Green River Rendezvous Site, On Green River above and below Daniel, Daniel vicinity, 10/15/66, A, NHL, 66000763

Wardell Buffalo Trap, Address Restricted, Big Piney vicinity, 8/12/71, D, 71000892

Sweetwater County

Araphoe and Lost Creek Site (48SW4882), Address Restricted, Hadsell Cabin vicinity, 3/12/86, A, D, 86000352

City Hall, 4th and B Sts., Rock Springs, 5/15/80, A, C, 80004053

Dug Springs Station Site, Address Restricted, Rock Springs vicinity, 9/22/77, A, D, 77001384

ETD Bridge over Green River [Vehicular Truss and Arch Bridges in Wyoming TR], Cty. Rd. CN4-8SS, Fontenelle, 2/22/85, A, C, 85000439

ETR Big Island Bridge [Vehicular Truss and Arch Bridges in Wyoming TR], Cty. Rd. CN4-4, Green River vicinity, 2/22/85, A, C, 85000440

Eldon—Wall Terrace Site (48SW4320), Address Restricted, Westvaco vicinity, 12/13/85, D, 85003223

Expedition Island, S of Union Pacific RR bridge, near E bank of the Green River, Green River, 11/24/68, A, B, NHL, 68000056

First National Bank Building, 502 S. Main St., Rock Springs, 3/13/80, A, C, 80004054

Granger Station, In Granger, Granger, 2/26/70, A, 70000678

Gras House, 616 W. Elias, Rock Springs, 3/13/86, C, 86000355

Laclede Station Ruin, Address Restricted, Rock Springs vicinity, 12/06/78, A, D, 78002833

Natural Corrals Archeological Site (48SW336), Address Restricted, South Superior vicinity, 8/17/87, D, 87000873

Parting of the Ways, 15 mi. NE of Farson, Farson vicinity, 1/11/76, A, 76001962

Point of Rocks Stage Station, Off I-80, Rock Springs vicinity, 4/03/70, A, 70000679

Red Rock, SW of Rawlins, Rawlins vicinity, 11/21/78, A, 78002832

Reliance School and Gymnasium, 1321 Main St., Reliance, 5/13/88, A, C, 87002303

Reliance Tipple, E of US 187, Reliance, 5/23/91, A, 91000619

Rock Springs Elks' Lodge No. 624, 307 C St., Rock Springs, 12/10/93, C, 93001383

South Superior Union Hall, Main and Bridge Sts., South Superior, 11/25/83, A, C, 83004305

Stewart, Elinore Pruitt, Homestead, Off UT 414, McKinnon vicinity, 4/25/85, A, B, 85000871

Sweetwater Brewery, 48 W. Railroad Ave., Green River, 11/01/82, A, C, 82001838

Teton County

4 Lazy F Dude Ranch [Grand Teton National Park MPS], Off Teton Park Rd., Moose vicinity, 4/23/90, A, NPS, 90000611

AMK Ranch [Grand Teton National Park MPS], Off US 89/27, Moran vicinity, 4/23/90, C, NPS, 90000615

Administrative Area Historic District, Old [Grand Teton National Park MPS], Off Teton Park Rd., Moose vicinity, 4/23/90, C, NPS, 90000621

Bar B C Dude Ranch [Grand Teton National Park MPS], Off Teton Park Rd., Moose vicinity, 4/23/90, A, B, NPS, 90000624

Brinkerhoff, The [Grand Teton National Park MPS], Teton Park Rd., Moose vicinity, 4/23/90, A, C, g, NPS, 90000622

Chambers, Andy, Ranch Historic District [Grand Teton National Park MPS], Mormon Row E of Moose, Moose vicinity, 4/23/90, A, NPS, 90000623

Chapel of the Transfiguration, Grand Teton National Park, Moose vicinity, 4/10/80, A, C, a, 80004055

Cunningham Cabin, NE of Moose off U.S. 26/89/187 in Grand Teton National Park, Moose vicinity, 10/02/73, A, C, NPS, 73000225

Gap Puche Cabin, Gros Ventre R. Rd. E of Grizzly Lake, Jackson vicinity, 6/18/90, A, B, b, 90000889

Huckleberry Mountain Fire Lookout, Off US 89/287, Teton National Forest vicinity, 7/08/83, A, C, g, 83003365

Jackson Lake Ranger Station [Grand Teton National Park MPS], Off Teton Park Rd., Moose vicinity, 4/23/90, A, NPS, 90000620

Jenny Lake Ranger Station Historic District [Grand Teton National Park MPS], Jenny Lake Rd., Moose vicinity, 4/23/90, A, B, C, NPS, 90000610

Kimmel Kabins [Grand Teton National Park MPS], Off Teton Park Rd., Moose vicinity, 4/23/90, A, NPS, 90000612

Teton County—Continued

Lake Hotel, NW shore of Lake Yellowstone, Yellowstone National Park, 5/16/91, A, C, NPS, 91000637

Leek's Lodge, 10 mi. NW of Moran in Grand Teton National Park off U.S. 89/287, Moran vicinity, 9/05/75, B, C, g, NPS, 75000216

Leigh Lake Ranger Patrol Cabin [Grand Teton National Park MPS], Off Teton Park Teton Rd. at Lehigh Lake, Moose vicinity, 4/23/90, A, C, NPS, 90000618

Madison Museum [Yellowstone National Park MRA], Yellowstone National Park, Madison Junction, 7/09/82, A, C, NHL, NPS, 82001720

Menor's Ferry, Across Snake River just above park headquarters, Grand Teton National Park, Moose, 4/16/69, A, e, NPS, 69000016

Miller Cabin, 1 mi. NE of Jackson, Jackson vicinity, 4/16/69, A, B, 69000195

Moose Entrance Kiosk [Grand Teton National Park MPS], Teton Park Rd., Moose, 4/23/90, C, b, NPS, 90000619

Murie Residence [Grand Teton National Park MPS], Off Moose Wilson Rd., Moose vicinity, 4/23/90, B, g, NPS, 90000616

Old Faithful Historic District [Yellowstone National Park MRA], Both sides of Grand Loop Rd. at Old Faithful Geyser, Yellowstone National Park, 12/07/82, A, C, g, NPS, 82001839

Old Faithful Inn, W of West Thumb at Old Faithful on Grand Loop Rd., West Thumb vicinity, 7/23/73, A, C, NHL, NPS, 73000226

Rosencrans Cabin Historic District, 9 mi. E of Moran, Moran vicinity, 8/06/80, B, C, 80004056

Squirrel Meadows Guard Station, Forest Rd. 20031, City Unavailable, 10/04/90, C, 90000149

St. John's Episcopal Church and Rectory, 132 N. Glenwood, Jackson, 12/01/78, A, C, a, 78002834

String Lake Comfort Station [Grand Teton National Park MPS], Off Teton Park Rd. at String Lake, Moose vicinity, 4/23/90, C, b, NPS, 90000617

White Grass Dude Ranch [Grand Teton National Park MPS], Off Moose Wilson Rd., Moose vicinity, 4/23/90, A, NPS, 90000613

White Grass Ranger Station Historic District [Grand Teton National Park MPS], Off Moose Wilson Rd., Moose vicinity, 4/23/90, C, NPS, 90000614

Uinta County

Bridger Antelope Trap, Address Restricted, Evanston vicinity, 1/21/71, D, 71000893

Downtown Evanston Historic District, Roughly bounded by Center, 9th 11th, and Front Sts., Evanston, 11/25/83, A, 83004307

ERT Bridge over Black's Fork [Vehicular Truss and Arch Bridges in Wyoming TR], Cty. Rd. CN19-217, Fort Bridger vicinity, 2/22/85, A, C, 85000441

Fort Bridger, On Black's Fork of Green River, near the town of Fort Bridger, Fort Bridger vicinity, 4/16/69, A, 69000197

Piedmont Charcoal Kilns, 14 mi. NE of Hilliard, Hilliard vicinity, 6/03/71, A, 71000894

Quinn, A. V., House, 1049 Center St., Evanston, 9/13/84, A, 84003712

St. Paul's Episcopal Church, 10th and Sage Sts., Evanston, 11/17/80, A, C, a, 80004057

Triangulation Point Draw Site District (48UT114; 48UT377; 48UT392; 48UT440), Address Restricted, Verne vicinity, 9/16/86, D, 86002320

US Post Office—Evanston Main [Historic US Post Offices in Wyoming, 1900–1941, TR], 221 Tenth St., Evanston, 5/19/87, A, B, C, 87000790

Uinta County Courthouse, Courthouse Sq., Evanston, 7/14/77, A, 77001385

Union Pacific Railroad Complex, Main and 15th Sts., Evanston, 2/26/85, A, 85000685

Young, Brigham, Oil Well, Address Restricted, Evanston vicinity, 4/25/85, A, 85000872

Washakie County

Ainsworth House, Spring Creek Rd., Big Trails, 9/11/86, B, C, 86002321

Ten Sleep Mercantile, Second and Pine Sts., Ten Sleep, 9/11/86, A, 86002324

Worland House, 520 Culbertson, Worland, 2/27/86, B, C, 86000310

Worland Ranch, Jct. of US 20 and Wy 433, Worland, 3/05/92, B, 92000123

Weston County

Cambria Casino, N of Newcastle, Newcastle vicinity, 11/18/80, A, C, 80004058

Jenney Stockade Site, Off US 16, Newcastle vicinity, 9/30/69, A, 69000198

US Post Office—Newcastle Main [Historic US Post Offices in Wyoming, 1900–1941, TR], W. Main St. and Sumner Ave., Newcastle, 5/19/87, A, B, C, 87000791

The ELY Wind River Diversion Dam Bridge (ca. 1924–25) in Fremont County is an outstanding Wyoming example of a steel, multi-span Warren pony truss, and is uniquely constructed as an integral part of the dam. (Clayton B. Fraser, 1982).